Radio Times
Guide to **Films**

Introduction by **Barry Norman**

Edited by Kilmeny Fane-Saunders
BBC WORLDWIDE LIMITED

Published by BBC Worldwide Limited 80 Wood Lane London W12 0TT
ISBN 0 563 53710 8
First published in the United Kingdom 2000
Copyright © 2000 BBC Worldwide Limited

Text designed by Ben Cracknell Studios
Typesetting by Polestar Whitefriars
Printed in the United Kingdom by Polestar Wheatons
Cover design by CDT Limited

Back cover picture credits Amadeus *Moviestore Collection* ● Lawrence of Arabia *Aquarius Library* ● Cabaret *Ronald Grant Archive* ● Rear Window *Kobal Collection* ● To Have and Have Not *Aquarius Library* ● The Jungle Book *Moviestore Collection / Disney Enterprises, Inc.* ● Jean de Florette *Moviestore Collection* ● Some Like It Hot *Moviestore Collection* ● Chicken Run *Pathe* ● Citizen Kane *Aquarius Library* ● Kes *Aquarius Library* ● The Phantom of the Opera *Kobal Collection* ● Gone with the Wind ● Pulp Fiction *Aquarius Library* ● The Railway Children *Kobal Collection* ● Seven Samurai *Ronald Grant Archive* ● The Searchers *Aquarius Library* ● Star Wars *Aquarius Library* ● Withnail and I

Contents

Introduction
by Barry Norman

What's on the telly then? Well, on any given night you can bet your life there'll be a movie – several movies in fact, some of which you may already have seen, many of which you won't. If you're foolish enough, perish the thought, not to have ordered your *Radio Times* the business of deciding which of them to view becomes a matter of trial and error – switch on, watch for a few minutes, mutter "Oh, God, who needs this rubbish?" and switch off.

A different scenario. There's nothing on the box that takes your fancy (a common complaint in my experience) and everything showing at the local multiplex is juvenile tosh (an even more common complaint in my experience). But you'd still like to see a film – something newish, something that has yet to appear on TV, something good. No problem: down to the video store, where you are immediately confronted by a multiplicity of options, each nestling in an oblong box whose lurid cover gives little, if any, indication of what the contents are like. And here, alas, the *Radio Times* can't help you, Sundance.

Until, that is, now.

Now we have the present spanking new, to say nothing of imposing, volume, a comprehensive guide to something like 20,000 films, the good, the bad, the ugly, the indifferent, the great and the dreadful. And the best advice I can offer is: never leave home without it – not when you're going to the video shop, anyway.

What it offers, along with comprehensive information about who made each film and where and when, is crisp, lucid reviews by the team of *Radio Times* critics. These people are good; I know they're good because, as someone who has contributed a regular column and reviews of current releases for more years than I can remember, I read the magazine every week. Mind you, I don't always agree with my colleagues' verdicts and neither will you, because you are obviously perceptive and thoughtful individuals with views of your own. And that is as it should be. Criticism is not brain surgery, after all; it's not an exact science. A professional critic, no matter how knowledgeable he/she may be or how many films he/she

Introduction

has seen, is still merely expressing a personal opinion and opinions are like belly buttons – we all have them.

If a movie works (or doesn't work) for you then that's that and it doesn't really matter what anybody else thinks. But that's only true after the event, after you've seen it. It's before you've seen it that a guide such as this one can be invaluable. Let me put it this way: a film is not necessarily good simply because A or B or C directed it and X, Y and Z are in it. The advertising hype will try to persuade us that all cinematic geese are really swans but it ain't necessarily so. We know that perfectly well; what we don't know, unless we have advice, is whether it's worth our while to rent the films being so aggressively promoted to us. We all need help from time to time – especially now when cinema, especially mainstream cinema, seems to be in a state of craven confusion.

I honestly don't know which is my favourite movie era but I do know that the last decade isn't it. The great William Goldman (writer of *Butch Cassidy and the Sundance Kid* and *All the President's Men*) has described the nineties as the worst decade in cinema history and I think he's right.

It was the decade in which Hollywood anyway – though not, God bless it, the independent sector in America and elsewhere – seemed to show a cynical disregard for literate, well-written screenplays and concentrated almost exclusively on action and special effects. In this it was abetted by hitherto respected stars and directors who were capable of much better work but who were, perforce, obliged to go with the flow if they wanted to continue in lucrative employment. Merely to help sort the bones out of the mess of expensive, glossy, noisy and empty movies

that resulted is alone a justification for books such as the *Radio Times Guide to Films*.

But that's only a part of it. The cinema did not – as, alas, so many people seem to believe nowadays – begin with *Star Wars*; hundreds of wonderful films were made not only long before *Star Wars* was a glimmer in George Lucas's eye but before he himself was even a glimmer in his parents' eyes. Because television and video have kept them alive those films are in this volume, too, and the advice of the *Radio Times* critics should prove essential to younger viewers who are interested in the cinema generally and wish to put contemporary movies into some kind of historical perspective.

In case you're wondering, this is not to say that I agree with those who mutter: "Ah, they don't make 'em like that any more" because I do not. I believe that the best of modern films are as good as, and technically superior to, anything that has gone before, while the worst are quite as bad as their predecessors. And that even goes for the nineties, too.

But if there was a Worst Decade was there also a Golden Age of the cinema as well? Some people maintain there was and cite the thirties or forties or seventies to prove the point but I'm not convinced. Some periods may seem better than others but in every era you can be sure there are good films and bad films – and this is the book that can help you sort out t'other from which.

How to use this guide

The starting point for this guide to more than 20,000 films was the excellent archive of the *Radio Times* film unit, with film billings of those shown on TV dating from 1991 and reviews from 1995. Naturally, the television schedules for those years determined the content of this archive of roughly 10,000 movies. When we decided to make this outstanding collection of reviews available in book form, the first task of the editorial team was to double the total number of films and fill in significant gaps.

We've included a wide range of films, not just limiting our selection to mainstream UK and US movies, but also including European films, significant and interesting works of World Cinema, and even underground and experimental films – a cross-section of 20th- (and 21st-) century cinema, rather than a comprehensive guide to a narrower range of movies. This isn't a book for completists – film series may be represented here selectively to give you a feel for their character and style.

This is a "work in perpetual progress", for we've not only been preparing a book, but building a reference database for film enthusiasts. In addition to enjoying and using this guide, you can also access the film database (in its entirety) via the *Radio Times* website: **www.radiotimes.com/film.**

We'd like to hear your comments and suggestions about what you want to see on the database and in any future editions of this book and other related film books. You can write to: *Radio Times Guide to Films*, Room A1189, BBC Worldwide Ltd, 80 Wood Lane, London, W12 0TT, or e-mail us at films.radiotimes@bbc.co.uk.

The A–Z entries

TITLE

Films are listed under the titles by which we consider them to be best known in the United Kingdom and these titles are listed as they appear on screen. While many foreign-language movies are listed under their English title, others are listed under their original title, especially if they are particularly famous, or were released theatrically or on video under that title.

Alternative titles If you cannot find the film you are looking for in the main A–Z section, refer to the appendix of alternative titles at the back of the book. You should find a cross-reference to the film you're seeking there. The alternative-title appendix is not a complete index of all the alternative titles and/or foreign-language titles by which a film might be known – it is a selective appendix, designed to help you find the film you're looking for.

Alphabetisation Titles are listed alphabetically, ignoring definite and indefinite articles (a, the, an, including foreign-language articles such as les, das, il, el, place names being the exception, eg Los Angeles, El Dorado). Titles are also listed alphabetically by word, with initials counting as an individual word. For example, *Back to the Future* comes before *Backdraft*; *LA Confidential* before *Labyrinth*.

STAR RATING

The star rating assigned a film reflects the opinion of the reviewer. Many older films may be considered "difficult" (*The Battleship Potemkin*) or offensive (Leni Riefenstahl's *Triumph of the Will*) by today's audiences but will still have a high star rating because of their importance and/or their technical excellence.

The star ratings also help rank a movie within its genre. For example, a TV movie may be granted five stars in comparison to other TV movies (*The Autobiography of Miss Jane Pittman* versus *Beverly Hills Madam*); but you wouldn't compare it to *Citizen Kane*. Action film *True Lies* rates four stars when compared to *Delta Force 2*, but you wouldn't compare it to *Kiss Me Kate*. And, within each star rating (since we don't give half stars) there may be a band of quality, some two-star movies being better than others. (The handful of "lost films" included in this guide have no star rating, as no prints exist.)

As a guideline, the star ratings mean:

★ poor

★★ fair/average

★★★ good/better than average

★★★★ very good

★★★★★ outstanding

BRITISH BOARD OF FILM CLASSIFICATION CERTIFICATES

Where possible we give the current BBFC video certificate. For post-1982 films not on video in the UK, we list the original UK cinema certificate. Definitions of the current certificates appear at the foot of each page in the A–Z section of films. We haven't included older cinema certificates (X, AA, A), since we consider them no longer a useful guide. However, films that received a U certificate pre-1982 are listed with that certificate (once a U always a U, but the fact that *Abbott and Costello Meet Dr Jekyll and Mr Hyde* rated an X back in 1953 is amusing but not very helpful). There may be no certificate at all for foreign-language films, made-for-TV movies and films that received only a festival, rather than a theatrical, release in this country.

GENRE

Set by our editorial team to give you some indication of the type of film – this is a guideline only.

YEAR

Wherever possible, this is the copyright year of the film, not the year in which it was released. When we have been unable to confirm a copyright year, we have used the year of production; if that cannot be confirmed, we have used the year of first release.

COLOUR

This refers to the original colour of the film, ie the colour in which it was made: black and white, colour, tinted, sepia or a combination of these. Films that were originally made in black and white but now exist in colourised versions will still be listed as "BW", ie black and white.

RUNNING TIME

Where there is a certificate, the running time relates to that certificate: that is, a video running time if the film is available on video in the UK, or the theatrical running time if not. Made-for-TV movies, unless they have been released on video, are not given with a running time; and for some more obscure films, it may not have been possible to ascertain the running time so none has been given. In the case of some silent films, we may only have been able to obtain information regarding the number of reels; and since the actual running length could vary dramatically depending on the speed at which the film is screened, no running time is listed.

REVIEWS

These have been written by our team of reviewers, and the opinions expressed in them are their own, based on their expertise and critical judgement.

LANGUAGE INFORMATION

Where applicable, language information has been added to the end of the review. If we have been able to confirm whether a film is available in subtitled or dubbed versions, we have specified. If we have been unable to confirm this information, or if different versions of a film may be available, we have given the language of the film only (ie "A German language film", versus "In French with English subtitles" and "Italian dialogue dubbed into English").

FAMILY VIEWING

Where available and appropriate, we have included a content warning at the end of the review. Where no advice as to the film's suitability has been given, please be guided by the BBFC certificate and the content of the review itself. For example, no content advice has been added to the end of the crime thriller *Bodily Harm* (1995), but the film does have an 18 certificate and the reviewer mentions "a steamy affair". For those films without a certificate, the reviewers' comments should give an indication of the content of the movie.

VIDEO AND DVD AVAILABILITY

▭ = available on video

DVD = available on DVD

The information is correct at the time of going to press and is based on availability in the UK only. Video availability means that at some point the film was released on video and does not mean that it is currently on a distributor's list. More detailed information can be found via www.radiotimes.com/film, or in your local video store.

Encryption technology means that videos and DVDs released in other countries may not be playable on standard equipment in the United Kingdom.

CAST LIST

For each film we have included a selected cast list of actors followed by the characters they play (where known). Famous people, when playing themselves in a film, appear with no character name. Very rarely, and mostly in the case of less mainstream foreign films, we have been unable to obtain the character names. Documentaries do not, in most cases, include a cast list.

Some actors are occasionally credited in different ways on different films. For example, early in his career, Charles Bronson used his real surname and was credited as Charles Buchinski. In these cases, we have printed the actor's name as he/she was credited on that film, followed in square brackets by the name under which that actor is listed in our index: eg Charles Buchinski [Charles Bronson].

In the case of animated films, it is assumed that the actor credited to a character is providing the voice only.

COUNTRY OF ORIGIN

The country, or countries, of origin is determined by which country/countries financed the film, not where it was made.

List of abbreviations

US - United States
UK - United Kingdom
Alg - Algeria
Arg - Argentina
Arm - Armenia
Aus - Austria
Ausl - Australia
Ban - Bangladesh
Bel - Belgium
Bra - Brazil
Bul - Bulgaria
Can - Canada
Chi - China
Chil - Chile
Col - Colombia
Cos R - Costa Rica
Cro - Croatia
Cub - Cuba
Cur - Curaçao
Cyp - Cyprus
Cz - Czechoslovakia (up to 1993)
Cz Rep - Czech Republic (1993 and onwards)
Den - Denmark
E Ger - East Germany (1945–90)
Egy - Egypt
Fin - Finland
Fr - France
Ger - Germany (pre-1945, post-1990)
Gr - Greece
HK - Hong Kong
Hun - Hungary
Ind - India
Ire - Republic of Ireland
Is - Israel
It - Italy

Iv C - Ivory Coast
Jam - Jamaica
Jap - Japan
Kaz - Kazakhstan
Ken - Kenya
Lux - Luxembourg
Mex - Mexico
Nep - Nepal
Neth - Netherlands
NZ - New Zealand
Nic - Nicaragua
Nor - Norway
Pak - Pakistan
Pan - Panama
Phil - Philippines
Pol - Poland
Por - Portugal
P Ric - Puerto Rico
Rus - Russia (pre-1922, post-1996)
S Afr - South Africa
S Kor - South Korea
Ser - Serbia
Slov - Slovakia (since 1993)
Sp - Spain
Swe - Sweden
Swi - Switzerland
Tai - Taiwan
Thai - Thailand
Tun - Tunisia
Tur - Turkey
Urug - Uruguay
USSR - Soviet Union (post-1922, pre-1996)
Viet - Vietnam
W Ger - West Germany (1945–90)
Yug - Yugoslavia
Zim - Zimbabwe

CREDITS

Each entry includes a director credit and a writer credit. In a small number of cases, we were unable to confirm the writer credit, and so none appears. In some cases we have given additional names of those who have contributed to a screenplay, such as the person responsible for the adaptation or for additional dialogue.

There may also be additional credits for cinematography, music, costume design, art direction and others. These have been included if the reviewer has singled out this aspect of a film for special commendation, or if it received an award. Again, if a person was credited on a particular film in a variation of the name by which they are best known, then their printed credit appears first, followed in square brackets by their "real" or best-known name.

DIRECTORS' AND ACTORS' INDEXES

These are indexes to the films of the actors and directors that appear in this book, not complete filmographies. If an actor does not appear in the cast list for a film in the A–Z, then that film will not appear after the actor's name in the index. And if an actor or a director has only one film listed in the A–Z, his or her name has not been included in the index.

APPENDIX OF AWARDS

International awards covered are the British Academy of Film and Television Arts Awards (Bafta), Academy Awards ("Oscars"), Golden Globe Awards (Hollywood Foreign Press Association), Cannes Film Festival and the Berlin Film Festival. Categories in the appendix are: best film, best foreign-language film, best director, best actress, best actor, best supporting actor, best supporting actress and best screenplay. For the Academy Awards, Baftas and Golden Globes, the year of the award relates to the year of the films, not the event. For the Cannes and Berlin festivals, it is the year of the event.

For the Baftas and the Oscars we have included both winners and nominees, for the others winners only.

Principal reviewers

DAVID PARKINSON has been reviewing for *Radio Times* since 1995 and is currently compiling a comprehensive dictionary of world cinema. Specialising in foreign-language films, he is also a contributing editor on *Empire* and broadcasts regularly on BBC national and local radio. Among his books are *A History of Film*, *The Young Oxford Book of Cinema* and *Mornings in the Dark: the Graham Greene Film Reader*.

DAVE ALDRIDGE is a former crime reporter who decided he preferred screen violence to the real thing. He has spent the past 25 years watching square and rectangular screens. A former editor of *Film Review* magazine, he is currently film and video reviewer for BBC Radio 5 Live and a regular contributor to *Radio Times* and other entertainment magazines.

RONALD BERGAN has lectured on literature, theatre and film. A regular contributor to *The Guardian*, his numerous books on the cinema include biographies of the Coen Brothers, Sergei Eisenstein, Jean Renoir, Dustin Hoffman, Anthony Perkins, Francis Ford Coppola and Katharine Hepburn, as well as *The United Artist Story* and *The Great Theatres of London*.

JOANNA BERRY began her career as a film journalist at the age of 18, writing for *Time Out* and *Film Review* before becoming reviews editor for *Empire* magazine. Since leaving *Empire* in 1992, she has written movie features and reviews, and interviewed celebrities for a variety of magazines and newspapers, as well as writing scripts for MTV's movie show *Cinematic*. She is currently film critic for *Eve* and *Sainsbury's the Magazine*, and is a regular contributor to the *Daily Express*.

MAJ CANTON is the author of the definitive *Complete Reference Guide to Movies and Miniseries Made for TV and Cable 1984–1994* and a second volume covering the years 1994–99. She started her career as a TV comedy writer and is now an independent producer, having completed two TV movies for ABC. She lives in Los Angeles with her two VCRs.

ALLEN EYLES is a film historian who has written career studies of such stars as Humphrey Bogart, Rex Harrison, James Stewart and John Wayne, and is at work on a two-volume history of the Odeon cinema circuit. He founded the historical magazine *Focus on Film*, was a former editor of *Films and Filming*, and currently edits *Picture House*.

JOHN FERGUSON has worked in video publishing since 1987 and is currently editor of *Video Home Entertainment* magazine. He also spent a year at the London office of *Billboard* and has freelanced for the both the *Daily Mail* and *Daily Express*. His association with *Radio Times* goes back to 1991.

DICK FIDDY is a freelance writer/researcher and was the creator and writer of Channel 4's archive specials *The A–Z of TV* and *1001 Nights of TV*. He is currently employed by the BFI as a member of the programming team at the National Film theatre, specialising in the areas of film comedy and television. He was also a major contributor to the *Radio Times Guide to TV Comedy*.

LORIEN HAYNES is a freelance film journalist who reviews and interviews for *Elle*, *Red* and *Film Review* among other publications. A part-time actress, she has also written a screen adaptation of Elizabeth Gaskell's *North and South*, and two years ago was shortlisted for the LWT Drama Awards for her drama pilot *W11*.

TOM HUTCHINSON has been reviewing films for newspapers and trade magazines for 30 years. He worked with director J Lee Thompson on several scripts, including *The Men in the Cage*, has presented a programme about movies for Southern Television, and was a specialist question-setter for *Mastermind* on BBC TV and BBC Radio 4. His most recent book is *Rod Steiger: Memoirs of a Friendship*.

ALAN JONES has reviewed fantasy, horror and sci-fi movies for *Radio Times* since 1995 and is also London correspondent for the American magazine *Cinefantastique*. He has researched and written numerous programmes for television, including two Film Four documentaries on the Italian horror directors Mario Bava and Dario Argento. He also reviews films regularly on TV and radio.

ROBYN KARNEY is a former critic and interviewer for *Empire* magazine. She was editor-in-chief of *The Chronicle of the Cinema*, supervising and contributing editor of *Who's Who in Hollywood*, editor of the Octopus series of studio histories, including *The Hollywood Musical*, and of Ronald Bergan's biographies of Jean Renoir and Sergei Eisenstein. Her own books include *The Foreign Film Guide* with Ronald Bergan, *A Star Danced: the Life of Audrey Hepburn* and *A Singular Man: Burt Lancaster*.

ROBERT SELLERS is a lover of the horror, science-fiction, fantasy and action movie genres. He has written biographies of Sean Connery, Tom Cruise, Sigourney Weaver and Harrison Ford and has worked as a contributor for many newspapers and magazines including *NME*, *The Guardian*, *Film Review* and *She*.

TONY SLOMAN is a regular *Radio Times* film reviewer, but his vast historical film knowledge is most actively deployed in the film industry itself, where he works as a producer, screenwriter, editor and occasionally director. His film credits range from *Radio On*, *Cross of Iron* and *Chitty Chitty Bang Bang* to the cult TV series *The Prisoner*. Sloman is also a lecturer and broadcaster, and has recently completed a ten-year period as a governor of the British Film Institute. In addition, he holds a rare life membership of Bafta.

Contributing reviewers

Keith Bailey, Brian Baxter, Jason Caro, Angie Errigo, Peter Freedman, John Gammon, Scott Hamilton and Chris Holland, Sue Heal, Frances Lass, David McGillivray, John Marriott, Simon Rose, Tom Vallance

Editorial team

Edited by Kilmeny Fane-Saunders
Consulting editors Sue Oates, David Parkinson
Sub-editors Jane Anderson, Jeremy Aspinall, Caroline Bullough, Nick Funnell, David Oppedisano, Neil Smith, Susannah Straughan
Database designed by Mark Ginns

Sources

Certain data published under licence from Baseline II Inc.
Certain data published under licence from the British Board of Film Classification.
Some material is verified from the *Motion Picture Guide*, published by Cinebooks, New York, with kind permission.

A–Z of films

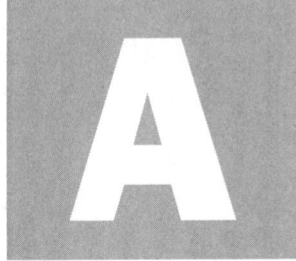

A Bout de Souffle ★★★★★ PG

Drama   1959 · Fr · BW · 86mins

Inspired by *Gun Crazy*, Joseph H Lewis's B-movie *film noir*, and made with the assistance of François Truffaut and Claude Chabrol, this was the keystone of the French New Wave. A homage to such fatalistic heroes as Jean Gabin and Humphrey Bogart, Jean-Luc Godard's masterpiece employed just about every cinematic trick associated with the *nouvelle vague*: location shooting, direct sound, hand-held footage (masterfully shot by Raoul Coutard), jump cuts, in-jokes and visual tributes to master film-makers. Jean-Paul Belmondo is superbly shambolic as the petty thief whose brief dalliance with American newspaper vendor Jean Seberg precipitates his demise. Costing just F90,000, the film's influence is incalculable. In French with English subtitles. 🎦

Jean-Paul Belmondo *Michel Poiccard/Laszlo Kovacs* • Jean Seberg *Patricia Franchini* • Van Doude *Journalist* • Daniel Boulanger *Police Inspector* • Henri-Jacques Huet *Antonio Berrutti* • Liliane Robin *Minouche* • Claude Mansard *Claudius Mansard* • Roger Hanin *Carl Zombach* • Jean-Pierre Melville *Parvulesco* • Richard Balducci *Tolmatchoff* • Jean-Luc Godard *Informer* ■ *Dir* Jean-Luc Godard • *Scr* Jean-Luc Godard, from a story by François Truffaut • *Cinematographer* Raoul Coutard

A la Place du Coeur ★★ 15

Romantic drama   1998 · Fr · Colour · 112mins

Adapted from James Baldwin's novel *If Beale Street Could Talk*, Robert Guédiguian's follow-up to his acclaimed breakthrough picture, *Marius et Jeannette*, came as a surprise to many. Yet, for all its good intentions and the committed naturalism of the performances, this slice-of-life tale, about a white teenager (Laure Raoust) who embarks on an affair with a jailed young black (Alexandre Ogou), rings hollow. Guédiguian is reunited with regular co-stars Ariane Ascaride and Gérard Meylan, and the themes of tolerance and reformation are worth exploring. However, there's an insistent preachiness to this interracial romance, which not only has nothing new to say but takes a long time saying it. In French with English subtitles. Contains swearing, nudity and sexual references.

Ariane Ascaride *Marianne* • Christine Brucher *Francine* • Jean-Pierre Darrousian *Joel* • Gérard Meylan *Franck* • Alexandre Ogou *Bébé* • Laure Raoust *Clim* ■ *Dir* Robert Guédiguian • *Scr* Jean-Louis Milesi, Robert Guédiguian, from the novel *If Beale Street Could Talk* by James Baldwin

A Nous la Liberté ★★★

Satire   1931 · Fr · BW · 96mins

Director René Clair's classic satire on modern life tells of an escaped convict who ends up running a gramophone factory and is then blackmailed by his cell-mate. Both end up as vagabonds. Made during the Depression, it chimed with audiences at the time who loved its mixture of music, comedy and radical politics. Clair's imagery of mass production with human automatons, led to the film to being banned by the left-wing government of Hungary and the right-wing government of Portugal. It was also the inspiration for Chaplin's *Modern Times*, and when Clair's producer wanted to take out a legal action for plagiarism, the director refused, saying he felt flattered rather than the victim of stylistic burglary. In French with English subtitles.

Henri Marchand *Emile* • Raymond Cordy *Louis* • Rolla France *Jeanne* • Paul Olivier *Paul Imaque* • Shelly Jacques *Paul* • André Michaud *Foreman* • Germaine Aussey *Maud* • Alexandre D'Arcy [Alex D'Arcy] *Gigolo* ■ *Dir/Scr* René Clair

A Propos de Nice ★★★★

Silent experimental documentary
1930 · Fr · BW · 27mins

At a time when documentarists across Europe were making "city symphonies", the French director Jean Vigo produced this delightful Riviera rhapsody. Vigo was one of the great screen poets, but the inspiration for this playful portrait clearly comes from the montage experiments of cinematographer Boris Kaufman's older brother, Dziga Vertov, the Polish director of the hugely influential *Man with a Movie Camera*. Brilliantly using transitions and parallel cutting, Vigo throws in some superb sequences, such as the sunbather turning into a skeleton and promenaders becoming strutting animals. Most famously, he employed a series of dissolves to strip a woman, a scene that was originally cut by British censors.

Dir/Scr Jean Vigo • *Cinematographer* Boris Kaufman

A Toute Vitesse ★★ 18

Drama   1996 · Fr · Colour · 81mins

Gaël Morel's directorial debut adheres closely to the theme of disaffected youth that inspired the film in which he made his name, André Téchiné's *Les Roseaux Sauvages*. He even recruits his co-star, Elodie Bouchez, to hold together a picture that admirably captures the language and attitudes of modern teenagers, before opting for some disappointingly formulaic resolutions. Pascal Cervo, as the Lyons adolescent embarking upon his first novel, is upstaged by the more abrasive Stéphane Rideau, who bitterly resents Meziane Bardadi, the gay Algerian Cervo plans to immortalise in print. Patchy, but occasionally provocative. In French with English subtitles. Contains swearing, nudity and violence.

Elodie Bouchez *Julie* • Pascal Cervo *Quentin* • Stéphane Rideau *Jimmy* • Meziane Bardadi *Samir* • Romain Auger *Rick* • Salim Kechiouche *Jamel* ■ *Dir* Gaël Morel • *Scr* Gaël Morel, Catherine Corsini

Aaron Loves Angela ★★★

Romance   1975 · US · Colour · 99mins

The son of one of African-American cinema's leading pioneers, Gordon Parks Jr was best known for *Superfly* when he took this unexpected detour from hard hitting blaxploitation. Set in Harlem, its combination of star-crossed romance, gang rivalry and urban deprivation invites comparisons with *West Side Story*, especially as the girl is a Puerto Rican. But the focus isn't restricted to Irene Cara and her black beau, Kevin Hooks, as the director adds coarse comedy, the music of Jose Feliciano and uncompromising action to the explosive mixture. Parks was killed in 1979 in a plane crash while scouting locations in Kenya. In French with English subtitles.

Kevin Hooks *Aaron* • Irene Cara *Angela* • Moses Gunn *Ike* • Robert Hooks *Beau* • Ernestine Jackson *Cleo* • Leon Pinkney *Willie* ■ *Dir* Gordon Parks Jr • *Scr* Gerald Sanford

Abandon Ship! ★★★

Drama   1957 · US · Colour · 99mins

Known as *Seven Waves Away* in the UK, this seaborne drama has Tyrone Power in charge of a lifeboat filled to the gunwhales with people who survive the sinking of a liner in the South Atlantic. Power decides that the injured and helpless must be thrown overboard and this makes him a hero until a rescue ship appears, when everyone feels guilty at what has happened. Like Hitchcock's earlier *Lifeboat*, it's set entirely at sea with moral problems floating like flotsam among the cast of familiar British stalwarts such as Gordon Jackson, Moira Lister and Noel Willman.

Tyrone Power *Alec Holmes* • Mai Zetterling *Julie* • Lloyd Nolan *Frank Kelly* • Stephen Boyd *Will McKinley* • Moira Lister *Edith Middleton* • James Hayter *"Cookie" Morrow* • Marie Lohr *Mrs Knudson* • Moultrie Kelsall *Daniel Cane* • Noel Willman *Aubrey Clark* • Gordon Jackson *John Merritt* • Clive Morton *Major General Barrington* • Laurence Naismith *Captain Darrow* • John Stratton *"Sparks" Clary* • Victor Maddern *Willie Hawkins* ■ *Dir/Scr* Richard Sale

ABBA The Movie ★★★ U

Music documentary
1977 · Swe/Ausl · Colour · 96mins

With the release of *The Adventures of Priscilla, Queen of the Desert*, *Muriel's Wedding*, numerous bestselling books and expert fakers Bjorn Again constantly gigging, the 1974 Eurovision Song Contest winners enjoyed a real revival in the nineties. This visual record of the Swedish superstars' 1977 Australian tour shows why they were billed as the most popular group in the world and became the pinnacle of kitsch glam. There is a story, involving a journalist desperate to secure an interview with the band, but really it's just an excuse to hear every major hit, from *Waterloo* to *Dancing Queen*. Sing along and say, "Thank you for the music". test *amrk* test. 🎦

Robert Hughes *Ashley* • Tom Oliver *Bodyguard/Bartender/Taxi driver* • Bruce Barry *Radio station manager* • Stig Anderson *Manager* ■ *Dir/Scr* Lasse Hallström

Abbott and Costello in Society ★★

Comedy   1944 · US · BW · 75mins

This very average Abbott and Costello flick relies too much on slapstick gags which don't seem as funny today as they did during the war. The same can be said for the plot, which has Bud and Lou as two dumb plumbers who gatecrash a posh weekend party. There's some charming fluff involving forties vocalist Marion Hutton (Betty's sister) as a taxi driver with the hots for Kirby Grant. Generally, however, the picture totters from one gag routine to the next, while it's disturbing to discover that substantial footage from the WC Fields classic *Never Give a Sucker an Even Break* was hijacked to boost the production values of the chase sequences.

Bud Abbott *Eddie Harrington* • Lou Costello *Albert Mansfield* • Marion Hutton *Elsie Hammerdingle* • Kirby Grant *Peter Evans* • Anne Gillis [Ann Gillis] *Gloria Winthrop* • Arthur Treacher *Pipps the butler* • Thomas Gomez *Drexel* • George Dolenz *Baron Sergei* ■ *Dir* Jean Yarbrough • *Scr* John Grant, Edmund L Hartmann, Hal Fimberg, Sid Fields, from a story by Hugh Wedlock Jr, Howard Snyder

Abbott and Costello in Hollywood ★★ U

Comedy   1945 · US · BW · 82mins

This typical Abbott and Costello vehicle offers some interesting behind-the-scenes glimpses of MGM at work; the film also includes guest appearances by the likes of Lucille Ball, Jackie "Butch" Jenkins and director Robert Z Leonard. The plot has Bud and Lou as a barber and shoeshine boy respectively, attempting to be Hollywood agents, though it's just a peg on which to hang a series of comic routines. The pace is smart and the running time is short. but if you don't like the duo it won't make any difference.

Bud Abbott *Buzz Kurtis* • Lou Costello *Abercrombie* • Frances Rafferty *Claire Warren* • Robert Stanton *Jeff Parker* • Jean Porter *Ruthie* • Warner Anderson *Norman Royce* • Mike Mazurki *Klondike Pete* ■ *Dir* S Sylvan Simon • *Scr* Nat Perrin, Lou Breslow

Abbott and Costello Meet Frankenstein ★★★

Comedy   1948 · US · BW · 83mins

Bud and Lou often just weren't funny enough by themselves. So Universal International set up a series of confrontations from the horror films that had been such a success for the studio in the thirties. This was one of the naively funniest, with the boys delivering crates to a wax museum (of course) unaware that their consignment contains Count Dracula and Frankenstein's monster. Bela Lugosi and Lon Chaney Jr as the Wolf Man play it straight enough to be naturally comic, so the real comedians end up as stooges.

Bud Abbott *Chick* • Lou Costello *Wilbur* • Lon Chaney Jr *Lawrence Talbot/the Wolf Man* • Bela Lugosi *Dracula* • Glenn Strange *The Monster* • Lenore Aubert *Sandra Mornay* • Jane Randolph *Joan Raymond* • Frank Ferguson *Mr McDougal* • Charles Bradstreet *Dr Steven* ■ *Dir* Charles T Barton [Charles

   U = SUITABLE FOR ALL   Uc = SUITABLE FOR ALL, ESPECIALLY FOR YOUNG CHILDREN (VIDEO ONLY)   PG = PARENTAL GUIDANCE

Barton] • *Scr* Robert Lees, Frederic Rinaldo, John Grant, from the novel *Frankenstein* by Mary Shelley

Abbott and Costello Meet the Killer, Boris Karloff ★★

Comedy mystery   1949 · US · BW · 94mins

This sort of title really should have caught on. Picture, if you will, "Bill and Ted Meet the Terminator, Arnold Schwarzenegger". The only snag is that Boris Karloff is not the killer. In fact, he's scarcely in the movie at all, although his charlatan swami does have the best scenes, notably the one in which he urges the mesmerised Lou Costello to top himself. The rest of this wobbly whodunit revolves around bellboy Lou being scared out of his ample skin by clues that have vanished before hotel detective Bud Abbott lays eyes on them. Worth a watch for Boris.

Bud Abbott *Casey Edwards* • Lou Costello *Freddie Phillips* • Boris Karloff *Swami Talpur* • Lenore Aubert *Angela Gordon* • Gar Moore *Jeff Wilson* ■ *Dir* Charles T Barton [Charles Barton] • *Scr* Hugh Wedlock Jr, John Grant, Howard Snyder

Abbott and Costello in the Foreign Legion ★★ U

Comedy   1950 · US · BW · 79mins

Between meeting Bela Lugosi and the Invisible Man, Abbott and Costello took time out to cavort on existing sets on Universal's backlot, and they could well have done with some scriptwriting help. The duo were also beginning to show their age physically, and Lou in particular was starting to look a little grotesque. The target audience for this outing seems younger than usual, and small fry will certainly enjoy all those mirage gags. Adults might not be quite so undemanding. Double bill fare, really.

Bud Abbott *Jonesy* • Lou Costello *Lou Hotchkiss* • Patricia Medina *Nicole* • Walter Slezak *Axmann* • Douglass Dumbrille *Hamud El Khalid* ■ *Dir* Charles Lamont • *Scr* Leonard Stern, John Grant, Martin Ragaway, from a story by DD Beauchamp

Abbott and Costello Meet the Invisible Man ★★ U

Comedy   1951 · US · BW · 82mins

Bungling private eyes Bud and Lou are hired by boxer Arthur Franz to get him off a murder rap in this acceptable timepasser from the team's regular director Charles Lamont. There is a modicum of mystery beneath the thin layer of comedy, and the highlight is a boxing bout in which Bud gets an invisible hand to hold off the champ.

Bud Abbott *Bud Alexander* • Lou Costello *Lou Francis* • Nancy Guild *Helen Gray* • Arthur Franz *Tommy Nelson* • Adele Jergens *Boots Marsden* • Sheldon Leonard *Morgan* • William Frawley *Detective Roberts* • Gavin Muir *Dr Philip Gray* ■ *Dir* Charles Lamont • *Scr* Robert Lees, Frederic I Rinaldo, John Grant, from the novel *The Invisible Man* by HG Wells

Abbott and Costello Meet Captain Kidd ★★ U

Comedy   1952 · US · Colour · 70mins

A rare colour outing for Bud and Lou as they are shanghaied by pirate Charles Laughton in his race for buried loot with Hillary Brooke's Anne Bonney. Slapsticking way below even their usual standard, the boys are as much use on the treasure hunt as a map without an X, while Laughton shamelessly spoofs his performance as Captain Bligh in the 1935 version of *Mutiny on the Bounty*.

Bud Abbott *Rocky Stonebridge* • Lou Costello *Oliver "Puddin' Head" Johnson* • Charles Laughton *Captain Kidd* • Hillary Brooke *Captain Bonney* • Fran Warren *Lady Jane* • Bill Shirley *Bruce Martingale* • Leif Erickson *Morgan* ■ *Dir* Charles Lamont • *Scr* Howard Dimsdale, John Grant

Abbott and Costello Go to Mars ★ U

Comedy   1953 · US · BW · 76mins

Bud and Lou actually go to Venus – not Mars. Having run out of exotic backgrounds on earth, the duo board a spaceship and think they've landed on Mars when they're in the middle of the New Orleans Mardi Gras. Hijacked by a couple of bank robbers, they escape to Venus, which is populated solely by former Miss Universe contestants under Mari Blanchard as Queen Allura. No matter how far they travelled, the stars' comic inventiveness was at a standstill and the tired routines won't have improved with age.

Bud Abbott *Lester* • Lou Costello *Orville* • Robert Paige *Dr Wilson* • Mari Blanchard *Allura* • Martha Hyer *Janie* • Horace McMahon *Mugsy* • Jack Kruschen *Harry* • Jean Willes *Captain* • Joe Kirk *Dr Orvilla* • Jack Tesler *Dr Holtz* • Anita Ekberg *Venusian woman* ■ *Dir* Charles Lamont • *Scr* DD Beauchamp, John Grant, from a story by Howard Christie, DD Beauchamp

Abbott and Costello Meet Dr Jekyll and Mr Hyde ★★★

Comedy   1953 · US · BW · 76mins

It sounds like the double date from hell, but this is one of Bud and Lou's livelier outings. The boys play a couple of sacked cops who hope to impress Inspector Reginald Denny by capturing the monster that is terrorising London. There are even a couple of laughs in the wax museum and rooftop chase scenes, although the romance between Helen Wescott and Craig Stevens slows things down a touch. Boris Karloff juicily hams up the roles of the mad scientist and his alter ego, making Jekyll seem every bit as sinister as Hyde.

Bud Abbott *Slim* • Lou Costello *Tubby* • Boris Karloff *Dr Jekyll/Mr Hyde* • Helen Wescott *Vicky Edwards* • Craig Stevens *Bruce Adams* • Reginald Denny *Inspector* ■ *Dir* Charles Lamont • *Scr* Lee Loeb, John Grant, from the novel *The Strange Case of Dr Jekyll and Mr Hyde* by Robert Louis Stevenson

Abbott and Costello Meet the Keystone Cops ★★ U

Comedy   1955 · US · BW · 78mins

A meeting some might want to miss. Intimidating Bud and slaphappy Lou are sold a rundown film studio in the early days of Hollywood, though they turn out to be better stuntmen than producers. Inept timing stifles the gags, but the chase finale is up there with the best of the original Keystones. However, the real interest lies in a guest appearance from Mack Sennett – the comedy giant from a time when silence really was golden.

Bud Abbott *Harry Pierce* • Lou Costello *Willie Piper* • Fred Clark *Joseph Gorman/Sergei Trumanoff* • Lynn Bari *Leota Van Cleef* • Frank Wilcox *Snavely* • Maxie Rosenbloom *Hinds* • Henry Kulky *Brakeman* • Sam Flint *Conductor* • Mack Sennett ■ *Dir* Charles Lamont • *Scr* John Grant, from a story by Lee Cobb

Abbott and Costello Meet the Mummy ★ U

Comedy   1955 · US · BW · 79mins

Abbott and Costello ended 15 years at Universal with this dismal low-budget attempt to excavate some humour from a story of buried treasure in Egypt. Having run through the rest of the studio's horror gallery earlier, Bud and Lou now stir up the Mummy (here played by minor actor Eddie Parker) who's a rather lifeless figure compared to the likes of Dracula and the Wolf Man. At least veteran character actress Marie Windsor brings waspish authority to her role of villainess.

Bud Abbott *Peter* • Lou Costello *Freddie* • Marie Windsor *Madame Rontru* • Michael Ansara *Charlie* • Dan Seymour *Josef* • Kurt Katch *Dr Zomer* • Richard Karlan *Hetsut* • Richard Deacon *Semu* • Eddie Parker *Klaris, the mummy* ■ *Dir* Charles Lamont • *Scr* John Grant, from a story by Lee Loeb

Abby ★★

Blaxploitation horror
1974 · US · Colour · 89mins

Noted Shakespearean actor William Marshall (*Blacula*) unleashes the evil African spirit of Eshu in this virtual copy of *The Exorcist*, made for the blaxploitation market by hack director William Girdler. Following Marshall to America, Eshu possesses minister's wife Carol Speed, who predictably starts talking dirty, sleeping around and vomiting. Speed's ridiculous make-up allows her to scream and flail about but little else, and everything is played with such a straight face that the film soon becomes unintentionally hilarious. (Check out the disco exorcism!) Successful legal action by Warner Bros makes this sluggish addition to the black-slanted genre a difficult-to-see seventies artefact.

William Marshall *Bishop Garnet Williams* • Carol Speed *Abby Williams* • Terry Carter *Reverend Emmett Williams* • Austin Stoker *Cass Potter* • Juanita Moore *Mama Potter* ■ *Dir* William Girdler • *Scr* G Cornell Layne, from a story by William Girdler, Gordon C Layne [G Cornell Layne]

The Abdication ★★

Historical drama
1974 · UK · Colour · 100mins

Liv Ullmann steps into Garbo's shoes by playing Queen Christina, who abdicates the Swedish throne and heads for Rome, wanting to be accepted as a Catholic and undergoing a searching inquisition from Cardinal Peter Finch. Having already played Pope Joan and fresh from *Lost Horizon*, Ullmann looks as if she's about to break into a schmaltzy song. Anthony Harvey directs, presumably in the hope of turning this piece of stodge into another *Lion in Winter*.

Peter Finch *Cardinal Azzolino* • Liv Ullmann *Queen Christina* • Cyril Cusack *Oxenstierna* • Graham Crowden *Cardinal Barberini* • Michael Dunn *The Dwarf* • Lewis Fiander *Father Dominic* • Kathleen Byron *Queen Mother* • James Faulkner *Magnus* • Ania Marson *Ebba Sparre* ■ *Dir* Anthony Harvey • *Scr* Ruth Wolff, from her play

Abduction ★★

Erotic crime drama
1975 · US · Colour · 94mins

A low-budget curiosity, mainly because of its striking similarities with the real-life Patty Hearst case. In this one, Judith-Marie Bergan is a poor little rich girl who gets a radical makeover when she is kidnapped by American urban terrorists. It's exploitational fare, with politics largely taking a back seat, and it's not exactly a high point in the careers of movie veterans Dorothy Malone and Lawrence Tierney.

Judith-Marie Bergan *Patricia* • David Pendleton *Dory* • Gregory Rozakis *Frank* • Leif Erickson *Mr Prescott* • Dorothy Malone *Mrs Prescott* • Lawrence Tierney *FBI agent* • Presley Caton *Angie* • Catherine Lacy *Carol* ■ *Dir* Joseph Zito • *Scr* Kent E Carroll, from the book *Black Abductor* by Harrison James

Abduction of Innocence ★★ 12

Drama   1996 · US · Colour · 86mins

There are shades of *A Life Less Ordinary* and *Excess Baggage* in the plot of this otherwise routinely bland TV thriller, in which a ruthless businessman is shocked to discover that his precious daughter has been kidnapped. However, is she really in danger, or is daddy being led up the garden path? Fans of TV's *The A-Team* may be curious to see how Dirk Benedict has aged here, but there is little in the way of suspense or thrills. Contains some swearing. ▭

Dirk Benedict *Robert Steves* • Lucie Arnaz *Helen Steves* • Katie Wright *Clare* • Lochlyn Munro *Eddie Spencer* • Conor O'Farrell *Loomis* ■ *Dir* James A Contner • *Scr* Derek Marlowe

Abe Lincoln in Illinois ★★★

Historical drama   1940 · US · BW · 110mins

Henry Fonda had just played the young Abraham Lincoln in John Ford's movie. Now it was the turn of Raymond Massey, who repeats his stage performance from the popular Robert Sherwood play. The 30-year span of the story rather lumbers along but Massey conveys the private complexity of the man as well as his public eloquence, though the film was an expensive flop at the box office. Massey played Lincoln again – ever so briefly – in *How the West Was Won*.

Raymond Massey *Abraham Lincoln* • Gene Lockhart *Stephen Douglas* • Ruth Gordon *Mary Todd Lincoln* • Mary Howard *Ann Rutledge* • Dorothy Tree *Elizabeth Edwards* • Harvey Stephens *Ninian Edwards* • Minor Watson *Joshua Speed* • Alan Baxter *Billy Herndon* ■ *Dir* John Cromwell • *Scr* Grover Jones, Robert E Sherwood, from the play by Robert E Sherwood

Abel ★★★ 15

Black comedy 1986 · Neth · Colour · 102mins

Abel, played by writer/director Alex van Warmerdam, is a 31-year-old man who has never left home – literally. After

failing to make progress with doctors and psychiatrists, his strict father attempts to teach him basic social skills by introducing a female into the household. Abel is accused of having an affair and gets thrown out on to the streets, where he meets a kind-hearted stripper. This weird Dutch film about obsessive family values comes across as a more benign version of cult favourite *Bad Boy Bubby*, resulting in a classy rite-of-passage comedy full of whimsical amusement. In Dutch with English subtitles.

Alex van Warmerdam *Abel* • Henri Garcin *Abel's father* • Olga Zuiderhoek *Abel's mother* • Annet Malherbe • Loos Luca ■ *Dir/Scr* Alex van Warmerdam

Abel Gance's Beethoven ★★★

Biographical romance 1936 · Fr · BW · 115mins

Abel Gance, the great Romantic of French cinema, idolised Ludwig van Beethoven, the great Romantic of German music. Unfortunately, the loss of sound for Beethoven and the coming of sound for Gance were almost equally agonising. Gance was not at his best with dialogue, as this rather leaden biopic demonstrates. But it does have the expected visual flourishes, such as the poignant sequence when the hero loses his hearing, revealed by the silent shots of violins, bells and birds singing. Originally titled *The Life and Loves of Beethoven*, the film relates how the composer loves a girl who ignores him; then another wins his heart. The powerful actor Harry Baur is well cast as Beethoven. A French language film.

Harry Baur *Ludwig van Beethoven* • Annie Ducaux *Thérèse de Brunswick* • Jany Holt *Giulietta Glucciardi* • Jean-Louis Barrault *Karl* • Jane Marken *Esther* • Jean Debucourt *Le Comte Gallenberg* ■ *Dir* Abel Gance • *Scr* Steve Passeur, Abel Gance

Aberration ★★ 18

Science-fiction horror thriller 1997 · Ausl/NZ · Colour · 89mins

New Zealand has produced more than its fair share of cult horror favourites (Peter Jackson's early films, *The Ugly*, *Jack Be Nimble*), but this chiller about lethal lizards is a more formulaic affair. The setting is a remote wooded area, where the local wildlife has has been wiped out by a mysterious force. The culprits turn out to be cunning, mutant reptiles who soon start tucking into human meat as well. Only Pamela Gidley and Simon Bossell stand in their way. Director Tim Boxell lays on lashings of gags and gore, but it is all very derivative. Contains some swearing, nudity and violence.

Pamela Gidley *Amy* • Simon Bossell *Marshall* • Valery Nikolaev *Uri* • Norman Forsey *Mr Peterson* • Helen Moulder *Mrs Miller* ■ *Dir* Tim Boxell • *Scr* Darrin Oura, Scott Lew

Abie's Irish Rose ★★ U

Silent comedy 1928 · US · BW · 108mins

A maudlin silent version of Anne Nichols's hit Broadway play about an Irish girl who marries a Jewish boy and starts up a feud between their two families. Directed by Victor Fleming, who would make *Gone with the Wind* a decade later, the film was mightily berated by the *New Yorker*, whose critic, the waspish Dorothy Parker, wrote: "They gave me the best view... they put me behind a post."

Jean Hersholt *Solomon Levy* • Charles Rogers *Abie Levy* • Nancy Carroll *Rosemary Murphy* • J Farrell MacDonald *Patrick Murphy* • Bernard Gorcey *Isaac Cohen* • Ida Kramer *Mrs Isaac Cohen* • Nick Cogley *Father Whalen* • Camillus Pretal *Rabbi Jacob Samuels* ■ *Dir* Victor Fleming • *Scr* Julian Johnson, Herman Mankiewicz, from the play by Anne Nichols

Abie's Irish Rose ★★ U

Comedy 1946 · US · BW · 96mins

Eighteen years after Victor Fleming's silent version, this tale of a Jewish boy and an Irish girl who fall in love seems even more dumb and sluggish in this mawkish makeover from producer Bing Crosby and director Edward Sutherland. Joanne Dru, Richard Norris and Michael Chekhov head the cast, while the screenplay is by the original playwright, Anne Nichols – not that it helps, though.

Joanne Dru *Rosemary* • Richard Norris *Abie* • Michael Chekhov *Solomon Levy* • JM Kerrigan *Patrick Murphy* • George E Stone *Isaac Cohen* • Vera Gordon *Mrs Cohen* • Emory Parnell *Father Whalen* • Art Baker *Rabbi Samuels* • Eric Blore *Hotel manager* ■ *Dir* Edward Sutherland [A Edward Sutherland] • *Scr* Anne Nichols, from her play • *Producer* Bing Crosby

Abigail's Party ★★★★★ PG

Comedy 1977 · UK · Colour · 102mins

A quintessential probe into the stiff British middle classes from director Mike Leigh, who cuts a scalpel-sharp swathe through seventies social mores and pretensions. Alison Steadman gives a masterful portrayal as Beverly, the hostess with the mostest neuroses, who invites some neighbours over for drinks and then proceeds to needle and cajole them with insensitive remarks as she gets drunker and more self-pitying. Painful, agonising and absolutely hilarious, the tension rises as Beverly plays Demis Roussos songs, shows off her spit roast oven and emasculates her snob workaholic husband with obnoxious glee. Although ultimately depressing, this fascinating portrait of suburban angst is a bittersweet masterpiece of manners and seething emotions.

Alison Steadman *Beverly* • Tim Stern *Laurence* • Janine Duvitski *Angela* • John Salthouse *Tony* • Harriet Reynolds *Susan* ■ *Dir* Mike Leigh • *Scr* Mike Leigh, from his play

Abilene Town ★★★

Western 1945 · US · BW · 91mins

Randolph Scott made virtually nothing but westerns after the Second World War and in this early example he's the marshal of Abilene, the town where the cattle drives end. Bringing prosperity as well as trouble, the rowdy cowboys dare to disturb the church service with their six-gun salute to Ann Dvorak's singing in the local saloon. Based on a novel by Ernest Haycox (who also co-wrote the screenplay for *Stagecoach*), it's a lively stew of rather familiar confrontations, with a spirited Rhonda Fleming as the grocer's daughter who tries to keep Scott from doing what a man has to do.

Randolph Scott *Dan Mitchell* • Ann Dvorak *Rita* • Edgar Buchanan *Bravo Trimble* • Rhonda Fleming *Sherry Balder* • Lloyd Bridges *Henry Dreiser* • Helen Boice *Big Annie* • Howard Freeman *Ed Balder* • Richard Hale *Charlie Fair* • Jack Lambert *Jet Younger* ■ *Dir* Edwin L Marin • *Scr* Harold Shumate, from the novel *Trail Town* by Ernest Haycox

The Abominable Dr Phibes ★★★★ 15

Horror 1971 · UK · Colour · 90mins

Vincent Price's role as an ex-vaudevillian madman living in a secret underground mechanical world is his only self-originated monster and is superbly tailored for the horror maestro. Phibes is a deformed maniac with a florid sense of style and an inclination to ham, who concocts a divinely ingenious revenge, gruesomely inspired by ancient plagues, on the surgeons he holds responsible for the death of his wife. Full of gaudy Art Deco excess, surprise charm and sardonic violence, this deadpan send-up is a classy delight. Originally billed with the tag-line "Love means never having to say you're ugly"!

Vincent Price *Dr Anton Phibes* • Joseph Cotten *Dr Vesalius* • Hugh Griffith *Rabbi* • Terry-Thomas *Dr Longstreet* • Virginia North *Vulnavia* • Aubrey Woods *Goldsmith* • Susan Travers *Nurse Allan* • Alex Scott *Dr Hargreaves* • Peter Gilmore *Dr Kitaj* • Edward Burnham *Dr Dunwoody* • Peter Jeffrey *Inspector Trout* • Maurice Kaufman *Dr Whitcombe* ■ *Dir* Robert Fuest • *Scr* James Whiton, William Goldstein

The Abominable Snowman ★★★

Horror 1957 · UK · BW · 90mins

Based on Nigel (*Quatermass*) Kneale's television play, this subtle Hammer horror follows two men with opposing views who go on a Yeti expedition to the Himalayas. Gun-runner Forrest Tucker plans to capture and exploit the legendary creature, while botanist Peter Cushing thinks research is more important. The man-beast turns out to have a surprise for both in this gripping slice of monster macabre. Tensely directed by Val Guest, the film uses eerie claustrophobia to convey a taut paranoid atmosphere that makes you overlook the fakeness of the studio-built mountains.

Forrest Tucker *Tom Friend* • Peter Cushing *Dr John Rollason* • Maureen Connell *Helen Rollason* • Richard Wattis *Peter Fox* • Robert Brown *Ed Shelley* • Michael Brill *Andrew McNee* ■ *Dir* Val Guest • *Scr* Nigel Kneale, from his TV play

About Last Night... ★★★ 18

Comedy drama 1986 · US · Colour · 108mins

Rob Lowe and Demi Moore star in this eighties look at the lifestyles and lovestyles of young city professionals, directed by Edward Zwick, who went on to make *Glory* and *Legends of the Fall*. The film is based on David Mamet's play *Sexual Perversity in Chicago*, though you'd hardly know it, since it is a far slicker affair than Mamet would ever produce. Yet it does retain at least some of the playwright's insight and intelligence, while also providing its ration of entertainment. Lowe and Moore do well as the on-again, off-again partners, although it is James Belushi, in an over-the-top supporting performance his brother John would have been proud of, who all but walks off with the show. Contains swearing and nudity. DVD

Rob Lowe *Danny Martin* • Demi Moore *Debbie Sullivan* • James Belushi *Bernie Litko* • Elizabeth Perkins *Joan* • George DiCenzo *Mr Favio* • Michael Alldredge *Mother Malone* • Robin Thomas *Steve Carlson* • Donna Gibbons *Alex* ■ *Dir* Edward Zwick • *Scr* Tim Kazurinsky, Denise DeClue, from the play *Sexual Perversity in Chicago* by David Mamet

About Mrs Leslie ★★ U

Romantic drama 1954 · US · BW · 103mins

Broadway star Shirley Booth had won the best actress Oscar for re-creating her stage role in *Come Back, Little Sheba* opposite a far-too-young Burt Lancaster, and it was a good two years before this follow-up vehicle appeared. The melodramatic tale tells the story in flashback of a couple of lovers who meet sporadically, spending time together once a year. Trouble is, he's the marvellously rugged Robert Ryan, and audiences may well wonder what on earth he sees in her. Distinguished film historian David Shipman called this "a very special film", but, despite the quality of the playing, this soap opera takes a lot of believing.

Shirley Booth *Mrs Vivien Leslie* • Robert Ryan *George Leslie* • Marjie Millar *Nadine Roland* • Alex Nicol *Ian McKay* • Sammy White *Harry Willey* • James Bell *Mr Poole* • Virginia Brissac *Mrs Poole* • Eileen Janssen [Eilene Janssen] *Pixie* ■ *Dir* Daniel Mann • *Scr* Ketti Frings, Hal Kanter, from the novel by Vina Delmar

About Sarah ★★★

Drama 1998 · US · Colour

Mary Steenburgen, Kellie Martin (Lucy Knight in *ER*) and Marion Ross (*Happy Days*) star in a family drama about Sarah, a mentally disabled, unmarried woman who lives with her devoted mother. When her parent suddenly dies, Sarah's daughter becomes her legal guardian – a dramatic turn of events that is not only challenged in court by an aunt, but may also prevent her daughter from attending medical school. A family dealing with mental disability is a TV movie staple, but if you like the stars you won't mind the journey. Steenburgen was nominated for a Screen Actors Guild award for her moving performance.

Kellie Martin *Mary Beth* • Mary Steenburgen *Sarah* • Diane Baker *Lila* • Nick Searcy *Johnny* • Steven Gilborn *Lew Roth* • Marion Ross *Rose* • Karen Rauch *Grace* ■ *Dir* Susan Rohrer • *Scr* Susan Rohrer, Nancey Silvers, from a story by Susan Rohrer

Above and Beyond ★

Second World War drama 1952 · US · BW · 122mins

Robert Taylor is given the job of dropping the Bomb on Hiroshima while his amour, Eleanor Parker, is moved into an army camp for security reasons, though she moves out because the laundry facilities aren't up to scratch. Poor dear, she hasn't been told what hubby's up to. It's all quite pathetic, really, trivialising a major historic event and patronising to women even in 1952.

16

U = SUITABLE FOR ALL Uc = SUITABLE FOR ALL, ESPECIALLY FOR YOUNG CHILDREN (VIDEO ONLY) PG = PARENTAL GUIDANCE

Robert Taylor (1) *Col Paul Tibbets* • Eleanor Parker *Lucy Tibbets* • James Whitmore *Maj Uanna* • Larry Keating *Maj Gen Vernon C Brent* • Larry Gates *Capt Parsons* • Marilyn Erskine *Marge Bratton* • Stephen Dunne *Maj Harry Bratton* • Robert Burton *Gen Samuel E Roberts* ■ *Dir* Melvin Frank, Norman Panama • *Scr* Beirne Lay Jr, Frank Panama

Above Suspicion ★★★★

Spy drama   1943 · US · BW · 90mins

Joan Crawford's presence is, for once, rather muted in this entertaining spy drama. Not only does she have to share star-billing with Fred MacMurray – they're honeymooning Americans caught up in espionage in pre-war Germany – but she also has to compete with the heel-clicking dynamism of Conrad Veidt and a marvellously villainous Basil Rathbone. So the star who could even upstage herself is considerably controlled, allowing the plot to gain proper prominence. The result is terrifically enjoyable escapism.

Joan Crawford *Frances Myles* • Fred MacMurray *Richard Myles* • Conrad Veidt *Hassert Seidel* • Basil Rathbone *Sig Von Aschenhausen* • Reginald Owen *Dr Mespelbrunn* • Richard Ainley *Peter Galt* • Cecil Cunningham *Countess* • Ann Shoemaker *Aunt Ellen* ■ *Dir* Richard Thorpe • *Scr* Keith Winter, Melville Baker, Patricia Coleman, from the novel by Helen MacInnes

Above Suspicion ★★★ 18

Crime drama   1995 · US · Colour · 91mins

An uncomfortable example of art imitating life in this classy straight-to-video thriller. Filmed before his tragic accident, Christopher Reeve plays a detective who becomes wheelchair bound after a bungled drugs raid. Together with wife Kim Cattrall, he plots an intricate insurance scam but things don't go according to plan. With the ever reliable Joe Mantegna in support, it's an enjoyably convoluted tale and director Steven Schachter handles the twists and turns with some skill. 🖵

Christopher Reeve *Dempsey* • Joe Mantegna *Rhinehart* • Kim Cattrall *Gail* • Edward Kerr *Nick* • Geoffrey Rivas *Enrique* • Finola Hughes *Iris* • William H Macy *Prosecutor (DA)* ■ *Dir* Steven Schachter • *Scr* Jerry Lazarus, William H Macy, Steven Schachter

Above the Rim ★★ 15

Sports drama   1994 · US · Colour · 93mins

Every hackneyed cliché is depressingly frog-marched before the camera in this sports-themed "gangsta ghetto" fare telling the tired tale of talented high school basketball player Duane Martin, torn between two friends on opposing sides of the law. One is drug-dealer Tupac Shakur who wants him playing on his tough inner-city team. The other is reluctant coach Leon, a former champion haunted by the death of his best friend. Crime or college? Which path will he choose? With no originality to commend it, director Jeff Pollack's saccharine saga relies on increasingly energetic basketball action to give it some pep. 🖵

Duane Martin *Kyle* • Leon *Shep* • Tupac Shakur *Birdie* • David Bailey *Rollins* • Tonya Pinkins *Mailika* • Marlon Wayans *Bugaloo* • Bernie Mac *Flip* • Byron Minns *Monroe* ■ *Dir*

Jeff Pollack • *Scr* Jeff Pollack, Barry Michael Cooper, from a story by Jeff Pollack, Benny Medina

Above Us the Waves ★★ U

Second World War drama
1955 · UK · BW · 95mins

Having failed with torpedoes, John Mills and his rookie crew set out in midget submarines to try and sink the German battleship *Tirpitz* in this rather disappointing Second World War action adventure. Riddled with stiff-upper-lipped stereotypes, this is one of those proud re-creations of an "against the odds" mission that were the staple of postwar British cinema. However, by opting to examine the cramped conditions of his characters rather than go overboard on their heroic exploits, director Ralph Thomas kills the pace of the picture, which he never recovers, even though the attack on Trondheim harbour should be a nail-biter. 🖵 **DVD**

John Mills *Commander Frazer* • John Gregson *Lieutenant Alec Duffy* • Donald Sinden *Lieutenant Tom Corbett* • James Robertson-Justice *Admiral Ryder* • Michael Medwin *Smart* • James Kenney *Abercrombie* • OE Hasse *Tirpitz Captain* • William Russell *Ramsey* • Thomas Heathcote *Hutchins* • Lee Patterson *Cox* • Theodore Bikel *German officer* • Anthony Newley *X2 engineer* ■ *Dir* Ralph Thomas • *Scr* Robin Estridge, from a story by CET Warren, James Benson

Abraham Lincoln ★★★ U

Drama   1930 · US · Tinted · 97mins

The last gasp of genius from the great silent film-maker, DW Griffith, this biopic of the American president has too much explanatory detail but boasts some remarkable visual set pieces. Written by Stephen Vincent Bené and Gerrit Lloyd, it stars Walter Huston as Lincoln and Una Merkel as his wife, and shows how the great man entered small-town politics before rising to the highest office in the land. Griffith was accused of racism in *The Birth of a Nation*; here, he shows a capacity for tolerance that beggars belief.

Walter Huston *Abraham Lincoln* • Una Merkel *Ann Rutledge* • Kay Hammond *Mary Todd Lincoln* • E Alyn Warren *Stephen Douglas* • Hobart Bosworth *Gen Robert E Lee* • Fred Warren *Gen US Grant* • Henry B Walthall *Col Marshall* • Frank Campeau *Gen Sheridan* ■ *Dir* DW Griffith • *Scr* Stephen Vincent Bené, Gerrit Lloyd • *Cinematographer* Karl Struss

Abraham Valley ★★★ PG

Drama   1993 · Por/Fr/Swi · Colour · 188mins

Manoel de Oliveira reworks Gustave Flaubert's *Madame Bovary* in this typically stylised outing from Europe's oldest active film-maker. In translating the story to a wine-growing region of modern day Portugal, novelist Augustina Bessa-Luis draws on her own acquaintances for inspiration. However, this is still very much the director's film, sprawling over its three hour duration like an epic cinematic poem. As the lame adulteress whose amours scandalise her staid community, Leonor Silveira is deliciously dolorous, while Luís Miguel Cintra is doggedly decent as the doctor she marries after a troubled childhood. In Portuguese with English subtitles.

Mário Barroso *Narrator* • Leonor Silveira *Ema Cardeano* • Cecile Sanz de Alba *Young Ema* • Luis Miguel Cintra *Carlos Paiva* • Rui de Carvalho *Paulino Cardeano* ■ *Dir* Manoel de Oliveira • *Scr* Manoel de Oliveira, from the novel *Vale Abraao* by Augustina Bessa-Luis

Abraxas ★ 15

Science-fiction adventure
1991 · Can · Colour · 86mins

Wrestler-turned-politician Jesse "the Body" Ventura is a 10,000-year-old law enforcer from the future in this cut-rate *Terminator*. His quest is to find renegade cop Sven-Ole Thorsen (doing a terrible Arnold Schwarzenegger impersonation) before he can kill his son who holds the key to universal peace. Aside from a lot of grunting, fighting and laser-gun shoot-outs in snowy landscapes, there's little on offer to either engage or entertain in this Canadian-made time-waster. 🖵

Jesse Ventura *Abraxas* • Sven-Ole Thorsen *Secundus* • Damian Lee *Dar* • Jerry Levitan *Hite* • Marjorie Bransfield *Sonia* • Ken Quinn *Carl* ■ *Dir* Damian Lee • *Scr* Damian Lee, David Mitchell

Abroad with Two Yanks ★★ U

Comedy   1944 · US · BW · 81mins

The two Yanks are loveable William Bendix and straight-up Dennis O'Keefe, and abroad is Australia, where the two marines find themselves competing for the attentions of the same woman, Helen Walker, best remembered today for her roles in *Nightmare Alley* and *The Big Combo*. It's likeable, lightweight stuff, without much substance, given great pace and comedic style by veteran Allan Dwan, director of over 400 features (some sources say 500!), who hit a very profitable period with star O'Keefe and such popular titles as *Up in Mabel's Room*, *Brewster's Millions* and *Getting Gertie's Garter*. Their partnership helped turn O'Keefe into a favourite of the forties.

William Bendix *Biff Koraski* • Helen Walker *Joyce Stuart* • Dennis O'Keefe *Jeff Reardon* • John Loder *Cyril North* • George Cleveland *Roderick Stuart* • Janet Lambert *Alice* • James Flavin *Sergeant Wiggins* • Arthur Hunnicutt *Arkie* ■ *Dir* Allan Dwan • *Scr* Charles Rogers, Wilkie Mahoney, Ted Sills

Absence of Malice ★★★ PG

Drama   1981 · US · Colour · 111mins

Tabloid hacks will probably ignore the attacks made on their profession in this big-issue drama, in which Miami reporter Sally Field defames honest businessman Paul Newman, mainly because it's too sluggishly worthy to make any real impact. Sydney Pollack's direction is simply monotonous, even if ex-newspaperman Kurt Luedtke's script makes all the right liberal noises as Sally Field's journalist is manipulated by government leaks about Newman's Mafia relatives. However, Melinda Dillon's performance as Newman's frightened alibi and the Newman–Field confrontation still make this well worth the time. Contains some strong language. 🖵

Paul Newman *Michael Gallagher* • Sally Field *Megan Carter* • Bob Balaban *Elliot Rosen* •

Melinda Dillon *Teresa* • Luther Adler *Malderone* • Barry Primus *Waddell* • Josef Sommer *McAdam* • John Harkins *Davidek* ■ *Dir* Sydney Pollack • *Scr* Kurt Luedtke

The Absent-Minded Professor ★★★ U

Fantasy comedy   1961 · US · BW · 98mins

With its second remake, *Flubber*, now released on video, here's a chance to see the original, a warm-hearted slice of Walt Disney-style Americana starring likeable Fred MacMurray as the inventor of flying rubber. Wicked Keenan Wynn wants to steal it, and that's about the nub of the flub. As always in Disney films of this period, there's much pleasure to be had from the supporting cast, which includes veteran clown Ed Wynn (father of Keenan), *Meet Me in St Louis's* Leon Ames and Elliott Reid, the long-forgotten leading man of *Gentlemen Prefer Blondes*. It's a shame the budget didn't stretch to colour, but the marvellous black-and-white image of the flubber-driven family car crossing the moon so inspired a young Steven Spielberg that he copied it to provide the most potent shot in *ET*, and eventually used it as the logo of his company, Amblin.

Fred MacMurray *Professor Ned Brainard* • Nancy Olson *Betsy Carlisle* • Keenan Wynn *Alonzo Hawk* • Tommy Kirk *Bill Hawk* • Leon Ames *Rufus Daggett* • Elliott Reid *Shelby Ashton* • Edward Andrews *Defence Secretary* • Wally Brown *Coach Elkins* ■ *Dir* Robert Stevenson • *Scr* Bill Walsh, from a story by Samuel W Taylor

Absent without Leave ★★★

Drama based on a true story
1993 · NZ · Colour · 95mins

This youngsters-on-the-run New Zealand road movie, set in 1942, has some sharp observations and unexpected insights to keep it from sagging into cliché. Conscript Craig McLachlan is rushed into marriage with pregnant girlfriend Katrina Hobbs and decides to take her on a hitch-hiking trip to her father 400 miles away. The army, though, takes a dim view of his desertion and pursues the couple. Sentimentality is never absent for very long, though the performances have a caring sensibility that keeps us rooting for the runaways.

Craig McLachlan *Ed* • Katrina Hobbs *Daisy* • Tony Barry *Peter* • Judie Douglass *Ella* • Robyn Malcolm *Betty* • David Copeland *Claude* ■ *Dir* John Laing • *Scr* James Edwards, Graeme Tetley

Absolute Beginners ★★ 15

Musical   1986 · UK · Colour · 102mins

A dismal attempt to turn Colin MacInnes's cult novel about the birth of the teenage nation in Britain into an eighties *Expresso Bongo* without the talents of Cliff Richard. Will fashion designer Patsy Kensit choose romance with trendy photographer Eddie O'Connell or toff couturier James Fox in this highly stylised view of fifties pop culture and changing social mores? You won't care in another rock 'n' roll swindle perpetrated by director Julien Temple. But songs by David Bowie, Ray Davies, Sade and the Style Council do help lighten the lively, if vacuous, load. And where else could you see the Notting Hill riots set to music! Contains some swearing.

Eddie O'Connell *Colin Young* • Patsy Kensit *Crepe Suzette* • David Bowie *Vendice Partners* • James Fox *Henley of Mayfair* • Ray Davies *Arthur* • Mandy Rice-Davies *Mum* • Steven Berkoff *Fanatic* • Sade *Athene Duncannon* ■ *Dir* Julien Temple • *Scr* Richard Burridge, Christopher Wicking, Don MacPherson, Michael Hamlyn, from the novel by Colin MacInnes

Absolute Power ★★★ 15

Crime drama   1996 · US · Colour · 116mins

Clint Eastwood had so much faith in this tale of absolute power corrupting absolutely that he directed, starred and co-wrote the music (with Lennie Niehaus). Clint plays veteran burglar Luther Whitney, who, during one last job, sees President Gene Hackman indulging in a spasm of sadistic sex that leads to a young woman's death. All the president's men try to track down Luther and his estranged daughter (Laura Linney), but he stays one step ahead of his pursuers. This ego trip gained unexpected topicality due to subsequent White House revelations. Contains some swearing, violence and nudity. ▭ **DVD**

Clint Eastwood *Luther Whitney* • Gene Hackman *President Richmond* • Ed Harris *Seth Frank* • Laura Linney *Kate Whitney* • Scott Glenn *Bill Burton* • Dennis Haysbert *Tim Collin* • Judy Davis *Gloria Russell* • EG Marshall *Walter Sullivan* • Alison Eastwood *Art Student* • Kimber Eastwood *White House tour guide* ■ *Dir* Clint Eastwood • *Scr* William Goldman, from the novel by David Baldacci

Absolute Strangers ★★★ PG

Drama based on a true story
1991 · US · Colour · 88mins

Henry Winkler will for ever be remembered for playing the Fonz, the epitome of cool, in the sitcom *Happy Days*. In this TV movie he makes an effective stab at a more serious role, a moving story about a man forced to choose between saving the life of his pregnant wife, comatose after a car crash, and their unborn child, while anti-abortionists do their bit by taking the matter to the courts. An intelligent screenplay by Robert Anderson that's based on a true case makes the most of his plight.

Henry Winkler *Marty Klein* • Jennifer Hetrick *Nancy Klein* • Karl Malden *Fred Zusselman* • Audra Lindley *Anne Zusselman* • Cassy Friel *Arielle Klein* • Richard Kiley *Dr RJ Cannon* • Patty Duke *Judge Carol Ray* ■ *Dir* Gilbert Cates • *Scr* Robert Anderson

The Absolute Truth ★★

Political drama   1997 · US · Colour

Once destined for movie stardom, both Jane Seymour and William Devane have made the most of their TV options. However, not even they can bring much suspense to this tacky political thriller. All designer suits and nail polish, Seymour barely convinces as the producer of a hard-hitting news show who sets out to expose Devane's presidential candidate, after she's informed by old friend Linda Purl that he's guilty of sexual harassment. Lacking the drama of the real thing, this is slick, but shallow.

Jane Seymour *Alison Reid* • Bruce Greenwood *Jake Slaughter* • William Devane *Senator*

Emmett Hunter • Linda Purl *Jean Dalton* ■ *Dir* James Keach • *Scr* Selma Thompson, Harriet N Francis

Absolution ★ 15

Thriller   1978 · UK · Colour · 91mins

Lashings of Catholic guilt pervade this totally bonkers pot-boiler, with Richard Burton as the priest in a Catholic boarding school for boys whose protégé, Dominic Guard, runs away with hippie Billy Connolly and turns into a killer. His confessions to Burton drive the priest insane, and he goes into the woods to dig up the corpses. Unlike red wine, the three years this movie spent on the shelf did not improve it, and it might never have been released had it not been for the star presence of Burton, the film's only point of interest. ▭

Richard Burton *Father Goddard* • Dominic Guard *Benjie Stanfield* • Billy Connolly *Blakey* • Andrew Keir *Headmaster* • Dai Bradley *Arthur Dyson* • Willoughby Gray *Brigadier Walsh* • Preston Lockwood *Father Hibbert* • Brook Williams *Father Clarence* ■ *Dir* Anthony Page • *Scr* Anthony Shaffer

The Abyss ★★★ 15

Science-fiction thriller
1989 · US · Colour · 163mins

For some, prior to *Titanic*, this was James Cameron's *Waterworld*, a bloated, sentimental epic from the king of high-tech thrillers. Some of the criticism was deserved, but it remains a fascinating folly. Ed Harris is the leader of an underwater team working for an oil company which is pressed into service to rescue the crew of a crippled submarine. But they soon begin to wonder if they are the only life-forms in the vicinity. Harris is in a rare leading man role and there is first-rate support from Mary Elizabeth Mastrantonio as his estranged partner. Cameron excels in cranking up the tension within the cramped quarters, while at the same time the effects are awe-inspiring and deservedly won an Oscar. It's only marred by being overlong and by its sentimental attachment to aliens. Contains violence and swearing. ▭

Ed Harris *Bud Brigman* • Mary Elizabeth Mastrantonio *Lindsey Brigman* • Michael Biehn *Lieutenant Coffey* • Leo Burmester *Catfish De Vries* • Todd Graff *Alan "Hippy" Carnes* • John Bedford Lloyd *Jammer Willis* • JC Quinn *"Sonny" Dawson* • Kimberly Scott *Lisa "One Night" Standing* • Captain Kidd Brewer Jr *Lew Finler* • George Robert Klek *Wilhite* • Christopher Murphy *Schoenick* • Adam Nelson *Ensign Monk* ■ *Dir/Scr* James Cameron • *Special Effects* Joe Unsinn, Joseph Viskocil

Acapulco Gold ★ 15

Action adventure 1976 · US · Colour · 87mins

Marjoe Gortner, a former evangelist turned actor, made his screen debut alongside American TV stalwart Robert Lansing in this barely watchable yarn about drug smugglers. (The title refers to one of the narcotics on offer, though the film itself was made in Hawaii.) Gortner went on to appear in the very first *Kojak* film, *The Marcus-Nelson Murders*, but he is best remembered for his role as the psychotic religious freak in *Earthquake*. After that, he became a rather unlikely

leading man of cheaply-made action movies and thrillers. ▭

Marjoe Gortner *Ralph* • Robert Lansing *Carl Solborg* • Ed Nelson *Hollister* • Randi Oakes *Sally* • John Harkins *Morgan Frye* • Lawrence Casey [Lawrence P Casey] *Gordon* ■ *Dir* Burt Brinckerhoff • *Scr* Don Enright, O'Brian Tomalin, from a story by David Lees, Stan Berkowitz

Accattone ★★★★ 15

Drama   1961 · It · BW · 111mins

Pier Paolo Pasolini made his directorial debut with this uncompromising study of life on the mean streets of Rome. Using a cast of actors drawn mostly from the city's slums, he manages to find a raw poetry in the dealings of the pimps, prostitutes and petty thieves who populate a world with which he was very familiar. Franco Citti brings an indolent charm to his portrayal of Accattone, a wastrel who's reluctant to work, yet insufficiently ruthless to live by crime. However, it's Pasolini's ability to re-create the teeming urban bustle, which he ironically counterpoints with the music of Bach, that gives this ultimately tragic tale its authenticity and power. In Italian with English subtitles. ▭

Franco Citti *Vittorio Accattone* • Franca Pasut *Stella* • Silvana Corsini *Maddalena* • Paolo Guidi *Ascenza* • Adriana Asti *Amore* • Renato Capogna *Renato* ■ *Dir/Scr* Pier Paolo Pasolini

Accent on Youth ★★★

Romance   1935 · US · BW · 77mins

Paramount made two subsequent versions of Samson Raphaelson's hit Broadway comedy – *Mr Music* (1950) and *But Not for Me* (1959) – though neither had the sparkle of the first, directed with style by Wesley Ruggles (one of the original Keystone Kops). Sylvia Sidney escapes from her usual tragic roles to play a young secretary who falls for her middle-aged employer (the mellifluous-voiced Herbert Marshall). It is rather wordy, but fortunately most of those words are witty and crisply delivered.

Sylvia Sidney *Linda Brown* • Herbert Marshall *Steven Gaye* • Philip Reed *Dickie Reynolds* • Astrid Allwyn *Genevieve Lang* • Holmes Herbert *Frank Galloway* • Catherine Doucet *Eleanor Darling* • Ernest Cossart *Flogdell* • Donald Meek *Orville* ■ *Dir* Wesley Ruggles • *Scr* Herbert Fields, Claude Binyon, from the play by Samson Raphaelson

Acceptable Risks ★★ 15

Thriller   1986 · US · Colour · 88mins

One of the revered kings of the TV movie, Brian Dennehy tries his best to bring some class to this overly worthy and technical drama about a chemical plant that poses a threat to a new housing development nearby. Unfortunately, this subject matter has been handled better, in the based-on-a-true-story vein with films such as *A Civil Action* (in which John Travolta tries to prove years of waste-dumping has brought cancer to the children of a local town). ▭

Brian Dennehy *Don Sheppard* • Cicely Tyson *Janet Framm* • Kenneth McMillan *Wes Boggs* • Christine Ebersole *Lee Snyder* ■ *Dir* Rick Wallace • *Scr* Norman Strum

Accident ★★★★★ PG

Drama   1967 · UK · Colour · 100mins

Shimmeringly photographed by Gerry Fisher, Oxford and its surrounding countryside have never looked as beautiful as in this delicious exercise in character assassination. Dirk Bogarde and Stanley Baker seize upon every opportunity presented in Harold Pinter's merciless script, in which donnish civility only thinly veils the disappointment, lust and cruelty of unfulfilled middle-age. Michael York, Delphine Seyrig and Vivien Merchant also give impeccable performances as those unfortunate enough to be caught up in Bogarde and Baker's mind games. Preying on their weaknesses, Joseph Losey's relentless direction leaves the characters with few hiding places, particularly during the squirmingly uncomfortable Sunday supper. Quite brilliant.

Dirk Bogarde *Stephen* • Stanley Baker *Charley* • Jacqueline Sassard *Anna* • Delphine Seyrig *Francesca* • Alexander Knox *Provost* • Michael York *William* • Vivien Merchant *Rosalind* • Harold Pinter *Bell* • Ann Firbank *Laura* • Brian Phelan *Police Sergeant* ■ *Dir* Joseph Losey • *Scr* Harold Pinter, from the novel by Nicholas Mosley

Accidental Hero ★★★★ 15

Comedy drama 1992 · US · Colour · 113mins

Another of Stephen Frears's box-office failures, this was originally released as *Hero* in the States. Clearly influenced by Billy Wilder's *Ace in the Hole*, Frears's film is seriously under-rated, a drama about a plane crash in which Geena Davis's TV reporter is saved by a mystery Good Samaritan. We know it's Dustin Hoffman, but when Andy Garcia claims to be the "Angel of Flight 104" he's swept up in the media hysteria. Sometimes funny, often deeply cynical and pessimistic, it's a clever and brave picture, with Hoffman reprising his Ratso Rizzo role from *Midnight Cowboy*, Garcia playing a slimeball to perfection, and Davis convincing as the journalist. Contains some swearing. ▭ **DVD**

Dustin Hoffman *Bernie Laplante* • Geena Davis *Gale Gayley* • Andy Garcia *John Bubber* • Joan Cusack *Evelyn* • Kevin J O'Connor *Chucky* • Maury Chaykin *Winston* • Stephen Tobolowsky *Wallace* • Christian Clemenson *Conklin* • Tom Arnold *Chick* • Warren Berlinger *Judge Goines* ■ *Dir* Stephen Frears • *Scr* David Webb Peoples, from a story by Laura Ziskin, Alvin Sergent, David Webb Peoples

Accidental Meeting ★★ 15

Crime thriller   1994 · US · Colour · 86mins

As a gender-switched update of Alfred Hitchcock's great murder-swap thriller *Strangers on a Train*, this TV production may think it's being audacious, but is all too predictable. Linda Gray (Sue Ellen in *Dallas* for so many years) and Linda Purl are the women bound together in an anti-male complicity that begins as a joke and ends in jeopardy when a man is killed. The result is Hitchcock at half-cock. Contains violent moments. ▭

Linda Gray *Jennifer Parris* • Linda Purl *Maryanne Belman* • Leigh J McCloskey [Leigh McCloskey] *Richard* • Ernie Lively *Obrenski* • David Hayward *Jonathan Holtman* • Kent McCord *Jack Parris* • Lorna Scott *Lynn* •

Nancy Hochman *Julie* ■ *Dir* Michael Zinberg • *Scr* Pete Best, Christopher Horner, from a story by Pete Best

The Accidental Tourist
★★★★ **PG**

Comedy drama · 1988 · US · Colour · 116mins

The Big Chill may be the crowd-pleaser from director Lawrence Kasdan's portfolio, but this under-rated story remains one of his best. William Hurt is wonderful as the travel writer whose life falls apart when his young son dies and his wife (Kathleen Turner) leaves him; an Oscar-winning Geena Davis is the loopy dog trainer who helps him recover. While there are plenty of laughs along the way, an air of melancholy hangs over the piece as Kasdan movingly probes the emotions Hurt has so successfully buried. ▭

William Hurt *Macon Leary* • Kathleen Turner *Sarah Leary* • Geena Davis *Muriel Pritchett* • Amy Wright *Rose Leary* • Bill Pullman *Julian Edge* • Robert Gorman [Robert Hy Gorman] *Alexander Pritchett* • David Ogden Stiers *Porter Leary* • Ed Begley Jr *Charles Leary* • Bradley Mott *Mr Loomis* • Seth Granger *Ethan Leary* ■ *Dir* Lawrence Kasdan • *Scr* Frank Galati and Lawrence Kasdan, from the novel by Anne Tyler

Acción Mutante
★★ **18**

Science-fiction horror
1993 · Sp · Colour · 94mins

A terminally camp paella of *Battle beyond the Stars* and Patty Hearst, Spanish director Alex de la Iglesia's debut feature begins in crackerjack comic book style as members of a disabled terrorist group in 2012 kidnap a debutante's daughter and hold her to ransom on a distant mining planet. But although gory, nasty and sexy in equal proportion, this Pedro Almodóvar-produced trash peters out into science-fiction on the verge of a nervous breakdown. By the time the dragged-out ending is reached, de la Iglesia has scraped the bottom of the *Spacehunter* barrel once too often in the effort to disguise his intergalactic *No Orchids for Miss Blandish*. In Spanish with English subtitles.

Antonio Resines *Ramón Yarritu* • Alex Angulo *Alex* • Frédérique Feder *Patricia Orujo* • Fernando Guillén *Orujo* • Enrique San Francisco *Novio Ultrajado* ■ *Dir* Alex de la Iglesia • *Scr* Alex de la Iglesia, Jorge Guerricaechevarria

L'Accompagnatrice
★★★★ **PG**

Second World War drama
1992 · Fr · Colour · 111mins

With the notable exception of Louis Malle's *Lacombe Lucien*, French cinema has mostly steered clear of the subject of the Nazi occupation in the Second World War. Here it provides the backdrop for this compelling, but not always convincing, story of a young pianist, who finds herself playing accompanist both on and off stage to her glamorous employer. François Truffaut's protégé Claude Miller has always excelled at directing young actresses and here he coaxes a bewitching performance from Romane Bohringer, who judges the differing shades of devotion, jealousy, timidity and regret to perfection. Elena Safonova has a ball as the singer torn

between her collaborator husband and her Resistance hero lover. In French with English subtitles.

Richard Bohringer *Charles Brice* • Elena Safonova *Irène Brice* • Romane Bohringer *Sophie Vasseur* • Bernard Verley *Jacques Ceniat* • Samuel Lebarthe *Jacques Fabert* • Nelly Borgeaud *Madame Vasseur* • Julien Rassam *Benoit Weizman* • Jean-Pierre Kohut Svelko *General Heller* • Claude Rich *Minister* ■ *Dir* Claude Miller • *Scr* Claude Miller, Luc Béraud, from the novel by Nina Berberova

Account Rendered
★

Crime drama · 1957 · UK · BW · 61mins

Griffith Jones plays a city banker who is apparently knocked unconscious when his two-timing wife, Ursula Howells, is murdered. We've heard that one before, say the men from Scotland Yard, so it's up to the hapless Jones to prove his innocence. This sub-standard B-movie, directed by the tireless Peter Graham Scott, lasts a mere hour and is notable only for an early screen appearance by Honor Blackman, who went on to star as Cathy Gale in TV's *The Avengers* and Pussy Galore in *Goldfinger*.

Honor Blackman *Sarah Hayward* • Griffith Jones *Robert Ainsworth* • Ursula Howells *Lucille Ainsworth* • Ewen Solon *Inspector Marshall* ■ *Dir* Peter Graham Scott • *Scr* Barbara S Harper, from the book by Pamela Barrington

Accused
★★

Crime drama · 1936 · UK · BW · 87mins

In this backstage murder mystery, set in Paris, Douglas Fairbanks Jr and Dolores Del Rio star as a married couple who perform one of those acts in which the man is tied to a revolving table and the woman throws knives at him. There's a whiff of adultery in the air, and the show's spiteful star (Florence Desmond) winds up with a dagger in her heart. Well, who do *you* think "dunnit"? It's a modestly enjoyable effort that features Googie Withers in a minor role.

Douglas Fairbanks Jr *Tony Seymour* • Dolores Del Rio *Gaby Seymour* • Florence Desmond *Yvette Delange* • Basil Sydney *Eugene Roget* • Athole Stewart *President of Court* • Cecil Humphreys *Prosecuting counsel* • Esme Percy *Morel* • Edward Rigby *Alphonse* • George Moore Marriott *Dubec* • Cyril Raymond *Guy Henry* • Googie Withers *Ninette* ■ *Dir* Thornton Freeland • *Scr* Zoe Akins, George Barraud

The Accused
★★★

Crime drama · 1949 · US · BW · 100mins

Loretta Young stars as the emotionally frigid professor of psychology who kills one of her students after he attempts to seduce her on a beach. Making the death look like a drowning accident, Young takes sleeping pills then heads for hospital where a serious case of flashback syndrome assails her, together with the cops and her lawyer. Hollywood was then at the height of its Freudian phase and you need to know what "cyclothymia" means to get the most out of this *noir*-ish melodrama.

Loretta Young *Wilma Tuttle* • Robert Cummings *Warren Ford* • Wendell Corey *Lt Ted Dorgan* • Sam Jaffe *Dr Romley* • Douglas Dick *Bill Perry* • Suzanne Dalbert *Susan Duval* • George Spaulding *Dean Rhodes* • Sara

Allgood *Mrs Conner* ■ *Dir* William Dieterle • *Scr* Ketti Frings, from the novel *Be Still, My Love* by June Truesdell

The Accused
★★★★ **18**

Drama · 1988 · US · Colour · 105mins

Jodie Foster won her first Oscar for her performance as Sarah Tobias, a white-trash waitress who is raped in a bar, in this controversial movie which raised a storm of protest on its release from those who believed its content veered too close to gratuitous voyeurism. After reducing the charges against Sarah's actual attackers, her lawyer (Kelly McGillis) pushes for the prosecution of the men who stood by and watched. Both Foster and McGillis are superb and the film raises some pointed questions about an emotive subject, but one can't help but be deeply if necessarily shocked by the explicit rape scene. Sexual situations, violence, swearing and nudity. ▭

Jodie Foster *Sarah Tobias* • Kelly McGillis *Kathryn Murphy* • Bernie Coulson *Kenneth Joyce* • Leo Rossi *Cliff "Scorpion" Albrecht* • Ann Hearn *Sally Fraser* • Carmen Argenziano *Da Paul Rudolph* • Steve Antin *Bob Joiner* • Tom O'Brien *Larry* • Peter Van Norden *Attorney Paulsen* ■ *Dir* Jonathan Kaplan • *Scr* Tom Topor

Ace Eli and Rodger of the Skies
★★

Adventure · 1973 · US · Colour · 92mins

Stunt pilot Cliff Roberston teaches his hero-worshipping son Eric Shea the tricks of his trade during the Roaring Twenties in this mediocre action adventure, notable for being based on a story by Steven Spielberg and for marking the screen debut of Broadway diva Bernadette Peters. Dogged by production problems and re-edited against director John Erman's wishes (the reason the name "Bill Sampson" appears on the credits), it's only worth catching for the breathtaking aerial photography.

Cliff Robertson *Eli* • Pamela Franklin *Shelby* • Eric Shea *Rodger* • Rosemary Murphy *Hannah* • Bernadette Peters *Allison* • Alice Ghostley *Sister Lite* • Kelly Jean Peters *Rachel* • Don Keefer *Mr Parsons* ■ *Dir* Bill Sampson [John Erman] • *Scr* Chips Rosen [Claudia Salte], from a story by Steven Spielberg

Ace in the Hole
★★★★★

Satirical drama · 1951 · US · BW · 111mins

"I've met some hard-boiled eggs in my time," says Jan Sterling to Kirk Douglas. "But you – you're 20 minutes!" Sterling's husband is a fat, slobbery sap who gets trapped in a cave; Douglas is the on-the-skids journalist who prolongs the man's agony while turning the accident into a major human interest story. Sterling co-operates with the scheme, making dough from the crowds who show up to watch the rescue operation. Few movies are as tough as this one, which is probably why it flopped at the box office – audiences don't like having their noses rubbed in their own dirt. However, it's one of Hollywood's great masterpieces, filled with Wilder's caustic wit and Douglas's trademark intensity.

Kirk Douglas *Chuck Tatum* • Jan Sterling *Lorraine* • Bob Arthur *Herbie Cook* • Porter

Hall *Jacob Q Boot* • Frank Cady *Mr Federber* • Richard Benedict *Leo Minosa* • Ray Teal *Sheriff* • Lewis Martin *McCardle* • John Berkes *Papa Minosa* • Frances Dominguez *Mama Minosa* ■ *Dir* Billy Wilder • *Scr* Billy Wilder, Lesser Samuels, Walter Newman

Ace of Aces
★★★

First World War drama
1933 · US · BW · 75mins

This is one of several powerful deglamourisations of war from the pen of John Monk Saunders, who served in the Army Air Corps and won an Oscar for the story of *The Dawn Patrol* (1930). Richard Dix is the sculptor with pacifist leanings, goaded by his girlfriend (Elizabeth Allan) into becoming a First World War pilot. He turns into a cold-blooded ace of the air until a meeting with Allan in Paris leaves him disillusioned and resigned to his fate. Skilfully directed by J Walter Ruben, it may not be subtle but it still reverberates with feeling.

Richard Dix *Lt Rex Thorne* • Elizabeth Allan *Nancy Adams* • Ralph Bellamy *Major Blake* • Theodore Newton *Lt Foster Kelly* • Bill Cagney [William Cagney] *Lt Meeker* • Clarence Stroud *Lt Carroll Winstead* ■ *Dir* J Walter Ruben • *Scr* John Monk Saunders, HW Hanemann, from the story *Bird of Prey* by John Monk Saunders

Ace Ventura: Pet Detective
★★★★ **12**

Comedy · 1993 · US · Colour · 82mins

Doctor Dolittle meets *The Crying Game* in the smash hit that made Jim Carrey an overnight comedy sensation. The rubber-faced star plays a bumbling, Hawaiian-shirted detective hired to find the kidnapped dolphin mascot of the Miami Dolphins football team in this fast and furious farce. Your reaction to the film will largely depend on whether you find Carrey's distinctive style of extremely physical comedy – often compared to that of Jerry Lewis – stupidly hilarious or downright annoying. Tom Shadyac directs with anarchic energy and quirky imagination. Contains some mild swearing. ▭ **DVD**

Jim Carrey *Ace Ventura* • Sean Young *Lieutenant Lois Einhorn* • Tone Loc *Emilio* • Dan Marino • Noble Willingham *Riddle* • Troy Evans *Podacter* • Raynor Scheine *Woodstock* • Udo Kier *Camp* • Frank Adonis *Vinnie* • Tiny Ron *Roc* • Courteney Cox *Melissa* ■ *Dir* Tom Shadyac • *Scr* Jack Bernstein, Tom Shadyac, Jim Carrey, from a story by Jack Bernstein

Ace Ventura: When Nature Calls
★★ **PG**

Comedy · 1995 · US · Colour · 88mins

Even though Jim Carrey has as many detractors as supporters, there's no denying his breakthrough hit *Ace Ventura: Pet Detective* exuded a barmy charm, but this silly sequel is often just plain irritating. For this adventure, Ace is off to Africa where he gets mixed up with warring tribes and the hunt for a rare bat. The slim plot is just the flimsiest of excuses for Carrey's wacky grimaces, while the slapstick is relentlessly juvenile and director Steve Oedekerk's direction lacks the surreal inspiration of the original. Visiting Britons Ian McNeice and Simon Callow struggle to bring a

little dignity to the proceedings.
DVD

Jim Carrey *Ace Ventura* • Ian McNeice *Fulton Greenwall* • Simon Callow *Vincent Cadby* • Maynard Eziashi *Ouda* • Bob Gunton *Burton Quinn* • Sophie Okonedo *Princess* • Tommy Davidson *Tiny warrior* • Adewale Hitu ■ *Dir/Scr* Steve Oedekerk

Aces and Eights ★★ U

Western 1936 · US · BW · 55mins

Poker fans will recognise the title immediately – the infamous "dead man's hand", held by Wild Bill Hickock as he was shot in the back and killed by gambler Jack McCall on the night of 2 August 1876 in Deadwood City. It's an incident that's been immortalised many times on celluloid, and mostly in better movies than this one. This version features a movie star who actually knew the West – the estimable Tim McCoy, who is fine as Gentleman Tim Madigan, a gambler trying to clear himself of murder. McCoy may defeat the villains, but not the programme-filler plot and slim production values of this run-of-the-mill western. Still, for cowboy fans, here's a real touch of sagebrush authenticity.

Tim McCoy *Gentleman Tim Madigan* • Luana Walters *Juanita Hernandez* • Rex Lease *Jose Hernandez* • Wheeler Oakman *Ace Morgan* • Charles Stevens *Capt Felipe* • Earl Hodgins [Earle Hodgins] *Marshal* ■ *Dir* Sam Newfield • *Scr* Arthur Durlan

Aces High ★★★ PG

First World War action drama
1976 · UK · Colour · 108mins

Jack Gold's stout anti-war statement actually takes its cue from an early sound film, 1930's *Journey's End*, but transposes the action from the trenches to the skies. It is here that the film finds its conviction, in the form of dogfight sequences that succeed in being both thrilling and horrifying. Back at base, however, where young and eager First World War flier Peter Firth gradually comes to understand the cynicism of his superior, Malcolm McDowell, events are not as well realised. Moments of emotional isolation work well, but a visit to a brothel is simply trite. Still, the film generally soars.

Malcolm McDowell *Gresham* • Christopher Plummer *Sinclair* • Simon Ward *Crawford* • Peter Firth *Croft* • John Gielgud *Headmaster* • Trevor Howard *Lieutenant Colonel Silkin* • Richard Johnson *Colonel Lyle* • Ray Milland *Brigadier Whale* ■ *Dir* Jack Gold • *Scr* Howard Barker, from the film *Journey's End* by James Whale, from the play by RC Sherriff

Aces: Iron Eagle III ★★ 15

Action adventure 1992 · US · Colour · 94mins

How else would you defeat a nasty Nazi, but with reconditioned Second World War planes? A far cry from its predecessors, this was John Glen's first feature after directing five James Bond movies, and the sense of anticlimax is there for all to see. Yet this vaguely silly enterprise is not without its pleasures. Louis Gossett Jr returns as the USAF ace who recruits his pals at a flying circus to deliver a South American village from the clutches of a ruthless drug baron. Old favourites Christopher Cazenove and Horst Buchholz feature in a solid supporting cast that also includes body-building champion, Rachel McLish. Contains swearing and violence.

Louis Gossett Jr *Colonel Charles "Chappy" Sinclair* • Rachel McLish *Anna* • Christopher Cazenove *Palmer* • Sonny Chiba *Horikoshi* • Horst Buchholz *Leichman* • Paul Freeman *Kleiss* • Ray Mancini *Chico* • Mitchell Ryan *Simms* ■ *Dir* John Glen • *Scr* Kevin Elders, from characters created by Kevin Elders, Sidney J Furie

Achilles ★★ U

Action adventure 1962 · It · Colour · 117mins

This Italian-made, would-be epic stars Hollywood hunk Gordon Mitchell – a sort of low-rent Steve Reeves – as Achilles, and Gallic "boeufcake" Jacques Bergerac as his arch rival, Hector. If one turns a blind eye to the performances and a deaf ear to the Anglo-American dubbing, this is quite a handsome breeze through parts of Homer's *Iliad*, with some decent battles and nice location work. That said, Achilles rather lets his guard slip when a simpering, supine slave girl takes his mind off the Trojan War. Italian dialogue dubbed into English.

Gordon Mitchell *Achilles* • Jacques Bergerac *Hector* • Enio Girolami *Patrocles* • Mario Petri *Agamemnon* • Cristina Gajoni *Briseyde* • Gloria Milland *Griseyde* • Eleonora Bianchi *Andromache* ■ *Dir* Marino Girolami • *Scr* Gino De Santis, Vladimiro Cajoli

The Acid House ★★ 18

Dark cult drama 1998 · UK · Colour · 106mins

This trio of very dark tales from Irvine Welsh's anthology has a great cast (including Ewen Bremner and Kevin McKidd from the superlative *Trainspotting*), but these stories are too wild, weird and unpleasant to appeal to anybody other than hardcore fans of Welsh's book. Although the stories – a downtrodden teen meets God and is transformed into a fly, nice guy suffers from the neighbour from hell, and an acid-taking clubber swops bodies with a newborn baby – all offer dramatic potential, they seem more calculated to shock and offend with graphic sex and in-your-face nastiness than to actually entertain. Contains swearing, nudity and violence.
DVD

Stephen McCole *Boab* • Maurice Roëves *God* • Garry Sweeney *Kev ("The Granton Star Cause")* • Jenny McCrindle *Evelyn* • Kevin McKidd *Johnny* • Ewen Bremner *Coco* • Martin Clunes *Rory* • Simon Weir *Tambo* • Alex Howden *Boab Snr* ■ *Dir* Paul McGuigan • *Scr* Irvine Welsh, from his short stories

Acquasanta Joe ★★

Spaghetti western 1971 · It · Colour · 94mins

At the end of the American Civil War Confederate soldiers have their cannon stolen by bandits, who use it to pull off a series of bank raids. But then they make the mistake of stealing the loot stashed by a bounty hunter, who is a staunch disbeliever in the concept of finders keepers and chases after them. The resultant action is a muddled round of ambushes and escapes, thefts and recoveries as all and sundry try to make off with the dough. Director Mario Gariazzo obviously knows his spaghetti, but this is a sloppily served helping. Italian dialogue dubbed into English.

Lincoln Tate *Acquasanta Joe* • Ty Hardin *Donovan* • Silvia Monelli *Estella* ■ *Dir* Mario Gariazzo • *Scr* Franco Poggi, Mario Gariazzo

Across 110th Street ★★ 18

Blaxploitation crime thriller
1972 · US · Colour · 97mins

In New York, the demarcation line between squalor and style, war and peace, was always 110th Street. Below the line was Central Park, above it was Harlem and mayhem. Even if that isn't the case today, in this movie crooked cop Anthony Quinn has a lot of hardware to deal with Harlem's racketeers. Quinn wanted Sidney Poitier, Sammy Davis Jr and Harry Belafonte as his co-stars; he got Yaphet Kotto as his police partner, and Antonio Fargas, Ed Bernard and Paul Benjamin as bank robbers when the Black Panthers vetoed the others because they lacked street cred. Director Barry Shear's picture tries to be hard-edged and aim for realism, but doesn't always succeed. Contains swearing and violence.

Anthony Quinn *Captain Frank Mattelli* • Yaphet Kotto *Detective Lieutenant Pope* • Anthony Franciosa *Nick D'Salvio* • Paul Benjamin *Jim Harris* • Ed Bernard *Joe Logart* • Richard Ward *Doc Johnson* • Norma Donaldson *Gloria Roberts* • Antonio Fargas *Henry J Jackson* ■ *Dir* Barry Shear • *Scr* Luther Davis, from the novel by Wally Ferris

Across the Bridge ★★★★

Thriller 1957 · UK · BW · 103mins

Rod Steiger takes on the ultimate scene-stealer – a small dog – and just about wins in this thriller, adapted from a Graham Greene story. Steiger plays a fraudster on the run who murders a man and assumes his identity, only to discover his victim is also a fugitive. His attempts to escape are further hampered when he becomes attached to the dead man's mangy mongrel. There was friction between director Ken Annakin and his star during production, with Spanish exteriors standing in for Latin American locations. Nevertheless, Steiger gives one of his best and most poignant performances.

Rod Steiger *Carl Schaffner* • David Knight *Johnny* • Marla Landi *Mary* • Noel Willman *Chief of Police* • Bernard Lee *Chief Inspector Hadden* • Bill Nagy *Paul Scarff* • Eric Pohlman [Eric Pohlmann] *Police Sergeant* • Alan Gifford *Cooper* ■ *Dir* Ken Annakin • *Scr* Guy Elmes, Denis Freeman, from a story by Graham Greene

Across the Great Divide ★★ U

Western 1977 · US · Colour · 96mins

Following the success of *The Adventures of the Wilderness Family*, producer Arthur R Dubs and director Stewart Raffill returned to the Rocky Mountains for this old-fashioned rites of passage picture. As the orphans risking all to claim their estate in Salem, Oregan, Heather Rattray and Mark Edward Hall give spirited performances, although conman Robert F Logan hogs nearly all their scenes. However, he's upstaged himself by the scenery and the adorable, if dangerous, wildlife. For all its visual splendour, the film lacks a sense of period (it's set in 1876) and the perils faced by the trio are predictable and too easily overcome.

Robert Logan *Zachariah Coop* • Heather Rattray *Holly Smith* • Mark Edward Hall *Jason Smith* • George "Buck" Flower *Ben* • Hal Bokar *Sternface* ■ *Dir/Scr* Stewart Raffill • *Producer* Arthur R Dubs

Across the Pacific ★★★ U

Spy drama 1942 · US · BW · 96mins

A wartime melodrama that reunited the cast and crew of *The Maltese Falcon*. The original script, written in 1941, described a Japanese plan to attack Pearl Harbor and when that really happened the script was rewritten, set near the Panama Canal and peopled with sundry spies, adventurers and mystery women. Humphrey Bogart plays a spy ordered to keep tabs on Sydney Greenstreet. What happens is purely formulaic, and enjoyable only because of the interplay between Bogart, Greenstreet and Mary Astor. John Huston directed all but the final scenes: ordered into the Signal Corps, he was replaced by Vincent Sherman.

Humphrey Bogart *Rick Leland* • Mary Astor *Alberta Marlow* • Sydney Greenstreet *Dr Lorenz* • Charles Halton *Av Smith* • Victor Sen Yung *Joe Totsuiko* • Roland Got *Sugi* ■ *Dir* John Huston, Vincent Sherman • *Scr* Richard Macaulay, from the serial *Aloha Means Goodbye* by Robert Carson in *The Saturday Evening Post*

Across the Tracks ★★ 15

Drama 1990 · US · Colour · 96mins

Fresh from his unfortunate experience on the short-lived TV series *Glory Days*, Brad Pitt got one of his first opprtunities to lead from the front in this below-par tale of sibling rivalry. He certainly looks the part as a clean-cut running star who tries to save cynical brother Rick Schroder from drug peddling by encouraging him to take up athletics. Few demands are made of Pitt's acting ability, as writer/director Sandy Tung's script is awash with clichéd situations and unconvincing sports sequences. However, it's fascinating to watch Pitt and Schroder competing with each other in the acting stakes. Contains swearing and scenes of substance abuse.

Rick Schroder *Billy Maloney* • Brad Pitt *Joe Maloney* • Carrie Snodgress *Rosemary Maloney* • David Anthony Marshall *Louie* • Thomas Mikal Ford *Coach Walsh* • John Linton *Brad* • Cyril O'Reilly *Coach Ryder* • Jack McGee *Frank* ■ *Dir/Scr* Sandy Tung

Across the Wide Missouri ★★★ U

Western adventure
1951 · US · Colour · 78mins

A great example of the use of Technicolor (cameraman William C Mellor), as vast landscapes are bloodied by the advance of "civilisation" in the shape of pioneers in the Rocky Mountains of the 1820s. Clark Gable seems uncomfortably cast as real-life trapper Flint Mitchell, and the complex dialogue scenes with the Indians severely hinder the plot's progression, but the movie has genuine scale. It would have been

20 U = SUITABLE FOR ALL Uc = SUITABLE FOR ALL, ESPECIALLY FOR YOUNG CHILDREN (VIDEO ONLY) PG = PARENTAL GUIDANCE

interesting had MGM left director William A Wellman's epic vision untouched, but after unfavourable previews this movie was hacked down to its current length and a narration was added, which, despite being superbly delivered by an off-screen Howard Keel, only serves to diminish and simplify a movie of real grandeur. The score is outstanding.

Clark Gable *Flint Mitchell* • Ricardo Montalban *Ironshirt* • John Hodiak *Brecan* • Adolphe Menjou *Pierre* • Maria Elena Marques *Kamiah* • J Carrol Naish *Looking Glass* • Jack Holt *Bear Ghost* • Alan Napier *Captain Humberstone Lyon* • Howard Keel *Narrator* ■ *Dir* William Wellman [William A Wellman] • *Scr* Talbot Jennings, from a story by Talbot Jennings, Frank Cavett, from a novel by Bernard DeVoto • *Music* David Raksin

Act of Love ★★★
Drama   1953 · US · BW · 109mins
Along with stars such as Alan Ladd, Kirk Douglas took full advantage of the postwar tax breaks available to American actors working in Europe, and this intense adult romance, scripted by *The Young Lions* author Irwin Shaw from Alfred Hayes's novel *The Girl on the Via Flaminia*, is a prime example of his output during that period. The late Dany Robin is the girl Douglas falls for, while other cast members include Gene Kelly's *Happy Road* co-star Barbara Laage, and a pretty, pouting youngster awaiting discovery called Brigitte Bardot. An intelligent, mature movie from director Anatole Litvak.

Kirk Douglas *Robert Teller* • Dany Robin *Lisa* • Barbara Laage *Nina* • Robert Strauss *Blackwood* • Gabrielle Dorziat *Adele* • Grégoire Aslan *Commissaire* • Marthe Mercadier *Young woman* • Brigitte Bardot *Mimi* ■ *Dir* Anatole Litvak • *Scr* Irwin Shaw, from the novel *The Girl on the Via Flaminia* by Alfred Hayes

Act of Necessity ★★★
Documentary drama
1991 · Ausl · Colour · 90mins
Although it seems a bit gimmicky to play the trial before a real judge and jury to get an authentic verdict, this docudrama is anything but a contrived melodrama. Angie Milliken gives a towering performance as the young mother who takes on the farmers and the chemical companies of Australia's cotton belt when she realises that the pesticides used in crop-spraying are responsible for her daughter's leukaemia. Passionately scripted by Pamela Williams and directed with Ken Loach-like realism by Ian Munro, this is hard-hitting stuff.

Angie Milliken ■ *Dir* Ian Munro • *Scr* Pamela Williams

Act of Piracy ★★ 18
Action thriller   1990 · US · Colour · 100mins
Gary Busey is a popular draw in the straight-to-video stakes nowadays, and this is a typically no-nonsense slice of action hokum. Here he's a Vietnam vet who fights back when Ray Sharkey and some terrorist pals seize his yacht with his children on board. There are echoes of Busey's *Under Siege* in the ocean-bound plotting, but it's not in the same class as that action spectacular. Nevertheless, Busey and Sharkey spark off each other nicely

and it makes for undemanding entertainment. Contains swearing, violence and nudity. ▣
Gary Busey *Ted Andrews* • Belinda Bauer *Sandy Andrews* • Ray Sharkey *Jack Wilcox* ■ *Dir* John "Bud" Cardos • *Scr* Hal Reed

Act of the Heart ★★★
Religious drama
1970 · Can · Colour · 103mins
An obsessive love affair within an obsessive religious faith lifts this Canadian movie out of the ordinary. while the acting elevates it even further. Country girl Geneviève Bujold falls desperately in love with priest Donald Sutherland when she goes to his urban parish to sing in the choir. The film is darker in hue than the surface gloss suggests, though non-religious audiences may wonder why everything is so intense.

Geneviève Bujold *Martha Hayes* • Donald Sutherland *Father Michael Ferrier* • Monique Leyrac *Johane Foss* • Bill Mitchell *Russell Foss* ■ *Dir/Scr* Paul Almond

Act of Vengeance ★★★ 18
Crime drama   1974 · US · Colour · 87mins
A surprisingly hard-edged slice of B-movie exploitation that manages to come up with a different spin on the familiar vigilante theme. Jo Ann Harris leads a band of rape victims who decide to take the law into their own hands and gain revenge against a serial attacker. The largely unknown cast – *Dallas* regular Steve Kanaly is probably the most recognisable face – gives sterling performances and director Robert Kelljchian succeeds in avoiding the more sensationalist aspects of the story. Contains violence and swearing. ▣

Jo Ann Harris *Linda* • Peter Brown *Jack* • Jennifer Lee *Nancy* • Lisa Moore *Karen* • Connie Strickland *Teresa* • Patricia Estrin *Angie* • Lada Edmund Jr *Tiny* • Steve Kanaly *Tom* ■ *Dir* Robert Kelljchian [Bob Kelljan] • *Scr* Betty Conklin, HR Christian

Act of Vengeance ★★★
Drama based on a true story
1986 · Can/US · Colour · 94mins
Charles Bronson will never ditch the wooden *Death Wish* tag but, given the right material, he can deliver beautifully understated performances. In this tough drama, Bronson plays an honest union man running for office against the villainous incumbent Wilford Brimley, who uses every dirty trick in the book to hold on to his power. The star is ably supported by the likes of Ellen Burstyn, Hoyt Axton and a young Ellen Barkin, and the no-frills direction of *The Long Good Friday*'s John MacKenzie is quietly effective. Look out, too, for a pre-stardom appearance by Keanu Reeves.

Charles Bronson *Jock Yablonski* • Ellen Burstyn *Margaret Yablonski* • Wilford Brimley *Tony Boyle* • Hoyt Axton *Silhous Huddleston* • Robert Schenkkan *Paul Gilly* • Ellen Barkin *Annette Gilly* • Maury Chaykin *Claude Vealy* • Keanu Reeves *Buddy Palmer* ■ *Dir* John Mackenzie • *Scr* Scott Spencer, from the book by Trevor Armbrister

Act of Violence ★★★
Film noir   1949 · US · BW · 82mins
A fine *film noir* melodrama from MGM, allowing its talented young contract director Fred Zinnemann to flex his creative muscles. There's a superb cast, including two of Hollywood's finest second league heavyweights, Robert Ryan and Van Heflin, the latter particularly brilliant as an officer who, while he was a prisoner of war, betrayed his men. Ryan is his fellow prisoner who seeks revenge. Janet Leigh is wasted as Heflin's worried wife, but there's a remarkable performance from the redoubtable Mary Astor as a bar-room prostitute. All told, a grim but satisfying movie that never quite rises above its co-feature status; indeed, on its original British release it was double-billed with Abraham Polonsky's *Force of Evil* starring John Garfield.

Van Heflin *Frank R Enley* • Robert Ryan *Joe Parkson* • Janet Leigh *Edith Enley* • Mary Astor *Pat* • Phyllis Thaxter *Ann* • Berry Kroeger *Johnny* • Taylor Holmes *Gavery* • Harry Antrim *Fred* • Connie Gilchrist *Martha* ■ *Dir* Fred Zinnemann • *Scr* Robert L Richards

Act One ★
Biographical drama 1963 · US · BW · 110mins
The best-selling autobiography of playwright Moss Hart who, with George S Kaufman, wrote some of the best comedies ever to come out of America, such as *Once in a Lifetime* and *The Man Who Came to Dinner*, makes a glitteringly entertaining and fascinating read. This attempt to film it, however, is an abject failure. Written, produced and directed by former MGM production chief Dore Schary, with George Hamilton as Hart and Jason Robards as Kaufman, the film doesn't find a way of translating Hart's genial account into a suitable narrative, leaving only a series of static scenes and a lot of Broadway name-dropping.

George Hamilton *Moss Hart* • Jason Robards Jr *George S Kaufman* • Jack Klugman *Joe Hyman* • Sam Levene *Richard Maxwell* • Ruth Ford *Beatrice Kaufman* • Eli Wallach *Warren Stone* • Joseph Leon *Max Siegel* • George Segal *Lester Sweyd* ■ *Dir* Dore Schary • *Scr* Dore Schary, from the autobiography by Moss Hart

Action in the North Atlantic ★★★
Second World War drama
1943 · US · BW · 127mins
Humphrey Bogart made this Second World War flag-waver immediately after *Casablanca*. It began as one of many Warner Bros short films designed to salute various aspects of the war effort, this time the merchant marine, but was quickly expanded into a full-length feature, with Bogart and Raymond Massey sailing from the USA to the Soviet Union, dodging German U-boats every league of the way. Ruth Gordon, meanwhile, keeps the home fires burning. Bogart and Massey make a convincing pair of heroes and the action sequences, filmed in the studio tank, are just as impressive as those in Noël Coward and David Lean's earlier *In Which We Serve*.

Humphrey Bogart *Joe Rossi* • Raymond Massey *Captain Steve Jarvis* • Alan Hale

Boats O'Hara • Julie Bishop *Pearl* • Ruth Gordon *Mrs Jarvis* • Sam Levene *Chips Abrams* • Dane Clark *Johnny Pulaski* ■ *Dir* Lloyd Bacon • *Scr* John Howard Lawson, from the novel by Guy Gilpatric

Action Jackson ★★★ 18
Action thriller   1988 · US · Colour · 91mins
Rocky star Carl Weathers is smart Detroit cop Jericho "Action" Jackson (he's even got a Harvard law degree!) out to nail evil auto magnate Craig T Nelson in this loud *Commando* clone liberally dosed with outlandish explosions, huge car crashes and stylish knock-outs. Fast and furiously directed by Craig R Baxley, the stunt director of television's *The A-Team*, singer Vanity plays a junkie whore crooning "Undress Me" to camera and there's an early appearance by Sharon Stone. Illogical and incomprehensible it may be most of the time, but the memorable high octane action more than makes up for its plot deficiencies. Contains graphic violence, nudity, sexual situations and swearing ▣

Carl Weathers *Jericho "Action" Jackson* • Craig T Nelson *Peter Dellaplane* • Vanity *Sydney Ash* • Sharon Stone *Patrice Dellaplane* • Thomas F Wilson *Officer Kornblau* • Bill Duke *Captain Armbruster* • Robert Davi *Tony Moretti* • Jack Thibeau *Detective Kotterwell* ■ *Dir* Craig R Baxley • *Scr* Robert Reneau

Action of the Tiger ★★ U
Adventure   1957 · US · Colour · 96mins
Van Johnson plays an adventurer who smuggles Martine Carol into Albania where the secret police are holding her father. What makes this B-movie rather more interesting now than it was in 1957 is the presence of Sean Connery, who plays Johnson's romantic rival and gets beaten up for his trouble. Director Terence Young thought the film was "dreadful, very badly directed", and Johnson (always a rather weak leading man) is no match for Sean's hulking sexuality. Young promised to make it up to him one day, and in 1962 he did – with a little number called *Dr No*.

Van Johnson *Carson* • Martine Carol *Tracy* • Herbert Lom *Trifon* • Gustavo Rojo *Henri* • Tony Dawson [Anthony Dawson] *Security officer* • Anna Gerber *Mara* • Yvonne Warren [Yvonne Romain] *Katina* • Helen Haye *The Countess* • Sean Connery *Mike* ■ *Dir* Terence Young • *Scr* Robert Carson, from a novel by James Wellard

Actors and Sin ★★★
Comedy drama   1952 · US · BW · 85mins
Two featurettes, glued together: the first is about a grand actor who makes the suicide of his vain, hateful daughter look like murder. The second is a satire about a Hollywood agent who sells a script that everyone thinks is brilliant and turns out to be written by a nine-year-old. Ben Hecht puts all available cynicism into this project but the second story is rivetingly weird as Hecht casts his own daughter as the moppet writer and her lack of acting ability is excruciatingly obvious.

Edward G Robinson *Maurice* • Marsha Hunt *Marcia* • Dan O'Herlihy *Alfred O'Shea* • Eddie Albert *Orlando Higgens* • Tracey Roberts *Miss Flannigan* • Jenny Hecht *Daisy Marcher* ■ *Dir/ Scr* Ben Hecht

An Actor's Revenge
★★★★ PG

Drama   1963 · Jap · Colour · 108mins

Having starred in the 1935 version, veteran actor Kazuo Hasegawa reprises the dual role of Yukinojo the female impersonator and Yamitaro, the bandit who befriends him. Revelling in his scheme to destroy the triumvirate responsible for the suicide of his parents – he starts by seducing the daughter of one of the men – Hasegawa gives a performance of rare immersion and control. While remaining faithful to Daisuke Ito's 1935 original, director Kon Ichikawa creates a nice sense of nostalgia and irony by re-creating not only the conventions of Kabuki theatre, but also the look of Japanese painting and the films of the early sound era. In Japanese with English subtitles. ▣

Kazuo Hasegawa *Yamitaro/Yukinojo* • Fujiko Yamamoto *Ohatsu* • Ayako Wakao *Namiji* • Ganjiro Nakamura *Sansai Dobe* ■ *Dir* Kon Ichikawa • *Scr* Teinosuke Kinugasa, Daisuke Ito, Natto Wada

The Actress
★★★★ U

Drama   1953 · US · BW · 90mins

Keeping up with the Jones girl is some feat! As Ruth Jones, aspiring thespian and would-be star, Jean Simmons is an obstinate and headstrong teenager demanding her theatrical rights despite opposition from Spencer Tracy as her seafaring father. Every dad will have his day, but not for very long, in this endearing adaptation of actress Ruth Gordon's play about her Broadway-bound early days in a Massachusetts small town. Anthony Perkins makes a rather timid debut as Ruth's boyfriend, but it's Tracy's movie, although Simmons does stand up to him remarkably well.

Spencer Tracy *Clinton Jones* • Jean Simmons *Ruth Gordon Jones* • Teresa Wright *Annie Jones* • Anthony Perkins *Fred Whitmarsh* • Ian Wolfe *Mr Bagley* • Kay Williams *Hazel Dawn* • Mary Wickes *Emma Glavey* • Norma Jean Nilsson *Anna* • Dawn Bender *Katherine* ■ *Dir* George Cukor • *Scr* Ruth Gordon, from her play *Years Ago*

Actresses
★★★ 15

Drama   1996 · Sp · Colour · 87mins

Intimacy and intensity are the bywords for Ventura Pons's adaptation of JM Benet I Jornet's acclaimed play about the encounters between an ambitious drama student and a legendary diva's favourite pupils. However, such is his emphasis on the mood and language of this essentially theatrical piece, that Pons neglects the cinematic potential of the allusions to *Rashomon* and *All about Eve* that arise as the truth slowly emerges from the embittered trio's well-practised reminiscences. The performances, however, are impeccable, with Rosa Maria Sarda's blowsy sitcom star just shading in over Núria Espert's drama queen and Anna Lizaran's voice-over artist. In Catalan and Spanish with English subtitles. Contains swearing.

Núria Espert *Gloria Marc* • Rosa Maria Sarda *Assumpta Roca* • Anna Lizaran *Maria Caminal* • Mercè Pons *Girl* ■ *Dir* Ventura Pons • *Scr* Ventura Pons, JM Benet I Jornet, from the play *ER* by JM Benet I Jornet

Acts of Love
★★ 18

Romantic drama
1995 · US · Colour · 104mins

It's hard to swallow Dennis Hopper as a shy, pipe-smoking teacher, married (unhappily) to Amy Irving, who lives on a farm with his sick mother (Julie Harris). The plot doesn't get any more credible when his character gets a new lease of life through an affair with a student (Amy Locane). Because of a childhood accident, Hopper lurches around with a limp, though that's nothing compared to Ed Jones's script. Contains some swearing and sexual situations. ▣

Dennis Hopper *Joseph Svenden* • Amy Irving *Rosealee Henson* • Amy Locane *Catherine Wheeler* • Julie Harris *Joseph's mother* • Gary Busey *Major Nathan Wheeler* • Hal Holbrook *Dr Evans* • Christopher Pettiet *Robert Henson* • Priscilla Pointer *Lily Henson* ■ *Dir* Bruno Barreto • *Scr* Ed Jones, from the novel *Farmer* by Jim Harrison

Ada
★★★

Drama   1961 · US · Colour · 108mins

Susan Hayward stars as former prostitute Ada, the fiery wife of southern politician Dean Martin, in an MGM rags-to-riches tale. Wilfrid Hyde White is Martin's scheming political adviser, who threatens to expose Hayward's colourful past if she continues to appear at her husband's side. Martin Balsam is also effective as Martin's press agent. A mesmerising melodrama from the studio's post-*Ben-Hur* period, when chances were taken with unusual casts and subjects, this was directed with a knowing hand by skilled craftsman Daniel Mann.

Susan Hayward *Ada* • Dean Martin *Bo Gillis* • Wilfrid Hyde White *Sylvester Marin* • Ralph Meeker *Colonel Yancey* • Martin Balsam *Steve Jackson* • Frank Maxwell *Ronnie Hallerton* • Connie Sawyer *Alice Sweet* • Ford Rainey *Speaker* • Charles Watts *Al Winslow* • Larry Gates *Joe Adams* ■ *Dir* Daniel Mann • *Scr* Arthur Sheekman, William Driskill, from the novel *Ada Dallas* by Wirt Williams

Adalen 31
★★★

Period drama 1969 · Swe · Colour · 114mins

Those familiar with *Elvira Madigan* will know that Bo Widerberg has an eye for lyrical imagery. But such pictorialism seems out of place in the reconstruction of a key moment in Swedish labour history. The 1931 protracted strike by the paper mill workers in an isolated northern town resulted in five people being killed by panicked soldiers. The violence is all the more shocking for the beauty of the visuals. But while we know everything about the striker's son and the plant manager's pregnant daughter, we get little insight into the political development of the pickets, or the hardships suffered by their families. A little more influence from *Battleship Potemkin* would not have gone amiss on this occasion. In Swedish with English subtitles.

Peter Schildt *Kjell Andersson* • Kerstin Tidelius *Kjell's mother* • Roland Hedlund *Harald Andersson* • Stefan Feierbach *Åke* • Martin Widerberg *Martin* • Marie De Geer *Anna* ■ *Dir/Scr* Bo Widerberg

Adam
★★★★ 15

Drama based on a true story
1983 · US · Colour · 91mins

Based on a true story, this moving and classy TV movie stars Daniel J Travanti (*Hill Street Blues*) and JoBeth Williams (*The Big Chill*) as parents who suffer the anguish of having their son kidnapped. In the hope of helping other families with missing children, the couple lobby Congress to give parents access to the FBI's national crime computer. Subtly and movingly performed, this is above average, and earned an Emmy nomination for outstanding drama.

Daniel J Travanti *John Walsh* • JoBeth Williams *Reve Walsh* • Martha Scott *Gram Walsh* • Richard Masur *Jay Howell* • Paul Regina *Joe Walsh* • Mason Adams *Ray Mellette* ■ *Dir* Michael Tuchner

Adam and Evelyne
★★★

Romantic melodrama
1949 · UK · BW · 82mins

Stewart Granger and Jean Simmons, who married in real life a year later, first played opposite each other in this pleasing comedy (although they both appeared three years earlier in *Caesar and Cleopatra*). He's a professional gambler who pretends to be a banker; she's an orphan who thinks he's her father but soon learns differently. Jest, not incest, is the name of this game, exuberantly performed by its two stars. The only thing that lets it down is the stodgy, stagey direction by Harold French.

Stewart Granger *Adam Black* • Jean Simmons *Evelyne Wallace* • Edwin Styles *Bill Murray* • Raymond Young *Roddy Black* • Helen Cherry *Moira* • Beatrice Varley *Mrs Parker* • Joan Swinstead *Molly* • Wilfrid Hyde White *Colonel Bradley* • Irene Handl *Manageress* • Dora Bryan *Store assistant* ■ *Dir* Harold French • *Scr* Noel Langley, Lesley Storm, George Barraud, Nicholas Phipps

Adam at 6 AM
★★ 15

Drama   1970 · US · Colour · 90mins

A young Michael Douglas overcomes miscasting with an acceptable performance as a West Coast professor in search of himself and a simpler life in rural America. The film, which offers neither a pulsating plot nor sparkling dialogue, flopped on its first outing. But it does have a certain offbeat appeal, as well as an authentic feel for its Missouri locations, and a strong performance by Joe Don Baker as the foreman of a crew of labourers who employs Douglas. ▣

Michael Douglas *Adam Gaines* • Lee Purcell *Jerri Jo Hopper* • Joe Don Baker *Harvey Gavin* • Charles Aidman *Mr Hooper* • Marge Redmond *Cleo* • Louise Latham *Mrs Hopper* • Grayson Hall *Inez Treadley* • Carolyn Conwell *Mavis* • Dana Elcar *Van* • Meg Foster *Joyce* ■ *Dir* Robert Scheerer • *Scr* Stephen Karpf, Elinor Karpf

Adam Had Four Sons
★★★

Melodrama 1941 · US · BW · 108mins

A powerful melodrama revolving around Ingrid Bergman as a governess hired to look after Warner Baxter's family after the death of their mother, with totally predictable consequences. There's a cracking turn from up-and-coming Susan Hayward as the girl you wouldn't

want to bring home to your parents, but otherwise this would-be sincere drama suffers from serious undercasting. Bergman's star quality keeps you watching and caring, even if you know exactly what's going to happen next.

Ingrid Bergman *Emilie Gallatin* • Warner Baxter *Adam Stoddard* • Susan Hayward *Hester* • Fay Wray *Molly Stoddard* • Helen Westley *Cousin Phillipa* • Richard Denning *Jack Stoddard* • Johnny Downs *David Stoddard* ■ *Dir* Gregory Ratoff • *Scr* William Hurlbut, Michael Blankfort, from the novel *Legacy* by Charles Bonner

Adam: His Song Continues
★★ 15

Drama based on a true story
1986 · US · Colour · 89mins

This unnecessary sequel to the moving original follows the parents of kidnapped Adam after the successful formation of the Missing Children's Bureau. Daniel J Travanti and JoBeth Williams reprise their roles as the campaigning parents, though *Adam* director Michael Tuchner hands over the reins to Robert Markowitz, best known for TV movies such as *The Tuskegee Airmen* and *Murder in the Heartland*. Unfortunately, it lacks the dramatic weight or human interest of the first TV movie.

Daniel J Travanti *John Walsh* • JoBeth Williams *Reve Walsh* • Martha Scott *Gram Walsh* • Richard Masur *Jay Howell* • Paul Regina *Joe Walsh* ■ *Dir* Robert Markowitz

Adam's Rib
★★★★★ U

Classic comedy 1949 · US · BW · 96mins

This witty and refreshing "battle of the sexes" comedy is a peerless joy. Tailor-made for Spencer Tracy and Katharine Hepburn, it gave the roles of a lifetime to an enduring partnership which first flourished on screen in the 1942 comedy *Woman of the Year*. They face each other as married lawyers on opposing sides in court, as Hepburn defends and Tracy prosecutes Judy Holliday. She almost puts the star couple in the shade as the dizzy blonde accused of a shooting involving her philandering husband Tom Ewell. Here the delightful Oscar-nominated screenplay by Ruth Gordon and Garson Kanin brings out the best in the talented stars, and the subtle direction of George Cukor shows him to be a master of his craft – watch how he handles the long takes, letting the performances take the flow, especially in the scene where Hepburn visits Holliday in jail. The sexual politics of the piece are as relevant now as they were prescient then, and the movie stands as a glorious tribute to all involved. ▣

Spencer Tracy *Adam Bonner* • Katharine Hepburn *Amanda Bonner* • Judy Holliday *Doris Attinger* • Tom Ewell *Warren Attinger* • David Wayne *Kip Lurie* • Jean Hagen *Beryl Caighn* • Hope Emerson *Olympia La Pere* • Eve March *Grace* • Polly Moran *Mrs McGrath* • Clarence Kolb *Judge Reiser* ■ *Dir* George Cukor • *Scr* Ruth Gordon, Garson Kanin

Adam's Woman
★★

Adventure 1970 · Ausl · Colour · 116mins

This well-intentioned drama compromised by the casting of Beau

Bridges as an American sailor wrongly sentenced to transportation to the penal colony that is now known as Australia. Bridges is there to lure the American audience (there wasn't one) while alienating the British audience (there wasn't one of those, either, since the film was never released to cinemas). John Mills appears briefly as the Governor and Jane Merrow as the love interest.

Beau Bridges *Adam* • Jane Merrow *Bess* • James Booth *Dyson* • Andrew Keir *O'Shea* • Tracy Reed *Duchess* • Peter O'Shaughnessy *Barrett* • John Mills *Sir Philip* ■ *Dir* Philip Leacock • *Scr* Richard Fielder, from a story by Lowell Barrington

The Addams Family
★★★★ PG

Comedy horror   1991 · US · Colour · 95mins

Hollywood's plundering of classic TV series has produced its fair share of turkeys, but this is a glorious exception. This is partly owing to director Barry Sonnenfeld's wise decision to stick with the black humour of Charles Addams's original *New Yorker* cartoons and some inspired casting. Anjelica Huston and Raul Julia are note perfect as loving Morticia and Gomez, while Christopher Lloyd was equally born to play Fester. However, these stars are almost surpassed by the astonishingly agile Thing and by Christina Ricci's splendid performance as the young Wednesday. The plot of a confidence trickster (Lloyd) poses as Fester to steal the Addams fortune is a tad contrived, but Sonnenfeld makes a confident transition from cinematographer to director and the result is a witty family comedy that has enough sly humour to keep adults chuckling throughout. ▭

Anjelica Huston *Morticia Addams* • Raul Julia *Gomez Addams* • Christopher Lloyd *Uncle Fester Addams/Gordon Craven* • Dan Hedaya *Tully Alford* • Elizabeth Wilson *Abigail Craven* • Judith Malina *Granny* • Carel Struycken *Lurch* • Christina Ricci *Wednesday Addams* • Jimmy Workman *Pugsley Addams* • Dana Ivey *Margaret Alford* • Paul Benedict *Judge Womack* ■ *Dir* Barry Sonnenfeld • *Scr* Caroline Thompson, Larry Wilson, from characters created by Charles Addams

Addams Family Reunion
★ PG

Horror comedy   1998 · US · Colour · 87mins

Even the Addams family themselves would be turning in their graves over this one. Carel "Lurch" Struycken aside, none of the original stars of the excellent first two films is back for this cheap TV movie cash-in. Tim Curry and Daryl Hannah take on the Raul Julia and Anjelica Huston roles with enthusiasm, but they can't do anything with the unfunny, childish script, and their spirited performances are further hampered by the slapdash special effects. ▭

Tim Curry *Gomez Addams* • Daryl Hannah *Morticia Addams* • Nicole Marie Fugere *Wednesday Addams* • Jerry Messing *Pugsley Addams* • Ray Walston *Walter* • Kevin McCarthy *Grandpa Addams* • Ed Begley Jr *Phillip Adams* ■ *Dir* David Payne [Dave Payne] • *Scr* Scott Sandin, Rob Krechner, from characters created by Charles Addams

Addams Family Values
★★★★ PG

Comedy horror   1993 · US · Colour · 90mins

A delightful follow-up to *The Addams Family*, with a more expansive plot and blessed with an even blacker vein of humour than the original. This time, Gomez and Morticia (Raul Julia and Anjelica Huston) have a new baby, much to the displeasure of their other children, while Fester has fallen under the spell of the youngster's new black widow nanny (Joan Cusack). Once again, the playing is faultless, but it is Christina Ricci who effortlessly steals the show, whether trying to bump off her new sibling or creating havoc at an all-American summer camp. The sets are wonderful, the cinematography exquisite and Barry Sonnenfeld's direction exhilarating. The perfect antidote to more traditional family fare. Contains cartoonish violence and some swearing.

Anjelica Huston *Morticia Addams* • Raul Julia *Gomez Addams* • Christopher Lloyd *Uncle Fester* • Joan Cusack *Debbie Jellinsky* • Christina Ricci *Wednesday Addams* • Carol Kane *Granny* • Jimmy Workman *Pugsley Addams* • Kristin Hooper *Pubert Addams* • Carel Struycken *Lurch* ■ *Scr* Paul Rudnick, from characters created by Charles Addams

Addicted to His Love ★★ PG

Drama   1988 · US · Colour · 93mins

A fun drama, also known as *Sisterhood*, about a group of women who discover they have one thing in common – a con man (Barry Bostwick) who has made money out of romancing each one of them. The adventure really starts when they decide to bring about his downfall in this moderately enjoyable vengeance tale, which also stars Polly Bergen (*The Winds of War*), Erin Gray (*Buck Rogers in the 25th Century*) and Dee Wallace Stone (*ET*). ▭

Barry Bostwick *Larry Hogan* • Polly Bergen *Vivien Langford* • Colleen Camp *Ellie* • Erin Gray *Jenny Barrett* • Linda Purl *Cassie Robbins* • Dee Wallace Stone *Betty Ann Brennan* ■ *Dir* Arthur Allan Seidelman

Addicted to Love
★★

Science-fiction thriller
1995 · US · Colour · 96mins

Jeff Fahey is zapped back to *The Lawnmower Man* territory in this intriguing, if flawed, sci-fi chiller. Depressed by the death of his girlfriend, Fahey employs a sinister new invention in an attempt to summon up a foolproof re-creation of his dead partner. However, he soon discovers that the path of computer-generated love runs far from smoothly. Sadly, despite the playing of the ever-reliable Fahey, the project is let down by the formulaic direction of Paul Ziller.

Jeff Fahey *Liam Bass* • Ami Dolenz *Laura* • Meshach Taylor *Rich Anderson* • Carrie Genzel *Paris* ■ *Dir* Paul Ziller • *Scr* William Widmaier, Michelle Gambel Bisley, Paul Ziller

Addicted to Love   ★★★ 15

Romantic black comedy
1997 · US · Colour · 96mins

A surprisingly dark romantic comedy vehicle for the usually sweetness-and-light Meg Ryan, this casts her as a vengeful ex-girlfriend who spends her waking hours thinking up ways of making life hell for the man who dumped her (Tcheky Karyo). This involves teaming up with the more straight-laced Matthew Broderick, whose childhood sweetheart has dumped him for Meg's ex. An almost vindictive tale of love gone sour from actor-turned-director Griffin Dunne (best known as the harassed lead in Scorsese's *After Hours*), this has an enjoyably acidic bite normally absent from romantic comedies, and a rare nasty turn from Ryan. Contains swearing and some sexual situations. ▭ **DVD**

Meg Ryan *Maggie* • Matthew Broderick *Sam* • Kelly Preston *Linda Green* • Tcheky Karyo *Anton Depeaux* • Maureen Stapleton *Nana* • Nesbitt Blaisdell *Ed Green* • Remak Ramsay *Professor Wells* • Lee Wilkof *Carl* ■ *Dir* Griffin Dunne • *Scr* Robert Gordon

The Addiction   ★★★ 18

Horror   1994 · US · BW · 82mins

Shot in black and white for that Andy Warhol feel, Abel Ferrara's New Wave tale is his most idiosyncratic film to date. Lili Taylor is the New York University philosophy student-turned-vampire who spends as much time pondering the Nietzschean significance of her gory deeds as she does shooting up blood. Intriguing and stylish, if pretentiously over-intellectualised, the film is hard-hitting if you're in the right frame of mind and can cope with such arch dialogue as "Do you want an apology for ethical relativism?". Otherwise, you should approach with caution.

Lili Taylor *Kathleen Conklin* • Christopher Walken *Peina* • Annabella Sciorra *Casanova* • Edie Falco *Jean* • Paul Calderon *Professor* • Fredro Starr *Black* ■ *Dir* Abel Ferrara • *Scr* Nicholas St John

The Adding Machine   ★★★

Fantasy drama
1969 · US/UK · Colour · 104mins

This grim, symbolic fantasy was adapted from Elmer Rice's agitprop play of the twenties. Milo O'Shea is Mr Zero, an oppressed office drudge who murders his boss, is executed and sent not to hell, but to a heavenly waiting area populated by other killers en route to a new life. Directed by Jerome Epstein, with luminous photography by Water Lassally, it lacks the Expressionist edge that such an allegory needs. There are memorable performances from Phyllis Diller, as the nagging wife, and Sydney Chaplin.

Phyllis Diller *Mrs Zero* • Milo O'Shea *Zero* • Billie Whitelaw *Daisy* • Sydney Chaplin *Lieutenant Charles* • Julian Glover *Shrdlu* • Raymond Huntley *Smithers* • Phil Brown *Don* • Libby Morris *Ethel* • Hugh McDermott *Harry* • Paddie O'Neil *Mabel* • Carol Cleveland *Judy* ■ *Dir* Jerome Epstein • *Scr* Jerome Epstein, from the play by Elmer Rice

Address Unknown   ★

Second World War drama
1944 · US · BW · 72mins

Paul Lukas plays a German-American art dealer who returns to Germany in 1939 and becomes a card-carrying Nazi. However, his position changes when the Jewishness of his partner's daughter is discovered. Lukas overacts terribly in what is a slow and rather worthy slice of wartime propaganda. Director William Cameron Menzies is better known as the production designer who worked on such classics as *Invaders from Mars* (which he also directed) and *Gone with the Wind*.

Paul Lukas *Martin Schulz* • Carl Esmond *Baron von Friesche* • Peter Van Eyck *Heinrich Schulz* • Mady Christians *Elsa* • Morris Carnovsky *Max Eisenstein* • KT Stevens *Griselle* • Mary Young *Mrs Delaney* ■ *Dir* William Cameron Menzies • *Scr* Herbert Dalmas, from a story by Kressman Taylor

Adios Amigo   ★

Comedy western   1975 · US · Colour · 87mins

Former football star Fred Williamson stars in, writes, directs and produces this blaxploitation pic, a sort of western about a pair of hopelessly inefficient con artists. As Williamson's partner in crime, Richard Pryor mugs shamelessly, only sometimes revealing an unwillingness to show up Williamson's obvious lack of acting ability. The fact that he can't write or direct very well is beside the point. ▭

Richard Pryor *Sam* • Fred Williamson *Ben* • Thalmus Rasulala *Noah* • James Brown (2) • Robert Phillips • Mike Henry ■ *Dir/Scr* Fred Williamson

Adios Gringo   ★

Western   1965 · It/Fr/Sp · Colour · 99mins

Spaghetti western staple Guiliano Gemma (usually billed as Montgomery Wood) can always be relied on to bring a touch of class to even the most routine cowboy drama. This one needs him more than most. He plays gunslinger Brett Landers, who goes on the run after almost being lynched for a murder he didn't commit. En route he rescues damsel in distress Evelyn Stewart before taking revenge on the cattle rustlers responsible for his plight. An Italian western with a Hollywood feel.

Montgomery Wood [Guiliano Gemma] *Brent Landers* • Evelyn Stewart *Lucy Tillson* • Roberto Camardiel *Dr Barfield* • Jesus Puente *Tex Slaughter* • Max Dean *Avery Ranchester* ■ *Dir* George Finlay [Georgio Stegani] • *Scr* Georgio Stegani, Jose Luis Jerez, Michele Villerot

The Adjuster   ★★★ 18

Drama   1991 · Can · Colour · 97mins

Preoccupied with images and the way in which we perceive them, Atom Egoyan is one of the most intriguing directors working today. Elias Koteas and Arsinée Khanjian are perhaps the perfect Egoyan couple. He studies accident scenes and photographs to assess insurance claims, while she is a porn film censor. He sleeps with his clients, she secretly records the scenes she is paid to withhold from the public. Nothing is what it seems in this teasing film, in which the full picture is as likely to emerge in a close-up as it is in a long shot. Contains sex scenes and nudity. ▭

Elias Koteas *Noah Render* • Arsinée Khanjian *Hera Render* • Maury Chaykin *Bubba* • Gabrielle Rose *Mimi* • Jennifer Dale *Arianne* • David Hemblen *Bert* • Rose Sarkisyan *Seta* ■ *Dir/Scr* Atom Egoyan

The Admirable Crichton
★★★ **U**

Comedy 1957 · UK · Colour · 93mins

An agreeably dated version of JM Barrie's play, about the butler to Lord Loam taking over as master when the family is shipwrecked. It's a splendid vehicle for Kenneth More's genial urbanity, though it's Cecil Parker, as the bemused peer, who seems more in touch with turn-of-the-century times. Diane Cilento (Jason Connery's mother) and Sally Ann Howes are the charmers vying for Crichton's impeccable affections.

Kenneth More *Crichton* • Diane Cilento *Tweeny* • Cecil Parker *Lord Loam* • Sally Ann Howes *Lady Mary* • Martita Hunt *Lady Brocklehurst* • Jack Watling *Treherne* • Peter Graves (2) *Brocklehurst* • Gerald Harper *Ernest* ■ *Dir* Lewis Gilbert • *Scr* Vernon Harris, from the play by JM Barrie

The Admiral Was a Lady
★★ **U**

Comedy 1950 · US · BW · 86mins

A sometimes droll, but mostly dull, attempt to make a comedy of sexual manners out of seafaring Wanda Hendrix's hold over four disparate but somewhat dissolute men. Hendrix is good fun and Edmond O'Brien is eminently watchable as always, but, despite a decent cast which struggles vainly with the extremely poor material, this one fails to ignite from reel one. With a brief nod to female emancipation here, and a doffed cap to chauvinism there, this is a film which does not recognise the need to play the gender game.

Edmond O'Brien *Jimmie Stevens* • Wanda Hendrix *Jean Madison* • Rudy Vallee *Peter Pettigrew* • Johnny Sands *Eddie* • Steve Brodie *Mike* • Richard Erdman *Ollie* • Hillary Brooke *Mrs Pettigrew* ■ *Dir* Albert S Rogell • *Scr* Sidney Salkow, John O'Dea

Adolf Hitler – My Part in His Downfall
★★★

Comedy 1972 · UK · Colour · 102mins

Spike Milligan doesn't write the script or play himself in this adaptation of his bestselling wartime memoir; Johnny Byrne does the honours in the first department, while Jim Dale portrays the future Goon. (Milligan puts in a cameo appearance as his own father.) It must have been a near impossible task to turn Milligan's priceless prose into a coherent movie, but this is a pretty fair effort that's bound to ring bells with anyone who survived basic training. The shifts between absurd comedy and sudden tragedy are neatly handled, and the supporting cast more than pass muster.

Jim Dale *Spike Milligan* • Arthur Lowe *Major Drysdale* • Bill Maynard *Sergeant Ellis* • Windsor Davies *Sergeant Mackay* • Tony Selby *Bill* • Geoffrey Hughes *Larry* • Jim Norton *Pongo* • David Belcher *Smith* • Spike Milligan *Spike's father* • Pat Coombs *Spike's mother* ■ *Dir* Norman Cohen • *Scr* Johnny Byrne, from the memoir by Spike Milligan

Adorable Lies
★★★★

Drama 1991 · Cub · Colour · 108mins

Robert Redford's Sundance Institute helped with the funding for this scathing Cuban satire, which then ran into difficulties with the Communist censors. It's hardly surprising, considering the barbed implications of this seemingly innocent story about a frustrated screenwriter (Luis Alberto Garcia) who loses touch with reality when his passion for wannabe actress Isabel Santos turns to obsession. Constantly switching the cinematic point-of-view and littering the action with allegorical references and sight gags, Gerardo Chijona has produced a film almost on a par with the early works of those master satirists Tomás Gutiérrez Alea and Humberto Solás. In Spanish with English subtitles.

Isabel Santos • Luis Alberto Garcia • Mirtha Ibarra [Mirta Ibarra] ■ *Dir* Gerardo Chijona • *Scr* Senel Paz

Adrenalin: Fear the Rush
★★ **18**

Science-fiction action thriller
1995 · US · Colour · 93mins

Species babe Natasha Henstridge and *Highlander* star Christopher Lambert (credited here as Christophe) join forces as two cops on the trail of a plague-infected serial killer in a so-so science-fiction effort scripted and directed by direct-to-video master Albert Pyun. As viral thrillers go it's an average action package, but the two photogenic stars add solid weight to the budget bravado. Contains swearing and violence. ▭

Christophe Lambert [Christopher Lambert] *Lemieux* • Natasha Henstridge *Delon* • Norbert Weisser *Cuzo* • Elizabeth Barondes *Wocek* • Xavier Declie *Volker* • Craig Davis *Suspect* • Nicholas Guest *Rennard* • Andrew Divoff *Sterns* ■ *Dir/Scr* Albert Pyun

Aduefue, the Lords of the Street
★★★

Crime drama 1988 · IvC/Fr · Colour

Sijiri Bakaba's fascinating film offers a stern warning about the perils facing Africa if the pace of progress is not controlled. Set in 1972 in the capital of the fictional republic of Nagban, the action follows Georges T Benson as he seeks to satisfy the "get rich quick" ambitions he developed while visiting France. Although Bakaba's bustling film concentrates on Benson's plans for an audacious robbery, it also touches on traditional morality and the way Western culture is undermining long-held social values. In French with English subtitles.

Georges T Benson • Pierre-Loup Rajot • Mory Traore • Sijiri Bakaba • Alpha Blondy ■ *Dir* Sijiri Bakaba

Advance to the Rear
★★★

Comedy western 1964 · US · BW · 96mins

This sweet-tempered send-up of Civil War heroics from *Destry Rides Again* director George Marshall has a company of Union misfits sent out of the reach of battle, but still managing to capture a rebel spy (Stella Stevens) and save a vast pay-out in gold. The situations are fairly obvious, certainly, but Glenn Ford injects an amused authority into the action so the result is gentle satire that saddles up the usual clichés but for different reasons.

Glenn Ford *Captain Jared Heath* • Stella Stevens *Martha Lou* • Melvyn Douglas *Colonel Claude Brackenby* • Jim Backus *General Willoughby* • Joan Blondell *Jenny* ■ *Dir* George Marshall • *Scr* Samuel A Peeples, William Bowers, from the novel *The Company of Cowards* by Jack Schaefer

Adventure
★

Adventure drama 1945 · US · BW · 128mins

Clark Gable had famously gone off to fight in the Second World War, and was decorated after flying bomb runs over Germany. But in 1945 he returned to Hollywood and made *Adventure*, giving MGM the dreamy advertising slogan, "Gable's back and Garson's got him!". But the movie, so anticipated, was a syrupy romance between a merchant sailor and a priggish bookworm. It might have worked at 70 minutes; at nearly double that, it's an endurance test.

Clark Gable *Harry Patterson* • Greer Garson *Emily Sears* • Joan Blondell *Helen Melohn* • Thomas Mitchell *Mudgin* • Tom Tully *Gus* • John Qualen *Model T* • Richard Haydn *Limo* ■ *Dir* Victor Fleming • *Scr* Frederick Hazlitt Brennan, Vincent Lawrence, from a novel by Clyde Brion Davis

An Adventure for Two ★★ **15**

Drama 1979 · Fr · Colour · 112mins

This rarely seen feature is one of writer/director Claude Lelouch's more puzzling offerings. So much of it seems to have been designed to vex the viewer, particularly in terms of its stuttering structure, its pernickety attention to minor detail and its often dubious incidents. Yet, Lelouch makes arresting use of locations in both the US and Canada and draws credible performances from Jacques Dutronc and Catherine Deneuve as a runaway gangster and his hostage who eventually become lovers. Usually keen to comment on sexual chemistry, Lelouch, for once, has little that's original or interesting to say. In French with English subtitles. ▭

Catherine Deneuve *Françoise* • Jacques Dutronc *Simon* • Jacques Villeret *Tonton* • Gerard Caillaud *Bliche* • Paul Preboist *Inspector Mimile* • Bernard Crommbey [Bernard Crombey] *Inspector Alain* • Gilberte Genait *Zézette* ■ *Dir/Scr* Claude Lelouch

Adventure in Baltimore
★★ **U**

Comedy 1949 · US · BW · 88mins

A vehicle supposedly tailored for the rapidly maturing Shirley Temple, who was soon to retire from the screen, perhaps as a result of movies like this. The extraordinarily (by today's standards) reactionary plotline has Temple submit to the conservative ways of her pastor father Robert Young, who was soon to immortalise the phrase "Father Knows Best" as the title of his popular long-running television series. The star copes well enough, but most will find her teenage cuteness rather galling. ▭

Robert Young *Dr Sheldon* • Shirley Temple *Dinah Sheldon* • John Agar *Tom Wade* • Albert Sharpe *Mr Fletcher* • Josephine Hutchinson *Mrs Sheldon* • Charles Kemper *Mr Steuben* • Johnny Sands *Gene Sheldon* ■ *Dir* Richard Wallace • *Scr* Lionel Houser, from a story by Lesser Samuels, Christopher Isherwood

Adventure in the Hopfields
★★ **U**

Adventure drama 1954 · UK · BW · 60mins

In days of yore, the poor folk of South London flocked to Kent and went hop-picking. But this adventure is no bucolic idyll. Made for the Children's Film Foundation, and starring popular child actor Mandy Miller, this exciting tale offers bullying, theft and a climactic lightning storm. A little piece of British social history from the future director of *The Towering Inferno*.

Mandy Miller *Jenny Quin* • Mona Washbourne *Mrs McBain* • Hilda Fenemore *Mrs Quin* • Russell Waters *Mr Quin* • Melvyn Hayes *Reilly* • Harold Lang *Sam Hines* • Wallas Eaton *Postman* • Jane Asher ■ *Dir* John Guillermin • *Scr* John Cresswell, from the novel *The Hop Dog* by Nora Lavin, Molly Thorp

The Adventure of Sherlock Holmes' Smarter Brother
★★ **PG**

Comedy 1975 · UK · Colour · 87mins

Gene Wilder's directorial debut owes much to his slapdash, slapstick mentor Mel Brooks, with its hit-and-miss array of jokes. Wilder also stars as a wonderfully supercilious Sigerson Holmes, taking over a blackmail case, involving Madeline Kahn and opera star Dom DeLuise, from his more famous brother Sherlock (Douglas Wilmer), and then becoming entangled with stolen state secrets. In a Victorian London that's a set designer's over-cluttered dream, the best humour – the members of a drugged operatic chorus collapsing one after the other – is very funny indeed, but, apart from that, the whimsy can be rather tiresome. It's all a bit too elementary. Contains swearing. ▭

Gene Wilder *Sigerson Holmes* • Madeline Kahn *Jenny* • Marty Feldman *Orville Sacker* • Dom DeLuise *Gambetti* • Leo McKern *Moriarty* • Roy Kinnear *Moriarty's aide* • John Le Mesurier *Lord Redcliff* • Douglas Wilmer *Sherlock Holmes* • Thorley Walters *Dr Watson* • George Silver *Bruner* • Susan Field *Queen Victoria* ■ *Dir/Scr* Gene Wilder

The Adventurers
★★ **U**

Adventure 1950 · UK · BW · 77mins

Not the 1970 Harold Robbins fiasco, but a sturdy British would-be action drama set in South Africa about the squabbling members of an expedition searching for a cache of diamonds. Jack Hawkins, on his way to major stardom, is cast against type as a villain, who enlists an unconvincing Dennis Price, a young Peter Hammond and Grégoire Aslan to help him recover the treasure. This could have been quite stirring if it hadn't been morbidly under-directed at a snail's pace by David MacDonald. In the US it ran 12 minutes shorter and was twice retitled, as *The Great Adventure* and *Fortune in Diamonds*. ▭

Jack Hawkins *Pieter Brandt* • Peter Hammond *Hendrik Von Thaal* • Dennis Price *Clive Hunter* • Grégoire Aslan *Dominic* • Charles Paton *Barman* • Siobhan McKenna *Anne Hunter* • Bernard Lee *O'Connell* ■ *Dir* David MacDonald • *Scr* Robert Westerby

U = SUITABLE FOR ALL **Uc** = SUITABLE FOR ALL, ESPECIALLY FOR YOUNG CHILDREN (VIDEO ONLY) **PG** = PARENTAL GUIDANCE

The Adventurers ★★ U

Action adventure
1968 · Fr/It · Colour · 101mins

The "adventurers" of the title are Alain Delon and Lino Ventura, whose partnership here was a huge European casting coup that was only topped by Brigitte Bardot and Jeanne Moreau in *Viva Maria!* and by Delon and Jean-Paul Belmondo in *Borsalino*. Delon and Ventura play a daredevil and inventor respectively who team up for stunts involving fast cars and a plane they plan to fly under the Arc de Triomphe. Joanna Shimkus briefly introduces a touch of *Jules et Jim* into the proceedings, before they become dominated by a race against the Mafia for hidden treasure. French dialogue dubbed into English.

Alain Delon *Manu* • Lino Ventura *Roland* • Joanna Shimkus *Letitia* ■ *Dir* Robert Enrico • *Scr* Robert Enrico, Pierre Pelegri, José Giovanni, from the novel *Les Aventuriers* by José Giovanni

The Adventurers ★ 18

Action adventure
1970 · US · Colour · 163mins

Lewis Gilbert directs this monumentally bad adaptation of Harold Robbins's potboiler about South American revolution, torrid sex and macho posturing. Bekim Fehmiu, a Yugoslavian actor whose career was deservedly short-lived, is at the top of a bewildering list of international stars, ranging from Olivia de Havilland and Candice Bergen, to Rossano Brazzi and Lois Maxwell (Miss Moneypenny in the James Bond films). The film's mishmash of orgies, violence, Freudian psycho-babble and jet-set locations makes for entertaining viewing – for the first hour. Alas, there's still two more to go. ▣

Bekim Fehmiu *Dax Xenos* • Alan Badel *Rojo* • Candice Bergen *Sue Ann Daley* • Ernest Borgnine *Fat Cat* • Leigh Taylor-Young *Amparo* • Fernando Rey *Jaime Xenox* • Charles Aznavour *Marcel Campion* • Olivia de Havilland *Deborah Hadley* • John Ireland *Mr Hadley* • Rossano Brazzi *Baron de Coyne* • Sydney Tafler *Colonel Gutierrez* • Peter Graves (1) *Trustee banker* • Jaclyn Smith *Belinda* • Lois Maxwell *Woman at Fashion Show* ■ *Dir* Lewis Gilbert • *Scr* Lewis Gilbert, Michael Hastings, from the novel by Harold Robbins

Adventures of a Plumber's Mate ★ 18

Sex comedy 1978 · UK · Colour · 84mins

An example of the British blue-comedy boom of the seventies, this tatty tale from Stanley Long (who made two other, similarly-titled movies) presents wife-beating as slapstick. Christopher Neil is singularly unappealing as the titular hero, whose attempts to settle his debts bring him into contact with endless sex-starved women and gangster William Rushton. The promotion material for the film attempted to cash in on Elaine Page's *Evita* fame (she won the 1978 West End Theatre Award for best performance in a musical) by splashing her name across the poster, even though she only plays a barmaid. Contains swearing, sex scenes and nudity. ▣

Christopher Neil *Sid South* • Arthur Mullard *Crapper* • Elaine Paige *Susie* • Anna Quayle *Loretta Proudfoot* ■ *Dir* Stanley Long • *Scr* Stephen D Frances, Aubrey Cash

Adventures of a Private Eye ★ 18

Sex comedy 1977 · UK · Colour · 92mins

Although he saw action in the "nudie cutie" business for over 25 years, Stanley Long only directed seven features and this was his penultimate big screen outing. Following on from the surprisingly profitable *Adventures of a Taxi Driver*, this smutty romp sticks to the same formula. Christopher Neil, in the title role, strips at regular intervals to satisfy a blackmailer's demand that he sleep with every pretty girl he meets. Comic stalwarts like Harry H Corbett and Irene Handl are joined by Jon Pertwee and the glamorous Diana Dors, Suzy Kendall and Liz Fraser, but this is really no more than soft-core pulp. ▣

Christopher Neil *Bob West* • Suzy Kendall *Laura Sutton* • Harry H Corbett *Sydney* • Liz Fraser *Violet* • Irene Handl *Miss Friggin* • Ian Lavender *Derek* • Jon Pertwee *Judd Blake* • Adrienne Posta *Lisa Moroni* • Anna Quayle *Medea* • William Rushton *Wilfred* • Diana Dors *Mrs Horne* ■ *Dir* Stanley Long • *Scr* Michael Armstrong

Adventures of a Taxi Driver ★★ 18

Sex comedy 1975 · UK · Colour · 89mins

Back in the seventies, smutty comedies such as this entry in the *Adventures* series were the order of the day for comedy actors trying to break into movies. Robert Lindsay, Liz Fraser, Ian Lavender and Henry McGee are among the familiar faces who probably squirmed with embarrassment at their performances in this bawdy comedy. Barry Evans, who came to prominence in the *Doctor* TV series, is the nominal leading man, adding new meaning to the familiar drivers' refrain, "You'll never guess who I had in the back of the cab?" Contains swearing, sex scenes, drug abuse and nudity.

Barry Evans *Joe North* • Judy Geeson *Nikki* • Adrienne Posta *Carol* • Diana Dors *Mrs North* • Liz Fraser *Maisie* • Ian Lavender *Ronald* • Stephen Lewis *Doorman* • Robert Lindsay *Tom* • Henry McGee *Inspector Rogers* ■ *Dir* Stanley A Long [Stanley Long] • *Scr* Suzanne Mercer

The Adventures of Baron Munchausen ★★★★ PG

Fantasy adventure
1988 · UK/W Ger · Colour · 121mins

John Neville plays the legendary liar to perfection in Terry Gilliam's sumptuous revision of the Rudolph Erich Raspe stories, which gives a delicious contemporary relevance to the infamous Baron's outlandish exploits as he reunites his four fantastically talented friends to fight the Turkish army. Gilliam's grandiose masterpiece visualises a warped world of chaotic Pythonesque extremes that extends from the moon (with the lunar king played by Robin Williams) to Mount Etna (where Oliver Reed gives a brilliant performance). An opulent odyssey balancing romance, comedy and thrills in one glittering, and constantly surprising, package. Contains mild swearing and brief nudity. ▣ **DVD**

John Neville *Baron Munchausen* • Eric Idle *Desmond/Berthold* • Sarah Polley *Sally Salt* • Oliver Reed *Vulcan* • Charles McKeown *Rupert/Adolphus* • Winston Dennis *Bill Albrecht* • Jack Purvis *Jeremy/Gustavus* • Valentina Cortese *Queen Ariadne/Violet* • Jonathan Pryce *Horatio Jackson* • Uma Thurman *Venus/Rose* • Bill Paterson *Henry Salt* • Sting *Heroic officer* • Alison Steadman *Daisy* • Robin Williams *King of the moon* ■ *Dir* Terry Gilliam • *Scr* Charles McKeown, Terry Gilliam, from the stories by Rudolph Erich Raspe

The Adventures of Barry McKenzie ★★★ 15

Comedy 1972 · Ausl · Colour · 101mins

Scrappy but often hilarious screen version of the *Private Eye* comic strip, with Barry Crocker escorting his Aunt Edna Everage through England's grottiest highways and dirtiest byways, and ending with Humphries "flashing his nasty" in front of Joan Bakewell on a late-night TV show. Words like "chunder" and "tubes of beer" entered the English language and, frankly possums, a lot of it is disgusting. To think that that lovely Bruce Beresford went on to make *Driving Miss Daisy*. ▣

Barry Crocker *Barry McKenzie* • Barry Humphries *Edna Everage/Hoot/Dr Meyer de Lamphrey* • Paul Bertam *Curly* • Dennis Price *Mr Gort* • Avice Landone *Mrs Gort* • Peter Cook *Dominic* • Mary Anne Severne *Lesley* • Dick Bentley *Detective* • Spike Milligan *Landlord* ■ *Dir* Bruce Beresford • *Scr* Bruce Beresford, Barry Humphries, from the comic strip *The Wonderful World of Barry McKenzie* by Barry Humphries

The Adventures of Buckaroo Banzai across the 8th Dimension ★★★ 15

Science-fiction comedy
1984 · US · Colour · 97mins

Comic book hero and rock star Banzai (Peter Weller) crashes his Jet Car through the eighth dimension and unwittingly opens a hole in time. Unless he and his weirdo team of Hong Kong Cavaliers close it, evil aliens will overrun the Earth. Far too clever and quirky for its own good, this esoteric cult movie (the directing debut of WD Richter) is a wacky spaced-out oddity. Watching it is like being on the outside of a gigantic in-joke trying desperately to understand what's so funny. An amazing cast, including Ellen Barkin, Jeff Goldblum, Christopher Lloyd and John Lithgow try their best to keep it all accessible but it wilfully degenerates into a huge impenetrable mess. ▣

Peter Weller *Buckaroo Banzai* • John Lithgow *Dr Emilio Lizardo/Lord John Whorfin* • Ellen Barkin *Penny Priddy* • Jeff Goldblum *New Jersey* • Christopher Lloyd *John Bigboote* • Lewis Smith *Perfect Tommy* • Robert Ito *Professor Hikita* ■ *Dir* WD Richter • *Scr* Earl Mac Rauch

The Adventures of Bullwhip Griffin ★★★ U

Comedy adventure
1967 · US · Colour · 105mins

Adapted from Sid Fleischman's novel, *By the Great Horn Spoon*, this lively Western spoof would have been even more entertaining if the mediocre songs had been dropped and director James Neilson had kept a tighter rein on the action. Roddy McDowall has a ball as the staid Boston butler who gains a reputation as a boxer after he unwillingly joins his young master, Bryan Russell, on the California gold rush. Karl Malden, who has stolen Richard Haydn's treasure map, relishes the chance to play a wicked master of disguise, but Suzanne Pleshette is wasted in romantic support. ▣

Roddy McDowall *Bullwhip Griffin* • Suzanne Pleshette *Arabella Flagg* • Karl Malden *Judge Higgins* • Harry Guardino *Sam Trimble* • Bryan Russell *Jack Flagg* • Richard Haydn *Quentin Bartlett* • Liam Redmond *Captain Swain* • Hermione Baddeley *Irene Chesney* • Cecil Kellaway *Mr Pemberton* ■ *Dir* James Neilson • *Scr* Lowell S Hawley, from the novel *By the Great Horn Spoon* by Sid Fleischman

Adventures of Don Juan ★★★ PG

Period adventure
1948 · US · Colour · 106mins

By the late forties, Errol Flynn's career was at a low ebb, caused by too much of everything. Warner Bros gave him one last chance as Don Juan (whom he emulated in real life, becoming infamous in 1942 when he was charged with and later acquitted of having under-age sex with two teenage girls), and Flynn somehow revived the athleticism and charm of his thirties' swashbucklers such as *The Adventures of Robin Hood*. Director Vincent Sherman tactfully photographed him from angles that disguised the facial ravages of booze, drugs and women. But, despite some fine swordplay and decent acting, the film bombed in America, though it was a hit in Europe. ▣

Errol Flynn *Don Juan* • Viveca Lindfors *Queen Margaret* • Robert Douglas *Duke De Lorca* • Alan Hale *Leporello* • Romney Brent *King Phillip III* • Ann Rutherford *Donna Elena* • Robert Warwick *Count De Polan* • Jerry Austin *Don Sebastian* ■ *Dir* Vincent Sherman • *Scr* George Oppenheimer, Harry Kurnitz, from a story by Herbert Dalmas

The Adventures of Elmo in Grouchland ★★★ U

Children's musical adventure
1999 · US · Colour · 73mins

Sesame Street has always aimed to entertain adults while teaching children, though this big-screen adaptation – concerning Elmo the muppet chasing his runaway blanket to Grouchland and finding both under the thumb of the selfish Mr Huxley (Mandy Patinkin) – is almost exclusively aimed at the five-and-under crowd. What's left over for grown-ups mostly consists of a few hilarious one-liner and Bert and Ernie's pleasing appearances; perhaps the next *Sesame Street* movie should focus on them.

Vanessa L Williams *Queen of Trash* • Mandy Patinkin *Huxley* • Kevin Clash *Elmo/Pestie/ Grouch jailer/Grouch cab driver* • Fran Brill *Zoe/Pestie/Prairie Dawn* • Sonia Manzano *Maria* • Roscoe Orman *Gordon* • Stephanie D'Abruzzo *Grizzy/Pestie* ■ *Dir* Gary Halvorson • *Scr* Mitchell Kriegman, Joseph Mazzarino, from a story by Mitchell Kriegman

The Adventures of Ford Fairlane ★★ 🔞

Action comedy 1990 · US · Colour · 97mins

Controversial sexist comic Andrew Dice Clay crashed and burned in an awkward misstep from action director Renny Harlin. The over-hyped Clay plays a rock 'n' roll detective investigating the death of a Heavy Metal singer on stage in this crude adventure, big on empty spectacle but very low on honest laughs. Robert Englund (Freddy Krueger in the *Nightmare on Elm Street* opus) turns up as a killer with a bad English accent while Priscilla Presley and Wayne Newton send themselves up as usual. A little Clay does go a long, long way. 🔲

Andrew Dice Clay *Ford Fairlane* • Wayne Newton *Julian Grendel* • Priscilla Presley *Colleen Sutton* • Morris Day *Don Cleveland* • Lauren Holly *Jazz* • Maddie Corman *Zuzu Petals* • Gilbert Gottfried *Johnny Crunch* • David Patrick Kelly *Sam* • Robert Englund *Smiley* ■ *Dir* Renny Harlin • *Scr* Daniel Waters, James Cappe, David Arnott, from the characters created by Rex Weiner

The Adventures of Gerard ★★

Historical adventure 1970 · UK/It/Swi · Colour · 91mins

Based on the stories of Sir Arthur Conan Doyle, this free-spirited romp through the Napoleonic Wars might well puncture a few inflated ideas about military glory, but even devotees of historical adventures like *Sharpe* will find it heavy going. Director Jerzy Skolimowski seems to have embarked on this campaign with little or no strategy – the jokes are haphazard, the acting veers between the astute and the theatrical, period detail is flouted with flippancy but not always with purpose, and the battle scenes are more shambolic than satire intended.

Peter McEnery *Colonel Etienne Gerard* • Claudia Cardinale *Countess Teresa* • Eli Wallach *Napoleon* • Jack Hawkins *Millefleurs* • Mark Burns *Colonel Russell* • Norman Rossington *Sgt Papilette* • John Neville *Wellington* ■ *Dir* Jerzy Skolimowski • *Scr* HAL Craig, Henry Lester, Gene Gutowski and Jerzy Skolimowski, from the stories by Sir Arthur Conan Doyle

The Adventures of Hajji Baba ★★

Adventure 1954 · US · Colour · 79mins

An unintentionally hilarious *Arabian Nights*-style fantasy, with the late John Derek, husband of Bo, as scantily clad as all the ladies of the harem. Whether or not Hajji is a relative of Ali Baba isn't clear; but because he's a barber, there's a phonetic logic to it all. Anyway, there's a lot of dashing about, plenty of kissing, some fine carpets, a little torture and, weirdest of all, Nat King Cole crooning on the soundtrack whenever the strapping Mr Derek makes an appearance.

John Derek *Hajji Baba* • Elaine Stewart *Princess Fawzia* • Thomas Gomez *Osman Aga* • Paul Picerni *Nur-el-din* • Amanda Blake *Banah* • Rosemarie Bowe *Ayesha* ■ *Dir* Don Weis • *Scr* Richard Collins

The Adventures of Hal 5 ★ 🆄

Adventure 1958 · UK · BW · 58mins

Later a key figure at Hammer, Tasmanian director Don Sharp found himself behind the camera for only the second time with this featurette from the Children's Film Foundation. It suffers hugely from a lack of resources, but even so, the tale of a villainous garage owner who tries to swindle a family out of their beloved old car typifies the patronising nature of most British children's pictures in the fifties and sixties. Ageing child star John Charlesworth, who was to commit suicide two years later, leads the rearguard, which seems very tame in this post-*Home Alone* era.

Peter Godsell *Charles* • William Russell *Vicar* • John Glyn Jones *Mr Goorlie* • Janina Faye *Moira* • John Charlesworth *Ralph* • Edwin Richfield *Cooper* • David Morrell *Dicey* ■ *Dir* Don Sharp • *Scr* Don Sharp, from the novel *Hal 5 and the Haywards* by Henry Donald

The Adventures of Huck Finn ★★★ 🅿🅶

Adventure 1993 · US · Colour · 107mins

This is one of at least eight film versions of Mark Twain's celebrated novel, but this Disney offering can hold its head much higher than several of its predecessors. With his wide eyes and refreshingly uncontrived manner, Elijah Wood gives a good account of himself in the title role, learning about racial tolerance along the way, thanks to his friendship with Jim, an escaped slave played with great finesse by Courtney B Vance. If writer/director Stephen Sommers occasionally soft-soaps and over-modernises in an attempt to connect with his audience, he still gets fine performances from a brutish Ron Perlman, and the roguish duo of Jason Robards and Robbie Coltrane. 🔲 **DVD**

Elijah Wood *Huck Finn* • Courtney B Vance *Jim* • Robbie Coltrane *The Duke* • Jason Robards [Jason Robards Jr] *The King* • Ron Perlman *Pap Finn* • Dana Ivey *Widow Douglas* • Anne Heche *Mary Jane Wilks* • James Gammon *Deputy Hines* • Paxton Whitehead *Harvey Wilks* • Tom Aldredge *Dr Robinson* ■ *Dir* Stephen Sommers • *Scr* Stephen Sommers from the novel by Mark Twain

The Adventures of Huckleberry Finn ★★★ 🅄

Comedy drama 1939 · US · BW · 90mins

In Hollywood's golden year of 1939, a showcase for MGM's popular and versatile male star Mickey Rooney, who was Oscar-nominated the same year for *Babes in Arms*. Although lacking the lavish Technicolor of David O Selznick's earlier *The Adventures of Tom Sawyer*, this film does benefit from producer Joseph L Mankiewicz's insistence on filming on authentic river locations. The members of the cast look perfect, as if they had just stepped out of Mark Twain's pages, particularly Rex Ingram (the genie in *The Thief of Bagdad*) as Jim the slave

and Elizabeth Risdon as the Widow Douglass.

Mickey Rooney *Huckleberry Finn* • Walter Connolly *The King* • William Frawley *The Duke* • Rex Ingram *Jim* • Lynne Carver *Mary Jane* • Jo Ann Sayers *Susan* • Minor Watson *Captain Brandy* • Elisabeth Risdon *Widow Douglass* • Clara Blandick *Miss Watson* ■ *Dir* Richard Thorpe • *Scr* Hugo Butler, from the novel by Mark Twain

The Adventures of Huckleberry Finn ★★★ 🅄

Adventure 1960 · US · Colour · 106mins

For all its Mississippi locations, this version of the great Mark Twain novel – primal source of much American literature – doesn't sweep us along in the torrential way it should. Maybe Eddie Hodges, as the mischievous Huck, is too prim, or perhaps director Michael Curtiz cut too many of the book's grimmer aspects. It's still an enjoyable epic, however, with Tony Randall as a superbly roguish con man and lively cameos by Buster Keaton and Andy Devine. As the slave, Archie Moore, former light heavyweight boxing world champion, is a knockout. Well, one wouldn't dare say anything else!

Tony Randall *The King* • Eddie Hodges *Huckleberry Finn* • Archie Moore *Jim* • Patty McCormack *Joanna* • Neville Brand *Pap* • Mickey Shaughnessy *The Duke* • Judy Canova *Sheriff's wife* • Andy Devine *Mr Carmody* • Buster Keaton *Lion tamer* ■ *Dir* Michael Curtiz • *Scr* James Lee, from the novel by Mark Twain

The Adventures of Ichabod and Mr Toad ★★★ 🅄

Animated adventure 1949 · US/UK · Colour · 65mins

This Disney feature begins with a whimsical version of the Washington Irving story *The Legend of Sleepy Hollow*. The tale of put-upon schoolmaster Ichabod Crane is pleasingly told by Bing Crosby, but it's the adventures of Toad of Toad Hall that capture the imagination. Basil Rathbone provides the narration, while Toad is superbly voiced by Eric Blore, best known as the butler in many of the Rogers–Astaire musicals. 🔲

Bing Crosby *Narrator* • Basil Rathbone *Narrator* • Eric Blore *Mr Toad* ■ *Dir* Jack Kinney, Clyde Geronimi, James Algar • *Scr* Erdman Penner, Winston Hibler, Joe Rinaldi, Ted Sears, Homer Brightman, Harry Reeves, from the story *The Legend of Sleepy Hollows* by Washington Irving and from the novel *The Wind in the Willows* by Kenneth Grahame

The Adventures of Marco Polo ★★ 🅄

Historical adventure 1938 · US · BW · 99mins

Gary Cooper is the most unlikely Marco Polo, but that didn't stop producer Samuel Goldwyn from casting him in this would-be tongue-in-cheek spectacular. Trouble is, it's not funny enough, nor at all spectacular, and, with cheesy art direction that cries out for Technicolor, the end result is both silly and dull. Also surprisingly dull is villain Basil Rathbone as Ahmed, his character not helped by director Archie Mayo's lack of imagination. Altogether a misfire, but there's still an appreciative audience for both Cooper and Hollywood at its most ridiculous,

and Lana Turner fans should watch for her brief appearance as a handmaiden. 🔲

Gary Cooper *Marco Polo* • Sigrid Gurie *Princess Kukachin* • Basil Rathbone *Ahmed* • Ernest Truex *Binguccio* • George Barbier *Kublai Khan* • Binnie Barnes *Nazama* • Alan Hale *Kaidu* • Lana Turner *Maid* ■ *Dir* Archie Mayo • *Scr* Robert E Sherwood, from a story by NA Pogson

The Adventures of Mark Twain ★★★

Biographical drama 1944 · US · BW · 130mins

Fredric March plays the title role in this workmanlike screen biography of Samuel Clemens, alias Mark Twain, America's greatest humorist. Twain, of course, was the creator of Huckleberry Finn, Tom Sawyer and half the entries in any decent book of quotations. He also found time to have an eventful life, which in turn makes an enjoyable enough film, despite a script which at times suggests that rumours of Twain's wit must have been greatly exaggerated.

Fredric March *Samuel Clemens/Mark Twain* • Alexis Smith *Olivia Langdon* • Donald Crisp *JB Pond* • Alan Hale *Steve Gillis* • C Aubrey Smith *Oxford Chancellor* • John Carradine *Bret Harte* • William Henry *Charles Langdon* • Robert Barrat *Horace E Bixby* ■ *Dir* Irving Rapper • *Scr* Alan LeMay, Harry Chandlee

The Adventures of Michael Strogoff ★★

Adventure drama 1937 · US · BW · 83mins

Before this version, Jules Verne's story had already been filmed twice in the silent era; in addition to this American adaptation, it was filmed four more times in Europe. Anton Walbrook here makes his Hollywood debut as a dashing emissary of the Tsar who is sent from St Petersburg to the frozen wastes of Siberia. The journey involves clashes with Tartars, romantic interludes and an interview with a British journalist. Despite some decent scenes and some lavish detail, what the movie really needs is a director like Michael Curtiz to bring it to life.

Anton Walbrook *Strogoff* • Elizabeth Allan *Nadia* • Akim Tamiroff *Ogareff* • Margot Grahame *Zangarra* • Eric Blore *Blount* • Edward Brophy *Packer* • Paul Guilfoyle *Vasiloff* ■ *Dir* George Nichols Jr • *Scr* Mortimer Offner, Anthony Veiller, Anne Morrison Chapin from the novel by Jules Verne

The Adventures of Milo and Otis ★★★ 🅄

Adventure 1986 · Jap · Colour · 71mins

Anyone, of any age, who has ever been won over by the wonderful sheep pig *Babe* should immediately tick off this Japanese live-action animal tale as essential viewing. Owing a huge debt to Disney's 1963 film *The Incredible Journey*, this is far superior to the studio's own 1993 remake *Homeward Bound: the Incredible Journey*, as the cat and dog of the title don't "speak" for themselves, making their perilous exploits seem all the more thrilling. Dudley Moore might not have been everyone's choice as narrator, but his lively voice-over gives the action sequences a bit more bite and prevents the gentler moments lapsing into whimsy. 🔲

Dudley Moore *Narrator* ■ *Dir* Masanori Hata • *Scr* Mark Saltzman, from a story by Masanori Hata

The Adventures of Pinocchio ★★ U

Fantasy adventure
1996 · UK/Fr/Ger/Cz Rep · Colour · 90mins

Despite state-of-the-art digital technology and creatures from the Jim Henson workshop, this is a disappointing rendition of Carlo Collodi's enchanting morality tale. Martin Landau brings some melancholic gravitas to the proceedings as Geppetto the woodcarver, and Udo Kier is suitably sinister as the puppeteer who lures little boys to his terrifying theme park. Director Steve Barron overplays his hand, however, so the film often feels like a glorified pantomime. The sequences at John Sessions's school and Dawn French's bakery will delight most youngsters, but it's all too brash and loud to be magical. 🖳

Martin Landau *Geppetto* • Jonathan Taylor Thomas *Pinocchio* • Udo Kier *Lorenzini* • Bebe Neuwirth *Felinet* • Rob Schneider *Volpe* • Corey Carrier *Lampwick* • Marcello Magni *Baker* • Dawn French *Baker's wife* • Griff Rhys Jones *Tino* • John Sessions *Schoolmaster* ■ *Dir* Steve Barron • *Scr* Sherry Mills, Steve Barron, Tom Benedek, Barry Berman, from the novel by Carlo Collodi

The Adventures of Priscilla, Queen of the Desert ★★★★ 15

Comedy drama　1994 · Ausl · Colour · 98mins
The nineties have been very good to Australian cinema. *Strictly Ballroom* and *Muriel's Wedding* were both released to great acclaim, but nothing's had quite the same impact as this wondrously camp classic. Tossing the niceties of sexual politics out of the window of a speeding bus, director Stephan Elliott sets about exposing the soft underbelly of the Australian male. Two drag queens and a transsexual travel across the outback in a dilapidated coach for a gig in that bastion of machismo, Alice Springs, en route finding themselves in all manner of hilarious fish-out-of-water situations. Ingeniously cast against type, Terence Stamp is a revelation as the hard-drinking transsexual. Brilliantly bitchy, fabulously photographed and wonderfully played, this frock opera (the costumes won a well-deserved Oscar) addresses serious issues with satirical accuracy and profound insight. Contains swearing 🖳 **DVD**

Terence Stamp *Bernadette* • Hugo Weaving *Tick/Mitzi* • Guy Pearce *Adam/Felicia* • Bill Hunter *Bob* • Sarah Chadwick *Marion* • Mark Holmes *Benjamin* • Julia Cortez *Cynthia* • Ken Radley *Frank* ■ *Dir/Scr* Stephan Elliott • *Cinematographer* Brian Breheny • *Costume Designer* Lizzy Gardiner, Tim Chappel

The Adventures of Quentin Durward ★★★★ U

Period drama　1955 · US · Colour · 116mins
This marvellous CinemaScope romp gave a new lease of life to the mature Robert Taylor and his career. Based on Sir Walter Scott's novel, and clearly an attempt to emulate the success of

Ivanhoe (same star, same director, same fiery stunt-packed climax), this is deliberately more tongue-in-cheek. Taylor is charmingly witty as the noble Durward, dignified by a moustache and a trimmed beard, and is the only American in a prestige mainly British cast, including Robert Morley and Martin Clunes's distinguished father Alec.

Robert Taylor (1) *Quentin Durward* • Kay Kendall *Isabelle* • Robert Morley *King Louis XI* • Alec Clunes *Charles, Duke Of Burgundy* • Marius Goring *Count Philip de Creville* • Wilfrid Hyde White *Master Oliver* • Ernest Thesiger *Lord Crawford* • George Cole *Hayraddin* ■ *Dir* Richard Thorpe • *Scr* Robert Ardrey, George Froeschel, from the novel by Sir Walter Scott

The Adventures of Robin Hood ★★★★★ U

Classic swashbuckling adventure
1938 · US · Colour · 101mins
Everyone's favourite swashbuckler, an action picture that, over 60 years on, still delights people of all ages, even youngsters weaned on CD-Rom. Shot in bright-as-a-button Technicolor, it was intended to star James Cagney but seems tailor-made for Errol Flynn as Sherwood's noblest outlaw, wooing Olivia de Havilland and crossing swords with Basil Rathbone's Sir Guy of Gisbourne and Claude Rains's Prince John, while Erich Wolfgang Korngold's music goes brassily heraldic. A few weeks into production, studio boss Jack Warner thought the rushes lacked sparkle and replaced director William Keighley with Michael Curtiz. The result was a box-office smash and Oscars for the score, editing and interior decoration. 🖳

Errol Flynn *Robin Hood* • Olivia de Havilland *Maid Marian* • Basil Rathbone *Guy of Gisbourne* • Claude Rains *Prince John* • Patric Knowles *Will Scarlet* • Eugene Pallette *Friar Tuck* • Alan Hale *Little John* • Melville Cooper *High Sheriff of Nottingham* • Ian Hunter *King Richard* • Una O'Connor *Bess* ■ *Dir* Michael Curtiz, William Keighley • *Scr* Norman Reilly Raine, Seton I Miller, from the novel *Ivanhoe* by Sir Walter Scott, from the operetta *Robin Hood* by De Koven-Smith • *Cinematographer* Sol Polito, Tony Gaudio, W Howard Greene • *Editor* Ralph Dawson • *Music* Erich Wolfgang Korngold • *Art Director* Carl Jules Weyl

The Adventures of Robinson Crusoe ★★★★ U

Adventure　1952 · US · Colour · 89mins
Considering what director Luis Buñuel did with *Wuthering Heights*, this is an astonishingly restrained adaptation of Daniel Defoe's classic castaway tale. Gone is the surrealism one expects of Buñuel, and in its place comes a heartfelt optimism about the salvation of humanity. Dan O'Herlihy received an Oscar nomination for his portrayal of the privileged man who comes to a greater understanding of life through his unbearable isolation. The arrival of Friday (Jaime Fernandez), offers an even more strenuous test and he finds himself reverting to his old ways. A Spanish language film.

Dan O'Herlihy *Robinson Crusoe* • Jaime Fernandez *Man Friday* • Felipe da Alba *Captain Oberzo* • Chel Lopez *Bosun* • Jose Chavez *Mutineer* • Emilio Garibay *Mutineer* ■ *Dir* Luis Buñuel • *Scr* Luis Buñuel, Philip Ansell Roll [Hugo Butler], from the novel by Daniel Defoe

The Adventures of Sherlock Holmes ★★★★ PG

Crime mystery　1939 · US · BW · 81mins
The second teaming of Basil Rathbone and Nigel Bruce as Holmes and Watson (and their last for Fox before the series moved to Universal) is one of the master detective's best screen cases. Borrowing from the stories of Sir Arthur Conan Doyle and the stage play by William Gillette, the film superbly re-creates the atmosphere of 221B Baker Street and Victorian London. Holmes never had a more devilish adversary than George Zucco as Moriarty or a more daring plot to foil than the theft of the Crown Jewels. The highlight has to be the disguised Rathbone singing *Oh, I Do Like to Be beside the Seaside*. 🖳

Basil Rathbone *Sherlock Holmes* • Nigel Bruce *Dr Watson* • Ida Lupino *Ann Brandon* • Alan Marshal *Jerrold Hunter* • Terry Kilburn *Billy* • George Zucco *Professor Moriarty* • Henry Stephenson *Sir Ronald Ramsgate* • EE Clive *Inspector Bristol* • Arthur Hohl *Bassick* • May Beatty *Mrs Jameson* ■ *Dir* Alfred Werker • *Scr* Edwin Blum, William Drake, from the play by William Gillette, from the stories of Sir Arthur Conan Doyle

The Adventures of Tartu ★★

Second World War spy drama
1943 · UK · BW · 112mins
In order to sabotage a Nazi nerve gas factory, Robert Donat goes undercover in Czechoslovakia as a Romanian ex-diplomat. Valerie Hobson is also undercover, though she's posing as a Nazi. Harold S Bucquet's film is solidly made and reasonably tense, but the casting of Donat can't help reminding viewers of the far superior *The Thirty-Nine Steps*. Apparently, the exotic-sounding title was a ploy to suggest to audiences that it wasn't just another wartime propaganda effort – by 1943, such pictures had run out of steam at the box office.

Robert Donat *Captain Terence Stevenson* • Valerie Hobson *Maruschka* • Walter Rills *Inspector Otto Vogel* • Glynis Johns *Paula Palacek* • Phyllis Morris *Anna Palacek* ■ *Dir* Harold S Bucquet • *Scr* Howard Emmet Rogers, John Lee Mahin, Miles Malleson, from a story by John C Higgins

The Adventures of the Wilderness Family ★★ U

Adventure　1975 · US · Colour · 98mins
Echoes of *Swiss Family Robinson* reverberate around this encounter with the great outdoors, as an identically named family quits Los Angeles to set up home in the Colorado Rockies. Robert F Logan is a construction worker, so building a cabin poses few problems. However, the marauding wildlife, suspicious locals and unyielding flora soon prove as irksome as the crime and pollution they have left behind. Writer/director Stewart Raffill makes the most of his breathtaking locations, but the survivalist angle is all too familiar.

Robert F Logan [Robert Logan] *Skip* • Susan Damante Shaw *Pat* • Hollye Holmes *Jenny* • Ham Larsen *Toby* ■ *Dir/Scr* Stewart Raffill

The Adventures of Tom Sawyer ★★★★ U

Adventure　1938 · US · Colour · 90mins
Despite the Disney studio's valiant attempt to retell this most beloved and arcane slice of Americana in 1993's *The Adventures of Huck Finn*, this superb David O Selznick production the year before he gave the world *Gone with the Wind* remains the most entertaining, and most faithful, of all screen adaptations of Mark Twain's tale. The nightmare sequences in the caverns are brilliantly executed, and the use of early Technicolor particularly effective. The pace is fast, the running time taut and the casting impeccable: apart from the two decent boy leads, who could fail to warm to a period romp featuring such character delights as Walter Brennan, May Robson and Victor Jory.

Tommy Kelly *Tom Sawyer* • Jackie Moran *Huckleberry Finn* • Ann Gillis *Becky Thatcher* • May Robson *Aunt Polly* • Walter Brennan *Muff Potter* • Victor Jory *Injun Joe* • David Holt *Sid Sawyer* • Victor Kilian *Sheriff* • Nana Bryant *Mrs Thatcher* • Olin Howland *Schoolmaster* • Donald Meek *Superintendent* • Charles Richman *Judge Thatcher* ■ *Dir* Norman Taurog • *Scr* John VA Weaver, from the novel by Mark Twain

The Adversary ★★★

Drama　1970 · Ind · BW · 100
Following his father's death, young Dhritiman Chatterjee is forced to abandon his studies and find work to support his family, but cannot compete in the scuttling rat race. Satyajit Ray paints a perceptive portrait of an educated but listless and unappealing character attempting to manage life in the stressful environment of Calcutta. The supporting characters are also incisively drawn in this sharply observed tale, at once amusing, poignant and bitter, from India's master auteur. A Bengali language film.

Dhritiman Chatterjee *Siddhartha* • Krishna Bose *Sutapa* • Jaysree Roy *Keya* • Debraj Roy *Tunu* ■ *Dir* Satyajit Ray • *Scr* Satyajit Ray, from the novel *Pratidwandi* by Sunil Ganguly • *Music* Satyajit Ray

Advice to the Lovelorn ★★

Comedy drama　1933 · US · BW · 62mins
Lee Tracy was never a frontline star and his fast-talking style (which made him something of a second division James Cagney) has not travelled well down the years. Nevertheless, his films were rarely dull. Here journalist Tracy alienates his rich fiancée and breaks up a drugs ring after being relegated to the lonely-hearts column of his local paper. This mixes comedy, tragedy and thrills, with capable performers such as Sally Blane and Jean Adair left in Tracy's dynamic slipstream.

Lee Tracy *Toby Prentiss* • Sally Blane *Louise Boley* • Sterling Holloway *Benny* • Jean Adair *Mrs Prentiss* • Paul Harvey *Gaskell* • Matt Briggs *Richards* • Charles Levison [Charles Lane (1)] *Circulation Manager* • Isabel Jewell *Rose* ■ *Dir* Alfred Werker • *Scr* Leonard Praskins, from the novel *Miss Lonelyhearts* by Nathanael West

Advise and Consent ★★★★

Political drama 1962 · US · BW · 138mins

Otto Preminger's superb study of political shenanigans in Washington provides marvellous roles for Henry Fonda as the liberal politician that ailing president Franchot Tone wants to promote and, especially, Charles Laughton, in his last film, as the southern senator opposed to the appointment. This was all but unique among Hollywood movies of the time in using homosexuality as a plot device, and, although it may seem a little tame today, it was significant and shocking enough on its release.

Henry Fonda *Robert Leffingwell* • Charles Laughton *Sen Seabright "Seb" Cooley* • Don Murray *Sen Brigham Anderson* • Walter Pidgeon *Sen Bob Munson* • Peter Lawford *Sen Lafe Smith* • George Grizzard *Sen Fred Van Ackerman* • Gene Tierney *Dolly Harrison* • Franchot Tone *President* • Lew Ayres *Vice-President* • Burgess Meredith *Herbert Gelman* ■ *Dir* Otto Preminger • *Scr* Wendell Mayes, from the novel by Allen Drury

The Affair ★★ PG

Romantic drama 1973 · US · Colour · 70mins

Made for American television, this trifling melodrama was shown theatrically in Europe, where its threadbare production values were painfully obvious. Nevertheless, this tale of a young woman disabled since childhood who finds romance with a sophisticated lawyer is given poignancy by the casting of Natalie Wood opposite her real-life husband, Robert Wagner. Director Gilbert Cates occasionally comes up with a few insights amid the tosh but, while Wagner and Wood clearly relish performing together, he's just not in her league. ▭

Natalie Wood *Courtney Patterson* • Robert Wagner *Marcus Simon* • Bruce Davison *Jamie Patterson* • Jamie Smith-Jackson *Jennifer* • Pat Harrington *Frank* ■ *Dir* Gilbert Cates • *Scr* Barbara Turner • *Producer* Aaron Spelling, Leonard Goldberg

The Affair ★★ 15

Second World War romantic drama 1995 · US/UK · Colour · 100mins

Executive produced by Harry Belafonte and directed by Paul Seed (*House of Cards*), this absorbing true story portrays the plight of black soldiers in wartime Britain. In a small English town in 1944, a lonely married woman, whose officer husband is away in the navy, finds herself having an affair with a black American soldier. When her husband returns and discovers them together, he charges the GI with rape, threatening to take their young son away unless his wife goes along with the story. Courtney B Vance and Kerry Fox give effective performances as the lovers trapped by the conventions of a bygone era. Contains some swearing, sex scenes and violence. ▭

Courtney B Vance *Travis Holloway* • Kerry Fox *Maggie* • Ciaran Hinds *Edward Leyland* • Leland Gantt *Barrett* • Beatie Edney *Esther* • Bill Nunn *Sgt Rivers* • Ned Beatty *Colonel Banning* • Fraser James *Sonny* • Adrian Lester *Ray* ■ *Dir* Paul Seed • *Scr* Pablo F Fenjves, Bryan Goluboff, from a story by Walter Bernstein, Pablo F Fenjves

Affair in Havana ★★

Crime drama 1957 · US · BW · 77mins

John Cassavetes plays a songwriter who goes to Cuba in search of great music and instead finds Sara Shane, the wife of repulsive plantation owner Raymond Burr. Shane falls for Cassavetes and is all set to run off with him when Burr promises her his $20 million fortune. Tired of waiting for him to die of natural causes, she shoves him into the swimming pool. Directed by Laslo Benedek, who made *Death of a Salesman* and *The Wild One*, this B-movie melodrama was partly financed by Cuba's tottering government in return for some travelogue footage of the island's scenery and music clubs.

John Cassavetes *Nick* • Raymond Burr *Mallabee* • Sara Shane *Lorna* • Lila Lazo *Fina* ■ *Dir* Laszlo Benedek [Laslo Benedek] • *Scr* Burton Lane, Maurice Zimm, from a story by Janet Green

Affair in Trinidad ★★★

Spy drama 1952 · US · BW · 98mins

Rita Hayworth and Glenn Ford, stars of that electric *film noir Gilda*, are re-united here in yet another spy drama set in a far-flung international Hollywood hotspot. The plot is some nonsense about spy rings, with Ford helping Hayworth find her husband's killer, but who cares when the stars strike such sparks from each other? Alexander Scourby makes an effective villain, and veteran director Vincent Sherman is in his element with this kind of material. Despite its flaws, this is highly entertaining, and Hayworth is simply ravishing in her return to the screen after a four-year break following her marriage to Prince Aly Khan.

Rita Hayworth *Chris Emery* • Glenn Ford *Steve Emery* • Alexander Scourby *Max Fabian* • Valerie Bettis *Veronica* • Torin Thatcher *Inspector Smythe* • Howard Wendell *Anderson* ■ *Dir* Vincent Sherman • *Scr* Oscar Saul, James Gunn, from a story by Virginia Van Upp, Berne Giler

An Affair to Remember ★★★★★ U

Romantic drama 1957 · US · Colour · 109mins

A wonderfully frothy fifties confection, which has inspired many a comic moment, as well as the climax on top of the Empire State Building in the much-loved Tom Hanks/Meg Ryan film *Sleepless in Seattle*. The incomparable Cary Grant is at his slickly arch and urbane best as a wealthy, idle womaniser who meets his match in self-contained, sassy Deborah Kerr aboard a luxury liner. Director Leo McCarey dresses his sophisticated comedy of sexual manners in an atmosphere of rhinestone-encrusted dresses, impeccably pressed dinner suits and raised champagne glasses. The second half slips off the boil somewhat, but, thanks to Grant and Kerr, this remains a cinematic object lesson in the perfect rapier delivery of cut-and-thrust dialogue. ▭

Cary Grant *Nickie Ferrante* • Deborah Kerr *Terry Mckay* • Richard Denning *Kenneth* • Neva Patterson *Lois* • Cathleen Nesbitt *Grandmother* • Robert Q Lewis *Announcer* • Charles Watts *Hathaway* • Fortunio Bonanova

Courbet ■ *Dir* Leo McCarey • *Scr* Delmer Daves, Donald Ogden Stewart (uncredited), Leo McCarey, from a story by Leo McCarey, Mildred Cram

Affair with a Stranger ★★★ U

Romantic drama 1953 · US · BW · 86mins

A lesson in how not to handle a disintegrating relationship from a well cast Victor Mature and Jean Simmons as a warring couple who adopt a child as their union collapses. Director Roy Rowland brings out the best in the stars, who make this barmy arrangement credible by sheer strength of acting and emotional depth. However, the film ultimately goes nowhere having set everything up, Rowland seems unsure about the direction his characters should take. Watching this is rather like opening a tempting box of chocolates and finding half are missing.

Jean Simmons *Carolyn Parker* • Victor Mature *Bill Blakeley* • Mary Jo Tarola *Dolly Murray* • Monica Lewis *Janet Boothe* • Jane Darwell *Ma Stanton* • Dabbs Greer *Happy Murray* • Wally Vernon *Joe* • Nicholas Joy *George Craig* ■ *Dir* Roy Rowland • *Scr* Richard Flournoy

The Affairs of Annabel ★★★ U

Satire 1938 · US · BW · 67mins

Good-natured, fast-moving semi-satire on the film industry, with wacky Lucille Ball as a star and rueful, loveable Jack Oakie as her inept press agent, who's always cooking up stunts that don't work. With nice support from the always welcome Ruth Donnelly and the instantly recognisable Fritz Feld, the film was popular enough in its day to inspire a limp sequel, *Annabel Takes a Tour*, with the same cast but a different director. Lucille Ball would eventually derive personal satisfaction from buying RKO, the studio where she filmed this trifle, and renaming it Desilu, where *I Love Lucy* was recorded for posterity.

Lucille Ball *Annabel Allison* • Jack Oakie *Lanny Morgan* • Ruth Donnelly *Josephine* • Bradley Page *Webb* • Fritz Feld *Vladimir* • Thurston Hall *Major* • Elisabeth Risdon *Mrs Fletcher* • Granville Bates *Mr Fletcher* ■ *Dir* Ben Stoloff [Benjamin Stoloff] • *Scr* Bert Granet, Paul Yawitz from a story by Charles Hoffman

The Affairs of Cellini ★★

Comedy 1934 · US · BW · 84mins

Hopelessly dated, this saunter through a Hollywood Florence initially offers some pleasure, largely thanks to director Gregory La Cava's sense of fun. In the title role, a bearded Fredric March proves he was one of the few stars of the time who looked truly comfortable in costume, and a top-billed Constance Bennett and Oscar-nominated Frank Morgan are enjoyable enough to watch. This was made in the wake of Britain's triumphant *The Private Life of Henry VIII*, so the farcical tone does become irritating. Still, this is adequate fare, and quite saucy in its own pre-censorship way. Watch out for an early appearance from Lucille Ball.

Constance Bennett *Duchess of Florence* • Fredric March *Benvenuto Cellini* • Frank Morgan *Alessandro, Duke of Florence* • Fay

Wray *Angela* • Vince Barnett *Ascanio* • Jessie Ralph *Beatrice* • Louis Calhern *Ottaviano* • Lucille Ball *Lady-in-waiting* ■ *Dir* Gregory La Cava • *Scr* Bess Meredyth, from the play *The Firebrand* by Edwin Justus Mayer

The Affairs of Dobie Gillis ★★★ U

Musical comedy 1953 · US · Colour · 72mins

It's youthful love at first sight when Debbie Reynolds and Bobby Van meet at the inaugural Freshmen's get-together at Grainbelt College – motto: learn, learn, learn; work, work, work. She's there to do just that, he's there to have fun... A good-natured and increasingly silly, semi-musical college caper in which true love faces numerous obstacles, especially Reynolds's tyrannical father, Hanley Stafford. The appealing and talented Van dances up a storm, as do Reynolds, Bob Fosse before he became famous, and Barbara Ruick.

Debbie Reynolds *Pansy Hammer* • Bobby Van *Dobie Gillis* • Barbara Ruick *Lorna Ellingboe* • Bob Fosse *Charlie Trask* • Hanley Stafford *Mr Hammer* • Lurene Tuttle *Mrs Hammer* • Hans Conried *Professor Amos Pomfritt* • Charles Lane (1) *Professor Obispo* ■ *Dir* Don Weis • *Scr* Max Shulman

The Affairs of Susan ★★★

Comedy 1945 · US · BW · 109mins

This is a sort of *Citizen Kane/ Rashomon* multi-sided type of comedy. Actress Susan Darell, portrayed by a very effervescent Joan Fontaine, gets to reveal four different personae during a series of flashbacks at fiancé Walter Abel's bachelor party, where he has invited two other suitors (one millionaire, one writer) plus Susan's previous husband, George Brent. This is a witty and classy Hal Wallis production, which rightly garnered an Oscar nomination for best original story. The real surprise is La Fontaine, who proves what a capable actress she is, offering a charming and utterly beguiling star performance in an unfairly neglected comedy.

Joan Fontaine *Susan Darell* • George Brent *Roger Berton* • Dennis O'Keefe *Bill Anthony* • Don DeFore *Mike Ward* • Rita Johnson *Mona Kent* • Walter Abel *Richard Aiken* • Byron Barr *Chick* • Mary Field *Nancy* • Francis Pierlot *Uncle Jimmy* ■ *Dir* William A Seiter • *Scr* Laszlo Gorog, Richard Flournoy, Thomas Monroe, from a story by Laszlo Gorog, Thomas Monroe

Affectionately Yours ★★

Comedy 1941 · US · BW · 87mins

Top news correspondent Dennis Morgan rushes home from an overseas assignment to win back his wife Merle Oberon. Rita Hayworth appears as "the other woman", and she's the best thing in a supposed marital comedy that misfires in every direction. Ralph Bellamy is fine as a rival for Oberon's affections, but neither of the stars has the right personality or touch to rescue the feeble material, while director Lloyd Bacon contributes little to the embarrassing proceedings.

Merle Oberon *Sue Marberry* • Dennis Morgan Richard *"Rickey" Mayberry* • Rita Hayworth *Irene Malcolm* • Ralph Bellamy *Owen Wright* • George Tobias *Pasha* • James Gleason *Chester Phillips* • Hattie McDaniel *Cynthia* • Jerome Cowan *Cullen* • Alexis Smith *Guest* •

Butterfly McQueen *Butterfly* • *Dir* Lloyd Bacon • *Scr* Edward Kaufman, from a story by Fanya Foss, Aileen Leslie

Affliction ★★★ 🔞

Drama 1997 · US · Colour · 109mins

Part thriller, part examination of a man in midlife crisis. this is a bleak but well-performed adaptation of the Russell Banks novel. Nick Nolte plays a traffic cop in a small, snow-covered New England town. When his friend Jack (Jim True) returns from a hunting expedition claiming the businessman he took with him died from a self-inflicted wound, Nolte seeks an escape from his damning ex-wife by turning detective. His subsequent mental disintegration is both painful and powerful to watch. Too black to be mainstream, this is nevertheless a tour de force for Nolte, though it was James Coburn who won the Oscar for his portrayal of Nolte's abusive father. Contains swearing and violence. 📼

Nick Nolte *Wade Whitehouse* • Sissy Spacek *Margie Fogg* • James Coburn *Glen Whitehouse* • Willem Dafoe *Rolfe Whitehouse* • Mary Beth Hurt *Lillian* • Jim True *Jack Hewitt* • Marian Seldes *Alma Pittman* ■ *Dir* Paul Schrader • *Scr* Paul Schrader, from the novel by Russell Banks

Afraid of the Dark ★★★ 🔞

Psychological thriller
1991 · UK/Fr · Colour · 87mins

The directorial debut of Mark Peploe, a regular scriptwriter for his brother-in-law, Bernardo Bertolucci, this is an eerily effective exercise in suspense. The always watchable James Fox is a cop trying to protect his small son and his blind wife (Fanny Ardant) from the attentions of a neighbourhood psycho, who may be window cleaner and pornographer Paul McGann. It's a quirky blend of *Wait until Dark* and Michael Powell's shocker *Peeping Tom* that throws up as many surprises as it does artistic pretensions. 📼

James Fox *Frank* • Fanny Ardant *Miriam* • Paul McGann *Tony Dalton* • Clare Holman *Rose* • Robert Stephens *Dan Burns* • Susan Woolridge *Lucy Trent* • Ben Keyworth *Lucas* ■ *Dir/Scr* Mark Peploe

Afraid to Dance ★★

Crime drama 1988 · Ausl · Colour · 90mins

Despite the title, there isn't much toe-tapping going on in this drama and perhaps a few *Footloose*-style numbers might have saved it from being yet another guy-and-gal on the run piece of tedium. Nique Needles is the teenage boy who is having a bad day after being fired from his job and then robbed. Naturally – at least, in this type of movie – he decides to steal a car. Instead, he gets tangled up with the owner (Rosey Jones) and the pair start their own miniature crime wave.

Nique Needles *The Male* • Rosey Jones *The Female* • Grigor Taylor *Jim Pratt* • Tina Bursill *Driving woman* • Tom Richards *Don Chapman* ■ *Dir* Denny Lawrence • *Scr* Paul Cockburn

Africa Screams ★★ 🅤

Comedy 1949 · US · BW · 78mins

Abbott and Costello find themselves at the mercy of rampaging lions, cheeky chimps and hostile locals when

bookseller Bud persuades explorer Frank Buck that Lou is the big game hunter he needs for his safari. Using every convention of the *Tarzan* movies, this forgettable comedy is as dense as the jungle, with the biggest laughs being Lou's name (Stanley Livingston) and the scene in which he fights off a frisky kitten. 📼

Bud Abbott *Buzz Johnson* • Lou Costello *Stanley Livingston* • Hillary Brooke *Diana Emerson* • Max Baer *Boots* • Buddy Baer *Grappler* ■ *Dir* Charles Barton • *Scr* Earl Baldwin

Africa – Texas Style ★★ 🅤

Adventure 1967 · US/UK · Colour · 108mins

In this unashamed attempt to replicate Howard Hawks's classic *Hatari!* – John Mills even plays a character called Howard Hayes! – Hugh O'Brian, then moderately famous as TV's Wyatt Earp, is the Texan cowboy hired by settler Mills to round up the Kenyan wildlife. Second unit maestro Andrew Marton, who directed the *Ben-Hur* chariot race and the D-Day landings for *The Longest Day*, has a field day with rhinos, but can't overcome the banal script. Mills's daughter, Hayley, is glimpsed at the airport.

Hugh O'Brian *Jim Sinclair* • John Mills *Wing Commander Hayes* • Nigel Green *Karl Bekker* • Tom Nardini *John Henry* • Adrienne Corri *Fay Carter* • Ronald Howard *Hugo Copp* • Charles Malinda *Sampson* • Honey Wamala *Mr Oyondi* • Hayley Mills *Girl at airport* ■ *Dir* Andrew Marton • *Scr* Andy White

The African Queen ★★★★★ 🅤

Classic First World War drama
1951 · UK · Colour · 100mins

What an inspired pairing! And to think, Charlie Allnutt and Rose Sayer were nearly played by David Niven and Bette Davis. Initially, all was not well between Katharine Hepburn and Humphrey Bogart but, from the moment she began basing her character on Eleanor Roosevelt, the elements fused into a unique screen chemistry, and a gentle humour (that was noticeably absent from the shooting script) began to seep into the action. With director John Huston preoccupied with extracurricular safaris, the location work was clearly a strain look at Bogie's face as he pulls the *Queen* through the leech-infested water. Yet the discord and discomfort resulted in a classic and a long overdue Oscar for Bogart. 📼

Humphrey Bogart *Charlie Allnutt* • Katharine Hepburn *Rose Sayer* • Robert Morley *Reverend Samuel Sayer* • Peter Bull *German Captain* • Theodore Bikel *German First Officer* • Walter Gotell *German Second Officer* • Gerald Onn *Petty Officer* ■ *Dir* John Huston • *Scr* James Agee, John Huston, from the novel by CS Forester • *Producer* SP Eagle [Sam Spiegel] • *Cinematographer* Jack Cardiff

After Dark, My Sweet ★★★★ 🔞

Crime thriller 1990 · US · Colour · 111mins

A suitably bleak slice of pulp fiction, which is taken from a Jim Thompson novel, with a brooding central performance from Jason Patric. He plays a washed up former boxer who gets entangled in a kidnapping being planned by Bruce Dern (as barmy as

ever) and sultry Rachel Ward (a revelation). Director James Foley (*At Close Range*) resists the temptation to put his foot on the throttle and is content to coolly watch the characters as they become locked in a doomed dance of greed and betrayal. Contains violence, swearing, nudity, sex scenes and substance abuse. 📼

Jason Patric *Kevin "Collie" Collins* • Rachel Ward *Fay Anderson* • Bruce Dern *Uncle Bud* • George Dickerson *Doc Goldman* • James Cotton *Charlie* • Corey Carrier *Jack* • Rocky Giordani *Bert* • Jeanie Moore *Nanny* ■ *Dir* James Foley • *Scr* Bob Redlin, from the novel by Jim Thompson

After Darkness ★★ 🔞

Psychological drama
1985 · UK/Swi · Colour · 103mins

Despite the best efforts of a hard-working cast, this psychological thriller never overcomes the flimsiness of its plot and the transparency of the principal protagonists. In delivering younger brother Julian Sands from an asylum, anthropologist John Hurt seems interested solely in helping him deal with the memory of his twin's death. When student Victoria Abril comes between them, however, it soon becomes clear which sibling is the more troubled. Writer/directors Sergio Guerraz and Dominique Othenin-Girard litter the action with haunting dreams and mysterious pronouncements, but the resultant melodramatics are far from persuasive. 📼

John Hurt *Peter Huninger* • Julian Sands *Laurence Huninger* • Victoria Abril *Pascale* • Pamela Salem *Elisabeth Huninger* • William Jacques *Dr Coles* ■ *Dir/Scr* Dominique Othenin-Girard, Sergio Guerraz

After Hours ★★★★ 🔞

Black comedy 1985 · US · Colour · 93mins

Griffin Dunne plays the angst-ridden Everyman to manic perfection in director Martin Scorsese's brilliantly original black comedy, where New York's SoHo district becomes a Kafkaesque labyrinth, stylishly populated by avant-garde crazies, bloodthirsty gangsters and flaky *Alice in Wonderland*-style headcases. A spiralling tale of nightmarish persecution and paranoia, Dunne's date with unhinged Rosanna Arquette becomes a roller-coaster ride into urban hell. Weird, wonderful and wildly funny, and Scorsese won the best director prize at Cannes for his efforts. Contains violence, swearing and nudity. 📼

Griffin Dunne *Paul Hackett* • Rosanna Arquette *Marcy Franklin* • Verna Bloom *June* • Thomas Chong [Tommy Chong] *Pepe* • Linda Fiorentino *Kiki* • Teri Garr *Julie* • John Heard *Tom the bartender* • Richard "Cheech" Marin *Neil* ■ *Dir* Martin Scorsese • *Scr* Joseph Minion • *Cinematographer* Michael Ballhaus

After Life ★★★★

Drama 1998 · Jap · Colour · 118mins

Japanese director Hirokazu Koreeda's vision of heaven has an irresistible simplicity to match its subtle ingenuity. Set in a spartan transit camp, the action focuses on a celestial film unit as it tries to help various recently departed souls re-create the favourite memory that will be their sole solace in eternity. Beautifully acted by a cast

that includes several non-professionals, this is a sublime celebration of life and the everyday joys that make it so worthwhile. But it is also tinged with regret, as some struggle to find anything meaningful in their seemingly mundane existence. Wise, warm and visually inventive, this is one to treasure. In Japanese with English subtitles.

Arata Takashi Mochizuki • Erika Oda *Shiori Satonaka* • Susumu Terajima *Satoru Kawashima* • Takashi Naito *Takuro Sugie* ■ *Dir/Scr* Hirokazu Koreeda

After Midnight ★★★ 🔞

Horror 1989 · US · Colour · 88mins

A better-than-average horror anthology featuring three stories which provide a fourth climax. Each tale of terror is told by students on a "psychology of fear" course and involve a haunted mansion, killer dogs, mysterious phone calls (the best section) and zombies. Produced, written and directed by Ken and Jim Wheat the genre's answer to the Coen brothers the classic *Dead of Night* format is stirred up with some very convincing special effects to leave the viewer suitably shaken. 📼

Ramy Zeda *Professor Derek* • Jillian McWhirter *Allison* • Pamela Segall *Cheryl* • Nadine Van Der Velde *Joan* • Marc McClure *Kevin* • Marg Helgenberger *Alex* • Billy Ray Sharkey *Ray* ■ *Dir/Scr* Ken Wheat, Jim Wheat

After Midnight ★★

Drama 1990 · UK · Colour · 90mins

A bitter comic cocktail with a dark dramatic chaser, this tale of a drunken Dublin hotel nightwatchman starts and ends reasonably well, but too much of what director Shani Grewal serves up in between is misjudged and muddled. The estimable Saeed Jaffrey turns in a mischievously maudlin performance as the writer whose reasons for abandoning his craft lie in a closely guarded secret. However, while the majority of his crooked schemes are amusing enough, his treatment of receptionist Hayley Mills and a Chinese prostitute is every bit as objectionable as his racist rivalry with Egyptian night manager Vladek Sheybal. Contains some swearing.

Saeed Jaffrey *Jas* • Hayley Mills *Sally* • Vladek Sheybal *El-Alfi* • Dhirendra *Ranj* • Ian Dury • Maurice O'Donaghue • Patrick Condren • Gerard Byrne ■ *Dir* Shani Grewal [Shani S Grewal] • *Scr* Shani Grewal

After Office Hours ★★★

Crime comedy drama
1935 · US · BW · 71mins

Back at his home studio, MGM, after his Oscar-winning success in *It Happened One Night*, Clark Gable was cast as another newspaper man who, with the aid of his glamorous society-girl-cum-reporter (Constance Bennett), solves a murder. A solidly entertaining example of the then fashionable newsroom genre, when papers were papers and reporters played detective, it was written by Herman J Mankiewicz (later to script *Citizen Kane* with Orson Welles) and directed by one of the studio's slickest craftsmen, Robert Z Leonard. The result is a sparky, witty and fast-moving comedy melodrama.

Constance Bennett *Sharon Norwood* • Clark Gable *Jim Branch* • Stuart Erwin *Hank Parr* • Billie Burke *Mrs Norwood* • Harvey Stephens *Tommy Bannister* • Katherine Alexander *Mrs Patterson* • Hale Hamilton *Mr Patterson* • Henry Travers *Cap* ■ *Dir* Robert Z Leonard • *Scr* Herman J Mankiewicz, from a story by Laurence Stallings, Dale Van Every

After Pilkington ★★ 15

Comedy drama 1986 · UK · Colour · 98mins

Miranda Richardson persuades childhood sweetheart Bob Peck, now an Oxford professor, to help track down a missing archaeologist. Christopher Morahan directs this airless little drama without much sense of purpose, though Miranda Richardson puts meaning into muddle and gives it the urgency it so requires, while Peck is believable as the besotted professor. ▭

Bob Peck *James Westgate* • Miranda Richardson *Penny* • Gary Waldhorn *Boris* • Barry Foster *Derek* • Reina James *Amanda* • Richard Brenner *Wilkins* • Mary Miller *Deirdre* • John Gill *Pottsy* • Richard Grant *Young James* ■ *Dir* Christopher Morahan • *Scr* Simon Gray

After the Fox ★★★ U

Comedy 1966 · US/UK/It · Colour · 103mins

In a switch from the bungling of Inspector Clouseau, here's Peter Sellers as a heist-fumbling supercrook, a master of disguise but not of his criminal career, breaking from jail to handle the smuggling of loot and to save his film-starlet sister's honour. The pretence of conning police and villagers into landing stolen gold during a movie "shoot" is a hoot, but the script collapses because the writing styles of New Yorker Neil Simon and Italian Cesare Zavattini clash awkwardly. However, the best joke of all is Victor Mature as a fading beefcake star, sending up his own image - corsets and all.

Peter Sellers *Aldo Vanucci* • Victor Mature *Tony Powell* • Britt Ekland *Gina Romantica* • Martin Balsam *Harry* • Akim Tamiroff *Okra* • Paolo Stoppa *Polio* • Tino Buazzeli *Siepi* • Mac Ronay *Carlo* ■ *Dir* Vittorio De Sica • *Scr* Neil Simon, Cesare Zavattini

After the Glory ★★ PG

Drama 1992 · US · Colour · 99mins

This is a tale of the American dream gone sour, especially for a group of Second World War veterans returning to their roots. Because their small-town paradise has been overrun by bigotry and corruption, they decide to try to win the local elections. Despite the presence of able actors like Brad Johnson and Kathleen Quinlan, the film's episodic nature means that it is often weighed down by plot. Had the story put more emphasis on developing the characters, this might have taken off. ▭

Brad Johnson *George Meade* • Kathleen Quinlan *Hope Tyler* • Tom Sizemore *Jesse Meadows* • Josef Sommer *Henry Meade* • GW Bailey *Tom Cantrell* • Patricia Clarkson *Barbara Meade* • David Labiosa *Juan Medina* • Lisa Blount *Becky Meadows* ■ *Dir* John Gray • *Scr* John Gray, from a story by Lemuel Pitkin, Paul Donald Snowe

After the Promise ★★★ PG

Drama based on a true story 1987 · US · Colour · 89mins

A refreshingly gritty made-for-TV drama, set against the backdrop of the Depression. Mark Harmon ditches his pretty-boy image to play an unschooled worker who battles bureaucracy in an attempt to be reunited with his children who have been taken into care following the death of his wife. Harmon is admirably low-key in the lead role and there is effective support from the likes of Diana Scarwid and Mark Hildreth. British director Diana Greene stylishly and accurately re-creates the desolation of the period. Contains some swearing ▭

Mark Harmon *Elmer Jackson* • Diana Scarwid *Anna* • Rosemary Dunsmore *Florence* • Donnelly Rhodes *Dr Northfield* ■ *Dir* David Greene • *Scr* Robert Lenski, from the story by Sebastian Milito

After the Rehearsal ★★★

Drama 1984 · Swe · Colour · 72mins

Echoes of August Strindberg's *Dream Play* ring around this chamber drama, which was originally filmed for television before finally receiving a theatrical release two years into Ingmar Bergman's "retirement". Dozing on a stage dressed for his production of the play, Erland Josephson has encounters with former mistress Ingrid Thulin and aspiring actress, Lena Olin. It is Olin who hopes an affair will further her career, despite the revelation her mother once had an affair with the director. Sven Nykvist's tight angles intensify the intrigue, as we wonder how autobiographical Bergman's insights into art and emotion really are. Superbly acted and directed with disciplined economy, but this is very much a minor Bergman work. In Swedish with English subtitles.

Erland Josephson *Henrik Vogler* • Ingrid Thulin *Rakel Egerman* • Lena Olin *Anna Egerman* ■ *Dir/Scr* Ingmar Bergman • *Cinematographer* Sven Nykvist

After the Storm ★★★ U

Drama 1990 · Arg/Sp · Colour · 60mins

Realism doesn't get much more brutal than this. In depicting the grinding poverty suffered by a rural family, Argentinian director Tristán Bauer refuses to allow petty sentiment to cloud the issue. Nor does he permit his cast the luxury of easy outbursts of bitterness. Lorenzo Quinteros is the proud working man who would rather tear down the doors of his home than send his father to the grave in an unfinished coffin. It isn't all gloom and doom, as Ruben Alvarez's script suggests better times lie ahead, but few will forget the misery they have witnessed. In Spanish with English subtitles.

Lorenzo Quinteros • Patricio Contreras • Ana Maria Picchio ■ *Dir* Tristán Bauer • *Scr* Tristán Bauer, Ruben Alvarez, Graciela Maglie

After the Thin Man ★★★

Detective comedy 1936 · US · BW · 112mins

The sequel to *The Thin Man* has William Powell, Myrna Loy and Asta the dog once more waltzing through high society. Dashiell Hammett's story and the script by Frances Goodrich and Albert Hackett have our intrepid trio solving three murders between cocktails and sharing bedroom scenes that put witty repartee before any hanky-panky. There's a minor twist with James Stewart playing a meek and mild ex-lover who suddenly loses his rag, but it might seem far too slight and slow for modern audiences. This was, however, a big hit in 1936 and the stars still have a considerable amount of charm.

William Powell *Nick Charles* • Myrna Loy *Nora Charles* • James Stewart *David Graham* • Elissa Landi *Selma Landis* • Joseph Calleia *Dancer* • Jessie Ralph *Aunt Katherine* • Alan Marshal *Robert* • Teddy Hart *Caspar* ■ *Dir* WS Van Dyke • *Scr* Frances Goodrich, Albert Hackett, from a story by Dashiell Hammett

Afterburn ★★★ 15

Drama based on a true story 1992 · US · Colour · 102mins

This drama based on a true story is lifted by Laura Dern's tough, moving performance as the widow of a pilot (Vincent Spano) accused of "human error" following the crash of his plane. Director Robert Markowitz skilfully builds the tension as clues to the reason for the tragedy are painstakingly uncovered. Dern is very convincing as a woman driven to the end of her tether by the tortuous struggle to discover the truth and clear her husband's name. ▭

Laura Dern *Janet Harduel* • Vincent Spano *Ted Harduel* • Robert Loggia *Robert Leonetti* • Michael Rooker *Casey Zankowski* ■ *Dir* Robert Markowitz • *Scr* Elizabeth Chandler

Afterglow ★★★★ 15

Drama 1997 · US · Colour · 109mins

Writer/director Alan Rudolph here delivers a by turns moving and funny tale of love, loss and relationships for which Julie Christie was nominated for an Oscar. She plays a former B-movie actress who embarks on an affair with a younger man in response to her philandering husband's (Nick Nolte) string of younger lovers. *Twin Peaks* graduate Lara Flynn Boyle and *Trainspotting* co-star Jonny Lee Miller are the younger couple caught in their own web of adultery and lies, but the show truly belongs to the more seasoned stars, the mesmerising Nolte and Christie, whose performances will wrench your heart and move you to tears. Contains swearing, sexual situations and some mild violence. ▭

Nick Nolte *Lucky "Fix-It" Mann* • Julie Christie *Phyllis Mann* • Lara Flynn Boyle *Marianne Byron* • Jonny Lee Miller *Jeffrey Byron* • Jay Underwood *Donald Duncan* • Domini Blythe *Helene Pelletier* • Yves Corbeil *Bernard Omay* • Alan Fawcett *Count Falco/Jack Dana* ■ *Dir/Scr* Alan Rudolph • *Producer* Robert Altman

Against a Crooked Sky ★ U

Western 1975 · US · Colour · 88mins

This western was criticised on its limited release for its perceived racism in the age of native American awareness, such liberal westerns as *Little Big Man* and revisionist studies like *Bury My Heart at Wounded Knee*. *Variety*, for instance, complained the film was more upset at the killing of a pet dog than by the vengeful slaughter of hundreds of Indians. The movie starts with an Indian raid and the kidnapping of a white girl, à la *The Searchers*. Gnarled fur trapper Richard Boone and teenager Stewart Petersen head off in pursuit across the desert; the usual stuff happens. ▭

Henry Wilcoxon *Cut Tongue* • Richard Boone *Russian* • Stewart Petersen *Sam Sutter* • Jewel Blanch *Charlotte Sutter* • Gordon Hanson *Shumeki* • Geoffrey Land *Temkai* ■ *Dir* Earl Bellamy • *Scr* Douglas C Stewart, Eleanor Lamb

Against All Flags ★★★ U

Adventure 1952 · US · Colour · 83mins

Errol Flynn is on top late-career form as a British naval officer who gets involved with beautiful buccaneer Maureen O'Hara in a Madagascan pirate stronghold ruled over by the scowling Anthony Quinn. This rollicking costume adventure is generally good fun, with rich Technicolor giving O'Hara's red hair and green eyes an even greater lustre. Though the credited director is George Sherman, it is a little-known fact that Douglas Sirk actually undertook most of the work behind the camera. Remade, utterly pointlessly, as *The King's Pirate* with Doug McClure, using footage from this original.

Errol Flynn *Brian Hawke* • Maureen O'Hara *Spitfire Stevens* • Anthony Quinn *Captain Roc Brasiliano* • Mildred Natwick *Miss MacGregor* • Alice Kelley *Princess Patma* • Robert Warwick *Captain Kidd* ■ *Dir* George Sherman • *Scr* Aeneas MacKenzie, Joseph Hoffman, from a story by Aeneas MacKenzie

Against All Odds ★★★ 18

Thriller 1984 · US · Colour · 116mins

A loose remake of the Robert Mitchum/Jane Greer *film noir* classic *Build My Gallows High*, with Jeff Bridges in the pay of, then on the run from minor mobster James Woods. Greer herself appears as the mother of her original character, now played by Rachel Ward, and Richard Widmark, another hero from the *film noir* era, also makes a welcome appearance. Taylor Hackford's moody direction keeps the picture moving, taking in the streets of Los Angeles and the spectacular Mayan ruins of Mexico. Phil Collins's theme song received an Oscar nomination. Contains violence and sex scenes. ▭ **DVD**

Rachel Ward *Jessie Wyler* • Jeff Bridges *Terry Brogan* • James Woods *Jake Wise* • Alex Karras *Hank Sully* • Jane Greer *Mrs Wyler* • Richard Widmark *Ben Caxton* • Saul Rubinek *Steve Kirsch* • Swoosie Kurtz *Edie* • Dorian Harewood *Tommy* • Pat Corley *Ed Phillips* ■ *Dir* Taylor Hackford • *Scr* Eric Hughes, from the film and novel *Build My Gallows High* by Geoffrey Homes [Daniel Mainwaring]

Against Her Will ★★★ PG

Courtroom drama 1991 · US · Colour · 89mins

Subtitled *An Incident in Baltimore*, this stars Walter Matthau, returning to the role he created so memorably in the 1990 TV movie *The Incident*, once again fighting bigotry in forties' America. He plays an attorney who ruffles more than a few feathers when he takes up the case of a young woman from Greece who has been

declared insane by the state government. As with the previous film, there's considerable charm in both the delightful playing of Matthau – though he's matched by Harry Morgan as a crusty judge – and the leisurely direction of veteran Delbert Mann, who made the Oscar-winning *Marty*. 💾

Walter Matthau *Harmon Cobb* • Harry Morgan *Judge Stoddard Bell* • Susan Blakely *Billie Cobb* • Ariana Richards *Nancy* • Barton Heyman *Donald* ■ *Dir* Delbert Mann • *Scr* Michael Norell, James Norell

Against Her Will: the Carrie Buck Story ★★★

Drama based on a true story
1994 · US · Colour

Marlee Matlin, who won an Oscar for her tour de force performance in *Children of a Lesser God*, stars alongside Melissa Gilbert (*Little House on the Prairie*) in this made-for-TV drama. In 1927 Virginia, an unwed, mentally disabled woman is involved in the landmark Supreme Court decision legalising the enforced sterilisation of feeble-minded women. A young female law student fights against a prominent physician and a politically motivated attorney in order to help disadvantaged young women stand up for their rights. Matlin and Gilbert deliver earnest performances in a richly filmed piece that delivers a piece of compelling American history.

Marlee Matlin *Carrie Buck* • Melissa Gilbert *Melissa Prentice* • Peter Frechette *Adam White* • Pat Hingle ■ *Dir* John David Coles • *Scr* Brian Ross

Against the Wall ★★★ 18

Prison drama based on a true story
1994 · US · Colour · 110mins

The true story of the Attica prison break in the seventies is turned into a trim, taut and suspenseful pseudo-documentary thanks to John Frankenheimer's solid direction and great performances by Samuel L Jackson and Kyle MacLachlan. Taking the perspective of a rookie warden appalled by the awful treatment of prisoners in the facility, Frankenheimer accents the convicts' grievances concerning liberation rights by having the do-gooder held hostage by rioters. Gritty and realistic, this TV movie raises hard questions and makes for compelling viewing. 💾

Kyle MacLachlan *Michael Smith* • Samuel L Jackson *Jamaal* • Harry Dean Stanton *Hal* • Anne Heche *Sharon* • Clarence Williams III *Chaka* • Frederic Forrest *Weisbad* • Philip Bosco *Corrections Commissioner Russell Oswald* • Tom Bower *Ed* ■ *Dir* John Frankenheimer • *Scr* Ron Hutchinson

Against the Wind ★★★

Spy drama
1947 · UK · BW · 94mins

Although he is best known as the screenwriter of several classic Ealing comedies, including *The Lavender Hill Mob* and *Passport to Pimlico*, TEB Clarke could turn his hand to several genres, as this tale of spy-school treachery, co-written with Michael Pertwee, proves. Paying tribute to the contribution of saboteurs to the war effort, the film owes a debt to the pseudo-documentary style of such Hollywood thrillers as *The House on*

92nd Street and *13 Rue Madeleine*. Jack Warner and Simone Signoret stand out in a cast packed with dependable character actors, although they are slightly hampered by director Charles Crichton's preoccupation with authentic detail.

Robert Beatty *Father Phillip* • Simone Signoret *Michele* • Jack Warner *Max Cronk* • Gordon Jackson *Johnny Duncan* • Paul Dupuis *Jacques Picquart* • Gisele Preville [Giselle Preville] *Julie* • John Slater *Emile Meyer* • Peter Illing *Andrew* • James Robertson-Justice *Ackerman* ■ *Dir* Charles Crichton • *Scr* TEB Clarke, Michael Pertwee, from a story by J Elder Wills

Agatha ★★

Drama   1978 · UK/US · Colour · 100mins

Dustin Hoffman and Vanessa Redgrave are the mismatched leads in this story of the real-life disappearance of Agatha Christie in 1926, which gave rise to a nationwide hunt and laid suspicion at the door of her husband. An imaginative "solution" brings an American journalist Hoffman. He traces her to a health resort, just as another link in the chain of events is being forged. Redgrave is a very credible Christie, but director Michael Apted, who's great on the style of the time, runs out of plot and loses any sense of suspense. To that extent, he hasn't a clue. 💾

Vanessa Redgrave *Agatha Christie* • Dustin Hoffman *Wally Stanton* • Timothy Dalton *Archie Christie* • Helen Morse *Evelyn* • Celia Gregory *Nancy Neele* • Tony Britton *William Collins* • Timothy West *Kenward* • Alan Badel *Lord Brackenbury* ■ *Dir* Michael Apted • *Scr* Kathleen Tynan, Arthur Hopcraft, from a story by Kathleen Tynan

Agatha Christie's A Caribbean Mystery ★★ PG

Murder mystery   1983 · US · Colour · 92mins

Helen Hayes appears as Miss Marple in a mystery based on one of Agatha Christie's weaker whodunits, in which the spinster sleuth investigates the death of an elderly major the morning after he revealed a sensational tale of greed and murder to her. Making the best of her miscasting, the 83-year-old Hayes still compares unfavourably with Margaret Rutherford and Joan Hickson, but the film benefits from not having the all-star cast that spoils the guessing game in so many other Christie adaptations. Don't be fooled by the "exotic" locations, this TV movie was shot on the cheap in California. 💾

Helen Hayes *Miss Jane Marple* • Barnard Hughes *Mr Rafiel* • Jameson Parker *Tim Kendall* • Season Hubley *Molly Kendall* • Swoosie Kurtz *Ruth Walters* • Cassie Yates *Lucky Dyson* • Zakes Mokae *Captain Daventry* • Stephen Macht *Greg Dyson* ■ *Dir* Robert Lewis • *Scr* Sue Grafton, Steven Humphrey, from the novel by Agatha Christie

Agatha Christie's Murder Is Easy ★★ PG

Murder mystery   1982 · US · Colour · 95mins

What you get is precisely what you see – there are no hidden depths to plummet here in this conveyor-belt made-for-TV movie. Bill Bixby is a computer expert who finds himself caught up in murderous events beyond

his ken, while there's a solid supporting cast, plus Lesley-Anne Down as co-star. This updated version of Agatha Christie's mystery *Easy to Kill* is, easy, undemanding entertainment. 💾

Bill Bixby *Luke Williams* • Lesley-Anne Down *Bridget Conway* • Olivia de Havilland *Honoria Waynflete* • Helen Hayes *Lavinia Fullerton* • Patrick Allen *Major Horton* • Shane Briant *Dr Thomas* • Freddie Jones *Constable Reed* • Leigh Lawson *Jimmy Lorrimer* • Jonathan Pryce *Mr Ellsworthy* ■ *Dir* Claude Whatham • *Scr* Carmen Culver, from the novel *Easy to Kill* by Agatha Christie

Agatha Christie's Murder with Mirrors ★★★ PG

Murder mystery
1985 · US/UK · Colour · 93mins

Director Dick Lowry makes an efficient job of adapting the Queen of Crime's 1952 thriller, *They Do It With Mirrors*. Making her second appearance as Miss Marple, Helen Hayes brought down the curtain on a 75-year screen career by deducing which of the gallery of eccentrics, gathered at a rambling English mansion, intends bumping off John Mills's beloved wife, Bette Davis. Although not one of Christie's best mysteries, it's certainly one of the busiest with countless characters to keep track of and a rather contrived conclusion. With Leo McKern hamming it up as the baffled inspector, it's enjoyable nonetheless. 💾

Helen Hayes *Miss Jane Marple* • Bette Davis *Carrie Louise* • John Mills *Lewis Serrocold* • Leo McKern *Inspector Curry* • Dorothy Tutin *Mildred* • Anton Rodgers *Dr Max Hargrove* • Frances de la Tour *Ms Bellaver* • Tim Roth *Edgar* ■ *Dir* Dick Lowry • *Scr* George Eckstein, from the novel *They Do It With Mirrors* by Agatha Christie

Agatha Christie's Murder in Three Acts ★★★

Murder mystery   1986 · US · Colour

The action may have been shifted from the quiet English resort of Loomouth to Acapulco, but this is still just about recognisable as the novel *Three Act Tragedy*, with vicars and neurologists falling like flies, even Hercule Poirot isn't convinced foul play is afoot until he discovers the dangers of colourless nicotine. A splendid cast of suspects lines up for this TV movie, with Tony Curtis, Lisa Eichhorn and Emma Samms giving nothing away. Peter Ustinov engages the "little grey cells" in what isn't a classic Christie, but it should keep you guessing.

Peter Ustinov *Hercule Poirot* • Tony Curtis *Charles Cartwright* • Emma Samms *Jennifer "Egg" Eastman* • Jonathan Cecil *Hastings* • Fernando Allende *Ricardo Montoya* • Pedro Armendariz *Colonel Mateo* • Lisa Eichhorn *Cynthia Dayton* • Dana Elcar *Dr Walter Strange* ■ *Dir* Gary Nelson • *Scr* Scott Swanton, from the novel *Three Act Tragedy* by Agatha Christie

Agatha Christie's Sparkling Cyanide ★★ PG

Murder mystery   1983 · US · Colour · 91mins

One of the attractions for Agatha Christie's American fans is her essential Englishness, so it seems odd to transfer the action to Pasadena. (At least Anthony Andrews is on hand to import some *Brideshead Revisited*

class.) With a couple of fatal toasts as its high points, the twisting plot will certainly keep you guessing. However, the tinkering with the original makes the mystery feel forced, and the resolution is not one of the author's most satisfying. 💾

Anthony Andrews *Tony Browne* • Deborah Raffin *Iris Murdoch* • Pamela Bellwood *Ruth Lessing* • Nancy Marchand *Lucilla Drake* • Josef Sommer *George Barton* • David Huffman *Stephan Farraday* • Christine Belford *Rosemary Barton* • June Chadwick *Sandra Farraday* ■ *Dir* Robert Michael Lewis [Robert Lewis] • *Scr* Robert Malcolm Young, Sue Grafton, Steven Humphrey, from the novel by Agatha Christie

L'Age d'Or ★★★★★

Satire   1930 · Fr · BW · 62mins

Having determinedly avowed that *Un Chien Andalou*, his previous collaboration with co-writer and surrealist artist Salvador Dali, meant nothing at all, Luis Buñuel declared that this second surrealist outing was "a desperate and passionate call to murder". He certainly got his wish, as the film caused riots when it premiered in Paris and was eventually banned at the insistence of the French fascists for 49 years. Exploring the themes that would sustain his entire career, Buñuel mercilessly pillories the bourgeoisie, with virtually every scene touching on the conflict between sexual desire and religious and political repression. The satire is both erotic and hilarious and still has the power to provoke. In French with English subtitles.

Lya Lys *The woman* • Gaston Modot *The man* • Max Ernst *Bandit Chief* • Pierre Prévert *Péman, a bandit* ■ *Dir* Luis Buñuel • *Scr* Luis Buñuel, Salvador Dali • *Cinematographer* Albert Duverger

Age Isn't Everything ★★★

Comedy drama   1991 · US · Colour · 91mins

A twist on the body-swap theme that was so popular in the eighties has Jonathan Silverman (*Brighton Beach Memoirs*, *Weekend at Bernie's*) as a disgruntled 25-year-old office worker who turns overnight into an octagenarian with a Yiddish accent. Thoroughly rattled, the young man in an old man's body goes to a host of doctors (including American health guru Dr Joyce Brothers) to see if the effects can be reversed. A strong cast of supporting players, whose faces will be familiar to you even if their names are not, make this dark, if sometimes sentimental, comedy a touch above the average.

Jonathan Silverman *Seymour* • Paul Sorvino *Max* • Rita Moreno *Rita* • Robert Prosky *Seymour's grandfather* • Rita Karlin *Seymour's grandmother* • Dr Joyce Brothers ■ *Dir/Scr* Douglas Katz

Age of Consent ★★★

Romance   1932 · US · BW · 106mins

Not to be confused with Michael Powell's 1969 Australian romp, this is an earnest look at the age-old problem of sex before marriage. Campus student Richard Cromwell wants to do it with his girlfriend, Dorothy Wilson (a non-actress who was discovered in the RKO typing pool). When she refuses, he does it instead with local waitress

Arline Judge. Director Gregory La Cava keeps it all extremely tasteful and makes you feel a very real angst on Cromwell's part. Worth a look.

Dorothy Wilson *Betty* • Richard Cromwell *Michael* • Eric Linden *Duke* • Arline Judge *Dora* • John Halliday *David* • Aileen Pringle *Barbara* • Reginald Barlow *Swale* ■ *Dir* Gregory La Cava • *Scr* Sarah Y Mason, Francis Cockrell, from the play *Cross Roads* by Martin Flavin

Age of Consent ★★★ 15
Romantic drama
1969 · Ausl · Colour · 95mins

Michael Powell's final feature film is about an artist (James Mason) who runs out of inspiration and retreats to the Great Barrier Reef with his young model (Helen Mirren). "The film was full of nudity," wrote Powell, "but it is a painter's nudity." Filmed mainly on Dunk Island (now the Reef's priciest resort), it is undeniably beautiful and filled with engaging characters. Mirren is not the only actress who takes her clothes off; so does Clarissa Kaye, who later married James Mason. ▣

James Mason *Bradley Morahan* • Helen Mirren *Cora* • Jack MacGowran *Nat Kelly* • Neva Carr-Glyn *Ma Ryan* • Andonia Katsaros *Isabel Marley* • Michael Boddy *Hendricks* • Harold Hopkins *Ted Farrell* • Clarissa Kaye *Meg* ■ *Dir* Michael Powell • *Scr* Peter Yeldham, from the novel by Norman Lindsay

The Age of Innocence ★
Period romantic melodrama
1934 · US · BW · 71mins

A rising young lawyer in late 19th-century New York falls in love with a woman in the throes of a divorce. Prevented from marrying her by high society's moral constraints, he marries someone else, but continues to see his true love. John Boles and Irene Dunne, who made such a hit together in the wonderfully sudsy *Back Street*, star in this bowdlerisation of Edith Wharton's famous novel, which is reduced to a small-scale and dreary melodrama under the first-time direction of Philip Moeller. Those who know the novel and/or Martin Scorsese's superb film version should avoid it at all costs.

Irene Dunne *Countess Ellen Olenska* • John Boles *Newland Archer* • Lionel Atwill *Julius Beaufort* • Laura Hope Crews *Mrs Welland* • Helen Westley *Granny Mingott* • Julie Haydon *May Welland* • Herbert Yost *Mr Welland* • Theresa Maxwell Conover *Mrs Archer* ■ *Dir* Philip Moeller • *Scr* Sarah Y Mason, Victor Heerman, from the novel by Edith Wharton • *Music* Max Steiner

The Age of Innocence ★★★★ U
Period romantic drama
1993 · US · Colour · 132mins

Eyebrows were raised when Martin Scorsese announced he was going to adapt Edith Wharton's Pulitzer Prize-winning novel about polite New York society in the 1870s. Yet, influenced by *The Heiress* and *The Magnificent Ambersons*, this is a directorial triumph, with the camera unobtrusively accumulating the small details that help make the story of Newland Archer and the Countess Olenska so compelling. Credit must also go here to cinematographer Michael Ballhaus

and production designer Dante Ferretti. Unfortunately, some of the cast, notably Winona Ryder, seem a little stiff; Daniel Day-Lewis and Michelle Pfeiffer, however, excel in conveying the conflict between their passion and their breeding. ▣

Daniel Day-Lewis *Newland Archer* • Michelle Pfeiffer *Ellen Olenska* • Winona Ryder *May Welland* • Alexis Smith *Louisa Van Der Luyden* • Geraldine Chaplin *Mrs Welland* • Mary Beth Hurt *Regina Beaufort* • Alec McCowen *Sillerton Jackson* • Richard E Grant *Larry Lefferts* • Miriam Margolyes *Mrs Mingott* • Robert Sean Leonard *Ted Archer* • Sian Phillips *Mrs Archer* • Joanne Woodward *Narrator* ■ *Dir* Martin Scorsese • *Scr* Jay Cocks, Martin Scorsese, from the novel by Edith Wharton • *Cinematographer* Michael Ballhaus

Agency ★★
Drama 1981 · Can · Colour · 94mins

It is one of the tragedies of cinema that movie producers failed to find roles worthy of the great Robert Mitchum in his latter years, when his craggy, sleepy-eyed features cried out for a decent film. Here the great Mitch plays a dodgy politician trying to corrupt the world by inserting subliminal messages in TV programmes. Directed by George Kaczender, this is a non-starter, despite a likeable turn from *Six Million Dollar Man*-star Lee Majors as the good guy and two undercast cult actresses, Valerie Perrine and Alexandra Stewart, in support.

Robert Mitchum *Ted Quinn* • Lee Majors *Philip Morgan* • Valerie Perrine *Brenda Wilcox* • Saul Rubinek *Sam Goldstein* • Alexandra Stewart *Mimi* • Hayward Morse *Tony* • Anthony Parr *Charlie* ■ *Dir* George Kaczender • *Scr* Noel Hynd, from the novel by Paul Gottlieb

The Ages of Lulu ★★★ 18
Erotic thriller 1990 · Sp · Colour · 93mins

Adapted from the novel by Almudena Grandes, this was the first film by Bigas Luna to make an international impact. Having already been rejected by numerous actresses, he found Italian star Francesca Neri willing to accept the challenge of playing the innocent who embarks upon a journey of sexual discovery that takes her into the darkest recesses of her psyche. So explicit it was dismissed by many as tasteless porn, this is a surprisingly moral, if ironic, film which makes for fascinating comparison with the director's studies of macho posturing, *Jamon Jamon* and *Golden Balls*. A Spanish language film. Contains coarse language, sex scenes and violence. ▣

Francesca Neri *Lulu* • Oscar Ladoire *Pablo* • Maria Barranco *Ely* • Fernando Guillen-Cuervo • Rosana Pastor • Javier Bardem ■ *Dir* Bigas Luna • *Scr* Bigas Luna, Almudena Grandes, from the novel by Almudena Grandes

Agnes Browne ★★★ 15
Period drama 1999 · Ire · Colour · 91mins

Anjelica Huston both directs and stars in this quirky little movie, set in Dublin in 1967. When her husband dies prematurely, Huston and her seven children are catapulted into an emotional maelstrom. Ekeing out an existence selling fruit and veg in the local market, she borrows cash from unpleasant loan shark Ray Winstone

and dreams of attending an upcoming Tom Jones concert. Despite being too cute and rather bizarre – it's hard to imagine Huston harbouring fantasies about Jones, for example – this is a watchable slice of Oirish whimsy.

Anjelica Huston *Agnes Browne* • Ray Winstone *Mr Billy* • Niall O'Shea *Mark Browne* • Ciaran Owens *Frankie Browne* • Marion O'Dwyer *Marion Monks* • Tom Jones ■ *Dir* Anjelica Huston • *Scr* John Goldsmith, Brendan O'Carroll, from the novel *The Mammy* by Brendan O'Carroll

Agnes of God ★★★ 15
Drama 1985 · US · Colour · 94mins

An odd, adult drama from *Moonstruck* director Norman Jewison, which promises more than it delivers. Jane Fonda is her usual forthright self as the court psychiatrist investigating the case of a novice nun (the waif-like Meg Tilly) accused of murdering her baby. It is thanks to the three lead performances Tilly, Fonda and always dependable Anne Bancroft as the convent's Mother Superior that this sustains interest for as long as it does, but even they cannot cover up what is essentially a rather disappointing ending. Contains some swearing. ▣

Jane Fonda *Dr Martha Livingston* • Anne Bancroft *Mother Miriam Ruth* • Meg Tilly *Sister Agnes* • Anne Pitoniak *Dr Livingston's Mother* • Winston Rekert *Detective Langevin* • Gratien Gelinas *Father Martineau* • Guy Hoffman *Justice Joseph Leveau* • Gabriel Arcand *Monsignor* ■ *Dir* Norman Jewison • *Scr* John Pielmeier, from his play

Agnus Dei ★★★
Religious drama 1997 · Den · Colour · 90mins

Danish cinema's aptitude for depicting childhood is again to the fore in this wonderfully wide-eyed study of the enticements and terrors of religion. Temporarily abandoned by her mother, pre-teenager Amalie Dollerup is forced to rely on the God in whom she doesn't believe to help her through the trials of late-fifties convent life, which include encounters with a bullying senior and a stigmatic nun. Although director Caecilia Holbek Trier deals for the most part in stereotypes, she admirably captures the atmosphere of discipline and devotion, which makes the mysteries of spirituality and sex all the more seductive and bemusing. A Danish language film.

Amalie Dollerup *Johanne* • Bodil Jørgensen *Augustina* • Nastja Arcel *Mother* • Cecilia Eliasson *Ingrid* • Helle Fagralid *Marianne* ■ *Dir/Scr* Caecilia Holbek Trier

Agony ★★★
Epic 1975 · USSR · Colour and BW · 148mins

Elem Klimov's take on the last days of the Tsar and the baleful influence of Rasputin blends newly shot colour scenes with archive black-and-white footage from 1916-17. The movie manages to be both documentary and speculation, though that didn't stop the Soviet authorities from banning it in 1975. They allowed it to be shown at the 1981 Moscow Film Festival, however, where it inevitably created a sensation. Klimov went on to run the Russian film studios. In Russian with English subtitles.

Alexei Petrenko *Rasputin* • Velta Linei *Tsarina Alexandra* • Alisa Freindlikh *Anna Vyrubova* • Anatoly Romashin *Tsar Nicholas II* • A Romantsov *Prince Felix* ■ *Dir* Elem Klimov • *Scr* Semion Lungin, Ilya Nusinov

The Agony and the Ecstasy ★★ U
Historical drama
1965 · US · Colour · 130mins

It's easy to make facile jokes about this monumental epic, based on Irving Stone's biography about Michelangelo and the painting of the Sistine Chapel ceiling, but there's little doubt of the sincerity of those involved in its making. This is particularly evident in the playing, notably a self-effacing performance from Charlton Heston. Rex Harrison's Pope Julius II is more Rex than pontiff, and his constant querying of the painter "When will you make an end?" may well be echoed by this film's viewers. Shot impressively in the Todd-AO widescreen process, the movie includes a documentary prologue on Michelangelo's works themselves, after which, sadly, the whole of director Carol Reed's overlong opus seems utterly negligible. ▣

Charlton Heston *Michelangelo* • Rex Harrison *Pope Julius II* • Diane Cilento *Contessina De Medici* • Harry Andrews *Bramante* • Alberto Lupo *Duke of Urbino* • Adolfo Celi *Giovanni De Medici* • Venantino Venantini *Paris De Grassis* • John Stacy *Sangallo* ■ *Dir* Carol Reed • *Scr* Philip Dunne, from the novel by Irving Stone • *Cinematographer* Leon Shamroy

Aguirre, Wrath of God ★★★★★ PG
Drama 1972 · W Ger · Colour · 90mins

One of the crowning achievements of the New German Cinema, this movie is a typically haunting Werner Herzog picture in which an eccentric character pursues an overpowering obsession in the most inhospitable of environs. Klaus Kinski dominates the action as the 16th-century conquistador who ruinously rebels against his commander in order to continue his fanatical search for the legendary city of El Dorado. As if shooting in the depths of the Peruvian jungle wasn't difficult enough, the cast were never permitted to see the script, and it says much for their improvisational powers that there isn't a single weak performance in the film. In German with English subtitles. ▣

Klaus Kinski *Don Lope de Aguirre* • Cecilia Rivera *Flores* • Ruy Guerra *Lieutenant Ursua* • Helena Rojo *Inez* • Del Negro *Brother Gaspar* • Peter Berling *Guzman* • Armando Polanah *Armando* • Daniel Ades *Perucho* • Edward Roland *Okello* ■ *Dir/Scr* Werner Herzog

Ah, Wilderness ★★★
Comedy 1935 · US · BW · 97mins

Typical piece of MGM homespun, directed by Clarence "Capability" Brown from Eugene O'Neill's play that enshrines small-town values and concentrates on a boy's first love affair and the advice he gets from his pop, Lionel Barrymore. Since Mickey Rooney is in the cast as Linden's annoying younger brother, this looks like a dry run for the Andy Hardy series, which started two years later. It was remade in 1948 as the musical, *Summer*

Holiday, in which Rooney takes over the starring role as the lovestruck Richard Miller.

Lionel Barrymore *Nat Miller* • Aline MacMahon *Lily Davis* • Eric Linden *Richard Miller* • Cecilia Parker *Muriel McComber* • Spring Byington *Essie Miller* • Mickey Rooney *Tommy Miller* • Charles Grapewin [Charley Grapewin] *Mr McComber* ■ *Dir* Clarence Brown • *Scr* Albert Hackett, Frances Goodrich, from the play by Eugene O'Neill

A-Haunting We Will Go
★★ **U**

| Comedy | 1942 · US · BW · 63mins |

This is the second of the five indifferent pictures Laurel and Hardy made for 20th Century-Fox in the early forties. As the script was written while they were on tour, Laurel was denied the opportunity to add some much needed comic genius to this tiresome tale of crooks and coffins. Only the scene in which they are conned into buying a money-making machine and their exchanges with Dante the magician alleviate the sense of despair you feel as cinema's finest comedy team are reduced to such a mediocre level.

Stan Laurel *Stan* • Oliver Hardy *Ollie* • Harry A Jansen *Dante the magician* • Sheila Ryan *Margo* • John Shelton *Tommy White* • Don Costello *Doc Lake* • Elisha Cook Jr *Frank Lucas* ■ *Dir* Alfred Werker • *Scr* Lou Breslow, from a story by Lou Breslow, Stanley Rauh

Ailsa
★★

Psychological drama
1994 · Ire/Ger/Fr · Colour · 78mins

Having won awards for his short film, *A Stone of the Heart*, Paddy Breathnach broke into features with this tale of obsession and indecision. Working from his own short story, screenwriter Joe O'Connor makes liberal use of flashback and off-screen narration to chronicle the passion of young husband Brendan Coyle for Juliette Gruber, the American stranger who moves into a flat in his rundown Dublin townhouse. Rather than empathising with Coyle's torment, it's easier to feel sorry for his deceived wife, Andrea Irvine, and Gruber, who has no idea that he's stealing her mail, let alone fantasising about her. Moody, but ultimately insubstantial.

Brendan Coyle *Miles* • Andrea Irvine *Sara* • Juliette Gruber *Campbell* • Anne McGeown *Mrs Foley* • Darragh Kelly *Sean* • Blanaid Irvine *Vera* • Des Spillane *Old Mr Johnson* • Gary Lydon *Jack* ■ *Dir* Paddy Breathnach • *Scr* Joe O'Connor, from his short story

Ain't Misbehavin'
★★ **U**

Musical comedy 1955 · US · Colour · 81mins

Rory Calhoun, the rugged and handsome star of many a western, co-stars with Piper Laurie in this somewhat flimsy excuse for a musical with an unmistakeable nod in the direction of *Pygmalion*. He's a millionaire, she's a chorus girl determined to acquire some education and social polish. Edward Buzzell directs, with Jack Carson, Mamie Van Doren and Barbara Britton on hand to inject extra life into the forgettable but agreeable proceedings. Best of the otherwise long-forgotten songs is Fats

Waller's famous number, from which the movie takes its title.

Rory Calhoun *Kenneth Post* • Piper Laurie *Sarah Hatfield* • Jack Carson *Hal North* • Mamie Van Doren *Jackie* • Reginald Gardiner *Piermont Rogers* • Barbara Britton *Pat* • Dani Crayne *Millie* • Harris Brown *Randall* ■ *Dir* Edward Buzzell • *Scr* Edward Buzzell, Philip Rapp, Devery Freeman, from the story *Third Girl from the Right* by Robert Carson

Air America
★★★ **15**

Action comedy 1990 · US · Colour · 107mins

This was originally conceived as a blackly satirical comedy by *The Stunt Man* director Richard Rush, but that idea went out the window in favour of a more obviously commercial approach. Roger Spottiswoode took over the directorial reins and the result was an amiable, if somewhat patchy, action comedy. Set in Laos during the Vietnam War, the story follows the adventures of a CIA-organised air freight organisation, which was actually smuggling heroin on behalf of the local drug barons. As the amoral head pilot, Mel Gibson reprises his *Lethal Weapon* role of the ever-so-slightly bonkers tough guy, with Robert Downey Jr as his wild-card sidekick. The flying sequences are neatly staged and Gibson fans will lap it up but, given the source material (it was loosely based on true events), this has got to go down as a missed opportunity. Contains some swearing ▭

Mel Gibson *Gene Ryack* • Robert Downey Jr *Billy Covington* • Nancy Travis *Corinne Landreaux* • Ken Jenkins *Major Donald Lemond* • David Marshall Grant *Rob Diehl* • Lane Smith *Senator Davenport* • Art La Fleur [Art LaFleur] *Jack Neely* • Ned Eisenberg *Pirelli* ■ *Dir* Roger Spottiswoode • *Scr* John Eskow, Richard Rush, from the book by Christopher Robbins

Air Bud
★★★ **U**

Sports adventure
1997 · US/Lux/Can · Colour · 93mins

Meet Air Bud, the energetic nineties version of Lassie, in this cute family adventure about a sporty dog who is promoted from team mascot to basketball player. While parents will be more impressed by the animal acrobatics, youngsters will be entertained by the main plot, in which a lonely young boy and the dog's abusive owner fight for custody of the talented pooch. With a canine story that's both appealing and amusing, this is particularly suitable for younger viewers. Contains some strong language. ▭

Michael Jeter *Norm Snively* • Kevin Zegers *Josh Framm* • Wendy Makkena *Jackie Framm* • Bill Cobbs *Arthur Chaney* • Eric Christmas *Judge Cranfield* • Jay Brazeau *Referee No 1* • Nicola Cavendish *Principal Pepper* ■ *Dir* Charles Martin Smith • *Scr* Paul Tamasy, Aaron Mendelsohn, from the character created by Kevin DiCicco

Air Bud: Golden Receiver
★★★

Sports comedy
1998 · US/Can · Colour · 90mins

Kids who didn't get enough of the basketball-playing dog in the first film will probably get a kick out of this adventure, in which our canine friend and his owner, Josh (Kevin Zegers),

take up the honourable pastime of American football. Adults will probably roll their eyes at the goofy animal-abduction subplot masterminded by Nora Dunn, who could learn some things about acting from the dog. The film needs more emphasis on the sports, and less on Zeger's opposition to his widowed mother's love life.

Kevin Zegers *Josh Framm* • Cynthia Stevenson *Jackie Framm* • Gregory Harrison *Patrick Sullivan* • Nora Dunn *Natalya* • Perry Anzilotti *Popov* • Robert Costanzo *Coach Fanelli* • Shayn Solberg *Tom* • Tim Conway *Fred Davis* ■ *Dir* Richard Martin • *Scr* Paul Tamasy, Aaron Mendelsohn, from the character created by Kevin DiCicco

Un Air de Famille
★★★★ **15**

Comedy drama 1996 · Fr · Colour · 105mins

After the zestful chic of *When the Cat's Away*, this bourgeois comedy is something of a departure for director Cédric Klapisch. Adapted by Jean-Pierre Bacri and Agnès Jaoui from their own play, it focuses on the spiteful sparring of three siblings unable to shoulder the responsibility for their own disappointments. Cleverly exploiting his claustrophonic set by keeping camera movements to a minimum, Klapisch relies on neat touches rather than grand flourishes, while his use of reflective surfaces recalls the films of Douglas Sirk and Rainer Werner Fassbinder. The performances are uniformly excellent, though the tipsy Catherine Frot steals the show. In French with English subtitles. Contains some swearing and violence. ▭

Jean-Pierre Bacri *Henri Menard* • Agnès Jaoui *Betty Menard* • Jean-Pierre Darroussin *Denis* • Catherine Frot *Yolande, Philippe's wife* • Claire Maurier *Mother* • Wladimir Yordanoff *Philippe Menard* ■ *Dir* Cédric Klapisch • *Scr* Cédric Klapisch, Agnès Jaoui, Jean-Pierre Bacri, from the play by Agnès Jaoui, Jean-Pierre Bacri

Air Force
★★★★ **PG**

Second World War drama
1943 · US · BW · 119mins

A marvellous Second World War drama from one of Hollywood's greatest directors, Howard Hawks. While not as famous as his *Scarface*, *Only Angels Have Wings*, *The Big Sleep* or *Rio Bravo*, *Air Force* is still a major achievement, the story of the Mary Ann, a Flying Fortress, and the men who operated her in the war against the Japanese. The action sequences are excitingly filmed, though it is the quieter moments, when the members of the crew express their excitement and their fears, that give the film its strength as a study of comradeship in adversity. The cast includes John Garfield, Harry Carey and Arthur Kennedy, all fine actors but not glamorous movie stars, which gives the film a rare authenticity. ▭ **DVD**

John Ridgely *Captain Mike Quincannon* • Gig Young *Lieutenant Bill Williams* • Arthur Kennedy *Lieutenant Tommy McMartin* • Charles Drake *Lieutenant Munchauser* • Harry Carey *Sergeant Robby White* • George Tobias *Corporal Weinberg* • Ward Wood *Corporal Peterson* • John Garfield *Sergeant Joe Winocki* ■ *Dir* Howard Hawks • *Scr* Dudley Nichols

Air Force One
★★★★ **15**

Action thriller 1997 · US · Colour · 119mins

The Americans do love their president, and Hollywood loves putting him in its movies. So who better to play him as an action hero than Indiana Jones himself, Harrison Ford? When the First Family is held hostage on Air Force One by a gang of ruthless terrorists, President James Marshall decides to fight back. If you liked *Die Hard 2*, you'll love the mid-air mayhem that ensues in a stunt-filled thriller brimming with nasty villains and daring deeds. Gary Oldman, who makes a mint playing rogues in Tinseltown, is back again playing the leader of the band of baddies. Contains swearing and violence. **DVD**

Harrison Ford *President James Marshall* • Gary Oldman *Ivan Korshunov* • Glenn Close *Vice President Kathryn Bennett* • Wendy Crewson *Grace Marshall* • Liesel Matthews *Alice Marshall* • Paul Guilfoyle *Chief of Staff Lloyd Shepherd* • Xander Berekeley *Agent Gibbs* • William H Macy *Major Caldwell* • Dean Stockwell *Defense Secretary Walter Dean* • Jürgen Prochnow *General Alexander Radek* ■ *Dir* Wolfgang Petersen • *Scr* Andrew W Marlowe

Air Mail
★★

Adventure 1932 · US · BW · 83mins

Director John Ford is more famous for his westerns, but this is his tribute to the pilots who flew the early air mail service across the West. In fact, this remains a typical Ford western in terms of theme and plot, with planes replacing the old Pony Express. Like the best Ford movies, there's lots of hard drinking and bonhomie on the ground and heroics in the air. Reviewing it, the *Hollywood Reporter* gushed, "Oil up the cash register! Here, boys and girls, is a honey, a wow, a smash and seven kinds of knock-out. Anybody who can't make dough with this should retire." Despite that glowing recommendation, it's all pretty routine stuff.

Pat O'Brien *Duke Talbot* • Ralph Bellamy *Mike Miller* • Gloria Stuart *Ruth Barnes* • Lillian Bond *Irene Wilkins* • Russell Hopton *Dizzy Wilkins* • Slim Summerville *Slim McCune* • Frank Albertson *Tommy Bogan* ■ *Dir* John Ford • *Scr* Dale Van Every, Frank W Wead, from a story by Frank W Wead

The Air up There
★★ **PG**

Sports comedy 1993 · US · Colour · 103mins

This so-so basketball movie received only the briefest of theatrical releases in Britain. Kevin Bacon is the ambitious coach who heads for Africa to sign up exceptional athlete Charles Gitonga Maina. However, the latter is a local prince and is more interested in protecting his village than shooting hoops. The blueprint seems to be a basketball equivalent of *Cool Runnings*, but the film is low on belly laughs, despite the plucky playing of Bacon, and the serious bits are just plain mawkish. On the plus side, *Starsky and Hutch* star-turned-director Paul Michael Glaser stages the basketball sequences with some style. Contains some swearing ▭

Kevin Bacon *Jimmy Dolan* • Charles Gitonga Maina *Jimmy Saleh* • Yolanda Vazquez *Sister Susan* • Winston Ntshona *Urudu* • Mabutho

"Kid" Sithole *Nyaga* • Sean McCann *Coach Ray Fox* • Dennis Patrick *Father O'Hara* ■ *Dir* Paul Michael Glaser • *Scr* Max Apple

Airborne ★★ PG
Sports drama   1993 · US · Colour · 86mins

Forced to move with his family from California to Cincinnati, laid-back dude Shane McDermott swaps surfing the waves for rollerblading in the streets to impress his arch-enemy's sister. Formula teen comedy stuff is given a welcome makeover by a likeable cast and some thrilling stunt work, including a hair-raising downhill rollerblade chase through heavy traffic. 📼

Shane McDermott *Mitchell Goosen* • Seth Green *Wiley* • Brittney Powell *Nikki* • Chris Conrad *Jack* • Edie McClurg *Aunt Irene* • Patrick O'Brien *Uncle Louie* ■ *Dir* Rob Bowman • *Scr* Bill Apablasa, from a story by Stephen McEveety, Bill Apablasa

Airborne ★ 18
Action thriller   1997 · Can · Colour · 89mins

Come back *Police Academy*, all is forgiven. In a laughable piece of miscasting, Steve Guttenberg gets all mean and moody as the head of an elite squad of commando types, who is assigned to track down an international crook threatening to hold the world the ransom with some sort of secret virus. However, can they trust their own employers? Don't spend any time puzzling over that – this is excruciating tosh from the start. Sean Bean manages to stay out of sight for most of the movie, but the rest of the cast aren't so lucky. Contains violence and some swearing.

Steve Guttenberg *Bill McNeil* • Kim Coates *Bob Murdoch* • Torri Higginson *Sara Gemmel* • Philip Akin *Romeo Cortez* • David Fraser *Mr Samuels* • Sean Bean *Dave Toombs* ■ *Dir* Julian Grant • *Scr* Tony Johnston, Julian Grant

Airheads ★★★ 15
Comedy   1994 · US · Colour · 88mins

A dumb heavy metal band finds fame by hijacking a local radio station in director Michael Lehmann's broad *Wayne's World*-style comedy that lacks the goofy cleverness of the blockbuster hit. Brendan Fraser ably heads the head-banging brigade, with amusing support from dimwitted Adam Sandler and long-haired Steve Buscemi, exchanging Bill and Ted-like ripostes over the airwaves. Never quite as funny as it thinks it is – it needs the lighter touch Lehmann showed in *Heathers* – the amiable anarchy does sometimes hit the screwball spot thanks to a handful of great one-liners. 📼

Brendan Fraser *Cazz* • Steve Buscemi *Rex* • Adam Sandler *Pip* • Chris Farley *Wilson* • Joe Mantegna *Ian* • Michael McKean *Milo* • Judd Nelson *Jimmie Wing* • Ernie Hudson *Sergeant Omalley* • Amy Locane *Kayla* • Nina Siemaszko *Suzzi* ■ *Dir* Michael Lehmann • *Scr* Rich Wilkes

Airplane! ★★★★★ PG
Disaster movie spoof
1980 · US · Colour · 84mins

The first, and still the best, of Zucker, Zucker and Abrahams's wonderful movie send-ups. There's hardly a second that passes without an assault

by a wickedly accurate spoof, cringe-inducing pun or inspired sight gag, and the years have not diminished its dumb appeal. Robert Hays and Julie Hagerty are the nominal stars, but the most fun is had by the distinguished supporting cast. It's the film that made a comedy star out of Leslie ("don't call me Shirley") Nielsen, but a whole troupe of veteran character actors also have a hugely enjoyable time sending up their screen personae. And, best of all, it drove a large nail into the coffin of what was becoming a very tired Hollywood institution, the *Airport* series. Contains some swearing. 📼

Robert Hays *Ted Striker* • Julie Hagerty *Elaine Dickinson* • Leslie Nielsen *Dr Rumack* • Lloyd Bridges *McCroskey* • Robert Stack *Rex Kramer* • Kareem Abdul-Jabbar *Roger Murdock* • Peter Graves (1) *Captain Oveur* ■ *Dir/Scr* Jim Abrahams, David Zucker, Jerry Zucker

Airplane II: the Sequel ★★ 15
Comedy   1982 · US · Colour · 80mins

Airplane! was always going to be a hard act to follow and this time the scattergun approach to the script carries more misfires and duds than normal. Still, the two leads from the original (Robert Hays and Julie Hagerty) are back on board again and the endless silliness of it all should win people over in the end. This time the flimsy storyline revolves around the first commercial flight to the Moon. Newcomers include William Shatner, Sonny Bono, Chuck Connors and Raymond Burr, although it is two stars from the original, Lloyd Bridges and Peter Graves, who once again shine. Contains some swearing and brief nudity. 📼

Robert Hays *Ted Striker* • Julie Hagerty *Elaine* • Lloyd Bridges *McCroskey* • Peter Graves (1) *Captain Oveur* • William Shatner *Murdock* • Chad Everett *Simon* • Sonny Bono *Bomber* • Raymond Burr *Judge* • Chuck Connors *Sarge* • Jack Jones *Singer* ■ *Dir/Scr* Ken Finkleman

Airport ★★★ PG
Disaster movie   1970 · US · Colour · 128mins

After *Airplane!*, it's almost impossible to keep a straight face through this sprawling drama, particularly since it features George Kennedy, who these days tends to specialise in sending up the sort of role he played here, most memorably in the *Naked Gun* series. But he and the rest of the starry cast (including Burt Lancaster, Dean Martin and an Oscar-winning Helen Hayes) are commendably serious throughout. A competent soapy concoction. 📼

Burt Lancaster *Mel Bakersfeld* • Dean Martin *Vernon Demerest* • Jacqueline Bisset *Gwen* • Jean Seberg *Tanya Livingston* • George Kennedy *Joe Patroni* • Helen Hayes *Ada Quonsett* • Van Heflin *Do Guerrero* • Maureen Stapleton *Mrs Guerrero* ■ *Dir* George Seaton, from the novel by Arthur Hailey

Airport 1975 ★★★ PG
Disaster movie   1974 · US · Colour · 101mins

When a light aircraft makes an unscheduled landing in the cockpit of a jumbo jet – the 747 being aloft at the time – it causes something of a panic among the surviving crew and passengers. Stewardess Karen Black

takes the controls while Gloria Swanson, Myrna Loy and Sid Caesar gibber quietly in the back, and a sick child (played by *The Exorcist's* Linda Blair) is soothed by a singing nun. Meanwhile, on the ground, George Kennedy talks into a microphone (his wife just happens to be on board) and Charlton Heston prepares to... Well, parting the Red Sea was nothing compared to this stunt. Mind-boggling stuff. Contains some swearing 📼

Charlton Heston *Alan Murdoch* • Karen Black *Nancy* • George Kennedy *Joseph Patroni* • Gloria Swanson • Helen Reddy *Sister Ruth* • Efrem Zimbalist Jr *Captain Stacy* • Sid Caesar *Barney* • Linda Blair *Janice Abbott* • Dana Andrews *Scott Freeman* • Myrna Loy *Mrs Devaney* ■ *Dir* Jack Smight • *Scr* Don Ingalls

Airport '77 ★★★ PG
Disaster movie   1977 · US · Colour · 108mins

The third in the popular mid-air disaster series and one of the best, thanks to a stellar cast led by Jack Lemmon, James Stewart, Joseph Cotten and Olivia de Havilland. The veterans simply sit around and look classy, but Lemmon has to work a tad harder as he tackles a hijack attempt led by co-pilot Robert Foxworth. Quite why the Academy felt it needed to nominate the art directors for designing the inside of a plane or Edith Head for some pretty standard costumes is anyone's guess. It's not the most nail-biting film you'll ever see, but it's stylish entertainment. 📼

Jack Lemmon *Don Gallagher* • Lee Grant *Karen Wallace* • Brenda Vaccaro *Eve Clayton* • Joseph Cotten *Nicholas St Downs III* • Olivia de Havilland *Emily Livingston* • Darren McGavin *Stan Buchek* • Christopher Lee *Martin Wallace* • James Stewart *Philip Stevens* • George Kennedy *Joe Patroni* • Robert Foxworth *Chambers* ■ *Dir* Jerry Jameson • *Scr* Michael Scheff, David Spector, from a story by HAL Craig, Charles Kuenstle

Airport: the Concorde ★★ PG
Disaster movie   1979 · US · Colour · 108mins

The fourth *Airport* movie goes supersonic and has more disaster-packed moments than the average genre entry. Taking a chance with the usual inedible in-flight food, pilots George Kennedy and Alain Delon also have to deal with a missile chasing the plane, an emergency landing with no brakes, various explosions and doors coming off, and a crash-landing into snow. It's very silly, of course, but the starry cast (Robert Wagner, Sylvia Kristel, Eddie Albert) manages to be as over-the-top as the effects, making this a fun if incredibly mindless way to spend a couple of hours. Contains some swearing 📼

Alain Delon *Captain Paul Metrand* • Robert Wagner *Dr Kevin Harrison* • Susan Blakely *Maggie Whelan* • Sylvia Kristel *Isabelle* • George Kennedy *Joe Patroni* • Eddie Albert *Eli Sande* • Bibi Andersson *Francine* • Charo *Margarita* ■ *Dir* David Lowell Rich • *Scr* Eric Roth, Jennings Lang

Ake and His World ★★★★
Drama   1984 · Swe · Colour · 99mins

The terrors that intrude upon the idylls of childhood are explored in this charming tale of village life, set in 1930s Sweden. Martin Lindström is outstanding as the six-year-old boy

convinced by the portent of an extinguished candle that he'll be severely punished for accidentally endangering the life of a neighbour's son. It's not all slavering wolves, river spooks and fanatical pastors, however, as Ake is doted on by a family that includes a pipe-smoking grandmother and an eccentric sister. As in *Elvira Madigan*, Jörgen Persson's glossy photography romanticises the action, but this doesn't diminish the film's genuine warmth and humanity. In Swedish with English subtitles.

Martin Lindström *Ake* • Loa Falkman *Father* • Gunnel Fred *Mother* • Katja Blomquist *Sister* • Ulla Sjoblom *Grandma* • Suzanne Ernrup *Anne-Marie* • Bjorn Gustafson *Bergstrom* • Alexander Skarsgård *Kalle* • Stellan Skarsgård *Ebenholtz* ■ *Dir* Allan Edwall • *Scr* Allan Edwall, from the novel by Bertil Malmberg

Akenfield ★★
Documentary drama
1974 · UK · Colour · 97mins

Sir Peter Hall, one of modern theatre's more innovative directors, clearly felt up to adapting Ronald Blythe's testimonial memoir of life in a sleepy Suffolk farming community for a full-length film. But while the largely non-professional cast provides some fascinating insights, the contrasts with their Edwardian ancestors often feel laboured and undermine the otherwise laudably realistic approach. Moreover, Ivan Strasberg's lyrical widescreen imagery and Michael Tippett's lush score seem unsuited to such a simple tale. It's a bold experiment, but too stylised and sentimental to succeed.

Garrow Shand *Tom Rouse/Old Tom* • Peggy Cole *Dulcie Rouse* • Barbara Tilney *Jean Quantrill* • Lyn Brooks *Charlotte Rouse* • Ida Page *Aunt Ida* • Ted Dedman *Ted* • Charlie Cornish *Charlie* ■ *Dir* Peter Hall • *Scr* Ronald Blythe, from his book

Akira ★★★★ 15
Animated science-fiction fantasy
1988 · Jap · Colour · 119mins

One of the jewels of the genre, this is perhaps the best known *manga* movie in this country. Directed, co-scripted and designed by Katsuhiro Otomo from his own comic-strip, it's a pacey, unrelentingly violent post-apocalyptic adventure, in which a gang of Neo-Tokyo slum kids attempts to counter the telekinetic machinations of a rogue buddy. Yet, for all its futuristic elements, this is also a dark and disturbing portrait of contemporary urban life that seeks to expose the lack of empathy between the establishment and modern youth. The cityscapes are awesome, the camerawork is dizzying. If you're new to *manga*, prepare to be converted. In Japanese with English subtitles. Contains swearing. 📼

Dir Katsuhiro Otomo • *Scr* Izo Hashimoto, Katsuhiro Otomo

Akira Kurosawa's Dreams ★★ PG
Fantasy drama   1990 · Jap · Colour · 114mins

This is one of the Japanese master's weakest films, though still demonstrating the stylistic versatility and genius for composition that characterises his previous works. Here, the 80-year-old Kurosawa reveals a regrettable tendency towards self-indulgence and political naivety. Although his environmentalism is heart-felt, the messages contained in the eight vignettes that make up the film are muddled and often pompously expressed. There is great beauty to be found, however, notably in the vibrant colours of the *Crows* segment (featuring Martin Scorsese as Vincent Van Gogh) and in the haunting tune accompanying the funeral procession during the concluding *Village of the Watermills*. In Japanese with English subtitles. ▣

Akira Terao *"I"* • Mitsuko Baisho *Mother of "I"* • Mieko Harada *Snow fairy* • Yoshitaka Zushi *Private Noguchi* • Martin Scorsese *Vincent Van Gogh* • Toshie Negishi *Mother carrying child* • Chosuke Ikariya *Weeping demon* • Chishu Ryu *103-year-old man* ▪ *Dir/Scr* Akira Kurosawa

Al Capone ★★★★ 15
Crime drama   1959 · US · BW · 104mins
Rod Steiger was a natural to play Al Capone: he had played a gangster masquerading as a lawyer in *On the Waterfront* and a gangster masquerading as a Hollywood mogul in *The Big Knife*. And Capone was a businessman, finally imprisoned for tax evasion rather than slaughter on the streets of Chicago. Steiger, of course, brings all his Method mannerisms to play and it's fascinating to compare his portrayal with later ones by Jason Robards (*The St Valentine's Day Massacre*) and Robert De Niro (Brian De Palma's *The Untouchables*). Directed by Richard Wilson, a former associate of Orson Welles, the picture revived interest in Capone, led to the TV series of *The Untouchables*.

Rod Steiger *Al Capone* • Fay Spain *Maureen Flannery* • Martin Balsam *Keely* • James Gregory *Tom Schaeffer* • Murvyn Vye *Bugs Moran* • Nehemiah Persoff *Johnny Torrio* • Joe De Santis *Big Jim Colosimo* • Lewis Charles *Hymie Weiss* ▪ *Dir* Richard Wilson • *Scr* Marvin Wald, Henry Greenberg

Aladdin ★ PG
Fantasy   1986 · It · Colour · 91mins
Released in Italy as *SuperFantaGenio*, this was one of the last films directed by Bruno Corbucci, who was returning to his origins in costume fantasy after making crime dramas such as *Crime at Porta Romana* (1980). It's pretty much a bargain basement affair, although it does allow Italian star Bud Spencer to gnaw at the scenery as the Genie who is released by the young Luca Venantini from the magic lamp found in a junk shop. Desperately corny and gushingly sentimental, this won't impress viewers who expect their cartoons to be of Disney standard. An Italian language film. ▣

Bud Spencer *Genie* • Luca Venantini *Al Haddin* • Janet Agren *Mrs Haddin* • Umberto Raho • Julian Voloshin *Jeremiah* • Daimy Spencer *Patricia* ▪ *Dir* Bruno Corbucci • *Scr* Mario Amendola, Marcello Fondato, Bruno Corbucci

Aladdin ★★★★ U
Animated musical adventure
1992 · US · Colour · 86mins
For a full-length cartoon featuring some remarkably hip animation, it's amazing how Robert Williams's performance as

the Genie steals the show, his ad-lib vocals a perfect match for the beautifully constructed Disney visuals. In this *Arabian Nights* tale, Aladdin (voiced by Scott Weinger) is the street urchin who uses a magical oil lamp and its wish-granting genie to win the love of Princess Jasmine (Linda Larkin, Lea Salonga singing) and defeat the evil Jafar (Jonathan Freeman). Kids will be enchanted by this captivating fable, while adults will appreciate the film's delightful songs and numerous sophisticated references. In the end, though, it's Williams's movie. ▣

Scott Weinger *Aladdin* • Robin Williams *Genie* • Linda Larkin *Jasmine* • Jonathan Freeman *Jafar* • Frank Welker *Abu/Narrator* • Gilbert Gottfried *Iago* • Douglas Seale *Sultan* • Lea Salonga *Jasmine (singing voice)* ▪ *Dir* John Musker, Ron Clements • *Scr* Ron Clements, John Musker, Ted Elliot, Terry Rossio

Aladdin and the King of Thieves ★★★ U
Animated fantasy 1996 · US · Colour · 78mins
A second sequel to the 1992 Disney animated adventure *Aladdin*, the first being *The Return of Jafar*. Robin Williams returns to give the same sharp voice characterisation to the Genie (Dan Castellaneta of *The Simpsons* fame did the honours in the first sequel), helping young Aladdin when he discovers that his father is actually the leader of the infamous ''40 thieves''. Adults will be just as entertained as the youngsters this is aimed at, thanks to a well thought-out plot and witty vocals from a cast which also includes Jerry Orbach (Jennifer Grey's dad in *Dirty Dancing*) and character actor John Rhys-Davies (*Raiders of the Lost Ark*). ▣ **DVD**

Robin Williams *Genie* • Gilbert Gottfried *Iago* • Jerry Orbach *Sa'luk* • John Rhys-Davies *Cassim* • Linda Larkin *Jasmine* • Scott Weinger *Aladdin* • Val Bettin *Sultan* • Frank Welker *Abu* ▪ *Dir* Tad Stones • *Scr* Mark McCorkle, Robert Schooley

The Alamo ★★★★★ PG
Historical western
1960 · US · Colour · 202mins
That giant of westerns, John Wayne, produced, directed and starred (as Colonel David Crockett) in this classic of the genre. The rhetoric in the cause of freedom seems anachronistic in a film made in 1960, and the historical events concerning the siege of the eponymous fort have since been reassessed. However, this epic remains a great achievement with powerful performances, notably by Wayne and Richard Widmark, and a fine script from James Edward Grant that has moments of wit and humour between the more dramatic speeches. Wayne was helped by an uncredited input from his friend John Ford in the battle scenes. ▣ **DVD**

John Wayne *Colonel David Crockett* • Richard Widmark *Colonel James Bowie* • Laurence Harvey *Colonel William Travis* • Richard Boone *General Sam Houston* • Frankie Avalon *Smitty* • Patrick Wayne *Captain James Butler Bonham* • Linda Cristal *Flaca* • Joan O'Brien *Mrs Dickinson* • Chill Wills *Beekeeper* • Joseph Calleia *Juan Sequin* ▪ *Dir* John Wayne • *Scr* James Edward Grant

Alamo Bay ★★★ 15
Drama based on a true story
1985 · US · Colour · 94mins
French director Louis Malle made a better study of racism in his acclaimed 1987 film *Au Revoir les Enfants*, but he also tackled the subject to decent effect two years earlier. This English-language movie examines the conflict between a group of Vietnamese refugees and a Texan shrimp-fishing community, whose members feel threatened by the competition from the hard-working newcomers. Amy Madigan stands out as the on-again, off-again girlfriend (and real-life wife) of chief racist thug Ed Harris, in this new variation on an old story. Contains some swearing. ▣

Amy Madigan *Glory Scheer* • Ed Harris *Shang Pierce* • Nguyen Ho Dinh • Donald Moffat *Wally Scheer* • Tran Truyen V *Ben* • Rudy Young *Skinner* • Cynthia Carle *Honey* • Martino Lasalle *Luis* • William Frankfather *Mac* • Lucky Mosley *Ab Crankshaw* • Bill Thurman *Sheriff* ▪ *Dir* Louis Malle • *Scr* Alice Arlen

Alan & Naomi ★★ PG
Drama   1992 · US · Colour · 91mins
A small but touching film in which youngsters Lukas Haas (*Witness*) and newcomer Vanessa Zaoui are two Jewish children in 1940s New York. Haas is instructed to befriend new neighbour Zaoui, deeply disturbed since she was forced to watch her father's death at the hands of the Nazis. He is initially resistant, but the two children develop a lasting and emotional friendship. Debut director Sterling Van Wagenen handles the largely unknown cast with ease and the result is poignant if a little stagey. ▣

Lukas Haas *Alan Drucker Silverman* • Vanessa Zaoui *Naomi Kirschenbaum* • Michael Gross *Sol Silverman* • Amy Aquino *Ruth Silverman* • Kevin Connolly *Shaun Kelly* ▪ *Dir* Sterling Van Wagenen • *Scr* Jordan Horowitz, from a novel by Myron Levoy

The Alarmist ★★ 15
Comedy crime drama
1997 · US · Colour · 91mins
Arriving with little fanfare, Evan Dunsky's indie comedy tries desperately to be wackily black. But uncertain pacing and a surfeit of plot padding make it feel like a neat short that unnecessarily sprawled into mediocrity. Mugging madly, David Arquette is way below his *Scream* form as a home security salesman who becomes convinced that crooked boss Stanley Tucci is responsible for the break-in death of his girlfriend (Kate Capshaw). Tucci revels in his Terry-Thomas villainy, but even he can't enliven the clumsy kidnap finale. Contains swearing, moderate sex and violence.

David Arquette *Tommy Hudler* • Stanley Tucci *Heinrich Grigoris* • Kate Capshaw *Gale Ancona* • Mary McCormack *Sally* • Ryan Reynolds *Howard Ancona* • Tricia Vessey *April* • Ruth Miller *Mrs Fielding* • Hoke Howell *Mr Fielding* • Lewis Arquette *Bruce Hudler* • Richmond Arquette *Andrew Hudler* ▪ *Dir* Evan Dunsky • *Scr* Evan Dunsky, from the play *Life During Wartime* by Keith Reddin

Alaska ★★★ PG
Adventure   1996 · US · Colour · 104mins
Fraser Heston directs his father Charlton for the second time (they first worked together on *Treasure Island*) in this well-made family adventure about a young brother and sister searching for their missing dad (played by *The A-Team's* Dirk Benedict) in the Alaskan wilderness. Instead they discover an adorable baby polar bear that's being hunted by a ruthless poacher (Heston Sr). Breathtaking scenery, a deliciously evil portrayal from Chuck and energetic performances from the kids (Thora Birch and Vincent Kartheiser) make this a thoroughly enjoyable adventure. Some scenes of (simulated) cruelty to the bears may upset younger viewers; for that reason *Alaska* was given a PG certificate. ▣

Thora Birch *Jessie Barnes* • Vincent Kartheiser *Sean Barnes* • Dirk Benedict *Jake Barnes* • Charlton Heston *Perry* • Duncan Fraser *Koontz* • Gordon Tootoosis *Ben* • Ben Cardinal *Charlie* • Ryan Kent *Chip* ▪ *Dir* Fraser C Heston • *Scr* Andy Burg, Scott Myers

Alaska Seas ★★ U
Adventure drama   1954 · US · BW · 76mins
A fight brews among the cannery men of Alaska, with bad guy Gene Barry opposed to good guys Robert Ryan and Brian Keith, who has just spent time in prison for poaching salmon. It's not clear if his sentence would have been longer had he fried them or grilled them. Jan Sterling is the girl in the middle, later upstaged by an iceberg that arrives to sort things out. The actors dress up warmly and huddle about, even though they are obviously in a Hollywood studio in front of a back projection screen.

Robert Ryan *Matt Kelly* • Jan Sterling *Nicky* • Brian Keith *Jim Kimmerly* • Gene Barry *Verne Williams* • Richard Shannon *Tom Erickson* • Ralph Dumke *Jackson* • Ross Bagdasarian *Joe* ▪ *Dir* Jerry Hopper • *Scr* Geoffrey Homes [Daniel Mainwaring], Walter Doniger, from a story by Barrett Willoughby

Albert, RN ★★★ U
Second World War drama
1953 · UK · BW · 88mins
A POW drama about a mannequin nicknamed Albert which supposedly stands in for escaped prisoners. A huge hit at the time, it still has bags of charm and a degree of tension, though a starrier cast than the wooden Anthony Steel and American expats like William Sylvester would have helped considerably. One looks in vain for Jack Hawkins and Dickie Attenborough. But all is not lost: Anton Diffring plays a Nazi.

Anthony Steel *Lt Geoffrey Ainsworth* • Jack Warner *Capt Maddox* • Robert Beatty *Lt Jim Reid* • William Sylvester *Lt ''Texas''Norton* • Michael Balfour *Lt Henry Adams* • Guy Middleton *Capt Barton* • Anton Diffring *Hauptmann Schultz* ▪ *Dir* Lewis Gilbert • *Scr* Vernon Harris, Guy Morgan, from the play by Guy Morgan, Edward Sammis

Albino Alligator ★★ 18
Crime drama   1996 · US/Fr · Colour · 92mins
Highly acclaimed *Usual Suspects* actor Kevin Spacey turns director in this far too theatrical and cerebral hostage thriller. An amateur gang, led by Matt

Dillon, flee a gone-wrong heist and hole up in Dino's Last Chance all-night bar. Tension rises and tempers fray among the low-lifes and drunks being tended to by barmaid Faye Dunaway as the police surround the place and wait for the criminals to buckle. The over-ripe dialogue, full of endless philosophical ramblings, and the claustrophobic confines of the stagey scenario soon become stifling. Contains swearing and violence. ▭

Matt Dillon *Dova* • Faye Dunaway *Janet Boudreaux* • Gary Sinise *Milo* • Viggo Mortensen *Guy Foucard* • Joe Mantegna *GD Browning* • M Emmet Walsh *Dino* • John Spencer *Jack* • William Fichtner *Law* • Skeet Ulrich *Danny Boudreaux* ■ *Dir* Kevin Spacey • *Scr* Christian Forte

The Alchemist ★ 18
Horror   1981 · US · Colour · 83mins

The gates of hell are opened when an old woman incants an ancient spell to free her father from the curse of eternal youth. And what's on the other side? Two men running around wearing dodgy demon rubber masks and a couple of awful special effects! Exploitation king director Robert Ginty stars in this tedious occult nonsense from straight-to-video horror maestro Charles Band. The virtually incoherent plot includes a splatter of gore in a vain effort to keep the interest, but it's a rock-bottom item off Band's schlock conveyor belt.

Lucinda Dooling *Lenora* • Robert Ginty *Aaron* • Robert Glaudini *DenGatto* • John Sanderford • Viola Kate Stimpson ■ *Dir* Charles Band • *Scr* Alan J Adler

Aldrich Ames: Traitor Within ★★★ PG
Spy drama based on a true story
1998 · US · Colour · 97mins

A fascinating account of one of the USA's most notorious double agents, who betrayed the CIA for years for money. Frustrated by lack of promotion and ridden with debt, Aldrich Ames (Timothy Hutton) starts selling agents' names to the enemy. Joan Plowright is the methodical investigator on his tail, while Elizabeth Peña plays his unsuspecting wife. British director John Mackenzie cranks up the suspense, but this is really Hutton's show. His subtly intense performance makes for a fascinating companion piece to his earlier role in the similarly themed *The Falcon and the Snowman*. Contains some mild swearing. ▭

Timothy Hutton *Aldrich Ames* • Elizabeth Pena *Rosario Ames* • Joan Plowright *Jeanne Vertefeuille* • Eugene Lipinski *Vlad* • Robert Benedetti *Chief of Operations* • C David Johnson *Brooks* • Patricia Carroll Brown *Connie Dru* ■ *Dir* John Mackenzie • *Scr* Michael Burton

Alex and the Gypsy ★★
Melodrama   1976 · US · Colour · 98mins

Jack Lemmon stars as a bail-bond dealer who falls for one of his clients, gypsy Geneviève Bujold, accused of nearly killing her husband. It's a story of two of society's drop-outs and, in some respects, sits comfortably within the counter-culture era. Lemmon seems to be reprising his Oscar-winning performance in *Save the Tiger*,

while Bujold is no less of a cliché, that of the European free spirit. It might have worked better had it been played for black comedy instead of schmaltz.

Jack Lemmon *Alexander Main* • Geneviève Bujold *Maritza* • James Woods *Crainpool* • Gino Ardito *Golfer* • Robert Emhardt *Judge* • Joseph X Flaherty *Morgan* • Todd Martin *Roy Blake* • Victor Pinhiero *Sanders* ■ *Dir* John Korty • *Scr* Lawrence B Marcus, from the novella *The Bailbondsman* by Stanley Elkin

Alex in Wonderland ★★
Comedy   1970 · US · Colour · 111mins

After minting a fortune at the box office with *Bob & Carol & Ted & Alice*, MGM allowed director Paul Mazursky to make any film he wanted. The result was this horribly self-indulgent and self-conscious bomb about the far-out dilemma of a hippie director searching for a follow-up to his first successful movie. Donald Sutherland plays the navel-gazing *auteur* who takes LSD for inspiration, pokes fun at sixties Hollywood and then fantasises about meeting Fellini (who appears as himself, along with Jeanne Moreau). Mazursky tried being autobiographical again in the equally dire *The Pickle*.

Donald Sutherland *Alex* • Ellen Burstyn *Beth* • Federico Fellini • Jeanne Moreau • Meg Mazursky *Amy* • Glenna Sergent *Nancy* • Viola Spolin *Mother* • Andre Philippe *André* ■ *Dir* Paul Mazursky • *Scr* Larry Tucker, Paul Mazursky

Alexander Nevsky ★★★★ PG
War drama   1938 · USSR · BW · 104mins

The Soviet equivalent to Olivier's *Henry V*, this historical epic aimed to serve as propaganda against Hitler's Reich. However, just as Sergei Eisenstein completed the story of the Teutonic invasion of Russia in the 13th century, Stalin and Hitler signed a non-aggression pact, so the film was withdrawn. Then, when Hitler broke the treaty, Stalin ordered it released. The film is famous for two things – the battle at the frozen lake, filmed in high summer, and Prokofiev's score. Both live up to their reputations but one must also endure much turgid story-telling and some excessively theatrical acting. In Russian with English subtitles. ▭

Nikolai Cherkassov *Prince Alexander Yaroslavich Nevsky* • Nikolai P Okhlopkov *Vassily Buslai* • Alexandr L Abrikossov *Gavrilo Olexich* • DN Orlov *Ignat Master Armourer* ■ *Dir* Sergei Eisenstein • *Scr* Sergei Eisenstein, Pyotr Pavlenko • *Cinematographer* Edouard Tissé

Alexander the Great ★★ U
Epic historical drama
1956 · US/Sp · Colour · 129mins

An epic that promises more than it delivers, though the blond-bewigged Richard Burton makes a fair stab at depicting the conqueror of half the known world, but remains no match for Fredric March's fiery bearded Philip of Macedonia, Alexander's father. The use of early CinemaScope is superb, as is the deployment of the armies of extras and the key scene of slicing the Gordian knot, but writer/director Robert Rossen's long and static movie is wordy and ponderous, and there's little for the classy female contingent of Claire Bloom and Danielle Darrieux to

do. Audiences will do, too, except when dynamic star-in-the-making Stanley Baker is on screen. ▭

Richard Burton *Alexander* • Fredric March *Philip of Macedonia* • Claire Bloom *Barsine* • Danielle Darrieux *Olympias* • Barry Jones *Aristotle* • Harry Andrews *Darius* • Stanley Baker *Attalus* • Peter Cushing *Memnon* • Michael Hordern *Demosthenes* ■ *Dir/Scr* Robert Rossen

Alexander's Ragtime Band ★★★ U
Musical   1938 · US · BW · 101mins

It doesn't matter that handsome Tyrone Power shows no sense of rhythm, or that the plot is pure hokum, or that the First World War is over in a montage that's quicker than a wink. No… what matters is that this is a glorious Irving Berlin songfest, with Alice Faye and a young Ethel Merman belting out some of Tin Pan Alley's best and brightest. Unfortunately, there is a plot, and it's 20th Century-Fox's old triangular one: guess who gets Alice: Ty or his best friend, Don Ameche? Puhleeze… Just relax, and revel in the music. ▭

Tyrone Power *Roger Grant* • Alice Faye *Stella Kirby* • Don Ameche *Charlie Dwyer* • Ethel Merman *Jerry Allen* • Jack Haley *Davey Lane* • Jean Hersholt *Professor Heinrich* • Helen Westley *Aunt Sophie* • John Carradine *Taxi driver* ■ *Dir* Henry King • *Scr* Kathryn Scola, Lamar Trotti

Alexandria Encore ★★★★
Documentary drama
1990 · Fr/Egypt · Colour · 100mins

Youssef Chahine cinema-inspired work is a dazzling, if occasionally self-indulgent, treatise on the process of film-making. Chahine stars as a director assessing his achievements during a period of creative block brought on by a row with the star of his proposed production of *Hamlet*. With a Hollywood song-and-dance spectacular recalling the night he triumphed at Berlin, and flashbacks to an unrealised musical homage to Alexander the Great, this is a witty yet wistful exploration of age, authorship, cinematic art and popular taste. Superbly staged and photographed, this is an elegant and engaging piece of entertainment. In Arabic with English subtitles.

Youssef Chahine • Yousra • Hussein Fahmy • Amr Abdel Guelil ■ *Dir/Scr* Youssef Chahine

Alexandria Why? ★★★★
Second World War drama
1979 · Egypt/Algeria · Colour · 132mins

Directed by Youssef Chahine, Egypt's most respected film-maker and the man who "discovered" Omar Sharif, a stylish wartime tale, which won the Special Jury prize at Berlin, it focuses on a movie-mad schoolboy (Moshen Mohiedine), obsessed with Hollywood musicals at a time when everyone else is preoccupied with the advance of Rommel. Packed with cinematic references, the highlights of this pleasing study of starstruck ambition include a wonderfully fouled-up school play and Mohiedine's touching friendship with a Jewish girl, Nagla Fathi. In Arabic with English subtitles.

Mohsen Mohiedine *Yehia* • Nagla Fathi *Sarah* • Gerry Sundquist *Tommy* ■ *Dir* Youssef Chahine • *Scr* Youssef Chahine, Mohsen Zayed

Alfie ★★★★ 15
Comedy drama   1966 · UK · Colour · 109mins

Receiving five Oscar nominations and rave reviews, this was one of the most talked-about British films of the sixties. The frank discussion of pre-marital sex, adultery and illegitimacy might now raise fewer eyebrows and the chirpy cockney banter might sound more than a little old hat, but this knowing drama still has much to say about how differently men and women view intimate relationships, and the abortion scene is particularly harrowing. Michael Caine has rarely bettered his performance here, conveying, particularly in his monologues, a charm and a naivety that is as troubling as it is accomplished. Of the wronged women, Julia Foster and Vivien Merchant are outstanding. Contains swearing ▭

Michael Caine *Alfie* • Shelley Winters *Ruby* • Millicent Martin *Siddie* • Julia Foster *Gilda* • Jane Asher *Annie* • Shirley Anne Field *Carla* • Vivien Merchant *Lily* • Eleanor Bron *Doctor* • Denholm Elliott *Abortionist* ■ *Dir* Lewis Gilbert • *Scr* Bill Naughton, his play

Alfie Darling ★★ 18
Comedy drama   1975 · UK · Colour · 97mins

This follow-up to the Oscar-nominated *Alfie* (1966) finds pop singer Alan Price replacing Michael Caine as the cockney Casanova, with director Ken Hughes taking over from Lewis Gilbert. This time around Alfie is a truck driver involved with the usual bevy of beauties, none of whom makes any impact apart from Jill Townsend. Although the description "soft porn" seems appropriate, it's not as bad as all that. It certainly lacks much of the verve and pathos of the original. Harmless and charmless. ▭

Alan Price *Alfie* • Jill Townsend *Abby* • Joan Collins *Fay* • Rula Lenska *Louise* • Hannah Gordon *Dora* • Vicki Michelle *Bird* • Annie Ross *Claire* • Sheila White *Norma* ■ *Dir* Ken Hughes • *Scr* Ken Hughes, from the character created by Bill Naughton

Alfred the Great ★★★
Historical drama
1969 · UK · Colour · 122mins

Sixties' trendy David Hemmings is a rather implausible Prince of Wessex, later the only British king to be called "great", in director Clive Donner's story of the man who not only burnt the cakes but also built the boats to create the British navy. In Donner's film, Alfred is portrayed as someone whose greatness was thrust upon him, a deep thinker who had once wanted to take holy orders. An interesting theme, but true epic status somehow eludes the movie.

David Hemmings *Alfred* • Michael York *Guthrum* • Prunella Ransome *Aelhswith* • Colin Blakely *Asher* • Julian Glover *Athelstan* • Ian McKellen *Roger* • Alan Dobie *Ethelred* • Peter Vaughan *Buhrud* • Julian Chagrin *Ivar* • Barry Jackson *Wulfstan* • Vivien Merchant *Freda* • Christopher Timothy *Cedric* • Michael Billington *Offa* ■ *Dir* Clive Donner • *Scr* Ken Taylor, James R Webb

Alfredo Alfredo ★★
Comedy 1971 · It · Colour · 97mins

Ever the Method actor, Dustin Hoffman took the trouble to learn the Italian dialogue for this laborious comedy, only for director Pietro Germi to shoot in English and then dub all the voices in post-production into Italian. A dubbed English version then went on general release in the States. Germi veers between cruel slapstick and broad satire as he chronicles Hoffman's doomed relationship with the demanding Stefania Sandrelli. While there's some vigour about the courtship sequences, the action gets bogged down once the focus shifts to the vagaries of the Italian legal system. Italian dialogue dubbed into English.

Dustin Hoffman *Alfredo* • Stefania Sandrelli *Mariarosa* • Carla Gravina *Carolina* • Clara Colosimo *Carolina's mother* • Daniele Patella *Carolina's father* • Danika La Loggia *Mariarosa's mother* • Saro Urzi *Mariarosa's father* ■ *Dir* Pietro Germi • *Scr* Leo Benvenuti, Piero De Bernardi, Tullio Pinelli, Pietro Germi

Alf's Button Afloat ★★★ U
Fantasy comedy 1938 · UK · BW · 89mins

The upstaging talents of "The Crazy Gang" – Bud Flanagan, Chesney Allen, Jimmy Nervo, Teddy Knox, Charles Naughton and Jimmy Gold – have never been in doubt. However, Alastair Sim easily surpasses them as the genie they encounter in this umpteenth version of WA Darlington's famous farce. As buskers serving in the Marines, the Gang work hard at their music hall routines. In contrast, the bumbling Sim steals the show – without even trying, it seems.

Bud Flanagan [Dennis O'Keefe] *Alf Higgins* • Chesney Allen *Ches* • Jimmy Nervo *Cecil* • Teddy Knox *Teddy* • Charlie Naughton *Charlie* • Jimmy Gold *Jimmy* • Alastair Sim *Eustace* • Wally Patch *Sergeant Hawkins* • Peter Gawthorne *Captain Driscol* • Glennis Lorimer *Frankie Driscol* ■ *Dir* Marcel Varnel • *Scr* Marriott Edgar, Val Guest, Ralph Smart, from the play *Alf's Button* by WA Darlington

Algiers ★★★
Crime drama 1938 · US · BW · 97mins

This loose remake of the Jean Gabin movie *Pépé le Moko*, has Charles Boyer and Hedy Lamarr clinching in the Casbah, the scene of innumerable shady goings-on from the supporting cast. The hard-boiled dialogue by James M Cain, author of *Double Indemnity*, and the lustrous black-and-white photography give this movie irresistible glamour, the virtual definition of Hollywood artifice. Producer Hal B Wallis saw how successful it was and immediately ordered a title change to his new production at Warners called *Everybody Comes to Rick's*. The new title? Why, *Casablanca*, of course.

Charles Boyer *Pépé le Moko* • Sigrid Gurie *Ines* • Hedy Lamarr *Gaby* • Joseph Calleia *Slimane* • Gene Lockhart *Regis* • Alan Hale *Grandpère* ■ *Dir* John Cromwell • *Scr* John Howard Lawson, James M Cain, from the novel *Pépé le Moko* by Detective Roger D'Ashelbe [Henri La Barthe]

Ali Baba and the Forty Thieves ★★ U
Adventure 1944 · US · Colour · 86mins

Baghdad… and the Mongols have landed, throwing everyone into slavery, except young Master Baba, who escapes into the desert and finds said number of thieves. He grows up to be Jon Hall, and falls for Maria Montez as a princess with attitude. Made by Universal as a follow-up to the money-spinning *Arabian Nights*, this take on an old story has its tongue in its cheek and delivers its cheapo action thrills quite efficiently. Montez is a hoot, Hall a rather tedious hero and Andy Devine injects a touch of the Wild West into the Exotic East. And when the thieves ride out singing *40 Thieves and One for All*, you'll wish it was a musical.

Maria Montez *Amara* • Jon Hall *Ali Baba* • Turhan Bey *Jamiel* • Andy Devine *Abdullah* • Kurt Katch *Hulagu Khan* • Frank Puglia *Cassim* • Fortunio Bonanova *Baba* • Moroni Olsen *Caliph* • Ramsay Ames *Nalu* ■ *Dir* Arthur Lubin • *Scr* Edmund L Hartmann

Alias Jesse James ★★★ U
Comedy western 1959 · US · Colour · 92mins

Bob Hope stars in yet another western spoof, this time playing an incompetent insurance salesman determined to retrieve the policy he unwittingly sold to outlaw Jesse James (Wendell Corey). Hope provides the jokes, while Rhonda Fleming supplies the pulchritude. The best moments are in the finale, though, when a host of cowboy stars (Roy Rogers, James Garner, Fess Parker) protect Bob from the killers.

Bob Hope *Milford Farnsworth* • Rhonda Fleming *Cora Lee Collins* • Wendell Corey *Jesse James* • Jim Davis *Frank James* • Gloria Talbott *Indian maiden* • Will Wright *Titus Queasley* • James Arness *Matt Dillon* • Ward Bond *Major Seth Adams* • Gary Cooper • Bing Crosby • Gail Davis *Annie Oakley* • Hugh O'Brian *Wyatt Earp* • Fess Parker *Davy Crockett* • Roy Rogers • Jay Silverheels *Tonto* • Gene Autry • James Garner *Bret Maverick* ■ *Dir* Norman Z McLeod • *Scr* William Bowers, Daniel D Beauchamp, from a story by Robert St Aubrey, Bert Lawrence

Alibi ★★
Crime drama 1929 · US · BW · 75mins

This early and rather primitive gangster movie was made by the maverick independent Roland West who later made *The Bat Whispers*. Now long forgotten, *Alibi* has been credited with being the first film to simultaneously record the sound and show the destruction caused by a tommy-gun. Two interrogation scenes are especially shocking, showing the sadistic techniques used by the cops as utterly normal. Chester Morris, in his first starring role, was among those nominated for the second Oscar ceremony.

Chester Morris *Chick Williams* • Harry Stubbs *Buck Bachman* • Mae Busch *Daisy Thomas* • Eleanor Griffith *Joan* • Irma Harrison *Toots* • Regis Toomey *Danny McGann* • Al Hill *Brown* • James Bradbury Jr *Blake* ■ *Dir* Roland West • *Scr* Roland West, C Gardner Sullivan, from the play *Nightstick* by John Wray, JC Nugent, Elaine S Carrington

Alice ★★★ PG
Animated fantasy
1988 · UK/Swi/W Ger · Colour · 82mins

This stunning modern-day version of the Lewis Carroll story from Czech director, animator and surrealist Jan Svankmajer uses every live-action technique in the special effects manual, and contains dashes of startling eroticism. The absurdist universe created by the Prague native plays around liberally with the source material, yet remains remarkably true to its spirit. Flesh-and-blood actress Kristyna Kohoutova shares the screen with a host of scary fish, skeleton birds and, most unusually, perambulating raw meat. 🎞

Kristyna Kohoutova *Alice* ■ *Dir* Jan Svankmajer • *Scr* from the novel *Alice's Adventures in Wonderland* by Lewis Carroll

Alice ★★★ 15
Fantasy comedy 1990 · US · Colour · 101mins

When *Alice* was originally released, several critics attacked Woody Allen for making the same film over and over again. But is there another Allen picture in which a woman is helped to confront her past with the help of Chinese herbal teas, gets to meet the ghost of an old flame and spy on her family and friends while invisible? What gives *Alice* that "oh-so-familiar" feel is the all too predictable and stylised performance of Mia Farrow, whose bored Manhattan underachiever undoes a lot of the good work by co-stars William Hurt and Joe Mantegna and the excellent supporting cast. Contains swearing. 🎞

Mia Farrow *Alice* • William Hurt *Doug* • Alec Baldwin *Ed* • Joe Mantegna *Joe* • Cybill Shepherd *Nancy Brill* • Blythe Danner *Dorothy* • Bernadette Peters *Muse* • Gwen Verdon *Alice's mother* • Patrick O'Neal *Alice's father* ■ *Dir/Scr* Woody Allen

Alice Adams ★★★★ U
Comedy drama 1935 · US · BW · 95mins

Brilliant Hollywood director George Stevens dates this small-town opus as the real start of his career, conveniently neglecting the early comedies that he cut his teeth on. Understandable, really, since his technique, coupled with a magnificent performance from Katharine Hepburn as Booth Tarkington's titular heroine, make this unforgettable. The dinner table scene, where beau Fred MacMurray comes visiting, is rightly famous, and is a brilliant example of the film-maker's craft, albeit aided by superb casting (in particular Hattie McDaniel's slovenly maid). This is, in fact, a remake of a 1923 silent version which had Florence Vidor in the lead, but it's Hepburn's version that's remembered. 🎞

Katharine Hepburn *Alice Adams* • Fred MacMurray *Arthur Russell* • Fred Stone *Mr Adams* • Evelyn Venable *Mildred Palmer* • Frank Albertson *Walter Adams* • Ann Shoemaker *Mrs Adams* • Charles Grapewin [Charley Grapewin] *Mr Lamb* • Grady Sutton *Frank Dowling* • Hedda Hopper *Mrs Palmer* • Hattie McDaniel *Malena* ■ *Dir* George Stevens • *Scr* Dorothy Yost, Mortimer Offner, from the novel by Booth Tarkington

Alice Doesn't Live Here Anymore ★★★★ 15
Drama 1974 · US · Colour · 107mins

Martin Scorsese's much maligned follow-up to his critically acclaimed *Mean Streets* is an expertly played drama in which bruised widow Ellen Burstyn hits the road with her brattish son in order to find herself, dreaming of a new beginning as a singer. The Oscar-winning Burstyn brilliantly conveys the vulnerability that forces Alice first into the arms of the brutal Harvey Keitel and then of taciturn rancher Kris Kristofferson. Scorsese just about keeps the sprawling road movie segment on track, but the film really comes to life when Alice allies with a sassy diner waitress played by Oscar-nominated Diane Ladd. Contains swearing and some violence 🎞

Ellen Burstyn *Alice Hyatt* • Kris Kristofferson *David Barrie* • Billy Green Bush *Donald Hyatt* • Diane Ladd *Flo* • Lelia Goldoni *Bea* • Lane Bradbury *Rita* • Vic Tayback *Mel* • Jodie Foster *Audrey* • Harvey Keitel *Ben Eberhart* • Alfred Lutter *Tom Hyatt* ■ *Dir* Martin Scorsese • *Scr* Robert Getchell

Alice et Martin ★★★ 12
Drama 1998 · Fr/Sp/US · Colour · 124mins

Fourteen years after *Rendez-vous*, Juliette Binoche and André Téchiné reunite for this coolly assured but coldly uninvolving film, which is further undermined by improbable characterisation and contrived plotting. At the mercy of her emotions, Binoche is never less than persuasive as the violinist who sacrifices everything for Alexis Loret, an undeserving narcissus. Aided by crisp photography and a lovely score, Téchiné deftly captures the fragility of the relationship, but refuses to allow us to delve too deeply. In French with English subtitles.

Juliette Binoche *Alice* • Alexis Loret *Martin Sauvagnac* • Mathieu Amalric *Benjamin Sauvagnac* • Carmen Maura *Jeanine Sauvagnac* • Jean-Pierre Lorit *Frédéric* • Marthe Villalonga *Lucie* • Pierre Maguelon *Victor Sauvagnac* ■ *Dir* André Téchiné • *Scr* André Téchiné, Gilles Taurand, Olivier Assayas • *Cinematographer* Caroline Champetier • *Music* Philippe Sarde

Alice in Acidland ★
Spoof documentary
1968 · US · BW and Colour

Great title, lousy movie. A cautionary quasi-documentary, this hopeless farrago has lurid scenes of sex, drugs and rock 'n' roll accompanied by censor-busting dire warnings. The confused premise is held together by a psychiatrist relating the sad tale of college student Alice Trenton who hits the decadent skids and turns into a weed-smoking twilight hippie after a pool party. Hilarious dialogue aside ("Let me eat the flowers"), this slice of lava lamp lunacy gets very boring pretty fast.

Patty Roberts *Alice* ■ *Dir* Cheshire Cat

Alice in the Cities ★★★★ U
Drama 1974 · W Ger · BW · 107mins

Introducing themes that would recur in *Wrong Move*, *Kings of the Road* and *Paris, Texas*, Wim Wenders's road movie provides an amusing, affectionate and yet quietly critical portrait of seventies America. Often employing a subjective camera technique, Wenders places the viewer at the heart of the odyssey so that we can experience the sights and sounds of the eastern seaboard exactly as photo-journalist Rüdiger Vogler and his nine-year-old companion Yella Rottlander see them. The search for the girl's grandmother is virtually irrelevant, as it is how this odd couple react to each other and their ever-changing environment that is important. Wenders's regular cameraman, Robby Müller, provides the superb photography. In German with English subtitles. ▭

Rüdiger Vogler *Philip Winter* • Yella Rottlander *Alice Van Damm* • Elisabeth Kreuzer *Lisa Van Damm* • Edda Kochl *Edda* • Didi Petrikat *Girl* • Ernest Bohm *Policeman* • Sam Presti *Car salesman* • Lois Moran *Airline girl* ■ *Dir* Wim Wenders • *Scr* Wim Wenders, Veith von Fürstenberg • *Cinematographer* Robby Müller

Alice in Wonderland ★★ U

Fantasy 1933 · US · BW · 79mins

This laboured attempt to include a vast range of Lewis Carroll's characters from both *Alice's Adventures in Wonderland* and *Alice through the Looking Glass* is of most interest for the appearance of Paramount's top stars. However, because they're clad in masks and costumes based on the John Tenniel drawings, the actors are only really recognisable by their voices.

Charlotte Henry *Alice* • Richard Arlen *Cheshire Cat* • Roscoe Ates *Fish* • William Austin *Gryphon* • Gary Cooper *White Knight* • Jack Duffy *Leg of Mutton* • Leon Errol *Uncle Gilbert* • Louise Fazenda *White Queen* • WC Fields *Humpty Dumpty* • Cary Grant *Mock Turtle* • Edward Everett Horton *Mad Hatter* • Edna May Oliver *Red Queen* • Charlie Ruggles [Charles Ruggles] *March Hare* ■ *Dir* Norman Z McLeod • *Scr* Joseph L Mankiewicz, William Cameron Menzies, from the books by Lewis Carroll

Alice in Wonderland ★★★ U

Animated fantasy 1951 · US · Colour · 72mins

A brash, colourful and undemanding animated feature, comprising the best-loved episodes from the Lewis Carroll classic. Where it scores over its live action rivals is in the depiction of the more fantastic figures like the White Rabbit, the Caterpillar, the Cheshire Cat, the March Hare and the Dormouse, which, while always more Disney than Carroll, are all engaging creations. Of the humans, Alice resembles her Tenniel original, but the Mad Hatter, the weedy King and the blustering Queen of Hearts are more imaginative and great fun. Not among the studio's best, but it is certainly well worth a watch. ▭ *DVD*

Kathryn Beaumont *Alice* • Ed Wynn *Mad Hatter* • Richard Haydn *Caterpillar* • Sterling Holloway *Cheshire Cat* • Jerry Colonna *March Hare* • Verna Felton *Queen of Hearts* • Pat O'Malley *Walrus/Carpenter/Tweedledee/Tweedledum* • Bill Thompson *White Rabbit/Dodo* ■ *Dir* Clyde Geronimi, Hamilton Luske, Wilfred Jackson • *Scr* from the books by Lewis Carroll

Alice's Adventures in Wonderland ★★ U

Fantasy 1972 · UK · Colour · 101mins

This all-star version of the Lewis Carroll classic has syrupy music and lyrics by John Barry and Don Black and casts Fiona Fullerton as Alice. Fullerton had already done a couple of movies and was promoted as a new Julie Andrews, but she has a hard time not being upstaged by her co-stars: Michael Hordern, Ralph Richardson and Spike Milligan. Peter Sellers, who plays the March Hare, caused a minor stir by peevishly slagging the film off before it opened.

Fiona Fullerton *Alice* • Peter Sellers *March Hare* • Michael Crawford *White Rabbit* • Robert Helpmann *Mad Hatter* • Michael Hordern *Mock Turtle* • Michael Jayston *Dodgson* • Spike Milligan *Gryphon* • Dudley Moore *Dormouse* • Ralph Richardson *Caterpillar* • Flora Robson *Queen of Hearts* ■ *Dir* William Sterling • *Scr* William Sterling, from the books by Lewis Carroll

Alice's Restaurant ★★★ 15

Comedy drama 1969 · US · Colour · 106mins

Not so much the story of the restaurant in question as an anti-Vietnam hymn celebrating dropouts, this stars folk singer Arlo Gurthrie. It is based on his lengthy (more than 18 minutes) hit recording in which he detailed some of his experiences of trying to dodge the draft for a war that he and his comrades didn't believe in. Directed with visual authority by Arthur Penn, it has some saving humour, but its narcissistic self-regard detracts from its undoubted sincerity, which reflects the mood of *Easy Rider*, made in the same year. ▭

Arlo Guthrie *Arlo* • Pat Quinn *Alice* • James Broderick *Ray* • Michael McClanathan *Shelly* • Geoff Outlaw *Roger* • Tina Chen *Mari-Chan* • Kathleen Dabney *Karin* • William Obanhein *Officer Obie* • M Emmet Walsh *Group W sergeant* ■ *Dir* Arthur Penn • *Scr* Venable Herndon, Arthur Penn, from the song *The Alice's Restaurant Massacre* by Arlo Guthrie

Alien ★★★★ 18

Science-fiction thriller 1979 · US/UK · Colour · 116mins

Top-notch acting (super-astronaut Sigourney Weaver), imaginative bio-mechanical production design (with the alien created by Swiss artist HR Giger), plus director Ridley Scott's eye for detail and brilliant way of alternating false scares with genuine jolts, all succeed in flattering a script culled from many cult sci-fi movies including *It! The Terror from beyond Space* and *Planet of the Vampires*. As a seamless blend of gothic horror and harrowing science fiction, this revolutionary "haunted house in space" thrill-ride is the classic business, stunning you with shock after shock, even when the fascinating creature is exposed in all its hideous glory. Contains violence and swearing. ▭ *DVD*

Sigourney Weaver *Ripley* • Tom Skerritt *Captain Dallas* • Veronica Cartwright *Lambert* • Harry Dean Stanton *Brett* • John Hurt *Kane* • Ian Holm *Ash* • Yaphet Kotto *Parker* • Helen Horton *"Mother"* ■ *Dir* Ridley Scott • *Scr* Dan O'Bannon, from a story by Dan O'Bannon, Ronald Shusett

Alien[3] ★★★ 18

Science-fiction horror 1992 · US · Colour · 109mins

Given that the first two films stand up as sci-fi classics in their own right, *Se7en* director David Fincher, in his feature film debut, had a virtually impossible act to follow with this second sequel. He makes a surprisingly good fist of it, developing the maternal themes of first sequel *Aliens* and providing an exhilarating final showdown. Sigourney Weaver returns as Ripley, who this time crash-lands on a prison colony where another lethal alien is let loose. A familiar cast of Brits (Charles Dance, Paul McGann, Brian Glover) provides the alien food and, while it isn't in the same class as the first two films, this provides a satisfactory addition to the series. Contains violence and swearing. ▭ *DVD*

Sigourney Weaver *Ripley* • Charles S Dutton *Dillon* • Charles Dance *Clemens* • Paul McGann *Golic* • Brian Glover *Superintendent Andrews* • Ralph Brown *Aaron* • Danny Webb [Daniel Webb] *Morse* • Christopher John Fields *Rains* • Holt McCallany *Junior* • Lance Henriksen *Bishop II* ■ *Dir* David Fincher • *Scr* David Giler, Walter Hill, Larry Ferguson, from a story by Vincent Ward, from characters created by Dan O'Bannon, Ronald Shusett

The Alien Dead ★

Science-fiction horror 1980 · US · Colour · 73mins

The first movie directed by hack-meister Fred Olen Ray was Buster Crabbe's last. It couldn't be a sadder epitaph for the thirties *Flash Gordon* star if it tried. Crabbe investigates a crash-landed meteorite in Florida, apparently responsible for turning a houseboat full of teens into raving ghouls – with predictably dire consequences. A pretty awful load of old zombie nonsense, complete with cheap special effects and amateur-hour direction.

Buster Crabbe [Larry "Buster" Crabbe] *Sheriff Kowalski* • Ray Roberts *Tom Corman* • Linda Lewis *Shawn Michaels* • George Kelsey *Emmett Michaels* • Mike Bonavia *Miller Haze* ■ *Dir* Fred Olen Ray • *Scr* Martin Alan Nicholas, Fred Olen Ray

The Alien Factor ★

Science-fiction thriller 1977 · US · Colour · 80mins

A rock-bottom alien invasion disaster made on a shoestring budget on 16mm by Baltimore film-maker Don Dohler. Three outer space monsters terrorise the Perry Hill area when they escape from their spaceship bound for an intergalactic zoo. The local authorities attempt a *Jaws*-type cover-up – difficult when locals keep turning up mutilated. Pitiful special effects, lousy acting and a droning synthesiser soundtrack make it a chore to sit through. One of the creatures looks like a furry toy wearing platform boots!

Tom Griffith *Ben Zachary* • Richard Dyszol *Mayor Wicker* • Tom Griffith *Sheriff* • Mary Mertens *Edie* ■ *Dir/Scr* Don Dohler

Alien Nation ★★★★ 18

Science-fiction thriller 1988 · US · Colour · 86mins

This is the ultimate in buddy-buddy cop movies, but with a difference, as this time the mismatched detectives come from different planets. In the near future, an alien race has been uncomfortably integrated into American society and, against this backdrop, earthling cop James Caan and alien cop Mandy Patinkin are reluctantly paired together to track down the killers of Caan's old partner. Director Graham Baker expertly combines the sci-fi and thriller elements and is well served by the two leads, particularly Patinkin, who manages to create a moving character while operating under a ton of latex. The movie inspired a rather more humdrum but still popular TV series. Contains violence, swearing, drug abuse and sex scenes. ▭

James Caan *Matthew Sykes* • Mandy Patinkin *Sam Francisco, "George"* • Terence Stamp *William Harcourt* • Kevyn Major Howard *Rudyard Kipling* • Leslie Bevis *Cassandra* • Peter Jason *Fedorchuk* • George Jenesky *Quint* • Jeff Kober *Josh Strader* ■ *Dir* Graham Baker • *Scr* Rockne S O'Bannon

Alien Nation: Dark Horizon ★★ 12

Science-fiction 1994 · US · Colour · 89mins

The "newcomers" who arrived on Earth in the 1988 blockbuster and helped us police the planet are wearing out their welcome in this science-fiction-meets-soap-opera TV movie. Well, according to the fascist "purists", they are. This bludgeoning parody of the neo-Nazi movement has a rival though as the "newcomers" worst enemy – the leader of an alien heavy mob who's on his way from the stars to round them up and return them to their previous status as slaves to the "overseers". A reasonably engaging romp through the stamping ground of the award-winning TV series, with much the same cast. ▭

Gary Graham *Detective Matthew Sikes* • Eric Pierpoint *George Francisco* • Michele Scarabelli *Susan Francisco* • Lauren Woodland *Emily Francisco* • Sean Six *Buck Francisco* • Terri Treas *Cathy Frankel* • Jeff Marcus *Albert Einstein* ■ *Dir* Kenneth Johnson • *Scr* Andrew Schneider, Diane Frolov, from characters created by Rockne S O'Bannon

Alien: Resurrection ★★★ 18

Science-fiction action thriller 1997 · US · Colour · 104mins

This enticing helter-skelter trip through space opera cliché cleverly conceals the fact there really isn't anything new of note here, just neat tangents off the basic *Alien* concept: nasty ETs relentlessly stalking their human prey through a deserted spaceship. Sigourney Weaver's Ripley is cloned 200 years after the action of *Alien*[3] because she's carrying a queen foetus. French director Jean-Pierre Jeunet's shock thrill-ride showcases such scintillating set pieces as an underwater battle and a gallery of grotesque clones-gone-wrong. Tense, mordantly funny, very graphic and bloody, with Weaver on great form as clone number eight who's gained some interesting alien influences on her personality. ▭ *DVD*

U = SUITABLE FOR ALL   Uc = SUITABLE FOR ALL, ESPECIALLY FOR YOUNG CHILDREN (VIDEO ONLY)   PG = PARENTAL GUIDANCE

Sigourney Weaver *Ripley* • Winona Ryder *Call* • Dominique Pinon *Vriess* • Ron Perlman *Johner* • Gary Dourdan *Christie* • Michael Wincott *Elgyn* • Kim Flowers *Hillard* • Dan Hedaya *General Perez* ■ *Dir* Jean-Pierre Jeunet • *Scr* Joss Whedon, from characters created by Dan O'Bannon, Ronald Shusett

Alien Space Avenger ★★★

Science-fiction comedy adventure
1989 · US · Colour · 80mins

This fun B-movie from director Richard W Haines melds science-fiction, soft-core porn, gangster chronicle and prison saga together for a cleverly constructed action thriller packed with gore, laughs and quirky acting. Outlaw aliens take over a pair of flapper-era couples in the thirties, hide out in a space sphere for 50 years, then emerge in late eighties Manhattan looking for plutonium to return home. As intergalactic bounty hunters close in, a comic-book artist uses their exploits for inspiration in a "Space Avenger" series. A hugely entertaining collision of fantasy and reality, paying homage to fifties cult movies in the deftest, and daftest, fashion.

Robert Prichard • Mike McClerie • Charity Staley • Gina Mastrogiacomo • Angela Nicholas ■ *Dir* Richard W Haines • *Scr* Richard W Haines, Linwood Sawyer, Leslie Delano

Alien Terror ★★ 18

Science-fiction thriller
1969 · Mex/US · Colour · 73mins

The last movie made by veteran horror icon Boris Karloff was also the last of a shoddily assembled quartet of creature features made back-to-back in Los Angeles and Mexico. Barely directed by schlock maestro Jack Hill (the Mexico scenes were the work of Juan Ibanez) and badly edited – Karloff is clearly emoting to actors in another time and country – the film involves a molecular ray gun which freaks out observing aliens when its inventor (Boris) accidentally blows a hole in his laboratory roof. Enter a blond ET in a silver lurex suit who inhabits the body of a psycho killer to stop humanity committing suicide. A weird and wacky mess that has to be seen to be believed. ▭

Boris Karloff *Professor John Meyer* • Enrique Guzman *Paul* • Christa Linder *Laura* • Yerye Beirute *Convict* • Maura Monti *Isabel* ■ *Dir* Jack Hill • *Scr* Karl Schanzer, Luis Vergara

The Alien Within ★★ 18

Science-fiction horror
1995 · US · Colour · 82mins

The Thing goes underwater in this fun, if rather hackneyed, production from veteran genre maestro Roger Corman. Roddy McDowall heads the scientific team fighting a parasitic alien during the construction of a deep sea colony. Lots of cheap thrills ensue as his crew (which includes William Shatner's daughter Melanie) tries to discover who's hiding the shape-shifter. ▭

Roddy McDowall *Dr Henry Lazarus* • Alex Hyde-White *Jedidiah Pickett* • Melanie Shatner *Catherine Harding* • Roger Halston *Wyatt* • Emile Levisetti *Brill* • Richard Biggs *Samuel Hawkes* • Sha-Ri Pendleton *Loretta Fife* • Don Stroud *Louis* ■ *Dir* Scott P Levy [Scott Levy] • *Scr* Alex Simon, from a story by Rob Kerchner • *Executive Producer* Roger Corman

Aliens ★★★★★ 18

Science-fiction action thriller
1986 · US · Colour · 131mins

Director James Cameron's sequel to Ridley Scott's outer-space nightmare is an outstanding science-fiction thriller that surpasses the original in terms of sheer spectacle. Sigourney Weaver wakes up 57 years after the original events unfolded, only to be told that the planet where she first met the alien predator has been colonised. When all contact with the inhabitants is lost, she's sent in with a crack squad of marines, and hurtles headlong into a high-tech house of horrors that delivers super shocks and nail-biting suspense. Masterfully controlling the tension and moving the involving plot at a lightning pace, Cameron exploits everyone's worst fears and carries them to the riveting extreme in his consummate Oscar-winning fright-fest. Contains violence and swearing. ▭ DVD

Sigourney Weaver *Ripley* • Carrie Henn *Rebecca Jorden, "Newt"* • Michael Biehn *Corporal Hicks* • Paul Reiser *Carter J Burke* • Lance Henriksen *Bishop* • Bill Paxton *Private Hudson* • William Hope *Lieutenant Gorman* • Jenette Goldstein *Private Vasquez* • Al Matthews *Sergeant Apone* ■ *Dir* James Cameron • *Scr* James Cameron, from a story by James Cameron, David Giler, Walter Hill, from characters created by Dan O'Bannon, Ronald Shusett

Alison's Birthday ★★ 15

Horror
1979 · Ausl · Colour · 94mins

In this muddled hybrid of *Carrie, The Exorcist* and *Rosemary's Baby*, Joanne Samuel is warned by her dead father during a seance to leave home before her 19th birthday. She doesn't and a female black magic cult try to transfer her soul into the remains of a dead witch so she'll become their leader. Trite, routine and poorly directed by Ian Coughlan, who also wrote this crass concoction and appears in the cast. ▭

Joanne Samuel *Alison Findlay* • Margie McCrae *Chrissie Willis* • Martin Vaughan *Mr Martin* • Robyn Gibbes *Helen McGill* • Lou Brown *Pete Healey* ■ *Dir/Scr* Ian Coughlan

Alive ★★ 15

Drama based on a true story
1992 · US · Colour · 121mins

This harrowing true story of a South American rugby team whose plane crash-lands in the Andes. It's a case of survival by dire measures as they start to eat their dead. What should have been a triumph of the human spirit droops into all-pervading gloom, and you can't help but keep your emotional distance from their dreadful dilemma because the atmosphere of the film is so suicidally glum and without momentum. The mountaintop plane crash, though, is an unexpected and terrifyingly convincing sequence of special effects. Contains swearing. ▭

Ethan Hawke *Nando Parrado* • Vincent Spano *Antonio Balbi* • Josh Hamilton *Roberto Canessa* • Bruce Ramsay *Carlitos Paez* • John Haymes Newton *Tintin* • David Kriegel *Gustavo Zerbino* • Kevin Breznahan *Roy Harley* • Sam Behrens *Javier Methol* • Illeana Douglas *Lilliana Methol* ■ *Dir* Frank Marshall • *Scr* John Patrick Shanley, from the book by Piers Paul Read

Alive and Kicking ★★★

Comedy
1958 · UK · BW · 94mins

Sybil Thorndike, Kathleen Harrison and Estelle Winwood are a joy to behold as three old ladies who escape from a home and set themselves up on an isolated island as the relatives of millionaire Stanley Holloway. Eyes twinkling with mischief as they carve a niche in the local knitwear trade, they are easily on a par with those other matronly menaces, Josephine Hull and Jean Adair in *Arsenic and Old Lace*. Director Cyril Frankel's engaging piece of Irish whimsy is slight but diverting, and also notable as the film debut of Richard Harris.

Sybil Thorndike *Dora* • Kathleen Harrison *Rosie* • Estelle Winwood *Mabel* • Stanley Holloway *MacDonagh* • Liam Redmond *Old man* • Marjorie Rhodes *Old woman* • Richard Harris *Lover* • Olive McFarland *Lover* • John Salew *Solicitor* • Eric Pohlmann *Captain* ■ *Dir* Cyril Frankel • *Scr* Denis Cannan

Alive and Kicking ★★★ 15

Drama
1996 · UK · Colour · 94mins

This is a spirited, if not always cinematic, tale by acclaimed dramatist Martin Sherman (*Bent*). Although rooted in the grand old kitchen sink tradition, director Nancy Meckler's grimly comic film never allows the grit to scratch the fading shine off a story that is both clichéd and insightful, sad and uplifting. As the ballet dancer coping with the closure of his company and his HIV-positive status, Jason Flemyng gives an unexpectedly poignant performance. But who could compete with Anthony Sher on top form as the paunchy, bald alcoholic who offers him love? Contains swearing. ▭

Jason Flemyng *Tonio* • Antony Sher *Jack* • Dorothy Tutin *Luna* • Anthony Higgins *Ramon* • Bill Nighy *Tristan* • Philip Voss *Duncan* • Diane Parish *Millie* • Aiden Waters *Vincent* • Natalie Roles *Catherine* • Freddy Douglas *Luke* ■ *Dir* Nancy Meckler • *Scr* Martin Sherman

All about Eve ★★★★★ U

Classic drama
1950 · US · BW · 132mins

"Fasten your seat belts it's going to be a bumpy night!", and with the acerbic talents of multi-Oscar-winning writer/director Joseph L Mankiewicz and his magnificent cast – the superb Bette Davis (replacing, thankfully, an ailing Claudette Colbert), the acid-tongued George Sanders, Celeste Holm, Thelma Ritter, Marilyn Monroe – it certainly is. On its original release, this tale of the theatre was criticised in some quarters for being over-wordy and relentlessly arch, though today's audiences tend to revel in its wit and cynicism. The dialogue is especially clever and the performances are first-rate. If the framing flashback structure seems a little contrived, or if Anne Baxter's Eve doesn't quite have the killer instinct required for the role, these are minor blemishes in a classic movie. ▭

Bette Davis *Margo* • Anne Baxter *Eve* • George Sanders *Addison De Witt* • Celeste Holm *Karen* • Gary Merrill *Bill Simpson* • Hugh Marlowe *Lloyd Richards* • Thelma Ritter *Birdie* • Marilyn Monroe *Miss Casswell* • Gregory Ratoff *Max Fabian* • Barbara Bates *Phoebe* ■

Dir Joseph L Mankiewicz • *Scr* Joseph L Mankiewicz, from the story *The Wisdom of Eve* by Mary Orr

All about My Mother ★★★★★ 15

Comedy drama
1999 · Sp/Fr · Colour · 101mins

Mature and moving aren't words usually associated with "King of Kitsch" Pedro Almodóvar, but they certainly apply to this inspired reworking of the old Bette Davis vehicle *All about Eve*. Devastated by the death of her son, hospital worker Cecilia Roth finds a whole new purpose in tending to a pregnant HIV-positive nun (Penelope Cruz) and a *grande dame* of the stage nearing the end of her career (Marisa Paredes). This fond, deliciously flamboyant study of womanhood and friendship is intense without ever being overbearing, touching but never sentimental. It's by far the Spanish director's finest achievement and picked up numerous awards, including the Oscar for best foreign language film. In Spanish with English subtitles. Contains swearing and sexual situations.

Cecilia Roth *Manuela* • Marisa Paredes *Huma Rojo* • Candela Peña *Niña* • Antonia San Juan *"La Agrado"* • Penelope Cruz *Sister Rosa* • Rosa Maria Sarda *Rosa's mother* • Toni Cantó *Lola, "la Pionera"* • Eloy Azorin *Esteban* ■ *Dir/Scr* Pedro Almodóvar

The All American ★★ U

Drama
1953 · US · BW · 82mins

Tony Curtis stars as a sports hero whose confidence is shaken when his parents are killed en route to watching him play, causing him to abandon glory for serious study – for a time. An unpretentious little film that effectively combines the ingredients of the rah-rah college football movie with a more intimate drama, it showcases the famous pretty-boy good looks that made Curtis a major star. Blonde siren Mamie Van Doren supplies a disruptive female presence, Lori Nelson a regenerative one, and the movie is competently directed by the little known Jesse Hibbs, himself a former professional of the gridiron.

Tony Curtis *Nick Bonelli* • Lori Nelson *Sharon Wallace* • Richard Long *Howard Carter* • Mamie Van Doren *Susie Ward* • Gregg Palmer *Cameron* • Paul Cavanagh *Prof Banning* • Herman Hickman *Jumbo* • Stuart Whitman *Zip Parker* ■ *Dir* Jesse Hibbs • *Scr* DD Beauchamp, Robert Yale Libett, from a story by Leonard Freeman

The All-American Boy ★

Sports drama
1973 · US · Colour · 118mins

Jon Voight made this clinker just before his breakthrough in *Midnight Cowboy*, though it sat on the Warner Bros shelf for four years before they re-edited it and released it to an indifferent world. Voight plays a small-town boxer and the movie is artfully structured into six rounds; however, most audiences will having trouble going the distance. Set in northern California, it has a thirties look and feel to it, yet Voight's extreme diffidence – he chucks his career just when it gets going – is symptomatic of the existentialism and counterculture mentality of the sixties.

Jon Voight *Vic Bealer* • EJ Peaker *Janelle Sharkey* • Ned Glass *Arty* • Anne Archer *Drenna Valentine* • Art Metrano *Jay* • Bob Hastings *Ariel* • Carol Androsky [Carole Androsky] *Rodine* • Gene Borkan *Rockoff* ■ *Dir/Scr* Charles Eastman

All Ashore ★★ Ⓤ

Musical comedy 1953 · US · Colour · 79mins

In the year of *Lili, Call Me Madam, Gentlemen Prefer Blondes* and, best of all, Vincente Minnelli's *The Band Wagon*, this cut-price imitation of the classic musical *On the Town* was hardly likely to make much impression. Directed by Richard Quine from a screenplay he wrote with Blake Edwards, the movie focuses on the shore-leave escapades of three sailors – Mickey Rooney, Dick Haymes, Ray McDonald – and their romantic involvements with Peggy Ryan, Jody Lawrence and Barbara Bates. It falls almost entirely to the diminutive, multi-talented Rooney, as the patsy of the seafaring trio, to provide the fun.

Mickey Rooney *Francis "Moby" Dickerson* • Dick Haymes *Joe Carter* • Ray McDonald *Skip Edwards* • Peggy Ryan *Gay Night* • Barbara Bates *Jane Stanton* • Jody Lawrence [Jody Lawrance] *Nancy Flynn* • Fay Roope *Commodore Stanton* • Jean Willes *Rose* ■ *Dir* Richard Quine • *Scr* Blake Edwards, Richard Quine, from a story by Robert Wells, Blake Edwards

All Coppers Are... ★

Comedy 1972 · UK · Colour · 87mins

You can complete the title yourself, but it won't improve this comedy misfire about a small-time crook (Nicky Henson) and a naive police constable (Martin Potter) who both fancy Julia Foster. This situation is supposed to be funny but isn't, and none of the ensuing complications raise a smile either. The supporting cast of TV regulars – look out for David Essex in a small role – grin and bear it.

Martin Potter *Joe* • Julia Foster *Sue* • Nicky Henson *Barry* • Wendy Allnutt *Peg* • Sandra Dorne *Sue's mother* • Ian Hendry *Sonny Wade* • David Baxter *Fancy Boy* • Glynn Edwards *Jock* • Carmel McSharry *Mrs Briggs* • Queenie Watts *Mrs Malloy* • Eddie Byrne *Malloy* • David Essex *Ronnie Briggs* ■ *Dir* Sidney Hayers • *Scr* Allan Prior

All Creatures Great and Small ★★★

Drama 1974 · UK · Colour · 91mins

Well, of course, we all know the animals are incidental in this screen prequel to TV's well-loved memoirs of vet James Herriot: what really matters is the Yorkshire folk whose emotions are brought out from behind those gruff exteriors by what happens to their creatures' comfort. Inevitably episodic, and fairly sentimental, it has warm-hearted performances by Simon Ward as the young Herriot, Lisa Harrow as his future wife Helen and Anthony Hopkins as local vet Siegfried Farnon, before he went on to win an Oscar for silencing lambs.

Simon Ward *James Herriot* • Anthony Hopkins *Siegfried Farnon* • Lisa Harrow *Helen Alderson* • Brian Stirner *Tristan Farnon* • Freddie Jones *Cranford* • TP McKenna *Soames* • Brenda Bruce *Miss Harbottle* • John Collin *Mr*

Alderson • Christine Buckley *Mrs Hall* ■ *Dir* Claude Whatham • *Scr* Hugh Whitemore, from the books by James Herriot

All Dogs Go to Heaven ★★★ Ⓤ

Animated adventure 1989 · Ire · Colour · 81mins

Another chance for younger viewers to get to know Charlie B Parkin and his canine chums, who became very popular with previous toddler generations. In fact, it's mutt ado about nothing, even though then box-office topper Burt Reynolds voices heroic hound Charlie. Co-producer/director Don Bluth (whose *The Pebble and the Penguin* was equally popular with young audiences) began his career at Disney so, as you would expect, the animation is mostly excellent, but the story is still rather clumsily told. Watchable, although you might want to turn the sound down for the songs. 🖭

Burt Reynolds *Charlie* • Dom DeLuise *Itchy* • Vic Tayback *Carface* • Judith Barsi *Anne-Marie* • Loni Anderson *Flo* • Melba Moore *Whippet Angel* • Charles Nelson Reilly *Killer* • Daryl Gilley *Dog Caster* • Candy Devine *Vera* • Rob Fuller *Harold* • Earleen Carey *Kate* ■ *Dir* Don Bluth • *Scr* David Weiss

All Dogs Go to Heaven 2 ★★ Ⓤ

Animated musical adventure 1996 · US/UK · Colour · 79mins

So much plot, so little time. But, sadly, there's also precious little quality in this disappointing sequel to Don Bluth's animated musical. Tired of eternity, Charlie (this time voiced by Charlie Sheen) heads back to earth with his faithful pal Itchy to retrieve Gabriel's Horn, which has fallen into evil hands. There's enough going on to amuse younger viewers but, excepting the energetic villainy of Ernest Borgnine's Carface, it's a pretty scrappy affair. 🖭

Charlie Sheen *Charlie* • Sheena Easton *Sasha* • Ernest Borgnine *Carface* • Dom DeLuise *Itchy Itchiford* • George Hearn *Red* • Bebe Neuwirth *Anabelle* ■ *Dir* Paul Sabella, Larry Leker • *Scr* Arne Olsen, Kelly Ward, Mark Young, from a story by Mark Young, Kelly Ward

All Fall Down ★★★★

Drama 1962 · US · BW · 110mins

The opening shots in Warren Beatty's career – *Splendor in the Grass, The Roman Spring of Mrs Stone* and *All Fall Down* – created his image as a Hollywood lothario. In *All Fall Down*, an intense family saga, he's a loner and a womaniser, idolised by his younger brother Brandon de Wilde, the boy who had idolised Shane and who would later idolise Paul Newman as Hud. Their father, Karl Malden, hits the bottle; their mother, Angela Lansbury, henpecks. And when lodger Eva Marie Saint falls for Beatty, de Wilde looks on, almost eager for a hard lesson in life. Directed by John Frankenheimer and scripted by playwright William Inge, it is now rather dated, but the cast is matchless.

Eva Marie Saint *Echo O'Brien* • Warren Beatty *Berry-Berry Willart* • Karl Malden *Ralph Willart* • Angela Lansbury *Annabel Willart* • Brandon

de Wilde *Clinton Willart* • Constance Ford *Mrs Mandel* • Barbara Baxley *Schoolteacher* • Evans Evans *Hedy* • Jennifer Howard *Myra* ■ • *Scr* William Inge, from the novel by James Leo Herlihy

All for Mary ★★ Ⓤ

Comedy 1955 · UK · Colour · 79mins

In this unfunny comedy, Nigel Patrick and David Tomlinson are rival suitors for the hand of Jill Day, but they contract chickenpox and are forced into quarantine in a Swiss chalet at the mercy of ageing nanny Kathleen Harrison. The invalids become infants as the grown men are brought under control by a dominant female. Sadly, director Wendy Toye takes the joke no further, so all we get is a feeble production that only weakly echoes its successful West End stage origins.

Nigel Patrick *Clive Morton* • Kathleen Harrison *Nannie Cartwright* • David Tomlinson *Humpy Miller* • Jill Day *Mary* • David Hurst *M Victor* • Leo McKern *Gaston Nikopopoulos* • Nicholas Phipps *General* • Lionel Jeffries *Maitre d'hotel* ■ *Dir* Wendy Toye • *Scr* Peter Blackmore, Paul Soskin, from the play by Harold Brooke, Kay Bannerman

All Hands on Deck ★★ Ⓤ

Musical comedy 1961 · US · Colour · 98mins

Director Norman Taurog – never one to over-tax the grey matter – ensures this lightweight shipboard comedy has a smooth passage. With Lieutenant Pat Boone excused duties to warble a few inoffensive songs, the time passes pleasantly enough. Given that the chief source of hilarity is the romance between Buddy Hackett's turkey and a passing pelican, though, it's not surprising the film sometimes goes adrift. However, things perk up back in dock as Boone steers visiting admiral Gale Gordon away from both his reporter girlfriend Barbara Eden and the world's first turkey-pelican egg.

Pat Boone *Lt Donald* • Buddy Hackett *Screaming Eagle Garfield* • Dennis O'Keefe *Lt Cdr O'Gara* • Barbara Eden *Sally Hobson* • Warren Berlinger *Ensign Rush* • Gale Gordon *Cdr Bintle* • David Brandon *Lt Kutley* • Joe E Ross *Bosun* • Bartlett Robinson *Lt Cdr Anthony* ■ *Dir* Norman Taurog • *Scr* Jay Sommers, from the novel by Donald R Morris

All I Desire ★★

Period drama 1953 · US · BW · 79mins

Barbara Stanwyck finds herself in a town she left long ago, and pays an unfortunate visit to what's left of her family. Since they're played by the likes of Richard Carlson and Lori Nelson, it's hard to care, though both Lyle Bettger and a lovely but wasted Maureen O'Sullivan have their moments. This slight tosh is under-directed by melodrama favourite Douglas Sirk, who totally fails to rein in Stanwyck's excesses, so losing all sympathy for her character. Since producer Ross Hunter shows no concern for establishing the period, this never rises above its double-bill status and, despite the extravagant claims made by Sirk fans, it's really rather tiresome.

Barbara Stanwyck *Naomi Murdoch* • Richard Carlson *Henry Murdoch* • Lyle Bettger *Dutch Heineman* • Marcia Henderson *Joyce Murdoch* • Lori Nelson *Lily Murdoch* • Maureen O'Sullivan *Sara Harper* • Richard Long *Russ*

Underwood • Billy Gray *Ted Murdoch* • Lotte Stein *Lena Engstrom* ■ *Dir* Douglas Sirk • *Scr* James Gunn, Robert Blees, Gina Kaus, from the novel *Stopover* by Carol Brink • *Producer* Ross Hunter

All I Want for Christmas ★★ Ⓤ

Seasonal comedy 1991 · US · Colour · 88mins

A rather ham-fisted attempt to spice up a children's Christmas movie with a more "mature" theme. The only thing Ethan Randall and Thora Birch want for Christmas is for their separated parents to be reconciled. Will they never learn? Lauren Bacall is way over the top as their batty but bountiful granny and everything creaks along, coated liberally in sentiment. This is not meant for cynical adults, but is aimed nearer the 12-year-old market, where it will probably be received as a passable hoot. However, it bombed in its day. 🖭

Harley Jane Kozak *Catherine O'Fallon* • Jamey Sheridan *Michael O'Fallon* • Ethan Randall [Ethan Embry] *Ethan O'Fallon* • Kevin Nealon *Tony Boer* • Thora Birch *Hallie O'Fallon* • Lauren Bacall *Lillian Brooks* • Leslie Nielsen *Santa* ■ *Dir* Robert Lieberman • *Scr* Richard Kramer, Thom Eberhardt, Gail Parent, Neal Israel

All in a Night's Work ★★★

Comedy 1960 · US · Colour · 94mins

Some may be enchanted by this glossily produced, one-gag trifle; others may find it simply smutty. Luckily the bright sheen of sixties Technicolor makes the shenanigans watchable, despite director Joseph Anthony's occasional lapses of pace and humour. Dean Martin and Shirley MacLaine are both exceedingly adept at this sort of sexy caper, and a fine veteran supporting cast come along for the ride. Cliff Robertson, meanwhile, makes the most of his thankless role as MacLaine's put-upon fiancé. 🖭

Dean Martin *Tony Ryder* • Shirley MacLaine *Katie Robbins* • Charles Ruggles *Dr Warren Kingsley Sr* • Cliff Robertson *Warren Kingsley Jr* • Norma Crane *Marge Coombs* • Gale Gordon *Oliver Dunning* • Jerome Cowan *Sam Weaver* • Jack Weston *Lasker* ■ *Dir* Joseph Anthony • *Scr* Edmund Beloin, Maurice Richlin, Sidney Sheldon, from a play by Owen Elford, from a story by Margit Veszi

All Lies End in Murder ★★★

Crime drama 1997 · US · Colour

An intriguing spin on police corruption, this time largely seen through the eyes of the wife of a policeman. Kim Delaney stars as the spouse who's shocked to discover that her husband Jamey Sheridan has his fingers in the till. But should she stand by her man and turn a blind eye to his activities or report him to the authorities? It's capably performed by the two leads and competently handled by director Andy Wolk; a cut above the usual made-for-TV police thrillers.

Kim Delaney *Meredith Sciallo* • Jamey Sheridan *Danny Sciallo* • Peter Dobson *Phil Paxton* • Robin Bartlett *Annie Roth* ■ *Dir* Andy Wolk • *Scr* Lynn Mamet

Ⓤ = SUITABLE FOR ALL Ⓤᴄ = SUITABLE FOR ALL, ESPECIALLY FOR YOUNG CHILDREN (VIDEO ONLY) ᴾᴳ = PARENTAL GUIDANCE

All Men Are Mortal ★★ 15

Romance
1995 · UK/Neth/Fr · Colour · 86mins

A sixties-style art movie, based on the novel by Simone de Beauvoir, about a temperamental, very actressy actress (Irène Jacob) who abandons her black musician lover for a mysterious stranger, played by Stephen Rea, who reveals himself as a 700-year-old immortal prince. It's all very metaphysical, existential, philosophical and, for many viewers, downright pretentious and snooze-inducing. Set in France in the late forties, it was filmed in Hungary. 🎦

Stephen Rea *Fosca* • Irène Jacob *Regina* • Colin Salmon *Chas* • Marianne Sägebrecht *Annie* • Maggie O'Neill *Florence* • Steve Nicolson *Laforet* • Chiara Mastroianni *Françoise* ■ *Dir* Ate de Jong • *Scr* Ate de Jong, Olwen Wymark, Steven Gaydos, from the novel by Simone de Beauvoir

All My Good Countrymen ★★★★

Drama 1968 · Cz · Colour · 126mins

One of four films "banned for ever" by the Czech authorities in the wake of the Prague Spring, this is an acerbic and acutely observed satire that won Vojtech Jasny the best director prize at Cannes. With its intricate blend of comedy, tragedy, fantasy and bitter reality, it chronicles events in a Moravian village from the end of the Second World War to the spring of 1968, exposing the excesses of communist rule by means of four shocking and suspicious deaths that periodically shatter the rural idyll. Played and directed with consummate skill, this provocative picture is as poetic as it is powerful. In Czech with English subtitles.

Vladimir Mensik *Jozka Pyrk* • Radoslav Brozobohaty *Frantisek* • Vlastimil Brodsky *Ocenas* • Vlaclav Babka *Franta Lampa* • Ilja Prachal *Plecmera* • Pavel Pavlovsky *Postman* ■ *Dir/Scr* Vojtech Jasny

All My Sons ★★★

Drama 1948 · US · BW · 93mins

The film of Arthur Miller's first play stars Burt Lancaster as the young man who makes the painful discovery that his father, tycoon Edward G Robinson, knowingly sold the US Air Force defective parts for their planes in the Second World War. Seized on by the right-wing as communist propaganda, the movie seems far less contentious today, and its moral debate rather open and shut. Very likely, too, as if no one dared cut a comma from Miller's text.

Edward G Robinson *Joe Keller* • Burt Lancaster *Chris Keller* • Mady Christians *Kate Keller* • Louisa Horton *Ann Deever* • Howard Duff *George Deever* • Frank Conroy *Herbert Deever* • Lloyd Gough *Jim Bayliss* • Arlene Francis *Sue Bayliss* ■ *Dir* Irving Reis • *Scr* Chester Erskine, from the play by Arthur Miller

All My Sons ★★★

Drama 1986 · US · Colour

Not the original 1948 film version of Arthur Miller's powerful play, starring Edward G Robinson and Burt Lancaster, but a more-than-acceptable TV-movie remake with James Whitmore as the guilt-ridden Joe Keller and Aidan Quinn as his war-hero son. The story of the father whose war profiteering prompts his son's suicide is uncomfortable to watch, and the showdowns between Whitmore and Quinn have an intensity rare in a TV script. There's also solid support from Michael Learned as Quinn's mother and Joan Allen as the daughter of the partner Whitmore tried to ruin.

James Whitmore *Joe Keller* • Aidan Quinn *Chris Keller* • Michael Learned *Kate Keller* • Joan Allen *Ann Deever* • Zeljko Ivanek *George Deever* • Joanna Miles ■ *Dir* Jack O'Brien • *Scr* from the play by Arthur Miller

All Neat in Black Stockings ★

Drama 1969 · UK · Colour · 105mins

There's little to recommend this cheesy mix of peek-a-boo nudity and bawdy humour, even though it boasts that icon of swinging sixties sex appeal, Susan George. The pairing of TV playwright Hugh Whitemore (who was so prolific he was nicknamed "Hugh Writemore") and director Christopher Morahan (who would later produce TV's *Jewel in the Crown*) produces little merit. At least they went on to better things.

Victor Henry *Ginger* • Susan George *Jill* • Jack Shepherd *Dwyer* • Clare Kelly *Mother* • Anna Cropper *Sis* • Harry Towb *Issur* • Vanessa Forsyth *Carole* ■ *Dir* Christopher Morahan • *Scr* Jane Gaskell, Hugh Whitemore, from the novel by Jane Gaskell

All Night Long ★★

Drama 1961 · UK · Colour · 91mins

The producer/director team of Michael Relph and Basil Dearden had already brought their rather smug, stolid approach to Britain's growing black community in *Sapphire*. Here they tackle the jazz scene, overlaid with a plot about sexual jealousy that culture vultures may recognise as *Othello*. At the centre of it all is jazz singer Marti Stevens, married to Paul Harris and desired by Patrick McGoohan, jazzmen both. It's shot like a moody *film noir* and its main appeal is the chance to spot hot jazzmen such as Dave Brubeck, Charles Mingus, Tubby Hayes and Britain's own Johnny Dankworth in the frequent musical interludes. The main incongruity is Richard Attenborough as a man about town.

Patrick McGoohan *Johnny Cousin* • Marti Stevens *Delia Lane* • Betsy Blair *Emily* • Keith Michell *Cass Michaels* • Richard Attenborough *Rod Hamilton* • Paul Harris *Aurelius Rex* ■ *Dir* Basil Dearden • *Scr* Nel King, Peter Achilles [Paul Jarrico]

All Night Long ★★★

Comedy 1981 · US · Colour · 88mins

Gene Hackman drops his usual intimidating manner to play the confused, middle-aged night-manager of a suburban supermarket, who decides to rebel against his staid existence by having an affair with the kooky wife of his cousin, played by Barbra Streisand. Directed by Frenchman Jean-Claude Tramont, the film's strange domestic focus creates an offbeat view of American city life, though some sequences lack continuity and coherence, and the whole makes for unusual viewing. Contains some swearing

Gene Hackman *George Dupler* • Barbra Streisand *Cheryl Gibbons* • Diane Ladd *Helen Dupler* • Dennis Quaid *Freddie Dupler* • Kevin Dobson *Bobby Gibbons* • William Daniels *Richard H Copleston* • Hamilton Camp *Buggams* • Ann Doran *Grandmother Gibbons* ■ *Dir* Jean-Claude Tramont • *Scr* WD Richter

All of Me ★★★ 15

Comedy 1984 · US · Colour · 87mins

A promising idea and a dynamic performance from Steve Martin aren't enough to distract from this film's shortage of genuinely funny moments and a lazy over-reliance on half-baked resolutions. As the lawyer whose body is taken over by the soul of deceased millionairess Lily Tomlin, Martin has never been so effective, combining his trademark exasperation with some amazingly energetic slapstick. Tomlin makes the most of appearing almost exclusively in reflection and Richard Libertini as a quack swami. But Victoria Tennant hams shamelessly, while director Carl Reiner (a regular Martin collaborator) cracks almost every gag with a mallet. Pity. Contains violence and swearing. 🎦

Steve Martin *Roger Cobb* • Lily Tomlin *Edwina Cutwater* • Victoria Tennant *Terry Hoskins* • Madolyn Smith *Peggy Schuyler* • Richard Libertini *Prahka Lasa* • Dana Elcar *Burton Schuyler* • Jason Bernard *Tyrone Wattell* • Selma Diamond *Margo* ■ *Dir* Carl Reiner • *Scr* Phil Alden Robinson

All over Me ★★★ 15

Drama 1996 · US · Colour · 89mins

A haunting, uncompromising snapshot of urban adolescent life, this exceptional debut never gained the same exposure as the similarly themed *kids*, but packs the same raw power to shock. Written and directed (respectively) by Sylvia and Alex Sichel, the film offers a portrait of two teenage girls: Tara Subkoff is hopelessly in love with drug-taking loser Cole Hauser, while Alison Folland is struggling to come to terms with her own sexuality. A brutal murder in their neighbourhood puts the two friends on a collision course. The cast of unknowns is superb, and the brutally frank script helps create a troubled vision of modern American life. Contains swearing and sex scenes 🎦

Alison Folland *Claude* • Tara Subkoff *Ellen* • Cole Hauser *Mark* • Wilson Cruz *Jesse* • Leisha Hailey *Lucy* • Pat Briggs *Luke* ■ *Dir* Alex Sichel • *Scr* Sylvia Sichel

All over Town ★★ U

Comedy 1937 · US · BW · 71mins

There's no denying that the comic team of Ole Olsen and Chic Johnson always were an acquired taste, and today the duo are best remembered for their wacky surreal classic of 1941, *Hellzapoppin'*, based on their Broadway success. But they were always very funny, both on stage and screen, and commanded a huge following in their day. This haunted theatre flick has a great deal of typical humour, and should please fans and make converts, even if the Republic studio production values are pretty ropey.

Ole Olsen *Olsen* • Chic Johnson *Johnson* • Mary Howard *Joan Eldridge* • Harry Stockwell *Don Fletcher* • Franklin Pangborn *Costumer* • James Finlayson *MacDougal* • Eddie Kane *Bailey* • Stanley Fields *Slug* ■ *Dir* James Horne [James W Horne] • *Scr* Jack Townley, Jerome Chodorov, from a story by Richard English

All Quiet on the Western Front ★★★★★ PG

Classic war drama
1930 · US · BW and Tinted · 125mins

Today's audiences may feel films such as *Platoon* and *Apocalypse Now* are the definitive war movies, but this classic Oscar-winning tale has lost none of its ability to shock and involve. As a study of the inhumanity of war, it retains all the impact of the novel by Erich Maria Remarque upon which it is so faithfully based. This epic saga of German schoolboys called up during the First World War marked the coming of age of the war movie, and of Carl Laemmle Jr's Universal Studios which produced it. It also demonstrated, as an early talkie, the flexibility of the new technique, with staggering trench sequences brilliantly filmed by director Lewis Milestone, who received his second Academy Award for his work. The performances are also exemplary, but it is primarily a film of great moments – the climactic sequence of the young conscript reaching out for a butterfly in the sun – that, once seen, are never forgotten. 🎦 **DVD**

Lew Ayres *Paul Baumer* • Louis Wolheim *Katczinsky* • John Wray *Himmelstoss* • Raymond Griffith *Gérard Duval* • George "Slim" Summerville [Slim Summerville] *Tjarden* • Russell Gleason *Müller* • William Bakewell *Albert* • Scott Kolk *Leer* • Walter Browne Rogers *Behm* • Beryl Mercer *Kemmericher* ■ *Dir* Lewis Milestone • *Scr* Del Andrews, Maxwell Anderson, George Abbott, from the novel by Erich Maria Remarque • *Producer* Carl Laemmle Jr • *Cinematographer* Arthur Edeson

All Quiet on the Western Front ★★★ PG

First World War drama
1979 · US · Colour · 122mins

It's a brave man who dares to remake what is still regarded as the most powerful pacifist statement ever committed to celluloid. However, director Delbert Mann does a fine job of adapting Erich Maria Remarque's harrowing study of life in the trenches. In addition to winning Emmys for its editing and special effects, this sprawling TV movie also brought nominations for Mann, Patricia Neal and Ernest Borgnine, here cast as the wizened veteran who puts Richard Thomas and his fellow recruits through their paces. While it lacks the immediacy of the 1930 version, this is still a compelling and affecting insight into the hellishness of war. 🎦

Richard Thomas *Paul Baumer* • Ernest Borgnine *Stanislaus Katczinsky* • Ian Holm *Himmelstoss* • Donald Pleasence *Kantorek* • Patricia Neal *Paul's mother* • Mark Drewry *Tjaden* • Michael Sheard *Paul's Father* ■ *Dir* Delbert Mann • *Scr* Paul Monash, from the novel by Erich Maria Remarque

All She Ever Wanted ★★ 🔞

Drama   1996 · US · Colour · 90mins

This TV movie is a real heart-tugger, which manages to combine both a "disease of the week" scenario with the responsibilities and traumas of parenthood. *Melrose Place*'s Marcia Cross plays a woman suffering from a rare mental disorder that can only be treated by drugs. She wants to have a baby but her medication is known to cause irreversible birth defects; is she prepared to risk her own health and sanity to have the baby she so craves? Overflowing with sentimentality, the result is so over the top that it is actually quite compelling. 📺

Marcia Cross *Rachel Stockman* • James Marshall *Tom Stockman* • Leila Kenzie *Jessie Frank* • Bruce Kirby *Bob* • Carrie Snodgress *Alma* • CCH Pounder *Dr Marilyn Tower* ■ *Dir* Michael Scott • *Scr* David Hill

All That Heaven Allows
★★★ 🇺

Melodrama   1955 · US · Colour · 88mins

A soapy follow-up to the same team's successful *Magnificent Obsession*, which had made a star out of Rock Hudson the previous year. This is almost as daft, but it's revered in some critical circles as director Douglas Sirk's serious commentary on fifties' American values. To Sirk though, this was just another job handed to him by Universal producer Ross Hunter, and he makes the romance between widow Jane Wyman and her gardener Hudson entirely unlikely. She's too old and boring, and he's patently none too bright. Nevertheless, the Technicolor photography by Russell Metty is sumptuous, Hudson is remarkably good, and Agnes Moorehead brings some much-needed acerbity to the tale.

Jane Wyman *Cary Scott* • Rock Hudson *Ron Kirby* • Agnes Moorehead *Sara Warren* • Conrad Nagel *Harvey* • Virginia Grey *Alida Anderson* • Gloria Talbot *Kay Scott* • William Reynolds *Ned Scott* • Jacqueline de Wit *Mona Flash* • Charles Drake *Mick Anderson* ■ *Dir* Douglas Sirk • *Scr* Peggy Fenwick, from a story by Edna Lee, from a story by Harry Lee

All That Jazz ★★★★ 🔞

Musical drama   1979 · US · Colour · 123 mins

Besides being the only musical featuring a surgical operation, this is unique in being heavily autobiographical about its director and co-writer, Bob Fosse. The talented choreographer closely resembles the lead character, Broadway dance-maestro Joe Gideon, whose philandering with women is only surpassed by his flirtations with the Angel of Death – the symbol of self-destructiveness that will eventually kill him. Jessica Lange and Ann Reinking are the women in his angst-fuelled life but it's Roy Scheider, as the driven Joe, who dominates in a film that's as brilliantly egotistical as it is flashily self-indulgent. 📺

Roy Scheider *Joe Gideon* • Jessica Lange *Angelique* • Ann Reinking *Kate Jagger* • Leland Palmer *Audrey Paris* • Cliff Gorman *Davis Newman* • Ben Vereen *O'Connor Flood* • Erzsebet Foldi *Michelle* • Michael Tolan *Dr Ballinger* • Sandahl Bergman *Dancer* ■ *Dir*

Bob Fosse • *Scr* Bob Fosse, Robert Alan Arthur • *Choreography* Bob Fosse • *Cinematographer* Giuseppe Rotunno • *Editor* Alan Heim • *Music Director* Ralph Burns • *Art Director* Philip Rosenberg, Tony Walton • *Costume Designer* Albert Wolsky

All the Brothers Were Valiant ★★

Adventure   1953 · US · Colour · 95mins

This is a watery yarn about whalers, mutiny, dusky South Seas maidens and exotic pearls. All that's missing is a giant squid and a tidal wave! Robert Taylor and Stewart Granger are on good form as the eponymous siblings, while Lewis Stone – Andy Hardy's dad – puts in an appearance in what was to prove his final film. (He died tragically from a heart attack that same year.)

Robert Taylor (1) *Joel Shore* • Stewart Granger *Mark Shore* • Ann Blyth *Priscilla Holt* • Betta St John *Native girl* • Keenan Wynn *Silva* • James Whitmore *Fetcher* • Kurt Kasznar *Quint* • Lewis Stone *Captain Holt* ■ *Dir* Richard Thorpe • *Scr* Harry Brown, from the novel by Ben Ames Williams • *Producer* Pandro S Berman

All the Fine Young Cannibals ★★

Drama   1960 · US · Colour · 122mins

A bizarre blend of teenage angst movie and Cassavetes-style drama that has Robert Wagner as Chet Baker in all but name. Jazz trumpeter and protégé of dipso Pearl Bailey, he's also the father of Natalie Wood's baby – though Wood marries George Hamilton when Wagner jilts her. Having Michael Anderson, the British director who made *The Dam Busters* and *Around the World in 80 Days*, at the helm ensures a blander ride than the subject merits.

Robert Wagner *Chad Bixby* • Natalie Wood *Salome Davis* • Susan Kohner *Catherine McDowall* • George Hamilton *Tony McDowall* • Pearl Bailey *Ruby Jones* • Jack Mullaney *Putney Tinker* • Onslow Stevens *Joshua Davis* • Anne Seymour *Mrs Bixby* ■ *Dir* Michael Anderson • *Scr* Robert Thom, from the novel *The Bixby Girls* by Rosamond Marshall

All the King's Horses ★★

Musical comedy   1935 · US · BW · 84mins

This musical variation of a show that was a cross between *The Prince and the Pauper* and *The Prisoner of Zenda* failed to set the screen alight, and did no favours to the movie careers of popular Carl Brisson or Ivor Novello's leading lady Mary Ellis. They look awkward and stiff in this under-directed Ruritanian farrago about a film star who takes the place of a king, the dual roles both played by Brisson. Slow and dull, this would-be romance even manages to make a trip to Vienna seem tedious. Camp Edward Everett Horton and rotund Eugene Pallette keep it just about watchable whenever they're on the screen.

Carl Brisson *Carl Rocco/King Rudolph* • Mary Ellis *Queen Elaine* • Edward Everett Horton *Peppi* • Katherine DeMille *Mimi* • Eugene Pallette *Con Conley* • Arnold Korff *Baron Kraemer* ■ *Dir* Frank Tuttle • *Scr* Frank Tuttle, Frederick Stephani, from the operetta by Laurence Clark, Max Gersberg

All the King's Men ★★★★ 🇺

Political drama   1949 · US · BW · 105mins

A blistering and powerful political drama that deservedly won the best picture Oscar, with the best actor award going to gruff Broderick Crawford in the performance of a lifetime as Willie Stark, a thinly disguised portrait of Louisiana demagogue "Kingfish" Huey Long. Mercedes McCambridge is also superb as a political aide, gaining another well-deserved Oscar as best supporting actress. Today this movie may seem a tad hysterical and over-performed, but it's important to view it in the context of when it was made – a time of extreme corruption and bigotry. Editor (and later director) Robert Parrish was responsible for restructuring director Robert Rossen's cut, based on Robert Penn Warren's unfilmable book. Parrish added new scenes and dialogue, making the film worthy of its Oscar nod, and at the same time winning the undying respect of Columbia boss Harry Cohn. 📺

Broderick Crawford *Willie Stark* • Joanne Dru *Anne Stanton* • John Ireland *Jack Burden* • John Derek *Tom Stark* • Mercedes McCambridge *Sadie Burke* • Shepperd Strudwick *Adam Stanton* • Ralph Dumke *Tiny Duffy* • Anne Seymour *Lucy Stark* • Katharine Warren *Mrs Burden* • Raymond Greenleaf *Judge Stanton* ■ *Dir* Robert Rossen • *Scr* Robert Rossen, from the novel by Robert Penn Warren

All the Little Animals
★★★ 🔞

Drama   1998 · UK · Colour · 112mins

British producer Jeremy Thomas makes his directorial debut with this odd little drama featuring one of John Hurt's patented quirky performances. Christian Bale (*American Psycho*) stars as Bobby, a mentally-impaired young man who runs away from his sinister stepfather (*Murder One*'s husky-voiced Daniel Benzali) and ends up in Cornwall, helping an eccentric hermit (Hurt, of course) collect and bury animals that have been hit by cars. While Thomas never quite settles on a consistent tone, this is nonetheless interesting, mainly thanks to the presence of Benzali and Hurt; Bale, however, seems somewhat overwhelmed in their company. Contains some violence.

John Hurt *Mr Summers* • Christian Bale *Bobby* • Daniel Benzali *De Winter* • James Faulkner *Mr Whiteside* • John O'Toole *Lorry driver* • Amanda Royle *Des* • Amy Robbins *Bobby's mother* • John Higgins *Dean* ■ *Dir* Jeremy Thomas • *Scr* Eski Thomas, from the novel by Walker Hamilton

All the President's Men
★★★★★ 🔞

Political thriller   1976 · US · Colour · 132mins

Alan J Pakula's Oscar-winning thriller about the Watergate burglary, with Robert Redford and Dustin Hoffman as the two *Washington Post* reporters (Bob Woodward and Carl Bernstein) whose stubborn digging ultimately brings down President Nixon. William Goldman's script brilliantly clarifies the multi-layered labyrinth of corruption, while Pakula's tense direction draws telling parallels between the blazing white, open-plan offices of the *Post* (no

secrets here) and the dark, murky world of Washington politics. Great support, too, from Jason Robards as the *Post*'s editor, Ben Bradlee, and Hal Holbrook as the creepy informant "Deep Throat". Along with *The Best Man* and *The Manchurian Candidate*, this is one of the best movies ever made about American politics. Contains swearing. 📺 *DVD*

Robert Redford *Bob Woodward* • Dustin Hoffman *Carl Bernstein* • Jack Warden *Harry Rosenfeld* • Martin Balsam *Howard Simons* • Hal Holbrook *Deep Throat* • Jason Robards [Jason Robards Jr] *Ben Bradlee* • Jane Alexander *Book-keeper* • Meredith Baxter *Debbie Sloan* • Ned Beatty *Dardis* • Stephen Collins *Hugh Sloan Jr* ■ *Dir* Alan J Pakula • *Scr* William Goldman, from the book by Bob Woodward, Carl Bernstein • *Cinematographer* Gordon Willis • *Editor* Robert L Wolfe • *Art Director* George Jenkins

All the Right Moves ★★★ 🔞

Sports drama   1983 · US · Colour · 86mins

Respected cinematographer, Michael Chapman made his directorial debut with this authentic portrait of college life. Indeed, it's such a well-rounded film that it makes his decision to resume lensing after the cool reception afforded *The Clan of the Cave Bear* all the more disappointing. The rivalry between the supposedly mutually dependent footballer Tom Cruise and coach Craig T Nelson is as convincingly established as the rather sweet relationship between Cruise and his girlfriend, Lea Thompson. Even the gridiron action smacks of the real thing, as does the sense of just how much college ball games mean to the local community. 📺

Tom Cruise *Stef Djordjevic* • Craig T Nelson *Vern Nickerson* • Lea Thompson *Lisa Lietske* • Charles Cioffi *Pop* • Paul Carafotes *Salvucci* • Christopher Penn *Brian* • Sandy Faison *Suzie* ■ *Dir* Michael Chapman • *Scr* Michael Kane

All the Vermeers in New York ★★★★

Romantic drama   1990 · US · Colour · 87mins

Virtually ignored on its original release, this is a subtle and often moving story of unfulfilled love, in which the pace and emptiness of modern life is contrasted with the serenity and beauty of the paintings by Dutch artist Jan Vermeer hanging in New York's art galleries. Proving that the auteur is not yet extinct, versatile Jon Jost not only wrote and directed the film, but also shot, designed and edited it. Jost's imaginative contrasts between art and life and his stylish compositions will linger longest in the memory, and Stephen Lack's passion for Emmanuelle Chaulet will leave you slightly misty-eyed.

Emmanuelle Chaulet *Anna* • Katherine Bean *Nicole* • Grace Phillips *Felicity* • Laurel Lee Kiefer *Ariel Ainsworth* • Gracie Mansion *Gracie Mansion* • Gordon Joseph Weiss *Gordon* • Stephen Lack *Mark* ■ *Dir/Scr* Jon Jost

All the Way Home ★★★★

Drama   1963 · US · BW · 97mins

Barely released in cinemas in the UK, this magnificently acted movie is actually an adaptation of James Agee's autobiographical *A Death in the Family*, coming to the big screen via a TV

movie and a Broadway version by playwright Tad Mosel. The tale of bereavement and its effect on the young Agee in Tennessee in 1915 is seen through the eyes of a boy, played by Michael Kearney, as his father is suddenly and accidentally killed. Jean Simmons is very moving in the role of the mother, and Robert Preston, as the father, also demonstrates what a fine and subtle actor he could be given the right material.

Jean Simmons *Mary* • Robert Preston *Jay* • Pat Hingle *Ralph* • Aline MacMahon *Aunt Hannah* • Thomas Chalmers *Joel* • John Cullum *Andrew* • Ronnie Claire Edwards *Sally* • Michael Kearney *Rufus* ■ Dir Alex Segal • Scr Philip Reisman Jr, from the play by Tad Mosel, from the novel *A Death in the Family* by James Agee

All the Young Men ★★
War drama   1960 · US · BW · 86mins

A desperately tedious Korean War tale, despite its interesting cast, produced and directed by one of Hollywood's true unsung mavericks, Hall Bartlett, probably best remembered, if at all, for filming *Jonathan Livingston Seagull*. It's sad to see Alan Ladd, well past his prime, struggling to hold the screen against sturdy Sidney Poitier and a cast of young Columbia contract artists such as James Darren and Glenn Corbett. Satirist Mort Sahl makes an acceptable conscript, but boxing champion Ingemar Johansson is embarrassing and should have stayed in the ring. For collectors only.

Alan Ladd *Kincaid* • Sidney Poitier *Towler* • James Darren *Cotton* • Glenn Corbett *Wade* • Mort Sahl *Crane* • Ana St Clair *Maya* • Joe Gallison *Jackson* • Ingemar Johansson *Torgil* ■ Dir/Scr Hall Bartlett

All Things Bright and Beautiful ★★★★
Comedy drama
1994 · UK/Ire · Colour · 90 mins

Innocence is next to godliness in this tender Irish yarn about a ten-year-old choirboy (Ciaran Fitzgerald) who meets an IRA fugitive (Gabriel Byrne), mistakes him for Barabbas, and then declares he's heard the Virgin Mary speak to him in church. The plot has vague echoes of *Whistle down the Wind*, but writer/director Barry Devlin has an unsentimental eye for the irony of a country filled with murder and miracles – an Ireland where ancient myth merges so completely with contemporary brutality you can't tell one from the other.

Ciaran Fitzgerald *Barry O'Neill* • Tom Wilkinson *Father McAteer* • Kevin McNally *Tommy O'Neill* • Gabrielle Reidy *Maeve O'Neill* • Lorraine Pilkington *Eileen O'Neill* • Gabriel Byrne *The Good Thief* ■ Dir/Scr Barry Devlin

All Things Fair ★★★ 15
Romantic drama
1995 · Swe/Den · Colour · 124mins

Winner of the Silver Bear at Berlin and recipient of an Oscar nomination for best foreign film, this was something of a return to form for Bo Widerberg, who remains best known outside his native Sweden for *Elvira Madigan*. Set in neutral Malmö during the Second World War, it tells of a lonely teenager who begins an affair with one of his teachers, seemingly with the consent of her drunken husband. The director's son, Johan, takes the lead, and his amenable performance and the customary beauty of the imagery are the main reasons for watching this often incoherent account of first love. In Swedish with English subtitles. Contains swearing, sex scenes and some mild violence. ▭

Johan Widerberg *Stig* • Marika Lagercrantz *Viola* • Tomas von Brömssen *Kjell* • Karin Huldt *Lisbet* • Björn Kjellman *Sigge* • Frida Lindholm *Olga* ■ Dir/Scr Bo Widerberg

All This, and Heaven Too ★★★★ U
Romantic drama   1940 · US · BW · 134mins

A sumptuous Warner Bros period melodrama with Bette Davis as a governess in Paris causing marital problems for her employer Charles Boyer. There's a veritable series of tragedies in scriptwriter Casey Robinson's torrid adaptation of the first half of Rachel Lyman Field's once-popular doorstop *roman à clef*, but Davis is remarkably restrained, and therefore doubly effective, in what must rank as one of her finest screen performances. Despite the length, Anatole Litvak's detailed pacing and Max Steiner's magnificent score render this one unmissable. Settle down with a good box of chocolates and the Kleenex. ▭

Bette Davis *Henriette Deluzy Desportes* • Charles Boyer *Duke De Praslin* • Jeffrey Lynn *Reverend Henry Field* • Barbara O'Neil *Duchesse De Praslin* • Virginia Weidler *Louise* • Walter Hampden *Pasquier* • Harry Davenport *Pierre* • Fritz Leiber *Albe* ■ Dir Anatole Litvak • Scr Casey Robinson, from the novel by Rachel Lyman Field

All through the Night ★★★
Spy drama   1942 · US · BW · 106mins

A standard piece of Warner Bros wartime propaganda, with Humphrey Bogart as a Broadway gambler who discovers a gang of Nazis plotting to sink a US battleship anchored in New York. The tone of the film is rather jokey, though it was released a year after the bombing of Pearl Harbor and consequently no one thought it was very funny. But Bogart is decent enough form and the usual suspects including Conrad Veidt and Peter Lorre lurk in the shadows as they often did in these vehicles. And while there's no Mary Astor or Ingrid Bergman to provide a shoulder for the hero to cry on, little-known Kaaren Verne does well as the solitary love interest.

Humphrey Bogart *Gloves Donahue* • Conrad Veidt *Hall Ebbing* • Kaaren Verne *Leda Hamilton* • Jane Darwell *Ma Donahue* • Frank McHugh *Barney* • Peter Lorre *Pepi* • Judith Anderson *Madame* • William Demarest *Sunshine* • Jackie Gleason *Starchie* • Phil Silvers *Waiter* • Wallace Ford *Spats Hunter* • Barton MacLane *Marty Callahan* ■ Dir Vincent Sherman • Scr Leonard Spigelgass, Edwin Gilbert, from a story by Leonard Spigelgass, Leonard Ross

All Tied Up ★★ 15
Romantic comedy
1994 · US · Colour · 90mins

One of the skeletons from Teri Hatcher's film closet before she found fame in TV's *The New Adventures of Superman*, this strained comedy centres on the adventures of serial womaniser Zach Galligan, who gets his comeuppance when he is kidnapped by a trio of young women after he dumps one of them. Hatcher, Lara Harris and Tracy Griffith (Melanie's younger sister) get to model a nice line in lingerie but that's about it: there is precious little in the way of laughs and director John Mark Robinson shows no interest in exploring the darker aspects of the plot.

Zach Galligan *Brian* • Teri Hatcher *Linda* • Tracy Griffith *Sharon* • Lara Harris *Kim* • Edward Blatchford *Detective Frank Steinham* ■ Dir John Mark Robinson • Scr Robert Madero, I Markie Lane, Laura Louden

Allan Quatermain and the Lost City of Gold ★ PG
Adventure   1987 · US · Colour · 95mins

A sequel to *King Solomon's Mines*, again with Richard Chamberlain and Sharon Stone slogging through the jungle in search of lost treasure. If the first film was a remake of a remake that ripped off *Raiders of the Lost Ark*, this one is a remake that rips off *Romancing the Stone*. Lazy direction and hilariously cheap special effects aren't quite awful enough to make it a candidate for the Ed Wood award. ▭

Richard Chamberlain *Allan Quatermain* • Sharon Stone *Jesse Huston* • James Earl Jones *Umslopogaas* • Henry Silva *Agon* • Cassandra Peterson *Sorais* • Robert Donner *Swarma* ■ Dir Gary Nelson • Scr Gene Quintano, Lee Reynolds, from the novel *Quatermain* by H Rider Haggard

Allegro non Troppo ★★★ PG
Animated musical comedy
1976 · It · BW and Colour · 74mins

Part parody, part homage to Disney's *Fantasia*, Bruno Bozzetto's third feature combines animation and live-action to generally amusing effect. Divided by sections featuring composer Maurizio Nichetti, the best vignettes show the serpent suffering the agony of Eden's apple to the strains of Stravinsky's *Firebird*, a weird menagerie of alien life forms struggling forth from a discarded Coke bottle to Ravel's *Bolero*, and Vivaldi's *Concerto in C Minor* forming the backdrop to a bee's pursuit of pollen in the presence of a courting couple. However, the showpiece is Sibelius's *Valse Triste*, which accompanies a melancholy cat on its nostalgic journey through the ruins of a bombed-out city. An Italian language film. ▭

Dir Bruno Bozzetto • Scr Bruno Bozzetto, Guido Manuli, Maurizio Nichetti • Animator Bruno Bozzetto, Guido Manuli

Alligator ★★★★ 15
Horror   1980 · US · Colour · 87mins

The old urban myth about baby alligators thriving in city sewers after being discarded as pets becomes a turbo-driven eco-chiller, thanks to the genuine wit and sardonic wisdom of John Sayles's superb script. Just as he did with *Piranha* and *The Howling* (written with Terence H Winkless), Sayles crafts a monster-on-the-loose scenario that's better than the best of the fifties movies it resembles. The cast (especially tough detective Robert Forster) is highly believable and treats the in-jokes with the right amount of tongue-in-cheek deference. Director Lewis Teague (*Cujo*) brings subtle irony to the carnage and infuses the whole radical re-packaging of mutant monster clichés with an immensely likeable sense of insolent fun. ▭ **DVD**

Robert Forster *Detective David Madison* • Robin Riker *Marisa Kendall* • Dean Jagger *Slade* • Michael Gazzo [Michael V Gazzo] *Police Chief Clark* • Sidney Lassick [Sydney Lassick] *Lou* • Jack Carter *Mayor Ledoux* • Perry Lang *Kelly* • Henry Silva *Col Brock* ■ Dir Lewis Teague • Scr John Sayles

Alligator II: the Mutation ★★ 15
Science-fiction horror
1991 · US · Colour · 90mins

The original *Alligator* was a cult delight: John Sayles had a hand in the witty dialogue, while the actors kept theirs tongues firmly in cheek. This sequel reprises the basic plot – mutant reptile wreaks havoc in suburbia – but it's tame stuff, despite a pretty good cast (Joseph Bologna, Dee Wallace Stone, Richard Lynch). The creature isn't particularly scary, either. ▭

Joseph Bologna *David Hodges* • Brock Peters *Chief Speed* • Dee Wallace Stone *Christine Hodges* • Woody Brown *Rich Harmon* • Holly Gagnier *Sheri* • Richard Lynch *Hawkins* • Bill Daily *Anderson* • Steve Railsback *Vincent Brown* ■ Dir Jon Hess • Scr Curt Allen

Alligator Eyes ★★★ 15
Thriller   1990 · US · Colour · 96mins

A modest but quietly menacing thriller that niftily subverts the woman-in-peril scenario. Annabelle Larsen stars as a blind woman who ensnares a trio of holiday-makers in a dangerous web of revenge. Director John Feldman, a documentary film-maker making his feature debut, conjures up an air of brooding suspense and sexual tension, and is rewarded with impressive performances particularly Larsen's from a largely unknown cast. Classical composer Sheila Silver provides a perfectly cold-blooded score. Contains violence, swearing and nudity. ▭

Annabelle Larsen *Pauline* • Roger Kabler *Robbie* • John Mackay *Peterson* • Mary McLain *Marjorie* • Allen McCulloch *Lance* ■ Dir/Scr John Feldman

An Alligator Named Daisy ★★★ U
Comedy   1955 · UK · Colour · 88mins

A bright, if silly, Rank comic romp for sexy Diana Dors and pompous Donald Sinden, with one of those compulsively watchable period character casts (keep an eye out for guest stars Frankie Howerd, Gilbert Harding and Jimmy Edwards). J Lee Thompson's hand lies a little too heavy over the proceedings (the director of *Cape Fear* and *The Guns of Navarone* never slummed lightly) and Pinewood's attempt to match Hollywood in pace and style doesn't happen. But Dors reveals a nice sense of comic timing and Stephen Boyd, who is best known for playing Messala in *Ben-Hur*, makes an early impact.

Donald Sinden *Peter Weston* • Diana Dors *Vanessa Colebrook* • Jean Carson *Moira* •

James Robertson-Justice *Sir James* • Stanley Holloway *General* • Margaret Rutherford *Prudence Croquet* • Roland Culver *Colonel Weston* • Stephen Boyd *Albert* • Richard Wattis *Hoskins* ■ *Dir* J Lee Thompson • *Scr* Jack Davies

The Alligator People ★★
Science-fiction horror
1959 · US · BW · 74mins

Fifties "creature features" don't come any sillier or more insane than this last-gasp effort from former musicals director Roy Del Ruth. Down in the Louisiana swamplands, doctor George Macready experiments with an alligator serum intended to help amputee victims grow new limbs. Bruce Bennett is a wounded man who takes the serum and turns into an upright reptile, with the help of an ill-fitting scaly rubber suit. Inept in practically every area, Del Ruth's ill-at-ease direction simply makes matters worse as the heavies slowly turn into walking handbags. That said, Beverly Garland does her usual spunky heroine routine to perfection.

Beverly Garland *Jane Marvin* • Bruce Bennett *Dr Erik Lorimer* • Lon Chaney Jr *Mannon* • George Macready *Dr Mark Sinclair* • Frieda Inescort *Mrs Henry Hawthorne* • Richard Crane *Paul Webster* ■ *Dir* Roy Del Ruth • *Scr* Orville H Hampton, from a story by Charles O'Neal, Orville H Hampton

The Allnighter ★★ PG
Comedy
1987 · US · Colour · 91mins

An attempt to turn The Bangles singer Susanna Hoffs into a movie star, that failed because she's not a very good actress, and the film isn't that great either. Hoffs and co-star Dedee Pfeiffer (Michelle's sister) are out of their depth, but the performances of the more experienced Joan Cusack and Michael Ontkean help make this a passable, slightly saucy comedy. ▣

Susanna Hoffs *Molly* • Dedee Pfeiffer *Val* • Joan Cusack *Gina* • John Terlesky *CJ* • James Anthony Shanta *Killer* • Michael Ontkean *Mickey Leroi* • Pam Grier *Sgt MacLeish* • Phil Brock *Brad* ■ *Dir/Scr* Tamar Simon Hoffs

All's Fair ★ 15
Comedy
1989 · US · Colour · 85mins

George Segal, once the credible embodiment of harassed middle America, must have been desperate when he agreed to star in this tosh. As chauvinist businessmen take on their wives and female colleagues at a weekend war game, this metaphor for the battle of the sexes is never less than clumsy. A no-laughs comedy saddled with slack direction throughout. Contains swearing. ▣

George Segal *Colonel* • Sally Kellerman *Florence* • Robert Carradine *Mark* • Jennifer Edwards *Ann* • Jane Kaczmarek *Linda* • John Kapelos *Eddy* • Lou Ferrigno *Klaus* ■ *Dir* Rocky Lang • *Scr* Randee Russell, John Finegan, Tom Rondinella, William Pace, from a story by Watt Tyler, John Finegan

Almost ★ PG
Romantic comedy
1990 · Ausl · Colour · 81mins

Rosanna Arquette is a wacky housewife regressing into uninspired fantasy through a combination of sheer boredom and constant arguments with

her uncaring husband. Short on wit and long on limp laughs, director Michael Pattinson's whimsically challenged, unremarkable comedy features Hugo Weaving, who later worked on much better material in The Adventures of Priscilla, Queen of the Desert. The film was also released as *Wendy Cracked a Walnut*. Contains some swearing and brief nudity. ▣

Rosanna Arquette *Wendy* • Bruce Spence *Ronnie* • Hugo Weaving *Jake* • Kerry Walker *Deidre* • Doreen Warburton *Elsie* • Desiree Smith *Cynthia* • Susan Lyons *Caroline* ■ *Dir* Michael Pattinson • *Scr* Suzanne Hawley

Almost an Angel ★★ PG
Comedy
1990 · US · Colour · 91mins

Poor Paul Hogan is simply lost away from his "Crocodile" Dundee persona and his Fosters ads. Here he plays a crook-turned-angel in what is anything but a divine comedy. He only has himself to blame for the feeble wisecracks and fortune cookie philosophy as he wrote the script, and one suspects that he had as much control over the direction as credited John Cornell. Hogan ambles through the action as if his mind was elsewhere, only perking up when joined by real-life wife Linda Kozlowski, who gives a half-decent performance, as does Elias Koteas as her disabled brother. Contains some swearing ▣

Paul Hogan *Terry Dean* • Linda Kozlowski *Rose Garner* • Elias Koteas *Steve Garner* • Doreen Lang *Mrs Garner* • Robert Sutton *Guido* • Travis Venable *Bubba* • Douglas Seale *Father* • Charlton Heston *God* ■ *Dir* John Cornell • *Scr* Paul Hogan

Almost Golden: the Jessica Savitch Story ★★ 15
Drama based on a true story
1995 · US · Colour · 87mins

In the early eighties, Jessica Savitch made American television headlines when she became one of the first women to anchor a major network news programme. However, she found the pressure that came with this success almost impossible to handle and, in a haze of drink and drugs, her career came to a juddering halt one night while live on air. This is a very different Savitch from the one depicted in that highly romanticised film *Up Close and Personal*, with Sela Ward here giving a much grittier performance than Michelle Pfeiffer did as Tally Atwater. A tragic life, but an unremarkable film. Contains some slight violence and brief nudity. ▣

Sela Ward *Jessica Savitch* • Ron Silver *Ron Kershaw* • Judith Ivey *Laura McCormick* • Jeffrey DeMunn *Mel Korn* • William Converse-Roberts *Dr Donald Payne* • Sean McCann *Mack Stevens* ■ *Dir* Peter Werner • *Scr* Gwenda Blair, from the biography *Almost Golden* by Neil Roach

Almost Heroes ★★ 12
Historical comedy adventure
1998 · US · Colour · 86mins

Final screen outing for loveable slob Chris Farley – a sort of John Belushi for the nineties, right down to his tragic early death. Here he is paired with Matthew Perry as 19th-century rivals of the legendary explorers Lewis and Clark. Determined to put their

names in the history books, they end up falling foul of Indians, the rugged wilderness and each other. Farley is as energetically crude as ever, but both Perry and director Christopher Guest, who was behind the classic *This Is Spinal Tap*, look uncomfortable with the material. Contains some mild swearing and nudity. ▣

Chris Farley *Bartholomew Hunt* • Matthew Perry *Leslie Edwards* • Bokeem Woodbine *Jonah* • Eugene Levy *Guy Fontenot* • Kevin Dunn *Hidalgo* • Lisa Barbuscia *Shaquinna* • Steven M Porter *Higgins* • David Packer *Bidwell* • Lewis Arquette *Merchant* ■ *Dir* Christopher Guest • *Scr* Boyd Hale, Mark Nutter, Tom Wolfe

An Almost Perfect Affair ★★ 15
Romantic comedy
1979 · US · Colour · 87mins

Michael Ritchie – whose *Smile* was a marvellous satire on Miss Young America beauty pageants – here casts his eye on the Cannes Film Festival. Keith Carradine plays an independent film director who comes to Cannes touting his movie about condemned murderer Gary Gilmore. It's seized by customs, released by Monica Vitti, then bought by an exploitation king who changes the title from *Choice of Ending* to *Shoot Me Before I Kill Again*. There are some nice jokes, but it needs more stars in cameo roles à la *The Player*. ▣

Keith Carradine *Hal* • Monica Vitti *Maria* • Raf Vallone *Freddie* • Christian De Sica *Carlo* • Dick Anthony Williams *Jackson* • Henri Garcin *Lieutenant Montand* • Anna Maria Horsford *Amy Zon* ■ *Dir* Michael Ritchie • *Scr* Walter Bernstein, Don Peterson, from a story by Michael Ritchie, Don Peterson

The Almost Perfect Bank Robbery ★★★
Comedy
1996 · US · Colour

Brooke Shields as an ex-Navy SEAL? That miscasting aside, this TV movie is a likeable enough crime caper. Dylan Walsh is the strait-laced cop whose thoughts turn to robbery when he realises that he can't keep new girlfriend Shields in the luxury she expects. The two leads are lightweight, but Rip Torn puts in an engaging supporting performance and the mix of comedy and thrills bustles along quite nicely.

Brooke Shields *Cyndee LaFrance* • Dylan Walsh *Frank Syler* • Rip Torn *Royce* • Sherie Rene Scott *Freddie* • Alessandro Nivola ■ *Dir* Ted Post • *Scr* Adam Greenman

Almost Summer ★★
Romantic drama
1977 · US · Colour · 88mins

High-school elections, the teenage dating game and a feelgood soundtrack combine for an initially bright and breezy satire about youth values. It's when the tone gets too serious and preachy that restlessness is likely to set in. Beach Boy Brian Wilson is credited for the title tune and *It's OK*, while fellow group member Mike Love penned and sings *Cruisin* and *Sad, Sad Summer*. While no great addition to the rock cinema genre, this is good natured enough to get by.

Bruno Kirby *Bobby DeVito* • Lee Purcell *Christine Alexander* • John Friedrich *Darryl*

Fitzgerald • Didi Conn *Donna DeVito* • Thomas Carter *Dean Hampton* • Tim Matheson *Kevin Hawkins* ■ *Dir* Martin Davidson • *Scr* Judith Berg, Sandra Berg, Martin Davidson, Marc Reid Rubel

Almost You ★★ 15
Romantic drama
1984 · US · Colour · 92mins

Griffin Dunne stars as the unhappy husband whose wife Brooke Adams is injured in a car accident. It's not long before he's having an affair with nurse Karen Young, hired to look after her, in a drama which suffers from the fact that few of the characters come across as remotely sympathetic. This would be a huge problem were it not for the performance of Dunne, who manages to give his character some credibility and keeps you watching. ▣

Brooke Adams *Erica Boyer* • Griffin Dunne *Alex Boyer* • Karen Young *Lisa Willoughby* • Marty Watt *Kevin Danzig* • Christine Estabrook *Maggie* • Josh Mostel *David* • Laura Dean *Jeannie* • Dana Delany *Susan McCall* ■ *Dir* Adam Brooks • *Scr* Mark Horowitz, from a story by Adam Brooks

Aloha, Bobby and Rose ★★★
Crime melodrama 1975 · US · Colour · 88mins

After making an impact with his role in George Lucas's *American Graffiti*, Paul LeMat starred in this crime melodrama from director Floyd Mutrux. This is just the kind of rock 'n' roll chase movie that influenced Quentin Tarantino and paved the lethal path towards Oliver Stone's *Natural Born Killers*. Note the use of rock standards and an early appearance from Edward James (billed here as "Eddie") Olmos. Mutrux went on to achieve further success with his Alan Freed biopic, *American Hot Wax*, with *Aloha*'s Tim McIntire as Freed. Contains some violence and swearing.

Paul LeMat *Bobby* • Dianne Hull *Rose* • Tim McIntire *Buford* • Leigh French *Donna Sue* • Noble Willingham *Uncle Charlie* • Martine Bartlett *Rose's mother* • Robert Carradine *Moxey* • Eddie Olmos [Edward James Olmos] ■ *Dir/Scr* Floyd Mutrux

Aloha Summer ★★★ PG
Drama
1988 · US · Colour · 92mins

The secret of surf movies is to ensure there is plenty of sun and sand, and as many shots of muscular, tanned, teen bodies arching through the breakers as decency will allow. Director Tommy Lee Wallace resists the temptation to tamper with what, essentially, is a winning formula, ensuring that this surfing sextet pass through their rites of passage in an orderly fashion to the sound of rock hits of the day. This being Hawaii in 1959, he is able to slip in a few novel touches, such as the Japanese kid who, while thinking his homeland was hard done by in the war, can't accept his father's traditional code. ▣

Chris Makepeace *Mike Tognetti* • Yuji Okumoto *Kenzo Konishi* • Don Michael Paul *Chuck Granville* • Tia Carrere *Lani Kepoo* • Sho Kosugi *Yukinaga Konishi* ■ *Dir* Tommy Lee Wallace • *Scr* Mike Greco, Bob Benedetto, from a story by Mike Greco

Alone in the Dark ★★ 🔞

Horror   1982 · US · Colour · 89mins

Donald Pleasence is the head of a New Jersey lunatic asylum keeping its really dangerous criminal inmates – among them Jack Palance and Martin Landau – under electronic surveillance. When a power failure occurs, the violent psychos break out and head to the home of the asylum doctor. This is a repetitive mishmash of stalk-and-slash themes and jump cuts. Aside from a promising opening dream sequence, a fleeting apparition (created by gore veteran Tom Savini) and an interesting "who's really crazy?" denouement set at a punk rock concert, the debut horror feature from director Jack Sholder (*The Hidden*) is a below-par maniacs-on-the-loose saga. 🎞

Jack Palance *Frank Hawkes* • Erland Van Lidth Ronald "Fatty" Elster • Deborah Hedwall *Nell Potter* • Phillip Clark *Tom Smith/Skagg* • Martin Landau *Bryon "Preacher" Sutcliff* • Dwight Schultz *Dan Potter* ■ *Dir* Jack Sholder • *Scr* Jack Sholder, from a story by Robert Shaye, Michael Harpster, Jack Sholder

Alone on the Pacific ★★★

Adventure   1963 · Jap · Colour · 104mins

In all his major films, from *The Burmese Harp* to *Tokyo Olympiad*, Kon Ichikawa is concerned with men pushed to extremes. Here, a young yachtsman takes three months to sail from Osaka to San Francisco on a 19-foot craft. Based on the true adventures of Kenichi Horie, it seems an impossible subject for a film. But Ichikawa, using widescreen to magnificent effect and integrating flashbacks to the sailor's life on shore, makes even the dull bits of the voyage interesting. The climactic scene, as the Golden Gate bridge looms out of the mist, is genuinely moving. In Japanese with English subtitles.

Yujiro Ishihara *The youth* • Kinuyo Tanaka *His mother* • Masayuki Mori *His father* • Ruriko Asoka *His sister* • Hajime Hana *His friend* ■ *Dir* Kon Ichikawa • *Scr* Natto Wada, from the logbook of Kenichi Horie

Along Came Jones ★★★

Comedy western   1945 · US · BW · 89mins

Fans of the Coasters' immortal fifties record *Along Came Jones* should check out this undervalued film, in which amiable cowpoke Gary Cooper is mistaken for outlaw Dan Duryea. It's a likeable compendium of western clichés, ably handled by former editor Stuart Heisler, who would later direct "Coop" in *Dallas* (1950). There's much to enjoy here, not least a lovely performance from Loretta Young. (She was hand-picked by Cooper, who was also the film's producer.) The title passed into western movie folklore.

Gary Cooper *Melody Jones* • Loretta Young *Cherry de Longpre* • William Demarest *George Fury* • Dan Duryea *Monte Jarrad* • Frank Sully *Cherry's brother* • Russell Simpson *Pop de Longpre* • Arthur Loft *Sheriff* ■ *Dir* Stuart Heisler • *Scr* Nunnally Johnson, from a story by Alan LeMay

Along the Great Divide ★★

Western   1951 · US · BW · 87mins

Standard revenge western that Kirk Douglas, in his memoirs, remembered with some distaste. "I hated *Along the Great Divide*," he wrote, "I did it just to get my one picture a year obligation [to Warners] out of the way." Douglas recalled the cruelty to the horses, the risks the stuntmen were forced to take and the sadism of the director, Raoul Walsh: "Critics talk about how Walsh movies have such great pace. They have great pace because they are always in a hurry to finish them."

Kirk Douglas *Len Merrick* • Virginia Mayo *Ann Keith* • John Agar *Billy Shear* • Walter Brennan *Pop Keith* • Ray Teal *Lou Gray* • Morris Ankrum *Ed Roden* • James Anderson *Dan Roden* • Charles Meredith *The Judge* ■ *Dir* Raoul Walsh • *Scr* Walter Doniger, Lewis Meltzer, from a story by Walter Doniger • *Cinematographer* Sid Hickox

Along the Rio Grande ★★ 🆄

Western   1941 · US · BW · 64mins

One of cowboy star Tim Holt's RKO pre-war series of westerns, featuring a routine plot wherein Tim and two pals join up with an outlaw gang to avenge the murder of their boss. Mind you, it takes some intervention from Sheriff Hal Taliaferro to help our heroes bring the villains to book, but the script is above par for this sort of western. Ray Whitley plays Holt's ongoing sidekick Smokey, while leading lady Betty Jane Rhodes is a pert plus.

Tim Holt *Jeff* • Ray Whitley *Smokey* • Betty Jane Rhodes *Mary* • Emmett Lynn *Whopper* • Robert Fiske *Doc Randall* • Hal Taliaferro *Sheriff* ■ *Dir* Edward Killy • *Scr* Arthur V Jones, Morton Grant, from a story by Stuart Anthony

Alpha Beta ★★★

Drama   1973 · UK · Colour · 66mins

EA Whitehead's play marked Albert Finney's return to the London stage after a six-year absence. The play is a two-hander, and Finney's co-star was Rachel Roberts, who last acted with him in *Saturday Night and Sunday Morning*. In three lacerating acts, the play defines modern marriage as a battlefield; there is caustic wit, bruising, a lot of metaphorical blood and ample opportunity for great acting. Financed by Finney himself and directed by Anthony Page, who also helmed the original Royal Court production, this is a valuable record of the stage original.

Albert Finney *Man* • Rachel Roberts *Woman* ■ *Dir* Anthony Page • *Scr* EA Whitehead, from his play

The Alpha Incident ★

Science-fiction   1977 · US · Colour · 92mins

A microbe from Mars terrorises people at a rural Wisconsin railroad depot managed by dim-witted Ralph Meeker. Only in sleep does the alien germ take control and destroy the body, so they must stay awake by playing cards and having sex. A micro-budget bore from director Bill Rebane, he of *The Giant Spider Invasion* and *Monster a-Go-Go* infamy, so you can't say you weren't warned. Apart from Meeker's messy death scene where his head turns to

jelly, there's little worth commenting on in this over-talky feeble fable.

John Alderman *Dr Rogers* • John F Goff *Jack Tiller* • Ralph Meeker *Charlie* • Stafford Morgan *Ted Sorenson* • Carol Irene Newell *Jenny* ■ *Dir* Bill Rebane • *Scr* Ingrid Neumayer

Alphabet City ★★ 🔞

Crime drama   1984 · US · Colour · 85mins

The most mainstream movie directed by underground film-maker Amos (*Subway Riders*) Poe has style in abundance and a great performance by Vincent Spano but virtually no plot. Tough Spano is a Lower East Side drug dealer with plans to retire until mobsters force him to go on the run. When Spano is centre stage this violent slice-of-life drama crackles with menacing intensity. Otherwise, it's a rather bland affair that goes over too much familiar ground. The music is by Nile Rodgers of Chic fame. 🎞

Vincent Spano *Johnny* • Kate Vernon *Angela* • Michael Winslow *Lippy* • Zohra Lampert *Mama* • Jami Gertz *Sophia* • Ray Serra *[Raymond Serra] Gino* • Daniel Jordano *Juani* ■ *Dir* Amos Poe • *Scr* Amos Poe, Gregory K Heller, Robert Seidman, from a novel by Gregory K Heller

The Alphabet Murders ★ 🆄

Comedy mystery   1966 · UK · BW · 95mins

Having met with cinematic success with Agatha Christie's Miss Marple as played by Margaret Rutherford, MGM turned to another of Christie's detectives, Hercule Poirot, here incarnated in the unlikely personage of Tony Randall. The film's an unfortunate mess, which is doubly sad since talented satirist director Frank Tashlin should be capable of getting a handle on the whole affair. Poirot stalks a killer who is bumping off victims in alphabetical order. Rutherford makes a guest appearance, but even that fails to enliven the proceedings. Poirot would be better served by Albert Finney and Peter Ustinov a decade later.

Tony Randall *Hercule Poirot* • Anita Ekberg *Amanda Beatrice Cross* • Robert Morley *Hastings* • Maurice Denham *Inspector Japp* • Guy Rolfe *Duncan Doncaster* • Sheila Allen *Lady Diane* • Margaret Rutherford *Miss Marple* ■ *Dir* Frank Tashlin • *Scr* David Pursall, Jack Seddon, from the novel by Agatha Christie

Alphaville ★★★★ 🅿🅶

Futuristic detective drama   1965 · Fr · BW · 94mins

The winner of the prestigious Golden Bear at the Berlin Festival, this assured blend of sci-fi and *film noir* is perhaps Jean-Luc Godard's most accessible picture: a chilling peek into the future inspired as much by poetry and mythology as pulp fiction. Playing fast and loose with genre conventions, Godard explores themes more readily associated with Michelangelo Antonioni, as world-weary private eye Eddie Constantine searches the far-off metropolis of Alphaville for missing scientist Akim Tamiroff. Anna Karina is genuinely affecting as the robot who discovers emotion, while cinematographer Raoul Coutard miraculously turns Paris into a soulless hell. A French language film. 🎞

Eddie Constantine *Lemmy Caution* • Anna Karina *Natacha Von Braun* • Akim Tamiroff

Henri Dickson • Howard Vernon *Professor Leonard Nosferatu/Von Braun* • Laszlo Szabo *Chief engineer* • Michel Delahaye *Von Braun's assistant* ■ *Dir/Scr* Jean-Luc Godard

Alpine Fire ★★★ 🔞

Drama   1985 · Swi · Colour · 118mins

Fredi M Murer adapts his own novel with a directorial style as stark as the Alpine landscape, and a power and subtlety usually missing from films about incest. Had the performances not been so innocent and unabashed, however, the realism would have seemed embarrassingly phoney. Johanna Lier impresses as the teenage daughter of a Swiss hill farmer, but it's Thomas Nock who compels as the pubescent deaf-mute who relieves his frustrations by constructing a network of stone monuments in the isolated high ground. This isn't an easy film, but it's certainly a hypnotic one. In Swiss German with English subtitles.

Thomas Nock *Boy* • Johanna Lier *Belli* • Dorothea Moritz *Mother* • Rolf Illig *Father* • Tilli Breidenbach *Grandmother* • Joerg Odermatt *Grandfather* ■ *Dir* Fredi M Murer • *Scr* Fredi M Murer, from his novel

Alsino and the Condor ★★★

Political drama
1982 · Nic/Cub/Mex/Cos R · Colour · 89mins

It's somewhat apt that the first feature produced in Nicaragua under the Sandinistas should have been directed by a Chilean who'd fled the Pinochet regime. Leavening his stylised portrait of the brutal civil war with juvenile escapades and magic realism, Miguel Littin succeeds in fashioning an allegory that, in spite of its anti-American sentiment, received an Oscar nomination for best foreign film. Personifying his nation's need to come of political age, Alan Esquivel is superb as the 12-year-old orphan whose dreams of flying high above the surrounding jungle sustain him through physical injury and the savagery of the conflict. In Spanish with English subtitles.

Dean Stockwell *Frank* • Alan Esquivel *Alsino* • Carmen Bunster *Alsino's grandmother* • Alejandro Parodi *The Major* ■ *Dir* Miguel Littin • *Scr* Miguel Littin, Isidora Aguirre, Tomas Perez Turrent

Altered States ★★★ 🔞

Horror fantasy   1980 · US · Colour · 98mins

Scientist William Hurt tinkers with tribal drug rituals and sensory deprivation tanks until they cause him to regress to a primitive killer-simian state of altered consciousness. The deer-eating Neanderthal man mid-section may seem too over-the-top considering the deliberately excessive whole, but, in general, director Ken Russell power-drives his mad doctor update with trademark visual excess. Even if celebrated screenwriter Paddy Chayefsky, who also wrote the novel on which this is based, removed his name from the film in disgust, Russell's razzle-dazzle hallucinogenic style certainly scores the freaked-out bullseye. Contains violence, swearing and nudity. 🎞

William Hurt *Eddie Jessup* • Blair Brown *Emily Jessup* • Bob Balaban *Arthur Rosenberg* •

Charles Haid *Mason Parrish* • Thaao Penghlis *Eccheverria* • Miguel Godreau *Primal Man* • Dori Brenner *Sylvia Rosenberg* • Peter Brandon *Hobart* • Drew Barrymore *Margaret Jessup* ■ *Dir* Ken Russell, Sidney Aaron [Paddy Chayefsky] • *Scr* Sidney Aaron [Paddy Chayefsky], from his novel

Alvarez Kelly ★★★ PG

Western 1966 · US · Colour · 105mins

An oddball American Civil War western, with William Holden as a rancher who delivers a herd of cattle to the Union army and is then kidnapped by the Confederates whose colonel, Richard Widmark, wants Holden to steal back the herd in order to feed his own soldiers. At first it's jokey; then Widmark shoots one of Holden's fingers off and things get rather more serious. Waywardly plotted, it's held together by the terrific rivalry and enmity whipped up by Holden and Widmark, two of Hollywood's finest. Contains violence and some swearing. 🖭

William Holden (1) *Alvarez Kelly* • Richard Widmark *Colonel Tom Rossiter* • Janice Rule *Liz Pickering* • Patrick O'Neal *Major Albert Stedman* • Victoria Shaw *Charity Warwick* • Roger C Carmel *Captain Angus Ferguson* ■ *Dir* Edward Dmytryk • *Scr* Franklin Coen, Elliot Arnold, from a story by Franklin Coen

Alvin Purple ★★

Comedy 1973 · Ausl · Colour · 97mins

In this lacklustre Australian romp, Graeme Blundell is so much the sex-object of women's desires – from schoolgirls to bored housewives to kinky ladies – that he's constantly on the run. Eventually, he ends up as a gardener in a convent. The innuendos come thick and fast, but director Tim Burstall's gaudily titled comedy never quite lives up to its promising premise. The film was a box-office blockbuster in its home country, however.

Graeme Blundell *Alvin Purple* • Jill Forster *Mrs Horwood* • Elli MacLure *Tina Donovan* • Penne Hackforth-Jones *Dr Liz Sort* • George Whaley *Dr McBurney* • Noel Ferrier *Judge* ■ *Dir* Tim Burstall • *Scr* Alan Hopgood

Always ★★★ 15

Comedy 1985 · US · Colour · 105mins

Not to be confused with the romantic melodrama Steven Spielberg made four years later, this distinctive comedy of manners probes the meaning of love and marriage by focusing on three couples, each at different stages of their relationship. Writer/director Henry Jaglom and his former wife Patrice Townsend co-star as a couple about to get divorced; Alan Rachins and Joanna Frank, their best friends in real life, play their best friends on screen; while shooting took place in the house that Jaglom and Townsend shared when they were married. Charming, witty and often perceptive, the film is probably too unconventional in structure to have more than a limited appeal.

Henry Jaglom *David* • Patrice Townsend *Judy* • Joanna Frank *Lucy* • Alan Rachins *Eddie* • Melissa Leo *Peggy* • Jonathan Kaufer *Maxwell* • Bud Townsend *Judy's father* • Bob Rafelson *David's neighbour* ■ *Dir/Scr* Henry Jaglom

Always ★★★ PG

Romantic fantasy 1989 · US · Colour · 117mins

This was Steven Spielberg's attempt to make a more grown-up fantasy, after he was criticised for pandering to the child in all of us with *ET* and *Raiders of the Lost Ark*. It's effectively an update of the Spencer Tracy film *A Guy Named Joe*, with Richard Dreyfuss as the firefighter pilot who returns from the dead to watch over the love of his life Holly Hunter. Best pal John Goodman steals the show, and Audrey Hepburn (in her last screen role) gives him a run for his money as an angelic guide, while Hunter and Dreyfuss manage to stave off the syrup to produce a romantic tale of everlasting love. 🖭

Richard Dreyfuss *Pete Sandich* • Holly Hunter *Dorinda Durston* • Brad Johnson *Ted Baker* • John Goodman *Al Yackey* • Audrey Hepburn *Hap* • Roberts Blossom *Dave* • Keith David *Powerhouse* • Ed Van Nuys *Nails* ■ *Dir* Steven Spielberg • *Scr* Jerry Belson, Diane Thomas, from the film *A Guy Named Joe* by Dalton Trumbo, Frederick Hazlitt Brennan, Chandler Sprague, David Boehm

Always Goodbye ★★

Melodrama 1938 · US · BW · 75mins

This remake of *Gallant Lady* (1934), which starred Ann Harding and Clive Brook, now stars Barbara Stanwyck and Herbert Marshall in the story of an unwed mother who sacrifices her child but then wants him back. Unfortunately, despite the ever-admirable Stanwyck and all the ingredients for a delicious wallow, the movie is directed by Sidney Lanfield with such a heavy overlay of treacle and unsubtle use of close-ups that it ends up an inferior and uninvolving example of the genre.

Barbara Stanwyck *Margot Weston* • Herbert Marshall *Jim Howard* • Ian Hunter *Phillip Marshall* • Cesar Romero *Count Giovanni Corini* • Lynn Bari *Jessica Reid* ■ *Dir* Sidney Lanfield • *Scr* Kathryn Scola, Edith Skouras, from a story by Gilbert Emery, Douglas Doty, from the film *Gallant Lady* by Gilbert Emery, Franc Rhodes, Sam Mintz

Always Leave Them Laughing ★★★ U

Comedy 1949 · US · BW · 115mins

"Uncle" Milton Berle's big feature starring role was not a success in its day, but Miltie went on to greater celebrity in the Golden Era of American television. His face in grimace was not, in truth, well-suited to leading roles on the big cinema screen, but he was perfectly (type-) cast in this wry saga of a vaudeville comic who becomes a TV star. There was considerable on-screen competition, though, from vaudeville great Bert Lahr, playing the comedian whose shoes Berle aspires to step into, and who immortalises one of his most famous routines in this movie.

Milton Berle *Kip Cooper* • Virginia Mayo *Nancy Egan* • Ruth Roman *Fay Washburn* • Bert Lahr *Eddie Egan* • Alan Hale *Mr Washburn* • Grace Hayes *Mrs Washburn* • Jerome Cowan *Elliot Montgomery* ■ *Dir* Roy Del Ruth • *Scr* Jack Rose, Mel Shavelson

Always Outnumbered ★★★ 15

Drama 1998 · US · Colour · 103mins

In this stark drama, paroled murderer Laurence Fishburne ekes out an existence on the ghetto streets of Los Angeles and becomes a latter-day angel of mercy. Whether steering youngsters away from gangs, saving the marriage of troubled neighbours or getting medical help for down-and-out friends, Fortlow uses his intimidating presence to get results. It's a rather humourless and depressing picture of urban poverty and homelessness, but the outstanding script and Michael Apted's firm direction make it compelling viewing. Contains swearing, violence and nudity. 🖭

Laurence Fishburne *Socrates Fortlow* • Bill Cobbs *Right Burke* • Natalie Cole *Iula Brown* • Laurie Metcalf *Halley Grimes* • Alan Wilder *Anton Crier* • Bill Nunn *Howard M'Shalla* • Cicely Tyson *Luvia* ■ *Dir* Michael Apted • *Scr* Walter Mosley, from his book *Always Outnumbered, Always Outgunned*

Always Remember I Love You ★★ U

Drama 1990 · US · Colour · 93mins

Stephen Dorff best known here for his role as "fifth Beatle" Stuart Sutcliffe in *Backbeat* is the teenager who discovers that, not only was he adopted, he was kidnapped from his real parents. The cast, including Patty Duke Astin, *Knots Landing*'s Joan Van Ark and Richard Masur, manages to keep this made-for-TV tale of the youngster searching for his mother and father surprisingly moving, despite the familiarity of some of the "I love you but I have to find out about myself" plot twists.

Patty Duke Astin [Patty Duke] *Ruth Monroe* • Joan Van Ark *Martha Mendham* • Richard Masur *Earl Monroe* • Stephen Dorff *Robert Mendham* • David Birney *Philip Mendham* • Sam Wanamaker *Philip Mendham Sr* ■ *Dir* Michael L Miller [Michael Miller] • *Scr* Vivienne Radkoff

Ama ★★ 15

Fantasy drama 1991 · UK/Gha · Colour · 105mins

This confused film bravely attempts to transport African mythology to suburban London, but fails to work as either an offbeat drama or a discourse on cultural assimilation. Young Georgina Ackerman receives dire warnings young from her Ghanian ancestors on a golden computer disc – a neat touch – but other promising plot leads are left unpursued. In spite of a feel-good finale at the Notting Hill carnival, this rare British venture into magic realism is an opportunity missed.

Thomas Baptiste *Babs* • Anima Misa *Corri* • Roger Griffiths *Joe* • Nii Oma Hunter *Uk* • Joy Elias-Rilwan *Araba* • Georgina Ackerman *Ama* ■ *Dir* Kwesi Owusu, Kwate Nee-Owoo • *Scr* Kwesi Owusu

Amadeus ★★★★★ PG

Biographical drama 1984 · US · Colour · 153mins

The winner of eight Oscars and an unexpected box-office smash, *Amadeus* is simply one of the finest biographical dramas ever made. Reworked rather than simply adapted by Peter Shaffer from his own hit play, the film is as much about the mediocrity and envy of the composer Antonio Salieri as it is about the eccentric genius of his rival Mozart. There is, therefore, a sort of poetic justice in the fact that F Murray Abraham – for those with an interest in biographical minutiae, the "F" stands for Fahrid – pipped Tom Hulce for the best actor award. Returning to Prague (standing in for Vienna) for the first time since the Soviet invasion in 1968, director Milos Forman and his regular cinematographer Miroslav Ondricek revel in the beauty of the city, but credit must also go to Patrizia von Brandenstein for her superb sets and inspired choice of location interiors. As one would expect, the music is majestic, thanks largely to Neville Marriner's outstanding interpretation of everything from gypsy dances to *Don Giovanni*. Contains some swearing. 🖭

DVD

F Murray Abraham *Antonio Salieri* • Tom Hulce *Wolfgang Amadeus Mozart* • Elizabeth Berridge *Constanze Mozart* • Simon Callow *Emanuel Schikaneder* • Roy Dotrice *Leopold Mozart* • Christine Ebersole *Katerina Cavalieri* • Jeffrey Jones *Emperor Joseph II* • Charles Kay *Count Orsini-Rosenberg* ■ *Dir* Milos Forman • *Scr* Peter Shaffer, from his stage play

Les Amants du Pont-Neuf ★★ 15

Drama 1990 · Fr · Colour · 120mins

This is a classic example of the kind of flashy French film whose MTV-inspired visuals and sound-bite dialogue earned them the nickname *cinéma du look* for the emphasis on style over content. Writer/director Léos Carax strains to make a grand statement, but ends up trapped between his attempts to explore the social realities of France during the bicentenary of its Revolution, and his genius for opulent set pieces, like the water-skiing sequence with its glorious firework accompaniment. The scenes on Paris's oldest bridge between Juliette Binoche, an artist losing her sight, and injured fire-eater Denis Lavant are more often pretentious than touching, but the film is still worth a look. In French with English subtitles. Contains some violence and nudity. 🖭

Juliette Binoche *Michèle* • Denis Lavant *Alex* • Klaus-Michael Gruber *Hans* • Daniel Buain *Clochard's friend* • Marion Statens *Marion* • Chrichan Larson *Julien* • Paulette Berthonnier *Sailor* • Roger Berthonnier *Sailor* ■ *Dir/Scr* Léos Carax

Amarcord ★★★★★

Comedy drama 1973 · It · Colour · 123mins

Deftly tainting childhood memory with adult insight, Federico Fellini's dazzling blend of autobiography, fantasy and wickedly precise satire won an Oscar for best foreign film. Set in a seaside town not dissimilar to the director's native Rimini, *Amarcord* ("I remember") assembles a wonderful cast of characters, as human as they are grotesque, while mocking Mussolini's regime, Roman Catholicism and the prejudices and peculiarities of the parochial bourgeoisie. Touching, coarse and

U = SUITABLE FOR ALL   Uc = SUITABLE FOR ALL, ESPECIALLY FOR YOUNG CHILDREN (VIDEO ONLY)   PG = PARENTAL GUIDANCE

comic, this is a must for fans and, for those yet to be converted, a superb introduction to the work of a great artist. In Italian with English subtitles.

Puppela Maggio *Gradisca* • Magali Noel *Gradisca* • Bruno Zanin *Titta Biondi* • Armando Brancia *Aurelio Biondi* • Ciccio Ingrassia *Uncle Teo* • Nandino Orfei *Dud Coin* • Luigi Rossi *Lawyer* • Gianfilippo Carcano *Don Baravelli* ■ *Dir* Federico Fellini • *Scr* Federico Fellini, Tonino Guerra • *Cinematographer* Giuseppe Rotunno • *Art Director* Danilo Donati • *Costume Designer* Danilo Donati • *Music* Nino Rota

The Amateur ★★ 15

Spy thriller 1981 · Can · Colour · 106mins

When terrorists take over the US consulate in Munich and kill a female hostage, the girl's boyfriend – computer boffin John Savage – starts plotting revenge. Despite some well-filmed action scenes, the plotting in this espionage thriller is slow and never plausible, while the performances range from the adequate to the laughable. (Christopher Plummer's Czech security chief is a case in point.) This Euro-pudding was produced by Carolco, which hit pay dirt with the *Rambo* films before going bust. ▭

John Savage *Charles Heller* • Christopher Plummer *Professor Lakos* • Marthe Keller *Elisabeth* • Arthur Hill *Brewer* • Nicholas Campbell *Schraeger* • George Coe *Rutledge* • John Marley *Molton* • Jan Rubes *Kaplan* • Ed Lauter *Anderson* ■ *Dir* Charles Jarrott • *Scr* Robert Littell, Diana Maddox, from the novel by Robert Littell

Amateur ★★★★ 15

Drama 1994 · Fr/UK/US · Colour · 100mins

Given that the central characters are an ex-nun turned professional pornographer and a professional pornographer now suffering from amnesia, it doesn't take a genius to recognise that you are in the world of Hal Hartley, a place where humour is so deadpan it makes *Twin Peaks* look like a celebration of slapstick. Isabelle Huppert gives a marvellous performance of wide-eyed innocence that surely mocks the role in *The Lacemaker* that made her a star, while Martin Donovan retains that unique expression he saves for Hartley films, one that implies he can't quite fathom why everyone else finds his normal behaviour so eccentric. This is in a league (let alone a world) of its own. Contains violence, swearing and sex scenes. ▭

Isabelle Huppert *Isabelle* • Martin Donovan *Thomas* • Elina Lowensohn *Sofia* • Damian Young *Edward* • Chuck Montgomery *Jan* • David Simonds *Kurt* • Pamela Stewart *Officer Melville* ■ *Dir/Scr* Hal Hartley

Amazing Adventure ★★

Comedy 1936 · UK/US · BW · 70mins

An idle millionaire accepts a challenge to earn his living for a year without touching his own means. He takes a serious of humble jobs – greengrocer, chauffeur, salesman and so on – though he decides to lose the bet when his girlfriend's invalid sister needs an operation. A mildly enjoyable, lightweight and light-hearted British film, competently directed by Alfred Zeisler, with the main appeal (then and now) being the presence of imported star Cary Grant. Mary Brian is Grant's girl, while the supporting players include Ralph Richardson.

Cary Grant *Ernest Bliss* • Mary Brian *Frances* • Peter Gawthorne *Sir James Aldroyd* • Henry Kendall *Lord Honiton* • Leon M Lion *Dorrington* • John Turnbull *Masters* • Arthur Hardy *Crawley* • Iris Ashley *Clare* ■ *Dir* Alfred Zeisler • *Scr* from the novel *The Amazing Quest of Ernest Bliss* by E Phillips Oppenheim

The Amazing Captain Nemo ★ U

Fantasy adventure 1978 · US · Colour · 98mins

Seven writers (including Robert Bloch, who penned the original *Psycho* novel) without a worthwhile idea between them collaborated on the script for this ludicrous movie, edited down from a three-part TV series. José Ferrer brings nothing new to the part of the captain, who is awakened after a century in suspended animation and pitched into battle with a mad professor (Burgess Meredith) bent on world domination. Although Meredith had extensive experience of playing arch villains (having excelled as the Penguin in the *Batman* TV series), even he is upstaged by his robot crew. ▭

José Ferrer *Captain Nemo* • Burgess Meredith *Professor Waldo Cunningham* • Tom Hallick *Commander Tom Franklin* • Burr DeBenning *Lieutenant Jim Porter* • Lynda Day George *Kate* • Mel Ferrer *Dr Robert Cook* • Horst Buchholz *King Tibor* ■ *Dir* Alex March • *Scr* Norman Katkov, Preston Wood, Robert C Dennis, William Keys, Mann Rubin, Robert Bloch, Larry Alexander

The Amazing Colossal Man ★ PG

Science-fiction 1957 · US · BW · 79mins

After being exposed to plutonium radiation, Lieutenant Colonel Glen Langan grows ten feet taller per day and rampages through cardboard miniatures on the way to Las Vegas. Truly amazing, because this shoddy *Incredible Shrinking Man* in reverse is considered supremo schlock producer/director Bert I Gordon's best effort. And colossal, because that's exactly what it is – a colossal bore – although the giant syringe will raise hoots of derisive laughter. Sadly, little else will. The colonel was back a year later (played by Dean Parkin) in the even worse *War of the Colossal Beast*. ▭

Glen Langan [Glenn Langan] *Lieutenant Colonel Glenn Manning* • Cathy Downs *Carol Forrest* • William Hudson *Dr Paul Lindstrom* • James Seay *Colonel Hallock* • Larry Thor *Dr Eric Coulter* • Russ Bender *Richard Kingman* • Lyn Osborn *Sergeant Taylor* ■ *Dir* Bert I Gordon • *Scr* Bert I Gordon, Mark Hanna

The Amazing Dobermans ★★

Crime caper 1976 · US · Colour · 96mins

Fred Astaire, in one of his last films, plays a reformed con man who leads five Doberman pinschers plus one undercover treasury agent (James Franciscus) on the trail of racketeers. This was the final film in a series that began in 1972 with *The Doberman Gang* and continued with *The Daring Dobermans* the following year. All offer the sort of family entertainment Disney churned out in the sixties; by the seventies, however, they seemed strangely anachronistic. After this third outing, director Byron Ross Chudnow and his producer brother David ran out of dogs and disappeared.

Fred Astaire *Daniel Hughes* • James Franciscus *Lucky Vincent* • Barbara Eden *Justine Pirot* • Jack Carter *Solly Kramer* ■ *Dir* Byron Ross Chudnow • *Scr* Michael Kraike, William Goldstein, Richard Chapman, from a story by Michael Kraike, William Goldstein

The Amazing Dr Clitterhouse ★★★

Crime drama 1938 · US · BW · 87mins

Edward G Robinson has a ball in this ingenious gangster picture, co-written by John Huston and directed by Anatole Litvak. Robinson plays a psychiatrist whose study of the criminal mind turns him into a criminal himself, while Humphrey Bogart is the gang leader he studies, emulates and subsequently plans to murder. Morality is clearly very much to the fore, but this is also a first-rate entertainment. Huston later reunited the three stars in 1948 for his own *Key Largo*.

Edward G Robinson *Dr Clitterhouse* • Claire Trevor *Jo Keller* • Humphrey Bogart *Rocks Valentine* • Gale Page *Nurse Randolph* • Donald Crisp *Inspector Lane* • Allen Jenkins *Okay* • Thurston Hall *Grant* • Susan Hayward ■ *Dir* Anatole Litvak • *Scr* John Wesley, John Huston, from the play by Barre Lyndon

Amazing Grace and Chuck ★★ PG

Drama 1987 · US · Colour · 110mins

A little league baseball player convinces major athletes on both sides of the Iron Curtain to stop playing sports as a protest over the nuclear arms race in *Four Weddings* director Mike Newell's simple-minded Capra-esque fable. Gregory Peck, as the US President, lends his support to the peacenik effort in a well-intentioned but ultimately squirm-inducing treatise. Jamie Lee Curtis and Boston Celtics player Alex English contribute to the overall embarrassment. ▭

Jamie Lee Curtis *Lynn Taylor* • Alex English *Amazing Grace Smith* • Gregory Peck *President* • William L Petersen [William Petersen] *Russell* • Joshua Zuehlke *Chuck Murdock* • Dennis Lipscomb *Johnny B Goode* • Lee Richardson *Jeffries* ■ *Dir* Mike Newell • *Scr* David Field

The Amazing Mr Blunden ★★★ U

Fantasy mystery 1972 · UK · Colour · 98mins

In his later years, character actor Lionel Jeffries has enjoyed a secondary career as a sympathetic director of films made for and about young people, notably *The Railway Children*. This Antonia Barber period ghost story is perfectly suitable for adult viewing as well: there's much to enjoy, especially in the ripe performances from Laurence Naismith in the title role, and from the splendid Diana Dors as Mrs Wickens, gross and warty and every young child's nightmare. Good work, too, from character actors Dorothy Alison (Nurse Brace in *Reach for the Sky*) and James Villiers.

Laurence Naismith *Mr Blunden* • Lynne Frederick *Lucy Allen* • Garry Miller *Jamie Allen* • Dorothy Alison *Mrs Allen* • Diana Dors *Mrs Wickens* • James Villiers *Uncle Bertie* • Madeline Smith *Bella* • Rosalyn Landor *Sarah* ■ *Dir* Lionel Jeffries • *Scr* Lionel Jeffries, from the story *The Ghosts* by Antonia Barber

The Amazing Mr Williams ★★ U

Comedy drama 1939 · US · BW · 84mins

This late arrival in the screwball comedy-mystery cycle presents Melvyn Douglas as the over-conscientious detective whose workload gets in the way of his romance with long-suffering fiancée Joan Blondell. To keep one date, Douglas arrives with a murderer in tow, and later he is forced into drag to trap a lady killer, which is the most amazing he gets. Though Blondell and Douglas mesh beautifully on their third pairing, the story has a mechanical feel which is not helped by Alexander Hall's uninspired direction.

Melvyn Douglas *Kenny Williams* • Joan Blondell *Maxine Carroll* • Clarence Kolb *McGovern* • Ruth Donnelly *Effie* • Edward Brophy *Moseby* • Donald MacBride *Bixler* • Don Beddoe *Deever* • Jonathan Hale *Mayor* • John Wray *Stanley* ■ *Dir* Alexander Hall • *Scr* Dwight Taylor, Sy Bartlett, from a story by Sy Bartlett

The Amazing Mrs Holliday ★★

Musical adventure 1943 · US · BW · 97mins

The fact that Jean Renoir, the great French director exiled in the US, was considered to be the right man for this sentimental vehicle for the wholesome singing star Deanna Durbin is an example of the mysterious way in which Hollywood works. However, after four weeks work, Renoir decided to withdraw diplomatically on grounds of health. What remains is a superficial film that exploits the theme of war orphans for entertainment. Yet Durbin does well in the role of an American missionary in China who smuggles nine Chinese children back to the States.

Deanna Durbin *Ruth* • Edmond O'Brien *Tom* • Barry Fitzgerald *Timothy* • Arthur Treacher *Henderson* • Harry Davenport *Commodore* ■ *Dir* Bruce Manning • *Scr* Frank Ryan, John Jacoby, from a story by Boris Ingster, Leo Townsend

The Amazing Panda Adventure ★★ PG

Adventure 1995 · US · Colour · 80mins

The panda is cute and the Chinese countryside is gorgeous, but that's all that can be said in this family film's favour. Ryan Slater (Christian's brother) is incredibly annoying as a spoiled American boy who travels to China to visit his father on a panda reserve. Somewhat better is Yi Ding as the young Chinese girl he teams up with to protect a baby panda from poachers. What's really amazing about this long slog in the woods is that the movie has the gall to reuse the same camera shots and few bars of music repeatedly. Contains some violence and swearing. ▭

Stephen Lang *Dr Michael Tyler* • Ryan Slater *Ryan Tyler* • Yi Ding *Ling* • Wang Fei *Chu* ■

Dir Chris Cain [Christopher Cain] • *Scr* Jeff Rothberg, Laurice Elehwany, from a story by John Wilcox, Steven Alldredge

Amazon Women on the Moon ★★ 15

Comedy   1987 · US · Colour · 80mins

This collection of comedy sketches spoofing commercials, sexual mores, tabloid television and old movies misses more targets than it hits. However, it's the fabulous cast of cult icons (director Russ Meyer), camp starlets (Sybil Danning) and Hollywood veterans (Ralph Bellamy) that makes this follow-up to *Kentucky Fried Movie* such a delight for cinema trainspotters. Ed Begley Jr plays a naked Invisible Man in the funniest segment, while other highlights include the post-credits medical parody, *Sexual Madness*. ▭

Michelle Pfeiffer *Brenda* • Rosanna Arquette *Karen* • Steve Guttenberg *Jerry* • Steve Forrest *Captain Nelson* • Joey Travolta *Butch* • David Alan Grier *Don Simmons* • Archie Hahn *Harvey Pitnik* • Ed Begley Jr *Griffin* • Matt Adler *George* • Ralph Bellamy *Mr Gower* • Carrie Fisher *Mary Brown* • Sybil Danning • Russ Meyer ■ *Dir* Joe Dante, Carl Gottlieb, Peter Horton, John Landis, Robert K Weiss • *Scr* Michael Barrie, Jim Mulholland

The Ambassador ★★ 18

Political thriller   1984 · US · Colour · 95mins

Elmore Leonard's novel, *52 Pick-Up*, is oddly transposed to Israel where middle-eastern politics, PLO guerrillas and CIA murkiness are added to the cocktail of adultery and blackmail. It's an overstuffed package, though not without its benefits – most of which come in the shape of Robert Mitchum's cuckolded and blackmailed US ambassador. Rock Hudson plays a security expert in what turned out to be his final film. Two years later, John Frankenheimer adapted this Leonard novel, rather more faithfully. ▭

Robert Mitchum *Peter Hacker* • Ellen Burstyn *Alex Hacker* • Rock Hudson *Frank Stevenson* • Donald Pleasence *Eretz* • Fabio Testi *Mustapha Hashimi* ■ *Dir* J Lee Thompson • *Scr* Max Jack, from the novel *52 Pick-Up* by Elmore Leonard

The Ambassador's Daughter ★★★ U

Romantic comedy
1956 · US · Colour · 103mins

This old-fashioned comedy, with a plot so featherlight it's in danger of blowing away, is thoroughly enjoyable thanks to glamorous Paris locations, some witty lines and a polished cast that includes Myrna Loy. Written, produced and directed by Norman Krasna, it deals with the adventures that befall the daughter (Olivia de Havilland) of the ambassador (Edward Arnold) when she sets out to disprove visiting senator Adolphe Menjou's contention that the GIs stationed in the city constitute a moral danger. De Havilland is years too old for the role, but carries it off with stylish conviction; and John Forsythe supplies the romancing.

Olivia de Havilland *Joan* • John Forsythe *Danny* • Myrna Loy *Mrs Cartwright* • Adolphe Menjou *Senator Cartwright* • Tommy Noonan *Al* • Francis Lederer *Prince Nicholas Obelski* • Edward Arnold *Ambassador Fiske* ■ *Dir/Scr* Norman Krasna

Ambition ★ 15

Psychological drama
1991 · US · Colour · 94mins

Some years after his Oscar-winning role in *The Killing Fields* (1984), Haing S Ngor is the best thing in this rambling indulgence written by and starring Lou Diamond Phillips as a ruthless writer who teams up with a mass murderer. It's almost impossible to suspend disbelief in a wild story that looks as though it was initially intended for television. ▭

Lou Diamond Phillips *Mitchell* • Clancy Brown *Albert Merrick* • Cecilia Peck *Julie* • Richard Bradford *Jordan* • Willard Pugh *Freddie* • Grace Zabriskie *Mrs Merrick* • Katherine Armstrong *Roseanne* • JD Cullum [John David Cullum] *Jack* • Haing S Ngor *Tatay* ■ *Dir* Scott D Goldstein • *Scr* Lou Diamond Phillips

The Ambulance ★★★★ 15

Black comedy thriller
1990 · US · Colour · 91mins

A terrific urban paranoia thriller dosed with engaging black comedy, this marvellous B-movie gem from director Larry (*It's Alive*, *Q – the Winged Serpent*) Cohen is a fright delight. A vintage ambulance roams Manhattan looking for the stricken and injured, only to whisk them off to psychotic surgeon Eric Braeden for illegal medical research. Eric Roberts is the comic artist plunged into a medical nightmare when the girl he's trying to date disappears into thin air. Witty repartee, unpredictable plot twists, Cohen's fast and furious direction and some superb action set-pieces (such as Roberts's ride through the city streets strapped to a mobile stretcher) make this an instant remedy for boredom and one shock treatment worth undergoing. ▭

Eric Roberts *Josh Baker* • James Earl Jones *Lieutenant Spencer* • Red Buttons *Elias* • Megan Gallagher *Sandy Malloy* • Janine Turner *Cheryl* • Richard Bright *Detective* • Eric Braeden *Doctor* • Stan Lee *Stan Lee, Marvel comics editor* ■ *Dir/Scr* Larry Cohen

Ambush ★★★ U

Western   1949 · US · BW · 88mins

Robert Taylor took up making westerns regularly after this cavalry-versus-Indians story showed how steely-eyed and determined he looked in the saddle. Here he's the scout easily persuaded by glamorous Arlene Dahl to help the army look for her young sister who's been abducted by Apaches. The plot proves cumbersome at times, delving into marital strife at the fort (where Jean Hagen's unhappy wife is carrying on with Don Taylor's lieutenant), but the film scores in its graphic depiction of the Apaches as cunning and merciless enemies. Veteran director Sam Wood does a capable job on his final picture.

Robert Taylor (1) *Ward Kinsman* • John Hodiak *Capt Ben Lorrison* • Arlene Dahl *Ann Duverall* • Don Taylor *Lt Linus Delaney* • Jean Hagen *Martha Conovan* • Bruce Cowling *Tom Conovan* • Leon Ames *Maj Beverly* • John McIntire *Frank Holly* ■ *Dir* Sam Wood • *Scr* Marguerite Roberts, from a story by Luke Short

Ambush at Tomahawk Gap ★★

Western adventure
1953 · US · Colour · 72mins

Featuring John Hodiak and John Derek, this has a formula plot in which four ex-cons seek lost loot in a ghost town. There aren't enough sharp twists in the story or characterisations to shake it up, but the swoop of the Apaches is well done. A standard western, certainly, but with some surprising lumps in the usual porridge.

John Hodiak *McCord* • John Derek *The Kid* • David Brian *Egan* • Ray Teal *Doc* • Maria Elena Marques *Indian girl* • John Qualen *Jonas P Travis* • Otto Hulett *Stranton* ■ *Dir* Fred F Sears • *Scr* David Lang

Ambush Bay ★★

Second World War adventure
1966 · US · Colour · 109mins

A snare too far and too late for this stalled action movie about a group of US Marines trying to escape a Japanese-controlled island in the Philippines in 1944. Hugh O'Brian and Mickey Rooney at least look as though they mean it, but James Mitchum, son of Robert, gives a performance as lacklustre as that of the film.

Hugh O'Brian *First Sergeant Steve Corey* • Mickey Rooney *Sergeant Ernest Wartell* • James Mitchum *Private First Class James Grenier* • Peter Masterson *Sergeant William Maccone* • Harry Lauter *Corporal Alvin Ross* ■ *Dir* Ron Winston • *Scr* Marve Feinberg, Ib Melchior

Ambushed ★ 18

Action thriller   1998 · US · Colour · 95mins

A black cop (Courtney B Vance) and a racist juvenile (Jeremy Lelliott), the son of a murdered Klansman, find themselves on the run together after an ambush by police and white supremacists. Although his film is billed as an incisive look at the effects of racism and corruption in American society, director Ernest R Dickerson goes more for shock thrills and gunfire action, to the detriment of the story. As a result, there's a cynical edge to the climax's syrupy liberalism, while Andrew Miles's script is full of laboured clichés. Contains swearing and violence. ▭

Courtney B Vance *Jerry Robinson* • Jeremy Lelliott *Eric Natter* • Virginia Madsen *Lucy Monroe* • William Forsythe *Mike Organski* • David Keith *Deputy Lawrence* • Bill Nunn *Watts Fatboy* • Charles Hallahan *Sheriff Carter* ■ *Dir* Ernest R Dickerson • *Scr* Andrew Miles

The Ambushers ★★ PG

Spy spoof   1967 · US · Colour · 97mins

Dean Martin's third Matt Helm romp takes him to Mexico to rescue a kidnapped pilot (Janice Rule) who has lost her flying saucer, a top secret gizmo that's vital to western security. Kurt Kasznar is the comic cut-out villain – he brews beer for a living – while Senta Berger is the object of Martin's main romantic dalliance. The film is a mixture of James Bond-style gadgets, Martin's gimlet-eyed quips, studio sets and back-projected scenery, and the result is a very jaded movie indeed. ▭

Dean Martin *Matt Helm* • Senta Berger *Francesca* • Janice Rule *Sheila* • James Gregory *MacDonald* • Albert Salmi *Ortega* • Kurt Kasznar *Quintana* • Beverly Adams *Lovey Kravezit* ■ *Dir* Henry Levin • *Scr* Herbert Baker, from the novel by Donald Hamilton

Amelia Earhart: the Final Flight ★★ PG

Biographical drama
1994 · US · Colour · 90mins

A curious TV movie, this was conceived for the small screen but with an ambitious plot and a high-class cast that cry out for the big screen treatment. Diane Keaton was extremely keen to play pioneer American aviator Amelia Earhart, aiming to convey a detailed portrait of a complex woman, but the finished product is less than scintillating. There is something a shade flat about Keaton's portrayal, and Rutger Hauer strides around the place looking mean and moody, but contributing little of solid value. Passable, but it could have been so much more. Contains some swearing ▭

Diane Keaton *Amelia Earhart* • Bruce Dern *George Putnam* • Rutger Hauer *Fred Noonan* • Paul Guilfoyle *Paul Mantz* • Denis Arndt *Joseph Laughlin* • David Carpenter *Harry Manning* ■ *Dir* Yves Simoneau • *Scr* Anna Sandor, from the book *Amelia Earhart: a Biography* by Doris L Rich

America ★★★

Silent historical epic
1924 · US · BW · 135mins

Set during the American War of Independence, DW Griffith's failed attempt to repeat the success of *The Birth of a Nation* (1915) is little more than a ponderous patriotic pageant. Claims to historical accuracy are undermined by having George Washington play cupid to a bland pair of lovers (Neil Hamilton and Carol Dempster, Griffith's then-inamorata). But the battle scenes were filmed magnificently by a team of photographers headed by Billy Bitzer and Hendrik Sartov, demonstrating that Griffith had not lost his eye for the grandiose.

Neil Hamilton *Nathan Holden* • Erville Alderson *Justice Montague* • Carol Dempster *Nancy Montague* • Charles Emmett Mack *Charles Philip Edward Montague* • Lee Beggs *Samuel Adams* • John Dunton *John Hancock* • Arthur Donaldson *King George III* • Charles Bennett *William Pitt* • Downing Clarke *Lord Chamberlain* • Lionel Barrymore *Captain Walter Butler* ■ *Dir* DW Griffith • *Scr* John LE Pell, from a story by Robert W Chambers

America ★★

Satirical comedy 1986 · US · Colour · 83mins

In the seventies, Robert Downey – now probably better known as the father of troubled actor and sometime con Robert Downey Jr – delivered some enjoyably jaundiced swipes at American institutions. Alas, he lost his way with this amateurish send-up of cable culture. The story focuses on a cheap cable TV station that is propelled on to the international broadcasting stage when its signal gets mistakenly bounced off the Moon. The likes of Michael J Pollard and Richard Belzer give their all, but the satirical barbs are misdirected

U = SUITABLE FOR ALL   Uc = SUITABLE FOR ALL, ESPECIALLY FOR YOUNG CHILDREN (VIDEO ONLY)   PG = PARENTAL GUIDANCE

Zack Norman *Terrence Hackley* • Tammy Grimes *Joy Hackley* • Michael J Pollard *Bob Jolly* • Richard Belzer *Gypsy Beam* • Monroe Arnold *Floyd Praeger* • Liz Torres *Dolores Frantico* • Pablo Ferro *Hector Frantico* • David Kerman *Mr Management* • Robert Downey Jr ■ *Dir* Robert Downey • *Scr* Robert Downey, Sidney Davis

America, America ★★★ PG

Drama   1963 · US · Colour · 161mins

Writer/director Elia Kazan based this would-be epic on the experiences of his uncle, who fled a perilous existence within the Ottoman empire to start afresh in New York. Whether Stathis Giallelis has the wherewithal to surmount the problems encountered en route is open to debate. Such is the authenticity of everything around him, however, that the hesitancy of his performance almost becomes an advantage. Gene Callahan's turn-of-the-century designs thoroughly deserved their Oscar, while the supporting turns of Paul Mann, Linda Marsh and the wicked Lou Antonio are exemplary. 🎬

Stathis Giallelis *Stavros Topouzoglou* • Frank Wolff *Vartan Damadian* • Harry Davis *Isaac* • Elena Karam *Vasso* • Estelle Hemsley *Grandmother* • Gregory Rozakis *Hohanness Gardashian* • Lou Antonio *Abdul* • Salem Ludwig *Odysseus* ■ *Dir* Elia Kazan • *Scr* Elia Kazan, from his book

America 3000 ★ 15

Science-fiction comedy
1986 · US · Colour · 89mins

A typical example of the sub-standard exploitation product Cannon Films cranked out in the mid-eighties when the market for low-budget movies was at its highest. Essentially, this is an update of those chauvinistic all-female tribe movies of the fifties, with women in charge of the post-apocalypse society and treating men as slaves. Although billed as a comedy, most of it is taken so unenergetically and seriously that there's hardly any fun to be found. The few attempts there are at humour are remarkably heavy-handed, while redundant narration from a secondary character points to a last-ditch effort at saving the movie in the editing room. 🎬

Chuck Wagner *Korvis* • Laurene Landon *Vena* • Camilla Sparv *Rhea* • Victoria Barrett *Lakella* • William Wallace *Gruss* • Sue Giosa *Morha* • Galyn Gorg *Lynka* • Shai K Ophir *Lelz* ■ *Dir/ Scr* David Engelbach

American Beauty ★★★★★ 18

Black comedy   1999 · US · Colour · 116mins

British theatre director Sam Mendes makes an astonishing film debut with this sublime black comedy about midlife crises, starring Kevin Spacey and Annette Bening as a bored couple in suburban America. The sexually frustrated Bening begins an affair with estate agent Peter Gallagher; Spacey, meanwhile, fantasises about Mena Suvari, a bimbette friend of his daughter's. Their disparate needs result in a comic tragedy of misunderstanding that combines acute observations with side-splitting scenarios. A truly sublime film, that deservedly picked up a clutch of Oscars including best picture, best director and best actor. 🎬

Kevin Spacey *Lester Burnham* • Annette Bening *Carolyn Burnham* • Thora Birch *Jane Burnham* • Wes Bentley *Ricky Fitts* • Mena Suvari *Angela Hayes* • Peter Gallagher *Buddy Kane* • Allison Janney *Barbara Fitts* • Scott Bakula *Jim Olmeyer* • Sam Rabards *Jim Berkley* • Chris Cooper *Colonel Fitts* ■ *Dir* Sam Mendes • *Scr* Alan Ball

American Blue Note ★★★ 15

Comedy drama   1989 · US · Colour · 88mins

One would normally associate movies about jazz bands searching for the unique sound that will take them to the top with the forties, but this quaint little film shows that the struggle went on long into the rock 'n' roll era. Neatly capturing the atmosphere of dingy rehearsal rooms and smoky clubs, director Ralph Toporoff strikes the perfect balance between music and drama, and draws a performance of some sensitivity from Peter MacNicol (*Sophie's Choice*) as the bandleader given a year to make it big or settle for a lifetime of disappointment. Striking all the right notes, this is like *The Commitments* in a minor key. Contains some swearing. 🎬

Peter MacNicol *Jack* • Charlotte D'Amboise *Benita* • Carl Capotorto *Jerry* • Tim Guinee *Bobby* • Bill Christopher-Myers *Lee* • Jonathan Walker *Tommy* • Zohra Lampert *Louise* ■ *Dir* Ralph Toporoff • *Scr* Gilbert Girion, from a story by Ralph Toporoff

American Boyfriends ★★★ 15

Comedy drama   1989 · Can · Colour · 91mins

The stars and writer/director of the engagingly quirky *My American Cousin* are reunited for this witty sequel. This time, Canadian Margaret Langrick is grappling with adolescence as she heads back to the US to attend her cousin John Wildman's wedding. The two leads once again deliver pleasing performances and writer/director Sandy Wilson demonstrates a keen understanding of teenage rites, although the tone here is more melancholy than in the earlier film. 🎬

Margaret Langrick *Sandy Wilcox* • John Wildman *Butch Wilcox* • Jason Blicker *Marty Kaplan* • Liisa Repo-Martel *Julie La Belle* • Delia Brett *Lizzie* • Michelle Bardeaux *Thelma* • Troy Mallory *Spider* • Scott Anderson *Daryl* ■ *Dir/Scr* Sandy Wilson

American Buffalo ★★★ 15

Drama   1995 · US/UK · Colour · 83mins

Dustin Hoffman returns to the skid row of *Midnight Cowboy*'s Ratso Rizzo for this talkfest, scripted by David Mamet from his stage play and directed by Michael Corrente. Hoffman's an aggressive petty thief who decides to muscle in on the burglary plans of ghetto junk dealer Dennis Franz (of *NYPD Blue* fame), at the expense of Franz's teenage sidekick, Sean Nelson. The plot disappears into the Pinteresque pauses, but the dialogue has such power, the acting such conviction, you hang on every word however obscene it is. Contains swearing and some violence. 🎬

Dustin Hoffman *Teach* • Dennis Franz *Donny Dubrow* • Sean Nelson *Bobby* ■ *Dir* Michael Corrente • *Scr* David Mamet, from his play

An American Dream ★★★

Drama   1966 · US · Colour · 103mins

This Warner Bros adaptation of one of Norman Mailer's lesser novels is enjoyable enough to watch, despite the ham-fisted direction from actor Robert Gist (you'd recognise him from *Strangers on a Train* or *The Band Wagon*). It's all Technicolor gloss when it should be lean and mean, though it did receive an X certificate for its release in Britain as *See You in Hell, Darling*. Stuart Whitman is most unappealing as the talk-show host who murders his wife and tries to pass her death off as a suicide. Janet Leigh, as his nosey ex-girlfriend, is much better, and there's also good work from Barry Sullivan (as the unfortunate wife) and Lloyd Nolan. Contains some swearing

Stuart Whitman *Stephen Rojack* • Eleanor Parker *Deborah Kelly Rojack* • Janet Leigh *Cherry McMahon* • Barry Sullivan *Roberts* • Lloyd Nolan *Barney Kelly* • Murray Hamilton *Arthur Kabot* • JD Cannon *Sergeant Leznicki* • Susan Denberg *Ruta* ■ *Dir* Robert Gist • *Scr* Mann Rubin, from the novel by Norman Mailer

American Dreamer ★★★ PG

Comedy adventure
1984 · US · Colour · 105mins

Though similar to the Kathleen Turner/ Michael Douglas adventure *Romancing the Stone*, this sprightly comedy is enormously enjoyable from beginning to end. JoBeth Williams throws herself into the part of a bored housewife who bumps her head and regains consciousness convinced that she is the heroine of her own thrill-a-minute tale of romance and intrigue. Tom Conti perhaps overdoes the bemusement as the man she insists is her faithful sidekick, but Giancarlo Giannini looks suitably shifty as her supposed adversary. Simply enter into the spirit and have fun. 🎬

JoBeth Williams *Cathy Palmer/Rebecca Ryan* • Tom Conti *Alan McMann* • Giancarlo Giannini *Victor Marchand* • Coral Browne *Margaret McMann* • James Staley *Kevin Palmer* • CD Barnes [Christopher Daniel Barnes] *Kevin Palmer Jr* • Huckleberry Fox *Karl Palmer* • Pierre Santini *Klaus* ■ *Dir* Rick Rosenthal • *Scr* Jim Kouf, David Greenwalt, from a story by Ann Biderman

American Flyers ★★★ PG

Action drama   1985 · US · Colour · 107mins

Much more earthbound than its title suggests, this tale of rival cycling siblings competing in a Rocky Mountains endurance race is complicated by David Grant's antagonism towards his sports doctor older brother Kevin Costner. Other distractions in the plot are an anti-Soviet diversion and a terminal illness that Grant may be suffering from. Writer Steve Tesich achieved better results with his more successful *Breaking Away*, also on the cycling theme, for which he won an Oscar. Contains swearing and brief nudity. 🎬

Kevin Costner *Marcus Sommers* • David Grant [David Marshall Grant] *David Sommers* • Rae Dawn Chong *Sarah* • Alexandra Paul *Becky* • Luca Bercovici *Muzzin* • Robert Townsend *Jerome* • John Amos *Dr Conrad* • John Garber *Belov* • Janice Rule *Mrs Sommers* • Jennifer Grey *Leslie* ■ *Dir* John Badham • *Scr* Steve Tesich

The American Friend ★★★★ 15

Drama   1977 · W Ger/Fr · Colour · 120mins

There are enough *film noir* tricks and dark philosophical insights in this adaptation of Patricia Highsmith's novel *Ripley's Game* for German director Wim Wenders to turn a bleak road movie into a dazzling psychological thriller. Bruno Ganz is the simple Swiss picture framer who, believing he's dying from a blood disease, is lured into killing Mafia kingpins by shady loner Dennis Hopper. Soon the two men from opposite ends of the human spectrum bond, allowing Wenders to explore his existentialist subtext with exciting wit and enjoyable wisdom. Reminiscent of Alfred Hitchcock's *Strangers on a Train* (also based on a Highsmith novel), the film features cameos from directors Samuel Fuller and Nicholas Ray, to whom Wenders pays visual homage. 🎬

Dennis Hopper *Ripley* • Bruno Ganz *Jonathan Zimmermann* • Lisa Kreuzer *Marianne Zimmermann* • Gérard Blain *Raoul Minot* • Nicholas Ray *Derwatt* • Samuel Fuller *American mobster* • Peter Lilienthal *Marcangelo* • Daniel Schmid *Ingraham* ■ *Dir* Wim Wenders • *Scr* Wim Wenders, from the novel *Ripley's Game* by Patricia Highsmith • *Cinematographer* Robby Müller

American Friends ★★★ PG

Romantic drama   1991 · UK · Colour · 91mins

A delightful, understated personal project from Michael Palin, who stars as a romantically awkward Oxford don, allegedly based on his great-grandfather. The stuffy, frock-coated formality of Victorian varsity life is atmospherically conjured up by director Tristram Powell, making good use of an affecting, insightful script. There are some lovely performances, particularly from Trini Alvarado as Palin's bouncy teenage love interest and a consummate Connie Booth as her guardian. A feel-good movie that gently sways along. Contains nudity. 🎬

Michael Palin *Rev Francis Ashby* • Connie Booth *Miss Caroline Hartley* • Trini Alvarado *Miss Elinor Hartley* • Alfred Molina *Oliver Syme* • David Calder *Pollitt* • Simon Jones *Anderson* • Robert Eddison *Rushden* • Alun Armstrong *Dr Weeks* • Sheila Reid *Mrs Weeks* • Edward Rawle-Hicks *John Weeks* • Roger Lloyd Pack *Dr Butler* • Jonathan Firth *Cable* ■ *Dir* Tristram Powell • *Scr* Michael Palin, Tristram Powell

American Gigolo ★★★ 18

Erotic thriller   1980 · US · Colour · 111mins

Richard Gere romped his way to stardom in this glossy and controversial (for its time) story of a Los Angeles stud who services the bored wives of Beverly Hills. His detached view of life is threatened, however, when he gets caught up in murder and politics. This is probably still director Paul Schrader's biggest hit but, sadly, it hasn't dated well, and it now comes across as a beautifully designed but ultimately transparent walk on the wild side. Contains swearing, sex scenes and nudity. 🎬

Richard Gere *Julian Kay* • Lauren Hutton *Michelle Stratton* • Hector Elizondo *Detective Sunday* • Nina Van Pallandt *Anne* • Bill Duke

Leon Jaimes • Brian Davies *Charles Stratton* • Patti Carr *Judy Rheiman* • Tom Stewart *Mr Rheiman* ■ *Dir/Scr* Paul Schrader

American Gothic ★ 🔞

Horror   1987 · UK/Can · Colour · 88mins

An uneasy mix of old-fashioned off-screen splatter and humour that's supposed to be black (but ends up being merely ludicrous), this vaguely sick shocker is the worst movie from British-born horror director John Hough. Rod Steiger and Yvonne De Carlo are backwoods nutcases who live on a remote island with their three retarded adult children. The suspense refuses to build from the moment six campers arrive on the island and become victims of the monstrous brood right up until the laughable twist ending. A lousy melodrama, this was dogged by production difficulties that are apparent throughout. Among the tepid surprises and scenery chewing from Steiger and Z-movie staple Michael J Pollard, only De Carlo is good value.

Rod Steiger *Pa* • Yvonne De Carlo *Ma* • Sarah Torgov *Cynthia* • Michael J Pollard *Woody* • Fiona Hutchison *Lynn* • William Hootkins *Teddy* ■ *Dir* John Hough • *Scr* John Hough, Terry Lens, Bert Wetanson, Michael Vines

American Graffiti ★★★★★🅿🅶

Comedy drama 1973 · US · Colour · 107mins

A summer night in the lives of a group of small-town Californian teenagers following their graduation from high school in 1962 is brilliantly captured by director George Lucas in this classic coming-of-age saga that virtually invented juke-box nostalgia. Based on Lucas's own youthful exploits, the wall-to-wall golden oldie soundtrack is a perfect counterpoint to the sharp and tender comedy, engagingly played out by Richard Dreyfuss and Ronny (Ron) Howard, two of a number of future stars in the cast. Wonderfully evoking the feel and spirit of the era, this is one of those rare movies you live through rather than watch. Contains swearing. 🎬

Richard Dreyfuss *Curt Henderson* • Ronny Howard [Ron Howard] *Steve Bolander* • Paul LeMat *John Milner* • Charles Martin Smith *Terry Fields* • Cindy Williams *Laurie* • Candy Clark *Debbie* • Mackenzie Phillips *Carol* • Wolfman Jack *Disc Jockey* • Harrison Ford *Bob Falfa* • Bo Hopkins *Joe* • Manuel Padilla Jr *Carlos* ■ *Dir* George Lucas • *Scr* George Lucas, Gloria Katz, Willard Huyck

An American Guerrilla in the Philippines ★★🆄

Second World War action adventure
1950 · US · Colour · 103mins

Retitled *I Shall Return* for the UK market, this ultra-patriotic flag-waver is almost unwatchable today, save for the striking fifties Technicolor and the star presence of Tyrone Power, whose dramatic energy alone goes a long way to saving the Filipinos, as he shows them how to build radio stations and organise their resistance against the Japanese. Director Fritz Lang never seemed happy at 20th Century-Fox, and this movie, despite its pacey action sequences, is rather too slow, especially in the dialogue scenes between naval officer Power and French import Micheline Presle.

Tyrone Power *Ensign Chuck Palmer* • Micheline Presle *Jeanne Martinez* • Tom Ewell *Jim Mitchell* • Bob Patten *Lovejoy* • Tommy Cook *Miguel* • Juan Torena *Juan Martinez* • Jack Elam *Speaker* • Robert Barrat *General Douglas Macarthur* • Carleton Young *Colonel Phillips* ■ *Dir* Fritz Lang • *Scr* Lamar Trotti, from the novel by Ira Wolfert

American Heart ★★🄸🄵

Drama   1992 · US · Colour · 109mins

Top-class performances by Jeff Bridges and Edward Furlong add a glossy sheen to this two-dimensional material from Peter Silverman, a writer on the TV shows *Hill Street Blues* and *Moonlighting*. Bridges plays a no-hope drifter who, when released from prison, tries bonding with his alienated teenage son (Furlong), with tragic results. By turns poignant, hard-hitting and annoying, it's only the stars who make director Martin Bell's strained relationship movie work. 🎬

Jeff Bridges *Jack Kelson* • Edward Furlong *Nick Kelson* • Lucinda Jenny *Charlotte* • Don Harvey *Rainey* • Tracey Kapisky *Molly* • Shareen Mitchell *Diane* • Christian Frizzell *Rollie* • Maggie Welsh *Freddie* ■ *Dir* Martin Bell • *Scr* Peter Silverman, from a story by Martin Bell, Peter Silverman, Mary Ellen Mark

American History X ★★★★🔞

Drama   1998 · US · Colour and BW · 113mins

Director Tony Kaye's tough, powerful and uncompromising cautionary tale takes a brutal look at the depths of racial prejudice and the roots of violent hate crimes. Teenager Edward Furlong has been keeping the faith of his older brother Edward Norton, a neo-Nazi white supremacist recently released from jail. However, Norton has undergone a radical transformation through his friendship with a black prison inmate and the moral clarity of solitude. Told in colour with black-and-white flashbacks, Kaye's cutting-edge treatise is a shock to the system filled with unforgettable moments, seriously handled issues and superb acting by Norton, who was deservedly Oscar-nominated. Definitely not for the squeamish. Contains swearing, nudity and violence. 🎬 **DVD**

Edward Norton *Derek Vinyard* • Edward Furlong *Danny Vinyard* • Beverly D'Angelo *Doris Vinyard* • Jennifer Lien *Davina Vinyard* • Ethan Suplee *Seth* • Fairuza Balk *Stacey* • Avery Brooks *Dr Robert Sweeney* • Elliott Gould *Murray* ■ *Dir* Tony Kaye • *Scr* David McKenna

American Hot Wax ★★★

Biographical drama
1977 · US · Colour · 91mins

DJ Alan Freed was the man credited with introducing white American teenagers to the sounds that their parents considered the Devil's music. With Tim McIntire solid enough as "the Pied Piper of Rock 'n' Roll", this pleasing pop picture makes a fair fist of re-creating the era when clean-cut kids became rebels whose only cause was twisting the night away. You can forgive director Floyd Mutrux for calling on the services of Chuck Berry and Jerry Lee Lewis, but, while their music might be timeless, they are not, and their obvious age and over-polished performances detract from the aura of amateur authenticity.

Tim McIntire *Alan Freed* • Fran Drescher *Sheryl* • Jay Leno *Mookie* • Laraine Newman *Louise* • Jeff Altman *Lennie Richfield* • Moosie Drier *Artie Moress* • John Lehne *District Attorney Coleman* • Stewart Steinberg *Stone* ■ *Dir* Floyd Mutrux • *Scr* John Kaye, Art Linson, from a story by John Kaye

An American in Paris ★★★★🆄

Musical   1951 · US · Colour · 113mins

In its day, this was the archetypal glamorous MGM musical – a just winner of six Oscars, including best picture, collected by genius producer Arthur Freed, with a special Oscar presented to star Gene Kelly for advancing the art of choreography on screen. It still generally looks pretty good today, with marvellous Technicolored design, athletic dancing from Kelly and a superb Gershwin score, but some sequences have dated. The climactic 17-minute ballet on the theme of the French Impressionists looks a little precious and over-staged today. But much of the movie remains delightful – if you've never seen it, don't miss. 🎬

Gene Kelly *Jerry Mulligan* • Leslie Caron *Lise* • Oscar Levant *Adam Cook* • Georges Guetary *Henri Baurel* • Nina Foch *Milo Roberts* • Eugene Borden *George Mattieu* • Martha Bamattre *Mathilde Mattieu* ■ *Dir* Vincente Minnelli • *Scr* Alan Jay Lerner • *Cinematographer* John Alton, Alfred Gilks • *Art Director* Cedric Gibbons, Preston Ames • *Costume Designer* Walter Plunkett, Irene Sharaff

American Madness ★★★★🆄

Period drama   1932 · US · BW · 73mins

Frank Capra was a master of the "feel-good factor", long before the phrase was coined. Populist and simplistic it may be, but this dry-run for the financial dilemma of *It's a Wonderful Life* is one of his American fantasies, showing how the "little people" can save big institutions. All bank bosses are perhaps not as dynamic as Walter Huston's Thomas Dickson, and it's unlikely that small depositors would rally round in real life as they do here, but with Capra you take it on trust. 🎬

Walter Huston *Thomas Dickson* • Pat O'Brien *Matt* • Kay Johnson *Mrs Dickson* • Constance Cummings *Helen* • Gavin Gordon *Cluett* ■ *Dir* Frank Capra • *Scr* Robert Riskin

American Me ★★★🔞

Drama   1992 · US · Colour · 120mins

This vivid exploration of three generations of a Hispanic-American family growing up in violence-torn Los Angeles marks the directing debut of actor Edward James Olmos. Low self-esteem and abject poverty inspire the criminal behaviour of Santana, a Chicano underworld kingpin whom Olmos plays as an adult. Against the background of the 1943 Pachuco riots, Santana controls the streets from behind bars in this fact-based drama. Olmos gives the action a brutally violent and raw realism to create a companion piece to Taylor Hackford's 1993 film *Blood In Blood Out*.

Edward James Olmos *Santana* • William Forsythe *JD* • Pepe Serna *Mundo* • Danny De La Paz *Puppet* • Evelina Fernandez *Julie* •

Cary-Hiroyuki Tagawa *El Japo* • Daniel Villarreal *Little Puppet* ■ *Dir* Edward James Olmos • *Scr* Floyd Mutrux, Desmond Nakano, from a story by Floyd Mutrux, Desmond Nakano

American Ninja ★★🔞

Martial arts   1985 · US · Colour · 91mins

At one time Michael Dudikoff was seen as a successor to Chuck Norris, and was a big favourite on tape at the height of the eighties video boom. This was the one that made his name, and went on to spawn a fair few sequels, most of which didn't stray too far from the blueprint established here. Dudikoff, along with chum Steve James, are the martial arts experts who take time off from their GI duties to tackle evil drug dealers. There are some nice fight scenes, but the acting is about as mindless as the action sequences. 🎬

Michael Dudikoff *Joe* • Guich Koock *Hickock* • Judie Aronson *Patricia* • Steve James *Jackson* • Don Stewart *Ortega* • John LaMotta *Rinaldo* ■ *Dir* Sam Firstenberg • *Scr* Paul de Mielche, from a story by Avi Kleinberger, Gideon Amir

American Ninja 2: The Confrontation ★ 🔞

Martial arts   1987 · US · Colour · 85mins

More formulaic martial arts mayhem, with army buddies Michael Dudikoff and Steve James reuniting to fight even more black clad ninja hoods. Why more? Well, the bad guys have come up with a cloning machine to produce endless numbers of robotic martial arts experts, and are kidnapping American marines for their nasty experiments. The performances are as wooden as ever, but the real disappointment is in the clumsy direction of the all-important biffing scenes. 🎬

Michael Dudikoff *Joe* • Steve James *Jackson* • Larry Poindexter *Sergeant Charlie McDonald* • Gary Conway *Leo "The Lion" Burke* ■ *Dir* Sam Firstenberg • *Scr* Gary Conway, James Booth, from a story by Gary Conway, from characters created by Avi Kleinberger, Gideon Amir

American Ninja 3: Blood Hunt ★★🔞

Martial arts   1989 · US · Colour · 84mins

A marked improvement on the first sequel, with David Bradley proving to be a more than adequate replacement for Michael Dudikoff. In both the plot and the fighting, it's back to basics: as a young boy Bradley's father is murdered during a robbery at a martial arts contest; son swears revenge and grows up to be a ninja. Steve James, who appeared in the first two, pops up again, but this is Bradley's show, and the non-stop action will please genre fans. 🎬

David Bradley (2) *Sean* • Steve James *Curtis Jackson* • Marjoe Gortner *Cobra* • Michele Chan *Chan Lee* • Yehuda Efroni *Andreas* • Calvin Jung *Izumo* • Adrienne Pearce *Minister's secretary* • Evan J Klisser *Dexter* ■ *Dir* Cedric Sundstrom • *Scr* Cedric Sundstrom, from a story by Gary Conway, from characters created by Avi Kleinberger, Gideon Amir

American Perfekt ★★★ 15

Psychological road movie drama
1997 · US · Colour · 99mins

The one-letter mis-spelling in the title aims to convey the imperfections of the American Dream in this weird road movie. Amanda Plummer has a bizarre accident on her way to the town of Peachblossom. Rescued by Robert Forster, a doctor, she hitches a lift from David Thewlis who was responsible for the original crash. From there, the plot corkscrews into mania and murder as Plummer's sister Fairuza Balk tries to re-trace her movements. Terrific performances add colour and momentum, but Paul Chart's lacklustre direction blunts the point and slackens the tension. Contains swearing, violence and sexual situations.

Fairuza Balk *Alice Thomas* • Robert Forster *Dr Jake Gordon Nyman* • Amanda Plummer *Sandra Thomas* • Paul Sorvino *Sheriff Frank Noonan* • David Thewlis *Ernest Santini* • Geoffrey Lewis *Willy* • Chris Sarandon *Deputy Sheriff Sammy Goodall* • Joanna Gleason *Shirley Dutton* • Jay Patterson *Bernie* ■ *Dir* Paul Chart • *Scr* Paul Chart

American Pie ★★★★ 18

Comedy   1999 · US · Colour · 129mins

If you thought *Dumb and Dumber* or *There's Something about Mary* plumbed the depths of grossness, hold on to your lunch – you ain't seen nothing yet. This laughter-packed comedy about four teenage boys who pledge to lose their virginity before prom night has enough stomach-churning, moral majority-offending gags to satisfy the most demanding farce fans. Yet it also boasts some on-the-money performances from a hip young cast which includes Chris Klein, Mena Suvari, Tara Reid and Natasha Lyonne. Definitely not one to take granny to, but must-see fare for those not easily offended. Contains strong sexual references. ▭ *DVD*

Jason Biggs *Jim* • Chris Klein *Screenplay* • Natasha Lyonne *Jessica* • Thomas Ian Nicholas *Kevin* • Tara Reid *Vicky* • Mena Suvari *Heather* • Eugene Levy *Jim's dad* • Jennifer Coolidge *Stifler's mom* • Seann William Scott *Stifler* ■ *Dir* Paul Weitz • *Scr* Adam Herz

The American President ★★★★ 15

Romantic comedy
1995 · US · Colour · 109mins

A gleaming, witty and irresistible romantic comedy, this was one of several White House-based movies made in the wake of Bill Clinton's election. Michael Douglas is President Andrew Shepherd, recently widowed and the father of a young daughter, he is in need of female company at official functions. Annette Bening, an eco-lobbyist, fits the bill and, after he dances with her in public, the press go into speculative overdrive. Douglas walks and talks presidentially and his partner, Bening, is also terrific, combining a briefcase full of nineties politically correct attitudes with Lauren Bacall's slinky sophistication and Jean Arthur's bubbly wit. Perfect entertainment from Reiner that often harks back to the films of Frank Capra. Contains some swearing ▭

Michael Douglas *Andrew Shepherd* • Annette Bening *Sydney Ellen Wade* • Michael J Fox *Lewis Rothschild* • David Paymer *Leon Kodak* • Martin Sheen *AJ MacInerney* • Anna Deavere Smith *Robin McCall* • Samantha Mathis *Janie Basdin* • Richard Dreyfuss *Senator Rumson* • John Mahoney *Leo Solomon* • Shawna Waldron *Lucy Shepherd* ■ *Dir* Rob Reiner • *Scr* Aaron Sorkin

American Psycho ★★★ 18

Satirical horror
2000 · US/Can · Colour · 101mins

Director Mary Harron fought tooth and nail for Christian Bale to play Bret Easton Ellis's smooth yuppie killer (Leonardo DiCaprio was the studio's choice), and her decision is totally vindicated. Bale is brilliant, boasting a flawless American accent and an impressively sculptured physique as the wealthy, successful and psychotic Patrick Bateman. Despite the novel's skin-crawling reputation, most of the violence takes place off-screen. Moreover, the film's satirical swipes at the materialistic eighties provide laughs amid the carnage, as does Bale's cheesy, game-show host delivery of Bateman's eccentric cultural observations. Aside from a graphic threesome, this is an admirably restrained adaptation, although its cold, aloof tone somehow lessens the impact of Bateman's actions.

Christian Bale *Patrick Bateman* • Willem Dafoe *Donald Kimball* • Jared Leto *Paul Allen* • Reese Witherspoon *Evelyn Williams* • Samantha Mathis *Courtney Rawlinson* • Chloë Sevigny *Jean* • Justin Theroux *Timothy Bryce* • Josh Lucas *Craig McDermott* • Guinevere Turner *Elizabeth* ■ *Dir* Mary Harron • *Scr* Guinevere Turner, Mary Harron, from the novel by Bret Easton Ellis • *Music* John Cale

An American Romance ★★ U

Drama   1944 · US · Colour · 150mins

Two years in the preparatory shooting, a year in the editing and weighing in at a long two-and-a-half hours, this epic film by the great pioneering director of the American cinema, King Vidor, is impressive in both scale and technical expertise. Unfortunately, the tale of a European immigrant's rise to the top of industry is an extraordinarily dull affair, curiously devoid of drama or passion. The lead roles are played by the competent but uncharismatic Brian Donlevy and unknown Australian Ann Richards, neither of whose shoulders are big enough to shoulder the weight.

Brian Donlevy *Steve Dangos* • Ann Richards *Anna* • Walter Abel *Howard Clinton* • John Qualen *Anton Dubechek* ■ *Dir* King Vidor • *Scr* Herbert Dalmas, William Ludwig, from a story by King Vidor

American Roulette ★ 15

Political thriller   1988 · UK · Colour · 97mins

Tatty political thriller about a deposed Latin American president living in exile in London and the perils he faces, not just from a pursuing death squad, but also from the conflicting demands of the KGB and CIA. It's talky, over-padded and has more plot holes than the average London street. Andy Garcia stars, while Robert Stephens and Susannah York provide stronger support than the film merits. ▭

Andy Garcia *Carlos Quintas* • Kitty Aldridge *Kate* • Al Matthews *Morrisey* • Alfredo Michelsen *Ramon* • Robert Stephens *Screech* • Carola Palacios *Inez* • Christopher Rozycki *Vladimir* • Boris Isarov *Nickolai* • Susannah York ■ *Dir/Scr* Maurice Hatton

The American Soldier ★★★★ 15

Crime   1970 · W Ger · BW · 76mins

A homage to the visual style of American gangster movies, this is often regarded as the prototype Fassbinder film. Bordering on pastiche, it follows Vietnam veteran Karl Scheydt as he dispassionately assassinates a gypsy rent boy, a pornographer and his own girlfriend before being wiped out by corrupt cops. Fassbinder was clearly more interested in creating a mood and referencing such film-makers as Samuel Fuller and Rosa von Praunheim than storytelling or social analysis. Yet this brooding non-drama is still highly revelatory of the director's preoccupations: sex and violence are chillingly equated, while emotion and morality are dismissed as fatal flaws. In German with English subtitles. ▭

Karl Scheydt *Ricky* • Elga Sorbas *Rosa von Praunheim* • Jan George *Jan* • Margarethe von Trotta *Maid* • Hark Bohm *Doc* • Ingrid Caven *Singer* • Eva-Ingeborg Scholz *Ricky's mother* • Kurt Raab *Ricky's brother* • Rainer Werner Fassbinder *Franz Walsh* • Ulli Lommel *Gypsy* ■ *Dir/Scr* Rainer Werner Fassbinder

American Strays ★★★

Black comedy crime thriller
1996 · US · Colour · 93mins

Occupying the same surreal niche as the offbeat work of David Lynch, this is a mordantly funny and intensely bizarre study of the meaning of life – and death. It all revolves around Red's Desert Oasis diner, where surly waitress Jennifer Tilly dishes up the very average food and where strangers, travelling salesmen and drifters meet their destinies in anything but average ways. Working on a hyper-real emotional level rather than relying on logical plotting, this is a compelling – if perplexing – mystery. By turns violent and hilarious, it is always intriguing and often likeable.

Jennifer Tilly *Patty Mae* • Eric Roberts *Martin* • John Savage *Dwayne* • Luke Perry *Johnny* • Carol Kane *Helen* • Joe Viterelli *Gene* • James Russo *Harv* • Vonte Sweet *Mondo* • Sam Jones *Exterminator* ■ *Dir/Scr* Michael Covert

The American Success Company ★★

Black comedy drama
1979 · US · Colour · 90mins

Corporate drone Jeff Bridges gives the "success at any price" business world a taste of its own medicine in this offbeat black comedy about ethics and karma. Director William Richert's follow-up to *Winter Kills* is wildly uneven and caustically toned in a way some may find off-putting. When he does hit his targets, however, Richert really pulls no punches. Bianca Jagger's name in the cast list might give you some idea of just how quirky this American Dream satire is.

Jeff Bridges *Harry* • Belinda Bauer *Sarah* • Ned Beatty *Mr Elliot* • Steven Keats *Rick Duprez* • Bianca Jagger *Corinne* • John Glover

Ernst • Mascha Gonska *Greta* • Michael Durrell *Herman* ■ *Dir* William Richert • *Scr* William Richert, Larry Cohen, from a story by Larry Cohen • *Music* Maurice Jarre

An American Tail ★★★★ U

Animated fantasy 1986 · US · Colour · 77mins

Directed by ex-Disney animator Don Bluth and with Steven Spielberg as co-executive producer, this handsome feature has the look and feel of a master cartoonist at work. It's the story of the Mousekewitz family who leave 1880s Russia for the United States because they've heard that the country has no cats and every wall has a mousehole on it. This ties in nicely with Bluth's stunning animation and, in true Disney tradition, the Oscar-nominated song *Somewhere out There* is a major highlight. Children everywhere will love it.

Phillip Glasser *Fievel* • Dom DeLuise *Tiger* • Nehemiah Persoff *Papa Mousekewitz* • Erica Yohn *Mama Mousekewitz* • Madeline Kahn *Gussie Mausheimer* • Christopher Plummer *Henri* • Cathianne Blore *Bridget* ■ *Dir* Don Bluth • *Scr* Judy Freudberg, Tony Geiss, from a story by David Kirschner, Judy Freudberg, Tony Geiss • *Executive Producer* Steven Spielberg

An American Tail: Fievel Goes West ★★ U

Animated adventure
1991 · US · Colour · 71mins

Any parent still labouring under the delusion that you can plonk your kids down in front of any old cartoon and they'll be happy, might wish to observe them during this lacklustre feature following the further adventures of Fievel, the little Russian immigrant mouse. The storyline is practically nonexistent, the songs are unimaginative, and the animation could easily have been done in the forties, such is its flat traditionalism. That said, the voice-overs of James Stewart, John Cleese and Dom DeLuise are excellent and they alone earn this poor production its second star. ▭

Phillip Glasser *Fievel* • James Stewart *Wylie Burp* • Erica Yohn *Mama Mousekewitz* • John Cleese *Cat R Waul* • Dom DeLuise *Tiger* • Jon Lovitz *TR Chula* • Amy Irving *Miss Kitty* • Nehemiah Persoff *Papa Mousekewitz* • Cathy Cavadini *Tanya Mousekewitz* ■ *Dir* Phil Nibbelink, Simon Wells • *Scr* Flint Dille, from the story by Charles Swenson, from characters created by David Kirschner

An American Tragedy ★★★

Romantic melodrama
1931 · US · BW · 96mins

This is the first film version of Theodore Dreiser's novel about a social climber who murders his pregnant low-born sweetheart when a society girl makes eyes at him. The story is a classic critique of the American Dream, so Hollywood bravely imported the Soviet Union's greatest director and chief propagandist, Sergei Eisenstein, to write and direct it. But Paramount rejected his script and got Sternberg to take over, much to Dreiser's fury. Sternberg, of course, treats the story as pure melodrama and it's most notable for Sylvia Sidney's touching performance. Fascinating to compare it to the 1951 remake, *A Place in the Sun*.

12 15 18 = PASSED FOR PEOPLE OF THESE AGES AND OVER   ▭ = RELEASED ON VIDEO   *DVD* = RELEASED ON DVD

Phillips Holmes *Clyde Griffiths* • Sylvia Sidney *Roberta Alden* • Frances Dee *Sondra Finchley* • Irving Pichel *Orville Mason* • Frederick Burton *Samuel Griffiths* • Claire McDowell *Mrs Samuel Griffiths* ■ *Dir* Josef von Sternberg • *Scr* Samuel Hoffenstein, from the novel by Theodore Dreiser

An American Werewolf in London ★★★★ 18

Horror comedy 1981 · US · Colour · 92mins

Director John Landis (*The Blues Brothers*) pulls off the difficult trick of revitalising the horror genre while parodying it at the same time. Funny, scary and extremely gory – Griffin Dunne's gradual decomposition is an absolute hoot – this lycanthropic lampoon is also a splendid satire on British life, as seen through American eyes. The special effects and Rick Baker's Oscar-winning make-up established new trends in monster metamorphoses: after this revolutionary movie, no horror transformation was ever the same again. Contains swearing. ▭

David Naughton *David Kessler* • Jenny Agutter *Alex Price* • Griffin Dunne *Jack Goodman* • John Woodvine *Dr Hirsch* • Brian Glover *Chess player* • Rik Mayall *Second chess player* • David Schofield *Darts player* • Lila Kaye *Barmaid* ■ *Dir/Scr* John Landis • *Make-Up* Rick Baker

An American Werewolf in Paris ★★★ 15

Horror comedy
1997 · US/Lux/Fr/UK · Colour · 94mins

Made as a belated sequel to the classic *An American Werewolf in London*, director Anthony Waller's watered-down lycanthrope lampoon is frustratingly devoid of the edgy suspense, biting humour and keen visual style of that comedy horror landmark. Three American students go to Paris to bungee jump off the Eiffel Tower and find themselves inducted into a tortured twilight world of full-moon parties. Despite the presence of the lovely Julie Delpy as a werewolf whose mutating biorhythms are kept in check by an experimental serum, Waller's low-key special effects extravaganza lacks the well-chosen fairy-tale quality director John Landis infused into his original. Contains violence and swearing, with some sexual situations. ▭

Tom Everett Scott *Andy* • Julie Delpy *Sérafine* • Vince Vieluf *Brad* • Phil Buckman *Chris* • Julie Bowen *Amy* • Pierre Cosso *Claude* • Thierry Lhermitte *Dr Pigot* • Tom Novembre *Inspector Leduc* ■ *Dir* Anthony Waller • *Scr* Tim Burns, Tom Stern, Anthony Waller, from characters created by John Landis

American Yakuza ★★ 18

Action 1994 · US · Colour · 95mins

Hollywood is always on the lookout for new bad guys, which explains its recent fascination with the Yakuza gangs of Japan. In this hard-edged thriller, Viggo Mortensen is FBI man Nick Davis, dispatched to Los Angeles to infiltrate and dismantle the American arm of the Japanese underworld. Adopted by a powerful crime family, he rises through the ranks. Inevitably, however, he finds his loyalties strained between the forces of law and order, his new-found

colleagues in the Yakuza and the established Mafia, who don't take kindly to interlopers from the other side of the Pacific. ▭

Viggo Mortensen *Nick Davis* • Ryo Ishibashi • Michael Nouri • Robert Forster • Franklyn Ajaye ■ *Dir* Frank Cappello • *Scr* Max Strom, John Allen Nelson

American Yakuza 2: Back to Back ★★★ 18

Action 1996 · US · Colour · 87mins

Outside the presence of the excellent Ryo Ishibashi, this quirky and stylish take on what happens when Japanese gangsters run amok in California bears little resemblance to *American Yakuza* (1994). However, it does feature cult comic and *Police Academy* series regular Bobcat Goldthwait, in a brief but bonkers role as a bank-robbing nutcase. The mood is darkly hip as two Yakuza – one with an Elvis fixation, the other (Ishibashi) cool and dangerous – hit town on a revenge mission that is thwarted when Goldthwait takes them and a downbeat cop (Michael Rooker) hostage. Slick, explosive and surprisingly original. ▭

Michael Rooker *Bob Malone* • Ryo Ishibashi *Koji* • Danielle Harris *Chelsea* • John Laughlin *Dusseco* • Koh Takasugi *Hideo* • Tim Thomerson *Thomas* • Stephen Furst *Jimmy* • Vincent Schiavelli *Leonardo* • Bobcat Goldthwait *Psycho* ■ *Dir* Roger Nygard • *Scr* Roger Nygard, Lloyd Keith

Americana ★★★ 15

Drama 1981 · US · Colour · 86mins

Shot in 1973, when David Carradine and Barbara Hershey (then known as Seagull) were in the middle of their torrid affair, this allegory on faith, morality and the American Way lay in the vaults for several years before post-production was completed. Although some of its relevance had, by then, been lost, there is still much to admire in this portrait of Mid-West, small-town life. Carradine is laudably restrained as the Vietnam veteran who arouses the ire of the locals when he decides to recondition a neglected merry-go-round. As the director, his camera strategies are less inhibited, while Hershey's mute flittings are more irritating than enigmatic. ▭

David Carradine *Soldier* • Barbara Hershey *Girl* • Michael Greene *Garage man* • John Blyth Barrymore *Jack* • Greg Walker *Greg* ■ *Dir* David Carradine • *Scr* Richard Carr, David Carradine, from the novel *The Perfect Round* by Henry Morton Robinson

The Americanization of Emily ★★★★

Comedy drama 1964 · US · BW · 115mins

A surprisingly acerbic and adult comedy from the usually glossy MGM studio. Shot in black and white in England and written by the brilliant Paddy Chayefsky from the William Bradford Huie novel, it's quite simply magnificently cast. Julie Andrews, in arguably her finest screen role, stars as an English war widow given to comforting US servicemen. James Garner is the cynically-treated Yank coward to whom Julie ministers and the superb supporting players include a very funny James Coburn, obsessed Admiral Melvyn Douglas, plus the

venerable Joyce Grenfell, perfectly cast as Julie's mum. This is director Arthur Hiller's best work, and his own personal favourite. ▭

James Garner *Lt Cmdr Charles Madison* • Julie Andrews *Emily Barham* • Melvyn Douglas *Admiral William Jessup* • James Coburn *Lt Cmdr "Bus" Cummings* • Joyce Grenfell *Mrs Barham* • Liz Fraser *Sheila* • Edward Binns *Admiral Thomas Healy* • Keenan Wynn *Old Sailor* • William Windom *Capt Harry Spaulding* ■ *Dir* Arthur Hiller • *Scr* Paddy Chayefsky, from the novel by William Bradford Huie

The Americano ★★ PG

Western 1955 · US · Colour · 81mins

Glenn Ford goes down South America way and meets Frank Lovejoy and Cesar Romero in this amiable western variant, though the Brazilian setting that was a novelty when the film came out may well have lost its appeal by now. Chief points of interest (beyond Ford's attractive naturalistic style that would soon turn him into one of Hollywood's biggest international stars) are the co-starring Ursula Thiess, once married to Robert Taylor, and the fact that this mainstream effort was directed by schlock horror maestro William Castle, who also produced *Rosemary's Baby*. ▭

Glenn Ford *Sam Dent* • Frank Lovejoy *Bento Hermanny* • Cesar Romero *Manoel* • Ursula Thiess *Marianna Figuerido* • Abbe Lane *Teresa* • Rodolfo Hoyos Jr [Rodolfo Hoyos] *Christino* • Salvador Baguez *Captain Gonzales* • Tom Powers *Jim Rogers* ■ *Dir* William Castle • *Scr* Guy Trosper, from a story by Leslie T White

Americanski Blues ★★

Thriller 1993 · US · Colour · 91mins

This Moscow-set crime thriller is clearly a present sent to himself from Russia with love by actor/director Wayne Crawford. Appearing unfeasibly heroic at all times, he plays a workaholic cop whose first vacation in years goes horribly wrong when he is mistaken for the FBI agent intent on thwarting gangster Daniel Quinn's power-crazed schemes. Complete with a couple of local beauties on hand, this loud and increasingly ludicrous adventure evidently aspires to be a Bond movie. But, for all its shaking, this humourless hokum will stir no one. An English/Russian language film.

Wayne Crawford *Elmo Legrange* • Ashley Laurence *Gina* • Daniel Quinn *Franco* • William Katt *Dr Dell Martin* • Olga Vodin *Katerina* ■ *Dir* Wayne Crawford • *Scr* Carlos Brooks

Americathon ★★ PG

Comedy 1979 · US · Colour · 80mins

Despite a talented, eclectic cast and an inspired premise – the United States is now so poor it will have to stage a telethon to bail itself out – this has to go down as a major disappointment. Written by Neal Israel, the man who gave the world *Police Academy*, the film lacks the necessary focus and fails to make the most of its satirical promise. Still, there's fun to be had watching Mel Brooks regular Harvey Korman, future chat-show king Jay Leno and Elvis Costello. ▭

Peter Riegert *Eric* • Harvey Korman *Monty Rushmore* • Fred Willard *Vanderhoff* • Zane Buzby *Mouling Jackson* • Nancy Morgan *Lucy*

Beth • John Ritter *Chet Roosevelt* • Elvis Costello *Earl Manchester* • Jay Leno *Larry Miller* • Meat Loaf *Oklahoma Roy* ■ *Dir* Neal Israel • *Scr* Neal Israel, Michael Mislove, Monica Johnson, from a play by Peter Bergman, Philip Proctor

Le Amiche ★★★★

Drama 1955 · It · BW · 104mins

After enjoying success as a fashion designer in Rome, Eleonora Rossi Drago returns to her native Turin and becomes involved in the affairs of four of her upper-middle-class girlfriends. Adapted from a story by Cesare Pavese, the film manages to hold ten characters in almost flawless equilibrium, while simultaneously attending to their individuality and oscillating relationships. The elaborate social groupings and Michelangelo Antonioni's gift for positioning actors meaningfully against landscapes is well-demonstrated, notably in an extended afternoon beach sequence. A prizewinner at Venice, the film demonstrates that Antonioni's greatness was already in evidence before the famous *L'Avventura* five years later. An Italian language film.

Eleonora Rossi-Drago *Clelia* • Valentina Cortese *Nene* • Yvonne Furneaux *Momina De Stefani* • Gabriele Ferzetti *Lorenzo* • Franco Fabrizi *Cesare Pedoni, the architect* • Ettore Manni *Carlo* • Madeleine Fischer *Rosetta Savoni* • Anna Maria Pancani *Mariella* ■ *Dir* Michelangelo Antonioni • *Scr* Michelangelo Antonioni, Suso Cecchi D'Amico, Alba De Céspedes, from the story *Tra Donne Sole* by Cesare Pavese

La Amiga ★★★

Drama 1988 · Arg/W Ger · Colour · 110mins

Classical myth, Nazi Germany and the Argentinian junta come together in this rather unfocused drama from Jeanine Meerapfel. As children, Liv Ullmann and Cipe Lincovsky wanted to be actresses, but, while the latter gets to play Antigone on stage, the former takes on the role in real life as she becomes a prominent figure in the "Mothers of the Disappeared". The comparison between the two political situations is adequately made, but, for all her good intentions, Meerapfel doesn't always appear to be in control of her material. The performances, however, are strong and assured, with Ullmann's transformation from passivist to activist particularly impressive. In Spanish with English subtitles.

Liv Ullmann *Maria* • Cipe Lincovsky *Raquel* • Federico Luppi *Pancho* • Victor Laplace *Diego* • Harry Baer *Raquel's friend in Berlin* • Lito Cruz *Chief of Police Tito* • Greger Hansen *"Aleman"* • Nicolas Frei *Chief of Special Commandos* ■ *Dir* Jeanine Meerapfel • *Scr* Jeanine Meerapfel, Alcides Chiesa

Amistad ★★★ 15

Period courtroom drama
1997 · US · Colour · 148mins

In 1839, a shipload of slaves heading for America overpower their captors, killing all but two crew members needed to navigate them back to Africa. Betrayed, intercepted and charged with murder, the slaves' only hope for justice lies with the Abolitionist movement and an inexperienced lawyer. In this lengthy courtroom drama, director Steven Spielberg fails to ignite the same moral outrage his *Schindler's List* poignantly evoked, despite an all-star cast, an amazing debut by Djimon Hounsou (playing the slaves' leader) and moments of pure visual poetry. Although flawed, this chilling portrayal of outright racism further reveals Spielberg's skill as an expert film-maker unafraid of tackling heavy political issues. Contains violence, and some nudity and swearing. 🖵

Anthony Hopkins *John Quincy Adams* • Matthew McConaughey *Roger Baldwin* • Morgan Freeman *Theodore Joadson* • Djimon Hounsou *Sengbe Pieh, "Cinque"* • Nigel Hawthorne *Martin Van Buren* • David Paymer *Secretary Forsyth* • Pete Postlethwaite *Holabird* • Stellan Skarsgård *Tappan* • Anna Paquin *Queen Isabella* • Jeremy Northam *Judge Coglin* ■ *Dir* Steven Spielberg • *Scr* David Franzoni

Amityville II: the Possession ★★★ 18

Horror　　　1982 · US · Colour · 99mins

Much better overall than the dull first outing, this prequel to *The Amityville Horror* is given a neat European atmosphere by Italian director Damiano Damiani. It tells the full story of the vicious multiple murders that happened a year prior to the Lutz family's infamous tenancy-turned-bestselling book. Standard haunted-house shocks are combined with prowling camerawork for maximum involvement, while unusual imagery and spectacular make-up and special effects place this handsomely crafted effort a cut above normal exploitation fare. Contains swearing and violence 🖵 **DVD**

Burt Young *Anthony Montelli* • Rutanya Alda *Dolores Montelli* • James Olson *Father Adamsky* • Jack Magner *Sonny Montelli* • Diane Franklin *Patricia Montelli* • Andrew Prine *Father Tom* • Leonardo Cimino *Chancellor* • Danny Aiello *First removal man* ■ *Dir* Damiano Damiani • *Scr* Tommy Lee Wallace, from the book *Murder in Amityville* by Hans Holzer

Amityville III: the Demon ★★★ 15

Horror　　　1983 · US · Colour · 89mins

After exposing a pair of phoney spiritualists based in the notorious Long Island town, journalist Tony Roberts laughs at the legends and moves into the famous cursed Amityville house. Almost immediately, strange manifestations occur, resulting in unexplained deaths among his work mates and family, as he eventually uncovers a gateway to hell in the cellar. Decent special effects – originally in highly effective 3-D – dovetail neatly with director Richard Fleischer's generation of a creepy, claustrophobic atmosphere. 🖵

Tony Roberts *John Baxter* • Tess Harper *Nancy Baxter* • Robert Joy *Elliot West* • Candy Clark *Melanie* • John Beal *Harold Caswell* • Leona Dana *Emma Caswell* • John Harkins *Clifford Sanders* • Lori Loughlin *Susan Baxter* • Meg Ryan *Lisa* ■ *Dir* Richard Fleischer • *Scr* William Wales

Amityville Dollhouse ★★ 18

Horror　　　1996 · US · Colour · 92mins

This adds nothing new to the supernatural series which itself merely delivers bland and unremarkable horror homages to innumerable – and far better – efforts in the genre. The Martin family desert the big city rat race for a quiet life in the country. But, when they find a beautifully ornate doll house in their new home, and give it to their daughter, it begins exerting an evil influence over the family – the effects of which will come as little surprise to anyone familiar with the original haunted house shocker. 🖵

Robin Thomas *Bill Martin* • Starr Andreeff *Claire* • Allen Cutler *Todd Martin* • Rachel Duncan *Jessica Martin* ■ *Dir* Steve White • *Scr* Joshua Michael Stern

The Amityville Horror ★★ 15

Supernatural chiller
1979 · US · Colour · 113mins

Marginally watchable schlock horror based on Jay Anson's allegedly true bestseller about the Lutz family and their Long Island dream house possessed by ghostly squatters. Oozing black mud in the cellar and swarms of flies in the parlour signal a few harrowing moments as valiant James Brolin and Margot Kidder continually battle evil spirits. Meanwhile, an overblown religious subplot unfolds starring Rod Steiger. Although a baffling box-office hit, director Stuart Rosenberg's tepid chiller never matches the flesh-crawling terror contained in Anson's book. 🖵

James Brolin *George Lutz* • Margot Kidder *Kathleen Lutz* • Rod Steiger *Father Delaney* • Don Stroud *Father Bolen* • Natasha Ryan *Amy* • KC Martel *Greg* • Meeno Peluce *Matt* • Michael Sacks *Jeff* • Helen Shaver *Carolyn* ■ *Dir* Stuart Rosenberg • *Scr* Sandor Stern, from the book by Jay Anson

Amityville 1992: It's About Time ★★ 18

Horror　　　1992 · US · Colour · 91mins

They just wouldn't let it lie. Having given up on creepy houses, this dire direct-to-video offering in the long-running series puts all the blame on an antique clock that is the essence of pure evil or something. Anyway, said clock ends up with new owners and starts making them act in rather strange ways. Cult actor Dick Miller makes a brief appearance, but the acting on the whole is undistinguished, and even experienced genre director Tony Randel struggles with the stale formula. Contains violence, swearing and nudity. 🖵

Stephen Macht *Jacob Sterling* • Shawn Weatherly *Andrea* • Megan Ward *Lisa* • Damon Martin *Rusty* • Jonathan Penner *Leonard* • Nita Talbot *Mrs Wheeler* • Dean Cochran *Andy* • Dick Miller *Mr Andersen* ■ *Dir* Tony Randel • *Scr* Christopher DeFaria, Antonio Toro, from a story by John G Jones

Amityville: the Evil Escapes ★★ 18

Horror　　　1989 · US · Colour · 95mins

The title conjures up a wonderful image of a detached bungalow loping down the highways to find a new town to terrorise. But, sadly, no, it's only

the evil that moves to California, leaving the original house in peace in this third sequel in a series that had long lost its power to shock. Director Sandor Stern, who scripted the first film, delivers some neat set pieces, but he is hampered by the constraints of the TV movie format. 🖵

Patty Duke *Nancy Evans* • Jane Wyatt *Alice Leacock* • Norman Lloyd *Father Manfred* • Frederic Lehne [Fredric Lehne] *Father Kibbler* • Brandy Gold *Jessica Evans* • Aron Eisenberg *Brian Evans* • Geri Betzler *Amanda Evans* ■ *Dir/Scr* Sandor Stern

Amnesia ★★★★

Thriller　　　1994 · Chil · Colour · 90m

Set in an unspecified country (that is patently Chile around the time of the 1973 coup), this powerful political thriller flashes back to a desert concentration camp and catalogues the crimes of the brutal regime against the inmates. Switching back to the present, a sadistic sergeant becomes the victim of a revenge plot. Seen only by a few privileged festival audiences, but a big box-office hit in Chile, Gonzalo Justiniano's uncompromising picture was cited as one of the ten best films ever made in Chile in a poll specially commissioned for the centenary of cinema. In Spanish with English subtitles.

Julio Jung *Zuniga* • Pedro Vicuna *Ramirez* • Nelson Villagra *The Captain* • Jose Secall *Carrasco* ■ *Dir* Gonzalo Justiniano • *Scr* Gonzalo Justiniano, Gustavo Frias

Amnesia ★★

Thriller　　　1996 · US · Colour · 87mins

A small-town minister and his son's schoolteacher carry on an affair at a local motel. But unbeknownst to the adulterers, they are being watched by the unhinged motel manageress who develops a fixation on the minister. When he eventually suffers a bout of amnesia, she pounces and makes him her sex slave prisoner. A couple of twists, but few surprises, are on offer in an average conspiracy thriller which coasts by on the unfulfilled promise of titillation.

Ally Sheedy *Martha Keller* • John Savage *Tim Bishop* • Sally Kirkland *Charlene Hunt* • Nicholas Walker *Paul Keller* • Dara Tomanovich *Veronica Dow* • Vincent Berry *Edgar Keller* ■ *Dir* Kurt Voss • *Scr* David Henry, Chris Belden, Kurt Voss, from a story by David Henry, Chris Belden

Among Giants ★★★ 15

Romantic drama　1998 · UK · Colour · 94mins

It may not have quite the same feel-good comedy spin as his hit *The Full Monty*, but writer Simon Beaufoy's latest look at unemployed Sheffield friends making do buzzes along thanks to his excellent ear for dialogue and his unerring eye for gritty truthfulness. This time, amateur mountain climber Pete Postlethwaite gets the lads to help him paint pylons in the wilds of northern England against an impossible deadline, for cash in hand. When sexy Australian backpacker Rachel Griffiths joins the team, however, romantic competition starts a rift between Postlethwaite and his best mate James Thornton. This is an always engaging ensemble piece,

tightly held together by the mature insight of *This Life* director Sam Miller. Contains swearing, nudity and sexual situations. 🖵

Pete Postlethwaite *Ray* • Rachel Griffiths *Gerry* • James Thornton *Steve* • Lennie James *Shovel* • Andy Serkis *Bob* • Rob Jarvis *Weasel* • Alan Williams *Frank* ■ *Dir* Sam Miller • *Scr* Simon Beaufoy

Among the Living ★★★

Drama　　　1941 · US · BW · 69mins

Albert Dekker is an actor destined to be remembered for the gruesome manner of his death in 1968. (He died of asphyxiation, but his body was found covered in obscenities, with a hypodermic needle stuck in each arm.) In *Dr Cyclops* and this movie, however, he displayed a remarkable talent that only manifested itself on those rare occasions when he was aptly cast. As a demented twin let loose in a sophisticated world, he is both disturbed and disturbing; ultimately, however, he is let down by the poor production values. Today the film's most interesting elements are its two leading ladies: a nascent Susan Hayward and the tragedy-strewn Frances Farmer, both of whom are excellent.

Albert Dekker *John Raden/Paul Raden* • Susan Hayward *Millie Pickens* • Harry Carey *Dr Ben Saunders* • Frances Farmer *Elaine Raden* • Gordon Jones *Bill Oakley* • Jean Phillips *Peggy Nolan* • Maude Eburne *Mrs Pickens* • Frank M Thomas *Sheriff* ■ *Dir* Stuart Heisler • *Scr* Lester Cole, Garrett Fort, from a story by Brian Marlowe, Lester Cole

Amongst Friends ★★ 18

Crime drama　　1993 · US · Colour · 83mins

This junior league *Mean Streets* marks a promising enough debut from Rob Weiss, who also appears. The main twist here is that the surly teens are actually from nice wealthy families, who are nevertheless sucked into the world of teenage gangs. It's not long before they are in over their heads, leading to a bloody finale. The young leads (Joseph Lindsey, Patrick McGaw and Steve Parlavecchio) acquit themselves well, although the film is now more notable for providing an early screen role for Mira Sorvino. 🖵

Joseph Lindsey *Billy* • Patrick McGaw *Trevor* • Steve Parlavecchio *Andy* • Mira Sorvino *Laura* • Michael Artura *Michael* • Rob Weiss *Bobby* • Chris Santos *Young Andy* • Michael Leb *Young Trevor* • Frank Medrano *Vic* • Louis Lombardi *Eddie* ■ *Dir/Scr* Rob Weiss

El Amor Brujo ★★★

Drama　　　1986 · Sp · Colour · 100mins

The concluding part of the "flamenco trilogy" that began with *Blood Wedding* and *Carmen* may be the least successful of the three, but there is still much to admire in Carlos Saura's highly stylised production. His use of artifice is particularly strong, and he deploys only a handful of props to transform a deserted sound stage into a vibrant shanty town. Against this background, a tale of doomed gypsy romance unfolds, with a woman torn between the spirit of her dead husband and the attentions of his convicted murderer. Teo Escamilla's photography enhances both Gerardo

Vera's costume designs and Antonio Gades's choreography, but the non-musical passages are heavy-going. In Spanish with English subtitles.

Antonio Gades *Carmelo* • Cristina Hoyos *Candela* • Laura Del Sol *Lucia* • Juan Antonio Jimenez *José* • Emma Penella *Hechicer* • La Polaca *Pastora* • Gomez De Jerez *El Lobo* ■ *Dir* Carlos Saura • *Scr* Antonio Gades, Carlos Saura, from a ballet by Manuel De Falla • *Music* Manuel De Falla

L'Amore ★★★
Drama 1948 · It · BW · 79mins

This film, from director Roberto Rossellini, comprising two separate tales, is a paean to the breathtaking talents of Anna Magnani, whose presence is the reason for watching it. The first half, an adaptation of Jean Cocteau's famous one-woman stage monologue *The Human Voice*, has the star as an abandoned society lady attempting to reconcile herself with her lover on the telephone; in *The Miracle*, she is a devout peasant woman seduced by a man, played by Federico Fellini, who claims to be St Joseph. Rossellini's somewhat over-theatrical departure from neorealism was originally banned in New York on grounds of blasphemy. In Italian with English subtitles.

Anna Magnani *The woman/Nannina* • Federico Fellini *St Joseph* ■ *Dir* Roberto Rossellini • *Scr* Roberto Rossellini, Tullio Pinelli, from the play *La Voix Humaine* by Jean Cocteau and from a story by Federico Fellini

Amore! ★★
Romantic comedy
1993 · US · Colour · 93mins

A starry supporting cast enlivens this otherwise insubstantial slice of movie fluff. Jack Scalia plays a wealthy businessman who rather bizarrely changes his identity and attempts to make it in Hollywood. The plot is ludicrous and Scalia is unconvincing in the lead role, but a string of delightful supporting turns from old troupers such as George Hamilton, Katherine Helmond and Elliott Gould almost make it worthwhile.

Jack Scalia *Saul Schwartz* • Kathy Ireland *Taylor Christopher* • George Hamilton *Rudolfo Carbonera* • Norm Crosby • Elliott Gould • Katherine Helmond ■ *Dir/Scr* Lorenzo Doumani

L'Amore Molesto ★★★ 15
Thriller 1995 · It · Colour · 98mins

Italian stage star Anna Bonaiuto is directed by her longtime partner Mario Martone in this atmospheric Neapolitan thriller, which was adapted from the acclaimed novel by Elena Ferrante. Returning to investigate the suspicious death of her elderly mother, Bonaiuto is forced to reacquaint herself with the city of her birth and delve into some long suppressed emotions in order to make sense of the clues. Although there is much to intrigue in the Freudian flashbacks and the encounters with the dead woman's male friends, the film's main interest lies in Martone's neorealist portrait of Naples. In Italian with English subtitles. Contains some swearing, sex scenes and nudity.

Anna Bonaiuto *Delia* • Angela Luce *Amalia* • Carmela Pecoraro *Delia as a child* • Licia Maglietta *Young Amalia* • Gianni Cajafa *Uncle Filippo* • Anna Calato *Mrs De Riso* • Giovanni Viglietti *Nicola Polledro, "Caserta"* ■ *Dir* Mario Martone • *Scr* Mario Martone, from the novel by Elena Ferrante

The Amorous Adventures of Moll Flanders ★★
Comedy 1965 · UK · Colour · 132mins

After *Tom Jones* cleaned up at the box office and the Oscars, this rollicking 18th-century yarn was rushed into production, using the same composer (John Addison) with James Bond's director, Terence Young, at the helm. Adapted from the novel by Daniel Defoe, it's a Hollywood concoction that rarely comes off, while Kim Novak isn't anyone's idea of the English workhouse girl who sleeps her way to the gallows and beyond. Hugh Griffith, so memorable as Squire Western in *Tom Jones*, also makes an appearance here as Novak's prison governor.

Kim Novak *Moll Flanders* • Claire Ufland *Young Moll* • Richard Johnson *Jemmy* • Angela Lansbury *Lady Blystone* • Vittorio De Sica *The Count* • Leo McKern *Squint* • George Sanders *The banker* • Lilli Palmer *Dutchy* • Hugh Griffith *Prison governor* ■ *Dir* Terence Young • *Scr* Denis Cannan, Roland Kibbee, from the novel *Moll Flanders* by Daniel Defoe

The Amorous Milkman ★ 18
Comedy 1974 · UK · Colour · 86mins

Actor Derren Nesbitt's one and only venture behind the camera is as cheap and cheerful as any soft-core comedy made in the seventies. It clearly owes its inspiration to the Timothy Lea *Confessions* books, but it has none of the cheeky charm of the Robin Askwith films, even though Brendan Price does his best to rattle his pintas with panache. The most significant thing about this bawdy trash is what it says about the state of the British film industry at the time – it's sad that this was the only worthwhile work Diana Dors, Roy Kinnear and other talented actors could find. Contains sex scenes and nudity. ▣

Diana Dors *Rita* • Brendan Price *Davy* • Julie Ege *Diana* • Bill Fraser *Gerald* • Roy Kinnear *Sergeant* ■ *Dir* Derren Nesbitt • *Scr* Derren Nesbitt, from his story

The Amorous Prawn ★★★ U
Comedy 1962 · UK · BW · 91mins

Nice to find two of the stars of *Kind Hearts and Coronets* reteamed here, as Dennis Price plays the title role (the film was retitled *The Amorous Mr Prawn* in the US), and velvet-voiced Joan Greenwood plays the actual lead. Greenwood is the general's wife who converts his HQ into a hotel in his absence to fleece visiting Americans and raise some cash. Director Anthony Kimmins also wrote the original play and hasn't really opened it out too much for the cinema, wasting the talents of the hugely popular Ian Carmichael, who was the Hugh Grant of his day.

Joan Greenwood *Lady Fitzadam* • Cecil Parker *General Fitzadam* • Ian Carmichael *Corporal Sidney Green* • Robert Beatty *Larry Hoffman* • Dennis Price *Prawn* • Liz Fraser *Suzie Tidmarsh* • Reg Lye *Uncle Joe* • Bridget Armstrong *Biddy O'Hara* • Derek Nimmo *Willie*

Maltravers ■ *Dir* Anthony Kimmins • *Scr* Anthony Kimmins, Nicholas Phipps, from the play by Anthony Kimmins

Amos ★★★ PG
Drama 1985 · US · Colour · 90mins

Director Michael Tuchner's defection from the ailing UK feature film industry to the US made-for-TV circuit is Britain's artistic loss. A talented director with a warm heart, his work has embraced such superb dramas as *Adam* and *Summer of My German Soldier*. Here, Kirk Douglas finally gets to play an elderly version of Randle P McMurphy, the protagonist of *One Flew over the Cuckoo's Nest*. (Douglas memorably played the role on Broadway, but age forced him to relinquish the part to Jack Nicholson in the Oscar-winning 1975 film.) Elizabeth Montgomery (*Bewitched*) plays against type as the Nurse Ratched figure, and there's a welcome appearance by lovely veteran Dorothy McGuire. ▣

Kirk Douglas *Amos Lasher* • Elizabeth Montgomery *Daisy Daws* • Dorothy McGuire *Hester Farrell* • Pat Morita *Tommy Tanaka* • James Sloyan *Sheriff John Thomas* • Ray Walston *Johnny Kent* • Jerry Hausner *Sol Kessler* • Don Keefer *Winston Beard* ■ *Dir* Michael Tuchner • *Scr* Richard Kramer, from the novel by Stanley West

Amos & Andrew ★★ 15
Comedy 1993 · US · Colour · 90mins

This silly, offbeat comedy begins as a satire of racial stereotyping before stumbling clumsily into buddy-movie territory. Samuel L Jackson is a successful, politically active author who moves into a wealthy (and very white) neighbourhood. His narrow-minded neighbours assume he's a burglar, cops surround the house, and police chief Dabney Coleman comes up with a hair-brained scheme involving small-time criminal Nicolas Cage that might salvage the situation. Writer/director E Max Frye's interesting anti-racist angle is lost in a comic treatment of the issues that totally misses the mark. Despite engaging characterisations from the two stars, the escalating plot is just too much to swallow. ▣

Nicolas Cage *Amos Odell* • Samuel L Jackson *Andrew Sterling* • Michael Lerner *Phil Gillman* • Margaret Colin *Judy Gillman* • Dabney Coleman *Chief of Police Cecil Tolliver* • Brad Dourif *Officer Donnie Donaldson* • Chelcie Ross *Earl* ■ *Dir/Scr* E Max Frye

L'Amour Fou ★★★★
Drama 1968 · Fr · BW · 256mins

Of all the French New Wave directors, Jacques Rivette has remained the most uncompromising. He usually goes in for exceptionally long movies, and this one, shot in both 35mm and 16mm, was originally 256 minutes. (The producers, however, initially distributed it in a two-hour version that the director disowned.) Like many of Rivette's pictures, it is about the art of creation: in this case, a theatre group preparing to stage Racine's *Andromaque* while being filmed by a TV team. There is a fascinating interplay between the characters and the play itself, but Rivette's austere style and cerebral preoccupations require some

effort on the part of the viewer. A French language film.

Jean-Pierre Kalfon *Sébastien* • Bulle Ogier *Claire* • André Labarthe [AndréS Labarthe] *André* • Josée Destoops *Marta* ■ *Dir* Jacques Rivette • *Scr* Jacques Rivette, Marilu Tonilini

L'Amour par Terre ★★
Drama 1984 · Fr · Colour · 125mins

A decade after *Celine and Julie Go Boating*, Jacques Rivette returned to similar territory – two women forced to play various roles in a strange house – but with less rewarding results. The director's interest in theatre and literature provides some pleasure (Geraldine Chaplin and Jane Birkin share their names with the Brontë sisters, Charlotte and Emily), as does the chateau setting, but the game-playing becomes tedious after a while. The film is short by Rivette's standards (a mere 125 minutes). In French with English subtitles.

Geraldine Chaplin *Charlotte* • Jane Birkin *Emily* • André Dussollier *Paul* • Jean-Pierre Kalfon *Clément Roquemaure* • Facundo Bo *Silvano* • Laszlo Szabo *Virgil* • Sandra Montaigu *Eléonore* • Isabelle Linnartz *Béatrice* ■ *Dir* Jacques Rivette • *Scr* Pascal Bonitzer, Marilù Parolini, Jacques Rivette, Suzanne Schiffman

The Amsterdam Kill ★★ 15
Thriller 1978 · HK · Colour · 86mins

Robert Mitchum sleepwalks through this Hong Kong-financed thriller about a modern opium war fought out in the Far East and Amsterdam. As a former Drug Enforcement Agency man who was fired for corruption, Mitchum is wholly convincing even when the plot is underdeveloped. Co-stars Bradford Dillman and Leslie Nielsen are given little to work with – beyond counting corpses – and the Chinese actors, stars on their home turf, seem frankly amateurish. Boringly predictable, except for Mitchum. ▣

Robert Mitchum *Quinlan* • Bradford Dillman *Odums* • Richard Egan *Ridgeway* • Leslie Nielsen *Riley Knight* • Keye Luke *Chung Wei* • eorge Kee Cheung [George Cheung] *Jimmy Wong* • Chen Hsing *Assassin* ■ *Dir* Robert Clouse • *Scr* Robert Clouse, Gregory Leifer

Amsterdamned ★★★ 18
Action thriller 1988 · Neth · Colour · 113mins

A maniac frogman, horribly scarred after exposure to toxic chemicals during a botched salvage operation, is haunting Amsterdam's canals to take revenge on the uncaring society he's judged responsible for his plight. The grim opening (a suspended body trailing blood over a glass-topped boat) sets the tone for Dick Maas's thriller, an unusual mix of police procedural and American stalk-and-slash conventions. Maas – Holland's answer to John Carpenter – both scripts and scores the film, but it's his efficient, no-nonsense direction and humorously etched character studies that set this nuanced Dutch treat apart. Dutch dialogue dubbed into English. ▣

Huub Stapel *Eric Visser* • Monique van de Ven *Laura* • Serge-Henri Valcke *Vermeer* • Tanneke Hartsuiker *Potter* • Wim Zomer *John* • Hidde Maas *Martin* • Lou Landré *Chief* ■ *Dir/Scr* Dick Maas • *Music* Dick Maas

U = SUITABLE FOR ALL   Uc = SUITABLE FOR ALL, ESPECIALLY FOR YOUNG CHILDREN (VIDEO ONLY)   PG = PARENTAL GUIDANCE

Amy ★★ 🅄

Period drama 1981 · US · Colour · 90mins

Disney's inability to resist coating the pill undermines this otherwise sincere insight into the educational needs of sight- and hearing-impaired children. Still grieving after the death of her deaf son, Jenny Agutter leaves domineering husband Chris Robinson to work with doctor Barry Newman at a special school, even though such independence was hardly expected of women in the early 1900s. Although aimed at younger viewers, Vincent McEveety's carefully made, but over-earnest drama might have benefitted from some of the emotional intensity of either *Mandy* or *The Miracle Worker*. Certainly it would have been no worse without its upbeat football finale. 🖭

Jenny Agutter *Amy Medford* • Barry Newman *Dr Ben Corcoran* • Kathleen Nolan *Helen Gibbs* • Chris Robinson *Elliot Medford* • Lou Fant *Lyle Ferguson* • Margaret O'Brien *Hazel Johnson* • Nanette Fabray *Malvina* • Otto Rechenberg *Henry Watkins* ■ *Dir* Vincent McEveety • *Scr* Noreen Stone

The Amy Fisher Story ★★

Crime drama based on a true story
1993 · US · Colour · 90mins

Amy Fisher was a *cause célèbre* in the early nineties and her case achieved a level of public notoriety that was unusual considering no one was actually killed. Fisher shot the wife of her older lover and became prime front-page fodder. The scandal had repercussions: on three different US TV networks, three different made-for-TV movies of the case premiered within six days of each other. This one is by far the best of the batch, with Drew Barrymore as the sexpot Amy, and Anthony John Denison as her lover, one Joey Buttafuoco.

Drew Barrymore *Amy Fisher* • Anthony John Denison *Joey Buttafuoco* • Laurie Paton *Mary Jo Buttafuoco* • Harley Jane Kozak *Amy Pagnozzi* • Linda Darlow *Roseann Fisher* • Ken Pogue *Elliot Fisher* ■ *Dir* Andy Tennant • *Scr* Janet Brownell

Amy Foster ★★ 🅸🅵

Romantic melodrama
1997 · UK/US/Fr · Colour · 108mins

Also known as *Swept from the Sea*, this is a wildly misjudged adaptation of the haunting Joseph Conrad novel. Director Beeban Kidron goes for the overblown romantic (and very heavy-handed) touch in this melodramatic tale of silent Rachel Weisz who falls in love with Vincent Perez, the sole survivor of a shipwreck. However, no amount of craggy scenery, violent storms and mournful looks from the duo can disguise the fact that Kidron has delivered a plodding tragedy that fails to move. Contains some swearing and violence, and a brief sex scene. 🖭 **DVD**

Rachel Weisz *Amy Foster* • Vincent Perez *Yanko* • Ian McKellen *Dr James Kennedy* • Kathy Bates *Miss Swaffer* • Joss Ackland *Mr Swaffer* • Tony Haygarth *Mr Smith* • Fiona Victory *Mrs Smith* • Tom Bell *Isaac Foster* • Zoë Wanamaker *Mary Foster* ■ *Dir* Beeban Kidron • *Scr* Tim Willocks, from the story by Joseph Conrad

Anaconda ★★★ 🅸🅵

Horror adventure 1997 · US · Colour · 85mins

A low-brow fifties monster movie concept is given a blockbuster makeover in director Luis Llosa's cheerful slither-fest. With predictable stupidity, the film shows how a documentary film crew sailing up the Amazon gets used as snake-bait by deranged explorer Jon Voight in his obsessive quest to capture a legendary, 40-foot anaconda. As the competent cast fight a computer-generated garden hose with fangs, and as Voight's performance goes into camp overdrive, the scaly scares shrink while the screams of laughter increase. Daft fun. Contains swearing and violence. 🖭 **DVD**

Jennifer Lopez *Terri Flores* • Ice Cube *Danny Rich* • Jon Voight *Paul Sarone* • Eric Stoltz *Dr Steven Cale* • Jonathan Hyde *Warren Westridge* • Owen Wilson *Gary Dixon* • Kari Wuhrer *Denise Kalberg* • Vincent Castellanos *Mateo* • Danny Trejo *Poacher* ■ *Dir* Luis Llosa • *Scr* Hans Bauer, Jim Cash, Jack Epps Jr

Analyze This ★★★★ 🅸🅵

Crime comedy 1999 · US · Colour · 99mins

"Honey, I shrunk the godfather!" Robert De Niro gives one of his best performances in a feel-good Mafia comedy from *Groundhog Day* director Harold Ramis. De Niro is a Manhattan mob boss whose stressful lifestyle causes him to seek undercover therapy from psychiatrist Billy Crystal. The laughs come thick and fast, with De Niro's deadpan responses to the Freudian dissections, while the soon-to-be-married Crystal becomes ever more entangled in the "family" business. Although aided by a clever script packed with fresh repartee, *GoodFellas* gags and hilarious moments of joyous farce, Ramis's skilled comic timing mainly lets the humour evolve from the two dynamic central turns for memorably mirthful impact. Contains swearing and sexual references. 🖭 **DVD**

Billy Crystal *Ben Sobol* • Robert De Niro *Paul Vitti* • Lisa Kudrow *Laura MacNamara* • Joe Viterelli *Jelly* • Chazz Palminteri *Primo Sindone* • Bill Macy *Isaac Sobel* • Molly Shannon *Caroline* • Max Casella *Nicky Shivers* ■ *Dir* Harold Ramis • *Scr* Peter Tolan, Harold Ramis, Kenneth Lonergan, from a story by Kenneth Lonergan, Peter Tolan

Anari ★★★ 🅄

Drama 1959 · Ind · BW · 156mins

Ever the underdog, Raj Kapoor takes the lead in this outspoken attack on capitalism and medical irresponsibility. It focuses on the plight of a painter, who is accused of murdering his landlady, even though a medicine produced by the company he works for is really to blame. Nutan is charming as the company owner's niece who poses as her own maid to prevent Raj from discovering the extent of her wealth. But the emphasis is clearly as much on the social issues as on escapism, prompting many critics to suggest that Kapoor had as much to do with the direction as Hrishikesh Mukherjee. In Hindi and Urdu with English subtitles.. 🖭

Raj Kapoor *Raj* • Nutan *Aarti* • Lalita Pawar *Mrs D'Sa* • Motilal *Ramnath* ■ *Dir* Hrishikesh Mukherjee • *Scr* Ander Raj Anand

Anastasia ★★★★ 🅄

Period drama 1956 · US · Colour · 100mins

An exceptional performance from Ingrid Bergman won her an Oscar in this gripping tale of a refugee passed off as the Romanov Grand Duchess by cunning Yul Brynner. A clever, insightful script puts flesh on the bones of an already intriguing mystery, but it is Bergman who makes this one a minor classic. She portrays vulnerability and dignity in equal measure with a rare screen intelligence, and Helen Hayes is also very fine as Anastasia's grandmother. 🖭

Ingrid Bergman *Anastasia* • Yul Brynner *Bounine* • Helen Hayes *Empress* • Akim Tamiroff *Chernov* • Martita Hunt *Baroness Von Livenbaum* • Felix Aylmer *Russian Chamberlain* • Sacha Pitoeff *Petrovin* • Ivan Desny *Prince Paul* • Natalie Schafer *Lissenskaia* • Gregoire Gromoff *Stepan* • Karel Stepanek *Vlados* ■ *Dir* Anatole Litvak • *Scr* Arthur Laurents, from the play by Marcelle Maurette, adapted by Guy Bolton

Anastasia ★★★ 🅄

Animated fantasy 1997 · US · Colour · 90mins

History buffs will despair at the liberal use of fiction in this animated adventure set around the time of the Russian Revolution. Little girls, however, will be enchanted by the tale of Anastasia, the Tsar's young daughter and the only one to survive after the evil Rasputin puts a curse on her family. Ten years later, orphaned and without any recollection of her past, she meets her grandmother and discovers her heritage – but Rasputin is lurking in the wings... 🖭

Meg Ryan *Anastasia* • John Cusack *Dimitri* • Kelsey Grammer *Vladimir* • Christopher Lloyd *Rasputin* • Hank Azaria *Bartok* • Bernadette Peters *Sophie* • Kirsten Dunst *Young Anastasia* • Angela Lansbury *Dowager Empress Marie* ■ *Dir* Don Bluth, Gary Goldman • *Scr* Susan Gauthier, Bruce Graham, Bob Tzudiker, Noni White

Anastasia: the Mystery of Anna ★★ 🅿🅶

Period drama 1986 · US · Colour · 187mins

Directed by Marvin J Chomsky, who made a far superior TV movie about Ted Bundy called *The Deliberate Stranger*, this umpteenth version of the Anastasia tale was originally a TV mini-series. Amy Irving (*Carrie*) is out of her depth as the mysterious woman who claims to be the presumed-dead daughter of the Russian Tsar, but Rex Harrison, Edward Fox, Olivia de Havilland and Omar Sharif inject some much needed class. This edited-down version is slightly jarring, but it's still worth a look for all fans of period romps. (The costumes are particularly magnificent.) 🖭

Amy Irving *Anna Anderson* • Rex Harrison *Grand Duke Cyril Romanov* • Olivia de Havilland *Dowager Empress Maria* • Omar Sharif *Tsar Nicholas II* • Claire Bloom *Tsarina Alexandra* • Elke Sommer *Isabel Von Hohenstauffen* • Edward Fox *Dr Hauser* • Angela Pleasence *Madwoman* • Julian Glover *Kobylinski* • Tim McInnerny *Yourkov* • Christian Bale *Alexis* ■ *Dir* Marvin J Chomsky • *Scr* James Goldman, from the non-fiction book *Anastasia: The Riddle of Anna Anderson* by Peter Kurth • *Costume Designer* Jane Robinson

Anatomy of a Murder ★★★★★ 🅸🅵

Classic courtroom drama
1959 · US · BW · 153mins

Probably the greatest courtroom drama ever made, this stars the great James Stewart in one of his finest screen performances. Controversial in its day for using words like "panties" and "spermatogenesis", its story about a rape and murder is based on a novel by Robert Traver, the pen name of retired judge John D Voelker. As the country hick lawyer (and jazz fan) Paul Biegler, Stewart is drawn into the case, suckered by it, and comes up against big-town prosecutor George C Scott. Their courtroom duels and stunts are mesmerising as they show us America leaving its traditional old-time moral values behind: this is the America not of apple pie but of *Lolita*. That Stewart's character loves jazz was a neat excuse to bring in the great Duke Ellington to write the soundtrack, and Ellington even appears in one scene in a club, playing a duet with Stewart. 🖭

James Stewart *Paul Biegler* • Lee Remick *Laura Manion* • Ben Gazzara *Lt Frederick Manion* • Arthur O'Connell *Parnell McCarthy* • Eve Arden *Maida* • George C Scott *Claude Dancer* • Kathryn Grant *Mary Pilant* • Joseph N Welch *Judge Weaver* • Duke Ellington *Pie-Eye* ■ *Dir* Otto Preminger • *Scr* Wendell Mayes, from the novel by Robert Traver [John D Voelker]

Anatomy of an Illness ★★★

Drama based on a true story
1984 · US · Colour · 98mins

Ed Asner, whose career has probably suffered as a consequence of his humanitarian politics, must have savoured the delicious irony of being cast in this TV movie as a determined humanitarian. Bringing on board all that rugged decency and gruff sensitivity so familiar from *Lou Grant*, Asner magnetically interprets the real-life Norman Cousins, a man hellbent on overcoming a degenerative spinal condition.

Edward Asner [Ed Asner] *Norman Cousins* • Eli Wallach *Dr William Hitzig* • Millie Perkins *Ellen Cousins* • David Ogden Stiers *Cleveland Amory* • Lelia Goldoni *Mrs Farelli* ■ *Dir* Richard T Heffron • *Scr* Lawrence Roman, from the book by Norman Cousins

Anchor Zone ★★

Science-fiction adventure
1994 · Can · Colour · 82mins

An obscure sci-fi thriller that is reminiscent of 1997's critically acclaimed futuristic chiller *Gattaca*. Nicole Stoffman plays a member of a privileged young elite trained into the ways of the sinister corporation that controls all aspects of life in the near future. However, in time-honoured fashion, she begins to rebel against her regimented life, and falls in with a group of young runaways, one of whom is escaping from an experiment. In a largely unknown cast, Henry Czerny, of *Clear and Present Danger* fame, is suitably menacing in a smoothly villainous role.

Henry Czerny *Lawson Hughes* • Nicole Stoffman *Robin* • Mark Critch *Radd* • Phelim Martin *Dogface* ■ *Dir* Andrée Pelletier • *Scr* Michael Luke, TH Hatte

Anchoress ★★ 12

Historical drama
1993 · UK/Bel · BW · 108mins

Based on letters written by a genuine anchoress in 1325, director Chris Newby's film chronicles the gruesome fate of peasant girl Natalie Morse. Seeking solace from her medieval family and tiny hovel, Morse becomes obsessed with the Virgin Mary and seeks to serve her ad infinitum by being walled up for life in her local church. Almost becoming a deity herself, she is fed by the villagers and sought after as a form of 14th-century guidance counsellor. When her mother is tried and convicted of witchcraft, however, she digs her way out of imprisonment and stands to pay for the action with her life. A haunting film shot in striking monochrome that offers a apt period metaphor for contemporary teenage rebellion.

Natalie Morse *Christine Carpenter* • Eugene Bervoets *[Gene Bervoets] Reeve* • Toyah Willcox *Pauline Carpenter* • Peter Postlethwaite *[Pete Postlethwaite] William Carpenter* • Christopher Eccleston *Priest* • Brenda Bertin *Meg Carpenter* • Annette Badland *Mary* ■ *Dir* Chris Newby • *Scr* Christine Watkins, Judith Stanley-Smith

Anchors Aweigh ★★★ U

Musical 1945 · US · Colour · 133mins

The musical in which Gene Kelly dances with cartoon mouse Jerry, and Kelly and Frank Sinatra don those oh-so-cute sailor suits, prior to *On the Town*. At times it's schmaltzy and overlong, with cloying moments involving Kathryn Grayson's quest for an interview with conductor José Iturbi, embarrassingly playing himself. However, none of that matters when Kelly and Sinatra are on the screen. They're a joy to watch, either together or separately, and Sinatra, though not known as a dancer, acquits himself well in his pairings with Kelly. The Technicolor is ravishing, George Sidney's direction is technically clever and assured, and that key moment when Gene shows the second most famous cartoon mouse how to dance is a stroke of genius. 🔲

Gene Kelly *Joseph Brady* • Frank Sinatra *Clarence Doolittle* • Kathryn Grayson *Susan Abbott* • Dean Stockwell *Donald Martin* • Pamela Britton *Girl from Brooklyn* • Rags Ragland *Police sergeant* • Billy Gilbert *Cafe manager* • Henry O'Neill *Admiral Hammond* • José Iturbi ■ *Dir* George Sidney • *Scr* Isobel Lennart, from a story by Natalie Marcin

And Baby Makes Six ★★★

Comedy drama 1979 · US · Colour · 100mins

Versatile stage, screen and TV actress Colleen Dewhurst portrays a mature woman who finds herself pregnant in the later years of her life. She and her husband, who have three grown-up children, face criticism and hostility from their friends and family once they announce they are going to have the baby. This emotionally-charged drama was ahead of its time and it's certain to polarise viewers. Timothy Hutton and Warren Oates co-star; Waris Hussein directs. A sequel, *Baby Comes Home* followed a year later.

Colleen Dewhurst *Anna Cramer* • Warren Oates *Michael Cramer* • Maggie Cooper

Elizabeth Winston • Al Corley *Franklyn Cramer* • Timothy Hutton *Jason Cramer* ■ *Dir* Waris Hussein • *Scr* Shelley List

And Baby Makes Three ★★

Comedy 1949 · US · BW · 83mins

Barbara Hale is in the family way and about to marry anew, but really wants to stay with divorced first husband Robert Young. Need you ask more? What you could ask is how such a topic appeased the strict US censor's Breen Office, and then enjoy the amazing number of euphemisms used to describe Hale's condition. This is a trifle, nicely played by Barbara Hale in her pre-Della Street Columbia contractee days, but its tale of a pregnant wife trying to get out of a second marriage to get her first hubby back leaves a strange taste in the mouth. Not without charm, but a tad muddled.

Robert Young *Vernon Walsh* • Barbara Hale *Jacqueline Walsh* • Robert Hutton *Herbert Fletcher* • Janis Carter *Wanda York* • Billie Burke *Mrs Fletcher* • Nicholas Joy *Mr Fletcher* • Lloyd Corrigan *Dr William Parnell* ■ *Dir* Henry Levin • *Scr* Lou Breslow, Joseph Hoffman

And God Created Woman ★★★

Drama 1956 · Fr · Colour · 90mins

This was not Brigitte Bardot's first movie, but it was the one that turned her into the world's ultimate sex symbol. Directed by Roger Vadim, her then husband, the film also turned the little fishing village of St Tropez into a glamorous resort – the kind of place where girls leave their bikini tops on the ironing board, pose provocatively in CinemaScope and go with anything in trousers. Curt Jurgens, Jean-Louis Trintignant and Christian Marquand are three of Bardot's conquests in a movie whose funny attitude towards sex made it seem all the more risqué in the fifties. Vadim directed a Hollywood remake (of sorts) in 1988. In French with English subtitles.

Brigitte Bardot *Juliette Hardy* • Curt Jurgens *Eric Carradine* • Jean-Louis Trintignant *Michel Tardieu* • Christian Marquand *Antoine Tardieu* • Georges Poujouly *Christian Tardieu* • Jean Tissier *M Vigier-Lefranc* • Jeanne Marken *Mme Morin* • Marie Glory *Mme Tardieu* ■ *Dir* Roger Vadim • *Scr* Roger Vadim, Raoul J Lévy

And God Created Woman ★ 18

Drama 1988 · US · Colour · 90mins

Director Roger Vadim's sad attempt to reclaim his past *Nouvelle Vague* glory is a tedious and trite retooling of the sensational 1956 original which made Brigitte Bardot an international sex symbol. Rebecca De Mornay is hardly in the same "sex kitten" class as an aspiring rock star who sleeps with electrician Vincent Spano and sundry other high-powered men to get out of jail and achieve her aim. Without Bardot's brand of sexual dynamism – De Mornay disrobes to little erotic effect – Vadim's contrived fable collapses into a cliché-ridden heap of "women behind bars" melodrama and "rags to riches" farce.

Rebecca De Mornay *Robin Shay* • Vincent Spano *Billy Moran* • Frank Langella *James*

Tiernan* • Donovan Leitch *Peter Moran* • Judith Chapman *Alexandra Tiernan* • Jaime McEnnan *Timmy Moran* • Benjamin Mouton *Blue* ■ *Dir* Roger Vadim • *Scr* RJ Stewart

...And God Spoke ★★

Spoof documentary 1993 · US · Colour · 83m

Though there are some laughs to be had in this mock documentary about two skin flick merchants who decide to make a biblical epic on the cheap – *Spinal Tap* it ain't. Clueless duo Michael Riley and Stephen Rappaport have no idea what they're letting themselves in for, and it's fun to see them treat the Bible like a Jackie Collins bestseller and hire such actors as *The Incredible Hulk*'s Lou Ferrigno and Eve Plumb from *The Brady Bunch*. The best scene is the one where no one can remember how many apostles Jesus had, but the gags are few and far between, and the film peters out alarmingly well before the end.

Michael Riley *Clive Walton* • Stephen Rappaport *Marvin Handleman* • Josh Trossman *Ray/Jesus* • Lou Ferrigno *Cain* • Andy Dick *Abel* • Eve Plumb *Mrs Noah* • Fred Kaz *Noah* • Soupy Sales *Moses* ■ *Dir* Arthur Borman • *Scr* Gregory S Malins, Michael Curtis, from a story by Arthur Borman, Mark Borman

And Hope to Die ★★★

Crime 1972 · Fr/US · Colour · 126mins

The penultimate film from veteran French director René Clément is a gangster thriller, filmed mainly in Canada, where fugitive Jean-Louis Trintignant inadvertently finds himself with a million bucks in cash, the price paid by a crime baron (Robert Ryan) to have a state witness assassinated. The plot gets even more complicated when Trintignant is kidnapped by the gang, though flashbacks to France and scenes of children playing – symbolising the childish but deadly antics of the gangsters – complicate things still further. Clearly intended to rival the crime dramas made by Jean-Pierre Melville, it's undeniably gripping, but not quite in that exalted league. An English/French language film.

Robert Ryan *Charley* • Jean-Louis Trintignant *Tony* • Aldo Ray *Mattone* • Lea Massari *Sugar* • Tisa Farrow *Pepper* • Jean Gaven *Rizzio* • Nadine Nabokov *Majorette* • Andre Lawrence *Gypsy* • Daniel Breton *Paul* ■ *Dir* René Clément • *Scr* Sebastien Japrisot

...And Justice for All ★★★ 15

Courtroom drama 1979 · US · Colour · 116mins

Later seen as a sinister legal eagle in *Devil's Advocate* with Keanu Reeves, Al Pacino's earlier essay in lawyerdom was this drama, which goes from case to case and then delivers its verdict: the American justice system is rotten to the core. Pacino's attorney, first seen in prison where he's serving time for contempt, is a crusader, fighting corruption within his profession with a zeal that real-life lawyers can only dream of. The writing by the then husband-and-wife team of Valerie Curtin and Barry Levinson is, on the whole, solid enough, but the direction by Norman Jewison is rather bloated. Watch out for a nice cameo by Lee Strasberg, the legendary Method acting

teacher who starred as Pacino's Jewish mobster rival in *The Godfather, Part II*.

Al Pacino *Arthur Kirkland* • Jack Warden *Judge Rayford* • John Forsythe *Judge Fleming* • Lee Strasberg *Grandpa Sam* • Jeffrey Tambor *Jay Porter* • Christine Lahti *Gail Packer* • Sam Levene *Arnie* ■ *Dir* Norman Jewison • *Scr* Valerie Curtin, Barry Levinson

And Life Goes On... ★★★

Documentary drama
1991 · Iran · Colour · 108mins

In keeping with the rest of Iranian director Abbas Kiarostami's canon, this is a deceptively simple study of the enduring link between cinema and life. Following an earthquake in northern Iran, a director (Ferhed Kherdamend representing Kiarostami) travels to see whether the cast of his 1987 film *Where Is the Friend's Home?*, survived the disaster. Taking a precarious mountain route, and in the company of his son, he arrives to discuss with the peoples of Rudbar and Rostamabad their plans for the future and how God could have allowed such suffering. Combining simple narrative with unobtrusive documentary, this is a humane, deeply affecting work. In Farsi with English subtitles.

Ferhed Kherdamend *Film director* • Buba Bayour *Film director's son* ■ *Dir/Scr* Abbas Kiarostami

And Millions Will Die! ★★

Science-fiction thriller
1973 · US · Colour · 93mins

An undistinguished thriller from the days when Leslie Nielsen's air of authority was still used for dramatic rather than comic purposes. He joins another TV regular, Richard Baseheart (*Voyage to the Bottom of the Sea*), in this story of an unknown force which threatens to unleash poison gas upon the population of Hong Kong. It attempts to cash in on the early seventies demand for disaster movies, but there is little in the way of either star charisma or suspense.

Richard Basehart *Dr Pruitt* • Leslie Nielsen *Gallagher* • Joseph First *Franz Kessler* • Susan Strasberg *Heather Kessler* • Alwyn Kurts *Dr Mitchell* • Shariff Medon *Postman* ■ *Dir* Leslie Martinson [Leslie H Martinson] • *Scr* Michael Fisher

And Now for Something Completely Different ★★★★ PG

Comedy 1971 · UK · Colour · 84mins

Not all that different, though, for British enthusiasts of *Monty Python's* comic madness, as it's a recycling of some sketches earlier seen on TV. But this first cinematic celebration was really aimed at American innocents, hitherto ignorant of such items as the "Upper Class Twit of the Year Race" and "Hell's Grannies", with Graham Chapman, John Cleese and Terry Gilliam giving vent to their wilfully superior form of surrealism. The Americans took it all to their hearts, bless 'em. Perhaps they thought that the "Townswomen's Guild Reconstruction of Pearl Harbor" was for real. Contains swearing. 🔲

Graham Chapman • John Cleese • Terry Gilliam • Eric Idle • Terry Jones • Michael

U = SUITABLE FOR ALL   Uc = SUITABLE FOR ALL, ESPECIALLY FOR YOUNG CHILDREN (VIDEO ONLY)   PG = PARENTAL GUIDANCE

Palin • Carol Cleveland • Connie Booth ■ *Dir* ian MacNaughton • *Scr* Graham Chapman, John Cleese, Terry Gilliam, Eric Idle, Terry Jones, Michael Palin • *Animation* Terry Gilliam

And Now Miguel ★★ U

Drama   1966 · US · Colour · 94mins

An old-style family entertainment about a little boy in New Mexico who wants to be a shepherd, just like his dad. Much time is spent on what it's like to be a sheep in this part of the world: you stand around, bleat a bit and get sheared once a year. (The humans seem to do much the same thing, only on two legs.) An attack by a pack of wolves comes not a moment too soon. Director James B Clark, a former editor, specialised in this sort of thing, having previously cranked out *Flipper* and *Island of the Blue Dolphins.*

Pat Cardi *Miguel* • Michael Ansara *Blas* • Guy Stockwell *Perez* • Clu Gulager *Johnny* • Joe De Santis *Padre de Chavez* • Pilar Del Rey *Tomasita* • Peter Robbins *Pedro* • Emma Tyson *Faustina* ■ *Dir* James B Clark • *Scr* Ted Sherdeman, Jane Klove, from the novel by Joseph Krumgold

And Now My Love ★★

Drama   1974 · Fr/It · Colour · 121mins

A flamboyant folly from director/co-writer Claude Lelouch that astonishingly earned an Oscar nomination for best original screenplay. Wildly overlong and hopelessly self-indulgent, this mammoth picture is interminably dull from our first encounter with a pioneering movie cameraman (Charles Denner) at the turn of the century right through to the moment his granddaughter (Marthe Keller) sets her roguish beau (André Dussollier) on the straight and narrow. As if the sprawling narrative and woefully one-dimensional characters weren't bad enough, we also have to suffer the sentimental singing of Gilbert Bécaud. In French with English subtitles.

Marthe Keller *Sarah/Her mother/Her grandmother* • André Dussollier *Simon Duroc* • Charles Denner *Cameraman/Sarah's father/Sarah's grandfather* • Carla Gravina *Sarah's Italian friend* • Charles Gerard *Charlot*, *Simon's friend* • Gilbert Bécaud *Gilbert Bécaud* ■ *Dir* Claude Lelouch • *Scr* Claude Lelouch, Pierre Uytterhoeven

And Now the Screaming Starts! ★★ 15

Horror   1973 · UK · Colour · 85mins

Stephanie Beacham (who cut her soap-acting teeth on numerous horrors like this) marries Ian Ogilvy and is menaced by a dismembered hand, an axe-wielding farmer and other apparitions thanks to an ancient family curse. The presence of horror veterans Peter Cushing and Herbert Lom gives this formula haunted house material a much needed lift, but there's very little action and too few surprises before the screaming well and truly stops and the yawning starts.

Peter Cushing *Doctor Pope* • Herbert Lom *Henry Fengriffen* • Patrick Magee *Doctor Whittle* • Ian Ogilvy *Charles Fengriffen* • Stephanie Beacham *Catherine Fengriffen* • Geoffrey Whitehead *Silas Jr/Sr* • Guy Rolfe *Maitland* • Rosalie Crutchley *Mrs Luke* ■ *Dir* Roy Ward Baker • *Scr* Roger Marshall, from the novel *Fengriffen* by David Case

And Quiet Rolls the Dawn ★★★★

Drama   1979 · Ind · Colour · 90mins

Less politically strident than his earlier work, this intense treatise on the role of women in Indian society demonstrates Mrinal Sen's total mastery of his art. Moving between the vast courtyard of a Calcuttan tenement and the crowded apartment in which Satya Bannerjee and his family of seven live, Sen uses the overnight absence of a hard-working daughter to expose the family's indolent dependence on her wage. Interspersing dramatic scenes with speeches to camera, he compels and provokes as he relentlessly probes their middle-class pride and prejudices, as each strives to conceal a concern inspired more by fiscal than familial motives. A Bengali language film.

Satya Bannerjee *Hrishikesh Sen Gupta* • Gita Sen *Mother* • Mamata Shankar *Chinu* • Sreela Majumdar *Minu* • Tapan Das *Tapu* • Umanath Bhattacharya *Landlord* • Arun Mukherjee *Shyamal, the neighbour* ■ *Dir* Mrinal Sen • *Scr* Mrinal Sen, from the story *Abiroto Chene Mukh* by Amalendu Chakravarty

And So They Were Married ★★★

Romantic comedy   1936 · US · BW · 68mins

Widower Melvyn Douglas and his young son Jackie Moran meet widow Mary Astor and her daughter Edith Fellows while vacationing at a winter resort. After a sticky start, the adults fall for each other, but their children set out to sabotage the relationship. A short, neat romantic comedy, directed by the excellent Elliott Nugent, in which the classy expertise of Douglas and Astor is almost buried by the engaging antics of the juveniles. A very pleasing way to spend 68 minutes.

Melvyn Douglas *Hugh "Stephen" Blake* • Mary Astor *Edith Farnham* • Edith Fellows *Brenda Farnham* • Jackie Moran *Tommy Blake* • Donald Meek *Hotel manager* • Dorothy Stickney *Miss Alma Peabody* • Romaine Callender *Mr Ralph P Shirley* • Douglas Scott *Horace* ■ *Dir* Elliott Nugent • *Scr* Doris Anderson, Joseph Anthony, A Laurie Brazee

And So They Were Married ★★ U

Comedy   1944 · US · BW · 73mins

The versatile Joe May was one of the directors who pulled German cinema up by its bootstraps in the aftermath of the First World War. Yet after he moved to Hollywood to escape the Nazi threat, his movies were, for the most part, routine. Reworking the plot of the previous year's *The More the Merrier*, this piece of romantic fluff is another comedy about tenants sharing their apartments with strangers. Simone Simon is typically charming as the career girl who suddenly finds her friend's flat being invaded by the pals to whom he's given keys. James Ellison might steal Simone's heart, but it's the laconic Robert Mitchum who steals the show in the final reel.

Simone Simon *Kathie Aumont* • James Ellison *Mike O'Brien* • Robert Mitchum *CPO Jeff Daniels* • William Terry *Johnny Moore* • Minna Gombell *Mrs Collins* • Chick Chandler *Jack* ■ *Dir* Joe May • *Scr* Philip Yordan, John H Kafka, from a story by Alice Means Reeve

And Soon the Darkness ★★

Thriller   1970 · UK · Colour · 99mins

One would have thought that writers Brian Clemens (who made his name on series such as *Danger Man* and *The Avengers*) and Terry Nation (doyen of *Doctor Who* scripters) would have come up with something more memorable than this nasty chiller. The voyeuristic approach to both the killer's crimes and the peril in which nurses Pamela Franklin and Michele Dotrice find themselves as they cycle through a French wood is most regrettable, if not downright objectionable. Director Robert Fuest ensures that it's also an uncomfortable watch from the suspense point of view, but it's not a film one can view with much pleasure.

Pamela Franklin *Jane* • Michele Dotrice *Cathy* • Sandor Eles *Paul* • John Nettleton *Gendarme* • Clare Kelly *Schoolmistress* • Hana-Maria Pravda *Madame Lassal* • John Franklyn *Old man* ■ *Dir* Robert Fuest • *Scr* Brian Clemens, Terry Nation

And the Band Played On ★★★ 15

Documentary drama
1993 · US · Colour · 135mins

This made-for-cable adaptation of Randy Shilts's monumental history of Aids is distractingly overloaded with stars, all too willing to prove their political correctness – Alan Alda, Ian McKellen, Richard Gere, Anjelica Huston, Steve Martin. But, taken as a detective story, this is still a gripping narrative in which French and American scientists search to isolate the virus and seek to find the airline employee who may have brought it from Africa. Matthew Modine's clear-sighted visionary provides the necessary human focus, keeping his integrity while others lose theirs. Director Roger Spottiswoode is hemmed in by too many statistics, yet still manages to produce a memorable and absorbing docudrama. Contains some swearing.
▣

Matthew Modine *Dr Don Francis* • Ian McKellen *Bill Kraus* • Lily Tomlin *Dr Selma Dritz* • Richard Gere *Choreographer* • Alan Alda *Dr Robert Gallo* • Glenne Headly *Mary Guinan* • Phil Collins *Eddie Papasano* • Anjelica Huston *Dr Betsy Reisz* • Saul Rubinek *Dr Jim Curran* • Steve Martin *Brother* • Charles Martin Smith *Dr Harold Jaffe* • Elizabeth Taylor ■ *Dir* Roger Spottiswoode • *Scr* Arnold Schulman, from the non-fiction book by Randy Shilts

And the Beat Goes On: the Sonny and Cher Story ★★★ PG

Drama   1999 · US · Colour · 85mins

Based on Sonny Bono's controversial autobiography, this biopic of the sixties odd couple is enjoyably camp without veering too far into the cheap and tacky. Cher – still topping the charts on a regular basis – is played with finesse and respect by lookalike Renee Faia, while Sonny's infectious enthusiasm is ably put across by Jay Underwood. Fans will enjoy the clever soundtrack, which mixes original music from the period with some skilled re-creations.
▣

Jay Underwood *Sonny Bono* • Renee Faia *Cher* • Jim Pirri *Buddy Black* • Laura Johnson

Georgia LaPierre • Christian Leffler *Phil Spector* • Walter Franks *Little Richard* • Bruce Nozick *Art Rupe* • Marie Wilson *Mary Bono* ■ *Dir* David Burton Morris • *Scr* Ellen Weston, from the autobiography by Sonny Bono

And the Same to You ★★ U

Comedy   1960 · UK · BW · 87mins

Any film boasting Sid James, Tommy Cooper and Brian Rix in the cast has to be worth a look, but there are few laughs to be had in this screen version of a popular stage farce. Rix stars as a singularly hopeless boxer who has to keep his career hidden from his disapproving archdeacon uncle. John Paddy Carstairs (who guided Norman Wisdom to fame) co-wrote the script with John Junkin, but every punch is pulled and not even Rix and James who had done well together on *Dry Rot* make it worth going the distance.

Brian Rix *Dickie Dreadnought* • William Hartnell *Wally Burton* • Tommy Cooper *Horace Hawkins* • Dick Bentley *George Nibbs* • Vera Day *Cynthia* • Sidney James *Sammy Gatt* • Leo Franklyn *Vicar* • Renee Houston *Mildred* • Miles Malleson *Bishop* ■ *Dir* George Pollock • *Scr* John Paddy Carstairs, John Junkin, from a play by AP Dearsley

And the Ship Sails On ★★★ PG

Comedy drama   1983 · It/Fr · Colour · 128mins

Federico Fellini's idea was to create the last voyage of the old Europe before it was snuffed out by the First World War. So in his mind he builds an ocean liner and lets it sail upon a phoney sea, laden with human cargo – aristocrats, diplomats and a band of opera singers who want to bury a great soprano on an offshore island. As usual, the director concocts some simply stunning moments of surreal beauty and impish humour, and the sudden arrival of Balkan refugees has the required impact, However, the film is still an awkward mishmash, much too long and unevenly acted. Italian dialogue dubbed into English. ▣

Freddie Jones *Mister Orlando* • Barbara Jefford *Ildebranda Cuffari* • Victor Poletti *Aureliano Fuciletto* • Peter Cellier *Sir Reginald Dongby* • Elisa Mainardi *Teresa Valegnani* • Janet Suzman *Edmea Tetua* ■ *Dir* Federico Fellini, Mike Hodges • *Scr* Federico Fellini, Tonino Guerra, Catherine Breillat

And Then There Was One ★★ 15

Drama based on a true story
1994 · US · Colour · 90mins

Amy Madigan and Dennis Boutsikaris star as comedy scriptwriters whose baby girl is diagnosed as HIV positive. Based on a true story, of course, and predictably gut-churning as both parents learn that they, too, are infected with the HIV virus. The questions are, how, why, and what to do about it? Directed by David Jones, its chief virtue is Madigan, a charming and talented actress best known for *Field of Dreams* and *Twice in a Lifetime* for which she was nominated for an Oscar. ▣

Amy Madigan *Roxy Ventola* • Dennis Boutsikaris *Vinnie Ventola* • Jane Daly *Lorrie Shapiro* • Steven Flynn *Jack* • John Robinson *Marvin Wilkes* • Jennifer Hetrick *Janet Wilkes* ■ *Dir* David Jones • *Scr* Rama Laurie Stagner

And Then There Were None ★★

Crime mystery   1945 · US · BW · 97mins

Agatha Christie's *Ten Little Niggers* was retitled *Ten Little Indians* when it arrived on Broadway. This stagey, ossified film version – the first of many – is a bit of a trial as the cast, marooned in an off-shore island mansion, begins to whittle down in number. Everyone overacts outrageously and what was a star cast in 1945 is no longer, while French wartime exile René Clair directs it like the chore it undoubtedly was.

Barry Fitzgerald *Judge Quincannon* • Walter Huston *Dr Armstrong* • Louis Hayward *Philip Lombard* • Roland Young *Blore* • June Duprez *Vera Claythorne* • C Aubrey Smith *Gen Mandrake* • Judith Anderson *Emily Brent* • Mischa Auer *Prince Starloff* ■ *Dir* René Clair • *Scr* Dudley Nichols, from the novel *Ten Little Niggers* by Agatha Christie

And Then There Were None ★★★ 🅿🄶

Crime mystery drama
1974 · Fr/Sp/W Ger/It · Colour · 93mins

This third film version of Agatha Christie's whodunit *Ten Little Niggers* assembles strangers at an isolated Persian palace and bumps them off one by one in retribution. It is lushly filmed by director Peter Collinson in pre-revolutionary Iran, but stars such as Richard Attenborough, Oliver Reed, Elke Sommer and Herbert Lom are given the task of propping up a dubious proposition, helped by the disembodied voice of narrator Orson Welles, who lends the project more weight than it deserves. ▭

Oliver Reed *Hugh Lombard* • Richard Attenborough *Judge Cannon* • Elke Sommer *Vera Clyde* • Gert Frobe *Wilhelm Blore* • Adolfo Celi *General Soule* • Stéphane Audran *Ilona Bergen* • Charles Aznavour *Michel Raven* • Herbert Lom *Dr Armstrong* • Orson Welles ■ *Dir* Peter Collinson • *Scr* Erich Krohnke, from the novel *Ten Little Niggers* by Agatha Christie

And Women Shall Weep ★★

Drama   1960 · UK · BW · 65mins

This little British B-movie is given great strength by the leading performance of veteran TV character actress Ruth Dunning. The actress, who was Mrs Grove in British television's first soap *The Grove Family*, stars as a widow trying to keep her young son Richard O'Sullivan on the straight and narrow. However, her older son Max Butterfield is beyond help and she ultimately hands him over to the police herself. Slight and overplayed, this would have been better as a live TV drama, but at least it's an honest attempt to take the justly maligned British second feature out of its perpetual cops 'n' robbers arena and into something vaguely resembling New Wave "kitchen sink" drama.

Ruth Dunning *Mrs Lumsden* • Max Butterfield *Terry Lumsden* • Gillian Vaughan *Brenda Wilkes* • Richard O'Sullivan *Godfrey Lumsden* • Claire Gordon *Sadie MacDougall* ■ *Dir* John Lemont • *Scr* John Lemont, Leigh Vance

And You Thought Your Parents Were Weird ★★ 🅿🄶

Science-fiction fantasy
1991 · US · Colour · 87mins

A low-budget and fairly weak family sci-fi comedy, rehashing a variety of ideas and gimmicks familiar from films including *Star Wars*, *Short Circuit* and *Forbidden Planet*. The action focuses on two boys who build a multi-talented robot from everyday household items, only to find it contains the spirit of their late father. Inoffensive, but ultimately mediocre.

Marcia Strassman *Sarah Carson* • Joshua Miller *Josh Carson* • Edan Gross *Max Carson* • John Quade *Irwin Kotzwinkle* • Sam Behrens *Steve Franklin* • Richard Libertini *Matthew Carson* • Alan Thicke *Newman the Robot* ■ *Dir/Scr* Tony Cookson

Andaz ★★★★ 🅿🄶

Drama   1949 · Ind · BW · 150mins

Also known as *A Matter of Style*, this concluded the string of forties classics that established Mehboob Khan as one of the key figures in Indian cinema. An allegorical warning to the newly independent state not to lose sight of traditional values, it is a typically knotty melodrama, with ambitious young executive Dilip Kumar coming between his heiress boss Nargis and her feckless husband, Raj Kapoor. The film turned Kumar into a superstar, while also reinforcing the status of his co-stars as the sub-continent's favourite romantic team. In addition to being a major box-office success, *Andaz* spawned several hit songs. In Hindi with English subtitles.

Raj Kapoor *Rajan* • Dilip Kumar *Dilip* • Nargis *Neeta* • Sapru *Badriprasad* ■ *Dir* Mehboob Khan • *Scr* S Ali Raza

The Anderson Tapes ★★★ 🄸🄵

Crime drama   1971 · US · Colour · 94mins

An "I spy" version of *The League of Gentlemen*, American-style. Sean Connery sets out to burgle a luxury apartment block helped by some notable eccentrics, unaware that his every move is under surveillance from various law enforcement agencies. The implicit ironies – that the agents can't see the larger picture of a major robbery for all their attention to the smaller details – are never quite forged into the intended satire, but director Sidney Lumet does manage to achieve a certain sarcastic humour. Christopher Walken makes one of his first major film appearances, and *The Wizard of Oz*'s Wicked Witch Margaret Hamilton (who was nearing 70) appears in one of her final roles. Contains swearing. ▭

Sean Connery *Duke Anderson* • Dyan Cannon *Ingrid Everleigh* • Martin Balsam *Tommy Haskins* • Ralph Meeker *Delaney* • Alan King *Pat Angelo* • Christopher Walken *The Kid* • Val Avery *Parelli* • Dick Williams [Dick Anthony Williams] *Spencer* • Margaret Hamilton *Miss Kaler* ■ *Dir* Sidney Lumet • *Scr* Frank R Pierson, from the novel by Lawrence Sanders

Andre ★★★ 🅄

Adventure   1994 · US · Colour · 90mins

Set in the early sixties, this perfect family fare tells the story of the rather cute seal of the title, which is adopted by precocious newcomer Tina Majorino, playing the animal-loving daughter of harbour master Keith Carradine. The local fishing community is worried that Andre will put a blight on its employment, which leads to the inevitable conflict. It's sickly sweet stuff, but Andre (actually played by a sea-lion) is undoubtedly endearing, and it's nice to see Carradine in an atypical role. Director George Miller (not the *Mad Max* man) milks the sentimentality for all it is worth, but that won't bother the youngsters, who will be enraptured by it. ▭

Keith Carradine *Harry Whitney* • Tina Majorino *Toni Whitney* • Chelsea Field *Thalice Whitney* • Shane Meier *Steve Whitney* • Aidan Pendleton *Paula Whitney* • Shirley Broderick *Mrs McCann* • Andrea Libman *Mary May* • Joshua Jackson *Mark Baker* ■ *Dir* George Miller (1) • *Scr* Dana Baratta, from the non-fiction book *A Seal Called Andre* by Harry Goodridge, Lew Dietz

Andrei Rublev ★★★★★ 🄸🄵

Historical drama
1966 · USSR · Colour and BW · 174mins

Divided into eight episodes and majestically photographed by Vadim Yusov, this is a remarkable study of the artist Andrei Rublev's struggle to overcome both his own doubts, and the poverty and cruelty of his time, to create works of inspirational power and outstanding beauty. Anatoli Solonitsyn plays the 15th-century icon painter as a sort of wandering mystic who takes a vow of silence in protest at conditions in Russia under the Tartars. Andrei Tarkovsky includes too much impenetrable symbolism, but the battle, the balloon flight, the snow crucifixion, the casting of the bell and the colour montage from Rublev's work are stunning. In Russian with English subtitles. ▭

Anatoly Solonitsin [Anatoli Solonitsyn] *Andrei Rublev* • Ivan Lapikov *Kirill* • Nikolai Grinko *Daniel Chorny* • Nikolai Sergeyev *Theophanes the Greek* • Irma Rausch *Idiot girl* • Nikolai Burlyaev *Boris* • Yuri Nazarov *The Grand Prince/His brother* ■ *Dir* Andrei Tarkovsky • *Scr* Andrei Tarkovsky, Andrei Mikhalkov-Konchalovsky • *Cinematographer* Vadim Yusov

Androcles and the Lion ★★ 🅄

Satirical comedy   1952 · US · BW · 96mins

George Bernard Shaw's Roman fable proved to be an interesting and quirky one-off when brought to the screen by producer Gabriel Pascal, who fetched up in Hollywood after the costly fiasco of *Caesar and Cleopatra*. Under the oppressive regime of Howard Hughes, this RKO movie was a long time in the making, and stars Victor Mature and Jean Simmons found greater success with their next foray into Roman history together, *The Robe*. The imported British supporting cast, including Robert Newton, behave like fish out of water under Chester Erskine's shambolic direction.

Jean Simmons *Lavinia* • Alan Young *Androcles* • Victor Mature *Captain* • Robert Newton *Ferrovius* • Maurice Evans *Caesar* • Elsa Lanchester *Megaera* • Reginald Gardiner *Lentulus* • Gene Lockhart *Menagerie keeper* • Alan Mowbray *Editor* ■ *Dir* Chester Erskine • *Scr* Chester Erskine, Ken Englund, from the play by George Bernard Shaw

Android ★★★ 🄸🄵

Science-fiction fantasy
1982 · US · Colour · 76mins

Three space convicts upset the plans of mad scientist Klaus Kinski to replace his companion android, Max 404, with a perfect female version in a low-key slice of cult science-fiction from the Roger Corman factory. Don Opper's portrayal of Max as a nerdy movie buff clone adds extra pop culture playfulness to the enjoyably exciting and charming proceedings, which were filmed on the same sets as *Battle beyond the Stars*. Neat suspense, a few final reel twists and another eccentric Kinski performance make this low-budget gem a winner. Contains some swearing and violence. ▭

Klaus Kinski *Dr Daniel* • Don Opper *Max 404* • Brie Howard *Maggie* • Norbert Weisser *Keller* • Crofton Hardester *Mendes* • Kendra Kirchner *Cassandra* ■ *Dir* Aaron Lipstadt • *Scr* Don Opper, James Reigle

The Android Affair ★★ 🄸🄶

Science-fiction thriller
1995 · US · Colour · 85mins

Director Richard Kletter plumbs new depths of slow-moving mediocrity in bringing his short story – co-written with sci-fi legend Isaac Asimov – to the screen. In a depressingly predictable futuristic tale, gorgeous robotics expert Harley Jane Kozak falls in love with an android called Teach 905 under the watchful eye of evil professor Ossie Davis and his assistant Saul Rubinek (wearing a ludicrous wig). Don't blame the cast, though: it gamely struggles with the mediocre script, especially Griffin Dunne as the android, but tedium wins out in the end. Contains some violence. ▭

Harley Jane Kozak *Dr Karen Garret* • Griffin Dunne *Teach 905* • Ossie Davis *Dr Winston* • Saul Rubinek *Fiedler* • Peter Outerbridge *Thomas Benti* • Natalie Radford *Rachel Tyler* • Chandra Galasso *Alexx* ■ *Dir* Richard Kletter • *Scr* Richard Kletter, from a short story by Isaac Asimov, Richard Kletter

The Andromeda Strain ★★★★ 🅿🄶

Science-fiction thriller
1970 · US · Colour · 123mins

Way before the similarly themed *Outbreak* and his own blockbuster *Jurassic Park*, novelist Michael Crichton came up with a super combination of high-tech thrills and against-the-clock suspense. Robert Wise's near-documentary direction keeps tension mounting as desperate scientists race to isolate a fatal alien virus from a fallen satellite. More science fact than fiction, and still powerfully relevant, it's a remarkably faithful account of Crichton's biological invasion bestseller, layered with sophisticated special effects by Douglas Trumbull, who had helped Stanley Kubrick towards a special effects Oscar two years earlier for *2001: a Space Odyssey*. ▭

Arthur Hill *Dr Jeremy Stone* • David Wayne *Dr Charles Dutton* • James Olson *Dr Mark Hall* • Kate Reid *Dr Ruth Leavitt* • Paula Kelly *Karen Anson* • George Mitchell *Jackson* • Ramon Bieri *Major Mancheck* • Richard O'Brien *Grimes* ■ *Dir* Robert Wise • *Scr* Nelson Gidding, from the novel by Michael Crichton

Andy Hardy Comes Home ★★ U

Comedy drama   1958 · US · BW · 79mins

A dozen years after his last appearance as Andy Hardy, Mickey Rooney returns to the small town of Carvel and finds himself embroiled in a dishonest property deal over an aircraft factory. Trading heavily on the audience's nostalgia for the series – clips from earlier films are featured – this was intended to herald a brand new run of Andy Hardy movies. Proudly waiting to take up the reins was none other than Mickey's son, Teddy; the series, however, ended here.

Mickey Rooney *Andy Hardy* • Patricia Breslin *Jane Hardy* • Fay Holden *Mother Hardy* • Cecilia Parker *Marian* • Sara Haden *Aunt Milly* • Jerry Colonna *Doc* • Frank Ferguson *Mayor Benson* • Teddy Rooney *Andy Hardy Jr* ■ *Dir* Howard W Koch • *Scr* Edward Everett Hutshing, Robert Morris Donley, from characters created by Aurania Rouverol

Andy Hardy Gets Spring Fever ★★ U

Comedy drama   1939 · US · BW · 85mins

Seventh in the series with a new director to marshal the action and those "man to man" talks between Judge Lewis Stone and Mickey Rooney. This time round, Rooney falls for a drama teacher and when it's revealed she's engaged, Andy's regular Ann Rutherford is still there for him. The teacher is played by Helen Gilbert who was a cellist in the MGM studio orchestra until someone gave her a screen test.

Lewis Stone *Judge James K Hardy* • Mickey Rooney *Andy Hardy* • Cecilia Parker *Marian Hardy* • Ann Rutherford *Polly Benedict* • Fay Holden *Mrs Emily Hardy* • Sara Haden *Aunt Milly* • Helen Gilbert *Rose Meredith* ■ *Scr* Kay Van Riper, from characters created by Aurania Rouverol

Andy Hardy Meets Debutante ★★ U

Comedy drama   1940 · US · BW · 87mins

The ninth film in the series sees Mickey Rooney in the Big Apple trying to secure a meeting with a debutante whose photograph he's seen in a magazine. It isn't all Hollywood pap, however: Andy's dad (Lewis Stone) is also in town, tending to the affairs of an orphanage. This entry is notable only for the appearance of Judy Garland, who sings *Alone* and *I'm Nobody's Baby*. She also gives Mickey a peck on the cheek.

Lewis Stone *Judge James K Hardy* • Mickey Rooney *Andy Hardy* • Fay Holden *Mrs Emily Hardy* • Cecilia Parker *Marian Hardy* • Judy Garland *Betsy Booth* • Sara Haden *Aunt Milly* • Ann Rutherford *Polly Benedict* • Tom Neal *Aldrich Brown* ■ *Dir* George B Seitz • *Scr* Annalee Whitmore, Thomas Seller, from characters created by Aurania Rouverol

Andy Hardy's Blonde Trouble ★★ U

Comedy drama   1944 · US · BW · 107mins

Mickey Rooney stars in the 14th and penultimate *Andy Hardy* comedy (not counting the straggler made in 1958). As the eternal, archetypal teenager, Rooney enrols in his dad's alma mater but gets into trouble by paying too much attention to girls, mainly Bonita Granville and twin blondes who fancy him and make his life a misery. Awash with those rather cloying MGM family values, plus a few songs, this was the final film of director George B Seitz, a veteran of all but two of the series.

Lewis Stone *Judge James K Hardy* • Mickey Rooney *Andy Hardy* • Fay Holden *Mrs Emily Hardy* • Sara Haden *Aunt Milly* • Bonita Granville *Kay Wilson* • Jean Porter *Katy Henderson* • Keye Luke *Dr Lee* • Herbert Marshall *Dr MJ Standish* ■ *Dir* George B Seitz • *Scr* Harry Ruskin, William Ludwig, Agnes Christine Johnston, from characters created by Aurania Rouverol

Andy Hardy's Double Life ★★ U

Comedy drama   1942 · US · BW · 92mins

This was one of the last films in this ever-popular series, as MGM couldn't stop Mickey Rooney from growing older. Andy Hardy finally gets to go to college, where he naturally gets embroiled with the opposite sex. (Look out for stars-to-be Esther Williams and Susan Peters, both of whom went on to better things.) Rooney's mugging and the sentimental home-town feel was beginning to wear thin by the Second World War, and there would be only two more films in the series, not including *Andy Hardy Comes Home* in 1958.

Mickey Rooney *Andy Hardy* • Lewis Stone *Judge James K Hardy* • Esther Williams *Sheila Brooks* • Ann Rutherford *Polly Benedict* • Fay Holden *Mrs Emily Hardy* • Cecilia Parker *Marian Hardy* • Sara Haden *Aunt Milly* • William Lundigan *Jeff Willis* ■ *Dir* George B Seitz • *Scr* Agnes Christine Johnston, from characters created by Aurania Rouverol

Andy Hardy's Private Secretary ★★ U

Comedy drama   1941 · US · BW · 100mins

The gang's all here for this tenth outing, plus 18-year-old Kathryn Grayson making an early screen appearance as the girl Mickey Rooney hires as his secretary as he is about to graduate from high school. He ends up helping him pass his English exam and getting him through high school at the second attempt. Grayson gets to sing and show her star potential (MGM had been grooming her as a rival to Universal's Deanna Durbin), but the formula already shows signs of running out of steam.

Lewis Stone *Judge James K Hardy* • Mickey Rooney *Andy Hardy* • Fay Holden *Mrs Emily Hardy* • Ian Hunter *Steven Land* • Ann Rutherford *Polly Benedict* • Kathryn Grayson *Kathryn Land* • Todd Karns *Harry Land* • John Dilson *Mr Davis* ■ *Dir* George B Seitz • *Scr* Jane Murfin, Harry Ruskin, from characters created by Aurania Rouverol

Angel ★★

Drama   1937 · US · BW · 90mins

Marlene Dietrich was already labelled box-office poison when she made this movie for Ernst Lubitsch, a tale of sexual deception that's halfway between romantic melodrama and sophisticated comedy. Dietrich is married to Herbert Marshall, but she still fancies former boyfriend Melvyn Douglas. Things get bogged down by plot and, without Josef von Sternberg's exotic camerawork, Dietrich often looks like a plain Jane. The film's failure took her by surprise, and she dropped out of movies for two years, before making a triumphant return in *Destry Rides Again* (1939).

Marlene Dietrich *Maria Barker* • Herbert Marshall *Sir Frederick Barker* • Melvyn Douglas *Anthony Halton* • Edward Everett Horton *Graham* • Ernest Cossart *Walton* • Laura Hope Crews *Grand Duchess Anna Dmitrievna* • Herbert Mundin *Greenwood* • Ivan Lebedeff *Prince Vladimir Gregorovitch* ■ *Dir* Ernst Lubitsch • *Scr* Samson Raphaelson, Guy Bolton, Russell Medcraft, Melchior Lengyel, from the play by Melchior Lengyel

Angel ★★★★ 15

Crime thriller   1982 · Ire · Colour · 88mins

In Neil Jordan's remarkable first feature, Stephen Rea plays a saxophonist who embarks on a bloody trail of revenge after his business manager and a mute girl are gunned down by Irish gangsters. While the Troubles and the sectarian divide are always in the background, Jordan steers a hypnotic and often surreal path through Ulster's underworld, while Rea – "the Stan Getz of South Armagh" – is perfect as the equivocal hero whose quest becomes almost Arthurian. The actor would later star in Jordan's 1992 Oscar-winner *The Crying Game*. 📼

Stephen Rea *Danny* • Alan Devlin *Bill* • Veronica Quilligan *Annie* • Peter Caffrey *Ray* • Honor Heffernan *Deirdre* • Ray McAnally *Bloom* ■ *Dir/Scr* Neil Jordan

Angel ★★

Crime   1984 · US · Colour · 92mins

Writer/director Robert Vincent O'Neil tosses some offbeat comedy and a teenage temptress angle into this tacky follow-up to *Vice Squad*. Dick Shawn serves up the former as a gregarious drag queen, while Donna Wilkes does her best to provide the latter as the class-topping student who becomes a fallen angel by night. Other lowlifes include Rory Calhoun as a former cowboy star, Susan Tyrell as a lesbian and John Diehl as the psycho being pursued by no-nonsense cop Cliff Gorman.

Cliff Gorman *Lt Andrews* • Susan Tyrell *Mosler* • Dick Shawn *Mae* • Rory Calhoun *Kit Carson* • John Diehl *Billy Boy* • Donna Wilkes *Angel/Molly* • Robert Acey *Driver/John* ■ *Dir* Robert Vincent O'Neil • *Scr* Robert Vincent O'Neil, Joseph Michael Cala

Angel and the Badman ★★★ U

Western   1947 · US · BW · 95mins

As Republic's one major star, John Wayne flexed his power to make a producing debut with this absorbingly offbeat western on which he promoted his writer buddy, James Edward Grant, to the director's chair (second unit specialist Yakima Canutt handled the striking action scenes). Wayne stars as the injured gunman, nursed back to health by Quakers, who falls for the sensitive daughter of the house, Gail Russell. Can Wayne embrace their peaceful ways and avoid firing his six-gun despite the continuing provocation of Bruce Cabot's bad guy? Fortunately, Grant's screenplay delivers some gratifying and ingenious twists en route. 📼 *DVD*

John Wayne *Quirt Evans* • Gail Russell *Penelope* • Harry Carey *Wistful McClintock* • Bruce Cabot *Laredo Stevens* • Irene Rich *Mrs Worth* • Lee Dixon *Randy McCall* • Stephen Grant *Johnny Worth* • Tom Powers *Dr Mangrum* ■ *Dir/Scr* James Edward Grant

Angel, Angel Down We Go ★★

Crime drama   1969 · US · Colour · 93mins

This attempt by American International Pictures (the home of cheesy fifties sci-fi, Roger Corman horrors and violent biker movies) to go up-market turned into an infamous cult movie disaster. Director Robert Thom's staggering folly stars Hollywood legend Jennifer Jones as a porn-movie actress, Roddy McDowall as a rock group member and future soul singer Lou Rawls. It finds rock star Jordan Christopher moving in on a wealthy Hollywood family only to seduce and kill them. Although startlingly similar to actual events in the Charles Manson murder case, the film was made before that real-life tragedy. Rarely seen at the time, even less so in the interim, this is worth catching if only because it's so warped, strange and ridiculous.

Jennifer Jones *Astrid Steele* • Jordan Christopher *Bogart* • Roddy McDowall *Santoro* • Holly Near *Tara Nicole Steele* • Lou Rawls *Joe* • Charles Aidman *Willy Steele* • Davey Davison *Anna Livia* ■ *Dir/Scr* Robert Thom

An Angel at My Table ★★★★★ 15

Biography
1990 · NZ/Ausl/UK · Colour · 151mins

Director Jane Campion went on to win a screenplay Oscar for *The Piano*, but this perceptive film biography of New Zealand author Janet Frame had already served notice of her remarkable talent. Based on Frame's autobiographies and put together from a three-part TV mini-series it charts the writer's difficult life, including the eight years she spent in a mental hospital after being wrongly diagnosed as schizophrenic. So tenderly is the story told and so full of insight is the observation that what could so easily have become a sensationalist exposé of mental shock treatment comes across as a small masterpiece about one woman's triumph in breaking out of life's straitjacket. *Shallow Grave's* Kerry Fox and Karen Fergusson give superb performances as the grown-up and teenage Janet. Contains swearing and nudity. 📼

Kerry Fox *Janet Frame* • Karen Fergusson *Teenage Janet* • Alexia Keogh *Young Janet* • Melina Bernecker *Myrtle Frame* • Glynis Angell *Isabel Frame* • Samantha Townsley *Teenage Isabel* • Katherine Murray-Cowper *Young Isabel* • Sarah Smuts-Kennedy *June Frame* ■ *Dir* Jane Campion • *Scr* Laura Jones, from the autobiographal books by Janet Frame

Angel Baby ★★★

Drama   1961 · US · BW · 97mins

Notable as Burt Reynolds's big-screen debut, this is a steely look at the effects of a no-holds-barred evangelical ministry on the deeply suspicious backwoods population of America's southern states. There's plenty of hootin', hollerin' and speakin' in tongues, but the movie cleverly avoids the obvious targets, choosing instead to concentrate on what happens to people within their own community when a collective subconscious is uncommonly rattled. Watch for two fine performances from Mercedes McCambridge and Joan Blondell.

George Hamilton *Paul Strand* • Mercedes McCambridge *Sarah Strand* • Salome Jens *Angel Baby* • Joan Blondell *Mollie Hays* • Henry Jones *Ben Hays* • Burt Reynolds *Hoke Adams* • Roger Clark *Sam Wilcox* • Dudley Remus *Otis Finch* ■ *Dir* Paul Wendkos • *Scr* Orin Borsten, Paul Mason, Samuel Roeca, from the novel *Jenny Angel* by Elsie Oaks Barber

Angel Baby ★★ 15
Romantic drama
1995 · Ausl · Colour · 100mins

A tale of doomed love starring John Lynch and Jacqueline McKenzie as two psychiatric patients who get on the couch together (as it were). Deciding to live together, the two lovers hit the bottom of mental hell, bouncing off the walls as well as each other and the prognosis does not suggest a happy ending. Compelling only for a teenage audience, the film suffers from the fact that the two leads sadly lack the depth to pull it off. It's as hard to watch as a particularly difficult session with your therapist. Contains some coarse language, nudity and a traumatic childbirth scene. ▭

John Lynch *Harry* • Jacqueline McKenzie *Kate* • Colin Friels *Morris* • Deborra-Lee Furness *Louise* • Daniel Daperis *Sam* • David Argue *Dave* • Geoff Brooks *Rowan* • Humphrey Bower *Frank* ■ *Dir/Scr* Michael Rymer

Angel Dust ★★★ 15
Thriller 1987 · Fr · Colour · 91mins

Seven years after he made his remarkable debut with *Anthracite*, Edouard Niermans resumed his directorial career with this downbeat homage to the Hollywood *film noir*. However, there's also a smattering of the Catholic symbolism that informed his earlier outing, as world-weary cop Bernard Giraudeau pulls his life together to investigate the part played by his wife's new lover in the murder of a prostitute. Trudging through Bernard Lutic's atmospheric cityscapes, Giraudeau gives a suitably hard-boiled performance. But there is plenty of wit here, too, plus a little angelic mystery provided by the victim's impish daughter, Fanny Bastien. In French with English subtitles. Contains violence ▭

Bernard Giraudeau *Simon Blount* • Fanny Bastien *Violetta* • Fanny Cottençon *Martine* • Michel Aumont *Florimont* • Jean-Pierre Sentier *Georges Landry* • Luc Lavandier *Gabriel Spielmacher* ■ *Dir* Edouard Niermans • *Scr* Jacques Audiard, Alain Le Henry, Edouard Niermans, Didier Haudepin • *Cinematographer* Bernard Lutic

Angel Face ★★★★
Crime drama 1953 · US · BW · 91mins

Jean Simmons was never happy under contract to Howard Hughes, who made her chop her hair off and obliged her to wear a wig. She also felt Otto Preminger brutalised her during the

making of *Angel Face*, taking rather too much enjoyment in showing Robert Mitchum how to slap her around. The film, however, is a near classic, in which Simmons's beauty is a mask for psychopathy. In this Freudian melodrama, she bumps off her dad and stepmother before turning her sights on the chauffeur (Mitchum). Passion has rarely been depicted so chillingly.

Robert Mitchum *Frank Jessup* • Jean Simmons *Diane Tremayne* • Mona Freeman *Mary* • Herbert Marshall *Mr Tremayne* • Leon Ames *Fred Barrett* • Barbara O'Neil *Mrs Tremayne* • Kenneth Tobey *Bill* • Raymond Greenleaf *Arthur Vance* • Jim Backus *Judson* ■ *Dir* Otto Preminger • *Scr* Frank Nugent, Oscar Millard, from a story by Chester Erskine

Angel Heart ★★★ 18
Mystery thriller 1987 · US · Colour · 108mins

Alan Parker's unpleasant if tense thriller, set in fifties New Orleans, where New York private detective Mickey Rourke is trying to locate a missing person for sinister client Robert De Niro. The trail leads towards voodoo rites and other gumbo jumbo. Rourke's naked romp with Lisa Bonet, as blood drips from the ceiling, caused considerable controversy and led to the film being cut in America. You might think the things that really need a good snip are De Niro's fingernails. The story is utter nonsense, dressed up by Parker with much visual hype and with Rourke, De Niro and Charlotte Rampling contributing performances just the right side of self-parody. Contains violence and swearing. ▭

Mickey Rourke *Harry Angel* • Robert De Niro *Louis Cyphre* • Lisa Bonet *Epiphany Proudfoot* • Charlotte Rampling *Margaret Krusemark* • Stocker Fontelieu *Ethan Krusemark* • Brownie McGhee *Toots Sweet* • Michael Higgins *Doctor Fowler* • Elizabeth Whitcraft *Connie* ■ *Dir* Alan Parker • *Scr* Alan Parker, from the novel *Falling Angel* by William Hjortsberg

Angel in Exile ★★★ PG
Western 1948 · US · BW · 86mins

Ex-convict John Carroll heads for Mexico to recover a cache of stolen gold hidden in a disused mine. Plans to work a scam go awry when his "discovery" convinces the local peasantry that God has worked a miracle for their prosperity. Co-directed by veteran Allan Dwan and Philip Ford, with a cast that includes Thomas Gomez as the village doctor and Adele Mara as his daughter, this modest western has an unusual, ironic and appealing message to accompany its otherwise stock ingredients. ▭

John Carroll *Charlie Dakin* • Adele Mara *Raquel Chavez* • Thomas Gomez *Dr Esteban Chavez* • Barton MacLane *Max Giorgio* • Alfonso Bedoya *Ysidro Alvarez* • Grant Withers *Sheriff* • Paul Fix *Carl Spitz* • Art Smith *Ernie Coons* ■ *Dir* Allan Dwan, Philip Ford • *Scr* Charles Larson

Angel in My Pocket ★★
Comedy 1968 · US · Colour · 105mins

Andy Griffith was at his disturbing best in the box-office failure *A Face in the Crowd*, but he seldom went beyond the safe character he developed in his TV series. This lightweight trifle is an extension of that soft-hearted soul, though Griffith is acted off the screen

by Jerry Van Dyke's performance as the most revolting brother-in-law in movie history. The tale of a new minister trying to win over his resentful new community is given some scale by the Techniscope process, but it's very American in theme and outlook and will only be enjoyed by those who like this particular territory.

Andy Griffith *Samuel D Whitehead* • Jerry Van Dyke *Bubba* • Kay Medford *Racine* • Edgar Buchanan *Axel Gresham* • Gary Collins *Art Shields* • Lee Meriwether *Mary Elizabeth* • Henry Jones *Will Sinclair* • Parker Fennelly *Calvin* ■ *Dir* Alan Rafkin • *Scr* James Fritzell, Everett Greenbaum

The Angel Levine ★★
Fantasy drama 1970 · US · Colour · 105mins

An exhaustingly tiresome parable about a Jewish tailor (Zero Mostel), forever complaining to God about his bad luck, who finds that black angel (Harry Belafonte) has been assigned to his case. But even the heavenly presence gets bored with the grumbles – as do we. Some admirable performances, but as an affirmation of faith it comes across in a very negative fashion.

Zero Mostel *Morris Mishkin* • Harry Belafonte *Alexander Levine* • Ida Kaminska *Fanny Mishkin* • Milo O'Shea *Dr Arnold Berg* • Gloria Foster *Sally* • Barbara Ann Teer *Welfare lady* • Eli Wallach *Store clerk* ■ *Dir* Jan Kadar • *Scr* Bill Gunn, Ronald Ribman, from the story by Bernard Malamud

Angel of Desire ★★★ 18
Erotic thriller 1993 · US · Colour · 92mins

Model-turned-actress Joan Severance has tended to find herself typecast in erotic thrillers such as *Lake Consequence* and *Red Shoe Diaries II*, but here she gets the chance to do something other than just disrobe in this effective police thriller. She and Anthony John Denison play detectives on the trail of a serial killer. The prime suspect is John Allen Nelson, son of a wealthy politician, but the investigation gets complicated when Severance falls for the dangerous charmer. It went straight to video here, but director Donna Deitch works hard to keep viewers guessing and is rewarded with convincing performances from the leads. Contains swearing, violence, sex scenes and nudity. ▭

Joan Severance *Det Melanie Hudson* • John Allen Nelson *Connor Ashcroft* • Anthony John Denison *Det Nathan Leonard* • Wolfgang Bodison *Det Jordan Monroe* • David Labiosa *Verutti* ■ *Dir* Donna Deitch • *Scr* Max Strom, John Allen Nelson

Angel of Fury ★ 18
Martial arts horror 1991 · US · Colour · 90mins

Along with *24 Hours to Midnight*, this may be one of Cynthia Rothrock's worst efforts to date. She plays a security agent attempting to safely deliver a high-tech computer from an evil terrorist (described twice in the film as, "Bolt – the terrorist that strikes like lightning"). Rothrock can certainly fight and she looks great in those tight-fitting clothes, but extensive editing ruins the brawling scenes. ▭

Cynthia Rothrock *Nancy Bollins* • Chris Barnes • Peter O'Brian • Roy Marten • Tanaka • Jurek Klyne ■ *Dir* Ackyl Anwary • *Scr* Christopher Mitchum, from a story by Deddy Armand

Angel of Mercy ★★
Romantic war drama 1993 · Cz · Colour · 95mins

With a fine classical score and stylishly filmed by Vladimir Hollos, this period piece might have been more convincing had it not succumbed to melodramatic contrivance. Not that Miloslav Luther's film is without its plus points. Ingrid Timkova is particularly impressive as the loyal wife whose shock at finding her soldier husband suffering from extensive burns drives her into the arms of Juraj Simko, a PoW at the military hospital where she nurses. But while the action touches on the physical and mental cost of war, it dwells too long on the doomed nature of the illicit affair. In Czech with English subtitles.

Ingrid Timkova *Anezka* • Juraj Simko *Krystof* • Josef Vajnar *Horecky* • Peter Simun *Fero* • Juraj Mokry *Sylvio* ■ *Dir* Miloslav Luther • *Scr* Vladimir Korner, Marian Puobis

Angel on My Shoulder ★★★
Fantasy drama 1946 · US · BW · 101mins

One of those whimsical fantasies beloved of Hollywood in the forties, this time with Paul Muni as a murdered gangster sent back to Earth to seek revenge in a deal with ultra-urbane Devil Claude Rains. The uncharacteristically cast Muni enjoys himself in the brash leading role, and Anne Baxter is simply delightful as the confused fiancée of the crusading judge whom Rains is trying to discredit. Veteran director Archie Mayo keeps the action moving along and makes good use of the story by Harry Segall.

Paul Muni *Eddie Kagle/Judge Parker* • Anne Baxter *Barbara Foster* • Claude Rains *Nick/the Devil* • Onslow Stevens *Dr Matt Higgins* • George Cleveland *Albert* • Hardie Albright *Smiley Williams* • James Flavin *Bellamy* • Erskine Sanford *Minister* ■ *Dir* Archie Mayo • *Scr* Harry Segall, Roland Kibbee, from the story *Here Comes Mr Jordan* by Harry Segall • *Music* Dimitri Tiomkin [Dmitri Tiomkin]

Angel Sharks ★★★★ 15
Romantic drama 1997 · Fr · Colour · 93mins

Echoes of Jacques Demy and Pier Paolo Pasolini ring teasingly around this tale of teenage driftwood. Yet Manuel Pradal's imagery and structuring are so singular, and his handling of the non-professional cast so impressive, that such comparisons do him a disservice. Not only does the writer/director refuse to sanitise the actions of Frédéric Malgras and his fellow "angel sharks"; he also avoids patronising him when he hooks up with the equally dispossessed Vahina Giocante, who's been rejected by both the local kids and the American sailors she hoped to exploit. Peering into the darker coves of the Côte d'Azur, this is as raw as it is poetic. In French with English subtitles. Contains swearing and a scene of sexual assault.

Nicolas Welbers *Goran* • Amira Casar *Young woman* • Swan Carpio *Jurec* • Jamie Harris *Jimmy* • Frédéric Malgras *Orso* • Vahina Giocante *Marie* • Andrew Clover *Andy* ■ *Dir/Scr* Manuel Pradal

Angel Square ★★

Adventure · 1990 · Can · Colour · 106m

Jeremy Radick stars as a schoolboy who sets out to uncover the truth behind the assault of his best friend's father in this likeable movie, set during the Christmas of 1945. Veteran Hollywood character actor Ned Beatty is a familiar face, and among the cast of youngsters both Radick and Marie Stefan Guadry give pleasing performances. The attention to period detail is also commendable, and, despite the *Boys' Own* plot, the film still manages to push all the right liberal buttons, making it particularly suitable family viewing.

Ned Beatty *Officer Ozzie O'Driscoll/Santa Claus* • Jeremy Radick *Tommy Doyle* • Marie Stefane Gaudry *Fleurette* • Guillaume Lemay Thivierge *Coco* • Leon Pownall *Blue Cheeks* • Nicola Cavendish *Aunt Dottie* • Sarah Meyette *Loretta* • Michel Barrette *Frank* ■ *Dir* Anne Wheeler • *Scr* James DeFelice, Anne Wheeler

The Angel Who Pawned Her Harp ★★ U

Fantasy comedy · 1954 · UK · BW · 76mins

In one of her first roles, Australian actress Diane Cilento plays an angel sent on a goodwill mission to earth. Landing in the Angel, Islington, she pawns her harp, wins some dosh on the greyhounds and sets about sorting out the romantic, economic and housing problems of the ordinary folk she encounters. What this dash of whimsy needs is a modicum of tension or humour, but it hopes to survive purely on charm and the attractiveness of Miss Cilento, who later became Mrs Sean Connery. Based on the novel by Charles Terrot, it also has an overt Jewishness unusual for British movies of the time.

Diane Cilento *The Angel* • Felix Aylmer *Joshua Webman* • Jerry Desmonde *Parker* • Robert Eddison *The Voice* • Sheila Sweet *Jenny Lane* • Alfie Bass *Lennox* • Joe Linnane *Ned Sullivan* • Philip Guard *Len Burrows* ■ *Dir* Alan Bromly • *Scr* Charles Terrot, Sidney Cole, from the novel by Charles Terrot

The Angel Wore Red ★★

Romantic drama · 1960 · US · BW · 98mins

One of the few features to deal with the Spanish Civil War, this improbable romantic drama suffers from confused ideas and unsuitable casting; no wonder it barely saw the light of day in cinemas, being released a year or so after it was filmed. Still, for lovers of this kind of tosh, Dirk Bogarde is the priest who falls for prostitute Ava Gardner but, despite their off-screen friendship, no real romantic sparks are struck and as a result the movie suffers a crippling blow. Colour would also have livened things up a bit, though Joseph Cotten and Vittorio de Sica do lend the film gravitas.

Ava Gardner *Soledad* • Dirk Bogarde *Arturo Carrera* • Joseph Cotten *Hawthorne* • Vittorio De Sica *General Clave* • Aldo Fabrizi *Canon Rota* • Arnoldo Foà *Insurgent Major* • Finlay Currie *Bishop* • Rossana Rory *Mercedes* ■ *Dir/Scr* Nunnally Johnson

Angela ★★

Drama · 1955 · US/It · BW · 91mins

Hollywood actor Dennis O'Keefe found himself increasingly in Europe towards the end of his career, and it was there that he wrote, directed and starred in this low-key combination of *Double Indemnity* and *The Postman Always Rings Twice*. Shot entirely on location in Rome, it was one of the movies that brought Italian heart-throb Rossano Brazzi to the attention of the world. O'Keefe does a workmanlike job, and he has a real chemistry with sexy Mara Lane in the title role. Though marred by poor dubbing of the Italian actors in minor roles, this now passes the time quite adequately.

Dennis O'Keefe *Steve Catlett* • Mara Lane *Angela Towne* • Rossano Brazzi *Nino* • Arnoldo Foà *Captain Ambrosi* • Galeazzo Benti *Gustavo Venturi* • Enzo Fiermonte *Sergeant Collins* • Nino Crisman *Bertolati* ■ *Dir* Dennis O'Keefe • *Scr* Jonathan Rix [Dennis O'Keefe], Edoardo Anton, from a story by Steven Carruthers

Angela's Ashes ★★ 15

Biographical drama · 1999 · US/Ire · Colour · 105mins

Great books don't necessarily translate into great movies, and here's a prime example. Frank McCourt's bestselling, Pulitzer Prize-winning memoir is brought vividly to the screen by Alan Parker with a good cast and top-of-the-line production values. Alas, the result is a motionless, boring movie. Parker's decision to film the terrible poverty of the McCourt family with artistic, anaesthetising cinematography is misguided, as is Robert Carlyle's ineffectual casting as Frank's alcoholic dad. Although McCourt's early memories of school and church provide some humorous respite, it's hard not to feel manipulated by the film's endless exhibition of misery and despair. ▭ *DVD*

Emily Watson *Angela* • Robert Carlyle *Dad* • Joe Breen *Young Frank* • Ciaran Owens *Middle Frank* • Michael Legge *Older Frank* • Ronnie Masterson *Grandma Sheehan* • Pauline McLynn *Aunt Aggie* • Liam Carney *Uncle Pa Keating* • Eanna MacLiam *Uncle Pat* ■ *Dir* Alan Parker • *Scr* Laura Jones, Alan Parker, from the book by Frank McCourt • *Music* John Williams • *Cinematographer* Michael Seresin

The Angelic Conversation ★★ PG

Experimental drama · 1985 · UK · Colour and BW · 77mins

Gay icon director Derek Jarman takes Shakespeare's sonnets back to their homoerotic roots in his highbrow rumination on the objectivity of desire. As young male figures wash, decorate and make love to each other on rocky seaside coastlines, a female narrator (Judi Dench) explores the subtext of the playwright's poetry in gay terms. Beautifully shot with painterly textures, Jarman's academic treatise will either bore or delight, depending on one's openness to the subject matter. ▭

Judi Dench *Narrator* ■ *Dir* Derek Jarman • *Music* Benjamin Britten, Coil

Angels ★★ U

Sports fantasy · 1994 · US · Colour · 93mins

This was a hit in the US, but the baseball theme limited its appeal here and it went straight to video. It is a flimsy, overly sentimental family comedy that wastes the talents of such respected performers as Danny Glover, Christopher Lloyd and Brenda Fricker. The nominal star is young Joseph Gordon-Levitt who calls in a bit of divine intervention to help a struggling baseball team win the championship in an attempt to get back his estranged father (Dermot Mulroney). Sickly sweet, but undemanding kids may lap it up.

Danny Glover *George Knox* • Brenda Fricker *Maggie Nelson* • Tony Danza *Mel Clark* • Christopher Lloyd *Al the Angel* • Ben Johnson *Hank Murphy* • Jay O Sanders *Ranch Wilder* • Joseph Gordon-Levitt *Roger* • Milton Davis Jr *J P* • Matthew McConaughey *Ben Williams* • Dermot Mulroney *Roger's Father* ■ *Dir* William Dear • *Scr* Dorothy Kingsley, George Wells, Holly Goldberg Sloan

Angels and Insects ★★ 18

Period drama · 1995 · UK/US · Colour · 112mins

The British film industry is justly proud of its reputation for meticulously crafted costume dramas. However, the slightest misjudgement can result in disaster, as in the case of this precious adaptation of AS Byatt's novella *Morpho Eugenia*. Although director Philip Haas and his co-writer Belinda Haas have got some pretty tricky ideas to convey (such as Darwinism and the notion that humans are little more than specimens in a celestial laboratory), they do so in such a pompous manner that the already stilted performances of Mark Rylance and Patsy Kensit on the comic. Only Kristin Scott Thomas, playing against type as a mousey governess, emerges with any credit. ▭

Mark Rylance *William Adamson* • Patsy Kensit *Eugenia Alabaster* • Saskia Wickham *Rowena Alabaster* • Chris Larkin *Robin Swinnerton* • Douglas Henshall *Edgar Alabaster* • Annette Badland *Lady Alabaster* • Kristin Scott Thomas *Matty Crompton* • Jeremy Kemp *Sir Harald Alabaster* ■ *Dir* Philip Haas • *Scr* Philip Haas, Belinda Haas, from the novella *Morpho Eugenia* by AS Byatt

Angels in the Outfield ★★ U

Comedy · 1951 · US · BW · 98mins

The rough-tongued and ill-tempered manager of a baseball team in need of success calls on celestial help; Paul Douglas heads a cast that includes Janet Leigh. An odd mix of comedy, whimsy and fantasy, this may appeal to those who like their laughs laced with sentimentality. It's directed by the distinguished Clarence Brown, veteran of seven successful Garbo films and other heavyweight offerings, but his expertise is wasted on the material.

Paul Douglas *Guffy McGovern* • Janet Leigh *Jennifer Paige* • Keenan Wynn *Fred Bayles* • Donna Corcoran *Bridget White* • Lewis Stone *Arnold P Hapgood* • Spring Byington *Sister Edwitha* • Bruce Bennett *Saul Hellman* • Marvin Kaplan *Timothy Durney* ■ *Dir* Clarence Brown • *Scr* Dorothy Kingsley, George Wells, from a story by Richard Conlin

Angels One Five ★★★ U

Second World War drama · 1952 · UK · BW · 93mins

Jack Hawkins, John Gregson and Michael Denison do well in this low-key, surprisingly intelligent Second World War drama, which attempts to show the reality of service life during the Battle of Britain. Director George More O'Ferrall draws on his first-hand knowledge of the subject gained during his own wartime RAF service to probe the emotions behind the British stiff upper lip. A big hit in its day, and still worth the time now. ▭

Jack Hawkins *Group Captain "Tiger" Small* • Michael Denison *Squadron Leader Peter Moon* • Dulcie Gray *Nadine Clinton* • John Gregson *Pilot Officer "Septic" Baird* • Cyril Raymond *Squadron Leader Barry Clinton* • Veronica Hurst *Betty Carfax* • Harold Goodwin *Wailes* • Norman Pierce *Bonzo* ■ *Dir* George More O'Ferrall • *Scr* Derek Twist, from a story by Pelham Groom

Angels over Broadway ★★★ U

Drama · 1940 · US · BW · 75mins

An intriguing, tongue-in-cheek blackly comic drama, in which Douglas Fairbanks Jr tries to embroil a suicidal con man in a poker game with the frantically paced help of Rita Hayworth (in her glamorous heyday) and Thomas Mitchell, playing a mouthy alcoholic with a big idea. The whole film is not as good as the sum of its many diverse parts, although Mitchell gives a truly terrific performance and takes over the screen whenever he appears. This is a laudable attempt to make something a little more sophisticated and complex than the "all cheeky chappies together" comedy of the time. ▭

Douglas Fairbanks Jr *Bill O'Brien* • Rita Hayworth *Nina Barona* • Thomas Mitchell *Gene Gibbons* • John Qualen *Charles Engle* • George Watts *Hopper* • Ralph Theodore *Dutch Enright* • Eddie Foster *Louie Artino* • Jack Roper *Eddie Burns* ■ *Dir* Ben Hecht, Lee Garmes • *Scr* Ben Hecht

Angels Wash Their Faces ★★★

Drama · 1939 · US · BW · 85mins

A follow-up, as you might have guessed from the rather arch title, to the previous year's classic *Angels with Dirty Faces*, though sadly bereft of that film's stars James Cagney and Pat O'Brien, not to mention director Michael Curtiz. So here's Ann Sheridan, who appeared in the original but in a different role, trying to keep her brother away from those pesky Dead End Kids in a moderately sentimental social opus. Still, this is from Warner Bros in a golden period, and it's expertly made, nattily paced and beautifully acted. Oh, and if you've never seen ex-American President Ronald Reagan in his acting heyday, he's actually well worth tuning in for.

Ann Sheridan *Joy Ryan* • Ronald Reagan *Pat Remson* • Billy Halop *Billy Shafter* • Bonita Granville *Peggy Finnigan* • Frankie Thomas *Gabe Ryan* • Bobby Jordan *Bernie* • Bernard Punsley *Sleepy Arkelian* • Leo Gorcey *Lee Finegan* • Huntz Hall *Huntz* • Gabriel Dell *Luigi* • Henry O'Neill *Mr Remson Sr* ■ *Dir* Ray Enright • *Scr* Michael Fessier, Niven Busch, Robert Buckner, from a idea by Jonathan Finn

Angels with Dirty Faces ★★★★★ PG

Classic crime drama 1938 · US · BW · 84mins

This is the definitive Warner Bros gangster movie, starring James Cagney in his image-defining role. It's a knockdown, knockout, fast-paced gritty melodrama, which, though much copied and even parodied, has never been bettered. The tale of two men one good, one bad is given extra weight by the casting of the Dead End Kids, headed by Leo Gorcey and Huntz Hall, as Cagney's would-be disciples, and the moral of the story is still valid today. Michael Curtiz directs with great élan, and the ending, as Cagney walks the famous last "mile" to his execution, is particularly well acted and directed. 🖵

James Cagney *"Rocky" Sullivan* • Pat O'Brien *Jerry Connelly* • Humphrey Bogart *James Frazier* • Ann Sheridan *Laury Ferguson* • George Bancroft *Mac Keefer* • Billy Halop *"Soapy"* • Bobby Jordan *"Swing"* • Leo Gorcey *"Bim"* • Gabriel Dell *"Pasty"* • Huntz Hall *"Crab"* ■ *Dir* Michael Curtiz • *Scr* John Wexley, Warren Duff, from a story by Rowland Brown

Les Anges du Péché ★★★★★

Drama 1943 · Fr · BW · 73mins

Robert Bresson's remarkable directorial debut set the tone for his entire career. It's an intense study of spirituality about a young novice (Renée Fauré) who sacrifices herself for the moral redemption of an ex-prisoner (Jany Holt) who murders her lover immediately on release. Set mainly in the confines of a convent, the film details the devotional aspects of the nuns' lives while depicting the relationship between the two women, one damned, the other divine. Bresson's later work became increasingly pared-down and austere, but this first outing is almost melodramatic; and, while nothing specifically sexual occurs, it's suffused with an eerie, unspoken eroticism. In French with English subtitles.

Renée Fauré *Anne-Marie* • Jany Holt *Thérèse* • Sylvie *Prioress* • Mila Parely *Madeleine* • Marie-Hélène Dasté *Mother St John* ■ *Dir* Robert Bresson • *Scr* Robert Bresson, Jean Giraudoux, RL Brückberger

Angi Vera ★★★★ 12

Political drama 1980 · Hun · Colour · 92mins

Set in 1948, as Stalinism tightened its grip on Hungary, this handsome drama provides an unsettling insight into political indoctrination. Veronika Papp is wholly convincing as the spirited teenage nurse who is sentenced to a Party correction centre after complaining about hospital conditions and then slowly succumbs to the allure of belonging and the illusion of status. The ease with which she betrays both her ideals and her lover is chilling, but Pal Gabor's stealthy direction leaves no doubt where the blame lies. In Hungarian with English subtitles. 🖵

Veronika Papp *Vera Angi* • Erzsi Pasztor *Anna Trajan* • Eva Szabo *Maria Muskat* • Tamas Dunai *Istvan Andre* • Laszlo Halasz *Comrade Sas* ■ *Dir* Pal Gabor • *Scr* Pal Gabor, from the novel by Endre Veszi

Angie ★★ 15

Comedy drama 1994 · US · Colour · 103mins

This should have been the perfect showcase for the talents of Geena Davis. However, Todd Graff's script is such an unconvincing blend of episode and narrative, comedy and melodrama, that she often seems to be acting in a vacuum. Her search for the mother who abandoned her as a child robs the plot of any momentum gained from the ruckus that occurs when she ditches longtime fiancé James Gandolfini for new beau Stephen Rea. Rea does a charming turn, but Davis's exchanges with best friend Aida Turturro are the only time the picture truly comes to life. Contains swearing and nudity. 🖵

Geena Davis *Angie Scacciapensieri* • Stephen Rea *Noel* • James Gandolfini *Vinnie* • Aida Turturro *Tina* • Philip Bosco *Frank* • Jenny O'Hara *Kathy* • Michael Rispoli *Jerry* • Betty Miller *Joanne* ■ *Dir* Martha Coolidge • *Scr* Todd Graff, from the novel *Angie, I Says* by Avra Wing

The Angry Hills ★★

Second World War spy drama 1959 · UK · BW · 114mins

This adaptation of Leon Uris's novel casts Robert Mitchum as an American war correspondent trapped in a Nazi advance in Greece after agreeing to spy for British intelligence. Most of the time he poses in front of olive groves, tries to avoid Gestapo officer Stanley Baker and dallies with Gia Scala. Apart from Mitchum's unavoidable and irrepressible charisma, this war frolic has little to commend it.

Robert Mitchum *Mike Morrison* • Stanley Baker *Konrad Heisler* • Elisabeth Mueller *Lisa Kyriakides* • Gia Scala *Eleftheria* • Theodore Bikel *Tassos* • Sebastian Cabot *Chesney* • Peter Illing *Leonides* • Leslie Phillips *Ray Taylor* ■ *Dir* Robert Aldrich • *Scr* AI Bezzerides, from the novel by Leon Uris

The Angry Red Planet ★★ PG

Science-fiction 1959 · US · Colour · 79mins

A female astronaut under the influence of drugs recalls an expedition to Mars where her team are greeted by giant man-eating plants, three-eyed Martians, Cyclopean blobs, giant bat-spiders and assorted bad vibes. The cartoon-like, expressionistic special effects are red-tinted thanks to the film process "Cinemagic" to approximate the distorted, dream-like quality of Nora Hayden's drug-addled reminiscences. Renowned science fiction director Ib Melchior gives a diverting spin to the familiar Saturday morning serial antics.

Gerald Mohr *O'Banion* • Nora Hayden *Iris Ryan* • Les Tremayne *Professor Gettell* • Jack Kruschen *Sergeant Jacobs* • Paul Hahn *General Treegar* • J Edward McKinley *Professor Weiner* • Tom Daly *Dr Gordon* • Edward Innes *General Prescott* ■ *Dir* Ib Melchior • *Scr* Ib Melchior, Sid Pink, from a story by Sid Pink

The Angry Silence ★★★ PG

Drama 1960 · UK · BW · 90mins

Although this fascinating melodrama was made over 35 years ago, its attitudes to trade unionism and industrial action are curiously contemporary. Bryan Forbes explores a range of political issues in his Oscar-nominated screenplay, but the practised rhetoric sounds false in the mouths of the rank and file, and, consequently, the best moments are not the confrontations between strike-breaker Richard Attenborough and his workmates, but those depicting the disintegration of his marriage. Attenborough gives a sterling performance, but the acting honours go to Pier Angeli as his distraught wife and Alfred Burke as the devious *agent provocateur* behind the strike. 🖵

Richard Attenborough *Tom Curtis* • Pier Angeli *Anna Curtis* • Michael Craig *Joe Wallace* • Bernard Lee *Bert Connolly* • Alfred Burke *Travers* • Geoffrey Keen *Davis* • Laurence Naismith *Martindale* • Oliver Reed *Mick* ■ *Dir* Guy Green • *Scr* Bryan Forbes, from a story by Michael Craig, Richard Gregson

Angus ★★★ 12

Comedy drama 1995 · US · Colour · 86mins

It may not be a classic, but there's no way you can watch this charming rites-of-passage picture and not end up smiling. Perfectly pitched without a hint of condescension, this will be an inspiration to all those children who have suffered at school because of their weight. Charlie Talbert gives a truly vibrant performance as the amiable, resilient teenager, who not only overcomes the snide teasing of physique fascist James Van Der Beek, but also steals his girl at the prom. With George C Scott growling out grandfatherly advice, this is funny, touching and hugely reassuring. 🖵

George C Scott *Ivan* • Chris Owen *Troy Wedberg* • Ariana Richards *Melissa Lefevre* • Anna Thomson [Anna Levine] *April Thomas* • Charlie Talbert *Angus* • Kathy Bates *Meg* • Rita Moreno *Madame Rulenska* • Lawrence Pressman *Principal Metcalf* ■ *Dir* Patrick Read Johnson • *Scr* Jill Gordon, from a short story by Chris Crutcher

Anhonee ★★★ PG

Romantic melodrama 1951 · Ind · BW · 136mins

There's double delight for Nargis fans in this convoluted melodrama, as she plays both the half-sisters competing for the attentions of lawyer Raj Kapoor. Directing only his third feature, one-time film critic KA Abbas achieves a unique brand of social realism by mixing stylistic elements from both the Soviet silent maestro Vsevelod Pudovkin and Frank Capra. Moreover, there's a healthy musical quota, too. In Urdu and Hindi with English subtitles. 🖵

Raj Kapoor • Nargis ■ *Dir* KA Abbas • *Scr* Moshin Abdullah, VP Sathe, KA Abbas

Animal Behavior ★★ PG

Romantic comedy 1989 · US · Colour · 88mins

An excellent cast can do little with this weak romantic comedy set on a college campus. Karen Allen is the psychologist studying animal communication who finds it more difficult to get on with her own species, particularly musician Armand Assante. Sadly, there appears to be little chemistry between Allen and Assante and they are hardly helped by the indecisive script and ill-focused direction. The supporting cast, which includes a pre-fame Holly Hunter, also has few opportunities to shine. Contains some swearing 🖵

Karen Allen *Alex Bristow* • Armand Assante *Mark Mathias* • Holly Hunter *Coral Grable* • Josh Mostel *Mel Gorsky* • Richard Libertini *Dr Parrish* • Alexa Kenin *Sheila Sandusky* • Jon Mathews *Tyler Forbes* • Nan Martin *Mrs Norton* ■ *Dir* H Anne Riley [Jenny Bowen], H Anne Riley [Kjehl Rasmussen] • *Scr* Susan Rice

Animal Crackers ★★★★ U

Comedy 1930 · US · BW · 92mins

"Hooray for Captain Spaulding, the African explorer!". "Did someone call me schnorrer?" asks Groucho Marx, making one the movies' greatest entrances. This was the Marx Brothers' first Hollywood movie (the earlier two were both shot in New York; one's now lost), and is a relatively straightforward film version of their Broadway hit of the same name. The requirements of early sound recording render the action somewhat static, but the clowning is irresistible and Margaret Dumont is a perfect foil (did she really not know the film was a comedy?). 🖵

Groucho Marx *Captain Jeffrey Spaulding* • Harpo Marx *Professor* • Chico Marx *Signor Emanuel Ravelli* • Zeppo Marx *Horatio Jamison* • Lillian Roth *Arabella Rittenhouse* • Margaret Dumont *Mrs Rittenhouse* ■ *Dir* Victor Heerman • *Scr* Morris Ryskind, from the play by Morris Ryskind, George S Kaufman

Animal Farm ★★★★ U

Animation 1954 · UK · Colour · 69mins

Made by the award-winning husband-and-wife team of John Halas and Joy Batchelor, this adaptation of George Orwell's searing political allegory was the first feature-length cartoon produced in Britain. Having decided to target an adult audience, the directors had to create characters that were not only faithful to the novel, but were also capable of arousing emotions without resorting to Disney cuteness. Their success in bringing to life the dictatorial Napoleon, the idealistic Snowball and the noble Boxer is aided by the amazingly individual voices provided by one man, Maurice Denham. This provocative and polished production is an all-too-rare attempt to make an intelligent and entertaining animation for adults. 🖵

Maurice Denham *Voices* • Gordon Heath *Narrator* ■ *Dir* John Halas, Joy Batchelor • *Scr* John Halas, Joy Batchelor, Lothar Wolff, Borden Mace, Philip Stapp, from the novel by George Orwell

Animal Instincts ★★ 18

Erotic thriller 1992 · US · Colour · 97mins

The thriller that made Shannon Whirry a favourite of the top-shelf brigade, and one which went some way to establishing a template for the whole erotic thriller genre. This sleazy study of voyeurism has Maxwell Caulfield playing a sexually frustrated policeman who discovers he would rather videotape his wife (Whirry) in bed with other men and women than sleep with her himself. Director Gregory Hippolyte, who became one of the genre's leading directors, presents the many couplings with some panache, but he can't hide the fact that this is really just *Emmanuelle* for the nineties. 🖵

Maxwell Caulfield *David Cole* • Jan-Michael Vincent *Fletcher Ross* • Mitch Gaylord *Rod Tennison* • Shannon Whirry *Joanne Cole* • Delia Sheppard *Ingrid* • John Saxon *Otto Van Horne* • David Carradine *Lamberti* • Tom Reilly *Ken* ■ *Dir* Gregory Hippolyte • *Scr* Georges Des Esseintes

The Animal Kingdom ★★★★

Drama   1932 · US · BW · 90mins

This highly sophisticated piece might almost be called a "drawing-room drama". A wealthy and unconventional publisher (Leslie Howard), marries an unsuitably conventional and shallow wife (Myrna Loy) to the detriment of his ideals, his lifestyle and his most precious relationship, with an artist (Ann Harding). An unusual approach and the lightest of touches elevates a seemingly well-worn storyline to something special. Credit is due to the impeccable screenplay, the elegance of the accomplished cast, David O Selznick's A-grade production values, and Edward H Griffith's direction.
Ann Harding *Daisy Sage* • Leslie Howard *Tom Collier* • Myrna Loy *Cecilia Henry* • Neil Hamilton *Owen* • William Gargan *Regan* • Henry Stephenson *Rufus Collier* • Ilka Chase *Grace* • Leni Stengel *Franc* • Donald Dillaway *Joe* ■ *Dir* Edward H Griffith • *Scr* Horace Jackson, from the play by Philip Barry

Animalympics ★★ U

Animated comedy
1979 · US · Colour · 78mins

A cartoon feature that spoofs the Olympics by having animals as athletes. It's a good idea, but the dull story could have done with more jokes and a little less preaching about taking part being more important than winning. Uninspired animation means that the characters are a pretty resistible bunch and not even the voices of Gilda Radner and Billy Crystal can liven them up. 🎞
Dir Steven Lisberger

Ann Vickers ★★★

Drama   1933 · US · BW · 74mins

Expertly directed by the always reliable John Cromwell as a starring vehicle for Irene Dunne, this adaptation of the novel by Sinclair Lewis manages to combine themes of feminism, social conscience, political comment and romance to absorbing effect. Dunne, dignified as ever, shines as a reforming social worker who surmounts life's knocks to gain fame for her humane approach to prison reform, while Walter Huston manages to win her heart despite a resistance to men that stems from a damaging love affair. Edna May Oliver is also splendid as an influential doctor friend who guides Dunne through a series of crises. Gritty entertainment, albeit with an element of soapy melodrama – though that, too, has its appeal.
Irene Dunne *Ann Vickers* • Walter Huston *Barney Dolphin* • Conrad Nagel *Lindsay* • Bruce Cabot *Resnick* • Edna May Oliver *Malvina* • Sam Hardy *Russell Spaulding* • Mitchell Lewis *Capt Waldo* • Helen Eby-Rock *Kitty Cignac* • Gertrude Michael *Mona Dolphin* ■ *Dir* John Cromwell • *Scr* Jane Murfin, from the novel by Sinclair Lewis

Anna ★★★ 15

Drama   1987 · US · Colour · 95mins

Sally Kirkland landed an Oscar nomination for her performance as a fading Czech actress in this beautifully observed but little seen film. Scripted by the Polish director Agnieszka Holland, it is essentially a reworking of *All about Eve*, with some shrewd (and clearly autobiographical) observations about living in exile thrown in for good measure. Kirkland does a nice line in mournful self-effacement, but she's nowhere near as convincing once she becomes jealous of the adoring hopeful (played by debuting supermodel Paulina Porizkova) she has turned into a star. Director Yurek Bogayevicz handles the cast well, but rather loses his grip on the story. Contains swearing and nudity. 🎞
Sally Kirkland *Anna* • Robert Fields *Daniel* • Paulina Porizkova *Krystyna* • Gibby Brand *1st director* • John Robert Tillotson *2nd director* • Julianne Gilliam *Woman author* • Joe Aufiery *Stage manager* • Charles Randall *Agent* • Mimi Wedell *Agent's secretary* • Larry Pine *Baskin* ■ *Dir* Yurek Bogayevicz • *Scr* Agnieszka Holland, from a story by Yurek Bogayevicz, Agnieszka Holland

Anna and the King ★★★ 12

Period romantic drama
1999 · US · Colour · 142mins

With so many versions of this tale already on film – including the limp animated adaptation released earlier in the same year – who doesn't know the story of the Victorian widow who travels with her son to tutor the children of the King of Siam? This time we have Jodie Foster, boasting an immaculate English accent as the plucky governess who melts the heart of the king, played by a surprisingly sweet-natured Chow Yun-Fat. With a heavy emphasis on complicated political machinations and the odd gruesome scene, it's hardly suitable for young ones. Nonetheless, this is a heartwarming yarn that builds to a great action climax. 🎞
Jodie Foster *Anna Leonowens* • Chow Yun-Fat *King Mongkut* • Bai Ling *Tuptim* • Tom Felton *Louis Leonowens* • Alwi Syed *The Kralahome* • Randall Duk Kim *General Alak* • Lim Kay Siu *Prince Chowfa* • Melissa Campbell *Princess Fa-Ying* ■ *Dir* Andy Tennant • *Scr* Peter Krikes, Steve Meerson, from diaries of Anna Leonowens

Anna and the King of Siam ★★★

Drama based on a true story
1946 · US · BW · 128mins

Before Deborah Kerr and Yul Brynner starred in the musical version of the story, Irene Dunne and Rex Harrison were Mrs Anna and her king in a stolid (if expensive) 20th Century-Fox adaptation of Margaret Landon's bestseller about English schoolteacher Anna Leonowens. While Dunne was born to play a governess, Harrison is miscast, with facial features more appropriate to Hampstead than Thailand (James Mason was the original choice). John Cromwell's direction suffers in comparison to the liveliness of the musical version and the art direction is relentlessly Hollywood Siam, but the sets won an

Oscar, as did Arthur Miller's camerawork.
Irene Dunne *Anna* • Rex Harrison *The King* • Linda Darnell *Tuptin* • Lee J Cobb *Kralahome* • Gale Sondergaard *Lady Thiang* • Mikhail Rasumny *Alak* • Dennis Hoey *Sir Edward* • Tito Renaldo *Prince, as a man* • Richard Lyon *Louis Owens* • William Edmunds *Monshee* • Mickey Roth *Prince, as a boy* ■ *Dir* John Cromwell • *Scr* Talbot Jennings, Sally Benson, from the non-fiction book by Margaret Landon • *Set Designer* Lyle Wheeler, William Darling, Thomas Little, Frank E Hughes

Anna Boleyn ★★★★

Silent historical drama
1920 · Ger · Tinted · 100mins

Recently restored with the original colour tinting, this sumptuous film has a fine cast headed by Henny Porten, Germany's first superstar, and the mighty Emil Jannings as a sensual and cruel Henry VIII. Before German-born Ernst Lubitsch went to Hollywood in 1923, he made his reputation with several ironic historical romances like this one, which led to his first being described as having the "Lubitsch Touch".
Henny Porten *Anne Boleyn* • Emil Jannings *King Henry VIII* • Paul Hartmann *Sir Henry Norris* • Ludwig Hartau *Duke of Norfolk* • Aud Egede Nissen *Jane Seymour* • Hedwig Pauly *Queen Catherine* • Hilde Müller *Princess Marie* ■ *Dir* Ernst Lubitsch • *Scr* Norbert Falk [Fred Orbing], Hans Kräly

Anna Christie ★★ U

Drama   1930 · US · BW · 85mins

"Gif me a vhiskey, ginger ale on the side – and don't be stingy, baby.'' These were the first words spoken on the screen in this, her first talkie, by the great Greta Garbo. She's perfectly cast as Eugene O'Neill's lady with a past in this turgid seafront drama, which plays more than a little creaky today. The Swedish *grande dame* also talked in the simultaneously-shot but shorter German language version of this film, and director Jacques Feyder was much more in sympathy with her European angst than was this version's director, Clarence Brown, with the result that the Feyder version rings truer. The American version does however boast the wonderful Marie Dressler as an old sea lag. 🎞
Greta Garbo *Anna Christie* • Charles Bickford *Matt Burke* • George F Marion *Producer* • Marie Dressler *Marthy Owen* • James T Mack [James Mack] • Lee Phelps *Larry, barman* ■ *Dir* Clarence Brown • *Scr* Frances Marion, from the play by Eugene O'Neill

Anna Karenina ★★★★ U

Period romantic drama
1935 · US · BW · 89mins

The great Greta Garbo in one of her best-remembered roles, a fine mating of artist and character. This was her second attempt at *Karenina*, having starred with John Gilbert in a notable silent version of the tale in 1927, retitled *Love*, and also for MGM ("Garbo and Gilbert in *Love*"). This is very much a *Reader's Digest* version of the great novel, paring the plot down to the bone (and completely eliminating all subplots); it is also overdependent on a splendid, but sometimes disconcertingly multi-accented, cast: Fredric March, Basil

Rathbone and Freddie Bartholomew. Garbo's favourite cameraman William Daniels gives a dynamic sheen to the famous final station scene, but the noted MGM production values look a shade creaky today. Still, for many, Garbo is the definitive screen Anna. 🎞
Greta Garbo *Anna Karenina* • Fredric March *Vronsky* • Freddie Bartholomew *Sergei* • Maureen O'Sullivan *Kitty* • May Robson *Countess Vronsky* • Basil Rathbone *Karenin* • Reginald Owen *Stiva* • Reginald Denny *Yashvin* • Phoebe Foster *Dolly* • Gyles Isham *Levin* ■ *Dir* Clarence Brown • *Scr* Clemence Dane, Salka Viertel, SN Behrman, from the novel by Leo Tolstoy • *Production Designer* Cedric Gibbons • *Costume Designer* Adrian

Anna Karenina ★★★

Period romantic drama
1947 · UK · BW · 139mins

The sumptuous production values of this film, directed by Julien Duvivier and photographed by Henri Alekan, even combined with the dazzling beauty of Vivien Leigh as Tolstoy's famously doomed heroine, are not enough to prevent it being ultimately a disappointment. It is too long to support the screenplay and the miscasting of a pretty but dull Kieron Moore as Vronsky robs the drama of weight and conviction. Leigh does her best and there are some affecting moments (notably the scenes between Anna and her child), but only Ralph Richardson, superbly unbending as Karenin, has the measure of the material. 🎞
Vivien Leigh *Anna Karenina* • Ralph Richardson *Alexei Karenin* • Kieron Moore *Count Vronsky* • Sally Ann Howes *Kitty Scherbatsky* • Niall MacGinnis *Levin* • Martita Hunt *Princess Betty Tversky* • Marie Lohr *Princess Scherbatsky* • Michael Gough *Nicholai* • Hugh Dempster *Stefan Oblonsky* ■ *Dir* Julien Duvivier • *Scr* Jean Anouilh, Guy Morgan, Julien Duvivier, from the novel by Leo Tolstoy • *Costume Design* Cecil Beaton

Anna Karenina ★★★ PG

Period romantic drama
1985 · US · Colour · 129mins

It can't be easy following in the footsteps of Greta Garbo and Vivien Leigh, but Jacqueline Bisset has a decent stab at it in this lavish made-for-TV version of Tolstoy's classic. Bisset has always been a rather nervy performer, conscious of her beauty, and this helps her portrayal of the neurotic heroine who falls for dashing Count Vronsky (Christopher Reeve) and abandons her boring husband (Paul Scofield), with tragic consequences. The cast is impressive, and James Goldman provides a literate compression of the novel's vast expanses. 🎞
Jacqueline Bisset *Anna* • Christopher Reeve *Count Vronsky* • Paul Scofield *Karenin* • Ian Ogilvy *Stiva* • Anna Massey *Betsy* • Joanna David *Dolly* • Judi Bowker *Kitty* • Valerie Lush *Annushka* • Judy Campbell *Countess Vronsky* ■ *Dir* Simon Langton • *Scr* James Goldman, from the novel by Leo Tolstoy

Anna Karenina ★★ 12

Period romantic drama
1997 · US · Colour · 103mins

Despite being the first film adaptation to benefit from authentic locations in

St Petersburg and Moscow, this is a fairly negligible version of the classic novel. The problem lies in the leaden script – which misguidedly incorporates the subplot about Levin's love for Anna's sister-in-law – and the Euro-pudding casting, which undermines the notion that Tolstoy's characters come out of the same Tsarist bottle. Sophie Marceau is pretty but vacuous in the lead, and only James Fox creates any lasting impression as her cuckolded husband.

Sophie Marceau *Anna Karenina* • Sean Bean *Vronsky* • Alfred Molina *Levin* • Mia Kirshner *Kitty* • James Fox *Karenin* • Fiona Shaw *Lydia* • Danny Huston *Stiva* • Phyllida Law *Vronskaya* ■ *Dir* Bernard Rose • *Scr* Bernard Rose, from the novel by Leo Tolstoy

Anna Lucasta ★★★

Melodrama 1949 · US · BW · 85mins

This film version of a long-running, much revived play by Philip Yordan stars the luscious Paulette Goddard as Anna, gone to the bad in Brooklyn after being thrown out by her Polish immigrant father (Oscar Homolka). She is lured back to her coarse, poor and feckless family in the Midwest who plot to marry her off for money, but the plans go awry... Directed with a sure hand by Irving Rapper and there's a standout supporting performance from Broderick Crawford as her scheming brother-in-law. It's good, solid entertainment that deftly signals the subtexts of incestuous desire and prostitution.

Paulette Goddard *Anna Lucasta* • William Bishop *Rudolf Strobel* • Oscar Homolka *Joe Lucasta* • John Ireland *Danny Johnson* • Broderick Crawford *Frank* • Will Geer *Noah* • Gale Page *Katie* • Mary Wickes *Stella* • Whit Bissell *Stanley* ■ *Dir* Irving Rapper • *Scr* Philip Yordan, Arthur Laurents, from the play by Philip Yordan

Anna Lucasta ★★

Drama 1958 · US · BW · 96mins

Philip Yordan's Broadway play, about a girl whose shady past as a sailors' whore catches up with her and almost destroys her chance of a fresh start, was originally staged with an all-black cast. Columbia filmed it in 1949 as an all-white drama, starring Paulette Goddard as the daughter of Polish immigrants, who becomes a prostitute in New York. Here, United Artists had Yordan adapt it again, and cast Eartha Kitt as Anna, this time plying her trade at the San Diego naval base, with an all-black cast featuring Rex Ingram, Henry Scott and Sammy Davis Jr. Kitt acquits herself reasonably well, but Arnold Laven's direction is stagey and the film is utterly lacking in conviction.

Eartha Kitt *Anna Lucasta* • Sammy Davis Jr *Danny Johnson* • Frederick O'Neal *Frank* • Henry Scott *Rudolph Slocum* • Rex Ingram *Joe Lucasta* • Georgia Burke *Theresa* • James Edwards *Eddie* • Rosetta Le Noire *Stella* ■ *Dir* Arnold Laven • *Scr* Philip Yordan, from his play

Annabel Takes a Tour ★★ U

Comedy 1938 · US · BW · 66mins

Earlier in 1938, RKO's *The Affairs of Annabel* launched a proposed B-comedy series for Lucille Ball, starring her as a giddy movie actress whose press agent (Jack Oakie) dreams up a series of screwball publicity stunts. Bright, breezy and fast-moving, the movie drew the punters, and this first sequel followed hot on its heels. It was also the last. No more than a laboured and less amusing retread of the first film, plotted on an identical premise with Ball on a promotional tour for her latest film, it lost money and the studio cancelled the series. However, Ball's always high-octane appeal is intact, and provides the main appeal here.

Lucille Ball *Annabel* • Jack Oakie *Lanny Morgan* • Ruth Donnelly *Josephine* • Bradley Page *Webb* • Ralph Forbes *Viscount* • Frances Mercer *Natalie* • Donald MacBride *Thompson* ■ *Dir* Lew Landers • *Scr* Bert Granet, Olive Cooper, from a story by Joe Bigelow, from characters created by Charles Hoffman

Annabelle Partagée ★ 18

Drama 1990 · Fr · Colour · 76mins

Although it made censorship history after the BBFC decided to pass the startling opening image of an ejaculating penis, this dreary mélange is the kind of movie that gives arthouse a bad name. Like Catherine Breillat's controversial *Romance*, the film – about a provincial in Paris who toys with both an architect friend of her father's and a handsome layabout – insists its aim is to depict a woman taking control of her own sexual destiny. But writer/director Francesca Comencini succeeds only in subjecting Delphine Zingg's body to the camera's dispassionate gaze, and the viewer to some interminably dull conversations about the meaning of life. In French with English subtitles.

Delphine Zingg *Annabelle* • François Marthouret *Richard* • Jean-Claude Adelin *Luca* ■ *Dir/Scr* Francesca Comencini

An Annapolis Story ★★★

Wartime romance
1955 · US · Colour · 81mins

Director Don Siegel makes the most of this tale of two brothers (John Derek and Kevin McCarthy), both cadets at the Annapolis naval academy, who fall out over a girl (Diana Lynn). Their relationship is temporarily poisoned, but the boys eventually settle their differences while on active service in Korea. The personal drama is lent veracity by authentic location filming at Annapolis (complete with flag-waving passing-out parades) and on board a real aircraft carrier.

John Derek *Tony Scott* • Diana Lynn *Peggy Lord* • Kevin McCarthy *Jim Scott* • Alvy Moore *Willie* • Pat Conway *Dooley* • LQ Jones *Watson* • John Kirby *Macklin* • Barbara Brown *Mrs Scott* ■ *Dir* Don Siegel • *Scr* Daniel B Ullman, Geoffrey Homes [Daniel Mainwaring], from a story by Daniel B Ullman

Anne and Muriel ★★★★ 15

Romantic drama 1971 · Fr · Colour · 124mins

Inspired by his fascination with the Brontës, François Truffaut reverses the situation in *Jules et Jim* – also adapted from a novel by Henri-Pierre Roché – with this elegiac tale of doomed love. An unbearably sad film, this is as much about the passion of creativity as it is about romance, as Jean-Pierre Léaud's art critic is capable only of appreciating the beauty of English sisters Kika Markham and Stacey Tendeter rather than being captivated by it. Shot in desaturated colour to convey the turn-of-the-century atmosphere, the film also employs written material, voice-overs and a range of cinematic devices to enhance the intimacy of the story. In French with English subtitles.

Jean-Pierre Léaud *Claude Roc* • Kika Markham *Anne Brown* • Stacey Tendeter *Muriel Brown* • Sylvia Marriott *Mrs Brown* • Marie Mansart *Madame Roc* • Philippe Léotard *Diurka* • François Truffaut *Narration* ■ *Dir* François Truffaut • *Scr* Jean Gruault, François Truffaut, from the novel by Henri-Pierre Roché

Anne Devlin ★★★ PG

Historical drama 1984 · Ire · Colour · 121mins

Pat Murphy's film is a fitting tribute to Anne Devlin, the peasant's daughter who, as Robert Emmett's confidante, played a key role in the struggle for Irish independence in the early 19th century. Brid Brennan certainly gives a committed performance, but comparisons with Renée Falconetti in Carl Dreyer's silent masterpiece *The Passion of Joan of Arc* are a little flattering. Deftly equating political liberation with female emancipation, Murphy is content to focus on character rather than events, and she's helped by the affecting simplicity of Thaddeus O'Sullivan's photography. Her pacing is a touch too deliberate, however.

Brid Brennan *Anne Devlin* • Bosco Hogan *Robert Emmett* • Des McAleer • Gillian Hackett ■ *Dir* Pat Murphy • *Scr* Pat Murphy, from journals by Anne Devlin

Anne of Green Gables ★★★ U

Drama 1934 · US · BW · 77mins

This is the definitive movie version (it had been filmed before in 1919) of LM Montgomery's popular tale about the teenage orphan. Child actress Dawn O'Day changed her professional name to that of the film's character, and as Anne Shirley delivered an exquisite, utterly charming performance. This is a real one-off: the 1940 sequel *Anne of Windy Poplars* is feeble by comparison, and Shirley was not nearly as beguiling as a grown-up, though she did continue a useful, if not striking, screen career.

Dawn O'Day [Anne Shirley] *Anne Shirley* • Tom Brown *Gilbert Blythe* • OP Heggie *Matthew Cuthbert* • Helen Westley *Marilla Cuthbert* • Sara Haden *Mrs Barry* • Murray Kinnell *Mr Phillips* • Gertrude Messinger *Diana* • June Preston *Mrs Blewett's daughter* • Charley Grapewin *Dr Tatum* • Hilda Vaughn *Mrs Blewett* ■ *Dir* George Nichols Jr • *Scr* Sam Mintz, from the novel by LM Montgomery

Anne of the Indies ★★★ U

Swashbuckling adventure
1951 · US · Colour · 79mins

Aha, me hearties, 'tis rollicking Jean Peters as the swashbuckling scourge of the Caribbean, surrounded by old reliables James Robertson-Justice as the first mate, Herbert Marshall as the rummy doc and Thomas Gomez as Blackbeard himself. Louis Jourdan is the dashing Frenchman who is forced into luring the pirate queen into a treasure-baited trap, while fifties icon Debra Paget plays Jourdan's kidnapped wife. Director Jacques Tourneur is best known for such classic horror movies as *Cat People* and *Night of the Demon*, but he seems more than comfortable with this splendid seafaring tale.

Jean Peters *Anne* • Louis Jourdan *Captain Pierre François La Rochelle* • Debra Paget *Molly* • Herbert Marshall *Dr Jameson* • Thomas Gomez *Blackbeard* • James Robertson-Justice *Red Dougal* • Francis Pierlot *Herkimer* • Sean McClory *Hackett* • Holmes Herbert *English sea captain* ■ *Dir* Jacques Tourneur • *Scr* Phillip Dunne, Arthur Caesar, from a story by Herbert Ravenel Sass

Anne of the Thousand Days ★★★ PG

Historical drama
1969 · US · Colour · 139mins

Producer Hal Wallis's inventive and flamboyant slice of English history was a surprising hit, reviving a moribund genre and providing marvellous showcases for Richard Burton, as a roistering but soulful Henry VIII, and Geneviève Bujold, touchingly well-cast as Anne Boleyn. The period interiors, largely re-created at Shepperton studios, are beautifully designed, though much of the attention to detail is lost on television. Margaret Furse's costumes rightly won an Oscar; a shame, then, that Charles Jarrott's direction is insipid and poorly paced. Nevertheless, this is a respectable piece of film-making.

Richard Burton *King Henry VIII* • Geneviève Bujold *Anne Boleyn* • Irene Papas *Catherine of Aragon* • Anthony Quayle *Cardinal Wolsey* • John Colicos *Cromwell* • Michael Hordern *Thomas Boleyn* • Katharine Blake *Elizabeth Boleyn* • Peter Jeffrey *Norfolk* • William Squire *Thomas More* • Valerie Gearon *Mary Boleyn* • Elizabeth Taylor *Courtesan* ■ *Dir* Charles Jarrott • *Scr* Bridget Boland, John Hale, Richard Sokolove (adaptation), from the play by Maxwell Anderson • *Cinematographer* Arthur Ibbetson • *Art Director* Maurice Carter, Lionel Couch, Patrick McLoughlin

Anne of Windy Poplars ★★ U

Drama 1940 · US · BW · 85mins

Six years after the charming film version of author LM Montgomery's popular *Anne of Green Gables* came this routine sequel, with the now grown-up Anne teaching in one of those small towns where everyone (except kindly old folks) is hypocritical or corrupt, or both. Anne Shirley is once again played by Anne Shirley, the former Dawn O'Day, who cannily changed her name to that of her character.

Anne Shirley *Anne Shirley* • James Ellison *Tony Pringle* • Henry Travers *Matey* • Patric Knowles *Gilbert Blythe* • Slim Summerville *Jabez Monkman* • Elizabeth Patterson *Rebecca* • Louise Campbell *Katherine Pringle* • Joan Carroll *Betty Grayson* ■ *Dir* Jack Hively • *Scr* Michael Kanin, Jerry Cady, from the novel by LM Montgomery

Anne Trister ★★★

Drama 1986 · Can · Colour · 115mins

Partly inspired by her own experiences, Léa Pool's second feature follows an aspiring painter from her Swiss home to Montreal, where she fulfils both her artistic and emotional destinies.

64
U = SUITABLE FOR ALL Uc = SUITABLE FOR ALL, ESPECIALLY FOR YOUNG CHILDREN (VIDEO ONLY) PG = PARENTAL GUIDANCE

Liberated from the influence of her father and her boyfriend (Hugues Quester), Albane Guilhe embarks upon a vast mural that reflects her growing attraction to Louise Marleau, the psychologist with whom she is living. Using Marleau's relationship with a young patient to comment on the burgeoning age-gap romance, Pool successfully gets under the skins of her characters, although her pacing is occasionally ponderous. In French with English subtitles. Contains sex scenes.

Albane Guilhe *Anne Trister* • Louise Marleau *Alix* • Lucie Laurier *Sarah* • Guy Thauvette *Thomas* • Hugues Quester *Pierre* • Nuvit Ozdogru *Simon* ■ *Dir* Léa Pool • *Scr* Léa Pool, Marcel Beaulieu

Anne Tyler's Saint Maybe ★★★

Drama   1998 · US · Colour

Thomas McCarthy stars as a young teenager disturbed by the past, whose suspicions about his sister-in-law's infidelity set in motion a chain of tragic events that are sure to have you reaching for the Kleenex. While this TV drama is quite predictable, the sterling performances of Mary-Louise Parker, Blythe Danner (Gwyneth Paltrow's mum) and Edward Hermann help overcome any shortcomings, and director Michael Pressman (*The Practice, Chicago Hope*) wrings every last tear from the unashamedly sentimental material. Ideal for rainy Sunday afternoons, as long as you have chocolate biscuits and a box of tissues by your side.

Thomas McCarthy *Ian Bedloe* • Mary-Louise Parker *Lucy* • Blythe Danner *Bee Bedloe* • Edward Herrmann *Doug Bedloe* • Jeffrey Nordling *Danny Bedloe* • Melina Kanakaredes *Rita DiCarlo* ■ *Dir* Michael Pressman • *Scr* Robert W Lenski, from the novel by Anne Tyler

Annie ★★★🅤

Musical   1982 · US · Colour · 122mins

John Huston was the wrong director for this long-winded version of the Broadway musical based on the popular American comic strip. He lacks the necessary light touch that might have made this the equal of the stage production, and he's not helped by the casting of heavyweight Albert Finney as bald Daddy Warbucks and grimacing Tim Curry as a villain. However, Carol Burnett is a zesty Miss Hannigan and Aileen Quinn is appealing as the moppet of the title, while real class is brought to the proceedings by Broadway divas Bernadette Peters and Ann Reinking. Dip in and enjoy the marvellous songs. 📼

Albert Finney *Daddy Warbucks* • Carol Burnett *Miss Hannigan* • Bernadette Peters *Lily* • Ann Reinking *Grace Farrell* • Tim Curry *Rooster* • Aileen Quinn *Annie* • Geoffrey Holder *Punjab* • Roger Minami *Asp* ■ *Dir* John Huston • *Scr* Carol Sobieski, from the book by Thomas Meehan, Charles Strouse, Martin Charnin, from the comic strip *Little Orphan Annie* by Harold Gray

Annie ★★★

Musical   1999 · US · Colour

The musical that gives thousands of showbiz mums the chance to push their little darlings on the stage gets the Walt Disney treatment in this occasionally saccharine but enjoyably bumptious TV movie. Newcomer Alicia Morton is little orphan Annie, who gradually thaws the heart of millionaire Daddy Warbucks (Victor Garber). As usual, though, it's the baddie who steals the show, and Kathy Bates is a memorable Miss Hannigan. (She received a Golden Globe nomination for her performance.) British actor Alan Cumming also scores, while Rob Marshall's zippy direction means youngsters won't get bored.

Victor Garber *Daddy Warbucks* • Kathy Bates *Miss Hannigan* • Audra McDonald *Grace Farrell* • Kristin Chenoweth *Lily* • Alan Cumming *Rooster* • Alicia Morton *Annie* ■ *Dir* Rob Marshall • *Scr* Irene Mecchi, from the musical by Thomas Meehan, Charles Strouse, Martin Charnin, from the comic strip *Little Orphan Annie* by Harold Gray

Annie: a Royal Adventure ★★🅤

Drama   1995 · US · Colour · 88mins

Most sequels are disappointing, but few plumb the depths of this right royal mess. Devoid of the cheerful songs that made *Annie* so popular, it is forced to rely on a preposterous plot in which the flame-haired heroine comes to London to see Daddy Warbucks receive his knighthood and ends up taking on the evil aristocrat who plans to blow up Buckingham Palace. Poor fare, but credit to the producers for casting Joan Collins. 📼

Ashley Johnson *Annie* • George Hearn *"Daddy" Oliver Warbucks* • Joan Collins *Lady Edwina Hogbottom* • Ian McDiarmid *Professor Eli Eon* • Emily Ann Lloyd *Hannah Apple* • Camilla Belle *Molly* • Crispin Bonham-Carter *Rupert* • Perry Benson *Murphy* • George Wood [G Wood] *Michael Webb* ■ *Dir* Ian Toynton • *Scr* Trish Soodik, from the comic strip *Little Orphan Annie* by Harold Gray

Annie Get Your Gun ★★★★★🅤

Musical western   1950 · US · Colour · 107mins

MGM's wonderfully zesty film of Irving Berlin's Broadway smash stars a perfectly cast Betty Hutton as Annie Oakley, borrowed from Paramount to replace an ailing (and, to tell the truth, unsuitable) Judy Garland. George Sidney's bravura direction gets the most out of a marvellous score, which includes such classics as *Anything You Can Do (I Can Do Better)* and, of course, *There's No Business Like Show Business*. Handsome newcomer Howard Keel makes an impressive movie musical debut as sharp-shooting Frank Butler, and the Technicolor and costume design are particularly ravishing. It's hard to see how this could have been any better.

Betty Hutton *Annie Oakley* • Howard Keel *Frank Butler* • Louis Calhern *Buffalo Bill* • J Carrol Naish *Chief Sitting Bull* • Edward Arnold *Pawnee Bill* • Keenan Wynn *Charlie Davenport* • Benay Venuta *Dolly Tate* • Clinton Sundberg *Foster Wilson* ■ *Dir* George Sidney • *Scr* Sidney Sheldon, from the play by Herbert Fields, Dorothy Fields • *Cinematographer* Charles Rosher • *Music/Lyrics* Irving Berlin • *Music* Adolph Deutsch, Roger Edens

Annie Hall ★★★★★ 🔞15

Romantic comedy
1977 · US · Colour · 89mins

Although Woody Allen had still to acquire great technical strength as a film-maker, this was the movie where he found his own singular voice, a voice that echoes across events with a mixture of exuberance and introspection. Peppered with hilarious, snappy insights into the meaning of life, love, psychiatry, ambition, art and New York, this comic delight also gains considerably from the spirited playing of Diane Keaton as the kooky innocent from the Midwest, and Woody himself as the fumbling New York neurotic. The narrative runs parallel to the real-life relationship between the two leads (Keaton's father's name was Hall), and the film scooped four Oscars, including best film and screenplay (co-written with Marshall Brickman) for Allen, and best actress for Keaton. Contains mild swearing. 📼 *DVD*

Woody Allen *Alvy Singer* • Diane Keaton *Annie Hall* • Tony Roberts *Rob* • Carol Kane *Allison* • Paul Simon *Tony Lacey* • Shelley Duvall *Pam* • Janet Margolin *Robin* • Colleen Dewhurst *Mom Hall* • Christopher Walken *Duane Hall* • Donald Symington *Dad Hall* • Helen Ludlam *Grammy Hall* • Mordecai Lawner *Producer* • Joan Newman *Alvy's Mom* • Jonathan Munk *Alvy aged nine* ■ *Dir* Woody Allen • *Scr* Woody Allen, Marshall Brickman

Annie Laurie ★★★

Silent romantic melodrama
1927 · US · BW and Colour

Because Lillian Gish's sweet image was out of step with the vogue for flappers and jazz babies, it was said that MGM humiliated her by giving her this, which one critic called "soggy haggis". It's true this tale of clan warfare, in which a governor's daughter has to choose between a Campbell and a MacDonald, is rather tritely handled. Yet Gish is as radiant as ever, there is some splendid camerawork, and the recently restored two-tone Technicolor scenes are lovely to look at. The picture was a failure, however, and Gish's career started to decline.

Lillian Gish *Annie Laurie* • Norman Kerry *Ian MacDonald* • Creighton Hale *Donald* • Joseph Striker *Alastair* • Hobart Bosworth *The MacDonald Chieftain* • Patricia Avery *Enid* • Russell Simpson *Sandy* • Brandon Hurst *The Campbell Chieftain* ■ *Dir* John S Robertson • *Scr* Josephine Lovett, Marian Ainslee (titles), Ruth Cummings (titles), from a story by Josephine Lovett • *Cinematographer* Jack Parker

Annie Oakley ★★★🅤

Western   1935 · US · BW · 86mins

The story of America's most famous female sharpshooter here becomes a vehicle for Barbara Stanwyck. It was her first western, and she copes well enough, though she seems far too contemporary in looks and attitude for the fiesty Ms Oakley. However, this is a still a thoroughly enjoyable early work from George Stevens, who went on to direct such classics as *A Place in the Sun* (1951), *Shane* (1953) and *Giant* (1956). Suave Melvyn Douglas and handsome Preston Foster both score highly in a film that studiously ignores history throughout. 📼

Barbara Stanwyck *Annie Oakley* • Preston Foster *Toby Walker* • Melvyn Douglas *Jeff Hogarth* • Moroni Olsen *Buffalo Bill* • Pert Kelton *Vera Delmar* • Andy Clyde *Macivor* • Chief Thundercloud *Sitting Bull* • Margaret Armstrong *Mrs Oakley* • Delmar Watson *Wesley Oakley* ■ *Dir* George Stevens • *Scr* Joel Sayre, John Twist, from a story by Joseph A Fields, Ewart Adamson

Annie's Coming Out ★★🅿🅖

Drama based on a true story
1984 · Ausl · Colour · 88mins

A cerebral palsy victim is confined to a state mental institution despite being highly intelligent, and has to fight to prove she is more than a vegetable. An interesting premise – based on a true story – ends up as TV-movie-of-the-week fodder thanks to a cumbersome soundtrack and an annoying tendency to raise questions without actually providing any answers to them. While it never quite rises above a run-of-the-mill weepie, this nonetheless features solid performances from leads Angela Punch McGregor and Drew Forsythe. 📼

Angela Punch McGregor *Jessica Hathaway* • Drew Forsythe *David Lewis* • Tina Arhondis *Annie O'Farrell* • Monica Maughan *Vera Peters* • Mark Butler *Dr John Monroe* • Philippa Baker *Sister Waterman* ■ *Scr* Dir Gil Brealey • *Scr* John Patterson, Chris Borthwick, from the book by Rosemary Crossley

The Annihilator ★★★ 🔞15

Science-fiction thriller
1986 · US · Colour · 89mins

This is a pilot for a TV series that never saw the light of day. Directed by Michael Chapman, whose work as a cinematographer includes Martin Scorsese's *Taxi Driver* and *Raging Bull*, this suitably sinister story centres on the discovery by newspaper editor Mark Lindsay Chapman that his girlfriend has been possessed by killer humanoids during a routine flight from Hawaii. Susan Blakely and Lisa Blount lead a respectable supporting cast, which also contains the ever-dubious Brion James and Geoffrey Lewis. 📼

Mark Lindsay Chapman *Richard Armour* • Susan Blakely *Layla* • Lisa Blount *Cindy* • Brion James *Alien leader* • Earl Boen *Sid* • Geoffrey Lewis *Professor Alan Jeffries* • Catherine Mary Stewart *Angela Taylor* • Nicole Eggert *Elyse* ■ *Dir* Michael Chapman • *Scr* Roderick Taylor, Bruce A Taylor

The Anniversary ★★★

Black comedy   1968 · UK · Colour · 93mins

Britain's Hammer studios took a break from monsters and ghoulies of the past to produce contemporary chillers for a brief period. Here, Hollywood *grande dame* Bette Davis provides the scares, and some laughs, as an eyepatch-wearing virago ruling an ill-assorted family in England's suburbia. The rest of the cast is no match for Davis, but Sheila Hancock, Jack Hedley and, particularly, James Cossins hold their own. This slice of *Grand Guignol* was based on a play and, despite *Brighton Rock* cinematographer Harry Waxman's excellent colour photography, the atmosphere is resolutely theatrical. Still, Davis is always watchable, even if one has the decided impression that she regarded this film as slumming, despite the fact that she had quite a say in the production.

Bette Davis *Mrs Taggart* • Sheila Hancock *Karen Taggart* • Jack Hedley *Terry Taggart* • James Cossins *Henry Taggart* • Christian Roberts *Tom Taggart* • Elaine Taylor *Shirley Blair* • Timothy Bateson *Mr Bird* • Arnold Diamond *Headwaiter* ■ *Dir* Roy Ward Baker • *Scr* Jimmy Sangster, from the play by Bill MacIlwraith

Another Country ★★★★ 15

Drama 1984 · UK · Colour · 86mins

This is the film that should have made Rupert Everett a bigger star than he is. His electrifying performance, as a homosexual public schoolboy barred from an exclusive prefects' society, is at once endearing and arrogant. Directed by Marek Kanievska, from Julian Mitchell's adaptation of his own play about the background to the Burgess/MacLean spy scandal, the tale only clicks into credibility when Everett goes into outsider mode. A wonderfully flamboyant exposure of what makes a traitor, this deserved more acclaim and box-office receipts than it got.

Rupert Everett *Guy Bennett* • Colin Firth *Tommy Judd* • Michael Jenn *Barclay* • Robert Addie *Delahay* • Anna Massey *Imogen Bennett* • Betsy Brantley *Julie Schofield* • Rupert Wainwright *Devenish* • Tristan Oliver *Fowler* • Cary Elwes *Harcourt* ■ *Dir* Marek Kanievska • *Scr* Julian Mitchell, from the play by Julian Mitchell

Another Dawn ★★

Romantic adventure 1937 · US · BW · 74mins

Errol Flynn made some classic adventure movies in the thirties, but this isn't one of them. Everyone involved seems to be treading water: his co-star this time is Kay Francis, a former secretary and estate agent, who became one of Warner's highest paid female stars until Bette Davis came on the scene. The story is a love triangle, with Francis marrying Ian Hunter yet lusting after Flynn, a British army officer. The Arabs, meanwhile, cause the Empire problems whenever the story gets bogged down, which is often, and sort out Francis's dilemma in violent fashion.

Errol Flynn *Captain Denny Roark* • Kay Francis *Julia Ashton* • Ian Hunter *Colonel John Wister* • Frieda Inescort *Grace Roark* • Herbert Mundin *Wilkins* • Billy Bevan *Hawkins* • Kenneth Hunter *Sir Charles Benton* ■ *Dir* William Dieterle • *Scr* Laird Doyle

Another Day in Paradise ★★★★ 18

Drama 1998 · US · Colour · 101mins

Director Larry Clark's compelling glimpse into outlaw life in the American Midwest during the seventies is nowhere near as controversial as his first feature, *kids*, but it's just as grim and gritty. In this disturbing look at thug bravado and emotional vulnerability, a charismatic drugs dealer (James Woods) persuades a teenage runaway (Vincent Kartheiser) and his junkie girlfriend (Natalie Wood's daughter Natasha Gregson Wagner) to help him pull a bank heist. It's when things go horribly wrong and the dysfunctional "family" is torn apart that this devastating road movie really

hits home. As Woods's heroin-addicted lover, Melanie Griffith gives the performance of her career in a sobering and shocking tale. Contains swearing, scenes of drug abuse, violence and sexual situations. 🄳
DVD

James Woods *Mel* • Melanie Griffith *Sid* • Vincent Kartheiser *Bobbie* • Natasha Gregson Wagner *Rosie* • James Otis *Reverend* • Branden Williams *Danny* • Brent Briscoe *Clem* • Peter Sarsgaard *Ty* • Lou Diamond Phillips *Jules* ■ *Dir* Larry Clark • *Scr* Christopher Landon, Stephen Chin, from the novel by Eddie Little

Another 48 HRS ★★ 18

Comedy thriller 1990 · US · Colour · 91mins

And another largely pointless reprise from the Hollywood mill. Although original stars Eddie Murphy and Nick Nolte are reunited with director Walter Hill, all three seem to be going through the motions. Nolte is the same rough and ready cop who is forced to team up again with con Murphy, this time in a bid to salvage his own career. Ironically, that seems to be the reason for this sequel in real life for Murphy; whereas in the original he was electrifying, here he verges on self-parody. The action is spectacular enough, though, and Hill makes sure he uses up his much bigger budget with increasingly ludicrous set pieces. Contains swearing, violence and nudity. 🄳

Eddie Murphy *Reggie Hammond* • Nick Nolte *Jack Cates* • Brion James *Ben Kehoe* • Kevin Tighe *Blake Wilson* • Ed O'Ross *Frank Cruise* • David Anthony Marshall *Willy Hickok* • Andrew Divoff *Cherry Ganz* • Bernie Casey *Kirkland Smith* ■ *Dir* Walter Hill • *Scr* John Fasano, Jeb Stuart, Larry Gross, from a story by Fred Braughton, from characters created by Roger Spottiswoode, Walter Hill, Larry Gross, Steven E de Souza

Another Man, Another Chance ★★★★

Drama 1977 · Fr/US · Colour · 127mins

This French take on the American western by Claude Lelouch is also a retake, 11 years on, of his most romantic movie of the sixties, *A Man and a Woman*, as the lives of widow Geneviève Bujold, a 19th-century French settler, and widower James Caan, a Yankee vet, intersect. A bit long for what it has to say, but there are some deliciously wry moments Caan demonstrating he's a worse shot than his young son, for example and a feeling that people are worth the effort.

James Caan *David Williams* • Geneviève Bujold *Jeanne* • Francis Huster *Francis Leroy* • Jennifer Warren *Mary* • Susan Tyrrell *Debbie/ "Miss Alice"* • Rossie Harris *Simon* • Linda Lee Lyons *Sarah* ■ *Dir/Scr* Claude Lelouch

Another Man's Poison ★

Crime melodrama 1951 · UK · BW · 90mins

Bette Davis crossed the Atlantic with her *Now, Voyager* director Irving Rapper and her husband Gary Merrill for this tale of a lady novelist residing on the Yorkshire moors. Engaged in an affair with her secretary's fiancé (Anthony Steel), she is provoked by her husband's return into murdering him. She then dispatches his accomplice (Merrill) with a dose of horse serum. It

defies belief that Davis, even in villainess mode, could appear in such drivel. She copes with the material by pulling out her entire bag of histrionic tricks on a scale that leaves us either gasping in shock or laughing hysterically – rather like Bette herself during her climactic death scene.

Bette Davis *Janet Frobisher* • Gary Merrill *George Bates* • Emlyn Williams *"Dr" Henderson* • Anthony Steel *Larry Stevens* • Barbara Murray *Chris Dale* • Reginald Beckwith *Mr Bigley* • Edna Morris *Mrs Bunting* ■ *Dir* Irving Rapper • *Scr* Val Guest, from a play by Leslie Sands

Another Nine ½ Weeks ★★ 18

Erotic drama 1997 · US · Colour · 100mins

Mickey Rourke returns to the role that made him (in)famous but he really shouldn't have bothered – this is an utterly pointless and flaccid affair. Here, moody rich bloke (it's still not explained what Rourke's character actually does for a living) John is still pining for Elizabeth (Kim Basinger in the original) and travels to Paris where he hooks up with a fashion designer (Angie Everhart). Director Anne Goursaud gives it a glossy surface sheen, but Rourke sleepwalks through the film and there is an embarrassingly camp cameo from Steven Berkoff. Contains swearing, violence and sexual scenes. 🄳

Mickey Rourke *John* • Angie Everhart *Lea* • Agathe de la Fontaine *Claire* • Steven Berkoff *Vittorio* • Dougray Scott *Charlie* ■ *Dir* Anne Goursaud • *Scr* Michael Davis, from a character created by Elizabeth McNeil

Another Pair of Aces: Three of a Kind ★★ 15

Western drama 1991 · US · Colour · 89mins

Kris Kristofferson and Willie Nelson, both crusty, charming mavericks in real life, are ideally cast here; in fact, the sparks produced by their on-screen relationship are the film's only source of life. This sequel to *Pair of Aces* again takes its cue from *48 HRS*, with Kristofferson's Texas ranger joining forces with Nelson's safecracker to prove a friend (Rip Torn) innocent of murder. This contemporary western ambles along in its wearisome, obvious way, relaxed in the knowledge that it has two charismatic players to offset the predictability. 🄳

Willie Nelson *Billy Roy Barker* • Kris Kristofferson *Captain Rip Metcalf* • Rip Torn *Jack Parsons* • Joan Severance *Susan Davis* • Dan Kamin *Sheriff Sheedy* • Sammy Allred *Radio personality* • Ken Farmer *Gary Bud Hoffner* ■ *Dir* Bill Bixby • *Scr* Rob Gilmer

Another Part of the Forest ★★

Drama 1948 · US · BW · 106mins

Lillian Hellman's prequel to *The Little Foxes* (which was filmed in 1941), shows how the awful Hubbard brood clawed and insinuated their way into Southern high society. The movie's stage origins are evident in every static scene, while the social criticism points to left-wing views for which director Michael Gordon was later blacklisted. There are some good performances, though, notably from Fredric March as

the family's patriarch, and from Ann Blyth in the role Bette Davis played seven years earlier.

Fredric March *Marcus Hubbard* • Ann Blyth *Regina Hubbard* • Edmond O'Brien *Ben Hubbard* • Florence Eldridge *Lavinia Hubbard* • Dan Duryea *Oscar Hubbard* • John Dall *John Bagtry* • Dona Drake *Laurette* ■ *Dir* Michael Gordon • *Scr* Vladimir Pozner, from the play by Lillian Hellman

Another Shore ★★

Comedy 1948 · UK · BW · 91mins

Based on the novel by Kenneth Reddin, this is one of the least distinguished films produced by Ealing during its golden age. Part of the problem lies in the unbearable whimsy of the plot, in which customs official Robert Beatty's dreams of living on a South Sea island are brought within touching distance by rich dipsomaniac Stanley Holloway. However, the real problem is the failure of Charles Crichton and his design team to re-create the atmosphere of postwar Dublin. Georges Auric's sloppy score doesn't help much either.

Robert Beatty *Gulliver Shiels* • Stanley Holloway *Alastair McNeil* • Moira Lister *Jennifer Stockley* • Michael Medwin *Yellow Bingham* • Maureen Delaney *Mrs Gleason* • Fred O'Donovan *Coghlan* • Sheila Manahan *Nora* • Wilfrid Brambell *Moore* ■ *Dir* Charles Crichton • *Scr* Walter Meade, from the novel by Kenneth Reddin

Another Stakeout ★★ PG

Action comedy 1993 · US · Colour · 104mins

Richard Dreyfuss and Emilio Estevez are reteamed for a sequel to the box office smash *Stakeout*, released six years earlier, but here the chemistry is missing. Once again, the two bickering cops find themselves on surveillance duty, this time watching a potential witness in a mob trial, played by *Raging Bull*'s Cathy Moriarty, and with feisty Assistant DA Rosie O'Donnell along for the ride. The comic playing between the three leads can't be faulted, and there's even a brief appearance by Dreyfuss's love interest from the original, Madeleine Stowe, but director John Badham can't bring anything new to a winning formula. Contains violence and swearing. 🄳

Richard Dreyfuss *Chris Lecce* • Emilio Estevez *Bill Reimers* • Rosie O'Donnell *Gina Garrett* • Madeleine Stowe *Maria* • Dennis Farina *Brian O'Hara* • Marcia Strassman *Pam O'Hara* • Cathy Moriarty *Lu Delano* • Miguel Ferrer *Tony Castellano* ■ *Dir* John Badham • *Scr* Jim Kouf, from his characters

Another Thin Man ★★

Detective comedy drama
1939 · US · BW · 102mins

The third in the massively popular series appeared after a two-year gap in which star William Powell had been absent from MGM through illness. This reunion with Myrna Loy, Asta the dog and director WS Van Dyke, is very much the formula as before – witty and sophisticated Nick and Nora Charles trade wisecracks in between solving a few murders – with the addition of a baby, Nick Jr, over whom the couple occasionally coo. Lacking the edge and, of course, the novelty, of its predecessors, it signals the decline of the series (there are three more to

🅄 = SUITABLE FOR ALL 🅄🄲 = SUITABLE FOR ALL, ESPECIALLY FOR YOUNG CHILDREN (VIDEO ONLY) 🄿🄶 = PARENTAL GUIDANCE

come). Nonetheless, Powell and Loy are hard to resist.

William Powell *Nick Charles* • Myrna Loy *Nora Charles* • Virginia Grey *Lois MacFay* • Otto Kruger *Van Slack* • C Aubrey Smith *Colonel MacFay* • Ruth Hussey *Dorothy Waters* • Nat Pendleton *Lt Guild* • Patric Knowles *Dudley Horn* ■ *Dir* WS Van Dyke • *Scr* Frances Goodrich, Albert Hackett, from a story by Dashiell Hammett

Another Time, Another Place ★

Second World War melodrama
1958 · UK · BW · 98mins

Veteran screenwriter Lenore Coffee began writing romantic melodramas for the screen in 1919. This tale, adapted from her novel, cast the glamorous Lana Turner as an unlikely American news reporter in England during the Second World War, who becomes embroiled in a love affair with married war correspondent Sean Connery (yet to find stardom). Tragedy strikes, and Lana spends the rest of director Lewis Allan's turgid film consoling his widow (Glynis Johns) in the unconvincing setting of a Cornish village.

Lana Turner *Sara Scott* • Sean Connery *Mark Trevor* • Barry Sullivan *Carter Reynolds* • Glynis Johns *Kay Trevor* ■ *Dir* Lewis Allen • *Scr* Stanley Mann, from the novel by Lenore Coffee

Another Time, Another Place ★★★★ 15

Second World War drama
1983 · UK · Colour · 91mins

This was one of the first *Film on Four*s, and it set a precedent for the innovative work to come. It also marked the directorial debut of Michael Radford, whose glorious *Il Postino* was nominated for a slew of Oscars in 1996. This fascinating, thoughtful Second World War drama takes a sharp but sympathetic look at a lonely young woman who becomes fascinated by the Italian prisoners of war incarcerated nearby. Phyllis Logan and Gregor Fisher (better known as Rab C Nesbitt) give sterling performances in a film that subtly avoids the story's obvious pitfalls. ▦

Phyllis Logan *Janie* • Giovanni Mauriello *Luigi* • Gian Luca Favilla *Umberto* • Claudio Rosini *Paolo* • Paul Young *Dougal* • Gregor Fisher *Beel* • Tom Watson *Finlay* • Jennifer Piercey *Kirsty* • Denise Coffey *Meg* • Yvonne Gilan *Jess* ■ *Dir* Michael Radford • *Scr* Michael Radford, from the novel by Jessie Kesson

Another Woman ★★★★ PG

Drama   1988 · US · Colour · 77mins

One of the few Woody Allen movies to have disappeared swiftly on release, this complex, highly structured look at the great questions of life, love and death contains a stunning performance from Gena Rowlands as a rather smug, self-absorbed college professor who is forced to question her assumed truths. This is Allen at his most serious, often verging on pretentiousness, but there is plenty of food for thought and some able support from Ian Holm, Gene Hackman and, of course, Mia Farrow before the infamous parting. ▦

Gena Rowlands *Marion Post* • Mia Farrow *Hope* • Ian Holm *Ken Post* • Blythe Danner *Lydia* • Gene Hackman *Larry* • Betty Buckley

Kathy • Martha Plimpton *Laura Post* • John Houseman *Marion's father* • Sandy Dennis *Claire* • David Ogden Stiers *Young Marion's father* ■ *Dir/Scr* Woody Allen

Another You ★ 15

Comedy   1991 · US · Colour · 90mins

Richard Pryor, who has a well-documented history of substance abuse, and who also has multiple sclerosis, looks very ill indeed in this lame comedy. This is one of those hare-brained efforts where all concerned cross their fingers and hope the combined talents of the stars can paper over a nondescript plot and lacklustre dialogue. There are numerous tasteless jokes about mental illness – Wilder has just been released from the local sanatorium – but nothing can disguise Pryor's deep-seated problems. Contains swearing. ▦

Gene Wilder *George/Abe Fielding* • Richard Pryor *Eddie Dash* • Mercedes Ruehl *Elaine/Mimi Kravitz* • Stephen Lang *Dibbs* • Vanessa Williams [Vanessa L Williams] *Gloria* • Jerry Houser *Tim* • Kevin Pollak *Phil* ■ *Dir* Maurice Phillips • *Scr* Ziggy Steinberg

Anthony Adverse ★★★★

Historical swashbuckling drama
1936 · US · BW · 142mins

A mammoth epic based on an even more mammoth popular novel, this splendid Warner Bros period melodrama offers many rewards, most notably the spectacle of a studio in its prime using all its facilities to the utmost. Unsurprisingly, this movie won Oscars for best cinematography, best editing and best score. Apply those elements to a rousing swashbuckler about a hero (an effective Fredric March) whose one true love (Olivia de Havilland at her peak) is swept away from him, and the result is very satisfying. The tale takes its time to unfold, but stick with it, especially for Gale Sondergaard's Oscar-winning debut performance.

Fredric March *Anthony Adverse* • Olivia de Havilland *Angela Guessippi* • Edmund Gwenn *John Bonnyfeather* • Claude Rains *Don Luis* • Anita Louise *Maria* • Louis Hayward *Denis Moore* • Gale Sondergaard *Faith Paleologus* • Steffi Duna *Neleta* • Billy Mauch *Anthony as a child* • Donald Woods *Vincent Nolte* • Akim Tamiroff *Carlo Cibo* • Rollo Lloyd *Napoleon Bonaparte* ■ *Dir* Mervyn LeRoy • *Scr* Sheridan Gibney, from the novel by Hervey Allen • *Music* Erich Wolfgang Korngold • *Cinematographer* Tony Gaudio • *Editor* Ralph Dawson

Antonia & Jane ★★★

Comedy drama   1990 · UK · Colour · 75mins

Beeban Kidron is one of the most underestimated female directors around and this film is yet another jewel in her crown. Saskia Reeves is the gorgeous and confident Antonia, whose streamlined life contrasts with the goofiness of her friend, plain Jane Imelda Staunton (her sad life is represented by the fact that to get her nutty boyfriend to sleep with her, she has to read him Iris Murdoch in bed). Cue plenty of clashes and tearful reunions, woven together with a great soundtrack.

Imelda Staunton *Jane Hartman* • Saskia Reeves *Antonia McGill* • Patricia Leventon

Rosa Gluberman • Alfred Hoffman *Harry Rosenthal* • Maria Charles *Sylvia Pinker* • John Bennett *Irwin Carlinsky* • Brenda Bruce *Therapist* • Alfred Marks *Uncle Vladimir* ■ *Dir* Beeban Kidron • *Scr* Marcy Kahan

Antonia's Line ★★★ 15

Drama   1995 · Bel/UK/Neth · Colour · 98mins

Combining pastoral fantasy and magic realism, feminist polemic and humanist compassion, Marleen Gorris's vibrant drama won the Oscar for best foreign film, albeit in a poor year. Sprawling over five decades, the action boasts a spirited start, in which Willeke van Ammelrooy returns to her home village after the war and introduces us to a gallery of eccentric characters. The tale then loses its way, partly owing to the dullness of Antonia's descendents, but mostly because the opening's life-affirming joy is gradually replaced with a stiff sense of moral rectitude. Poignant and pertinent, perhaps, but ultimately somewhat self-satisfied. In Dutch with English subtitles. Contains some moderate swearing and violence ▦

Willeke van Ammelrooy *Antonia* • Els Dottermans *Danielle, Antonia's daughter* • Jan Decleir *Bas* • Marina de Graaf *Deedee* • Mil Seghers *Crooked Finger* • Fran Waller Zeper *Olga* • Jakob Beks *Farmer Daan* • Jan Steen *Loony Lips* ■ *Dir/Scr* Marleen Gorris

Antonio das Mortes ★★★★

Political drama   1969 · Bra · Colour · 100mins

Returning to the barren *sertao* plain, Glauber Rocha's sequel to *Black God, White Devil* (1964) was one of the key films in the second phase of the Brazilian *cinema nôvo* revival, known as "cannibal-tropicalist" for its heavy emphasis on allegorical symbolism. Rocha won the best director prize at Cannes for his first colour feature, but the decision to turn Antonio (Maurício do Valle) from an establishment assassin into a revolutionary hero of the downtrodden peasantry did not impress the junta, and he was hounded into decade-long European exile. Almost politicising the spaghetti western, this is highly stylised yet highly effective film-making. In Portuguese with English subtitles.

Maurício do Valle *Antonio das Mortes* • Hugo Carvana *Police Chief Mattos* • Odete Lara *Laura* • Othon Bastos *Professor* • Jofre Soares *Colonel Horacio* • Lorival Pariz *Coirana* ■ *Dir/Scr* Glauber Rocha

Antony and Cleopatra ★★★ U

Historical drama
1972 · UK · Colour · 158mins

Charlton Heston played Mark Antony in 1949, then again in 1970, both times in film versions of *Julius Caesar*. Here he begs comparisons with Olivier by directing and starring in an adaptation of the other Shakespeare play in which the character appears. Heston's long experience in epic movies holds him in good stead: the picture has an undeniable grandeur, while the English cast members are all excellent. Chuck's Antony is a bit of a pontificating bore, however, and Hildegard Neil isn't up to the role of Cleopatra. Buffs will notice that Heston

raids *Ben-Hur* for some footage of Roman sea battles. ▦

Charlton Heston *Antony* • Hildegard Neil *Cleopatra* • Eric Porter *Enobarbus* • John Castle *Octavius Caesar* • Fernando Rey *Lepidus* • Juan Luis Galiardo *Alexas* • Carmen Sevilla *Octavia* • Freddie Jones *Pompey* • Jane Lapotaire *Charmian* ■ *Dir* Charlton Heston • *Scr* Charlton Heston, from the play by William Shakespeare

Antz ★★★★ PG

Animation   1998 · US · Colour · 79mins

A hugely charming and witty animated adventure that's perhaps even more appealing to adults than it is to children, who are nevertheless sure to be enchanted. Woody Allen is the perfect choice for the voice of Z, an ant who feels insignificant among millions. He sets out to achieve something in his life by winning the heart of the colony's Princess Bala (sexily voiced by Sharon Stone). Helping him in his quest for fulfilment is a butch soldier ant (Sylvester Stallone), while Gene Hackman and Christopher Walken give voice to the sinister General Mandible and his sidekick Cutter, who are plotting dastardly things for the colony. Beautifully produced by DreamWorks and with a sparkling script, *Antz* is not to be confused with the other enjoyable (but more juvenile) insect-themed film of 1998, *A Bug's Life*. ▦

Woody Allen *Z* • Sharon Stone *Bala* • Sylvester Stallone *Weaver* • Gene Hackman *Mandible* • Christopher Walken *Cutter* • Jane Curtin *Muffy* • Jennifer Lopez *Azteca* • John Mahoney *Drunk Scout* • Paul Mazursky *Psychologist* • Anne Bancroft *Queen* • Dan Aykroyd *Chip* • Danny Glover *Barbatus* ■ *Dir* Eric Darnell, Tim Johnson • *Scr* Todd Alcott, Chris Weitz, Paul Weitz

Any Given Sunday ★★★★ 15

Sports drama   1999 · US · Colour · 150mins

Oliver Stone offers his multi-camera perspective on American football in this bruising "us and them" drama. Essentially it's *North Dallas Forty* with a racial subtext, coated in *Jerry Maguire* feel-good. But this ensemble masterclass is also a hybrid of *Platoon* and *Wall Street*, with Al Pacino even delivering a teamwork variation on Michael Douglas's "Greed is Good" speech. It's no accident that the tin-helmeted players thunder into encounters resembling the beach sequence in *Saving Private Ryan*. For Stone considers them the cannon fodder in a militaristic strategem, to be patched up and returned to the front by generals stationed safely away from the conflict. Tight as a scrimmage, but with moments of explosive inspiration.

Al Pacino *Tony D'Amato* • Cameron Diaz *Christina Pagniacci* • Dennis Quaid *Jack "Cap" Rooney* • James Woods *Dr Harvey Mandrake* • Jamie Foxx *Willie Beamen* • LL Cool J *Julian Washington* • Matthew Modine *Dr Ollie Powers* • Jim Brown *Montezuma Monroe* • Charlton Heston *AFFA football commissioner* • Ann-Margret *Margaret Pagniacci* • Aaron Eckhart *Nick Crozier* ■ *Dir* Oliver Stone • *Scr* John Logan, Oliver Stone, from a story by Daniel Pyne, John Logan

Any Man's Death ★★ 15

Drama 1990 · SAfr · Colour · 104mins

Dull morality drama with John Savage as a journalist who, while working in Africa, stumbles upon a scientist who once masterminded medical experiments in the Nazi death camps. But the doctor's work now helps humanity. What's a poor reporter to do? Mia Sara and Ernest Borgnine help Savage wrestle with his conscience. The result is a film that raises pertinent questions, but cops out of answering them. ▭

John Savage *Leon* • William Hickey *Schiller* • Mia Sara *Gerline* • Ernest Borgnine *Gantz* • Michael Lerner *Denner* • James Ryan *Caplan* • Damarob *Oskar* • Tobie Cronje *Johann* ▪ *Dir* Tom Clegg • *Scr* Iain Roy, Chris Kelly

Any Number Can Play ★★★

Drama 1949 · US · BW · 102mins

Clark Gable runs a casino, much to the embarrassment of his son – until he starts winning, of course. Director Mervyn LeRoy's movie seems to say that gambling will make a man of you and cure family problems. Since it won't do much for your heart condition, however, quit now while you're ahead. There's a weird moral here, though the gangster subplot is more conventional. The solid supporting cast includes Mary Astor and Lewis Stone.

Clark Gable *Charley Enley Kyng* • Alexis Smith *Lon Kyng* • Wendell Corey *Robbin Elcott* • Audrey Totter *Alice Elcott* • Frank Morgan *Jim Kurstyn* • Mary Astor *Ada* • Lewis Stone *Ben Gavery Snelerr* • Barry Sullivan *Tycoon* ▪ *Dir* Mervyn LeRoy • *Scr* Richard Brooks, from the novel by Edward Harris Heth

Any Number Can Win ★★★

Crime drama 1963 · Fr/It · BW · 112mins

Despite the rise of the French New Wave, such competent directors as Henri Verneuil continued to make traditional genre movies like this entertaining, albeit familiar heist yarn. This time the Cannes casino is the target of an ageing ex-con and a younger crook. What made it a hit in France was the co-starring of Jean Gabin, a huge box-office star of the thirties, with Alain Delon, as big a name in the sixties. Those who now know their classic French cinema will also recognise Viviane Romance, who had played opposite Gabin nearly three decades previously. In French with English subtitles.

Jean Gabin *Charles* • Alain Delon *Francis* • Viviane Romance *Ginette* • Maurice Biraud *Louis* • Carla Marlier *Brigitte* • José-Luis De Vilallonga *Grimp* • Germaine Montero *Francis's mother* ▪ *Dir* Henri Verneuil • *Scr* Albert Simonin, Michel Audiard, Henri Verneuil, from the novel *The Big Grab* by John Trinian

Any Wednesday ★★★

Comedy 1966 · US · Colour · 109mins

From the bimbo Barbarella via political activist to mogul-mate Jane Fonda has been a moll for all seasons. This is an eager-to-please sex farce with Jason Robards as the married executive whose mid-weekly liaisons with mindless mistress Fonda have become a ritual even his wife (Rosemary Murphy) knows about. Dean Jones, seeking true love, tries to find a way to break the habit so that it all ends happily. Originally cut and called *Bachelor Girl Apartment*, it works better with the risqué bits back in.

Jane Fonda *Ellen Gordon* • Jason Robards Jr *John Cleves* • Dean Jones *Cass Henderson* • Rosemary Murphy *Dorothy Cleves* • Ann Prentiss *Miss Linsley* • Jack Fletcher *Felix* • Kelly Jean Peters *Girl in Museum* ▪ *Dir* Robert Ellis Miller • *Scr* Julius J Epstein, from the play *Son of Any Wednesday* by Muriel Resnik

Any Which Way You Can ★★★ 15

Action comedy 1980 · US · Colour · 110mins

This 1980 sequel to *Every Which Way but Loose* typifies the kind of lightweight, disposable comic vehicles that paid Clint Eastwood's rent in the late seventies and early eighties. Short on plot, tall on slapstick humour and featuring real-life girlfriend Sondra Locke as his love interest and the always likeable Geoffrey Lewis as his best buddy, it has a lightweight charm that makes up for the insignificance of the story. Eastwood plays a car repair mechanic pushed back into bare-knuckle boxing for one last fight by the mafia. Destructive orang-utan Clyde steals scenes like an old pro. Contains some violence and swearing. ▭

Clint Eastwood *Philo Beddoe* • Sondra Locke *Lynn Halsey-Taylor* • Geoffrey Lewis *Orville Boggs* • William Smith *Jack Wilson* • Harry Guardino *James Beekman* • Ruth Gordon *Ma Boggs* • Michael Cavanaugh *Patrick Scarfe* ▪ *Dir* Buddy Van Horn • *Scr* Stanford Sherman, from characters created by Jeremy Joe Kronsberg

Anybody's Woman ★★★

Romantic comedy 1930 · US · BW · 80mins

A case has been made for this movie's seeming honesty because it was directed by a woman, Dorothy Arzner, who empathised with the plight of a woman who married an alcoholic. The film's strengths are in its depiction of the couple's sleaze-ridden life, and the remarkably strong performances of the fine Clive Brook as the drunken lawyer and the splendid Ruth Chatterton as the cheap stripper he marries. Age has not worn this film well, but it retains its inherent interest and – dare one say it? – its topicality.

Ruth Chatterton *Pansy Gray* • Clive Brook *Neil Dunlap* • Paul Lukas *Gustav Saxon* • Huntley Gordon *Grant Crosby* • Virginia Hammond *Katherine Malcolm* • Tom Patricola *Eddie Calcio* • Juliette Compton *Ellen* • Cecil Cunningham *Dot* ▪ *Dir* Dorothy Arzner • *Scr* Zoe Akins, Doris Anderson, from a story by Gouverneur Morris • *Cinematographer* Charles Lang • *Editor* Jane Loring

Anything Can Happen ★★ U

Comedy 1952 · US · BW · 96mins

Two years after his Oscar-winning performance as Cyrano de Bergerac, José Ferrer played a Russian immigrant in this comedy of manners and language, based on the real-life experiences of George and Helen Papashvily. Falling for a court stenographer (Kim Hunter), Ferrer follows her to California, gets married and starts an orange farm. Director George Seaton's film offers some episodic, fitfully amusing entertainment, though its real aim is to portray America as a haven for the dispossessed of Eastern Europe.

José Ferrer *Giorgi* • Kim Hunter *Helen Watson* • Kurt Kasznar *Nuri Bey* • Eugenie Leontovich *Anna Godiedze* • Oscar Karlweis *Uncle Besso* • Oscar Beregi *Uncle John* • Mikhail Rasumny *Tariel Godiedze* • Nick Dennis *Chancho* ▪ *Dir* George Seaton • *Scr* George Seaton, George Oppenheimer, from the memoirs of George Papashvily, Helen Papashvily

Anything Goes ★★★ U

Musical 1936 · US · BW · 91mins

PG Wodehouse (who co-wrote the original stage show) was one of the writers who collaborated in adapting this Cole Porter smash for the screen. In the end, this shipboard story of a romantic stowaway who's forced to pose as a criminal is pretty lightweight, but there's still plenty to enjoy, particularly with Ethel Merman repeating her Broadway triumph by belting out such classic tunes as *I Get a Kick Out of You* and the title song. A relaxed Bing Crosby and a radiant Ida Lupino play the lovers, while Charles Ruggles enjoys himself enormously as "Public Enemy #13".

Bing Crosby *Billy Crocker* • Ethel Merman *Reno Sweeney* • Charlie Ruggles [Charles Ruggles] *Rev Dr Moon* • Ida Lupino *Hope Harcourt* • Grace Bradley *Bonnie Le Tour* • Arthur Treacher *Sir Evelyn Oakleigh* • Robert McWade *Elisha J Whitney* • Richard Carle *Bishop Dobson* ▪ *Dir* Lewis Milestone • *Scr* Howard Lindsay, Russel Crouse, Guy Bolton, PG Wodehouse, from the musical by PG Wodehouse, Guy Bolton • *Music* Cole Porter, Hoagy Carmichael, Frederick Hollander, Richard A Whiting

Anything Goes ★★ U

Musical 1956 · US · Colour · 105mins

Having already starred in the 1936 film version of Cole Porter's hit musical, Bing Crosby came aboard this Sidney Sheldon-scripted reworking, which is far too loose to be considered a genuine remake. Donald O'Connor co-stars as the vaudevillian who hires showgirl Mitzi Gaynor, unaware that Crosby has already signed up Zizi Jeanmaire. In his farewell to Paramount (after nearly 25 years), Crosby revels in the exceptional Porter songbook, which was supplemented by songs from Jimmy Van Heusen and Sammy Cahn, while Jeanmaire impresses in a ballet choreographed by her husband, Roland Petit. Yet it all remains stubbornly flat.

Bing Crosby *Bill Benson* • Donald O'Connor *Ted Adams* • Zizi Jeanmaire *Gaby Duval* • Mitzi Gaynor *Patsy Blair* • Phil Harris *Steve Blair* • Kurt Kasznar *Victor Lawrence* ▪ *Dir* Robert Lewis • *Scr* Sidney Sheldon, from the musical by PG Wodehouse, Guy Bolton • *Music* Cole Porter, Van Heusen • *Lyrics* Cole Porter, Sammy Cahn

Anywhere but Here ★★★ 12

Comedy drama 1999 · US · Colour · 114mins

Flighty Susan Sarandon and her rebellious daughter Natalie Portman go on a turbulent voyage of self-discovery in an old-fashioned tear-jerker from director Wayne Wang that pays dramatic lip-service to such classic weepies as *Stella Dallas*. Familial tension mounts as they drive to Hollywood to fulfil the acting dreams Sarandon has for her embarrassed daughter, though the sudsy script eventually allows its emotional themes to bubble to the surface. Portman breathes fresh life into the over-familiar, soap-opera plot with grace, charm and wit. Her star is clearly ascending to future Oscar glory, but there's little else on offer here that hasn't been seen in a hundred other relationship/road movies. ▭

Susan Sarandon *Adele August* • Natalie Portman *Ann August* • Eileen Ryan *Lillian* • Ray Baker *Ted* • John Diehl *Jimmy* • Shawn Hatosy *Benny* • Bonnie Bedelia *Carol* • Faran Tahir *Hisham* ▪ *Dir* Wayne Wang • *Scr* Alvin Sargent, from the book by Mona Simpson

Anzio ★★ PG

Second World War drama 1968 · It · Colour · 112mins

In this epic Second World War drama, Robert Mitchum stars as an American war correspondent covering the Allied Forces' landing at Anzio Beach in Italy and their costly and bloody march on Rome. This is one of those war movies that poses thunderous moral questions at every turn and gives ordinary Joes statements rather than dialogue. It's a long haul, in every respect. Predictably, Mitchum and the odd cameo by the likes of Robert Ryan and Arthur Kennedy are the only things worth your attention. ▭

Robert Mitchum *Dick Ennis* • Peter Falk *Corporal Rabinoff* • Arthur Kennedy *General Lesly* • Robert Ryan *General Carson* • Earl Holliman *Sergeant Stimler* • Mark Damon *Richardson* • Reni Santoni *Movie* • Joseph Walsh *Doyle* • Thomas Hunter *Andy* • Giancarlo Giannini *Cellini* • Anthony Steel *General Marsh* ▪ *Dir* Edward Dmytryk • *Scr* Harry AL Craig, from the novel by Wynford Vaughan-Thomas, adapted by Frank DeFelitta, Duilio Coletti, Giuseppe Mangione, Canestri

Apa ★★★★

Drama 1966 · Hun · Colour · 91mins

Described by sophomore director István Szabó as "the autobiography of a generation", this is a visually audacious, yet highly personal, study of the uneasy relationship between postwar Hungary and its past. Bearing the influence of both neorealism and the *nouvelle vague*, the fragmentary structure enables Szabó to explore the themes of reputation, heroism and paternalism as student Andras Balint gradually discovers the truth about his deceased partisan father. Committedly played and meticulously constructed, the film gains additional power and authenticity from cinematographer Sándor Sára's inspired photographic pastiches of *film noir* and State-sponsored newsreel. In Hungarian with English subtitles.

Miklos Gabor *Father* • Klari Tolnay *Mother* • Andras Balint *Tako* • Dani Erdelyi *Tako, as a child* ▪ *Dir/Scr* István Szabó

Apache ★★★★ U

Western 1954 · US · Colour · 87mins

This courageous (for its day) film was an early feature from Burt Lancaster's production outfit, Hecht-Lancaster, which would go on to produce such classics as *Marty* and *Sweet Smell of Success*. The direction was entrusted to newcomer and former assistant director Robert Aldrich, who rose to the challenge and turned in a fine and

intelligent western with splendid set pieces. He is helped immeasurably by the dynamic athletic presence of Lancaster in the lead as Massai, the last noble Apache, who tried to hold out against the overwhelming forces of the US Army, and so passed into legend. The showing of the so-called growth of western civilisation through Massai's eyes is superbly directed, and the film, though brutal, presents a realistic and wholly sympathetic viewpoint, despite being compromised by the happy ending insisted upon by the distributors; Harold Hecht and Lancaster wanted their hero to be needlessly shot by the cavalry. ▭

Burt Lancaster *Massai* • Jean Peters *Nalinle* • John McIntire *Al Sieber* • Charles Buchinsky [Charles Bronson] *Hondo* • John Dehner *Weddle* • Paul Guilfoyle *Santos* • Ian MacDonald *Clagg* • Walter Sande *Lieutenant Colonel Beck* • Morris Ankrum *Dawson* • Monte Blue *Geronimo* ■ *Dir* Robert Aldrich • *Scr* James R Webb, from the novel *Bronco Apache* by Paul I Wellman

Apache Drums ★★★ U

Western 1951 · US · Colour · 74mins

That this is a dark western is perhaps not too surprising since it was the last film of horror producer Val Lewton, not exactly renowned for his contribution to the genre. Stephen McNally is excellent as the ne'er-do-well who's run out of town, then returns to help defend the community from an Apache attack, and *Red River's* Coleen Gray also acquits herself well. Argentinian director Hugo Fregonese was to prove excellent at depicting themes of courage (*Harry Black and the Tiger*) and divided loyalties (*The Raid*) and isn't daunted by the movie's obviously low budget. The short running time helps keep the tension taut.

Stephen McNally *Sam Leeds* • Coleen Gray *Sally* • Arthur Shields *Rev Griffin* • Willard Parker *Joe Madden* • James Griffith *Lt Glidden* • Armando Silvestre *Pedro-Peter* • Georgia Backus *Mrs Keon* • Clarence Muse *Jehu* ■ *Dir* Hugo Fregonese • *Scr* David Chandler, from the story *Stand at Spanish Boot* by Harry Brown

Apache Rifles ★ U

Western drama 1964 · US · Colour · 91mins

Provoked by gold miners invading their homeland, the Apaches go on the warpath. Audie Murphy's cavalry captain brings about a peace that lasts until the murder of a new Indian agent is blamed on the tribe and the ruthless tactics of commanding officer (John Archer) make matters worse. Murphy turns from hating Indians to helping them and ultimately proposes marriage to Linda Lawson's half-breed. Not as polished as earlier Audie Murphy westerns, with a weak supporting cast.

Audie Murphy *Jeff Stanton* • Michael Dante *Red Hawk* • Linda Lawson *Dawn Gillis* • LQ Jones *Mike Greer* • Ken Lynch *Hodges* • Joseph Vitale *Victorio* • Robert Brubaker *Sergeant Cobb* • J Pat O'Malley *Captain Thatcher* • John Archer *Colonel Perry* ■ *Dir* William Witney • *Scr* Charles B Smith, from a story by Kenneth Gamet, Richard Schayer, from the 1951 film *Indian Uprising* by Richard Schayer

Apache Trail ★★ U

Western 1942 · US · BW · 65mins

Routine but reliable B-western about a pair of estranged brothers (William Lundigan and Lloyd Nolan) who are thrown together by an Apache uprising. Donna Reed provides the love interest, while Chill Wills supplies the corncob philosophising, but there are very few surprises on this well-rutted cowboy trail. Richard Thorpe's film was remade ten years later as *Apache War Smoke*.

Lloyd Nolan *Trigger Bill* • Donna Reed *Rosalia Martinez* • William Lundigan *Tom Folliard* • Ann Ayars *Constance Selden* • Connie Gilchrist *Senora Martinez* • Chill Wills *"Pike" Skelton* • Miles Mander *James V Thorne* ■ *Dir* Richard Thorpe • *Scr* Maurice Geraghty, from a story by Ernest Haycox

Apache Uprising ★ U

Western 1965 · US · Colour · 91mins

Curiosity may have drawn audiences in 1965 to see what had become of stars like Rory Calhoun, Corinne Calvet, Lon Chaney Jr, Richard Arlen and Johnny Mack Brown. Unfortunately it's an utterly routine affair which pits hero Calhoun against Apaches and outlaws. John Russell makes an excellent deep-dyed villain, and DeForest Kelley also scores as a paranoid henchman, but it would be kinder to catch the others when they were in their prime.

Rory Calhoun *Jim Walker* • Corinne Calvet *Janice MacKenzie* • John Russell *Vance Buckner* • Lon Chaney [Lon Chaney Jr] *Charlie Russell* • Gene Evans *Jess Cooney* • Richard Arlen *Captain Gannon* • Arthur Hunnicutt *Bill Gibson* • DeForest Kelley *Toby Jack Saunders* • Johnny Mack Brown *Sheriff Ben Hall* • Jean Parker *Mrs Hawkes* • Donald Barry *Henry Belden* ■ *Dir* RG Springsteen • *Scr* Harry Sanford, Max Lamb, from the novel *Way Station* by Max Steeber, Harry Sanford

Apache War Smoke ★★ U

Western 1952 · US · BW · 67mins

It was said that MGM's B-pictures looked like other studios' A-features, and this is a good example, with only the absence of star names giving away its modest pretensions. This features an assortment of stage passengers and Apaches on the warpath. Charismatic bandit Gilbert Roland joins the group under siege at a way station run by his long-lost son, Robert Horton. Ace editor Harold Kress, on one of his occasional turns at directing, draws a virile performance from Horton, while veterans Gene Lockhart and Glenda Farrell take care of themselves.

Gilbert Roland *Peso* • Glenda Farrell *Fanny Webson* • Robert Horton *Tom Herrera* • Barbara Ruick *Nancy Dekker* • Gene Lockhart *Cyril R Snowden* • Henry Morgan [Harry Morgan] *Ed Cotten* • Douglas Dumbrille [Douglass Dumbrille] *Maj Dekker* ■ *Dir* Harold Kress • *Scr* Jerry Davis, from a story by Ernest Haycox

Apache Woman ★★ U

Western 1955 · US · Colour · 83mins

Celebrated B-movie producer/director Roger Corman is perhaps best known for his sixties' adaptations of Edgar Allan Poe stories such as *The Masque of the Red Death* and *The Fall of the House of Usher*. Corman also made notable, if often tacky, contributions to

the sci-fi and gangster genres, but westerns like this weren't really his thing, although the story in which Lloyd Bridges is a government agent sent to investigate crimes supposedly committed by a group of renegade Apaches has some surprises.

Lloyd Bridges *Rex Moffet* • Joan Taylor *Anne Libeau* • Lance Fuller *Armand* • Morgan Jones *Macey* • Paul Birch *Sheriff* ■ *Dir* Roger Corman • *Scr* Lou Rusoff

Aparajito ★★★★ U

Drama 1956 · Ind · BW · 104mins

This central part of Satyajit Ray's celebrated Apu trilogy won the Golden Lion at the Venice Film Festival. Continuing the story started in *Pather Panchali*, it focuses on Apu's relationship with his mother and the sharp contrasts between his simple country background and the bustle of city life. With his camera scarcely still for a second, Ray paints a fascinating picture of Indian life, considering the clash between western and traditional ideas with the same humanism that characterises all his work. While it lacks some of the poignancy of its predecessor, this is still a remarkable and deeply felt film. In Bengali with English subtitles.

Pinaki Sen Gupta *Apu, as a boy* • Smaran Ghoshal *Apu, as an adolescent* • Karuna Bannerjee *Mother* • Kanu Bannerjee *Father* ■ *Dir* Satyajit Ray • *Scr* Satyajit Ray, from the novels by Bibhutibhushan Bannerjee

The Apartment ★★★★★ PG

Comedy drama 1960 · US · BW · 119mins

When he saw David Lean's classic *Brief Encounter*, director Billy Wilder was intrigued by the man who gave Trevor Howard the use of his flat. That germ of an idea eventually led to *The Apartment*, in which Jack Lemmon is a schmuck who loans his home to his philandering bosses in return for promotion. With its marvellous script and flawless performances by Lemmon, elevator girl Shirley MacLaine and slimy boss Fred MacMurray this satire of office life has real bite as well as a feel-good glow. A timeless classic that won five Oscars, including best picture, direction and screenplay. ▭

Jack Lemmon *CC Baxter* • Shirley MacLaine *Fran Kubelik* • Fred MacMurray *JD Sheldrake* • Ray Walston *Mr Dobisch* • David Lewis *Mr Kirkeby* • Jack Kruschen *Dr Dreyfuss* • Joan Shawlee *Sylvia* • Edie Adams *Miss Olsen* ■ *Dir* Billy Wilder • *Scr* Billy Wilder, IAL Diamond • *Cinematographer* Joseph LaShelle • *Editor* Daniel Mandell • *Art Director* Alexandre Trauner

Apartment for Peggy ★★★

Drama 1948 · US · Colour · 96mins

Jeanne Crain and William Holden star as married youngsters trying to find a place to live in the era of postwar housing shortages in this shamelessly sentimental opus. Crain and Holden play off each other nicely, but both leads are given a run for their money by loveable veterans Edmund Gwenn and Gene Lockhart. Elderly professor Gwenn's transformation from suicidal depressive into hopeful optimist does take some swallowing, though the movie's worth perservering with for the

period Technicolor and the charming performances.

Jeanne Crain *Peggy* • William Holden (1) *Jason* • Edmund Gwenn *Professor Henry Barnes* • Gene Lockhart *Professor Edward Bell* • Griff Barnett *Dr Conway* • Randy Stuart *Dorothy* ■ *Dir/Scr* George Seaton

Apartment Zero ★★ 15

Psychological thriller 1988 · UK · Colour · 119mins

Look away, all those who prefer their Colin Firth wrapped in the soaked shirt guise of Mr Darcy, for you ain't gonna like what you see here. As the frustrated manager of a Buenos Aires cinema, he is twitchy, timid and totally unconvincing, as he falls under the spell of dynamic lodger Hart Bochner. Director Martin Donovan obviously knows his films, but this occasionally intriguing mix of *The Lady from Shanghai* and *The Servant* is often too clever for its own good, and runs out of steam long before the inevitable "housemate from hell" plot kicks in. Contains swearing and nudity. ▭

Colin Firth *Adrian LeDuc* • Hart Bochner *Jack Carney* • Dora Bryan *Margaret McKinney* • Liz Smith *Mary Louise McKinney* • Fabrizio Bentivoglio *Carlos Sanchez-Verne* • James Telfer *"Vanessa"* • Mirella D'Angelo *Laura Werpachowsky* • Juan Vitali *Alberto Werpachowsky* ■ *Dir* Martin Donovan • *Scr* Martin Donovan, David Koepp, from a story by Martin Donovan

A.P.E.X. ★★★ 15

Science-fiction action 1994 · US · Colour · 98mins

The Terminator sparked a rash of cash-ins, but this video hit is one of the better ones. Richard Keats is a well-meaning scientist whose dabbling with time travel creates a horrific futureworld where superior robots are gradually eliminating the war-ravaged human race. Director Phillip J Roth certainly gets his money's worth out of the relatively tiny effects budget and, while it isn't as good as that other *Terminator*-inspired cult success, *Trancers*, it's an enjoyable enough ride. ▭

Richard Keats *Nicholas Sinclair* • Mitchell Cox *Shepherd* • Lisa Ann Russell *Natasha Sinclair* • Marcus Aurelius *Taylor* • Adam Lawson *Rasheed* • David Jean Thomas *Dr Elgin* • Brian Richard Peck *Desert Rat* • Anna B Choi *Mishima* ■ *Dir* Phillip J Roth • *Scr* Phillip J Roth, Ronald Schmidt, from a story by Gian Carlo Scandiuzzi, Phillip J Roth

Aphrodite Goddess of Love ★★

Drama 1957 · It · Colour · 94mins

Mario Bonnard began directing in 1917 and had trotted out dozens of adaptations and costume dramas by the time he came to this sword-and-sandal adventure. It will come as a shock to many to learn that the great Sergio Leone had a hand in the script for this overwrought melodrama set in Corinth in the reign of the Emperor Nero. While corrupt officials sell the poor into slavery to acquire a new canal for their valley, two women, one rich and the other a Christian, vie for the attentions of a handsome artist. The stars look good, but they can't act. In Italian with English subtitles.

Isabelle Corey • Irene Turc • Ivo Garrani • Anthony Steffen ■ *Dir* Mario Bonnard • *Scr* Damiano Damiani

Apocalypse Now ★★★★★ 18

Epic war drama 1979 · US · Colour · 147mins

Apocalypse Now was started by writer John Milius who planned a modest comment about the Vietnam War, to be shot in Vietnam itself. The title mocked the "Peace Now!" badges worn by the flower people. But Francis Coppola inherited the project and turned Vietnam into a phantasmagorical ride as Martin Sheen travels up the Mekong river to terminate "with extreme prejudice" Marlon Brando's rebel command. Made under difficult conditions in the Philippines and running way over budget, Coppola delivered a harrowing masterwork that bursts with malarial, mystical images, such as *Playboy* playmates in the jungle and the Wagnerian helicopter attack which ends with marines surfing and Robert Duvall saying, "I love the smell of napalm in the morning." There are some notable faces in support, including Harrison Ford and Dennis Hopper, the latter playing a photographer among the fanatical Brando followers. Contains violence and swearing.

Martin Sheen *Captain Willard* • Marlon Brando *Colonel Kurtz* • Robert Duvall *Lieutenant Colonel Kilgore* • Frederic Forrest *Chef* • Albert Hall *Chief* • Sam Bottoms *Lance* • Larry Fishburne [Laurence Fishburne] *Clean* • Dennis Hopper *Photo journalist* • GD Spradlin *General* • Harrison Ford *Colonel* • Scott Glenn *Civilian* • Bill Graham *Agent* ■ *Dir* Francis Coppola [Francis Ford Coppola] • *Scr* Francis Coppola [Francis Ford Coppola], John Milius, from the novella *Heart of Darkness* by Joseph Conrad • *Cinematographer* Vittorio Storaro

Apollo 13 ★★★★ PG

Historical adventure
1995 · US · Colour · 140mins

In April 1970, astronaut Jim Lovell contacted mission control with the words: "Houston, we have a problem." It was a classic understatement, signalling a huge, complex problem to be solved. Lovell and his crew, Jack Swigert and Fred Haise, were bound for the Moon when an oxygen tank exploded in their craft, leaving them potentially marooned. It gave Nasa's scientists the biggest headache of the space-age so far and kept Americans – by then blasé about the space programme – glued to their TVs. It is the ultimate rescue story, paying due tribute to the bravery of the astronauts as well as American know-how. Lovell is played by Tom Hanks, whose very ordinariness – blandness, some would say – is the essence of astronaut-man, while Kevin Bacon and Bill Paxton offer welcome contrast, as does the superb Ed Harris as the chain-smoking mission controller. Filmed in genuine weightless conditions, Ron Howard's movie is a technical tour de force. Contains swearing ▣ *DVD*

Tom Hanks *Jim Lovell* • Bill Paxton *Fred Haise* • Kevin Bacon *Jack Swigert* • Gary Sinise *Ken Mattingly* • Ed Harris *Gene Kranz* • Kathleen Quinlan *Marilyn Lovell* • Mary Kate Schellhardt *Barbara Lovell* • Emily Ann Lloyd *Susan Lovell* • Joe Spano *Nasa director* • Xander Berkeley

Henry Hurt ■ *Dir* Ron Howard • *Scr* William Broyles Jr, Al Reinert, from the non-fiction book *Lost Moon* by Jim Lovell, Jeffrey Kluger

Apology ★★★ 15

Thriller 1986 · US · Colour · 93mins

An above-average made-for-cable chiller that makes some telling points about the nature of voyeurism. Lesley Ann Warren plays an artist in search of inspiration who starts a confession line, where people are asked to phone through anonymous details of their misdemeanours. However, it backfires when she finds herself stalked by a psycho. Robert Bierman, who went on to direct the weird Nicolas Cage horror movie *Vampire's Kiss*, sustains an air of menace throughout and delivers enough quirky touches to keep viewers guessing. Warren is good as the slightly pretentious artist, and there's fine support from Peter Weller and John Glover. ▣

Lesley Ann Warren *Lily McGuire* • Peter Weller *Rad Hungate* • George Loros *Frank Lestall* • John Glover *Philip Purness* • Jimmie Ray Weeks *Claude Kenley* • Harvey Fierstein *Derelict* • Charles S Dutton *Assistant DA* ■ *Dir* Robert Bierman • *Scr* Mark Medoff

The Apostle ★★★★ 12

Drama 1997 · US · Colour · 128mins

Robert Duvall writes, produces, directs and stars in this beautifully detailed character study of a Pentecostal preacher on a quest for atonement. The journey begins when his wife Farrah Fawcett has an affair with a younger minister, forcing him to take a long, hard look at his own life, the rural Texan community he serves and the Word of God itself. Expertly using little-seen Bible Belt locations and a great supporting cast (including Miranda Richardson and Billy Bob Thornton), Duvall then proceeds to act everybody else off the screen. The result is an engrossing labour of love and a literal tour de force. Contains some mild swearing and violence. ▣

Robert Duvall *Euliss "Sonny" Dewey, the Apostle EF* • Farrah Fawcett *Jessie Dewey* • Todd Allen *Horace* • John Beasley *Brother Blackwell* • June Carter Cash *Mrs Dewey Sr* • Walton Goggins *Sam* • Billy Joe Shaver *Joe* • Billy Bob Thornton *Troublemaker* • Miranda Richardson *Toosie* ■ *Dir/Scr* Robert Duvall

The Appaloosa ★★★ PG

Western 1966 · US · Colour · 94mins

Marlon Brando and his much-prized Appaloosa horse become the target for a Mexican bandit chief in this very sixties western, flashily directed by Sidney J Furie. Brando is at his mumbliest, moodiest and most masochistic, having already been on the revenge trail with his own superior western *One-Eyed Jacks*. The highlight is an absurd arm-locking duel fought between Brando and John Saxon over a pair of scorpions – the loser gets stung – and the whole movie has an operatic, parodic quality not unlike Sergio Leone's films. ▣

Marlon Brando *Fletcher* • Anjanette Comer *Trini* • John Saxon *Chuy Medina* • Emilio Fernandez *Lazaro* • Alex Montoya *Squint Eye* ■ *Dir* Sidney J Furie • *Scr* James Bridges, Roland Kibbee, from the novel by Robert MacLeod

L'Appartement ★★★★ 15

Romantic mystery drama
1996 · Fr/Sp/It · Colour · 111mins

One of the most visually audacious French films of the nineties, this intricate thriller clearly owes a debt to Hitchcock and Truffaut. Debutant writer/director Gilles Mimouni isn't just a cinematic magpie, however, as these homages are an ingenious means of making us identify with Vincent Cassel's high-flying executive. Suspecting that a long-vanished girlfriend has reappeared, he's duped into a web of deceit and desire, with every icon and flashback drawing him deeper into the mystery. We follow not so much out of a desire to solve the puzzle, but more because we're spellbound by the dazzling imagery. In French with English subtitles. Contains sex scenes. ▣

Romane Bohringer *Alice* • Vincent Cassel *Max* • Jean-Philippe Ecoffey *Lucien* • Monica Bellucci *Lisa* • Sandrine Kiberlain *Muriel* • Olivier Granier *Daniel* • Paul Pavel *Jeweller* ■ *Dir/Scr* Gilles Mimouni

Applause ★★★★

Musical drama 1929 · US · BW · 80mins

This very early talkie should be seen for the heart-rending performance of the legendary stage singer Helen Morgan. Not yet 30, she allowed herself, in her first dramatic film role, to be deglamourised and aged to play the boozy burlesque artiste who sacrifices herself for her teenage daughter. Imaginatively directed by Rouben Mamoulian, *Applause* remains equally notable for being one of the first films to throw off the restrictions on camera movement that the microphone had imposed and to use sound creatively, mixing dialogue with atmospheric background noise.

Helen Morgan *Kitty Darling* • Joan Peers *April Darling* • Fuller Mellish Jr *Hitch Nelson* • Henry Wadsworth *Tony* • Jack Cameron *Joe King* ■ *Dir* Rouben Mamoulian • *Scr* Garrett Fort, from the novel by Beth Brown

The Apple ★

Science-fiction musical
1980 · US · Colour · 91mins

Written and directed by Menahem Golan and co-produced with his longtime partner, Yoram Globus, this is one of the low points of Cannon's chequered history. Set in the New York of the future (well, 1994) and borrowing shamelessly from *The Rocky Horror Picture Show*, it follows the foot-tapping efforts of tunesmiths Catherine Mary Stewart and George Gilmour to deliver the world from drug-peddling villain Mr Boogalow and his demonic dance craze, the "Bim". This discordant drivel is best forgotten.

Catherine Mary Stewart *Bibi* • George Gilmour *Alphie* • Grace Kennedy *Pandi* • Alan Love *Dandi* • Joss Ackland *Mr Topps* • Vladek Sheybal *Mr Boogalow* • Ray Shell *Shake/Snake* • Miriam Margolyes *Landlady* ■ *Dir* Menahem Golan • *Scr* Menahem Golan, Coby Recht, Iris Recht, from a story by Coby Recht, Iris Recht

The Apple ★★★★ PG

Drama 1998 · Iran/Fr · Colour · 81mins

Scripted by her director father, Mohsen Makhmalbaf, 17-year-old Samirah

Makhmalbaf's first feature is a quietly ambitious assault on social injustice and sexual discrimination. Inspired by a scandal that shocked Iran, the tale of twin sisters who finally experience the world after a lifetime's imprisonment at the hands of their ultra-conservative father is re-enacted by the actual people involved. Demonstrating an astonishing ease before the camera, Zahra and Massoumeh Naderi stand in wonderfully mischievous contrast to the shame and regret of their gnarled father, Ghorban Ali-Naderi. However, while the film is defiantly affirmative, it doesn't attempt to disguise the family's crippling poverty. In Farsi with English subtitles. ▣

Massoumeh Naderi • Zahra Naderi • Ghorban Ali-Naderi • Zahra Saghrisaz • Amir Hossein Khosrojerdi • Azizeh Mohamadi • *Dir* Samirah Makhmalbaf • *Scr* Mohsen Makhmalbaf

The Apple Dumpling Gang ★★★ U

Comedy western 1974 · US · Colour · 96mins

A charming comedy western from the Disney stable, driven by some fine comic performances. Bill Bixby, best known for his TV roles in *The Magician* and *The Incredible Hulk*, heads a cast full of amiable and refreshingly believable characters. An inferior sequel *The Apple Dumpling Gang Rides Again* was made in 1979. ▣

Bill Bixby *Russel Donovan* • Susan Clark *Magnolia Dusty Clydesdale* • Don Knotts *Theodore Ogelvie* • Tim Conway *Amos Tucker* • David Wayne *Colonel Tr Clydesdale* • Slim Pickens *Frank Stillwell* • Harry Morgan *Sheriff Homer McCoy* • John McGiver *Leonard Sharpe* • Brad Savage *Clovis Bradley* ■ *Dir* Norman Tokar • *Scr* Don Tait, from the novel by Jack M Bickham

The Apple Dumpling Gang Rides Again ★ U

Comedy western 1979 · US · Colour · 85mins

Don Knotts and Tim Conway, who formed an enduring Disney partnership in the original *Apple Dumpling* adventure, return as the "Hash Knife Outfit" in this substandard sequel. Their buffoonery raises the odd smile, but there's little else to recommend this tiresome tale, in which the gang reforms (albeit with different actors) to foil a smuggling ring threatening the existence of a cavalry fort. ▣

Tim Conway *Amos* • Don Knotts *Theodore* • Tim Matheson *Private Jeff Reid* • Kenneth Mars *Marshall* • Elyssa Davalos *Millie* • Jack Elam *Big Mac* • Robert Pine *Lt Ravencroft* • Harry Morgan *Major Gaskill* ■ *Dir* Vincent McEveety • *Scr* Don Tait

The Appointment ★

Melodrama 1968 · US · Colour · 114mins

Abandoning the New York he later represented so well in films such as *Serpico* and *Dog Day Afternoon*, Sidney Lumet went all Euro-arty for this dismal melodrama, quite the worst film he ever made. Omar Sharif plays a lawyer in Rome and Anouk Aimée is his wife who may or may not be a high-class call girl. This leads to a thriller of sorts in which Sharif becomes insanely jealous and worries about the meaning of love and existence as if he's seen one too many Michelangelo Antonioni

U = SUITABLE FOR ALL   Uc = SUITABLE FOR ALL, ESPECIALLY FOR YOUNG CHILDREN (VIDEO ONLY)   PG = PARENTAL GUIDANCE

movies. Lumet, quite out of his depth in the shallows, piles on the angst, while John Barry's violins saw away to the gobsmackingly awful climax.

Omar Sharif *Federico Fendi* • Anouk Aimée *Carla* • Lotte Lenya *Emma Valadier* • Fausto Tozzi *Renzo* • Ennio Balbo *Ugo Perino* • Didi Perego *Nany* ■ *Dir* Sidney Lumet • *Scr* James Salter, from a story by Antonio Leonviola

The Appointment ★

Thriller 1981 · UK · Colour · 90m

Not to be confused with the Sidney Lumet melodrama of the same name, this is an underfunded British possession thriller in which any sense of suspense is undermined by the amateurishness of the special effects. However, the director Lindsey C Vickers is primarily responsible for this being such a lacklustre picture, with many of the incidents during classical musician Samantha Weyson's murderous reign of terror bordering on the risible. Edward Woodward tries to bring a bit of steel to the proceedings, but this is further proof of our inability to make credible chillers.

Edward Woodward *Ian Fowler* • Jane Merrow *Diane Fowler* • Samantha Weyson *Joanne Fowler* ■ *Dir/Scr* Lindsey C Vickers

Appointment for a Killing ★★★ 15

Thriller based on a true story
1993 · US · Colour · 87mins

Corbin Bernsen stars in this TV movie about a St Louis dentist who dispatches a number of unfortunates over 22 years until his suspicious wife Markie Post hatches a plan with the authorities to trap him. Bernsen's smooth plausibility is unnervingly right for his role as the killer, while Kelsey Grammer brings his familiar intensity to his portrayal of the detective on his trail. Contains swearing and nudity. ⊞

Markie Post *Joyce Benderman* • Corbin Bernsen *Dr Stan Benderman* • Kelsey Grammer *Ron McNally* • Don Swayze *Duke* ■ *Dir* William A Graham • *Scr* Karen Clark, from the non-fiction book by Susan Crain Bakos

Appointment for Love ★★ U

Romantic comedy 1941 · US · BW · 88mins

Hollywood's favourite Frenchman of the forties, Charles Boyer, and the luminously talented and touching Margaret Sullavan (who would die of an overdose at the age of 49), star in this romantic comedy about a playwright (he) and a doctor (she) who marry, only to be plunged into near-terminal misunderstandings and suspicion. They have separate apartments on honeymoon, and only meet once a day, at 7am. Thin and superficial, the movie gets by thanks to the polished expertise of the stars, and William A Seiter's glossy direction.

Charles Boyer *Andre Casall* • Margaret Sullavan *Jane Alexander* • Rita Johnson *Nancy Benson* • Eugene Pallette *George Hastings* • Ruth Terry *Edith Meredith* • Reginald Denny *Michael Dailey* • Cecil Kellaway *OLeary* • JM Kerrigan *Timothy* ■ *Dir* William A Seiter • *Scr* Bruce Manning, Felix Jackson, from the story by Ladislaus Bus-Fekete

Appointment in Honduras ★★★ U

Adventure 1953 · Colour · 79mins

A furiously fast, all-action jungle drama with Glenn Ford at his most nobly heroic, bristling with brio and derring-do as an adventurer en route to save the president of Honduras. Director Jacques Tourneur fashions an intelligent, multi-layered romp, which on first sight may appear to be little more than "man wrestles baddies and requisite troop of snarling beasts", but opens out to display great performances from all concerned, particularly Ford, and Ann Sheridan as one half of a married couple inadvertently caught up in the mayhem. You can almost smell the stifling humidity and the tension could be cut with a knife. Great stuff.

Glenn Ford *Corbett* • Ann Sheridan *Sylvia Sheppard* • Zachary Scott *Harry Sheppard* • Rodolfo Acosta *Reyes* • Jack Elam *Castro* • Ric Roman *Jiminez* ■ *Dir* Jacques Tourneur • *Scr* Karen de Wolfe

Appointment in London ★★ U

Second World War drama
1952 · UK · BW · 92mins

A routine mission for the reliable Dirk Bogarde, who is slightly off-form as a Second World War pilot grounded on doctor's orders. His determination to continue flying is deflected momentarily by his love for naval intelligence widow Dinah Sheridan and the disappearance of comrade Bryan Forbes after he's caught tinkering with a code machine. It's all much as you'd expect, but a little more insight into the lives of the air crews would have filled in the gaps left by the absence of flag-waving propaganda. ⊞

Dirk Bogarde *Wing Commander Tim Mason* • Ian Hunter *Captain Logan* • Dinah Sheridan *Eve Canyon* • Bill Kerr *Flight Lieutenant Bill Brown* • Bryan Forbes *Pilot Officer Greeno* • William Sylvester *Mac* ■ *Dir* Philip Leacock • *Scr* John Wooldridge, Robert Westerby

Appointment with Danger ★★★

Film noir 1950 · US · BW · 89mins

This nifty little B-thriller finds Alan Ladd working for the Post Office's detective branch, tracking down the murderers of a colleague and foiling a robbery by posing as a corrupt cop. Phyllis Calvert plays a nun on the run who witnessed the murder. Moodily shot by master cameraman John F Seitz, the *film noir* proceedings are smartly handled by Lewis Allen, who directed that minor classic, *Suddenly*.

Alan Ladd *Al Goddard* • Phyllis Calvert *Sister Augustine* • Paul Stewart *Earl Boettiger* • Jan Sterling *Dodie* • Jack Webb *Joe Regas* • Stacy Harris *Paul Ferrar* • Henry Morgan [Harry Morgan] *George Soderquist* • David Wolfe *David Goodman* ■ *Dir* Lewis Allen • *Scr* Richard Breen, Warren Duff

Appointment with Death ★★ PG

Crime mystery 1988 · US · Colour · 98mins

Peter Ustinov as Hercule Poirot travels to Palestine where a murder awaits a twist of his waxed moustache. The usual assortment of glamorous suspects are on hand, including John Gielgud and Lauren Bacall. Michael Winner was the director, so a good time was probably had by the stars, but with Ustinov making his sixth appearance as Poirot, the formula looks stale to say the least, though some mild amusement can be had from the cast and trying to guess whodunit. Contains violence ⊞

Peter Ustinov *Hercule Poirot* • Lauren Bacall *Lady Westholme* • Carrie Fisher *Nadine Boynton* • John Gielgud *Colonel Carbury* • Piper Laurie *Mrs Emily Boynton* • Hayley Mills *Miss Quinton* • Jenny Seagrove *Dr Sarah King* • David Soul *Jefferson Cope* ■ *Dir* Michael Winner • *Scr* Anthony Shaffer, Peter Buckman, Michael Winner, from the novel by Agatha Christie

Appointment with Venus ★★★ U

Second World War comedy adventure
1951 · UK · BW · 87mins

Venus is a pedigree cow who has to be shipped off the German-occupied Channel Island of Armorel by major David Niven, with help from Glynis Johns, during the Second World War. If you can forget the real-life horrors, this light comedy adventure is more than passable. The supporting cast is a *Who's Who* of British cinema, with Kenneth More, in an early role, showing real star potential. The US title was *Island Rescue*, which rather gives away the ending, but then who really thought they wouldn't save Venus from the nasty Nazis?

David Niven *Major Valentine Morland* • Glynis Johns *Nicola Fallaize* • George Coulouris *Captain Weiss* • Kenneth More *Lionel Fallaize* • Noel Purcell *Trawler Langley* • Barry Jones *Provost* • Bernard Lee *Brigadier* • Richard Wattis *Higher executive* ■ *Dir* Ralph Thomas • *Scr* Nicholas Phipps, from the novel *Transit of Venus* by Jerrard Tickell Black

Apprentice to Murder ★★ 15

Mystery thriller
1988 · US/Can · Colour · 88mins

Fire and brimstone preacher Donald Sutherland – known locally as the Pow Wow Doctor – is sure a hex has been placed on him by Knut Husebo as an emissary from Satan. With help from the young Chad Lowe, who he's training to detect such evil, the maniac mystic kills Husebo. Both religious fanatics are then given a jail sentence. Loosely based on a true-life murder case, this is initially intriguing, but it's very slow in presenting the offbeat facts of the story. Norwegian locations stand in for rural Pennsylvania. ⊞

Donald Sutherland *John Reese* • Chad Lowe *Billy Kelly* • Mia Sara *Alice Spangler* • Knut Husebo *Lars Hoeglin* • Rutanya Alda *Elma Kelly* • Eddie Jones *Tom Kelly* • Adrian Sparks *Irwin Meyers* ■ *Dir* RL Thomas [Ralph L Thomas] • *Scr* Alan Scott, Wesley Moore

The Apprenticeship of Duddy Kravitz ★★★★ 15

Drama 1974 · Can · Colour · 120mins

After notable appearances in *Dillinger* and *American Graffiti*, Richard Dreyfuss confirmed his star quality in this adaptation of Mordecai Richler's novel. As Duddy, a no-holds-barred hustler in 1948 Montreal, he alienates friends and family in his quest to get rich and make his mark. Directed by former TV director Ted Kotcheff, the comic highlights include Denholm Elliott's down-at-heel film director setting up a bar mitzvah as an artsy-fartsy work of art. ⊞

Richard Dreyfuss *Duddy* • Micheline Lanctot *Yvette* • Jack Warden *Max* • Randy Quaid *Virgil* • Joseph Wiseman *Uncle Benjy* • Denholm Elliott *Friar* • Henry Ramer *Dingleman* • Joe Silver *Farber* ■ *Dir* Ted Kotcheff • *Scr* Mordecai Richler, Lionel Chetwynd, from the novel by Mordecai Richler

Les Apprentis ★★★ 15

Comedy 1995 · Fr · Colour · 93mins

Long, lithe and languorous, Guillaume Depardieu gave notice that he had finally emerged from the shadow of his famous father Gérard with this César-winning performance. As Fred, the indolent flatmate, he brings some much-needed sanity to the proceedings, as his neurotic buddy François Cluzet comes close to madness wrestling with his literary aspirations. Considerably more restrained than Pierre Salvadori's debut feature, *Wild Target*, this odd-couple comedy may be short on incident, but it's packed with quirky humour and sly insights into the character of the modern French male. In French with English subtitles. Contains violence, swearing and nudity. ⊞

François Cluzet *Antoine* • Guillaume Depardieu *Fred* • Judith Henry *Sylvie* • Claire Laroche *Agnes* • Philippe Girard *Nicolas* • Bernard Yerles *Patrick* • Jean-Pol Brissard *Magazine editor* • Marie Trintignant *Lorette* ■ *Dir* Pierre Salvadori • *Scr* Pierre Salvadori, Philippe Harel

Après l'Amour ★★★ 15

Drama 1992 · Fr · Colour · 100mins

An air of detached amusement hangs over this assured discourse on the sexual mores of today's sophisticated Parisians, exemplified by novelist Isabelle Huppert and architect Bernard Giraudeau and pop star Hippolyte Girardot. Employing her trademark mix of naturalism and keen social insight, director Diane Kurys suggests that, where love is concerned, liberation is just another form of entanglement. Occasionally struggling for significance, the film is perhaps too insular and the characters too self-obsessed to engross. The casting is apposite, however, and Huppert (who also starred in Kurys's *Entre Nous*) is outstanding. In French with English subtitles. ⊞

Isabelle Huppert *Lola* • Bernard Giraudeau *David* • Hippolyte Girardot *Tom* • Lio *Marianne* • Yvan Attal *Romain* • Judith Reval *Rachel* • Ingrid Held *Anne* ■ *Dir* Diane Kurys • *Scr* Diane Kurys, Antoine Lacomblez

The April Fools ★★★★

Romantic drama 1969 · US · Colour · 94mins

The oddball teaming of Jack Lemmon, the quintessential neurotic American, with Catherine Deneuve, the epitome of cool French charm, might seem like a seasonal hoax played on cinema audiences. But it works extraordinarily well, with the two stars playing refugees from tedious New York marriages escaping to Paris and self-discovery. Stuart Rosenberg's direction desperately tries to be sixties' trendy, but there's dramatic poignancy to be experienced all the same.

Jack Lemmon *Howard Brubaker* • Catherine Deneuve *Catherine Gunther* • Peter Lawford *Ted Gunther* • Jack Weston *Potter Shrader* • Myrna Loy *Grace Greenlaw* • Charles Boyer *André Greenlaw* • Harvey Korman *Benson* • Sally Kellerman *Phyllis Brubaker* • Melinda Dillon *Leslie Hopkins* • Kenneth Mars *Don Hopkins* • David Doyle *Walters* ■ *Dir* Stuart Rosenberg • *Scr* Hal Dresner

April Fool's Day ★★★ 18

Horror 1986 · US · Colour · 85mins

Responsible for the seminal stalk-and-slash movie *When a Stranger Calls*, director Fred Walton made a belated return to the much-maligned genre he helped create with this amusing diversion, inspired more by Agatha Christie than by *Friday the 13th*. Who's the insane maniac gruesomely reducing the ranks of practical joker Deborah Foreman's college pals as they party on her island retreat? The answer comes courtesy of a surprising twist in the tail of this wittily inventive whodunit. Contains swearing, violence and sex scenes. [cc]

Deborah Foreman *Muffy St John/Buffy* • Deborah Goodrich *Nikki* • Ken Olandt *Rob* • Griffin O'Neal *Skip* • Mike Nomad *Buck* • Leah King Pinsent [Leah Pinsent] *Nan* • Clayton Rohner *Chaz* ■ *Dir* Fred Walton • *Scr* Danilo Bach

April in Paris ★ U

Musical comedy romance
1952 · US · Colour · 95mins

This is a leaden would-be romance that never gets off the backlot. The film pairs a hard-working Doris Day (she sings, she dances, she smiles) with a most unlikely leading man in Ray Bolger (not typically attractive and too old for the star) and the pair are lumbered with such a numbskull of a plot that it doesn't bear thinking about, let alone watching. No wonder she eventually rebelled. The fifties Technicolor is attractive, but the art direction is garish, the dumb script wastes every opportunity for wit or satire, and the songs are weak. [cc]

Doris Day *Ethel Dynamite Jackson* • Ray Bolger *S Winthrop Putnam* • Claude Dauphin *Philippe Fouquet* • Eve Miller *Marcia* • George Givot *François* • Paul Harvey *Secretary Sherman* • Herbert Farjeon *Joshua Stevens* • Wilson Millar *Sinclair Wilson* ■ *Dir* David Butler • *Scr* Jack Rose, Melville Shavelson

April Love ★★★

Romantic musical
1957 · US · Colour · 99mins

Harmless remake of *Home in Indiana*, one of a seemingly endless stream of 20th Century-Fox films featuring horses. This musical romance is dressed up as a star vehicle for fifties' teen heart-throb Pat Boone, once considered a serious threat to Elvis Presley. The controversy at the time was that clean-livin' Boone wouldn't take part in love scenes, and, true to form, the moment when he actually plants a peck on co-star Shirley Jones doesn't exactly raise the temperature. However, Boone and Jones make a very likeable pair and the overall impression mighty pleasant, though

can you imagine presenting this as a teen flick today?

Pat Boone *Nick Conover* • Shirley Jones *Liz Templeton* • Dolores Michaels *Fran* • Arthur O'Connell *Jed* • Matt Crowley *Dan Templeton* • Jeanette Nolan *Henrietta* • Brad Jackson *Al Turner* ■ *Dir* Henry Levin • *Scr* Winston Miller, from the novel by George Agnew Chamberlain

April One ★★

Thriller based on a true story
1993 · Can · Colour

This quota quickie of the television era is based on a true story. The absence of familiar faces, with the exception of David Strathairn who played Meryl Streep's husband in *The River Wild*, adds credibility to this account of the hostage crisis at the Bahamian High Commission that gripped Ottawa in 1986. Contains some swearing.

Stephen Shellen *David Maltby* • Djanet Sears *Jane Briscoe* • David Strathairn *Don McCowan* • Shannon Lawson *Sally Conway* • Monique Spaziani *Lucie Rivette* • Pierre Curzi *Jean Leduc* • Gordon Clapp *Sergeant Gordon Davies* ■ *Dir/Scr* Murray Battle

Aprile ★★★ 15

Comedy drama 1998 · It/Fr · Colour · 77mins

Having reinforced his auteur status with *Dear Diary*, Nanni Moretti opted for more of the same in this teasing blend of fact and fiction. Musing on aspects of his own life, as well as the state of Italian politics, this is more calculated and less charming than its predecessor, with the highly personal insights into nationhood, fatherhood and the frustrations of being a film director making for intriguing viewing. The genial honesty of the project keeps you hooked until the bizarre finale, in which Moretti finally succeeds in mounting part of his musical about a politicised pastry cook. In Italian with English subtitles. Contains a scene of drug abuse.

Nanni Moretti • Andrea Molaiolo • Silvio Orlando • Silvia Nono • Pietro Moretti • Nuria Schoenberg ■ *Dir/Scr* Nanni Moretti

Apt Pupil ★★★★ 15

Drama 1997 · US/Fr · Colour · 107mins

The third work taken from Stephen King's 1982 anthology *Different Seasons* is almost the equal of the other two, *Stand by Me* and *The Shawshank Redemption*, in terms of artfulness and sheer storytelling power. Outlining the terrible consequences of a gifted Californian teenager's obsession with the Holocaust and his strange relationship with a Nazi war criminal living in secret in his home town, *The Usual Suspects* director Bryan Singer uses smart visual fluency to suggest the shocking nature of his core story. King's chiller deals with the horror of human nature and melancholic dread, and this adaptation keeps close to the author's original intentions, only rarely crossing the bad-taste barrier, while Ian McKellen's stupendous performance as the disgraced SS officer provides unsettling, blood-curdling viewing. Contains swearing and some violence. [cc] **DVD**

Brad Renfro *Todd Bowden* • Ian McKellen *Kurt Dussander* • Joshua Jackson *Joey* • Mickey Cottrell *Sociology teacher* • Michael Reid

MacKay *Nightmare victim* • Ann Dowd *Monica Bowden* • Bruce Davison *Richard Bowden* • James Karen *Victor Bowden* • David Schwimmer *Edward French* ■ *Dir* Bryan Singer • *Scr* Brandon Boyce, from the novella by Stephen King

The Arab ★★★

Silent adventure 1924 · US · BW

Having played a key part in the emergence of Rudolph Valentino by directing *The Four Horsemen of the Apocalypse*, Irish firebrand director Rex Ingram drew inspiration from the silent superstar's best-known film, *The Sheik*, for this tempestuous desert romance. However, he had to settle for Hollywood's second-string Latin lover Ramon Novarro, instead of Valentino, to play the disgraced son of a Bedouin chief, now a tour guide, who smoulders missionary Alice Terry into submission. Unusually for the time, this overwrought Metro melodrama was shot on location in North Africa.

Ramon Novarro *Jamil Abdullah Azam* • Alice Terry *Mary Hilbert* • Gerald Robertshaw *Dr Hilbert* • Maxudian *Governor* • Count Jean de Limur *Hossein, governor's aide* ■ *Dir* Rex Ingram • *Scr* Rex Ingram, from the play by Edgar Selwyn

Arabella ★★★

Comedy 1967 · US/It · Colour · 87mins

This bizarre and often very funny comedy has Virna Lisi – a minor goddess of the sixties – trying to raise money so that her eccentric grandmother (Margaret Rutherford) can pay a fortune in back taxes. Naturally, Lisi hasn't the slightest intention of raising the cash legally. It's all done in episodic fashion with quite a flourish, mainly due to the cast. Rutherford is a cigar-chomping joy, and so is Terry-Thomas in each of his four roles.

Virna Lisi *Arabella Danesi* • James Fox *Giorgio* • Margaret Rutherford *Princess Ilaria* • Terry-Thomas *Hotel manager/General/Duke/Insurance agent* • Paola Borboni *Duchess Moretti* • Antonio Casagrande *Filberto* ■ *Dir* Mauro Bolognini • *Scr* Adriano Baracco

Arabesque ★★★

Spy drama 1966 · US · Colour · 105mins

In the wake of the box-office smash *Charade*, here's a glamorous trawl through sixties international post-Bond espionage from the same director, Stanley Donen. This film stars eternally-puzzled Gregory Peck (Cary Grant would have been better), and the lovely Sophia Loren, lit by ace cinematographer Chris Challis in ravishing Panavisioned Technicolor. The plot is some nonsense about Arab espionage (hence the punning title) which doesn't really matter, but Alan Badel and Kieron Moore provide fine support. This is lush, mindless and expertly-crafted matinée fare.

Sophia Loren *Yasmin Azir* • Gregory Peck *David Pollock* • Alan Badel *Beshraavi* • Kieron Moore *Yussef Kassim* • Carl Duering *Hassan Jena* • John Merivale *Sloane* • Duncan Lamont *Webster* • George Coulouris *Ragheeb* ■ *Dir* Stanley Donen • *Scr* Julian Mitchell, Stanley Price, Pierre Martin, from the novel *The Cipher* by Gordon Cotler

Arabian Adventure ★★ U

Fantasy adventure
1979 · US · Colour · 93mins

Former editor-turned-director Kevin Connor here lacks the imagination needed to conjure up the magic of the *Arabian Nights* tales, and he's not helped by a weak turn from Oliver Tobias as the prince battling Christopher Lee's wicked caliph. Nevertheless, if you're too young to remember the splendours of Alexander Korda's 1940 *The Thief of Bagdad* or those Universal fifties B-features with Piper Laurie, this might just pass muster. The eclectic cast keeps it watchable, but the special effects look cheap and rather let down the whole affair. [cc]

Christopher Lee *Alquazar* • Milo O'Shea *Khasim* • Oliver Tobias *Prince Hasan* • Emma Samms *Princess Zuleira* • John Ratzenberger *Achmed* • Peter Cushing *Wazir Al Wuzara* • Capucine *Vahishta* • Mickey Rooney *Daad El Shur* • Athar Malik [Art Malik] *Mahmoud* ■ *Dir* Kevin Connor • *Scr* Brian Hayles

Arabian Knight ★

Animated fantasy 1995 · UK · Colour · 81mins

The quirky, jagged style of this animated feature will probably not appeal to younger viewers. Unfortunately, that's the audience this simple tale is aimed at. It's a bit of a Disney wannabe, peppered with a few forgettable songs, about a young princess who falls for a rather unexciting cobbler. The pair then set out to save the kingdom from the evil Zigzag (who thinks of these names?) and his army of one-eyed soldiers. Only notable for featuring one of the last vocal performances by Vincent Prince, this is eminently missable – especially compared with all the other cartoons appearing these days.

Vincent Price *Zigzag* • Matthew Broderick *Tack the Cobbler* • Jennifer Beals *Princess Yum Yum* • Eric Bogosian *Phido* • Toni Collette *Nurse/Witch* • Jonathan Winters *The Thief* • Clive Revill *King Nod* • Kevin Dorsey *One-Eye* • Donald Pleasence *Additional voice* ■ *Dir* Richard Williams • *Scr* Richard Williams, Margaret French

Arabian Nights ★★★

Adventure 1942 · US · Colour · 86mins

This piece of Hollywood exotica, made to cash in on the success of *The Thief of Bagdad*, stars Jon Hall as the Caliph, Sabu as his best buddy and Maria Montez as his suitor. The actors have their tongues firmly in their cheeks and the whole show is on the brink of send-up, which is exactly where it should be. Producer Walter Wanger was one of Tinseltown's more enterprising independents, though he was later brought to his knees by the crippling costs of *Cleopatra*.

Jon Hall *Haroun al Raschid* • Sabu *Ali Ben Ali* • Maria Montez *Sherazad* • Leif Erickson *Kamar* • Shemp Howard *Sinbad* • "Wee Willie" Davis *Valda* • John Qualen *Aladdin* • Turhan Bey *Captain* • Richard Lane *Corporal* ■ *Dir* John Rawlins • *Scr* Michael Hogan, True Boardman, from stories by Sir Richard Burton

The Arabian Nights ★★★★
Fantasy adventure
1974 · It/Fr · Colour · 130mins

Italian director Pier Paolo Pasolini took almost two years to complete this final, and most polished, offering in his trilogy of great story cycles, the others being *The Decameron* (1970) and *The Canterbury Tales* (1971). *The Arabian Nights* features ten interwoven stories of love, potions and betrayal, connected by the tale of Mur-El-Din (Franco Merli) searching for his kidnapped slave girl. Filmed in Eritrea, Iran, Nepal and Yemen, it reveals the captivating beauty of those countries, while the ribald spirit of the original tales remains thankfully unshackled by Freudian or religious guilt. Italian dialogue dubbed in English.

Ninetto Davoli *Aziz* • Ines Pellegrini *Zumurrud* • Franco Citti *Demon* • Franco Merli *Mur-El-Din* ■ *Dir* Pier Paolo Pasolini • *Scr* Pier Paolo Pasolini, Danilo Donati

Arachnophobia ★★★★ PG
Comedy horror 1990 · US · Colour · 104mins

Steven Spielberg's longtime producer Frank Marshall turned director for this tongue-in-cheek creepy-crawly about deadly tropical spiders invading the small California town where phobic doctor Jeff Daniels has just started up a practice. Marshall shows much of his mentor's touch (Spielberg acted as co-executive producer with Marshall), spinning a tension-laden web full of solid scares and well-timed wit in what is virtually *The Birds* with eight legs. The black humour mixes with the black widows surprisingly well (John Goodman's exterminator provides some lovely moments) even if the shudder content will remain sky high for those suffering from symptoms of the title. Contains violence. ▣ **DVD**

Jeff Daniels *Dr Ross Jennings* • Harley Jane Kozak *Molly Jennings* • John Goodman *Delbert McClintock* • Julian Sands *Dr James Atherton* • Stuart Pankin *Sheriff Parsons* • Brian McNamara *Chris Collins* • Mark L Taylor *Jerry Manley* • Henry Jones *Dr Sam Metcalf* ■ *Dir* Frank Marshall • *Scr* Don Jakoby, Wesley Strick, from a story by Don Jakoby, Al Williams

Arcade ★★ 15
Science-fiction 1993 · US · Colour · 80mins

A hot new virtual-reality video game over at the Dante's Inferno arcade, run by sinister John DeLancie, feeds on teenage souls and traps them in a seven-level hell. In straight-to-video director Albert Pyun's cheap take on *Tron*, Megan Ward and Peter Billingsley must work their way to the final level of the game in order to save their friends. An assortment of digitally enhanced landscapes and a computer brain uttering Freddy Krueger-style lines stop Pyun's cyberspace snoozer from being a complete dead loss.

Peter Billingsley *Nick* • John DeLancie *Difford* • Megan Ward *Alex Manning* • Sharon Farrell *Alex's Mom* • Seth Green *Stilts* • Humberto Ortiz *Boy* • Jonathan Fuller *Arcade* • Norbert Weisser *Albert* ■ *Dir* Albert Pyun • *Scr* David S Goyer, from an idea by Charles Band

Arch of Triumph ★ U
Romantic drama 1948 · US · BW · 126mins

This adaptation of an Erich Maria Remarque bestseller should have been a successful movie, blessed as it was with the reteaming of the two stars of *Gaslight* (Ingrid Bergman and Charles Boyer) and the directorial skills of Lewis Milestone, who turned Remarque's *All Quiet on the Western Front* into a screen classic. As it turned out, the film was a costly failure, sinking its distinguished production company (Enterprise) and failing to find an audience in any of its many re-edited or shortened versions. Whatever the version, it's clear to see there's no chemistry between Bergman and Boyer, while the overall pace is deadly and that the re-creation of Paris is totally without atmosphere. ▣

Ingrid Bergman *Joan Madou* • Charles Boyer *Dr Ravic* • Charles Laughton *Haake* • Louis Calhern *Morosow* • Ruth Warrick *Kate Hegstroem* • Roman Bohnen *Dr Weber* • Stephen Bekassy *Alex* • Ruth Nelson *Madame Fessier* ■ *Dir* Lewis Milestone • *Scr* Harry Brown, Lewis Milestone, from the novel by Erich Maria Remarque

Are You Being Served? ★ PG
Comedy 1977 · UK · Colour · 91mins

Grace Brothers opened for business as part of the BBC's *Comedy Playhouse* in the early seventies, but never in its ten-year history were the shelves as bare as they are in this feeble feature. Abandoning the clothing department for the Costa Plonka, the staff are soon engaging in the usual smutty banter as sun, sand and booze take their toll. Why did the makers of these spin-offs always insist on breaking with the winning sitcom formula? It's even more puzzling here, as it was the petty shop-floor rivalries and tacky sales gimmicks that provided most of the laughs. Ten times worse than *Carry On Abroad*. ▣

Mollie Sugden *Mrs Slocombe* • John Inman *Mr Humphries* • Frank Thornton *Captain Peacock* • Trevor Bannister *Mr Lucas* • Wendy Richard *Miss Brahms* • Arthur Brough *Mr Grainger* • Nicholas Smith *Mr Rumbold* • Arthur English *Harman* • Harold Bennett *Young Mr Grace* • Andrew Sachs *Don Bernardo* ■ *Dir* Bob Kellett • *Scr* Jeremy Lloyd, David Croft

Are You Lonesome Tonight ★★ 15
Suspense thriller 1992 · US · Colour · 88mins

Jane Seymour plunges into the murky world of phone sex in this passable TV thriller. Armed only with tapes of some kinky conversations, she teams up with detective Parker Stevenson to locate her missing husband, only to discover he's got himself into an even more sinister mess. Plausibility is clearly low on screenwriter Wesley Moore's list of priorities, while director EW Swackhamer frequently allows the tension to slacken. The resolution is well executed, however, and Seymour has a presence that more than compensates for her limited range. ▣

Jane Seymour *Adrienne Welles* • Parker Stevenson *Mat Henderson* • Beth Broderick *Laura* • Joel Brooks *Gary Nussbaum* • Robert Pine *Supervisor Mandel* ■ *Dir* EW Swackhamer • *Scr* Wesley Moore

Arena ★★
Western drama 1953 · US · Colour · 83mins

Sadly no gladiators, for this melodrama concerns itself with rodeo riders and bucking broncos. Gig Young is the seasoned rodeo star thinking of quitting, but thinking mostly about his girlfriend and his wife who wants a divorce. Then his best mate gets killed in the arena and Gig gets very gloomy indeed. Filmed in 3-D – hence the frequency of shots in which the bulls snort into the camera lens – it's not a patch on the Robert Mitchum/Nicholas Ray effort, *The Lusty Men*, made the year before.

Gig Young *Bob Danvers* • Jean Hagen *Meg Hutchins* • Polly Bergen *Ruth Danvers* • Henry Morgan [Harry Morgan] *Lew Hutchins* • Barbara Lawrence *Sylvia Morgan* • Robert Horton *Jackie Roach* • Lee Van Cleef *Smitty* ■ *Dir* Richard Fleischer • *Scr* Harold Jack Bloom, from a story by Arthur Loew Jr

L'Argent ★★★ PG
Drama 1983 · Fr/Swi · Colour · 80mins

Robert Bresson's most devoted disciples called this, his last film, a masterpiece, and the 76-year-old director won a prize for his screenplay at Cannes. However, those unmoved by Bresson's pared-down style and his use of non-professional actors may find the picture a baffling experience. The story starts when a schoolboy gets rid of a forged banknote, unwittingly initiating a downward spiral of robbery, murder and imprisonment. Bresson films peoples' hands obsessively, gives a weird spin to everyday incidents and ends his fable on a note of pure cinematic horror. In French with English subtitles. ▣

Christian Patey *Yvon Targe* • Sylvie van den Elsen *Woman* • Michel Briguet *Woman's father* • Caroline Lang *Elise Targe* • Vincent Risterucci *Lucien* ■ *Dir* Robert Bresson • *Scr* Robert Bresson, from the story *The False Note* by Leo Tolstoy

Argentine Nights ★★ U
Comedy musical 1940 · US · BW · 74mins

A low-budget B-musical with the focus fairly divided by some cheerful but largely unremembered songs and a clutch of fairly crude comic turns. A trio of girl singers, accompanied by their managers (conveniently also numbering three) decamp to Argentina to escape their creditors. Notable for marking the screen debut of immensely popular vocalists the Andrews Sisters, and the Universal debut of former Fox stars, the Ritz Brothers.

Maxine Andrews *Maxine* • Patty Andrews *Patty* • La Verne Andrews *La Verne* • Al Ritz *Al* • Harry Ritz *Harry* • Jimmy Ritz *Jimmy* • Constance Moore *Bonnie Brooks* • George Reeves *Eduardo* • Peggy Moran *Peggy* • Anne Nagel *Linda* • Kathryn Adams *Carol* ■ *Dir* Albert S Rogell • *Scr* Arthur T Horman, Ray Golden, sid Kuller

L'Arche du Désert ★★★ 12
Political drama 1997 · Alg/Fr/Ger/Swi · Colour · 89mins

There's a depressing universality about this tale of bigotry, which valiantly puts the case for co-operation to a world seemingly hellbent on conquest as the only form of co-existence. Ironically, it's love that proves the undoing of this particular interdependent desert community, as Myriam Aouffen and Messaouda Adami's forbidden romance sets the various tribes on a pitiless path to self-destruction. Fascinating in its anthropological detail but weak in its characterisation, Mohamed Chouikh's powerful film pulls no punches in its depiction of the senseless violence. In Algerian with English subtitles.

Myriam Aouffen *Myriam* • Messaouda Adami *Houria du Ksar* • Hacen Abdou *Amin* • Shyraz Aliane *Cousin* • Amin Chouikh *The child* • Abdelkader Belmokadem *Sage Omar* • Fatyha Nesserine *Myriam's mother* • Lynda Fares *Myriam's aunt* ■ *Dir/Scr* Mohamed Chouikh

Archipelago ★★
Drama 1991 · Chil · Colour · 85mins

Drawing comparisons between the Chono Indians slaughtered by 16th-century conquistadores and protestors killed while demonstrating against present day political repression, this is an earnest, but heavy handed example of Third Cinema. Cross-cutting between time frames, director Pablo Perelman overloads his imagery with oblique angles to reinforce the dislocation experienced by archaology professor Sergio Schmied, who, escapes from Santiago to an archipelago currently undergoing deforestation to facilitate the building of a bridge to the mainland. In Spanish with English subtitles.

Hector Noguera *Architect* • Sergio Schmied *Professor* ■ *Dir/Scr* Pablo Perelman

Arctic Blue ★★ 15
Action adventure 1993 · US/Can · Colour · 91mins

Video king Rutger Hauer enlivens this proficient but mundane thriller, set in the bleak snowy wastes of Alaska. Dylan Walsh plays a part-time policeman who reluctantly agrees to nursemaid a killer (Hauer) to the city. When their plane crashes en route, Walsh finds both the environment and his prisoner against him. Hauer is as charismatic as ever, while the effective direction is by Peter Masterson, sometime actor and father of Mary Stuart Masterson. ▣

Rutger Hauer *Ben Corbett* • Dylan Walsh *Eric Desmond* • Rya Kihlstedt *Anne Marie* • Jon Cuthbert *Lemalle* • John Bear Curtis *Mitchell* • Bill Croft *"Viking" Bob Corbett* • Richard Bradford *Wilder* ■ *Dir* Peter Masterson • *Scr* Ross Lamanna

Aria ★★★ 18
Opera anthology 1987 · UK · Colour · 85mins

This is the cinematic equivalent of the *Three Tenors* concerts: hummable slices of opera, here interpreted visually by an eclectic selection of film directors. Understandably, it's an uneven affair but, although the true opera buff will be horrified, there are some little gems. The pick of the vignettes is Franc Roddam's take on the *Liebestod* from Wagner's *Tristan und Isolde*, with Bridget Fonda (in her film debut) and James Mathers as a pair of beautiful, tragic lovers. Honourable mention, too, for Robert Altman's segment from *Les Boréades* (with the camera focused entirely on an audience seemingly made up of inmates from an asylum) and Julien Temple's trashy and kitsch version of Verdi's *Rigoletto*, with Buck Henry and Anita Morris as the adulterous Hollywood couple. Jean-Luc Godard's segment is the silliest, while non-opera fans will be drawn to the Bruce Beresford section in which Elizabeth Hurley disrobes in the picturesque setting of Bruges. Contains sex scenes and nudity.

John Hurt • Sophie Ward • Theresa Russell • Jack Kyle • Marianne McLoughlin • Buck Henry • Beverly D'Angelo • Anita Morris • Elizabeth Hurley • Peter Birch • Julie Hagerty • Genevieve Page • Bridget Fonda • James Mathers • Linzi Drew • Andreas Wisniewski • Tilda Swinton ■ *Dir* Nicolas Roeg, Jean-Luc Godard, Robert Altman, Derek Jarman, Charles Sturridge, Julien Temple, Bruce Beresford, Franc Roddam, Ken Russell, Bill Bryden • *Scr* Nicolas Roeg, Jean-Luc Godard, Robert Altman, Derek Jarman, Charles Sturridge, Julien Temple, Bruce Beresford, Franc Roddam, Ken Russell, Bill Bryden, Don Boyd

Ariane ★★★

Drama 1931 · Ger · BW · 78mins

The sixth collaboration between the soon-to-be husband-and-wife team of Hungarian director Paul Czinner and Polish-born actress Elizabeth Bergner was their first venture into talkies. She is positively radiant as the Russian émigrée who is distracted from her studies by sophisticated businessman Rudolf Forster, whose boast that he prefers experienced women prompts her to invent a string of affairs that only alienate his affections. Filmed in both German and English (as *The Loves of Ariane*) and adapted from a novel by Claude Anet, the action is as deliciously light as Billy Wilder's 1957 remake *Love in the Afternoon*. In German with English subtitles.

Elisabeth Bergner *Ariane* • Rudolf Forster *Konstantin* • Annemarie Steinsieck *Tante Warwara* • Hertha Guthmar *Olga* • Theodor Loos *The teacher* • Nikolas Wassilieff *The student* • Alfred Gerasch *The doctor* ■ *Dir* Paul Czinner • *Scr* Paul Czinner, Carl Mayer, from a novel by Claude Anet

Ariel ★★★★ 15

Comedy drama 1988 · Fin · Colour · 69mins

Aki Kaurismäki puts his habitually offbeat slant on the *film noir* road movie in this second instalment of the "working life" trilogy that brought him to international fame. Quitting Lapland in his Cadillac to seek pastures new, tin miner Turo Pajala makes a typically lugubrious Kaurismäki hero, stumbling into increasingly dangerous situations almost as accidentally as he takes up with single-mom meter maid Susanna Häävisto. The deceptively simple style may seem to subvert traditional social realism, but there's a barbed satirical intent at work here, which blends with the subtle character comedy to pass copious pertinent comments on modern-day Finland. In Finnish with English subtitles. Contains some swearing and moderate violence.

Turo Pajala *Taisto Kasurinen* • Susanna Häävisto *Irmeli* • Matti Pellonpää *Mikkonen* • Eetu Hilkamo *Riku* • Erkki Pajala *Miner* • Matti Jaaranen *Mugger* ■ *Dir/Scr* Aki Kaurismäki

Arise, My Love ★★★★

Wartime romantic comedy
1940 · US · BW · 111mins

Claudette Colbert and Ray Milland co-star in this superior comedy-drama-romance from Paramount, which won several Oscar nominations and the award itself for its story, although not, surprisingly for the polished and admirably topical screenplay by the 18-carat team of Billy Wilder and Charles Brackett. It audaciously combines wit and a love story with headline events of the Spanish Civil War and then the Second World War, both of which Paris-based newswoman Colbert is reporting while becoming involved with Milland. The film is sophisticated and gripping entertainment with a serious theme, and Mitchell Leisen's direction, backed by the resources of Paramount, perfectly catches the nuances.

Claudette Colbert *Augusta Nash* • Ray Milland *Tom Martin* • Dennis O'Keefe *Shep* • Walter Abel *Phillips* • Dick Purcell *Pink* • George Zucco *Prison Governor* • Frank Puglia *Father Jacinto* ■ *Dir* Mitchell Leisen • *Scr* Charles Brackett, Billy Wilder, from the story by Benjamin Glazer, John S Toldy

The Aristocats ★★★★ U

Animated adventure
1970 · US · Colour · 75mins

The last of the Disney animated features to be personally supervised by Walt, the delight in Wolfgang Reitherman's turn-of-the-century movie, set in a charmingly detailed Paris, is the brilliant matching of voices to visuals. Hermione Baddeley plays the aristo-owner of elegant feline Eva Gabor who, with her three kittens, is rescued from a nasty fate by Phil Harris's alley cat. The man responsible, butler Edgar (Roddy Maude-Roxby), has good reason for resentment – the old lady was going to leave everything to the cats in her will – but we're always on the side of the animals in a Disney film.

Phil Harris *J Thomas O'Malley* • Eva Gabor *Duchess* • Sterling Holloway *Roquefort* • Scatman Crothers *Scat Cat* • Paul Winchell *Chinese Cat* • Tim Hudson *English Cat* • Vito Scotti *Italian Cat* • Thurl Ravenscroft *Russian Cat* • Hermione Baddeley *Madame Bonfamille* • Roddy Maude-Roxby *Butler* ■ *Dir* Wolfgang Reitherman • *Animation Director* Frank Thomas

Arizona ★★★ U

Western 1940 · US · BW · 116mins

Director Wesley Ruggles, who had won his western spurs and a best picture Oscar with the early talkie epic *Cimarron* (1931), was responsible for this account of pioneering life in Tucson. The focus is firmly on Jean Arthur as the first lady settler there, battling it out with the rogues trying to control her rail freight business. Femininity asserts itself when she falls in love with William Holden (in his first western), passing through on his travels. Distinguished by Arthur's performance and outstanding photography and action set-pieces which reflect the film's then massive production budget, it contains all the ingredients that became standard to the frontier western.

Jean Arthur *Phoebe Titus* • William Holden (1) *Peter Muncie* • Warren William *Jefferson Carteret* • Porter Hall *Lazarus Ward* • Paul Harvey *Solomon Warner* • George Chandler *Haley* • Byron Foulger *Pete Kitchen* • Regis Toomey *Grant Oury* ■ *Dir* Wesley Ruggles • *Scr* Claude Binyon, from a story by Clarence Budington Kelland • *Cinematographer* Joseph Walker, Harry Hallenberger, Fayte Browne

Arizona Bushwhackers ★

Western 1968 · US · Colour · 87mins

Producer AC Lyles's series of plodding westerns stuffed with veteran stars was looking as tired as its principal players when this entry hobbled into release. Lyles coaxed James Cagney out of retirement to speak the narration and the film also introduced Roy Rogers Jr in a small supporting role. Otherwise, there's little pleasure now in the convoluted plot about gunrunning in Arizona during the Civil War under the anonymous direction of Lesley Selander.

Howard Keel *Lee Travis* • Yvonne De Carlo *Jill Wyler* • John Ireland *Dan Shelby* • Marilyn Maxwell *Molly* • Scott Brady *Tom Rile* • Brian Donlevy *Major Smith* • Barton MacLane *Sheriff Grover* • James Craig *Ike Clanton* • Roy Rogers Jr *Roy* • James Cagney *Narrator* ■ *Dir* Lesley Selander • *Scr* Steve Fisher, from a story by Steve Fisher, Andrew Craddock

Arizona Dream ★★★ 15

Drama 1991 · Fr · Colour · 134mins

Talented European directors often fail to succeed in transferring their specific view of life to English-language cinema, and this sprawling eccentric drama from Bosnian film-maker Emir Kusturica is a case in point; Kusturica, director of the acclaimed *Time of the Gypsies* and *When Father Was Away on Business*, fails to do himself justice. Nevertheless, it remains mesmerisingly watchable, largely owing to the superb performances of an eclectic cast, particularly the marvellous Faye Dunaway in one of her best roles as the emotional wreck that drifter Johnny Depp falls for, and the cleverly cast Jerry Lewis as Depp's very practical uncle. Cult favourites Vincent Gallo and Lili Taylor also emerge with credit. Despite their efforts, it still doesn't really work. Contains swearing.

Johnny Depp *Axel Backmar* • Jerry Lewis *Leo Sweetie* • Faye Dunaway *Elaine Stalker* • Lili Taylor *Grace Stalker* • Paulina Porizkova *Millie* • Vincent Gallo *Paul Backmar* • Michael J Pollard *Fabian* ■ *Dir* Emir Kusturica • *Scr* David Atkins, Emir Kusturica

The Arizona Kid ★★

Western 1939 · US · BW · 61mins

In 1939, Roy Rogers became the third most popular western star in America; Gene Autry came top, while William "Hopalong Cassidy" Boyd was second. With his trademark white hat, twin holsters and gee-tar, Rogers rode, shot and crooned his way through scores of B-westerns like this one: a Civil War yarn in which our hero, a Confederate captain, must kill his best friend when he realises they have been fighting on the wrong side of the moral fence. Rogers's longtime pardner, George "Gabby" Hayes, is in attendance, while Sally March provides the romantic interest.

Roy Rogers *Roy* • George "Gabby" Hayes *Gabby Whittaker* • Sally March *Laura Radford* • Stuart Hamblen *McBride* • Dorothy Sebastian *Bess Warren* • Earl Dwire *Dr Radford* ■ *Dir* Joseph Kane • *Scr* Luci Ward, Gerald Geraghty, from a story by Luci Ward

Arizona Legion ★ U

Western 1939 · US · BW · 58mins

In this routine series western for RKO, George O'Brien goes undercover as the leader of a band of secret agents known as the Arizona Rangers and infiltrates the outlaw gang who have taken over a town. Of course, his activities lead to problems with girlfriend Laraine Johnson, (who would become a big star as Laraine Day). By contrast, O'Brien's career had seen much better days.

George O'Brien *Boone Yeager* • Laraine Johnson [Laraine Day] *Letty Meade* • Carlyle Moore Jr *Lt Ives* • Chill Wills *Whopper Hatch* • Edward Le Saint *Judge Meade* • Harry Cording *Whiskey Joe* ■ *Dir* David Howard • *Scr* Oliver Drake, from a story by Bernard McConville

Arizona Raiders ★★

Western 1965 · US · Colour · 89mins

Audie Murphy and Ben Cooper are convicted members of Quantrill's Raiders, who agree to help Buster Crabbe and the newly-formed Arizona Rangers round up the remainder of the gang who are still on the loose and causing mayhem. This by-the-numbers western is a new version of the 1951 George Montgomery picture *The Texas Rangers*, which helps explain why it seems so old-hat.

Audie Murphy *Clint* • Michael Dante *Brady* • Ben Cooper *Willie Martin* • Buster Crabbe [Larry "Buster" Crabbe] *Captain Andrews* • Gloria Talbott *Martina* • Ray Stricklyn *Danny Bonner* ■ *Dir* William Witney • *Scr* Alex Gottlieb, Willard Willingham, Mary Willingham, from a story by Frank Gruber, Richard Schayer

The Arizona Ranger ★★

Western 1948 · US · BW · 64mins

Tim Holt, who had just proved once again what a fine actor he was as one of the gold prospectors in John Huston's *The Treasure of the Sierra Madre*, returns to the world of formula B-westerns in this RKO feature. Here at least there was some added interest as Tim was cast as the son of his real-life father, the former western star Jack Holt (who had an uncredited role in *The Treasure of the Sierra Madre*). Holt Jr falls in love with the wife of abusive Steve Brodie, before reconciling with Dad and returning to the family ranch.

Tim Holt *Bob Wade* • Jack Holt *Rawhide* • Nan Leslie *Laura Butler* • Richard Martin *Chito Rafferty* • Steve Brodie *Quirt* ■ *Dir* John Rawlins • *Scr* Norman Houston

The Arizonian ★★★ U

Western 1935 · US · BW · 75mins

An excellent screenplay by Dudley Nichols (who also wrote *Stagecoach*) enlivens a western which these days rather shows its age. Richard Dix, on his way down after the giddy heights of *Cimarron* (1931), is a marshal working with reformed outlaw Preston Foster to rid Silver City of corrupt Louis Calhern. (This was years before Calhern assumed the patriarchal style of villainy he brought to films such as *The Asphalt Jungle*.) Nichols won a best screenplay Oscar for his next film, *The Informer*, which also featured *The Arizonian*'s English-born heroine, Margot Grahame, in a supporting role.

74

U = SUITABLE FOR ALL   Uc = SUITABLE FOR ALL, ESPECIALLY FOR YOUNG CHILDREN (VIDEO ONLY)   PG = PARENTAL GUIDANCE

Richard Dix *Clay Tallant* • Margot Grahame *Kitty Rivers* • Preston Foster *Tex Randolph* • Louis Calhern *Jake Mamien* • James Bush *Orin Tallant* • Ray Mayer *McClosky* ■ *Dir* Charles Vidor • *Scr* Dudley Nichols

Arlington Road ★★★★ 15

Thriller   1998 · US/UK · Colour · 113mins

Is college professor Jeff Bridges's new next-door neighbour Tim Robbins a white supremacist urban terrorist planning to bomb a government target? Or is it just that his nervous paranoia stems from the fact that his FBI agent wife was killed in suspicious circumstances? Director Mark Pellington audaciously chips away at the American psyche to deliver a gripping thriller with a stunning twist ending. The tautly-built suspense comes from never letting the viewer in on the supposed conspiracy theory and a totally sympathetic and believable performance by Bridges. Seat-edge stuff. ▭ **DVD**

Jeff Bridges *Michael Farady* • Tim Robbins *Oliver Lang* • Joan Cusack *Cheryl Lang* • Hope Davis *Brooke Wolf* • Robert Gossett *FBI Agent Whit Carver* • Mason Gamble *Brady Lang* • Spencer Treat Clark *Grant Farady* • Stanley Anderson *Dr Archer Scobee* ■ *Dir* Mark Pellington • *Scr* Ehren Kruger

Armageddon ★★ 12

Science-fiction action adventure
1998 · US · Colour · 144mins

Bruce Willis leads a crack crew of astronauts (including Ben Affleck, Will Patton and Steve Buscemi) into space to blow up an asteroid threatening Earth's existence in a typically gung-ho action juggernaut from producer Jerry Bruckheimer (*Con Air*). The script is scarcely believable and contains zero characterisation, so director Michael Bay (*Bad Boys*, *The Rock*) tries to make up for these deficiencies with incessant special effects and ever more bombastic and outlandish set-pieces. The result is a numbing visual assault that is completely devoid of imagination. The acting is corny, the story pure hokum and the comic strip dialogue gets tiresome very quickly. The result is a testosterone-laden, intergalactic *Top Gun* that makes a very shallow impact. Contains some swearing and violence. ▭ **DVD**

Bruce Willis *Harry S Stamper* • Billy Bob Thornton *Dan Truman* • Ben Affleck *AJ Frost* • Liv Tyler *Grace Stamper* • Keith David *General Kimsey* • Chris Ellis *Walter Clark* • Jason Isaacs *Ronald Quincy* • Will Patton *Charles "Chick" Chapple* • Steve Buscemi *Rockhound* • Ken Campbell *Max Lennert* • Charlton Heston *Narrator* ■ *Dir* Michael Bay • *Scr* Jonathan Hensleigh, Jeffrey Abrams, from a story by Jonathan Hensleigh, Robert Roy Pool, adapted by Tony Gilroy, Shane Salerno

Armed and Dangerous ★ 15

Comedy   1986 · US · Colour · 83mins

John Candy often showed very suspect judgement when it came to leading roles and this moronic comedy was a depressingly familiar waste of his talents. Teaming up with old chum Eugene Levy, this finds the unlikely duo causing chaos at a private security company and coming up against cartoonish gangster Robert Loggia. The spectre of *Police Academy* looms large, but this even lacks the grossness of

that series, while director Mark L Lester, usually a proficient handler of action material, messes up the few chase sequences. Meg Ryan would probably like to draw a discreet veil over this one as well. ▭

John Candy *Frank Dooley* • Eugene Levy *Norman Kane* • Robert Loggia *Michael Carlino* • Kenneth McMillan *Clarence O'Connell* • Meg Ryan *Maggie Cavanaugh* • Brion James *Anthony Lazarus* • Jonathan Banks *Clyde Klepper* • Don Stroud *Sergeant Rizzo* ■ *Dir* Mark L Lester • *Scr* Harold Ramis, Peter Torokvei, from a story by Brian Grazer, Harold Ramis, James Keach

Armed and Innocent ★★ 15

Thriller based on a true story
1994 · US · Colour · 93mins

Given the rash of tragic incidents in the USA in the nineties involving youngsters abusing the people's constitutional right to bear arms, this drama based on a true story may raise a few eyebrows. In this case, a young boy shoots and kills two burglars attempting to rob his parents' home, only to find himself tracked remorselessly by their accomplice who wants revenge. The dubious message aside, this is pretty formulaic stuff that's not helped by the casting of two familiar TV faces, Gerald McRaney and Kate Jackson. Contains violence.

Gerald McRaney *Bobby Lee Holland* • Kate Jackson *Patsy Holland* • Cotter Smith *Lonnie* • Andrew Starnes *Chris Holland* • Jim Haynie *Brad St Clair* ■ *Dir* Jack Bender • *Scr* Danielle Hill

Armed Response ★★ 18

Action crime drama
1986 · US · Colour · 82mins

Hardworking Fred Olen Ray is best known for such cheap and sleazy exploitation hits as *Hollywood Chainsaw Hookers*, but this early effort is a much more mainstream affair. David Carradine teams up with spaghetti western icon Lee Van Cleef to play a father and son who go head to head with the Japanese Yakuza, led by Mako. The supporting players include Michael Berryman, Roger Corman favourite Dick Miller and Laurene Landon, so it's light years ahead of Ray's normal fare. Easily-pleased action fans will lap up the numerous explosions, fight scenes and car smashes. ▭

David Carradine *Jim Roth* • Lee Van Cleef *Burt Roth* • Mako *Akira Tanaka* • Lois Hamilton *Sara Roth* • Ross Hagen *Cory Thorton* • Brent Huff *Tommy Roth* • Laurene Landon *Deborah Silverstein* • Dick Miller *Steve* • Michael Berryman *FC* ■ *Dir* Fred Olen Ray • *Scr* TL Lankford, from a story by Paul Hertzberg, Fred Olen Ray, TL Lankford

L'Armée des Ombres ★★★★★

Second World War drama
1969 · Fr/It · Colour · 143mins

Jean-Pierre Melville's reputation rests largely on American-style gangster movies such as *Le Deuxième Souffle* and *Le Samouraï*, but *L'Armée des Ombres* may be his greatest film. In this long but utterly mesmerising vengeance thriller, set during the Second World War, Lino Ventura plays a Resistance fighter searching for the man who betrayed him to the Nazis.

With its superb cast, moody photography, marvellous use of Lyons locations and doom-laden flashbacks, this is a war drama *par excellence* that draws on the director's own experience as a member of the Maquis.

Lino Ventura *Philippe Gerbier* • Paul Meurisse *Luc Jardie* • Simone Signoret *Mathilde* • Jean-Pierre Cassel *Jean-François* • Claude Mann *Le Masque* • Christian Barbier *Le Bison* • Serge Reggiani *Barber* • Alain Libolt *Paul Dounat* • Paul Crauchet *Felix* ■ *Dir* Jean-Pierre Melville • *Scr* Jean-Pierre Melville, from the novel *Army of Shadows* by Joseph Kessel • *Cinematographer* Pierre Lhomme

Armored Car Robbery ★★

Crime drama   1950 · US · BW · 67mins

This B-movie thriller about a robbery that goes horribly wrong vaguely resembles *The Asphalt Jungle*, which was made the same year, while its ironic climax was copied by Stanley Kubrick for his 1956 effort, *The Killing*. Director Richard Fleischer is clearly working on a shoestring, but that doesn't hinder his creation of suspense or atmosphere. The cast, alas, is distinctly third-rate: Charles MacGraw comes across as a neanderthal version of Ernest Borgnine.

Charles McGraw *Cordell* • Adele Jergens *Yvonne* • William Talman *Purvus* • Douglas Fowley *Benny* • Steve Brodie *Mapes* • Don McGuire *Ryan* • Don Haggerty *Cuyler* ■ *Dir* Richard Fleischer • *Scr* Earl Fenton, Gerald Drayson Adams, from a story by Robert Angus, Robert Leeds

Armored Command ★★

Second World War spy drama
1961 · US · BW · 98mins

A potentially interesting but bungled Second World War drama, with Tina Louise as a sort of Mata Hari figure who infiltrates a group of GIs to discover the Allied Forces' strength and tactics. The soldiers squabble for her favours, but the leader remains sceptical. Louise looks good but lacks the dramatic range to carry off the demanding role, and she's not helped by a script that deals strictly in clichés. The film also offers a non-musical starring role for Howard Keel. "He should've sung," wrote sixth-billed Burt Reynolds. "We needed all the help we could get."

Howard Keel *Colonel Devlin* • Tina Louise *Alexandra Bastegar* • Warner Anderson *Lieutenant Colonel Wilson* • Earl Holliman *Sergeant Mike* • Carleton Young *Captain Macklin* • Burt Reynolds *Skee* • Marty Ingels *Pinhead* ■ *Dir* Byron Haskin • *Scr* Ron W Alcorn, Ernest Haller

The Armour of God ★★ 15

Martial arts adventure
1986 · HK · Colour · 84mins

Although he has never reached the kung fu heights of Bruce Lee, Jackie Chan's high-vaulting, low-swiping action movies – especially those made on his Hong Kong home soil – have an endearing humour that almost amounts to wit. Sadly, this *Raiders of the Lost Ark* rip-off exports him to Europe, where he seeks out a crusader's relic and battles some lethal monks. As director as well as star, his style is not so much cramped

as numbed. Cantonese dialogue dubbed into English. ▭

Jackie Chan *Jackie* • Alan Tam *Alan* • Rosamund Kwan *Lorelei* • Lola Forner *May* • Bozidar Smilianic *Bannon* • Ken Boyle *Grand Wizard* • John Ladalski *Chief Lama* • Robert O'Brien *Witch doctor* ■ *Dir* Jackie Chan • *Scr* Edward Tang, Szeto Chuek-Hun, Ken Lowe, John Sheppard, from a story by Barry Wong

Arms and the Man ★★ U

Comedy   1958 · W Ger · Colour · 86mins

Although Jacques Tati's *Mon Oncle* would have won the Oscar for best foreign film in just about any year, only a shortage of suitable submissions could explain why this stilted West German adaptation of George Bernard Shaw's play was even nominated. While undeniably superior to British director Cecil Lewis's 1932 version of this Balkan War comedy, it's still a highly stagebound production, with Franz Peter Wirth restricting his camera to spectating rather than playing an active part in the encounter between fleeing Swiss mercenary OW Fischer and Lisolette Pulver, the fiancée of his adversary. Respectful, but dull. A German language film.

OW Fischer *Captain Bluntschli* • Liselotte Pulver *Raina Petkoff* • Ellen Schwiers *Louka* • Jan Hendriks *Sergius Saranoff* • Ljuba Welitsch *Katharina* • Kurt Kasznar *Petkoff* • Manfred Inger *Nicola* ■ *Dir* Franz Peter Wirth • *Scr* Johanna Sibelius, Eberhard Keindorff, from the play by George Bernard Shaw

Army of Darkness ★★

Horror fantasy comedy
1993 · US · Colour · 81mins

As a loose remake of *A Connecticut Yankee in King Arthur's Court* filmed in the style of the Three Stooges, director Sam Raimi's hopelessly juvenile effort just about scrapes by as a humdrum knockabout parody. As the second sequel to his classic *Evil Dead*, however, it's a vapid exercise in watered-down horror kitsch that betrays the whole ethos of the sublime original. After a recap of the first two movies, Bruce Campbell battles with pit monsters, sword-wielding skeletons and his evil clone to find the sacred "Book of the Dead" that will help him escape the Dark Ages and return to the present. This cardboard comic book fantasy has plenty of in-jokes for the discerning horror buff but little actual horror.

Bruce Campbell *Ash/Evil Ash* • Embeth Davidtz *Sheila/Evil Sheila* • Marcus Gilbert *Arthur* • Ian Abercrombie *Wiseman* • Richard Grove *Duke Henry* • Michael Earl Reid *Gold Tooth* • Bridget Fonda *Linda* • Ivan Raimi *Fake Shemp* ■ *Dir* Sam Raimi • *Scr* Sam Raimi, Ivan Raimi

Army of One ★★ 18

Action thriller   1993 · US · Colour · 96mins

Geoffrey Lewis (father of Juliette) has made a nice living playing second string to some of Hollywood's top action heroes. Here he's teamed with Dolph Lundgren in a slam-bam adventure that also goes under the title of *Joshua Tree*. While it may be meat and drink to Lewis, George Segal is definitely slumming in a movie that seems to have been designed solely to exhibit the strapping Lundgren's fighting skills. Seeking the man who framed him, he rips through the American Southwest like one of Ray Harryhausen's stop-motion animated statues. Strictly for fans. Contains swearing, violence and nudity. ▭

Dolph Lundgren *Wellman Santee* • George Segal *Severence* • Kristian Alfonso *Rita* • Geoffrey Lewis *Cepeda* • Michelle Phillips *Esther* • Matt Battaglia *Michael Agnos* ■ *Dir* Vic Armstrong • *Scr* Steven Pressfield

The Arnelo Affair ★

Mystery melodrama 1947 · US · BW · 87mins

The guilty party in this glossy but less than hypnotic mystery is writer/director Arch Oboler, whose radio background explains the emphasis on talk and the static camera set-ups. The lacklustre line-up of MGM's second-rank stars doesn't help: John Hodiak as a shady nightclub proprietor, George Murphy as a Chicago attorney and Frances Gifford as his neglected wife, whose affair with Hodiak involves her in murder.

John Hodiak *Tony Arnelo* • Frances Gifford *Anne Parkson* • George Murphy *Ted Parkson* • Dean Stockwell *Ricky Parkson* • Eve Arden *Vivian Delwyn* • Lowell Gillmore *Avery Border* ■ *Dir/Scr* Arch Oboler

Arnold ★★ 15

Comedy thriller 1973 · US · Colour · 90mins

The oddball cast is the sole attraction here. Stella Stevens plays a gold-digger who marries an aristocrat for his money. The thing is, the poor man is lying in his coffin throughout the ceremony! This makes the reading of the will a rather tricky business, and wastrel brother Roddy MacDowall and sister Elsa Lanchester are miffed to say the least. Others involved in this black comedy are Farley Granger, Victor Buono and British cabaret singer Shani Wallis as the dead aristocrat's widow. Left out of the will, she gets to sing the title number instead. ▭

Stella Stevens *Karen* • Roddy McDowall *Robert* • Elsa Lanchester *Hester* • Shani Wallis *Jocelyn* • Farley Granger *Evan Lyons* • Victor Buono *Governor* • John McGiver *Governor* ■ *Dir* Georg Fenady • *Scr* Jameson Brewer, John Fenton Murray

Around the World in 80 Days ★★★★ U

Adventure 1956 · US · Colour · 187mins

An epic much of its time, this vastly entertaining star-studded travelogue was produced (with some difficulty) by the great showman Michael Todd (one of Elizabeth Taylor's many husbands), who was awarded the best picture Oscar for his considerable pains. The cast, led by the ultra-urbane David Niven, couldn't be bettered, nor could the use of worldwide locations – 13 countries in all. Todd persuaded 46 guest stars to appear in supporting roles, and spotting them is a delight. ▭

David Niven *Phileas Fogg* • Cantinflas *Passepartout* • Shirley MacLaine *Princess Aouda* • Robert Newton *Inspector Fix* • Noël Coward *Minister* • Hermione Gingold • Marlene Dietrich • Trevor Howard • Peter Lorre • John Mills • Robert Morley • George Raft • Frank Sinatra • Buster Keaton • John Gielgud *Foster* ■ *Dir* Michael Anderson • *Scr* SJ Perelman, from the novel by Jules Verne

Around the World under the Sea ★★ U

Adventure 1966 · US · Colour · 110mins

Lloyd Bridges, master scuba diver in the TV series *Sea Hunt*, spits into his mask again before investigating a series of underwater volcanic eruptions. There's some scientific chat about earthquakes and the end of the world, but mostly it's a daft yarn with a giant squid, a friendly dolphin and Shirley Eaton as the only woman in sight. It was filmed on the Great Barrier Reef and in the Bahamas by veteran director Andrew Marton, the man responsible for the chariot race sequence in *Ben-Hur*.

Lloyd Bridges *Dr Doug Standish* • Shirley Eaton *Dr Maggie Hanford* • Brian Kelly *Dr Craig Mosby* • David McCallum *Dr Phil Volker* • Keenan Wynn *Hank Stahl* • Marshall Thompson *Dr Orin Hillyard* ■ *Dir* Andrew Marton • *Scr* Arthur Weiss, Art Arthur

Around the World with Dot ★★ Uc

Part-animated adventure 1982 · Ausl · Colour · 70mins

With their blend of animation and live-action nature footage, the films about tiny Australian redhead Dot and her animal friends are usually as educational as they are entertaining. But with this early entry in the long-running series, director Yoram Gross pushed his luck too far. Even before he had exhausted the wonderful land of Oz, he sends Dot out into the big wide world in search of her runaway pet kangaroo. The creatures she encounters have some charm, but enlisting the help of Father Christmas is more a sign of desperation than inspiration. ▭

Dir Yoram Gross • *Scr* John Palmer, Yoram Gross

The Arousers ★★

Horror 1970 · US · Colour · 75mins

Fifties dreamboat Tab Hunter plays the Catherine Deneuve role in a rehash of Polanski's classic psycho shocker, *Repulsion*. Hunter is compelling as a personal trainer who is not the stud he appears, but an impotent, mother-fixated psychopath who kills whenever sex rears its head. The film is an early soft-core slasher with lots of female victims naked and dead. Unusually, though, there is always something kinky bubbling beneath the surface.

Tab Hunter *Eddie Collins* • Cherie Latimer *Lauren Powers* • Linda Leider *Vickie* • Isabel Jewell *Mrs Cole* • Nadyne Turney *Barbara* ■ *Dir/Scr* Curtis Hanson

The Arrangement ★★ 15

Drama 1969 · US · Colour · 120mins

A rather distasteful film from director Elia Kazan, taken from his own novel, about a successful New York advertising man, played by Kirk Douglas, who becomes totally disenchanted with his cosy, privileged world and decides to jettison work, marriage and respectability in one foul swoop. A starry cast struggles with a rather old-fashioned premise: Kazan appears to espouse the principles of free love, but actually promotes the abdication of all personal responsibility

and seems to give gung-ho approval to stomping over the feelings of others. Contains swearing ▭

Kirk Douglas *Eddie Anderson* • Faye Dunaway *Gwen* • Deborah Kerr *Florence Anderson* • Richard Boone *Sam Anderson* • Hume Cronyn *Arthur* • Michael Higgins *Michael* • John Randolph Jones *Charles* ■ *Dir* Elia Kazan • *Scr* Elia Kazan, from his novel

The Arrival ★★★ 18

Science-fiction thriller 1996 · US · Colour · 103mins

Charlie Sheen goes on the run after discovering an extraterrestrial conspiracy in a Mexican power plant to change the earth's climate and prepare it for colonisation. Although not in the same league as *Independence Day* or *The X Files*, director David N Twohy skilfully reworks a number of science fiction clichés (as well as ideas from his *Waterworld* and *The Fugitive* scripts) to deliver a highly polished entry in the alien invasion sweepstakes. Sheen faces stylish computer-generated effects at every turn, but still emerges as the winner in this pleasing, if low-key B-movie. ▭

Charlie Sheen *Zane Ziminski* • Ron Silver *Gordian* • Lindsay Crouse *Ilana Green* • Teri Polo *Char* • Richard Schiff *Calvin* • Tony T Johnson *Kiki* ■ *Dir* David Twohy [David N Twohy] • *Scr* David Twohy

Arrow in the Dust ★★ U

Western 1954 · US · Colour · 80mins

Prolific director Lesley Selander was one of the unsung heroes of the western, whose feature output embraced such cowboy icons as Buck Jones, Hopalong Cassidy and Tim Holt. This perfectly workmanlike programme filler stars Sterling Hayden as a deserter masquerading as an officer to help out a wagon train. Lee Van Cleef makes an early appearance, and *Red River*'s Coleen Gray is the female lead. The footage from the 1951 Lew Ayres picture *New Mexico* doesn't really match, though.

Sterling Hayden *Bart Laish* • Coleen Gray *Christella* • Keith Larsen *Lt King* • Tom Tully *Crowshaw* • Jimmy Wakely *Carqueville* • Tudor Owen *Tillotson* • Lee Van Cleef *Crew boss* ■ *Dir* Lesley Selander • *Scr* Don Martin, from the novel by LL Foreman

Arrowhead ★★ U

Western 1953 · US · Colour · 105mins

This western packs considerable force from the sheer intensity of the hatred between Charlton Heston, as the army scout who was raised by the Apaches, and Jack Palance as Toriano, the son of the chief. The government wants peace but Heston is sure the Apaches can't be trusted, and in hand-to-hand combat eventually proves that Palance is not the invincible new leader he claims to be. While Palance is chillingly ruthless, Heston remains monotonously grim. The film as a whole, crudely written and directed by Charles Marquis Warren, is distinctly unpleasant.

Charlton Heston *Ed Bannon* • Jack Palance *Toriano* • Katy Jurado *Nita* • Brian Keith *Capt North* • Mary Sinclair *Lela Wilson* • Milburn Stone *Sandy MacKinnon* • Richard Shannon *Lieutenant Kirk* • Lewis Martin *Col Weybright*

■ *Dir* Charles Marquis Warren • *Scr* Charles Marquis Warren, from the novel *Adobe Walls* by WR Burnett

Arrowsmith ★★★

Drama 1931 · US · BW · 102mins

John Ford wasn't, perhaps, the ideal director for the work of Sinclair Lewis, but this sturdy adaptation of Lewis's novel benefits from a marvellous performance by Ronald Colman as the idealistic doctor of the title who's seeking a cure for bubonic plague. Colman brings a vivid, idealistic freshness to the part and single-handedly justifies this Samuel Goldwyn production. Helen Hayes suffers nobly as his wife and a pre-stardom Myrna Loy excels as the bored society girl with whom Colman has a fling.

Ronald Colman *Dr Martin Arrowsmith* • Helen Hayes *Leora* • AC Anson *Professor Gottlieb* • Richard Bennett *Sondelius* • Claude King *Dr Tubbs* • Beulah Bondi *Mrs Tozer* • Myrna Loy *Joyce Lanyon* • Russell Hopton *Terry Wickett* ■ *Dir* John Ford • *Scr* Sidney Howard, from the novel by Sinclair Lewis

The Arsenal Stadium Mystery ★★★ PG

Crime drama 1939 · UK · BW · 82mins

This far from baffling murder mystery may not be premier league stuff, but it has become something of a cult item in arthouse circles. There's plenty to enjoy as maverick Scotland Yard inspector Leslie Banks tries to find out who murdered star player Anthony Bushell during a friendly match, not least the chance to see members of the 1937/38 Arsenal championship-winning side in action. Working from Leonard Gribble's novel, director Thorold Dickinson reveals a talent for authentic detail; there's also a pleasing lightness about the action, which stands in stark contrast to his later films such as *Gaslight* and *The Queen of Spades*. ▭

Leslie Banks *Inspector Slade* • Greta Gynt *Gwen Lee* • Ian Maclean *Sergeant Clinton* • Esmond Knight *Raille* • Liane Linden *Inga* • Brian Worth *Philip Morring* • Anthony Bushell *Jack Dyce* ■ *Dir* Thorold Dickinson • *Scr* Thorold Dickinson, Donald Bull, from the novel by Leonard Gribble

Arsene Lupin ★★★

Comedy thriller 1932 · US · BW · 84mins

The names of John and Lionel Barrymore sharing the marquee guaranteed big audiences for this well-upholstered version of Maurice LeBlanc and Francis de Croisset's play about a master criminal. It was the first time the two brothers had starred together on film and that prospect created fireworks in 1932, though today the picture inevitably lacks that resonance and creaks a little. John plays the thief, Lionel the detective on his trail, and director Jack Conway, at the behest of the studio bosses, sacrifices plot (the theft of the Mona Lisa from the Louvre) for some elaborate thesping. A sequel, *Arsene Lupin Returns*, was made in 1938 without the Barrymores.

John Barrymore *Duke of Charmerace* • Lionel Barrymore *Guerchard* • Karen Morley *Sonia* • John Miljan *Prefect of Police* • Tully Marshall *Gourney-Martin* ■ *Dir* Jack Conway • *Scr* Carey

U = SUITABLE FOR ALL   Uc = SUITABLE FOR ALL, ESPECIALLY FOR YOUNG CHILDREN (VIDEO ONLY)   PG = PARENTAL GUIDANCE

Wilson, Bayard Veiller, Lenore Coffee, from the play by Maurice LeBlanc, Francis de croiset [François Wiener]

Arsene Lupin Returns ★★★
Comedy thriller   1938 · US · BW · 80mins

He needn't have bothered, really. The glamorous criminal was first personified by John Barrymore in 1932, memorably pitted against his brother Lionel, and the ultra-sophisticated thief went down a treat with American audiences. Six years later the same studio, MGM, decided to revive him, this time played by the equally debonair Melvyn Douglas. Trouble is, the quintessential French flavour of the original has been relentlessly Americanised here, with a plot involving Warren William as an overly publicity conscious ex-FBI man. Still, there's much to enjoy, especially in the early Franz Waxman score.

Melvyn Douglas *Rene Farrand* • Virginia Bruce *Lorraine Degrissac* • Warren William *Steve Emerson* • John Halliday *Count Degrissac* • Nat Pendleton *Joe Doyle* • Monty Woolley *Georges Bouchet* • EE Clive *Alf* • George Zucco *Prefect of Police* ■ *Dir* George Fitzmaurice • *Scr* James Kevin McGuiness, Howard Emmett Rogers, George Harmon Coxe

Arsenic and Old Lace
             ★★★★★ PG
Classic comedy   1944 · US · BW · 113mins

From the moment he saw Joseph Kesselring's hit play, Frank Capra was determined to bring this frantic comedy to the screen. Although forced to settle for Raymond Massey after he failed to get Boris Karloff to repeat his stage triumph, Capra was blessed with a sparkling cast. Cary Grant only agreed to take the lead as it gave him the chance to reunite with Jean Adair, who had once nursed him through a nasty bout of rheumatic fever. However, he then proceeded to insist on changes to the script, costumes, sets and the lighting. Grant ended up donating his fee to a range of war charities and rarely spoke of the picture with any fondness. A shame, really, as he hurls himself into the part of the decent nephew who discovers that his respectable aunts (played with hilarious dottiness by Josephine Hull and Adair) are serial killers. Spookily lit and very funny, the film is unmissable, with Grant's wonderful double-takes lightening the pitch-black humour. 📼

Cary Grant *Mortimer Brewster* • Priscilla Lane *Elaine Harper* • Raymond Massey *Jonathan Brewster* • Jack Carson *O'Hara* • Edward Everett Horton *Mr Witherspoon* • Peter Lorre *Dr Einstein* • James Gleason *Lieutenant Rooney* • Josephine Hull *Abby Brewster* • Jean Adair *Martha Brewster* • John Alexander *"Teddy Roosevelt" Brewster* • Grant Mitchell *Reverend Harper* ■ *Dir* Frank Capra • *Scr* Julius J Epstein, Philip G Epstein, from the play by Joseph Kesselring • *Cinematographer* Sol Polito

Art Deco Detective   ★★
Detective comedy
1994 · US · Colour · 102mins

John Dennis Johnson is Art Deco, a hard-boiled gumshoe who becomes embroiled in a terrorist conspiracy set-up while investigating the murder of movie star Rena Riffel in which he is implicated as the killer. A game cast is

wasted in a lame satire on Hollywood fame and wheeler-dealing. It was written and directed by the Australian director of a couple of *Howling* sequels, Philippe Mora.

John Dennis Johnston *Arthur "Art" Decowitz* • Stephen McHattie *Hyena* • Brion James *Jim Wexler* • Joe Santos *Detective Guy Lean* • Rena Riffel *Julie/Meg Hudson* • Sonia Cole *Irina Bordat* ■ *Dir/Scr* Philippe Mora

Art of Love   ★★★ U
Comedy   1965 · US · Colour · 98mins

Glossy, very silly but nonetheless enjoyable example of the Technicolor Universal sixties style as produced by Ross Hunter. Like his *Pillow Talk*, this is bedecked with likeable stars and is a jolly pleasant way to pass the time. The would-be adult plot involves James Garner and Dick Van Dyke as struggling artists in Paris, with the ultra-glamorous Angie Dickinson and Elke Sommer as their chicks and the great Ethel Merman as a singing madame. What's really strange, though, is how the undeniably talented Norman Jewison's direction is just so, well, anonymous.

James Garner *Casey* • Dick Van Dyke *Paul* • Elke Sommer *Nikki* • Angie Dickinson *Laurie* • Ethel Merman *Madame Coco* • Carl Reiner *Rodin* • Pierre Olaf *Carnot* ■ *Dir* Norman Jewison • *Scr* Carl Reiner, from a story by Richard Alan Simmons, William Sackheim

Artemisia   ★★★ 18
Historical biographical drama
1997 · Fr/Ger/It · Colour · 95mins

The first significant female figure in western art, 17th-century painter Artemisia Gentileschi emerges from this sumptuous biopic as the doomed heroine of a Gothic melodrama rather than a courageous artist who challenged the conventions of her day. However, while director Agnès Merlet's approach has appalled purists and feminists alike, she has nevertheless produced a moving portrayal that captures both the flavour of the times and the tragic fate of a passionate artist. Valentina Cervi conveys sensuality rather than creative zest in the title role but, thanks to Michel Serrault and Miki Manojlovi's generous support, this succeeds in being a vibrant portrait. In French and Italian with English subtitles. Contains nudity and sex scenes.

Michel Serrault *Orazio Gentileschi* • Valentina Cervi *Artemisia Gentileschi* • Miki Manojlovic *Agostino Tassi* • Luca Zingaretti *Cosimo* • Brigitte Catillon *Tuzia* • Frédéric Pierrot *Roberto* ■ *Dir* Agnès Merlet • *Scr* Agnès Merlet, Christine Miller, from their story

Arthur   ★★★★ 15
Comedy   1981 · US · Colour · 93mins

While Dudley Moore's drunken millionaire is outclassed by John Gielgud's disdainful butler, he's not the dud he might have been in this boozy variation on Jeeves and Wooster. As he tries to change his layabout lifestyle for love of working girl Liza Minnelli, Moore displays the charm and timing that helped to make *10* a hit, though his character is sometimes too clichéd. The ever-adaptable Gielgud delivers his lines with such wonderful aplomb that he

won an Oscar; the veteran actor was tempted back to the role seven years later for a brief appearance in the inferior sequel. Contains some swearing. 📼 **DVD**

Dudley Moore *Arthur Bach* • Liza Minnelli *Linda Marolla* • John Gielgud *Hobson* • Geraldine Fitzgerald *Martha Bach* • Jill Eikenberry *Susan Johnson* • Stephen Elliot *Burt Johnson* • Ted Ross *Bitterman* ■ *Dir/Scr* Steve Gordon

Arthur 2: On the Rocks ★ PG
Romantic comedy
1988 · US · Colour · 108mins

Seven years after that charming if one-joke movie *Arthur*, Dudley Moore ill-advisedly returned to the role of the drunken millionaire in this disastrous comedy sequel. After a financial takeover by the father of his former girlfriend, Arthur is left penniless and has to save his marriage to Liza Minnelli and regain his fortune before the end credits. You know things are getting bad when John Gielgud is resurrected as a ghost (well, the ploy worked for Alec Guinness in the *Star Wars* sequels). Believe it or not, things get even worse as the film moves towards the predictable happy ending. You have been warned. Contains some swearing 📼

Dudley Moore *Arthur Bach* • Liza Minnelli *Linda Marolla Bach* • John Gielgud *Hobson* • Geraldine Fitzgerald *Martha Bach* • Stephen Elliott *Burt Johnson* • Paul Benedict *Fairchild* • Kathy Bates *Mrs Canby* ■ *Dir* Bud Yorkin • *Scr* Andy Breckman, from characters created by Steve Gordon

Arthur Miller's The American Clock   ★★★
Drama   1993 · US · Colour

An adaptation of Arthur Miller's 1980 play, which Miller described as "a mural of American society in the Depression crisis." This TV adaptation is a three-stranded sprawl, dealing with a powerful family of bankers gone bust, a songwriter faced by eviction and a rich New Yorker whose journey to the rural heartland transforms him into a Marxist. Directed by Bob Clark, whose career has taken in *Porky's* and *Murder by Decree*, it has an impressive cast featuring David Strathairn, Mary McDonnell, JT Walsh, Estelle Parsons and Kelly Preston.

Mary McDonnell *Rose Baumler* • Darren McGavin *Older Arthur Huntington* • Kelly Preston *Diana Marley* • David Strathairn *Young Arthur Huntington* • Eddie Bracken *Grandpa* • Tony Roberts *Jesse Livermore* • Jim Dale *Ted Quinn* • Estelle Parsons *Older Doris* ■ *Dir* Bob Clark • *Scr* Frank Galati, from the play by Arthur Miller, from the book *Hard Times* by Studs Terkel

Arthur's Hallowed Ground   ★★
Drama   1985 · UK · Colour · 84mins

Not to be confused with anything to do with Camelot, this is a slight, David Puttnam-produced film. The Arthur of the title (Jimmy Jewel) is an indispensable school groundsman whose main ambition in life is to create the perfect cricket pitch. Cue much fiddling with antiquated machinery, which is as slow-moving as the film itself. This is the directorial

debut of 82-year-old Freddie Young, a distinguished cinematographer who worked on David Lean's *Doctor Zhivago*, *Ryan's Daughter* and *Lawrence of Arabia*. Unfortunately such experience doesn't seem to have helped him succeed as director.

Jimmy Jewel *Arthur* • Jean Boht *Betty* • David Swift *Lionel* • Michael Elphick *Len* • Derek Benfield *Eric* • Vas Blackwood *Henry* • John Flanagan *Norman* • Bernard Gallagher *George* ■ *Dir* Freddie Young • *Scr* Peter Gibbs

Article 99   ★ 15
Comedy drama   1992 · US · Colour · 96mins

This comedy drama sets out with three aims, but fails to accomplish any one of them. Firstly, it wants to make us angry that Washington neglects the war veterans in its hospitals. Secondly, it seeks to reproduce the gallows humour of *MASH* by having the cast quip endlessly throughout each and every crisis. And, finally, it sets out to prove that Ray Liotta has a gift for comedy. In the face of such unrelieved failure, the best one can do is acknowledge that John Mahoney and Kiefer Sutherland do all they can in support, but it's easier to accept that this was dead on arrival. Contains violence and swearing. 📼

Ray Liotta *Dr Richard Sturgess* • Kiefer Sutherland *Dr Peter Morgan* • Forest Whitaker *Dr Sid Handleman* • Lea Thompson *Dr Robin Van Dorn* • John C McGinley *Dr Rudy Bobrick* • John Mahoney *Dr Henry Dreyfoos* • Keith David *Luther Jerome* • Kathy Baker *Dr Diane Walton* • Eli Wallach *Sam Abrams* ■ *Dir* Howard Deutch • *Scr* Ron Cutler

Artists and Models   ★★★ U
Musical   1937 · US · BW · 97mins

Jack Benny's first starring vehicle, which has nothing to do with the Dean Martin and Jerry Lewis flick of the same name, was made at the height of his radio fame. While the Louis Armstrong and Martha Raye blackface sequences seem tasteless and offensive today, this is a raucous funfest that fairly zips along under Raoul Walsh's canny direction. There's a lovely pitch-driving performance from young co-star Ida Lupino that's a joy to watch, and sturdy Richard Arlen also registers strongly. A sequel, *Artists and Models Abroad*, followed in 1938.

Jack Benny *Mac Brewster* • Ida Lupino *Paula* • Richard Arlen *Alan Townsend* • Gail Patrick *Cynthia* • Ben Blue *Jupiter Pluvius* • Judy Canova *Toots* • Cecil Cunningham *Stella* • Donald Meek *Dr Zimmer* • Louis Armstrong • Martha Raye ■ *Dir* Raoul Walsh • *Scr* Walter DeLeon, Francis Martin, from a story by Sig Herzig, Gene Thackrey • *Choreographer* Vincente Minnelli, LeRoy Prinz • *Music* Victor Young

Artists and Models
            ★★★★ U
Musical comedy 1955 · US · Colour · 108mins

A superior Dean Martin and Jerry Lewis vehicle, gloriously photographed in some of the most brilliant Technicolor that you're ever likely to see. Of course, appreciation really depends on how one feels about Martin and Lewis, here expertly cast as a cartoonist and wacky fantasist, respectively, Dean using Jerry's dreams for inspiration. What gives this lunacy credence is that it's the work of Frank Tashlin, himself a noted cartoon artist. As in Tashlin's masterpiece, *The Girl Can't Help It*, the humour may seem sexist today.

Dean Martin *Rick Todd* • Jerry Lewis *Eugene Fullstack* • Shirley MacLaine *Bessie Sparrowbush* • Dorothy Malone *Abigail Parker* • Eddie Mayehoff *Mr Murdock* • Eva Gabor *Sonia* • Anita Ekberg *Anita* • George Winslow *Richard Stilton* • Jack Elam *Ivan* ■ *Dir* Frank Tashlin. • *Scr* Frank Tashlin, Hal Kanter, Herbert Baker, from a play by Norman Lessing, Michael Davidson • *Cinematographer* Daniel L Fapp

Artists and Models Abroad
★★

Musical   1938 · US · BW · 90mins

This follow-up to Paramount's 1937 hit musical comedy *Artists and Models* is more of the same, only with a French setting. Jack Benny schemes to save his untalented American theatrical troupe when it becomes stranded in Paris, but the story's merely a link between songs and fashion shows. The four Yacht Club Boys have a lively speciality number, while Joan Bennett, Mary Boland and Fritz Feld lend able support.

Jack Benny *Buck Boswell* • Joan Bennett *Patricia Harper* • Mary Boland *Mrs Isabel Channing* • Charley Grapewin *James Harper* • Joyce Compton *Chickie* ■ *Dir* Mitchell Leisen • *Scr* Howard Lindsay, Russell Crouse, Ken England, from a story by Howard Lindsay, from an idea by JP McEvoy • *Costume Designer* Edith Head

As Good as Dead
★★ PG

Thriller   1995 · US · Colour · 84mins

Horror specialist Larry Cohen plunges into the world of TV-movie thrillers with this unpleasant case of mistaken identity. The trouble starts when Crystal Bernard agrees to swap identities with her make-up artist buddy, Traci Lords. This is so that Lords can undergo emergency surgery, with disastrous consequences. Convinced she herself is in danger, Bernard decides to team up with stranger Judge Reinhold to determine the truth. This hardly pushes back the frontiers of originality, but Cohen has always had a way with unnerving atmosphere and makes the most of a distinctly ropey plot. ▣

Judge Reinhold *Ron Riverton* • Crystal Bernard *Susan Warfield* • Traci Lords *Nicole Grace* • George Dickerson *Edgar Warfield* • Carlos Carrasco *Eddie Garcia* • Jerry Bernard *Funeral director* ■ *Dir/Scr* Larry Cohen

As Good As It Gets
★★★★ 15

Romantic comedy drama
1997 · US · Colour · 132mins

Ostensibly, James L Brooks's movie is about Jack Nicholson. He plays Melvin Udall, a racist, homophobic bigot who insults everyone, lives alone, writes trashy novels for a living and has an obsessive-compulsive disorder. However, the movie is really about Helen Hunt, who plays that corniest of Hollywood characters – the lonely, frustrated waitress with a problem child. Yet Hunt, who was offered the role when Holly Hunter turned it down and, like Nicholson, won an Oscar for her pains, breathes life into the part,

trouncing her co-star and his trademark grouchy act. The picture, though, is a mixed blessing: a romantic comedy of sorts, shot on oddly retro studio sets and featuring Greg Kinnear in the clichéd role of a homosexual artist with a pet dog. It's lazily directed and far too long, but Hunt is a revelation and the reason we stick with the film. Contains some swearing and a violent scene. ▣ *DVD*

Jack Nicholson *Melvin Udall* • Helen Hunt *Carol Connelly* • Greg Kinnear *Simon Bishop* • Cuba Gooding Jr *Frank Sachs* • Skeet Ulrich *Vincent* • Shirley Knight *Beverly* • Yeardley Smith *Jackie* • Lupe Ontiveros *Nora* ■ *Dir* James L Brooks • *Scr* Mark Andrus, James L Brooks, from a story by Mark Andrus

As If It Were Raining
★★

Thriller   1963 · Fr/Sp · BW · 84mins

Shamefully wasting the beauties of Madrid and allowing the action to amble along rather than involve and confuse us, José Luis Monter has made rather a mess of this Franco-Spanish co-production. French film icon Eddie Constantine plays an American author whose chance encounter with a damsel in distress leads to his involvement in shady, and ultimately deadly, dealings. In addition to a deficiency of mystery, this picture is not helped by the cast, who plod through the proceedings with evident disinterest. French and Spanish dialogue dubbed into English.

Eddie Constantine *Eddie* • Silvia Solar *Rosa* • Maria Silva *Wilma* • Jacinto San Emerito *Coll* • Elisa Montes *Esperanza* ■ *Dir* José Luis Monter • *Scr* Niels Larsen

As Long as They're Happy
★★ U

Comedy   1955 · UK · Colour · 90mins

A moderately amusing all-British comedy, with some music, inspired by the fifties craze for sob singer Johnny Ray. The plot has an American crying crooner (Jerry Wayne) causing havoc in an English family with whom he stays. Jack Buchanan plays the unamused head of the household and the father of three daughters (Janette Scott, Jean Carson and Susan Stephen) obsessed with the visitor. J Lee Thompson directs a large cast of familiar faces.

Jack Buchanan *John Bentley* • Janette Scott *Gwen* • Jean Carson *Pat* • Susan Stephen *Corinne* • Brenda de Banzie *Stella* • Jerry Wayne *Bobby Denver* • Diana Dors *Pearl* • Joan Sims *Linda* • Dora Bryan *Mavis* ■ *Dir* J Lee Thompson • *Scr* Alan Melville, from the play by Vernon Sylvaine

As Summers Die
★★★ 15

Drama   1986 · US · Colour · 83mins

The setting for this drama – based on the novel by Winston Groom, who also wrote *Forrest Gump* – is a small town in America's Deep South during the fifties. An old-style colonial family is trying to deprive a black woman of her rightful land, and Scott Glenn is the crusading lawyer who attempts to help her. Jean-Claude Tramont's predictable TV movie rises above the norm thanks to the performances of Glenn, Jamie Lee Curtis and the ageing but still wonderful Bette Davis. ▣

Jamie Lee Curtis *Whitsey* • Scott Glenn *Willie Croft* • Bette Davis *Aunt Hannah* • CCH

Pounder *Priscilla* • Beah Richards *Elvira* • John Randolph *Augustus Tompkins* ■ *Dir* Jean-Claude Tramont • *Scr* Jeff Andrus, Ed Namzug, from the novel by Winston Groom

As Time Goes By
★

Science-fiction drama
1987 · Ausl · Colour · 96m

When the Australian film industry does science-fiction well, it comes up with classics like the *Mad Max* series. But when it misses by miles, the result is something akin to this "adult" sci-fi spoof depicting a surfer's close encounter with an alien travelling in a UFO disguised as a forties diner. Max Gillies plays extra-terrestrial Joe Bogart, spouting lines from old fifties movies and doing impressions of famous Hollywood actors. As a one-joke premise stretched extremely thinly, this quickly outstays its welcome. Contains mild swearing.

Bruno Lawrence *Ryder* • Max Gillies *Joe Bogart* • Nique Needles *Mike* • Ray Barrett *JL Weston* • Marcelle Schmitz *Connie Stanton* • Deborah Force *Cheryl* ■ *Dir/Scr* Barry Peak

As You Desire Me
★★★

Melodrama   1932 · US · BW · 69mins

It may be slow moving and a shade creaky today, but this Greta Garbo vehicle positively smoulders, and contains some of the most overt sensuality you're likely to see in a Hollywood movie of the period. It's a classy MGM production, with George Fitzmaurice directing from a Pirandello play and Melvyn Douglas and Erich von Stroheim as Garbo's co-stars. The scenes between the blonde, fashionably bobbed Garbo and the handsome Douglas have an unusually charged eroticism: can't be just acting, surely? Watch for Hollywood gossip queen Hedda Hopper, and the first Mr Mary Pickford, Owen Moore, brightening the doom and gloom with a winningly jaunty performance.

Greta Garbo *Zara* • Melvyn Douglas *Count Bruno Varelli* • Erich von Stroheim *Carl Salter* • Owen Moore *Tony* • Hedda Hopper *Madame Mantari* • Rafaela Ottiano *Lena* ■ *Dir* George Fitzmaurice • *Scr* Gene Markey, from the play by Luigi Pirandello

As You Like It
★★ U

Romance comedy drama
1936 · UK · BW · 96mins

With her German accent and mispronunciations, Elisabeth Bergner is unintentionally hilarious as Rosalind in this lavish film version of Shakespeare's comedy, directed and produced by her husband Paul Czinner. Laurence Olivier speaks beautifully but seems awkward as Orlando in his first screen venture into Shakespeare, which led him to the (temporary) conclusion that the Bard and the movies should stay clear of each other. JM Barrie adds a whimsical edge to the adaptation.

Elisabeth Bergner *Rosalind* • Laurence Olivier *Orlando* • Sophie Stewart *Celia* • Henry Ainley *Exiled Duke* • Leon Quartermaine *Jacques* • Mackenzie Ward *Touchstone* • Richard Ainley *Sylvius* • Felix Aylmer *Duke Frederick* • John Laurie *Oliver* ■ *Dir* Paul Czinner • *Scr* JM Barrie, Robert Cullen, from the play by William Shakespeare

As You Like It
★ U

Romance   1992 · UK · Colour · 112mins

This ill-fated version of one of the Bard's finest comedies finds the forest of Arden transposed into a contemporary urban environment. Peopled by strays in cardboard boxes, the tale of Orlando's passion for the banished Rosalind misfires conceptually compared to other recent Shakespearean interpretations (Richard Loncraine's *Richard III*, Baz Luhrmann's *Romeo + Juliet*). The talents of Cyril Cusack, James Fox and Miriam Margolyes are as lost as the viewer, though the film's nondescript box-office performance may be compensated by its subsequent use in the classroom. ▣

Emma Croft *Rosalind* • Andrew Tiernan *Orlando/Oliver* • James Fox *Jaques* • Griff Rhys Jones *Touchstone* • Cyril Cusack *Adam* • Miriam Margolyes *Audrey* • Don Henderson *The Dukes* • Celia Bannerman *Celia* • Ewen Bremner *Silvius* ■ *Dir* Christine Edzard • *Scr* from the play by William Shakespeare

As Young as You Feel
★★★ U

Comedy   1951 · US · BW · 76mins

This 20th Century-Fox comedy is still relevant today and provides a marvellous vehicle for *The Man Who Came to Dinner's* Monty Woolley, here playing a 65-year-old print worker who refuses to go quietly when he is asked to retire. The acerbic tale is an early work by writer Paddy Chayefsky, who earned great acclaim in the golden years of TV drama and went on to win Oscars for *Marty*, *The Hospital* and *Network*. The supporting cast is particularly fine, most notably Thelma Ritter and Constance Bennett, but pay attention to that scene-stealing contract blonde: a certain Marilyn Monroe in an early role.

Monty Woolley *John Hodges* • Thelma Ritter *Della Hodges* • David Wayne *Joe* • Jean Peters *Alice Hodges* • Constance Bennett *Lucille McKinley* • Marilyn Monroe *Harriet* ■ *Dir* Harmon Jones • *Scr* Lamar Trotti, from a story by Paddy Chayefsky

The Ascent
★★★★ PG

Second World War drama
1976 · USSR · BW · 104mins

Filmed in harsh monochrome by Vladimir Chukhnov, this was Larissa Shepitko's fourth feature in a career than spanned 20 years; it was also the last she completed before her fatal car crash. It is clearly the work of an inspired film-maker, though, as she imbues this award-winning tale of desperate survival with a biblical spirit that further ennobles the deeds of the partisans who fought to liberate Belorussia. Refusing to toe the socialist realist line on the Second World War, Shepitko depicts such unpatriotic acts as cowardice and collaboration, as well as suggesting that the Russian climate was as dangerous an enemy as the Nazis. A Russian language film. ▣

Boris Plotnikov • Vladimir Gostukhin • Sergei Jakovlev • Anatoli Solinitzin ■ *Dir* Larissa Shepitko • *Scr* Yuri Klepikov, Larissa Shepitko, from a novel by Vassil Bykov • *Cinematographer* Vladimir Chukhnov

The Ascent ★★

Second World War adventure
1994 · US · Colour · 96mins

An offbeat Second World War adventure, based loosely on one of those "stranger than fiction" tales that are usually the preserve of the TV movie. This feature, set in Africa well away from the front line, centres on a PoW camp where the largely Italian inmates and their British guards get involved in a bizarre challenge to see who can climb a treacherous mountain peak nearby. Ben Cross and John DeVeillers are flying the Union Jack; Vincent Spano is the PoW with more than just mountain-climbing on his mind. The stunning locations and the oddness of the tale don't really compensate for the uneven script.

Vincent Spano *Franco* • Ben Cross *Major Farrell* • Rachel Ward *Patricia* • Tony LoBianco *Aldo* • Mark Ingall *Sergeant Thomas* ■ *Dir* Donald Shebib • *Scr* David Wiltse

Ash Wednesday ★★ 15

Drama   1973 · US · Colour · 94mins

To save her ailing marriage to Henry Fonda, Elizabeth Taylor decides to fly to Italy for a face-lift. Looking beautiful again, she has a fling with Euro-stud Helmut Berger. Sadly this isn't a comedy, but a heavy drama which shows the agonies of plastic surgery in unremitting detail before turning to the emotional pain of a splintering relationship. Playing 55, Taylor was a mere 40-year-old when she made the picture, and she looks utterly ravishing – and that's *before* the surgery scenes. The film can be regarded as autobiographical, in that it looks at what it takes to be a movie star. ▭

Elizabeth Taylor *Barbara Sawyer* • Henry Fonda *Mark Sawyer* • Helmut Berger *Erich* • Keith Baxter *David* • Maurice Teynac *Dr Lambert* ■ *Dir* Larry Peerce • *Scr* Jean-Claude Tramont

Ashanti ★★ 15

Adventure   1979 · Swi/US · Colour · 112mins

Michael Caine and Beverly Johnson are married doctors, working for the World Health Organisation in a small West African village, when Johnson is kidnapped by slave-trader Peter Ustinov for wealthy prince Omar Sharif. Caine sets off to track her down, a journey as heavy-going as tap-dancing on sand thanks to Richard Fleischer's leisurely direction and Ustinov's lack of menace. William Holden and Rex Harrison put in cameo appearances as though performing a duty, while Caine is inanimate and inadequate. Contains swearing and violence. ▭

Michael Caine *Dr David Linderby* • Peter Ustinov *Suleiman* • Beverly Johnson *Dr Anansa Linderby* • Kabir Bedi *Malik* • Omar Sharif *Prince Hassan* • Rex Harrison *Brian Walker* • William Holden (1) *Jim Sandell* ■ *Dir* Richard Fleischer • *Scr* Stephen Geller, from the novel *Ebano* by Alberto Vasquez-Figueroa

Ashes and Diamonds
★★★★★ 12

Drama   1958 · Pol · BW · 99mins

The concluding part of Andrzej Wajda's "lost generation" trilogy made an overnight star of Zbigniew Cybulski, who was hailed by some as the Polish James Dean. Set on the last day of the Second World War, the film follows an underground guerrilla as he plots to assassinate a communist leader whose views he despises, but whose humanity he admires. Cybulski is quite magnificent as the resistance fighter, whether debating where to draw the line between military and moral duty, romancing barmaid Ewa Krzyzanowska, or paying bitterly for his indecision. Demonstrating a mastery of location shooting, symbolism, characterisation and camera technique, this is Wajda's masterpiece. In Polish with English subtitles. ▭

Zbigniew Cybulski *Maciek* • Ewa Krzyzanowska *Krystyna* • Adam Pawlikowski *Andrzej* • Waclaw Zastrzezynski *Szczuka* • Bogumil Kobiela *Drewnowski* ■ *Dir* Andrzej Wajda • *Scr* Andrzej Wajda, Jerzy Andrzejewski, from the novel by Jerzy Andrzejewski • *Cinematographer* Jerzy Wojcik

Ashik Kerib ★★★★

Fantasy drama 1988 · USSR · Colour · 78mins

This was the last film completed by the extraordinarily talented Georgian filmmaker Sergei Paradzhanov. Although actor Dodo Abashidze shares the directorial credit, the astonishing beauty and complexity of the imagery is so reminiscent of such earlier Paradjanov pictures as *The Colour of Pomegranates* that the film's authorship is never in doubt. Loosely based on a story by the Russian writer Mikhail Lermontov, the action follows a poor minstrel on his 1001-day exile from his true love. Drawing on Azerbaijani folk culture and subtly commenting on the plight of artists under Soviet rule, this is cinematic poetry. In Azerbaijani with Georgian voice-over and English subtitles.

Yuri Mgoyan *Ashik Kerib* • Veronika Metonidze • Levan Natroshvili • Sofiko Chiaureli • R Chkhikvadze ■ *Dir* Dodo Abashidze, Sergei Paradjanov • *Scr* Giya Badridze, from the story *Ashik Kerib the Lovelorn Minstrel* by Mikhail Lermontov

Ask a Policeman ★★★ U

Comedy   1938 · UK · BW · 74mins

Will Hay had a thing about spooky crooks. Just as the villains in *Oh, Mr Porter!* exploited a local legend to keep snoopers at bay, so the smugglers in this corking comedy play on the myth of the headless horseman to go about their business undisturbed. The setting is a sleepy coastal berg where the police station is in danger of being closed down because Sergeant Dudfoot (Hay) claims there is no crime. Naturally, he and his accomplices (Graham Moffatt and Moore Marriott) are on the fiddle. ▭

Will Hay *Sgt Dudfoot* • Graham Moffatt *Albert* • Moore Marriott *Harbottle* • Glennis Lorimer *Emily* • Peter Gawthorne *Chief Constable* • Charles Oliver *Squire* • Herbert Lomas *Coastguard* • Pat Aherne *Motorist* ■ *Dir* Marcel Varnel • *Scr* Marriott Edgar, Val Guest, from a story by Sidney Gilliat

Ask Any Girl ★★ U

Comedy   1959 · US · Colour · 97mins

Joe Pasternak's musical unit at MGM never reached the heights of the one headed by colleague Arthur Freed, often lacking both the budgets and star names, and being forced to make do with mostly mediocre material. This comedy is a case in point. For once the cast is topnotch, but George Wells's script is merely good-natured and, while it occasionally bubbles, it's still definitely sparkling wine rather than champagne. Shirley MacLaine is wide-eyed and lovely as a waif with a glut of suitors, who are played with typical aplomb by David Niven, Gig Young and Rod Taylor.

David Niven *Miles Doughton* • Shirley MacLaine *Meg Wheeler* • Gig Young *Evan Doughton* • Rod Taylor *Ross Taford* • Jim Backus *Mr Maxwell* • Claire Kelly *Lisa* • Elisabeth Fraser *Jeannie Boyden* ■ *Dir* Charles Walters • *Scr* George Wells, from the novel by Winifred Wolfe

Aspen Extreme ★ 15

Drama   1993 · US · Colour · 113mins

It's rather apt that this movie is about skiing, because it really is downhill all the way. They say you should write about what you know, and that's exactly what writer/director Patrick Hasburgh has done: he was once a ski instructor in Aspen, Colorado, and if this is an example of his daily routine you can see why he changed jobs. Quitting Detroit for a life on the piste, Peter Berg is quickly on the slide, while his buddy Paul Gross slaloms between Teri Polo and Finola Hughes. Save yourself a bumpy ride and go straight to the credits. ▭

Paul Gross *TJ Burke* • Peter Berg *Dexter Rutecki* • Finola Hughes *Bryce Kellogg* • Teri Polo *Robin Hand* • William Russ *Dave Ritchie* • Trevor Eve *Karl Stall* • Martin Kemp *Franc Hauser* ■ *Dir/Scr* Patrick Hasburgh

Asphalt ★★★★

Silent drama   1928 · Ger · BW · 114mins

Making exceptional use of sequence montage, superimpositions, neon lighting and meticulously re-created interiors, Joe May brings a gritty realism to what is essentially a melodramatic tale of petty crime, seduction and misplaced loyalty. Betty Amann is beguiling as the jewel thief who uses her charms to silence eager policeman Gustav Fröhlich, whose slavish devotion causes him to kill her lover. Combining the visual dynamism of the "city symphony" with the dramatic authenticity of the "street film", this is an astute summation of the styles dominating German cinema at the end of the silent era.

Gustav Fröhlich *Police Constable Albert Holk* • Betty Amann *Else Kramer* • Albert Steinrück *Police Sergeant Holk* • Else Heller *Mrs Holk* • Hans Adalbert von Schlettow *Lagen* ■ *Dir* Joe May • *Scr* Fred Majo, Hans Szekely, Rolf E Vanloo • *Cinematographer* Günther Rittau

The Asphalt Jungle
★★★★★ PG

Crime thriller   1950 · US · Colour · 112mins

Shot with an almost documentary realism, John Huston's exceptional *film noir* continues to influence heist movies to this day. This really does have everything you could ask of a thriller, from a scintillating plot (co-scripted with Ben Maddow by Huston from WR Burnett's novel), in which the perfect plan unravels with compelling inevitability; the seminal criminal mastermind performance from Oscar-nominated Sam Jaffe; totally convincing ensemble playing from his bungling gang (including Sterling Hayden and Anthony Caruso); and superb moll supports from Jean Hagen and Marilyn Monroe. Add this to Miklos Rozsa's atmospheric score and Harold Rosson's gritty photography and you have a masterpiece.

Sterling Hayden *Dix Handley* • Louis Calhern *Alonzo D Emmerich* • Jean Hagen *Doll Conovan* • James Whitmore *Gus Ninissi* • Sam Jaffe *Doc Erwin Riedenschneider* • John McIntire *Police Commissioner Hardy* • Marc Lawrence *Cobby* • Barry Kelley *Lieutenant Ditrich* • Anthony Caruso *Louis Ciavelli* • Marilyn Monroe *Angela Phinlay* ■ *Dir* John Huston • *Scr* Ben Maddow, John Huston, from the novel by WR Burnett

The Asphyx ★★★★ 15

Drama   1972 · UK · Colour · 82mins

A thoughtful and convincing British horror oddity exploring aspects of immortality with a unique sci-fi spin. The title refers to a soul-snatching being from another dimension that approaches the body at the moment of death. Photographer Robert Stephens captures one such life form in the hope he can claim eternal life. Morbid, intriguing and acted with sensitive conviction, director Peter Newbrook's cerebral chiller is a wordy Gothic drama masquerading as a supernatural terroriser. ▭

Robert Stephens *Hugo Cunningham* • Robert Powell *Giles Cunningham* • Jane Lapotaire *Christina Cunningham* • Alex Scott *President* • Ralph Arliss *Clive Cunningham* • Fiona Walker *Anna Cunningham* • Terry Scully *Pauper* ■ *Dir* Peter Newbrook • *Scr* Brian Comfort

The Assam Garden ★★ U

Drama   1985 · UK · Colour · 90mins

Deborah Kerr's first film since 1969 is a mild, inconsequential affair. Returning from Assam to England, Kerr tends her recently deceased husband's eastern garden as a way of cherishing his memory. This, and her friendship with neighbour Madhur Jaffrey, are the means by which she tries to heal her grief. Kerr is as delightful as ever, but the film – written by Elisabeth Bond – lacks real substance.

Deborah Kerr *Helen* • Madhur Jaffrey *Ruxmani Lal* • Alec McCowen *Mr Philpott* • Zia Mohyeddin *Mr Lal* • Anton Lesser *Mr Sutton* • Iain Cuthbertson *Arthur* • Tara Shaw *Sushi* ■ *Dir* Mary McMurray • *Scr* Elisabeth Bond

Assassin ★★

Spy drama   1973 · UK · Colour · 82mins

Without the extraneous style and a couple of the more extended scenes, this might have made a decent half-hour TV thriller. Instead, director Peter Crane piles on the flashy visuals in an attempt to turn a humdrum espionage caper into a meaningful tract on the state's dispassionate sanctioning of murder and the isolation of the professional killer. Amid the directorial pyrotechnics, however, Ian Hendry is highly effective as the disillusioned hitman ordered to liquidate an Air Ministry mole.

Ian Hendry *Assassin* • Edward Judd *MI5 Control* • Frank Windsor *John Stacey* • Ray

Brooks *Edward Craig* • John Hart Dyke *Janik* • Verna Harvey *Girl* • Mike Pratt *Matthew* ■ *Dir* Peter Crane • *Scr* Michael Sloan

Assassin ★★ PG

Science-fiction adventure
1986 · US · Colour · 90mins

A rather dated mix of sci-fi and thrills, with Robert Conrad as the ageing agent on the trail of a robotic killer who has been reprogrammed to eliminate lots of important people. Karen Austin is the scientist whose creature has been put to misuse. Conrad does his best, but he is hardly helped by an uncharismatic supporting cast and insipid direction from TV-movie specialist Sandor Stern. Contains some violence. ▭

Robert Conrad *Henry Stanton* • Karen Austin *Mary Casallas* • Richard Young *Robert Golem* • Jonathan Banks *Earl Dickman* • Robert Webber *Calvin Lantz* • Ben Frank *Franklin* • Jessica Nelson *Ann Walsh* • Nancy Lenehan *Grace Decker* ■ *Dir/Scr* Sandor Stern

The Assassin ★★ 18

Thriller 1993 · US · Colour · 103mins

Another example of Hollywood's unfortunate tendency to take fine Continental fare and rework it into sensationalist pap. The original by French director Luc Besson, called *Nikita* and starring the luminous Anne Parillaud, was a throbbing, stylish look at a convicted murderess who receives secret government training as a hired gun. Remade here with a plodding hand by John Badham and featuring a seemingly ill-at-ease Bridget Fonda, what was once witty, if somewhat vacuous entertainment has been reduced to a series of one-dimensional thrills. Though the supporting cast, including Gabriel Byrne and Harvey Keitel, is substantial, this ends up, nonetheless, as a gutless piece. Contains violence, swearing, sex scenes and nudity. ▭ **DVD**

Bridget Fonda *Maggie* • Gabriel Byrne *Bob* • Dermot Mulroney *J P* • Miguel Ferrer *Kaufman* • Anne Bancroft *Amanda* • Olivia D'Abo *Angela* • Richard Romanus *Fahd Bahktiar* • Harvey Keitel *Victor the cleaner* ■ *Dir* John Badham • *Scr* Robert Getchell, Alexandra Seros, from the film *Nikita* by Luc Besson

Assassin for Hire ★★

Crime drama 1951 · UK/US · BW · 66mins

A dependable supporting player in British prestige productions and programme fillers alike, Sydney Tafler was always on the verge of the action as a sneaky crook or a disreputable nightclub owner. Here he has one of his rare opportunities in a leading role and he acquits himself very ably as a professional killer, under pressure from an enterprising detective. There's a typically dignified performance from Ronald Howard as the policeman, while director Michael McCarthy gets a surprising amount of suspense from the slightest of stories.

Sydney Tafler *Antonio Riccardi* • Ronald Howard *Inspector Carson* • John Hewer *Guiseppi Riccardi* • Kathryn Blake [Katharine Blake] *Maria Riccardi* • Gerald Case *Sergeant Scott* • Ian Wallace *Charlie* • Martin Benson *Catesby* ■ *Dir* Michael McCarthy • *Scr* Rex Rientis

Assassin of the Tsar ★★★ 15

Psychological drama
1991 · Rus/UK · Colour · 100mins

Malcolm McDowell stars as a psychiatric patient who believes he assassinated the Tsar and his family in 1918. From his hospital bed in present-day Moscow, McDowell is taken back to the past by his psychiatrist, Oleg Yankovsky (who also plays the Tsar), in an attempt to free him of his delusion. Shot in Moscow and Leningrad in both English and Russian versions, its flaws are obvious. However, McDowell's portrait of schizophrenia is often disturbing, and the whole picture is a fascinating and gripping study of madness seen through the vortex of history. Russian dialogue dubbed into English. ▭

Malcolm McDowell *Timofeev/Yurovsky* • Oleg Yankovsky *Dr Smirnov/Tsar Nicholas Ii* • Armen Dzhigarkhanyan *Alexander Egorovich* • Iurii Sherstnev *Kozlov* • Angela Ptashuk *Marina* • Viktor Seferov *Voikov* ■ *Dir* Karen Shakhnazarov • *Scr* Aleksandr Borodianskii, Karen Shakhnazarov

Assassination ★★ 15

Thriller 1986 · US · Colour · 84mins

Charles Bronson is the minder to the American president's wife (here played by Bronson's own wife, Jill Ireland) who goes on the run with her when killers threaten. It has its moments of tension – director Peter Hunt made the James Bond film *On Her Majesty's Secret Service*, after all – but the relationship never achieves much credibility. Bronson dozes off in scene one and doesn't even begin to stir before the end. Contains mild swearing and violence.

Charles Bronson *Jay Killian* • Jill Ireland *Lara Royce Craig* • Stephen Elliott *Fitzroy* • Jan Gan Boyd *Charlotte Chang* • Randy Brooks *Tyler Loudermilk* • Michael Ansara *Senator Hector Bunsen* • Erik Stern *Reno Bracken* ■ *Dir* Peter Hunt • *Scr* Richard Sale

The Assassination Bureau ★★★★

Black comedy 1969 · UK · Colour · 111mins

A dry period comedy, with Diana Rigg as a journalist infiltrating a gang of professional killers whose members only accept contracts on those who "deserve" to die. Rigg persuades the gang's leader, Oliver Reed, to allow himself to become a target as a challenge to his professionalism. It's a clever twist in a madcap yarn by Jack London and Robert Fish, and director Basil Dearden has infused the tale with joyous glee and no little character insight. Fresh from his triumph in as Bill Sikes in the musical *Oliver!*, Reed is wonderfully malevolent.

Oliver Reed *Ivan Dragomiloff* • Diana Rigg *Sonya Winter* • Telly Savalas *Lord Bostwick* • Curt Jurgens *General von Pinck* • Philippe Noiret *Lucoville* • Warren Mitchell *Weiss* • Beryl Reid *Madame Otero* • Clive Revill *Cesare Spado* ■ *Dir* Basil Dearden • *Scr* Michael Relph, from the novel *The Assassination Bureau Limited* by Jack London, Robert Fish

The Assassination of Trotsky ★★

Historical drama
1972 · Fr/It · Colour · 102mins

A botched drama about the Russian revolutionary Leon Trotsky, who was gruesomely murdered on Stalin's orders in Mexico City in 1940. Despite being shot on authentic locations, Joseph Losey's movie is often dull and fatally lacking in both historical perspective and on-screen drama. Richard Burton acts his socks off as Trotsky, a role previously offered to Dirk Bogarde, Marlon Brando, George C Scott and Topol. However, while Alain Delon has a certain menace as the assassin, he's never a flesh-and-blood character. The film was a flop everywhere and initiated its director's long and slow decline following the triumph of *The Go-Between*.

Richard Burton *Leon Trotsky* • Alain Delon *Frank Jacson* • Romy Schneider *Gita* • Valentina Cortese *Natasha* • Luigi Vannucchi *Ruiz* • Duilio Del Prete *Felipe* • Simone Valere *Mrs Rosmer* ■ *Dir* Joseph Losey • *Scr* Nicholas Mosley, Masolino D'Amico

Assassins ★★★ 15

Action thriller 1995 · US · Colour · 127mins

There are more holes in this plot than there are in the floor of the hotel overlooking the bank that is the setting for the slowest showdown in movie history. Yet there's something intriguing about the rivalry that develops between hit men Sylvester Stallone and Antonio Banderas, especially when Stallone becomes enamoured of their target, hacker Julianne Moore. Director Richard Donner lets Banderas get away with a lazy performance, but Stallone has rarely been so interesting. Contains swearing and violence. ▭ **DVD**

Sylvester Stallone *Robert Rath* • Antonio Banderas *Miguel Bain* • Julianne Moore *Electra* • Anatoly Davydov *Nicolai* • Muse Watson *Ketcham* • Stephen Kahan *Alan Branch* • Kelly Rowan *Jennifer* ■ • *Scr* Andy Wachowski, Larry Wachowski, Brian Helgeland, from a story by Andy Wachowski, Larry Wachowski

Assault ★★ 18

Thriller 1970 · UK · Colour · 90mins

Made by *Carry On* producer Peter Rogers, this drama stars Suzy Kendall as an art teacher whose pupils are being targeted by a killer/rapist. Hoping to trap the murderer before he strikes again, she offers herself to the police as a decoy. Apart from its rather leery approach to the subject matter, this is a resolutely old-fashioned whodunit, complete with a gallery of not-so-likely suspects, a series of mini-skirted would-be victims and a baffled cop played by Frank Finlay. David Essex can be spotted in a chemist's shop, while Leslie-Anne Down plays the killer's traumatised first victim. ▭

Suzy Kendall *Julie West* • Frank Finlay *Det Chief Supt John Velyan* • James Laurenson *Dr Gregory Lomax* • Lesley-Anne Down *Tessa Hurst* • Freddie Jones *Denning* • Tony Beckley *Leslie Sanford* • Dilys Hamlett *Mrs Sanford* ■ *Dir* Sidney Hayers • *Scr* John Kruse, from the novel *The Ravine* by Kendal Young

The Assault ★★★ PG

Drama 1986 · Neth · Colour · 120mins

Winner of the Oscar for best foreign film, this is a harrowing study of how a victim of the Nazi occupation of Holland is continually reminded of the horrific night when his entire family was arrested and executed in reprisal for the death of a collaborator. Derek De Lint conveys some of the survivor's pain and resilience, but the impact of this shocking incident is rather lost as the film comes up to date, with neither De Lint's encounters with others who were involved in the "assault" nor his moments of crushing guilt and depression having quite the same dramatic intensity. In Dutch with English subtitles. ▭

Derek De Lint *Anton Steenwijk* • Marc Van Uchelen *Anton as a boy* • Monique van de Ven *Truus Coster/Saskia De Graaff* • John Kraaykamp *Cor Takes* • Elly Weller *Mrs Beumer* • Ina Van Der Molen *Karin Korteweg* ■ *Dir* Fons Rademakers • *Scr* Gerard Soeteman, from the novel by Harry Mulisch

Assault at West Point: the Court Martial of John Whittaker ★★★

Historical courtroom drama
1994 · US · Colour · 94mins

Based on John F Marszalek's minutely researched book, this is a well-mounted re-creation of one of the most shameful episodes in US military history. At the tail end of the last century, Johnson Whittaker became the first black cadet at the famed academy, only to be charged with beating himself unconscious (while tied to his bunk) in order to frame his racist persecutors. There are a couple of explosive courtroom sequences featuring Sam Waterston and Samuel L Jackson, but some power is lost thanks to Seth Gilliam's lacklustre performance in the title role.

Samuel L Jackson *Richard Greener* • Sam Waterston *Daniel Chamberlain* • Seth Gilliam *Cadet Johnson Whittaker* • Mason Adams *Hyde* • Val Avery *General Sherman* ■ *Dir* Harry Moses • *Scr* Harry Moses, from the non-fiction book *The Court-Martial of Johnson Whittaker* by John F Marszalek

Assault on a Queen ★ U

Crime caper 1966 · US · Colour · 106mins

In *Ocean's Eleven*, Frank Sinatra and his cronies held up five casinos in Las Vegas. In this follow-up, Ol' Blue Eyes and even more cronies raise a U-boat from the ocean shallows to plunder the *Queen Mary* and its well-heeled passengers. While Sinatra and co make with the action-man stuff, European sex symbol Virna Lisi has little to do except pose in a bikini. It's heavy-handed in all departments, with leaden direction by Jack Donohue, a former choreographer to Shirley Temple and Esther Williams.

Frank Sinatra *Mark Brittain* • Virna Lisi *Rosa Lucchesi* • Tony Franciosa [Anthony Franciosa] *Vic Rossiter* • Richard Conte *Tony Moreno* • Alf Kjellin *Eric Lauffnauer* • Errol John *Linc Langley* ■ *Dir* Jack Donohue • *Scr* Rod Serling, from the novel by Jack Finney

Assault on Devil's Island
★ **15**

Action adventure 1997 · US · Colour · 90mins

Mind-bogglingly bad action adventure, which looks suspiciously like an intended pilot for a TV series for wrestler Hulk Hogan. He plays Mike McBride, the leader of an elite army force, in a plot involving the rescue of a group of American gymnasts held prisoner on Devil's Island. Hulk is assisted in his heroics by Carl Weathers and drugs agent Shannon Tweed. The performances are uniformly awful, and the cheapskate direction of Jon Cassar hardly helps. Contains violence, brief nudity and some swearing. ▣

Terry "Hulk" Hogan [Hulk Hogan] *Mike McBride* • Carl Weathers *Roy Brown* • Shannon Tweed *Hunter Wiley* • Martin Kove *Andy Powers* • Trevor Goddard *Fraker* • Billy Drago *Gallindo* • Vivienne Sendaydiego *Carol* ■ *Dir* Jon Cassar • *Scr* Cal Clements Jr, from a story by Michael Berk, Douglas Schwartz, Steven McKay, Cal Clements Jr

Assault on Precinct 13
★★★★ **18**

Thriller 1976 · US · Colour · 90mins

Cult director John Carpenter's hybrid of *Rio Bravo* and *Night of the Living Dead* is a model of expert, low-budget filmmaking and ranks as one of the best B-movies ever made in the urban horror/action genre. In this gripping thriller, a nearly abandoned police station in the worst neighbourhood in Los Angeles is placed under siege for harbouring the killer of a street gang's fearless leader. Paranoia abounds as Austin Stoker and his motley crew of quipping cops are attacked from all sides with no escape route. The shocking ice-cream van sequence is the best thing Carpenter has ever done; he also supplies a taut synthesiser score which adds untold atmosphere to this minor gem. ▣

Austin Stoker *Ethan Bishop* • Darwin Joston *Napoleon Wilson* • Laurie Zimmer *Leigh* • Martin West *Lawson* • Tony Burton *Wells* • Kim Richards *Kathy* ■ *Dir/Scr* John Carpenter

The Assignment
★★★ **18**

Thriller 1997 · Can/US · Colour · 114mins

The Day of the Jackal dawns again thanks to director Christian Duguay's ace take on the real-life story behind Frederick Forsyth's bestseller and the hit movie it spawned. Suspense and intrigue register high as Duguay dishes up a steady stream of graphic action. Aidan Quinn plays a dual role, as the Jackal himself and an American naval officer with a remarkable resemblance to the wanted terrorist. Donald Sutherland plays a CIA veteran obsessed with getting revenge for past humiliation; Ben Kingsley is a Mossad agent eager to rid the world of the assassin responsible for ending scores of Israeli lives. Together they train Quinn to take part in a daring sting, but the plan spirals dangerously out of control. Contains nudity, coarse language and violence. ▣ **DVD**

Aidan Quinn *Annibal Ramirez/Carlos* • Donald Sutherland *Jack Shaw/Henry Fields* • Ben Kingsley *Amos* • Claudia Ferri *Maura Ramirez* • Celine Bonnier *Carla* • Vlasta Vrana *KGB*

Head officer • Liliana Komorowska *Agnieszka* • Von Flores *Koj* ■ *Dir* Christian Duguay • *Scr* Dan Gordon, Sabi H Shabtai

Assignment K
★★ **U**

Spy drama 1968 · UK · Colour · 90mins

Having cut his teeth on comedy, writer and director Val Guest latterly gravitated towards sci-fi and thrillers. Here he's unable to bring to life a moribund espionage tale, crucially failing to come close to the strong sense of disillusion that characterises Martin Ritt's *The Spy Who Came in from the Cold*. Stephen Boyd gives a charmless performance as a spy working undercover as a toy manufacturer. Slowly he comes to realise that almost everyone he has trusted has deceived him. Camilla Sparv is adequate as his German girlfriend, but Michael Redgrave, as his loyal lieutenant, and Leo McKern, as his nemesis, contribute little. ▣

Stephen Boyd *Philip Scott* • Camilla Sparv *Toni Peters* • Michael Redgrave *Harris* • Leo McKern *Smith* • Jeremy Kemp *Hal* • Robert Hoffmann *Paul Spiegler* • Jane Merrow *Martine* ■ *Dir* Val Guest • *Scr* Val Guest, Bill Strutton, Maurice Foster, from the novel *Department K* by Hartley Howard

Assignment – Paris
★★ **U**

Spy drama 1952 · US · BW · 84mins

This unremarkable Cold War thriller, based on a story by Paul and Pauline Gallico, stars Dana Andrews as a reporter in the Paris office of the *New York Herald Tribune* who uncovers a conspiracy in Budapest. The communists throw him in jail and shoot him full of truth drugs; his editor (George Sanders) tries to forget that Andrews stole his girlfriend (Marta Toren) and fights for his release. Critics at the time thought the whole thing far-fetched; nowdays, however, it's just rather ho-hum.

Dana Andrews *Jimmy Race* • Marta Toren *Jeanne Moray* • George Sanders *Nick Strang* • Audrey Totter *Sandy Tate* • Sandro Giglio *Grischa* • Donald Randolph *Anton Borvitch* • Herbert Berghof *Andreas Ordy* ■ *Dir* Robert Parrish • *Scr* William Bowers, Paul Gallico, Jack Palmer White, from the story *Trial by Terror* by Paul Gallico, Pauline Gallico

Assignment Redhead
★

Crime drama 1956 · UK · BW · 80mins

Aficionados of low-budget British quickies know Maclean Rogers as the prolific director of some of the lousiest pictures ever made. Also known as *Million Dollar Manhunt*, this dismal thriller has all the hallmarks of a Butcher's production: shoddy script, cheap settings and a cast of has-beens and no-hopers. Ronald Adam can just about hold his head up as the crook intent on blagging $12 million worth of counterfeit Nazi cash. But Richard Denning as the agent on his tail and Carole Mathews as the singer who switches sides are so inept their performances have a ghoulish must-see quality about them.

Richard Denning *Keen* • Carole Mathews *Hedy* • Ronald Adam *Scammel/Dumetrius* • Danny Green *Yottie* • Brian Worth *Ridgeway* • Jan Holden *Sally* • Hugh Moxey *Sergeant Coutts* ■ *Dir* Maclean Rogers • *Scr* Maclean Rogers, from the novel *Requiem for a Redhead* by Al Bocca

Assignment to Kill
★★

Crime drama 1968 · US · Colour · 99mins

International intrigue abounds in this tale of an insurance investigator on the trail of a dodgy European bigwig whose ships have a habit of going belly-up. The hero is played by Patrick O'Neal, while his prey is none other than a busking John Gielgud, whose lilting tones add a touch of class to the proceedings. Peter Van Eyck and Herbert Lom play heavies, Eric Portman is a corrupt civil servant, while Oscar Homolka pops up as an apoplectic Swiss policeman.

Patrick O'Neal *Richard Cutting* • Joan Hackett *Dominique Laurant* • John Gielgud *Curt Valayan* • Herbert Lom *Matt Wilson* • Eric Portman *Notary* • Peter Van Eyck *Walter Green* • Oscar Homolka *Inspector Ruff* ■ *Dir/Scr* Sheldon Reynolds

The Assisi Underground
★ **PG**

Second World War drama 1985 · It/US · Colour · 109mins

Underground is where this Second World War drama should have stayed. Its truth-based story of an Assisi-centred network, smuggling disguised Jewish refugees out of Italy via Franciscan monasteries, needed its own lifeline of credibility but didn't get it from a muddled script and banal direction. Ben Cross and James Mason are among those wasted in an important story that deserved better treatment. ▣

Ben Cross *Padre Rufino* • James Mason *Bishop Nicolini* • Irene Papas *Mother Giuseppina* • Maximilian Schell *Colonel Mueller* • Karl-Heinz Hackl *Captain von Velden* ■ *Dir* Alexander Ramati • *Scr* Alexander Ramati, from his novel

The Associate
★★ **PG**

Comedy drama 1996 · US · Colour · 108mins

A weak vehicle for comedian Whoopi Goldberg, in which she plays a Wall Street analyst who can't move up the career ladder because she's a woman. Taking the rather radical action of setting up her own company with a fictitious male partner, matters are further complicated when her excuses for her absences run out and she actually has to produce the mystery man. Despite fun performances from Goldberg, Dianne Wiest and Bebe Neuwirth from *Cheers*, there just aren't enough jokes in Donald Petrie's film to keep the audience interested until the end credits. ▣

Whoopi Goldberg *Laurel* • Dianne Wiest *Sally* • Eli Wallach *Fallon* • Tim Daly [Timothy Daly] *Frank* • Bebe Neuwirth *Camille* • Austin Pendleton *Aesop* • Lainie Kazan *Cindy Mason* • George Martin *Manchester* ■ *Dir* Donald Petrie • *Scr* Nick Thiel, from the novel *El Socio* by Jenaro Prieto

Asterix and Obelix Take on Caesar
★★ **U**

Comedy fantasy adventure 1999 · Fr/Ger/It · Colour · 110mins

The most expensive French movie ever made might have put most of its 274 million franc budget up on the screen, but Claude Zidi's live-action romp has none of the wit or charm of the earlier animated adaptations, let alone that of Albert Uderzo and René Goscinny's original comic books. With Christian Clavier and Gérard Depardieu well cast as the indomitable Gauls and Roberto Benigni milking every gag as a scheming centurion, the acting is suitably pantomimic. But the tired plot of kidnapping the village druid and the inability of Terry Jones (who penned the English language script and dubbed Depardieu) to duplicate Goscinny's sublime linguistic games undermine the cast's efforts. French dialogue dubbed into English. ▣

Christian Clavier *Astérix* • Gérard Depardieu *Obélix* • Roberto Benigni *Detritus* • Marianne Sägebrecht *Bonnemine* • Gottfried John *César* • Laetitia Casta *Falbala* • Michel Galabru *Abaracourcix* • Claude Piéplu *Panoramix* ■ *Dir* Claude Zidi • *Scr* Claude Zidi, Gérard Lauzier, from the comic books by René Goscinny, Albert Uderzo

Asterix and the Big Fight
★★ **U**

Animated adventure 1989 · Fr/W Ger · Colour · 76mins

For fans of the Goscinny/Uderzo comic books, this is a bit of a letdown. Here, the wily Asterix tries to restore the memory of the village soothsayer so that his powers can be used in the fight against the Romans. The animation is rather stilted, though, and the British voices (Bill Oddie, Bernard Bresslaw, Ron Moody) are too well-known to let the characters speak for themselves. The puns and Latin tags are still great fun, however. This also comes in a French language version . ▣

Bill Oddie *Asterix* • Bernard Bresslaw *Obelix* • Ron Moody *Prolix* • Brian Blessed *Caous* • Sheila Hancock *Impedimenta* • Andrew Sachs *Ardeco* ■ *Dir* Philippe Grimond • *Scr* George Roubicek, from the comic books *Asterix and the Big Fight* and *Asterix and the Soothsayer* by René Goscinny, Albert Uderzo

Asterix Conquers America
★★ **U**

Animated adventure 1994 · Ger · Colour · 81mins

Asterix's adventures are hardly the most politically correct at the best of times, but this adaptation is guilty of some unforgivable racist lapses. The story of Getafix's rescue from the New World is not the strongest in the series, though the anachronistic gags are as sharp as ever, while the familiar drawing style atones for the rather uninspired voice-overs. This also comes in a German language version . ▣

John Rye *Narrator* • Craig Charles *Asterix* • Howard Lew Lewis *Obelix* • Henry McGee *Caesar* • Christopher Biggins *Lucullus* • Geoffrey Bayldon *Getafix* ■ *Dir* Gerhard Hahn • *Scr* Thomas Platt, Rhett Rooster, from an idea by Pierre Tchernia, Albert Uderzo, from the comic book *Asterix and the Great Crossing* by René Goscinny, Albert Uderzo

Asterix in Britain
★★★ **U**

Animated adventure 1986 · Fr · Colour · 75mins

By Jupiter! How superbus! Another animated movie to be lifted from the text and drawings of Goscinny and Uderzo's books retells the adventures of our pun-struck Gallic heroes battling Romans in 50 BC, this time helping out a village in Britain which has just

been invaded. The wily Asterix and the galumphing Obelix are on hand to satirise national stereotypes, and the puns are enough to make "wincemeat" of us all. The line may sometimes be weak, but the spirit is decidedly strong. This also comes in a French language version . ▣

Jack Beaber *Asterix* • Bill Kearns [Billy Kearns] *Obelix* • Graham Bushnell *Anticlimax* • Herbert Baskind *Totalapsus* • Jimmy Shuman *Chateaupetrus* • Ed Marcus *Stratocumulus* • Sean O'Neil *General Motus* • Gordon Heath *Ceasar* ▪ *Dir* Pino Van Lamsweerde • *Scr* Pierre Tchernia, from the comic book by René Goscinny, Albert Uderzo

Asterix the Gaul ★★★ U
Animated adventure
1967 · Bel/Fr · Colour · 65mins

Almost a decade after the publication of René Goscinny and Albert Uderzo's first comic book, Asterix and his indomitable friends found their way on to the big screen. Made in Belgium by Ray Goossens, this is pretty much an introductory exercise, as the secret of Getafix's magic potion, the story behind Obelix's ludicrous strength and the reasons why Caesar's legions can't conquer a tiny Gaullish village are all explained. But there's also plenty of action as Asterix and his menhir-carrying chum set out to rescue their druid from an ambitious centurion. French dialogue dubbed into English. ▣

Dir/Scr René Goscinny, Albert Uderzo

The Asthenic Syndrome ★★★★
Drama
1989 · USSR · Colour and BW · 153mins

Kira Muratova has made only eight features in her 30-year career, and this uncompromising study of the last days of the USSR shows why she had so much trouble with the Soviet censors and why she's ranked among the most important of all women film-makers. The winner of the Special Jury Prize at the Berlin film festival, the film suggests that Communist rule has subjected the entire population to asthenia, a condition that induces dejected passivity in times of stress. The pain of the opening monochrome sequence and the stark realism of the Moscow scenes make for most uncomfortable yet compelling viewing. In Russian with English subtitles.

Sergei Popov *Nikolai* • Olga Antonova *Natasha* • Natalia Busko *Mascha, the brunette* • Galina Sakurdaeva *Mascha, the blonde* • Aleksandra Ovenskaia *Lehrerin* • Pavel Polischnuk • Natalia Rallewa ▪ *Dir* Kira Muratova • *Scr* Kira Muratova, Sergei Popov, Aleksandr Chernitch, Vladimir Pankov

The Astonished Heart ★
Romantic drama
1949 · UK · BW · 87mins

Noël Coward stars a psychiatrist whose understanding wife (Celia Johnson) attempts to condone his adultery with her beautiful best friend (Margaret Leighton). A low point in the career of all three principals and co-director Terence Fisher, it sank into almost immediate obscurity, and there it should perhaps remain, but for curiosity value. (This film was adapted by the "Master" from one of his weakest and least known plays.) The one star is for Celia Johnson, who cannot avoid being wonderful as a best-of-British middle-class wife.

Noël Coward *Christian Faber* • Celia Johnson *Barbara Faber* • Margaret Leighton *Leonora Vail* • Joyce Carey *Susan Birch* • Graham Payn *Tim Verney* • Amy Veness *Alice Smith* • Ralph Michael *Philip Lucas* • Michael Hordern *Ernest* ▪ *Dir* Terence Fisher, Anthony Damborough • *Scr* Noël Coward, from his play

The Astounding She-Monster ★★
Science-fiction horror
1958 · US · BW · 59mins

A super-tall female alien in a skin-tight metallic spacesuit, spangled tights and high heels lands on earth and uses her glow-in-the-dark touch to kill. A group of loyal citizens band together to fight the intergalactic menace in a prime example of ultra-cheap fifties trash, which is so bad it's actually quite good fun. Pitiful special effects and deadly dull nocturnal strolls through the forest by the extraordinary-looking She-Monster (Shirley Kilpatrick) add to its camp charm. Astounding it certainly is!

Robert Clarke *Dick Cutler* • Kenne Duncan *Nat Burdell* • Marilyn Harvey *Margaret Chaffee* • Jeanne Tatum *Esther Malone* • Shirley Kilpatrick *Monster* • Ewing Brown *Brad Conley* ▪ *Dir* Ronnie Ashcroft • *Scr* Frank Hall

The Astronaut's Wife ★★★★ 18
Science-fiction psychological thriller
1999 · US · Colour · 109mins

A postmodern update of classic fifties "creature features", Rand Ravich's directorial debut is a psychological thriller refreshingly free of the usual baggage associated with *Quatermass*-inspired science-fiction. Charlize Theron is wonderful as Johnny Depp's distressed and puzzled spouse, who notices alarming differences in her husband's behaviour after he survives a space mission accident. Detonating key plot details to powerful and cumulative effect, Ravich successfully accents the interior terrors of the well-worn premise. Enhanced by inventive camera angles, masses of style and stunning production design (by *Gattaca*'s Jan Roelfs), this beautifully appointed entry into insidious invasion territory is an engrossing nightmare that remains alarmingly believable. Contains sex scenes and swearing.

Johnny Depp *Spencer Armacost* • Charlize Theron *Jillian Armacost* • Joe Morton *Sherman Reese* • Clea DuVall *Nan* • Samantha Eggar *Doctor* • Donna Murphy *Natalie Streck* • Nick Cassavetes *Alex Streck* • Gary Grubbs *NASA director* ▪ *Dir/Scr* Rand Ravich • *Cinematographer* Allen Daviau

Asya's Happiness ★★★★★ PG
Drama
1967 · USSR · BW · 97mins

Suppressed by the Communist authorities because of the critical political opinions expressed by some of the male characters and not released abroad until the late eighties, this film exemplifies why director Andrei Mikhalkov-Konchalovsky was one of the USSR's premier directors before decamping to Hollywood and taking on more commercial fare (as plain Andrei Konchalovsky). The magnificent Iya Savvina, supported by a largely non-professional and extraordinarily natural cast, stars in this account of life in a rural village, with its attendant hardships, its community attitudes, and the personal suffering and indomitable courage of Asya herself. This absorbing and moving film is rich in detail, authentic atmosphere and honesty. In Russian with English subtitles.

Iya Savvina *Asya Klyachinka* • Lyubov Sokolova • Alexander Surin • Gennady Yegorychev ▪ *Dir* Andrei Mikhalkov-Konchalovsky [Andrei Konchalovsky] • *Scr* Ivan Petrov, Yuri Klepikov

Asylum ★★★ 15
Horror
1972 · UK · Colour · 88mins

A rippingly good terror anthology of *Psycho* author Robert Bloch's tales, showcasing reanimated, dismembered limbs, a magic suit, homicidal split personalities and tiny murdering robots. With an ingenious linking device each story is a mental patient's case history building to a *Grand Guignol* twist finale, the excellent cast (including Robert Powell, Herbert Lom and Peter Cushing) wrings every ounce of horror from a clever script. Adroitly directed by shock veteran Roy Ward Baker, the underplayed black humour is a welcome bonus. ▣

Peter Cushing *Smith* • Britt Ekland *Lucy* • Herbert Lom *Byron* • Patrick Magee *Dr Rutherford* • Barry Morse *Bruno* • Barbara Parkins *Bonnie* • Robert Powell *Dr Martin* • Charlotte Rampling *Barbara* • Sylvia Syms *Ruth* • Richard Todd *Walter* ▪ *Dir* Roy Ward Baker • *Scr* Robert Bloch, from his stories

At Close Range ★★★★ 15
Drama based on a true story
1985 · US · Colour · 110mins

A strong and powerful drama about crime and misguided family loyalties. Sean Penn turns in a magnificent performance as the bored son lured into the world of gangsters by evil dad Christopher Walken. Downbeat and very tough going in parts, the grim tale is even more compelling and chilling for being true. Opting to shoot his movie with documentary realism is one of director James Foley's major stylistic achievements, giving the gripping chain of events a pervasive atmosphere of simmering violence that's tremendously effective. Contains swearing and violence. ▣

Sean Penn *Brad Whitewood Jr* • Christopher Walken *Brad Whitewood Sr* • Mary Stuart Masterson *Terry* • Christopher Penn *Tommy Whitewood* • Millie Perkins *Julie Whitewood* • Eileen Ryan *Grandmother* • Kiefer Sutherland *Tim* ▪ *Dir* James Foley • *Scr* Nicholas Kazan, from a story by Elliott Lewitt, Nicholas Kazan • *Cinematographer* Juan Ruiz-Anchia

...At First Sight ★★★
Romantic comedy
1995 · US · Colour · 90 mins

Jonathan Silverman stars as a loveable schmuck who's dating the lovely Rhonda (Allison Smith). But his pal Joey (Dan Cortese) bullies him into more adventurous romantic escapades. Funny in parts, this feels like a warm-up for Silverman's *Single Guy* TV series, which began the same year. Like its main characters, however, it doesn't really go anywhere. The film features a hilarious cameo from voice actress Pamela Segall as a wallflower turned vamp.

Dan Cortese *Joey Fortone* • Jonathan Silverman *Lenny Kaminski* • Allison Smith *Rhonda Glick* • Monte Markham *Lester Glick* • Kathleen Freeman *Grandma* • Susan Walters *Cindy One* • Pamela Segall *Tracy* ▪ *Dir* Steven Pearl • *Scr* Ken Copel

At First Sight ★★★ 12
Drama
1998 · US · Colour · 123mins

Although also drawn from the casebook of Dr Oliver Sacks, this medical melodrama is less dramatically satisfying and markedly less well acted than *Awakenings*. However, the tale of courage originally told in his essay *To See or Not to See* is so remarkable that any filming of it would seem trite and sentimental. Certainly Val Kilmer's infuriatingly mannered performance doesn't help matters. But, as the sister and the lover respectively of Kilmer's small-town masseur who briefly has his sight restored, Kelly McGillis and Mira Sorvino deflect any comparisons with a formulaic disease-of-the-week TV movie. No classic, but thoughtful and solidly crafted. Contains some mild swearing and nudity. ▣ DVD

Val Kilmer *Virgil Adamson* • Mira Sorvino *Amy Benic* • Kelly McGillis *Jennie Adamson* • Steven Weber *Duncan Allanbrook* • Bruce Davison *Dr Charles Aaron* • Nathan Lane *Phil Webster* • Ken Howard *Virgil's father* • Laura Kirk *Betsy Ernst* • Jack Dodick *Dr Goldman* • Oliver Sacks *Reporter* • Claude Ravier *Reporter* ▪ *Dir* Irwin Winkler • *Scr* Steve Levitt, from the article *To See and Not See* from *An Anthropologist on Mars* by Oliver Sacks

At Gunpoint ★★
Western
1955 · US · Colour · 80mins

Mysteriously shortened to *Gunpoint* for its UK release, this is a very average Allied Artists western owing much to *High Noon* in its plotting. It stars a very glum Fred MacMurray, but the ever-glamorous Dorothy Malone (seemingly born to play frontierswomen) is the main attraction here, doing sterling work as Fred's wife. Walter Brennan's in there, too, for western authenticity, and the whole benefits from being filmed in CinemaScope. However, director Alfred Werker's pace is just too slow for comfort.

Fred MacMurray *Jack Wright* • Dorothy Malone *Martha Wright* • Walter Brennan *Doc Lacy* • Tommy Rettig *Billy* • John Qualen *Livingstone* • Irving Bacon *Ferguson* • Skip Homeier *Bob* • Jack Lambert *Kirk* ▪ *Dir* Alfred Werker • *Scr* Daniel B Ullman

At Long Last Love ★★ U
Musical romance
1975 · US · Colour · 114mins

Despite predictions that this spoof on thirties' musicals would become a cult classic to look back on with affection, it's still stuck in the mire of embarrassment at the way aspiration became affectation. Playboy Burt Reynolds, icy-blonde Cybill Shepherd, Broadway star Madeline Kahn and gambler Duilio Del Prete find contrivances to weave in and out of 16 Cole Porter songs, and get lost in the process. Director/producer/writer Peter

Bogdanovich insisted the principals sing the words while acting to eliminate post-synching. He needn't have bothered.

Burt Reynolds *Michael Oliver Pritchard III* • Cybill Shepherd *Brooke Carter* • Madeline Kahn *Kitty O'Kelly* • Duilio Del Prete *Johnny Spanish* • Eileen Brennan *Elizabeth* • John Hillerman *Rodney James* • Mildred Natwick *Mabel Pritchard* • Quinn Redeker *Phillip* • M Emmet Walsh *Harold* ■ *Dir/Scr* Peter Bogdanovich ■ *Music* Cole Porter

At Play in the Fields of the Lord ★★ 15
Adventure drama
1991 · US · Colour · 178mins

Hector Babenco's Amazonian rainforest saga has the virtue of a good cast. Unless you're fascinated by the ecological issues raised, however, it's unlikely to sustain your interest throughout the mammoth three-hour running time. There's no doubting the sincerity of this tale of religious, emotional and physical conflict in one of the most beautiful vistas on earth, while Aidan Quinn, Kathy Bates and Tom Berenger give fiercely committed performances. Alas, the unsympathetic characters, rambling plot and extreme length are hurdles Babenco is ultimately unable to overcome. ▭

Tom Berenger *Lewis Moon* • John Lithgow *Leslie Huben* • Daryl Hannah *Andy Huben* • Aidan Quinn *Martin Quarrier* • Tom Waits *Wolf* • Kathy Bates *Hazel Quarrier* • Stenio Garcia *Boronai* • Nelson Xavier *Father Xantes* ■ *Dir* Hector Babenco • *Scr* Jean-Claude Carrière, Hector Babenco, from the novel by Peter Matthiessen

At the Circus ★★★ U
Comedy
1939 · US · BW · 83mins

This picture marked the start of the Marx Brothers' fall from grace, as their humorous anarchy was severely restricted by MGM's big-studio regulations. Here Groucho plays a shyster lawyer who teams up with Harpo and Chico to save a circus from bankruptcy. There are some great moments – Groucho's elephantine flirtations with the monumental Margaret Dumont and his rendition of "Lydia the Tattooed Lady" – but the exuberance has been clearly toned down. The terrible trio also seem reluctant to follow the plot, especially if it means being on the same bill as crooner Kenny Baker. ▭

Groucho Marx *Attorney Loophole* • Chico Marx *Antonio* • Harpo Marx *Punchy* • Kenny Baker (2) *Jeff Wilson* • Eve Arden *Peerless Pauline* • Margaret Dumont *Mrs Dukesbury* • Florence Rice *Julie Randall* • Nat Pendleton *Goliath* ■ *Dir* Edward Buzzell • *Scr* Irving Brecher

At the Earth's Core ★ PG
Science-fiction adventure
1976 · UK · Colour · 86mins

Victorian explorer Doug McClure and fidgety scientist Peter Cushing encounter all manner of rubber monsters as they burrow through the earth with a giant boring device – yes, there is another apart from the film itself – to the subterranean kingdom of Pellucidar. This childish and chintzy Edgar Rice Burroughs adaptation would be an even bigger patience-tester if not for sultry heroine Caroline Munro and the truly awful man-in-suit special

effects, which will inspire hoots of laughter rather than the intended sense of wonder. ▭

Doug McClure *David Innes* • Peter Cushing *Dr Abner Perry* • Caroline Munro *Dia* • Cy Grant *Ra* • Godfrey James *Ghak* • Sean Lynch *Hooja* ■ *Dir* Kevin Connor • *Scr* Milton Subotsky, from the novel by Edgar Rice Burroughs

At the Midnight Hour ★★
Mystery thriller　　1995 · Can · Colour

A would-be Gothic thriller, which unsuccessfully attempts to re-create the brooding atmosphere of classics like *Rebecca*. Patsy Kensit is the innocent young nanny employed to look after the son of scientist Simon MacCorkindale, whose wife died in suspicious circumstances. Kensit gradually falls under the widower's spell even though he could possibly be a murderer. Director Charles Jarrott's TV movie is hardly helped by the bland playing of the leads and, despite its Gothic pretentions, it remains a very average melodrama.

Patsy Kensit *Elizabeth Guinness* • Simon MacCorkindale *Richard Keaton* • Keegan Macintosh *Keaton's son* • Lindsay Merrithew *Blaine* • Cynthia Dale *Jillian* ■ *Dir* Charles Jarrott • *Scr* Joe Wiesenfeld

At War with the Army ★★★ U
Comedy　　1950 · US · BW · 91mins

A massive early success for the comedy team of Dean Martin and Jerry Lewis in their third film. It's their first starring vehicle for producer Hal Wallis at Paramount, consolidating their screen images (Martin's the smoothie, Lewis is the nerd) and ensuring their success throughout a generation.This is slapdash film-making, but also very funny, and a scene involving a soda machine is simply priceless. Dean croons three songs as he enjoins Jerry to help him out of female trouble, and Polly Bergen makes a very attractive movie debut. ▭

Dean Martin *Sergeant Puccinelli* • Jerry Lewis *Private Korwin* • Mike Kellin *Sergeant McVey* • Jimmie Dundee *Eddie* • Dick Stabile *Pokey* • Tommy Farrell *Corporal Clark* • Frank Hyers *Corporal Shaughnessy* • Dan Dayton *Sergeant Miller* • Polly Bergen *Helen* ■ *Dir* Hal Walker • *Scr* Fred F Finklehoffe, from the play by James B Allardice

L'Atalante ★★★★★ PG
Romantic drama　　1934 · Fr · BW · 85mins

Few films can claim to have inspired two revolutions. Jean Vigo's masterpiece not only established the visual style of thirties' poetic realism, but was also one of the key influences on the New Wave of the late fifties. It's a simple, almost uneventful picture, chronicling barge captain Jean Dasté's first days of marriage to Dita Parlo. Yet it becomes a mesmerising personal vision thanks to Vigo's sophisticated blend of fairy-tale romance, documentary realism, surrealist fantasy, bawdy humour and song. Michel Simon's scene-stealing improvisation and Boris Kaufman's exceptional cinematography further enhance the pleasure to be derived from one of the most completely cinematic pictures ever made. In French with English subtitles. ▭

Michel Simon *Père Jules* • Jean Dasté *Jean* • Dita Parlo *Juliette* • Gilles Margaritis *Pedlar* • Louis Lefèvre *Cabin boy* • Fanny Clar *Juliette's mother* • Raphael Diligent *Juliette's father* • Charles Goldblatt *Thief* • René Bleck *Best man* ■ *Dir* Jean Vigo • *Scr* Jean Vigo, Jean Guinée, Albert Riera

Athena ★★ U
Musical　　1954 · US · Colour · 95mins

An unusual idea is let down by a paper-thin plot and screenplay in this musical starring Jane Powell and Debbie Reynolds as two of seven sisters who belong to a family of health and exercise fanatics. Crooner Vic Damone and cardboard cut-out Edmund Purdom are their suitors, Louis Calhern and Evelyn Varden the brood's eccentric vegetarian grandparents, and Mr Universe-turned-movie-star Steve Reeves is on hand to support the theory about healthy living ensuring the body beautiful. Some pleasant singing and dancing livens up the otherwise routine proceedings.

Jane Powell *Athena* • Debbie Reynolds *Minerva* • Virginia Gibson *Niobe* • Nancy Kilgas *Aphrodite* • Dolores Starr *Calliope* • Jane Fischer *Medea* • Cecile Rogers *Ceres* • Edmund Purdom *Adam Calhorn Shaw* • Vic Damone *Johnny Nyle* • Louis Calhern *Grandpa Mulvain* • Steve Reeves *Ed Perkins* ■ *Dir* Richard Thorpe • *Scr* William Ludwig, Leonard Spigelgass

Atlantic Adventure ★★
Crime drama　　1935 · US · BW · 68mins

From the days when reporters (rather than private detectives and spies) were heroic figures, comes this lively B-picture about a journalist involved in murderous intrigue and intriguing murder aboard an ocean liner. Lloyd Nolan and Nancy Carroll make the best of a not-so-bad job, but silent film enthusiasts should look out for a baby-faced character actor, the great Harry Langdon, the film comedian who never made it into the talkies other than in movies like this. A decline and fall has rarely been so pitiful.

Nancy Carroll *Helen* • Lloyd Nolan *Dan* • Harry Langdon *Snapper* • Arthur Hohl *Frank* • Robert Middlemass *Van Dieman* • John Wray *Mitts* • EE Clive *McIntosh* • Dwight Frye *Spike* • Nana Bryant *Mrs Van Dieman* ■ *Dir* Albert S Rogell • *Scr* John T Neville, Nat Dorfman, from a story by Diana Bourbon

Atlantic City ★★★ U
Musical　　1944 · US · BW · 87mins

A surprise offering from the poverty row studio Republic, this agreeable little musical chronicles the professional trials, personal tribulations and eventual triumphs of a young impresario (Brad Taylor) as he pursues his ambition to make Atlantic City into a world-class entertainment playground. The plus factors include the presence of Paul Whiteman and Louis Armstrong with their orchestras, some good musical numbers, a top-starred Constance Moore lending the turbulent romantic interest, and Charley Grapewin and Jerry Colonna in the lively supporting cast.

Brad Taylor [Stanley Brown] *Brad Taylor* • Constance Moore *Marilyn Whitaker* • Charley Grapewin *Jake Taylor* • Jerry Colonna *Professor* • Robert B Castaine *Carter Graham* • Adele Mara *Barmaid* • Louis Armstrong •

Paul Whiteman • Dorothy Dandridge • Belle Baker ■ *Dir* Ray McCarey • *Scr* Doris Gilbert, Frank Gill Jr, George Carleton Brown, from a story by Arthur Caesar

Atlantic City USA ★★★★★ 15
Crime drama
1980 · US/Can · Colour · 104mins

A wonderfully bizarre and beguiling study of small-time losers, the best film French director Louis Malle made in America has Burt Lancaster slumping his imposing personality into round-shouldered seediness as a voyeuristic, over-the-hill hood reduced to running a gambling racket and living off fake memories of days with famous gangsters of yesteryear. Paradoxically, this role became one of his career's towering performances, suitably matched by that of Susan Sarandon as the woman with whom he becomes involved when a stash of drugs is stolen from the Mafia. Hard to define, it's neither a thriller nor a love story – the only thing for sure is that it's a gangster movie with a totally unexpected and abundant Gallic charm. Contains violence, swearing and brief nudity. ▭

Burt Lancaster *Lou* • Susan Sarandon *Sally* • Kate Reid *Grace* • Michel Piccoli *Joseph* • Hollis McLaren *Chrissie* • Robert Joy *Dave* • Al Waxman *Alfie* • Robert Goulet *Singer* ■ *Dir* Louis Malle • *Scr* John Guare

Atlantis ★★★ U
Documentary　　1991 · Fr · Colour · 80mins

After making *Nikita*, director Luc Besson returned to the ocean depths of *The Big Blue* for a stunningly shot but boring documentary on undersea life that proved he was no Jacques Cousteau. Barely released outside his native France, Besson's camera highlights dugongs eating plankton, seals mating, a turtle swimming underwater, a shark feeding frenzy, a crab scuttling along the sea floor, waves rolling in slow motion and a pan over the Great Barrier Reef. Concentration lapses are numerous for such a short film, which is best described as a marine *Microcosmos* without the natural drama. A French language film.

Dir Luc Besson

Atlantis, the Lost Continent ★★
Fantasy adventure
1961 · US · Colour · 90mins

Famed producer/director George Pal came unstuck with this silly fantasy adventure after winning praise for his *The War of the Worlds* and *The Time Machine*. Anthony Hall is the young Greek sailor facing danger, intriguing animal men and atomic death rays in the final days of the fabled city before it slips into the deep, thanks to a volcanic eruption. Even the special effects are below sea level in this uneasy mix of comic-book science fiction and tacky sand-and-sandal epic. Set at the time of the Roman Empire so Pal could borrow footage from *Quo Vadis* to pep up his visuals, the entire film is an unappetising mixture of eclectic styles and weird notions only the early sixties could spawn.

Anthony Hall [Sal Ponti] *Demetrios* • Joyce Taylor *Antillia* • John Dall *Zaren* • Bill Smith [William Smith] *Captain of the guard* • Edward Platt *Azor* • Frank DeKova *Sonoy* • Berry Kroeger *Surgeon* ■ *Dir* George Pal • *Scr* Daniel Mainwaring, from a play by Gerald Hargreaves

Atlas ★★ U

Fantasy adventure
1960 · US · Colour · 78mins

Muscles and baloney combine in this early outing from exploitation director Roger Corman, here trawling through Greek myths and dredging up risible rubbish about an Olympic champion (Michael Forest) who, despite being bribed by Praximedes (Frank Wolff), opts for democracy and fighting on behalf of the ordinary citizen. The solitary saving grace is that the film was shot in Greece.

Michael Forest *Atlas* • Barboura Morris *Candia* • Frank Wolff *Praximedes* • Walter Maslow *Garnis* • Christos Exarchos *Indros* • Andreas Philippides *Talectos* ■ *Dir* Roger Corman • *Scr* Charles Griffith

The Atomic Café ★★★

Satirical political documentary
1982 · US · Colour and BW · 92mins

An absorbing documentary, assembled from an amazing array of fifties government and educational films, that reveals how Americans were eased into the atomic era and the threat of possible nuclear annihilation. The film shows soldiers being subjected to A-bomb tests, while schoolchildren are taught how to ''duck and cover'' under their desks to avoid the harmful effects of fallout. The naive assumption that an atomic war would be survivable is one of the many shocking facts to emerge from this worthwhile nostalgia trip, which manages to be at once scary and hilarious, informative and compelling.

Dir Jayne Loader, Kevin Rafferty, Pierce Rafferty

The Atomic Kid ★★ U

Science-fiction comedy
1954 · US · BW · 85mins

Made at a time when nuclear power could be treated as a joke, this happy-go-lucky tosh has Mickey Rooney as a prospector who survives an atomic test in the desert and finds he's immune to radiation. His special powers come in handy when he helps the FBI catch a ring of communist spies. The story is by Blake Edwards, who went on to make such comic gems as *10*; this film, however, is more of a four.

Mickey Rooney *Blix Waterberry* • Robert Strauss *Stan Cooper* • Elaine Davis *Audrey Nelson* • Bill Goodwin *Dr Rodell* • Whit Bissell *Dr Edgar Pangborn* ■ *Dir* Leslie H Martinson • *Scr* Benedict Freedman, John Fenton Murray, from a story by Blake Edwards

The Atomic Submarine ★★ PG

Science-fiction drama
1960 · US · BW · 67mins

Endearing hokum about an underwater alien, with a nicely sustained tense atmosphere from director Spencer Gordon Bennet. But the real star of this B-movie is producer Alex Gordon, who assembled a memorable cast for

movie buffs. The nominal star is Arthur Franz (*The Sniper*, *Invaders from Mars*) and in support are a veritable clutch of familiar faces, all past their sell-by date, including amiable veteran Dick Foran from *The Petrified Forest*, George Sanders's older brother Tom Conway and former cowboy star Bob Steele. The obligatory blonde is Frank Sinatra's one-time girlfriend Joi Lansing.

Arthur Franz *Reef* • Dick Foran *Wendover* • Brett Halsey *Carl* • Tom Conway *Sir Ian Hunt* • Paul Dubov *Dave* • Bob Steele *Griff* • Victor Varconi *Kent* • Joi Lansing *Julie* ■ *Dir* Spencer G Bennet [Spencer Gordon Bennet] • *Scr* Orville H Hampton

Attack! ★★★★ PG

Second World War drama
1956 · US · BW · 103mins

Director Robert Aldrich didn't have much time for human aspirations, and never less so than in this US Army shocker about a cowardly captain (Eddie Albert) endangering the lives of his men during the Second World War's Battle of the Bulge. As the heroic platoon leader, Jack Palance has never been better, and neither has Lee Marvin as the colonel presiding over the whole affair. In Aldrich's macho view, war is only hell because men make it so, but his true skill is that he makes these unattractive characters convincing and understandable. Contains mild swearing and violence

Jack Palance *Lieutenant Costa* • Eddie Albert *Captain Cooney* • Lee Marvin *Colonel Bartlett* • Robert Strauss *Private Bernstein* • Richard Jaeckel *Private Snowden* • Buddy Ebsen *Sergeant Tolliver* • William Smithers *Lieutenant Woodruff* ■ *Dir* Robert Aldrich • *Scr* James Poe, from the play *The Fragile Fox* by Norman Brooks

Attack Force Z ★★ 15

Second World War drama
1981 · Ausl/Tai · Colour · 89mins

John Phillip Law is the nominal star of this fifties-style war yarn, now more notable for featuring an early performance from Mel Gibson, with able support from Sam Neill. The story is the usual *Guns of Navarone/ Cockleshell Heroes* stuff about a commando group sent on an impossible mission to rescue the survivors of a plane wreck on a Japanese island. Some decent action scenes (filmed in Taiwan), typically dry humour and Law's trademark teak-forest performance keep the interest going, though the script quickly runs out of ideas. Only released abroad when Gibson became a major star, the film was heavily cut from its original running time.

John Phillip Law *Lt JA Veitch* • Mel Gibson *Capt PG Kelly* • Sam Neill *Sgt DJ Costello* • Chris Haywood *Able Seaman AD Bird* • John Waters *Sub Lt EP King* ■ *Dir* Tim Burstall • *Scr* Roger Marshall, Lee Robinson

Attack of the Crab Monsters ★★★

Science-fiction horror
1957 · US · BW · 62mins

Atomic testing on a remote Pacific island causes the crab population to mutate into giant monsters in one of cult director Roger Corman's earliest

successes. The crustaceans look shoddy and laughable (you can often glimpse the stuntmen's feet under the costumes), but Charles Griffith's compact script successfully mines the concept for keen menace and gruesome shock. (The crabs decapitate victims and eat the heads in order to assimilate their brain power.) Lunatic but fast-moving fun.

Richard Garland *Dale Drewer* • Pamela Duncan *Martha Hunter* • Russell Johnson *Hank Chapman* • Leslie Bradley *Dr Karl Weigand* • Mel Welles *Jules Deveroux* • Richard Cutting *Dr James Carson* ■ *Dir* Roger Corman • *Scr* Charles Griffith

Attack of the 50 Foot Woman ★★

Science-fiction
1958 · US · BW · 65mins

Originally seen as an incompetent example of low-budget fifties sci-fi, this poverty row cheapie has since become a legendary absurd classic. Viewed from a modern feminist perspective, wealthy Allison Hayes is right to teach her cheating husband a well-deserved lesson after a bald alien turns her into a giant. However, with the effects at their least special and camp at its highest, Hayes's accelerating voluptuousness exerts a curious fascination that is anything but politically correct. It only goes to show that size *isn't* everything.

Allison Hayes *Nancy Archer* • William Hudson *Harry Archer* • Roy Gordon *Dr Cushing* • Yvette Vickers *Honey Parker* • Ken Terrell *Jessup Stout* • George Douglas *Sheriff Dubbitt* ■ *Dir* Nathan Hertz • *Scr* Mark Hanna

Attack of the 50 Ft Woman ★★

Cult science-fiction
1993 · US · Colour · 89mins

A pointless revamp of the beloved 1958 cult classic that often looks cheesier than its inspiration. Daryl Hannah narrates and stars as the rich, unhappy wife, abused by both her unfaithful husband and her uncaring father, who takes revenge when she grows to monstrous proportions after being zapped by an alien ray. Christopher Guest directs half-heartedly, fluffing the humour, overdoing the women's lib angle and the fifties' sci-fi homages, and missing more satirical targets than he hits in a rather desperate attempt to match the fun incompetence of the original. Contains mild swearing and brief nudity.

Daryl Hannah *Nancy Archer* • Daniel Baldwin *Harry Archer* • William Windom *Hamilton Cobb* • Frances Fisher *Dr Cushing* • Christi Conaway *Honey* • Paul Benedict *Dr Loeb* • O'Neal Compton *Sheriff Denby* • Victoria Haas *Deputy Charlie Spooner* ■ *Dir* Christopher Guest • *Scr* Joseph Dougherty, from the 1958 film

Attack of the Giant Leeches ★

Horror
1960 · US · BW · 62mins

A small town in the swampy South is terrorised by bloodthirsty giant leeches (the stuntmen barely covered by their ill-fitting rubber suction-cup suits) in this thankfully short cheapie produced by cult director Roger Corman. Uninspired trash with a lousy script and inept direction it may be, but

starlet Yvette Vickers is good value as bartender Bruno VeSota's trampy, two-timing wife.

Ken Clark *Steve Benton* • Yvette Vickers *Liz Walker* • Jan Shepard *Nan Greyson* • Michael Emmet *Cal Moulton* • Tyler McVey *Doc Greyson* • Bruno VeSota *Dave Walker* • Gene Roth *Sheriff Kovis* ■ *Dir* Bernard L Kowalski • *Scr* Leo Gordon

Attack of the Killer Tomatoes ★ PG

Horror comedy
1978 · US · Colour · 86mins

Behind an irresistible title lurks one of the worst movies ever made. Deliberately planned as a bad movie from the start, the fact that director John DeBello totally achieves his aim is the only good thing to say about this dire spoof, in which giant tomatoes rampage through San Diego to avenge fruit mistreatment. It's all downhill after the fun title song, as intentionally awful special effects (the tomatoes are beach balls), ludicrous dialogue and low camp turns this parody of monster movies into a mind-numbing splatter bore. Still, it did spawn three sequels (one of which starred George Clooney) and a television cartoon show.

David Miller *Mason Dixon* • George Wilson *Jim Richardson* • Sharon Taylor *Lois Fairchild* • Jack Riley *Agricultural official* • Rock Peace *Wilbur Finletter* • Eric Christmas *Senator Polk* • Al Sklar *Ted Swan* ■ *Dir* John DeBello • *Scr* Costa Dillon, John DeBello, Steve Peace

Attack on the Iron Coast ★★ U

Second World War drama
1968 · US/UK · Colour · 89mins

As a cinema actor, the late Lloyd Bridges never really rose above B-movies, despite (or perhaps because of) his long-running starring role on TV in *Sea Hunt*, but he is a useful presence in this Second World War action adventure. The film was shot in England, and a supporting cast of British TV names such as Mark Eden and Andrew Keir does what is expected of it, but the overall style is curiously flat considering the director is Paul Wendkos of *Angel Baby* fame, obviously slumming with this material.

Lloyd Bridges *Major James Wilson* • Andrew Keir *Captain Owen Franklin* • Sue Lloyd *Sue Wilson* • Mark Eden *Lt Commander Donald Kimberley* • Maurice Denham *Sir Frederick Grafton* • Glyn Owen *Lt Forrester* ■ *Dir* Paul Wendkos • *Scr* Herman Hoffman, from a story by John C Champion

The Attic: the Hiding of Anne Frank ★★★★

Drama based on a true story
1988 · US/UK · Colour · 95mins

Like the room in question, this is near the top of the many film versions of the story of the Frank family, who were forced to hide from the Jew-hunting Gestapo. Told from an unusual perspective – that of Miep Gies – it relates how the courageous Dutch woman (played by the wonderful Mary Steenburgen) gave shelter to her employer Otto Frank (Paul Scofield) and his family, including his daughter Anne. A TV movie, directed by John Erman, it successfully conveys a sense of the claustrophobia of the situation

and the courage of the family – refugees in their own country.

Mary Steenburgen *Miep Gies* • Paul Scofield *Otto Frank* • Lisa Jacobs *Anne Frank* • Eleanor Bron *Edith Frank* • Frances Cuka *Petronella van Daan* • Victor Spinetti *Herman van Daan* • Ian Sears *Peter van Daan* • Georgia Slowe *Margot Frank* • Jeffrey Robert *Albert Dussel* ■ Dir John Erman • Scr William Hanley, from the non-fiction book *Anne Frank Remembered* by Miep Gies, Allison Leslie Gold

Au Hasard, Balthazar
★★★★★ PG

Drama   1966 · Fr/Swe · BW · 91mins

Robert Bresson's extraordinary film is the story of a donkey named Balthazar who is, at various times, an adored children's playmate, a circus performer and a harsh mill owner's slave. Finally, and fatefully, he carries smugglers' contraband over the mountains. The film is, clearly, a religious parable, with the donkey – like Jesus – taking the sins of the world upon his back. It is also one of the great masterpieces of world cinema: austere, warm, grim, surreal, shocking and heartbreaking. In French with English subtitles. ▦

Anne Wiazemsky *Marie* • François Lafarge *Gerard* • Philippe Asselin *Marie's father* • Nathalie Joyaut *Marie's mother* • Walter Green *Jacques* • Jean-Claude Guilbert *Arnold* • Pierre Klossowski *Merchant* • François Sullerot *Baker* ■ Dir/Scr Robert Bresson

Au Revoir les Enfants
★★★★ PG

Second World War drama
1987 · Fr · Colour · 100mins

As a reminiscence of bigotries past, French director Louis Malle's autobiographical memoir has a discreet integrity rare among films dealing with anti-Semitism. A 12-year-old boy at a strict Carmelite convent school in 1944 wonders why a newcomer is treated so differently – bullied by other boys, shielded by teachers. The arrival of the Gestapo shows why – the boy is Jewish. It all works so extremely well because Malle never sentimentalises friendships or cruelty, and the result is a powerful tract in miniature. In French with English subtitles. ▦

Gaspard Manesse *Julien Quentin* • Raphael Fejtö *Jean Bonnet* • Francine Racette *Mme Quentin* • Stanislas Carréde Malberg *François Quentin* • Philippe Morier-Genoud *Father Jean* • François Berléand *Father Michel* ■ Dir/Scr Louis Malle

Audrey Rose
★★★ 15

Supernatural thriller
1977 · US · Colour · 108mins

Before *The Silence of the Lambs* revitalised his career, Anthony Hopkins hammed it up in less successful movies like this. Directed by Robert Wise whose credits include *The Sound of Music*, *The Andromeda Strain* and *Somebody Up There Likes Me* this cashes in on the seventies' post-*Exorcist* interest in possession and the supernatural, with a tale about a young girl who may in fact be a reincarnation of Hopkins's deceased daughter. The cast (including Marsha Mason and John Beck as the girl's understandably concerned parents) is capable, but in

the end it's let down by the drawn-out plot and the unlikely ending. ▦

Anthony Hopkins *Elliot Hoover* • Marsha Mason *Janice Templeton* • John Beck *Bill Templeton* • Susan Swift *Ivy Templeton/ Audrey Rose* • Norman Lloyd *Dr Steven Lipscomb* ■ Dir Robert Wise • Scr Frank De Felitta, from his novel

August
★★★ PG

Period drama   1995 · UK · Colour · 89mins

Chekhov's *Uncle Vanya* is relocated to 19th-century Wales in Anthony Hopkins's handsomely shot directorial debut. Although the new setting and a British cast that includes Leslie Phillips and Kate Burton (the late great Richard Burton's daughter) lend some appeal, the slow pacing and not terribly sympathetic characters will be a turn-off for some. Hopkins gives an energetic performance as the estate manager Ieuan/Vanya, whose unrequited feelings for Burton and frustration with his lot are fuelled by bouts of drinking. Probably best appreciated as a showcase for Hopkins's talent (he also composed the score) rather than as a period drama in the Merchant–Ivory mould. Contains some violence. ▦

Anthony Hopkins *Ieuan Davies* • Kate Burton *Helen Blathwaite* • Leslie Phillips *Professor Alexander Blathwaite* • Gawn Grainger *Dr Michael Lloyd* • Rhian Morgan *Sian Blathwaite* • Hugh Lloyd *Thomas "Pocky" Prosser* • Rhoda Lewis *Mair Davies* • Menna Trussler *Gwen* ■ Dir Anthony Hopkins • Scr Julian Mitchell, from the play *Uncle Vanya* by Anton Chekhov, from the play *August* by Julian Mitchell • Cinematographer Robin Vidgeon

August in the Water
★★★

Fantasy   1995 · Jap · Colour · 117mins

As Fukuoka city swelters in drought-inducing heat and its citizens fall prey to a mysterious epidemic, champion diver Rena Komine emerges from a coma and begins to experience visions of a rock face which resembles the meteorites that have recently been falling to earth. A hybrid of Leni Riefenstahl's *Olympia* and Andrei Tarkovsky's *Solaris*, Sogo Ishii's visually sumptuous sci-fi puzzle could all too easily be dismissed as mystical tosh. It's certainly leisurely and self-consciously obscure. In an age where so many films hammer home their messages, however, it's rather refreshing to watch something that makes you search for enlightenment. A Japanese language film.

Shinsuke Aoki *Mao* • Rena Komine *Izumi* • Reiko Matsuo *Miki* • Masaaki Takarai *Ukiya* • Naho Toda *Yo* ■ Dir/Scr Sogo Ishii

Aunt Julia and the Scriptwriter
★★★ 15

Comedy   1990 · US · Colour · 102mins

Mario Vargas Llosa's novel is translated to the big screen by *Sommersby* director Jon Amiel, while the action is transported from Peru to 1950s New Orleans. Barbara Hershey is the aunt of the title, Keanu Reeves plays her gullible nephew, and Peter Falk steals the show as the gruff, obsessive radio scriptwriter who has more going on than meets the eye. It's enjoyably quirky stuff, adapted by William Boyd and played beautifully by

an impressive cast that includes Richard Portnow, Elizabeth McGovern and Hope Lange. ▦

Barbara Hershey *Aunt Julia* • Keanu Reeves *Martin Loader* • Peter Falk *Pedro Carmichael* • Bill McCutcheon *Puddler* • Patricia Clarkson *Aunt Olga* • Richard Portnow *Uncle Luke* • Dan Hedaya *Robert Quince* • Elizabeth McGovern *Elena Quince* • Hope Lange *Margaret Quince* ■ Dir Jon Amiel • Scr William Boyd, from the novel by Mario Vargas Llosa

Aunt Sally
★★ U

Musical comedy   1933 · UK · BW · 80mins

A vehicle for the irrepressible comedian and musical comedy star Cicely Courtneidge, this good-natured and thoroughly silly little British musical has her pretending to be a French nightclub star in order to get a job, only to find herself dealing with gangsters with a grudge against the club's owner (Sam Hardy). Directed by Tim Whelan, this is a romp for addicts of thirties English nostalgia who will enjoy the numbers performed by such forgotten acts of the time. ▦

Cicely Courtneidge *Mademoiselle Zaza/Sally Bird* • Sam Hardy *Michael "King" Kelly* • Phyllis Clare *Queenie* • Billy Milton *Billy* • Hartley Power *"Gloves" Clark* • Ben Weldon *Casion* • Enrico Naldi *Little Joe* ■ Dir Tim Whelan • Scr Tim Whelan, Guy Bolton, AR Rawlinson

Auntie Lee's Meat Pies ★★

Horror comedy   1991 · US · Colour · 100mins

Satanist Karen Black fills her tasty meat pies with the flesh of men lured by her gorgeous nieces, all played by *Playboy* models, in this homespun take on the *Sweeney Todd* story. This is surprisingly low on titillation considering the director Joseph F Robertson is famous for his porno movies (he used the alias Adele Robbins for those) and it's laughably bad in the horror special effects department. A very odd obscurity, it's made even stranger by yet another off-the-wall performance by Black, and a Heavy Metal soundtrack. This is too lame for horror buffs and too sexless for the stag brigade.

Karen Black *Auntie Lee* • Pat Morita *Chief Koal* • Kristine Anne Rose *Fawn* • Michael Berryman *Larry* • Pat Paulsen *Minister* • Huntz Hall *Farmer* • Ava Fabian *Magnolia* • Teri Weigel *Coral* ■ Dir Joseph F Robertson • Scr Joseph F Robertson, Gerald M Steiner

Auntie Mame
★★★★

Comedy   1958 · US · Colour · 143mins

"Life is a banquet. Most poor suckers are starving to death," sums up the philosophy of Patrick Dennis's flamboyant aunt, and this film is the definitive version of her fantastical life, following a successful stage show based on Dennis's book. Rosalind Russell is simply fabulous in the outrageous leading role, filling the Technirama and Technicolor screen with an ebullience equalled only by Robert Preston in director Morton Da Costa's other Warner Bros hit, *The Music Man*. Forget Bea Lillie (who played the role in London) and all of those musical "Mames" – Russell *is* Auntie Mame.

Rosalind Russell *Mame Dennis* • Forrest Tucker *Beauregard Burnside* • Coral Browne

Vera Charles • Roger Smith *Patrick Dennis* • Fred Clark *Mr Babcock* • Peggy Cass *Agnes Gooch* • Patric Knowles *Lindsay Woolsey* ■ Dir Morton Da Costa • Scr Betty Comden, Adolph Green, from the play by Jerome Lawrence, Robert E Lee, from the novel *Mame* by Patrick Dennis

Aurora
★★★ PG

Comedy drama   1984 · US · Colour · 90mins

For the record, this TV movie is about a woman duping the ex-lovers – who could possibly be the father of her son – out of money to fund his eye operation. But, considering the slack-paced momentum, what really matters is the cast: it's headed by Sophia Loren and her own 13-year-old son Edoardo, with a small role for her niece, Allesandra Mussolini (Il Duce's granddaughter and Italian politician). Then there's Ricky Tognazzi son of Ugo (of *La Cage aux Folles* fame) and now a top Italian actor/director and Anna Strasberg, widow of acting guru Lee and stepmother of actress Susan Strasberg. It's a family affair that must have made co-stars Daniel J Travanti and Philippe Noiret feel as much outsiders as the audience. The producer is Loren's stepson, Alex Ponti. ▦

Sophia Loren *Aurora* • Daniel J Travanti *David Ackermann* • Edoardo Ponti *Ciro* • Angela Goodwin *Nurse* • Ricky Tognazzi *Michele Orcini* • Marisa Merlini *Teresa* • Anna Strasberg *Angela Feretti* • Franco Fabrizi *Guelfo* • Philippe Noiret *Dr Andre Feretti* • Allesandra Mussolini *Bride* ■ Dir Maurizio Ponzi • Scr John McGreevey, Franco Ferrini, Gianni Menon, Maurizio Ponzi

The Aurora Encounter
★★★ U

Science-fiction drama
1985 · US · Colour · 86mins

Good performances and some neat special effects lift this drama from being yet another run-of-the-mill alien-on-earth fantasy. It's the Old West at the end of the 19th century when a powerful but cute little alien turns up to give the locals a scare. Not exactly brain-straining stuff, but an entertaining watch for fantasy fans just the same. Contains mild swearing. ▦

Jack Elam *Charlie* • Peter Brown *Sheriff* • Carol Bagdasarian *Alain* • Dottie West *Irene* • Will Mitchell *Ranger* • Charles B Pierce *Preacher* • Mickey Hays *Aurora spaceman* • Spanky McFarland *Governor* ■ Dir Jim McCullough Sr • Scr Jim McCullough Jr

Austin Powers: International Man of Mystery
★★★★ 15

Spy spoof   1997 · US · Colour · 90mins

Mike Myers's Swinging Sixties spy spoof is a fast, furious and fabulously funny ride which expertly mocks every groovy fad, psychedelic fashion and musical style of the period. Myers is brilliant as the secret agent-cum-fashion photographer cryogenically frozen so he can foil the world domination plans of his arch nemesis Dr Evil (Myers again) in the nineties. Witty, sophisticated and hysterically stupid by turns, the side-splitting humour arises from clever culture-clash comedy, knockabout farce, Austin's catchphrases ("Oh, behave!") and

countless references to 007, Matt Helm and Our Man Flint. Even Elizabeth Hurley is fantastic as ersatz Bond girl, Vanessa Kensington. Shagadelic, baby! Contains swearing and sexual references, with some violence. ▣ **DVD**

Mike Myers *Austin Powers/Dr Evil* • Elizabeth Hurley *Vanessa Kensington* • Michael York *Basil Exposition* • Mimi Rogers *Mrs Kensington* • Robert Wagner *Number Two* • Seth Green *Scott Evil* • Fabiana Udenio *Alotta Fagina* • Mindy Sterling *Frau Farbissina* • Burt Bacharach ▪ *Dir* Jay Roach • *Scr* Mike Myers

Austin Powers: The Spy Who Shagged Me ★★★★ 12

Spy spoof   1999 · US · Colour · 95mins

If you liked the International Man of Mystery's first adventure, then you'll love this shagadelic sequel. *The Spy Who Shagged Me* sends Powers (Mike Myers) back to the sixties to reclaim his ''mojo'' which has been stolen by his nemesis Dr Evil (also played by Myers). While the star and his returning director, Jay Roach, revisit the same free-for-all secret agent spoofing of the original, they do it with just the right degree of retro style, knowing geniality and complete lack of taste and restraint. Heather Graham is an adequate replacement for Elizabeth Hurley as Powers's mini-skirted sidekick, and the result is a lava lamp lampoon as stupid and (for Powers fans) as sophisticated as the first excursion. Contains sexual references.

Mike Myers *Austin Powers/Dr Evil/Fat Bastard* • Heather Graham *Felicity Shagwell* • Michael York *Basil Exposition* • Robert Wagner *Number Two* • Seth Green *Scott Evil* • Mindy Sterling *Frau Farbissina* • Rob Lowe *Young Number Two* • Gia Carides *Robin Swallows* • Verne Troyer *Mini-Me* • Elizabeth Hurley *Vanessa Kensington* • Kristen Johnston *Ivana Humpalot* • Burt Bacharach • Elvis Costello ▪ *Dir* Jay Roach • *Scr* Mike Myers, Michael McCullers, from characters created by Mike Myers

Australia ★★ U

Romantic drama
1989 · Fr/Bel/Swi · Colour · 118mins

Set in southern Australia and the Belgian town of Verviers in the fifties, this plodding drama of sheep farming and adultery instantly pulls the wool over our eyes, and is quite content to let it remain there. Director Jean-Jacques Andrien would have us believe that glossy visuals, authentic period trappings, a stately pace and the presence of such stars as Jeremy Irons and Fanny Ardant are compensation for the fact that virtually nothing happens. Irons is horribly off-form and saddled with an awful French accent, while Ardant's character is sketched too thinly to make up for it.

Jeremy Irons *Edouard Pierson* • Fanny Ardant *Jeanne Gauthier* • Tcheky Karyo *Julien Pierson* • Agnès Soral *Agnès Decker* • Hélène Surgère *Madame Pierson* • Maxime Laloux *François Gauthier* • Patrick Bauchau *André Gauthier* ▪ *Dir* Jean-Jacques Andrien • *Scr* Jean-Jacques Andrien, Jean Gruault, Jacques Audiard

Author! Author! ★★ PG

Comedy   1982 · US · Colour · 104mins

An ill-cast but effective Al Pacino (the role needed a Jack Lemmon) is having a slew of domestic troubles as his new play opens on Broadway, and unlikely

director Arthur Hiller is having a tough time finding the requisite lightness of touch to make all the shenanigans convincing. There is, though, a sort of rough-edged charm to the piece, largely thanks to the blissful performances of clever Dyan Cannon and the sublime Tuesday Weld as the gals in Pacino's life, but the material involving the threesome's respective offspring is extraordinarily tasteless. This was written by New York playwright Israel Horovitz, now better known as Winona Ryder's uncle and the father of the lead singer of the Beastie Boys. ▣

Al Pacino *Ivan Travalian* • Dyan Cannon *Alice Detroit* • Tuesday Weld *Gloria* • Alan King *Kreplich* • Bob Dishy *Finestein* • Bob Elliott *Patrick Dicker* • Eric Curry *Igor* • Elva Leff *Bonnie* ▪ *Dir* Arthur Hiller • *Scr* Israel Horovitz

Autobiography of a Princess ★★★ PG

Drama   1975 · UK · Colour · 58mins

An early (and short) Merchant–Ivory offering in their traditional reserved vein, scripted as ever by Ruth Prawer Jhabvala. James Mason and Madhur Jaffrey star as a former secretary to a maharajah and the maharajah's daughter who meet up in London. Through watching old home movies of India they begin to share caustic reminiscences of their time there and of past relationships. An insubstantial but touching and well-observed study of age, looking back on life with some bitterness.

James Mason *Cyril Sahib* • Madhur Jaffrey *The princess* • Keith Varnier *Delivery man* • Diane Fletcher *Seductress* • Timothy Bateson *Blackmailer* • Nazruh Rahman *Papa* ▪ *Dir* James Ivory • *Scr* Ruth Prawer Jhabvala • *Producer* Ismail Merchant

The Autobiography of Miss Jane Pittman ★★★★★

Drama   1974 · US · Colour · 109mins

The winner of nine Emmys, this ambitious adaptation of Ernest J Gaines's novel is one of the finest TV movies ever made. As the 110-year-old Southern women who has experienced both the abolition of slavery at the end of the Civil War and the start of the sixties civil rights movement, Cicely Tyson gives a towering performance. We see her progress from timid innocent to sassy senior citizen, no longer prepared to tolerate the injustices of a supposedly civilised society. Tracy Keenan Wynn's script is occasionally unfocused and over-relies on journalist Michael Murphy to link the episodes. Nonetheless, this makes for compelling viewing.

Cicely Tyson *Jane Pittman* • Michael Murphy *Quentin Lerner* • Richard Dysart *Master Bryant* • Collin Wilcox-Horne [Collin Wilcox Paxton] *Mistress Bryant* • Thalmus Rasulala *Ned* • Dean Smith *Ned aged 15* • Odetta *Big Laura* • Barbara Chaney *Amma Dean* ▪ *Dir* John Korty • *Scr* Tracy Keenan Wynn, from the novel by Ernest J Gaines

Autobus ★★★★ 15

Drama   1991 · Fr · Colour · 93mins

Presenting all-aboard thrills well before Sandra Bullock bought a ticket downtown, Eric Rochant's compelling drama might not be able to compete with *Speed*'s high-octane stunts, but it

more than compensates in terms of tension and performance. Yvan Attal is outstanding as the emotionally unstable man who hijacks a school bus in the hope of impressing girlfriend Charlotte Gainsbourg, veering between menace and confusion as he gets to know teacher Kristin Scott Thomas and the little charmers in her charge. Steering a steady course, Rochant makes the most of the cramped confines and perfectly judges the shifts in tone. In French with English subtitles. ▣

Yvan Attal *Bruno* • Kristin Scott Thomas *Teacher* • Marc Berman *Driver* • Charlotte Gainsbourg *Juliette* • Renan Mazeas *Bruno's brother* • Francine Olivier *Bruno's mother* • Michèle Foucher *Juliette's mother* • Aline Still *Headmistress* • Daniel Milgram *Brigadier* ▪ *Dir/Scr* Eric Rochant

Automatic ★★★ 15

Science-fiction action
1994 · US · Colour · 86mins

A cutting-edge electronics corporation tries to hush up a homicidal fault which develops within its top secret prototype, a cyborg bodyguard/servant called J269 (Oliver Gruner), by sending in a SWAT team to eliminate it. Unfortunately lowly secretary (Daphne Ashbrook) has witnessed the murderous glitch and will have to be erased, too. An effective, well-mounted action thriller in the *Die Hard* mould that treads old ground with fresh verve and rarely a dull moment. Contains swearing and violence. ▣

Olivier Gruner *J269* • Daphne Ashbrook *Nora Rochester* • John Glover *Goddard Marx* • Jeff Kober *Major West* • Penny Johnson *Julia Rodriguez* • Marjean Holden *Epsilon leader* • Dennis Lipscomb *Raymond Hammer* ▪ *Dir* John Murlowski • *Scr* Susan Lambert, Patrick Highsmith

An Autumn Afternoon ★★★★★

Drama   1962 · Jap · Colour · 112mins

Yasujiro Ozu, one of film's great artists, signed off with this typically gentle study of family obligation and the relentless advance of life. Making only his second film in colour, Ozu keeps his camera still and at its customarily low angle, giving us the freedom to explore the meticulously composed frame. It also allows us to concentrate on Chishu Ryu's touching performance as the widowed bookkeeper who reluctantly convinces his daughter (Shima Iwashita) that it's her duty to wed and leave him to the companionship of his drinking buddies. Suffused with genial humanity, this warm, wise tale is both pure cinema and a sheer delight. In Japanese with English subtitles.

Chishu Ryu *Shuhei Hirayama* • Shima Iwashita *Michiko Hirayama* • Shinichiro Mikami *Kazuo Hirayama* • Keiji Sada *Koichi Hirayama* • Mariko Okada *Akiko Hirayama* ▪ *Dir* Yasujiro Ozu • *Scr* Yasujiro Ozu, Kogo Noda

The Autumn Heart ★★

Drama   1998 · US · Colour · 110mins

An adequate family saga – and wannabe weepy – starring Tyne Daly and Ally Sheedy. Daly is a school bus driver who, after suffering a heart attack asks her daughters to search

out their estranged brother. The brother was taken by their father when he deserted the family 16 years previously and the sisters discover that, while they have been on the breadline, their father has become extremely rich and their brother is living it up at Harvard. A working-class/middle-class culture clash ensues with warm and funny results. Nevertheless, this remains a chick flick in the conventional mould.

Ally Sheedy *Deb* • Tyne Daly *Ann* • Davidlee Willson *Daniel* • Marceline Hugot *Donna* • Jack Davidson *Lee* • Marla Sucharetza *Diane* • Willy O'Donnell • Julian Sands ▪ *Dir* Steven Maler • *Scr* Davidlee Willson

Autumn Leaves ★★★

Melodrama   1956 · US · BW · 108mins

Oh dear, Joan Crawford has married her toyboy and now discovers that he's a little, shall we say, disturbed, if not totally deranged. Given an X certificate for its release in the UK, this dark melodrama features all the hallmarks of director Robert Aldrich: misogyny, misanthropy and murderous intent, a trio of themes he would happily reprise with Crawford in *What Ever Happened to Baby Jane?* Cliff Robertson puts in a distinguished performance as Crawford's dangerous other half, although his naturalistic acting style clashes somewhat with Crawford's all-stops-out performance.

Joan Crawford *Milly* • Cliff Robertson *Burt Hanson* • Vera Miles *Virginia* • Lorne Greene *Mr Hanson* • Ruth Donnelly *Liz* • Shepperd Strudwick *Dr Couzzens* • Selmer Jackson *Mr Wetherby* • Maxine Cooper *Nurse Evans* ▪ *Dir* Robert Aldrich • *Scr* Jack Jevne, Lewis Metzer [Jean Rouverol], Robert Blees

Autumn Marathon ★★★

Comedy   1979 · USSR · Colour · 92mins

Georgian director Georgi Danelia described this satire on Leningrad academe as a ''sad comedy'', because a reasonably decent cove manages to drive everyone to distraction through his inability to finish what he started. Only Norbert Kukhinke, the Danish professor with whom he goes jogging, has any sympathy for literary translator Oleg Basilashvili, whose innocent bungling and lapses of memory alienate both his wife, Natalia Gundareva, and mistress, Marina Neyelova. Wittily scripted by Alexander Volodin and played by Basilashvili with a finely judged blend of self-obsession, incompetence and pathos, this won't generate any guffaws, but there'll be wry smiles aplenty. In Russian with English subtitles.

Oleg Basilashvili *Andrei* • Natalia Gundareva *Nina* • Marina Neyelova *Alla* • Yevgeny Leonov *Vasily* • Norbert Kukhinke ▪ *Dir* Georgi Danelia • *Scr* Alexander Volodin

Autumn Moon ★★★★

Drama   1992 · HK/Jap · Colour · 108mins

Set during the days when Hong Kong's post-colonial destiny had been determined but was still some time off, this is an elegant and intelligent exploration of the differences between two of Asia's most vibrant economies. Li Pui Wai is a teenager whose experience of first love eases the worry of her grandmother's illness, while Masatoshi Nagase, as the Japanese visitor she befriends, finds his past flirtations no longer satisfy him. Directed with delicious understatement by Clara Law from a subtle script, this is a thoughtful, intimate drama, made all the more intriguing by the fact that much of the dialogue is delivered in faltering English. In Japanese and English with subtitles.

Masatoshi Nagase *Tokio* • Li Pui Wai *Wai* • Choi Siu Wan *Granny* • Maki Kiuchi *Miki* • Suen Ching Hung *Wai's boyfriend* • Sung Lap Yeung *Wai's father* • Tsang Yust Guen *Wai's mother* • Chu Kit Ming *Wai's brother* ■ *Dir* Clara Law • *Scr* Ling Ching Fong

Autumn Sonata ★★★ 🔢

Drama 1978 · Swe/W Ger · Colour · 88mins

Originally intended as a four-hour feature, the sole collaboration between Ingrid and Ingmar Bergman was born of a troubled shoot, with her Hollywood emoting constantly clashing with his ensemble sensibilities. However, this is still an astonishingly honest study of the personal regret of the public artist, which eerily recalls Ingrid's own decision in the late forties to leave her family to set up home with Roberto Rossellini. Her mix of unrepentant pride and misplaced resentment earned her an Oscar nomination. Without the calm dignity of Liv Ullmann as her abandoned daughter, though, this intense chamber drama would have seriously overbalanced. In Swedish with English subtitles. 📼

Ingrid Bergman *Charlotte* • Liv Ullmann *Eva* • Lena Nyman *Helena* • Halvar Bjork *Viktor* • Arne Bang-Hansen *Uncle Otto* • Gunnar Björnstrand *Paul* • Erland Josephson *Josef* • Georg Lokkeberg *Leonardo* • Linn Ullmann *Eva as a Child* ■ *Dir/Scr* Ingmar Bergman • *Producer* Lew Grade, Martin Starger

An Autumn Tale ★★★★ 🅤

Romantic comedy drama 1998 · Fr · Colour · 111mins

Eric Rohmer is one of the few contemporary directors still interested in people. The final part of his *Four Seasons* series is a typically intimate human drama, in which bookish Marie Rivière becomes overly involved with the lonely heart date (Alain Libolt) she has arranged for her wine-growing friend (Béatrice Romand). This deft, meticulously paced exploration of emotional confusion develops into a delightful comedy of errors, with Rohmer mirroring the plight of his middle-aged leads in the romantic tangles of teenager Alexia Portal. Drawing us inexorably into the lives of characters whose foibles are instantly recognisable, *An Autumn Tale* is a triumph of literate cinema. In French with English subtitles.

Marie Rivière *Isabelle* • Béatrice Romand *Magali* • Alain Libolt *Gérard* • Didier Sandre *Etienne* • Alexia Portal *Rosine* • Stéphane Darmon *Léo* • Aurélia Alcaïs *Emilia* • Mathieu Davette *Grégoire* • Yves Alcaïs *Jean-Jacques* ■ *Dir/Scr* Eric Rohmer

Avalanche ★★ 🅤

Adventure 1975 · UK · Colour · 55mins

One of the Children's Film Foundation's more ambitious projects, this family featurette will seem tame to today's youngsters. Yet Frederic Goode

makes good use of the Austrian Alps to fashion an adventure that should still quicken the odd pulse. Michael Portman and David Ronder do well as the brothers who slope away from a school skiing trip in a bid to climb Mount Elpha. Common sense plays no part in their rivalry, though, as it takes a perilous rescue mission to bring them back from the brink of disaster. Pacey and action-packed, but disappointingly short on surprises.

Michael Portman *David* • David Ronder *Rob* • Norbert Gleirscher *Hans* • Ann Mannion *Sheena* • Bernadette Winship *Pam* • David Dundas *Mr Goring* • Karl Span *Karl Muller* ■ *Dir* Frederic Goode • *Scr* Wally Bosco

Avalanche ★★ 🔢

Disaster movie 1978 · US · Colour · 86mins

Cult director Roger Corman turned producer for this cut-rate disaster movie coasting on the seventies' fascination with a genre popularised by Irwin Allen (*The Towering Inferno*, *The Poseidon Adventure*). Rich developer Rock Hudson opens a ski resort during avalanche season and watches as the low-rent celebrities fall foul of the "six million tons of icy terror" promised in the ads. Poor effects match the acting in what was supposed to be Corman's ticket to mainstream respectability. Its lacklustre box-office performance quickly sent him back to B-movie territory. 📼

Rock Hudson *David Shelby* • Mia Farrow *Caroline Brace* • Robert Foster *Nick Thorne* • Jeanette Nolan *Florence Shelby* • Rick Moses *Bruce Scott* • Steve Franken *Henry McDade* • Barry Primus *Mark Elliott* ■ *Dir* Corey Allen • *Scr* Corey Allen, Claude Pola

Avalanche ★★

Thriller 1994 · US · Colour · 110mins

A change of both scenery and character for *Baywatch*'s David Hasselhoff as he swaps the sea and surf for snow and ice and his nice-guy persona for that of a villain. He plays a jewel smuggler who bails out over Alaska after double-crossing his partners and triggers a massive avalanche. Saved by the holidaying Michael Gross and his two children, he then plots to dump his saviours. Hasselhoff is too much of a square-jawed hero to be that bad, but Gross acquits himself well and director Paul Shapiro makes good use of the Canadian settings. Contains some violence.

David Hasselhoff *Snyder* • Michael Gross *Brian Kemp* • Deanna Milligan *Deirdre* • Myles Ferguson *Max* • Ben Cardinal *Hunter* • Don Davis [Don S Davis] *Whitney* • George Josef *Major* ■ *Dir* Paul Shapiro • *Scr* Tim Redman

Avalanche Express ★★ 🅟🄶

Spy drama 1979 · Ire · Colour · 84mins

A Cold War thriller, in which brutal and ruthless CIA agent Lee Marvin uses defector Robert Shaw to entrap Soviet scientist Maximilian Schell. Set on a cross-border train impeded by blizzards, the film suffered its own tragedies when both Shaw and director Mark Robson died before production was completed. The repair job on what was left doesn't quite hide the joins, though the acting has an impressive energy. 📼

Robert Shaw *General Marenkov* • Lee Marvin *Colonel Harry Wargrave* • Linda Evans *Elsa Lang* • Maximilian Schell *Nikolai Bunin* • Mike Connors *Haller* • Joe Namath *Leroy* • Horst Buchholz *Scholten* • David Hess *Geiger* ■ *Dir* Mark Robson • *Scr* Abraham Polonsky, from the novel by Colin Forbes

Avalon ★★★ 🅤

Epic drama 1990 · US · Colour · 122mins

Director Barry Levinson's lengthy family epic – a sort of *Godfather* without guns – is saved from schmaltz by a wonderfully assured and generous performance by Armin Mueller-Stahl. He plays Sam Krichinsky, the head of an immigrant clan who arrives in America on 4 July, 1914. Four generations of family loving and feuding follow, with the bulk of the film taking place just after the Second World War. While Joan Plowright and Elizabeth Perkins are featured, it's primarily a movie about men, though everyone is so talkily eloquent they eventually become tiresome. 📼

Aidan Quinn *Jules Krichinsky* • Elizabeth Perkins *Ann Kaye* • Armin Mueller-Stahl *Sam Krichinsky* • Leo Fuchs *Hymie Krichinsky* • Eve Gordon *Dottie Kirk* • Lou Jacobi *Gabriel Krichinsky* • Joan Plowright *Eva Krichinsky* • Kevin Pollak *Izzy Krichinsky* • Elijah Wood *Michael Kaye* ■ *Dir/Scr* Barry Levinson

Avanti! ★★★★★ 🔢

Comedy 1972 · US · Colour · 138mins

Billy Wilder is deservedly celebrated for corrosive dramas and scintillating comedies such as *Double Indemnity*, *Sunset Boulevard*, *Some Like It Hot* and *The Apartment*. *Avanti!*, however, is perhaps his most neglected masterpiece. It's a sublime romantic comedy which spins on one of Wilder's favourite themes: the confrontation between the brashness of America, where he worked, and the sophistication of Europe, where he was born. Jack Lemmon's harried business executive flies from Baltimore to Italy to collect his father's corpse. Juliet Mills arrives from England to pick up her mother's body, and before you can say "espresso", the odd couple are re-enacting their parents' affair, first for the hotel staff, then for real. To watch Lemmon, in his best screen performance, shed his clothes and his finger-snapping rudeness, slowly unwind and renew himself spiritually and physically is both moving and wonderfully witty. The picture is long (justifiably), impeccably plotted and brimming with marvellous characters, from Clive Revill's hotel manager to Edward Andrews as a CIA agent whose last-minute appearance serves to show the distance Lemmon has travelled. A desert island movie if ever there was one. Contains swearing and some nudity. 📼

Jack Lemmon *Wendell Armbruster* • Juliet Mills *Pamela Piggott* • Clive Revill *Carlo Carlucci* • Edward Andrews *JJ Blodgett* • Gianfranco Barra *Bruno* • Franco Angrisano *Arnold Trotta* • Pippo Franco *Mattarazzo* • Franco Acampora *Armando Trotta* ■ *Dir* Billy Wilder • *Scr* Billy Wilder, IAL Diamond, from the play by Samuel Taylor

The Avengers ★ 🔢

Action comedy thriller 1998 · US · Colour · 85mins

The cult sixties TV series gets royally shafted by Hollywood in a stunningly designed blockbuster that's stunningly awful in every other department. Ralph Fiennes and Uma Thurman couldn't be more miscast as John Steed and Emma Peel, here trying to stop villainous Sir August de Wynter (Sean Connery playing himself again) holding the world's weather to ransom and freezing London to an arctic standstill. Ruthlessly edited before release and packed with arch one-liners, bad puns and vulgar double entendres, this is misguided and misbegotten to a simply staggering degree, while Jeremiah Chechik's mannered direction screeches the action to an unexciting halt at every flat turn. Contains moderate violence and strong language. 📼 **DVD**

Ralph Fiennes *John Steed* • Uma Thurman *Doctor Emma Peel* • Sean Connery *Sir August De Wynter* • Jim Broadbent *Mother* • Fiona Shaw *Father* • Eddie Izzard *Bailey* • Eileen Atkins *Alice* • Shaun Ryder *Donavan* • Patrick Macnee *Invisible Jones* ■ *Dir* Jeremiah Chechik • *Scr* Don MacPherson • *Production Designer* Stuart Craig

Avenging Angel ★ 🔞

Crime drama 1985 · US · Colour · 93mins

Taking on the role played by Donna Wilkes in the original film, *Angel*, Betsy Russell here puts her streetwalking days behind her to pound the beat down Hollywood way in search of the killers of the cop who saved her from prostitution. It's a noble enough aim, but the way in which director Robert Vincent O'Neil goes about telling her story is less laudable. Little more than an excuse for some cheap sex and violence, this is only of interest to western fans curious to see what happened to Rory Calhoun.

Betsy Russell *Angel/Molly Stewart* • Rory Calhoun *Kit Carson* • Robert F Lyons *Detective Andrews* • Susan Tyrrell *Solly Mosier* • Ossie Davis *Captain Moradian* • Barry Pearl *Johnny Glitter* • Ross Hagen *Ray Mitchell* ■ *Dir* Robert Vincent O'Neil • *Scr* Robert Vincent O'Neil, Joseph M Cala

The Avenging Angel ★★★ 🔢

Historical western 1995 · US · Colour · 92mins

There's no little irony in finding Charlton Heston, president of the National Rifle Association, starring in a film with a pronounced anti-gun message. Yet, he brings copious gravitas to the role of Mormon leader Brigham Young in this earnest TV movie about the violent factions of the religion's early years. Tom Berenger also shows strongly as Miles Utley, the outcast who uncovers a conspiracy within the Mormon hierarchy after he is falsely accused of trying to assassinate its founder. In bidding to play down the religious content, director Craig Baxley succeeds in producing a whodunit western that holds the attention without ever being really compelling. 📼

Tom Berenger *Miles Utley* • Fay Masterton *Miranda Young* • Kevin Tighe *Elder Rigby* • Charlton Heston *Brigham Young* • James

Coburn *Porter Rockwell* ■ *Dir* Craig Baxley [Craig R Baxley] • *Scr* Dennis Nemec, from a novel by Gary Stewart

Avenging Force ★★ 18
Martial arts action thriller
1986 · US · Colour · 98mins

It's too bad that Steve James exits this movie halfway through. He is not only a much better actor than top-billed Michael Dudikoff, but he shows he had the stuff to be a big action star. Still, even when he's gone, this slick production delivers the goods for action fans. Dudikoff plays a retired secret agent who lends his aspiring politician buddy (James) a hand when a Neo-Nazi group makes him a target. The danger proves too much, and in the second half Dudikoff goes through another retelling of *The Hounds of Zaroff* in the Louisiana bayou. The fight scenes are exciting and brutal, but the disturbing and tasteless violence leaves a bad impression. ▭

Michael Dudikoff *Matt Hunter* • Steve James *Larry Richards* • James Booth *Admiral Brown* • John P Ryan *Glastenbury* • Bill Wallace *Delaney* • Karl Johnson *Wallace* • Marc Alaimo *Lavall* • Allison Gereighty *Sarah Hunter* ■ *Dir* Sam Firstenberg • *Scr* James Booth

The Avenging Hand ★
Thriller
1936 · UK · BW · 66mins

Staying in a gloomy English hotel, Chicago gangster Noah Beery tracks down the killer of an old match-seller with the help of a hotel clerk and then disappears back to America. Running at not much more than an hour, this somewhat confused thriller is feeble, forgettable and largely forgotten. Beery is a bright spark in the midst of the murk and an obscure British supporting cast.

Noah Beery *Lee Barwell* • Kathleen Kelly *Gwen Taylor* • Louis Borell *Pierre Charrell* • James Harcourt *Sam Hupp* • Charles Oliver *Toni Visetti* • Reginald Long *Charles Mason* ■ *Dir* Victor Hanbury • *Scr* Akos Talney, Reginald Long

Aventure Malgache ★★★ PG
Second World War adventure
1944 · UK · BW · 29mins

The second of the two wartime shorts that Alfred Hitchcock made for the Ministry of Information was prompted by the feuding between the Free French who had worked on the first, *Bon Voyage*. Co-scripting with Angus MacPhail, ''Hitch'' introduced a note of levity that was unusual for propaganda films of the time to help encourage co-operation between partisans of all regional, personal and political persuasions. Yet the anecdote told by an exiled amateur actor about his Resistance activities against the Vichy regime on Madagascar didn't meet with the approval of Whitehall, and the film was never shown. In French with English subtitles. ▭

Dir Alfred Hitchcock • *Scr* Angus MacPhail, Alfred Hitchcock

The Aviator ★★ PG
Period drama
1985 · US · Colour · 92mins

This is a typical outing for two performers with a talent for finding themselves in forgettable films.

Christopher Reeve, as a pilot haunted by the crash that killed his buddy, is ordered to fly rebellious Rosanna Arquette to college to avoid an adultery scandal. It's loathe at first sight, but their bickering ceases when they are forced down in a mountain wilderness. The need to survive brings about the sort of change of heart that only happens in thinly-plotted movies. Director George Miller (*The Man from Snowy River*) obviously hoped for fireworks of the Clark Gable/Jean Harlow variety, but Reeve and Arquette barely raise a spark. ▭

Christopher Reeve *Edgar Anscombe* • Rosanna Arquette *Tillie Hansen* • Jack Warden *Moravia* • Sam Wanamaker *Bruno Hansen* • Scott Wilson *Jerry Stiller* • Tyne Daly *Evelyn Stiller* • Marcia Strassman *Rose Stiller* ■ *Dir* George Miller (1) • *Scr* Marc Norman, from the novel by Ernest K Gann

The Aviator's Wife ★★★★
Comedy
1980 · Fr · Colour · 106mins

Eric Rohmer launched his *Comedies and Proverbs* series with this shrewd tale of tortured emotions, deceptive appearances and missed opportunities. Wracked by the sight of girlfriend Marie Rivière leaving her apartment with pilot Mathieu Carrière, postal worker Philippe Marlaud begins to pursue his rival, enlisting the assistance of amused schoolgirl Anne-Laure Meury. Although Bernard Lutic's photography glories in the parks and backstreets of Paris, this is still a typically garrulous picture, with Marlaud's bemusing ramblings and Rivière's self-pitying rant being delivered to perfection. However, it's Rohmer's sympathy for these lost souls that makes everything so engaging. In French with English subtitles.

Philippe Marlaud *François* • Marie Rivière *Anne* • Anne-Laure Meury *Lucie* • Mathieu Carrière *Christian* • Philippe Caroit *Friend* • Coralie Clément *Colleague* • Lisa Heredia *Girlfriend* ■ *Dir/Scr* Eric Rohmer

L'Avventura ★★★★★ PG
Classic drama
1959 · It/Fr · BW · 142mins

Booed at Cannes (where it still won the Special Jury Prize) and branded immoral by the American National League of Decency, Michelangelo Antonioni's masterpiece is a mystery without a solution. Shot in real time, this adventure in cinematic technique is a brilliant and troubling study of alienation, privileged indolence and psychological sterility, in which the search for a missing woman gradually becomes irrelevant as her lover and best friend are drawn into an unsatisfying relationship of their own. Antonioni coaxes memorable performances from Monica Vitti and Gabriele Ferzetti, while he uses cinematographer Aldo Scavarda's exceptional views of both island and mainland landscapes to reveal his characters' emotional states. Timeless genius. In Italian with English subtitles.

Gabriele Ferzetti *Sandro* • Monica Vitti *Claudia* • Lea Massari *Anna* • Dominique Blanchar *Giulia* • James Addams *Carrado* • Lelio Luttazzi *Raimondo* • Esmeralda Ruspoli *Patrizia* • Renzo Ricci *Anna's father* ■ *Dir* Michelangelo Antonioni • *Scr* Michelangelo Antonioni, Elio Bartolini, Tonino Guerra, from a story by Michelangelo Antonioni

Awake to Danger ★★
Psychological thriller
1995 · US · Colour

Beverly Hills 90210 star Tori Spelling attempts to flex her acting muscles in this routine TV thriller. Locked in a coma for more than a year following a robbery that resulted in the death of her mother, she awakens to find herself the target of the killer, who wants her removed before her memory returns. Spelling lacks credibility in the lead role, but the solid performances of Michael Gross and John Getz make this passable fare. ▭

Tori Spelling *Aimee McAdams* • Michael Gross *Ben McAdams* • John Getz *Steve Murdock* • Reed Diamond *Jeff Baker* • Laura Johnson *Renee McAdams* • Shae D'Lyn *Lorette McAdams* ■ *Dir* Michael Tuchner • *Scr* April Campbell Jones, from the novel *The Other Side of Dark* by Joan Lowery Nixon

The Awakening ★ 15
Horror
1980 · UK/US · Colour · 95mins

This adaptation of Bram Stoker's *The Jewel of Seven Stars* (which had previously inspired a Hammer horror, *Blood from the Mummy's Tomb*) is a dreadful plod. Surprising, given the film's credentials – two of the screenwriters, Allan Scott and Chris Bryant, wrote Nicolas Roeg's masterpiece *Don't Look Now*, the cinematography's by the great Jack Cardiff and promising British director Mike Newell (who later made *Four Weddings and a Funeral*) is behind the camera. The symbolism is heavy-handed, Susannah York merely looks pretty and Charlton Heston reads the script as if it were the Ten Commandments, forgetting Cecil B DeMille's 11th commandment: Thou Shalt Not Bore. ▭

Charlton Heston *Matthew Corbeck* • Susannah York *Jane Turner* • Jill Townsend *Anne Corbeck* • Stephanie Zimbalist *Margaret Corbeck* • Patrick Drury *Paul Whittier* • Nadim Sawalha *Dr El Sadek* • Miriam Margolyes *Kadira* ■ *Dir* Mike Newell • *Scr* Allan Scott, Chris Bryant, Clive Exton, from the novel *The Jewel of Seven Stars* by Bram Stoker

The Awakening ★★
Romantic drama
1995 · Can/US/Ger · Colour

Intended as a rousing adventure with plenty of simmering romance, this sanitised made-for-TV romp has about as much passion as a convent outing. Mousey landlady Cynthia Geary is the daydreaming damsel hurtled by writer Maria Nation and director George Bloomfield through a series of lacklustre encounters as she and bounty hunter David Beecroft set off in search of antiquities smugglers. Harmless enough.

Cynthia Geary *Sara* • David Beecroft *Flynn* • Sheila McCarthy *Maurice Godin* • David Ferry ■ *Dir* George Bloomfield • *Scr* Maria Nation

Awakenings ★★★★ 15
Drama based on a true story
1990 · US · Colour · 115mins

Robert De Niro and Robin Williams star in a powerful dramatisation of neurologist Oliver Sacks's book, based on his real-life success in ''awakening'' patients who had been trapped in a comatose state for over 30 years after contracting sleeping sickness in the twenties. Williams

shows his versatility by playing the shy scientist, though it was De Niro who got the Oscar nomination. Too upbeat for some tastes, Penny Marshall's film got mixed reviews on its release, but also earned an Oscar nomination for best picture. An absorbing treatment of an intriguing subject. Contains some swearing. ▭ **DVD**

Robert De Niro *Leonard Lowe* • Robin Williams *Dr Malcolm Sayer* • Julie Kavner *Eleanor Costello* • Ruth Nelson *Mrs Lowe* • John Heard *Dr Kaufman* • Penelope Ann Miller *Paula* • Alice Drummond *Lucy* • Judith Malina *Rose* • Max von Sydow *Dr Peter Ingham* ■ *Dir* Penny Marshall • *Scr* Steven Zaillian, from the book by Oliver Sacks

Away All Boats ★★★ U
Second World War drama
1956 · US · Colour · 113mins

A movie with the kind of gung-ho heroism now rarely seen, simply because today's cynicism would blow it out of the water which is what nearly happens to the wartime attack transport boat *Belinda*. Jeff Chandler is the inevitably unyielding captain who has to spark a fighting spirit among his dispirited crew. It takes him all his time, and ours, too, though the action scenes pass the time spectacularly enough, while there's a very young Clint Eastwood to be spotted. Otherwise, its flag-waving patriotism makes it a curio from a bygone era.

Jeff Chandler *Captain Jebediah Hawks* • George Nader *Lieutenant MacDougall* • Lex Barker *Commander Quigley* • Julie Adams *Lieutenant MacDougall* • Keith Andes *Dr Bell* • Richard Boone *Lieutenant Fraser* • William Reynolds *Kruger* • Clint Eastwood ■ *Dir* Joseph Pevney • *Scr* Ted Sherdeman, from a novel by Kenneth M Dodson

The Awful Dr Orloff ★★
Horror
1962 · Sp/Fr · BW · 90mins

Trash-meister Jess Franco's incredible directing career took off with this graphic Spanish shocker (which credits the director as Norbert Moutier, one of many pseudonyms he has taken to avoid France's strict quota laws), in which demented Howard Vernon kidnaps starlets to perform skin-graft operations on his disfigured daughter. Clearly borrowing elements from the Edgar Wallace tale *Dark Eyes of London* and Georges Franju's *Eyes without a Face*, Franco's early gore landmark is rather talky by today's standards, but the expressionistic black-and-white photography still impresses even if the tacky tinsel terror charts familiar sixties territory. It spawned four sequels. Contains violence and nudity.

Howard Vernon *Dr Orloff* • Conrado San Martin *Inspector Tanner* • Diana Lorys *Wanda Bronsky* • Perla Cristal *Arne* • Maria Silva *Dany* • Ricardo Valle *Morpho* • Mara Lasso *Irma Gold* • Venancio Muro *Jean Rousseau* • Felix Dafauce *Inspector* ■ *Dir* Norbert Moutier [Jesus Franco] • *Scr* Jesus Franco, from the novel *Gritos en la Noche* by David Khune [Jesus Franco]

The Awful Truth ★★★★★ U
Classic comedy
1937 · US · BW · 87mins

A wonderful example of Cary Grant at his screwball comic best as one half of a sniping, divorcing couple, who trade insults like gunfire and seek to spoil

U = SUITABLE FOR ALL   **Uc** = SUITABLE FOR ALL, ESPECIALLY FOR YOUNG CHILDREN (VIDEO ONLY)   **PG** = PARENTAL GUIDANCE

each other's future plans. Irene Dunne is the superb foil for Grant's laconic asides, and the two leads are ably assisted by a great supporting cast, which includes Ralph Bellamy and Molly Lamont. Leo McCarey's assured and fluid direction was rightly rewarded with an Oscar. Many stars, including Tom Hanks and Hugh Grant, have laid claim to Grant's mantle, but this classic movie illustrates once again that they are light years away from the man at his best.

Irene Dunne *Lucy Warriner* • Cary Grant *Jerry Warriner* • Ralph Bellamy *Daniel Leeson* • Alexander D'Arcy [Alex D'Arcy] *Armand Duvalle* • Cecil Cunningham *Aunt Patsy* • Molly Lamont *Barbara Vance* • Esther Dale *Mrs Leeson* • Joyce Compton *Dixie Belle Lee/Toots Binswanger* ■ *Dir* Leo McCarey • *Scr* Vina Delmar, from the play by Arthur Richman

An Awfully Big Adventure
★★★ 15

Black comedy　1994 · UK · Colour · 107mins

Under-rated on its release by those upset that the latest pairing of director Mike Newell and star Hugh Grant hadn't produced another *Four Weddings and a Funeral*, this watchable and moderately entertaining adaptation of Beryl Bainbridge's jet-black comedy novel hits the right cynical notes. Focusing on the romantic intrigues involving the members of a British repertory theatre as they prepare to mount a production of *Peter Pan* in the late forties, the film has Grant cast against type as the egomaniacal director, while Alan Rickman's charismatic and stylish portrayal of the ageing matinée idol steals the handsomely mounted show. Contains swearing and brief nudity.

Alan Rickman *PL O'Hara* • Hugh Grant *Meredith Potter* • Georgina Cates *Stella* • Alun Armstrong *Uncle Vernon* • Peter Firth *Bunny* • Prunella Scales *Rose* • Rita Tushingham *Aunt Lily* • Nicola Pagett *Dotty Blundell* ■ *Dir* Mike Newell • *Scr* Charles Wood, from the novel by Beryl Bainbridge

AWOL
★★ 18

Action thriller　1990 · US · Colour · 103mins

Although Jean-Claude Van Damme gawps blankly, as if trying to remember the simplest lines is a particularly tricky task, at least his director Sheldon Lettich knows how to move the action along in this mildly efficient thriller. Balancing most of the tale between the sentimental, the risible and the hysterically overacted, Van Damme provides volleys of well crafted fisticuffs, and somehow manages to bring a certain humanity to his punch-drunk protagonist, a French legionnaire who's deserted to the States. Contains violence, swearing and nudity.

Jean-Claude Van Damme *Lyon Gaultier* • Harrison Page *Joshua* • Deborah Rennard *Cynthia* • Lisa Pelikan *Helene* • Ashley Johnson *Nicole* • Brian Thompson *Russell* • Voyo *Sergeant Hartog* • Michel Qissi *Moustafa* ■ *Dir* Sheldon Lettich • *Scr* Sheldon Lettich, Jean-Claude Van Damme, RN Warren, from a story by Jean-Claude Van Damme

Ay, Carmela!
★★★ 15

War drama　1990 · Sp/It · Colour · 98mins

As a tragicomedy in the rose-tinted nostalgic style of the Oscar-winning

Belle Epoque, this is a highly enjoyable and eventually moving story of a vaudevillian couple's contact with the opposing sides in the Spanish Civil War. As a political satire, it is markedly less successful, with both the Falangists and the Republicans being drawn as broad caricatures, while the pokes at military bureaucracy, cynical survivalism and the macho nature of Spanish society are as gentle as they are obvious. Nevertheless, director Carlos Saura re-creates the period admirably and coaxes fine performances from Andres Pajares and the astonishing Carmen Maura. In Spanish with English subtitles.

Carmen Maura *Carmela* • Andres Pajares *Paulino* • Gabino Diego *Gustavete* • Maurizio De Razza *Lieutenant Ripamonte* • Miguel Angel Rellan *Interrogating lieutenant* • Edward Zentara *Polish officer* • Mario Decandia *Bruno* • Jose Sancho *Artillery captain* • Antonio Fuentes *Artillery subaltern* ■ *Dir* Carlos Saura • *Scr* Carlos Saura, Rafael Azcona, from the play by Jose Sanchis Sinisterra

B

The BFG
★★★ U

Animated adventure　1989 · UK · Colour · 88mins

Based on Roald Dahl's classic tale, this animated feature boasts the vocal talents of David Jason as the Big Friendly Giant and Amanda Root as Sophie, the little girl he befriends while delivering dreams to children. The two team up to defeat the bad giants, with a little help from the Queen of England (voiced by Angela Thorne). Cute and pleasing, and great for kids.

David Jason *BFG* • Amanda Root *Sophie* • Angela Thorne *Queen of England* • Ballard Berkeley *Head of the Army* • Michael Knowles *Head of the Air Force* • Don Henderson *Giants/Sergeant* ■ *Dir* Brian Cosgrove • *Scr* John Hambley, from the novel by Roald Dahl

BF's Daughter
★★

Drama　1948 · US · BW · 107mins

Or Polly Fulton, as she was better known in Britain, where "BF" was common slang for "bloody fool" in the late forties. John P Marquand's novel was a serious study in social mores, but the film adaptation became little more than a vehicle for Barbara Stanwyck, who over-emotes as only she can as the rich man's daughter who destroys her weak liberal husband, Van Heflin. It's not very interesting, and director Robert Z Leonard's pacing is sluggish, yet Stanwyck fans won't want to miss this. She looks stunning (the cameraman is Joseph Ruttenberg) and is dressed by Irene, the consummate MGM designer.

Barbara Stanwyck *Polly Fulton* • Van Heflin *Thomas W Brett* • Richard Hart *Robert S Tasmin* • Charles Coburn *BF Fulton* • Keenan Wynn *Martin Delwyn Ainsley* • Margaret Lindsay *Apples Sandler* • Spring Byington *Gladys Fulton* ■ *Dir* Robert Z Leonard • *Scr* Luther Davis, from the novel by John P Marquand

BMX Bandits
★★ PG

Adventure　1983 · Ausl · Colour · 86mins

This lively but very ordinary adventure story would probably be gathering dust in some TV station by now if it weren't for the presence of a pre-stardom Nicole Kidman. She and her chums get mixed up with a gang of crooks who might have got away with it if it weren't for those darned BMX bikes. It lacks the charm of similar Children's Film Foundation stories.

David Argue *Duane Whitey* • John Ley "Moustache" • Nicole Kidman *Judy* • James Lugton *Goose* • Bryan Marshall *The Boss* • Angelo D'Angelo *PJ* ■ *Dir* Brian Trenchard-Smith • *Scr* Patrick Edgeworth, from a screenplay by Russell Hagg

B Monkey
★★★ 18

Romantic thriller　1996 · UK/US · Colour · 88mins

Tired of her life of crime, sexy jewel thief Asia Argento (known as B Monkey) decides to go straight. But as romance with schoolteacher Jared Harris beckons, can she really give up the guns, drugs and glamorous danger of London's underworld? Distinctly old-fashioned with echoes of early seventies British caper movies, this fast-moving thriller from director Michael (*Il Postino*) Radford also pays obvious homage to French films such as *Nikita* and *Betty Blue*. The well-drawn characters help smooth over the bumpier plot jolts. Argento – in her English-language debut – glows with charisma.

Asia Argento *Beatrice (B Monkey)* • Jared Harris *Alan* • Rupert Everett *Paul* • Jonathan Rhys-Meyers *Bruno* • Tim Woodward *Frank* • Ian Hart *Steve* ■ *Dir* Michael Radford • *Scr* Chloe King, Michael Radford, Michael Thomas, from the novel by Andrew Davies

Baazigar
★★★ 15

Psychological drama　1993 · Ind · Colour · 173mins

Not since George Raft has a bad guy been able to trip the light fantastic as well as Shahrukh Khan. One of the most popular villains in recent Bollywood history, he turns in an impeccable performance of malevolent charm in this psychological masala from directing duo Abbas/Mustan. Equally impressive is Kajol, as the beauty who discovers that the supposedly deceased killer of her sister is alive, well and on her trail. The music is every bit as important as the melodrama, but a little more suspense might not have gone amiss. In Hindi with English subtitles.

Shahrukh Khan • Kajol • Shilpa Shetty • Dalip Tahil • Siddharth • Johnny Lever • Krish Malik • Anant ■ *Dir* Abbas, Mustan • *Scr* Robin Bhatt, Javed Sidique, Akash Khurana

Bab El-Oued City
★★★

Drama　1994 · Alg · Colour · 93mins

Although established as his country's leading film-maker, Merzak Allouache took a considerable risk in painting so graphic a portrait of Muslim Algeria. He not only suggests that the heroes of the 1988 protests were gangsters using religion as a pretext for their activities, but also reveals Algiers to be a city teaming with prostitutes and petty crooks for whom the teachings of the Koran mean next to nothing. Mohamed Ourdache's thuggish performance lacks shading, but Hassan Abdou is more credible as the wastrel whose theft of some loudspeakers from the mosque invites the ire of the fundamentalists. In Arabic with English subtitles.

Hassan Abdou *Boualem* • Nadia Kaci *Yamina* • Nadia Samir *Ouardya* • Mohamed Ourdache *Said* ■ *Dir/Scr* Merzak Allouache

The Babe
★★★ PG

Sports biography　1992 · US · Colour · 109mins

This was only released on video in the UK, perhaps because it was felt we would rather count sheep than watch baseball. It is, however, a character study of a flawed talent, baseball legend Babe Ruth, rather than a sports film centred on endless action. John Goodman, capitalising on the success of the TV series *Roseanne*, perfectly captures the hero's enthusiasm, insecurity and weaknesses, and helps distract from the fact that the film is episodic. Contains some swearing. 🔲

John Goodman *George Herman "Babe" Ruth* • Kelly McGillis *Claire Hodgson-Ruth* • Trini Alvarado *Helen Woodford-Ruth* • Bruce Boxleitner *Jumpin' Joe Dugan* • Peter Donat *Harry Frazee* • James Cromwell *Brother Mathias* ▪ *Dir* Arthur Hiller • *Scr* John Fusco

Babe ★★★★ U
Comedy adventure
1995 · Ausl · Colour · 88mins

This Australian family comedy came out of nowhere to enchant millions around the world. The "babe" of the title is an orphaned piglet adopted by a family of Border collies who learns how to handle sheep under the patient training of soft-hearted farmer James Cromwell. The mixture of live action and animatronics brings the animals magically to life (the film won an Oscar for visual effects). A delight from start to finish that will captivate children and melt the heart of even the grumpiest adult. 🔲 DVD

James Cromwell *Farmer Arthur Hoggett* • Magda Szubanski *Esme Hoggett* • Christine Cavanaugh *Babe* • Miriam Margolyes *Fly* • Danny Mann *Ferdinand* • Hugo Weaving *Rex* • Miriam Flynn *Maa* • Roscoe Lee Browne *Narrator* ▪ *Dir* Chris Noonan • *Scr* Chris Noonan, George Miller, from the novel *The Sheep-Pig* by Dick King-Smith

Babe: Pig in the City
★★★ U
Comedy   1998 · US/Ausl · Colour · 91mins

This sequel isn't anywhere near the equal of the endearing original, in which the delightful talking pig-hero entered a sheepdog trial and went on to win hearts as well as prizes. Here, Babe finds himself in an urban environment as he attempts to save the farm after Farmer Hoggett is injured and unable to work, and he's in constant danger with his animal companions. The action is taken at too frantic a pace to let the personalities come through, but the work with the animals is still wonderful. 🔲 DVD

James Cromwell *Farmer Hoggett* • Magda Szubanski *Esme Hoggett* • Mickey Rooney *Fugly Floom* • Mary Stein *Landlady* • Julie Godfrey *Neighbour* • EG Daily [*Elizabeth Daily*] *Babe* • Glenne Headly *Zootie* • Steven Wright *Bob* • Miriam Margolyes *Fly* • Hugo Weaving *Rex* ▪ *Dir* George Miller (2) • *Scr* George Miller, Judy Morris, Mark Lamprell, from characters created by Dick King-Smith

Babes in Arms ★★★★ U
Musical   1939 · US · BW · 95mins

Not much of Rodgers and Hart's Broadway score was left in this MGM film version, but that didn't matter to audiences who turned out in force to watch Judy Garland and Mickey Rooney. They were brought together in the very first musical produced by genius Arthur Freed, whose later work would include such classics as *On the Town*. Rooney is magnificent, earning an Oscar nomination but losing to

Robert Donat. He's a perfect foil for Garland, her wayward vulnerability contrasting with his brashness. Just sit back and enjoy their obvious pleasure in singing *Good Morning*. It's just a "putting on the show right here" musical, but it was one of the first and it's still one of the best.

Mickey Rooney *Mickey Moran* • Judy Garland *Patsy Barton* • Charles Winninger *Joe Moran* • Guy Kibbee *Judge Black* • June Preisser *Rosalie Essex* • Grace Hayes *Florrie Moran* ▪ *Dir* Busby Berkeley • *Scr* Jack McGowan, Kay Van Riper, from the musical by Richard Rodgers, Lorenz Hart

Babes in Toyland ★★★★ U
Musical fantasy   1934 · US · BW · 77mins

Fairy-tale whimsy with Laurel and Hardy! What could be better for children of all ages? Victor Herbert's light operetta was adapted – to the extent there's nothing left of the original – with Stan and Ollie as incompetent assistants to Santa Claus. They order 100 six-foot wooden soldiers instead of 600 foot-tall militants. But the combatants come in handy when miser Barnaby pesters Tom-Tom from his beloved Bo-Peep. Simple-minded joy. DVD

Stan Laurel *Stanley Dum* • Oliver Hardy *Oliver Dee* • Charlotte Henry *Little Bo-Peep* • Felix Knight *Tom-Tom* • Henry Kleinbach [*Henry Brandon*] *Evil Silas Barnaby* • Florence Roberts *Widow Peep* • Ferdinand Munier *Santa Claus* ▪ *Dir* Gus Meins, Charles Rogers • *Scr* Nick Grinde, Frank Butler, from the operetta *Babes in Toyland* by Victor Herbert, Glen MacDonough

Babes in Toyland ★★ U
Musical fantasy   1961 · US · Colour · 101mins

The second of three film adaptations of Victor Herbert's light opera, this earned a couple of Oscar nominations but it isn't a patch on the classic Laurel and Hardy version. Personally produced by Walt Disney, this was the studio's first live-action musical, but there's a distinct lack of magic. The special effects that allow Tommy Sands to lead an army of toy soldiers to rescue Annette Funicello from the grasp of evil Ray Bolger are clever enough, but Jack Donohue's direction is uninspired. 🔲

Ray Bolger *Barnaby* • Tommy Sands *Tom Piper* • Annette Funicello *Mary Contrary* • Ed Wynn *Toymaker* • Tommy Kirk *Grumio* • Kevin Corcoran *Boy Blue* • Henry Calvin *Gonzorgo* ▪ *Dir* Jack Donohue • *Scr* Ward Kimball, Joe Rinaldi, Lowell S Hawley, from the operetta by Victor Herbert, Glen MacDonough

Babes in Toyland ★ U
Musical fantasy
1986 · US/W Ger · Colour · 91mins

The old Laurel and Hardy picture of 1934 was remade by Disney in 1961, with two TV versions in between. This further TV remake is only of minor interest, even for fans of Drew Barrymore and Keanu Reeves: she was 11, and towards the end of her first flush of success, while he was 21, and yet to find his. The original songs by Victor Herbert and Glen McDonough have been replaced by gooey items by Leslie Bricusse, who wrote *Scrooge* and *Doctor Dolittle*. 🔲

Drew Barrymore *Lisa Piper* • Richard Mulligan *Bernie/Barnaby Barnacle* • Eileen Brennan

Mrs Piper/Widow Hubbard • Keanu Reeves *Alex/Jack Be Nimble* • Jill Schoelen *Margaret/ Mary Contrary* • Pat Morita *Toymaster* ▪ *Dir* Clive Donner • *Scr* Paul Zindel

Babes on Broadway ★★★ U
Musical   1941 · US · BW · 117mins

An appallingly contrived, sentimental mishmash created to suit the talents of its stars, but when those particular stars are the incomparable Judy Garland and the ineffable Mickey Rooney, frankly they could have dispensed with the plot entirely. As it is, the fabulous twosome manage to repeat their earlier successes in this third Busby Berkeley-directed musical, and the arch plot structure enables them to go though their paces – Rooney performs an amazing Carmen Miranda impression and Judy pretends to be Sarah Bernhardt. But be warned: the minstrel number seems incredibly tasteless today and there's an air of corny wartime patriotism that hasn't worn well.

Mickey Rooney *Tommy Williams* • Judy Garland *Penny Morris* • Fay Bainter *Miss Jones* • Virginia Weidler *Barbara Jo* • Ray McDonald *Ray Lambert* • Richard Quine *Morton Hammond* • Donald Meek *Mr Stone* • Alexander Woollcott ▪ *Dir* Busby Berkeley • *Scr* Fred F Finklehoffe, Elaine Ryan, from the story by Burton Lane

Babette's Feast ★★★★★ U
Period drama   1987 · Den · Colour · 103mins

A Danish film with a French star, directed by Gabriel Axel, that deservedly won the best foreign film Oscar and transcended the barriers of subtitles to capture the imagination of cinemagoers everywhere. Set in the 1870s, the story unfolds against the background of the grim Jutland peninsula, where two spinster sister (Bodil Kjer, Birgitte Federspiel), daughters of the former pastor, continue his work in leading the religious sect he founded. Into their lives comes Babette (Stéphane Audran), seeking refuge from war-torn Paris, who becomes their housekeeper. Her presence gradually effects changes in the austere community, culminating in a magnificent feast that she cooks 14 years later, which serves as a profoundly cathartic event in the lives of all. Faithfully and brilliantly adapted by Axel from the story by Isak Dinesen (Karen Blixen), this highly original and deeply poignant tale, leavened with well-judged humour is that rare thing – a perfect work. In Danish with English subtitles. 🔲

Stéphane Audran *Babette Hersant* • Jean-Philippe Lafont *Achille Papin* • Gudmar Wivesson *Young Lorenz Lowenhielm* • Jarl Kulle *Old Lorenz Lowenhielm* • Bibi Andersson *Swedish court lady-in-waiting* • Hanne Stensgaard *Young Philippa* ▪ *Dir* Gabriel Axel • *Scr* Gabriel Axel, from a story by Isak Dinesen [Karen Blixen]

Babies ★★ 15
Drama   1990 · US · Colour · 89mins

Every year, thousands of women in their thirties have babies. But none of them makes such a meal of it as the trio in this tiresome TV movie. Armed with a medical textbook and a fortune-cookie approach to psychology,

scriptwriter Lynn Roth has managed to squeeze in every conceivable cliché. Lindsay Wagner, Dinah Manoff (one of the "Pink Ladies" in *Grease*) and Marcy Walker play every scene with excruciating earnestness. 🔲

Lindsay Wagner *Yvonne* • Dinah Manoff *Laura* • Marcy Walker *Cindy* • Adam Arkin *David* • Valerie Landsburg *Andrea* • John Walcott *Jake* ▪ *Dir* Michael Ray Rhodes • *Scr* Lynn Roth, from a story by Lynn Roth, Helena Hacker, Frank Swertlow

Babul ★★ U
Romantic drama   1950 · Ind · BW · 124mins

A huge hit at the Indian box office, this Indian romance not only takes tragedy to new heights, but also comes pretty close to crossing the boundaries of credibility. It's intrigue all the way as the new village postman becomes the subject of a tug-of-war between his boss's daughter and the spoilt sibling of the local landowner. Critics will tell you that Dilip Kumar broke all sorts of cinematic conventions by jilting Nargis and opting for the resistible Munawar Sultana, but what they fail to comment on is the ludicrousness of the finale. You won't know whether to laugh or cry. In Hindi with English subtitles. 🔲

Dilip Kumar *Ashok* • Nargis *Bela* • Munawar Sultana *Usha* ▪ *Dir* SU Sunny • *Scr* Azm Bazidpuri

The Baby ★★★
Horror   1973 · US · Colour · 85mins

Kept in nappies by his man-hating mother, taunted by his psycho sister and desired by a well-meaning social worker, life has been anything but easy for teenager David Manzy, but it's going to get worse. Best known for his collaborations with Clint Eastwood (*Hang 'Em High* and *Magnum Force*), director Ted Post makes a decent fist of this bizarre horror film, although his use of footage showing real mentally disabled children is in poor taste. The trio of terrible women (Ruth Roman, Marianna Hill and Anjanette Comer) makes this well worth a look.

Ruth Roman *Mrs Wadsworth* • Anjanette Comer *Ann Gentry* • Marianna Hill *Germaine* • Suzanne Zenor *Alba* • Beatrice Manley Blau *Judith* • David Manzy *Baby* ▪ *Dir* Ted Post • *Scr* Abe Polsky

The Baby and the Battleship ★★ U
Comedy   1956 · UK · Colour · 95mins

It was in Malta, when shooting this picture, that Bryan Forbes coined his nickname for Richard Attenborough. "Bunter" he called him and "Bunter" he remained, owing to Attenborough's addiction to chocolate. Nowadays that little piece of trivia is of rather more significance than the movie, which is a juvenile comedy about an Italian baby smuggled aboard HMS *Gillingham* while the ship is docked in Naples. Joining Attenborough and Forbes in the cast are John Mills (of course) and Michael Hordern as the captain. It's all too twee for words and the single joke is stretched almost beyond endurance.

John Mills *Puncher Roberts* • Richard Attenborough *Knocker White* • Bryan Forbes *Professor* • Harold Siddons *Whiskers* • Clifford Mollison *Sails* • Lionel Jeffries *George* • Gordon Jackson *Harry* • Michael Howard *Joe* •

U = SUITABLE FOR ALL   Uc = SUITABLE FOR ALL, ESPECIALLY FOR YOUNG CHILDREN (VIDEO ONLY)   PG = PARENTAL GUIDANCE

Michael Hordern *Captain* • Ernest Clark *Commander Digby* • Lisa Gastoni *Maria* • Martyn Garrett *Baby* ■ *Dir* Jay Lewis • *Scr* Jay Lewis, Gilbert Hackforth-Jones, from the novel by Anthony Thorne

Baby Boom ★★★ PG

Comedy   1987 · US · Colour · 105mins

Diane Keaton stars as a ruthless New York executive whose business ambitions falter when she's forced to foster a dead relative's baby girl. The men in her life – boss Sam Wanamaker and lover Harold Ramis – aren't sympathetic to her new working mother status, so she buys a money-pit mansion in the country and tries to make it on her own, with local veterinarian Sam Shepard popping in to borrow an egg or two. Allegedly pro-feminist, it still defines a woman by the males who influence her, though with its mix of cuteness and acuteness, it's one of Keaton's most likeable films. Contains some swearing and brief nudity.

Diane Keaton *JC Wiatt* • Harold Ramis *Steven Buchner* • Sam Wanamaker *Fritz Curtis* • Sam Shepard *Dr Jeff Cooper* • James Spader *Ken Arrenberg* • Pat Hingle *Hughes Larrabee* • Britt Leach *Vern Boone* • Kristina Kennedy *Elizabeth Wiatt* • Michelle Kennedy *Elizabeth Wiatt* • Kim Sebastian *Robin* ■ *Dir* Charles Shyer • *Scr* Nancy Meyers, Charles Shyer

Baby Brokers ★★

Drama   1994 · US · Colour · 87mins

Mimi Leder (who's gone from directing episodes of *ER* to films such as *The Peacemaker*) was responsible for this slight TV movie starring Cybill Shepherd. Shepherd plays a wealthy LA doctor whose wish to adopt a child is about to be realised, but the dream turns into a nightmare. The role gives Shepherd a bit more range than usual, but the film gets bogged down by its predictable plot and the run-of-the-mill performances from the cast.

Cybill Shepherd *Debbie Freeman* • Nina Siemaszko *Leeanne* • Tom O'Brien *Frankie* • Anna Maria Horsford *Randi* • Jeffrey Nordling *John* • Joseph Maher *Leo* • Shirley Knight *Sylvia* • Gary Werntz *Dick Plager* ■ *Dir* Mimi Leder • *Scr* Susan Nanus

The Baby Dance ★★★

Drama   1998 · US · Colour · 95mins

In this moving examination of surrogacy and adoption, Laura Dern and Richard Lineback play a poor couple expecting their fifth child who agree to give their baby to infertile, middle-class Stockard Channing and Peter Riegert. However, the deal soon turns sour and a bitter battle ensues. The ever reliable Channing delivers a bravura performance and writer/director Jane Anderson, adapting her own play, invests the project with a gritty realism that is rarely seen in TV movies. Jodie Foster serves as co-executive producer.

Laura Dern *Wanda LeFauve* • Stockard Channing *Rachel Luckman* • Peter Riegert *Richard Luckman* • Richard Lineback *Al LeFauve* • Sandra Seacat *Doreen* • Wally Dalton *Ron Callaway* • Stephen E Miller *Dr Selby* • Heather McEwen *Patricia* ■ *Dir* Jane Anderson • *Scr* Jane Anderson, from her play

Baby Doll ★★★ PG

Melodrama   1956 · US · BW · 109mins

The film that scandalised America has been tamed by the passage of some four decades. It is hard to keep a smile off one's face at the thought of millions of respectable citizens being pinned back in their seats by the emotional G-force emanating from the screen and their own sense of delicious guilt. Yet Tennessee Williams's screenplay is not without its highlights, thanks to the skilled direction of his favourite film-maker, Elia Kazan, notably the scene on a swing in which Eli Wallach, in his film debut, seeks revenge on arsonist Karl Malden by seducing his bride. 📺

Karl Malden *Archie* • Carroll Baker *Baby Doll* • Eli Wallach *Silva Vacarro* • Mildred Dunnock *Aunt Rose Comfort* • Lonny Chapman *Rock* • Eades Hogue *Town Marshall* • Noah Williamson *Deputy* ■ *Dir* Elia Kazan • *Scr* Tennessee Williams, from his story

Baby Face ★★★

Drama   1933 · US · BW · 68mins

A tour-de-force performance from the incomparable Barbara Stanwyck enlivens this tale of a small-town girl who makes it to the mansion by using and abusing every gullible schmuck who crosses her silk-stockinged path. This is essentially a pretty ordinary movie – everything moves along predictably and the clichés have been shared out even-handedly – made extraordinary by its star who is in her sashaying, gimlet-eyed, "don't mess with me" prime. Keep an eye out for a youthful John Wayne, but everyone is acted off the screen by Stanwyck.

Barbara Stanwyck *Lily "Baby Face" Powers* • George Brent *Trenholm* • Donald Cook *Stevens* • Arthur Hohl *Sipple* • John Wayne *Jimmy McCoy* • Henry Kolker *Mr Carter* • Margaret Lindsay *Ann Carter* • Theresa Harris *Chico* ■ *Dir* Alfred E Green • *Scr* Gene Markey, Kathryn Scola, from a story by Mark Canfield [Darryl F Zanuck]

Baby Face Morgan ★★

Crime comedy   1942 · US · BW · 60mins

PRC was the quintessential Poverty Row studio, grinding out B-movies with speed but little else. Today, there's a perverse charm in watching these hour-long films. In this would-be gangster comedy the camerawork is so inept and the sets so obviously cheap that the very incompetence of the production makes for compulsive viewing. Richard Cromwell plays the title mobster's son who gets embroiled in an insurance scam. This is poor quality stuff, but it's enlivened by sterling work from a cast headed by perpetual B-movie girl Mary Carlisle and King Kong's discoverer, Robert Armstrong.

Mary Carlisle *Virginia Clark* • Richard Cromwell *"Baby Face" Morgan* • Robert Armstrong *"Doc" Rogers* • Chick Chandler *Oliver Harrison* • Charles Judels *"Deacon" Davis* • Warren Hymer *Wise Willie* ■ *Dir* Arthur Dreifuss • *Scr* Edward Dein, Jack Rubin, from a story by Oscar Brodney, Jack Rubin

Baby Face Nelson ★★★

Film noir crime drama   1957 · US · BW · 84mins

Casting Mickey Rooney, the baby face of all those cutesy MGM movies, was a wonderfully subversive idea, and Rooney turns in an energetic, scary and convincing performance as the thirties' principal psychotic. Falling in with Leo Gordon's gang, Rooney goes bonkers and becomes America's Public Enemy Number One. Carolyn Jones is the girlfriend who finally puts him out of his misery. What really distinguishes this movie is its refusal to moralise: it's a slick, sick celebration of anti-social behaviour.

Mickey Rooney *Lester "Baby Face Nelson" Gillis* • Carolyn Jones *Sue* • Cedric Hardwicke *Doc Saunders* • Chris Dark *Jerry* • Emile Meyer *Mac* • Tony Caruso [Anthony Caruso] *Hamilton* • Leo Gordon *John Dillinger* • Dan Terranova *Miller* • Elisha Cook Jr *Van Meter* ■ *Dir* Don Siegel • *Scr* Irving Shulman, Geoffrey Homes [Daniel Mainwaring], from a story by Irving Shulman

Baby Geniuses ★ PG

Comedy fantasy adventure   1999 · US · Colour · 94mins

This rotten, infantile comedy makes *Baby's Day Out* look the height of grown-up sophistication and signals a new career low for that talented actress, Kathleen Turner. She plays a nasty children's magnate who is carrying out tests on a host of brainy litte nippers on the shaky premise that infants can actually converse in a secret language. However, she meets her match in twins, played irritatingly by triplets Leo, Myles and Gerry Fitzgerald. The grown-ups look like they want to get the ordeal over as soon as possible, while the artlessly staged slapstick will amuse only toddlers. Contains mild swearing.

Kathleen Turner *Elena* • Christopher Lloyd *Heep* • Kim Cattrall *Robin* • Peter MacNicol *Dan* • Dom DeLuise *Lenny* • Ruby Dee *Margo* • Kyle Howard *Dickie* • Kaye Ballard *Mayor* ■ *Dir* Bob Clark • *Scr* Bob Clark, Greg Michael, from a story by Steven Paul, Francisca Matos, Robert Grasmere

Baby It's You ★★★ 15

Romantic comedy drama   1983 · US · Colour · 100mins

One of the earlier films of the determinedly independent writer/director John Sayles, this is a slice-of-life drama set in 1960s New Jersey. It centres on the bid by an Italian Catholic boy (Vincent Spano) to romance a middle-class Jewish girl (Rosanna Arquette). Sayles's talents weren't yet fully formed, and the film rather runs out of steam in the later stages. But the attention to detail, plus some bursts of typically sharp Sayles dialogue, are indicative of the movie mastery he would exhibit in later films such as *Matewan* and *Lone Star*. Matthew Modine has his film debut and there's an early appearance by Robert Downey Jr. 📺

Rosanna Arquette *Jill Rosen* • Vincent Spano *"Sheikh" Capadilupo* • Joanna Merlin *Mrs Rosen* • Jack Davidson *Dr Rosen* • Nick Ferrari *Mr Capadilupo* • Dolores Messina *Mrs Capadilupo* • Robert Downey Jr *Stewart* ■ *Dir* John Sayles • *Scr* John Sayles, from a story by Amy Robinson

The Baby Maker ★★ 18

Drama   1970 · US · Colour · 104mins

An early investigation into surrogate motherhood, as childless couple Sam Groom and Collin Wilcox-Horne hire hippy Barbara Hershey to have a child by the husband. An explosive situation – Hershey falls for the husband, while lover Scott Glenn gets jealously uptight – is played for all it's worth, but the characters are so self-centred they cast no social shadows, other than their own emotional dilemmas. What might have been a compelling comment on surrogacy becomes obscured by soapy lather. Following this, director Bridges made *The Paper Chase* and *The China Syndrome*. 📺

Barbara Hershey *Tish Gray* • Collin Wilcox-Horne *Suzanne Wilcox* • Sam Groom *Jay Wilcox* • Scott Glenn *Ted Jacks* • Jeannie Berlin *Charlotte* • Lili Valenty *Mrs Culnick* ■ *Dir/Scr* James Bridges

Baby Makes Three ★

Romantic comedy   1988 · US · Colour · 100mins

Three may also be the number of people who will be able to sit through this nonsense until the end. Jane Curtin (*Third Rock from the Sun*) is the middle-aged woman who decides she wants to have a baby with her 57-year-old husband Dabney Coleman. But he is happy as he is, and she has a career and a packed social life, so expect many supposedly amusing moments as the pair try to cope with parenthood. This weak tale would have fared marginally better condensed into a half-hour sitcom episode.

Dabney Coleman *Hal Maxwell* • Jane Curtin *Julia Maxwell* • Julia Duffy *Casey* • David Bowe *Mark* • Florence Stanley *Ebba* • Peter Michael Goetz *Mayor Maneri* ■ *Dir* Tom Moore • *Scr* Jane Kovalcik

Baby Monitor: Sound of Fear ★ 15

Thriller   1998 · US · Colour · 85mins

An unhappily married businessman (Jason Beghe) falls in love with his child's nanny and soon the illicit lovers are contemplating a possible future together, while he makes plans to end his marriage. When his wife learns of the affair, she decides to take revenge. The unsuspecting nanny (*Melrose Place*'s Josie Bissett) overhears a murderous plot on the baby monitor and discovers that she is the intended victim. Clichéd characterisation and dull plotting by writer/director Walter Klenhard make this cheesy US cable movie a disappointment.

Josie Bissett *Ann* • Jason Beghe *Matt Whitten* • Barbara Tyson *Carol Whitten* • Jeffrey Noah *Peter Whitten* ■ *Dir* Walter Klenhard • *Scr* Walter Klenhard, from the film *Babyfon* by Edgar Van Cossart

The Baby of Macon ★★★ 18

Period drama   1993 · UK · Colour · 121mins

There's a certain irony in the fact that a film about the deceptiveness of appearance should itself glitter without ever being golden. Thanks to Sacha Vierny's sumptuous photography, this is a visual if disturbing delight, but director Peter Greenaway allows his twin penchants for thematic controversy and stylistic contrivance to run away with him. In deriding the faith and rituals of Christianity, he finds himself unable to resist the visual temptations offered by its art and architecture, while the theatricality of the action sits uncomfortably with Greenaway's highly cinematic style. A British film, this was made with money from almost every European country. Contains violence and nudity. ▣

Julia Ormond *Daughter* • Ralph Fiennes *Bishop's son* • Philip Stone *Bishop* • Jonathan Lacey *Cosimo Medici* • Don Henderson *Father Confessor* • Celia Gregory *Mother Superior* • Jeff Nuttall *Major Domo* ■ *Dir/Scr* Peter Greenaway

Baby on Board ★★ PG
Romantic comedy thriller
1993 · Can · Colour · 86mins

Beware the innocent title: there are precious few cuddly moments in this thriller, and the dribbling chin shots are confined to a posse of Brylcreemed mafiosos who follow taxi driver Judge Reinhold and passengers Carol Kane and her young daughter. This is basically one very long and very predictable chase movie, in which squealing brakes and interior car shots dominate so exclusively that the entire cast could have shot this trouserless and we'd be none the wiser. ▣

Judge Reinhold *Ernie* • Carol Kane *Maria* • Geza Kovacs *Carmine* • Alex Stapley *Angelica* • Conrad Bergschneider *Lorenzo* • Lou Pitoscias *Vincenzo* • Jason Blicker *Frankie* • Holly Stapley *Angelica* ■ *Dir* Francis A Schaeffer • *Scr* Damian Lee, James Shavick, from a story by Doug Moore

Baby: Secret of the Lost Legend ★★★ PG
Comedy adventure
1985 · US · Colour · 88mins

Despite looking really cheesy compared to more modern *Jurassic Park*-style fare, Disney's old-fashioned adventure fantasy is a pleasant enough tale about palaeontologist Sean Young and her sports writer husband William Katt discovering a brontosaurus family in Africa. Scientist Patrick McGoohan is the villain of the prehistoric puff piece who wants the baby bronto brought back to civilisation. Veering from cute to violent, an unevenness matched by Bill L Norton's direction, this reworked *Lost World* tale is too bland to properly satisfy. Yet kids will love the huggable Baby, for all its winsome plasticity. Contains some nudity. ▣

William Katt *George Loomis* • Sean Young *Susan Matthews-Loomis* • Patrick McGoohan *Dr Erick Kiviat* • Julian Fellowes *Nigel Jenkins* • Kyalo Mativo *Cephu* • Hugh Quarshie *Kenge Obe* • Edward Hardwicke *Dr Pierre Dubois* ■ *Dir* Bill Norton [Bill L Norton] • *Scr* Clifford Green, Ellen Green

The Baby-Sitter's Club ★★★
Comedy drama drama
1995 · US · Colour · 85mins

Based on the Ann M Martin novels for young girls (positive pre-teen bibles in the US, but relatively unknown in the UK), this has former *thirtysomething* star Melanie Mayron in the director's chair. It's an agreeable story concerning a group of young girls

dealing with parents, romance and baby-sitting while earning extra money looking after kids at a day camp. Sissy Spacek's daughter, Schuyler Fisk, appeared in her first starring role and, despite a nice performance, has done very little since. Her co-star Rachael Leigh Cook has had more success in the teen romance *She's All That*.

Schuyler Fisk *Kristy* • Bre Blair *Stacey* • Rachael Leigh Cook *Mary Anne* • Larisa Oleynik *Dawn* • Tricia Joe *Claudia* • Stacey Linn Ramsower *Mallory* • Zelda Harris *Jessi* • Vanessa Zima *Rosie Wilder* • Bruce Davison *Watson* • Ellen Burstyn *Mrs Haberman* ■ *Dir* Melanie Mayron • *Scr* Dalene Young, from the novels story by Ann M Martin

Baby Snatcher ★★ PG
Thriller 1992 · US · Colour · 88mins

An emotionally charged, headline-making true story is given the thriller treatment by director Joyce Chopra, who turns here to TV movies following limited success with cinema-released features. Veronica Hamel, best known for her role as lawyer Joyce Davenport in the TV series *Hill Street Blues*, plays a woman who plans to abduct a baby following her miscarriage. Michael Madsen, the ear-slicing Mr Blonde in *Reservoir Dogs*, plays Hamel's husband, while *X Files* star David Duchovny also puts in an appearance. A fair attempt at a tough subject. ▣

Veronica Hamel *Bianca Hudson* • Nancy McKeon *Karen Williams* • Michael Madsen *Cal Hudson* • David Duchovny *David* ■ *Dir* Joyce Chopra • *Scr* Susan Rhinehart

Baby, Take a Bow ★★ U
Crime drama 1934 · US · BW · 75mins

This was Shirley Temple's first starring vehicle after Fox signed her to a seven-year contract. She had her sixth birthday while making it and enchanted critics and audiences with her performance as the daughter of an ex-convict (James Dunn) who saves him from false accusations of theft. Temple and Dunn perform the song *On Account-a I Love You*, while Claire Trevor plays her mother and Alan Dinehart is a crooked detective. American women's groups winced at such a young child being seen mixed up with criminals.

Shirley Temple *Shirley Ellison* • James Dunn *Eddie Ellison* • Claire Trevor *Kay Ellison* • Alan Dinehart *Welch* • Ray Walker *Larry Scott* • Dorothy Libaire *Jane* ■ *Dir* Harry Lachman • *Scr* Philip Klein, Ee Paramore Jr, from the play *Square Crooks* by James P Judge

Baby the Rain Must Fall ★★★
Drama 1965 · US · BW · 98mins

The great Steve McQueen in one of his sombre roles, fresh out of jail and reunited with his wife, played by Lee Remick, and the daughter he has never seen. He has a nothing job by day but sings with a band at night, though any hopes he has of fame are dashed by his foster mother, a domineering woman who becomes the catalyst for later events. McQueen and Remick are both excellent, while Robert Mulligan's direction not only eschews any easy melodramatics, but also beautifully evokes the flatness and deadness of small-town Texas, all

of which acts as a tinderbox for McQueen's pent-up emotions.

Lee Remick *Georgette Thomas* • Steve McQueen *Henry Thomas* • Don Murray *Slim* • Paul Fix *Judge Ewing* • Josephine Hutchinson *Mrs Ewing* • Ruth White *Miss Clara* • Charles Watts *Mr Tillman* • Carol Veazie *Mrs Tillman* • Estelle Hemsley *Catherine* ■ *Dir* Robert Mulligan • *Scr* Horton Foote

Babycakes ★★★
Romantic comedy 1989 · US · Colour

Ricki Lake is perhaps better known to most viewers today as a chat-show host than as the kooky actress who made her name in the movies of trash king John Waters. Although she's her usual lively self here, she has a hard act to follow in this TV-movie remake of German director Percy Adlon's cult hit *Sugarbaby*, since the outsize and outlandish Marianne Sägebrecht gave such a fine performance as the lovesick mortician in the original. Director Paul Schneider elicits attractive performances from Lake and her co-star Craig Sheffer, but it's still not a patch on the first movie. Contains some swearing.

Ricki Lake *Grace Johnson* • Craig Sheffer *Rob* • John Karlen *Grace's father* • Betty Buckley *Grace's stepmother* • Nada Despotovich *Keri* ■ *Dir* Paul Schneider • *Scr* Joyce Eliason

Babyfever ★★★
Comedy drama 1994 · US · Colour · 110mins

Constantly threatening to outstay its welcome, yet always managing to come up with another worthwhile line of inquiry, Henry Jaglom's typically talky treatise on babies was clearly inspired by the fact he had just fathered a second child with his wife, the film's star Victoria Foyt. As Gena, Foyt is so tormented by the ticking of her biological clock that she can barely make a rational choice between dull, worthy boyfriend Matt Salinger and her reckless ex, Eric Roberts. The verbosity of the baby-shower scene will alienate many, but some of the insights are disarmingly honest – if not particularly original. Contains swearing.

Victoria Foyt *Gena* • Matt Salinger *James* • Dinah Lenney *Roz* • Eric Roberts *Anthony* • Frances Fisher *Rosie* • Elaine Kagan *Milly* • Zack Norman *Mark* ■ *Dir* Henry Jaglom • *Scr* Henry Jaglom, Victoria Foyt

Babylon ★★★
Drama 1980 · UK · Colour · 94mins

This ground-breaking British film about contemporary black life in London was not the first of its kind, but it was the first to give white audiences an insight into the significance of such things as "sound systems", the Stop-and-Search Law and Rastafarianism. The action revolves around young garage mechanic Blue, who is trying to take part in a sound-system contest while dealing with domestic, racial and cultural pressures. Natural performances and desolate locations give a vivid impression of south London life prior to the real-life riots, only a year ahead. In English and Jamaican patois with subtitles.

Karl Howman *Ronnie* • Trevor Laird *"Beefy"* • Brian Bovell *"Spark"* • Victor Evans Romero *"Lover"* • David N Haynes *Errol* • Archie Pool *"Dreadhead"* • T Bone Wilson *Wesley* • Mel

Smith *Alan* • Bill Moody *Man on balcony* ■ *Dir* Franco Rosso • *Scr* Martin Stellman, Franco Rosso

Babymother ★★ 15
Musical comedy drama
1998 · UK · Colour · 78mins

Writer/director Julian Henriques's feature debut has in its favour an undeniable energy and a gutsy performance from Anjela Lauren Smith, as the mother of two battling against the odds and the indifference of her partner to become a reggae singer. Yet too often the narrative is hijacked by musical interludes, which, with the exception of the final gig, do little to further our understanding of either Smith's tangled personal history or the chauvinism of the record business. It has a *Secrets and Lies* feel, but there's insufficient dramatic focus. Contains swearing, some mild violence and a sex scene. ▣

Anjela Lauren Smith *Anita* • Caroline Chikezie *Sharon* • Jocelyn Esien *Yvette* • Wil Johnson *Byron* • Don Warrington *Luther* • Tameka Empson *Dionne* • Diane Bailey *Bee* • Vas Blackwood *Caesar* • Andrea Francis *Yvette's Sister* ■ *Dir* Julian Henriques • *Scr* Julian Henriques, Vivienne Howard

Baby's Day Out ★★★ PG
Comedy 1994 · US · Colour · 94mins

Love him or hate him, John Hughes certainly hit upon a winning formula with *Home Alone*. Here he comes up with another successful spin on the small-things-humiliating-adults theme, with a wee baby standing in for Macaulay Culkin. The little tot – the precious child of a wealthy family – is snatched by a bungling trio of kidnappers and blithely proceeds to make their life hell. Unsurprisingly, wit and subtlety are hardly to the fore. However, the action does rip along at a cracking pace, the comic set pieces are executed with precision, and Joe Mantegna, Joe Pantoliano and Brian Haley are good fun as the crooks. ▣

Joe Mantegna *Eddie Mauser* • Lara Flynn Boyle *Laraine Cotwell* • Joe Pantoliano *Norby Leblaw* • Brian Haley *Veeko Riley* • Cynthia Nixon *Gilbertine* • Fred Dalton Thompson *FBI Agent Grissom* ■ *Dir* Patrick Read Johnson • *Scr* John Hughes

The Babysitter ★ 18
Thriller 1995 · US · Colour · 85mins

It's hard to see how this trashy drama could have come from such a respectable source as a short story by Robert Coover. What's less surprising is why this litany of tired sex fantasies went straight to video. Indeed, we might never have heard of it at all had not Alicia Silverstone scored such a huge hit in the same year with *Clueless*. She has little to do here but look alluring as her employers and their neighbours contemplate soft-core encounters in a series of daydreams that only rarely rise above the squalid. George Segal and JT Walsh, in particular, should have known better. Contains violence, swearing, substance abuse and nudity. ▣

Alicia Silverstone *Jennifer* • Jeremy London *Jack* • JT Walsh *Harry Tucker* • Lee Garlington *Dolly Tucker* • Nicky Katt *Mark* • Lois Chiles

Bernice Holsten • George Segal *Bill Holsten* ■ *Dir* Guy Ferland • *Scr* Guy Ferland, from the short story by Robert Coover

The Babysitters ★ PG

Action comedy · 1994 · US · Colour · 88mins

Fortunately, not all American phenomenons are embraced enthusiastically over here. This is a case in point: twins Peter and David Paul, AKA the Barbarian Brothers, were wrestling stars who had a pop at breaking into the movies (they had at least half a dozen goes). This has the muscley morons in *Home Alone* territory as they are given the job of minding spoilt twins. The slapstick will leave most viewers stone-faced while the Barbarians' acting abilities make Hulk Hogan look like Kevin Spacey. Look out for George Lazenby in a cameo role. ▢

David Paul *David Falcone* • Peter Paul *Peter Falcone* • Christian Cousins *Bradley* • Joseph Cousins *Steven* • George Lazenby *Stromm* ■ *Dir/Scr* John Paragon

The Babysitter's Seduction ★★★

Thriller · 1996 · US · Colour · 85mins

Babysitters get some rough treatment in American films (remember Jamie Lee Curtis in *Halloween*?), and this intriguing TV-movie thriller is no exception. Keri Russell is the teenager who finds herself in all sorts of trouble when the wife of one of her employers turns up dead; detective Phylicia Rashad, better known as Bill Cosby's other half in *The Cosby Show*, suspects foul play and Russell is her prime suspect. Director David Burton Morris maintains the suspense throughout and the denouement will provoke gasps of surprise.

Stephen Collins *Bill Bartrand* • Keri Russell *Michelle Winston* • Phylicia Rashad *Detective Kate Jacobs* • Tobin Bell *Frank O'Keefe* • John D'Aquino *Paul Richards* • Linda Kelsey *Alice Winston* ■ *Dir* David Burton Morris • *Scr* Shirley Tallman, Nancy Hersage

The Bacchantes ★★

Drama · 1960 · Fr/It · Colour · 100mins

Euripides receives the sword-and-sandal treatment in this rattling ancient adventure that, like so many of its ilk, is a little hit and myth. Akim Tamiroff, the selfless support in many a Hollywood picture, gets his moment in the sun as Tiresias, who predicts disaster when the people of Thebes abandon their faith in the city's god, Bacchus. Over-plotted, overplayed, and not over quickly enough. In Italian with English subtitles.

Taina Elg *Dirce* • Pierre Brice *Dionysus* • Alessandra Panaro *Manto* • Alberto Lupo *Pentheus* • Akim Tamiroff *Tiresias* ■ *Dir* Giorgio Ferroni • *Scr* Giorgio Stegani, Giorgio Ferroni, from the play *The Bacchae* by Euripides

Bach and Broccoli ★★★ U

Comedy drama · 1986 · Can · Colour · 95mins

A box-office sensation in its native Quebec, the *Tales for All* series of children's films won over 100 international awards. This third entry brought about a reunion between producer Rock Demers and André Melançon, who directed the first film in the series, *The Dog Who Stopped the War*. Mahée Paiement is hugely impressive as the 11-year-old orphan who arrives with her pet skunk, Bottine (or Broccoli), to disrupt the ordered life of her uncle, Raymond Legault. Maintaining a light touch, Melançon doesn't labour his life lessons. French dialogue dubbed into English.

Mahée Paiement *Fanny* • Raymond Legault *Jonathan* • Harry Marciano *Sean* • Andrée Pelletier *Bernice* ■ *Dir* André Melançon • *Scr* Bernadette Renaud, André Melançon

The Bachelor ★★★

Romantic drama · 1990 · It · Colour · 105mins

Roberto Faenza directs Keith Carradine, Miranda Richardson and Kristin Scott Thomas in a drama about loss and love, adapted from Arthur Schnitzler's novel. Carradine, a middle-class, middle-aged doctor who has never married, is devastated when his close sibling (Richardson) commits suicide. He subsequently embarks on a string of sexual liaisons with three women, one of whom is played by Richardson in a secondary role. This understated and atmospheric drama about midlife crisis and masculinity is a fine example of good European cinema – an all-too-rare occurrence in the age of the Europudding.

Keith Carradine *Dr Emil Grasler* • Miranda Richardson *Frederica/Widow* • Kristin Scott Thomas *Sabine* • Sarah-Jane Fenton *Katerina* • Max von Sydow *Von Schleheim* ■ *Dir* Roberto Faenza • *Scr* Enrico DeConcini, Roberto Faenza, Hugh Fleetwood (English language version), from the novel *Dr Grasler, Spa Physician* by Arthur Schnitzler • *Music* Ennio Morricone

The Bachelor ★★ 12

Romantic comedy · 1999 · US · Colour · 101mins

This weak update of Buster Keaton's 1925 classic *Seven Chances* stars Chris O'Donnell as a young man who must get married by his 30th birthday (just 24 hours away) if he is to inherit $100 million dollars from his deceased grandfather. His girlfriend (Renee Zellweger) has already given up on him, so it's up to O'Donnell to try all his ex-girlfriends. Unfortunately, no matter how pretty his face is, O'Donnell lacks both the charisma and comic timing to hold this unfunny film together. Despite a nicely bitchy turn from Brooke Shields and the well-choreographed scene in which O'Donnell is chased through San Francisco by a horde of wedding dress-wearing women, this has few touching or amusing moments.

Chris O'Donnell *Jimmy Shannon* • Renee Zellweger *Anne* • Hal Holbrook *O'Dell* • James Cromwell *Priest* • Artie Lange *Marco* • Edward Asner [Ed Asner] *Gluckman* • Marley Shelton *Natalie* • Sarah Silverman *Carolyn* • Peter Ustinov *Grandad* • Mariah Carey *Ilana* • Brooke Shields *Buckley* ■ *Dir* Gary Sinyor • *Scr* Steve Cohen, from the film *Seven Chances* by Clyde Bruckman, Jean Havez, Joseph A Mitchell, from the play by Roi Cooper Megrue

Bachelor Apartment ★★★

Drama · 1931 · US · BW · 77mins

It's always interesting to see a Hollywood sex comedy from before when the puritanical Hays Code pooped the party. Here Lowell Sherman, who made a speciality of playing lecherous lovers, is the confirmed bachelor with three women on the go simultaneously. They are ladylike Irene Dunne (in one of her first films), vampish Mae Murray (in one of her last films) and innocent Claudia Dell. It's a trifle theatrical, but Sherman directs smoothly enough; he also directed Mae West's naughty *She Done Him Wrong*.

Lowell Sherman *Wayne Carter* • Irene Dunne *Helene Andrews* • Mae Murray *Agatha Carraway* • Ivan Lebedeff *Henri De Maneau* • Norman Kerry *Lee Graham* • Noel Francis *Janet* • Claudia Dell *Lita Andrews* ■ *Dir* Lowell Sherman • *Scr* John Howard Lawson, J Walter Ruben (adaptation and dialogue)

Bachelor Bait ★★

Romantic comedy · 1934 · US · BW · 74mins

A mediocre little programme filler of interest mainly as an early full-length feature directed by the great George Stevens (later to make his name with *A Place in the Sun*, *Shane* and *Giant*). Stevens, who cut his teeth on Laurel and Hardy shorts, does well by this RKO comedy about a marriage bureau called Romance, Incorporated. It stars the amiable Stuart Erwin and the sexy Rochelle Hudson (imported from Fox), and pert Pert Kelton scores as a gold-digger, but there's little else of real note. No wonder Stevens prefered to view the following year's *Alice Adams* as his directorial debut.

Stuart Erwin *Wilbur Fess* • Rochelle Hudson *Linda* • Pert Kelton *Allie Summers* • Skeets Gallagher *Van Dusen* • Berton Churchill *Big Barney* • Grady Sutton *Don Belden* • Clarence H Wilson [Clarence Wilson] *District Attorney* ■ *Dir* George Stevens • *Scr* Glenn Tryon, from a story by Edward Halperin, Victor Halperin

The Bachelor Father ★★★

Comedy · 1931 · US · BW · 91mins

A rather nice vehicle for the venerable C Aubrey Smith, best known today as a crusty old actor in supporting roles embodying stiff-upper-lippery in such films as the 1937 *Prisoner of Zenda* and the unforgettable 1939 version of *The Four Feathers*. Although Marion Davies and Ralph Forbes are billed above Sir C, this is his picture all the way. He plays the titular role of a man searching for his three grown-up children. Director Robert Z Leonard stands back and just lets the old ham get on with it. He does achieve some genuinely touching moments, but fails to completely disguise the film's theatrical origins. Watch out for Ray Milland in his second screen role.

Marion Davies *Tony Flagg* • Ralph Forbes *John Ashley* • C Aubrey Smith *Sir Basil Winterton* • Ray Milland *Geoffrey Trent* • Guinn "Big Boy" Williams [Guinn Williams] *Dick Berney* • David Torrence *Doctor MacDonald* ■ *Dir* Robert Z Leonard • *Scr* Lawrence E Johnson, from the play by Edward Childs Carpenter

Bachelor Flat ★★★ U

Comedy · 1961 · US · Colour · 91mins

A former cartoonist, director Frank Tashlin scored cinematic bull's-eyes with his colourfully trenchant and hysterical satires, most famously *Son of Paleface* and *The Girl Can't Help It*. Here he cocks an anti-English snoot at California-style education, as girls run hot and cold through professor Terry-Thomas's beachside apartment. Terry-Thomas has had far better scripts than this to get his gapped teeth into; nevertheless he's compulsively watchable, though sadly co-star Celeste Holm is wasted.

Tuesday Weld *Libby Bushmill* • Richard Beymer *Mike Pulaski* • Terry-Thomas *Professor Bruce Patterson* • Celeste Holm *Helen Bushmill* • Francesca Bellini *Gladys* • Howard McNear *Dr Bowman* • Ann Del Guercio *Liz* ■ *Dir* Frank Tashlin • *Scr* Frank Tashlin, Bud Grossman, from the play by Bud Grossman

Bachelor in Paradise ★★★

Comedy · 1961 · US · Colour · 108mins

A typical relic of the Eisenhower era, this breezy satire on American lifestyle and morals stars Bob Hope as a famous travel-writer-cum-sociologist who, for tax reasons, adopts a phoney identity and settles down in a model housing development called "Paradise". The film's targets are marriage (Hope causes three divorces) and modern household gadgetry; the result is like a Jacques Tati version of *The Stepford Wives*. Hope quips his way through the jubilantly sexist material and cop-out ending.

Bob Hope *Adam J Niles* • Lana Turner *Rosemary Howard* • Janis Paige *Dolores Jynson* • Jim Hutton *Larry Delavane* • Paula Prentiss *Linda Delavane* • Don Porter *Thomas W Jynson* • Virginia Grey *Camille Quinlaw* ■ *Dir* Jack Arnold • *Scr* Valentine Davies, Hal Kanter, from a story by Vera Caspary

Bachelor Knight ★★★ U

Comedy · 1947 · US · BW · 95mins

Teenager Shirley Temple has a crush on womaniser Cary Grant (who wouldn't?), so her sister, judge Myrna Loy, orders Grant to wine and dine Temple until she grows sick of him. It's a thin premise for Grant's 50th movie, but sparkling playing and sheer starpower, not to mention Sidney Sheldon's Oscar-winning original screenplay, turned this trifle into one of the top box-office hits of its day. Time hasn't dented its appeal.

Cary Grant *Dick* • Myrna Loy *Margaret* • Shirley Temple *Susan* • Rudy Vallee *Tommy* • Ray Collins *Beemish* • Harry Davenport *Thaddeus* • Johnny Sands *Jerry* • Don Beddoe *Tony* • Lillian Randolph *Bessie* ■ *Dir* Irving Reis • *Scr* Sidney Sheldon

Bachelor Mother ★★★ U

Comedy · 1939 · US · BW · 78mins

Although Ginger Rogers and David Niven are top-billed in this contrived but hugely enjoyable comedy, the real star is that cuddly curmudgeon Charles Coburn. As the department store tycoon who threatens to dismiss Rogers from the toy counter after she finds an abandoned baby, he times every disapproving look to perfection before melting like the big softy he was. Felix Jackson's story earned an Oscar nomination, but it's Norman Krasna's screenplay that merits the praise, along with the slick direction of Garson Kanin. ▢

Ginger Rogers *Polly Parrish* • David Niven *David Merlin* • Charles Coburn *JB Merlin* •

Frank Albertson *Freddie Miller* • EE Clive Butler ■ *Dir* Garson Kanin • *Scr* Norman Krasna, from a story by Felix Jackson

Bachelor of Hearts ★★★ U

Comedy   1958 · UK · Colour · 94mins

Rank flirted with a series of German actors in the fifties, and achieved particular success with Hardy Kruger in *The One That Got Away*. This is Kruger's follow-up to his hit, a rather charming romantic comedy, lovingly photographed on Cambridge locations by the great cameraman Geoffrey Unsworth, directed by the talented Wolf Rilla, and aided by a lovely performance from co-star Sylvia Syms. Today these gauche student antics look a little daft, but they belong to a bygone era, a time depicted here by a pair of young screenwriters who have since become much more famous: Leslie Bricusse, distinguished co-writer of *Stop the World I Want to Get Off*, and Frederic Raphael, who collected an Oscar for *Darling*.

Hardy Kruger *Wolf* • Sylvia Syms *Ann* • Ronald Lewis *Hugo* • Jeremy Burnham *Adrian* • Peter Myers • Philip Gilbert *Conrad* • Charles Kay *Tom* ■ *Dir* Wolf Rilla • *Scr* Leslie Bricusse, Frederic Raphael

The Bachelor Party ★★★★

Drama   1957 · US · BW · 94mins

Screenwriter Paddy Chayefsky's gift for realism-as-fable was never grittier than in this adaptation of his own TV play, in which a bawdy stag-night becomes an odyssey in which the American male's inherent fear of women is brilliantly explored – from porn movies to strip-show to hooker confrontation – all floated along on a river of alcohol. Nervous groom-to-be Philip Abbott is counterbalanced by Don Murray, the married man wondering if he did the right thing, while office bachelor Jack Warden presents a cheery persona to hide his own loneliness. As a companion piece to *Marty*, two years earlier, it has some profound things to say about the macho psyche.

Don Murray *Charlie Samson* • EG Marshall *Walter* • Jack Warden *Eddie* • Philip Abbott *Arnold* • Larry Blyden *Kenneth* • Patricia Smith *Helen Samson* • Carolyn Jones *Existentialist* • Nancy Marchand *Julie* • Karen Norris *Hostess* ■ *Dir* Delbert Mann • *Scr* Paddy Chayefsky, from his TV play

Bachelor Party ★★ 18

Comedy   1984 · US · Colour · 101mins

Chaos ensues as Tom Hanks's bachelor binge degenerates into a bawdy riot, in a plot similar to the formula used in *National Lampoon's Animal House* and *Porky's*. Writer/ director Neal Israel's bid to produce a riotous comedy doesn't really hit the mark, and while Hanks's presence is welcome, he won't be looking back on this as a career highlight. ▭

Tom Hanks *Rick Gassko* • Tawny Kitaen *Debbie Thompson* • Adrian Zmed *Jay O'Neill* • Robert Prescott *Cole Whittier* • George Grizzard *Mr Thompson* • Barbara Stuart *Mrs Thompson* • William Tepper *Dr Stan Gassko* ■ *Dir* Neal Israel • *Scr* Neal Israel, Pat Proft, from a story by Bob Israel

Back Door to Heaven ★★★

Crime drama   1939 · US · BW · 73mins

In its day, this grim 20th Century-Fox melodrama was much-discussed – it's a sort of *Cathy Come Home* about how the underprivileged drift into crime. A teacher awaits the return of former pupils, but one of them has ended up in reform school. Although the nominal star is sturdy Wallace Ford, the most interesting cast member is young Van Heflin as the errant student. Three movies after this one Van Heflin won an Oscar at MGM for *Johnny Eager*.

Aline MacMahon *Miss Williams* • Jimmy Lydon [James Lydon] *Frankie as a boy* • Anita Magee *Carol* • William Harrigan *Mr Rogers* • Jane Seymour (2) *Mrs Rogers* • Robert Wildhack *Rudolph Herzing* • Van Heflin *John Shelley as an adult* ■ *Dir* William K Howard • *Scr* William K Howard, John Bright, Robert Tasker

Back Door to Hell ★★

Second World War drama   1964 · US/Phil · BW · 69mins

The first of four films Jack Nicholson made with director Monte Hellman is a sparse war drama, shot in the Philippines at the same time as *Flight to Fury* and costing around $80,000. Nicholson plays one of three marines who reconnoitre a Japanese-held island ahead of the American invasion force. The jungle location eventually hospitalised everyone with tropical bugs. As far as Nicholson is concerned, the film allows us to see him learning as he goes along without giving any inkling that a major star was in the process of being born.

Jimmie Rodgers *Lieutenant Craig* • Jack Nicholson *Burnett* • John Hackett *Jersey* • Annabelle Huggins *Maria* • Conrad Maga *Paco* • Johnny Monteiro *Ramundo* • Joe Sison *Japanese captain* ■ *Dir* Monte Hellman • *Scr* Richard A Guttman, John Hackett, from a story by Richard A Guttman

Back from Eternity ★★★

Drama   1956 · US · BW · 97mins

Director John Farrow waited 17 years to remake his movie, *Five Came Back* and, if anything, the idea works even better the second time around. Rod Steiger and Robert Ryan star in this story of a plane that crash-lands in cannibal country, using every trick of the acting trade to up-stage each other. It's still an obvious situation, but the budget is better than it was for the 1939 original and the treatment more spectacular. Worth waiting for.

Robert Ryan *Bill* • Anita Ekberg *Rena* • Rod Steiger *Vasquel* • Phyllis Kirk *Louise* • Keith Andes *Joe* • Gene Barry *Ellis* • Fred Clark *Crimp* • Beulah Bondi *Martha* ■ *Dir* John Farrow • *Scr* Jonathan Latimer, from a story by Richard Carroll

Back Home ★★

Drama   1990 · UK/US · Colour

Dripping with Disney sentimentality, yet also benefiting from the studio's customarily impeccable production values, this TV movie will probably prove more popular with grandparents than youngsters. That's because it's set in the postwar period when families were reunited and austerity was briefly forgotten. However young Hayley Carr has nothing to celebrate for, having spent the war in the States,

she no longer feels she belongs in Blighty, especially as mother Hayley Mills is more preoccupied with her husband's homecoming. Decently played by a cast of familiar faces, this has the comforting sweetness of a good mint humbug.

Hayley Mills *Peggy* • Hayley Carr *Rusty* • Rupert Frazer *Roger* • Adam Stevenson *Charlie* • George Clark *Lance* • Mac McDonald *Mitch* • Carol Gillies *Miss Bembridge* • Brenda Kempner *Miss Bullivant* ■ *Dir* Piers Haggard • *Scr* David Wood, from the novel by Michelle Magorian

Back in Action ★★ 18

Action thriller   1993 · Can · Colour · 79mins

When a nasty drug dealer guts his partner, cop Roddy Piper sets his sights on eliminating the gang. At the same time, cabbie Billy Blanks attempts to shelter his uncooperative sister from the same gang, who want her rubbed out because she witnessed the killing. Inevitably the two men work together, though not before butting heads – literally. An incredibly brutal film that boasts about one shoot-out or bone-breaking fight every ten minutes but, to its credit, it doesn't take itself that seriously, and it's sure to please action fans looking for some dumb, violent fun. ▭

"Rowdy" Roddy Piper [Roddy Piper] *Frank Rossi* • Billy Blanks *Billy* • Kai Soremekun *Tara* • Damon D'Oliveria *Gantry* ■ *Dir* Steve DiMarco • *Scr* Karl Schiffman

Back in Business ★★ 18

Action thriller   1997 · US · Colour · 89mins

A watchable action thriller starring Brian Bosworth, a former American football player who made a passable transition to acting. Bosworth is an ex-policeman who gets involved in a sting operation that brings him up against the corrupt cops who got him booted off the force. Philippe Mora specialises in middling second-stringers: he also directed the sci-fi thriller *Communion* and two of the *Howling* sequels. Contains swearing, violence and sex scenes. ▭

Brian Bosworth *Joe Elkhart* • Joe Torry *Tony Dunbar* • Dara Tomanovich *Natalie Waler* • Alan Scarfe *David Ashby* • Aubrey Beavers *Remy* • Brion James *Emery Ryker* ■ *Dir* Philippe Mora • *Scr* George Zateslo, Rick Natkin, David Fuller

Back in the USSR ★ 15

Romantic thriller   1992 · US/Rus · Colour · 83mins

This uninspiring thriller propels Frank Whaley from support roles (where he should, quite frankly, have stayed) to lead protagonist as an American getting lost in the Russian underworld. Encountering the feisty Natalya Negoda (sadly no more impressive a performance), Whaley is drawn into the black market and soon finds himself on the run from the Russian mafia and the police. Negoda and Whaley become romantically entwined but far from generating excitement, their relationship makes the film about as unappealing as a piece of tripe. ▭

Frank Whaley *Archer Sloan* • Natalya Negoda *Lena* • Roman Polanski *Kurilov* • Andrew Divoff *Dimitri* • Dey Young *Claudia* • Ravil Issyanov *Georgi* • Harry Ditson *Whittier* • Brian

Blessed *Chazov* ■ *Dir* Deran Sarafian • *Scr* Lindsay Smith, from a story by Lindsay Smith, Ilmar Taska

Back of Beyond ★★ 15

Romantic crime thriller   1995 · Ausl · Colour · 81mins

This Australian thriller was inspired by the Quentin Tarantino-scripted *True Romance*. However, even though Michael Robertson was a film school contemporary of Peter Weir and Philip Noyce, there's nothing particularly inventive about his blend of outback realism, petty crime and aboriginal spiritualism. Paul Mercurio reveals why we've heard so little of him since *Strictly Ballroom*, as the garage owner still shaken by the death of his sister in a motorcycle accident. Meanwhile a blonde Colin Friels gives a risible rendition of paranoid villainy as he tries to cool the ardour of fellow diamond thief Dee Smart. ▭

Paul Mercurio *Tom* • Colin Friels *Connor* • Dee Smart *Charlie* • John Polson *Nick* • Bob Maza *Gilbert* • Rebekah Elmaloglou *Susan* ■ *Dir* Michael Robertson • *Scr* Richard J Sawyer, Paul Leadon, AM Brooksbank

Back Roads ★★ 15

Comedy drama   1981 · US · Colour · 94mins

A big-hearted hooker in the Deep South falls in love with an unsuccessful boxer who is unable to pay for her services. Together they take to the road to seek better times. Starring Sally Fields and Tommy Lee Jones and directed by Martin Ritt (who helped Fields win an Oscar for *Norma Rae*), this cutesy road movie, dealing with the couple's adventures en route to California, is a journey to nowhere: a collection of outmoded clichés and an awful waste of its talented leads, whose relationship you don't believe in for a minute. ▭

Sally Field *Amy Post* • Tommy Lee Jones *Elmore Pratt* • David Keith *Mason* • Miriam Colon *Angel* • Michael V Gazzo *Tazio* • Dan Shor *Spivey* • M Emmet Walsh *Arthur* ■ *Dir* Martin Ritt • *Scr* Gary DeVore

Back Room Boy ★★ U

Second World War comedy   1942 · UK · BW · 82mins

How many flag-waving British comedies during the Second World War rehashed the old "haunted house full of spies" plot? The year after Will Hay used the premise in *The Ghost of St Michael's*, his regular sidekicks Graham Moffatt and Moore Marriott cropped up in this inferior version set on an Orkney island lighthouse, tailored for the talents of Arthur Askey. The main problem is the film's insistence on hammering home every gag, with Askey particularly at fault. There are compensations, however, notably the by-play between Moffatt and Marriott, and the performance of Googie Withers.

Arthur Askey *Arthur Pilbeam* • Googie Withers *Bobbie* • Moore Marriott *Jerry* • Graham Moffatt *Albert* • Vera Frances *Jane* • Joyce Howard *Betty* ■ *Dir* Herbert Mason • *Scr* Val Guest, Marriott Edgar

Back Stab ★★ 18

Crime thriller
1990 · Can/US · Colour · 87mins

This is one of many ''bunny boiler'' movies made in the wake of *Fatal Attraction*. Most were more fatal than attractive – and this is no exception. James Brolin plays an architect bidding to build a relationship with a woman he's fallen for. But, rather like Michael Douglas's doomed bunny, Brolin soon finds himself embroiled in a hotpot – of murder and mayhem. Meg Foster co-stars. 📼

James Brolin *Cliff Murphy* • Dorothée Berryman *Juliet Powell* • Meg Foster *Sara Rudnik* • June Chadwick *Caroline Chambers* • Brett Halsey *Ken Updike* • Isabelle Truchon *Jennifer* • Robert Morelli *Steve Howe* ■ *Dir* Jim Kaufman • *Scr* Paul Koval

Back Street ★★

Romantic melodrama
1932 · US · BW · 84mins

Adapted from a bestselling novel by the queen of woman's weepies, Fannie Hurst, this tale of the self-sacrificing mistress of a married man, who comes to grief after over 20 years of ''backstreet'' fidelity, would be filmed twice more (in 1941 and 1961) to be wept over by successive generations. This first version, directed by John M Stahl, is the least successful, due to a stilted script and an even more stilted and unattractive performance from John Boles. Ladylike and long-suffering, the accomplished Irene Dunne does, however, radiate her usual sweetness.

Irene Dunne *Ray Schmidt* • John Boles *Walter Saxel* • June Clyde *Freda Schmidt* • George Meeker *Kurt Schendler* • ZaSu Pitts *Mrs Dole* • Shirley Grey *Francine* • Doris Lloyd *Mrs Saxel* ■ *Dir* John M Stahl • *Scr* Gladys Lehman, Lynn Starling, from the novel by Fannie Hurst

Back Street ★★★★

Romantic melodrama
1941 · US · BW · 88mins

This remake of the 1932 film of Fannie Hurst's tear-jerking bestseller about the long-standing mistress of a married man, whose understanding, discretion and fidelity lead only to heartbreak, stars the luminous Margaret Sullavan, who waits in vain for her wealthy banker lover, played by the smoothly sexy Charles Boyer. Both stars pull out all the stops in conveying their different areas of torment under the expert direction of Robert Stevenson and with a little help from an excellent supporting cast. An irresistible period romance, requiring a handy box of Kleenex for a totally enjoyable wallow.

Charles Boyer *Walter Saxel* • Margaret Sullavan *Ray Smith* • Richard Carlson *Curt Stanton* • Frank McHugh *Ed Porter* • Frank Jenks *Harry Niles* • Tim Holt *Richard Saxel* • Peggy Stewart *Freda Smith* • Samuel S Hinds *Felix Darren* ■ *Dir* Robert Stevenson • *Scr* Bruce Manning, Felix Jackson, from the novel by Fannie Hurst

Back Street ★★★★

Romantic melodrama
1961 · US · Colour · 105mins

The third and final version of the three-handkerchief weepie about a long-running and painful love affair between a married man and his mistress

updates the story and gives it the full Ross Hunter treatment. This time the suffering pair are cast for glamour, with Susan Hayward languishing in luxury and sumptuous clothes by Jean Louis, and the glossily good-looking John Gavin playing the object of her tormented affections. David Miller directs efficiently, while Vera Miles supplies an entertaining turn as Gavin's alcoholic wife. It may lack some of the class and poignancy of the 1941 version, but this is nonetheless a shameless and wildly enjoyable melodrama.

Susan Hayward *Rae Smith* • John Gavin *Paul Saxon* • Vera Miles *Liz Saxon* • Charles Drake *Curt Stanton* • Virginia Grey *Janie* • Reginald Gardiner *Dalian* • Tammy Marihugh *Caroline Saxon* • Robert Eyer *Paul Saxon Jr* ■ *Dir* David Miller • *Scr* Eleanore Griffin, William Ludwig, from the novel by Fannie Hurst

Back to Bataan ★★★ PG

Second World War drama
1945 · US · BW · 87mins

MGM scored a tremendous success with the then-topical war film *Bataan* back in 1943, so it was a Hollywood inevitability that the Philippines would be revisited. However, instead of the searing campaign study that was expected, RKO plumped for a routine action film starring John Wayne. Still exciting for all that, the plot features a surprisingly subdued Duke as a colonel leading his unit of guerrillas in an undercover mission through the rather obvious studio foliage to victory. Anthony Quinn fights alongside Wayne, and handles the romantic chores, and it's all expertly directed by former editor Edward Dmytryk. 📼

John Wayne *Colonel Madden* • Anthony Quinn *Captain Andres Bonifacio* • Beulah Bondi *Miss Bertha Barnes* • Fely Franquelli *Dalisay Delgado* • Richard Loo *Major Hasko* • Philip Ahn *Colonel Kuroki* • ''Ducky'' Louie *Maximo* ■ *Dir* Edward Dmytryk • *Scr* Ben Barzman, Richard Landau, from a story by Aeneas MacKenzie, William Gordon

Back to God's Country ★★★

Adventure
1953 · US · Colour · 77mins

One of those tremendously enjoyable Universal co-features that always provided terrific value for money. These films were often used to showcase new talent, and here Rock Hudson makes a splendid job of starring in this rugged James Oliver Curwood story set in the far Canadian north. Hudson is a sea captain, married to the rather colourless Marcia Henderson, who has to face up to the tough weather and an even tougher Steve Cochran. Hudson tackles his plight splendidly, or at least well enough to convince his bosses at Universal he was ready for promotion to A-features: next came *Taza, Son of Cochise*, then his star-making performance in *Magnificent Obsession*.

Rock Hudson *Peter Keith* • Marcia Henderson *Dolores Keith* • Steve Cochran *Paul Blake* • Hugh O'Brian *Frank Hudson* • Chubby Johnson *Billy Shorter* • Tudor Owen *Fitzsimmons* • John Cliff *Joe* ■ *Dir* Joseph Pevney • *Scr* Tom Reed, from the novel by James Oliver Curwood

Back to Hannibal: the Return of Tom Sawyer and Huckleberry Finn ★★ U

Period drama
1990 · US · Colour · 88mins

In this harmless TV movie made for the Disney Channel, the grown-up Huckleberry Finn, now a reporter, and Tom Sawyer, a lawyer, return to Hannibal, Missouri, to come to the aid of ex-slave Jim, falsely accused of murdering Becky Thatcher's husband. Veteran TV director Paul Krasny does an admirable job re-creating the look and feel of small-town life in the late 1800s. However, while screenwriter Roy Johansen tries to capture the style and tone of the original classic, he is no Mark Twain. 📼

Raphael Sbarge *Tom Sawyer* • Megan Follows *Becky Thatcher* • Mitchell Anderson *Huckleberry Finn* • Shea Farrell *Lyle Newman* • Zachary Bennett *Marcus* • Ned Beatty *Duke of Bridgewater* • Paul Winfield *Jim Watson* ■ *Dir* Paul Krasny • *Scr* Roy Johansen, from the characters created by Mark Twain

Back to School ★★ 15

Comedy
1986 · US · Colour · 92mins

Co-written by Harold Ramis, of *Groundhog Day* fame, this ham-fisted comedy has echoes of the Bing Crosby picture *High Time*, in which a wealthy middle-aged man returns to college to prove there's life in the old dog yet. Rodney Dangerfield takes the Bing role here and drives in every gag with the subtlety of a steam hammer. Keith Gordon and Robert Downey Jr try hard as Dangerfield's weedy son and his radical pal, but the standouts are English teacher Sally Kellerman and coach M Emmett Walsh. 📼

Rodney Dangerfield *Thornton Melon* • Keith Gordon *Jason Melon* • Sally Kellerman *Diane Turner* • Burt Young *Lou* • Robert Downey Jr *Derek* • Paxton Whitehead *Philip Barbay* • Terry Farrell *Valerie Desmond* • M Emmett Walsh *Coach Turnbull* ■ *Dir* Alan Metter • *Scr* Steven Kampmann, Will Porter, Peter Torokvei, Harold Ramis, from a story by Rodney Dangerfield, Greg Fields, Dennis Snee

Back to the Future ★★★★★ PG

Comedy adventure
1985 · US · Colour · 111mins

This irresistible combination of dazzling effects and sly comedy propelled Michael J Fox to stardom and Robert Zemeckis to the front rank of Hollywood directors. And time has not robbed it of any of its vitality. Fox plays the young student who travels back in time to the fifties and acts as matchmaker for his future parents. It's beautifully played by the cast (honourable mentions to Christopher Lloyd, Lea Thompson and Crispin Glover), making the most of an ingenious script, which finds time to poke fun at fifties icons between the bouts of time travelling. Zemeckis's direction is equally adroit and he never lets the effects swamp the film. Contains some swearing. 📼

Michael J Fox *Marty McFly* • Christopher Lloyd *Dr Emmett Brown* • Lea Thompson *Lorraine Baines* • Crispin Glover *George McFly* • Thomas F Wilson *Biff Tannen* • Claudia Wells *Jennifer Parker* • Marc McClure *Dave McFly* •

Wendie Jo Sperber *Linda McFly* ■ *Dir* Robert Zemeckis • *Scr* Robert Zemeckis, Bob Gale • *Special Effects* Kevin Pike

Back to the Future Part II ★★★ PG

Comedy adventure
1989 · US · Colour · 103mins

After the success of the first time-travelling caper a sequel was inevitable, although this time around director Robert Zemeckis is guilty of over-gilding the lily. Stars Michael J Fox and Christopher Lloyd are back, along with Lea Thompson and Thomas F Wilson, but the script is too clever for its own good and the film gets bogged down by trying to cram in too many ideas and settings (past, future, alternative universes). The effects, however, are even better than those in the first film. Contains some swearing and violence. 📼

Michael J Fox *Marty McFly/Marty McFly Jr/ Marlene McFly* • Christopher Lloyd *Dr Emmett Brown* • Lea Thompson *Lorraine* • Thomas F Wilson *Biff Tannen/Griff Tannen* • Harry Waters Jr *Marvin Berry* • Charles Fleischer *Terry* • Elisabeth Shue *Jennifer* ■ *Dir* Robert Zemeckis • *Scr* Bob Gale, from a story by Bob Gale, Robert Zemeckis

Back to the Future Part III ★★★★ PG

Comedy adventure
1990 · US · Colour · 113mins

Director Robert Zemeckis's blockbusting trilogy went slightly off the rails with the second segment, but it got right back on track with the concluding instalment. Shot back-to-back with *Part II*, the film is set predominantly in the old West and, as before, the plot revolves around the need to tinker with time and the problem of how to power the trusty DeLorean car so that Fox can get back to the present. Once more Gale and Zemeckis have come up with an ingenious plot and a clutch of in-jokes, including the casting of western favourites Dub Taylor, Harry Carey Jr and Pat Buttram as a trio of old timers in the saloon. The inimitable Fox is again on cracking form and Christopher Lloyd's romance with Mary Steenburgen is surprisingly touching. Contains some swearing. 📼

Michael J Fox *Marty McFly/Seamus McFly* • Christopher Lloyd ''*Doc*'' *Emmett Brown* • Mary Steenburgen *Clara Clayton* • Thomas F Wilson *Buford ''Mad Dog'' Tannen/Biff Tannen* • Lea Thompson *Maggie McFly/Lorraine McFly* • Elisabeth Shue *Jennifer* • Richard Dysart *Barbed wire salesman* • Pat Buttram *Saloon old timer* • Harry Carey Jr *Saloon old timer* • Dub Taylor *Saloon old timer* ■ *Dir* Robert Zemeckis • *Scr* Bob Gale, from a story by Bob Gale, Robert Zemeckis

BackBeat ★★★ 15

Biographical drama
1993 · UK · Colour · 96mins

While a huge improvement on the dismal TV movie *Birth of the Beatles*, Iain Softley's account of the Fab Four's Hamburg days is rather like their music of the time: loud, raw and full of energy. It also betrays a lack of experience, leaving too much to enthusiasm and carrying the audience along on euphoria. Focusing primarily on the relationship between John

Lennon and "Fifth Beatle" Stuart Sutcliffe, it descends into tacky melodrama once Sutcliffe falls for photographer Astrid Kirchherr. Ian Hart is solid enough in another of his outings as Lennon (he played the Beatle in *The Hours and Times*), but Stephen Dorff and Sheryl Lee only occasionally convince as the star-crossed lovers. Contains violence, swearing, drug abuse and nudity.

Sheryl Lee *Astrid Kirchherr* • Stephen Dorff *Stuart Sutcliffe* • Ian Hart *John Lennon* • Gary Bakewell *Paul McCartney* • Chris O'Neill *George Harrison* • Scot Williams *Pete Best* • Kai Wiesinger *Klaus Voormann* • Jennifer Ehle *Cynthia Powell* ■ *Dir* Iain Softley • *Scr* Iain Softley, Michael Thomas, Stephen Ward

Backdraft ★★★★ 15

Action drama 1991 · US · Colour · 131mins

Director Ron Howard has become one of the most accomplished of Hollywood craftsmen, and this sturdy star-studded fare was deservedly a mainstream hit. Kurt Russell and William Baldwin are the two warring, firefighting brothers who have to cope with a rash of fires sparked by a seemingly deranged arsonist, whose lethal "backdrafts" are resulting in death and destruction. The plot is hardly original, but Howard marshals the sprawling elements with great finesse and the fire footage, if harrowing at times, is genuinely exhilarating. Contains swearing, sex scenes and nudity. DVD

Kurt Russell *Stephen McCaffrey* • William Baldwin *Brian McCaffrey* • Robert De Niro *Donald Rimgale* • Jennifer Jason Leigh *Jennifer Vaitkus* • Scott Glenn *John Adcox* • Rebecca De Mornay *Helen Mccaffrey* • Jason Gedrick *Tim Krizminski* • JT Walsh *Martin Swayzak* • Donald Sutherland *Ronald Bartel* ■ *Dir* Ron Howard • *Scr* Gregory Widen

Backfield in Motion ★★ 18

Romantic comedy
1991 · US · Colour · 95mins

Roseanne took a break from her dysfunctional sitcom family for this rare TV-movie outing, but unfortunately left most of her bark behind. She plays a suburban mother, who recruits fellow mums into an American football team that takes on the local high school. Barr's then husband Tom Arnold provides the comic support, but Barr steals the best gags. However, be warned: the sentimentality that started to seep into episodes of *Roseanne* is allowed to run riot here.

Roseanne Arnold [Roseanne] *Nancy Seavers* • Tom Arnold *Howard Peterman* • Colleen Camp *Laurie* ■ *Dir* Richard Michaels • *Scr* Gene O'Neill, Noreen Tobin, Janet Brownell, from a story by Gene O'Neill

Backfire ★

Mystery 1950 · US · BW · 91mins

With Gordon MacRae and Virginia Mayo in the leads, this ought to have been a musical. As an ex-soldier just released from hospital and his obliging nurse, they're clearly unsuited to serious detective work as they investigate the disappearance of Edmond O'Brien, a friend of MacRae's wanted for murder. Too many writers cooked up the convoluted story, with its excess of flashbacks, and Vincent Sherman's direction fails to liven the pace.

Virginia Mayo *Julie Benson* • Gordon MacRae *Bob Corey* • Edmond O'Brien *Steve Connolly* • Dane Clark *Ben Arno* • Viveca Lindfors *Lysa Randolph* • Ed Begley *Capt Garcia* ■ *Dir* Vincent Sherman • *Scr* Larry Marcus, Ivan Goff, Ben Roberts

Backfire ★★ 18

Mystery thriller 1987 · US · Colour · 88mins

Occasionally, films get better performances than they deserve. Here it's Karen Allen and Keith Carradine who rise above the predictable plotting. Allen is pretty convincing, although her plan to bump off husband Jeff Fahey and share his loot with lover Dean Paul Martin is gruyère-like in its feasibility. Things perk up a bit when stranger Keith Carradine gives her a taste of her own hallucinogenic medicine, but Gilbert Cates's direction is too deliberate for any genuine surprises.

Karen Allen *Mara* • Keith Carradine *Reed* • Jeff Fahey *Donnie* • Bernie Casey *Clint* • Dean Paul Martin *Jake* ■ *Dir* Gilbert Cates • *Scr* Larry Brand, Rebecca Reynolds

Background ★★

Drama 1953 · UK · BW · 82mins

This stiff little picture is supposed to be a grown-up drama about the need to adopt a responsible attitude to divorce. However, by overplaying the "for the sake of the children" angle and allowing Valerie Hobson and Philip Friend to bicker in clipped BBC accents, director Daniel Birt succeeds only in drawing unintentional laughs. The question of why anyone would want to stay together for the sake of children as unappealing as those portrayed by Jeremy Spenser and Mandy Miller is never broached.

Valerie Hobson *Barbie Lomax* • Philip Friend *John Lomax* • Norman Wooland *Bill Ogden* • Janette Scott *Jess Lomax* • Mandy Miller *Linda Lomax* • Jeremy Spenser *Adrian Lomax* ■ *Dir* Daniel Birt • *Scr* Warren Chetham Strode, Don Sharp, from the play by Warren Chetham Strode

Background to Danger ★★★

Second World War spy drama
1943 · US · BW · 79mins

One of the few starring roles not turned down by Warner Bros contract artist George Raft (he allegedly said no to *The Maltese Falcon* and *Casablanca* among others), this is a rattling good action film, with smoothie Raft battling Nazis in a studio-bound Turkey (the *Casablanca* sets revamped?). Warner stalwarts and *Casablanca* veterans Sydney Greenstreet and Peter Lorre are on welcome stand-by, but Brenda Marshall (then married to actor William Holden) is unfortunately a rather glamour-less leading lady.

George Raft *Joe Barton* • Brenda Marshall *Tamara* • Sydney Greenstreet *Colonel Robinson* • Peter Lorre *Zaleshoff* • Osa Massen *Ana Remzi* • Turhan Bey *Hassan* • Willard Robertson *McNamara* ■ *Dir* Raoul Walsh • *Scr* WR Burnett, from the novel *Uncommon Danger* by Eric Ambler

Backlash ★★★

Western 1956 · US · Colour · 84mins

A bizarre western with a superbly neurotic Richard Widmark as the gunfighter searching for gold and the sole survivor of a mining party, including his father, that was massacred by Indians. Made just before John Sturges directed the classic *Gunfight at the OK Corral*, this develops into a heavily symbolic, Oedipal and Freudian story that has to be seen to be believed. Intended for director Anthony Mann, it has Mann's regular producer and writer, Aaron Rosenberg and Borden Chase.

Richard Widmark *Jim Slater* • Donna Reed *Karyl Orton* • William Campbell *Johnny Cool* • John McIntire *Jim Bonniwell* • Barton MacLane *George Lake* • Edward Platt *Sheriff Marson* ■ *Dir* John Sturges • *Scr* Borden Chase, from a novel by Frank Gruber

Backlash ★★★

Road movie 1986 · Ausl · Colour · 90mins

Produced, scripted and directed by experienced documentarist Bill Bennett, this highly distinctive road movie gradually builds up suspense through improvised dialogue, off-screen cries in the dead of night, and the disconcerting contrasts between the claustrophobic confines of a police car and the untamed vastness of the Australian outback. The alliances between veteran cop David Argue, rookie Gia Carides and their Aboriginal prisoner Lydia Miller shift a little too slowly at times. The performances are credible, however, and Bennett's use of locations is often inspired. Contains violence, swearing and some nudity.

David Argue *Trevor Darling* • Gia Carides *Nikki Iceton* • Lydia Miller *Kath* • Brian Syron *Executioner* • Anne Smith *Mrs Smith* • Don Smith *Mr Smith* ■ *Dir/Scr* Bill Bennett

Backsliding ★★

Psychological thriller
1991 · Ausl/UK · Colour · 88mins

Made with the backing of FilmFour, this little-seen Australian thriller begins promisingly, only to descend rapidly and irreversibly into clichéd chaos. Director Simon Target handles the set pieces with confidence, but his grasp of character and atmosphere leaves a lot to be desired. Unfortunately, he's given little assistance from a cast headed by Tim Roth, as the drifter whose arrival at an outback gas plant sparks tension between born-again ex-convict Jim Holt and his holier-than-thou wife, Odile LeClezio.

Tim Roth *Tom Whitton* • Jim Holt *Jack Tyson* • Odile LeClezio *Alison Tyson* • Ross McGregor *Pastor* ■ *Dir* Simon Target • *Scr* Simon Target, Ross Wilson

Backstreet Dreams ★★ 18

Drama 1990 · US · Colour · 95mins

Jason O'Malley has no one to blame but himself as he co-produced, wrote and stars in this self-indulgent, contrived tale. It mixes elements of crime and family dramas to no logical effect, and an interesting cast that includes Burt Young and Nick Cassavetes can do little but flounder. O'Malley plays a small-time crook with an autistic child who finds an unlikely friend in PhD psychology student Brooke Shields when his wife (Sherilyn Fenn) leaves him. Contains violence, swearing and drug abuse.

Brooke Shields *Stephanie Bloom* • Jason O'Malley *Dean Costello* • Sherilyn Fenn *Lucy Costello* • Tony Fields *Manny Santana* • Burt Young *Luca Garibaldi* • Anthony Franciosa *Angelo Carnivale* ■ *Dir* Rupert Hitzig • *Scr* Jason O'Malley

Bad ★★★ 18

Comedy 1976 · US · Colour · 58mins

Camp icon Carroll Baker (*Baby Doll*) pulls out all the stops as a Queens housewife using her electrolysis business as a front for a freelance assassination operation. Very funny and very sick (the scene where a baby is thrown out of a window is justly infamous), director Jed Johnson's absurdist excursion into John Waters territory is a hugely satisfying satire on rotten seventies society. Not for those of a nervous disposition.

Carroll Baker *Mrs Aiken* • Perry King *LT* • Susan Tyrrell *Mary Aiken* • Stefania Casini *PG* • Cyrinda Foxe *RC* • Mary Boylan *Grandmother* ■ *Dir* Jed Johnson • *Scr* Pat Hackett, George Abagnalo

The Bad and the Beautiful ★★★★ PG

Drama 1952 · US · BW · 113mins

Riven by political investigation, competition from TV and the realisation that the Golden Age had passed, Hollywood produced a series of withering self-portraits in the early fifties that revealed, beneath the tinsel, a sordidness worthy of Dorian Gray. Full of insider gags, Vincente Minnelli's fizzing melodrama touches more than a few raw nerves as it charts the decline and fall of a movie mogul (Kirk Douglas) through the eyes of a writer (Dick Powell), a director (Barry Sullivan) and an actress (Lana Turner). Allegedly an amalgam of David O Selznick and Val Lewton, the character of Jonathan Shields is made truly detestable by Douglas, who obviously relishes a role rejected by Clark Gable.

Kirk Douglas *Jonathan Shields* • Lana Turner *Georgia Lorrison* • Walter Pidgeon *Harry Pebbel* • Dick Powell *James Lee Bartlow* • Barry Sullivan *Fred Amiel* • Gloria Grahame *Rosemary Bartlow* • Vanessa Brown *Kay Amiel* ■ *Dir* Vincente Minnelli • *Scr* Charles Schnee, from a story by George Bradshaw

Bad Attitudes ★ PG

Comedy 1991 · US · Colour · 88mins

This TV movie rip-off of *Home Alone* might appeal to children under ten, though even they may find it only mildly entertaining. Five precocious summer camp escapees stow away on a billionaire's private jet and find themselves in the middle of a hijacking attempt by a pair of bumbling kidnappers. Richard Gilliland and Maryedith Burrell do their best as the stupid terrorists; since the film revolves around the kids making fun of the adults, however, don't look for scintillating dialogue. Surprisingly, this opus was written by bestselling author Caleb Carr (*The Alienist*).

Richard Gilliland *Jurgen* • Maryedith Burrell *Katyana* • Ethan Randall [Ethan Embry] *Cosmo Coningsby* • Jack Evans *Dabney Mitchell* • Ellen Blain *Jenny* • Eugene Byrd *James* • Meghann Haldeman *Angela* ■ *Dir* Alan Myerson • *Scr* Caleb Carr

U = SUITABLE FOR ALL, Uc = SUITABLE FOR ALL, ESPECIALLY FOR YOUNG CHILDREN (VIDEO ONLY) PG = PARENTAL GUIDANCE

Bad Bascomb ★★ 🔳

Western   1946 · US · BW · 110mins

MGM tried to perk up the career of ageing Wallace Beery by putting him opposite rising moppet Margaret O'Brien as well as teaming him again with character actress Marjorie Main. It's another case of Beery the badman being reformed – this time by O'Brien and Main as members of a Mormon wagon train. Produced to excessive length by the unfortunately named OO Dull, it has its sickly moments but the action pieces of Indian attack and O'Brien's escape from drowning in a swollen river are well enough handled.

Wallace Beery *Zeb Bascomb* • Margaret O'Brien *Emmy* • Marjorie Main *Abbey Hanks* • J Carrol Naish *Bart Yancy* • Frances Rafferty *Dora* • Marshall Thompson *Jimmy Holden* ■ *Dir* Sylvan Simon [S Sylvan Simon] • *Scr* William Lipman, Grant Carrett, from a story by DA Loxley

Bad Behaviour ★★ 🔳

Comedy drama   1992 · UK · Colour · 99mins

A slightly eccentric British comedy of the new Mike Leigh school of movie-making; in other words, wry, improvised, rooted in social nuance and wholly dependent on the audience's recognition of character types. Director Les Blair has fashioned an amusing look at the external stresses that can crack a seemingly idyllic partnership, with Stephen Rea and Sinead Cusack as the oddly cast but affecting pair. Blair doesn't have Leigh's unerring eye for human fallibility, but neither has he the maestro's unfortunate habit of using the working class for target practice. This bobs along pleasingly enough but with a curious lack of soul. Contains drug abuse. 🔲

Stephen Rea *Gerry McAllister* • Sinead Cusack *Ellie McAllister* • Philip Jackson *Howard Spink* • Clare Higgins *Jessica Kennedy* • Phil Daniels *The Nunn Brothers* • Mary Jo Randle *Winifred Turner* • Saira Todd *Sophie Bevan* • Amanda Boxer *Linda Marks* ■ *Dir/Scr* Les Blair

Bad Blood ★★★★ 🔳

Crime drama based on a true story
1982 · UK/NZ · Colour · 109mins

This has been rightly hailed as a key release in New Zealand cinema – even if many of those involved are foreign imports. Based on a notorious murder case, it stars Australian Jack Thompson as a reclusive farmer who refuses to surrender his weapons to the authorities during the Second World War, leading to a violent manhunt. British director Mike Newell keeps the tension simmering, while managing to look sympathetically at the farmer's plight. Thompson is superb, but veteran New Zealand character actor Martyn Sanderson steals the show. 🔲

Jack Thompson *Stanley Graham* • Carol Burns *Dorothy Graham* • Denis Lill *Ted Best* • Donna Akersten *Doreen Bond* • Martyn Sanderson *Les North* • Marshall Napier *Trev Bond* ■ *Dir* Mike Newell • *Scr* Andrew Brown, from the book *Manhunt: The Story of Stanley Graham* by Howard Willis

Bad Boy Bubby ★★★ 🔳

Horror comedy
1993 · Ausl/It · Colour · 109mins

A brave, interesting at times, yet hugely discomforting modern-day *Candide*, this experimental attempt at the cinema of the grotesque will not be to everyone's taste. It's the grim and controversial story of an imprisoned, abused, childlike 35-year-old who has never encountered another human being other than his mother, and what happens when the outside world finally crashes in on his squalid existence. Using differing cinematic styles to relate each of Bubby's peculiar adventures, director Rolf De Heer lets the viewer feel some of Bubby's disorientation. Hugely effective at best, irritating and shocking at worst, you won't ever have seen anything quite like this one. Contains swearing and sex scenes. 🔲

Nicholas Hope *Bubby* • Claire Benito *Mom* • Ralph Cotterill *Pop* • Carmel Johnson *Angel* • Syd Brisbane *Yobbo* • Nikki Price *Screaming woman* • Norman Kaye *Scientist* • Paul Philpot *Paul* ■ *Dir/Scr* Rolf De Heer

Bad Boys ★★★ 🔳

Prison drama   1983 · US · Colour · 104mins

Not the fun Will Smith/Martin Lawrence action comedy, but a far more serious affair about troubled youth starring Sean Penn as a young street thug who tries to steal a pile of drugs from a rival gang, only for it all to go horribly wrong. Penn ends up serving time in the same correctional facility as the rival he tried to cheat. Littered with violence (a revenge rape, shootings, fights) and flashy direction from Rick Rosenthal (*Halloween II*), this can be hard to stomach, but does boast an early strong and neurotic performance from Penn. **DVD**

Sean Penn *Mick O'Brien* • Reni Santoni *Ramon Herrera* • Jim Moody *Gene Daniels* • Eric Gurry *Horowitz* • Esai Morales *Paco Moreno* • Ally Sheedy *JC Walenski* ■ *Dir* Richard L Rosenthal [Rick Rosenthal] • *Scr* Richard DiLello

Bad Boys ★★★★ 🔳

Action comedy thriller
1995 · US · Colour · 114mins

Michael Bay obviously likes blowing things up: in *Armageddon*, the director destroys Paris; in *The Rock* Alcatraz goes up in smoke; here, in his debut, he has to settle for demolishing large chunks of Miami real estate. Of course, there is more to Bay than just an affinity for explosives and *Bad Boys* is a perfect example of his slick directorial abilities. In fact, this is probably the best buddy movie in years, with Bay's eye for cool ultra-violence enhanced by the inspired double-act of Will Smith and Martin Lawrence. The plot revolves around the audacious robbery of a huge cache of heroin. Enter our two heroes: Smith as the womanising bachelor and Lawrence as his married strait-laced partner, who are forced to swap lifestyles to fool the only witness to the crime (Téa Leoni). Contains violence and swearing. 🔲

Martin Lawrence *Marcus Burnett* • Will Smith *Mike Lowrey* • Téa Leoni *Julie Mott* • Tcheky Karyo *Fouchet* • Theresa Randle *Theresa Burnett* • Marg Helgenberger *Alison Sinclair* • Nestor Serrano *Detective Sanchez* ■

Michael Bay • *Scr* Michael Barrie, Jim Mulholland, Doug Richardson, from a story by George Gallo

Bad Company ★★★★ 🔳

Western   1972 · US · Colour · 88mins

An oddball take on the American Civil War, with Jeff Bridges as the leader of runaways from conscription. He's joined by Barry Brown, and the crew become outlaws, drifting towards the Mississippi. (David Huddleston plays the massive menace, Big Joe Simmons.) As an evocation of past times, it's a remarkably successful venture for first-time director Robert Benton, a Robert Altman protégé, who co-wrote *Bonnie and Clyde*. Woody Allen's onetime cinematographer, Gordon Willis, provides the autumnal mood that gives the idea an elegaic resonance. 🔲

Jeff Bridges *Jake Rumsey* • Barry Brown *Drew Dixon* • Jim Davis *Marshal* • David Huddleston *Big Joe* • John Savage *Loney* • Jerry Houser *Arthur Simms* • Damon Cofer *Jim Bob Logan* • Joshua Hill Lewis *Boog Bookin* ■ *Dir* Robert Benton • *Scr* David Newman, Robert Benton • *Cinematographer* Gordon Willis

Bad Company ★★ 🔳

Thriller   1995 · US · Colour · 103mins

On paper this must have looked foolproof – a sexy, serious spin on *Sneakers* – with the two charismatic leads, Laurence Fishburne and Ellen Barkin, capable of generating a fair amount of on-screen steam. However, the plodding direction and an unnecessarily convoluted script put paid to any high expectations, and this went straight to video in Britain. Fishburne plays the newest recruit to a shadowy organisation specialising in industrial espionage, who becomes romantically involved with one of his colleagues (Barkin). The accomplished cast means it is always watchable, but, ultimately, it's a missed opportunity. 🔲

Ellen Barkin *Margaret Wells* • Laurence Fishburne *Nelson Crowe* • Frank Langella *Vic Grimes* • Spalding Gray *Walter Curl* • Michael Beach *Tod Stapp* • Gia Carides *Julie Ames* ■ *Dir* Damian Harris • *Scr* Ross Thomas

Bad Day at Black Rock ★★★★★ 🔳

Western   1955 · US · Colour · 78mins

It is one of the great Oscar travesties that Ernest Borgnine won the best actor award (for *Marty*) in the same year that Spencer Tracy turned in his monumental performance in *Bad Day at Black Rock*. Tracy is at the peak of his powers as the one-armed Second World War veteran who comes to a small town to present a Japanese farmer with his son's posthumous medal, only to discover a dark secret that puts his life in danger. Robert Ryan is also on career-best form as the leader of the rednecks, whose menacing of Tracy is brought to a chilling climax by director John Sturges.

Spencer Tracy *John J Macreedy* • Robert Ryan *Reno Smith* • Anne Francis *Liz Wirth* • Dean Jagger *Tim Horn* • Walter Brennan *Doc Velie* • John Ericson *Pete Wirth* • Ernest Borgnine *Coley Trimble* • Lee Marvin *Hector David* • Russell Collins *Mr Hastings* ■ *Dir* John

Sturges • *Scr* Millard Kaufman, from a story by Howard Breslin • *Cinematographer* William C Mellor

Bad for Each Other ★

Drama   1954 · US · BW · 82mins

Doctor Charlton Heston returns from patching up wounded soldiers in Korea and must decide between a practice in the rich area of Pittsburgh or the nearby mining community. He chooses money and Lizabeth Scott until a catastrophe at the mine makes him rethink his priorities. Made before Heston acquired his epic-hero status, this moral medico-melo was panned by critics and was a major flop.

Charlton Heston *Dr Tom Owen* • Lizabeth Scott *Helen Curtis* • Dianne Foster *Joan Lasher* • Mildred Dunnock *Mrs Mary Owen* • Arthur Franz *Dr Jim Crowley* • Ray Collins *Dan Reasonover* ■ *Dir* Irving Rapper • *Scr* Irving Wallace, Horace McCoy, from the story *Scalpel* by Horace McCoy

Bad Girl ★★★ 🔳

Melodrama   1931 · US · BW · 90mins

A misleading title for the account of a year in the life of a young working-class couple, from their meeting to their marriage and the birth of their first child. James Dunn is a hardworking lad from the tenements intent on bettering himself, Sally Eilers the girl he loves, and Minna Gombell her best friend and his verbal sparring partner. Frank Borzage, as you would expect from the director of *Seventh Heaven*, brings realism, tenderness and humour to this depiction of life in a more innocent era when, despite the Depression, aspirations remained intact. Dunn and Eilers, in the first of several teamings, make a very attractive and convincing pair.

Sally Eilers *Dorothy Haley* • James Dunn *Eddie Collins* • Minna Gombell *Edna Driggs* • Frank Darien *Lathrop* • William Pawley *Jim Haley* ■ *Dir* Frank Borzage • *Scr* Edwin Burke, from the novel *Bad Girl* by Viña Delmar, Eugene Delmar, from the play by Viña Delmar, Brian Marlowe

Bad Girls ★★ 🔳

Western   1994 · US · Colour · 95mins

You can almost see the pitch now: *Young Guns*, but with babes. It's actually not a bad idea, but sadly it's let down by a weak, ill-focused script that can't seem to make up its mind whether it should be a feminist reworking of the western genre, or just an old-fashioned ''girls' own'' adventure. The bad girls of the title are four prostitutes (Andie MacDowell, Madeleine Stowe, Drew Barrymore and Mary Stuart Masterson) who find a price on their heads when Stowe shoots a disagreeable client. On the trail of the cowgirls are a mixed bag of cowboys, including bad James Russo and nice Dermot Mulroney. The ladies handle the traditional western duties with aplomb, but, despite their spirited performances, the biggest problem is that none of them (not even Barrymore) is particularly bad. Contains violence, swearing and nudity. 🔲

Madeleine Stowe *Cody Zamora* • Mary Stuart Masterson *Anita Crown* • Andie MacDowell *Eileen Spenser* • Drew Barrymore *Lilly Laronette* • James Russo *Kid Jarrett* • James LeGros *William Tucker* • Robert Loggia *Frank Jarrett* • Dermot Mulroney *Josh McCoy* ■ *Dir*

Jonathan Kaplan • Scr Ken Friedman, Yolande Finch, from a story by Albert S Ruddy, Charles Finch, Gary Frederickson

Bad Guys ★★ PG
Comedy 1986 · US · Colour · 86mins

A dreadful early attempt to cash-in on the huge popularity of wrestling, this bottom-of-the-barrel affair has a young Adam Baldwin and Mike Jolly as a pair of bumbling policeman who turn to the ring when they lose their day jobs. However, their bid to become wrestling stars soon arouses emnity among the professional wrestling community. Wrestling stars of the eighties – Chief Jay Strongbow, Count Billy Varga, Professor Toru Tanaka – put in appearances but, like this film, they probably won't be of much interest to today's audiences ▭

Adam Baldwin *Skip Jackson* • Mike Jolly *Dave Atkins* • Michelle Nicastro *Janice Edwards* • Ruth Buzzi *Petal McGurk* • James Booth *Lord Percy* • Gene LeBell *Turk McGurk* ■ *Dir* Joel Silberg • *Scr* Brady W Setwater, Joe Gillis

Bad Influence ★★ 18
Mystery thriller 1990 · US · Colour · 94mins

This "should-have-gone-straight-to-video" thriller stars ex-Brat Packer Rob Lowe and James Spader. In a wildly implausible scenario, a stranger befriends a down-at-heel suit, and the friendship soon turns into a cat-and-mouse game of psychological manipulation. What starts as a promising, taut thriller soon disintegrates into beyond-believable pulp. It's a waste of the exceptionally talented Spader, and Lowe should stick to *Austin Powers* and his Robert Wagner impressions. ▭

Rob Lowe *Alex* • James Spader *Michael Boll* • Lisa Zane *Claire* • Christian Clemenson *Pismo Boll* • Kathleen Wilhoite *Leslie* • Tony Maggio *Patterson* • Marcia Cross *Ruth Fielding* • David Duchovny *Clubgoer* ■ *Dir* Curtis Hanson • *Scr* David Koepp

Bad Jim ★★★
Western 1989 · US · Colour · 90mins

An affectionate, cosily paced western that succeeds in coming up with a different spin on the story of Billy the Kid. Now it's the late outlaw's horse that is the focus of attention, with the film tracing the stallion's adventures as it falls into the hands of a trio of cowboys. Clyde Ware's direction is perhaps too unhurried, but he is rewarded with some amiable performances from a line-up that is headed by James Brolin and Richard Roundtree and features Clark Gable's son, John Clark Gable, making his film debut. The cast also includes the western character actors Harry Carey Jr, Ty Hardin and Rory Calhoun.

James Brolin *BD Sweetman* • Richard Roundtree *July* • John Clark Gable *JT Coleman* • Harry Carey Jr *CJ Lee* • Ty Hardin *Tom Jefford* • Rory Calhoun *Sam Harper* • Pepe Serna *Virgilio* • Suzanne Wouk *Elizabeth* ■ *Dir/Scr* Clyde Ware

Bad Lands ★★
Western 1939 · US · BW · 70mins

This has a stronger script than most B-pictures, being RKO's unacknowledged re-make in western dress of its 1934

desert war drama *The Lost Patrol*, which was powerfully directed by the great John Ford. Here the British soldiers of the original become a posse trapped in the desert by Apaches and picked off one by one. A lacklustre cast, headed by Robert Barrat and Noah Beery Jr, includes Douglas Walton from the earlier version, who survives far longer time this time around, as well as John Ford's actor brother, Francis, perhaps retained for good luck.

Robert Barrat *Sheriff* • Noah Beery Jr *Chile Lyman* • Guinn "Big Boy" Williams [Guinn Williams] *Billy Sweet* • Douglas Walton *Mulford* • Andy Clyde *Cliff* • Addison Richards *Rayburn* • Robert Coote *Eaton* • Paul Hurst *Curley Tom* • Francis Ford *Garth* ■ *Dir* Lew Landers • *Scr* Clarence Upson Young

The Bad Liaisons ★★
Drama 1955 · Fr · BW · 90mins

Although he made several films, Alexandre Astruc is better known as the critic who devised the *caméra-stylo* concept that underlays auteur theory. This second feature clearly bears the director's thematic trademarks, though he would later denounce the excessively stylised imagery. Anouk Aimée is suitably enigmatic as she talks about the various men she has encountered since arriving in Paris with inspector Yves Robert, who is investigating her links with abortionist Claude Dauphin. With its voiceover narration and reliance on flashbacks, this once controversial drama now seems contrived and stilted. A French language film.

Anouk Aimée *Catherine Racan* • Jean-Claude Pascal *Blaise Walter* • Claude Dauphin *Doctor Danieli* • Philippe Lemaire *Alain Bergere* • Yves Robert *Commissaire Forbin* ■ *Dir* Alexandre Astruc • *Scr* Alexandre Astruc, Roland Laudenbach, from the novel *Cette Sacrée Salade* by Cecil Saint-Laurent

Bad Lieutenant ★★★★ 18
Drama 1992 · US · Colour · 96mins

When director Abel Ferrara's films are good, they are exceptionally good, as proved by *King of New York*, *Ms 45* and this highly controversial tale of a corrupt cop (Harvey Keitel) getting one last chance at redemption when he investigates the rape of a nun. The problem is that she has forgiven her attackers and therefore refuses to name them. This depiction of one man's vice-ridden hell is sexually explicit and brutally violent to an extreme degree, but the intention to shock audiences out of their complacency is the point of Ferrara's furious walk on the wild side. Keitel gives the bravest performance of his career so far as the lapsed Catholic in serious debt and even worse moral and ethical chaos. Contains swearing, drug abuse and nudity.

Harvey Keitel *Lieutenant* • Victor Argo *Beat Cop* • Paul Calderone [Paul Calderon] *Cop* • Leonard Thomas *Cop* • Robin Burrows *Ariane* • Frankie Thorn *Nun* • Victoria Bastel *Bowtay* ■ *Dir* Abel Ferrara • *Scr* Zoe Tamarlaine Lund, Abel Ferrara

The Bad Lord Byron ★★
Biographical drama 1949 · UK · BW · 84mins

Released at a time when hopes were high that British cinema would be able to compete with Hollywood, this historical fantasy was massacred by the critics. It hasn't really improved with age, although it provided Dennis Price with a useful run-through for the role of the equally caddish Louis Mazzini in the following year's classic *Kind Hearts and Coronets*. There is precious little biography on display, but the way in which the script whizzes you round the celebrities of the day is fun.

Dennis Price *Lord Byron* • Mai Zetterling *Teresa Guiccioli* • Joan Greenwood *Lady Caroline Lamb* • Linden Travers *Augusta Leigh* • Sonia Holm *Arabella Millbank* • Raymond Lovell *John Hobhouse* • Leslie Dwyer *Fletcher* ■ *Dir* David MacDonald • *Scr* Terence Young, Anthony Thorne, Peter Quennell, Lawrence Kitchen, Paul Holt

Bad Man of Brimstone ★★
Western 1938 · US · BW · 88mins

Ugly mug Wallace Beery stars in this western about a gunfighter redeemed when he meets his long-lost son, a boxer turned lawyer played by Dennis O'Keefe. (This was the first time O'Keefe used that name; up to this point, he was billed as Bud Flanagan.) It's the sort of morality tale that only MGM could make, with a message about the evil of violence and the importance of society that comes courtesy of a script co-written by future Bond scribe Richard Maibaum.

Wallace Beery *"Trigger" Bill* • Virginia Bruce *Loretta Douglas* • Dennis O'Keefe *Jeffrey Burton* • Joseph Calleia *Ben* • Lewis Stone *Mr Jack Douglas* • Guy Kibbee *"Eight Ball" Harrison* ■ *Dir* J Walter Reuben • *Scr* Cyril Hume, Richard Maibaum, from a story by J Walter Reuben, Maurice Rapf

Bad Manners ★★★ PG
Psychological drama
1998 · US · Colour · 60mins

Jonathan Kaufer was briefly regarded as one of a promising young talent around Hollywood in the eighties but his career never seemed to get into gear. This caustic drama offers a glimpse of what we have been missing. A bitter take on academic and sexual jealousy, it finds David Strathairn and Bonnie Bedelia as married lecturers crossing psychological swords with the latter's former lover (Saul Rubinek) and his young girlfriend (Caroleen Feeney). It's a claustrophobic affair but it's beautifully played, written and directed. ▭

David Strathairn *Wes Westlund* • Bonnie Bedelia *Nancy Westlund* • Saul Rubinek *Matt Carroll* • Caroleen Feeney *Kim Matthews* • Julie Harris *Professor Harper* ■ *Dir* Jonathan Kaufer • *Scr* David Gilman, from his play *Ghost in the Machine*

Bad Man's River ★★
Comedy western
1971 · Sp/It/Fr · Colour · 91mins

What might be called a spaghetti-paella western, flavoured with garlic. It's a production with Italian/Spanish/French influences that's as indigestible as it sounds, with the somewhat bizarre casting of Lee Van Cleef,

James Mason and Gina Lollobrigida in a story about an attempt to blow up a Mexican arms arsenal for revolutionary reasons only the inscrutable Mason knows much about. Director Gene (Eugenio) Martin succumbs too often to freeze-frame fever, and there's very little else to raise the temperature.

Lee Van Cleef *Roy King* • James Mason *Montero* • Gina Lollobrigida *Alicia* • Simon Andreu *Angel Sandos* • Diana Lorys *Dolores* • John Garko *Ed Pace* • Lone Ferk *Conchita* ■ *Dir* Gene Martin [Eugenio Martin] • *Scr* Gene Martin [Eugenio Martin], Philip Yordan

Bad Medicine ★★ 15
Comedy 1985 · US · Colour · 93mins

After hitting it big with *Police Academy* and *Cocoon*, Steve Guttenberg came a cropper with this dim medical comedy. Guttenberg is the lazy student who winds up in a dodgy medical school in Latin America – run by Alan Arkin, complete with preposterous accent – only to discover something approaching a conscience. Director Harvey Miller serves up an unappealing menu of old medical jokes and toilet humour, and then compounds the problem by getting all sentimental on us at the end. ▭

Steve Guttenberg *Jeff Marx* • Alan Arkin *Dr Ramon Madera* • Julie Hagerty *Liz Parker* • Bill Macy *Dr Gerald Marx* • Curtis Armstrong *Dennis Gladstone* • Candy Milo *Maria Morales* ■ *Dir* Harvey Miller • *Scr* Harvey Miller, from the novel *Calling Dr Horowitz* by Steven Horowitz, Neil Offen

Bad Moon ★ 18
Horror thriller 1996 · US · Colour · 76mins

Director Eric Red put a unique spin on vampire lore as one of the writers of *Near Dark*, but he has less success with the werewolf genre. Michael Paré is mauled by a beast in Nepal and returns home to sister Mariel Hemmingway and her son, in the hope their love will stop him having to wear one of the most ill-fitting fur suits in cinematic history. It's up to the family dog to sniff out the truth – and plug the plot holes. Contains violence, nudity and sexual situations. ▭

Mariel Hemingway *Janet* • Michael Paré *Ted Harrison* • Mason Gamble *Brett* ■ *Dir* Eric Red • *Scr* Eric Red, from the novel *Thor* by Wayne Smith

The Bad News Bears ★★★ PG
Sports comedy 1976 · US · Colour · 97mins

Walter Matthau is on fine form in one of the first sports comedies to use the now familiar "underdogs taking on the big boys" scenario. He plays a boozy coach trying to lick a bunch of no-hoper Little League baseball misfits into shape, with a little help from star-pitcher Tatum O'Neal. As in *A League of Their Own*, it's the relationship between coach and team that pulls you in, while the child actors are more than a match for old pro Matthau – especially O'Neal, who has more screen presence than dad Ryan ever had. A small winner.

Walter Matthau *Coach Morris Buttermaker* • Tatum O'Neal *Amanda Whurlizer* • Vic Morrow *Roy Turner* • Joyce Van Patten *Cleveland* • Ben Piazza *Councilman Whitewood* • Jackie

U = SUITABLE FOR ALL   **Uc** = SUITABLE FOR ALL, ESPECIALLY FOR YOUNG CHILDREN (VIDEO ONLY)   **PG** = PARENTAL GUIDANCE

Earle Haley *Kelly Leak* • Alfred W Lutter [Alfred Lutter] *Ogilvie* • *Dir* Michael Ritchie • *Scr* Bill Lancaster

The Bad News Bears Go to Japan ★

Sports comedy 1978 · US · Colour · 91mins

Aside from Tony Curtis's star turn as a greedy hustler who takes charge of the titular Little Leaguers, there's little to say about this lifeless, pointless second sequel. Curtis sees a lucrative dollar opportunity in a tour of Japan, which involves the kids taking on the National Champions. The actor must have also been doing this diamond dud purely for the money, while return engagements from the first movie's writer and director (the latter now producing) seem to have had little positive effect.

Tony Curtis *Marvin Lazar* • Jackie Earle Haley *Kelly Leak* • Matthew Douglas Anton *ERW Tillyard III* • Erin Blunt *Ahmad Rahim* • George Gonzales *Miguel Agilar* • Brett Marx *Jimmy Feldman* • David Pollock *Rudy Stein* ■ *Dir* John Berry • *Scr* Bill Lancaster

The Bad Seed ★★★★

Psychological horror
1956 · US · BW · 128mins

This is an adaptation of playwright Maxwell Anderson's Broadway and West End success about an irredeemably evil eight-year-old child, played on stage and here on screen by the brilliant Patty McCormack. Also imported from the Broadway production are Nancy Kelly as the girl's mother, Eileen Heckart, as the mother of one of the girl's school friends, and a particularly effective Henry Jones as the venal caretaker. This is *Grand Guignol* stuff, really, but veteran Mervyn LeRoy directs effectively. The film was X-certificated on its release here, but watch out for an unbelievable censor-placating ending.

Nancy Kelly *Christine* • Patty McCormack *Rhoda* • Henry Jones *LeRoy* • Eileen Heckart *Mrs Daigle* • Evelyn Varden *Monica* • William Hopper *Kenneth* • Paul Fix *Bravo* • Jesse White *Emory* ■ *Dir* Mervyn LeRoy • *Scr* John Lee Mahin, from the play by Maxwell Anderson and the novel by William March

Bad Sister ★★ U

Drama 1931 · US · BW · 69mins

An extrovert and flirtatious small-town girl (Sidney Fox) falls for a big-city swindler (Humphrey Bogart). The couple elopes, with unhappy consequences for her, but her actions lead to the happy union of her respectable rejected suitor (Conrad Nagel) and her demure sister (Bette Davis). This flaccid drama, directed by Hobart Henley for Universal, is notable only as marking Davis's screen debut – though it gives little intimation of the fact that she wouldn't be playing the subsidiary good girl for long.

Conrad Nagel *Dr Dick Lindley* • Sidney Fox *Marianne* • Bette Davis *Laura* • ZaSu Pitts *Minnie* • Slim Summerville *Sam* • Charles Winninger *Mr Madison* • Emma Dunn *Mrs Madison* • Humphrey Bogart *Corliss* ■ *Dir* Hobart Henley • *Scr* Raymond L Schrock, Tom Reed, Edwin H Knopf, from the novel *The Flirt* by Booth Tarkington

The Bad Sleep Well ★★ PG

Crime drama 1960 · Jap · BW · 127mins

In this drama about corporate corruption in postwar Japan, Toshiro Mifune lays down his samurai sword to play a housing company employee who marries the boss's daughter purely to expose his new father-in-law, whom he believes was responsible for his own father's "suicide". Akira Kurosawa turns what should have been a taut thriller into a rather sombre exercise in morality, with Shakespearean themes of revenge and remorse. The film flopped in Japan (critiques of the economic recovery were rare) and led to the eventual collapse of the director's production company. In Japanese with English subtitles. ▣

Toshiro Mifune *Koichi Nishi* • Takeshi Kato *Itakura* • Masayuki Mori *Iwabuchi* • Takashi Shimura *Moriyama* • Akira Nishimura *Shirai* ■ *Dir* Akira Kurosawa • *Scr* Akira Kurosawa, Shinobu Hashimoto, Hideo Oguni, Ryuzo Kikushima, Eijiro Hisaita

Bad Taste ★★★ 18

Horror comedy 1987 · NZ · Colour · 87mins

Director Peter Jackson is currently working on his epic *Lord of the Rings* trilogy, but his career began with this cheerfully disgusting Kiwi sickie, made over a four-year period. Directed in chaotic fashion, with epic quantities of gore, flying viscera, macabre humour and wild special effects, Jackson's man-eating alien invasion film remained the bloody benchmark of sci-fi horror, though he topped it five years later with *Braindead*. The title says it all, so those of a sensitive disposition should steer clear. ▣

Peter Jackson *Derek/Robert* • Mike Minett *Frank* • Peter O'Herne *Barry* • Terry Potter *Ozzy* • Craig Smith *Giles* • Doug Wren *Lord Crumb* ■ *Dir/Scr* Peter Jackson

Bad Timing ★★★★ 18

Drama 1980 · UK · Colour · 117mins

One to admire or abhor, director Nicolas Roeg's case history of a sexual obsession dazzles with flashbacks and disturbs with "What if?" sidetracks. Art Garfunkel is the psycho-psychiatrist involved with Theresa Russell in a sadistic affair, which starts with the girl's suicide attempt and ends with even nastier revelations about their relationship. Seven years after his poignantly creepy *Don't Look Now*, Roeg piles on angst-ridden chic to the detriment of human values and sympathy, but, for what he achieves in complexity and conviction, it's well worth watching. Contains swearing, sex scenes and nudity. ▣

Art Garfunkel *Dr Alex Linden* • Theresa Russell *Milena Flaherty* • Harvey Keitel *Inspector Netusil* • Denholm Elliott *Stefan Vognic* • Dana Gillespie *Amy* • Daniel Massey *Foppish man* ■ *Dir* Nicolas Roeg • *Scr* Yale Udoff

Bad to the Bone ★★ 12

Crime drama 1997 · US · Colour · 86mins

Kristy Swanson (*Buffy the Vampire Slayer*) is Francesca, a psycho teen who learns that her stepfather left an estate of half a million dollars that will come to her if her mother isn't around. Mom is soon found dead, but Swanson cleverly uses her boyfriend (David Chokachi from *Baywatch*) as an alibi. Two years later, she gets her brother (*Party of Five*'s Jeremy London) to kill the boyfriend after taking out an insurance policy on his life... The premise may be totally improbable, but Swanson is spellbinding as the seductive sociopath whose only true skill is the ability to manipulate men. Contains moderate violence, sexual references and some swearing. ▣

Kristy Swanson *Francesca Wells* • Jeremy London *Danny Wells* • David Chokachi *Waldo* • Patti D'Arbanville [Patti D'Arbanville-Quinn] *Marilyn Wells* • Christine Tucci *Martina Dobbs* • Ben Browder *Brent Rohrbach* ■ *Dir* Bill L Norton • *Scr* Rob Fresco

Badge 373 ★★ 15

Crime drama 1973 · US · Colour · 110mins

The real-life New York cop who inspired *The French Connection* was called Eddie Egan, and he served as this film's technical adviser. Presumably, then, he endorsed Robert Duvall's portrait of a bigoted, racist thug with a badge. Here Egan (renamed Ryan) is up against the Puerto Ricans and tends to shoot or punch first and ask questions later, if ever. It's not unlike *The French Connection* in its equivocal stance towards its hero, though a chase with a school bus seems to mimic another maverick cop classic, *Dirty Harry*. ▣

Robert Duvall *Eddie Ryan* • Verna Bloom *Maureen* • Henry Darrow *Sweet William* • Eddie Egan *Scanlon* • Felipe Luciano *Ruben* • Tina Cristiani *Mrs Caputo* ■ *Dir* Howard W Koch • *Scr* Pete Hamill

Badge of Betrayal ★★ 12

Crime drama 1996 · US · Colour · 87mins

TV-movie regular Sandor Stern puts a professional directorial sheen on this otherwise formulaic crime drama. Michele Greene plays a single mother who moves to a small town and gets hired as a deputy sheriff; Harry Hamlin is her boss, who may not be all he seems. Hamlin relishes the opportunity to play against type and Greene proves to be a feisty foil, but there are few surprises. Contains violence. ▣

Michele Greene *Annie Walker* • Harry Hamlin *Sheriff Dave Ward* • Linda Doucett *Patty Renault* ■ *Dir* Sandor Stern • *Scr* Julia Minsky

Badge of the Assassin
★★★ 15

Crime drama based on a true story
1985 · US · Colour · 94mins

Another tough-guy role for James Woods, though in this hard-edged and controversial film he's on the right side of the law for a change. As assistant district attorney Robert K Tanenbaum, it's his job to find the men responsible for the murder of two police officers. Woods's powerful performance, the strong supporting cast and the tense, fact-based plotline add up to an entertaining TV-movie package. ▣

James Woods *Robert K Tanenbaum* • Yaphet Kotto *Cliff Fenton* • Alex Rocco *Bill Butler* • David Harris *Lester May* • Steven Keats *Skelton* • Larry Riley *Herman Bell* • Pam Grier *Alie* • Rae Dawn Chong *Christine* • Richard Bradford *Delsa* ■ *Dir* Mel Damski • *Scr* Lawrence Roman, from the book by Robert K Tanenbaum, Philip Rosenberg

The Badlanders ★★★

Western 1958 · US · Colour · 83mins

A decent western, directed by the reliable Delmer Daves and starring Alan Ladd and Ernest Borgnine as ex-convicts who emerge from prison in Yuma with a plan to rob a gold mine. Since this involves blowing up a mountain and escaping with half a ton of rock, it takes some organising. The picture is actually less a western than a suspense thriller, a remake of John Huston's classic 1950 crime drama *The Asphalt Jungle* on horseback, with plenty of surprises, a thrilling chase through a carnival and some excellent performances, notably from Nehemiah Persoff – best known for his mobster role in *Some Like It Hot* – as the gunpowder expert.

Alan Ladd *Peter Van Hock* • Ernest Borgnine *John McBain* • Katy Jurado *Anita* • Claire Kelly *Ada Winton* • Kent Smith *Cyril Lounsberry* • Nehemiah Persoff *Vincente* • Robert Emhardt *Sample* • Anthony Caruso *Comanche* • Adam Williams *Leslie* ■ *Dir* Delmer Daves • *Scr* Richard Collins, from the novel *The Asphalt Jungle* by WR Burnett

Badlands ★★★★ 18

Crime drama 1973 · US · Colour · 89mins

The *Natural Born Killers* of its day, reclusive director Terrence Malick's reprise of the infamous Charlie Starkweather murders in the fifties is a moodily disturbing and deadpan cult item. Martin Sheen is the alienated serial killer on a psychopathic rampage through the American Midwest accompanied by his loyal teenage girlfriend, Sissy Spacek, and the series of horrific events is depicted in Malick's dazzling and daring romance novel style. Sheen and Spacek are highly effective as the apathetic and icy duo holed up in the eponymous Badlands of Montana and it's the matter-of-fact dreamy approach, defying convention by leaving loose ends, that makes it a truly scary experience. ▣

Martin Sheen *Kit Carruthers* • Sissy Spacek *Holly* • Warren Oates *Father* • Ramon Bieri *Cato* • Alan Vint *Deputy* • Gary Littlejohn *Sheriff* • John Carter *Rich man* • Bryan Montgomery *Boy* • Gail Threlkeld *Girl* ■ *Dir/Scr* Terrence Malick

Badman's Territory ★★★ U

Western 1946 · US · BW · 97mins

An excellent Randolph Scott western, featuring such tried-and-tested supporting players as grizzled George "Gabby" Hayes and the great Chief Thundercloud. Rather like those Universal horror movies that gathered together Dracula, Frankenstein's monster and the Wolf Man, this RKO special has Jesse and Frank James, Sam Bass, Belle Starr and the Dalton gang as opponents to Scott, as he attempts to turn the Oklahoma territory into a full-grown state. Cleverly directed by Tim Whelan, who doesn't let the clutter of characters spoil the flow.

Randolph Scott *Mark Rowley* • Ann Richards *Henryette Alcott* • George "Gabby" Hayes *Coyote* • Steve Brodie *Bob Dalton* • Ray Collins *Colonel Farewell* • Lawrence Tierney *Jesse James* • Tom Tyler *Frank James* • Nestor Paiva *Sam Bass* • Isabel Jewell *Belle Starr* • William Moss *Bill Dalton* ■ *Dir* Tim Whelan • *Scr* Jack Natteford, Luci Ward, Clarence Upson Young, Bess Taffel

Bagdad Café ★★★★ PG

Comedy drama 1987 · W Ger · Colour · 87mins

Co-written and co-produced with his wife Eleanore and starring his regular favourite Marianne Sägebrecht, German director Percy Adlon's first American feature is a hypnotic blend of feminist fantasy and Capraesque feel-good. Set in a run-down diner in the middle of the Arizona desert, the action centres on the impact Sägebrecht has on the claustrophobic local community, in particular on café boss CCH Pounder and an ageing hippy artist, played with an instinctive comic touch by the undervalued Jack Palance. Although there are some shrewd asides on racial division, this is still the kind of gentle comedy you can simply sink into your armchair and enjoy. Contains some mild swearing and nudity.

Marianne Sägebrecht *Jasmin Münchgstettner* • CCH Pounder *Brenda* • Jack Palance *Rudi Cox* • Christine Kauffman *Debby* • Monica Calhoun *Phyllis* • Darron Flagg *Sal Junior* • George Aguilar *Cahuenga* • G Smokey Campbell *Sal* • Hans Stadlbauer *Münchgstettner* • Alan S Craig *Eric* ■ *Dir* Percy Adlon • *Scr* Percy Adlon, Eleonore Adlon

Bagh Bahadur ★★★

Drama 1989 · Ind · Colour · 91mins

Bengali poet Buddhadev Dasgupta gave up his job as an economics lecturer at Calcutta University to direct films, starting with realist studies of city life such as *Dooratwa*. However, this tragic tale, also known as *The Tiger Dancer*, is set in a small village and is closer in tone to a folk tale. Pavan Malhotra stars as a quarry worker who returns home to dance in a traditional festival and marry his sweetheart, only to lose both his place of honour and his girl when a circus troupe sets up camp nearby. He's upstaged by a beautiful caged leopard. In Hindi with English subtitles.

Pavan Malhotra *Ghunuram* • Archana *Radha* • Vasudev Rao *Sibal* • Rajeshwari Roy Choudhury ■ *Dir/Scr* Buddhadev Dasgupta

Baiju Bawra ★★★ U

Epic romantic musical 1952 · Ind · BW · 154mins

Although set in the Mughal court, this melodrama owes about as much to historical fact as such Western classical music biopics as *Song of Love*. Director Vijay Bhatt is primarily concerned with the clash of personalities between court composer Surendra and itinerant musician Bharat Bhushan, who go head to head in a tuneful showdown after the latter's father is murdered by palace guards. However, it was Ali Naushad who took most of the plaudits for the songs that made this a box-office hit and turned Meena Kumari into a major star after 12 years in Bollywood as Baby Meena. In Hindi with English subtitles.

Meena Kumari *Gauri* • Bharat Bhushan *Baiju* • Surendra *Tansen* • Bipin Gupta *Akbhar* ■ *Dir* Vijay Bhatt • *Scr* RS Choudhry, Ramchandra Thakur

The Bait ★★★★ 15

Crime drama 1995 · Fr · Colour · 111mins

Shot in the same uncompromising manner as his policier *L.627*, Bertrand Tavernier's lowlife thriller is darker than the average *film noir* as both the crime and the violence are so chillingly pitiless. Driven by an ambition to open a chain of boutiques in the States, shopgirl-cum-model Marie Gillain agrees to distract her wealthy male contacts while they're burgled by boyfriend Olivier Sitruk and his doltish buddy Bruno Putzulu. The resolution is never in doubt, but the action remains engrossing as Tavernier, aided by a grittily credible cast, strips the daydreams down to their seedy reality. In French with English subtitles. ▭

Marie Gillain *Nathalie* • Olivier Sitruk *Eric* • Bruno Putzulu *Bruno* • Richard Berry *Alain* • Philippe Duclos *Antoine* • Marie Ravel *Karine* • Clotilde Courau *Patricia* • Jean-Louis Richard *Restaurant owner* ■ *Dir* Bertrand Tavernier • *Scr* Colo Tavernier O'Hagan, Bertrand Tavernier, from a book by Morgan Sportes

The Baited Trap ★★★

Crime thriller 1959 · US · Colour · 86mins

Also known as *The Trap*, this tense suspense film from writer/director Norman Panama – a man more usually known for his comedies – is a better movie than it ought to be thanks to an above-average cast. Lawyer Richard Widmark returns to his small home town of Tula to help villainous Lee J Cobb escape into Mexico. There he must deal with his father (Carl Benton Reid) and his ex-girlfriend (Tina Louise), who's now married to Widmark's brother.

Richard Widmark *Ralph Anderson* • Lee J Cobb *Victor Massonetti* • Earl Holliman *Tippy Anderson* • Tina Louise *Linda Anderson* • Carl Benton Reid *Sheriff Anderson* • Lorne Greene *Davis* ■ *Dir* Norman Panama • *Scr* Richard Alan Simmons, Norman Panama

Baja Oklahoma ★★★ PG

Romantic comedy 1988 · US · Colour · 99mins

A host of country stars were assembled for this appealing comedy about an aspiring songwriter (Lesley Ann Warren) who is desperately searching for her big Nashville break. The shenanigans of the country music business are sketched out with some affection by Dan Jenkins and director Bobby Roth. Cameos from the likes of Willie Nelson and Emmylou Harris (as themselves) add the requisite authenticity, and strong support from such fine character actors as Anthony Zerbe, Swoosie Kurtz and Peter Coyote helps the cause.

Lesley Ann Warren *Juanita Hutchins* • Peter Coyote *Slick* • Swoosie Kurtz *Doris Steadman* • Anthony Zerbe *Old Jeemy* • William Forsythe *Tommy Earl Brownlee* • Billy Vera *Lonnie Slocum* • Julia Roberts *Candy Hutchins* • John M Jackson *Lee Steadman* ■ *Dir* Bobby Roth • *Scr* Bobby Roth, Dan Jenkins, from the novel by Dan Jenkins

Baker's Hawk ★★★

Western 1976 · US · Colour · 96mins

Clint Walker only enjoyed brief stardom, but this family western shows what a capable actor he could be. Here he plays the father of Lee H

Montgomery, a young boy who helps recluse Burl Ives and his pet hawk escape from hooligans. It could be an episode of the TV series *Cheyenne*, which made Walker's name before that other Clint (Eastwood) moseyed along. However, Lyman D Dayton's direction gives the film a moral dimension that lifts it out of the ordinary.

Clint Walker *Dan Baker* • Burl Ives *Mr McGraw* • Diane Baker *Jenny Baker* • Lee H Montgomery *[Lee Montgomery] Billy Baker* • Alan Young *Mr Carson* • Taylor Lacher *Sweeney* • Bruce M Fischer *Blacksmith* ■ *Dir* Lyman D Dayton *[Lyman Dayton]* • *Scr* Dan Greer, Hal Harrison Jr, from the novel by Jack Bickham

The Baker's Wife ★★★★

Comedy 1938 · Fr · BW · 118mins

While Marcel Pagnol's style may be regarded as hopelessly old-fashioned by many post-New Wave critics, there's no escaping the wit and warmth of this tale of simple Provençal folk. Villagers have to band together to disrupt the romance between a shepherd (Charles Moulin) and a faithless wife (Ginette Leclerc) to encourage their cuckolded baker to make bread again. One of the screen's finest comic actors, Raimu is superb as the broken-hearted *boulanger*. But what makes the film so irresistible is Pagnol's attention to detail and mastery at creating the close-knit communal atmosphere. In French with English subtitles.

Raimu *Aimable, the baker* • Ginette Leclerc *Aurelie, the wife* • Charles Moulin *Dominique, the shepherd* • Robert Vattier *The priest* • Robert Bassac *The schoolteacher* ■ *Dir* Marcel Pagnol • *Scr* Marcel Pagnol, from the novel *Jean le Bleu* by Jean Giono

Le Bal ★★★ PG

Musical 1983 · Alg/Fr/It · Colour · 107mins

In addition to landing a best foreign film Oscar nomination, Ettore Scola won the best director prize at Berlin for this stylised adaptation of Jean-Claude Penchenat's experimental stage play. Original members of the Théâtre du Campagnol cast re-enact routines inspired by events in France from 1936 to the early 1980s. But while their expertise is undeniable and Vladimir Cosma's score cleverly plays on the popular tunes of the different periods, the action says more about Scola's ingenuity than the incidents on which it's supposed to be commenting. Packed with allegorical allusions, this is visually mesmerising but intellectually frustrating. A French language film. ▭

Etienne Guichard *Provincial student* • Régis Bouquet *Ballroom owner* • Francesco de Rosa *Toni* • Nani Noël *Goodtime girl* • Liliane Delval *Girl with long hair* • Arnault Lecarpentier *Young printer* • Martine Chauvin *Flower girl* ■ *Dir* Ettore Scola • *Scr* Ettore Scola, Ruggero Maccari, Furio Scarpelli, Jean-Claude Penchenat, from the Théâtre du Campagnol stage production, from an original idea by Jean-Claude Penchenat

Balalaika ★ U

Musical 1939 · US · BW · 102mins

This monumentally boring and incredibly dull MGM adaptation of Eric Maschwitz's popular West End operetta, retains only the title song from the original (*At the Bal-a-laika*) and turns the Russian setting into something vaguely Ruritanian. Nelson Eddy and Ilona Massey (amazingly originally billed as "The New Dietrich") are the supremely uninteresting leads, and Reinhold Schunzel's direction is truly uninspired, if not actually incompetent. The usual MGM production gloss glues the whole daft farrago together and, for those who care, Eddy and an MGM male chorus sing not only the *Song of the Volga Boatmen* but also the likes of *God Save the Czar* and *O Chichornya*.

Nelson Eddy *Prince Peter Karagin* • Ilona Massey *Lydia Pavlovna Marakova* • Charlie Ruggles *[Charles Ruggles] Private Nicki Popoff* • Frank Morgan *Ivan Danchenoff* • Lionel Atwill *Professor Marakov* • C Aubrey Smith *General Karagin* • Dalies Frantz *Dimitri Marakov* ■ *Dir* Reinhold Schunzel • *Scr* Leon Gordon, Charles Bennett, Jacques Deval, from the operetta by Eric Maschwitz, George Posford, Bernard Grun

La Balance ★★★★ 18

Detective thriller 1982 · Fr · Colour · 101mins

An American in Paris was responsible for this hard-as-nails thriller, which won several Césars including best picture and best actor and best actress. Stylishly exploiting the seedy streets of Belleville, Bob Swaim brings an unswerving authenticity to this tale of a pimp (Philippe Léotard) who agrees to inform on neighbourhood thug Maurice Ronet to prevent detective Richard Berry from harming the whore he adores. Although Swaim makes the most of action sequences, such as the traffic jam ambush, the film's real strength lies in the conviction of the performances. Nathalie Baye's hardened hooker is a revelation. In French with English subtitles. ▭

Nathalie Baye *Nicole* • Philippe Léotard *Dede* • Richard Berry *Inspector Paluzzi* • Christophe Malavoy *Tintin* • Jean-Paul Connart *The Belgian* • Bernard Freyd *The Captain* • Albert Dray *Carlini* • Florent Pagny *Simoni* • Maurice Ronet *Roger Massina* ■ *Dir/Scr* Bob Swaim

The Balanced Particle Freeway ★★

Fantasy adventure 1997 · Ausl · Colour

Two children stumble upon a gateway to a magical world in director Paul Moloney's ambitious fantasy adventure. Good fun for youngsters with excellent visual effects and puppet models that belie the modest television budget, but the simplistic storyline won't hold the attention of older children for very long.

Molly McCaffrey *Lili* • Damien Bode *Bede* • Trudy Hellier *Helen* • Doug Bowles *Drew* ■ *Dir* Paul Moloney • *Scr* Carole Wilkinson

Balboa ★★ 15

Melodrama 1982 · US · Colour · 91mins

Eighties glitz and big-business scheming is rather unoriginally rehashed in this disjointed pseudo-soap. Tony Curtis goes over the top as the villainous tycoon, while everyone around him is busy with sexual intrigue. The supporting cast includes Sonny Bono, Steve Kanaly (Ray Krebbs in *Dallas*) and even a lost-looking Chuck Connors. While ludicrous, this does nonetheless have moments of inane delight for those connoisseurs of the decade. ▭

Tony Curtis *Ernie Stoddard* • Carol Lynley *Erin Blakely* • Jennifer Chase *Kathy Love* • Chuck Connors *Alabama Dern* • Lupita Ferrer *Rita Carlo* • Sonny Bono *Terry Carlo* • Catherine Campbell *Cindy Dern* • Steve Kanaly *Sam Cole* ■ *Dir* James Polakof • *Scr* James Polakof, Gail Willumsen, Nicki Lewis

The Balcony ★★★

Drama fantasy 1963 · US · BW · 85mins

A fascinating film of Jean Genet's controversial late-fifties play set in a brothel. While the revolutionaries occupy the streets below, the brothel becomes the headquarters of the government, the state police, religion and the media. The brothel itself is designed like a film studio, with different sets, lighting and even back projection to add "reality" to the clients' sexual fantasies. Deeply allegorical, it captures the off-Broadway ambience of the period.

Shelley Winters *Madame Irma* • Peter Falk *Police chief* • Lee Grant *Carmen* • Ruby Dee *Thief* • Peter Brocco *Judge* • Jeff Corey *Bishop* • Joyce Jameson *Penitent* • Arnette Jens *Horse* • Leonard Nimoy *Roger* ■ *Dir* Joseph Strick • *Scr* Ben Maddow, from a play by Jean Genet • *Music* Igor Stravinsky

Ball of Fire ★★★★ U

Comedy 1941 · US · BW · 106mins

A scintillating and hysterically funny update of *Snow White and the Seven Dwarfs*, featuring Barbara Stanwyck as Sugarpuss O'Shea, a moll on the run who falls in with a group of wacky academics working on a language dictionary. Gawky, loveable Gary Cooper is the professor quizzing fireball Babs (hence the title) about contemporary slang. Genius director Howard Hawks creates a minor comic masterpiece from the witty screenplay by Billy Wilder and Charles Brackett, and all the performances are spot-on. There's also a treat as Stanwyck performs *Drum Boogie* with percussion king Gene Krupa. [video]

Gary Cooper *Professor Bertram Potts* • Barbara Stanwyck *Sugarpuss O'Shea* • Oscar Homolka *Professor Gurkakoff* • Henry Travers *Professor Jerome* • SZ Sakall *Professor Magenbruch* • Tully Marshall *Professor Robinson* • Leonid Kinsky *Professor Quintana* ■ *Dir* Howard Hawks • *Scr* Charles Brackett, Billy Wilder, from the story *From A to Z* by Thomas Monroe, Billy Wilder

Ballad in Blue ★★ U

Drama 1966 · UK · BW · 88mins

A starring vehicle for singer Ray Charles, playing himself, in a mawkish London-filmed melodrama about a blind entertainer who befriends a blind child. Suffice to say that the singer, styled "The Genius", performs such greats as *What'd I Say* and *I Got a Woman* and benefits from terrific support from Dawn Addams and Mary Peach. *Now, Voyager* actor-turned-director Paul Henreid, certainly no stranger to melodrama, can't do much with this codswallop. Called *Blues for Lovers* in the US.

Ray Charles • Tom Bell *Steve Collins* • Mary Peach *Peggy Harrison* • Piers Bishop *David Harrison* • Dawn Addams *Gina Graham* • Betty McDowall *Helen Babbidge* • Lucy Appleby *Margaret Babbidge* • Joe Adams *Fred Parker* ■ *Dir* Paul Henreid • *Scr* Burton Wohl, from a story by Paul Henreid, Burton Wohl

Ballad of a Soldier ★★★★ U

War drama 1959 · USSR · BW · 87mins

The winner of the special jury prize at Cannes, Grigori Chukhrai's picaresque home-front drama is a classic example of the socialist-realist style films that dominated postwar Soviet cinema. As much a statement about the resilience of Stalin's citizenry as a pacifist tract, this is a surprisingly sentimental tale, in which the naive hero (Vladimir Ivashov) encounters a series of people as he travels to spend a four-day leave with his mother. Particularly striking is the contrast between the pitiable infidelity of a comrade's frightened wife and Ivashov's brief romance with peasant girl Shanna Prokhorenko. A Russian film with English subtitles.

Vladimir Ivashov *Alyosha* • Shanna Prokhorenko *Shura* • Antonina Maximova *Alyosha's mother* • Nikolai Kruchkov *General* ■ *Dir* Grigori Chukhrai • *Scr* Grigori Chukhrai, Valentin Yoshov

The Ballad of Cable Hogue ★★★★ PG

Comedy western 1970 · US · Colour · 116mins

A sublime movie from master director Sam Peckinpah, tender and ironic by turns, this contains marvellous performances from a whimsical Jason Robards (arguably a career best) in the title role as Hogue, and sexy Stella Stevens as the hooker who becomes his lady. This tale of the itinerant prospector who "found water where there wasn't" is a beautifully crafted and very funny film, an elegy for the old west, and, like Peckinpah's earlier and more explicitly violent *The Wild Bunch*, leaves an audience with nostalgic pangs for a lifestyle that perhaps only existed in motion pictures. It was severely truncated for release in Britain – the fabulously complete two-hour version includes the lilting ballad link *Tomorrow Is the Song I Sing*. Contains swearing. [video]

Jason Robards [Jason Robards Jr] *Cable Hogue* • Stella Stevens *Hildy* • David Warner *Joshua* • Strother Martin *Bowen* • Slim Pickens *Ben* • LQ Jones *Taggart* • Peter Whitney *Cushing* ■ *Dir* Sam Peckinpah • *Scr* John Crawford, Edmund Penney

The Ballad of Gregorio Cortez ★★★ 15

Western based on a true story
1983 · US · Colour · 105mins

An unusual Western based on the true story of Mexican cowhand Cortez, who was mistakenly arrested by Texas Rangers in 1901. He kills a sheriff in the struggle to escape from a situation he can't comprehend and leads the posse after him on a merry dance for nearly a fortnight. Shot in the locations where the real Cortez was actually imprisoned and tried, this gripping saga of racial bigotry and language barriers gains drama by being told from multiple perspectives. Edward James Olmos makes a sympathetic Cortez, even if the overall film is a trifle worthy at times. [video]

Edward James Olmos *Gregorio Cortez* • James Gammon *Sheriff Frank Fly* • Tom Bower *Boone Choate* • Bruce McGill *Bill Blakely* • Brion James *Captain Rogers* • Alan Vint *Mike Trimmell* • Timothy Scott *Sheriff Morris* ■ *Dir* Robert M Young • *Scr* Victor Villasenor, Robert M Young, from the novel *With His Pistol in His Hands* by Americo Paredes

The Ballad of Josie ★★ U

Comedy western
1968 · US · Colour · 101mins

Bland is too strong a word for this tepid flick, which never really catches fire despite being directed by western ace Andrew V McLaglen. Doris Day is good, even though by this stage in her career she was becoming hard to cast, but the men are desperately uninteresting – only Andy Devine brings a sense of authenticity to this western where the jeans look newly ironed and the faces are too well scrubbed. This was the first Day movie to play as a co-feature, and the writing was on the wall – she made only two more films.

Doris Day *Josie Minick* • Peter Graves (1) *Jason Meredith* • George Kennedy *Arch Ogden* • Andy Devine *Judge Tatum* • William Talman *Charlie Lord* • David Hartman *Fonse Pruitt* • Guy Raymond *Doc* ■ *Dir* Andrew V McLaglen • *Scr* Harold Swanton

The Ballad of Little Jo ★★★ 15

Western 1993 · US · Colour · 116mins

This is the flip side of the more glamorous excursions into the gals-out-west genre – *Bad Girls*, *The Quick and the Dead* – presented by director Maggie Greenwald through a sobering, beautifully understated portrait of a woman alone in the west. Suzy Amis is superb as the socialite, driven into exile after a scandal, who is forced to pose as a man to survive in a wild frontier town. Greenwald makes some telling points about the chauvinistic attitudes prevalent and creates a believable picture of the harshness of western life. Amis is well supported by an eclectic cast. Contains violence, swearing and nudity. [video]

Suzy Amis *Josephine Monaghan* • Bo Hopkins *Frank Badger* • Ian McKellen *Percy Corcoran* • David Chung *Tinman Wong* • Carrie Snodgress *Ruth Badger* • René Auberjonois *Streight Hollander* • Heather Graham *Mary Addie* • Sam Robards *Jasper Hill* • Tom Bower *Lyle* ■ *Dir/Scr* Maggie Greenwald

The Ballad of Narayama ★★★

Historical drama 1958 · Jap · Colour · 98mins

Five years after becoming the first Japanese woman to director a feature (*Love Letter*, 1953), Kinuyo Tanaka gave a remarkable rendition of stoic resignation by starring in this stylised adaptation of Shichiro Fukazawa's novels. Focusing on the custom of abandoning the elderly to die on a mountain top, Keisuke Kinoshita's heart-breaking drama is consciously played in a Kabuki manner against theatrical settings to remove any vestige of realism and thus increase the folkloric nature of a practice that will seem barbaric to most Western observers. Aided by Teiji Takahashi as her son, Tanaka sublimely recaptures the brilliance that characterised her collaborations with Kenji Mizoguchi. A Japanese language film.

Kinuyo Tanaka *Orin* • Teiji Takahashi *Tatsuhei* • Yuko Mochizuki *Tama-yan* • Danko Ichikawa *Kesakichi* • Keiko Ogasawara *Mutsu-yan* • Seiji Miyaguchi *Mata-yan* • Yunosuke Ito *Mata-yan's Son* • Ken Mitsuda *Teru-yan* ■ *Dir* Keisuke Kinoshita • *Scr* Keisuke Kinoshita, from the novels by Shichiro Fukazawa

The Ballad of Narayama ★★★★

Drama 1983 · Jap · Colour · 130mins

A far cry from Keisuke Kinoshita's earlier adaptation, Shohei Imamura's Palme d'Or-winning reworking of Shichiro Fukazawa's novels dispassionately places humanity in the context of the natural world, with all its seemingly callous acts of survivalism. Thus, rape, infant mortality and death by burial are presented as nothing more sensational than scrabbling for subsistence in a famine. Stoically accepting the tradition of the elderly being left on a mountain top to ease the communal burden, Sumiko Sakamoto goes about settling her affairs with a calculation that contrasts with the brutality of the daily grind and the abjection of her final journey. In Japanese with English subtitles.

Ken Ogata *Tatsuhei* • Sumiko Sakamoto *Orin-yan* • Tonpei Hidari *Risuke, "Smelly"* • Takejo Aki *Tama-yan* • Shoichi Ozawa *Shozo* • Mitsuaki Fukamizu *Tada-yan* • Seiji Kurasaki *Kesakichi* • Junko Takada *Matsu-yan* ■ *Dir* Shohei Imamura • *Scr* Shohei Imamura, from the novels by Shichiro Fukazawa

The Ballad of the Sad Café ★★ 15

Drama 1991 · US/UK · Colour · 100mins

A critical success but commercial flop on release, this sometimes brutal directorial debut by actor Simon Callow takes a bizarre but wonderfully written book by Carson McCullers and, by way of Edward Albee's stage version, gives it the enclosed, soundstage-on-a-shoestring-budget treatment. Its toe-curling pretentiousness knows no bounds, crowned by an execrable over-the-top performance by Vanessa Redgrave who attacks her role with full rolling-eyed abandon. More directorial control would have prevented this movie from being the luvvie-in it is. [video]

Vanessa Redgrave *Miss Amelia Evans* • Keith Carradine *Marvin Macy* • Cork Hubbert *Cousin Lymon* • Rod Steiger *Reverend Willin* • Austin Pendleton *Lawyer Taylor* • Beth Dixon *Mary Hale* • Lanny Flaherty *Merlie Ryan* ■ *Dir* Simon Callow • *Scr* Michael Hirst, from the play by Edward Albee, from the novel by Carson McCullers

Balloon Farm ★★

Fantasy 1999 · US · Colour · 92mins

This whimsical Disney TV movie, based on a popular children's book, is strictly for the kiddies. If you watch it with them, however, you might just be charmed. A mysterious stranger (Rip Torn) comes to a farming community suffering from a seemingly endless drought and begins to grow balloons. Not just any balloons, either: as 12-year-old Willow (Mara Wilson from *Mrs Doubtfire*) discovers, they have magical properties... A well-directed fantasy from William Dear, in which everyone lives happily ever after.

Rip Torn *Harvey Potter* • Laurie Metcalf *Casey Johnson* • Mara Wilson *Willow Johnson* • Roberts Blossom *Whezzle Mayfield* • Fredric Lane [Fredric Lehne] *Jake* • Richard Riehle

Earl • Ernie Lively *Tom Williams* • Arnetia Walker *Crystal* ■ *Dir* William Dear • *Scr* Steven M Karczynski, from the novel *Harvey Potter's Balloon Farm* by Jerdine Nolen

Balmaa ★★ PG
Drama 1993 · Ind · Colour · 132mins

The subcontinent's controversial marital customs have inspired countless melodramas down the years. But few have contained such dark undercurrents as Lawrence D'Souza's drama about an orphan who begins to have doubts about marriage when her best friend is murdered shortly after setting up home with her seemingly charming husband. With Ayesha Jhulka impressive as the imperilled innocent and a typically assured supporting performance from Saeed Jaffrey, this may have the plotline of a straight-to-video thriller, but the setting gives it a certain curio value. In Hindi with English subtitles. 🎬

Avinash Wadhawan • Ayesha Jhulka • Saeed Jaffrey • Anjana Mumtaz • Shammi ■ *Dir* Lawrence D'Souza • *Scr* Talat Rekhi

The Baltimore Bullet ★★ 15
Comedy 1980 · US · Colour · 98mins

The Hustler for wimps, with James Coburn and protégé Bruce Boxleitner touring the pool halls of America and taking on the sharks. A big tournament lies ahead, for which Coburn needs a minimum stake of $20,000 if he is to take on the Deacon (Omar Sharif in the old Jackie Gleason role). Subplots about local gangsters and the drug trade juggle for screen time with the rather repetitive pool games, though the film just about gets by on the charm of its two stars. 🎬

James Coburn *Nick Casey* • Omar Sharif *Deacon* • Ronee Blakely *Carolina Red* • Bruce Boxleitner *Billie Joe Robbins* • Jack O'Halloran *Max* • Michael Lerner *Paulie* • Calvin Lockhart *Snow White* ■ *Dir* Robert Ellis Miller • *Scr* John Brascia, Robert Vincent O'Neill

Balto ★★★ U
Animated adventure
1995 · US/UK · Colour · 77mins

Executive produced by Steven Spielberg, this well-crafted cartoon tells the story of an outcast sled dog who tries to save the children of the isolated Alaskan town of Nome during a diphtheria epidemic in 1925. Kevin Bacon's voice turns the wolf-dog crossbreed into a no-nonsense hero with a sense of duty that far outweighs the pride of his deadly rival, Steele, while Bob Hoskins's eccentric Russian goose provides the comedy. A touch darker than most animated features.

Kevin Bacon *Balto* • Bob Hoskins *Boris* • Bridget Fonda *Jenna* • Jim Cummings *Steele* • Phil Collins *Muk/Luk* • Jack Angel *Nikki* ■ *Dir* Simon Wells • *Scr* Cliff Ruby, Elana Lesser, David Steven Cohen, Roger SH Schulman, from a story by Elana Lesser, Cliff Ruby

La Bamba ★★★ 15
Biographical drama
1986 · US · Colour · 104mins

Most pop biopics are tepid affairs, but the same cannot be said for director Luis Valdez's engrossing re-creation of Ritchie Valens's short life. Los Angeles band Los Lobos perform impassioned versions of the young man's songs, and their playing is mirrored by Lou Diamond Phillips's intense performance, which brings the fifties rock 'n' roll star to life with a lot of vibrant detail while generally avoiding the usual clichés of the genre. As Ritchie's bad-boy half-brother, Esai Morales also contributes to the authenticity. Contains swearing and some nudity. 🎬

Lou Diamond Phillips *Ritchie Valens/Richard Valenzuela* • Esai Morales *Bob Morales* • Rosana De Soto *Connie Valenzuela* • Elizabeth Pena *Rosie Morales* • Danielle Von Zerneck *Donna Ludwig* • Joe Pantoliano *Bob Keene* ■ *Dir/Scr* Luis Valdez

Bambi ★★★★★ U
Animation 1942 · US · Colour · 66mins

A classic for all age-groups and all time. The Disney animation of Felix Salten's book is peerless. It's about a young deer growing up in the forest alongside a timid skunk and a scene-stealing rabbit, Thumper, a ground-drumming creature – just as the film is a ground-breaker for its filming of shades of black on black. The death of Bambi's mother is still a heart-piercing event. However, musical numbers such as *Love Is a Song* and *Little April Showers* lift the heart with an affirmation for life that supervising director David Hand maintains throughout. 🎬

Bobby Stewart *Bambi* • Peter Behn *Thumper* • Stan Alexander *Flower* • Cammie King *Phylline* ■ *Dir* David D Hand [David Hand] • *Scr* Perce Pearce, Larry Morey, from a story by Felix Salten, from his novel

Banana Ridge ★★
Comedy 1941 · UK · BW · 87mins

Along with Ralph Lynn and Tom Walls, Robertson Hare was one of the stalwarts of the Aldwych farces in the twenties. He reprises one of his stage roles in this creaky comedy by the great Ben Travers. Set on a Malaysian rubber plantation, the story of gold digging, guilty secrets and disputed paternity follows the farce formula to the last letter, but it lacks the pace and complexity essential for a first-class comedy. The ever-flustered Hare and Alfred Drayton rush around gamely, but they are ultimately defeated by Walter C Mycroft's plodding direction.

Robertson Hare *Willoughby Pink* • Alfred Drayton *Mr Pound* • Isabel Jeans *Sue Long* • Nova Pilbeam *Cora Pound* • Adele Dixon *Mrs Pound* • Patrick Kinsella *Jones* • Valentine Dunn *Mrs Pink* ■ *Dir* Walter C Mycroft • *Scr* Lesley Storm, Walter C Mycroft, Ben Travers, from the play by Ben Travers

Bananas ★★★ 15
Comedy 1971 · US · Colour · 78mins

With a title that refers to both banana republics and the Marx Brothers film *Cocoanuts*, Woody Allen's second picture as director and star is one of his least convincing outings. Packed with nods to cinematic maestros such as Eisenstein, Chaplin, Buñuel and Bergman, it's the work of a comic delighting in his gags rather than a director in control of his material. A touch of political satire might have helped stem the endless flow of throwaway lines and surreal incidents, as well as giving the plot a little more focus. Inconsistent it may be, but when *Bananas* is funny, it's a riot. 🎬

Woody Allen *Fielding Mellish* • Louise Lasser *Nancy* • Carlos Montalban *General Emilio M Vargas* • Natividad Abascal *Yolanda* • Jacobo Morales *Esposito* • Miguel Suarez [Miguel Angel Suarez] *Luis* • Sylvester Stallone *Subway thug* ■ *Dir* Woody Allen • *Scr* Woody Allen, Mickey Rose

Band of Angels ★★
Period drama 1957 · US · Colour · 114mins

After the death of her father, a beautiful Southern belle is not only left without a cent to her name, but also unearths the startling fact that her mother was a slave. As a result she's sold as a slave to millionaire Clark Gable, whose mistress she becomes. Directed by the veteran Raoul Walsh, who must have been forced into it, and with Sidney Poitier as a slave, this utter tosh strains credibility to the limits and has little to recommend it other than De Carlo's glamour and the occasional disconcerting echo of better pre-Civil War epics.

Clark Gable *Hamish Bond* • Yvonne De Carlo *Amantha Starr* • Sidney Poitier *Rau-Ru* • Efrem Zimbalist Jr *Ethan Sears* • Rex Reason *Seth Parton* • Patric Knowles *Charles de Marigny* • Torin Thatcher *Captain Canavan* ■ *Dir* Raoul Walsh • *Scr* John Twist, Ivan Goff, Ben Roberts, from the novel by Robert Penn Warren

Band Waggon ★★★ U
Musical comedy 1939 · UK · BW · 85mins

The radio spin-off movie may be unheard of today, but they were all the rage in the thirties. Although it only ran for some two years, *Band Waggon*, with its quirky characters and rapid-fire humour, was hugely popular. Here, the script restricts the fabled ad-libbing of Arthur Askey and Richard "Stinker" Murdoch, but it's still good fun as the pair stray from their famous flat in the eaves of Broadcasting House only to encounter spies in a haunted castle – a plot familiar to director Marcel Varnel from his time with Will Hay. Hay's toothless sidekick Moore Marriott also makes a welcome appearance.

Arthur Askey *Big Hearted Arthur* • Richard Murdoch *Stinker* • Jack Hylton *Jack Hylton* • Pat Kirkwood *Pat* • Moore Marriott *Jasper* • Peter Gawthorne *Claude Pilkington* • Wally Patch *Commissionaire* ■ *Dir* Marcel Varnel • *Scr* Marriott Edgar, Val Guest, from the radio series by Harry S Pepper, Gordon Crier, Vernon Harris

The Band Wagon ★★★★★ U
Musical 1953 · US · Colour · 107mins

A clever and witty backstage musical, with a great Arthur Schwartz/Howard Dietz score. A screen original from writers Betty Comden and Adolph Green (the *Singin' in the Rain* team), it boasts brilliant direction from Vincente Minnelli. To many, this is the peak of Fred Astaire's screen work. He's stunning as he partners the gorgeous Cyd Charisse in Michael Kidd and Oliver Smith's superb choreography to *Dancing in the Dark* and the Mickey Spillane parody *The Girl Hunt* ballet. British veteran Jack Buchanan is cleverly cast, and Oscar Levant and Nanette Fabray effectively play Green and Comden themselves. As good as musicals get. 🎬

Fred Astaire *Tony Hunter* • Cyd Charisse *Gaby Berard* • Jack Buchanan *Jeffrey Cordova* • Oscar Levant *Lester Marton* • Nanette Fabray *Lily Marton* • James Mitchell *Paul Byrd* • Robert Gist *Hal Benton* • Ava Gardner *Movie star* ■ *Dir* Vincente Minnelli • *Scr* Betty Comden, Adolph Green • *Lyrics* Howard Dietz • *Music* Arthur Schwartz

Bande à Part ★★★★
Crime drama 1964 · Fr · Colour · 95mins

A playful effort from Jean-Luc Godard in which his then wife, the radiant Anna Karina, teams up with a couple of petty crooks – Sami Frey and Claude Brasseur – in a hair-brained scheme to rob her aunt. In characteristic fashion, Godard drops the plot at every opportunity to indulge in homages to various Hollywood genres – the thriller, the musical and so on – and to allow his camera to idolise Karina's beauty. Some may find it irritating beyond endurance, but in its day its freshness was greeted like rain in a drought. Thirty years later, a certain Quentin Tarantino rediscovered the film and liked it so much he named his production company "A Band Apart". A French language film. 🎬 **DVD**

Anna Karina *Odile* • Claude Brasseur *Arthur* • Sami Frey *Franz* • Louisa Colpeyn *Madame Victoria* • Danièle Girard *English teacher* • Ernest Menzer *Arthur's uncle* • Chantal Darget *Arthur's aunt* ■ *Dir* Jean-Luc Godard • *Scr* Jean-Luc Godard, from the novel *Fool's Gold (Pigeon Vole)* by Dolores Hitchens

Bandido ★★ U
Western 1956 · US · Colour · 91mins

This routine fifties western adventure stars Robert Mitchum as an American soldier of fortune who joins forces with a rebel leader in a bid to intercept a shipment of arms during the Mexican Revolution. Mitchum is better than the script, but the film still offers action, sufficient intrigue and picturesque landscapes. You could do worse.

Robert Mitchum *Wilson* • Ursula Thiess *Lisa* • Gilbert Roland *Escobar* • Zachary Scott *Kennedy* • Rodolfo Acosta *Sebastian* • Henry Brandon *Gunther* • Douglas Fowley *McGee* • Jose I Torvay *Gonzalez* • Victor Junco *Lorenzo* ■ *Dir* Richard Fleischer • *Scr* Earl Felton

The Bandit of Sherwood Forest ★★ U
Swashbuckling adventure
1946 · US · Colour · 86mins

Cornel Wilde stars in this swashbuckler as Robin Hood's son, who tries to save the Magna Carta and Britain from the constitutional ravages of Henry Daniell's royal schemer, the wayward Regent. It's really just a western in weird costumes with added peasantry, shot on the Columbia backlot in bright-as-a-button Technicolor. Not a patch on Errol Flynn's classic *The Adventures of Robin Hood*, this is an enjoyable romp just the same.

Cornel Wilde *Robert of Nottingham* • Anita Louise *Lady Catherine Maitland* • Jill Esmond *Queen Mother* • Edgar Buchanan *Friar Tuck* • Henry Daniell *Regent* • George Macready *Fitz-Herbert* • Russell Hicks *Robin Hood* • John Abbott *Will Scarlet* • Ray Teal *Little John* ■ *Dir*

George Sherman, Henry Levin • *Scr* Wilfred H Pettit, Melvyn Levy, from the novel *Son of Robin Hood* by Paul A Castleton

The Bandit of Zhobe ★★ 🄴

Action adventure 1959 · UK · Colour · 81mins

Very silly Northwest Frontier romp, with Victor Mature in dark make-up as Kasim Khan, a fearsome but noble Indian leader whose family has been massacred by red-coated Brits. There ensues much pillage (but little rape), a lot of smirking by Mature, romantic interest from forgotten starlet Anne Aubrey and some wince-inducing comic mugging from Anthony Newley. Quite a lot of money was thrown at it, but this remains a B-movie at heart. Producer Albert R Broccoli, source writer Richard Maibaum and cameraman Ted Moore would all be more profitably employed on the Bond films.

Victor Mature *Kasim Khan* • Anne Aubrey *Zena Crowley* • Anthony Newley *Corporal Stokes* • Norman Wooland *Major Crowley* • Dermot Walsh *Captain Saunders* • Walter Gotell *Azhad* ■ *Dir* John Gilling • *Scr* John Gilling, from a story by Richard Maibaum

Bandit Queen ★★★★ 🄸

Biographical drama
1994 · Ind/UK · Colour · 114mins

Released to a storm of protest throughout the subcontinent and the displeasure of its subject, Phoolan Devi herself, this is a damning condemnation of both the caste system and the subservience of women in modern Indian society. Director Shekhar Kapur deserves great credit for depicting provocative events without the slightest hint of sensationalism, whether it is Devi's gang-rape at the hands of some Uttar Pradeshi bandits or her merciless revenge, which culminated in the Behmai massacre of 1981. Seema Biswas is superb as the folkloric figure who avoided capture for five years before surrendering in 1983. In Hindi with English subtitles.

Seema Biswas *Phoolan Devi* • Nirmal Pandey *Vikram Mallah* • Manoj Bajpai *Man Singh* • Rajesh Vivek *Mustaquim* • Raghuvir Yadav *Madho* • Govind Namdeo *Sriram* • Saurabh Shukla *Kailash* • Aditya Srivastava *Puttilal* ■ *Dir* Shekhar Kapur • *Scr* Mala Sen

The Bandits of Corsica ★ 🄴

Adventure 1953 · US · BW · 80mins

The 1942 Douglas Fairbanks Jr swashbuckler *The Corsican Brothers* was only loosely based on the characters created by Alexandre Dumas, but this sequel is even further removed. Every expense seems to have been spared in the mounting of this clumping adventure, in which Richard Greene manages to give two poor performances, as the heroic gypsy Mario and as his wicked twin, Carlos. Raymond Burr is suitably bombastic as the island's tyrannical ruler, but director Ray Nazarro seems more interested in the bizarre telepathy between the twins, particularly once Carlos makes a move on Mario's missus. More dumb than Dumas.

Richard Greene *Mario/Carlos* • Paula Raymond *Christina* • Raymond Burr *Jonatto* • Dona Drake *Zelda* • Raymond Greenleaf *Paoli*

• Lee Van Cleef *Nerva* • Frank Puglia *Riggio* ■ *Dir* Ray Nazarro • *Scr* Richard Schayer, from a story by Frank Burt

Bandolero! ★★★ 🄸

Western 1968 · US · Colour · 101mins

One of a slew of colourful, handsomely mounted westerns made by 20th Century-Fox during the sixties, this would-be rollicking adventure suffers from chronic miscasting. All-time good guys James Stewart and Dean Martin are a pair of outlaw brothers who hold a peculiarly accented Raquel Welch hostage after she loses her husband in a botched bank raid. The actual good guy, surprisingly, is George Kennedy, no match for these particular baddies. The uneven mixture of contemporary violence and traditional western values is uncomfortably directed by Andrew V McLaglen, whose father, Victor, appeared in many of the best of the westerns directed by the great John Ford. A mess, but not unenjoyable. ▢

James Stewart *Mace Bishop* • Dean Martin *Dee Bishop* • Raquel Welch *Maria* • George Kennedy *Sheriff Johnson* • Andrew Prine *Roscoe Bookbinder* • Will Geer *Pop Chaney* • Clint Richie *Babe* • Denver Pyle *Muncie Carter* ■ *Dir* Andrew V McLaglen • *Scr* James Lee Barrett, from a story by Stanley L Hough

Bang ★★★ 🄸

Drama 1995 · US · Colour · 94mins

A struggling Japanese-American actress (Darling Narita) steals an LA cop's uniform and motorcycle and finds that she is treated differently by everyone she meets. Her newly found status also enables her to take revenge on the producer who tried to molest her. Written and directed by London-born Ash (real name Ashley Baron Cohen), this ambitious US indie was made for just $20,000 with hand-held cameras and no permits. Peter Greene (*Pulp Fiction*) plays a homeless man who becomes embroiled in the unnamed heroine's curious social experiment. Contains swearing, violence and sex scenes. ▢

Darling Narita *The girl* • Peter Greene *Adam* • Michael Newland *Officer Rattler* • David Allen Graf [David Alan Graf] *Peter Fawcette, the producer* • Everlast *Pimp* • Art Cruz *Juan* • Luis Guizar *Jezuz* ■ *Dir* Ash • *Scr* Ash

Bang the Drum Slowly

★★★★

Sports drama 1973 · US · Colour · 98mins

Until *Field of Dreams* came along, director John Hancock's moving buddy drama held the title of the best baseball movie ever made. Telling the engrossing tale of how New York pitcher Michael Moriarty helps his terminally-ill catcher Robert De Niro through one more season, this fifties-set heartbreaker resonates with emotional truths while evoking nostalgia for a more innocent era. It's superlatively performed by De Niro (then unknown) and Moriarty, with excellent support from Vincent Gardenia, as his manager (he was nominated for an Oscar). The underlying theme of people coming through for each other in times of dire trouble is expertly handled by Hancock from a first-class script by Mark Harris.

Robert De Niro *Bruce Pearson* • Vincent Gardenia *Dutch Schnell* • Phil Foster *Joe Jaros* • Ann Wedgeworth *Katie* • Patrick McVey *Pearson's father* • Heather MacRae *Holly Wiggin* • Selma Diamond *Tootsie* ■ *Dir* John Hancock • *Scr* Mark Harris, from his novel

Bang! You're Dead ★★

Crime drama 1954 · UK · BW · 88mins

Simply because the plot revolves around a young boy finding a gun and accidentally killing a much detested local man, only for the victim's most outspoken detractor to be arrested for murder, this minor British crime drama has been compared to both 1949's *The Window* and 1952's *The Yellow Balloon*. Yet there's considerably less insight into the boy's guilt-stricken torment than in either of those films, with director Lance Comfort settling for a mildly suspenseful countdown to the predictable climax.

Jack Warner *Mr Bonsell* • Derek Farr *Detective Grey* • Veronica Hurst *Hilda* • Michael Medwin *Bob Carter* • Gordon Harker *Mr Hare* • Anthony Richmond *Cliff Bonsell* • Sean Barrett *Willy* ■ *Dir* Lance Comfort • *Scr* Guy Elmes, Ernest Borneman

Banjo on My Knee ★★★

Musical drama 1936 · US · BW · 95mins

Here's feisty Barbara Stanwyck in one of her early tours de force. After being abandoned by new husband Joel McCrea, Stanwyck, as riverboat moll Pearl, takes over the whole show: she dances with Buddy Ebsen, sings with Tony Martin and even gets into a fight with Katherine DeMille, adopted daughter of the legendary Cecil B. John Cromwell's direction is perfunctory, but the supporting players (Walter Brennan, Helen Westley, Walter Catlett) are a joy, and the movie paved the way for Stanwyck's triumph the following year in *Stella Dallas*.

Barbara Stanwyck *Pearl* • Joel McCrea *Ernie Holley* • Helen Westley *Grandma* • Buddy Ebsen *Puddy* • Walter Brennan *Newt Holley* • Walter Catlett *Warfield Scott* • Tony Martin *Chick Bean* • Minna Gombell *Ruby* • Katherine DeMille *Leota Long* ■ *Dir* John Cromwell • *Scr* Nunnally Johnson, from the novel by Harry Hamilton

The Bank Dick ★★★★ 🄴

Comedy 1940 · US · BW · 72mins

Scripted by WC Fields under the name of Mahatma Kane Jeeves, this is one of his finest comedies. Playing the wonderfully named Egbert Souse, Fields growls and grumbles his way through some inspired routines as the indolent passer-by who is rewarded with the post of bank detective after inadvertently foiling a raid. Even though several gags are rehashed from his celebrated shorts, they are done to a crisp by Fields and a superb supporting cast, in which Cora Witherspoon, Una Merkel and Jessie Ralph are outstanding as the women who delight in wearily pointing out the shortcomings he considers his assets. ▢

WC Fields *Egbert Souse* • Cora Witherspoon *Agatha Souse* • Una Merkel *Myrtle Souse* • Evelyn Del Rio *Elsie May Adele Souse* • Jessie Ralph *Mrs Hermisillo Brunch* • Franklin Pangborn *J Pinkerton Snoopington* • Shemp Howard *Joe Guelpe* ■ *Dir* Edward Cline • *Scr* Mahatma Kane Jeeves [WC Fields]

Bank Holiday ★★★

Comedy drama 1938 · UK · BW · 86mins

While today it may look slightly laboured, in 1938 this neat comedy drama was acclaimed for its naturalism, restraint and shrewd characterisation. Following a group of day trippers to Brighton, the film is smoothly directed by Carol Reed, who sustains interest in a variety of stock figures by flitting between them in the style of a soap opera instalment. Margaret Lockwood wins sympathy as a nurse who is distracted from a dirty weekend by her concern for a grieving widow, but the stand-out performances come from Kathleen Harrison as a prim Cockney wife and Wilfrid Lawson as a world-weary police desk sergeant.

John Lodge *Stephen Howard* • Margaret Lockwood *Catherine* • Hugh Williams *Geoffrey* • René Ray *Doreen* • Merle Tottenham *Milly* • Linden Travers *Ann Howard* • Wally Patch *Arthur* • Kathleen Harrison *May* • Garry Marsh *Manager* ■ *Dir* Carol Reed • *Scr* Rodney Ackland, Roger Burford, from a story by Hans Wilhelm, Rodney Ackland

The Bank Raiders ★ 🄴

Crime thriller 1958 · UK · BW · 60mins

A dismal B-movie about a bank robber who spends his swag too quickly and attracts the rozzers, obliging him to turn kidnapper. Designed as something to have on the screen while the queue was being let in to the cinema, it's cheap and cheerless wallpaper, though connoisseurs of early TV sitcoms might relish the sight of heavyweight Arthur Mullard, who usually turned in performances as the village idiot.

Peter Reynolds *Terry* • Sandra Dorne *Della* • Sydney Tafler *Sholton* • Lloyd Lamble *Inspector Mason* • Rose Hill *Mrs Marling* • Arthur Mullard *Linders* ■ *Dir* Maxwell Munden • *Scr* Brandon Fleming

Bank Robber ★★★ 🄸

Crime comedy 1993 · US · Colour · 89mins

A modern-day version of the Robin Hood legend, with further twists provided by the fact that this outlaw not only steals from the rich, but also gets shafted by the poor. Most of the action takes place in one room in writer/director Nick Mead's conceptually interesting mix of dark comedy, surreal action and extreme social significance. With the exception of a bland Patrick Dempsey, the cast rises to the offbeat occasion, providing exuberant fun and some seriously sexy moments. ▢

Patrick Dempsey *Billy* • Lisa Bonet *Priscilla* • Judge Reinhold *Officer Gross* • Forest Whitaker *Officer Battle* • Olivia D'Abo *Selina* • Mariska Hargitay *Marisa Benoit* • Joe Alaskey *2nd night clerk* ■ *Dir/Scr* Nick Mead

Bank Shot ★★ 🄿🄶

Comedy caper 1974 · US · Colour · 80mins

Directed by Gower Champion of Hollywood's Marge and Gower Champion dance team, this bizarre outing for George C Scott is a far cry from his magnificent performance four years earlier in the Second World War biopic *Patton: Lust for Glory*. This feeble comedy caper too often stretches credibility as escaped convict Scott literally steals a bank by lifting it up and dragging it off. Although there are some neat gags and shrewd ideas, such as the final shots of Scott, the result is all at sea. ▭

George C Scott *Walter Ballantine* • Joanna Cassidy *El* • Sorrell Booke *Al G Karp* • G Wood *FBI Agent Andrew Constable* • Clifton James *Frank ''Bulldog'' Streiger* • Robert Balaban [Bob Balaban] *Victor Karp* • Bibi Osterwald *Mums* • Harvey J Goldenberg *First policeman* ■ *Dir* Gower Champion • *Scr* Wendell Mayes, from the novel by Donald E Westlake

B.A.P.S. ★ 15

Comedy   1997 · US · Colour · 92mins

If George Bernard Shaw could see this, he'd be doing cartwheels in his coffin. A lame, ludicrous African-American *Pygmalion*, it stars Halle Berry and Natalie Desselle as a couple of garishly-dressed Georgia dreamers auditioning for a music video in LA, who are offered cash to brighten up the last days of dying millionaire Martin Landau by posing as relatives of his long-lost love. The scenario that introduces these ''Black American Princesses'' would be insulting enough, if the movie didn't believe it had a message – apparently black women can reach for the skies, and white people can listen to rap music, too. Not cute or clever, just clueless.

Halle Berry *Nisi* • Martin Landau *Mr Blakemore* • Ian Richardson *Manley* • Natalie Desselle *Mickey* • Troy Beyer *Tracy* • Luigi Amodeo *Antonio* • Jonathan Fried *Isaac* • Pierre *Ali* • AJ Johnson [Anthony Johnson] *James* ■ *Dir* Robert Townsend • *Scr* Troy Beyer

Bar Girls ★ 18

Romantic comedy
1994 · US · Colour · 94mins

On its release, this was well received at various festivals, including Toronto and Berlin, but it must have been part of a very bad batch. The criticism that dares not speak its name has to say that if this was about eight heterosexuals in a bar – and not eight upfront lesbians – the movie probably would not have been considered for selection. Good grief, do these women witter. This self-indulgent film fails to sufficiently flesh out either the characters or screenplay. ▭

Nancy Allison Wolfe *Loretta* • Liza D'Agostino *Rachel* • Camila Griggs *JR* • Michael Harris *Noah* • Justine Slater *Veronica* • Lisa Parker *Annie* • Pam Raines *Celia* ■ *Dir* Marita Giovanni • *Scr* Lauran Hoffman, from her play

Barabbas ★★★ PG

Epic biblical drama
1961 · It · Colour · 127mins

An impressive quasi-biblical epic, produced by Dino De Laurentiis on a grand scale and directed with a fine sense of period by Richard Fleischer. It's best remembered today, however, for the fact that the Crucifixion was photographed against an actual eclipse of the sun. Anthony Quinn does well in the title role as the murderer and thief pardoned in place of Christ, and the climactic arena sequences involving Jack Palance are splendid. However, as a whole, it's overlong and dull, like the novel on which it is based. ▭

Anthony Quinn *Barabbas* • Silvana Mangano *Rachel* • Arthur Kennedy *Pontius Pilate* • Katy

Jurado *Sara* • Harry Andrews *Peter* • Vittorio Gassman *Sahak* • Jack Palance *Torvald* • Ernest Borgnine *Lucius* ■ *Dir* Richard Fleischer • *Scr* Christopher Fry, from the novel by Par Lagerkvist

Baraka ★★ PG

Documentary   1992 · US · Colour · 92mins

Shot on Todd-AO 70mm stock, so that every image positively shimmers, Ron Fricke's heartfelt film is, sadly, a wasted opportunity. The ecological points he makes are blatant and laboured, while his over-reliance on snazzy editing and time-lapse photography draws too much attention to technique at the expense of the visual content. The contrasts between urban jungles and the areas of natural beauty they imperil do, occasionally, strike home, but, while it's easy to look at these often beautiful moving postcards, Fricke presents locations without identifying them, so most viewers will quickly find themselves lost and overwhelmed. ▭

Dir Ron Fricke • *Music* Michael Stearns

Barb Wire ★ 18

Science-fiction adventure
1995 · US · Colour · 100mins

''Don't call me babe!'' scowls Pamela Anderson, as she roves around Steel Harbor zapping agents of the Congressional Directorate. OK, providing you don't ask us to call this insulting reworking of *Casablanca* a film. Betraying his pop-video background, director David Hogan clearly isn't interested in storytelling, which is just as well as he doesn't have much of a tale to tell. Even amid the devastation of a second American civil war, surely more will stand between the people and tyranny than magical contact lenses? Despite being treated like a computer generated cartoon, Pam takes it all in surprisingly good part. Contains violence, swearing and nudity. ▭

Pamela Anderson Lee [Pamela Anderson] *Barb Wire* • Temuera Morrison *Axel Hood* • Victoria Rowell *Cora D* • Jack Noseworthy *Charlie* • Xander Berkeley *Alexander Willis* • Steve Railsback *Colonel Pryzer* • Udo Kier *Curly* ■ *Dir* David Hogan • *Scr* Chuck Pfarrer, Ilene Chaiken, from the story by Ilene Chaiken

Barbara Taylor Bradford's Everything to Gain ★

Mystery   1996 · US · Colour · 87mins

Sean Young (*No Way Out*) stars as a woman who tries to rebuild her life after her loving husband and two children are murdered. Alone and depressed, she joins forces with a gritty detective (Jack Scalia) to find the thugs responsible for the crime. Unless you're a rabid fan of Barbara Taylor Bradford, you have nothing to gain from this preposterous story. How on earth did those talented actresses Joanna Miles and Samantha Eggar get mixed up in this drivel?

Sean Young *Mallory Jordan* • Jack Scalia *Detective DeMarco* • Charles Shaughnessy *Andrew Keswick* • Joanna Miles *Jessica Jordan* • Samantha Eggar *Diana Keswick* ■ *Dir* Michael Miller • *Scr* Cathleen Young, from the novel by Barbara Taylor Bradford

Barbara Taylor Bradford's Love in Another Town ★

Romantic drama   1997 · US · Colour · 88mins

When her husband leaves her after 22 years of marriage, a middle-aged designer (former *Dallas* diva Victoria Principal) moves to a new town and falls in love with a younger man (Adrian Pasdar). She doesn't know he's still married and is soon carrying his child. Complications ensue, but true love conquers all in this sappy, soapy melodrama. Watch this only if you're a fan of overwrought acting, mundane dialogue and vapid characters.

Victoria Principal *Maggie Sorrell* • Adrian Pasdar *Jake Cantrell* • Mary Kay Place *Sam* • Terence Knox *Mike* • Finn Carter *Amy* ■ *Dir* Lorraine Senna [Lorraine Senna Ferrara] • *Scr* H Haden Yelin, from the novel by Barbara Taylor Bradford

Barbara Taylor Bradford's Her Own Rules ★★ PG

Romantic drama   1998 · US · Colour · 86mins

This frothy confection was made for American TV, set in England and apparently filmed in Ireland, though that's hardly likely to bother Barbara Taylor Bradford's legion of fans. Melissa Gilbert exchanges the Little House on the Prairie for a string of luxury hotels as a wealthy woman who's seeking the truth about her traumatic past. Jean Simmons leads a distinguished supporting cast in a soapy melodrama that won't disappoint fans of the original. ▭

Melissa Gilbert *Meredith Sanders* • Jeremy Sheffield *Lucas Kent* • Jean Simmons *Britta Smith* ■ *Scr* Cathleen Young, from the novel by Barbara Taylor Bradford

Barbarella ★★★ 15

Cult science-fiction fantasy
1967 · Fr/It · Colour · 93mins

The famed French comic strip comes to glorious life in director Roger Vadim's 40th-century space opera. Once you get past Jane Fonda's infamous anti-gravity striptease, however, the script turns rather dull. The imaginative sets steal the whole show, as Fonda's nubile intergalactic bimbo experiences close encounters of the sexually bizarre kind. A pleasure machine, cannibalistic dolls and Anita Pallenberg's Black Queen help ease the verbal vacuum in Vadim's relentless visual assault, which is sure to delight some and prove tiresome to others. Contains violence and sex scenes. ▭

Jane Fonda *Barbarella* • John Phillip Law *Pygar* • Anita Pallenberg *Black Queen* • Milo O'Shea *Concierge/Durand-Durand* • David Hemmings *Dildano* • Marcel Marceau *Professor Ping* • Ugo Tognazzi *Mark Hand* • Claude Dauphin *President of Earth* • Catherine Chevalier *Stomoxys* ■ *Dir* Roger Vadim • *Scr* Terry Southern, Brian Degas, Claude Brulé, Jean-Claude Forest, Clement Biddle Wood, Tudor Gates, Vittorio Bonicelli, Roger Vadim, from the comic by Jean-Claude Forest

The Barbarian ★★★

Romance   1933 · US · BW · 82mins

Made when screen idol Ramon Novarro was nearing the end of the peak of his career and Myrna Loy was at the start of hers, this kind of hot-blooded desert

romance was already somewhat old hat. Wisely, the screenplay does not take things too seriously. When tourist Loy is cautioned by her uncle that she is hiring as a guide a man she knows nothing about, she replies, ''But look at that profile!'' Dashing Novarro sings *Love Songs of the Nile*; sparkling Loy takes an on-screen bath and relishes the risqué pre-code dialogue. Taken in the right spirit, it is great fun.

Ramon Novarro *Jamil* • Myrna Loy *Diana* • Reginald Denny *Gerald* • Louise Closser Hale *Powers* • C Aubrey Smith *Cecil* • Edward Arnold *Achmed* • Blanche Frederici *Mrs Hume* ■ *Dir* Sam Wood • *Scr* Anita Loos, Elmer Harris, from the story by Edgar Selwyn

The Barbarian and the Geisha ★ U

Historical drama
1958 · US · Colour · 100mins

Tough-guy director John Huston teamed up with John Wayne for the first and last time to make this historical drama about Townsend Harris, America's first consul to Japan. Huston cast Wayne because he would physically and metaphorically tower over the Japanese, while Wayne was attracted to the role because it got him out of westerns and showed America's historical influence over their wartime enemy. Wayne and Huston loathed each other from day one, however, and the movie was an unmitigated disaster – from the indulgent casting of Huston's Oriental girlfriend, Eiko Ando, to a riot after a special-effects fire nearly wrecked a fishing village. ▭

John Wayne *Townsend Harris* • Eiko Ando *Okichi* • Sam Jaffe *Henry Heusken* • So Yamamura *Tamura* • Norman Thomson *Ship captain* • James Robbins *Lieutenant Fisher* • Morita *Prime minister* • Kodaya Ichikawa *Daimyo* ■ *Dir* John Huston • *Scr* Charles Grayson, from a story by Ellis St Joseph

Barbarians at the Gate ★★★★ 15

Satirical drama based on a true story
1993 · US · Colour · 102mins

A true-life tale that disproves Gordon Gekko's famous *Wall Street* quote ''Greed is good. Greed works!''. Based on Bryan Burrough and John Helyar's bestseller, this superior TV movie recounts one of the most vicious takeover deals in American business history. James Garner is admirable as the head of multinational power player RJR Nabisco, who tries to buy the company when he realises its smokeless cigarette project isn't going to catch light. Stealing the show, however, is Jonathan Pryce as the wheeler-dealer determined to block him. The script is razor-sharp and Glenn Jordan's direction red hot. Contains swearing. ▭

James Garner *F Ross Johnson* • Jonathan Pryce *Henry Kravis* • Peter Riegert *Peter Cohen* • Joanna Cassidy *Linda Robinson* • Fred Dalton Thompson *Jim Robinson* • Leilani Ferrer *Laurie Johnson* • Matt Clark *Ed Horrigan* • Jeffrey DeMunn *John Greenieus* ■ *Dir* Glenn Jordan • *Scr* Larry Gelbart, from the book *Barbarians at the Gate: the Fall of RJR Nabisco* by Bryan Burrough, John Helyar

U = SUITABLE FOR ALL   Uc = SUITABLE FOR ALL, ESPECIALLY FOR YOUNG CHILDREN (VIDEO ONLY)   PG = PARENTAL GUIDANCE

Barbarosa ★★★ PG

Western   1982 · US · Colour · 86mins

Just as rock stars lend the status of myth to their movies (Mick Jagger in *Ned Kelly*, David Bowie in *The Man Who Fell to Earth*), so country-and-western star Willie Nelson was chosen by director Fred Schepisi to be this film's western legend. But it doesn't work as well as intended, despite Nelson's endearing partnership with goofy farmboy Gary Busey, because the idea of an ageing outlaw forever on the lam is not only predictable but monotonous. However, the Rio Grande scenery is as spectacular as the movie should have been. ▣

Willie Nelson *Barbarosa* • Gary Busey *Karl* • Gilbert Roland *Don Braulio* • Isela Vega *Josephina* • Danny De La Paz *Eduardo* • Alma Martinez *Juanita* • George Voskovec *Herman Pahmeyer* • Sharon Compton *Hilda* ■ *Dir* Fred Schepisi • *Scr* William D Wittliff

Barbary Coast ★★★ PG

Drama   1935 · US · BW · 86mins

This rowdy action drama, directed by Howard Hawks, was scripted by Ben Hecht and Charles MacArthur, who wrote *The Front Page* as well as Hawks's earlier masterpiece *Scarface*. But Hawks rewrote the script and Hecht and MacArthur wanted to have their names taken off the credits. Miriam Hopkins plays a gold-digger who arrives in San Francisco intending to marry a rich man but, when she discovers he's dead, she switches her affections to crime boss Edward G Robinson. Then Joel McCrea shows up and confuses the issue. Sharp performances make this an enjoyable romp, which was significant for making a star out of Walter Brennan. ▣

Miriam Hopkins *Mary Rutledge* • Edward G Robinson *Louis Charnalis* • Joel McCrea *James Carmichael* • Walter Brennan *Old Atrocity* • Frank Craven *Colonel Marcus* • Brian Donlevy *Knuckles* ■ *Dir* Howard Hawks • *Scr* Ben Hecht, Charles MacArthur

Barbary Coast Gent ★★ U

Western   1944 · US · BW · 86mins

The main attraction of this Gold Rush rough-and-tumble is Wallace Beery, starring as a San Francisco con man gloriously named Honest Plush Brannon, who is forced out of town after a shooting fracas with his enemy John Carradine. Waved goodbye to by his understanding girlfriend Binnie Barnes, he makes for Nevada and strikes gold, but that's not the end of the story. Directed by Roy Del Ruth, it features a cast of familiar character actors, including Chill Wills, Noah Beery and Louise Beavers, and was produced appropriately by Orville Dull.

Wallace Beery *Honest Plush Brannon* • Binnie Barnes *Lil Damish* • John Carradine *Duke Cleat* • Bruce Kellogg *Bradford Bellamy III* • Frances Rafferty *Portia Adair* • Chill Wills *Sheriff Hightower* • Noah Beery Sr [Noah Beery] *Pete Hannibal* • Louise Beavers *Bedelia* ■ *Dir* Roy Del Ruth • *Scr* William R Lipman, Grant Garrett, Harry Ruskin

The Barber of Seville ★★★ U

Opera   1946 · It · BW · 96mins

Director Mario Costa will go down in film history as the man who discovered Gina Lollobrigida. Yet he also handled several operatic adaptations in the forties which, while not particularly inventive in visual terms, do adequate justice to both the music and its performance. Without quite overcoming the stagebound setting, American journalist Deems Taylor (who narrated Disney's *Fantasia*) reworked the libretto for the screen to enable Costa to place the emphasis firmly on Rossini's memorable score. As Figaro, the barber who matchmakes lovesick count Ferruccio Tagliavini and miser's ward Nelly Corradi, the flamboyant Tito Gobi is in fine fettle. In Italian with English subtitles.

Ferruccio Tagliavini *Count Almaviva* • Tito Gobbi *Figaro* • Nelly Corradi *Rosina* • Vito de Tarranto *Don Bartolo* • Italo Tajo *Don Basilio* • Natalia Nicolini *Berta* • Nino Mazziotti *Fiorello* ■ *Dir* Mario Costa • *Scr* Deems Taylor, from the opera by Giacomo Rossini

The Barber of Siberia ★★ 12

Period drama   1999 · Rus · Colour · 177mins

Staged with a grandeur that undermines his trademark intimacy, Nikita Mikhalkov's Tsarist epic suffers from thematic imprecision, uncertainty of tone and excessive length. The lack of spark between American Julia Ormond and soldier Oleg Menshikov further strains the credibility of this long-cherished project, which inexplicably lurches from comedy to melodrama partway through. Thanks to Pavel Lebeshev's glorious photography, the evocation of the 1880s is impeccable. But with forestry inventor Richard Harris and bashful general Alexei Petrenko too often sidelined, what should have been enchanting becomes a test of endurance. In English and Russian with subtitles.

Julia Ormond *Jane Callahan* • Richard Harris *Douglas McCracken* • Oleg Menshikov *Andre Tolstoy* • Alexei Petrenko *General Radlov* • Alexander Yakovlev *Maximich* • Marat Bacharov *Polievsky* • Daniel Olbrychski *Kopnovsky* ■ *Dir* Nikita Mikhalkov • *Scr* Nikita Mikhalkov, Rustam Ibragimbekov, Rospo Pallenberg, from a story by Nikita Mikhalkov

The Barber Shop ★★★★ U

Comedy   1933 · US · BW · 20mins

WC Fields engaged in surrealist experimentation in his last two-reeler for comic king Mack Sennett. A cello has a romance, a fat man is steamed skeletally thin and a dog develops a taste for severed ears as Fields reworks material that had served him since his vaudeville days. The plotline – about the bungled capture of a fleeing bank robber – is almost an irrelevance; the real interest lies in Fields as he absentmindedly wields a razor and deals with the various eccentrics who enter his shop. Arthur Ripley, Harry Langdon's old director, is nominally in charge, but there's only one creative force at work here. ▣

WC Fields *Cornelius O'Hare* ■ *Dir* Arthur Ripley • *Scr* WC Fields

Barcelona ★★★★ 12

Comedy drama   1994 · US · Colour · 96mins

Louche observation, tart dialogue and droll wit are director Whit Stillman's hallmarks, and they're all astutely called on in this sophisticated rumination on the sex and social lives of two American cousins living in the cosmopolitan Spanish city during the eighties. Solemn salesman Taylor Nichols and loudmouth navy officer Christopher Eigeman clash with each other as much as the foreign culture, while roaming the Ramblas and seducing the senoritas in a spot-on view of the Eurotrash disco scene. Crafted with care for the literary-minded and covering an interesting political canvas, Stillman's modern comedy of manners comes between *Metropolitan* and *The Last Days of Disco* in his urban romance trilogy. Contains some violence, swearing, nudity and substance abuse. ▣

Taylor Nichols *Ted Boynton* • Christopher Eigeman [Chris Eigeman] *Fred Mason* • Tushka Bergen *Montserrat* • Mira Sorvino *Marta Ferrer* • Pep Munne *Ramon* • Hellena Schmied *Greta* • Nuria Badia *Aurora* • Thomas Gibson *Dickie Taylor* ■ *Dir/Scr* Whit Stillman

Bare Essentials ★★ 18

Romantic comedy
1991 · US · Colour · 94mins

This silly TV movie has little going for it other than its sun-drenched setting. Mark Linn-Baker and Lisa Hartman are the wealthy couple on a tropical holiday who are washed up on a remote island inhabited by Gregory Harrison and his native girlfriend Charlotte Lewis. Gradually learning to be nicer people, the city folk develop an attraction for their hosts. Director Martha Coolidge seems to be going through the motions. ▣

Gregory Harrison *Bill* • Lisa Hartman *Sydney* • Mark Linn-Baker *Gordon* • Charlotte Lewis *Tarita* • Manu Tupou *Emile* ■ *Dir* Martha Coolidge • *Scr* Allen Estrin, Mark Estrin

The Barefoot Contessa ★★★★ PG

Drama   1954 · US · Colour · 125mins

''The world's most beautiful animal,'' shrieked the ads for this mordant satire on the movie biz and, unsurprisingly, nobody disputed the fact, for ''the animal'' was none other than Ava Gardner in her prime, playing a character based on Rita Hayworth. Humphrey Bogart plays her cynical director: ''I made her,'' he snarls, and you believe him. Director/writer Joe Mankiewicz had satirised Broadway in the multi-Oscar winning *All about Eve*, and this is similar, but far less theatrical. Edmond O'Brien collected an Oscar here as the sweaty publicist, and there's a star-making performance from Rossano Brazzi. The bare feet belonged not to Gardner but to Margo Lorenz, who was also the foot-double for Ava in *The Little Hut*. ▣

Humphrey Bogart *Harry Dawes* • Ava Gardner *Maria Vargas* • Edmond O'Brien *Oscar Muldoon* • Marius Goring *Alberto Bravano* • Valentina Cortesa [Valentina Cortese] *Eleanora Torlato-Favrini* • Rossano Brazzi *Vincenzo Torlato-Favrini* • Elizabeth Sellars *Jerry* ■ *Dir/Scr* Joseph L Mankiewicz • *Cinematographer* Jack Cardiff

The Barefoot Executive ★★★ U

Comedy   1971 · US · Colour · 91mins

Blue Peter with a cutting edge? This children-aimed dollop of Disney may blunt some of its point with whimsy, but it's nonetheless an enjoyable spoof of TV ratings, when it's discovered that the best television programmer is a chimpanzee. Kurt Russell looks bewildered, but the hip ape going hip-hop with commercial forecasts proves what the rest of us have always known about scheduling: it's just monkey business about the money business. ▣

Kurt Russell *Steven Post* • Joe Flynn *Francis X Wilbanks* • Harry Morgan *EJ Crampton* • Wally Cox *Mertons* • Heather North *Jennifer Scott* • Alan Hewitt *Farnsworth* • Hayden Rourke *Clifford* • John Ritter *Roger* ■ *Dir* Robert Butler • *Scr* Joseph L McEveety, from a story by Lila Garrett, Bernie Kahn, Stewart C Billett

The Barefoot Executive ★★

Comedy   1995 · US · Colour

In this inoffensive TV remake of the 1971 Disney feature film, an ambitious television-network mailroom clerk, who is dating a pretty animal trainer, discovers that her monkey has an uncanny ability to pick hit shows. Armed with sure-fire results, he moves up the corporate ladder to vice president of development – but when his scam is exposed, he must choose between Hollywood and his integrity. Director Susan Seidelman (*Desperately Seeking Susan*) shows her ability at satire instead of the madcap animal mayhem that is typical of the genre.

Jason London • Eddie Albert • Jay Mohr ■ *Dir* Susan Seidelman • *Scr* Tracy Newman, Jonathan Stark, Tim Doyle, from the 1971 film

Barefoot in the Park ★★★★ PG

Comedy   1967 · US · Colour · 101mins

A delightful comedy, adapted by Neil Simon from his hit Broadway show. Robert Redford (who appeared in the stage play) and Jane Fonda are the young married couple attempting to achieve newly wedded bliss, while Mildred Natwick almost steals the show as Fonda's mother. It's handled well by director Gene Saks (he also made *The Odd Couple*), who only lets the humour slacken about half an hour from the end, and Redford is a joy in a reasonably rare comic role. ▣

Robert Redford *Paul Bratter* • Jane Fonda *Corie Bratter* • Charles Boyer *Victor Velasco* • Mildred Natwick *Mrs Ethel Banks* • Herbert Edelman *Telephone man* • James Stone *Delivery man* • Ted Hartley *Frank* ■ *Dir* Gene Saks • *Scr* Neil Simon, from his play

Barfly ★★ 18

Comedy drama   1987 · US · Colour · 95mins

Confirming the notion that there's no one more boring than a drunk, *Barfly* gives Mickey Rourke and Faye Dunaway the chance to slur their words and blur their meaning for 90-odd minutes. Written by Charles Bukowski from his own experiences propping up a bar in a dimly-lit dive in some lost zone of Los Angeles, the story puts the casualties of life who think they are poets or romantics, or both, on display. It all seems very fifties, man. ▭

Mickey Rourke *Henry Chinaski* • Faye Dunaway *Wanda Wilcox* • Alice Krige *Tully Sorenson* • Jack Nance *Detective* • JC Quinn *Jim* • Frank Stallone *Eddie* • Sandy Martin *Janice* • Roberta Bassin *Lilly* • Gloria LeRoy *Grandma Moses* • Joe Unger *Ben* ■ *Dir* Barbet Schroeder • *Scr* Charles Bukowski

The Bargee ★★★ PG

Comedy 1964 · UK · Colour · 101mins

Having failed to make a movie headliner out of Tony Hancock with *The Rebel*, Ray Galton and Alan Simpson tried to fashion a star-making film comedy for their *Steptoe and Son* protégé Harry H Corbett. However, in spite of the presence of such comic luminaries as Eric Sykes, Ronnie Barker, Derek Nimmo and Richard Briers, the result is disappointing. The poverty of the plot (in which Corbett's Lothario of the Locks is duped into matrimony) is nothing next to its intrinsic sexism. Corbett tuts and shrugs with characteristic melancholy, but to little effect. ▭

Harry H Corbett *Hemel* • Hugh Griffith *Joe* • Eric Sykes *The mariner* • Ronnie Barker *Ronnie* • Julia Foster *Christine* • Miriam Karlin *Nellie* • Eric Barker *Foreman* • Derek Nimmo *Dr Scott* • Norman Bird *Waterways supervisor* • Richard Briers *Tomkins* ■ *Dir* Duncan Wood • *Scr* Ray Galton, Alan Simpson

The Barker ★★

Silent drama 1928 · US · BW · 86mins

Starring Milton Sills as a fairground barker, this movie captures the colourful milieu of the tent-show world and boasts a cast that includes silent stars Betty Compson and Dorothy Mackaill. With direction by George Fitzmaurice and superior photography from Lee Garmes, it promises good if modest entertainment. Unfortunately, however, it was made as a silent with some sound subsequently added. This is of such poor quality that it becomes a pain instead of a pleasure to watch the film. Recommended for silent era specialists.

Milton Sills *Nifty Miller* • Dorothy Mackaill *Lou* • Betty Compson *Carrie* • Douglas Fairbanks Jr *Chris Miller* • Sylvia Ashton *Ma Benson* • George Cooper *Hap Spissel* ■ *Dir* George Fitzmaurice • *Scr* Benjamin Glazer, Joseph Jackson, Herman J Mankiewicz (titles), from the play by Kenyon Nicholson

The Barkleys of Broadway ★★★ U

Musical 1949 · US · Colour · 104mins

This movie was originally intended as a vehicle for the successful *Easter Parade* team, but in fact resulted in the reteaming of Ginger Rogers and Fred Astaire after a ten-year break, with Rogers replacing an ailing Judy Garland. Fred is as chirpy and debonair as ever, but time hasn't been kind to Ginger, who has lost her freshness – and she's not helped by some of the hokey situations. Cherishable, but a bit disappointing. ▭

Fred Astaire *Josh Barkley* • Ginger Rogers *Dinah Barkley* • Oscar Levant *Ezra Miller* • Billie Burke *Mrs Belney* ■ *Dir* Charles Walters • *Scr* Betty Comden, Adolph Green • *Choreography* Hermes Pan • *Music* Harry Warren • *Lyrics* Ira Gershwin

Barnabo of the Mountains ★★ 12

Drama 1994 · Fr/It/Swi · Colour · 124mins

Loosely adapted from a novel by Dino Buzzati, this earnest blend of nature documentary and Christian allegory is so painfully slow that it quickly alienates even the most temperate viewer. Lingering over every glance and gesture, director Mario Brenta treats his non-professional cast like emotionless puppets, as he relates the story of the Dolomite mountain ranger whose refusal to kill either man or beast costs him the respect of locals plagued by smugglers. In Italian with English subtitles.

Marco Pauletti *Barnabo* • Duilio Fontana *Berton* • Carlo Caserotti *Molo* • Antonio Vecellio *Marden* • Angelo Chiesura *Del Colle* • Alessandra Milan *Ines* • Elisa Gasperini *Grandmother* ■ *Dir* Mario Brenta • *Scr* Angelo Pasquini, Mario Brenta, Francesco Alberti, Enrico Soci, from a novel by Dino Buzzati

Barnacle Bill ★ U

Comedy 1957 · UK · BW · 85mins

The last of the Ealing comedies, written by TEB Clarke, who scripted so many of the studio's comic classics, this is a wearisome affair that tries every trick it knows to recall past glories. There are echoes of *Kind Hearts and Coronets* (with Alec Guinness playing his ancestors in several contrived flashbacks), and the action brims over with eccentric characters who could be refugees from any of the film's more illustrious predecessors. But it's all in vain, as this is an unfunny and slightly embarrassing bore.

Alec Guinness *Captain Ambrose/His Ancestors* • Irene Browne *Mrs Barrington* • Percy Herbert *Tommy* • Harold Goodwin *Duckworth* • Maurice Denham *Crowley* • Victor Maddern *Figg* • George Rose *Bullen* • Jackie Collins *June* • Warren Mitchell *Artie White* • Donald Pleasence *Teller* ■ *Dir* Charles Frend • *Scr* TEB Clarke

Barney's Great Adventure ★★★ U

Fantasy 1998 · US · Colour · 73mins

Television's popular purple dinosaur magically appears to teach three vacationing youngsters all about the worlds of the farmyard and the circus as they undertake a quest to find a nearly-hatched alien egg. Devoid of all the usual Hollywood special effects razzmatazz, but not so sugary sweet that it will cause tooth decay, this colourful, energetic and endurable nursery rhyme-style fantasy will have children hitting the rewind button from now until for ever. ▭

George Hearn *Grandpa Greenfield* • Shirley Douglas *Grandma Greenfield* • Trevor Morgan *Cody Newton* • Kyla Pratt *Marcella* ■ *Dir* Steve Gomer • *Scr* Stephen White, from a story by Sheryl Leach, Dennis DeShazer, Stephen White, from characters created by Kathy Parker, Sheryl Leach, Dennis DeShazer

Barnum ★★★ U

Biographical drama 1986 · US/Can · Colour · 111mins

Burt Lancaster's past as a circus acrobat comes in handy for his role here as the charismatic 19th-century

showman who coined the phrase ''The Greatest Show on Earth''. Among Barnum's discoveries were the ''Smallest Man Alive'', General Tom Thumb and the ''Swedish Nightingale'', Jenny Lind. Narrated in flashback by the ageing showman, this TV movie's plot leaves much to be desired, but, with Queen Victoria and Jumbo the Elephant having walk-on roles, there's plenty to enjoy. ▭

Burt Lancaster *PT Barnum* • Hanna Schygulla *Jenny Lind* • John Roney *Young Barnum* • Sandor Raski *Young Tom Thumb* • Patty Maloney *Older Tom Thumb* • Laura Press *Charity* • Kirsten Bishop *Nancy* • Lorena Gale *Joyce Heth* • Bronwen Mantel *Queen Victoria* ■ *Dir* Lee Philips • *Scr* Michael Norell, from a story by Michael Norell, Andy Siegel

The Baron and the Kid ★★ PG

Drama 1984 · US · Colour · 90mins

One of a small group of films owing their existence to a hit song, this TV movie features the great Johnny Cash in a film based on his song *The Baron*. He plays a legendary pool player who has to confront his destiny across the green baize, *Hustler*-style, by beating a young upstart played by Greg Webb. As viewers of Cash's previous screen outing *A Gunfight* will recall, the old boy's no actor, but on screen, as on stage, he's a mighty presence, and on TV you don't really notice his shortcomings. ▭

Johnny Cash *Will ''Baron'' Addington* • Darren McGavin *Jack ''Streamer'' Beamer* • Greg Webb *Billy Joe ''The Cajun Kid''* • Tracy Pollan *Mary Beth Phillips* • June Carter Cash *Dee Dee Stanley* • Richard Roundtree *Walter Frost* • Dan Albright *Barney* ■ *Dir* Gary Nelson • *Scr* William Stratton, from the song *The Baron* by Paul Richey, Billy Sherrill, Jerry Taylor, performed by Johnny Cash

Baron Münchhausen ★★★

Fantasy 1943 · Ger · Colour · 134mins

The eponymous Baron, described as ''the greatest liar of all time'', was a real-life character who lived in Germany and became an 18th-century folk hero with his outrageous stories. None of them were true; all of them were entertaining. He has formed the basis of three feature films. This first version, directed by the Hungarian Josef von Baky, is an extraordinary technical achievement, the equal of that other forties fantasy, *The Thief of Bagdad*. The film was commissioned by Joseph Goebbels to celebrate the 25th anniversary of the UFA studios in Berlin. A German language film.

Hans Albers *Baron Münchhausen* • Brigitte Horney *Catherine the Great* • Wilhelm Bendow *The Man in the Moon* • Michael Bohnen *Prince Karl of Brunswick* • Hans Brausewetter *Frederick von Hartenfeld* • Marina von Ditmar *Sophie von Riedesel* ■ *Dir* Josef von Baky • *Scr* Berthold Bürger [Erich Kästner]

Baron Munchhausen ★★★

Fantasy adventure 1961 · Cz · Colour · 81mins

Czech animator Karel Zeman tackled the fantastic adventures of the notorious mythomaniac by using puppets, cartoons, special effects and live action against painted backdrops. Zeman's inspiration sprang from the 1862 edition of Gottfried Burger's

novel, with its drawings by Gustave Doré, and the turn of the century films of conjurer and cinema pioneer Georges Méliès. Yet, fascinating as it is visually, it is rather stilted and uninvolving. Both the sumptuous 1943 German epic and Terry Gilliam's overblown but under-rated 1988 version are more enjoyable. A Czech language film.

Milos Kopecky *Baron Munchhausen* • Jana Brejchova *Bianca* • Rudolf Jelinek *Tonik* • Jan Werich *Captain of Dutch ship* • Rudolf Hrusinsky *Sultan* • Eduard Kohout *Commander of the fortress* • Karel Hoger *Cyrano de Bergerac* • Karel Effa *Officer of the guard* ■ *Dir* Karel Zeman • *Scr* Karel Zeman, Jiri Brdecka, Josef Kainar, from the novel *Baron Prásil* by Gottfried Burger and the illustrations by Gustave Doré

The Baron of Arizona ★★

Western 1950 · US · BW · 96mins

The second film of maverick writer/ director Samuel Fuller, this low-budget, fact-based drama tells the story of a land office clerk in the 19th century who forges documents to prove himself the ''Baron of Arizona''. Unfortunately, the forger is played rather ponderously by Vincent Price and the film becomes bogged down in detail. It also lacks the vitality of Fuller's *Forty Guns*.

Vincent Price *James Addison Reavis* • Ellen Drew *Sofia Peralta-Reavis* • Vladimir Sokoloff *Pepito* • Reed Hadley *Griff* • Robert Barrat *Judge Adams* • Robin Short *Lansing* • Tina Rome *Rita* ■ *Dir/Scr* Samuel Fuller

Barquero ★★★ 15

Western 1970 · US · Colour · 104mins

A violent American western in the European style, and here that's a recommendation, especially since this is one of the few movies to give a decent co-starring role to the estimable Warren Oates. Here, a black-clad Oates is pitted mercilessly against Lee Van Cleef as the tenacious ferryman of the title. There's a moral of sorts amid all the slaughter, and it's interesting to see how veteran western director Gordon Douglas adapts himself to the new freer style, post Sam Peckinpah and Sergio Leone. Contains violence and swearing. ▭

Lee Van Cleef *Travis* • Warren Oates *Jake Remy* • Forrest Tucker *Mountain Phil* • Kerwin Mathews *Marquette* • Mariette Hartley *Anna* • Marie Gomez *Nola* • Brad Weston *Driver* • Craig Littler *Pitney* ■ *Dir* Gordon Douglas • *Scr* George Schenck, William Marks

The Barretts of Wimpole Street ★★★★ U

Period drama 1934 · US · BW · 109mins

One of the great triumphs of producer Irving G Thalberg's reign at MGM, this managed to be both intelligent in execution and a commercial success. As Elizabeth Barrett, Norma Shearer (Mrs Thalberg) is superb, but the real star is Charles Laughton as Elizabeth's tyrannical father, whose incestuous love for his daughter is hinted at but never addressed. In fact, he was only a year older than his ''daughter'' Shearer and two years younger than Fredric March, uncomfortably cast as poet Robert Browning.

U = SUITABLE FOR ALL   Uc = SUITABLE FOR ALL, ESPECIALLY FOR YOUNG CHILDREN (VIDEO ONLY)   PG = PARENTAL GUIDANCE

Fredric March *Robert Browning* • Norma Shearer *Elizabeth Barrett* • Charles Laughton *Edward Moulton Barrett* • Maureen O'Sullivan *Henrietta Barrett* • Katherine Alexander *Arabel Barrett* • Una O'Connor *Wilson* • Ian Wolfe *Harry Bevan* ■ *Dir* Sidney Franklin • *Scr* Ernest Vajda, Claudine West, Donald Ogden Stewart, from the play by Rudolf Besier

The Barretts of Wimpole Street ★★ U

Period drama 1957 · UK · Colour · 105mins

This recounts the story of the love affair between the invalid poetess Elizabeth Barrett and Robert Browning, with whom she elopes to escape the rigid and frightening control of her father (John Gielgud). Sidney Franklin, who directed the 1934 Hollywood version, also directed this British remake. Although stylish and sober-minded, with a Freudian take on Barrett's relationship with his daughters (Virginia McKenna is featured as the other victim of his wrath), the film emerges as slow, heavy-handed and uninvolving.

Jennifer Jones *Elizabeth* • John Gielgud *Barrett* • Bill Travers *Robert Browning* • Virginia McKenna *Henrietta* • Susan Stephen *Bella* ■ *Dir* Sidney Franklin • *Scr* John Dighton, from the play by Rudolf Besier

Barricade ★★

Western 1950 · US · Colour · 75mins

This exercise in rough brutality features Raymond Massey as the owner of a mine in the middle of nowhere who slave-drives his labourers with sadistic cruelty, until nemesis arrives in the form of a fugitive from justice (Dane Clark). Both the screenplay and Peter Godfrey's direction are undistinguished, and the romantic interest supplied by Ruth Roman inconsequential, but as a merciless depiction of violence in a different era the movie has its moments.

Ruth Roman *Judith Burns* • Dane Clark *Bob Peters* • Raymond Massey *"Boss" Kruger* • Robert Douglas *Aubry Milburn* • Morgan Farley *Judge* • Walter Coy *Benson* • George Stern *Tippy* • Robert Griffin *Kirby* ■ *Dir* Peter Godfrey • *Scr* William Sackheim

Barry Lyndon ★★★★★ PG

Period drama 1975 · UK · Colour · 177mins

This awesome work might be retitled *1789: a Georgian Odyssey*, for Stanley Kubrick gives to the past what he gave to the future in *2001: a Space Odyssey*, providing this film with an authentic 18th-century look and a unique atmosphere that totally convinces. This is a period film like no other, a slow and utterly hypnotic tale of an Irish youth whose adventures and misfortunes take in the Seven Years' War, the gambling clubs of Europe and marriage into the English aristocracy. In Kubrick's scheme of things, character means less than context, so Ryan O'Neal may appear bloodless and Marisa Berenson wholly vacant, but this turns out to be a strength, not a weakness. Anyway, there are fine turns by Leonard Rossiter, Hardy Kruger and, best of all, Leon Vitali as O'Neal's stepson. There is also a definitive climactic duel scene, a confiding narration by Michael Hordern and ravishing photography. Contains some violence. ▭

Ryan O'Neal *Barry Lyndon* • Marisa Berenson *Lady Lyndon* • Patrick Magee *The Chevalier* • Hardy Kruger *Captain Potzdorf* • Steven Berkoff *Lord Ludd* • Gay Hamilton *Nora* • Leonard Rossiter *Captain Quin* • Godfrey Quigley *Captain Grogan* • Marie Kean *Barry's mother* ■ *Dir* Stanley Kubrick • *Scr* Stanley Kubrick, from the novel by William Makepeace Thackeray • *Cinematographer* John Alcott • *Art Director* Ken Adam

Barry McKenzie Holds His Own ★★ 18

Comedy adventure 1974 · Ausl · Colour · 93mins

When Dame Edna is mistaken for the Queen, she and her nephew Barry are whisked off to Transylvania by Count Plasma. A lot of this sequel to *The Adventures of Barry McKenzie* is naff, lazily shot and rather boring. But when the actors get fired up and the Aussie slang starts flowing, it's splendidly vulgar and even subversive in its trouncing of racial stereotypes and political hypocrisy. Gough Whitlam, Australia's prime minister at the time, makes a guest appearance, while the vampire is slain with a crucifix made from beer cans. ▭

Barry Crocker *Barry McKenzie/Ken McKenzie* • Barry Humphries *Buck-toothed Englishman/ Edna Everage/Senator Douglas Manton/Dr Meyer de Lamphrey* • Donald Pleasence *Erich, Count Plasma* • Roy Kinnear *Bishop of Paris* • John Le Mesurier *English emigrant* • Tommy Trinder *Arthur McKenzie* • Dick Bentley *Colonel Lucas* ■ *Dir* Bruce Beresford • *Scr* Barry Humphries, Bruce Beresford, from the comic strip *The Wonderful World of Barry McKenzie* by Barry Humphries

Bartleby ★★★

Drama 1971 · UK · Colour · 78mins

Herman Melville's short story makes for a unremittingly downbeat yet fascinating movie, mainly due to the riveting interplay between its two stars. John McEnery plays Bartleby, a reclusive, diffident accounts clerk who simply won't accept he has been fired by Paul Scofield. Instead, he carries on accounting until he achieves his ultimate aim, which is total exclusion from society – in other words, death. A mysterious, chilling allegory, this was a labour of love for all concerned. There was a remake in 1976 made by French actor/director Maurice Ronet.

Paul Scofield *The accountant* • John McEnery *Bartleby* • Thorley Walters *The colleague* • Colin Jeavons *Tucker* • Raymond Mason *Landlord* • Charles Kinross *Tenant* • Neville Barber *First client* ■ *Dir* Anthony Friedman • *Scr* Anthony Friedman, Rodney Carr-Smith, from the story *Bartleby the Scrivener* by Herman Melville

Barton Fink ★★★★ 15

Drama 1991 · US · Colour · 111mins

This is the most brilliantly observed Hollywood put-down since *Day of the Locust*. Only the Coen brothers would dare to make such a vitriolic attack on the industry supporting them and actually get away with it. Part David Lynch, part Kafka and wholly demanding, this tale features John Turturro as the social realist playwright snapped up by forties Hollywood to script a Wallace Beery wrestling picture. But, even as his life collapses around him, and his next door

neighbour (*Roseanne*'s John Goodman) turns serial killer, he just can't sacrifice his ideals on the altar of commercialism. A gorgeously designed paranoid parable packed with sharp detail and great in-jokes. Contains violence and swearing. ▭

John Turturro *Barton Fink* • John Goodman *Charlie Meadows* • Judy Davis *Audrey Taylor* • Michael Lerner *Jack Lipnick* • John Mahoney *WP Mayhew* • Tony Shalhoub *Ben Geisler* • Jon Polito *Lou Breeze* • Steve Buscemi *Chet* ■ *Dir* Joel Coen • *Scr* Joel Coen, Ethan Coen

The Base ★★

Action 1999 · US · Colour · 97mins

Despite the casting of Mark Dacascos in the lead role, martial arts takes a back seat here. Director Mark L Lester instead goes for suspense, as high-ranked soldier Dacascos goes undercover in Tim Abell's squadron to confirm rumours of corruption. Lester's forte has always been action, and he proves it again here. The sporadic thrills provide relief in a serviceable treatment of a familiar story.

Mark Dacascos *Major John Murphy/Captain John Dalton* • Tim Abell *Sergeant Gammon* • Paula Trickey *Lieutenant Kelly Andrews* • Noah Blake *Captain Castellano* ■ *Dir* Mark L Lester • *Scr* Jeff Albert, Hesh Rephun

Based on an Untrue Story ★★ 15

Comedy 1993 · US · Colour · 89mins

It's almost impossible to spoof something that already borders on parody, but a choice cast does its best to mock the clichés of the "true-story" TV movie in this eager satire. The plot outline is a gem, with perfume tycoon Morgan Fairchild learning from mentor Dyan Cannon that she was parted at birth from fellow triplets Ricki Lake and Victoria Jackson, only to discover that, while they hold the genetic key to saving her sense of smell, both sisters are psychopaths. Unfortunately, here the deft details that make the *Naked Gun* films so hilarious are not just unsubtle, but also unfunny. ▭

Morgan Fairchild *Satin Chow* • Dyan Cannon *Varda Gray* • Robert Goulet *Remo* • Ricki Lake *Velour* • Victoria Jackson *Corduroy* • Dan Hedaya *Caprawolski* • Harvey Korman *Dr Meir* ■ *Dir* Jim Drake • *Scr* George McGrath

BASEketball ★★★ 15

Sports comedy 1998 · US · Colour · 103mins

Unfairly pulled from a British cinema release after a disastrous US showing, this sports spoof from director David Zucker (who made *Airplane*, and the first two *Naked Guns*) is wildly offensive fun. It stars *South Park* creators Trey Parker and Matt Stone, who play a pair of infantile slobs who invent a popular new game that combines the hoops of basketball with the runs of baseball – and a few sick twists of their own. There are more hits than misses in the slapstick gags, ultra-crude humour and numerous nods to sport, movies and *South Park*. An eclectic cast includes Robert Vaughn, *Baywatch*'s Yasmine Bleeth and Ernest Borgnine. Contains swearing and coarse language.

Trey Parker *Joseph Cooper* • Matt Stone *Doug Remer* • Robert Vaughn *Baxter Cain* • Ernest Borgnine *Theodore Denslow* • Dian Bachar

Kenny "Squeak" Scolari • Yasmine Bleeth *Jenna Reed* • Jenny McCarthy *Yvette Denslow* ■ *Dir* David Zucker • *Scr* David Zucker, Robert LoCash, Jeff Wright, Lewis Friedman

Basic Instinct ★★★ 18

Thriller 1992 · US · Colour · 122mins

Director Paul Verhoeven's reputation is built on his wonderful lack of taste and restraint, and these "qualities" are fully to the fore in this controversial but massively successful thriller. Sharon Stone became a sex symbol for the nineties with her cool playing of the predatory novelist who may or may not be a murderer, but who enjoys tormenting policeman Michael Douglas all the same. Writer Joe Eszterhas shamelessly reworks themes he had earlier exploited in films such as *Jagged Edge*, but Verhoeven's overheated direction makes this an over-the-top delight. Contains swearing, violence, sex scenes and nudity. ▭

Michael Douglas *Detective Nick Curran* • Sharon Stone *Catherine Tramell* • George Dzundza *Gus* • Jeanne Tripplehorn *Dr Beth Garner* • Denis Arndt *Lieutenant Walker* • Leilani Sarelle *Roxy* ■ *Dir* Paul Verhoeven • *Scr* Joe Eszterhas

Basil ★★

Period drama 1998 · US · Colour · 102mins

Writer/director Radha Bharadwaj, whose previous film was the 1991 thriller *Closet Land*, here delivers a stiff costume drama, based on the novel by Wilkie Collins. Jared Leto (*Girl, Interrupted*) is miscast as rich man's son Basil, who offends his father by marrying the mysterious Julia (*Meet Joe Black*'s Claire Forlani) and befriending commoner John (Christian Slater). This being a tale of oppression, love and revenge, you'd expect some twists in the tale and bumps along the path to true love. However, Bharadwaj signposts each one so obviously that you know what the characters are up to almost before they do. This is watchable – if only for the chance to see Leto and Slater attempt English accents.

Jared Leto *Basil* • Christian Slater *John Mannion* • Jack Wild *Peddler* • Claire Forlani *Julia Sherwin* • Derek Jacobi *Basil's father, Frederick* • David Ross *Mr Sherwin* • Crispin Bonham-Carter *Ralph* ■ *Scr* Radha Bharadwaj, from the novel *Basil: a Story of Modern Life* by Wilkie Collins

Basil the Great Mouse Detective ★★★ U

Animated adventure 1986 · US · Colour · 71mins

An attractive idea, but rather crudely done for Disney animation, this is about a young mouse devotee of Sherlock Holmes who helps to investigate the disappearance of a mouse toymaker and a plot against the Mouse Queen. It's notable for Vincent Price's wonderfully arch voice-over as the master scoundrel Professor Ratigan – as rat-like a monster as ever drew sibiliant breath – proving that villains have all the best lines. ▭

Vincent Price *Professor Ratigan* • Barrie Ingham *Basil/Bartholomew* • Val Bettin *Dr David Q Dawson/Thug guard* • Diana Chesney *Mrs Judson* • Candy Candido *Fidget* • Susanne Pollatschek *Olivia Flaversham* • Eve

Brenner *The Mouse Queen* ■ *Dir* Ron Clements, Dave Michener, John Musker, Burny Mattinson • *Scr* Eve Titus, Paul Galdone

Basket Case ★★★★ 18

Horror 1982 · US · Colour · 85mins

This gore-drenched, gutter-trash classic is one of the key horror movies of the eighties. It tells the bizarre story of the Bradley brothers – normal Duane (Kevin Van Hentenryck) and his hideously deformed Siamese twin Belial, whom he carries around in a wicker basket – and how they wreak revenge on the quack doctor who separated them years before. Graphic blood-letting is juxtaposed with comic relief in cult director Frank Henenlotter's distorted version of *ET*, but lurking behind its cruel and crude façade is an accomplished shocker laced with great artistry and pathos.

Kevin Van Hentenryck *Duane Bradley* • Terri Susan Smith *Sharon* • Beverly Bonner *Casey* • Robert Vogel *Hotel manager* • Diana Browne *Dr Judith Kutter* • Lloyd Pace *Dr Harold Needleman* • Bill Freeman *Dr Julius Lifflander* • Joe Clarke *Brian "Mickey" O'Donovan* ■ *Dir/Scr* Frank Henenlotter

Basket Case 2 ★★ 18

Horror comedy 1990 · US · Colour · 86mins

The saga of Duane and Belial, his grotesque Siamese twin, continues as they both escape from hospital and media attention to hide out in a Staten Island shelter for freaks. Suffering from latex monster overkill and with too many references to Tod Browning's *Freaks* for comfort, director Frank Henenlotter's poor follow-up is nothing more than a cynical and calculated cash-in. It's also missing the gruesome high notes, sharp satire and sympathetic characterisations of the first film.

Kevin Van Hentenryck *Duane Bradley* • Annie Ross *Granny Ruth* • Kathryn Meisle *Marcie Elliott* • Heather Rattray *Susan* • Jason Evers *Lou the editor* • Ted Sorel *Phil* • Matt Mitler *Artie* ■ *Dir/Scr* Frank Henenlotter

Basket Case 3: the Progeny ★★★ 18

Horror comedy 1992 · US · Colour · 85mins

Director Frank Henenlotter's second sequel to his inspired original is a far less depressing experience than *Basket Case 2*. Dealing more in edgy cartoon craziness than gory splatter, the film follows the Bradley twins, Duane and Belial, as they accompany Granny Ruth to the redneck Deep South. It's where Belial's flesh-hungry offspring are stolen by the police department that Henenlotter's frenzied rubber romp takes off. Belial's mechanical *Aliens*-style harness is the wacky highlight.

Kevin Van Hentenryck *Duane Bradley* • Annie Ross *Granny Ruth* • Dan Biggers *Uncle Hal* • Gil Roper *Sheriff Griffith* • James O'Doherty *Little Hal* ■ *Dir* Frank Henenlotter • *Scr* Frank Henenlotter, Robert Martin

The Basketball Diaries ★★ 18

Drama 1995 · US · Colour · 97mins

This dates from the time when Leonardo DiCaprio was still a promising actor rather than a teenage fantasy icon. Based on the autobiographical writings of Jim Carroll, it attempts to plumb the depths of adolescent despair but, ultimately, only betrays the pop-video limitations of debut director Scott Kalvert. DiCaprio occasionally comes close to real pathos as the hoop dreamer wallowing in a mire of sex, drugs and squalor, but there's no real torment in his pain. Best buddy Mark Wahlberg and desperate mum Lorraine Bracco are more persuasive. Contains swearing, nudity and violence.

Leonardo DiCaprio *Jim Carroll* • Bruno Kirby *Swifty* • Lorraine Bracco *Jim's mother* • Ernie Hudson *Reggie Porter* • Patrick McGaw *Neutron* • James Madio *Pedro* • Mark Wahlberg *Mickey* • Juliette Lewis *Diane Moody* ■ *Dir* Scott Kalvert • *Scr* Brian Goluboff, from the memoirs of Jim Carroll

Basquiat ★★★ 15

Biographical drama 1996 · US · Colour · 106mins

The true story of black artist Jean Michel Basquiat (Jeffrey Wright) as told by his friend and contemporary, director Julian Schnabel. Basquiat went from being an angry graffiti artist to one of Andy Warhol's close circle before overdosing on heroin in the late eighties. Schnabel's aim is to show how Basquiat was uncomfortable being lionised by the bourgeoisie he so despised. But he comes off more as a tiresome anti-hero in this well-meaning biopic, which fails to reveal why he's more deserving of martyrdom than any other Warhol satellite. Benicio Del Toro is good as Basquiat's put-upon best friend and, as Warhol, David Bowie even better. Contains swearing and some violence.

Jeffrey Wright *Jean Michel Basquiat* • Michael Wincott *René Ricard* • Benicio Del Toro *Benny Dalmau* • Claire Forlani *Gina Cardinale* • David Bowie *Andy Warhol* • Dennis Hopper *Bruno Bischofberger* • Gary Oldman *Albert Milo* • Courtney Love *Big Pink* • Tatum O'Neal *Cynthia Kruger* ■ *Dir* Julian Schnabel • *Scr* Julian Schnabel, from a story by Lech J Majewski, John Bowe

Bastard out of Carolina ★★★

Drama 1996 · US · Colour · 101mins

The mixed fortunes of a young mother (Jennifer Jason Leigh) and her illegitimate daughter are brought to screen with authority and authenticity in actress Anjelica Huston's solid directorial debut. Making optimum use of a uniformly talented cast, the fifties setting and fluid camera moves, Huston delineates the economic and emotional dependence of single mothers. From the casual cruelty of other children and uncaring bureaucracies to physical and sexual abuse at the hands of adults, it's an engrossing and involving drama.

Jennifer Jason Leigh *Anney Boatwright* • Ron Eldard *Glen Waddell* • Jena Malone *Bone* • Glenne Headly *Ruth* • Lyle Lovett *Wade* • Dermot Mulroney *Lyle Parsons* • Christina Ricci *Dee Dee* • Laura Dern *Narrator* ■ *Dir* Anjelica Huston • *Scr* Anne Meredith, from a novel by Dorothy Allison

The Bat ★★

Mystery thriller 1959 · US · BW · 80mins

Intrepid mystery writer Agnes Moorehead rents a country mansion for the summer, only to be terrorised by a mad hooded killer called "The Bat". Money is stolen, a real bat turns up and Vincent Price becomes the prime suspect in a creaky, improbable thriller in the *Old Dark House* mould. This fourth screen version of Avery Hopwood and Mary Roberts Rinehart's comedy chiller is sluggishly paced and old-fashioned in the extreme, yet it nevertheless has a comfortably nostalgic appeal.

Vincent Price *Dr Malcolm Wells* • Agnes Moorehead *Cornelia Van Gorder* • Gavin Gordon *Lieutenant Anderson* • John Sutton *Warner* • Lenita Lane *Lizzie Allen* • Elaine Edwards *Dale Bailey* ■ *Dir* Crane Wilbur • *Scr* Crane Wilbur, from the play by Mary Roberts Rinehart, Avery Hopwood, from their novel *The Circular Staircase*

BAT-21 ★★ 15

War drama 1988 · US · Colour · 100mins

Set during the Vietnam War, this drama stars Gene Hackman as Lieutenant Colonel Hambleton (codenamed BAT-21), who crashes behind enemy lines and is brought face to face with the human misery of the conflict. Hackman makes the career soldier a strongly believable character, while Danny Glover is excellent as as the helicopter pilot trying to track him down. However, the episodic nature of the tale never allows a sense of urgency to surface, while director Peter Markle backs off from real commitment to the situation's dramatic irony. Contains violence and swearing.

Gene Hackman *Lieutenant Colonel Iceal Hambleton* • Danny Glover *Captain Bartholomew Clark* • Jerry Reed *Colonel George Walker* • David Marshall Grant *Ross Carver* • Clayton Rohner *Sergeant Harley Rumbaugh* ■ *Dir* Peter Markle • *Scr* William C Anderson, George Gordon, from the novel by William C Anderson

The Bat Whispers ★★★ U

Mystery thriller 1930 · US · BW · 84mins

Roland West's talkie remake of his own 1926 silent film *The Bat* is by far the best movie adaptation of the stock spoof horror play set in a creepy mansion. It's also a superior chiller in its own right. Sure, it's a dusty antique, but the impressively surreal imagery is unusual for the period, making it well worth a look. Using remarkable special effects and miniature sets, the fluid camera darts about as much as the titular caped criminal for a fun combination of screams and laughs.

Chester Morris *Detective Anderson* • Grayce Hampton *Cornelia Van Gorder* • Chance Ward *Police lieutenant* • Richard Tucker *Mr Bell* • Wilson Benge *The butler* • Maude Eburne *Lizzie Allen* ■ *Dir* Roland West • *Scr* Roland West, from the play *The Bat* by Mary Roberts Rinehart, Avery Hopwood, from their novel *The Circular Staircase*

Bataan ★★

Second World War drama 1943 · US · BW · 114mins

Arnold Schwarzenegger was not the originator of the phrase, "I'll be back". It was General MacArthur after he was forced to abandon the Philippines to the Japanese during the Second World War, and this scrappy piece of patriotic action re-creates one of the battles before the pull-out. Robert Taylor and Barry Nelson (the screen's first James Bond) are among those caught in the jungled MGM backlot, exchanging bullets and sanctimonious dialogue. MacArthur did go back and so did John Wayne, in *Back to Bataan*.

Robert Taylor (1) *Sergeant Bill Dane* • George Murphy *Lieutenant Steve Bentley* • Thomas Mitchell *Corporal Jake Feingold* • Lloyd Nolan *Corporal Barney Todd/Danny Burns* • Lee Bowman *Captain Lassiter* ■ *Dir* Tay Garnett • *Scr* Robert D Andrews

La Bataille du Rail ★★★

War drama 1946 · Fr · BW · 87mins

Director René Clément's directing debut is about the war waged by the French railway workers against their Nazi oppressors. Using a largely amateur cast of genuine railway personnel (an introduction and narration by Charles Boyer was added for foreign release), Clément depicts in great detail the various acts of sabotage and subtle route changes that were to cause havoc to the German supply lines. The film's influence on John Frankenheimer's 1964 film *The Train* is obvious. In French with English subtitles.

Jean Daurand *Railroad worker* • Jacques Desagneaux *Maquis Chief* • Leroy *Station master* • Redon *Mechanic* • Pauléon *Station master at St André* • Charles Boyer *Narrator* ■ *Dir* René Clément • *Scr* Colette Audry, René Clément, Jean Daurand, from stories by Colette Audry

Bates Motel ★ 15

Horror 1987 · US · Colour · 90mins

Think Norman had problems? What about the executive who thought *Psycho* could be turned into a television series? This is the pilot for that disastrously misconceived project, with shy, nervous asylum inmate Bud Cort inheriting the notorious motel and discovering that it hasn't lost its horrific reputation. It's nice to see *Harold and Maude*'s Cort back on the screen, and there's a solid support cast, but Alfred Hitchcock must have turned in his grave over this sanitised fluff. Contains violence.

Bud Cort *Alex West* • Lori Petty *Willie* • Moses Gunn *Henry Watson* • Gregg Henry *Tom Fuller* • Kerrie Keane *Barbara Peters "Sally"* ■ *Dir/Scr* Richard Rothstein

Bathing Beauty ★★★ U

Musical 1944 · US · Colour · 101mins

MGM contractee Esther Williams became a star overnight in this, the first ever of her many swimfests, and who could ever forget her as she steps on to the MGM diving board? Esther had a robust, sexy aura that director George Sidney knew exactly how to exploit, although this movie actually started life as a Red Skelton vehicle, one of those school romps about romance among the co-eds. The film's a little too long, but Esther's worth every single Technicolored frame.

Red Skelton *Steve Elliott* • Esther Williams *Caroline Brooks* • Basil Rathbone *George Adams* • Bill Goodwin *Willis Evans* • Ethel Smith *Organist* • Jean Porter *Jean Allenwood* • Carlos Ramirez *Carlos* • Donald Meek *Chester Klazenfrantz* • *Dir* George Sidney • *Scr* Dorothy Kingsley, Allen Boretz, Frank Waldman, Joseph Schrank, from a story by Kenneth Earl, MM Musselman

Batman ★★★★ U
Action fantasy 1966 · US · Colour · 104mins

This is the movie spin-off from the hit TV series of the sixties, with Adam West as the Caped Crusader and Burt Ward as the Boy Wonder. Lee Meriwether, the least well known of the three actresses who played Catwoman on TV (the others were Julie Newmarr and Eartha Kitt), reprises her role. Director Leslie H Martinson has the pace slacken occasionally, but Lorenzo Semple Jr's script overflows with the kind of throwaway gags that Joel Schumacher's *Batman and Robin* cried out for. 📺

Adam West *Batman/Bruce Wayne* • Burt Ward *Robin/Dick Grayson* • Lee Meriwether *Catwoman/Kitka* • Cesar Romero *Joker* • Burgess Meredith *Penguin* • Frank Gorshin *Riddler* • Alan Napier *Alfred* • *Dir* Leslie H Martinson • *Scr* Lorenzo Semple Jr, from characters created by Bob Kane

Batman ★★★★★ 15
Action fantasy 1989 · US · Colour · 121mins

Only director Tim Burton could take the caped crusader into the darkest realms of comic-strip nightmare yet still manage to weave an arresting tale full of doomy Shakespearean irony. From the camera crawling around the Bat symbol under the opening credits to the *Hunchback of Notre Dame*-inspired finale, Burton's captures the spirit of artist Bob Kane's creation to produce a sophisticated *film noir*. With Michael Keaton's brooding Batman/Bruce Wayne and Jack Nicholson's superlative Joker/Jack Napier on the knife-edge of good and evil, Burton's cleverly places both tragic characters within the same psychotic bracket, making the film the *Blue Velvet* of superhero movies. This marvellous original is still the best of the entire series, knocking the dismal sequels into a cocked cape. Contains some swearing. 📺 *DVD*

Michael Keaton *Batman/Bruce Wayne* • Jack Nicholson *Joker/Jack Napier* • Kim Basinger *Vicki Vale* • Robert Wuhl *Alexander Knox* • Pat Hingle *Commissioner Gordon* • Billy Dee Williams *Harvey Dent* • Michael Gough *Alfred* • Jack Palance *Carl Grissom* • Jerry Hall *Alicia* ■ • *Scr* Sam Hamm, Warren Skaaren, from a story by Sam Hamm, from characters created by Bob Kane • *Production Designer* Anton Furst

Batman and Robin ★★ U
Action fantasy 1997 · US · Colour · 245mins

By 1997 the Batman franchise was becoming decidedly tired, and was already on to Caped Crusader Mark 3 in the shape of *ER*'s George Clooney. He does not actually disgrace himself in a wild special-effects extravaganza that is as close to a cartoon adventure

as director Joel Schumacher could get. Compared to the first two *Batman* films, though, this is a major disappointment. 📺 *DVD*

Arnold Schwarzenegger *Mr Freeze/Dr Victor Fries* • George Clooney *Batman/Bruce Wayne* • Chris O'Donnell *Robin/Dick Grayson* • Uma Thurman *Poison Ivy/Pamela Isley* • Alicia Silverstone *Batgirl/Barbara Wilson* • Michael Gough *Alfred Pennyworth* ■ *Dir* Joel Schumacher • *Scr* Akiva Goldsman, from characters created by Bob Kane

Batman Forever ★★★★ PG
Action fantasy 1995 · US · Colour · 114mins

Although it performed well at the box office, the critics were less than convinced by the gloomy turn taken by *Batman Returns*. So, when Tim Burton said no to a third outing, Warners brought in the flamboyant Joel Schumacher. This entry is nowhere near as dark as its predecessors, even though the brooding Val Kilmer took over the Dark Knight's mantle from Michael Keaton. It's easily the funniest of the quartet to date and also the fastest, with the action hurtling along at a breakneck pace. With the special effects team including the legendary John Dykstra and Oscar-nominated photography from Stephen Goldblatt, it's a rousingly undemanding piece of popcorn fodder. Contains some swearing. 📺 *DVD*

Val Kilmer *Batman/Bruce Wayne* • Tommy Lee Jones *Harvey Two-Face/Harvey Dent* • Jim Carrey *The Riddler/Edward Nygma* • Nicole Kidman *Dr Chase Meridian* • Christopher O'Donnell *Robin/Dick Grayson* ■ *Dir* Joel Schumacher • *Scr* Lee Batchler, Janet Scott Batchler, Akiva Goldsman, from a story by Lee Batchler, Janet Scott Batchler, from characters created by Bob Kane

Batman: Mask of the Phantasm ★★★★ PG
Animated adventure 1993 · US · Colour · 73mins

Released in cinemas months after the TV animated series took off, this cartoon feature expertly captures the feel of the comics. The Phantasm is a formidable vigilante who painstakingly executes Gotham's most powerful criminals. After both the police and the underworld mistakenly hold the Dark Knight responsible, Batman must unmask the real culprit. Stylishly drawn and with a strong cast of voices including Stacy Keach and *Star Wars*'s Mark Hamill, it's a spirited riposte to the live-action film series. 📺

Kevin Conroy *Batman/Bruce Wayne* • Dana Delany *Andrea Beaumont* • Hart Bochner *Councilman Arthur Reeves* • Stacy Keach *Phantasm/Carl Beaumont* • Abe Vigoda *Salvatore Valestra* • Dick Miller *Chuckie Sol* ■ *Dir* Eric Radomski, Bruce W Timm • *Scr* Alan Burnett, Paul Dini, Martin Pasko, Michael Reaves, from a story by Alan Burnett, from characters created by Bob Kane

Batman Returns ★★★★ 15
Action fantasy 1992 · US · Colour · 121mins

Director Tim Burton refused to lighten up for the second of the Batman movies and the result is another moody, gloomy and occasionally perverse portrait of the Dark Knight. The sets are stunning and, while action may not be Burton's strongest suit, there are still some dazzling set

pieces and a range of new gadgets. The only real problem is that all the best lines are bagged by the villains – Danny DeVito's tragic Penguin, Michelle Pfeiffer in *that* suit as Catwoman. It's still impressive stuff. Contains some violence. 📺 *DVD*

Michael Keaton *Batman/Bruce Wayne* • Danny DeVito *Oswald Cobblepot/The Penguin* • Michelle Pfeiffer *Catwoman/Selina Kyle* • Christopher Walken *Max Shreck* • Michael Gough *Alfred* • Michael Murphy *Mayor* ■ *Dir* Tim Burton • *Scr* Daniel Waters, from a story by Daniel Waters, Sam Hahm, from characters created by Bob Kane

Bats ★ 15
Horror 1999 · US · Colour · mins

Genetically enhanced killer bats are released upon an unsuspecting Texas town by a mad scientist. A perky zoologist, her cowardly sidekick and the town's sheriff fight desperately to fend off the flying monsters in this by-the-numbers monster movie, in which the lead characters never say or do anything of any interest. The bats could make effective villains in a better-made movie.

Lou Diamond Phillips *Emmett Kimsey* • Dina Meyer *Dr Sheila Casper* • Bob Gunton *Dr Alexander McCabe* • Leon *Jimmy Sands* ■ *Dir* Louis Morneau • *Scr* John Logan

*batteries not included ★★★ PG
Science-fiction fantasy 1987 · US · Colour · 102mins

The presence of Hume Cronyn and Jessica Tandy makes this retread of *Cocoon* worth watching. They play residents of a doomed New York block of flats, who find the unlikeliest of allies in the shape of a friendly group of aliens. It's made by Steven Spielberg's production company, Amblin, but there is little of his magic touch here and director Matthew Robbins lets sentimentality run supreme. Nevertheless, Cronyn and Tandy rise above it all. 📺

Hume Cronyn *Frank Riley* • Jessica Tandy *Faye Riley* • Frank McRae *Harry Noble* • Elizabeth Pena *Marisa* • Michael Carmine *Carlos* • Dennis Boutsikaris *Mason* • Tom Aldredge *Sid* ■ *Dir* Matthew Robbins • *Scr* Brad Bird, Matthew Robbins, Brent Maddock, SS Wilson, from a story by Mick Garris, Steven Spielberg

The Battle at Apache Pass ★★★ U
Western 1952 · US · Colour · 85mins

Universal contract star Jeff Chandler created a tremendous impression as the native American chief Cochise in the remarkably liberal (for its time) *Broken Arrow*. Here he reprises the role in another sympathetic western, which deals primarily with Apache warrior Geronimo, played by native American actor Jay Silverheels, who is best known as the Lone Ranger's sidekick Tonto. Intelligent writing and performances make up for the lack of political depth and there's a splendid staging of the battle. Western fans won't be disappointed.

Jeff Chandler *Cochise* • John Lund *Major Jim Colton* • Beverly Tyler *Mary Kearny* • Bruce Cowling *Neil Baylor* • Susan Cabot *Nono* •

John Hudson *Lieutenant George Bascom* • Jay Silverheels *Geronimo* ■ *Dir* George Sherman • *Scr* Gerald Drayson Adams

Battle beneath the Earth ★★ U
Science-fiction 1968 · UK · Colour · 91mins

The Red Chinese have dug a series of tunnels beneath the United States. In go Chinese H-bombs and lasers, and in after them goes Kerwin Matthews, the Harrison Ford of British cinema back in the sixties, to do a job even 007 might have found taxing. Everyone takes it very seriously and, as a result, it's hugely enjoyable rubbish.

Kerwin Mathews *Commander Jonathan Shaw* • Viviane Ventura *Tila Yung* • Robert Ayres *Admiral Felix Hillebrand* • Peter Arne *Arnold Kramer* • Al Mulock *Sergeant Marvin Mulberry* • Martin Benson *General Chan Lu* ■ *Dir* Montgomery Tully • *Scr* Lance Z Hargreaves

Battle beyond the Stars ★★★ PG
Science-fiction adventure 1980 · US · Colour · 98mins

This entertaining slice of hokum from Roger Corman production company is great B-movie fodder. Essentially it's *The Magnificent Seven* in space; Corman even manages to rope in one of the original cast, Robert Vaughn, to take his place alongside the likes of John Saxon (as the baddie), George Peppard and Richard Thomas from *The Waltons*. The knowing script is by John Sayles, now better known as the writer/director of such critically acclaimed films as *Passion Fish* and *Lone Star*. 📺

Richard Thomas *Shad* • Robert Vaughn *Gelt* • John Saxon *Sador* • George Peppard *Cowboy* • Darlanne Fluegel *Nanelia* • Sybil Danning *St Exmin* • Sam Jaffe *Dr Hephaestus* • Morgan Woodward *Cayman* • Steve Davis *Quopeg* ■ *Dir* Jimmy T Murakami • *Scr* John Sayles, from a story by John Sayles, Ann Dyer

Battle beyond the Sun ★
Science-fiction 1959 · USSR · Colour · 67mins

This version of the space race to Mars between the Russians and the Americans was constructed by cult director Roger Corman out of special effects and footage from an existing Russian sci-fi movie, *Nebo Sovyot*, combined with new footage. This includes the major highlight – a notoriously kitsch battle between a penis-shaped monster and a vagina-shaped alien. Otherwise it's a deadly dull combination of conflicting styles and hastily matched edits.

Edd Perry [Ivan Pereverzev] *Kornev* • Andy Stewart [A Shvorin] *Gordiyenko* • Kirk Barton [K Bartashevich] *Klark* • Gene Tonner [G Tonunts] *Verst* • Barry Chertok [V Chernyak] *Somov* ■ *Dir* Thomas Colchart [A Kozyr], M Karyukov • *Scr* M Karyukov, Nicholas Colbert [A Sazonov], Edwin Palmer [Yevgeny Pomeshchikov], Francis Ford Coppola (English version adaptation)

Battle Circus ★★
War drama 1953 · US · BW · 90mins

Humphrey Bogart coasts through this movie, playing the commanding officer of a US Army surgical unit during the Korean War, who falls in love with idealistic nurse June Allyson between dodging bullets and indulging in blokeish camaraderie. This was Bogart's second film for writer/director Richard Brooks (they had just made *Deadline USA*), who wanted to call this one *MASH 66*, but the studio thought the title was unsuitable. Released six months before the Korean war ended, it doesn't have much to say about the conflict and seems cliché ridden for a director of Brooks's talent.

Humphrey Bogart *Major Jeb Webbe* • June Allyson *Ruth McCara* • Keenan Wynn *Sergeant Orvil Statt* • Robert Keith *Lt Col Hillary Whalters* • William Campbell *Captain John Rustford* • Perry Sheehan *Lt Lawrence* • Patricia Tiernan *Lt Rose Ashland* ■ *Dir* Richard Brooks • *Scr* Richard Brooks, from a story by Allen Rivkin, Laura Kerr

Battle Cry ★★★★ PG
Second World War drama
1955 · US · Colour · 142mins

It may seem dated today, but this impressive Warner Bros drama based on Leon Uris's semi-fictional account of his own wartime experiences still packs a terrific emotional punch. It is exceptionally well cast, with a key star-making role for Tab Hunter, though top-billed Van Heflin has little to do but act gritty as the leader of "Huxley's Harlots". Watch out, too, for Justus E McQueen as LQ Jones, who took his professional name from the character he portrays here. There's also a rousing Oscar-nominated score by the great Max Steiner. □

Van Heflin *Major Huxley* • Aldo Ray *Andy* • Mona Freeman *Kathy* • Nancy Olson *Pat* • James Whitmore *Sergeant Mac* • Raymond Massey *General Snipes* • Tab Hunter *Danny* • Justus E McQueen [LQ Jones] *LQ Jones* ■ *Dir* Raoul Walsh • *Scr* Leon Uris, from his novel

Battle for the Planet of the Apes ★ PG
Science-fiction adventure
1973 · US · Colour · 83mins

This is the fifth, final and least effective entry in the *Planet of the Apes* series. It's good apes versus guerrilla gorillas as our heroes attempt to restore racial harmony to Earth and make humans social equals. Spotting who's who under the hairy masks will while away the time as this threadbare monkey business wends its time-warp way back to the beginning of the original film. Endless action can't disguise the cheapness of the production or the lack of novelty and story values. □

Roddy McDowall *Caesar* • Claude Akins *Aldo* • John Huston *Lawgiver* • Natalie Trundy *Lisa* • Severn Darden *Kolp* • Lew Ayres *Mandemus* • Paul Williams *Virgil* • Austin Stoker *MacDonald* • Noah Keen *Teacher* ■ *Dir* J Lee Thompson • *Scr* John William Corrington, Joyce Hooper Corrington, from a story by Paul Dehn, from characters created by Pierre Boulle

Battle Hymn ★★★ U
War drama based on a true story
1957 · US · Colour · 108mins

From the producer-director team of Ross Hunter and Douglas Sirk, responsible for glossy remakes of classic weepies such as *Imitation of Life* and *Magnificent Obsession*, comes this earnest biopic about Dean Hess. As a combat flyer he accidentally bombed a German orphanage in the

Second World War; how, as a minister in the Korean war, Hess heroically atones for this mistake, forms the stuff of this starring vehicle for Rock Hudson. Among those helping him tug at our heartstrings are Dan Duryea, unusually playing a good guy, the lovely Anna Kashfi, and an assembly of Korean war orphans.

Rock Hudson *Colonel Dean Hess* • Anna Kashfi *En Soon Yang* • Dan Duryea *Sgt Herman* • Don DeFore *Capt Skidmore* • Martha Hyer *Mary Hess* • Jock Mahoney *Major Moore* • Alan Hale *Mess Sergeant* • James Edwards *Lt Maples* ■ *Dir* Douglas Sirk • *Scr* Charles Grayson, Vincent B Evans, from the memoirs of Colonel Dean Hess

The Battle of Algiers ★★★★★ 15
War drama 1965 · Alg/It · BW · 116mins

Although directed by Italian Gillo Pontecorvo, this stark and compelling drama about the rise of the Front de Libération Nationale was the first indigenous feature shot in Algeria. Beside the simplicity of the visuals, the film's great strength is its even-handedness. French and Algerian rhetoric is given equal airing, actions are neither condemned nor condoned and the characters on each side are depicted as committed combatants caught in the tide of history. Although it won the Golden Lion at Venice, the picture was banned in France and torture scenes were cut for its UK release. In French and Arabic with English subtitles. □

Yacef Saadi *Saari Kader* • Jean Martin *Colonel Mathieu* • Brahim Haggiag *Ali la Pointe* • Tommaso Neri *Captain Dubois* • Michèle Kerbash [Samia Kerbash] *Fathia* ■ *Dir* Gillo Pontecorvo • *Scr* Franco Solinas, from a story by Franco Solinas, Gillo Pontecorvo

The Battle of Austerlitz ★★ U
Historical drama
1960 · Fr/It/Yug · Colour · 122mins

Although watching international superstars of the likes of Orson Welles, Claudia Cardinale and Jean Marais re-enact Napoleon's greatest victory might seem a pleasant enough way of passing the time, it's sad to realise that this rather tawdry epic is the penultimate feature of veteran French director Abel Gance. By 1960, Gance was still eking out a living from the cinema, having spent his early years virtually inventing it, and this series of tableaux is barely recognisable as the work of the director of the masterpiece *Napoléon*. French and Italian dialogue dubbed into English.

Pierre Mondy *Napoleon Bonaparte* • Jean Mercure *Talleyrand* • Jack Palance *General Weirother* • Orson Welles *Robert Fulton* • Martine Carol *Josephine* • Leslie Caron *Mademoiselle de Vaudey* • Claudia Cardinale *Pauline* • Jean Marais *Carnot* ■ *Dir* Abel Gance • *Scr* Abel Gance, Roger Richebe

Battle of Britain ★★★ PG
Second World War epic
1969 · UK · Colour · 126mins

This worthy tribute to "the few" has spectacular air battles, a memorable re-creation of the Blitz and a terrific cast. It is interesting today to watch so

many great names in the twilight of their careers: not just knights Ralph Richardson, Michael Redgrave and Laurence Olivier, but also Trevor Howard, Robert Shaw, Kenneth More and Curt Jurgens. Most of Sir William Walton's original score was dumped and replaced by Ron Goodwin's, but a tantalising fragment remains in the air battles. A special word of praise, too, for sound editor James Shields, who came up with the authentic engine noises for the reconstituted aeroplanes. □

Laurence Olivier *Air Chief Marshal Sir Hugh Dowding* • Robert Shaw *Squadron Leader Skipper* • Christopher Plummer *Squadron Leader Colin Harvey* • Susannah York *Section Officer Maggie Harvey* • Ian McShane *Sergeant Pilot Andy* • Michael Caine *Squadron Leader Canfield* • Kenneth More *Group Captain Baker* • Trevor Howard *Air Vice-Marshal Keith Park* • Ralph Richardson *British Minister in Switzerland* • Curd Jürgens [Curt Jurgens] *Baron von Richter* • Michael Redgrave *Air Vice-Marshal Evill* ■ *Dir* Guy Hamilton • *Scr* James Kennaway, Wilfred Greatorex, from the book *The Narrow Margin* by Derek Wood, Derek Dempster

The Battle of El Alamein ★★ PG
Second World War drama
1968 · It/Fr · Colour · 101mins

This might have been an intriguing, alternative account of the battle that marked a turning point in the war in North Africa. Viewing the conflict from the Axis perspective, it reveals an uneasy alliance, in which the Italian Division Folgore ("Thunderbolt Division") is left high and dry by Rommel's grand design. As the rival field marshals, Robert Hossein and Michael Rennie (presented as the villain of the piece) are adequate, but this is something of a wasted opportunity. Italian dialogue dubbed into English. □

Michael Rennie *Field Marshal Montgomery* • Robert Hossein *Field Marshal Rommel* • George Hilton *Lieutenant Graham* • Ira Furstenberg *Marta* • Enrico Maria Salerno *Captain Hubert* • Frederick Stafford *Lieutenant Claudio Borri* ■ *Dir* Calvin Jackson Padget [Giorgio Ferroni] • *Scr* Ernesto Gastaldi

The Battle of Elderbush ★★★
Silent western 1914 · US · BW · 29mins

This very early western was the last two-reeler made by DW Griffith before embarking on America's first feature-length films. For this simple tale of Indians attacking a settlement, Griffith constructed a complete three-dimensional town in the San Fernando Valley. Brilliantly shot by Billy Bitzer, the short becomes more and more compelling towards its climax, as a baby whose parents have been killed escapes the shelter of her cabin and must be rescued by a posse. The baby, who was actually black and was selected by Griffith from a foundling home for her photogenic eyes, curiously grows up to be the white Blanche Sweet.

Mae Marsh *The waif* • Alfred Paget *Her uncle* • Charles H Mailes [Charles Hill Mailes] *The ranch owner* • Lillian Gish *Young wife* • Robert Harron *Young husband* • Kate Bruce *Settler* • W Chrystie Miller [Walter Miller] *Settler* • Blanche Sweet *Child* ■ *Dir/Scr* DW Griffith

The Battle of Midway ★★★★ PG
Second World War documentary
1942 · US · Colour · 18mins

One of a striking series of Second World War documentaries made by the world's greatest film directors – this time John Ford, uncredited, for the US Navy. Ford did some of the camerawork himself and, despite being wounded in the eye, captured the searing, tragic sense of destruction in a battle that marked a turning point in the war against Japan. In the cutting rooms, aided by Robert Parrish and some familiar voices (you'll easily recognise Henry Fonda) Ford wove a structure around his material and, with his original 16mm Technicolor blown up to 35mm, made a superb propagandist tract. It became the subject of a fictionalised Sensurround epic in 1976, but this all-too-brief colour featurette is the one with the ring of truth. □

Henry Fonda • Jane Darwell • Donald Crisp • Irving Pichel ■ *Dir* John Ford • *Cinematographer* John Ford • *Music* Alfred Newman • *Editor* Robert Parrish

Battle of Midway ★★★
Second World War action drama
1976 · US · Colour · 131mins

Charlton Heston juts his jaw aggressively and Henry Fonda falters reflectively, but to no avail. Their acting techniques are blown away by the big guns in this blockbuster drama about the events leading up to the decisive battle fought between the navies of the US and Japan. Originally filmed in ear-blasting Sensurround, its din has been diminished to clarify the narrative, as star performers share the screen with stock footage. □

Charlton Heston *Capt Matt Garth* • Henry Fonda *Adm Chester W Nimitz* • James Coburn *Capt Vinton Maddox* • Glenn Ford *Rear Adm Raymond A Spruance* • Hal Holbrook *Cmdr Joseph Rochefort* • Toshiro Mifune *Adm Isoroku Yamamoto* • Robert Mitchum *Adm William F Halsey* • Cliff Robertson *Cmdr Carl Jessop* • Ed Nelson *Adm Harry Pearson* ■ *Dir* Jack Smight • *Scr* Donald S Sanford

The Battle of Neretva ★★
Second World War adventure
1969 · Yug/US/It/W Ger · Colour · 175mins

A sluggish vanity project for the Yugoslavian dictator General Tito, who lavished US$12 million on the story of how the partisan army overthrew the Nazis and Italians in Western Bosnia. It's pitched as the Balkan equivalent to *The Longest Day* or *Battle of Britain*, with an all-star cast that includes Orson Welles, and the Russian Sergei Bondarchuk, who had made the nine-hour *War and Peace*. *The Battle for Neretva* originally ran at three hours long, but was later cut by an hour for international release.

Yul Brynner *Vlado* • Hardy Kruger *Colonel Kranzer* • Franco Nero *Captain Riva* • Sylva Koscina *Danica* • Orson Welles *Senator* • Curt Jurgens *General Löhring* • Antony Dawson *General Morelli* • Milena Dravic *Girl* • Sergei Bondarchuk *Artillery Man Martin* ■ *Dir* Veljko Bulajic • *Scr* Ugo Pirro, Ratko Durovic, Stevan Bulajic, Veljko Bulajic

U = SUITABLE FOR ALL   Uc = SUITABLE FOR ALL, ESPECIALLY FOR YOUNG CHILDREN (VIDEO ONLY)   PG = PARENTAL GUIDANCE

The Battle of Russia ★★
Second World War documentary
1943 · US · BW · 80mins

Lt Col Frank Capra, Lt Col Anatole Litvak and other ranking Hollywood soldiers made this documentary, one of a series of seven designed to show Americans what the Second World War was all about. This one's about the ally Russia, from the time of Alexander Nevsky to the Nazi invasion. The vast amount of documentary footage is accompanied by soundtrack composer Dimitri Tiomkin's copious borrowings from Prokofiev, Tchaikovsky and Shostakovich.

Walter Huston *Narrator* • Anthony Veiller *Narrator* ■ *Dir* Frank Capra, Anatole Litvak • *Scr* Anatole Litvak

Battle of the Bulge ★★★★ PG
Second World War action drama
1965 · US · Colour · 149mins

A truly spectacular war epic, though its original widescreen impact is sorely diminished when shown on TV. Based on the last German offensive of the war, when thousands of tanks smashed their way through the snowy pine forests of the Ardennes, it's a study of resolve on both the American and the German sides. Representing Uncle Sam are Robert Ryan and Dana Andrews, with Henry Fonda as the only man who sees the German tactic months before it happens. But the picture is dominated by Robert Shaw as the German colonel, a riveting portrait of military genius infested with paranoia. The climax is pure *High Noon* with tanks. 🖾

Henry Fonda *Lieutenant Colonel Kiley* • Robert Shaw *Colonel Hessler* • Robert Ryan *General Grey* • Dana Andrews *Colonel Pritchard* • George Montgomery *Sergeant Duquesne* • Ty Hardin *Schumacher* • Pier Angeli *Louise* • Barbara Werle *Elena* • Charles Bronson *Wolenski* ■ *Dir* Ken Annakin • *Scr* Philip Yordan, Milton Sperling, John Melson

The Battle of the River Plate ★★ U
Second World War adventure
1956 · UK · Colour · 114mins

The Royal Performance film of its year promised much, its story based on one of the most exciting tales of the Second World War, the pursuit of the German pocket battleship *Graf Spee* by three British cruisers masquerading as a task force. It was directed, written and produced by Michael Powell and Emeric Pressburger, with photography by Christopher Challis in Technicolor. But what emerged was a dull, characterless, documentarist study, marred by appalling Pinewood mock-up and model shots, its cast enlivened only by Peter Finch's swashbuckling German captain. 🖾 **DVD**

John Gregson *Captain Bell* • Anthony Quayle *Commodore Harwood* • Peter Finch *Captain Langsdorff* • Ian Hunter *Captain Woodhouse* • Jack Gwillim *Captain Barry* • Bernard Lee *Captain Dove* • Lionel Murton *Mike Fowler* • Anthony Bushell *Mr Millington-Drake* • Peter Illing *Dr Guani* • Michael Goodliffe *Captain McCall* • Patrick Macnee *Lt Comdr Medley* • John Chandos *Dr Langmann* • Douglas Wilmer *M Desmoulins* ■ *Dir/Scr* Michael Powell, Emeric Pressburger

The Battle of the Sexes ★★★
Silent drama   1914 · US · BW · 50mins

Long thought lost, this is a five-reeler made by the great film pioneer DW Griffith halfway between the four-reel success *Judith of Bethulia* and the ground-breaking 12 reels of *The Birth of a Nation*, one of his amazing total of 495 movies. Like many of Griffith's morality playlets from this period, this drama of a father demanding that his daughter live a moral life to which he himself does not aspire may prove hard to watch today, but there is no denying the sheer creativity at work in the storytelling. Here are close-ups, here, too, a moving camera – tools of the trade we now take for granted. A hand-picked cast includes the great Lillian Gish, plus Donald Crisp, Mary Alden and Owen Moore.

Lillian Gish *Jane Andrews* • Owen Moore *Andrews, Frank* • Mary Alden *Mrs Frank Andrews* • Fay Tincher *Cleo* • Robert Harron *The son* • Donald Crisp • WE Lawrence ■ *Dir* DW Griffith • *Scr* by Daniel Carson Goodman

The Battle of the Sexes ★★★ U
Comedy   1960 · UK · BW · 80mins

Shakily expanded from a James Thurber story *The Catbird Seat* this, nevertheless, has one of the most under-rated performances by Peter Sellers. He plays a Scottish accountant revenging himself on efficiency expert Constance Cummings, who wants his firm to get rid of old-fashioned impedimenta like him. There's an industrial message that's still relevant today, though director Charles Crichton (who went on to make *A Fish Called Wanda* 28 years later) never seems to be enough in control to make it matter. Perhaps he was too overawed by Sellers's accent, which makes Billy Connolly sound almost English! 🖾

Peter Sellers *Mr Martin* • Robert Morley *Robert MacPherson* • Constance Cummings *Angela Barrows* • Ernest Thesiger *Old MacPherson* • Jameson Clark *Andrew Darling* • Moultrie Kelsall *Graham* • Alex Mackenzie *Robertson* • Roddy McMillan *MacLeod* ■ *Dir* Charles Crichton • *Scr* Monja Danischewsky, from the short story *The Catbird Seat* by James Thurber

The Battle of the Villa Fiorita ★★ U
Romance   1964 · UK · Colour · 111mins

Hankies out for this slick weepie. Shamelessly emulating the glossy soap-opera style of Douglas Sirk, writer/director Delmer Daves makes the most of the gorgeous Italian scenery, as runaway wife Maureen O'Hara and her composer lover Rossano Brazzi are dogged by the disapproval of her children. Brazzi is suavity personified, but O'Hara's flame-haired ebullience is disappointingly buried beneath an unexpected veneer of suffering. There's also plenty of British support on duty, notably Richard Todd as O'Hara's husband and Phyllis Calvert as a shameless gossip.

Maureen O'Hara *Moira* • Rossano Brazzi *Lorenzo* • Richard Todd *Darrell* • Phyllis Calvert *Margot* • Martin Stephens *Michael* • Elizabeth Dear *Debby* • Olivia Hussey *Donna* •

Maxine Audley *Charmian* • Ursula Jeans *Lady Anthea* ■ *Dir* Delmer Daves • *Scr* Delmer Daves, from the novel by Rumer Godden

Battle Shock ★★
Psychological drama 1956 · US · BW · 88mins

Directed by the actor Paul Henreid – better known as the Resistance leader in *Casablanca* – this thriller, released in the States as *A Woman's Devotion*, finds artist Ralph Meeker and wife Janice Rule snarled up in a murder hunt while holidaying in Mexico. Meeker had played Mike Hammer the previous year in *Kiss Me Deadly*; Rule would later become Mrs Ben Gazzara.

Ralph Meeker *Trevor Stevenson* • Janice Rule *Stella Stevenson* • Paul Henreid *Captain Henrique Monteros* • Rosenda Monteros *Maria* • Fanny Schiller *Senora Reidl* • Jose Torvay *Gomez* • Yerye Beirute *Amigo Herrera* ■ *Dir* Paul Henreid • *Scr* Robert Hill

Battle Taxi ★ U
War drama   1955 · US · BW · 80mins

In this Korean war drama, Sterling Hayden plays the commander of a unit of rescue helicopters who's getting trouble from Arthur Franz, a former jet pilot who resents his present assignment and starts launching attacks in his unarmed chopper. Hayden was way too good an actor for this dime-budget stuff, which has precious little time for character development beyond the odd frown. The picture mostly comprises shots of helicopters and stock footage from the real war, glued together by director Herbert L Strock – the man who made the gobsmacking *Gog*.

Sterling Hayden *Captain Russ Edwards* • Arthur Franz *Lieutenant Pete Stacy* • Marshall Thompson *2nd Lieutenant Tim Vernon* • Leo Needham *Staff Sergeant Slats Klein* • Jay Barney *Lieutenant Colonel Stoneham* ■ *Dir* Herbert L Strock • *Scr* Malvin Wald, from a story by Art Arthur, Malvin Wald

Battlefield Earth ★ 12
Science-fiction action
2000 · US · Colour · 117mins

Based on the novel by L Ron Hubbard, founder of Scientology, this expensive stinker is very much a labour of love for its producer and star, John Travolta. In the year 3000, Earth is controlled by ten-foot-tall aliens from the planet Psychlo; the few remaining humans either hide out in the mountains or live and die as slaves. One man, Jonnie Goodboy Tyler (Barry Pepper), dares to rebel against the invaders, a course of action that brings him into conflict with fearsome chief of security Terl (a dreadlocked Travolta). With futuristic designs redolent of *Blade Runner* and *Independence Day*-style space battles, Roger Christian's epic looks and sounds like your average sci-fi blockbuster. Yet the emphasis placed on indoctrination, enslavement and superior alien intelligence bring the film troublingly close to subliminal propaganda, while the script is so unfeasibly banal you'd have to be brainwashed to enjoy it.

John Travolta *Terl* • Barry Pepper *Jonnie Goodboy Tyler* • Forest Whitaker *Ker* • Kim Coates *Carlo* • Richard Tyson *Robert the Fox* • Sabine Karsenti *Chrissie* • Michael Byrne

Parson Staffer ■ *Dir* Roger Christian • *Scr* Corey Mandell, JD Shapiro, from the novel by L Ron Hubbard

Battleflag ★
First World War drama
1977 · W Ger/Aus/Sp · BW · 120mins

A terrible clinker made in West Germany but intended as an international epic. Simon Ward looks hopelessly lost as the soldier fighting for the old Austro-Hungarian Empire at the end of the First World War, who also falls in love. The politics of the time, always messy, are downright confusing and, despite some striking locations, the movie botches almost all the issues it attempts to deal with. German dialogue dubbed into English.

Simon Ward *Fahnrith Menis* • Siegfried Rauch *Bottenlauben* • Wolfgang Preiss *Colonel* • Peter Cushing *Baron Hackenberg* • Jon Finch *Charbinsky* • Viktor Staal *Anton* • Verónica Forqué *Resa* • Robert Hoffmann *Klein* ■ *Dir* Ottokar Runze • *Scr* Herbert Asmodi

Battleground ★★★★ PG
Second World War drama
1949 · US · BW · 113mins

This grimy and authentic-looking study of wartime close combat comes, surprisingly, from MGM, fabled home of glamour and glossy production values. The studio supplied an all-star cast, and then proceeded to make the likes of Van Johnson, George Murphy and Ricardo Montalban virtually unrecognisable in combat duds as members of a US Army infantry unit trapped during the siege of Bastogne in 1944. Writer Robert Pirosh actually served at Bastogne, and his screenplay was taken to Metro by new head of production Dore Schary and made in the face of opposition from studio boss Louis B Mayer. It won an Oscar, as did Paul C Vogel's cinematography, though director William A Wellman lost out to Joseph L Mankiewicz. Even those who aren't fans of war movies might find much to appreciate in this one.

Van Johnson *Holley* • John Hodiak *Jarvess* • Ricardo Montalban *Roderigues* • George Murphy *Pop Stazak* • Marshall Thompson *Jim Layton* • Jerome Courtland *Abner Spudler* • Don Taylor *Standiferd* • Bruce Cowling *Wolowicz* • James Whitmore *Kinnie* ■ *Dir* William Wellman [William A Wellman] • *Scr* Robert Pirosh

The Battleship Potemkin ★★★★★ PG
Silent historical drama
1925 · USSR · BW · 65mins

Originally planned as a brief episode in an epic history of the 1905 Revolution, Eisenstein's silent classic remains one of the most influential films ever made. A masterpiece of editorial dexterity, it proved that symbolic imagery could have the same emotional and intellectual impact on an audience as a straightforward narrative. You don't need a working knowledge of Russian history, Marxist dialectic, Japanese pictographs or the techniques of ''montage'' to appreciate the power of the plate smashing that sparks the mutiny, the fog scene and the massacre on the Odessa Steps. Don't be put off by its highbrow reputation, this is essential cinema. 🖾

Mikhail Gomarov *Sailor* • Repnikova *Woman on the steps* • Aleksander Antonov *Vakulinchuk the sailor* • Grigori Aleksandrov *Chief Officer Gilyarovsky* • Vladimir Barsky *Captain Golikov* • Alexander Lyovshin *Petty officer* • Beatrice Vitoldi *Mother with baby carriage* • I Bobrov *Humiliated soldier* ■ *Dir* Sergei Eisenstein • *Scr* Sergei Eisenstein, Nina Agadzhanova-Shutko

Battlestar Galactica ★★ PG

Science-fiction 1978 · US · Colour · 119mins

This feature film spin-off consists of two episodes from the short-lived TV series, cloned from *Star Wars* and unsuccessfully sued for plagiarism by the makers of that blockbuster hit. Lorne Greene stars as the commander of a fleet of starships trying to return to Earth after it has virtually been wiped out by the Cylons, a robot race programmed to destroy mankind. The result is a tacky, juvenile and derivative space opera with a gee-whiz aesthetic. Sometimes, though, it accidentally manages to evoke a comfortable sense of wonder. ▭

Lorne Greene *Commander Adama* • Richard L Hatch [Richard Hatch] *Captain Apollo* • Dirk Benedict *Lieutenant Starbuck* • Maren Jensen *Athena* • Herb Jefferson Jr [Herbert Jefferson Jr] *Lieutenant Boomer* • Terry Carter *Colonel Tigh* • Jane Seymour *Serina* • Noah Hathaway *Boxey* ■ *Dir* Richard A Colla • *Scr* Glen A Larson

Battletruck ★★★ 15

Science-fiction 1982 · US · Colour · 88mins

Lone warrior hero Michael Beck takes on bloodthirsty pirates and their super truck after 21st-century oil wars cause a fuel shortage. Further friction occurs when Annie McEnroe, the villain's daughter, is caught between the opposing camps. This may be a rather juvenile *Mad Max* clone, but director Harley Cokliss ensures that the subtle ecological messages don't get in the way of the fast-paced mayhem. The New Zealand locations provide an intriguingly atmospheric background to the irony and sharp wit of the screenplay. ▭

Michael Beck *Hunter* • Annie McEnroe *Corlie* • James Wainwright *Straker* • John Ratzenberger *Rusty* • Randolph Powell *Judd* • Bruno Lawrence *Willie* • Diana Rowan *Charlene* • John Bach *Bone* ■ *Dir* Harley Cokliss • *Scr* Irving Austin, Harley Cokliss, John Beech

Battling Butler ★★★

Silent comedy 1926 · US · BW · 80mins

Although this was Buster Keaton's most profitable silent film (and one he once cited as his favourite), it is generally rated among his weaker ventures. The pioneering use of deep-focus photography gives it a certain historical value, but there is too little comic business to relish. Keaton plays a wealthy milksop who is sent into the woods to toughen up, only to be mistaken for a prizefighter by mountain girl Sally O'Neil. The duck shoot is ingeniously staged, and there are a couple of amusing training camp gags, but what lingers longest is the brutality of the final boxing bout.

Buster Keaton *Alfred Butler* • Sally O'Neil *Mountain girl* • Snitz Edwards *His valet* • Francis McDonald *Alfred "Battling Butler"* • Mary O'Brien *His wife* • Tom Wilson *The trainer* • Eddie Borden *His manager* • Walter

James *The girl's father* ■ *Dir* Buster Keaton • *Scr* Albert Boasberg, Paul Gerard Smith, Lex Neal, Charles Smith, from the musical by Stanley Brightman, Austin Melford

Battling for Baby ★★ PG

Drama 1992 · US · Colour · 89mins

How did hokum like this attract luminaries such as Debbie Reynolds, Suzanne Pleshette and Courteney Cox, not to mention such persistent underachievers as Doug McClure? The story is pure cornball, involving a couple of long-estranged schoolfriends whose feud to monopolise their grandchild threatens their children's marriage. You might be tempted to watch to see a pre-fame Cox, but otherwise only devotees of mawkish melodrama need spare the time. ▭

Suzanne Pleshette *Marie Peters* • Debbie Reynolds *Helen Jeffries* • Courteney Cox *Katherine Jeffries* • John Terlesky *Phillip Jeffries* • Doug McClure *David* • Mary Jo Catlett *Mrs Capello* • Leigh Lawson *Allen* • Jeff Olson *Doctor* ■ *Dir* Art Wolff • *Scr* Nancey Silvers, Walter Lockwood

Baxter ★★★

Drama 1973 · UK · Colour · 104mins

Actor-turned-director Lionel Jeffries never puts a foot wrong through the quagmire of clichés that can so often swamp stories of ill-adjusted youngsters. The 12-year-old hero (Scott Jacoby) is being treated for his lisp by speech therapist Patricia Neal, which seems to put him at odds with his friends and compounds the problem of his parents splitting up. The acting throughout lives up to the gravitas of the film's theme.

Patricia Neal *Dr Clemm* • Jean-Pierre Cassel *Roger Tunnell* • Britt Ekland *Chris Bentley* • Lynn Carlin *Mrs Baxter* • Scott Jacoby *Robert Baxter* • Sally Thomsett *Nemo* • Paul Eddington *Mr Rawling* • Paul Maxwell *Mr Baxter* • Ian Thomson *Dr Walsh* ■ *Dir* Lionel Jeffries • *Scr* Reginald Rose

Bay Boy ★★★ 15

Drama 1984 · Can/Fr · Colour · 96mins

Kiefer Sutherland's first starring role was in this downbeat but interesting film from Canada. He plays a Nova Scotia lad destined for the priesthood who witnesses the murder of a Jewish couple and keeps quiet about it because he knows the killer, a cop who also happens to be the father of the girl he fancies. Set in 1937, Daniel Petrie's tale is semi-autobiographical and rather low key for its subject matter. Even so, Sutherland is appealing and his problems with his mother (Liv Ullmann) are often touching. There's some strong support from Alan Scarfe as the killer cop, and a brief appearance from Stéphane Audran, the classy heroine of countless Claude Chabrol thrillers. Contains swearing and nudity. ▭

Liv Ullmann *Mrs Jennie Campbell* • Kiefer Sutherland *Donald Campbell* • Alan Scarfe *Sergeant Tom Coldwell* • Peter Donat *Mr Will Campbell* • Mathieu Carrière *Father Chaisson* • Chris Wiggins *Chief Charles McInnes* • Isabelle Mejias *Mary McNeil* • Leah Pinsent *Saxon Coldwell* • Stéphane Audran *Blanche* ■ *Dir/Scr* Daniel Petrie

Bay Cove ★★ 15

Supernatural thriller 1987 · US · Colour · 95mins

This is a rather silly tale about a couple who discover that their new neighbours belong to a coven of witches and want them to join in. Despite the poor plot and lack of chills, there are plenty of familiar faces to be seen, including Tim Matheson and Pamela Sue Martin as the newlyweds and Woody Harrelson, the former star of TV's *Cheers* who's made a successful transition to Hollywood leading man. This rehash of *Rosemary's Baby*-style clichés is sadly devoid of director Carl Schenkel's usual glossy style. Contains violence. ▭

Tim Matheson *Jerry LeBon* • Pamela Sue Martin *Linda LeBon* • Barbara Billingsley *Beatrice Gower* • Jeff Conaway *Josh McGwin* • Woody Harrelson *Theodore Slater* • Susan Ruttan *Debbie McGwin* • James Sikking [James B Sikking] *Nicholas Kline* ■ *Dir* Carl Schenkel • *Scr* R Timothy Kring

The Bay of Saint Michel ★★

Adventure 1963 · UK · BW · 73mins

That marvellous French monument, Le Mont-Saint-Michel, with its broad sweep of sandy bay, makes a spectacular location for this unassuming little thriller about a commando unit that reforms after the Second World War and sets about finding some buried Nazi loot. The treasure map is in three bits, each of which needs finding first. Yet it's only when the treasure itself looks like being found that the screenplay reveals the first of several sudden twists. American star Keenan Wynn is in charge of the operation, while Mai Zetterling, a Swedish actress who made many movies in Britain, plays a mystery Frenchwoman.

Keenan Wynn *Nick Rawlings* • Mai Zetterling *Helene Bretton* • Ronald Howard *Bill Webb* • Rona Anderson *Pru Lawson* • Trader Faulkner *Dave Newton* • Edward Underdown *Col Harvey* • Michael Peake *Capt Starkey* • Rudolph Offenbach *Father Laurent* ■ *Dir* John Ainsworth • *Scr* Christopher Davis

Baywatch: Panic at Malibu Pier ★ 15

Adventure drama 1989 · US · Colour · 97mins

Here it is, folks, the pilot that started it all. The American TV series *Baywatch* features sand-blown stories about the romances, family lives and daredevil aquatic rescues of a group of buff and busty LA lifeguards. David Hasselhoff and Parker Stevenson star alongside Erika Eleniak (sorry, fans, Pamela Anderson came to the beach a bit later). This TV movie started an international tidal wave: the series went on to become the number one syndicated show around the world. ▭

David Hasselhoff *Mitch Bucannon* • Parker Stevenson *Craig Pomeroy* • Bill Warlock [Billy Warlock] *Eddie Krammer* • Monte Markham *Captain Thorpe* • Shawn Weatherly *Jill Riley* • Erika Eleniak *Shauni McClain* • Richard Jaeckel *Al Gibson* ■ *Dir* Richard Compton • *Scr* Douglas Schwartz, Michael Berk, from a story by Gregory J Bonann, Douglas Schwartz

Baywatch the Movie: Forbidden Paradise ★★

Adventure drama 1995 · US · Colour · 90mins

David Hasselhoff and his sillicone-enchanced lifesavers swap the polluted shores of California for an undeserved Hawaiian break in the usual banal mix of soap, surf and sun. The regulars – Alexandra Paul, Pamela Anderson, David Charvet, Yasmine Bleeth, Jaason Simmons – all get their own little subplots. But they are there basically to be photographed against the tourist delights of the islands and to be seen in something other than those familiar red cossies. Real-life surfer Gerry Lopez appears as himself.

David Hasselhoff *Mitch* • David Charvet *Matt* • Pamela Anderson *CJ* • Alexandra Paul *Stephanie* • Yasmine Bleeth *Caroline* • Jaason Simmons *Logan* ■ *Dir* Douglas Schwartz

The Beach ★★★★ 15

Adventure thriller 2000 · US/UK · Colour · 118mins

Many movies have taken us down the hippy trail, with wildly varying success. *The Beach*, based on Alex Garland's bestseller, is better than most. The latest film from the *Trainspotting* team takes a tour round the mind of Richard (Leonardo DiCaprio), a young backpacker seeking adventure in Thailand who gets more than he bargained for when drug-crazed madman Daffy (Robert Carlyle) tells him the location of a secret beach. John Hodge's clever, witty script keeps the narrative firmly on track, while leaving director Danny Boyle ample room to luxuriate in the Orient's visual delights. With DiCaprio giving his most mature, multi-layered performance to date, and French actress Virginie Ledoyen a great find as the love interest, *The Beach* achieves the near impossible by evoking in us the same feelings of longing and regret experienced by the film's characters.

Leonardo DiCaprio *Richard* • Tilda Swinton *Sal* • Virginie Ledoyen *Françoise* • Guillaume Canet *Etienne* • Robert Carlyle *Daffy* • Paterson Joseph *Keaty* • Lars Arentz Hansen *Bugs* • Daniel York *Hustler* ■ *Dir* Danny Boyle • *Scr* John Hodge, from the novel by Alex Garland

Beach Blanket Bingo ★★

Comedy 1965 · US · Colour · 100mins

A mindless, pointless title for a mindless, pointless movie, unless you happen to be a fan of American-International's stream of post-*Beach Party* teen films, many of which never played at cinemas in the UK. For those who care, this yet again features those oh-so-nice singing stars Frankie Avalon and Annette Funicello, and it's sad to see the great Buster Keaton paying the rent with a walk-on cameo. The music is utter drivel and the direction nonexistent. An extraordinary time capsule to look and wonder at.

Frankie Avalon *Frankie* • Annette Funicello *Dee Dee* • Deborah Walley *Bonnie Graham* • Harvey Lembeck *Eric Von Zipper* • John Ashley *Steve Gordon* • Jody McCrea *Bonehead* • Donna Loren *Donna* • Linda Evans *Sugar Kane* • Buster Keaton ■ *Dir* William Asher • *Scr* Sher Townsend, Leo Townsend

Beach Party ★★★ U

Comedy   1963 · US · Colour · 97mins

The first, and best, of AIP's phenomenally successful surfin' series. These naive frolics proved to a British audience that America, post-Beatles, was positively archaic. Viewed charitably (is there any other way?), this teen-slanted Frankie Avalon/ Annette Funicello beach romp is not without charm, though the inclusion of grown-ups Bob Cummings and Dorothy Malone wastes two usually likeable screen performers in a sub-plot of astounding banality that looks as though it was filmed separately from the rest of the movie.

Bob Cummings [Robert Cummings] *Professor Sutwell* • Dorothy Malone *Marianne* • Frankie Avalon *Frankie* • Annette Funicello *Dolores* • Harvey Lembeck *Eric Von Zipper* • Jody McCrea *Deadhead* • John Ashley *Ken* • Morey Amsterdam *Cappy* ■ *Dir* William Asher • *Scr* Lou Rusoff

Beach Red ★★★★ 12

Second World War drama
1967 · US · Colour · 99mins

Former beefcake star Cornel Wilde, best remembered for *The Greatest Show on Earth* and his role as Chopin in *A Song to Remember*, became a maverick director to reckon with in later life, producing self-starring vehicles, invariably also featuring his wife, Jean Wallace, as co-star. This ferocious Pacific war opus is one of his better efforts, an uncompromising movie with minimal narrative, adapted from a wartime novel written in 1945. The film's editing, by *Bullitt's* Frank P Keller, is stunning, and was rightly Oscar nominated, and the depiction of war's savagery is truly remarkable: no one who has seen this film will ever forget the shot of the soldier leaving his arm behind on the beach. Contains violence and nudity. ▭

Cornel Wilde *Captain MacDonald* • Rip Torn *Sergeant Honeywell* • Dewey Stinger III *Mouse* • Patrick Wolfe *Cliff* • Burr DeBenning *Egan* • Jean Wallace *Julie MacDonald* • Linda Albertano *Girl in Baltimore* • Jan Garrison *Susie* • Gene Blakely *Goldberg* ■ *Dir* Cornel Wilde • *Scr* Clint Johnston, Donald A Peters, Jefferson Pascal, from the novel *Sunday Red Beach* by Peter Bowman

The Beachcomber ★★ U

Drama   1954 · UK · Colour · 78mins

W Somerset Maugham's story of the drunken derelict who is reformed by a prissy missionary had been filmed under its original title, *Vessel of Wrath*, in 1938 with Charles Laughton and Elsa Lanchester in the leads. Robert Newton had also appeared in the 1938 version and seems so aware of the stature of Laughton's performance that he allows his own to lapse into a slurred variation on Long John Silver, whom he had played four years earlier. Newton's blustering blows poor Glynis Johns and the rest of a decent cast off the screen. ▭

Robert Newton *Ted* • Glynis Johns *Martha* • Donald Sinden *Ewart Gray* • Paul Rogers *Owen* • Donald Pleasence *Tromp* • Walter Crisham *Vederala* • Michael Hordern *Headman* • Auric Lorand *Alfred* • *Dir* Muriel Box • *Scr* Sydney Box, from the story *Vessel of Wrath* by W Somerset Maugham

Beaches ★★★ 15

Drama   1988 · US · Colour · 118mins

A movie about a lifetime friendship between two women makes a refreshing change, especially when it stars powerhouse Bette Midler and Barbara Hershey. They both make the most of their roles as two girls from completely different backgrounds who meet as 11-year-olds and, despite various setbacks, remain friends over the years. *Pretty Woman's* Garry Marshall directs slickly and Hershey is very appealing as a poor little rich girl, but the movie belongs to the astonishing Midler, playing a brash, selfish singer. It's at its best when Midler gives free rein to her character rather than when it slips into schmaltz. Contains some swearing ▭

Bette Midler *CC Bloom* • Barbara Hershey *Hillary Whitney Essex* • John Heard *John Pierce* • Spalding Gray *Dr Richard Milstein* • Lainie Kazan *Leona Bloom* • James Read *Michael Essex* • Grace Johnston *Victoria Essex* ■ *Dir* Garry Marshall • *Scr* Mary Agnes Donoghue, from the novel by Iris Rainer Dart

Beachhead ★★

Second World War drama
1954 · US · Colour · 89mins

Tony Curtis served in the US Navy during the Second World War and saw action in the South Pacific; he was then stationed on Guam, where many Japanese were imprisoned. Perhaps that explains why he got rather emotionally involved in this otherwise unexceptional war movie, set in the Solomon Islands. Curtis is one of a group of marines who go behind enemy lines on a spying mission, prior to a bombing raid on a Japanese base. The plot is identical to *South Pacific*, without the songs and all that *Bali H'ai* stuff; as in that film, the Hawaiian island of Kauai doubles for Melanesia.

Tony Curtis *Burke* • Frank Lovejoy *Sergeant Fletcher* • Mary Murphy *Nina* • Eduard Franz *Bouchard* • Skip Homeier *Reynolds* • John Doucette *Major Scott* • Alan Wells *Biggerman* ■ *Dir* Stuart Heisler • *Scr* Richard Alan Simmons, from the novel *I've Got Mine* by Richard G Hubler

Bean ★★★★ PG

Comedy   1997 · UK · Colour · 85mins

A very enjoyable American outing for Rowan Atkinson's celebrated TV character, as he jets off to the States to oversee the unveiling of the newly acquired Whistler's Mother. There are some familiar sketches, but writers Richard Curtis and Robin Driscoll and director Mel Smith have skilfully slotted them into a cohesive, engaging and fast-moving story perfectly suited to Atkinson's singular style of physical comedy – his close encounter with "America's greatest painting" is an absolute riot. Peter MacNicol's anxiety-ridden American host is the perfect foil to Atkinson and Burt Reynolds is, well, Burt Reynolds in a general's uniform. The film was a massive international hit and deservedly so. The UK video contains 20 minutes of additional scenes, including Bean's mini taking a detour through Harrods. Contains some mild swearing and sexual references. ▭ DVD

Rowan Atkinson *Mr Bean* • Peter MacNicol *David Langley* • Pamela Reed *Alison Langley* •

Harris Yulin *George Grierson* • Burt Reynolds *General Newton* • Larry Drake *Elmer* • Chris Ellis *Detective Butler* • Johnny Galecki *Stingo Wheelie* ■ *Dir* Mel Smith • *Scr* Richard Curtis, Robin Driscoll, from the character created by Rowan Atkinson, Richard Curtis

The Beans of Egypt, Maine ★★★ 18

Drama   1994 · US · Colour · 95mins

Also known as *Forbidden Choices*, this drama – co-produced for TV's *American Playhouse* – is based on the novel by Carolyn Chute and follows the life and loves of the Bean family, who live in the small town of Egypt. Focusing particularly on randy young Beal (Patrick McGaw) and his relationship with a feisty neighbour (Martha Plimpton, who narrates the tale), this doesn't quite capture the full depth of the novel, but features nice performances from Plimpton, Kelly Lynch and Rutger Hauer. ▭

Martha Plimpton *Earlene Pomerleau* • Kelly Lynch *Roberta Bean* • Rutger Hauer *Reuben Bean* • Patrick McGaw *Beal Bean* • Michael MacRae *Cole Deveraux* • Ariana Lamon-Anderson *Bonnie Loo* ■ *Dir* Jennifer Warren • *Scr* Bill Phillips, from the novel by Carolyn Chute

Beanstalk ★★ U

Comedy fantasy   1994 · US · Colour · 77mins

This is a routine update of the Jack and the beanstalk story, with a kid tossing some beans out of the window, and discovering that the sky's the limit for the stalk that grows from them. It's more ho-hum than fe-fi-fo-fum – even the kids it's aimed at won't be overly impressed by the corny humour and the crumby special effects. The cast includes Margot Kidder (Lois Lane in the *Superman* films) and David Naughton of *An American Werewolf in London*. Both must have been wondering how they'd suddenly become such has-beans.

JD Daniels *Jack Taylor* • Amy Stock-Poynton *Rebecca* • Patrick Renna *Danny* • Margot Kidder *Dr Kate Winston* • Richard Moll *Leatch* ■ *Dir* Michael Paul Davis [Michael Davis] • *Scr* Michael Paul Davis

The Bear ★★★★ PG

Adventure   1988 · Fr · Colour · 89mins

A (tooth)ripping yarn by director Jean-Jacques Annaud, this tells of the aventures of a small bear, befriended by a larger cousin who is a tempting target for a couple of trappers. It's filmed with enormous expertise and the eco-warrior case is put with great sympathy, but its anthropomorphism makes it seem like a glossy and more symbolic version of the Disney real-life stories that used to be all the rage in the sixties. ▭

Jack Wallace *Bill* • Tcheky Karyo *Tom* • André Lacombe *Joseph, the dog handler* ■ *Dir* Jean-Jacques Annaud • *Scr* Gérard Brach, John Brownjohn, Alexander Whitelaw, from the novel *The Grizzly King* by James Oliver Curwood • *Cinematographer* Philippe Rousselot

Bear Island ★ PG

Action thriller
1979 · UK/Can · Colour · 102mins

Few authors have been as frequently translated to the big screen with as

little success as Alistair MacLean. In a competitive field, this is among the worst adaptations. Obviously unimpressed by the story of fascists bidding for world domination by means of meteorological mastery, director Don Sharp rejects plot in favour of a series of earnest conversations in ludicrous accents and a glut of action sequences which never threaten to set pulses racing. Consequently, character specialists like Donald Sutherland, Vanessa Redgrave and Richard Widmark are as out of place as a bikini in the Arctic. Contains some swearing and violence. ▭

Donald Sutherland *Frank Lansing* • Vanessa Redgrave *Hedi Lindquist* • Richard Widmark *Otto Gerran* • Christopher Lee *Lechinski* • Barbara Parkins *Judith Ruben* • Lloyd Bridges *Smithy* • Lawrence Dane *Paul Hartman* • Patricia Collins *Inge Van Zipper* ■ *Dir* Don Sharp • *Scr* David Butler, Murray Smith, Don Sharp, from the novel by Alistair MacLean

The Bears and I ★★ U

Adventure   1974 · US · Colour · 88mins

In attempting to follow in his father John's footsteps, Patrick Wayne set himself a mission impossible. A decade after he appeared in the last in a series of westerns with the Duke himself, Patrick struck out on his own in this passable live-action adventure from Disney. Playing a Vietnam veteran who settles in a national park, he finds himself with the dual problem of preventing native American land from falling into the hands of racist rednecks and of raising a trio of mischievous bear cubs. Wayne and Chief Dan George give pleasing performances, but the story plays second fiddle to the adorable bears.

Patrick Wayne *Bob Leslie* • Chief Dan George *Chief A-Tas-Ka-Nay* • Andrew Duggan *Commissioner Gaines* • Michael Ansara *Oliver Red Fern* • Robert Pine *John McCarten* • Val DeVargas *Sam Eagle Speaker* ■ *Dir* Bernard McEveety • *Scr* John Whedon, from the novel by Robert Franklin Leslie

The Beast ★★★

Erotic fantasy drama
1975 · Fr · Colour · 102mins

The perverse sexual content of this erotic fairy tale earned it a notoriety that detracted from its value as a savage social satire and a film of painterly beauty. Echoing the soft-core irony of his earlier films, *Blanche* and *Contes Immoraux*, Polish-born former animator Walerian Borowczyk errs frequently on the wrong side of political correctness in contrasting the experiences of an 18th-century bride and an American heiress, both about to marry into the same aristocratic horse-breeding family. The bestial nature of some of the dream-diary sequences might cause offence, but there is an undeniable playfulness about the eccentric couplings and the upstairs/downstairs relationships. In French with English subtitles.

Sirpa Lane *Romilda* • Lisbeth Hummel *Lucy* • Elizabeth Kaza *Virginia* • Pierre Benedetti *Mathrurin* • Guy Tréjan *Pierre* • Marcel Dalio *Duc* • Roland Armontel *Priest* ■ *Dir/Scr* Walerian Borowczyk • *Cinematographer* Bernard Daillencourt, Marcel Grignon

The Beast ★★★★ 18

War drama   1988 · US · Colour · 105mins

Yet another movie to prove, as if we didn't know, that war is hell. And yet, with its exotic locations and intense relationships, director Kevin Reynolds's carefully balanced drama brings its message home with a fierce urgency. Set in 1981 during the second year of the Soviet-Afghan war, the beast of the title is a Soviet tank that has helped raze a village to the ground and, becoming separated from its unit, is trapped in a mountainous dead-end by guerrillas bent on reprisals. Emotions within the tank are just as overheated, with paranoid commander George Dzundza at odds with crew member Jason Patric. Reynolds (*Waterworld*) handles the action well and directs with a keen awareness of the claustrophobic settings. In English and Pashtu (Afghan dialect) with subtitles. Contains violence and swearing. ▢

George Dzundza *Daskal* • Jason Patric *Koverchenko* • Steven Bauer *Taj* • Stephen Baldwin *Golikov* • Don Harvey *Kaminski* • Kabir Bedi *Akbar* • Erick Avari *Samad* ■ *Dir* Kevin Reynolds • *Scr* William Mastrosimone, from his play *Nanawatai*

Beast from Haunted Cave ★★

Horror   1959 · US · BW · 67mins

Crooks hiding out in a ski resort get their comeuppance at the paws of a cave-dwelling snow beast. This is a painless, cost-conscious effort typical of producer Roger Corman, made by his company and filmed in Deadwood, South Dakota. Yet it is infused with flair and imagination by director Monte Hellman. Hellman later directed the cult westerns *Ride in the Whirlwind* (1965) and *The Shooting* (1967), and this unusual mobster versus monster melange shows his early promise.

Michael Forest *Gill* • Sheila Carol *Gypsy* • Frank Wolff *Alex* • Richard Sinatra *Marty* • Wally Campo *Byron* • Linne Ahlstrand *Natalie* ■ *Dir* Monte Hellman • *Scr* Charles B Griffith

The Beast from 20,000 Fathoms ★★★★

Science-fiction adventure
1953 · US · BW · 79mins

The first prehistoric-monster-on-the-rampage feature and arguably the best. It marked the solo debut of special effects genius Ray Harryhausen, who would refine his stop-motion puppetry in the Sinbad fantasies and *Jason and the Argonauts*. Freed from a prehistoric hibernation by an atomic blast at the North Pole, the monster tramples through New York and ends up taking a bite out of the Coney Island roller coaster. Tense and ferocious, this was the *Jurassic Park* of its day and spawned countless imitations.

Paul Christian *Tom Nesbitt* • Paula Raymond *Lee Hunter* • Cecil Kellaway *Professor Elson* • Kenneth Tobey *Colonel Evans* • Jack Pennick *Jacob* • Donald Woods *Captain Jackson* • Lee Van Cleef *Corporal Stone* • Steve Brodie *Sergeant Loomis* ■ *Dir* Eugène Lourié • *Scr* Lou Morheim, Fred Freiberger, from the story *The Fog Horn* by Ray Bradbury

The Beast in the Cellar ★

Horror   1970 · UK · Colour · 87mins

Two sinister sisters hide a dark secret in their basement in this ponderously talky attempt at a modern HP Lovecraft-style horror tale. With the title revealing all, writer/director James Kelly has nowhere interesting to go and what little atmosphere he initially conjures up is soon dissipated in a pretty tedious, badly constructed and unsuspenseful affair. Quite what induced Beryl Reid and Flora Robson to get involved in such a pointless exercise is a mystery, but they are the only reason for watching this forgettable filler.

Beryl Reid *Ellie Ballantyne* • Flora Robson *Joyce Ballantyne* • Tessa Wyatt *Joanna Sutherland* • John Hamill *Corporal Alan Marlow* • TP McKenna *Superintendent Paddick* • David Dodimead *Dr Spencer* • Christopher Chittell *Baker* ■ *Dir/Scr* James Kelly

The Beast Must Die ★★ 15

Horror   1974 · UK · Colour · 87mins

A clumsily contrived variation on the old dark house whodunit, in which one of the guests invited to eccentric Calvin Lockhart's hunting lodge is not merely a murderer but a werewolf to boot. Even with the lame "werewolf break" gimmick (the film suddenly stops and viewers are asked to guess the lurking lycanthrope's identity), it all boils down to the same horror clichés, with the wolf rather too obviously played by a dressed-up dog. Ever-reliable Peter Cushing turns in top work as a Nordic professor whose long folklore lectures lazily disguise the clues to the wolf's identity, should you wish to enter into the spirit of things and play along. ▢

Calvin Lockhart *Tom Newcliffe* • Peter Cushing *Dr Christopher Lundgren* • Charles Gray *Bennington* • Anton Diffring *Pavel* • Marlene Clark *Caroline Newcliffe* • Ciaran Madden *Davina Gilmore* • Tom Chadbon *Paul Foote* • Michael Gambon *Jan Jarmokowski* ■ *Dir* Paul Annett • *Scr* Michael Winder, from the story *There Shall Be No Darkness* by James Blish

The Beast of Hollow Mountain ★★

Science-fiction western
1956 · US · Colour · 46mins

A full 13 years before his story *Valley of the Mist*, on which this film was based, turned up posthumously in *The Valley of Gwang* (executed by his disciple Ray Harryhausen), Willis O'Brien tried out his cowboys versus prehistoric monster idea in this hokey dud shot in Mexico. Sadly, the low-budget producers couldn't afford to hire O'Brien, the animator on the original *King Kong*, to animate the combat scenes between Guy Madison and the tyrannosaurus once they'd bought the story. When it finally makes its long-awaited appearance, within a typically fifties western scenario about greedy land barons, the dinosaur is sub-standard and a crashing disappointment.

Guy Madison *Jimmy Ryan* • Patricia Medina *Sarita* • Eduardo Noriega *Enrique Rios* • Carlos Rivas *Felipe Sanchez* ■ *Dir* Edward Nassour, Ismael Rodriguez • *Scr* Robert Hill, Jack DeWitt, from the story *Valley of the Mist* by Willis H O'Brien

The Beast of the City ★★★

Crime drama   1932 · US · BW · 86mins

In direct response to a request by President Herbert Hoover that the police be glorified on screen rather than gangsters, MGM turned out this crusading drama with Walter Huston well cast as the incorruptible police chief waging war on Jean Hersholt's big shot and his empire of crime. Jean Harlow puts in a torrid appearance as the gangster's moll who proves irresistible to Huston's younger brother, played by Wallace Ford. A lively precursor of *The Untouchables* (and a seeming influence on *Kiss of Death* among many other crime films), this climaxes rather curiously in a western-style shoot-out that claims far more police casualties than necessary.

Walter Huston *Jim Fitzpatrick* • Jean Harlow *Daisy* • Wallace Ford *Edward Fitzpatrick* • Jean Hersholt *Sam Belmonte* • Dorothy Peterson *Mary Fitzpatrick* • Tully Marshall *Michaels* • John Miljan *District attorney* • Emmett Corrigan *Chief of Police* • Sandy Roth *Mac* • Mickey Rooney *Mickey Fitzpatrick* ■ *Dir* Charles Brabin • *Scr* John Lee Mahin, from the story by WR Burnett

The Beast with Five Fingers ★★★★ 15

Horror   1946 · US · BW · 84mins

Peter Lorre acts deliciously deranged, as only he can, when the severed hand of a dead concert pianist returns from the grave to haunt his tortured soul. Or is he just imagining it? Lorre steals the show with a masterfully bravura performance in a superior slice of psychological horror, marshalling the sinister staples of mythic madness and macabre music into a satisfying scare-fest. Give a big hand to Robert Florey for his adept direction, and to the key special effect itself (which Luis Buñuel had a hand in), a marvellously nightmarish image. ▢

Robert Alda *Bruce Conrad* • Andrea King *Julie Holden* • Peter Lorre *Hilary Cummins* • Victor Francen *Francis Ingram* • J Carrol Naish *Ouidio Castanio* • Charles Dingle *Raymond Arlington* • John Alvin *Donald Arlington* • David Hoffman *Duprex* ■ *Dir* Robert Florey • *Scr* Curt Siodmak, from a story by William Fryer Harvey

The Beast Within ★★★

Psychological drama
1995 · Den · Colour · 79mins

This unstinting rite-of-passage picture established the Nimbus company, which transformed Danish cinema through its sponsorship of Dogma 95. Bemused by his mother's relationships with her husband, the vicar and his headmaster, Cyron Bjorn Melville seeks sinister solace in assuming the demonic personality secretly summoned in the woods by his mischievous friends. Often resembling Alex Van Warmerdam's *The Northerners* in its revelation of the darker side of an outwardly respectable community, Carsten Rudolf's strikingly composed comedy benefits from exceptional support playing from Jens Okking as the boy's taxidermist "dad" and Soren Pilmark as the cleric with a broken heart. A Danish language film.

Cyron Bjorn Melville *Frederik* • Jens Okking *Otto Steppe* • Michelle Bjorn-Andersen *Marie Andersen* • Soren Pilmark *Vicar* ■ *Dir/Scr* Carsten Rudolf

The Beastmaster ★★★ 15

Fantasy action adventure
1982 · US · Colour · 113mins

A daft sword-and-sorcery fantasy adventure from director Don Coscarelli of *Phantasm* fame. Muscleman Marc Singer is Dar, a prehistoric Doctor Dolittle, who can telepathically talk to jungle animals and uses them to battle evil magician Maax (an over-the-top Rip Torn), the plunderer of his barbarian village. Lots of glitzy special effects, zombie guards in bondage gear and some amazing animal stunts spice up the broad proceedings, and ex-*Charlie's Angel* Tanya Roberts features as a decorative slave girl. There's also a laugh to be had from Dar's two cute ferret pals, which hang from his loin cloth. Contains violence and brief nudity. ▢

Marc Singer *Dar* • Tanya Roberts *Kiri* • Rip Torn *Maax* • John Amos *Seth* • Josh Milrad *Tal* • Rod Loomis *Zed* • Ten Hammer *Young Dar's father* • Ralph Strait *Sacco* • Billy Jacoby *Young Dar* ■ *Dir* Don Coscarelli • *Scr* Don Coscarelli, Paul Pepperman, from the novel by Andre Norton

Beastmaster 2: through the Portal of Time ★★ PG

Fantasy action adventure
1991 · US · Colour · 102mins

This better-than-average sequel to *The Beastmaster* has benevolent barbarian Dar (Marc Singer) following evil ruler Arklon (Wings Hauser) through a time gate, opened by sorceress Sarah Douglas, to modern-day Los Angeles. Arklon wants the "neutron detonator" to secure world domination; Dar – aided by his trusty eagle, tiger and two ferrets – tries to stop him. It's a likeable, comic book fantasy tinged with light camp comedy. ▢

Marc Singer *Dar* • Wings Hauser *Arklon* • Sarah Douglas *Lyranna* • Kari Wuhrer *Jackie Trent* • James Avery *Captain Coberly* • Robert Fieldsteel *Bendowski* • Robert Z'Dar *Zavik* ■ *Dir* Sylvio Tabet • *Scr* Jim Wynorski, RJ Robertson, Sylvio Tabet, Ken Hauser, Doug Miles, from the story by Jim Wynorski, RJ Robertson, from the characters created by Paul Pepperman, Don Coscarelli, from the novel *The Beastmaster* by Andre Norton

Beastmaster III: the Eye of Braxus ★★ PG

Fantasy action adventure
1995 · US · Colour · 87mins

Production values and special effects wizardry are downsized in this continuing adventures of blond warrior Dar (the ever likeable Marc Singer) and his animal menagerie, as he tries to save his kidnapped brother from torture by the evil Lord Agon and retrieve an all important gem known as the Eye of Braxus. Sandra Hess and Lesley-Anne Downe lend fun support, but the cheap trappings of this fantasy adventure make it a firmly fair-to-middling entry in the series. ▢

Marc Singer *Dar* • Tony Todd *Seth* • Keith Coulouris *Bey* • Sandra Hess *Shada* • Casper Van Dien *King Tal* • Patrick Kilpatrick *Jaggard* • Lesley-Anne Down *Morgana* • David Warner

U = SUITABLE FOR ALL   Uc = SUITABLE FOR ALL, ESPECIALLY FOR YOUNG CHILDREN (VIDEO ONLY)   PG = PARENTAL GUIDANCE

Lord Agon ■ Dir Gabrielle Beaumont • Scr David Wise, from the characters created by Dan Coscarelli, Paul Pepperman

The Beat Generation ★★

Psychological detective drama
1959 · US · BW · 94mins

This is one of those mesmerisingly bad productions with a sordid storyline and a compulsively watchable eclectic period cast. Here we've got tough detective Steve Cochran on the hunt for a sex killer, along the way meeting the likes of blonde sexpot Mamie Van Doren, sex kitten Fay Spain and sexy Maggie Hayes. Males on the side include Mamie's real-life hubbie bandleader Ray Anthony, and the great Louis Armstrong. All this in gritty black-and-white CinemaScope. Talented director Charles Haas manages to make the grim goings-on compulsive viewing though, without much conviction.

Steve Cochran *Dave Culloran* • Mamie Van Doren *Georgia Altera* • Ray Danton *Stan Hess* • Fay Spain *Francee Culloran* • Louis Armstrong • Maggie Hayes *Joyce Greenfield* • Jackie Coogan *Jake Baron* • Jim Mitchum [James Mitchum] *Art Jester* • Ray Anthony *Harry Altera* • Vampira [Maila Nurmi] *Poetess* • Charles Chaplin Jr *Lover Boy* ■ Dir Charles Haas • Scr Richard Matheson, Lewis Meltzer

Beat Girl ★★12

Drama
1960 · UK · BW · 88mins

Beatnik parties in backstreet sin cellars, nights in sleazy Soho strip joints, unsupervised drag racing and the youth generation wild for kicks – it's easy to see why this raucous juvenile-delinquency romp raised eyebrows and scared adults back in 1960. But the failed attempt to launch Adam Faith as yet another of Britain's answers to Elvis Presley is now a great pop history lesson in teenage attitudes and rock 'n' roll rebellion, complete with cool jive talk and swinging sounds from the John Barry Seven. Contains mild swearing and brief nudity.

David Farrar *Paul Linden* • Noelle Adam *Nichole* • Christopher Lee *Kenny* • Gillian Hills *Jennifer* • Adam Faith *Dave* • Shirley Anne Field *Dodo* • Peter McEnery *Tony* • Claire Gordon *Honey* • Oliver Reed *Plaid shirt* ■ Dir Edmond T Gréville • Scr Dail Ambler

Beat Street ★★15

Musical dance drama
1984 · US · Colour · 101mins

Although it trades in such eighties phenomena as break-dancing, rapping and graffiti, this exploitative teen pic proves only that the "puttin' on a show" formula has changed little since the days of Judy Garland and Mickey Rooney. Director Stan Lathan doggedly attempts to depict the degradation in which many inner-city black Americans are forced to live. But DJ Guy Davis and spray-can artist Jon Chardiet are stereotypes and, while the latter's subway murder is effectively handled, the former's romance with student Rae Dawn Chong is unconvincing. Co-producer Harry Belafonte helped compose the songs. 📼

Rae Dawn Chong *Tracy* • Guy Davis *Kenny* • Jon Chardiet *Ramon* • Leon W Grant *Chollie* • Saundra Santiago *Carmen* • Robert Taylor (2) *Lee* • Lee Chamberlin *Alicia* • Mary Alice *Cora*

■ Dir Stan Lathan • Scr Andrew Davis, David Gilbert, Paul Golding, from a story by Steven Hager • Music Harry Belafonte, Arthur Baker

Beat the Devil ★★★U

Comedy thriller   1953 · UK/It · BW · 89mins

This sophisticated international romp (co-scripted by Truman Capote and John Huston) must have been more fun to make than to watch. Nevertheless, the splendid cast ensures that the jokes play and the romance works. Peter Lorre and Humphrey Bogart work again here with Huston, with support from Jennifer Jones as the wife of oh-so-English Edward Underdown, and goonish gangsters Robert Morley and Ivor Barnard. Not terribly well appreciated in its day, this quirky one-off has achieved something of a cult status, and is well worth catching up with. 📼

Humphrey Bogart *Billy Dannreuther* • Jennifer Jones *Gwendolen Chelm* • Gina Lollobrigida *Maria Dannreuther* • Robert Morley *Petersen* • Peter Lorre *O'Hara* • Edward Underdown *Harry Chelm* • Ivor Barnard *Major Ross* • Bernard Lee *CID Inspector* ■ Dir John Huston • Scr John Huston, Truman Capote, from the novel by James Helvick

Beatrice Cenci ★★★

Historical tragedy   1969 · It · Colour · 99mins

Italian director Lucio Fulci regarded this blend of costume melodrama and stylised horror as his finest film. Opening on the morning of the Cenci family's execution, the action is constructed from a series of flashbacks that slowly reveals the fate of the brutal patriarch, George Wilson. But while the torture scenes deter the squeamish, they serve to highlight the unswerving loyalty of Tomas Milian as he seeks to prevent the unworldly Adrienne Larussa from suffering the consequences of her justifiable act of revenge. In stark contrast stands the duplicity of the Catholic Church. Gruesome, but handsomely staged. Italian dialogue dubbed into English.

Tomas Milian *Olimpio* • Adrienne Larussa *Beatrice Cenci* • George Wilson *Cenci* • Raymond Pellegrin *Cardinal Lanciani* ■ Dir Lucio Fulci • Scr Lucio Fulci, Roberto Gianviti, from the play *The Cenci* by Percy Bysshe Shelley

Beau Brummell ★★★U

Historical drama
1954 · US · Colour · 111mins

Robert Morley had the distinction of playing the late-18th century's two unhappiest monarchs: Louis XVI of France (in *Marie Antoinette*, for which he earned an Oscar nomination) and George III in this over-inflated historical pageant. Nevertheless, Stewart Granger cuts a dashing figure as the Regency fop, whose life, loves and dress sense set tongues wagging. Faced with the exuberance of Morley, Granger and Peter Ustinov (deliciously affected as the Prince of Wales), Elizabeth Taylor seems a little daunted.

Stewart Granger *Beau Brummell* • Elizabeth Taylor *Lady Patricia* • Peter Ustinov *Prince of Wales* • Robert Morley *King George III* • James Donald *Lord Edwin Mercer* • James Hayter *Mortimer* • Rosemary Harris *Mrs Fitzherbert* • Paul Rogers *William Pitt* ■ Dir Curtis Bernhardt • Scr Karl Tunberg, from the play by Clyde Fitch

Beau Geste ★★★★

Silent adventure   1926 · US · BW · 101mins

One of the most popular films of the silent era and still a ripping yarn, thanks to the irresistible appeal of PC Wren's story and the flamboyance of the performances. Ronald Colman, Ralph Forbes and Neil Hamilton are the three English brothers who join the Foreign Legion in search of a family heirloom, the Blue Water diamond. The story unfolds in a series of flashbacks and revelations – quite complex and innovative for the time – and director Herbert Brenon has the knack of combining epic tragedy with lightweight adventure. Noah Beery has a field day as the sadistic sergeant-major and there's a seemingly endless supply of shifty Arabs to attack their fort.

Ronald Colman *Michael "Beau" Geste* • Neil Hamilton *Digby Geste* • Ralph Forbes *John Geste* • Alice Joyce *Lady Brandon* • Mary Brian *Isobel* • Noah Beery *Sgt Lejaune* • Norman Trevor *Maj de Beaujolais* • William Powell *Boldini* • Victor McLaglen *Hank* ■ Dir Herbert Brenon • Scr Paul Schofield, John Russell, from the novel by PC Wren

Beau Geste ★★★★★PG

Classic adventure   1939 · US · BW · 108mins

The definitive version of PC Wren's *Boys' Own* classic saga of the Foreign Legion and the events surrounding Fort Zinderneuf. Gary Cooper makes a perfect Beau, while Ray Milland and Robert Preston are well cast as his brothers John and Digby. Also watch out for a very young Donald O'Connor as Beau as a boy. Discerning viewers (and silent movie fans) will spot that this is virtually a shot-for-shot remake of the Ronald Colman version, but a major plus here (apart from sound) is the casting of Brian Donlevy as the evil Sergeant Markoff, who garnered an Oscar nomination. The heroic and romantic attitudes on display may now seem out of date, but that's the fault of the times, not the story. 📼

Gary Cooper *Beau Geste* • Ray Milland *John Geste* • Robert Preston *Digby Geste* • Brian Donlevy *Sgt Markoff* • Susan Hayward *Isobel Rivers* • J Carrol Naish *Rasinoff* • Albert Dekker *Schwartz* • Broderick Crawford *Hank Miller* • Charles Barton *Buddy McMonigal* ■ Dir William A Wellman • Scr Robert Carson, from the novel by PC Wren

Beau Geste ★★

Adventure   1966 · US · Colour · 104mins

This is the third – and by far the least impressive – version of PC Wren's foreign legion yarn. Guy Stockwell isn't in the same league as Ronald Colman and Gary Cooper, and only Telly Savalas as the sadistic sergeant major comes close to matching his predecessors. Writer/director Douglas Heyes takes several liberties with the original story, most notably reducing the three Geste brothers to two and changing their nationality from English to American. The action scenes are well handled, however, and Bud Thackery's colour photography of the desert is eye-catching.

Telly Savalas *Sergeant Major Dagineau* • Guy Stockwell *Beau* • Doug McClure *John* • Leslie Nielsen *Lieutenant De Ruse* • Robert Wolders *Fouchet* • David Mauro *Boldini* • Leo Gordon *Krauss* ■ Dir Douglas Heyes • Scr Douglas Heyes, from the novel by PC Wren

Beau Ideal ★★

Adventure   1931 · US · BW · 82mins

Beau Geste was such a huge success in 1926 that Paramount knocked out a quickie sequel, *Beau Ideal*, two years later. *Beau Ideal* is the second sequel to the original film and is also based on a PC Wren story; Ralph Forbes returns as John Geste, as does original director Herbert Brenon. This time around, John meets up with his childhood buddy in the foreign legion. Loretta Young is the girl back in England who keeps their hearts fluttering and perpetuates their romantic rivalry.

Frank McCormack *Carl Neyer* • Ralph Forbes *John Geste* • Lester Vail *Otis Madison* • Otto Matieson *Jacob Levine* • Don Alvarado *Ramon Gonzales* • Bernard Siegel *Ivan Radinoff* • Irene Rich *Lady Brandon* • Myrtle Stedman *Mrs Frank Madison* • Loretta Young *Isobel Brandon* ■ Dir Herbert Brenon • Scr Elizabeth Meehan, from the novel by PC Wren

Beau James ★★★★

Biographical drama
1957 · US · Colour · 106mins

Bob Hope had been successful in a sentimental semi-comic role in *The Seven Little Foys*, and here he is reunited with the under-rated writer/director Melville Shavelson for this sparkling biopic of New York's flamboyant former mayor Jimmy Walker. Hope is superb, effortlessly capturing the cynicism and brashness of this son of the Roaring Twenties, and there's a fine support cast. Walter Winchell, the narrator of *The Untouchables* on TV, narrated the American version, with Alistair Cooke, his equivalent in Britain, lending an authenticity belied by the largely glamorised and inaccurate screen story.

Bob Hope *Jimmy Walker* • Vera Miles *Betty Compton* • Paul Douglas *Chris Nolan* • Alexis Smith *Allie Walker* • Darren McGavin *Charley Hand* • Joe Mantell *Bernie Williams* • Horace McMahon *Prosecutor* • Richard Shannon *Dick Jackson* ■ Dir Melville Shavelson • Scr Jack Rose, Melville Shavelson, from the book by Gene Fowler

Le Beau Mariage ★★★★PG

Comedy drama   1982 · Fr · Colour · 95mins

Having impressed as an adolescent in *Claire's Knee*, Béatrice Romand is reunited with director Eric Rohmer for this bittersweet treatise on the clash between feminist and old-fashioned ideals, winning the Best Actress prize at Venice. In the second in the "Comedies and Proverbs" series, the action flits between Paris and Le Mans as Romand's art student decides to quit the romantic rat race and find a husband. However, it soon becomes clear that lawyer André Dussolier is immune to her charms and humiliation is in the offing. Bristling with life, Rohmer's slyly witty film is as chatty and keenly observed as ever. In French with English subtitles. 📼

Béatrice Romand *Sabine* • André Dussollier *Edmond* • Arielle Dombasle *Clarisse* • Feodor Atkine *Simon* • Huguette Faget *Antique dealer* • Thamila Mezbah *Mother* • Sophie Renoir *Lise* ■ Dir/Scr Eric Rohmer

12 15 18 = PASSED FOR PEOPLE OF THESE AGES AND OVER   📼 = RELEASED ON VIDEO   DVD = RELEASED ON DVD

Beau Sabreur ★★★

Silent adventure 1928 · US · BW · 67mins

In this silent movie, Gary Cooper elegantly disports himself in the desert, as a French legionnaire who is sent to the Sahara to negotiate a treaty with an oil-rich sheik and falls in love with Evelyn Brent on the way. It followed *Beau Geste* (1926), and was meant to use up pieces of leftover location film from the first movie. Cooper went on to star in the sound version of *Beau Geste* in 1939.

Gary Cooper *Major Henri de Beaujolais* • Evelyn Brent *May Vanbrugh* • Noah Beery Sr [Noah Beery] *Sheikh El Hamel* • William Powell *Becque* • Mitchell Lewis *Suleiman the Strong* • Frank Reicher *Gen de Beaujolais* • Oscar Smith *Djikki* ■ *Dir* John Waters • *Scr* Tom J Geraghty (story), Julian Johnson (titles), from the story by PC Wren

Le Beau Serge ★★★★

Drama 1958 · Fr · BW · 97mins

Traditionally hailed as the first feature of the French New Wave, Claude Chabrol's inconsistent debut was made while he was still working as a film critic, with a small sum inherited by his wife. The picture's American title, *Bitter Reunion*, sums up the story, in which Jean-Claude Brialy returns home to find that his gifted childhood friend Gérard Blain has destroyed his life through drink. Shunning the directorial pyrotechnics associated with contemporaries such as Godard and Truffaut, Chabrol coaxes intelligent performances from his leads and makes effective use of Sardent, the town where he spent part of his own youth. In French with English subtitles.

Gérard Blain *Serge* • Jean-Claude Brialy *François Bayon* • Michèle Meritz *Yvonne* • Bernadette Lafont *Marie* • Edmond Beauchamp *Glomaud* • Claude Cerval *The curé* • AndréDino *The doctor* ■ *Dir/Scr* Claude Chabrol

Beau Travail ★★★★ 15

Psychological drama 1999 · Fr · Colour · mins

Translating Herman Melville's *Billy Budd* from the 18th-century Royal Navy to the modern Foreign Legion, Claire Denis has produced a simmering study of petty tyranny, fatuous duty and homoerotic repression. Spurning the barked histrionics of American boot camp pictures, she uses stylised audiovisual rhythms to convey the ennui endured by an isolated unit in Djibouti. As the sergeant seized by a pathological hatred of new recruit Grégoire Colin, Denis Lavant gives a remarkable, almost wordless performance that culminates in some astonishing disco gyrations. In French with English subtitles.

Denis Lavant *Galoup* • Michel Subor *Commander* • Grégoire Colin *Sentain* • Richard Courcet *Legionnaire* ■ *Dir* Claire Denis • *Scr* Claire Denis, Jean-Pol Fargeau, from the novella *Billy Budd, Sailor* by Herman Melville

Beaumarchais l'Insolent ★★★ 15

Historical biographical drama 1996 · Fr · Colour · 96mins

Edouard Molinaro directs this breathless biopic of one of France's most dashing heroes, Beaumarchais. When evoking the theatrical milieu, his allusions to *Les Enfants du Paradis* and *Cyrano de Bergerac* give the action a true sense of pageant, place and purpose. Yet, in chronicling the playwright's more picturesque activities, from law reform to arms dealing and espionage, the fact and fantasy become entangled and there's barely room to mention his love life, let alone celebrate his literary achievement. However, Fabrice Luchini's vibrant performance ensures this isn't merely a series of elegant tableaux. A French language film.

Fabrice Luchini *Pierre-Augustin Caron de Beaumarchais* • Manuel Blanc *Gudin* • Sandrine Kiberlain *Marie-Thérèse* • Michel Serrault *Louis XV* • Jacques Weber *Duc de Chaulnes* • Michel Piccoli *Prince de Conti* • Jean-François Balmer *Sartine* ■ *Dir* Edouard Molinaro • *Scr* Edouard Molinaro, Jean-Claude Brisville, from a play by Sacha Guitry

La Beauté du Diable ★★★

Fantasy drama 1949 · Fr/It · BW · 95mins

René Clair is arguably the finest director of comic fantasy in screen history. Though he does not quite hit the heights here, this is still a sparkling and highly individual version of the Faust legend. The picture uses stylised sets similar to those of pioneer film-maker Georges Méliès and poet-director Jean Cocteau to create a world touched more by magic than evil. Clair's cutest trick, however, is to have Michel Simon and Gérard Philipe swap places after the former sells his soul in return for the latter's devilish good looks. In French with English subtitles.

Michel Simon *Old Mephistopheles/Faust* • Gérard Philipe *Young Faust/Mephistopheles* • Simone Valère *Princess* • Nicole Besnard *Marguerite* • Carlo Ninchi *Prince* • Paolo Stoppa *Prosecutor* ■ *Dir* René Clair • *Scr* René Clair, Armand Salacrou

The Beautician and the Beast ★★ PG

Romantic comedy 1997 · US · Colour · 102mins

Fran Drescher made her name as the "hostess with the mostest" in *This Is Spinal Tap*, but these days she's probably better know as the star of US TV sitcom *The Nanny*. This was intended to kickstart her career on the big screen, but unfortunately it was consigned to the straight-to-video bin here. It's actually not too bad – Drescher is the very "Nu Yawk" beautician who mistakenly winds up as governess to the family of the president (Timothy Dalton) of an Eastern European country and gradually melts his heart. Simplistic but fun. Contains some mild swearing and sexual references.

Fran Drescher *Joy Miller* • Timothy Dalton *Boris Pochenko* • Ian McNeice *Grushinsky* • Patrick Malahide *Kleist* • Lisa Jakub *Katrina* • Michael Lerner *Jerry Miller* • Phyllis Newman *Judy Miller* • Adam LaVorgna *Karl* ■ *Dir* Ken Kwapis • *Scr* Todd Graff

The Beautiful Blonde from Bashful Bend ★★★★

Comedy western 1949 · US · Colour · 76mins

Though one of Betty Grable's better vehicles, this burlesque western was considered to be one of the major catastrophes of 1949 – a setback for its talented writer/director Preston Sturges, who had acquired a reputation for churning out wacky and risqué comedies. Viewed today, however, this farce can be regarded as a comedy triumph for both star and director. Fabulously photographed in that gloriously garish forties Technicolor, the film features a terrific cameo from daffy Hugh Herbert as a myopic quack.

Betty Grable *Freddie* • Cesar Romero *Blackie Jobero* • Rudy Vallee *Charles Hingleman* • Olga San Juan *Conchita* • Sterling Holloway *Basserman Boy* • Hugh Herbert *Doctor* • El Brendel *Mr Jorgenson* • Porter Hall *Judge O'Toole* ■ *Dir* Preston Sturges • *Scr* Preston Sturges, from a story by Earl Felton • *Cinematographer* Harry Jackson

Beautiful but Dangerous ★★ U

Comedy drama 1954 · US · BW · 88mins

Having bought RKO in 1948, Howard Hughes took a shine to Jean Simmons and imported her from England, casting her opposite Robert Mitchum in Otto Preminger's torrid *Angel Face*. Since the on-screen chemistry between the two stars was combustible, this second rendezvous was concocted; the mistake was to make it a comedy. Simmons plays an heiress with a guilt complex and Mitchum is the local doctor who rumbles her. Intended as a satire on small-town hypocrisy, the sort of thing Frank Capra churned out in the thirties, it's stilted and slackly directed by Lloyd Bacon.

Robert Mitchum *Doc Sellars* • Jean Simmons *Corby Lane* • Arthur Hunnicutt *Otey* • Edgar Buchanan *Ad Meeker* • Wallace Ford *Joe* • Raymond Walburn *Judge Holbert* ■ *Dir* Lloyd Bacon • *Scr* DD Beauchamp, William Bowers, Richard Flournoy, from the story *Enough for Happiness* by DD Beauchamp

Beautiful but Dangerous ★★

Romantic drama 1955 · It/Fr · Colour · 102mins

This pallid period piece, shot in Italy (where it was known as *The World's Most Beautiful Woman*), was one of the last pictures made by Robert Z Leonard, who made his directorial debut back in 1914. Gina Lollobrigida plays Lina Cavalieri, the 19th-century opera singer who finds love with Prince Sergei Bariatine (Vittorio Gassman), the Russian royal whom she had encountered many years before. As with much of Leonard's other work, the result is a polished but plodding affair. Italian dialogue dubbed into English.

Gina Lollobrigida *Lina Cavalieri* • Vittorio Gassman *Prince Sergei Bariatine* • Robert Alda *Doria* • Tamara Lees *Manolita* • Anne Vernon *Carmela* ■ *Dir* Robert Z Leonard • *Scr* Cesare Cavagna, Liana Ferri, Frank Gervasi, Mario Monicelli, Luciano Martino, Piero Pierotti, Franco Solinas, Giovanna Soria, from a story by Maleno Malenotti

Beautiful Dreamers ★★ 15

Period drama based on a true story 1990 · Can · Colour · 103mins

The under-rated Rip Torn gives a tour de force performance as legendary American poet Walt Whitman who, while visiting the London Asylum for the Insane in Ontario, encounters psychiatrist Dr Maurice Bucke (Colm Feore). The pair proceed to make waves with their revolutionary ideas on the treatment of mental illness. A little trite and predictable in places, this is more of a Disney-style history lesson than a dissection of Victorian attitudes towards madness.

Colm Feore *Dr Maurice Bucke* • Rip Torn *Walt Whitman* • Wendel Meldrum *Jessie Bucke* • Sheila McCarthy *Molly Jessop* • Colin Fox *Rev Randolph Haines* • David Gardner *Dr Lett* ■ *Dir/Scr* John Kent Harrison

The Beautiful End of This World ★★

Thriller 1983 · W Ger · Colour · 90mins

For all their good intentions, films in the "Green Screen" tradition tend to approach their themes so earnestly that they often pay scant attention to the dramatic storylines that would make their propagandist message both more palatable and effective. This thriller, about a German chemical executive whose conscience is pricked while planning to build a chemical plant in the Australian wilds, is a sort of *Local Hero* without the laughs. Director Rainer Erler fails to capitalise on the abundant local colour and lays on his ecological ideas with a trowel. Wolfgang Grasshoff's impressive photography offers some consolation. German dialogue dubbed into English.

Robert Atzorn *Dr Michael Brandt* • Claire Oberman *Elaine* • Gotz George *Craig* • Judy Winter *Ursula* ■ *Dir/Scr* Rainer Erler

Beautiful Girls ★★★ 15

Comedy drama 1996 · US · Colour · 107mins

An ensemble piece combining what should have been the dependable talents of Matt Dillon, Timothy Hutton, Mira Sorvino and Uma Thurman, this is an unoriginal high-school reunion flick. Pianist Hutton returns home from New York and is depressed to discover all his schoolmates stuck in dead-end jobs. The men relentlessly and stereotypically talk sex over beers, while the women are wasted as similarly two dimensional figures. Only Natalie Portman, as Hutton's mature teenage neighbour, shows great promise and their relationship is touching. Contains swearing, sexual references and a violent scene.

Matt Dillon *Tommy "Birdman" Rowland* • Noah Emmerich *Michael "Mo" Morris* • Annabeth Gish *Tracy Stover* • Lauren Holly *Darian Smalls* • Timothy Hutton *Willie Conway* • Rosie O'Donnell *Gina Barrisano* • Martha Plimpton *Jan* • Natalie Portman *Marty* • Michael Rapaport *Paul Kirkwood* • Mira Sorvino *Sharon Cassidy* • Uma Thurman *Andera* • David Arquette *Bobby Conway* ■ *Dir* Ted Demme • *Scr* Scott Rosenberg

Beautiful People ★★★ U

Comedy drama 1999 · UK · Colour · 93mins

Jasmin Dizdar's debut feature is a creditable achievement, especially bearing in mind it cost a mere £1.1 million. It includes snippets from an affair between a Tory MP's doctor daughter and an exiled war criminal, and follows a TV reporter filming a football hooligan's accidental transformation into a hero. These diverse plot strands ambitiously attempt to meld romance, black comedy and political critique. Ultimately, both character and thematic depth are sacrificed to plot contrivance, but the ensemble cast (including Charlotte Coleman and Siobhan Redmond) brings commitment and wit to the proceedings, which, while rarely credible, are certainly never dull.

Rosalind Ayres *Nora Thornton* • Charlotte Coleman *Portia Thornton* • Edin Dzandzanovic *Pero Guzina* • Nicholas Farrell *Doctor Mouldy* • Siobhan Redmond ◼ *Dir/Scr* Jasmin Dizdar

Beautiful Stranger ★

Crime drama   1954 · UK · BW · 89mins

Ginger Rogers, moving inexorably towards her sell-by date, stars in this British-made thriller set on the French Riviera and directed by David Miller. She plays a woman who, let down by her wealthy and married racketeer lover Stanley Baker, contemplates killing herself but, instead, hooks up with Frenchman Jacques Bergerac and finds herself implicated in murder. This is a labyrinthine, depressing and unconvincing melodrama, although the always interestingly suave Herbert Lom makes a welcome appearance in a supporting role.

Ginger Rogers *Johnny Victor* • Herbert Lom *Emil Landosh* • Stanley Baker *Louis Galt* • Jacques Bergerac *Pierre Clement* • Margaret Rawlings *Marie Galt* • Eddie Byrne *Luigi* • Ferdy Mayne *Chief of Police* • Coral Browne *Helen* ◼ *Dir* David Miller • *Scr* Robert Westerby, Carl Nystrom, from a story by Rip Van Ronkel, David Miller

Beautiful Thing ★★★ 15

Drama   1995 · UK · Colour · 87mins

Two teenage neighbours on a London council estate discover they are gay in director Hettie MacDonald's urban fairy tale based on Jonathan Harvey's West End stage success. How the boys deal with their sexual awakening is endearingly explored via a rough kitchen-sink backdrop, camp one-liners and a soundtrack leaning heavily on hits from Mama Cass. Newcomers Glen Berry and Scott Neal give purposely raw-edged performances to match their on-screen naivety, but it's Linda Henry, making the most of the familiar sitcom moments, who shines as the indomitable single mother trying to understand her son. Contains violence, swearing and nudity. 📼 *DVD*

Glen Berry *Jamie Gangel* • Linda Henry *Sandra Gangel* • Scott Neal *Ste Pearce* • Ben Daniels *Tony* • Tameka Empson *Leah* • Meera Syal *Miss Chauhan* ◼ *Dir* Hettie MacDonald • *Scr* Jonathan Harvey, from his play

Beauty ★ PG

Romance   1998 · US · Colour

Based on the book by Susan Wilson, this soapy romance stars Janine Turner (*Northern Exposure*) as a beautiful artist commissioned to paint the portrait of a wealthy, reclusive mystery writer (Jamey Sheridan). She falls in love with him (naturally) in spite of his disfiguring bone disorder and his belief that his appearance dooms him to unhappiness. This tedious TV-movie remake of *Beauty and the Beast* is neither fresh nor distinctive enough to make it worth your time.

Janine Turner *Alix Miller* • Hal Holbrook *Alexander Miller* • Jamey Sheridan *Lee Crompton* • Shirley Broderick *Mrs Greaves* • Malcolm Stewart *Father McClellan* ◼ *Dir* Jerry London • *Scr* Selma Thompson, from the novel by Susan Wilson

Beauty and Denise ★★★ 15

Comedy thriller   1989 · US · Colour · 92mins

This also went by the equally daft name of *The Cover Girl and the Cop*, but don't hold either title against it. It's actually a reasonably fair drama about a woman (Julia Duffy) who is assigned tough cop Dinah Manoff to look after her when she witnesses the murder of a Washington politician. You'll probably be able to work out who's doing what to whom before the leads do, but, thanks to entertaining performances from supporting cast members David Carradine and *Star Trek: the Next Generation*'s Jonathan Frakes, this is worth sticking with. 📼

Dinah Manoff *Denise Danielovitch* • Julia Duffy *Jackie Flanders* • John Karlen *Charlie Wingo* • Parker Stevenson *Cabell Hayward* • David Carradine *Slade* • Jonathan Frakes *Josh Boyland* ◼ *Dir* Neal Israel • *Scr* Michael Norell, from a story by Les Alexander, Steve Ditlea, Don Enright, James Norell

Beauty and the Beast ★★★ U

Fantasy   1976 · UK/US · Colour · 90mins

Oscar-winner George C Scott, best known for his portrayal of General Patton, stars with his then wife, actress Trish Van Devere, in this lavish production of the classic fairy tale about a beautiful young woman who agrees to marry an ugly beast in order to save her father's life. No dancing candlesticks or singing teapots here; just solid performances, majestic costumes and magical make-up.

George C Scott *Beast* • Trish Van Devere *Belle* • Virginia McKenna *Lucy* • Bernard Lee *Beaumont* • Michael N Harbour *Anthony* • William Relton *Nicholas* ◼ *Dir* Fielder Cook • *Scr* Sherman Yellen, from the fairy tale by Mme Leprince de Beaumont

Beauty and the Beast ★★ U

Fantasy   1987 · US · Colour · 89mins

In another reworking of the classic tale of the young woman taken hostage by a half-man, half-beast whom she eventually falls in love with, Rebecca De Mornay (*The Hand that Rocks the Cradle*) is bland as Beauty, while John Savage (*The Deer Hunter*) is gruffly enjoyable as the Beast. But they both flounder during the duff song and dance numbers in the middle. 📼

Rebecca De Mornay *Beauty* • John Savage *Beast/Prince* • Yossi Graber *Father* • Michael Schneider *Kuppel* • Carmela Marner *Bettina* • Ruth Harlap *Isabella* • Joseph Bee *Oliver* ◼ *Dir* Eugene Marner • *Scr* Carole Lucia Satrina

Beauty and the Beast ★★★★★ U

Animated musical fantasy
1991 · US · Colour · 80mins

The first feature-length cartoon to be nominated for the best picture Oscar, this is one of the most ambitious films ever produced by Disney. Three and a half years in the making, the movie was one of the first animations to include computer-generated imagery, seen to best advantage during the ballroom and Be Our Guest sequences. With visuals based on such French artists as Fragonard and a storyline inspired by Madame Leprince de Beaumont's famous fairy tale, the film also boasts the vocal talents of Angela Lansbury (who sings the Oscar-winning title song), Paige O'Hara as Beauty and Robby Benson as Beast. 📼

Paige O'Hara *Belle* • Robby Benson *Beast* • Rex Everhart *Maurice* • Richard White *Gaston* • Jesse Corti *Le Fou* • Angela Lansbury *Mrs Potts* • Jerry Orbach *Lumiere* • David Ogden Stiers *Cogsworth/Narrator* • Bradley Michael Pierce [Bradley Pierce] *Chip* ◼ *Dir* Gary Trousdale, Kirk Wise • *Scr* Linda Woolverton, from a story by Brenda Chapman, Burny Mattinson, Brian Pimental, Joe Ranft, Kelly Asbury, Christopher Sanders, Kevin Harkey, Bruce Woodside, Tom Ellery, Robert Lence, from the fairy tale by Mme Leprince de Beaumont

Beauty and the Beast: the Enchanted Christmas ★★★ U

Animation   1997 · US · Colour · 67mins

A made-for-video sequel to the wonderful 1991 Disney animated movie *Beauty and the Beast*, this takes place while Belle is still a prisoner in the Beast's castle as she attempts to convince the Beast to celebrate Christmas. While many of the cast return to lend their voices, this doesn't quite have the production values or charm of the original, but it should enchant young children if not their more fussy parents. The child actor Haley Joel Osment, now best known for his Oscar-nominated performance in *The Sixth Sense*, provides the voice of Chip. 📼 *DVD*

Paige O'Hara *Belle* • Robby Benson *Beast* • Jerry Orbach *Lumiere* • David Ogden Stiers *Cogsworth* • Bernadette Peters *Angelique* • Tim Curry *Forte* • Haley Joel Osment *Chip* • Paul Reubens *Fife* • Angela Lansbury *Mrs Potts* ◼ *Dir* Andy Knight • *Scr* Flip Kobler, Cindy Marcus, Bill Motz, Bob Roth

Beauty for the Asking ★★

Drama   1939 · US · BW · 68mins

Leaving Lucille Ball's outstanding comic gifts on the back burner, RKO cast her to play straight in this plodding and uncertain tale of a beautician who, after being jilted by smooth Patric Knowles, comes up with a new face cream that makes millions. It's directed without distinction by Glenn Tryon, but there's some fun to be had from the backroom bitching in the cosmetics industry, and the cast is fine.

Lucille Ball *Jean Russell* • Patric Knowles *Denny Williams* • Donald Woods *Jeffrey Martin* • Frieda Inescort *Flora Barton* • Inez Courtney *Gwen Morrison* • Leona Maricle *Eva*

Harrington • Frances Mercer *Patricia Wharton* • Whitney Bourne *Peggy Ponsby* ◼ *Dir* Glenn Tryon • *Scr* Doris Anderson, Paul Jerrico

The Beauty Jungle ★★

Drama   1964 · UK · Colour · 114mins

Portraying the seedier side of beauty contests in the early sixties, this is a bustling but predictable rise-and-fall story, in which Janette Scott discovers that fame sometimes doesn't even last 15 minutes. Charting her progress to the Miss Globe title, Val Guest's film unerringly descends upon the tawdry and the fake, whether exposing the cattiness behind the catwalk or the emptiness behind celebrity. Scott is suitably naive, while Ian Hendry and Edmund Purdom reek of insincerity as the men promising her stardom.

Ian Hendry *Don Mackenzie* • Janette Scott *Shirley* • Ronald Fraser *Walter* • Edmund Purdom *Carrick* • Jean Claudio *Armand* • Kay Walsh *Mrs Freeman* • Norman Bird *Freeman* • Janina Faye *Elaine* • Tommy Trinder *Charlie Dorton* • David Weston *Harry* ◼ *Dir* Val Guest • *Scr* Robert Muller, Val Guest

Beavis and Butt-head Do America ★★★ 12

Animated comedy
1996 · US · Colour · 77mins

Given that the moronic animated duo spend most of their time in their TV spot rooted to the couch, a full-length feature might seem to be hopelessly ambitious. But unbelievably it works. Beavis and Butt-head (voiced again by creator and director Mike Judge) snigger away as usual, oblivious to a dramatic plot that sees them being chased cross-country after become the unwitting carriers of a lethal chemical weapon. Bruce Willis and Demi Moore score as the villains, while Robert Stack is spot on as the head of the FBI. Contains mild swearing, sexual references and some mild violence. 📼

Mike Judge *Beavis/Butt-head* • Cloris Leachman *Old woman on plane and bus* • Robert Stack *Agent Flemming* • Eric Bogosian *Ranger* • Richard Linklater *Tour bus driver* • Bruce Willis *Muddy Grimes* • Demi Moore *Dallas Grimes* ◼ *Dir* Mike Judge • *Scr* Mike Judge, Joe Stillman

Bebe's Kids ★★★ PG

Animated musical comedy
1992 · US · Colour · 69mins

Based on the characters invented by comedian Robin Harris and scripted by Reginald Hudlin, this was the only animated feature released during the black cinema boom of the early nineties. Some of the snipes at African-American and white culture are predictable, others are way off beam. Yet when they do hit the target, they are both sassy and funny. The gruff voice of baby Pee-Wee is provided by rap singer Tone Loc. 📼

Faizon Love *Robin Harris* • Vanessa Bell Calloway *Jamika* • Wayne Collins Jr *Leon* • Jonell Greene *LaShawn* • Marques Huston *Kahlil* • Tone Loc *Pee-Wee* • Myra J *Dorothea* • Nell Carter *Vivian* • Reynaldo Rey *Lush* ◼ *Dir* Bruce Smith • *Scr* Reginald Hudlin, from characters created by Robin Harris

Because He's My Friend ★★

Drama 1978 · Ausl · Colour · 91mins

This Australian-made TV movie, about a retarded boy and the couple who adopt him, offers a twist on the familiar storyline: rather than bringing the couple together, the child threatens to wreck their marriage. Karen Black and Kier Dullea – the astronaut who was reborn in *2001: a Space Odyssey* – make an interesting team, while director Ralph Nelson has a facility for this sort of material, having directed Cliff Robertson in the Oscar-winning *Charly* (1968).

Karen Black *Anne* • Keir Dullea *Eric* • Warwick Poulsen *Peter* • Jack Thompson *Geoff* • Tom Oliver *Ian* • Barbara Stephens *Meg* ■ *Dir* Ralph Nelson • *Scr* Peter Schreck

Because Mommy Works ★★

Drama based on a true story
1994 · US · Colour

A routine but nicely played courtroom TV drama that centres around a custody battle. Anne Archer is the single mother who finds an unexpected legal battle on her hands when her ex-husband sues for custody of their son, arguing that she can't work and look after the child at the same time. Archer and John Heard bring considerable force to their roles as the warring couple, but the direction from Robert Markowitz is a tad stilted and there are few surprises. Contains swearing.

Anne Archer *Abby Forman* • John Heard *Ted Forman* • Ashley Crow *Claire Forman* • Tom Amandes *Eric Donovan* ■ *Dir* Robert Markowitz • *Scr* Lynn Mamet Weisberg, Judith Paige-Mitchell

Because of Him ★★★ U

Musical romance 1946 · US · BW · 87mins

Ten years after she arrived as a teenage singing star to save Universal studios from bankruptcy and two years before her retirement from the screen at the age of 27, Deanna Durbin starred in this ''grown-up'' version of her previous adolescent-dream-come-true movies. The plot has waitress Durbin determinedly seeking the help of famous actor Charles Laughton to establish her stage career and overcoming his resistance with her rendition of *Danny Boy*. Franchot Tone is the playwright who is initially immune to her charms. Director Richard Wallace exploits the sugar content of the formula.

Deanna Durbin *Kim Walker* • Franchot Tone *Paul Taylor* • Charles Laughton *Sheridan* • Helen Broderick *Nora* • Stanley Ridges *Charlie Gilbert* • Donald Meek *Martin* • Charles Halton *Mr Dunlap* ■ *Dir* Richard Wallace • *Scr* Edmund Beloin, from the story by Edmund Beloin, Sig Herzig

Because They're Young ★★★

Drama 1960 · US · Colour · 98mins

This little Columbia teenage angst flick. was given street credibility by the starring presence of *American Bandstand* host Dick Clark, who unfortunately proved to be no thespian. At the helm was superior cult director Paul Wendkos, perhaps best-remembered for *Gidget* (1959). The film is actually based on a paperback bestseller of its day by John Farris, and the student cast is a teen dream: here's Tuesday Weld and James Darren (who also recorded the theme song), plus *Cat Ballou*'s Michael Callan and *Blue Denim*'s Warren Berlinger.

Dick Clark *Neil* • Michael Callan *Griff* • Tuesday Weld *Anne* • Victoria Shaw *Joan* • Roberta Shore *Ricky* • Warren Berlinger *Buddy* • Doug McClure *Jim* • Linda Watkins *Frances McCalla* • Duane Eddy • The Rebels ■ *Dir* Paul Wendkos • *Scr* James Gunn, from the novel *Harrison High* by John Farris

Because You're Mine ★★ U

Musical comedy 1952 · US · Colour · 103mins

Amazingly selected as the 1953 Royal Command Film, this Mario Lanza vehicle is memorable today as the feeble follow-up to his biggest success, *The Great Caruso*. This is a thankless affair, with Lanza as an opera star conscripted into the army who falls for his sergeant's sister, less than winningly played by Broadway *Kismet* star Doretta Morrow. Lanza's big hit song from 1950's *Toast of New Orleans*, *Be My Love*, makes a welcome reappearance, and the rest of the film is peppered with opera extracts. However, apart from the rich period Technicolor, there's little to sing about in this lacklustre MGM musical.

Mario Lanza *Renaldo Rossano* • Doretta Morrow *Bridget Batterson* • James Whitmore *Sgt Batterson* • Dean Miller *Ben Jones* • Paula Corday [Rita Corday] *Francesca Landers* • Jeff Donnell *Patty Ware* • Spring Byington *Mrs Montville* • Curtis Cooksey *Gen Montville* ■ *Dir* Alexander Hall • *Scr* Karl Tunberg, Leonard Spigelgass, from a story by Ruth Brooks Flippen, Sy Gomberg • *Music* Sammy Cahn

Becket ★★★★ PG

Historical drama
1964 · UK · Colour · 141mins

This is distinguished by overwhelmingly historic histrionics, with a double-whammy of charismatic performances by Richard Burton and Peter O'Toole. Edward Anhalt's Oscar-winning script from Jean Anouilh's stage play tells of the friendship, at the 12th century court, between Henry II (O'Toole) and Archbishop Becket (Burton) – here seen as friends from childhood. The motivational insights into their power struggle are more modern than medieval, but they make for a wholly engrossing portrayal of the past. 🖼

Richard Burton *Thomas Becket* • Peter O'Toole *King Henry II* • John Gielgud *King Louis VII of France* • Donald Wolfit *Bishop Folliot* • Martita Hunt *Queen Matilda* • Pamela Brown *Queen Eleanor* • Paolo Stoppa *Pope Alexander III* • Gino Cervi *Cardinal Zambelli* • Sian Phillips *Gwendolen* ■ *Dir* Peter Glenville • *Scr* Edward Anhalt, from the play *Becket, ou l'Honneur de Dieu* by Jean Anouilh • *Producer* Hal B Wallis • *Cinematographer* Geoffrey Unsworth • *Costume Designer* Margaret Furse

Becky Sharp ★★★

Period drama 1935 · US · Colour · 84mins

Rouben Mamoulian's picture is notable as the first full-length feature in three-strip Technicolor. And what exquisite colour it is! The costumes are dazzling – bright and beautiful, yet soft-edged like an 18th-century painting – and are seen at their best in the ball scenes on the eve of Waterloo. Francis Edward Faragoh's script focuses on the famous central character from Thackeray's *Vanity Fair*, romping at high speed through her rise and fall in a breathtakingly audacious bowdlerisation and distortion of the original. An Oscar-nominated Miriam Hopkins makes a spirited if unsubtle and hoydenish Becky, while most of the supporting characters are reduced to fleeting cardboard cut-outs or caricatures. Cedric Hardwicke's Marquis of Steyne and Nigel Bruce's Josh Sedley are splendid, though, and the film is never dull.

Miriam Hopkins *Becky Sharp* • Frances Dee *Amelia Sedley* • Cedric Hardwicke *Marquis of Steyne* • Billie Burke *Lady Bareacres* • Alison Skipworth *Miss Crawley* • Nigel Bruce *Joseph Sedley* ■ *Dir* Rouben Mamoulian • *Scr* Francis Edward Faragoh, from a play by Langdon Mitchell, from the novel *Vanity Fair* by William Makepeace Thackeray • *Cinematographer* Ray Rennahan

Becoming Colette ★★ 18

Biographical drama
1991 · Ger/UK/Fr · Colour · 96mins

A stilted account of the life and early career of the French author who wrote as Colette (Mathilda May), this details her transformation from a naive country girl to a Paris socialite, her disastrous marriage to Henri Gauthier-Villars (Klaus Maria Brandauer) and her sexual awakening. A rather superficial and empty period piece with indifferent performances from the lead actors, including Virginia Madsen as the lesbian Polaire, this proves director Danny Huston is no match for his father John Huston. 🖼

Klaus Maria Brandauer *Henri Gauthier-Villars* • Mathilda May *Sidonie Gabrielle Colette* • Virginia Madsen *Polaire Sorel* • Paul Rhys *Chapo* • John Van Dreelen *Albert* • Jean-Pierre Aumont *Captain* • Lucienne Hamon *Sido* • Georg Tryphon *Creditor* ■ *Dir* Danny Huston • *Scr* Ruth Graham, Burt Weinshanker

Bed and Board ★★★ PG

Comedy drama 1970 · Fr · Colour · 93mins

Antoine Doinel, the hero of *The 400 Blows*, is now married to Claude Jade but still can't settle down. He has an affair with a Japanese girl and enters a ludicrous Zen period; after a variety of pointless jobs, he appears to mature by writing a novel and becoming a father. While *Bed and Board* is not in the same class as its gorgeous predecessor, *Stolen Kisses*, the gentle comedy and romance make for an utterly charming film, shot through with Truffaut's trademark optimism about human nature. Buffs will delight in the fleeting glimpse of Mr Hulot at a Metro station and the send-up of *Last Year at Marienbad*. A French language film. 🖼

Jean-Pierre Léaud *Antoine Doinel* • Claude Jade *Christine Doinel* • Hiroko Berghauer *Kyoko* • Daniel Ceccaldi *Lucien Darbon* • Claire Duhamel *Madame Darbon* • Daniel Boulanger *Tenor* • Barbara Laage *Monique* ■ *Dir* François Truffaut • *Scr* François Truffaut, Claude de Givray, Bernard Revon

Bed & Breakfast ★★★ 15

Romantic comedy
1992 · US · Colour · 88mins

On one of those rare occasions when Roger Moore has been caught acting, this very modest comedy has him as a con man who arrives at a lodging house run by a widow and charms all the women there – Talia Shire, Colleen Dewhurst and Nina Siemaszko. Directed by Robert Ellis Miller, it's pleasantly unusual and self-effacing – which is more than Roger Moore is as he directs the full force of his personality at everyone in sight. 🖼

Roger Moore *Adam* • Talia Shire *Claire* • Colleen Dewhurst *Ruth* • Nina Siemaszko *Cassie* • Ford Rainey *Amos* • Stephen Root *Randolph* • Jamie Walters *Mitch* ■ *Dir* Robert Ellis Miller • *Scr* Cindy Myers

Bed of Lies ★★ 15

Drama based on a true story
1991 · US · Colour · 90mins

Susan Dey, of *The Partridge Family* and *LA Law* fame, deserves better material than this true-life Texan tragedy, in which she plays a waitress whose affair with political hotshot Chris Cooper leads not only to his disgrace, but also ultimately to his murder after he becomes abusive towards her and her children. Both Dey and Cooper (one of John Sayles's stock company of actors) give solid performances, but TV-movie specialist William A Graham overdoes the melodrama.

Susan Dey *Vickie* • Chris Cooper *Price Daniel Jr* • Fred Dalton Thompson • Mary Kay Place • Dollie Cole ■ *Dir* William A Graham • *Scr* John Ireland, from a story by Steve Salerno

Bed of Roses ★★ PG

Romantic comedy drama
1995 · US · Colour · 84mins

Life isn't always rosy in this uncertain attempt to combine realism and romance. Christian Slater is a florist whose wife died giving birth. Grieving madly (and rather badly), he gradually falls for ''suit'' Mary Stuart Masterson. As their relationship develops, both attempt to heal past wounds and Masterson reveals that she was abused by her adoptive father. Although well meaning, this is a wilting rose rather than a blooming one. 🖼

Christian Slater *Lewis* • Mary Stuart Masterson *Lisa* • Pamela Segall *Kim* • Josh Brolin *Danny* • Gina Torres *Francine* • Ally Walker *Wendy* ■ *Dir/Scr* Michael Goldenberg

The Bed Sitting Room ★★★

Comedy 1969 · UK · Colour · 91mins

One of comic genius Spike Milligan's two great West End hits, this anti-war play by Milligan and John Antrobus seemed ideal screen material. It's set three years after the great nuclear holocaust and the cast gradually transmutes into various altered physical states – Arthur Lowe becomes a parrot. Ralph Richardson stars, joined by a cast full of priceless British eccentrics, including Milligan's *Goon Show* pal Harry Secombe, Peter Cook and Dudley Moore. Richard Lester is quite at home in this surreal world, but despite its undoubted originality, *The Bed Sitting Room* failed to transfer successfully from stage to screen.

Watch carefully for Marty Feldman in his movie debut.

Ralph Richardson *Lord Fortnum* • Rita Tushingham *Penelope* • Peter Cook *Inspector* • Dudley Moore *Sergeant* • Arthur Lowe *Father* • Roy Kinnear *Plastic Mac Man* • Mona Washbourne *Mother* • Michael Hordern *Captain Bules Martin* • Spike Milligan *Mate* • Harry Secombe *The Shelter Man* • Jimmy Edwards *Nigel* • Marty Feldman *Nurse Arthur* ■ *Dir* Richard Lester • *Scr* John Antrobus, from the play by Spike Milligan, John Antrobus

Bedazzled ★★★ PG

Comedy 1967 · UK · Colour · 99mins

From the days when London was swinging and Peter Cook and Dudley Moore were a partnership made in comedy heaven, this Faustian fantasy has Dud as a cook lusting after waitress Eleanor Bron and being granted seven wishes by Pete, as a drawlingly engaging Devil hungry for Dud's soul. A briefly clad, briefly glimpsed Raquel Welch is one of the Deadly Sins, while Barry Humphries turns in a typically hilarious performance as Envy. By electing to have Cook play Satan as a prankster rather than the incarnation of evil, director Stanley Donen settles for quirky comedy instead of razor-sharp satire, and his determinedly trendy direction means that the film ends up being as patchy as Raquel's outfit. [video]

Peter Cook *George Spiggot* • Dudley Moore *Stanley Moon* • Raquel Welch *Lillian Lust* • Eleanor Bron *Margaret* • Alba *Vanity* • Robert Russell *Anger* • Barry Humphries *Envy* • Parnell McGarry *Gluttony* • Danielle Noel *Avarice* • Howard Goorney *Sloth* ■ *Dir* Stanley Donen • *Scr* Peter Cook, Dudley Moore, from a story by Peter Cook • *Music* Dudley Moore

Bedelia ★★

Crime drama 1946 · UK · BW · 89mins

Made when Britain's glamorous and highly popular "wicked lady" Margaret Lockwood was at the peak of her stardom, the postwar public flocked to this tale of a classy married woman who, having poisoned three husbands, is planning to dispose of the present one (Ian Hunter). Lance Comfort directed this utter drivel, which offers a nice twist ending, photography by Frederick A Young (who would go on to better things such as *Lawrence of Arabia*), and a giggly frisson for Lockwood fans.

Margaret Lockwood *Bedelia Carrington* • Ian Hunter *Charlie Carrington* • Barry K Barnes *Ben Chaney* • Anne Crawford *Ellen Walker* • Jill Esmond *Nurse Harris* • Barbara Blair *Sylvia Johnstone* ■ *Dir* Lance Comfort • *Scr* Vera Caspary, Herbert Victor, from the novel by Vera Caspary

Bedevilled ★

Crime drama 1955 · US · Colour · 85mins

This dreadful quasi-religious thriller was made to use some of MGM's funds locked in France. That fine actress Anne Baxter is wasted as a nightclub singer on the run who finds refuge in a church and the sensitive arms of priest-to-be Steve Forrest, who gives a terribly wooden performance. The production itself was bedevilled with so many problems that MGM chief Dore Schary fired director Mitchell Leisen towards the end of shooting and had John Sturges take over.

Anne Baxter *Monica Johnson* • Steve Forrest *Gregory Fitzgerald* • Victor Francen *Father Du Rocher* • Simone Renant *Francesca* • Maurice Teynac *Trevelle* • Robert Christopher *Tony Lugacetti* • Ina De La Hye *Mama Lugacetti* • Joseph Tomelty *Father Cunningham* ■ *Dir* Mitchell Leisen • *Scr* Jo Eisinger

The Bedford Incident ★★★★ PG

Adventure 1965 · UK · BW · 101mins

A superior Cold War sea drama-cum-chase movie, directed by Stanley Kubrick's one-time producer James B Harris, and exploring similar nuclear fears to Kubrick's *Dr Strangelove*, but in more sober fashion. Richard Widmark gives a notable performance as the captain of a nuclear-armed American naval destroyer, with the job of hunting Russian subs, who has a perhaps excessive zeal for the task. Sidney Poitier plays a journalist who comes along for what turns out to be an exciting ride. [video]

Richard Widmark *Captain Eric Finlander* • Sidney Poitier *Ben Munceford* • James MacArthur *Ensign Ralston* • Martin Balsam *Lieutenant Commander Chester Potter* • Wally Cox *Sonar operator* • Eric Portman *Commander Wolfgang Schrepke* • Michael Kane *Commander Allison* • Donald Sutherland *Pharmacist's mate* ■ *Dir* James B Harris • *Scr* James Poe, from the novel by Mark Rascovich

Bedknobs and Broomsticks ★★★ U

Musical fantasy 1971 · US · Colour · 133mins

Directed by Robert Stevenson, this was a conscious effort on the part of Disney to repeat the success of *Mary Poppins*. Angela Lansbury is splendidly dotty as amateur witch Eglantine Price, but neither David Tomlinson nor the trio of cockney evacuees offer her much support. But then neither does the story, cobbled together from a couple of Mary Norton novels, in which the Nazi invasion of Britain is repelled by magic. The animated sequences are easily the highlights of the film, which is now available in full (for many years we had to make do with a 98-minute version that cut several of the Sherman brothers' songs). [video]

Angela Lansbury *Eglantine Price* • David Tomlinson *Emelius Browne* • Roddy McDowall *Mr Jelk* • Sam Jaffe *Bookman* • John Ericson *Colonel Heller* • Bruce Forsyth *Swinburne* • Reginald Owen *General Teagler* • Tessie O'Shea *Mrs Hobday* ■ *Dir* Robert Stevenson • *Scr* Bill Walsh, Don DaGradi, from the books *The Magic Bed-Knob* and *Bonfires and Broomsticks* by Mary Norton

Bedlam ★★★

Horror 1946 · US · BW · 79mins

Was there ever a star who played sadistic men with as much relish as Boris Karloff? He's given ample room to snarl here as an asylum boss in 18th-century London who interns an innocent woman to stop her from exposing his harsh rule. Intelligently written and acted, with its production design modelled on Hogarth's engravings, this atmospheric chiller from the Val Lewton stable is let down by Mark Robson's rather pedestrian direction. Despite the attention paid to historical detail, its talky approach will no doubt turn off fans raised on a diet of Freddy and Jason.

Boris Karloff *Master Sims* • Anna Lee *Nell Bowen* • Billy House *Lord Mortimer* • Jason Robards *Oliver Todd* • Richard Fraser *Hannay* • Glenn Vernon *The gilded boy* • Ian Wolfe *Sidney Long* • Leyland Hodgson *John Wilkes* ■ *Dir* Mark Robson • *Scr* Carlos Keith [Val Lewton], Mark Robson, from the engravings by William Hogarth • *Cinematographer* Nicholas Musuraca

Bedroom Eyes ★★ 18

Erotic thriller 1984 · Can · Colour · 89mins

A fitfully entertaining blend of comedy and mystery, this is a considerable improvement on the usual B-movie fare churned out by director William Fruet, the man who brought the risible *Spasms* and *Blue Monkey* to the screen. Kenneth Gilman gives a willing performance as a stockbroker who begins to jog with increased enthusiasm after he starts spying on a beautiful woman through her bedroom window. After she's murdered, however, the Peeping Tom is forced to turn detective, having become the prime suspect. [video]

Kenneth Gilman *Harry Ross* • Dayle Haddon *Alixe Barnes* • Barbara Law *Jobeth* • Christine Cattell *Caroline* • Jane Catling *Marry Kittricke* ■ *Dir* William Fruet • *Scr* Michael Alan Eddy

The Bedroom Window ★★★ 15

Thriller 1987 · US · Colour · 108mins

Steve Guttenberg must have seen this thriller as a means of escaping being typecast in he zany *Police Academy* series. Unfortunately, for all his efforts, he comes off second best to his female co-stars, Elizabeth McGovern and Isabelle Huppert. Writer/director Curtis Hanson who made the brilliant Oscar-winning *LA Confidential* keeps this bright and entertaining, but he eventually runs into trouble when he tries to resolve the many intrigues and plot twists. Contains swearing, sex scenes and nudity. [video]

Steve Guttenberg *Terry Lambert* • Elizabeth McGovern *Denise Connelly* • Isabelle Huppert *Sylvia Wentworth* • Paul Shenar *Collin Wentworth* • Carl Lumbly *Detective Quirke* • Wallace Shawn *Henderson's attorney* ■ *Dir* Curtis Hanson • *Scr* Curtis Hanson, from the novel *The Witnesses* by Anne Holden

Bedrooms and Hallways ★★★ 15

Romantic comedy
1998 · UK · Colour · 91mins

More commercial than her debut film *Go Fish*, Rose Troche's second feature is an intelligent and funny examination of nineties sexuality. Kevin McKidd, a quiet homosexual, starts exploring his masculinity in an overly serious men's group. There McKidd meets James Purefoy and, embarking on a relationship with him, is distraught to discover Purefoy is the boyfriend of his first love and good friend Jennifer Ehle. The web woven, this ensemble piece comes to a climax on McKidd's birthday. Impressive in its open attitude, where the characters' sexual bent is not as important as their essential humanity, this is a funny and perceptive film. Contains swearing and sexual scenes. [video]

Kevin McKidd *Leo* • Jennifer Ehle *Sally* • Simon Callow *Keith* • Hugo Weaving *Jeremy* • Christopher Fulford *Adam* • Julie Graham *Angie* • Tom Hollander *Darren* • Harriet Walter *Sybil* • James Purefoy *Brendan* ■ *Dir* Rose Troche • *Scr* Robert Farrar

Bedside Manner ★★

Romantic comedy 1945 · US · BW · 78mins

Ruth Hussey stars as a doctor who, on her way to Chicago, stops off at the small-town surgery of her uncle Charles Ruggles to lend a helping hand. There, her brilliant powers of diagnosis and treatment of every kind of complaint prove nothing short of miraculous, until the faked head injury of romantically smitten John Carroll confounds her. An idiotic screenplay, pedestrian direction and a less than glittering cast ensure that this unconvincing attempt at romantic comedy remains firmly second rate.

John Carroll *Morgan Hale* • Ruth Hussey *Hedy Fredericks* • Charles Ruggles *Doc Fredericks* • Ann Rutherford *Lola* • Claudia Drake *Tanya* • Renee Godfrey *Stella* • Esther Dale *Gravitt* • Grant Mitchell *Mr Pope* ■ *Dir* Andrew L Stone • *Scr* Frederick Jackson, Malcolm Stuart Boylan, from the story by Robert Carson

Bedtime for Bonzo ★★ U

Comedy 1951 · US · BW · 83mins

Apart from the fact that this wretched farce starred an actor destined to be President of the United States – Ronald Reagan – this nature-versus-nurture joke has little going for it. The story, which looks at how environment shapes personality, is about a chimpanzee being brought up as a human baby and the monkey business which ensues. It's an amiable idea, perhaps, if you find a simian in nappies at all funny, but director Frederick de Cordova's cramped style of approach affords it little room for comic manouevre – rather like that be-nappied monkey.

Ronald Reagan *Professor Peter Boyd* • Diana Lynn *Jane* • Walter Slezak *Professor Hans Neumann* • Lucille Barkley *Valerie Tillinghast* • Jesse White *Babcock* • Herbert Heyes *Dean Tillinghast* • Herb Vigran *Lt Daggett* ■ *Dir* Frederick De Cordova • *Scr* Val Burton, Lou Breslow, from a story by Raphael David Blau [Raphael Blau], Ted Berkman

Bedtime Story ★★★

Comedy 1942 · US · BW · 84mins

Sparks fly when the starry actress wife (Loretta Young) of a theatre-obsessed playwright (Fredric March) insists on retiring from the stage. A rather over-extended one-joke situation is enlivened by sporadically successful attempts at screwball comedy, but eventually it wears a bit thin and the formidable March is somewhat unsympathetic. The ravishing Young holds it together, however, with the aid of an excellent supporting cast, notably Allyn Joslyn as her stuffed-shirt suitor and the sublime Eve Arden, who assists March in one of his schemes to lure his wife back into his new play.

Fredric March *Lucius Drake* • Loretta Young *Jane Drake* • Robert Benchley *Eddie Turner* • Allyn Joslyn *William Dudley* • Eve Arden *Virginia Cole* • Helen Westley *Emma Harper* • Joyce Compton *Beulah* • Tim Ryan *Mac* ■ *Dir* Alexander Hall • *Scr* Richard Flournoy, from a story by Horace Jackson, Grant Garrett

Bedtime Story ★★★★

Comedy   1964 · US · Colour · 98mins

Marlon Brando – the ultimate method actor – and David Niven – the ultimate exponent of relaxed, intuitive style – make for an unlikely double act, but the results are absolutely hilarious. They play two rival con men on the French Riviera who try and trick TV soap star Shirley Jones out of her riches. Besides Niven's irresistible debonair charm, we have Brando's extraordinary catalogue of accents and disguises, notably his Ruritanian prince Ruprecht. It's marred by some phoney sets and back projection, but it deserves to be known in its own right rather than just as the basis for the Michael Caine/Steve Martin remake, *Dirty Rotten Scoundrels*.

Marlon Brando *Freddy Benson* • David Niven *Lawrence Jameson* • Shirley Jones *Janet Walker* • Dody Goodman *Fanny Eubank* • Aram Stephan *Andre* • Parley Baer *Colonel Williams* • Marie Windsor *Mrs Sutton* • Rebecca Sand *Miss Trumble* ■ *Dir* Ralph Levy • *Scr* Stanley Shapiro, Paul Henning

The Bee Keeper ★★★ 18

Drama   1986 · Gr/Fr · Colour · 121mins

Marcello Mastroianni is an elderly schoolteacher, at the end of his life and his tether, who sets out to visit his beloved beehives, family and old friends before his intended suicide. Along the road he picks up a teenage hitchhiker (Nadia Mourouzi) who may or may not revive him spiritually and sexually. As usual with Theo Angelopoulos's work, this is a beautifully shot, but over-extended allegory, though Mastroianni delivers a wonderfully detailed and very moving performance. The actor had to endure three days of bee attack for the final sequence. In Greek with English subtitles.

Marcello Mastroianni *Spyros* • Nadia Mourouzi *Girl* • Serge Reggiani *Sick man* • Jenny Roussea *Spyros's wife* • Dinos Iliopoulos *Spyros's friend* ■ *Dir* Theodoros Angelopoulos [Theo Angelopoulos] • *Scr* Thodoros Angelopoulos, Dimitris Nollas, Tonino Guerra • *Cinematographer* Yorgos Arvanitis

Beer ★ 15

Comedy   1985 · US · Colour · 79mins

An old-fashioned and rather naive satire on the Madison Avenue advertising industry, which strains to be funny and credible but ends up being bland and unsubtle. Aggressive executive Loretta Swit comes up with an outrageous advertising campaign for Norbecker beer which upsets various minority groups due to the sleazy, sexist and camp approach taken by its alcoholic director, Rip Torn.

Loretta Swit *BD Tucker* • Rip Torn *Buzz Beckerman* • Kenneth Mars *AJ Norbecker* • David Alan Grier *Elliot Morrison* • William Russ *Merle Draggett* • Saul Stein *Frankie Falcone* • Peter Michael Goetz *Harley Feemer* • Dick Shawn *Talk show host* ■ *Dir* Patrick Kelly • *Scr* Allan Weisbecker

Bees in Paradise ★★

Musical comedy   1943 · UK · BW · 75mins

Co-scripted by director Val Guest and gagsmith Marriott Edgar, who wrote for Will Hay and the Crazy Gang and penned some of Stanley Holloway's famous monologues, this is one of Arthur Askey's lesser-known vehicles. This may be because there's a sauciness to the dialogue and lyrics that makes it rather risqué for its time. As one of four pilots stranded on a South Sea island, Askey revels in the attentions of the local maidens, only to discover that it's traditional for husbands to commit suicide once the honeymoon is over.

Arthur Askey *Arthur Tucker* • Anne Shelton *Rouana* • Peter Graves (2) *Peter Lovell* • Max Bacon *Max Holer* • Jean Kent *Jani* • Ronald Shiner *Ronald Wild* • Antoinette Cellier *Queen* • Joy Shelton *Almura* ■ *Dir* Val Guest • *Scr* Val Guest, Marriott Edgar

Beethoven ★★★★ U

Comedy   1992 · US · Colour · 83mins

This is a cute family comedy about an adorable St Bernard dog named Beethoven and the effect he has on an American family. Charles Grodin (best known for his performance opposite Robert De Niro in *Midnight Run*) is the father who ends up with a puppy he doesn't want, which turns into a huge eating and slobbering machine. *The Flintstones* director Brian Levant keeps the comedy coming fast and furious so this never lapses into soppy territory, while Beethoven is gorgeous enough to soften even the hardest dog-hater's heart. Watch out for David Duchovny as the sleazy yuppy who reckons he's a coffee connoisseur.

Charles Grodin *George Newton* • Bonnie Hunt *Alice Newton* • Dean Jones *Dr Varnick* • Nicholle Tom *Ryce* • Christopher Castile *Ted* • Sarah Rose Karr *Emily* • Oliver Platt *Harvey* • Stanley Tucci *Vernon* • David Duchovny *Brad* • Patricia Heaton *Brie* ■ *Dir* Brian Levant • *Scr* Edmond Dantes, Amy Holden Jones

Beethoven's 2nd ★★★ U

Comedy   1993 · US · Colour · 84mins

With the paw prints of *One Hundred and One Dalmatians* all over it, this cosy sequel sees the Newton children trying to hide a litter of ultra-cute St Bernard puppies from their still dog-shy father, Charles Grodin. While all eyes will be on the four pups (who were played by over 100 pooches at various times), let's not forget the amiable performances of Grodin and Bonnie Hunt, and the Cruella-like villainy of scheming Debi Mazar, who dognaps Missy (Beethoven's beloved) to use as a pawn in her divorce. The holiday finale is hopelessly contrived, but what the heck? The song *The Day I Fall in Love* was Oscar nominated.

Charles Grodin *George Newton* • Bonnie Hunt *Alice Newton* • Nicholle Tom *Ryce* • Christopher Castile *Ted* • Sarah Rose Karr *Emily* • Debi Mazar *Regina* • Chris Penn [Christopher Penn] *Floyd* • Ashley Hamilton *Taylor* • Danny Masterson *Seth* ■ *Dir* Rod Daniel • *Scr* Len Blum

Beetle Juice ★★★★ 15

Comedy horror   1988 · US · Colour · 88mins

Tim Burton's refreshingly flakey fantasy is a landmark in supernatural comedy, ingeniously showcasing monstrously zany special effects, demonic one-liners and off-beat performances. Michael Keaton is amazing as the unstable freelance exorcist, who is called in to help recently deceased Geena Davis and Alec Baldwin rid their new home of human pests. Burton's imaginative view of the afterlife as a ghoulish extension of mundane earthbound problems is a visionary masterstroke crammed with wit and invention. Weird, wonderful and dead funny. Contains some swearing

DVD

Michael Keaton *Betelgeuse* • Geena Davis *Barbara Maitland* • Alec Baldwin *Adam Maitland* • Catherine O'Hara *Delia Deetz* • Winona Ryder *Lydia Deetz* • Jeffrey Jones *Charles Deetz* • Robert Goulet *Maxie Dean* • Sylvia Sidney *Juno* ■ *Dir* Tim Burton • *Scr* Michael McDowell, Warren Skaaren, from a story by Michael McDowell, Larry Wilson

Before and After ★★ 12

Drama   1996 · US · Colour · 103mins

Meryl Streep and Liam Neeson's lives are irrevocably changed when their son is accused of murdering his girlfriend in director Barbet Schroeder's unfocused pseudo-thriller. A turgid pace coupled with poor plotting stretches credibility to breaking point in a bland morality melodrama, notable only for Streep's fine, suitably distressed performance. None of the other actors, especially sullen Edward Furlong as the possible killer, match up to her calibre. Sentimentality, not harsh reality, is the driving force of this fudged dilemma, while Schroeder is less interested in the final verdict than in the ripples it causes.

Meryl Streep *Carolyn Ryan* • Liam Neeson *Ben Ryan* • Edward Furlong *Jacob Ryan* • Julia Weldon *Judith Ryan* • Alfred Molina *Panos Demeris* • Daniel Von Bargen *Fran Conklin* • John Heard *Wendell Bye* • Ann Magnuson *Terry Taverner* ■ *Dir* Barbet Schroeder • *Scr* Ted Tally, from the book by Rosellen Brown

Before He Wakes ★★ PG

Drama   1998 · US · Colour · 92mins

The lovely Jaclyn Smith plays the heavy in this uninspired TV movie, which revolves around Bridgette (Smith), who returns to her home town with her young son after her husband dies in an "accidental" shooting. She soon remarries, but her mounting debts point to only one way out – her second husband's life insurance policy. Will she kill again? Do we care? It's all so utterly inane you won't believe it's supposedly based on fact.

Jaclyn Smith *Bridgette Smith Michaels* • Diana Scarwid *Joanne* • Timothy Carhart *Ron Michaels* • Ron Canada *Detective Cochran* • Barbara Tarbuck *Diane Michaels* • Hope Lange *Helen* • Michael Flynn *Ken Young* ■ *Dir* Michael Scott • *Scr* Selma Thompson, from the book by Jerry Bledsoe

Before I Hang ★★★

Horror   1940 · US · BW · 62mins

A short and sweet programme filler allowing Boris Karloff to veer superbly between brilliant scientist and rabid madman. This time he's dabbling in serums to combat old age and uses a criminal's blood for some behind bars experimentation after he's imprisoned for a "mercy killing". There's loads of fun psychobabble about medicine being for the good of mankind, but what it – like many of the King of Horror's potboilers from the period – eventually turns into is another twist on the *Frankenstein* theme. Yet Karloff glues it all together as ever.

Boris Karloff *Dr John Garth* • Evelyn Keyes *Martha Garth* • Bruce Bennett *Dr Paul Ames* • Edward Van Sloan *Dr Ralph Howard* • Ben Taggart *Warden Thompson* ■ *Dir* Nick Grinde • *Scr* Robert D Andrews

Before Sunrise ★★★★ 15

Romantic drama   1995 · US · Colour · 97mins

When American slacker Ethan Hawke meets French student Julie Delpy on a train to Vienna, the romantic sparks fly and they spend one eventful night together in director Richard Linklater's exhilarating drama. Announcing his presence as a major talent after grabbing attention with *Dazed and Confused*, Linklater's understated use of gorgeous Viennese backgrounds, coupled with a smart, funny and touching script, make this ultra-modern romance hip yet timeless. With engaging Hawke and free-spirited Delpy delivering confident chemistry, this contemporary brief encounter is a real winner. Contains swearing.

Ethan Hawke *Jesse* • Julie Delpy *Céline* • Andrea Eckert *Wife on train* • Hanno Poschl *Husband on train* • Karl Bruckschwaiger *Guy on bridge* • Tex Rubinowitz *Guy on bridge* • Erni Mangold *Palm reader* • Dominik Castell *Street poet* ■ *Dir* Richard Linklater • *Scr* Richard Linklater, Kim Krizan

Before the Night ★★ 18

Erotic thriller   1995 · US · Colour · 93mins

Talk about keeping it in the family. Talia Shire makes her directorial debut with this instantly forgettable erotic thriller, but just to bolster her confidence ex-husband David Shire composed the score, while older brother Francis Ford Coppola and his mentor Roger Corman also helped out behind the scenes. Coppola regular Frederic Forrest even crops up as the father whose daughter may or may not have been murdered by A Martinez, the very man with whom lonely Ally Sheedy has a one-night stand. Coppola's first commercial film was the soft-core feature *Tonight for Sure*, so this straight-to-video offering is akin to continuing a family tradition. Contains swearing, sex scenes and nudity

Ally Sheedy *Michelle Sanderson* • A Martinez *Jack Gillman* • Frederic Forrest *Josslyn* • Don Novello *Warren Miller* ■ *Dir* Talia Shire • *Scr* Marty Casella

Before the Rain ★★★ 15

Portmanteau drama
1994 · Mac/UK/Fr · Colour · 108mins

Winner of the Golden Lion at Venice and nominated for the best foreign film Oscar, this was the first film produced in the newly formed Republic of Macedonia. Director Milcho Manchevski brings an imposing portentousness to this portmanteau picture, but too often he mistakes ponderousness for gravity, particularly in "Words", in which monk Grégoire Colin breaks his vows to help refugee Labina Mitevska. In Macedonian, Albanian and English with subtitles.

Josif Josifovski *Father Marko* • Rade Serbedzija *Aleksandar* • Grégoire Colin *Kiril* • Labina Mitevska *Zamira* • Boris Delcevski *Petre* • Dejan Velkov *Mate* • Kiril Ristoski

U = SUITABLE FOR ALL   **Uc** = SUITABLE FOR ALL, ESPECIALLY FOR YOUNG CHILDREN (VIDEO ONLY)   **PG** = PARENTAL GUIDANCE

Father Damjan • Mladen Krstevski *Trifun* • Dzemail Maksut *Kuzman* • Katrin Cartlidge *Anne* • Phyllida Law *Anne's mother* • Jay Villiers *Nick* ■ *Dir/Scr* Milcho Manchevski

Before the Revolution ★★★ 15

Political drama 1964 · It · BW · 106mins

The second feature from Bernardo Bertolucci, director of *Last Tango in Paris* and *The Last Emperor*, tells of a young man whose involvement with radical politics and affair with an aunt is countered by his need to conform and settle down with a pretty girl. Bertolucci refined these themes over and over again, notably in his masterpiece *The Conformist* (1969). This is a fascinating apprentice effort, even if it is full of dated, gimmicky effects apparently borrowed from Jean-Luc Godard. In Italian with English subtitles. ▣

Adriana Asti *Gina* • Francesco Barilli *Fabrizio* • Morando Morandini *Cesare* • Allen Midgette *Agostino* • Cristina Pariset *Clelia* • Domenico Alpi *Fabrizio's father* ■ *Dir/Scr* Bernardo Bertolucci

Before Winter Comes ★★★

Drama 1968 · UK · Colour · 107mins

Instead of merrily fiddling on the roof, here's Topol cheerfully trifling with the truth. He plays a Russian deserter, masquerading as a Slav interpreter who speaks 13 languages, helping major David Niven run a displaced persons camp in Austria at the end of the Second World War. Both are in conflict over local girl Anna Karina, but J Lee Thompson's relaxed direction fails to generate sufficient tension. Niven's punctilious dignity is as memorable as ever, however.

David Niven *Major Giles Burnside* • Topol *Janovic* • Anna Karina *Maria Holz* • John Hurt *Lieutenant Francis Pilkington* • Anthony Quayle *Brigadier-General Bewley* • Ori Levy *Captain Kamenev* • John Collin *Sergeant Woody* • Karel Stepanek *Count Derassy* ■ *Dir* J Lee Thompson • *Scr* Andrew Sinclair, from the story *The Interpreter* by Frederick L Keefe

Before Women Had Wings ★★★ 15

Drama 1997 · US · Colour · 88mins

Once you get past the naff title, there's actually some decent drama to be found in this TV movie "presented by" Oprah Winfrey. The film stars Oprah (of course) as the kindly woman who takes in the children of downtrodden mother Ellen Barkin. While Winfrey goes for melodrama, Barkin adds much needed class and grit and is backed up by nice performances from young Tina Majorino and hot young actress Julia Stiles (*10 Things I Hate about You*). ▣

Oprah Winfrey *Miss Zora* • Ellen Barkin *Glory Marie Jackson* • Tina Majorino *Bird* • Julia Stiles *Phoebe Jackson* • John Savage *Billy Jackson* • Burt Young *Mr Ippolito* • William Lee Scott *Hank* • Louis Crugnali *LJ Ippolito* • David Hart *Sheriff* ■ *Dir* Lloyd Kramer • *Scr* Connie May Fowler, from her novel

Beg, Borrow or Steal ★★ U

Comedy thriller 1973 · US · Colour · 71mins

Having directed Chuck Connors in *Set This Town on Fire* earlier in the year, David Lowell Rich teamed up with Chuck's namesake Mike on this decidedly dodgy heist thriller. Like his fellow conspirators in this exploitative exercise, Connors once starred as a TV detective. But here, he plays a legless thief who allies with Kent McCord (who has no eyes) and Michael Cole (who lacks hands) to crack a maximum security museum. In fairness, the robbery is tense and well-staged, but the premise in Paul Playdon's teleplay is hard to accept as novelty entertainment in these more politically correct times.

Mike Connors *Victor Cummings* • Kent McCord *Lester Yates* • Michael Cole *Cliff Norris* • Joel Fabiani *Kevin Turner* • Henry Beckman *Hal Cooper* • Russell Johnson *Alex Langley* • Logan Ramsey *Walter Beal* • Ron Glass *Ray Buren* ■ *Dir* David Lowell Rich • *Scr* Paul Playdon, from a story by Grant Sims, Paul Playdon

Beggars of Life ★★★

Drama 1928 · US · BW · 80mins

After killing her brutal stepfather, farm girl Louise Brooks, disguised as a boy, flees into hiding in company with youthful hobo Richard Arlen. Much of the action famously has them hopping freight trains and dossing down in a community of tramps, where Wallace Beery is top dog. Director William A Wellman, filming on location on railways and in the Californian desert, creates strong atmosphere and Brooks is beguiling, but the film is disappointingly slow and sketchy after its explosive opening scenes and it's left to Beery to give life to the proceedings. It was filmed as a silent movie, but some snatches of dialogue and a music track were added to qualify it, a little dubiously, as Paramount's first talkie feature.

Wallace Beery *Oklahoma Red* • Louise Brooks *Nancy* • Richard Arlen *Jim* • Edgar Blue Washington *Mose* • HA Morgan [Horace Morgan] *Skinny* • Andy Clark *Skelly* • Mike Donlin *Bill* ■ *Dir* William A Wellman • *Scr* Benjamin Glazer, Jim Tully, from the story by Jim Tully

The Beggar's Opera ★★★ U

Operetta 1953 · US · Colour · 94mins

What with Laurence Olivier launching into lilting vocals as highwayman MacHeath, and Dorothy Tutin in exasperated voice as Polly Peachum, the first movie of radical stage producer Peter Brook's had some distinguished credentials for success. But John Gay's satirical operetta, full of whores and hangmen, comes across as stagey and stilted, despite music arranged by Sir Arthur Bliss and script by playwrights Dennis Cannan and Christopher Fry. It now looks less patronisingly styled for the plebs, and has some visual and harmonious delights that, at least, make it an intriguing spectacle. ▣

Laurence Olivier *Capt MacHeath* • Stanley Holloway *Lockit* • George Devine *Peachum* • Mary Clare *Mrs Peachum* • Athene Seyler *Mrs Trapes* • Dorothy Tutin *Polly Peachum* • Daphne Anderson *Lucy Lockit* • Hugh Griffith *The Beggar* • Margot Grahame *The actress* ■

Dir Peter Brook • *Scr* Dennis Cannan, Christopher Fry, from the comic opera by John Gay • *Cinematographer* Guy Green

Beginning of the End ★

Science-fiction horror 1957 · US · BW · 72mins

Rubbishy schlock horror about an atomic radiation leak that kills off scores of farmers in the Midwest and produces giant grasshoppers that march in formation on hapless Chicago, slaughtering everyone who stands in their way. Peter Graves is the baffled boffin, while Peggy Castle plays a boggled journalist. Cheesy effects and hammy performances may delight fans of the genre, but 15 minutes is as much as most people can take before boredom sets in.

Peggie Castle *Audrey* • Peter Graves (1) *Ed Wainwright* • Morris Ankrum *General Hanson* • Richard Benedict *Corporal Mathias* • James Seay *Captain Barton* ■ *Dir* Bert I Gordon • *Scr* Fred Freiberger, Lester Gorn

The Beginning or the End ★★★ U

Second World War drama 1947 · US · BW · 111mins

MGM's dramatisation of America's development of the atom bomb is a portentous and turgid, yet absolutely fascinating, relic of the Cold War era. Hume Cronyn plays the scientist, J Robert Oppenheimer, while a cast of dozens play other real-life personages, including Einstein, Roosevelt and Harry Truman. Charting the science and the politics thatled to the bomb being dropped on Japan, the movie celebrates Yankee know-how, but also wonders if the invention might herald an apocalyptic dawn and wipe out humanity for good. Thus the romantic subplots seem more inane than usual, and there's a framing device, about a time capsule to be opened in the year 2446, that's simply mind-boggling.

Brian Donlevy *Maj-Gen Leslie R Groves* • Robert Walker *Col Jeff Nixon* • Tom Drake *Matt Cochran* • Beverly Tyler *Ann Cochran* • Audrey Totter *Jean O'Leary* • Hume Cronyn *Dr J Robert Oppenheimer* • Hurd Hatfield *Dr John Wyatt* • Godfrey Tearle *President Roosevelt* • Ludwig Stossel *Dr Albert Einstein* • Art Baker *President Truman* ■ *Dir* Norman Taurog • *Scr* Frank Wead

The Beguiled ★★★★ 15

Western drama 1971 · US · Colour · 99mins

An eccentric change of pace for Clint Eastwood and action director Don Siegel who successfully collaborated on *Dirty Harry*, this could be entitled "Sex and the Single Girls". For it is the frustrated sexuality of the young ladies in the Southern school run by Geraldine Page that leads to the downfall of Eastwood's wounded Unionist soldier, whom they nurse and protect. It might have played better as a languid black comedy – Siegel's camera is too energetic for its own good – but it's still effective melodrama, despite an undercurrent of misogyny. Contains some nudity. ▣

Clint Eastwood *John McBurney* • Geraldine Page *Martha Farnsworth* • Elizabeth Hartman *Edwina Dabney* • Jo Ann Harris *Carol* • Darleen Carr *Doris* • Mae Mercer *Hallie* • Pamelyn Ferdin *Amy* • Melody Thomas *Abigail*

• Peggy Drier *Lizzie* ■ *Dir* Don Siegel • *Scr* John B Sherry, Grimes Grice, from the novel by Thomas Cullinan

Behind Closed Doors ★★

Thriller 1994 · US · Colour

The main point of interest here is an early appearance by Lisa Kudrow (before *Friends*). Otherwise this is a feverishly plotted but rather empty throwback to *film noir* hampered by its TV origins. Barry Bostwick conspires against his wealthy wife Lesley-Anne Down, who becomes involved in a web of blackmail and deceit. Fortunately, the cast, which includes Michael Gross and Matt McCoy, doesn't take things too seriously, but the direction is strictly by numbers. Contains swearing, violence and nudity.

Barry Bostwick *Philip Donovan* • Lesley-Anne Down *Jean Donovan* • Michael Gross *Howard Epstein* • Teresa Hill *Casey Stevens* • Lisa Kudrow *Teller* ■ *Dir* Catherine Cyran • *Scr* Travis Rink

Behind Enemy Lines ★

Action adventure 1996 · US · Colour · 89mins

Before the studio's demise in 1996, there were several features that Orion Pictures never got around to releasing theatrically; this is the worst. Sadly, it turned up on video, with Thomas Ian Griffiths gives an utterly empty and blank-faced performance as a special ops member who returns to Vietnam to rescue an old buddy. Griffiths is so inept, he ends up getting captured himself. It's up to his Hawaiian-shirt-wearing buddies to break him out, getting into countless slow-motion shoot-outs along the way.

Thomas Ian Griffin *Mike Weston* • Chris Mulkey *Jones* • Mark Carlton *Colonel Wolfe* • Mushond Lee *Luther* • Hillary Matthews *Kat* ■ *Dir* Mark Griffiths • *Scr* Dennis Cooley, Andrew Osborne, from a story by Andrew Osborne

Behind the Forbidden City ★★★★

Drama 1996 · Chi/Fr/Neth · Colour · 94mins

Announced as the first Chinese film to tackle homosexuality, this intense interrogation drama is also an allegory on the complex relationship between the people and the forces of law and order. There's something of *The Usual Suspects* in the way Si Han uses flashbacked episodes from his life to force a sexually ambivalent cop, Hu Jun, to confront his own preferences. Set around the public toilets on the edge of Tiananmen Square, which gives the film its slang title, this controversial drama led to the confiscation of Zhang Yuan's passport and the formation of the Film Bureau to outlaw production of unapproved independent pictures. In Mandarin with English subtitles.

Si Han *A-Lan* • Hu Jun *Shi Xiaohua* ■ *Dir* Zhang Yuan • *Scr* Yuan Zhang, Xiaobo Wang

Behind the Headlines ★★★

Drama 1937 · US · BW · 58mins

Having played Hildy Johnson on Broadway in the jewel of newsroom dramas, *The Front Page*, Lee Tracy was frequently cast as fast-talking, sharp-witted reporters on screen. This superior B-melodrama finds him playing

just such a character. Good at getting scoops, Tracy finds his relationship with his reporter girlfriend (Diana Gibson) threatened by their rivalry, though circumstances eventually require him to rescue her from danger. Well directed by Richard Rosson, with good performances from the leads, a solid supporting cast and quality cinematography, it's much better than it sounds on paper.

Lee Tracy *Eddie Haines* • Diana Gibson *Mary Bradley* • Donald Meek *Potter* • Paul Guilfoyle *Art Martin* • Philip Huston *Bennett* • Frank M Thomas *Naylor* ■ *Dir* Richard Rosson • *Scr* J Robert Bren, Edmund I Hartman, from a story by Thomas Ahearn

Behind the Headlines ★★ U
Thriller   1956 · UK · BW · 67mins
This is elevated above the morass of British crime B-movies by a sure sense of newsroom atmosphere that owes more to Hollywood than Pinewood. This tale of showgirls, blackmail and murder presents an unromanticised view of journalism – although the intrepid reporter always stays one step ahead of the doltish flatfoot – and there's a convincing seediness about the backstage milieu thanks to Geoffrey Faithfull's unfussy photography. It may lack suspense and newsman Paul Carpenter is short on charisma, but there's admirable support from the likes of Adrienne Corri, Hazel Court and Alfie Bass.

Paul Carpenter *Paul Banner* • Adrienne Corri *Pam Barnes* • Hazel Court *Maxine* • Ewen Solon *Supt Faro* • Alfie Bass *Sammy* • Harry Fowler *Alfie* • Tom Gill *Creloch* ■ *Dir* Charles Saunders • *Scr* Allan MacKinnon, from the novel by Robert Chapman

Behind the Mask ★★
Medical drama   1958 · UK · Colour · 108mins
This potboiling hospital drama suffers from the fact that much of its incident and nearly all its characters have now become over familiar thanks to endless TV programmes about feuding surgeons, put-upon housemen and devoted nurses. As much of the story is taken up with a dispute between Michael Redgrave and Niall MacGinnis over the management of their hospital, there is as much boardroom chat as there is action in the wards. Director Brian Desmond Hurst seems unable to choose between realism and melodrama, leaving his actors unsure how to pitch their performances.

Michael Redgrave *Sir Arthur Benson Gray* • Tony Britton *Philip Selwood* • Carl Mohner *Dr Carl Romek* • Niall MacGinnis *Neil Isherwood* • Vanessa Redgrave *Pamela Gray* • Ian Bannen *Alan Crabtree* • Brenda Bruce *Elizabeth Fallon* • Lionel Jeffries *Walter Froy* • Ann Firbank *Mrs Judson* ■ *Dir* Brian Desmond Hurst • *Scr* John Hunter, from the novel *The Pack* by John Rowan Wilson

Behind the Mask ★★
Drama based on a true story
1999 · US · Colour
Donald Sutherland plays a doctor who suffers a heart attack while running a facility for the disabled in this TV movie. When a mentally challenged janitor (Matthew Fox) saves his life, he becomes the doctor's surrogate son – much to the chagrin of Sutherland's own son, who has long felt neglected

by his father. Fox and Sutherland deliver honest performances under Tom McLoughlin's steady direction, while the emotional power of this sometimes maudlin true-life story ensures it's never boring.

Donald Sutherland *Dr Bob Shushan* • Matthew Fox *James Jones* • Bradley Whitford *Brian Shushan* • Sheila Larken *Dana* • Lorena Gale *Mrs Flowers* • Currie Graham *Geller* • Mary McDonnell *Mary Shushan* ■ *Dir* Tom McLoughlin • *Scr* Gregory Goodell

Behind the Rising Sun ★★
Second World War drama
1943 · US · BW · 87mins
''Know your enemy'' is the motto behind this propaganda exercise, which sets out to show how cruel and ruthless the Japanese are. The writer and director had already performed a similar job on the Germans with *Hitler's Children*. This time a Japanese diplomat's son (Tom Neal) is forced to join the army, where he sees the horrors of the inhuman soldiers for himself and falls in love with Margo (a Mexican actress playing Japanese), while his dad does the honourable thing and kills himself. A huge hit in 1943 – but not good for Japanese-American relations today.

Margo *Tama* • Tom Neal *Taro* • J Carrol Naish *Publisher* • Robert Ryan *Lefty* • Gloria Holden *Sara* • Don Douglas *O'Hara* • George Givot *Boris* • Adeline De Walt Reynolds *Grandmother* ■ *Dir* Edward Dmytryk • *Scr* Emmett Lavery Sr, from a book by James R Young

Behind the Screen ★★★★
Silent satire   1916 · US · BW · 15mins
At a time when movies had scarcely moved out of the freak-show stage, the novelty of Charlie Chaplin's sophisticated slapstick made a star of him. In this Biograph silent, he satisfied the public's curiosity about the new medium by taking us behind the scenes at a movie studio. Also known as *The Pride of Hollywood*, its story is simple – Charlie, in Little Tramp guise, sneaks into a studio where a film is being made, only to be pursued by the usual burly, wild-eyed nemesis of Eric Campbell. Several film personalities, such as producer Hal Roach, can be seen in passing and, although very dated, it is a fascinating glimpse of a bygone age and art.

Charles Chaplin *David, a stagehand* • Eric Campbell *Goliath, his boss* • Edna Purviance *Girl seeking film job* • Frank J Coleman *Assistant director* • Albert Austin *A stagehand* • Henry Bergman *Dramatic director* • Lloyd Bacon *Comedy director* ■ *Dir* Charles Chaplin • *Scr* Charles Chaplin

Behold a Pale Horse ★★★
Drama   1964 · US · BW · 119mins
As an exiled former Spanish Civil War guerrilla, Gregory Peck is drawn into a confrontation years later with brutal police chief Anthony Quinn, in a story based on a novel by Emeric Pressburger. Director Fred Zinnemann continues his *High Noon* tradition of combining moral dilemmas with violent action, and the film contains one of Peck's finest – and least heroic – performances. Omar Sharif is miscast as a young priest, however, spouting

the message of virtue versus vengeance a little too blatantly.

Gregory Peck *Manuel Artiguez* • Anthony Quinn *Captain Vinolas* • Omar Sharif *Father Francisco* • Mildred Dunnock *Pilar* • Raymond Pellegrin *Carlos* • Paolo Stoppa *Pedro* • Daniela Rocca *Rosanna* • Christian Marquand *Lieutenant Zaganar* ■ *Dir* Fred Zinnemann • *Scr* JP Miller, from the novel *Killing a Mouse on Sunday* by Emeric Pressburger

Beijing Bastards ★★★
Musical drama
1993 · HK/Chi · Colour · 88mins
Director Zhang Yuan first fell foul of the Chinese authorities with *Mama*, a sensitive tale about a mother and her mentally handicapped son, and he was hardly likely to atone with *Beijing Bastards*, which resulted in his blacklisting. This semi-documentary study of teenage delinquency focuses on the disillusion of post-Tiananmen Square youth with the party hierarchy and the social system it maintains, and features subversive pop icon Cui Jian. Zhang's aggressive direction adds to the pace and punch of the picture, but style too often counts for more than content, and his preoccupation with provocative images makes it hard to identify with the characters. In Mandarin with English subtitles.

Wei Li *Karzi* • Cui Jian *Rock singer* ■ *Dir* Zhang Yuan • *Scr* Cui Jian, Tang Dalian, Zhang Yuan

Being at Home with Claude ★★★ 18
Drama   1992 · Can · Colour · 85mins
Based on the esteemed play by René-Daniel Dubois, this stylised blend of romantic drama and mystery thriller makes the most of its claustrophobic setting to focus our attention on the motive for the crime committed in the arresting opening sequence. Cutting between a series of graphic black and white flashbacks and the intense interview between a gay hustler (Roy Dupuis), and police inspector Jacques Godin, director Jean Beaudin slowly reveals why Dupuis loved his partner to death – literally. Although occasionally self-indulgent, this is a well staged and impeccably acted film that took New Queer Cinema into previously unchartered, controversial territory. In French with English subtitles. ▭

Roy Dupuis *Yves* • Jacques Godin *Inspector* • Jean-François Pichette *Claude* • Gaston Lepage *Stenographer* • Hugo Dube *Policeman* • Johanne-Marie Tremblay *Inspector's wife* ■ *Dir* Jean Beaudin • *Scr* Jean Baudin, from the play by René-Daniel Dubois

Being Human ★★★ 15
Comedy drama
1994 · UK/US · Colour · 116mins
While Robin Williams went on to greater things, this unclassifiable picture very nearly spelled the end for director Bill Forsyth. Shelved after its disastrous US opening, the film re-emerged with a narrative by Theresa Russell that was supposed to tie together the five tales spanning 6,000 years. For all the ingenious interaction of recurrent themes and motifs, none of these understated and mournfully anti-climactic stories is particularly memorable in itself. Yet watched with

an open mind, this is a thoughtful, if obscure, experiment, with Williams endlessly inventive as a caveman, a Roman slave, a medieval wanderer, a 17th-century nobleman and a modern-day New Yorker. ▭

Robin Williams *Hector* • John Turturro *Lucinnius* • Kelly Hunter *Deirdre* • Anna Galiena *Beatrice* • Vincent D'Onofrio *Priest* • Jonathan Hyde *Francisco* • Lizzy McInnerny *Ursula* • Hector Elizondo *Dom Paulo* • Ewan McGregor *Alvarez* • Helen Miller *Betsy* • Lindsay Crouse *Janet* • Lorraine Bracco *Anna* • William H Macy *Boris* • Theresa Russell *The Storyteller* ■ *Dir/Scr* Bill Forsyth • *Producer* David Puttnam, Robert F Colesberry

Being John Malkovich ★★★★★ 15
Fantasy comedy 1999 · US · Colour · 112mins
Spike Jonze's crazy, surreal comedy consistently dazzles with superior invention while never losing its grip on unreality. Yet this daringly original, metaphysical fantasy still finds time to pose hard-hitting questions about the human status quo, sexual gender and identity. Down-on-his-luck street puppeteer John Cusack takes a job at a strange Manhattan firm, where a small door hidden behind a filing cabinet reveals a dark tunnel that leads into the head of movie star John Malkovich. When he tells co-worker Catherine Keener about his celebrity joy ride, they form a business partnership that offers jaded New Yorkers the chance to be the actor for 15 minutes at $200 a time. Super-smart, hip and darkly subversive, Jonze's Kafkaesque mind trip is so far-out in conservative Hollywood terms it's a real shock to the system.

John Cusack *Craig Schwartz* • Cameron Diaz *Lotte Schwartz* • Catherine Keener *Maxine* • John Malkovich *John Horatio Malkovich* • Orson Bean *Dr Lester* • Mary Kay Place *Floris* • Carlos Jacott *Larry the agent* • Charlie Sheen *[Charlie Sheen] Charlie* • Brad Pitt • Sean Penn ■ *Dir* Spike Jonze • *Scr* Charlie Kaufman

Being There ★★★★ 15
Fantasy   1979 · US · Colour · 123mins
A satirical parable on the way the US surrenders itself to homespun evangelicals, this gives Peter Sellers the role of a lifetime as the naive, illiterate gardener thrust into a world that takes his ignorance for philosophical depth. So much so that he's soon poised for the Presidency. TV-nurtured, his comment to a seductive Shirley MacLaine that he likes watching gives her entirely the wrong idea. Veteran Melvyn Douglas won an Oscar for best supporting actor and deserved it, not just for a lifetime's achievement, but for managing not to be upstaged by Sellers. ▭

Peter Sellers *Chance* • Shirley MacLaine *Eve Rand* • Melvyn Douglas *Benjamin Rand* • Jack Warden *President, ''Bobby''* • Richard Dysart *Dr Robert Allenby* • Richard Basehart *Vladimir Skrapinov* • Ruth Attaway *Louise* • Dave Clennon *[David Clennon] Thomas Franklin* ■ *Dir* Hal Ashby • *Scr* Jerzy Kosinski, from his novel

U = SUITABLE FOR ALL   Uc = SUITABLE FOR ALL, ESPECIALLY FOR YOUNG CHILDREN (VIDEO ONLY)   PG = PARENTAL GUIDANCE

Bejewelled ★★★

Adventure   1990 · UK/US · Colour · 95mins

Dynasty's Emma Samms stars in this intriguing yarn, based on the novel *Bejewelled Death*. A curator, travelling by plane to England with a collection of priceless jewels, encounters murder, mayhem and mystery in her efforts to deliver the gems to a London museum. Twists and turns abound in a TV movie originally made for the Disney Channel. The interesting cast includes Denis Lawson, Jerry Hall and Jean Marsh from *Upstairs, Downstairs*.

Emma Samms *Stacey* • Denis Lawson *Alistair* • Dirk Benedict *Gordon* • Jerry Hall *Imelda* • Jean Marsh *Barbara* • Frances de la Tour *Beatrice* • John Bird *Eustace* ■ *Dir* Terry Marcel • *Scr* Tom J Astle, from the novel *Bejewelled Death* by Marion Babson

The Belarus File ★★ PG

Crime drama   1985 · US · Colour · 90mins

Telly Savalas returns to the role that made him a seventies household name for this bowdlerisation of John Loftus's spy novel, *The Belarus Secret*. While he sucks his lollipops and cracks his trademark one-liners with practised ease, Kojak somehow seems the wrong person to go on the track of a murderer who is bumping off Russian survivors of a Nazi concentration camp. Max von Sydow and Suzanne Pleshette soldier on with material that is quite clearly beneath them, receiving little help from the ponderous direction of the usually dependable Robert Markowitz. All in all, a sadly misguided enterprise. 🖿

Telly Savalas *Theo Kojak* • Suzanne Pleshette *Dana Sutton* • Max von Sydow *Peter Barak* • Herbert Berghof *Buchardt* • Dan Frazer *Frank McNeil* • Betsy Aidem *Elissa Barak* • Alan Rosenberg *Lustig* • Charles Brown *Captain Julius Gay* • George Savalas *Stavros* ■ *Dir* Robert Markowitz • *Scr* Albert Ruben, from novel *The Belarus Secret* by John Loftus

Believe in Me ★★

Drama   1971 · US · Colour · 87mins

Michael Sarrazin is the New York hospital intern, Jacqueline Bisset his live-in partner; together they slip into the outer limits of drug addiction. It's the long hours and constant pressure of his job that are to blame, and she just gets dragged along. Eventually, Bisset sees sense, leavining Sarrazin just as heroin looks like taking over from amphetamines. Less of an "entertainment" than the director and writer's previous effort, *The Strawberry Statement*, this is more of a stern health warning aimed at the audience of the time, who habitually turned up stoned to watch a movie.

Michael Sarrazin *Remy* • Jacqueline Bisset *Pamela* • Jon Cypher *Alan* • Allen Garfield *Stutter* • Kurt Dodenhoff *Matthew* • Marcia Jean Kurtz *ER nurse* • Kevin Conway *Clancy* • Roger Robinson *Angel* • Antonio Fargas *Boy* ■ *Dir* Stuart Hagmann • *Scr* Israel Horovitz

The Believers ★★★ 18

Horror   1987 · US · Colour · 109mins

Had anyone else but John Schlesinger, who was responsible for *Marathon Man* and *Midnight Cowboy*, directed this tale of a voodoo cult holding Manhattan in a grip of terror, the result would have been an unpretentious

horror potboiler. But, because Schlesinger clearly feels the material based on Nicholas Conde's bestseller is beneath him, he tries upgrading it to a *Rosemary's Baby*-style exercise in paranoia. Wrong choice. Despite the presence of the ever-dependable Martin Sheen, as a police psychiatrist trying to save his son from Satan, and a very polished style, this uninspired suspense tale is ultimately more depressing than chilling. Contains swearing and violence. 🖿

Martin Sheen *Cal Jamison* • Helen Shaver *Jessica Halliday* • Harley Cross *Chris Jamison* • Robert Loggia *Lieutenant Sean McTaggert* • Elizabeth Wilson *Kate Maslow* • Harris Yulin *Donald Calder* • Lee Richardson *Dennis Maslow* • Richard Masur *Marty Wertheimer* ■ *Dir* John Schlesinger • *Scr* Mark Frost, from the novel *The Religion* by Nicholas Conde

Belizaire the Cajun ★★★

Historical drama
1985 · US · Colour · 101mins

Not so much a western as a "Deep Southern", this American indie effort dramatises the persecution of French-speaking Cajuns by landowners and their henchmen in the 1850s. The main characters are Armand Assante as a Cajun herbalist, Gail Youngs as his former girlfriend and Will Patton as her common-law husband. All are happy to farm the land and keep themselves to themselves, but are inexorably caught up in the violence and necktie parties. The film was developed at Robert Redford's Sundance Institute with the active support of Robert Duvall, who makes a cameo appearance as a preacher at a funeral. Contains some violence and strong language.

Armand Assante *Belizaire Breaux* • Gail Youngs *Alida Thibodaux* • Michael Schoeffling *Hypolite Leger* • Stephen McHattie *James Willoughby* • Will Patton *Matthew Perry* • Nancy Barrett *Rebecca* • Robert Duvall *Preacher* ■ *Dir/Scr* Glen Pitre

Bell, Book and Candle ★★★ U

Comedy   1958 · US · Colour · 102mins

The fun side of *Rosemary's Baby* was a theatre hit for the elegant pairing of Rex Harrison and Lilli Palmer. James Stewart and Kim Novak are pleasant enough in this screen version, but they are left struggling in a lush but charmless adaptation sadly lacking the right witches' brew. Novak was director Richard Quine's muse (and lover), but both did better work apart, particularly Quine, who also directed this film's co-stars Jack Lemmon and Ernie Kovacs to far better effect in *Operation Mad Ball*. Still, the Oscar-nominated art direction/set decoration is strikingly effective, there's a fine performance from Pyewacket the cat, and rival witches Hermione Gingold and Elsa Lanchester are good fun.

James Stewart *Shepherd Henderson* • Kim Novak *Gillian Holroyd* • Jack Lemmon *Nicky Holroyd* • Ernie Kovacs *Sidney Redlitch* • Hermione Gingold *Mrs De Pass* • Elsa Lanchester *Queenie* • Janice Rule *Merle Kittridge* ■ *Dir* Richard Quine • *Scr* Daniel Taradash, from the play by John Van Druten • *Art Director* Cary Odell • *Set Designer* Louis Diage

Bell-Bottom George ★★ U

Second World War comedy
1943 · UK · BW · 97mins

This wartime comedy is so full of tired plot that it could easily have been assembled after a recce of the cutting room floor. George Formby is rejected by the armed forces only to find himself in the thick of the action after he puts on a handy uniform. Like so many British flag-wavers, the storyline concerns a nest of Nazi spies that has confounded the entire secret service. They're no match for an amiable oaf like Formby, however, who even has time for a couple of numbers on the ukelele.

George Formby *George* • Anne Firth *Pat* • Reginald Purdell *Birdie Edwards* • Peter Murray Hill *Shapley* • Charles Farrell *Jim Benson* • Eliot Makeham *Johnson* • Manning Whiley *Church* ■ *Dir* Marcel Varnel • *Scr* Peter Fraser, Edward Dryhurst, from a story by Richard Fisher, Peter Cresswell

A Bell for Adano ★★★

Second World War drama
1945 · US · BW · 103mins

The prolific American director Henry King was always a safe pair of hands but rarely an inspired artist in a film career that spanned half a century, and *A Bell for Adano* is a typical example of his work. No masterpiece, in other words, but still a gentle and engaging Second World War tale about a US Army unit that occupies an Italian town and wins over the locals by, among other things, providing them with a new bell after the old one had been melted down for the war effort.

Gene Tierney *Tina* • John Hodiak *Major Victor Joppolo* • William Bendix *Sergeant Borth* • Glenn Langan *Lieutenant Livingstone* • Richard Conte *Nicolo* • Stanley Prager *Sergeant Trampani* • Henry Morgan [Harry Morgan] *Captain Purvis* ■ *Dir* Henry King • *Scr* Lamar Trotti, Norman Reilly Raine, from the novel by John Hersey

The Bell Jar ★★

Drama   1979 · US · Colour · 112mins

A disappointingly dull adaptation of Sylvia Plath's autobiographical novel, published pseudonymously in 1963 and then under her own name in 1966. The heroine, Esther Greenwood, lives with her widowed mother in comfortable, middle-class fifties America before becoming a journalist in Boston. Bright and pretty, she's also self-absorbed, neurotic, sexually disturbed and suicidal. Greenwood/Plath is played by Marilyn Hassett, a briefly shining star of the seventies; her domineering, repressed mother is respected Broadway actress Julie Harris.

Marilyn Hassett *Esther* • Julie Harris *Mrs Greenwood* • Anne Jackson *Dr Nolan* • Barbara Barrie *Jay Cee* • Robert Klein *Lenny* • Donna Mitchell *Joan* • Mary Louise Weller *Doreen* ■ *Dir* Larry Peerce • *Scr* Marjorie Kellogg, from the novel by Sylvia Plath

The Bellboy ★★★ U

Comedy   1960 · US · BW · 71mins

After 17 films with partner Dean Martin, and a further seven solo, Jerry Lewis persuaded Paramount to let him take on the directorial duties for the first time in one of his own films. Little

more than a series of sketches set in the famous Fontainebleau Hotel in Miami, this very funny movie (which Lewis also produced and wrote) confirmed a clear directorial style, and proved Lewis well capable of continuing the tradition of American comedy auteurs. Unfortunately, this talent has only really been recognised in France; most British critics still loathe Lewis's humour. 🖿

Jerry Lewis *Stanley* • Alex Gerry *Manager* • Bob Clayton *Bell Captain* • Herkie Styles *Bellboy* • Sonny Sands *Bellboy* • Eddie Shaeffer *Bellboy* • David Landfield *Bellboy* ■ *Dir/Scr* Jerry Lewis

Belle de Jour ★★★★★ 18

Psychological drama
1967 · Fr/It · Colour · 95mins

Luis Buñuel embarked on this picture convinced it would be his last. However, the receipt of the Golden Lion at Venice and universal critical acclaim persuaded him to undertake five further features, each one a masterpiece. Stunningly photographed by Sacha Vierny, this complex parable on social, sexual and emotional repression flits between dream and reality with such deft sleights of hand that we are never sure whether we are watching episodes from Catherine Deneuve's life or sharing her fantasies. Deneuve is utterly beguiling as the housewife who seeks escape in prostitution, but the director is the film's true star. In French with English subtitles. Contains sex scenes and some swearing and violence. 🖿

Catherine Deneuve *Séverine Serizy* • Jean Sorel *Pierre Serizy* • Geneviève Page *Mme Anais* • Michel Piccoli *Henri Husson* • Macha Meril *Renee* • Francisco Rabal *Hyppolite* • Pierre Clémenti *Marcel* ■ *Dir* Luis Buñuel • *Scr* Luis Buñuel, Jean-Claude Carrière, from the novel by Joseph Kessel

Belle Epoque ★★★★ 15

Comedy drama
1992 · Sp/Por/Fr · Colour · 104mins

Winner of the best foreign language film Oscar, this charming picture recalls not only a key moment in Spanish history, at the dawning of the short-lived Republic, but also a golden age in film-making when romantic comedies were about innocence, discovery and love. Director Fernando Trueba claims his only mentor is Billy Wilder, but there is more than a touch of Buñuel about the opening sequences and the down-to-earth-with-a-bump finale. Although the romantic entanglements involving army deserter Jorge Sanz and the four bewitching sisters hold centre stage, the film is stolen by Fernando Fernán Gómez as their anarchist artist father. In Spanish with English subtitles. Contains some swearing and sex scenes. 🖿

Fernando Fernan Gomez *Manolo* • Jorge Sanz *Fernando* • Maribel Verdu *Rocio* • Ariadna Gil *Violeta* • Miriam Diaz-Aroca *Clara* • Penelope Cruz *Luz* • Mary Carmen Ramirez *Amalia, Manola's wife* • Gabino Diego *Juanito* ■ *Dir* Fernando Trueba • *Scr* Rafael Azcona, from a story by Rafael Azcona, José Luis García Sanchez , Fernando Trueba

La Belle Équipe ★★★★
Drama   1936 · Fr · BW · 101mins

Jean Renoir was originally to make this classic example of the poetic realist style that dominated French cinema under the Popular Front. However, Julien Duvivier makes a fine job of juggling the quirks and concerns of the five nobodies who decide to invest their lottery winnings in a rundown riverside inn. Jean Gabin is outstanding, as cameraderie turns to contempt and the pals fall out over the renovation and the beguiling Viviane Romance. A revised ending is now generally shown, although it's widely considered that the pessimistic version is more revealing about the fragility of happiness. In French with English subtitles.

Jean Gabin *Jean, "Jeannot"* • Charles Vanel *Charles, "Charlot"* • Raymond Aimos *Raymond, "Tintin"* • Charles Dorat *Jacques* • Raphael Medina *Mario* • Micheline Cheirel *Huguette* • Viviane Romance *Gina* • Marcelle Géniat *The grandmother* • Raymond Cordy *Drunk* ■ *Dir* Julien Duvivier • *Scr* Charles Spaak, Julien Duvivier

La Belle et la Bête
★★★★★ PG

Fantasy   1946 · Fr · BW · 93mins

Although René Clément got a co-directing credit for his technical assistance, this adaptation of Mme Leprince de Beaumont's timeless fairy tale is clearly the work of the poet-director Jean Cocteau. With interiors that owe much to the paintings of Doré and Vermeer, this visual feast is enhanced by the magical realism of Henri Alekan's photography, exquisite costumes and Georges Auric's audacious score. Josette Day is a delight as Beauty, while Jean Marais, in his dual role as the Beast and the Prince, manages to be truly touching beneath the superb make-up. In French with English subtitles.

Jean Marais *Avenant/The Beast/The Prince* • Josette Day *Beauty* • Marcel André *The Merchant* • Mila Parely *Adelaide* • Nane Germon *Felice* • Michel Auclair *Ludovic* ■ *Dir* Jean Cocteau, René Clément • *Scr* Jean Cocteau • *Costume Designer* Christian Bérard, Antonio Castillo, Marcel Escoffier

Une Belle Fille Comme Moi
★★ 15

Black comedy   1973 · Fr · Colour · 93mins

François Truffaut so misjudges the tone of this black comedy that brusque becomes strident and risqué becomes tasteless. Returning to the one woman against five men scenario of the 1957 short *Les Mistons* and *The Bride Wore Black* (1967), he has Bernadette Lafont recall in flashback to sociologist André Dussolier the experiences that landed her in jail. Stuffing the action with in-jokes, autobiographical snippets and cinematic allusions, Truffaut succeeds only in making singer Guy Marchand, ratcatcher Charles Denner and lawyer Claude Brasseur seem as one-dimensional as the satire. A French language film. ▭

Bernadette Lafont *Camille Bliss* • Claude Brasseur *Monsieur Murène* • Charles Denner *Arthur* • Guy Marchand *Sam Golden* • André Dussollier *Stanislas Previne* • Philippe Léotard *Clovis Bliss* • Michel Delahaye *Marchal* ■ *Dir*

François Truffaut • *Scr* François Truffaut, Jean-Loup Dabadie, from the novel *Such a Gorgeous Kid* by Henry Farrell

La Belle Noiseuse ★★★★★ 15
Drama   1991 · Fr · Colour · 228mins

In its full form (as opposed to the 125-minute *Divertimento*), this is a majestic study of art and the agonies of creation from one of the masters of the French New Wave, Jacques Rivette. The sophisticated seduction games played by artist Michel Piccoli as he sketches his new model Emmanuelle Béart make for fascinating viewing, but it will be some time before you see anything as compelling as the artist's hand at work. The sight of the drawing taking shape and the sound of the charcoal or nib scratching paper are hypnotic. This is a courageous and thoroughly rewarding masterpiece. In French with English subtitles. Contains nudity. ▭

Michel Piccoli *Frenhofer* • Jane Birkin *Liz* • Emmanuelle Béart *Marianne* • David Bursztein *Nicolas* • Marianne Denicourt *Julienne* • Gilles Arbona *Porbus* • Bernard Dufour *The painter* ■ *Dir* Jacques Rivette • *Scr* Pascal Bonitzar, Christine Laurent, from the story *Le Chef d'Oeuvre Inconnu* by Honoré de Balzac

The Belle of New York
★★★★ U

Musical   1952 · US · Colour · 80mins

Utterly charming , this MGM Technicolor musical stars the inimitable Fred Astaire in an idle playboy role perfectly suited to his louche screen persona, and the often under-rated Vera-Ellen as the social worker he falls for. If the hoary plot seems familiar, it's because it's not so different from that of *Guys and Dolls* or *Grease*. The film offers many delights along the way, notably Astaire's superb *Shoes with Wings On* number and his *I Wanna Be a Dancin' Man*. Vera-Ellen dazzles in partnership (with vocals dubbed by an uncredited Anita Ellis), and unfairly neglected director Charles Walters turns this elderly Broadway show into a tiptop Metro musical.

Fred Astaire *Charlie Hill* • Vera-Ellen *Angela Bonfils* • Marjorie Main *Mrs Phineas Hill* • Keenan Wynn *Max Ferris* • Alice Pearce *Elsie Wilkins* • Clinton Sundberg *Gilfred Spivak* • Gale Robbins *Dixie McCoy* • Lisa Ferraday *Frenchie* • Henry Slate *Clancy* ■ *Dir* Charles Walters • *Scr* Robert O'Brien, Irving Elinson, Chester Erskine (adaptation), from a play by Hugh Morton

Belle of the Nineties ★★★
Comedy melodrama   1934 · US · BW · 71mins

Following her smash-hits *She Done Him Wrong* and *I'm No Angel*, queen of the double entendre Mae West returned with more of the same in a lavish production under Leo McCarey's expert direction. The screenplay – originally entitled *It Ain't No Sin* until the Hays Office said no – was penned by the buxom star herself. It's no great shakes (St Louis saloon singer engages in two romances simultaneously, while fending off a third) and the men (Roger Pryor, John Mack Brown) are no substitute for Cary Grant, but the innuendos flow, and Mae's musical numbers, which include

My Old Flame, are backed up by Duke Ellington and his Orchestra.

Mae West *Ruby Carter* • Roger Pryor *Tiger Kid* • John Mack Brown [Johnny Mack Brown] *Brooks Claybourne* • John Miljan *Ace Lamont* • Katherine DeMille *Molly Brant* • James Donlan *Kirby* • Stuart Holmes *Dirk* ■ *Dir* Leo McCarey • *Scr* Mae West

Belle of the Yukon ★★
Musical western   1944 · US · Colour · 84mins

This musical Western set in the gold rush days stars Randolph Scott as a con man, so convincing that he is dubbed "Honest John" by the Klondike miners who entrust their gold dust to his safekeeping. Scott's plans are hindered by his romance with the Belle of the title, played by famous stripper Gypsy Rose Lee, while another love affair has singer Dinah Shore falling for William Marshall's piano player. Some nice tongue-in-cheek comedy, lively performances and Shore warbling *Like Someone in Love* contribute to the sporadic pleasures of an over complicated screenplay.

Randolph Scott *Honest John Calhoun* • Gypsy Rose Lee *Belle Devalle* • Dinah Shore *Lettie Candless* • Charles Winninger *Pop Candless* • Bob Burns *Sam Slade* • Florence Bates *Viola* • Guinn Williams *Marshall Maitland* • William Marshall *Steve* ■ *Dir* William A Seiter • *Scr* James Edward Grant, from a story by Houston Branch

Belle Starr ★★
Western   1941 · US · Colour · 87mins

The inexperience of the breathtakingly beautiful Gene Tierney, relatively early in her career, shows through in her unconvincing, one-note performance as a Missouri slave-owner determined to see off the Yankees. This shameless rewriting of history converts America's famous 19th-century female bandit into a Southern plantation owner, complete with loyal "mammy" (Louise Beavers) and a husband (Randolph Scott) who leads guerilla actions against the North under Major Dana Andrews. Short on action and characterisation, the weak script defeats both the cast and director Irving Cummings.

Randolph Scott *Sam Starr* • Gene Tierney *Belle Starr* • Dana Andrews *Major Thomas Crall* • John Shepperd [Shepperd Strudwick] *Ed Shirley* • Elizabeth Patterson *Sarah* • Chill Wills *Blue Duck* • Louise Beavers *Mammy Lou* • Olin Howlin *Jasper Tench* ■ *Dir* Irving Cummings • *Scr* Lamar Trotti, from a story by Niven Busch, Cameron Rogers

Belle Starr's Daughter
★★ U

Western   1948 · US · BW · 85mins

In the 1941 original, Belle Starr was a real six-gun sizzler, as portrayed by Gene Tierney. Seven years later, 20th Century-Fox made this lacklustre sequel. Ruth Roman, playing Belle's daughter, chases marshal George Montgomery who she thinks (wrongly, of course) shot and killed her mother. Not much more than an average co-feature, it's of interest today as one of the higher-budgeted westerns directed by Lesley Selander, who made almost 200 such films for the big screen and spent his declining years turning out 40 episodes of the TV series *Laramie*,

George Montgomery *Tom Jackson* • Rod Cameron *Bob "Bittercreek" Yauntis* • Ruth Roman *Rose of Cimarron* • Wallace Ford *Bailey* • Charles Kemper *Gaffer* • William Phipps *Yuma* • Edith King *Mrs Allen* • Jack Lambert *Brone* • Isabel Jewell *Belle Starr* ■ *Dir* Lesley Selander • *Scr* WR Burnett

Les Belles de Nuit ★★★★
Fantasy drama   1952 · Fr · BW · 89mins

From writer/director René Clair, one of the great stylists of European cinema, comes this wistful, ironic and sexy fantasy about a shy young man who escapes his bleak life by dreaming of adventure and romantic encounters in different places at different historical periods. The star is the devastatingly handsome Gérard Philipe, one of France's great actors as well as the premier matinee idol of his generation. The main purveyors of feminine pulchritude are Gina Lollobrigida and Martine Carol. Strangely and sadly, both Philipe and Carol died prematurely, she at 45, he a week before his 37th birthday. They are marvellous together in this dreamlike film. In French with English subtitles.

Gérard Philipe *Claude* • Gina Lollobrigida *Leila* • Magali Vendeuil *Suzanne* • Marilyn Buferd *Bonny* • Raymond Cordy *Gaston* • Martine Carol *Edmée* ■ *Dir/Scr* René Clair

The Belles of St Trinian's
★★★ U

Comedy   1954 · UK · BW · 86mins

Most people's memory of the *St Trinian's* films dates from their own youth, when the wonderful indiscipline of the tearaways and the debauched indifference of the staff had them longing for their own school to be run along similar lines. In 1954 nothing had ever been seen to compare with this anarchic adaptation of Ronald Searle's cartoons, which turned traditional ideas of female gentility on their heads. Alastair Sim's Miss Fritton and George Cole's Flash Harry became icons of British comic lore, but the real star of the film is Joyce Grenfell. ▭

Alastair Sim *Millicent Fritton/Clarence Fritton* • Joyce Grenfell *Sergeant Ruby Gates* • George Cole *Flash Harry* • Vivienne Martin *Arabella* • Eric Pohlmann *Sultan of Makyad* • Lorna Henderson *Princess Fatima* • Hermione Baddeley *Miss Drownder* • Betty Ann Davies *Miss Waters* ■ *Dir* Frank Launder • *Scr* Frank Launder, Sidney Gilliat, Val Valentine, from the drawings by Ronald Searle

Belles on Their Toes ★★★ U
Comedy   1952 · US · Colour · 89mins

A delightful and equally popular sequel to *Cheaper by the Dozen*, with a lascivious Edward Arnold romancing newly widowed Myrna Loy but not wanting to take her extraordinarily large family with him to the altar. Jeanne Crain heads up the brood and Clifton Webb appears briefly, so don't blink in the finale. Loy battles hard on her own in this early feminist tract, backed by a typical fifties cast, including Debra Paget and Jeffrey Hunter. There's a change of director from the first movie (Henry Levin for Walter Lang), but these films are really a tribute to the unchanging house style at Darryl F Zanuck's 20th Century-Fox.

U = SUITABLE FOR ALL   Uc = SUITABLE FOR ALL, ESPECIALLY FOR YOUNG CHILDREN (VIDEO ONLY)   PG = PARENTAL GUIDANCE

Jeanne Crain *Ann Gilbreth* • Myrna Loy *Mrs Lillian Gilbreth* • Debra Paget *Martha* • Jeffrey Hunter *Dr Bob Grayson* • Edward Arnold *Sam Harper* • Hoagy Carmichael *Tom Bracken* • Barbara Bates *Ernestine* • Robert Arthur *Frank Gilbreth* ■ *Dir* Henry Levin • *Scr* Phoebe Ephron, Henry Ephron, from a novel by Frank B Gilbreth Jr, Ernestine Gilbreth Carey

Bellissima ★★★ U
Drama　　　　　1951 · It · BW · 103mins

Italian aristocrat Luchino Visconti is best known for his sumptuous, operatic approach in films such as *Senso* and *The Leopard*. His early career, however, saw him as a pioneer of neorealism, focusing on the harsh reality of working-class life. In this, his third feature film, the powerful, uninhibited Anna Magnani plays a mother from the slums attempting to get her small daughter into a film at Rome's Cinecittà studios. The only operatic element of the film is the noise, much of it made by the star, but the portrayal of life in the contrasting worlds of the tenements and the film studio is fascinating. In Italian with English subtitles. 🎞

Anna Magnani *Maddalena Cecconi* • Walter Chiari *Alberto Annovazzi* • Tina Apicella *Maria Cecconi* • Gastone Renzelli *Spartaco Cecconi* ■ *Dir* Luchino Visconti • *Scr* Suso Cecchi D'Amico, Francesco Rosi, Luchino Visconti, from the story by Cesare Zavattini

Bellman & True ★★★ 15
Crime thriller　1987 · UK · Colour · 116mins

A low-budget British crime thriller that proves that there's sentiment, if not honour, among thieves. Bernard Hill is the alcoholic computer ace, forever telling bedtime stories to his small stepson (Kieran O'Brien), who's leaned on by villains (Derek Newark, Richard Hope) to hack into a bank prior to a heist. Despite stereotypes – the sinisterly silken chief crook calls victims "Dear Heart" – this includes some great moments of tension, especially the tragi-comic break-in. 🎞

Bernard Hill *Hiller* • Derek Newark *Guv'nor* • Richard Hope *Salto* • Ken Bones *Gort* • Frances Tomelty *Anna* • Kieran O'Brien *Boy* • John Kavanagh *The Donkey* • Arthur Whybrow *The Peterman* ■ *Dir* Richard Loncraine • *Scr* Desmond Lowden, Richard Loncraine, Michael Wearing, from a novel by Desmond Lowden

Bells Are Ringing ★★★ U
Musical comedy　1960 · US · Colour · 125mins

Judy Holliday's Broadway performance was enshrined for ever when she repeated it in this sophisticated but lacklustre Vincente Minnelli musical. By the time this was made, MGM had lost its magic touch and it was a case of *The Party's Over* for its stylish brand of musical tonic. But there is still much pleasure to be had in watching the radiant Holliday in her last screen appearance before her tragically early death from cancer in 1965.

Judy Holliday *Ella Peterson* • Dean Martin *Jeffrey Moss* • Fred Clark *Larry Hastings* • Eddie Foy Jr *J Otto Prantz* • Jean Stapleton *Sue* • Ruth Storey *Gwynne* • Dort Clark *Inspector Barnes* • Frank Gorshin *Blake Barton* ■ *Dir* Vincente Minnelli • *Scr* Betty Comden, Adolph Green, from the musical play by Betty Comden, Adolph Green, Jule Styne

The Bells Go Down ★★ U
Comedy drama　1943 · UK · BW · 85mins

From wartime days, when British film-makers thought the lower orders all spoke cockney and made cups of tea in times of crisis, comes this uneasy Ealing chronicle of the work of a London firefighting unit, which still fascinates for its social documentation and class conflict. As a tribute to the Auxiliary Fire Service, it has an embarrassingly contrived plot, but comedian Tommy Trinder and James Mason still manage to convince by sheer force of personality. 🎞

Tommy Trinder *Tommy Turk* • James Mason *Ted Robbins* • Philip Friend *Bob* • Mervyn Johns *Sam* • Billy Hartnell [William Hartnell] *Bookes* • Finlay Currie *Dist Officer MacFarlane* • Philippa Hiatt *Nan* • Meriel Forbes *Susie* ■ *Dir* Basil Dearden • *Scr* Roger MacDougall, from the novel by Stephen Black

Bells of Rosarita ★★★
Western　　　1945 · US · BW · 68mins

According to this somewhat offbeat Roy Rogers picture, cowboy stars are just as resourceful in real life as they are up there on screen. Rogers is quietly making a western on location at a circus when he finds out the pretty owner (Dale Evans) is in danger of being cheated out of her property. Roy summons five of his fellow Republic stars – "Wild Bill" Elliott, Allan "Rocky" Lane, Don "Red" Barry, Robert Livingston and Sunset Carson – to stage a benefit on her behalf and they end up corralling the bad guys.

Roy Rogers • George "Gabby" Hayes *Baggy Whittaker* • Dale Evans *Sue Farnum* • Adele Mara *Patty Phillips* • William Elliott • Allan Lane • Donald Barry • Robert Livingston • Sunset Carson ■ *Dir* Frank McDonald • *Scr* Jack Townley

The Bells of St Mary's ★★★ U
Musical drama　1945 · US · BW · 125mins

A massively popular success in its day, this pairs Bing Crosby with beautiful *Casablanca* star Ingrid Bergman. Crosby reprises the role that won him a coveted Oscar statuette, that of wise and loveable Father O'Malley from *Going My Way*. Today, Crosby's priest seems rather insufferable as he helps Sister Ingrid fix up her rundown mission with a bit of song and a lot of charm. Crosby fans will brook no arguments, of course, but others may feel director Leo McCarey has his tongue well and truly in his cheek and only made this for the money. Still, it may work for you, and Bergman looks wonderful in a wimple. 🎞

Bing Crosby *Father O'Malley* • Ingrid Bergman *Sister Benedict* • Henry Travers *Mr Bogardus* • Joan Carroll *Patsy* • Martha Sleeper *Patsy's mother* • William Gargan *Joe Gallagher* • Ruth Donnelly *Sister Michael* ■ *Dir* Leo McCarey • *Scr* Dudley Nichols, from a story by Leo McCarey

Bells of San Angelo ★★ U
Western　　　1947 · US · Colour · 77mins

This was the Republic studio movie intended to toughen up the image of Roy Rogers, whose hand-tailored outfits had never previously shown any signs of dirt, and whose ethics

outweighed his screen presence. Here, villain John McGuire actually beats up our hero, and, at last, in the fight sequences there's a realistic feeling of characters being hurt. Indeed, Rogers himself moves as comfortably in the action sequences as he does wielding a guitar. He was also obviously comfortable with leading lady Dale Evans because he married her the same year. The tougher strain continued in subsequent Rogers movies.

Roy Rogers • Dale Evans *Lee Madison* • Andy Devine *Cookie* • John McGuire *Rex Gridley* • Olaf Hytten *Lionel Bates* ■ *Dir* William Witney • *Scr* Sloan Nibley

Belly ★★ 18
Crime thriller　1998 · US · Colour · 95mins

This frenetic thriller, as directed by rap video film-maker Hype Williams, is all stuttering edits and flash visuals, as it tells of the decline and fall of two violent young black men (played by rap musicians Nas and DMX) in the last weeks of 1999. The film has dubious credentials, having been banned by an American cinema chain on the grounds that "it raises concerns about the film's overwhelmingly negative and violent depiction of African-Americans, as well as its potential to create disruptive situations in our theatres". Despite its dramatic explosiveness, this is a movie that's going nowhere. Contains swearing and violence.

Nas [Nasir Jones] *Sincere* • DMX [Earl Simmons] *Tommy Brown* • Taral Hicks *Kisha* • Tionne "T-Boz" Watkins *Tionne* • Method Man [Clifford Smith] *Shameek* • Tyrin Turner *Big* • Hassan Johnson *Mark* • Power [Oliver Grant] *Knowledge* ■ *Dir* Hype Williams • *Scr* Hype Williams, from a story by Anthony Bodden, Nas [Nasir Jones]

The Belly of an Architect ★★★ 15
Psychological drama
1987 · It/UK · Colour · 113mins

This features Peter Greenaway's trademark strongly visual approach and multiple referencing to birth, death and the insubstantial human condition. Brian Dennehy stars as a self-obsessed American architect travelling to Italy to supervise an exhibition about an 18th-century French architect. His work is subverted by his preoccupation with his own stomach pains (cue a scene where he photocopies his belly obsessively) and with his wife Chloe Webb's attempts to conceive. This won't disappoint Greenaway fans – but dissenters may prefer to avoid it. 🎞

Brian Dennehy *Stourley Kracklite* • Chloe Webb *Louisa Kracklite* • Lambert Wilson *Caspasian Speckler* • Sergio Fantoni *Io Speckler* • Stefania Casini *Flavia Speckler* • Vanni Corbellini *Frederico* • Alfredo Varelli *Julio* • Geoffrey Copleston *Caspetti* • Francesco Carnelutti *Pastarri* ■ *Dir/Scr* Peter Greenaway

Beloved ★★ 15
Period drama　1998 · US · Colour · 164mins

Director Jonathan Demme translates Toni Morrison's acclaimed novel to the screen with mixed results, garnering a strong lead performance from Oprah Winfrey, but ultimately getting bogged down in a laborious attempt to make

something worthy. Winfrey is the ex-slave who killed her own daughter to prevent her being taken into slavery, only to have a young, childlike woman (an overcooked performance from Thandie Newton) turn up on her doorstep years later who seems to have all the characteristics of the child she killed. Winfrey is surprisingly moving and is given solid support by Danny Glover, but they can't save this from ending up as a successful cure for insomnia. Contains violence and some nudity. 🎞

Oprah Winfrey *Sethe* • Danny Glover *Paul D* • Thandie Newton *Beloved* • Kimberly Elise *Denver* • Beah Richards *Baby Suggs* • Lisa Gay Hamilton *Younger Sethe* • Albert Hall *Stamp Paid* • Irma P Hall *Ella* ■ *Dir* Jonathan Demme • *Scr* Akosua Busia, Richard LaGravenese, Adam Brooks, from the novel by Toni Morrison

Beloved Enemy ★★★ U
Romantic drama　1936 · US · BW · 82mins

An odd subject for the movie debut of director HC ("Hank") Potter, the Yale Drama School graduate best remembered for comedies such as *Hellzapoppin'* and *Mr Blandings Builds His Dream House*. One of the few mainstream Hollywood movies to deal with the political upheaval in Ireland in the early part of this century, this features top-billed Merle Oberon falling for Irish rebel leader Brian Aherne. Though the title's of literary derivation, the plot clearly isn't. Nevertheless, it's an intelligent and well-made romantic drama, politics aside. Watch for future star David Niven in a supporting role. 🎞

Merle Oberon *Helen Drummond* • Brian Aherne *Dennis Riordan* • Karen Morley *Cathleen* • Theodore von Eltz *O'Brian* • Jerome Cowan *O'Rourke* • David Niven *Gerald Preston* • John Burton *Hall* ■ *Dir* HC Potter • *Scr* John Balderston, Rose Franken, William Brown Meloney, David Hart, from a story by John Balderston

Beloved Infidel ★★★
Romantic drama
1959 · US · Colour · 122mins

This screen version of Sheilah Graham's bestselling memoir is sunk by the staggering miscasting of Gregory Peck as F Scott Fitzgerald, though Deborah Kerr makes a brave stab at Graham. Director Henry King concentrates on the period feel, and the CinemaScope photography is stunning, but to no avail. Legend has it that Peck was annoyed that the first edit of the film favoured Kerr, and summoned brilliant film editor William Reynolds to see him. "Why do you think they pay me a fortune to do this?" demanded Peck. "I really can't imagine," replied Reynolds.

Gregory Peck *F Scott Fitzgerald* • Deborah Kerr *Sheilah Graham* • Eddie Albert *Carter* • Philip Ober *John Wheeler* • Herbert Rudley *Stan Harris* • John Sutton *Lord Donegal* • Karin Booth *Janet Pierce* • Ken Scott *Robinson* ■ *Dir* Henry King • *Scr* Sy Bartlett, from the book by Sheilah Graham, Gerold Frank

Beloved/Friend ★★★
Drama　　　1998 · Sp · Colour · 91mins

Catalan director Ventura Pons is renowned for ensemble pieces in which emotions are revealed through earnest conversation. Such is the case here, as a group of friends fall out over the contents of a dying academic's will. Adapted from his own play, *Testament*, by Josep M Benet i Jornet (who also scripted *Actresses* for Pons), the action retains a staginess that enhances the airless atmosphere of this enclosed world. However, it's the intensity of the performances that really gives the intricate drama its fascination. In particular, Josep Maria Pou excels as the medievalist forced to confront both his own fears and the expectations of others. In Catalan with English subtitles.

Josep Maria Pou [Jose Maria Pou] *Jaume Clara* • Rosa Maria Sarda *Fanny* • Mario Gas *Pere Roure* • David Selvas *David Vila* • Irene Montala *Alba* ■ *Dir* Ventura Pons • *Scr* Josep M Benet i Jornet from his play *Testament*

The Belstone Fox ★★PG

Drama 1973 · UK · Colour · 98mins

Nice guys finish last is the moral of this workmanlike adaptation of David Rook's novel. Eric Porter is the huntsman who adopts an abandoned fox cub and rears it with a litter of puppy hounds. When the hunting season starts, the fox reverts to its traditional role as quarry and Porter lives to regret his moment of weakness. Porter and Rachel Roberts acquit themselves adequately but the film ultimately impresses more for its wildlife photography than for its dramatic interest. ▣

Eric Porter *Asher* • Rachel Roberts *Cathie* • Jeremy Kemp *Kendrick* • Bill Travers *Tod* • Dennis Waterman *Stephen* • Heather Wright *Jenny* ■ *Dir* James Hill • *Scr* James Hill, from the novel *Ballad of the Belstone Fox* by David Rook • *Cinematographer* John Wilcox, James Allen

Ben ★★

Horror 1972 · US · Colour · 94mins

This sequel to *Willard* is probably best known for its theme song (which was a hit for Michael Jackson), as few horror aficionados have much time for its unconvincing blend of gore and gushing sentimentality. Yet it's a polished piece of work, with director Phil Karlson exercising the restraint he brought to his fifties crime films, while the experience of 150-plus features is readily apparent in the atmospheric photography of Russell Metty (shooting his penultimate picture). Moreover, Lee Harcourt Montgomery is fine as the kid sheltering the rodent hordes, and Joseph Campanella business-like as the pursuing cop who discovers who is leading a pack of killer rats.

Lee Harcourt Montgomery [Lee Montgomery] *Danny Garrison* • Joseph Campanella *Cliff Kirtland* • Arthur O'Connell *Bill Hatfield* • Rosemary Murphy *Beth Garrison* • Meredith Baxter *Eve Garrison* • Kaz Garas *Joe Greer* • Paul Carr *Kelly* • Richard Van Fleet *Reade* ■ *Dir* Phil Karlson • *Scr* Gilbert A Ralston, from characters created by Stephen Gilbert

Ben-Hur ★★★★★PG

Historical epic 1959 · US · Colour · 217mins

The epic *di tutti epics*, and, at the time, the most costly movie ever made. Many believe that it is not a match for the twenties' silent version, while it certainly lasts almost as long

as the Roman Empire itself. Nor will it ever win any prizes for experimental film-making. But never mind the quality of the at-times ponderous script, enjoy Charlton Heston's chariot-driving, galley-rowing and toga-wearing and, above all, feel the vital statistics. A thousand-strong force toiled for a year to construct the 18-acre chariot arena, which was eventually filled with 8,000 extras for the 20-minute race that forms the famous climax. The film, in all, used over 300 sets, 40,000 tons of sand (for the chariot track) and swept up 11 Oscars, a record-breaking total that was equalled in 1998 by James Cameron's *Titanic*. ▣

Charlton Heston *Judah Ben-Hur* • Stephen Boyd *Messala* • Haya Harareet *Esther* • Jack Hawkins *Quintus Arrius* • Hugh Griffith *Sheik Ilderim* • Martha Scott *Miriam* • Cathy O'Donnell *Tirzah* • Frank Thring *Pontius Pilate* • Sam Jaffe *Simonides* ■ *Dir* William Wyler • *Scr* Karl Tunberg, from the novel by Lew Wallace • *Music* Miklos Rozsa • *Cinematographer* Robert L Surtees [Robert Surtees] • *Special Effects* A Arnold Gillespie, Robert MacDonald, Milo Lory • *Music* Miklos Rozsa • *Art Director* Edward Carfagno, William A Horning • *Costume Designer* Elizabeth Haffenden • *Editor* Ralph E Winters, John Dunning

Ben-Hur: a Tale of Christ ★★★★★

Silent biblical epic 1925 · US · BW and Colour · 143mins

A landmark movie in every respect. Its story of the friendship and hatred between a Jew and a Roman allowed for plenty of moralising as well as rousing action scenes. Lewis Wallace's novel – a Victorian potboiler – had been a Broadway hit and MGM almost broke the bank buying the rights. Filming was due to begin in Italy with George Walsh as Ben-Hur, under the direction of Charles Brabin. But the footage was so terrible MGM junked everything and fired Walsh. He was replaced by Ramon Novarro, and Fred Niblo took over as director. The footage was better, but filming the sea battle claimed the lives of at least three Italian extras. The result flabbergasted critics and audiences alike, but its final cost of $4 million was too much to see any profit. Even today, the scale of the picture is staggering, and the occasional static, over-pious scenes are a small price to pay for so much stunning spectacle.

Ramon Novarro *Ben-Hur* • Francis X Bushman *Messala* • May McAvoy *Esther* • Betty Bronson *Mary* • Claire McDowell *Princess of Hur* • Kathleen Key *Tirzah* • Carmel Myers *Iras* ■ *Dir* Fred Niblo • *Scr* Bess Meredyth, Carey Wilson, June Mathis, from the novel by Lew Wallace

Bend of the River ★★★★

Western 1952 · US · Colour · 90mins

Originally known in the UK as *Where the River Bends*, this is a magnificent western, one of a superb postwar series of films starring James Stewart and directed by Anthony Mann. Here, Stewart is a wagon train scout trying to hide his past, pitted against former partner Arthur Kennedy in a story that takes on the dimensions of Greek tragedy. Watch, too, for an early star-making performance from Rock Hudson, who forms a bond with

reformed outlaw Stewart. A satisfying work, with action sequences and performances that repay several viewings.

James Stewart *Glyn McLyntock* • Arthur Kennedy *Cole Garett* • Rock Hudson *Trey Wilson* • Julia Adams [Julie Adams] *Laura Baile* • Lori Nelson *Marjie* • Jay C Flippen *Jeremy Baile* • Stepin' Fetchit [Stepin Fetchit] *Adam* ■ *Dir* Anthony Mann • *Scr* Borden Chase, from the novel *Bend of the Snake* by Bill Gulick

Beneath the Planet of the Apes ★★★15

Science-fiction adventure 1969 · US · Colour · 90mins

The first sequel to the enormously successful *Planet of the Apes* is also the best. Less subtle and profound than its predecessor, it's still an exciting and colourful action adventure. This time out, astronaut James Franciscus and chimpanzee scientist Kim Hunter search for Charlton Heston (star of the first film) in the nuclear-devastated future, evading militaristic apes only to stumble upon an underground community of mutant, telepathic humans. It ends somewhat hammily in the buried ruins of Grand Central Station, but the destruction of the world didn't stop three more progressively silly sequels from appearing. Contains violence. ▣

Charlton Heston *George Taylor* • James Franciscus *Brent* • Kim Hunter *Dr Zira* • Maurice Evans *Dr Zaius* • Linda Harrison *Nova* • Paul Richards (1) *Mendez* • Victor Buono *Fat Man* • James Gregory *Ursus* ■ *Dir* Ted Post • *Scr* Paul Dehn, Mort Abrahams, from characters created by Pierre Boulle

Beneath the 12-Mile Reef ★★U

Adventure 1953 · US · Colour · 100mins

Having already shot the Crucifixion (*The Robe*) and Marilyn Monroe (*How to Marry a Millionaire*) in CinemaScope, 20th Century-Fox took its new wonder process underwater for this scuba-frolic. Robert Wagner gives a dash as a sponge diver, Gilbert Roland is his dad, Terry Moore is the love interest, Richard Boone the heavy and an octopus shows up when the plot begins to leak like... well, like a sponge. When the guys get into frogman mode, you can't tell who's who, and on the surface you don't much care.

Robert Wagner *Tony Petrakis* • Gilbert Roland *Mike Petrakis* • J Carrol Naish *Soak* • Richard Boone *Thomas Rhys* • Harry Carey Jr *Griff Rhys* • Terry Moore *Gwyneth Rhys* • Peter Graves (1) *Arnold* • Angela Clarke *Mama* ■ *Dir* Robert D Webb • *Scr* Al Bezzerides

Beneath the Valley of the Ultra Vixens ★★★

Cult erotic comedy 1979 · US · Colour · 85mins

This quintessential sex comedy is Russ Meyer's last movie to date as director, and it's all here: comic violence, insatiable mega-busty women, religion, necrophilia, impotent bumbling men, chainsaws and Martin Bormann. The plot revolves around stripper "Kitten" Natividad's attempts to steer her husband away from perversion, with Anne Marie and Uschi

Digard along for the roller coaster ride through Meyer's lusty small-town landscape. The director plays himself in this satirical semi-autobiography, which has a strong moral code at its soft-core centre.

Francesca "Kitten" Natividad *Lavonia/Lola Langusta* • Anne Marie *Eufaula Roop* • Ken Kerr *Lamar Shedd* • June Mack *"Junk-yard" Sal* • Uschi Digard *Supersoul* ■ *Dir* Russ Meyer • *Scr* Roger Ebert, Russ Meyer

Benefit of the Doubt ★★★18

Thriller 1993 · US/Ger · Colour · 87mins

A modest, occasionally gripping little thriller that manages some neat variations on a familiar theme. An almost unrecognisable Amy Irving is the struggling single mum who is less than enamoured when she learns that her father (Donald Sutherland) is about to be released from prison, particularly because it was her testimony as a child that convicted him of the murder of her mother. The two leads, particularly the ambivalent Sutherland, are good and there is solid support from Graham Greene as the local sheriff, but the film is let down by a half-hearted climax. Contains violence, swearing and nudity. ▣

Donald Sutherland *Frank Braswell* • Amy Irving *Karen Braswell* • Rider Strong *Pete Braswell* • Christopher McDonald *Dan* • Graham Greene *Sheriff Calhoun* • Theodore Bikel *Gideon Lee* • Gisele Kovach *Susanna* • Ferdinand Mayne [Ferdy Mayne] *Mueller* • Julie Hasel *Young Karen* ■ *Dir* Jonathan Heap • *Scr* Christopher Keyser, Jeffrey Polman, Michael Lieber

Bengal Brigade ★★U

Period adventure 1954 · US · Colour · 87mins

Straight after *Death of a Salesman* and *The Wild One*, director Laslo Benedek cranked out this North-West Frontier caper. Rock Hudson plays a British Army captain who is framed and court-martialled, and resigns his commission. He becomes a big-game hunter yet still manages to suss out rebel plans, win the girl and keep the British Raj running. The Indians in this case wear turbans rather than feathers.

Rock Hudson *Jeff Claybourne* • Arlene Dahl *Vivian Morrow* • Ursula Thiess *Latah* • Torin Thatcher *Colonel Morrow* • Arnold Moss *Rajah Karam Jee* • Dan O'Herlihy *Captain Ronald Blaine* • Michael Ansara *Major Puran Singh* ■ *Dir* Laslo Benedek • *Scr* Richard Alan Simmons, from the novel by Hall Hunter

Bengazi ★★

Adventure 1955 · US · BW · 79mins

Richard Conte here makes the most of a script that seems content to rehash a job-lot of clichés and assorted deadends. Recalling his peak of fame as a hard-nut gangster, Conte is energetically gritty playing an unsavoury character trying to unearth hidden gold in North Africa. Sadly, director John Brahm's laudable attempts at style are punctured by moments of unplanned hilarity, including Richard Carlson's beyond-ludicrous attempts at a Scottish accent. Mediocre.

Richard Conte *Gilmore* • Victor McLaglen *Donovan* • Richard Carlson *Levering* • Mala Powers *Aileen Donovan* • Richard Erdman *Selby* • Hillary Brooke *Nora* • Maury Hill *Peters*

• Jay Novello *Basim* • Albert Carrier *MacMillan* ■ *Dir* John Brahm • *Scr* Endre Bohem, Louis Vittes, from a story by Jeff Bailey

Benji   ★★★ 🄵

Adventure   1974 · US · Colour · 85mins

So what if the production values are shoddy, the kids can't act and the plot was old hat when Rin Tin Tin was a pup. This is a cheer-to-the-rafters adventure, thanks to the exuberant ingenuity and adorably expressive face of a mongrel called Higgins. A veteran of TV's *Petticoat Junction*, the 18-year-old dog was brought out of retirement for this role of a lifetime, as the family pet who foils a kidnapping attempt. Aided by his dainty assistant Tiffany, Benji pulls off a series of truly amazing tricks that won him the Georgie for the animal act of the year. 🄳

Peter Breck *Dr Chapman* • Edgar Buchanan *Bill* • Patsy Garrett *Mary* • Allen Fiuzat *Paul* • Cynthia Smith *Cindy* ■ *Dir/Scr* Joe Camp

Benji the Hunted   ★★

Adventure   1987 · US · Colour · 89mins

A litter of cuddly cougar cubs comes close to upstaging our cute hero in the final film (to date) in the Benji series. It was made seven years after *Oh, Heavenly Dog!*, but the passage of time did little to refresh director Joe Camp's imagination, as the plot is nothing more than a cross-breed between a Lassie movie and Disney adventures such as *The Incredible Journey*. However, with a shipwreck, a trek through the wilderness and a series of murderous attacks, it's packed with enough incident to retain the interest even of children with short attention spans.

Red Steagall *Hunter* • Nancy Francis *Newscaster* • Frank Inn • Mike Francis *TV cameraman* ■ *Dir/Scr* Joe Camp

Benny and Joon   ★★★ 🄵🄵

Comedy drama   1993 · US · Colour · 94mins

You'll either find this so-so romantic fable a whimsical joy or annoyingly eccentric, as beguiling man-child Johnny Depp woos mentally unstable Mary Stuart Masterson, much to her brother Aidan Quinn's concern. It's one of those "lunatics are saner than the rest of us" polemics, admittedly heartfelt but, ultimately, too underwritten to put its message across properly. However, the performances do wonders in papering over the credibility gaps, and Depp's silent movie skills, much in evidence because his character is besotted with Buster Keaton and Charlie Chaplin, are truly remarkable. 🄳

Johnny Depp *Sam* • Mary Stuart Masterson *Joon Pearl* • Aidan Quinn *Benny Pearl* • Julianne Moore *Ruthie* • Oliver Platt *Eric* • CCH Pounder *Doctor Garvey* • Dan Hedaya *Thomas* • Joe Grifasi *Mike* • William H Macy *Randy Burch* ■ *Dir* Jeremiah Chechik • *Scr* Barry Berman, from a story by Barry Berman, Leslie McNeil

The Benny Goodman Story   ★★ 🄵

Musical biography
1955 · US · Colour · 116mins

Universal had a surprise smash hit with *The Glenn Miller Story* and this

forlorn follow-up proved that lightning doesn't strike twice, despite the great Benny himself playing clarinet to Steve Allen's miming. Trouble is, TV chat show host Allen lacks both the screen charisma and acting experience to make this involving, even though he's surrounded by ace real-life musicians and has Donna Reed as co-star. Inexperienced director Valentine Davies (best remembered for penning the Oscar-winning *Miracle on 34th Street*) can't manage the pace or the mood, and, of course, there's no tragic ending, either. The Technicolor's nice to look at, though.

Steve Allen *Benny Goodman* • Donna Reed *Alice Hammond* • Berta Gersten *Mom Goodman* • Herbert Anderson *John Hammond* • Robert F Simon [Robert Simon] *Pop Goodman* • Sammy Davis Sr *Fletcher Henderson* • Dick Winslow *Gil Rodin* ■ *Dir/Scr* Valentine Davies

Bent   ★★★ 🄵🄸

Drama   1996 · UK/US/Jap · Colour · 100mins

Lothaire Bluteau and Clive Owen star as fellow prisoners and lovers against the background of the appallingly cruel conditions of the Nazi concentration camps. Martin Sherman adapted his own West End play about Nazi homophobia and persecution, while theatre stalwart Sean Mathias directs. Mathias fails to give the film any emotional urgency – even in the opening Berlin party scenes in which Mick Jagger intrudes to no real purpose – so it's the actors, including Ian McKellen, who have to carry the main burden. They stagger a bit, but provide the impetus the direction lacks. Contains violence, swearing and sex scenes. 🄳

Lothaire Bluteau *Horst* • Clive Owen *Max* • Ian McKellen *Uncle Freddie* • Mick Jagger *Greta/ George* • Brian Webber *Rudy* • Nikolaj Waldau *Wolf* • Jude Law *Stormtrooper* ■ *Dir* Sean Mathias • *Scr* Martin Sherman

Bequest to the Nation   ★★

Historical drama
1972 · UK · Colour · 116mins

Although the tone is far too lofty for playwright Terence Rattigan's account of the relationship between Lord Nelson and Lady Hamilton to be called the Trafalgar hero's "little bit on the side", that's exactly what it is – and it matters about as much as that derogatory description. Fine performances by Peter Finch as Nelson and Glenda Jackson as Hamilton do little to animate the walking-waxworks style of what amounts to video history.

Glenda Jackson *Lady Emma Hamilton* • Peter Finch *Lord Horatio Nelson* • Michael Jayston *Captain Hardy* • Anthony Quayle *Lord Minto* • Margaret Leighton *Lady Frances Nelson* • Dominic Guard *Master George Matcham Jr* • Nigel Stock *George Matcham Sr* • Barbara Leigh-Hunt *Catherine "Catty" Matcham* ■ *Dir* James Cellan Jones • *Scr* Terence Rattigan, from his play

Berkeley Square   ★★★★ 🄤

Period romantic fantasy
1933 · US · BW · 89mins

Peter Standish (Leslie Howard) is so entranced by the early 18th-century diaries of his namesake ancestor that he takes on his identity and finds himself transported back to a

periwigged past, where he consorts with the likes of Sir Joshua Reynolds. This quaint and delightful fantasy, ornamented with immaculate and sumptuous period detail, has Howard repeating the role he created on Broadway with all the polished elegance and poetic presence that made him a revered star of stage and screen. Heather Angel plays the love interest for both Standishes and the accomplished direction is by Scottish-born veteran Frank Lloyd.

Leslie Howard *Peter Standish* • Heather Angel *Helen Pettigrew* • Valerie Taylor *Kate Pettigrew* • Irene Browne *Lady Ann Pettigrew* • Beryl Mercer *Mrs Barwick* • Colin Keith-Johnston *Tom Pettigrew* • Alan Mowbray *Maj Clinton* • Lionel Belmore *Innkeeper* ■ *Dir* Frank Lloyd • *Scr* Sonya Levien, John L Balderston, from the play by John L Balderston

Berlin Alexanderplatz   ★★★

Drama   1931 · Ger · BW · 90mins

With sound still in its infancy, it was the visual aspect of this adaptation of Alfred Döblin's sprawling novel that made the greatest impression, even though the author co-wrote the screenplay. Clearly influenced by the "city symphony" style so popular in the late silent era, director Phil Jutzi captures the sights and rhythms of Berlin with a vibrancy that stands in stark contrast to the grim Depression existence of reformed criminal Heinrich George, whose obsession with Margarete Schlegel prompts him to return to his wicked ways. Something of the book's scope would be restored in Rainer Werner Fassbinder's magisterial 13-part television version. In German with English subtitles.

Heinrich George *Franz Bieberkopf* • Bernhard Minetti *Reinhold* • Margarete Schlegel *Mieze* • Albert Florath *Pums* • Paul Westermeier *Henschke* ■ *Dir* Phil Jutzi • *Scr* Alfred Döblin, Hans Wilhelm, from the novel by Alfred Döblin

Berlin Alexanderplatz

★★★★★

Drama   1980 · W Ger/It · Colour · 921mins

Originally screened as a 13-part TV series, this epic study of sexual obsession is far superior to Phil Jutzi's 1931 version, even though Alfred Döblin, who wrote the source novel, was among that film's scriptwriters. The book was Rainer Werner Fassbinder's lifelong inspiration and his fascination with its themes and central character, Franz Biberkopf, is evident from the deeply personal epilogue. As played by Günther Lamprecht, Biberkopf is the plaything of a callous society that would rather destroy him than allow him to thrive as an individual. A remarkable undertaking that has to be seen. In German with English subtitles.

Hanna Schygulla *Eva* • Günther Lamprecht [Günter Lamprecht] *Franz Biberkopf* • Franz Buchrieser *Meck* • Gottfried John *Reinhold* • Barbara Sukowa *Mieze* • Peter Kolleck *Nachum* • Elisabeth Trissenaar *Lina* • Brigitte Mira *Frau Bast* • Hans Zander *Eliser* • Mechthild Grossmann *Paula* • Karin Baal *Minna* ■ *Dir* Rainer Werner Fassbinder • *Scr* Rainer Werner Fassbinder, from the novel by Alfred Doblin

Berlin Correspondent   ★★ 🄤

Second World War spy drama
1942 · US · BW · 69mins

A routine, low-budget wartime espionage drama, set in the days before Pearl Harbor, with Dana Andrews as an American radio journalist in Berlin whose broadcasts contain coded information about Nazi plans. He is rumbled by beautiful Virginia Gilmore who, don't you know it, is about to forsake her Nazi beliefs. A hazardous flight to Switzerland ensues. This takes some believing, as do Andrews's attempts to mimic German officers without his accent ever leaving his native Mississippi.

Virginia Gilmore *Karen Hauen* • Dana Andrews *Bill Roberts* • Mona Maris *Carla* • Martin Kosleck *Captain von Rau* • Sig Rumann [Sig Ruman] *Dr Dietrich* • Kurt Katch *Weiner* • Erwin Kalser *Mr Hauen* • Hans Schumm *Gunther* ■ *Dir* Eugene Forde • *Scr* Steve Fisher, Jack Andrews

Berlin Express   ★★★

Spy thriller   1948 · US · BW · 86mins

The average, nondescript title masks a really tense suspense tale from talented cult director Jacques Tourneur, in his *film noir* period before he hit his swashbuckling stride with *The Flame and the Arrow* and *Anne of the Indies*. Paul Lukas is the suave German democrat kidnapped by an underground group of nasty Nazis opposed to the unification of their country. Merle Oberon who forms part of a symbolic Big Four world powers casting coup, of which Robert Ryan is genuinely impressive. The Nazis are strictly clichéd, but there's an authentic documentarist view of postwar Germany and Tourneur keeps up the tension throughout.

Merle Oberon *Lucienne Mirbeau* • Robert Ryan *Robert Lindley* • Charles Korvin *Henri Perrot* • Paul Lukas *Dr Heinrich Bernhardt* • Robert Coote *James Sterling* • Reinhold Schunzel *Johann Walther* • Roman Toporow *Lieutenant Maxim* • Peter Von Zerneck *Hans Schmidt* ■ *Dir* Jacques Tourneur • *Scr* Harold Medford, from a story by Curt Siodmak

Berlin Jerusalem   ★★★

Drama
1989 · Fr/Is/Neth/UK · Colour · 89mins

Israeli director Amos Gitai's film, which he also co-wrote, may be an uphill struggle for many viewers, but it's still a fascinating attempt to depict the lives and friendship of two little-known, real-life women in the twenties and thirties: the German poet Else Lasker-Schüler and the Russian revolutionary Tania Shochat. The ambition often outpaces the technique, but Gitai is helped immeasurably by the sheer artistry of the great French cinematographer Henri Alekan. Lisa Kreuzer, Rivka Neuman and veteran character actor Vernon Dobtcheff try to bring life to the interweaving stories, but the production values and uncertain pace do no service to the film. In German and Hebrew with English subtitles.

Lisa Kreuzer *Else* • Rivka Neuman *Tania* • Markus Stockhausen *Ludwig* • Vernon Dobtcheff *Editor* • Veronica Lazare [Veronica

Lazar] *Secretary* • Bernard Eisenschitz *Man in Berlin café* ■ *Dir* Amos Gitai • *Scr* Amos Gitai, Gudie Lawaeyz

Berlin: Symphony of a Great City ★★★★★

Experimental silent documentary
1927 · Ger · BW · 77mins

As with so much in German silent cinema, this artistic masterpiece was conceived by the screenwriter Carl Mayer, who was to disassociate himself from the project when director Walter Ruttman opted for an abstract, rather than a sociological, approach. Applying still novel theories of montage to Karl Freund's vibrant imagery, Ruttman created a rhythmical portrait of the city, which seems to last a day, but was, in fact, the product of 18 months of candid photography. Dropping in on various workplaces and night spots, the film pulses with life and remains as inventive and viscerally thrilling as it must have seemed to audiences in 1927.

Dir Walter Ruttmann • *Scr* Walter Ruttmann, Karl Freund, from an idea by Carl Mayer

The Bermuda Mystery ★★

Crime mystery   1944 · US · BW · 65mins

This watchable little forties B-movie is the usual mixture of murder and money, featuring the rather too stolid Preston Foster in the lead and an interesting support cast. Ann Rutherford, perhaps best known as Polly Benedict in the Andy Hardy films, makes a charming leading lady, while the rather camp Charles Butterworth gives added value. While director Benjamin Stoloff's picture is nothing special, it's very characteristic of its type.

Preston Foster *Steve Carromond* • Ann Rutherford *Constance Martin* • Charles Butterworth *Dr Tilford* • Helene Reynolds *Angela* • Jean Howard *Mrs Tilford* • Richard Lane *Detective Donovan* • Roland Drew *Mr Best* ■ *Dir* Benjamin Stoloff • *Scr* W Scott Darling, from a story by John Larkin

Berserk ★★ 12

Mystery melodrama
1967 · US · Colour · 92mins

After their successful teaming in the Gothic monstrosity *What Ever Happened to Baby Jane?*, both Bette Davis and Joan Crawford found twilight career success in a run of chillers of varying standards. Here Crawford stars in a tale about murderous goings-on in a circus, which is at least marginally better than her caveman fiasco *Trog*. She's backed up by some interesting faces, ranging from Ty Hardin to Diana Dors, but, sadly, it just isn't any good. It's a shame to watch an actress of Crawford's stature gawking at such explicit sadism, for many that is this tawdry flick's main appeal.

Joan Crawford *Monica Rivers* • Ty Hardin *Frank Hawkins* • Diana Dors *Matilda* • Michael Gough *Dorando* • Judy Geeson *Angela Rivers* • Robert Hardy *Supt Brooks* • Geoffrey Keen *Comm Dalby* ■ *Dir* Jim O'Connor • *Scr* Aben Kandel, Herman Cohen

Bert Rigby, You're a Fool ★★ 15

Musical comedy   1989 · US · Colour · 90mins

American director Carl Reiner was so impressed by Robert Lindsay in a West End show that he wrote this wish-fulfilling fable for him. He's a striking miner, whose impersonations of Gene Kelly and Fred Astaire take him to Hollywood stardom, and collisions with clichéd characters such as Anne Bancroft, portraying the frustrated wife of a film producer. It's like *Little Voice* with a social attitude. Songs by Cole Porter and Irving Berlin do their best to enliven the idea, but fail. ▭

Robert Lindsay *Bert Rigby* • Anne Bancroft *Meredith Perlestein* • Corbin Bernsen *Jim Shirley* • Robbie Coltrane *Sid Trample* • Cathryn Bradshaw *Laurel Pennington* • Jackie Gayle *II Perlestein* • Bruno Kirby *Kyle DeForest* • Liz Smith *Mrs Rigby* ■ *Dir/Scr* Carl Reiner

Besieged ★★ PG

Drama   1998 · It · Colour · 93mins

Echoes of director Bernardo Bertolucci's previous work – notably *Last Tango in Paris* and *Tragedy of a Ridiculous Man* – abound. Originally intended as a 60-minute TV drama, the tale of a timid pianist's obsession with his housekeeper is intriguing without ever being wholly engaging. Thandie Newton is solid enough as the medical student forced into service to make ends meet after fleeing a tyrannical African regime, but David Thewlis is wildly erratic as her besotted benefactor. Such a slender, sedate story demands subtle direction, but Bertolucci's restless camera movements and elliptical edits undermine the narrative. A very minor work. Contains brief nudity. ▭

Thandie Newton *Shandurai* • David Thewlis *Jason Kinsky* • Claudio Santamaria *Agostino* • John C Ojwang *Singer* • Cyril Nri *Priest* • Massimo De Rossi *Patient* • Andrea Quercia *Child pianist* • Mario Mazzetti Di Pietralata *Piano buyer* ■ *Dir* Bernardo Bertolucci • *Scr* Clare Peploe, Bernardo Bertolucci, from a story by James Lasdun

Best ★★ 15

Sports biography
1999 · UK · Colour · 106mins

There's nothing like a good film, and this shoddy biography of soccer genius George Best is nothing like a good film. Normally, it's the match scenes that let football films down: you either have actors who can't play, or players who can't act. Ironically, though, *Best*'s match scenes, a blend of grainy original footage and cleverly integrated re-creations, are one of its few plus points. The bulk of the film, however, focuses on George's downward spiral into alcoholism and unfulfilled potential. It's muddled in structure, melodramatic in direction and boringly repetitive. Worse still, it offers no real insight into George's flawed genius.

John Lynch *George Best* • Ian Bannen *Sir Matt Busby* • Jerome Flynn *Bobby Charlton* • Ian Hart *Nobby Stiles* • Patsy Kensit *Anna* • Cal MacAninch *Paddy Crerand* • Linus Roache *Denis Law* • Roger Daltrey *Rodney Marsh* ■ *Dir* Mary McGuckian • *Scr* Mary McGuckian, John Lynch, George Best (script consultant)

Best Boy ★★★★ 18

Documentary   1979 · US · Colour · 104mins

Disregarding the documentarist's supposed duty to remain impartial, Ira Wohl directly influences the action in this life-affirming Oscar winner, as he prizes his 52-year-old cousin, Philly, away from the parents who have devotedly cossetted him on account of his mental incapacity. Realising that they are ageing (indeed, the father is dying), Wohl attempts to prepare Philly for life on his own. Nonetheless, he remains sensitive to the fact that each small accomplishment is as much a source of regret as of pride for the selfless people witnessing their son's dependence on them diminishing. This is movingly inspirational, with only the much-vaunted backstage meeting with Zero Mostel ringing false. ▭

Dir/Scr Ira Wohl

Best Defense ★★ 15

Comedy   1984 · US · Colour · 92mins

This anti-establishment comedy from the writers of *Indiana Jones and the Temple of Doom* was filmed as a Dudley Moore vehicle, but the result pleased nobody. After previews, the movie was recalled, rewritten and partially reshot, incorporating a very expensive Eddie Murphy (hot from *Beverly Hills Cop*), billed awkwardly as "Strategic guest star". It still doesn't work, but it's fascinating to see how Murphy was filmed without interfacing with the rest of the existing cast and action. The anti-Russian material is tasteless and the comedy unfunny, but Kate Capshaw and Helen Shaver make it watchable to a degree. Contains some swearing, sex scenes and brief nudity.

Dudley Moore *Wylie Cooper* • Eddie Murphy *Landry* • Kate Capshaw *Laura* • George Dzundza *Loparino* • Helen Shaver *Claire Lewis* • Mark Arnott *Brank* • Peter Michael Goetz *Frank Joyner* ■ *Dir* Willard Huyck • *Scr* Gloria Katz, Willard Huyck, from the novel *Easy and Hard Ways Out* by Robert Grossbach

Best Foot Forward ★★★ U

Musical   1943 · US · Colour · 95mins

This early MGM Technicolor musical was produced by the great Arthur Freed, who would later redefine the genre with such classics as *An American in Paris* and *Gigi*. It's a movie adaptation of a famous George Abbott Broadway show, and is notable for importing many of the Broadway cast to MGM. Although the feeble leading men didn't stay the course, Hollywood fell for peppy June Allyson and zesty Nancy Walker. The plot, originally purchased for Lana Turner, revolves around movie star Lucille Ball visiting a military academy. The glamorous Gloria DeHaven steals every scene in which she appears. Period nonsense, but watchable.

Lucille Ball • William Gaxton *Jack O'Riley* • Virginia Weidler *Helen Schlessenger* • Tommy Dix *Elwood* • Nancy Walker *Nancy* • Gloria DeHaven *Minerva* • Kenny Bowers *Dutch* • June Allyson *Ethel* ■ *Dir* Edward Buzzell • *Scr* Irving Brecher, Fred F Finklehoffe

Best Friends ★★★ PG

Comedy   1982 · US · Colour · 104mins

Before he became the director of such hits as *Rain Man* and *Disclosure*, Barry Levinson worked as a scriptwriter, often in collaboration with his first wife, Valerie Curtin. Proving that the couple who write together also fight together, this overexcitable comedy is a dramatic exaggeration of their real-life relationship. Burt Reynolds and Goldie Hawn are well-matched as the Hollywood scriptwriters whose marriage puts a strain on their working relationship. Once the bickering begins, they hurl their lines at each other with some enthusiasm, but this only partly atones for the fact that they are never particularly funny. ▭

Burt Reynolds *Richard Babson* • Goldie Hawn *Paula McCullen* • Jessica Tandy *Eleanor McCullen* • Barnard Hughes *Tim McCullen* • Audra Lindley *Ann Babson* • Keenan Wynn *Tom Babson* • Ron Silver *Larry Weisman* • Carol Locatell *Nellie Ballou* ■ *Dir* Norman Jewison • *Scr* Valerie Curtin, Barry Levinson

Best Friends for Life ★★

Drama   1998 · US · Colour

Two women, best friends since childhood, face uncertain futures after the sudden deaths of their husbands. One starts her own business and becomes romantically involved with a doctor, but the other is unable to adjust to her loss and is later diagnosed with a serious illness. With an accomplished cast including Gena Rowlands, Linda Lavin (*Alice*) and Richard Farnsworth (Oscar-nominated for *The Straight Story*) this is a melodramatic TV tear-jerker aimed squarely at the female viewer.

Gena Rowlands *Harriet* • Linda Lavin *Sarah* • Helen Slater *Pammy* • Richard Farnsworth *Will* • Gwen Verdon *Edith* ■ *Dir* Michael Switzer • *Scr* Cynthia Whitcomb, from the novel *Life Estates* by Shelby Hearon

Best Intentions ★★★★ PG

Drama   1992 · Swe · Colour · 173mins

Although a six-hour version was made for Swedish TV, director Bille August here settled on half that time to explore the tempestuous early relationship of Ingmar Bergman's parents. The great film-maker's script returns to the theme of troubled young love that informed so many of his early features, but there's also plenty of the spiritual and emotional angst that characterised much of his later work. The difficulties facing Henrik (Samuel Froler) and Anna (Pernilla August, Bille's wife) provide plenty of dramatic interest, especially when they come in the form of Anna's disapproving father, magisterially played by Max von Sydow. In Swedish with English subtitles. ▭

Samuel Froler *Henrik Bergman* • Pernilla August *Anna Akerblom* • Max von Sydow *Johan Akerblom* • Ghita Norby *Karin Akerblom* • Mona Malm *Alma Bergman* • Lena Endre *Frida Strandberg* • Keve Hjelm *Fredrik Bergman* • Björn Kjellman *Ernst Akerblom* • Börje Ahlstedt *Carl Akerblom* ■ *Dir* Bille August • *Scr* Ingmar Bergman

Best Laid Plans ★★★ 15

Heist drama   1999 · US · Colour · 89mins

The set-up is ingenious: Alessandro Nivola (Nicolas Cage's brother in *Face/*

Off) is called to Josh Brolin's house in the middle of the night where his friend confesses that he has been accused of raping a girl he had picked up earlier at a bar (Reese Witherspoon). To make matters worse, it turns out she is only 16 and Brolin, panicking, has her tied up downstairs. All is not what it seems, however. British director Mike Barker, who made *The James Gang*, creates a complex tale of robbery and deception, and displays a sympathetic eye for the small-town, blue-collar backdrop to the film. Although the tone is uneven, the charismatic performances, particularly Nivola's, more than compensate for the odd uncertain moment. Contains swearing and sex scenes. ⊞

Alessandro Nivola *Nick* • Reese Witherspoon *Lissa* • Josh Brolin *Bryce* • Rocky Carroll *Bad ass dude* • Michael G Hagerty *Charlie* • Terrence Howard *Jimmy* • Jamie Marsh *Barry* ■ *Dir* Michael Barker [Mike Barker] • *Scr* Ted Griffin

The Best Little Whorehouse in Texas ★★★ 15

Musical comedy 1982 · US · Colour · 109mins

A lightweight version of the much grittier long-running Broadway musical with Dolly Parton and Burt Reynolds, two performers noted for their sex appeal, failing to ignite the proper sparks. Parton plays the madam of the Chicken Ranch brothel, who comes to blows with her sheriff lover (Reynolds) when TV evangelist Dom DeLuise tries to close the place down. Some great routines augmented with new songs (the first movie appearance of *I Will Always Love You*, which Whitney Houston sang in *The Bodyguard*, here sung by Parton) keeps everything on a lively and likeable keel. ⊞

Burt Reynolds *Sheriff Dodd* • Dolly Parton *Miss Mona* • Dom DeLuise *Melvin* • Charles Durning *Governor* • Jim Nabors *Deputy Fred* • Robert Mandan *Senator Wingwood* • Lois Nettleton *Dulci Mae* ■ *Dir* Colin Higgins • *Scr* Larry L King, Peter Masterson, Colin Higgins, from the musical by Peter Masterson

The Best Man ★★★★

Political drama 1964 · US · BW · 101mins

Political satire is a tough subject to convey successfully in a movie, but director Franklin J Schaffner (*Planet of the Apes, Patton*) succeeded brilliantly with Gore Vidal's scabrous look at the underbelly of Washington. Not surprisingly a commercial failure, this brilliantly cast, superbly acted drama got lost on its release alongside the similar but more expensive, and therefore in Hollywood terms more prestigious, *Advise and Consent* and *Dr Strangelove*, both now recognised classics. But this movie is easily their equal. Daring in its day – two political rivals have dark and deep secrets in their past – this is a mature and satisfying work, and contains an almost career-best performance from the great Henry Fonda.

Henry Fonda *William Russell* • Cliff Robertson *Joe Cantwell* • Edie Adams *Mabel Cantwell* • Margaret Leighton *Alice Russell* • Shelley Berman *Sheldon Bascomb* • Lee Tracy *Art Hockstader* • Ann Sothern *Mrs Gamadge* • Gene Raymond *Dan Cantwell* • Kevin

McCarthy *Dick Jensen* ■ *Dir* Franklin Schaffner [Franklin J Schaffner] • *Scr* Gore Vidal, from his play

The Best Man ★★

Comedy drama 1986 · UK · Colour

A showboating performance from Seamus Ball holds together this raucous comedy from writer/director Joe Mahon. As the northern Irish gadabout whose aversion to commitment is matched only by his fondness for a tipple and a flutter, he bestrides the proceedings, as he not only seeks refuge from his own problems, but also tries to lead astray his impressionable best mate, Denis McGowan, whose marriage to Mairead Mullan is heading for the rocks. Relegating the Troubles to the background, this decidedly unromantic take on matrimony makes up in perceptive bitterness what it lacks in consistent quality.

Seamus Ball *Billy Maguire* • Denis McGowan *Jamsie McDaid* • Mairead Mullan *Maureen McDaid* • Jean Flagherty *Mrs Maguire* • Mickey McGowan *Joe McLaughlin* • Aiden Heaney *Pat McIntyre* • Hugh McIntyre *Professor* ■ *Dir/Scr* Joe Mahon

Best Man ★★

Documentary 1997 · Colour · 88mins

A follow-up to 1979's Oscar-winning documentary *Best Boy*, which director Ira Wohl shot over three years while persuading the elderly parents of his mentally disabled 52-year-old cousin, Philly, that they should allow their son more freedom. Here Philly is 70, and preparing for his bar mitzvah with the help of caretaker Frances Reiss. For those who remember the marvellous original, this sequel will provide a welcome update.

Philly Wohl ■ *Dir/Scr* Ira Wohl

The Best Man ★★ 15

Comedy drama 1999 · US · Colour · mins

In this first feature from writer/director Malcolm D Lee (cousin of Spike), Taye Diggs discovers that his debut novel, as yet unpublished, has been leaked to his friends as they prepare to reunite for a wedding. Since the book is drawn from his own experiences, they're none too pleased with his representation of them. The great soundtrack features Stevie Wonder and Lauren Hill, but the dud script undermines the considerable talents of Diggs and his co-star, Nia Long.

Nia Long *Jordan* • Taye Diggs *Harper* • Morris Chestnut *Lance* • Terrence Howard *Quentin* • Harold Perrineau Jr [Harold Perrineau] *Murch* • Sanaa Lathan *Robin* • Monica Calhoun *Mia* • Melissa De Sousa *Shelby* • Victoria Dillard *Anita* ■ *Dir/Scr* Malcolm D Lee

Best Men ★ 15

Crime comedy drama 1997 · US · Colour · 86mins

Just released from prison, and on his way to his wedding with Drew Barrymore, Luke Wilson finds himself in trouble when one of the friends driving him to church makes an unscheduled stop to rob a bank. In predictable fashion, the bungled heist quickly escalates into a full-scale hostage situation. It's a ridiculous

story, made worse by clueless direction from Tamra Davis. ⊞ **DVD**

Drew Barrymore *Hope* • Dean Cain *Sergeant Buzz Thomas* • Andy Dick *Teddy Pollack* • Sean Patrick Flanery *Billy Phillips* • Mitchell Whitfield *Sol Jacobs* • Luke Wilson *Jesse Chandler* • Fred Ward *Sheriff Bud Phillips* ■ *Dir* Tamra Davis • *Scr* Art Edler Brown, Tracy Fraim

The Best of Enemies ★★ PG

Second World War comedy 1962 · UK/It · BW · 99mins

This Anglo-Italian co-production boasts exceptional talent both before and behind the camera. As the rival commanders, David Niven and Alberto Sordi are given admirable support by such stalwarts as Michael Wilding, Harry Andrews and Bernard Cribbins. The great Nino Rota composed the score, while Fellini's regular cameraman, Giuseppe Rotunno, provides some stunning visuals. Yet, in spite of Guy Hamilton's steady direction and the odd amusing moment, this account of the misadventures of a British army unit in Abyssinia in the early forties never really gathers much momentum. ⊞

David Niven *Major Richardson* • Michael Wilding *Lt Burke* • Harry Andrews *Capt Rootes* • Noel Harrison *Lt Hilary* • Ronald Fraser *Cpl Prefect* • Bernard Cribbins *Pvt Tanner* • Duncan Macrae *Sgt Trevethan* ■ *Dir* Guy Hamilton • *Scr* Jack Pulman, Age Scarpelli [Agenore Incrocci and Furio Scarpelli] (adaptation), Suso Cecchi D'Amico (adaptation), from a story by Luciano Vincenzoni

The Best of Everything ★★

Romantic drama 1959 · US · Colour · 120mins

"We've proven romance is still the best of everything," croons Johnny Mathis over the titles, but this preposterous 20th Century-Fox tosh is not really a romance: it's a steamy melodrama about power and glamour, based on Rona Jaffe's bestseller about the New York publishing jungle. An ageing and predatory Joan Crawford chews the scenery with aplomb, making mincemeat of Fox's young contract players Hope Lange, Suzy Parker and Diane Baker, all of whom nowadays add to the period charm. Stephen Boyd seems cast adrift, but watch out for Robert Evans, later the producer of such blockbusters as *Chinatown* and *Marathon Man*.

Joan Crawford *Amanda Farrow* • Hope Lange *Caroline Bender* • Stephen Boyd *Mike* • Louis Jourdan *David Savage* • Suzy Parker *Gregg* • Martha Hyer *Barbara* • Diane Baker *April* • Brian Aherne *Mr Shalimar* • Robert Evans *Dexter Key* ■ *Dir* Jean Negulesco • *Scr* Edith Sommer, Mann Rubin, from the novel by Rona Jaffe

Best of the Badmen ★★ U

Western 1951 · US · Colour · 83mins

A collection of noted western outlaws ride together in this innocuous RKO film. Robert Ryan is top billed as a former Confederate colonel pitted against a rather bland Robert Preston, while *Stagecoach* veteran Claire Trevor and Jack Buetel provide able support. *Red River's* Walter Brennan makes the most of a then-topical role as an ex-Quantrill's raider who wonders why

there's now a price on his head for doing something which brought him glory in the Civil War. Too talky and not terribly interesting, the film is only notable today because of its cast.

Robert Ryan *Jeff Clanton* • Claire Trevor *Lily* • Jack Buetel *Bob Younger* • Robert Preston *Matthew Fowler* • Walter Brennan *Doc Butcher* • Bruce Cabot *Cole Younger* • John Archer *Curley Ringo* • Lawrence Tierney *Jesse James* • Barton MacLane *Joad* ■ *Dir* William D Russell • *Scr* Robert Hardy Andrews, John Twist, from a story by Robert Hardy Andrews

Best of the Best ★★ 15

Martial arts sports drama 1989 · US · Colour · 93mins

The US karate team take on the mighty Koreans in a slick "against the odds" martial arts drama that alternates between body blows and tugs on the heartstrings. Formulaic in the extreme, with nice fighter Eric Roberts given every possible reason to triumph (his son's in a coma after a traffic accident *and* he has a nasty shoulder injury), this compendium of clichés is undone by sentimentality and paper-thin characterisation. ⊞

Eric Roberts *Alex Grady* • James Earl Jones *Coach Couzo* • Sally Kirkland *Catherine Wade* • Phillip Rhee *Tommy Lee* • Christopher Penn *Travis Brickley* ■ *Dir* Robert Radler • *Scr* Paul Levine, from a story by Phillip Rhee, Paul Levine

Best of the Best II ★★ 18

Action thriller 1992 · US · Colour · 95mins

The original *Best of the Best* was a glossy, straight-to-video action tale that benefited from a surprisingly good cast. There's no James Earl Jones this time around, but Eric Roberts, Christopher Penn and martial arts expert Phillip Rhee are reunited for another bout of mindless but hugely entertaining biffing. *Rocky*-style trimmings are absent as the karate fighters find themselves ensnared in a private competition, hosted by evil Wayne Newton, where there are no rules. ⊞

Eric Roberts *Alex Grady* • Phillip Rhee *Tommy Lee* • Edan Gross *Walter Grady* • Ralph Moeller *Brakus* • Christopher Penn *Travis Brickley* • Sonny Landham *James* • Wayne Newton *Weldon* • Meg Foster *Sue* ■ *Dir* Robert Radler • *Scr* Max Strom, John Allen Nelson, from characters created by Paul Levine

Best of the Best 3: No Turning Back ★★ 15

Martial arts action 1995 · US · Colour · 93mins

No Eric Roberts or Christopher Penn this time, but this boisterous follow-up to *Best of the Best II* still manages to attract a better than average cast. This time the supporting players include Christopher McDonald, Gina Gershon and Dee Wallace Stone. However, the spotlight rightly falls on martial arts master Phillip Rhee, who also directs. The storyline may be negligible – a mysterious stranger helps defend a town against racists – but the fight scenes are stylishly staged. ⊞

Phillip Rhee *Tommy Lee* • Christopher McDonald *Jack Banning* • Gina Gershon *Margo Preston* • Mark Rolston *Donnie Hanson* • Peter Simmons *Owen Tucker* • Cristina Anzu

Lawson *Karen Banning* • Dee Wallace Stone *Georgia* • Michael Bailey Smith *Tiny* ■ *Dir* Phillip Rhee • *Scr* Barry Gray, Deborah Scott

Best of the Best: Without Warning ★

Martial arts   1998 · US · Colour · 90mins

Star/director Phillip Rhee returns as Tommy Lee, though he has a different background here: now he's living in LA and has a previously unmentioned daughter, who only seems to be on hand so that she can get kidnapped. The film pits Lee against the Russian Mafia after he's unwittingly slipped a CD-Rom they were using for their counterfeit operation. The photography has improved, but the action sequences are sluggish and, at times, downright laughable.

Phillip Rhee *Tommy Lee* • Ernie Hudson *Detective Gresko* • Tobin Bell *Lukass Stava* • Thure Riefenstein *Yuri Stava* • Jessica Collins *Karlina* • Christopher Lemmon [Chris Lemmon] *Detective Jarvis* • Paul Gleason *Father G* ■ *Dir* Phillip Rhee • *Scr* Phillip Rhee, Fred Vicarel

The Best of Times ★★ 15

Comedy drama   1986 · US · Colour · 99mins

All-American whimsy, set in small-town California, where Robin Williams and Kurt Russell are two of life's failures. Williams is a banker, living in the shadow of a missed pass at a high school football game; Russell was the school's star quarterback, now also on the skids. When Williams decides the town needs a little encouragement and some moral fibre, we're into a rehash of *It's a Wonderful Life*, except that the characters are one dimensional, there aren't any jokes, and the tone set by writer Ron Shelton and director Roger Spottiswoode is glutinous in the extreme. Contains swearing. ▢

Robin Williams *Jack Dundee* • Kurt Russell *Reno Hightower* • Pamela Reed *Gigi Hightower* • Holly Palance *Elly Dundee* • Donald Moffat *The Colonel* • Margaret Whitton *Darla* • M Emmet Walsh *Charlie* • Donovan Scott *Eddie* ■ *Dir* Roger Spottiswoode • *Scr* Ron Shelton

The Best Pair of Legs in the Business ★

Comedy drama   1972 · UK · Colour · 87mins

Taking a break from the buses, Reg Varney finds himself at a holiday camp in this old-fashioned seaside comedy. Although he's the world's worst entertainer, our Reg is convinced that the big time is just a soft-shoe shuffle away. But his ambition blinds him to the fact that his wife, Diana Coupland, is playing away from home with his boss. A trouper through and through, Varney always tries to make the most of even the lowest grade material, yet even he struggles to pep up this maudlin mess. Contains some swearing.

Reg Varney *"Sherry" Sheridan* • Diana Coupland *Mary Sheridan* • Jean Harvey *Emma* • Lee Montague *Charlie* • David Lincoln *Ron* • George Sweeney *Dai* ■ *Dir* Christopher Hodson • *Scr* Kevin Laffan

Best Revenge ★★ 18

Thriller   1983 · Can · Colour · 91mins

John Heard can be electric in a part with some depth, but here he is saddled with a film that has none.

Instead, he is required to wrestle with the obviously episodic story of a small-potatoes drugs runner who is arm-twisted into undertaking a larger errand when a friend is taken hostage. As he tries to bring unseemly quantities of cannabis from Morocco to America, all the regulation nastiness is given full rein. *Midnight Express* it ain't. ▢

John Heard *Charlie Grainger* • Levon Helm *Bo* • Alberta Watson *Dinah* • Stephen McHattie *Brett Munro* • Moses Znaimer *Leo Ellis* • John Rhys-Davies *Mustapha* • Benjamin Gordon *Willy* ■ *Dir* John Trent • *Scr* David Rothberg, Rick Rosenthal, Logan N Danforth, from a story by David Rothberg

Best Seller ★★★★ 18

Thriller   1987 · US · Colour · 91mins

In between making his own quirky horror films, Larry Cohen turned his writing attention to the crime genre and the result was this ingenious, electric thriller. Brian Dennehy is the policeman turned writer who forms an uneasy alliance with hit man James Woods, who has promised to put him back on the bestseller lists. Cohen delivers a typically witty script and director John Flynn is a dab hand at the action set pieces. However, it's the performances that really count: Dennehy is as dependable as ever, while Woods mesmerises as the strangely likeable killer. Contains some swearing and violence. ▢

Brian Dennehy *Dennis Meechum* • James Woods *Cleve* • Victoria Tennant *Roberta Gillian* • Allison Balson *Holly Meechum* • Paul Shenar *David Madlock* • George Coe *Graham* • Ann Pitoniak [Anne Pitoniak] *Mrs Foster* • Mary Carver *Cleve's mother* • Sully Boyar *Monks* ■ *Dir* John Flynn • *Scr* Larry Cohen

Best Shot ★★★★ PG

Sports drama   1986 · US · Colour · 115mins

People from Indiana are known as "Hoosiers", which was this film's US title – it was renamed *Best Shot* for UK audiences. It's a story about a former army man, played with great swagger and insight by Gene Hackman, who is invited by a friend and high-school principal to train the school's basketball team. And while Hackman's turning the team around, he also gets to work on the town drunk, Dennis Hopper, and fellow teacher Barbara Hershey. Set in 1951, it's a finely drawn study of postwar American mores, evocatively scored by Jerry Goldsmith and sharply directed by first-timer David Anspaugh, a TV director whose credits include *Hill Street Blues* and *St Elsewhere*. ▢

Gene Hackman *Norman Dale* • Barbara Hershey *Myra Fleener* • Dennis Hopper *Shooter* • Sheb Wooley *Cletus Summers* • Fern Persons *Opal Fleener* • Maris Valainis *Jimmy Chitwood* • Brad Boyle *Whit* • Steve Hollar *Rade* • Brad Long *Buddy* ■ *Dir* David Anspaugh • *Scr* Angelo Pizzo

The Best Things in Life Are Free ★★★★ U

Musical biographical drama
1956 · US · Colour · 104mins

Director Michael Curtiz's stirring musical biopic is about the songwriting team of BG De Sylva, Ray Henderson and Lew Brown. It matters not a jot if you've never heard of them, since

they're played with tremendous verve by Gordon MacRae, Dan Dailey and Ernest Borgnine. Fresh from winning a best actor Oscar for the previous year's *Marty*, Borgnine clearly enjoys his very different role here. Sheree North simply sizzles in two superb dance routines, a vibrant (and definitive) *Birth of the Blues* with the great Jacques d'Amboise and a very snazzy *Black Bottom*.

Gordon MacRae *BG "Buddy" De Sylva* • Dan Dailey *Ray Henderson* • Ernest Borgnine *Lew Brown* • Sheree North *Kitty* • Tommy Noonan *Carl* • Murvyn Vye *Manny* • Phyllis Avery *Maggie Henderson* • Jacques d'Amboise *Speciality dancer* ■ *Dir* Michael Curtiz • *Scr* William Bowers, Phoebe Ephron, from a story by John O'Hara

The Best Years of Our Lives ★★★★★ U

Drama   1946 · US · BW · 163mins

Undoubtedly one of the finest and most satisfying achievements in American cinema, this Samuel Goldwyn production now tends, regrettably, to be overlooked by film scholars. Despite its length, it still retains its capacity to move an audience. The tale of three returning GIs adjusting to civilian life after the Second World War may have lost some relevance post-Vietnam, but there's no denying the magnificent craftsmanship as director William Wyler and photographer Gregg Toland (*Citizen Kane*) bring Robert E Sherwood's vivid screenplay to life. Stars Fredric March, Myrna Loy and Dana Andrews are at their postwar peaks here, but it is the performance of real-life wartime amputee Harold Russell that is most touching, and he rightly won two Academy Awards for his role (a special award for bringing hope to other veterans along with that of best supporting actor). Awarded six other Oscars, this movie is hard to overpraise. ▢

Myrna Loy *Milly Stephenson* • Fredric March *Al Stephenson* • Dana Andrews *Fred Derry* • Harold Russell *Homer Parrish* • Teresa Wright *Peggy Stephenson* • Virginia Mayo *Marie Derry* • Cathy O'Donnell *Wilma Cameron* • Hoagy Carmichael *Butch Engle* ■ *Dir* William Wyler • *Scr* Robert E Sherwood, from the blank verse novella *Glory for Me* by MacKinlay Kantor • *Cinematographer* Gregg Toland • *Editor* Daniel Mandell • *Music* Hugo Friedhofer

La Bête Humaine ★★★★★ PG

Drama   1938 · Fr · BW · 98mins

Zola's dark, fatalistic novel of the railway tracks was turned by Jean Renoir into one of the classics of pre-war French cinema. The incomparable Jean Gabin stars as the train driver who acquires a young mistress, and together they plot to murder her husband. Hollywood would use Zola's yarn as a template for many pulp fictions and *films noirs* (*The Postman Always Rings Twice*, *Double Indemnity*) but Renoir's film is every inch their equal. It's a wonderful, painterly evocation of the railway – belching steam and rain making the tracks glitter – and a poetic drama that just gets grimmer and grimmer. Fritz Lang remade it in Hollywood as *Human Desire* with Glenn Ford and Gloria Grahame, a dead ringer for this film's pathetic heroine, Simone Simon. In French with English subtitles. ▢

Jean Gabin *Jacques Lantier* • Simone Simon *Séverine* • Fernand Ledoux *Roubaud, Séverine's husband* • Julien Carette *Pecqueux* • Blanchette Brunoy *Flore* • Jean Renoir *Cabuche, the poacher* • Gerard Landry *Dauvergne's son* • Jenny Helia *Philomene* ■ *Dir* Jean Renoir • *Scr* Jean Renoir, from the novel by Emile Zola

Bethune: the Making of a Hero ★★★ 15

Biographical drama
1990 · Can/Fr/Chi · Colour · 111mins

Having already played controversial Canadian doctor Norman Bethune in Eric Till's 1977 biopic, Donald Sutherland returned to the role for this troubled co-production. As before, he gives a warts-and-all portrayal of the surgeon whose avowed detestation of fascism led him first to participate in the Spanish Civil War, and then to assist Mao Tse-tung on his famous Long March. Strikingly filmed by Mike Molloy and Raoul Coutard, the scenery makes an imposing impression. There is generous support from Helen Mirren, as Bethune's long-suffering wife, Helen Shaver as his mistress and Harrison Liu as his loyal aide. ▢

Donald Sutherland *Dr Norman Bethune* • Helen Mirren *Frances Penny Bethune* • Helen Shaver *Ms Dowd* • Colm Feore *Chester Rice* • James Pax *Mr Tung* • Ronald Pickup *Alan Coleman* • Da Guo *Dr Chian* • Harrison Liu *Dr Fong* • Anouk Aimée *Marie-France Coudaire* ■ *Dir* Phillip Borsos • *Scr* Ted Allan

Betrayal ★★★★ 15

Romantic drama   1982 · UK · Colour · 91mins

This film version of Harold Pinter's 1978 play has Patricia Hodge married to Ben Kingsley but having an affair with Jeremy Irons. The story – a sort of sexual charade – starts at the end and works backwards, dealing with a sequence of betrayals between the three friends. Razor sharp in its depiction of a rather pretentious literary London, it includes an unforgettable scene in a restaurant when Kingsley goes ballistic. This was producer Sam Spiegel's final film, ending a distinguished career that encompassed such classics as *On the Waterfront* and *Lawrence of Arabia*. Contains swearing. ▢

Jeremy Irons *Jerry* • Ben Kingsley *Robert* • Patricia Hodge *Emma* • Avril Elgar *Mrs Banks* • Ray Marioni *Waiter* • Caspar Norman *Sam* ■ *Dir* David Jones • *Scr* Harold Pinter, from his play

Betrayal from the East ★★

Second World War drama
1945 · US · BW · 82mins

Lee Tracy is enlisted by the Japanese in 1941 to spy for them. In particular they want the defence plans for the Panama Canal, which they apparently hope to destroy. But Tracy, though broke, isn't morally bankrupt, and intends to trick the Japanese with the help of double agent Nancy Kelly. Made when victory in Europe was secure and victory over the Japanese just months away, this cheapo war drama isn't the expected flag waver. It suddenly springs a shock ending and epilogue that is intended to warn Americans against getting caught on the hop by another Pearl Harbor.

Lee Tracy *Eddie* • Nancy Kelly *Peggy* • Richard Loo *Tanni* • Abner Biberman *Yamato* • Regis Toomey *Scott* • Philip Ahn *Kato* • Addison Richards *Capt Bates* • Bruce Edwards *Purdy* ■ *Dir* William Berke • *Scr* Kenneth Gamet, Aubrey Wisberg, from the book by Alan Hynd

Betrayal of the Dove ★★ 15

Thriller 1993 · US · Colour · 89mins

Great things were expected of Robby Benson as an actor in the seventies, but he's had his fair share of credits behind the camera since then, including the screenplay of this thriller. He's clearly seen plenty of other thrillers in which Mr Right turns out to be anything but; in fact, he's probably seen too many. Surprises are thin on the ground here as single mum Helen Slater begins to suspect that best friend Kelly LeBrock had ulterior motives in sending her on a blind date with dishy doctor Billy Zane. Slightly less raunchy than many of its kind, it turns quite nasty towards the end. Contains swearing, violence, sex scenes and nudity. [video]

Helen Slater *Ellie* • Billy Zane *Dr Jesse Peter* • Kelly LeBrock *Una* • Alan Thicke *Jack West* • Harvey Korman *Sid* • Stuart Pankin *Gabe* • David L Lander *Norman* ■ *Dir* Strathford Hamilton • *Scr* Robby Benson, Karla De Vito

Betrayal of Trust ★★★ 15

Drama based on a true story
1994 · US · Colour · 88mins

Judd Hirsch is excellently cast against type in this sensationalist, yet gripping, TV drama. Hirsch plays a respected psychiatrist who is seen in a new light when one of his patients (Judith Light) accuses him of raping her repeatedly while she was under sedation. The leads are excellent and there's a sterling roster of character actors in support, including Betty Buckley, Kevin Tighe and John Getz. George Kaczender's direction is plodding, but the tabloid-style story will keep viewers riveted. [video]

Judith Light *Barbara Noel* • Judd Hirsch *Dr Jules Masserman* • Betty Buckley *Dr Jan Galanti* • Jeff De Munn *Dick* • Kevin Tighe *Bill Carroll* • Holland Taylor *Mary* • Nicholas Campbell *Richard Noel* • John Getz *Curt* ■ *Dir* George Kaczender • *Scr* Suzette Couture, from the book *You Must Be Dreaming* by Barbara Noel, Kathryn Watterson

Betrayed ★★★

Thriller 1944 · US · BW · 67mins

An effective, moody B-thriller that was originally titled *When Strangers Marry* but was quickly changed to *Betrayed* when people expected a marital comedy. It stars Kim Hunter as the latest wife of Dean Jagger, whom she suspects may be a murderer. Hunter's fears are calmed by her former boyfriend Robert Mitchum, whose hulking, laconic presence dominates the picture. Philip Yordan, who later wrote *Johnny Guitar* and epics for producer Samuel Bronston, has a hand in the script, and the taut direction is by William Castle, later famous as the schlock-meister who wired up cinema seats to give audiences a shock during screenings of his 1959 horror film *The Tingler* and the inspiration for John Goodman's producer in *Matinee*.

Robert Mitchum *Fred* • Kim Hunter *Millie* • Dean Jagger *Paul* • Neil Hamilton *Blake* • Lou Lubin *Houser* • Milton Kibbee *Charlie* • Dewey Robinson *News stand man* • Claire Whitney *Middle-aged woman* ■ *Dir* William Castle • *Scr* Philip Yordan, Dennis J Cooper, from a story by George V Moscov

Betrayed ★★ U

Second World War spy drama
1954 · US · Colour · 108mins

Directed by Gottfried Reinhardt at MGM's British studios, this old-fashioned, plodding film about spies, Resistance workers and traitors is chiefly notable for marking the end of Clark Gable's 22-year tenure with the studio, before he went lucratively freelance for his remaining years. Co-starring with Victor Mature and Lana Turner, the ageing "King" of Hollywood was hardly challenged by this outmoded melodrama. He is surrounded by a supporting cast that includes British actors Wilfrid Hyde White, Ian Carmichael, Roland Culver and Nora Swinburne.

Clark Gable *Colonel Pieter Deventer* • Lana Turner *Carla Van Oven* • Victor Mature *"The Scarf"* • Louis Calhern *General Ten Eyck* • OE Hasse *Colonel Helmuth Dietrich* • Wilfrid Hyde White *General Charles Larraby* • Ian Carmichael *Captain Jackie Lawson* • Niall MacGinnis *"Blackie"* • Nora Swinburne *"The Scarf's" Mother* • Roland Culver *General Warsleigh* ■ *Dir* Gottfried Reinhardt • *Scr* Ronald Millar, George Froeschel

Betrayed ★★★ 18

Political thriller 1988 · US · Colour · 121mins

An intelligent and intriguing political thriller from director Costa-Gavras about an undercover FBI agent – played by the excellent Debra Winger – sent to investigate a Midwest farmer who's suspected of having links with a white supremacist organisation. Tom Berenger is suitably charming and chilling as Winger's prey, but Costa-Gavras gives the convoluted plot such a plethora of twists and turns that cohesive tension is ultimately lost. The performances and set pieces raise it up, but this film is simply too long. Contains violence and swearing. [video]

Debra Winger *Cathy Weaver/Katie Phillips* • Tom Berenger *Gary Simmons* • John Heard *Michael Carnes* • Betsy Blair *Gladys Simmons* • John Mahoney *Shorty* • Ted Levine *Wes* • Jeffrey DeMunn *Flynn* • Albert Hall *Al Sanders* • David Clennon *Jack Carpenter* ■ *Dir* Costa-Gavras • *Scr* Joe Eszterhas

Betrayed: a Story of Three Women ★★

Drama 1995 · US · Colour

As TV movie plots go, this is one of the better ones, with longtime pals Meredith Baxter and Swoosie Kurtz falling out after Baxter discovers her husband is sleeping with Kurtz's 19-year-old daughter. The story's plausibility is the film's greatest asset, but much of its credibility is frittered away by the larger-than-life performances and overblown emotions more in keeping with a glitzy soap opera than an intimate drama. Clare Carey scores as the teenage temptress, but cheating husband John Terry is made to look such a heel that it's hard to understand why they're bothering to fight over him.

Meredith Baxter *Amanda Nelson* • Swoosie Kurtz *Joan Bixler* • Clare Carey *Dana Bixler* • John Terry *Rob Nelson* • John Livingston *Paul Nelson* • Breckin Meyer *Eric Nelson* ■ *Dir* William A Graham • *Scr* James Duff

Betrayed by Love ★★★ 15

Drama based on a true story
1994 · US · Colour · 84mins

Based on a highly unusual case from the files of the FBI, this superior TV movie is also known as *The Susan Daniels Smith Murder*. As the bored Kentucky wife seeking to escape from the monotony of poverty by flirting with a bureau agent, Mare Winningham creates a character as worthy of sympathy as censure. But every bit as impressive is Steven Weber's cynical agent, who ruthlessly exploits her despair to investigate her husband's role in a bank robbery. With Patricia Arquette providing unassuming support, this is as much a study of "trailer trash" as it is a turbulent crime drama. [video]

Mare Winningham *Dana* • Steven Weber *Jeff Avery* • Patricia Arquette *Deanne Wilson* • Perry Lang *Earl McNally* • Ned Vaughn *Harry Hill* • Christopher Curry *Captain Stevenson* ■ *Dir* John Power • *Scr* Alan Sharp, from the book *The FBI Killer* by Aphrodite Jones

The Betsy ★★ 18

Drama 1978 · US · Colour · 120mins

It was said when this film was first released that it was too up-market to be a successful adaptation of a Harold Robbins novel. Well, if your idea of sophistication is the sight of Laurence Olivier bouncing around on a bed, then director Daniel Petrie's full-throttle tale of cars, lust and greed will be right up your street. Ageing 50 years over a series of flashbacks, Olivier acts up a storm, and is joined at the ham counter by Tommy Lee Jones and Lesley-Anne Down. There's more restrained playing from Robert Duvall, but it's rather out of place in a film so clearly devoted to excess. Contains swearing and nudity. [video]

Laurence Olivier *Loren Hardeman Sr* • Robert Duvall *Loren Hardeman III* • Katharine Ross *Sally Hardeman* • Tommy Lee Jones *Angelo Perino* • Jane Alexander *Alicia Hardeman* • Lesley-Anne Down *Lady Bobby Ayres* • Joseph Wiseman *Jake Weinstein* • Kathleen Beller *Betsy Hardeman* ■ *Dir* Daniel Petrie • *Scr* Walter Bernstein, William Bast, from the novel by Harold Robbins

Betsy's Wedding ★★★ 15

Comedy 1990 · US · Colour · 90mins

A movie directed by Alan Alda always means a touch of Woody Allen meets vaudeville and that's the case with this tale of a group of eccentric New Yorkers all trying to get Betsy married off according to their own agendas. Molly Ringwald is neatly understated as the title gal who wishes to make an honest man of a nice boy who is neither Jewish like Ringwald's mom (an excellent Madeline Kahn) nor makes breakfast seem like a scene from *Tosca*, as does her Italian dad (Alda, at his best). The cast is faultless, right down to the minor roles. Contains violence and swearing. [video]

Alan Alda *Eddie Hopper* • Madeline Kahn *Lola Hopper* • Molly Ringwald *Betsy Hopper* • Ally Sheedy *Connie Hopper* • Anthony LaPaglia *Stevie Dee* • Joe Pesci *Oscar Henner* • Catherine O'Hara *Gloria Henner* • Joey Bishop *Eddie's father* • Samuel L Jackson *Mickey, taxi dispatcher* ■ *Dir/Scr* Alan Alda

Better Late Than Never ★★ PG

Comedy 1983 · UK · Colour · 91mins

Great talent, shame about the script. David Niven and Art Carney are a couple of con-men competing for the affections of a ten-year-old heiress (Kimberley Partridge). Her grandmother (Maggie Smith) is a dithering amnesiac, so it's up to the girl to decide which one is her true grandfather. Writer/director Bryan Forbes is as flat-footed here as he was with *International Velvet*. [video]

David Niven *Nick Cartland* • Art Carney *Charley Dunbar* • Maggie Smith *Anderson* • Kimberley Partridge *Bridget* • Catherine Hicks *Sable* • Lionel Jeffries *Hargreaves* • Melissa Prophet *Marlene* ■ *Dir/Scr* Bryan Forbes

Better Off Dead ★★ 15

Comedy 1985 · US · Colour · 92mins

It seems like every teen romantic comedy made in the mid- to late-eighties starred John Cusack as a loveable loser. In this one, Cusack is suicidal after being dumped by his beautiful but shallow girlfriend (Amanda Wyss) – and that's just the start of his problems. Writer/director Savage Steve Holland (who re-teamed with Cusack the following year for *One Crazy Summer*) surrounds the always engaging star with a variety of quirky neighbourhood characters and slapstick sight gags. Closer in spirit to an *Airplane!*-style spoof than a John Hughes movie, this is pretty lightweight compared to such classier Cusack comedies as *The Sure Thing*. [video]

John Cusack *Lane Myer* • David Ogden Stiers *Al Myer* • Kim Darby *Jenny Myer* • Demian Slade *Johnny Gasparini* • Scooter Stevens *Badger Myer* • Diane Franklin *Monique Junet* ■ *Dir/Scr* Savage Steve Holland

Better Off Dead ★★★

Crime drama 1993 · US · Colour

Executive produced by feminist Gloria Steinem and skilfully directed by Neema Barnette, this thought-provoking TV movie explores the issue of capital punishment. Tyra Ferrell plays a former district attorney who fights to save the life of a female Death Row inmate (Mare Winningham giving a stand-out performance), whom she prosecuted in a cop-killing case seven years earlier. A strong bond develops between the women as they race against time to win a stay of execution. Screenwriter Marlane X Meyers provides intelligent dialogue and some genuinely gripping scenes.

Mare Winningham *Kit Kellner* • Tyra Ferrell *Cutter Dubuque* • Kevin Tighe *John Byron* • Don Harvey *Del Collins* • Reed McCants *Sam* • Marilyn Coleman *Rene Dubuque* • Robert Nadir ■ *Dir* Neema Barnette • *Scr* Marlane X Meyer, from a story by Randy C Baer

A Better Tomorrow ★★★★ 18

Action thriller 1986 · HK · Colour · 90mins

One of the defining films in Hong Kong action cinema, this not only made names out of director John Woo and star Chow Yun-Fat, but also exerted a considerable influence over one Quentin Tarantino. Chow takes his now familiar role as the lethal but honorable crook – in this case a counterfeiter who, with his weary partner in crime (Ti Lung), attempts to go straight but is led back into a battle to the death with a ruthless gangster. Inspired by the respected sixties Hong Kong crime drama *True Colours of a Hero*, this also has nods to the ultra-cool French thrillers of Jean Melville. However, the artfully choreographed scenes of slow-motion destruction are all Woo's and more than compensate for the occasional lapses into clumsy sentimentality. This is available on video in both dubbed and subtitled versions, although the latter is unintentionally funny because of dubious translation. A Cantonese language film. 🖵 **DVD**

Chow Yun-Fat *Mark* • Ti Lung *Ho* • Leslie Cheung *Kit Sung* • Lee Waise *Shing* ■ *Dir/Scr* John Woo

A Better Tomorrow II

Action thriller   1987 · HK · Colour · 94mins   ★★★ 18

Less a sequel than a remake, this nevertheless consolidated John Woo's reputation as the hippest of Hong Kong's action directors. Most of the stars of the original are back on board: Chow Yun-Fat this time plays the brother of the master counterfeiter of the first film, while Ti Lung and Leslie Cheung return as the two brothers from different sides of the law. All three are drawn back into bloody violence when an old criminal associate, also trying to go straight, falls foul of a new crime lord. The childish attempts at humour will leave western audiences embarrassed. But once again the set pieces, in particular the awesome finale, are stunning. In Cantonese with English subtitles. 🖵

Chow Yun-Fat *Ken* • Ti Lung *Ho* • Leslie Cheung *Kit* • Dean Shek *Lung* ■ *Dir* John Woo • *Scr* John Woo, Tsui Hark • *Producer* Tsui Hark

A Better Tomorrow III ★★ 18

Action thriller   1989 · HK · Colour · 106mins

John Woo jumped ship after the first two *Better Tomorrow* films, so producer Tsui Hark took over the directorial reins. Given the death toll of the first two – and the fact there is a limit to how many identical brothers you can dig up – this one is actually a prequel, although it bares only a passing resemblance to the first two. Chow Yun-Fat is back on board, although his co-star Tony Leung takes centre stage, as he attempts to bring his relatives out of South Vietnam as the communists move in. While this is not in the same league as the first two movies, Tsui Hark is no slouch when it comes to extravagant destruction, so fans of Hong Kong cinema won't be disappointed. In Cantonese with English subtitles. 🖵

Chow Yun-Fat *Cheung Chi-Keung (Mark)* • Anita Mui *Chow Ying-Kit (Kitty Chow)* • Tony Kar-Fai Leung [Tony Leung (2)] *Cheung Chi Mun (Mun)* • Saburo Tokito *Ho Cheung-Ching* • Cheng Wai Lan *Pat* • Shek Kin *Uncle* • Maggie Cheung *Ling* ■ *Dir* Tsui Hark • *Scr* Tai Fu-Ho, Leung Yiu-Ming

Betty Blue

★★★★★ 18

Drama   1986 · Fr · Colour · 116mins

Blessed with a beautiful score by Gabriel Yared, this is the finest example of the type of French film known, rather snipingly, as *cinéma du look*. The usual accusation of all style and no content simply can't be aimed at Jean-Jacques Beineix's Oscar-nominated return to form after *Moon in the Gutter*. The tragic relationship of Betty and Zorg is as compelling as it is chic. Béatrice Dalle is unbelievably vibrant as the waitress living on the edge of her passions, but Jean-Hugues Anglade does manage to keep up as the would-be novelist coping with her exhilarating highs and destructive lows. In French with English subtitles. Contains violence, swearing, sex scenes and nudity. 🖵

Béatrice Dalle *Betty* • Jean-Hugues Anglade *Zorg* • Consuelo de Haviland *Lisa* • Gérard Darmon *Eddy* • Clementine Celarié *Annie* • Jacques Mathou *Bob* • Claude Confortes *Zorg's boss* ■ *Dir* Jean-Jacques Beineix • *Scr* Jean-Jacques Beineix, from the novel by Philippe Dijan

The Betty Ford Story ★★★

Biographical drama
1987 · US · Colour · 96mins

Gena Rowlands gives a stunning performance as the president's wife who battled an addiction to prescription drugs and alcohol in this powerful TV movie, based on Mrs Ford's autobiography. The story is told with candour and the film offers an intimate view of the emotional pain Ford and her family suffered because of her destructive behaviour. The drama is bolstered by strong acting from the supporting cast, especially Josef Sommer as Gerald Ford.

Gena Rowlands *Betty Ford* • Josef Sommer *President Gerald Ford* • Nan Woods *Susan Ford* • Concetta Tomei *Jan* • Jack Radar *First doctor* • Joan McMurtrey *Diane* • Kenneth Tigar *Dr Lukash* • Laura Leigh Hughes *Gayle Ford* ■ *Dir* David Greene • *Scr* Karen Hall, from the autobiography *The Times of My Life* by Betty Ford, Chris Chase

Between Friends ★★★ 15

Drama   1983 · US · Colour · 95mins

Forget the old hat story and enjoy watching two great stars strut their stuff as middle-aged divorcees from different backgrounds who meet by accident and help each other through their mid-life crises. In a neat twist, Carol Burnett plays the object of all men's desire, while Elizabeth Taylor can't even get close to a boyfriend. The two leads give incandescent performances in this cable television movie, adapted from Shelley List's novel, and are the sole reason for its success. 🖵

Elizabeth Taylor *Deborah Shapiro* • Carol Burnett *Mary Catherine Castelli* • Barbara Bush *Francie Castelli* • Henry Ramer *Sam Tucker* • Bruce Gray *Malcolm Hollan* • Charles Shamata [Chuck Shamata] *Dr Seth Simpson* • Lally Cadeau *Lolly James* ■ *Dir* Lou Antonio • *Scr* Shelley List, Jonathan Estrin, from the novel *Nobody Makes Me Cry* by Shelley List

Between Heaven and Hell

★★

Second World War drama
1956 · US · Colour · 93mins

A routine 20th Century-Fox feature from Richard Fleischer, the skilled director of such classics as *The Vikings* and *Compulsion*. The plot favours the fifties psychological approach, as rich southern recruit Robert Wagner suffers in combat under psychotic bully Broderick Crawford, but the structure is messy and confused, and Wagner's brilliantined hairstyle is well out of the Second World War period.

Robert Wagner *Sam Gifford* • Terry Moore *Jenny* • Broderick Crawford *Waco* • Buddy Ebsen *Willie* • Robert Keith *Colonel Gozzens* • Brad Dexter *Joe Johnson* • Mark Damon *Terry* • Ken Clark *Morgan* ■ *Dir* Richard Fleischer • *Scr* Harry Brown, from the novel *The Day the Century Ended* by Francis Gwaltney

Between Love and Honor

★★ 12

Drama based on a true story
1995 · US · Colour · 86mins

Set in the seventies, this true story stars *Melrose Place* hunk Grant Show as Brooklyn photographer Steve Collura, recruited by the police to go undercover and infiltrate the Gambino crime family. He wins the Don over but, to his dismay, falls in love with Maria Caprefoli (Maria Pitillo), Gambino's goddaughter. Robert Loggia and Pitillo offer astute performances, but Show is rather dull as the besotted informer. Though at times absorbing, this TV movie is not a patch on *Donnie Brasco*. Contains violence and some swearing. 🖵

Grant Show *Steve Collura* • Robert Loggia *Carlo Gambino* • Cloris Leachman *Anna Collura* • Michael Nouri *Joey Gallo* • Maria Pitillo *Maria Caprefoli* • Steve Allie Collura *Detective Cellini* • Joseph Scoren *Danny* ■ *Dir* Sam Pillsbury • *Scr* Arnold Margolin

Between the Devil and the Deep Blue Sea ★★

Drama   1995 · Bel/Fr/UK · Colour · 92mins

Stephen Rea is an unlikely choice to play a Greek-Irish radio operator whose ship is stranded in Hong Kong when the company goes bust. While he's waiting to move on, he befriends a ten-year-old Chinese girl who cooks and cleans for him in order to care for her blind father. Made by a Belgian director, this anecdotal tale gets a mite pretentious when letters from Rea's girlfriend are heard over the soundtrack (read by Jane Birkin).

Stephen Rea *Nikos* • Chu Ling *Li* • Adrian Brine *Captain* • Maka Kotto *African sailor* • Mischa Aznavour *Young sailor* • Jane Birkin *Woman's voice* ■ *Dir* Marion Hänsel • *Scr* Marion Hänsel, Louis Grospierre, from a short story by Nikos Kavvadias

Between the Lines

★★★★ 15

Comedy   1977 · US · Colour · 101mins

A warm-hearted character comedy revolving around staff members of a Boston underground newspaper just before it's sold to a profit-minded publisher. The perceptive humour comes from the last bastion of sixties political radicalism taking on corporate

thinking, coupled with a brilliant ensemble cast milking every moment for wit and poignancy. Rock critic Jeff Goldblum's ad-libbed music lecture is a hoot, while photographer Lindsay Crouse's feminist rapport with stripper Marilu Henner is another highlight. Utterly engrossing and believable, this is a spirited satire full of real people involved in real situations. 🖵

John Heard *Harry* • Bruno Kirby *David* • Lindsay Crouse *Abbie* • Gwen Welles *Laura* • Jeff Goldblum *Max* • Stephen Collins *Michael* • Jill Eikenberry *Lynn* • Michael J Pollard *Hawker* • Marilu Henner *Stripper* ■ *Dir* Joan Micklin Silver • *Scr* Fred Barron, from a story by Fred Barron, David Helpern

Between Two Worlds ★★★

Fantasy drama   1944 · US · BW · 111mins

This is a revamped and updated version (it begins with an air raid) of Sutton Vane's allegorical play *Outward Bound*, which was filmed in 1930. It has a shipload of "dead" Warner Bros contract players en route to the next world, some going on to Heaven and others to Hell. Rather turgid stuff, it has good performances from Isobel Elsom, as a dreadful snob, Edmund Gwenn, as the steward, and Sydney Greenstreet as God's great divider, which make it worth watching. Paul Henreid and Eleanor Parker have a more difficult time as a couple who have committed suicide and John Garfield (in the role played by Leslie Howard in the 1930 film) overacts.

John Garfield *Tom Prior* • Paul Henreid *Henry* • Sydney Greenstreet *Thompson* • Eleanor Parker *Ann* • Edmund Gwenn *Scrubby* • George Tobias *Pete Musick* • George Coulouris *Lingley* • Faye Emerson *Maxine* ■ *Dir* Edward A Blatt • *Scr* Daniel Fuchs, from the play *Outward Bound* by Sutton Vane

The Beverly Hillbillies ★★ PG

Comedy   1993 · US · Colour · 89mins

Apparently stuck for ideas, Hollywood loves rehashing old TV shows into movies. This nineties' transfer of the sixties' show to the big screen seems just as pointless as the others of its ilk, despite Penelope Spheeris's direction, which tries hard to put a modern edge on nostalgia. The cast, including Dabney Coleman and Cloris Leachman, mainly mimic their predecessors, while Dolly Parton and Zsa Zsa Gabor make guest appearances. For fans of the TV show, the only highlight is a cameo from Buddy Ebsen, star of the original. 🖵

Jim Varney *Jed Clampett* • Diedrich Bader *Jethro/Jethrine* • Erika Eleniak *Elly May* • Cloris Leachman *Granny* • Lily Tomlin *Miss Hathaway* • Dabney Coleman *Mr Drysdale* • Lea Thompson *Laura* • Rob Schneider *Tyler* • Dolly Parton • Buddy Ebsen *Barnaby Jones* • Zsa Zsa Gabor ■ *Dir* Penelope Spheeris • *Scr* Lawrence Konner, Mark Rosenthal, Jim Fisher, Jim Staahl, Rob Schneider, Alex Herschlag, from a story by Lawrence Konner, Mark Rosenthal, from the TV series by Paul Henning

Beverly Hills Brats ★★ 15

Comedy   1989 · US · Colour · 91mins

The much revered Sheen clan (here Martin stars, with son Ramon in the cast and daughter Janet as associate producer) often displays an earnestness in their work that too often gives way to pretentiousness.

🅤 = SUITABLE FOR ALL   🆄c = SUITABLE FOR ALL, ESPECIALLY FOR YOUNG CHILDREN (VIDEO ONLY)   **PG** = PARENTAL GUIDANCE

And that's exactly what happens here in a film that, in attempting to expose the self-obsession of privileged Californians, purports to be satire but soon becomes a superficial and empty imitation. However, the film benefits greatly from the polished performance of Sheen the elder. Contains some swearing and nudity. 🎞

Martin Sheen *Jeffrey Miller* • Burt Young *Clive* • Terry Moore *Veronica Miller* • Peter Billingsley *Scooter Miller* • Ramon Sheen *Sterling Miller* • Cathy Podewell *Tiffany* ■ *Dir* Dimitri Sotirakis • *Scr* Linda Silverthorn, from a story by Terry Moore, Jerry Rivers

Beverly Hills Connection ★ 15

Thriller   1985 · US · Colour · 90mins

Billed as a light-hearted thriller, this foolish TV movie is pure rubbish. Lisa Hartman, (*Knots Landing* vixen and wife of country singer Clint Black) plays a Wyoming policewoman who goes to Beverly Hills to investigate the murder of a childhood friend, whom she discovers to have been a diamond-smuggling prostitute. James Brolin has the misfortune of playing a Los Angeles cop who helps her solve the case. Originally aired in the US as *Beverly Hills Cowgirl Blues*. 🎞

James Brolin *Harry Wilde* • Lisa Hartman *Amanda Ryder* • David Hemmings *Ian Blaze* • Stuart Whitman *Josh Ryder* • Irena Ferris *Christine Woodward* • Michael C Gwynne *Jimmy Blue* • Alexa Hamilton *Karen Moore* ■ *Dir* Corey Allen • *Scr* Rick Husky

Beverly Hills Cop ★★★★ 15

Action comedy 1984 · US · Colour · 100mins

This is the blockbuster that propelled Eddie Murphy to superstardom, when his brash, confident swagger still appeared fresh and he hadn't descended into caricature. In the first and best of the trilogy, he's the Detroit street cop who causes major upset in posh Beverly Hills when he turns up to investigate the murder of an old friend. Director Martin Brest orchestrates the senseless set pieces with slick precision and Brit Steven Berkoff takes the money and runs as the villain of the piece. Contains swearing. 🎞

Eddie Murphy *Axel Foley* • Judge Reinhold *Detective Billy Rosewood* • Lisa Eilbacher *Jenny Summers* • Steven Berkoff *Victor Maitland* • John Ashton *Sergeant Taggart* • Ronny Cox *Lieutenant Bogomil* • James Russo *Mikey Tandino* • Jonathan Banks *Zack* • Bronson Pinchot *Serge* ■ *Dir* Martin Brest • *Scr* Daniel Petrie Jr, from a story by Daniel Petrie Jr, Danilo Bach

Beverly Hills Cop II ★★ 15

Action comedy 1987 · US · Colour · 98mins

Eddie Murphy was back, the set pieces were even more spectacular and there were even some foreigners on board to ham it up as villains. Shame that they forgot about the script. This blockbusting sequel replays the plot of the original – Murphy returns to Los Angeles's swankiest suburb, this time to foil a gang of designer robbers who have wounded an old colleague – but any wit goes largely by the wayside and Murphy's mugging becomes increasingly irritating. Jürgen Prochnow and Brigitte Nielsen, as the obligatory accented baddies, fail to make much

impact, while Tony Scott's direction is flashy and superficial. Contains swearing and violence 🎞

Eddie Murphy *Axel Foley* • Judge Reinhold *Billy Rosewood* • Jürgen Prochnow *Maxwell Dent* • Ronny Cox *Andrew Bogomil* • John Ashton *John Taggart* • Brigitte Nielsen *Karla Fry* • Allen Garfield *Harold Lutz* • Dean Stockwell *Charles "Chip" Cain* ■ *Dir* Tony Scott • *Scr* Larry Ferguson, Warren Skaaren, from a story by Eddie Murphy, Robert D Wachs, from characters created by Danilo Bach, Daniel Petrie Jr

Beverly Hills Cop III ★★ 15

Action comedy 1994 · US · Colour · 99mins

Eddie Murphy and Judge Reinhold go through their paces for a third time, beginning once again on Murphy's home turf in Detroit and moving to Beverly Hills and a theme park called Wonder World. Even ardent advocates of recycling garbage might query the principle as shown here, though John Landis, who also directed Murphy in *Trading Places* and *Coming to America*, does pull off the occasional visual joke and an impressive set-piece car chase. While Murphy looks bored, that fine character actor Hector Elizondo adds some genuine quirkiness. 🎞

Eddie Murphy *Axel Foley* • Judge Reinhold *Billy Rosewood* • Hector Elizondo *Jon Flint* • Timothy Carhart *Ellis Dewald* • Stephen McHattie *Steve Fulbright* • Theresa Randle *Janice* • John Saxon *Orrin Sanderson* • Bronson Pinchot *Serge* ■ *Dir* John Landis • *Scr* Steven E De Souza, from characters created by Danilo Bach, Daniel Petrie Jr

Beverly Hills Family Robinson ★★

Comedy adventure 1997 · US · Colour · 88mins

Directed by Troy Miller (*Jack Frost*), this is a disappointing comic attempt to update Johann David Wyss's famous novel, *The Swiss Family Robinson*. Dyan Cannon stars as a TV cook who finds it hard to ditch her LA creature comforts when her clan's South Seas vacation goes badly wrong. Her young co-star, Sarah Michelle Gellar, would soon afterwards shoot to fame playing the title role in the hit TV series *Buffy the Vampire Slayer*.

Dyan Cannon *Marsha Robinson* • Martin Mull *Doug Robinson* • Sarah Michelle Gellar *Jane Robinson* • Ryan O'Donohue *Roger Robinson* • Josh Picker *Digger* ■ *Dir* Troy Miller • *Scr* TC Smith, from the novel *The Swiss Family Robinson* by Johann David Wyss

Beverly Hills Madam ★ 15

Drama 1986 · US · Colour · 92mins

An international cast that includes Faye Dunaway, Donna Dixon and the dashing Louis Jordan is the only point of interest in this trashy TV movie. The story follows a glamorous yet motherly madam whose high-priced call girls tend to fall in love with their clients. Faye's career must have been in a serious slump for her to make this one, though there is just enough seediness to make it almost worth watching. 🎞

Faye Dunaway *Lil Hutton* • Louis Jordan *Douglas Corbin* • Robin Givens *April Baxter* • Donna Dixon *Wendy Nelson* • Terry Farrell *Julie Taylor* • Melody Anderson *Claudia Winston* • Marshall Colt *Steven Beck* ■ *Dir* Harvey Hart • *Scr* Nancy Sackett

Beverly Hills 90210 ★★ PG

Drama 1990 · US · Colour · 92mins

Quite how Tim Hunter, director of bleak teen flicks such as *River's Edge*, ended up with the ever so perfect rich kids of Beverly Hills defies belief. Still, it remains a hoot, if only for the fact that the series – this was the pilot – hasn't aged particularly well. The then unknowns, Jason Priestley and Shannen Doherty, are the Midwest kids trying to make their way in Beverly Hills's bitchy high-school society. Most of the regulars from the series are present and correct (no Luke Perry, though) and fans will enjoy seeing how the various characters were individually conceived. Non-devotees will find it hard to keep a straight face. 🎞

Jason Priestley *Brandon Walsh* • Shannen Doherty *Brenda Walsh* • James Eckhouse *Jim Walsh* • Carol Potter *Cindy Walsh* • Jennie Garth *Kelly Taylor* • Ian Ziering *Steve Sanders* • Gabrielle Carteris *Andrea* • Brian Austin Green *David Silver* • Tori Spelling *Donna Martin* ■ *Dir* Tim Hunter • *Scr* Darren Star

Beverly Hills Ninja ★★★ 12

Martial arts comedy
1997 · US · Colour · 84mins

A box-office number one in the States, *Beverly Hills Ninja* comes from the producers of no-brainer classics *Dumb and Dumber* and *Kingpin* and features one of the last performances of chubby comic Chris Farley. An American baby washes up on the shores of Japan and is brought up by a clan of martial arts masters. Now Haru (Farley), a willing but clumsy pupil, must journey with a skilled sidekick (Robin Shou) to the "Hills of Beverly" to rescue a beautiful American girl from Yakuza counterfeiters. Slapstick fun for the undemanding. Contains some mild swearing and sexual references. 🎞

Chris Farley *Haru* • Nicollette Sheridan *Alison* • Robin Shou *Gobei* • Nathaniel Parker *Tanley* • Soon-Tek Oh [Soon-Teck Oh] *Sensei* • Keith Cooke Hirabayashi *Nobu* • Chris Rock *Joey* • François Chau *Izumo* • John Farley *Policeman* • Kevin Farley *Policeman* ■ *Dir* Dennis Dugan • *Scr* Mark Feldberg, Mitch Klebanoff

Beware, My Lovely ★★★

Drama 1952 · US · BW · 76mins

In this tense drama, vulnerable widow Ida Lupino hires craggy handyman Robert Ryan to help her prepare for Christmas, only to discover that he's a psychopath. Director Harry Horner creates such a claustrophobic atmosphere of pervasive nastiness that this film was rightly given an X certificate for its cinema release in Britain. Much disliked by the critics of the day, this is tough stuff, indeed. It was produced by Lupino's second husband, Collier Young.

Ida Lupino *Helen Gordon* • Robert Ryan *Howard Wilton* • Taylor Holmes *Mr Armstrong* • Barbara Whiting *Ruth Williams* • James Willmas *Mr Stevens* • OZ Whitehead *Mr Franks* ■ *Dir* Harry Horner • *Scr* Mel Dinelli, from his story and play *The Man*

Beware of a Holy Whore ★★★

Comedy 1970 · W Ger/It · Colour · 103mins

Inspired by Rainer Werner Fassbinder's own unhappy experience of shooting

Whity in Spain, this is a real eye-opener for those who doggedly believe in cinema as a glamorous business. A brutally honest – if self-indulgent – auto-critique, this is as much about the frustration of failing to find a means of expression as the dangerous vanity of artists. Yet there is still much satirical fun to be had at the expense of director Lou Castel, his bolshy film crew and the preening star, played with conscious irony by Eddie Constantine, the washed-up American actor and singer who became a sixties Euro icon. In German with English subtitles.

Lou Castel *Jeff, the director* • Eddie Constantine *Eddie Constantine, lead actor* • Marquard Böhm *Ricky, lead actor* • Hanna Schygulla *Hanna, lead actress* • Rainer Werner Fassbinder *Sascha Berling, production manager* • Margarethe von Trotta *Babs, production secretary* ■ *Dir* Rainer Werner Fassbinder • *Scr* Rainer Werner Fassbinder

Beware of Pity ★★

Romantic drama 1946 · UK · BW · 102mins

Several books by the Austrian novelist Stefan Zweig were adapted for the screen. However, while this one is infinitely inferior to *Letter from an Unknown Woman* (made two years later by Max Ophüls), it's not without its dark fascination. Lilli Palmer is touchingly vulnerable as the disabled baroness whose happiness with army officer Albert Lieven is jeopardised when she discovers the real motive for his attentions. Having learnt his trade in the silent era, director Maurice Elvey can't resist overplaying the melodrama, but the cast – particularly doctor Cedric Hardwicke and his wife, Gladys Cooper – keep things on track.

Lilli Palmer *Baroness Edith* • Albert Lieven *Lt Anton Marek* • Cedric Hardwicke *Dr Albert Condor* • Gladys Cooper *Klara Condor* • Linden Travers *Ilona Domansky* • Ernest Thesiger *Baron Emil de Kekesfalva* • Peter Cotes *Cusma* • Freda Jackson *Gypsy* ■ *Dir* Maurice Elvey • *Scr* WP Lipscomb, from the novel by Stefan Zweig

Beware! The Blob ★ 15

Science-fiction horror
1971 · US · Colour · 86mins

Noteworthy only for being directed by Larry (*Dallas*) Hagman – it was re-released in the eighties with the tag line "The film that JR shot!" – this pointless sequel to the 1958 classic rehashes virtually the same plot, but dumbs it down with amateurish special effects and strained acting. Godfrey Cambridge brings a globule of alien jelly back from the Arctic, which thaws out to become a homicidal protoplasm that increases its size by attacking partygoers and bowling alleys. The interesting cameo cast exists solely to get eaten by the pulsating red mass. Not scary or campy – just boring. 🎞

Robert Walker Jr *Bobby Hartford* • Gwynne Gilford *Lisa Clark* • Godfrey Cambridge *Chester* • Richard Stahl *Edward Fazio* • Richard Webb *Sheriff Jones* • Carol Lynley *Leslie* • Shelley Berman *Hairdresser* • Larry Hagman *Cop* ■ *Dir* Larry Hagman • *Scr* Anthony Harris, Jack Woods, from a story by Richard Clair, Anthony Harris

Bewitched ★★
Suspense drama   1945 · US · BW · 65mins

Arch Oboler, a radio producer who turned to movies, is nowadays best known, if at all, for his groundbreaking 3-D feature *Bwana Devil*. This adaptation of his story *Alter Ego* was the first of a series of films that invariably featured bizarre or supernatural themes. Phyllis Thaxter plays a woman suffering from a dual personality disorder, an unusual subject for this period. Edmund Gwenn offers sympathetic support, but the sheer talkiness betrays the writer/director's background in radio.

Phyllis Thaxter *Joan Alris Ellis* • Edmund Gwenn *Dr Bergson* • Henry H Daniels Jr *Bob Arnold* • Addison Richards *John Ellis* • Kathleen Lockhart *Mrs Ellis* • Francis Pierlot *Dr George Wilton* ■ *Dir* Arch Oboler • *Scr* Arch Oboler, from his story *Alter Ego*

Beyond a Reasonable Doubt ★★★★ PG
Film noir   1956 · US · BW · 80mins

While perhaps overdependent on coincidence and contrivance, Fritz Lang's Hollywood swan song is, nonetheless, a deft thriller that guards its secret right to the end. Some of the credit must go to stars Dana Andrews, who brings a chilling calculation to the part of the journalist whose crusade against circumstantial evidence results in a murder rap, and Joan Fontaine, as the loyal fiancée who campaigns to prove his innocence. But it is Lang's teasing direction that keeps the viewer guessing as his camera alights on seemingly inconsequential details that are just as likely to be red herrings as vital clues. ▦

Dana Andrews *Tom Garrett* • Joan Fontaine *Susan Spencer* • Sidney Blackmer *Austin Spencer* • Philip Bourneuf *Roy Thompson* • Shepperd Strudwick *Wilson* • Arthur Franz *Bob Hale* • Edward Binns *Lt Kennedy* ■ *Dir* Fritz Lang • *Scr* Douglas Morrow

Beyond Bedlam ★ 18
Psychological thriller
1993 · UK · Colour · 85mins

Clockwork Mice showed Vadim Jean to be a director of some talent, but there's little of it on display in this convoluted, violent and ineffectual thriller. The cat-and-mouse tale involves a detective (Craig Fairbrass) who stumbles upon a scientist (Elizabeth Hurley) conducting gross experiments on serial killer Keith Allen. The B-list British cast – which includes erstwhile soap stars Anita Dobson and Jesse Birdsall – doesn't bode well in a film we wouldn't even advise you to buy for 50p at a car boot sale. ▦

Craig Fairbrass *Terry Hamiltorn* • Elizabeth Hurley *Stephanie Lyell* • Keith Allen *Marc Gilmour* • Anita Dobson *Judith Hamilton* • Craig Kelly *Matthew Hamilton* • Georgina Hale *Sister Romulus* • Jesse Birdsall *Scott* ■ *Dir* Vadim Jean • *Scr* Rob Walker, Vadim Jean, from the novel *Bedlam* by Harry Adam Knight

Beyond Forgiveness ★★ 18
Action thriller
1994 · US/Pol · Colour · 89mins

Action star Thomas Ian Griffith tones down the skull-cracking and kick-boxing in this American-Polish thriller. Griffith plays a Chicago cop, whose lust for revenge following the brutal murder of his younger brother sends him off on a dangerous mission to his father's homeland – Poland – in a bid to track down the killer. Teaming up with a portly policeman played by John Rhys-Davies (*Raiders of the Lost Ark*), he soon uncovers a sinister trade in human organs masterminded by the evil Dr Lem (Rutger Hauer). ▦

Thomas Ian Griffith *Frank Wushinsky* • Rutger Hauer *Dr Lem* • John Rhys-Davies *Zmuda* • Artur Zmijewski *Marty* • Bozena Szymanska *Patty* • Jerzy Karaszkiewicz *Stan the barman* • Cezary Poks *Courier* • Aleksander Wysocki *Scarface* • Ryszard Ronczewski *Chicago priest* ■ *Dir* Bob Misiorowski • *Scr* Charles Cohen, from a story by Anatoly Niman

Beyond Mombasa ★★ U
Action adventure   1957 · US · Colour · 90mins

This safari adventure has Cornel Wilde's plans to mine uranium hampered by a leopard-worshipping tribe who have already flayed his brother alive. Wilde later directed and starred in *The Naked Prey*, one of the most distinctive African yarns ever made. However, this effort is content to roll out every cliché – from blowpipes and missionaries turned mad by malaria and greed, to the obligatory damsel in distress (played by Donna Reed). The nice location photography by Freddie Young was completed just as Kenya itself was enduring the terrorism of the Mau Mau, which resulted in British troops being sent to defend the Empire.

Cornel Wilde *Matt Campbell* • Donna Reed *Ann Wilson* • Leo Genn *Ralph Hoyt* • Ron Randell *Elliott Hastings* • Christopher Lee *Gil Rossi* • Eddie Calvert *Trumpet player* • Dan Jackson *Ketimi* • Macdonald Parke *Tourist* ■ *Dir* George Marshall • *Scr* Richard English, Gene Levitt, from the story *The Mark of the Leopard* by James Eastwood

Beyond Obsession ★★
Drama based on a true story
1994 · US · Colour

Making the best of what little material they've got, Emily Warfield and Henry Thomas are credible enough in this TV movie as teenagers driven to murder. The idea of *Dallas*'s Victoria Principal as an abusive mother is, however, stretching things too far. Director David Greene struggles to prevent the domestic discord from descending into melodrama, but still fails to inject much tension into the courtroom scenes.

Emily Warfield *Traci DiCarlo* • Henry Thomas *John Thompson* • Joe Regalbuto *Jake Meletti* • Donnelly Rhodes *Bill Richardson* • Victoria Principal *Eleanor DiCarlo* • Garry Chalk *Lieutenant Bartell* • Alex Bruhanski *Roger Horn* • Linda Darlow *Dr Janet Lytton* ■ *Dir* David Greene • *Scr* Eugenia Bostwick-Singer, Raymond Singer, from the non-fiction book by Richard Leiterman

Beyond Rangoon ★★★★ 15
Drama   1995 · US · Colour · 99mins

John Boorman's powerful indictment of Burma's oppressive military regime stars Patricia Arquette as a naive American doctor who becomes embroiled in the country's problems. She finds herself drawn to the campaign of the democratic leader under house arrest, Aung San Suu Kyi. Filmed in neighbouring Malaysia (whose government was shrewdly misled about the film's content), it follows *The Year of Living Dangerously* and *The Killing Fields* by using a westerner as its protagonist: "Some people have found that her grief is in some sense trivial against the horrors of a nation's bloodshed," said Boorman, "but my feeling was that this woman shares the audience's ignorance... she's drawn into it and learns about it as we do."

Patricia Arquette *Laura Bowman* • U Aung Ko • Frances McDormand *Andy* • Spalding Gray *Jeremy Watt* • Tiara Jacquelina *Desk clerk* • Kuswadinath Bujang *Colonel* • Victor Slezak *Mr Scott* • Jit Murad *Sein Htoo* • Ye Myint Zaw Win • Adelle Lutz *Aung San Suu Kyi* ■ *Dir* John Boorman • *Scr* Alex Lasker, Bill Rubenstein

Beyond Reasonable Doubt ★★★★ PG
Drama based on a true story
1980 · NZ · Colour · 103mins

David Hemmings gives his best performance since he became a Swinging Sixties' sensation in *Blow Up*, playing a malicious New Zealand cop planting evidence to put a noose around the neck of a feeble-minded farmer (John Hargreaves) accused of a husband-and-wife murder. The farmer went for two trials, was found guilty and then pardoned, a chilling sequence of events that led British writer David Yallop to research the book on which the film is based. John Laing directs without any sense of urgency, but the fact that it's a true story makes it memorable. Contains some violence ▦

David Hemmings *Inspector Hutton* • John Hargreaves *Arthur Allen Thomas* • Martyn Sanderson *Lem Demler* • Tony Barry *Detective John Hughes* • Grant Tilly *David Morris* • Diana Rowan *Vivien Thomas* ■ *Dir* John Laing • *Scr* David Yallop, from his non-fiction book

Beyond Silence ★★★ 12
Drama   1996 · Ger · Colour · 113mins

More interested in the problem of living with deaf people than with deafness itself, this is still an ambitious attempt to combine the problem picture and the tear-jerker, within the confines of the European art movie. Caroline Link makes evocative use of sound throughout as she shows how a young girl finds release in music from the routine of signing for her deaf-mute parents. Both Tatjana Trieb and Sylvie Testud excel as the maturing Lara, although the latter is forced to deal with a melodramatic plotline when she becomes torn between her father and her friends in Berlin. In German with English subtitles. Contains a mild sex scene.

Sylvie Testud *Lara* • Tatjana Trieb *Lara as a child* • Howie Seago *Martin* • Emmanuelle Laborit *Kai* • Sibylle Canonica *Clarissa* • Matthias Habich *Gregor* • Alexandra Bolz *Marie* • Hansa Czypionka *Tom* ■ *Dir* Caroline Link • *Scr* Caroline Link, Beth Serlin

Beyond Suspicion ★★
Thriller   1994 · US · Colour · 98mins

This is another of those forgettable thrillers, in which the amnesiac victim only ever manages to remember key points one at a time to ensure that 40-seconds-worth of plot sprawls out to fill the running time. Here, Stepfanie Kramer is a little foggy about the facts of a murder case, but she's nowhere near as blocked as crooked cop Jack Scalia thinks she is and she feigns ignorance to lure him into a trap. Scalia is a nasty piece of work and, scheming though Kramer is, she just doesn't have what it takes to give him a run for his money. Contains violence, swearing, sex scenes and nudity.

Stepfanie Kramer *Karen Reikhart* • Jack Scalia *Detective Sergeant Vince Morgan* • Howard GH Dell [Howard Dell] *Capt Townsend* • Lily Shavick *Sara* ■ *Dir* Paul Ziller • *Scr* Simon Abbott

Beyond the Blue Horizon ★★★
Musical comedy   1942 · US · Colour · 76mins

Sporting her trademark sarong in yet another of her popular South Seas movies, Dorothy Lamour stars as an orphan who has grown up living native on a tropical isle with a tiger and a chimp for company. Richard Denning supplies the romance, while Dottie's discovery that she's a millionairess peps up the plot. Treated as the fantastical nonsense it is by director Alfred Santell, who squeezes as much amusement as possible from GoGo the chimp and Jack Haley (*The Wizard of Oz*'s Tin Man), this is gloriously tongue-in-cheek, escapist fare.

Dorothy Lamour *Tama* • Richard Denning *Jakra* • Jack Haley *Squidge* • Walter Abel *Thornton* • Helen Gilbert *Carol* • Patricia Morison *Sylvia* • Frances Gifford *Charlotte* • Elizabeth Patterson *Mrs Daly* ■ *Dir* Alfred Santell • *Scr* Frank Butler, from a story by E Lloyd Sheldon, Jack DeWitt

Beyond the Call ★★★
Drama   1996 · US · Colour · 101mins

Dead Man Walking meets *Born on the Fourth of July* in this affecting TV movie, with a cast a good few notches above the norm. Sissy Spacek plays a housewife who becomes involved in a battle to save the life of David Strathairn, a former beau and Vietnam vet on death row after murdering a policeman. She learns that the tragedy was the result of post-traumatic shock syndrome, but her campaign puts her own marriage to Arliss Howard in jeopardy. The performances are first rate and the direction from Tony Bill is sympathetically understated. Contains violence and swearing.

Sissy Spacek *Pam O'Brien* • David Strathairn *Russell Gates* • Arliss Howard *Keith O'Brien* • Janet Wright *Fran* • Lindsay Murrell *Rebecca O'Brien* • Andrew Sardella *Mark O'Brien* ■ *Dir* Tony Bill • *Scr* Doug Magee

Beyond the Clouds ★★ 18
Drama   1995 · It/Ger/Fr · Colour · 104mins

At the age of 82 and in poor health, Michelangelo Antonioni filmed this quartet of short stories, linked by John Malkovich as a film director looking for his next idea. At times the visuals betray the presence of a master filmmaker, but otherwise this is a flimsy and rather sad enterprise that has the look of a dying man's last breath. Antonioni was helped by his friend and admirer, Wim Wenders, and lots of actors look in and pay tribute. They include Marcello Mastroianni and Jeanne Moreau, the stars of Antonioni's *La Notte*. An English/Italian/French language film. Contains swearing and nudity. ▭

Ines Sastre *Carmen* • Kim Rossi Stuart *Silvano* • Sophie Marceau *Young woman* • John Malkovich *The Director* • Irène Jacob *Girl* • Vincent Perez *Boy* • Fanny Ardant *Patricia* • Peter Weller *Husband* • Chiara Caselli *Olga* • Jean Reno *Carlo* • Marcello Mastroianni *Maestro* • Jeanne Moreau *Woman* ▪ *Dir* Michelangelo Antonioni • *Scr* Michelangelo Antonioni, Wim Wenders, Tonino Guerra, from the short story collection *That Bowling Alley on the River Tiber* by Michelangelo Antonioni

Beyond the Curtain ★ ▣
Thriller 1960 · UK · BW · 91mins

This shoddy propaganda piece is the kind of bargain-basement nonsense that gives low-budget features a bad name. It stars Richard Greene as a pilot who drops behind the Iron Curtain to prise air hostess Eva Bartok out of the clutches of the communists. They seem to think her kidnapping will give them match point in the Cold War. Faced with a dismal script and locations that would shame poverty row, the unfortunate cast doesn't even try to convince. It's quite a comedown for *The Seventh Veil* director Compton Bennett.

Richard Greene *Captain Jim Kyle* • Eva Bartok *Karin von Seefeldt* • Marius Goring *Hans Koertner* • Lucie Mannheim *Frau von Seefeldt* • Andrée Melly *Linda* • George Mikell *Pieter* • John Welsh *Turner* • Dennis Shaw [Denis Shaw] *Krumm* ▪ *Dir* Compton Bennett • *Scr* John Cresswell, Compton Bennett, from the novel *Thunder Above* by Charles F Blair

Beyond the Forest ★★
Melodrama 1949 · US · BW · 76mins

The great Bette Davis occasionally teetered on the edge of farce, only saved from producing a parody of herself by a strong directorial hand on the tiller. Sadly, King Vidor does not provide it here. Davis is the disenchanted wife of a hick doctor – a competent Joseph Cotten – stuck in a small town and soon embroiled in a murder puzzle. Vidor tries too hard and fails miserably to engender an atmosphere of tension and menace between a triangle consisting of Davis, Cotten and rich neighbour David Brian. Davis at her most arch and uncontained is not a pretty sight.

Bette Davis *Rosa Moline* • Joseph Cotten *Dr Lewis Moline* • David Brian *Neil Latimer* • Ruth Roman *Carol* • Minor Watson *Moose* • Dona Drake *Jenny* • Regis Toomey *Sorren* • Sara Selby [Sarah Selby] *Mildred* • Mary Servoss *Mrs Welch* ▪ *Dir* King Vidor • *Scr* Lenore Coffee, from the novel by Stuart Engstrand

Beyond the Law ★★
Spaghetti western
1967 · It/W Ger · BW · 85mins

It's the details that make this routine and rather anaemic Spaghetti western fun. Lee Van Cleef plays a bandit who undergoes a miraculous change of heart when he becomes the sheriff of a one-horse town, while Gordon Mitchell is the villain who comes up against his ex-partner when he tries to

rob the local mine of its payroll. Moody Van Cleef's shifting allegiances add an extra frisson to the predictability. Italian dialogue dubbed into English.

Lee Van Cleef *Cudlipp* • Gordon Mitchell *Burton* • Antonio Sabato *Ben Novack* • Lionel Stander *Preacher* • Graziella Granata *Sally* • Ann Smyrner *Lola* ▪ *Scr* Warren Kiefer [Lorenzo Sabatini], Fernando DiLeo, Mino Roli, Giorgio Stegani, from a story by Warren Kiefer [Lorenzo Sabatini]

Beyond the Law ★★★ ▣
Detective drama 1968 · US · BW · 85mins

This abrasive second film from novelist-turned-director Norman Mailer shows the off-duty hours of three Manhattan cops. Mailer himself plays the senior detective, while his colleagues are all racist bigots who bend the rules in their quest for a collar. In some senses, it's a forerunner to *Dirty Harry* and *The French Connection*. The style is strictly *cinéma vérité*, however – the cameraman is noted documentarist DA Pennebaker – and the script consists of improvised dialogue made up on the spot. It's a grubby, shambolic movie with some terrible scenes, but there's also some powerful stuff here, most of it involving Rip Torn as a hippie accused of murder.

Rip Torn *Popcorn* • George Plimpton *Mayor* • Norman Mailer *Lieutenant Francis Xavier Pope* • Mickey Knox *Mickey Berk* • Buzz Farbar *Rocco Gibraltar* • Beverly Bentley *Mary Pope* • Mara Lynn *Ilse Fuchs* • Marcia Mason *Marcia Stillwell* ▪ *Dir/Scr* Norman Mailer

Beyond the Poseidon Adventure ★★ ▣
Drama 1979 · US · Colour · 109mins

The movie that, until *Independence Day* came along, effectively finished off the disaster movie genre, and the career of its king Irwin Allen. Michael Caine (possibly at one of the lowest ebbs in his career) Sally Field and Karl Malden are the salvage team who come to the rescue of the sunken *Poseidon* passenger liner and find themselves fighting off villainous Telly Savalas, who is after the ship's valuable secret cargo. Peter Boyle, Shirley Knight, Veronica Hamel and Mark Harmon are among the stars who probably wished they hadn't survived the sinking, and even the effects aren't up to much. ▭

Michael Caine *Captain Mike Turner* • Sally Field *Celeste Whitman* • Telly Savalas *Stefan Svevo* • Peter Boyle *Frank Mazzetti* • Jack Warden *Harold Meredith* • Shirley Knight *Hannah Meredith* • Shirley Jones *Gina Rowe* • Karl Malden *Wilbur Hubbard* • Veronica Hamel *Suzanne Constantine* • Slim Pickens *Tex* • Mark Harmon *Larry Simpson* ▪ *Dir* Irwin Allen • *Scr* Nelson Gidding, from the novel by Paul Gallico

Beyond the River ★★
Drama 1956 · US · Colour · 88mins

The original American title, *The Bottom of the Bottle*, should alert you to the content of this maudlin adaptation of a Georges Simenon novel. The physically similar Van Johnson and Joseph Cotten are well cast as psychologically mismatched brothers, one an alcoholic fugitive, the other a respected attorney. Despite veteran director

Henry Hathaway's expert handling, the story barely fills the CinemaScope screen; it would have worked better as a tight, black-and-white production. Jack Carson steals the show in a supporting role, but Ruth Roman is wildly inadequate as the hysterical leading lady.

Van Johnson *Donald Martin* • Joseph Cotten *PM* • Ruth Roman *Nora Martin* • Jack Carson *Hal Breckinridge* • Margaret Hayes *Lil Breckinridge* • Bruce Bennett *Brand* • Brad Dexter *Stanley Miller* • Peggy Knudsen *Ellen Miller* ▪ *Dir* Henry Hathaway • *Scr* Sidney Boehm, from a novel by Georges Simenon

Beyond the Stars ★★★ ▣
Drama 1988 · Can/US · Colour · 87mins

A very young looking Christian Slater is the teenager who dreams of becoming an astronaut in this charming drama. His life changes for ever when he discovers that a reclusive neighbour (Martin Sheen) actually took part in a Moon landing, and the two form an uneasy friendship. Both Slater and Sheen are delightful in this enjoyable tale, and they are joined by an impressive cast, which includes F Murray Abraham, Robert Foxworth and a pre-*Basic Instinct* Sharon Stone. Contains mild swearing. ▭

Martin Sheen *Paul Andrews* • Christian Slater *Eric Mason* • Robert Foxworth *Richard Michaels* • Sharon Stone *Laurie McCall* • Olivia D'Abo *Mara Simons* • F Murray Abraham *Harry* ▪ *Dir/Scr* David Saperstein

Beyond the Valley of the Dolls ★★★★ ▣
Cult satirical comedy
1970 · US · Colour · 104mins

Dubbed "BVD" by die-hard trash lovers, soft-core porn king Russ Meyer's hilarious exposé of Hollywood sex, drugs and rock 'n' roll is platinum-plated cult camp. Telling the fabulous rags-to-bitches story of all-girl band the Carrie Nations as they scale the dizzy heights of rock-star fame and then crash-land into decadent sleaze, Meyer's pneumatic parody flashes between soap-opera morality, caricature deviance, flower-power lunacy and shock horror with such breathless audacity that you'll watch it in open-mouthed disbelief. All this and music by the Strawberry Alarm Clock, too. Contains swearing and nudity. ▭

Dolly Read *Kelly MacNamara* • Cynthia Myers *Casey Anderson* • Marcia McBroom *Pertonella Danforth* • John LaZar *Z-Man* • Michael Blodgett *Lance Rocke* • David Gurian *Harris Allworth* • Edy Williams *Ashley St Ives* • Erica Gavin *Roxanne* • Charles Napier *Baxter Wolfe* ▪ *Dir* Russ Meyer • *Scr* Roger Ebert

Beyond the Walls ★★ ▣
Prison drama 1984 · Is · Colour · 98mins

An Israeli contender for the best foreign film Oscar, this overload and hysterical prison drama typifies all that can be wrong with Israeli cinema. Though well intentioned it's over-directed, horrendously derivative and emotionally strident. The plot is naive beyond measure: in a maximum security jail an Israeli criminal and an Arab terrorist team up to start a prison strike and stop the escalation of violence between inmates and guards. The cast – headed by Arnon Zadok and

Muhamad Bakri – plays with sincerity, which ironically reinforces director Uri Barbash's simplistic premise that these Israeli-Arab prison relationships serve as a metaphor for the Middle East conflict. In Hebrew with English subtitles. ▭

Arnon Zadok *Uri* • Muhamad Bakri *Issam* • Assi Dayan *Assaf* • Hilel Ne'eman *Hershko, the security officer* • Rami Danon *Fittusi* • Boaz Sharaabi *"The Nightingale"* • Adib Jahashan *Malid* • Roberto Polak *Yechiel* • Naffi Salach *Sanji* ▪ *Dir* Uri Barbash, Arnon Zadok, Muhamad Bakri, Rudy Cohen • *Scr* Benny Barbash, Eran Preis, Uri Barbash

Beyond Therapy ★★★ ▣
Comedy 1987 · US · Colour · 89mins

With his customary scatter-gun style, director Robert Altman tends to miss as many targets as he hits. So it proves in this weirdly wacky love story, in which bisexual Jeff Goldblum's relationship with neurotic Julie Hagerty is helped and hindered by their respective psychiatric agony aunts. Glenda Jackson intimidates everyone within reach and there are some great one-liners, though this exercise in disconnected thinking might have worked better with a more coherent approach. Adapted from the play by Christopher Durang, the film achieves a wan poignancy at best. ▭

Julie Hagerty *Prudence* • Jeff Goldblum *Bruce* • Glenda Jackson *Charlotte* • Tom Conti *Dr Stuart Framingham* • Christopher Guest *Bob* • Genevieve Page *Zizi* • Cris Campion *Andrew* • Sandrine Dumas *Cindy* ▪ *Dir* Robert Altman • *Scr* Christopher Durang, Robert Altman, from the play by Christopher Durang

Beyond This Place ★★
Drama 1959 · UK · BW · 90mins

Cameraman-turned-director Jack Cardiff was still finding his feet with this, his second film. It's a rather turgid adaptation of AJ Cronin's tale, about a grown-up wartime evacuee who returns to England to clear his dad of murder. Anglophile Van Johnson is not an ideal lead, though he furrows his brow nicely, but there's a fine British supporting cast. The budget limitations are obvious, despite the presence of US import Vera Miles (previously teamed with Johnson in the superior *23 Paces to Baker Street*) and a brief location shoot in Liverpool. Movie buffs should look out for production manager Vincent Winter, playing the Van Johnson character as a boy.

Van Johnson *Paul Mathry* • Vera Miles *Lena Anderson* • Emlyn Williams *Enoch Oswald* • Bernard Lee *Patrick Mathry* • Jean Kent *Louise Birt* • Leo McKern *McEvoy* • Rosalie Crutchley *Ella Mathry* • Vincent Winter *Paul, as a child* ▪ *Dir* Jack Cardiff • *Scr* Kenneth Taylor, from a novel by AJ Cronin

Bezubaan ★★★
Drama 1981 · Ind · Colour

Loosely based on Tamil director SP Muthuraman's *Mayangurikal Oru Madhu* (1975), this Bollywood drama explores the constraints placed upon women within Indian society. As the happily married wife whose bliss is threatened by the return of a former lover, Reena Roy does extremely well to hold her own alongside her more illustrious co-stars Shashi Kapoor and Naseeruddin Shah. Best known for retelling classical myths in contemporary settings, Bapu directs his cast well, but the conventions of Indian cinema prevent him from tackling the theme of pre-marital chastity with the required realism. In Hindi and Urdu with English subtitles.

Reena Roy • Shashi Kapoor • Naseeruddin Shah • Raj Kiran • Reeta Bhaduri ■ *Dir* Bapu

Bhaji on the Beach ★★★ 15
Comedy drama   1993 · UK · Colour · 96mins

Gurinder Chadha's debut feature is an astute look at what it means to be Asian, female and British. Following a group of Brummies on a day trip to Blackpool, the film's great strength is the way it interweaves the different plot strands so that each one develops into a fascinating little story in its own right before being neatly brought together at the end. Chadha and scriptwriter Meera Syal were a touch overambitious in trying to tackle so many themes, but whether discussing the clash between Indian traditions and modern values or the racial prejudice that exists between Britain's different ethnic groups, their insights are often provocative. Contains violence and swearing. 🖵

Kim Vithana *Ginder* • Jimmi Harkishin *Ranjit* • Sarita Khajuria *Hashida* • Mo Sesay *Oliver* • Lalita Ahmed *Asha* • Shaheen Khan *Simi* • Zohra Segal *Pushpa* • Amer Chadha-Patel *Amrik* • Nisha Nayar [Nisha K Nayar] *Ladhu* ■ *Dir* Gurinder Chadha • *Scr* Meera Syal, from a story by Meera Syal, Gurinder Chadha

Bhowani Junction ★★★
Drama   1956 · US · Colour · 109mins

Director George Cukor's record with action was far from enviable when he set off for Pakistan to shoot this adaptation of John Masters's novel about inflamed political and romantic passions in the last days of the Raj. Yet, surprisingly, the crowd scenes and the acts of Communist terror are the best parts of this rather turgid melodrama, in which Cukor (known as a "woman's director") fails to coax any kind of performance out of Ava Gardner, who was about to divorce then husband Frank Sinatra and leave Hollywood for the high life in Europe. Stewart Granger and Bill Travers are scarcely more animated.

Ava Gardner *Victoria Jones* • Stewart Granger *Colonel Rodney Savage* • Bill Travers *Patrick Taylor* • Abraham Sofaer *Surabhai* • Francis Matthews *Ranjit Kasel* • Marne Maitland *Govindaswami* • Peter Illing *Ghanshyam* • Edward Chapman *Thomas Jones* ■ *Dir* George Cukor • *Scr* Sonya Levien, Ivan Moffat, from the novel by John Masters

The Bible...in the Beginning ★★ U
Biblical epic   1966 · US/It · Colour · 218mins

Even though screenwriter Christopher Fry consulted with eminent bible scholars and producer Dino DeLaurentiis threw pots of money at the project, this is a reverential but onerous adaptation of the first 22 chapters of Genesis. Director John Huston makes a lovely job of the Creation, but the stellar casting too often works against the drama, most notably in the case of Richard Harris's Cain, Stephen Boyd's Nimrod and Ava

Gardner's Sarah. George C Scott is imposing as Abraham, however, while Huston himself makes a suitably humble Noah. Giuseppe Rotunno's photography is striking, but Toshiro Mayuzumi's Oscar-nominated score is somewhat overbearing.

Michael Parks *Adam* • Ulla Bergryd *Eve* • Richard Harris *Cain* • John Huston *Noah* • Stephen Boyd *Nimrod* • George C Scott *Abraham* • Ava Gardner *Sarah* • Peter O'Toole *Three Angels* • Franco Nero *Abel* ■ *Dir* John Huston • *Scr* Christopher Fry, Jonathan Griffin, Ivo Perilli, Vittorio Bonicelli

Bicentennial Man ★★ 12
Science-fiction comedy
1999 · US · Colour · 125mins

Based on the work of two of science fiction's literary giants, Isaac Asimov and Robert Silverberg, this admirably treats its robot hero as a suitable case for dramatic treatment. Unfortunately, Robin Williams plays for tears as Andrew, the android butler assembled to serve one family over four generations. Andrew is treated well by his owner (Sam Neill), but later has himself reconstructed as a human being for the sake of his true love (Embeth Davidtz). Directed by Chris Columbus, the film makes Andrew irritatingly cute (as does the star), undermining Asimov's original analogy with black outsiders. With marvellous effects and ideas scuppered by sentimentality, it's enough to make a mechanical man weep. 📀

Robin Williams *Andrew* • Embeth Davidtz *Little Miss/Portia* • Sam Neill *Sir* • Oliver Platt *Rupert Burns* • Wendy Crewson *Ma'am* • Hallie Kate Eisenberg *Little Miss, 7 years old* • Stephen Root *Dennis Mansky* • Kiersten Warren *Galatea robotic/Human* ■ *Dir* Chris Columbus • *Scr* Nicholas Kazan, from sshort story by Isaac Asimov and from the novel *The Positronic Man* by Isaac Asimov, Robert Silverberg

Les Biches ★★★★ 15
Erotic drama   1968 · Fr/It · Colour · 94mins

New Wave director Claude Chabrol entered a new phase – which would ultimately lead to such masterpieces as *Le Boucher* – with this cool study of a *ménage à trois* between rich lesbian Stéphane Audran, her penniless young plaything Jacqueline Sassard, and handsome architect Jean-Louis Trintignant. Set on the Riviera, the movie has a marvellously fluid style that matches the seesawing sexuality of the characters and builds towards a startling climax. The picture is also a showcase for Audran, who was then Chabrol's wife and the star of most of his major films. In French with English subtitles. 🖵

Jean-Louis Trintignant *Paul* • Jacqueline Sassard *Why* • Stéphane Audran *Frederique* • Nane Germon *Violetta* • Henri Attal *Robeque* • Dominique Zardi *Riais* • Claude Chabrol *Film-maker* ■ *Dir* Claude Chabrol • *Scr* Claude Chabrol, Paul Gégauff

Bicycle Thieves ★★★★★ U
Drama   1948 · It · BW · 88mins

Scripted by Cesare Zavattini and directed by Vittorio De Sica, this urban parable is the masterwork of the neorealist movement. Exploring the response of ordinary people to the socio-political changes sweeping

postwar Italy, the film adopts a "flow of life" structure, comprising vignettes of differing emotional intensity as it follows long-unemployed Lamberto Maggiorani and his son, Enzo Staiola, around Rome in search of the stolen bicycle on which the family depends for its livelihood. Alternating travelling shots of poetic symbolism with stark close-ups of his non-professional leads, De Sica achieves an ironic humanism that can't fail to touch the heart. In Italian with English subtitles.

Lamberto Maggiorani *Antonio Ricci* • Lianella Carell *Maria Ricci* • Enzo Staiola *Bruno Ricci* • Elena Altieri *The Lady* • Vittorio Antonucci *The Thief* ■ *Dir* Vittorio De Sica • *Scr* Cesare Zavattini, Suso Cecchi d'Amico, Vittorio De Sica, Oreste Biancoli, Adolfo Franci, Gherardo Gherardi, Guerrier Gerardo, from a novel by Luigi Bartolini • *Cinematographer* Carlo Montuori

Big ★★★★ PG
Comedy   1988 · US · Colour · 99mins

Tom Hanks, winner of best actor Oscars for his roles in 1993's *Philadelphia* and the following year's *Forrest Gump* only got an Oscar nomination for this, one of his finest performances to date as a 12-year-old boy transplanted by a carnival wishing contraption into a man's body. In fact, his role as a simple but sincere guy in a cynical world foreshadows his portrayal of Gump. *Big* may well be a formula fantasy movie, but Penny Marshall's polished direction combined with Hanks's gauche charm make it the best of the spate of body-swap movies that were turned out by Hollywood in the late eighties. Contains some swearing. 🖵

Tom Hanks *Josh Baskin* • Elizabeth Perkins *Susan Lawrence* • Robert Loggia *"Mac" MacMillan* • John Heard *Paul Davenport* • Jared Rushton *Billy Kopeche* • David Moscow *Young Josh* • Jon Lovitz *Scotty Brennen* • Mercedes Ruehl *Mrs Baskin* ■ *Dir* Penny Marshall • *Scr* Gary Ross, Anne Spielberg

Big Bad Mama ★★★
Crime drama   1974 · US · Colour · 84mins

Angie Dickinson comes on strong in a typical early-seventies B-movie from the Roger Corman production line, clearly based on *Bonnie and Clyde* and *Bloody Mama*. Dickinson plays a high-spirited widow in thirties Texas who goes on a bank-robbing spree with her two nubile daughters when the Depression bites. Full of sex, violence, machine guns and banjo music, it's a rambunctious quickie effortlessly touching each exploitation base that able action director Steve Carver sets his sights on. *Star Trek's* William Shatner turns up to romance Dickinson, and her eye-popping nude scenes have made this one a cult favourite.

Angie Dickinson *Wilma McClatchie* • William Shatner *William J Baxter* • Tom Skerritt *Fred Diller* • Susan Sennett *Billy Jean McClatchie* • Robbie Lee *Polly McClatchie* • Noble Willingham *Barney* • Joan Prather *Jane Kingston* • Royal Dano *Reverend Johnson* • William O'Connell *Preacher* • Dick Miller *Bonny* ■ *Dir* Steve Carver • *Scr* William Norton, Frances Doel

Big Bad Mama II ★★★ 18
Crime drama   1987 · US · Colour · 80mins

A cheap and cheerful follow-up – albeit 13 years later – to Roger Corman's cult gangster hit, with Angie Dickinson reviving her role as the gun-toting matriarch. In this adventure, she takes time off from her bank-robbing activities to do battle with slimy politician Bruce Glover, with journalist Robert Culp also on her trail. Although this lacks the knockabout charm and the eclectic casting of the original, director Jim Wynorski, who was also responsible for *The Return of Swamp Thing*, is a protégé of Corman and delivers a lightweight, knowing slice of exploitation. Contains violence, swearing and nudity. 🖵

Angie Dickinson *Wilma McClatchie* • Robert Culp *Daryl Pearson* • Danielle Brisebois *Billie Jean McClatchie* • Julie McCullough *Polly McClatchie* • Bruce Glover *Crawford* • Jeff Yagher *Jordan Crawford* ■ *Dir* Jim Wynorski • *Scr* RJ Robertson, Jim Wynorski

The Big Bang ★★★ 18
Documentary   1989 · US · Colour · 73mins

Among the most unconventional directors in modern American cinema, James Toback usually has something to say in his films. But here, he contented himself with a few appeals for cash to potential backers and leaves the serious talking to an eloquent and refreshingly candid cast in this compelling documentary on life, the universe and everything. An artist, an astronomer, a basketball player and a gangster are among those with an option to share. But the most poignant "talking head" is Barbara Traub, an Auschwitz survivor whose thoughts have much greater resonance than all the others, particularly those of successful film producer Don Simpson. Contains swearing. 🖵

Dir/Scr James Toback

The Big Bird Cage ★★
Crime drama   1972 · US · Colour · 88mins

The sequel to *The Big Doll House* is more of the same – a blaxploitation mix of broad humour, random violence and dodgy politics. Anitra Ford is jailed in a bamboo sugar mill for knowing too much about a banana republic's revolutionary government and gets imprisoned in the titular torture device. Sid Haig, meanwhile, swoops in to rescue his girlfriend (Pam Grier) and incite a bloody insurrection. This is predictable escapist mayhem with the accent on laughs – especially when Haig acts fey to become friendly with the gay guards. 🖵

Pam Grier *Blossom* • Anitra Ford *Terry* • Candice Roman *Carla* • Teda Bracci *Bull Jones* • Carol Speed *Mickie* • Karen McKevic *Karen* • Sid Haig *Django* ■ *Dir/Scr* Jack Hill

The Big Blue ★★★★ 15
Romantic adventure
1988 · US · Colour · 114mins

Action director Luc Besson (*The Fifth Element*) pays homage to the ocean-exploring documentaries of Jacques Cousteau with this stunning, if long and slightly pretentious, underwater cult epic. The story – about two rival deep-sea divers (Besson regular Jean

Reno and Jean-Marc Barr) who are crazy about dolphins – is a little shallow, and Rosanna Arquette's role, as a New York insurance investigator who meets Barr in Peru, does seem rather like an afterthought. But Reno mines great humour from his macho mother's boy role, Barr looks impossibly handsome, and the sensational ocean photography is absolutely magnificent – the first plunge into the watery alien blackness is pure cinematic magic. ▣

Rosanna Arquette *Joanna Cross* • Jean-Marc Barr *Jacques Mayol* • Jean Reno *Enzo Molinari* • Paul Shenar *Dr Laurence* • Sergio Castellitto *Novelli* • Jean Bouise *Uncle Louis* • Marc Duret *Roberto* • Griffin Dunne *Duffy* ■ *Dir* Luc Besson • *Scr* Luc Besson, Robert Garland, Marilyn Golding, Jacques Mayol, Marc Perrier, from a story by Luc Besson

The Big Boss ★★★ 18
Martial arts drama
1971 · HK · Colour · 94mins

Bruce Lee's Hong Kong film breakthrough may be a bit rough around the edges, but it remains an electrifying example of the martial-arts master at work. The plot is fairly perfunctory: Lee is a young man who travels to Thailand, promising to keep out of trouble only to find himself caught up with a drugs ring. However, his graceful charisma shines throughout and director Lo Wei and fight co-ordinator Han Ying-Chieh (who also plays the villain of the piece) orchestrate some stunning set pieces, most notably a fight in the ice factory. You may know this film better under its two other release titles, *Fists of Fury* and *Tang Shan Da Xiong*. Cantonese dialogue dubbed into English. Contains violence. ▣

Bruce Lee *Cheng Chao-An* • Maria Yi *Lin Hau-Mei* • James Tien *Hsu Chien* • Nora Miao *Prostitute* • Hang Ying-Chieh ■ *Dir* Lo Wei • *Scr* Lo Wei

The Big Bounce ★
Crime drama
1969 · US · Colour · 102mins

Ryan O'Neal makes his big screen debut as a cucumber picker who jumps in and out of bed with various women and ends up accused of murder. One of his dalliances (Leigh Taylor-Young) likes having sex in graveyards; another (Lee Grant) commits suicide. Made in 1969, this adaptation of an Elmore Leonard novel is one of those "youth movies" that's full of hippie characters, free sex, "daring" nudity and a general air of social rebellion. O'Neal and Taylor-Young were the stars of the TV series *Peyton Place* and were married in real life.

Ryan O'Neal *Jack Ryan* • Leigh Taylor-Young *Nancy Barker* • Van Heflin *Sam Mirakian* • Lee Grant *Motel resident* • James Daly *Ray Richie* • Robert Webber *Bob Rogers* • Cindy Eilbacher *Cheryl* ■ *Dir* Alex March • *Scr* Robert Dozier, from a novel by Elmore Leonard

The Big Brawl ★★ 15
Martial arts comedy
1980 · US · Colour · 91mins

This was an early tilt at the American market from Jackie Chan – although he would have to wait for more than a decade before breaking through. Chan plays a martial arts star in 1930s America who decides to take part in a no-holds barred fighting competition, bringing him into conflict with local gangsters. Robert Clouse directed Bruce Lee in *Enter the Dragon* and he expertly stages the many fight sequences, although even then Chan was putting equal emphasis on comedy. The period trappings add a fresh flavour to the otherwise predictable plotting. ▣

Jackie Chan *Jerry* • José Ferrer *Dominici* • Kristine DeBell *Nancy* • Mako *Herbert* • Ron Max *Leggetti* • David Sheiner *Morgan* • Rosalind Chao *Mae* • Lenny Montana *John* ■ *Dir* Robert Clouse • *Scr* Robert Clouse, from a story by Fred Weintraub, Robert Clouse

The Big Broadcast ★★★★
Musical comedy
1932 · US · BW · 83mins

Radio was huge in the thirties and families listening in at home was starting to pose a threat to cinema, so Paramount cleverly exploited the trend by making this vehicle for radio stars on the big screen. The paper-thin plot has Stuart Erwin taking over a failing radio station run by George Burns and – guess what? – putting on an all-star show. So successful was this flick that three sort-of sequels followed, all successful. Somehow they lack the quaint and specific charm of the original, which even manages to bring some fresh cleverness to its familiar triangle subplot. The stars on display, including Bing Crosby at his peak singing such gems as *Here Lies Love*, are priceless.

Bing Crosby *Bing Hornsby* • Stuart Erwin *Leslie McWhinney* • Leila Hyams *Anita Rogers* • Sharon Lynne *Mona* • George Burns *George* • Gracie Allen *Gracie* • George Barbier *Clapsaddle* • Ralph Robertson *Announcer* ■ *Dir* Frank Tuttle • *Scr* George Marion Jr, from the play *Wild Waves* by William Ford Manley

The Big Broadcast of 1936 ★★★ U
Musical comedy
1935 · US · BW · 94mins

In this second of Paramount's all-star collections of radio stars on the silver screen the linking plot seems strangely prophetic, as Gracie Allen's alleged uncle invents a device called television that can send pictures of artistes performing to anywhere in the world. Jack Oakie is the nominal star, as a radio station owner. But more importantly this is your opportunity to catch such major period names as Amos 'n' Andy (Freeman Gosden and Charles Correll, blackfaced), Ethel Merman, the great Bill Robinson and the Vienna Boys' Choir. All this and Bing Crosby superbly crooning the enchanting *I Wished on the Moon* with lyrics by Dorothy Parker.

Jack Oakie *Spud* • George Burns *George* • Gracie Allen *Gracie* • Fayard Nicholas *Dash* • Harold Nicholas *Dot* • Akim Tamiroff *Boris* • Bing Crosby • Ethel Merman • Amos 'n' Andy • Bill Robinson ■ *Dir* Norman Taurog • *Scr* Walter DeLeon, Francis Martin, Ralph Spence

The Big Broadcast of 1937 ★★★ U
Musical comedy
1936 · US · BW · 104mins

The third of Paramount's showcases for big radio names ostensibly stars the great George Burns and Gracie Allen, but actually teams Gracie with the incorrigible Jack Benny, to great (and utterly hilarious) effect. There is a plot of sorts involving Ray Milland and Shirley Ross going on the town. But, as ever, this is really just an excuse for some of the biggest stars of the day to strut their stuff – those on show include the volatile, big-mouthed Martha Raye, whose *Vote for Mr Rhythm* number is the film's highlight. Watch out, too, for Benny Goodman and conductor Leopold Stokowski.

Jack Benny *Jack Carson* • George Burns *Mr Platt* • Gracie Allen *Mrs Platt* • Bob Burns *Bob Black* • Frank Forest *Frank Rossman* • Ray Milland *Bob Miller* • Shirley Ross *Gwen Holmes* • Martha Raye *Patsy* • Benny Goodman • Leopold Stokowski ■ *Dir* Mitchell Leisen • *Scr* Walter DeLeon, Francis Martin, from a story by Barry Trivers, Arthur Kober, Erwin Gelsey

The Big Broadcast of 1938 ★★ U
Musical comedy
1937 · US · BW · 90mins

The last and frankly weakest of Paramount's all-star series is missing George Burns and Gracie Allen, but benefits from starring the great WC Fields. Though nearly crippled by a dumb plot about racing ocean liners, the film does include a moment that bequeaths immortality upon it – a radio comic called Bob Hope, making his film debut, joins star Shirley Ross in a specially written bittersweet duet entitled *Thanks for the Memory*. The song rightfully won an Oscar and became Bob Hope's theme song.

WC Fields *T Frothingill Bellows/SB Bellows* • Martha Raye *Martha Bellows* • Dorothy Lamour *Dorothy Wyndham* • Shirley Ross *Cleo Fielding* • Russell Hicks *Capt Stafford* • Dorothy Howe *Joan Fielding* • Lionel Pape *Lord Droopy* • Bob Hope *Buzz Fielding* • Kirsten Flagstad ■ *Dir* Mitchell Leisen • *Scr* Walter DeLeon, Francis Martin, Ken Englund, Howard Lindsay, Russel Crouse, from a story by Frederick Hazlitt Brennan

Big Brown Eyes ★★
Crime drama
1936 · US · BW · 76mins

This crime drama sought to emulate the success of *The Thin Man* in its teaming of Cary Grant and Joan Bennett, but it has rather more violence and action, including the accidental shooting of a baby. Grant is a little awkward as the two-fisted detective who finds his vaudeville past as a ventriloquist useful in a tight spot, but Bennett is on top form as the wisecracking hotel manicurist turned reporter, who helps him collar Walter Pidgeon's suave racketeer. Director and co-writer Raoul Walsh keeps it brief and breezy.

Cary Grant *Danny Barr* • Joan Bennett *Eve Fallon* • Walter Pidgeon *Richard Morey* • Lloyd Nolan *Russ Cortig* • Alan Baxter *Cary Butler* • Marjorie Gateson *Mrs Cole* • Isabel Jewell *Bessie Blair* • Douglas Fowley *Benny Bottle* ■ *Dir* Raoul Walsh • *Scr* Raoul Walsh, Bert Hanlon, from the short stories *Hahsit Babe* and *Big Brown Eyes* by James Edward Grant

Big Bully ★ PG
Comedy
1996 · US · Colour · 86mins

Chances are you've never heard of this awful comedy from horror specialist Steve Miner, and for good reason. The plot is unappealing (boy bullied at school grows up to be Rick Moranis and continues to be tormented by Tom Arnold), the black humour falls flat and the notion that disenchanted Arnold can find renewed meaning in his life through thuggery is vaguely offensive. Writer Mark Steven Johnson tackled a similar feuding scenario with far more success in *Grumpy Old Men*, mainly because you felt something for Jack Lemmon and Walter Matthau's old coots. Here, who cares? ▣

Rick Moranis *David Leary* • Tom Arnold *Rosco Bigger (Fang)* • Julianne Phillips *Victoria* • Carol Kane *Faith* • Jeffrey Tambor *Art* • Curtis Armstrong *Clark* • Faith Prince *Betty* ■ *Dir* Steve Miner • *Scr* Mark Steven Johnson

The Big Bus ★ PG
Disaster movie spoof
1976 · US · Colour · 84mins

In this intended parody of the seventies disaster movie genre, the usual bunch of misfits climb aboard the world's first nuclear-powered coach, travelling from New York to Denver. More like *The Big Blunderbuss* in its scatter-gun attack on its targets; the likes of Joseph Bologna, Stockard Channing and Ned Beatty make a lot of noise to negligible comic effect. Embarrassingly archaic, it's less amusing than most "serious" disaster movies of the period. ▣

Joseph Bologna *Dan Torrance* • Stockard Channing *Kitty Baxter* • John Beck *Shoulders* • René Auberjonois *Father Kudos* • Ned Beatty *Shorty Scotty* • Bob Dishy *Dr Kurtz* • José Ferrer *Ironman* • Ruth Gordon *Old lady* • Harold Gould *Professor Baxter* • Larry Hagman *Parking lot doctor* • Sally Kellerman *Sybil Crane* ■ *Dir* James Frawley • *Scr* Fred Freeman, Lawrence J Cohen

Big Business ★★★★★
Silent comedy
1929 · US · BW · 19mins

Hailed by some critics as the greatest Laurel and Hardy comedy ever filmed, this has the dynamic duo fighting back in an orgy of reciprocal destruction. They're door-to-door salesmen selling Christmas trees in sunny California, up against their ever-wrathful stooge, James Finlayson – he of the pop-eyes and belligerent moustache – as a householder driven to take apart, bit by bit, their car, while they tear up his house and garden. Stan's crocodile tears win over the on-guard policeman, but Ollie's giveaway grin ruins any chance of a happy-ever-after finale. Even from them this is outstanding.

Stan Laurel *Stan* • Oliver Hardy *Ollie* • James Finlayson *Homeowner* • Tiny Sandford *Policeman* • Lyle Tayo *Husbandless woman* • Retta Palmer *Neighbor* ■ *Dir* James W Horne • *Scr* Leo McCarey, HM Walker (titles)

Big Business ★★ PG
Comedy
1988 · US · Colour · 93mins

One of those frenetic double-role efforts, this strains the talents and energy levels of Bette Midler and Lily Tomlin to breaking point, along with the audience, who are asked to not so much suspend disbelief as leave their brains on the sideboard during viewing. This could have been enormous fun – a brace of old comedy pros playing two sets of identical twins juggled at birth and meeting years later in a posh New York hotel. But director Jim Abrahams jettisons all semblance of coherent narrative in favour of giving his leads enough rope to hang themselves amid the irritating sound of constantly banging doors. ▭

Bette Midler *Sadie Shelton/Sadie Ratliff* • Lily Tomlin *Rose Shelton/Rose Ratliff* • Fred Ward *Roone Dimmick* • Edward Herrmann *Graham Sherbourne* • Michele Placido *Fabio Alberici* • Daniel Gerroll *Chuck* • Barry Primus *Michael* • Michael Gross *Dr Jay Marshall* • Deborah Rush *Binky Shelton* ■ *Dir* Jim Abrahams • *Scr* Dori Pierson, Marc Rubel

The Big Caper ★★★

Heist drama 1957 · US · BW · 84mins

Rory Calhoun is part of a motley gang of fruitcakes and no-hopers, who plan to be a million dollars richer by robbing a bank. Things don't quite go to plan, however. This dime-budget thriller is based on a book by Lionel White, whose novel *Clean Break* had been filmed the previous year as *The Killing*. That picture was a modest success and made the young Stanley Kubrick's career. United Artists clearly saw *The Big Caper* in the same light, handing it to another young director, Robert Stevens, who maintains the tension and evokes the small-town atmosphere rather well.

Rory Calhoun *Frank Harber* • Mary Costa *Kay* • James Gregory *Flood* • Robert Harris *Zimmer* • Corey Allen *Roy* • Roxanne Arlen *Doll* • Paul Picerni *Harry* • Pat McVey [Patrick McVey] *Sam Loxley* ■ *Dir* Robert Stevens • *Scr* Martin Berkeley, from a novel by Lionel White

The Big Chance ★ U

Crime drama 1957 · UK · BW · 61mins

Adapted by director Peter Graham Scott from the novel by Pamela Barrington, this is an efficient but hackneyed variation on the well-worn movie notion that crime must never pay. From the moment travel agent William Russell claps eyes on foxy socialite Adrienne Corri and decides to abandon his humdrum married existence for a life of South American excess, we know it will end in tears. Mercifully, events move at such a pace that there's scarcely time to notice either the poverty of the plot or the stiffness of the acting.

Adrienne Corri *Diana Maxwell* • William Russell *Bill Anderson* • Ian Colin *Adam Maxwell* • Penelope Bartley *Betty* • Ferdy Mayne *Alpherghies* • John Rae *Jarvis* • Douglas Ives *Stan Willett* ■ *Dir* Peter Graham Scott • *Scr* Peter Graham Scott, from the novel by Pamela Barrington

The Big Chill ★★★★ 15

Drama 1983 · US · Colour · 100mins

At one time a cult movie among twentysomethings, this chic comedy is now better known as the picture from which Kevin Costner had all his scenes cut. Smartly written by director Lawrence Kasdan and Barbara Benedek, the Oscar-nominated script clearly owes a debt to John Sayles's overlooked and superior reunion drama *The Return of the Secaucus Seven*. However, there are still plenty of original insights into both sixties' counterculture and the pretensions of the chattering classes. There's a dream cast, although Meg Tilly upstages her more famous co-stars, while the soundtrack is packed with the anthems of an age. Overclever, but very slick. Contains swearing and brief nudity. ▭ *DVD*

Kevin Kline *Harold Cooper* • Glenn Close *Sarah Cooper* • William Hurt *Nick* • Jeff Goldblum *Michael* • Tom Berenger *Sam* • Meg Tilly *Chloe* • JoBeth Williams *Karen* • Mary Kay Place *Meg* • Don Galloway *Richard* ■ *Dir* Lawrence Kasdan • *Scr* Lawrence Kasdan, Barbara Benedek

The Big Circus ★★★ U

Adventure 1959 · US · Colour · 103mins

Minor league studio Allied Artists attempted a huge leap upwards with this colourful and gritty circus film, directed superbly in CinemaScope by cult favourite Joseph M Newman. Co-writer/producer Irwin Allen – now famous for *The Towering Inferno* and *The Poseidon Adventure* – assembled a fine, though slightly second-rung, cast. It's headed by world-weary Victor Mature and features such stars as Peter Lorre (as a neurotic clown) and Gilbert Roland (as the tightrope walker). Although clearly hindered by budget limitations, this is a worthy attempt by the studio to break new ground, and rejects the phoney romanticism of *The Greatest Show on Earth* to good effect. Though not the box-office hit it so desperately wanted to be, this remains a treat. ▭

Victor Mature *Hank Whirling* • Red Buttons *Randy Sherman* • Rhonda Fleming *Helen Harrison* • Kathryn Grant *Jeannie Whirling* • Vincent Price *Hans Hagenfeld* • David Nelson *Tommy Gordon* • Gilbert Roland *Zach Colino* • Peter Lorre *Skeeter* ■ *Dir* Joseph M Newman • *Scr* Irwin Allen, Charles Bennett, Irving Wallace, from a story by Irwin Allen

Big City ★★

Drama 1937 · US · BW · 79mins

Rival New York cab companies are at loggerheads but you'd think that the Third World War had broken out, so overwrought is this movie. Cabs get smashed, faces get smashed, the unions march in and then bombs go off and the city teeters on anarchy. Spencer Tracy, as one of the cabbies, tries to stay calm, while his pregnant Russian immigrant wife, Luise Rainer, is accused of causing explosions. She, rather absurdly, has to say, "Excuse me, do you mind if I have my baby?" in the last scene. Just awful, but compulsive viewing.

Spencer Tracy *Joe Benton* • Luise Rainer *Anna Benton* • Charley Grapewin *Mayor* • Janet Beecher *Sophie Sloane* • Eddie Quillan *Mike Edwards* • Victor Varconi *Paul Roya* • Oscar O'Shea *John C Andrews* ■ *Dir* Frank Borzage • *Scr* Dore Schary, Hugo Butler, from a story by Norman Krasna

The Big City ★★★★ U

Drama 1963 · Ind · BW · 131mins

Satyajit Ray won the best director prize at Berlin for this, the first of his films with a contemporary setting. Although thematically related to the "salaryman" comedies of Yasujiro Ozu, the style remains that blend of elements from Jean Renoir and neorealism that characterised Ray's earliest work. Touching on the mores of Anglo-Indians, the film deals primarily with the social role of women, as it traces Madhabi Mukherjee's progress from traditional housewife to middle-class heroine. Minutely observed and flawlessly acted, this gently satirical study of the changing face of Calcutta was typical of Ray's wry approach to all things political. In Bengali with English subtitles.

Madhabi Mukherjee *Arati* • Anil Chatterjee *Subrata Mazumdar* • Haradhan Bannerjee *Mukherjee* • Haren Chatterjee *Father* • Vicky Redwood *Edith Simmons* • Jaya Bhaduri *Sister* ■ *Dir* Satyajit Ray • *Scr* Satyajit Ray, from novel Narendranath Mitra's *Abataranika*

The Big Clock ★★★

Film noir 1948 · US · BW · 95mins

An excellent second-eleven *film noir* with Charles Laughton as a publisher who murders his mistress and then gets one of his employees, crime editor Ray Milland, to investigate. What Laughton doesn't know is that Milland shared the same girlfriend, so lots of juicy complications ensue, especially as Milland hates Laughton for his oppressive business practices. With the huge office clock ticking away like a countdown to doom, and Laughton looking every ugly inch a caseload of neuroses, this is a highly effective movie, which was loosely remade in 1987 as *No Way Out* with Gene Hackman and Kevin Costner.

Ray Milland *George Stroud* • Charles Laughton *Earl Janoth* • Maureen O'Sullivan *Georgette Stroud* • George Macready *Steven Hagen* • Rita Johnson *Pauline York* • Elsa Lanchester *Louise Patterson* • Harold Vermilyea *Don Klausmeyer* • Dan Tobin *Ray Cordette* ■ *Dir* John Farrow • *Scr* Jonathan Latimer, from the novel by Kenneth Fearing

The Big Combo ★★★★ PG

Film noir 1955 · US · BW · 87mins

This is as tough and nasty as they come – and that's a recommendation. Cult director Joseph H Lewis trawls the mean streets as his lead character, cop Cornel Wilde, turns over the local rocks to see what slime crawls out from underneath. A co-feature on its original release, and barely noticed, this movie was accorded a reissue in repertory cinemas in the eighties, bringing it to the attention of a new audience, which responded to the amorality and the raw violence, delighting in the twisted viciousness of evil Richard Conte and positively revelling in the demise of Brian Donlevy.

Cornel Wilde *Diamond* • Richard Conte *Brown* • Brian Donlevy *McClure* • Jean Wallace *Susan* • Robert Middleton *Peterson* • Lee Van Cleef *Fante* • Ted De Corsia *Bettini* • Helen Walker *Alicia* ■ *Dir* Joseph H Lewis • *Scr* Philip Yordan

The Big Country ★★★★★ PG

Western 1958 · US · Colour · 159mins

Unfairly neglected today, this major western is a film of truly epic dimensions, utilising Technirama widescreen to the full. It tells the tale of a greenhorn sent to the wide-open spaces, a role to which star (and co-producer) Gregory Peck is particularly suited. Peck is one of the few actors whose innate pacifism rings true. Thanks to the combination of top director William Wyler and a superb cast – including Jean Simmons, Charlton Heston and an Oscar-winning performance from big Burl Ives - the film never palls, despite its length. It also features a great theme tune, a

triumph for composer Jerome Moross. Though misused by a score of commercials, when heard in context, the music rightfully lifts this distinguished movie to the realm of screen classic. ▭

Gregory Peck *James McKay* • Jean Simmons *Julie Maragon* • Carroll Baker *Patricia Terrill* • Charlton Heston *Steve Leech* • Burl Ives *Rufus Hannassey* • Charles Bickford *Major Henry Terrill* • Alfonso Bedoya *Ramon* • Chuck Connors *Buck Hannassey* ■ *Dir* William Wyler • *Scr* James R Webb, Robert Wilder, Sy Bartlett, Robert Wyler, from the novel by Donald Hamilton, adapted by Jessamyn West, Robert Wyler • *Cinematographer* Franz Planer

The Big Cube ★

Drama 1969 · US/Mex · Colour · 98mins

A sad coda to the great Lana Turner's career. Three years after her last glamorous Ross Hunter/Universal production, *Madame X*, the trade was screened this underfinanced farrago that was mercifully undershown. Co-stars George Chakiris, Richard Egan and Dan O'Herlihy – all well past their prime – lend this demented melodrama a camp attraction. But its sheer ineptitude combined with Turner's ravaged looks and (to be kind) uncertain performance make it hard to watch, let alone take seriously. Genuinely sad.

Lana Turner *Adriana Roman* • George Chakiris *Johnny Allen* • Richard Egan *Frederick Lansdale* • Dan O'Herlihy *Charles Winthrop* • Karin Mossberg *Lisa Winthrop* • Pamela Rodgers *Bibi* ■ *Dir* Tito Davison • *Scr* William Douglas Lansford, from a story by Tito Davison, Edmundo Baez

Big Daddy ★★★★ 12

Comedy 1999 · US · Colour · 89mins

A perfect example of how a sparkling central performance can make even the most crudely sentimental fluff hilariously palatable, this adoption-by-proxy comedy works like a charm, thanks to slacker superstar Adam Sandler and his infectious goofball sweetness. The story springs few surprises: lazy loafer takes his flatmate's love-child under his wing; they bond; and the parental challenges change him sufficiently to win the hand of Miss Right (Joey Lauren Adams). Yes, it's contrived, mawkish and manipulative. But *Happy Gilmore* director Dennis Dugan's effortless handling of the tale and Sandler's confident puppy-dog demeanour ensures it delivers huge laughs along with a touchingly neat wrap-up. Contains mild swearing, and sexual and drug references. ▭ *DVD*

Adam Sandler *Sonny Koufax* • Joey Lauren Adams *Layla* • Jon Stewart *Kevin* • Cole Sprouse *Julian* • Dylan Sprouse *Julian* • Josh Mostel *Mr Brooks* • Leslie Mann *Corinne* • Allen Covert *Phil* • Rob Schneider *Delivery guy* • Kristy Swanson *Vanessa* • Joe Bologna *Mr Koufax* • Steve Buscemi *Homeless guy* ■ *Dir* Dennis Dugan • *Scr* Steve Franks, Tim Herlihy, Adam Sandler, from a story by Steve Franks

Big Deal at Dodge City ★★★ U

Comedy western 1966 · US · Colour · 95mins

This amiable comedy western was originally devised as a 50-minute TV programme. Although there are a few visible stretch marks, screenwriter

Sidney Carroll and director Fielder Cook have done a creditable job in filling it out to feature length. With echoes of both *The Sting* and *Maverick*, it is slickly played by Henry Fonda, Joanne Woodward, Jason Robards, Charles Bickford and Burgess Meredith. It remains a mystery why the American title *A Big Hand for the Little Lady* was changed on its British release – especially as the town of Laredo provides the backdrop for the plot.

Henry Fonda *Meredith* • Joanne Woodward *Mary* • Jason Robards [Jason Robards Jr] *Henry Drummond* • Charles Bickford *Benson Tropp* • Burgess Meredith *Doc Scully* • Kevin McCarthy *Otto Habershaw* • Robert Middleton *Dennis Wilcox* • Paul Ford *Ballinger* ■ *Dir* Fielder Cook • *Scr* Sidney Carroll, from his teleplay *Big Deal at Laredo*

Big Deal on Madonna Street ★★★★

Heist comedy 1958 · It · BW · 91mins

A smashing comedy, mainly a send-up of *Rififi*, about a band of incompetent layabouts and petty crooks who plan a major heist by breaking into an empty flat and drilling through to the bank vault next door. The plan goes slightly awry and leads to a hilarious twist in the tale. Made quickly and cheaply, it stars Marcello Mastroianni and Vittorio Gassman, the latter made up to hide his Latin lover image completely, and features an early performance by Claudia Cardinale. Louis Malle remade it in 1984 as *Crackers*; it was loosely remade again in 1995 as *Palookaville*. An Italian language film.

Vittorio Gassman *Peppe* • Marcello Mastroianni *Tiberio* • Totò *Dante* • Renato Salvatori *Mario* • Carla Gravina *Nicoletta* • Claudia Cardinale *Carmelina* • Memmo Carotenuto *Cosimo* • Tiberio Murgia *Ferribotte* ■ *Dir* Mario Monicelli • *Scr* Mario Monicelli, Suso Cecchi D'Amico, Age Scarpelli [Agenore Incrocci and Furio Scarpelli]

The Big Doll House ★ 18

Prison drama 1971 · US · Colour · 89mins

An early example of the women-in-prison picture, a seventies genre that was generally regarded as too hot for UK audiences. In this one, the extremely popular Pam Grier and four other tough ladies generally do what is expected of them (fight, have showers, try to escape). Roger Corman protégé Jack Hill shot it cheaply in the Philippines, the location for many exploitation films of the period. Unwatchable trash or a cult classic, depending on your attitude. [video]

Judy Brown *Collier* • Roberta Collins *Alcott* • Pam Grier *Grear* • Brooke Mills *Harrad* • Pat Woodell *Bodine* • Sid Haig *Harry* • Christiane Schmidtmer *Miss Dietrich* ■ *Dir* Jack Hill • *Scr* Don Spencer

Big Dreams & Broken Hearts: the Dottie West Story ★★ PG

Biographical drama
1995 · US · Colour · 88mins

A string of cameos from real-life country legends including Kenny Rogers and Dolly Parton enlivens this otherwise rather pedestrian biopic. *Knots Landing* star Michele Lee takes the title role of Dottie West, billed as the wild woman of country music. Although she's not quite a household name, she certainly had a life story packed to the gunnels with hardship and tragedy, which should have made her a perfect TV movie subject. Disappointingly, despite the presence of such distinguished Nashville greats, Bill D'Elia's movie is light on the music side and the result is a rather syrupy and formulaic rags-to-riches tale. [video]

Michele Lee *Dottie West* • William Russ *Bill West* • David James Elliot *Byron Metcalf* • Lisa Akey *Shelly West* • Kenny Rogers • Larry Gatlin • Tere Myers *Patsy Cline* • Ben Browder *Al Winters* • Chet Atkins • Kris Kristofferson • Loretta Lynn • Willie Nelson • Dolly Parton ■ *Dir* Bill D'Elia • *Scr* Theresa Rogerton

The Big Easy ★★★★ 15

Crime thriller 1986 · US · Colour · 96mins

After watching this sizzling crime thriller, you will be at a loss to explain why director Jim McBride and stars Dennis Quaid and Ellen Barkin failed to go on and take Hollywood by storm. Rather than the start of something big, this was the career peak of all three, but what heights they attained! Sparks fly from the moment cop Quaid and assistant district attorney Barkin come together to investigate a New Orleans Mob killing, but their conflicting moral codes threaten to take the heat out of their steamy affair. Ned Beatty and John Goodman provide gritty support, while McBride brings the unique quality of the city to throbbing life. Contains violence and swearing. [video]

Dennis Quaid *Remy McSwain* • Ellen Barkin *Anne Osborne* • Ned Beatty *Jack Kellom* • Ebbe Roe Smith *Detective Dodge* • John Goodman *Detective DeSoto* • Lisa Jane Persky *Detective McCabe* • Charles Ludlam *Lamar* • Thomas O'Brien *Bobby* ■ *Dir* Jim McBride • *Scr* Daniel Petrie Jr, Jack Baran

The Big Fisherman ★★ U

Biblical drama 1959 · US · Colour · 166mins

Howard Keel is competent enough as Simon Peter in this biblical saga, based on Lloyd C Douglas's bestselling novel. Directed by Frank Borzage, an Oscar-winning veteran of the twenties and thirties, the film is handsomely mounted and photographed, as befits the epic genre. But it's still a plodding and interminable bore, the main excitement in which comes from a princess (Susan Kohner) out to kill Herod (Herbert Lom) and a prince (John Saxon) who is hopelessly in love with her.

Howard Keel *Simon Peter* • Susan Kohner *Fara* • John Saxon *Voldi* • Martha Hyer *Herodias* • Herbert Lom *Herod Antipas* • Ray Stricklyn *Deran* • Marian Seldes *Arnon* ■ *Dir* Frank Borzage • *Scr* Howard Estabrook, Rowland V Lee, from a novel by Lloyd C Douglas

The Big Fix ★★★ 15

Comedy detective drama
1978 · US · Colour · 103mins

Richard Dreyfuss turned actor/producer for this off-the-wall private eye thriller that takes in the demise of sixties radicalism, Latino tensions and what might be summed up as post-Watergate disenchantment. Dreyfuss plays the Jewish gumshoe Moses Wine, a former campus activist with an ex-wife, two kids and a heap of debt. Then the plot kicks in – something about dirty tricks during a political campaign – and quickly gets very complicated. But this is principally a character study, superbly portrayed by Dreyfuss. Sadly it flopped, putting paid to plans for a series based on the novels of Roger L Simon. [video]

Richard Dreyfuss *Moses Wine* • Susan Anspach *Lila* • Bonnie Bedelia *Suzanne* • John Lithgow *Sam Sebastian* • Ofelia Medina *Alora* • Nicolas Coster *Spitzler* • F Murray Abraham *Eppis* • Fritz Weaver *Oscar Procari Sr* • Mandy Patinkin *Pool man* ■ *Dir* Jeremy Paul Kagan • *Scr* Roger L Simon, from his novel

The Big Gamble ★★ U

Adventure 1961 · US · Colour · 100mins

Stephen Boyd teamed up with Juliette Greco for this plodding adventure about truck drivers in equatorial Africa. Boyd and Greco start off in Dublin, where they raise the cash for their trip and, after a comic interlude with aunt Sybil Thorndike, head for the dark continent. Obviously inspired by Henri-Georges Clouzot's suspense classic *The Wages of Fear* and shot on location in the Ivory Coast, this must have been murder to make. Sadly, it delivers only modest thrills.

Stephen Boyd *Vic Brennan* • Juliette Greco *Marie Brennan* • David Wayne *Samuel Brennan* • Sybil Thorndike *Aunt Cathleen* • Gregory Ratoff *Daltenberg* • Harold Goldblatt *Father Frederick* • Philip O'Flynn *John Brennan* • Maureen O'Dea *Margaret Brennan* • Marie Kean *Cynthia* ■ *Dir* Richard Fleischer, Elmo William • *Scr* Irwin Shaw

Big Girls Don't Cry... They Get Even ★★ PG

Comedy 1992 · US · Colour · 100mins

The problems of trying to survive in an overextended family form the basis of director Joan Micklin Silver's over-long and mawkish comedy. Disgruntled 13-year-old Hillary Wolf decides to run away to stepbrother Dan Futterman's lakeside cabin, following a row at home. Unfortunately, far from escaping her dysfunctional family – consisting of numerous stepmothers, stepfathers and step-siblings – Wolf's disappearance makes them converge on the cabin. Despite the presence of Griffin Dunne, there isn't much in the way of sense, wit or bittersweet meaning to be found in this overly cute and schematic tale. [video]

Hillary Wolf *Laura Chartoff* • David Strathairn *Keith Powers* • Margaret Whitton *Melinda Powers* • Griffin Dunne *David Chartoff* • Patricia Kalember *Barbara Chartoff* • Adrienne Shelly *Stephanie Miller* • Dan Futterman *Josh Powers* • Ben Savage *Sam* • Trenton Teigen *Kurt* ■ *Dir* Joan Micklin Silver • *Scr* Frank Mugavero, from a story by Mark Goddard, Melissa Goddard, Frank Mugavero

The Big Green ★★ U

Sports comedy 1995 · US · Colour · 95mins

After the success of kids ice hockey movie *The Mighty Ducks* (which, with the help of likeable Emilio Estevez, spawned two sequels), it probably seemed a good idea to use the same ingredients (little team does good and the players learn more about themselves and each other in the process) for other sports. However, here the plot is rehashed for a movie about soccer, and Estevez is replaced by a man whose career is even further in the dumpster, *Police Academy*'s Steve Guttenberg. Unengaging and not a patch on the *Ducks*. [video]

Steve Guttenberg *Sheriff Tom Palmer* • Olivia D'Abo *Anna Montgomery* • Jay O Sanders *Jay Huffer* • John Terry *Edwin V Douglas* • Chauncey Leopardi *Evan Schiff* • Patrick Renna *Larry Musgrove* • Billy L Sullivan *Jeffrey Luttrell* • Yareli Arizmendi *Marbelly Morales* ■ *Dir/Scr* Holly Goldberg Sloan

The Big Hangover ★★★ U

Comedy drama 1950 · US · BW · 82mins

An engaging comedy with Van Johnson working for a law firm and trying to conceal an allergy to alcohol brought on during the war when the cellar he was hiding in flooded with brandy. This is where Elizabeth Taylor comes in. She's the boss's daughter and an amateur shrink, who sets out to cure our hero of his allergy. There's also a subplot about Johnson deciding whether to become a rich man's brief or take up arms for the poor. You'd think that prissy old MGM would not wish to encourage boozing, though Taylor, in her first adult role, could probably persuade any man to overcome any phobia.

Van Johnson *David* • Elizabeth Taylor *Mary Belney* • Percy Waram *John Belney* • Fay Holden *Martha Belney* • Leon Ames *Carl Bellcap* • Edgar Buchanan *Uncle Fred Mahoney* • Selena Royle *Kate Mahoney* ■ *Dir/Scr* Norman Krasna

The Big Heat ★★★★ 15

Film noir 1953 · US · BW · 85mins

Glenn Ford crusades against mob-led civic corruption and hunts for vengeance in this classic *film noir* from director Fritz Lang. Its most famous scene, when moll Gloria Grahame is scalded by hot coffee hurled by crook Lee Marvin, was trimmed by the censors before the movie could be released in Britain, with an X certificate. Now fully restored, it's tame by today's standards, but still packs a punch. Ford is excellent as the cop with a mission – his character was based on the investigators who uncovered the bile in US cities during the televised fifties' Estes Kefauver Senate investigations – and Lang gives the vicious exposé a sleek and glossy surface. [video]

Glenn Ford *Dave Bannion* • Gloria Grahame *Debby Marsh* • Jocelyn Brando *Katie Bannion* • Alexander Scourby *Mike Lagana* • Lee Marvin *Vince Stone* • Jeanette Nolan *Bertha Duncan* • Peter Whitney *Tierney* • Willis Bouchey *Lieutenant Wilkes* ■ *Dir* Fritz Lang • *Scr* Sydney Boehm, from the serial in *The Saturday Evening Post* by William P McGivern • *Cinematographer* Charles B Lang [Charles Lang]

The Big Hit ★★ 15

Action thriller 1998 · US · Colour · 88mins

A second rate rip-off of humorous hit-man gem *Grosse Pointe Blank*, this tries very hard to be offbeat and quirky, but ends up as merely dumb and annoying. Performances vary from good (a sensitive Mark Wahlberg) to appalling (an arrogant Lou Diamond Phillips). Despite a dazzling pair of slam-bang action bookends from director Kirk Wong, this isn't clever, funny or engaging enough to be the exercise in killer cool it clearly craves to be. ▣ *DVD*

Mark Wahlberg *Melvin Smiley* • Lou Diamond Phillips *Cisco* • Christina Applegate *Pam Shulman* • Avery Brooks *Paris* • Bokeem Woodbine *Crunch* • Antonio Sabato Jr *Vince* • China Chow *Keiko Nishi* • Lainie Kazan *Jeanne Shulman* • Elliott Gould *Morton Shulman* • Sab Shimono *Jiro Nishi* ■ *Dir* Che-Kirk Wong [Kirk Wong] • *Scr* Ben Ramsey

The Big House ★★★★

Prison drama   1930 · US · BW · 84mins

This powerful exposé of conditions in a men's prison, prompted by newspaper headlines of rioting convicts, was such as a smash hit that it served as a template for dozens of pictures. Robert Montgomery is the new inmate, a well-bred weakling sentenced for manslaughter, who has to share a cell with Wallace Beery's tough gangster and Chester Morris's repentant forger. Co-written by a leading female screenwriter, Frances Marion, and directed by her husband, George Hill, the film vividly evokes the grimness of prison life, from overcrowded cells to a spell in solitary. The long take down the empty corridor of the solitary wing as the inmates call out to each other for company is unforgettable.

Chester Morris *John Morgan* • Wallace Beery *Butch Schmidt* • Lewis Stone *Warden James Adams* • Robert Montgomery *Kent Marlowe* • Leila Hyams *Ann Marlowe* • George F Marion *Pop Riker* • JC Nugent *Mr Marlowe* • Karl Dane *Olsen* ■ *Dir* George Hill • *Scr* Frances Marion, Joe Farnham, Martin Flavin • *Cinematographer* Harold Wenstrom

Big House, USA ★★★

Action crime drama 1955 · US · BW · 82mins

A tight, compressed thriller about a kidnapped boy, some buried ransom money and the heavies and psychos who break out of jail intending to dig it up. All the while, FBI man Reed Hadley lies in wait. A strong cast of B-movie regulars – Broderick Crawford, Charles Bronson and Ralph Meeker, as the kidnapper – contribute some agreeably cheesy characterisations, while the impressive location shooting was done in Colorado's Royal George Park, where the high suspension bridge, built in 1929, exists solely as a tourist attraction. Director Howard W Koch became Paramount's head of production in 1965.

Broderick Crawford *Rollo Lamar* • Ralph Meeker *Jerry Barker* • Reed Hadley *James Madden* • Randy Farr *Nurse Emily Evans* • William Talman *Machinegun Mason* • Lon Chaney Jr *Alamo Smith* • Charles Bronson *Benny Kelly* • Peter Votrian *Danny Lambert* ■ *Dir* Howard W Koch • *Scr* John C Higgins

Big Jack ★★

Black comedy western
1949 · US · BW · 84mins

Wallace Beery was another good-hearted rogue in his last picture, released shortly after his death at the age of 64. Marjorie Main played opposite him for the seventh time, as his wife, in this comedy western. Beery's Big Jack, the feared leader of outlaws in the early 19th century, befriends Richard Conte's young physician and offers a supply of bodies for his medical experiments. Sadly, the

black humour isn't forceful enough to overcome the tedium.

Wallace Beery *Big Jack Horner* • Richard Conte *Dr Alexander Meade* • Marjorie Main *Flapjack Kate* • Edward Arnold *Mayor Mahoney* • Vanessa Brown *Patricia Mahoney* • Clinton Sundberg *C Patronius Smith* • Charles Dingle *Mathias Taylor* • Clem Bevans *Saltlick Joe* ■ *Dir* Richard Thorpe • *Scr* Gene Fowler, Marvin Borowsky, Osso Van Eyss, from a story by Robert Thoeren

Big Jake ★★15

Western   1971 · US · Colour · 109mins

It might just as well have been titled *Big John*, because that's all it is, really: close-ups of the grizzled John Wayne, in the twilight of his career, nostalgically paired (for the fifth and last time) with an elegantly ageing Maureen O'Hara. There's precious little plot, though, and George Sherman's direction is lazy and untidy. Still, William Clothier's outdoor photography is worth a look and Richard Boone makes a fine larger-than-life baddie. But the whole sad enterprise is altogether too routine, and the leads just look too old. ▣

John Wayne *Jacob McCandles* • Richard Boone *John Fain* • Maureen O'Hara *Martha McCandles* • Patrick Wayne *James McCandles* • Chris Mitchum [Christopher Mitchum] *Michael McCandles* • Bobby Vinton *Jeff McCandles* • Bruce Cabot *Sam Sharpnose* ■ *Dir* George Sherman • *Scr* Harry Julian Fink, Rita M Fink

Big Jim McLain ★U

Spy drama   1952 · US · BW · 86mins

1952 was a bit late in the day to be sticking up for the likes of Senator Joe McCarthy, but nevertheless John Wayne produced and starred in this nasty piece of anti-Red propaganda in which he and James Arness, as House Un-American Activities Committee investigators, rout out communist spies in Hawaii. The astonishingly crude script portrays communists as inadequate human beings who behave like gangsters and make stupid mistakes. If Wayne hoped to make the subject more palatable by dressing it up as standard action fare, he was to be disappointed. Moviegoers smelled a rat, and it performed poorly. ▣

John Wayne *Big Jim McLain* • Nancy Olson *Nancy Vallon* • James Arness *Mal Baxter* • Alan Napier *Sturak* • Veda Ann Borg *Madge* • Gayne Whitman *Dr Gelster* • Hal Baylor *Poke* ■ *Dir* Edward Ludwig • *Scr* James Edward Grant, Richard English, Eric Taylor

The Big Job ★★★U

Comedy   1965 · UK · BW · 84mins

A breezy comedy from the *Carry On* people, played with evident relish by several series regulars. As ever, Sid James is the life and soul, as the leader of a gang of incompetent crooks who discover a police station has been built on the site where they stashed the loot from their last robbery. Partners-in-crime Sylvia Syms, Dick Emery and Lance Percival bungle his recovery plans with practised buffoonery, but they are often reduced to slapstick props. In contrast, Joan Sims's landlady, Jim Dale's goofy plod and Deryck Guyler's idle desk sergeant are much more fully developed comic creations. ▣

Sidney James *George Brain* • Sylvia Syms *Myrtle Robbins* • Dick Emery *Fred "Booky" Binns* • Lance Percival *Tim "Dipper" Day* • Joan Sims *Mildred Gamely* • Jim Dale *Harold* • Edina Ronay *Sally Gamely* • Deryck Guyler *Police sergeant* ■ *Dir* Gerald Thomas • *Scr* Talbot Rothwell

The Big Knife ★★★★

Drama   1955 · US · BW · 113mins

An intelligent, haunting film full of wonderful performances, particularly from Jack Palance (never better) and Rod Steiger as, respectively, the movie star coming apart at the seams and the studio boss who wants to cover up the paranoia at any price. This is one of the more successful films that Hollywood has made about itself, blessed with a marvellously literate script from the play by Clifford Odets and able direction from Robert Aldrich. A great movie suffused with realistic tension and lacerating satire.

Jack Palance *Charles Castle* • Ida Lupino *Marion Castle* • Shelley Winters *Dixie Evans* • Wendell Corey *Smiley Coy* • Jean Hagen *Connie Bliss* • Rod Steiger *Stanley Hoff* ■ *Dir* Robert Aldrich • *Scr* James Poe, from the play by Clifford Odets

The Big Land ★★★U

Western   1957 · US · Colour · 92mins

Called *Stampede* in the UK, this was one of star Alan Ladd's production ventures, made by his own company Jaguar under a releasing deal at Warner Bros. Ladd's wife and agent, former actress Sue Carol, often chose these projects, and cocooned her husband with quality factors. In this case he is reunited with Virginia Mayo and Gordon Douglas, his co-star and director respectively from *The Iron Mistress* (1952). Ladd is now sadly unfashionable and almost forgotten, but there was much more to him than *Shane*. Watch how effortlessly he turns this ordinary western into an impressively comfortable star vehicle.

Alan Ladd *Chad Morgan* • Virginia Mayo *Helen* • Edmond O'Brien *Jagger* • Anthony Caruso *Brog* • Julie Bishop *Kate Johnson* • John Qualen *Sven Johnson* • Don Castle *Draper* • David Ladd *David Johnson* ■ *Dir* Gordon Douglas • *Scr* David Dortort, Martin Rackin, from an adaptation by David Dortort of the novel *Buffalo Grass* by Frank Gruber

Big Leaguer ★★U

Sports drama   1953 · US · BW · 53mins

Robert Aldrich made his directing debut with this baseball drama, shot in 16 days in the area of Florida that was to become Cape Canaveral. Edward G Robinson stars as real-life John B Lobert, who ran a training camp for the New York Giants' potential recruits. Vera-Ellen (in a non-singing and non-dancing role) plays Robinson's niece, while Richard Jaeckel is among the young hopefuls. Most of the story is concerned with the kids' social background – rich and poor, cocky and shy, Cuban and American – and paints Robinson's character as one of the world's kindest people.

Edward G Robinson *John B "Hans" Lobert* • Vera-Ellen *Christy* • Jeff Richards *Adam Polachuk* • Richard Jaeckel *Bobby Bronson* • William Campbell *Julie Davis* • Carl Hubbell •

Paul Langton *Brian McLennan* ■ *Dir* Robert Aldrich • *Scr* Herbert Baker, from a story by John McNulty, Louis Morheim

The Big Lebowski ★★★★18

Comedy   1997 · US/UK · Colour · 112mins

While not in the same class as the Coen Brothers' previous film, *Fargo*, this goofy tribute to Raymond Chandler and *film noir* still comes gift-wrapped with enough good lines, ingenious plot twists and eccentric characters to satisfy the siblings' dedicated army of fans. There are in fact two Lebowskis: the first is leftover hippy Jeff Bridges, who gets bounced into kidnapping the other Lebowski by his ten-pin bowling chums (Steve Buscemi and John Goodman). What follows is an insane labyrinth of plot and counter-plot that encompasses the drug and porn underworlds, Busby Berkeley fantasies and bathtime with a savage marmot, sharply edited by the Cohens (under the pseudonym of Roderick Jaynes). Bridges, Buscemi and Goodman all give marvellous performances. Contains swearing, sexual references and some violence. *DVD*

Jeff Bridges *Jeff "The Dude" Lebowski* • John Goodman *Walter Sobchak* • Julianne Moore *Maude Lebowski* • Steve Buscemi *Donny* • David Huddleston *The Big Lebowski* • Philip Seymour Hoffman *Brandt* • Tara Reid *Bunny Lebowski* • John Turturro *Jesus Quintana* ■ *Dir* Joel Coen • *Scr* Ethan Coen, Joel Coen • *Producer* Ethan Coen

The Big Lift ★★★

Drama   1950 · US · BW · 120mins

The talented and tragic Montgomery Clift only completed 17 features, but each movie is of supreme interest. That's because Clift was the forerunner of today's naturalistic school of screen acting, predating Brando's film debut by a good couple of years. *The Big Lift* is one of five films Clift made with a German or militarist theme – a propagandist piece celebrating the airlift from post-war Berlin. It benefits from location shooting in Frankfurt and Berlin, with a supporting cast recruited from the military stationed there. Paul Douglas plays the blustering mouthpiece for American policy, and Cornell Borchers charmingly smooches with Clift in a dance club. Watch Clift try to upstage Douglas in their scenes together – Douglas soon stopped his tricks by treading on his foot.

Montgomery Clift *Danny MacCullough* • Paul Douglas *Hank* • Cornell Borchers *Frederica* • Bruni Lobel *Gerda* • OE Hasse *Stieber* ■ *Dir/ Scr* George Seaton

The Big Man ★18

Sports drama   1990 · UK · Colour · 111mins

What a shame that Liam Neeson got his first starring role in this ham-fisted drama. He plays an unemployed Scottish miner who becomes a bare-knuckle fighter, a Spartacus for corrupt businessman Ian Bannen. Joanne Whalley-Kilmer, Hugh Grant and a not particularly comic Billy Connolly complete the interesting cast. Set in a small Scottish mining town, the script turns cartwheels to gain resonance from Mrs Thatcher's duel with the miners, but to little avail – the picture is "pumped-up" yet irredeemably dull.

U = SUITABLE FOR ALL   Uc = SUITABLE FOR ALL, ESPECIALLY FOR YOUNG CHILDREN (VIDEO ONLY)   PG = PARENTAL GUIDANCE

A resounding flop, it was quickly withdrawn from cinemas and hastened the demise of the ailing Palace Pictures. Contains violence and swearing. ▭

Liam Neeson *Danny Scoular* • Joanne Whalley-Kilmer [Joanne Whalley] *Beth Scoular* • Billy Connolly *Frankie* • Ian Bannen *Matt Mason* • Maurice Roëves *Cam Colvin* • Hugh Grant *Gordon* • Kenny Ireland *Tony* ■ *Dir* David Leland • *Scr* Don MacPherson, from the novel by William McIlvanney

Big Man on Campus ★★
Spoof   1989 · US · Colour · 102mins

Allan Katz, who also wrote the script, steals the show here as "Bob Maloogalooga-Loogaloogalooga" – mainly because, for all his grunts and rampaging, he never forgets to make his wild man character loveable. Mr Looga is a feral man discovered living secretly on a Californian university campus. Melora Hardin plays the student who volunteers to civilise him, investing her role with a sweetness that's both fresh and convincing. As engaging as the film is, it's more pleasant than laugh-out-loud funny. The serious moments almost seem tacked on, and there are clear signs the original cut was significantly longer.

Allan Katz *Bob* • Corey Parker *Alex Kaminsky* • Cindy Williams *Diane Girard* • Melora Hardin *Cathy* • Tom Skerritt *Dr Webster* • Jessica Harper *Dr Fisk* • Gerrit Graham *Stanley Hoyle* ■ *Dir* Jeremy Paul Kagan • *Scr* Allan Katz

The Big Money ★★Ⓤ
Comedy   1956 · UK · Colour · 86mins

There are too many British comedies in which the talents of a superb cast are wasted by an inferior script. This offering is a case in point, though it does boast a decent story about a family of crack crooks whose eldest son couldn't pass a counterfeit note in a game of Monopoly. Ian Carmichael is perfectly cast in the lead, and who could ask for more than Kathleen Harrison, James Hayter and Leslie Phillips in support? But director John Paddy Carstairs hammers every gag into place. Staying the course soon begins to seem like a life sentence.

Ian Carmichael *Willie Frith* • Belinda Lee *Gloria* • Kathleen Harrison *Mrs Frith* • Robert Helpmann *The Reverend* • James Hayter *Mr Frith* • George Coulouris *The Colonel* • Jill Ireland *Doreen Frith* • Renee Houston *Bobby* • Leslie Phillips *Receptionist* ■ *Dir* John Paddy Carstairs • *Scr* John Baines

The Big Mouth ★
Comedy   1967 · US · Colour · 107mins

Comedian Jerry Lewis opens his mouth to the usual embarrassingly idiotic effect as a less-than-aggressive little guy who is the double of a gangster and becomes involved in a search for stolen diamonds. Directed, produced and co-written by Lewis, the film focuses almost continually on the star, which is a pity. Sadly, he does little here to convince non-devotees that he's an acquired taste worth acquiring.

Jerry Lewis *Gerald Clamson* • Harold J Stone *Thor* • Susan Bay *Suzie Cartwright* • Buddy Lester *Studs* • Del Moore *Mr Hodges* • Paul Lambert *Moxie* • Leonard Stone *Fong* •

Jeannine Riley *Bambi Berman* ■ *Dir* Jerry Lewis • *Scr* Jerry Lewis, Bill Richmond, from a story by Bill Richmond

Big News ★★★
Crime drama   1929 · US · BW · 75mins

This early talkie entry in the popular reporter-turned-detective cycle is directed with a good feel for authenticity by Gregory La Cava and is marked by some witty exchanges and a breezy leading performance from Robert Armstrong. He plays a reckless newspaper reporter with a taste for drinking in speakeasies, who courts trouble in his determination to nail a narcotics gang. Playing his journalist wife, Carole Lombard – not yet a star – demonstrates why she became one.

Robert Armstrong *Steve Banks* • Carole Lombard *Margaret Banks* • Tom Kennedy *Sgt Ryan* • Warner Richmond *Phelps* • Wade Boteler *O'Neil* • Sam Hardy *Joe Reno* • Louis Payne *Hensel* • James Donlan *Deke* • Cupid Ainsworth *Vera Wilson* • Lew Ayres *Copy Boy* ■ *Dir* Gregory La Cava • *Scr* Walter DeLeon, Jack Jungmeyer, from the play *For Two Cents* by George S Brooks

The Big Night ★★Ⓤ
Drama   1951 · US · BW · 73mins

When sports columnist Howard St John beats up widowed ex-boxer Preston Foster for no apparent reason, the victim's young son John Barrymore Jr goes on a night-long quest for the attacker through murky nightclubs, bars and hotels. He is rewarded with an unwelcome revelation. Flashily directed (and co-written) by Joseph Losey, who offers a compendium of nightlife underbelly clichés, and featuring a 19-year-old lead in Barrymore Jr who lacks the weight of his famous father, this is nonetheless a vivid and quite enjoyable little movie. Dorothy Comingore, of *Citizen Kane* fame, makes her final screen appearance.

John Barrymore Jr [John Drew Barrymore] *George La Main* • Preston Foster *Andy La Main* • Joan Lorring *Marion Rostina* • Howard St John *Al Judge* • Philip Bourneuf *Dr Lloyd Cooper* • Howland Chamberlin *Flanagan* • Emil Meyer [Emile Meyer] *Packingpaugh* ■ *Dir* Joseph Losey • *Scr* Stanley Ellin, Joseph Losey, from the novel *Dreadful Summit* by Stanley Ellin

Big Night ★★★★⑮
Comedy drama   1996 · US · Colour · 104mins

Actors Campbell Scott and Stanley Tucci impress as promising and sensitive directors in this small-scale fifties tale, a gastronomic dream for all lovers of fine Italian food that offers a crisp chianti of comedy as accompaniment. Brothers Tony Shalhoub and Stanley Tucci run a not particularly successful restaurant in New Jersey. Their constant competitiveness reaches a crescendo with the prospect that entertainer Louis Prima will come to dinner and help resurrect their failing business. Isabella Rossellini and Minnie Driver supply the love interest. Contains swearing. ▭

Tony Shalhoub *Primo* • Stanley Tucci *Secondo* • Marc Anthony *Cristiano* • Campbell Scott *Bob* • Minnie Driver *Phyllis* • Isabella Rossellini *Gabriella* • Larry Block *Man in restaurant* • Caroline Aaron *Woman in*

restaurant • Ian Holm *Pascal* ■ *Dir* Stanley Tucci, Campbell Scott • *Scr* Joseph Tropiano, Stanley Tucci

The Big Noise ★★★
Silent comedy   1928 · US · BW

Former vaudevillian, circus clown and Keystone Kop, Chester Conklin, a great comedy favourite of the silent era, stars in this efficiently made romp combining farce and satire. Sporting his trademark moustache, Conklin plays an ineffectual New York subway guard who accidentally falls on the track in front of an oncoming express. When a daily tabloid turns the incident into a heroic deed, he temporarily becomes a "big noise". It's a bit creaky now, but it has its moments for fans of the early comic style.

Chester Conklin *John Sloval* • Alice White *Sophie Sloval* • Bodil Rosing *Ma Sloval* • Sam Hardy *Philip Hurd* • Jack Egan *Bill Hedges* • Ned Sparks *William Howard* • David Torrence *Managing editor* ■ *Dir* Allan Dwan • *Scr* Thomas J Geraghty, George Marion (titles), from a story by Ben Hecht

The Big Noise ★★Ⓤ
Comedy   1944 · US · BW · 73mins

...but only a faint cackle to greet the comic genius of Laurel and Hardy. The duo are on the skids in this incompetently staged story of two dumb-luck detectives, hired to guard an inventor's new bomb – the titular "Big Noise". Biggest laughs are in the performance of Jack Norton, whose "drunk" routine has its moments. The rest, though, has scarcely any.

Stan Laurel *Stan* • Oliver Hardy *Ollie* • Doris Merrick *Evelyn* • Arthur Space *Hartley* • Louis Arco *German officer* • Beal Wong *Japanese officer* • Veda Ann Borg *Mayme* • Bobby Blake *Egbert* • Jack Norton *Drunk* ■ *Dir* Malcolm St Clair • *Scr* Scott Darling

The Big Operator ★★★
Crime drama   1959 · US · BW · 90mins

It's small beer today, but in 1959 this was a real toughie, beginning with a man being chucked into a cement mixer. It stars Mickey Rooney as a sadistic racketeer who takes the fifth while under investigation by the Senate. Rooney had already essayed Baby Face Nelson, and here he creates another memorable and plausible psycho in the fictional Little Joe Braun. Co-star Mamie Van Doren adds allure as the wife of Steve Cochran, whom Rooney has tortured, while Mel Tormé cruises along nicely until Mickey has him torched. It's tempting to see the whole film as an allegory about the McCarthy witch hunts.

Mickey Rooney *Little Joe Braun* • Steve Cochran *Bill Gibson* • Mamie Van Doren *Mary Gibson* • Mel Tormé *Fred McAfee* • Ray Danton *Oscar Wetzel* • Jim Backus *Cliff Heldon* • Ray Anthony *Slim Clayburn* • Jackie Coogan *Ed Brannell* • Charles Chaplin Jr *Bill Tragg* ■ *Dir* Charles Haas • *Scr* Robert Smith, Allen Rivkin, from a story by Paul Gallico

The Big Parade ★★★★★Ⓤ
Silent war drama   1925 · US · BW and Colour · 137mins

Rich industrialist's idle son John Gilbert enlists in the army when America enters the First World War and

is sent to France. Billeted in a village, he meets and falls in love with French farm girl Renée Adorée before going to the front. A simple synopsis doesn't begin to convey the beauty of the love story, the poignancy of comradeship among men almost certainly facing death, or the authentic power and horror of the battle. Director King Vidor's approach to his subject, and his great artistry in executing it, has given us one of the great anti-war films – an unqualified masterpiece, enacted by a uniformly first-class cast. The parting of the lovers as Gilbert is swept away to the front in the "big parade" is one of the most unforgettable set pieces in cinema history. The astonishing battle sequences demonstrate that film-making, at its best, has not really advanced much since the twenties. ▭

John Gilbert *James Apperson* • Renée Adorée *Mélisande* • Hobart Bosworth *Mr Apperson* • Claire McDowell *Mrs Apperson* • Claire Adams *Justyn Reed* • Robert Ober *Harry* • Tom O'Brien *Bull* • Karl Dane *Slim* • Rosita Marstini *French mother* ■ *Dir* King Vidor • *Scr* Henry Behn, Joseph Farnham (titles), from a story by Laurence Stallings • *Cinematographer* John Arnold, Henrik Sartov

The Big Parade ★★★★Ⓤ
Drama   1986 · Chi · Colour · 137mins

Thanks to the imposing finale, filmed with suitable pomp and scale by Zhang Yimou, this study of soldiers preparing for China's National Day parade was embraced by the authorities as a fitting tribute to the People's Liberation Army. Yet Chen Kaige was ordered to add this triumphant ending to lessen the impact of the gruelling training sequences, which were criticised for glorifying the achievements of the individual rather than extolling the virtues of communal endeavour. Chen's main aim is clearly a critique of the communist system, but this is also a powerful paean to the indomitability of the human spirit. In Mandarin with English subtitles. ▭

Wang Xueqi *Li Weicheng* • Sun Chun *Sun Fang* • Lu Lei *Jiang Junbiao* • Wu Ruofu *Lu Chun* • Guan Qiang *Liu Guoqiang* • Kang Hua Hao *Xiaoyuan* ■ *Dir* Chen Kaige • *Scr* Lili Gao

The Big Parade of Comedy ★★★Ⓤ
Comedy   1964 · US · BW · 89mins

This patchy celebration of MGM's comic past is another of the compilation films assembled by producer Robert Youngson. There are a couple of funny episodes featuring Laurel and Hardy and Buster Keaton, but neither did their best work for the studio and we are forced to spend too long in the company of performers such as Wallace Beery and Marie Dressler, whose brand of humour is now very dated. The high points are provided by William Powell, Myrna Loy, Jean Harlow and Marion Davies, who was a much better actress than critics at the time gave her credit for.

Dir Robert Youngson

The Big Picture ★★★★ 15

Satire 1989 · US · Colour · 96mins

Three years before *The Player*, this criminally neglected satire hit the same Hollywood targets first. But what else would you expect from director Christopher Guest and his *This Is Spinal Tap* co-writer Michael McKean? Hilariously detailing just how much film student Kevin Bacon is willing to compromise his integrity to get his first feature made, Guest smartly dissects the movie industry with malicious glee, film buff in-jokes and gentle humour, while also providing a fascinating insight into its power plays and studio politics. In the uniformly excellent cast – peppered with cameos from the likes of John Cleese and Elliott Gould – Martin Short steals the show as a smarmy talent agent. Contains some swearing and nudity. 📼

Kevin Bacon *Nick Chapman* • Emily Longstreth *Susan Rawlings* • JT Walsh *Allen Habel* • Jennifer Jason Leigh *Lydia Johnson* • Martin Short *Neil Sussman* • Michael McKean *Emmett Sumner* • Kim Miyori *Jenny Sumner* • Teri Hatcher *Gretchen* • John Cleese *Bartender* • Gould Elliott *Attorney* ■ *Dir* Christopher Guest • *Scr* Michael Varhol, Christopher Guest, Michael McKean, from a story by Michael Varhol, Christopher Guest

The Big Pond ★★★

Romantic musical 1930 · US · BW · 78mins

This vehicle for Maurice Chevalier is not in the same class as the previous year's hit *The Love Parade*, though he received a joint Oscar nomination for both films in 1929/1930. (This was the era of split-year Academy Awards.) The featherbrained screenplay (with additional dialogue from future master of satire Preston Sturges) has the star as a French tour guide in Venice falling for wealthy American tourist Claudette Colbert, but her father, a chewing gum millionaire, disapproves of the alliance. Although no Lubitsch, Hobart Henley directs competently enough, and Chevalier, oozing his usual Gallic charm, sings a clutch of excellent songs.

Maurice Chevalier *Pierre Mirande* • Claudette Colbert *Barbara Billings* • George Barbier *Mr Billings* • Marion Ballou *Mrs Billings* • Elaine Koch *Jennie* • Nat Pendleton *Pat O'Day* • Frank Lyon *Ronnie* • Andrée Corday *Toinette* ■ *Dir* Hobart Henley • *Scr* Robert Presnell, Garrett Fort, Preston Sturges, from a story by George Middleton, AE Thomas

Big Red ★ U

Adventure 1962 · US · Colour · 85mins

A Disney wildlife adventure about an Irish setter called Big Red and the young orphan boy who trains him. Their friendship is put to the test when old curmudgeon Walter Pidgeon decides to split them up. Romantic interest is provided by a female Irish setter, reinforcing the impression that the dogs are far more human than anything on two legs. Set in Quebec along the St Lawrence river, this is a movie of unspeakable treacliness. 📼

Walter Pidgeon *James Haggin* • Gilles Payant *René Dumont* • Emile Genest *Emile Fornet* • Janette Bertrand *Terese Fornet* • George Bouvier *Baggageman* • Doris Lussier *Farmer Mariot* • Roland Bedard *Conductor* ■ *Dir* Norman Tokar • *Scr* Louis Pelletier, from the novel by Jim Kjelgaard

The Big Red One ★★★★ 15

Second World War drama
1980 · US · Colour · 108mins

Samuel Fuller's skills had been blunted by working in American TV in the sixties, but the director returned to form on the big screen with this war movie, arguably one of his most accomplished features. Fuller had, in fact, regularly tried to make this picture for about 30 years. Drawing on his graphic memories of life as a crime reporter and infantryman in the Second World War, he produces a powerful and, at times, poetic tale of five soldiers who experience the brutal realities of combat. Lee Marvin, a perfect choice as the tight-jawed, bullish, growling sergeant, is reminiscent of Fuller himself. Contains violence and some swearing. 📼

Lee Marvin *Sergeant* • Mark Hamill *Griff* • Robert Carradine *Zab* • Bobby DiCicco *Vinci* • Kelly Ward *Johnson* • Siegfried Rauch *Schroeder* • Stéphane Audran *Walloon* • Serge Marquand *Rensonnet* • Charles Macaulay *General/Captain* ■ *Dir/Scr* Samuel Fuller

The Big Risk ★★★

Crime drama 1960 · Fr/It · BW · 111mins

A very early feature by Claude Sautet, this is clearly influenced as much by the gangster thrillers of Jean-Pierre Melville as earlier Hollywood models. Lino Ventura plays a gangster hiding out in Nice with his two children. His former associates in Paris hire a hitman to kill him but the two men become friends. Ventura – so good in the Melville films – is a sort of French Bogart and carries a romantic sense of doomy heroism. As the killer who switches allegiances Jean-Paul Belmondo is all youth and recklessness; he was about to turn the French cinema upside-down with his starring role in Jean-Luc Godard's *A Bout de Souffle*. The film was initially released in a dreadful dubbed version. A French language film.

Lino Ventura *Abel Davos* • Sandra Milo *Liliane* • Jean-Paul Belmondo *Eric Stark* • Marcel Dalio *Arthur Gibelin* • Jacques Dacqmine *Blot* • Claude Cerval *Raoul Fargier* ■ *Dir* Claude Sautet • *Scr* José Giovanni, Claude Sautet, Pascal Jardin, from the novel *Classe Tous Risques* by José Giovanni

The Big Shot ★★★

Crime drama 1942 · US · BW · 81mins

This was one of the movies Humphrey Bogart made just before *Casablanca* that consolidated the cynical, hard-boiled, louche image he had established in 1941's *The Maltese Falcon* – and would endearingly perpetuate in those later great Howard Hawks and John Huston pictures. It comes as no surprise, then, to discover that this flick is little more than a standard Warner Bros potboiler, albeit with a slightly more clever exposition than most, with Bogie reverting to contract type as self-styled three-time loser framed after a heist. Bogart virtually carries the movie single-handedly, but Irene Manning is interesting as a former girlfriend, and tragic Susan Peters (seriously disabled in a riding accident in 1944) makes a fetching ingénue.

Humphrey Bogart *Duke Berne* • Irene Manning *Lorna Fleming* • Richard Travis *George Anderson* • Susan Peters *Ruth Carter* • Stanley Ridges *Martin Fleming* • Minor Watson *Warden Booth* • Chick Chandler *Dancer* ■ *Dir* Lewis Seiler • *Scr* Bertram Millhauser, Abem Finkel, Daniel Fuchs

The Big Show ★★★ U

Drama 1961 · US · Colour · 112mins

When 20th Century-Fox got hold of a good story they sure as heck milked it to death with remakes. The publicity for this lavish circus epic wouldn't tell you, but this is yet another version of 1949's *House of Strangers*, itself westernised (and Oscared for original story!) in 1954 as *Broken Lance*. This time out Nehemiah Persoff is the troubled patriarch. The top-billed star is, however, the fabulous Esther Williams, her MGM swimming pool days behind her and her Amazonian physique now deployed on the high wire. Esther is super to watch, as is the young star she has the hots for, Cliff Robertson. While it doesn't quite come off, the European circus background is enthralling.

Esther Williams *Hillary Allen* • Cliff Robertson *Josef Everard* • Nehemiah Persoff *Bruno Everard* • Robert Vaughn *Klaus Everard* • Margia Dean *Carlotta Martinez* • David Nelson *Eric Solden* • Carol Christensen *Garda Everard* ■ *Dir* James B Clark • *Scr* Ted Sherdeman

The Big Showdown ★★

Spaghetti western
1972 · It/W Ger/Fr · Colour · 94mins

Although he was Sergio Leone's assistant on both *The Good, the Bad and the Ugly* and *Once upon a Time in the West*, there's little of the great man's influence in Giancarlo Santi's directorial debut. However, he does manage to blur the moral lines between gunslingers Lee Van Cleef and Horst Frank, which leaves us unsure where to place our sympathies as they head for the inevitable shootout. Further clouding the issue is Peter O'Brien, the maverick kid whom Van Cleef helps escape a trumped-up murder charge. The staging is hesitant, though, and composer Luis Enriquez Bacalov is no Ennio Morricone. Italina dialogue dubbed into English.

Lee Van Cleef *Sheriff Clayton* • Bob Clark *Deputy* • Horst Frank *David Saxon* • Peter O'Brien *Newland* • Sandra Cardini *Anita* • Dominique Darel *Elisabeth* • Alberto Dentice *Philipp Wermeer* • Klaus Grünberg *Adam Saxon* ■ *Dir* Giancarlo Santi • *Scr* Ernesto Gastaldi

The Big Silence ★★★

Spaghetti western 1967 · It/Fr · Colour

What do you get when you cross an Italian director with a German villain and a French hero? The answer is a thumping good spaghetti western from director Sergio Corbucci, best known for the cult classic *Django*. Klaus Kinski stars as a bounty hunter waiting to pick off the outlaws hiding in the Sierra Madre as the severe winter of 1896 drives them into the border villages. But mute gunfighter Jean-Louis Trintignant stands in his way. Blessed with stunning shots of the snow-covered mountains, this is a forerunner of such ghostly avenger westerns as Clint Eastwood's *High Plains Drifter* and *Pale Rider*. Italian dialogue dubbed into English.

Jean-Louis Trintignant *Silenzio* • Klaus Kinski *Tigrero* • Vonetta McGee *Pauline* ■ *Dir* Sergio Corbucci • *Scr* Sergio Corbucci, Vittoriano Petrilli, Mario Amendola, Bruno Corbucci • *Music* Ennio Morricone

The Big Sky ★★★★ U

Western 1952 · US · BW · 121mins

An eventful epic western, directed with great flair by maestro Howard Hawks, which could have been a great one with better casting. Kirk Douglas in the lead, good though he is, looks too urbane, not to mention intense, for this particular role, while his co-stars are not up to the splendour of Dudley Nichols's fine screenplay. There's a problem of taste, too – the finger amputation scene is played for laughs – but the film overall is so satisfying you'll forgive its faults. 📼

Kirk Douglas *Jim Deakins* • Dewey Martin *Boone Caudill* • Arthur Hunnicutt *Zeb* • Elizabeth Threatt *Teal Eye* • Steven Geray *Jourdonnais* • Buddy Baer *Romaine* • Hank Worden *Poordevil* • Jim Davis *Streak* ■ *Dir* Howard Hawks • *Scr* Dudley Nichols, from the novel by AB Guthrie

The Big Sleep ★★★★★ PG

Classic film noir 1946 · US · BW · 114mins

The second classic screen pairing of real-life lovers Humphrey Bogart and Lauren Bacall, this ultra-witty romantic thriller from maestro director Howard Hawks is one of the great pleasures of the silver screen. Its original release was delayed to give Hawks time to exploit and build up the Bogie–Bacall scenes, and as a result the movie sizzles with sexual chemistry as each exchange hides a censor-baiting double – or triple – entendre. The Raymond Chandler plot is infamously confusing, and ultimately irrelevant, but the delights are many: Martha Vickers's sexy Carmen ("She tried to sit in my lap when I was standing up"); Dorothy Malone's bookshop flirt; Elisha Cook Jr's sad fall guy. The pace never lets up, and this is a timeless, much-loved classic. 📼 DVD

Humphrey Bogart *Philip Marlowe* • Lauren Bacall *Vivian* • John Ridgely *Eddie Mars* • Louis Jean Heydt *Joe Brody* • Elisha Cook Jr *Jones* • Regis Toomey *Bernie Ohls* • Charles Waldron *General Sternwood* • Sonia Darren *Agnes* • Martha Vickers *Carmen* • Dorothy Malone *Girl in bookshop* ■ *Dir* Howard Hawks • *Scr* William Faulkner, Jules Furthman, Leigh Brackett, from the novel by Raymond Chandler • *Cinematographer* Sid Hickox • *Music* Max Steiner

The Big Sleep ★★ 15

Detective drama 1978 · UK · Colour · 95mins

Having given an excellent account of himself in *Farewell, My Lovely*, Robert Mitchum returned to the role of Philip Marlowe for this curious reworking of Raymond Chandler's hard-boiled novel. Shifted to seventies London, the action loses nearly all of its *noirish* atmosphere and, although Michael Winner sticks closer to the book than the writers responsible for Howard Hawks's seminal 1946 version, he's not in the same class as Leigh Brackett or Jules Furthman, let alone William Faulkner. The all-star cast is fun to watch, but only Mitchum and

Candy Clark seem to be playing characters involved in the story. ▱

Robert Mitchum *Philip Marlowe* • Sarah Miles *Charlotte Regan* • Richard Boone *Lash Canino* • Candy Clark *Camilla Sternwood* • Joan Collins *Agnes Lozelle* • Edward Fox *Joe Brody* • John Mills *Inspector Carson* • James Stewart *General Sternwood* • Oliver Reed *Eddie Mars* • Harry Andrews *Norris* ■ *Dir* Michael Winner • *Scr* Michael Winner, from the novel by Raymond Chandler

The Big Squeeze ★★

Crime comedy   1996 · US · Colour · 107mins

A lukewarm black comedy, with a hint of *noir* skulduggery thrown in for good measure. There's a couple of original twists offered – barmaid Lara Flynn Boyle schemes to con money out of her estranged, religious-nut husband rather than having him meet with an accident – and the quirky plotting separates it from more conventional "con" movies. Unfortunately, it's far less plausible than others of its ilk, and the "miracle tree" scam is plain silly. The casting is dubious too, with Boyle and conman Peter Dobson cutting unconvincing figures. It's a nice-looking movie, but there's less here than meets the eye.

Peter Dobson *Benny O'Malley* • Lara Flynn Boyle *Tanya Mulhill* • Luca Bercovici *Henry Mulhill* • Danny Nucci *Jesse* • Teresa Dispina *Cece* • Sam Vlahos *Father Sanchez* • Valente Rodriguez *Father Arias* • Michael Chieffo *Inspector* ■ *Dir/Scr* Marcus DeLeon

The Big Stampede ★ U

Western   1932 · US · BW · 51mins

The second of six B-westerns John Wayne dashed off for Warner Bros early in his career, this remake of the 1927 silent Ken Maynard vehicle, *The Land Beyond the Law*, is tailored to make use of that film's action highlights. Its big studio pedigree puts it a cut above Wayne's subsequent poverty row efforts, and it has character actor Berton Churchill as New Mexico Governor Lew Wallace dispatching John Wayne's deputy sheriff on his white horse to deal with cattle rustlers. They are led by Noah Beery, masquerading as a prosperous businessman. As usual, Wayne works hard, but the thin plot and characterisations defeat him. ▱

John Wayne *John Steele* • Noah Beery *Sam Crew* • Mae Madison *Ginger Malloy* • Luis Alberni *Sonora Joe* • Berton Churchill *Gov Lew Wallace* • Paul Hurst *Arizona* • Sherwood Bailey *Pat Malloy* ■ *Dir* Tenny Wright • *Scr* Kurt Kempler, from a story by Marion Jackson

The Big Steal ★★★ PG

Film noir   1949 · US · BW · 71mins

Reuniting the stars of the classic *Build My Gallows High*, and also going down Mexico way, Don Siegel's third feature is a thriller with more mirth than menace, and the sexual banter between Robert Mitchum and Jane Greer sometimes rivals that of Bogart and Bacall. The plot is simple – $300,000 of army payroll money has gone missing – and the extended chase throws up a great deal of subplots and shifty characters, notably Ramon Novarro as a lazy police chief. Real locations, rather than studio backdrops, are an asset, and Siegel (*Invasion of the Body Snatchers*, *Dirty*

Harry) never lets the pace sag or the shoestring budget show. ▱

Robert Mitchum *Lieutenant Duke Halliday* • Jane Greer *Joan Graham* • William Bendix *Captain Vincent Blake* • Patric Knowles *Jim Fiske* • Ramon Novarro *Colonel Ortega* • Don Alvarado *Lieutenant Ruiz* • John Qualen *Julius Seton* • Pascual Garcia Pena *Manuel* ■ *Dir* Don Siegel • *Scr* Geoffrey Homes [Daniel Mainwaring], Gerald Drayson Adams, from the story *The Road to Carmichael's* by Richard Wormser

The Big Steal ★★★ 15

Comedy   1990 · Ausl · Colour · 96mins

Fans of the 1986 Australian comedy *Malcolm* will enjoy this equally quirky offering from the husband-and-wife team of director Nadia Tass and writer/cameraman David Parker. This comedy of cars and romance stars Ben Mendelsohn (*The Year My Voice Broke*) as a shy teenager who craves a Jaguar so that he can woo a local beauty. When his dad gives him a battered old Nissan, our hero gets involved with shady car dealers and a 1973 Jag of dubious provenance. It's a slight but charming movie that takes its time to get on the road. ▱

Ben Mendelsohn *Danny Clark* • Claudia Karvan *Joanna Johnson* • Steve Bisley *Gordon Farkas* • Marshall Napier *Desmond Clark* • Damon Herriman *Mark Jorgensen* • Angelo D'Angelo *Vangeli Petrakis* • Tim Robertson *Desmond Johnson* • Maggie King *Edith Clark* • Sheryl Munks *Pam Schaeffer* ■ *Dir* Nadia Tass • *Scr* David Parker, Max Dunn

The Big Store ★★★★ U

Comedy   1941 · US · BW · 79mins

The last of five MGM comedies by the Marx Brothers, this has more plot than is usual for them. They play ramshackle detectives hired to guard a vast emporium in which customers take second place to the various under-the-counter shenanigans, in which the Brothers participate. As usual, Groucho woos massive Margaret Dumont, with insult amounting to injury but, more unusually, the romantic subplot is let loose, and allows Tony Martin to sing *Tenement Symphony*. Corny, but confident. ▱

Groucho Marx *Wolf J Flywheel* • Chico Marx *Ravelli* • Harpo Marx *Wacky* • Tony Martin *Tommy Rogers* • Virginia Grey *Joan Sutton* • Margaret Dumont *Martha Phelps* • William Tannen *Fred Sutton* ■ *Dir* Charles Riesner • *Scr* Sid Kuller, Hal Fimberg, Ray Golden, from a story by Nat Perrin

The Big Street ★★★

Comedy melodrama   1942 · US · BW · 88mins

Writer Damon Runyon produced this movie version of his own short story, *Little Pinks*, which has an adult cast Henry Fonda playing the busboy with a crush on moll Lucille Ball. Fonda and Ball are an unlikely couple – and would remain so when they next appeared together, 26 years later, in *Yours, Mine and Ours*. They're a great pleasure to watch, however, and Runyon's world is a delight to dip into: you'll emerge talking the jargon just like all dose guys 'n' dolls. Slight but fun.

Henry Fonda *Little Pinks* • Lucille Ball *Gloria* • Barton MacLane *Case Ables* • Eugene Pallette *Nicely Nicely Johnson* • Agnes Moorehead *Violette* • Sam Levene *Horsethief* • Ray

Collins *Professor B* • Marion Martin *Mrs Venus* ■ *Dir* Irving Reis • *Scr* Leonard Spiegelglass, from the short story *Little Pinks* by Damon Runyon

The Big Swap ★★ 18

Erotic drama   1997 · UK · Colour · 116mins

An ambitious but ultimately doomed British look at modern sexual politics and relationships. The set-up is promising: a large group of thirtysomethings, all of whom have partners, decide to spice up their lives by randomly swapping their respective boyfriends and girlfriends via the old car keys lottery. However, what seemed like a bit of harmless fun soon opens huge fissures between all the participants. It's raunchy stuff, but the performances from the largely unknown cast fail to convince. Contains swearing, sex scenes and some violence. ▱

Antony Edridge *Jack* • Sorcha Brooks *Ellen* • Richard Cherry *Hal* • Julie-Ann Gillitt *Liz* • Kevin Howarth *Julian* • Alison Egan *Eve* • Mark Caven *Michael* • Clarke Hayes *Fi* • Jackie Sawiris *Sydney* • Thierry Harcourt *Tony* • Mark Adams *Sam* ■ *Dir/Scr* Niall Johnson

The Big TNT Show ★★★★

Music concert documentary   1966 · US · Colour · 93mins

Shot in Electrovision (an early version of video) on November 29, 1965 at the Moulin Rouge nightclub in Hollywood, this fabulous concert film delivers one legendary performance after another and captures the precise moment old school rock 'n' roll turned hippy. The happy-go-lucky atmosphere is infectious as the Byrds, Petula Clark, Bo Diddley, the Ronettes, the Lovin' Spoonful, Roger Miller and other contemporary acts sock out their hits and drive the crowd wild, with the orchestra swelling under Phil Spector's giant production. A superb pop time capsule and an ideal companion piece to the earlier (and very similar) *The T.A.M.I. Show*.

Dir Larry Peerce • *Producer* Phil Spector

The Big Tease ★★ 15

Comedy   1999 · US/UK · Colour · 103mins

It's blow-dryers at dawn in director Kevin Allen's limp-wristed follow-up to *Twin Town*. Gay Scottish crimper Craig Ferguson believes that, thanks to his talent with the curling tongs, he's been invited to Los Angeles to take part in an international hairdressing competition. His hopes are dashed, however, when he realises he's only been summoned to appear in the celebrity audience. Refusing to curl up and dye, he charms his way into the contest via hard-nosed Hollywood agent Frances Fisher, millionaire sponsor Charles Napier and the usual bunch of Tinseltown eccentrics. The result is an intermittently amusing wash-and-go affair – having Ferguson's exploits filmed by a fly-on-the-wall documentary crew is an awkward device – although the actual competition, complete with bitchy rivals, conditioner sabotage and ludicrous hairdos, is a cut above the rest. Contains swearing.

Craig Ferguson *Crawford Mackenzie* • Frances Fisher *Candace "Candy" Harper* • Mary

McCormack *Monique Geingold* • Donal Logue *Eamonn McGarvey* • Larry Miller *Dunston Cactus, hotel manager* • Charles Napier *Senator Warren Crockett* • Michael Paul Chan *Clarence* • David Hasselhoff ■ *Dir* Kevin Allen • *Scr* Sacha Gervasi, Craig Ferguson

Big Time ★ PG

Music documentary   1988 · US · Colour · 92mins

Put together by singer/songwriter Tom Waits, his wife Kathleen Brennan and Levis 501 commercials director Chris Blum, this indulgent concert documentary was shot during the raspy lounge lizard's 1987 tour and contains all, or snatches of, 22 songs in his haphazard repertoire. The bittersweet meditations *Time, Innocent When You Dream* and *Cold Cold Ground* are covered, but the main focus of this vanity production – with Waits often in extreme close-up as he sings – are the three dull Island Records albums recorded prior to the tour. Anyone other than the ardent fan will find *Big Time* a hard time. ▱

Dir Chris Blum • *Scr* Tom Waits, Kathleen Brennen, Chris Blum

The Big Tip Off ★

Crime drama   1955 · US · BW · 78mins

In one of Hollywood's first efforts to discredit its burgeoning rival, television, journalist Richard Conte is duped by gangster Bruce Bennett who diverts funds from a charity telethon into his own pocket. The telethon scam is only one of several strands in a baffling plot. The treatment is decidedly lacklustre, and the minor stars are generally a wan bunch. Conte looks more like a gangster than Bennett, while love interest Constance Smith simply looks longingly at both chaps until she nearly gets murdered. The sole spark of interest is the brief appearance by George Sanders.

Richard Conte *Johnny Denton* • Constance Smith *Penny Conroy* • Bruce Bennett *Bob Gilmore* • Cathy Downs *Sister Joan* • James Millican *Lt East* • Dick Benedict *First hood* • Sam Flint *Father Kearney* • Mary Carroll *Sister Superior* • George Sanders ■ *Dir* Frank McDonald • *Scr* Steve Fisher

Big Top Pee-wee ★★★ U

Comedy   1988 · US · Colour · 85mins

As a bizarre star, he blazed only briefly in this and *Pee-wee's Big Adventure* before his career was abruptly halted by ignominy. But Pee-wee Herman, alias Paul Reubens, and his childish eccentricity of manner and dress contrived an odd originality, at least in this account of his funny farm – a hot-dog tree is the least of it – into which Kris Kristofferson's circus is blown during a storm. The talking pig is amusingly oinkish, but for most of the time the film has all the eerie fascination of a freak show – with Pee-wee as the main exhibit.

Pee-wee Herman [Paul Reubens] *Pee-wee Herman* • Kris Kristofferson *Mace Montana* • Penelope Ann Miller *Winnie* • Valeria Golino *Gina* • Susan Tyrrell *Midge Montana* • Albert Henderson *Mr Ryan* • Jack Murdock *Otis* ■ *Dir* Randal Kleiser • *Scr* Paul Reubens, George McGrath

The Big Town ★★ 15

Drama 1987 · US · Colour · 105mins

Matt Dillon plays an extremely sulky would-be high-roller in this formulaic, sepia-toned, crap-shooting movie. Director Ben Bolt ladles on the fug and finger snappin' with a heavy-handed trowel, but this remains a fruitless, sterile exercise with deep pretentions to style but little discernible substance. That said, there are solid performances from the always interesting Tommy Lee Jones and the pouting Diane Lane, as a deeply unsavoury couple who inveigle Dillon into further naughty doings. Contains some swearing. ▭

Matt Dillon *JC Cullen* • Diane Lane *Lorry Dane* • Tommy Lee Jones *George Cole* • Bruce Dern *Mr Edwards* • Lee Grant *Ferguson Edwards* • Tom Skerritt *Phil Carpenter* • Suzy Amis *Aggie Donaldson* • David Marshall Grant *Sonny Binkley* ■ *Dir* Ben Bolt • *Scr* Robert Roy Pool, from the novel *The Arm* by Clark Howard

The Big Trail ★★★★ U

Western 1930 · US · BW · 109mins

Fox made this truly epic western to celebrate the centenary of a famous pioneers' trek from Independence, Missouri. Under director Raoul Walsh, the cast and crew arduously re-created the highlights of that journey, lowering wagons and horses down cliff-faces, fighting heat, blizzards, raging rivers and Indians, giving the film an amazing documentary look. It was shot for both 70mm widescreen (the shortlived Fox Grandeur process) and for standard 35mm. A then unknown John Wayne took the lead: some of his lines are awkwardly spoken but he makes an authoritative figure of the wagon train scout. Unfairly, he took most of the flack for the film's failure, and was relegated to minor parts for a while.

John Wayne *Breck Coleman* • Marguerite Churchill *Ruth Cameron* • El Brendel *Gussie* • Tully Marshall *Zeke* • Tyrone Power [Tyrone Power Sr] *Red Flack* • David Rollins *Dave Cameron* • Ian Keith *Bill Thorpe* • Frederick Burton *Pa Bascom* • Russ Powell *Windy Bill* ■ *Dir* Raoul Walsh • *Scr* Jack Peabody, Marie Boyle, Florence Postal, Fred Sersen, from a story by Hal G Evarts, Raoul Walsh

The Big Trees ★★★

Drama 1952 · US · Colour · 89mins

A saga about a forest of giant redwood trees that lumberjack Kirk Douglas wants to cut down, much to the horror of the local Quaker community. Cue drama and romance with a demure Quaker girl, played by Eve Miller. For Douglas, still chasing after real stardom, this low-budget movie was a way out of a stifling contract with Warner Bros: he did the picture for nothing and earned his independence. Warners also saved money by using footage from an earlier lumberjack drama, *Valley of the Giants*. Filmed in Oregon, the picture is routinely exciting and delivers a powerful environmental message for the time.

Kirk Douglas *John Fallon* • Eve Miller *Alicia Chadwick* • Patrice Wymore *Daisy Fisher* • Edgar Buchanan *Yukon Burns* • John Archer *Frenchy Lecroix* • Alan Hale Jr *Tiny* ■ *Dir* Felix Feist • *Scr* John Twist, James R Webb, from a story by Kenneth Earl

Big Trouble ★★★ 15

Comedy 1986 · US · Colour · 89mins

An odd switch of tactics for the great improvisational director, John Cassavetes – a blandly contrived take-off of *Double Indemnity*, with insurance man Alan Arkin conniving with Beverly D'Angelo to take out a lethal kind of insurance policy on her husband Peter Falk. So far, so conventional. But there are enough off-the-wall surprises to raise it just above the average spoof thriller – one of which is that Arkin needs the money to send his trio of musical children to Yale. Contains some violence and swearing. ▭

Peter Falk *Steve Rickey* • Alan Arkin *Leonard Hoffman* • Beverly D'Angelo *Blanche Rickey* • Charles Durning *O'Mara* • Paul Dooley *Noozel* • Robert Stack *Winslow* • Valerie Curtin *Arlene Hoffman* • Richard Libertini *Dr Lopez* ■ *Dir* John Cassavetes • *Scr* Warren Bogle

Big Trouble in Little China ★★ 15

Action adventure 1986 · US · Colour · 95mins

Horror maestro John Carpenter is clearly in awe of Hong Kong movies, but this brave attempt to fuse martial-arts action with a westernised adventure story sadly doesn't gel. Kurt Russell makes an amiably inept hero as the dense lorry driver who gets mixed up with ancient Chinese magic when he ventures beneath the streets of San Francisco. The fight scenes are surprisingly stodgy, however, and in the end the special effects take over. ▭

Kurt Russell *Jack Burton* • Kim Cattrall *Gracie Law* • Dennis Dun *Wang Chi* • James Hong *Lo Pan* • Victor Wong *Egg Shen* • Kate Burton *Margo* • Donald Li *Eddie Lee* • Carter Wong *Thunder* ■ *Dir* John Carpenter • *Scr* Gary Goldman, David Z Weinstein, WD Richter

Big Wednesday ★★★★ PG

Drama 1978 · US · Colour · 114mins

It's easy to dismiss this Malibu surfing saga as pretentious nonsense, with beach bums Jan-Michael Vincent, William Katt and Gary Busey forever seeking the great Californian wave that will give meaning to their lives. However, director John Milius – who went on to script *Apocalypse Now* – shows a personal commitment to all the mystical bonding. The finished result rises above the pseudo-intellectual twaddle to make a poignant statement about the lack of purpose in the sixties, and the way Vietnam forced even infantile hunks such as these to take on responsibility. ▭

Jan-Michael Vincent *Matt Johnson* • William Katt *Jack Barlow* • Gary Busey *Leroy Smith* • Patti D'Arbanville [Patti D'Arbanville-Quinn] *Sally Johnson* • Lee Purcell *Peggy Gordon* • Darrell Fetty *Jim "Waxer" King* • Sam Melville *"The Bear"* • Barbara Hale *Mrs Barlow* ■ *Dir* John Milius • *Scr* John Milius, Dennis Aaberg

The Big Wheel ★★ U

Sports drama 1949 · US · BW · 92mins

Tough guy Mickey Rooney gets back into the racing car seat again, this time to prove he's as good as his old man, who, of course, died on the track. Clichéd stuff, but done with confidence and bravura, though alas without much style. Rooney continues to amaze, giving real credence to the duffest dialogue and situations, and he's ably backed-up by veteran stalwarts Thomas Mitchell, Spring Byington, and Allen Jenkins. Worth a look, but don't expect too much.

Mickey Rooney *Billy Coy* • Thomas Mitchell *Red Stanley* • Michael O'Shea *Vic Sullivan* • Mary Hatcher *Louise Riley* • Spring Byington *Mary Coy* • Lina Romay *Dolores Raymond* • Steve Brodie *Happy* • Allen Jenkins *George* ■ *Dir* Edward Ludwig • *Scr* Robert Smith

The Bigamist ★★★ PG

Drama 1953 · US · BW · 79mins

A gritty but far-fetched tale, directed by and co-starring Ida Lupino, in which feckless travelling salesman Edmond O'Brien ends up with two wives – Lupino and the suffering Joan Fontaine. This is adult material, originally released with an X certificate in the UK, and director Lupino really makes you believe in O'Brien's dilemma. It's an unusual and serious subject that is given a dramatic outing for a change. The only weakness is in the framing story, with loveable Edmund Gwenn as an investigator. ▭

Edmond O'Brien *Harry Graham* • Joan Fontaine *Eve Graham* • Ida Lupino *Phyllis Martin* • Edmund Gwenn *Mr Jordan* • Jane Darwell *Mrs Connelley* • Kenneth Tobey *Tom Morgan* • John Maxwell *Judge* ■ *Dir* Ida Lupino • *Scr* Collier Young, from a story by Larry Marcus, Lou Schor

Bigfoot ★★ U

Adventure 1987 · US · Colour · 89mins

Director Danny Huston, with a hard act to follow as the son of director John Huston, has a brief, rather mundane track-record to date. Unlike his father, who would surely have brought a dark comic twist to the material here, Danny only manages an efficient stab at this pleasant Disney outing. Most of the creativity, in fact, is down to make-up artist Robert Schiffer. His work is evident in the look of the sasquatch, the hairy, manlike creature that enter the lives of two plucky kids and a surly anthropologist. ▭

James Sloyan *Dr Zack Emerson* • Gracie Harrison *Laura Davis* • Adam Carl *Kevin Emerson* • Candace Cameron *Samantha Oneger* • Joseph Maher *Jack Kendrix* • Bernie White *Lazlo Whitefeather* • Colleen Dewhurst *Gladys Samcoe* • Dawan Scott *"Albert"* ■ *Dir* Danny Huston • *Scr* John Groves

Bigfoot and the Hendersons ★★ PG

Comedy 1987 · US · Colour · 106mins

A tale that resembles a watered-down, terrestrial remake of *ET*, produced by Steven Spielberg's company Amblin Entertainment. A Seattle family adopts America's answer to the abominable snowman and suffers the ludicrous consequences, while trying to keep it a secret from the neighbours. It's cosier, cutesier and even more sentimental than the Spielberg norm – perhaps the reason why it became a short-lived TV sitcom. However, seven foot two actor Kevin Peter Hall (the alien in *Predator* opposite Arnold Schwarzenegger) works miracles in Chewbacca drag as Harry the Missing Link. Contains some strong language. ▭

John Lithgow *George Henderson* • Melinda Dillon *Nancy Henderson* • Margaret Langrick *Sarah Henderson* • Joshua Rudoy *Ernie Henderson* • Kevin Peter Hall *Harry* • David Suchet *Jacques Lafleur* • Lainie Kazan *Irene Moffitt* • Don Ameche *Dr Wallace Wrightwood* • M Emmet Walsh *George Henderson Sr* ■ *Dir* William Dear • *Scr* William Dear, William E Martin, Ezra D Rappaport

A Bigger Splash ★★

Biographical documentary 1974 · UK · Colour · 104mins

The winner of a number of festival prizes, Jack Hazan's documentary portrait of artist David Hockney admirably captures the visual style of the artist, without ever quite breaking through his defences. Touching on the closeness of his friendships and his penchant for revisiting favourite haunts, the action mostly concerns his relationship with his latest sitter, Peter Schlesinger. Revealing the considerable personal stake Hockney invests in each new project, the film is less concerned with his methods than with the way in which he relates to his model and how he copes with the completion of his work. Precious, but illuminating. ▭

Dir Jack Hazan • *Scr* Jack Hazan, David Mingay

Bigger than Life ★★★★

Melodrama 1956 · US · Colour · 95mins

One of those legendary fifties melodramas, this was treated as a routine release in America and Britain, but hailed as a major work of art by the French (notably Jean-Luc Godard and François Truffaut) because it is a film by Nicholas Ray, the director of *Rebel without a Cause* and *They Live by Night*. James Mason, in one of his best roles, is a mild-mannered teacher whose career and marriage are wrecked by his addiction to cortisone, which turns him into a monster. Made in CinemaScope and famous for its dramatic colour scheme (New York cabs are at their yellowest), it is a real humdinger. And it features Walter Matthau, too.

James Mason *Ed Avery* • Barbara Rush *Lou* • Walter Matthau *Wally* • Robert Simon *Dr Norton* • Christopher Olsen *Richie Avery* • Roland Winters *Dr Rurich* • Rusty Lane *La Porte* • Rachel Stephens *Nurse* ■ *Dir* Nicholas Ray • *Scr* Cyril Hume, Richard Maibaum, from the article *Ten Feet Tall* by Berton Roueche • *Cinematographer* Joseph MacDonald

The Biggest Bundle of Them All ★★

Crime comedy 1968 · US/It · Colour · 107mins

Robert Wagner kidnaps rival mobster Vittorio De Sica. When no one offers to pay the ransom, De Sica takes over the gang and proposes stealing $5 million of valuable platinum. The resulting caper is a little too frantic for its own good; since it all ends in a big chase, the film resembles a gangster version of director Ken Annakin's earlier hit, *Those Magnificent Men in Their Flying Machines*. However, Edward G Robinson is on excellent form as the mastermind who plans the heist, while Raquel Welch has a lot of fizz as Wagner's moll.

U = SUITABLE FOR ALL Us = SUITABLE FOR ALL, ESPECIALLY FOR YOUNG CHILDREN (VIDEO ONLY) PG = PARENTAL GUIDANCE

Vittorio De Sica *Cesare Celli* • Raquel Welch *Juliana* • Robert Wagner *Harry* • Godfrey Cambridge *Benny* • Edward G Robinson *Professor Samuels* • Davy Kaye *Davey* • Francesco Mule *Tozzi* • Victor Spinetti *Captain Giglio* ■ *Dir* Ken Annakin • *Scr* Sy Salkowitz, Josef Shaftel, Riccardo Aragno, from a story by Josef Shaftel

Biggles ★ PG

Science-fiction adventure
1986 · UK · Colour · 88mins

A hero to a generation of young readers, Captain WE Johns's immortal flying ace is made to look very foolish in this ghastly spoof, directed with a leaden touch by John Hough. Neil Dickson does his best to give Biggles his customary gung-ho cheeriness, but his efforts are shot to pieces by a shambles of a story in which burger-bar boss Alex Hyde-White is whisked from modern America back to the First World War to join his time-twin, the flying ace on a secret mission. However, the saddest aspect of this sorry episode is that it was Peter Cushing's final film. Not even one for entertaining the children.

Neil Dickson *James "Biggles" Bigglesworth* • Alex Hyde-White *Jim Ferguson* • Fiona Hutchison *Debbie Stevens* • Peter Cushing *Colonel Raymond* • Marcus Gilbert *Eric von Stalhein* • William Hootkins *Chuck* • Michael Siberry *Algy* ■ *Dir* John Hough • *Scr* John Groves, Ken Walwin, from characters created by Captain WE Johns

Bike Boy ★

Underground satire
1967 · US · Colour · 96mins

Put your average sixties American stud, Joe Spencer, in various calculated situations with a bevy of screeching Andy Warhol superstars. Stand back, shoot on 16mm and see what happens. Not a lot does in this desperate Factory fiasco, which really is like watching proverbial paint dry. Will Viva get Joe's trousers off before the film runs out to reward voyeurs with another scene like the tacked-on shower prologue? Few will last the mind-numbingly boring course to find out. One of those underground movies that should have remained so, despite the chic Warhol imprint.

Joe Spencer *The motorcyclist* • Ed Wiener *His buddy* • Viva *Girl on couch* • Vera Cruz *Other cyclist* • George Ann *Salesman* • Bruce Ann *Salesman* ■ *Dir/Scr* Andy Warhol

Bill ★★★★

Drama based on a true story
1981 · US · Colour · 93mins

Almost 60 years after making his showbiz debut, mini-dynamo Mickey Rooney turns in what many rate a career-best performance, playing a mentally retarded man who has to learn to survive on his own in New York City after spending almost half a century in institutions. The film teeters on the edge of over-sentimentality. But, thanks to the sheer class of Rooney's performance, it never quite topples over. Made for TV, *Bill* earned Rooney an Emmy. Had it been made for the cinema, it might well have earned him an Oscar. Dennis Quaid co-stars in this true story, which spawned a sequel, *Bill: On His Own*.

Mickey Rooney *Bill Sackter* • Dennis Quaid *Barry Morrow* • Largo Woodruff *Bev Morrow* • Harry Goz *Thomas Walz* • Anna Maria Horsford *Marge Keating* • Kathleen Maguire *Florence Archer* • Jenny Rebecca Dweir *Amy Hill* • Tony Turco *Dr Peters* ■ *Dir* Anthony Page • *Scr* Corey Blechman, from a story by Barry Morrow

Bill & Ted's Bogus Journey ★★★★ PG

Cult comedy 1991 · US · Colour · 89mins

Wayne's World heroes Wayne and Garth may have won out at the box office, but Bill and Ted remain the original and best dudes. This time around the two airheads (played with enormous energy by Alex Winter and Keanu Reeves) are still trying to get their band together when they're murdered by their robotic doppelgängers, sent from the future by the evil Joss Ackland. They must then face the Grim Reaper if they are to become the saviours of mankind. This sequel lacks the inspired stupidity of the first, but it is still a hoot, especially the knowing nods to Ingmar Bergman's classic *The Seventh Seal* as the gormless duo play battleships with the Reaper. Reeves and Winter are once again cheerfully inept, and British director Peter Hewitt stages the spectacular set pieces with some panache. Contains swearing.

Keanu Reeves *Ted/Evil Ted* • Alex Winter *Bill/Evil Bill* • George Carlin *Rufus* • Joss Ackland *De Nomolos* • Sarah Trigger *Joanna* • Annette Azcuy *Elizabeth* • Hal Landon Jr *Captain Logan* • William Sadler *Grim Reaper* ■ *Dir* Peter Hewitt • *Scr* Ed Solomon, Chris Matheson

Bill & Ted's Excellent Adventure ★★★★ PG

Cult comedy 1988 · US · Colour · 85mins

A nonstop giggle from start to finish, this beguiling grab-bag of time-travel clichés, hard-rock music and Valley-speaking cool dudes is a flawless, purpose-built junk movie. Director Stephen Herek's scattershot style perfectly complements the wayward cosmic capers, and Keanu Reeves (in his pre-sex symbol days) bravely takes on comedian Alex Winter in competing for the "Most Witlessly Appealing Airhead" crown. Reeves resembles a moronic puppet with loose strings ambling amiably through this happy-go-lucky voyage into the short circuits of history. Engaging to the max. Contains some swearing.

Keanu Reeves *Ted "Theodore" Logan* • Alex Winter *Bill S Preston* • George Carlin *Rufus* • Terry Camilleri *Napoleon* • Dan Shor *Billy the Kid* • Tony Steedman *Socrates* • Rod Loomis *Sigmund Freud* • Al Leong *Genghis Khan* • Jane Wiedlin *Joan of Arc* ■ *Dir* Stephen Herek • *Scr* Chris Matheson, Ed Solomon

A Bill of Divorcement ★★★ U

Drama 1932 · US · BW · 68mins

More of interest for its place in cinema history than its dramatic content, this film features Katharine Hepburn's screen debut and introduced Hepburn to her favourite director, George Cukor, later responsible for such Hepburn delights as *The Philadelphia Story* and *Adam's Rib*. The Clemence Dane original is a hoary old thing, but star John Barrymore, though prone to ham,

is extraordinarily moving as the former mental asylum inmate reunited with his family, including daughter Hepburn. Billie Burke – Glinda the Good Witch in *The Wizard of Oz* – is also effective as Barrymore's wife, but many of today's viewers may find both the acting style and proscenium-based direction very creaky.

John Barrymore *Hilary Fairfield* • Katharine Hepburn *Sydney Fairfield* • Billie Burke *Margaret Fairfield* • David Manners *Kit Humphrey* • Elizabeth Patterson *Aunt Hester* • Paul Cavanagh *Gray Meredith* • Henry Stephenson *Dr Alliot* ■ *Dir* George Cukor • *Scr* Howard Estabrook, Harry Wagstaff Gribble, from the play by Clemence Dane

A Bill of Divorcement ★★★ PG

Drama 1940 · US · BW · 74mins

Confined to an asylum for 20 years and unaware that his wife has divorced him and is to remarry, Adolphe Menjou suddenly regains sanity and unexpectedly returns to the family home, precipitating emotional havoc. The 1932 version of the Clemence Dane play marked the screen debut of Katharine Hepburn and was a box-office hit. This straight remake was unfavourably compared to the original but, sacrilegious as it might be to say this, stands up better for a modern audience. It creaks in the same places, but offers a stunning performance from Maureen O'Hara. Menjou convinces and the supporting cast is superb, especially Dame May Whitty as the unbending sister of the ill man. John Farrow (father of Mia) directs with depth and sensitivity.

Maureen O'Hara *Sydney Fairfield* • Adolphe Menjou *Hilary Fairfield* • Fay Bainter *Margaret Fairfield* • Herbert Marshall *Gray Meredith* • Dame May Whitty *Hester Fairfield* • Patric Knowles *John Storm* • C Aubrey Smith *Dr Alliot* • Ernest Cossart *Dr Pumphrey* ■ *Dir* John Farrow • *Scr* Dalton Trumbo, from the play by Clemence Dane

Billie ★★★ U

Comedy musical 1965 · US · Colour · 86mins

An Oscar-winner at 16 for her startling performance as the young Helen Keller in *The Miracle Worker* (1962), Patty Duke returned to the screen three years later to play a tomboy whose astonishing prowess at athletics humiliates her male team-mates, bruises her beau's ego and embarrasses her mayoral candidate father. Directed with a pleasingly light touch by Don Weis, with good support from Jim Backus as Billie's male chauvinist dad, Jane Greer as her mom and Warren Berlinger as her boyfriend, this high-school comedy is both innocuous and entertaining.

Patty Duke *Billie Carol* • Jim Backus *Howard G Carol* • Jane Greer *Agnes Carol* • Warren Berlinger *Mike Benson* • Billy De Wolfe *Mayor Davis* • Charles Lane (1) *Coach Jones* • Dick Sargent *Matt Bullitt* • Susan Seaforth *Jean Matthews* • Ted Bessell *Bob Matthews* ■ *Dir* Don Weis • *Scr* Ronald Alexander, from the play *Time Out for Ginger* by Ronald Alexander

Billion Dollar Brain ★★ PG

Spy thriller 1967 · UK · Colour · 104mins

This is the least of the sixties Harry Palmer pictures, with a story that

smacks of substandard Bond, as Michael Caine travels to Finland to infiltrate Ed Begley's secret organisation and prevent him from taking over the world. Ken Russell was perhaps an unlikely choice as director, but his exuberance prevents the plot from lapsing into predictability. Catherine Deneuve's sister Françoise Dorléac impresses in her last performance before she was killed in a car smash. In 1995, Harry Palmer was brought put of retirement for the fourth and fifth films in the series, *Bullet to Beijing* and *Midnight in St Petersburg*.

Michael Caine *Harry Palmer* • Karl Malden *Leo Newbigin* • Françoise Dorléac *Anya* • Oscar Homolka *Colonel Stok* • Ed Begley *General Midwinter* • Guy Doleman *Colonel Ross* • Vladek Sheybal *Dr Eiwort* • Milo Sperber *Basil* ■ *Dir* Ken Russell • *Scr* John McGrath, from the novel by Len Deighton

The Billion Dollar Hobo ★★

Comedy 1978 · US · Colour · 96mins

In this wish fulfilment fable, Tim Conway discovers he'll only inherit a vast fortune if he duplicates his benefactor's experiences during the Depression. Stuart E McGowan's film intends to be make satirical points about unemployment and its consequences, but the vagrant script (co-written by Conway) wanders away from dramatic issues. For a far better movie on the same theme, see Preston Sturges's classic comedy *Sullivan's Travels* (1941).

Tim Conway *Vernon Praiseworthy* • Will Geer *Choo Choo Trayne* • Eric Weston *Steve* • Sydney Lassick *Mitchell* • John Myhers *Leonard Cox* • Frank Sivero *Ernie* • Sharon Weber *Jen* • Sheela Tessler *Rita* ■ *Dir* Stuart E McGowan • *Scr* Stuart E McGowan, Tim Conway, Roger Beatty

Billion Dollar Threat ★★

Spy drama 1979 · US · Colour · 96mins

Written by Hammer scribe Jimmy Sangster and produced as a TV pilot, this cheapskate Bond wannabe ends up being unintentionally hilarious in an Austin Powers sort of way. Dale Robinette is hung out to dry by a ludicrous plot that sees his groovy agent sent to investigate a series of UFO sightings. The esteemed Ralph Bellamy crops up as Dale's spymaster, but it's Patrick Macnee who dominates proceedings as an eco-terrorist who threatens to destroy the ozone layer unless his demands are met.

Dale Robinette *Robert Sands* • Ralph Bellamy *Miles Larson* • Patrick Macnee *Horatio Black* • Keenan Wynn *Ely* • Robert Tessier *Benjamin* • Beth Specht *Holly* • Ronnie Carol *Marcia Buttercup* • Stephen Keep *Harold Darling* ■ *Dir* Barry Shear • *Scr* Jimmy Sangster

A Billion for Boris ★★ PG

Comedy 1984 · US · Colour · 90mins

Based on the novel by Mary Rodgers, this comedy has a great idea at its core. Unfortunately it isn't followed through, and the whole thing ends up a bit of a mess. The story tells of a ten-year-old electronics expert who fixes a TV set so it can show the next day's programmes, much to the delight of his sister's boyfriend, who sees it as a great way of making money. What could have been an interesting piece of whimsy if given a heavy-handed treatment by director Alex Grasshoff and the cast, which includes Lee Grant. A missed opportunity.

Scott Tiler *Boris Harris* • Mary Tanner *Annabel Andrews* • Seth Green *Ape-Face* • Lee Grant *Sascha Harris* • Tim Kazurinsky *Bartholomew Bacon* ■ *Dir* Alex Grasshoff • *Scr* Sandy Gartin, from the novel by Mary Rodgers

Billy Bathgate ★★★ 15
Crime drama 1991 · US · Colour · 102mins

An only partially successful exercise in re-creating the world of the gangland vendetta from director Robert Benton, in which visual flair jostles uneasily with supremacy with a complicated narrative. Dustin Hoffman as infamous mobster Dutch Schultz gives one of his more over-egged performances, pulling all his tics, shrugs and grimacing rabbits out of the bag, but Nicole Kidman is sterling in support as a society moll. The credentials of this mahogany-toned movie are pretty impressive – original novel by EL Doctorow, script by Tom Stoppard – and there is an obvious intelligence that shines through the many nasty killings on offer. But, where the book meanders, the movie all too often mystifies and confuses. Contains violence, swearing and nudity. ▭

Dustin Hoffman *Dutch Schultz* • Nicole Kidman *Drew Preston* • Loren Dean *Billy Bathgate* • Bruce Willis *Bo Weinberg* • Steven Hill *Otto Berman* • Steve Buscemi *Irving* • Billy Jaye *Mickey* • John Costelloe *Lulu* ■ *Dir* Robert Benton • *Scr* Tom Stoppard, from the novel by EL Doctorow • *Cinematographer* Nestor Almendros

Billy Budd ★★★ U
Adventure drama
1962 · UK/US · BW · 124mins

Although this allegory about good versus evil is more suited to declamatory opera than cinema, writer/director Peter Ustinov's adaptation of Herman Melville's novel about life aboard an 18th-century British warship has a cannonade of powerful performances, notably from Ustinov as the indecisive captain, Robert Ryan as the sadistic Master-at-Arms, and an Oscar-nominated Terence Stamp as the innocent Billy. The film backs off from the fable that Melville intended, but the actors lift the rather plodding treatment to emotional heights reached by Benjamin Britten in his earlier operatic version.

Terence Stamp *Billy Budd* • Peter Ustinov *Captain Edward Fairfax Vere* • Robert Ryan *Master-at-Arms John Claggart* • Melvyn Douglas *The Dansker* • Ronald Lewis *Jenkins* • David McCallum *Lieutenant Wyatt* • John Neville *Lieutenant John Ratcliffe* • Ray McAnally *O'Daniel* ■ *Dir* Peter Ustinov, DeWitt Bodeen, Robert Rossen, from the novel *Billy Budd, Foretopman* by Herman Melville, from a play by Louis O Coxe, Robert H Chapman

Billy Galvin ★★★ PG
Drama 1986 · US · Colour · 90mins

A pleasingly gritty blue-collar drama, held together by a powerful performance from screen veteran Karl Malden, best known for his starring role opposite Michael Douglas in the seventies' TV series *The Streets of*

San Francisco. In a neat twist on a familiar story, he plays a stubborn construction worker who doesn't want his rebellious son Lenny Von Dohlen to join him on the scaffolding. There are believable performances from the largely unknown supporting cast and John E Gray's direction is admirably low key. Contains swearing. ▭

Karl Malden *Jack Galvin* • Lenny Von Dohlen *Billy Galvin* • Joyce Van Patten *Mae* • Toni Kalem *Nora* • Keith Szarabajka *Donny* • Alan North *Georgie* • Paul Guilfoyle *Nolan* • Barton Heyman *Kennedy* ■ *Dir* John E Gray [John Gray] • *Scr* John E Gray

Billy Jack ★★★ 18
Action drama 1971 · US · Colour · 109mins

Directing himself (under the name of TC Frank), Tom Laughlin stars as a mixed-race Vietnam veteran who comes to the aid of a school that is being harassed by a group of racists. Very much a family affair – co-star and co-scriptwriter Delores Taylor is Laughlin's wife – this achieved a surprisingly good return at the box office in spite of its humble origins and its apparent advocation of achieving peace through violence. Contains violence, swearing and nudity.

Tom Laughlin *Billy Jack* • Delores Taylor *Jean Roberts* • Clark Howat *Sheriff Cole* • Bert Freed *Posner* • David Roya *Bernard* • Julie Webb *Barbara* • Kenneth Tobey *Deputy* • Victor Izay *Doctor* ■ *Dir* TC Frank [Tom Laughlin] • *Scr* TC Frank [Tom Laughlin], Teresa Christina [Delores Taylor]

Billy Jack Goes to Washington ★
Drama 1977 · US · Colour · 155mins

The Billy Jack saga (introduced in *Born Losers* and continued through *Billy Jack* and the first sequel *The Trial of Billy Jack*) reaches a humdrum conclusion in star/writer/director Tom Laughlin's disastrous vanity production. The half-breed hapkido expert and former Green Beret hero takes his idealistic hippy causes to the White House and ends up fighting political corruption in this bland, out-of-step, Capraesque retread. Preachy, incredibly naive and well past its love-and-peace sell-by date even when it was first released.

Tom Laughlin *Billy Jack* • Delores Taylor *Jean Roberts* • EG Marshall *Senator Joseph Paine* • Teresa Laughlin *Staff worker* • Sam Wanamaker *Bailey* • Lucie Arnaz *Saunders McArthur* • Dick Gautier *Governor Hubert Hopper* ■ *Dir* TC Frank [Tom Laughlin] • *Scr* TC Frank [Tom Laughlin], Teresa Christina [Delores Taylor], from the film *Mr Smith Goes to Washington* by Sidney Buchman, from a novel by Lewis R Foster • *Producer* Frank Capra Jr

Billy Liar ★★★★★ PG
Comedy drama 1963 · UK · BW · 93mins

A hit on page and stage, Keith Waterhouse and Willis Hall's *Billy Liar* was brought to the screen by John Schlesinger as a faultless blend of social realism and satirical fantasy. Tom Courtenay is at his career best – so far – as the undertaker's assistant who escapes from his mundane existence into the neverland of Ambrosia, where he is supreme dictator. The performances are all first

rate, notably Julie Christie and Helen Fraser as two of the three women in his life, Wilfred Pickles and Mona Washbourne as his long-suffering parents, and Leonard Rossiter as his humourless boss. A must-see. ▭

Tom Courtenay *Billy Fisher* • Julie Christie *Liz* • Wilfred Pickles *Geoffrey Fisher* • Mona Washbourne *Alice Fisher* • Ethel Griffies *Florence, grandmother* • Finlay Currie *Duxbury* • Rodney Bewes *Arthur Crabtree* • Helen Fraser *Barbara* • Leonard Rossiter *Shadrack* ■ *Dir* John Schlesinger • *Scr* Keith Waterhouse, Willis Hall, from their play and the novel by Keith Waterhouse

Billy Madison ★★★ PG
Comedy 1995 · US · Colour · 85mins

Your enjoyment of this gimmicky comedy will depend on your feelings about the low-brow comedy of Adam Sandler. He plays an infantile loser who won't be given control of his father's billion dollar business empire unless he agrees to repeat his school education in just 24 weeks. Exploiting the star's talent for slapstick stupidity, this has some entertaining moments as he clashes with junior classmates and falls for his pretty teacher (Bridgette Wilson). Not in the same league as *The Wedding Singer*, but enjoyably dumb fun for Sandler supporters. ▭

Adam Sandler *Billy Madison* • Darren McGavin *Brian Madison* • Bridgette Wilson *Veronica* • Bradley Whitford *Eric Gordon* • Josh Mostel *Max Anderson* • Norm MacDonald *Frank* • Mark Beltzman *Jack* • Larry Hankin *Carl Alphonse* ■ *Dir* Tamra Davis • *Scr* Tim Herlihy, Adam Sandler

Billy Rose's Diamond Horseshoe ★★★ U
Musical 1945 · US · Colour · 100mins

Probably the best of the Betty Grable vehicles. For once, she had a decent director in George Seaton, who ensured that the garish 20th Century-Fox production was well appointed – check those wacky condiment costumes – and that the songs were well above the usual recycled standard of the period. This is the film that introduced the endearing hit *The More I See You*. Grable and co-star Dick Haymes are well supported by troupers Phil Silvers and Margaret Dumont, but the plot's as meagre as usual. ▭

Betty Grable *Bonnie Collins* • Dick Haymes *Joe Davis Jr* • Phil Silvers *Blinky Walker* • William Gaxton *Joe Davis Sr* • Beatrice Kay *Claire Williams* • Margaret Dumont *Mrs Standish* • Roy Benson *Harper* • George Melford *Pop* • Hal K Dawson *Carter* ■ *Dir* George Seaton • *Scr* George Seaton, from a play by John Kenyon Nicholson • *Music* Alfred Newman, Charles Henderson • *Costume Designer* Kay Nelson, Rene Hubert, Sascha Brastoff, Bonnie Cashin

Billy Rose's Jumbo ★★★★ U
Musical comedy 1962 · US · Colour · 123mins

A wonderfully warm-hearted MGM musical about circus rivalries, this is based on showman Billy Rose's Broadway extravaganza, which actually featured an elephant on stage. Star Doris Day is, sadly, too old and wise to play the ingénue here, but she delivers the lovely Rodgers and Hart songs

superbly, especially the sublime *My Romance*. Unlikely co-star Stephen Boyd, still hot from *Ben-Hur*, also acquits himself surprisingly well, but then he does get to sing a lilting *The Most Beautiful Girl in the World*. However, the real joys are veterans Martha Raye and Jimmy Durante, whose "What elephant?" line from this movie has rightly become classic.

Doris Day *Kitty Wonder* • Stephen Boyd *Sam Rawlins* • Jimmy Durante *Pop Wonder* • Martha Raye *Lulu* • Dean Jagger *John Noble* • Joseph Waring *Harry* • Lynn Wood *Tina* • Charles Watts *Ellis* ■ *Dir* Charles Walters • *Scr* Sidney Sheldon, from the musical by Ben Hecht, Charles MacArthur • *Choreography* Busby Berkeley

Billy the Kid ★★★★
Western 1930 · US · BW · 95mins

The first sound film about Billy the Kid tells a now familiar story of his friendship with a kindly British rancher and his relentless pursuit of the man's killers who have the law in their pocket. It shows its age at times, but director King Vidor presents the story in an austere, anti-romantic fashion, with a realistic regard for the effects of hunger and thirst on men under siege – and for the pain and finality of violent death, as when the previously comical Roscoe Ates is riddled with bullets in a valiant attempt to bring water to Billy and others. Johnny Mack Brown makes an excellent Kid, while Wallace Beery is restrained and believable as the fair-minded sheriff Pat Garrett. The film was shot with alternative endings, tragic and upbeat; it is the latter which is now usually shown.

John Mack Brown [Johnny Mack Brown] *Billy* • Wallace Beery *Barrett* • Kay Johnson *Claire* • Karl Dane *Swenson* • Wyndham Standing *Tunston* • Russell Simpson *McSween* • Blanche Frederici *Mrs McSween* ■ *Dir* King Vidor • *Scr* Wanda Tuchock, Laurence Stallings, Charles Macarthur, from the novel *The Saga of Billy the Kid* by Walter Noble Burns

Billy the Kid ★★★
Western 1941 · US · Colour · 94mins

The superb use of three-strip Technicolor doesn't altogether compensate for a certain dullness in this portrayal of the west's most famous outlaw, played by Robert Taylor dressed entirely in black. It's an image of the Kid that endured for another two decades as boys all over the world followed his black-clad comic book adventures in the Thriller Picture Library. First-time feature director and former editor David Miller has the benefit of the MGM production process, but, despite Gene Fowler's literate and inventive screenplay, which makes Billy and his nemesis Pat Garrett (here renamed Jim Sherwood) childhood friends, fans of this oft-told tale will be disappointed.

Robert Taylor (1) *Billy Bonney* • Brian Donlevy *Jim Sherwood* • Ian Hunter *Eric Keating* • Mary Howard *Edith Keating* • Gene Lockhart *Dan Hickey* • Lon Chaney Jr *Spike Hudson* • Henry O'Neill *Tim Ward* • Guinn "Big Boy" Williams [Guinn Williams] *Ed Bronson* ■ *Dir* David Miller • *Scr* Gene Fowler, from a story by Howard Emmett Rogers, Bradbury Foote, suggested by the book *The Saga of Billy the Kid* by Walter Noble Burns

U = SUITABLE FOR ALL, Uc = SUITABLE FOR ALL, ESPECIALLY FOR YOUNG CHILDREN (VIDEO ONLY) PG = PARENTAL GUIDANCE

Billy the Kid Returns ★★ U

Western   1938 · US · BW · 55mins

This starring vehicle for Roy Rogers has him playing Billy the Kid. After the outlaw is killed by sheriff Pat Garrett (Wade Boteler), Roy Rogers uses his strong resemblance to Billy to carry on the good work of protecting homesteaders and merchants from the machinations of a local rancher. Seven songs are packed into the brief running time, delivered by Rogers and sidekick Smiley Burnette. Leading lady Lynne Roberts made six subsequent appearances opposite Rogers.

Roy Rogers *Billy the Kid* • Smiley Burnette *Frog* • Lynne Roberts *Ellen* • Morgan Wallace *Morganson* • Fred Kohler Sr [Fred Kohler] *Matson* • Wade Boteler *Garrett* • Edwin Stanley *Miller* ■ *Dir* Joseph Kane • *Scr* Jack Natteford

Billy Two Hats ★★★

Western   1973 · UK/US · Colour · 99mins

An example of how Hollywood's elder statesmen (here Gregory Peck) tried to connect with the new "youth" audience of the seventies by co-starring with fresh talent, in this case Desi Arnaz Jr, best known for being the son of Desi Arnaz and Lucille Ball. It's a British-financed western about a bungled robbery, filmed in Israel, which looks like Spain pretending to be New Mexico. Co-produced by Norman Jewison with a screenplay by talented Alan Sharp, the writer of *Ulzana's Raid*, *Night Moves* and *Rob Roy*, it offers some decent action sequences and the novelty of the usually presidential Peck ostensibly playing a baddie. Contains swearing.

Gregory Peck *Deans* • Desi Arnaz Jr *Billy* • Jack Warden *Gifford* • Sian Barbara Allen *Esther* • David Huddleston *Copeland* • John Pearce *Spencer* • Dawn Littlesky *Squaw* ■ *Dir* Ted Kotcheff • *Scr* Alan Sharp

Billy's Hollywood Screen Kiss ★★★ 15

Romantic comedy
1997 · US · Colour · 92mins

An amiable valentine to the delicious ache of true love, frothy Doris Day romances and Petula Clark golden oldies, director Tommy O'Haver's farce and furious gay comedy drama serves up some disarmingly honest truths about confused passion in a camp cascade of glossy style, glamorous drag queens and glorious vamping. As wannabe LA photographer Sean P Hayes shoots homoerotic portraits based on famous Hollywood kisses and falls in lust with one of his models, the sexually confused Brad Rowe. Although never quite scalpel-sharp or profound enough to put it in the *Priscilla, Queen of the Desert* category, O'Haver's classy confection is nevertheless an engaging enough diversion held together by Hayes's central turn. Contains swearing and sexual references.

Sean P Hayes *Billy* • Brad Rowe *Gabriel* • Meredith Scott Lynn *Georgiana* • Richard Ganoung *Perry* • Armando Valdes-Kennedy *Fernando* • Paul Bartel *Rex Webster* • Matthew Ashford *Whitey* • Carmine Giovinazzo *Gundy* ■ *Dir/Scr* Tommy O'Haver

Biloxi Blues ★★★★ 15

Second World War comedy
1988 · US · Colour · 102mins

Playwright Neil Simon's semi-autobiographical trilogy began with *Brighton Beach Memoirs* (1986) and ended with *Broadway Bound* (1991), but this second instalment is the most entertaining of the three. Matthew Broderick plays Simon's altered ego Eugene Jerome, whose army boot camp training involves him in the lives of the various soldiers around him – from Christopher Walken's surprisingly desolate sergeant to Matt Mulhern's dumb-ox bully boy. Adapted from Simon's Broadway play, the film is dense with dialogue and dilemmas. (Should the recruits visit the local brothel? How many press-ups can they fake?) Director Mike Nichols makes up for the lack of momentum with character-revealing conversation and the result is comic and poignant. ▣

Matthew Broderick *Eugene* • Christopher Walken *Sgt Toomey* • Matt Mulhern *Wykowski* • Corey Parker *Epstein* • Markus Flanagan *Selridge* • Casey Siemaszko *Carney* • Michael Dolan *Hennessey* • Penelope Ann Miller *Daisy* • Park Overall *Rowena* ■ *Dir* Mike Nichols • *Scr* Neil Simon, from his play

Bingo ★★ PG

Adventure   1991 · US · Colour · 86mins

One to make WC Fields turn in his tomb, with acres of syrup oozing forth, this involves one small boy's tearful wish to hold on to his small dog. Every cliché in the "youngsters and canines" lexicon is dragged out, and the whole exercise in moribund sentimentality and occasional vulgarity is enough to put even the most dedicated *Blue Peter* fan off pets and children for life. Parents beware: this may strongly appeal to the very young. Contains swearing, and some violence. ▣

Cindy Williams *Natalie Devlin* • David Rasche *Hal Devlin* • Robert J Steinmiller Jr *Chuckie Devlin* • Kurt Fuller *Lennie* • Joe Guzaldo *Eli* • David French *Chickie Devlin* • Glenn Shadix *Duke* • Suzie Plakson *Ginger* ■ *Dir* Matthew Robbins • *Scr* Jim Strain, from the film *The Littlest Hobo* by Dorrell McGowan

The Bingo Long Travelling All-Stars and Motor Kings ★★★★

Period sports comedy
1976 · US · Colour · 110mins

This sports comedy set in 1939 takes a less than serious look at the issue of racial prejudice. Billy Dee Williams and James Earl Jones are the stars of a black baseball team, who decide to set up their own club in defiance of Negro League manager Ted Ross. Needless to say the bosses don't like it and try to put the All-Stars out of business. In this crowd-pleasing mix of skill and farce, Richard Pryor almost steals the show with his attempts to crash the race barrier.

Billy Dee Williams *Bingo Long* • James Earl Jones *Leon* • Richard Pryor *Charlie Snow* • Rico Dawson *Willie Lee* • Sam "Birmingham" Briston *Louis* • Jophery Brown *Champ Chambers* • Leon Wagner *Fat Sam* • Tony Burton *Isaac* ■ *Dir* John Badham • *Scr* Hal Barwood, Matthew Robbins, from a novel by William Brashler

Bio-Dome ★ 12

Comedy   1996 · US · Colour · 90mins

Excruciatingly awful comedy about a couple of crude, lewd and generally nauseating brothers (Pauly Shore and Stephen Baldwin) who accidentally gatecrash a year-long science bio-dome experiment. Naturally, they trash the place. The film aims for a goofy *Wayne's World* type vibe, but the brain-dead brothers' juvenile antics grate and the plotting is an insult – the boys invite hundreds of revellers to a dome party, yet nobody tries to stop them. Even the expected last-minute change of heart rings hollow. ▣

Pauly Shore *Bud Macintosh* • Stephen Baldwin *Doyle Johnson* • William Atherton *Dr Noah Faulkner* • Denise Dowse *Olivia Biggs* • Dara Tomanovich *Mimi Simkins* • Kevin West *TC Romulus* • Kylie Minogue *Petra Von Kant* • Joey Adams [Joey Lauren Adams] *Monique* • Patricia Hearst *Doyle's mother* • Roger Clinton *Professor Bloom* ■ *Dir* Jason Bloom • *Scr* Kip Koenig, Scott Marcano, from a story by Adam Leff, Mitchell Peck, Jason Blumenthal

Bionic Ever After? ★★ PG

Science-fiction adventure
1994 · US · Colour · 86mins

If you're looking for undemanding viewing, this frivolous TV movie reuniting Six Million Dollar Man Lee Majors with Bionic Woman Lindsay Wagner is just the ticket. The story has the bionic duo coming out of retirement to foil a terrorist who is about to launch a nuclear-tipped missile; they also must free the ambassador to the Bahamas, whose embassy has been hijacked. After the daring heroics, the couple finally get hitched. Fans of the TV shows will like seeing how their heroes have aged, but this sombre version is lacking in the originals' comic-book elements. ▣

Lee Majors *Steve Austin* • Lindsay Wagner *Jaime Sommers* • Richard Anderson *Oscar Goldman* • Farrah Forke *Kimberly* • Martin E Brooks *Dr Rudy Wells* • Alan Sader *John McNamara* • Geordie Johnson *Miles Kendrick* ■ *Dir* Stephen Stafford • *Scr* Michael Sloan, Norman Morill, from a story by Michael Sloan

Bionic Showdown: the Six Million Dollar Man and the Bionic Woman ★★★ PG

Science-fiction adventure
1989 · US · Colour · 92mins

Before you start worrying, Lee Majors and Lindsay Wagner are not about to beat the bionic daylights out of each other. After all, if you remember, they were once lovers before his disastrous test flight and her sky-diving mishap. No, the bionic baddie belongs to a secret government organisation intent on disrupting the Russian/American unity games. What with Steve Austin's eyes, Jaime Sommers's ears, a couple of phenomenal right arms and four of the fastest legs on the planet, who's going to bet against them? Keep those eyes peeled for a young hopeful by the name of Sandra Bullock. ▣

Lee Majors *Steve Austin* • Lindsay Wagner *Jaime Sommers* • Richard Anderson *Oscar Goldman* • Martin E Brooks *Dr Rudy Wells* • Sandra Bullock *Kate Mason* • Jeff Yagher *Jim Goldman* • Geraint Wyn Davies *Devlin* • Robert Lansing *General McAllister* • Josef Sommer

Esterman ■ *Dir* Alan J Levi • *Scr* Michael Sloan, Ted Mann, from a story by Michael Sloan, Robert DeLaurentiis

Birch Interval ★★★★

Drama   1976 · US · Colour · 103mins

Not shown in British cinemas, this marvellous film is touching and sensitive in its telling of the story of a young American girl growing up in the midst of an Amish community. It's finely directed by Delbert Mann, who is best remembered for the 1950s Paddy Chayefsky-scripted trilogy *Marty* (for which Mann won the best director Oscar), *The Bachelor Party* and *Middle of the Night* but has of late been lost to TV movies. An exceptionally strong cast is headed by veterans Eddie Albert and Rip Torn, and this marks a last return to film by blacklisted Oscar-winner Anne Revere. Little seen and little known, this is a minor classic in search of recognition.

Eddie Albert *Pa Strawacher* • Rip Torn *Thomas* • Ann Wedgeworth *Marie* • Susan McClung *Jesse* • Brian Part *Samuel* • Jann Stanley *Esther* • Bill Lucking [William Lucking] *Charlie* • Anne Revere *Mrs Tanner* • Joanna Crawford *Lady on Bus* ■ *Dir* Delbert Mann • *Scr* Joanna Crawford, from her novel

Bird ★★★★ 15

Biographical drama
1988 · US · Colour · 154mins

Charlie Parker, the black American alto saxophonist who was the driving force behind the bebop jazz revolution, sacrificed his well-being, and that of his lover, to the tempting whirlwind of his music. As Parker, Forest Whitaker gives a pumping performance. He's required to be arrogant but unsteady, cocksure of his muse, yet hooked on drugs. Diane Venora is no second best as his hapless lady, a woman who goes from strutting dancer to empty soul. Director Clint Eastwood is perfectly in tune with his subject, giving the film a claustrophobic atmosphere as it portrays the anarchy of bebop, though he overextends the sequences about Parker's personality. The innovative soundtrack, enhancing Parker's recordings using present-day musicians, is a perfect accompaniment. Contains swearing. ▣

Forest Whitaker *Charlie "Yardbird" Parker* • Diane Venora *Chan Richardson* • Michael Zelniker *Red Rodney* • Samuel E Wright *Dizzy Gillespie* • Keith David *Buster Franklin* • Michael McGuire *Brewster* • James Handy *Esteves* • Damon Whitaker *Young Bird* ■ *Dir* Clint Eastwood • *Scr* Joel Oliansky

Bird of Paradise ★★★

Romantic adventure   1932 · US · BW · 81mins

Producer David O Selznick wheeled in the big guns at RKO for this romance about love across the racial divide on a Polynesian island, sending Joel McCrea and the luscious Dolores Del Rio and distinguished director King Vidor off to locations in Hawaii. Appalling weather plagued the shoot, but can't be blamed for the turgid and messy screenplay, which deadens the drama. The production values are first-rate, though, while the doom-laden tale is played with conviction by the subtle and beautiful Del Rio and the attractive McCrea, is undeniably atmospheric.

12 15 18 = PASSED FOR PEOPLE OF THESE AGES AND OVER   ▣ = RELEASED ON VIDEO   **DVD** = RELEASED ON DVD

Delores Del Rio *Luana* • Joel McCrea *Johnny Baker* • John Halliday *Mac* • Richard "Skeets" Gallagher *Chester* • Creighton Chaney [Lon Chaney Jr] *Thornton* • Bert Roach *Hector* • Napoleon Pukui *The King* • Sofia Ortega *Mahumahu* ■ *Dir* King Vidor • *Scr* Wells Root, Leonard Praskins, Wanda Tuchok, from a play by Richard Walton Tully

Bird of Paradise ★

Romantic adventure
1951 · US · Colour · 100mins

Bird of Paradise was originally filmed in black and white by RKO in 1932, with stellar leads, a top-class director and loads of authentic atmosphere. This pointless Technicolor remake from Fox has no merit, despite being written and directed by the usually reliable Delmer Daves. As the white South Seas adventurer and the exotic native girl who fall disastrously in love, brooding Frenchman Louis Jourdan and tough girl Debra Paget are no match for their predecessors. The over-lush visuals engulf the human drama, and much of the film descends into idiotic fake ritual.

Louis Jourdan *Andre Laurence* • Debra Paget *Kalua* • Jeff Chandler *Tenga* • Everett Sloane *The beachcomber* • Maurice Schwartz *The Kahuna* • Jack Elam *The trader* • Prince Leilani *Chief* • Otto Waldis *Skipper* ■ *Dir* Delmer Daves • *Scr* Delmer Daves, from a play by Richard Walton Tully

Bird of Prey ★★ 15

Thriller 1995 · US/Bul · Colour · 96mins

Richard Chamberlain as a murderous drug dealer? It just doesn't seem right. Nonetheless he acquits himself reasonably well in this starry, if erratic, straight-to-video thriller. Boyan Milushev plays a man seeking revenge on Chamberlain, who murdered his father. Together with photographer Lenny Von Dohlen, he decides to get at him through the two women in the crime boss's life – wife Lesley Ann Warren and daughter Jennifer Tilly. Predictably nothing goes to plan. There are a few stylish moments, but mediocrity rules. [video]

Jennifer Tilly *Kily Griffith* • Boyan Milushev *Nikolai Milev* • Richard Chamberlain *Jonathan Griffith* • Lesley Ann Warren *Claire* • Robert Carradine *Eric Parker* • Lenny Von Dohlen *Johnny* ■ *Dir* Temistocles Lopez • *Scr* Boyan Milushev, James J Mellon, Tracy Hall Adams, Lynette Prucha, from a story by Boyan Milushev

Bird on a Wire ★★★ 15

Comedy action thriller
1990 · US · Colour · 105mins

Mel Gibson has another crack at a drugs-related role (first seen in *Tequila Sunrise*), although this time the mood is considerably lighter. He plays a former small-time drugs runner who has been in hiding since turning state's evidence, but who ends up on the run with an old flame (Goldie Hawn) when his cover is broken. It's frothy nonsense for the most part, but expertly packaged by director John Badham, and it does boast the rare sight of macho Mel impersonating a camp hairdresser. Hawn is an able, if sometimes irritating, foil, while David Carradine, Bill Duke (best known now as the director of films such as *Deep Cover* and *A Rage in Harlem*) and Stephen Tobolowsky are an entertaining trio of villains. Contains swearing and violence. [video] DVD

Mel Gibson *Rick Jarmin* • Goldie Hawn *Marianne Graves* • David Carradine *Eugene Sorenson* • Bill Duke *Albert Diggs* • Stephen Tobolowsky *Joe Weyburn* • Joan Severance *Rachel Varney* • Harry Caesar *Marvin* • Jeff Corey *Lou Baird* • Alex Bruhanski *Raun* ■ *Dir* John Badham • *Scr* David Seltzer, Louis Venosta, Eric Lerner, from a story by Louis Venosta, Eric Lerner

The Bird with the Crystal Plumage ★★★★ 18

Thriller 1969 · It/W Ger · Colour · 95mins

Who is the new Jack the Ripper holding Rome in a grip of terror? American author Tony Musante knows he's witnessed a vital clue to the chilling conundrum – but what is it exactly? Dario Argento's *giallo* trendsetter (*giallo*, or "yellow", being a term for all Italian thrillers more concerned with the modus operandi of the bloody murders than their whodunit aspect) is a glossy, cosmopolitan and jagged mystery firmly entrenched in Hitchcockian paranoia. A seminal work, it shows Argento's visual flair for horrific set pieces and introduced the trademark themes he'd develop in such subsequent violent nightmares as *Suspiria* and *Opera*. Italian dialogue dubbed into English. [video]

Tony Musante *Sam Dalmas* • Suzy Kendall *Julia* • Eva Renzi *Monica* • Enrico Maria Salerno *Morosini* • Mario Adorf *Berto* • Renato Romano *Dover* • Umberto Rano *Ranieri* ■ *Dir/Scr* Dario Argento • *Music* Ennio Morricone • *Cinematographer* Vittorio Storaro

The Birdcage ★★★ 15

Comedy 1996 · US · Colour · 114mins

The knives were out for this camp comedy from the start. Film snobs were convinced it would besmirch the memory of *La Cage aux Folles*, and the gay lobby denounced the making of such a cosy film in the Aids era. Yet, in the end, nearly everyone was pleasantly surprised by a picture that trivialised neither its source nor its sensitive issues. While not a patch on the original, it is a marked improvement on some of the other disastrous Hollywood remakes of Gallic favourites. Robin Williams underplays sensibly, Nathan Lane almost matches the peerless Michel Serrault, and Gene Hackman shows again what a deft comic he can be. Less assured, however, is director Mike Nichols and writer Elaine May's clumsy political satire at the expense of the American right. Contains swearing. [video] DVD

Robin Williams *Armand Goldman* • Gene Hackman *Senator Keeley* • Nathan Lane *Albert* • Dianne Wiest *Louise Keeley* • Dan Futterman *Val Goldman* • Calista Flockhart *Barbara Keeley* • Hank Azaria *Agador* • Christine Baranski *Katherine* ■ *Dir* Mike Nichols • *Scr* Elaine May, from the film *La Cage aux Folles* by Jean Poiret, Francis Veber, Edouard Molinaro, Marcello Danon, from the play *La Cage aux Folles* by Jean Poiret

Birdman of Alcatraz ★★★★ PG

Biographical drama 1962 · US · BW · 142mins

Real-life killer Robert Stroud was apparently quite unlike the tough, taciturn inmate portrayed by Burt Lancaster in director John Frankenheimer's thought-provoking study of one man's attempt to survive an unforgiving prison system. Stroud used his years in solitary confinement to become a world authority on ornithology, despite the cruel injustices meted out by the prison warden (convincingly played by Karl Malden). Lancaster was Oscar-nominated for a performance that is ranked by many to be one of the finest of his career, and he is well supported by fellow nominees Telly Savalas and Thelma Ritter, and by undervalued *Streets of San Franscisco* star Malden. Burnett Guffrey's claustrophobic black-and-white photography is masterly. [video]

Burt Lancaster *Robert Stroud* • Karl Malden *Harvey Shoemaker* • Thelma Ritter *Elizabeth Stroud* • Betty Field *Stella Johnson* • Neville Brand *Bull Ransom* • Edmond O'Brien *Tom Gaddis* • Hugh Marlowe *Roy Comstock* • Telly Savalas *Feto Gomez* • Crahan Denton *Kramer* ■ *Dir* John Frankenheimer • *Scr* Guy Trosper, from the book by Thomas E Gaddis

The Birds ★★★★★ 15

Classic black comedy horror
1963 · US · Colour · 113mins

A black comedy moonlighting as a genuinely unsettling, horrific allegory, this Hitchcock classic somehow strayed from favour for awhile. Yet in the realm of popular mythology, it is now rivalled only by *Psycho*. Set in the remote California coastal town of Bodega Bay, the story concerns a small group of unsatisfied creatures. Two women and a young girl are all fixed on one man (Rod Taylor), and when a fourth arrives from San Francisco with a certain determination in her heart, a menacing populace of birds descends on the town, wreaking terror and havoc, right up until the film's inscrutable ending. But as ever, Hitchcock is also having a laugh. The cast has Jessica Tandy and Suzanne Pleshette going for it, and, in an exceptional use of an otherwise unusable actress, Tippi Hedren. [video]

Tippi Hedren *Melanie Daniels* • Rod Taylor *Mitch Brenner* • Suzanne Pleshette *Annie Hayworth* • Jessica Tandy *Lydia Brenner* • Veronica Cartwright *Cathy Brenner* • Ruth McDevitt *Mrs MacGruder* • Ethel Griffies *Mrs Bundy* • Charles McGraw *Sebastian Sholes* ■ *Dir* Alfred Hitchcock • *Scr* Evan Hunter, from the short story by Daphne du Maurier

The Birds II: Land's End ★ 15

Thriller 1994 · US · Colour · 82mins

Unhappily married Brad Johnson and Chelsea Field take their two kids on vacation to Gull Island, only to become pecking targets in this vapid TV movie sequel to Alfred Hitchcock's classic 1963 shocker. More concerned with soap-opera squabbles than any avian horror, this padded-out slice of schlock offers an ecological explanation of the bird attacks that simply doesn't ring true. Tippi Hedren supplies a cameo, to little effect, while director Rick Rosenthal was so distressed by the whole farrago that he used the significant "bad movie" pseudonym, Alan Smithee, on the credits. [video]

Brad Johnson *Ted Hocken* • Chelsea Field *May Hocken* • James Naughton *Frank Irving* • Tippi Hedren *Helen Matthews* • Jan Rubes *Karl* • Megan Gallacher *Joanna Hocken* • Stephanie Milford *Jill Hocken* ■ *Dir* Alan Smithee [Rick Rosenthal] • *Scr* Ken Wheat, Jim Wheat, Robert Eisele, from the short story by Daphne du Maurier

The Birds and the Bees ★★ U

Comedy 1956 · US · Colour · 94mins

Preston Sturges's *The Lady Eve* was one of the smash hits of 1941 and is now regarded as an enduring gem of screwball comedy. Played by a trio of polished heavyweights (Barbara Stanwyck, Henry Fonda and Charles Coburn), this story of a father-daughter duo of cardsharps who fleece a gullible millionaire remains a magic amalgam of satire, farce, slapstick and romance. This Technicolor remake, directed by Norman Taurog with Mitzi Gaynor, David Niven and George Gobel, is a direct copy: mildly amusing, short on charm and entirely pointless.

George Gobel *George Hamilton* • Mitzi Gaynor *Jean Harris* • David Niven *Colonel Harris* • Reginald Gardiner *Gerald* • Fred Clark *Mr Hamilton* • Harry Bellaver *Marty Kennedy* • Hans Conried *Duc Jacques de Montaigne* • Margery Maude *Mrs Hamilton* ■ *Dir* Norman Taurog • *Scr* Sidney Sheldon, Preston Sturges, from a story by Monckton Hoffe

The Birds, the Bees, and the Italians ★★

Comedy 1965 · Fr/It · BW · 115mins

Bursting with Italianate gusto, director Pietro Germi's film is one of the many compendium works from Italy with sex as the subject of their intentionally humorous tales. This contribution, in which Virna Lisi is the best-known name, offers three episodes dealing variously with: a deceived husband; a henpecked husband who rebels; and an underage girl who is the favoured bed-mate of most of the male population of her village. Efficient enough, it now seems rather dated and tedious, though American and British audiences found it hilarious in its day. An Italian language film.

Virna Lisi *Milena Zulian* • Gastone Moschin *Osvaldo Bisigato* • Nora Ricci *Gilda Bisigato* • Alberto Lionello *Toni Gasparini* • Olga Villi *Ippolita Gasparini* • Franco Fabrizi *Lino Benedetti* • Beba Loncar *Noemi Castellan* • Gigi Ballista *Giancinato Castellan* ■ *Dir* Pietro Germi • *Scr* Age Scarpelli [Agenore Incrocci and Furio Scarpelli], Luciano Vincenzoni, Pietro Germi, from a story by Age Scarpelli [Agenore Incrocci and Furio Scarpelli], Pietro Germi

Birdy ★★★★ 15

Drama 1984 · US · Colour · 115mins

An engrossing psychological drama with powerful performances from Matthew Modine and Nicolas Cage as two young friends since childhood who are scarred by the trauma of fighting in Vietnam. Director Alan Parker, probably better known for such films as *Fame*, *The Commitments* and *Evita*, shows his versatility by adapting William Wharton's complex novel with sensitivity and skill, while Modine is exceptional as the boy who believes he's a bird. It deservedly won the Special Grand Jury Prize at the 1985 Cannes film festival. Contains violence, swearing and sex scenes. [video] DVD

Matthew Modine *Birdy* • Nicolas Cage *Al Columbato* • John Harkins *Dr Weiss* • Sandy

U = SUITABLE FOR ALL Uc = SUITABLE FOR ALL, ESPECIALLY FOR YOUNG CHILDREN (VIDEO ONLY) PG = PARENTAL GUIDANCE

Baron *Mr Columbato* • Karen Young *Hannah Rourke* • Bruno Kirby *Renaldi* • Nancy Fish *Mrs Prevost* • George Buck *Birdy's father* • Dolores Sage *Birdy's mother* ■ *Dir* Alan Parker • *Scr* Sandy Kroopf, Jack Behr, from the novel by William Wharton

The Birth of a Nation ★★★★ 15

Silent historical epic
1915 · US · BW · 192mins

This colossal, majestic Civil War epic from pioneer director DW Griffith is one of the most successful films of all time. In terms of film history, the film was groundbreaking: a long and epic narrative telling a complex tale interweaving two families' fortunes, with dramatic reconstructions of key events including the assassination of Abraham Lincoln, not to mention accurate (and costly) re-creations of Civil War battlefields. But – and it's a very big "but" – the source material is fervently and distressingly racist, and Griffith remains true to his source. It's hard to applaud a film where the Ku Klux Klan rides triumphantly to the rescue, and this, alas, undoes all the sterling work put in earlier and the wonderful performances from Lillian Gish, Mae Marsh, Henry B Walthall and, especially, Robert Harron. Griffith tried to make amends with *Intolerance*, but the damage was done. ▣

Lillian Gish *Elsie Stoneman* • Mae Marsh *Flora Cameron* • Henry B Walthall *Ben Cameron* • Miriam Cooper *Margaret Cameron* • Mary Alden *Lydia Brown* • Ralph Lewis *Hon Austin Stoneman* • George Siegmann *Silas Lynch* • Walter Long *Gus* ■ *Dir* DW Griffith • *Scr* DW Griffith, Frank E Woods, from the novel and the play *The Clansman* and the novel *The Leopard's Spots* by Thomas Dixon Jr • *Cinematographer* Billy Bitzer

Birth of the Beatles ★★

Musical biographical drama
1979 · US · Colour · 103mins

In comparison to the real thing, the wilder imaginings and flawed period atmosphere of this made-in-Britain TV movie are all the more cruelly exposed. John, Paul, George and Ringo are so familiar that it is almost impossible to accept imitations, even if they are as skilful as those in the 1993 film *BackBeat*. The quartet assembled here don't even bear a passing resemblance to the Fab Four and the accents are atrocious. Still, the Cavern/Hamburg period is fascinating and the passable music (performed by the band Rain) provides welcome relief from the acting. Contains mild swearing and brief nudity.

Stephen Mackenna *John Lennon* • Rod Culbertson *Paul McCartney* • John Altman *George Harrison* • Ray Ashcroft *Ringo Starr* • Ryan Michael *Pete Best* • David Wilkinson *Stu Sutcliffe* • Brian Jameson *Brian Epstein* • Wendy Morgan *Cynthia Lennon* ■ *Dir* Richard Marquand • *Scr* John Kurland, Jacob Eskendar, from a story by John Kurland • *Beatles Music* Rain

The Birth of the Blues ★★★ U

Musical
1941 · US · BW · 86mins

Bing Crosby, Brian Donlevy, Mary Martin and real-life trombonist Jack Teagarden head the line-up in this rather flimsy fiction about a pioneering

group who progress from being street entertainers to taking New Orleans by storm as the original Dixieland jazz band. Plot and characterisation, however, are secondary to such great numbers as *St Louis Blues*, *Melancholy Baby* and DeSylva, Henderson and Brown's title number. A supposed history of the blues, it's a good-natured, well-directed film that will delight fans of the music.

Bing Crosby *Jeff Lambert* • Mary Martin *Betty Lou Cobb* • Brian Donlevy *Memphis* • Carolyn Lee *Aunt Phoebe* • Eddie "Rochester" Anderson *Louie* • Jack Teagarden *Pepper* • J Carrol Naish *Blackie* • Warren Hymer *Limpy* ■ *Dir* Victor Schertzinger • *Scr* Harry Tugend, Walter DeLeon, from a story by Harry Tugend ▣

The Birthday Party ★★★ 15

Drama 1968 · UK · Colour and BW · 118mins

Directing only his second film, William Friedkin opted for a safe and rather uncinematic approach to Harold Pinter's first full-length play. This is all about text and performance, and, compelling though the action is, it's clearly diminished by the loss of the immediacy you get in the theatre. Robert Shaw is too sturdy an actor to convince as the frightened mystery man hiding away in a seaside B&B. Veterans Sydney Tafler and Dandy Nichols are left to steal the show with performances that suggest both had been rather wasted during their earlier movie careers. ▣

Robert Shaw *Stanley Weber* • Patrick Magee *Shamus McCann* • Dandy Nichols *Meg Bowles* • Sydney Tafler *Nat Goldberg* • Moultrie Kelsall *Petey Bowles* ■ *Dir* William Friedkin • *Scr* Harold Pinter, from his play

The Birthday Present ★★ U

Drama 1957 · UK · BW · 99mins

Pat Jackson was hailed by many critics in the mid-forties as one of the possible saviours of the floundering British film industry. However, by the time he came to make this doleful, overlong slice of surburban life, he had lost faith in the documentary style of film-making with which he had made his name and accepted the grim realities of the bargain basement. Tony Britton shows why he never made it as even a minor movie star, playing a toy salesman whose world falls apart when he is arrested for smuggling a wrist watch. Sylvia Syms, as the long-suffering wife who can take no more, deserves better than this.

Tony Britton *Simon Scott* • Sylvia Syms *Jean Scott* • Jack Watling *Bill Thompson* • Walter Fitzgerald *Sir John Dell* • Geoffrey Keen *Colonel Wilson* • Howard Marion-Crawford *George Bates* • John Welsh *Chief customs officer* • Lockwood West *Mr Barraclough* ■ *Dir* Pat Jackson • *Scr* Jack Whittingham

The Biscuit Eater ★★ U

Adventure 1972 · US · Colour · 86mins

Although this Disney remake of a minor 1940 hit is typically sugar-coated, watching a dog bounding through the undergrowth with a bird in its mouth is not likely to be everyone's idea of wholesome family entertainment. As the pals who overcome the racial prejudices of the adults around them to transform a wild hunting dog into a champion, Johnny

Whitaker and George Spell avoid the winsome boyishness usually portrayed in Hollywood outdoor adventures. But director Vincent McEveety tub-thumps the liberal American values and allows sentiment to turn to mush. ▣

Earl Holliman *Harve McNeil* • Lew Ayres *Mr Ames* • Godfrey Cambridge *Willie Dorsey* • Patricia Crowley *[Pat Crowley] Mrs McNeil* • Beah Richards *Charity Tomlin* • Johnny Whitaker *Lonnie McNeil* • George Spell *Text Tomlin* • Clifton James *Mr Eben* ■ *Dir* Vincent McEveety • *Scr* Lawrence Edward Watkin

The Bishop's Wife ★★★ U

Fantasy comedy 1947 · US · BW · 105mins

David Niven plays an irritable, materialistic bishop, Loretta Young his wife and Cary Grant an angel who descends from heaven to put their marriage in order and to raise money for a new church. Tensions on the set arose as Grant clashed with Young and director Henry Koster since he thought the script, co-written by Robert E Sherwood, was substandard. However, the playing from all three stars is enjoyable and there are some memorable moments – the festive setting allows Grant to trim a Christmas tree with the flick of a finger. His best line, "The only people who grow old are people who were born old to begin with," might well have been his own epitaph. ▣

Cary Grant *Dudley* • David Niven *Henry Brougham* • Loretta Young *Julia Brougham* • Monty Woolley *Professor Wutheridge* • James Gleason *Sylvester* • Gladys Cooper *Mrs Hamilton* • Elsa Lanchester *Matilda* • Sara Haden *Mildred Cassaway* ■ *Dir* Henry Koster • *Scr* Robert E Sherwood, Leonardo Bercovici, from the novel *In Barleyfields* by Robert Nathan

A Bit of Scarlet ★★★ 12

Documentary
1996 · UK · Colour and BW · 74mins

While not as good as its recent American counterpart *The Celluloid Closet*, this miscellany of gay and lesbian clips culled from British movies of the past 60 years has a fun time contrasting its stereotypical images with the supposed rules of the genre: all relationships must end with broken hearts; you will not be the main character; go to public school. The usual suspects are all here – *The Killing of Sister George*, *Victim*, Charles Hawtrey, *Carry On Spying* – and though it's somewhat messily assembled, it's narrated with ironic aplomb by Ian McKellen.

Ian McKellen *Narrator* ■ *Dir* Andrea Weiss • *Scr* Andrea Weiss, Stuart Marshall

The Bit Part ★

Comedy 1987 · Ausl · Colour · 87mins

A low-budget Australian comedy, this features Nicole Kidman before she had become Mrs Tom Cruise and established her own Hollywood stardom. Career counsellor Chris Haywood takes his own advice and tries to become a Shakespearean actor, with predictably miserable results. He befriends actress Kidman, who then makes it big in Hollywood. Who says it can only happen in the movies? This is interesting only for the presence of a pre-Cruise era Kidman.

Chris Haywood *Michael Thornton* • Nicole Kidman *Mary McAllister* • Katrina Foster *Helen Thornton* • John Wood *John Bainbridge* • Maurie Fields *Peter* • Brian Mannix *Barry* • Deborra-Lee Furness *Acting teacher* • Maggie Miller *Molly* • Maureen Edwards *Bev Howard* ■ *Dir* Brendan Maher • *Scr* Ian McFadyen

The Bit Player ★★★

Comedy 1973 · Fr · Colour · 96mins

Marcello Mastroianni stars as a bit-part actor, separated from his wife (Carla Gravina) and children, and living with his jealous mistress (Françoise Fabian). When she leaves him, he tries to go back to his wife, who is now carrying another man's child. Directed by Yves Robert, who undermines the sardonic comedy with a dollop of sentimentality, the film depends for its appeal on Mastroianni's entertaining, melancholy performance, and that of Jean Rochefort as his friend. The film certainly attempts to explore the less glamorous aspects of show business, but the female characters are woefully underwritten. French dialogue dubbed into English.

Marcello Mastroianni *Nicolas* • Françoise Fabian *Peggy* • Jean Rochefort *Clement* • Carla Gravina *Elizabeth* ■ *Dir* Yves Robert • *Scr* Jean-Loup Dabadie, Yves Robert

The Bitch ★★★ 18

Erotic drama 1979 · UK · Colour · 88mins

This kitsch classic follows the further adventures of promiscuous club owner Fontaine Khaled (Joan Collins), as she goes through a messy divorce and tries to get her London disco back in the celebrity limelight: Add a jewel robbery, handsome con men, horse racing and glamorous parties, and this sequel to *The Stud* is the usual Jackie Collins cocktail of sexy sleaze, camp hysteria and trashy dance routines. Collins's demon diva performance led to *Dynasty* and her golden years as TV's supreme super-bitch. ▣

Joan Collins *Fontaine Khaled* • Michael Coby *Nico Cantafora* • Kenneth Haigh *Arnold Rinstead* • Ian Hendry *Thrush Feather* • Carolyn Seymour *Polly* • Sue Lloyd *Vanessa* • Mark Burns *Leonard* • John Ratzenberger *Hal* ■ *Dir* Gerry O'Hara • *Scr* Gerry O'Hara, from the novel by Jackie Collins

Bite the Bullet ★★★ PG

Adventure 1975 · US · Colour · 125mins

Nine years after his hit western *The Professionals*, writer/director Richard Brooks released this gripping, allegorical drama about a 700-mile horse race. Entrants include Gene Hackman, James Coburn, Candice Bergen, Ben Johnson, Ian Bannen and Jan-Michael Vincent, pitting old-school values against the shallowness of capitalism. Filmed amid the stunning scenery of Nevada, Colorado and New Mexico, the picture is perhaps too long, with too many trough-stops for discourses about machismo and the motives of the competitors. But on the hoof it's an excellent adventure with a splendid cast and some spectacular turn-of-the-century settings. Contains some swearing. ▣

Gene Hackman *Sam Clayton* • Candice Bergen *Miss Jones* • James Coburn *Luke Matthews* • Ben Johnson *Mister* • Jan-Michael Vincent *Carbo* • Ian Bannen *Norfolk* • Mario Arteaga *Mexican* ■ *Dir/Scr* Richard Brooks

Bits and Pieces ★★★ 15

Drama   1995 · It · Colour · 109mins

With over 130 speaking parts and 30 different storylines, there's little wonder Antonello Grimaldi's ambitious film was dubbed "a Roman *Short Cuts*". Yet the roving style of Robert Altman is not the only influence on a picture that most vividly recalls the portmanteau compilations of short stories that were so popular in the sixties. Shot over a period of 18 months, the action is naturally fragmented and some characters pass us by before we've even noticed them. There are neat vignettes, however, featuring Dario and Asia Argento, Margherita Buy (as a vindictive traffic warden) and Enrico Lo Verso as a lovesick postman. In Italian with English subtitles. Contains violence, swearing and sex scenes.

Asia Argento *Teenage cousin* • Luca Barbareschi *Shyster* • Margherita Buy *Traffic warden* • Roberto Citran *Businessman* • Enrico Lo Verso *Postman* • Ivano Marescotti *Jogger* • Dario Argento *Man confessing to Franciscan monk* • Silvio Orlando *Mechanic* ■ *Dir* Antonello Grimaldi • *Scr* Daniele Cesarano, Paolo Marchesini

Bitter Harvest ★★

Drama   1963 · UK · Colour · 100mins

Having broken into Disney films in the late 1950s, Janet Munro suffered from typecasting for much of her tragically brief career (she died at just 38). Consequently, she was too rarely offered gutsier assignments like this adaptation of Patrick Hamilton's novel *The Street Has a Thousand Skies*. As the young Welsh innocent who is abused by various London ne'er-do-wells, she exhibits not only a touching vulnerability but also a credible inner reserve, which sustains her after she herself exploits a kindly barman (John Stride). Scripted by Ted Willis, this lacks the bite of contemporary examples of social realism, but it's solidly made.

Janet Munro *Jeannie Jones* • John Stride *Bob Williams* • Anne Cunningham *Ella* • Alan Badel *Karl Denny* • Vanda Godsell *Mrs Pitt* • Norman Bird *Mr Pitt* • Terence Alexander *Andy* • Richard Thorp *Rex* ■ *Dir* Peter Graham Scott • *Scr* Ted Willis, from the novel *The Street Has a Thousand Skies* by Patrick Hamilton

Bitter Harvest ★★ 18

Erotic crime thriller
1993 · US · Colour · 93mins

If you've ever wanted to watch beautiful women throwing themselves at Stephen Baldwin for no apparent reason, *Bitter Harvest* is for you. Baldwin plays Travis, a young man who has just inherited his father's house. And it's not a coincidence that, at the same time as he takes possession of the house, two attractive blondes start hanging around and trying to seduce him at every opportunity. Baldwin has made a career out of these kinds of sleazy roles – the very next year he would make *Threesome*. ▣

Patsy Kensit *Jolene* • Stephen Baldwin *Travis Graham* • Jennifer Rubin *Kelly Ann* • M Emmet Walsh *Sheriff Bob* • Adam Baldwin *Bobby* ■ *Dir* Duane Clark • *Scr* Randall Fontana

Bitter Moon ★★★ 18

Drama   1992 · Fr/UK · Colour · 133mins

It's not often that you see a film that needs therapy more than the characters that appear in it. But Roman Polanski's slickly told psychological drama – set on board a liner – is just such a film, trying to make sexual sadism into a metaphor for human relationships. Innocents Hugh Grant and Kristin Scott Thomas become entangled in the fantasies of paralysed writer Peter Coyote and Emmanuelle Seigner (Polanski's wife). It should have been played as a Buñuel-esque comedy, but it's no laughing matter, and ponderous solemnity finally makes it seem too much like a psychiatric casebook of the kind only Polanski could love. Contains violence, swearing, sex scenes and nudity. ▣

Peter Coyote *Oscar* • Emmanuelle Seigner *Mimi* • Hugh Grant *Nigel Dobson* • Kristin Scott Thomas *Fiona Dobson* • Victor Bannerjee [Victor Banerjee] *Mr Singh* • Sophie Patel *Amrita* • Patrick Albenque *Steward* • Stockard Channing *Beverly* ■ *Dir* Roman Polanski • *Scr* Roman Polanski, Gérard Brach, John Brownjohn, from the novel *Lunes de Fiel* by Pascal Bruckner

Bitter Rice ★★★

Drama   1949 · It · BW · 107mins

This Italian film about a woman (Silvana Mangano) who comes from the city each year to labour in the rice fields of the Po valley and falls in love with a macho petty villain (Vittorio Gassman), who is planning to steal the crop, caused a sensation in its day. The reason was not, however, the Academy Award-nominated original story, but the presence of the then 19-year-old, voluptuous beauty Mangano, clad in skimpy shorts and emanating sexuality from every pore. The story is no longer original, but the steamy eroticism is intact. Giuseppe De Santis directed for producer Dino De Laurentiis, who married his breathtaking young star later that year. In Italian with English subtitles.

Silvana Mangano *Silvana* • Doris Dowling *Francesca* • Vittorio Gassman *Walter* • Raf Vallone *Marco* • Checco Rissone *Aristide* • Nico Pepe *Beppe* • Adriana Sivieri *Celeste* • Lia Croelli *Amelia* ■ *Dir* Giuseppe De Santis • *Scr* Giuseppe De Santis, Carlo Lizzani, Gianni Puccini, from a story by Giuseppe De Santis, Carlo Lizzani

Bitter Springs ★★★ U

Adventure   1950 · Ausl/UK · BW · 88mins

Dismissed by many critics as a mere Outback western, this is a typical Ealing attempt to humanise a pressing social problem. In this case, it's the relationship between Australia's white and Aboriginal populations. There is an adventure element to the clash over water rights between pioneer Chips Rafferty and tribesman Henry Murdoch. However, while the action is set in the early 1900s, it has an obvious contemporary resonance – right down to the uncomfortable truce. Tommy Trinder is the nominal (and unlikely) star, but it's Michael Pate who makes a telling contribution as the itinerant soldier advocating indigenous rights.

Tommy Trinder *Tommy* • Chips Rafferty *Wally King* • Gordon Jackson *Mac* • Jean Blue *Ma*

King • Charles "Bud" Tingwell [Charles Tingwell] *John King* • Nonnie Piper *Emma King* • Nicky Yardley *Charlie* • Michael Pate *Trooper* ■ *Dir* Ralph Smart • *Scr* WP Lipscomb, Monja Danischewsky, from a story by Ralph Smart • *Producer* Michael Balcon

Bitter Sweet ★★

Operetta   1933 · UK · BW · 94mins

Produced, directed and partly written by Herbert Wilcox from Noël Coward's operetta, and starring his future wife Anna Neagle, this wistful period piece recounts the tale of a girl who elopes with her music teacher to 1870s Vienna. They live in happy poverty until tragedy strikes – but the movie's message is optimistically romantic. The Belgian actor Fernand Gravey, billed as "Graavey" for pronunciation reasons and later to make a Hollywood career as Gravet, made his English-speaking film debut as the lover. MGM remade it as a ludicrously sumptuous vehicle for Jeanette MacDonald and Nelson Eddy in 1940.

Anna Neagle *Sari Linden* • Fernand Graavey [Fernand Gravet] *Carl Linden* • Esme Percy *Hugh Devon* • Clifford Heatherley *Herr Schlick* • Ivy St Helier *Manon La Crevette* • Miles Mander *Captain August Lutte* • Pat Paterson *Dolly* ■ *Dir* Herbert Wilcox • *Scr* Herbert Wilcox, Lydia Hayward, Monckton Hoffe, from the operetta by Noël Coward

Bitter Sweet ★★★ U

Operetta   1940 · US · Colour · 93mins

One of the greatest of Noël Coward's scores, lavishly redone by MGM in the heart of their golden era. Deciding to photograph in sumptuous and expensive three-strip Technicolor was a clear indication of how highly studio boss Louis B Mayer prized his team of songbirds (not even Garbo rated colour), the legendary "Iron Butterfly" Jeanette MacDonald and her partner, the now-almost-unwatchable Nelson Eddy. The songs are fabulous; other pleasures include a very funny turn from Herman Bing, and distinguished Brits George Sanders and Ian Hunter, as a Viennese officer and an English lord respectively, lending a touch of class to the heavyweight American leads.

Jeanette MacDonald *Sarah Millick* • Nelson Eddy *Carl Linden* • George Sanders *Baron Von Tranisch* • Ian Hunter *Lord Shayne* • Felix Bressart *Max* • Edward Ashley *Harry Daventry* • Lynne Carver *Dolly* • Diana Lewis *Jane* ■ *Dir* WS Van Dyke II [WS Van Dyke] • *Scr* Lesser Samuels, from the operetta by Noël Coward

The Bitter Tea of General Yen ★★★★ PG

Drama   1933 · US · BW · 83mins

A genuinely exotic oddity, superbly performed by stars Barbara Stanwyck and the Swedish actor Nils Asther, and magnificently directed by a young Frank Capra. The first film ever to play the famous Radio City Music Hall, New York, this deeply sensuous movie was banned throughout the UK and the Commonwealth for dealing so blatantly with the then taboo subject of miscegenation. Stanwyck is magnificent, and the final close-up of her face deserves to be as well-known in cinema annals as the similar shot of Garbo at the end of *Queen Christina*. There's brilliant editing (by Edward

Curtiss) at work here, too, notably a classically cut dialogue scene between Stanwyck and Walter Connolly, in an early screen role. Sensual and disturbing, this film is a revelation to those who know its director only as a purveyor of "Capra-corn". ▣

Barbara Stanwyck *Megan Davis* • Nils Asther *General Yen* • Gavin Gordon *Dr Robert Strike* • Lucien Littlefield *Mr Jackson* • Toshia Mori *Mah-Li* • Richard Loo *Captain Li* • Clara Blandick *Mrs Jackson* • Walter Connolly *Jones* ■ *Dir* Frank Capra • *Scr* Edward Paramore, from the novel by Grace Zaring Stone • *Editor* Edward Curtiss

The Bitter Tears of Petra von Kant ★★★★ 15

Melodrama   1972 · W Ger · Colour · 118mins

Inspired by both his own experiences as a gay man and Joseph L Mankiewicz's *All About Eve*, this is Rainer Werner Fassbinder's tribute to the Hollywood "woman's picture". Petra von Kant (Margit Carstensen) is the fashion designer who embarks on a stormy lesbian affair with her model Hanna Schygulla. Fassbinder shows the classic relationship issues of dominance, submission and jealousy are just as prevalent in homosexual affairs as straight ones. The production is heavily stylised but such is the elegance of the gliding camerawork and the symbolic kitsch of the furnishings that the action never feels stagey. Expertly played, this is soap par excellence. In German with English subtitles.

Margit Carstensen *Petra von Kant* • Hanna Schygulla *Karin Thimm* • Irm Hermann *Marlene* • Katrin Schaake *Sidonie von Grasenabb* • Eva Mattes *Gabriele von Kant* • Gisela Fackeldey *Valerie von Kant* ■ *Dir/Scr* Rainer Werner Fassbinder • *Cinematographer* Michael Ballhaus

Bitter Vengeance ★★ 15

Thriller   1994 · US · Colour · 86mins

A slow-paced made-for-TV thriller that wastes the talents of Virginia Madsen, whose career seems to have gone very quiet of late. Here she plays the long-suffering wife of security guard Bruce Greenwood, who decides to rob the bank he is meant to be guarding. However, unbeknown to her, she doesn't figure in his plans for a new life as a millionaire – in fact, she is going to be the patsy for the whole caper. Madsen is as charismatic as ever, but the direction of Stuart Cooper is plodding and there is little in the way of surprises. Contains some violence and sex scenes. ▣

Virginia Madsen *Annie Westford* • Bruce Greenwood *Jack Westford* • Kristen Hocking *Isabella Martens* • Eddie Velez *Harry Carver* ■ *Dir* Stuart Cooper • *Scr* Pablo F Fenjves

Bitter Victory ★★★

Second World War adventure
1957 · Fr/US · BW · 105mins

In this taut and fraught war drama, Richard Burton and Curt Jurgens lead an assault on Rommel's HQ. Jurgens cracks up under the strain, and tries to kill Burton. Everything stems from an affair Burton has had with Jurgens's wife. The picture veers from realism to surrealism (Jurgens watching a scorpion crawling over Burton) and then to overblown melodrama. Jurgens is an impressive fraudulent hero (and a German to boot) and Burton comes across as a sort of TE Lawrence figure, the neurotic scholar-soldier. It was filmed in Libya and heavily cut for American release.

Richard Burton *Captain Leith* • Curt Jurgens *Major Brand* • Ruth Roman *Mrs Brand* • Raymond Pellegrin *Makron* • Anthony Bushell *General Paterson* • Alfred Burke *Lt Col Callander* • Christopher Lee *Sergeant Barney* ◼ *Dir* Nicholas Ray • *Scr* Rene Hardy, Nicholas Ray, Gavin Lambert, from the novel by Rene Hardy

Bittersweet Love ★★

Drama 1976 · US · Colour · 90mins

Meredith Baxter and Scott Hylands fall in love. She becomes pregnant. Then they discover they're half-siblings as a result of the one-night stand of her mother (Lana Turner) and his father (Robert Lansing) who are married, respectively, to Robert Alda and Celeste Holm. Starting from a not uninteresting idea, this degenerates into an endless debate about whether Patricia should have an abortion. An inadequate screenplay that sidesteps the issues and David Miller's limp direction make this a damp squib of a movie.

Lana Turner *Claire* • Robert Lansing *Howard* • Celeste Holm *Marian* • Robert Alda *Ben* • Meredith Baxter Birney [Meredith Baxter] *Patricia* • Scott Hylands *Michael* • Gail Strickland *Roz* ◼ *Dir* David Miller • *Scr* Adrian Morrall, DA Kellogg

The Black Abbot ★

Crime comedy thriller
1934 · UK · BW · 56mins

Julius Hagen acquired Twickenham Studios in 1928 with the express purpose of turning out quota quickies. This is a typical example of these low-budget programme fillers, as it hurtles through a pot-holed plot with little regard for character development or cinematic invention. Richard Cooper struggles to convince as the nobleman who proves more than a match for his kidnapper John Stuart. Director George A Cooper does little more than point the camera at the action, which is staged on as few sets as possible to keep the costs down.

John Stuart *Frank Brooks* • Judy Kelly *Sylvia Hillcrest* • Richard Cooper *Lord Jerry Pilkdown* • Ben Welden *Charlie Marsh* • Drusilla Wills *Mary Hillcrest* • Edgar Norfolk *Brian Heslewood* • Farren Souter *John Hillcrest* • Cyril Smith *Alf Higgins* • John Turnbull *Inspector Lockwood* ◼ *Dir* George A Cooper • *Scr* H Fowler Mear, from the novel *The Grange Mystery* by Phillip Godfrey

Black and White ★★★

Drama 1999 · US · Colour · 98mins

A group of affluent white teens obsessed with hip-hop culture are at the heart of writer/director James Toback's provocative look at race relations in contemporary America. A web of tenuously connected storylines covers everything from blackmail to documentary film-making and there's an eclectic cast that includes Robert Downey Jr, Claudia Schiffer, boxer Mike Tyson, and Oli "Power" Grant (from Wu-Tang Clan), as a thug trying to go legit as a rap music producer.

The largely improvised script gives the film a raw energy at the expense of a cohesive narrative. Tyson, portraying himself, gives a performance that's funny and surprisingly wise.

Scott Caan *Scotty* • Robert Downey Jr *Terry* • Stacy Edwards *Sheila King* • Allan Houston *Dean* • Gaby Hoffman *Raven* • Kidada Jones *Jesse* • Jared Leto *Casey* • Marla Maples *Muffy* • Power [Oli "Power" Grant] *Rich Bower* • Claudia Schiffer *Greta* • Brooke Shields *Sam* • Mike Tyson ◼ *Dir/Scr* James Toback

Black and White in Color ★★★

First World War satire
1976 · Fr/IvC/Swi · Colour · 91mins

Set in a remote trading post in a French colony in West Africa on the outbreak of the First World War, this Ivory Coast co-production deals with a group of French colonists, who mobilise the natives to attack a German fort. A rather specious satire on colonialism, it certainly has many amusing moments, but most of the humour is largely dependent on racist and sexist stereotypes. In fact, the French title of *La Victoire en Chantant* is the most witty thing about the picture. The debut feature of former TV-commercials director Jean-Jacques Annaud, it won the Oscar for the best foreign film in a bad year. In French with English subtitles.

Jean Carmet *Sergeant Bosselet* • Jacques Dufilho *Paul Rechampot* • Catherine Rouvel *Marinette* • Jacques Spiesser *Hubert Fresnoy* • Dora Doll *Maryvonne* • Maurice Barrier *Caprice* • Claude Legros *Jacques Rechampot* • Jacques Monnet *Père Simon* ◼ *Dir* Jean-Jacques Annaud • *Scr* Georges Conchon, Jean-Jacques Annaud

Black Angel ★★

Film noir 1946 · US · BW · 80mins

Following impressive supporting roles in two Fritz Lang movies – *The Woman in the Window* and *Scarlet Street* – Dan Duryea was given star billing in this darkish thriller. He plays a songwriter whose wife is strangled, presenting him with any number of suspects. It turns out she had been blackmailing someone, and then... well, it gets a little too complicated for its own good. Duryea's profession as a tunesmith is merely an excuse to cram in some musical sequences with June Vincent, set mainly in Peter Lorre's nightclub. The film is anonymously directed by Roy William Neill, and Duryea doesn't really have leading man appeal. In fact, he comes across as a bit of a chump.

Dan Duryea *Martin Blair* • June Vincent *Catherine* • Peter Lorre *Marko* • Broderick Crawford *Captain Flood* • Wallace Ford *Joe* • Hobart Cavanaugh *Jake* • Constance Dowling *Marvis Marlowe* • Freddie Steele *Lucky* ◼ *Dir* Roy William Neill • *Scr* Roy Chanslor, from a novel by Cornell Woolrich

The Black Arrow ★★ 🆄

Historical adventure 1948 · US · BW · 75mins

There's trouble brewing in Ye Olde House of York, as Louis Hayward discovers when he returns from the War of the Roses. Uncle George Macready has seized power, hacking off many heads in the process, including that of Hayward's father.

Loosely based (they used the title) on Robert Louis Stevenson's novel, it's moderately entertaining, with Hayward looking fetching in shining armour, behaving with the utmost chivalry and cooing over demure little Janet Blair, a nightclub singer who subsequently quit Hollywood to star in a touring production of *South Pacific*.

Louis Hayward *Richard Shelton* • Janet Blair *Joanna Sedley* • George Macready *Sir Daniel Brackley* • Edgar Buchanan *Lawless* • Lowell Gilmore *Duke of Gloucester* • Russell Hicks *Sir Harry Shelton* ◼ *Dir* Gordon Douglas • *Scr* Richard Schayer, David P Sheppard, Thomas Seller, from the novel by Robert Louis Stevenson

Black Beauty ★★ 🆄

Melodrama 1933 · US · BW · 47mins

Fans of Anna Sewell's famous horsey tale didn't get a decent talkie version until 1994, when writer/director Caroline Thompson followed the book's format of having the narrative recounted by the horse. This version is a very average low-budgeter, competently directed by studio hack Phil Rosen, with former silent star Esther Ralston topping a largely forgettable cast. The horse sequences may look vaguely familiar, since they went into the studio stock library and used material featured in many other films of that time. 🎬

Esther Ralston *Leila Lambert* • Alexander Kirkland *Henry Cameron* • Hale Hamilton *Bledsoe* • Gavin Gordon *Captain Jordan* • Don Alvarado *Renaldo* • George Walsh *Junk man* ◼ *Dir* Phil Rosen • *Scr* Charles Logue, from the novel by Anna Sewell

Black Beauty ★★ 🆄

Drama 1946 · US · BW · 73mins

An early score from ace composer Dimitri Tiomkin, best known for *Giant* and *The Alamo*, distinguishes this pallid version of Anna Sewell's equine classic. Although this is set in England, none of the cast seriously modify their Yank accents. Ingénue Mona Freeman would appear in many horse operas later on, but is perhaps best remembered as Miriam Wilkins in the very forties trilogy *Dear Ruth*. Handsome leading man Richard Denning never really made first rank either. A moderate low-budget film, drably directed by Polish expatriate Max Nosseck (*Dillinger*).

Mona Freeman *Anne Wendon* • Richard Denning *Bill Dixon* • Evelyn Ankers *Evelyn Carrington* • Charles Evans *Squire Wendon* • JM Kerrigan *John* • Moyna MacGill *Mrs Blake* • Terry Kilburn *Joe* • Tom Dillon [Thomas P Dillon] *Skinner* ◼ *Dir* Max Nosseck • *Scr* Lillie Hayward, Agnes Christine Johnston, from the novel by Anna Sewell

Black Beauty ★★ 🅿🅶

Drama
1971 · UK/W Ger/Sp · Colour · 101mins

Anna Sewell's classic children's story has had no shortage of film adaptations. This version doesn't really hit the mark, despite starring the winsome Mark Lester. Director James Hill obviously knows how to work with animals, having made both *Born Free* and *The Belstone Fox*, and screenwriter Wolf Mankowitz also had a hand in many notable British films from the late fifties onwards. But their

combined talents couldn't save this muddled and undistinguished Euro-pudding, produced at German and Spanish studios with a pan-European cast, but made in English.

Mark Lester (1) *Joe* • Walter Slezak *Hackenschmidt* • Peter Lee Lawrence *Gervaise* • Ursula Glas *Marie* • Patrick Mower *Sam Greene* • John Nettleton *Sir William* • Maria Rohm *Anne* • Eddie Golden *Evans* ◼ *Dir* James Hill • *Scr* Wolf Mankowitz, from the novel by Anna Sewell

Black Beauty ★★★ 🆄

Drama 1994 · UK/US · Colour · 84mins

This glossy reworking of Anna Sewell's much-filmed classic marked the directorial debut of Caroline Thompson, a writer whose successes include *Edward Scissorhands* and *The Addams Family*. She's no stranger to animals, either, having co-scripted *Homeward Bound*, Disney's remake of *The Incredible Journey*, and that experience is utilised to good effect here – the horses look superb and Beauty even sounds convincing, thanks to Alan Cumming's clever voice-over. The largely British cast does its bit, too, with Sean Bean and David Thewlis revealing previously unsuspected soft centres, but the acting honours go to Peter Cook and Eleanor Bron, as Lord and Lady Wexmire. 🎬

Sean Bean *Farmer Grey* • David Thewlis *Jerry Barker* • Jim Carter *John Manly* • Peter Davison *Squire Gordon* • Alun Armstrong *Reuben Smith* • John McEnery *Mr York* • Eleanor Bron *Lady Wexmire* • Peter Cook *Lord Wexmire* • Andrew Knott *Joe Green* • Alan Cumming *Voice of Black Beauty* ◼ *Dir* Caroline Thompson • *Scr* Caroline Thompson, from the novel by Anna Sewell

Black Belt Jones ★★ 🔞

Martial arts crime thriller
1974 · US · Colour · 80mins

Having pulled off a major box office coup with *Enter the Dragon*, producers Fred Weintraub and Paul Heller were denied the services of their recently deceased star, Bruce Lee. So they turned to karate champion Jim Kelly for this rollicking (albeit overplotted) mixture of blaxploitation and kung fu. Reuniting with *Dragon* director, Robert Clouse, Kelly teams up with Scatman Crothers and his daughter (Gloria Hendry) to prevent property developer Malik Carter and mobster Andre Phillipe from taking over their rundown martial arts school. Robert Wall's fight sequences are slickly choreographed, and there's even a romantic subplot. Alas, lightning didn't strike twice. 🎬

Jim Kelly *Black Belt Jones* • Gloria Hendry *Sydney* • Scatman Crothers *Pop* • Alan Weeks *Tippy* • Eric Laneuville *Quincy* • Andre Philippe *Don Steffano* • Vincent Barbi *Big Tuna* • Nate Esformes *Roberts* ◼ *Dir* Robert Clouse • *Scr* Oscar Williams, from a story by Alex Rose, Fred Weintraub • *Choreographer* Robert Wall

The Black Bird ★★★

Silent crime drama 1926 · US · BW

In seedy Limehouse, a master criminal known as the Black Bird covers his crimes by assuming the identity of his disabled "twin" and uses a charity mission house as an elaborate front. Thanks to a brilliant performance by Lon Chaney, kept in a deliberate and darkly fantastic key by director Tod

Browning, a preposterous premise is transformed into convincing entertainment. There's a nasty sting in the tall tale – Chaney's villain is actually paralysed in a police raid and dies having truly become his false persona – and the plot's essential irrationalities are masked by Browning's masterful direction, as he distracts viewer attention by remaining on the dangerous side of farce. An exaggerated vision of the shadowy underworld from two seminal masters of silent shock.

Lon Chaney *The Blackbird/The Bishop of Limehouse* • Renée Adorée *Fifi* • Owen Moore *West End Bertie* • Doris Lloyd *Limehouse Polly* • Andy MacLennan *The Shadow* • William Weston *Red* • Eric Mayne *A Sightseer* • Sidney Brace *Bertie's No 1 Man* • Ernie S Adams *Bertie's No 2 Man* ■ *Dir* Tod Browning • *Scr* Waldemar Young, from the story *The Mockingbird* by Tod Browning

The Black Bird ★★
Detective spoof 1975 · US · Colour · 97mins

This sequel to (and send-up of) *The Maltese Falcon* has Sam Spade Jr (George Segal) discovering the priceless statuette among his dad's old files. It's a nice idea, thoroughly botched – it simply isn't funny, tense or even nostalgic, despite appearances from the original's Lee Patrick and Elisha Cook Jr. There is, however, one clever in-joke. Anxious to raise some money for the falcon, Segal takes it to a pawnbroker named Kerkorian, who offers him a paltry $15. This is a reference to Kirk Kerkorian, who owned MGM at the time and sold off its most famous props. There is also a silly *Jaws* rip-off scene at the end, which wasn't shot by the director David Giler.

George Segal *Sam Spade Jr* • Stéphane Audran *Anna Kemidov* • Lionel Stander *Gordon Andre Jackson Immerman* • Lee Patrick *Effie* • Elisha Cook Jr *Wilmer* • Felix Silla *Litvak* • Signe Hasso *Dr Crippen* • John Abbot *DuQuai* • Howard Jeffrey *Kerkorian* ■ *Dir* David Giler • *Scr* David Giler, from a story by Don M Mankiewicz, Gordon Cotler, from characters created by Dashiell Hammett

Black Caesar ★★★ 18
Blaxploitation crime drama
1973 · US · Colour · 89mins

Tried and tested gangster themes from *Little Caesar* and *Scarface* are updated using elements of the early seventies blaxploitation genre in B-movie maestro Larry Cohen's funky inner-city thriller. Former American football star Fred Williamson gives one of his best performances as the shoeshine boy who rises through the mobster ranks to become Harlem's crime lord. Violent heroics clash with relative morality, but in its quieter moments this spirited action pic offers tender moments brimming with emotional truth. Williamson and Cohen returned for the sequel *Hell Up in Harlem*. Contains swearing, violence and nudity.

Fred Williamson *Tommy Gibbs* • Phillip Roye *Joe Washington* • Gloria Hendry *Helen* • Julius W Harris [Julius Harris] *Mr Gibbs* • Val Avery *Cardoza* • Minnie Gentry *Mama Gibbs* • Art Lund *John McKinney* • D'Urville Martin *Reverend Rufus* ■ *Dir/Scr* Larry Cohen

The Black Cat ★★★★ 15
Horror 1934 · US · BW · 62mins

One of the landmark horror films of the thirties, this was the first feature to double bill Boris Karloff and Bela Lugosi, both of whom were given reverential sole surname billing on the credits. Karloff is the satanist playing chess with doctor Lugosi for innocent lives. More Aleister Crowley than the Edgar Allan Poe story it's actually based on, it's a triumph of bizarre Art Deco sets, innovative style, classical music and eerie tension. This timeless classic is superbly directed by Edgar G Ulmer before his career lurched into the quickie arena. Lugosi has never been so sympathetic or Karloff so evil and the heady finale, where the former flays the latter after a black mass, is incredibly potent stuff for the era.

Boris Karloff *Hjalmar Poelzig* • Bela Lugosi *Dr Vitus Verdegast* • David Manners *Peter Allison* • Jacqueline Wells [Julie Bishop] *Joan Allison* • Lucille Lund *Karen* • Egon Brecher *Majordomo* • Henry Armetta *Sergeant* • Albert Conti *Lieutenant* ■ *Dir* Edgar G Ulmer • *Scr* Edgar G Ulmer, Peter Ruric, from the story by Edgar Allan Poe • *Cinematographer* John J Mescall • *Art Director* Charles D Hall

The Black Cat ★★
Horror 1941 · US · BW · 70mins

It's sad to see such great horror icons as Bela Lugosi, Basil Rathbone and Gale Sondergaard in this unremarkable creepie which is based on a story by Edgar Allan Poe. Real-estate promoter Broderick Crawford and dizzy antiques collector Hugh Herbert gate-crash the reading of a will. To make up for the film's simple-mindedness the old dark house atmosphere is elegantly photographed by Stanley Cortez, who went on to film Orson Welles's acclaimed *The Magnificent Ambersons*. Alan Ladd makes a brief appearance.

Dir Albert S Rogell • *Scr* Robert Lees, Fred Rinaldo, Eric Taylor, Robert Neville, from story by Edgar Allan Poe

Black Cat, White Cat ★★★★ 15
Comedy drama
1998 · Fr/Ger/Ser · Colour · 128mins

Vowing to quit after the savage press reception for his Cannes Palme d'Or winner *Underground*, director Emir Kusturica returns with this riotous blend of crime, comedy and romance. Originally planned as a documentary about gypsy musicians, this is a scattershot affair, with offbeat hilarity competing with coarse slapstick. The network of fictional relationships between the various Romany families takes time to establish but, once all are assembled for the wedding, this gleeful romp goes into overdrive. Yet, amid the barnyard chaos, there are lyrical moments. Awarded the Silver Lion for best direction at the Venice film festival, Kusturica's celebration of gypsy culture is far from subtle but, thanks to exuberant storytelling and a magnificent non-professional cast, it is irresistible. In Serbo-Croat and Romany with English subtitles. Contains swearing and drug abuse.

Bajram Severdzan *Matko Destanov* • Florijan Ajdini *Zare Destanov* • Jasar Destani *Grga Veliki* • Sabri Sulejmani *Grga Pitic* • Srdjan

Todorovic *Dadan Karambolo* • Salija Ibraimova *Afrodita* ■ *Dir* Emir Kusturica • *Scr* Gordan Mihic, Emir Kusturica

The Black Cauldron ★★★ U
Animated adventure
1985 · US · Colour · 78mins

The most distinguished element of this medium-rated Disney animation, from a Tolkien-like series by Lloyd Alexander, is the solemn intonation of narrator John Huston. Otherwise, it's standard stuff about likeable teenagers (of course!) trying to stop the Horned King from using a magic cauldron to raise an Army of the Dead. As swords-and-sorcery, it's potboiling stuff.

John Huston *Narrator* • Grant Bardsley *Taran* • Susan Sheridan *Princess Eilonwy* • Freddie Jones *Dallben* • Nigel Hawthorne *Fflewddur* • Arthur Malet *King Eidilleg* • John Byner *Gurgi/Doli* • John Hurt *Horned King* ■ *Dir* Ted Berman, Richard Rich • *Scr* David Jonas, Vance Gerry, Ted Berman, Richard Rich, Al Wilson, Roy Morita, Peter Young, Art Stevens, Joe Hale, from the book series *The Chronicles of Prydain* by Lloyd Alexander

Black Christmas ★★★★
Horror 1974 · Can · Colour · 97mins

An under-rated holiday horror that pre-dated the *Halloween* slasher cycle and practically established the genre's hard-and-fast rules. A maniac is on the loose in a closed-for-Christmas girls' boarding school. Director Bob Clark's neat little chiller scores scares thanks to stylish visuals, fiendishly inventive slaughter and unexpected twists. Promoted at the time with the wicked tag line "If this picture doesn't make your skin crawl, it's on too tight!", the film also features above-average performances from Olivia Hussey and Margot Kidder. Clark went on to direct *Porky's* and the minor Yuletide classic *A Christmas Story*. Contains swearing.

Olivia Hussey *Jess* • Keir Dullea *Peter* • Margot Kidder *Barb* • Andrea Martin *Phyl* • John Saxon *Lieutenant Fuller* • Marian Waldman *Mrs Mac* • Art Hindle *Chris* • Lynne Griffin *Clare Harrison* • James Edmond *Mr Harrison* ■ *Dir* Bob Clark • *Scr* Roy Moore

Black Day Blue Night ★★
Crime thriller 1995 · US · Colour · 96mins

A convoluted and slow-paced crime drama in the style of Quentin Tarantino but completely lacking that director's quirky and assured touch. JT Walsh is a cop on the trail of armoured-car robbers, one of whom fatally shot his partner. How wronged wife Mia Sara, on the road with her husband's lover Michelle Forbes, and their mysterious hitchhiker (Gil Bellows) fit into the puzzle is barely worth the effort of watching. With lots of twists, but few surprises, this lame erotic thriller features plenty of nudity on Sara's part – the trio don't hide in a canyon with hot springs for nothing!

Gil Bellows *Dodge* • Michelle Forbes *Rinda Wooley* • Mia Sara *Hallie Schrag* • JT Walsh *Lt John Quinn* • Tim Guinee *Bo Schrag* • John Beck *Chief Reed* ■ *Dir/Scr* JS Cardone

Black Death ★★★ 15
Thriller 1992 · US · Colour · 92mins

New York inhabitants love to make you believe they're living in a war zone. In this TV movie, they're galvanised by

the threat of bubonic plague, brought back to the city by a young girl after a camping trip. Chaos reigns as the medics receive no official help and the press feeds off the drama. Director Sheldon Larry is a dab hand at this kind of thing, but he rarely pushes his cast to the limit. Kate Jackson, as the doctor in charge, is only energetic and concerned, while the mayor (played by Al Waxman) is a near-caricature, who's only anxious about the effect of the plague on tourism.

Kate Jackson *Dr Nora Hart* • Howard Hesseman *Congressman Calvin Phillips* • Jerry Orbach *Vincent Callafato* • Jeffrey Nordling *Dr Jake Prescott* • Al Waxman *Mayor Andrew Carmichael* • Chip Zien *Dr Alan Katz* • Barbara Williams *Charlene* • David Hewlett *Myles Chapman* ■ *Dir* Sheldon Larry • *Scr* Ic Rappaport, from a story by Gwyneth Cravens, from the book *The Black Death* by John S Marr

Black Dog ★★★ 12
Action road movie
1998 · US · Colour · 84mins

Movie-goers weren't quite ready for a *Dukes of Hazzard* revival, and, as a result, this similarly themed Patrick Swayze vehicle was waved into the straight-to-video lane in Britain. It's a shame, because this action drama is entertaining enough in a rough-hewn kind of way. Swayze is the ex-convict trucker caught up in a feud with a religious zealot (Meat Loaf) after he is duped into delivering a cargo of stolen weapons. It's not subtle, but the vehicular destruction will bring a nostalgic tear to the eyes of *Smokey and the Bandit* fans. While not exactly the career reviver Swayze hoped for, this could have been worse. Contains some swearing and violence.

Patrick Swayze *Jack Crews* • Randy Travis *Earl* • Meat Loaf *Red* • Gabriel Casseus *Sonny* • Brian Vincent *Wes* • Brenda Strong *Melanie* • Graham Beckel *Cutler* • Charles S Dutton *Agent Ford* ■ *Dir* Kevin Hooks • *Scr* William Mickelberry, Dan Vining

Black Eagle ★★★ 15
Martial arts thriller
1988 · US · Colour · 89mins

Malta is the location for this Jean-Claude Van Damme martial-arts thriller. Remember the Cold War? CIA and KGB agents hurtling around the globe in pursuit of top secret weapons? Well, there is nothing hush-hush about this action fest, in which the Muscles from Brussels plays a Soviet killing machine intent on seizing a laser device lost in a plane crash, before high-kicking hero Sho Kosugi can lay his mitts on it. Directed with maximum noise by Eric Karson, this take on the spy thriller is a far cry from the world of passwords and microdots. Contains swearing and violence. *DVD*

Sho Kosugi *Ken Tani* • Jean-Claude Van Damme *Andrei* • Doran Clark *Patricia Parker* • Vladimir Skomarovsky *Vladimir Klimenko* • Bruce French *Father Joseph Bedelia* • Dorota Puzio *Natasha* • Jan Triska *Valery* • William Bassett *Dean Rickert* ■ *Dir* Eric Karson • *Scr* AE Peters, Michael Gonzales, from a story by Shimon Arama

Black Eyes ★★

Drama   1939 · UK · BW · 75mins

Creaking more with each frame, this only passable melodrama was adapted from the 1935 French film *Dark Eyes* by Russian director Victor Tourjansky. The story concerns a father who is forced to lead a double life to prevent his proud daughter from discovering that, rather than being a high-flying tycoon, he is merely a waiter at a posh restaurant. Frank Capra told a similar story with considerably more charm in *Lady for a Day* and, try as he might, Otto Kruger is too stuffy to be sympathetic.

Otto Kruger *Petroff* • Mary Maguire *Tania* • Walter Rilla *Roudine* • John Wood *Karlo* • Marie Wright *Miss Brown* ■ *Dir* Herbert Brenon • *Scr* Dudley Leslie

The Black Fox ★★★

Documentary   1962 · US · BW · 89mins

The winner of the Oscar for best documentary feature, this is a fascinating exploration of the historical factors that led to the rise (and fall) of Adolf Hitler. Narrated by Marlene Dietrich (who refused Nazi overtures to make a triumphant return to the Fatherland), Louis Clyde Stoumen's film resorts to some overly familiar newsreel footage. But it also offers some perceptive insights into the general European situation and the nature of the German people, who so readily accepted a fascist dictatorship. Less successful are the references to Goethe's retelling of the medieval fable of *Reynard the Fox*.

Marlene Dietrich *Narrator* ■ *Dir* Louis Clyde Stoumen • *Scr* Louis Clyde Stoumen, suggested by the story *Reynard the Fox* by Johann Wolfgang Von Goethe

Black Fox ★★★

Western   1995 · US · Colour · 92mins

Tipping a respectful hat to the excellent *Lonesome Dove*, this is a glossy but always watchable slice of western drama that offers a fresh spin on the American Civil War. Christopher Reeve and *Candyman*'s Tony Todd are the mismatched pair – one a former plantation owner, the other an ex-slave – who set off for a new life in Texas. However, as war breaks out, they find themselves facing an unexpected foe – two native American tribes who seize the opportunity to drive the white man out of the state. Planned as the first in a trilogy, this is a good-looking if sometimes hackneyed adventure that is further lifted by the amiable performances of the two leads. Contains violence and swearing.

Christopher Reeve *Alan Johnson* • Tony Todd *Britt Johnson* • Raoul Trujillo *Running Dog* • Chris Wiggins *Ralph Holtz* • Kim Coates *Natchez John Dunn* • Kelly Rowan *Hallie Russell* • Janet Bailey *Mary Johnson* • Nancy Sorel *Sarah Johnson* • Chris Benson *Tom Fitzpatrick* ■ *Dir* Steven Hilliard Stern • *Scr* Jeb Rosebrook, Joe Byrne, John Binder, Michael Michaelian, from the stories by John Binder, from the novel and characters created by Matt Braun

Black Fury ★★

Drama based on a true story   1935 · US · BW · 93mins

A committed social melodrama torn, as Warner Bros was wont to say, from the headlines, about a mine worker who falls victim to corrupt employers and racketeers. Based on a true story, it's also a reworking of key elements from *I Am a Fugitive from a Chain Gang*. Paul Muni's presence guarantees some "serious" acting and serious make-up, but there are compensations, notably Michael Curtiz's characteristically pacy direction and an extraordinary full-scale underground mine built on the Warner Bros ranch. A box-office flop, it was banned in Pennsylvania where the main industry is coal mining.

Paul Muni *Joe Radek* • Karen Morley *Anna Novak* • William Gargan *Slim* • Barton MacLane *McGee* • John Qualen *Mike Shemanski* • J Carrol Naish *Steve Croner* • Vince Barnett *Kubanda* • Henry O'Neill *JW Hendricks* ■ *Dir* Michael Curtiz • *Scr* Abem Finkel, Carl Erickson, from the play *Bohunk* by Henry R Irving and the story *Jan Volkanik* by Judge MA Musmanno

Black Girl ★★★

Drama   1972 · US · Colour · 96mins

Lurking behind the catchpenny, blaxploitation title is a rather perceptive and thought-provoking study of foster parenting and the integration of children within a caring family unit. Louise Stubbs is the put-upon mother trying to cope with her two daughters and their new half-sister, who aspires to be a dancer and makes life intolerable in the process. Astutely directed by actor Ossie Davis, it has a ring of truth rarely achieved by other contemporary dramas commenting on the African-American experience.

Brock Peters *Earl* • Leslie Uggams *Netta* • Claudia McNeil *Mu' Dear* • Louise Stubbs *Mama Rosie* • Gloria Edwards *Norma* • Loretta Greene *Ruth Ann* • Kent Martin *Herbert* • Peggy Pettit *Billie Jean* ■ *Dir* Ossie Davis • *Scr* JE Franklin, from his play

Black God, White Devil ★★★★

Drama   1964 · Bra · BW · 120mins

Glauber Rocha was one of the driving forces behind Brazilian *cinema nôvo*. Set in the forties and exhibiting both indigenous cultural and international filmic influences, this *sertao* western epitomises the movement's initial preoccupation with the politicisation of the peasantry. Alternately presented in long takes and montage sequences, the action follows Geraldo d'el Rey as he veers between bandit Othon Bastos and his sworn enemy Maurício de Valle. In so doing, Rocha illustrates how difficult it was for uneducated farmhands to know where to place allegiance in the struggle against the oppression of the pitiless landowners. De Valle would return in the sequel, *Antonio das Mortes* (1969). In Portuguese with English subtitles.

Yona Magalhaes *Rosa* • Geraldo D'el Rey *Manuel* • Othon Bastos *Sebastian* • Maurício de Valle *Antonio* • Lidio Silva *Corisco* • Sonia dos Humildes *Dada* ■ *Dir/Scr* Glauber Rocha

The Black Hand ★★

Film noir   1950 · US · BW · 90mins

A potentially fascinating study of the roots of the Mafia in turn-of-the-century New York is not helped by its odd casting and by the MGM studio gloss that, although usually welcome, makes this feature look artificial. When the studio had actors like Ricardo Montalban under contract, precisely why casting directors thought Gene Kelly should play the young Italian seeking to avenge his father's death is beyond comprehension. The Pittsburgh-Irish Kelly is quite wrong, and his earnest manner grates throughout, especially in the company of character actors such as J Carrol Naish and Marc Lawrence. Richard Thorpe's not the director for this kind of material, either, and the whole seems a rare miscalculation, though Kelly devotees may find it interesting.

Gene Kelly *Johnny Columbo* • J Carrol Naish *Louis Lorelli* • Teresa Celli *Isabella Gomboli* • Marc Lawrence *Caesar Xavier Serpi* • Frank Puglia *Carlo Sabballera* • Barry Kelley *Captain Thompson* • Mario Siletti *Benny Danetta* • Carl Milletaire *George Allani* ■ *Dir* Richard Thorpe • *Scr* Luther Davis, from a story by Leo Townsend

The Black Hole ★★★

Science-fiction adventure   1979 · US · Colour · 97mins

It seems strange now, but there was a time in the seventies when Disney seemed to have lost its magic touch, and this unwieldy sci-fi epic didn't really succeed in halting the decline of the period. It's actually not too bad, boasting some stunning special effects and an intriguing story about a disturbed scientist (Maximilian Schell) who is about to go boldly where no man has been before into a black hole in space. The cast is dependable – Anthony Perkins, Ernest Borgnine, Yvette Mimieux – but it's a bit staid.

Maximilian Schell *Dr Hans Reinhardt* • Anthony Perkins *Dr Alex Durant* • Robert Forster *Captain Dan Holland* • Joseph Bottoms *Lieutenant Charles Pizer* • Yvette Mimieux *Dr Kate McCrae* • Ernest Borgnine *Harry Booth* • Tommy McLoughlin *Captain STAR* ■ *Dir* Gary Nelson • *Scr* Jeb Rosebrook, Gerry Day, from a story by Bob Barbash, Richard Landau, Jeb Rosebrook • *Special Effects* Peter Ellenshaw, Art Cruickshank, Eustace Lycett, Danny Lee, Harrison Ellenshaw, Joe Hale

Black Horse Canyon ★★ U

Western   1954 · US · Colour · 81mins

Joel McCrea may be top billed in this fitfully entertaining Universal western, but his limelight is stolen by a superb wild stallion called Outlaw who won the 1955 Patsy Award of Excellence for animal actors. Here, Outlaw plays the horse that McCrea's co-stars Mari Blanchard and Mervyn Vye want to capture for breeding purposes – and that's about it as far as the plot is concerned. It's directed by Jesse Hibbs from a warm-hearted screenplay by the prolific Geoffrey Homes, who's better known as the writer of *film noir* classics such as *Build My Gallows High* and *The Big Steal*.

Joel McCrea *Del Rockwell* • Mari Blanchard *Aldia Spain* • Race Gentry *Ti* • Murvyn Vye *Jennings* • Irving Bacon *Doc* • Ewing Mitchell

Sheriff • John Pickard *Duke* • Pilar Del Rey *Juanita* ■ *Dir* Jesse Hibbs • *Scr* Daniel Mainwaring, from the novel *The Wild Horse* by Les Savage Jr, adapted by David Lang

Black Jack ★★

Drama   1952 · US/Fr · BW · 101mins

Julien Duvivier was one of the finest exponents of the poetic realist style, which laid bare the soul of France in the thirties. However, he never recovered his assured sense of atmosphere and place after a wartime sojourn in Hollywood. Co-scripted by Duvivier and his longtime collaborator Charles Spaak, this wearying tale of duplicity among the idle rich of the Riviera is never as frothy or intricate as the makers intend it to be. Usually proficient performers such as George Sanders, Agnes Moorehead and Herbert Marshall are left high and dry in what amounts to a *Trouble in Paradise* for the less discerning.

George Sanders *Mike Alexander* • Patri`c` Roc *Ingrid* • Herbert Marshall *James* • Agnes Moorehead *Emily* • Marcel Dalio *Captain* ■ *Dir* Julien Duvivier • *Scr* Julien Duvivier, Charles Spaak

Black Jack ★★

Satirical comedy   1972 · US · Colour · 87mins

Produced by exploitation hive American International Pictures, this demented Cold War satire is a sort of poor man's *Dr Strangelove*. Georg Stanford Brown and Brandon de Wilde star as a couple of escaped peaceniks who hijack a B-52 so they can drop an atom bomb on Fort Knox. William T Naud wrote, directed, produced and edited this scattershot portrait of a nation torn apart by Vietnam fallout. However, its main significance is that it marked the last appearance of 30-year-old de Wilde, who never really capitalised on the Oscar nomination he received for the classic western, *Shane*.

Georg Stanford Brown *Lynch* • Brandon de Wilde *Josh* • Keenan Wynn *General Harry Gobohare* • Tim O'Connor *Senator Bob Recker* • Dick Gautier *Diver* • Robert Lansing *Major Reason* • Larry Hovis *Captain Breen* • Bernie Kopell *Penrat* ■ *Dir* William T Naud • *Scr* Dick Gautier, William T Naud, from a story by Peter Marshall, Dick Gautier, William T Naud

Black Jack ★★★★ U

Adventure   1979 · UK · Colour · 109mins

Burt Lancaster wanted to play the hero, but director Ken Loach's aversion to stars meant that French actor Jean Franval took the role of the 18th-century rogue. His escape from hanging – by lodging a bullet in his throat – means escape and involvement with a young boy (Stephen Hirst) and girl (Louise Cooper). Adapted from the novel by Leon Garfield, its free-market mood of moralities mislaid and greed revealed is brilliantly established, but a real star might have made it more coherent.

Jean Franval *Black Jack* • Stephen Hirst *Tolly* • Andrew Bennet *Hatch* • Louise Cooper *Belle* • Packie Byrne *Dr Carmody* • John Young *Dr Hunter* • Russell Waters *Dr Jones* • Pat Wallis *Mrs Gorgandy* • William Moore *Mr Carter* ■ *Dir* Kenneth Loach [Ken Loach] • *Scr* Kenneth Loach, from the novel by Leon Garfield

Black Joy ★★
Comedy   1977 · UK · Colour · 97mins

Although Anthony Simmons's film tries to say something significant about the experience of being black in Brixton in the mid-seventies, he and co-writer Jamal Ali fail to achieve a consistent tone, as they veer between back-street realism and front-line comedy. There are a few rough-hewn gems hidden in the dialogue, but the acting is as variable as the writing, with only Norman Beaton (as a wily waster) and Trevor Thomas (as the young Guyanan he dupes) convincing throughout. It's the soundtrack, however, with snippets from a wide range of Afro-Caribbean music, that makes this worth a look. Contains swearing and sex scenes.

Norman Beaton *Dave King* • Trevor Thomas *Benjamin Jones* • Floella Benjamin *Miriam* • Dawn Hope *Saffra* • Oscar James *Jomo* • Paul Medford *Devon* • Shango Baku *Raastaman* ■ *Dir* Anthony Simmons • *Scr* Anthony Simmons, Jamal Ali, from the play *Dark Days and Light Nights* by Jamal Ali

The Black Knight ★★★ U
Historical drama
1954 · UK/US · Colour · 86mins

An under-rated Alan Ladd vehicle, released a year after his leading role in the classic western *Shane*. Skilled director Tay Garnett brings a fair amount of boisterous charm to this not-to-be-taken-seriously studio-bound Arthurian romp. The fifties' Technicolor is absolutely splendid and the supporting cast of British stalwarts, such as Peter Cushing and Harry Andrews, is a joy to behold. A better script wouldn't really have helped – and doesn't really matter.

Alan Ladd *John* • Patricia Medina *Linet* • André Morell *Sir Ontzlake* • Harry Andrews *Earl of Yeonil* • Peter Cushing *Sir Palamides* • Anthony Bushell *King Arthur* • Laurence Naismith *Major Domo* • Patrick Troughton *King Mark* ■ *Dir* Tay Garnett • *Scr* Alec Coppel

The Black Legion ★★★
Crime drama   1937 · US · BW · 83mins

A young Humphrey Bogart stars as a devoted family man and factory worker who becomes hopelessly and tragically embroiled with a Ku Klux Klan-style secret society, which is dedicated to "cleansing" America of so-called foreigners. Straight from the heart of Warner Bros' social conscience cycle, the drama is grim and the moral message against intolerance strong. Basically a B-picture, it's elevated by its subject and some compelling supporting performances, notably from Dick Foran as the friend who tries to save Bogart from himself.

Humphrey Bogart *Frank Taylor* • Dick Foran *Ed Jackson* • Erin O'Brien-Moore *Ruth Taylor* • Ann Sheridan *Betty Grogan* • Robert Barrat *Brown* • Helen Flint *Pearl Davis* • Joseph Sawyer [Joe Sawyer] *Cliff Moore* • Addison Richards *Prosecuting Attorney* ■ *Dir* Archie Mayo • *Scr* Abem Finkel, William Wister Haines, from a story by Robert Lord

Black Like Me ★★
Biographical drama 1964 · US · BW · 107mins

This relates the real-life experiences of white writer John Howard Griffin, who decided to pose as a black man in the South. The consequences of this and the racial discrimination that he suffers are wholly predictable. James Whitmore and the supporting cast, most notably Clifton James and Roscoe Lee Browne, try to make a slack script taut but, despite good intentions, this never convinces other than as a piece of sixties anti-racist propaganda.

James Whitmore *John Finley Horton* • Clifton James *Eli Carr* • Lenka Peterson *Lucy Horton* • Roscoe Lee Browne *Christopher* • Sorrell Booke *Doctor Jackson* ■ *Dir* Carl Lerner • *Scr* Gerda Lerner, Carl Lerner, from the book by John Howard Griffin

Black Magic ★★
Swashbuckling drama
1949 · US · BW · 105mins

Orson Welles's hobby was conjuring, but no sleight of hand can disguise the ramshackle nature of this swashbuckler, one of those low-grade acting jobs he took to raise funds to make his Shakespearian films, *Macbeth* and *Othello*. It's based on the novel *Joseph Balsamo* by Alexandre Dumas about a notorious court magician around the time of the French Revolution, who becomes part of a plot to switch Marie Antoinette for a servant girl (both played by Nancy Guild). Welles seems to be toying with the role, but director Gregory Ratoff is deadly serious. The result is ponderous rubbish, though Welles manages to be a compelling ham.

Orson Welles *Cagliostro* • Nancy Guild *Marie Antoinette/Lorenza* • Akim Tamiroff *Gitano* • Frank Latimore *Gilbert* • Valentina Cortesa [Valentina Cortese] *Zoraida* • Margot Grahame *Madame Dubarry* • Stephen Bekassy *DeMontagne* • Berry Kroeger *Alexandre Dumas Sr* • Raymond Burr *Alexandre Dumas Jr* ■ *Dir* Gregory Ratoff • *Scr* Charles Bennett, from the novel *Joseph Balsamo* by Alexandre Dumas

Black Magic ★★★ 15
Supernatural thriller
1992 · US · Colour · 89mins

Writer/director Daniel Taplitz has crafted a droll supernatural thriller relying more on satire then screams. Judge Reinhold (*Beverly Hills Cop*) plays a young New Yorker who is tormented by ghostly visions of his dead cousin (Anthony LaPaglia). Bewitched by his relative's ex-girlfriend (Rachel Ward), Reinhold's attempts to reclaim his sanity plunge him into a conspiracy of murder, greed, jealousy and revenge. A capable cast in a pleasingly wicked TV movie.

Rachel Ward *Lillian Blatman* • Judge Reinhold *Alex Gage* • Anthony LaPaglia *Ross Gage* • Brion James *Tom McKay* • Wendy Makkena *Sally Rowe* ■ *Dir/Scr* Daniel Taplitz

Black Mama, White Mama ★★ 18
Blaxploitation action adventure
1972 · US · Colour · 81mins

The Defiant Ones changes sex and gets the blaxploitation treatment in hack Filipino director Eddie Romero's trashy action filler. Hooker Pam Grier and guerrilla fighter Margaret Markov are the chicks in chains who escape from a prison and, disguised as nuns, flee from the police, counter-revolutionaries and a criminal gang. Complete with cat fights, shower scenes and gun battles, this was the movie (amazingly from a story co-written by future director Jonathan Demme) that apparently convinced future black superstar Grier to become a full-time actress – so it wasn't a complete waste of everyone's time. Contains violence, and some swearing and nudity. ▢

Pam Grier *Lee Daniels* • Margaret Markov *Karen Brent* • Sid Haig *Ruben* • Lynn Borden *Densmore* • Zaldy Zshornack *Ernesto* • Laurie Burton *Logan* ■ *Dir* Eddie Romero • *Scr* HR Christian, from a story by Joseph Viola, Jonathan Demme

The Black Marble ★★★ 15
Romantic comedy
1980 · US · Colour · 105mins

Dognapping would hardly seem to be the stuff of riveting drama. Yet this cop thriller, taken from Joseph Wambaugh's bestseller, is a thoughtful look at the human side of police work. Transferred from the homicide department after a gruelling child murder case, burnt-out Robert Foxworth teams up with Paula Prentiss to investigate animal burglary. Love rears its head between the partners as they close in on the debt-ridden culprit (Harry Dean Stanton). Strong acting takes up the trivial slack, especially from Barbara Babcock, as a lonely widow whose whole life revolves around her prize-winning show dog. ▢

Robert Foxworth *Sgt Valnikov* • Paula Prentiss *Sgt Natalie Zimmerman* • James Woods *Fiddler* • Harry Dean Stanton *Philo* • Barbara Babcock *Madeline Whitfield* • John Hancock *Clarence Cromwell* • Raleigh Bond *Capt Hooker* • Judy Landers *Pattie Mae* • Pat Corley *Itchy Mitch* ■ *Dir* Harold Becker • *Scr* Joseph Wambaugh, from his novel

Black Market Baby ★★ PG
Drama   1977 · US · Colour · 96mins

It's a long road that takes a director from guiding Boris Karloff along the *Corridors of Blood* and coaxing Tony Hancock into being *The Rebel* to making tacky TV movies like this one. But that was the route taken by the prolific Robert Day. Here he teams up again with Desi Arnaz Jr, with whom he'd made another TV movie, *Having Babies*, the previous year. The story of a couple of college kids struggling to prevent their baby from being farmed out on the adoption black market tugs at every heartstring without coming close to genuine emotion. Day deserves better material than this. ▢

Linda Purl *Anne Macarino* • Desi Arnaz Jr *Steve Aletti* • Jessica Walter *Louise Carmino* • David Doyle *Joseph Carmino* • Tom Bosley *Dr Brantford* • Bill Bixby *Herbert Freemont* • Lucille Benson *Mrs Krieg* • Annie Potts *Linda Cleary* ■ *Dir* Robert Day • *Scr* Andrew P Marin, from the novel *A Nice Italian Girl* by Elizabeth Christman

Black Mask ★★★★ 18
Martial arts action thriller
1996 · HK · Colour · 83mins

This was the film that introduced UK audiences to Jet Li, now best known as the sleek villain from *Lethal Weapon 4*. The deliriously bonkers plot has Li as a former member of an elite group of assassins who, after radical nerve surgery, feel neither pain nor emotion. He escapes to take up a new life – as a librarian! – but is forced back into action, as the mysterious ''Black Mask'', when he begins to suspect his old chums are behind an attempt to wipe out all of Hong Kong's triads. Director Daniel Lee takes the action sequences to mind-boggling new extremes with some jaw-dropping ultra-violence, while Li gets to showcase the full range of his dazzling physical talents. Only the typically clunky dubbing lets the side down. Cantonese dialogue dubbed into English. Contains violence and some swearing. ▢

Jet Li *Tsui* • Lau Ching Wan *Shi* • Karen Mok *Tracy* • Françoise Yip *Yu Lan* • Patrick Lung-Kang *Commander Hung* ■ *Dir* Daniel Lee • *Scr* Hark Tsui, Hui Kuan, Teddy Chen, Joe Ma

Black Moon ★★★
Fantasy drama   1974 · Fr · Colour · 100mins

Beautifully photographed by Sven Nykvist, Louis Malle's first film in English is a weird, futuristic fantasy set in a countryside where symbols abound. Not all of this enigmatic movie comes off, but Malle's Wonderland is full of surprising things, including talking rats, unicorns and ex-Andy Warhol hunk Joe Dallesandro. Cathryn Harrison, Rex's granddaughter, is adequate as the Alice figure; the title refers to the time of chaos that preludes some cataclysmic change.

Cathryn Harrison *Lily* • Thérèse Giehse *The old lady* • Alexandra Stewart *Sister* • Joe Dallesandro *Brother* ■ *Dir* Louis Malle • *Scr* Louis Malle, Ghislain Uhry, Joyce Buñuel

Black Moon Rising ★★ 18
Action thriller   1985 · US · Colour · 94mins

Director Harley Cokliss plays too safe, here sticking to a standard action-thriller format. Similarly, there are solid but not outstanding performances from the cast, with the exception of the ever-excellent Tommy Lee Jones, who for once comes off the sidelines as the hero. Linda Hamilton, who made her mark in the *Terminator* movies, and Robert Vaughn (*The Man from UNCLE*) provide able support, but even they are not at their best. Co-written (with Desmond Nakano and William Gray) by John Carpenter from his own story, it could have been so much better with him as director. Contains violence, swearing and nudity. ▢

Tommy Lee Jones *Quint* • Linda Hamilton *Nina* • Robert Vaughn *Ryland* • Richard Jaeckel *Earl Windom* • Lee Ving *Marvin Ringer* • Bubba Smith *Johnson* • Dan Shor *Billy Lyons* • William Sanderson *Tyke Thayden* • Keenan Wynn *Iron John* • Nick Cassavetes *Luis* ■ *Dir* Harley Cokliss • *Scr* John Carpenter, Desmond Nakano, William Gray, from a story by John Carpenter

Black Narcissus ★★★★★ PG
Classic drama   1946 · UK · Colour · 100mins

Winner of Oscars for art design and cinematography, Michael Powell and Emeric Pressburger's adaptation of Rumer Godden's simmering novel is one of the most striking examples of studio-controlled artifice in film history. Jack Cardiff's lush colour images not only enhance the beauty of the stylised Himalayan scenery, but also bring a certain grandeur to the melodramatic events at a remote mountain mission, where the visit of English agent David

Farrar is causing passions to run dangerously out of control. Kathleen Byron's eye-rolling jealousy awakens the occasionally sleepy plot and her scene with Deborah Kerr on the bell-tower is a true classic. Sabu, as a wealthy local general, and Jean Simmons, as the nubile native girl he's trying to seduce, provide a little eastern spice. ▭

Deborah Kerr *Sister Clodagh* • Sabu *Dilip Rai* • David Farrar *Mr Dean* • Flora Robson *Sister Philippa* • Esmond Knight *General* • Jean Simmons *Kanchi* • Kathleen Byron *Sister Ruth* • Jenny Laird *Sister Honey* ▪ *Dir* Michael Powell, Emeric Pressburger • *Scr* Michael Powell, Emeric Pressburger, from the novel by Rumer Godden • *Cinematographer* Jack Cardiff • *Art Director* Alfred Junge

The Black Orchid ★★ U
Drama 1959 · US · BW · 98mins

Hollywood, on the whole, gave the luscious Sophia Loren a raw deal, leaving her native Italy to provide worthy vehicles for her talent. Without her, and Anthony Quinn's excellent co-starring performance, this New York-based saga about a widower (Quinn) fighting his children's opposition to his marrying a gangster's widow (Loren) would hardly be worth staying in for. Nonetheless, the Italian star won the acting award at the Venice Film Festival for her sterling efforts.

Sophia Loren *Rose Bianco* • Anthony Quinn *Frank Valente* • Ina Balin *Mary Valente* • Mark Richman [Peter Mark Richman] *Noble* • Jimmy Baird *Ralphie Bianco* • Virginia Vincent *Alma Gallo* • Naomi Stevens *Guilia Gallo* • Frank Puglia *Henry Gallo* ▪ *Dir* Martin Ritt • *Scr* Joseph Stefano

Black Orpheus ★★★ PG
Romance 1958 · Fr/Br/It · Colour · 102mins

The winner of the Oscar for best foreign film and the Palme d'Or at Cannes, this transposition of the myth of Orpheus and the Underworld to Rio de Janeiro at Carnival time is a riot of exotic colour and dynamic movement. Yet there's also an overweening sentimentality about trolleybus conductor Breno Mello's doomed affair with Marpessa Dawn (who was the director's wife). Director Marcel Camus is guilty of a certain naïveté in his political symbolism and of failing to compensate for the limitations of his inexperienced cast. Yet, this remains a visually exhilarating and – thanks, largely, to a superb score – vibrant experience. In Portuguese with English subtitles. ▭

Breno Mello *Orpheus* • Marpessa Dawn *Eurydice* • Lourdes de Oliveria *Mira* • Lea Garcia *Serafina* • Ademar da Silva *Death* • Alexandro Constantino *Hermes* • Waldetar de Souza *Chico* • Jorge dos Santos *Benedito* ▪ *Dir* Marcel Camus • *Scr* Jacques Viot, Marcel Camus, from the play *Orfeu da Conceicao* by Vinicius DeMoraes • *Cinematographer* Jean Bourgoin • *Music* Antonio Carlos Jobim, Luiz Bonfa

The Black Pirate ★★★★ PG
Silent swashbuckling adventure
1926 · US · Colour · 97mins

Hailed as the first full-length feature to be made in two-tone Technicolor, this was one of the most spectacular swashbucklers undertaken by Douglas Fairbanks (who also took a story credit

as Elton Thomas). It was a stormy production, with co-star Donald Crisp being ousted from the director's chair in favour of the more malleable Albert Parker. Yet what emerged was a ripsnorting adventure, in which the aristocratic Fairbanks joins a pirate band to avenge the death of his father. Underwater battles and the rescue of princess Billie Dove maintained the tempo, but it was the knife-blade descent down a billowing sail that thrilled audiences. ▭

Douglas Fairbanks *The Black Pirate* • Billie Dove *The Princess* • Anders Randolf *Pirate leader* • Donald Crisp *McTavish* • Tempe Pigott *Duenna* • Sam De Grasse *Pirate* • Charlie Stevens [Charles Stevens] *Powder man* • Charles Belcher *Chief passenger* ▪ *Dir* Albert Parker • *Scr* Lotta Woods, Jack Cunningham, from a story by Elton Thomas [Douglas Fairbanks]

Black Rain ★★★★ PG
Drama 1988 · Jap · BW · 122mins

From its devastating re-creation of the atomic bombing of Hiroshima, this intense and affecting drama exercises the fiercest of grips. Set mainly five years on from the blast, the story focuses on a woman whose marriage prospects have been dashed because the male population of her country village fear she contracted radiation sickness. Yoshiko Tanaka gives an exceptional performance, as does Keisuke Ishida as the tormented stonemason with whom she strikes up an uneasy relationship. However, the powerful insights into the social and psychological aftermath of the bomb make this very much director Shohei Imamura's film. In Japanese with English subtitles.

Yoshiko Tanaka *Yasuko* • Kazuo Kitamura *Shigematsu Shizuma* • Etsuko Ichihara *Shigeko Shizuma* • Shoichi Ozawa *Shokichi* ▪ *Dir* Shohei Imamura • *Scr* Shohei Imamura,Toshiro Ishido, from the novel by Masuji Ibuse

Black Rain ★★★ 18
Thriller 1989 · US · Colour · 120mins

A tense, glossy and violent thriller, with bad cop Michael Douglas and good cop Andy Garcia transferred from New York to Japan where Yakuza gangsters wield razor-sharp swords and where Kate Capshaw hangs out in a nightclub à la Marlene Dietrich. This being a Ridley Scott film, the atmosphere is so hyped up that the picture threatens to burst an artery every second, and Jan De Bont's photography (he went on to direct *Speed* and *Twister*) delights in the neon-lit locations and makes the city of Osaka look like a vision of hell. Beneath all this is a very conventional cop thriller, plus the odd bit of moralising about Japan's economic miracle after Hiroshima. Contains violence and swearing.

Michael Douglas *Nick Conklin* • Andy Garcia *Charlie Vincent* • Ken Takakura *Masahiro Matsumoto* • Kate Capshaw *Joyce Kingsley* • Yusaku Matsuda *Sato* • Tomisaburo Wakayama *Sugai* • Shigeru Koyama *Ohashi* • John Spencer *Oliver* ▪ *Dir* Ridley Scott • *Scr* Craig Bolotin, Warren Lewis

Black Rainbow ★★★★ 15
Supernatural thriller
1989 · UK · Colour · 98mins

Achieving a ring of truth very few fantasies aspire to, Mike Hodges's most personal movie is an intriguing psychic thriller containing numerous eerie surprises. One of the main shocks is Rosanna Arquette, in her finest role to date, as the Doris Stokes-type medium who can plug into the link between this world and the spiritual one – the ''black rainbow'' of the title. And when she successfully predicts a murder, the unusual scene is set for a clairvoyant cat-and-mouse chase through previously uncharted suspense territory. Contains swearing and brief nudity. ▭

Rosanna Arquette *Martha Travis* • Jason Robards [Jason Robards Jr] *Walter Travis* • Tom Hulce *Gary Wallace* • Mark Joy *Lloyd Harley* • Ron Rosenthal *Detective Irving Weinberg* • John Bennes *Ted Silas* • Linda Pierce *Mary Kuron* • Olek Krupa *Tom Kuron* ▪ *Dir/Scr* Mike Hodges

The Black Rider ★★
Crime caper 1954 · UK · BW · 66mins

First there was the *The Ghost Train* and then *Oh, Mr Porter!*. This amiable low-budget crime caper also takes the idea of using spooks to cover a smuggling operation and adds a dash of *Famous Five* exuberance to create a formula familiar to fans of the cartoon series *Scooby Doo*. The plot zips along like one of the motorbikes owned by the club members who expose the villains with the help of a crusading journalist. Director Wolf Rilla was the author of a manual called *A-Z of Making Movies*, and this is very much film-making by the book, but it's a pleasing time-passer.

Jimmy Hanley *Jerry Marsh* • Rona Anderson *Mary* • Leslie Dwyer *Robert* • Beatrice Varley *Mrs Marsh* • Lionel Jeffries *Brennan* • Valerie Hanson *Karen* • Vincent Ball *Ted Lintott* ▪ *Dir* Wolf Rilla • *Scr* AR Rawlinson

Black Robe ★★★ 15
Historical drama
1991 · Can/Ausl · Colour · 96mins

Adapted by Brian Moore from his own novel, this saga about the clash between native Americans and Jesuits in the 17th century invites comparison with *The Mission* as well as *Dances with Wolves*. Directed by Bruce Beresford amid stunning forest scenery in Quebec, it's an austere, small-scale epic that turns on the sexuality of the Indians and the morality of organised, colonialist religion. It's a dark, intense piece, partly subtitled and powerfully acted by Lothaire Bluteau (*Jesus of Montreal*) as the head priest, and Sandrine Holt as the chief's daughter who falls in love with a Frenchman. In English and French with subtitles. ▭

Lothaire Bluteau *Father Laforgue* • Aden Young *Daniel* • Sandrine Holt *Annuka* • August Schellenberg *Chomina* • Tantoo Cardinal *Chomina's wife* • Billy Two Rivers *Ougebmat* • Lawrence Bayne *Neehatin* • Harrison Liu *Awondoie* • Wesley Cote *Oujita* ▪ *Dir* Bruce Beresford • *Scr* Brian Moore, from his novel

The Black Room ★★★
Horror 1935 · US · BW · 68mins

Two Boris Karloffs for the price of one! The gentle horror giant plays 19th-century twins in a standard Gothic melodrama in which an evil brother murders the good one and impersonates him until an ancient family curse comes true. Generally effective, with the ''black room'' debauchery, sadism and torture implied rather than shown, it's primarily a showcase for Karloff to display his acting range between ''hateful'' and ''sympathetic''. He does it brilliantly in a choice item from the horror hero's work.

Boris Karloff *Baron Gregor de Berghmann/Anton de Berghmann* • Marian Marsh *Thea Hassel* • Robert Allen *Lieutenant Albert Lussan* • Thurston Hall *Colonel Hassel* • Katherine DeMille *Mashka* • John Buckler *Beran* • Henry Kolker *Baron Frederick de Berghmann* ▪ *Dir* Roy William Neill • *Scr* Arthur Strawn, Henry Myers, from a story by Arthur Strawn

The Black Room ★★
Erotic horror 1983 · US · Colour · 87mins

This low-budget chiller gets points for trying to generate horror while largely eschewing blood and gore. A pair of siblings rent out a black decorated room in their home to swingers, secretly murdering select customers and draining their blood in an attempt to cure the brother's blood disease. Superior Steadicam work and careful lighting create a sense of creepiness and eroticism, while the voyeuristic elements add a kinky edge. The script is quite underwritten, though, and mostly focuses on the boring life of one adulterer and his unknowing wife.

Stephen Knight *Jason* • Cassandra Gaviola *Bridget* • Jim Stathis *Larry* • Clara Perryman *Robin* • Geanne Frank *Sandy* • Charlie Young *Lisa* • Christopher McDonald *Terry* • Linnea Quigley *Milly* ▪ *Dir* Elly Kenner, Norman Thaddeus Vane • *Scr* Norman Thaddeus Vane

The Black Rose ★★ U
Romantic adventure
1950 · UK · Colour · 120mins

Filmed in England and North Africa, this sweeping yarn set in the 13th century stars Tyrone Power as the bastard son of a Saxon nobleman who travels from England to the Far East. On the way to Cathay, he rescues a blonde slave girl (the diminutive French actress Cécile Aubry) and confronts a Mongolian warlord (Orson Welles, hamming it up under heavy Oriental make-up). The film looks good, but most of the dialogue is so bad it's painful to listen to. The fur coat worn by Welles was so heavy it took two wardrobe men to help him into it.

Tyrone Power *Walter of Gurnie* • Orson Welles *Bayan* • Cécile Aubry *Maryam* • Jack Hawkins *Tristram* • Michael Rennie *King Edward* • Finlay Currie *Alfgar* • Herbert Lom *Anthemus* • Mary Clare *Countess of Lessford* ▪ *Dir* Henry Hathaway • *Scr* Talbot Jennings, from the novel by Thomas B Costain

Black Sabbath ★★★★

Portmanteau horror
1963 · US/Fr/It · BW · 95mins

A chillingly effective portmanteau piece from the Italian master of horror and suspense Mario Bava. Veteran Boris Karloff, acting as master of ceremonies, introduces three classic tales heralding from such literary heavyweights as Tolstoy. In the first a woman steals a ring from a corpse only to be subsequently haunted by her spirit. In the second a prostitute is terrified by a phantom telephone caller and lastly Karloff himself turns in one of his creepiest performances as a vampire cursed to chew only upon his own family. Pictorially stunning, this also has a script of above average intelligence for a horror movie. Bava imbues every scene with darkly imposing atmosphere and conjures up some truly terrifying set pieces. For horror buffs, this marked the only occasion in nearly 60 years of films that Karloff played a vampire; two versions of the film exist – in Italian and English – with slight variations. Some dialogue dubbed into English.

Jacqueline Pierreux [Jacqueline Soussard] *Helen Corey* • Milli Monti *Maid* • Michèle Mercier *Rosy* • Lydia Alfonsi *Mary* • Gustavo de Nardo *Frank* • Boris Karloff *Gorka* • Mark Damon *Vladimir D'Urfe* • Susy Anderson *Sdenka* ■ *Dir* Mario Bava • *Scr* Marcello Fondato, Alberto Bevilacqua, Mario Bava • *Cinematographer* Ubaldo Terzano

The Black Scorpion ★★★

Science-fiction drama
1957 · US · BW · 87mins

The slumber of giant scorpions is disturbed due to volcanic activity, in director Edward Ludwig's low-budget sci-fi drama. The leader of the angry arachnids takes one look at the desert and heads straight for Mexico City and a showdown with a cast headed by B-movie regulars Richard Denning and Mara Corday. Special effects come courtesy of Willis O'Brien, who helped give life to King Kong, and there's a scene in the insects' lair that might have provided some inspiration for *Starship Troopers*. The film's climax, in the Mexico City stadium, is wonderfully schlocky.

Richard Denning *Henry Scott* • Mara Corday *Teresa* • Carlos Rivas *Arturo Ramos* • Mario Navarro *Juanito* • Carlos Muzquiz *Doctor Velasco* • Pascual Garcia Pena *Jose de la Cruz* ■ *Dir* Edward Ludwig • *Scr* David Duncan, Robert Blees, from a story by Paul Yawitz

Black Scorpion ★★

Action drama
1995 · US · Colour · 92mins

A cheap, campy cartoon cash-in, which actually is quite fun. Joan Severance is the hero of the title – cop by day, masked avenger at night – who sets out to catch bad, mad professor Casey Siesmaszko who has a fiendish plot to poison the population. Severance is her usual wooden self but looks quite fetching in her catsuit while Siesmaszko and former *Saturday Night Live* regular Garrett Morris, as the Scorpion's sidekick, are wildly over the top. The low budget occasionally shows but, as you would expect from a Roger Corman production, it's very hard to dislike it.

Joan Severance *Darcy Walker/Black Scorpion* • Bruce Abbott *Michael Russo* • Stephen Lee *Captain Strickland* • Terri J Vaughn *Tender Lovin* • Michael Wiseman *Hacksaw* • Bradford Tatum *Razor* • Casey Siemaszko *Dr Noah Goddard/Breathtaker* • Garrett Morris *Argyle* ■ *Dir* Jonathan Winfrey • *Scr* Craig J Nevius • *Executive Producer* Roger Corman

Black Scorpion: Ground Zero ★★

Action drama
1996 · US · Colour · 85mins

No one is better than Roger Corman at cashing in on trends, and, after creating a new superhero in the shape of Joan Severance in *Black Scorpion*, this sequel was quickly on its way. This time around cop-turned-masked avenger Severance finds herself up against jokey villain Gangster Prankster (played by Stoney Jackson), who is out to get his hands on money earmarked for earthquake relief. Stephen Lee and Garrett Morris are back from the original, alongside newcomer Whip Hubley. Not quite as good as the first, but fun all the same. Contains swearing, violence and nudity.

Joan Severance *Darcy Walker/Black Scorpion* • Whip Hubley *Michael Russo* • Garrett Morris *Argyle* • Sherrie Rose *Ursula Undershaft/Aftershock* • Stoney Jackson *Gangster Prankster* ■ *Dir* Jonathan Winfrey • *Scr* Craig Nevius

Black Sheep ★★☒

Comedy
1996 · US · Colour · 86mins

Wayne's World director Penelope Spheeris continues her erratic career with this mindless vehicle for double act Chris Farley and David Spade. Farley is the overweight, accident-prone brother of would-be State Governor Tim Matheson. To get Mike out of the way the caustic Spade is enlisted to "baby-sit", and everything that the large one comes into contact with is flattened or destroyed. There's undeniable chemistry between Farley and Spade, the ex-*Saturday Night Live* partnership, but the jokes are uninspired and so obviously sign-posted that it quickly becomes very tiresome.

Chris Farley *Mike Donnelly* • David Spade *Steve Dodds* • Tim Matheson *Al Donnelly* • Christine Ebersole *Governor Tracy* • Gary Busey *Drake Sabitch* • Grant Heslov *Robbie Mieghem* • Timothy Carhart *Roger Kovary* • Bruce McGill *Neuschwander* • "Gypsy" Spheeris *Pocket pool lady* • Kevin P Farley [Kevin Farley] *Bouncer* • John Farley *Bouncer* ■ *Dir* Penelope Spheeris • *Scr* Fred Wolf

The Black Sheep of Whitehall ★★★★☒

Comedy
1941 · UK · BW · 80mins

Co-directing, as well as starring, Will Hay is at his blithering best as the incompetent principal of a correspondence college. He stumbles across a dastardly plot involving Nazi Felix Aylmer masquerading as a famous economist so that he and treacherous journalist Basil Sydney can disrupt a vital trade pact between Britain and South America. Adopting a series of hilariously transparent disguises, Hay and sole pupil John Mills finally capture the villains in a corking chase sequence, with Hay (dressed as a nurse) being dragged along in a Bath chair. This wonderful wartime comedy is the neglected classic in the Hay canon.

Will Hay *Professor Davis* • John Mills *Bobby* • Basil Sydney *Costello* • Henry Hewitt *Professor Davys* • Felix Aylmer *Crabtree* • Frank Cellier *Innsbach* • Joss Ambler *Sir John* • Frank Allenby *Onslow* ■ *Dir* Will Hay, Basil Dearden • *Scr* Angus Macphail, John Dighton

The Black Shield of Falworth ★★☒

Swashbuckling adventure
1954 · US · Colour · 98mins

Janet Leigh and Tony Curtis made six films together during their marriage, though curiously Curtis, in his highly readable autobiography, claims this was the first and last. Selective memory aside, the glam couple cavort across Ye Merrie Olde Englande (or the Universal backlot) and save Henry IV from a fate worse than a Kenneth Branagh remake. This swashbuckler features suave Herbert Marshall, decent sword fights, early CinemaScope photography and some wonderful Brooklyn accents, including the infamous line when Curtis says, "Yonder lies the castle of my fodda."

Tony Curtis *Myles Falworth* • Janet Leigh *Lady Anne* • David Farrar *Earl of Alban* • Barbara Rush *Meg Falworth* • Herbert Marshall *Earl of Mackworth* • Torin Thatcher *Sir James* • Dan O'Herlihy *Prince Hal* • Rhys Williams *Diccon Bowman* • Ian Keith *King Henry IV* ■ *Dir* Rudolph Maté • *Scr* Oscar Brodney, from the novel *Men of Iron* by Howard Pyle

The Black Sleep ★

Horror thriller
1956 · US · BW · 82mins

In order to cure his wife's catalepsy, mad doctor Basil Rathbone performs surgery on innocent victims to unlock the secrets of the brain. His failed lobotomy experiments eventually escape their cellar prison and rebel against him. Aside from the unique spectacle of seeing such horror heavies as Rathbone, Bela Lugosi, Lon Chaney Jr, John Carradine, Tor Johnson and Akim Tamiroff, this wasted opportunity is barely watchable.

Basil Rathbone *Sir Joel Cadman* • Akim Tamiroff *Odo* • Lon Chaney Jr *Mungo* • John Carradine *Bohemond* • Bela Lugosi *Casimir* • Herbert Rudley *Dr Gordon Ramsay* • Patricia Blake *Laurie* • Tor Johnson *Curry* ■ *Dir* Reginald Le Borg • *Scr* John C Higgins

Black Spurs ★★☒

Western
1965 · US · Colour · 81mins

A routine western with Rory Calhoun as a bounty hunter buying up a nice little town and turning it into his own fiefdom. However, when the local sheriff is tarred and feathered, Calhoun starts to rethink his anti-social behaviour. Not much more here than you'll find in an average episode of *Gunsmoke* or *Wyatt Earp*, though the film does include a musical interlude. Lon Chaney Jr is the heavy, while Linda Darnell plays the local saloon owner and madame. The movie was released shortly after her tragic death in a domestic fire.

Rory Calhoun *Santee* • Terry Moore *Anna* • Linda Darnell *Sadie* • Scott Brady *Tanner* • Lon Chaney Jr *Kile* • Bruce Cabot *Henderson* • Richard Arlen *Pete* • Patricia Owens *Clare Grubbs* • James Best *Sheriff Elkins* ■ *Dir* RG Springsteen • *Scr* Steve Fisher

The Black Stallion ★★★★★ U

Adventure
1979 · US · Colour · 112mins

Adapted by Melissa Mathison (who wrote the script for *ET* and is married to Harrison Ford), Jeanne Rosenberg and William Witliff from the novel by Walter Farley, this is among the most magical children's films ever made. Making his debut as director, Carroll Ballard blends stunning visuals with a heartwarming story in which a small boy trains the horse he rescued from a shipwreck. The storm and the desert island scenes are breathtaking, and, if the training and racing sequences have all been done before, they have an energy and an eye-catching splendour that more than compensates. Mickey Rooney earned an Oscar nomination as a has-been trainer, but the true stars are 11-year-old Kelly Reno and the horse Cass-ole. ▭

Mickey Rooney *Henry Dailey* • Kelly Reno *Alec Ramsey* • Teri Garr *Alec's mother* • Clarence Muse *Snoe* • Hoyt Axton *Alec's father* • Michael Higgins *Jim Neville* • Ed McNamara *Jake* • Doghmi Larbi *Arab* ■ *Dir* Carroll Ballard • *Scr* Melissa Mathison, Jeanne Rosenberg, William Witliff, from the novel by Walter Farley • *Executive Producer* Francis Ford Coppola • *Cinematographer* Caleb Deschanel • *Editor* Robert Dalva

The Black Stallion Returns ★★ U

Adventure
1983 · US · Colour · 98mins

Having edited Carroll Ballard's original film, Robert Dalva made his directorial debut with this substandard sequel, which is short on both fantasy and charm. Although the action is handsomely photographed by Carlo Di Palma and Caleb Deschanel, too few risks are taken with the storyline, which again sees Kelly Reno and his superb horse (Cass-ole) overcome all manner of trials to reunite in time for a big race. Reno underplays admirably, but there's a disturbing amount of stereotyping (particularly on the part of Allen Garfield) in how the Arabs who steal the stallion and smuggle it away to the Sahara are depicted. ▭

Hoyt Axton *Narrator* • Kelly Reno *Alec Ramsay* • Vincent Spano *Raj* • Allen Goorwitz [Allen Garfield] *Kurr* • Woody Strode *Meslar* • Ferdy Mayne *Abu Ben Ishak* • Jodi Thelen *Tabari* • Teri Garr *Alec's mother* ■ *Dir* Robert Dalva • *Scr* Richard Kletter, Jerome Kass, from the novel by Walter Farley • *Executive Producer* Francis Ford Coppola • *Cinematographer* Carlo Di Palma, Caleb Deschanel

Black Sunday ★★★★☒

Crime thriller
1976 · US · Colour · 137mins

John Frankenheimer is on top form with this thriller based on the novel by Thomas Harris, author of *The Silence of the Lambs*, about terrorists planning to cause mayhem at a Super Bowl football game. Manics on both sides of the law (Robert Shaw and Bruce Dern) explain their motives, but it's the violent action that makes the film so fraught and yet so exciting. The clash between police helicopters and a hijacked blimp is the highlight of the outstanding set pieces it's the sort of thing that Frankenheimer can do with one hand tied behind his back. Contains swearing. ▭

U = SUITABLE FOR ALL   **Uc** = SUITABLE FOR ALL, ESPECIALLY FOR YOUNG CHILDREN (VIDEO ONLY)   **PG** = PARENTAL GUIDANCE

Robert Shaw *Major Kabakov* • Bruce Dern *Michael Lander* • Marthe Keller *Dahlia Iyad* • Fritz Weaver *Corley* • Steven Keats *Robert Moshevsky* • Bekim Fehmiu *Fasil* • Michael V Gazzo *Muzi* • William Daniels *Pugh* • Tom McFadden *Farley* ■ *Dir* John Frankenheimer • *Scr* Ernest Lehman, Kenneth Ross, Ivan Moffat, from the novel by Thomas Harris

The Black Swan ★★★★

Swashbuckling adventure
1942 · US · Colour · 81mins

The kind of movie they used to make before they stopped making them like that any more, this is a rip-roaring tale of swashbuckling, buccaneering and damsel-wooing, starring Tyrone Power in the sort of role normally reserved for Errol Flynn or Douglas Fairbanks Jr. Power plays a reformed sea wolf, whose former partner in piracy (Laird Cregar) is made governor of Jamaica. They join forces to rid the neighbourhood of assorted rogues and one-eyed knaves. Much swordplay – plus intermittent courtship of Maureen O'Hara by Power – ensues, all captured by Oscar-winning colour cinematography. Vintage stuff.

Tyrone Power *James Waring* • Maureen O'Hara *Margaret Denby* • Laird Cregar *Captain Henry Morgan* • Thomas Mitchell *Tommy Blue* • George Sanders *Captain Billy Leech* • Anthony Quinn *Wogan* • George Zucco *Lord Denby* • Edward Ashley *Roger Ingram* ■ *Dir* Henry King • *Scr* Ben Hecht, Seton I Miller, from the novel by Rafael Sabatini • *Cinematographer* Leon Shamroy

The Black Tent ★★ U

Second World War drama
1956 · UK · Colour · 92mins

Brian Desmond Hurst had proved with *The Malta Story* that he could spin a decent war yarn and, with *Simba*, that he could make the most of exotic locations. But he failed to bring those skills to bear on this contrived piece of stiff-upper-lippery, in which wounded officer Anthony Steel joins with Bedouin sheikh André Morell to confound the Nazis. The romance with Anna-Maria Sandri sits awkwardly alongside the action, while Donald Sinden's clipped bravado as Steel's brother occasionally borders on the comic. The script by Robin Maugham and Bryan Forbes is undistinguished.

Anthony Steel *David Holland* • Donald Sinden *Charles Holland* • Anna-Maria Sandri *Mabrouka* • André Morell *Sheikh Salem* • Ralph Truman *Croft* • Donald Pleasence *Ali* • Anthony Bushell *Baring* • Michael Craig *Faris* • Anton Diffring *German officer* ■ *Dir* Brian Desmond Hurst • *Scr* Robin Maugham, Bryan Forbes

The Black Torment ★★ 15

Gothic horror 1964 · UK · Colour · 82mins

This barnstorming period horror is no longer the marrow-chiller it once was. Nevertheless, it has a surprisingly literate script and still delivers some mild shocks as it wheels out a time-honoured tale of suicide, gloomy castles, mad relatives locked in the attic and ghosts on horseback. It's directed by Robert Hartford-Davis, a criminally unsung hero of British horror and actors John Turner and Heather Sears work miracles in making this Gothic melodrama as believable as possible. ▭

John Turner *Sir Richard Fordyke* • Heather Sears *Lady Elizabeth* • Ann Lynn *Diane* • Peter Arne *Seymour* • Raymond Huntley *Colonel Wentworth* • Annette Whiteley *Mary* • Norman Bird *Harris* • Roger Croucher *Apprentice* • Joseph Tomelty *Sir Giles* • Patrick Troughton *Ostler* • Edina Ronay *Lucy Judd* ■ *Dir* Robert Hartford-Davis • *Scr* Donald Ford, Derek Ford

The Black Tulip ★★

Historical adventure
1963 · Fr · Colour · 57mins

French superstar Alain Delon stars in this Alexandre Dumas tale about the exploits of *La Tulipe Noire*, a sort of Robin Hood figure of 18th-century France. He also has a twin brother, so it's as much a dual role as a duelling one. Virna Lisi makes a glamorous heroine, and Akim Tamiroff hams away as the local big *fromage*. Filmed in 70mm and originally shown in Britain and America in Superpanorama, it's slackly directed by Christian-Jaque, who shows none of the style that won him the best director award at Cannes for the Gérard Philipe swashbuckler, *Fanfan la Tulipe*. French dialogue dubbed into English.

Alain Delon *Guillaume de Saint-Preux/Julien de Saint-Preux* • Virna Lisi *Caroline* • Dawn Addams *Marquise de Vigogne* • Francis Blanche *Plantin* • Akim Tamiroff *Marquis de Vigogne* • Robert Manuel *Prince Alexander de Grassilach* • Adolfo Marsillach *La Mouche* • Laura Valenzuela *Lisette* ■ *Dir* Christian-Jaque • *Scr* Henri Jeanson, from the novel *La Tulipe Noire* by Alexandre Dumas

A Black Veil for Lisa ★

Crime thriller
1969 · It/W Ger · Colour · 87mins

One of John Mills's lowest career points, this is a Euro-pudding cop thriller that dredges up every cliché of the British B-movie, relocates them to Hamburg and adds some nudity and violence. Mills is a detective more concerned with the infidelities of his wife (Luciana Paluzzi) than solving the various high-profile drug trafficking cases on his desk. Then Mills plots to have his wife bumped off by an underworld hitman. Filmed by an obscure tax shelter outfit with an Italian director, it hardly passes muster in any department. Some dialogue dubbed into English.

John Mills *Bulon* • Luciana Paluzzi *Lisa* • Robert Hoffmann *Max* • Renata Kasche *Marianne* • Tullio Altamura *Ostermeyer* • Carlo Hintermann *Mansfeld* • Enzo Fiermonte *Siegert* • Loris Bazzocchi *Kruger* ■ *Dir* Massimo Dallamano • *Scr* Giuseppe Belli, Vittoriano Petrilli, Massimo Dallamano, Audrey Nohra, from a story by Giuseppe Belli

The Black Watch ★★ U

Adventure 1929 · US · BW · 9mins

Just before the Fox company took up talking pictures, John Ford had directed a visually striking and fast-paced adventure story starring Victor McLaglen as a British army officer in India who feigns desertion to win the affection of Myrna Loy's goddess of the tribes and thus avert a rebellion. Then one of the supporting players, Lumsden Hare, was engaged to add talking sequences, mainly love scenes between McLaglen and Loy, which held up the picture and had audiences laughing at the stilted dialogue. The

same story was later used to serve another technical revolution – forming the basis of 1953's *King of the Khyber Rifles*, one of the first productions in CinemaScope.

Victor McLaglen *Capt Donald Gordon King* • Myrna Loy *Yasmini* • David Rollins *Lt Malcolm King* • Lumsden Hare *Colonel of the Black Watch* • Roy D'Arcy *Rewa Ghunga* • Mitchell Lewis *Mohammed Khan* • Cyril Chadwick *Maj Twynes* • David Torrence *Field Marshall* ■ *Dir* John Ford • *Scr* John Stone, James Kevin McGuinness, from the novel *King of the Khyber Rifles* by Talbot Mundy

Black Widow ★★

Murder mystery 1954 · US · Colour · 94mins

A starry cast, a decent build-up of tension and a surprise denouement overcome a slow start and a superficial screenplay in this moderately enjoyable murder mystery. Van Heflin is the producer suspected of killing a young Broadway hopeful, and Ginger Rogers his poisonous leading lady; the glamorous Gene Tierney plays another stage star, while George Raft is the purposeful investigating detective. Writer/director Nunnally Johnson's movie also benefits from Reginald Gardner's performance as Rogers's ineffectual kept husband, who boosts his ego with illicit liaisons, including one with the murder victim.

Ginger Rogers *Lottie* • Van Heflin *Peter* • Gene Tierney *Iris* • George Raft *Detective Bruce* • Peggy Ann Garner *Nancy Ordway* • Reginald Gardiner *Brian* • Virginia Leith *Claire Amberly* • Otto Kruger *Ling* ■ *Dir* Nunnally Johnson • *Scr* Nunnally Johnson, from the novel by Patrick Quentin [Hugh Wheeler]

Black Widow ★★★ 15

Thriller 1987 · US · Colour · 97mins

It's not quite in the same league as his dense psychological dramas from the early seventies, for example *Five Easy Pieces*, but this intriguing thriller marked a return to form for Bob Rafelson. Theresa Russell is the black widow of the title, a female Bluebeard who specialises in bumping off a starry list of wealthy millionaires, including Dennis Hopper and Nicol Williamson. Debra Winger is the uptight FBI agent who sets out to bring her to justice. The cat-and-mouse games played by Winger and Russell crackle with tension and there is a lovely twist at the end. The two leads are magnificent and they are well supported by a distinguished cast. Contains violence, swearing and nudity. ▭

Debra Winger *Alexandra Barnes* • Theresa Russell *Catharine* • Sami Frey *Paul Nuytten* • Dennis Hopper *Ben Dumers* • Nicol Williamson *William Macauley* • Terry O'Quinn *Bruce* • James Hong *Shin* • Diane Ladd *Etta* ■ *Dir* Bob Rafelson • *Scr* Ronald Bass

Black Widow Murders ★★★

Crime drama based on a true story
1993 · US · Colour · 92mins

Elizabeth Montgomery proved once again that she could do more than comedies such as *Bewitched* with her convincing performance in this TV crime drama. She stars as Blanche Taylor Moore, a North Carolina widow respected in the community, who hides the secrets of childhood abuse and her resultant anger against all men. However, when two of her suitors die

in similar ways, the town realises Blanche may not be all she seems. Tautly directed, this is a gripping story made all the more so by Montgomery's portrayal and the truth of the tale.

Elizabeth Montgomery *Blanche Taylor Moore* • David Clennon *Reverend Dwight Moore* • John M Jackson *Raymond Reid* • Grace Zabriskie *Ethel* • Bruce McGill *Morgan* • Mark Rolston *O'Keefe* • Guy Boyd *Kevin Denton* ■ *Dir* Alan Metzger • *Scr* Judith Paige Mitchell, from the book *Preacher's Girl* by Jim Schutze

The Black Windmill ★★

Spy thriller 1974 · UK · Colour · 106mins

A disappointing thriller from *Dirty Harry* director Don Siegel, with Michael Caine as an agent whose son is kidnapped by a mysterious military organisation, which demands diamonds in return for his release. Like all good fictional heroes, Caine finds himself the number one suspect and thus spends as much time keeping out of the clutches of the law as he does tracking down the real culprits. The plot is over-thickened with cat-and-mouse sequences and Siegel's acclaimed naturalistic style is intrusive here, but the performances are fine. Contains swearing.

Michael Caine *Major John Tarrant* • Joseph O'Conor *Sir Edward Julyan* • Donald Pleasence *Cedric Harper* • John Vernon *McKee* • Janet Suzman *Alex Tarrant* • Delphine Seyrig *Ceil Burrows* • Joss Ackland *Chief Superintendent Wray* • Clive Revill *Alf Chesterman* ■ *Dir* Don Siegel • *Scr* Leigh Vance, from the novel *Seven Days to a Killing* by Clive Egleton

Blackbeard the Pirate ★★ U

Swashbuckling adventure
1952 · US · Colour · 94mins

RKO producer Val Lewton had, at one time, planned this swashbuckler as a vehicle for Boris Karloff and, in view of the outlandish performance by Robert Newton, one can only lament the fact that he didn't take the starring role. Fresh from playing Long John Silver for Disney, Newton throws in every cliché ever used by a pantomime pirate and occasionally comes close to making this vigorous adventure almost unwatchable. Fortunately, director Raoul Walsh's sure handling of the action sequences (Lewton had died the previous year), Torin Thatcher's wonderfully wicked Henry Morgan, Linda Darnell's feisty heroine and William Bendix's burly good humour keep the thing afloat.

Robert Newton *Blackbeard* • Linda Darnell *Edwina* • William Bendix *Worley* • Keith Andes *Maynard* • Torin Thatcher *Sir Henry Morgan* • Irene Ryan *Alvina* • Alan Mowbray *Noll* ■ *Dir* Raoul Walsh • *Scr* Alan LeMay, from a story by DeVallon Scott

Blackbeard's Ghost ★★★ U

Comedy 1967 · US · Colour · 102mins

With a plot along the same lines as *The Canterville Ghost* (the 1944 comedy starring Charles Laughton), this Disney caper is overlong and short on inspiration, but it does have a lively lead in the incomparable Peter Ustinov as the buccaneer condemned to wander in limbo until he performs a good deed. Poaching the picture from him, however, is Elsa Lanchester, as one of the old dears he must save from gambling gangsters. It's corny and over the top, but it's better than Hollywood's more recent ventures into piracy, such as *CutThroat Island*. ▭

Peter Ustinov *Captain Blackbeard* • Dean Jones *Steve Walker* • Suzanne Pleshette *Jo Anne Baker* • Elsa Lanchester *Emily Stowecroft* • Joby Baker *Silky Seymour* • Elliott Reid *TV commentator* • Richard Deacon *Dean Wheaton* • Norman Grabowski *Virgil* ■ *Dir* Robert Stevenson • *Scr* Bill Walsh, Don DaGradi, from the novel by Ben Stahl

Blackbelt ★★ 18

Martial arts action
1992 · US · Colour · 83mins

Apart from the novelty value of seeing *West Side Story* star Richard Beymer play a crooked record producer, there's little in this martial arts action thriller to get excited about. Don ''The Dragon'' Wilson is an ex-cop-turned-bodyguard hired to protect singer Deidre Imershein from the deranged attentions of psycho Vietnam veteran Matthias Hues. Numerous famous martial artists also pop up to play assorted bad guys in the Philippines-set off-shoot of Wilson's better *Bloodfist* series. ▭

Don ''The Dragon'' Wilson *Jack Dillon* • Richard Beymer *Eddie DiAngelo* • Deidre Imershein *Shanna* • Alan Blumenfeld *Will Sturges* • ''Bad'' Brad Hefton *Frank Ellis* • Ernest Simmons *Mercanary* • Mitch Borrow *Rene* ■ *Dir/Scr* Charles Philip Moore

The Blackboard Jungle ★★★ 12

Drama
1955 · US · BW · 96mins

A teenage angst picture, following hot on the heels of James Dean's *Rebel without a Cause*, with Glenn Ford as the gauche schoolteacher who wonders why his class beat him up and ''don't wanna loin nuthin''''. Anne Francis offered him a shoulder to cry on, while American parents everywhere sobbed in sympathy. Filmed in sombre black and white (as against *Rebel's* colour and Scope), director Richard Brooks's film rams home his message without much subtlety. It has a footnote in history, though, for introducing rock music to mainstream cinema, courtesy of Bill Haley's *Rock around the Clock* which is played over the credit titles. When South London teddy boys heard that, they trashed the cinemas. ▭

Glenn Ford *Richard Dadier* • Anne Francis *Anne Dadier* • Louis Calhern *Jim Murdock* • Margaret Hayes *Lois Judby Hammond* • John Hoyt *Mr Warneke* • Richard Kiley *Joshua Y Edwards* • Emile Meyer *Mr Halloran* • Warner Anderson *Dr Bradley* ■ *Dir* Richard Brooks • *Scr* Richard Brooks, from the novel by Evan Hunter • *Cinematographer* Russell Harlan

Blackjack ★★ 18

Action thriller
1998 · US/Can · Colour · 108mins

Other than the star power of Dolph Lundgren and a few flashes of slow-mo gunplay, this is a depressingly ordinary action movie from *Face/Off* director John Woo. The mishmash of a plot finds ex-bodyguard Lundgren coming out of retirement to protect a supermodel from a psychotic failed actor, while overcoming a bizarre phobia about the colour white (tricky really, particularly when he gets caught up in a fight in a milk factory). Despite the presence of Saul Rubinek and Fred

Williamson, this is really only for die-hard Woo fans. Contains violence, and some mild swearing. ▭

Dolph Lundgren *Jack Devlin* • Kate Vernon *Doctor Rachel Stein* • Phillip MacKenzie *Rory James* • Fred Williamson *Tom Hastings* • Kam Heskin *Cinder James* • Saul Rubinek *Thomas* • Padraigin Murphy *Casey* ■ *Dir* John Woo • *Scr* Peter Lance

Blackmail ★★★ PG

Thriller
1929 · UK · BW · 81mins

Alfred Hitchcock's first talking picture was also the earliest in which he used a famous landmark to stage the finale. The visuals are eerily expressionistic, the trick photography in the British Museum sequence is first class and the recurrence of the word ''knife'' on the soundtrack is amusingly ghoulish. But the restrictions placed on film-makers by primitive sound recording techniques render the action and the acting fatally stilted. There is a predominantly silent version of this film, which is infinitely better. Although most film histories claim this to be the first British talkie, the honour actually goes to Arthur Maude's *The Clue of the New Pin*. ▭

Anny Ondra *Alice White* • John Longden *Frank Webber* • Donald Calthrop *Tracy* • Sara Allgood *Mrs White* • Charles Paton *Mr White* • Cyril Ritchard *Artist* • Harvey Braban *Inspector* • Phyllis Monkman *Gossip* • Hannah Jones *Landlady* ■ *Dir* Alfred Hitchcock • *Scr* Alfred Hitchcock, Benn W Levy, Charles Bennett, from the play by Charles Bennett • *Cinematographer* Jack Cox

Blackmail ★★★

Crime drama
1939 · US · BW · 80mins

Edward G Robinson fights fires on Oklahoma's oil fields but serves time on a chain-gang for a crime he did not commit, and is then blackmailed by Gene Lockhart. MGM was trying to splice two genres here – the social drama, such as *I Am a Fugitive from a Chain Gang*, and the sexy melodrama. It works, sort of, mainly due to the powerful performances of Robinson and Lockhart, as well as some well-handled scenes of burned-out oil-rigs and burned-out convicts. ▭

Edward G Robinson *John Ingram* • Ruth Hussey *Helen Ingram* • Gene Lockhart *William Ramey* • Bobs Watson *Hank Ingram* • Guinn Williams *Moose McCarthy* • John Wray *Diggs* • Arthur Hohl *Rawlins* • Esther Dale *Sarah* • Joe Whitehead *Anderson* ■ *Dir* HC Potter • *Scr* David Hertz, William Ludwig, from a story by Endre Bohem, from a story by Dorothy Yost

Blackout ★★

Thriller
1950 · UK · BW · 73mins

Directed by Robert S Baker, this is a fanciful projects, about a blind man (Maxwell Reed) who recovers his sight in time to tackle a counterfeiting ring led by supposed air-crash victim Kynaston Reeves. Written by future horror director John Gilling, this is a by-the-numbers thriller, although the photography is seedily atmospheric.

Maxwell Reed *Chris Pelley* • Dinah Sheridan *Patricia Dale* • Eric Pohlmann *Otto* • Patric Doonan *Chalky* • Michael Brennan *Mickey* • Michael Evans *Sinclair* • Annette Simmonds *Lila Drew* • Campbell Singer *Inspector* ■ *Dir* Robert S Baker • *Scr* Robert S Baker, John Gilling • *Cinematographer* Monty Berman

Blackout ★★ 18

Crime thriller
1985 · US · Colour · 93mins

Richard Widmark and Keith Carradine star in this average TV thriller, in which an ex-detective learns of a man with amnesia who may just be the same guy who killed his family several years before. Unfortunately, there are no real surprises in store for the detective or for the audience, who can figure out every plot twist at least half an hour before any of the characters do. ▭

Richard Widmark *Joe Steiner* • Keith Carradine *Allen Devlin* • Kathleen Quinlan *Chris Graham* • Michael Beck *Mike Patterson* • Don Hood *Phil Murphy* • Martina Deignan *Pauline* ■ *Dir* Douglas Hickox • *Scr* David E Ambrose, from a story by David Ambrose, from a story by Richard Parks, Richard Smith, Les Alexander

The Blackout ★★ 18

Thriller
1997 · US/Fr · Colour · 94mins

Less an entertainment, more an endurance test – as *enfant terrible* Abel Ferrara uses a rather blunt scalpel to expose the living hell of Hollywood stardom in another of his typically unrestrained rants. Matty (played with autobiographical candour by Matthew Modine) is a high-living movie celebrity who can't curtail his booze and drug lifestyle despite it causing him to endure increasing blackouts. Did he commit murder during one such bout of unconsciousness? Sleazy nightclub owner Dennis Hopper helps him sift through the truth. Contains swearing, violence, drug abuse and sex scenes. ▭

Matthew Modine *Matty* • Claudia Schiffer *Susan* • Béatrice Dalle *Annie 1* • Sarah Lassez *Annie 2* • Dennis Hopper *Mickey Wayne* • Steven Bauer *Mickey's studio actor* ■ *Dir* Abel Ferrara • *Scr* Abel Ferrara, Marla Hanson, Christ Zois

Blackwater Trail ★★★ 18

Thriller
1995 · Ausl · Colour · 95mins

Judd Nelson hasn't enjoyed much success since the heyday of the Brat Pack in the eighties. This Australian thriller provides him with one of his strongest roles as a writer who returns to his home town for the funeral of an old friend, a policeman who had been involved in the case of a serial killer. Nelson continues the investigation undeterred by opposition from the town's establishment. The imported star is well supported by a galaxy of familiar Aussie soap stars. Although the plotting is contrived, director Ian Barry delivers some genuinely scary jolts. Contains violence, and some swearing. ▭

Judd Nelson *Matt Curran* • Dee Smart *Cathy* • Peter Phelps *Dr Frank Jamison* • Mark Lee *Chris* • Brett Climo *Father Michael* • Rowena Wallace *Beth* • Gabrielle Fitzpatrick *Sandra* ■ *Dir* Ian Barry • *Scr* Andrew Russell

Blacula ★★★ 15

Blaxploitation horror
1972 · US · Colour · 89mins

This is one of the better novelty blaxploitation horror romps, despite its eventual turn toward predictable genre conventions in the last half. Noted Shakespearean actor William Marshall raised a few eyebrows when he took on the role of an African prince turned

into a vampire by Count Dracula two centuries earlier, who arrives in his coffin in contemporary Los Angeles and starts cleaning up the ghetto by putting the bite on drug dealers, pimps and homosexuals. Thalmus Rasulala is the nemesis who finally stakes him out. Marshall's dignity contrasted with the tongue-in-cheek humour makes this undead shocker undemanding fun. Contains some swearing and sexual references. ▭

William Marshall *Blacula* • Vonetta McGee *Tina* • Denise Nicholas *Michelle* • Thalmus Rasulala *Gordon Thomas* • Gordon Pinsent *Lieutenant Peters* • Charles McCauley *Dracula* • Emily Yancy *Nancy* • Lance Taylor Sr *Swenson* ■ *Dir* William Crain • *Scr* Joan Torres, Raymond Koenig

Blade ★★★ 18

Fantasy action adventure
1998 · US · Colour · 115mins

Wesley Snipes is the half-mortal, half-vampire who hunts down creatures of the night in this flashy action adventure based on the popular comic. Aided by gruff-and-tough Kris Kristofferson, he finally meets his match when he flashes fangs at vampire Stephen Dorff, whose evil plans include running a nightclub that will entice humans in so his fiendish pals can feed on them. Daft stuff indeed, but snappily paced and performed with tongue firmly placed in cheek. Plus Snipes looks great in a leather coat and strides. Contains swearing and violence. ▭ *DVD*

Wesley Snipes *Blade* • Stephen Dorff *Frost* • Kris Kristofferson *Whistler* • Kevin Patrick Walls *Krieger* • N'Bushe Wright *Karen* • Donal Logue *Quinn* • Arly Jover *Mercury* • Udo Kier *Dragonetti* • Traci Lords *Raquel* ■ *Dir* Stephen Norrington • *Scr* David S Goyer, from characters created for Marvel Comics by Marv Wolfman, Gene Colan

Blade Runner ★★★★★ 15

Science-fiction thriller
1982 · US · Colour · 112mins

A super Philip K Dick story, about superdick Harrison Ford battling rebellious replicants, translates here into a violent eye-popper, based in a futuristic American Chinatown, which set the acid rain/neon-drenched metropolis design standard for eighties' sci-fi. As influential as *2001: a Space Odyssey* and *Star Wars*, and as thought provoking as the Kubrick classic, Ridley Scott's atmospheric downer is a compelling *noir* thriller pleading for harmony between man and machine. Rutger Hauer is exceptional as the blond humanoid who, like the others, has been implanted with memories of a nonexistent youth. The Director's Cut, which drops Ford's voice-over, actually adds more depth to the 1982 original, so the full masterpiece can shine through. Contains violence, swearing and brief nudity. ▭ *DVD*

Harrison Ford *Rick Deckard* • Rutger Hauer *Roy Batty* • Sean Young *Rachael* • Edward James Olmos *Gaff* • M Emmet Walsh *Bryant* • Daryl Hannah *Pris* • William Sanderson *Sebastian* • Brion James *Leon* ■ *Dir* Ridley Scott • *Scr* Hampton Fancher, David Peoples, from the story *Do Androids Dream of Electric Sheep?* by Philip K Dick • *Cinematographer*

U = SUITABLE FOR ALL   Uc = SUITABLE FOR ALL, ESPECIALLY FOR YOUNG CHILDREN (VIDEO ONLY)   PG = PARENTAL GUIDANCE

Jordan Cronenweth • *Music* Vangelis • *Production Design* Lawrence G Paull • *Special Effects* Douglas Trumbull

The Blair Witch Project

★★ 15

Supernatural horror
1998 · US · Colour and BW · 77mins

Fantastic hype, shame about the dull little home movie that has engendered it. Three amateur film-makers go into the woods to shoot a documentary on a supernatural Maryland legend. They get lost, bicker endlessly, hear strange noises; one disappears, the other two argue some more – and that's it! Supposedly an exercise in mounting dread, this deliberately artless fly-on-the-wall con trick, using grainy footage, jerky hand-held camerawork and video inserts, couldn't be less scary or uninvolving if it tried. The awesome Internet reputation this complete dud has garnered, and the media frenzy it has whipped up, are the only mysteries worth contemplating here. Contains swearing. 🖭 *DVD*

Heather Donahue • Michael Williams • Joshua Leonard • Bob Griffith *Interviewee* • Jim King *Interviewee* • Sandra Sanchez *Interviewee* • Ed Swanson *Interviewee* ■ *Dir* Daniel Myrick, Eduardo Sanchez • *Scr* Eduardo Sanchez, Daniel Myrick

Blame It on Rio

★★ 15

Comedy 1984 · US · Colour · 95mins

Michael Caine and Joseph Bologna may give decent enough performances as best friends on a spree in Rio, but the romance that develops between Caine and Bologna's teenage daughter (Michelle Johnson) is just too leery for comfort. The holiday atmosphere is well evoked, but the bad taste from director Stanley Donen, who made such stylish nonsense as *On the Town* and *Charade*, is an unpleasant surprise, while, for Caine, this misfiring comedy was one of a series of disasters about this time. Contains swearing and nudity. 🖭

Michael Caine *Matthew Hollis* • Joseph Bologna *Victor Lyons* • Valerie Harper *Karen Hollis* • Michelle Johnson *Jennifer Lyons* • Demi Moore *Nicole Hollis* • Jose Lewgoy *Eduardo Marques* • Lupe Gigliotti *Signora Botega* • Michael Menaugh *Peter* ■ *Dir* Stanley Donen • *Scr* Charlie Peters, Larry Gelbart, from the film *Un Moment d'Egarement* by Claude Berri

Blame It on the Bellboy

★★★ 15

Comedy 1992 · UK · Colour · 75mins

A bellboy (Bronson Pinchot in a wonderfully farcical turn) is responsible for a series of mistaken identity mix-ups at a hotel in this rather daft but nonetheless fun slapstick-style comedy. Dudley Moore, Bryan Brown and Patsy Kensit are among the people getting confused in this intermittently hilarious tale, which owes much of its charm to the supporting performances from Richard Griffiths, Penelope Wilton and the always reliable Alison Steadman. Contains some swearing. 🖭

Dudley Moore *Melvyn Orton* • Bryan Brown *Charlton Black/Mike Lawton* • Richard Griffiths *Maurice Horton* • Patsy Kensit *Caroline Wright* • Andreas Katsulas *Scarpa* • Alison Steadman

Rosemary Horton • Penelope Wilton *Patricia Fulford* • Bronson Pinchot *Bellboy* • Jim Carter *Rossi* ■ *Dir/Scr* Mark Herman

Blame It on the Night

★★ PG

Drama 1984 · US · Colour · 84mins

Of most note since the screenplay is based on an original story by director Gene Taft and rock legend Mick Jagger, this shoddy, misbegotten family drama also showcases rock stars Billy Preston and Merry Clayton. Nick Mancuso plays an ageing rock star trying to buy the affections of his illegitimate son and one can only suppose that the plot has resonance for Mr Jagger, because there's little here for any audience. Former fifties teen-pic icon Richard Bakalyan (*The Cool and the Crazy*) makes a welcome appearance, but this is tatty and ludicrous if well intentioned. 🖭

Nick Mancuso *Chris Dalton* • Byron Thames *Job Dalton* • Leslie Ackerman *Shelly* • Dick Bakalyan [Richard Bakalyan] *Manzini* • Leeyan Granger *Melanie* • Rex Ludwick *Animal* • Michael Wilding Jr *Terry* • Merry Clayton • Billy Preston ■ *Dir* Gene Taft • *Scr* Len Jenkin, from a story by Gene Taft, Mick Jagger

Blanche Fury

★★★★ PG

Melodrama 1948 · UK · Colour · 90mins

A wonderful-looking, dark, brooding tale, set on a large, rambling English estate, with Stewart Granger impressive as the maverick groom. Granger is pitted against the best that British melodrama had to offer at the time, including Valerie Hobson in the title role, Maurice Denham and Michael Gough. The late forties saw many examples of this type of movie, set amid the backdrop of iron gates, with stooped retainers and timely thunderstorms. This also has the benefit of an excellent screenplay and some taut direction from Marc Allégret. Yet it's the distinctive atmosphere that lingers in the memory. 🖭 *DVD*

Valerie Hobson *Blanche Fury* • Stewart Granger *Philip Thorn* • Walter Fitzgerald *Simon Fury* • Michael Gough *Lawrence Fury* • Maurice Denham *Major Frazer* • Sybilla Binder *Louisa* • Edward Lexy *Colonel Jenkins* • Allan Jeayes *Wetherby* ■ *Dir* Marc Allégret • *Scr* Audrey Erskine Lindop, Hugh Mills, Cecil McGivern, from the novel by Joseph Shearing • *Cinematographer* Guy Green, Geoffrey Unsworth

Blank Cheque

★★ PG

Comedy 1994 · US · Colour · 89mins

Clearly hoping to cash in on the success of *Home Alone*, Disney seemingly produced this kiddie comedy with nothing but the urgency of the release date in mind. The story of how pre-teen Brian Bonsall forges a cheque, sets himself up in the lap of luxury and then defends his patch is patently ludicrous – but with a little more imagination it might have made an entertaining romp. As it is, most of the gags feel reheated and, hard though he tries, Bonsall boasts too meagre a repertoire of awestruck gushings and swaggering gestures to succeed in doing anything but try the patience. For the bored or undemanding only. 🖭 *DVD*

Brian Bonsall *Preston Waters* • Karen Duffy *Shay Stanley* • James Rebhorn *Fred Waters* •

Jayne Atkinson *Sandra Waters* • Michael Faustino *Ralph Waters* • Chris Demetral *Damian Waters* • Miguel Ferrer *Quigley* • Michael Lerner *Biderman* ■ *Dir* Rupert Wainwright • *Scr* Blake Snyder, Colby Carr

Blankman

★★★ 12

Comedy 1994 · US · Colour · 91mins

Nerdy inventor Damon Wayans creates a bulletproof fabric, fashions a ridiculous superhero costume from it and becomes an inept crimefighter battling ghetto gangsters in this above-average comedy. Despite having no superpowers and with only his daft inventions and luck on his side, Wayans sets out to beat underworld kingpin Jon Polito and get the girl – TV news reporter Robin Givens. Semi-succeeding where Robert Townsend's similar satire *The Meteor Man* failed dismally, this leans heavily on parodies of the sixties *Batman* series and Wayans's funky humour. A pleasant – if juvenile – diversion. 🖭

Damon Wayans *Darryl Walker/Young Kevin Walker* • David Alan Grier *Kevin Walker* • Robin Givens *Kimberly Jonz* • Christopher Lawford *Mayor Marvin Harris* • Lynne Thigpen *Grandma Walker* • Jon Polito *Michael "The Suit" Minelli* • Nicky Corello *Sammy the Blade* • Jason Alexander *Mr Stone* • Michael Wayans *Young Darryl* • Greg Kinnear *Talk show host* • Arsenio Hall ■ *Dir* Mike Binder, Mike Binder • *Scr* JF Lawton, Damon Wayans, from a story by Damon Wayans

Blast

★★ 18

Action adventure 1996 · US · Colour · 94mins

Die Hard at the Olympics is the pitch for this entertainingly shameless action thriller from prolific straight-to-video specialist Albert Pyun. Andrew Divoff plays a terrorist who kidnaps the American women's swimming team at the 1996 Atlanta Olympics. However, he hasn't reckoned on the resourcefulness of janitor and martial-arts champ Linden Ashby and disabled anti-terrorist expert Rutger Hauer. Dumb fun if you can get over the fact that the action looks like it's taking place at your local sports centre. Contains swearing and violence. 🖭

Linden Ashby *Jack Bryant* • Andrew Divoff *Omado* • Kimberly Warren *Diane Colton* • Rutger Hauer *Leo* • Norbert Weisser *Commando rescuer* ■ *Dir* Albert Pyun • *Scr* Hannah Blue

Blast from the Past

★★ 12

Comedy 1998 · US · Colour · 108mins

Convinced that an atomic bomb is about to drop on sixties America, married couple Sissy Spacek and Christopher Walken seal themselves in an elaborate fallout shelter for 35 years. What will their naive son (Brendan Fraser) make of the cynical nineties when he's sent out into the world for the first time? Not quite enough, unfortunately, in Hugh Wilson's somewhat laboured "culture clash" romantic comedy, as Fraser enlists the aid of streetwise Alicia Silverstone in his quest for supplies. Though the tone is sweet, the gags fail to bite and there's little innovation on offer beyond the initial premise. But it's pleasant enough, with Fraser's goofy charm particularly winning. Contains swearing and some mild sexual references. *DVD*

Brendan Fraser *Adam* • Christopher Walken *Calvin* • Sissy Spacek *Helen* • Alicia Silverstone *Eve* • Dave Foley *Troy* • Joey Slotnick *Soda jerk* • Rex Linn *Dave* ■ *Dir* Hugh Wilson • *Scr* Bill Kelly, Hugh Wilson, from a story by Bill Kelly

Blaze

★★★ 15

Biographical drama
1989 · US · Colour · 112mins

The story of the passionate love affair between feisty Louisiana governor Earl Long and infamous New Orleans stripper Blaze Starr in the straight-laced fifties is sanitised in director Ron Shelton's sometimes insightful look into the dangerous and volatile mix of sex and politics. Paul Newman has fun moments as the uninhibited maverick who advocated black voting rights and Lolita Davidovich gives a memorable performance as the well-endowed hillbilly burlesque queen. While the combination of truth and comedy doesn't quite work, the two stars deliver a fair account of the tabloid scandal, and the real Blaze appears as backstage stripper Lily in a tiny cameo. Contains swearing and nudity. 🖭

Paul Newman *Earl Kemp Long* • Lolita Davidovich *Fannie Belle Flirtey/Blaze Starr* • Jerry Hardin *Thibodeaux* • Gailard Sartain *LaGrange* • Jeffrey DeMunn *Tuck* • Garland Bunting *Doc Ferriday* • Richard Jenkins *Times-Picayune Reporter* • Brandon Smith *Arvin Deeter* ■ *Dir* Ron Shelton • *Scr* Ron Shelton, from the autobiography *Blaze Starr: My Life as Told to Huey Perry* by Blaze Starr, Huey Perry

Blaze of Glory

★★★ 15

Crime drama based on a true story
1997 · US · Colour · 86mins

A fascinating, alternative take on the real-life story that also inspired the much under-rated thriller *Normal Life* from John McNaughton. Bruce Campbell plays a former marine and cop who takes up a life of crime with his wife Lori Loughlin to help pay the bills. Problem is that Loughlin starts to develop a taste for the Bonnie and Clyde lifestyle. Part of the rightly acclaimed *In the Line of Duty* TV-movie series, it lacks the psychological depth McNaughton brought to his version of the story, but it remains a gripping ride and the performances from the leads are spot on. Contains some mild swearing and violence. 🖭

Lori Loughlin *Jill Erickson* • Bruce Campbell *Jeff Erickson* • Brad Whitford [Bradley Whitford] *Tom LaSalle* • Brad Sullivan *Mike LaSalle* • Susanna Thompson *Sylvia* • Mariangela Pino *Dr Anspach* • Victor A Morris *Roderick* • Shannon Day *Cindy* ■ *Dir* Dick Lowry • *Scr* Susan Rhinehart, Stephen Harrigan, from a story by Susan Rhinehart

Blaze of Noon

★★

Adventure drama 1947 · US · BW · 90mins

William Holden, returning to civvy street and Paramount studios after four years of active service, stars in this tale of stunt-circus flying brothers who switch to the commercial world of airmail delivery. Set in the twenties and adapted from a novel by Ernest K Gann, it was directed by John Farrow for maximum excitement in the air – it collapses on the ground thanks to the turgidly scripted, drawn-out relationship between Holden and Anne Baxter, and the predictable crises that beset the fliers. The perfomances are competent.

Anne Baxter *Lucille Stewart* • William Holden (1) *Colin McDonald* • William Bendix *Porkie* • Sonny Tufts *Roland McDonald* • Sterling Hayden *Tad McDonald* • Howard Da Silva *Gafferty* • Johnny Sands *Keith McDonald* • Jean Wallace *Poppy* • Edith King *Mrs Murphy* ■ *Dir* John Farrow • *Scr* Frank Wead, Arthur Sheekman, from the novel by Ernest K Gann

Blazing Saddles ★★★★ 15

Spoof western 1974 · US · Colour · 88mins

Mel Brooks's all-singing, all-belching western spoof remains one of his finest creations. Cleavon Little is the railway worker who is appointed the first black sheriff to a hell-raising western town; Gene Wilder is the drunken gunman who helps him out. The two stars are great, but there are even better performances from Madeline Kahn (sending up Marlene Dietrich) and the crazed Harvey Korman. There's not a lot of subtlety, but loads of slapstick, and even more jokes about bodily functions. Contains swearing. DVD

Cleavon Little *Bart* • Gene Wilder *Jim, the Waco Kid* • Slim Pickens *Taggart* • Harvey Korman *Hedley Lamarr* • Madeline Kahn *Lili Von Shtupp* • Mel Brooks *Governor Lepetoma/Indian chief* • David Huddleston *Olson Johnson* • Liam Dunn *Rev Johnson* • Alex Karras *Mongo* ■ *Dir* Mel Brooks • *Scr* Mel Brooks, Norman Steinberg, Andrew Bergman, Richard Pryor, Alan Uger, from a story by Andrew Bergman

Bleak Moments ★★★★ PG

Drama 1971 · UK · Colour · 106mins

Written and directed by Mike Leigh and produced and edited by Leslie Blair, this may be the work of two dedicated realists, but it isn't quite the depressing prospect suggested by the title. However, it is an unflinching look at the everyday difficulties facing people leading quietly extraordinary lives. Among them is Anne Raitt, who struggles to communicate with those she knows, from her mentally disabled sister and her daydreaming office-mate to the hippie in her garage and her kindly teacher boyfriend. Everyone remembers the Chinese meal, but it's the aggregate of little episodes that makes this drama so moving.

Anne Raitt *Sylvia* • Sarah Stephenson *Hilda* • Eric Allan *Peter* • Joolia Cappleman *Pat* • Mike Bradwell *Norman* • Liz Smith *Pat's mother* ■ *Dir/Scr* Mike Leigh

Bleeder ★★★ 18

Drama 1999 · Den · Colour · 97mins

Questioning the truism that movies are responsible for societal violence, and containing one of the most sadistic modes of execution ever witnessed on screen, this raw melodrama has much in common with Nicolas Winding Refn's debut feature, *Pusher*. However, while Kim Bodnia's abusive relationship with pregnant girlfriend Rikke Louise Andersson is sickening in the extreme, there's a hint of optimism in video geek Mads Mikkelsen's timid regard for waitress Liv Corfixen. Indeed, this study of emasculated self-loathing is much more effective when it departs from the Tarantino-esque antics and concentrates on the characters' very real problems. Flawed but provocative. A Danish language film. Contains extreme violence.

Kim Bodnia *Leo* • Mads Mikkelsen *Lenny* • Rikke Louise Andersson *Louise* • Liv Corfixen *Lea* • Levino Jensen *Louis* • Zlatko Buric *Kitjo* • Claus Flyggare *Joe* ■ *Dir/Scr* Nicolas Winding Refn

Bless the Beasts and Children ★★

Drama 1971 · US · Colour · 101mins

An environmental fable about six adolescent boys, all from broken families, who rescue a herd of buffalo destined for the slaughterhouse. Since this is a movie from Stanley Kramer, purveyor of such big message pictures as *On the Beach* and *Guess Who's Coming to Dinner*, the story is milked for every drop of meaning, symbolism and Biblical parallel. Years ahead of the eco-movement, the film draws one's admiration and sympathy. A pity it's so heavy-handed and contrived.

Bill Mumy *Teft* • Barry Robins *Cotton* • Miles Chapin *Shecker* • Darel Glaser *Goodenow* • Bob Kramer *Lally I* • Marc Vahanian *Lally II* • Elaine Devry *Cotton's mother* • Jesse White *Shecker's father* ■ *Dir* Stanley Kramer • *Scr* Mac Benoff, from a novel by Glendon Swarthout

Bless This House ★★ U

Comedy 1972 · UK · Colour · 85mins

In the seventies, there was a misguided belief among British film-makers that successful sitcoms could be transferred to the big screen. The majority unsurprisingly proved to be huge disappointments, and this was no exception, although it did have one saving grace: the presence of the incomparable Sidney James. He is the grouchy father, married to Diana Coupland, who is trying to come to grips with his teenage children and his neighbours (the almost obligatory Terry Scott and June Whitfield). There is no shortage of familiar faces, but there are more laughs in the naff seventies' fashions, than in the script.

Sidney James *Sid Abbot* • Diana Coupland *Jean Abbot* • Sally Geeson *Sally Abbot* • Terry Scott *Ronald Baines* • June Whitfield *Vera Baines* • Peter Butterworth *Trevor Lewis* • Robin Askwith *Mike Abbot* • Bill Maynard *Oldham* • Wendy Richard *Carol* ■ *Dir* Gerald Thomas • *Scr* Dave Freeman

Blind Adventure ★★ U

Mystery 1933 · US · BW · 62mins

An American in London (Robert Armstrong) gets mixed up with a bunch of criminal rogues that includes a charming burglar (Roland Young). Helen Mack is the heroine of this routine programme filler, which adopts a comic tone but is defeated by a tediously muddled plot. The surprise is that it was written by Ruth Rose and directed by her husband Ernest B Schoedsack, in the same year she co-wrote and he co-directed one of the American cinema's landmark films, *King Kong*. Judging from this minor diversion, they didn't have their minds fully on the job.

Robert Armstrong *Richard Bruce* • Roland Young *Burglar* • Ralph Bellamy *Jim Steele* • Helen Mack *Rose Thorne* • Laura Hope Crews *Lady Rockingham* ■ *Dir* Ernest B Schoedsack • *Scr* Ruth Rose

Blind Alley ★★★

Crime thriller 1939 · US · BW · 69mins

Remade in 1948 with William Holden as *The Dark Past*, this adaptation of James Warwick's play keeps the original Broadway title. Chester Morris, two years before he took on the role of "Boston Blackie", is interestingly cast as a thug who holds a psychologist prisoner, getting himself analysed in the process. (This was one of the first films to offer a Freudian explanation for a character's behaviour.) Likeable Ralph Bellamy is extremely sympathetic as the shrink hostage, while director Charles Vidor calls on his experience as an apprentice at Berlin's UFA studios in an early forerunner to his masterwork, *Gilda*.

Chester Morris *Hal Wilson* • Ralph Bellamy *Dr Shelby* • Ann Dvorak *Mary* • Joan Perry *Linda Curtis* • Melville Cooper *George Curtis* • Rose Stradner *Doris Shelby* • John Eldredge *Dick Holbrook* • Ann Doran *Agnes* • Marc Lawrence *Buck* ■ *Dir* Charles Vidor • *Scr* Phillip MacDonald, Michael Blankfort, Albert Duffy, from the play by James Warwick

Blind Alley ★★★ 18

Thriller 1984 · US · Colour · 87mins

The start of Larry Cohen's film plays a similar tune to the 1985 Harrison Ford hit *Witness*, in that it has a young boy witnessing a murder. The similarities end there, though, and what follows is a smart romantic thriller whose different plot strands come together neatly at the climax. Anne Carlisle (*Liquid Sky*) plays the boy's mother, while Brad Rijn plays the Mafia hitman with whom she becomes involved.

Anne Carlisle *Sally* • Brad Rijn *Johnny* • John Woehrle *Fred* • Matthew Stockley *Matthew* • Stephen Lack *Burns* • Ann Magnuson *Maida* • Zachary Hains *Maletti* • Otto von Wernherr *Private eye* ■ *Dir/Scr* Larry Cohen

Blind Date ★★★

Crime drama 1959 · UK · BW · 94mins

This usually overlooked entry in the Joseph Losey canon is actually quite a daring and sophisticated investigation into British attitudes towards sex, class and the Establishment in the late fifties. Adapted from Leigh Howard's novel, the story is pretty unremarkable, but Losey's assured handling of character and location forces you to share the plight of Dutch painter Hardy Kruger, as he becomes embroiled in a political scandal after the mistress he shares with the French ambassador in London is murdered. Stanley Baker investigates with quiet efficiency.

Hardy Kruger *Jan van Rooyen* • Stanley Baker *Inspector Morgan* • Micheline Presle *Jacqueline Cousteau* • Robert Flemyng *Sir Brian Lewis* • Gordon Jackson *Police sergeant* • John Van Eyssen *Westover* • Jack MacGowran *Postman* • Lee Montague *Sergeant Farrow* ■ *Dir* Joseph Losey • *Scr* Ben Barzman, Millard Lampell, from the novel by Leigh Howard

Blind Date ★ 18

Crime thriller 1984 · US · Colour · 99mins

Blind Joseph Bottoms is able to see again after doctor Keir Dullea fits him up with a computer implant. But what's the link between him and a mad serial killer into surgical splatter? You won't care in this Greece-set slasher that's so high on tortuous logic and so low on conviction that only the scriptwriters could swallow it. Writer/director Nico Mastorakis gets it wrong in every area, especially the shockingly inane dialogue. The Greeks have a word for it – rubbish.

Joseph Bottoms *Jonathon Ratcliffe* • Kirstie Alley *Claire Simpson* • James Daughton *Dave* • Lana Clarkson *Rachel* • Keir Dullea *Dr Steiger* • Charles Nicklin *Robert* • Michael Howe *Subway gang member* • Marina Sirtis *Hooker* ■ *Dir* Nico Mastorakis • *Scr* Nico Mastorakis, Fred C Perry

Blind Date ★★ 15

Comedy 1987 · US · Colour · 91mins

When Bruce Willis's feature debut was released, it was mauled by the critics and some predicted he would join the many TV stars who had attempted to cross over into Hollywood and failed miserably. The film's box-office success and the subsequent career of the former *Moonlighting* actor have proved the critics wrong, but this would-be comedy hasn't improved with age. An example of the yuppy nightmare tales so popular at the end of the eighties, this finds Willis fixed up with the blind date from hell in the shape of Kim Basinger. Despite warnings to the contrary, he lets her have a drink and then watches her create havoc. The two leads are likeable enough, although the best performance comes from John Larroquette as Basinger's psychotic ex. Blake Edwards's direction, however, is typically crass and chaotic. Contains some swearing.

Bruce Willis *Walter Davis* • Kim Basinger *Nadia Gates* • John Larroquette *David Bedford* • William Daniels *Judge Harold Bedford* • George Coe *Harry Gruen* • Mark Blum *Denny Gordon* • Phil Hartman *Ted Davis* ■ *Dir* Blake Edwards • *Scr* Dale Launer

Blind Faith ★★★

Courtroom drama
1998 · US · Colour · 107mins

Ernest R Dickerson made his name as Spike Lee's cinematographer but, as a director, he has usually opted for genre films such as *Tales from the Crypt: Demon Knight* and *Surviving the Game*. However, this intense, moving courtroom drama proves he is equally at home with more controversial material. The always excellent Courtney B Vance plays a struggling black lawyer in the 1950s. He comes up against white legal establishment when he agrees to defend his nephew, who has been accused of murdering a young white man. Although most of the action is confined to the courtroom, Dickerson never lets that hamper him and he is rewarded with superb performances from Vance and Charles S Dutton, as the boy's father.

Charles S Dutton *Charles Williams* • Courtney B Vance *John Williams* • Lonette McKee *Carol Williams* • Kadeem Hardison *Eddie Williams* • Garland Whitt *Charles Williams Jr* • Karen Glave *Anna Huggins* • Jeff Clarke *Timothy* ■ *Dir* Ernest R Dickerson • *Scr* Frank Military

Blind Fury ★★★ 18

Action thriller 1990 · US · Colour · 82mins

Two years after he hit the big time with the fabulous *Dead Calm*, Australian director Phillip Noyce made this nifty

U = SUITABLE FOR ALL Uc = SUITABLE FOR ALL, ESPECIALLY FOR YOUNG CHILDREN (VIDEO ONLY) PG = PARENTAL GUIDANCE

martial arts saga, in which blind Vietnam veteran Rutger Hauer rescues his buddy's son from evil gangsters and then hits the road, bonding with the boy while fending off the bad guys at every available opportunity. It's a gimmicky, but above-average, action adventure (based on the hugely popular Japanese *Zatoichi* film series). Hauer does his best to cover up the lack of substance with some split-second samurai stunts. A smattering of well placed tongue-in-cheek humour helps the time pass in reasonably entertaining fashion. Contains violence and swearing. [VIDEO]

Rutger Hauer *Nick Parker* • Terrance O'Quinn [Terry O'Quinn] *Frank Devereaux* • Brandon Call *Billy Devereaux* • Lisa Blount *Annie Winchester* • Randall "Tex" Cobb *Slag* • Noble Willingham *MacCready* • Meg Foster *Lynn Devereaux* • Sho Kosugi *Assassin* ■ *Dir* Phillip Noyce • *Scr* Charles Robert Carner

The Blind Goddess ★★

Drama 1947 · UK · BW · 87mins

Nobody can do decent coves caught in a dilemma quite like Michael Denison and he's perfectly cast again in this screen version of Patrick Hastings's hit stage play as a secretary who shops his embezzling boss. But, unfortunately, this reunion with director Harold French (after the same year's *My Brother Jonathan*) suffers from some uncertain handling, with the courtroom scenes in particular sapped of the suspense that made them so compelling in the theatre. However, Eric Portman brings some much-needed authority to the proceedings. This was something of a family affair, with Betty Box producing and Sydney and Muriel Box writing the script.

Eric Portman *Sir John Dearing* • Anne Crawford *Lady Brasted* • Hugh Williams *Lord Brasted* • Michael Denison *Derek Waterhouse* • Nora Swinburne *Lady Dearing* • Claire Bloom *Mary Dearing* • Raymond Lovell *Mr Mainwaring* • Frank Cellier *Judge* • Maurice Denham *Butler* ■ *Dir* Harold French • *Scr* Muriel Box, Sydney Box, from the play by Patrick Hastings

Blind Hate ★★★

Drama based on a true story
1991 · US · Colour

LA Law's Corbin Bernsen swaps glitzy divorces for a legal battle against the Ku Klux Klan in this well-meaning TV drama, based on a true story. Bernsen plays Morris Dees, a liberal lawyer in the Deep South who decides to tackle the race hate organisation through the courts following the murder of a black youth. The gritty subject matter and the committed playing make it eminently watchable, and look out for Angela Bassett in a supporting role.

Corbin Bernsen *Morris Dees* • Jenny Lewis *Ellie Dees* • Sandy Bull *Bill Stanton* • John M Jackson *Evan Curtis* • Angela Bassett *Pat Clark* • James Staley *Danny Welch* • Casey Biggs *Howard Lee* • Harold Sylvester *John Gilbert* ■ *Dir* John Korty • *Scr* James G Hirsch, Charles Rosin

Blind Husbands ★★★★

Silent melodrama 1919 · US · BW · 129mins

After the First World War, when Erich von Stroheim's "Horrible Hun" roles were no longer in demand, he persuaded Universal to let him direct this cynical, witty and erotic drama set in the Alps. Stroheim also wrote the script, designed the sets and played the lead role of the dashing Lieutenant von Steuben, who seduces a bored American wife on holiday. With its careful attention to detail in the decor and costumes, and the acute psychological observation of the characters, Stroheim's debut movie prefigured his later, more mature work. The picture was a commercial and critical success; it was also the only one of his films to be released without considerable studio interference.

Sam De Grasse *Dr Robert Armstrong* • Francelia Billington *Margaret Armstrong* • Erich von Stroheim *Lieutenant von Steuben* • TH Gibson-Gowland [Gibson Gowland] *Sepp* • Fay Holderness *Vamp waitress* • Ruby Kendrick *"A Village Blossom"* ■ *Dir* Erich von Stroheim • *Scr* Erich von Stroheim, Lillian Ducey (titles), from the story *The Pinnacle* by Erich von Stroheim • *Cinematographer* Ben Reynolds

Blind Judgement: Seduction in Travis County ★★★ 15

Thriller based on a true story
1991 · US · Colour · 87mins

A proficient TV psycho-thriller, loosely based on a true story, this provides its fair share of excitement. Peter Coyote (still probably best known for playing the scientist Keys in *ET*) is a lawyer who has it all – a high-flying career, a marvellous wife and political aspirations – until he lands the task of defending a suspected murderer (Lesley Ann Warren). He sets to the job with his usual brilliance, but then his client's irrational behaviour begins to jeopardise the case. [VIDEO]

Lesley Ann Warren *Melanie Evans* • Peter Coyote *Frank Maguire* • Jean Smart *Karen Maguire* • Matt Clark *Buck Dobbs* • Don Hood *Herman Ray* • Freda Ramsey Williams *Connie* • Marco Perella *Clancey Pogue* • Brandon Smith *Skyler Freemont* • Jerry Cotton *JT Gibbs* ■ *Dir* George Kaczender • *Scr* Christopher Canaan, Jan Meins, from the book *Murder in Little Rock* by George Laszlo

Blind Justice ★★ 15

Western 1994 · US · Colour · 88mins

Followers of Elisabeth Shue's erratic career prior to her best actress Oscar nomination for *Leaving Las Vegas* may be interested in this Sergio Leone-inspired spaghetti western. It's doubtful, however, that anyone else will find much to enjoy in the rather ordinary shoot-'em-up action plot. Armand Assante is wasted as the blind gunfighter caught up in a battle between (ex-Bond villain) Robert Davi's vicious bandits and a US cavalry detachment guarding a consignment of silver. Very predictable, with a highly manufactured feel, this cable movie is merely ho-hum horse opera. Contains violence, swearing and nudity. [VIDEO]

Armand Assante *Canaan* • Elisabeth Shue *Caroline* • Robert Davi *Alacran* • Danny Nucci *Roberto* • Ian McElhinney *Father Malone* • Adam Baldwin *Sgt Hastings* • MC Gainey *Bull* • Titus Welliver *Sumner* • Jack Black *Private* ■ *Dir* Richard Spence • *Scr* Daniel Knauf

Blind Side ★★★ 18

Thriller 1993 · US · Colour · 93mins

The Hitcher provided Rutger Hauer with one of his more memorable roles and he's back in the same sort of territory for this taut, intelligent made-for-cable thriller. Ron Silver and Rebecca De Mornay are the couple involved in a hit-and-run accident abroad and all seems to be OK until Hauer turns up on their doorstep with knowledge of the incident. The cat-and-mouse games are expertly captured by New Zealand director Geoff Murphy and the talented leads deliver enjoyably overblown performances. Contains swearing, violence and sex scenes. [VIDEO]

Rutger Hauer *Shell* • Rebecca De Mornay *Lynn Kaines* • Ron Silver *Doug Kaines* • Jonathan Banks *Aaron* • Mariska Hargitay *Melanie* • Tamara Clatterbuck *Barbara Hall* ■ *Dir* Geoff Murphy • *Scr* Stewart Lindh, Solomon Weingarten, John Carlen, from a story by Stewart Lindh, Solomon Weingarten

Blind Spot ★★★

Drama 1993 · US · Colour · 120mins

Joanne Woodward earned an Emmy nomination for her formidable performance in this solid TV movie about drug abuse among the well-to-do. She's a politician who finds a new cause to fight for when she discovers that her daughter's cocaine addiction was to blame for her son-in-law's death in a car crash. It's not quite a one-woman show, however, with Laura Linney making the suffering sibling seem more than just a refugee from a glitzy soap opera. Neither provocative nor compelling, it is at least sober and sincere. Contains drug abuse.

Joanne Woodward *Nell Harrington* • Laura Linney *Phoebe* • Reed Diamond *Charlie* • Fritz Weaver *Simon* • Patti D'Arbanville [Patti D'Arbanville-Quinn] *Lucinda* • Cynthia Martells *Holly* • Patti Yasutake *Dr Charbonneau* • Mark Anthony Wade *Adam* ■ *Dir* Michael Toshiyuki Uno • *Scr* Nina Shengold

Blind Terror ★★ 15

Thriller 1971 · UK · Colour · 83mins

Blind Mia Farrow splashes mud on a young drifter's cowboy boots while travelling to her uncle's isolated mansion. In revenge, he slaughters her entire family and relentlessly pursues her around the old dark house. Written by Brian Clemens (*The Avengers*) on what must clearly have been an off-day, Richard Fleischer's cumbersome chiller combines elements of *Psycho* and *Wait until Dark* for minimal shocks and suspense. Farrow tries her best to convince, but the half-baked premise is too full of ridiculous red herrings to be even remotely believable. [VIDEO]

Mia Farrow *Sarah* • Robin Bailey *George Rexton* • Dorothy Alison *Betty Rexton* • Norman Eshley *Steve Reding* • Diane Grayson *Sandy Rexton* • Paul Nicholas *Jacko* • Christopher Matthews *Frost* • Brian Rawlinson *Barker* • Michael Elphick *Gypsy Tom* ■ *Dir* Richard Fleischer • *Scr* Brian Clemens

Blind Vengeance ★★ 15

Psychological drama
1990 · US · Colour · 88mins

Touching a topical racial nerve, this TV movie about a father taking revenge on white supremacists acquitted of killing his student son pushes all the right vigilante buttons but never quite succeeds. That's because the plot looks limited by budgetary considerations and the dialogue is too heavily laden with slogans that are as obvious as they are shallow. Contains swearing. [VIDEO]

Gerald McRaney *"Gar" Garland Hager Sr* • Lane Smith *Colonel Blanchard* • Don Hood *Sheriff Drumm* • Thalmus Rasulala *Reverend Abraham Mace* • James Parks *Willis Sharkey* • Richard Lineback *Edwin Rentzel* • Grand Bush [Grand L Bush] *Deputy Jones* • Marg Helgenberger *Virginia Whitelaw* ■ *Dir* Lee Philips • *Scr* Henri Simoun, Curt Allen, Jerry McNeely

Blind Vision ★★★

Thriller 1992 · US · Colour · 90mins

Attempting to recapture the eerie voyeurism present in many of Hitchcock's best films, *Blind Vision* is about a man who becomes a murder suspect when the boyfriend of the woman he is watching ends up dead. The voyeur is played by Lenny Von Dohlen and the object of his desire is Deborah Shelton. Most eyes will, however, be on the supporting cast: Louise Fletcher, an Oscar-winner for *One Flew over the Cuckoo's Nest*, Ned Beatty and the wondrously smarmy Robert Vaughn. Co-writer and director Shuki Levy offers a standard mix of thriller fare. Contains swearing, violence, sex scenes and brief nudity.

Lenny Von Dohlen *William Dalton* • Deborah Shelton *Leanne Dunaway* • Ned Beatty *Sergeant Dave Logan* • Robert Vaughn *Mr X* • Louise Fletcher *Virginia Taylor* • Stoney Jackson *Tony Davis* • Catherine McGoohan *Gloria Byers* ■ *Dir* Shuki Levy • *Scr* Shuki Levy, Winston Rickard

Blind Witness ★★ 15

Thriller 1989 · US · Colour · 87mins

This is a rather mindless TV-movie vehicle for *Dallas's* Victoria Principal, who puts up a better battle against banality than others have before her in a woman-in-jeopardy role. She plays a blind wife seeking revenge after her husband is murdered in front of her by burglars. Sadly, the film is as inspirationally challenged as she is visually challenged, though director Richard Colla does manage to produce the occasional moment of tension from the predictable material. Contains violence. [VIDEO]

Victoria Principal *Maggie Kemlich* • Paul LeMat *Detective Mike Tuthill* • Stephen Macht *Gordon Kemlich* • Matt Clark *Lieutenant Schapper* • Tim Choate *Remy* ■ *Dir* Richard Colla [Richard A Colla] • *Scr* Edmond Stevens, from a story and teleplay by Tom Sullivan, Robert Carrington

Blindfold ★★★ U

Comedy thriller 1966 · US · Colour · 101mins

Had co-writer-director Philip Dunne resisted the temptation to parody Hitchcock, this might have been a first-rate thriller. The levity undercuts the tension that develops as society psychiatrist Rock Hudson begins to realise that Alejandro Rey (the patient he's been seeing in such secrecy that he's blindfolded to and from their consultations) is actually in grave danger. The sequence in which Hudson attempts to retrace his journey to the kidnapper's bayou hideout using only ambient sound to guide him is neatly realised. But the romance with Rey's sister Claudia Cardinale and some uncomfortable slapstick prevent the action from being genuinely nail-biting.

Rock Hudson *Dr Bartholomew Snow* • Claudia Cardinale *Vicki* • Jack Warren *General Pratt* • Guy Stockwell *Fitzpatrick* • Brad Dexter *Det Harrigan* • Anne Seymour *Smitty* • Alejandro Rey *Arthur Vincenti* • Hari Rhodes *Capt Davis* ■ *Dir* Philip Dunne • *Scr* Philip Dunne, WH Menger, from the novel by Lucille Fletcher

Blindfold: Acts of Obsession ★★ [18]

Erotic thriller 1994 · US · Colour · 85mins

The fact that former *Beverly Hills 90210* star Shannen Doherty takes her clothes off is probably the sole point of interest in this bland TV-movie thriller. Doherty is a bored wife who, on the advice of therapist Judd Nelson, sets about spicing up her sex life, only to find that this somehow attracts the attention of a murderer. For an erotic thriller, it's surprisingly devoid of either eroticism or thrills, and Doherty is even less convincing as an actress with her kit off. Contains violence, swearing and nudity.

Judd Nelson *Dr Jennings* • Shannen Doherty *Madeleine Dalton* • Kristian Alfonso *Chris Madigan* • Michael Woods *Mike Dalton* • Tony Griffin *Thin man* • Drew Snyder *Lieutenant Alex Saunders* • Shell Danielson *Young female addict* ■ *Dir/Scr* Lawrence L Simeone

Blindsided ★★★ [15]

Thriller 1993 · US · Colour · 88mins

Nowadays, Jeff Fahey is one of the most under-rated of video stars. Although he has made respectable features, including *White Hunter, Black Heart* with Clint Eastwood, it's in the world of straight-to-rental that he really shines. He moves easily between being a goodie and a villain, and here he is in typically ambivalent form as an ex-cop, blinded when betrayed during a robbery and nursed back to health by *femme fatale* Mia Sara. Writer/director Tom Donnelly manages to avoid the usual TV-movie clichés and comes up with a suitably twisting plot.

Jeff Fahey *Frank McKenna* • Mia Sara *Chandler Strange* • Rudy Ramos *Jessy Aruna* • Jack Kehler *Waco Dean* • Brad Hunt *Lee* • Ben Gazzara *Ira Gold* • Michael Ornstein *Detective Sartucci* • Glenn Ash *J Willy Gault* ■ *Dir* Tom Donnelly [Thomas Michael Donnelly] • *Scr* Tom Donnelly

Blink ★★★ [18]

Thriller 1994 · US · Colour · 101mins

The concept is not exactly new – blind woman in peril fights back – but, thanks to a winning, sassy performance from Madeleine Stowe, this effortlessly rises above the routine. Stowe is a folk fiddle player recovering from an operation that will eventually allow her to see again. For the time being, she gets fleeting moments of vision and during one of these periods she catches sight of a murderer, thereby putting her own life in danger. Aidan Quinn is the sceptical policeman assigned to watch over her, and there is reliable support from the likes of Laurie Metcalf and James Remar. Director Michael Apted competently cranks up the tension, and Stowe's faltering flashes of sight are brilliantly realised. Contains violence, swearing and nudity.

Madeleine Stowe *Emma Brody* • Aidan Quinn *Detective John Hallstrom* • James Remar *Thomas Ridgely* • Peter Friedman *Doctor Ryan Pierce* • Bruce A Young *Lieutenant Mitchell* • Laurie Metcalf *Candice* • Matt Roth *Crowe* • Paul Dillon *Neal Booker* ■ *Dir* Michael Apted • *Scr* Dana Stevens

Bliss ★★★ [18]

Black comedy 1985 · Aus · Colour · 107mins

An Australian movie of great charm and style this concentrates on the hoary old "cheating death and rediscovering life" chestnut, but gives it some fresh and funny topspin. The performances, particularly from frenzied Barry Otto as a hapless advertising executive, are universally excellent, but it is Ray Lawrence's adroit and deft direction that turns a simple and oft-told tale – about a man who dramatically changes his life after a heart attack – into a miniature comic tour de force. Another example of the small but witty features Australian cinema has become famous for. Contains swearing.

Barry Otto *Harry Joy* • Lynette Curran *Bettina Joy* • Helen Jones *Honey Barbara* • Miles Buchanan *David Joy* • Gia Carides *Lucy Joy* • Tim Robertson *Alex Duval* • Jeff Truman *Joel* • Bryan Marshall *Adrian* • Jon Ewing *Aldo* ■ *Dir* Ray Lawrence • *Scr* Ray Lawrence, Peter Carey, from the novel by Peter Carey

Bliss ★★ [18]

Erotic drama 1997 · US · Colour · 99mins

Despite the high production values, a quality cast and a wordy script, this is not very different from the *Indecent Behaviour* and *Animal Instinct* films that clutter up the top shelves of your local video shop. Craig Sheffer and Sheryl Lee are a young, newly married couple whose sex life is proving to be a damp squib. In desperation they turn to therapist Terence Stamp, who opens them up to a new world of sexual experience. The latter steals the show since the two young leads fail to convince and while writer/director Lance Young takes the subject matter seriously, the soft-focus direction constantly undermines his worthy intentions. Contains swearing and sex scenes.

Terence Stamp *Baltazar Vincenza* • Craig Sheffer *Joseph* • Sheryl Lee *Maria* • Spalding Gray *Alfred* • Casey Siemaszko *Tanner* • Ken Camroux *Hank* • Pamela Perry *Dottie* • Blu Mankuma *Nick* ■ *Dir/Scr* Lance Young

The Bliss of Mrs Blossom ★★

Comedy 1968 · UK · Colour · 93mins

Shirley MacLaine stars in this otherwise all-British comedy, written by Alec Coppel and Denis Norden and directed by Joseph McGrath. She plays the wife of a brassière manufacturer (Richard Attenborough), who manages to conceal her lover (James Booth), one of her husband's employees, in the attic for three years before her husband tumbles to the situation... A kind of screwball farce, it is played with evident gusto by MacLaine and a cast that features Freddie Jones, Patricia Routledge, Bob Monkhouse and William Rushton, who, defying the total absurdity of the situation, manage to ellicit some laughs.

Shirley MacLaine *Harriet Blossom* • Richard Attenborough *Robert Blossom* • James Booth *Ambrose Tuttle* • Freddie Jones *Detective Sergeant Dylan* • William Rushton *Dylan's assistant* • Bob Monkhouse *Doctor Taylor* • Patricia Routledge *Miss Reece* • John Bluthal *Judge* • Barry Humphries *Art dealer* • Clive Dunn *Man* • John Cleese *Clerk* ■ *Dir* Joseph McGrath • *Scr* Alec Coppel, Denis Norden, from the story by Josef Shaftel, from the play *A Bird in the Nest* by Alec Coppel

Blithe Spirit ★★★★ [U]

Comedy fantasy 1945 · UK · Colour · 91mins

A polished adaptation of Noël Coward's comedy, with widower Rex Harrison happily remarried to Constance Cummings and visited by the ghost of his first wife, Kay Hammond (the ghost was modelled on Gertrude Lawrence who had left Coward's stock company for Broadway). The architect of this event is a dotty old medium, played by the unforgettable Margaret Rutherford. David Lean directed – Coward was away in America and the great British director was worried he was the wrong man for the job. According to Kevin Brownlow's monumental biography of Lean, Coward attended the first preview and was distinctly unimpressed. The critics lapped it up, though, and the dainty special effects won an Oscar.

Rex Harrison *Charles Condomine* • Constance Cummings *Ruth Condomine* • Kay Hammond *Elvira* • Margaret Rutherford *Madame Arcati* • Hugh Wakefield *Dr Bradman* • Joyce Carey *Mrs Bradman* • Jacqueline Clark *Edith* ■ *Dir* David Lean • *Scr* Anthony Havelock-Allan, David Lean, Ronald Neame, from the play by Noël Coward • *Cinematographer* Ronald Neame • *Special Effects* Thomas Howard

The Blob ★★★★★ [15]

Science-fiction 1958 · US · Colour · 82mins

Steve McQueen got his first starring role in this musty delight about a giant red alien jelly terrorising small-town America and absorbing the population. A quintessential fifties classic (which spawned a successful 1988 remake), the gaudy colours, self-mocking tone and the neat title creature add up to loads of unsettling fun. The scene where the outer space ooze invades a local cinema has become one of science-fiction cinema's key images. Note the title song, which is an early composition by those kings of easy listening, Burt Bacharach and Hal David.

Steve McQueen *Steve* • Aneta Corseaut *Judy* • Earl Rowe *Police Lieutenant* • Olin Howlin *Old man* • Stephen Chase • John Benson • Vince Barbi • Tom Ogen • Julie Cousins • Ralph Roseman ■ *Dir* Irvin S Yeaworth Jr • *Scr* Irvin S Yeaworth Jr, Theodore Simonson, Ruth Phillips, from an idea by Irvine H Millgate

The Blob ★★★★ [18]

Science-fiction 1988 · US · Colour · 90mins

The Space Sponge returns in a super remake of the cult monster movie from sci-fi's golden era. As with John Carpenter and his remake of *The Thing*, director Chuck Russell (*The Mask*) gets his revamp exactly right. By re-interpreting all the potent moments from the Steve McQueen original in today's sophisticated special-effects terms, and updating the plot to include contemporary mores and political issues, Russell creates a breakneck monster-on-the-loose crowd-pleaser with a fun nostalgic pulse.

Shawnee Smith *Meg Penny* • Donovan Leitch *Paul Taylor* • Kevin Dillon *Brian Flagg* • Ricky Paull Goldin *Scott Jeskey* • Billy Beck *Can man* • Jeffrey DeMunn *Sheriff Herb Geller* • Candy Clark *Fran Hewitt* • Beau Billingslea *Moss Woolsey* ■ *Dir* Chuck Russell • *Scr* Chuck Russell, Frank Darabont

Block Busters ★★ [U]

Comedy 1944 · US · BW · 60mins

Before the East Side Kids became the Bowery Boys, there was a pleasing rough edge to their comedy, and here (yup, that's a pun in the title) a new French kid on the block proves to be the very model of international camaraderie as he helps the boys win their local baseball game. Symbolic, you betcha! Back in the dark days of the Second World War, this was a lesson in how to be good neighbours for all audiences. Watch carefully for silent screen genius Harry Langdon, sadly here reduced to a walk-on part.

Leo Gorcey *Muggs* • Huntz Hall *Glimpy* • Gabriel Dell *Skinny* • Billy Benedict *Butch* • Jimmy Strand *Danny* • Bill Chaney *Tobey* • Minerva Urecal *Amelia* • Roberta Smith *Jinx* • Noah Beery Sr [Noah Beery] *Judge* • Harry Langdon *Higgins* ■ *Dir* Wallace Fox • *Scr* Houston Branch

Blockade ★★

War drama 1938 · US · BW · 85mins

The Spanish Civil War, that curtain-raiser to the Second World War, was a crusade for many Hollywood liberals and one might have expected a screenwriter like John Howard Lawson, later one of the original Hollywood Ten, to have produced something less lily-livered than this. The picture tells us that war is wrong and nothing else. Henry Fonda and Madeleine Carroll are mixed up in it – he's a peasant, she's one of dozens of spies – but the story is hopelessly muddled.

Henry Fonda *Marco* • Madeleine Carroll *Norma* • Leo Carrillo *Luis* • John Halliday *Andre* • Vladimir Sokoloff *Basil* • Robert Warwick *General Vallejo* ■ *Dir* William Dieterle • *Scr* John Howard Lawson

Blockheads ★★★★ [U]

Classic comedy 1938 · US · BW · 56mins

Stan Laurel, left to guard a trench in 1917, is discovered two decades later with a pile of empty bean cans, still on guard. Ollie takes the trench hero home, where they become involved in a farcical situation with jealous big-game hunter Billy Gilbert. One to relish for its innuendos and sight gags, John G Blystone's remake of the short *Unaccustomed as We Are* is one of Laurel and Hardy's most domestic comedies.

Stan Laurel *Stan* • Oliver Hardy *Ollie* • Billy Gilbert *Mr Gilbert* • Patricia Ellis *Mrs Gilbert* • Minna Gombell *Mrs Hardy* • James Finlayson *Mr Finn* ■ *Dir* John G Blystone • *Scr* Felix Adler, Arnold Belgard, Harry Langdon, James Parrott, Charles Rogers

The Blockhouse ★★★

Second World War drama
1973 · UK · Colour · 103mins

An almost unseen Peter Sellers movie, this features the star in a rare straight

role. In wartime Germany, slave workers from all over Europe are used to build German coastal fortifications while the Allies bombard the sites. Several workers take refuge in a network of underground tunnels and are subsequently sealed in. Although the bunkers contain ample supplies, the workers undergo a tortuous time in their subterranean prison. This grim movie based on real-life events (two men were discovered in 1951, having been trapped for six years in a similar situation). This difficult film sat on the shelf for several years after its completion, before surfacing briefly in 1978.

Peter Sellers *Rouquet* • Charles Aznavour *Visconti* • Per Oscarsson *Lund* • Peter Vaughan *Aufret* • Jeremy Kemp *Grabinski* • Leon Lissek *Kozhek* • Nicholas Jones *Kramer* • Alfred Lynch *Larshen* ■ *Dir* Clive Rees • *Scr* John Gould, Clive Rees, from the novel *Le Blockhaus* by Jean Paul Clebert

Blond Cheat ★ U

Comedy   1938 · US · BW · 62mins

Intended as a farce with an English slant, this miserable offering from RKO and director Joseph Santley needed five writers to dream up the tale of a British millionaire (Cecil Kellaway) who offers to finance a new show for an actress (Joan Fontaine, before her career took off with *Rebecca*) on condition she breaks up the romance between his daughter (Lilian Bond) and a smooth socialite (Derrick DeMarney). There is little to recommend it.

Joan Fontaine *Julie Evans* • Derrick DeMarney *Michael Ashburn* • Cecil Kellaway *Mr Trent* • Cecil Cunningham *Mrs Trent* • Lillian Bond *Roberta Trent* • Robert Coote *Gilbert Potts* • Olaf Hytten *Paul Douglas* ■ *Dir* Joseph Santley • *Scr* Viola Brothers Shore, Harry Segall, Charles Kaufman, Paul Yawitz, from a story by Aladar Lazlo

Blonde Bombshell ★★★★

Comedy   1933 · US · BW · 90mins

A chance to see Jean Harlow in the movie that originally opened – and still plays world cinematheques – as *Bombshell*. It's a perceptive yet affectionate satire on Hollywood itself, with the peroxide sex symbol playing movie sexpot Lola Burns, desperate for a life away from the cameras. It's quite a wacky farce with some biting observations, and Harlow really proves her worth, keeping sentimentality at bay while revealing a warm yet snappy comedic style that would serve her well in her next film, the all-star classic *Dinner at Eight*. This movie is directed by one of Hollywood's most under-rated craftsmen, Victor Fleming of *Gone with the Wind* and *The Wizard of Oz* fame, who squeezes every inch of mileage out of a plot one suspects he understood very well.

Jean Harlow *Lola* • Lee Tracy *Space* • Frank Morgan *Pops* • Franchot Tone *Gifford Middleton* • Pat O'Brien *Brogan* • Una Merkel *Mae* • Ted Healy *Junior* • Ivan Lebedeff *Marquis* • Mary Forbes *Mrs Middleton* ■ *Dir* Victor Fleming • *Scr* Jules Furthman, John Lee Mahin, from the play by Caroline Francke, Mack Crane

Blonde Crazy ★★★

Crime drama   1931 · US · BW · 78mins

Fast-talking James Cagney's follow-up to his smash hits *Public Enemy* and *Smart Money* was this nifty little melodrama, shown in the UK as *Larceny Lane*. Cagney and Joan Blondell were on Broadway together and had a professional rapport long before Warner Bros brought them out to the West Coast, where they both epitomised the Depression era in a series of pacey, smartly dialogued frolics. Here, he's a con man and she's his business partner/girlfriend who marries a relative newcomer to Hollywood, a startlingly young looking Ray Milland. Jim plays everything, from convict to bellboy and back again, and the pace never lets up. The success of this movie forced boss Jack Warner to up Cagney's salary to a richly deserved $1,000 per week after the star threatened to go elsewhere.

James Cagney *Bert Harris* • Joan Blondell *Ann Roberts* • Louis Calhern *Dapper Dan Barker* • Noel Francis *Helen Wilson* • Guy Kibbee *A Rupert Johnson Jr* • Ray Milland *Joe Reynolds* • Polly Walters *Peggy* • Charles Lane (1) *Four-eyes, the Desk Clerk* ■ *Dir* Roy Del Ruth • *Scr* Kubec Glasmon, John Bright

Blonde Fever ★★

Comedy drama   1944 · US · BW · 60mins

Based on Ferenc Molnar's play *Delila*, this familiar tale of a married man falling for the charms of a gold-digger needed a Lubitsch but instead got the uninspired direction of Richard Whorf. It remains watchable due to the MGM production gloss, Gloria Grahame, in her screen debut as the scheming waitress, and a beautiful performance by veteran Mary Astor, as the wife. She was only three years on from *The Maltese Falcon*, but was already settling into character roles.

Philip Dorn *Peter Donay* • Mary Astor *Delilah Donay* • Felix Bressart *Johnny* • Gloria Grahame *Sally Murfin* ■ *Dir* Richard Whorf • *Scr* Patricia Coleman, from the play *Delila* by Ferenc Molnar

Blonde Fist ★ 15

Comedy drama   1991 · UK · Colour · 98mins

Real-life brother and sister Frank and Margi Clarke showed promise as, respectively, writer and star of the 1985 hit *Letter to Brezhnev*, but conspicuously failed to live up to it, as, the writer/director and star of this lumbering *Film on Four* about a working-class woman with a mess of a life but a socking right hook, inherited from her bare-knuckle boxing dad. When she needs cash to rebuild her life, she only knows one way to amek money – by joining the women's boxing circuit. One to duck. Contains violence and swearing. ▭

Margi Clarke *Ronnie O'Dowd* • Carroll Baker *Lovelle Summers* • Ken Hutchinson *John O'Dowd* • Sharon Power *Mary* • Angela Clarke *Brenda Doyle* • Lewis Bester *Young Tony* • Gary Mavers *Tony Bone* • Jeff Weatherford *Dan* ■ *Dir/Scr* Frank Clarke

A Blonde in Love ★★★★

Romantic comedy   1965 · Cz · BW · 80mins

Combining sly situation comedy with charming observation, Milos Forman's second feature thoroughly merited its Oscar nomination – all the more so considering the inexperienced cast improvised much of its dialogue. Hana Brejchova is superb as the small-town factory girl whose earnest (and one-sided) pursuit of pianist Vladimir Pucholt comes to a head when she follows him to his parents' house in Prague. Full of the affectionate irony that characterises Forman's early studies of naive youth, this is also a subtly acerbic social satire, though there's a more openly mocking tone to the scenes dealing with the older generation, sexual manners and the military. In Czech with English subtitles.

Hana Brejchova *Andula* • Vladimir Pucholt *Milda* • Vladimir Mensik *Vacovsky* • Milada Jezkova *Milda's mother* • Josef Sebanek *Milda's father* • Ivan Kheil *Manas* • Jiri Hruby *Burda* • Marie Salacova *Marie* ■ *Dir* Milos Forman • *Scr* Milos Forman, Jaroslav Papousek, Ivan Passer

Blonde Venus ★★★

Drama   1932 · US · BW · 91mins

The fourth of the six American films from Josef von Sternberg and Marlene Dietrich's partnership, this is by far the poorest in content. It's the one where cabaret entertainer Marlene makes a dramatic entrance in a gorilla skin to sing *Hot Voodoo*. The storyline – which charts Dietrich's degradation after her husband (Herbert Marshall) learns she has acquired the money for his medical treatment from her rich lover Cary Grant – is unremitting drivel, evoking more sniggers than sympathy. However, von Sternberg's undisputed mastery of atmosphere and his handling of his star make the film compulsive, even as one scoffs.

Marlene Dietrich *Helen Faraday* • Herbert Marshall *Edward Faraday* • Cary Grant *Nick Townsend* • Dickie Moore *Johnny Faraday* • Francis Sayles *Charlie Blaine* • Gene Morgan *Ben Smith* • Rita Laroy *"Taxi Belle" Hooper* • Robert Emmett O'Connor *O'Connor* ■ *Dir* Josef von Sternberg • *Scr* Jules Furthman, SK Lauren, from a story by Josef von Sternberg • *Cinematographer* Bert Glennon

Blondie ★★★ U

Comedy   1938 · US · BW · 69mins

This was the first in the long-running series of films about the chaotic household of Blondie and Dagwood Bumstead, based on the strip cartoon by Chic Young. In this introduction to the family, Dagwood loses his job; his attempts to keep this a secret cause Blondie to suspect him of infidelity. Penny Singleton's delightfully dippy housewife makes an amusing mate for the bumbling Arthur Lake, while the audience of the time could readily identify with the family's dilemmas.

Penny Singleton *Blondie* • Arthur Lake *Dagwood Bumstead* • Larry Simms *Baby Dumpling* • Gene Lockhart *CP Hazlip* • Ann Doran *Elzie Hazlip* • Jonathan Hale *JC Dithers* • Irving Bacon *Mailman* ■ *Dir* Frank R Strayer • *Scr* Richard Floumoy, from the comic strip by Chic Young

Blondie Meets the Boss ★★★ U

Comedy   1939 · US · BW · 72mins

The second episode in the *Blondie* series, derived from Chic Young's cartoon strip, finds Dagwood (Arthur Lake) minding the home after Blondie (Penny Singleton) takes over his job. The hapless Dagwood ends up in deep water after he deserts his post for a spot of fishing. This ongoing comedy of small predicaments spanned 28 films; back then, candyfloss like this was the equivalent of today's soap operas.

Penny Singleton *Blondie* • Arthur Lake *Dagwood* • Larry Simms *Baby Dumpling* • Jonathan Hale *JC Dithers* • Don Beddoe *Marvin* • Dorothy Comingore *Francine* • Danny Mummert *Alvin* ■ *Dir* Frank R Strayer • *Scr* Richard Floumoy, from a story by Kay Van Riper, Richard Floumoy, from the comic strip by Chic Young

Blondie of the Follies ★★★

Musical comedy   1932 · US · BW · 91mins

The plotline of this musical comedy must have titillated those in the know at the time. Scorned by nice young Robert Montgomery, Blondie becomes the kept plaything of older man Douglass Dumbrille. Since Marion Davies played the title role and she was the mistress of newspaper magnate William Randolph Hearst, whose Cosmopolitan film company funded this opus, one wonders what could be inferred. Parallels aside, this is a likeable rags-to-riches romp, which really centres on Davies and Billie Dove (both, incidentally, real-life Ziegfeld Follies graduates) vying for Montgomery's affections. It features an especially wicked take-off by Davies and the great Jimmy Durante of Greta Garbo and John Barrymore in *Grand Hotel*. The screenplay, co-written by Anita Loos, allows for some attractive song and dance numbers in which Miss Davies acquits herself surprisingly well.

Marion Davies *Blondie McClune* • Robert Montgomery *Larry Belmont* • Billie Dove *Lottie Callahan* • Jimmy Durante *Jimmy* • James Gleason *Pa McClune* • ZaSu Pitts *Gertie* • Sidney Toler *Pete* • Douglass Dumbrille *Murchenson* ■ *Dir* Edmund Goulding • *Scr* Frances Mario, Anita Loos

Blondie Takes a Vacation ★★

Comedy   1939 · US · BW · 69mins

In the third feature version of cartoonist Chic Young's famous comic strip characters, the screen images of Blondie and Dagwood Bumstead (not to mention Larry Simms as Baby Dumpling) were still new and inventive. Thanks also to the perfectly cast Penny Singleton and Arthur Lake, the hackneyed plot about the urban Bumsteads helping out in a mountain lodge and Dagwood rescuing an elderly couple from losing their savings seems new and refreshing (just). As the series lurched into the forties, the freshness wore off and the plots became strained. These early flicks are, however, delightful time-passers.

Penny Singleton *Blondie* • Arthur Lake *Dagwood* • Larry Simms *Baby Dumpling* • Danny Mummert *Alvin Fuddle* • Donald Meek *Jonathan Gillis* • Elizabeth Dunne *Mrs*

Dickerson • Robert Wilcox *John Larkin* • Irving Bacon *Mailman* ■ *Dir* Frank R Strayer • *Scr* Richard Flournoy, from a story by Karen DeWolf, Robert Chapin, Richard Flournoy, from the comic strip by Chic Young

Blood Alley ★★ U

Adventure 1955 · US · Colour · 110mins

The first film to be made by John Wayne's production company, Batjac, *Blood Alley* began shooting with Robert Mitchum playing the American seafarer who leads 180 villagers in an escape from Communist William A Wellman clashed and Wayne was obliged to fire Mitchum. When Gregory Peck and Humphrey Bogart's demands for high fees were turned down, Wayne himself stepped in as Mitchum's replacement, squeezing the picture in between his honeymoon and *The Searchers*. It's a typical piece of Yellow Peril propaganda, sluggish and predictable, with Lauren Bacall and Anita Ekberg as cross-country refugees.

John Wayne *Wilder* • Lauren Bacall *Cathy* • Paul Fix *Mr Tso* • Joy Kim *Susu* • Berry Kroeger *Old Feng* • Mike Mazurki *Big Han* • Anita Ekberg *Wei Long* • Henry Nakamura *Tak* • WT Chang *Mr Han* ■ *Dir* William Wellman [William A Wellman] • *Scr* AS Fleischmann, from his novel

Blood and Sand ★★★

Silent epic 1922 · US · Tinted · 90mins

Hot on the heels of the previous year's *Four Horsemen of the Apocalypse* and *The Sheik* came this third smash hit for superstar Rudolph Valentino. This time, the first and sleekest of the screen's Latin lovers plays a matador led into temptation by a decadent vamp (Nita Naldi). Almost gored to death in the bull ring, he recovers through the tender loving care of his wife (Lila Lee). Fred Niblo's film defies modern criticism, so far are we from its exaggerated histrionics and early techniques. However, it's clear why Valentino's potent presence captured the female hearts of a generation.

Rudolph Valentino *Juan Gallardo* • Lila Lee *Carmen* • Rosa Rosanova *Senora Augustias* • George Periolat *Marquise de Guevera* • Nita Naldi *Doña Sol* • Walter Long *Plumitas* • Rosita Marstini *El Carnacione* ■ *Dir* Fred Niblo • *Scr* June Mathis, from the play *Blood and Sand* by Tom Cushing, from the novel *Sangre y Arena* by Vicente Blasco Ibanez

Blood and Sand ★★★ PG

Adventure 1941 · US · Colour · 119mins

An expensively mounted 20th Century-Fox treatment of Vicente Blasco Ibanez's famous melodramatic novel about a young matador, as sexy as forties censorship would allow. Rita Hayworth, in a star-making performance, taunts unlikely bullfighter Tyrone Power, handsome but totally miscast (and a poor substitute for Rudolph Valentino, who created the role in the 1922 silent version). Linda Darnell fumes on the sidelines, and only Alla Nazimova and Anthony Quinn emerge with acting *olés*. The pace is slow and the attitudes astoundingly naive, but there is a fine lushness and a wonderful symbolic use of Technicolor that gives the film a rare distinction, and, for admirers of Hollywood melodramas, the sheer soppiness of the whole enterprise is breathtakingly endearing.

Tyrone Power *Juan Gallardo* • Linda Darnell *Carmen Espinosa* • Rita Hayworth *Dona Sol des Muire* • Anthony Quinn *Manolo de Palma* • Alla Nazimova *Senora Augustias* • J Carrol Naish *Garabato* • John Carradine *Nacional* • Laird Cregar *Natalio Curro* • Lynn Bari *Encarnacion* ■ *Dir* Rouben Mamoulian • *Scr* Jo Swerling , from the novel *Sangre y Arena* by Vincente Blasco Ibanez • *Choreographer* Budd Boetticher

Blood and Sand ★★ 18

Drama 1989 · Sp/US · Colour · 96mins

Sharon Stone stars in the third – and weakest – screen version of Vicente Blasco Ibanez's novel. Juan (Christopher Rydell) is happily married to Carmen (Ana Torrent) and nurses a burning ambition to become a famous toreador. A rehearsal with a dangerous bull the night before a big fight backfires, and it is left to Stone, playing the stunning daughter of a Spanish landowner, to show him the ropes. Juan falls in love with her, causing his career and marriage to go down the pan. Lacking the gusto of a real bullfight, this Spanish drama is a piece of Euro-pudding nonsense.

Christopher Rydell *Juan Gallardo* • Sharon Stone *Doña Sol* • Ana Torrent *Carmen* • Antonio Flores *Chiripa* • Simon Andreu *Juan's uncle* • Albert Vidal ■ *Dir* Javier Elorrieta • *Scr* Rafael Azcona, Ricardo Franco, Thomas Fucci, from the novel *Sangre y Arena* by Vicente Blasco Ibanez

Blood and Wine ★★★ 15

Crime thriller
1996 · US/UK/Fr · Colour · 96mins

A smart, engrossing adult thriller filled with dark twists and excellent performances. Paired for the first time, Jack Nicholson and Michael Caine are supremely sleazy as a couple of businessmen/thieves who steal a costly necklace from one of wine dealer Nicholson's affluent Florida clients. They make a delicious double act: Jack is, well, Jack and Caine, with dyed black hair and an alarming cough, creates his vilest villain since *Mona Lisa*. Stephen Dorff and Jennifer Lopez offer sexy support as unwitting flies in the duo's ointment, while director Bob Rafelson stylishly juggles the complexities of characters and plot. Contains swearing and violence.

Jack Nicholson *Alex Gates* • Stephen Dorff *Jason* • Jennifer Lopez *Gabriela* • Judy Davis *Suzanne Gates* • Michael Caine *Victor Spansky* • Harold Perrineau Jr [Harold Perrineau] *Henry* • Robyn Peterson *Dina* • Mike Starr *Mike* • John Seitz *Frank* ■ *Dir* Bob Rafelson • *Scr* Nick Villiers, Alison Cross, from a story by Bob Rafelson, Nick Villiers

Blood Beach ★★

Horror 1981 · US · Colour · 89mins

What's sucking sun-worshippers and concerned locals under the sand on a south California beach? Nothing more than a stock papier-mâché monster in this workmanlike update of a formula fifties B-movie. A little atmosphere is created when heroine Mariana Hill finds the creature's lair by accident, but elsewhere director Jeffrey Bloom's first foray into the horror genre is familiar territory, all the way from harbour patrol officer David Huffman's initial disappearance to obnoxious cop Burt Young blowing the left-over *Doctor Who* beast to smithereens in a less than thrilling climax.

David Huffman *Harry Caulder* • Mariana Hill [Marianna Hill] *Catherine* • John Saxon *Captain Pearson* • Otis Young *Lieutenant Piantadosi* • Stefan Gierasch *Dr Dimitrios* • Burt Young *Sergeant Royko* • Darrell Fetty *Hoagy* ■ *Dir* Jeffrey Bloom • *Scr* Jeffrey Bloom, from a story by Steven Nalevansky, Jeffrey Bloom

The Blood Beast Terror ★

Horror 1967 · UK · Colour · 87mins

Peter Cushing considered this clumsy chiller the worst picture he ever made. In many respects he was right. He's the policeman investigating vampiristic murders carried out by a giant death's-head moth masquerading as the "daughter" of a renowned Victorian entomologist. (It must have seemed a good idea at the time!) Vernon Sewell's direction barely papers over the pedestrian cracks in an equally moth-eaten screenplay decked out with a catalogue of dodgy horror clichés.

Peter Cushing *Inspector Quennell* • Robert Flemyng *Professor Mallinger* • Wanda Ventham *Clare Mallinger* • Vanessa Howard *Meg Quennell* • Roy Hudd *Morgue attendant* • David Griffin *William* • Kevin Stoney *Grainger* • Glynn Edwards *Sergeant Allan* ■ *Dir* Vernon Sewell • *Scr* Peter Bryan

Blood Brothers ★★

Drama 1994 · US · Colour · 80mins

Also known as *Silent Witness: What a Child Saw*, this TV movie is a toned-down version of the kind of racial tension drama that emerged during the African-American new wave of the early nineties. Set in Los Angeles, it tells of the dilemma facing a young boy who knows that his brother was one of the gang responsible for the murder of a Korean couple. Director Bruce Pittman generates sufficient suspense, but there's none of the aggression or authenticity we have come to expect from more socially committed film-makers such as Spike Lee and John Singleton. Contains some violence.

Mia Korf *Carol Lee-Rembrandt* • Bill Nunn *William Crawford* • Clark Johnson *Glenn James* • Richard Chevolleau *Sylvester Crawford* • Richard Yearwood *T-Bear* • Amir Jamal Williams *Darryl Crawford* • Ron White *Archer* • Nderhu Roberts *Li'l Puppet* • Timothy D Stickney *Toke* ■ *Dir* Bruce Pittman • *Scr* Paris Qualles, from a story by Charles Rosin

Blood Feud ★

Drama 1979 · It · Colour · 112mins

In the mid-seventies, Italian director Lina Wertmuller became a sensation in America, mainly because *Seven Beauties* (1976) made her the first woman ever to be nominated for a best director Oscar. After that, Wertmüller cashed in on her fame by making increasingly pretentious films with increasingly long titles. The original title of this effort means "A Bloody Event between Two Men because of a Widow... Political Motivations Are Suspected". So there you have it. Set in Sicily at the birth of fascism, it has Marcello Mastroianni and Sophia Loren making their umpteenth film together and probably regretting every second of it. Italian dialogue dubbed into English.

Sophia Loren *Titina Paterno* • Marcello Mastroianni *Spallone* • Giancarlo Giannini *Nick* • Turi Ferro *Baron* ■ *Dir/Scr* Lina Wertmuller

Blood for Dracula ★★★ 18

Horror 1974 · It · Colour · 98mins

In contrast to this film's Andy Warhol-produced companion piece, *Flesh for Frankenstein* in 3-D, The Factory's in-house director Paul Morrissey here accents wit over gore in a clever twist on the vampire myth. Udo Kier is tragicomic as the anaemic Transylvanian Count looking for "wirgin" blood in an Italian household of females. Trouble is, sexy handyman Joe Dallesandro keeps deflowering his prospective prey. Heavy bloodshed is lightened by the consistently humorous tone of the tale, which hilariously ends with Kier having his arms and legs hacked off. Directors Vittorio De Sica and Roman Polanski put in telling cameos in this funny fang farce.

Joe Dallesandro *Mario* • Udo Kier *Dracula* • Vittorio De Sica *Marquis* • Maxime McKendry *Marquisa* • Arno Juerging *Anton* • Milena Vukotic *Esmeralda* • Dominique Darel *Saphiria* • Stefania Casini *Rubinia* • Roman Polanski • Vittorio De Sica ■ *Dir/Scr* Paul Morrissey • *Producer* Carlo Ponti, Andy Warhol

Blood from the Mummy's Tomb ★★★ 15

Horror 1971 · UK · Colour · 89mins

Statuesque Valerie Leon is possessed by the spirit of an ancient Egyptian queen in a cult Hammer horror based on Bram Stoker's *The Jewel of Seven Stars*. With hardly a bandage in sight, director Seth Holt tried to radically rethink the mummy genre, and largely succeeded in creating a fascinating fantasy with a uniquely menacing atmosphere dripping in delicious irony. Sadly, Holt died during shooting; Hammer boss Michael Carreras took over and the film is not as interesting as it should have been. The same story was the basis for *The Awakening* in 1980.

Andrew Keir *Professor Fuchs* • Valerie Leon *Margaret/Tera* • James Villiers *Corbeck* • Hugh Burden *Dandridge* • George Coulouris *Berigan* • Mark Edwards *Tod Browning* • Rosalie Crutchley *Helen Dickerson* • Aubrey Morris *Dr Putnum* • David Markham *Dr Burgess* ■ *Dir* Seth Holt, Michael Carreras • *Scr* Christopher Wicking, from the novel *The Jewel of Seven Stars* by Bram Stoker

Blood, Guts, Bullets & Octane ★★ 15

Action comedy 1997 · US · Colour · 86mins

A wordy title for a wordy film. This quirky, Tarantino-type thriller is about two motor-mouthed used car salesmen who get embroiled in a bizarre plot to smuggle rare blood supplies across the Mexican/American border. The film starts strongly, with some super-fast one-take talk scenes that are neatly scripted and cleverly acted. Once the plot kicks in, though, it is marked by the irritating and wilful quirkiness that mars so many independent movies. Interest is maintained, at least, by snappy direction and oodles of oddball plot twists. But somehow this is rather

164

U = SUITABLE FOR ALL Uc = SUITABLE FOR ALL, ESPECIALLY FOR YOUNG CHILDREN (VIDEO ONLY) PG = PARENTAL GUIDANCE

less than the sum of its parts. Contains swearing and violence.

Mike Maas *Victor Drub* • Nick Fenske *Mechanic* • Mark Priolo *Frank Priolo* • Joe Carnahan *Sid French* • Andrew Fowler *Mike Carbuyer* • Gloria Gomez *Julie Carbuyer* • Dan Leis *Bob Melba* • Josephine Arreola *Elda* ■ *Dir/Scr* Joe Carnahan

Blood In Blood Out ★★ 18

Drama 1992 · US · Colour · 172mins

Co-written by poet Jimmy Santiago Baca, this is based on his real-life experiences. Director Taylor Hackford blunts his treatise on the cultural ties that bind through excessive length and off-putting violence. Three Chicano cousins take the viewer on a gruelling journey through the Latino experience, as they go from the gang-run streets of East LA to the brutal inter-racial confines of San Quentin prison. The unknown leads turn in strong performances and Hackford intermittently packs the sermonising saga with a powerfully emotional punch. But, despite it oozing unquestionable integrity, the profound often becomes ponderous through overstatement.

Damian Chapa *Miklo* • Jesse Borrego *Cruz* • Benjamin Bratt *Paco* • Enrique J Castillo [Enrique Castillo] *Montana* • Victor Rivers *Magic Mike* • Delroy Lindo *Bonafide* • Tom Towles *Red Ryder* • Carlos Carrasco *Popeye* ■ *Dir* Taylor Hackford • *Scr* Jimmy Santiago Baca, Jeremy Iacone, Floyd Mutrux, from a story by Ross Thomas

Blood Money ★★

Martial arts western
1974 · It/HK/Sp · Colour · 99mins

Run Run Shaw, one of the key figures in Hong Kong cinema, produced this unappetising mix of spaghetti western and chop-socky action movie. Lee Van Cleef snarls in the accustomed manner as a bounty hunter seeking four women who have the clues to buried treasure tattooed on their bodies. However, Italian director Antonio Margheriti (billed under the pseudonym Anthony M Dawson) struggles to sustain the blistering pace expected of a martial-arts movie. That said, he doesn't shy away from the brutality of the fight sequences, which are definitely not for the faint-hearted.

Lee Van Cleef *Dakota* • Lo Lieh *Wang Ho Kiang* • Karen Yeh *Yeh Ling Chih/Lia Hua* • Julian Ugarte *Deacon Yancy Hobbitt* • Goyo Peralta *Indio* • Al Tung *Wang* ■ *Dir* Anthony M Dawson [Antonio Margheriti] • *Scr* Barth Jules Sussman

Blood Money ★★★

Crime thriller 1980 · Ausl · Colour · 63mins

Bryan Brown never quite gets the proper credit for performances such as this one. Perhaps it's because he appears so often in movies from Australia that we get used to his presence (just like Chips Rafferty in the past). Yet this can be counted as one of his most notable Australian films. He's a former international criminal who returns Down Under to try to redeem his name and die with dignity. But even such a simple endeavour causes problems, both legal and emotional. Christopher Fitchett directs, Chrissie James is the girl who's unconvinced by the crook's best endeavours, while John Flaus is the man who believes him – but doesn't care. This is short but poignant in what it has to say – especially when Bryan Brown says it.

John Flaus *Pete Shields* • Bryan Brown *Brian Shields* • Chrissie James *Jeannie Shields* • Peter Stratford *Curtis* • Peter Curtain *Dan* • Sue Jones *Doctor* • John Proper *Jack* ■ *Dir* Christopher Fitchett • *Scr* Christopher Fitchett, John Ruane, Ellery Ryan

Blood Money ★★ 15

Political thriller 1988 · US · Colour · 90mins

This sweaty, muddled political thriller is notable mainly for the presence of two actors on the cusp of stardom: Andy Garcia and Ellen Barkin. Garcia is a petty crook who gets way out of his depth when he starts sniffing around a scheme to smuggle guns to the Contra rebels in Nicaragua. The star is a touch over-the-top, but Barkin is sympathetic as a prostitute who also gets caught up in the plot. There is also an impressive supporting turn from Morgan Freeman, another star of the future.

Andy Garcia *Clinton Dillard* • Ellen Barkin *Nadine Powers* • Morgan Freeman *Dorsey Pratt* • Michael Lombard *James Conrad* • John C McGinley *Turner* • Brad Sullivan *General John Anson* • Alan North *Detective Rayburn* ■ *Dir* Jerry Schatzberg • *Scr* Robert Foster

Blood Money ★★ 18

Thriller 1996 · US · Colour · 88mins

A flimsily plotted crime thriller that comes in at under 90 minutes but feels considerably longer. James Brolin, Billy Drago and Traci Lords head exactly the sort of cast you'd expect to find in thick-ear stuff of this sort, though it's hard to imagine anyone doing much with such dire scripting and clueless direction. The action sequences are watchable, but they're nothing to write home about. Contains swearing, sexual situations and violence.

James Brolin *Lieutenant Kincaid* • Traci Lords *Wendy Monroe* • Billy Drago *Agent Pierce* • Dean Tarrolly *Stuart/Hank* • Sonny Carl Davis *Lester Grisam* • Katherine Armstrong *Cindy* • Bentley Mitchum *Dexter* ■ *Dir* John Shepphird • *Scr* Steve Jankowski, John Shepphird

Blood Oath ★★★★ 15

Courtroom drama
1990 · Ausl · Colour · 103mins

Before he took to commercials as a car tout, Bryan Brown was a considerable lean and leathery presence in Australian movies, notably in this courtroom drama in which he's the Aussie officer prosecuting an Oxford-educated Japanese commander (George Takei) for war crimes. His task is complicated by Americans wanting a "not guilty" verdict for reasons of political expediency. Brown's role is based on the experiences of the father of co-scriptwriter Brian A Williams, and Brown brings a sardonic edge to the search for motives. Contains violence and swearing.

Bryan Brown *Captain Robert Cooper* • George Takei *Vice-Admiral Baron Takahashi* • Terry O'Quinn *Major Tom Beckett* • John Bach *Major Frank Roberts* • Toshi Shioya *Lieutenant Hideo Tanaka* • John Clarke *Mike Sheedy* • Deborah Unger [Deborah Kara Unger] *Sister Carol Littell* • Jason Donovan *Private Talbot* • Russell Crowe *Lieutenant Jack Corbett* ■ *Dir* Stephen Wallace • *Scr* Denis Whitburn, Brian A Williams

The Blood of a Poet ★★★ PG

Experimental drama 1930 · Fr · BW · 49mins

Jean Cocteau's first film – made when he was 41, his fame already established as a writer, poet and artist – follows the dream-like encounters and observations of a young poet as he views the world on the other side of a mirror. Highly experimental and devoid of any conventional narrative, the film offers a series of arresting images (executions, hermaphrodites, opium smokers), and exerted a strong influence on the American avant garde. The surreal symbolism is inaccessible to the majority of viewers, however, who are more likely to appreciate Cocteau's ravishing *La Belle et la Bête*, made 16 years later. In French with English subtitles.

Lee Miller *The statue* • Pauline Carton *Child's tutor* • Odette Talazac • Enrico Rivero *The poet* • Jean Desbordes *The friend in Louis XV costume* • Fernand Dichamps • Lucien Jager • Féral Benga *The black angel* • Barbette *Spectator in lodge* • Jean Cocteau *Narrator* ■ *Dir/Scr* Jean Cocteau • *Cinematographer* Georges Périnal

Blood of Dracula ★★

Horror 1957 · US · BW · 69mins

Although a routine fifties' "schlock 'n' roller", this female counterpart to *I Was a Teenage Werewolf* is great drive-in movie trash. As is so often the case in these morality-tinged horrors, carnal thoughts equal out-of-control monsterhood, as staid college girl Sandra Harrison turns tramp vamp when hypnotised by a magic amulet owned by her evil chemistry teacher. The solemn intensity Harrison brings to her ludicrous tight-sweater role is a joy to behold. And so is her undead "babe" look. She can hardly close her mouth for fangs and surely she can't have enough combs for all that facial hair! A scream, but not quite in the way anyone intended.

Sandra Harrison *Nancy Perkins* • Louise Lewis *Miss Branding* • Gail Ganley *Myra* • Jerry Blaine *Tab* • Heather Ames *Nola* • Malcolm Atterbury *Lieutenant Dunlap* • Mary Adams *Mrs Thorndyke* • Thomas B Henry [Thomas Browne Henry] *Mr Perkins* • Don Devlin *Eddie* ■ *Dir* Herbert L Strock • *Scr* Ralph Thornton

Blood of Dracula's Castle ★

Gothic horror 1967 · US · Colour · 84mins

This dreadful attempt by exploitation maverick Al Adamson to update the Dracula myth finds high-class vampires Alex D'Arcy and Paula Raymond living in a castle in modern California. A half-wit hunchback keeps the cellar stocked with nubile victims, who are drained of blood for gruesome cocktail hours and occasionally sacrificed to the god Luna. Even by Adamson's half-baked horror standards, this is a rock-bottom cheapie, which displays his moribund penchant for S&M-tinged tacky terror.

John Carradine *George* • Paula Raymond *Countess Townsend* • Alex D'Arcy *Count Townsend* • Robert Dix *Johnny* • Gene O'Shane *Glen Cannon* • Barbara Bishop *Liz* ■ *Dir* Al Adamson • *Scr* Rex Carlton

The Blood of Fu Manchu ★★ 15

Horror
1968 · US/UK/Sp/W Ger · Colour · 89mins

Actually more like a western, thanks to its Brazilian setting and bandit subplot, the fourth outing for Christopher Lee as Sax Rohmer's insidious Oriental is cheaply made horror exotica. Lee's stiff performance doesn't help the daft story, as Fu Manchu endows ten gorgeous girls with the "kiss of death" via an Inca poison deadly only to the male and programmes them to kill any influential power-broker who touches their passionate lips. *Goldfinger* beauty Shirley Eaton is chief amongst these black widows in hack director Jess Franco's easy-on-the-eye, even easier on the brain horror travesty. Contains some violence and mild swearing.

Christopher Lee *Fu Manchu* • George Gotz *Carl Janson* • Richard Greene *Nayland Smith* • Howard Marion-Crawford *Dr Petrie* • Tsai Chin *Lin Tang* • Maria Rohm *Ursula* • Shirley Eaton *Black Widow* ■ *Dir* Jess Franco [Jesus Franco] • *Scr* Harry Alan Towers

The Blood of Others ★★ 15

Second World War drama
1984 · Can/Fr · Colour · 130mins

Adapted from the novel by Simone De Beauvoir, and with additional dialogue by the Irish-Canadian author, Brian Moore, this wartime drama efficiently captures the claustrophobic paranoia of Occupied Paris, without ever involving us in the fate of its protagonists. Torn between her loyalty to imprisoned Resistance fighterMichael Ontkean and a love of luxury that draws her towards pro-Nazi businessman, Sam Neill, Jodie Foster gives one of her least credible performances. The supporting cast, including such stalwarts as Stéphane Audran and Micheline Presle, is disappointingly marginalised.

Jodie Foster *Hélène* • Michael Ontkean *Jean Blomart* • Sam Neill *Bergman* • Lambert Wilson *Paul* • Stéphane Audran *Gigi* • Jean-Pierre Aumont *AndréBlomart* • Micheline Presle *Denise* ■ *Dir* Claude Chabrol • *Scr* Brian Moore, from the novel *Le Sang des Autres* by Simone de Beauvoir

Blood of the Vampire ★★

Horror 1958 · UK · Colour · 85mins

Universal nabbed Hammer's gore theatrics along with their resident scriptwriter, Jimmy Sangster, in the effort to beat the House of Horror at their own game. The result is enjoyable hokum with, for the era, some edgily gruesome torture chamber scenes . Thespian legend Sir Donald Wolfit goes predictably over the top as Doctor Callistratus, who needs blood to stay alive and uses victims from his insane asylum for the grisly transfusion purpose. Hammer heroine Barbara Shelley adds the glamour, while Victor Maddern wears the daftest make-up imaginable as Carl, the scarred cripple servant of the mad doctor. Serviceable shocks pepper the crisp period atmosphere, neatly laced with an ever-present sense of doom.

Donald Wolfit *Dr Callistratus* • Vincent Ball *Dr John Pierre* • Barbara Shelley *Madeleine* • Victor Maddern *Carl* • William Devlin *Kurt Urah* • Andrew Faulds *Wetzler* • Hal Osmond *Sneak*

thief • Bernard Bresslaw *Sneak thief* • John Le Mesurier *Chief Justice* ■ *Dir* Henry Cass • *Scr* Jimmy Sangster

Blood on My Hands ★★

Crime drama 1948 · US · BW · 77mins

Originally released as *Kiss the Blood off My Hands*, the lurid title of its source novel, this downbeat melodrama was star Burt Lancaster's first stab at being involved in production through the company named after his wife, Norma Productions. Set in a Hollywood studio re-creation of postwar London, it stars Lancaster as the violent war veteran who accidentally kills a man in a pub and goes on the run. He's blackmailed by a witness (played with exaggerated relish by Robert Newton) and befriended by a nurse (Joan Fontaine in her most sensitive mode). Despite some visual flair from Norman Foster's direction and Russell Metty's photography, plus one of Miklos Rozsa's best scores, this is mostly tedious and unbelievable.

Joan Fontaine *Jane Wharton* • Burt Lancaster *Bill Saunders* • Robert Newton *Harry Carter* • Lewis L Russell *Tom Widgery* • Aminta Dyne *Landlady* • Grizelda Hervey *Mrs Paton* • Jay Novello *Sea captain* • Colin Keith-Johnston *Judge* ■ *Dir* Norman Foster • *Scr* Leonardo Bercovici, Walter Bernstein, Hugh Gray, Ben Maddow, from the novel *Kiss the Blood off My Hands* by Gerald Butler

Blood on Satan's Claw ★★★

Horror 1970 · UK · Colour · 100mins

Devil-worshipping children in 17th-century England cause havoc for their local village community in this super-stylish supernatural shocker with a strong period flavour. While this is more sensational, violent and crude than its obvious model *Witchfinder General*, Piers Haggard's tense direction keeps the cauldron of fiendish orgies, demonic tortures and Linda Hayden's sultry turn as the devil's advocate bubbling at an even terror temperature until the satanic slow-motion climax. Vintage British horror at its lip-smacking, exploitative best.

Patrick Wymark *Judge* • Linda Hayden *Angel* • Barry Andrews *Ralph* • Michele Dotrice *Margaret* • Wendy Padbury *Cathy* • Anthony Ainley *Reverend Fallowfield* • Charlotte Mitchell *Ellen* • Tamara Ustinov *Rosalind* ■ *Dir* Piers Haggard • *Scr* Robert Wynne

Blood on the Moon ★★★ U

Western 1948 · US · BW · 87mins

If there's such a thing as "western *noir*", then this is it, as editor-turned-director Robert Wise and distinguished black-and-white photographer Nicholas Musuraca team up again (following 1944's *The Curse of the Cat People*) for this psychological take on the genre. Robert Mitchum brings some weighty experience to his role as a drifter forced to turn against his one-time mentor (an oily Robert Preston before his Broadway stardom). The mood is satisfyingly dark. The actual confrontation scene is masterly, set in a saloon where light only leaks through sporadically, and there's a protracted chase across snowy, clearly studio-located mountains. Indeed, there's no real sense of the wide west, just deep internal conflicts, which give way to a violence that's surprising for the time.

Robert Mitchum *Jim Garry* • Barbara Bel Geddes *Amy Lufton* • Robert Preston *Tate Riling* • Walter Brennan *Kris Barden* • Phyllis Thaxter *Carol Lufton* • Frank Faylen *Jake Pindalest* • Tom Tully *John Lufton* • Charles McGraw *Milo Sweet* ■ *Dir* Robert Wise • *Scr* Willie Hayward, from an adaptation by Harold Shumate of the novel *Gunman's Chance* by Luke Short

Blood on the Sun ★★★ PG

Drama 1945 · US · BW · 93mins

The Cagney brothers chose a formidable subject for their second independent production, with Bill producing and Jimmy starring as an aggressive editor of an American newspaper in Tokyo, who daringly publishes the Japanese Master Plan for world domination. This doesn't go down too well with Colonel Tojo, nor did the film with the public when it was released. As scripted by blacklisted left-wing Hollywood Ten veteran Lester Cole, the movie packs a powerhouse message, appropriate in its day and still worth heeding. But the propaganda content overwhelms the drama and, despite the valiant efforts of Cagney, Sylvia Sidney and Robert Armstrong (*King Kong*), the melodrama doesn't really catch fire. Today it's more than interesting for its subject matter and the Cagneys' choice of director, Frank Lloyd. DVD

James Cagney *Nick Condon* • Sylvia Sidney *Iris Hilliard* • Wallace Ford *Ollie Miller* • Rosemary De Camp *Edith Miller* • Robert Armstrong *Colonel Tojo* • John Emery *Premier Tanaka* • Leonard Strong *Hijikata* • Frank Puglia *Prince Tatsugi* • John Halloran *Captain Oshima* ■ *Dir* Frank Lloyd • *Scr* Lester Cole, from a story by Garrett Fort

Blood Orange ★★

Crime 1953 · UK · BW · 80mins

Made for Hammer's B-movie outlet, Exclusive, this is an unremarkable offering from director Terence Fisher, who went on to make some of the studio's best horrors. Jan Read's tepid story about a retired FBI agent who gets involved with jewel thieves following the murder of model Delphi Lawrence gives him little to work with. The real problem, however, is Tom Conway's lacklustre performance. Almost a decade after he scored in Val Lewton's RKO chillers and took over from brother George Sanders in the *Falcon* series, he looks like a man interested only in his pay cheque.

Tom Conway *Conway* • Mila Parely *Helen Pascall* • Naomi Chance *Gina* • Eric Pohlmann *Mercedes* • Andrew Osborn *Captain Simpson* • Richard Wattis *Macleod* • Margaret Halstan *Lady Marchant* • Eileen Way *Fernande* • Delphi Lawrence *Chelsea* ■ *Dir* Terence Fisher • *Scr* Jan Read

The Blood Oranges ★

Erotic drama 1997 · US · Colour · 93mins

Unintentionally hilarious, this is another peepshow masquerading as a profound statement from Philip Haas, director of the far more interesting – if equally daft – *Angels and Insects*. Sheryl Lee and Charles Dance are holidaying hippies who tempt another couple into a sexual foursome. Soon the usual mix of jealousy and dark secrets ruin their blood-orange strewn love nest. Even the uncomfortable two leads look embarrassed having to utter such ridiculous dialogue as "tasting the love lunch". Overlong, self-indulgent and completely unconvincing, this deeply dippy, nonsense gives art movies a bad name.

Charles Dance *Cyril* • Sheryl Lee *Fiona* • Laila Robins *Catherine* • Colin Lane *Hugh* • Rachael Bella *Meredith* • Aida Lopez *Rosella* ■ *Dir* Philip Haas • *Scr* Philip Haas, Belinda Haas, from the novel by John Hawkes

Blood Red ★ 15

Period action drama
1988 · US · Colour · 87mins

Immigrant Sicilian grape farmers try to stop tycoon Dennis Hopper from building a railroad through the Napa Valley wine country of the late 19th century in this weak action adventure with low production values. It's interesting for two reasons: future Hollywood superstar Julia Roberts makes her screen debut; and it's the only film she's ever made with her brother Eric (she plays his sister). The supporting cast is above average with Burt Young, Giancarlo Giannini and Susan Anspach holding their own against an over-ripe script that quickly withers on the vine.

Eric Roberts *Marco Collogero* • Giancarlo Giannini *Sebastian Collogero* • Dennis Hopper *William Bradford Berrigan* • Burt Young *Andrews* • Carlin Glynn *Miss Jeffreys* • Lara Harris *Angelica* • Francesca De Sapio *Rosa Collogero* • Julia Roberts *Maria Collogero* • Michael Madsen *Enzio* • Elias Koteas *Silvio* ■ *Dir* Peter Masterson • *Scr* Ron Cutler

Blood Relatives ★★★ 18

Crime drama 1977 · Can/Fr · Colour · 90mins

Adapted from an Ed McBain novel, this is directed by the French master Claude Chabrol with a sharp eye for the middle-class hypocrisies of a Canadian community. Donald Sutherland is the detective investigating the assault and murder of a young Montreal girl, with accusations and confessions flying thick and fast, though it's only in the film's final section that there's any real tension. The rest of the drama is – astonishingly for Chabrol – actually a little wooden and flat. Contains violence and swearing. DVD

Donald Sutherland *Steve Carella* • Aude Landry *Patricia Lowery* • Lisa Langlois *Muriel* • Laurent Malet *Andy Lowery* • Stéphane Audran *Mrs Lowery* • Donald Pleasence *Doniac* • David Hemmings *Jack Armstrong* • Walter Massey *Mr Lowery* ■ *Dir* Claude Chabrol • *Scr* Claude Chabrol, Sydney Banks, from the novel by Evan Hunter [Ed McBain]

Blood River ★★ PG

Western 1991 · US · Colour · 88mins

John Carpenter's long-gestating western script finally surfaced here as a TV movie, a vehicle for the now grown-up Rick Schroder (formerly little Ricky, who starred in the 1979 tear-jerker *The Champ*) and loveable character actor Wilford Brimley. Surprisingly, for such an avowed devotee of western maestro Howard Hawks, there's little real substance to Carpenter's screenplay, at least as realised by director Mel Damski. Still, there's a welcome guest appearance by Adrienne Barbeau and some likeable minor characters. One for John Carpenter completists – and probably that's about its only audience.

Rick Schroder *Perls* • Wilford Brimley *Culler* • John P Ryan *Logan* • Mills Watson *Jake* • Henry Beckman *Sheriff Webber* • Dwight McFee *Squints* • Adrienne Barbeau *Georgina* ■ *Dir* Mel Damski • *Scr* John Carpenter

Blood Simple ★★★★ 18

Thriller 1983 · US · Colour · 94mins

A jealous Texas husband hires a sleazy private eye to murder his adulterous wife and her lover in the Coen Brothers' feature debut. Blending elements of James M Cain, *film noir*, Hitchcock thrillers and contemporary horror movies, this dark morality tale deviates imaginatively from the forties' murder mysteries it evokes. The acting is first rate (the long road to Frances McDormand's Oscar for *Fargo* started here) and the atmosphere appropriately brooding. The Coens' use of light and space is impressive, and the innovative camera work (by *Men in Black* director Barry Sonnenfeld) to increase the suspense is breathtaking. A modern classic. Contains violence, swearing and sex scenes.

John Getz *Ray* • Frances McDormand *Abby* • Dan Hedaya *Julian Marty* • M Emmet Walsh *Visser* • Samm-Art Williams *Maurice* • Deborah Neumann *Debra* • Raquel Gavia *Landlady* • Van Brooks *Man from Lubbock* ■ *Dir* Joel Coen • *Scr* Ethan Coen, Joel Coen • *Cinematographer* Barry Sonnenfeld

Blood Ties ★★ 15

Horror thriller 1991 · US · Colour · 89mins

This ordinary horror thriller, in which a family of vampires unleashes its power on a centuries-old enemy that's threatening its very existence, marked director Jim McBride's entry into the world of the TV movie. Sadly, the fizz and style that distinguish McBride's earlier feature films, such as *Breathless*, *The Big Easy* and *Great Balls of Fire!*, are missing here, and this lacklustre effort is never more than predictable. Contains some violence and swearing.

Harley Venton *Harry Martin* • Kim Johnston-Ulrich *Amy Lawrence* • Michelle Johnson *Celia* • Jason London *Cody Puckett* • Patrick Bauchau *Eli Chelarin* • Salvator Xuereb *Butch* • Bo Hopkins *Chief Hunter* • Michael C Gwynne *Marvin* • Grace Zabriskie *The woman* ■ *Dir* Jim McBride • *Scr* Richard Shapiro

Blood Wedding ★★★★ U

Dance drama 1981 · Sp · Colour · 70mins

Setting the minimalist tone that persisted through *Carmen* and *El Amor Brujo*, the first of Carlos Saura's "flamenco trilogy" is an exhilarating blend of passionate choreography and rhythmic camerawork. By setting the action on a bare stage with the minimum of props, Saura focuses our attention on the intricacy and symbolism of the dance. As well as designing the flamboyant routines, Antonio Gades stars as one of the troupe rehearsing a musical version of the celebrated play by Federico Garcia Lorca, in which a jilted husband pursues the wife who abandoned him

at the altar. In Spanish with English subtitles. ▭

Antonio Gades *Leonardo* • Cristina Hoyos *Bride* • Juan Antonio Jimenez *Groom* • Pilar Cardenas *Mother* • Carmen Villena *Wife* • Pepe Blanco *Wedding guest* • Lario Diaz *Wedding guest* • Enrique Esteve *Wedding guest* ■ *Dir* Carlos Saura • *Scr* Carlos Saura, from a play by Federico Garcia Lorca • *Choreographer* Antonio Gades • *Cinematographer* Teo Escamilla

Bloodbath at the House of Death ★ 18

Horror comedy 1983 · UK · Colour · 87mins

Lampoons of everything from *Carrie* and *ET* to *Star Wars* and *Friday the 13th* are dragged screaming through this painfully thin comedy starring Kenny Everett and Pamela Stephenson as paranormal researchers investigating Vincent Price's devil-worshipping cult at Headstone Manor. Nothing more than an excuse for Everett and his chums to indulge in low-grade lavatorial humour and fart jokes with gory punchlines, this sad embarrassment makes even the worst *Carry On* film look like a masterpiece. In the best possible taste? Hardly! ▭

Kenny Everett *Dr Lucas Mandeville* • Pamela Stephenson *Dr Barbara Coyle* • Vincent Price *Sinister man* • Gareth Hunt *Elliot Broome* • Don Warrington *Stephen Wilson* • John Fortune *John Harrison* • Sheila Steafel *Sheila Finch* • John Stephen Hill *Henry Noland* • Cleo Rocos *Deborah Kedding* • Barry Cryer *Police inspector* • Ray Cameron *Policeman* ■ *Dir* Ray Cameron • *Scr* Ray Cameron, Barry Cryer

Bloodbrothers ★★

Drama 1978 · US · Colour · 116mins

Richard Gere is surprisingly good in the unlikely role of aspiring social worker Stony DeCoco in this familiar tale of conflict in an Italian-American family. Gere wants to work with children but Dad (Tony LoBianco) and appropriately named uncle Chubby (Paul Sorvino) want him to stay in the macho world of construction. Unfortunately, any insights are diverted by way of narrative short cuts, though it's interesting to see how good Gere was before he became a big name. Director Robert Mulligan re-cut this for TV, which is probably where it belongs.

Paul Sorvino *Chubby DeCoco* • Tony LoBianco *Tommy DeCoco* • Richard Gere *Stony DeCoco* • Lelia Goldoni *Marie* • Yvonne Wilder *Phyllis* • Kenneth McMillan *Banion* • Floyd Levine *Doctor Harris* • Marilu Henner *Annette* ■ *Dir* Robert Mulligan • *Scr* Walter Newman, from the novel by Richard Price

Bloodfist ★ 18

Martial arts action
1989 · US · Colour · 82mins

Three times world kickboxing champion Don "The Dragon" Wilson plays it safe in his first major role cast as – yes, you've guessed it – a kickboxer who travels from Los Angeles to Manila to avenge the death of his brother by competing in a fight tournament. Director Terence H Winkless offers nothing new to the martial-arts genre, serving up uninspired fight sequences with the stunt guys missing each other's jaws by miles. This must rank even below a poor Chuck Norris or Jean-Claude Van Damme vehicle. Although Wilson demonstrates little

screen presence, he went on to star in all of the *Bloodfist* sequels. ▭

Don "The Dragon" Wilson *Jake Raye* • Joe Mari Avellana *Kwong* • Michael Shaner *Baby Davies* • Riley Bowman *Nancy* • Rob Kaman *Raton* • Billy Blanks *Black Rose* • Kris Aguilar *Chin Woo* • Vic Diaz *Detective* ■ *Dir* Terence H Winkless • *Scr* Robert King

Bloodhounds of Broadway ★★★ U

Musical 1952 · US · Colour · 89mins

This enjoyable 20th Century-Fox musical, gives the marvellous Mitzi Gaynor the chance to sing such super numbers as *I Wish I Knew*, in a whirl of Damon Runyon-inspired nonsense. Another Mitzi vies for screen time, however – comedian Mitzi Green, who shines in support. Gaynor's co-star is *Johnny Guitar* tough guy Scott Brady, and watch out for a typecast Charles Buchinski (later Charles Bronson). This was remade in 1989 with an all-star cast including Madonna and Matt Dillon, but that film only received a limited release. This version is both breezier and bawdier, and much closer to Runyon in spirit. ▭

Mitzi Gaynor *Emily Ann Stackerlee* • Scott Brady *Numbers Foster* • Mitzi Green *Tessie Sammis* • Marguerite Chapman *Yvonne* • Michael O'Shea *Inspector McNamara* • Wally Vernon *Poorly Sammis* • Henry Slate *Dave the Dude* • George E Stone *Ropes McGonigle* ■ *Dir* Harmon Jones • *Scr* Sy Gomberg, from the short stories by Damon Runyon

Bloodhounds of Broadway ★★ PG

Comedy drama 1989 · US · Colour · 83mins

Not to be confused with the (better) 1952 musical of the same name, this is an adaptation of a collection of short stories by Damon Runyon. Set in New York on New Year's Eve, 1928, it traces the ins and outs of a group of Mafia gangsters and their molls. Madonna, Jennifer Grey, Matt Dillon, Randy Quaid and Rutger Hauer star, but even their combined efforts fail to make Howard Brookner's film anything more than a lacklustre amalgam of tales and cabaret. Compared to *The Cotton Club*, it's paste to a Tiffany diamond. ▭

Josef Sommer *Waldo Winchester* • Madonna *Hortense Hathaway* • Tony Azito *Waiter* • Jennifer Grey *Lovey Lou* • Tony Longo *Crunch Sweeney* • Rutger Hauer *The Brain* • Matt Dillon *Regret* • Stephen McHattie *Red Henry* • Randy Quaid *Feet Samuels* • Steve Buscemi *Whining Willie* ■ *Dir* Howard Brookner • *Scr* Howard Brookner, Colman deKay, from the short stories by Damon Runyon

Bloodknot ★★

Thriller 1995 · US · Colour · 98mins

The idea of an opportunist exploiting a bereaved family was well depicted by Barbara Stanwyck's deception in *No Man of Her Own* and is one that occasionally hits the headlines in real life. So don't be too surprised to see cupboards disgorging skeletons at an alarming rate once stranger Kate Vernon has convinced the grieving Margot Kidder that she is the heartbroken girlfriend of Kidder's son, who has been killed in a military accident. Patrick Dempsey and Craig Sheffer give the supporting cast some

clout, but it's the vicious Vernon who hogs centre stage. This was a step up for director Jorge Montesi after the previous year's *Omen IV: the Awakening* but not much of one. Contains violence, swearing, sex scenes and nudity.

Margot Kidder *Evelyn Reeves* • Patrick Dempsey *Tom* • Kate Vernon *Kay Everett* • Craig Sheffer *Mike* • Krista Bridges *Julie* • Allan Royal *Arthur* ■ *Dir* Jorge Montesi • *Scr* Randy Kornfield

Bloodline ★★ 18

Mystery melodrama
1979 · US/W Ger · Colour · 111mins

An anaemic script pumps little in the way of drama into this tedious thriller, adapted from Sidney Sheldon's novel. Audrey Hepburn is the heiress to a pharmaceutical conglomerate, who takes control of the company only to find that she's in fear for her life. James Mason, Ben Gazzara and Omar Sharif try for some smoothly silken menace, but it comes across as hair-shirt denim. Ennio Morricone's music is probably best appreciated without the accompanying dialogue. ▭

Audrey Hepburn *Elizabeth Roffe* • Ben Gazzara *Rhys Williams* • James Mason *Sir Alec Nichols* • Claudia Mori *Donatella* • Irene Papas *Simonetta Palazzi* • Michelle Phillips *Vivian Nichols* • Maurice Ronet *Charles Martin* • Romy Schneider *Helene Martin* • Omar Sharif *Ivo Palazzi* ■ *Dir* Terence Young • *Scr* Laird Koenig, from the novel by Sidney Sheldon

Bloodsport ★★ 18

Martial arts action
1988 · US · Colour · 88mins

This is the one that consolidated Jean-Claude Van Damme's standing in the martial-arts film world and was a big UK video hit. Loosely based on a true story, it stars Van Damme as the first western fighter to enter a lethal martial-arts tournament in Hong Kong. The always frightening Bolo Yeung is the man standing in his way. The Belgian star unsurprisingly merits even fewer acting plaudits than usual (it was early on in his career), but director Newt Arnold wisely concentrates on the increasingly violent bouts. ▭

Jean-Claude Van Damme *Frank Dux* • Donald Gibb *Ray Jackson* • Leah Ayres *Janice* • Norman Burton *Helmer* • Forest Whitaker *Rawlins* • Roy Chiao *Senzo "Tiger" Tanaka* • Philip Chan *Captain Chen* • Pierre Rafini *Young Frank* • Bolo Yeung *Chong Li* ■ *Scr* Sheldon Lettich, Christopher Cosby, Mel Friedman, from a story by Sheldon Lettich

Bloodsport II: The Next Kumite ★★ 18

Martial arts action
1996 · US · Colour · 82mins

The original *Bloodsport* catapulted Jean-Claude Van Damme to stardom, but the sequel didn't do the same for fellow biffer Daniel Bernhardt. He plays a gentleman thief who ends up in a Thai jail and discovers that his only passport out is to fight in the legendary *kumite*, a last-man-standing martial arts championship. In an unusual role reversal, James Hong plays his patient teacher, while Pat Morita (*The Karate Kid*) is a villainous millionaire. There's plenty of bone-crunching action, but the plotting and

acting is strictly average. Another sequel followed. ▭ *DVD*

Daniel Bernhardt *Alex* • Pat Morita *Leung* • Donald Gibb *Tiny* • Lori Lynn Dickerson *Janine* • Philip Tan *John* • James Hong *Sun* • Nick Hill *Sergio* • Ron Hall *Cliff* ■ *Dir* Alan Mehrez • *Scr* Jeff Schechter

Bloodsuckers ★★ 18

Horror 1970 · US · Colour · 73mins

Based on Simon Raven's cult novel *Doctors Wear Scarlet*, this rare oddity clearly fails to surmount its numerous production problems. The low budget ran out in Cyprus and planned re-shoots never happened, so it was hastily patchworked together and subsequently disowned by horror maestro director Robert Hartford-Davis, who signed it Michael Burrowes. Yet flashes of imagination shine through the fiasco as Patrick Macnee helps doomed starlet Imogen Hassall save her fiancé Patrick Mower from Greek satanists. Vampirism being an extension of sexual perversion is one of the potent issues raised in this horror collector's curio.

Patrick Macnee *Major Derek Longbow* • Peter Cushing *Dr Goodrich* • Alex Davion *Tony Seymour* • Patrick Mower *Richard Fountain* • Imogen Hassall *Chriseis Constandindi* • Johnny Sekka *Bob Kirby* • Madeline Hinde *Penelope* • Edward Woodward *Holmstrom* • William Mervyn *Honeydew* ■ *Dir* Michael Burrowes [Robert Hartford-Davis] • *Scr* Julian More, from the novel *Doctors Wear Scarlet* by Simon Raven

Bloody Angels ★★★ 18

Crime thriller 1998 · Nor/UK · Colour · 99mins

An Oslo detective travels to a snowbound backwater to investigate a killing in Karin Julsrud's dour thriller, which, like Erik Skjoldbjaerg's *Insomnia*, uses the forbidding Scandinavian landscape to underpin its *Deliverance*-style tale. With his flash Jag and open contempt for the hicks, Reidar Sorensen's big city cop has little hope of identifying the masked vigilantes who drowned a local lad suspected of the rape and murder of a mentally handicapped girl. He has even less chance of halting the cycle of violence that leads to the brutal victimisation of the dead man's angelic younger brother. Ingmar Bergman meets David Lynch in an austere whodunit where everyone is corrupted. In Norwegian with English subtitles.

Reidar Sorensen *Nicholas Ramm* • Jon Oigarden *Baste Hartmann* • Gaute Skjegstad *Niklas Hartmann* • Trond Hovik *Holger* • Stig Henrik Hoff *Dwayne Karlson* • Laila Goody *Victoria* • Simon Northon *Cato* • Kjersti Holmen *Andrea Hartmann* ■ *Dir* Karin Julsrud • *Scr* Kjetil Indregard

The Bloody Brood ★

Crime drama 1959 · Can · BW · 69mins

Peter Falk would undoubtedly prefer to forget his early appearance in this cheap Canadian crime melodrama. He's the only member of the cast to have become well known, and he's the only reason for watching it. In fact, he's quite effective in a ridiculous part, giving a cold, emotionless performance as the psychopathic gangleader who feeds a youngster a deadly hamburger containing ground-up glass. The dead man's brother seeks revenge by infiltrating the film's bizarre world of beatniks and weirdos. Director Julian Roffman benefits from having the great cameraman of *The Hustler*, Eugen Schüfftan, to make this look rather better than it is.

Peter Falk *Nico* • Jack Betts *Cliff* • Ronald Hartman *Francis* • Barbara Lord *Ellie* • Robert Christie *Detective McLeod* • William Brydon *Studs* • George Sperdakos *Ricky* • Ron Taylor (2) *Dave* ■ *Dir* Julian Roffman • *Scr* Elwood Ullman, Ben Kerner, from a story by Anne Howard Bailey

Bloody Mama ★★★ 18

Crime drama   1970 · US · Colour · 89mins

Shelley Winters is the quintessential Ma Barker in cult director Roger Corman's psychological gangster movie about her infamous bank-robbing brood who terrorised the thirties. A satisfyingly sleazy salute to Middle American family values – the family that slays together, stays together – Corman's supposedly true-crime saga is a riotous stew of sentimental blood-bonding and perverse bloody violence. In one of his earliest appearances, Robert De Niro is electrifying as the drug-addicted son.

Shelley Winters *Kat "Ma" Barker* • Pat Hingle *Sam Pendlebury* • Don Stroud *Herman Barker* • Diane Varsi *Mona Gibson* • Bruce Dern *Kevin Kirkman* • Clint Kimbrough *Arthur Barker* • Robert Walden *Fred Barker* • Robert De Niro *Lloyd Barker* ■ *Dir* Roger Corman • *Scr* Robert Thom, from a story by Robert Thom, Don Peters

Bloomfield ★ PG

Sports drama   1969 · UK/Is · Colour · 91mins

Richard Harris made a disastrous directorial debut with this curious blend of soccer and sentiment. Whereas he once made a fearsome rugby league player (in *This Sporting Life*), at 39 he looked less imposingly athletic as the Israeli footballer who, though well past his sell-by date, goes a game too far because he's been offered a car to fix the result. There are a couple of blazing rows with sculptress girlfriend Romy Schneider, but they fail to distract from the poorly staged soccer sequences and the achingly dull vista that accompany ten-year-old Yossi Yadin on his trek to Jaffa to see his hero's farewell.

Richard Harris *Eitan* • Romy Schneider *Nira* • Kim Burfield *Nimrod* • Maurice Kaufmann *Yasha* • Yossi Yadin *Weiner* • Shraga Friedman *Chairman* • Aviva Marks *Teddy* ■ *Dir* Richard Harris • *Scr* Wolf Mankowitz, from a story by Joseph Gross

Blossoms in the Dust ★★★

Biographical drama
1941 · US · Colour · 100mins

All the MGM gloss in the world can't hide the fact that this is a tear-jerker of the first order, but director Mervyn LeRoy and stars Greer Garson and Walter Pidgeon embrace the subject head-on and, knowingly create a fine biopic, enhanced by Oscar-winning interior decoration and some first-rate Technicolor. This is the tale of Wisconsin-born Edna Gladney, who started the Texas Children's Home and Aid Society of Fort Worth, caring for orphans and strays. Nobody could be better equipped to play her than Oscar-nominated Garson. Trouble is, there

are far too many children to keep track of, and, despite the film's undoubted worthiness, Garson's stubborn refusal to age alongside the narrative reduces the drama to bathos. It's worth dipping into, though, especially for admirers of MGM's ultra-high production standards.

Greer Garson *Edna Gladney* • Walter Pidgeon *Sam Gladney* • Felix Bressart *Dr Max Breslar* • Marsha Hunt *Charlotte* • Fay Holden *Mrs Kahly* • Samuel S Hinds *Mr Kahly* • Kathleen Howard *Mrs Keats* • George Lessey *Mr Keats* ■ *Dir* Mervyn LeRoy • *Scr* Anita Loos, from a story by Ralph Wheelwright • *Cinematographer* Karl Freund, W Howard Greene • *Set Designer* Cedric Gibbons, Urie McCleary, Edwin B Willis

Blow Out ★★★★ 18

Thriller   1981 · US · Colour · 107mins

Long before *Pulp Fiction*, John Travolta's best role was in Brian De Palma's audio version of Michelangelo Antonioni's *Blow Up*, laced with the director's usual quota of Hitchcockian black humour and startling suspense. Travolta is marvellous as the cheesy horror flick sound-effects man who accidentally tapes events leading to the Chappaquiddick-style drowning of a presidential candidate. Nothing is what it seems, in a paranoid mystery deliciously overflowing with De Palma's trademark high style and cinematic technique right up until the knockout, downbeat ending. Contains violence, swearing and nudity. ▭

John Travolta *Jack Terry* • Nancy Allen *Sally Badina* • John Lithgow *Burke* • Dennis Franz *Manny Karp* • John Aquino *Detective Mackey* • Peter Boyden *Sam* • Curt May *Donahue* • John McMartin *Lawrence Henry* • Deborah Everton *Hooker* ■ *Dir/Scr* Brian De Palma

Blow Up ★★★ 15

Thriller   1966 · UK/It · Colour · 106mins

One of the true tests of a great work of art is its ability to transcend time. Film can have the shortest shelf life of any art form. Michelangelo Antonioni's first English language feature is a case in point. Hailed in its day as a work of genius, an intriguing, if self-indulgent, challenge to the idea that the camera never lies, this might-be murder mystery is now often dismissed as ostentatious and exploitative. Antonioni is usually sound on the theme of urban alienation, but he tries too hard for arty style and manages to miss the beat of swinging London. Sarah Miles walked out during production, leaving Vanessa Redgrave to strip off, look gawky and fidget while Hemmings puts on a jazz record. There is no more cringe-inducing scene in the history of the cinema, but if you can ignore such pretensions, this does contain fleeting moments of brilliance. Contains swearing and nudity. ▭

David Hemmings *Co-producer* • Vanessa Redgrave *Jane* • Sarah Miles *Patricia* • Jane Birkin *Girl in studio* • Gillian Hills *Girl in studio* • Peter Bowles *Ron* • Harry Hutchinson *Antiques dealer* • John Castle *Painter* • Jill Kennington *Model* • Melanie Hampshire *Model* • Ann Norman *Model* • Rosaleen Murray *Model* ■ *Dir* Michelangelo Antonioni • *Scr* Michelangelo Antonioni, Tonino Guerra, Edward Bond, from a story by Julio Cortazar

Blowing Wild ★★★

Drama   1953 · US · BW · 89mins

"Marina mine..." belted out ol' leather-lungs Frankie Laine over the opening titles of this thirties-set oil-rig melodrama (and so secured himself a substantial hit). Marina is played by Barbara Stanwyck. She's married to tycoon Anthony Quinn, but has the hots (and who can blame her?) for former lover Gary Cooper, a wildcatter from her past who turns up in her life just when he shouldn't. Tosh, of course, and summarily dismissed by contemporary critics. But fans of the latter-day Coop and Stanwyck certainly get their money's worth. Director Hugo Fregonese, an Argentinian working in Hollywood, makes the most of the Mexican locations, even though he seems incapable of reining in his stars, who emote at full throttle.

Barbara Stanwyck *Marina Conway* • Gary Cooper *Jeff Dawson* • Ruth Roman *Sal* • Anthony Quinn *Paco Conway* • Ward Bond *Dutch Peterson* • Juan Garcia *El Gavilan* • Ian MacDonald *Jackson* ■ *Dir* Hugo Fregonese • *Scr* Phillip Yordan

Blown Away ★★ 18

Thriller   1992 · Can · Colour · 92mins

At one time it seemed that the two Coreys (Feldman and Haim) were joined at the hip. This teen *film noir* is one of their better efforts. The latter plays a teenager working at a ski resort who is seduced by poor little rich girl Nicole Eggert (*Baywatch*). She then starts to plant murderous thoughts in his head about her nasty dad (a creepy Jean LeClerc). The young cast give a passable account of themselves, while director Brenton Spencer brings a bit of style to the rather predictable plot. ▭

Corey Haim *Rich* • Nicole Eggert *Megan* • Corey Feldman *Wes* • Gary Farmer *Anderson* • Kathleen Robertson *Darla* • Jean LeClerc *Cy* • Jason Hopley *Rody* ■ *Dir* Brenton Spencer • *Scr* Robert Cooper

Blown Away ★★ 15

Thriller   1994 · US · Colour and BW · 115mins

A bungled high-tech thriller, with Jeff Bridges as a bomb disposal expert and Tommy Lee Jones as his former colleague who wants Bridges blown away. To show us just why he does, the film takes us back to Northern Ireland (always a risky subject for Hollywood). This aspect of the movie is neither interesting nor particularly relevant to the main thrust, which aims to deliver a tense sequence every 15 minutes or so. Bridges and Jones, two of the best around, can make nothing of the thinly written, often tasteless, material, while Lloyd Bridges and Forest Whitaker are completely wasted. Unsurprisingly, this bombed at the box office. Contains violence, swearing and brief nudity. ▭ **DVD**

Jeff Bridges *Jimmy Dove* • Tommy Lee Jones *Ryan Gaerity* • Suzy Amis *Kate* • Lloyd Bridges *Max O'Bannon* • Forest Whitaker *Anthony Franklin* • Stephi Lineburg *Lizzy* • John Finn *Captain Roarke* • Caitlin Clarke *Rita* • Chris De Oni *Cortez* ■ *Dir* Stephen Hopkins • *Scr* Joe Batteer, John Rice, from a story by John Rice, Joe Batteer, M Jay Roach

Blue ★★

Western   1968 · US · Colour · 112mins

Strikingly photographed by Stanley Cortez, who also shot *The Magnificent Ambersons* and *The Night of the Hunter*, this is an otherwise undistinguished western from Canadian director Silvio Narizzano. As the adopted son of Mexican bandit Ricardo Montalban, Terence Stamp rescues respectable Karl Malden and his daughter Joanna Pettet only to learn the hard facts of life in the Old West. Attempting to reproduce the sort of steely-eyed smouldering you'd expect of Franco Nero, Stamp opts for striking a series of poses rather than giving a rounded performance. Archly acted and heavy-handed in its symbolism, this is a long haul for little reward.

Terence Stamp *Blue/Azul* • Joanna Pettet *Joanne Morton* • Karl Malden *Doc Morton* • Ricardo Montalban *Ortega* • Anthony Costello *Jess Parker* • Joe De Santis *Carlos* • Stathis Giallelis *Manuel* • Carlos East *Xavier* ■ *Dir* Silvio Narizzano • *Scr* Meade Roberts, Ronald M Cohen, from the story by Ronald M Cohen

Blue ★★★★ 15

Experimental   1993 · UK · Colour · 75mins

Derek Jarman's work has been overpraised by critics desperate for an original voice in British cinema, but there is no doubting the courage and sincerity of this deeply moving swansong. The screen remains a shimmering shade of blue for the entire film, while Nigel Terry, John Quentin, Tilda Swinton and the director himself read extracts from Jarman's diary and other writings to the accompaniment of Simon Fisher Turner's imaginative score. The meditations might meander now and then, but there is no self-pity or bitterness in his comments on Aids, the loss of his friends, his own blindness and the inevitability of death. A bold farewell from an irreplaceable talent. Contains swearing. ▭

Derek Jarman • John Quentin • Nigel Terry • Tilda Swinton ■ *Dir/Scr* Derek Jarman • *Music* Simon Fisher Turner

The Blue Angel ★★★★ PG

Drama   1930 · Ger · BW · 106mins

Contrary to popular myth, 28-year-old Marlene Dietrich had already appeared in almost 20 (admittedly minor) films in her native Germany when Josef von Sternberg cast her as Lola, the sensual cabaret singer who enslaves, humiliates and finally destroys middle-aged professor Emil Jannings. The film did, however, bring about the famous von Sternberg/Dietrich Hollywood collaboration. Jannings, making his first talking picture, has some wonderful moments in an uneven performance. But it was the cruel and seductive Dietrich, in top hat and black stockings, perched on a bar stool and huskily singing *Falling in Love Again*, that became one of the cinema's great iconic images. The film was pointlessly and inadequately remade in 1959 with Curt Jurgens and May Britt. In German with English subtitles. ▭ **DVD**

Emil Jannings *Professor Immanuel Rath* • Marlene Dietrich *Lola Frohlich* • Kurt Gerron *Kiepert, a magician* • Rosa Valette *Guste Kiepert, his wife* • Hans Albers *Mazeppa* •

Eduard Von Winterstein *School principal* • Reinhold Bernt *The clown* • Hans Roth *Beadle* ■ *Dir* Josef von Sternberg • *Scr* Carl Zuckmayer, Karl Vollmöller, Robert Liebmann, from the novel *Professor Unrat* by Heinrich Mann • *Music* Friedrich Hollän, der

The Blue Angel ★

Drama   1959 · US · Colour · 107mins

A seriously misguided attempt by 20th Century-Fox to remake Josef von Sternberg's thirites German classic, about a cabaret singer who destroys the middle-aged professor obsessionally in love with her. Placed in a modern setting and filmed in CinemaScope, this is truly awful, losing the atmosphere, resonance and credibility of the original. Curt Jurgens and May Britt are the unfortunate substitutes for Emil Jannings and Marlene Dietrich.

Curt Jurgens *Professor Immanuel Rath* • May Britt *Lola-Lola* • Theodore Bikel *Klepert* • John Banner *Principal Harter* • Fabrizio Mioni *Rolf* • Ludwig Stossel *Professor Braun* • Wolfe Barzell *Clown* • Ina Anders *Gussie* ■ *Dir* Edward Dmytryk • *Scr* Nigel Balchin, from the film by Carl Zuckmayer, Karl Vollmöller, Robert Liebmann, from the novel *Professor Unrat* by Heinrich Mann

Blue Bayou ★★ 18

Crime drama   1990 · US · Colour · 67mins

This is yet another pilot for a series that never happened. Talented actress Alfre Woodard (*Grand Canyon*, *Passion Fish*) is sadly wasted in the stereotyped role of a lawyer who moves with her troublesome son from Los Angeles to New Orleans, in order to be near the boy's police officer father who left her 15 years earlier. Both Woodard and co-star Mario Van Peebles are excellent, but there's really nothing said here that hasn't already turned up in every family drama of the past ten years. ▭

Alfre Woodard *Jessica Filley* • Keith Williams *Nick Filley* • Mario Van Peebles *Jay Filley* • Elizabeth Ashley *Lolly Fontenot* • Roy Thinnes *Barney Fontenot* • Pamela Gidley *Deanie Fontenot Serulla* • Maxwell Caulfield *Phil Serulla* • Ashley Crow *Morgan Fontenot* • Carmen DeLavallade *Frosine* ■ *Dir* Karen Arthur • *Scr* Terry Louise Fisher

The Blue Bird ★★★ U

Fantasy   1940 · US · Colour · 82mins

Twentieth Century-Fox's answer to MGM's *The Wizard of Oz* was this lavish version of the Maurice Maeterlinck play about a woodcutter's daughter, played by Shirley Temple, seeking the blue bird of happiness. Enjoy the fantastic settings and the fine Technicolor and be thankful it's not longer, for the characters never come to life and the handling is too literal. Confined by a foreign character and setting, and fast losing her precocious appeal at 11, this was Temple's first box-office flop and her career never really recovered. Gale Sondergaard, though, is splendid, playing the treacherous family cat.

Shirley Temple *Mytyl* • Spring Byington *Mummy Tyl* • Nigel Bruce *Mr Luxury* • Gale Sondergaard *Tylette* • Eddie Collins *Tylo, the dog* • Edwin Maxwell *Oak* • Thurston Hall *Father Time* ■ *Dir* Walter Lang • *Scr* Ernest Pascal, Walter Bullock, from the play *L'Oiseau Bleu* by Maurice Maeterlinck

The Blue Bird ★★ U

Fantasy   1976 · US/USSR · Colour · 97mins

Patsy Kensit is in the glittering company of Liz Taylor, Ava Gardner and Jane Fonda in this retelling of the Maeterlinck theatrical fairy tale. Two children, Mytyl (Kensit) and her brother Tyltyl (Todd Lookinland), set out on a journey to find the blue bird of happiness accompanied by the human manifestations of, among others, a dog, a cat, a loaf of bread and fire. Despite the starry cast, this first ever US/Soviet co-production is a turgid and silly affair and is doubtful entertainment, even for the children it's aimed at.

Elizabeth Taylor *Mother/Light/Maternal Love/ Witch* • Jane Fonda *Night* • Cicely Tyson *Cat* • Ava Gardner *Luxury* • Patsy Kensit *Mytyl* • Todd Lookinland *Tyltyl* • Mona Washbourne *Grandmother* • George Cole *Dog* • Robert Morley *Father Time* • Harry Andrews *Oak* ■ *Dir* George Cukor • *Scr* Hugh Whitemore, Alfred Hayes, Alexei Kapler, from the play *L'Oiseau Bleu* by Maurice Maeterlinck

Blue Black Permanent ★★★★ PG

Drama   1992 · UK · Colour · 85mins

A stunning feature debut from Margaret Tait, who also wrote the script. We watch, moved, as Scottish photographer Celia Imrie tells her boyfriend Jack Shepherd the heartrending story of her mother's death when she was a child, coming to realise as she does so just how much the event has shaped her life. Superbly performed, this is an unusual and thought-provoking drama about coping with loss and the guilt that comes with it, filled with unusual imagery that punctuates each emotion. While it doesn't always work, this is nonetheless an interesting film full of emotion and meaning.

Celia Imrie *Barbara Thorburn* • Jack Shepherd *Philip Lomax* • Gerda Stevenson *Greta Thorburn* • James Fleet *Jim Thorburn* • Sean Scanlan *Andrew Cunningham* • Hilary Maclean *Wendy* • Walter Leask *Sam Kelday* • Sheana Marr *Mrs Kemp* • Eoin MacDonald *Dan of Fea* ■ *Dir/Scr* Margaret Tait

Blue Blood ★ 18

Drama   1973 · UK · Colour · 78mins

It's hard to find the words to express just how abysmal this reworking of *The Servant* really is. Based on Alexander Thynne's psychological shocker *The Carry-Cot*, it is directed with revolting enthusiasm by Andrew Sinclair who, unsurprisingly, has not been entrusted with many features since. As the vicious butler intent on destabilising his weak-kneed aristocratic employer (Derek Jacobi), Oliver Reed gesticulates and rolls his eyes in a manner more befitting villainous Eric Campbell in a Charlie Chaplin short than a figure of menace in a supposedly literate tale of manipulation and witchcraft. So dire, it's not even a curio. ▭

Oliver Reed *Tom* • Derek Jacobi *Gregory* • Fiona Lewis *Lily* • Anna Gael *Carlotta* • Meg Wynn Owen *Beate Krug* • John Rainer *Clurman* • Richard Davies *Jones* • Gwyneth Owen *Agnes* ■ *Dir* Andrew Sinclair • *Scr* Andrew Sinclair, from the novel *The Carry-Cot* by Alexander Thynne

Blue Canadian Rockies ★★ U

Western   1952 · US · Sepia · 57mins

This Saturday morning fare is only for die-hard fans of the immensely popular singing cowboy Gene Autry. Along with his rival Roy Rogers, Autry was responsible for instilling in youngsters a valuable sense of ethics, now forgotten and impractical, via his "Cowboy's Code of the West". This programmer is a typical vehicle, with Autry's regular sidekick Pat Buttram also along for the ride. The real co-star, though, is Champion, who went on to become the only cowboy horse to have his own TV series.

Gene Autry • Pat Buttram *"Rawhide" Buttram* • Gail Davis *Sandra Higbee* • Carolina Cotton • Ross Ford *Todd Markley* ■ *Dir* George Archainbaud • *Scr* Gerald Geraghty

Blue Chips ★★★ 15

Sports drama   1994 · US · Colour · 103mins

Ron Shelton is probably the finest writer of sports movies Hollywood has produced. Although not up there with *Bull Durham*, this is still a perceptive take on the machinations of the American sporting industry. This time the target is basketball, with Nick Nolte as the honourable college coach under pressure to succumb to the dodgy practices of his peers by secretly paying for young stars to join his team. Nolte is excellent as the good man who learns that, when it comes to sport, money controls everything. He is helped out by an excellent supporting cast that includes JT Walsh and Mary McDonnell, with real-life basketball star Shaquille O'Neal surprisingly good in a key role. Director William Friedkin, better known for his action thrillers, films the basketball set pieces with his usual aplomb. Contains swearing. ▭

Nick Nolte *Pete Bell* • Mary McDonnell *Jenny* • JT Walsh *Happy* • Ed O'Neill *Ed* • Alfre Woodard *Lavada McRae* • Bob Cousy *Vic* • Shaquille O'Neal *Neon* • Anfernee "Penny" Hardaway *Butch* • Matt Nover *Ricky* • Louis Gossett Jr *Father Dawkins* ■ *Dir* William Friedkin • *Scr* Ron Shelton

Blue City ★★ 18

Thriller   1986 · US · Colour · 79mins

Though the sublime Ry Cooder supplies part of the soundtrack, this is an overwrought, largely forgettable, crime drama, in which Judd Nelson attempts to discover the truth behind the death of his father. Nelson and Ally Sheedy, who starred together the year before in *The Breakfast Club*, look out of their depth while the other familiar faces in the cast (David Caruso, Anita Morris) are wasted. Only the ever-reliable Paul Winfield emerges from this mess with reputation intact. Contains swearing and violence. ▭

Judd Nelson *Billy Turner* • Ally Sheedy *Annie Rayford* • David Caruso *Joey Rayford* • Paul Winfield *Luther Reynolds* • Scott Wilson *Perry Kerch* • Anita Morris *Malvina Kerch* • Luis Contreras *Lieutenant Ortiz* • Julie Carmen *Debbie Torez* ■ *Dir* Michelle Manning • *Scr* Lukas Heller, Walter Hill, from the novel by Ross MacDonald

Blue Collar ★★★★ 18

Drama   1978 · US · Colour · 108mins

After writing the scripts for *Taxi Driver* and an early version of *Close Encounters of the Third Kind*, Paul Schrader made his directorial debut with *Blue Collar*, a rare Hollywood feature in that it deals with America's industrial relations in a factory, more the province of British realist pictures of the sixties. It's the grinding boredom of the production line that interests Schrader and how his three workers – Richard Pryor, Harvey Keitel, Yaphet Kotto – plan to break free of it by robbing their union. It's tough, convincing and littered with ripe language, capturing the atmosphere of the streets and domestic lives with the same sort of pulse as *Taxi Driver*. Contains swearing, drug abuse and brief nudity. ▭

Richard Pryor *Zeke Brown* • Harvey Keitel *Jerry Bartowski* • Yaphet Kotto *Smokey* • Ed Begley Jr *Bobby Joe* • Harry Bellaver *Eddie Johnson* • George Memmoli *Jenkins* • Lucy Saroyan *Arlene Bartowski* ■ *Dir* Paul Schrader • *Scr* Paul Schrader, Leonard Schrader, from source material by Sydney A Glass

The Blue Dahlia ★★★★

Film noir   1946 · US · BW · 100mins

A terrifically taut thriller, written for the screen from his own original story by the great Raymond Chandler, with lines and whole scenes as hard-boiled and witty as in the better known *films noirs*, *The Big Sleep* or *Double Indemnity*. Steely-eyed, super-cool Alan Ladd returns from the war to find wife Doris Dowling cheating and then dead, with himself as the chief murder suspect. He meets sultry Veronica Lake, and their scenes together simply sizzle. Under George Marshall's expert direction, the fight sequences are unusually realistic and brutal for a movie made by Paramount, a studio better known for lighter entertainment. The classy score's by Victor Young, the costumes are by Edith Head, the cutting's by Billy Wilder's editor Arthur Schmidt: with a pedigree like that, this one could hardly fail.

Alan Ladd *Johnny Morrison* • Veronica Lake *Joyce Harwood* • William Bendix *Buzz Wanchek* • Howard Da Silva *Eddie Harwood* • Doris Dowling *Helen Morrison* • Tom Powers *Captain Hendrickson* • Hugh Beaumont *George Copeland* • Howard Freeman *Corelli* ■ *Dir* George Marshall • *Scr* Raymond Chandler, from his story • *Cinematographer* Lionel Lindon

Blue Denim ★★★

Drama   1959 · US · BW · 89mins

Considered shocking in its day, Philip Dunne's drama stands in stark contrast to the more frivolous teen pictures produced in the late fifties. There's an undeniable sweetness about the way alienated high school kids Brandon de Wilde and Carol Lynley fall in love, which makes their need to visit an abortionist all the more distressing. However, this being Hollywood under the Production Code, what would have been the inevitable conclusion in life is hijacked by moral rectitude as the boy's parents intervene. Both principals are outstanding; it's a pity that time has weakened the impact of the scenario.

Carol Lynley *Janet Willard* • Brandon de Wilde *Arthur Bartley* • Macdonald Carey *Maj Malcolm Bartley, Ret* • Marsha Hunt *Jessie Bartley* • Warren Berlinger *Ernie* • Buck Class *Axel Sorenson* • Nina Shipman *Lillian Bartley* ■ *Dir* Philip Dunne • *Scr* Edith Sommer, Philip Dunne, from the play by James Leo Herlihy, William Noble

Blue Fire Lady ★★
Drama   1977 · Ausl · Colour · 96mins

Made in those forgettable seventies when Australia was just emerging from years of this type of anthropomorphic nonsense, this is the story of a girl and her love for a racehorse who, amazingly, seems to know her every whim and mood. Starring Cathryn Harrison as the smitten youngster and Mark Holden as a ubiquitous square-jawed presence, this is a film with so much soft focus you'll think your screen has misted up. The young will love it, but cynical adults beware.

Cathryn Harrison *Jenny Grey* • Mark Holden *Barry* • Peter Cummins *McIntyre* • Marion Edward *Mrs Gianini* • Lloyd Cunnington *Mr Grey* • Irene Hewitt *Mrs Bartlett* • Wyd Conabere *Mr Bartlett* ■ *Dir* Ross Dimsey • *Scr* Bob Maumill

Blue Flame ★ 15
Science-fiction drama
1995 · US · Colour · 87mins

A hard-boiled detective goes on a search-and-destroy mission when two aliens kidnap his daughter, in the writing/directing debut of former William Morris agent Cassian Elwes. With its threadbare plot and terrible dialogue, this excruciating low-budget disaster is bearable only thanks to cinematographer Daniele Massaccesi, who at least makes it visually interesting. The story apparently came to Elwes while he was high on medicinal drugs during an operation – worth bearing in mind if you're considering whether to watch this psychedelic-tinged fiasco.

Brian Wimmer *Flemming* • Kerri Green *Rain* • Jad Mager *Fire* • Cecilia Peck *Jessie* ■ *Dir/Scr* Cassian Elwes

The Blue Gardenia ★★★
Film noir   1953 · US · BW · 90mins

Director Fritz Lang, one of the great expressionists and innovators of cinema (*Metropolis*, *M*) fled the Nazis in 1936 and made a second career in Hollywood. Reined in by studio executives who tampered with his vision, he nonetheless established himself as a master of *film noir*. This modest offering stars Anne Baxter who, duped into drunkenness by baddie Raymond Burr, comes to in his apartment, finds him dead and flees the scene. Co-star Richard Conte is a powerful newspaper columnist who invites the unknown killer to surrender. The plot and the denouement are incredible, but it's made with Langian flair. It features Nat King Cole singing the title song and there's a terrific supporting performance from Ann Sothern. Entertaining.

Anne Baxter *Norah Larkin* • Richard Conte *Casey Mayo* • Ann Sothern *Crystal Carpenter* • Raymond Burr *Harry Prebble* • Jeff Donnell *Sally Ellis* • Richard Erdman *Al* • George Reeves *Police Captain Haynes* • Ruth Storey

Rose Miller ■ *Dir* Fritz Lang • *Scr* Charles Hoffman, from the story *Gardenia* by Vera Caspary

Blue Hawaii ★★★ PG
Musical   1961 · US · Colour · 96mins

Though one of Elvis Presley's biggest successes, this movie was directly responsible for turning him from the new James Dean into the king of pap. Confronted with the huge box office grosses, Elvis's controllers – venal manager Colonel Tom Parker and film producer Hal Wallis – decided that every movie their boy made from then on would be the same mix of girls, songs and exotic locations. Thirty films later, they'd sacrificed both their audience and Presley's screen credibility. For all that, this is colourful, amiable fluff, with some nice near-jailbait, Angela Lansbury as Elvis's mom, and such beautifully performed songs as the title number and *Can't Help Falling in Love*. 🔲

Elvis Presley *Chad Gates* • Joan Blackman *Maile Duval* • Nancy Walters *Abigail Prentice* • Roland Winters *Fred Gates* • Angela Lansbury *Sarah Lee Gates* • John Archer *Jack Kelman* • Howard McNear *Mr Chapman* • Flora Hayes *Mrs Manaka* ■ *Dir* Norman Taurog • *Scr* Hal Kanter, from a story by Allan Weiss

Blue Heat ★★★ 15
Police action drama
1990 · US · Colour · 101mins

Brian Dennehy looks fearsome enough to go off like a one-man firework display, but also kindly enough to play Santa Claus down at your local store. This odd ability is put to good use in this action drama, in which Dennehy co-stars with Joe Pantoliano, Jeff Fahey and Bill Paxton as a member of an elite unit working for the Los Angeles Police Department. Though it strives to be a political allegory, any resemblance to the Iran-Contra affair is a bit too sketchy and the story works better as a tale of Dennehy and his unit against the drugs barons, even when the action sequences fall flat. Contains swearing, violence and drug abuse. 🔲

Brian Dennehy *Frank Daly* • Joe Pantoliano *Wayne Gross* • Jeff Fahey *Ricky Rodriguez* • Bill Paxton *Howard "Hojo" Jones* • Michael C Gwynne *Anthony Reece* • Henry Stolow *Stant* • Guy Boyd *RJ Norringer* • Henry Darrow *Captain Joe Torres* • Deborra-Lee Furness *Linda Daly* ■ *Dir* John Mackenzie • *Scr* Jere Cunningham, Thomas Lee Wright, George Armitage, from a story by Jere Cunningham

Blue Ice ★★ 18
Thriller   1992 · US/UK · Colour · 68mins

Michael Caine, apparently believing that the British film industry meant no audience, decided to make a film for Americans set in Britain, which people might actually want to see. Unfortunately, a thriller featuring a central character who resembles a warmed-up version of *The Ipcress File*'s Harry Palmer (Caine, naturally), a performance from Sean Young that is all mannerism and no depth, and direction from Russell Mulcahy that is all gloss and no suspense did not stir the public. Still, at least a London of dark encounters and ne'er-do-wells looks properly seedy. Contains swearing, violence and nudity. 🔲

Michael Caine *Harry Anders* • Sean Young *Stacy Mansdorf* • Ian Holm *Sir Hector* • Bobby Short *Buddy* • Alun Armstrong *Det Sgt Osgood* • Sam Kelly *George* • Jack Shepherd *Stevens* • Philip Davis *Westy* ■ *Dir* Russell Mulcahy • *Scr* Ron Hutchinson, from the character created by Ted Allbeury

The Blue Iguana ★ 15
Crime comedy   1988 · US · Colour · 86mins

An off-target attempt to satirise gumshoe pictures, B-movies and *film noir*, this is directed by John Lafia, who has subsequently worked on more populist fare, such as *Child's Play 2*. Displaying precious little idea of how to mount satire through situation or character and no grasp of basic comic timing, Lafia wades into the mire and remains stuck there throughout. The story, for what it's worth, concerns a hopeless bounty hunter who heads south of the border to retrieve $20 million in drug money from a Latin American bank. Contains violence, swearing and drug abuse. 🔲

Dylan McDermott *Vince Holloway* • Jessica Harper *Cora* • James Russo *Reno* • Pamela Gidley *Dakota* • Yano Anaya *Yano* • Flea *Floyd* ■ *Dir/Scr* John Lafia

Blue in the Face ★★★ 15
Comedy drama   1995 · US · Colour · 80mins

A funny thing happened once Wayne Wang wrapped *Smoke*, the director and novelist Paul Auster's excellent look at Brooklyn life distilled through Harvey Keitel's cigar shop. They realised that they had the set for another week and since the actors had had such a good time making the film, they didn't want to go home. Hence this bookend, which features mainly improvised scenes from the likes Madonna, Roseanne, Jim Jarmusch and Lou Reed on the power of the weed, mixed in with video documentary footage. Self-indulgent at times, and distinctly different from its companion piece, this is, in its own small way, equally entertaining. Contains swearing and occasional sexual references. 🔲

Harvey Keitel *Auggie Wren* • Michael J Fox *Peter* • Roseanne Barr [Roseanne] *Dot* • Mel Gorham *Violet* • Lily Tomlin *Derelict* • Madonna *Singing telegram girl* • Jim Jarmusch • Lou Reed ■ *Dir/Scr* Wayne Wang, Paul Auster

Blue Jean Cop ★★★ 18
Action crime drama
1988 · US · Colour · 92mins

Forget the implausibilities in the dumb plot of this *Lethal Weapon* copy and marvel at how director James Glickenhaus (*The Exterminator*) choreographs the truly spectacular stuntwork. With highlights such as undercover cop Sam Elliott swinging off 42nd Street cinema balconies like an urban Tarzan and the frenetic Coney Island roller-coaster chase, this kinetic sleaze-fest delivers the action goods. In the mind-engaging department, however, there's little of substance. Contains violence and swearing. 🔲

Peter Weller *Roland Dalton* • Sam Elliott *Richie Marks* • Richard Brooks *Michael Jones* • Jude Ciccolella *Patrick O'Leary* • Tom Waites [Thomas G Waites] *Officer Kelly* • George Loros *Officer Varelli* • Daryl Edwards *Dr Watson* • Antonio Fargas *Nicky Carr* ■ *Dir/Scr* James Glickenhaus

Blue Juice ★★ 15
Comedy drama   1995 · UK · Colour · 94mins

What's this? A British movie about surfing! Since it's set on the rocky, chilly beaches of Cornwall, it's no wonder you see little of the sport itself. Instead, director Carl Prechezer focuses on the less interesting dilemma facing surfer Sean Pertwee. Terrified of turning 30, he must choose between his woman (Catherine Zeta-Jones) and the waves. One look at the weather throughout this contrived melodrama – which could have been made in the sixties, starring Cliff Richard – and there's no contest. Ewan McGregor's drug-popping psycho places this old-fashioned emotional whirlpool in the nineties. Contains substance abuse. 📀 DVD

Sean Pertwee *JC* • Catherine Zeta-Jones *Chloe* • Ewan McGregor *Dean Raymond* • Steven Mackintosh *Josh Tambini* • Peter Gunn *Terry Colcott* • Heathcote Williams *Shaper* • Colette Brown *Junior* • Michelle Chadwick *Sarah* • Keith Allen *Mike* ■ *Dir* Carl Prechezer • *Scr* Peter Salmi, Carl Prechezer, from an idea by Peter Salmi, Carl Prechezer, Tim Veglio

The Blue Kite ★★★★ 12
Drama   1992 · HK/Chi · Colour · 134mins

Banned by the Chinese authorities, this is a rich and courageous study of the impact that the policies pursued by the Communist Party between 1949 and 1967 had on ordinary people. Based on Tian Zhuangzhuang's memories and the stories told to him by family and friends, this tough film combines strident criticisms of Mao's regime with moments of great personal drama as careers, romances, friendships and rivalries are affected by momentous political and historical events. As in many features by "Fifth Generation" film-makers, the betrayals and brutalities of the Cultural Revolution are depicted with devastating power, while the playing is utterly convincing. In Mandarin with English subtitles. 🔲

Yi Tian *Director* • Zhang Wenyao *Tietou as a child* • Chen Xiaoman *Tietou as a teenager* • Lu Liping *Mum (Chen Shujuan)* • Pu Quanxin *Dad (Lin Shaolong)* • Guo Baochang *Stepfather (Lao Wu)* • Zhong Ping *Chen Shusheng* ■ *Dir* Tian Zhuangzhuang • *Scr* Xiao Mao

The Blue Knight ★★★
Police drama   1973 · US · Colour · 102mins

This police drama was originally made for American television, ran at nearly four hours and was shown on four consecutive nights. After it won several awards, it was cut by two-thirds and released in cinemas in Britain. Based on the bestselling book by former cop Joseph Wambaugh, it's set among the drug dealers and low-lifes of Los Angeles, but concentrates on the character of weary, craggy patrolman William Holden, who is obsessed with finding the killer of a prostitute. Lee Remick is the schoolteacher who offers the chance of marriage and a way out of the sewer.

William Holden (1) *"Bumper" Morgan* • Lee Remick *Cassie* • Joe Santos *Sergeant Cruze* • Eileen Brennan *Glenda* • Emile Meyer *Bartender* • Sam Elliott *Homicide detective* • Ernest Esparza III *Rudy Garcia* • Anne Archer

U = SUITABLE FOR ALL   Uc = SUITABLE FOR ALL, ESPECIALLY FOR YOUNG CHILDREN (VIDEO ONLY)   PG = PARENTAL GUIDANCE

Call-girl • Vic Tayback *Retired cop* ■ *Dir* Robert Butler • *Scr* E Jack Neuman, from the novel by Joseph Wambaugh

The Blue Lagoon ★★★

Romantic adventure
1949 · UK · Colour · 103mins

An immensely popular and very likeable British version of the sexy little tale by Henry Devere Stacpoole about two children marooned on a desert island paradise, growing up to discover sex and their attraction to each other. The book had to be slightly modified to meet the needs of the censor (a problem not encountered by the ludicrous 1980 remake with Brooke Shields). Here the castaways are played with great charm by Donald Houston and lovely Jean Simmons, the latter on the brink of international stardom. Geoffrey Unsworth's Technicolor location photography is extremely satisfying.

Jean Simmons *Emmeline Foster* • Susan Stranks *Emmeline as child* • Donald Houston *Michael Reynolds* • Peter Jones *Michael as child* • Noel Purcell *Paddy Button* • James Hayter *Dr Murdoch* • Cyril Cusack *James Carter* • Nora Nicholson *Mrs Stannard* ■ *Dir* Frank Launder • *Scr* Frank Launder, John Baines, Michael Hogan, from the novel by Henry Devere Stacpoole

The Blue Lagoon ★★ 15

Romantic adventure
1980 · US · Colour · 100mins

An adolescent fantasy that is a remake of a 1949 British film directed by Frank Launder, in which two children are shipwrecked on a deserted island. In this update, teenage self-discovery and love ensue as Brooke Shields and co-star Christopher Atkins grow up isolated from the world in a Swiss Family Robinson-style shack. It's beautifully shot and there's much nudity and suggested sex, but it's all very, very silly, as the lovebirds conform to traditional marriage-and-baby values – strange for a couple with no sociological context to draw on. For the under-twenties only. Contains sex scenes and nudity. ▭

Brooke Shields *Emmeline* • Christopher Atkins *Richard* • Leo McKern *Paddy Button* • William Daniels *Arthur Lestrange* • Elva Josephson *Young Emmeline* • Glenn Kohan *Young Richard* • Alan Hopgood *Captain* • Gus Mercurio *Officer* ■ *Dir* Randal Kleiser • *Scr* Douglas Day Stewart, from the novel by Henry Devere Stacpoole

The Blue Lamp ★★★★ PG

Crime drama 1949 · UK · BW · 80mins

Jack Warner rose from the dead to star in TV's *Dixon of Dock Green* after his character was bumped off by petty crook Dirk Bogarde in this crime classic. Produced by Michael Balcon and scripted by TEB Clarke (a former policeman who penned many an Ealing comedy), the film yet again revealed the influence of the documentary on postwar British cinema, with its realistic depiction of the austere times that drove people to crime. Jimmy Hanley is a touch lightweight as Warner's police colleague who brings Bogarde to book, but the rest of director Basil Dearden's cast is outstanding. ▭

Jack Warner *PC George Dixon* • Jimmy Hanley *PC Andy Mitchell* • Dirk Bogarde *Tom Riley* • Robert Flemyng *Sergeant Roberts* • Gladys Henson *Mrs Dixon* • Bernard Lee *Inspector Cherry* • Peggy Evans *Diana Lewis* • Patric Doonan *Spud* • Bruce Seton *Constable Campbell* ■ *Dir* Basil Dearden • *Scr* TEB Clarke

The Blue Light ★★★★

Drama 1932 · Ger · BW · 77mins

The mountain film was hugely popular with German audiences in the thirties. Having starred in four features for the master of the genre, Dr Arnold Fanck, Leni Riefenstahl made her directorial debut with this tale of a Dolomite villager who is denounced as a witch for her ability to climb the unscaleable Mount Cristallo. As the maiden who plunges to her death after her lover removes the peak's magic crystals, Riefenstahl does a steady job. However, it's the stylised beauty of her direction that takes this simple moral fable on to a higher plane and landed her the post of Hitler's film-maker. An Italian/German language film.

Leni Riefenstahl *Junta* • Mattias Weimann *Vigo* • Max Holzboer *Innkeeper* • Beni Führer *Tonio* • Franz Maldacea *Guzzi* • Martha Mair *Lucia* ■ *Dir* Leni Riefenstahl • *Scr* Leni Riefenstahl, Béla Balázs • *Cinematographer* Hans Schneeberger

The Blue Lightning ★★ 15

Action adventure 1986 · US · Colour · 92mins

Sam Elliott, who's becoming more grizzled and perplexed as time goes on, is the American private eye who finds himself in the Australian outback on the trail of a valuable gem in this patchy action adventure tale. Unfortunately, Elliott is more capable as a supporting actor in movies such as *Road House* and *Sibling Rivalry* than as a leading man, especially in a film that is quite obviously a rip-off of every other adventure movie (*Raiders of the Lost Ark*, *Romancing the Stone*) made in the early eighties. ▭

Sam Elliott *Harry Wingate* • Rebecca Gilling *Kate McQueen* • Robert Culp *Lester McInally* • John Meillon *Dr William Giles* • Robert Coleby *Ninian* • Max Phipps *Brutus Cathcart* • Ralph Cotterill *Words* • Glen Boswell *Verna* ■ *Dir* Lee Philips • *Scr* William Kelley

The Blue Max ★★★★ PG

First World War drama
1966 · US · Colour · 137mins

A film about the short lives and lengthy lusts of German First World War fighter aces – it sounds luridly sensational, but action director John Guillermin makes it a rare treat of aerial excitement. George Peppard is the reckless go-it-alone high-flier who endangers his comrades and beds Ursula Andress, wife of commander James Mason. The love story is unconvincingly staged and compares badly with the camaraderie of men under stress. What really matters is steely James Mason, honour bound to ensure Peppard gets his comeuppance, and the in-flight photography, which reveals the grit as well as the glamour of such manic escapades. ▭

George Peppard *Bruno Stachel* • James Mason *Count von Klugermann* • Ursula Andress *Countess Kasti* • Jeremy Kemp *Willi*

von Klugermann • Karl Michael Vogler *Heidemann* • Carl Schell *Richthofen* • Loni von Friedl *Elfi Heidemann* • Anton Diffring *Holbach* ■ *Dir* John Guillermin • *Scr* David Pursall, Jack Seddon, Gerald Hanley, from the novel by Jack D Hunter • *Cinematographer* Douglas Slocombe

Blue Monkey ★★★

Horror thriller 1987 · US · Colour · 98mins

Silly, scary and lots of fun, director William Fruet's throwback to fifties monster movies offers knowing chuckles and disturbing horror in roughly equal proportion. A gardener cuts himself on an exotic plant and promptly vomits up a larva, and steroids turn the insect into a giant mutant bug, in this nostalgia-tinged hokum unashamedly stealing ideas from *Aliens*, *Jaws* and *The Fly*. Hard-boiled detective Steve Railsback creeps through dark tunnels to eradicate the latest threat to mankind. Camp dialogue ("We still have a few bugs to iron out"), cardboard creatures and gleeful schlock combine to make this an enjoyably slime-encrusted B-movie.

Steve Railsback *Detective Jim Bishop* • Gwynyth Walsh *Dr Rachel Carson* • Susan Anspach *Dr Judith Glass* • John Vernon *Roger Levering* • Joe Flaherty *George Baker* • Robin Duke *Sandra Baker* • Don Lake *Elliot Jacobs* • Sandy Webster *Fred Adams* ■ *Dir* William Fruet • *Scr* George Goldsmith

Blue Murder at St Trinian's ★★★ U

Comedy 1957 · UK · BW · 82mins

While hugely enjoyable, the second of Frank Launder and Sidney Gilliat's adaptations of Ronald Searle's popular cartoons is something of a disappointment after the riotous success of *The Belles of St Trinian's*. The main problem is that there's only a fleeting glimpse of Alastair Sim as Miss Fritton, but the plot – about a tour of Europe and some stolen gems – is also somewhat under par. The flirting between coach company owner Terry-Thomas and undercover cop Joyce Grenfell is a comic delight, but too many gags fall flat. ▭

Joyce Grenfell *Sergeant Gates* • Terry-Thomas *Romney* • George Cole *Flash Harry* • Alastair Sim *Miss Fritton* • Sabrina *Virginia* • Lionel Jeffries *Joe Mangan* • Lloyd Lamble *Superintendent* • Raymond Rollett *Chief Constable* ■ *Dir* Frank Launder • *Scr* Sidney Gilliat, Frank Launder, Val Valentine, from the drawings by Ronald Searle

The Blue Parrot ★★

Crime drama 1953 · UK · BW · 71mins

This features an unoriginal plot and a title that irresistibly recalls the Graham Greene-inspired thriller *The Green Cockatoo*. The budget was clearly tight and the story, about an American cop who solves a case and falls for a pretty English girl while on secondment to Scotland Yard, is hardly riveting stuff. Dermot Walsh does his best with some lacklustre material, and John Le Mesurier turns up in a supporting slot, but there's little else to recommend it.

Dermot Walsh *Bob Herrick* • Jacqueline Hill *Maureen* • Ballard Berkeley *Supt Chester* • Ferdy Mayne *Stevens* • Valerie White *Eva West* • John Le Mesurier *Henry Carson* •

Richard Pearson *Quinney* • June Ashley *Gloria* ■ *Dir* John Harlow • *Scr* Alan Mackinnon, from the story *Gunman* by Percy Hoskins

The Blue Peter ★★★ U

Comedy drama 1955 · UK · Colour · 94mins

Group 3 was a government-backed British film production company set up to make low-budget projects utilising new talent. This adventure romp was co-written by talented director Don Sharp and directed by equally talented writer Wolf Rilla. It brought Irish hunk Kieron Moore back from Hollywood to play a Korean War veteran teaching Aberdovey students at an outdoor camp. The youngsters include Anthony Newley and Harry Fowler, and the cast is brimming with welcome period faces, including Aussies Vincent Ball and Russell Napier and Indian dance maestro Ram Gopal.

Kieron Moore *Mike Merriworth* • Greta Gynt *Mary Griffith* • Sarah Lawson *Gwyneth Thomas* • Mervyn Johns *Captain Snow* • John Charlesworth *Andrew Griffin* • Harry Fowler *Charlie Barton* • Mary Kerridge *Mrs Snow* • Ram Gopal *Dr Tigara* • Russell Napier *Raymond Curtiss* • Anthony Newley *Sparrow* • Vincent Ball *Digger* ■ *Dir* Wolf Rilla • *Scr* Don Sharp, John Pudney

Blue Rodeo ★★★ PG

Drama 1996 · US · Colour · 87mins

After early years as a vulnerable female lead in features such as *Carnal Knowledge*, Ann-Margret is now more often seen in TV movies. In this drama she stars as the mother of a resentful teenager (Corbin Allred), who blames her for the accident that caused his deafness. Her growing love for cowboy Kris Kristofferson exacerbates the boy's anger and leads to a rather too obviously signposted emotional showdown. That Ann-Margret still makes the mother's character sympathetic is a tribute to her acting ability – and staying power. Contains some mild swearing.

Ann-Margret *Maggie Yearwood* • Kris Kristofferson *Owen Whister* • Corbin Allred *Peter Yearwood* • Jade Herrera *Bonnie Tsotsie* ■ *Dir* Peter Werner • *Scr* Paul Lussier, from the novel by Jo-Ann Mapson

Blue Scar ★★★ U

Drama 1947 · UK · BW · 102mins

A year after her outstanding documentary study of postwar Plymouth, *The Way We Live*, Jill Craigie made her fiction debut with this openly political drama. Craigie, who was married to ex-Labour leader Michael Foot, and producer William MacQuitty raised the budget themselves and shot much of the action in a converted cinema in the valleys of South Wales. The director later dismissed the tale of mining engineer Emrys Jones's visit to London as "amateurish". The acting of the largely nonprofessional cast is certainly stilted, but this is still a bold attempt to present a truthful portrait of late-forties life.

Emrys Jones *Tom Thomas* • Gwyneth Vaughan Olwen Williams • Rachel Thomas *Gweneth Williams* • Anthony Pendrell [Tony Pendrell] *Alfred Collins* • Prysor Williams *Ted Williams* • Madoline Thomas *Granny* • Jack James *Dai Morgan* • Kenneth Griffith *Thomas Williams* ■ *Dir/Scr* Jill Craigie

Blue Skies ★★★ U

Musical 1946 · US · Colour · 106mins

When dancer Paul Draper turned out to be unsuitable, Paramount called up the great Fred Astaire to replace him opposite crooner Bing Crosby in this garishly Technicolored Irving Berlin songfest. Beside the divine Astaire, Crosby looks like a galumphing oaf as they declare that they're *A Couple of Song and Dance Men*. The undoubted highlight is Astaire's classic solo dance routine during *Puttin' On the Ritz*. The girls are weak, the comedy's patchy, the plot's paper thin, but who cares when Astaire's on screen dancing to Berlin?

Fred Astaire *Jed Potter* • Bing Crosby *Johnny Adams* • Joan Caulfield *Mary O'Hara* • Billy De Wolfe *Tony* • Olga San Juan *Nita Nova* • Mikhail Rasmuny *François* • Carol Andrews *Dolly* • Dorothy Barrett *Showgirl* • Robert Benchley *Businessman* ■ *Dir* Stuart Heisler • *Scr* Arthur Sheekman, Allan Scott (adaptation), from an idea by Irving Berlin

Blue Sky ★★★★ 15

Drama 1991 · US · Colour · 96mins

This fragmented yet compelling drama is distinguished by Jessica Lange's merciless, Oscar-winning performance as a wife who's a walking nervous breakdown. Tommy Lee Jones matches her every spasm as her US Army husband, an atomic scientist facing the risk of meltdown in both his work and his marriage when Lange sets her sights on commanding officer Powers Boothe. Set in the early sixties, veteran British director Tony Richardson's final film uses the couple's personal crises to echo the nation's nuclear dilemma, but you can forget the symbolism – it's the people who matter. Contains violence, swearing and nudity.

Jessica Lange *Carly Marshall* • Tommy Lee Jones *Hank Marshall* • Powers Boothe *Vince Johnson* • Carrie Snodgress *Vera Johnson* • Amy Locane *Alex Marshall* • Chris O'Donnell *Glenn Johnson* • Mitchell Ryan *Ray Stevens* • Dale Dye *Colonel Mike Anwalt* ■ *Dir* Tony Richardson • *Scr* Rama Laurie Stagner, Arlene Sarner, Jerry Leichtling, from a story by Arlene Stagner

Blue Steel ★★ U

Western 1934 · US · BW · 54mins

A programme filler made for Monogram Studios, thios stars John Wayne before he had managed to break free from such routine fare. There's not a lot to commend here: George "Gabby" Hayes makes a watchable tobacco-chewing sheriff (he would soon advance to playing Wayne's sidekick), and Yakima Canutt, a mainstay of this series, appears as the quaintly monikered Polka Dot Bandit. The plot's that old chestnut about the marshal disguising himself to nail the baddies, and there's little artistry in Robert N Bradbury's perfunctory direction. For fans of the Duke only.

John Wayne *John Beaumont* • Eleanor Hunt *Betty Mason* • George "Gabby" Hayes *Sheriff Jake* • Ed Peil Sr [Edward Peil Sr] *Melgrove* • Yakima Canutt *Danti, The Polka Dot Bandit* • George Cleveland *Hank* • George Nash *Bridegroom* ■ *Dir/Scr* Robert N Bradbury

Blue Steel ★★★★ 18

Thriller 1990 · US · Colour · 97mins

Made a year before the male-dominated *Point Break*, this intelligent, provocative thriller from director Kathryn Bigelow stars Jamie Lee Curtis as the rookie police officer who tries to prevent an armed robbery in a supermarket. Ron Silver is the businessman and firearms nut who picks up the robber's gun and embarks on a chilling game of cat and mouse with her. Curtis is outstanding as the harassed officer and Silver is genuinely creepy, while there is strong support from a cast that includes Philip Bosco, Louise Fletcher and Tom Sizemore. Bigelow skilfully defines the almost fetishistic attraction of weaponry, and stages some exhilarating action set pieces. Contains violence, swearing and sex scenes.

Jamie Lee Curtis *Megan Turner* • Ron Silver *Eugene Hunt* • Clancy Brown *Nick Mann* • Elizabeth Pena *Tracy Perez* • Louise Fletcher *Shirley Turner* • Philip Bosco *Frank Turner* • Kevin Dunn *Assistant Chief Stanley Hoyt* • Tom Sizemore *Wool cap* ■ *Dir* Kathryn Bigelow • *Scr* Kathryn Bigelow, Eric Red

Blue Streak ★★★ 12

Crime comedy 1999 · US · Colour · 91mins

Emerging from prison, thief Martin Lawrence is horrified to find that the construction site where he hid a stolen jewel is now a police station. Joining the boys in blue, his "wrong side of the law" approach to crime-solving yields some extraordinary results. Unlike so many action comedies, Les Mayfield's film boasts an intricate and cleverly structured plot, though the tension is undermined by Lawrence's wild overacting. Highly reminiscent of Eddie Murphy's early (funny) movies, this may be unashamedly lowbrow entertainment, but it's great fun nonetheless.

Martin Lawrence *Miles Logan* • Luke Wilson *Carlson* • Peter Greene *Deacon* • Dave Chappelle *Tulley* • Nicole Ari Parker *Melissa Green* • Graham Beckel *Rizzo* • Robert Miranda *Glenfiddith* • Olek Krupa *LaFleur* ■ *Dir* Les Mayfield • *Scr* Michael Berry, John Blumenthal, Steve Carpenter

Blue Suede Shoes ★★

Music documentary 1980 · UK · Colour · 95mins

Some critics will tell you that the truest form of documentary is one in which the director resists the temptation either to participate or impose an editorial slant. However, the simple recording of events without any spin invariably makes for very dull viewing. This is a film brimming with personalities as director Curtis Clark poses the question, "Why do these people dress in long outmoded threads and hurl themselves around to music the devil no longer seems to have a use for?" But Clark doesn't really bother to find an answer, opting to shoot this seaside rock revival with all the vibrance of a Pat Boone B-side.

Dir Curtis Clark

Blue Thunder ★★★ 15

Action thriller 1983 · US · Colour · 105mins

Directed by John Badham (*Saturday Night Fever*, *Stakeout*), this is a *Boys' Own*-style action drama involving a super-helicopter, complete with high-tech surveillance gadgets and mega-weapons, belonging to the LA police and flown by cop Roy Scheider. It's a slick if somewhat predictable adventure that was spun off into a TV series of the same name, starring James Farentino and *Wayne's World*'s Dana Carvey. Contains violence, swearing and nudity. ▭ **DVD**

Roy Scheider *Frank Murphy* • Malcolm McDowell *Colonel Cochrane* • Candy Clark *Kate* • Warren Oates *Captain Braddock* • Daniel Stern *Lymangood* • Paul Roebling *Icelan* • David Sheiner *Fletcher* • Ed Bernard *Sergeant Short* ■ *Dir* John Badham • *Scr* Dan O'Bannon, Don Jakoby

Blue Tiger ★★★ 18

Action crime thriller 1994 · US · Colour · 84mins

Japanese gangsters were briefly in vogue in the mid-nineties, mainly on the back of *Rising Sun*. This, along with *American Yakuza*, is the pick of the straight-to-video bunch, thanks to a charismatic turn from Virginia Madsen in the lead role. She plays a mother who, after her son is killed during a gun battle, goes gunning for the Yakuza by getting a blue tiger tattoo and posing as a member of the fraternity. Norbeto Barba keeps the foot firmly on the accelerator and serves up some slick scenes of ultra-violence, while there's a nice cameo from the forever world-weary Harry Dean Stanton. ▭

Virginia Madsen *Gina Hayes* • Toru Nakamura *Seiji* • Dean Hallo *Henry Soames* • Ryo Ishibashi *Gan* • Sal Lopez *Luis* • Yuji Okumoto *Sakagami* • Harry Dean Stanton *Smith* • Brenda Varda *Emily* ■ *Dir* Norberto Barba • *Scr* Joel Soisson, from a story by Taka Ichise

The Blue Veil ★★★★

Romantic drama 1951 · US · BW · 108mins

Already an Oscar-winner for *Johnny Belinda* and a best actress nominee for *The Yearling*, Jane Wyman arrived at RKO on loan from Warner Bros to make this effective remake of a French original. She picked up another nomination and delivered a massive profit for the small and often troubled studio. Wyman plays a woman who devotes her life to caring for the children of others and winning their devotion, only to descend into lonely poverty. That's not the end of the story, though. The star's convincing and dignified portrayal, together with an exceptional set of supporting performances from Joan Blondell (also Oscar-nominated), Charles Laughton, Agnes Moorehead and 13-year-old Natalie Wood, makes for a thoroughly satisfying, high-class tear-jerker.

Jane Wyman *Louise Mason* • Charles Laughton *Fred K Begley* • Joan Blondell *Annie Rawlins* • Richard Carlson *Gerald Kean* • Agnes Moorehead *Mrs Palfrey* • Don Taylor *Dr Robert Palfrey* • Audrey Totter *Helen Williams* • Cyril Cusack *Frank Hutchins* • Natalie Wood *Stephanie Rawlins* ■ *Dir* Curtis Bernhardt • *Scr* Norman Corwin, from a story by François Campaux

Blue Velvet ★★★★★ 18

Cult mystery thriller 1986 · US · Colour · 115mins

The most complete of David Lynch's films, this was made before his disturbingly sombre vision of small-town American life veered into self-parody. The dark tone is set from the opening sequence, which starts with white picket fences and cheery volunteer firemen, and ends with a man suffering a stroke and a shot of seething insect life. Lynch regular Kyle MacLachlan is the young innocent who gets sucked into the bizarre sadomasochistic relationship between a nightclub singer (Isabella Rossellini) and the monstrous local crime boss (Dennis Hopper). The latter resurrected his career with its crazed portrait of evil. Listening to Roy Orbison's *In Dreams* will never be the same again. Contains swearing. ▭ **DVD**

Kyle MacLachlan *Jeffrey Beaumont* • Isabella Rossellini *Dorothy Vallens* • Dennis Hopper *Frank Booth* • Laura Dern *Sandy Williams* • Hope Lange *Mrs Williams* • Dean Stockwell *Ben* • George Dickerson *Detective Williams* • Brad Dourif *Raymond* • Jack Nance *Paul* ■ *Dir/Scr* David Lynch • *Cinematographer* Frederick Elmes • *Music* Angelo Badalamenti

The Blue Villa ★★★

Drama 1994 · Bel/Fr/Swi · Colour · 100mins

More than 30 years after electrifying world cinema with his screenplay for *Last Year at Marienbad*, Alain Robbe-Grillet was still playing intellectual games with structure and perception in this contrived thriller. Shuffling dreams, memory and reality, Robbe-Grillet and co-director Dimitri de Clercq ally us with a Greek policeman, as he tries to decide whether a returning sailor (who could be a ghost) was responsible for the murder of the daughter of an alcoholic screenwriter – or whether she is still alive and a resident of the local brothel. The control is as admirable as it's arch. The endless sleights of hand will either delight or infuriate. In French with English subtitles.

Fred Ward *Frank* • Arielle Dombasle *Sarah-Blonde* • Charles Tordjman *Edouard Nordmann* • Sandrine Le Berre *Santa* • Dimitri Poulikakos *Thieu* • Christian Maillet *The Father* • Muriel Jacobs *Kim* ■ *Dir/Scr* Alain Robbe-Grillet, Dimitri de Clercq

Blue Water, White Death ★★★ U

Documentary 1971 · US · Colour · 98mins

Four years before *Jaws* made seaside swimming seem a hazardous occupation for tourists, director Peter Gimbel mined the same deep-water fears in this outstanding documentary. Using the device of divers searching for the hunting grounds of the Great White Shark, Gimbel's cameras get unflinchingly up close and dangerously personal with the ocean's eating machines. Yet the film manages to avoid the clichés that have become the norm since the success of Steven Spielberg's shocker. Fans of wildlife programmes will love it.

Dir Peter Gimbel, James Lipscomb • *Scr* Peter Gimbel

U = SUITABLE FOR ALL, Uc = SUITABLE FOR ALL, ESPECIALLY FOR YOUNG CHILDREN (VIDEO ONLY), PG = PARENTAL GUIDANCE

The Blue Yonder ★★ U

Fantasy adventure
1985 · US · Colour · 86mins

Made in the same year as *Back to the Future*, this time travel TV-movie adventure did not receive quite the same attention as the Michael J Fox blockbuster. In this one, a young boy zips back in time to find out more about his late grandfather, a legendary pilot in the twenties. Worth a look if only for the dependable playing of Peter Coyote and Art Carney. ▭

Peter Coyote *Max Knickerbocker* • Huckleberry Fox *Jonathan Knicks* • Art Carney *Henry Coogan* • Dennis Lipscomb *Finch* ■ *Dir/Scr* Mark Rosman

Bluebeard ★★★

Horror
1944 · US · BW · 71mins

It wasn't often that poverty row studio PRC (Producers Releasing Corporation) came up with a film worth watching, but it did give the highly talented director Edgar G Ulmer some low-budget artistic freedom. Here he coaxes a beautifully restrained performance from the flamboyant character actor John Carradine, in one of his few starring roles, as the artist and puppeteer in 19th-century Paris who has an irresistible urge to murder his models. With strong support from Jean Parker and Nils Asther, and production values that transcend the low budget, this is a small miracle of polished film-making.

John Carradine *Gaston* • Jean Parker *Lucille* • Nils Asther *Insp Lefevre* • Ludwig Stossel *Lamarte* • George Pembroke *Insp Renard* • Teala Loring *Francine* • Sonia Sorel *Renee* • Iris Adrian *Mimi* ■ *Dir* Edgar G Ulmer • *Scr* Pierre Gendron, from a screenplay by Arnold Phillips, Werner H Furst

Bluebeard ★★★

Drama drama
1962 · Fr/It · Colour · 115mins

Claude Chabrol gave Charles Denner his first leading film role in this true story of Landru, a man who charmed a number of unsuspecting women and then murdered them. The magnetic Denner, with bald dome, bushy eyebrows and black beard, was an ideal interpreter of Chabrol's characteristic acid wit. But the screenplay by novelist Françoise Sagan lacks the sympathy or depth that Charlie Chaplin brought to the same subject in *Monsieur Verdoux* (1947). However, the photography, the sets, and the bevy of beautiful actresses – including Michèle Morgan, Danielle Darrieux and Hildegarde Neff looking attractive in their period costumes – are pleasing to the eye. French dialogue dubbed into English.

Michèle Morgan *Celestine Buisson* • Danielle Darrieux *Berthe Heon* • Charles Denner *Henri-Désire Landru* • Hildegarde Knef [Hildegarde Neff] *Madame Ixe* • Juliette Mayniel *Anna Colomb* • Stéphane Audran *Fernande Segret* • Mary Marquet *Madame Guillin* ■ *Dir* Claude Chabrol • *Scr* Françoise Sagan, Claude Chabrol • *Cinematographer* Jean Rabier • *Costume Designer* Maurice Albray

Bluebeard ★

Crime thriller
1972 · It/Fr/W Ger · Colour · 123mins

This take on the infamous serial killer is likely to offend almost everyone. The execution is so ham-fisted, and the murders so exploitative, that the film is oddly repugnant – the sort of movie Bluebeard himself might have liked. Richard Burton apparently took the role because he fancied a trip to Budapest, while his female victims (Raquel Welch, Virna Lisi, Nathalie Delon) are encouraged to strip and camp it up before they meet their untimely ends.

Richard Burton *Baron Von Sepper* • Raquel Welch *Magdalena* • Joey Heatherton *Anne* • Virna Lisi *Elga* • Nathalie Delon *Erika* • Marilu Tolo *Brigitte* • Karin Schubert *Greta* • Agostina Belli *Caroline* ■ *Dir* Edward Dmytryk • *Scr* Ennio Di Concini, Edward Dmytryk, Maria Pia Fusco, from a story by Ennio Di Concini, Edward Dmytryk, Maria Pia Fusco

Bluebeard's Eighth Wife ★★

Romantic comedy
1938 · US · BW · 84mins

An impoverished daughter of the French nobility becomes the eighth wife of a millionaire who finds he has finally met his match. Marking the first screenplay collaboration of Charles Brackett and Billy Wilder, and directed by Ernst Lubitsch, this romantic comedy promises much but, alas, delivers little. After the delightful opening sequence, in which the stars "meet cute" in a store's pyjama department, the famous "Lubitsch touch" disappears and gives way to increasing tedium. It ended Lubitsch's brilliant tenure at Paramount; he left for MGM, where he immediately regained his form with the brilliant *Ninotchka*.

Claudette Colbert *Nicole de Loiselle* • Gary Cooper *Michael Brandon* • Edward Everett Horton *de Loiselle* • David Niven *Albert De Regnier* • Elizabeth Patterson *Aunt Hedwige* • Herman Bing *Monsieur Pepinard* • Charles Halton *Monsieur de la Coste* • Barlowe Borland *Uncle Fernandel* • Warren Hymer *Kid Mulligan* • Franklin Pangborn *Assistant hotel manager* ■ *Dir* Ernst Lubitsch • *Scr* Charles Brackett, Billy Wilder, from the translation by Charlton Andrews of the play *La Huitiéme Femme de Barbe-bleu* by Alfred Savoir

Blueberry Hill ★★ 15

Drama
1988 · US · Colour · 88mins

Though set in the mid-fifties, this dysfunctional-family drama is far less rock 'n' roll than the time-frame and Fats Domino-derived title might suggest. Carrie Snodgress plays an overwound mum and Jennifer Rubin is the daughter who discovers the twin secrets about her dad's death and her inheritance of his honkytonk piano-playing skills. Matt Lattanzi co-stars. For five minutes back in the late-eighties, Lattanzi was being touted as the next big thing. Like this film, he's been little heard of since. ▭

Carrie Snodgress *Becca Dane* • Margaret Avery *Hattie Cale* • Jennifer Rubin *Ellie Dane* • Matt Lattanzi *Denny Logan* • Tommy Swerdlow *Ray Porter* ■ *Dir* Strathford Hamilton • *Scr* Lonon F Smith

Blueberry Hill ★★★

Drama
1989 · Bel · Colour · 90mins

Awash with nostalgia, yet never guilty of descending into mawkishness, this admirable rite-of-passage picture from Belgian director Robbe de Hert expertly evokes an era and its attitudes. Accompanied by a throbbing soundtrack of fifties jukebox hits, this semi-autobiographical tale touches on everything from teenage rebellion and first love to authoritarianism and Catholic hypocrisy. Michael Pas is hugely impressive as the bright kid who would rather hang around a jumping nightclub than pore over his books, and it's his romantic entanglements and defiant defence of a bullied classmate that gives the film both its charm and its backbone. In Flemish with English subtitles.

Michael Pas *Robin De Hert* • Babette Van Veen *Cathy* • Hilde Heijnen *Jeanine* • Frank Aendenboom *Verbist* • Myriam Meszieres *Suzanne Claessens* • Ronny Coutteure *Valère* ■ *Dir* Robbe de Hert • *Scr* Robbe de Hert, Noel Degeling, Walter Van Den Broeck

The Blues Brothers ★★★★ 15

Musical comedy 1980 · US · Colour · 127mins

A wonderful sprawling mess of a movie that remains one of the best musical comedies of modern times. John Belushi and Dan Aykroyd are the criminally minded brothers on a mission from God, who resurrect their old rhythm-and-blues band to raise money for their old church. The skimpiest of plots provides the excuse for a string of rousing musical numbers and cameo appearances from music legends such as Ray Charles, Aretha Franklin and Cab Calloway. When the music runs out, director John Landis stages a ludicrously spectacular car chase involving the massed forces of law and order, a rabid country-and-western band and neo-Nazis. The supporting cast includes Carrie Fisher as a miffed lover, Twiggy and Steven Spielberg. Contains swearing. ▭

John Belushi *"Joliet" Jake Blues* • Dan Aykroyd *Elwood Blues* • Kathleen Freeman *Sister Mary Stigmata* • James Brown (1) *Reverend Cleophus James* • Cab Calloway *Curtis* • Carrie Fisher *Mystery woman* • Ray Charles *Ray* • Aretha Franklin *Soul food café owner* • John Candy *Burton Mercer* • Henry Gibson *Nazi leader* • Steven Spielberg *Cook county clerk* • Twiggy *Chic lady* ■ *Dir* John Landis • *Scr* John Landis, Dan Aykroyd

Blues Brothers 2000 ★★★ PG

Comedy 1998 · US · Colour · 118mins

It took 18 years for actor Dan Aykroyd and director John Landis to "get the band back together". Although viewers will miss the marvellous slapstick slobbishness of the late John Belushi, this sequel is still a lot of fun. The wafer-thin plot has Elwood Blues (Aykroyd) hooking up with the band's former musicians. But the movie's *raison d'être* are the irresistible R 'n' B numbers performed by Aykroyd, his co-star John Goodman and dynamic performers such as Aretha Franklin, BB King and James Brown. It's definitely worth catching if you can forgive Landis's self-indulgent touches. Contains some mild swearing and sexual references. ▭

Dan Aykroyd *Elwood Blues* • John Goodman *Mighty Mack McTeer* • Joe Morton *Cabel Chamberlain* • J Evan Bonifant *Buster* • Aretha Franklin *Mrs Murphy* • James Brown (1) *Reverend Cleophus James* • BB King *Malvern Gasperon* • Steve Cropper *Steve "The Colonel" Cropper* • Donald Dunn *Donald*

Blues in the Night ★★

Musical drama 1941 · US · BW · 87mins

A tough, interesting Warner Bros drama, purporting to deal honestly with the life of itinerant jazz musicians, with murky direction by Anatole Litvak. The film almost works, but the pivotal role of a musician bent on self-destruction is played by the bland, amorphous Richard Whorf – John Garfield or even Victor Mature would have been better – who would swiftly switch to directing at MGM. The support, though, is excellent, and includes a young, acting Elia Kazan playing (or miming) the clarinet. But, despite the gritty look and those wonderful much-copied Warner Bros montages, the film never quite hangs together. Lovers of trash melodrama may enjoy it.

Priscilla Lane *Ginger* • Betty Field *Kay Grant* • Richard Whorf *Jigger Pine* • Lloyd Nolan *Del Davis* • Jack Carson *Leo Powell* • Wally Ford [Wallace Ford] *Brad Ames* • Elia Kazan *Nickie Haroyan* ■ *Dir* Anatole Litvak • *Scr* Robert Rossen, from the play by Edwin Gilbert

Blume in Love ★★★★ 15

Comedy drama 1973 · US · Colour · 110mins

One of the best sex comedies from the fast-and-loose seventies, with a wonderfully warm performance from George Segal as a lawyer whose harassed humour endears us to his infidelities. His wife (Susan Anspach), alas, feels differently, throwing him out on his ear to repent at leisure and ponder passions past. Writer/director Paul Mazursky – who made *Bob & Carol & Ted & Alice* four years earlier – indulges his usual predilection for lengthy exposition, while the Italian locations add more travelogue gloss than emotional point. Segal's characterisation makes it all worthwhile, however. ▭

George Segal *Blume* • Susan Anspach *Nina Blume* • Kris Kristofferson *Elmo* • Marsha Mason *Arlene* • Shelley Winters *Mrs Cramer* • Donald F Muhich *Analyst* • Paul Mazursky *Blume's partner* ■ *Dir/Scr* Paul Mazursky

Boardwalk ★★

Drama 1979 · US · Colour · 100mins

American theatre luminaries Lee Strasberg and Ruth Gordon star as David and Becky Rosen, a happily married Jewish couple approaching their golden wedding whose lives – and those of their friends – are blighted by the disintegration of their Brooklyn neighbourhood. Violent gangs roam the Coney Island boardwalk, their best friends gas themselves in despair, and their forlorn middle-aged daughter (Janet Leigh) makes a loveless marriage to escape spinsterhood. Such is the framework of writer/director Steven Verona's relentlessly depressing and ineptly-made film, which offers no insight into the problems it exaggeratedly depicts.

Ruth Gordon *Becky Rosen* • Lee Strasberg *David Rosen* • Janet Leigh *Florence* • Joe Silver *Leo* • Eli Mintz *Mr Friedman* • Eddie Barth *Eli Rosen* • Merwin Goldsmith *Charlie* • Michael Ayr *Peter* ■ *Dir* Stephen Verona • *Scr* Stephen Verona, Leigh Chapman

The Boatniks ★★ 🆄

Comedy adventure
1970 · US · Colour · 99mins

Rocking the boat with his outrageous mugging, Phil Silvers eventually capsizes this unremarkable Disney comedy. As a smart-talking, but decidedly minor league, jewel thief, he fails to outwit the equally gormless Robert Morse, who, up to that point, had been carving his little niche as the worst-ever coastguard in the history of California's Newport harbour. A much firmer hand was needed on the tiller than that applied by director Norman Tokar, but there are a couple of neat set pieces, and no film featuring Don Ameche can be all bad.

Robert Morse *Ensign Thomas Garland* • Stefanie Powers *Kate Fairchild* • Phil Silvers *Harry* • Norman Fell *Max* • Mickey Shaughnessy *Charlie* • Don Ameche *Commander Taylor* • Wally Cox *Jason Bennett* ■ *Dir* Norman Tokar • *Scr* Arthur Julian, from a story by Marty Roth

Bob & Carol & Ted & Alice ★★★★ 🔟

Comedy 1969 · US · Colour · 100mins

As dated as flared trousers, this flower power piece of permissiveness alarmed some at the time because of promised revelations, but disappointed others because romance got in the way. Natalie Wood, Robert Culp, Elliott Gould and Dyan Cannon make up the two Californian couples who go in for group therapy and confessing to extra-marital sex. Trouble is, they're such chatterboxes (so, too many words and too little action) because director Paul Mazursky (who was Oscar-nominated for the screenplay along with co-writer Larry Tucker) makes films that way. There's an intimidating sentimentality, too, but the film was still an important landmark in its day. 🔲

Natalie Wood *Carol* • Robert Culp *Bob* • Elliott Gould *Ted* • Dyan Cannon *Alice* • Horst Ebersberg *Horst* • Lee Bergere *Emelio* • Donald F Muhich *Psychiatrist* • Noble Lee Holderread Jr *Sean* • KT Stevens *Phyllis* ■ *Dir* Paul Mazursky • *Scr* Paul Mazursky, Larry Tucker • *Cinematographer* Charles Lang

Bob Le Flambeur ★★★★ 🅿🅶

Crime drama 1955 · Fr · BW · 97mins

This little-known classic counts as one of Jean-Pierre Melville's very best. It's a bizarre heist movie that spins on a delicious irony: Bob plans to rob the casino at Deauville but wins the money at the tables. There are tragic overtones, but this is still an absurdist comedy with bags of atmosphere, romance, jazz music, pretentious dialogue, great locations and a wonderfully brooding performance from Roger Duchesne. In French with English subtitles. 🔲

Roger Duchesne *Bob* • Isabelle Corey *Anne* • Daniel Cauchy *Paolo* • Howard Vernon *McKimmie* • Gérard Buhr *Marc* • André Garret *Roger* • Guy Decomble *Inspector* ■ *Dir* Jean-Pierre Melville • *Scr* Jean-Pierre Melville, Auguste Le Breton

The Bob Mathias Story ★ 🆄

Biographical sports drama
1954 · US · BW · 70mins

Although his achievement of becoming the first decathlete to retain his

Olympic title was laudable, Bob Mathias is hopelessly miscast in this sanctimonious biopic. Neither he nor his wife Melba have the charisma to overcome either their dramatic inexperience or the platitudes in Richard Collins's gushingly patriotic screenplay. The sense of triumphalism is quickly out of the blocks, as coach Ward Bond guides the 17-year-old to victory at the 1948 London Games. But that's nothing compared to the blaring jingoism that leads him to come out of retirement in order to beat the Russkies at Helsinki in 1952.

Bob Mathias • Ward Bond *Coach Jackson* • Melba Mathias • Paul Bryar *Andrews* • Ann Doran *Mrs Mathias* • Howard Petrie *Dr Mathias* • Diane Jergens *Pat Mathias* ■ *Dir* Francis D Lyon • *Scr* Richard Collins

Bob Roberts ★★★★ 🔟

Spoof political documentary
1992 · US · Colour · 99mins

1992 was the year of Tim Robbins. Not only did he star in Robert Altman's savage Hollywood satire *The Player* but he also starred in, wrote and directed this hilarious pseudo-documentary about a folk-singing right-wing politician running for the US Senate. Taking its style from *This Is Spinal Tap* with a deliberate on-screen homage to the Bob Dylan tour movie *Don't Look Back*, *Bob Roberts* is both witty and wickedly pointed, if a shade smug at times. Immaculately cast, with telling performances from Alan Rickman, Gore Vidal and John Cusack, the film was a notable and substantial achievement for its young *auteur*, who has gone on to become one of the movie names of the nineties. Contains swearing 🔲

Tim Robbins *Bob Roberts* • Giancarlo Esposito *Bugs Raplin* • Ray Wise *Chet MacGregor* • Rebecca Jenkins *Delores Perrigrew* • Harry J Lennix *Franklin Dockett* • John Ottavino *Clark Anderson* • Robert Stanton *Bart Macklerooney* • Alan Rickman *Lukas Hart III* • Gore Vidal *Senator Brickley Paiste* • James Spader *Chuck Marlin* • Helen Hunt *Rose Pondell* • Susan Sarandon *Tawna Titan* • John Cusack *TV host* ■ *Dir/Scr* Tim Robbins

Bob, Son of Battle ★★ 🆄

Drama 1947 · US · Colour · 103mins

Clean-cut Lon McCallister, who romanced the horses in *Home in Indiana*, is in love with his dog this time, in a movie directed by Louis King, the younger brother of director Henry and famed for such animal sagas as *Smoky* and *Thunderhead Son of Flicka*. Peggy Ann Garner is sweet, Edmund Gwenn watchable as ever and the scenery attractive but, unless you particularly enjoy boy-and-dog movies, you may want to give it a miss – it's not up to *Old Yeller* or those early Lassie features.

Edmund Gwenn *Adam McAdam* • Lon McCallister *David McAdam* • Peggy Ann Garner *Maggie Moore* • Reginald Owen *James Moore* • Charles Irwin *Long Kirby* • Dave Thursby *Samuel Thornton* • John Rogers *Mackenzie* ■ *Dir* Louis King • *Scr* Jerome Cady, from the novel by Alfred Ollivant

Bobbikins ★ 🆄

Fantasy comedy 1959 · UK · BW · 89mins

Even die-hard Max Bygraves fans will be hard pressed to squeeze much enjoyment out of this cinematic lemon.

Impoverished entertainer Bygraves becomes rich after his 14-month-old baby begins picking up financial titbits from his park bench conversations with Chancellor Charles Carson. Preposterous, you might think. But this tot has got his head screwed on and knows what to do when he sees the filthy lucre coming between dad and mum Shirley Jones. It's hard to imagine who felt more peeved – Jones for crossing the Atlantic for this fiddle-faddle, or Fox for funding it.

Max Bygraves *Benjamin Barnaby* • Shirley Jones *Betty Barnaby* • Steven Stacker *Bobbikins* • Billie Whitelaw *Lydia* • Barbara Shelley *Valerie* • Colin Gordon *Dr Phillips* • Charles Tingwell *Luke* • Lionel Jeffries *Gregory Mason* • Rupert Davies *Jock Fleming* ■ *Dir* Robert Day • *Scr* Oscar Brodney

Bobby ★★★ 🅿🅶

Musical romance
1973 · Ind · Colour · 160mins

Movie references abound in this colourful masala, which is not only packed with memorable songs, but also manages to tack a happy ending on to the *Romeo and Juliet* story. Director Raj Kapoor is in playful mood throughout, making many of the love scenes between his son Rishi and Dimple Kapadia mirror classic moments from his own on-screen teaming with future superstar Nargis. Moreover, he casts the hissible Prem Chopra as himself to act as the *deus ex machina*, whose abduction of Kapadia sees a cessation in the feud between her fisherman father and Rishi's rich relations. In Hindi with English subtitles. 🔲

Rishi Kapoor *Raj Nath* • Dimple Kapadia *Bobby* • Pran *Rishi's father* • Premnath *Bobby's father* • Prem Chopra ■ *Dir* Raj Kapoor • *Scr* KA Abbas, VP Sathe

Bobby Deerfield ★★★ 🅿🅶

Romantic drama
1977 · US · Colour · 118mins

A self-consciously arty (and often just plain dumb) yet strangely compelling melodrama, with Al Pacino as a Formula One racing driver who falls in love with a terminally ill Italian beauty, played by Marthe Keller. Thanks to Pacino's addiction to speed, there's a death sentence hanging over both of them, making this a peculiarly morbid experience. What makes it not quite laughable, and even bearable, is the quality of Pacino's performance and director Sydney Pollack's assured coverage of the races and use of the Florence locations. 🔲

Al Pacino *Bobby Deerfield* • Marthe Keller *Lillian Morelli* • Anny Duperey *Lydia* • Walter McGinn *Leonard* • Romolo Valli *Uncle Luigi* • Stephan Meldegg *Karl Holtzmann* • Jaime Sanchez *Delvecchio* ■ *Dir* Sydney Pollack • *Scr* Alvin Sargent, from the novel *Heaven Has No Favorites* by Erich Maria Remarque

The Bobo ★★

Comedy 1967 · UK · Colour · 103mins

Director Robert Parrish is both talented and under-rated, but you'd never guess it from his mishandling of this bizarre Peter Sellers vehicle. An alleged comedy, made when the sixties swung and Sellers was married to co-star Britt Ekland, this was one of a string of ill-chosen projects that tarnished

Sellers's reputation before he returned to the Clouseau role in the mid-seventies. Here, would you believe it, he plays an unsuccessful matador who has to seduce Barcelona's most desirable lady in order to get a booking as a singer. It's not very funny, but the locations are gorgeous, and the sublime Hattie Jacques is a treat.

Peter Sellers *Juan Bautista* • Britt Ekland *Olimpia Segura* • Rossano Brazzi *Carlos Matabosch* • Adolfo Celi *Francisco Carbonell* • Hattie Jacques *Trinity Martinez* • Alfredo Lettieri [Al Lettieri] *Eugenio* • Kenneth Griffith *Gamazo* • Marne Maitland *Castillo* ■ *Dir* Robert Parrish • *Scr* David R Schwartz, from his play

Boccaccio '70 ★★

Portmanteau comedy drama
1961 · It/Fr · Colour · 149mins

A compendium of three separate stories, each with a major director wasting his gifts on a contemporary *Decameron* that focuses on women in relation to different aspects of sex. Fellini directs Anita Ekberg as a billboard model taking a swipe at puritanism; Visconti's segment has Romy Schneider playing a wife who takes unexpected action on learning that her husband frequents brothels; Sophia Loren auctions herself as a raffle prize under Vittorio De Sica's guidance. The film veers between the vulgar, the boring and the intermittently amusing; only Loren's episode manages to be poignant. A fourth episode, directed by Mario Monicelli was dropped from versions shown outside Italy. In Italian with English subtitles.

Anita Ekberg *Anita* • Peppino De Filippo *Dr Antonio Mazzuolo* • Romy Schneider *Pupe* • Tomas Milian *The count* • Romolo Valli *The lawyer* • Sophia Loren *Zoe* • Luigi Giuliani *Gaetano* • Alfio Vita *The sexton* • Giacomo Furia • Alberto Sorrentino • Marisa Solinas *Luciana* • Germano Giglioli *Renzo* ■ *Dir* Federico Fellini, Vittorio De Sica, Luchino Visconti, Mario Monicelli • *Scr* Federico Fellini, Ennio Flaiano, Tullio Pinelli, Suso Cecchi D'Amico, Luchino Visconti, Cesare Zavattini, Giovanni Arpino, Italo Calvino, Mario Monicello

Bodies, Rest and Motion ★★★ 🔟

Drama 1993 · US · Colour · 94mins

An average "twentysomething" tale, similar to Cameron Crowe's *Singles* (but without the cool Seattle soundtrack). Phoebe Cates, Bridget Fonda, Tim Roth and Eric Stoltz bum around Arizona musing about life, love and shallow relationships that no one will particularly care about except them. A disappointment from director Michael Steinberg, who previously made, with Neal Jimenez, the moving and meaningful drama *The Waterdance*, which also starred Stoltz. Contains swearing.

Phoebe Cates *Carol* • Bridget Fonda *Beth* • Tim Roth *Nick* • Eric Stoltz *Sid* • Alicia Witt *Elizabeth* • Sandra Lafferty *Yard-sale lady* • Sidney Dawson *TV customer* • Jon Proudstar *Station attendant* ■ *Dir* Michael Steinberg • *Scr* Roger Hedden, from his play

Bodily Harm ★★ 🔞

Crime thriller 1995 · US · Colour · 87mins

Since her riveting performance in *The Last Seduction* Linda Fiorentino's career has too often included routine thrillers like this one. Fiorentino plays Rita Cates, a Las Vegas detective investigating the murders of two women linked with former copper Sam (Daniel Baldwin), who is also her ex-lover. True to form, Fiorentino renews her steamy affair with the prime suspect. While the star oozes sensuality, the script is plodding. Even the usually reliable Gregg Henry fails to lift this out of the ordinary. ▭

Linda Fiorentino *Rita Cates* • Daniel Baldwin *Sam McKeon* • Gregg Henry *JD Prejon* • Bill Smitrovich *Lt Darryl Stewart* • Troy Evans *Oscar Simpson* • Joe Regalbuto *Stan Geffen* • Millie Perkins *Dr Spencer* • Shannon Kenny *Krystal Lynn/Jacy Barclay* ▪ *Dir* James Lemmo • *Scr* Joseph Whaley, Ronda Barendse, James Lemmo

Body and Soul ★★
First World War spy drama
1931 · US · BW · 81mins

The principal interest today of this apparently lost First World War flying-and-spying drama is the brief appearance of Humphrey Bogart. He plays an American flyer in France who dies trying to shoot down a German observation balloon. After Bogey's demise, Charles Farrell falls for his dead pal's widow Elissa Landi, who comes under suspicion of being a spy. The arrival of Myrna Loy, also claiming to have been Bogart's dame, complicates matters. The script is by Jules Furthman, known for his work with directors Josef von Sternberg and Howard Hawks, but this was directed by the lesser known Alfred Santell.

Charles Farrell *Maj Andrews* • Elissa Landi *Carla* • Humphrey Bogart *Jim Watson* • Myrna Loy *Alice Lester* • Donald Dillaway *Tap Johnson* • Crawford Kent [Crauford Kent] *Major Burke* • Pat Somerset *Major Knowles* • Ian MacLaren *Gen Trofford Jones* ▪ *Dir* Alfred Santell • *Scr* Jules Furthman, from the play *Squadrons* by AE Thomas and the story *Big Eyes and Little Mouth* by Elliot White Springs

Body and Soul ★★★★★ PG
Film noir sports drama
1947 · US · BW · 100mins

The greatest boxing movie of all time, *Raging Bull* and *Champion* notwithstanding, James Wong Howe's in-the-ring photography set landmark standards, as he dispensed with tripods and roller skated with a hand-held camera. Robert Parrish's Oscar-winning editing (with Francis D Lyon) prefigured his directing career, as did Robert Aldrich's assistant direction. John Garfield is superb as the champ with an uncertain sense of ethics, and Lilli Palmer simply mouthwatering as his doll. There's a tautness in Robert Rossen's direction that would recapture 14 years later in his equally masterly *The Hustler*. ▭

John Garfield *Charlie Davis* • Lilli Palmer *Peg Born* • Hazel Brooks *Alice* • Anne Revere *Anna Davis* • William Conrad *Quinn* • Joseph Pevney *Shorty Polaski* • Canada Lee *Ben Chaplin* • Lloyd Goff *Roberts* ▪ *Dir* Robert Rossen • *Scr* Abraham Polonsky

Body and Soul ★★ 18
Sports drama　1981 · US · Colour · 93mins

This pallid remake of the powerful 1947 John Garfield boxing classic is remarkable for all the wrong reasons.

Hidden away near the bottom of the cast list are two of the most charismatic figures in popular culture: Muhammad Ali, playing himself in a brief cameo; and Rat Packer Peter Lawford, here cast, oddly enough, as a gangster. Leon Isaac Kennedy is in the Garfield role, but it's his then-wife, Jayne Kennedy, who acts the rest of the cast off the screen. That isn't much of an achievement, though, in a film that pulls all its punches. ▭

Leon Isaac Kennedy *Leon Johnson* • Jayne Kennedy *Julie Winters* • Michael V Gazzo *Frankie* • Peter Lawford *Big Man* • Perry Lang *Charles Golphin* • Kim Hamilton *Mrs Johnson* • Muhammad Ali ▪ *Dir* George Bowers • *Scr* Leon Isaac Kennedy

Body Armor ★★
Action thriller　1996 · US · Colour · 90mins

The cinematography of this action film is above average for a made-for-video movie, with crisp night photography and sharp colors, so even the most dreary locations look decent. Unfortunately, the cinematography can't improve the action sequences – the martial arts sequences have been edited too quickly and the car chases and shoot-outs suffer from being shot in a way that drains from them all suspense. Matt McColm plays an especially arrogant hero, muttering profanities under his breath as he smugly takes on an evil chemist (played by a bored Ron Perlman) after he's hired by his ex-girlfriend. The extremely silly ending does, however, almost make it worth sitting through.

Matt McColm *Ken Conway* • Annabel Schofield *Marisa* • Carol Alt *Agent Monica McBride* • Morgan Brittany *Sloane Matthews* • John Rhys-Davies *Rasheed* • Ron Perlman *Dr Ramsey Krago* ▪ *Dir* Jack Gill • *Scr* Stuart Beattie, Andrea Buck, Jack Gill, Duncan McLachlan, from a story by Paul Steven • *Cinematographer* Robert Hays

Body Bags ★★ 18
Horror comedy　1993 · US · Colour · 90mins

The involvement of two masters of modern horror, John Carpenter and Tobe Hooper, will spark some interest, but this is an otherwise routine gorefest. Carpenter, who also serves as a cadaverous host, directs the first two stories: one is about a woman threatened by an unknown psycho; the other's a fable about the perils of hiding a thinning crop. Hooper wraps up the proceedings with a story of a baseball player getting horrible visions when he has an eye transplant. The direction from the two old hands is fluid enough, but they are let down by weak scripts. On the plus side it boasts an interesting cast, plus cameos from horror directors Sam Raimi, Wes Craven and Roger Corman. Contains swearing, violence and a sex scene. ▭

John Carpenter (1) *Coroner* • Tom Arnold *First man* • Tobe Hooper *Second man* • Robert Carradine *Bill, attendant* • Wes Craven *Pasty-faced man* • Stacy Keach *Richard* • David Warner *Dr Lock* • Sheena Easton *Megan* • Mark Hamill *Brent* • Twiggy *Cathy* • Roger Corman *Dr Bregman* • Sam Raimi *Dead attendant (The Real Bill)* ▪ *Dir* John Carpenter, Tobe Hooper • *Scr* Billy Brown, Dan Angel

Body Chemistry ★★ 18
Erotic thriller　1990 · US · Colour · 80mins

An early entry in the erotic thriller stakes, and one which, like *Indecent Behaviour* and *Animal Instincts*, developed into a profitable video franchise. In this one, Lisa Pescia plays a doctor who gets mixed up in sexual mind games with one of her colleagues, video stalwart Marc Singer. It's the usual mix of sub-*noir* thrills and soft-core bonking, but it looks pretty enough. If you've never seen an erotic thriller before, this is as good a place as any to start. ▭

Marc Singer *Dr Tom Redding* • Mary Crosby *Marlee* • Lisa Pescia *Dr Claire Archer* • David Kagen *Freddie* • H Bradley Barneson *Jason* • Doreen Alderman *Kim* • Lauren Tuerk *Wendy* • Joseph Campanella *Doctor Pritchard* ▪ *Dir* Kristine Peterson • *Scr* Jackson Barr

Body Chemistry 2: Voice of a Stranger ★★ 18
Erotic thriller　1992 · US · Colour · 80mins

Lisa Pescia returns for another slice of sexy shenanigans from this profitable erotic thriller franchise. This time around, bad doctor Claire Archer has assumed a new identity as a radio therapist. She soon starts to spin a naughty web of intrigue around moody Gregory Harrison, who is, of course, hiding some deep, dark secrets of his own. By 1992 the video exploitation companies were churning out these sort of thrillers by the dozen; this one is remarkable only for a cameo from A-list director John Landis. Two further sequels followed. ▭

Gregory Harrison *Dan* • Lisa Pescia *Dr Claire Archer* • Robin Riker *Brenda* • Morton Downey Jr *Big Chuck* • Clint Howard *Larabee* • John Landis *Dr Edwards* ▪ *Dir* Adam Simon • *Scr* Jackson Barr, Christopher Wooden

Body Count ★★ 18
Crime drama　1997 · US/UK · Colour · 80mins

After the massive success of the first series of *NYPD Blue*, its star David Caruso seemed destined for bigger things. So far his big screen career hasn't gone quite to plan, though this is one of his better efforts. He's part of a bickering gang of robbers who, having just pulled off a multi-million dollar art heist, must now get to Miami to cash in their haul. With the likes of Ving Rhames, Linda Fiorentino, John Leguizamo and Donnie Wahlberg along for the ride, the performances can't be faulted. For all that, this is lower-league Tarantino. Contains swearing, sexual references and violence. ▭

David Caruso *Hobbs* • Linda Fiorentino *Natalie* • John Leguizamo *Chino* • Ving Rhames *Pike* • Donnie Wahlberg *Booker* • Forest Whitaker *Crane* • Michael Corrigan *Security officer no 1* • Michael Hunter *Security officer no 2* ▪ *Dir* Robert Patton-Spruill • *Scr* Theodore Witcher

Body Double ★★★★ 18
Erotic thriller　1984 · US · Colour · 109mins

No one is better at apeing Alfred Hitchcock than director Brian De Palma. In this engrossingly sly shocker, he combines the master's predilection for kinky storytelling with his own engaging high style and taste for designer violence. Little does B-movie horror actor Craig Wasson know

when he spies on Deborah Shelton undressing in her Hollywood home that it will lead him to witnessing murder and seeking clues to who perpetrated such a shocking crime in Tinseltown's sex industry. Tense, deliciously sleazy and blackly comic – and sporting a gorgeous Pino Donaggio score – De Palma's *Rear Window* update is his most outrageous and voyeuristic suspense film to date. Contains violence, swearing, sex scenes and nudity. ▭ **DVD**

Craig Wasson *Jake* • Melanie Griffith *Holly* • Gregg Henry *Sam* • Deborah Shelton *Gloria* • Guy Boyd *Jim McClean* • Dennis Franz *Rubin* • David Haskell *Drama teacher* • Rebecca Stanley *Kimberly* ▪ *Dir* Brian De Palma • *Scr* Brian De Palma, Robert Avrech, from a story by Brian De Palma

Body Heat ★★★★ 18
Thriller　1981 · US · Colour · 108mins

The likes of *Basic Instinct* writer Joe Eszterhas have given the term "erotic thriller" a bad name of late, but this dazzling directorial debut from Lawrence Kasdan still packs a steamy punch. William Hurt is the small-town lawyer who falls for *femme fatale* Kathleen Turner only to find himself ensnared in a tortuous plot to murder her wealthy husband (Richard Crenna). Kasdan respectfully tips his hat to classics such as *Double Indemnity*, but the intricate plotting and sly humour ensure that his film stands in its own right. The performances are first rate, too. Turner positively sizzles, while Hurt is excellent as the ordinary Joe getting increasingly out of his depth. There's also a creepy cameo from Mickey Rourke and a jolly supporting role for the then-unknown Ted Danson. Contains violence, swearing, sex scenes and nudity. ▭ **DVD**

William Hurt *Ned Racine* • Kathleen Turner *Matty Walker* • Richard Crenna *Edmund Walker* • Ted Danson *Peter Lowenstein* • JA Preston *Oscar Grace* • Mickey Rourke *Teddy Lewis* • Kim Zimmer *Mary Ann* • Jane Hallaren *Stella* • Lanna Sanders *Roz Kraft* ▪ *Dir/Scr* Lawrence Kasdan

Body Language ★★★ PG
Thriller　1992 · US · Colour · 88mins

Dynasty and *Melrose Place* actress Heather Locklear stars in this slightly raunchy tale of a businesswoman who hires a super-efficient secretary to sort out her life, unaware that her new employee has a rather sinister side and may do more than just reorganise her Filofax. Silly stuff, indeed, but entertainingly presented, with Locklear, Linda Purl and Edward Albert all having fun with their roles. Director Arthur Allan Seidelman keeps the pace fast enough to hide holes in the plot. ▭

Heather Locklear *Betsy Frieze* • Linda Purl *Norma* • James Acheson *Victor* • Edward Albert *Charles Stella* • Gary Bisig *Detective Gordon* • Jeff Kizer *Richie* • Denise Dal Vera *Clothing store clerk* ▪ *Dir* Arthur Allan Seidelman • *Scr* Dan Gurskis, Brian Ross, from the book by Brian Ross

Body Language ★ 18
Erotic thriller　1995 · US · Colour · 95mins

The usually competent Tom Berenger (*Platoon*) stars in this overwrought sexual thriller about a mob lawyer who courts disaster for himself and his

Mafia boss when he's fatally distracted by stripper Nancy Travis. Her seductive web of manipulation draws him into a deadly plan to free her from her abusive partner. A turgid, suspenseless melodrama. ▢

Tom Berenger *Gavin St Clair* • Nancy Travis *TJ Harlow* • Heidi Schanz *Dora Circe* ▪ Dir George Case • Scr Eric Harlacher

Body Melt ★★ 18
Horror comedy 1993 · Ausl · Colour · 79mins

Inhabitants of a suburban Melbourne cul-de-sac become unwitting guinea pigs for a new body enhancement drug in this splatter satire from Australian director Philip Brophy. Exploding genitalia, kangaroo cannibalism and placentas taking on lives of their own are a few of the over-the-top gross-outs in this corrosive stomach-churner. Hysterical acting and pointless horror homages (one minor character is named Gino Argento) lessen the confrontational nature of Brophy's slime-encrusted *Knots Landing* in Hell. However, while every body fluid is called into action, the end result of this ingenious vision about the modern obsession with physical fitness is only mildly offensive.

Gerard Kennedy *Det Sam Phillips* • Andrew Daddo *Johnno* • Ian Smith *Dr Carrera* • Vincent Gil *Pud* • Regina Gaigalas *Shaan* ▪ Dir Philip Brophy • Scr Philip Brophy, Rod Bishop

Body of Evidence ★★ 18
Thriller 1988 · US · Colour · 89mins

Sadly, this is not the hilarious 1992 Madonna movie of the same name, but a rather predictable thriller in which *Superman*'s Margot Kidder entertains the suspicion that her husband, a police pathologist, is a serial killer. Although there are some tense moments as Kidder moves towards major paranoia, this has all been done before (and better) in such movies as *Suspicion* and *Jagged Edge*. ▢

Margot Kidder *Carol Dwyer* • Barry Bostwick *Alex Dwyer* • Tony LoBianco *Evan Campbell* • Caroline Kava *Jean Fowler* • Jennifer Barbour *Jessie* • Debbie Carr *Lisa* • David Hayward *Jack* ▪ Dir Roy Campanella II • Scr Cynthia Whitcomb, Roy Campanella II

Body of Evidence ★★★ 18
Erotic thriller 1992 · US · Colour · 96mins

With this erotic thriller, director Uli Edel (*Last Exit to Brooklyn*) attempted to out-steam the same year's *Basic Instinct*, but, although it makes for rather hokey fun, it lacks the outrageous flair of Paul Verhoeven's notorious hit. Madonna is the *femme fatale* accused of killing her elderly millionaire boyfriend; Willem Dafoe is the lawyer who gets seduced into a dangerous affair with his client. The story is absolute rot, of course, and it's more interesting to guess how much of the erotic footage survived the snip. Madonna proves adept at shedding her clothes and handling candle wax, while Dafoe goes through the film largely on autopilot. However, the distinguished supporting cast adds some much needed class to the proceedings. Contains swearing, violence, sex scenes and nudity. ▢

Madonna *Rebecca Carlson* • Willem Dafoe *Frank Dulaney* • Joe Mantegna *Robert Garrett* • Anne Archer *Joanne Braslow* • Julianne Moore *Sharon Dulaney* • Stan Shaw *Charles Biggs* • Jürgen Prochnow *Dr Alan Paley* ▪ Dir Uli Edel • Scr Brad Mirman

Body of Influence ★★
Erotic thriller 1993 · US · Colour · 92mins

Soft-core king Gregory Hippolyte is reunited once again with Shannon Whirry (*Animal Instincts*) in this steamy tale of sexy shenanigans on the psychiatrist's couch. She's the sultry *femme fatale* claiming to be suffering from amnesia who gets her hooks into gullible psychiatrist Nick Cassavetes. Also along for the ride are the likes of Don Swayze, Sandahl Bergman and Richard Roundtree (*Shaft*). Don't expect the thriller elements to tax the brain. Contains nudity, sexual situations and some swearing.

Nick Cassavetes *Dr Jonathon Brooks* • Shannon Whirry *Laura/Lana* • Sandahl Bergman *Clarissa* • Don Swayze *Biker* • Anna Karin *Beth* • Diana Barton *Jennifer* • Richard Roundtree *Harry Reams* ▪ Dir Gregory Hippolyte • Scr David Schreiber

Body of Influence 2 ★ 18
Erotic thriller 1996 · US · Colour · 89mins

This lazy sequel to the erotic thriller makes the original seem like *Basic Instinct*. Set against that ever popular setting for erotic thrillers – a psychiatrist's office – this has Daniel Anderson as a shrink who gets a little too involved with one of his patients, Jodie Fisher, who insists that her life is being threatened by her S&M-hooked partner. The level of suspense rarely rises above zero, while even the sex scenes are heavy-handed. ▢

Jodie Fisher *Leza Watkins* • Daniel Anderson *Dr Thomas Benson* • Jonathan Goldstein *Rick Benson* • Pat Brennan *Walter Watkins* • Stephen Poletti *Lieutenant Murphy* • Cheryl Lawyer *Carrie* • Clive Rees *Nicky Diamond* ▪ Dir/Scr Brian J Smith

Body Parts ★★★ 18
Horror thriller 1991 · US · Colour · 84mins

From the writers of novels that inspired the film classics *Diabolique* and *Vertigo* comes this not-so-classic sci-fi horror, blending high-tech surgery with low-grade shocks. After a car accident, prison psychiatrist Jeff Fahey has the arm of an executed killer grafted on to his shoulder, which develops a murderous life of its own. Then he meets other recipients of the psycho's body parts suffering similar symptoms. *Near Dark* screenplay writer Eric Red directs all this sinister lunacy with a sure hand – but is it his own? An outrageously ghoulish thriller if you can keep a straight face. Contains swearing and violence. ▢

Jeff Fahey *Bill Chrushank* • Lindsay Duncan *Dr Webb* • Kim Delaney *Karen Chrushank* • Brad Dourif *Remo Lacey* • Zakes Mokae *Detective Sawchuk* • Peter Murnik *Mark Draper* • Paul Ben-Victor *Ray Kolberg* • John Walsh *Charlie Fletcher* ▪ Dir Eric Red • Scr Eric Red, Norman Snider, from a story by Patricia Herskovic, Joyce Taylor, from the novel *Choice Cuts* by Thomas Narcejac, Pierre Boileau

Body Shot ★★ 18
Erotic crime thriller 1994 · US · Colour · 93mins

Not many people would root for a member of the paparazzi, but at least the unlikely hero lends a novel twist to an otherwise by-the-numbers thriller. A blond Robert Patrick plays a sleazy snapper who is obsessed with reclusive rock superstar Michelle Johnson. Things go pear-shaped when he ends up framed for her murder. The plot stretches credibility to the limit, but the dependable cast makes it just about bearable. ▢

Robert Patrick *Mickey Dane* • Michelle Johnson *Danielle Wilde/Chelsea* • Ray Wise *Dwight Frye* • Jonathan Banks *Simon Deverau/Blake Donner* • Kim Miyori *Christine Wyler* • Peter Koch *Elmer Hatch* • William Steis *Curt Lomann* ▪ Dir Dimitri Logothetis • Scr Robert Ian Strauss

Body Shots ★★★ 18
Drama 1999 · US · Colour · 105mins

Michael Cristofer can finally shed the tag of "*Bonfire of the Vanities* screenwriter", for he has followed up with this debate-sparking study of twentysomething morality. It looks like we've a long night ahead of us as eight near-identical Los Angelenos go through their pre-club rituals. However, when wannabe actress Tara Reid accuses pro-footballer Jerry O'Connell of date rape, the fun stops and sides are taken. Snappily shot in hip image bites by Rodrigo Garcia and astutely structured by writer David McKenna (*American History X*), this breaks no new ground but still manages to tease, amuse and provoke.

Sean Patrick Flanery *Rick Hamilton* • Jerry O'Connell *Michael Penorisi* • Amanda Peet *Jane Bannister* • Tara Reid *Sara Olswang* • Ron Livingston *Trent Barber* • Emily Procter *Whitney Bryant* • Brad Rowe *Shawn Denigan* • Sybil Temchen *Emma Cooper* ▪ Dir Michael Cristofer • Scr David McKenna

The Body Snatcher ★★★★★ PG
Horror 1945 · US · BW · 78mins

Producer Val Lewton's magnificent version of Robert Louis Stevenson's Burke and Hare-like corpse-stealing short story is a horror masterpiece. Striking attention to historical authenticity and a magnificently evil performance from Boris Karloff as the vile cab driver supplying cadavers to desperate anatomist Henry Daniell, make for a grippingly literate and macabre shocker. Sinister support from Bela Lugosi and imaginative direction from Robert Wise give the tale a restrained ominousness and builds up a sense of unseen terror until the justifiably famous hallucination climax. ▢

Boris Karloff *John Gray* • Bela Lugosi *Joseph* • Henry Daniell *Dr MacFarlane* • Edith Atwater *Meg Camden* • Russell Wade *Donald Fettes* • Rita Corday *Mrs Marsh* • Sharyn Moffett *Georgina Marsh* • Donna Lee *Street singer* ▪ Dir Robert Wise • Scr Carlos Keith [Val Lewton], Philip MacDonald, from a short story by Robert Louis Stevenson

Body Snatchers ★★★★ 15
Science-fiction horror 1993 · US · Colour · 83mins

Those interstellar pods capable of duplicating humans return for a third sinister attempt on mankind's individual identities in director Abel Ferrara's masterly reinterpretation of the classic Jack Finney terror tale. Easily on an empathic par with the 1956 original chiller, *Invasion of the Body Snatchers*, this has – thanks to Ferrara's keen contemporary eye, controlled vision and heartless shock tactics – an underlying message that seems more pertinent and vital than ever. Meg Tilly and Gabrielle Anwar make indelible impressions as they take on the horrifying enemy infiltrating their military home base. Contains violence, swearing and nudity. ▢

Terry Kinney *Steve Malone* • Meg Tilly *Carole Malone* • Gabrielle Anwar *Marty Malone* • Forest Whitaker *Doctor Collins* • Reilly Murphy *Andy Malone* • Billy Wirth *Tim Young* • Christine Elise *Jenn Platt* • R Lee Ermey *General Platt* ▪ Dir Abel Ferrara • Scr Stuart Gordon, Dennis Paoli, Nicholas St John, from a story by Larry Cohen, Raymond Cistheri, from the novel *Invasion of the Body Snatchers* by Jack Finney

The Body Stealers ★
Science-fiction adventure 1969 · US/UK · Colour · 91mins

Parachutists pass through a red mist and disappear into thin air. And before long you will, too! There is little point in sticking around to find out it's alien Maurice Evans putting sky divers in suspended animation and substituting duplicates. A shame top agents Patrick Allen and Neil Connery (Sean's kid brother) don't reach the same conclusion after investigating a top secret space research lab, in this talky, laughably low-budget and hopelessly inept clone of *Invasion of the Body Snatchers*. What was George Sanders thinking of when he agreed to appear in this sci-fi belly flop?

George Sanders *General Armstrong* • Maurice Evans *Dr Matthews* • Patrick Allen *Bob Megan* • Neil Connery *Jim Radford* • Hilary Dwyer *Julie Slade* • Robert Flemyng *WC Baldwin* • Lorna Wilde *Lorna* • Allan Cuthbertson *Hindesmith* ▪ Dir Gerry Levy • Scr Mike St Clair, Peter Marcus

The Bodyguard ★★★ 15
Romantic thriller 1992 · US · Colour · 123mins

Kevin Costner and Whitney Houston fall in love, she trilling all the while, amid a highly charged atmosphere of jealousy and death threats in this hugely entertaining load of old baloney. Director Mick Jackson created a wildly successful film, much to several critics' snooty chagrin, by teaming two megastars and adding a daft but jaunty script, loud rock soundtrack and a few well-staged exciting moments. Costner is a trifle stern, but Houston makes a very creditable acting debut. Contains some violence and swearing. ▢ *DVD*

Kevin Costner *Frank Farmer* • Whitney Houston *Rachel Marron* • Gary Kemp *Sy Spector* • Bill Cobbs *Devaney* • Ralph Waite *Herb Farmer* • Tomas Arana *Portman* • Michele Lamar Richards *Nicki* • Mike Starr *Tony* ▪ Dir Mick Jackson • Scr Lawrence Kasdan, from his story

Boeing Boeing ★★★

Romantic comedy
1965 · US · Colour · 102mins

Marc Camoletti's hit play achieved astoundingly long theatrical runs throughout the world, so a screen version of this latter-day Feydeauesque farce was an inevitability. With a genuinely funny plot about a Casanova of the airlines skewed by modern technology, this is beautifully cast by skilled producer Hal Wallis and features two great comedians – the incorrigibly brash Tony Curtis and a disciplined and subdued Jerry Lewis – who work together impeccably. Thelma Ritter is the put-upon housekeeper and the trio of airline cuties are equally well cast. Director John Rich wisely opts for a proscenium approach and doesn't get in the way of the action, the pin-sharp photography is by the great Lucien Ballard and the period Paramount gloss helps.

Jerry Lewis *Robert Reed* • Tony Curtis *Bernard Lawrence* • Dany Saval *Jacqueline Grieux* • Christiane Schmidtmer *Lise Bruner* • Suzanna Leigh *Vicky Hawkins* • Thelma Ritter *Bertha* • Lomax Study *Pierre* • Françoise Ruggieri *Taxi driver* ■ *Dir* John Rich • *Scr* Edward Anholt, from the play by Marc Camoletti

The Bofors Gun ★

Drama
1968 · UK · Colour · 105mins

The setting for this drama of violent personal conflict is a British army camp in Germany; the year is 1954. David Warner plays an indecisive corporal in charge of a guard detail, while Nicol Williamson is the abrasive, self-despising Irish gunner under his command. Too talkative and claustrophobic by half, this unremittingly downbeat study of futility, weakness and hatred takes an inordinate time to reach its very predictable conclusion.

Nicol Williamson *O'Rourke* • Ian Holm *Flynn* • David Warner *Evans* • Richard O'Callaghan *Rowe* • Barry Jackson *Shone* • Donald Gee *Crawley* • John Thaw *Featherstone* • Peter Vaughan *Sergeant Walker* ■ *Dir* Jack Gold • *Scr* John McGrath, from his play *Events While Guarding the Bofors Gun*

Bogus ★★ PG

Fantasy comedy 1996 · US · Colour · 106mins

A tad disappointing all round. Director Norman Jewison (*Moonstruck*) has Whoopi Goldberg and Gérard Depardieu at his disposal, as well as *Sixth Sense* star Haley Joel Osment, and all he produces is sentimental codswallop. Osment, recently orphaned, ends up living with his child-loathing aunt (Goldberg). In order to survive the ordeal, he develops a relationship with an imaginary friend called Bogus (Depardieu). Trite stuff, though it may prove entertaining to the under-fives. ▭

Whoopi Goldberg *Harriet Franklin* • Gérard Depardieu *Bogus* • Haley Joel Osment *Albert* • Andrea Martin *Penny* • Nancy Travis *Lorraine* • Denis Mercier *M Antoine* • Ute Lemper *Babette* • Sheryl Lee Ralph *Ruth Clark* ■ *Dir* Norman Jewison • *Scr* Alvin Sargent, from a story by Jeff Rothberg, Francis X McCarthy

Bogus Bandits ★★ U

Comedy opera 1933 · US · BW · 88mins

A very dubious outing for Laurel and Hardy, this has the glorious boobies playing second fiddle to a *Desert Song*-style operetta. Dennis King is a dashing brigand in 18th-century Italy, wooing Thelma Todd, the neglected wife of lord James Finlayson. Stan and Ollie – here Stanlio and Olio – are vagrants trying to earn a living as bandits. There are some wonderful music-hall moments – Stan getting drunk on a barrel of wine is especially memorable. However, they scarcely get a chance to shine through the clichéd blackout of a ridiculous plot. ▭

Stan Laurel *Stanlio* • Oliver Hardy *Olio* • Dennis King *Fra Diavolo/Marquis de San Marco* • Thelma Todd *Lady Pamela* • James Finlayson *Lord Rocberg* • Lucille Browne *Zerlina* • Arthur Pierson *Lorenzo* • Henry Armetta *Matteo* ■ *Dir* Charles Rogers, Hal Roach • *Scr* Jeanie Macpherson, from the opera *Fra Diavolo* by Daniel F Auber

Bogwoman ★★★ 15

Drama 1997 · Ire · Colour · 77mins

This is a provocative study of how 1960s Northern Irish politics impacted on people's everyday lives. Rachel Dowling gives a mettlesome performance as the single mother who crosses the border to settle in Derry's Bogside and, having married, comes to realise she's capable of more than just slaving for her chauvinistic husband (Peter Mullan). Exploring the role of women in the Province in a much more credible way than Roger Michell's *Titanic Town*, Tom Collins's film is given added resonance by the fact that it ends on the eve of the Troubles, which dominated Ulster for the next 30 years. Contains swearing. ▭

Rachel Dowling [Rachael Dowling] *Maureen* • Sean McGinley *Mr D* • Peter Mullan *Barry* • Noelle Brown *Mrs D* ■ *Dir/Scr* Tom Collins

La Bohème ★★ U

Silent romantic drama
1926 · US · BW · 106mins

A characteristically soulful and touching Lillian Gish and an athletically exuberant and sincere John Gilbert are Mimi and Rodolfe, the lovers doomed to be parted by death in this silent enactment of the story familiar to those who know Puccini's popular opera. Director King Vidor (whose leading lady from *The Big Parade*, Renée Adorée, plays the ebullient Musette) expertly steers the changes of mood from the boisterous to the tragic in the Latin quarter of Paris. Despite its virtues, however, its style is too outmoded to hold much appeal for audiences now.

Lillian Gish *Mimi* • John Gilbert *Rodolphe* • Renée Adorée *Musette* • George Hassell *Schaunard* • Roy D'Arcy *Vicomte Paul* • Edward Everett Horton *Colline* • Karl Dane *Benoit* • Mathilde Comont *Madame Benoit* ■ *Dir* King Vidor • *Scr* Ray Doyle, Harry Behn, Fred De Gresac, William Conselman (titles), Ruth Cummings (titles), from the novel *Scènes de La Vie de Bohème (The Latin Quarter)* by Henri Murger

The Bohemian Girl ★★ U

Comedy 1936 · US · BW · 67mins

Not even the great Laurel and Hardy can lift the spirits of this damp adaptation of the operetta by Michael Balfe, about gypsies who, in revenge, kidnap a nobleman's daughter and bring her up as one of their own. Stan and Ollie are snatch-purses, not that it matters much. Their gags disappear in the banal and confused plot and they look as embarrassed as audiences feel. This was the last film of their regular co-star Thelma Todd, who made 40 films and died of carbon monoxide poisoning just after this film was completed. ▭

Stan Laurel *Stan* • Oliver Hardy *Ollie* • Thelma Todd *Gypsy Queen's daughter* • Antonio Moreno *Devilshoof* • Jacqueline Wells [Julie Bishop] *Arline* • Mae Busch *Mrs Hardy* • James Finlayson *Captain Finn* ■ *Dir* James W Horne, Charles Rogers • *Scr* Alfred Bunn, from the opera by Michael Balfe

Boiler Room ★★★★ 15

Drama 2000 · US · Colour · 119mins

Welcome to *Wall Street*: the Next Generation, an amorality tale of financial swizz-kids for whom greed is still good and who still think lunch is for wimps. The film focuses on a young chancer (Giovanni Ribisi) who's head-hunted by an "off-Broadway" brokerage firm that sells stocks in non-existent companies. Fuelled by equal measures of drink, drugs, adrenalin and *Boys' Own* testosterone, the young fiends of the firm's high-pressure "boiler room" are an obnoxious bunch. Writer/director Ben Younger worked in a real-life "boiler room" to research the film, and the result is a dynamite debut. There's great acting, too, from Ribisi, Vin Diesel and Ben Affleck, cameoing as the firm's Mr Motivator.

Giovanni Ribisi *Seth Davis* • Nia Long *Abby Halperin* • Vin Diesel *Chris* • Ben Affleck *Jim Young* • Tom Everett Scott *Michael* • Ron Rifkin *Marty Davis* • Nicky Katt *Greg* • Bill Sage *Agent Drew* ■ *Dir/Scr* Ben Younger

Boiling Point ★★★★ 18

Thriller 1990 · Jap · Colour · 92mins

Takeshi "Beat" Kitano followed up his excellent directorial debut, *Violent Cop*, with this equally assured mix of abrasive action and earthy humour. Set again in the sinister world of the Yakuza, the film focuses on the efforts of daydreaming greenhorn Masahiko Ono to protect his boss after he lands him in a gangster's bad books. As the manic former hood Ono hires to save the day, Takahito Iguchi gives a performance as hilarious as it is disturbing. This is essentially a samurai tale given an urban twist, and Kitano makes the city of Okinawa look a particularly forbidding place. Brutal, perhaps, but great fun, too. In Japanese with English subtitles. Contains violence and nudity. ▭

Masahiko Ono *Masaki* • Yuriko Ishida *Sayaka* • Takahito Iguchi *Takashi Iguchi* • Minoru Iizuka *Kazuo* • Makoto Ashikawa *Akira* • Hitoshi Ozawa *Kanai* • Hisashi Igawa *Otomo, gang boss* ■ *Dir/Scr* Takeshi Kitano

Boiling Point ★★★★ 15

Thriller 1993 · US · Colour · 88mins

On its cinema release, this was promoted as a straightforward action thriller, but it's far more intelligent than that. Wesley Snipes plays a treasury agent who hits the vengeance trail when his partner is killed during an undercover operation that goes horribly wrong. Dennis Hopper and Viggo Mortensen are his targets, who are also trying to keep one step ahead of the mob. While there are some excellently staged action set pieces, director James B Harris is more interested in exploring the relationships between the hunters and the hunted, and delivers a moody, melancholic tale of crime and punishment. Contains swearing, violence and sex scenes. ▭

Wesley Snipes *Jimmy Mercer* • Dennis Hopper *Red* • Lolita Davidovich *Vikki* • Viggo Mortensen *Ronnie* • Seymour Cassel *Leach* • Jonathan Banks *Max* • Christine Elise *Carol* • Tony LoBianco *Dio* • Valerie Perrine *Mona* • James Tolkan *Levitt* ■ *Dir* James B Harris • *Scr* James B Harris, from the novel *Money Men* by Gerald Petievich

The Bold and the Brave ★★

Second World War drama
1956 · US · BW · 87mins

If you can stand Mickey Rooney at full throttle, you may warm to this Second World War drama set on the front line in Italy. Rooney, as the soldier who wins a fortune in a marathon crap game, is contrasted with sensitive infantryman Wendell Corey, who fears he may have turned yellow, and Don Taylor, as the puritanical sergeant involved with Nicole Maurey, a local girl who hasn't been as good as she should have been. A well-staged reconnaisance mission sorts out who lives and who dies, in a film which plays down the heroics and doesn't run to major battle scenes.

Wendell Corey *Fairchild* • Mickey Rooney *Dooley* • Don Taylor *Preacher* • Nicole Maurey *Fiamma* • John Smith *Smith* • Race Gentry *Hendricks* • Ralph Votrian *Wilbur* ■ *Dir* Lewis R Foster • *Scr* Robert Lewin

Bolero ★★★

Romantic drama 1934 · US · BW · 82mins

A romantic drama with a good script, expertly directed by Wesley Ruggles, has stars George Raft and Carole Lombard as a dancing duo competing for attention with the hypnotic spell of Ravel's *Bolero*. He opens a smart nightclub in Paris, she goes off to marry a wealthy man, but they're reunited unexpectedly after the First World War, dancing to the aforementioned number as a lead-up to a dramatic climax. The film, which includes a number by the famous fan dancer Sally Rand, was a major hit at the 1934 box office and hasn't lost its capacity to entertain.

George Raft *Raoul DeBaere* • Carole Lombard *Helen Hathaway* • Sally Rand *Annette* • Frances Drake *Leona* • William Frawley *Mike DeBaere* • Ray Milland *Lord Robert Coray* • Gloria Shea *Lucy* • Gertrude Michael *Lady D'Argon* ■ *Dir* Wesley Ruggles • *Scr* Carey Wilson Kubec Glasmon, Horace Jackson (adaptation), from an idea by Ruth Ridenour • *Music* Ralph Rainger, Maurice Ravel

Bolero ★ 18

Period erotic drama
1984 · US · Colour · 100mins

One of the funniest bad movies ever made. Virginal heiress Bo Derek goes to the Sahara desert and Spain in search of pure sexual ecstasy, and ends up making love with a sheik and a bullfighter. Set in the twenties for no apparent reason, director John Derek's anti-erotic valentine to his wife is packed with hilariously awful encounters that are further undermined by insipid dialogue. See Bo ride a horse naked! See Bo writhe passionately in front of a red neon sign spelling out the film's title! See Bo covered in honey and licked clean in slow motion! See how badly a film goes wrong when a besotted husband thinks the world is ready for a Bo-peep tribute to a wife who may have a great body, but is one lousy actress. ▭

Bo Derek *Ayre McGillvary* • George Kennedy *Cotton* • Andrea Occhipinti *Angel Contreras* • Ana Obregon *Catalina* • Greg Bensen *Sheik* • Olivia D'Abo *Paloma* • Ian Cochrane *Robert Stewart* ■ *Dir/Scr* John Derek

Bolwieser ★★★

Drama 1977 · W Ger · Colour · 201mins

Based on the novel by Oskar Maria Graf, this bitter study of marital discord, social rigidity and incipient fascism was edited down from a two-part television film. Kurt Raab cuts a pathetically dignified figure as the genial stationmaster who is twice cuckolded by wife Elisabeth Trissenaar, whose desire for freedom ultimately results in her husband's imprisonment. In exploring the dispiriting notion that love has no place in the law, director Rainer Werner Fassbinder was also keen to show that, even in a supposedly patriarchal society, the female is the deadlier of the species. The result is subtlety symbolic, yet uncompromisingly bleak. In German with English subtitles.

Kurt Raab *Bolwieser* • Elisabeth Trissenaar *Frau Hanni* • Gustl Bayrhammer *Hanni's father* • Bernhard Helfrich *Merkl* • Udo Kier *Schaffthaler* • Volker Spengler *Mangst* ■ *Dir* Rainer Werner Fassbinder • *Scr* Rainer Werner Fassbinder, from the novel by Oskar Maria Graf

Bombardier ★★

Second World War adventure
1943 · US · BW · 98mins

An airborne propaganda picture, this follows a bomber crew on a mission to Japan. At times the picture has all the excitement of a technical manual – no switch, no scanner, no nut and bolt is ignored by the script – and it is, of course, a long haul across the Pacific to the target zone. Released after Japan's attack on Pearl Harbor – though production started before – the story is filled with vengeance and the Japanese are, of course, depicted as perpetrators of hideous cruelty, and lacking in military know-how. Routine, but lifted by a decent cast.

Pat O'Brien *Major Chick Davis* • Randolph Scott *Captain Buck Oliver* • Anne Shirley *Burt Hughes* • Eddie Albert *Tom Hughes* • Robert Ryan *Joe Connors* • Walter Reed *Jim Carter* • Barton MacLane *Sergeant Dixon* ■ *Dir* Richard Wallace • *Scr* John Twist, from a story by John Twist, Martin Rackin

Bombay ★★★ 12

Drama 1995 · Ind · Colour · 135mins

Shot in southern India and recalling the civil unrest that occurred in Bombay in the early nineties, this film achieved several things. It confirmed the reputation of Mani Rathnam as one of the most uncompromising contemporary Indian directors, while also sealing the celebrity of now red-hot composer AR Rahman. But, more importantly, this story of a couple's search for their missing children proved that masala musicals could be suitable vehicles for social comment. Indeed, the film was so effective that it was banned, yet its sheer polish made it a box-office smash. In Tamil and Hindi with English subtitles. ▭

Tinnu Anand • Manisha Koirala • Nazar • Arvind Swamy ■ *Dir/Scr* Mani Rathnam

Bombay Talkie ★★★

Romantic drama
1970 · Ind · Colour · 105mins

The sound of clashing cultures reverberates around many of James Ivory's films, but there's a hollow ring to this tale of the doomed romance between a self-centred western novelist and an image-conscious Bollywood star. The opening parody of masala musicals – complete with a chorus line dancing on the keys of a giant typewriter – creates something of a false impression. This is a melodrama of the old school, in which Jennifer Kendal toys in a callously destructive manner with the affections of Shashi Kapoor. It's a mediocre outing, although Pinchoo Kapoor as a celebrity guru and the night-time carriage drive are memorable.

Shashi Kapoor *Vikram* • Jennifer Kendal *Lucia Lane* • Zia Mohyeddin *Hari* • Aparna Sen *Mala* • Utpal Dutt *Bose* • Nadira *Anjana Devi* • Pincho Kapoor *Swamiji* ■ *Dir* James Ivory • *Scr* Ruth Prawer Jhabvala, James Ivory, from a story by Ruth Prawer Jhabvala • *Producer* Ismail Merchant

Bombers B-52 ★★ U

Drama 1957 · US · Colour · 106mins

Released in this country under the title *No Sleep till Dawn*, this is a clumsy melodrama directed with little sense of either drama or irony by Gordon Douglas. Karl Malden might not have had the greatest range in Hollywood, but he could fret like few others. Here he gets the chance to work himself into a right old lather as he considers a move into civvy street, as well as daughter Natalie Wood's romance with flashy flyboy Efrem Zimbalist Jr. Cinematographer William Clothier captures some nifty flying sequences, but the story seems to be permanently taxiing along the runway waiting for instructions to take off.

Natalie Wood *Lois Brennan* • Karl Malden *Sergeant Chuck Brennan* • Marsha Hunt *Edith Brennan* • Efrem Zimbalist Jr *Colonel Jim Herlihy* • Don Kelly *Sergeant Darren McKind* ■ *Dir* Gordon Douglas • *Scr* Irving Wallace, from a story by Sam Rolfe

Bomber's Moon ★★ U

Second World War drama
1943 · US · BW · 69mins

American pilot George Montgomery is shot down over Germany and thrown into a POW camp. As luck would have it, he shares his cell with a female Russian doctor, played by Annabella, the pertly pretty French actress best known for marrying Tyrone Power. Breaking out of the camp, Montgomery, Annabella and Kent Taylor head for England, dodging the enemy and generally behaving heroically, especially when Montgomery disguises himself as a German and hijacks a bomber for his getaway. No great shakes today, it probably felt just as average in 1943, when such movies were a dime a dozen.

George Montgomery *Captain Jeff Dakin* • Annabella *Lt Alexandra Zoreich* • Kent Taylor *Captain Paul Husnik* • Walter Kingsford *Friedrich Mueller* • Martin Kosleck *Major von Streicher* • Dennis Hoey *Major von Grunow* • Robert Barrat *Ernst* • Kenneth Brown *Karl* ■ *Dir* Charles Fuhr [Edward Ludwig], Harold Schuster • *Scr* Kenneth Gamet, Aubrey Wisberg, from a story by Leonard Lee

Bombshell ★

Science-fiction thriller
1997 · US · Colour · 95mins

Beware any film that has "bomb" in the title, as it may live up to its unfortunate moniker. That's the case with this lame sci-fi thriller. Henry Thomas is one of two scientists in the near future (the other being Frank Whaley). They are using nanotechnology to fight cancer, but discover that their miracle cure could actually cause the disease. Daft fare that was originally made for the Sci-Fi Channel in the US, this is actually quite insulting for sci-fi fans and boring twaddle for everyone else.

Henry Thomas *Buck Hogan* • Mädchen Amick *Angeline* • Frank Whaley *Malcolm* • Brion James *Donald* • Pamela Gidley *Melinda* • Michael Jace *Detective Jefferson* • Martin Hewitt *Adam* • David Packer *Brad* • Victoria Jackson *Waitress* ■ *Dir* Paul Wynne • *Scr* Paul Wynne, from a story by Vicky Pike, Paul Wynne

Bon Voyage ★★★ U

Spy drama 1944 · UK · BW · 25mins

Returning from Hollywood at the behest of the Ministry of Information, Alfred Hitchcock commanded a weekly rate of just £10 for this propaganda boost for the French Resistance. It also served to advocate general vigilance, as a superbly controlled flashback sequence reveals to doltish RAF pilot John Blythe the tell-tale signs he missed as he was escorted back from a PoW camp by a Gestapo agent masquerading as a Pole. With its shocking denouement, this provocative short was atmospherically shot by the exiled Günther Krampf, who'd also filmed such key expressionist silents as *Pandora's Box*. In French with English subtitles. ▭

John Blythe *John Dougall* ■ *Dir* Alfred Hitchcock • *Scr* JOC Orton, Angus McPhail, from an idea by Arthur Calder-Marshall

Bon Voyage! ★★★ U

Comedy 1962 · US · Colour · 126mins

There have been plenty of movies about Americans in Paris, but rarely one as bland as this family film from Disney. The family in question, headed by Fred MacMurray and Jane Wyman, have a series of comic misadventures you can see coming a mile off, while the open-mouthed awe with which they greet all things European is that of the simple-minded for the sophisticated. That said, the various twists and turns have a rather endearing innocence, and the costumes were nominated for an Academy Award. ▭

Fred MacMurray *Harry Willard* • Jane Wyman *Katie Willard* • Deborah Walley *Amy Willard* • Michael Callan *Nick O'Mara* • Jessie Royce Landis *La Comtesse* • Tommy Kirk *Elliot Willard* • Kevin Corcoran *Skipper Willard* ■ *Dir* James Neilson • *Scr* Bill Walsh, from the novel by Marrijane Hayes, Joseph Hayes • *Costume Designer* Bill Thomas

Bon Voyage, Charlie Brown ★★★ U

Animation 1980 · US · Colour · 72mins

Inspired by Charles Schulz's long-running *Peanuts* comic strip, this animated feature proves the gently sardonic tone that hooked millions is present and correct by appending the bracketed rider (*And Don't Come Back*) to the title. Heading to Europe for an exchange visit, the worldly-wise toddlers find themselves living it up in a French château at the expense of a mysterious patron. There are some nice cultural asides, but what makes this so enjoyable is the trademark philosophising – plus, of course, Snoopy who, after years of practice against the garage door, finally gets to play at Wimbledon. ▭

Dir Bill Melendez • *Scr* Charles M Schulz, from his comic strip *Peanuts*

Bonanza: the Next Generation ★★ PG

Western 1988 · US · Colour · 92mins

Like *Star Trek: the Next Generation*, this is a bid to renew a winning TV formula without any of the orginal stars. The pilot for an intended series, this TV movie might equally have been called son or, indeed, daughter of *Bonanza*, since the acting line-up includes two offspring of erstwhile cast members. (Michael Landon Jr plays Little Joe's screen son, and there's a romantic role for Gillian Greene, daughter of Lorne.) It's competent western fare, but it will only really appeal to *Bonanza* die-hards. ▭

John Ireland *Aaron Cartwright* • Robert Fuller *Charley Poke* • John Amos *Mr Mack* • Barbara Anderson *Annabelle Cartwright* • Peter Mark Richman *Cliel Dunston* • Michael Landon Jr *Benj Cartwright* • Brian A Smith *Josh Cartwright* • Gillian Greene *Jennifer* ■ *Dir* William F Claxton • *Scr* Paul Savage

Bonanza – the Return ★★

Western adventure 1993 · US · Colour ·

Made as a pilot for a new *Bonanza* series, this TV movie is something of a family affair. Michael Landon Jr follows his famous father (Little Joe in the original series) in the Cartwright tradition, while Dirk Blocker, the son of

Dan Blocker who played "Hoss", crops up as a sympathetic newspaper reporter. The Pondarosa Ranch is under threat from an unscrupulous land developer and it doesn't take a quantum leap to gather that villain of the piece Dean Stockwell isn't going to have things all his own way. The story is a little ponderous, but the supporting cast is to be treasured, with Richard Roundtree teaming up with such Wild West veterans as Ben Johnson and Jack Elam.

Michael Landon Jr *Benj Cartwright* • Dean Stockwell *Augustus Brandenburg* • Ben Johnson *Bronc Evans* • Linda Gray *Laredo Stimmons* • Emily Warfield *Sara Cartwright* • Alistair MacDougall *Adam Cartwright Jr* • Richard Roundtree *Jacob Briscoe* • Jack Elam *Buckshot Patterson* • Brian Leckner *Josh Cartwright* • Dirk Blocker ■ *Dir* Jerry Jameson • *Scr* Michael McGreevey, from a story by Michael McGreevey, Tom Brinson, Michael Landon Jr, David Dortort, from the characters created by Haskell Boggs

Bond Street ★★

Portmanteau drama
1948 · UK · BW · 109mins

Clearly inspired by *Tales of Manhattan*, in which dozens of guest stars helped director Julien Duvivier tell the life story of a tail coat, this portmanteau drama, set around the preparations for a wedding, works best when it's funny and drags when it's not. The stars of the show are undoubtedly Kathleen Harrison as a chirpy seamstress and Roland Young as the befuddled father of the bride. Kenneth Griffith is suitably hissable as disabled Patricia Plunkett's ne'er-do-well spouse, but Derek Farr is embarrassingly unconvincing as a twitchy killer. Producer/writer Anatole de Grunwald and co-scriptwriter Terence Rattigan would later dust off the formula for *The Yellow Rolls-Royce*.

Jean Kent *Ricki Merritt* • Roland Young *George Chester-Barrett* • Kathleen Harrison *Mrs Brawn* • Derek Farr *Joe Marsh* • Hazel Court *Julia Chester-Barrett* • Ronald Howard *Steve Winter* • Paula Valenska *Elsa* • Patricia Plunkett *Mary* ■ *Dir* Gordon Parry • *Scr* Anatole de Grunwald, Terence Rattigan, Rodney Ackland, from an idea by JG Brown

Bonds of Love ★★ 15

Romance based on a true story
1993 · US · Colour · 89mins

This weepy true story tells the plight of a twice-divorced woman, living in a small Kansas town, who falls in love with a sensitive, mentally disabled man. When his overprotective family and the social welfare department conspire to keep them apart, the couple starts an emotional legal battle. Treat Williams and Kelly McGillis give strong, convincing performances, but all the obstacles put in their way it detract from both the love story and the social issue. 📼

Treat Williams *Robby Smith* • Kelly McGillis *Rose Parks* • Hal Holbrook *Jim Smith* • Steve Railsback *Ken Smith* • Grace Zabriskie *Emma Smith* • RH Thomson *Jake Hobart* • Kenneth Welsh *Judge* • Gordon Pinsent *Leon* ■ *Dir* Larry Elikann • *Scr* Mary Gallagher

The Bone Collector ★★★ 15

Crime thriller 1999 · US · Colour · 118mins

A run-of-the-mill story is turned into an above-average thriller, thanks to

impressive central performances from Denzel Washington and Angelina Jolie as two very different cops who team up to track down a serial killer. Washington plays a decorated police officer now confined to his bed, virtually paralysed following an accident on the job. Jolie's the young rookie who's brought in to explore the deepest, darkest areas of Manhattan under his instruction as they follow the trail of a sadistic murderer who picks up his victims in a yellow taxi. Although the daft conclusion abandons all the logic painstakingly established in the previous scenes, this benefits from Phillip Noyce's fast-paced direction and sterling performances from Queen Latifah as Washington's nurse and Michael Rooker as his irascible superior. Proof of Washington's acting talent – especially as he spends the whole movie immobile.

Denzel Washington *Lincoln Rhyme* • Angelina Jolie *Amelia Donaghy* • Queen Latifah *Thelma* • Michael Rooker *Captain Howard Cheney* • Mike McGlone *Detective Kenny Solomon* • Luis Guzman *Eddie Ortiz* • Leland Orser *Richard Thompson* • John Benjamin Hickey *Dr Barry Lehman* • Ed O'Neill *Detective Paulie Sellitto* ■ *Dir* Phillip Noyce • *Scr* Jeremy Iacone, from the book by Jeffery Deaver

Bone Daddy ★★ 18

Crime thriller 1998 · US · Colour · 87mins

Ex-medical examiner Rutger Hauer writes a fictional bestseller about a serial killer, who then gets up to his old tricks again in this above-average horror thriller, clearly based on *The Silence of the Lambs*. Hauer is put back on the case when bones – removed from the still-living body of his literary agent – begin arriving at police headquarters. The suspects mount up with little sense of suspense or hope of a satisfying resolution, but Hauer acquits himself well in a role tailor-made for his talents. Contains violence and some swearing. 📼

Rutger Hauer *William Palmer* • Barbara Williams *Sharon Hewlett* • RH Thomson *Marshall Stone* • Joseph Kell *Peter Palmer* • Robin Gammell *Cobb* • Blu Mankuma *Trent* ■ *Dir* Mario Azzopardi • *Scr* Thomas Szollosi

The Bonfire of the Vanities ★★★ 15

Drama 1990 · US · Colour · 120mins

Brian De Palma's adaptation of Tom Wolfe's scathing attack on the yuppy lifestyles of the Wall Street rich and Park Avenue famous is, admittedly, a flawed satire (the casting of Tom Hanks and Melanie Griffith didn't help). Nonetheless, it's hardly the irredeemably awful disaster most critics led you to believe. And, anyway, even a lesser De Palma picture is a whole lot more interesting than many A-list directors' good ones. Purely from a technical standpoint, it's a marvel – the opening four-minute continuous shot, for example – and now that the glaring media spotlight has been turned off, its subtle entertainment values can gloriously shine through. Contains some violence, swearing and nudity. 📼 *DVD*

Tom Hanks *Sherman McCoy* • Bruce Willis *Peter Fallow* • Melanie Griffith *Maria Ruskin* • Kim Cattrall *Judy McCoy* • Saul Rubinek *Jed Kramer* • Morgan Freeman *Judge White* • F

Murray Abraham *Abe Weiss* • John Hancock *Reverend Bacon* • Kevin Dunn *Tom Killian* ■ *Dir* Brian De Palma • *Scr* Michael Cristofer, from the novel by Tom Wolfe • *Cinematographer* Vilmos Zsigmond

Le Bonheur ★★★★

Drama 1965 · Fr · Colour · 79mins

The under-rated Agnès Varda here produced one of new French cinema's most controversial films. Few could find fault with her elliptical narrative, elegant compositions and psychological use of colour. But debates raged over her motive for having an adulterous carpenter settle down happily with his mistress and children after his wife drowns herself, rather than accept a suggested *ménage à trois*. Irrespective of the film's mischievous morality, the romantic imagery and Mozart score provide an ironic contrast to the contentious sexual politics, which were given an added *je ne sais quoi* by the fact that Jean-Claude Drouot's screen kin were played by his own family. In French with English subtitles.

Jean-Claude Drouot *François* • Claire Drouot *Thérèse* • Sandrine Drouot *Gisou* • Olivier Drouot *Pierrot* • Marie-France Boyer *Emilie* ■ *Dir/Scr* Agnès Varda

Le Bonheur Est dans le Pré ★★★ 15

Comedy 1995 · Fr · Colour · 101mins

Etienne Chatiliez is no stranger to the themes of belonging and dislocation. But here he seems less interested in astute social observations than in relating the simple story of toilet king Michel Serrault, who seizes the opportunity presented by a case of mistaken identity to abandon his workshy employees and grasping wife, Sabine Azéma, to enjoy a rural idyll with Carmen Maura. Although an amiable picture, this lacks both the satirical edge of Chatiliez's *Life Is a Long Quiet River* and the black comedy of his *Tatie Danielle* and it would have benefited from a more enlightened view of women. In French with English subtitles. Contains some swearing and sexual references. 📼

Michel Serrault *Francis Bergeaud* • Eddy Mitchell *Gérard* • Sabine Azéma *Nicole Bergeaud* • Carmen Maura *Dolores Thivart* • François Morel *Pouillaud* • Eric Cantona *Lionel* ■ *Dir* Etienne Chatiliez • *Scr* Florence Quentin

Bonjour Tristesse ★★★ PG

Drama 1958 · US · BW and Colour · 89mins

Otto Preminger's romantic drama set on the Riviera stars David Niven as the widower whose affair with Deborah Kerr is subverted by his daughter, Jean Seberg. Loosely based on the novel by Françoise Sagan, it's fluffy stuff, enjoyable for Niven's deft playing and for Seberg, whose radiant performance caused a stir not unlike the one caused by Audrey Hepburn in *Roman Holiday*. It was a huge hit in France – Preminger was second only to God in the eyes of critics of the time, such as Jean-Luc Godard and François Truffaut. Seberg became an overnight cult sensation and starred in Godard's debut feature *A Bout de Souffle* the following year. 📼

Deborah Kerr *Anne Larsen* • David Niven *Raymond* • Jean Seberg *Cecile* • Mylene Demongeot *Elsa Mackenbourg* • Geoffrey Horne *Philippe* • Juliette Greco *Nightclub singer* • Walter Chiari *Pablo* ■ *Dir* Otto Preminger • *Scr* Arthur Laurents, from the novel by Françoise Sagan

Les Bonnes Femmes ★★★★

Drama 1960 · Fr/It · BW · 98mins

Meeting no great critical acclaim on its first release, this is now rated one of Claude Chabrol's early masterpieces and a major film of the French New Wave. The "good girls" of the title are four young Parisian women, who make up for the ennui of their working life in an electrical goods shop by regularly hitting the town in search of glamour and romance. Chabrol's mixture of documentary-style realism, slice-of-life drama and black humour combines with stunning black-and-white photography and fine performances to impressive effect. In French with English subtitles.

Bernadette Lafont *Jane* • Clothilde Joano *Jacqueline* • Lucile Saint-Simon *Rita* • Stéphane Audran *Ginette* • Mario David *André Lapierre* • Claude Berri *André* ■ *Dir* Claude Chabrol • *Scr* Paul Gégauff, Claude Chabrol • *Cinematographer* Henri Decaë

Bonnie and Clyde ★★★★★ 18

Crime drama 1967 · US · Colour · 106mins

"They're young! They're in love! And they kill people!" Not the slogan for Oliver Stone's notorious *Natural Born Killers*, but for one of the most stylish and uncompromising of gangster pictures, *Bonnie and Clyde*. Released when graphic screen violence was very rare, this influential film was misread by American critics on its release, many of whom dismissed it as a gimmicky, gory crime thriller. However, it proved to be the box-office hit of the year, and scooped ten Oscar nominations. Faye Dunaway and Warren Beatty excel as the gun-toting criminals who roamed the American Midwest during the Depression, while the sizzling script (originally offered to both François Truffaut and Jean-Luc Godard) and Arthur Penn's bravura direction are as fresh as ever. Contains violence. 📼 *DVD*

Warren Beatty *Clyde Barrow* • Faye Dunaway *Bonnie Parker* • Michael J Pollard *CW Moss* • Gene Hackman *Buck Barrow* • Estelle Parsons *Blanche* • Denver Pyle *Frank Hamer* • Dub Taylor *Ivan Moss* • Evans Evans *Velma Davis* • Gene Wilder *Eugene Grizzard* ■ *Dir* Arthur Penn • *Scr* David Newman, Robert Benton, Robert Towne (uncredited) • *Cinematographer* Burnett Guffey • *Costume Designer* Theadora Van Runkle

Bonnie and Clyde: the True Story ★★★ 15

Crime drama 1992 · US · Colour · 90mins

It is pointless comparing this TV movie with the classic 1967 account of the life and crimes of Bonnie Parker and Clyde Barrow, as Arthur Penn's flashy feature changed the face of Hollywood film-making. However, it holds its own with the biopic B-movies *Persons in Hiding* and *The Bonnie Parker Story*. Writer/director Gary Hoffman aimed for authenticity rather than insight by shooting on actual locations and casting teenage performers as the gruesome twosome. But, for all his efforts, we are never quite convinced by the period trappings or the characterisation. ▣

Dana Ashbrook *Clyde Barrow* • Tracey Needham *Bonnie Parker* • Doug Savant *Deputy Sheriff Ted Hinton* • Billy Morrissette *WD Jones* • Michael Bowen *Buck Barrow* • Michelle Joyner *Blanche Barrow* • Louanne Stephens *Mrs Barrow* • Betty Buckley *Mrs Parker* ▣ *Dir/Scr* Gary Hoffman

The Bonnie Parker Story ★★

Crime drama　　　1958 · US · BW · 75mins

Dorothy Provine stars as half of the infamous thirties' duo, Bonnie and Clyde, in this fictionalised account of their partnership. After her husband is sent to prison for 175 years, Bonnie Parker waits at tables and hangs out with undesirables, eventually teaming up with ruffian Guy Darrow (renamed as Clyde Barrow's family was still alive when the film was made) for a "lonesome ride on a one-way ticket". Unlike the later Faye Dunaway/Warren Beatty classic, this low-budget effort bravely steers away from glamorising the couple's murderous antics, while also laying off the heavy moralising.

Dorothy Provine *Bonnie Parker* • Jack Hogan *Guy Darrow* • Richard Bakalyan *Duke Jefferson* • Joseph Turkel *Chuck Darrow* • William Stevens *Paul* • Ken Lynch *Manager of restaurant* • Douglas Kennedy *Tom Steel* • Patt Huston *Chuck's girl* • Joel Colin *Bobby* ▣ *Dir* William Witney • *Scr* Stanley Shpetner

Bonnie Prince Charlie ★ U

Historical drama
1948 · UK · Colour · 139mins

Mauled by the British press on its original release, this shoddy costume drama must rank as one of the worst films ever made in this country. It was written by playwright Clemence Dane, but it contains some quite dreadful dialogue delivered in atrocious accents by an all-star cast led by a hopelessly miscast David Niven. The studio sets look home-made, but they are nowhere near as embarrassing as Ian Whyte's twee, cliché-ridden score. Only cinematographer Robert Krasker and Margaret Leighton (as Flora MacDonald) emerge with any credit. A very sorry episode indeed.

David Niven *Bonnie Prince Charlie* • Margaret Leighton *Flora MacDonald* • Judy Campbell *Clementine Walkinshaw* • Jack Hawkins *Lord George Murray* • Morland Graham *Donald* • Finlay Currie *Marquis of Tullibardine* • Elwyn Brook-Jones *Duke of Cumberland* • John Laurie *Blind Jamie* ▣ *Dir* Anthony Kimmins • *Scr* Clemence Dane

Bonnie Scotland ★★★★ U

Comedy　　　1935 · US · BW · 76mins

An overcomplicated plot – and some comedy routines from previous movies – can't prevent this from being one of the most delightful comedies from the "golden period" of the Laurel and Hardy series of laughter-makers. It includes a litter-picking exercise by the twosome that becomes a soft-shoe shuffle, which is a classic of fanciful timing. Stan and Ollie go to Scotland to claim Stan's inheritance, which turns out to be bagpipes and a snuff box, and from there they are

unwittingly recruited to the British Army in India. There's the added bonus of the pop-eyed, moustachioed James Finlayson, as a dastardly sergeant major, making up for the wan love interest provided by June Lang.

Stan Laurel *Stanley McLaurel* • Oliver Hardy *Ollie* • Anne Grey *Lady Violet Ormsby* • David Torrence *Mr Miggs* • June Lang *Lorna McLaurel* • William Janney *Alan Douglas* • James Mack *Butler* • James Finlayson *Sergeant Major* ▣ *Dir* James W Horne • *Scr* Frank Butler, Jefferson Moffitt

Booby Trap ★

Crime thriller　　　1957 · UK · BW · 72mins

A dire British B-feature, barely seen when it first came out. An absent-minded boffin (Tony Quinn) invents an explosive fountain pen, timed to go off on the first stroke of Big Ben. The pen falls into the hands of a drug peddler (Sydney Tafler) who, as it happens, hides his wares in fountain pens. While the denouement is explosive, the build-up is feeble and none of the characters engage one's interest.

Sydney Tafler *Hunter* • Patti Morgan *Jackie* • Tony Quinn *Professor Hasdane* • John Watson *Major Cunliffe* • Jacques Cey *Bentley* • Richard Shaw *Richards* • Harry Fowler *Sammy* ▣ *Dir* Henry Cass • *Scr* Peter Bryan, Bill Luckwell, from a novel by Peter Bryan

The Boogie Man Will Get You ★★★

Comedy horror　　　1942 · US · BW · 66mins

Here's a fun cast in a lively programme filler that cheered up many a wartime audience. Boris Karloff plays a demented (what else?) scientist who attempts to turn salesmen into supermen in a crazy plot, which also involves the wonderful Peter Lorre. Larry Parks is the juvenile lead, with Jeff Donnell aboard to add romantic interest. Lew Landers, who, as Louis Friedlander, made his directorial feature debut with the 1935 Karloff classic *The Raven*, successfully juggles the lunatic elements of plot and action.

Boris Karloff *Professor Nathaniel Billings* • Peter Lorre *Dr Lorentz* • Maxie Rosenbloom *Maxie* • Larry Parks *Bill Leyden* • Jeff Donnell *Winnie Leyden* • Maude Eburne *Amelia Jones* • Don Beddoe *J Gilbert Brampton* • George McKay *Ebenezer* • Frank Puglia *Silvio Baciagalupi* ▣ *Dir* Lew Landers • *Scr* Edwin Blum, Paul Gangelin (adaptation), from a story by Hal Fimberg, Robert E Hunt

Boogie Nights ★★★★★ 18

Drama　　　1997 · US · Colour · 149mins

Pornography, drugs and disco are the driving forces of director Paul Thomas Anderson's potent parable of the partying seventies. Spanning the height of the disco era, this Martin Scorsese-influenced rags-to-bitches allegory is a visually stunning and poignant exploration of the adult entertainment industry. Charting the rise, fall and rise again of busboy-turned-porn star Mark Wahlberg, Anderson's surreal take on the American Dream is as startling as it is highly entertaining. Burt Reynolds was Oscar nominated for his brilliant turn as sleaze-movie producer Jack Horner, the patriarch of an extended family of life's flotsam and jetsam. Scintillating support is provided by

Heather Graham and Julianne Moore, as Horner's wife and leading lady. The breathtaking opening Steadicam shot is justifiably famous. Contains swearing, drug abuse, sex scenes and violence. ▣ **DVD**

Mark Wahlberg *Eddie Adams/Dirk Diggler* • Burt Reynolds *Jack Horner* • Julianne Moore *Amber Waves* • John C Reilly *Reed Rothchild* • Melora Walters *Jessie St Vincent* • Robert Ridgely *The Colonel James* • Don Cheadle *Buck Swope* • Heather Graham *Rollergirl* • William H Macy *Little Bill* ▣ *Dir/Scr* Paul Thomas Anderson

The Book of Life ★★★★

Satirical black comedy
1998 · Fr/US · Colour · 63mins

Director Hal Hartley is never dull but he remains an acquired taste. Taking the millennium as potentially apocalyptic, Hartley films a discussion between Satan (Thomas Jay Ryan), Jesus (Martin Donovan) and Magdalena (PJ Harvey) on New Year's Eve, 1999, about the survival of the human race. Less pretentious and less flawed than *Dogma*, Kevin Smith's recent film with similar themes, and thankfully much shorter, this is a fascinating black comedy. We have Christ and his girl Friday wandering round JFK airport lamenting mortals and Satan getting drunk in a hotel bar. Bizarre, and yet at times brilliant.

Martin Donovan *Jesus Christ* • PJ Harvey *Magdalena* • Thomas Jay Ryan *Satan* • David Simonds *Dave* • Miho Nikaido *Edie* • DJ Mendel *Lawyer* ▣ *Dir/Scr* Hal Hartley

Book of Numbers ★★★ 15

Blaxploitation period drama
1972 · US · Colour · 81mins

Directed by its star, Raymond St Jacques, this is a rare blaxploitation venture into period drama. St Jacques joins with fellow city slacker Philip Thomas in an attempt to beat the Depression by setting up a numbers racket in a small Arkansas town. But can our roguish duo overcome the threat posed by racist gangster Gilbert Greene? Although budgetary constraints leave it looking a little ragged around the edges, this is a mostly entertaining caper movie, with St Jacques sneaking in a few social barbs between the gags. However, soul singer Freda Payne wins no band of gold for her supporting performance. Contains swearing and violence. ▣

Raymond St Jacques *Blueboy Harris* • Freda Payne *Kelly Simms* • Philip Thomas [Philip Michael Thomas] *Dave Greene* • Hope Clarke *Pigmeat Goins* • Willie Washington Jr *Makepeace Johnson* • Doug Finell *Eggy* • Sterling St Jacques *Kid Flick* • CL Williams *Blip Blip* ▣ *Dir* Raymond St Jacques • *Scr* Larry Spiegel, from the novel by Robert Deane Pharr

Boom ★★

Drama　　　1968 · UK/US · Colour · 112mins

A piece of preening self-indulgence by Richard Burton and Elizabeth Taylor – and director Joseph Losey – at a time when the two stars thought they could be forgiven anything. An adaptation by Tennessee Williams of his play *The Milk Train Doesn't Stop Here Anymore*, it clashes symbols with its study of life among the idle rich. Taylor is Flora, a six-times married virago, and Burton is

a freeloading poet. Noël Coward gives it all some semblance of life as Flora's confidant – but can't make up for the film's deficiencies.

Elizabeth Taylor *Flora Goforth* • Richard Burton *Chris Flanders* • Noël Coward *Witch of Capri* • Joanna Shimkus *Blackie* • Michael Dunn *Rudy* • Romolo Valli *Dr Luilo* • Veronica Wells *Simonetta* • Fernando Piazza *Giulio* • Howard Taylor *Journalist* ▣ *Dir* Joseph Losey • *Scr* Tennessee Williams, from his play *The Milk Train Doesn't Stop Here Anymore*

Boom Town ★★★★

Adventure drama　　　1940 · US · BW · 118mins

After the huge success of *San Francisco* and *Test Pilot*, Clark Gable and Spencer Tracy were reunited for another sprawling adventure, this time about two pioneers in the oil business. Although there were reports of behind-the-scenes tensions, the two stars give memorably larger-than-life performances and the female leads, Claudette Colbert and Hedy Lamarr, are on equally good form. Director Jack Conway stages some stunning set pieces (notably a burning oil field) and keeps the action roaring along.

Clark Gable *Big John McMasters* • Spencer Tracy *Square John Sand* • Claudette Colbert *Betsy Bartlett* • Hedy Lamarr *Karen Vanmeer* • Frank Morgan *Luther Aldrich* • Lionel Atwill *Harry Compton* • Chill Wills *Harmony Jones* ▣ *Dir* Jack Conway • *Scr* John Lee Mahin, from a story by James Edward Grant

Boomerang! ★★★★

Crime drama　　　1947 · US · BW · 85mins

A riveting 20th Century-Fox social thriller from a period in which *film noir* style and location shooting were combined in the safe hands of *March of Time* producer Louis de Rochemont. Quintessential forties' icon Dana Andrews heads a fine cast that includes Arthur Kennedy, Lee J Cobb and Sam Levene – all stage actors who flourished under New Yorker Elia Kazan's direction. This was Kazan's third feature film, having just completed *A Streetcar Named Desire* on Broadway. If the denouement seems contrived, remember this is based on a true story.

Dana Andrews *Henry L Harvey* • Jane Wyatt *Mrs Harvey* • Lee J Cobb *Chief Robinson* • Cara Williams *Irene Nelson* • Arthur Kennedy *John Waldron* • Sam Levene *Woods* • Taylor Holmes *Wade* • Robert Keith *McCreery* ▣ *Dir* Elia Kazan • *Scr* Richard Murphy, from the *Reader's Digest* article *The Perfect Case* by Anthony Abbott

Boomerang ★★★

Thriller　　　1976 · Fr · Colour · 100mins

Co-written and produced by Alain Delon with pulp novelist José Giovanni, who also directed, this under-rated film offers a shrewd mix of social comment and human drama. Although it adopts a preachy tone in its discussion of drug culture, the story of a businessman's determination to help his son following the murder of a cop – even though it will mean the exposure of his own criminal past – is told crisply and convincingly. Yet it's the acting of Delon, as the reformed gangster, Louis Julien as his suicidal son and Charles Vanel as their devoted lawyer that gives the action its

U = SUITABLE FOR ALL　　Uc = SUITABLE FOR ALL, ESPECIALLY FOR YOUNG CHILDREN (VIDEO ONLY)　　PG = PARENTAL GUIDANCE

authenticity. French dialogue dubbed into English.

Alain Delon *Jacques* • Charles Vanel *Lawyer* • Carla Gravina *Wife* • Louis Julien *Eddy* • Dora Doll *Mother* • Suzanne Flon *Widow* ■ *Dir* José Giovanni • *Scr* Alain Delon, José Giovanni

Boomerang ★★★ 15
Comedy   1992 · US · Colour · 111mins

After a few years in the wilderness, after flops such as *The Golden Child* and *Harlem Nights*, Eddie Murphy returned with this amiable – if slightly overlong comedy – from *House Party* director Reginald Hudlin. Murphy is on form as the womaniser who gets his comeuppance when he tries his smooth-talking ways on canny Robin Givens, who turns the tables when she treats him as a sex object. However, it is the supporting performances that really give the film a buzz. Grace Jones is, well, Grace Jones, playing a demanding supermodel with a penchant for removing her knickers in public, while Eartha Kitt is a scream as the ageing nymphomaniac. Contains swearing, sex scenes and nudity. 📼

Eddie Murphy *Marcus Graham* • Robin Givens *Jacqueline* • Halle Berry *Angela* • David Alan Grier *Gerard* • Martin Lawrence *Tyler* • Grace Jones *Strangé* • Geoffrey Holder *Nelson* • Eartha Kitt *Lady Eloise* • Chris Rock *Bony T* • Lela Rochon *Christie* ■ *Dir* Reginald Hudlin • *Scr* Barry W Blaustein, David Sheffield, from a story by Eddie Murphy

The Boost ★★★ 18
Drama   1988 · US · Colour · 90mins

Better known for the rumours behind the scenes than for the action in front of the camera (during the filming stars Sean Young and James Woods allegedly had an affair that ended rather bitterly in lawsuits), this overlooked drama from director Harold Becker, who also made the excellent *Sea of Love*, has moments of insight in between the screaming matches. The film catalogues a couple's descent into drug addiction. Although more time is spent banging home the anti-drug message than on developing character, both Woods and Young give gutsy enough performances to lift the film above the dismal and completely depressing. Contains violence, swearing, sex scenes, drug abuse and nudity. 📼

James Woods *Lenny Brown* • Sean Young *Linda Brown* • John Kapelos *Joel* • Steven Hill *Max Sherman* • Kelle Kerr *Rochelle* • John Rothman *Ned Leavis* • Amanda Blake *Barbara* • Grace Zabriskie *Sheryl* • Marc Poppel *Mark* ■ *Dir* Harold Becker • *Scr* Darryl Ponicsan, from the novel *Ludes* by Benjamin Stein

Das Boot ★★★ 12
Second World War action drama
1981 · W Ger · Colour · 199mins

This sprawling U-boat epic is based on actual incidents during the 1941 battle for the North Atlantic. Submarine warfare offers film-makers little in the way of variation, and the action inevitably alternates between tense periods of silent stalking and frantic moments of engagement (brilliantly captured by Jost Vacano's darting camera). Director Wolfgang Petersen adopts an understandably anti-Nazi tone and depicts the crew as courageous conscripts serving a cause

to which they are not wholeheartedly committed. However, his preoccupation with the terrors of their claustrophobic existence means that, apart from steely captain Jürgen Prochnow, few of the characters come alive. A German language film. Contains some violence and swearing. 📼 *DVD*

Jürgen Prochnow *Captain* • Herbert Grönemeyer *Lieutenant Werner/Correspondent* • Klaus Wennemann *Chief Engineer* • Hubertus Bengsch *First Lieutenant/Number One* • Martin Semmelrogge *Second Lieutenant* • Bernd Tauber *Chief Quartermaster* • Erwin Leder *Johann* ■ *Dir* Wolfgang Petersen • *Scr* Wolfgang Petersen, from the novel *Das Boot* by Lothar-Guenther Buchheim

Boot Hill ★★ PG
Spaghetti western 1969 · It · Colour · 91mins

As the vogue for spaghetti westerns began to wane, Italian actors Mario Girotti and Carlo Pedersoli created a sub-genre based on the new-found traditions, effectively imitating the imitators. They gave themselves the American-sounding names of Terence Hill and Bud Spencer respectively, and became immensely popular (and rich) primarily for a series of films featuring "Trinity" or "Nobody" in the titles. This movie pre-dates those, and Hill and Spencer haven't quite discovered the knockabout style that endeared them to unsophisticated audiences all over Europe. Non-fans will find the inept dubbing and poor story structure irritating. Italian dialogue dubbed into English. Contains violence. 📼

Bud Spencer *Hutch Bessy* • Woody Strode *Thomas* • Edward Ciannelli [Eduardo Ciannelli] *Boone* • Terence Hill *Cat Stevens* ■ *Dir/Scr* Giuseppe Colizzi

Boots! Boots! ★★ U
Musical   1934 · UK · BW · 87mins

Now here's a collector's item. If you ignore a 1915 film called *By the Shortest of Heads*, in which he appeared when he was only 11, George Formby made his proper screen debut in this cheap and cheerful hotel comedy. It's not hard to spot that much of the action was filmed in a single room above a Manchester garage, but what is of more interest is the fact that George's co-star is Beryl, the domineering wife who exerted such a firm grip on his career that she tried to prevent him from kissing any of his later heroines. Hopelessly dated, but a must for Formby fans.

George Formby *John Willie* • Beryl Formby *Beryl* • Arthur Kingsley *Manager* • Tonie Forde *Chambermaid* • Lilian Keyes *Lady Royston* • Donald Reid *Sir Alfred Royston* • Betty Driver *Betty* ■ *Dir* Bert Tracy • *Scr* George Formby, Arthur Mertz

Boots Malone ★★ U
Sports drama   1951 · US · BW · 103mins

Although William Holden had already made *Sunset Boulevard* and *Born Yesterday*, Paramount still loaned him out for rubbish like this family movie. It's an awfully sentimental tale, set at a racing stables where Johnny Stewart is a rich kid who loves horses. Holden is a jockey's agent who hasn't won a race in years but who thinks "The Kid" might change his luck. Veteran director William Dieterle had the chore of

calling the shots, and he relies heavily on Holden's innate charm.

William Holden (1) *Boots Malone* • Johnny Stewart *"The Kid"* • Stanley Clements *Stash Clements* • Basil Ruysdael *Preacher Cole* • Carl Benton Reid *John Williams* • Ralph Dumke *Beckett* • Ed Begley *Howard Whitehead* • Hugh Sanders *Matson* ■ *Dir* William Dieterle • *Scr* Milton Holmes, Harold Buchman (uncredited)

Booty Call ★★ 18
Comedy   1997 · US · Colour · 75mins

Friends Jamie Foxx and Tommy Davidson are absolutely determined to score with their girls before the night's out. But as they search for contraceptives, Vivica A Fox and Tamala Jones refuse to give in that easily in this lame battle-of-the-sexes comedy aimed squarely below the belt. If you find testicular surgery, baby urine and butt-sniffing remotely funny, then this deliberately raw gross-out will be just your *National Lampoon*-style cup of tea. Contains swearing.

Jamie Foxx *Bunz* • Tommy Davidson *Rushon* • Wiley Moore *Arguing man* • Vivica A Fox *Lysterine* • Scott LaRose *Singh* • Ric Young *Mr Chiu* • Tamala Jones *Nikki* • Art Malik *Akmed* ■ *Dir* Jeff Pollack • *Scr* Takashi Bufford, Bootsie

Bopha! ★★★ 15
Political drama 1993 · US · Colour · 113mins

Morgan Freeman made his directorial debut with this powerful study of apartheid, which presented South Africa from the viewpoint of the black population rather than white liberals. As the police sergeant torn between the comforts his career provides and the inescapable consequences of prejudice, Danny Glover gives one of his finest performances. Alfre Woodard is also impressive as his wife, while Maynard Eziashi shows great promise as the son whose support for active protest turns the family's world upside down. Malcolm McDowell keeps on just the right side of caricature as a sadistic Special Branch officer. Contains violence and swearing. 📼

Danny Glover *Micah Mangena* • Malcolm McDowell *De Villiers* • Alfre Woodard *Rosie Mangena* • Marius Weyers *Van Tonder* • Maynard Eziashi *Zweli Mangena* • Malick Bowens *Pule Rampa* ■ *Dir* Morgan Freeman • *Scr* Brian Bird, John T Wierick, from the play by Percy Mtwa

The Border ★★ 18
Drama   1981 · US · Colour · 103mins

It's good cop Jack Nicholson versus bad cop Harvey Keitel on the Tex-Mex border of El Paso, trying to stop "wetbacks" illegally entering America. Well-meaning Nicholson pities the poor immigrants and takes on the corrupt Keitel's smuggling operations, in director Tony Richardson's bland and simplistic human rights drama. Naturally, Nicholson is good as the cop with a crisis of conscience. However, it's a surprisingly limp look at what still remains a hot issue. The ending was changed in post-production to make Nicholson's character more heroic. 📼

Jack Nicholson *Charlie Smith* • Harvey Keitel *Cat* • Valerie Perrine *Marcy Smith* • Warren Oates *Red* • Elpidia Carrillo *Maria* • Shannon

Wilcox *Savannah* • Manuel Viescas *Juan* • Jeff Morris *JJ* ■ *Dir* Tony Richardson • *Scr* Deric Washburn, Walon Green, David Freeman

Border Incident ★★★
Film noir   1949 · US · BW · 95mins

This is one of Hollywood's early attempts to tackle the thorny topic of illegal immigration across the Mexican/American border, though the so-called "wetbacks" play second fiddle to a routine plot about racketeering. It was one of several *film noir*-style thrillers from director Anthony Mann, who later made a series of outstanding westerns with James Stewart, as well as two of the best epics ever made, *El Cid* and *The Fall of the Roman Empire*. This picture is intelligent and belies its low budget. It also has a fine performance from Ricardo Montalban, a handsome Mexican actor whom Hollywood would later groom into a "Latin lover".

Ricardo Montalban *Pablo Rodriguez* • George Murphy *Jack Bearnes* • Howard Da Silva *Owen Parkson* • James Mitchell *Juan Garcia* • Arnold Moss *Zopilote* • Alfonso Bedoya *Cuchillo* • Teresa Celli *Maria* ■ *Dir* Anthony Mann • *Scr* John C Higgins, from a story by John C Higgins, George Zuckerman

Border Radio ★
Musical drama   1987 · US · BW · 87mins

Allison Anders made her name as a director with the excellent *Gas, Food, Lodging*, but judging by the standard of this, her debut film, she was lucky to get a second chance behind the camera. Of course, she could always point an accusing finger at her co-writers and co-directors Dean Lent and Kurt Voss (an old film-school classmate) for this shambles – though, judging by her lacklustre contribution to *Four Rooms*, it's clear she has no alibis. In spite of the presence of B-movie icon Luana Anders, this punk road movie should have been parked on the hard shoulder and left there. Contains swearing.

Chris D *Jeff* • Luana Anders *Lu* • John Doe *Dean* • Chris Shearer *Chris* • Dave Alvin *Dave* • Iris Berry *Scenester* • Texacala Jones *Babysitter* • Devon Anders *Devon* • Chuck Shepard *Expatriot* • Craig Stark *Thugs* ■ *Dir/Scr* Allison Anders, Dean Lent, Kurt Voss

Border Shootout ★★
Western   1990 · US · Colour · 110mins

You don't expect a western from big-city writer Elmore Leonard (*Get Shorty*). But the plot, adapted from his novel, is the best thing in this morality tale, about townsfolk who elect an unworldly farmer as deputy sheriff to ageing lawman Glenn Ford so that they can go vigilante lynching. There's an intriguing set-up, but the production is as simple-minded as the deputy and even Ford is subdued. Contains mild swearing.

Glenn Ford *Sheriff Danahar* • Cody Glenn *Kirby Frye* • Charlene Tilton *Edith Hanasain* • Jeff Kaake *Phil Sundeen* • Danny Nelson *Harold Mendez* • Michael Ansara *Chuluka* • Sergio Calderone [Sergio Calderon] *Juaquin* ■ *Dir* Chris McIntyre • *Scr* Chris Mcintyre, from the novel *The Law at Randado* by Elmore Leonard

Borderline ★★ 15

Crime drama 1980 · US · Colour · 98mins

This conventional thriller has Charles Bronson as a patrolman on the US-Mexican border out to thwart those who make a profit out of illegal immigrants. Ed Harris, in his first major role, is outstanding as the chief baddie, but Bronson can't smuggle an expression of any kind onto that Mount Rushmore face of his. Director Jerrold Freedman tries valiantly to squeeze fresh blood from the script's tired collection of clichés. 💷

Charles Bronson *Jeb Maynard* • Bruno Kirby *Jimmy Fante* • Bert Remsen *Carl Richards* • Michael Lerner *Henry Lydell* • Kenneth McMillan *Malcolm Wallace* • Ed Harris *Hotchkiss* • Karmin Murcelo *Elena Morales* • Enrique Castillo *Arturo* ■ *Dir* Jerrold Freedman • *Scr* Steve Kline, Jerrold Freedman

Borderline ★★

Drama 1994 · Gr/Ger/UK · Colour · 85mins

An odd co-production between Channel 4, German television and the Greek film industry, this is a complex drama about the corrupting influences of city life and how little we ultimately know about the people closest to us. Co-written and directed by Panos Karkanevatos, the film focuses on two brothers from a remote mining village who are parted when the older of the two engineers fakes his own death only to be found later, alive and well, by his police officer sibling. For all its pretensions, this is a rather inconsequential picture, with neither of the leading actors arousing our interest. In Greek with English subtitles.

Aris Lebassopoulos *Yannis Markou* • Stavros Zalmas *Stelios* • Christos Kalavrouzos *Father* • Yannis Bofilios • Efi Drossou • Dinos Karydis • Maria Kiriaki • Patis Koutsaftis ■ *Dir* Panos Karkanevatos • *Scr* Panos Karkanevatos, Yannis Xanthopoulos

Bordertown ★★★

Crime drama 1935 · US · BW · 90mins

A super-pacey melodrama from Warner Bros, this stars Paul Muni as a disbarred lawyer who heads south to the US-Mexico border in search of work. There he finds sex in the form of playgirl Margaret Lindsay and hotblood Bette Davis. Davis's role, which culminates in a tremendous trial sequence, is actually quite sympathetic, since her lust for Muni is presented as entirely understandable because she's married to the gross Eugene Pallette. Daring then, and still stirring now, despite Muni's hamminess, it's essentially a love-triangle drama with social pretensions, and none the worse for that.

Paul Muni *Johnny Ramirez* • Bette Davis *Marie Roark* • Margaret Lindsay *Dale Elwell* • Eugene Pallette *Charlie Roark* • Soledad Jiminez *Mrs Ramirez* • Robert Barrat *Padre* • Gavin Gordon *Brook Mandillo* ■ *Dir* Archie Mayo • *Scr* Laird Doyle, Wallace Smith, from the novel by Carroll Graham

Bordertown Cafe ★★★

Comedy drama 1991 · Can · Colour · 101mins

A wry, warm-hearted Canadian comedy drama that takes an affectionate look at the relationship between a divorced woman and her troubled adolescent

son. Susan Hogan is a larger-than-life owner of a café, something of an embarrassment to her teenage offspring who longs for a normal existence. There are shades of *Bagdad Café* in the rich mix of eccentric characters, but director Norma Bailey also succeeds in making some telling points about the generation gap. Contains swearing.

Susan Hogan *Marlene* • Janet Wright *Maxime* • Lora Schroeder *Linda* • Gordon Michael Woolvett • Sean McCann • Nicholas Campbell ■ *Dir* Norma Bailey • *Scr* Kelly Rebar

Born Again ★ PG

Biographical drama 1978 · US · Colour · 104mins

A weird appendage to the Watergate scandal, this chronicles the rise of White House employee Charles Colson, who served time in prison for his involvement in the affair and became a born-again Christian. This movie version doesn't compare well with TV mini-series such as *Washington behind Closed Doors* and *Blind Ambition*, let alone the masterly *All the President's Men*. Former blues singer (and born-again) Christian Dean Jones plays Colson. Anne Francis is his wife, Patty, and several people appear who claim to be Nixon, Kissinger, Haldeman et al while looking nothing like them. The cringe factor is high. 💷

Dean Jones *Charles Colson* • Anne Francis *Patty Colson* • Jay Robinson *David Shapiro* • Dana Andrews *Tom Phillips* • Raymond St Jacques *Jimmy Newsom* • George Brent *Judge Gerhard Gesell* • Harry Spillman *President Richard M Nixon* • Peter Jurasik *Henry Kissinger* • Richard Caine *HR Haldeman* ■ *Dir* Irving Rapper • *Scr* Walter Bloch

Born Bad ★★★

Action crime thriller 1996 · US · Colour · 88 mins

A surprisingly thoughtful spin on the crime thriller, this provides a good guy role for James Remar, best known for his villainous turns in *48 Hours* and *The Cotton Club*. The setting is a bank where a raid staged by a bunch of bored teens has gone horribly wrong; they are forced to take hostages while sheriff Remar attempts to prevent bloodshed. There are good performances from Remar, Corey Feldman and Justin Walker, while the direction from Jeff Yonis is adequate.

Justin Walker *Brian* • Corey Feldman *Marco* • James Remar *Sheriff Larabee* • Ryan Francis *Craig* • Heidi Noelle Lenhart [Heidi Lenhart] *Laura* ■ *Dir/Scr* Jeff Yonis

Born Free ★★★★ U

Adventure drama based on a true story 1966 · US · Colour · 91mins

Beautifully shot and sensitively staged by director James Hill, this charming adaptation of Joy Adamson's bestseller is one of the great animal films. It goes without saying that all eyes will be on Elsa the lioness whenever she is on the screen, with her reluctance to take the first steps back into the wild bringing a lump to every throat. But the human performances are also first rate, with Virginia McKenna and Bill Travers bringing real warmth, rather than easy sentimentality, to their roles, while Geoffrey Keen excels as the

kindly commissioner who persuades them to part with their pet. 💷

Virginia McKenna *Joy Adamson* • Bill Travers *George Adamson* • Geoffrey Keen *Kendall* • Peter Luckoye *Nuru* • Omar Chambati *Makkede* • Bill Godden *Sam* • Bryan Epsom *Baker* • Robert Cheetham *Ken* ■ *Dir* James Hill • *Scr* Gerald LC Copley [Lester Cole], from the books by Joy Adamson • *Cinematographer* Ken Talbot

Born Free: A New Adventure ★★ U

Adventure drama 1996 · US · Colour · 92mins

Bearing only the slightest resemblance to the 1966 Oscar-winning feature film, this TV movie fails to evoke the pathos so memorable in the original. Filmed on location in South Africa, this pale sequel tells of a widowed research scientist (Christopher Noth) who moves his family to Africa after receiving a grant to study viruses. His teenage son resents being uprooted, but soon befriends a tame lioness and the young girl who has raised her. Unless the two youths can help acclimatise her to the wild, however, the local game warden will have to place the now-mature lioness in a zoo. Noth does his best in a lacklustre role, while Jonathan Brandis and Ariana Richards (*Jurassic Park*) play the dedicated animal lovers with syrupy conviction. 💷

Jonathan Brandis *Rand* • Christopher Noth *David Thompson* • Ariana Richards *Val Porter* • Linda Purl *Ellie Porter* • Lea Moreno *Jena Thompson* • John Matshikiza ■ *Dir* Tommy Lee Wallace • *Scr* John McGreevey

Born in East LA ★★ 15

Comedy drama 1987 · US · Colour · 80mins

Based on Cheech Marin's parody of Bruce Springsteen's rock anthem *Born in the USA*, this weak-kneed effort lacks the wit of the Marin recording and cannot even muster a fraction of the Boss's own power. This tale of a third-generation Hispanic American who is wrongly deported to Tijuana starts by taking a handful of amiable pot shots, but eventually allows itself to be smothered by blandness. Nonetheless Marin, who writes, directs and stars in the film, supplies a comfortable comic presence. Contains swearing. 💷

Cheech Marin [Richard "Cheech" Marin] *Rudy Robles* • Daniel Stern *Jimmy* • Paul Rodriguez *Javier* • Kamala Lopez *Dolores* • Jan-Michael Vincent *McCalister* • Lupe Ontiveros *Rudy's mother* • Urbanie Lucero *Rudy's sister* • Chastity Ayala *Rudy's niece* ■ *Dir* Richard Marin [Richard "Cheech" Marin] • *Scr* Richard Marin [Richard "Cheech" Marin]

Born in Flames ★★★ 15

Drama 1983 · US · Colour · 79mins

In a futuristic New York, ten years after a peaceful revolution has made all men equal, three feminists from different backgrounds (the army, radio and performance arts) join together to fight for the rights of women irrespective of their race or sexual preference. A classic women's rights movie that utilises an in-your-face, *cinéma vérité* style, poignant arguments and razor-sharp humour to put across the hopeful fantasy of liberation against oppression. Among

the cast is future director Kathryn (*Strange Days*) Bigelow.

Honey • Adele Bertei *Isabel* • Jeanne Satterfield *Adelaide* • Flo Kennedy *Zella* • Pat Murphy *Newspaper editor* • Kathryn Bigelow *Newspaper editor* • Becky Johnston *Newspaper editor* • Hillary Hurst *Leader of women's army* ■ *Dir* Lizzie Borden • *Scr* Hisa Tayo, from a story by Lizzie Borden

Born Losers ★★★ 18

Crime drama 1967 · US · Colour · 106mins

Don't be fooled by the credits for director TC Frank, screenwriter E James Lloyd and producer Donald Henderson – they are all pseudonyms for Tom Laughlin, the rough-and-ready auteur who also starred in this bruising encounter between a half-breed ex-Green Beret and a sadistic biker gang. Nowadays it's hard to fathom why this crude exploitation flick was one of the sixties highest grossers. But the rescue of Elizabeth James was attended by such sickening violence that audiences were shocked to the edge of their seats. Over the next decade, Laughlin would revive the Billy Jack character for three disappointing sequels. 💷

Tom Laughlin *Billy Jack* • Elizabeth James *Vicky Barrington* • Jane Russell *Mrs Shorn* • Jeremy Slate *Danny Carmody* • William Wellman Jr *Child* • Robert Tessier *Cue Ball* • Jeff Cooper *Gangrene* • Edwin Cook *Crabs* ■ *Dir* TC Frank [Tom Laughlin] • *Scr* E James Lloyd [Tom Laughlin]

Born of Fire ★★

Horror 1987 · UK · Colour

British concert flautist Peter Firth heads to Turkey for a musical duel with a supernatural magician in a puzzling and hallucinatory mystical adventure about the power of religion. Heavy symbolism and paradoxical events are the mainstay of this beautifully photographed cautionary tale, which also finds astronomer Suzan Crowley mating with a deformed dwarf and giving birth to an insect. Meanwhile a genie appears in various animal guises to throw further spokes in a confusing wheel of parallel universes, weird imagery and a James Galway-style soundtrack. Vagueness has never been given a more esoteric or disturbing sheen.

Peter Firth *Paul Bergson* • Suzan Crowley *Woman astronomer* • Oh-Tee *Master Musician* • Nabil Shaban *Silent One* • Stefan Kalipha *Bilal* ■ *Dir* Jamil Dehlavi • *Scr* Raficq Abdulla • *Cinematographer* Bruce McGowan

Born on the Fourth of July ★★★★★ 18

Biographical drama 1989 · US · Colour · 138mins

The second film in director Oliver Stone's Vietnam trilogy is a masterpiece, on a much broader canvas than its predecessor *Platoon*. It stars Tom Cruise as Ron Kovic, the all-American boy who enlists in the marines because he loves his country. The Stars and Stripes flies proudly in his home town. Then he is hideously wounded, endures the rat-infested hell of a veterans' hospital and comes home to find the Stars and Stripes being burned in the streets. He drops out in druggy Mexico, then returns to

America to conduct an antiwar campaign from his wheelchair. The story is based on the autobiography of Ron Kovic; Stone himself did two tours of duty in Vietnam and the movie fairly reeks of their experience and regret. Stone had won the director's Oscar for *Platoon* and he won it again for his work here. Sadly, Cruise had to settle for a nomination, but Cruise's transformation from golden boy to a ravaged and embittered paraplegic is utterly convincing. Contains swearing, sex scenes and nudity. [video] DVD

Tom Cruise *Ron Kovic* • Kyra Sedgwick *Donna* • Raymond J Barry *Mr Kovic* • Caroline Kava *Mrs Kovic* • Willem Dafoe *Charlie* • Josh Evans *Tommy Kovic* • Jamie Talisman *Jimmy Kovic* • Tom Berenger *Recruiting sergeant* • Oliver Stone *News reporter* ■ *Dir* Oliver Stone • *Scr* Oliver Stone, Ron Kovic, from Ron Kovic's autobiography

Born Reckless ★★

Crime drama 1930 · US · BW · 73mins

A Little Italy gangster, arrested for robbery, is given the opportunity to serve his country rather than serve a prison sentence. He accepts and becomes a hero on the battlefield but, home again, he's drawn back into the underworld and gets involved in bootlegging. An early example of a film containing many of the elements Warner Bros would soon make into a classic genre with stars such as Paul Muni, Edward G Robinson and James Cagney, this offering from Fox suffers from a miscast Edmund Lowe and, more seriously, an inept screenplay. However, it's also an early example of John Ford's work before he became the premier director of westerns, and, as such, is of some cinematic interest.

Edmund Lowe *Louis Beretti* • Catherine Dale Owen *Joan Sheldon* • Lee Tracy *Bill O'Brien* • Marguerite Churchill *Rosa Beretti* • Warren Hymer *Big Shot* • William Harrigan *Good News Brophy* • Frank Albertson *Frank Sheldon* • Eddie Gribbon *Bugs* ■ *Dir* John Ford • *Scr* Dudley Nichols, from the novel *Louis Beretti* by Donald Henderson Clarke

Born Reckless ★

Crime drama 1937 · US · BW · 60mins

Racing driver Brian Donlevy becomes a cabbie, but finds the cab company under threat from ruthless racketeer Barton MacLane who wants to own it and turns nasty when he's thwarted. Donlevy joins forces with MacLane's moll (Rochelle Hudson) to collect evidence that will get the heavy put behind bars. Directed by Malcolm St Clair, this crime drama is so pointless and feeble that it caused the *New York Times* critic to dismiss it as "a little cinematic starveling". The passing of decades hasn't improved it.

Rochelle Hudson *Sybil Roberts* • Brian Donlevy *Bob "Hurry" Kane* • Barton MacLane *Jim Barnes* • Robert Kent *Les Martin* • Harry Carey *Dad Martin* • Pauline Moore *Dorothy Collins* • Chick Chandler *Windy Bowman* • William Pawley *Mac* ■ *Dir* Malcolm St Clair • *Scr* John Patrick, Robert Ellis, Helen Logan, from a story by Jack Andrews

Born Reckless ★★

Musical drama 1959 · US · BW · 79mins

The same title was used for an early John Ford failure about bootlegging, and again in 1937 for a programme-filler about taxi wars. This time around, it's used for a feeble musical with a western theme. The almost non-existent plot has a luckless rodeo cowboy (Jeff Richards) taking to the road with his old-timer pal and partner (Arthur Hunnicutt) and a sexy blonde trick rider (Mamie Van Doren). This slim premise gives rise to several songs that have probably never been heard again.

Mamie Van Doren *Jackie Adams* • Jeff Richards *Kelly Cobb* • Arthur Hunnicutt *Cool Man* • Carol Ohmart *Liz* • Tom Duggan *Wilson* • Tex Williams • Don "Red" Barry [Donald Barry] *Oakie* • Nacho Galindo *Papa Gomez* ■ *Dir* Howard W Koch • *Scr* Richard Landau, from a story by Aubrey Schenck, Richard Landau

Born to Be Bad ★★ PG

Drama 1950 · US · BW · 89mins

Unfortunately for RKO, Joan Fontaine was put on this earth to be timid and twee on screen, if not in real life, and acting bad did not come easily. The film had already been postponed in 1946 and again in 1948, when Barbara Bel Geddes was offered the lead. The publicity people obviously knew they had a struggle selling this when they came up with the tag line "a cross between Lucretia Borgia and Peg o' My Heart" to describe Fontaine's callous character. [video]

Joan Fontaine *Christabel Caine* • Robert Ryan *Nick Bradley* • Zachary Scott *Curtis Carey* • Joan Leslie *Donna Foster* • Mel Ferrer *Gobby* • Harold Vermilyea *John Caine* • Virginia Farmer *Aunt Clara* ■ *Dir* Nicholas Ray • *Scr* Edith Sommer, Robert Soderberg, George Oppenheimer, Charles Schnee (adaptation), from the novel *All Kneeling* by Anne Parrish

Born to Be Wild ★★ U

Adventure 1995 · US · Colour · 94mins

Movie-mad youngsters just can't be fobbed off with cheap special effects any more. Consequently, only the youngest viewers will fail to spot that animal star Katie is nothing more than a fur-covered collection of gears and wires in this simian reworking of *Free Willy*. Which is a shame, as the story of a lonely kid who befriends a three-year-old gorilla in a behavioural study lab is actually quite entertaining, at least until it reaches the ponderous courtroom sequences. Wil Horneff interacts surprisingly well with the animatronic ape, while Peter Boyle comes up with some deliciously hammed-up villainy. [video]

Wil Horneff *Rick Heller* • Helen Shaver *Margaret Heller* • John C McGinley *Max Carr* • Peter Boyle *Gus Charnley* • Jean Marie Barnwell *Lacey Carr* • Marvin J McIntyre *Bob the paramedic* • Gregory Itzin *Walter Mallinson* ■ *Dir* John Gray • *Scr* Paul Young, John Bunzel, from a story by Paul Young

Born to Dance ★★★ U

Musical 1936 · US · BW · 105mins

A vintage MGM musical, in which a young and lovable James Stewart croons (in his own inimitable voice) to Eleanor Powell – she of the mesmerising tap shoes – who manages to bring this movie to a memorable climax with an intoxicating (and patriotic) nautical finale. Stewart is especially amiable, but there's also talented support from loose-limbed Buddy Ebsen and lovely Virginia Bruce, and the fine Cole Porter score includes the classic *I've Got You under My Skin*. Those glossy MGM production values give a rare sheen to the proceedings and the black and white is positively luminous, making you care less about the extremely silly plot.

Eleanor Powell *Nora Paige* • James Stewart *Ted Barker* • Virginia Bruce *Lucy James* • Una Merkel *Jenny Saks* • Sid Silvers *Gunny Saks* • Frances Langford *Peppy Turner* • Raymond Walburn *Captain Dingby* • Alan Dinehart *McKay* ■ *Dir* Roy Del Ruth • *Scr* Jack McGowan, Sid Silvers, from a story by Jack McGowan, Sid Silvers, BG DeSylva • *Cinematographer* Ray June

Born to Ride ★★ PG

Second World War action adventure
1991 · US · Colour · 85mins

Mechanic John Stamos joins the army to help phase in the use of motorbikes, but he only succeeds in upsetting those in command. To make matters worse, both he and his superior (John Stockwell) fall for the commanding officer's daughter (Teri Polo). Stamos – star of US TV sitcom *Full House* – can't handle himself or his bike one iota as well as Steve McQueen did in *The Great Escape*, in this rather unappealing mix of romance and wartime adventure. Contains swearing. [video]

John Stamos *Grady* • John Stockwell *Hassler* • Teri Polo *Beryl Ann* • Thom Mathews *Willis* • Dean Yacalis *Tony* • Salvator Xuereb *Levon* • Justin Lazard *Brooks* • Keith Cooke *Broadwater* ■ *Dir* Graham Baker • *Scr* Janice Hickey, Michael Patridge

Born to Run ★★ 18

Drama 1993 · US · Colour · 92mins

Unlike Johnny Depp, his fellow teen idol in the eighties television series *21 Jump Street*, Richard Grieco has never made the transition to Hollywood star, and now seems to divide his time between straight-to-video features and made-for-TV fodder. Here he's a moody hot-rod racer who gets caught up with the Mafia when his brother starts mixing in the wrong circles. Albert Magnoli, best known for the Prince movie *Purple Rain*, directs flashily, but to little effect. [video]

Richard Grieco *Nicky Donatello* • Jay Acovone *Richie* • Shelli Lether *Sally* • Joe Cortese *Phil* • Christian Campbell *Jamie* • Brent Stait *Raymond* • Martin Cummins *Art* • Wren Roberts *Tattoo* ■ *Dir* Albert Magnoli • *Scr* Frank Bitetto, Tobias Schliessler, Randall M Badat [Randall Badat]

Born to Win ★★

Black comedy 1971 · US · Colour · 90mins

Robert De Niro appeared in more than ten movies before his real breakthrough parts in *Mean Streets* and *The Godfather Part II*. One of his early films, directed by Czech émigré Ivan Passer, this deals lightly with the New York drug scene. George Segal is the shaggy-haired ex-crimper who needs $100 a day to pay for his heroin habit, but can't even seem to rob a diner successfully. Among the supporting cast, Hector Elizondo plays a big-time dealer, Paula Prentiss appears for less than five minutes and British actress Sylvia Syms crops up as a cashier in the diner. De Niro shows little star potential.

George Segal *Jay Jay* • Karen Black *Parm* • Jay Fletcher *Billy Dynamite* • Hector Elizondo *The Geek* • Marcia Jean Kurtz *Marlene* • Robert De Niro *Danny* • Paula Prentiss *Veronica* • Sylvia Syms *Cashier* ■ *Dir* Ivan Passer • *Scr* David Scott Milton, Ivan Passer

Born Too Soon ★★★ 15

Drama based on a true story
1993 · US · Colour · 92mins

It's amazing what a shrewd piece of casting can do for even the most mundane material. This true-life TV movie is raised several notches above the norm by the assured performances of Michael Moriarty and Pamela Reed, as a couple of fortysomething careerists who are willing to sacrifice everything they have worked for to save their premature baby daughter. Admittedly, the film occasionally resorts to a shameless tug at the heartstrings, but it also has some interesting things to say about the motivations of people who have encountered nothing but success. [video]

Michael Moriarty *Fox Butterfield* • Pamela Reed *Elizabeth Mehren* • Terry O'Quinn *Dr Friedman* • Joanna Gleason *Annemarie* • Mariangela Pino *Leslie* • Elizabeth Ruscio *Tina* • Christianne Hirt *Carol* • Christine Avila *Mrs Diaz* ■ *Dir* Noel Nosseck • *Scr* Susan Baskin, from Elizabeth Mehren's autobiography

Born Yesterday ★★★★★ U

Comedy 1950 · US · BW · 98mins

Forget the 1993 remake with Melanie Griffith, this is the original, a wonderfully funny look at Washington corruption and the age-old battle between the sexes. As Billie Dawn, mistress to Broderick Crawford's junk trader-made-good, Judy Holliday affects a voice that could curdle cream and a persona that will melt your heart. It's a measure of her performance that she beat both Bette Davis (for *All About Eve*) and Gloria Swanson (for *Sunset Boulevard*) to the best actress Oscar. Garson Kanin's dialogue is acid on toast and director George Cukor cleverly knows when to let the action play in splendid long takes – the gin rummy scene is cinematic perfection. As the nice guy, William Holden demonstates the subtle charm that soon made him a movie legend. [video]

Judy Holliday *Billie Dawn* • Broderick Crawford *Harry Brock* • William Holden (1) *Paul Verrall* • Howard St John *Jim Devery* • Frank Otto *Eddie* • Larry Oliver *Norval Hedges* • Barbara Brown *Mrs Hedges* • Grandon Rhodes *Sanborn* ■ *Dir* George Cukor • *Scr* Albert Mannheimer, from the play by Garson Kanin • *Cinematographer* Joseph Walker

Born Yesterday ★★★ PG

Comedy 1993 · US · Colour · 96mins

It's a brave man who tampers with a classic and Luis Mandoki's remake of George Cukor's Oscar-winning charmer predictably brought howls of protest. However, if you can put the original to the back of your mind, this makes for an amiable, easy-going journey. Melanie Griffith takes the Judy Holliday role of the sassy, deceptively smart girlfriend of rich businessman John Goodman. He wants her smartened up for Washington, so he hires jaded journalist Don Johnson. It was

intended as a vehicle for the then-married Johnson and Griffith, and they are the main problem: the former *Miami Vice* man looks uncomfortable with light comedy, while Griffith lacks Holliday's razor-sharp comic timing. However, John Goodman, as always, is a delight and Mandoki (*White Palace*) keeps the proceedings bubbling along. Contains violence and swearing. 🖭

Melanie Griffith *Billie Dawn* • John Goodman *Harry Brock* • Don Johnson *Paul Verrall* • Edward Herrmann *Ed Devery* • Max Perlich *JJ* • Michael Ensign *Philippe* • Benjamin C Bradlee *Secretary Duffee* ■ *Dir* Luis Mandoki • *Scr* Douglas McGrath, from the play by Garson Kanin

The Borrower ★★★ 18
Science-fiction horror thriller
1989 · US · Colour · 87mins
John McNaughton's follow-up to the hugely controversial *Henry: Portrait of a Serial Killer* finds him in more straightforward sci-fi horror territory. The story tracks an alien creature with a penchant for ripping the heads off unsuspecting humans and plonking them on his own neck. Rae Dawn Chong and Don Gordon are the puzzled detectives on its trail. McNaughton has some fun playing around with genre conventions and, while it's a long way from the bleak dread of *Henry*, it offers enough scares to keep horror fans happy. It's co-written by Richard Fire and the cast includes Tom Towles, both of whom collaborated with McNaughton on *Henry*. Contains swearing and sexual situations. 🖭

Rae Dawn Chong *Diana Pierce* • Don Gordon *Charles Krieger* • Antonio Fargas *Julius Caesar Roosevelt* • Tom Towles *Bob Laney* • Neil Giuntoli *Scully* • Pam Gordon *Connie* • Mädchen Amick *Megan* • Larry Pennell *Captain Scarcelli* ■ *Dir* John McNaughton • *Scr* Sam Egan [Mason Nage], Richard Fire, from a story by Sam Egan [Mason Nage]

The Borrowers ★★★ U
Fantasy adventure
1997 · UK · Colour · 83mins
Mary Norton's charming children's stories about a family of minute people (the ''Borrowers'' of the title) are here turned into a delightful family film. Jim Broadbent is the head of the tiny brood while John Goodman is the oafish tycoon they encounter. However, it's really the special effects that steal the show from the human cast (miniature or otherwise). Peter Hewitt (*Bill & Ted's Bogus Journey*) directs this fun kids' adventure. 🖭 *DVD*

John Goodman *Ocious P Potter* • Jim Broadbent *Pod Clock* • Mark Williams *Exterminator Jeff* • Celia Imrie *Homily Clock* • Hugh Laurie *Officer Steady* • Ruby Wax *Town Hall Clerk* • Bradley Pierce *Pete Leender* • Flora Newbigin *Arietty Clock* ■ *Dir* Peter Hewitt • *Scr* Gavin Scott, John Kamps, from the novels by Mary Norton • *Special Effects* Digby Milner, Lyn Nicholson, Peter Chiang, Tim Field

Borsalino ★★★★ 15
Crime thriller 1970 · Fr/It · Colour · 119mins
Jean-Paul Belmondo and Alain Delon are in top serio-comic form as two small-time hoodlums breaking into the Marseilles criminal underworld of the thirties. The superb period detailing and Claude Bolling's hum-along score are additional delights in Jacques

Deray's bloody gangster pastiche, which liberally borrows ideas from the work of Howard Hawks and Jean-Pierre Melville, among others. It's *The Public Enemy*, Gallic-style, with engaging tongue-in-cheek wit and a cheeky comic-strip atmosphere. In French with English subtitles. 🖭

Jean-Paul Belmondo *Capella* • Alain Delon *Siffredi* • Michel Bouquet *Rinaldi* • Catherine Rouvel *Lola* • Françoise Christophe *Mme Escarguel* • Corinne Marchand *Mme Rinaldi* ■ *Dir* Jacques Deray • *Scr* Jean-Claude Carrière, Claude Sautet, Jacques Deray, Jean Cau, from the book *Bandits à Marseille* by Eugène Soccomare

Borsalino and Co ★★
Thriller 1974 · Fr/It/W Ger · Colour · 110mins
Gangster Alain Delon fights heroin addiction and his mob enemies for control of the criminal underworld in thirties Marseille in a hackneyed rehash of the far superior *Borsalino*. While clearly taking pointers from *French Connection II*, it fails to do anything interesting with them. Despite the sleazy dockside glamour setting, director Jacques Deray's lazy sequel is for Delon completists only. French dialogue dubbed into English.

Alain Delon *Roch Siffredi* • Riccardo Cucciolla *Volpone* • Reinhardt Kolldehoff *Sam* • Lionel Vitrant *Lionel* • Catherine Rouvel *Lola* • Daniel Ivernel *Fanti* ■ *Dir* Jacques Deray • *Scr* Jacques Deray, Pascal Jardin

Le Bossu ★★
Swashbuckling adventure adventure
1959 · Fr/It · Colour · 101mins
This French swashbuckler stars Jean Marais as an adventurer who cares for a small girl when her nobleman father is murdered. As the dashing hero, Marais avenges his friend's death by infiltrating the enemy camp disguised as a hunchback. Based on Paul Féval's much-filmed novel, it's all a bit *Three Musketeers* – not surprising, since director André Hunebelle had already adapted the Dumas classic in 1953, while Marais himself played D'Artagnan in *Le Masque de Fer* (1962). French dialogue dubbed into English.

Jean Marais *Chevalier de Legardère* • André Bourvil [Bourvil] *Passepoil* • Sabina Sesselmann *Aurore de Nevers, Isabelle de Caylus* • Hubert Noël *Duc de Nevers* • François Chaumette *Gonzague* • Jean Le Poulain *Monsieur de Peyrolles* • Paulette Dubost *Dame Marthe* ■ *Dir* André Hunebelle • *Scr* Jean Halain, Pierre Foucaud, from the novel by Paul Féval

Le Bossu ★★★ 15
Swashbuckling adventure
1997 · Fr/It/Ger · Colour · 123mins
This most recent version of Paul Féval's classic adventure and, like its predecessors, it feels more like a serial than a seamless narrative. That said, this pacey and polished picture is never anything less than sabre-rattling entertainment. Although not known for action heroics, Daniel Auteuil emerges from this rousing romp with flying colours, as he hones his fencing skills and assumes the disguise of a hunchback to avenge the murder of Vincent Perez by scheming financier Fabrice Luchini. Director Philippe de Broca is a master swashbuckler, but

his handling of Auteuil's romance with Marie Gillain is less assured. A French language film. Contains some violence and swearing. 🖭

Daniel Auteuil *Lagardère/The Hunchback (Le Bossu)* • Fabrice Luchini *Gonzague* • Vincent Perez *Duc de Nevers* • Marie Gillain *Aurore* • Yann Colette *Peyrolles* • Jean-François Stévenin *Cocardasse* • Didier Pain *Passepoil* • Charles Nelson *Aesop* • Philippe Noiret *Philippe d'Orléans* ■ *Dir* Philippe de Broca • *Scr* Philippe de Broca, Jean Cosmos, Jérôme Tonnerre, from the novel by Paul Féval

Boston Kickout ★★★ 18
Black comedy 1995 · UK · Colour · 100mins
Youthful exuberance and an affectionate eye for suburban life help paper over the technical deficiencies of this oddball black comedy. It was the first film that introduced John Simm (*Human Traffic*, *The Lakes*) to a wider audience. He plays a confused teen desperate to get out of his dead-end life in dead-end Stevenage, as his friends drift improbably into crime. It's a bit erratic but there are some nice lines, plus a memorably psychotic turn from Marc Warren (*The Vice*, *Game On*). Contains swearing, violence and sex scenes. 🖭

John Simm *Phil* • Emer McCourt *Shona* • Andrew Lincoln *Ted* • Nathan Valente *Matt* • Richard Hanson *Steve* • Marc Warren *Robert* • Derek Martin *Ray* ■ *Dir* Paul Hills • *Scr* Paul Hills, Diane Whitley, Roberto Troni, from a story by Paul Hills

The Boston Strangler ★★★★ 18
Biographical crime drama
1968 · US · Colour · 109mins
A suspenseful, often disturbing re-creation of the crimes, capture and psychoanalysis of Albert DeSalvo (played by Tony Curtis), who charmed his way behind the bolted doors of Bostonian women in the early sixties by pretending to be a plumber. Director Richard Fleischer deftly captures the pensive atmosphere of a frightened city with a stark, documentary-style approach that makes good use of split-screen sequences, as an all-star line-up of lawmen tighten the net around the elusive maniac. Curtis proved beyond doubt he could act with this nuanced performance of considerable depth and power. 🖭

Tony Curtis *Albert DeSalvo* • Henry Fonda *John S Bottomly* • George Kennedy *Phil Di Natale* • Mike Kellin *Julian Soshnick* • Hurd Hatfield *Terence Huntley* • Murray Hamilton *Frank McAfee* • Jeff Corey *John Asgeirsson* • Sally Kellerman *Dianne Cluny* ■ *Dir* Richard Fleischer • *Scr* Edward Anhalt, from the book by Gerold Frank • *Cinematographer* Richard H Kline

The Bostonians ★★ PG
Period drama 1984 · UK · Colour · 116mins
A Merchant-Ivory production adapted from the Henry James novel by Ruth Prawer Jhabvala. Vanessa Redgrave stars as the Bostonian suffragette who gets involved with a faith healer's daughter, while Christopher Reeve appears out of his depth as the lumbering cousin who falls for the girl. James is notoriously difficult to convey on film and the film moves at a snail's pace; as a result it's a tad dull, despite the loving attention paid to

period detail. Director James Ivory might have benefited from the contemporary energy brought to recent adaptations of James's works, such as *The Portrait of a Lady* and *The Wings of the Dove*. 🖭

Christopher Reeve *Basil Ransome* • Vanessa Redgrave *Olive Chancellor* • Madeleine Potter *Verena Tarrant* • Jessica Tandy *Miss Birdseye* • Nancy Marchand *Mrs Burrage* • Wesley Addy *Dr Tarrant* • Barbara Bryne *Mrs Tarrant* • Linda Hunt *Dr Prance* ■ *Dir* James Ivory • *Scr* Ruth Prawer Jhabvala, from the novel by Henry James

Botany Bay ★★★
Adventure 1952 · US · Colour · 93mins
Alan Ladd is a medical student unjustly transported to Australia, and James Mason is the sadistic captain of the prison ship that takes him there. While Ladd and Mason square up to each other, Patricia Medina sets both their hearts fluttering. In the end, after some flogging, snogging and an outbreak of plague, they all arrive Down Under, where a tribe of savage Aborigines sort out the unresolved plotlines. It's all a bit *Mutiny on the Bounty*, having been adapted from a similar potboiling novel by Charles Nordhoff and James Norman Hall, and Ladd and Mason have clearly been told to act up like Clark Gable and Charles Laughton. Together, they do put gloss on the dross.

Alan Ladd *Hugh Tallant* • James Mason *Capt Paul Gilbert* • Patricia Medina *Sally Munroe* • Cedric Hardwicke *Governor Phillips* • Murray Matheson *Rev Thynne* • Malcolm Lee Beggs *Nick Sabb* • Jonathan Harris *Tom Oakley* • Dorothy Patten *Mrs Nellie Garth* ■ *Dir* John Farrow • *Scr* Jonathan Latimer, from the novel by Charles Nordhoff , James Norman Hall

Bottle Rocket ★★★ 15
Comedy crime drama
1996 · US · Colour · 87mins
The debut feature from Wes Anderson, who impressed with his quirky and sophisticated comedy *Rushmore*, this is an agreeably eccentric affair about a dopey trio (Luke and Owen Wilson, Robert Musgrave) who bewilderingly think they are cut out for a life in crime. Anderson observes their bungling antics and personality disorders with obvious affection, while continually taking the episodic tale in unexpected directions. The largely unknown leads deliver expertly judged performances and there's a nice cameo from James Caan. 🖭

Luke Wilson *Anthony Adams* • Robert Musgrave *Bob Mapplethorpe* • Owen C Wilson [Owen Wilson] *Dignan* • Lumi Cavazos *Inez* • James Caan *Mr Henry* • Andrew Wilson *Future Man* • Ned Dowd *Dr Nichols* • Shea Fowler *Grace* ■ *Dir* Wes Anderson • *Scr* Owen C Wilson, Wes Anderson

Bottoms Up ★★ U
Comedy 1959 · UK · BW · 88mins
Frank Muir, Denis Norden and Michael Pertwee collaborated on the script for this school-based comedy, which sought to cash in on the successful Jimmy Edwards *Whack-O!* TV series. Leslie Howard's brother Arthur again plays stooge to Jimmy's cane-wielding headmaster, as he tries to raise the profile of his academy by passing off his bookie's son as eastern royalty.

The strong supporting cast makes a solid contribution to an otherwise hit-and-miss comedy, which comes a poor third behind the much more original Will Hay or St Trinian's films. ▭

Jimmy Edwards *Professor Jim Edwards* • Arthur Howard *Oliver Pettigrew* • Martita Hunt *Lady Gore-Willoughby* • Sydney Tafler *Sid Biggs* • Raymond Huntley *Garrick Jones* • Reginald Beckwith *Bishop Wendover* • Vanda Hudson *Matron* • Richard Briers *Colbourne* • Melvyn Hayes *Cecil Biggs* ■ *Dir* Mario Zampi • *Scr* Michael Pertwee, with additional dialogue by Frank Muir, Denis Norden

Le Boucher ★★★★
Psychological drama
1969 · Fr · Colour · 94mins

One of Claude Chabrol's most accomplished and celebrated films has the director returning to the provincial world of his first film *Le Beau Serge* a decade later. Chabrol's then wife, Stéphane Audran plays a village schoolteacher who gradually comes to realise that her new friend, a shy butcher (Jean Yanne), is the sex murderer the police are searching for. With certain nods to Chabrol's idol Alfred Hitchcock, the film is much more than a thriller – it's a sympathetic psychological study of sexual frustration. Supported by the actual inhabitants of the town in Périgord in which it is set, the two leads are superb. The film is brilliantly shot by Jean Rabier, Chabrol's usual cinematographer. In French with English subtitles.

Stéphane Audran *Hélène* • Jean Yanne *Popaul* • Antonio Passalia *Angelo* • Mario Beccaria *Léon Hamel* • Pasquale Ferone *Père Cahrpy* • Roger Rudel *Police Inspector Grumbach* ■ *Dir/Scr* Claude Chabrol

Boudu, Saved from Drowning ★★★★PG
Comedy
1932 · Fr · BW · 84mins

Jean Renoir's classic farce-cum-satire of bourgeois ways will seem familiar to anyone who has seen Paul Mazursky's *Down and Out in Beverly Hills*. The latter was Hollywood's retelling of the same story about a particularly smelly and ill-natured tramp, who is saved from suicide in the Seine by a nice, middle-class gent, and shows his gratitude by staying with the chap's family and wreaking havoc on their lives. A neat idea, executed to fine comic effect by a master film-maker. In French with English subtitles.

Michel Simon *Boudu* • Charles Grandval *Monsieur Lestingois* • Marcella Hainia *Madame Lestingois* • Séverine Lerczynska *Anne-Marie* • Jean Dasté *Student* • Max Dalban *Godin* • Jean Gehret *Vigour* • Jacques Becker *Poet on bench* ■ *Dir* Jean Renoir • *Scr* Jean Renoir, from the play by René Fauchois

Boulevard ★★18
Crime drama
1994 · US · Colour · 95mins

Despite a better-than-average cast, this still lands on the wrong side of the exploitation/gritty drama divide. Kari Wuhrer plays a young victim of domestic violence who heads to the city and drifts into the seamier side of life, despite the best attentions of prostitute Rae Dawn Chong. Lou Diamond Phillips is way over the top as a vicious pimp; Lance Henriksen

also pops up as a tough but fair cop. Director Penelope Buitenhuis has a good eye for the mean streets, but loses the fight against the sleazier elements of the story. ▭

Rae Dawn Chong *Ola* • Kari Wuhrer *Jennefer* • Joel Bissonnette *J-Rod* • Lance Henriksen *McClaren* • Lou Diamond Phillips *Hassan* • Judith Scott *Sheila* ■ *Dir* Penelope Buitenhuis • *Scr* Rae Dawn Chong

Boulevard Nights ★★18
Drama
1979 · US · Colour · 97mins

Despite wearing its social conscience blatantly on its sleeve, this story of two Mexican Americans in downtown Los Angeles is ultimately rather a bore. Danny De La Paz is compelling enough as the Chicano trying to extricate his brother (Richard Yniguez) from the clutches of the local gang and there's lots of hard-breathing atmosphere and rebel-with-a-cause angst. But director Michael Pressman never manages to raise much impetus or interest. He also directed *Teenage Mutant Ninja Turtles II: the Secret of the Ooze*, which may say something. ▭

Richard Yniguez *Raymond Avila* • Danny De La Paz *Chuco Avila* • Marta DuBois *"Shady" Landeros* • James Victor *Gil Moreno* • Betty Carvalho *Mrs Avila* • Carmen Zapata *Mrs Landeros* • Gary Cervantes *"Big Happy"* • Victor Millan *Mr Landeros* ■ *Dir* Michael Pressman • *Scr* Desmond Nakano

Boulevard of Broken Dreams ★★
Drama
1988 · Ausl · Colour · 95mins

Pino Amenta, best known for directing episodes of TV series such as *The Sullivans*, *The Flying Doctors* and cult hit *Farscape*, here directs a mediocre drama about a successful screenwriter (John Waters) who realises he has lost his soul and abandoned the dreams he had earlier in his career. The Hollywood scene has been captured better in films such as *Swimming with Sharks* and *The Player*, and Amenta's film covers no new ground.

John Waters *Tom Garfield* • Penelope Stewart *Helen Garfield* • Kim Gyngell *Ian McKenzie* • Nicki Paull *Suzy Daniels* • Andrew McFarlane *Jonathan Lovell* • Kevin Miles *Geoff Bormann* • Ross Thompson *Cameron Wright* ■ *Dir* Pino Amenta • *Scr* Frank Howson

Bound ★★★★18
Crime thriller
1996 · US · Colour · 104mins

An original and intensely black comedy thriller from Larry and Andy Wachowski, who hit the A-list big time in 1999 with *The Matrix*. Jennifer Tilly and Gina Gershon co-star as lesbian lovers who seek to outwit a hefty Mafia outfit. Not simply lipstick titillation, the pair form a convincing *Thelma and Louise*-style team and take the punches like men. Visually dynamic, stylish, refreshing and funny, this dispels any doubts that the Wachowski brothers deserve to be heralded as highly influential auteurs. Contains swearing, violence and sexual situations. ▭ **DVD**

Jennifer Tilly *Violet* • Gina Gershon *Corky* • Joe Pantoliano *Ceasar* • John P Ryan *Mickey Malnato* • Christopher Meloni *Johnny Marconi* • Richard C Sarafian *Gino Marzzone* • Barry Kivel *Shelly* • Mary Mara *Bartender* ■ *Dir/Scr* Larry Wachowski, Andy Wachowski

Bound and Gagged: a Love Story ★★★18
Black comedy
1992 · US · Colour · 89mins

More a road movie than the love story the title suggests, this focuses on Ginger Lynn Allen, who escapes her thuggish husband by beginning an affair with another woman. However, this romance takes on a bizarre turn when her lover kidnaps her after Allen refuses to divorce her husband, and takes her on a journey through the badlands of Minnesota. It's strange and often funny stuff, capably handled by director Daniel B Appleby, and featuring two strong lead performances from Allen and Elizabeth Saltarrelli as Leslie's lover. ▭

Ginger Lynn Allen *Leslie* • Karen Black *Carla* • Chris Denton *Cliff* • Elizabeth Saltarrelli *Elizabeth* • Mary Ella Ross *Lida* • Chris Mulkey *Steve* ■ *Dir/Scr* Daniel B Appleby

Bound for Glory ★★★★PG
Biography
1976 · US · Colour · 142mins

This is a moving account of the folk singer Woody Guthrie, a real-life rebel who travelled through the Dust Bowl during the Depression years, singing and whingeing as he went along. David Carradine, who provides his own vocals, makes a credible Guthrie, while director Hal Ashby creates many a vivid composition lit by flashes of real insight. Guthrie influenced many of today's balladeers; watching this, it's not hard to see why. ▭

David Carradine *Woody Guthrie* • Ronny Cox *Ozark Bule* • Melinda Dillon *Mary Guthrie* • Gail Strickland *Pauline* • John Lehne *Locke* • Ji-Tu Cumbuka *Slim Snedeger* • Randy Quaid *Luther Johnson* • Elizabeth Macey *Liz Johnson* ■ *Dir* Hal Ashby • *Scr* Robert Getchell, from Woody Guthrie's autobiography

Boundaries of the Heart ★★
Romantic drama
1988 · Ausl · Colour · 105mins

An Australian movie that takes the small-town theme and runs with it to exhaustion point, like a rugby player desperate for a try. Wendy Hughes is nicely feisty and manipulative as Stella, the town's man-eater, but John Hargreaves is a shade too vacuous in the chief supporting role. There is much rumour-mongering and townsfolk muttering behind their hands, which effectively gives the movie an enclosed, claustrophobic feel, but overall the story goes nowhere very much. Contains some swearing.

Wendy Hughes *Stella Marsden* • John Hargreaves *Andy Ford* • Norman Kaye *WH (Billy) Marsden* • Michael Siberry *Arthur Pearson* • Julie Nihill *June Thompson* • Max Cullen *Blanco White* • John Clayton *Riley* • Vivienne Garrett *Freda* • Beverley Shaw *Millie* ■ *Dir* Lex Marinos • *Scr* Peter Yeldham

The Bounty ★★★★15
Historical drama
1984 · UK · Colour · 127mins

Although this is the third Hollywood account of the infamous 1789 mutiny, it's not a remake. Unlike the Charles Laughton/Clark Gable and Trevor Howard/Marlon Brando versions, this sticks closely to historical fact. Consequently, Lieutenant – as he was at the time of the mutiny – William

Bligh emerges as a gentleman bound by duty and loyalty who expected nothing less of his crew, while Fletcher Christian comes across as a man driven by heartfelt but half-digested notions of liberty and romance. It was undoubtedly a bold move for Mel Gibson to play such an anti-hero, but, despite his efforts, he is acted off the screen by the magnificent Anthony Hopkins, whose dignity and determination hold together Roger Donaldson's highly intelligent film. ▭

Mel Gibson *Fletcher Christian* • Anthony Hopkins *Lieutenant William Bligh* • Laurence Olivier *Admiral Hood* • Edward Fox *Captain Greetham* • Daniel Day-Lewis *John Fryer* • Bernard Hill *Cole* • John Sessions *Smith* • Philip Davis *Young* • Liam Neeson *Churchill* ■ *Dir* Roger Donaldson • *Scr* Robert Bolt, from the non-fiction book *Captain Bligh and Mr Christian* by Richard Hough

The Bounty Hunter ★★★PG
Western
1954 · US · Colour · 75mins

A straightforward yet satisfying Randolph Scott western, in which the stone-faced one sets out after three marauding bank robbers, all of whom are in disguise as respectable townsfolk, making Randy's job a little difficult. This is gripping stuff from director Andre De Toth, who formed a working relationship with Scott that preceded Scott's remarkable series of westerns with the better-known director Budd Boetticher. These De Toth horse operas were screened as co-features, often with a minor musical or thick-ear thriller (this one partnered the original *Dragnet* on its release), and provided satisfactory, value-for-money programming. ▭

Randolph Scott *Jim Kipp* • Dolores Dorn *Julie Spencer* • Marie Windsor *Alice* • Howard Petrie *Sheriff Brand* • Harry Antrim *Dr Spencer* • Robert Keys *George Williams* • Ernest Borgnine *Rachin* • Dub Taylor *Danvers* ■ *Dir* Andre De Toth • *Scr* Winston Miller, from a story by Winston Miller, Finlay McDermid

The Bounty Hunters ★★★
Western adventure
1970 · It · Colour · 105mins

This is a lesser known but nonetheless competent spaghetti western, set in 19th-century Mexico and starring Yul Brynner. He plays Sabata, the archetypal gunslinger supreme, who teams up with a band of Mexican revolutionaries. Brynner made the film during his time in Switzerland – he became a Swiss citizen in the late sixties, but returned to Hollywood in 1972. This is a quite acceptable offering of its kind, with a few original touches added to the usual body count. Italian dialogue dubbed into English.

Yul Brynner *Sabata* • Dean Reed *Ballantine* • Pedro Sanchez *Escudo* • Gerard Herter *Colonel Skimmel* • Sal Borgese *Septiembre* • Franco Fantasia *Ocano* • Gianni Rizzo *Folgen* • Salvatore Billa *Manuel* • Massimo Carocci *Juan* ■ *Dir* Frank Kramer [Ginafranco Parolini] • *Scr* Renato Izzo, Gianfranco Parolini

Bounty Hunters ★★15
Action comedy
1996 · US · Colour · 93mins

Action man Michael Dudikoff was one of the first popular video stars in Britain and although by the nineties he had been overtaken by a fresh batch of martial arts maestros, he still managed to churn out popular lightweight vehicles like this no-brain thriller. Here he plays a high-bounty hunter who teams up with feisty rival tracker Lisa Howard to bring in a ruthless mobster. The duo set off down a well-worn, wisecracking path through car stunts and gun battles to a satisfyingly explosive – if routine – denouement.

Michael Dudikoff *Jersey* • Lisa Howard *BB* ■ *Dir* George Erschbamer • *Scr* George Erschbamer, Michael Ellis

The Bounty Killer ★★
Western drama 1965 · US · Colour · 92mins

This B-western has Dan Duryea as an easterner who, by accident, becomes a vicious bounty hunter out west and only meets his match when a young bounty hunter (played by Duryea's son, Peter) appears to settle the score. The director, former stuntman Spencer G Bennet, was a veteran of sagebrush operas and serials such as *Superman* and *Batman and Robin*. For this effort, one of his last films, he gathered a nostalgic supporting cast.

Dan Duryea *Willie Duggan* • Audrey Dalton *Carole Ridgeway* • Fuzzy Knight *Luther* • Rod Cameron *Johnny Liam* • Richard Arlen *Ridgeway* • Buster Crabbe [Larry ''Buster'' Crabbe] *Mike Clayman* • Johnny Mack Brown *Sheriff Green* • Bob Steele *Red* ■ *Dir* Spencer G Bennet [Spencer Gordon Bennet] • *Scr* R Alexander, Leo Gordon

Bounty Tracker ★★ 18
Martial arts action 1993 · US · Colour · 86mins

This mechanical straight-to-video action thriller competently, if unimaginatively, plunders every cliché in the book. Moody Lorenzo Lamas is the hard-as-nuts bounty hunter, who goes seeking revenge when his brother is murdered by a mobster trying to cover up his money-laundering activities. Undemanding genre fans will warm to the copious amount of explosions, shoot-outs and car chases, but the performances are anonymous and it is ploddingly predictable throughout.

Lorenzo Lamas *Johnny Damone* • Matthias Hues *Erik Gauss* • Cyndi Pass *Jewels* • Paul Regina *Paul Damone* • Brooks Gardner *Max Talton* • Eugene Robert Glazer *Sarazin* • Anthony Peck *Jerry Greco* • Eddie Frias *Tony* ■ *Dir* Kurt Anderson • *Scr* Caroline Olson

The Bowery ★★★
Drama 1933 · US · BW · 94mins

Loveable Wallace Beery and child star Jackie Cooper had a huge public and critical success in *The Champ* (1931), and here they're reunited in a film based on some romantic legends of old New York. Tough guy George Raft is Steve Brodie, who (in)famously jumped off the Brooklyn Bridge in 1886 (an incident shown to dramatic effect here), while Beery plays his sparring partner in this fast-paced Raoul Walsh production, complete with colourful Bowery language and even more colourful Bowery characters. This was one of eleven pictures ''scream queen'' Fay Wray made in 1933 (*King Kong* was another).

Wallace Beery *Chuck Connors* • George Raft *Steve Brodie* • Jackie Cooper *Swipes McGurk*

• Fay Wray *Lucy Calhoun* • Pert Kelton *Trixie Odbray* • George Walsh *John L Sullivan* • Oscar Apfel *Mr Herman* ■ *Dir* Raoul Walsh • *Scr* Howard Estabrook, James Gleason, from the novel *Chuck Connors* by Michael L Simmons, Bessie Ruth Solomon

The Bowery Boys Meet the Monsters ★★★
Comedy horror 1954 · US · BW · 65mins

In 1946 surviving members of the Dead End Kids, who'd come to prominence in films such as in *Angels with Dirty Faces*, became the Bowery Boys to conveyor-belt feed the nation's adolescents with juvenile slapstick comedies of which this was the most commercially successful. A monster spoof, in the vein of those perpetrated by Abbott and Costello, this has the Boys running foul of a family that makes the Addams clan look like something out of Enid Blyton. Although not particularly funny, it's directed by Edward Bernds, who'd previously worked with the Three Stooges, at such a pace that boredom doesn't get a look in.

Leo Gorcey *Slip* • Huntz Hall *Sach* • Bernard Gorcey *Louie* • Lloyd Corrigan *Anton* • Ellen Corby *Amelia* • John Dehner *Derek* • Laura Mason *Francine* ■ *Dir* Edward Bernds • *Scr* Elwood Ullman, Edward Bernds

Bowery Champs ★★★
Comedy 1944 · US · BW · 61mins

This is one of the more amusing entries in the *East Side Kids* series, thanks to a super in-joke that has former *Dead End Kid* Bobby Jordan playing himself. The running gag is threaded throughout this daft tale of Muggs (Leo Gorcey) getting himself involved – yet again – in a murder hunt. Journeyman director William Beaudine keeps the pace up; he became a regular helmer for the *Bowery Boys* series that subsequently grew out of this picture. Watch for distinguished character actor Ian Keith (*Queen Christina*) and former silent star Evelyn Brent in one of her last screen appearances.

Leo Gorcey *Muggs* • Huntz Hall *Glimpy* • Billy Benedict *Skinny* • Jimmy Strand *Danny* • Bobby Jordan *Kid* • Bud Gorman *Shorty* • Anne Sterling *Jane* • Gabriel Dell *Jim* ■ *Dir* William Beaudine • *Scr* Earle Snell

Bowfinger ★★★★ 12
Comedy 1999 · US · Colour · 93mins

A bang-on-target satire of low-budget Hollywood film-making featuring Steve Martin's best comic performance since *Dirty Rotten Scoundrels*. He's an ambitious but financially challenged producer/director who can't get A-list action star Eddie Murphy for his new sci-fi project. So he follows the actor around, setting up various silly scenarios and filming Murphy's shocked reactions. Martin – who also wrote the hilarious screenplay – is immensely engaging, and there's sparkling support from Murphy (in dual roles) and Heather Graham, as a talentless actress who's quite happy to sleep her way to a larger role. While *The Player* was a snarling, sharp-toothed beast, director Frank Oz's lively send-up of Tinseltown is a far more cute and cuddly companion.

Contains some strong language. ▭
DVD

Steve Martin *Bowfinger* • Eddie Murphy *Kit Ramsey/Jeff Ramsey* • Heather Graham *Daisy* • Christine Baranski *Carol* • Jamie Kennedy *Dave* • Barry Newman *Kit's agent* • Adam Alexi-Malle *Afrim* • Terence Stamp *Terry Stricter* • Robert Downey Jr *Jerry Renfro* ■ *Dir* Frank Oz • *Scr* Steve Martin

Box of Moon Light ★★★★ 15
Comedy 1996 · US · Colour · 106mins

An immensely enjoyable, warm and relevant human comedy about the quality of life. Electrical engineer John Turturro lives by the clock, plays by the book and is as boring as hell, until the day he hears what his co-workers truly think of him and decides to go back to the lake where he spent his childhood. There he meets Sam Rockwell, a free spirit who lives in a dilapidated trailer and steals garden gnomes for a living. How his new companion's chaotic existence changes Turturro's attitudes is highly engaging, very affecting and always amusing. Beautifully shot and scripted, with director Tom DiCillo supplying a weird, yet welcome, atmosphere, this allegorical fairy tale is a box of sheer delights. Contains swearing, some sexual references and one violent scene. ▭

John Turturro *Al Fountain* • Sam Rockwell *Bucky, ''Kid''* • Catherine Keener *Floatie Dupre* • Lisa Blount *Purlene Dupre* • Annie Corley *Deb Fountain* • Rica Martens *Doris* • Ray Aranha *Soapy* • Alexander Goodwin *Bobby Fountain* • Dermot Mulroney *Wick* ■ *Dir/Scr* Tom DiCillo

Boxcar Bertha ★★★ 18
Biographical crime drama 1972 · US · Colour · 88mins

Director Martin Scorsese broke into the big time with this Roger Corman-produced bloodfest that clearly signalled he was a major film-maker in waiting. Based on the autobiography of Bertha Thompson, this is a good girl-gone-bad picture, with Barbara Hershey as the farmer's daughter driven to crime by misfortune and an uncaring system. There's the occasional bravura shot and some coal-black humour, but essentially Scorsese is bound too tightly by Corman's usual exploitation formula to have space for such luxuries as character development. Hershey is outshone by her then beau David Carradine and his tireless father John. Negligible in itself, but fascinating in its context. Contains swearing, violence and nudity. ▭

Barbara Hershey *Boxcar Bertha* • David Carradine *Big Bill Shelley* • Barry Primus *Rake Brown* • Bernie Casey *Von Morton* • John Carradine *H Buckram Sartoris* • Victor Argo *One of the McIvers* • David R Osterhout *One of the McIvers* • Michael Powell *Chicken Holleman* • Emeric Pressburger *Graham Pratt* ■ *Dir* Martin Scorsese • *Scr* Joyce H Corrington, John William Corrington, from characters in *Sister of the Road, the Autobiography of Boxcar Bertha Thompson* by Bertha Thompson, Dr Ben L Reitman • *Producer* Roger Corman

The Boxer ★★★ 15
Political drama 1997 · Ire/UK/US · Colour · 108mins

A knock-out performance by Daniel Day-Lewis embellishes this otherwise

under-nourished tale that seems at times to be a polemic for the Irish Republican cause. He plays an IRA prisoner who returns to his former profession of boxing and establishes a gym, giving delinquents the chance to pummel their way to a better life. Directed and co-written by Jim Sheridan, it feels as sweatily authentic as the inside of a boxing glove, but the flatness of the narrative makes it seem rather dull. Contains swearing and some violence. ▭

Daniel Day-Lewis *Danny Flynn* • Emily Watson *Maggie* • Brian Cox *Joe Hamill* • Ken Stott *Ike Weir* • Gerard McSorley *Harry* • Eleanor Methven *Patsy* • Ciaran Fitzgerald *Liam* • David McBlain *Sean* ■ *Dir* Jim Sheridan • *Scr* Jim Sheridan, Terry George

Boxing Helena ★★ 18
Erotic thriller 1993 · US · Colour · 100mins

Infamous for provoking a feminist controversy and a lawsuit (Kim Basinger was sued for backing out of the lead role), the directorial debut of Jennifer Lynch is a fudged allegorical fantasy about aberrant human behaviour and sexual complexes. Sick surgeon Julian Sands falls in love with Sherilyn Fenn and, after she has a car accident, removes her legs and arms to keep her captive on a pedestal. This is by turns macabre and silly – Lynch is clearly aiming for the surreal atmosphere of her director father David's work, but fails to capture it. Fenn is great as the chastised bitch but Sands's performance is too superficial to evoke the dark side of his character's subconscious. ▭

Julian Sands *Dr Nick Cavanaugh* • Sherilyn Fenn *Helena* • Bill Paxton *Ray O'Malley* • Kurtwood Smith *Dr Alan Harrison* • Art Garfunkel *Dr Lawrence Augustine* • Betsy Clark *Anne Garrett* • Nicolette Scorsese *Fantasy lover/Nurse* • Meg Register *Marion Cavanaugh* ■ *Dir* Jennifer Lynch [Jennifer Chambers Lynch] • *Scr* Jennifer Chambers Lynch, from the story by Philippe Caland

A Boy, a Girl and a Bike ★★
Comedy drama 1949 · UK · BW · 91mins

A minor, good-natured British comedy romance that follows the adventures and love affairs of the youthful members of a Yorkshire cycling club. Future Avenger Honor Blackman is the girl whose affections are vied for by humble Patrick Holt and rich boy John McCallum, while Anthony Newley and Diana Dors play other members of the group. Among the older generation, the incomparable Thora Hird runs the club's ''café''. Ted Willis supplies the screenplay, Ralph Smart directs, and the whole cosy enterprise demonstrates why, with certain superior exceptions, the public preferred American films.

John McCallum *David Howarth* • Honor Blackman *Susie Bates* • Patrick Holt *Sam Walters* • Diana Dors *Ada Foster* • Maurice Denham *Bill Martin* • Leslie Dwyer *Steve Hall* • Anthony Newley *Charlie Ritchie* • Megs Jenkins *Nan Ritchie* • Thora Hird *Mrs Bates* ■ *Dir* Ralph Smart • *Scr* Ted Willis, from a story by Ralph Keene, John Sommerfield

A Boy and His Dog ★★★★ U
Science-fiction black comedy
1975 · US · Colour · 87mins

Featuring a very early screen appearance by Don Johnson, this film remains one of his best. He's actually not particularly brilliant in it as he is upstaged by his canine co-star, but this offbeat sci-fi comedy has deservedly become a cult favourite. Set in a post-apocalyptic world, the story follows the adventures of Johnson and his super intelligent dog when they get mixed up with a strange subterranean community, unable to reproduce sexually. Director LQ Jones (best known as a western character actor) works wonders with a tiny budget and maintains a pleasingly black tone throughout.

Don Johnson *Vic* • Susanne Benton *Quilla June* • Jason Robards [Jason Robards Jr] *Mr Craddock* • Alvy Moore *Dr Moore* • Helene Winston *Mez* • Charles McGraw *Preacher* • Hal Baylor *Michael* • Ron Feinberg *Fellini* • Mike Rupert *Gary* ■ *Dir* LQ Jones • *Scr* LQ Jones, from the novella by Harlan Ellison

A Boy Called Hate ★★★ 15
Road movie　　1995 · US · Colour · 93mins

Scott Caan makes his film debut alongside his more famous dad, James, in this intriguing road movie. Caan Jr plays a delinquent teenager who comes to the aid of would-be rape victim Missy Crider (best known for her role in the second series of *Murder One*) and ends up on the run from both the law and the girl's guardian. First-time director Mitch Marcus coaxes intense performances out of his two young leads, while Caan Sr and Elliott Gould add class and experience to the proceedings. Contains swearing, violence and sex scenes. 📼

Scott Caan *Steve "Hate" Bason* • Missy Crider *Cindy* • James Caan *Jim* • Elliott Gould *Richard* • Adam Beach *Billy Little Plume* ■ *Dir/Scr* Mitch Marcus

Boy, Did I Get a Wrong Number ★★ U
Comedy　　1966 · US · Colour · 98mins

Not even an ageing Hope can save this cheapskate, dumbed-down comedy, in which he plays an estate agent who becomes involved with sexy starlet Elke Sommer after she runs away from the set of her latest film. It's hard to believe that director George Marshall is the same man who directed such classics as *The Blue Dahlia* and *Destry Rides Again*. Phyllis Diller has her moments as Bob's wacky maid.

Bob Hope *Tom Meade* • Elke Sommer *Didi* • Phyllis Diller *Lily* • Cesare Danova *Pepe* • Marjorie Lord *Martha Meade* • Kelly Thordsen *Schwartz* • Benny Baker *Regan* • Terry Burnham *Doris Meade* ■ *Dir* George Marshall • *Scr* Burt Styler, Albert E Lewin, George Kennett, from a story by George Beck

The Boy Friend ★★★ U
Musical comedy 1971 · UK · Colour · 104mins

Indebted to the Warner Bros classic *42nd Street*, this is an energetic and invigorating adaptation of Sandy Wilson's stage success, in which the members of a provincial rep company discover their true selves in the process of putting on a show. A warm-hearted tribute to master choreographer Busby Berkeley, the film unsurprisingly lacks his inspiration. Yet Ken Russell makes a fair fist of the song and dance numbers, while Twiggy is ideally cast as the willing gofer who gets the chance to become a star when the lead (an uncredited Glenda Jackson) injures an ankle. 📼

Twiggy *Polly Browne* • Christopher Gable *Tony Brockhurst* • Barbara Windsor *Hortense* • Moyra Fraser *Mme Dubonnet* • Bryan Pringle *Percy Parkhill* • Max Adrian *Max* • Catherine Willmer *Lady Brockhurst* • Vladek Sheybal *De Thrill* • Tommy Tune *Tommy* ■ *Dir* Ken Russell • *Scr* Ken Russell, from a play by Sandy Wilson

The Boy from Mercury ★★★★ PG
Drama　　1996 · UK /Fr/ Ire · Colour · 83mins

Martin Duffy made his debut as a writer/director with this semi-autobiographical tale set at the dawn of the space age. Paying homage to both fifties sci-fi and sixties kitchen sink drama, Duffy not only gets the fashions and furnishings right, but also re-creates the cinematic look of the period thanks to Seamus Deasy's ingeniously faded photography. James Hickey is magnificent as the eight-year-old who compensates for the loss of his dad by adopting Flash Gordon as his hero and claiming interstellar ancestry. Sean O'Flanagain is equally engaging as his bullied, cowboy-crazy pal, while there are expert cameos from Rita Tushingham and Tom Courtenay. All in all, a gem. 📼

James Hickey *Harry* • Tom Courtenay *Uncle Tony* • Rita Tushingham *Harry's mother* • Hugh O'Conor *Paul* • Joanne Gerard *Sarah, Paul's girlfriend* • Sean O'Flanagain *Sean McCarthy* ■ *Dir/Scr* Martin Duffy

The Boy from Oklahoma ★★ U
Western　　1954 · US · Colour · 88mins

Michael Curtiz had directed Will Rogers Jr with some success two years earlier, when Jr played Sr in a faithful biopic of the well-loved star (Jr was facially a dead ringer). Warner Bros decided to pair director and star one more time, and this pleasant western was the result. It's a minor film with Rogers Jr as a law student who becomes the peace-loving sheriff of Bluerock. Rogers Jr didn't have what it took to become a star, but a minor cowboy player in this movie did become one of America's most famous chat-show hosts: watch out for Merv Griffin in his early incarnation as an actor.

Will Rogers Jr *Tom Brewster* • Nancy Olson *Katie Brannigan* • Lon Chaney Jr *Crazy Charlie* • Anthony Caruso *Barney Turlock* • Wallace Ford *Wally Higgins* • Clem Bevans *Pop Pruty* • Merv Griffin *Steve* • Louis Jean Heydt *Paul Evans* ■ *Dir* Michael Curtiz • *Scr* Frank Davis, Winston Miller, from a story in *The Saturday Evening Post* by Michael Fessier

The Boy in Blue ★★ 15
Biographical sports drama
1986 · Can · Colour · 93mins

This Canadian curio is not the most compelling picture Nicolas Cage has ever been in. But a screen biography of Ned Hanlan, the Ontario-based ne'er-do-well who held the world speed sculling title towards the end of the last century, was never likely to be. Cage deserves some credit for involving us in Hanlan's struggles, but it's mostly dispiriting stuff and the rowing scenes are largely devoid of energy and tension. Contains swearing and nudity. 📼

Nicolas Cage *Ned* • Christopher Plummer *Knox* • Cynthia Dale *Margaret* • David Naughton *Bill* • Sean Sullivan *Walter* • Melody Anderson *Dulcie* • Walter Massey *Mayor* ■ *Dir* Charles Jarrott • *Scr* Douglas Bowie, from an original idea by John Trent

Boy Meets Girl ★★★
Comedy　　1938 · US · BW · 87mins

When you see the picture, you'll discover that the title isn't as corny at as it sounds, but ironic. For this is a frenetic screwball comedy with James Cagney and Pat O'Brien as screenwriters who take the strut out of an arrogant star (Dick Foran) by casting him opposite a scene-stealing infant. As always, Cagney's presence is highly combustible, even having exchanged a machine gun for a typewriter, and the direction by Lloyd Bacon (of *42nd Street* fame) is suitably breezy. It seems likely that the writing pair were based on Ben Hecht and Charles MacArthur. Real-life radio announcer Ronald Reagan is played by... Ronald Reagan.

James Cagney *Robert Law* • Pat O'Brien *J Carlyle Benson* • Marie Wilson *Susie* • Ralph Bellamy *E Elliott Friday* • Dick Foran *Larry Toms* • Frank McHugh *Rosetti* • Bruce Lester *Rodney Bevan* • Ronald Reagan *Announcer* ■ *Dir* Lloyd Bacon • *Scr* Samuel Spewack, Bella Spewack, from their Broadway play

A Boy Named Charlie Brown ★★★ U
Animated musical comedy
1969 · US · Colour · 79mins

The first of four feature-length films starring Charles M Schulz's much-loved *Peanuts* gang finds the eternal no-hoper Charlie Brown filled with anxiety as he prepares for a national spelling competition and the opening day of baseball season. Director Bill Melendez, a veteran of the Disney and Warner Bros animation studios and countless animated commercials, puts his expertise to charming and imaginative effect, though the gentle antics and excruciatingly twee songs – Oscar-nominated at the time – have dated badly. Small children and life-long *Peanuts* fans probably won't mind in the least, however. 📼

Peter Robbins *Charlie Brown* • Pamelyn Ferdin *Lucy Van Pelt* • Glenn Gilger *Linus Van Pelt* • Andy Pforsich *Schroeder* • Sally Dryer *Patty* • Anne Altieri *Violet* • Erin Sullivan *Sally* • Linda Mendelson *Frieda* ■ *Dir* Bill Melendez • *Scr* Charles M Shulz, from his comic strip *Peanuts*

Boy on a Dolphin ★ U
Adventure　　1957 · US · Colour · 106mins

A dreary mismatch of the voluptuous Sophia Loren, in her first film for a Hollywood studio, with the ageing Alan Ladd, a last-minute replacement for Robert Mitchum. She's a Greek sponge diver, he's an American archaeologist, and the slight but protracted story is about the raising of a priceless statue from the bed of the Aegean. Loren towered over Ladd, so the island where filming took place was riddled with trenches to even up their heights. Clifton Webb does what he can as the supercilious villain. 📼

Alan Ladd *Dr James Calder* • Sophia Loren *Phaedra* • Clifton Webb *Victor Parmalee* • Jorge Mistral *Rhif* • Laurence Naismith *Dr Hawkins* • Alexis Minotis *Government Man* • Piero Giagnoni *Niko* ■ *Dir* Jean Negulesco • *Scr* Ivan Moffat, Dwight Taylor, from the novel by David Divine

Boy Slaves ★★★
Drama　　1938 · US · BW · 66mins

This oddity stems from the period when RKO's B-unit was instructed by corporate president Leo Spitz to produce tougher material. However, the public didn't warm to such fare, preferring to leave social issues to Warner Bros. This was the last of Spitz's legacy, a drama about forced labour on the turpentine farms of the South during the Depression. Anne Shirley is excellent as a victim trapped by the system and, in a largely unknown cast, teen-gang leader James McCallion and runaway Roger Daniel are stand-outs. This is harrowing stuff, melodramatic and preachy by turns, but credit should go to producer/director PJ Wolfson for managing to get it made at all.

Anne Shirley *Annie* • Roger Daniel *Jesse* • James McCallion *Tim* • Alan Baxter *Graff* • Johnny Fitzgerald *Knuckles* • Walter Ward *Miser* • Charles Powers *Lollie* • Walter Tetley *Pee Wee* ■ *Dir* PJ Wolfson • *Scr* Albert Bein, Ben Orkow, from a story by Albert Bein

The Boy Who Caught a Crook ★★ U
Crime adventure　　1961 · US · BW · 72mins

Having debuted in *A Dog's Best Friend*, Roger Mobley was joined by another canine companion in his second feature. He's also accompanied by a genial hobo, which is just as well as the excitable newsboy spends much of the action being menaced by a villain desperate to recover a briefcase containing $100,000 in stolen loot. With some 50 B-movies to his credit, director Edward L Cahn knew exactly which buttons to push. Unfortunately any suspense that he manages to create is rather undermined by screenwriter Nathan Juran's choice of title. Mobley tries hard, but Don Beddoe is the pick of the cast.

Wanda Hendrix *Laura* • Roger Mobley *Kid* • Don Beddoe *Colonel* • Richard Crane *Connors* • Johnny Seven *Rocky Kent* • Robert J Stevenson *Sergeant* • William Walker *Keeper* • Henry Hunter *Flannigan* ■ *Dir* Edward L Cahn • *Scr* Nathan Juran

The Boy Who Could Fly ★★★ PG
Fantasy drama 1986 · US · Colour · 103mins

With a touch more imagination and a little less saccharine, this fledgling version of Alan Parker's *Birdy* could have been one of the best family films of the eighties, but writer/director Nick Castle couldn't resist the flights of fancy that hijack the action. It's a touching tale about an autistic boy, whose attempts to fly from the roof of his house attract the attention of a girl who has moved to the neighbourhood after her father's suicide. Jay Underwood and Lucy Deakins are splendid as the teenage friends, while Bonnie Bedelia and Colleen Dewhurst provide sympathetic adult support. 🖵

Lucy Deakins *Milly Michaelson* • Jay Underwood *Eric Gibb* • Bonnie Bedelia *Charlene Michaelson* • Fred Savage *Louis Michaelson* • Colleen Dewhurst *Mrs Sherman* • Fred Gwynne *Uncle Hugo* • Mindy Cohen *Geneva* • Janet MacLachlan *Mrs D'Gregario* ■ *Dir/Scr* Nick Castle

The Boy Who Cried Bitch ★★★

Psychological drama
1991 · US · Colour · 101mins

Disturbed adolescent Harley Cross is expelled from prep school, and ends up in a psychiatric hospital where he threatens his room-mate, torches the hallway and has convulsions in the classroom. Eventually his mother brings him home, where he leads his brothers astray and threatens her with a gun. Argentine director Juan Jose Campanella builds up an all-too believable scenario in his desire to show what Charles Manson, and other similar mass murderers, were probably like as children.

Harley Cross *Dan Love* • Karen Young *Candice Love* • Jesse Bradford *Mike Love* • JD Daniels *Nick Love* • Gene Canfield *Jim Cutler* • Moira Kelly *Jessica* • Adrien Brody *Eddy* • Dennis Boutsikaris *Orin Fell* ■ *Dir* Juan Jose Campanella • *Scr* Catherine May Levin

The Boy Who Drank Too Much ★★★

Drama
1980 · US · Colour · 99mins

This gutsy, and at times compelling, TV movie follows a high school ice hockey star's grim battle against alcoholism. Scott Baio, best known for starring in the sitcom *Happy Days* and its short-lived spin-off *Joanie Loves Chachi*, gives a convincing performance as the troubled teenager, while the hard-hitting script is confidently handled by seasoned television director Jerrold Freedman. The result is a forceful study of a problem faced by countless American teenagers.

Scott Baio *Buff Saunders* • Lance Kerwin *Billy Carpenter* • Ed Lauter *Gus Carpenter* • Mariclare Costello *Louis Carpenter* • Don Murray *Ken Saunders* • Stephen Davies *Alan* • Toni Kalem *Tina* • Katherine Pass *Donna Watson* ■ *Dir* Jerrold Freedman • *Scr* Edward DeBlasio, from the novel by Shep Greene

The Boy Who Had Everything ★ 18

Drama
1984 · Ausl · Colour · 90mins

Chariots of Fire meets *Oedipus Rex* in this inconsequential tale of overachieving college student Jason Connery. He's caught between his mother (Diane Cilento, his real mother), a blonde girlfriend and loyalty to a private school where sadistic humiliation rites are the norm, despite his athletic ability. Awkwardly acted and preciously directed, Stephen Wallace's old-fashioned melodrama has little to say about relationships and growing up. 🖵

Jason Connery *John* • Diane Cilento *Mother* • Laura Williams *Robin* • Lewis Fitz-Gerald *Vandervelt* • Ian Gilmour *Pollock* • Nique

Needles *Cummerford* • Michael Gow *Kaplin* • Mark Wignall *McPhee* • Monroe Reimers *Afferson* ■ *Dir/Scr* Stephen Wallace

The Boy Who Stole a Million ★★ U

Comedy
1960 · UK · BW · 84mins

Although many critics have compared this hard-times drama to Vittorio De Sica's neorealist classic *Bicycle Thieves*, it is, in fact, much closer in spirit to the Graham Greene-penned tale *The Fallen Idol*. Co-written by director Charles Crichton and one-time documentarist John Eldridge, the story of a Spanish boy who steals from a bank to help his impoverished family is supposed to be gnawingly realistic. However, not even the drab photography or the run-down locations can increase the authenticity of the protracted pursuit by some sniffy bank officials and a gang of sneaky criminals. A cloying and unconvincing disappointment.

Virgilio Texera [Virgilio Texeira] *Miguel* • Maurice Reyna *Paco* • Marianne Benet *Maria* • Harold Kasket *Luis* • George Coulouris *Bank manager* • Bill Nagy *Police chief* • Warren Mitchell *Pedro* • Tutte Lemkow *Mateo* ■ *Dir* Charles Crichton • *Scr* Charles Crichton, John Eldridge, from a story by Neils West Larsen, Antonio de Leon

The Boy Who Turned Yellow ★★

Science-fiction fantasy
1972 · UK · Colour · 55mins

It is a film-making tragedy that, after 1960's *Peeping Tom*, director Michael Powell's reputation took a serious nose dive. This peculiar little film for children, which was the final teaming of Powell with longtime collaborator Emeric Pressburger, sadly did nothing to resurrect the great man's career. Here, schoolboy John (Mark Dightman) takes a trip to the Tower of London and loses his pet mouse. Sent home from school later for falling asleep in a class on electricity, he dreams (or does he?) that the people on the tube and in the street have turned yellow.

Mark Dightman *John* • Robert Eddison *Nick* • Helen Weir *Mrs Saunders* • Brian Worth *Mr Saunders* • Esmond Knight *Doctor* • Laurence Carter *Schoolteacher* • Patrick McAlinney *Supreme Beefeater* ■ *Dir* Michael Powell • *Scr* Emeric Pressburger

The Boy with Green Hair ★★★ U

Fantasy drama
1948 · US · Colour · 82mins

One of the last pictures studio chief Dore Schary made at RKO, this somewhat clumsy mix of whimsy and allegory marked the Hollywood feature debut of director Joseph Losey. Howard Hughes ordered wholesale changes to the film when he bought the studio, but the tolerance theme that he detested so much remained largely intact. Dean Stockwell does well as the orphan whose hair changes colour, and there's some expert support by the likes of Walter Catlett, Samuel S Hinds and Regis Toomey. Most notable, however, are the splendid against-type performances of Robert Ryan and Pat O'Brien.

Robert Ryan *Dr Evans* • Dean Stockwell *Peter* • Pat O'Brien *Gramp* • Barbara Hale *Miss*

Brand • Richard Lyon *Michael* • Walter Catlett *"The King"* • Samuel S Hinds *Dr Knudson* • Regis Toomey *Mr Davis* ■ *Dir* Joseph Losey • *Scr* Ben Barzman, Alfred Lewis Levitt, from a story by Betsy Beaton

Boyfriends ★★★ 18

Drama
1996 · UK · Colour · 81mins

Co-directors Neil Hunter and Tom Hunsinger's promising feature debut shows consummate skill in getting under the skin of homosexual neuroses, as it follows the exploits of three troubled gay couples on a weekend in the country. An amalgam of *The Big Chill*, *Peter's Friends* and *A Little Night Music*, this shining example of British low-budget film-making accurately scrutinises gay sex and love in the nineties. James Dreyfus from the TV comedy series *The Thin Blue Line* plays one of the lovelorn Londoners. Contains swearing, sex scenes and nudity. 🖵

James Dreyfus *Paul* • Mark Sands *Ben* • Andrew Ableson *Owen* • Michael Urwin *Matt* • David Coffey *Will* • Darren Petrucci *Adam* • Michael McGrath *James* • Russell Higgs *Mark* ■ *Dir/Scr* Neil Hunter, Tom Hunsinger

The Boys ★★

Courtroom drama
1961 · UK · BW · 123mins

This badly dated courtroom drama from Sidney J Furie was originally, somewhat incongruously, sandwiched between the Cliff Richard vehicle, *The Young Ones*, and that moody study of juvenile delinquency, *The Leather Boys*. Although proving that some things never change – Jess Conrad, Dudley Sutton and their pals are suspected of murder simply because they're young and rebellious – the film becomes both patronising and predictable as with-it lawyer Richard Todd champions the lads' cause.

Richard Todd *Victor Webster* • Robert Morley *Lewis Montgomery* • Felix Aylmer *Judge* • Dudley Sutton *Stan Coulter* • Ronald Lacey *Billy Herne* • Tony Garnett *Ginger Thompson* • Jess Conrad *Barney Lee* • Wilfrid Brambell *Robert Brewer* • Wensley Pithey *Mr Coulter* ■ *Dir* Sidney J Furie • *Scr* Stuart Douglas

The Boys ★★★ PG

Black comedy
1991 · US · Colour · 90mins

Based on the careers of William Link and Richard Levinson, this is a film *à clef*, in other words a biopic with the names changed to allow a little dramatic latitude. Link and Levinson were the writing duo behind such TV hits as *Columbo* and *Murder, She Wrote*, until the latter died from cancer contracted from inhaling the former's cigarette smoke. Written by Link, the film is directed without mawkishness by Glenn Jordan. It's the inspired teaming of those undervalued actors James Woods and John Lithgow, however, that lifts this TV movie a notch above the pack. 🖵

James Woods *Walter Farmer* • John Lithgow *Artie Margulies* • Joanna Gleason *Marie Margulies* • Eve Gordon *Amanda Freeman* • Alan Rosenberg *Psychiatrist* • Rosemary Dunsmore *Helene Farmer* • John Vickery *Dr Simon* • Ebbe Roe Smith *Sokalow* ■ *Dir* Glenn Jordan • *Scr* William Link

Boys ★★ 15

Romantic drama 1995 · US · Colour · 82mins

A flimsy but watchable teen drama with Lukas Haas (the boy from *Witness*) as the boarding school boy whose friends discover sexy and mysterious Winona Ryder unconscious in a field. He decides to smuggle her back to his dormitory. Unfortunately, the unravelling secrets of her past aren't quite as thrilling as one would hope for. But both Haas and Ryder give good turns, and there are nice supporting performances from John C Reilly, Skeet Ulrich and Chris Cooper. Contains some swearing, drug use, and mild violence and sexual references. 🖵

Winona Ryder *Patty Vare* • Lukas Haas *John Baker Jr* • Skeet Ulrich *Bud Valentine* • John C Reilly *Officer Kellogg Curry* • Bill Sage *Officer Bill Martone* • Matt Malloy *Bartender* • Wiley Wiggins *John Phillips* • Russell Young *John Van Slieder* • Marty McDonough *Teacher* • Charlie Hofheimer *John Cooke* • James LeGros *Fenton Ray* • Chris Cooper *Mr John Baker* ■ *Dir* Stacy Cochran • *Scr* Stacy Cochran, from the short story *Twenty Minutes* by James Salter

The Boys ★★★★ 18

Drama 1998 · Ausl/UK · Colour · 85mins

Adapted from Gordon Graham's play, this is the bleak, disorientating flipside to *Neighbours*. David Wenham, just released from prison, returns to his suburban home, where he immediately begins to torment girlfriend Toni Collette (Oscar nominated for *The Sixth Sense*), his sleazy weak-willed brothers, their girlfriends and even his long-suffering mother. Although confined largely to one set, director Rowan Woods sustains an almost suffocating air of menace, which is further heightened by dislocating flash-forwards to an unknown future crime. An almost unrecognisable Collette demonstrates once again her range, but the real star here is Wenham, who delivers frighteningly believable portrait of a monstrous sociopath. Contains violence and swearing.

David Wenham *Brett Sprague* • Toni Collette *Michelle* • Lynette Curran *Sandra Sprague* • John Polson *Glenn Sprague* • Jeanette Cronin *Jackie* • Anthony Hayes *Stevie Sprague* • Anna Lise *Nola* • Pete Smith *George "Abo"* ■ *Dir* Rowan Woods • *Scr* Stephen Sewell, from the play by Gordon Graham

The Boys Club ★★★ 15

Thriller 1996 · Can · Colour · 87mins

Similar in feel to James Foley's under-rated *At Close Range*, this disturbing crime drama also offers a well-deserved lead role for Chris Penn. He plays a mysterious stranger with a bullet in his leg who is found sheltering in a deserted shack used by three disaffected teenagers. Penn claims to be a cop on the run from corrupt colleagues and the three boys immediately warm to his bluff charm and macho wisdom. But is he who he says he is? It's a dark coming-of-age fable, and all the more chilling for it. As good as Penn is, he is actually eclipsed by the talented young supporting cast. 🖵

Chris Penn [Christopher Penn] *Luke* • Dominic Zamprogna *Kyle* • Stuart Stone *Brad* • Devon Sawa *Eric* • Amy Stewart *Megan* • Jarred

🅄 = SUITABLE FOR ALL   🆄c = SUITABLE FOR ALL, ESPECIALLY FOR YOUNG CHILDREN (VIDEO ONLY)   🅿🅶 = PARENTAL GUIDANCE

Blancard *Jake* • Nicholas Campbell *Kyle's dad* ■ *Dir* John Fawcett • *Scr* Peter Wellington, from a story by Doug Smith

Boys Don't Cry ★★★ 18

Drama based on a true story
1999 · US · Colour · 116mins

The tragic true-life case history of Teena Brandon, a young girl from Nebraska who disguised herself as a man and was brutally raped and murdered in 1993, is compassionately brought to the screen by writer/director Kimberly Peirce. While Oscar-winner Hilary Swank gives a remarkable performance as the hero(ine), there's an exploitative sordidness to the enterprise that limits our sympathy. (Brandon's girlfriend Lana, portrayed here by Chloë Sevigny, tried to stop the film's release.) Not since *The Accused* has rape been shown so savagely on screen – though that's hardly a recommendation. Indeed, the ugliness of the film's conclusion is severely at odds with the genuinely touching scenes between Swank and Sevigny that precede it. Still, it's a brave and important work.

Hilary Swank *Teena Brandon/Brandon Teena* • Peter Sarsgaard *John* • Chloë Sevigny *Lana* • Brendan Sexton III *Tom* • Alison Folland *Kate* • Alicia Goranson *Candace* • Matt McGrath *Lonny* • Rob Campbell *Brian* • Jeannetta Arnette [Jeanetta Arnette] *Lana's mom* ■ *Dir* Kimberly Peirce • *Scr* Kimberly Peirce, Andy Bienen

The Boys from Brazil ★★★ 18

Thriller 1978 · US · Colour · 118mins

Ira Levin's ingenious novel about the cloning of Hitler's body tissue into identical little boys who would revive the Third Reich is given the epic treatment by director Franklin J Schaffner. Masterminding the genetic engineering is the infamous Dr Mengele, played by Gregory Peck in a convincing departure from his usual good-guy roles. James Mason is his accomplice and Laurence Olivier is the Nazi hunter modelled on Simon Wiesenthal who tracks them down. More plausible now than it was in the late seventies and still an accomplished, globe-trotting thriller, with the added appeal of Peck, Mason and Olivier scoring points off each other. Contains violence.

Gregory Peck *Dr Josef Mengele* • Laurence Olivier *Ezra Lieberman* • James Mason *Eduard Seibert* • Lilli Palmer *Esther Lieberman* • Uta Hagen *Frieda Maloney* • Rosemary Harris *Herta Doring* • Jeremy Black *Bobby/Jack/Erich/Simon* • Steve Guttenberg *Barry Kohler* ■ *Dir* Franklin J Schaffner • *Scr* Heywood Gould, from the novel by Ira Levin

The Boys from Syracuse ★★★ U

Musical comedy 1940 · US · BW · 73mins

Undercast (and in desperate need of colour) this jolly romp is the film of Rodgers and Hart's Broadway hit, itself based on Shakespeare's *Comedy of Errors*, and boasting two of the all-time great popular standards *This Can't Be Love* and *Falling in Love with Love*. Only Martha Raye and Joe Penner seem to capture the requisite Broadway brashness, and a wan Allan

Jones in the lead looks uncomfortable and strained. Many of the "ancient" jokes pre-date similar humoresques in *The Flintstones*, and period comedians Charles Butterworth and Eric Blore have a camp old time mining the gags.

Allan Jones *Antipholus of Ephesus/Antipholus of Syracuse* • Martha Raye *Luce* • Joe Penner *Dromio of Ephesus/Dromio of Syracuse* • Rosemary Lane *Phyllis* • Charles Butterworth *Duke of Ephesus* • Irene Hervey *Adriana* • Alan Mowbray *Angelo* • Eric Blore *Pinch* • Samuel S Hinds *Aegon* ■ *Dir* Edward Sutherland [A Edward Sutherland] • *Scr* Leonard Spigelgass, Charles Grayson, from the play by George Abbott, with music and lyrics by Richard Rodgers, Lorenz Hart, from the play *Comedy of Errors* by William Shakespeare

The Boys in Blue ★ PG

Comedy 1983 · UK · Colour · 93mins

In a packed field, this is a serious contender for the unwanted title of worst British film ever made. Over 40 years after he helped adapt Sidney Gilliat's story for the Will Hay vehicle *Ask a Policeman*, director Val Guest returned to the scene of the crime for this shudderingly awful remake, with TV comedy duo Tommy Cannon and Bobby Ball as the bumpkin bobbies whose station is reprieved when a gang of villains moves into their manor. The supporting cast contains such usual suspects as Roy Kinnear, Eric Sykes and Jon Pertwee, all of whom might have been better occupied doing community service.

Bobby Ball *Police Constable Bobby Ball* • Tommy Cannon *Sergeant Tommy Cannon* • Suzanne Danielle *Kim* • Roy Kinnear *Hector Lloyd* • Eric Sykes *Chief Constable* • Jack Douglas *Chief Superintendent* • Edward Judd *Hilling* • Jon Pertwee *Coastguard* • Arthur English *Farmer* ■ *Dir* Val Guest • *Scr* Val Guest, from Sidney Gilliat's story for the film *Ask a Policeman*

Boys in Brown ★★★

Crime drama 1949 · UK · BW · 85mins

Former variety comedian Jack Warner brings quiet conviction to one of the avuncular roles that brought him film fame in the forties. This time he's the governor of a boys' reformatory who does his best to convert his charges to the straight and narrow. Based on a play by Reginald Beckwith, this is a taut tale with a gallery of fine players including Richard Attenborough, Barbara Murray and Thora Hird. The most unregenerate of the delinquents is played by Dirk Bogarde, who was to menace Warner again when he shot dead PC Dixon (Warner) in the classic thriller *The Blue Lamp*.

Jack Warner *Governor* • Richard Attenborough *Jackie Knowles* • Dirk Bogarde *Alfie Rawlins* • Jimmy Hanley *Bill Foster* • Barbara Murray *Kitty Hurst* • Patrick Holt *Tigson* • Andrew Crawford *Casey* • Thora Hird *Mrs Knowles* ■ *Dir* Montgomery Tully • *Scr* Montgomery Tully, from a play by Reginald Beckwith

The Boys in Company C ★★★

War drama 1978 · US/HK · Colour · 125mins

A Vietnam war drama financed in Hong Kong and designed as a quickie to cash in on the then-imminent release of *Apocalypse Now*. Following a bunch of raw recruits played by a largely

unknown cast, the movie explores the ideas and moral terrain later refined by *Platoon*. But this tour of duty ends surprisingly with a soccer match between GIs and a Vietnamese team, effectively reducing the war to an absurdist symbol. Veterans of Vietnam movies might spot Lee Ermey, later the drill instructor in *Full Metal Jacket*.

Stan Shaw *Tyrone Washington* • Andrew Stevens *Billy Ray Pike* • James Canning *Alvin Foster* • Michael Lembeck *Vinnie Fazio* • Craig Wasson *Dave Bisbee* • Scott Hylands *Captain Collins* • James Whitmore Jr *Lieutenant Archer* • Lee Ermey [R Lee Ermey] *Sergeant Loyce* ■ *Dir* Sidney J Furie • *Scr* Rick Natkin, Sidney J Furie

The Boys in the Band ★★★ 15

Comedy drama 1970 · US · Colour · 114mins

The first and most famous Hollywood film on the subject of male homosexuality, director William Friedkin's stagey version of Mart Crowley's off-Broadway hit captures early glimmers of gay liberation while dealing with the self-hating, straight-acting and overly camp stereotypes of the era. Eight gay men gather for a Manhattan birthday party and a heterosexual visitor from the host's past turns up, only to add more game-playing therapy sessions and vicious bitchiness to the awkward proceedings. It's all very dated and it gives the impression that all gay men are miserable, tragic, venomous queens. Some of the lines are still hilarious, though, while Leonard Frey's performance as the Jewish birthday boy is a kitsch classic.

Kenneth Nelson *Michael* • Leonard Frey *Harold* • Frederick Combs *Donald* • Cliff Gorman *Emory* • Reuben Greene *Bernard* • Robert La Tourneaux *Cowboy* • Laurence Luckinbill *Hank* • Keith Prentice *Larry* • Peter White *Alan* ■ *Dir* William Friedkin • *Scr* Mart Crowley, from his play

The Boys Next Door ★★ 18

Crime drama 1985 · US · Colour · 86mins

Penelope Spheeris, best known for *Wayne's World*, directs this tough, grim drama about two 18-year-olds (played by Maxwell Caulfield and Charlie Sheen) who embark upon a series of brutal murders for no apparent reason. Although a sometimes shocking look at teen violence, the film eventually seems too slick for its own good, and any message Spheeris may have been trying to get across is lost in a cacophony of flashiness and moody glares from the two leads.

Maxwell Caulfield *Roy Alston* • Charlie Sheen *Bo Richards* • Christopher McDonald *Woods* • Hank Garrett *Detective Ed Hanley* • Patti D'Arbanville-Quinn *Angie* ■ *Dir* Penelope Spheeris • *Scr* Glen Morgan, James Wong

The Boys Next Door ★★★

Comedy drama 1996 · US · Colour · 99mins

A high-class made-for-TV drama, which grabbed a bag of award nominations in the US. The feel-good tale focuses on four men – Nathan Lane, Robert Sean Leonard, Courtney B Vance and Michael Jeter – with mental health disorders watched over by a sympathetic social worker (Tony Goldwyn), who is helping them learn to

how fend for themselves. Based on the play by Tom Griffin, it is sensitively acted by the top-notch cast – special plaudits for the Emmy-nominated Mare Winningham. While it occasionally gets too syrupy, only the most cynical will fail to be moved.

Nathan Lane *Norman Bulansky* • Robert Sean Leonard *Barry Klemper* • Tony Goldwyn *Jack Palmer* • Michael Jeter *Arnold Wiggins* • Courtney B Vance *Lucien P Singer* • Mare Winningham *Sheila* ■ *Dir* John Erman • *Scr* William Blinn, from the play by Tom Griffin

Boys' Night Out ★★ 18

Comedy 1962 · US · Colour · 58mins

A bachelor and his three married friends decide to rent an apartment with a dishy blonde inside and use it, and her, for a week each. What they don't know is that the lady of the night is actually a sociology student doing her thesis on the American male, and she is singularly inimpressed with the men's ability to sustain a playboy lifestyle. Following films such as *The Seven Year Itch*, *The Apartment*, *Pillow Talk* and *Bachelor Party*, this may be revealing of early sixties sexual mores but falls absolutely flat as a comedy. Once Oscar Homolka appears as a sociologist spouting theories, it becomes singularly embarrasssing.

Kim Novak *Cathy* • James Garner *Fred Williams* • Tony Randall *George Drayton* • Howard Duff *Doug Jackson* • Janet Blair *Marge Drayton* • Patti Page *Joanne McIllenny* • Jessie Royce Landis *Ethel Williams* • Oscar Homolka *D Prokosch* ■ *Dir* Michael Gordon • *Scr* Ira Wallach, Marion Hargrove (adaptation), from a story by Marvin Worth, Arne Sultan

The Boys of Paul Street ★★★ U

Comedy drama 1968 · US/Hun · Colour · 104mins

Previously filmed in Hollywood by Frank Borzage as *No Greater Glory* in 1934, this Oscar-nominated adaptation by Zoltán Fábri of Ferenc Molnár's autobiographical novel returned to its original Budapest locations. Although intended as an allegory on the futility of war, the feud between two rival gangs over an unclaimed patch of land also has a Party angle, as it's the benevolent forces of authority that eventually claim the lot for building work. This is slightly unusual for a director who prided himself on his critical realism, but the film still has the freshness that typified most Eastern European cinema in the mid-sixties. A Hungarian/English language film.

Anthony Kemp *Nemecsek* • William Burleigh *Boka* • Julien Holdaway *Feriats* • Peter Delmar *Older Pasztor* • Andras Avar *Szabo* • Mari Torocsik *Nemecsek's mother* • Sandor Pecsi *Professor Racz* ■ *Dir* Zoltan Fabri • *Scr* Zoltán Fábri, Endre Bohém, from the novel *A Pal Utcai Fiuk* by Ferenc Molnár

Boys of the City ★★

Crime comedy 1940 · US · BW · 68mins

The first in the series featuring the East Side Kids, after they were the Dead End Kids and before they were the Bowery Boys, was typical of the films of the streetwise gang – whatever they were called. The crude farce (also known as *The Ghost Creeps*) has the lads, headed by Leo Gorcey and Bobby Jordan, sent to the country where they get involved with murder in a haunted house. The ghost footage was added at the last minute in an effort to parody *Rebecca*. The director Joseph H Lewis went on to make *film noir* classics such as 1949's *Gun Crazy*.

Bobby Jordan *Danny* • Leo Gorcey *Muggs* • Dave O'Brien *Knuckles Dolan* • George Humbert *Tony* • Hally Chester *Boy* • ''Sunshine Sammy'' Morrison *Morrison Scruno* ■ *Dir* Joseph H Lewis • *Scr* William Lively, from his story

Boys on the Side ★★★★ 15

Drama   1995 · US/Fr · Colour · 112mins

Starting out as a comfortable *Thelma and Louise* retread before settling down into harder-edged *Fried Green Tomatoes at the Whistle Stop Cafe* territory, director Herbert Ross's emotional rollercoaster ride has three crackerjack central performances oiling its unconventional fugitive tale. Lesbian Whoopi Goldberg, HIV-positive Mary-Louise Parker and pregnant Drew Barrymore head for California, but find themselves grounded in Arizona when Parker falls ill. It's a tender drama that's smart, sassy and really quite special and when Roy Orbison's *You Got It* strikes up, there won't be a dry eye in the house. Contains violence, swearing and nudity.

Whoopi Goldberg *Jane DeLuca* • Mary-Louise Parker *Robin Nickerson* • Drew Barrymore *Holly* • Matthew McConaughey *Abe Lincoln* • James Remar *Alex* • Billy Wirth *Nick* • Anita Gillette *Elaine* • Dennis Boutsikaris *Massarelli* • Estelle Parsons *Louise* • Amy Aquino *Anna* ■ *Dir* Herbert Ross • *Scr* Don Roos

Boys Town ★★★

Biographical drama 1938 · US · BW · 92mins

This incredibly corny and manipulative tear-jerker was just the type of film that reduced MGM boss Louis B Mayer to tears. Spencer Tracy is Father Flanagan, a Nebraskan priest who wants to set up a sanctuary for society's lost causes, and Mickey Rooney is one of the juvenile delinquents he tries to save. When the picture opened, the real Father Flanagan complained about the studio gloss and how that had affected donations since people assumed his refuge was rolling in money. Mayer went on the radio saying, ''Boys Town does need your money, so keep it coming, Americans!'' Tracy won his second consecutive Oscar for this film and dedicated it to Flanagan.

Spencer Tracy *Father Edward Flanagan* • Mickey Rooney *Whitey Marsh* • Henry Hull *Dave Morris* • Leslie Fenton *Dan Farrow* • Addison Richards *Judge* • Edward Norris *Joe Marsh* • Gene Reynolds *Tony Ponessa* • Minor Watson *Bishop* ■ *Dir* Norman Taurog • *Scr* John Meehan, Dore Schary, from a story by Dore Schary, Eleanore Griffin

Boys Will Be Boys ★★★ U

Comedy   1935 · UK · BW · 72mins

Although Will Hay had included the ''Fourth Form at St Michael's'' sketch in his music-hall act since the early twenties, this was the first time he donned the familiar mortar board, gown and pince-nez on the screen. He plays Dr Alec Smart, whose rogue's progress takes him from a prison

classroom to the headmaster's study of that school for crooks, Narkover. The script is based on characters invented by JB Morton for the legendary ''Beachcomber'' newspaper column, and Hay retains the inimitable blend of bluff, bluster and dishonesty that makes his films irresistible. ▭

Will Hay *Dr Alec Smart* • Gordon Harker *Faker Brown* • Claude Dampier *Theo P Finch* • Jimmy Hanley *Cyril Brown* • Davy Burnaby *Colonel Crableigh* • Norma Varden *Lady Korking* • Charles Farrell *Louis Brown* • Percy Walsh *Governor* ■ *Dir* William Beaudine • *Scr* Will Hay, Robert Edmunds, from the characters created by JB Morton

Boyz N the Hood ★★★★ 15

Drama   1991 · US · Colour · 107mins

Alongside Quentin Tarantino's *Reservoir Dogs*, this was the most astonishing and hard-hitting directorial debut of the nineties. John Singleton was a mere 23 when he wrote and directed this powerhouse picture about growing up black in inner-city America. Rougher and readier than Spike Lee on the same subject, Singleton largely avoids sermonising to present a brutally candid view of the realities of LA street life. Cuba Gooding Jr and co-stars Morris Chestnut and Ice Cube impress as the friends for whom the future looks uncertain (if not downright unlikely), while Larry (now Laurence) Fishburne is outstanding as Gooding's disciplinarian father. Credible roles for women are usually at a premium in African-American cinema, but the boys' mothers are beautifully observed and sensitively played by Angela Bassett and Tyra Ferrell. Singleton deservedly received Oscar nominations as both writer and director. Contains violence and swearing.

Larry Fishburne [Laurence Fishburne] *Furious Styles* • Ice Cube *Doughboy Baker* • Cuba Gooding Jr *Tre Styles* • Nia Long *Brandi* • Morris Chestnut *Ricky Baker* • Tyra Ferrell *Mrs Baker* • Angela Bassett *Reva Styles* • Redge Green *Chris* ■ *Dir/Scr* John Singleton

The Brady Bunch Movie ★★★ 12

Comedy   1995 · US · Colour · 84mins

In the nineties, Hollywood studios have desperately ransacked their old TV archives for cinema remakes, with very mixed results. This one is probably the most innovative of the lot, even if it doesn't always work. If anyone can't remember, the Brady bunch were a cute-as-pie American family suffering the mildest of seventies' domestic discord every week. And in this remake, the same applies, except that everyone else is now living in the nineties. A cue, then, for loads of postmodernist laughs, expertly served up by a cast headed by Shelley Long and Gary Cole. Essential viewing for fans of flares and anything else kitsch. Contains some swearing. ▭

Shelley Long *Carol Brady* • Gary Cole *Mike Brady* • Michael McKean *Mr Dittmeyer* • Christine Taylor *Marcia Brady* • Christopher Daniel Barnes *Greg Brady* • Jennifer Elise Cox *Jan Brady* • Paul Sutera *Peter Brady* • Olivia Hack *Cindy Brady* • Jesse Lee *Bobby Brady* • Henriette Mantel *Alice* ■ *Dir* Betty Thomas • *Scr* Laurice Elehwany, Rick Copp, Bonnie Turner, Terry Turner, from characters created by Sherwood Schwartz

The Brain ★★ 12

Science-fiction
1962 · W Ger/UK · BW · 83mins

Hammer Horror veteran Freddie Francis does a decent job directing this version of Curt Siodmak's *Donovan's Brain*. Peter Van Eyck is the scientist controlled by the power-crazed organ of a sadistic tycoon kept alive after a plane crash. More of a mystery than an all-stops-out horror, the moody tale has some eerie moments and is efficiently involving. A competent cast, including producer Raymond Stross's wife Anne Heywood, injects new life into a familiar story. ▭

Anne Heywood *Anna* • Peter Van Eyck *Doctor Peter Corrie* • Cecil Parker *Stevenson* • Bernard Lee *Frank Shears* • Ellen Schwiers *Ella* • Maxine Audley *Marion* • Jeremy Spenser *Martin* • Ann Sears *Secretary* ■ *Dir* Freddie Francis • *Scr* Robert Stewart, Phil Macki, from the novel *Donovan's Brain* by Curt Siodmak

The Brain ★ PG

Comedy caper
1969 · Fr/US/It · Colour · 95mins

Despite sterling work by David Niven as a master criminal, this frenetic French comedy needs a brain transplant in the script department. Put in charge of security for the transportation of NATO's military funds – which he intends to snatch – Niven finds himself competing for the loot with two French rogues (Jean-Paul Belmondo and Bourvil) as well as with the Mafia. Written and directed by Gérard Oury, it has a Keystone Kops pace without the simplicity of those silent comedians. The result is a mess which not even Niven can save. French dialogue dubbed into English. ▭

David Niven *The Brain* • Jean-Paul Belmondo *Arthur* • Bourvil *Anatole* • Eli Wallach *Scannapieco* • Silvia Monti *Sofia* • Fernand Valois *Bruno* • Raymond Gerome *Le Commanissaire* • Jacques Balutin *Pochet* ■ *Dir* Gérard Oury • *Scr* Gérard Oury, Marcel Julian, Daniele Thompson

Brain Damage ★★★★ 18

Horror comedy 1988 · US · Colour · 85mins

An outrageously gory and excessively violent fable infused with the junk culture and trash aesthetic of cult director Frank Henenlotter's demented imagination. *The Muppet Show* meets *The Tingler* in this spaced-out gore joke about Elmer, the all-singing, all-dancing alien parasite, who injects a euphoric hallucinogenic fluid into his host, Rick Herbst, in return for donors it can suck brains from. The more Herbst gets addicted to Elmer's secretion, the more dangerous the risks he's prepared to take to satisfy his vicious pet's bloodlust. Quirky, inventive and completely offensive – some death scenes deliberately use pornographic imagery – this wickedly humorous slice of warped genius couldn't have come from anyone other than the perpetrator of *Basket Case*. ▭

Rick Herbst *Brian* • Gordon MacDonald *Mike* • Jennifer Lowry *Barbara* • Theo Barnes *Morris Ackerman* • Lucille Saint-Peter *Martha Ackerman* • Vicki Darnell *Blonde in Hell Club* • Joe Gonzales *Guy in shower* • Bradlee Rhodes *Night watchman* • Don Henenlotter *Policeman* ■ *Dir/Scr* Frank Henenlotter

Brain Dead ★★★ 15

Psychological horror
1990 · US · Colour · 80mins

Neurologist Bill Pullman is blackmailed by business friend Bill Paxton into studying the case history of paranoid accountant-turned-serial killer Bud Cort in order to unlock the secrets in his mind. After brain surgery and shock therapy, however, Cort switches personalities with Pullman, turning director Adam Simon's enjoyably quirky *Twilight Zone* update into a crazed splatter romp. Dreams within dreams, nightmare flashbacks, terrifying visions and people running around with brains in jars keep the pace lively and interesting even if it is hard to follow exactly what's going on. ▭

Bill Pullman *Rex Martin* • Bill Paxton *Jim Reston* • Bud Cort *Jack Halsey* • Patricia Charboneau *Dana Martin* • Nicholas Pryor *Conklin/Ramsen* • George Kennedy *Vance* • Brian Brophy *Ellis* ■ *Dir* Adam Simon • *Scr* Charles Beaumont, Adam Simon, from a story by Charles Beaumont

Brain Donors ★ PG

Comedy   1992 · US · Colour · 76mins

Modelled on *A Night at the Opera*, but with little of the Marx Brothers's witty invention on display, director Dennis Dugan's flat face has the occasional flash of high-energy outrageousness, but little else to commend it. Shyster lawyer John Turturro and his two wacky assistants, Bob Nelson and Mel Smith, take over rich widow Nancy Marchand's ballet company, with suitably dire consequences. Short but not very sweet, Dugan's laboured burlesque throws every tired and tested gag into the frantic action hoping it hits the fan – sorry, screen.

John Turturro *Roland T Flakfizer* • Bob Nelson *Jacques* • Mel Smith *Rocco Melonchek* • Nancy Marchand *Lillian Oglethorpe* • John Savident *Lazlo* • George De La Pena ''*The Great*'' *Volare* • Spike Alexander *Alan* • Juli Donald *Lisa* • Teri Copley *Blonde* ■ *Dir* Dennis Dugan • *Scr* Pat Proft

The Brain Eaters ★★ PG

Science-fiction adventure
1958 · US · BW · 60mins

An uncredited adaptation of Robert Heinlein's landmark alien invasion novel *The Puppet Masters*, this routine B-movie exemplifies the atomic-era paranoia genre. Despite the laughable, hairy, neck-burrowing parasites and the stock scientist-versus-the-military scenario, director Bruno VeSota creates an imaginatively bleak atmosphere through tilted camera angles and crisp black-and-white photography. Though no great shakes, this sci-fi adventure is only an hour long and *Star Trek* fanatics can see Leonard Nimoy in an early role. ▭

Edwin Nelson *Dr Kettering* • Joanna Lee *Alice* • Jody Fair *Elaine* • Alan Frost *Glenn* • Jack Hill *Senator Powers* • David Hughes *Dr Wyler* • Robert Ball *Dan Walker* • Greigh Phillips *Sheriff* • Orville Sherman *Cameron* • Leonard Nimoy *Protector* ■ *Dir* Bruno VeSota • *Scr* Gordon Urquhart

The Brain from Planet Arous ★★ PG

Science-fiction 1958 · US · BW · 70mins

An all-time camp schlock classic, with bad-movie icon John Agar an absolute hoot as the nuclear physicist possessed by a floating alien brain called Gor, in its first step towards Earth domination. Soon Agar is sporting silver contact lenses and setting model planes on fire with a glance, while his pet dog is taken over by Gor's rival for the final axe battle. Unsurprisingly, director Nathan Hertz changed his name to Nathan Juran for *The 7th Voyage of Sinbad* later the same year. 🎞

John Agar *Steve* • Joyce Meadows *Sally Fallon* • Robert Fuller *Dan* • Thomas Browne Henry *John Fallon* • Henry Travis *Colonel Grogley* • Ken Terrell *Colonel* • Tim Graham *Sheriff Paine* • E Leslie Thomas *General Brown* • Bill Giorgio *Russian* ■ *Dir* Nathan Hertz [Nathan Juran] • *Scr* Ray Buffum

The Brain Machine ★★ U

Crime thriller 1954 · UK · BW · 79mins

This British B-movie begins, promisingly, in sci-fi mode but soon lapses into routine thrillerdom – a typical product of the old Merton Park studios. The machine of the title, known as an "electroencephalograph", is attached to an accident victim who may also be a psychopath. Despite its cheap production values and leaden acting from Patrick Barr, Elizabeth Allan and Maxwell Reed, the picture has a trashy energy that can be enjoyed if you disengage your own brain. Writer/director Ken Hughes went on to bigger things, such as *The Trials of Oscar Wilde* and *Cromwell*.

Patrick Barr *Dr Geoffrey Allen* • Elizabeth Allan *Dr Philippa Roberts* • Maxwell Reed *Frank Smith* • Russell Napier *Inspector Durham* • Gibb McLaughlin *Spencer Simon* • Edwin Richfield *Ryan* • Neil Hallett *Sergeant John Harris* • Vanda Godsell *Mae* • Bill Nagy *Charlie* ■ *Dir/Scr* Ken Hughes

Brain Smasher... a Love Story ★★ PG

Comedy action adventure 1993 · US · Colour · 84mins

In straight-to-video director Albert Pyun's mildly amusing action comedy, bouncer Andrew Dice Clay joins supermodel Teri Hatcher and her botanist sister to stop a sacred mystical lotus flower, which holds the key to unlimited power over matter, from falling into the hands of a suave band of Chinese ninja monks. Although described as Rambo, Superman and the Terminator all rolled into one, wild comedian Clay prefers dropping one-liners to participating in any kick-boxing fight. The romance between Clay and Hatcher looms larger than any of the anticipated "brain smashing" mayhem. 🎞

Andrew Dice Clay *Ed Malloy* • Teri Hatcher *Samantha Crain* • Deborah Van Valkenburgh • Yuji Okamoto • Brion James • Tim Thomerson • Charles Rocket ■ *Dir/Scr* Albert Pyun

The Brain That Wouldn't Die ★★

Horror thriller 1959 · US · BW · 0mins

After decapitating his fiancée Virginia Leith in a car crash, demented surgeon Jason Evers decides to transplant her still living head onto the body of a facially scarred stripper. But Leith wants to die and telepathically manipulates the giant pinhead mutant locked up in Evers's cupboard to go on the rampage. This rock-bottom fantasy exploitation pic reaches high levels of engaging absurdity through poverty-row production values and ludicrous, blood-soaked action. Left on the shelf for three years (Evers had changed his name from Herb to Jason by then), this appalling cheapie has nonetheless become a brainless cult classic.

Jason Evers *Dr Bill Cortner* • Leslie Daniel *Kurt* • Paula Maurice *B-Girl* • Virginia Leith *Jan Compton* • Adele Lamont *Doris* • Bruce Brighton *Doctor* • Lola Mason *Donna Williams* • Audrey Devereau *Jeannie* ■ *Dir* Joseph Green • *Scr* Joseph Green, from a story by Rex Carlton, Joseph Green

Braindead ★★★★★ 18

Horror comedy 1992 · NZ · Colour · 99mins

The ultimate gore movie. Kiwi director Peter Jackson's horrendously funny gross-out shocker is a brilliant black comedy, which piles on dismembered limbs, bloody slaughter and perverse dementia to deliciously tasteless excess. Timothy Balme's mother gets bitten by a Sumatran rat-monkey carrying a living-dead virus and turns into a rabid zombie with terrible table manners. Cue zombie sex, kung fu priests, reanimated spinal columns and half-eaten craniums, all building towards a final, gore-drenched massacre. Using welters of blood instead of custard pies and a rich vein of eccentric humour veering between razor-sharp satire and toilet humour, Jackson's outrageously sick groundbreaker is a virtuoso *Grand Guignol* masterpiece. 🎞

Timothy Balme *Lionel* • Diana Penalver *Paquita* • Liz Moody *Mum* • Ian Watkin *Uncle Les* • Brenda Kendall *Nurse McTavish* • Stuart Devenie *Father McGruder/Zombie McGruder* • Jed Brophy *Void* • Elizabeth Brimilcombe *Zombie mum* • Peter Jackson *Undertaker's assistant* ■ *Dir* Peter Jackson • *Scr* Peter Jackson, Stephen Sinclair, Francis Walsh

Brainscan ★★★ 15

Science-fiction horror 1994 · Can/US/UK · Colour · 90mins

Misfit loner Edward Furlong sends off for the virtual reality game *Brainscan*, advertised as the ultimate in terror, only to wake up with memory loss and a severed foot in the refrigerator. Frank Langella is the cop on his trail. But will he believe the murder is really the work of the Trickster, a vile demon who represents the dark side of anybody playing the game? Despite some inferior special effects, this unusually bleak and intense chiller is one of the best horror films to use the virtual reality hook. 🎞

Edward Furlong *Michael Brower* • Frank Langella *Detective Hayden* • T Rider-Smith *Trickster* • Amy Hargreaves *Kimberly* • Jamie Marsh *Kyle* • Victor Ertmanis *Martin* • David

Hemblen *Dr Fromberg* • Vlasta Vrana *Frank* ■ *Dir* John Flynn • *Scr* Andrew Kevin Walker, from a story by Brian Owens

Brainstorm ★★★★ 15

Science-fiction thriller 1983 · US · Colour · 101mins

In more recent films such as *The Lawnmower Man* and *Strange Days*, it's called virtual reality. But when *2001: a Space Odyssey* special effects genius Douglas Trumbull directed this film (which turned out to be Natalie Wood's last), he termed it "telepathic engineering". Louise Fletcher (giving a stand-out performance) and Christopher Walken invent a headset enabling the wearer to experience the sensory recordings of others. Then Fletcher has a coronary and leaves behind a recording of her death experience, which the military seizes for its own misuse. Although flawed and naive, Trumbull's metaphysical odyssey is a technically dazzling triumph packing the same pseudo-religious punch as *Close Encounters of the Third Kind*. 🎞

Christopher Walken *Michael Brace* • Natalie Wood *Karen Brace* • Cliff Robertson *Alex Terson* • Louise Fletcher *Lillian Reynolds* • Donald Hotton *Landon Marks* • Joe Dorsey *Hal Abramson* • Darrell Larson *Security technician* ■ *Dir* Douglas Trumbull • *Scr* Robert Statzel, Phillip Frank Messina, from a story by Bruce Joel Rubin

Brainwaves ★★ 18

Science-fiction thriller 1982 · US · Colour · 76mins

This suffers from a combination of a low budget and some clumsy writing and direction. Suzanna Love plays a woman who regains consciousness after a coma only to discover that, thanks to some ground-breaking surgery, she has inherited the brainwaves of a murdered woman. There are some nifty moments but the main point of interest is the eclectic casting – as well as Vera Miles and Keir Dullea (*2001: a Space Odyssey*), there is Tony Curtis in a ripe cameo as an improbable brain surgeon. 🎞

Keir Dullea *Julian Bedford* • Suzanna Love *Kaylie Bedford* • Vera Miles *Marian* • Percy Rodrigues *Dr Robinson* • Tony Curtis *Dr Clavius* • Paul Wilson [Paul Willson] *Dr Schroder* • Ryan Seitz *Danny Bedford* • Nicholas Love *Willy Meiser* ■ *Dir* Ulli Lommel • *Scr* Ulli Lommel, Suzanna Love

Bram Stoker's Burial of the Rats ★

Horror 1995 · US · Colour · 79mins

A cult of Rat Women, led by queen Adrienne Barbeau, kidnap the young Bram Stoker (Kevin Alber) and force him to write about their exploits. A borderline ludicrous cable movie from cult producer Roger Corman, this throws everything into the horror melting-pot and hopes for the best. Aside from the wholesale slaughter climax and the appearance of scream queens Linnea Quigley and Nikki Fritz as Rat Women, there's very little to recommend in this slight shocker.

Adrienne Barbeau *The Queen* • Maria Ford *Madeleine* • Kevin Alber *Bram Stoker* • Olga Kabo *Anna* • Eduard Plaxin *Mr Stoker* • Vladimir Kuleshov *Constable* • Leonid Timtsunik *Verlaine* • Linnea Quigley *Rat*

woman • Nikki Fritz *Rat woman* ■ *Dir* Dan Golden • *Scr* SP Somtow, Adrien Hein, Tara McCann, from a story by Bram Stoker

Bram Stoker's Dracula ★★★★ 18

Horror 1992 · US · Colour · 121mins

Eerie, romantic and operatic, Francis Ford Coppola's exquisitely mounted revamp of the undead legend is a supreme artistic achievement. Taking a grandiose visual approach and using every cinematic trick – from the basic atmospheric lighting of the silent era to today's more sophisticated techniques – Coppola accentuates the poetic sensuality of Stoker's chiller rather than the more exploitative blood-sucking elements, to mine a new vein of high horror adventure. Keanu Reeves's acting talents may not be to everyone's taste, but, as the tired count who has overdosed on immortality, Gary Oldman's towering performance holds centre stage and burns itself into the memory. 🎞

Gary Oldman *Dracula* • Winona Ryder *Mina Murray/Elisabeta* • Anthony Hopkins *Professor Abraham Van Helsing* • Keanu Reeves *Jonathan Harker* • Richard E Grant *Doctor Jack Seward* • Cary Elwes *Lord Arthur Holmwood* • Bill Campbell *Quincey P Morris* • Sadie Frost *Lucy Westenra* • Tom Waits *RM Renfield* • *Dir* Francis Ford Coppola • *Scr* James V Hart, from the novel by Bram Stoker • *Cinematographer* Michael Ballhaus

Bram Stoker's Legend of the Mummy ★★ 18

Horror 1998 · US · Colour · 96mins

A familiar cocktail of ancient curses and dusty bandages from B-movie veteran Jeffrey Obrow. When her father incurs the wrath of the reanimated Queen Tera, Margaret (Amy Locane) enlists the aid of retired tomb raider Louis Gossett Jr to return the Egyptian ruler to eternal rest. Much more a Hammer homage to *Blood from the Mummy's Tomb* than an adaptation of Bram Stoker's *Jewel of the Seven Stars* tale, this blunt-edged chiller features the least believable mummy make-up in horror history. Contains swearing and nudity. 🎞 **DVD**

Louis Gossett Jr *Corbeck* • Amy Locane *Margaret Trelawny* • Eric Lutes *Robert Wyatt* • Mark Lindsay Chapman *Daw* • Lloyd Bochner *Abel Trelawny* • Mary Jo Catlett *Mrs Grant* • Aubrey Morris *Dr Winchester* • Laura Otis *Lily* ■ *Dir* Jeffrey Obrow • *Scr* Jeffrey Obrow, Lars Hauglie, John Penney, from the novel *The Jewel of the Seven Stars* by Bram Stoker

Bram Stoker's Shadowbuilder ★ 18

Horror 1997 · US/Can · Colour · 96mins

A demon tries to open the gates of hell by sacrificing an innocent child during a solar eclipse. A renegade, chain-smoking priest must stop the ancient prophecy coming true in a silly, sexed-up shocker that has more to do with Jackie Collins than Bram Stoker. Despite solid acting and a respectable pace, this death, darkness and blasphemy-fuelled wash-out wants to be another *Omen*. Instead, with its topless demons pole-dancing in cemeteries, it ends up more like *Showgirls*. Contains some swearing, violence and nudity. 🎞 **DVD**

Kevin Zegers *Chris Hatcher* • Tony Todd *Evert Covey* • Michael Rooker *Father Vassey* ■ *Dir* Jamie Dixon • *Scr* Michael Stokes, from the short story by Bram Stoker

The Bramble Bush ★★

Drama 1960 · US · Colour · 93mins

Richard Burton is ill at ease here as a New England doctor who returns to his Cape Cod home town and falls in love with his dying friend's wife. Adapted from a bestseller by Charles Mergendahl, it's a soap opera lacking in strong characters and situations, though corruption and adultery figure as prominently as ever. Barbara Rush and the great Jack Carson are suitably angst-ridden for the material, but Burton looks all at sea.

Richard Burton *Guy Montford* • Barbara Rush *Mar McFie* • Jack Carson *Bert Mosley* • Angie Dickinson *Fran* • James Dunn *Stew Schaeffer* • Henry Jones *Parker Welk* • Tom Drake *Larry McFie* • Frank Conroy *Dr Kelsey* • Carl Benton Reid *Sam McFie* ■ *Dir* Daniel Petrie • *Scr* Milton Sperling, Philip Yordan, from the novel by Charles Mergendahl

Branches of the Tree ★★

Drama 1990 · Fr/Ind · Colour · 120mins

Satyajit Ray's penultimate film as a director is anything but the work of a master. He may well have written the script 25 years earlier, but there's no doubt that his own heart problems had a bearing on the action. Mostly set in a single room, the film explores the relationship between a wealthy man who has a heart attack and his four sons, one of whom is mentally disturbed. As the declamatory speeches become longer and more turgid, each brother rejects his upbringing and the values of a bygone era. The overwrought acting is certainly off-putting, but it's Ray's theatrical staging that is so dismaying. In Hindi with English subtitles.

Ajit Bannerjee *Ananda Majumdar* • Haradhan Bannerjee *Probodh* • Soumitra Chatterjee *Prashanto* • Dipankar De • Ranjit Mullick • Lily Chakravarty • Mamata Shankar ■ *Dir/Scr* Satyajit Ray • *Co-Producer* Gérard Depardieu

Branded ★★★

Western 1950 · US · Colour · 94mins

More psychological than most westerns – and the better for it – this lavish Paramount picture stars Alan Ladd as the gunman who is persuaded to impersonate the long-lost son of wealthy rancher Charles Bickford. Predictably, Ladd becomes sick of the deception when he comes under the warm and loving embrace of a family that includes Mona Freeman as the beautiful daughter. Putting director Rudolph Maté, previously an outstanding cinematographer, with one of Hollywood's finest practising cameramen, Charles Lang, results in a visually arresting western in glorious Technicolor. Robert Keith has a colourful turn as the real villain of the piece and Ladd shows what an under-rated actor he was.

Alan Ladd *Choya* • Mona Freeman *Ruth Lavery* • Charles Bickford *Mr Lavery* • Robert Keith *Leffingwell* • Joseph Calleia *Rubriz* • Peter Hansen *Tonio* • Selena Royle *Mrs Lavery* • Milburn Stone *Dawson* • Tom Tully *Ransome* •

John Berkes *Tattoo* ■ *Dir* Rudolph Maté • *Scr* Sydney Boehm, Cyril Hume, from the novel by Evan Evans

Branded to Kill ★★★★ 18

Thriller 1967 · Jap · Colour · 87mins

Filming the year after the surreal crime comedy *Tokyo Drifter* and the uncompromising political drama *Elegy to Violence*, director Seijun Suzuki outdid himself with this astonishing blend of yakuza movie, *film noir* and *nouvelle vague*. The picture starts off in classic crime mode, with a ruthless hit man goaded by a *femme fatale* into a confrontation with his deadliest rival. As our hero begins to lose his grip, however, the tone changes completely and we are bombarded with a dizzying array of cinematic tricks. A puzzle that resists an easy solution, the film represented a controversial peak for the director's style and resulted in his being fired by his baffled superiors. In Japanese with English subtitles. Contains violence and nudity. ▭

Jo Shishido *Goro Hanada* • Mariko Ogawa *Mami Hanada* • Koji Nanbara *Number One Killer* • Mari Annu *Nakajo Misako* ■ *Dir* Seijun Suzuki • *Scr* Hachiro Guryu

Brandy for the Parson ★★ U

Comedy 1951 · UK · BW · 78mins

This comedy has a distinctly Ealing feel and a touch of realism about it. Working from the novel by Geoffrey Household, director John Eldridge makes leisurely use of the coastal locations as holidaymakers James Donald and Jean Lodge become entangled with genial smuggler Kenneth More. A few more comic set pieces wouldn't have gone amiss, but this is still an amiable entertainment, with More in particular shining alongside such stalwarts as Alfie Bass and Charles Hawtrey.

Kenneth More *Tony Rackman* • James Donald *Bill Harper* • Jean Lodge *Petronella Brand* • Frederick Piper *Customs Inspector* • Charles Hawtrey *George Crumb* • Michael Trubshawe *Redworth* • Alfie Bass *Dallyn* • Wilfred Caithness *Mr Minch* ■ *Dir* John Eldridge • *Scr* John Dighton, Walter Meade, from the novel by Geoffrey Household

Brannigan ★★★

Crime drama 1975 · UK · Colour · 110mins

John Wayne's in town and Richard Attenborough is the Scotland Yard police officer whose job it is to make sure he plays things by the book. It's essentially a western transported to London, with red double-deckers instead of stagecoaches and hangovers from swinging London. It is also a blatant rip-off of Clint Eastwood's *Coogan's Bluff* and *Dirty Harry*, which Wayne bitterly regretted turning down after seeing the film. Contains some violence and swearing. ▭

John Wayne *Jim Brannigan* • Richard Attenborough *Commander Swann* • Judy Geeson *Jennifer Thatcher* • Mel Ferrer *Mel Fields* • Del Henney *Drexel* • Lesley-Anne Down *Luana* • Barry Dennen *Julian* • John Vernon *Larkin* • Daniel Pilon *Gorman* • John Stride *Traven* ■ *Dir* Douglas Hickox • *Scr* Christopher Trumbo, Michael Butler, William P McGivern, William Norton, from a story by Christopher Trumbo, Michael Butler

Branwen ★★ 15

Political drama 1994 · UK · Colour · 101mins

Unbalanced by its political indignation and undone by its ludicrous plot contrivances, this is one of Welsh cinema's few misfires since it reached maturity in the early nineties. Director Ceri Sherlock never comes close to convincing us that the hostility felt by the Welsh towards the English is on a par with the sentiments harboured by Irish Republicans. But where the film really falls flat is by pitting Branwen and her Northern Irish husband against her adopted soldier brother, who has just been wounded in Bosnia. The performances are committed, but the material is naive. In Welsh, Gaelic and English with subtitles.

Morfudd Hughes *Branwen Roberts* • Richard Lynch *Kevin McCarthy* • Jo Roberts *Llion Roberts* • Robert Gwyn Davies *Mathonwy Roberts* • Allin Elidyr *Peredur Roberts* ■ *Dir* Ceri Sherlock • *Scr* Gareth Miles, Angela Graham, Ceri Sherlock, from a play by Gareth Miles

The Brass Bottle ★★

Comedy 1964 · US · Colour · 89mins

Tony Randall never seems to get a chance to show off his comedic talents, though this witless farce – adapted from F Anstey's perennial bestseller – tries to do so. Randall is a naive architect who opens an antique brass bottle and releases a genie that makes threats and offers to grant wishes. There's good back-up from Burl Ives and Barbara Eden (from the TV series *I Dream of Jeannie*). But the material is too thin to stretch very far and it soon splits disastrously.

Tony Randall *Harold Ventimore* • Burl Ives *Fakrash* • Barbara Eden *Sylvia* • Edward Andrews *Professor Kenton* • Ann Doran *Martha Kenton* • Kamala Devi *Tezra* • Lulu Porter *Belly dancer* • Philip Ober *William Beevor* ■ *Dir* Harry Keller • *Scr* Oscar Brodney, from the novel by F Anstey

The Brass Legend ★★★

Western 1956 · US · BW · 79mins

An impressive B-western with Raymond Burr as the psychotic killer captured by Arizona lawman Hugh O'Brian, who then has to deal with various factions within the town and keep Burr from escaping. Critics at the time admired the showdown between the two antagonists, which was filmed like a medieval joust with the two men facing each other down on charging horses. However, the whole movie has an admirable tension and a neatly dovetailed gallery of characters. Burr was a popular screen heavy, and he contrasts well with the tall, languid presence of O'Brian.

Hugh O'Brian *Sheriff Wade Adams* • Nancy Gates *Linda* • Raymond Burr *Tris Hatten* • Reba Tassell *Millie* • Donald MacDonald *Clay* • Robert Burton *Gipson* • Eddie Firestone *Shorty* • Willard Sage *Tatum* ■ *Dir* Gerd Oswald • *Scr* Don Martin, from a story by George Zuckerman, Jess Arnold

The Brass Monkey ★★

Comedy thriller 1948 · UK · BW · 81mins

This is a bizarre combination of a Saki-esque parable and a vehicle for radio talent scout Carroll Levis. Here he's pitted against an evil connoisseur bent

on obtaining the titular Buddhist artefact. This was the penultimate film (not released until 1951) of tragic Hollywood actress Carole Landis, who committed suicide after breaking up with the married Rex Harrison.

Carole Landis *Kay Sheldon* • Carroll Levis • Herbert Lom *Peter Hobart* • Avril Angers • Ernest Thesiger *Ryder-Harris* • Henry Edwards *Inspector Miller* • Edward Underdown *Max Taylor* ■ *Dir* Thornton Freeland • *Scr* Alec Coppel, Thornton Freeland, C Denis Freeman, from the story by Alec Coppel

Brass Target ★★ 15

Thriller 1978 · US · Colour · 106mins

Thick layers of plot make for a very thin enterprise in a film that lacks any central focus point. It's the kind of picture that is so mesmerised by the detail of its basic idea – what if General Patton was killed just after the war in the course of his investigation into a gold bullion heist? – that it allows class performers to wander in and out of the story, spouting slabs of dialogue rather than developing their roles. Sophia Loren is the prime victim. Contains violence and swearing. ▭

Sophia Loren *Mara* • John Cassavetes *Major Joe De Lucca* • George Kennedy *Gen George S Patton Jr* • Robert Vaughn *Colonel Donald Rogers* • Patrick McGoohan *Colonel Mike McCauley* • Bruce Davison *Colonel Robert Dawson* • Edward Herrmann *Colonel Walter Gilchrist* • Max von Sydow *Shelley/Webber* • Ed Bishop *Colonel Stewart* ■ *Dir* John Hough • *Scr* Alvin Boretz, from the novel *The Algonquin Project* by Frederick Nolan

Brassed Off ★★★★ 15

Drama 1996 · UK/US · Colour · 103mins

It was almost inevitable that comparisons would be made between *Brassed Off* and *The Full Monty*. But whereas *The Full Monty* was an unashamedly feel-good movie, *Brassed Off* is a much less cosy affair, in which the future of an entire community is at stake. There's a certain Ealing-like quality in the way the mining town of Grimley rallies around the colliery's brass band as it progresses to the national finals amid talk of pit closures and redundancies. But there's no coy comedy here. The humour is acerbic and near the knuckle. Also missing is the Capra-esque last act in which the everyday folk triumph over adversity. Instead, there's only the promise of more struggle and the grim realisation that a way of life has gone forever. But the edgy pace writer/director Mark Herman brings to the drama and his presentation of the musical sequences can't be faulted, and he draws remarkable performances from a strong cast. Contains swearing. ▭
DVD

Pete Postlethwaite *Danny* • Tara FitzGerald *Gloria* • Ewan McGregor *Andy* • Stephen Tompkinson *Phil* • Jim Carter *Harry* • Ken Colley [Kenneth Colley] *Greasley* • Peter Gunn *Simmo* • Mary Healey *Ida* • Melanie Hill *Sandra* • Sue Johnston *Vera* ■ *Dir/Scr* Mark Herman

The BRAT Patrol ★★ U

Adventure 1986 · US · Colour · 87mins

Having made his name in *The Goonies* the year before, Sean Astin landed the lead in this resistible family drama from Disney. It's a typical example of

the "I'd have got away with it, if it hadn't been for you meddling kids" school of adventure, with Astin and his pals forced to take on the villains when the top brass refuses to believe that weapons are about to be stolen from an army base. No one in the gang is particularly worth rooting for and even the most undemanding child would ask for a little more from a movie than this. ▣

Sean Astin *Leonard Kinsey* • Timothy Thomerson [Tim Thomerson] *Major Dan Hackett* • Jason Presson *Raymond McGeorge* • Joe Wright *Chuck Newmeyer* • Dustin Berkovitz *Darryl "Squeaker" Malloy* • Dylan Kussman *Danny "Bug" Malloy* • Nia Long *Darla Perkins* • Brian Keith *General Newmeyer* • Stephen Lee *Phillips* • John Quade *Knife* ■ *Dir* Mollie Miller • *Scr* Chris C Carter, Michael Patrick Goodman

The Bravados ★★ PG
Western   1958 · US · Colour · 93mins

A psychological western in which Gregory Peck tracks down a gang he thinks raped and murdered his wife. But after he kills three of them he realises he's been obsessively pursuing the wrong gang. This is intended as a parable about revenge that shows Peck descending into madness and seeking religious salvation at the end. It's a good story, but the treatment needs far more emotional conviction than either Peck or director Henry King give it. Joan Collins stars as Peck's love interest in an underwritten role. ▣

Gregory Peck *Jim Douglas* • Joan Collins *Josefa Velarde* • Stephen Boyd *Bill Zachary* • Albert Salmi *Ed Taylor* • Henry Silva *Lujan* • Kathleen Gallant *Emma* • Barry Coe *Tom* • Lee Van Cleef *Alfonso Parral* ■ *Dir* Henry King • *Scr* Philip Yordan, from the novel by Frank O'Rourke

The Brave ★★
Drama   1997 · US · Colour · 123mins

Johnny Depp's eclectic career has seen collaborations with a host of deeply idiosyncratic directors, from Jim Jarmusch and Tim Burton to Roman Polanski and Emir Kusturica. His own directing debut, however, displays little of their flair. It's a muddled and pretentious affair about a native American (played by Depp) who agrees to star in a real-life snuff film in order to provide for his family. Marlon Brando, who appeared alongside Depp in *Don Juan DeMarco*, co-stars in a movie that premiered at the 1997 Cannes Film Festival and quickly sunk without trace.

Johnny Depp *Raphael* • Marlon Brando *McCarthy* • Marshall Bell *Larry* • Elpidia Carrillo *Rita* • Clarence Williams III *Father Stratton* • Frederic Forrest *Lou Sr* • Max Perlich *Lou Jr* ■ *Dir* Johnny Depp • *Scr* Paul McCudden, Johnny Depp, DP Depp, from the novel by Gregory McDonald

The Brave Bulls ★★
Drama   1951 · US · BW · 112mins

This is a fraught exploration of the psychology of a bullfighter (Mel Ferrer), whose fear before a fight intensifies after his girlfriend dies in a car crash. The girl is played by Czech actress Miroslava, who committed suicide soon after the film's release. Co-star Anthony Quinn, who plays Ferrer's

personal manager, claims the film as one of his personal favourites but blamed its lack of commercial success on the studio, which dumped it when director Robert Rossen was named a communist in the McCarthy hearings. As a result of being made by a "Red", the film never found a large following, but it's pretty average stuff.

Mel Ferrer *Luis Bello* • Miroslava *Linda de Calderon* • Anthony Quinn *Raul Fuentes* • Eugene Iglesias *Pepe Bello* • Jose Torvay *Eladio Gomez* • Charlita *Raquelita* • Jose Luis Vasquez *Yank Delgado* • Alfonso Alvirez *Loco Ruiz* ■ *Dir* Robert Rossen • *Scr* John Bright, from a novel by Tom Lea

The Brave Don't Cry ★★
Disaster drama   1952 · UK · BW · 89mins

Having pioneered the cause of screen realism in the thirties, one-time documentarist John Grierson and socially conscious director John Baxter joined forces to produce this deliberately downbeat reconstruction of a true-life Scottish mining disaster. Philip Leacock, Grierson's former assistant, admirably captures the stoicism of the hundred or so men trapped in a suffocating chamber following a landslide. However, he is less successful in eliciting credible performances from the non-professionals who make up the worried villagers, as prodigal miner John Gregson leads an audacious rescue. Despite the use of actual locations, this is markedly less affecting than GW Pabst's studio-realist classic *Kameradschaft*.

John Gregson *John Cameron* • Meg Buchanan *Margaret Wishart* • John Rae *Donald Sloan* • Fulton Mackay *Dan Wishart* • Andrew Keir *Charlie Ross* • Wendy Noel *Jean Knox* • Russell Walters *Hughie Aitken* • Jameson Clark *Dr Andrew Keir* ■ *Dir* Philip Leacock • *Scr* Montagu Slater

The Brave Little Toaster ★★★★ U
Animated adventure   1987 · US · Colour · 90mins

This is probably the best animated feature Disney never made. So it's hardly surprising that so many ex-Disney personnel were involved in crafting this unofficial remake of Disney favourite *The Incredible Journey*, which substitutes household appliances for the animals in the classic Disney cartoon house style. The final irony is that Disney snapped it up for release on its video label in America. The songs are a bit of a letdown, but otherwise the sharp humour and heart-warming sentiments make it marvellous fun for all the family. ▣

Jon Lovitz *Radio* • Tim Stack [Timothy Stack] *Lampy* • Timothy E Day *Blanky* • Thurl Ravenscroft *Kirby* • Deanna Oliver *Toaster* • Phil Hartman *Air conditioner/hanging lamp* • Joe Ranft *Elmo St Peters* ■ *Dir* Jerry Rees • *Scr* Jerry Rees, Joe Ranft, from a story by Jerry Rees, Joe Ranft, Brian McEntee, from the novella by Thomas M Disch

The Brave One ★★★ U
Drama   1956 · US · Colour · 94mins

Owing to the anti-communist blacklist that operated in Hollywood throughout the fifties, Dalton Trumbo had to wait

until 1975 to collect the best story Oscar he won (under the pseudonym of Robert Rich) for this charming tale of childlike innocence and loyalty. Transposing events that occurred in Barcelona in the mid-thirties to Mexico allows the screenplay to concentrate on the peasant sensibility of Michel Ray, the farm boy who doggedly follows his pet bull all the way to the Plaza de Mexico. Director Irving Rapper may not stage the arena action with the panache of Budd Boetticher, but the melodrama is touchingly handled.

Michel Ray *Leonardo* • Rodolfo Hoyos *Rafael Rosillo* • Elsa Cardenas *Maria* • Carlos Navarro *Don Alejandro* • Joi Lansing *Marion Randall* • George Trevino *Salvador* • Carlos Fernandez *Manuel* ■ *Dir* Irving Rapper • *Scr* Harry Franklin, Merrill G White, from a story by Robert Rich [Dalton Trumbo]

Braveheart ★★★★ 15
Historical drama   1995 · US · Colour · 179mins

Mel Gibson's 13th-century saga of Scottish revolt against English tyranny was not only an international box-office hit, it also caught the nationalistic mood of the moment. Scotland for the Scots is the theme of this epic, which Gibson himself directed with a claymore-like flourish, defying the criticism that there are moments as bogus as plastic haggis. Gibson's rebel leader and rabble-rouser William Wallace is an intrepid champion from the mould of Hollywood heroics, made credible by the grace of the star. However, Patrick McGoohan, as the villainous King Edward "Longshanks", is a jeering, sneering cliché too far. As director, Gibson's control over thousands of extras, in the swift succession of gruesome hand-to-hand battles, is effective. But when the action moves in for the emotional kill, it loses credibility. Nonetheless, it succeeds in bringing to life the reality of Scottish patriotism and brilliantly captures the spirit of a revolution. Little wonder it won an Oscar for best picture. Contains violence, swearing and some nudity. ▣

Mel Gibson *William Wallace* • Sophie Marceau *Princess Isabelle* • Patrick McGoohan *Longshanks King Edward I* • Catherine McCormack *Murron* • Brendan Gleeson *Hamish* • James Cosmo *Campell* • David O'Hara *Stephen* • Angus MacFadyen *Robert the Bruce* • Ian Bannen *Leper* • Peter Hanly *Prince Edward* ■ *Dir* Mel Gibson • *Scr* Randall Wallace

Brazil ★★★ U
Musical comedy   1944 · US · BW · 91mins

A Brazilian composer (Tito Guizar) takes exception to an uncomplimentary book called *Why Marry a Latin?* and sets out to put the record straight with its attractive American author (Virginia Bruce). A big-budget musical from a little studio (Republic), Joseph Santley's film doesn't set the world on fire, but it is pleasing and lively. The songs include the pulsating title number and *Hands across the Border*, warbled in a guest appearance by the studio's famous resident cowboy, Roy Rogers. Speciality dancer Aurora Miranda (Carmen's sister) and Edward Everett Horton are in it, too.

Virginia Bruce *Nicky Henderson* • Tito Guizar *Miguel "Mike" Soares* • Edward Everett

Horton *Everett St John Everett* • Robert Livingston *Rod Walker* • Richard Lane *Edward Graham* • Roy Rogers • Aurora Miranda *Speciality dancer* ■ *Dir* Joseph Santley • *Scr* Frank Gill Jr, Laura Kerr, from a story by Richard English

Brazil ★★★★★ 15
Science-fiction fantasy   1985 · US/UK · Colour · 137mins

It's 1984 with knobs on in Terry Gilliam's extraordinary vision of a futuristic bureaucratic hell. Jonathan Pryce is the Orwellian hero, a permanently harrassed clerk at the all-seeing Department of Information Retrieval who is only kept sane by his vivid daydreams, which see him as a heroic flying warrior coming to the aid of a beautiful woman (Kim Griest). Dazzling, daring and even depressing, Gilliam gives this the sort of unpredictable off-the-wall creativity he brought to his Monty Python animations, but it's multiplied by a thousand in a weird world where Robert De Niro is an SAS-style repairman. The movie's sledgehammer conclusion gave studio executives sleepless nights. Expect the same. ▣

Jonathan Pryce *Sam Lowry* • Robert De Niro *Archibald "Harry" Tuttle* • Katherine Helmond *Mrs Ida Lowry* • Ian Holm *Mr Kurtzmann* • Bob Hoskins *Spoor* • Michael Palin *Jack Lint* • Ian Richardson *Mr Warrenn* • Peter Vaughan *Mr Eugene Helpmann* • Kim Greist *Jill Layton* • Jim Broadbent *Dr Jaffe* ■ *Dir* Terry Gilliam • *Scr* Terry Gilliam, Tom Stoppard

Breach of Conduct ★★ 15
Thriller   1994 · US · Colour · 89mins

As Georgia in *Ally McBeal*, all Courtney Thorne-Smith had to worry about was whether her husband was still in love with his old flame. But in this nightmarish TV movie, she's forced to follow the orders of her officer husband's lustful commander, Peter Coyote. Also known as *Tour of Duty*, this hugely derivative melodrama is directed by actor Tim Matheson, who wastes an interesting idea by littering the action with outbursts of violence that leave a nasty taste. ▣

Peter Coyote *Colonel Andrew Chase* • Courtney Thorne-Smith *Helen Lutz* • Tom Verica *Lieutenant Ted Lutz* • Keith Amos *Corporal Reed* • Beth Toussaint *Paula White* • Tom McFadden *Deputy sheriff* ■ *Dir* Tim Matheson • *Scr* Scott Abbott

Breach of Faith: Family of Cops II ★★
Crime drama   1996 · US/Can · Colour

The word "craggy" might have been invented to describe Charles Bronson in this so-so TV crime drama. The tough guy shuffles once more into action as head of the Fein clan, juggling policework and domestic disputes with the minimum of facial expression. Sebastian Spence and Barbara Williams reprise roles from the first movie, and Diane Ladd makes a welcome appearance as a Fein family aunt, but it does make one yearn for Bronson in *Death Wish*-vigilante mode. Contains violence.

Charles Bronson *Paul Fein* • Angela Featherstone *Jackie Fein* • Barbara Williams *Kate Fein* • Sebastian Spence *Eddie Fein* • Diane Ladd *Aunt Shelly (Fein)* ■ *Dir* David Green • *Scr* Joel Blasberg

Bread, Love and Dreams ★★★

Comedy 1953 · It · BW · 97mins

Dated now, this is a typically frothy Italian comedy of the postwar years, set in a mountain village and dominated by the presence of Gina Lollobrigida. "La Lollo" plays the wild beauty lustily in love with a young policeman. She also catches the eye of Vittorio De Sica, playing the newly arrived police chief, who locks her up in his jail. Village elders and the priest frown at the sexual intrigue. A huge hit in Italy and released widely abroad, it led to a quickie sequel, *Bread, Love and Jealousy*, which reunited the cast and director. An Italian language film.

Vittorio De Sica *The marshal* • Gina Lollobrigida *The girl/"Frisky"* • Marisa Merlini *The midwife/"Annarella"* • Roberto Risso *The carabiniere/"Stelluti"* • Virgilio Riento *Priest "/Dom Emidio"* • Maria Pia Casilio *Priest's niece/"Paoletta"* • Memmo Carotenuto *Another carabiniere* • Tina Pica *Housekeeper/"Caramel"* ■ *Dir* Luigi Comencini • *Scr* Ettore Margadonna, Luigi Comencini, from a story by Ettore Margadonna

The Break ★★12

Mystery thriller 1962 · UK · BW · 100mins

Films such as *Tomorrow at Ten* proved that Lance Comfort could make tense B-thrillers to compete with the best. Unfortunately, his touch completely deserted him while shooting this plodding whodunit, in which a detective, a novelist, a fleeing crook and his sister stumble upon dark deeds on a Devon farm. Tony Britton does his best in the lead, while Sonia Dresdel, Robert Urquhart and Eddie Byrne provide the familiar faces in the supporting cast. But the mystery isn't likely to put too much strain on your little grey cells. 🖵

Tony Britton *Greg Parker* • William Lucas *Jacko Thomas* • Eddie Byrne *Judd Tredegar* • Robert Urquhart *Pearson* • Sonia Dresdel *Sarah* • Edwin Richfield *Moses* • Gene Anderson *Jean Tredegar* ■ *Dir* Lance Comfort • *Scr* Pip Baker, Jane Baker

Break in the Circle ★★🅄

Adventure drama 1955 · UK · BW · 90mins

An adventurer (Forrest Tucker) is hired by a wealthy foreign baron (Marius Goring) to smuggle a Polish scientist out of East Germany. However, he is nabbed in Hamburg by the gang who are holding the boffin captive. The glamorous Eva Bartok comes to his rescue, but things are not what they seem. Written and directed by Val Guest, this is an efficient and energetic British thriller, not without the odd moment of humour, but it's of only passing interest now.

Forrest Tucker *Skip Morgan* • Eva Bartok *Lisa* • Marius Goring *Baron Keller* • Eric Pohlmann *Emile* • Guy Middleton *Hobart* • Arnold Marle *Kudnic* • Fred Johnson *Farquarson* • Reginald Beckwith *Dusty* ■ *Dir* Val Guest • *Scr* Val Guest, from the novel by Philip Lorraine

Break of Dawn ★★★★

Biographical drama 1988 · US · Colour

A strong, affecting TV biopic that tells the story of a courageous, unsung Los Angeles folk hero. Pedro J Gonzalez, played by Mexican actor/singer Oscar

Chavez, was the city's first Hispanic radio host who, instead of opting to play a few mariachi songs and recommending taco outlets, tried to rouse his compatriots into nonviolent political action. Through the use of an intelligent script, a merciful lack of clichés and Chavez's fine performance, we come to understand the man and the hornet's nest he stirred up. In English and Spanish with subtitles.

Oscar Chavez *Pedro J Gonzalez* • Maria Rojo *Maria Gonzalez* • Tony Plana *Gene Rodriguez* • Pepe Serna *Hector Gonzalez* • Peter Henry Schroeder *Kyle Mitchell* • Socorro Valdez *Matilde Gonzalez* • Kamala Lopez *Linda Galvan* ■ *Dir/Scr* Isaac Artenstein

Break of Day ★★

Romantic drama 1977 · Ausl · Colour · 112mins

This Australian drama, set in the aftermath of the First World War's Gallipoli landings, can't make up its mind whether it's a romance or a rite-of-passage story – or both. Andrew McFarlane plays a shell-shocked soldier who is trying to pick up where he left off before the war. He is the editor of a small-town paper, but finds it difficult to settle down again. In walks painter Sara Kestleman, with whom he falls in love. When she leaves, he has to come to terms with his past, present and future.

Sara Kestelman *Alice* • Andrew McFarlane *Tom* • Ingrid Mason *Beth* • Tony Barry *Joe* • Eileen Chapman *Susan* • Malcolm Phillips *Robbie* • Ben Gabriel *Mr Evans* ■ *Dir* Ken Hannam • *Scr* Cliff Green

Break of Hearts ★★★🅄

Romantic drama 1935 · US · BW · 77mins

This is one of a string of RKO features that lead to cinema exhibitors listing Katharine Hepburn as box-office poison. She plays a struggling young composer in Greenwich Village who falls for a famous international conductor, played by French heart-throb Charles Boyer. They both suffer unmercifully and he becomes a lush. Of course, she nurses him. Taken in the right spirit, on a wet matinée afternoon, this tosh has pleasure to offer, but the story is so familiar that there are no real surprises in store. However, though it may not have been apparent at the time, Hepburn is positively stunning, and there's real on-screen chemistry between her and Boyer. Watch it for star power alone.

Katharine Hepburn *Constance Roberti* • Charles Boyer *Fritz Roberti* • John Beal *Johnny* • Jean Hersholt *Talma* • Sam Hardy *Marx* • Inez Courtney *Miss Wilson* • Helene Millard *Sylvia* ■ *Dir* Phillip Moeller • *Scr* Sarah Y Mason, Anthony Veiller, Victor Heerman, from a story by Lester Cohen

Breakdance ★★🅿🅶

Musical drama 1984 · US · Colour · 82mins

Adolfo "Shabba-Doo" Quinones and Michael "Boogaloo Shrimp" Chambers teach white waitress Lucinda Dickey their moves so that she can win a dance contest in a film that was rush-released to cash in on the short-lived breakdance craze. Great street choreography comes a poor second to the yawn-inducing, youth-versus-establishment plot with *Flashdance*

trappings. Still, this dance culture is where hip-hop and rap found their acceptable public face, so file it under "World Music History Lesson". 🖵

Lucinda Dickey *Kelly* • Adolfo "Shabba-Doo" Quinones *Ozone* • Michael "Boogaloo Shrimp" Chambers *Turbo* • Phineas Newborn III *Adam* • Christopher McDonald *James* ■ *Dir* Joel Silberg • *Scr* Allen DeBevoise, from a story by Allen DeBevoise, Charles Parker

Breakdance 2 – Electric Boogaloo ★★🅿🅶

Musical drama 1984 · US · Colour · 89mins

The super-quick sequel to *Breakdance* finds the same lead characters using their dance talents once more to save their rundown community centre. Just as Judy Garland and Mickey Rooney did in the thirties, Adolfo "Shabba-Doo" Quinones and Michael "Boogaloo Shrimp" Chambers put on a show to raise cash and halt the urban developers who want to turn the centre into a shopping mall. A standard-issue follow-up with stereotypical humour undercutting its happy-go-lucky breeziness. 🖵

Lucinda Dickey *Kelly* • Adolfo "Shabba-Doo" Quinones *Ozone* • Michael "Boogaloo Shrimp" Chambers *Turbo* • Susie Bono *Rhonda* • Harry Caesar *Byron* • Jo De Winter *Mrs Bennett* • John Christy Ewing *Mr Bennett* ■ *Dir* Sam Firstenberg • *Scr* Jan Ventura, Julie Reichert, from the characters created by Charles Parker, Allen DeBevoise

Breakdown ★★★★15

Thriller 1997 · US · Colour · 89mins

A gripping thriller starring Kurt Russell and Kathleen Quinlan as a city couple moving west, whose car breaks down in the middle of nowhere. Trucker J T Walsh gives Quinlan a lift to the nearest phone, but when she subsequently vanishes he denies ever seeing her. This is enjoyably old-fashioned (it's reminiscent of Steven Spielberg's *Duel*), with Russell giving his most engaging performance since *Escape from New York* and director Jonathan Mostow twisting the knife with a certain taut flair. The explanation for Quinlan's disappearance isn't as clever as you might think, but you'll be too busy chewing your cuticles to really care. Contains coarse language and violence. 🖵

Kurt Russell *Jeff Taylor* • JT Walsh *Red Barr* • Kathleen Quinlan *Amy Taylor* • MC Gainey *Earl* • Jack Noseworthy *Billy* • Rex Linn *Sheriff Boyd* • Ritch Brinkley *Al* • Moira Harris *Arleen* ■ *Dir* Jonathan Mostow • *Scr* Sam Montgomery, Jonathan Mostow, from a story by Jonathan Mostow

Breaker Morant ★★★★🅿🅶

War drama based on a true story 1979 · Ausl · Colour · 102mins

Director Bruce Beresford has never quite matched the impact he made here with this true story of three soldiers (led by Edward Woodward) fighting the Boers, who are court-martialled by the British in need of scapegoats for war crimes. What Beresford sometimes lacks in subtlety, he makes up for in an impassioned sense of injustice and he draws powerful performances from

Woodward, reluctant counsel Jack Thompson and Bryan Brown. 🖵

Edward Woodward *Lt Harry Harbord "Breaker" Morant* • Jack Thompson *Major JF Thomas* • John Waters *Captain Alfred Taylor* • Bryan Brown *Lt Peter Handcock* • Charles Tingwell *Lt Col Denny* • Terence Donovan *Captain Simon Hunt* • Vincent Ball *Colonel Ian "Johnny" Hamilton* • Chris Haywood *Corporal Sharp* ■ *Dir* Bruce Beresford • *Scr* Jonathan Hardy, David Stevens, Bruce Beresford, from the play by Kenneth Ross and the book *The Breaker* by Kit Denton

Breakfast at Tiffany's ★★★★★🅿🅶

Romantic drama 1961 · US · Colour · 109mins

Audrey Hepburn's Holly Golightly has passed, happily, into cinematic folklore. Director Blake Edwards's hymn to New York high style and high living, with its charming heroineand those wonderful Johnny Mercer *Moon River* lyrics, has hardly dated in the four decades since its release. Originally a creation of writer Truman Capote, Holly, as written for the screen by George Axelrod and portrayed by Hepburn, is quite enchanting, even though period censorship makes it rather unclear what she actually does for a living. Despite the presence of handsome George Peppard and Patricia Neal, this is Hepburn's movie, her black dress and long cigarette holder ready to start a fashion revolution. Only Mickey Rooney's phoney caricature of a Japanese gent seems out of kilter in what is otherwise a thoroughly entertaining and wonderfully escapist movie. 🖵

Audrey Hepburn *Holly Golightly* • George Peppard *Paul Varjak* • Patricia Neal *"2-E"* • Buddy Ebsen *Doc Golightly* • Martin Balsam *OJ Berman* • Mickey Rooney *Mr Yunioshi* • Vilallonga *Jose* • Dorothy Whitney *Mag Wildwood* • John McGiver *Tiffany's clerk* ■ *Dir* Blake Edwards • *Scr* George Axelrod, from the novella by Truman Capote • *Cinematographer* Franz Planer • *Music* Henry Mancini

The Breakfast Club ★★★★15

Drama 1985 · US · Colour · 92mins

One of the high-water marks of the eighties teenpic, John Hughes's Saturday detention comedy has lost some of its freshness in the face of time and endless inferior imitations. Yet this chat-fest still rings true often enough to be relevant to both overgrown teenagers and the disgruntled kids of today. Brat Packers Emilio Estevez, Judd Nelson and Ally Sheedy are joined by teen favourite of the time, Molly Ringwald, and the underestimated Anthony Michael Hall in this mix of justified grievances, self-pitying whinges and hard-hitting home truths. The girls easily outshine the boys, but everyone manages to breathe a little life into their essentially clichéd characters. Contains swearing and drug abuse. 🖵

Emilio Estevez *Andrew Clark* • Molly Ringwald *Claire Standish* • Paul Gleason *Richard Vernon* • Anthony Michael Hall *Brian Johnson* • John Kapelos *Carl* • Judd Nelson *John Bender* • Ally Sheedy *Allison Reynolds* • Perry Crawford *Allison's father* • John Hughes *Brian's father* ■ *Dir/Scr* John Hughes

🅄 = SUITABLE FOR ALL   🅄ᴱ = SUITABLE FOR ALL, ESPECIALLY FOR YOUNG CHILDREN (VIDEO ONLY)   🅿🅶 = PARENTAL GUIDANCE

Breakfast for Two ★★★ U

Comedy   1937 · US · BW · 67mins

A little known screwball comedy that gives Barbara Stanwyck and Herbert Marshall plenty of opportunities to strike sparks off each other. She's a Texan heiress and he's a playboy, who prefers the bottle to facing up to his responsibilities as heir to a shipping line. Stanwyck buys the company as part of her plan to reform and marry him. Running at barely over an hour, the picture has bags of energy and decent support from the likes of Eric Blore, Donald Meek and Glenda Farrell.

Barbara Stanwyck *Valentine Ransome* • Herbert Marshall *Jonathan Blair* • Glenda Farrell *Carol Wallace* • Eric Blore *Butch* • Etienne Girardot *Meggs* • Donald Meek *Justice of the peace* • **Dir** Alfred Santell • **Scr** Charles Kaufman, Paul Yawitz, Viola Brothers Shore

Breakfast of Champions ★ 15

Black comedy   1999 · US · Colour · 109mins

As the richest man in a small town, Bruce Willis is having an existential crisis in this tedious adaptation of the Kurt Vonnegut Jr novel. He spends most of the movie contemplating ending it all and, after enduring two hours of this mess, you might too. An able cast – including Nick Nolte, Albert Finney and Barbara Hershey – supports Willis, but they are hindered by an incoherent script and schizophrenic direction by Alan Rudolph. Nolte in a dress is not a pretty sight.

Bruce Willis *Dwayne Hoover* • Albert Finney *Kilgore Trout* • Barbara Hershey *Celia Hoover* • Nick Nolte *Harry Le Sabre* • Glenne Headly *Francine Pefko* • Lukas Haas *Bunny Hoover* • Omar Epps *Wayne Hoobler* • Buck Henry *Fred T Barry* • **Dir** Alan Rudolph • **Scr** Alan Rudolph, from the novel by Kurt Vonnegut Jr

Breakheart Pass ★★ PG

Western murder mystery
1976 · US · Colour · 91mins

This inconsequential Alistair MacLean caper has Charles Bronson on the trail of gun-runners and running into a murder mystery. And, if that wasn't enough, the plot is thickened by an outbreak of diphtheria. There are more red herrings than a chef could wave a skillet at, for this is really Agatha Christie in western garb, replete with a wonderful old steam train that steals every scene in which it appears. A pity that it stars Bronson, not Burt Reynolds – this pretty daft enterprise should have sent itself up. Ben Johnson, Jill Ireland and Richard Crenna coast through it. ▭

Charles Bronson *John Deakin* • Ben Johnson *Nathan Pearce* • Richard Crenna *Richard Fairchild* • Jill Ireland *Marcia Scoville* • Charles Durning *Frank O'Brien* • Ed Lauter *Major Claremont* • David Huddleston *Dr Molyneux* • Roy Jenson *Banlon* • **Dir** Tom Gries • **Scr** Alistair MacLean, from his novel

Breaking Away ★★★★ PG

Comedy drama   1979 · US · Colour · 96mins

Director Peter Yates's delightfully unpredictable comedy uses a local bicycle race to uncover the sexual, class and economic tensions within an all-American community. The Oscar-winning script by Steve Tesich has a wry wit and great sensitivity. The performances are marvellous, especially from Dennis Quaid and, more particularly, Dennis Christopher, who plays a character so enamoured of the Italian cycling team that he speaks with an Italian accent, bursts into Verdi arias and re-names his cat Fellini. Costing a mere $2.4 million to make, it was destined to be dumped by the studio, but became a huge box-office success, initiating the scores of brat-pack, rite-of-passage pictures of the eighties. Contains swearing. ▭

Dennis Christopher *Dave Stohler* • Dennis Quaid *Mike* • Daniel Stern *Cyril* • Jackie Earle Haley *Moocher* • Barbara Barrie *Mrs Stohler* • Paul Dooley *Mr Stohler* • Robyn Douglass *Katherine* • Hart Bochner *Rod* • Amy Wright *Nancy* • **Dir** Peter Yates • **Scr** Steve Tesich

Breaking Glass ★★ 15

Musical drama   1980 · UK · Colour · 99mins

Singer Hazel O'Connor claws her way into the charts, with help from spiv promoter Phil Daniels, only to find the glitter tarnished and the pressures of fame unbearable. Efficiently directed by Brian Gibson, this hopelessly dated musical is completely formulaic, yet intriguing from a New Wave nostalgia perspective. O'Connor, who wrote all the songs, hit the Top Ten with *Eighth Day* before fading into obscurity. The "life imitating art" subtext adds another level of interest to what is basically a morose chronicle of music-biz clichés. ▭

Phil Daniels *Danny Price* • Hazel O'Connor *Kate Crawley* • Jon Finch *Bob Woods* • Jonathan Pryce *Ken* • Peter-Hugo Daly *Mick Leaf* • Mark Wingett *Tony* • Paul McCartney • Rod Stewart • **Dir/Scr** Brian Gibson

Breaking In ★★★ 15

Comedy   1989 · US · Colour · 90mins

An overoptimistic title for Scottish director Bill Forsyth, who was making his second attempt at a Hollywood breakthrough after the British success of *Gregory's Girl* and *Local Hero*. Burt Reynolds, as an ageing burglar teaching his skills to a younger man (Casey Siemaszko), suits the humorous style, but John Sayles's script stresses mildness at the expense of momentum. The resulting shaggy-dog story possesses a measure of charm, but more bite would have helped. Contains swearing. ▭

Burt Reynolds *Ernie Mullins* • Casey Siemaszko *Mike Lefebb* • Sheila Kelley *Carrie* • Lorraine Toussaint *Delphine* • Albert Salmi *Johnny Scat* • Harry Carey *Shoes* • Maury Chaykin *Tucci* • Stephen Tobolowsky *District attorney* • **Dir** Bill Forsyth • **Scr** John Sayles

The Breaking Point ★★★

Drama   1950 · US · BW · 97mins

Ernest Hemingway's short novel, *To Have and Have Not*, became a classic movie in 1944, starring Humphrey Bogart and Lauren Bacall . This version, directed by Michael Curtiz, who made that other Bogart classic *Casablanca*, co-stars John Garfield and Patricia Neal. Hawks's version at least used Hemingway's title. This movie doesn't even bother to do that, replacing the tale of wartime gun-running with one of peacetime smuggling, but retaining its core relationship about an unlucky guy, a bunch of hoodlums and a girl in the middle. It's efficient, if forgettable. The story was rehashed again in 1958 as *The Gun Runners*.

John Garfield *Harry Morgan* • Patricia Neal *Leona Charles* • Phyllis Thaxter *Lucy Morgan* • Juano Hernandez *Wesley Park* • Wallace Ford *Duncan* • Edmond Ryan [Edmon Ryan] *Rogers* • Ralph Dumke *Hannagan* • Guy Thomajan *Danny* • William Campbell *Concho* • **Dir** Michael Curtiz • **Scr** Ranald MacDougall, from the novel *To Have and Have Not* by Ernest Hemingway

The Breaking Point ★ U

Thriller   1961 · UK · BW · 58mins

If stars were awarded for plot contrivance, this low-budget thriller would be well into double figures. There's a bank note printer with a gambling debt, revolutionaries with a counterfeiting plan, an armed robbery, a bomb, a touch of adultery and a speeding plane finale. All of this is breathlessly crammed into under an hour of screen time, with not one character ringing true nor one fragment of the storyline seeming the least bit credible. Director Lance Comfort deserves a pat on the back for trying to film such nonsense. That he fails is neither surprising nor to his demerit.

Peter Reynolds *Eric Winlatter* • Dermot Walsh *Robert Wade* • Joanna Dunham *Cherry Winlatter* • Lisa Gastoni *Eva* • Brian Cobby *Peter De Savory* • Jack Allen *Ernest Winlatter* • Geoffrey Denton *Debt collector* • Arnold Diamond *Telling* • Richard Golding *Mintos* • **Dir** Lance Comfort • **Scr** Peter Lambert, from a novel by Laurence Meynell

Breaking Point ★

Crime drama   1976 · Can · Colour · 91mins

Bo Svenson, a sort of expressionless forerunner of fellow Swede Dolph Lundgren, takes the stand against the Mafia and is set up with another identity by decent cop Robert Culp. But the Mafia soon sniff Svenson out and threaten his family and then we're into *Death Wish* vigilante land. Fortunately, Svenson is a judo instructor and is well equipped to take on the mob. To begin with, he uses fists and feet, then he graduates to guns and, finally, he resorts to a bulldozer – apparently the ultimate solution to dealing with troublesome gangsters.

Bo Svenson *Michael McBain* • Robert Culp *Frank Sirrianni* • John Colicos *Vincent Karbone* • Belinda Montgomery [Belinda J Montgomery] *Diana McBain* • Stephen Young *Peter Stratis* • Linda Sorenson *Helen McBain* • Jeffrey Lynas *Andy Stratis* • **Dir** Bob Clark • **Scr** Roger Swaybill, Stanley Mann, from a story by Roger Swaybill

Breaking Point ★★ 15

Second World War thriller
1989 · US · Colour · 90mins

Don't expect much from this TV movie from director Peter Markle (*Wagons East!*). Here, *LA Law*'s Corbin Bernsen is an American officer in the Second World War who's captured by the Nazis just before D-Day. They cunningly try to convince him that he's in a US hospital and the war has already ended in an attempt to discover the invasion plans. The idea is not very original – the story is from the 1964 James Garner film *36 Hours* – and it's also handled too messily to be entirely effective. ▭

Corbin Bernsen *Major Jefferson Pike* • Joanna Pacula *Anna* • John Glover *Dr Walter Gerber* • David Marshall *Grant Colonel Osterman* • Lawrence Pressman *General Smith* • Ken Jenkins *Colonel Lowe* • **Dir** Peter Markle • **Scr** Stanley Greenberg

Breaking the Rules ★

Road movie comedy drama
1992 · US · Colour · 100mins

Since his promising starring debut in Francis Ford Coppola's *The Outsiders*, C Thomas Howell has appeared to harbour a career death wish, appearing in increasingly bad movies. He hit the jackpot with this misconceived disease-of-the-week pic about a leukaemia sufferer who takes his two best mates (Howell and Jonathan Silverman) on a van trip to California so he can appear on TV's *Jeopardy* before croaking. As hard as this tries to tug at the heartstrings, the combination of appalling dialogue, completely divorced from the way real people talk, and emotional barreness ends up trivialising the subject matter.

Jason Bateman *Phil Stepler* • C Thomas Howell *Gene Michaels* • Jonathan Silverman *Rob Konigsberg* • Annie Potts *Mary Klingsmith* • Kent Bateman *Mr Stepler* • Shawn Phelan *Young Phil* • Jackey Vinson *Young Gene* • **Dir** Neal Israel • **Scr** Paul Shapiro

Breaking the Silence ★★★ 15

Drama   1992 · US · Colour · 89mins

A routine but watchable made-for-television courtroom drama, which succeeds in putting a fresh spin on a familiar story. Gregory Harrison is the hotshot attorney who is persuaded by old flame Stephanie Zimbalist to defend a young teenager accused of murdering his father. As the case unfolds, Harrison realises he has more in common with the defendant than he thinks. Director Robert Iscove, who also made the gripping war drama *Mission of the Shark*, elicits good performances from a strong cast and manages to avoid most of the clichés of the genre. ▭

Gregory Harrison *Paul Danner* • Stephanie Zimbalist *Janey Kirkland* • Chris Young *Kenny Becker* • Kevin Conway *Jack Hastings* • Kelly Rutherford *Cheryl* • Fran Bennett *Richards* • TC Warner *Shirley* • David Ackroyd *Berringer* • **Dir** Robert Iscove • **Scr** Adam Greenman

Breaking the Waves ★★★★★ 18

Romantic drama
1996 · D-en/Swe/Fr/Neth/Nor · Colour · 152mins

A wrenching central theme – the meaning of true love – coupled with a staggeringly honest performance from newcomer Emily Watson makes Danish director Lars von Trier's first English-language film a moving testament to the human spirit. Set in the remote Scottish wilds, and shot in pseudo home-video style to keep the profound events real and exposed, it tells the heartbreaking tale of a devoutly religious young woman who sacrifices everything for the man she adores. An often uncompromising and uncomfortable saga of faith, hope and charity, this will have you sobbing well before the unforgettable climax. [=]

Emily Watson *Bess* • Stellan Skarsgård *Jan* • Katrin Cartlidge *Dodo* • Jean-Marc Barr *Terry* • Udo Kier *Man on the trawler* • Adrian Rawlins *Doctor Richardson* • Jonathan Hackett *The minister* • Sandra Voe *Bess's mother* • Mikkel Gaup *Pits* ■ *Dir* Lars von Trier • *Scr* Lars Von Trier, Peter Asmussen

Breaking Up ★ 15
Romantic drama 1996 · US · Colour · 85mins

The talented Russell Crowe and Salma Hayek are both completely wasted in this low-budget, endlessly drawn-out explanation of a marriage. The pair reminisce about years' worth of relationship ups and downs, breaking up and getting back together so many times you really don't care if they live happily ever after or end up killing each other. Scriptwriter Michael Cristofer obviously had a great deal of emotional baggage to sort through; perhaps he should've kept it to himself. Contains swearing and sexual references. [=]

Russell Crowe *Steve* • Salma Hayek *Monica* • Abraham Alvarez *Minister* ■ *Dir* Robert Greenwald • *Scr* Michael Cristofer

Breakout ★★★
Action adventure 1975 · US · Colour · 95mins

In this off-target thriller, adventurer Charles Bronson rescues Robert Duvall from the Mexican prison he's been languishing in since being framed by father-in-law John Huston. As directed by Tom Gries (who made the formidable *Will Penny*), the film starts rather slowly, but the tension builds as Duvall seeks revenge. Jill Ireland – Bronson's real-life wife, who die of cancer in 1990 – is third-billed as Duvall's yearning spouse. Huston is nearly as villainous as he was in *Chinatown*, though the best work in the movie comes from Randy Quaid, Sheree North and Alejandro Rey in supporting roles.

Charles Bronson *Nick Colton* • Robert Duvall *Ray Wagner* • Jill Ireland *Ann Wagner* • John Huston *Harris Wagner* • Randy Quaid *Hawk Hawkins* • Sheree North *Myrna* • Alejandro Rey *Sanchez* • Paul Mantee *Cable* ■ *Dir* Tom Gries • *Scr* Howard B Kreitsek, Marc Norman, Elliott Baker, from the novel *Ten Second Jailbreak* by Warren Hinckle, William Turner, Eliot Asinof

Breakthrough ★ 15
Second World War drama
1978 · W Ger · Colour · 92mins

A sorry sequel to Sam Peckinpah's classic war drama *Cross of Iron*, this tawdry affair has Richard Burton as Sergeant Steiner, the role so magnificently created by James Coburn in the original, and features a totally wasted all-star support cast, including Robert Mitchum, Rod Steiger and Curt Jurgens. Burton doesn't seem interested in making his character believable, and it's hard to disguise the severe lack of both production values and a decent script. Clearly a film that all involved – particularly director Andrew V McLaglen – would rather forget.

Richard Burton *Sergeant Steiner* • Rod Steiger *General Webster* • Robert Mitchum *Colonel*

Rogers • Curt Jurgens *General Hoffmann* • Helmut Griem *Major Stransky* • Michael Parks *Sergeant Anderson* • Klaus Loewitsch [Klaus Löwitsch] *Corporal Krueger* • Veronique Vendell *Yvette* • Joachim Hansen *Captain Kirstner* ■ *Dir* Andrew V McLaglen • *Scr* Tony Williamson

Breast Men ★★★ 18
Black comedy 1997 · US · Colour · 91mins

A racy, frequently hilarious history of the fake boob industry. David Schwimmer, relishing his first major chance since *Friends* not to be entirely lovable, and Chris Cooper play the pioneering surgeons who make a fortune through their silicon implants in the drug-fuelled seventies, only to fall out. There's a talented support cast (Emily Procter, Matt Frewer, Louise Fletcher, Lyle Lovett) while Lawrence O'Neil's witheringly cynical direction offers up a mordant picture of beauty-obsessed America. Contains nudity, and some swearing. [=]

David Schwimmer *Dr Christopher Saunders/Kevin Saunders* • Chris Cooper *Dr William Larson* • Emily Procter *Laura Pierson* • Matt Frewer *Gerald* • Terry Quinn *Hersch Lawyer* • Kathleen Wilhoite *Timmi-Jean Lindsey* • John Stockwell *Robert Renaud* • Louise Fletcher *Mrs Saunders* • Lyle Lovett *Research scientist* ■ *Dir* Lawrence O'Neil • *Scr* John Stockwell

A Breath of Scandal ★★
Romance 1960 · US/It · Colour · 97mins

The costumes are nice, the colour's lovely and Sophia Loren looks gorgeous. But there's little ace *Casablanca* director Michael Curtiz can do to make this somewhat misguided version of Molnar's hoary old play *Olympia* sparkle, especially when wooden John Gavin is cast as the light in Loren's eye. Still, two refugees from *Gigi*, Maurice Chevalier and Isabel Jeans, delight both eye and ear and Angela Lansbury is Loren's lying arch rival, so there's some pleasure to be had among the tedium.

Sophia Loren *Princess Olympia* • John Gavin *Charlie Foster* • Maurice Chevalier *Prince Philip* • Isabel Jeans *Princess Eugenie* • Angela Lansbury *Countess Lina* • Tullio Carminati *Albert* • Roberto Risso *Aide* • Carlo Hintermann *Prince Ruprecht* • Milly Vitale *Can-can girl* ■ *Dir* Michael Curtiz • *Scr* Walter Bernstein, Ring Lardner Jr, Sidney Howard, from the play *Olympia* by Ferenc Molnar

Breathing Lessons ★★★
Drama 1994 · US · Colour

Joanne Woodward and James Garner star in this made-for-TV adaptation of Anne Tyler's novel about a bickering married couple who drive from Baltimore to a funeral in Pennsylvania. As far as road movies go, this one only lasts a day and doesn't take in the great sweep of America, but as the couple married for 29 years, Woodward (a rather bossy meddler) and Garner (inured to his wife's ways) make several breaks in their journey and learn a lot about each other. Their performances are as good as one could wish for.

James Garner *Ira Moran* • Joanne Woodward *Maggie Moran* • Kathryn Erbe *Fiona* • Joyce Van Patten *Serena* • Eileen Heckart *Mabel* • Paul Winfield *Mr Otis* • Henry Jones *Ira's father* ■ *Dir* John Erman • *Scr* Robert W Lenski, from the novel by Anne Tyler

Breathless ★★★ 18
Crime drama 1983 · US · Colour · 95mins

A remake of Jean-Luc Godard's 1959 classic *A Bout de Souffle*, this suffers greatly in comparison. But judged on its own merits, it's a fair attempt at an on-the-run-style drama. Driving a stolen car, Richard Gere kills a cop and then heads into the arms of Valerie Kaprisky, a French student with whom he's had a brief affair. As the police close in, our romantic lead seems oblivious to anything other than Kaprisky's rather obvious (and oft displayed) charms and Jim McBride (*The Big Easy*) seems most interested in getting both his actors to display as much flesh as possible. It's stylish but shallow, and Gere fits his superficial role like a glove. Contains violence, swearing and nudity. [=]

Richard Gere *Jesse Lujack* • Valérie Kaprisky *Monica* • Art Metrano *Birnbaum* • John P Ryan *Lieutenant Parmental* • William Tepper *Paul* • Robert Dunn *Sergeant Enright* • Garry Goodrew *Berutti* • Lisa Persky [Lisa Jane Persky] *Salesgirl* ■ *Dir* Jim McBride • *Scr* McBride, LM "Kit" Carson, from the film *A Bout de Souffle* by Jean-Luc Godard, from a story by François Truffaut

A Breed Apart ★★ 15
Drama 1984 · US · Colour · 91mins

Rutger Hauer plays a damaged and eccentric Vietnam veteran who's chosen to live as a recluse on a remote island. There he turns into a bird fancier and is pitted against Powers Booth, who has been hired by a rich egg collector to steal from Rutger's nest of eagles. Add to this unlikely scenario Kathleen Turner, who initiates an improbable love triangle, and you have a picture as risible as the moment when Hauer rides his white steed across the island, dressed as a pirate and carrying a crossbow (kidding you not). [=]

Rutger Hauer *Jim Malden* • Kathleen Turner *Stella Clayton* • Powers Boothe *Michael Walker* • Donald Pleasence *Whittier* • Jayne Bentzen *Amy Rollings* • Adam Fenwick *Adam Clayton* • John Dennis Johnston *Peyton* • Brion James *Miller* • Jayne Bentzen *Amy Rollings* ■ *Dir* Philippe Mora • *Scr* Paul Wheeler • *Music* Maurice Gibb

Breezy ★★★
Drama 1973 · US · Colour · 107mins

In 1973, this gentle, middle-age romance marked a real departure for Clint Eastwood as director, though he stopped short of taking the main role himself. Instead the craggy and irresistibly charming William Holden plays the cynical divorcee who becomes infatuated with a young girl named Breezy, the sort of hippy who says, "I love being horizontal." There are vague echoes of the heyday of Ernst Lubitsch, Leo McCarey and Billy Wilder, along with some echoes of Eastwood's private life (he tested Sondra Locke for the part but gave it to the younger Kay Lenz). But it's really a directorial try-out and a slightly soppy interlude – there's an injured dog in there, too – between *High Plains Drifter* and *Magnum Force*.

William Holden (1) *Frank Harmon* • Kay Lenz *Breezy* • Roger C Carmel *Bob Henderson* •

Marj Dusay *Betty Tobin* • Joan Hotchkis *Paula Harmon* • Jamie Smith Jackson *Marcy* ■ *Dir* Clint Eastwood • *Scr* Jo Heims

Brenda Starr ★★ PG
Fantasy adventure
1989 · US · Colour · 98mins

This cheap and cheerful comic-strip adaptation is let down by a plastic performance from Brooke Shields in the title role. She is the annoyingly intrepid ace reporter on the trail of a mad inventor and pursued by a posse of rival journalists and baddies. It's the latter that are the most fun: the bumbling crooks include Diana Scarwid, and Jeffrey Tambor, while Timothy Dalton is the smooth romantic interest. There are some camp moments but sadly it is not really trashy enough to be truly enjoyable. Contains swearing and violent moments. [=]

Brooke Shields *Brenda Starr* • Timothy Dalton *Basil St John* • Tony Peck *Mike Randall* • Diana Scarwid *Libby "Lips" Lipscomb* • Nestor Serrano *José, seaplane pilot* • Jeffrey Tambor *Vladimir* • June Gable *Luba* • Charles Durning *Francis I Livright, editor* ■ *Dir* Robert Ellis Miller • *Scr* Noreen Stone, James David Buchanan, Delia Ephron, from a story by Noreen Stone, James David Buchanan, from the comic strip by Dale Messick

Brennus – Enemy of Rome
★ U

Historical adventure
1963 · It · Colour · 90mins

Anyone who has seen the engaging Australian spoof *Hercules Returns* won't be able to keep a straight face through this sort of costume epic. That said, the vast majority of them were beyond parody anyway, and this ludicrous tale of marauding Gauls and brave Romans is no exception. The inevitable dubbing will have you in fits, as will the desperately straight-faced performances of the international cast. Italian dubbed into English.

Gordon Mitchell *Brennus* • Ursula Davis *Nisia* • Massimo Serato *Camillus* • Erno Crisa *Vatinius* ■ *Dir* Giacomo Gentilomo • *Scr* De Riso Scolaro, Arpad De Riso

Brewster McCloud ★★ 15
Comedy 1970 · US · Colour · 105mins

Robert Altman had just made *MASH* and was deluged by offers from the major studios. He chose to make this eccentric movie with Bud Cort as a modern-day Icarus, who kits himself out with wings and wants to fly in the Houston Astrodome (then recently completed and a modern wonder of the world). Altman probably felt he had a giant symbol on his hands – an allegory for freedom. In fact, he simply had a Disney-ish story without the layers of syrup. Making things even wackier is Shelley Duvall – Altman met Duvall at a party in Houston and promptly offered her her first film role. She made a further six films with the director. Contains swearing and nudity. [=]

Bud Cort *Brewster McCloud* • Sally Kellerman *Louise* • Michael Murphy *Frank Shaft* • William Windom *Sheriff Weeks* • Shelley Duvall *Suzanne* • René Auberjonois *Lecturer* • Stacy Keach *Abraham Wright* • John Schuck *Policeman Johnson* ■ *Dir* Robert Altman • *Scr* Doran William Cannon

Brewster's Millions ★★ U

Comedy   1945 · US · BW · 79mins

The idea of a young man who must spend a million to inherit many times that amount is one of the most popular comedy plots, with seven film versions dating back almost to the dawn of cinema. This time Dennis O'Keefe is the guy who finds it harder to spend his loot than he expects. Although only sporadically amusing, this fast-paced farce is still probably the funniest take on the tale.

Dennis O'Keefe *Monty Brewster* • Helen Walker *Peggy Gray* • Eddie "Rochester" Anderson *Jackson* • June Havoc *Trixie Summers* • Gail Patrick *Barbara Drew* • Mischa Auer *Michael Michaelovich* ■ *Dir* Allan Dwan • *Scr* Sig Herzig, Charles Rogers, Wilkie Mahoney [Wilkie C Mahoney], from the novel by George Barr McCutcheon, from the play by Winchell Smith, Byron Ongley

Brewster's Millions ★★ PG

Comedy   1985 · US · Colour · 96mins

Director Walter Hill and comedy are always an uneasy combination, and this hackneyed, overlong tale glaringly proves the point. Add the manic, rolling-eyed Richard Pryor, a taste never really acquired by British audiences, and you have a major disappointment that fell flat even when it was made. This was the seventh time the story had been filmed – man left millions in will but first has to spend large amount in 30 days – which should have sounded a note of caution all round, but didn't. As usual, Pryor overacts wildly. Contains mild swearing. 📺

Richard Pryor *Montgomery Brewster* • John Candy *Spike Nolan* • Lonette McKee *Angela Drake* • Stephen Collins *Warren Cox* • Jerry Orbach *Charley Pegler* • Pat Hingle *Edward Roundfield* • Tovah Feldshuh *Marilyn* • Hume Cronyn *Rupert Horn* • Rick Moranis *Morty King* • Reni Santoni *Vin Rapelito* ■ *Dir* Walter Hill • *Scr* Herschel Weingrod, Timothy Harris, from the novel by George Barr McCutcheon

Brian's Song ★★★★ PG

Sports drama based on a true story
1971 · US · Colour · 74mins

This tragic true story brought a new respectability to that despised genre, the TV movie, proving that real quality was possible. James Caan finally achieved stardom (his next role would be Sonny in *The Godfather*) as Brian Piccolo, a Chicago Bears football star dying of cancer. This moving story was based on the real-life account entitled *I Am Third* written by Piccolo's friend Gale Sayers, here played by Billy Dee Williams. Under-rated director Buzz Kulik (*Warning Shot*) displays a remarkable sensitivity, and Michel Legrand's score is wonderful. 📺

James Caan *Brian Piccolo* • Billy Dee Williams *Gale Sayers* • Jack Warden *Coach George Halas* • Shelley Fabares *Joy Piccolo* • Judy Pace *Linda Sayers* • Bernie Casey *JC Caroline* • David Huddleston *Ed McCaskey* • Ron Feinberg *Doug Atkins* ■ *Dir* Buzz Kulik • *Scr* William E Blinn, from the book *I Am Third* by Gale Sayers with Al Silverman • *Music* Michel Legrand

The Bribe ★★★

Crime drama   1949 · US · BW · 97mins

This was as close as that home of gloss, MGM, got to making a genuine *film noir*. Federal agent Robert Taylor heads south of the border to encounter a cleverly cast assortment of genre clichés, including ailing crook John Hodiak and sultry singer Ava Gardner. Villains Charles Laughton and Vincent Price are both seemingly well out of directorial control, which is perhaps not surprising as the movie was started by arch stylist Vincente Minnelli and finished by the credited director Robert Z Leonard. *The Bribe* would probably be barely remembered today but for the Steve Martin vehicle *Dead Men Don't Wear Plaid*, which included great chunks of the movie to great effect.

Robert Taylor (1) *Rigby* • Ava Gardner *Elizabeth Hintten* • Charles Laughton *JJ Bealler* • Vincent Price *Carwood* • John Hodiak *Tug Hintten* • Samuel S Hinds *Dr Warren* • John Hoyt *Gibbs* • Tito Renaldo *Emilio Gomez* • Martin Garralaga *Pablo Gomez* ■ *Dir* Robert Z Leonard • *Scr* Marguerite Roberts, from the short story by Frederick Nebel

The Bridal Path ★★ U

Comedy   1959 · UK · Colour · 95mins

Frank Launder and Sidney Gilliat's powers were clearly on the wane in this slipshod romantic comedy adapted from Nigel Tranter's lightweight novel. Bill Travers presents only a slight variation on his performance in the same team's earlier film *Geordie*, as a tetchy Scottish giant whose doltish unwillingness to come to terms with modern life precipitates what is intended to be all manner of rib-tickling confusion. However, the act here wears as thin as the plot, in which he crosses from the Hebrides in search of the perfect wife only to be arrested as a poacher. Hamming gleefully, George Cole and Gordon Jackson only emphasise Travers's one-dimensional performance.

Bill Travers *Ewan McEwan* • Alex Mackenzie *Finlay* • Eric Woodburn *Archie* • Jack Lambert *Hector* • John Rae *Angus* • Roddy McMillan *Murdo* • Jefferson Clifford *Wallace* • Nell Ballantyne *Jessie* • George Cole *Sergeant Bruce* • Gordon Jackson *Constable Alec* ■ *Dir* Frank Launder • *Scr* Frank Launder, Geoffrey Willans, Nigel Tranter, from the novel by Nigel Tranter

The Bride ★★ 15

Gothic horror drama   1985 · US · Colour · 114mins

This is one of the more unnecessary versions of Mary Shelley's man-makes-monster story. A bizarre cast has Sting as Baron Frankenstein, bringing Jennifer Beals to life (now *that* takes some doing!) under the watchful gaze of monster number one Clancy Brown, whose touching scenes with the late David Rappaport effortlessly steal the movie. Michael Seymour's production design is lush and impressive, as is Maurice Jarre's score, but despite the dextrous efforts of editor Michael Ellis, this one is a nonstarter. More humour might have helped. 📺

Sting *Baron Frankenstein* • Jennifer Beals *Eva* • Anthony Higgins *Clerval* • Clancy Brown *Viktor* • David Rappaport *Rinaldo* • Geraldine Page *Mrs Baumann* • Alexei Sayle *Magar* •

Phil Daniels *Bela* • Veruschka [Veruschka Von Lehndorff] *Countess* • Quentin Crisp *Dr Zalhus* ■ *Dir* Franc Roddam • *Scr* Lloyd Fonvielle, from characters created by Mary Shelley • *Music* Maurice Jarre • *Editor* Michael Ellis • *Production Designer* Michael Seymour

The Bride and the Beast ★ PG

Psychological horror   1958 · US · BW · 73mins

What else could this painfully cheap *King Kong* variant be but junk, when its author is Ed Wood Jr, the world's worst director? On their wedding night, Charlotte Austin is curiously attracted to hubby Lance Fuller's pet ape. Under hypnosis, she learns that in a previous incarnation she was queen of the gorillas. So it's off on an African safari (cue endless stock footage) to meet her hairy destiny. Tapping into the popular fifties theme of semi-naked women in monkey suit embrace, this laughably inept sleaze flick is for Wood completists only. 📺

Charlotte Austin *Laura* • Lance Fuller *Dan* • Johnny Roth *Taro* • Steve Calvert *Beast* • William Justine *Dr Reiner* • Jeanne Gerson *Marka* • Gil Frye *Captain Cameron* ■ *Dir* Adrian Weiss • *Scr* Edward D Wood Jr, from a story by Adrian Weiss

Bride by Mistake ★★

Comedy   1944 · US · BW · 81mins

Lovely Laraine Day nearly achieved stardom in the mid-forties, having built up a following as Mary Lamont in MGM's popular *Dr Kildare* series. Eventually she secured leads in major movies, playing opposite Gary Cooper in *The Story of Dr Wassell* and Cary Grant in *Mr Lucky*. This film followed those two major roles, but did little for her career. A minor feature that showcased her charms, it led to co-starring roles supporting Lana Turner and John Wayne. Films such as this are pleasant enough time-passers, but the slight material would barely get by as a TV sitcom nowadays.

Alan Marshal *Tony Travis* • Laraine Day *Norah Hunter* • Marsha Hunt *Sylvia* • Allyn Joslyn *Phil Vernon* • Edgar Buchanan *Connors* • Michael St Angel *Corey* • Marc Cramer *Ross* • William Post Jr *Donald* • Bruce Edwards *Chaplain* ■ *Dir* Richard Wallace • *Scr* Phoebe Ephron, Henry Ephron, from a story by Norman Krasna

The Bride Came C.O.D. ★★★ U

Comedy   1941 · US · BW · 91mins

The unlikely comic pairing of movie greats James Cagney and Bette Davis may seem a mite arch, but they seem to enjoy each other's company. The plot is a heavily diluted comic caper about mistaken identities and runaway brides – he's a flier, she's an heiress and, for some obscure reason, they spend a lot of time together marooned in a desert ghost town. Cagney manages to give Davis a pretty good run for her money and is better at the farcical moments, especially as most of the jokes involve Davis losing her dignity. Still, Davis was a born trouper, and rises above this nonsense with style and grace. Jack Carson and Eugene Pallette have their moments, too, but if ever a movie was a vehicle for its stars, it's this one. Without

them, this would have been forgettable, yet they really are superb.

James Cagney *Steve* • Bette Davis *Joan Winfield* • Stuart Erwin *Tommy Keenan* • Jack Carson *Allen Brice* • George Tobias *Peewee* • Eugene Pallette *Lucius K Winfield* • Harry Davenport *Pop Tolliver* • William Frawley *Sheriff McGee* ■ *Dir* William Keighley • *Scr* Julius J Epstein, Philip G Epstein, from a story by Kenneth Earl, MM Musselman

The Bride Comes Home ★★★ U

Comedy   1935 · US · BW · 82mins

Having chalked up a success by pairing Claudette Colbert and newcomer Fred MacMurray in the romantic comedy *The Gilded Lily* (1935), Paramount recycled the formula – same stars, same director (Wesley Ruggles) and the same screenwriter (Claude Binyon). Once again the delightful Colbert is in a tug of war between two suitors. She's now an impoverished but feisty heiress involved in a magazine-publishing venture with mega-rich and sweet-natured Robert Young. MacMurray is Young's ill-tempered, and poor, sidekick, with whom Colbert engages in pre-feminist era, battle-of-the-sexes verbal sparring that provides the comedy. No prizes for guessing which man she chooses in the end.

Claudette Colbert *Jeanette Desmereau* • Fred MacMurray *Cyrus Anderson* • Robert Young *Jack Bristow* • William Collier Sr *Alfred Desmereau* • Donald Meek *The judge* • Richard Carle *Frank* • Johnny Arthur *Otto* ■ *Dir* Wesley Ruggles • *Scr* Claude Binyon, from a story by Elizabeth Sanxay Holding

Bride for Sale ★★★

Romantic comedy   1949 · US · BW · 87mins

Although her career would extend another two decades, this was the last comedy made by the sparkling Claudette Colbert. It's slight stuff – a romance that finds her torn between sturdy George Brent and cheerful Robert Young – made watchable by its attractive stars. Though released by RKO, the film was made by the independent producer Jack Skirball, best known for his work with Hitchcock on *Saboteur* and *Shadow of a Doubt*. Colbert's next role was to have been Margo Channing in *All about Eve*, but she injured her back.

Claudette Colbert *Nora Shelly* • Robert Young *Steve Adams* • George Brent *Paul Martin* • Max Baer *Litka* • Gus Schilling *Timothy* • Charles Arnt *Dobbs* • Mary Bear *Miss Stone* • Ann Tyrrell *Miss Swanson* ■ *Dir* William D Russell • *Scr* Bruce Manning, Islin Auster, from a story by Joseph Fields

The Bride in Black ★★ PG

Thriller   1990 · US · Colour · 90mins

American daytime soap star Susan Lucci plays a woman whose whirlwind courtship ends in tragedy when her lover is killed outside the church where they have just been married. She vows to track down the killers and, of course, discovers that her late hubby may not have been all that he seemed. Unfortunately, this movie has all the impact of an adaptation of a Danielle Steel novel rather than the tense thriller it would like to be. Star attractions in the cast are David Soul

and Reginald VelJohnson, who played Bruce Willis's police patrolman ally in *Die Hard*.

Susan Lucci *Rose D'Amore* • David Soul *Owen Malloy* • Reginald VelJohnson *Barry Gates* • Finola Hughes *Cybil Cobb* • Melissa Leo *Mary Margaret* • Tom Signorelli *Ray D'Amore* • Angela D'Ambrosia *Ginny D'Amore* • Irma St Paule *Nonna* ■ *Dir* James Goldstone • *Scr* Claire Labine, from the novel *The Bride Wore Black* by Cornell Woolrich

The Bride Is Much Too Beautiful ★★

Romantic comedy 1956 · Fr · BW · 93mins

This slight Brigitte Bardot vehicle was made when the pouty little minx could break your heart with a look. It's a mild comedy of manners that was dubbed on release; unsurprisingly, it works better in the original French. Pairing the "sex kitten" with handsome Louis Jourdan, the film has Bardot as a girl from the sticks who becomes a top model after she is spotted by the publishers of a chic Paris magazine. Micheline Presle brings class to the silly proceedings, which involve a phoney wedding, in a lightweight offering that is not regarded as one of BB's better movies. French dialogue dubbed into English.

Brigitte Bardot *Chouchou* • Micheline Presle *Judith* • Louis Jourdan *Michel* • Marcel Amont *Tom* • Jean-François Calvé *Patrice* • Roger Dumas *Marc* • Madeleine Lambert *Aunt Agnès* • Marcelle Arnold *Madame Victoire* ■ *Dir* Pierre Gaspard-Huit • *Scr* Philippe Agostini, Odette Joyeux, Juliette Saint-Giniez, from a story by Odette Joyeux

Bride of Chucky ★★★ 18

Horror spoof 1998 · US · Colour · 85mins

This fourth encounter with devilish doll Chucky is the most entertaining of the *Child's Play* series, thanks to Ronny Yu's colourful direction, a wickedly humorous tone and the irresistible presence of Jennifer Tilly. Clearly inspired by the tongue-in-cheek playfulness of *Scream*, there's more laughter than slaughter as Chucky and new dolly girl Tiffany plot to escape their diminutive frames. Although the story is lightweight even by the standards of a horror spoof, the witty references to horror classics of past and present and the hilarious interplay (and intercourse) between the rubber lovers resurrect this series from its movie grave. Contains swearing and violence. DVD

Jennifer Tilly *Tiffany* • Brad Dourif *Chucky* • Katherine Heigl *Jade* • Nick Stabile *Jesse* • Alexis Arquette *Damien Baylock* • Gordon Michael Woolvett *David* • John Ritter *Chief Warren Kincaid* • Lawrence Dane *Lieutenant Preston* ■ *Dir* Ronny Yu • *Scr* Don Mancini

Bride of Frankenstein ★★★★★ PG

Classic horror 1935 · US · BW · 74mins

James Whale's extravagantly produced sequel to his own *Frankenstein* still ranks as one of horrordom's greatest achievements. From his wittily eccentric direction and Elsa Lanchester's electric hairdo, to Ernest Thesiger's ingenious portrayal of the perverse Dr Pretorius and Boris Karloff's alternately poignant and pushy monster, it's a class act from amazing start to religious-slanted finish. They don't get any better than this one and some scenes – the unveiling of the bride to the sound of wedding bells, the miniature people in bell jars – are of classic status.

Boris Karloff *The monster* • Colin Clive *Henry Frankenstein* • Valerie Hobson *Elizabeth* • Ernest Thesiger *Doctor Pretorius* • Elsa Lanchester *Mary Shelley/The bride* • Gavin Gordon *Lord Byron* • Douglas Walton *Percy Bysshe Shelley* • Una O'Connor *Minnie* ■ *Dir* James Whale • *Scr* William Hurlbut, John L Balderston, from the novel *Frankenstein* by Mary Shelley • *Cinematographer* John Mescall • *Art Director* Charles D Hall • *Special Effects* John P Fulton • *Make-up* Jack Pierce

Bride of Re-Animator ★★ 18

Horror comedy 1991 · US · Colour · 92mins

Nowhere near as impactful, witty or fresh as the original HP Lovecraft-based cult movie *Re-Animator*, director Brian Yuzna's gloriously gory sequel (he produced the first outing) sadly ventures more into standard Frankenstein territory. Jeffrey Combs is good value as Herbert West, the mad doctor with the luminous green serum that revives dead tissue to create a living woman out of assorted body parts (the feet of a ballet dancer, the womb of virgin and so on). This has the usual dire consequences. Gruesomely over-the-top, with a nightmarishly surreal climax. Contains violence, and some swearing.

Jeffrey Combs *Herbert West* • Bruce Abbott *Dan Cain* • Claude Earl Jones *Lieutenant Leslie Chapham* • Fabiana Udenio *Francesca Danelli* • David Gale *Doctor Carl Hill* • Kathleen Kinmont *Gloria –The Bride* ■ *Dir* Brian Yuzna • *Scr* Woody Keith, Rick Fry, from a story by Brian Yuzna, Woody Keith, Rick Fry, from the story *Herbert West – the Re-Animator* by HP Lovecraft

Bride of the Monster ★ PG

Horror 1955 · US · BW · 68mins

Many will know about this movie purely because Tim Burton expertly re-created key scenes in his superb *Ed Wood* biopic. The movie itself is pure torture to watch, but has to be seen to be believed. Bela Lugosi, in his only true starring role in an Ed Wood exploiter, is a fugitive Russian scientist trying to create a race of super-beings in his swamp-based hideout. *Plan 9 from Outer Space* star Tor Johnson is his moronic, mute assistant, while bland hero Tony McCoy only got the role because his Arizona rancher father financed the film. The whole sorry affair comes complete with light-bulb special effects and the infamous pit fight between Lugosi and a lifeless rubber octopus stolen from a John Wayne movie.

Bela Lugosi *Dr Eric Vornoff* • Tor Johnson *Lobo* • Tony McCoy *Lieutenant Dick Craig* • Loretta King *Janet Lawton* • Harvey Dunn *Captain Robbins* • George Becwar *Professor Strowski* • Paul Marco *Kelton* • Don Nagel *Martin* ■ *Dir* Edward D Wood Jr • *Scr* Edward D Wood Jr, Alex Gordon

Bride of Vengeance ★

Drama 1949 · US · BW · 92mins

The Borgias get up to all sorts of shady dealings in Renaissance Italy, especially Lucretia, who is sent out to kill a man, but falls in love with him. This was a disaster for all concerned – even Ray Milland who refused to appear in it and was suspended by the studio. Director Mitchell Leisen loathed the script and concentrated on the flamboyant decor – he was originally an art director – but it should have been in colour. So bad were the reviews, and so thin was the box office, that Paramount sacked its contract star, Paulette Goddard.

Paulette Goddard *Lucretia Borgia* • John Lund *Alfonso D'Este* • Macdonald Carey *Cesare Borgia* • Albert Dekker *Vanetti* • John Sutton *Bisceglie* • Raymond Burr *Michelotto* • Charles Dayton *Bastino* • Donald Randolph *Tiziano* • Billy Gilbert *Beppo* ■ *Dir* Mitchell Leisen • *Scr* Cyril Hume, Michael Hogan, Clemence Dane, from a story by Michael Hogan

The Bride Walks Out ★★★

Comedy 1936 · US · BW · 80mins

A Barbara Stanwyck vehicle in which the star demonstrated that, without a strong director and clever script, comedy was not her forte. She tries hard as a model who becomes a housewife, but the material defeats her and her co-star, bland Gene Raymond. Yet, there's still pleasure to be had in watching a cast that includes such super character players as Ned Sparks, Helen Broderick and Hattie McDaniel.

Barbara Stanwyck *Carolyn Martin* • Robert Young *Hugh McKenzie* • Gene Raymond *Michael Martin* • Ned Sparks *Mr Dodson* • Helen Broderick *Mrs Dodson* • Billy Gilbert *Donovan* • Willie Best *Smokie* • Hattie McDaniels [Hattie McDaniel] *Maime* ■ *Dir* Leigh Jason • *Scr* PJ Wolfson, Philip G Epstein, from a story by Howard Emmett Rogers

The Bride Wore Black ★★★★

Mystery 1967 · Fr/It · Colour · 107mins

In adapting Cornell Woolrich's novel and hiring Bernard Herrmann for the score, François Truffaut paid his most conscious tribute to Alfred Hitchcock. Yet this tale of relentless revenge also owes much to the style of Truffaut's other mentor, Jean Renoir. Jeanne Moreau gives a chameleon-like performance as the widow seeking retribution from the quintet who accidentally killed her husband on their wedding day. Each of them is an archetype of male boorishness, yet their deaths invoke a mixture of emotions and calculated flashbacks, which reveal the extent of Moreau's, loss temper the callousness of her crimes. In French with English subtitles.

Jeanne Moreau *Julie Kohler* • Jean-Claude Brialy *Corey* • Michel Bouquet *Coral* • Charles Denner *Fergus* • Claude Rich *Bliss* • Daniel Boulanger *Holmes/Delvaux* • Michael Lonsdale [Michel Lonsdale] *Rene Morane* • Serge Rousseau *David* ■ *Dir* François Truffaut • *Scr* François Truffaut, Jean-Louis Richard, from the novel by William Irish [Cornell Woolrich] • *Cinematographer* Raoul Coutard

The Bride Wore Boots ★★

Comedy 1946 · US · BW · 86mins

A comedy of marital disharmony, with Barbara Stanwyck detesting husband Robert Cummings's interest in the Civil War and he detesting her love of horses. There's a divorce, a horse that's in love with Cummings and a championship steeplechase. And that's about it, really, with both stars making the most of their modest material, especially Cummins. A very young Natalie Wood plays one of two precocious by-products of the marriage.

Barbara Stanwyck *Sally Warren* • Robert Cummings *Jeff Warren* • Diana Lynn *Mary Lou Medford* • Patric Knowles *Lance Gale* • Peggy Wood *Grace Apley* • Robert Benchley *Tod Warren* • Willie Best *Joe* • Natalie Wood *Carol Warren* ■ *Dir* Irving Pichel • *Scr* Dwight Michael Wiley, from a story by Dwight Michael Wiley, from a play by Harry Segall

The Bride Wore Red ★★★ U

Drama 1937 · US · BW · 103mins

A fairly typical, though slightly more eccentric than most, Joan Crawford vehicle. The star plays a cabaret singer who gets to travel to the obviously studio-bound and back-projected Austrian Tyrol and can't choose between handsome and dashing playboy Robert Young or handsome and dashing postman Franchot Tone. Not, of course, that it matters one jot in this entertaining tosh. This tale was directed by the only woman director in mainstream Hollywood at the time, Dorothy Arzner; it's just a shame that she wasn't more talented. Billie Burke and Reginald Owen lend a spurious dignity to the proceedings.

Joan Crawford *Anni* • Franchot Tone *Giulio* • Robert Young *Rudi Pal* • Billie Burke *Contessa di Milano* • Reginald Owen *Admiral Monti* • Lynne Carver *Magdalena Monti* • George Zucco *Count Armalia* • Mary Phillips [Mary Philips] *Maria* ■ *Dir* Dorothy Arzner • *Scr* Tess Slesinger, Bradbury Foote, from the play *The Girl from Trieste* by Ferenc Molnar

The Brides of Dracula ★★★★

Horror 1960 · UK · Colour · 85mins

While Christopher Lee worried about typecasting, Hammer went ahead anyway with this sequel (in name only) to its huge 1958 hit *Dracula*. Anaemic David Peel as Baron Meinster is a poor substitute for Lee's more full-blooded undead Count, but that's the only point of contention in a classic Terence Fisher-directed shocker. The marvellous atmosphere drips with a lingering Gothic ghoulishness, the sexuality is remarkably upfront for its time, and the climax set in the shadow of a moonlit windmill is the stuff of fairy-tale nightmare.

Peter Cushing *Dr Van Helsing* • Martita Hunt *Baroness Meinster* • Yvonne Monlaur *Marianne* • Freda Jackson *Greta* • David Peel *Baron Meinster* • Miles Malleson *Dr Tobler* • Henry Oscar *Herr Lang* • Mona Washbourne *Frau Lang* ■ *Dir* Terence Fisher • *Scr* Jimmy Sangster, Peter Bryan, Edward Percy, from characters created by Bram Stoker

The Brides of Fu Manchu ★★ U

Crime drama 1966 · UK · Colour · 90mins

The second outing for Christopher Lee as Sax Rohmer's East-Asian mastermind was the first step down the slippery slope of inadequate stories and deteriorating quality for the series. In this bid for world domination, Fu Manchu kidnaps the daughters of 12 international diplomats to cause

political chaos. The plot was born out of a limp publicity stunt involving a beauty contest in which the winners won movie roles. Don Sharp's direction rarely lives up to his surname and even the death ray in Fu Manchu's secret temple fails to raise excitement, although Lee's performance is as entertaining as always. ▭

Christopher Lee *Fu Manchu* • Douglas Wilmer *Nayland Smith* • Marie Versini *Marie Lentz* • Heinz Drache *Franz Baumer* • Howard Marion-Crawford *Dr Petrie* • Kenneth Fortescue *Sergeant Spier* • Joseph Furst *Otto Lentz* • Carole Gray *Michele* ■ *Dir* Don Sharp • *Scr* Peter Welbeck [Harry Alan Towers], from characters created by Sax Rohmer

The Bridge ★★★★

Second World War drama
1959 · W Ger · BW · 106mins

Although many German features in the fifties tackled the aftermath of the Second World War (the so-called "rubble films"), few dealt with the conflict itself. Actor Bernhard Wicki made his debut as writer/director with this docudramatic reconstruction of an actual incident involving seven teenage recruits who were ordered to defend a strategically irrelevant bridge in the last days of the American advance. Rarely has the rigidity of Nazi discipline or the futility of war been as powerfully exposed as in this Oscar-nominated drama, which is not only forcibly directed, but also impeccably played by its suitably inexperienced cast. In German with English subtitles.

Volker Bohnet *Hans Scholten* • Fritz Wepper *Albert Mutz* • Michael Hinz *Walter Forst* • Frank Glaubrecht *Jurgen Borchert* • Karl Michael Balzer *Karl Horber* • Volker Lechtenbrink *Klaus Hager* • Gunther Hoffmann *Sigi Bernhard* ■ *Dir* Bernhard Wicki • *Scr* Michael Mansfeld, Karl-Wilhelm Vivier, from the novel *Die Brucke* by Manfred Gregor

The Bridge ★★ 15

Period drama 1990 · UK · Colour · 97mins

A heritage cast-off from the Merchant-Ivory school, this genteel British period piece lacks both subtlety and dynamism. The brilliant Saskia Reeves is underused as a bored wife who falls head over heels for a young artist (David O'Hara) while on holiday with her children. Even with the acting clout of Joss Ackland, Geraldine James and Rosemary Harris behind him, director Sydney MacCartney simply doesn't have the artistry of James Ivory. ▭

Saskia Reeves *Isobel Hetherington* • David O'Hara *Philip Wilson Steer* • Joss Ackland *Smithson* • Rosemary Harris *Aunt Jude* • Anthony Higgins *Reginald Hetherington* • Geraldine James *Mrs Todd* • Tabitha Allen *Emma Hetherington* • Dominique Rossi *Mary* ■ *Dir* Sydney Macartney • *Scr* Adrian Hodges, from the novel by Maggie Hemingway

The Bridge ★★★

Drama 1999 · Fr · Colour · 88mins

Screenwriter François Dupeyron, who directed Gérard Depardieu in *A Strange Place to Meet*, again explores the randomness of attraction in this measured drama, which the actor co-directed with Frédéric Auburtin. In a bid to reinforce his themes, Depardieu archly cast his off-screen lover, Carole Bouquet, as the perfect wife who has an affair with Charles Berling, an

engineer working on the same bridge as her hard-up husband. Scrupulously refusing to apportion blame, the film is painfully truthful but slightly lacking in dramatic impetus. In French with English subtitles.

Gérard Depardieu *Georges* • Carole Bouquet *Mina* • Charles Berling *Matthias* • Stanislas Crevillen *Tommy* • Dominique Reymond *Claire Daboval* • Mélanie Laurent *Lisbeth* • Michèle Goddet ■ *Dir* Gérard Depardieu, Frédéric Auburtin • *Scr* François Dupeyron, from a novel by Alain LeBlanc

The Bridge at Remagen ★★★ PG

Second World War drama
1969 · US · Colour · 112mins

A great performance by George Segal, as a die-hard platoon leader, lifts this "war is hell" saga out of the ordinary. Filming in Czechoslovakia and interrupted by the actual Russian invasion, big-budget director John Guillermin was clearly trying to achieve something different by adding sober measures of cynical disenchantment to the conventional Second World War melodramatic mix. Epic explosions and razzle-dazzle camerawork ultimately win out over any such grandiose "thinking action man" ideas, however. An A for effort, though.

George Segal *Lieutenant Phil Hartman* • Robert Vaughn *Major Paul Kreuger* • Ben Gazzara *Sergeant Angelo* • Bradford Dillman *Major Barnes* • EG Marshall *Brigadier General Shinner* • Peter Van Eyck *General Von Brock* • Matt Clark *Colonel Jellicoe* • Fritz Ford *Colonel Dent* ■ *Dir* John Guillermin • *Scr* Richard Yates, William Roberts, from a story by Roger Hirson, from a novel by Ken Hechler

Bridge of Dragons ★★ 18

Action thriller 1999 · US · Colour · 87mins

Dolph Lundgren's star may have faded a little since the heady days of *Rocky IV* and *Universal Soldier*, but he remains a popular draw in video land and this won't disappoint his fans. Set in a post-apocalyptic future, it stars Lundgren as a programmed killing machine – an always helpful plot device since it explains the wooden acting. When he comes to the rescue of a princess, he incurs the wrath of evil warlord Cary-Hiroyuki Tagawa. While this offers plenty of high-quality biffing and loud explosions, it's the charismatic Tagawa who steals the show. ▭

Dolph Lundgren *Warchyld* • Cary-Hiroyuki Tagawa *Ruecheng* • Rachel Shane [Valerie Chow] *Halo* ■ *Dir* Isaac Florentine • *Scr* Carlton Holder

Bridge of Time ★ U

Science-fiction 1997 · US · Colour · 102mins

Forced to crash-land their plane, a UN relief worker (*LA Law*'s Susan Dey) her photojournalist ex-husband and an opportunistic fortune hunter are rescued and brought to a mystical city where the people live in harmony and youth springs eternal. Although the visitors are not held captive, their departure becomes increasingly complicated when the city's spiritual leader (Cicely Tyson) convinces them it is their destiny to be the custodians of the human race. A brainless TV movie

with terrible acting and really bad dialogue.

Susan Dey *Madeline Armstrong* • Cotter Smith *Robert Creighton* • Nigel Havers *Halek* • Cicely Tyson *Guardian* • Robert Whitehead *Maxwell Spring* • Kimberleigh Stark *Keza* • Todd Jensen *William* ■ *Dir* Jorge Montesi • *Scr* Drew Hunter, Christopher Canaan

The Bridge on the River Kwai ★★★★ PG

Second World War drama
1957 · UK · Colour · 155mins

Director David Lean's multi-Oscar-winning monument to saving face in a Japanese prisoner-of-war camp is wonderfully judged when it's concerned with British colonel Alec Guinness and his feud with his Japanese counterpart (Sessue Hayakawa). But it's strangely fudged when American escapee William Holden tries to destroy the strategic bridge Guinness and his men have built. Nevertheless, the film was rewarded with seven Academy Awards, including one for Jack Hildyard's stunning CinemaScope photography on Ceylon locations, and was a massive box-office hit. Upper lips were never stiffer – all the better to whistle the Colonel Bogey March. ▭

William Holden (1) *Shears* • Alec Guinness *Colonel Nicholson* • Jack Hawkins *Major Warden* • Sessue Hayakawa *Colonel Saito* • James Donald *Major Clipton* • Geoffrey Horne *Lieutenant Joyce* • André Morell *Colonel Green* • Peter Williams *Captain Reeves* ■ *Dir* David Lean • *Scr* Pierre Boulle (front for Carl Foreman, Michael Wilson), from the novel by Pierre Boulle • *Music* Malcolm Arnold • *Editor* Peter Taylor

Bridge to Silence ★★★ 15

Drama 1989 · US · Colour · 92mins

Lee Remick stars as a cold-hearted mother whose deaf daughter survives a car crash in which her son-in-law is killed. Remick's grandchild is caught in the middle. The script has obviously been processed through one of those computer programmes that offer story curves, road humps, fast straights and an emotional crash every ten minutes. It's standard TV-movie fodder, directed by Karen Arthur, who gained experience on TV's *Cagney and Lacey*. However, it's lifted by the performances of the late, lamented Remick (in her last film appearance) and, as her daughter, Marlee Matlin, an Oscar-winner for *Children of a Lesser God*. Contains some nudity. ▭

Marlee Matlin *Peg Lawrence* • Lee Remick *Marge Duffield* • Josef Sommer *Al Duffield* • Michael O'Keefe *Dan Burnell* • Allison Silva *Lisa Lawrence* • Candace Brecker *Mary Amblett* • Pat Hamilton *Betty Samuels* • Cec Linder *Sam Samuels* ■ *Dir* Karen Arthur • *Scr* Louisa Burns-Bisogno, from a story by Tom Bisogno, Tom Neuwirth

A Bridge Too Far ★★★ 15

Second World War drama
1977 · UK · Colour · 168mins

Richard Attenborough's epic retelling of one of the Second World War's biggest debacles is impressive enough, with its eye-catching list of stars, fabulous parachute drop sequences and superb Panavision photography from Geoffrey Unsworth. But the depressing nature of this story of human suffering and sacrifice makes for grim, unedifying

film-making, no matter how cleverly writer William Goldman has created drama from the event. Only Sean Connery and Edward Fox really shine in an all-star cast, though Hardy Kruger and Maximilian Schell emerge with credibility as Germans. ▭

Dirk Bogarde *Lieutenant General Frederick Browning* • James Caan *Staff Sergeant Eddie Dohun* • Michael Caine *Lieutenant Colonel Joe Vandeleur* • Sean Connery *Major General Robert Urquhart* • Edward Fox *Lieutenant General Brian Horrocks* • Elliott Gould *Colonel Bobby Stout* • Gene Hackman *Major General Stanislaw Sosabowski* • Anthony Hopkins *Lieutenant Colonel John Frost* • Hardy Kruger *Major General Ludwig* • Laurence Olivier *Dr Spaander* • Ryan O'Neal *Brigadier General James M Gavin* • Robert Redford *Major Julian Cook* • Maximilian Schell *Lieutenant General Bittrich* ■ *Dir* Richard Attenborough • *Scr* William Goldman, from the book by Cornelius Ryan

The Bridges at Toko-Ri ★★★★ U

War drama 1954 · US · Colour · 98mins

This glossy, star-laden Korean War movie that manages to be both superbly entertaining and extremely moving, thanks to solid direction from the under-rated Mark Robson. The source material is from the prolific writer James A Michener, and his view of the futility of the war in Korea is given expert emphasis by the fine performances of William Holden as a reserve officer recalled to service and Fredric March as a gruff admiral. Grace Kelly is simply luminous as Holden's navy wife. The movie won an Oscar for its special effects. ▭

William Holden (1) *Lieutenant Harry Brubaker* • Fredric March *Rear Admiral George Tarrant* • Grace Kelly *Nancy Brubaker* • Mickey Rooney *Mike Forney* • Robert Strauss *Beer Barrel* • Charles McGraw *Commander Wayne Lee* • Keiko Awaji *Kimiko* • Earl Holliman *Nestor Gamidge* • Richard Shannon *Lieutenant Olds* ■ *Dir* Mark Robson • *Scr* Valentine Davies, from a novel by James A Michener

The Bridges of Madison County ★★★★ 12

Romantic drama 1995 · US · Colour · 129mins

Clint Eastwood directs and stars in this *Brief Encounter* of the open spaces, taken from Robert James Waller's bestseller. Eastwood plays *National Geographic* photographer Robert Kincaid, a sensitive loner drawn into an intense love affair with rancher's wife Meryl Streep when he arrives in Iowa to take pictures of Madison County's covered bridges. Told in flashback after Streep's death, when her grown-up children discover a diary and realise how deeply affected their mother was by the experience. Eastwood's adult-orientated romance may be tear-driven but it avoids easy sentimentality in favour of a more complex exploration of family responsibility, marital fidelity and self denial. Contains some swearing. ▭ **DVD**

Clint Eastwood *Robert Kincaid* • Meryl Streep *Francesca Johnson* • Annie Corley *Carolyn Johnson* • Victor Slezak *Michael Johnson* • Jim Haynie *Richard* • Sarah Kathryn Schmitt *Young Carolyn* • Christopher Kroon *Young*

Michael • Phyllis Lyons *Betty* ■ *Dir* Clint Eastwood • *Scr* Richard LaGravenese, from the novel by Robert James Waller

Brief Encounter ★★★★★ PG

Classic romantic drama
1945 · UK · BW · 82mins

Co-adapted by Noël Coward from his own one-act play *Still Life*, this is one of the finest films ever made in Britain. What makes the illicit love between doctor Trevor Howard and housewife Celia Johnson so memorable is their sheer ordinariness – they really could be anybody sat in the dark or in the comfort of their armchair. That's why *Falling in Love*, the unofficial Hollywood remake, fell so flat: Robert De Niro and Meryl Streep simply weren't ordinary enough. Romancing to the strains of Rachmaninoff's Second Piano Concerto, the leads are outstanding, but credit should also go to the forgotten Cyril Raymond, whose decent dullness as Johnson's husband makes those stolen Thursdays seem so special. 🖭 *DVD*

Celia Johnson *Laura Jesson* • Trevor Howard *Dr Alec Harvey* • Cyril Raymond *Fred Jesson* • Stanley Holloway *Albert Godby* • Joyce Carey *Myrtle Bagot* • Everley Gregg *Dolly Messiter* • Margaret Barton *Beryl Waters* • Dennis Harkin *Stanley* • Irene Handl *Organist* ■ *Dir* David Lean • *Scr* Noël Coward, David Lean, Anthony Havelock-Allan, from the play *Still Life* by Noël Coward • *Cinematographer* Robert Krasker

Brief Encounter ★★ PG

Drama   1974 · UK/US · Colour · 99mins

A rather pointless update of Noël Coward's romantic tear-jerker *Still Life*, already given the classic treatment by David Lean in 1945. Richard Burton and Sophia Loren step uncomfortably into Trevor Howard and Celia Johnson's shoes as the married strangers drifting into a poignant affair. There's no denying the bittersweet source material still packs an emotional punch even in this lavish treatment. But the ever-gorgeous Loren, as an Italian housewife who married into the English middle class, barely convinces. This was shown in America as a TV movie. 🖭

Richard Burton *Alec Harvey* • Sophia Loren *Anna Jesson* • Jack Hedley *Graham Jesson* • Rosemary Leach *Mrs Gaines* • John Le Mesurier *Stephen* • Gwen Cherrell *Dolly* • Jumoke Debayo *Mrs Harris* • Madeline Hinde *Grace* ■ *Dir* Alan Bridges • *Scr* John Bowne, from the play *Still Life* by Noël Coward

A Brief History of Time ★★★

Documentary 1992 · US/UK · Colour · 80mins

Using computers and synthesizers to circumvent the devastating effects of amyotrophic lateral sclerosis, Stephen Hawking succeeded in transforming our notions about the formation of the universe and, through his bestseller *A Brief History of Time*, became the world's most famous theoretical physicist. Steering scrupulously clear of Hawking's then-complex love life, innovative documentarist Errol Morris delves into his past to discover a rebellious student whose mental faculties sharpened as his physical condition deteriorated. With stylised graphics illuminating the theories, and Philip Glass's score imbuing them with a suitable sense of awesomeness, this is a fascinating study of both the man and his ideas.

Dir Errol Morris • *Scr* Stephen Hawking, from his book

Brigadoon ★★★★ U

Musical   1954 · US · Colour · 103mins

A beguiling MGM version of Alan Jay Lerner and Frederick Loewe's magical stage musical about the Scottish village that comes to life every hundred years. It boasts a wonderful score and magnificent arrangements, plus an imaginative studio set. Yet the real heart of the film lies in the casting. The great Gene Kelly could not be bettered as the American in love in a faraway time and a foreign clime. His duet with Cyd Charisse, *The Heather on the Hill*, is enchanting (though, sadly, it was deleted from the British cinema version of the film) and, as Kelly's buddy-in-booze, Van Johnson positively shines. This is an overlooked and often derided movie in director Vincente Minnelli's canon – time has proved such harsh judgement unjustified. 🖭

Gene Kelly *Tommy Albright* • Van Johnson *Jeff Douglas* • Cyd Charisse *Fiona Campbell* • Elaine Stewart *Jane Ashton* • Barry Jones *Mr Lundie* • Hugh Laing *Harry Beaton* • Albert Sharpe *Andrew Campbell* • Virginia Bosler *Jean Campbell* ■ *Dir* Vincente Minnelli • *Scr* Alan Jay Lerner, from the musical by Alan Jay Lerner, Frederick Loewe • *Choreographer* Gene Kelly • *Art Director* Cedric Gibbons, Preston Ames • *Set Designer* Edwin B Willis, Keogh Gleason • *Costume Designer* Irene

Brigham Young ★★

Historical drama   1940 · US · BW · 112mins

It was jolly difficult to tell the true story of the Mormon trek westward when the censor forbade polygamy on the screen. Director Henry Hathaway gets around this by ignoring the facts and concentrating instead on such eye-catching events as an impressive locust attack on the Mormons' first spring crop. Tyrone Power and Linda Darnell are top billed, but the title role is played by Dean Jagger with his customary sense of rugged integrity and conviction. The sequence depicting the lynching of Joseph Smith (Vincent Price) is impressive, but the movie subsequently takes on a solemnity of tone from which it never really recovers.

Tyrone Power *Jonathan Kent* • Linda Darnell *Zina Webb* • Dean Jagger *Brigham Young* • Brian Donlevy *Angus Duncan* • Jane Darwell *Eliza Kent* • John Carradine *Porter Rockwell* • Mary Astor *Mary Ann Young* • Vincent Price *Joseph Smith* • Jean Rogers *Clara Young* ■ *Dir* Henry Hathaway • *Scr* Lamar Trotti, from the story by Louis Bromfield

Bright Angel ★★ 15

Road movie   1990 · US · Colour · 89mins

A heavenly cast are rather lost at sea in this over-stylised thriller from director Michael Fields. Mulroney plays a Montana boy inveigled by a runaway hippy (Lili Taylor) to go to Wyoming and find a man who will spring her brother from jail. A pair of innocents, their road trip places them up to their necks in unpleasant but interesting characters. Fans of *Drugstore Cowboy* may like this depressing examination of

Midwest life, drifters and "Generation X". 🖭

Dermot Mulroney *George Russell* • Lili Taylor *Lucy* • Sam Shepard *Jack Russell* • Valerie Perrine *Aileen Russell* • Burt Young *Art Falcone* • Bill Pullman *Bob* • Benjamin Bratt *Claude* • Mary Kay Place *Judy* • Delroy Lindo *Harley* ■ *Dir* Michael Fields • *Scr* Richard Ford

Bright Eyes ★★

Comedy   1934 · US · BW · 84mins

A must for Shirley Temple fans (but others beware) as here, at six years' old, she performs her most famous song, *On the Good Ship Lollipop*. In the last of some ten 1934 screen appearances, the hard-working moppet is the daughter of a maid killed in a road accident. Her mother's employers grudgingly look after Temple to keep in with a rich relative (Charles Sellon) who dotes on her. In memorable contrast to Hollywood's favourite moppet is Jane Withers in her first substantial role as a spoiled and sadistic brat. Two years older than Temple, she went on to become a child star in her own right.

Shirley Temple *Shirley Blake* • James Dunn *Loop Merritt* • Jane Darwell *Mrs Higgins* • Judith Allen *Adele Martin* • Lois Wilson *Mary Blake* • Charles Sellon *Uncle Ned Smith* • Walter Johnson *Thomas, the chauffeur* • Jane Withers *Joy Smythe* ■ *Dir* David Butler • *Scr* William Conselman, Edwin Burke, David Butler

Bright Leaf ★★

Drama   1950 · US · BW · 110mins

After appearing together in *The Fountainhead*, Gary Cooper and Patricia Neal were reunited for this turgid melodrama, adapted from Foster Fitz-Simons's slow-burning novel about rival tobacco barons. In the middle of a run of mundane movies and not in the best of health, Cooper gives a lazy performance that stands in stark contrast to Donald Crisp and Neal, who both overact wildly as the father and daughter who seek to ruin him. Director Michael Curtiz could scarcely coax better out of Lauren Bacall, but there's always Karl Freund's lush photography to help pass the time.

Gary Cooper *Brant Royle* • Lauren Bacall *Sonia Kovac* • Patricia Neal *Margaret Jane Singleton* • Jack Carson *Chris Malley* • Donald Crisp *Major James Singleton* • Gladys George *Rose* • Elizabeth Patterson *Tabitha Jackson* ■ *Dir* Michael Curtiz • *Scr* Ranald MacDougall, from the novel by Foster Fitz-Simons

Bright Lights, Big City ★★ 18

Drama   1988 · US · Colour · 102mins

The archetypal eighties movie, this has oodles of RayBans, credit cards, minimalist furniture, naked ambition and enough South American nose candy to make antihero Michael J Fox's coffee table look like Mount Kilimanjaro. At the time, though, it all creaked and groaned, largely due to Fox's inability to portray the complexities of an aspiring young New York novelist on the skids. Phoebe Cates turns in a pleasing performance as Fox's disillusioned wife, while two-time Oscar winner Dianne Wiest is predictably superb as his mother in the deathbed flashback scene. However, Fox and his grungy chum Kiefer

Sutherland are wholly unsympathetic. Contains swearing and drug abuse. 🖭

Michael J Fox *Jamie Conway* • Kiefer Sutherland *Tad Allagash* • Phoebe Cates *Amanda* • Swoosie Kurtz *Megan* • Frances Sternhagen *Clara Tillinghast* • Tracy Pollan *Vicky* • John Houseman *Mr Vogel* • Charlie Schlatter *Michael* • Jason Robards Jr *Alex Hardy* • Dianne Wiest *Mother* ■ *Dir* James Bridges • *Scr* Jay McInerney, from his novel

Bright Road ★★★ U

Drama   1953 · US · BW · 68mins

A modest second feature, this is about a pupil (Philip Hepburn) in an all-black school, emotionally troubled as a result of racism and a depressed home life, who overcomes his difficulties with the dedicated help of sympathetic teacher Dorothy Dandridge. It's a worthy, well-acted effort with some touching moments, but it's hampered by a screenplay that pulls its punches and deprives itself of dramatic opportunities.

Dorothy Dandridge *Jane Richards* • Philip Hepburn *CT Young* • Harry Belafonte *School principal* • Barbara Ann Sanders *Tanya* • Robert Horton *Dr Mitchell* • Maidie Norman *Tanya's mother* • Renee Beard *Booker T Jones* ■ *Dir* Gerald Mayer • *Scr* Emmett Lavery, from the short story *See How They Run* by Mary Elizabeth Vroman

Bright Victory ★★★

Drama   1951 · US · BW · 97mins

Blinded in the war, soldier Arthur Kennedy faces another kind of battle as he attempts to adjust to his disability, first in hospital, then back home, where his girlfriend Julia Adams is waiting for him. Further emotional complications arise through his relationship with Peggy Dow he meets while in hospital. A moving, if sentimental drama, this is lent added interest by its insight into the rehabilitation methods for the blind. Kennedy gives a superbly convincing performance that earned him a deserved Oscar nomination.

Arthur Kennedy *Larry Nevins* • Peggy Dow *Judy Greene* • Julia Adams [Julie Adams] *Chris Paterson* • James Edwards *Joe Morgan* • Will Geer *Mr Nevins* • Minor Watson *Mr Paterson* • Jim Backus *Bill Grayson* • Joan Banks *Janet Grayson* • Rock Hudson *Cpl John Flagg* ■ *Dir* Mark Robson • *Scr* Robert Buckner, from the novel *Lights Out* by Bayard Kendrick

A Brighter Summer Day ★★★★★

Drama   1991 · Tai · Colour · 185mins

Rather overshadowed by his better-known and much-lauded compatriot Hou Hsiao-Hsien on the international stage, director Edward Yang is still a remarkable film-maker in his own right. Sharing many of the themes of Hou's *A City of Sadness* (which Yang produced), this sprawling, stately epic presents a compelling portrait of growing up in a young nation that was itself struggling to find its identity after the break with China. Three years in the making, it was inspired by a true event encapsulated in the Taiwanese title that translates as *Incident of a Juvenile Murder on Ku Ling Street*. The gang war is less interesting than the social comment, but this is

undoubtedly the work of a master. In Mandarin with English subtitles.

Zhen Zhang *Xiao S'ir (Zhang Zhen)* • Lisa Yang *Ming (Liu Zhiming)* • Zhang Guozhu *Zhang Ju (Father)* • Elaine Jin *Mrs Zhang (Mother)* • Wang Juan *Juan (Eldest sister)* • Zhang Han *Lao Er (Elder brother)* • Jiang Xiuqiong *Qiong (Middle sister)* • Lai Fanyun *Yun (Youngest sister)* ■ *Dir* Edward Yang • *Scr* Edward Yang, Yan Hongya, Yang Shunqing, Lai Mingtang

Brighton Beach Memoirs
★★★ 15

Comedy drama 1986 · US · Colour · 104mins

Neil Simon is an expert at angst-ridden autobiography and loves to mine the seam of Jewish family life. Nobody does this particular brand of head-banging better, and this slice of strudel bakes a lovely, acerbic portrayal from Jonathan Silverman as Simon's adolescent doppelgänger, Eugene Jerome. However, Simon has failed to open out his original stage play enough for the film version to breathe. ▭

Jonathan Silverman *Eugene* • Blythe Danner *Kate* • Bob Dishy *Jack* • Brian Drillinger *Stanley* • Stacey Glick *Laurie* • Judith Ivey *Blanche* • Lisa Waltz *Nora* ■ *Dir* Gene Saks • *Scr* Neil Simon, from his play

Brighton Rock
★★★★ PG

Film noir 1947 · UK · BW · 88mins

Released in America as *Young Scarface*, this is one of the most sinister crime films ever made in Britain, and, but for several cuts by the censor, it would also have been one of the most shocking. However, Graham Greene, scripting from his own novel (not in collaboration with Terence Rattigan, as many sources state), also drew some of the film's teeth in a hugely contrived happy ending that was given a glutinously spiritual slant by director John Boulting. Richard Attenborough was never better as Pinkie the teenage gangster, and he is magnificently supported by William Hartnell and the under-rated Carol Marsh as Rose. ▭

Richard Attenborough *Pinkie Brown* • Hermione Baddeley *Ida Arnold* • William Hartnell *Dallow* • Carol Marsh *Rose* • Nigel Stock *Cubitt* • Wylie Watson *Spicer* • Harcourt Williams *Prewitt* • Alan Wheatley *Fred Hale/Kolley Kibber* ■ *Dir* John Boulting • *Scr* Graham Greene, from his novel

The Brighton Strangler
★★★

Thriller 1945 · US · BW · 67mins

Set in Britain during the Second World War, but filmed (extremely quickly and cheaply) in Hollywood, this intriguing little programme filler was directed by Max Nosseck, whose bizarre career ranges from directing Buster Keaton in French, through a notable Yiddish-language feature, *Overture to Glory*, to the fifties nudist comedy, *Garden of Eden*. This stars a rather wooden John Loder, who appears on stage as "the Brighton Strangler", and, after a blow to the head, begins to live out his stage role in real life. Cleverly done, and really quite eerie, this is well worth catching on a dark night. After a few more movies on this scale, John Loder returned to England and eventually

wrote a racy autobiography called *Hollywood Hussar*.

John Loder *Reginald/Edward* • June Duprez *April* • Michael St Angel *Bob* • Miles Mander *Allison* • Rose Hobart *Dorothy* • Gilbert Emery *Dr Manby* • Rex Evans *Shelton* • Matthew Boulton *Inspector Graham* ■ *Dir* Max Nosseck • *Scr* Arnold Phillips, Max Nosseck

Brighty of the Grand Canyon
★★

Western 1966 · US · Colour · 89mins

This is a harmless, fairly humorous family film about a clever mule who teams up with an elderly gold prospector, played by Dick Foran. Norman Foster's film, based on the novel by Marguerite Henry and shot on location, also features Joseph Cotten, while Karl Swenson plays Theodore Roosevelt. The real star, however, is the Grand Canyon itself.

Joseph Cotten *Jim* • Pat Conway *Jake Irons* • Dick Foran *Old Timer* • Karl Swenson *Theodore Roosevelt* • Dandy Curran *Homer Hobbs* ■ *Dir* Norman Foster • *Scr* Norman Foster, from the novel by Marguerite Henry

A Brilliant Disguise
★★ 18

Erotic thriller 1993 · US · Colour · 92mins

English TV star Lysette Anthony ditched her Goody Two-Shoes image when she crossed the Atlantic and ended up in a number of very naughty straight-to-video thrillers, such as this adequate but routine erotic caper. Anthony John Denison is the dupe who falls under the spell of the increasingly disturbed Ms Anthony; Corbin Bernsen is the shrink who may or may not have her best interests at heart. Pretty steamy at times, though not particularly convincing, this offers no real surprises in plotting or direction. Contains violence. ▭

Lysette Anthony *Michelle* • Anthony John Denison *Andy Minola* • Corbin Bernsen *Dr Martin* ■ *Dir* Nick Vallelonga • *Scr* Nick Vallelonga, Maurice Berger

Brilliant Lies
★★

Courtroom drama 1996 · Ausl · Colour · 93mins

Based on David Williamson's play and co-written by director Richard Franklin, this is a real battle between the sexes. It has a similar theme to David Mamet's *Oleanna* – here Gia Carides plays an embittered employee who accuses her boss Anthony LaPaglia of sexual harassment and unfair dismissal. The two take their case to court, inveigling the support of others along the way, and gradually the truth comes out. This is entertaining and engaging, and features some original filmic stylistics, but the problem is that both principles appear conniving and unsympathetic. By failing to evoke our sympathies, Franklin makes this a one-dimensional affair.

Gia Carides *Susy Connor* • Anthony LaPaglia *Gary Fitzgerald* • Zoe Carides *Katy Connor* • Ray Barrett *Brian Connor* • Michael Veitch *Paul Connor* • Catherine Wilkin *Marion Lee* • Neil Melville *Vince Williams* • Jennifer Jarman Walker *Ruth Miller* ■ *Dir* Richard Franklin • *Scr* Richard Franklin, Peter Fitzpatrick, from the play by David Williamson

Brimstone and Treacle
★★★

Black comedy thriller 1982 · UK · Colour · 86mins

The movie version of Dennis Potter's controversial television play (taped by the BBC, but then promptly banned) emerges as an uneven and theatrical thriller with dark religious underpinnings. Demonic Sting is the cunning stranger who worms his way into the household of an atheist hymn composer (Denholm Elliot), his devout wife (Joan Plowright) and their comatose daughter (Suzanna Hamilton) for nefarious reasons. It's persuasively performed and typical Potter – by turns unpleasant and thought-provoking – but director Richard Loncraine goes for mood and atmosphere above any sense of logic or reality. DVD

Sting *Martin Taylor* • Denholm Elliott *Thomas Bates* • Joan Plowright *Norma Bates* • Suzanna Hamilton *Patricia Bates* • Mary McLeod *Valerie Holdsworth* • Benjamin Whitrow *Businessman* ■ *Dir* Richard Loncraine • *Scr* Dennis Potter

Bring Me the Head of Alfredo Garcia
★★★ 18

Crime drama 1974 · US · Colour · 107mins

Sam Peckinpah's enormous talent was on the wane when he made this gruesome, grave-robbing Mexican crime drama. But, if you can bear to look beneath its gory exterior, as piano player Warren Oates becomes caught up with bounty hunters pursuing *that* head for a wealthy landowner, there are still enough moments when Peckinpah's greatness shines through. Excitingly told, this is like the *The Wild Bunch* – but even wilder. Contains swearing, violence and nudity. ▭

Warren Oates *Bennie* • Isela Vega *Elita* • Gig Young *Quill* • Robert Webber *Sappensly* • Helmut Dantine *Max* • Emilio Fernandez *El Jefe* • Kris Kristofferson *Paco* • Chano Urueta *One-armed bartender* ■ *Dir* Sam Peckinpah • *Scr* Sam Peckinpah, Gordon Dawson, from a story by Frank Kowalski

Bring Me the Head of Dobie Gillis
★★ U

Comedy 1988 · US · Colour · 93mins

Just when it seemed there was no film idea, television series or comic book hero that hadn't been dusted down, along came this film which, typically, puts nostalgia ahead of invention. *The Many Loves of Dobie Gillis* was a popular series that ran from 1959 to 1963, and fond memories secured a sizeable audience for this TV movie. Here Dobie (original star Dwayne Hickman) is buffeted between the attentions of the super-rich Thalia (Connie Stevens replacing Tuesday Weld) and his devoted wife Zelda (Sheila James). There's little chance of surprise, though the film does possess a degree of light charm. ▭

Dwayne Hickman *Dobie Gillis* • Bob Denver *Maynard G Krebs* • Connie Stevens *Thalia Menninger* • Sheila James *Zelda* • Scott Grimes *Georgie* • Tricia Leigh Fisher *Chatsie* ■ *Dir* Stanley Z Cherry • *Scr* Deborah Zoe Dawson, Victoria Johns, Stanley Z Cherry, from characters created by Max Schulman

Bring Me the Head of Mavis Davis
★ 15

Comedy 1997 · UK · Colour · 95mins

Another British comedy failure in the same vein as *Mad Cows*. Not even director John Henderson and actors Jane Horrocks and Danny Aiello can enliven a clumsy script and naff scenario. Rik Mayall overacts for England as a record producer who realises that his pride and joy, singer Horrocks, is worth more to him dead than alive. So he hires a hitman to do the dirty. Mayall's shouting and Horrocks's shrieking make earplugs a necessity, and there are some pretty unpleasant gags to boot. Contains swearing and violence.

Rik Mayall *Marty Starr* • Jane Horrocks *Marla Dorland* • Danny Aiello *Rathbone* • Ronald Pickup *Percy Stone* • Philip Martin Brown *Inspector Furse* • Ross Boatman *Rock star* • Paul Shearer *Presenter 1980* • Stuart Bunce *Aspirant* ■ *Dir* John Henderson • *Scr* Craig Strachan, from an idea by Joanne Reay

Bring on the Girls
★★

Romantic musical comedy 1945 · US · Colour · 91mins

A disingenuous millionaire (Eddie Bracken) joins the navy hoping that, as a humble sailor, he'll find a girl who'll love him for himself. Around such thin stuff is woven a feeble assembly-line musical comedy which, under Sidney Lanfield's dull direction, wastes the considerable talents of Bracken, star of such gems as *Hail the Conquering Hero*. Sonny Tufts plays Bracken's buddy; Veronica Lake and Marjorie Reynolds are the girls they hitch up with. Spike Jones and his City Slickers provide the musical high spot – if you like that sort of thing.

Veronica Lake *Teddy Collins* • Sonny Tufts *Phil North* • Eddie Bracken *J Newport Bates* • Marjorie Reynolds *Sue Thomas* • Grant Mitchell *Uncle Ralph* • Johnny Coy *Benny Lowe* • Peter Whitney *Swede* ■ *Dir* Sidney Lanfield • *Scr* Karl Tunberg, Darrell Ware, from a story by Pierre Wolff

Bring On the Night
★★ 15

Music documentary 1985 · UK · Colour · 96mins

As the brains behind TV's seminal *7 Up* series, Michael Apted is no stranger to documentary. But he fails to prevent this behind-the-scenes account of Sting's *Dream of the Blue Turtles* tour from becoming a pretentious, self-glorifying vehicle for the one-time Police front man. While it's fascinating to watch him rehearsing his new band in a palatial French mansion, the talking-head pieces (whether discussions of music or more serious issues) are less than inspiring. The songs, however, with their jazz-rock feel, are superb. But did he really have to end the film with the birth of his son to the accompaniment of the song *Russians*? ▭

Dir Michael Apted

Bring Your Smile Along
★★★

Musical comedy 1955 · US · Colour · 83mins

The dynamic singer Frankie Laine made five musicals for producer Jonie Taps in the fifties and this is the best, brightened by the assured comic touch of writer/director Blake Edwards, making his directorial debut. (*Breakfast at Tiffany's* and *The Pink Panther* were to follow several years later.) The plot, which has a timid schoolmarm venturing to the big city and writing the lyrics for a string of hit songs recorded by Laine, is an amusing trifle, filling the spaces between Frankie's electrifying musical renditions.

Frankie Laine *Jerry Dennis* • Keefe Brasselle *Martin Adams* • Constance Towers *Nancy Willows* • Lucy Marlow *Marge Stevenson* • William Leslie *David Parker* • Mario Siletti *Ricardo* • Ruth Warren *Landlady* • Jack Albertson *Jenson* ■ *Dir* Blake Edwards • *Scr* Blake Edwards, from a story by Blake Edwards, from a story by Richard Quine

Bringing out the Dead ★★★ 18

Drama 1999 · US · Colour · 115mins

Martin Scorsese lends his customary intensity and visual razzle-dazzle to this 72-hour insight into the exhausting lives of New York paramedics. The director reunites with his *Taxi Driver* collaborator Paul Schrader to conjure up a powerful, blackly comic and often hallucinatory portrait of this most emotionally demanding of careers. Nicolas Cage is perfectly cast as crumbling protagonist Frank Pierce. However, the other performances are so unhinged (mad medics Tom Sizemore and Ving Rhames especially), and the episodic encounters so overwrought, that the drama never really grabs as it should. Once again, though, Scorsese proves himself to be one of the most technically creative and thematically audacious film-makers on the planet. DVD

Nicolas Cage *Frank Pierce* • Patricia Arquette *Mary Burke* • John Goodman *Larry* • Ving Rhames *Marcus* • Tom Sizemore *Tom Wolls* • Marc Anthony *Noel* • Mary Beth Hurt *Nurse Constance* • Martin Scorsese *Dispatcher* ■ *Dir* Martin Scorsese • *Scr* Paul Schrader, from the novel by Joe Connelly

Bringing Up Baby ★★★★★ U

Comedy 1938 · US · BW · 102mins

How sublime can movies get? This is perfectly cast (Katharine Hepburn in a celebrated screwball role), brilliantly written by Hagar Wilde and *Stagecoach's* Dudley Nichols, and fabulously well directed by Howard Hawks. It's a genuinely funny original that repays repeated viewings, especially to marvel at the variety of subtle expressions on the face of "Professor" Cary Grant, in one of the most wonderful comic performances ever to grace the silver screen. Regarded as too wacky by half when it was released, this shimmering dissection of the male-female relationship is now regarded as a classic. By the way, "Baby" is a pet leopard.

Cary Grant *David Huxley* • Katharine Hepburn *Susan Vance* • May Robson *Aunt Elizabeth* • Charlie Ruggles [Charles Ruggles] *Major Horace Applegate* • Barry Fitzgerald *Mr Gogarty* • George Irving *Alexander Peabody* • Walter Catlett *Constable Slocum* • Fritz Feld *Dr Lehmann* ■ *Dir* Howard Hawks • *Scr* Dudley Nichols, Hagar Wilde, from a story by Hagar Wilde • *Cinematographer* Russell Metty • *Art Director* Van Nest Polglase

The Brink's Job ★★★ PG

Comedy crime 1978 · US · Colour · 98mins

Having hit the big time with *The French Connection* and *The Exorcist*, director William Friedkin opted for a distinct change of pace with this wild, but often hugely entertaining heist comedy. Re-creating what was then dubbed "the crime of the century", it stars Peter Falk as the leader of a gang of amateur crooks who knock over a Boston security firm to the tune of nearly $3 million. The art direction team notched up an Oscar nomination for their stylish period designs, but it's the cast that catches the eye, with Warren Oates a standout as Falk's doltish sidekick.

Peter Falk *Tony Pino* • Peter Boyle *Joe McGinnis* • Allen Goorwitz [Allen Garfield] *Vinnie Costa* • Warren Oates *Specs O'Keefe* • Gena Rowlands *Mary Pino* • Paul Sorvino *Jazz Maffie* • Sheldon Leonard *J Edgar Hoover* • Gerard Murphy *Sandy Richardson* ■ *Dir* William Friedkin • *Scr* Walon Green, from the book *Big Stick Up at Brink's* by Noel Behn • *Art Director* Dean Tavoularis, Angelo Graham • *Set Designer* George R Nelson, Bruce Kay

Britannia Hospital ★★★ 15

Black comedy 1982 · UK · Colour · 111mins

Director Lindsay Anderson's top-heavy symbolism all but crushes the satirical life out of this attempt to lampoon the state of the nation, with a run-down hospital expecting a royal visit to celebrate its 500th anniversary used as a metaphor for Britain's moral decay. Media hacks, strike-bent workers, bureaucratic chaos and sinister laboratory experiments are Anderson's targets, although the burlesque humour makes it seem closer to "Carry On Casualty". Malcolm McDowell, Anderson's favourite hero, is the journalist who wanders through NHS chaos in a film saved by some of Britain's finest character actors. Contains violence, swearing and nudity.

Leonard Rossiter *Potter* • Graham Crowden *Millar* • Malcolm McDowell *Mike* • Joan Plowright *Phyllis* • Marsha A Hunt *Amanda* • Frank Grimes *Fred* • Jill Bennett *MacMillan* • Robin Askwith • Peter Jeffrey • Fulton Mackay • John Moffatt • Dandy Nichols • Alan Bates ■ *Dir* Lindsay Anderson • *Scr* David Sherwin

Britannia Mews ★★★

Drama 1949 · UK · BW · 91mins

Twentieth Century-Fox made this interesting version of part of Margery Sharp's excellent but dour novel about Victorian class relationships to use up part of their frozen UK assets. It's a striking and original film, though undermined by the bizarre casting of the usually dependable Dana Andrews in a dual role as Maureen O'Hara's two husbands, in one of which he is rather weirdly revoiced. Nevertheless, O'Hara is striking as ever and the British contingent, which includes Dame Sybil Thorndike as a wretched hag, makes this sordid opus compulsively watchable.

Maureen O'Hara *Adelaide Culver* • Dana Andrews *Gilbert Lauderdale/Henry Lambert* • Sybil Thorndike *Mrs Mounsey* • June Allen *Adelaide as a child* • Anthony Tancred *Treff Culver* • Anthony Lamb *Treff as a child* • Wilfrid Hyde White *Mr Culver* • Fay Compton *Mrs Culver* ■ *Dir* Jean Negulesco • *Scr* Ring Lardner Jr, from the novel by Margery Sharp

British Agent ★★★ U

Historical drama 1934 · US · BW · 79mins

This historical drama dares to show ungentlemanly conduct on the part of the British Government, which is here shown trying to stop the Bolsheviks making peace with Germany in 1917. Leslie Howard stars as Britain's unofficial representative, who is readily betrayed when he becomes a political embarrassment to his country. Luckily, he has more on his mind than politics after meeting the delectable Kay Francis, who is – as she puts it – a woman first and a Russian agent second. Laird Doyle's screenplay is often tiresome, but director Michael Curtiz brings his usual pace and visual flair to the proceedings.

Leslie Howard *Stephen Locke* • Kay Francis *Elena* • William Gargan *Medill* • Phillip Reed [Philip Reed] *Gaston LaFarge* • Irving Pichel *Pavlov* • Walter Byron *Stanley* • Cesar Romero *Tito Del Val* • J Carrol Naish *Commissioner for War* ■ *Dir* Michael Curtiz • *Scr* Laird Doyle, from a novel by RH Bruce Lockhart

Broadcast News ★★★★ 15

Comedy drama 1987 · US · Colour · 126mins

The self-serving natures of three Washington-based TV journalists form the focus of James L Brooks's sweet-and-sour comedy of superegos pursuing serious news, but ending up with spurious glamour. Undervalued William Hurt, as a newscaster who can bring phoney tears to his eyes, is one corner of a romantic triangle; the underused Albert Brooks, as a seasoned investigator, is another. But it's Holly Hunter, as the hard-nosed producer and object of their attentions (long before her Oscar-winning role in *The Piano*) who really provokes the sorrow and the pity of lives at the mercy of their careers. Contains swearing and brief nudity.

William Hurt *Tom Grunick* • Albert Brooks *Aaron Altman* • Holly Hunter *Jane Craig* • Jack Nicholson *Bill Rorich, news anchor* • Lois Chiles *Jennifer Mack* • Joan Cusack *Blair Litton* • Peter Hackes *Paul Moore* • Christian Clemenson *Bobby* ■ *Dir/Scr* James L Brooks

Broadway ★★★

Musical melodrama
1929 · US · BW and Colour · 105mins

This film version of the Broadway stage hit is one of the most eye-catching of the early sound musicals, boasting elaborate settings for its production numbers. It also has an entertainingly suspenseful plot, in which a young Broadway dancer (Glenn Tryon) becomes unwittingly caught up in a murder. Robert Ellis is an effective villain, while Evelyn Brent scores as a chorus girl. Director Paul Fejos devised a versatile and high-speed crane specially for the film, and the climactic nightclub sequence is photographed in "natural" colour.

Glenn Tryon *Roy Lane* • Evelyn Brent *Pearl* • Merna Kennedy *Billie Moore* • Thomas E Jackson *Dan McCorn* • Robert Ellis *Steve Crandall* • Otis Harlan *"Porky" Thompson* • Paul Porcasi *Nick Verdis* • Marion Lord *Lil Rice* ■ *Dir* Paul Fejos • *Scr* Edward T Lowe Jr, Charles Furthman, from the play by Philip Dunning, George Abbott • *Cinematographer* Hal Mohr • *Choreographer* Maurice L Kusell

Broadway ★★★

Crime drama 1942 · US · BW · 91mins

George Raft stars in this remake of the 1929 musical, which was taken, in turn, from a 1927 Broadway hit. This version is a crime melodrama with a decent helping of snappy songs, some dance and the neat twist of having Raft play himself. As he reminisces about the Roaring Twenties, when bootleggers and mobsters were part of the New York showbiz scene, his memories fold into flashback to tell a tale of backstage murder in which he once found himself involved. Broderick Crawford is excellent as the villain of the piece, Janet Blair is Raft's girlfriend and dance partner, and Pat O'Brien plays a detective.

George Raft • Pat O'Brien *Dan McCorn* • Janet Blair *Billie* • Broderick Crawford *Steve Crandall* • Marjorie Rambeau *Lili* • Anne Gwynne *Pearl* • SZ Sakall *Nick* • Edward S Brophy [Edward Brophy] *Porky* ■ *Dir* William A Seiter • *Scr* Felix Jackson, John Bright, from the play by Philip Dunning, George Abbott

Broadway Bill ★★★ U

Drama 1934 · US · BW · 102mins

The title is the name of the racehorse bought by businessman Warner Baxter, who gives up everything to run the horse. Baxter's sister-in-law Myrna Loy believes in him, so therefore we all should. A Frank Capra movie, this is simply brimming over with nice people and good intentions – you may find a little of it goes a long way, but then you'd be being churlish. Capra remade it in 1950 as *Riding High* with Bing Crosby (who, unlike Warner Baxter, actually liked horses). He used great chunks of this film, even going so far as to cast some of the same character actors so that the scenes would match. Both versions are very likeable. Watch this closely and don't blink – that's a very young Lucille Ball handling the telephones.

Warner Baxter *Dan Brooks* • Myrna Loy *Alice Higgins* • Walter Connolly *JL Higgins* • Raymond Walburn *Colonel Pettigrew* • Clarence Muse *Whitey* • Helen Vinson *Margaret Brooks* • Douglass Dumbrille *Eddie Morgan* • Lynne Overman *Happy McGuire* ■ *Dir* Frank Capra • *Scr* Robert Riskin, from a story by Mark Hellinger, Lucille Ball

Broadway Bound ★★★ PG

Comedy drama 1991 · US · Colour · 89mins

Has any modern playwright made as many dramatic mountains out of his life's domestic molehills as Neil Simon? Made as a TV movie but shown in cinemas in Britain, this is the final segment – its predecessors were *Brighton Beach Memoirs* and *Biloxi Blues* – of an autobiographical trilogy. Here, Simon's alter ego Eugene makes it to the big time with his brother Stan, leaving behind a grumbling grandfather and an embattled mother and father. Jonathan Silverman, Anne Bancroft and Hume Cronyn skilfully put acting flesh on skeletal memory, but the material is thin.

Anne Bancroft *Kate Jerome* • Hume Cronyn *Ben* • Corey Parker *Eugene Morris Jerome* • Jonathan Silverman *Stan Jerome* • Jerry

Orbach *Jack Jerome* • Michele Lee *Blanche* • Marilyn Cooper *Mrs Pitkin* • Pat McCormick *Announcer* ■ *Dir* Paul Bogart • *Scr* Neil Simon, from his play

Broadway Danny Rose ★★★★ PG

Comedy   1984 · US · BW · 80mins

Romping gleefully rather than analysing deeply, Woody Allen as director, writer and star brings his own light touch to every frame of this film. Putting egotistical, arty Manhattan on hold, and cutting down on his verbal wit to boot, Allen rings the changes not only by taking us to the swamps of New Jersey but also by squeezing humour primarily from situation and character rather than dialogue. Allen the director keeps the caper aspect on a beautifully tight leash at all times and, as the star, he fairly sparkles with eccentricity as a small-fry showbiz agent, while Mia Farrow is amusingly, nasally blunt as a gangster's moll with daft hair. Contains some violence. 🎞

Woody Allen *Danny Rose* • Mia Farrow *Tina Vitale* • Nick Apollo Forte *Lou Canova* • Craig Vandenburgh *Ray Webb* • Herb Reynolds *Barney Dunn* • Paul Greco *Vito Rispoli* • Frank Renzulli *Joe Rispoli* • Edwin Bordo *Johnny Rispoli* ■ *Dir/Scr* Woody Allen

Broadway Limited ★ U

Comedy   1941 · US · BW · 75mins

Producer Hal Roach wasn't trying very hard with this weak farce. Like the John Barrymore classic, *Twentieth Century*, the film is named after a Chicago to New York express train and concerns showbiz shenanigans. Here they're provided by Leonid Kinskey's wily Russian film producer, Marjorie Woodworth as his hot young film star, ZaSu Pitts as the president of her fan club, and Patsy Kelly as her loyal secretary. Victor McLaglen appears as the railroad engineer who finds a baby for the star as a publicity stunt, and Dennis O'Keefe plays her true love. Woodworth was touted as the new Jean Harlow, but she doesn't make much of an impact.

Victor McLaglen *Mike* • Marjorie Woodworth *April* • Patsy Kelly *Patsy* • Dennis O'Keefe *Dr Harvey North* • ZaSu Pitts *Myra* • Leonid Kinskey *Ivan* ■ *Dir* Gordon Douglas • *Scr* Rian James

The Broadway Melody ★★★

Musical comedy   1929 · US · BW · 102mins

The first Hollywood musical, and the prototype for the backstage musical romance that grew, flourished and evolved to become a unique cinematic art form for some three decades. Bessie Love and Anita Page star as a vaudeville sister act, vying for the attentions of dancer Charles King. The drama is woven around a marvellous musical score that includes the enduring title number, as well as the even more ageless *Give My Regards to Broadway*. The movie was voted best picture at the 1928/1929 Oscar ceremony – only the second – with nominations for director Harry Beaumont and Love. Made by MGM, whose musicals would form a genre of their own in years to come, it seems stylistically dated and the staging, hampered by the early static camera,

looks primitive. But it's history, and there is much to enjoy.

Anita Page *Queenie* • Bessie Love *Hank* • Charles King *Eddie* • Jed Prouty *Uncle Jed* • Kenneth Thomson *Jock Warriner* • Edward Dillon *Stage manager* • Mary Doran *Blonde* • JE Beck *Bebe Hatrick* • Marshall Ruth *Stew* ■ *Dir* Harry Beaumont • *Scr* James Gleason, Norman Houston, Sarah Y Mason, from a story by Edmund Goulding • *Art Director* Cedric Gibbons

Broadway Melody of 1936 ★★★★ U

Musical comedy   1935 · US · BW · 100mins

A terrific, warm and wonderful MGM follow-up to its smash hit *The Broadway Melody*, this has a fabulous Arthur Freed and Nacio Herb Brown score, which includes most of those songs that you probably heard for the first time in *Singin' in the Rain*. Eleanor Powell is devastating as a dancer, and she is well backed by Jack Benny as a theatre columnist and handsome hero Robert Taylor. Taylor actually sings quite charmingly, though he's no threat to Bing Crosby. Powell taps up a storm, and her *I've Got a Feeling You're Fooling* picked up the dance direction Oscar for choreographer Dave Gould. This is swell stuff, and with numbers such as *Broadway Rhythm* and *You Are My Lucky Star*, who could ask for more?

Jack Benny *Bert Keeler* • Eleanor Powell *Irene Foster* • Robert Taylor (1) *Bob Gordon* • Una Merkel *Kitty Corbett* • Sid Silvers *Snoop* • Buddy Ebsen *Ted* • June Knight *Lillian Brent* • Vilma Ebsen *Sally* ■ *Dir* Roy Del Ruth • *Scr* Jack McGowan, Sid Silvers, Harry Cohn, from a story by Moss Hart • *Choreographer* Dave Gould • *Music Director* Alfred Newman

Broadway Melody of 1938 ★★★ U

Musical comedy   1937 · US · BW · 105mins

For connoisseurs, this contains some knockout routines from that fabulous tap dancer Eleanor Powell. On the singing side, there's Sophie Tucker putting her all into *Your Broadway and My Broadway*, but for fans of Judy Garland, it has something unforgettable – the song *Dear Mr Gable*. It was originally written to be performed at a birthday party on the MGM lot, sung by the young Garland to the tune of the standard *You Made Me Love You*, with additional lyrics by Roger Edens. When studio boss Louis B Mayer heard it, he ordered it to be filmed for posterity. This wonderful sequence is in itself a good reason for watching. 🎞

Robert Taylor (1) *Steve Raleigh* • Eleanor Powell *Sally Lee* • George Murphy *Sonny Ledford* • Binnie Barnes *Caroline Whipple* • Buddy Ebsen *Peter Trot* • Sophie Tucker *Alice Clayton* • Judy Garland *Betty Clayton* • Charles Igor Gorin *Nicki Papaloopas* ■ *Dir* Roy Del Ruth • *Scr* Jack McGowan, from a story by Jack McGowan, Sid Silvers • *Music Director* George Stoll

Broadway Melody of 1940 ★★★★★ U

Musical   1940 · US · BW · 101mins

The fourth and last of MGM's great *Broadway Melody* series is perfection in rhythm. Fred Astaire and George Murphy play sparring dance partners,

though together they perform terrifically; the seemingly effortless sophistication of *Please Don't Monkey with Broadway* is utterly beguiling. A masked Douglas McPhail introduces the Cole Porter classic *I Concentrate on You*, but the movie's undoubted highlight is Astaire sublimely performing a tap with toothy Eleanor Powell to Cole's *Begin the Beguine* on a glossy, highly polished black-and-white set. As Frank Sinatra said in *That's Entertainment!*: "You can wait around and hope, but you'll never see its like again."

Fred Astaire *Johnny Brett* • Eleanor Powell *Clara Bennett* • George Murphy *King Shaw* • Frank Morgan *Bob Casey* • Ian Hunter *Bert C Matthews* • Florence Rice *Amy Blake* • Lynne Carver *Emmy Lou Lee* • Ann Morriss *Pearl* ■ *Dir* Norman Taurog • *Scr* Leon Gordon, George Oppenheimer, from a story by Jack MacGowran, Dore Schary • *Music Director* Alfred Newman

Broadway Rhythm ★★ U

Musical   1944 · US · Colour · 114mins

George Murphy stars as a Broadway producer beset by various problems in mounting his extravagant new revue-style show. And that's about the size of it. This particular musical from the MGM stable is excessively lengthy, devoid of any appreciable narrative and directed without flair by Roy del Ruth. What it does offer is an excuse to parade a string of talented performers, including Lena Horne, Gloria DeHaven, Eddie "Rochester" Anderson and the Russ Brothers, an extraordinary trio of contortionists. There are some good songs too, including *Pretty Baby*, *Oh You Beautiful Doll*, *Ida, Sweet as Apple Cider* and Jerome Kern's glorious ballad *All the Things You Are*.

George Murphy *Johnnie Demming* • Ginny Simms *Helen Hoyt* • Charles Winninger *Sam Demming* • Gloria DeHaven *Patsy Demming* • Nancy Walker *Trixie Simpson* • Ben Blue *Felix Gross* • Lena Horne *Fernway De La Fer* • Eddie "Rochester" Anderson *Eddie* ■ *Dir* Roy Del Ruth • *Scr* Dorothy Kingsley, Harry Clark, from a story by Jack McGowan, from the musical *Very Warm for May* by Jerome Kern, Oscar Hammerstein II

Broadway Serenade ★★

Musical   1939 · US · BW · 113mins

Marital problems inevitably arise between a songwriter husband (Lew Ayres) and his singer wife (Jeanette MacDonald) when she soars to stardom and he doesn't. MacDonald, minus Nelson Eddy, doesn't fare too well in this opulent but otherwise leaden offering. She bravely warbles everything from Puccini to a couple of upbeat contemporary numbers, but it doesn't help a lumbering production in which even a grand finale choreographed by Busby Berkeley (his first assignment from MGM after his great Warner Bros years) goes horribly wrong. Robert Z Leonard directs.

Jeanette MacDonald *Mary Hale* • Lew Ayres *James Geoffrey Seymour* • Ian Hunter *Larry Bryant* • Frank Morgan *Cornelius Collier Jr* • Wally Vernon *Joey, the Jinx* • Rita Johnson *Judy Tyrrell* • Virginia Grey *Pearl* ■ *Dir* Robert Z Leonard • *Scr* Charles Lederer, from a story by Lew Lipton, from John Taintor Foote, Hans Kräly

Broadway through a Keyhole ★★★★

Musical   1933 · US · BW · 92mins

Famous New York gossip columnist Walter Winchell wrote the story, using himself and his broadcasts on the Broadway and gangland scenes as a framework for the plot. The story is simple: mobster Paul Kelly falls for decent Constance Cummings and gets her a job in Texas Guinan's nightclub, where the shows are directed by volatile Gregory Ratoff. Grateful Cummings tries to stay loyal, but falls in love with crooner Russ Columbo. Directed with style and pace by Lowell Sherman, with some production numbers clearly influenced by Busby Berkeley, this is a sharp peep into a thirties New York where showbiz and the mob overlap. A cynical and quirky homage to Broadway boasting a string of terrific performances, this musical romance is sophisticated, unusual and vastly entertaining, despite some sentimentality.

Constance Cummings *Joan Whelan* • Russ Columbo *Clark Brian* • Paul Kelly *Hank Rocci* • Blossom Seeley *Sybil Smith* • Gregory Ratoff *Max Mefooski* • Texas Guinan *Tex Kaley* • Hugh O'Connell *Chuck Haskins* ■ *Dir* Lowell Sherman • *Scr* Gene Towne, C Graham Baker, from a story by Walter Winchell • *Music Director* Alfred Newman

Broadway to Hollywood ★★★

Musical   1933 · US · BW and Colour · 87mins

The struggles of a show business family across three generations, with Ted the Third (Eddie Quillan) ending up as a Hollywood star almost half a century after his grandparents (Frank Morgan and the gutsy Alice Brady) started out on the hard road of vaudeville. Written and directed by Willard Mack, this is a very sentimental but extremely lively look at a vanished era. Featuring a 13-year-old Mickey Rooney, it marks the screen debut of Nelson Eddy and includes appearances by Jackie Cooper and Jimmy Durante. It incorporates colour sequences from *The March of Time*, a revue that MGM abandoned halfway through.

Alice Brady *Lulu Hackett* • Frank Morgan *Ted Hackett* • Madge Evans *Anne Ainslee* • Russell Hardie *Ted Hackett Jr* • Jackie Cooper *Ted Hackett Jr as a child* • Eddie Quillan *Ted the Third* • Mickey Rooney *Ted the Third as a child* • Tad Alexander *David* • Jimmy Durante *Hollywood character* • Nelson Eddy *John Sylvester* ■ *Dir* Willard Mack • *Scr* Willard Mack, Edgar Allan Woolf

Brokedown Palace ★★ 12

Prison drama   1999 · US · Colour · 97mins

If it weren't for sterling performances from Claire Danes and Kate Beckinsale, this would be yet another turgid rehash of the plot in which nice American kids get burnt by Bangkok drug laws. After high school, the two friends scoot to the Far East where they are framed for heroin possession. Slammed in a *Tenko*-style women's prison (whose most bizarre inmate is a cockney-accented Amanda de Cadenet), they pin their hopes on renegade lawyer Bill Pullman. The film, subsequently cold-shouldered by both stars, is entirely formulaic, predictable and dull. Given the all-too-evident abilities of Danes and Beckinsale, the true crime here is a flagrant waste of talent. Contains swearing.

Claire Danes *Alice Marano* • Bill Pullman *Henry "Yank Hank" Greene* • Kate Beckinsale *Darlene Davis* • Lou Diamond Phillips *Roy Knox* • Jacqueline Kim *Yon Greene* • Daniel LaPaine *Skip Kahn, "Nick Parks"* • Tom Amandes *Doug Davis* ■ *Dir* Jonathan Kaplan • *Scr* David Arata, from a story by Adam Fields, David Arata

Broken Arrow ★★★★ PG

Western 1950 · US · Colour · 88mins

Director Delmer Daves's massively influential western was among the first to tell the native American side of the story. James Stewart heads the cast as a war-weary scout who falls, controversially, for Apache maiden Debra Paget during his mission to negotiate a truce, while Jeff Chandler became an international star following his performance here as Cochise, a role he was to reprise twice. Michael Blankfort's screenplay from Elliott Arnold's novel *Blood Brother*, was nominated for an Oscar.

James Stewart *Tom Jeffords* • Jeff Chandler *Cochise* • Debra Paget *Sonseeahray* • Basil Ruysdael *General Howard* • Will Geer *Ben Slade* • Joyce MacKenzie *Terry* • Arthur Hunnicutt *Duffield* • Raymond Bramley *Colonel Bernall* • Jay Silverheels *Goklia* ■ *Dir* Delmer Daves • *Scr* Michael Blankfort [Albert Maltz], from the novel *Blood Brother* by Elliott Arnold

Broken Arrow ★★★ 15

Action thriller 1996 · US · Colour · 103mins

For his second Hollywood film after the Jean-Claude Van Damme vehicle *Hard Target*, hyper-kinetic Hong Kong director John Woo teams up with reinvented hard man John Travolta for a tepid techno-thriller. Despite rattling along at a breakneck pace, this cliché-ridden tale fails to demonstrate the intensity that elevated Woo's Asian classics such as *The Killer* above the norm. Yet Travolta charismatically milks his new-found icon status as an amoral stealth-bomber pilot, cleverly hijacking the nuclear cargo he's carrying for eventual sale to a foreign power. Christian Slater is an able good guy, pursuing his maniac adversary across the desert into ever more ludicrous action set pieces, while Samantha Mathis is refreshingly capable as Slater's sidekick. Contains violence and swearing. DVD

John Travolta *Vic Deakins* • Christian Slater *Riley Hale* • Samantha Mathis *Terry Carmichael* • Delroy Lindo *Colonel Max Wilkins* • Bob Gunton *Pritchett* • Frank Whaley *Giles Prentice* • Howie Long *Kelly* • Vondie Curtis-Hall *Lieutenant Colonel Sam Rhodes* • Jack Thompson *Chairman, Joint Chief of Staff* • Vyto Ruginis *Johnson* ■ *Dir* John Woo • *Scr* Graham Yost

Broken Badges ★★ 15

Crime drama 1990 · US · Colour · 94mins

A rare good guy role for Miguel Ferrer, who has carved a nice little niche in villainy (see the original *RoboCop* movie) in the last decade or so. Here he plays a maverick cop who, against his better judgement, decides to help a youngster who has been accused of murdering his own parents. Ferrer is as watchable as ever and there are strong supporting performances from Eileen Davidson and Jay Johnson. However, director Kim Manners, who was responsible for the dire *K-9* cash-in, *K-9000*, brings little style to the venture. Contains some swearing.

Miguel Ferrer *Beau Jack Bowman* • Eileen Davidson *JJ Tingreedes* • Ernie Hudson *Toby Baker* • Jay Johnson *Stanley Jones* ■ *Dir* Kim Manners • *Scr* Stephen J Cannell, Randall Wallace

Broken Blossoms ★★★★ PG

Silent drama
1919 · US · BW and Tinted · 94mins

Set in London's Limehouse, this melodrama is the last of director DW Griffith's undisputed masterpieces. Shot in just 18 days, the story of brutalised waif Lillian Gish's chaste relationship with noble Chinese merchant Richard Barthelmess was Griffith's most expensive film to date. It marked both his earliest experiment with tinted film stock and his first exclusive use of studio sets. The atmosphere of misty dilapidation was achieved by cinematographer Billy Bitzer and effects expert Hendrik Sartov, but it's the way in which Griffith exploits his seedy setting to enhance the ethereality of the romance between the battered girl and the merchant that makes the film so memorable.

Lillian Gish *Lucy* • Donald Crisp *"Battling" Burrows* • Arthur Howard *Burrows's manager* • Richard Barthelmess *Cheng Huan* • Edward Peil [Edward Peil Sr] *Evil Eye* • Norman Selby *A prizefighter* • George Beranger *The Spying One* • Ernest Butterworth ■ *Dir* DW Griffith • *Scr* DW Griffith, from the short story *The Chink and the Child* by Thomas Burke

Broken Blossoms ★★

Drama 1936 · UK · BW · 88mins

Five years after directing his last feature, DW Griffith – the father of narrative film – was invited by Twickenham Studios to remake his 1919 classic about doomed love in London's Limehouse. When he dropped out, Emlyn Williams hurriedly produced a script based on the Griffith original, and German exile John Brahm was hired to direct. The result is better than might be expected, with Brahm emulating the visual delicacy of the silent version. However, the dialogue is excruciating in places, Dolly Haas is no Lillian Gish, and Williams can't match Richard Barthelmess.

Dolly Haas *Lucy Burrows* • Emlyn Williams *Chen* • Arthur Margetson *Battling Burrows* • Gibb McLaughlin *Evil Eye* • Donald Calthrop *Old Chinaman* • Ernest Sefton *Manager* • Jerry Verno *Bert* • Bertha Belmore *Daisy* • Ernest Jay *Alf* ■ *Dir* John Brahm • *Scr* Emlyn Williams, from the story *The Chink and the Child* by Thomas Burke, from the 1919 film • *Cinematographer* Curt Courant

The Broken Chain ★★

Historical action drama
1993 · US · Colour · 76mins

One of a series of TV movies for TNT cable network about the history of the American Indian, this is an absorbing historical drama. In this film, the Iroquois Confederation, made up of six individual tribes, is torn apart because of conflicting loyalties during the 1700s. An English-educated warrior (Eric Schweig) eventually sees the white man as a threat to his people's way of life and fights to keep colonial settlers off his lands. Lamont Johnson's educational, entertaining drama captures the look and feel of the period, while Schweig, Buffy Sainte-Marie and Pierce Brosnan deliver impressive performances.

Pierce Brosnan *Sir William Johnson* • Buffy Sainte-Marie *Gesina* • Eric Schweig *Joseph Brant* • JC White Shirt *Lohaheo* ■ *Dir* Lamont Johnson • *Scr* Earl W Wallace

The Broken Cord ★★★ PG

Drama based on a true story
1992 · US · Colour · 88mins

Based on the book by Michael Dorris, this is a touching and troubling story about a man who discovers that his adopted child has Fetal Alcohol Syndrome. Dorris wrote about his experiences to publicise the plight of babies born to alcoholic mothers and Ken Olin's made-for-TV film plays down the melodrama in order to get the facts across. There's also a racial subtext, as the authorities try to prevent a brain-damaged native American child from going to a parent of mixed race. Jimmy Smits and Kim Delaney give admirable performances, but, for once, it's the good cause that takes centre stage.

Jimmy Smits *David Norwell* • Kim Delaney *Suzanne Lefever* • Fredrick Leader-Charge *First Adam* • Michael Spears *Second Adam* • Frank Burning *Third Adam* • Deborah Duchene *Allison Chapman* • Raoul Trujillo *Emil Bear Heart* • Billy Merasty *Frank Cree* ■ *Dir* Ken Olin • *Scr* Ann Beckett, Michael Dorris, from the book by Michael Dorris

Broken English ★★

Romantic drama 1981 · US · Colour · 93mins

Written and directed by Michie Gleason, this is a well-meaning but overly emphatic treatise on interracial marriage. Moving between Senegal, Tunisia and France, the action centres on Beverly Ross's relationship with black African Jacques Martial and the response of her family and friends. The attitudes are predictable, but there's a touching togetherness about the way the couple confront their detractors. However, the main point of interest in this little-seen film is the sole screen appearance of Oona Chaplin, who defied her playwright father, Eugene O'Neill, to marry Charlie Chaplin in 1943, despite an age gap of 36 years.

Beverly Ross *Sarah* • Jacques Martial *Maas* • Greta Rannigen *Leslie* • Mansour Sy *Cheekh* • Oona Chaplin *Sarah's mother* • Frankie Stein *Cecile* • Sandy Whitelaw *Arms dealer* • Serge Rynecki *Jacques* ■ *Dir/Scr* Michie Gleason

Broken English ★★★ 18

Romantic drama 1996 · NZ · Colour · 88mins

Having scored an international hit with *Once Were Warriors*, producer Robin Scholes returned to similar territory with this Auckland-based variation on the *Romeo and Juliet* story. Debutant director Gregor Nicholas lacks Lee Tamahori's flair, however, and his insights into the need for racial tolerance in a melting-pot society are frequently overstated in a bid to provoke. Moreover, the glossy visuals often detract from the authenticity of this otherwise downbeat drama. Yet Aleksandra Vujcic gives a memorable performance as the war-scarred Croatian exile who defies her boorishly patriotic father (Rade Serbeszija) to romance Maori chef Julian Arahanga. An English/Maori/Serbo-Croatian language film. Contains swearing, sex scenes and some violence.

Aleksandra Vujcic *Nina* • Julian Arahanga *Eddie* • Rade Serbedzija *Ivan* • Marton Csokas *Darko* • Madeline McNamara *Mira* • Elizabeth Mavric *Vanya* • Zhao Jing *Clara* • Li Yang *Wu* ■ *Dir* Gregor Nicholas • *Scr* Gregor Nicholas, Johanna Pigott, Jim Salter

Broken Harvest ★★

Historical epic
1994 · Ire · Colour and BW · 101mins

The period immediately following the Irish civil war has been relatively neglected by film-makers. However, Maurice O'Callaghan's study of the tensions that remained after independence admirably captures the atmosphere of retrenchment and remembrance that characterised the early De Valera years. Yet there's a predictability about the storyline, in which two men refuse to call a ceasefire in the feud that began decades before over a woman. Colin Lane and Niall O'Brien turn in creditable performances, but O'Callaghan isn't always in control of either the drama or the camera, with the result that the whole affair is rather rough and ready.

Colin Lane *Arthur O'Leary* • Niall O'Brien *Josie McCarthy* • Marian Quinn *Catherine O'Leary* • Darren McHugh *Jimmy O'Leary* • Joy Florish *Mary Finnegan* • Joe Jeffers *Willie Hogan* ■ *Dir* Maurice O'Callaghan • *Scr* Maurice O'Callaghan, Kate O'Callaghan, from the story *The Shilling* by Maurice O'Callaghan

Broken Journey ★★ U

Melodrama 1948 · UK · BW · 85mins

A plane full of mismatched characters comes down in the Alps. Guess what happens next? Watching painfully earnest tales like this makes you wonder why anyone bothers with disaster movies, and why it took so long for *Airplane!* to come along and mock them. From the moment the camera mingles with the passengers, it is woefully obvious who will be the selfless do-gooders and who will be the bad eggs. Director Ken Annakin, on his third picture, has little idea how to freshen up the stock situations, while there are few hidden depths in the overfamiliar characters.

Phyllis Calvert *Mary Johnstone* • Margot Grahame *Joanna Dane* • James Donald *Bill Haverton* • Francis L Sullivan *Anton Perami* • Raymond Huntley *Edward Marshall* • Derek Bond *Richard Faber* • Guy Rolfe *Captain Fox* • Sonia Holm *Anne Stevens* ■ *Dir* Ken Annakin • *Scr* Robert Westerby

Broken Lance ★★★★ U

Western 1954 · US · Colour · 92mins

This splendid 20th Century-Fox western stars a magnificently grizzled Spencer Tracy in the role he was born to play – King Lear. Even though the daughters have become sons, this is the (uncredited) westernisation of Shakespeare's tragedy about the royal patriarch and his disparate family. It's also a remake of *House of Strangers*, the Joseph L Mankiewicz crime drama

204

U = SUITABLE FOR ALL Uc = SUITABLE FOR ALL, ESPECIALLY FOR YOUNG CHILDREN (VIDEO ONLY) PG = PARENTAL GUIDANCE

that was also remade in the big-top setting of *The Big Show*. Still, despite the claims for Akira Kurosawa's *Ran*, this is the definitive screen version of the Bard's celebrated work, and the western setting provides a dimension of grandeur.

Spencer Tracy *Matt Devereaux* • Robert Wagner *Joe Devereaux* • Jean Peters *Barbara* • Richard Widmark *Ben* • Katy Jurado *Senora Devereaux* • Hugh O'Brian *Mike Devereaux* • Eduard Franz *Two Moons* • Earl Holliman *Denny Devereaux* • EG Marshall *Governor* ■ *Dir* Edward Dmytryk • *Scr* Richard Murphy, from a story by Philip Yordan

The Broken Land ★★

Western   1962 · US · Colour · 59mins

A B-western about a tyrannical sheriff who winds up committing rape, murder and sundry other offences while trying to wipe out anyone who can speak against him. Kent Taylor plays the vile man, Diana Darrin is his main accuser, and Jody McCrea (Joel's son) plays the good guy, who looks like dead meat from the start. Some reviewers at the time felt the script was written by a sixties shrink, since it's full of gestalt stuff about violent impulses and guilt. Now, though, the movie is likely to be viewed solely for an early appearance by Jack Nicholson. It was shot in ten days in Arizona.

Kent Taylor *Jim Kogan* • Diana Darrin *Marva Aikens* • Jody McCrea *Deputy Ed Flynn* • Robert Sampson *Gabe Dunson* • Jack Nicholson *Will Broicous* • Gary Sneed *Billy Bell* • Don Orlando ■ *Dir* John Bushelman • *Scr* Edward J Lakso, Dixie McCoy

Broken Pledges ★★ PG

Drama based on a true story
1994 · US · Colour · 88mins

The *Animal House* gang would be turning in their graves: two key elements of campus comedies (initiation tests and drinking) get rapped over the knuckles in this worthy TV movie. Former *Dallas* star Linda Gray ditches the glamour image to play the mum who attempts to stamp out "hazing" rites in student fraternities after her son dies from alcohol poisoning. Unfortunately, she lays it on a bit strong and the end result is a too-preachy and rather tedious melodrama.

Linda Gray *Eileen Stevens* • Leon Russom *Roy Stevens* • David Lipper *Chuck Stenzel* • Chris Martin *Scott Stevens* • Emily Perkins *Suzanne Stevens* • Laurie Grogan *Steven Stevens* ■ *Dir* Jorge Montesi • *Scr* Sandra Jennings

Broken Promise ★★ 15

Drama   1981 · US · Colour · 84mins

Directed by Don Taylor – the man Elizabeth Taylor married in 1950's *Father of the Bride* – this is a well-meaning TV movie that never quite comes off, in spite of a remarkably mature performance from Melissa Michaelsen. As the 11-year-old determined to keep her five brothers together after their parents have abandoned them, she has a conviction and a naturalism that is missing from her adult co-stars, who try too hard to compensate for their misgivings about this shamelessly sentimental story. Wholesome but hardly scintillating stuff. Contains violence.

Chris Sarandon *Bud Griggs* • Melissa Michaelsen *Patty Clawson* • George Coe *George Mathews* • McKee Anderson *Nancy Sloan* • David Haskell *Tom Parks* • Sondra West *Alice Parks* ■ *Dir* Don Taylor • *Scr* Stephen Kandel, from the book by Kent Hayes, Alex Lazzarino

Broken Trust ★★★ 12

Thriller   1995 · US · Colour · 92mins

A thoughtful, made-for-TV legal drama, this takes a hard-eyed look at corruption at the very top of the justice system. Tom Selleck plays a dedicated judge who is persuaded by FBI agent Elizabeth McGovern to go undercover, in order to expose senior legal figures on the take. However, he faces a tricky dilemma when he discovers that some of his closest friends may be implicated in the scandal. It's not in the same league as Sidney Lumet's classic films about legal corruption, but it's still an absorbing piece, benefiting from a mature performance by Selleck.

Tom Selleck *Tim Nash* • Elizabeth McGovern *Janice Diller* • William Atherton *Neil Roemer* • Marsha Mason *Ruth Fraser* • Charles Haid *Harold Ashley* • Stanley DeSantis *Vince Escobar* ■ *Dir* Geoffrey Sax • *Scr* Joan Didion, John Gregory Dunne, from the novel *Court of Honor* by William P Wood

Broken Vessels ★★★ 18

Medical drama   1998 · US · Colour · 90mins

Here's some advice. If you're ever taken ill in the States, get yourself to hospital. Do not, under any circumstances, call the paramedics. In Martin Scorsese's *Bringing Out the Dead*, a strung-out Nicolas Cage hallucinated his way through his own personal heart of darkness. Now Todd Field and Jason London do likewise in an edgy little indie drama, the low-tech, almost documentary style of which recalls those *Cops*-style "true life" TV programmes. Like its characters, *Broken Vessels* is unfocused and disjointed. Less of a triumph of style over content, it is, however, arguably a better film than Scorsese's.

Todd Field *Jimmy Warzniak* • Jason London *Tom Meyer* • Roxana Zal *Elizabeth* • Susan Traylor *Susy* • James Hong *Mr Chen* ■ *Dir* Scott Ziehl • *Scr* Scott Ziehl, David Baer, John McMahon

Broken Vows ★★★ 15

Thriller   1987 · US · Colour · 94mins

A priest gets involved with the former lover of a murder victim and becomes caught up in the subsequent homicide investigation in a thriller that emulates Hitchcock's *I Confess* in substance though not in key plot points or, of course, in style. Still, this is a reasonable enough TV movie, with a strong cast headed by the ever-excellent Tommy Lee Jones and the under-rated Annette O'Toole, while *Rhoda*'s David Groh and character actor M Emmet Walsh also shine. The forbidden love affair is well-drawn and delicately played by the two leads, and, with a bigger budget and a more adult treatment, this would have worked as a cinema release. Contains some violence.

Tommy Lee Jones *Father Joseph McMahon* • Annette O'Toole *Nim Fitzpatrick* • M Emmet Walsh *Detective Mulligan* • Milo O'Shea

Monsignor *Casey* • David Groh *Mason Drumm* ■ *Dir* Jud Taylor • *Scr* Ivan Davis, from the novel *Where the Dark Secrets Go* by Dorothy Salisbury Davis

Bronco Billy ★★★ PG

Comedy western
1980 · US · Colour · 111mins

This is reputedly Clint Eastwood's favourite of his own pictures, a small-scale charmer about a shoe sales clerk who dreams of being a cowboy and gathers around him a bunch of other no-hopers and oddballs, among them Sondra Locke, who launch a Wild West show with that singularly all-American optimism. It's *The Outlaw Josey Wales* without the spitting and shooting, as Eastwood deftly plays with his image as a solitary man of action, the loner who resents company but gets it all the same. Eastwood is a sure judge of tone, and there's sufficient edge and wit to keep bathos at bay in what is at times a rather cutesy, sentimental yarn. Contains some swearing.

Clint Eastwood *"Bronco Billy" McCoy* • Sondra Locke *Antoinette Lily* • Geoffrey Lewis *John Arlington* • Scatman Crothers *"Doc" Lynch* • Bill McKinney *"Lefty" Lebow* • Sam Bottoms *Leonard James* • Dan Vadis *Chief Big Eagle* • Sierra Pecheur *Lorraine Running Water* ■ *Dir* Clint Eastwood • *Scr* Dennis Hackin

Bronco Buster ★★ U

Western   1952 · US · Colour · 80mins

Standard rodeo spills and thrills come from this tale of a promising young rider, played by Scott Brady, who is groomed for stardom by John Lund's champ. Brady's success goes to his head and he becomes thoroughly obnoxious, even attempting to take Lund's girl (Joyce Holden) away from him. Several rodeo stars are featured, and director Budd Boetticher makes the most of the film's limited potential. For what could be done with the same basic rodeo story, look to *The Lusty Men* with Robert Mitchum, Arthur Kennedy and Susan Hayward, released only a few months after this film.

John Lund *Tom Moody* • Scott Brady *Bart Eaton* • Joyce Holden *Judy Bream* • Chill Wills *Dan Bream* • Don Haggerty *Dobie* • Dan Poore *Elliott* • Casey Tibbs *Rodeo rider* ■ *Dir* Budd Boetticher • *Scr* Horace McCoy, Lillie Hayward, from a story by Peter B Kyne

The Brontë Sisters ★★

Biographical drama
1979 · Fr · Colour · 115mins

The major – indeed, the only – interest in this alternative take on the literary sisters is provided by the casting of three of France's most talented actresses: the Isabelles Adjani and Huppert, and Marie-France Pisier. Director André Téchiné (who also co-wrote the script) seems to have a misplaced vision of the claustrophobic life lived by the famous family in their remote Yorkshire parsonage and, in concentrating on the tortured life of the sisters' doomed brother Branwell (Pascal Greggory) and their relationship with him, detracts from the carefully constructed period atmosphere. A laboured affair, not nearly as entertaining as a 1946 Hollywood version of the tale called *Devotion*. In French with English subtitles..

Isabelle Adjani *Emily* • Marie-France Pisier *Charlotte* • Isabelle Huppert *Anne* • Pascal Greggory *Branwell* • Patrick Magee *Father* • Hélène Surgère *Mrs Robinson* • Roland Bertin *Nicholls* ■ *Dir* André Téchiné • *Scr* Pascal Bonitzer, André Téchiné, Jean Gruault

A Bronx Tale ★★★★ 18

Drama   1993 · US · Colour · 116mins

Adapted by *The Usual Suspects*'s Chazz Palminteri from his own play, this is an intelligent portrait of a time (the sixties) and place (New York's Little Italy) that eschews some of the more extravagant sweeps of Martin Scorsese, probably cinema's most famous chronicler of Italian-American life. Goodness is a hard quality to depict without sentimentality, yet Robert De Niro manages to convey it well, as a bus driver whose impressionable young son is attracted to a sharp-dressing neighbourhood gangster (played by Palminteri). Lillo Brancato gives a good account of himself as the confused teenager, but it's De Niro's sense of place and pace (this was his directorial debut) and Palminteri's autobiographical insights into the neighbourhood that make this such a compelling picture. Contains swearing and violence.

Robert De Niro *Lorenzo Anello* • Chazz Palminteri *Sonny* • Lillo Brancato *Calogero Anello aged 17* • Francis Capra *Calogero Anello aged nine* • Taral Hicks *Jane* • Katherine Narducci *Rosina Anello* • Clem Caserta *Jimmy Whispers* • Alfred Sauchelli Jr *Bobby Bars* • Joe Pesci *Carmine* ■ *Dir* Robert De Niro • *Scr* Chazz Palminteri, from his play

The Brood ★★★★ 18

Horror   1979 · Can · Colour · 88mins

Oliver Reed, a doctor experimenting with the new science of psychoplasmics, persuades Samantha Eggar to "shape her rage" and give birth to deformed children with killer instincts in another of director David Cronenberg's disturbing shockers. An intriguing metaphor for both unexplained bodily changes and the mental abuse some parents heap on their offspring, this genuinely creepy and upsetting stomach churner is a modern horror classic. Eggar's performance gives a poignant emotional depth to Cronenberg's complex chiller. *DVD*

Oliver Reed *Dr Hal Raglan* • Samantha Eggar *Nola Carveth* • Art Hindle *Frank Carveth* • Cindy Hinds *Candice Carveth* • Nuala Fitzgerald *Julianna Kelly* • Henry Beckman *Barton Kelly* • Susan Hogan *Ruth Mayer* • Michael McGhee *Inspector Mrazek* ■ *Dir/Scr* David Cronenberg

A Brooklyn State of Mind ★★ 15

Crime drama
1997 · US/Can · Colour · 85mins

A predictable slice of thin-base Italian American life, this stars Vincent Spano as a nice guy in with the wrong crowd and Danny Aiello as the neighbourhood big guy. Although it's competently shot and performed, this sort of criminal community has been explored many times before and with far more conviction. *Il Postino*'s beautiful Maria Grazia Cucinotta has an unconvincing role as a documentary-maker, becoming both Spano's love interest and a catalyst for rather obvious revelations about his father's unsolved murder. Mired in criminal clichés, the very watchable cast are the sole virtue of this motionless movie. Contains swearing, and some violence. 🔲

Vincent Spano *Al Stanco* • Maria Grazia Cucinotta *Gabriella* • Abe Vigoda *Uncle Guy* • Morgana King *Aunt Rose* • Ricky Aiello [Rick Aiello] *Nicky Vetrino* • Danny Aiello *Danny Parente* ■ *Dir* Frank Rainone • *Scr* Frank Rainone, Frederick J Stroppel

Brother ★★★★ 15

Crime drama 1997 · Rus · Colour · 99mins

A controversial hit in Russia, Alexei Balabanov's unflinchingly naturalistic *noir* equates democratic St Petersburg with the Chicago of the twenties. Crime is as unavoidable as American consumerism, rabid nationalism, urban decay and dehumanising poverty, so ex-soldier Sergei Bodrov Jr has little option but to emulate his assassin brother, Viktor Sukhorukov, to survive. It's a perilous existence, though the wages of sin afford him the chance to rescue tram driver Svetlana Pismichenko from her abusive marriage and indulge his passion for pop heroes Nautilus. Matter of fact in its violence, scathing in its politics yet teeming with humanity, this is grimly impressive stuff. In Russian with English subtitles. 🔲

Sergei Bodrov Jr *Danila Bragov* • Viktor Sukhorukov *Viktor Bragov* • Svetlana Pismichenko *Sveta* ■ *Dir/Scr* Alexei Balabanov

The Brother from Another Planet ★★★ 15

Science-fiction satire
1984 · US · Colour · 108mins

A beguiling and thoughtful example of science fiction as social satire from independent writer/director John Sayles, the best purveyor of refreshingly new gritty comedies in the business. As the mute ET wandering Harlem streets in a daze, whose "magical touch" enables him to mend any household object, Joe Morton gives a tour de force performance. However, Sayles mainly uses his alien hero's inability to speak as an object lesson in human behaviour. The provocative device provides opportunities for a fine roster of supporting characters who can pour out their hearts and be spiritually "fixed". Contains violence, swearing and drug abuse. 🔲

Joe Morton *The Brother* • Daryl Edwards *Fly* • Steve James *Odell* • Leonard Jackson *Smokey* • Bill Cobbs *Walter* • Maggie Renzi *Noreen* • Tom Wright *Sam* • Ren Woods *Bernice* ■ *Dir* John Sayles • *Scr* John Sayles

Brother Future ★★ U

Fantasy drama 1991 · US · Colour · 103mins

Stand back or you may get hit by the large amounts of obvious moralising flying about this family film. Roy Campanella II directed this tale of an inner-city boy who learns about life the hard way when he is magically transported into the middle of a 19th-century slave uprising. While definitely well meaning, *Brother Future* is also heavy-handed and ultimately says less about racial problems than an average episode of *The Cosby Show*. 🔲

Phil Lewis *TJ* • Carl Lumbly *Denmark Vesey* • Frank Converse *Cooper* • Bernard Addison *Zeke* ■ *Dir* Alan Smithee [Roy Campanella II] • *Scr* Ann E Eskridge

Brother John ★★

Fantasy drama 1970 · US · Colour · 95mins

The title role is so admirably suited to the saintly-looking Sidney Poitier, it's almost a cliché in itself. A black man returns to his Alabama home town to see if racial tensions have eased over the years. It turns out he's an angel who's recording it all for the heavenly host. As a fantasy it's pleasant enough, but James Goldstone's film could have been been much more searching in its implications.

Sidney Poitier *John Kane* • Will Geer *Doc Thomas* • Bradford Dillman *Lloyd Thomas* • Beverly Todd *Louisa MacGill* • Ramon Bieri *Orly Ball* • Warren J Kemmerling [Warren Kemmerling] *George* ■ *Dir* James Goldstone • *Scr* Ernest Kinoy

Brother Orchid ★★★

Crime spoof 1940 · US · BW · 87mins

There is always a down side to Warner Bros gangster pictures – a rather out-of-place moral dimension, meant to counterbalance the fast-living world of guys and molls. The down side here, after the pleasure of watching Edward G Robinson and Humphrey Bogart as partners who fall out, is having to watch Robinson transform himself into a pious friar. But, before the picture takes on an unnecessarily religious tone, it keeps to the guidelines of the genre, with the two stars on good form as they run rival protection rackets and rub out the lesser names on the cast list. Ann Sothern adds a lot of humour as Robinson's girl – deliriously drunk in her best scene – and Lloyd Bacon directs with machine-gun speed.

Edward G Robinson *Little John Sarto* • Humphrey Bogart *Jack Buck* • Ann Sothern *Flo Addams* • Donald Crisp *Brother Superior* • Ralph Bellamy *Clarence Fletcher* • Allen Jenkins *Willie the Knife* • Charles D Brown *Brother Wren* • Cecil Kellaway *Brother Goodwin* • Morgan Conway *Philadelphia Powell* ■ *Dir* Lloyd Bacon • *Scr* Earl Baldwin, from the *Collier's Magazine*,article by Richard Connell

Brother Sun, Sister Moon ★ PG

Biographical religious drama
1972 · It/UK · Colour · 115mins

Avoid this insipid rendering of the early life of St Francis of Assisi. As seen by Franco Zeffirelli, Francesco di Bernadone was a prototype hippy with flowers in his hair who approved of free love (the only sort he could afford) and social equality. To play him, Zeffirelli first fancied the young Al Pacino, but the studio said "Who?". So Graham Faulkner, another unknown, was hired to star alongside the vacant Judi Bowker. Alec Guinness plays Pope Innocent III, and Britain's answer to Bob Dylan, the vapid Donovan, sings some songs. 🔲

Graham Faulkner *Francesco* • Judi Bowker *Clare* • Leigh Lawson *Bernardo* • Kenneth Cranham *Paolo* • Lee Montague *Pietro di Bernardone* • Valentina Cortese *Pica di Bernardone* • Alec Guinness *Pope Innocent III*

■ *Dir* Franco Zeffirelli • *Scr* Suso Cecchi D'Amico, Kenneth Ross, Lina Wertmuller, Franco Zeffirelli

The Brotherhood ★★

Crime drama 1968 · US · Colour · 96mins

Made before *The Godfather* revealed how fascinating and complex a subject the Mafia could be, this is a straightforward tale of generational conflict within the criminal "family". Kirk Douglas (who also produced) stars as the traditionalist at odds with his younger brother (Alex Cord), although the real drama arises when each has to carry out the role of executioner. There are the usual strong performances to be found in a Martin Ritt film, but it suffers as a result of failing to synthesise the good and bad aspects of Douglas's character.

Kirk Douglas *Frank Ginetta* • Alex Cord *Vince Ginetta* • Irene Papas *Ida Ginetta* • Luther Adler *Dominick Bertolo* • Susan Strasberg *Emma Ginetta* • Murray Hamilton *Jim Egan* ■ *Dir* Martin Ritt • *Scr* Lewis John Carlino

Brotherhood of Justice ★★ 15

Action drama 1986 · US · Colour · 93mins

Proving that everyone has to start somewhere, this high-school version of *Death Wish* finds a young Keanu Reeves, in one of his early roles, deciding to fight back against rising crime at school and in the city. However, it's not long before the junior vigilantes get out of control. This made-for-TV crime drama also provides early roles for such luminaries as Kiefer Sutherland and Billy Zane, so it's not without curiosity value – but it has little else to offer. 🔲

Keanu Reeves *Derek* • Lori Loughlin *Christie* • Kiefer Sutherland *Victor* • Joe Spano *Bob Grootemat* • Darren Dalton *Scottie* • Evan Mirand *Mule* • Billy Zane *Les* ■ *Dir* Charles Braverman • *Scr* Noah Jubelirer, Jeffrey Bloom, from a story by Noah Jubelirer

Brotherhood of Satan ★★★ 18

Horror 1970 · US · Colour · 88mins

Strother Martin heads a Californian devil cult kidnapping local children for soul transference purposes. This eerie witchcraft extravaganza packs an unsettling punch because of its ordinary setting and the imaginative and versatile use of its low-budget trappings. It's a great example of what can be achieved with very little, enhanced by uniformly good acting, classy direction by Bernard McEveety and clever small-scale special effects (for example, the kids' toys being enlarged to life-size) make this an unpretentious winner. 🔲

Strother Martin *Don Duncan* • LQ Jones *Sheriff* • Charles Bateman *Ben* • Anna Capri [Ahna Capri] *Nicky* • Charles Robinson *Priest* • Alvy Moore *Tobey* ■ *Dir* Bernard McEveety • *Scr* William Welch, from an idea by Sean MacGregor

Brotherhood of the Gun ★★★

Western 1992 · US · Colour · 88mins

We've had bawdy adventures set in 18th-century England and France, so it

was only a matter of time before we got a saucy view of the Wild West. Unfortunately, this being a TV movie, it has neither the dash nor the daring that might have made it something more than just a run-of-the-mill maverick tale. It also suffers from having the relatively unknown Brian Bloom in the lead, as it's much easier to identify with a loveable rogue if he is already a familiar face. However, villains James Remar and David Carradine are top notch.

Brian Bloom *Zach Hollister* • Jamie Rose *Kathryn Battle* • Jorge Cervera Jr *Sheriff Charlie Madera* • David Carradine *Artemis McBride* • James Remar *Frank Weir* • Mark Ballou *Tom Hollister* • Deborah Falconer *Allison McBride* • Shawn Levy *Teddy McBride* ■ *Dir* Vern Gillum • *Scr* Robert Ward

The Brothers ★★ PG

Drama 1947 · UK · BW · 87mins

Cecil B DeMille's one-time assistant David MacDonald returned to his native Scotland for this tempestuous melodrama co-written by the husband-and-wife team of Sydney and Muriel Box. While Stephen Dade's images of Skye are highly evocative, little passion is generated in the romance between orphaned Patricia Roc and Andrew Crawford, even though she's the housekeeper of his deadliest rival (Finlay Currie). Part of the problem is the straightlaced nature of postwar British cinema, which kept emotions firmly in check. Yet Roc is also miscast as the free-spirited waif whose charms melt the hearts of Currie's sons (Maxwell Reed and Duncan Macrae). 🔲

Patricia Roc *Mary* • Will Fyffe *Aeneas McGrath* • Maxwell Reed *Fergus Macrae* • Finlay Currie *Hector Macrae* • Duncan Macrae *John Macrae* • John Laurie *Dugald* • Andrew Crawford *Willie McFarish* • James Woodburn *Priest* ■ *Dir* David MacDonald • *Scr* Muriel Box, Sydney Box, Paul Vincent Carroll, David MacDonald, from a novel by L AG Strong

Brothers ★★

Prison drama based on a true story
1977 · US · Colour · 105mins

Films *à clef* are supposed to be fictionalised versions of real people's lives. However, screenwriters Edward and Mildred Lewis haven't bothered to rework too many of the events in this misguided drama inspired by the notorious relationship between black activist Angela Davis and San Quentin inmate George Jackson, whose brother and a judge were killed during an attempted breakout from the Marin County Courthouse. What makes this angry film so resistible, however, is the racial stereotyping of the prison sequences. While there's no denying the brutality of the regime, this really needed some shades of grey.

Bernie Casey *David Thomas* • Vonetta McGee *Paula Jones* • Ron O'Neal *Walter Nance* • Renny Roker *Lewis* • Stu Gilliam *Robinson* • John Lehne *McGee* ■ *Dir* Arthur Barron • *Scr* Edward Lewis, Mildred Lewis

Brothers and Relations ★★★

Drama 1988 · Viet · BW

Few films had been made in Vietnam before the civil war, when the majority of those produced were amateurish propaganda efforts made to boost morale. However, once the dust settled, indigenous directors took a more reflective look at the conflict and its impact. Set in the mid-1970s, this stark drama is still prone to a certain political naiveté, but there is undeniable poignancy in the tale of a wounded veteran who is forced to seek work and restore his self-esteem in Hanoi after he returns home to discover that his family has leased out his room presuming him dead. In Vietnamese with English subtitles.

Dang Viet Bao • Bui Bai Binh • Ngoc Bich • Ngoc Thu ■ *Dir* Tran Vu, Nguyen Huu Luyen • *Scr* Thu Huong Duong

Brothers in Arms ★★ 18
Action crime thriller
1988 · US · Colour · 87mins

In a crude cross between *The Texas Chain Saw Massacre* and *Deliverance*, brothers Todd Allen and Charles Grant find themselves crossing swords with a family of barmy backswoodmen who don't take kindly to strangers. Apart from Michelle Pfeiffer's sister Dedee and *The X Files* regular Mitch Pileggi, the cast is largely undistinguished. There is precious little suspense and even less imagination shown in the increasingly monotonous blood-letting.
⊡

Todd Allen *Joey* • Charles Grant *Dallas* • Dedee Pfeiffer *Stevie* • Jack Starrett *Father* • Mitch Pileggi *Caleb* • Dan Bell *Aaron* ■ *Dir* George Jay Bloom III • *Scr* Steve Fisher

Brothers in Arms ★★★
Political thriller
1990 · Fr · Colour

Not to be confused with the Todd Allen action movie of the same name, made two years earlier, this is a rather more interesting political thriller about terrorism and underworld crime on the mean streets of Paris. Added interest comes from the odd-couple pairing of a Jewish vice squad agent and an Arab undercover man on an assignment to hunt for the supplier of a killer drug. A French language film.

Richard Berry *Karim Hamida* • Patrick Bruel *Simon Atlan* • Corinne Dacla *Lisa* • Bruno Cremer *Joulin* • Said Amadis *Ali Radjani* ■ *Dir* Alexandre Arcady • *Scr* Daniel St-Hamont, Benedicte Kermadec, Pierre Aknine

Brothers in Law ★★★★ U
Comedy
1956 · UK · BW · 94mins

A delightfully witty follow-up to the Boulting brothers' smash hit *Private's Progress*, this features many of the same cast. Its source novel is by Henry Cecil, himself a distinguished QC and hopefully quite unlike the absent-minded QC played by Miles Malleson to whom our hero Ian Carmichael is apprenticed. Carmichael at this point in his career was as popular, and as stereotyped, as Hugh Grant is now. He is surrounded here by myriad character actors, including the splendid Terry-Thomas and the redoubtable Richard Attenborough as a smarmy barrister. Still funny, and still relevant.

Ian Carmichael *Roger Thursby* • Terry-Thomas *Alfred Green* • Richard Attenborough *Henry Marshall* • Miles Malleson *Kendall Grimes* • Eric Barker *Alec Blair* • Irene Handl *Mrs Potter* • John Le Mesurier *Judge Ryman* • Jill Adams

Sally Smith • Raymond Huntley *Tatlock* • Nicholas Parsons *Charles Poole* ■ *Dir* Roy Boulting • *Scr* Roy Boulting, Frank Harvey, Jeffrey Dell, from the novel by Henry Cecil

Brothers in Trouble ★★★ 15
Drama
1995 · UK · Colour · 97mins

Director Udayan Prasad betrays his inexperience with narrative in this well-meaning, but ultimately rather contrived, drama about illegal immigrants living in eighties' Britain. While making atmospheric use of the cramped house in which the 18 illegals live, Prasad also draws fine performances from Pavan Malhotra, Angeline Ball (*The Commitments*) and the leading Indian star Om Puri. But the story begins to disintegrate the moment the script abandons telling observation in favour of sensationalist melodrama. Flawed, perhaps, but definitely relevant and worthwhile. Contains swearing and nudity. ⊡

Om Puri *Hussein Shah* • Angeline Ball *Mary* • Pavan Malhotra *Amir* • Ahsen Bhatti *Irshad* • Bhasker *Gholam* • Pravesh Kumar *Sakib* • Lesley Clare O'Neill *Prostitute* • Kulvinder Ghir *Agent* • Badi Uzzaman *Old Ram* ■ *Dir* Udayan Prasad • *Scr* Robert Buckler, from the novel *Return Journey* by Abdullah Hussein

The Brothers Karamazov
★★★
Drama
1958 · US · Colour · 145mins

Most famous in its day for the fact that Marilyn Monroe wanted to play Grushenka – or so she breathily gasped in an assembled press – this rather stodgy but undeniably well-made MGM epic could well have benefited from such courageous casting, for, excellent though Maria Schell is, she just isn't Monroe. Nevertheless, the brothers themselves are superb, with Yul Brynner (with hair!) a dashing Dmitri, Richard Basehart as Ivan, and William Shatner, in his debut, as the young Alexey. Only Lee J Cobb topples over into ham, as the father whose death precipitates further chaos. Writer/director Richard Brooks's screenplay is both clever and literate, capturing the essence of Dostoyevsky without losing substance or tone. Although rather long, this is accessible, and should send those who enjoy it scurrying to the book.

Yul Brynner *Dmitri Karamazov* • Maria Schell *Grushenka* • Claire Bloom *Katya* • Lee J Cobb *Fyodor Karamazov* • Richard Basehart *Ivan Karamazov* • Albert Salmi *Smerdyakov* • William Shatner *Alexey Karamazov* • Judith Evelyn *Madame Anna Hohlakov* • Edgar Stehli *Grigory* ■ *Dir* Richard Brooks • *Scr* Richard Brooks, from the novel by Fyodor Dostoyevsky, adapted by Julius J Epstein, Philip G Epstein

The Brothers McMullen
★★★ 15
Comedy drama
1995 · US · Colour · 94mins

Edward Burns starred as handsome soldier Reiben in *Saving Private Ryan*, but he's better known as a noted director of quirky independent movies. He made his directorial debut with this endearing look at the mixed up romantic lives of three Irish Catholic brothers who share the family home in New York following their widowed mother's return to Ireland. Dealing with unusually heavyweight topics for a

comedy drama, such as religious ethics and sexual morality, the literate and amusing script keeps things bubbling along nicely as Burns establishes himself as a high-achiever on a low budget. ⊡

Edward Burns *Barry* • Mike McGlone *Patrick* • Jack Mulcahy *Jack* • Shari Albert *Susan* • Maxine Bahns *Audry* • Catharine Bolz *Mrs McMullen* • Connie Britton *Molly* • Peter Johansen *Marty* • Jennifer Jostyn *Leslie* • Elizabeth P McKay *Ann* ■ *Dir/Scr* Edward Burns

The Brothers Rico ★★★
Crime drama
1957 · US · BW · 91mins

As *film noir* disappeared in the late fifties, this crude example of the genre emerged. Richard Conte is the gangster turned successful businessman whose younger brothers have been earmarked for assassination by the mob. The *noir* element is provided by Conte's meaningless quest and the disorderly world around him, but director Phil Karlson piles on enough violence to flatten the subtleties of French writer Georges Simenon's original story.

Richard Conte *Eddie Rico* • Dianne Foster *Alice Rico* • Kathryn Grant *Norah* • Larry Gates *Sid Kubik* • Argentina Brunetti *Mrs Rico* • Lamont Johnson *Peter Malaks* • Harry Bellaver *Mike Lamotta* ■ *Dir* Phil Karlson • *Scr* Lewis Meltzer, Ben Perry, from the novella *Les Frères Rico* by Georges Simenon

The Browning Version
★★★★ U
Drama
1951 · UK · BW · 89mins

Infinitely superior to Mike Figgis's 1994 remake, this is another expert collaboration between writer Terence Rattigan and director Anthony Asquith. What makes this version of Rattigan's hit play so memorable is the mesmerising performance of Michael Redgrave as the classics teacher whose life is as redundant as his subject. The supporting cast is also first rate, with Jean Kent chillingly heartless as Redgrave's adulterous wife and Nigel Patrick suitably cocky as the man who cuckolds him. The shabby gentility of the school is neatly captured and the merciless revelation of each new woe is, thanks to Redgrave's dignified self-pity, agonising to watch. Only the optimistic conclusion fails to ring true. ⊡

Michael Redgrave *Andrew Crocker-Harris* • Jean Kent *Millie Crocker-Harris* • Nigel Patrick *Frank Hunter* • Wilfrid Hyde White *Frobisher* • Brian Smith *Taplow* • Bill Travers *Fletcher* • Ronald Howard *Gilbert* • Paul Medland *Wilson* ■ *Dir* Anthony Asquith • *Scr* Terence Rattigan, from his play • *Art Director* Carmen Dillon

The Browning Version
★★★ 15
Drama
1994 · UK · Colour · 93mins

The last film that Mike Figgis made prior to achieving long-overdue international recognition with *Leaving Las Vegas*, this version of Terence Rattigan's play is a polished, if slightly old-fashioned piece of work. However, it doesn't bear comparison with Anthony Asquith's 1951 adaptation, with Albert Finney giving a less finely shaded performance than Michael

Redgrave in the role of the timid, under-appreciated schoolmaster, Crocker-Harris. Jean Kent and Nigel Patrick were also much more callous than Greta Scacchi and Matthew Modine as the couple who cuckold him. A curious choice for its director, perhaps, but still an affecting tale. ⊡

Albert Finney *Andrew Crocker-Harris* • Greta Scacchi *Laura Crocker-Harris* • Matthew Modine *Frank Hunter* • Julian Sands *Tom Gilbert* • Michael Gambon *Dr Frobisher* • Ben Silverstone *Taplow* • Maryam D'Abo *Diana Rafferty* • James Sturgess *Bryant* ■ *Dir* Mike Figgis • *Scr* Ronald Harwood, from the play by Terence Rattigan

Brown's Requiem ★★ 18
Crime drama
1998 · US · Colour · 100mins

This competent adaptation of James Ellroy's first novel suffers from unavoidable comparisons with the superb film version of the author's *LA Confidential*. Michael Rooker (*Henry: Portrait of a Serial Killer*) has the appropriately intimidating frame and throaty voice for Fritz Brown, a low-rent, ex-alcoholic private investigator assigned to keeping an eye on a young girl who's involved with a local heavy. Although director/screenwriter Jason Freeland creates a convincing shady milieu, the flawed characters and cynical voiceover are pretty run of the mill. The under-rated Rooker does more for this inconsequential movie than it does for him. ⊡

Michael Rooker *Fritz Brown* • Selma Blair *Jane Baker* • Jack Conley *Richard Ralston* • Harold Gould *Solly K* • Tobin Bell *Stan the Man* • Brad Dourif *Edwards* • Brion James *Cathcart* ■ *Dir* Jason Freeland • *Scr* Jason Freeland, from the novel by James Ellroy

Brubaker ★★★★ 15
Prison drama
1980 · US · Colour · 124mins

Robert Redford is in reformist mode here, determined to combat brutality and corruption in a state prison farm. Director Stuart Rosenberg piles on the agony with sequences of bleak action, while the acting – especially from Jane Alexander and Yaphet Kotto – is formidable enough to take on all that social responsibility. A touch downbeat, and at times ponderous and sanctimonious, this prison drama still sends out an ominous message to those who care about what society does with its misfits. Contains violence and swearing. ⊡

Robert Redford *Henry Brubaker* • Yaphet Kotto *Richard "Dickie" Coombes* • Jane Alexander *Lillian Gray* • Murray Hamilton *Deach* • David Keith *Larry Lee Bullen* • Morgan Freeman *Walter* • Matt Clark *Purcell* • Tim McIntire *Huey Rauch* ■ *Dir* Stuart Rosenberg • *Scr* WD Richter, from the story by WD Richter, Arthur Ross, from a book by Thomas O Murton, Joe Hyams

The Bruce ★ 15
Historical adventure
1996 · UK · Colour · 106mins

This is a ramshackle historical drama about Robert the Bruce, the Scots hero who, according to legend, was inspired by the persistence of a stranded spider to renew his bid to expel the English from Scotland. Less low-budget than no-budget, the film was largely funded, like 1994's *Chasing the Deer* about the Battle of Culloden, by public subscriptions. One has to admire the bravehearts who at least got *The Bruce* made. Unfortunately, one can't much admire the film itself. File this under "Am-dram with ambitions". ▣

Sandy Welch *Robert the Bruce* • Brian Blessed *King Edward* • Michael van Wijk *De Bohun* • Oliver Reed *Bishop Wisharton* ■ *Dir* Bob Carruthers • *Scr* Bob Carruthers, Michael Leighton

Brute Force ★★★★
Prison drama   1947 · US · BW · 94mins

This is one of the great prison dramas, tough even by today's standards, the film's parallels to the Nazi concentration camps would have been obvious to the audience of the time. Hume Cronyn is a sadistic prison warden whose staff systematically brutalise their captives; Burt Lancaster, in his second picture, leads the prisoners in a *Spartacus*-style revolt. Apart from the flashbacks showing prisoners with their wives and girlfriends, the whole movie is a masterpiece of escalating violence, from the shocking moment when an informer is blowtorched to death, to the spectacular climax when Lancaster and his cohorts have a chance to win through. It's a disturbing, powerful picture, handled in an urgent, documentary style by Jules Dassin, who went on to make *The Naked City*.

Burt Lancaster *Joe Collins* • Hume Cronyn *Capt Munsey* • Charles Bickford *Gallagher* • Whit Bissell *Tom Lister* • Sam Levene *Louie* • John Hoyt *Spencer* • Yvonne De Carlo *Gina* • Ann Blyth *Ruth* • Ella Raines *Cora* • Anita Colby *Flossie* ■ *Dir* Jules Dassin • *Scr* Richard Brooks, from a story by Robert Patterson • *Cinematographer* William Daniels

El Bruto ★★★
Drama   1952 · Mex · BW · 82mins

This simmering drama is at least among his more interesting failures. Although he clearly has little sympathy with the worker who becomes a boss's lackey, Buñuel clearly demonstrates the desperate domestic situation that would compel a man to betray his class. Shot in a mere 18 days, the film looks rough, but this only reinforces the atmosphere of life around Mexico City's abattoirs. Katy Jurado is superb, as always, but Pedro Armendariz – Mexico's greatest actor – seems more interested in preserving his macho image than giving a germane performance. In Spanish with English subtitles.

Pedro Armendariz *Pedro* • Katy Jurado *Paloma* • Andres Soler *Andres* • Rosita Arena *Michette* ■ *Dir* Luis Buñuel • *Scr* Luis Buñuel, Luis Alcoriza

The Brylcreem Boys ★★★ 15
Second World War comedy drama
1996 · UK · Colour · 101mins

The Great Escape meets *Riverdance*? Not quite, but this is certainly one of the odder entries in that venerable old genre, the Second World War PoW saga. Loosely based on actual events, the film is set in the Republic of Ireland which, as a neutral country, was committed to interning both German and Allied personnel – in the same camp. Canadian flier Bill Campbell and German air ace Angus

MacFadyen are the two newest internees who come to blows over both the conflict and a local farm girl, played by *Riverdance*'s Jean Butler. There are pleasing supporting turns from John Gordon-Sinclair, William McNamara and, in particular, Gabriel Byrne, while director/co-writer Terence Ryan affably melds together the comic, romantic and dramatic elements of the tale. Contains swearing and some violence. ▣ **DVD**

Bill Campbell *Myles Keogh* • William McNamara *Sam Gunn* • Angus MacFadyen *Rudolph Von Stegenbek* • John Gordon-Sinclair *Richard Lewis* • Oliver Tobias *Hans Jorg Wolff* • Jean Butler *Mattie Guerin* • Joe McGann *Captain Deegan* • Hal Fowler *Bunty Winthrop* • Gabriel Byrne *Commandant O'Brien* ■ *Dir* Terence Ryan • *Scr* Terence Ryan, Jamie Brown, Susan Morrall

The Buccaneer ★★ U
Swashbuckling adventure
1938 · US · BW · 125mins

Cecil B DeMille's lavish juggernaut of a swashbuckler is set during the British-American war of 1812-15, but rather lacks the lightness and humour the genre needs. Fredric March plays the pirate Jean Lafitte, who sides with President Andrew Jackson and runs the British out of New Orleans. The leading lady whom March saves from drowning is Franciska Gaal, a Hungarian discovery of DeMille's who subsequently went home and vanished without a trace. Anthony Quinn, DeMille's son-in-law at the time, plays one of March's henchman. In 1958 Quinn remade the film, as his sole directorial effort.

Fredric March *Jean Lafitte* • Franciska Gaal *Gretchen* • Akim Tamiroff *Dominique You* • Margot Grahame *Annette* • Walter Brennan *Ezra Peavey* • Ian Keith *Crawford* • Spring Byington *Dolly Madison* • Douglass Dumbrille *Governor Claiborne* • Hugh Sothern *Andrew Jackson* • Anthony Quinn *Beluche* ■ *Dir* Cecil B DeMille • *Scr* Edwin Justus Mayer, Harold Lamb, C Gardner Sullivan, Jeanie Macpherson, from the book *Lafitte the Pirate* by Lyle Saxon

The Buccaneer ★★★ U
Swashbuckling adventure
1958 · US · Colour · 118mins

Cecil B DeMille had successfully filmed this tale of pirate Jean Lafitte in 1938 with Fredric March, but DeMille was ailing by the time of this remake, so direction was entrusted to his son-in-law, actor Anthony Quinn (his only film as director). It's a little long and drawn out, but splendid to watch in Technicolor and boasts quite a cast. This time a bewigged Yul Brynner is the dashing Lafitte and his women are Claire Bloom and Inger Stevens, while Charlton Heston appears as General Andrew Jackson. The most impressive sequence is a well-mounted but studio-bound Battle of New Orleans, immortalised by the Johnny Houston/Lonnie Donegan hit ballad. The anti-British sentiments might put off some viewers, but for students of American history and for fans of a Hollywood in decline this is worth a look.

Yul Brynner *Jean Lafitte* • Charlton Heston *General Andrew Jackson* • Claire Bloom *Bonnie Brown* • Charles Boyer *Dominique You* • Inger Stevens *Annette Claiborne* • Henry Hull *Ezra Peavey* • EG Marshall *Governor Claiborne* • Lorne Greene *Mercier* ■ *Dir* Anthony Quinn •

Scr Jesse L Lasky Jr, Bernice Mosk, from the 1938 film, from the book *Lafitte the Pirate* by Lyle Saxon

Buchanan Rides Alone ★★★
Western   1958 · US · Colour · 79mins

One of the colourful B-westerns co-produced by star Randolph Scott and Harry Joe Brown for their Ranown independent production company, and directed by the talented Budd Boetticher. This is an unusual entry in the cycle, since it's based on a novel in a cowboy series (the "Buchanan" books by Jonas Ward) and features a rather more cheerful, humorous hero than usually portrayed by the craggy, taciturn Scott. The myriad plot convolutions are mightily effective, too, but there are no stand-outs in the rather feeble supporting cast.

Randolph Scott *Buchanan* • Craig Stevens *Abe Carbo* • Barry Kelley *Lou Agry* • Tol Avery *Simon Agry* • Peter Whitney *Amos Agry* • Manuel Rojas *Juan* • LQ Jones *Pecos Bill* ■ *Dir* Budd Boetticher • *Scr* Charles Lang, from the novel *The Name's Buchanan* by Jonas Ward

Buck and the Preacher ★★★
Western   1972 · US · Colour · 102mins

Sidney Poitier's first film as director is a lively reworking of a *Wagon Train* idea, with Poitier as leader of a group of slaves, newly freed after the American Civil War, making their way through the wilderness despite harassment by white nightriders trying to take them back to the plantations. A mainly black cast notably avoids "hush-mah-mouth" clichés, while Harry Belafonte gives real edge to his con-man preacher whose slickness turns eventually to integrity. One of those rare movies in which the Indians, rather than the cowboys, ride to the rescue. Contains swearing.

Sidney Poitier *Buck* • Harry Belafonte *Preacher* • Ruby Dee *Ruth* • Cameron Mitchell *Deshay* • Denny Miller *Floyd* • Nita Talbot *Madame Esther* • John Kelly *Sheriff* • Tony Brubaker *Headman* • James McEachin *Kingston* ■ *Dir* Sidney Poitier • *Scr* Ernest Kinoy, from a story by Ernest Kinoy, Drake Walker

Buck Privates ★★★
Comedy   1941 · US · BW · 84mins

A decade after they first joined forces as a makeshift vaudeville act, Abbott and Costello went stellar with this, their second film. It's hard to see why the picture grossed over $10 million at the US box office – a phenomenal sum for the times – though it's amusing enough. Here Bud and Lou are drafted by accident and find themselves having to adjudicate in a military *ménage à trois* between Alan Curtis, Lee Bowman and Jane Frazee. The highlights are provided by the Andrews Sisters' renditions of some top-notch tunes, including the Oscar-nominated *Boogie Woogie Bugle Boy from Company B*.

Bud Abbott *Slicker Smith* • Lou Costello *Herbie Brown* • Lee Bowman *Randolph Parker III* • Alan Curtis *Bob Martin* • Jane Frazee *Judy Gray* ■ *Dir* Arthur Lubin • *Scr* Arthur T Horman, John Grant

Buck Privates Come Home ★ U
Comedy   1947 · US · BW · 77mins

After the huge success of Abbott and Costello's second feature, *Buck Privates*, a sequel was an inevitable. But Bud and Lou had packed 18 movies into the six years that separated the two films, and it's all too obvious to see how thinly the material has been spread. Borrowing heavily from Laurel and Hardy's *Pack Up Your Troubles*, the story sees the boys having to baby-sit a French orphan who has been smuggled home by their army buddy. The chase is frantic enough, but time weighs heavily for much of the rest.

Bud Abbott *Cpl Slicker Smith* • Lou Costello *Herbie Brown* • Tom Brown *Bill Gregory* • Joan Fulton *Sylvia Hunter* • Nat Pendleton *Sgt Collins* • Don Beddoe *Mr Roberts* • Don Porter *Captain* ■ *Dir* Charles Barton • *Scr* John Grant, Frederic I Rinaldo, Robert Lees, from a story by Richard Macauley, Bradford Ropes

Buck Rogers in the 25th Century ★★ 15
Science-fiction adventure
1979 · US · Colour · 88mins

Only American television could lavishly update a thirties' film serial and make it more trivial and corny than the original. Even funnier, in the post-*Star Wars* glow of space warriors, cute cyborgs and colourful spectacle, is the fact that people actually paid money to see this TV pilot in the cinema. Hunky Gil Gerard jockeys his way through the good versus evil pastiche, with added comedy relief, and the whole thing remains strictly intergalactic kids' stuff. Mel Blanc, man of a thousand voices (including Bugs Bunny's), supplies yet another, that of a diminutive robot called Twiki. ▣

Gil Gerard *"Buck" Rogers* • Pamela Hensley *Princess Ardala* • Erin Gray *Colonel Wilma Deering* • Henry Silva *Kane* • Tim O'Connor *Dr Huer* • Felix Silla *Twiki* • Mel Blanc *Twiki* • Joseph Wiseman *Draco* • Duke Butler *First Tigerman* ■ *Dir* Daniel Haller • *Scr* Glen Larson, Leslie Stevens, from characters created by Robert C Dille

A Bucket of Blood ★★★ 15
Horror comedy   1959 · US · BW · 64mins

Essential Roger Corman. Hopeless as a horror film, but priceless as a hip black comedy, this beatnik variation on *House of Wax* has coffee-bar worker Walter Paisley (wonderfully played by Corman regular Dick Miller) hailed as a cool "art" genius when he turns dead bodies into sculpture. Filmed in five days, Corman's cult sickie-quickie is a brilliant satire on the whole Beat Generation scene. ▣

Dick Miller *Walter Paisley* • Barboura Morris *Carla* • Antony Carbone *Leonard* • Julian Burton *Brock* • Ed Nelson *Art Lacroix* • John Brinkley *Will* • John Shaner *Oscar* ■ *Dir* Roger Corman • *Scr* Charles B Griffith

Buddy ★★★ U
Biographical period drama
1997 · US · Colour · 80mins

This sweet but missable film stars Rene Russo as Trudy Lintz, a woman in the twenties who became known for the collection of animals she looked

after at her Long Island home. The film focuses on Trudy's attempts to raise Buddy, a baby gorilla that she treats as if it were her own child. Alan Cumming (*Circle of Friends*) and Robbie Coltrane also turn up in Caroline Thompson's film. An ideal Sunday afternoon weepie.

Rene Russo *Trudy Lintz* • Robbie Coltrane *Dr Lintz* • Alan Cumming *Dick* • Irma P Hall *Emma* • Paul Reubens *Professor Spatz* • John Aylward *Mr Bowman* • Mimi Kennedy *Mrs Bowman* ■ *Dir* Caroline Thompson • *Scr* Caroline Thompson, from a story by William Joyce, Caroline Thompson, from the novel *Animals Are My Hobby* by Gertrude Davies Lintz

Buddy Buddy ★★ 15

Comedy   1981 · US · Colour · 91mins

Ever since their first film together Jack Lemmon and Walter Matthau have been the odd couple of the movies, as inseparable as Laurel and Hardy. But this farce marks the low point in their chalk-and-cheese collaboration, with slapstick usurping the biting wit of previous productions. Matthau is a hit man who's hampered in his job by a suicide-bent Lemmon. Adapted from the funnier French comedy, *A Pain in the A…!*, its jokes are ill-timed and the mutual admiration society of its two stars becomes tedious.

Jack Lemmon *Victor Clooney* • Walter Matthau *Trabucco* • Paula Prentiss *Celia Clooney* • Klaus Kinski *Dr Zuckerbrot* • Dana Elcar *Captain Hubris* • Miles Chapin *Eddie the bellhop* • Michael Ensign *Assistant manager* • Joan Shawlee *Receptionist* ■ *Dir* Billy Wilder • *Scr* Billy Wilder, Ial Diamond, from the story and play *A Pain in the A …* by Francis Veber

The Buddy Holly Story ★★★★ PG

Biography   1978 · US · Colour · 108mins

A stunningly well-made biopic of the legendary rock 'n' roller, who met his tragically premature end in a plane crash in 1959. Gary Busey has never matched the marvellous Oscar-nominated performance he gives here, contenting himself instead with a rogues' gallery of roles as cops and psychos ever since. Director Steve Rash has likewise never managed to recapture the verve he conjures up here. The movie is made doubly enjoyable by the knowledge that Busey and the movie's Crickets actually do their own singing and playing, generating their own very palpable raw energy in the process.

Gary Busey *Buddy Holly* • Don Stroud *Jesse Clarence* • Charles Martin Smith *Ray Bob Simmons* • William Jordan *Riley Randolph* • Maria Richwine *Maria Elena Santiago* • Conrad Janis *Ross Turner* • Albert Popwell *Eddie Foster* • Amy Johnston *Cindy Lou* ■ *Dir* Steve Rash • *Scr* Robert Gittler, from a story by Alan Swyer, from the biography *Buddy Holly His Life and Music* by John Coldrosen

The Buddy System ★★ PG

Romantic comedy drama
1984 · US · Colour · 105mins

From the doldrums of Richard Dreyfuss's movie career comes this pale imitation of *The Goodbye Girl*, in which he played a frustrated actor involved in an on/off relationship with a single mother and her precocious daughter. This time round he is a

frustrated writer, forced to take a security job at the local school where he pals up with single mom Susan Sarandon's precocious 11-year-old son. From then on, it's the "will they/won't they?" scenario. You'd think that such a cast would be box-office gold, but sadly the pair fail to sizzle. While *The Goodbye Girl* had Neil Simon's tart script, this harmless romantic comedy is pleasant rather than dynamic.

Richard Dreyfuss *Joe* • Susan Sarandon *Emily* • Nancy Allen *Carrie* • Jean Stapleton *Mrs Price* • Wil Wheaton *Tim* • Edward Winter *Jim Parks* • Keene Curtis *Dr Knitz* ■ *Dir* Glenn Jordan • *Scr* Mary Agnes Donoghue

Buddy's Song ★★ PG

Drama   1990 · UK · Colour · 102mins

The One and Only has turned out to be something of a self-fulfilling prophesy for Chesney Hawkes, for not only has he struggled to repeat the success of that hit single, but *Buddy's Song* is also his only movie of any note. And you can see why. Nigel Hinton has done his popular teen novel a major disservice with his clumsy adaptation that failed to convince the younger members of the audience, while boring the pants off their parents. Roger Daltrey gives a knowing and willing performance as Buddy's teddy boy dad, but Sharon Duce and Michael Elphick settle for caricatures. As for poor old Ches… Contains mild violence, swearing and brief nudity.

Roger Daltrey *Terry Clark* • Chesney Hawkes *Buddy* • Sharon Duce *Carol* • Michael Elphick *Des King* • Douglas Hodge *Bobby Rosen* • Paul McKenzie *Julius* • Lee Ross *Jason* • Nick Moran *Mike* ■ *Dir* Claude Watham • *Scr* Nigel Hinton, from his novel

Buena Vista Social Club ★★★★ U

Music documentary
1998 · Ger · Colour · 100mins

A charming tale to lift the heart and soothe the soul, director Wim Wenders's movie follows in the footsteps of the legendary record by influential guitarist Ry Cooder and catches, as he did, the rhythm and blues of a group of elderly Cuban musicians – the oldest over 90. All had been forgotten or banned in their own country, but can now be heard by a world that had consigned them to a bygone age. The visual style sometimes detracts from the lyrical substance – the camera keeps circling soloists to an irritating degree – but, despite that, it is still one of the greatest documentaries ever made on music and the strength of the human spirit. In English and Spanish with subtitles. *DVD*

Dir Wim Wenders

Buffalo Bill ★★★ U

Western   1944 · US · Colour · 90mins

You won't learn much about the real William Frederick Cody from this conventional and sentimental western, with a stalwart, though rather dull, Joel McCrea in the lead. Still, redhead Maureen O'Hara and the striking locations were made for Fox Technicolor – though these days you have to take Anthony Quinn and Linda Darnell made-up as Cheyenne Indians

with a pinch of salt. Director William A Wellman knows how to keep this film moving, but spends too much time on the romance in Buffalo Bill's life rather than on the building of his Wild West image abroad.

Joel McCrea *Buffalo Bill* • Maureen O'Hara *Louisa Cody* • Linda Darnell *Dawn Starlight* • Thomas Mitchell *Ned Buntline* • Edgar Buchanan *Sergeant Chips* • Anthony Quinn *Yellow Hand* • Moroni Olsen *Senator Frederici* • Frank Fenton *Murdo Carvell* ■ *Dir* William A Wellman • *Scr* Aeneas MacKenzie, Clements Ripley, Cecile Kramer, from a story by Frank Winch • *Cinematographer* Leon Shamroy

Buffalo Bill and the Indians, or Sitting Bull's History Lesson ★★ PG

Western   1976 · US · Colour · 118mins

Like so many of Robert Altman's pictures, this is a glorious, infuriating mess, a whirl of half-baked ideas, missed opportunities and startling moments. It started out, though, as a project to follow *Butch Cassidy and the Sundance Kid* for Paul Newman and director George Roy Hill. Newman remained on board and plays Buffalo Bill with golden locks and a twinkle in his eye, a phoney and a showman, a Hollywood producer before his time, who hires Sitting Bull for his travelling Wild West show. Co-stars Burt Lancaster, Joel Grey, Geraldine Chaplin and Harvey Keitel drift in and out of a picture driven solely by Altman's unfocused vision of a people on the edge of extinction and a country in turmoil. Contains mild swearing.

Paul Newman *Buffalo Bill* • Joel Grey *Nate Salsbury* • Burt Lancaster *Ned Buntline* • Kevin McCarthy *Major John Burke* • Harvey Keitel *Ed Goodman* • Allan Nicholls *Prentiss Ingraham* • Geraldine Chaplin *Annie Oakley* • John Considine *Frank Butler* • Frank Kaquitts *Sitting Bull* ■ *Dir* Robert Altman • *Scr* Alan Rudolph, Robert Altman, from the play *Indians* by Arthur Kopit

Buffalo '66 ★★★★ 15

Drama   1997 · Can/US · Colour · 109mins

Touted by actor/director Vincent Gallo as a self-styled masterpiece, this searing view of twentysomething disillusionment is indeed as arrogantly conceited as the man himself. But his grimy, ironic look at uncaring family life, and the emotional pain it causes, is also an amazing slice of neo-existentialism that takes breathtaking risks and breaks rules. Gallo plays the born loser desperate for a lucky break who unknowingly finds one when he kidnaps Christina Ricci to play his wife for an overdue family visit. Sharp dialogue and unusual flashbacks interrupting the main action inexorably lead to an uplifting pay-off that is well worth the wait. A minor gem, thanks mainly to Gallo's talent for making even the most unlikeable characters sympathetic. Contains swearing, and some violence.

Vincent Gallo *Billy Brown* • Christina Ricci *Layla* • Ben Gazzara *Jimmy Brown* • Mickey Rourke *The Bookie* • Rosanna Arquette *Wendy Balsam* • Jan-Michael Vincent *Sonny* • Anjelica Huston *Janet "Jan" Brown* ■ *Dir* Vincent Gallo • *Scr* Vincent Gallo, Alison Bagnall, from a story by Vincent Gallo • *Music* Vincent Gallo

Buffalo Soldiers ★★★ 15

Western war drama
1997 · US · Colour · 90mins

Based on actual events, this quality TV movie is well worth seeing. In post-Civil War New Mexico, an all-black cavalry troop under the leadership of a fearless ex-slave (Danny Glover) pursues an Apache warrior through the territory. The tight-knit group must also suffer the endless degradation heaped upon them by white officers in the segregated army. Glover gives a strong lead to the proceedings, and Charles Haid, who starred in the hit TV show *Hill Street Blues*, directs.

Danny Glover *Sergeant Wyatt* • Bob Gunton *Colonel Grierson* • Carl Lumbly *Horse* • Glynn Turman *Sergeant Joshua "Joju" Judges Ruth* • Mykel T Williamson *Corporal William Christy* • Lamont Bentley *Corporal Sea* • Tom Bower *General Pike* • Timothy Busfield *Major Robert Carr* ■ *Dir* Charles Haid • *Scr* Frank Military, Susan Rhinehart, from a story by Jonathan Klein, Frank Military

Buffet Froid ★★★ 15

Black comedy   1979 · Fr · Colour · 89mins

Not since *The Treasure of the Sierra Madre* has a son directed his father with such a mischievous sense of respect as in this savage black comedy. As the inspector inexorably drawn into a series of bizarre murders, Bernard Blier is given full rein by his son, Bertrand, who also coaxes a full-throttled display of blue collar boorishness from Gérard Depardieu as the casual killer caught up in the crimes of serial maniac Jean Carmet. For all its exuberance and insolence, though, the film does occasionally feel like a smorgasbord of leftovers from Buñuel and other absurdists. In French with English subtitles.

Gérard Depardieu *Alphonse Tram* • Bernard Blier *Inspector Morvandieu* • Jean Carmet *Murderer* • Genevieve Page *Widow* • Denise Gence *Hostess* • Carole Bouquet *Young girl* • Michel Serrault *Man in subway* ■ *Dir/Scr* Bertrand Blier

Buffy the Vampire Slayer ★★★ 15

Comedy horror   1992 · US · Colour · 81mins

Clueless meets *Dracula* in this engagingly silly, yet knowing, horror comedy that deserves cult status. Kristy Swanson is cheerfully dim-witted as LA teenager Buffy, who's surprised to discover that she is actually the only person who can save the city from suave Rutger Hauer and his fellow vampires. Director Fran Rubel Kuzui rightly plays it like a comic strip and draws perfectly judged performances from an eclectic cast that also includes teen heart-throb Luke Perry, Donald Sutherland, an unrecognisable Paul Reubens (Pee-wee Herman) and an uncredited appearance from Ben Affleck. Fun, but fans of the TV series starring Sarah Michelle Gellar will be disappointed.

Kristy Swanson *Buffy* • Donald Sutherland *Merrick* • Paul Reubens *Amilyn* • Rutger Hauer *Lothos* • Luke Perry *Pike* • Michele Abrams *Jennifer* • Hilary Swank *Kimberly* • Paris Vaughn *Nicole* • David Arquette *Benny* ■ *Dir* Fran Rubel Kuzui • *Scr* Joss Whedon

Bug ★★ 15

Horror   1975 · US · Colour · 95mins

The last film produced by William Castle, the king of gimmick cinema (*The Tingler*, *Macabre*), is one of his better efforts. An earthquake unleashes a swarm of fire-making insects and scientist Bradford Dillman mates them with the common cockroach in order to communicate with them. The initial nature-revenge plot tends to get lost once the routine mad-doctor thread takes over, but zestful direction and tongue-in-cheek acting eke out some decent thrills and chills from the implausible tale. Castle originally wanted to present this in "Feel-O-Vision", with windscreen wiper-style brushes attached to every cinema seat, but was deterred by the huge costs involved. ▢

Bradford Dillman *James Parmiter* • Joanna Miles *Carrie Parmiter* • Richard Gilliland *Metbaum* • Jamie Smith Jackson *Norma Tacker* • Alan Fudge *Mark Ross* • Jesse Vint *Tom Tacker* • Brenden Dillon *Charlie* ■ *Dir* Jeannot Szwarc • *Scr* Thomas Page, William Castle, from the novel *The Hephaestus Plague* by Thomas Page

Bugles in the Afternoon ★★ U

Western   1952 · US · Colour · 84mins

A disappointing, would-be stirring Warner Bros western, adapted from an excellent novel by Ernest Haycox, but seriously hampered by poor casting. The urbane Ray Milland looks uncomfortable out west and fails to convince as a disgraced coward, looking generally peeved rather than seething with inner rage. He's not helped by a sub-par supporting cast and a totally inadequate leading lady in Helena Carter. Nevertheless, the exterior Technicolor location photography is impressive, and the action scenes are well staged, within obvious budgetary limitations. Dmitri Tiomkin's score is nice, too.

Ray Milland *Kern Shafter* • Helena Carter *Josephine Russell* • Hugh Marlowe *Captain Edward Garnett* • Forrest Tucker *Private Donovan* • Barton MacLane *Captain Myles Moylan* • George Reeves *Lieutenant Smith* • James Millican *Sergeant Hines* • Gertrude Michael *May* ■ *Dir* Roy Rowland • *Scr* Geoffrey Homes [Daniel Mainwaring], Harry Brown, from a novel by Ernest Haycox • *Cinematographer* Wilfrid M Cline

Bugs ★★ 18

Horror   1990 · US · Colour · 85mins

Although this is a sequel in name only to the previous three Santa Claus gore sagas (it's also known as *Silent Night, Deadly Night 4: Initiation*) director Brian Yuzna still manages to pile on the unpleasantness in a sexy shocker with a high disgust factor. Satanic cult leader Maud Adams terrorises LA reporter Neith Hunter with all manner of creepy-crawlies in this weird insect spin on *Rosemary's Baby*, while Clint Howard, as Adams's lackey, commits nasty murders in return for bug feasts. ▢

Maud Adams *Fima* • Neith Hunter *Kim* • Tommy Hinkley *Hank* • Hugh Fink *Jeff* • Richard N Gladstein *Woody* • Reggie Bannister *Eli* • Allyce Beasley *Janice* • Clint Howard *Ricky* ■ *Dir* Brian Yuzna • *Scr* Woody Keith

Bugs Bunny 1001 Rabbit Tales ★★★

Animation compilation
1982 · US · Colour · 90mins

This slickly assembled compilation film was produced by Friz Freleng, the genius behind many of the most popular Warner Bros cartoon characters and a pioneer of the crash-bang style of animation known as "socko". Voiced, as ever, by the legendary Mel Blanc, Bugs Bunny and Daffy Duck here find themselves reliving some classic capers as they try to sell books to some highly resistant customers. As you would expect, the quality is inconsistent, but there are some cracking slapstick gags and lots of cringe-worthy puns.

Mel Blanc ■ *Dir* David Detiege, Art Davis, Bill Perez, Friz Freleng • *Scr* John Dunn, David Detiege, Friz Freleng

The Bugs Bunny/Road Runner Movie ★★★★ U

Animation compilation
1979 · US · Colour · 97mins

Not really a film in the true sense of the word, this is essentially the best of Bugs tenuously linked by the presence of the much loved rabbit. But as it brings together some of the most memorable shorts devised by animation legend Chuck Jones, who's complaining? Along with Bugs, his long-suffering adversaries Daffy Duck and Porky Pig get plenty of screen time, while Wile E Coyote gets to suffer endless humiliation at the hands of his nemesis Road Runner. You've probably seen most of the sketches on TV before, but that by no means lessens the enjoyment.

Mel Blanc ■ *Dir* Chuck Jones, Phil Monroe • *Scr* Chuck Jones, Michael Maltese

A Bug's Life ★★★★ U

Animated adventure
1998 · US · Colour · 93mins

Director John Lasseter broke new ground with the computer animation for Disney's *Toy Story* (1995). *A Bug's Life* improves upon that film's wondrous effects, although its insect characters are less beguiling than their predecessors. Flik (voiced by David Foley) is the outsider ant blamed for his colony for destroying the sacrifice regularly offered to the band of hostile grasshoppers led by bullying Hopper (Kevin Spacey). So Flik hires a flea circus of colourful eccentrics to scare off the terrorists. The result is a witty variation of *The Seven Samurai*, filled with verdant art and heart – though it lacks the social message of the similarly themed *Antz*, which appeared the same year. ▢ **DVD**

Kevin Spacey *Hopper* • Julia Louis-Dreyfus *Princess Atta* • Phyllis Diller *Queen* • Richard Kind *Molt* • Denis Leary *Francis* • Bonnie Hunt *Rosie* • Roddy McDowall *Mr Soil* • Dave Foley *Flik* ■ *Dir* John Lasseter • *Scr* Andrew Stanton, Donald Mcenery, Bob Shaw, from the story *The Ant and the Grasshopper* by Aesop

Bugsy ★★★★ 18

Crime drama   1991 · US · Colour · 130mins

While avoiding the usual gangster film clichés, director Barry Levinson also insists that Warren Beatty does more than coast through the movie on matinée idol looks and easy charm. Beatty is charismatically dangerous as gangster Benjamin "Bugsy" Siegel, switching unnervingly from flirtation to rage, even if his on-screen romance with Annette Bening never really catches fire (unlike their off-screen relationship, which led to marriage and parenthood). This double Oscar winner (for costume and art direction) is strong on pumping narrative, and strewn with memorable scenes and distinctive criminals. Contains violence and swearing. ▢ **DVD**

Warren Beatty *Benjamin "Bugsy" Siegel* • Annette Bening *Virginia Hill* • Harvey Keitel *Mickey Cohen* • Ben Kingsley *Meyer Lansky* • Elliott Gould *Harry Greenberg* • Joe Mantegna *George Raft* • Richard Sarafian [Richard C Sarafian] *Jack Dragna* • Bebe Neuwirth *Countess Di Frasso* ■ *Dir* Barry Levinson • *Scr* James Toback, from the book *We Only Kill Each Other: the Life and Bad Times of Bugsy Siegel* by Dean Jennings • *Art Director* Dennis Gassner • *Set Designer* Nancy Haigh • *Costume Designer* Albert Wolsky

Bugsy Malone ★★★★ U

Spoof gangster musical
1976 · UK · Colour · 89mins

Alan Parker's first feature, following a number of social-realist scripts for the BBC, was a deliberate attempt to get attention. And, by casting children as American gangsters whose Tommy guns fire gunk, Parker achieved his ambition: the movie was the buttered toast of the Cannes film festival and a flamboyant career was under way. Using techniques borrowed from old Hollywood movies, as well as the polish that he learned from his many TV commercials, Parker creates a vibrant pastiche that hovers just on the brink of cutesiness. The children have an edge to their performances that cuts through sentiment – most notably Jodie Foster, whose extraordinarily slinky speakeasy number, *My Name Is Tallulah*, is the film's memorable highlight. ▢ **DVD**

Scott Baio *Bugsy Malone* • Jodie Foster *Tallulah* • Florrie Dugger *Blousey* • John Cassisi *Fat Sam* • Martin Lev *Dandy Dan* • Paul Murphy *Leroy* • "Humpty" [Albin Jenkins *Fizzy* • Davidson Knight *Cagey Joe* ■ *Dir/Scr* Alan Parker • *Music/Lyrics* Paul Williams

Build My Gallows High ★★★★★ PG

Film noir   1947 · US · BW · 92mins

This classic forties' *film noir*, better known in the States as *Out of the Past*, has a memorably languid performance by Robert Mitchum as the ultra hard-boiled former private eye who falls for the doll (Jane Greer) he's been hired to track by gangster Kirk Douglas. It was remade in 1984 as *Against All Odds* (with Jeff Bridges and Rachel Ward), but nowhere near as effectively as this stylish, atmospheric, highly watchable and strongly recommended original from genre expert Jacques Tourneur, who also made horror classics *I Walked with a Zombie*, *Cat People* and *Night of the Demon*. The film's scriptwriter, Daniel Mainwaring (writing here under the name Geoffrey Homes), also penned the sci-fi gem *Invasion of the Body Snatchers*. ▢

Robert Mitchum *Jeff Bailey* • Jane Greer *Kathie Moffett* • Kirk Douglas *Whit Sterling* • Rhonda Fleming *Meta Carson* • Richard Webb *Jim* • Steve Brodie *Fisher* • Virginia Huston *Ann* • Paul Valentine *Joe* ■ *Dir* Jacques Tourneur • *Scr* Geoffrey Homes [Daniel Mainwaring], from his novel *Build My Gallows High* • *Cinematographer* Nicholas Musuraca

Bull Durham ★★★★ 18

Comedy drama   1988 · US · Colour · 103mins

Director Ron Shelton has proved more creative with baseball than most directors – he also brought *Cobb* to the big screen, in which Tommy Lee Jones thunders magnificently as the twisted baseball star. Shelton's first baseball winner was with *Bull Durham*, in which his detailed love of the sport never becomes the usual tired tale of the heart. Instead it propels a smart, witty character piece, featuring an electric love story between Susan Sarandon and Tim Robbins, with Kevin Costner brooding convincingly in the wings. All three actors make the picture really sizzle. Contains swearing. ▢

Kevin Costner *Crash Davis* • Susan Sarandon *Annie Savoy* • Tim Robbins *Ebby Calvin "Nuke" Laloosh* • Trey Wilson *Joe "Skip" Riggins* • Robert Wuhl *Larry Hockett* • William O'Leary *Jimmy* • David Neidorf *Bobby* • Danny Gans *Deke* ■ *Dir/Scr* Ron Shelton

The Bulldog Breed ★★ PG

Comedy   1960 · UK · BW · 93mins

There is no doubt where the fun lies in this merely adequate comedy – it's in the brief sight of hopefuls Michael Caine and Oliver Reed playing second fiddle to Norman Wisdom. Coming towards the end of his purple patch, Norman is not at his best as the fumbling shop assistant whose career in the navy culminates in an ill-fated moonshot. The script does him few favours, however, restricting the opportunities for sentimental slapstick in order to accommodate the surplus plot. Dependable stooges do all that is expected, with Edward Chapman at his bullying best as Norman's grocer boss. ▢

Norman Wisdom *Norman Puckle* • Ian Hunter *Admiral Sir Bryanston Blyth* • David Lodge *CPO Knowles* • Robert Urquhart *Commander Clayton* • Edward Chapman *Mr Philpots* • John Le Mesurier *Prosecuting counsel* • Michael Caine *Sailor* • Oliver Reed ■ *Dir* Robert Asher • *Scr* Jack Davies, Henry Blyth, Norman Wisdom

Bulldog Drummond ★★★

Mystery adventure   1929 · US · BW · 90mins

Suave Ronald Colman's first talkie revealed to movie-goers the dulcet tones and perfect enunciation that would become a model for all future screen matinée idols. As the ex-army adventure hero of a series of popular novels by "Sapper" (HC McNeile), Colman is splendidly cast. He provides a Drummond that others found impossible to better, while Claud Allister is the definitive Algy, Drummond's constant companion. This is an exceptionally well-mounted early talkie with much of value, though its creakiness can sometimes make it difficult to view.

Ronald Colman *Bulldog Drummond* • Joan Bennett *Phyllis Benton* • Lilyan Tashman *Erma Peterson* • Montagu Love *Carl Peterson* •

Lawrence Grant *Doctor Lakington* • Wilson Benge *Danny* • Claud Allister *Algy Longworth* ■ *Dir* F Richard Jones • *Scr* Wallace Smith, Sidney Howard, from the play by Sapper [HC McNeile], Gerald Du Maurier

Bulldog Drummond Strikes Back ★★★

Mystery adventure 1934 · US · BW · 0mins

Ronald Colman in his rarely seen second outing as super-sleuth and 007 precursor Bulldog Drummond, the clubland hero created by "Sapper" in 1919. The picture had a British rival called *The Return of Bulldog Drummond* starring Ralph Richardson and Ann Todd, which doubtless confused audiences at the time. Colman is suave, fearless and witty, while co-star Loretta Young is there to look pretty and to be kidnapped more than once. Nunnally Johnson's screenplay has a few sharp lines and Roy Del Ruth, best known for his breezy musicals, directs with dollar efficiency to disguise the dime budget.

Ronald Colman *Captain Hugh Drummond* • Loretta Young *Lola Field* • C Aubrey Smith *Inspector Nielsen* • Charles Butterworth *Algy Longworth* • Una Merkel *Gwen* • Warner Oland *Prince Achmed* • George Regas *Singh* • Mischa Auer *Hassan* ■ *Dir* Roy Del Ruth • *Scr* Nunnally Johnson, Henry Lehrman, from the novel by Sapper [HC McNeile]

Bulldog Drummond Strikes Back ★

Mystery adventure 1947 · US · BW · 64mins

One of the 20-odd movies to feature the James Bond forerunner Bulldog Drummond, created in 1919 by HC "Sapper" McNeile as a post-First World War clubland hero whose daring exploits sold in their millions. Kicked off in 1929 with Ronald Colman, the series quickly went down-market as various British and American studios bought and sold the franchise. This dismal entry stars Ron Randell, an Australian actor who played Drummond twice. Here he's involved in a stale plot about an inheritance, a peeved heiress and other cardboard cut-outs. For completists only.

Ron Randell *Bulldog Drummond* • Gloria Henry *Ellen Curtiss* • Pat O'Moore *Algy Longworth* • Anabel Shaw *Ellen Curtiss #2* • Holmes Herbert *Inspector McIver* • Wilton Graff *Cedric Mason* • Matthew Boulton *William Cosgrove* • Terry Kilburn *Seymour* ■ *Dir* Frank McDonald • *Scr* Edward Anhalt, Edna Anhalt, from the novel by Sapper [HC McNeile]

Bulldog Jack ★★★ U

Comedy crime drama
1934 · UK · BW · 69mins

British comedies have rarely travelled well across the Atlantic, but none has been so mistreated as this Gaumont spoof on the *Bulldog Drummond* myth, which was shown in the States as a straight thriller with all the gags removed! In his only screen teaming with his brother Claude, Jack Hulbert is all jutting chin and silly expressions as he pursues villainous Ralph Richardson and rescues thirties scream queen Fay Wray. Produced by Michael Balcon and co-scripted by Sidney Gilliat, the film also makes a sly dig at Alfred Hitchcock's fondness for finales at a famous landmark. ▦

Fay Wray *Ann Manders* • Jack Hulbert *Jack Pennington* • Claude Hulbert *Algy Longworth* • Ralph Richardson *Morelle* • Paul Graetz *Salvini* • Gibb McLaughlin *Denny* • Atholl Fleming *Bulldog Drummond* ■ *Dir* Walter Forde • *Scr* Sapper [HC McNeile], Gerard Fairlie, JOC Orton, Sidney Gilliat, from an idea by Jack Hulbert, from the character created by Sapper [HC McNeile]

Bullet ★ 18

Crime drama 1995 · US · Colour · 90mins

The first few moments of Mickey Rourke (in his late thirties) acting and dressing like a gang-banger must be some of the most unintentionally hilarious footage ever shot for a motion picture. Unfortunately, the laughs soon evaporate when he starts to mutter in his infamous style and his performance is enough to bury any other good impressions that this snail-paced movie could have generated. The meandering plot has Rourke being released from prison, teaming up with his Jewish homeboys and doing everything possible to shorten his chance of staying alive on New York's mean streets. This was shelved and was only released on video after co-star Tupac Shakur was murdered; despite his trumpeted appearance, he only appears for a few minutes. Contains swearing, sex scenes and violence. ▦

Mickey Rourke *Butch "Bullet" Stein* • Tupac Shakur *Tank* • Ted Levine *Louis* • Donnie Wahlberg *Big Balls* • John Enos III [John Enos] *Lester* • Adrien Brody *Ruby* ■ *Dir* Julien Temple • *Scr* Bruce Rubinstein, Sir Eddie Cook

Bullet for a Badman ★★★ PG

Western 1964 · US · Colour · 76mins

This is a rare decent role for Audie Murphy, and the baby-faced war hero rises to the occasion, making one regret that he had so few opportunities to fulfil his potential. This RG Springsteen western has Murphy vying with baddie Darren McGavin for Ruta Lee, as he heads a posse escorting McGavin back to town for justice. Photographed by the great Joe Biroc and featuring a marvellous supporting cast of familiar faces, this is a pleasure to watch. ▦

Audie Murphy *Logan Keliher* • Darren McGavin *Sam Ward* • Ruta Lee *Lottie* • Beverley Owen *Susan* • Skip Homeier *Pink* • George Tobias *Diggs* • Alan Hale Jr *Leach* • Berkeley Harris *Jeff* ■ *Dir* RG Springsteen • *Scr* Mary Willingham, Willard Willingham, from the novel by Marvin H Albert

A Bullet for Joey ★★

Spy crime drama 1955 · US · BW · 86mins

A disappointing reunion of Edward G Robinson and George Raft, this economically made crime melodrama revolves about a communist spy's use of an exiled gangster to kidnap an atomic scientist. Raft plays the gangster, while Robinson is the police inspector who uncovers the scheme. Their climactic encounter on a boat takes too long to materialise and feebly suggests that even mobsters are patriots when it comes to the Red menace. Audrey Totter and Peter Van Eyck deliver sharp performances as the moll who seduces the scientist, and the master spy, respectively.

Edward G Robinson *Inspector Raoul Leduc* • George Raft *Joe Victor* • Audrey Totter *Joyce Geary* • George Dolenz *Carl Macklin* • Peter Hanson *Fred* • Peter Van Eyck *Eric Hartman* ■ *Dir* Lewis Allen • *Scr* Geoffrey Homes [Daniel Mainwaring], Al Bezzerides, from a story by James Benson Nablo

A Bullet for Sandoval ★★★

Spaghetti western
1970 · It/Sp · Colour · 91mins

The three stars are principally there for the climax: a battle between four desperate gringos and hundreds of Mexican soldiers, all crowded into a bullring where they blast each other to pieces. It's the sort of deadly, crimson-coloured ballet that Sergio Leone made famous, and one which Julio Buchs stages with just as much arty brio. Until then, though, it's the usual overcooked spaghetti, with an American star (Ernest Borgnine) wading through a botched revenge plot and talking to badly dubbed Italian actors. Italian dialogue dubbed into English.

Ernest Borgnine *Don Pedro Sandoval* • George Hilton *Warner* • Alberto de Mendoza *Lucky boy* • Leo Anchoriz *Padre* • Antonio Pica *Sam* • Jose Manuel Martin *Cross-eyed man* • Manuel de Blas *Jose* • Manuel Miranda *Francisco* ■ *Dir* Julio Buchs • *Scr* Ugo Guerra, Jose Luis Martinez Molla, Federico De Urrutia, Julio Buchs, from a story by Jose Luis Martinez Molla, Federico De Urrutia

A Bullet for the General ★★★ 18

Spaghetti western
1966 · It · Colour · 112mins

Think spaghetti western and Sergio Leone will always spring to mind. Other directors who toyed with the form are generally overlooked, including Italian Damiano Damiani, whose film is a very decent stab at the genre. Capably instilling the violence with intelligent, probing moral concern, Damiani also casts Gian Maria Volonté and Klaus Kinski, both of whom star alongside Clint Eastwood in Leone's *For a Few Dollars More*. There is a creative tension throughout between introspection and exuberance. Italian dialogue dubbed into English. ▦

Gian Maria Volonté *El Chuncho* • Klaus Kinski *Santo* • Lou Castel *Bill Tate* • Jaime Fernandez *General Elias* • Andrea Checchi *Don Felipe* • Spartaco Conversi *Cirillo* • Joaquin Parra *Picaro* • Jose Manuel Martin *Raimundo* ■ *Dir* Damiano Damiani • *Scr* Salvatore Laurani, Franco Solinas

Bullet in the Head ★★★ 18

Crime drama 1990 · HK · Colour · 125mins

One of the more personal films in John Woo's canon and one which combines the highly stylised themes and motifs of his gangster films with a grittier than usual edge. Tony Leung, Jacky Cheung and Waise Lee play a trio of Hong Kong chums who see the chance to make a fortune in sixties Vietnam, but find their friendship pushed to the limit by the war. It's not without its flaws, but bravura direction from Woo carries the day and it provides a fascinating view of a conflict usually seen from a western perspective. In Cantonese with English subtitles. Contains violence and swearing. ▦

Tony Chiu-Wai Leung [Tony Leung (1)] *Ben* • Jacky Cheung *Frank* • Lee Waise *Paul* • Simon

Yam *Luke* • Fennie Yeun *Jane* ■ *Dir* John Woo • *Scr* John Woo, Patrick Leung, Janet Chung

A Bullet Is Waiting ★ U

Crime drama 1954 · US · Colour · 81mins

The audience is waiting, too – for something, *anything* to happen. The film starts with a plane crash that strands Stephen McNally's sheriff at a sheep ranch with his captive (Rory Calhoun), an alleged murderer. It becomes bogged down in endless talk as lonely shepherdess Jean Simmons takes a shine to Calhoun. The chat continues when her father, played by Brian Aherne, returns to contribute his views. With these four players making up the entire cast, it feels like a bad play that defeats all concerned, including director John Farrow.

Jean Simmons *Cally Canham* • Rory Calhoun *Ed Stone* • Stephen McNally *Sheriff Munson* • Brian Aherne *David Canham* ■ *Dir* John Farrow • *Scr* Thames Williamson, Casey Robinson, from a story by Thames Williamson

Bullet to Beijing ★★ 15

Spy thriller
1995 · UK/Can/Rus · Colour · 100mins

Thirty years after the film of Len Deighton's novel *The Ipcress File*, Michael Caine resurrects his British spy Harry Palmer. In this very average affort, Palmer is in Russia, working with former KGB agents to prevent North Korea from using biological weapons. Michael Gambon plays a Russian magnate and there's the casting in-joke of Jason Connery as a Russian agent, while Sue Lloyd makes a welcome appearance, reprising her role of Jean from *The Ipcress File*. Caine and Connery made a second Palmer movie, *Midnight in St Petersburg*, back to back with this one. Contains violence, swearing and brief nudity. ▦

Michael Caine *Harry Palmer* • Jason Connery *Nikolai* • Mia Sara *Natasha* • Michael Sarrazin *Craig* • Michael Gambon *Alexei* • John Dunn-Hill *Louis* • Lev Prygunov *Colonel Gradsky* • Burt Kwouk *Kim Soo* ■ *Dir* George Mihalka • *Scr* Peter Welbeck [Harry Alan Towers], from the novel by Len Deighton

Bulletproof ★ 15

Action adventure 1987 · US · Colour · 90mins

Perhaps best known for his bad boy roles in *Lethal Weapon* and *Under Siege*, the under-rated Gary Busey finds himself on the right side of the law in this preposterous action film that gives new meaning to the word derivative. He plays the indestructible Frank "Bulletproof" McBain, lured out of retirement by the government to retrieve a secret weapon captured by a terrorist group headed by veteran Henry Silva. Director Steve Carver fills the screen with enough comic-book characters to keep Marvel in business for years. ▦

Gary Busey *Frank McBain* • Darlanne Fluegel *Lieutenant Devon Shepard* • Henry Silva *Colonel Kartiff* • Thalmus Rasulala *Billy Dunbar* • LQ Jones *Sergeant O'Rourke* • Rene Enriquez *General Brogado* ■ *Dir* Steve Carver • *Scr* TL Lankford, Steve Carver, from a story by Fred Olen Ray, TL Lankford

Bulletproof ★ 18
Action comedy 1996 · US · Colour · 80mins

The secret of a good buddy movie is likeable characters, juicy dialogue and dynamic action sequences – think the *Lethal Weapon* series and *Midnight Run*. Director Ernest Dickerson (a brilliant cinematographer on Spike Lee's earlier movies) delivers some slick shoot-outs, but everything else here is all wrong. Undercover cop Damon Wayans and drug dealer Adam Sandler are utterly unappealing as ex-friends (things changed after Sandler shot Wayans in the head), forced to team up against crime lord James Caan. The performances are annoying, the tasteless jokes are lame and the violence is plain nasty. Contains swearing, sexual references and violence. ▣

Damon Wayans *Keats* • Adam Sandler *Moses* • James Caan *Colton* • Jeep Swenson *Bledsoe* • James Farentino *Captain Jensen* • Kristen Wilson *Traci* • Larry McCoy *Detective Sulliman* • Allen Covert *Detective Jones* ■ *Dir* Ernest R Dickerson • *Scr* Lewis Colick, Joe Gayton, from a story by Joe Gayton

Bullets or Ballots ★★★ PG
Crime drama 1936 · US · BW · 81mins

A taut and tough crime drama, with Edward G Robinson as a New York City cop who infiltrates the rackets run by Barton MacLane. Warner Bros churned this type of film out by the yard in the thirties, claiming they were good for the nation's morals, but the casts and the straightforward style makes them seem rather special nowadays. This one co-stars feisty Joan Blondell and Humphrey Bogart, who has a great showdown with Robinson and the director is William Keighley, a second-string contract director who usually got the job done well and on time. ▣

Edward G Robinson *Johnny Blake* • Joan Blondell *Lee Morgan* • Barton MacLane *Al Kruger* • Humphrey Bogart *Nick "Bugs" Fenner* • Frank McHugh *Herman* • Joseph King *Captain Dan McLaren* • Richard Purcell [Dick Purcell] *Ed Driscoll* ■ *Dir* William Keighley • *Scr* Seton I Miller, from a story by Martin Mooney

Bullets over Broadway ★★★★ 15
Comedy drama 1994 · US · Colour · 95mins

This is the final part of what might be called Woody Allen's "nostalgia" trilogy. Coming after his paeans to the movies (*The Purple Rose of Cairo*) and radio (*Radio Days*), this celebrates the heyday of New York's theatreland. As with the two earlier films, Allen remains behind the camera, giving his typically excellent ensemble cast its chance to shine in the spotlight. As the earnest playwright making his Broadway debut, John Cusack is in the unenviable position of playing a role a younger Allen would almost certainly have taken himself, and he rather fumbles some classic Woodyisms. Jennifer Tilly similarly fails to emerge from the shadow of Judy Holliday's Oscar-winning role in *Born Yesterday* as yet another mobster's moll forced to embrace culture. Dianne Wiest thoroughly deserved her best supporting actress Oscar for her performance as an amorous, alcoholic

actress, but Chazz Palminteri's Cheech, the gangster with a poet's soul, is, perhaps, even more remarkable, and he was decidedly unlucky to come up against Martin Landau's Oscar-winning turn in *Ed Wood*. Contains swearing.

John Cusack *David Shayne* • Jack Warden *Julian Marx* • Chazz Palminteri *Cheech* • Joe Viterelli *Nick Valenti* • Jennifer Tilly *Olive Neal* • Rob Reiner *Sheldon Flender* • Mary-Louise Parker *Ellen* • Dianne Wiest *Helen Sinclair* • Harvey Fierstein *Sid Loomis* • Jim Broadbent *Warner Purcell* ■ *Dir* Woody Allen • *Scr* Woody Allen, Douglas McGrath

The Bullfighter and the Lady ★★★
Drama 1951 · US · BW · 87mins

Director Budd Boetticher and his co-writer Ray Nazarro were Oscar-nominated for the story, but the story's the least of it. For the love of pretty senorita Joy Page, clean-cut, all-American guy Robert Stack goes to Mexico to become a bullfighter, ending up a hero in the final fade. On this flimsy and unconvincing premise, Boetticher builds a colourful and absorbing account of the training and art of the matador. Filming on location, he captures all the excitement of this bloody sport. Gilbert Roland, Katy Jurado and real-life matador Antonio Gomez lend authentic support.

Robert Stack *Chuck Regan* • Joy Page *Anita de la Vega* • Gilbert Roland *Manolo Estrada* • Virginia Grey *Lisbeth Flood* • John Hubbard *Barney Flood* • Katy Jurado *Chelo Estrada* • Antonio Gomez ■ *Dir* Budd Boetticher • *Scr* James Edward Grant, from a story by Budd Boetticher, Ray Nazarro

The Bullfighters ★ PG
Comedy 1945 · US · BW · 60mins

Laurel and Hardy's final Hollywood film was, as Stan said later, "a vast disappointment". Not only were their usual hairstyles changed and slicked down, but the studio (20th Century-Fox) only allowed a brief snatch of their "cuckoo theme" in the music. This time around they're private detectives in Mexico, where Stan finds he's the spitting image of a famous matador. There are some blissful moments – the doubling-up, for instance – but the climax, with Laurel and Hardy as heads on skeletons, is unpleasant. The studio really had it in for them. ▣

Stanley Laurel [Stan Laurel] *Stan* • Oliver Hardy *Ollie* • Margo Woods *Tangerine* • Richard Lane *Hot Shot Coleman* • Carol Andrews *Hattie Blake* ■ *Dir* Malcolm St Clair • *Scr* W Scott Darling

Bullitt ★★★★ 15
Crime thriller 1968 · US · Colour · 108mins

Steve McQueen did better work in his tragically shortened career, but this is one of the films that helped make him a screen icon – not just because of the famous San Francisco hill-bouncing car chase, but also for his deadpan cop-against-the-system routine. He's hired to protect a Chicago mobster who's a key witness against a crime syndicate, and a pawn in the political career of Robert Vaughn. Director Peter Yates gives it more of a sense of urban reality than the predictable script deserves. Frank P Keller got an Oscar

for his editing of *that* car chase. It's always McQueen's movie, however, and he's snappy, laconic and cynical in equal doses. Contains some violence and swearing. ▣ **DVD**

Steve McQueen *Bullitt* • Robert Vaughn *Chalmers* • Jacqueline Bisset *Cathy* • Don Gordon *Delgetti* • Robert Duvall *Weissberg* • Simon Oakland *Captain Bennett* • Norman Fell *Baker* • Georg Stanford Brown *Dr Willard* ■ *Dir* Peter Yates • *Scr* Alan R Trustman, Harry Kleiner, from the novel *Mute Witness* by Robert L Pike

Bullseye! ★ 15
Comedy thriller 1990 · US · Colour · 88mins

A hideously unfunny comedy of errors from Michael Winner that must rank as a career low for nearly all involved. Poor old Michael Caine and Roger Moore play con men who set out to steal gems from under the noses of their lookalikes. Neither seems comfortable for a second, with Caine particularly pained when called upon to essay a scientist. The glamorous locations and the glut of cameos barely plug the gaps in an awful script that is stuffed with irritating in-jokes. ▣

Michael Caine *Sidney Lipton/Dr Daniel Hicklar* • Roger Moore *Gerald Bradley-Smith/Sir John Bavistock* • Sally Kirkland *Willie Metcalfe* • Deborah Barrymore *Flo Fleming* • Lee Patterson *Darrell Hyde* • Mark Burns *Nigel Holden* ■ *Dir* Michael Winner • *Scr* Leslie Bricusse, Laurence Marks, Maurice Gran, from a story by Leslie Bricusse, Michael Winner, Nick Mead

Bullshot ★ PG
Spoof adventure 1983 · UK · Colour · 88mins

A risible spoof of the Bulldog Drummond stories, this stars Alan Shearman, Ron House and Diz White, who wrote the screenplay and the stage play on which it is based. Shearman plays the fearless "Bullshot" Crummond with all the subtlety of a salesman on commission. But he has left himself with little option as every pun and sight gag in this atrocious tale, of German cads pursuing a top secret formula, demands to be rammed home with steam-hammer finesse. Billy Connolly, Mel Smith and Nicholas Lyndhurst are among the celebrities whose cameos can't help the cause. Contains violence and mild swearing. ▣

Alan Shearman *"Bullshot" Crummond* • Diz White *Rosemary Fenton* • Ron House *Count Otto von Bruno* • Frances Tomelty *Fraulein Lenya Von Bruno* • Ron Pember *Dobbs* • Mel Smith *Crouch* • Michael Aldridge *Rupert Fenton* • Billy Connolly *Hawkeye McGillicuddy* • Nicholas Lyndhurst *Nobby Clark* ■ *Dir* Dick Clement • *Scr* Ron House, Alan Shearman, Diz White, from their play

Bullwhip ★★★ U
Western 1958 · US · Colour · 80mins

The bullwhip is wielded by gorgeous redhead Rhonda Fleming, no stranger to playing spirited tough-girl roles. She's a part-Cheyenne Indian with moneymaking ambitions in the fur trade, who needs to be married to own property and makes a deal with cowboy Guy Madison, who's about to be executed for another man's crime. He has a reprieve if he marries her and never sees her again, but his

curiosity is roused and he follows her. A rarely seen B-western, directed by Harmon Jones, it suffers from its over-the-top comedy elements, but it's an unusual little film, decently acted, and photographed in attractive Technicolor by John J Martin.

Guy Madison *Steve* • Rhonda Fleming *Cheyenne* • James Griffith *Karp* • Don Beddoe *Judge* • Peter Adams *Parnell* • Dan Sheridan *Podo* ■ *Dir* Harmon Jones • *Scr* Adele Buffington

Bulworth ★★★★ 18
Political comedy drama 1998 · US · Colour · 103mins

Warren Beatty's astonishingly fearless political satire is one of the boldest studio films to come out of Hollywood in years. Beatty, who writes and directs, also stars as a disillusioned liberal senator who takes out a contract on his own life, giving him three days to start saying what he really believes. Just when you think Beatty won't dare to be more radical than his acidic (and very funny) swipes at just about everybody, he re-invents himself as a street-wise urban rapper. Sharper and riskier than the more conventional political satires such as *Bob Roberts* or *Primary Colors*, the film succeeds as both a startlingly original comedy and a fang-baring assault on the American political system. Contains drug abuse, coarse language and sexual references. ▣

Warren Beatty *Jay Bulworth* • Halle Berry *Nina* • Paul Sorvino *Graham Crockett* • Christine Baranski *Constance Bulworth* • Kimberly Deauna Adams *Denisha* • Vinny Argiro *Debate director* • Sean Astin *Gary* • Kirk Baltz *Debate producer* • Laurie Metcalf *Mimi* ■ *Dir* Warren Beatty • *Scr* Warren Beatty, Jeremy Pikser, from a story by Warren Beatty

Bump in the Night ★★★ 15
Psychological thriller 1991 · US · Colour · 91mins

Every trauma possible is thrown into the mix of this TV thriller in which alcoholic, divorced investigative journalist Meredith Baxter Birney has to rescue her young son from a paedophile intent on selling the child to a porn film-maker. Director Karen Arthur manages to keep the tension mounting despite some less than plausible plot twists. She is ably abetted by a good cast that includes Christopher Reeve, Wings Hauser and Terrence Mann. Contains violence. ▣

Meredith Baxter Birney [Meredith Baxter] *Martha Tierney* • Christopher Reeve *Lawrence Miller* • Wings Hauser *Patrick Tierney* • Richard Bradford *Sergeant Pete Mooney* • Geraldine Fitzgerald *Mrs Beauchamps* • Shirley Knight *Katie Leonard* • Corey Carrier *Jonathan Tierney* ■ *Dir* Karen Arthur • *Scr* Christopher Lofton, from the novel by Isabelle Holland

Bunco Squad ★★
Crime drama 1950 · US · BW · 67mins

This is the penultimate movie of B-feature director Herbert I Leeds (dead a year later at the age of 42) who was taking a break from *Cisco Kid* and *Mr Moto* programme fillers. Here he niftily remakes part of the plot of a 1938 second feature called *Crime Ring*, this time with likeable Robert Sterling foiling a plot involving phoney psychics cheating Elisabeth Risdon, conned into parting with $2 million at a fake seance. Watch out for Ricardo Cortez as one of the fake psychics, and the real-life Dante the Magician.

Robert Sterling *Steve* • Joan Dixon *Grace* • Ricardo Cortez *Anthony Wells* • Douglas Fowley *McManus* • Elisabeth Risdon *Jessica Royce* • Marguerite Churchill *Barbara* • John Kellogg *Reed* • Bernadene Hayes *Liane* ■ *Dir* Herbert I Leeds • *Scr* George Callahan, from a story by Reginald Taviner

Bundle of Joy ★★ U

Musical comedy 1956 · US · Colour · 98mins

This is more of a social document than a film – a perfectly preserved slice of pop culture from a bygone era. This is a starring vehicle for "America's Sweethearts" Eddie Fisher, king of the pre-rock 'n' roll pop charts, and his new bride Debbie Reynolds, the little girl that moviegoers wouldn't let grow up. It's a trifling, slightly musicalised, remake of the popular Ginger Rogers movie *Bachelor Mother*, and would deserve to be forgotten, but for the social events that overwhelmed it. Within a year of the film's release, Eddie had left Debbie (and their daughter Carrie Fisher) for the wife of his best friend Mike Todd, the newly widowed Elizabeth Taylor. But even with that background, this is a silly, laboured farce and Fisher proved to be no film star.

Debbie Reynolds *Polly Parrish* • Eddie Fisher *Dan Merlin* • Adolphe Menjou *JB Merlin* • Tommy Noonan *Freddie Miller* • Nita Talbot *Mary* • Una Merkel *Mrs Dugan* • Melville Cooper *Adams* • Bill Goodwin *Mr Creely* ■ *Dir* Norman Taurog • *Scr* Norman Krasna, Robert Carson, Arthur Sheekman, from a story by Felix Jackson

Bunny Lake Is Missing ★★★

Mystery drama 1965 · US · BW · 107mins

Laurence Olivier (as a leaden-paced, raincoated British copper) and Noël Coward may have regarded this as a bit of slumming, judging by the way they camp it up. However, director Otto Preminger uses their archness to consolidate the nightmarish quality of this story about American Carol Lynley's illegitimate little girl being absent without mum's leave. Keir Dullea demonstrates that, even prior to *2001: a Space Odyssey*, he was an unconventional actor, and his performance reflects the illusory atmosphere of the movie. John and Penelope Mortimer wrote the screenplay, but it's Preminger's gimmickry that makes it such fun.

Laurence Olivier *Newhouse* • Carol Lynley *Ann* • Keir Dullea *Steven* • Noël Coward *Wilson* • Martita Hunt *Ada Ford* • Anna Massey *Elvira* • Clive Revill *Andrews* • Finlay Currie *Doll maker* • Richard Wattis *Shipping Clerk* ■ *Dir* Otto Preminger • *Scr* John Mortimer, Penelope Mortimer, from the novel by Evelyn Piper

Bunny O'Hare ★

Crime comedy 1971 · US · Colour · 92mins

In her golden years, veteran diva Bette Davis took on practically any role to prove she was still alive and a viable actress. But nothing can really explain why she sank as low as this dreadful gimmick flick, where she's a bored grandmother in hippie gear and a long blonde wig, who decides to rob banks

with ageing partner-in-crime Ernest Borgnine. So appalling, it must be seen to be believed.

Bette Davis *Bunny O'Hare* • Ernest Borgnine *Bill Green* • Jack Cassidy *Detective Greeley* • Joan Delaney *RJ Hart* • Jay Robinson *Banker* • Reva Rose *Lulu* ■ *Dir* Gerd Oswald • *Scr* Stanley Z Cherry, Coslough Johnson, from a story by Stanley Z Cherry

Buona Sera, Mrs Campbell ★★★

Comedy drama 1968 · It · Colour · 111mins

Gina Lollobrigida looks a treat in director Melvin Frank's rather tasteless comedy drama about an Italian single mother whose promiscuous wartime past comes back to haunt her. There's earnest support from Phil Silvers, Telly Savalas and suave Peter Lawford as the three American airmen who each believe they fathered Lollobrigida's child 20 years ago, and who have been paying child support ever since. If you're a fan of sixties farces and find comedy of the opening-and-shutting-door variety funny, this glossy romp may well pass muster.

Gina Lollobrigida *Carla* • Shelley Winters *Shirley Newman* • Phil Silvers *Phil Newman* • Peter Lawford *Justin Young* • Telly Savalas *Walter Braddock* • Lee Grant *Fritzie Braddock* • Janet Margolin *Gia* • Marian Moses *Lauren Young* ■ *Dir* Melvin Frank • *Scr* Melvin Frank, Sheldon Keller, Denis Norden

The 'Burbs ★★★★ PG

Comedy 1989 · US · Colour · 96mins

When the Klopeks move into a run down house in an otherwise spick-and-span suburb, Tom Hanks – playing a one-man neighbourhood watch scheme – starts to fret and frown. Just what are the Klopeks up to, digging in the garden and making all those clanking noises at night? Though light-hearted and often very funny indeed, this is an askew parable about small-town America, with Hanks as the ultimate conformist surrounded by weirdos. However, director Joe Dante, who made *Gremlins*, excels at this sort of thing and, even though it promises to stray into David Lynch territory but ultimately cops out, this is still a constantly intriguing picture. Bruce Dern and Carrie Fisher offer fine support to the affable Hanks. Contains swearing and violence. 📼

Tom Hanks *Ray Peterson* • Bruce Dern *Mark Rumsfield* • Carrie Fisher *Carol Peterson* • Rick Ducommun *Art Weingartner* • Corey Feldman *Ricky Butler* • Henry Gibson *Dr Werner Klopek* • Brother Theodore *Uncle Reuben Klopek* • Courtney Gains *Hans Klopek* ■ *Dir* Joe Dante • *Scr* Dana Olsen

Burden of Dreams ★★★★

Documentary 1982 · US · Colour · 37mins

A remarkable documentary by Les Blank about the appalling slog involved in making Werner Herzog's *Fitzcarraldo*. In telling the story of an opera lover (Klaus Kinski) who hauls a ship through the South American jungle to bring music to the natives, the visionary German director embarked upon an overtaxing labour of love that frayed tempers and stirred skirmishes with the locals. Rarely have the rigours

of location filming been so dramatically and painstakingly chronicled.

Dir Les Blank • *Scr* Michael Goodwin

Bureau of Missing Persons ★★★

Comedy thriller 1933 · US · BW · 73mins

A pacey action movie from Warner Bros, which is, in effect, a selection of different overlapping stories, tightly held together by the direction of Roy Del Ruth. (It's one of six films he made in 1933.) The central tale features Bette Davis, who may or may not have killed her husband, and tough-talking cop Pat O'Brien, who has to sort out the mystery. There's much pleasure to be had from watching Warners' hard-boiled rep company (Allen Jenkins, Ruth Donnelly, Glenda Farrell) go through their paces, but none of them can surpass Davis.

Bette Davis *Norma Phillips* • Lewis Stone *Captain Webb* • Pat O'Brien *Butch Saunders* • Glenda Farrell *Belle* • Allen Jenkins *Joe Musik* • Ruth Donnelly *Pete* • Hugh Herbert *Slade* • Alan Dinehart *Therme Roberts* ■ *Dir* Roy Del Ruth • *Scr* Robert Presnell, from the book *Missing Men* by John H Ayres, Carol Bird

The Burglar ★★★

Film noir 1956 · US · BW · 90mins

This little gem is the real thing, a sordid little flick with great style, directed with panache by cult favourite Paul Wendkos, who latterly has made some of the hardest edged TV movies. The cast is well worth tuning in for: Dan Duryea (the Richard Widmark of the Bs) is the disturbed titular crook, while Jayne Mansfield, early in her career, and seldom better, and *The Big Sleep's* Martha Vickers provide terrific female support. Bleak and bizarre, but give it a whirl.

Dan Duryea *Nat Harbin* • Jayne Mansfield *Gladden* • Martha Vickers *Della* • Peter Capell *Baylock* • Mickey Shaughnessy *Dohmer* • Wendell Phillips *Police Captain* • Phoebe Mackay *Sister Sara* ■ *Dir* Paul Wendkos • *Scr* David Goodis, from his novel

Burglar ★★ 15

Comedy thriller 1987 · US · Colour · 97mins

After the lukewarm reception for *Jumpin' Jack Flash*, Whoopi Goldberg made another attempt at a leading comedy role in this disappointing mix of humour and action. This time, the added talents of her fellow stand-up comedian Bob "Bobcat" Goldthwait and *Roseanne* star John Goodman seem to have little impact on the comedy. Goldberg is the burglar of the title who witnesses a murder and then finds herself suspected of the crime, but even the actress's comic timing and acting talents can't keep you from guessing what will happen way before her character does. Contains violence and swearing. 📼

Whoopi Goldberg *Bernice Rhodenbarr* • Bob Goldthwait [Bobcat Goldthwait] *Carl Hefler* • GW Bailey *Ray Kirschman* • Lesley Ann Warren *Dr Cynthia Sheldrake* • James Handy *Carson Verrill* • Anne DeSalvo *Detective Todras* • John Goodman *Detective Nyswander* ■ *Dir* Hugh Wilson • *Scr* Joseph Loeb III, Matthew Weisman, Hugh Wilson, from the books by Lawrence Block

The Burglars ★★ 18

Crime drama 1971 · Fr/It · Colour · 109mins

French director Henri Verneuil specialised in glossy crime movies at this stage of his career, and the worldwide success of *The Sicilian Clan* meant that he could call on an international cast and a high-powered location shoot for his next movie *Le Casse*, retitled *The Burglars* for export. Jean-Paul Belmondo and Omar Sharif co-star in this colourful remake of David Goodis's *noir* thriller, *The Burglar*, this time shot in sun-drenched Greece and containing some of the most irritating dubbing you're ever likely to hear in a film of such pedigree. Still, Hollywood female lead Dyan Cannon performs in her own native American, and there's a rattling good car chase, besides. French dialogue dubbed into English. 📼

Jean-Paul Belmondo *Azad* • Omar Sharif *Abel Zacharia* • Dyan Cannon *Lena* • Robert Hossein *Ralph* • Nicole Calfan *Hélène* • Renato Salvatori *Renzi* • José-Luis De Villalonga *Tasco* • Myriam Colombi *Mme Tasco* • Raoul Delfosse *Caretaker* • Steve Eckardt *Malloch* ■ *Dir* Henri Verneuil • *Scr* Henri Verneuil, Vahe Katcha, from the film an novel *The Burglar* by David Goodis

Buried Alive ★ 18

Horror 1990 · US · Colour · 86mins

This is a shoddy rehash of Edgar Allan Poe (misspelt Allen in the credits!) plonked down in South Africa, produced by veteran sleaze merchant Harry Alan Towers and directed by one-time porn film-maker Gerard Kikoine. Robert Vaughn runs the Ravenscroft Institute, populated by shady students (hardcore actress Ginger Lynn Allen among them) and eccentric teachers (including grey-wigged Donald Pleasence), where Poe's psychological horrors are made stupidly literal, with hands emerging from toilet bowls and death by food processor. John Carradine's appearance as a walled-up victim was his last and saddest. Contains swearing and violence. 📼

Robert Vaughn *Dr Gary* • Donald Pleasence *Dr Schaeffer* • Karen Witter *Janet* • John Carradine *Jacob* • Nia Long *Fingers* • Ginger Lynn Allen *Debbie* • Bill Butler *Tim* • Janine Denison *Shiro* ■ *Dir* Gérard Kikoine • *Scr* Jake Clesi, Stuart Lee, from stories by Peter Welbeck [Harry Alan Towers], Edgar Allan Poe

Buried Alive ★★★ 15

Thriller 1990 · US · Colour · 89mins

Not to be confused with another horror movie of the same name made, by sinister coincidence, in the same year. This is a superior TV movie, directed by Frank Darabont, who went on to greater things with *The Shawshank Redemption* and *The Green Mile*. Tim Matheson does well as the small-town construction manager who survives but not just poisoning but also burial by his adulterous wife (Jennifer Jason Leigh), to rise from the grave and take ingenious revenge. 📼

Tim Matheson *Clint Goodman* • Jennifer Jason Leigh *Joanna Goodman* • William Atherton *Cortland* • Hoyt Axton *Sheriff Sam* • Brian Libby *Earl* ■ *Dir* Frank Darabont • *Scr* Mark Carducci

---

Buried Loot ★
Crime   1934 · US · BW · 18mins

This two-reeler initiated MGM's *Crime Does Not Pay* series, which ran to 48 titles over 12 years, giving movie houses quality shorts and enabling the studio to try out new talent. Here the recently signed 23-year-old Robert Taylor was given the principal role of the thief who hides his loot, aiming to recover it after serving time in prison. What with a jailbreak, plastic surgery and a twist ending, it packed a full B-feature plot into 18 minutes. Taylor soon became a star, while later *Crime Does Not Pay* entries became informative exposés of rackets that were fooling the public.

Robert Taylor (1) *Al Douglas* • Robert Livingston ■ *Dir* George B Seitz • *Scr* George B Seitz, from a story by Marty Brooks

Burke and Wills ★★★
Biographical drama
1985 · Ausl · Colour · 140mins

Robert Burke and William Wills, who with two others were the first explorers to cross Australia from south to north, are here played with lantern-jawed determination and righteous zeal by Jack Thompson and Nigel Havers. The same team of explorers were spoofed by another version of the tale, *Wills and Burke*, released at roughly the same time but with a very different take on the tale. Indeed, even here there are certain grandiose moments that border on parody and so nudge the film towards unintended hilarity. Otherwise the extended scenes of bravery and endurance have an authentic period atmosphere and psychological resonance. Contains some violence and swearing.

Jack Thompson *Robert O'Hara Burke* • Nigel Havers *William John Wills* • Greta Scacchi *Julia Matthews* • Matthew Fargher *John King* • Ralph Cotterill *Charley Gray* • Drew Forsythe *William Brahe* ■ *Dir* Graeme Clifford • *Scr* Michael Thomas

The Burmese Harp ★★★★
War drama   1956 · Jap · BW · 116mins

Adapted from Michio Takeyama's novel by director Kon Ichikawa's wife, Natto Wada, this lyrical epic is among the most moving acts of atonement made by the postwar Japanese film industry. Yet the decision of a young musician (Shoji Yasui) to renounce his homeland and remain in Burma as a Buddhist monk is less an indictment of militarism and more a cry of anguish on behalf of all those who suffered during the Second World War. Ichikawa occasionally allows sincerity to lapse into sentimentality, but he clearly felt deeply about the story, which he remade (less memorably) in 1985. In Japanese with English subtitles.

Rentaro Mikuni *Captain Inoue* • Shoji Yasui *Private Yasuhiko* • Tatsuya Mihashi *Defence Commander* • Tanie Kitabayashi *Old woman* • Yunosuke Ito *Village head* ■ *Dir* Kon Ichikawa • *Scr* Natto Wada, from the novel by Michio Takeyama

The Burmese Harp ★★★
War drama   1985 · Jap · Colour · 132mins

Strikingly filmed in colour by Setsuo Kobayashi, Kon Ichikawa's remake of his 1956 classic lacks the original's contemporary resonance. This time, in seeking to expose the fanaticism and brutality of the militarist tendency, Ichikawa overdoes the humanist earnestness that inspires a soldier musician to remain in Burma after the Imperial Army's retreat and join the Buddhist monks in burying the dead. Still persuasive in its pacifism and its depiction of simple compassion, this is a deeply moving film that would, perhaps, have been more effective had it not been quite so deliberate. A Japanese language film.

Koji Ishizaka *Captain Inoue* • Kiichi Nakai *Private Mizushima* • Takuzo Kawatani *Sgt Ito* • Atsushi Watanabe *Pvt Kobayashi* • Fujio Tokita *Old man* • Tanie Kitabayashi *Old woman* • Bunta Sugawara *Commander of Sankaku Mountain Platoon* ■ *Dir* Kon Ichikawa • *Scr* Natto Wada, from the novel by Michio Takeyama

Burn! ★★★
Swashbuckling drama
1969 · Fr/It · Colour · 112mins

Even at the height of his stardom, Marlon Brando was prepared to take chances by accepting challenging roles. In this attack on colonial manipulation – a period swashbuckler with attitude – he plays a cynical British secret agent who ignites a Caribbean island revolution against the ruling Portuguese using slave labour on a sugar-cane plantation. It's clumsily handled at times by director Gillo Pontecorvo, who made the remarkable documentary-style epic *The Battle of Algiers*, but it still has scenes of enormous visual power. Brando is magnificent, and a lot slimmer than he is today.

Marlon Brando *Sir William Walker* • Evaristo Marquez *Jose Dolores* • Renato Salvatori *Teddy Sanchez* • Norman Hill *Shelton* • Tom Lyons *General Prada* • Wanani *Guarina* • Joseph Persaud *Juanito* • Giampiero Albertini *Henry* ■ *Dir* Gillo Pontecorvo • *Scr* Franco Solinas, Giorgio Arlorio, from a story by Gillo Pontecorvo, Franco Solinas, Giorgio Arlorio • *Cinematographer* Marcello Gatti

Burn Hollywood Burn ★ 15
Satirical comedy 1997 · US · Colour · 81mins

In this monumentally awful celebrity-packed Hollywood "mockumentary", Eric Idle plays Allan Smithee, the joke being that this is the pseudonym used by directors who don't want to have their real name credited on a movie. Sylvester Stallone, Jackie Chan and Whoopi Goldberg look embarrassed playing themselves, which is unsurprising given that the Joe Eszterhas script makes his *Showgirls* work read like Shakespeare. Unsubtle, unfunny and an unbelievable waste of time and money, this could well be the worst satire ever made. It's no surprise that director Arthur Hiller took the movie's plot to heart and let Mr Smithee take the blame. Contains coarse language. ▭

Ryan O'Neal *James Edmunds* • Coolio *Dion Brothers* • Chuck D *Leon Brothers* • Eric Idle *Alan Smithee* • Leslie Stefanson *Michelle Rafferty* • Sandra Bernhard *Ann Glover* • Cherie Lunghi *Myrna Smithee* • Harvey Weinstein *Sam Rizzo* • Naomi Campbell *Attendant no 2* • Sylvester Stallone • Whoopi

Goldberg • Jackie Chan • Robert Evans • Joe Eszterhas ■ *Dir* Alan Smithee [Arthur Hiller] • *Scr* Joe Eszterhas

The Burning ★ 18
Horror   1981 · US · Colour · 87mins

A highly derivative *Friday the 13th* clone that found itself on the infamous video nasty list that caused a furore in the early eighties. A horribly-burned summer camp caretaker returns with scissors and shears to take bloody vengeance on the promiscuous teens responsible for the joke-gone-wrong that caused his fiery scars. Despite the viciously effective gore, inept direction by Tony Maylam and a predictable script cause boredom to set in very early on. Future stars Jason Alexander (*Seinfeld*) and Holly Hunter make early screen appearances. ▭

Brian Matthews *Todd* • Leah Ayres *Michelle* • Brian Backer *Alfred* • Larry Joshua *Glazer* • Jason Alexander *Dave* • Ned Eisenberg *Eddy* • Fisher Stevens *Woodstock* • Holly Hunter *Sophie* ■ *Dir* Tony Maylam • *Scr* Peter Lawrence, Bob Weinstein, from a story by Harvey Weinstein, Tony Maylam, Brad Grey

The Burning Bed ★★★★ 15
Drama based on a true story
1984 · US · Colour · 91mins

Farrah Fawcett left her blonde bimbo *Charlie's Angels* image behind for ever with this superb performance as a battered wife who takes revenge on her husband by setting him on fire while he is sleeping. Based on a true story, this Emmy-nominated drama from Robert Greenwald – who also made the neglected *Sweet Hearts Dance* and the hilariously abysmal *Xanadu* – is carefully and sensitively handled, and never lapses into melodrama. Thought provoking, moving and exceptionally well played. ▭

Farrah Fawcett *Francine Hughes* • Paul LeMat *Mickey Hughes* • Richard Masur *Aryon Greydanus* • Grace Zabriskie *Flossie Hughes* • Penelope Milford *Gaby* • Christa Denton *Christy aged 12* • James Callahan *Berlin Hughes* • Gary Grubbs *District Attorney* ■ *Dir* Robert Greenwald • *Scr* Rose Leiman Goldemberg, from a book by Faith McNulty

The Burning Hills ★★ PG
Western   1956 · US · Colour · 88mins

This minor western has Tab Hunter setting out on a vengeance trail and finding Natalie Wood as a Mexican/American who nurses him when he's shot. Casting these two young and pretty things to star in a western was unusual in those days, a studio ploy to lure teenagers away from their dance halls and TV sets. Consequently, Hunter takes off his shirt while Wood takes on an interesting accent. Hunter proves himself a rather anaemic hero, though his popularity later gained him his own TV show. In the eighties, he appeared in several camp comedies starring alongside Divine. ▭

Tab Hunter *Trace Jordan* • Natalie Wood *Maria Colton* • Skip Homeier *Jack Sutton* • Eduard Franz *Jacob Lantz* • Earl Holliman *Mort Bayliss* • Claude Akins *Ben Hindeman* • Ray Teal *Joe Sutton* ■ *Dir* Stuart Heisler • *Scr* Irving Wallace, from the novel by Louis L'Amour

Burning Memory ★★★
War drama   1988 · Is · Colour · 93mins

This harrowing Israeli feature was based on debutant director Yossi Somer's experiences as a paramedic during the war with the Lebanon. A former assistant to Fred Zinnemann, Somer depicts Israel as a nation fraught with internal strife, which is only kept in check by the need to unite in the face of a common enemy. But, as one would expect from a film that went through three editors, the action is too often disjointed. Nevertheless, there is an affecting performance from Danny Roth as the shellshocked soldier, who knows he must return to the front as soon as he is cured. In Hebrew with English subtitles.

Danny Roth *Gary* • Shmuel Edelman *Tzvika* • Pauli Reshef *Alex* • Etti Ankri *Ruth* • Alon Oliarchick *Rubi* • Yossef El-Dror *Avram* • Reuven Dayan *Nissim* • Yahli Bergman *Momen* • Koby Hagoel *Tzukerman* • Avi Gilor *Amos* ■ *Dir* Yossi Somer • *Scr* Ami Amir, Yossi Somer

A Burning Passion: the Margaret Mitchell Story ★
Biographical drama   1994 · US · Colour

In a slight departure from her own wild life, Shannen Doherty stars in this sudsy biography of *Gone with the Wind* author Margaret Mitchell. The film spans the years 1918 to 1937, during which time Mitchell met, married and divorced her swaggering, bootlegging husband Red Upshaw (Dale Midkiff), who later became the inspiration for Rhett Butler. "Fiddle-dee-dee!" is all you can say for a clumsy TV melodrama that's short on facts and long on frivolous dialogue. Rue McClanahan provides a good turn as Grandma, while John Clark Gable, son of the actor who played Rhett, has a bit part as one of Mitchell's suitors.

Shannen Doherty *Margaret Mitchell* • Rue McClanahan *Grandma Stephens* • Dale Midkiff *Red Upshaw* • Matt Mulhern *John Marsh* • John Clark Gable ■ *Dir* Larry Peerce • *Scr* Robert Hamilton

The Burning Season ★★★★ 15
Drama based on a true story
1994 · US · Colour · 117mins

In one of his last roles before his tragically early death, Raul Julia is both committed and convincing as Chico Mendes, the Brazilian union leader who was assassinated in 1990. Superbly scripted, and directed with power by John Frankenheimer, this superior TV movie never allows its passionate support for Mendes and his cause (the preservation of the Amazon rainforests) to deteriorate into either hagiography or melodrama. Ably supported by Sonia Braga and Edward James Olmos, Julia commands the screen, whether rallying the local peasantry, battling with big business or challenging the corrupt administration. Green film-making at its best. Contains swearing and violence. ▭

Raul Julia *Chico Mendes* • Kamala Dawson *Ilzamar* • Edward James Olmos *Wilson Pinhairo* • Sonia Braga *Regina De Carvaiho* • Esai Morales *Jair* • Carmen Argenziano *Allredo Sezero* • Enrigue Novi *Nilo Sergio* • Jorge

U = SUITABLE FOR ALL   Uc = SUITABLE FOR ALL, ESPECIALLY FOR YOUNG CHILDREN (VIDEO ONLY)   PG = PARENTAL GUIDANCE

Zepeda *Thomas Sanjos* • Tomas Milian ■ *Dir* John Frankenheimer • *Scr* Michael Tolkin, Ron Hutchinson, William Mastrosimone

Sørensen *Harder* • Iris Johansen *Hedvik* ■ *Dir* Knut Erik Jensen • *Scr* Alf R Jacobsen, Knut Erik Jensen

Killer • Maureen Math • Joanne Moore Jordan • Marie Denn • Dennis Peabody • *Dir/Scr* Barbara Peeters

Lange *Elma* • Hans Conried *Life photographer* • Casey Adams [Max Showalter] *Life reporter* ■ *Dir* Joshua Logan • *Scr* George Axelrod, from the play by William Inge

Burning Secret ★★★ PG

Period drama
1988 · US/UK/W Ger · Colour · 103mins

Debutant feature director Andrew Birkin here shows the sure grasp of child psychology that made his later adaptation of Ian McEwan's *The Cement Garden* so engrossing. Expanding on a short story by Stefan Zweig, this is a thoughtful child's-eye view of the charged relationship that develops between an asthmatic boy's mother (Faye Dunaway) and a rakish Austrian baron (Klaus Maria Brandauer) during the youth's treatment at a mountain spa town after the First World War. Young David Eberts responds well to Birkin's sensitive direction and, if the pace occasionally slackens, there is always the consolation of the beauties of Prague (standing in for Vienna). ▭

Faye Dunaway *Sonya Tuchman* • Klaus Maria Brandauer *Baron Alexander Maria von Hauenschild* • David Eberts *Edmund Tuchman* • Ian Richardson *Father* • Martin Obernigg *Concierge* • John Nettleton *Dr Weiss* ■ *Dir* Andrew Birkin • *Scr* Andrew Birkin, from the short story *Brennendes Geheimnis* by Stefan Zweig

Burnt Barns ★★

Drama
1973 · Fr · Colour · 95mins

A dead woman is discovered on a farm, and suspicion falls on the son of Simone Signoret, a widowed matriarch who rules her family with a rod of iron. Alain Delon plays the local magistrate, who uncovers the sort of familial resentment that can only be put down to peasant tradition and in-breeding. The presence of Signoret and Delon made Jean Chapot's sombre film a sure-fire hit in France, although it's far too ordinary to be of much interest elsewhere. French dialogue dubbed into English.

Alain Delon *Larcher* • Simone Signoret *Rose* • Paul Crauchet *Pierre* • Catherine Allégret *Françoise* • Bernard Le Coq *Paul* • Miou-Miou *Monique* • Pierre Rousseau *Louis* • Renato Salvatori *Patron* ■ *Dir* Jean Chapot • *Scr* Sebastian Roulet, Frantz-Andre Burget

Burnt by Frost ★★

Spy drama
1997 · Nor · Colour and BW · 97mins

Having witnessed the heroism of the Red Army in liberating northern Norway from the Nazis, the enigmatic Stig Henrik Hoff agrees to spy for the Soviets. With Svein Krovel's carefully composed imagery conveying the isolation of Finnmark and the seductive splendour of Moscow, this should have been a fascinating exploration of a relatively neglected topic. However, Knut Erik Jensen's preoccupation with criss-crossing time zones renders the film fussy and confusing, when it should have been as complex and intriguing as Hoff's motives, as he risks both his relationship with his fellow fishermen and his marriage to Gørild Mauseth. A Norwegian/Russian/German/English language film.

Stig Henrik Hoff *Simon* • Gørild Mauseth *Lillian* • Yevgeni Sidikhin *Lasov* • Reidar

Burnt by the Sun ★★★★★ 15

Historical drama
1994 · Rus/Fr · Colour · 129mins

A daring plunge into the heart of darkness that was Stalin's Russia in the mid-thirties from director Nikita Mikhalkov. Mikhalkov also stars as Kotov, the complacent military hero of the Soviet Revolution, whose country house is visited unexpectedly by his young wife's former childhood sweetheart, Dmitrii. Against the backdrop of a lazy summer's day, the truth behind Stalin's rule and the reason for Dmitrii's visit become apparent as Kotov entertains his guest. Winner of the Oscar for best foreign film, this masterpiece of visual audacity – the vast balloon displaying an image of Stalin is a highlight – depicts, with vivid candour, a nation's paranoia grievously turned in upon itself. In Russian with English subtitles. Contains violence, swearing, sex scenes and nudity. ▭

Nikita Mikhalkov *Sergei Petrovich Kotov* • Oleg Menshikov *Dmitrii* • Ingeborga Dapkunaite *Marusia Kotov* • Nadia Mikhalkova *Nadia* • André Umansky *Philippe* • Vyacheslav Tikhonov *Vsevolod Konstantinovich* • Svetlana Kriuchkova *Mokhova* ■ *Dir* Nikita Mikhalkov • *Scr* Nikita Mikhalkov, Rustam Ibragimbekov, from a story by Nikita Mikhalkov • *Cinematographer* Vilen Kaliuta

Burnt Offerings ★

Horror
1976 · US · Colour · 115mins

In this *Amityville Horror*-style chiller, Karen Black, Oliver Reed and family take a house for the summer. The fact that the house is owned by that old fruitcake Burgess Meredith should have told them at the start that things will soon get very bumpy in the night. Dan Curtis's film is much too long and not at all scary by today's standards. It's also laughable in places, with Bette Davis as a dotty old biddy and especially in the scenes where Reed gets the heebie-jeebies.

Karen Black *Marian* • Oliver Reed *Ben* • Burgess Meredith *Brother* • Eileen Heckart *Roz* • Lee Montgomery *David* • Dub Taylor *Walker* • Bette Davis *Aunt Elizabeth* ■ *Dir* Dan Curtis • *Scr* William F Nolan, Dan Curtis, from the novel by Robert Marasco

Bury Me an Angel ★★

Action drama
1972 · US · Colour · 86mins

Dixie Peabody (who disappeared not long after this movie) plays a female biker who hits the road to find and kill the guy who blew off her brother's head with a shotgun. With a woman as writer/director, it isn't surprising the movie takes time to focus on Peabody and her sometimes interesting interactions with other characters. Sadly, the material between is slow, with not much action and not much sex, making it far from the "howling hellcat humping a hot steel hog on a roaring rampage of revenge" that the original ads promised. Peabody is stiff, but with time she could have been another Pam Grier.

Dixie Peabody *Dag* • Terry Mace *Jonsie* • Clyde Ventura *Bernie* • Stephen Whittaker

Bury Me in Niagara ★★

Supernatural comedy
1993 · US · Colour

As bizarre and as wacky as its title, this vehicle for Jean Stapleton, star of US TV sitcom *All in the Family*, is a supernatural comedy, with Stapleton playing a ghost who returns to Earth to tidy up a few affairs before she's granted her wings. There's also a stolen jewel to account for, a "my son the doctor" subplot and a confrontation with some Japanese gangsters. Tighter scripting, a stronger supporting cast and better direction would have helped, but this TV movie does have some originality and might raise a few smiles.

Jean Stapleton • Geraint Wyn Davies • Shae D'Lyn • Denis Akiyama • Jayne Eastwood • Zachary Bennett • Ed Sahely • Bernard Behrens ■ *Dir* Dave Thomas (1) • *Scr* Daniel Harris, Constantino Magnatta, Dave Thomas, from a story by Daniel Harris, Constantino Magnatta

Bus Riley's Back in Town ★★★

Drama
1965 · US · Colour · 93mins

As Bus Riley, Michael Parks shuffles and mumbles his way through this small-town melodrama. He's a former sailor twice jilted by the voluptuous Ann-Margret, who has married a sugar daddy but still fancies Bus. There are lots of secondary characters – Jocelyn Brando is Bus's mother, Janet Margolin the "nice" girl in town – all well knitted together by debutant director Harvey Hart. Parks is something of a weakness (the movie really needed a Robert Redford or a Warren Beatty) but this is a quiet, understated study of frustrated ambition. The original author, noted playwright William Inge, demanded his real name be removed from the credits and the movie bombed at the box office.

Ann-Margret *Laurel* • Michael Parks *Bus Riley* • Janet Margolin *Judy* • Brad Dexter *Slocum* • Jocelyn Brando *Mrs Riley* • Larry Storch *Howie* • Crahan Denton *Spencer* ■ *Dir* Harvey Hart • *Scr* Walter Gage [William Inge]

Bus Stop ★★★★ U

Comedy
1956 · US · Colour · 90mins

This was the film that proved Marilyn Monroe was a considerable screen actress, and capable of much, much more than her sexpot image indicated. Whether Monroe's performance is a result of director Joshua Logan's patience or Lee and Paula Strasberg's legendary coaching is irrelevant: she is simply superb as the down-at-heel saloon chanteuse young cowboy Don Murray (impressive in his film debut) decides to marry. Based on William Inge's stage play, this is a movie that rewards – especially memorable is Monroe's delivery of an off-kilter *That Old Black Magic* in an outfit that leaves little to the imagination. If you've ever wondered, this movie certainly shows what Monroe was all about. ▭

Marilyn Monroe *Cherie* • Don Murray *Bo* • Arthur O'Connell *Virgil* • Betty Field *Grace* • Eileen Heckart *Vera* • Robert Bray *Carl* • Hope

Bush Christmas ★★★ U

Adventure
1947 · Ausl/UK · BW · 61mins

The first film made for J Arthur Rank's Children's Cinema Club, this adventure was beautifully photographed in the sultry Blue Mountains of New South Wales with an all-Australian cast and crew. Chips Rafferty, at the time the only world-famous Australian actor, heads the cast in the tale of a group of dauntless children who trek through the bush in order to catch the rustlers who have stolen their father's horses. The exciting climax takes place in a ghost town, where the children use techniques taught to them by their Aborigine servants to get the better of the villains. The film does not talk down to its youthful audience and is fine family fare.

Chips Rafferty *Long Bill* • John Fernside *Jim* • Stan Tolhurst *Blue* • Pat Penny *Father* • Thelma Grigg *Mother* • Clyde Combo *Old Jack* • John McCallum *Narrator* • Helen Grieve *Helen* ■ *Dir/Scr* Ralph Smart • *Cinematographer* George Heath

Bush Christmas ★★★ U

Adventure
1983 · Ausl · Colour · 91mins

A remake of British director Ralph Smart's 1947 original, this amiable outdoor adventure is of primary interest for marking the screen debut of Nicole Kidman. Along with brother Mark Spain, English cousin James Wingrove and Aboriginal stablehand Manalpuy, she spends much of the film pursuing roguish horse thieves John Ewart and John Howard, whose need for a big racecourse win is as pressing as that of Kidman's farmer parents, Peter Sumner and Vineta O'Malley. Directed with a kid-friendly mix of humour and action by Henri Safran and splendidly shot by Malcolm Richards and Ross Berryman, this is family fare of a high order.

Nicole Kidman *Helen* • Mark Spain *John* • James Wingrove *Michael* • Manalpuy *Manalpuy* • John Ewart *John Howard (2)* • Sly • Vineta O'Malley *Kate Thompson* • Peter Sumner *Ben Thompson* ■ *Dir* Henri Safran • *Scr* Ted Roberts, from the film by Ralph Smart

The Bushido Blade ★★ 15

Historical action drama
1981 · US/UK · Colour · 90mins

Despite its handsome trappings, this is an unremarkable historical adventure. In his last film, Richard Boone is typically gruff as the American commander who leads an expedition to 19th-century Japan to recover a ceremonial sword that has been stolen by those opposed to the forces of westernisation, strengthened by a treaty between the two nations. The narrative is too episodic to engross, with long stretches of stilted dialogue merely delaying the inevitable scenes of flashing swordplay and high-flying kung fu. Kurosawa's favourite actor, Toshiro Mifune, lends a little class in the role he would reprise in a spin-off mini-series. ▭

Richard Boone *Matthew Perry* • Sonny Chiba *Prince Edo* • Frank Converse *Captain Hawk* • Laura Gemser *Edo's cousin* • James Earl

Jones *Harpooner* • Mako *Friend* • Toshiro Mifune *Shogun's commander* ■ *Dir* Tom Kotani • *Scr* William Overgard

Bushwhacked ★ PG

Comedy 1995 · US · Colour · 86mins

This calamitous comedy might appeal to those youngsters who thought that Daniel Stern being pummelled in *Home Alone* was hilariously funny. Here, Stern is a doltish delivery man who poses as a scout leader while trying to beat a murder rap. After just a couple of bruising mishaps, you begin to long for the infinitely more subtle slapstick of scoutmaster William Powell in *I Love You Again* or even Fred MacMurray's wholehearted dib-dobbing in *Follow Me, Boys!* It's as if, having been upstaged by Macaulay Culkin, Stern was determined not to let it happen again. Contains swearing. ▣

Daniel Stern *Max Grabelski* • Jon Polito *Agent Palmer* • Brad Sullivan *Jack Erickson* • Ann Dowd *Mrs Patterson* • Anthony Heald *Bragdon* • Tom Wood *Agent McMurrey* ■ *Dir* Greg Beeman • *Scr* John Jordan, Danny Byers, Tommy Swerdlow, Michael Goldberg, from a story by John Jordan, Danny Byers

A Business Affair ★★ 15

Romantic comedy
1993 · Fr/UK/Ger/Sp · Colour · 97mins

It's hard to believe the combined talents of Christopher Walken and Jonathan Pryce could make such a lacklustre film. Pryce plays a novelist whose writer's block is seriously aggravated when his wife Carole Bouquet achieves sudden success as a novelist. To make matters worse, she elopes with her husband's literary agent (Walken). Charlotte Brandstrom's film has everything going for it, but it's simply too fluffy for its heavyweight cast. It might have worked better had it been shot in French. ▣

Christopher Walken *Vanni Corso* • Carole Bouquet *Kate Swallow* • Jonathan Pryce *Alec Bolton* • Sheila Hancock *Judith* • Anna Manahan *Bianca* • Fernando Guillen-Cuervo *Angel* • Tom Wilkinson *Bob* ■ *Dir* Charlotte Brandstrom • *Scr* William Stadiem, from a story by Charlotte Brandstrom, William Stadiem, from the books *Tears Before Bedtime* and *Weep No More* by Barbara Skelton

Business as Usual ★★ 15

Drama 1987 · UK · Colour · 85mins

Lezli-An Barrett's debut feature has a tendency towards the didactic. Glenda Jackson, in her pre-Labour MP days, plays a Liverpool boutique manager who becomes a supporter of workers' rights when she's sacked by her boss for complaining about the sexual harassment of an employee. Very eighties and anti-Thatcher in its approach, the film is watchable thanks to the conviction of the cast, but not helped by the heavy-handed treatment of the subject matter. Barrett should save her ranting for Speakers' Corner. ▣

Glenda Jackson *Babs Flynn* • John Thaw *Kieran Flynn* • Cathy Tyson *Josie Patterson* • Mark McGann *Stevie Flynn* • Eamon Boland *Mr Barry* • James Hazeldine *Mark* • Buki Armstrong *Paula Douglas* • Stephen McGann *Terry Flynn* ■ *Dir/Scr* Lezli-An Barrett

Business for Pleasure ★★ 18

Erotic drama 1996 · US · Colour · 92mins

Another film from the seemingly inexhaustible sexual fantasy warehouse that is the mind of soft-core impresario Zalman King (writer/director of *The Red Shoe Diaries, Two Moon Junction*). As usual there is a better than average cast (Jeroen Krabbé, Joanna Pacula), high production values and a mild streak of kinkiness in an otherwise formulaic tale. Pacula plays an executive who ends up posing as a hooker to land a big business deal, only to find herself drawn into a very seamy world indeed. The young male lead, incidentally, is Gary Stretch, the UK's only martial arts video star. ▣

Caron Bernstein *Isabel* • Joanna Pacula *Anna* • Gary Stretch *Rolf* ■ *Dir* Rafael Eisenman • *Scr* Zalman King, Laline Paull, from a story by Zalman King

Busman's Honeymoon ★★

Crime thriller 1940 · UK · BW · 98mins

Lord Peter Wimsey gets married and vows to drop all his detective work until a corpse appears in his honeymoon hideaway in Devon. It's based on the novel by Dorothy L Sayers and you can almost hear the stage boards creaking. However, Robert Montgomery and Constance Cummings are delightful company as the lead couple and there's a host of stalwarts, such as Robert Newton and Googie Withers, to please fans of vintage British cinema. The clear camerawork is by Freddie Young, who later won Oscars for *Lawrence of Arabia* and *Doctor Zhivago*.

Robert Montgomery *Lord Peter Wimsey* • Constance Cummings *Harriet Vane* • Leslie Banks *Inspector Kirk* • Seymour Hicks *Bunter* • Robert Newton *Frank Crutchley* • Googie Withers *Polly* • Frank Pettingell *Puffett* • Joan Kemp-Welch *Aggie Twitterton* ■ *Dir* Arthur B Woods • *Scr* Monckton Hoffe, Angus MacPhail, Harold Goldman, from the novel by Dorothy L Sayers

Buster ★★★ 15

Biographical crime drama
1988 · UK · Colour · 98mins

Although he's best known as a musician, Phil Collins actually began his show-business career as a child actor. Here he takes on his first lead movie role, playing Buster Edwards, one of the gang involved in the Great Train Robbery. Julie Walters plays his wife and they make the most of their roles as loveably cheeky Cockney sparrers chirruping away in Acapulco after fleeing London. *EastEnders*-style clichés fall as thick and fast as the pair's "aitches", and, while Collins does his best, it's Walters who scores as a woman missing the comforts of home. Too squeaky clean to be believable, this is an entertaining but fairy-tale view of law-breaking. Contains swearing, violence and nudity. ▣

Phil Collins *Buster Edwards* • Julie Walters *June Edwards* • Larry Lamb *Bruce Reynolds* • Stephanie Lawrence *Franny Reynolds* • Ellen Beaven *Nicky Edwards* • Michael Attwell *Harry* • Ralph Brown *Ronnie* • Christopher Ellison *George* • Sheila Hancock *Mrs Rothery* ■ *Dir* David Green • *Scr* Colin Shindler

Buster and Billie ★★★ 18

Drama 1974 · US · Colour · 95mins

A rite of passage movie, set in rural Georgia in 1948, where local boys loaf about eying the girls and wonder how far they will go in a sexual relationship. The exception is Joan Goodfellow who lives in squalor on the other side of the tracks and entertains the boys at the drop of a hat. When Jan-Michael Vincent abandons his childhood sweetheart for her, things come to a head and end in a chain of murders. The movie should have been a potboiler – a sort of Tennessee Williams crossed with Roger Corman teenpic – but it's a bit too well behaved, too self-consciously "literate" and too preoccupied with period trappings to be more than just absorbing. ▣

Jan-Michael Vincent *Buster Lane* • Joan Goodfellow *Billie* • Pamela Sue Martin *Margie Hooks* • Clifton James *Jake* • Robert Englund *Whitey* • Jessie Lee Fulton *Mrs Lane* • JB Joiner *Mr Lane* • Dell C Payne *Warren* ■ *Dir* Daniel Petrie • *Scr* Ron Turbeville, from a story by Ron Baron, Ron Turbeville

The Buster Keaton Story ★ U

Biographical comedy drama
1957 · US · BW · 91mins

Blockbuster novelist Sidney Sheldon was responsible (as co-writer, co-producer and director) for this insult to the comic genius of the Great Stone Face. Even though Keaton himself supervised the re-created moments of peerless slapstick, he was so furious at the flagrant fictions littering the script that he almost walked out of the Hollywood premiere in disgust. In his defence, Donald O'Connor works overtime to re-create Keaton's screen presence. But, while his alcoholism is tactfully handled, the segments on his passion for the unattainable Rhonda Fleming and his doomed marriage to the long-suffering Ann Blyth are as tacky as they're inaccurate.

Donald O'Connor *Buster Keaton* • Ann Blyth *Gloria* • Rhonda Fleming *Peggy Courtney* • Peter Lorre *Kurt Bergner* • Larry Keating *Larry Winters* • Richard Anderson *Tom McAffee* • Dave Willock *Joe Keaton* • Claire Carleton *Myrna Keaton* • Jackie Coogan *Elmer Case* • Cecil B DeMille ■ *Dir* Sidney Sheldon • *Scr* Sidney Sheldon, Robert Smith

Buster's World ★★★

Comedy drama 1984 · Den · Colour · 77mins

This charming rite-of-passage picture is considerably more personal than Bille August's more internationally acclaimed study of childhood, *Pelle the Conqueror*. Mads Bugge Andersen gives a wonderfully eccentric performance as the daydreaming pre-teen who uses his grandfather's magic kit not only to ward off the bullies who threaten his crippled sister, but also to further his chances with the poor little rich girl he meets at the fair. Clearly influenced by the likes of *Kes*, this is an astute blend of pathos and comedy. The school football match and Buster's adventures on his delivery round are among the highlights. In Danish with English subtitles.

Mads Bugge Andersen *Buster* • Katerina Stenbeck *Buster's sister* • Peter Schrøder

Father • Kirsten Rolffes *Joanna's mother* • Berthe Qvistgaard *Mrs Larsen* • Buster Larsen *Shopkeeper* • Signe Dahl Madsen *Joanna* • Katja Miehe-Renard *Mother* ■ *Dir* Bille August • *Scr* Bjarne Reuther, from his novel

Bustin' Loose ★★★ 15

Comedy 1981 · US · Colour · 88mins

Richard Pryor wrote and co-produced this story of an ex-convict shepherding teacher Cicely Tyson and her class of maladjusted children to a rural retreat, revealing that sentiment was as much his line as deadpan wisecracks. The film took two years to complete, because it was interrupted by Pryor's near-fatal drug-related accident, and, as a result, theatre director Oz Scott, in his film debut, was left with insurmountable discrepancies in continuity. Despite a queasy mix of pratfalls and pathos, Pryor still comes across as hugely likeable. Contains swearing and violence. ▣

Richard Pryor *Joe Braxton* • Cicely Tyson *Vivian Perry* • Alphonso Alexander *Martin* • Kia Cooper *Samantha* • Edwin Deleon *Ernesto* • Jimmy Hughes *Harold* • Edwin Kinter *Anthony* ■ *Dir* Oz Scott • *Scr* Roger L Simon, Lonne Elder III, from a story by Richard Pryor

Busting ★★ 18

Crime drama 1974 · US · Colour · 87mins

An early attempt to show the Los Angeles police as corrupt, bureaucratic and just like any other government department. While Elliott Gould and Robert Blake are the vice detectives forced to crack down on minor drug dealers, top managers are taking pay-offs from high ranking mobsters. Peter Hyams's direction bustles farcically to make its case that the LAPD is lapdog to the Syndicate, but it's too raucous to make the point at all coherently. More fun than fact, but still worth watching. ▣

Elliott Gould *Michael Keneely* • Blake Robert *Patrick Farrell* • Allen Garfield *Carl Rizzo* • William Sylvester *Mr Weldman* • Logan Ramsey *Dr Berman* • Richard X Slattery *Desk sergeant* • John Lawrence *Sergeant Kenfick* ■ *Dir/Scr* Peter Hyams

The Busy Body ★★★

Black comedy 1967 · US · Colour · 101mins

A change of pace for William Castle, the schlockmeister who famously wired up cinema seats to give audiences a little extra shock during showings of *The Tingler*. This Castle offering, though, is a black comedy about Mafia folk and is based on the novel by Donald E Westlake, author of *Point Blank*. Sid Caesar is the Mafia employee suspected of stealing a bundle, Robert Ryan, always a joy to watch, is the *numero uno* mobster and there's rich support from Anne Baxter and Richard Pryor in his screen debut. Sloppy in places, this is nonetheless a delightful tongue-in-cheek piece for connoisseurs of the crime movie.

Sid Caesar *George Norton* • Robert Ryan *Charley Barker* • Anne Baxter *Margo Foster* • Kay Medford *Ma Norton* • Jan Murray *Murray Foster* • Richard Pryor *Whittaker* • Arlene Golonka *Bobbi Brody* • Dom DeLuise *Kurt Brock* ■ *Dir* William Castle • *Scr* Ben Starr, from the novel by Donald E Westlake

U = SUITABLE FOR ALL   Uc = SUITABLE FOR ALL, ESPECIALLY FOR YOUNG CHILDREN (VIDEO ONLY)   PG = PARENTAL GUIDANCE

But I'm a Cheerleader ★★

Satirical comedy 1999 · US · Colour · 81mins

This sugar-coated satire is continually sacrificing the important points it makes regarding homophobia and prejudice for the sake of an easy gag. Teenager Natasha Lyonne is suspected of being a lesbian by her friends and family, so she's shipped off to a rehabilitation camp that promises to "cure" her sexual preference. But there she meets the sexy Clea DuVall. Lyonne is good value and drag artist RuPaul is fun as the butch camp counsellor whose job it is to straighten the kids out. However, the initial spoofing of gay culture loses its edge after too many compromises and the film turns into a toothless sitcom-style plea for tolerance.

Natasha Lyonne *Megan* • Cathy Moriarty *Mary Brown* • Mink Stole *Nancy* • RuPaul Charles [RuPaul] *Mike* • Clea DuVall *Graham* • Bud Cort *Peter* • Eddie Cibrian *Rock* • Melanie Lynskey *Hilary* • Julie Delpy *Lipstick lesbian* ■ *Dir* Jamie Babbit • *Scr* Brian Wayne Peterson, from a story by Jamie Babbit

But Not for Me ★★★ U

Romantic comedy 1959 · US · BW · 104mins

Prior to this comedy, Paramount had already filmed two other versions of Samson Raphaelson's hit Broadway play, *Accent on Youth*: in 1935, with Herbert Marshall as a playwright and Sylvia Sidney as the youthful secretary who falls for him; and in 1950, as *Mr Music*, with Bing Crosby as a songwriter and Nancy Olson as the girl. Here Clark Gable stars as a fading theatre producer who almost succumbs to the charms and devotion of his new secretary (Carroll Baker). A pleasingly suitable vehicle for its ageing star, the film lacks effervescence, but Walter Lang directs with polish, while Lilli Palmer is ideal as the woman who boxes more to Gable's weight.

Clark Gable *Russell Ward* • Carroll Baker *Eleanor Brown* • Lilli Palmer *Kathryn Ward* • Lee J Cobb *Jeremiah MacDonald* • Barry Coe *Gordon Reynolds* • Thomas Gomez *Demetrios Bacos* • Charles Lane (1) *Atwood* • Wendell Holmes *Montgomery* ■ *Dir* Walter Lang • *Scr* John Michael Hayes, from the play *Accent on Youth* by Samson Raphaelson

Butch and Sundance: the Early Days ★★★ PG

Comedy western 1979 · US · Colour · 106mins

Completely inconsequential when measured against its phenomenally successful progenitor, this fictional version of the early outlaw careers of Butch Cassidy and the Sundance Kid is still an enjoyable romp. William Katt and Tom Berenger emit oodles of charm as the cowboy heroes' younger selves, and director Richard Lester laces the ambitious material with the same wit and irony he brought to *The Three Musketeers*. Worth seeing for the highly amusing train robbery and the extraordinary sight of a flooded western town. ▭

William Katt *Sundance Kid* • Tom Berenger *Butch Cassidy* • Jeff Corey *Sheriff Ray Bledsoe* • John Schuck *Harvey Logan* • Michael C Gwynne *Mike Cassidy* • Peter

Weller *Joe LeFors* • Brian Dennehy *OC Hanks* • Chris Lloyd [Christopher Lloyd] *Bill Carver* ■ *Dir* Richard Lester • *Scr* Allan Burns

Butch Cassidy and the Sundance Kid ★★★★★ PG

Classic western 1969 · US · Colour · 105mins

1969 was a vintage year for the western, with *The Wild Bunch* and *True Grit* joining this freewheeling fantasy among the year's releases. In many ways the western's answer to *Bonnie and Clyde*, George Roy Hill's film was one of the biggest box-office hits in the genre's history. Some of the credit must go to the Oscar-winning trio of William Goldman, Conrad Hall and Burt Bacharach for the witty script, luminous photography and jaunty score respectively. But the true charm of this ever-popular picture lies in the exhilarating performances of Paul Newman and Robert Redford, who turn the ruthless desperadoes of fact into loveable rogues and, ultimately, tragic heroes. Contains moderate violence and swearing. ▭

Paul Newman *Butch Cassidy* • Robert Redford *Sundance Kid* • Katharine Ross *Etta Place* • Strother Martin *Percy Garris* • Henry Jones *Bike salesman* • Jeff Corey *Sheriff Bledsoe* • George Furth *Woodcock* • Cloris Leachman *Agnes* ■ *Dir* George Roy Hill • *Scr* William Goldman

The Butcher Boy ★★★★

Silent comedy 1917 · US · BW · 30mins

Although the career of silent film comedian Roscoe "Fatty" Arbuckle was to end in scandal, this shows just how deft and delicate he could be in fast-moving farce. It's a simple-minded tale of love among the meat-hooks, the first of the Comique films he signed up for with Paramount's Joseph Schenck. The occasional vulgarity of his Keystone movies was left behind and, generously, he gave a first chance to one of his vaudeville friends whose routine with a coin and molasses in the film almost upstaged "Fatty" himself. The friend? Buster Keaton, who supported Arbuckle after scandal had ruined his career.

Roscoe "Fatty" Arbuckle • Josephine Stevens • Al St John • Buster Keaton ■ *Dir* Roscoe "Fatty" Arbuckle • *Scr* from a story by Roscoe "Fatty" Arbuckle, Joseph Anthony Roach

The Butcher Boy ★★★★ 15

Black comedy drama 1997 · Ire/US · Colour · 105mins

Novelist Patrick McCabe's portrait of small-town Irish life in the sixties is viewed through dark-tinted glasses in this shocking, often surreal adaptation by Neil Jordan. Armed only with comics, movies and visions of the Virgin Mary (Sinead O'Connor), Eamonn Owens excels as the breezy teenager whose grip on reality begins to loosen as he returns from a pitiless Catholic remand home to witness the descent of father Stephen Rea into alcoholism and mother Aisling O'Sullivan into madness. There's always an edge to his mischief, but nothing can prepare you for the brutal fate meted out to prurient neighbour Fiona Shaw. Contains swearing, violence and some sexual reference. ▭

Stephen Rea *Da Brady* • Fiona Shaw *Mrs Nugent* • Eamonn Owens *Francie Brady* • Ian Hart *Uncle Alo* • Aisling O'Sullivan *Ma Brady* • Sinead O'Connor *Our Lady/Colleen* • Ardal O'Hanlon *Mr Purcell* • Milo O'Shea *Father Sullivan* ■ *Dir* Neil Jordan • *Scr* Neil Jordan, Patrick McCabe, from the novel by Patrick McCabe

The Butcher's Wife ★★★ 15

Romantic comedy 1991 · US · Colour · 100mins

After the blockbuster success of *Ghost* in 1990, Demi Moore certainly chose some odd projects for the following year: there was the misfire *Nothing but Trouble*, the downbeat drama *Mortal Thoughts* and this quirky but quiet romantic comedy. Moore plays a blonde psychic who cheerfully tries to sort out the lives of her lonely neighbours in New York, who include besotted Jeff Daniels, Mary Steenburgen and Frances McDormand. Director Terry Hughes succeeds in conjuring up a bittersweet, magical atmosphere which is rarely cloying, and he is well served by a talented cast. However, it all proved a little too obscure for Moore's fans and the film didn't last long at the cinema. Contains some swearing. ▭

Demi Moore *Marina* • Jeff Daniels *Alex* • George Dzundza *Leo* • Mary Steenburgen *Stella* • Frances McDormand *Grace* • Margaret Colin *Robyn* • Max Perlich *Eugene* • Miriam Margolyes *Gina* ■ *Dir* Terry Hughes • *Scr* Ezra Litwak, Marjorie Schwartz

Butley ★★★

Drama 1973 · UK · Colour · 129mins

A tour de force for Alan Bates in a filmed play – made for the American Film Theatre – of Simon Gray's drama about an academic whose wit and know-all attitude lacerates those around him (Jessica Tandy, Richard O'Callaghan, Susan Engel). In the end, though, his self-destructiveness hurts no one but himself. Playwright Harold Pinter directs with a typically laconic style that has little to do with cinema.

Alan Bates *Ben Butley* • Jessica Tandy *Edna Shaft* • Richard O'Callaghan *Joey Keyston* • Susan Engel *Anne Butley* • Michael Byrne *Reg Nuttall* • Georgina Hale *Miss Heasman* ■ *Dir* Harold Pinter • *Scr* Simon Gray, from his play

The Butter Cream Gang ★★

Drama 1991 · US · Colour · 93mins

The said gang consists of four smashing boys, so full of sunshine and charity that their home town of Upbridge just adores them. But when one of them moves to Chicago, the Windy City proves to be a bad influence and, instead of helping old ladies up the stairs, he'd rather push them down. When he goes back to Upbridge and forms a new gang of yobs, the three he left behind take action. Jason Johnson, Michael D Weatherred, Brandon Blaser and Jason Glenn are the gang of four with very little between them to recommend watching. Despite being moral and upright, the tale itself is very mediocre.

Jason Johnson *Scott* • Michael D Weatherred *Pete* • Brandon Blaser *Eldon* • Jason Glenn *Larry* • Michael Scott *Reverend Wilde/Coach* • Stephanie Dees *Margaret* ■ *Dir* Bruce Neibaur • *Scr* Forrest S Baker III

Butterbox Babies ★★★ 15

Drama based on a true story 1995 · Can · Colour · 94mins

A well-made and interesting drama based on the true story of Lila and William Young, who ran a maternity home and adoption service in Nova Scotia during the Depression. Portrayed as a haven for unmarried mothers to be, it was actually a front for illegal adoptions, and many of the babies died in mysterious circumstances and were buried in boxes from the local creamery in the garden of the home. Stars Susan Clark, Peter MacNeill and Michael Riley, under the direction of Don McBrearty, manage to portray events with the minimum of hysteria, never lapsing into melodrama. ▭

Susan Clark *Lila Young* • Peter MacNeill *William Young* • Catherine Fitch *Iris* • Michael Riley *Russell Cameron* • Shannon Lawson *Nurse Ann O'Dwyer* • Nicholas Campbell *Clayton Oliver* • Corinne Conley *Mrs Chadway* • Cedric Smith *Dr Frank Davis* ■ *Dir* Don McBrearty • *Scr* Raymond Storey, from the book by Bette Cahill

The Buttercup Chain ★

Drama 1970 · UK · Colour · 94mins

Filled with the psycho-sexual babble of the Swinging Sixties, this awful movie has Hywel Bennett as the founder member of a group of four inseperable friends who swap partners, generally relate to each other and are clearly destined for an unhappy ending. Bennett is sullen throughout while Jane Asher and Leigh Taylor-Young model some short skirts as the story flits around Europe, picking up cardboard Swedish stud Sven-Bertil Taube en route.

Hywel Bennett *France* • Leigh Taylor-Young *Manny* • Jane Asher *Margaret* • Sven-Bertil Taube *Fred* • Clive Revill *George* • Roy Dotrice *Martin Carr-Gibbons* • Michael Elphick *Chauffeur* ■ *Dir* Robert Ellis Miller • *Scr* Peter Draper, from a novel by Janice Elliott

Butterfield 8 ★★★ 15

Drama 1960 · US · Colour · 108mins

Elizabeth Taylor's Oscar-winning performance as an up-market whore with a heart is the chief, if not only, interest of this otherwise weak and dated drama. Based on the thirties novel by John O'Hara, the film's attitude to sex was controversial on its release in 1960, but it is tepid stuff today. Eddie Fisher, Taylor's husband at the time, fails to convince as the call girl's long-time friend, while Laurence Harvey looks equally uncomfortable as the married man with whom she has a passionate affair. ▭

Elizabeth Taylor *Gloria Wandrous* • Laurence Harvey *Weston Liggett* • Eddie Fisher *Steve Carpenter* • Dina Merrill *Emily Liggett* • Mildred Dunnock *Mrs Wandrous* • Betty Field *Mrs Fanny Thurber* • Jeffrey Lynn *Bingham Smith* ■ *Dir* Daniel Mann • *Scr* Charles Schnee, John Michael Hayes, from the novel by John O'Hara

Butterflies Are Free ★★ PG

Drama 1972 · US · Colour · 104mins

Eileen Heckart won a best supporting actress Oscar for her role as blind Edward Albert's possessive mother, trying to protect her son from the advances of free spirit Goldie Hawn in this screen version of Leonard Gershe's Broadway hit. Unfortunately, this often laughably corny product of the flower power era hasn't dated well, but it may offer some nostalgic pleasure for those old enough to remember. Contains some swearing. 🖭

Goldie Hawn *Jill* • Edward Albert *Don* • Eileen Heckart *Mrs Baker* • Michael Glasser *Ralph* • Mike Warren [Michael Warren] *Roy* ■ *Dir* Milton Katselas • *Scr* Leonard Gershe, from his play

Butterfly ★★ 18

Drama   1982 · US · Colour · 103mins

James M Cain's tough and complex crime novel about silver mines, incest and murder becomes a patience-testing sexploitation thriller thanks to Matt Cimber's soft-focus direction and a mind-numbing, Lolita-style performance from low-rent starlet Pia Zadora. Stacy Keach plays Zadora's long-lost father who succumbs to her feminine wiles and ore-stripping scam – part of her plan to take revenge on the mine-owner's son who got her pregnant, then refused to marry her. Orson Welles cameos as a lecherous judge, while Ennio Morricone supplies the music. Too awful to be taken seriously, yet too camp to miss. 🖭

Stacy Keach *Jeff Tyler* • Pia Zadora *Kady* • Orson Welles *Judge Rauch* • Lois Nettleton *Belle Morgan* • Edward Albert *Wash Gillespie* • James Franciscus *Moke Blue* • Stuart Whitman *Rev Rivers* • Ed McMahon *Mr Gillespie* ■ *Dir* Matt Cimber • *Scr* Matt Cimber, John Goff, from the novel by James M Cain

The Butterfly Effect ★★★ 15

Comedy   1995 · Sp/Fr/UK · Colour · 108mins

Using chaos theory as the pretext for setting in motion a domino run of coincidences and catastrophes, this cleverly constructed comedy touches on everything from machismo and European unity to incest and *Star Trek*. Permitting each character their moment in the spotlight, director Fernando Colomo expertly picks his way through the maze of tangled relationships that forms after Coque Malla's mother sends him to visit her sister in London, in order to learn about life. Debunking cultural stereotypes at every plot turn, the film even has sufficient courage of its comic convictions to attempt an audacious socio-political finale. A Spanish language film.

Maria Barranco *Olivia* • Coque Malla *Luis* • Rosa Maria Sarda *Noelia* • James Fleet *Oswald* • Peter Sullivan *Duncan* • Cécile Pallas *Chantal* • Jose Maria Pou *Rafa* • John Faal *Nick* ■ *Dir* Fernando Colomo • *Scr* Joaquín Oristrell, Fernando Colomo

Butterfly Kiss ★★ 18

Drama   1994 · UK · Colour and BW · 87mins

Thelma and Louise meets *The Silence of the Lambs* in this weird British road movie that stars Amanda Plummer as a lesbian serial killer and Saskia Reeves as her willing associate. It's narrated by Reeves, who plays the extremely dense shop assistant picked up by punkette Plummer at a service station. They go to bed, hit the road

and the body count rises as Plummer seeks out a former lover. Instead of being shockingly original like, say, *Trainspotting* it's merely drab and depressing. It's directed by Michael Winterbottom (*Jude, Welcome to Sarajevo*). Contains violence, swearing, sex scenes and nudity. 🖭

Amanda Plummer *Eunice* • Saskia Reeves *Miriam* • Ricky Tomlinson *Robert* • Des McAleer *Eric* • Paul Bown *Gary* • Freda Dowie *Elsie* • Fine Time Fontayne *Tony* ■ *Dir* Michael Winterbottom • *Scr* Frank Cottrell Boyce, from an idea by Frank Cottrell Boyce, Michael Winterbottom

The Butterfly Murders ★★★

Martial arts mystery horror
1979 · HK · Colour · 88mins

Tsui Hark made his directorial debut with this eerie hybrid of the horror and swordplay genres. Edgar Allan Poe's *The Masque of the Red Death* is the clear inspiration for this elaborate tale of killer butterflies, hidden identities and fantastical contraptions. By reinforcing the claustrophobic atmosphere of the labyrinthine castle setting, Fan Jinyu's photography makes the explosive action all the more dynamic and ethereal as warrior/scholar Liu Zhaoming seeks to eradicate the lepidopteran peril. The characters may have names like "Thousand Hands" and "Green Shadow", but this is no mere heroic fantasy; a vein of Chinese nationalism runs through the narrative. In Mandarin with English subtitles.

Liu Zhaoming *Fang Hongye* • Michelle Mee *Green Shadow* • Huang Shutang *Tian Feng* • Zhang Guozhu *Shen Qing* • Chen Qiqi *Lady Shen* • Wang Jiang *Li "The Thousand Hands"* • Gao Ziong *Guo "The Magic Fire"* • Xu Xiaoling *Ah Zhi* • Xia Jiangli *Number 10 of the Red Flags* ■ *Dir* Tsui Hark • *Scr* Lin Fan

Buttoners ★★★★

Portmanteau drama
1997 · Cz Rep · Colour · 108mins

Although this ingeniously structured portmanteau picture often recalls the surrealist antics of Luis Buñuel, Petr Zelenka's astute mix of satire, sci-fi and historical supposition owes more to the eccentric strain of Czech comedy that also inspires the likes of Jan Svankmajer. Starting with the atomic assault on Hiroshima, Zelenka relates six stories which gradually link together to form a mischievous thesis on the role of chance, coincidence, fate and forgiveness in everyday life. Featuring a gallery of offbeat characters, including a man who spits at trains and another who snips buttons off furniture, this is a gleefully quirky and superbly controlled film. In Czech with English subtitles.

Pavel Zajicek *Radio 1 moderator* • Jan Haubert *Guest* • Seisuke Tsukahara *Japanese man with spectacles* • Frantisek Cerny *Franta, taxi driver* • Vladimir Dlouhy *Psychiatrist* • Jiri Kodet *Honza, host* • Rudolf Hrusinsky Jr *Unsuccessful man* • Mariana Stojlovova *Girl at seance* ■ *Dir/Scr* Petr Zelenka

Buy & Cell ★★ 15

Comedy   1988 · US · Colour · 92mins

Although filmed at the height of Wall Street's insider trading crisis, this slight comedy feels as if it could have been made in Britain in the late fifties,

with Ian Carmichael as the naive stockbroker taking the rap for his crooked boss and Lionel Jeffries as the disreputable prison warden. Instead, we have to settle for Robert Carradine and Malcolm McDowell, although the latter has his moments. As is so often the case, a good idea has been frittered away by a lacklustre script. Consequently, the satire is slapdash and the inmates are uninspired stereotypes. The title's awful, too. Contains swearing. 🖭

Malcolm McDowell *Warden Tennant* • Robert Carradine *Herbie Altman* • Michael Winslow *Sly* • Randall "Tex" Cobb *Wolf* • Ben Vereen *Shaka* • Lise Cutter *Dr Ellen Scott* ■ *Dir* Robert Boris • *Scr* Neal Israel, Larry Siegel

Bwana Devil ★

Action adventure 1952 · US · Colour · 79mins

The film that launched the 3-D craze of the fifties with its slogan "A lion in your lap! A lover in your arms!" did record business as a novelty attraction. However, writer/producer/director Arch Oboler's film was so flat dramatically that it saddled the stereoscopic process with the reputation of being all gimmick. Substandard colour didn't help, either. In fact, you end up feeling sorry for the hungry lions that devour the African natives as they lay tracks for a new railroad. Robert Stack plays the engineer turned great white hunter, while Barbara Britton is his scared leading lady.

Robert Stack *Bob Hayward* • Barbara Britton *Alice Hayward* • Nigel Bruce *Dr Angus Ross* • Ramsay Hill *Maj Parkhurst* • Paul McVey *Commissioner* • Hope Miller *Portuguese girl* ■ *Dir/Scr* Arch Oboler

By Candlelight ★★★

Romantic comedy   1934 · US · BW · 70mins

During a European train journey, a nobleman's manservant (Paul Lukas) is mistaken for his employer (Nils Asther) by a lovely woman (Elissa Landi) and he does nothing to disillusion her. In due course, the nobleman turns up and is taken for his servant. Universal Studios' James Whale, the star director of its famous horror cycle, trespasses here on territory more generally associated with Paramount and Ernst Lubitsch. While not quite up to the rival studio's standard of sophisticated romantic comedies peopled by aristocrats, this is a more than respectably assembled film, well directed and well acted, particularly by Lukas.

Elissa Landi *Marie* • Paul Lukas *Josef* • Nils Asther *Count von Bommer* • Dorothy Revier *Countess von Rischenheim* • Lawrence Grant *Count von Rischenheim* • Esther Ralston *Baroness von Ballin* • Warburton Gamble *Baron von Ballin* • Lois January *Ann* ■ *Dir* James Whale • *Scr* Hans Kräly, F Hugh Herbert, Karen de Wolf, Ruth Cummings, from the play *Candlelight* by Siegfried Geyer

By Dawn's Early Light ★★★ 15

Thriller   1990 · US · Colour · 96mins

Powers Boothe gives another powerful performance in this effective dramatisation of what might happen to bring about the Third World War. Like *Crimson Tide*, this successfully poses

the nuclear threat question, and, even though you could only really have one of two outcomes, director Jack Sholder manages to keep the tension building, helped by a solid cast which includes James Earl Jones, Martin Landau and Rip Torn. Contains swearing. 🖭

Powers Boothe *Cassidy* • Rebecca De Mornay *Moreau* • Martin Landau *US President* • James Earl Jones *Alice* • Rip Torn *Colonel Fargo* • Darren McGavin *Condor* • Peter MacNicol *Sedgewick* • Jeffrey DeMunn *Harpoon* • Nicolas Coster *Icarus* ■ *Dir* Jack Sholder • *Scr* Bruce Gilbert, from the novel *Trinity's Child* by William Prochnau

By Love Possessed ★★★★

Drama   1961 · US · Colour · 115mins

Meriting four stars for excess rather than consistent quality, this heavenly example of the sleazy, lurid and luxurious finds the gorgeous Lana Turner saddled with an impotent husband (Jason Robards) and an opulent wardrobe of designer gowns. So she drowns her sorrows in drink, riding and the willing arms of Robard's law partner (Efrem Zimbalist Jr). The latter's father-in-law (Thomas Mitchell) is an embezzler, while his son (George Hamilton) is up on a rape charge. And that's just for starters! The only normal person in director Jean Sturges's cast of characters is Barbara Bel Geddes as Zimbalist's estranged wife.

Lana Turner *Marjorie Penrose* • Efrem Zimbalist Jr *Arthur Winner* • Jason Robards Jr *Julius Penrose* • George Hamilton *Warren Winner* • Susan Kohner *Helen Detweiler* • Barbara Bel Geddes *Clarissa Winner* • Thomas Mitchell *Noah Tuttle* • Everett Sloane *Reggie* ■ *Dir* John Sturges • *Scr* John Dennis [Charles Schnee], from the novel by James Gould Cozzens • *Costume Designer* Bill Thomas

By the Law ★★★★

Silent drama   1926 · USSR · BW · 83mins

Inspired by Jack London's short story, *The Unexpected* (though the birthday scene was drawn from Dostoyevsky), this Alaskan-based drama remains the least expensive feature ever produced in Russia. Working on a single set erected in the studio courtyard, Lev Kuleshov choreographed each expression and gesture to attain maximum dramatic effect and intensity of performance. The director's wife, Alexandra Khokhlova, excels as the gold prospector's wife who insists that avaricious Irishman Sergei Komarov is tried according to the law for the murder of his companions. A masterly experiment in silent stylisation, this is also a fervent, claustrophobic human melodrama.

Alexandra Khokhlova *Edith* • Sergei Komarov *Hans* • Vladimir Fogel *Michael* ■ *Dir* Lev Kuleshov • *Scr* Lev Kuleshov, Viktor Shklovsky, from the story *The Unexpected* by Jack London

By the Light of the Silvery Moon ★★★ U

Musical comedy   1953 · US · Colour · 97mins

In the wake of MGM's popular nostalgic songfest *Meet Me in St Louis*, Warner Bros borrowed debonair star Leon Ames and gave him a brand-new singing household in *On Moonlight Bay*, fronted by the top Warners songbird, the fabulous Doris Day. This very loose reworking of the *Penrod* stories by Booth Tarkington, who also wrote *The Magnificent Ambersons*, was successful enough to warrant a sequel. Here the delightful Doris (her hair a slightly blonder shade) and her soldier sweetheart Gordon MacRae cope with life in the post-First World War twenties. The Technicolor styling is superb, the treatment of the old songs enchanting and veterans Ames and, particularly, Mary Wickes as the maid are fun to watch. ▭

Doris Day *Marjorie Winfield* • Gordon MacRae *William Sherman* • Leon Ames *George Winfield* • Rosemary DeCamp *Mrs Winfield* • Billy Gray *Wesley* • Mary Wickes *Stella* • Russell Arms *Chester Finley* • Maria Palmer *Miss LaRue* ■ *Dir* David Butler • *Scr* Robert O'Brien, Irving Elinson, from the *Penrod,stories by Booth Tarkington*

By the Sword ★★ 15

Sports drama
1992 · US · Colour and BW · 87mins

The sport of fencing has been largely overlooked by Hollywood, so this drama at least scores on curiosity value. Taking its lead from the *Karate Kid* movies, this has two teachers clashing on the honourable way of fighting: F Murray Abraham is the mysterious elderly pupil who turns up at the school run by undefeated Olympic champion Eric Roberts and the two are soon locked in a deeply personal battle. The plotting is confused and Roberts is typically over the top, but Abraham brings some dignity to the proceedings and the fencing sequences work surprisingly well. Contains swearing. ▭

F Murray Abraham *Max Suba* • Eric Roberts *Alexander Villard* • Mia Sara *Erin Clavelli* • Christopher Rydell *Jimmy Trebor* • Elaine Kagan *Rachel* • Brett Cullen *Danny Gallagher* • Doug Wert *Hobbs* • Stoney Jackson *Johnson* • Caroline Barclay *Tatiana* ■ *Dir* Jeremy Kagan [Jeremy Paul Kagan] • *Scr* John McDonald, James Donadio

Bye Bye Birdie ★★★★ U

Musical comedy 1963 · US · Colour · 110mins

A wonderfully energetic and colourful adaptation of the smash Broadway hit, satirising the traumatic induction of one Elvis Presley into the US Army. Named Conrad Birdie here (a reference to contemporary rock 'n' roll star Conway Twitty), this focuses on the legendary rocker bestowing "one last kiss" on a small-town girl – a gimmick started by the star's promoter, played by Dick Van Dyke re-creating his Broadway role. It's splendid stuff and, although the satire has dated, the sheer exuberance of veteran *Anchors Aweigh* director George Sidney's guiding hand endures. So does the talent of vivacious Ann-Margret, who gets a specially written musical prologue. There are lots of laughs along the way, especially from stage star Paul Lynde. Ironically, the "we love you, Conrad" chorus was later used to hail the Beatles.

Janet Leigh *Rosie DeLeon* • Dick Van Dyke *Albert Peterson* • Ann-Margret *Kim McAfee* • Maureen Stapleton *Mama* • Bobby Rydell *Hugo Peabody* • Jesse Pearson *Conrad Birdie* • Ed Sullivan *Ed Sullivan* • Paul Lynde *Mr McAfee* ■ *Dir* George Sidney • *Scr* Irving

Brecher, from the musical comedy by Michael Stewart, with music and lyrics by Charles Strouse, Lee Adams

Bye Bye Blues ★★★ PG

Romantic drama
1989 · Can · Colour · 116mins

Post-Second World War cinema was so intent on telling tales of male heroism or sympathising with the problems of returning veterans that it completely ignored the dilemmas facing women who had spread their wings while their men were away fighting and were reluctant to return meekly to their nests in peacetime. Based on the experiences of director Anne Wheeler's own mother, this tear-jerker shows just how much of an upheaval the war was for women and how cheated they must have felt when their courage and ingenuity seemed to vanish into thin air as the first troopships docked. Helped by a nostalgic dance band soundtrack, this is warm, wise and beautifully acted. Contains brief nudity.

Rebecca Jenkins *Daisy Cooper* • Luke Reilly *Max Gramley* • Michael Ontkean *Teddy Cooper* • Stuart Margolin *Slim Godfrey* • Wayne Robson *Pete* • Robyn Stevan *Frances Cooper* • Leon Pownall *Bernie Blitzer* • Sheila Moore *Doreen Cooper* ■ *Dir/Scr* Anne Wheeler

Bye Bye Braverman ★★★★

Drama 1968 · US · Colour · 94mins

This wickedly acerbic mid-life crisis comedy anticipates *The Big Chill* in plot and theme, as a group of New York intellectuals mourn a deceased childhood friend and reflect on the state of their own lives on the way to his funeral. Brilliantly acted by a cast headed by George Segal and *Dr No*'s Joseph Wiseman, with comedian Alan King superb as a rabbi, this deserves to be better known, though its mordant theme almost certainly restricted its initial theatrical release. Director Sidney Lumet is not usually recognised for lightness of touch, but acquits himself extremely well here.

George Segal *Morroe Rieff* • Jack Warden *Barnet Weiner* • Jessica Walter *Inez Braverman* • Phyllis Newman *Myra Mandelbaum* • Godfrey Cambridge *Taxi cab driver* • Joseph Wiseman *Felix Ottensteen* • Sorrell Booke *Holly Levine* • Alan King *Rabbi* ■ *Dir* Sidney Lumet • *Scr* Herbert Sargent, from the novel *To an Early Grave* by Wallace Markfield

Bye Bye Brazil ★★★

Adventure drama
1979 · Bra/Fr · Colour · 100mins

It's hard to imagine a more flamboyant picture with such a downbeat message. Traipsing through northern Brazil, magician Jose Wilker, dancer Betty Faria and strongman Fabio Junior become increasingly despondent. Not only has their brand of live entertainment gone out of fashion, they are also appalled at how traditional lifestyles have been corroded by the incursion of social and consumerist "progress". Making telling use of colour and the Amazonian landscapes, director Carlos Diegues is not as scathing in his political asides as he might be. Yet this is still a lively and poignant film. In Portuguese with English subtitles.

Betty Faria *Salome* • José Wilker *Lorde Cigano* • Fabio Junior *Cico* • Zaira Zambelli *Dasdo* • Principe Nabor *Swallow* ■ *Dir/Scr* Carlos Diegues

Bye Bye Love ★★ 12

Comedy 1995 · US · Colour · 101mins

Some ghastly slapstick and several clumsy social situations ruin any chance this smarmy comedy has of success. The premise of showing how three divorced fathers cope with life after marriage is essentially a sound one, but not only is the screenplay littered with lines begging to be cut, but director Sam Weisman also has a forte for playing each scene at precisely the wrong pace. Matthew Modine escapes relatively unscathed, but Randy Quaid comes off badly during his encounter with daunting date Janeane Garofalo, while Paul Reiser suffers in his scenes with distraught daughter Eliza Dushku. Contains some swearing and sexual references. ▭

Matthew Modine *Dave* • Randy Quaid *Vic* • Paul Reiser *Donny* • Janeane Garofalo *Lucille* • Amy Brenneman *Susan* • Eliza Dushku *Emma* • Ed Flanders *Walter* • Maria Pitillo *Kim* • Lindsay Crouse *Grace* • Rob Reiner *Dr Townsend* ■ *Dir* Sam Weisman • *Scr* Gary David Goldberg, Brad Hall

Bye Bye Monkey ★★★

Black comedy drama
1978 · It/Fr · Colour · 114mins

Euro director Marco Ferreri, who had an international hit with *La Grande Bouffe*, made this fable in New York with rising star Gérard Depardieu and old master Marcello Mastroianni. Depardieu keeps a pet chimpanzee and is an electrician in a radical theatre where he's raped; Mastroianni is an asthmatic eccentric who lives in a rat-infested hovel and is on the verge of suicide. Praised at Cannes but barely released, this follows the descent of man from ape to human, from tenderness into barbarism among the rotting skyscrapers of Manhattan. Mastroianni rated his performance among his best. Contains violence, nudity, sexual situations and swearing.

Gérard Depardieu *Gérard Lafayette* • Marcello Mastroianni *Luigi Nocello* • James Coco *Andreas Flaxman* • Gail Lawrence *Angelica* • Geraldine Fitzgerald *Toland* • Avon Long *Miko* ■ *Dir* Marco Ferreri • *Scr* Marco Ferreri, Gérard Brach, Rafael Azcona

CB4 ★★★ 18

Satire 1993 · US · Colour · 84mins

Although this comedy lacks cohesion and feels like a series of loosely-linked sketches, it takes several well-aimed pot shots at both gangsta rap and the culture that engendered it. Surprisingly, considering it was directed by a woman, it somewhat ducks the issue of sexism, but *Saturday Night Live* alumnus Chris Rock and his rappers clearly have a ball. Eddie Murphy's brother, Charlie, appears as the convict whom they inspire the band's name (*CB4* stands for Cell Block 4) and image. Contains swearing, sex scenes, drug abuse and nudity. ▭

Chris Rock *Albert* • Allen Payne *Euripides* • D Deezer *Otis* • Chris Elliott *A White* • Phil Hartman *Virgil Robinson* • Charlie Murphy *Gusto* • Ice-T • Flavor Flav • Shaquille O'Neal ■ *Dir* Tamra Davis • *Scr* Chris Rock, Nelson George, Robert LoCash, from a story by Chris Rock, Nelson George

CIA – Codename Alexa
★★ 18

Action thriller 1992 · US · Colour · 94mins

This is a strictly by-the-numbers affair which grafts some sci-fi elements on to a fairly standard action plot. Kathleen Kinmont is the top-notch terrorist courted by moody CIA agent Lorenzo Lamas, who wants her to betray crime boss Alex Cord. Director Joseph Merhi makes sure all the ingredients for a straight-to-video success are present and correct, though mainstream film fans are unlikely to be impressed. ▭

Lorenzo Lamas *Mark Graver* • Kathleen Kinmont *Alexa* • Alex Cord *Victor Mahler* • OJ Simpson *Nick Murphy* ■ *Dir* Joseph Merhi • *Scr* John Weidner, Ken Lamplugh

Cabaret ★★★★★ 15

Musical drama 1972 · US · Colour · 123mins

A tremendously effective and affecting adult musical version of writer Christopher Isherwood's Berlin memoirs. The tale is transformed here, through the Oscar-winning magic of director Bob Fosse (replacing first choice Gene Kelly) and star Liza Minnelli, into a lasting screen classic, sparing no punches as it depicts the rise of Hitler and the spread of anti-Semitism through the twilight world of the Berlin cabaret. As the emcee of the Kit-Kat club, Joel Grey positively exudes decadence, and also collected one of the movie's eight Oscars. Fosse achieves several compelling cinematic moments, notably a chilling crescendo of emotion as a young Nazi sings Kander and Ebb's hymnic *Tomorrow Belongs to Me*. If brash Minnelli seems a mite too talented for the Sally Bowles character, it really doesn't matter: she is, quite simply, magnificent in this role. 🖵

Liza Minnelli *Sally Bowles* • Joel Grey *Master of Ceremonies* • Michael York *Brian Roberts* • Helmut Griem *Maximilian von Heune* • Fritz Wepper *Fritz Wendel* • Marisa Berenson *Natalia Landauer* ■ *Dir* Bob Fosse • *Scr* Jay Presson Allen, from the musical by Joe Masteroff, from the play *I Am a Camera* by John Van Druten, from the short story collection *Goodbye to Berlin* by Christopher Isherwood • *Choreography* Bob Fosse • *Cinematographer* Geoffrey Unsworth • *Music* Ralph Burnes • *Editor* David Bretherton • *Art Director* Rolf Zehetbauer, Jurgen Kiebach

Cabeza de Vaca ★★
Historical epic　1990 · Mex · Colour · 111mins

With the exception of Werner Herzog's *Aguirre, Wrath of God*, films about the Spanish conquest of the New World have been hugely disappointing. This one recounts the extraordinary story of Alvar Nuñez Cabeza de Vaca, a 16th-century soldier who was shipwrecked off the coast of what is now Florida. Following a series of miraculous cures, he is hailed as a messiah by the local tribes. Nicolas Echevarria's epic makes some telling points but is too slow to fire the imagination. In Spanish with English subtitles.

Juan Diego • Daniel Gimenez Cacho • Roberto Sosa • Jose Flores ■ *Dir* Nicolas Echevarria • *Scr* Nicolas Echevarria, Guillermo Sheridan, from the autobiography *Shipwrecks* by Alvar Nuñez Cabeza de Vaca

Cabin Boy ★★🆖
Comedy　1994 · US · Colour · 76mins

This "fish out of water" comedy gets low marks for originality but succeeds in raising the odd laugh. Chris Elliott (*Groundhog Day*) plays Nathanial Mayweather, a spoilt brat who mistakes a fishing boat for a luxury cruise liner and gets a lesson in life from the salty crew. Elliott is fine in the lead role, and watch for some interesting cameos from John Waters regular Ricki Lake, *West Side Story*'s Russ Tamblyn and late-night chat show host David Letterman. 🖵

Chris Elliott *Nathanial Mayweather* • Ritch Brinkley *Captain Greybar* • James Gammon *Paps* • Brian Doyle-Murray *Skunk* • Brion James *Big Teddy* ■ *Dir* Adam Resnick • *Scr* Adam Resnick, from a story by Adam Resnick, Chris Elliott

Cabin in the Cotton ★★🆖
Drama　1932 · US · BW · 79mins

Caught between loyalty to his own people – poor tenant farmers – and the friendship of his plantation-owner boss, sharecropper Richard Barthelmess faces further problems when he betrays his sweetheart (Dorothy Jordan) by succumbing to the shameless advances of the boss's predatory daughter (Bette Davis). The dramatic tension is dissipated by a poor script, a lifeless and confused-looking Barthelmess, and run-of-the-mill direction by Michael Curtiz. Davis, however, rises above the circumstances with characteristically fiery commitment.

Richard Barthelmess *Marvin* • Dorothy Jordan *Betty* • Bette Davis *Madge* • Berton Churchill *Lane Norwood* • Walter Percival *Cleve Clinton*

• William LeMaire *Jake Fisher* ■ *Dir* Michael Curtiz • *Scr* Paul Green, from the novel by Harry Harrison Kroll

Cabin in the Sky ★★★★🆖
Musical　1943 · US · BW · 94mins

An all-black fable about heaven and hell fighting for one man's soul. Sounds patronising, doesn't it? Well, this little gem is one of the cinema's great surprises: a stunning directorial debut from Broadway import Vincente Minnelli, featuring a sublime score performed by such fabulous artistes as Lena Horne, Ethel Waters, Louis Armstrong and the Duke Ellington Orchestra. The film's theatrical origins are terrifically subsumed in Minnelli's clever and stylish direction, and Eddie "Rochester" Anderson's performance in the pivotal role of Joe is a revelation. A gentle word of warning: in these enlightened days, the humour and stereotypes on display here may be deemed offensive. 🖵

Ethel Waters *Petunia Jackson* • Eddie "Rochester" Anderson *Little Joe Jackson* • Lena Horne *Georgia Brown* • Louis Armstrong *Trumpeter* • Rex Ingram *Lucius/Lucifer Jr* • Kenneth Spencer *Rev Green/The General* • John "Bubbles" Sublett *Domino Johnson* ■ *Dir* Vincente Minnelli • *Scr* Joseph Schrank, from the musical play by Lynn Root • *Music Director* George Stoll

The Cabinet of Caligari ★★
Horror　1962 · US · BW · 102mins

This pseudo-Freudian nonsense may share the same title as the 1919 silent classic, but it possesses none of its artistic aspirations. Horror clichés abound as a young woman's car breaks down near a mansion and she is held prisoner by its sinister owner, played with exuberant vigour by Dan O'Herlihy. There are moments of well-handled delirium and suspense featuring scenes of murder and voyeurism, but mostly it's a bore.

Dan O'Herlihy *Paul/Caligari* • Glynis Johns *Jane* • Richard Davalos *Mark* • Lawrence Dobkin *David* • Constance Ford *Christine* ■ *Dir* Roger Kay • *Scr* Robert Bloch

The Cabinet of Dr Caligari
★★★★★🆖
Silent horror　1919 · Ger · BW · 48mins

Like Sergei Eisenstein's *Battleship Potemkin*, this venerable silent classic changed the way movies were made and appreciated. Adapting techniques from the German theatrical style known as Expressionism, it explores the world and mind of a psychotic fairground showman who hypnotises a sleepwalker to commit a murder for him. However, the sleepwalker abducts the intended victim instead. The use of lopsided sets, odd camera angles and general weirdness caused a sensation at the time, and still look amazing. However, modern audiences may find the exaggerated acting and stilted movements of the characters dated and rather laughable. 🖵

Werner Krauss *Dr Caligari* • Conrad Veidt *Cesare* • Friedrich Feher *Francis* • Lil Dagover *Jane* • Hans von Twardowski *Alan* • Rudolf Lettinger *Dr Olson* • Rudoph Klein-Rogge *A criminal* ■ *Dir* Robert Wiene • *Scr* Carl Mayer, Hans Janowitz

Cabiri ★★
Documentary drama　1990 · UK/Ken · Colour

This unusual film is a mix of dreams, mythology and music that's dialogue-free. Even though he'd lived among them for some time, director Michael Kohler had trouble persuading the Samburu tribe of Kenya to co-operate in the making of the film, as none of them had ever seen a movie before and they were deeply suspicious of the camera's power to capture their image. However, they make a striking contribution to this bold and often arresting attempt to explore the universality of myths through the symbolic use of imagery, sound and music.

Dir Michael Kohler • *Scr* Michael Kohler, Sally Kohler

Cabiria ★★★★
Silent epic　1914 · It · BW · 210mins

The international success of this Italian spectacle, the longest and most expensive motion picture made up to that date, allowed DW Griffith to gain support for his large-scale projects. The film, which took an unprecedented six months to shoot in studios and locations in Sicily, the Alps and Tunisia, follows the adventures of Cabiria, a kidnapped girl, and Maciste, her giant slave companion, during the Second Punic War. Giovanni Pastrone directed, but the lion's share of the credit went to Gabriele D'Annunzio, despite the fact that the latter's contribution was limited to the intertitles.

Italia Almirante Manzini *Sophonisba* • Vitale de Stefano *Massinissa* • Bartolomeo Pagano *Maciste* • Lidia Quaranta *Cabiria* • Umberto Mozzato *Fulvio Axilla* • Enrico Gemelli *Archimedes* • Ignazio Lupi *Arbace* ■ *Dir* Piero Fosco [Giovanni Pastrone] • *Scr* Giovanni Pastrone

The Cable Guy ★★★🆓
Satirical comedy　1996 · US · Colour · 91mins

Jim Carrey was afforded the opportunity to do something different in this jet-black satire on the power of television, and he responds with a performance that brings a dark edge to his wacky persona. Carrey is on top form as a manic cable television technician who takes a special interest in one of his customers (Matthew Broderick). Although merely over-friendly at first, psycho stalker Carrey starts invading every aspect of Broderick's life, with both hilarious and sobering results. Ben Stiller's film may suffer from dull patches, but it's much better than you've heard it is. Contains violence and swearing. 🖵 DVD

Jim Carrey *Chip Douglas* • Matthew Broderick *Steven Kovacs* • Leslie Mann *Robin* • Jack Black *Rick* • George Segal *Steven's father* • Diane Baker *Steven's mother* • Ben Stiller *Sam Sweet* • Eric Roberts • Janeane Garofalo *Waitress* ■ *Dir* Ben Stiller • *Scr* Lou Holtz Jr

Caboblanco ★★
Drama　1980 · US · Colour · 87mins

Everybody comes to Giff's, the seedy bar run by Giff Hoyt (Charles Bronson), a tough guy with a past who has washed up in Peru. There's Jason Robards as an ex-Nazi gangster,

Fernando Rey as a corrupt police chief, and Dominique Sanda as a mystery woman looking for her lover and $22 million in sunken treasure. With its tongue only half inside its cheek, this adventure yarn never quite gets going, though the exotic setting helps create an agreeably torpid atmosphere. DVD

Charles Bronson *Giff Hoyt* • Dominique Sanda *Marie Claire Allesandri* • Fernando Rey *Terredo* • Jason Robards [Jason Robards Jr] *Gunther Beckdorff* • Simon MacCorkindale *Lewis Clarkson* • Camilla Sparv *Hera* • Clifton James *Lorrimer* • Gilbert Roland *Dr Ramirez* ■ *Dir* J Lee Thompson • *Scr* Milton Gelman, Mort Fine [Morton S Fine]

Cactus ★★★🆓
Drama　1986 · Ausl · Colour · 91mins

Isabelle Huppert, on holiday Down Under, has a car crash and loses sight in one eye. Doctors recommend she has the eye removed to prevent sympathetic blindness in the other. Her choice is complicated when she falls in love with a blind man and contemplates total blindness. A painful topic is handled with naturalism and insight in a drama that weaves in and out of Huppert's life and the lives of her family and friends. 🖵

Isabelle Huppert *Colo* • Robert Menzies *Robert* • Norman Kaye *Tom* • Monica Maughan *Bea* • Banduk Marika *Banduk* • Sheila Florance *Martha* ■ *Dir/Scr* Paul Cox

Cactus Flower ★★★🆓
Comedy　1969 · US · Colour · 99mins

Goldie Hawn won a best supporting actress Oscar for converting her loveable *Laugh-In* bimbo into a believable screen persona as dentist Walter Matthau's young girlfriend. Matthau deflects Hawn's talk of marriage by presenting his receptionist Ingrid Bergman (in one of several screen comebacks) as his wife. Hawn is enchanting and Matthau is always watchable, but the material is wafer thin, and Bergman seems ill at ease in this glossy adaptation of Abe Burrows's play, itself based on a French boulevard time-passer. 🖵

Walter Matthau *Julian Winston* • Ingrid Bergman *Stephanie Dickinson* • Goldie Hawn *Toni Simmons* • Jack Weston *Harvey Greenfield* • Rick Lenz *Igor Sullivan* • Vito Scotti *Senor Sanchez* • Irene Hervey *Mrs Durant* ■ *Dir* Gene Saks • *Scr* IAL Diamond, from the play by Abe Burrows, from the French play by Barillet & Gredy

Cactus Jack ★★🆓
Comedy western　1979 · US · Colour · 85mins

This attempt at spoofing old westerns stars Arnold Schwarzenegger and Kirk Douglas in what sounds like a comic meeting of the two chins. Made before anyone had the wit to relaunch Arnie as a pneumatic self-parody, this is, sadly, an example of crass comic mistiming in the extreme. At least Ann-Margret looks as striking as ever. 🖵

Kirk Douglas *Cactus Jack* • Ann-Margret *Charming Jones* • Arnold Schwarzenegger *Handsome Stranger* • Paul Lynde *Nervous Elk* • Foster Brooks *Bank Clerk* • Ruth Buzzi *Damsel In Distress* • Jack Elam *Avery Simpson* • Strother Martin *Parody Jones* ■ *Dir* Hal Needham • *Scr* Robert G Kane

　🆄 = SUITABLE FOR ALL　🆄ᶜ = SUITABLE FOR ALL, ESPECIALLY FOR YOUNG CHILDREN (VIDEO ONLY)　🆓 = PARENTAL GUIDANCE

Caddie ★★

Drama   1976 · Ausl · Colour · 106mins

A worthy drama from Down Under about a woman who is forced to make radical changes to her lifestyle when she leaves her cheating husband. Helen Morse gives a dignified performance as the woman trying to make her own way in the very macho world of Australia between the wars, and Jack Thompson is as reliable as ever. Donald Crombie's direction, however, is uninspired.

Helen Morse *Caddie* • Takis Emmanuel *Peter* • Jack Thompson *Ted* • Jacki Weaver *Josie* • Melissa Jaffer *Leslie* • Ron Blanchard *Bill* • Deborah Kounnas *Ann Marsh aged 2* ■ *Dir* Donald Crombie • *Scr* Joan Long, from the autobiography by "Carrie"

The Caddy ★★ U

Comedy   1953 · US · BW · 95mins

Relying on the popularity and appeal of Dean Martin and Jerry Lewis, this hotch-potch of a comedy is chiefly memorable for spawning the Oscar-nominated smash hit, *That's Amore*. The unfocused screenplay has Lewis caddying for Martin, with predictably chaotic consequences. Donna Reed and Barbara Bates are the boys' girls, and golfers Sam Snead and Ben Hogan put in appearances.

Jerry Lewis *Harvey Miller* • Dean Martin *Joe Anthony* • Donna Reed *Kathy Taylor* • Barbara Bates *Lisa* • Joseph Calleia *Papa Anthony* • Clinton Sundberg *Charles* • Howard Smith *Golf official* • Marshall Thompson *Bruce Reeber* ■ *Dir* Norman Taurog • *Scr* Danny Arnold

Caddyshack ★★★ 15

Comedy   1980 · US · Colour · 93mins

A wonderfully crass comedy from *Groundhog Day* director Harold Ramis that wins no prizes for subtlety, yet breezes along in a cheerfully tasteless manner. Loud-mouth millionaire Rodney Dangerfield gets up snobbish Ted Knight's nose when he attempts to take over his golf club, setting the scene for a climactic contest on the links. There's an annoying subplot about caddies, presumably for the teens, and Chevy Chase is given little to do as the louche golf professional. Dangerfield reprises his stand-up persona to gloriously vulgar effect, however, and Bill Murray steals the show as a psychopathic groundsman continuing a running battle with the club's resident gophers. Contains swearing and nudity. ▭ *DVD*

Chevy Chase *Ty Webb* • Rodney Dangerfield *Al Czervik* • Ted Knight *Judge Smails* • Michael O'Keefe *Danny Noonan* • Bill Murray *Carl Spackler* • Sarah Holcomb *Maggie O'Hooligan* • Scott Colomby *Tony D'Annunzio* • Cindy Morgan *Lacey Underall* • Brian Doyle-Murray *Lou Loomis* ■ *Dir* Harold Ramis • *Scr* Brian Doyle-Murray, Harold Ramis, Douglas Kenney

Caddyshack II ★ 15

Comedy   1988 · US · Colour · 93mins

The first *Caddyshack* may have been funny, but take away some of the talent from the original – Bill Murray, Rodney Dangerfield, director Harold Ramis – and you're left with this mess. Instead you have Jackie Mason as a self-made millionaire who decides to take revenge when he's refused membership to an up-market country club. Meanwhile, Chevy Chase reprises his role of spaced-out golfer Ty Webb to little effect, while Dan Aykroyd runs around aimlessly, probably wondering why he agreed to appear in the first place. Contains swearing. ▭

Jackie Mason *Jack Hartounian* • Robert Stack *Chandler Young* • Dina Merrill *Cynthia Young* • Dyan Cannon *Elizabeth Pearce* • Jonathan Silverman *Harry* • Randy Quaid *Peter Blunt* • Chevy Chase *Ty Webb* • Dan Aykroyd *Captain Tom Everett* ■ *Dir* Allan Arkush • *Scr* Harold Ramis, Peter Torokvei

Cadillac Man ★★★ 15

Comedy drama   1990 · US · Colour · 93mins

After his success with *Good Morning, Vietnam*, Robin Williams was still having difficulty finding another star vehicle equal to his talents when he accepted the lead in this comedy from Roger Donaldson. The role of the sleazy car salesman having an incredibly bad day was not Williams's best career choice, but luckily his comedic skills give the film the life it needs. Also on hand to keep things going are Tim Robbins, playing a gun-toting husband who holds up the car lot, and, in smaller roles, Annabella Sciorra and Lori Petty. Contains swearing, violence and nudity.

Robin Williams *Joey O'Brien* • Tim Robbins *Larry* • Pamela Reed *Tina O'Brien* • Fran Drescher *Joy Munchack* • Zack Norman *Harry Munchack* • Annabella Sciorra *Donna* • Lori Petty *Lila* • Paul Guilfoyle *Little Jack Turgeon* • Bill Nelson *Big Jack Turgeon* • Eddie Jones *Benny* • Mimi Cecchini *Ma* ■ *Dir* Roger Donaldson • *Scr* Ken Friedman

Cadillac Ranch ★★ 15

Comedy   1996 · US · Colour · 98mins

Three sisters hit the road with some stolen loot in a muddled journey made palatable by likeable performances from Suzy Amis, Renee Humphrey and Caroleen Feeney. Lisa Gottlieb's *Thelma and Louise*-style movie has plenty going on – and that's the problem. Female bonding, a hint of idealised romance, reminiscences about their criminal dad and a killer on their trail make this a recipe with too many ingredients. Christopher Lloyd's former lawman is a villain by numbers, but Amis is great as the feistiest of the siblings. Contains swearing, mild violence and semi-nudity. ▭

Christopher Lloyd *Wood Grimes* • Suzy Amis *CJ Crowley* • Caroleen Feeney *Frances Crowley* • Renee Humphrey *Mary Katherine Crowley* • Jim Metzler *Travis Crowley* ■ *Dir* Lisa Gottlieb • *Scr* Jennifer Cecil

Caesar and Cleopatra ★★★ U

Historical drama   1945 · UK · Colour · 122mins

Legend has it that Hungarian producer Gabriel Pascal managed to convince George Bernard Shaw he was the only person who could do justice to the great man's plays. Unfortunately, Pascal wasn't content to be merely producer here: he also directed, with astounding ineptitude. The production went grossly over budget, which might account for both the film's excessive length and its failure to recoup its costs. There's no denying the Technicolor is splendid, but, despite the spirited efforts of Claude Rains and Vivien Leigh as the titular couple, there's no sexual chemistry at all. Stewart Granger smoulders, despite the boot-polish make-up, but Flora Robson is quite ludicrous as Ftatateeta. Still worth a look, though not to be taken too seriously. ▭

Vivien Leigh *Cleopatra* • Claude Rains *Caesar* • Stewart Granger *Apollodorus* • Flora Robson *Ftatateeta* • Francis L Sullivan *Pothinus* • Basil Sydney *Rufio* • Cecil Parker *Britannus* • Raymond Lovell *Lucius Septimius* • Anthony Eustrel *Achillas* • Ernest Thesiger *Theodotus* • Anthony Harvey *Ptolemy* ■ *Dir* Gabriel Pascal • *Scr* George Bernard Shaw, Majorie Deans, from the play by George Bernard Shaw

Cafe Flesh ★★

Cult erotic   1982 · US · Colour · 69mins

Although only a classy porn movie with artistic pretensions, Stephen Sayadian's cult classic (directed under his pseudonym Rinse Dream) is extraordinarily prophetic when viewed in an Aids-related context. Well-made and acted for a picture that features only one heavy-duty porn queen (Michelle Bauer, aka Pia Snow), initial intrigue in the plot soon wears off as genre clichés take over.

Andrew Nichols [Andy Nichols] *Max Melodramatic* • Paul McGibboney *Nick* • Pia Snow [Michelle Bauer] *Lana* • Marie Sharp *Angel* • Dondi Bastone *Spike* ■ *Dir* Rinse Dream [Stephen Sayadian] • *Scr* Rinse Dream [Stephen Sayadian], Herbert W Day [Jerry Stahl], FX Pope [Stephen Sayadian]

Cafe Society ★★★

Crime drama based on a true story   1995 · US · Colour · 104mins

A convincingly nasty and skilfully-made melodrama about the monied wasters who haunted the salacious New York nightclub scene of the fifties. The plot centres on a scandal that put the scene in the public spotlight, destroyed several lives and led to a major club clean-up. Frank Whaley, Peter Gallagher and Lara Flynn Boyle head the attractive young cast.

Frank Whaley *Mickey Jelke* • Peter Gallagher *Jack Kale* • John Spencer *Ray Davioni* • David Patrick Kelly *J Roland Sala* ■ *Dir/Scr* Raymond DeFelitta

Cage ★★★

Action drama   1989 · US · Colour · 101mins

Incredible Hulk star Lou Ferrigno gives his best performance in this violent exploitation movie. He and Reb Brown play Vietnam veterans who run a Los Angeles bar in an area where fixed, no-holds-barred fights are the latest illegal money-spinner. Ferrigno, brain-damaged after being shot in the head on manoeuvres, is conned into entering the bare-knuckle "cage" and putting his life on the line for Chinatown mobsters. Sleazy, obnoxiously racist and nasty it may be, but Lang Elliott's carnage caper sure delivers the goods in bloody excitement.

Lou Ferrigno *Billy Thomas* • Reb Brown *Scott Monroe* • Michael Dante *Tony Baccola* • Al Leong *Tiger Joe* • Mike Moroff *Mario* • James Shigeta *Tin Lum Yin* • Marilyn Tokuda *Morgan Garrett* • Branscombe Richmond *Diablo* ■ *Dir* Lang Elliott • *Scr* Hugh Kelley

Cage 2: the Arena of Death ★★ 18

Action drama   1994 · US · Colour · 94mins

After being painted green for all those years, this probably passes for a career progression for *Incredible Hulk* star Lou Ferrigno. In this sequel to a popular straight-to-video item, Ferrigno plays an ordinary sort of hulk whose bulging biceps attract the attention of a criminal gang that stages brutal cage fights. Reb Brown plays a chum who tries to come to his rescue. ▭

Lou Ferrigno *Billy Thomas* • Reb Brown *Scott* • James Shigeta *Tin Lum Yin* ■ *Dir* Lang Elliott • *Scr* Hugh Kelley

La Cage aux Folles ★★★★ 15

Comedy   1978 · Fr/It · Colour · 87mins

One of the most successful foreign films ever released, this frilly farce led to two sequels, a Broadway musical and a Hollywood remake starring Robin Williams. It's the remarkably inoffensive and non-threatening tale of what happens when the gay owners of a St Tropez transvestite club meet the straight parents of the daughter their heterosexual son (don't ask!) wants to marry. Cue much mistaken identity humour, mainly revolving around the exaggerated effeminacy of brilliant Michel Serrault as the highly-strung drag diva. In French with English subtitles. ▭

Michel Serrault *Albin, "Zaza"* • Ugo Tognazzi *Renato* • Michel Galabru *Charrier* • Claire Maurier *Simone* • Remi Laurent *Laurent* • Benny Luke *Jacob* • Carmen Scarpitta *Madame Charrier* • Luisa Maneri *Andrea* ■ *Dir* Edouard Molinaro • *Scr* Marcello Danon, Edouard Molinaro, Francis Veber, Jean Poiret, from the play by Jean Poiret

La Cage aux Folles II ★★

Comedy   1980 · Fr/It · Colour · 99mins

Michel Serrault and Ugo Tognazzi return as the bickering lovers in this so-so sequel to the 1978 camp classic. Complete with spies, corpses and secret microfilms, the espionage elements of the plot get in the way of the much more amusing character farce. However, director Edouard Molinaro makes the most of the unlikely situations, especially when Serrault has to pretend to be Tognazzi's bride to fool the latter's ultra-conservative mother. In French with English subtitles.

Michel Serrault *Albin, "Zaza"* • Ugo Tognazzi *Renato* • Marcel Bozzuffi *Broca* • Paola Borboni *Signora Baldi* • Giovanni Vettorazzo *Milan* • Glauco Onorato *Luigi* • Roberto Bisacco *Ralph* • Benny Luke *Jacob* • Michel Galabru *Charrier* ■ *Dir* Edouard Molinaro • *Scr* Jean Poiret, Francis Veber, Marcello Danon, from characters created by Jean Poiret

La Cage aux Folles III: "Elles" se Marient ★ 15

Comedy   1985 · Fr/It · Colour · 91mins

The second sequel to the popular French farce *La Cage aux Folles* finds drag queen nightclub owner Albin (Michel Serrault) forced to sire a child so he can inherit a fortune. His partner Renato (Ugo Tognazzi) can only stand back and watch the shrieking and high camp tantrums that this outrageous ultimatum precipitates. Georges Lautner replaces Edouard Molinaro, who directed the first two films in the gay series, and his handling of the material reveals little flair for comedy. It's all too strident, loud and silly. In French with English subtitles.

Michel Serrault *Albin, "Zaza"* • Ugo Tognazzi *Renato* • Michel Galabru *Charrier* • Benny Luke *Jacob* • Stéphane Audran *Matrimonia* • Antonella Interlenghi *Cindy* ■ *Dir* Georges Lautner • *Scr* Philippe Nicaud, Christine Carère, Marcello Danon, Jacques Audiard, Michel Audiard, Georges Lautner, Gérard Lamballe, from a story by Philippe Nicaud, Christine Carère, Marcello Danon, from characters created by Jean Poiret

Cage of Gold ★★
Crime drama　　1950 · UK · BW · 83mins

An overwrought melodrama from director Basil Dearden, with David Farrar cast somewhat against type as an RAF rogue who, having cheated on Jean Simmons with French singer Madeleine Lebeau during the war, deserts the pregnant Simmons shortly after their marriage in order to smuggle jewels for Paris club owner Herbert Lom. There are simply too many underdrawn characters flitting in and out of the increasingly preposterous plot for comfort or comprehension.

Jean Simmons *Judith Moray* • David Farrar *Bill Brennan* • James Donald *Alan Keane* • Herbert Lom *Rahman* • Madeleine Lebeau *Marie* • Maria Mauban *Antoinette* • Bernard Lee *Inspector Grey* ■ *Dir* Basil Dearden • *Scr* Jack Whittingham, Paul Stein, from a story by Jack Whittingham

A Cage of Nightingales ★★★ U
Musical drama　　1947 · Fr · BW · 88mins

A French film from director Jean Dréville in which a young working man (Noël-Noël) writes a novel about his life, which includes a spell in a reformatory. His past is revealed to his girlfriend (Micheline Francey) when she reads the book; we see the tale unfold in flashback as she does so. A neat blend of past and present, this modest film is a truthful, sober and understanding picture of juvenile delinquency, offering excellent performances and a positive message. In French with English subtitles.

Noël-Noël *Clément* • Micheline Francey *Martine* • George Biscot *Raymond* • René Genin *Maxence* • René Blancard *Rachin* • Marguerite Ducouret *Mme Martine* ■ *Dir* Jean Dréville • *Scr* Noël-Noël, René Wheeler

Caged ★★★
Melodrama　　1950 · US · BW · 91mins

A typical Warner Bros prison melodrama, only this time it's a women's prison. So instead of James Cagney, there's an unglamorous Eleanor Parker as the innocent victim who grows tougher after exposure to the brutality of life on the inside. There's an interesting censor-circumventing prison matron who clearly displays lesbian tendencies, played convincingly by Hope Emerson. Agnes Moorehead also registers strongly, as do Jan Sterling and Jane Darwell. It's a slow, absorbing work, and its very drabness renders it rather tedious for viewers. Watch it for the

under-rated Parker, a terrific actress who was never really given her due.

Eleanor Parker *Marie Allen* • Agnes Moorehead *Ruth Benton* • Ellen Corby *Emma* • Hope Emerson *Evelyn Harper* • Betty Garde *Kitty Stark* • Jan Sterling *Smoochie* • Lee Patrick *Elvira Powell* • Jane Darwell *Isolation Matron* • Sheila Stevens *Helen* ■ *Dir* John Cromwell • *Scr* Virginia Kellogg, Bernard C Schoenfeld

Caged Hearts ★ 18
Prison drama　　1995 · US · Colour · 83mins

Carrie Genzel and Tane McClure kill a man in self-defence, get framed by the justice system and are sent to prison, where they are forced into prostitution. With the help of their lawyer, they plot to expose the corrupt court officials who are responsible for their degradation. A formulaic "women in prison" saga, invested with little sense of reality from anyone either behind or in front of the camera. ▭ DVD

Carrie Genzel *Kate Paris* • Tane McClure *Sharon O'Neal* • Nick Wilder *Steve* • Dink O'Neal *George Delvin* • Brent Keast *Judge Winters* • Taylor Leigh *Warden Loren McBride* ■ *Dir* Henri Charr • *Scr* Taesung Yim, from a story by Henri Charr, Jess Mancilla

Caged Heat ★★★ 18
Drama　　1974 · US · Colour · 73mins

Jonathan Demme's debut as writer/director bears all the hallmarks of his mentor, exploitation maestro Roger Corman, who was making this kind of "babes behind bars" flick back in the late fifties. Horror icon Barbara Steele returns to the screen after a five-year absence to play the sadistic wheelchair-bound governor, a role that had been written specially for her. There's plenty of humour to leaven the story of naive Juanita Brown's struggle against the system, but the biggest laughs come from the tremendous seventies outfits. Contains violence, swearing and nudity. ▭

Juanita Brown *Maggie* • Roberta Collins *Belle Tyson* • Erica Gavin *Jacqueline Wilson* • Barbara Steele *Mcqueen* • Ella Reid *Pandora Williams* ■ *Dir/Scr* Jonathan Demme

Cagney & Lacey ★★★★ 15
Police drama　　1981 · US · Colour · 91mins

The pilot of the hugely popular TV series about two lady cops, here played by Tyne Daly (who continued her role in the series) and Loretta Swit of TV's *M*A*S*H* (who was replaced by Meg Foster and, subsequently, Sharon Gless). As many fans will remember, the series got a bit ropey in later years, but this pilot is a reminder of how great *Cagney & Lacey* was in the beginning. Daly looks youthful (well, it was 1981) and Swit is suitably tough-as-nails as her partner. One can only assume Gless was brought in to be a younger, more glamorous version of Chris Cagney when the producers realised the series would run for almost a decade. ▭

Loretta Swit *Christine Cagney* • Tyne Daly *Mary Beth Lacey* • Al Waxman *Detective Samuels* • Joan Copeland *Mrs Friedlander* • Ronald Hunter *Harvey* ■ *Dir* Ted Post • *Scr* Barbara Avedon

Cagney & Lacey: the Return ★★★ PG
Police drama　　1994 · US · Colour · 89mins

There's a certain irony that a need for fulfilling, well-paid work forces Mary Beth Lacey back on the beat in this TV movie reunion of the ever-popular cop duo. She needs employment because her husband has had a coronary, but it was a severe lapse in the professional health of Tyne Daly and Sharon Gless that surely prompted them to reteam six years after the ratings-topping series went off air. After a clutch of indifferent assignments, they look relieved to be playing once again the characters that made their names. ▭

Tyne Daly *Mary Beth Lacey* • Sharon Gless *Christine Cagney* • James Naughton *James Burton* • David Paymer *Deputy DA Feldberg* • Susan Anspach *Deborah Nelson* • John Karlen *Harvey Lacey* • Martin Kove *Isbecki* • Carl Lumbly *Marcus Petrie* • Vonetta McGee *Claudia Petrie* • Al Waxman *Lieutenant Samuels* ■ *Dir* James Frawley • *Scr* Terry Louise Fisher, from characters created by Barbara Avedon, Barbara Corday

Cagney & Lacey: the View through the Glass Ceiling ★★ 12
Police drama　　1995 · US · Colour · 88mins

It's good to see the dynamic duo of Tyne Daly and Sharon Gless together again in the third TV movie made after their popular series was cancelled. The plot has the two detectives working for the DA's office, where they investigate a case of police corruption. Cagney becomes increasingly interested in politics when her boss gets involved in the mayoral race, but her friendship with Lacey is threatened. The easy camaraderie between Cagney and Lacey, and the ease which the two actresses bring to their roles, makes this a pleasure for fans to watch. ▭

Tyne Daly *Mary Beth Lacey* • Sharon Gless *Christine Cagney* • John Karlen *Harvey Lacey* • George Coe *Dan Broadbent* • Chip Zien *Assistant District Attorney Trayne* • Lynne Thigpen *Captain Cardenas* ■ *Dir* John Patterson • *Scr* Michele Gallery, from characters created by Barbara Avedon, Barbara Corday

Cagney & Lacey: Together Again ★★ 12
Police drama　　1994 · US · Colour · 89mins

The hit TV series went off the air in the late eighties, but Mary Beth and Christine returned to the streets of New York several years later to investigate the murder of a menacing hobo who has been terrorising the residents of an apartment block. As usual, the case manages to hit close to home, as one of the chief suspects has connections with Lacey's builder husband, John Karlen. ▭

Tyne Daly *Mary Beth Lacey* • Sharon Gless *Christine Cagney* • John Karlen *Harvey Lacey* • David Paymer *Deputy DA Feldberg* • James Naughton *James Burton* • Paul Lieber *Romeo DeCarlo* ■ *Dir* Reza Badiyi • *Scr* Steve Brown, Terry Louise Fisher, from characters created by Barbara Avedon, Barbara Corday

Cagney & Lacey: True Convictions ★★ PG
Police drama　　1996 · US · Colour · 88mins

In their fourth TV movie outing, the quirky New York detectives investigate tainted evidence in a death penalty case. Cagney gets romantically involved with the father (Michael Moriarty) of a shooting victim; Lacey, meanwhile, fights with her husband (John Karlen). Smoothly directed by Lynne Littman and nicely scripted by Michele Gallery, the drama deals with controversial issues without becoming overwrought, while Tyne Daly and Sharon Gless are so brisk and convincing we believe everything they say and do. ▭

Tyne Daly *Mary Beth Lacey* • Sharon Gless *Christine Cagney* • Michael Moriarty *Matthew Wylie* • John Karlen *Harvey Lacey* • Chip Zien *Assistant DA Trayne* ■ *Dir* Lynne Littman • *Scr* Michele Gallery, from characters created by Barbara Avedon, Barbara Corday

Cahill, United States Marshal ★★★ 15
Western　　1973 · US · Colour · 97mins

Director Andrew V McLaglen could always be depended upon to hammer out gruff, good-looking westerns from the most unpromising material. Here he saddles up John Wayne and a skilled supporting cast for a parable on the extent to which modern youth had been corrupted while America was away solving the problems of the world. As a political statement, it's reactionary and naive, but it passes muster as a late Wayne western, with the Duke looking every day of his 66 years as the absentee father out to teach villainous George Kennedy a lesson for enticing his teenage sons into crime. Contains violence. ▭

John Wayne *JD Cahill* • George Kennedy *Abe Fraser* • Gary Grimes *Danny Cahill* • Neville Brand *Lightfoot* • Clay O'Brien *Billy Joe Cahill* • Marie Windsor *Mrs Green* • Morgan Paull *Struther* • Dan Vadis *Brownie* • Royal Dano *MacDonald* • Scott Walker *Ben Tildy* ■ *Dir* Andrew V McLaglen • *Scr* Harry Julian Fink, Rita M Fink, from a story by Barney Slater

Cain and Mabel ★★★ U
Musical comedy　　1936 · US · BW · 90mins

The penultimate movie of talented star Marion Davies, best known today for being the mistress and protégée of newspaper magnate William Randolph Hearst (the inspiration behind Orson Welles's *Citizen Kane*). It's an unfortunate way to remember the delightful actress, here woefully miscast as a Broadway star pretending to romance a boxer for publicity. Since the heavyweight is played by Clark Gable on specially requested loan to Warners from MGM just after the popular successes *Mutiny on the Bounty* and *San Francisco*, Davies has trouble holding the screen. Hearst and director Lloyd Bacon know this, so surround her with a clever cast, some witty dialogue and a production number of such unremitting vulgarity that it almost takes the breath away.

Clark Gable *Larry Cain* • Marion Davies *Mabel O'Dare* • Allen Jenkins *Dodo* • Roscoe Karns *Reilly* • Walter Catlett *Jake Sherman* • David

Carlyle *Ronny Cauldwell* • Hobart Cavanaugh *Milo* • *Dir* Lloyd Bacon • *Scr* Laird Doyle, from a story by HC Witwer

The Caine Mutiny ★★★ U

Drama   1954 · US · Colour · 119mins

Anything starring Humphrey Bogart is worth a peek, but this rather dourly scripted adaptation of Herman Wouk's Pulitzer Prize-winning novel veers spectacularly between the best high drama and plodding, explanatory narrative. A sterling cast (José Ferrer, Fred MacMurray, Van Johnson) brings the court-martial scenes vividly to life, but the film is let down considerably by lengthy speeches of unremitting moral rectitude. Bogart's snivelling Captain Queeg lacks much of the actor's former screen punch and, with hindsight, one can see the sad spectre of a sick man nearing the end of his career. This could have been a classic but ended up an also-ran. **DVD**

Humphrey Bogart *Captain Queeg* • José Ferrer *Lt Barney Greenwald* • Van Johnson *Lt Steve Maryk* • Fred MacMurray *Lt Tom Keefer* • EG Marshall *Lt Cmdr Challee* • Lee Marvin *Meatball* • *Dir* Edward Dmytryk • *Scr* Stanley Roberts, from the play and novel by Herman Wouk • *Music* Max Steiner

Cairo ★

Crime drama   1962 · US/UK · BW · 90mins

A sand-blown remake of just about every caper movie ever made – *The Asphalt Jungle, Rififi*, you name it. George Sanders plays a master thief who decides to steal Tutankhamen's jewels from the Cairo museum, so he forms a gang of rogues to execute his plan. Directed by Wolf Rilla, who made the exceptional science-fiction chiller *Village of the Damned*, this is a real letdown with some very listless patches of narrative.

George Sanders *Major Pickering* • Richard Johnson *Ali* • Faten Hamama *Amina* • John Meillon *Willy* • Ahmed Mazhar *Kerim* • Eric Pohlmann *Nicodemos* • Walter Rilla *Kuchuk* • Salah Nazmi *Commandant* • *Dir* Wolf Rilla • *Scr* Joan Scott, from the novel *The Asphalt Jungle* by WR Burnett

Cairo Road ★★ U

Crime drama   1950 · UK · BW · 86mins

A British B-movie about drug smuggling, with Eric Portman as an Egyptian detective and Laurence Harvey as his ambitious assistant. While Portman rather overplays his part, Harvey, giving one of his earliest screen performances, is fascinating to watch as a scene-stealing star on the rise. Despite some location sequences (a rarity for a low budget production), the action is fairly slow and routine. One minor footnote: the Egyptian technical adviser is Michel Talhami, who spent years trying to finance a film about Lawrence of Arabia before producer Sam Spiegel and director David Lean made their masterpiece ahead of him.

Eric Portman *Colonel Youssef Bey* • Laurence Harvey *Lieutenant Mourad* • Maria Mauban *Marie* • Anna Michelis *Camelia* • Harold Lang *Humble* • Coco Aslan *Lombardi* • *Dir* David MacDonald • *Scr* Robert Westerby

Cal ★★★★ 15

Romantic thriller   1984 · UK · Colour · 98mins

Pat O'Connor made his feature debut with this adaptation by Bernard MacLaverty of his own novel. At times treading a mite too carefully along the sectarian divide, this is nevertheless a credible and often compelling look at how the Troubles intrude upon what should be the events of everyday life. There's a genuine warmth in the relationship between widow Helen Mirren (who won Best Actress at Cannes) and John Lynch, the getaway driver on the IRA mission that resulted in the death of her RUC husband. But the tension amid which their romance blossoms is also well conveyed by O'Connor and his impressive supporting cast.

Helen Mirren *Marcella* • John Lynch *Cal* • Donal McCann *Shamie* • John Kavanagh *Skeffington* • Ray McAnally *Cyril Dunlop* • Stevan Rimkus *Crilly* • *Dir* Pat O'Connor • *Scr* Bernard MacLaverty, from his novel

Calamity Jane ★★★★★ U

Musical comedy   1953 · US · Colour · 96mins

The opening sequence of this wonderful musical is pure pleasure, as Doris Day rides the Deadwood stage across the screen and into our hearts. This isn't the real Wild West, of course, but Warner Bros's Technicolor riposte to MGM's *Annie Get Your Gun*: the studio even poached the same leading man, handsome Howard Keel, who is excellent here as Wild Bill Hickok. The specially commissioned score is a treat, but the strength of the movie is Day giving a marvellous musical comedy performance in her finest role, creating a warm, robust yet tender character. (Just marvel at her timing in *Just Blew In from the Windy City.*) *Secret Love*, recorded by Day in just one take, won the best song Oscar and is beautifully staged by choreographer Jack Donohue.

Doris Day *Calamity Jane* • Howard Keel *Wild Bill Hickok* • Allyn McLerie [Allyn Ann McLerie] *Katie Brown* • Philip Carey *Lt Gilmartin* • Dick Wesson *Francis Fryer* • Paul Harvey *Henry Miller* • Chubby Johnson *Rattlesnake* • Gale Robbins *Adelaide Adams* • *Dir* David Butler • *Scr* James O'Hanlon • *Music* Sammy Fain, Paul Francis Webster

Calamity Jane and Sam Bass ★★ U

Western   1949 · US · Colour · 85mins

Martha Jane Burke, Calamity Jane of western lore, was played by Jean Arthur for Cecil B DeMille, and would soon be immortalised by a ripsnortin' Doris Day in the Warner Bros musical. But here she's incarnated by exotic Yvonne De Carlo in a decidedly routine western that plays fast and loose with the facts. Former stage star Howard Duff is cast as Calamity's romantic interest, outlaw Sam Bass, whose character is whitewashed beyond all recognition in this censor-appeasing moralistic fable.

Yvonne De Carlo *Calamity Jane* • Howard Duff *Sam Bass* • Dorothy Hart *Katharine Egan* • Willard Parker *Sheriff Will Egan* • Norman Lloyd *Jim Murphy* • Lloyd Bridges *Joel Collins* • *Dir* George Sherman • *Scr* Maurice Geraghty, Melvin Levy, from a story by George Sherman

Calculated Risk ★

Crime drama   1963 · UK · BW · 71mins

The only thing of interest about this tatty little drama is a cameo from Warren Mitchell as a dodgy market trader who sells William Lucas the explosives he needs for his bank job. The story isn't a bad one – about a gang that comes across an unexploded Second World War bomb while tunnelling into a vault – but Norman Harrison directs with no sense of suspense at all and, instead of being nail-biting, the plight of the thieves becomes side-splittingly funny. Contains some swearing.

John Rutland *Kip* • William Lucas *Steve* • Dilys Watling *Julie* • Warren Mitchell *Simmie* • Shay Gorman *Dodo* • Terence Cooper *Nodge* • *Dir* Norman Harrison • *Scr* Edwin Richfield

Calcutta ★★★

Thriller   1947 · US · BW · 83mins

Clean-cut, good-looking Alan Ladd and pug-faced William Bendix, his frequent on-screen partner, trawl the threatening back alleys, colourful bazaars and sleazy hotels of India's teeming city (built on the Paramount backlot). There Ladd's search for whoever killed his friend gets them entangled with the underworld and its questionable inhabitants. The result is an old-fashioned, low-budget formula thriller, but one that makes for easy and entertaining viewing. Glamorous Gail Russell plays the female lead.

Alan Ladd *Neale Gordon* • William Bendix *Pedro Blake* • Gail Russell *Virginia Moore* • June Duprez *Marina* • Lowell Gilmore *Eric Lasser* • Edith King *Mrs Smith* • Paul Singh *Malik* • Gavin Muir *Kendricks* • *Dir* John Farrow • *Scr* Seton I Miller

The Calendar ★★

Drama   1948 · UK · BW · 79mins

British cinema was heavily dependent on the mysteries of Edgar Wallace in the early talkie era. Few of these creaky thrillers were ever remade, until someone at Gainsborough Productions felt the need to bring this veritable stage warhorse under starter's orders for a second time. It's all clipped accents and impossibly earnest hamming from the off, as trainer Greta Gynt tries to prove that owner John McCallum didn't throw a race to improve the odds of his horse at a later Ascot meeting. Fans of Dick Francis may find it amusing.

Greta Gynt *Wenda* • John McCallum *Garry* • Raymond Lovell *Willie* • Sonia Holm *Mollie* • Leslie Dwyer *Hillcott* • Charles Victor *John Dory* • Felix Aylmer *Lord Forlingham* • Diana Dors *Hawkins* • *Dir* Arthur Crabtree • *Scr* Geoffrey Kerr, from the play by Edgar Wallace

Calendar ★★★

Drama   1993 · Can/Arm · BW and Colour · 75mins

This fascinating treatise on communication, appreciation and the limits of the static image co-stars Armenian/Canadian director Atom Egoyan and real-life partner Arsinée Khanjian as a couple who drift apart during a visit to Armenia to photograph churches for a calendar. As one would expect of this most inventive of film-makers, Egoyan isn't content simply to tell his story through flashbacks, but uses video footage to recall the breakdown of his relationship and lush colour film to show how his life since then has been dominated by disappointing dinner dates and painful memories. Personal it may be, but it's also compelling viewing.

Arsinée Khanjian *Translator* • Ashot Adamian *Driver* • Atom Egoyan *Photographer* • *Dir/Scr* Atom Egoyan

Calendar Girl ★★ 15

Comedy drama   1993 · US · Colour · 87mins

A surprisingly understated big-screen appearance from Jason Priestley, making the most of his *Beverly Hills 90210* fame. Set in the early sixties, the story follows the adventures of a trio of teenagers who leave their small town to go to Hollywood to meet their idol Marilyn Monroe. Although it's marred by some *Animal House*-style slapstick, it remains an affectionate coming-of-age comedy, even if the teenagers would be arrested as celebrity stalkers were it set in modern times. Sadly, it didn't provide Priestley with the desired kick start to a big-screen career. Contains mild swearing, drug abuse and nudity.

Jason Priestley *Roy Darpinian* • Gabriel Olds *Ned Bleuer* • Jerry O'Connell *Scott "The Dood" Foreman* • Joe Pantoliano *Uncle Harvey Darpinian* • Kurt Fuller *Arturo Gallo* • Stephen Tobolowsky *Antonio Gallo* • *Dir* John Whitesell • *Scr* Paul W Shapiro

Calendar Girl Murders ★★★ 15

Crime thriller   1984 · US · Colour · 91mins

A chance to see Sharon Stone on the early road to stardom in this steamy tale of a serial killer with a penchant for bumping off centrefolds. Detective Tom Skerritt struggles successfully to keep a straight face in the eye of a storm of hoary clichés, as the meticulous killer works his way through the months like an over-zealous accountant. It's saved by a racy, stops-out denouement.

Tom Skerritt *Dan Stoner* • Sharon Stone *Cassie Bascomb* • Barbara Bosson *Nancy Stoner* • Robert Beltran *Mooney* • Pat Corley *Tony* • Robert Morse *Nat Couray* • Robert Culp *Richard Trainor* • *Dir* William A Graham • *Scr* Scott Swanton, Gregory S Dinallo, from a story by Gregory S Dinallo

California ★★

Western   1946 · US · Colour · 98mins

A routine Gold Rush western, with Ray Milland drinking too much (didn't *The Lost Weekend* teach him anything?) and Barbara Stanwyck shuffling stacked decks as the woman with a history. Directed by Mia's dad, John Farrow, in his customary no-nonsense manner, it breezes along nicely without seeming to get anywhere. Paramount lavished bright-as-a-button Technicolor on it, as well as a couple of songs mimed by Stanwyck and a good supporting cast: Barry Fitzgerald, George Coulouris, Albert Dekker and Anthony Quinn, who was offered $5,000 for a week's work and stubbornly held out for $15,000.

Ray Milland *Jonathan Trumbo* • Barbara Stanwyck *Lily Bishop* • Barry Fitzgerald *Michael Fabian* • George Coulouris *Pharoah*

Coffin • Albert Dekker *Mr Pike* • Anthony Quinn *Don Luis* ■ *Dir* John Farrow • *Scr* Frank Butler, Theodore Strauss, from the story by Boris Ingster

The California Dolls ★★ 18

Comedy drama 1981 · US · Colour · 108mins

Although this dismal final effort from Robert Aldrich purports to be about women's wrestling, it's actually a shameless plug for MGM's Grand Hotel in Reno, Nevada, the glitzy casino where much of the action takes place. What the picture needed was a light satirical touch, not Aldrich's heavy-handed approach which tends to leer when it should laugh. Even so, Peter Falk as the girls' manager and Burt Young as the shady promoter are in their seedy element and provide the few moments of interest. ▭

Peter Falk *Harry* • Vicki Frederick *Iris* • Laurene Landon *Molly* • Burt Young *Eddie Cisco* • Tracy Reed *Diane* • Ursaline Bryant-King *June* • Richard Jaeckel *Reno Referee* ■ *Dir* Robert Aldrich • *Scr* Mel Frohman

The California Kid ★★★ PG

Thriller 1974 · US · Colour · 70mins

This exciting blend of *Duel* and *The Wild One* has Vic Morrow as the small-town sheriff who doesn't issue tickets to people who break the speed limit; instead, he runs them off the road. When Joe Estevez gets killed, Martin Sheen (the actor's real-life brother) arrives in a very fast machine to take on the maverick cop. The result is a sharply made TV movie, with Nick Nolte – then a big TV star who was yet to make his cinema debut – offering strong support. ▭

Martin Sheen *Michael McCord* • Vic Morrow *Sheriff Roy Childress* • Stuart Margolin *Deputy* • Michelle Phillips *Maggie* • Nick Nolte *Buzz Stafford* • Janit Baldwin *Sissy* • Gary Morgan *Lyle Stafford* • Joe Estevez *Don McCord* ■ *Dir* Richard T Heffron • *Scr* Richard Compton

California Man ★★ PG

Comedy fantasy 1992 · US · Colour · 84mins

A belated attempt to cash in on *Bill and Ted*-style comic capers, although by this stage the Californian teen speak was becoming more irritating than funny. Sean Astin and Pauly Shore are the two nerdish teenagers who dig up a deep-frozen caveman (Brendan Fraser) and educate him in the ways of adolescent etiquette. There are some amusing moments, Fraser makes for a pleasingly gormless hunk and the reliable Richard Masur is among the supporting players. However, it lacks the winning stupidity of Bill and Ted's two adventures. Released in the USA as *Encino Man*. Contains drug use. ▭

Sean Astin *Dave Morgan* • Brendan Fraser *Link* • Pauly Shore *Stoney Brown* • Megan Ward *Robyn Sweeney* • Robin Tunney *Ella* • Michael DeLuise *Matt* • Patrick Van Horn *Phil* • Dalton James *Will* • Richard Masur *Mr Morgan* • Rose McGowan *Nora* ■ *Dir* Les Mayfield • *Scr* Shawn Schepps, from a story by Shawn Schepps, George Zaloom

California Split ★★★

Comedy 1974 · US · Colour · 108mins

Robert Altman's off-the-wall insight into macho men is too wordy, but still has

enough gambling action to hold the attention while leads Elliott Gould and George Segal drink themselves through casino-surfing romps. As the girls sidelined by the men's fixation with the tables, Ann Prentis and Gwen Welles give as bad as they get – Altman's women characters are always real people, not ciphers – but it's really the disintegration of the buddies' friendship that forms the core of a movie that is more rewarding than its initial scenes suggest.

George Segal *Bill Denny* • Elliott Gould *Charlie Walters* • Ann Prentiss *Barbara Miller* • Gwen Welles *Susan Peters* • Edward Walsh *Lew* • Joseph Walsh *Sparkie* • Jay Fletcher *Robber* ■ *Dir* Robert Altman • *Scr* Joseph Walsh

California Straight Ahead ★★★ U

Action adventure 1937 · US · BW · 68mins

Vintage chase flick made watchable by the casting of John Wayne, trapped in a career no-man's land in the decade between *The Big Trail* and *Stagecoach*. Wayne is Biff Smith, a partner in a trucking firm whose feud with business rivals gets out of hand. In a Depression-era precursor of *The Cannonball Run*, he's crossing the States in a terrific chase involving trucks and trains. Louise Latimer provides the romantic interest, and director Arthur Lubin keeps it all going at a rate of knots.

John Wayne *Biff Smith* • Louise Latimer *Mary Porter* • Robert McWade *Corrigan* • Theodore von Eltz *James Gifford* • Tully Marshall *Harrison* • Emerson Treacy *Charlie Porter* ■ *Dir* Arthur Lubin • *Scr* Scott Darling, from a story by Herman Boxer

California Suite ★★★★ 15

Comedy 1978 · US · Colour · 98mins

Playwright Neil Simon is at his most devilish and rapier-witted in this classy confection of oddball vignettes, set in the up-market Beverly Hills Hotel. The cast is a superior mix of old faithfuls, all acting their designer socks off. The stand-out turns are from Walter Matthau and Elaine May, whose frantically unbalanced antics almost take the movie into the surreal, and Maggie Smith, whose actress preparing for the Academy Awards ceremony deservedly won an Oscar. There is the merest hint of froth over substance as, once again, Simon shows us his repertoire of verbal conjuring tricks, but enter Jane Fonda stage left to give the film some moving gravitas. This isn't brain food, but it works. Contains some swearing. ▭

Alan Alda *Bill Warren* • Michael Caine *Sidney Cochran* • Bill Cosby *Dr Willis Panama* • Jane Fonda *Hannah Warren* • Walter Matthau *Marvin Michaels* • Elaine May *Millie Michaels* • Richard Pryor *Dr Chauncey Gump* • Maggie Smith *Diana Barrie* ■ *Dir* Herbert Ross • *Scr* Neil Simon, from his play

Caligula ★ 18

Historical drama 1979 · US/It · Colour · 98mins

This purports to be a biographical drama about the infamous Roman emperor, but it's nothing more than toga-dropping soft porn celebrating the most basic of human instincts. Malcolm McDowell glares balefully as

the lustful, unhinged emperor, embarking on an increasingly sadistic road to destruction. Italian director Tinto Brass couldn't quite plumb the depths demanded, so extra scenes of titillation were allegedly added. A milestone of smut and hugely controversial in its day, this is now worth only a giggle or two. Contains violence, sex scenes and nudity. ▭

Malcolm McDowell *Caligula* • Theresa Ann Savoy [Teresa Ann Savoy] *Drusilla* • Peter O'Toole *Tiberius* • John Gielgud *Nerva* • Helen Mirren *Caesonia* ■ *Dir* Tinto Brass [Giovanni Tinto Brass] • *Scr* Gore Vidal

Call Him Savage ★★★

Romantic comedy 1975 · Fr · Colour · 110mins

A flaky comedy that trades heavily on the appeal of its French megastars, Catherine Deneuve and Yves Montand. The story kicks off in South America where Deneuve walks out on her fiancé and into the arms of next door neighbour Montand, who is himself on the run from his wife. Together they sail to the South Seas, creating the sort of screwball romance that sustained Hollywood for decades with stars like Cary Grant and Katharine Hepburn. There's much to enjoy here, including a welcome appearance by Tony Roberts, best known as Woody Allen's best mate in several of the director's movies. French dialogue dubbed into English.

Catherine Deneuve *Nelly* • Yves Montand *Martin* • Luigi Vannucchi *Vittorio* • Tony Roberts *Alex* • Dana Wynter *Wife* ■ *Dir* Jean-Paul Rappeneau • *Scr* Jean-Paul Rappeneau, Elizabeth Rappeneau, Jean-Loup Dabadie

Call Me ★★ 18

Thriller 1988 · US · Colour · 90mins

A rather daft thriller, only notable for an early appearance by Steve Buscemi. Patricia Charbonneau is the New York journalist who gets all excited when she gets an obscene phone call, thinking it's from her boyfriend. Things change, however, when she learns that the guy at the other end is a cold-blooded killer. There are more holes than in a piece of Swiss cheese, and Charbonneau is stuck with a character who is so naive you can't believe she has survived in the big city this long, let alone land her own newspaper column. ▭

Patricia Charbonneau *Anna* • Patti D'Arbanville [Patti D'Arbanville-Quinn] *Cori* • Boyd Gaines *Bill* • Stephen McHattie *Jellybean* • John Seitz *Pressure* • David Strathairn *Sam* • Ernest Abuba *Boss* • Steve Buscemi *Switchblade* ■ *Dir* Sollace Mitchell • *Scr* Karyn Kay, from a story by Sollace Mitchell, Karyn Kay

Call Me Anna ★★ 15

Biographical drama 1990 · US · Colour · 94mins

Actress Patty Duke (an Academy Award winner for *The Miracle Worker*) stars as her adult self in this unflinching biopic based on her best-selling book. (Patty's given name is Anna.) Written by John McGreevey, this TV movie focuses on her years as a child star, her failed marriages and her long battle with manic depression. Ari Meyers and Jenny Robertson play Patty in her younger days and give strong, convincing performances. While

engrossing, the film's weakness is that it only offers highlights of the actress's troubled life and often jumps too quickly to the next segment. ▭

Patty Duke *Patty Duke* • Ari Meyers *Patty Duke aged 11-16* • Jenny Robertson *Patty Duke aged 18-30* • Ray Duke *John Patrick Duke* • Millie Perkins *Frances Duke* ■ *Dir* Gilbert Cates • *Scr* John McGreevey, from the non-fiction book *My Name Is Anna* by Patty Duke, Kenneth Turan

Call Me Bwana ★★★ U

Comedy adventure 1963 · US /UK · Colour · 93mins

Viewed as outrageously patronising nowadays, this comedy stars Bob Hope as a bogus, bumbling explorer who helps CIA agent Edie Adams find an American space capsule lost in deepest, darkest Africa. Anita Ekberg and Lionel Jeffries play the enemy spies trying to thwart the mission. Despite its political incorrectness, this isn't bad considering the rubbish Hope was churning out at the time. The film was produced by the James Bond team of Albert R Broccoli and Harry Saltzman, who gave it a plug in *From Russia with Love*.

Bob Hope *Matt Merriwether* • Anita Ekberg *Luba* • Edie Adams *Frederica Larsen* • Lionel Jeffries *Dr Ezra Mungo* • Arnold Palmer ■ *Dir* Gordon Douglas • *Scr* Nate Monaster, Johanna Harwood • *Producer* Harry Saltzman

Call Me Madam ★★★★ U

Musical comedy 1953 · US · Colour · 114mins

After 644 performances as ''the hostess with the mostest'' in Irving Berlin's hit Broadway show, Ethel Merman repeated her tour de force for the rest of the world's benefit. Acting and singing up a storm with her foghorn voice, whirlwind energy and larger-than-life personality, Merman dominates this lively, lavish movie. Yet she doesn't quite outdo the scintillating dancing of Donald O'Connor and Vera-Ellen; nor does she upstage the suave George Sanders, who steals Merman's heart and has his own musical number.

Ethel Merman *Mrs Sally Adams* • Donald O'Connor *Kenneth* • Vera-Ellen *Princess Maria* • George Sanders *Cosmo Constantine* • Billy De Wolfe *Pemberton Maxwell* • Walter Slezak *Tantinnin* ■ *Dir* Walter Lang • *Scr* Arthur Sheekman, from the musical by Howard Lindsay, Russel Crouse • *Music* Irving Berlin • *Choreographer* Robert Alton

Call Me Mister ★★★ U

Musical 1951 · US · Colour · 95mins

A long-running Broadway revue that 20th Century-Fox brought to the screen as a Betty Grable/Dan Dailey vehicle. It's pleasant enough and the dance routines are choreographed by the great Busby Berkeley, though he's well past his prime. The supporting cast is a veritable roster of rising stars, including Dale Robertson, Jeffrey Hunter and Richard Boone. The plot deteriorates into a ''putting on a show in an army camp'' piece of nothingness, but Grable is attractive and Dailey is, as ever, outstanding.

Betty Grable *Kay Hudson* • Dan Dailey *Shep Dooley* • Danny Thomas *Stanley* • Dale Robertson *Captain Johnny Comstock* • Benay Venuta *Billie Barton* • Richard Boone *Mess*

U = SUITABLE FOR ALL   Uc = SUITABLE FOR ALL, ESPECIALLY FOR YOUNG CHILDREN (VIDEO ONLY)   PG = PARENTAL GUIDANCE

Sergeant ■ *Dir* Lloyd Bacon • *Scr* Albert E Lewin, Burt Styler, from the musical by Harold J Rome, Arnold M Auerbach

Call Northside 777 ★★★★
Crime drama   1948 · US · BW · 110mins

James Stewart doesn't always convince as the investigating reporter trying to clear Richard Conte of a murder he didn't commit, but the growing sense of injustice carries you along in director Henry Hathaway's crime drama based on a real-life story. With producer Louis de Rochemont (who made his name with *The March of Time* newsreels), Hathaway had forged a new style of gritty movie-making that reconstructed true stories with a realism and attention to the details of police procedure that made them seem more like documentaries than thrillers. The technique soon became clichéd, but this still works as a crusading piece of film-making.

James Stewart *McNeal* • Richard Conte *Frank Wiecek* • Lee J Cobb *Brian Kelly* • Helen Walker *Laura McNeal* • Betty Garde *Wanda Skutnik* • Kasia Orzazewski *Tillie Wiecek* ■ *Dir* Henry Hathaway • *Scr* Jerome Cady, Jay Dratler, from articles by James P McGuire in the *Chicago Times,*, adapted by Leonard Hoffman, Quentin Reynolds • *Music* Alfred Newman

The Call of the Wild ★★★
Adventure   1935 · US · BW · 93mins

While not exactly true to Jack London's source novel, this is nevertheless an enjoyable 20th Century-Fox romantic adventure. It was during the making of this movie that Clark Gable had a brief affair with his co-star, the lovely Loretta Young, resulting in an illegitimate daughter who for years didn't know who her father was. The movie is tremendous fun, with a great sense of pace. Despite being filmed high on Washington State's Mount Baker, the snowbound locations still look suspiciously like the Fox backlot.

Clark Gable *Jack Thornton* • Loretta Young *Claire Blake* • Jack Oakie *Shorty Hoolihan* • Frank Conroy *John Blake* • Reginald Owen *Smith* • Sidney Toler *Groggin* ■ *Dir* William Wellman [William A Wellman] • *Scr* Gene Fowler, Leonard Praskins, from the novel by Jack London

The Call of the Wild ★ U_c
Adventure   1972 · UK · Colour · 67mins

Jack London's yarn about the Yukon gold rush was previously filmed in 1935 with Clark Gable. This version stars a husky dog and Charlton Heston, who, in his memoirs, considers it "the worst movie I ever made". Heston blames the mess on a British producer and the fact that finance came from Germany, France, Italy and Spain. "It was a United Nations of a movie," he wrote, "using actors according to nationality rather than ability." ▭

Charlton Heston *John Thornton* • Michèle Mercier *Calliope Laurent* • Raimund Harmstorf *Pete* • Jack Ken Annakin • *Scr* Peter Wellbeck [Harry Alan Towers], Wyn Wells, Peter Yeldman, from the novel by Jack London

Call of the Wild ★★
Adventure   1993 · US · Colour · 97 mins

Umpteenth version of the classic Jack London adventure set against the backdrop of the Klondike gold rush. Rick Schroder is the young innocent who heads north at the end of the 19th century and eventually links up with Buck, an Alsatian dog who is enjoying a perilous journey himself. Schroder makes for an earnest enough young adventurer and Mia Sara supplies the romantic interest, but the real stars of the show are the British Columbia locations and the four-legged canine hero.

Rick Schroder *John Thornton* • Gordon Tootoosis *Charlie* • Mia Sara *Jessie Gosseling* • Duncan Fraser *Red Fiske* • Richard Newman *Perrault* ■ *Dir* Alan Smithee [Michael Toshiyuki Uno] • *Scr* Christopher Lofton, from the novel by Jack London

Call Out the Marines ★★★ U
Musical comedy   1942 · US · BW · 67mins

Victor McLaglen and Edmund Lowe were one of the screen's great comic partnerships, co-starring as the roistering Captain Flagg and Sergeant Quirt in the 1926 silent war classic *What Price Glory?* and continuing on their merry way in a popular series of boisterous follow-ups. By the time they made this semi-musical spy story, however, they were both well past their sell-by date. Here the duo vie for the love of nightclub hostess Binnie Barnes, though movie buffs will be more interested in the fact that William Hamilton, the great RKO film editor, shares director's credit.

Victor McLaglen *McGinnis* • Edmund Lowe *Harry Curtis* • Binnie Barnes *Vi* • Paul Kelly *Jim Blake* • Robert Smith *Billy Harrison* • Dorothy Lovett *Mitzi* • Franklin Pangborn *Wilbur* • Corinna Mura *Rita* ■ *Dir/Scr* Frank Ryan, William Hamilton

Call to Glory ★★★ PG
Drama   1983 · US · Colour · 92mins

The sixties have gained the reputation as a time of peace and love, yet this was also one of the most turbulent decades in recent American history. This Cold War drama was made to launch a TV series showing how historical events could affect a typical family. As a USAF officer, Craig T Nelson finds himself in the thick of the Cuban Missile Crisis. However, director Thomas Carter is careful to show events from the perspective of his wife (Cindy Pickett) and their kids (Elisabeth Shue and Gabriel Damon). ▭

Craig T Nelson *Col Raynor Sarnac* • Cindy Pickett *Vanessa Sarnac* • Elisabeth Shue *Jackie Sarnac* • David Hollander *Wesley Sarnac* • Gabriel Damon *RH Sarnac* • Keenan Wynn *Carl Sarnac* ■ *Dir* Thomas Carter • *Scr* Diane English

Callan ★★★ 15
Spy drama   1974 · UK · Colour · 101mins

In 1967, James Mitchell turned his novel *A Red File for Callan* into an *Armchair Theatre* production called *A Magnum for Schneider*. This movie expands that play to feature-length status to cash in on the success of the popular TV series. Considering how well-established Callan and Hunter were, the film is disappointingly slow off the mark. But thanks to Don Sharp's slick direction, the pace eventually picks up, with Edward Woodward excelling as the ex-agent whose ruthless professionalism belies a highly developed conscience. Although the emphasis is more on character than action, the car chase is particularly memorable. ▭

Edward Woodward *Callan* • Eric Porter *Hunter* • Carl Mohner *Schneider* • Catherine Schell *Jenny* • Peter Egan *Meres* • Russell Hunter *Lonely* • Kenneth Griffith *Waterman* • Dave Prowse *Arthur* • Don Henderson *George* ■ *Dir* Don Sharp • *Scr* James Mitchell, from his TVplay *A Magnum for Schneider*, from his novel *A Red File for Callan*

Callaway Went Thataway ★★★ U
Comedy western   1951 · US · BW · 81mins

When the old movies of forgotten western star "Smoky" Callaway – whereabouts unknown – enjoy a resurgence of popularity on TV, publicists Fred MacMurray and Dorothy McGuire hire a dim-witted lookalike to impersonate him. In due course, the genuine article – now a washed-up drunk – materialises. Howard Keel plays both roles, though he's better as the fake "Smoky" than the real one.

Fred MacMurray *Mike Frye* • Dorothy McGuire *Deborah Patterson* • Howard Keel *"Stretch" Barnes/"Smoky" Callaway* • Jesse White *George Markham* • Fay Roope *Tom Lorrison* • Natalie Schafer *Martha Lorrison* • Clark Gable • Elizabeth Taylor • Esther Williams ■ *Dir/Scr* Norman Panama, Melvin Frank

Calle Mayor ★★★
Comedy drama   1956 · Sp/Fr · BW · 94mins

Things do not go according to plan when virile young Jose Suarez accepts a bet from his friends to court plain spinster Betsy Blair. Also known as *Main Street* and *The Love Maker*, this is one of the films that put the dissident Spanish film-maker Juan Antonio Bardem on the international map. Skilfully capturing the stifling atmosphere of Franco's Spain (indeed, Bardem was arrested and jailed while filming it), it is not an uninteresting comedy drama, with Lila Kedrova featured in the supporting cast. However, it's difficult to escape the feeling that the film sets out to capitalise on Betsy Blair's Oscar-nomination for a similar role in *Marty* the previous year. Spanish dialogue dubbed into English.

Betsy Blair *Isabelle* • Jose Suarez *Juan* • Yves Massard *Jean* • Dora Doll *Antonia* • Lila Kedrova *Mme Pepita* ■ *Dir/Scr* Juan Antonio Bardem

The Caller ★★ 18
Suspense drama   1987 · US · Colour · 92mins

Malcolm McDowell's early films for Anderson, Kubrick, Losey and Lester should have secured his future as a serious actor. Maybe it was the vilified *Caligula* that sealed his fate, but virtually any movie with McDowell in it rapidly became unseen, unshown and unshowable. *The Caller* – which premiered at Cannes and was hardly seen again – is a curious two-hander in which McDowell mysteriously shows up at Madolyn Smith's remote log cabin. As a TV play, this might have worked; as a movie, though, it never stood a chance. ▭

Malcolm McDowell *The caller* • Madolyn Smith *The girl* ■ *Dir* Arthur Allan Seidelman • *Scr* Michael Sloan

Calling Bulldog Drummond ★★ U
Mystery   1951 · UK · BW · 79mins

Bulldog Drummond had last been seen doing B-feature duties in a Hollywood series at Fox when MGM claimed him for this more substantial one-off picture, filmed at its British studios. Walter Pidgeon plays the sleuth who helps Scotland Yard nail a gang of thieves by going undercover, while the strong supporting cast includes Margaret Leighton as his police assistant. Freddie Young's photography lends class to Victor Saville's direction.

Walter Pidgeon *Hugh Drummond* • Margaret Leighton *Sergeant Helen Smith* • Robert Beatty *"Guns"* • David Tomlinson *Algy Longworth* • Peggy Evans *Molly* • Charles Victor *Inspector McIver* • Bernard Lee *Colonel Webson* ■ *Dir* Victor Saville • *Scr* Gerard Fairlie, Howard Emmett Rogers, Arthur Wimperis, from the story by Gerard Fairlie, from characters created by Sapper [HC McNeile] • *Cinematographer* Freddie Young

Calling Dr Gillespie ★★★
Drama   1942 · US · BW · 83mins

With the departure of Dr Kildare from Blair General, the focus of attention in MGM's popular medical series shifted on to the crotchety Dr Gillespie. Disguising his soft centre beneath a thick crust as usual, Lionel Barrymore rose to the challenge and carried the franchise for a further six cases. Here he puts his new Dutch assistant Philip Dorn through his paces, although the central plot strand involves the demented attempts of Phil Brown to dispatch the senior surgeon. Efficiently combining mystery with melodrama, director Harold S Bucquet also finds time to squeeze in a walk-on for a young Ava Gardner.

Lionel Barrymore *Dr Gillespie* • Philip Dorn *Dr Gerniede* • Donna Reed *Marcia Bradburn* • Phil Brown *Roy Todwell* • Nat Pendleton *Joe Wayman* • Alma Kruger *Molly Byrd* • Ava Gardner *Girl* ■ *Dir* Harold S Bucquet • *Scr* Willis Goldbeck, Harry Ruskin, from a story by Kubec Glasmon, from characters created by Max Brand

Calling Dr Kildare ★★
Medical drama   1939 · US · BW · 86mins

The second in MGM's hospital series finds Blair General intern James Kildare (Lew Ayres) packed off by crusty but kind-hearted Dr Gillespie (Lionel Barrymore) to a humble neighbourhood clinic for a lesson in life. This is well-made, pleasant and sanitised stuff, despite the intrusion of the criminal underworld and Lana Turner as a wounded gunman's glamorous sister. The movie cemented the formula and popularity of the series, though Lew Ayres only starred in nine of the 15 – the same number made by director Harold S Bucquet.

Lew Ayres *Dr James Kildare* • Lionel Barrymore *Dr Leonard Gillespie* • Laraine Day *Mary Lamont* • Nat Pendleton *Joe Wayman* •

Lana Turner *Rosalie* • Samuel S Hinds *Dr Stephen Kildare* • Walter Kingsford *Dr Walter Carew* • Alma Kruger *Molly Byrd* ■ *Dir* Harold S Bucquet • *Scr* Harry Ruskin, Willis Goldbeck, from a story by Max Brand

Caltiki, the Immortal Monster ★★

Science-fiction horror 1959 · It · BW · 76mins

Future horror maestro Mario Bava directed 70 per cent of this endearing Italian-style mixture of *The Quatermass Experiment* and *The Blob* when director Riccardo Freda walked off the film and left his cinematographer in confused charge. Freda was probably exaggerating when he stated he took such action to make the indecisive Bava take the plunge into directing. Yet this purported Mayan legend, about a radioactive monster unleashed when explorers defile its holy lair, nevertheless demonstrates how inventively Bava's technical genius overcame the micro-budgets he was to suffer throughout his long and illustrious career.

John Merivale *Dr John Fielding* • Didi Sullivan [Didi Perego] *Ellen Fielding* • Gerard Herter *Max Gunther* • Daniela Rocca *Linda* ■ *Dir* Robert Hampton [Riccardo Freda], Mario Bava • *Scr* Filippo Sanjust

Calypso Joe ★★ 🔲

Musical romance 1957 · US · BW · 75mins

Made by Allied Artists (formerly "Poverty Row" studio Monogram) to cash in on the short-lived calypso craze, this stars one-time Duke Ellington vocalist Herb Jeffries, who had a movie career in the thirties as the cowboy hero of a series of all-black westerns. His leading lady is sultry Angie Dickinson, a long way before her hit TV series *Police Woman*, and there are some wonderful numbers featuring such genuine Jamaican calypso stars as Lord Flea and the Duke of Iron. However, the real star of this little exploitation flick was the song *Marianne*, a chart-topping success all over the world.

Herb Jeffries *Joe* • Angie Dickinson *Julie* • Edward Kemmer *Lee Darling* • Stephen Bekassy *Rico Vargas* • Laurie Mitchell *Leah* • Claudia Drake *Astra Vargas* ■ *Dir* Edward Dein • *Scr* Edward Dein, Mildred Dein

Camelot ★★★★ 🔲

Musical 1967 · US · Colour · 175mins

Despite Joshua Logan's stodgy staging, this sumptuous screen version of the Arthurian musical by Lerner and Loewe still pierces the heart in *Excalibur* fashion. Vanessa Redgrave as Guenevere convincingly enthrals King Arthur (Richard Harris), Lancelot (Franco Nero) and us. The stars may not be exactly tuneful, but they compensate for that with their dramatic and moving interpretation of the glorious songs. 🖭 **DVD**

Richard Harris *King Arthur* • Vanessa Redgrave *Queen Guenevere* • Franco Nero *Lancelot Du Lac* • David Hemmings *Mordred* • Lionel Jeffries *King Pellinore* • Laurence Naismith *Merlyn* • Pierre Olaf *Dap* • Estelle Winwood *Lady Clarinda* ■ *Dir* Joshua Logan • *Scr* Alan J Lerner, from the musical by Alan J Lerner, Frederick Loewe, from the novel *The Once and Future King* by TH White

The Camels Are Coming ★★ 🔲

Comedy 1934 · UK · BW · 71mins

Directed by American Tim Whelan, this was hardly a feather in producer Michael Balcon's cap. But comedies of this kind went down a treat with audiences in the thirties and it was their success that later enabled Balcon to make the Gainsborough costume dramas and Ealing comedies. Star Jack Hulbert teamed with Guy Bolton and WP Lipscomb on the script, and he and Anna Lee make a pleasing partnership as they unmask desert drug smugglers. 🖭

Jack Hulbert *Jack Campbell* • Anna Lee *Anita Rodgers* • Hartley Power *Nicholas* • Harold Huth *Dr Zhiga* • Allan Jeayes *Sheikh* • Peter Gawthorne *Colonel Fairley* ■ *Dir* Tim Whelan • *Scr* Guy Bolton, Jack Hulbert, WP Lipscomb, from a story by Tim Whelan, Russell Medcraft

The Cameraman ★★★★★

Silent comedy 1928 · US · BW · 67mins

A superb example of Buster Keaton's comic genius. He's a street photographer who wants to become a newsreel cameraman to get close to Marceline Day. The film was remade for comedian Red Skelton as *Watch the Birdie* in 1950, but that went nowhere compared with the original. In one bit of knockabout Keaton hitches a ride on a fire engine to get a scoop, only to find it's returning from the fire.

Buster Keaton *Luke Shannon/Buster* • Marceline Day *Sally* • Harold Goodwin *Stagg* • Harry Gribbon *Cop* • Sidney Bracy *Editor* ■ *Dir* Edward Sedgwick • *Scr* Richard Schayer, Joseph Farnham (titles), from a story by Clyde Bruckman, Lew Lipton

Cameron's Closet ★ 🔞

Supernatural horror 1988 · UK · Colour · 83mins

This indigestible slice of eighties horror pulp centres on a boy whose telekinetic powers conjure up a red-eyed monster that resides in his closet. The result is an odd mix of mawkish family drama and graphic gore; fifties star Tab Hunter has the right idea when he exits this dull affair early on. When it arrives, the Carlo Rambaldi-designed creature wouldn't terrify a Muppets fan – a real letdown from the man who created ET. 🖭

Cotter Smith *Sam Talliaferro* • Mel Harris *Nora Haley* • Scott Curtis *Cameron Lansing* • Chuck McCann *Ben Majors* • Leigh McCloskey *Det Pete Groom* • Tab Hunter *Owen Lansing* ■ *Dir* Armand Mastroianni • *Scr* Gary Brandner

Camila ★★★ 🔢

Historical drama 1984 · Arg · Colour · 107mins

Such was the contemporary resonance of this true-life period drama that director Maria Luisa Bemberg was denied permission to film it for many years. Those pillars of Argentine society – the church, the state and the family – come in for pitiless barrage as Buenos Aires socialite Susu Pecoraro and Jesuit priest Imanol Arias briefly defy the conventions extant under the brutal de Rosas dictatorship to set up housekeeping in a remote country village. Although her lush visual style tends to romanticise the 1840s,

Bemberg shows that even the most overpowering passion cannot rob a woman of her individualism. In Spanish with English subtitles.

Susu Pecoraro *Camila O'Gorman* • Imanol Arias *Father Ladislao Gutierrez* • Hector Alterio *Adolfo O'Gorman* • Elena Tasisto *Dona Joaquina O'Gorman* • Carlos Munoz *Monsignor Elortondo* ■ *Dir* Maria Luisa Bemberg • *Scr* Maria Luisa Bemberg, Beda Docampo Feijo, Juan Batista Stagnaro

Camilla ★★★ 🔢

Drama 1993 · Can/UK · Colour · 94mins

It's impossible to watch this variation on the road-movie theme without getting a lump in your throat. In her final role, Jessica Tandy gives a performance of regal impudence that helps elevate a rather undistinguished film to something worth cherishing. The scenes she shares with husband of 51 years Hume Cronyn are exquisitely poignant, but they're over far too soon as Tandy and new-found buddy Bridget Fonda leave in pursuit of the latter's musical dream. A whiff of *Fried Green Tomatoes* lingers over the picture, which suffers from a haphazard structure and a dull subplot involving Tandy's son and Fonda's husband. Contains some swearing. 🖭

Bridget Fonda *Freda Lopez* • Jessica Tandy *Camilla Cara* • Elias Koteas *Vincent Lopez* • Maury Chaykin *Harold Cara* • Graham Greene *Hunt Weller* • Hume Cronyn *Ewald* • Ranjit Chowdhry *Kapur* • George Harris *Jerry* ■ *Dir* Deepa Mehta • *Scr* Paul Quarrington

Camille ★★

Silent romantic drama 1921 · US · BW · 72mins

The great Russian actress Alla Nazimova stars as Marguerite in an updated version of Alexandre Dumas's frequently filmed novel, which, unaccountably and unacceptably, removes Armand from the famous deathbed finale, leaving the consumptive heroine to expire in the company of her servants. The bob-haired star displays her considerable range of emotions to the full, and is well-partnered by an elegant, handsome and suitably restrained Rudolph Valentino.

Alla Nazimova *Camille/Marguerite Gautier* • Rudolph Valentino *Armand Duval* • Arthur Hoyt *Count de Varville* • Zeffie Tillbury *Prudence* • Rex Cherryman *Gaston* • Edward Connelly *Duke* ■ *Dir* Ray C Smallwood • *Scr* June Mathis, from the novel *La Dame aux Camélias* by Alexandre Dumas fils

Camille ★★★

Silent romantic drama 1927 · US · BW

Yet another in the string of silent adaptations of Dumas's famous novel, starring one of America's queens of the silent screen, Norma Talmadge, as the ill-fated Marguerite and a bland Gilbert Roland as her lover, Armand. This is, sadly, a lost film and is on the American Film Institute's "most wanted" list. However, along with previous attempts, it has been overshadowed by MGM's deathless sound version, made ten years later with Greta Garbo and Robert Taylor.

Norma Talmadge *Camille/Marguerite* • Gilbert Roland *Armand* • Lilyan Tashman *Olympe* • Maurice Costello *Monsieur Duval* • Harvey

Clark *The Baron* • Alec B Francis *The Duke* ■ *Dir* Fred Niblo • *Scr* Olga Printzlau, Chandler Sprague, Fred De Gresac, from the novel *La Dame aux Camélias* by Alexandre Dumas fils

Camille ★★★★ 🅿🅶

Romantic melodrama 1937 · US · BW · 104mins

Greta Garbo never won an Oscar for a specific role (she received a special one in 1954), but the New York film critics did give her their best actress gong for what is now one of her most famous performances, as the doomed heroine in George Cukor's sumptuous film of the younger Alexandre Dumas's classic play and novel. She certainly pulls out all the stops, whether expressing her love for young Armand (Robert Taylor), modelling a glamorous wardrobe, or finally breathing her last in one of cinema's most celebrated death scenes. Cukor handles the whole thing with confidence, but it is Garbo's movie all the way.

Greta Garbo *Marguerite* • Robert Taylor (1) *Armand* • Lionel Barrymore *Monsieur Duval* • Elizabeth Allan *Nichette* • Jessie Ralph *Nanine* • Henry Daniell *Baron De Varville* • Lenore Ulric *Olympe* • Laura Hope Crews *Prudence* • Rex O'Malley *Gaston* • Russell Hardie *Gustave* ■ *Dir* George Cukor • *Scr* Zoe Akins, Frances Marion, James Hilton, from the novel *La Dame aux Camélias* by Alexandre Dumas fils • *Costume Designer* Adrian

Camille Claudel ★★★ 🅿🅶

Biography 1988 · Fr · Colour · 167mins

It is fascinating to discover that Rodin's mistress Camille Claudel was a talented sculptress, and agonising to watch her sublimation beneath Rodin, who used her talent to further his own. Isabelle Adjani and Gérard Depardieu are well cast in this re-creation of the Rodin/Claudel relationship, which, in typical French style, makes the journey through the emotional maelstrom akin to walking barefoot over broken glass. Adjani was nominated for an Oscar, and her descent into self-destruction is moving. Overall, though, Bruno Nuytten's film tends towards the lengthy and tortuous. In French with English subtitles. 🖭

Isabelle Adjani *Camille Claudel* • Gérard Depardieu *Auguste Rodin* • Laurent Crevill *Paul Claudel* • Alain Cuny *Mr Claudel* • Madeleine Robinson *Madame Claudel* • Katrine Boorman *Jessie* ■ *Dir* Bruno Nuytten • *Scr* Marilyn Goldin, from a biography by Reine-Marie Paris, Bruno Nuytten

Camouflage ★★★

Comedy satire 1977 · Pol · Colour · 100mins

Made by Krzysztof Zanussi and considered by many to be a landmark of Polish cinema, this intelligent and subtly understated film explores the themes of bureaucratic pettiness and the crushing of idealism. Using a summer seminar for linguistic students, held at a palatial country estate, as his fulcrum, Zanussi addresses the concerns of the generation gap through a youthful protagonist, liberal professor Piotr Garlicki, who confronts the collective cynicism of the status quo, and a particular older colleague (Zbigniew Zapasiewicz). The divergence of opinion between the two men is manifested in a series of duologues,

some of the finer points of which are liable to be lost on a non-Polish-speaking audience, but which remain impressive. A Polish language film.

Piotr Garlicki *Jaroslaw Kruszynski* • Zbigniew Zapasiewicz *Jakub Szelestowski* • Christine Paul-Podlasky *Mary* • Mariusz Dmochowski *Vice-rector* ■ *Dir/Scr* Krzysztof Zanussi

Camp Nowhere ★★ PG

Comedy   1994 · US · Colour · 91mins

Every conceivable stereotype of American teenagehood is on display in this woefully unfunny slice of wish fulfilment, as a bunch of spoilt nerds set up their own summer camp with unemployed drama teacher Christopher Lloyd in nominal charge. There are one or two laughs when the suspicious parents show up for an open day, but the whole production has a "dashed-off" air to it. The children are both bratty and anaemic, and the film would benefit from less of them and more of reliable old hands M Emmet Walsh and Burgess Meredith.

Jonathan Jackson *Morris "Mud" Himmel* • Christopher Lloyd *Dennis Van Welker* • Andrew Keegan *Zack Dell* • Marne Patterson *Trish Prescott* • Melody Kay *Gaby Nowicki* • Raymond Baker [Ray Baker] *Norris Prescott* • Kate Mulgrew *Rachel Prescott* • M Emmet Walsh *TR Polk* • Burgess Meredith *Feln* ■ *Dir* Jonathan Prince • *Scr* Andrew Kurtzman, Eliot Wald

The Camp on Blood Island
★★★

Second World War drama
1958 · UK · BW · 82mins

The Hammer House of Horror took a rest from gothic gore to take a grim look at the real-life horrors of the Second World War. A sensation in its day, Hammer faced condemnation on all fronts for daring to tell the moving tale of British PoWs fearing a massacre after their cruel captors learn that the war has ended. Based on a true story, Hammer didn't flinch from the subject's pathos or its sadistic shock value. A sequel, *The Secret Of Blood Island*, followed in 1965.

Carl Mohner *Piet Van Elst* • André Morell *Colonel Lambert* ■ *Dir* Val Guest • *Scr* Jon Manchip White, Val Guest, from a story by Jon Manchip White

Campbell's Kingdom ★★ U

Adventure   1957 · UK · Colour · 97mins

An unconvincing adventure set in Canada, with Dirk Bogarde setting out to prove that he can stand up to mean Stanley Baker, who is out to swipe his land. There is some stunning location photography and a reliable British cast, but director Ralph Thomas looks out of his depth with this genre. □

Dirk Bogarde *Bruce Campbell* • Stanley Baker *Owen Morgan* • Michael Craig *Boy Bladen* • Barbara Murray *Jean Lucas* • James Robertson-Justice *James Macdonald* • John Laurie *Mac* • Sidney James *Driver* ■ *Dir* Ralph Thomas • *Scr* Robin Estridge, from the novel by Hammond Innes • *Cinematographer* Ernest Steward

Can-Can ★★ U

Musical   1960 · US · Colour · 124mins

When Soviet premier Khrushchev visited Hollywood, he was taken on to the set of this 20th Century-Fox musical and shown the can-can number being filmed. He commented: "The face of humanity is more beautiful than its backside." A very poor PR result, but then Fox did sometimes lack taste when it came to musicals. Although based on Cole Porter's Broadway hit, set in turn-of-the-century Paris, this movie manages to lose some of Porter's best material, notably the brilliant lyric to *Can-Can* itself, and remains resolutely anachronistic. The film is at its best in the intimate moments, but is simply too long. □

Frank Sinatra *François Durnais* • Shirley MacLaine *Simone Pistache* • Maurice Chevalier *Paul Barrière* • Louis Jourdan *Philippe Forrestier* • Juliet Prowse *Claudine* • Marcel Dalio *Head Waiter* ■ *Dir* Walter Lang • *Scr* Dorothy Kingsley, Charles Lederer, from the musical by Abe Burrows, Cole Porter

Can Heironymus Merkin Ever Forget Mercy Humppe and Find True Happiness?
★★

Musical comedy 1969 · UK · Colour · 117mins

Anthony Newley's sprawling musical fantasy, a Fellini-esque hotch-potch of dream-like sequences and irreverent whimsy, is a film that could only have been made in the sixties. Heironymus Merkin sits on a beach surrounded by the flotsam and jetsam of his life, including a film biography which he projects to his family. We learn his story from the vignettes contained in the film-within-the-film. Meanwhile, back in the present, the film company expresses its concern that this movie still has no ending. Joan Collins, Newley's wife at the time, shows off her assets, and there's a rare feature film appearance from Bruce Forsyth.

Anthony Newley *Heironymus Merkin* • Joan Collins *Polyester Poontang* • Milton Berle *Good Time Eddie Filth* • George Jessel *The Presence* • Stubby Kaye *Fat Writer* • Bruce Forsyth *Uncle Limelight* • Patricia Hayes *Grandma* • Victor Spinetti *Sharpnose* ■ *Dir* Anthony Newley • *Scr* Herman Raucher, Anthony Newley

Can She Bake a Cherry Pie? ★★★★ 15

Comedy   1983 · US · Colour · 86mins

Maverick director Henry Jaglom continues on his own sweet way with this entrancing tale of opposites attracting. Mostly improvising their lines, the leads are simply superb. When she's not belting out blues numbers, kooky Karen Black frets over her divorce and the impossibility of finding romance the second time around. Meanwhile, fussy, balding Michael Emil declaims at great length about anything and everything. Teetering on the brink of self-indulgence, this meticulously-paced picture allows us to get to know the characters, whose eccentricities and opinions inexorably reel us in and make us care. □

Karen Black *Zee* • Michael Emil *Eli* • Michael Margotta *Larry* • Frances Fisher *Louise* • Martin Harvey Friedberg *Mort* ■ *Dir/Scr* Henry Jaglom

Can You Feel Me Dancing?
★★ PG

Drama based on a true story
1986 · US · Colour · 94mins

Another sudsy slice of made-for-TV melodrama, which finds former *Family Ties* star Justine Bateman playing a blind adolescent determined to assert her independence. She gives a good account of herself and there is useful support from her real-life brother Jason (playing her brother here), Max Gail and Roger Wilson. However, as with many other TV productions, director Michael Miller over-sweetens the dish and the final product lapses into sentimentality. Contains violence. □

Justine Bateman *Karin Nichols* • Max Gail *Mel Nichols* • Jason Bateman *Larry Nichols* ■ *Dir* Michael Miller • *Scr* J Miyoko Hensley, Steven Hensley

Can You Keep It Up for a Week? ★★ 18

Sex comedy   1974 · UK · Colour · 88mins

Now here's a fascinating fact. Although the producer of this bawdy seventies romp is credited as Elton Hawke, this was the joint pseudonym of ITV wrestling commentator Kent Walton and Hazel Adair, the writer behind such pioneering soaps as *Compact* and *Crossroads*. Written by Robin Gough and directed by Jim Atkinson, it's one of the better-known British sex comedies of the period. The flesh count is high, but there are also some giggles along the way as Jeremy Bulloch tries to resist temptation and hang on to a job for a week so that his girlfriend will marry him. Contains sex scenes and nudity. □

Jeremy Bulloch *Gil* • Neil Hallett *Gerry Grimwood* • Jill Damas *Annette* • Joy Harrington *Mrs Grimwood* ■ *Dir* Jim Atkinson • *Scr* Robin Gough

Canadian Bacon ★★ PG

Satirical comedy 1995 · US · Colour · 90mins

Director Michael Moore impressed both with his satirical documentary *Roger and Me* and his small-screen series *TV Nation*, but he came a cropper with his feature debut. Reversing the old *The Mouse That Roared* idea, the story has US President Alan Alda declaring war on Canada to boost his popularity rating. This should have been the signal for some incisive cross-border comedy, but Moore too often goes for easy laughs and settles for national stereotypes instead of fully rounded characters. Contains swearing. □

Alan Alda *President* • John Candy *Bud B Boomer* • Rhea Perlman *Deputy Honey* • Kevin Pollak *Stuart Smiley* • Rip Torn *General Dick Panzer* • Kevin J O'Connor *Roy Boy* • Bill Nunn *Kabral* • Steven Wright *Niagara Mountie* • James Belushi *Charles Jackal* ■ *Dir/Scr* Michael Moore (2)

Canadian Pacific ★★ U

Western   1949 · US · Colour · 94mins

Randolph Scott drives the railroad through the Rocky mountains, fighting off Indians and trappers every inch of the way. Shot on authentic locations, this Fox effort can't quite match the scale and pomposity of *Union Pacific*, which Cecil B DeMille made ten years earlier. As the heroic railroad surveyor, Scott underplays everything, despite juggling two women – Nancy Olsen and doctor Jane Wyatt – and dodging various explosions. Outdoor action specialist Edwin L Marin directed Scott many times, most notably in *Colt .45*.

Randolph Scott *Tom Andrews* • Jane Wyatt *Dr Edith Cabot* • J Carrol Naish *Dynamite Dawson* • Victor Jory *Dirk Rourke* • Nancy Olson *Cecille Gautier* • Robert Barrat *Cornelius Van Horne* ■ *Dir* Edwin L Marin • *Scr* Jack DeWitt, Kenneth Gamet, from a story by Jack DeWitt

The Canadians ★★ U

Western   1961 · US · Colour · 85mins

Following the Battle of the Little Bighorn, 6,000 Sioux Indians flee to Canada. They live in peace until some cowboys from Montana cross the border looking for stolen horses. Canadian Mountie Robert Ryan, standing up for Sioux rights, bars their path. Some lovely location photography barely compensates for the solemn, self-righteous tone of this early "New Age" western, which follows the Canadian line that everything bad starts below the 49th parallel.

Robert Ryan *Inspector Gannon* • John Dehner *Frank Boone* • Torin Thatcher *Master Sgt McGregor* • Burt Metcalfe *Constable Springer* • John Sutton *Supt Walker* • Jack Creley *Greer* ■ *Dir/Scr* Burt Kennedy

Canary Murder Case ★★★

Mystery   1929 · US · BW · 80mins

This first of 15 films from SS Van Dine's novels featuring sophisticated sleuth Philo Vance had William Powell in the role (which he would play four times). It made a welcome change from the gallery of rogues for which the actor was becoming known and paved the way for his famously urbane detective, Nick Charles, in the *Thin Man* series. The "canary" of this case is Louise Brooks, an alluring beauty not above a bit of blackmail. When she is murdered, Vance investigates. Shot as a silent by Malcom St Clair, it was reworked by Frank Tuttle as a talkie before its release. Brooks, away in Europe, was dubbed by Margaret Livingston.

William Powell *Philo Vance* • Louise Brooks *Margaret O'Dell* • James Hall *Jimmy Spotswoode* • Jean Arthur *Alice LaFosse* • Gustav von Seyffertitz *Dr Ambrose Linquist* • Charles Lane (2) *Charles Sportswoode* ■ *Dir* Malcolm St Clair, Frank Tuttle • *Scr* Florence Ryerson, Albert S LeVino, Herman J Mankiewicz, from a novel by SS Van Dine

Cancel My Reservation ★★ U

Comedy western 1972 · US · Colour · 86mins

This incompetent farce from Bob Hope – one of the last he made – reprises so many themes from his earlier movies (*My Favorite Blonde* in particular) it feels like a remake. Hope does his cowardly lion routine as a TV talk show host who becomes entangled with murder and Eva Marie Saint while vacationing in Arizona. An uncredited guest appearance by Bing Crosby serves only to remind us of a time when such a sight caused delight – and laughter. Sadly, no longer.

Bob Hope *Dan Bartlett* • Eva Marie Saint *Sheila Bartlett* • Ralph Bellamy *John Ed* •

Forrest Tucker *Reese* • Anne Archer *Crazy* • Keenan Wynn *Sheriff Riley* ■ *Dir* Paul Bogart • *Scr* Arthur Marx, Robert Fisher, from the novel *The Broken Gun* by Louis L'Amour

The Candidate ★★★★ PG

Political drama 1972 · US · Colour · 105mins

Robert Redford's engaging performance breathes fresh life into the all-power-corrupts theme. Striving "to do an Abe Lincoln", Redford is the idealistic lawyer who succumbs to mass-merchandising politics when he sets out to be a senator. With a campaign engineered by party managers Peter Boyle and Allen Garfield, he ends up alienating his wife Karen Carlson and his principles. Director Michael Ritchie and Redford together made the skiing exposé *Downhill Racer* in 1969, and the word "downhill" could apply to the morality in this movie, to which the director gives a documentary-like credibility. ▣

Robert Redford *Bill McKay* • Peter Boyle *Lucas* • Don Porter *Senator Crocker Jarmon* • Allen Garfield *Howard Klein* • Melvyn Douglas *John J McKay* • Quinn Redeker *Rich Jenkin* • Michael Lerner *Paul Corliss* • Karen Carlson *Nancy* ■ *Dir* Michael Ritchie • *Scr* Jeremy Larner

Candlelight in Algeria ★★ U

Second World War spy drama 1943 · UK · BW · 85mins

Throughout the Second World War, Allied intelligence chiefs were worried that the image of the doltish Nazi depicted in films might make people underestimate the Germans as an enemy. Certainly, the officers on parade in this tepid potboiler pose few problems for James Mason as he attempts to steal the film that will betray the location of a top secret meeting. Well below his usual nasty best, Walter Rilla is confounded by Mason and sculptress Carla Lehmann with embarrassing ease, while director George King misses out on suspense and authenticity. A distinct comedown for Mason after *The Man in Grey*.

James Mason *Alan Thurston* • Carla Lehmann *Susan Foster* • Walter Rilla *Dr Muller* • Raymond Lovell *Von Alven* • Enid Stamp Taylor *Maritza* • Pamela Stirling *Yvette* ■ *Dir* George King • *Scr* Brock Williams, Katherine Strueby, from a story by Dorothy Hope

Candleshoe ★★★ U

Comedy 1977 · UK/US · Colour · 96mins

In her fifth outing for Disney, Jodie Foster is in fine fettle as a tomboy turning the tables on bungling crook Leo McKern. This is the kind of family entertainment that everyone seems to have forgotten how to make: good story, fine acting and no special effects. The star of the show is David Niven, who is clearly having a ball beneath his various disguises, but there's also solid support from Helen Hayes as the owner of a stately children's hostel that will be closed down unless some buried treasure is unearthed. ▣

Jodie Foster *Casey Brown* • Helen Hayes *Lady St Edmund* • David Niven *Priory* • Leo McKern *Harry Bundage* • Veronica Quilligan *Cluny* ■ *Dir* Norman Tokar • *Scr* David Swift, Rosemary Anne Sisson, from the novel *Christmas at Candleshoe* by Michael Innes

Candy ★

Comedy 1968 · US/It/Fr · Colour · 124mins

This is a sex farce of mind-boggling ineptitude. The impressive roster of co-stars were each paid $50,000 for a week's work, though it's such an shambolic, episodic mess that the movie seems a monument to the arrogance and indifference of stars tanked up on drugs, booze and undiluted ego. Marlon Brando, a close friend of director Christian Marquand and the film's prime mover, plays an Indian guru addicted to sex. It is the actor's all-time career low, though Richard Burton's Dylan Thomas take-off rivals it for sheer laziness.

Ewa Aulin *Candy* • Charles Aznavour *The hunchback* • Marlon Brando *Grindl* • Richard Burton *McPhisto* • James Coburn *Dr Krankeit* • John Huston *Dr Dunlap* • Walter Matthau *General Smight* • Ringo Starr *Emmanuel* • John Astin *Daddy, Uncle Jack* • Anita Pallenberg *Nurse Bullock* ■ *Dir* Christian Marquand • *Scr* Buck Henry, from the novel by Terry Southern

The Candy Man ★

Crime thriller 1969 · US · Colour · 97mins ■

A deservedly obscure kidnapping drama shot on location in Mexico City. George Sanders stars as a British drug pusher who decides to branch out by abducting the daughter of an American film star. Sanders's tired performance is typical of the boredom that drove him to suicide three years later; in contrast, Leslie Parrish over-emotes grief and worry as the frantic mother.

George Sanders *Sidney Carter* • Leslie Parrish *Julia Evans* • Manolo Fabregas *Lieutenant Garcia* • Gina Ronan *Greta Hansen* • Carlos Cortez *Rick Pierce* • Pedro Galvan *Roger West* ■ *Dir* Herbert J Leder • *Scr* Herbert J Leder, from a story by Francis Swann

Candy Mountain ★★★ 15

Road movie 1987 · US · Colour · 91mins

Ambitious musician Kevin J O'Connor pretends to know a legendary guitar-maker named Elmore Silk (Harris Yulin) in order to get a job with rocker David Johansen's band. When his bluff is finally called, he attempts to track Silk down via encounters with friends, lovers and relatives. The result is a quirky, if downbeat road movie that's more a celebration of the marginal than a straight story with a cohesive narrative. In a difficult role that requires him to put across a despairing ordinariness, O'Connor sustains the interest right up to the honest and uplifting pay-off.

Kevin J O'Connor *Julius Book* • Harris Yulin *Elmore Silk* • Tom Waits *Al Silk* • Bulle Ogier *Cornelia* • Roberts Blossom *Archie* • Leon Redbone *Huey* • Dr John *Henry* • Rita MacNeil *Winnie* • Joe Strummer *Mario* • Laurie Metcalf *Alice* • David Johansen *Keith* ■ *Dir* Robert Frank, Rudy Wurlitzer • *Scr* Rudy Wurlitzer

Candyman ★★★★ 18

Horror 1992 · US · Colour · 94mins

Horror maestro Clive Barker's short story *The Forbidden* is the inspiration for director Bernard Rose's electrifying shocker in which student Virginia Madsen, researching urban legends in Chicago, uncovers a hook-handed mythical killer who then catapults her into the chilling realms of dread and

destiny. Intelligent, gripping and refreshingly gimmick-free, this adult-orientated study in psychological fear is a breath of fresh scare. Madsen is terrific, giving a well-shaded performance as the emotionally abandoned heroine, and Rose's bold direction milks every terrifying moment of this compelling and atmospheric movie. Contains violence, swearing and nudity. ▣ **DVD**

Virginia Madsen *Helen Lyle* • Tony Todd *Candyman* • Xander Berkeley *Trevor Lyle* • Kasi Lemmons *Bernadette Walsh* • Vanessa Williams *Anne-Marie McCoy* • Dejuan Guy *Jake* • Marianna Eliott *Clara* • Ted Raimi *Billy* • Ria Pavia *Monica* • Mark Daniels *Student* ■ *Dir* Bernard Rose • *Scr* Bernard Rose, from the short story *The Forbidden* by Clive Barker

Candyman II: Farewell to the Flesh ★★ 18

Horror 1995 · US · Colour · 90mins

Director Bill Condon shows little of the flair or fluency he would bring to his Oscar-winning *Gods and Monsters* in this long-winded and utterly conventional sequel to a marvellous original. Tony Todd returns as the hook-handed slave spirit, this time terrorising New Orleans during Mardi Gras. Not even the colourful carnival backdrop makes up for the predictable plot, which eschews the spooky scares of *Candyman* for pure gruesome schlock as Condon tragically waters down the original's supernatural strength. Contains violence, swearing and brief nudity. ▣

Tony Todd *Candyman/Daniel Robitaille* • Kelly Rowan *Annie Tarrant* • Timothy Carhart *Paul McKeever* • Veronica Cartwright *Octavia Tarrant* • William O'Leary *Ethan Tarrant* • Fay Hauser *Pam Carver* • Bill Nunn *Reverend Ellis* ■ *Dir* Bill Condon • *Scr* Rand Ravich, Mark Kruger, from a story by Clive Barker

Cane Toads – an Unnatural History ★★★ PG

Cult documentary 1987 · Ausl · Colour · 46mins

Those who believe nature is rendered safe by the urbane explanations of David Attenborough might well be checking behind the sofa or under the bed after this rude shock. It's a wonderfully dotty history lesson about the wholesale import of cane toads into Australia in 1935 to annihilate the cane beetle, showing how the utter uselessness of the attempt bordered on the surreal. Not only were they unfit for the job, but the grubby beasts devoured everything in sight except for their appointed targets. They were also so highly sexed they were incessantly breeding and were quite happy to cosy up to some mud in the absence of anything more animate. ▣

Dir/Scr Mark Lewis

Cannery Row ★★★ 15

Drama 1982 · US · Colour · 115mins

Raquel Welch was originally cast in David S Ward's over-reverential production of two John Steinbeck novels, but was fired midway through filming. It's a pity, as her buxom sexuality might have roused this story of waterfront bums from its languor. Ward wrote *The Sting*, but his screenplay here lacks that movie's zip

and suffers from an episodic narrative. Debra Winger takes on the Welch role of a hooker who yearns for Nick Nolte, excellent as a baseball star turned marine biologist.

Nick Nolte *Doc* • Debra Winger *Suzy* • Audra Lindley *Fauna* • Frank McRae *Hazel* • M Emmet Walsh *Mack* • Tom Mahoney *Hughie* • John Malloy *Jones* • James Keane *Eddie* • John Huston *Narrator* ■ *Dir* David S Ward • *Scr* David S Ward, from the novels *Cannery Row* and *Sweet Thursday* by John Steinbeck

Cannibal! the Musical ★★★ 18

Spoof musical comedy 1993 · US · Colour · 97mins

Only the creators of *South Park*, Trey Parker and Matt Stone, could have come up with this an "all singing, all dancing, all flesh-eating" gore flick that's a weird yet quite wonderfully awful mix of western spoof, *Scream*-style horror and cod Hollywood musical joyfulness. *Oklahoma!* meets *Dawn of the Dead* in this demented satire in which the sole survivor of an ill-fated mining expedition tells how his taste for gold was replaced by one for human flesh while singing of gay love, horses and snowmen. Contains violence. ▣

Juan Schwartz *Alferd Packer* • Ian Hardin *Shannon Bell* • Matthew Stone *James Humphrey* • Jon Hegel *Israel Swan* • Jason McHugh *Frank Miller* • Dian Buchar *George Noon* ■ *Dir/Scr* Trey Parker

Cannibal Women in the Avocado Jungle of Death ★ 12

Comedy adventure 1989 · US · Colour · 85mins

Can any film with a title this great be any good? "No" is the short answer, as far as this deadpan feminist send-up is concerned. *Apocalypse Now* meets *Indiana Jones* as tough anthropologist Margo Hunt (former *Playboy* centrefold Shannon Tweed) is sent by the CIA on an expedition into the Californian wilderness to locate a legendary tribe of man-eating cannibal babes. Aided by bumbling mercenary Bill Maher and bimbo Karen Mistal (*Return of the Killer Tomatoes*), the safari is a mix of stupid sex farce and talky rhetoric on women's issues. Contains some nudity, swearing and violence. ▣

Shannon Tweed *Dr Margo Hunt* • Adrienne Barbeau *Dr Kurtz* • Bill Maher *Jim* • Karen Mistal *Bunny* • Brett Stimely *Jean-Pierre* ■ *Dir/Scr* JF Lawton

Cannon for Cordoba ★★ 12

Western 1970 · US · Colour · 99mins

The Wild Bunch it ain't, but this western adventure is still an entertaining affair. George Peppard is a suitably heroic lead, playing an American soldier battling Mexican bandits in the early 1900s, and there's enough action to satisfy fans. The director is Paul Wendkos, an experienced Hollywood hand who since the seventies has concentrated mainly on made-for-TV movies. Contains some mild swearing, sexual references and violence. ▣

U = SUITABLE FOR ALL   Uc = SUITABLE FOR ALL, ESPECIALLY FOR YOUNG CHILDREN (VIDEO ONLY)   PG = PARENTAL GUIDANCE

George Peppard *Captain Rod Douglas* • Giovanna Ralli *Leonora Cristobal* • Raf Vallone *Cordoba* • Peter Duel *Andy Rice* • Don Gordon *Sergeant Jackson Harkness* ■ *Dir* Paul Wendkos • *Scr* Stephen Kandel

Cannonball ★★

Adventure thriller
1976 · HK/US · Colour · 91mins

This is nothing more than a poor retread of director Paul Bartel's wilder and wittier *Death Race 2000*, with all the expensive futuristic trappings removed and loads more epic car crashes added. David Carradine is "Cannonball" Buckman, who signs up for the illegal Trans-American Grand Prix cross-country car race between Los Angeles and New York, where no rules apply and underhand sabotage is *de rigueur*. Great stunts, shame about the formula-one plot.

David Carradine *Coy "Cannonball" Buckman* • Bill McKinney *Cade Redman* • Veronica Hamel *Linda* • Gerrit Graham *Perman Waters* • Robert Carradine *Jim Crandell* • Belinda Balaski *Maryann* • Martin Scorsese *Mafioso* • Roger Corman • Sylvester Stallone • Joe Dante ■ *Dir* Paul Bartel • *Scr* Paul Bartel, Donald C Simpson

Cannonball Fever ★★ PG

Comedy 1989 · US · Colour · 91mins

Depressingly, this was not only one of Lee Van Cleef's final films, but also one of the most expensive movies ever filmed in Canada. It's impossible to see where all the money went, for this third instalment in the *Cannonball Run* series is so bad it's embarrassing. This time a bunch of minor celebrities find themselves behind the wheels after the original racers are jailed by sheriff Peter Boyle. John Candy manages to rise above the material and Brooke Shields sportingly makes fun of her image, but as for the rest... Contains some coarse language. ▭

John Candy *Charlie Cronyn* • Donna Dixon *Tiffany* • Matt Frewer *Alec* • Joe Flaherty *Vic* • Tim Matheson *Jack* • Mimi Kuzyk *Heather* • Melody Anderson *Lee* • Shari Belafonte *Margaret* • Peter Boyle *Chief Spiro T Edsel* • Lee Van Cleef *Grandfather* ■ *Dir* Jim Drake • *Scr* Michael Short

The Cannonball Run ★★ PG

Action comedy 1981 · US · Colour · 91mins

This big-budget take on the illegal coast-to-coast car race movie was made at the height of Burt Reynolds's stardom and Roger Moore's tenure as James Bond. Not surprisingly it was a global smash, but as entertainment it leaves a lot to be desired. There's not nearly enough pile-ups and too many duff jokes from a cameo-studded cast, who act as if they're all starring in each other's home movies. Dean Martin and Sammy Davis Jr offer a geriatric version of their Rat Pack routine; Farrah Fawcett makes Barbie look like Katharine Hepburn; and Jackie Chan's martial arts prowess is underused. You'd have thought Hal Needham would have learnt his lesson after *Smokey and the Bandit II*. ▭

Burt Reynolds *JJ McClure* • Roger Moore *Seymour* • Farrah Fawcett *Pamela* • Dom DeLuise *Victor* • Dean Martin *Jamie Blake* • Sammy Davis Jr *Fenderbaum* • Jack Elam *Doctor* • Adrienne Barbeau *Marcie* • Terry Bradshaw *Terry* • Jackie Chan *First Subaru*

driver • Jamie Farr *Sheik* • Peter Fonda *Chief biker* • Bianca Jagger *Sheik's sister* ■ *Dir* Hal Needham • *Scr* Brock Yates

Cannonball Run II ★ PG

Comedy 1983 · US · Colour · 103mins

One of the worst films ever made starring a plethora of old has-beens – Dean Martin, Sammy Davis Jr, Ricardo Montalban, Telly Savalas and, of course, Burt Reynolds – who try in vain to recapture the whimsical success of *The Cannonball Run*. This purports to be an all-action comedy, but should be approached with extreme caution; fluffing lines seems to be the order of the day. Contains some coarse language. ▭

Burt Reynolds *JJ McClure* • Dom DeLuise *Victor* • Dean Martin *Jamie Blake* • Sammy Davis Jr *Fenderbaum* • Jamie Farr *Sheik* • Telly Savalas *Hymie* • Shirley MacLaine *Veronica* • Jackie Chan *Jackie* • Frank Sinatra ■ *Dir* Hal Needham • *Scr* Hal Needham, Albert S Ruddy, Harvey Miller, from characters created by Brock Yates

Can't Buy Me Love ★★ PG

Comedy 1987 · US · Colour · 92mins

Fed up with his nerdy reputation at high school, Patrick Dempsey pays sexpot senior Amanda Peterson a hard-earned $1,000 to pose as his girlfriend for a month. The image-building works fine until she blows the gaff. A very predictable boy meets, hires and loses girl saga, this is given far too sentimental a spin to work well as romantic comedy in the "pretty woman goes to college" vein. Contains swearing. ▭

Patrick Dempsey *Ronald Miller* • Amanda Peterson *Cindy Mancini* • Courtney Gains *Kenneth Wurman* • Tina Caspary *Barbara* • Seth Green *Chuckie Miller* • Dennis Dugan *David Miller* ■ *Dir* Steve Rash • *Scr* Michael Swerdlick

Can't Hardly Wait ★★ 12

Romantic comedy
1998 · US · Colour · 96mins

Flat characters are stuck in underdeveloped situations in first-time directors Deborah Kaplan and Harry Elfont's attempt to recapture the mood of a John Hughes eighties teen comedy. Rather than crafting a post-modern *Breakfast Club*, they've made a bad *Porky's* retread instead. Set around a post-graduation party where couples meet, get drunk, indulge in bonding and gross slapstick, every stereotypical situation is pulled out of the old-hat formula plot to little effect. Contains swearing and sexual references. ▭ *DVD*

Jennifer Love Hewitt *Amanda Beckett* • Ethan Embry *Preston Meyers* • Charlie Korsmo *William Lichter* • Lauren Ambrose *Denise Fleming* • Peter Facinelli *Mike Dexter* • Melissa Joan Hart *Yearbook girl* ■ *Dir/Scr* Harry Elfont, Deborah Kaplan

Can't Help Singing ★★ U

Musical western 1944 · US · Colour · 90mins

An apt title indeed for this Deanna Durbin vehicle, and her devotees will doubtless embrace this western, vaguely influenced by the Broadway success of *Oklahoma!* (The film even includes a rip-off number entitled *Cal-i-for-ni-ay*.) Non-Durbin fans, however,

will struggle with the dumb plot (Deanna heads west to marry, then changes her mind), uncharismatic leading man Robert Paige and director Frank Ryan's non-existent grasp of simple film narrative.

Deanna Durbin *Caroline* • Akim Tamiroff *Gregory* • Robert Paige *Lawlor* • David Bruce *Latham* • Leonid Kinskey *Koppa* • Ray Collins *Senator Frost* • June Vincent *Miss MacLean* • Andrew Tombes *Sad Sam* ■ *Dir* Frank Ryan • *Scr* Lewis R Foster, Frank Ryan, from the novel *Girl of the Overland Trail* by Curtis B Warshawsky, Samuel J Warshawsky

Can't Stop the Music ★★★ PG

Musical 1980 · US · Colour · 117mins

Aspiring songwriter Steve Guttenberg and girlfriend Valerie Perrine scour Greenwich Village looking for singers to do justice to his music in this heavily fictionalised account of how disco sensation the Village People rose to fame. All references to the group's gay genesis were placed on the periphery for commercial safety, although much fun can be had spotting the deliberate clues planted by director Nancy Walker. Reviled at the time for being dishonest, coy and late, from a distance this camp catastrophe is great fun and sums up the entire hedonistic era. ▭

Valerie Perrine *Samantha Simpson* • Bruce Jenner *Ron White* • Steve Guttenberg *Jack Morell* • Paul Sand *Steve Waits* • Tammy Grimes *Sydney Channing* • June Havoc *Helen Morell* • Barbara Rush *Norma White* • Ray Simpson *Policeman* • David Hodo *Construction Worker* • Felipe Rose *Indian* • Randy Jones *Cowboy* • Glenn Hughes *Leatherman* • Alexander Briley *GI* ■ *Dir* Nancy Walker • *Scr* Bronte Woodard, Allan Carr

A Canterbury Tale ★★★★ U

Second World War drama
1944 · UK · BW · 119mins

Michael Powell and Emeric Pressburger's re-think of Chaucer is the most peculiar piece of wartime propaganda ever devised. Two army sergeants (one British, one American) and a girl arrive at a Kentish village which is within praying distance of Canterbury. The girls hereabouts fraternise with servicemen and one local yokel pours glue into their hair as punishment. While it's hard to convey the film's eerie shifts of mood, it impresses as a study of a community resistant to change. A far-sighted film, dismissed at the time, and lyrical in its celebration of a disappearing England. ▭ *DVD*

Eric Portman *Thomas Colpepper* • Sheila Sim *Alison Smith* • John Sweet *Bob Johnson* • Dennis Price *Peter Gibbs* • Charles Hawtrey *Thomas Duckett* • Hay Petrie *Woodcock* ■ *Dir/Scr* Michael Powell, Emeric Pressburger

The Canterbury Tales ★★★

Historical comedy drama
1971 · It/Fr · Colour · 104mins

Coming between *The Decameron* and *Arabian Nights* in Pier Paolo Pasolini's classic tales trilogy, this adaptation of Chaucer's masterpiece outraged the purists with its bawdy bowdlerisation. Reinforcing his status as auteur, Pasolini also guests as the poet accompanying the party of pilgrims, who relieve the tedium of their journey

to Beckett's shrine with a variety of tales. Glorying in the filth and vulgarity of medieval life and the grotesqueness of the characters, this is a film teeming with life and insight. An English/Italian language film.

Pier Paolo Pasolini *Geoffrey Chaucer* • Tom Baker *Jenkin* • Laura Betti *Wife of Bath* • JP Van Dyne *Cook* • Derek Deadman *Pardoner* • George Bethell Datch *Host of the Tabard* ■ *Dir* Pier Paolo Pasolini • *Scr* Pier Paolo Pasolini, from the stories by Geoffrey Chaucer

The Canterville Ghost ★★★

Supernatural comedy
1944 · US · BW · 95mins

An enjoyable MGM version of Oscar Wilde's story, with the wonderfully irascible Charles Laughton in the title role as the spirit who can only free himself from eternally roaming by performing one good deed. Made in the heat of wartime, this has dated owing to its emphasis on harmonising Anglo-American relationships. However, a super cast including talented moppet Margaret O'Brien, amiable Robert Young and suave Peter Lawford handle the stilted sentiments with aplomb.

Charles Laughton *Sir Simon De Canterville/ The Ghost* • Robert Young *Cuffy Williams* • Margaret O'Brien *Lady Jessica De Canterville* • William Gargan *Sergeant Benson* • Reginald Owen *Lord Canterville* • Peter Lawford *Anthony De Canterville* ■ *Dir* Jules Dassin • *Scr* Edwin Harvey Blum, from the story by Oscar Wilde

The Canterville Ghost ★★★

Supernatural comedy
1996 · US · Colour · 92mins

A fine adaptation of Oscar Wilde's fun fantasy about a cursed ghost and the young girl he befriends. This features *Star Trek: the Next Generation*'s Patrick Stewart (who also produced) and *Scream*'s Neve Campbell, who both deliver superb performances. The comedy side of the story is deliberately played down and the pathos brought centre stage, with touching results.

Patrick Stewart *Sir Simon De Canterville* • Neve Campbell *Virginia Otis* • Cherie Lunghi *Lucille Otis* • Donald Sinden *Mr Umney* • Joan Sims *Mrs Umney* • Leslie Phillips *Lord Henry* ■ *Dir* Sydney Macartney • *Scr* Robert Benedetti, from the story by Oscar Wilde

Canticle of the Stones ★★★

Documentary drama
1990 · Pal · Colour · 110mins

Following the acclaimed *Wedding in Galilee*, Michel Khleifi attempted to meld drama with archive footage in this study of life in Gaza between the riots of the sixties and the Intifada. The documentary material is particularly provocative, as various Palestinians recall the fighting that reduced their settlements to rubble and decimated a generation of their youth. The fictional segments, however, involving reunited lovers Bushra Karaman and Makram Khouri, are awash with pompous pronouncements which trivialise the genuine tragedy of this troubled region. Uncompromising in its politics yet naive in its execution, this is hard to watch but difficult to ignore. In Arabic with English subtitles.

Bushra Karaman • Makram Khouri ■ *Dir* Michel Khleifi

Canyon Passage ★★★★

Western   1946 · US · Colour · 91mins

Based on a novel by Ernest Haycox, author of *Stagecoach*, this routine story of harsh frontier life was one of the first mature postwar westerns. Director Jacques Tourneur makes wonderful use of the Oregon locations and lifts the material by his thoughtful staging of everything from a cabin-raising ceremony for a newly married couple to the saloon fight between hero Dana Andrews and heavy Ward Bond. Alas, Britain's Patricia Roc – making her bid for Hollywood fame – is no match for the fiery Susan Hayward.

Dana Andrews *Logan Stuart* • Brian Donlevy *George Camrose* • Susan Hayward *Lucy Overmire* • Patricia Roc *Caroline Marsh* • Ward Bond *Honey Bragg* • Andy Devine *Ben Dance* ■ *Dir* Jacques Tourneur • *Scr* Ernest Pascal, from the novel by Ernest Haycox

Cape Fear ★★★★ 15

Classic thriller   1962 · US · BW · 101mins

Not the slick Martin Scorsese remake, but the gripping original thriller about embittered ex-con Robert Mitchum terrorising the frightened family of the meek lawyer (Gregory Peck) who put him in prison. Great shocks increase the climactic suspense, with Mitchum giving a portrayal of villainy that's unforgettably vicious and sadistic. Director J Lee Thompson's skilful use of light and shadow enhances the uncomfortable mood, while Bernard Herrmann's score counterpoints the growing dread with deft precision. ▣

Gregory Peck *Sam Bowden* • Robert Mitchum *Max Cady* • Polly Bergen *Peggy Bowden* • Lori Martin *Nancy Bowden* • Martin Balsam *Mark Dutton* • Jack Kruschen *Dave Grafton* • Telly Savalas *Charles Sievers* ■ *Dir* J Lee Thompson • *Scr* James R Webb, from the novel *The Executioners* by John D MacDonald • *Cinematographer* Sam Leavitt

Cape Fear ★★★★ 18

Thriller   1991 · US · Colour · 122mins

Martin Scorsese has flirted with Hollywood in the past, but this remake of the Robert Mitchum classic is an unashamed bid for the mainstream. Regular collaborator Robert De Niro takes the Mitchum role, playing a psychotic ex-convict who torments his former attorney Nick Nolte. De Niro is way over the top as the Bible-babbling psychopath, but where Scorsese scores is in his portrayal of Nolte and his family (Jessica Lange, Juliette Lewis). Whereas in the original they were the embodiment of apple-pie American values, here they are falling apart at the seams. Scorsese brings a dazzling array of cinematic techniques to the party and only loses his way in a crowd-pleasing but ludicrous finale. The original stars Gregory Peck, Martin Balsam and Mitchum himself pop up in cameo roles, and there is also strong support from Joe Don Baker. Contains swearing and violence. ▣

Robert De Niro *Max Cady* • Nick Nolte *Sam Bowden* • Jessica Lange *Leigh Bowden* • Juliette Lewis *Danielle Bowden* • Joe Don Baker *Claude Kersek* • Robert Mitchum *Lieutenant Elgart* • Gregory Peck *Lee Heller* •

Martin Balsam *Judge* • Illeana Douglas *Lori Davis* ■ *Dir* Martin Scorsese • *Scr* Wesley Strick, from the 1962 film, from the novel *The Executioners* by John D MacDonald • *Cinematographer* Freddie Francis

Capone ★★★ 18

Biographical crime drama
1975 · US · Colour · 97mins

Ben Gazzara gained 20 pounds by eating spaghetti for the title role in this slick exploitation biography of Al Capone. Showing the rise of the iron-hearted, death-dealing kingpin of Chicago's machine-gun mobs in the Roaring Twenties, his fall at the hands of the tax men and descent into syphilitic madness, director Steve Carver emphasises fast-paced action, copious blood-letting and speakeasy atmospheres above the true facts. Sylvester Stallone plays Frank "The Enforcer" Nitti, Capone's treacherous lieutenant. ▣

Ben Gazzara *Al Capone* • Susan Blakely *Iris Crawford* • Harry Guardino *Johnny Torrio* • John Cassavetes *Frankie Yale* • Sylvester Stallone *Frank Nitti* ■ *Dir* Steve Carver • *Scr* Howard Browne

Cappuccino ★★★

Comedy   1989 · Ausl · Colour · 86mins

As with most cappuccinos, this Australian film is all froth and precious little substance. Yet there is something about this portrait of Sydney theatreland that keeps you going to the bitter end. It's certainly not the script, which lurches from chic café chit-chat to broad comedy, and from crime to frantic chase sequences with little cohesion. What saves this lukewarm offering are the performances, with Rowena Wallace as a stage star who wants to direct and viciously ambitious Cristina Parker the standouts. Contains swearing.

John Clayton *Max* • Rowena Wallace *Anna French* • Jeanie Drynan *Maggie Spencer* • Barry Quin *Larry* • Cristina Parker *Celia* • Ritchie Singer *Bollinger* • Simon Mathew *Nigel* ■ *Dir* Anthony Bowman [Antony J Bowman] • *Scr* Anthony Bowman

Caprice ★★★ U

Comedy thriller   1967 · US · Colour · 97mins

The later movies of Doris Day now look like period artefacts. Here she plays an agent working for an international cosmetics company in a confection co-produced by her then-husband, Martin Melcher. Director Frank Tashlin shows his usual deft hand with a daft plot and is skilled in getting the most out of the widescreen format, despite Day's apparent insistence that her close-ups were filmed through multi-layered gauze. Day's co-star is a quaintly cast Richard Harris, in the same year he made *Camelot*, whose own insistence on wearing blue eye shadow effectively sabotages his right to be taken seriously. Best viewed as a sixties period piece: not quite as chic and modish as it thinks it is, but by no means negligible either. ▣

Doris Day *Patricia Foster* • Richard Harris *Christopher White* • Ray Walston *Stuart Clancy* • Jack Kruschen *Matthew Cutter* • Edward Mulhare *Sir Jason Fox* • Lilia Skala *Madame Piasco* • Michael J Pollard *Barney* ■ *Dir* Frank Tashlin • *Scr* Jay Jayson, Frank Tashlin, from a story by Martin Hale

Capricious Summer ★★★★★

Period drama   1968 · Cz · Colour · 78mins

It's not often that you come across a method director, but Jiří Menzel learned to walk the tightrope for his role as an itinerant showman in this enchanting period comedy. He also manages to slip a little subversive allegory into the story of a trio of friends whose tranquil existence is shaken by the appearance of Menzel's stunning wife, Jana Drchalova. Although perfectly capturing the ambience of provincial life, the film's real strength is the impeccable performances of swimming pool boss Rudolf Hrusinsky, indolent mayor Vlastimil Brodsky and priest Frantisek Rehak. In Czech with English subtitles.

Rudolf Hrusinsky *Dura* • Vlastimil Brodsky *Major Hugo* • Mila Myslikova *Durova* • Frantisek Rehak *Abbé Roch* • Jana Drchalova *Anna* • Jiří Menzel *Arnostek* ■ *Dir* Jiří Menzel • *Scr* Jiří Menzel, from a novel by Vladislav Vancura, Vaclau Nyult

Capricorn One ★★★★ PG

Thriller   1978 · US · Colour · 118mins

Did the Americans really land on the Moon, or did they fake it in a TV studio? That's the premise of this ingenious thriller, in which three men are bound for Mars until there's a technical slip-up on the launch pad. The astronauts end up faking the mission to save face but their space capsule (which went without them) burns up on re-entry. Problem one: three embarrassingly alive astronauts. Problem two: their distraught families. Problem three: Elliott Gould as a nosey reporter. Directed by Peter Hyams with real flair, this is hugely enjoyable, all the way to the gripping finale with Telly Savalas relishing his fun role as an old-time crop-dusting pilot who's got the right stuff. ▣ **DVD**

Elliott Gould *Robert Caulfield* • James Brolin *Charles Brubaker* • Sam Waterston *Peter Willis* • Brenda Vaccaro *Kay Brubaker* • OJ Simpson *John Walker* • Hal Holbrook *Dr James Kelloway* • Karen Black *Judy Drinkwater* • Telly Savalas *Albain* ■ *Dir/Scr* Peter Hyams

The Captain ★★★

Period drama   1960 · Fr/It · Colour · 115mins

While it is hard to fault the period trappings and sense of time and place created by director André Hunebelle, this is a pale imitation of the kind of rousing swashbuckler that came from the pen of Alexandre Dumas. Set in 17th-century France, it concerns the plot of Marie de Medicis to murder her son, Louis XIII. Having just completed *The Testament of Orpheus*, Jean Marais is more statuesque than ever as a loyal courtier. Not even the attentions of Elsa Martinelli can rouse him from his lethargy. French dialogue dubbed into English.

Jean Marais *François de Capestang* • Elsa Martinelli *Gisele d'Angoulême* • Bourvil *Cogolin* • Arnoldo Foa *Concini* • Pierrette Bruno *Giuseppa* • Christian Fourçade *Louis XIII* ■ *Dir* André Hunebelle • *Scr* Jean Halain, André Hunebelle, Pierre Foucard, from the novel by Michel Zevaco

Captain America ★★ U

Fantasy adventure
1979 · US · Colour · 93mins

It's odd that the most patriotic superhero of all, in the United States at least, is the one who has failed to take off. In this TV movie, Reb Brown has the necessary physique but little else as he dons the stars-and-stripes costume to save Phoenix from being blown up by a neutron bomb. An even sillier sequel followed, and there was a movie version in 1990, but in both cases the concept failed to grab the public's imagination. ▣

Reb Brown *Steve Rogers/Captain America* • Len Birman *Dr Simon Mills* • Heather Menzies *Dr Wendy Day* • Steve Forrest *Lou Brackett* • Robin Mattson *Tina Hayden* ■ *Dir* Rod Holcomb • *Scr* Don Ingalls, from a story by Chester Krumholz, Don Ingalls

Captain America ★★ PG

Action adventure   1990 · US · Colour · 93mins

This is another botched attempt to revive the popular American cartoon character, with Matt Salinger battling the evil Red Skull. Albert Pyun is a competent director of sci-fi and martial arts action movies, but this tough, brooding comic-book fantasy suffers in comparison to other big-budget superhero adventures. There is, however, solid support from such old hands as Ned Beatty, Ronny Cox and Darren McGavin. Contains comic-book violence and mild swearing. ▣

Matt Salinger *Steve Rogers/Captain America* • Ned Beatty *Sam Kolawetz* • Scott Paulin *Red Skull* • Ronny Cox *President Tom Kimball* • Darren McGavin *General Fleming* • Melinda Dillon *Mrs Rogers* ■ *Dir* Albert Pyun • *Scr* Stephen Tolkin

Captain Apache ★★★

Western   1971 · US/Sp · Colour · 96mins

One of a series of ferociously violent westerns produced by a group of left-leaning American expatriates who fetched up in Spain in the late sixties and early seventies. Director Alexander Singer once made a now forgotten mini-masterpiece, *A Cold Wind in August*, but he seems less happy here. Nevertheless, there's some real tension generated amid the excellent use of the landscape, while English character actor Percy Herbert holds his own against such western stalwarts as Stuart Whitman and Lee Van Cleef. Contains swearing.

Lee Van Cleef *Captain Apache* • Carroll Baker *Maude* • Stuart Whitman *Griffin* • Percy Herbert *Moon* • Elisa Montes *Rosita* • Tony Vogel *Snake* • Charles Stalnaker *O'Rourke* • Charlie Bravo *Sanchez* ■ *Dir* Alexander Singer • *Scr* Milton Sperling, Philip Yordan, from the novel by SE Whitman

Captain Blood ★★★★ PG

Adventure   1935 · US · BW · 94mins

"Come, feel the wind that fills the sails that carry us all to freedom!" Errol Flynn, a last-minute substitute for asthma sufferer Robert Donat, stars as Peter Blood, doctor turned swashbuckler, in Michael Curtiz's enjoyable adventure. Flynn was never much of an actor, but the camera (and the ladies) loved his devil-may-care arrogance, and *Captain Blood* remains important as the first leading role of

one of the greatest movie legends. Today, though, it's a little long and creaks in places. 📺

Errol Flynn *Captain Blood* • Olivia de Havilland *Arabella Bishop* • Lionel Atwill *Colonel Bishop* • Basil Rathbone *Captain Levasseur* • Ross Alexander *Jeremy Pitt* • Guy Kibbee *Hagthorpe* ■ *Dir* Michael Curtiz • *Scr* Casey Robinson, from the novel by Rafael Sabatini

Captain Boycott ★★★

Historical drama   1947 · UK · BW · 92mins

A "serious comedy" from the team of Frank Launder and Sidney Gilliat about absentee British landowners in Ireland and their rebellious Irish workers. Set in the 1880s, it stars Stewart Granger and Kathleen Ryan, with Cecil Parker as the unpleasant Boycott, whose name entered the language after a failed attempt to collect the rent by force. Lavishly made, partly on location, it falls uneasily between historical adventure and political lampoon.

Stewart Granger *Hugh Davin* • Kathleen Ryan *Anne Killain* • Cecil Parker *Contessa Francesca De Cresci* • Angela Clarke *Serafina* • Richard Avonde *Count Carlo De Cresci* • Joseph Calleia *Dr Lunati* ■ *Dir* Mitchell Leisen • *Scr* Robert Thoeren, from the novel *After Midnight* by Martha Albrand

Captain Carey, USA ★★

Spy drama   1950 · US · BW · 82mins

Alan Ladd is the US army captain sent to an Italian town to root out Nazi collaborators who betrayed his compatriots during the Second World War. A promising premise, but the plot is a mass of confusion that defeats director Mitchell Leisen and leaves the viewer feeling as numb as Ladd looks. Wanda Hendrix plays the love interest effectively enough, but the only real success is the Oscar-winning song *Mona Lisa*, which sold a million copies for Nat King Cole.

Alan Ladd *Webster Carey* • Wanda Hendrix *Giula* • Celia Lovsky *Contessa Francesca De Cresci* • Angela Clarke *Serafina* • Richard Avonde *Count Carlo De Cresci* • Joseph Calleia *Dr Lunati* ■ *Dir* Mitchell Leisen • *Scr* Robert Thoeren, from the novel *After Midnight* by Martha Albrand

Captain Eddie ★★★ U

Biographical drama 1945 · US · BW · 107mins

The life and times of Eddie Rickenbacker, the First World War flying ace and racing driver, are re-created in this lavish biopic. The focal point is the time when he crashed his plane and nearly drowned in the middle of the Pacific, an event which makes his whole life pass in front of him – and us. Fred MacMurray handles the part with his customary charm; you really believe he's a hero who can handle everything with a shrug and a grin. The film is episodic and not without its dull stretches, but it's still a genuine slice of Americana.

Fred MacMurray *Eddie Rickenbacker* • Lloyd Nolan *Lieutenant Whittaker* • Charles Bickford *William Rickenbacker* • Thomas Mitchell *Ike Howard* • Lynn Bari *Adelaide Frost* • Mary Phillips *Elsie Rickenbacker* • Richard Conte *Bartek* ■ *Dir* Lloyd Bacon • *Scr* John Tucker Battle

Captain from Castile ★★★

Adventure   1947 · US · Colour · 139mins

An expansive and sumptuous 20th Century-Fox epic, set around the 16th-century conquest of Mexico by Cortez (one of Cesar Romero's best performances) and distinguished by one of the finest musical scores in Hollywood history. Today's audiences may be less tolerant of its length, and a miscast Tyrone Power grows ever more wooden as the tortuous tale of revenge and greed unfurls. Despite its shortcomings, though, this is diverting and colourful entertainment.

Tyrone Power *Pedro De Vargas* • Jean Peters *Catana Perez* • Cesar Romero *Hernando Cortez* • Lee J Cobb *Juan Garcia* • John Sutton *Diego De Silva* • Antonio Moreno *Don Francisco* ■ *Dir* Henry King • *Scr* Lamar Trotti, from the novel by Samuel Shellabarger

The Captain Hates the Sea ★★★

Comedy   1934 · US · BW · 84mins

Comedy tends to date more than any other genre, but there's still enjoyment to be had from this slightly wacky film based around the captain of an ocean liner, played by Walter Connolly. An episodic plot about some of the passengers includes an appearance by John Gilbert – ex-silent star, close companion of Garbo and notorious alcoholic – as a man trying to give up the bottle. Unusually for the time, the film was shot on location, and director Lewis Milestone keeps a tight rein on the various plot strands.

Victor McLaglen *Schulte* • Helen Vinson *Janet Grayson* • John Gilbert *Steve Bramley* • Alison Skipworth *Mrs Magruder* • Wynne Gibson *Mrs Jeddock* • Walter Connolly *Captain Helquist* ■ *Dir* Lewis Milestone • *Scr* Wallace Smith

Captain Horatio Hornblower ★★★ U

Swashbuckling adventure 1951 · UK · Colour · 116mins

Based on three separate CS Forester stories about the scourge of Napoleon's navy, this sprawling, handsome but flat feature suffers from too many shifts of emphasis between action adventure and psychological study. Gregory Peck (in a role originally meant for Errol Flynn) plays Hornblower as a high-principled stuffed shirt and thus confounds director Raoul Walsh's efforts to inject some pace. Virginia Mayo, as the Duke of Wellington's sister, further slows the proceedings as Horatio nurses her through a bout of fever. What should have been stirring stuff ends up becalmed.

Gregory Peck *Captain Horatio Hornblower* • Virginia Mayo *Lady Barbara Wellesley* • Robert Beatty *Lieutenant William Bush* • James Robertson-Justice *Quist* • Terence Morgan *Lieutenant Gerard* • Stanley Baker *Mr Harrison* • Christopher Lee *Captain* ■ *Dir* Raoul Walsh • *Scr* Ivan Goff, Ben Roberts, Aeneas MacKenzie, from the novels by CS Forester

Captain Hurricane ★★ U

Drama   1935 · US · BW · 71mins

RKO's investment in this much-vaunted adaptation of Sara Ware Bassett's long-forgotten seafaring novel *The Taming of Zenas Henry* did not bring the studio great success. Deprived of

action and saddled with dull minor characters, director John S Robertson soon found himself all at sea. But James Barton gives a good account of himself in his first talkie as the weather-beaten sailor whose retirement plans are shattered by the need to return to sea to pay his mortgage.

James Barton *Zenas Henry* • Helen Westley *Abbie* • Helen Mack *Matie* • Gene Lockhart *Capt Jeremiah* • Douglas Walton *Jimmy* • Henry Travers *Capt Ben* • Otto Hoffman *Silas Coffin* ■ *Dir* John S Robertson • *Scr* Joseph Lovett, from the novel *The Taming of Zenas Henry* by Sara Ware Bassett

Captain Jack ★★ PG

Comedy adventure
1998 · UK · Colour · 96mins

A slight but genial seafaring adventure, with Bob Hoskins playing the good captain of the title. Tiring of endless pleasure cruises, Jack decides to re-create the journey of an 18th-century whaler, Captain Scoresby, who sailed from Whitby to the Arctic. He assembles a disparate crew of loners and losers – including bickering sisters Gemma Jones and Anna Massey, Aussie drifter Peter McDonald and shy chip-shop worker Sadie Frost – and together they set off on the adventure of a lifetime. Jack Rosenthal's script lacks the sharpness of his best TV work, but the scenery is nice, the performances adept and the direction from Robert Young refreshingly uncynical. Contains mild swearing. 📺

Bob Hoskins *Captain Jack* • Anna Massey *Phoebe* • Gemma Jones *Eunice* • David Troughton *Emmett* • Peter McDonald *Andy* • Sadie Frost *Tessa* • Maureen Lipman *Miss Barbara Bostock* • Patrick Malahide *Mr Lancing* ■ *Dir* Robert Young • *Scr* Jack Rosenthal, from articles by Nick Davies

Captain January ★★★

Musical drama   1936 · US · BW · 78mins

This perky Shirley Temple vehicle casts her as a little girl rescued from a shipwreck that claims the life of her parents. Adopted by Guy Kibbee's kindly lighthouse keeper, she runs into trouble when the local truant officer, played by Sara Haden (later Aunt Milly of the Andy Hardy series), discovers her being taught how to spit into the wind and decides to dispatch her to boarding school. The highlight is Temple and Buddy Ebsen singing and dancing *At the Codfish Ball* to Jack Donahue's choreography. This was one of four 1936 releases that maintained Temple as the biggest box-office draw in America for the second year running.

Shirley Temple *Star* • Guy Kibbee *Captain January* • Slim Summerville *Captain Nazro* • June Lang *Mary Marshall* • Buddy Ebsen *Paul Roberts* • Sara Haden *Agatha Morgan* • Jane Darwell *Eliza Croft* ■ *Dir* David Butler • *Scr* Sam Hellman, Gladys Lehman, Harry Tugend, from a story by Laura E Richards

Captain Kidd ★★★

Swashbuckling adventure
1945 · US · BW · 89mins

Charles Laughton, his triumph as Captain Bligh in *Mutiny on the Bounty* behind him, takes to the high seas again in this period swashbuckler. The star is in barnstorming, picture-stealing form as the devious and bloodthirsty pirate, while his larger-than-life

posturings are both fearful and funny. Gilbert Roland and John Carradine make fine henchmen, Randolph Scott is the hero who nails Kidd, while Barbara Britton is the film's fleeting gesture towards romance.

Charles Laughton *Captain William Kidd* • Randolph Scott *Adam Mercy* • Barbara Britton *Lady Anne* • Reginald Owen *Cary Shadwell* • John Carradine *Orange Povey* • Gilbert Roland *Jose Lorenzo* • John Qualen *Bert Blivens* ■ *Dir* Rowland V Lee • *Scr* Norman Reilly Raine, from a story by Robert H Lee

Captain Kronos: Vampire Hunter ★★★

Horror   1972 · UK · Colour · 90mins

In a bid to revitalise the genre during the seventies, Hammer gave writer/director Brian Clemens, the brains behind *The Avengers*, carte blanche to bring new blood to the vampire myth. The result is a bright and breezy blend of horror, comedy, swashbuckler and Italian western that follows Captain Kronos (Horst Janson) as he tracks down aristocratic bloodsuckers, with a little help from a hunchback professor (John Carson) and an exotic gypsy dancer (Caroline Munro). A dead toad, buried in a box, will spring to life if a vampire walks over it – just one example of the undead rules introduced in a fun fear-frolic that became an instant Hammer cult.

Horst Janson *Captain Kronos* • John Carson *Dr Marcus* • John Cater *Professor Grost* • Shane Briant *Paul Durward* • Caroline Munro *Carla* • Ian Hendry *Kerro* • Wanda Ventham *Lady Durward* ■ *Dir/Scr* Brian Clemens

Captain Lightfoot ★★ U

Period adventure 1955 · US · Colour · 94mins

Rock Hudson stars as a 19th-century Irish rebel who joins an outfit led by Jeff Morrow to fight against the English. Morrow is wounded and leaves the heroics to Hudson, who, between battles, romances the boss's daughter (Barbara Rush). Authentic locations do little to rescue this dreary and basically uneventful adventure story, produced by Ross Hunter and directed by Douglas Sirk. Both men, and their handsome star, were clearly more at ease with such high-gloss soap operas as *Magnificent Obsession* and *All That Heaven Allows*.

Rock Hudson *Michael Martin* • Barbara Rush *Aga Doherty* • Jeff Morrow *John Doherty (Captain Thunderbolt)* • Kathleen Ryan *Lady Anne More* • Finlay Currie *Callahan* ■ *Dir* Douglas Sirk • *Scr* WR Burnett, Oscar Brodney, from a story by WR Burnett

Captain Nemo and the Underwater City ★ U

Fantasy adventure
1969 · UK · Colour · 105mins

MGM steered clear of Jules Verne novels after its disastrous early talkie adaptation of *Mysterious Island* in 1929. Undoubtedly, the success of Disney's *20,000 Leagues under the Sea* influenced this change of heart, but the 15-year gap between the films and the fact that this was made by MGM's British operation suggest that no one had any real faith in the project. Robert Ryan as Nemo looks as if experiencing the "bends" would be preferable to participating in the picture, which has barely adequate effects and a shoddy script made up of borrowed ideas.

Robert Ryan *Captain Nemo* • Chuck Connors *Senator Robert Fraser* • Nanette Newman *Helena* • John Turner *Joab* • Luciana Paluzzi *Mala* • Bill Fraser *Barnaby* • Kenneth Connor *Swallow* • Allan Cuthbertson *Lomax* • Christopher Hartstone *Philip* ■ *Dir* James Hill • *Scr* Jane Baker, R Wright Campbell, from characters created by Jules Verne

Captain Newman, MD ★★★

Comedy drama 1963 · US · Colour · 126mins

Gregory Peck is the military hospital psychiatrist dealing with three cases involving guilt. Corporal Bobby Darin believes himself to be a coward; colonel Eddie Albert feels responsible for the deaths of his men in combat; while Robert Duvall hates himself for hiding out in Nazi territory. The actors are good, with Peck in a role tailor-made for his earnest persona, and there are bonuses in the form of Tony Curtis as a hospital orderly and Angie Dickinson as a nurse. Directed by David Miller, it's entertaining up to a point, but suffers from its uncomfortable mix of drama, sentimentality and comedy.

Gregory Peck *Capt Josiah Newman* • Tony Curtis *Corporal Jackson Laibowitz* • Angie Dickinson *Lieutenant Francie Corum* • Eddie Albert *Colonel Bliss* • Bobby Darin *Corporal Jim Tompkins* • Robert Duvall *Captain Paul Cabot Winston* ■ *Dir* David Miller • *Scr* Richard L Breen, Phoebe Ephron, Henry Ephron, from a novel by Leo Rosten

Captain Nuke and the Bomber Boys ★★

Crime adventure 1995 · US · Colour · 87mins

A slight but amusing children's film, of interest to grown-ups thanks to the surprising quality of its cast. Martin Sheen, Rod Steiger, Joe Mantegna and *Star Trek: Voyager* star Kate Mulgrew lend their talents to this tale of a group of young boys who discover an old atomic bomb and use it to get the President to cancel school. In true *Home Alone* style, all the adults – including the FBI – spend their time bumbling around. This results in a few laughs, but one can't help thinking that such heavyweight talent is wasted in a kids' caper flick.

Martin Sheen *Jeff Snyder* • Joe Mantegna *Joey Franelli* • Joanna Pacula *Brenda Franelli* • Joe Piscopo *Mr Wareman* • Rod Steiger *The President* • Ryan Thomas Johnson *The Slug* • Joshua Schaefer *Mickey Boyle* • Michael Bower *Frank Pescoe* • Kate Mulgrew *Mrs Pesco* ■ *Dir/Scr* Charles Gale

Captain Ron ★★🅿🄶

Comedy 1992 · US · Colour · 95mins

There's not much worth noting in this Disney attempt at maritime comedy, in which Kurt Russell dons an eye-patch and something that looks like a bikini. When businessman Martin Short and his wife Mary Kay Place set sail with his sassy kids, they hire Russell for his supposed sailing expertise. Needless to say, their best-laid plans are soon up the creek without a paddle. Although the film contains some hilarious moments, they are too few and far between. Contains some coarse language. 📺

Kurt Russell *Captain Ron* • Martin Short *Martin Harvey* • Mary Kay Place *Katherine Harvey* • Benjamin Salisbury *Benjamin Harvey* • Meadow Sisto *Caroline Harvey* • Emmanuel Logrono *General Armando* • Jorge Luis Ramos *General's Translator* • JA Preston *Magistrate* ■ *Dir* Thom Eberhardt • *Scr* Thom Eberhardt, John Dwyer, from a story by John Dwyer

Captain Scarlett ★★🅄

Period action adventure 1953 · US · Colour · 75mins

The Mexican locations and supporting cast are a major stumbling block for this would-be swashbuckler that is actually set in post-Napoleonic France. Producer Howard Dimsdale should be applauded for refusing to settle for backlot "realism", but director Thomas Carr seems as indifferent to the location as he is to the pacing and content of the narrative. Mercifully, Richard Greene, warming up for his stint as TV's Robin Hood, is on noble form, as he returns from war to find his estates misappropriated by scheming duke Manolo Fabregas and princess Leonora Amar in the clutches of slavering count, Eduardo Noriega.

Richard Greene *Captain Scarlett* • Leonora Amar *Princess Maria* • Nedrick Young *Pierre DuCloux* • Manolo Fabregas *Duke of Corlaine* • Eduardo Noriega *Count Villiers* • Isobel del Puerto *Josephine* • Carlos Muzquiz *Etienne Dumas* • George Trevino *Friar* ■ *Dir* Thomas Carr • *Scr* Howard Dimsdale

Captains Courageous ★★★🅄

Adventure 1937 · US · BW · 111mins

Spencer Tracy landed an Oscar for the unlikely role of a Portuguese fisherman with a penchant for sea shanties in MGM's big-budget rendering of Rudyard Kipling's adventure tale. A pampered young toff (Freddie Bartholomew) falls off a liner and is scooped from the briny by a fishing crew, who teach him the basics of life. A box-office hit at the time, it now shows its age, while Tracy's Portuguese lilt takes a while to get used to. But the sum of the parts remains wholesome family entertainment.

Spencer Tracy *Manuel* • Freddie Bartholomew *Harvey* • Lionel Barrymore *Disko* • Melvyn Douglas *Mr Cheyne* • Mickey Rooney *Dan* • Charley Grapewin *Uncle Salters* • John Carradine *"Long Jack"* • Oscar O'Shea *Cushman* ■ *Dir* Victor Fleming • *Scr* John Lee Mahin, Marc Connelly, Dale Van Every, from the novel by Rudyard Kipling

Captains Courageous ★★

Adventure 1995 · US · Colour · 93 mins

Although it hasn't aged well, the Spencer Tracy version of *Captains Courageous* remains a family classic. This watered-down TV remake was never likely to challenge that status. Bland TV nice guy Robert Urich steps into the Tracy role as the grumpy fisherman who rescues spoilt brat Kenny Vadas from the sea and teaches him to be a better person. Director Michael Anderson provides a more believable portrait of life at sea than Victor Fleming did, but the Urich/Vadas double act is no substitute for the Tracy/Freddie Bartholomew pairing.

Robert Urich *Matt Troop* • Kenny Vadas *Harvey Cheyne Jr* • Kaj Erick-Eriksen *Dan*

Troop • Sandra Nelson *Mary Ann Troop* ■ *Dir* Michael Anderson • *Scr* John McGreevey, from the novel by Rudyard Kipling

Captains of the Clouds ★★★🅄

Second World War drama 1942 · US · Colour · 113mins

Happy to support the war effort, Warner Bros recruited some of their finest, led by James Cagney, to join the Royal Canadian Air Force and fight the Germans. Despite Cagney's initial cockiness (irritating to Canadians who knew there was more at stake than American machismo), the result was this patriotic propaganda piece, directed with his usual efficiency by Michael Curtiz who, the same year, made the more subtle and romantic anti-Nazi movie *Casablanca*.

James Cagney *Brian Maclean* • Dennis Morgan *Johnny Dutton* • Brenda Marshall *Emily Foster* • Alan Hale *Tiny Murphy* • George Tobias *Blimp Lebec* • Reginald Gardiner *Scrounger Harris* • Reginald Denny *Commanding Officer* ■ *Dir* Michael Curtiz • *Scr* Arthur T Horman, Richard Macaulay, Norman Reilly Raine, from a story by Arthur T Horman, Roland Gillette

The Captain's Paradise ★★★🅄

Comedy 1953 · UK · BW · 85mins

Alec Coppel received an Oscar nomination for the original story of this self-satisfied British comedy, in which bigamy is laughed off as the ideal solution to the sociosexual vacillation of an outwardly charming sea captain. Called upon to do little more than vegetate in Gibraltar and tango around Tangier, Alec Guinness cruises through this lightweight picture, which charts an even more predictable course than the ferry he commands. Yvonne De Carlo confuses noise with exoticism, but Celia Johnson is splendid as the mouse wife who discovers, in the bazaars of North Africa, that there is more to life than warming slippers. 📺

Alec Guinness *Captain Henry St James* • Yvonne De Carlo *Nita* • Celia Johnson *Maud* • Charles Goldner *Chief Officer Ricco* • Miles Malleson *Lawrence St James* • Bill Fraser *Absalom* • Tutte Lemkow *Principal Dancer* ■ *Dir* Anthony Kimmins • *Scr* Alec Coppel, Nicholas Phipps, from a story by Alec Coppel

The Captain's Table ★★🅄

Comedy 1958 · UK · Colour · 86mins

Richard Gordon's *Doctor* series had been the mainstay of the Rank Organisation in the fifties. This adaptation of another Gordon novel was obviously something of a gratuity for services rendered, as almost every scene seems like an out-take from *Doctor at Sea*. At the helm is John Gregson as a bluff sea cove whose colourful cargo-ship banter is hardly suitable for the passengers of the luxury liner he now commands. The class clash throws up the usual cosy gags, but there is little to smile about in the gold-digging of Peggy Cummins, Nadia Gray and Joan Sims. 📺

John Gregson *Captain Ebbs* • Peggy Cummins *Mrs Judd* • Donald Sinden *Shawe-Wilson* • Nadia Gray *Mrs Porteous* • Maurice Denham *Major Broster* • Reginald Beckwith *Burtweed* • Bill Kerr *Bill Coke* • Joan Sims *Maude*

Pritchett ■ *Dir* Jack Lee • *Scr* John Whiting, Bryan Forbes, Nicholas Phipps, from the novel by Richard Gordon

Captive ★★★🔞

Thriller 1986 · UK/Fr · Colour · 94mins

Wealthy heiress Irina Brook is kidnapped, brainwashed and eventually re-educated by terrorists to recognise the hollowness of her existence in a vague approximation of the Patty Hearst story. Multi-layered in thematic structure (as one would expect from writer/director Paul Mayersberg, who wrote the screenplay for Nicolas Roeg's *The Man Who Fell to Earth*), this is a constantly intriguing, if overly intellectual polemic on privilege and self-discovery. 📺

Irina Brook *Rowena Le Vay* • Oliver Reed *Gregory Le Vay* • Xavier Deluc *D* • Corinne Dacla *Bryony* • Hiro Arai *Hiro* • Nick Reding *Leo* • Annie Leon *Pine* ■ *Dir/Scr* Paul Mayersberg

Captive ★★🔞

Thriller based on a true story 1991 · US · Colour · 93mins

Joanna Kerns, Barry Bostwick and Rob Lowe's brother Chad star in this TV tale, about a married couple who are held captive by a pair of rather nasty escaped prisoners. Unfortunately, this has all been done before, and better, in William Wyler's 1955 film *The Desperate Hours*. Occasionally disturbing but eminently missable. 📺

Barry Bostwick *Paul Plunk* • Joanna Kerns *Kathy Plunk* • John Stamos *Robert Knott* • Chad Lowe *Frost* • Patricia Charbonneau *Karen* • Jaclyn Hazeldine *Katie Plunk* • Teddie Stidder [Ted Stidder] *Rudy Bruger* ■ *Dir* Michael Tuchner • *Scr* Leonie Sandercock

The Captive City ★★★

Crime drama 1952 · US · BW · 91mins

An exposé of organised crime, as seen through the eyes of a small-town newspaper editor (John Forsythe). Using the documentary approach, director Robert Wise creates an excellent atmosphere of corruption, and the lack of star names adds to the general authenticity. The story is framed in flashback during Forsythe's journey to Washington where he testifies to the Senate Crime Investigating Committee headed by Senator Kefauver (who makes a cameo appearance). Estes Kefauver was a feared figure in Hollywood, having criticised the studios' glamorising of crime, so films like *The Captive City* and *Hoodlum Empire* (in which Brian Donlevy played a clone of the senator) were made to redress the balance.

John Forsythe *Jim Austin* • Joan Camden *Marge Austin* • Harold J Kennedy *Don Carey* • Ray Teal *Chief Gillette* • Marjorie Crossland *Mrs Sirak* • Victor Sutherland *Murray Sirak* ■ *Dir* Robert Wise • *Scr* Karl Kamb, Alvin M Josephy Jr, from a story by Alvin M Josephy Jr

The Captive Heart ★★★★🅿🄶

Second World War drama 1946 · UK · BW · 94mins

British cinema produced many fine prisoner-of-war movies, but this, made within a year of the liberation of the camps, is the best. Both Graham Greene's novel *The Tenth Man* and Billy Wilder's film *Stalag 17* owe debts

🅄 = SUITABLE FOR ALL   🅄𝖈 = SUITABLE FOR ALL, ESPECIALLY FOR YOUNG CHILDREN (VIDEO ONLY)   🅿🄶 = PARENTAL GUIDANCE

to it. Perhaps the most notable thing about the production is the almost documentary-like re-creation of the boredom, frustration and claustrophobia of stalag life. Basil Dearden's meticulous direction keeps melodrama at bay, but the real power of the piece comes from the performance of Michael Redgrave, who is superb as the frightened Czech whose deceptions arouse the suspicions of friend and foe alike. 🖵

Michael Redgrave *Captain Karel Hasek* • Rachel Kempson *Celia Mitchell* • Frederick Leister *Mr Mowbray* • Mervyn Johns *Private Evans* • Rachel Thomas *Mrs Evans* • Jack Warner *Corporal Horsfall* • Gladys Henson *Mrs Horsfall* • Gordon Jackson *Lieutenant Lennox* ■ *Dir* Basil Dearden • *Scr* Angus MacPhail, Guy Morgan, from a story by Patrick Kirwan

Captive Heart: the James Mink Story ★★

Period drama 1996 · US · Colour · 91 mins

A delightfully convoluted tale that is so bizarre it must be true. Louis Gossett Jr plays a wealthy black Canadian, married to Kate Nelligan, whose mixed-race daughter (Rachael Crawford) is sold into slavery by her evil husband, Peter Outerbridge. The couple must then make a perilous journey posing as mistress and slave to rescue her from the Deep South. The stranger-than-fiction story is given credibility by the committed performances and Bruce Pittman's straight-faced direction. Contains violence.

Louis Gossett Jr *James Mink* • Kate Nelligan *Elizabeth Mink* • Rachael Crawford *Mary Mink* • Peter Outerbridge *William Johnson* • Winston Rekert *Sherman Clay* • Ruby Dee *Mammy* ■ *Dir* Bruce Pittman • *Scr* Brian Bird, John Wierick, from a story by Bryon White

Captive Hearts ★ 15

Drama 1988 · US · Colour · 96 mins

An American serviceman, imprisoned by the Japanese during the Second World War, falls for a local girl in this lame drama, co-written by star Noriyuki "Pat" Morita (*The Karate Kid*). The script's weak plea for universal tolerance and world unity reduces proceedings to the level of a cartoon. Laughter, therefore, is the unplanned result as we glaze over at this woefully undernourished, starchy endeavour, which is so wooden you can almost hear the entire cast creak. 🖵

Chris Makepeace *Robert* • Noriyuki "Pat" Morita [Pat Morita] *Fukushima* • Michael Sarrazin *McManus* • Mari Sato *Miyoko* • Seth Sakai *Takayama* ■ *Dir* Paul Almond • *Scr* Noriyuki "Pat" Morita, John A Kuri, from an unproduced • *Scr* by Sargon Tamimi

A Captive in the Land ★★

Action drama
1991 · USSR/US · Colour · 96mins

The concept is familiar – a mismatched duo must bury their differences to survive in a hostile environment – but the striking locations rise it above the norm. Sam Waterston is the American pilot who forms an unlikely alliance with a Russian flyer (Alexander Potapov) when the two become stranded in the Arctic wastes. Based on the novel by James Alridge, this is essentially a two-hander which recycles more than a couple of

well-worn clichés. However, director John Berry skilfully evokes the desolation of their predicament.

Sam Waterston *Royce* • Alexander Potapov *Averyanov* ■ *Dir* John Berry • *Scr* Lee Gold, from a novel by James Aldridge

Captive of the Desert ★★★★ PG

Biographical drama
1990 · Fr · Colour · 101mins

Anyone seduced by the beauties of the desert while watching *The English Patient* should give this remarkable true-life tale a try. Although hardly saying a word, Sandrine Bonnaire gives a powerful performance portraying the story of Françoise Claustre, the Frenchwoman who was kidnapped as a political protest by a tribe of nomadic rebels in Chad in 1975. Director Raymond Depardon captures Bonnaire's shift from desperation to acclimatisation with great subtlety, while he records the daily rituals of the desert people (actually the Chirfa, Orida and Djaba tribes of Niger) with a respectful curiosity that makes the mundane seem fascinating. In French with English subtitles.

Sandrine Bonnaire *Frenchwoman* • Dobi Kor • Fadi Taha • Dobi Wachink • Badei Barka • Atchi Wahi-li • Daki Kor • Isai Kor • Brahim Barka ■ *Dir/Scr* Raymond Depardon

Captive Rage ★★ 18

Action adventure 1988 · US · Colour · 87mins

Oliver Reed plays South American despot General Belmondo, whose son is thrown in jail by Robert Vaughn of America's Drug Enforcement Agency. Mucho miffed by this, Reed retaliates big time by hijacking a plane of lissome young gringos – including Vaughn's daughter. The hostages are then routinely abused, tortured and fed to Reed's pet piranhas. This isn't a particularly subtle movie, with a platoon of scantily-clad girls, every one of whom turns out to be Reed's worst nightmare. For obscure financial reasons, it was made in Africa and aimed at the home video market. 🖵

Oliver Reed *General Belmondo* • Robert Vaughn *Eduard Delacorte* • Claudia Udy *Chiga* • Deon Stewardson *Carlos Belmondo* ■ *Dir* Cedric Sundstrom • *Scr* Rick Marx, Cedric Sundstrom, Peter Welbeck [Harry Alan Towers]

Captives ★★★ 15

Drama 1994 · UK · Colour · 95mins

Made by the BBC and given a limited cinema release, *Captives* stars Tim Roth – so good in Quentin Tarantino's *Pulp Fiction* and *Reservoir Dogs*, and even better in *Rob Roy* – and Julia Ormond, the English actress who made it big in Hollywood with *Legends of the Fall*, *First Knight* and *Sabrina*. Roth's in prison for mysterious reasons; Ormond's a dental surgeon, recently divorced, who examines his teeth and falls in love with him. From this decidedly offbeat premise emerges a strange love story and suspense thriller, tightly directed by Angela Pope and sharply written by Frank Deasy. There's fine support, too, from Keith Allen, Siobhan Redmond and Kenneth Cope. Contains violence, swearing and sex scenes. 🖵

Tim Roth *Philip Chaney* • Julia Ormond *Rachel Clifford* • Keith Allen *Lenny* • Siobhan Redmond *Sue* • Peter Capaldi *Simon* • Colin Salmon *Towler* • Richard Hawley *Sexton* • Annette Badland *Maggie* • Jeff Nuttall *Harold* • Kenneth Cope *Dr Hockley* • Mark Strong *Kenny* ■ *Dir* Angela Pope • *Scr* Frank Deasy

The Capture ★★★

Drama 1950 · US · BW · 90mins

A nifty little flashback movie from the pen of Niven Busch, who was also responsible for that bubbling cauldron of overwrought emotion *Duel in the Sun*. Busch's then-wife, Teresa Wright, gives a typically adroit performance as the widow involved with oil executive Lew Ayres, blissfully unaware that he killed her husband during an investigation of a payroll robbery. The script is occasionally overcooked, but the leads and the ever-sinister Victor Jory are eminently watchable. Director John Sturges makes the most of the Mexican locations and draws on his experience as an editor to keep the action ticking over.

Lew Ayres *Vanner* • Teresa Wright *Ellen* • Victor Jory *Father Gomez* • Jacqueline White *Luanda* • Jimmy Hunt *Mike* • Barry Kelley *Mahoney* • Duncan Renaldo *Carlos* • William Bakewell *Tobin* • Edwin Rand *Tevlin* ■ *Dir* John Sturges • *Scr* Niven Busch

The Car ★★

Horror 1977 · US · Colour · 98mins

An unlikely subject for *Cat Ballou* and *The Happening* director Elliot Silverstein, this schlock horror about a demonic killer car is not particularly original (watch *Duel* and *Christine* for better examples of the genre), but is nonetheless surprisingly effective. What success it does achieve is largely owing to its excellent use of night shooting and a superb dramatic use of sound from dubbing editor John Stacy. The cast – James Brolin, John Marley, RG Armstrong – is interesting, but the star is really the car.

James Brolin *Deputy Sheriff Wade Parent* • Kathleen Lloyd *Lauren* • John Marley *Sheriff Everett Peck* • RG Armstrong *Amos* • John Rubinstein *John Morris* • Elizabeth Thompson *Margie* ■ *Dir* Elliot Silverstein • *Scr* Dennis Shryack, Michael Butler, Lane Slate, from a story by Dennis Shryack

Car 54 Where Are You? ★★ 15

Comedy 1991 · US · Colour · 84mins

Yet another Hollywood movie with its origins in a TV sitcom. Devised originally by Nat Hiken, creator of the *Sergeant Bilko* TV series, the show teamed Joe E Ross and Fred Gwynne as the doltish cops who brought chaos to New York's 53rd Precinct. David Johansen and John C McGinley step into their uniforms for this drab reworking, which sees the officers trying to protect Mafia informer Jeremy Piven. There's an appearance from the underappreciated Fran Drescher and a guest spot for Al Lewis, reprising his original role of Schnauzer, but it's easy to see why this went unreleased for three years. Contains violence. 🖵

David Johansen *Officer Gunther Toody* • John C McGinley *Officer Francis Muldoon* • Fran Drescher *Velma Velour* • Nipsey Russell *Captain Dave Anderson* • Rosie O'Donnell *Lucille Toody* • Daniel Baldwin *Don Motti* •

Jeremy Piven *Herbert Hortz* • Al Lewis *Patrolman Leo Schnauzer* ■ *Dir* Bill Fishman • *Scr* Eric Tarloff, Ebbe Roe Smith, Peter McCarthy, Peter Crabbe, from a story by Nat Hiken, from the TV series by Eric Tarloff

Car of Dreams ★★ U

Musical comedy 1935 · UK · BW · 72mins

The British film industry has never been renowned for its musicals, but this romantic frippery is made more palatable by the sight of John Mills doing a spot of crooning and hoofing. Mills plays the son of a musical instrument tycoon, who poses as a chauffeur to win the heart of factory girl Grete Mosheim after she sets her heart on a gleaming white Rolls-Royce. Based on a popular German picture, the film was co-directed by Austin Melford (who wrote the original story) and Graham Cutts. The songs are pretty dire, but the presence of J Robertson Hare more than compensates.

John Mills *Robert Miller* • Mark Lester (2) *Miller Sr* • Norah Howard *Anne Fisher* • J Robertson Hare [Robertson Hare] *Henry Butterworth* • Grete Mosheim *Vera Hart* • Margaret Withers *Mrs Hart* ■ *Dir* Graham Cutts, Austin Melford • *Scr* C Stafford Dickens, R Benson, from a story by Austin Melford

Car Trouble ★ 18

Comedy 1985 · UK · Colour · 89mins

No wonder British film comedy was an endangered species in the mid-eighties. This tale of an adulterous wife who steals her husband's beloved Jaguar and proceeds to get stuck, literally, in flagrante with an obsequious car dealer would barely have provided enough sniggers for a sitcom. But director David Green strings it out to an excruciating 90 minutes that tax even Julie Walters's comic ingenuity. At least she gets some vulgarity to work with; poor Ian Charleson has to resort to comic fuming to put flesh on the bones of his cuckold caricature. 🖵

Julie Walters *Jacqueline Spong* • Ian Charleson *Gerald Spong* • Stratford Johns *Reg Sampson* • Vincenzo Ricotta *Kevin* • Hazel O'Connor *Maureen* ■ *Dir* David Green • *Scr* James Whaley, AJ Tipping

Car Wash ★★★★ PG

Comedy 1976 · US · Colour · 92mins

A great little movie, made for small change and all the bacon butties the crew could eat, that deservedly erupted into a major hit. The premise is simple, but bursting with energy and high octane joy. A bevy of finger snappin', jive talkin' car wash attendants josh and joke their way through 24 hours in their downmarket establishment's precarious life. The young men keep up a continual, good-natured line in fantasy and patter, with the obscure cultural references only adding to the movie's frenetic delights. A largely unknown cast, a barely known director and one run-down location all add up to a minor movie classic. Watch out for the Pointer Sisters and a cameo from Richard Pryor. Contains swearing. 🖵

Franklyn Ajaye *TC* • Sully Boyar *Mr B* • Richard Brestoff *Irwin* • George Carlin *Taxi driver* • Professor Irwin Corey *Mad Bomber* • Bill Duke

Duane • Antonio Fargas *Lindy* • Richard Pryor *Daddy Rich* ■ *Dir* Michael Schultz • *Scr* Joel Schumacher

Les Carabiniers ★★★

War drama 1963 · Fr/It · BW · 79mins

Jean-Luc Godard's bleak semi-documentary follows two uncouth, unwashed peasant boys who sign up for war, commit terrible crimes and are stunned when they are not regarded as heroes. The movie adopts a casual approach to violence that is reflected in the attitudes of its main characters. Critical reaction was so hostile that the film was initially withdrawn, while modern audiences may be confused by Godard's habitual cultural teasing, typified by odd inserts and allusions to Greek and Shakespearean tragedy. That said, it remains one of the most provocative studies of war ever filmed. In French with English subtitles.

Marino Mase *Ulysses* • Albert Juross *Michel-Ange* • Genevieve Galea *Venus* • Catherine Ribero *Cleopatre* • Gerard Poirot *1st Carabinier* • Jean Brassat *2nd Carabinier* • Alvaro Gheri *3rd Carabinier* • Barbet Schroeder *Car Salesman* ■ *Dir* Jean-Luc Godard • *Scr* Jean-Luc Godard, Jean Gruault, Roberto Rossellini, from the play *I Carabinieri* by Benjamino Joppolo

Caravaggio ★★★★ 18

Biographical drama
1986 · UK · Colour · 88mins

With Nigel Terry excelling in the lead, this portrait of the artist as a gay man is Derek Jarman's most accessible, revealing and beautiful work. By slotting anachronistic details into a *mise en scène* that is almost mannerist in its solemn grandeur, Jarman frees himself from the constraints of the traditional biopic in order to investigate not just the painter's relationships with male model Sean Bean and his mistress, Tilda Swinton, but also the animus of his inspiration. Also, since this is a study of a visual medium, he constantly forces us to seek significance in gestures, silences and exquisitely reproduced tableaux.

Nigel Terry *Caravaggio* • Sean Bean *Ranuccio Thomasoni* • Tilda Swinton *Lena* • Garry Cooper *Davide* • Spencer Leigh *Jerusaleme* • Nigel Davenport *Giustiniani* • Robbie Coltrane *Scipione Borghese* • Michael Gough *Cardinal Del Monte* ■ *Dir/Scr* Derek Jarman • *Cinematographer* Gabriel Beristain

Caravan ★★★ U

Period romantic drama
1946 · UK · BW · 102mins

This period melodrama from Gainsborough Studios was a huge hit in 1946, Stewart Granger's bare chest being just the thing to take women's minds off food and clothes rationing. Granger plays an impoverished writer who dallies with Jean Kent's gypsy dancer, but whose heart is really set on Anne Crawford's lady of the manor. Dennis Price oozes caddishness from every pore as Granger's deadly rival, while Robert Helpmann grovels at his feet and plots murder. Set in Spain in the 1840s, it's overdressed, overheated and deliriously silly.

Stewart Granger *Richard* • Anne Crawford *Oriana* • Jean Kent *Rosal* • Dennis Price *Francis* • Robert Helpmann *Wycroft* • Gerard Heinz *Don Carlos* • Arthur Goullet *Suiza* • John Salew *Diego* ■ *Dir* Arthur Crabtree • *Scr* Roland Pertwee, from the novel by Lady Eleanor Smith

Caravan to Vaccares ★★ 15

Action adventure
1974 · UK/Fr · Colour · 93mins

Caravan to vacuity, more like, in this implausible adaptation of a far-fetched Alistair Maclean novel in which boorish American David Birney and seductress Charlotte Rampling team up to try to smuggle Hungarian scientist Michael Bryant from Provence to New York. The lush Camargue locations and co-star Michel Lonsdale's ironic asides are two meagre reasons to watch.

Charlotte Rampling *Lila* • David Birney *Neil Bowman* • Michael Lonsdale [Michel Lonsdale] *Duc De Croytor* • Marcel Bozzuffi *Henri Czerda* • Michael Bryant *Stefan Zuger* ■ *Dir* Geoffrey Reeve • *Scr* Paul Wheeler, from the novel by Alistair Maclean

Caravans ★★

Adventure 1978 · US/Iran · Colour · 123mins

A year before he was deposed by the Ayatollahs, the Shah of Iran financed this flabby epic, based on James Michener's novel. Set in 1948, this tale of American beauty Jennifer O'Neill who runs off with desert chieftain Anthony Quinn is not a patch on John Milius's *The Wind and the Lion*, let alone *The Searchers*, to which it owes much. However, it offers some breathtaking (not to mention unfamiliar) scenery, beautifully shot by British maestro Douglas Slocombe, while Quinn adds another nationality to his ethnic bag of tricks.

Anthony Quinn *Zulfigar* • Michael Sarrazin *Mark Miller* • Jennifer O'Neill *Ellen Jasper* • Christopher Lee *Sardar Khan* • Joseph Cotten *Crandall* • Behrooz Vosoughi *Nazrullah* ■ *Dir* James Fargo • *Scr* Nancy Voyles Crawford, Thomas A McMahon, Lorraine Williams, from the novel by James Michener

Carbine Williams ★★

Crime drama 1952 · US · BW · 91mins

James Stewart played several real-life people in his illustrious film career, including Glenn Miller and Charles Lindbergh. Here he stars as Marsh Williams, the inventor of the M-1 carbine, a weapon that revolutionised modern warfare. One interesting feature of this rather dour story, directed by Richard Thorpe in a pedestrian manner, was that Williams did his work on the rifle while in prison for bootlegging. Jean Hagen is good as his devoted wife, while Wendell Corey is sympathetic as the warden.

James Stewart *Marsh Williams* • Jean Hagen *Maggie Williams* • Wendell Corey *Capt HT Peoples* • Carl Benton Reid *Claude Williams* • Paul Stewart *"Dutch" Kruger* • Otto Hulett *Mobley* • Rhys Williams *Redwick Karson* • Herbert Heyes *Lionel Daniels* ■ *Dir* Richard Thorpe • *Scr* Art Cohn

Carbon Copy ★ 15

Comedy drama 1981 · US · Colour · 87mins

This tepid race satire drives its point home with sledgehammer subtlety. The usually dependable George Segal is wasted here as Walter Whitney, a successful business executive whose life falls apart following the sudden arrival of the son he never knew he had. Shock, horror – the boy (Denzel Washington) is black! Susan Saint James tries hard as Segal's wife, but the two-dimensional script makes it heavy-going for all concerned.

George Segal *Walter Whitney* • Susan Saint James *Vivian Whitney* • Jack Warden *Nelson Longhurst* • Denzel Washington *Roger Porter* • Dick Martin *Victor Bard* • Paul Winfield *Bob Garvey* • Vicky Dawson *Mary Ann* ■ *Dir* Michael Schultz • *Scr* Stanley Shapiro

The Card ★★★ U

Drama 1952 · UK · BW · 87mins

Adapted from Arnold Bennett's 1911 novel, this is a stylish, if rather empty, rags to riches story set in the author's beloved Five Towns. Eric Ambler's script is full of smart situations and witty lines, but Alec Guinness is hardly stretched as "Denry" Machin, the laundress's son who achieves wealth and respectability through his Machiavellian machinations. There is admirable support from Glynis Johns and Valerie Hobson as the women in his life, but the film suffers from the attempt to cast it in the Ealing comedy mould. It's solid stuff, but too many involved seem to be marking time.

Alec Guinness *Edward Henry "Denry" Machin* • Glynis Johns *Ruth Earp* • Valerie Hobson *Countess of Chell* • Petula Clark *Nellie Cotterill* • Edward Chapman *Mr Duncalf* • Joan Hickson *Mrs Codleyn* • Michael Hordern *Bank manager* ■ *Dir* Ronald Neame • *Scr* Eric Ambler, from the novel by Arnold Bennett

Cardboard Cavalier ★★ U

Comedy 1949 · UK · BW · 99mins

Popular music hall duo Sid Field and Jerry Desmonde team up for this eager historical comedy that, in spite of some spirited playing, soon outstays its welcome. Set during the Cromwellian Commonwealth, the story, in which Field's barrow boy carries secret messages for Desmonde's Royalist spy, has all the appearances of being a flag-waver left over from the war, with puritanism continuously being equated with fascism. Field's high-camp style is an acquired taste, but Margaret Lockwood, the belle of many a British period piece, hurls herself into the part of Nell Gwynne and Irene Handl is splendid as a castle ghost.

Sid Field *Sidcup Buttermeadow* • Margaret Lockwood *Nell Gwynne* • Jerry Desmonde *Lovelace* • Jack McNaughton *Uriah Croup* • Alfie Dean *Murdercasket* • Brian Worth *Tom Pride* • Irene Handl *Lady Agnes* ■ *Dir* Walter Forde • *Scr* Noel Langley

The Cardinal ★★★★

Epic drama 1963 · US · Colour · 75mins

A magnificent though awfully long adaptation of one of those American doorstop novels about faith, produced on a vast transworld scale by director Otto Preminger. Despite its sweep, scale and obvious intelligence, however, this failed to make a dent in both screen history and the box office. The blame lies in the serious miscasting of Tom Tryon in the pivotal title role, as he lacks both range and sympathy. But Preminger surrounds him with a superb supporting cast including John Huston, Carol Lynley and Burgess Meredith, while the Technicolor photography is truly impressive. There's an awkward Hollywood moment involving a choir, but the rest of the movie rings true.

Tom Tryon *Stephen Fermoyle* • John Huston *Cardinal Glennon* • Raf Vallone *Cardinal Quarenghi* • Romy Schneider *Annemarie* • Carol Lynley *Mona/Regina Fermoyle* • Dorothy Gish *Celia Fermoyle* • Burgess Meredith *Father Ned Halley* • Ossie Davis *Father Gillis* ■ *Dir* Otto Preminger • *Scr* Robert Dozier, from the novel by Henry Morton Robinson • *Cinematographer* Leon Shamray

Cardinal Richelieu ★★★ U

Biography 1935 · US · BW · 82mins

This diverting biopic stars George Arliss as Louis XIII's first minister, whose plans to unify France earned him the enmity of the disaffected nobility and the king's womenfolk. Director Rowland V Lee has a tenuous grasp of the period atmosphere, but this scarcely matters as the historical facts are little more than an excuse for a series of melodramatic intrigues from which Arliss emerges triumphant like some scarlet-caped crusader. The complexities of 17th-century court life and diplomacy are somewhat enlivened by the support playing, most notably that of Edward Arnold as Louis and Cesar Romero as André de Pons.

George Arliss *Cardinal Richelieu* • Edward Arnold *Louis XIII* • Halliwell Hobbes *Father Joseph* • Maureen O'Sullivan *Lenore* • Cesar Romero *André de Pons* • Douglass Dumbrille *Baradas* ■ *Dir* Rowland V Lee • *Scr* Maude Howell, Cameron Rogers, WP Lipscomb, from the play by Edward Bulwer-Lytton

The Care Bears Adventure in Wonderland ★★ U

Animated adventure
1987 · Can · Colour · 75mins

Following on from *The Care Bears Movie* and *The Care Bears Movie II: a New Generation*, this third instalment in the lives of those loving, caring and sharing animated bears follows their adventures with Alice through the looking glass in Wonderland. Younger children will no doubt be happy to watch this tale, but even the youngest critic will probably grumble that it isn't as good as the first two.

Bob Dermer *Grumpy Bear* • Eva Almos *Swift Heart Rabbit* • Dan Hennessey *Brave Heart Lion/Dum* • Jim Henshaw *Tender Heart Bear* ■ *Dir* Raymond Jafelice • *Scr* Susan Snooks, John De Klein, from a story by Peter Sauder

The Care Bears Movie ★★ U

Animated adventure
1985 · Can · Colour · 75mins

Only teen bands have shorter life cycles than children's television characters, so it will be interesting to see how a generation reared on the Teletubbies reacts to their eighties equivalents. Although sixties luminaries Carole King and John Sebastian supply some tunes, there's not much in this for adults, and the animation seems tame compared to the computer-generated wizardry of today. Nevertheless, the film struck a chord with kids, spawning two sequels and a TV series.

Mickey Rooney *Mr Cherrywood* • Jackie Burroughs *The Spirit* • Harry Dean Stanton

...ion • Sunny Besen Thrasher *Jason* • Georgia ...ngel *Love-a-Lot* ■ *Dir* Arna Selzick • *Scr* ...eter Sauder

The Care Bears Movie II: a New Generation ★★ U

Animated adventure
1986 · US · Colour · 73mins

Pleasingly animated and full of the values to which we hope our children will one day aspire, this is still nothing more than a feature-length commercial for a range of soft toys. Its very title betrays the fact that the film is intended to promote such new characters as True Heart Bear and his faithful companion, Noble Heart Horse. Their camp-site adventure with the dastardly Dark Heart will hit the spot with the very youngest of viewers, but any grown-ups watching will be irritated by the twee songs and the sponsors' shameless marketing ploys.

Maxine Miller *True Heart Bear* • Pam Hyatt *Noble Heart Horse* • Hadley Kay *Dark Heart/ The Boy* • Dan Hennessey *Brave Heart Lion* • Billie Mae Richards *Tender Heart Bear* • Chris Wiggins *Great Wishing Star* ■ *Dir* Dale Schott • *Scr* Peter Sauder

Career ★★★

Drama
1959 · US · BW · 106mins

Anthony Franciosa is excellent in this screen version of James Lee's Broadway play about an aspiring actor waiting for his big break in New York. Directed by Joseph Anthony with an A-list cast – Shirley MacLaine as Franciosa's alcoholic wife, Dean Martin as a stage director, Carolyn Jones as a talent scout – the movie is too long and a little plodding, but is redolent with the smell of the greasepaint and the lure of applause. Gritty and authentic, it earned cinematographer Joseph LaShelle an Oscar nomination.

Anthony Franciosa *Sam Lawson* • Dean Martin *Maury Novak* • Shirley MacLaine *Sharon Kensington* • Carolyn Jones *Shirley Drake* • Joan Blackman *Barbara* • Robert Middleton *Robert Kensington* • Donna Douglas *Marjorie Burke* • Frank McHugh *Charlie* ■ *Dir* Joseph Anthony • *Scr* James Lee, from his play

Career Girls ★★★★ 15

Comedy drama
1997 · UK · Colour · 83mins

Mike Leigh isn't cinema's foremost realist, but he's definitely its most perceptive people-watcher. The deceptively simple characters he favours reveal hidden depths that make them utterly fascinating. Here, arrogantly affected Katrin Cartlidge and twitchly timid Lynda Steadman are pretty resistible during the flashbacks to their college days. But they capture our sympathies during a series of low-key misadventures with three old friends and a detestable newcomer. With its tentatively optimistic ending, this may be a small, rather safe film, yet it's also funny, touching and plausible. Contains swearing and sexual references. **DVD**

Katrin Cartlidge *Hannah Mills* • Lynda Steadman *Annie* • Kate Byers *Claire* • Mark Benton *Richard "Ricky" Burton* • Andy Serkis *Mr Evans* • Joe Tucker *Adrian Spinks* • Margo Stanley *Ricky's Nan* • Michael Healy *Lecturer* ■ *Dir/Scr* Mike Leigh

Career Opportunities ★★ 15

Comedy
1991 · US · Colour · 79mins

Written by teen chronicler John Hughes (*Pretty in Pink*, *The Breakfast Club*), this unexciting story has Frank Whaley as a young, incompetent con man hired as night watchman at a department store. On his first night on the job, he finds the town beauty (Jennifer Connelly) asleep in a changing room and thwarts some would-be thieves. It might have worked with a touch of fantasy, but the straightforward treatment means Bryan Gordon's bland comedy is never elevated above the routine.

Frank Whaley *Jim Dodge* • Jennifer Connelly *Josie McClellan* • Dermot Mulroney *Nestor Pyle* • Kieran Mulroney *Gil Kinney* • John M Jackson *Bud Dodge* • Jenny O'Hara *Dotty Dodge* • Barry Corbin *Officer Don* • John Candy *Store manager* ■ *Dir* Bryan Gordon • *Scr* John Hughes

Carefree ★★ U

Musical comedy
1938 · US · BW · 79mins

One of the weakest of the Astaire/ Rogers features, but there is still enough to enjoy in this rather silly musical comedy. Fred looks uneasy as a psychiatrist charged by best pal Ralph Bellamy with finding a cure for the latter's dippy fiancée Ginger, and she looks positively mortified at having to endure hypnotic mischief sequences. As far as the songs go, *The Yam* is a far cry from *The Continental*, but *Change Partners* is pleasing and the dream dance *I Used to Be Colour Blind* is suitably surreal. The highlight, however, is Fred's exquisite golfing routine.

Fred Astaire *Tony Flagg* • Ginger Rogers *Amanda Cooper* • Ralph Bellamy *Stephen Arden* • Luella Gear *Aunt Cora* • Jack Carson *Connors* • Walter Kingsford *Dr Powers* • Kay Sutton *Miss Adams* ■ *Dir* Mark Sandrich • *Scr* Ernest Pagano, Allan Scott, from a story by Dudley Nichols, Hagar Wilde, Marian Ainslee, Guy Endore • *Music* Irving Berlin

Careful ★★★★

Black comedy drama
1992 · Can · Colour · 100mins

Director Guy Maddin is something of a cult figure in Canadian cinema and this costume curio is his most ambitious and enjoyable project to date. Shot to look like a twenties melodrama – complete with stylised silent acting, dialogue captions and whole scenes tinted in atmospheric colours – it tells of the secret passions that lurk behind the respectable façade of the Bavarian town of Tolzbad, which is in such peril from avalanches that everyone talks in whispers or in specially soundproofed rooms to prevent disaster. Kyle McCulloch and Gosia Dobrowolska lead a cast all tuning in to Maddin's offbeat intentions. Contains sex scenes and nudity.

Kyle McCulloch *Grigorss* • Gosia Dobrowolska *Zenaida* • Sarah Neville *Klara* • Brent Neale *Johann* • Paul Cox *Count Knotgers* • Victor Cowie *Herr Trotta* ■ *Dir* Guy Maddin • *Scr* Guy Maddin, George Toles

Careful, He Might Hear You ★★★★ PG

Drama
1983 · Ausl · Colour · 112mins

In adapting Sumner Locke Elliott's novel for the screen, Carl Schultz has been careful to ensure that much of the action is seen from orphan Nicholas Gledhill's perspective as his aunts struggle for custody. Yet he also emphasises several adult themes, among them Australia's relationship with the "mother country", the impact of the Depression on all strata of society, and the role of women in a repressive patriarchy. John Stoddart's sets and John Seale's photography give the film a nostalgic glow.

Wendy Hughes *Vanessa* • Robyn Nevin *Lila* • Nicholas Gledhill *PS* • John Hargreaves *Logan* • Geraldine Turner *Vere* • Isabelle Anderson *Agnes* • Peter Whitford *George* • Colleen Clifford *Ettie* • Julie Nihill *Diana* ■ *Dir* Carl Schultz • *Scr* Michael Jenkins, from the novel by Sumner Locke Elliott

Careful, Soft Shoulder ★★★★ U

Second World War comedy drama
1942 · US · BW · 69mins

An engaging and intelligently subversive movie from director Oliver HP Garrett, who co-scripted *Duel in the Sun* with David O Selznick. Virginia Bruce stars as a world-weary social butterfly who casually mentions at a cocktail party that she fancies spying for the Nazis. Aubrey Mather takes her up on it. Told primarily in flashback by Bruce, whom Garrett interestingly makes sympathetic, this is a classy film with a witty central performance. It's all the more remarkable when one considers the majority of gung-ho dross on offer over at the time.

Virginia Bruce *Connie Mathers* • James Ellison *Thomas Aldrich* • Aubrey Mather *Mr Fortune* • Sheila Ryan *Agatha Mathers* • Ralph Byrd *Elliot Salmon* • Sigurd Tor *Milo* • Charles Tannen *Joe* ■ *Dir/Scr* Oliver HP Garrett

The Caretaker ★★★★

Drama
1964 · UK · BW · 102mins

One of Harold Pinter's most famous plays – a study in sinister pauses and comic shifts of emphasis – is wonderfully given over to its fine cast of actors. Alan Bates and Robert Shaw play two brothers who give shelter to Davies (Donald Pleasence), a scruffy tramp forever on his way to Sidcup. Either a doomy allegory or a realistic drama with menaces, it's directed without fuss by Clive Donner. A memorable piece of theatre, if not particularly effective as cinema.

Donald Pleasence *Davies* • Alan Bates *Mick* • Robert Shaw *Aston* ■ *Dir* Clive Donner • *Scr* Harold Pinter, from his play

The Caretakers ★

Melodrama
1963 · US · BW · 97mins

Considering its subject matter and setting (a mental hospital), producer/ director Hall Bartlett's incident-packed melodrama is almost insulting in its lack of seriousness, accuracy or insight. However, it's the kind of awful film which, viewed decades later, entertains for all the wrong reasons – notably Joan Crawford as a senior psychiatric nurse, locked in disagreement with medic Robert Stack's compassionate approach to the disturbed inmates. Electric shock treatment, attempted rape and arson are rife in the institution, presided over by the mellifluously voiced Herbert Marshall, but Stack's methods eventually bear fruit in an act of heroism by patient Polly Bergen. Hysterical, in every sense of the word.

Robert Stack *Dr Donovan MacLeod* • Polly Bergen *Lorna Melford* • Joan Crawford *Lucretia Terry* • Janis Paige *Marion* • Herbert Marshall *Dr Jubal Harrington* • Robert Vaughn *Jim Melford* ■ *Dir* Hall Bartlett • *Scr* Henry F Greenberg, from a story by Hall Bartlett, Jerry Paris and a novel by Dariel Telfer

The Carey Treatment ★★ 15

Mystery drama
1972 · US · Colour · 96mins

It would have been an unsuitable case for treatment by Inspector Clouseau. Yet, as it is, it's Clouseau creator Blake Edwards who's out on a limb with a bizarre plot involving a hospital racket in body parts. Instead of Clouseau, it has hip Californian pathologist James Coburn, who swings like a stethoscope but does not convince as he disentangles a colleague from a murder frame-up. Neither can Edwards persuade us that he himself is at home with this sort of drama which, as the body count rises, veers towards self parody. Contains some swearing.

James Coburn *Peter Carey* • Jennifer O'Neill *Georgia Hightower* • Pat Hingle *Captain Pearson* • Skye Aubrey *Angela Holder* • Elizabeth Allen *Evelyn Randall* • John Fink *Murphy* • Dan O'Herlihy *JD Randall* ■ *Dir* Blake Edwards • *Scr* James P Bonner, from the novel *A Case of Need* by Jeffrey Hudson

The Cariboo Trail ★★ U

Western adventure
1950 · US · Colour · 79mins

A moderately interesting Randolph Scott vehicle, produced by western veteran Nat Holt and written by skilled Frank Gruber. Both Holt and Gruber were perhaps better known for the TV series *Tales of Wells Fargo*, whose star, Dale Robertson, appears here in a supporting role. Victor Jory is Scott's usual snarling foe, but the real interest lies in the use of primitive two-strip Cinecolor, a process that's a far cry from the Technicolor of Scott's distinguished Warner Bros and Columbia output.

Randolph Scott *Jim Redfern* • George "Gabby" Hayes *Grizzly* • Bill Williams *Mike Evans* • Karin Booth *Frances* • Victor Jory *Frank Walsh* • Douglas Kennedy *Murphy* • Jim Davis *Miller* • Dale Robertson *Will Gray* ■ *Dir* Edwin L Marin • *Scr* Frank Gruber, from a story by John Rhodes Sturdy

Carla's Song ★★★★ 15

Drama
1996 · UK/Ger/Sp · Colour · 119mins

Just before *The Full Monty*, Robert Carlyle made this more sombre story of love among the revolutionaries for director Ken Loach. Carlyle is the Glasgow bus driver who falls in love with exotic Oyanka Cabezas, a refugee from war-torn Nicaragua. He insists they go there so that she can confront her demons, only for him to learn just what she's had to suffer. The story runs out of steam once the action moves from Scotland, but Loach is a persuasive propagandist and Carlyle has enormous charm. In English and Spanish with subtitles. Contains some violence and swearing. ▢

Robert Carlyle *George* • Oyanka Cabezas *Carla* • Scott Glenn *Bradley* • Salvador Espinoza *Rafael* • Louise Goodall *Maureen* • Richard Loza *Antonio* • Gary Lewis *Sammy* • Subash Singh Pall *Victor* • Stewart Preston *McGurk* ■ *Dir* Ken Loach • *Scr* Paul Laverty

Carlito's Way ★★★★ 18

Gangster drama 1993 · US · Colour · 138mins

Ten years after *Scarface*, Al Pacino and director Brian De Palma reunited for another crime-doesn't-pay drama. Pacino plays Puerto Rican hoodlum Carlito Brigante, sprung from jail by his lawyer Sean Penn and determined to go straight. But Penn, who fancies himself as a gangster, scoffs at the idea, and when Pacino meets up with his old acquaintances, he's soon back in trouble. Combined with regular scriptwriter David Koepp's smart and funny script, De Palma's visual flair comes into its own in the seedy milieu of New York's clubs and backstreet dives. The set pieces – a pool-room fight, a 15-minute subway chase and shenanigans on a train-station escalator – are among the most thrilling De Palma has ever filmed, while Pacino's restrained performance as the leather-clad, gently lisping Pacino allows plenty of scope for the supporting cast to chew the scenery. Contains violence, swearing, sex scenes, drug abuse and nudity. ▢
DVD

Al Pacino *Carlito Brigante* • Sean Penn *Dave Kleinfeld* • Penelope Ann Miller *Gail* • John Leguizamo *Benny Blanco* • Ingrid Rogers *Steffie* • Luis Guzman *Pachanga* • James Rebhorn *Norwalk* • Joseph Siravo *Vinnie Taglialucci* • Viggo Mortensen *Lalin* ■ *Dir* Brian De Palma • *Scr* David Koepp, from the novels *Carlito's Way* and *After Hours* by Edwin Torres

Carlton-Browne of the FO ★★ U

Satire 1958 · UK · BW · 86mins

Slightly silly Boulting Brothers farce, with a talented cast, led by Terry-Thomas and Peter Sellers, put to disappointing use by a rather bizarre script about the world's worst diplomat dispatched to a faraway but suddenly mineral-rich British colony. His mission is to save the day for Blighty, but he blusters and blunders instead. ▢

Terry-Thomas *Cadogen De Vere Carlton-Browne* • Peter Sellers *Prime Minister* • Luciana Paluzzi *Princess Ilyena* • Thorley Walters *Colonel Bellingham* • Ian Bannen *Young king* • John Le Mesurier *Grand duke* ■ *Dir/Scr* Roy Boulting, Jeffrey Dell

Carmen ★★★★ U

Silent drama 1915 · US · BW · 62mins

One of the great Cecil B DeMille's biggest early hits, this was one of the movies actually responsible for popularising cinema itself. Unfairly vilified later for his naive and expansive film spectacles, DeMille was one of the film industry's pioneers, and the first to exploit the climate of the Californian orange grove known as Hollywood. As producer, he also pioneered the multiple picture contract;

starring here, in the first movie of a three-picture deal, is Metropolitan Opera soprano Geraldine Farrar. She is superb, but co-star Wallace Reid's career ended tragically, both life and stardom eroded by drug abuse. ▢

Geraldine Ferrar *Carmen* • Wallace Reid *Don José* ■ *Dir* Cecil B DeMille • *Scr* William C DeMille, from the novel by Prosper Mérimée and the opera by Georges Bizet

Carmen ★★★★ PG

Dance drama 1983 · Sp · Colour · 97mins

Coming between *Blood Wedding* and *El Amor Brujo*, this is the best-known segment of Carlos Saura's "flamenco trilogy". Bringing a new zest to the old cliché that life imitates art, Saura cross-cuts between rehearsals and performance as Antonio Gades becomes fatally bewitched with tempestuous co-star Laura del Sol. As Teo Escamilla's camera is choreographed as meticulously as the dancers, the action is at once joyous and tragic; while the blend of folk music and opera manages to both send up and celebrate Bizet's famous score. With its exemplary editing, this passionate picture is both kinetic and cinematic. In Spanish with English subtitles. ▢

Antonio Gades *Antonio* • Laura del Sol *Carmen* • Paco de Lucia *Paco* • Cristina Hoyos *Cristina* • Juan Antonio Jimenez *Juan* • Sebastian Moreno *Escamillo* • Jose Yepes *Pepe Giron* • Pepa Flores *Pepa Flores* ■ *Dir* Carlos Saura • *Scr* Carlos Saura, Antonio Gades, from the novel by Prosper Mérimée and the opera by Georges Bizet • *Cinematographer* Teo Escamila • *Editor* Pedro del Rey

Carmen ★★★★ PG

Opera 1984 · Fr/It · Colour · 148mins

Having been performed by an all-black cast and as a flamenco ballet, Georges Bizet's adaptation of Prosper Mérimée's novel is here cloaked in realism by Italian director Francesco Rosi. There's nothing stylised about the Andalusian settings in which the fiercely independent Julia Migenes-Johnson exploits her relationship with besotted soldier Placido Domingo. Poverty gnaws at the bones of everyone who works in the hellish cigarette factory, yet cinematographer Pasqualino De Santis's control of colour is so inspired that he manages to make the rundown buildings seem the perfect place for inflamed passion. A treat for both eye and ear. In French with English subtitles. ▢ *DVD*

Julia Migenes-Johnson *Carmen* • Placido Domingo *Don José* • Ruggero Raimondi *Escamillo* • Faith Esham *Micaëla* • Jean-Philippe Lafont *Dancaïre* • Gérard Garino *Remendado* • Lilian Watson *Frasquita* ■ *Dir* Francesco Rosi • *Scr* Francesco Rosi, Tonino Guerra, from the novel by Prosper Mérimée and the opera by Georges Bizet

Carmen Jones ★★★★ U

Musical melodrama 1954 · US · Colour · 100mins

Twentieth Century-Fox's all-black version of Bizet's opera *Carmen*, based on the Oscar Hammerstein II Broadway triumph. As the ultimate *femme fatale* Carmen Jones, Dorothy Dandridge sizzles on screen, although her singing voice was dubbed by the

then unknown Marilyn Horne. LeVern Hutcherson sings for handsome Harry Belafonte, but the rest of the cast largely sings for itself. The music has an enjoyable Hollywood zest and *Carmen* fans will warm to the wit of this interpretation: for example, Bizet's toreador becomes boxer Husky Miller. By the way, look closely into that store window during *Whizzin' Away along the Track* and you'll see the whole film crew captured in reflection. ▢

Dorothy Dandridge *Carmen* • Harry Belafonte *Joe* • Olga James *Cindy Lou* • Pearl Bailey *Frankie* • Diahann Carroll *Myrt* • Roy Glenn *Rum* • Nick Stewart *Dink* • Joe Adams *Husky* • Brock Peters *Sergeant Brown* • Sandy Lewis *T-Bone* ■ *Dir* Otto Preminger • *Scr* Harry Kleiner, from the musical by Oscar Hammerstein II

Carmen Miranda: Bananas Is My Business ★★★★

Documentary 1994 · US/Bra · Colour · 92mins

Born Maria do Carmo Miranda da Cunha near Lisbon in Portugal, Carmen Miranda became an international symbol of Brazilian pizzazz, and her sudden death at 46 was the cause of national mourning. A star of Brazilian films and Broadway before she conquered Hollywood, Miranda was unquestionably wasted by producers who thought that all she had to offer was a genius for mangling the English language and an exoticism that could brighten up an ordinary musical with a few colourful routines. As this revealing documentary tribute proves, she was capable of much more. A treat for fans and an eye-opener for the sceptical. In Portuguese and English with subtitles.

Cynthia Adler *Luella Hopper* • Erick Barreto *Carmen Miranda (fantasy sequences)* • Leticia Monte *Carmen Miranda (as a teenager)* • Helena Solberg *Narrator* ■ *Dir* Helena Solberg

Carnal Knowledge ★★★★ 18

Drama 1971 · US · Colour · 93mins

This seventies drama featured one of the roles which brought Jack Nicholson to international attention and was a precursor to the emerging debate into the price the sexual revolution had on personal relationships. Mike Nichols directs a tale of two old college chums traversing life with some incisive flair, and Ann-Margret is especially fine as a vulnerable partner eager to salvage honesty from the emotional debris. If Nicholson is a touch too vulpine and slavering (at times he teeters on the edge of caricature), the film admirably retains its edge and pace. Contains swearing. ▢

Jack Nicholson *Jonathan* • Arthur Garfunkel [Art Garfunkel] *Sandy* • Ann-Margret *Bobbie* • Candice Bergen *Susan* • Rita Moreno *Louise* • Cynthia O'Neal *Cindy* • Carol Kane *Jennifer* ■ *Dir* Mike Nichols • *Scr* Jules Feiffer

Carnegie Hall ★★★ U

Musical 1947 · US · BW · 144mins

That venerable New York institution is presented here in an over-stuffed, overlong pudding of a picture that has the sublime merit of featuring many of the greatest classical performers of its day, including Leopold Stokowski, Jascha Heifetz, Artur Rubinstein, Lily Pons and Rise Stevens. Big bandsters

Harry James and Vaughn Monroe provide some populist appeal, but the music is somewhat dissipated by the thin plot, which sees Marsha Hunt trying to get her offspring onto the concert stage. It is the most upmarket movie that cult B-movie director Edgar G Ulmer ever made.

Marsha Hunt *Nora Ryan* • William Prince *Tony Salerno Jr* • Frank McHugh *John Donovan* • Martha O'Driscoll *Ruth Haines* • Hans Yaray *Tony Salerno Sr* • Joseph Buloff *Anton Tribik* • Olin Downes • Emile Boreo *Henry* • Alfonso D'Artega *Tchaikovsky* ■ *Dir* Edgar G Ulmer • *Scr* Karl Kamb, from a story by Seena Owen

Carnival ★★

Romantic melodrama 1946 · UK · BW · 93mins

Ballet dancer Sally Gray falls in love with sculptor Michael Wilding, but refuses to compromise her honour by living with him. When he leaves her, she makes the unhappy mistake of marrying Cornish farmer Bernard Miles. All ends unhappily. Directed by Stanley Haynes with Stanley Holloway, Jean Kent and Catherine Lacey among the supporting cast, this British-made drama is a relentlessly morose and uninteresting film with a melodramatically tragic ending.

Michael Wilding *Maurice Avery* • Stanley Holloway *Charlie Raeburn* • Bernard Miles *Trewhella* • Jean Kent *Irene Dale* • Catherine Lacey *Florrie Raeburn* • Hazel Court *May Raeburn* ■ *Dir* Stanley Haynes • *Scr* Eric Maschwitz, Stanley Haynes, Peter Ustinov, Guy Green, from a story by Compton Mackenzie

Carnival in Flanders ★★★

Comedy 1935 · Fr/Ger · BW · 115mins

Directed and co-written by Jacques Feyder, this witty and sophisticated farce is set in 17th-century Flanders, wonderfully conjured up by Lazare Meerson's terrific sets and costumes. The beautiful and accomplished Françoise Rosay stars as the wife of a mayor whose small town is invaded by Spanish troops. The men take fright and go into hiding; the women enjoy the attentions of the occupiers. Although not nearly as daring as it seemed in the thirties, the film, which co-stars the great Louis Jouvet, remains a charming and amusing romp. In French with English subtitles.

Françoise Rosay *Madame Burgomaster* • Jean Murat *The Duke* • AndréAlerme *Burgomaster* • Louis Jouvet *The Priest* • Lynne Clévers *Fishmonger's wife* • Micheline Cheirel *Siska* ■ *Dir* Jacques Feyder • *Scr* Bernard Zimmer, Charles Spaak, Jacques Feyder, from a story by Charles Spaak

Carnival of Souls ★★★★ 15

Horror 1962 · US · BW · 74mins

A young church organist finds herself in a strange limbo, haunted by spectral ghouls, in the creepy cult classic that director George A Romero credits as being his major inspiration for *Night of the Living Dead*. Representing the ultimate triumph of talent over budget, Herk Harvey's sole film as director is a crude but compelling chiller evoking a genuinely eerie atmosphere. Harvey also plays the lead phantom pursuing the heroine, played by the excellent, if oddly named Candace Hilligoss. ▢

U = SUITABLE FOR ALL Uc = SUITABLE FOR ALL, ESPECIALLY FOR YOUNG CHILDREN (VIDEO ONLY) PG = PARENTAL GUIDANCE

andace Hilligoss *Mary Henry* • Herk Harvey he Man • Frances Feist *Landlady* • Sidney erger *John Linden* • Art Ellison *Minister* ■ *Dir* Herk Harvey • *Scr* John Clifford, from a tory by John Clifford, Herk Harvey

Carnival of Souls ★★★
Horror   1999 · US · Colour · 83 mins

he black-and-white 1962 original emains a genuinely creepy tale of ossession – fertile material for modern horror maestro Wes Craven. Sadly, though, he only served as executive producer on this slick update. Bobbie Phillips plays a young woman who is haunted by visions of er hated stepfather (comic actor Larry Miller in a surprisingly creepy performance), who she insists is trying o kill her. Problem is, the police insist e is already dead! Director Adam Grossman piles on some jolting shocks, but never manages to re-reate the haunting melancholy of Herk Harvey's cult classic.

Bobbie Phillips *Alex* • Larry Miller *Louis* • Shawnee Smith *Sandra* ■ *Dir/Scr* Adam Grossman

Carnival Story ★★
Drama   1954 · US · Colour · 94mins

Anne Baxter's career reached its peak with her role as the schemingly ambitious "fan" of Bette Davis in 1950's *All about Eve*. Alas, thereafter she was saddled with increasingly inferior material, as this tale of a German girl seeking refuge from unhappiness by joining a carnival demonstrates. Baxter falls prey to a lustful cad (Steve Cochran), marries the troupe's high-diver (Lyle Bettger) and... well, see for yourself. Made in Germany by co-writer and director Kurt Neumann and vaguely based on the 1925 expressionistic film *Variety*, this is tacky fare, but the erotic and suspenseful big-top atmosphere exerts its usual fascination.

Anne Baxter *Willie* • Steve Cochran *Joe Hammond* • Lyle Bettger *Frank Colloni* • George Nader *Vines* • Jay C Flippen *Charley* • Helene Stanley *Peggy* • Adi Berber *Groppo* ■ *Dir* Kurt Neumann • *Scr* Hans Jacoby, Kurt Neumann, from the story by Marcel Klauber, CB Williams

Carnosaur ★★
Science-fiction horror 1993 · US · Colour · 82mins

Executive producer Roger Corman's cheap answer to *Jurassic Park* finds evil scientist Diane Ladd developing a virus in chicken eggs that makes women give birth to savage dinosaurs. It's ably directed by Adam Simon, and delivers the copious blood and gore the child-friendly Steven Spielberg blockbuster couldn't. However, the dreadful model monsters, dodgy animatronics and overly talky script quickly and rightly made this extinct in movie houses.

Diane Ladd *Dr Jane Tiptree* • Raphael Sbarge "Doc" Smith • Jennifer Runyon *Thrush* • Harrison Page *Sheriff* • Clint Howard *Trucker* ■ *Dir* Adam Simon • *Scr* Adam Simon, from a novel by Harry Adam Knight

Carny ★★★★ 18
Drama   1980 · US · Colour · 102mins

Set behind the scenes of a travelling carnival, this very dark tale stars Robbie Robertson (of rock group The Band) as a con man and fixer, Gary Busey as an insane dimwit, and Jodie Foster as the teenage runaway who comes between them. The setting, complete with authentic sideshows and genuine freaks, gives an added creepiness to the proceedings, and, although director Robert Kaylor tries to concentrate on buddy bonding and life on the road, it's the strangeness of it all that leaves the biggest impression. Unusual, but also unmissable. Contains swearing. ▭

Jodie Foster *Donna* • Gary Busey *Frankie Chipman* • Robbie Robertson *Patch Beaudry* • Meg Foster *Gerta* • Kenneth McMillan *Heavy St John* • Elisha Cook [Elisha Cook Jr] "On Your Mark" • Tim Thomerson *Doubles* • Theodore Wilson [Teddy Wilson] *Nails* • John Lehne *Skeet* ■ *Dir* Robert Kaylor • *Scr* Thomas Baum, from a story by Phoebe Taylor, Robert Kaylor, Robbie Robertson

Carolina Skeletons ★★★ 18
Crime mystery 1991 · US · Colour · 93mins

Overshadowed by the similarly themed, bigger-budgeted *Mississippi Burning*, this is still an absorbing thriller that transcends its TV origins. Louis Gossett Jr is the soldier who returns to his small town to uncover the truth about his older brother, lynched over 30 years before following a brutal double murder. Gossett is as charismatic as ever and the powerful supporting cast includes Bruce Dern, Melissa Chessington Leo and GD Spradlin. Intelligently scripted by Tracy Keenan Wynn, this fascinating and moving drama is directed with a sensitive touch by John Erman. Contains violence and swearing. ▭

Louis Gossett Jr *Major James Bragg* • Bruce Dern *Sheriff Junior Stoker* • Melissa Chessington Leo [Melissa Leo] *Cassie* • GD Spradlin *Hiram Stoker* • Bill Cobbs *Elijah Crooks* • Paul Roebling *TJ Campbell* • Clifton James *Dexter Cody* ■ *Dir* John Erman • *Scr* Tracy Keenan Wynn, from the novel by David Stout

Caroline? ★★★
Mystery drama 1990 · US · Colour

Here's a made-for-TV movie that's way above average, transferring an old Hollywood standby plot to the glossy world of "movie of the week". Stephanie Zimbalist returns to claim her inheritance after – guess what? – her family thought she was dead. Of course, Anastasia-like, they don't think she's who she says she is. This won Emmy Awards for outstanding drama and the direction of Joseph Sargent, better known over here for his earlier TV work, including *The Man from UNCLE*, and the excellent feature *The Taking of Pelham One Two Three*.

Stephanie Zimbalist *Caroline* • Pamela Reed *Grace Carmichael* • George Grizzard *Paul Carmichael* • Shawn Phelan *Winston Carmichael* • Jenny Jacobs *Heidi Carmichael* • Patricia Neal • *Dir* Joseph Sargent • *Scr* Michael De Guzman, from the novel *Father's Arcane Daughter* by EL Konigsburg

Carousel ★★★★★ U
Musical   1956 · US · Colour · 123mins

A marvellous screen version of what is arguably Rodgers and Hammerstein's finest Broadway show, immaculately cast and filmed in part on glorious Maine locations. Some may find this tale of a reprobate's return to Earth to look out for his daughter arch in the extreme, but it is a tribute to the superb score and sensitive handling of the material that the film is exceptionally moving. Gordon MacRae and Shirley Jones, reunited after *Oklahoma!*, have the roles of their lives as Billy Bigelow and Julie Jordan, though they're done no favours by Henry King's static direction. However, the spirited *June Is Bustin' Out All Over* more than compensates. A treat. ▭

Gordon MacRae *Billy Bigelow* • Shirley Jones *Julie* • Cameron Mitchell *Jigger* • Barbara Ruick *Carrie* • Claramae Turner *Cousin Nettie* • Robert Rounseville *Mr Snow* • Gene Lockhart *Starkeeper* • Audrey Christie *Mrs Mullin* ■ *Dir* Henry King • *Scr* Phoebe Ephron, Henry Ephron, from the musical by Richard Rodgers, Oscar Hammerstein II, Benjamin F Glazer, Ferenc Molnar

The Carpetbaggers ★★★★
Drama   1964 · US · Colour · 150mins

With the lustre of age, nostalgia for its stars and that vanished art of story-telling know-how, this trashy tale has now acquired a certain fascination. Based on the Harold Robbins's potboiler, it sprawls across nearly three hours and as many decades, focusing on the life and loves of a tycoon (George Peppard in a role that James Dean might have played, had he lived.) Alan Ladd, as a cowboy star, makes his final screen appearance and Hollywood sexpot Carroll Baker drapes herself over both of them. It's lumpen, lavish and lascivious, a gripping cocktail of melodrama and moralising.

George Peppard *Jonas Cord Jr* • Alan Ladd *Nevada Smith* • Carroll Baker *Rina* • Bob Cummings [Robert Cummings] *Dan Pierce* • Martha Hyer *Jennie Denton* • Elizabeth Ashley *Monica Winthrop* • Martin Balsam *Bernard B Norman* • Lew Ayres *McAllister* • Tom Tully *Amos Winthrop* ■ *Dir* Edward Dmytryk • *Scr* John Michael Hayes, from the novel by Harold Robbins

Carpool ★ PG
Comedy   1996 · US · Colour · 85mins

The ex-Mr Roseanne Barr, Tom Arnold, won the "Razzie" award for worst actor for his performance in this annoying chase movie. Ironically, though, he's the only reason for watching it. His affably juvenile persona can be grating at times, but it suits his role here as a bumbling crook holding a carload of kids hostage. Filmed in Vancouver (standing in for Seattle) by Arthur Hiller, this runs out of gas way before the end, while the thin plot is entirely built around a succession of screeching tires and sexist gags. Contains some mild swearing and sexual references. ▭

Tom Arnold *Franklin Laszlo* • David Paymer *Daniel Miller* • Rhea Perlman *Martha* • Rod Steiger *Mr Hammerman* • Kim Coates *Detective Erdman* • Rachael Leigh Cook *Kayla* ■ *Dir* Arthur Hiller • *Scr* Don Rhymer

Carrie ★★★
Romantic melodrama 1952 · US · BW · 121mins

Not the Stephen King bloodbath, but a full-blown romance from the great William Wyler. Jennifer Jones stars as the small-town girl who gets seduced into a life of crime and passion in early 1900s Chicago, while Laurence Olivier is in fine form as the married man who whisks her off her feet. Based on Theodore Dreiser's novel *Sister Carrie*, the story veers between agony and ecstasy in the way that only a Hollywood melodrama can. It may not be vintage Wyler, but the pairing of Jones and Olivier is electric.

Jennifer Jones *Carrie Meeber* • Laurence Olivier *George Hurstwood* • Miriam Hopkins *Julia Hurstwood* • Eddie Albert *Charlie Drouet* • Basil Ruysdael *Mr Fitzgerald* • Ray Teal *Allan* • Barry Kelley *Slawson* ■ *Dir* William Wyler • *Scr* Ruth Goetz, Augustus Goetz, from the novel *Sister Carrie* by Theodore Dreiser

Carrie ★★★★★ 18
Horror   1976 · US · Colour · 93mins

Brian De Palma's modern Gothic fairy tale, based on Stephen King's bestseller, offers a tense and lyrical web of emotions. Sissy Spacek is heartbreaking as the telekinetic Cinderella turning her school prom into a bloody massacre after a macabre joke is played on her by vicious teens (including John Travolta). Piper Laurie as Spacek's religious fanatic mother is equally striking and her symbolic "crucifixion" is a thrilling highlight in an unforgettable package of pop psychology and psychic phenomena. Despite a much-copied plot and even more copied shock climax, De Palma's best movie remains a transfixing experience. Contains violence, swearing and nudity. ▭ **DVD**

Sissy Spacek *Carrie White* • Piper Laurie *Margaret White* • Amy Irving *Sue Snell* • William Katt *Tommy Ross* • John Travolta *Billy Nolan* • Nancy Allen *Chris Hargenson* • Betty Buckley *Miss Collins* • Priscilla Pointer *Mrs Snell* ■ *Dir* Brian De Palma • *Scr* Lawrence D Cohen, from the novel by Stephen King

La Carrière de Suzanne ★★★★
Drama   1963 · Fr · BW · 54mins

The second of Eric Rohmer's "Six Moral Tales" is a witty, wise and wonderfully-told story about the gulf in emotional maturity that exists between young men and women. The men behaving badly here are a medical student whose worthless friendship with his lothario buddy costs him not only his meagre supply of cash, but also his chance of romance with Suzanne, the interpreter who at first tolerates and then repudiates their childish games. No one films Paris better than Rohmer, and he coaxes such naturalistic performances from his young cast that you part from them only with the greatest reluctance. In French with English subtitles.

Catherine Sée *Suzanne* • Philippe Beuzen *Bertrand* • Christian Charrière *Guillaume* • Diane Wilkinson *Sophie* • Jean-Claude Biette *Jean-Louis* ■ *Dir/Scr* Eric Rohmer

Carrington ★★★★ 18

Biographical drama
1995 · UK · Colour · 117mins

The extraordinary romance between androgynous painter Dora Carrington and homosexual poet Lytton Strachey is captivatingly portrayed by Emma Thompson and Jonathan Pryce in the directing debut of Christopher Hampton, writer of *Dangerous Liaisons*. Few love stories have been so intense or unusual as this account of the non-sexual relationship between the Bloomsbury group twosome, who shared their nonconformist alliance with Carrington's husband and Strachey's occasional boyfriends. Hampton's fascinating account is beautifully crafted, wittily scripted and intelligently realised, with Pryce giving the Cannes award-winning performance of a lifetime. Costume drama is rarely this compelling or moving. ▣

Emma Thompson *Carrington* • Jonathan Pryce *Lytton Strachey* • Steven Waddington *Ralph Partridge* • Samuel West *Gerald Brenan* • Rufus Sewell *Mark Gertler* • Penelope Wilton *Lady Ottoline Morrell* • Janet McTeer *Vanessa Bell* • Peter Blythe *Phillip Morrell* • Jeremy Northam *Beacus Penrose* • Alex Kingston *Frances Partridge* ■ *Dir* Christopher Hampton • *Scr* Christopher Hampton, from the book *Lytton Strachey* by Michael Holroyd

Carrington VC ★★★ U

Courtroom drama 1954 · UK · BW · 100mins

David Niven had no formal acting training, but he was capable of giving performances of both subtlety and power. Unfortunately, producers typecast him in debonair roles and only rarely gave him the chance to tackle more demanding characters. Here he shows the depth of his instinctive talent as a war hero driven to theft by delays in repayments of his expenses. Niven's shifts between despair, dignity and determination are masterly, and he is well supported by Margaret Leighton as his shrewish wife. Director Anthony Asquith handles the trial scenes with great assurance, keeping the verdict in doubt.

David Niven *Major Carrington VC* • Margaret Leighton *Valerie Carrington* • Noelle Middleton *Captain Alison Graham* • Laurence Naismith *Major Panton* • Clive Morton *Lieutenant Colonel Huxford* • Maurice Denham *Lieutenant Colonel Reeve* ■ *Dir* Anthony Asquith • *Scr* John Hunter, from a play by Dorothy Christie, Campbell Christie

Carry On Abroad ★★ PG

Comedy 1972 · UK · Colour · 85mins

A disappointing outing that's every bit as jerry-built as the Elsbels Palace Hotel itself. With a stingy quota of jokes, the team's package holiday to Spain rapidly descends into predictable postcard innuendo and second-rate slapstick. There are one or two neat observations on the British abroad, but there is too little for the regulars to do, and it's a sad series swan song for the inimitable Charles Hawtrey. ▣

Sidney James *Vic Flange* • Kenneth Williams *Stuart Farquhar* • Charles Hawtrey *Tuttle* • Peter Butterworth *Pepe* • Joan Sims *Cora Flange* • Kenneth Connor *Stanley Blunt* • Jimmy Logan *Bert Conway* • Barbara Windsor *Sadie* • June Whitfield *Evelyn Blunt* • Hattie Jacques *Floella* • Bernard Bresslaw *Brother*

Bernard • Jack Douglas *Harry* • Patsy Rowlands *Miss Dobbs* • *Dir* Gerald Thomas • *Scr* Talbot Rothwell

Carry On Admiral ★★ U

Comedy 1957 · UK · BW · 78mins

Not one of the *Carry Ons*, but an unremarkable screen adaptation of an almost forgotten stage farce called *Off the Record*. Also known as *The Ship Was Loaded*, this comedy of errors has more in common with radio hit *The Navy Lark* than its saucier namesakes. David Tomlinson and Brian Reece goof gamely as the civil servant and the sailor whose identities get muddled, but it's AE Matthews (at the ripe old age of 87) who steals the show.

David Tomlinson *Tom Baker* • Peggy Cummins *Susan Lashwood* • Brian Reece *Peter Fraser* • Eunice Gayson *Jane Godfrey* • AE Matthews *Admiral Godfrey* • Joan Sims *Mary* ■ *Dir* Val Guest • *Scr* Val Guest, from the play *Off the Record* by Ian Hay, Stephen King-Hall

Carry On Again Doctor ★★★★ PG

Comedy 1969 · UK · Colour · 85mins

The 17th *Carry On* is easily the funniest of the medical capers. Rejoicing under the glorious name of Dr Nookey, Jim Dale holds centre stage with some aplomb, most notably matching Sid James gag for gag during the wonderfully sleazy Beatific Island scenes. Charles Hawtrey also has one of his better outings, hissing bitterly as the covetous Dr Stoppidge who is forced to resort to drag in order to discover the secret of Dale's revolutionary slimming tonic. As usual, Talbot Rothwell litters his script with wincingly witty one-liners. ▣ **DVD**

Kenneth Williams *Frederick Carver* • Jim Dale *Dr James Nookey* • Sidney James *Gladstone Screwer* • Charles Hawtrey *Dr Ernest Stoppidge* • Joan Sims *Ellen Moore* • Hattie Jacques *Matron* • Barbara Windsor *Goldie Locks* • Patsy Rowlands *Miss Fosdick* ■ *Dir* Gerald Thomas • *Scr* Talbot Rothwell

Carry On at Your Convenience ★★ PG

Comedy 1971 · UK · Colour · 86mins

"What a load of ballcocks!" Among the weakest of the *Carry Ons*, this is toilet humour in every sense of the phrase. Plumbing the depths of his imagination, screenwriter Talbot Rothwell throws up a spoof on "everybody out" trade unionism that is hardly flush with originality. To relieve the comic drought, he packs bosses and workers alike into a charabanc for a works outing that has all the appearance of a desperate time-filler. Sid James and Hattie Jacques have the best scenes with their racing tipster budgie, but the remaining regulars deserve better than being asked to wade knee-deep in mediocrity. ▣ **DVD**

Sidney James *Sid Plummer* • Kenneth Williams *Wc Boggs* • Charles Hawtrey *Charles Coote* • Joan Sims *Chloe Moore* • Hattie Jacques *Beattie Plummer* • Bernard Bresslaw *Bernie Hulke* • Patsy Rowlands *Miss Withering* • Bill Maynard *Fred Moore* • *Dir* Gerald Thomas • *Scr* Talbot Rothwell

Carry On Behind ★★ PG

Comedy 1975 · UK · Colour · 86mins

Sid James wasn't the only stalwart to bid farewell to the *Carry On* series in 1974, with scriptwriter Talbot Rothwell dying after notching up 20 titles in the series. Although his later efforts occasionally missed the mark, they were in a different league to this woeful effort from Dave Freeman. Essentially it's a caravan version of *Carry On Camping*, with regulars Bernard Bresslaw, Kenneth Connor and Joan Sims sadly restricted to supporting roles. The only fun comes from Kenneth Williams and Elke Sommer as archaeologists on a dig. Pity they couldn't have unearthed a decent script. ▣

Elke Sommer *Professor Anna Vrooshka* • Kenneth Williams *Professor Roland Crump* • Joan Sims *Daphne Barnes* • Bernard Bresslaw *Arthur Upmore* • Jack Douglas *Ernie Bragg* • Windsor Davies *Fred Ramsden* • Kenneth Connor *Major Leep* • Liz Fraser *Sylvia Ramsden* • Peter Butterworth *Barnes* ■ *Dir* Gerald Thomas • *Scr* Dave Freeman

Carry On Cabby ★★★ PG

Comedy 1963 · UK · BW · 87mins

The best of the black-and-white *Carry Ons* began life as a script by the then little known Talbot Rothwell entitled *Call Me a Cab*. Having just parted company with regular scriptwriter Norman Hudis, producer Peter Rogers brought Rothwell into the fold and he went on to pen the next 19 films in the series. Pitting Sid James against the long-suffering Hattie Jacques, the battle between Speedee Taxis and Glamcabs is packed with hilarious incidents and cracking performances, not least from Kenneth Connor and Esma Cannon as the respective loyal lieutenants and Charles Hawtrey as the hapless Pint-Pot. ▣

Sidney James *Charlie* • Hattie Jacques *Peggy* • Kenneth Connor *Ted* • Charles Hawtrey *Pint-Pot* • Liz Fraser *Sally* • Bill Owen *Smiley* • Milo O'Shea *Len* • Jim Dale *Small Man* • Amanda Barrie *Anthea* ■ *Dir* Gerald Thomas • *Scr* Talbot Rothwell, from a story by Sidney Green, Richard Hills

Carry On Camping ★★★ PG

Comedy 1969 · UK · Colour · 85mins

The 18th outing is one of the liveliest *Carry Ons*, with the cast making light of the fact that they were shooting in freezing temperatures in fields that were so muddy they were sprayed green to give the impression of high summer. Yet again, the big slapstick finale is a disappointment after all the wonderful double entendre incidents, but there is the compensation of Sid James as a hippy, while Peter Butterworth has his finest hour as the miserly site owner. ▣ **DVD**

Sidney James *Sid Boggle* • Kenneth Williams *Dr Soper* • Joan Sims *Joan Fussey* • Charles Hawtrey *Charlie Muggins* • Bernard Bresslaw *Bernie Lugg* • Terry Scott *Peter Potter* • Barbara Windsor *Babs* • Hattie Jacques *Miss Haggerd* • Peter Butterworth *Joshua Fiddler* ■ *Dir* Gerald Thomas • *Scr* Talbot Rothwell

Carry On Cleo ★★★★ PG

Comedy 1964 · UK · Colour · 87mins

Mercilessly mocking Elizabeth Taylor's disastrous *Cleopatra*, this is a corking ancient history lesson by the *Carry On* team at the peak of their powers. It's hard to know where to start lavishing the praise. Scriptwriter Talbot Rothwell never punned better ("infamy, infamy, they've all got it in for me!") and the sets are positively luxuriant. Amanda Barrie is exquisitely dippy in the title role, and Kenneth Connor and Jim Dale do well as the Britons in the imperial guard. But topping them all are Sid James's Mark Antony and Kenneth Williams's snivelling Caesar. ▣

Sidney James *Mark Antony* • Kenneth Williams *Julius Caesar* • Kenneth Connor *Hengist Pod* • Charles Hawtrey *Seneca* • Joan Sims *Calpurnia* • Jim Dale *Horsa* • Amanda Barrie *Cleo* • Sheila Hancock *Senna Pod* • Warren Mitchell *Spencius* ■ *Dir* Gerald Thomas • *Scr* Talbot Rothwell

Carry On Columbus ★★ PG

Comedy 1992 · UK · Colour · 87mins

Oh dear. With many of the original *Carry On* regulars no longer with us or (sensibly) otherwise engaged, it was left to more contemporary comedians like Alexei Sayle, Julian Clary, Rik Mayall and Tony Slattery to put the final nail in the *Carry On* coffin with a cacophony of puerile jokes and general atrociousness. This mainly fails because the *Carry On* films are part of British comedy nostalgia, and, like many other historic things (the three-day week, the Blitz), they are probably best remembered rather than re-created. ▣

Jim Dale *Christopher Columbus* • Peter Richardson *Bart* • Alexei Sayle *Achmed* • Sara Crowe *Fatima* • Julian Clary *Diego* • Bernard Cribbins *Mordecai Mendoza* • Richard Wilson *Don Felipe* • Keith Allen *Pepi* • Nigel Planer *Wazir* • Rik Mayall *Sultan* • Tony Slattery *Baba* • Maureen Lipman *Countess Esme* • Jon Pertwee *Duke of Costa Brava* • Leslie Phillips *King Ferdinand* • June Whitfield *Queen Isabella* • Martin Clunes *Martin* ■ *Dir* Gerald Thomas • *Scr* Dave Freeman

Carry On Constable ★★★ U

Comedy 1960 · UK · BW · 82mins

The fourth in the *Carry On* series is the first to feature the excellent Sid James, who stars as the sergeant detailed to vet nurse rookies Kenneth Williams, Leslie Phillips, Charles Hawtrey and Kenneth Connor. Having studied the policeman's lot at Slough, screenwriter Norman Hudis confessed he could find nothing funny about pounding the beat, but he still turned in a chucklesome script. The bungling bobbies have their moments, notably when Williams and Hawtrey don skirts to trap some shoplifters, but their thunder is stolen by seasoned supports Joan Hickson, Irene Handl and Esma Cannon, inevitably playing their usual eccentrics. ▣

Sidney James *Sergeant Frank Wilkins* • Kenneth Williams *Constable Benson* • Hattie Jacques *Sergeant Laura Moon* • Eric Barker *Inspector Mills* • Kenneth Connor *Constable Charlie Constable* • Charles Hawtrey *Special Constable Gorse* • Leslie Phillips *Constable Potter* • Joan Sims *Policewoman Gloria Passworthy* ■ *Dir* Gerald Thomas • *Scr* Norman Hudis, from an idea by Brock Williams

U = SUITABLE FOR ALL, Uc = SUITABLE FOR ALL, ESPECIALLY FOR YOUNG CHILDREN (VIDEO ONLY) PG = PARENTAL GUIDANCE

Carry On Cowboy ★★★ PG

Comedy   1965 · UK · Colour · 90mins

When Marshall P Knutt (Jim Dale) rides into Stodge City, Judge Burke (Kenneth Williams) is convinced that he is the lawman who will rid him of the Rumpo Kid (Sid James) and his band of desperadoes. But to a sanitary engineer like Knutt, cleaning up the town has a totally different meaning. Shot in the untamed wilds of Pinewood Studios, the 11th *Carry On* finds the team in mid-season form. All the regulars impress, but Charles Hawtrey steals the picture as the fire-water-swilling Chief Big Heap.

Sidney James *Rumpo Kid* • Kenneth Williams *Judge Burke* • Jim Dale *Marshall P Knutt* • Charles Hawtrey *Chief Big Heap* • Joan Sims *Belle* • Angela Douglas *Annie Oakley* • Bernard Bresslaw *Little Heap* • Peter Butterworth *Doc* • Jon Pertwee *Sheriff Earp* ■ *Dir* Gerald Thomas • *Scr* Talbot Rothwell

Carry On Cruising ★★★ U

Comedy   1962 · UK · Colour · 85mins

The first in colour and the last *Carry On* written by Norman Hudis, this is the most charming film in the series. Set aboard the SS *Happy Wanderer*, it charts the course of captain Sid James's tenth anniversary cruise, during which his new crew seek to find their sea legs. Kenneth Connor enjoys one of his best outings as the nervous ship's doctor and Lance Percival has fun as the cook-it-and-see chef. ▭

Sidney James *Captain Crowther* • Kenneth Williams *Leonard Marjoribanks* • Kenneth Connor *Arthur Binn* • Liz Fraser *Gladys Trimble* • Dilys Laye *Flo Castle* • Lance Percival *Wilfred Haines* ■ *Dir* Gerald Thomas • *Scr* Norman Hudis, from a story by Eric Barker

Carry On Dick ★★ PG

Comedy   1974 · UK · Colour · 86mins

Packed with more than the usual amount of smutty innuendo, this spoof on period adventures does not live up to the team's previous best. It is chiefly memorable for being the 19th and last *Carry On* to star Sid James, as the country vicar who masquerades as the feared highwayman Dick Turpin. Also leading a double life, Barbara Windsor gives one of her best performances of the series as Turpin's sidekick. ▭ **DVD**

Sidney James *Dick Turpin/Reverend Flasher* • Barbara Windsor *Harriet/Harry* • Kenneth Williams *Captain Desmond Fancey* • Hattie Jacques *Martha Hoggett* • Bernard Bresslaw *Sir Roger Daley* • Joan Sims *Madame Desiree* • Kenneth Connor *Constable* • Peter Butterworth *Tom "Doc" Scholl* • Jack Douglas *Sergeant Jock Strapp* ■ *Dir* Gerald Thomas • *Scr* Talbot Rothwell, from a treatment by Lawrie Wyman, George Evans

Carry On Doctor ★★★ PG

Comedy   1968 · UK · Colour · 90mins

After seven consecutive spoofs of other movies, the *Carry On* crew returned to the world of work for this lively comedy that virtually takes up from where *Carry On Nurse* left off. The timing of another hospital picture couldn't have been better for Sid James, who was genuinely bedridden for much of the production. Consequently, the majority of the workload falls upon Kenneth Williams

as a sneering consultant, Jim Dale as the clumsy Dr Kilmore, and Frankie Howerd, making an impressive series debut as a fussy faith healer. ▭

Frankie Howerd *Francis Bigger* • Sidney James *Charlie Roper* • Kenneth Williams *Dr Tinkle* • Charles Hawtrey *Mr Barron* • Jim Dale *Dr Kilmore* • Barbara Windsor *Sandra May* • Joan Sims *Chloe Gibson* • Hattie Jacques *Matron* • Bernard Bresslaw *Ken Biddle* • Peter Butterworth *Mr Smith* ■ *Dir* Gerald Thomas • *Scr* Talbot Rothwell

Carry On – Don't Lose Your Head ★★★★ PG

Comedy   1966 · UK · Colour · 86mins

Originally not intended to be a *Carry On*, this turns out to be one of the jewels of the series. Hilariously spoofing *The Scarlet Pimpernel*, Talbot Rothwell's script is stuffed with comic incidents and names ranging from Sir Rodney Ffing to the Duc de Pommfrit. Sid James is superb, whether camping it up as a society fop or cutting a dash as the Black Fingernail, while Kenneth Williams's Citizen Camembert is great as "the big cheese" of the French Revolution. ▭

Sidney James *Sir Rodney Ffing* • Kenneth Williams *Citizen Camembert* • Jim Dale *Lord Darcy* • Charles Hawtrey *Duc De Pommfrit* • Joan Sims *Desirée Dubarry* • Peter Butterworth *Citizen Bidet* ■ *Dir* Gerald Thomas • *Scr* Talbot Rothwell

Carry On Emmannuelle ★ 15

Comedy   1978 · UK · Colour · 84mins

Spoofing the long-running series of erotic movies starring Sylvia Kristel, this was the last *Carry On* made during the series' golden age. Sadly, it's the weakest of the lot. Lance Peters's script is a gag-free zone that is utterly dependent on smutty innuendo and severely taxes the talents of the few regulars on duty. Curiously, in a film lampooning porn, it's Kenneth Williams who bares the most, with Suzanne Danielle being the model of modesty in the lead. An embarrassment. ▭

Suzanne Danielle *Emmannuelle Prevert* • Kenneth Williams *Emile Prevert* • Kenneth Connor *Leyland* • Jack Douglas *Lyons* • Joan Sims *Mrs Dangle* • Peter Butterworth *Richmond* • Beryl Reid *Mrs Valentine* • Henry McGee *Harold Hump* ■ *Dir* Gerald Thomas • *Scr* Lance Peters

Carry On England ★ PG

Comedy   1976 · UK · Colour · 84mins

For all the attention paid to the wonderful casts, the real secret of the *Carry Ons* success was in the scriptwriting, which provided the actors with an endless supply of stinging ammunition. This woeful effort by Jack Seddon and David Pursall (ironically about a Battle of Britain anti-aircraft battery) leaves what is essentially a B-team with nothing to fire but blanks. Patrick Mower overdoes the mugging as a chirpy sergeant, Windsor Davies trots out all his *It Ain't Half Hot, Mum* parade ground mannerisms, while Kenneth Connor is wasted as the battery's CO. ▭

Kenneth Connor *Captain S Melly* • Windsor Davies *Sergeant Major "Tiger" Bloomer* • Patrick Mower *Sergeant Len Able* • Judy Geeson *Sergeant Tilly Willing* • Jack Douglas *Bombardier Ready* • Melvyn Hayes *Gunner*

Shorthouse • Joan Sims *Private Sharpe* • Peter Jones *Brigadier* • Peter Butterworth *Major Carstairs* ■ *Dir* Gerald Thomas • *Scr* David Pursall, Jack Seddon

Carry On Follow That Camel ★★ PG

Comedy   1967 · UK · Colour · 90mins

Originally released under the title *Follow That Camel*, this disappointing spoof on *Beau Geste* was only later added to the *Carry On* series and it sits uncomfortably alongside the rest. Although many of the regular team are on duty at Fort Zuassantneuf, the presence of Phil Silvers overbalances the story. There are comic oases along the way, however, with the Mustapha Leek joke being the most memorable, but too much emphasis is placed on Silvers's "Bilko of the Dunes" routine, while many of the other Foreign Legion gags are shamelessly borrowed from Laurel and Hardy's *Beau Hunks*. ▭

Phil Silvers *Sergeant Nocker* • Jim Dale *Bertram Oliphant West* • Peter Butterworth *Simpson* • Charles Hawtrey *Captain Le Pice* • Kenneth Williams *Commandant Burger* • Anita Harris *Corktip* • Joan Sims *Zigzig* • Bernard Bresslaw *Abdul* • Angela Douglas *Lady Jane Ponsonby* • John Bluthal *Corporal Clotski* ■ *Dir* Gerald Thomas • *Scr* Talbot Rothwell

Carry On Girls ★★ PG

Comedy   1973 · UK · Colour · 84mins

When councillor Sidney Fiddler (Sid James) decides that a beauty contest is the only way to put the sleepy seaside resort of Fircombe on the map, the local feminists are soon up in arms. The least focused of the *Carry On* series, this combines the gentle social satire of an Ealing comedy with the sniggering sauciness of a Donald McGill postcard. It's not one of Talbot Rothwell's best scripts, with the sabotage sequence more in keeping with St Trinian's. However, there are splendid supporting performances from Kenneth Connor as the feeble mayor and Patsy Rowlands as his newly liberated wife. ▭ **DVD**

Sidney James *Sidney Fiddler* • Joan Sims *Connie Philpotts* • Kenneth Connor *Frederick Bumble* • Barbara Windsor *Hope Springs* • Bernard Bresslaw *Peter Potter* • June Whitfield *Augusta Prodworthy* • Peter Butterworth *Admiral* • Jack Douglas *William* • Patsy Rowlands *Mildred Bumble* • Joan Hickson *Mrs Dukes* • Wendy Richard *Ida Downs* ■ *Dir* Gerald Thomas • *Scr* Talbot Rothwell

Carry On Henry ★★★ PG

Comedy   1971 · UK · Colour · 86mins

This raucous history lesson from the *Carry On* crew is something of an on-off affair. For once, Talbot Rothwell's script isn't as sharp as an executioner's axe, but there are still plenty of wicked one-liners and savage parodies. Sid James makes a suitably merry monarch, while Joan Sims gives her best performance of the series as his garlic-gobbling queen. Exceptional support is given by Kenneth Williams as Thomas Cromwell and Charles Hawtrey as the wonderfully named Sir Roger de Lodgerley. ▭

Sidney James *Henry VIII* • Kenneth Williams *Thomas Cromwell* • Charles Hawtrey *Sir Roger de Lodgerley* • Joan Sims *Queen Marie* • Terry Scott *Cardinal Wolsey* • Barbara Windsor

Bettina • Kenneth Connor *Lord Hampton of Wick* • Bill Maynard *Fawkes* ■ *Dir* Gerald Thomas • *Scr* Talbot Rothwell

Carry On Jack ★★ PG

Comedy   1963 · UK · Colour · 87mins

The innuendos continue as the *Carry On* crew takes to the seas in the first of the historical costume parodies tackled by the team. Alas, some of the regulars are missing, making it one of the less memorable productions in the series. Bernard Cribbins doesn't carry the same clout as Sid James, but director Gerald Thomas keeps the fun shipshape and Bristol fashion. ▭

Bernard Cribbins *Albert Poop-Decker* • Kenneth Williams *Captain Fearless* • Juliet Mills *Sally* • Charles Hawtrey *Walter* • Donald Houston *Howett* • Percy Herbert *Angel* ■ *Dir* Gerald Thomas • *Scr* Talbot Rothwell

Carry On Loving ★★ PG

Comedy   1970 · UK · Colour · 86mins

Containing more double entendres than an exhibition of smutty postcards, Talbot Rothwell's script for this patchy *Carry On* spends too much time in the company of Terry Scott and the other clients of the Wedded Bliss Marriage Bureau. Consequently, we get nowhere near enough of the bureau's proprietors: Hattie Jacques and Sid James, amorous spinster Joan Sims and marriage guidance counsellor Kenneth Williams. The sound you can hear during the slapstick wedding finale is barrels being scraped. ▭

Sidney James *Sidney Bliss* • Kenneth Williams *Percival Snooper* • Charles Hawtrey *James Bedsop* • Joan Sims *Esme Crowfoot* • Hattie Jacques *Sophie* • Terry Scott *Terence Philpot* • Bernard Bresslaw *Gripper Burke* • Patsy Rowlands *Miss Dempsey* • Joan Hickson *Mrs Grubb* • Bill Maynard *Mr Dreery* ■ *Dir* Gerald Thomas • *Scr* Talbot Rothwell

Carry On Matron ★★★ PG

Comedy   1972 · UK · Colour · 85mins

Subtitled *From Here to Maternity*, the fourth *Carry On* to be set in a hospital is the last in the series that manages to be consistently funny throughout. The regulars are all present and correct, with Hattie Jacques in the title role as the object of consultant Kenneth Williams's confused affections, while crooked Sid James leads a raid on the clinic where they work to steal contraceptive pills. Amid the innuendo, cross-dressing and crude slapstick, there are lovely cameos from Kenneth Connor as a dad-to-be and Joan Sims as an overdue mum. ▭

Sidney James *Sid Carter* • Kenneth Williams *Sir Bernard Cutting* • Charles Hawtrey *Dr Francis Goode* • Joan Sims *Mrs Tidey* • Hattie Jacques *Matron* • Bernard Bresslaw *Ernie* • Kenneth Cope *Cyril Carter* • Terry Scott *Dr Prodd* • Barbara Windsor *Nurse Susan Ball* • Kenneth Connor *Mr Tidey* • Bill Maynard *Freddy* • Patsy Rowlands *Evelyn Banks* ■ *Dir* Gerald Thomas • *Scr* Talbot Rothwell

Carry On Nurse ★★★ PG

Comedy   1959 · UK · BW · 82mins

The second film in the *Carry On* series overdoses on bedpan, large needle and inedible food gags, but, as most of them are funny, no one will mind in the slightest. Hattie Jacques is superb as the bullying matron whose clipped supervision of nurses Shirley Eaton and Joan Sims prompts Kenneth Connor, Leslie Phillips and Kenneth Williams to give her a taste of her own medicine, while Wilfrid Hyde White has fun as a lecherous colonel in a private ward. Loosely based on a forgotten play called *Ring for Catty*. ▣

Kenneth Connor *Bernie Bishop* • Charles Hawtrey *Mr Hinton* • Hattie Jacques *Matron* • Shirley Eaton *Dorothy Denton* • Wilfrid Hyde White *Colonel* • Bill Owen *Percy Hickson* • Leslie Phillips *Jack Bell* • Joan Sims *Stella Dawson* • Kenneth Williams *Oliver Reckitt* • Terence Longdon [Terence Longden] *Ted York* ■ *Dir* Gerald Thomas • *Scr* Norman Hudis, from the play *Ring for Catty* by Patrick Cargill, Jack Searle

Carry On Regardless
★★★ **PG**

Comedy 1960 · UK · BW · 86mins

The fifth *Carry On* is unique in that it does not have a single storyline, but consists of a loose collection of sketches linked by the "Helping Hands" employment agency, run by Sid James to tackle the oddest of jobs. The assignments vary in comic value, but the ones in which Joan Sims gets hammered at a snooty wine tasting and Kenneth Williams baby-sits a frolicsome chimpanzee stand out. The inimitable Esma Cannon simpers and sniggers superbly as Sid's assistant, but Charles Hawtrey and Kenneth Connor have little to do. ▣

Sidney James *Bert Handy* • Kenneth Connor *Sam Twist* • Kenneth Williams *Francis Courtenay* • Charles Hawtrey *Gabriel Dimple* • Joan Sims *Lily Duveen* • Liz Fraser *Delia King* • Bill Owen *Mike Weston* • Hattie Jacques *Frosty-Faced Sister* • Terence Longdon [Terence Longden] *Montgomery Infield-Hopping* • Joan Hickson *Matron* • Esma Cannon *Miss Cooling* ■ *Dir* Gerald Thomas • *Scr* Norman Hudis

Carry On Screaming
★★★★ **PG**

Comedy 1966 · UK · Colour · 92mins

This is one of the finest entries in Britain's most popular comedy series. Mocking that other bastion of British cinema in the sixties, the Hammer horror film, Talbot Rothwell's script positively bristles with classic one-liners, the most memorable being Kenneth Williams's gleeful "Frying tonight!" as he sinks into a bubbling cauldron. In his only *Carry On*, Harry H Corbett is superb as the Holmesian detective and Fenella Fielding revels in her role as a vampish vampire. ▣

Kenneth Williams *Dr Watt* • Harry H Corbett *Detective Sergeant Bung* • Fenella Fielding *Valeria* • Jim Dale *Albert Potter* • Charles Hawtrey *Dan Dann* • Joan Sims *Emily Bung* ■ *Dir* Gerald Thomas • *Scr* Talbot Rothwell

Carry On Sergeant ★★★ **U**

Comedy 1958 · UK · BW · 80mins

The first of a phenomenon. Like many of the early outings, it centres on an occupation at the heart of British life and is, therefore, closer to Ealing whimsy than the raucous fun of the later *Carry Ons*. Now most famous for being the first Doctor Who, William Hartnell stars as the sergeant determined to make soldiers out of his final batch of national service

conscripts. Alongside Bob Monkhouse, a handful of regulars are on duty, with Kenneth Connor splendid as a weedy hypochondriac, Kenneth Williams as a smarmy know-all, and Charles Hawtrey as the wonderfully named Private Golightly. ▣

William Hartnell *Sergeant Grimshawe* • Bob Monkhouse *Charlie Sage* • Shirley Eaton *Mary* • Eric Barker *Captain Potts* • Dora Bryan *Nora* • Bill Owen *Corporal Copping* • Charles Hawtrey *Peter Golightly* • Kenneth Connor *Horace Strong* • Kenneth Williams *James Bailey* • Hattie Jacques *Captain Clark* ■ *Dir* Gerald Thomas • *Scr* Norman Hudis, from the novel *The Bull Boys* by RF Delderfield

Carry On Spying ★★★ **U**

Spy spoof 1964 · UK · BW · 83mins

Mercilessly ribbing the Bond movies and Graham Greene's espionage entertainments, the ninth *Carry On* saw Barbara Windsor make her series debut as the most resourceful of a hamstrung quartet of agents sent to Vienna to recover a secret formula. The Casbah scenes rather slow things down, but the action picks up pace on the *Orient Express* and in STENCH's underground HQ (a wonderfully observed 007 send-up). Bernard Cribbins, Charles Hawtrey and Kenneth Williams are on form as Babs's weak-kneed accomplices and there are splendid turns from Jim Dale as a master of disguise and Eric Barker as a world-weary spymaster. ▣

Kenneth Williams *Desmond Simpkins* • Barbara Windsor *Daphne Honeybutt* • Bernard Cribbins *Harold Crump* • Charles Hawtrey *Charlie Bind* • Eric Barker *Chief* • Dilys Laye *Lila* • Jim Dale *Carstairs* ■ *Dir* Gerald Thomas • *Scr* Talbot Rothwell, Sid Colin

Carry On Teacher ★★★ **U**

Comedy 1959 · UK · BW · 82mins

The third in the *Carry On* series is a gentle comedy about the concerted efforts of both the pupils and staff of Maudlin Street School to dissuade headmaster Ted Ray from accepting a post elsewhere. The pranks are Bash Street Kids' calibre and raise few laughs, but the staff-room infighting is good value, with drama teacher Kenneth Williams and educational psychologist Leslie Phillips squabbling with maths teacher Hattie Jacques over corporal punishment, and gym mistress Joan Sims feuding with school assessor Rosalind Knight over weedy Kenneth Connor. ▣

Ted Ray *William Wakefield* • Kenneth Connor *Gregory Adams* • Charles Hawtrey *Michael Bean* • Leslie Phillips *Alistair Grigg* • Joan Sims *Sarah Allcock* • Kenneth Williams *Edwin Milton* • Hattie Jacques *Grace Short* • Rosalind Knight *Felicity Wheeler* ■ *Dir* Gerald Thomas • *Scr* Norman Hudis

Carry On Up the Jungle ★★★ **PG**

Comedy 1970 · UK · Colour · 86mins

One of the weaker of the genre spoofs, but there's still much to raise a titter as Frankie Howerd and Kenneth Connor lead an expedition to Africa (Pinewood sets at their most gloriously economical) in order to find the Oozalum bird. Along for the ride are Joan Sims in search of her long-lost son and Sid James seeking a rumble

in the jungle. The reception committee includes Terry Scott as an infantile Tarzan and Charles Hawtrey as the Great Tonka, a tribal chief with a guilty secret. Worth tagging along. ▣

Frankie Howerd *Professor Inigo Tinkle* • Sidney James *Bill Boosey* • Charles Hawtrey *Tonka/Walter* • Joan Sims *Lady Evelyn Bagley* • Terry Scott *Jungle Boy* • Kenneth Connor *Claude Chumley* • Bernard Bresslaw *Upsidasi* ■ *Dir* Gerald Thomas • *Scr* Talbot Rothwell

Carry On Up the Khyber
★★★★ **PG**

Comedy 1968 · UK · Colour · 85mins

Only the *Carry Ons* could get away with using a wooden gate in Snowdonia as the farthest flung outpost of the British Empire! Originally to be called *Carry On the Regiment*, this is rightly regarded as one of the best in the series. Affectionately mocking Hollywood's Raj adventures, Talbot Rothwell's script is stuffed with ludicrous names, classic one-liners and memorable moments, none better than the dinner under fire. Kenneth Williams is superb as the Khasi of Kalabar, but it's Sid James and Joan Sims who steal the show as the Ruff-Diamonds.

Sidney James *Sir Sidney Ruff-Diamond* • Kenneth Williams *Khasi of Kalabar* • Charles Hawtrey *Private James Widdle* • Roy Castle *Captain Keene* • Joan Sims *Lady Ruff-Diamond* • Bernard Bresslaw *Bungdit Din* • Terry Scott *Sergeant Major MacNutt* ■ *Dir* Gerald Thomas • *Scr* Talbot Rothwell

The Cars That Ate Paris
★★★★ **15**

Black comedy 1974 · Ausl · Colour · 84mins

Peter Weir's directorial debut could not be more different from such films as *Picnic at Hanging Rock* and *Witness*, with which he made his reputation. It's a darkly comic tale of a small Australian town that feeds on passing travellers for their car parts, with Terry Camilleri as the newcomer who decides to fight back. Rough edges notwithstanding, it's a sharp, vaguely unsettling affair and fortunately free of some of the portentous imagery that occasionally mars Weir's more recent works. Contains swearing. ▣

Terry Camilleri *Arthur* • John Meillon *Mayor* • Melissa Jaffa *Beth* • Kevin Miles *Dr Midland* • Max Gillies *Metcalfe* • Peter Armstrong *Gorman* ■ *Dir* Peter Weir • *Scr* Peter Weir, Keith Gow, Piers Davies

Carson City ★★★ **U**

Western 1952 · US · Colour · 86mins

Randolph Scott stars as a trouble-shooting railway foreman in director Andre De Toth's roistering western, leading the fight against slumming villain Raymond Massey and his gang of bandits. De Toth had a good rapport with Scott, and this is one of the best of their several westerns together. It's also notable for being one of the first movies filmed in Warnercolor, Warner Bros's short-lived rival to Technicolor.

Randolph Scott *Jeff Kincaid* • Lucille Norman *Susan Mitchell* • Raymond Massey *Big Jack Davis* • Richard Webb *Alan Kincaid* • Larry Keating *Jim Squires* • George Cleveland *William Sharon* ■ *Dir* Andre De Toth • *Scr* Sloan Nibley, Winston Miller, from a story by Sloan Nibley

Carthage in Flames ★ **U**

Historical adventure 1960 · It/Fr · Colour · 96mins

Rome puts Carthage to the torch and the natives run hither and thither, sorting out their petty romantic problems while the rival navies meet on the high seas. The actors, meanwhile, mouth Italian, having been badly dubbed into American. Italian epics are an acquired taste, and there isn't much to recommend this one. Carthage burns prettily, however, and former British beauty queen Anne Heywood swans around in some fetching Punic tunics. Italian dialogue dubbed into English. ▣

Anne Heywood *Fulvia* • Jose Suarez *Hiram* • Pierre Brasseur *Sidone* • Ilaria Occhini *Ophir* • Daniel Gelin *Phegot* ■ *Dir* Carmine Gallone • *Scr* Ennio De Concini, Duccio Tessari, Carmine Gallone, William De Lane Lea

The Cartier Affair ★★ **PG**

Comedy thriller 1984 · US · Colour · 91mins

Fans of kitsch will be in seventh heaven: not only does this boast Joan Collins at her most flamboyant, but her male lead is *Baywatch* star David Hasselhoff. He plays a charming rogue out to fleece his rich employer Collins, only to end up falling in love with her. Director Rod Holcomb tries to whip it all up into witty froth, but he is hampered by the ever-wooden Hasselhoff and a clumsy script. Collins, however, has a ball sending up her soap-queen image, while Telly Savalas makes a splendid villain. ▣

Joan Collins *Cartier Rand* • David Hasselhoff *Curt Taylor* • Telly Savalas *Phil Drexler* • Randi Brooks *Shirl* • Jordan Charney *Ben Foley* ■ *Dir* Rod Holcomb • *Scr* Eugenie Ross-Leming, Brad Buckner, from a story by Eugenie Ross-Leming, Brad Buckner, Michael Devereaux

Cartouche ★ **U**

Swashbuckling adventure 1954 · It/US · BW · 73mins

It's pre-Revolutionary France and Richard Basehart is in exile, trying to prove he didn't murder a prince while evading the various titled gents who want revenge. Basehart joins a troupe of travelling players and romances Patricia Roc; elsewhere, Akim Tamiroff can be found hamming away under a mountain of make-up. Filmed in Italy, this swashbuckler doesn't compare to *The Prisoner of Zenda* or *The Crimson Pirate*, made around the same time.

Richard Basehart *Jacques de Maudy* • Patricia Roc *Donna Violante* • Massimo Serato *Vaubranche* • Akim Tamiroff *Marchese di Salpiere* ■ *Dir* Steve Sekely, Gianni Vernuccio • *Scr* Louis Stevens, from a story by Tullio Pinelli, Gian Paolo Callegari

Cartouche ★★★ **15**

Swashbuckling comedy adventure 1961 · Fr/It · Colour · 110mins

Louis Dominique Bourguignon, alias Cartouche, was a Gallic cousin of Robin Hood. The subject of many plays in his own lifetime, he makes an irresistible hero, especially when played by Jean-Paul Belmondo with a dashing charm that even Errol Flynn would have envied. However, no true swashbuckler would be complete without an utterly unscrupulous enemy and a beautiful heroine. This one is

blessed with Philippe Lemaire as the slimy Chief of Police, and Claudia Cardinale as the newest addition to Belmondo's band of robbers. French dialogue dubbed into English.

Jean-Paul Belmondo *Cartouche* • Claudia Cardinale *Vénus* • Odile Versois *Isabelle de Ferrussac* • Philippe Lemaire *de Ferrussac* • Marcel Dalio *Malichot* • Noël Roquevert *Recruiting sergeant* • Jess Hahn *La Douceur* ■ *Dir* Philippe de Broca • *Scr* Philippe De Broca, Charles Spaak, Daniel Boulanger

Carve Her Name with Pride ★★★★ PG

Second World War spy drama
1958 · UK · BW · 113mins

Made by the same team of director Lewis Gilbert and co-writer Vernon Harris that had previously brought us the Douglas Bader biopic *Reach for the Sky*, this is another well-crafted biographical film inspired by real-life heroism beyond the call of duty in the Second World War. Virginia McKenna gives an understated performance as Violette Szabo, a glamorous young woman who, after her French officer husband was killed in action, became a British spy on the continent.

Virginia McKenna *Violette Szabo* • Paul Scofield *Tony Fraser* • Jack Warner *Mr Bushell* • Denise Grey *Mrs Bushell* • Alain Saury *Etienne Szabo* • Maurice Ronet *Jacques* • Bill Owen *NCO Instructor* • Billie Whitelaw *Winnie* • Michael Caine ■ *Dir* Lewis Gilbert • *Scr* Vernon Harris, Lewis Gilbert, from the novel by RJ Minney

Casablanca ★★★★★ U

Wartime romantic drama
1942 · US · BW · 102mins

"I came to Casablanca for the waters," says Rick. "What waters? We're in the desert," says Renault. "I was misinformed," says Rick. You must remember that, along with "Here's looking at you, kid", "Round up the usual suspects" and the famously misquoted "Play it, Sam." *Casablanca* was conceived in chaos (last-minute casting, an unfinished script), was born a masterpiece and struck a spark with wartime audiences who valued political and emotional commitment. It has Humphrey Bogart, Ingrid Bergman, Paul Henreid, Claude Rains and a marvellous array of fully developed supporting characters. Although its surviving writer dismissed it as just one of the 50 movies Warner Bros made that year, it was special then and always will be.

Humphrey Bogart *Rick Blaine* • Ingrid Bergman *Ilsa Lund* • Paul Henreid *Victor Laszlo* • Claude Rains *Captain Louis Renault* • Conrad Veidt *Major Strasser* • Sydney Greenstreet *Senor Ferrari* • Peter Lorre *Ugarte* • SZ Sakall *Carl* • Madeleine Lebeau *Yvonne* • Dooley Wilson *Sam* ■ *Dir* Michael Curtiz • *Scr* J Julius Epstein, G Philip Epstein, Howard Koch, from the play *Everybody Goes to Rick's* by Murray Burnett, Joan Alison • *Producer* Hal B Wallis • *Cinematographer* Arthur Edeson • *Music* Max Steiner

Casanova ★★★★

Silent drama
1927 · Fr · BW and Tinted · 132mins

Here's a rare treat: the life of the great Italian seducer, made in France but directed by and starring Russians! This jewel of the French silent cinema arrived to some controversy in Paris when it premiered in a censored version in 1931. Finished in 1927, the same year as Abel Gance's mighty *Napoléon*, it stars the great Russian émigré Ivan Mosjoukine, who makes a bold, if temperamental Casanova. This treasure, long unseen, is a fitting reminder of the glory of silent cinema.

Ivan Mosjoukine *Casanova* • Diana Karenne *Maria Mari* • Suzanne Bianchetti *Catherine II* • Jenny Jugo *Therese* • Rina De Liguro *Corticelli* • Nina Kochitz *Countess Vorontzoff* • Olga Day *Baroness Stanhope* ■ *Dir* Alexandre Volkoff • *Scr* Norbert Falk, Ivan Mosjoukine, Alexandre Volkoff

Casanova ★★★ 18

Biographical historical drama
1976 · It · Colour · 147mins

Federico Fellini variously considered this sprawling period fantasy to be the worst film he ever made and his "most complete, expressive and courageous" vision. As ever, the answer lies somewhere in between. Private distractions, labour disputes and a tense shoot, in which the director's relationship with Donald Sutherland deteriorated daily, hardly facilitated creative endeavour. Yet it was Fellini's determination to undermine accepted notions of romantic love and depict the legendary lothario as a pompous, decadent sex machine that rendered the action so cold and detached. Danilo Donati's costumes won an Oscar, while Nino Rota's score is a mocking delight.

Donald Sutherland *Giacomo Casanova* • Tina Aumont *Henriette* • Cicely Browne *Madame D'Urfe* • Carmen Scarpitta *Madame Charpillon* • Clara Algranti *Marcolina* • Margareth Clementi *Sister Maddalena* • Olimpia Carlisi *Isabella* ■ *Dir* Federico Fellini • *Scr* Federico Fellini, Bernardino Zapponi, from the autobiography *Histoire de Ma Vie* by Giacomo Casanova de Seingalt

Casanova '70 ★★★

Comedy
1965 · Fr/It · Colour · 112mins

Six writers contributed to the Oscar-nominated screenplay for this smug sex comedy from Mario Monicelli, which aimed to satirise the effect of female emancipation on the modern male. Marcello Mastroianni, on the other hand, signed up to play the NATO official who discovers he can only rise to the occasion in moments of peril in a bid to debunk the tired image of the Latin lover. Neither director nor star totally succeeded in their intentions, but Marcello exhibits all his Fellini-esque foibles, while Virni Lisi is quite enchanting. In Italian with English subtitles.

Marcello Mastroianni *Major Andrea Rossi-Colombetti* • Virna Lisi *Gigliola* • Michèle Mercier *Noelle* • Marisa Mell *Thelma* • Marco Ferreri *Count Ferreri* ■ *Dir* Mario Monicelli • *Scr* Furio Scarpelli, Agenore Incrocci, Suso Cecchi D'Amico, Mario Monicelli, from a story by Tonino Guerra, Giorgio Salvioni

Casanova & Co ★

Comedy
1976 · Aus/It/Fr/W Ger · Colour · 101mins

Tony Curtis's Casanova conceals his impotence by hiring a man of prodigious sexual appetite who also happens to be his exact double. Released soon after Fellini's sumptuous take on the notorious womaniser, this is really just a soft-core skin flick featuring an army of semi-naked women, among them Bond girl Britt Ekland and Marisa Berenson from *Barry Lyndon*. Hugh Griffith – so memorable in *Ben-Hur* and *Tom Jones* – also gets caught up in the farrago.

Tony Curtis *Giacomo Casanova/Giacomino* • Marisa Berenson *Calipha of Shiraz* • Hugh Griffith *Caliph of Shiraz* • Marisa Mell *Duchess Francesca* • Britt Ekland *Countess Trivulzi* ■ *Dir* François Legrand [Franz Antel] • *Scr* Joshua Sinclair, Tom Priman

Casanova Brown ★★

Comedy
1944 · US · BW · 91mins

About to marry for the second time, Casanova Brown (Gary Cooper) learns that his ex-wife (Teresa Wright) has given birth to his child and is about to have it adopted. Horrified, he spirits the baby away and hides out in a downmarket hotel. Sam Wood's film is not a fraught drama, but a rather undernourished comedy that raises no more than the occasional smile. Interesting, though, to see the screen's famously strong and silent hero figure battling with baby talk and indulging in infantile antics.

Gary Cooper *Casanova Brown* • Teresa Wright *Isabel Drury* • Frank Morgan *Mr Ferris* • Anita Louise *Madge Ferris* • Patricia Collinge *Mrs Drury* • Edmund Breon *Mr Drury* • Jill Esmond *Dr Zernerke* ■ *Dir* Sam Wood • *Scr* Nunnally Johnson, from the play *The Little Accident* by Floyd Dell, Thomas Mitchell

Casanova's Big Night ★★★ U

Musical comedy
1954 · US · Colour · 82mins

Bob Hope's self-created screen image always cast him as a *faux-naïf* – leching yet never leched after. It's interesting, then, to find him playing a Casanova substitute, perpetually mistaken for Vincent Price's genuine womaniser. The film is beautifully designed, and Paramount's Technicolor Venice capably stands in for the real thing. With Basil Rathbone as a suave arch villain, this is one of Hope's better comic vehicles.

Bob Hope *Pippo Popolino* • Joan Fontaine *Francesca Bruni* • Basil Rathbone *Lucio* • Raymond Burr *Bragadin* • Audrey Dalton *Elena* • Vincent Price *Casanova* • John Carradine *Minister Foressi* • Lon Chaney Jr *Emo* ■ *Dir* Norman Z McLeod • *Scr* Hal Kanter, Edmund Hartmann, from a story by Aubrey Wisberg

Casbah ★★★★

Musical drama
1948 · US · BW · 93mins

Thoroughly entertaining remake of *Algiers*, itself a reworking of the classic *Pépé le Moko*, with crooner Tony Martin stepping into the much-imitated shoes of Charles Boyer. This is enthrallingly romantic or excruciatingly corny, depending on your point of view, but there's no denying the pleasure afforded from the musical numbers by Harold Arlen and Leo Robin. Peter Lorre gives arguably his best ever Hollywood performance, there's the sultry allure of Yvonne De Carlo, and watch closely for the briefest glimpse of a young Eartha Kitt.

Yvonne De Carlo *Inez* • Tony Martin *Pépé le Moko* • Peter Lorre *Slimane* • Marta Toren *Gaby* • Hugo Haas *Omar* • Thomas Gomez *Louvain* • Douglas Dick *Carlo* • Eartha Kitt ■ *Dir* John Berry • *Scr* L Bus-Fekete, Arnold Manoff, from a story by Erik Charell, from the novel *Pépé le Moko* by Detective Roger D'Ashelbe [Henri La Barthe]

A Case for Murder ★★★ 15

Thriller
1993 · US · Colour · 89mins

Jennifer Grey's career never really took off after the blockbuster success of *Dirty Dancing*, and she now tends to stick to TV movies or straight-to-video work. It's a shame, because she is on good form here as a young lawyer who teams up with *Last Seduction* star Peter Berg to investigate the murder of a colleague. The latter's former wife is the prime suspect, but it soon becomes apparent that others would benefit from the death. Contains violence and sex scenes.

Jennifer Grey *Kate Weldon* • Peter Berg *Jack Hammett* • Belinda Bauer *Joanna Gaines* • Eugene Roche *Alan Nugent* • Samantha Eggar *Ellen Danvers* • Justine Arlin *Pattie Henderson* • David Hayward *Darren Gaines* ■ *Dir* Duncan Gibbins • *Scr* Pablo F Fenjves, Anthony Richmond, from a story by Duncan Gibbins

A Case for PC 49 ★

Crime drama
1950 · UK · BW · 78mins

Unfortunately, every expense was spared in relating this tale of models, millionaires and murder. Hardly fitting treatment for Brian Reece, British crime fiction's first uniformed hero, who solved over a hundred cases on the airwaves between 1947 and 1953. Such was his popularity that he starred in the *Eagle* comic and in his own board game, *Burglars*. However, thanks to director Francis Searle, he never appeared on screen again.

Brian Reece *Archibald Berkeley-Willoughby* • Joy Shelton *Joan Carr* • Christine Norden *Della Dainton* • Leslie Bradley *Victor Palantine* • Gordon McLeod *Inspector Wilson* • Campbell Singer *Sergeant Wright* • Jack Stewart *Cutler* • Michael Balfour *Chubby Price* ■ *Dir* Francis Searle • *Scr* Alan Stranks, Vernon Harris, from their radio series

The Case of Dr Laurent ★★★

Drama
1957 · Fr · Colour · 111mins

An intense yet sensitive performance from Jean Gabin holds together this medical melodrama from writer/director Jean-Paul Le Chanois. Quitting his Parisian practice for a rural village, Gabin tries to win the locals round to his ideas on natural childbirth. With opposition to the doctor's theories duly provided, the action could easily have lapsed into a typical "tradition vs progress" tirade. Thanks to Henri Alekan's evocative photography and Joseph Kosma's delicate soundtrack, however, the story has stealthily captured the imagination by the time Nicole Courcel has her baby. The birth was actually shown on screen and became a source of some controversy. In French with English subtitles.

Jean Gabin *Dr Laurent* • Nicole Courcel *Francine* • Sylvia Monfort *Catherine Loubet* • Arius *Dr Bastide* • Daxely *Simonet the baker* • Michel Barbey *André Loubet* • Yvonne Gamy *Midwife* ■ *Dir* Jean-Paul Le Chanois • *Scr* Jean-Paul Le Chanois, Rene Barjavel

The Case of the Black Cat ★★★

Mystery   1936 · US · BW · 66mins

The debonair, wise-cracking Warren William was replaced by Ricardo Cortez for this entry in the Perry Mason series, in which the puzzling death of a bedridden millionaire sets off a chain of killings. Directed by William McGann, this is one of the better Mason movies, even though Cortez is a poor actor and Della Street (June Travis) is reduced to a bit part.

Ricardo Cortez *Perry Mason* • June Travis *Della Street* • Jane Bryan *Wilma Laxter* • Craig Reynolds *Frank Oafley* • Carlyle Moore Jr *Douglas Keene* • Gordon Elliott *Sam Laxter* ■ *Dir* William McGann • *Scr* F Hugh Herbert, from the story *The Case of the Caretaker's Cat* by Erle Stanley Gardner

The Case of the Black Parrot ★★

Mystery   1941 · US · BW · 59mins

Having already been transferred to the stage, it was somewhat inevitable that Burton E Stevenson's novel *Mystery of the Boule Cabinet* would be filmed. Noel Smith's suspense-free thriller has intrepid reporter William Lundigan charging around a transatlantic liner in search of the diamonds stolen by an international criminal during a fake submarine alert. With a couple of murders thrown in to reduce still further the list of suspects, it wouldn't take Nancy Drew to identify the culprit.

William Lundigan *Jim Moore* • Eddie Foy Jr *Tripod* • Maris Wrixon *Sandy Vantine* • Paul Cavanagh *Max Armand* • Luli Deste *Madame de Charriere* • Cyril Thornton *Rogers* ■ *Dir* Noel M Smith • *Scr* Robert E Kent, from the play *In the Next Room* by Eleanor Belmont, Harriet Ford, from the novel *Mystery of the Boule Cabinet* by Burton E Stevenson

The Case of the Howling Dog ★★

Mystery   1934 · US · BW · 75mins

A year after Erle Stanley Gardner created him, Perry Mason made his screen debut in this teasing murder mystery. Although Warren William had just finished playing another detective, Philo Vance, his portrayal of the ingenious attorney owed more to William Powell's soused sleuth, Nick Charles, in cult hit *The Thin Man*. Alan Crosland (who made history as the director of *The Jazz Singer*) keeps the clues close to his chest and shifts suspicion between Mary Astor and her fellow suspects with some skill. It's curious to note that the film has no background music whatsoever.

Warren William *Perry Mason* • Mary Astor *Bessie Foley* • Helen Trenholme *Della Street* • Allen Jenkins *Sgt Holcomb* • Grant Mitchell *Claude Drumm* ■ *Dir* Alan Crosland • *Scr* Ben Markson, from a novel by Erle Stanley Gardner

The Case of the Lucky Legs ★★

Mystery   1935 · US · BW · 78mins

The law and Perry Mason are on the trail of a crooked sponsor of "best legs" contests. When he is found murdered, however, the hunt becomes one for his killer. Warren William, the best of the actors to play Erle Stanley

Gardner's lawyer/sleuth, stars in this entry, with Genevieve Tobin providing a vivacious Della Street. Alas, the script is so relentlessly jokey as to bury any possibility of excitement or interest in the over-complicated mystery.

Warren William *Perry Mason* • Genevieve Tobin *Della Street* • Patricia Ellis *Margie Clune* • Lyle Talbot *Dr Doray* • Allen Jenkins *Spudsy* • Barton MacLane *Bissonette* • Peggy Shannon *Thelma Bell* ■ *Dir* Archie Mayo • *Scr* Brown Holmes, Ben Markson, Jerome Chodorov, from a novel by Erle Stanley Gardner

The Case of the Mukkinese Battle Horn ★★★ U

Spoof mystery   1955 · UK · BW · 28mins

Dick Emery stands in for Harry Secombe in this pseudo-Goons picture. The theft of the eponymous instrument is of virtually no significance other than to give Peter Sellers the opportunity to play three characters – music-shop owner Henry Crun, Inspector Quilt and Assistant Chief Commissioner Sir Jervis Fruit. Spike Milligan also gets to reprise his beloved character, Eccles. The opening "Crime Does Not Pay" pastiche and the hilarious door-knocking sequence are the highlights, but there are plenty of other giggles along the way. 🖼

Peter Sellers • Spike Milligan • Dick Emery ■ *Dir* Joseph Sterling

The Case of the Stuttering Bishop ★★ U

Mystery   1937 · US · BW · 71mins

Lacking the enlivening presence of Warren William, the first and best of the Perry Masons, this run-of-the-mill episode stars Donald Woods as the investigative lawyer and Ann Dvorak as Della Street. The plot finds Mason having to determine whether the granddaughter of a millionaire is the genuine article or an impostor. The uninspiring action culminates – surprise, surprise – in the courtroom.

Donald Woods *Perry Mason* • Ann Dvorak *Della Street* • Anne Nagel *Janice Alma Brownley* • Linda Perry *Janice Seaton* • Craig Reynolds *Gordon Bixter* ■ *Dir* William Clemens • *Scr* Don Ryan, Kenneth Gamet, from the novel by Erle Stanley Gardner

The Case of the Velvet Claws ★★★

Mystery   1936 · US · BW · 64mins

One of the better entries in the Perry Mason series, featuring the urbane Warren William as Erle Stanley Gardner's lawyer/sleuth, which finds him actually married to his loyal secretary Della Street, played this time around by Claire Dodd. The honeymoon, however, is delayed when Mason is forced at gunpoint to take on a blackmail case. Moderately sinister, quite amusing and not much longer than a TV episode.

Warren William *Perry Mason* • Claire Dodd *Della Street* • Winifred Shaw *Eva Belter* • Gordon Elliott *Carl Griffin* • Joseph King *George C Belter* • Eddie Acuff *Spudsy* ■ *Dir* William Clemens • *Scr* Tom Reed, from a story by Erle Stanley Gardner

Casey's Shadow ★★★ PG

Drama   1978 · US · Colour · 92mins

A charming portrayal by Walter Matthau carries this fairly insubstantial family drama. Overlong (though trimmed considerably for its UK release) and relentlessly soft-hearted, it nevertheless offers the welcome sparring of horse-trainer Matthau with horse-breeder Alexis Smith, a former Warner Bros star and *Follies* veteran. The action is in the firm but sensitive hands of *Hud* director Martin Ritt, who knows just how much rope to hand out. In real-life Matthau has spent more than a pretty penny on the ponies, but here he's only concerned with getting the titular horsey through a big race. Contains some swearing. 🖼

Walter Matthau *Lloyd Bourdelle* • Alexis Smith *Sarah Blue* • Robert Webber *Mike Marsh* • Murray Hamilton *Tom Patterson* • Andrew A Rubin *[Andrew Rubin] Buddy Bourdelle* ■ *Dir* Martin Ritt • *Scr* Carol Sobieski, from the short story *Ruidoso* by John McPhee

Cash McCall ★★ U

Romantic comedy   1960 · US · Colour · 101mins

Warner Bros were enjoying commercial success at the time with glossy adaptations of popular novels (*Giant*, *A Summer Place*), but this film version of the bestseller by *Executive Suite* writer Cameron Hawley suffered from poor development on its way to the screen. Despite a good cast headed by a terrific James Garner and a radiant Natalie Wood in her first adult role, the end result is too superficial.

James Garner *Cash McCall* • Natalie Wood *Lory Austen* • Nina Foch *Maude Kennard* • Dean Jagger *Grant Austen* • EG Marshall *Winston Conway* • Henry Jones *Gil Clark* • Otto Kruger *Will Atherson* ■ *Dir* Joseph Pevney • *Scr* Lenore Coffee, Marion Hargrove, from the novel by Cameron Hawley

Casino ★★★★ 18

Crime drama   1995 · US · Colour · 170mins

GoodFellas goes to Las Vegas in Martin Scorsese's under-rated tale of power, money and depravity. Robert De Niro plays Sam "Ace" Rothstein, a master bookie turned big-shot casino manager whose head for business deserts him when he marries ex-hooker Ginger McKenna (Sharon Stone). But it's when Nicky Santoro (Joe Pesci), Ace's boyhood acquaintance, arrives in town with an ambitious agenda of his own that things take a further downward spiral. Written by Nicholas Pileggi, an Oscar nominee for *GoodFellas*, *Casino* goes for absorbing realism, intriguing subplots and expertly drawn characters, while Stone is an absolute revelation in her demanding role. A victim's head being squeezed in a vice is one of the more extreme examples of the graphic brutality that's on display in this unflagging and compelling study of how the mobsters drown in the sleaze of their own making. Contains violence, swearing, sex scenes, drug abuse and nudity. 🖼 DVD

Robert De Niro *Sam "Ace" Rothstein* • Sharon Stone *Ginger McKenna* • Joe Pesci *Nicky Santoro* • James Woods *Lester Diamond* • Don Rickles *Billy Sherbert* • Alan King *Andy Stone* • Kevin Pollak *Phillip Green*

■ *Dir* Martin Scorsese • *Scr* Nicholas Pileggi, Martin Scorsese, from the novel by Nicholas Pileggi

The Casino Murder Case ★★

Mystery   1935 · US · BW · 82mins

Several actors played SS Van Dine's popular sleuth Philo Vance. The first, and best, was William Powell, who made four films in the series; by 1935, Warren William and Basil Rathbone had each had an outing. This information is more interesting than the seventh film, which stars a miscast Paul Lukas on the trail of a mad poisoner who succeeds in killing three members of a bizarre family before Vance solves the case.

Paul Lukas *Philo Vance* • Rosalind Russell *Doris* • Alison Skipworth *Mrs Llewellyn* • Donald Cook *Lynn* • Arthur Byron *Kincaid* • Ted Healy *Sgt Heath* ■ *Dir* Edwin L Marin • *Scr* Florence Ryerson, Edgar Allan Woolf, from a novel by SS Van Dine

Casino Royale ★★ PG

Spy spoof   1967 · UK · Colour · 125mins

A leaden, toe-curlingly unfunny attempt to pastiche the 007 fluffery, with an ageing David Niven doing his urbane, tongue-in-cheek best with a script the consistency of celluloid suet. An all-star cast has been wheeled out – Orson Welles, Woody Allen, Deborah Kerr, Charles Boyer, Ursula Andress, William Holden et al – in a vain attempt to add a pinch of pizzazz, as the now retired Bond is hoicked from the Twilight Home for Terminally Confused Spies and ordered to smash SMERSH. Moral of this one: never spoof a spoof. 🖼

David Niven *Sir James Bond* • Peter Sellers *Evelyn Tremble* • Ursula Andress *Vesper Lynd* • Orson Welles *Le Chiffre* • Woody Allen *Jimmy Bond, Dr Noah* • Deborah Kerr *Agent Mimi, Lady Fiona McTarry* • William Holden (1) *Ransome* • Charles Boyer *Le Grand* • John Huston *McTarry* • Jean-Paul Belmondo *French Legionnaire* • George Raft • Barbara Bouchet *Moneypenny* • Peter O'Toole *Scotch Piper* • Geoffrey Bayldon *"Q"* • Ronnie Corbett *Polo* • Bernard Cribbins *Taxi driver* • Jacqueline Bisset *Miss Goodthighs* • Derek Nimmo *Hadley* ■ *Dir* John Huston, Ken Hughes, Val Guest, Robert Parrish, Joe McGrath *[Joseph McGrath]* • *Scr* Wolf Mankowitz, John Law, Michael Sayers (with uncredited contributions from Billy Wilder, Val Guest, Joseph Heller, Ben Hecht, Terry Southern), from the novel by Ian Fleming

Casper ★★★★ PG

Supernatural comedy drama   1995 · US · Colour · 95mins

With comic books and cartoon series full of muscle-bound superheroes vying for big-screen superstardom, it's nice to see a gentler character making such an impact in his first film outing. Here, Casper the Friendly Ghost is doing his bit to make Whipstaff Manor a homelier place for lonely Christina Ricci to live in, but it's his ghoulish uncles Stretch, Stinkie and Fatso who scare up all the fun in this enchanting family comedy. Although the movie is dominated by special effects, Cathy Moriarty nearly steals the show. Contains some swearing. 🖼

Christina Ricci *Kat Harvey* • Bill Pullman *Dr James Harvey* • Cathy Moriarty *Carrigan*

U = SUITABLE FOR ALL   **Uc** = SUITABLE FOR ALL, ESPECIALLY FOR YOUNG CHILDREN (VIDEO ONLY)   **PG** = PARENTAL GUIDANCE

Crittenden • Eric Idle *Dibs* • Malachi Pearson *Casper* • Joe Nipote *Stretch* • Joe Alaskey *Stinkie* • Brad Garrett *Fatso* • Clint Eastwood • Mel Gibson ■ *Dir* Brad Silberling • *Scr* Sherri Stoner, Deanna Oliver, from a story by Joseph Oriolo, Seymour Reit, from characters created by Joseph Oriolo • *Special Effects* Michael Lantieri

Casper: a Spirited Beginning ★★ U

Supernatural comedy
1997 · US · Colour · 91mins

The friendly ghost does a runner from the ghost training centre and makes friends with a bullied young boy (Brendon Ryan Barrett) in this charmless straight-to-video sequel. Steve Guttenberg is the boy's workaholic building contractor dad who pays him little attention, and toothy Lori Loughlin is Barrett's teacher who's trying to stop Guttenberg demolishing a local mansion to make way for a mini-mall. A cheesy concoction, clumsily mixing ghoulish humour, children's angst and high explosives. ▣

Brendon Ryan Barrett *Chris Carson* • Steve Guttenberg *Tim Carson* • James Earl Jones *Kibosh* • Pauly Shore *Snivel* • Michael McKean *Bill Case* • Rodney Dangerfield *Mayor Johnny Hunt* • James Ward *Stretch* • Bill Farmer *Stinkie* • Jeff Harnell *Fatso* • Jeremy Foley *Casper* ■ *Dir* Sean McNamara • *Scr* Jymn Magon, from characters created by Joseph Oriolo

Casper Meets Wendy ★ U

Supernatural comedy
1998 · US · Colour · 90mins

Teri Garr, Cathy Moriarty and Shelley Duvall reach career lowpoints as a trio of witches hiding away at a summer resort in a straight-to-video release that makes *Home Alone* look like an exercise in subtlety. Their niece Wendy (the helium-voiced Hilary Duff) is being sought by arched-eyebrow pantomime warlock George Hamilton, because he's been told she's a better witch than him. Somehow or other Casper and the other ghosts become involved, leading to an unbearably manic series of supernatural shenanigans. ▣

Hilary Duff *Wendy* • Jeremy Foley *Casper* • Shelley Duvall *Gabby* • Teri Garr *Fanny* • Cathy Moriarty *Geri* • George Hamilton *Desmond Spellman* ■ *Dir* Sean McNamara • *Scr* Jymn Magon, Rob Kerchner, from characters created by Joseph Oriolo

Casque d'Or ★★★★

Drama
1952 · Fr · BW · 97mins

Based on an actual *crime passionnel*, this is one of the jewels of that much-maligned strain of literate French filmmaking, cynically dubbed, by François Truffaut, the "tradition of quality". In re-creating the underworld Paris of the Impressionists, director Jacques Becker draws upon the poetic humanity of his mentor Jean Renoir and the glowing elegance of his painter father, Auguste, to create a vibrant world of amiable rogues and sensual delight. Radiant at its centre is Simone Signoret, whose golden beauty prompts the tragic rivalry between naive carpenter Serge Reggiani and calculating gangster Claude Dauphin. A French language film.

Simone Signoret *Marie* • Serge Reggiani *Manda* • Claude Dauphin *Felix Leca* •

Raymond Bussières *Raymond* • William Sabatier *Roland* • Gaston Modot *Danard* • Loleh Bellon *Billy* • Claude Castaing *Fredo* ■ *Dir* Jacques Becker, Jacques Becker • *Scr* Jacques Companeez

Cass Timberlane ★★★★

Romance
1947 · US · BW · 118mins

Cass Timberlane (Spencer Tracy) is a highly respected judge in a small Minneapolis town, beloved of the country club set but living alone since the death of his wife. When he falls passionately in love with a beautiful girl from the "wrong" side of town (Lana Turner), a series of shock waves, professional and personal, are unleashed. A good, old-fashioned drama that reveals Turner's often overlooked and mismanaged talent and offers Tracy at his magnificently nuanced best. Zachary Scott's womanising lawyer and Mary Astor's society bitch add extra bite.

Spencer Tracy *Cass Timberlane* • Lana Turner *Virginia Marshland* • Zachary Scott *Brad Criley* • Tom Drake *Jamie Wargate* • Mary Astor *Queenie Havock* • Albert Dekker *Boone Havock* ■ *Dir* George Sidney • *Scr* Donald Ogden Stewart, Sonya Levien, from the novel by Sinclair Lewis

Cassandra ★★★ 18

Supernatural thriller
1987 · Ausl · Colour · 89mins

An interesting little movie from Australia that belts along effectively enough, featuring Tessa Humphries as a young woman who discovers that her brother has been jailed for causing their mother's death. As if this isn't enough of a shock, her brother has escaped from prison. The jolts are expertly placed, the cast is nicely twitchy and, despite the fact that Humphries shows an uncommon stoicism in the face of alarming news, this film is intriguing stuff. Contains violence and nudity. ▣

Tessa Humphries *Cassandra* • Shane Briant *Steven Roberts* • Briony Behets *Helen Roberts* • Susan Barling *Libby* ■ *Dir* Colin Eggleston • *Scr* Colin Eggleston, John Ruane, Chris Fichett

The Cassandra Crossing ★ PG

Disaster thriller
1976 · UK/It/W Ger · Colour · 123mins

A terrorist has passed on a deadly plague to the passengers of a luxury express train, which has to be rerouted across a rickety bridge to a deserted concentration camp in order to prevent a worldwide epidemic. Burt Lancaster, the mastermind behind this cunning diversion, had the right idea when he suggested blowing the train to smithereens – ideally with the film inside. There were better effects and more thrills (if fewer laughs) in Gromit's train chase with the penguin in *The Wrong Trousers*. ▣

Richard Harris *Dr Jonathan Chamberlain* • Sophia Loren *Jennifer Rispoli Chamberlain* • Burt Lancaster *Col Stephen Mackenzie* • Ava Gardner *Nicole Dressler* • Martin Sheen *Robby Navarro* • Ingrid Thulin *Dr Elena Stradner* • Lee Strasberg *Herman Kaplan* • John Phillip Law *Major Stack* • Ann Turkel *Susan* • OJ Simpson *Father Haley* ■ *Dir* George Pan Cosmatos • *Scr* Tom Mankiewicz, Robert Katz, George Pan Cosmatos, from a story by Robert Katz, George Pan Cosmatos

Cast a Dark Shadow ★★★

Drama thriller
1957 · UK · BW · 82mins

After murdering his wife Mona Washbourne for her money, Dirk Bogarde marries a canny former barmaid Margaret Lockwood who proves less easy to dispose of. When he meets Kay Walsh, however, murder is back on the agenda. A modest but entertaining melodrama, directed by Lewis Gilbert with a stylish and proficient cast. Lockwood, who would return to the screen only once more two decades later, is particularly effective.

Dirk Bogarde *Edward Bare* • Mona Washbourne *Monica Bare* • Margaret Lockwood *Freda Jeffries* • Kay Walsh *Charlotte Young* • Kathleen Harrison *Emmie* ■ *Dir* Lewis Gilbert • *Scr* John Cresswell, from the play *Murder Mistaken* by Janet Green

Cast a Deadly Spell ★★★ 15

Thriller
1991 · US · Colour · 92mins

Also known as *Lovecraft*, this is a strange, quirky tale that tips its hat at the stories of horror writer HP Lovecraft. *Henry and June* star Fred Ward is a private eye in a kind of alternative Los Angeles of the forties, where everyone indulges in magic except him. He's hired by David Warner to get back the *Necronomicon*, which, as anyone who has seen *The Evil Dead* will know, is the ominous "Book of the Dead". It's not long before gory creatures are coming out of every nook and cranny. ▣

Fred Ward *H Phillip Lovecraft* • David Warner *Amos Hackshaw* • Julianne Moore *Connie Stone* • Clancy Brown *Harry Bordon* • Alexandra Powers *Olivia Hackshaw* • Arnetia Walker *Hypolite Kropotkin* ■ *Dir* Martin Campbell • *Scr* Joseph Dougherty

Cast a Giant Shadow ★★★ PG

War drama
1966 · US · Colour · 132mins

This expensive epic tells one of the great stories of the early days in Israel's struggle for independence. The role of American-born colonel David "Mickey" Marcus is ruggedly incarnated by Kirk Douglas, apt casting for the orthodox Jew, born Issur Danielovitch, later dubbed Stephen Demsky, and self-styled "Ragman's Son". Marcus's story is impressive enough without the array of guest stars (John Wayne, Yul Brynner, Frank Sinatra) writer/director Melville Shavelson assembled in a distracting attempt to ensure box office respectability. For an absolutely hilarious account of the filming, read Shavelson's own book, *How to Make a Jewish Movie*. ▣

Kirk Douglas *Colonel David "Mickey" Marcus* • Senta Berger *Magda Simon* • Angie Dickinson *Emma Marcus* • Gary Merrill *Pentagon Chief of Staff* • Haym Topol [Topol] *Abou Ibn Kader* • Frank Sinatra *Vince* • Yul Brynner *Asher Gonen* • John Wayne *General Mike Randolph* ■ *Dir* Melville Shavelson • *Scr* Melville Shavelson, from a biography by Ted Berkman

Cast a Long Shadow ★★ U

Western drama
1959 · US · Colour · 82mins

It's illegitimacy that casts the long shadow here, turning Audie Murphy's

cowpoke into an embittered, hard-drinking, gambling drifter. Then he inherits the estate of a wealthy rancher who may have been his father, whereupon he becomes an intolerant trail boss during an arduous cattle drive. The script sorts him out in due course, but leaves some irritating loose ends. Terry Moore plays his girl.

Audie Murphy *Matt Brown* • Terry Moore *Janet Calvert* • John Dehner *Chip Donohue* • James Best *Sam Mullen* • Rita Lynn *Hortensia* • Denver Pyle *Harrison* ■ *Dir* Thomas Carr • *Scr* Martin G Goldsmith, John McGreevey, from a novel by Wayne D Overholser, from a story by Martin G Goldsmith

Cast the First Stone ★★ 15

Drama based on a true story
1989 · US · Colour · 94mins

Jill Eikenberry (*LA Law*) plays former Roman Catholic novitiate, now a respected school teacher, who is brutally raped. Ashamed, she remains silent until she discovers that she is pregnant and decides to keep the baby. The school board, disbelieving her story of being attacked, fires her on the grounds of immoral conduct. Based on a true incident, this TV movie about one woman's battle against intolerance is still topical and timely. ▣

Jill Eikenberry *Diane Martin* • Richard Masur *Alan Refson* • Joe Spano *Bill Spencer* • Lew Ayres *Mr Martin* • Anne Schedeen *Elaine Stanton* ■ *Dir* John Korty • *Scr* Brian L Ross, from a story by Vickie Patik, Brian L Ross

Castaway ★★ 15

Drama based on a true story
1986 · UK · Colour · 112mins

Essentially an excuse for Oliver Reed and Amanda Donohoe to get their kit off, this is Nicolas Roeg's version of the real-life experiences of Lucy Irvine, who replied to a newspaper advert from Gerald Kingsland for a woman to join him for a year on a desert island. Both Donohoe and Reed cope well with their roles as the castaway and the sex-mad, middle-aged man who is her companion, but in the end you can't help feeling the nudity is only there to spice up a tale of two selfish people who probably deserved each other. Contains swearing, sex scenes and nudity. ▣

Oliver Reed *Gerald Kingsland* • Amanda Donohoe *Lucy Irvine* • Georgina Hale *Sister St Margaret* • Frances Barber *Sister St Winifred* ■ *Dir* Nicolas Roeg • *Scr* Allan Scott, from the books *Castaway* by Lucy Irvine and *The Islander* by Gerald Kingsland

The Castaway Cowboy ★★★ U

Western
1974 · US · Colour · 87mins

The ever-amiable James Garner is the best thing in this Disney family movie about the first big cattle ranch to be set up in the Hawaiian islands. Garner plays a Texan cowboy who helps pretty widow Vera Miles convert her land from potatoes to beef. Robert Culp is a shady operator and Garner's romantic rival, and there are various "noble savages" on hand to cause trouble. The main location is the island of Kauai, whose mountains and beaches are familiar to everyone thanks to *South Pacific* and *Blue Hawaii*. ▣

James Garner *Lincoln Costain* • Vera Miles *Henrietta MacAvoy* • Robert Culp *Bryson* • Eric Shea *Booton MacAvoy* • Elizabeth Smith *Liliha* • Manu Tupou *Kimo* • Gregory Sierra *Marrujo* • Nephi Hannemann *Malakoma* ■ Dir Vincent McEveety • Scr Don Tait, from a story by Don Tait, Richard Bluel, Hugh Benson

The Castilian ★ U

Historical adventure
1963 · US/Sp · Colour · 129mins

This uninvolving costume epic concerns the 10th-century legend of Fernan Gonzales, who tried to free Spain from the Moors. First, though, he has to unite Spain, despite fierce opposition from Broderick Crawford, the unwholesome King of Navarre. Plenty of swordplay and romance ensues. Produced by Sidney Pink (the man behind such gems as *Reptilicus* and *The Man from ORGY*), it's one of a clutch of second-rate pictures Crawford made between *Highway Patrol* and *The Private Files of J Edgar Hoover*.

Cesar Romero *Jeronimo* • Frankie Avalon *Jerifan* • Broderick Crawford *Don Sancho* • Alida Valli *Queen Teresa* • Spartaco Santoni *Fernan Gonzales* • Teresa Velazquez *Sancha* • Fernando Rey *Ramiro II, King of Leon* • George Rigaud *Saint Milan* ■ Dir Javier Seto • Scr Paulino Rodrigo Diaz, Javier Seto, Luis de los Arcos, Sidney Pink, from the epic poem by Fernan Gonzales

The Castle ★★★★★ 15

Comedy 1997 · Ausl · Colour · 81mins

Take the endearing stupidity of the Farrelly Brothers and the Coen Brothers' quirky eye for detail, and you're getting close to the appeal of this utterly splendid Aussie comedy. It didn't make a big impact in the UK, but don't let that deter you – although it flags a little at the end it remains one of the funniest films of the decade. Former soap stars Michael Caton (*The Sullivans*) and Anne Tenney (*A Country Practice*) are the engagingly dim heads of the Kerrigan family who are delighted with their dream home, which borders the runway of Melbourne's airport. When the airport authority decides to compulsorily purchase their property to make way for expansion, the bumbling Kerrigans go into battle against the authorities. Contains swearing. ▭

Michael Caton *Darryl Kerrigan* • Anne Tenney *Sal Kerrigan* • Stephen Curry *Dale Kerrigan* • Anthony Simcoe *Steve Kerrigan* • Sophie Lee *Tracey Kerrigan* • Wayne Hope *Wayne Kerrigan* ■ Dir Rob Stitch • Scr Rob Sitch, Santo Cilauro, Tom Gleisner, Jane Kennedy

Castle Freak ★★ 18

Horror 1995 · US · Colour · 89mins

Alcoholic Jeffrey Combs inherits a castle in Italy, only to find the previous tenant kept a deformed zombie with a taste for human flesh chained in the dungeon. Although this straight-laced horror comedy speeds along with enough splashy gore and weirdness to provide mild amusement, it's a minor effort from *Re-Animator* director Stuart Gordon. Eschewing the razor-sharp satire contained in his best work, Gordon focuses instead on screams, kinky sex and blood, paying scant attention to the wildly uneven performances or gaping plot-holes. ▭

Jonathan Fuller *Giorgio* • Jeffrey Combs *John Reilly* • Barbara Crampton *Susan Reilly* • Jessica Dollarhide *Rebecca Reilly* • Massimo Sarchielli *Giannetti* • Elisabeth Kaza *Agnese* ■ Dir Stuart Gordon • Scr Dennis Paoli, from a story by Stuart Gordon, Dennis Paoli

Castle Keep ★★★ 15

Second World War drama
1969 · US · Colour · 102mins

Sydney Pollack's fourth film as director is strange indeed: a heavily allegorical Second World War drama about a squad of American soldiers who defend a Belgian castle, its impotent count and art treasures from the approaching Germans. Often pretentious, often startling and rooted in symbol and unreality, it's as if maverick director Sam Fuller had remade *Last Year at Marienbad*. Contains swearing. ▭

Burt Lancaster *Major Abraham Falconer* • Peter Falk *Sergeant Orlando Rossi* • Patrick O'Neal *Captain Lionel Beckman* • Jean-Pierre Aumont *Henri Tixier, Comte De Maldorais* • Bruce Dern *Lieutenant Billy Byron Bix* ■ Dir Sydney Pollack • Scr Daniel Taradash, David Rayfiel, from the novel by William Eastlake

Castle of Evil ★

Horror 1966 · US · Colour · 80mins

Relatives of a dead, mad scientist gather in his creepy castle for the reading of the will, only to be systematically murdered by a robot fashioned in the image of the deceased. The result is a ridiculously bad mixture of Agatha Christie and schlock horror, featuring forties sex goddess Virginia Mayo as the madman's ex-mistress. A free funeral was promised if you died of fright while watching this amateur exploiter, though one is more likely to die laughing.

Scott Brady *Matt Granger* • Virginia Mayo *Sable* • Lisa Gaye *Carol Harris* • David Brian *Robert Hawley* • Hugh Marlowe *Dr Corozal* • William Thourlby *The robot* • Shelley Morrison *Lupe Tekal d'Esperanza* ■ Dir Francis D Lyon • Scr Charles A Wallace

The Castle of Fu Manchu ★ PG

Horror
1968 · W Ger/Sp/It/UK · Colour · 88mins

The appalling final entry in the series featuring Sax Rohmer's Oriental arch-villain has Christopher Lee once more plotting world domination on a shoestring budget. Richard Greene, of TV's *Robin Hood* fame, is Scotland Yard's Nayland Smith trying to halt the evil Asian's plan to turn oceans into ice from his base in Istanbul. Director Jess Franco is currently being lauded in some cineaste circles as an unsung demented genius. Judge for yourself with this atrocious turkey. ▭

Christopher Lee *Fu Manchu* • Richard Greene *Nayland Smith* • Howard Marion-Crawford *Dr Petrie* • Tsai Chin *Lin Tang* • Gunther Stoll *Curt* ■ Dir Jess Franco [Jesus Franco] • Scr Harry Alan Towers

Castle on the Hudson ★★★

Prison drama 1940 · US · BW · 74mins

The castle in question is Sing Sing penitentiary, where John Garfield is serving a long stretch for robbery. Girlfriend Ann Sheridan campaigns for his release; when she's injured in a

car crash, the prison warden (Pat O'Brien, who else?) goes soft and lets Garfield out. Despite this B-movie's relatively short running time, it still manages to veer off into a typical Warner Bros exposé of political expediency. It's breathless and dated, though Garfield's strengths as an actor still shine through.

John Garfield *Tommy Gordon* • Ann Sheridan *Kay* • Pat O'Brien *Warden Long* • Burgess Meredith *Steven Rockford* • Henry O'Neill *District Attorney* • Jerome Cowan *Ed Crowley* • Guinn "Big Boy" Williams [Guinn Williams] *Mike Cagle* ■ Dir Anatole Litvak • Scr Seton I Miller, Brown Holmes, Courteney Terrett, from the book *20,000 Years in Sing Sing* by Lewis E Lawes

Casual Sex? ★★★ 18

Comedy 1988 · US · Colour · 83mins

Based on Wendy Goldman and Judy Toll's stage play, this talky but likeable post-Aids comedy might equally have been called *Sex and the Single Girl*. The setting is an up-market health centre, where Lea Thompson and Victoria Jackson hope to bump into a hunky, healthy guy. While they're at it, they reflect on the new sexual realities of the late eighties. Comedian Andrew Dice Clay shows that he can be more than just an offensive stand-up with an amusing cameo as a New Jersey male with an attitude problem. ▭

Lea Thompson *Stacy* • Victoria Jackson *Melissa* • Stephen Shellen *Nick* • Jerry Levine *Jamie* • Andrew Dice Clay *Vinny* • Mary Gross *Ilene* ■ Dir Genevieve Robert • Scr Wendy Goldman, Judy Toll, from their play

Casualties ★★★ 18

Thriller 1997 · US · Colour · 82mins

After supporting roles in Hollywood movies such as *Disclosure* and *White Squall*, UK actress Caroline Goodall gets top billing in her own right in this creepy American indie chiller. She plays the abused wife of cop Jon Gries who strikes up a friendship with seemingly nice Mark Harmon, a fellow student in her cookery class. However, it quickly becomes apparent that her idealised "new man" is more than a couple of eggs short of an omelette. Alex Graves's direction is appreciably claustrophobic and he elicits strong performances from his two leads. ▭

Mark Harmon *Tommy Nance* • Caroline Goodall *Annie Summers* • Jon Gries [Jonathan Gries] *Bill Summers* • Michael Beach *Clark* ■ Dir Alex Graves • Scr Gary Preisler, Alex Graves

Casualties of Love: the Long Island Lolita Story ★★

Drama based on a true story
1993 · US · Colour · 95 mins

In 1992, 17-year-old Amy Fisher made headlines when she was tried for shooting and permanently disabling the wife of her lover. Long Island, known for its ritzy residents, went ape and so did the American press who dubbed Fisher the "Long Island Lolita". One of three TV movies that were rushed into production in the ensuing months, this is the sort of trashy, true-life crime drama that crops up all too often these days. This one stars Alyssa Milano and Jack Scalia and takes the victim's point of view.

Jack Scalia *Joey Buttafuoco* • Alyssa Milano *Amy Fisher* • Phyllis Lyons *Mary Jo Buttafuoco* • Leo Rossi *Bobby Buttafuoco* • JE Freeman *Detective Marty Alger* • Peter Van Norden *Mike Rindenow* ■ Dir/Scr John Herzfeld

Casualties of War ★★★★★ 18

War drama 1989 · US · Colour · 108mins

Not as well-known as *The Deer Hunter*, *Apocalypse Now* or *Platoon*, this Vietnam War tale is just as disturbing and probably more provocative. It has at its centre the fact-based story of a Vietnamese woman who is kidnapped and brutally raped by four GIs. While battle-scarred Sean Penn leads the assault, new recruit Michael J Fox stands back but doesn't help her. The film's compassion for the woman hits us directly, as does the way Brian De Palma sets up the episode by showing the brutalisation of Penn and his cohorts in the preceding scenes. Filmed with all of the director's technical bravura, it heads towards an epilogue that reaches an emotional precipice and then leaps confidently over it. Contains violence, swearing, sex scenes and nudity. ▭

Michael J Fox *Eriksson* • Sean Penn *Sergeant Tony Meserve* • Don Harvey *Corporal Thomas E Clark* • John C Reilly *Herbert Hatcher* • John Leguizamo *Diaz* • Le Thuy Thu *Oahn* • Erik King *Sergeant Frank Brown* • Jack Gwaltney *Rowan* • Ving Rhames *Lieutenant Reilly* ■ Dir Brian De Palma • Scr David Rabe, from the book by Daniel Lang

Cat and Mouse ★★★

Drama 1958 · UK · BW · 79mins

Adapted from Michael Halliday's novel, this claustrophobic thriller denies documentary director Paul Rotha the chance to demonstrate his facility with realism. Yet he still manages to generate a fair amount of suspense as Ann Sears finds herself caught between an American army deserter and the villains searching for the diamonds stolen by her recently executed father. With Hilton Edwards and Lee Paterson suitably imposing as her pursuers, this is vastly superior to the majority of British B-movies made at the time.

Lee Patterson *Rod Fenner* • Ann Sears *Ann Coltby* • Hilton Edwards *Mr Scruby* • Victor Maddern *Superintendent Harding* • George Rose *Dealer* ■ Dir Paul Rotha • Scr Paul Rotha, from the novel *Cat and Mouse* by Michael Halliday

The Cat and the Canary ★★★★

Silent mystery 1927 · US · BW · 82mins

Paul Leni was the first of the great expressionist German directors to go to Hollywood, and his debut film there was a strong influence on subsequent horror movies. Moodily shot, this classic "old dark house" picture is played mostly for laughs. The canary is a wealthy old man and the cat, or rather cats, are those who gather at midnight 20 years after his death to hear a reading of the will. It was remade with Bob Hope in 1939, and again in 1979. Leni died of blood poisoning two years later, aged 44.

Laura La Plante *Annabelle West* • Creighton Hale *Paul Jones* • Forrest Stanley *Charles Wilder* • Tully Marshall *Roger Crosby* •

Gertrude Astor *Cecily Young* • Arthur Edmund Carewe *Harry Blythe* • Flora Finch *Susan Sillsby* ■ *Dir* Paul Leni • *Scr* Robert F Hill, Alfred A Cohn, from the play by John Willard

The Cat and the Canary
★★★★

Mystery comedy 1939 · US · BW · 73mins

Unfairly neglected today, this also suffered on release from the fact that 1939 was the *annus mirabilis* of Hollywood's Golden Era. This is the definitive haunted-house movie, much copied, never bettered, in which Bob Hope cements his screen image: at once cowardly, lecherous, vulnerable and attractive. Lovely Paulette Goddard makes a fine foil for Hope; so successful were they together that they were immediately re-teamed in *The Ghost Breakers*, with which this film is often confused. This is a remake of an equally good silent version, and was itself remade by porn king Radley Metzger in 1979.

Bob Hope *Wally Campbell* • Paulette Goddard *Joyce Norman* • John Beal *Fred Blythe* • Douglass Montgomery *Charlie Wilder* • Gale Sondergaard *Miss Lu* • George Zucco *Lawyer Crosby* • Elizabeth Patterson *Aunt Susan* ■ *Dir* Elliott Nugent • *Scr* Walter De Leon, Lynn Starling, from the play by John Willard

The Cat and the Canary
★★ 15

Murder mystery 1979 · UK · Colour · 93mins

This remake is not a patch on either Paul Leni's silent original or Bob Hope's cornball 1939 reworking. An all-star British cast works incredibly hard to raise both laughs and the hairs on the back of your neck, but only succeeds in being annoying. The main reason is Radley Metzger's tepid direction, which almost completely misses the eerie "old dark house" atmosphere and the grisly graveyard humour that made John Willard's play such a natural for the screen. 🖵

Honor Blackman *Susan Sillsby* • Edward Fox *Hendricks* • Michael Callan *Paul Jones* • Wendy Hiller *Allison Crosby* • Olivia Hussey *Cicily Young* • Beatrix Lehmann *Mrs Pleasant* • Carol Lynley *Annabelle West* • Daniel Massey *Harry Blythe* • Peter McEnery *Charlie Wilder* • Wilfrid Hyde White *Cyrus West* ■ *Dir* Radley Metzger • *Scr* Radley Metzger, from the play by John Willard

The Cat and the Fiddle
★★★ U

Romantic musical
1934 · US · BW and Colour · 88mins

This wittily filmed version of the lightweight Jerome Kern/Otto Harbach Broadway show stars the actress who was undoubtedly queen of movie operetta, the "iron butterfly" Jeanette MacDonald. She's paired here with silent screen idol Ramon Novarro, whose matinée good looks and singing voice endured in talkies until his notorious private life led to a severe fall-off in screen popularity. This is good fun, with a sparkling script and the bonus of a last reel in early three-strip Technicolor. Director William K Howard doesn't have the lightness of touch for a bright and breezy musical, but the glossy production values help out immensely.

Ramon Novarro *Victor* • Jeanette MacDonald *Shirley* • Frank Morgan *Daudet* • Charles Butterworth *Charles* • Jean Hersholt *Professor* ■ *Dir* William K Howard • *Scr* Bella Spewack, Sam Spewack, from the musical by Jerome Kern, Otto Harbach

Cat Ballou
★★★★ PG

Comedy western 1965 · US · Colour · 92mins

Famous comedy western with Jane Fonda hiring a gunman to avenge her murdered father. The man she hires is Kid Shelleen, a long-haired, buckskinned gunfighter who wakes up sozzled and gets worse by the minute. Even his horse is a drunkard, leaning against a barn for support. This showpiece role won an Oscar for Lee Marvin, who also plays straight man to himself as Shelleen's psychotic brother, a killer with a silver nose. Nat King Cole and Stubby Kaye string along for a singalong in what is an amiable and literally hit-and-miss affair that paved the way for such films as Mel Brooks's *Blazing Saddles*.

Jane Fonda *Cat Ballou* • Lee Marvin *Kid Shelleen/Tim Strawn* • Michael Callan *Clay Boone* • Dwayne Hickman *Jed* • Tom Nardini *Jackson Two-Bears* • John Marley *Frankie Ballou* • Reginald Denny *Sir Harry Percival* • Arthur Hunnicutt *Butch Cassidy* ■ *Dir* Elliot Silverstein • *Scr* Frank Pierson, Walter Newman, from the novel by Roy Chanslor

Cat Chaser
★★ 18

Thriller 1989 · US · Colour · 86mins

With 1995's *Get Shorty*, director Barry Sonnenfeld seemed to have achieved what Elmore Leonard fans were beginning to think was impossible: a good film adaptation of one of his novels. Before that milestone, however, they had to make do with this tough political thriller, which is light years ahead of the likes of Burt Reynolds's *Stick*, but still remains a disappointment. Peter Weller is the ex-soldier who gets lured into an affair and dangerous intrigue with a former flame (Kelly McGillis), now the wife of a particularly nasty Latin American policeman. Weller is fine as the tormented hero and there is reliable support from Charles Durning and Frederic Forrest. However, McGillis is an unconvincing *femme fatale*, and director Abel Ferrara's heart doesn't seem to be in it. Contains swearing, violence, sex scenes and nudity. 🖵

Peter Weller *George Moran* • Kelly McGillis *Mary De Boya* • Charles Durning *Jiggs Scully* • Frederic Forrest *Nolan Tyner* • Tomas Milian *Andres De Boya* ■ *Dir* Abel Ferrara • *Scr* Elmore Leonard, James Borrelli, Alan Sharp, from the novel by Elmore Leonard

The Cat from Outer Space
★★ U

Comedy 1978 · US · Colour · 94mins

Harmless Disney matinée fodder, with alien feline "Jake" grounded on Earth and in need of human dexterity to repair its disabled spacecraft. Startling similarities to *ET* add an unforeseen layer of entertainment value to a bland package that could have done with a bit of Spielberg magic. Other than Jake's "wonder collar" that levitates people and places them in suspended animation, it's a pretty uninspired juvenile romp. 🖵

Ken Berry *Dr Frank Wilson* • Sandy Duncan *Dr Liz Bartlett* • Harry Morgan *General Stilton* • Roddy McDowall *Stallwood* • McLean Stevenson *Dr Carl Link* • Jesse White *Earnest Ernie* • Alan Young *Dr Wenger* ■ *Dir* Norman Tokar • *Scr* Ted Key

The Cat Gang
★★ U

Crime drama 1959 · UK · BW · 50mins

Based on a story by George Ewart Evans, this featurette might have kept kids amused in the late fifties. However, the demands of young audiences have changed dramatically since those more innocent times, and a tale of smuggling devoid of special effects will now have few takers. That said, their parents will no doubt be fascinated to see a youthful Francesca Annis among the gang assisting a grumpy customs officer in the recovery of some valuable contraband.

Francesca Annis *Sylvia* • John Pike *John* • Jeremy Bullock [Jeremy Bulloch] *Bill* • John Gabriel *Mason* • John Stacy *Dodds* • Paddy Joyce *Banks* ■ *Dir* Darrell Catling • *Scr* John Eldridge, from a story by G Ewart Evans [George Ewart Evans]

Cat on a Hot Tin Roof
★★★★ 15

Drama 1958 · US · Colour · 103mins

Tennessee Williams at his most overheated, with familial strife in the Deep South coming atmospherically alive in all its steamy, fly-blown glory. Elizabeth Taylor overdoes the Southern accent, though Paul Newman is splendid as the sullen but only upright member of a thoroughly dislikeable clan. The surprise plus is Burl Ives as the dying patriarch Big Daddy. One of the sounder screen adaptations of the playwright's work, even if the play's references to the homosexuality of Newman's character were watered down for the film. Contains some sexual references.

Elizabeth Taylor *Maggie Pollitt* • Paul Newman *Brick Pollitt* • Burl Ives *Big Daddy Pollitt* • Jack Carson *Gooper Pollitt* • Judith Anderson *Big Mama Pollitt* • Madeleine Sherwood *Mae Pollitt* • Larry Gates *Dr Baugh* • Vaughn Taylor *Deacon Davis* ■ *Dir* Richard Brooks • *Scr* Richard Brooks, James Poe, from the play by Tennessee Williams

Cat o'Nine Tails
★★★ 18

Thriller 1971 · Fr/It/W Ger · Colour · 107mins

Blind Karl Malden and journalist James Franciscus unravel a tortuous mystery combining industrial espionage, homosexuality and genetic dementia in director Dario Argento's visually creative study in psycho terror. Thrilling subjective camerawork masks the maniac's identity in a stunning triumph of style over content that marks the beginning of the director's obsession with eyes and blades. The train platform murder and the skylight finale are textbook examples of what Argento calls "violence as art". Some dialogue dubbed into English. 🖵

Karl Malden *Franco Arno* • James Franciscus *Carlo Giordani* • Catherine Spaak *Anna Terzi* • Cinzia De Carolis *Lori* • Carlo Alighiero *Dr Calabresi* • Vittorio Congia *Righetto* • Aldo Reggiani *Dr Casoni* ■ *Dir* Dario Argento • *Scr* Dario Argento, from a story by Luigi Collo, Dardano Sacchetti, Dario Argento • *Cinematographer* Erico Menczer

Cat People
★★★★ PG

Horror 1942 · US · BW · 72mins

Produced by Val Lewton and directed by the great Jacques Tourneur, this was one of the first Hollywood horrors to play on the audience's fears rather than expose them to ghouls and monsters. Simone Simon makes one of cinema's most sensual menaces as the sketch artist who turns into a panther as a result of an ancient Serbian curse. Apart from Simon, the acting's pretty ropey, but the film is packed with eerie moments. 🖵

Simone Simon *Irena Dubrovna* • Kent Smith *Oliver Reed* • Tom Conway *Dr Judd* • Jane Randolph *Alice Moore* • Jack Holt *Commodore* • Alan Napier *Carver* • Elizabeth Dunne *Miss Plunkett* • Mary Halsey *Blondie* ■ *Dir* Jacques Tourneur • *Scr* DeWitt Bodeen • *Cinematographer* Nicholas Musuraca

Cat People
★★★ 18

Horror 1982 · US · Colour · 112mins

Paul Schrader's stylish remake of producer Val Lewton's horror classic features a well-cast Nastassja Kinski (billed here as Nastassia) as one of the last survivors of a race of beings who transform into felines in the heat of passion. Malcolm McDowell is her kinky brother and John Heard the zookeeper unaware that not all of the animals are behind bars. Driven by nudity, gore and sensuality Schrader's emotionally cold fantasy begins well, but degenerates into a surrealistic, gruesome mess. Contains violence, swearing, sex scenes and nudity. 🖵

Nastassia Kinski [Nastassja Kinski] *Irena Gallier* • Malcolm McDowell *Paul Gallier* • John Heard *Oliver Yates* • Annette O'Toole *Alice Perrin* • Ed Begley Jr *Joe Creigh* ■ *Dir* Paul Schrader • *Scr* Alan Ormsby, from the story by DeWitt Bodeen

The Catamount Killing
★★★

Crime drama
1974 · W Ger/US · Colour · 97mins

Coming between those landmarks in Polish cinema, *Illumination* and *Camouflage*, this English language crime drama may seem something of an aberration on the part of Krzysztof Zanussi. Yet, as banker Horst Buchholz and his lover Ann Wedgeworth flee with the proceeds of their heist, it becomes clear the director's recurrent themes of moral decline and the disintegration of meaningful relationships are both present and correct. Surveying Vermont with the intuitive eye of the outsider, Zanussi might be accused of over-subjecting his characters to the caprices of fate. However, strong performances ensure the psychological ramifications are not lost.

Horst Buchholz *Mark Kalvin* • Ann Wedgeworth *Kit Loring* • Chip Taylor *Ken Travers* • Louise Clark *Iris Loring* • Patricia Joyce *Alice Craig* ■ *Dir* Krzysztof Zanussi • *Scr* Julien More, Sheila More, from the novel *I'd Rather Stay Poor* by James Hadley Chase

Catch Me a Spy
★★

Spy thriller 1971 · UK · Colour · 94mins

This lame spy thriller about missing secret files has a sometimes clever and witty script by the ace TV team of Dick Clement and Ian La Frenais. However, it's rather let down by

Clement's uncertain direction, while Kirk Douglas's peculiar intensity isn't best suited to a comedy. Trevor Howard and Tom Courtenay seem more at home with the spy spoof material, though.

Kirk Douglas *Andrej* • Marlène Jobert *Fabienne* • Trevor Howard *Sir Trevor Dawson* • Tom Courtenay *Baxter Clarke* • Patrick Mower *John Fenton* • Bernadette Lafont *Simone* • Bernard Blier *Webb* ■ *Dir* Dick Clement • *Scr* Dick Clement, Ian La Frenais, from the novel by George Marton, Tibor Meray

Catch My Soul ★

Musical 1973 · US · Colour · 95mins

Iago (Lance LeGault), the demonic leader of a desert-based religious commune, manipulates black preacher Othello (Richie Havens) into murdering his white hippy wife Desdemona (Season Hubley) in a fit of jealous rage. This updated musical version of Shakespeare's *Othello*, adapted for the screen by Jack Good, is to be avoided by all but the most dedicated fans of seventies rock operas. A noisy and inept bowdlerisation of the Bard, it succeeds in boring only where it doesn't infuriate.

Richie Havens *Othello* • Lance LeGault *Iago* • Season Hubley *Desdemona* • Tony Joe White *Cassio* • Susan Tyrrell *Emilia* ■ *Dir* Patrick McGoohan • *Scr* Jack Good, from the play *Othello* by William Shakespeare • *Music* Tony Joe White

Catch-22 ★★★ 15

War satire 1970 · US · Colour · 115mins

An adaptation of Joseph Heller's novel whose title, meaning a no-win situation, became part of the language. As black comedy, it lumbers when it should prance and slashes when it should pierce. For all that, Mike Nichols's direction of Buck Henry's script is an organisational tour de force. Alan Arkin is splendid as Captain Yossarian, the innocent abroad at a US Air Force base in the Mediterranean, coping with sham, hypocrisy and Orson Welles. More violent burlesque than tragi-farce, but it certainly draws attention to its hero's predicament.

Alan Arkin *Captain Yossarian* • Martin Balsam *Colonel Cathcart* • Richard Benjamin *Major Danby* • Jon Voight *Milo Minderbinder* • Martin Sheen *Lieutenant Dobbs* • Orson Welles *General Dreedle* • Art Garfunkel *Captain Nately* • Bob Newhart *Major Major* • Anthony Perkins *Chaplain Tappman* • Paula Prentiss *Nurse Duckett* ■ *Dir* Mike Nichols • *Scr* Buck Henry, from the novel by Joseph Heller

Catch Us If You Can ★★ PG

Musical 1965 · UK · BW · 87mins

Despite a run of jolly, sunny-sounding pop hits, the Dave Clark Five chose former documentarist John Boorman to direct this starkly black-and-white and unexpectedly bleak first feature. It's no *A Hard Day's Night*, but it paved the way for Boorman to make *Point Blank* and proved to be massively influential on such films as *Radio On* and *Two-Lane Blacktop*. Clark and the lads are singularly charmless and unskilled at thesping, but Barbara Ferris does a nice turn as a model on the lam.

Dave Clark *Steve* • Lenny Davidson *Lenny* • Rick Huxley *Rick* • Mike Smith *Mike* • Denis Payton *Denis* • Barbara Ferris *Dinah* • David Lodge *Louis* • Robin Bailey *Guy* ■ *Dir* John Boorman • *Scr* Peter Nichols

Catchfire ★★★ 15

Thriller 1990 · US · Colour · 98mins

Disowned by director Dennis Hopper (hence the Alan Smithee directorial credit), this remains an oddly watchable mess. Hopper also stars as the Mafia hit man who is ordered to assassinate a witness to a gangland killing (Jodie Foster), only to fall in love with his victim. It's an offbeat combination of black comedy and gangster thriller, but the tone is uneven and its disparate themes never successfully jell. However, Hopper and Foster spark off each other nicely, while a starry supporting cast keeps you hooked. There's even room for a lengthy but redundant uncredited cameo from Bob Dylan. Contains violence, swearing, sex scenes and nudity.

Jodie Foster *Anne Benton* • Dennis Hopper *Milo* • Dean Stockwell *John Luponi* • Vincent Price *Lino Avoca* • John Turturro *Pinella* • Joe Pesci *Leo Carelli* • Fred Ward *Pauling* • Charlie Sheen *Bob* ■ *Dir* Alan Smithee [Dennis Hopper] • *Scr* Rachel Kronstadt-Mann, Ann Louise Bardach, Stephen L Cotler, Lanny Cotler, from a story by Rachel Kronstadt-Mann

The Catered Affair ★★★ U

Comedy 1956 · US · BW · 93mins

Bette Davis is miscast as a downtrodden Bronx taxi driver's wife, but she used to glory in shedding the glamour now and then. A passably fine script from Gore Vidal and a good supporting cast (including Ernest Borgnine and Debbie Reynolds) made this a major hit in its day, though it's a B-league effort compared to the rest of Davis's cinematic work.

Bette Davis *Mrs Tom Hurley* • Ernest Borgnine *Tom Hurley* • Debbie Reynolds *Jane Hurley* • Barry Fitzgerald *Uncle Jack Conlon* • Rod Taylor *Ralph Halloran* • Robert Simon *Mr Halloran* • Madge Kennedy *Mrs Halloran* ■ *Dir* Richard Brooks • *Scr* Gore Vidal, from the TV play by Paddy Chayefsky

Catherine the Great ★★

Historical drama 1934 · UK · BW · 98mins

British-based movie mogul Alexander Korda produced this historical saga, hoping it would repeat the transatlantic success of *The Private Life of Henry VIII*. But it's all rather stuffy and lacks the humour of the previous year's royal romp. The director is Paul Czinner, whose wife, Elisabeth Bergner, plays the tsarina rather glumly, and Douglas Fairbanks Jr is the rakish Grand Duke who quickly goes off his troika.

Elisabeth Bergner *Catherine II* • Douglas Fairbanks Jr *Grand Duke Peter* • Flora Robson *Empress Elizabeth* • Gerald Du Maurier *Lecocq* • Irene Vanbrugh *Princess Anhalt-Zerbst* • Griffith Jones *Grigory Orlov* ■ *Dir* Paul Czinner • *Scr* Marjorie Deans, Arthur Wimperis, from the play *The Czarina* by Lajos Biro, Melchior Lengyel

Catholic Boys ★★★ 15

Comedy 1985 · US · Colour · 99mins

Angst, guilt and raging hormones combine to provide a fresh, affecting glimpse of life behind the steel doors of a Catholic boys' school – its regime is so strict that it makes the institutions envisioned by Dickens look positively luxurious. There are a clutch of strong performances, most notably from Andrew McCarthy and Kevin Dillon, while Donald Sutherland is at his brooding best as chief monk and administrator of major whackings. In his feature film debut, director Michael Dinner deals intelligently with a well-worn theme and injects some subtle nuances. Contains swearing.

Andrew McCarthy *Michael Dunn* • Kevin Dillon *Rooney* • Donald Sutherland *Brother Thadeus* • John Heard *Brother Timothy* • Mary Stuart Masterson *Danni* • Kate Reid *Grandma* • Wallace Shawn *Father Abruzzi* • Philip Bosco *Brother Paul* • Patrick Dempsey *Corbet* ■ *Dir* Michael Dinner • *Scr* Charles Purpura

Catholics ★★★ U

Drama 1973 · US · Colour · 83mins

Brian Moore reworked his own novel for this top-notch TV movie, released on video in Britain as *The Conflict*. Trevor Howard reins in the tendency to excess that marred so many of his later films, giving a magnificent performance as an Irish abbot who clings on to traditional doctrines in defiance of the Vatican. Martin Sheen is equally effective as the emissary sent by the reformist pope to make Howard and his brethren toe the line. Excellent support from Cyril Cusack and Raf Vallone will help those of a non-religious persuasion through the more overtly theological passages.

Trevor Howard *The Abbot* • Martin Sheen *Father Kinsella* • Raf Vallone *Father General* • Cyril Cusack *Father Manus* • Andrew Keir *Father Matthew* • Michael Gambon *Brother Kevin* • Leon Vitale *Brother Donald* ■ *Dir* Jack Gold • *Scr* Brian Moore, from his novel

Cathy's Child ★★★ PG

Drama based on a true story
1979 · Ausl · Colour · 84mins

Inspired by actual events, this provocative assault on the relevance of patriarchal jurisdiction to the modern state is also a rare tale of tabloid heroism, as a Sydney newspaper champions the cause of a young mother whose estranged husband has spirited their daughter away to Greece. With a visual and dramatic style redolent of kitchen sink realism, the film marked something of a departure for Donald Crombie after a couple of period pictures. However, he strikes the right tone of protest throughout and draws fine performances from Michele Fawdon and Alan Cassell.

Michele Fawdon *Cathy Baikis* • Alan Cassell *Dick Wordley* • Bryan Brown *Paul Nicholson* • Arthur Dignam *Minister* • Willie Fennel *Australian Consul* • Bob Hughes *Solicitor* ■ *Dir* Donald Crombie • *Scr* Ken Quinnell, from a non-fiction book by Dick Wordley

Catlow ★★ PG

Western 1971 · Sp · Colour · 92mins

Yul Brynner takes the title role, a cattle rustler caught between marshal Richard Crenna, who wants to lock him up, and bounty hunter Leonard Nimoy, who wants him dead. Filmed in Spain by the formerly blacklisted Sam Wanamaker, it's an unpretentious effort that veers more towards knockabout comedy than spaghetti-style ketchup. Silent movie aficionados will relish the brief appearance by Bessie Love.

Yul Brynner *Catlow* • Richard Crenna *Cowan* • Leonard Nimoy *Miller* • Daliah Lavi *Rosita* • Jo Ann Pflug *Christina* • Jeff Corey *Merridew* • Michael Delano *Rio* • Julian Mateos *Recalde* • Bessie Love *Mrs Frost* ■ *Dir* Sam Wanamaker • *Scr* Scot Finch [Scott Finch], JJ Griffith, from the novel by Louis L'Amour

Cats Don't Dance ★★ U

Animated musical comedy
1998 · US · Colour · 71mins

Like an MGM musical with animals instead of humans, this overly ambitious animated film is set in late thirties Hollywood. Danny (voiced by Scott Bakula from TV's *Quantum Leap*) is a Gene Kelly-type, small-town feline who discovers that animals are relegated to the background while the humans hog the movie limelight. Kelly himself acted as consultant for the film's sprightly dance choreography, but the characters are rather dull and Randy Newman contributes some disappointingly forgettable tunes.

Scott Bakula *Danny* • Jasmine Guy *Sawyer* • Natalie Cole *Sawyer* • Ashley Peldon *Darla Dimple* • Lindsay Rideway *Darla Dimple* • Kathy Najimy *Tillie* • John Rhys-Davies *Woolie* • George Kennedy *LB Mammoth* • René Auberjonois *Flanigan* • Hal Holbrook *Cranston* ■ *Dir* Mark Dindal • *Scr* Roberts Gannaway, Cliff Ruby, Elana Lesser, Theresa Pettengill, from a story by Rick Schneider, Robert Lence, Mark Dindal, Brian McEntee, David Womersley, Kelvin Yasuda

Cat's Eye ★★★ 15

Horror 1984 · US · Colour · 90mins

A generally entertaining trilogy of terror tales from the ubiquitous Stephen King, the Big Mac of horror literature. James Woods tries an unorthodox method of quitting smoking, *Airplane!'s* Robert Hays is forced into a deadly bet and Drew Barrymore comes under attack from a rather unappetising gnome-like monster in a swift-paced anthology that works more often than not because of strong casting and a refreshingly throwaway tone. Cameos from the *Christine* car and the *Cujo* dog add to the scary comic-book fun of one of the better King adaptations. Contains violence and swearing.

Drew Barrymore *Girl* • James Woods *Morrison* • Alan King *Dr Donatti* • Kenneth McMillan *Cressner* • Robert Hays *Norris* • Candy Clark *Sally Ann* • James Naughton *Hugh* • Tony Munafo *Junk* ■ *Dir* Lewis Teague • *Scr* Stephen King, from his short stories *Quitters Inc*, *The Ledge* and *The General*

The Cat's Paw ★★★ U

Comedy 1934 · US · BW · 101mins

Harold Lloyd, the silent comedian archivists usually overlook, stars in a comedy that shows off little of his acutely timed talents. He plays Ezekiel Cobb, a missionary's son raised in China who arrives in America to find himself up to his spectacles in corrupt politicians. From the man who used cliffhanger comedy so brilliantly in *Safety Last*, this film comes as something of a disappointment.

Harold Lloyd *Ezekiel Cobb* • Una Merkel *Petunia Pratt* • George Barbier *Jake Mayo* • Nat Pendleton *Strozzi* • Grace Bradley *Dolores Dace* • Alan Dinehart *Mayor Morgan* • Grant

Mitchell *"Silk Hat"McGee* ■ *Dir* Sam Taylor • *Scr* Sam Taylor, from a story by Clarence Budington Kelland

Cattle Annie and Little Britches ★★★
Western   1981 · US · Colour · 97mins

In this cheerful family western, never released in Britain, Diane Lane and Amanda Plummer play a pair of teenage girls intent on joining Burt Lancaster's gang of bank robbers, while Rod Steiger is the lawman determined to bring them all to justice. The scenes where he discusses changing times with Lancaster are the most memorable moments in Lamont Johnson's film, which manages to be quite enjoyable despite an irritating banjo-strumming soundtrack.

Burt Lancaster *Bill Doolin* • John Savage *Bittercreek Newcomb* • Rod Steiger *Tilghman* • Diane Lane *Jenny/Little Britches* • Amanda Plummer *Annie/Cattle Annie* • Scott Glenn *Bill Dalton* ■ *Dir* Lamont Johnson • *Scr* David Eyre, Robert Ward, from a story and novel by Robert Ward

Cattle Drive ★★★
Western   1951 · US · Colour · 83mins

Dean Stockwell, better known to today's audiences for TV's *Quantum Leap*, had a major career as a child star, and notably featured in *Anchors Aweigh* as well as playing the title roles in such films as *Kim* and *The Boy with Green Hair*. Here he gets to grow up out west as a spoiled rich brat alongside grizzled trail boss Joel McCrea, learning the cowboy ropes from the likes of veterans Chill Wills and Bob Steele. Kurt Neumann directs with warmth and understanding, and the Technicolor photography of the Death Valley locations is superb.

Joel McCrea *Dan Mathews* • Dean Stockwell *Chester Graham Jr* • Chill Wills *Dallas* • Leon Ames *Mr Graham* • Henry Brandon *Jim Currie* • Howard Petrie *Cap* • Bob Steele *Careless* • Griff Barnett *Conductor O'Hara* ■ *Dir* Kurt Neumann • *Scr* Jack Natteford, Lillie Hayward • *Cinematographer* Maury Gertsman

Cattle Empire ★★ U
Western   1958 · US · Colour · 82mins

Little more than a B-feature, this routine western dates from the twilight of veteran Joel McCrea's career, a period when his name could only guarantee co-feature status. McCrea lends real authority to the tale, and fans of fifties B-movies will welcome the presence of Gloria Talbott and Phyllis Coates. Watch out, too, for Kurt Russell's dad, Bing. But classic western fans will shy away from this Charles Marquis Warren confection, as he brings all the TV production values that enabled him to produce such long-running series as *Gunsmoke* and *Rawhide* quickly and economically.

Joel McCrea *John Cord* • Gloria Talbott *Sandy* • Don Haggerty *Ralph Hamilton* • Phyllis Coates *Janice Hamilton* • Bing Russell *Douglas Hamilton* • Paul Brinegar *Tom Jeffrey* • Hal K Dawson *George Jeffrey* • Duane Grey *Aruzza* ■ *Dir* Charles Marquis Warren • *Scr* Eric Norden, Endre Bohem, from a story by Daniel B Ullman

Cattle King ★★ U
Western   1963 · US · Colour · 89mins

His glory days as an MGM star long over, Robert Taylor drifts through this B-western, which tells an all-too-familiar story of Wyoming settlers who want to fence in their land and evil ranchers who think their cows should roam free. Guns come out, cattle stampede, and the dispute goes all the way to President Chester A Arthur (Larry Gates). The film is directed by Tay Garnett, a veteran who reached his peak with *The Postman Always Rings Twice* in 1946.

Robert Taylor (1) *Sam Brassfield* • Joan Caulfield *Sharleen* • Robert Loggia *Johnny Quatro* • Robert Middleton *Clay Matthews* • Malcolm Atterbury *Clevenger* ■ *Dir* Tay Garnett • *Scr* Thomas Thompson

Cattle Queen of Montana ★★★ PG
Western   1954 · US · Colour · 84mins

One of two low-budget westerns made by Barbara Stanwyck – the other was 1956's *The Maverick Queen* – before she found her glorious late-career stride with such titles as *Forty Guns* and TV's *The Big Valley*. Aided by thoughtful direction from the prolific and talented Allan Dwan, this movie now has great curiosity value, in that the leading man is former US president Ronald Reagan, a bland and colourless performer when pitted against screen villains Gene Evans and Jack Elam. The location scenery is very attractive, the action sequences well-staged, and Stanwyck as tough as ever: it's a shame the script didn't give her, or any of the cast for that matter, more opportunities.

Barbara Stanwyck *Sierra Nevada Jones* • Ronald Reagan *Farrell* • Gene Evans *Tom McCord* • Lance Fuller *Colorados* • Anthony Caruso *Natchakoa* • Jack Elam *Yost* • Yvette Dugay *Starfire* • Morris Ankrum *JI "Pop"Jones* • Chubby Johnson *Nat* ■ *Dir* Allan Dwan • *Scr* Robert Blees, Howard Estabrook, from a story by Thomas Blackburn

Caught ★★ U
Romantic drama   1949 · US · BW · 84mins

A trite soap opera in which the attractive wife (Barbara Bel Geddes) of a neurotic and unpleasant millionaire (Robert Ryan) falls in love with an idealistic doctor (James Mason). The only surprise is that this romantic melodrama is directed by the distinguished Max Ophüls, whose expertise and commitment bring some texture and gloss to the dour proceedings. The film marked Mason's Hollywood debut; he, Bel Geddes and Ryan almost succeed in rising above the unconvincing material.

James Mason *Larry Quinada* • Barbara Bel Geddes *Leonora Eames* • Robert Ryan *Smith Ohlrig* • Ruth Brady *Maxine* • Curt Bois *Franzi* • Frank Ferguson *Dr Hoffman* • Natalie Schafer *Dorothy Dale* • Art Smith *Psychiatrist* • Sonia Darrin *Miss Chambers* ■ *Dir* Max Ophüls • *Scr* Arthur Laurents, from the novel *Wild Calendar* by Libbie Bloch

Caught ★★★ 18
Drama   1996 · US · Colour · 105mins

A menacing adult drama bolstered by fine performances. Edward James

Olmos plays a New Jersey fish merchant who takes drifter Arie Verveen under his wing, only for the kid to strike up a steamy affair with his wife (Maria Conchita Alonso). Trouble brews when the couple's shifty son (Steven Schub) returns home unexpectedly and smells something fishy. It all ends in tears.

Edward James Olmos *Joe* • Maria Conchita Alonso *Betty* • Arie Verveen *Nick* • Steven Schub *Danny* • Bitty Schram *Amy* ■ *Dir* Robert M Young • *Scr* Edward Pomerantz

Caught in the Act ★★ PG
Thriller   1993 · US · Colour · 89mins

A video-friendly slice of *film noir* that won't tax the brain too much. Gregory Harrison stars as a struggling actor who gets mixed up in kidnapping and financial fraud when he falls for *femme fatale* Leslie Hope. Director Deborah Reinisch weaves an entertaining and complicated tale, but there's little special to mark this out from hundreds of other made-for-cable thrillers.

Gregory Harrison *Scott McNally* • Leslie Hope *Rachel* • Patricia Clarkson *Meg* • Kimberly Scott *Wilson* • Raye Birk *Sterling* ■ *Dir* Deborah Reinisch • *Scr* Ken Hixon, from a story by Andy Evanson, Ken Hixon

Caught in the Act ★★ PG
Comedy   1996 · UK · Colour · 92mins

Lucinda (Sara Crowe) has had a crush on variety agent Neville Goodenough (Paul Shelley) since she was 12. What better way to win his heart than enter an amateur talent show with her pals Katherine (Annette Badland) and Amanda (Nadia Sawalha)? Actually, there are probably quite a few better ways, but only this one offers director Mark Greenstreet the chance to have three perfectly talented actresses pretend to be talentless. Thankfully Leslie Phillips is on hand to supply some genuine comic flair.

Sara Crowe *Lucinda* • Annette Badland *Katherine* • Leslie Phillips *Sydney Fisher* • Paul Shelley *Neville Goodenough* • Guy Henry *Algie* ■ *Dir* Mark Greenstreet • *Scr* Mark Greenstreet, Caroline Hill

Caught in the Crossfire ★★ PG
Crime drama based on a true story
1994 · US · Colour · 85mins

The rumpled charisma of *NYPD Blue*'s Dennis Franz shines through this otherwise formulaic true story. Franz is as convincing as ever playing the unlikely hero, a journalist on the trail of the story of his life who finds himself caught up in the murkier side of FBI operations. The supporting cast (Daniel Roebuck, Alley Mills) is able enough and it's competently directed by Chuck Bowman, but ultimately this TV movie is an underwhelming affair.

Dennis Franz *Gus Payne* • Alley Mills *Royce Payne* • Daniel Roebuck *Randy Wood* • Anna Gunn *Alex King* • Ray McKinnon *Buddy Rivers* ■ *Dir* Chuck Bowman • *Scr* Victor D Hawkins, Tom Nelson, Dan Levine, from a story by Victor D Hawkins, Tom Nelson

Cauldron of Blood ★ 15
Horror   1967 · US/Sp · Colour · 94mins

This mad mixture of *House of Wax* and Roger Corman's *A Bucket of Blood* is

grisly tedium at its best. Boris Karloff plays a blind sculptor using real human bones in his statues – courtesy of his psychopathic spouse, who kills people and dumps them in an acid bath in the basement. Sounds like the perfect marriage! Filmed in 1967 but not released until 1971, two years after the star's death, this American/Spanish co-production offers few chills; indeed, the biggest shocks come from the cornball dialogue. For Karloff completists only. Spanish dialogue dubbed into English.

Jean-Pierre Aumont *Claude Marchand* • Boris Karloff *Franz Badulescu* • Viveca Lindfors *Tania Badulescu* • Jacqui Speed *Pilar* • Rosenda Monteros *Valerie* • Ruben Rojo *Lover* ■ *Dir* Edward Mann [Santos Alcocer] • *Scr* John Melson, Jose Luis Bayonas, Edward Mann, from a story by Edward Mann

Cause for Alarm ★★★
Film noir   1951 · US · BW · 73mins

This *film noir* has a blacker shade than usual, as finger-fluttering, saucer-eyed Loretta Young tries to retrieve a letter sent by her bedridden husband before his death that blames her for his demise. Director Tay Garnett may have been an MGM hack, but, despite some risibly optimistic touches, his craftsmanship is very evident. This was also the case in the first – and best – version of *The Postman Always Rings Twice* (1946).

Loretta Young *Ellen Jones* • Barry Sullivan *George Z Jones* • Bruce Cowling *Dr Grahame* • Margalo Gillmore *Mrs Edwards* • Bradley Mora *Billy* • Irving Bacon *Carston* • Georgia Backus *Mrs Warren* • Don Haggerty *Russell* ■ *Dir* Tay Garnett • *Scr* Tom Lewis, Mel Dinelli, from a story by Larry Marcus

Cavalcade ★★★ U
Historical drama   1933 · US · BW · 111mins

Noël Coward uses a well-to-do family as a microcosm in this look at British life down the years, from the Boer War to the Great Depression. Critics at the time loved this rather sanctimonious jaunt through history. Seen from the vantage point of post-Second World War egalitarianism, however, it all appears quaint and riddled with accepted class differences. While Coward, via director Frank Lloyd, pulls out all the stops, a modern audience will remain resolutely dry-eyed. Still, it's an interesting period piece.

Diana Wynyard *Jane Marryot* • Clive Brook *Robert Marryot* • Herbert Mundin *Alfred Bridges* • Una O'Connor *Ellen Bridges* • Ursula Jeans *Fanny Bridges* • Beryl Mercer *Cook* ■ *Dir* Frank Lloyd • *Scr* Reginald Berkeley, from the play by Noël Coward

Cavalry Scout ★★ U
Western   1951 · US · Colour · 77mins

This minor western, photographed in the elementary Cinecolor process, centres around the efforts of an army scout (granite-faced Rod Cameron) to prevent stolen Gatling guns from falling into the hands of hostile Indians. Audrey Long is the trader whose wagons are being surreptitiously used to transport weapons by villain James Millican. A nice touch is the deliberate destruction of the army's Gatlings so that they can't be used by either side.

Rod Cameron *Kirby Frye* • Audrey Long *Claire* • Jim Davis *Lt Spaulding* • James Millican *Martin Gavin* • James Arness *Barth* • John Doucette *Varney* • William Phillips [William "Bill" Phillips] *Sgt Wilkins* • Stephen Chase *Col Drumm* • Rory Mallinson *Corporal* ■ *Dir* Lesley Selander • *Scr* Dan Ullman, Thomas Blackburn

Cave of Outlaws ★★ U
Western   1951 · US · Colour · 75mins

Long before William Castle hit his stride as the maker of gimmick horror films and producer of the classic *Rosemary's Baby*, he cut his teeth directing B-features, invariably minor swashbucklers or routine westerns. This example of his work is a western whose only distinction is in its location usage of New Mexico's Carlsbad Caverns where the climactic shootout takes place. The Technicolor is rich, but Alexis Smith is wasted and MacDonald Carey is far too bland.

Macdonald Carey *Pete Carver* • Alexis Smith *Liz Trent* • Edgar Buchanan *Dobbs* • Victor Jory *Ben Cross* • Hugh O'Brian *Garth* • Housely Stevenson [Houseley Stevenson] *Cooley* ■ *Dir* William Castle • *Scr* Elizabeth Wilson

Caveman ★★★ PG
Comedy adventure
1981 · US · Colour · 87mins

Ringo Starr is perfectly cast as a hapless cave-dweller in an endearingly stupid prehistoric romp that introduced a couple of future stars to the world. The former Beatle is a caveman drummed out of his tribe for making eyes at the chief's woman (played by his real-life wife Barbara Bach). So he teams up with fellow misfits Shelley Long and Dennis Quaid to advance man's evolution. Writer/director Carl Gottlieb, better known as co-writer of the first three *Jaws* movies, relishes the opportunity to pile on the sort of dumb slapstick that will delight fans of the Farrelly Brothers' comedies. ▭

Ringo Starr *Atouk* • Dennis Quaid *Lar* • Shelley Long *Tala* • Barbara Bach *Lana* • John Matuszak *Tonda* • Avery Schreiber *Ock* • Jack Gilford *Gog* • Cork Hubbert *Ta* ■ *Dir* Carl Gottlieb • *Scr* Carl Gottlieb, Rudy De Luca

Ceiling Zero ★★★
Adventure   1935 · US · BW · 95mins

Director and erstwhile pilot Howard Hawks proved the ideal guiding hand for this version of flying expert and author Frank "Spig" Wead's Broadway play, filmed by Warner Bros the moment the curtain fell on the New York run. Hawks and Wead opened out the work and, though most of the activity takes place on the ground in the office of a commercial airline, the incidents and tensions never let up. However, despite a terrific performance from James Cagney as the daredevil pilot and knockout verbal sparring with Pat O'Brien, the movie creaks a bit today, with phoney back projection sky sequences and poor model shots.

James Cagney *Dizzy Davis* • Pat O'Brien *Jack Lee* • June Travis *Tommy Thomas* • Stuart Erwin *Texas Clark* • Henry Wadsworth *Tay Lawson* • Isabel Jewell *Lou Clark* • Barton MacLane *Al Stone* ■ *Dir* Howard Hawks • *Scr* Frank Wead, from his play

Celà s'Appelle l'Aurore ★★
Drama   1956 · Fr/It · BW · 102mins

Luis Buñuel adapted an Emmanuel Roblès novel for his first film in Europe after 23 years of exile, setting it in Corsica and casting the implacable and uncharismatic Georges Marchal as a doctor who falls in love with a widow (Lucia Bosé) in his wife's absence. Essentially a melodrama whose level is raised by the director's unmistakable social consciousness, the film is nevertheless little more than a solidly assembled but minor stepping stone towards the famously original and penetrating works of his lengthy career. A French language film.

Georges Marchal *Doctor Valerio* • Lucia Bosé *Clara* • Gianni Esposito *Sandro* • Julien Bertheau *Fasaro* • Nelly Bourgeaud *Angela* • Jean-Jacques Delbo *Gorzone* ■ *Dir* Luis Buñuel • *Scr* Jean Ferry, Luis Buñuel, from a novel by Emmanuel Roblès

Celebrity ★★★ 15
Comedy drama   1998 · US · BW · 113mins

After having his private life splashed all over the tabloids, writer/director Woody Allen uses his own cameras to probe the nature of celebrity. Kenneth Branagh steps up to play the Allen-esque "Ordinary Joe" who finds himself mixing with supermodels (Charlize Theron), spoiled stars (Leonardo DiCaprio) and oversexed actresses (Melanie Griffith), while his ex-wife (Judy Davis) tries to find her own identity as a TV presenter. While not vintage Allen, this black-and-white amusement has some choice moments – notably hooker Bebe Neuwirth teaching Davis how to improve her sexual skills – and some fun tongue-in-cheek performances. Contains drug use, sexual references and swearing.

Hank Azaria *David* • Kenneth Branagh *Lee Simon* • Joe Mantegna *Tony Gardella* • Judy Davis *Robin Simon* • Winona Ryder *Nola* • Leonardo DiCaprio *Brandon Darrow* • Famke Janssen *Bonnie* • Melanie Griffith *Nicole Oliver* • Charlize Theron *Supermodel* • Bebe Neuwirth *Hooker* ■ *Dir/Scr* Woody Allen

Celia ★★
Crime drama   1949 · UK · BW · 66mins

Not much more than an hour in length, this small-scale, low-budget and largely forgotten British thriller may be wildly old-fashioned, but it's perfectly competent, whimsical and not without a certain degree of charm and humour. Directed by Francis Searle and based on a BBC radio serial, it concerns an actress (Hy Hazell) who, short of money, does a stint as a private detective. Disguised as her aunt, she foils a murderous scheme.

Hy Hazell *Celia* • Bruce Lister *Larry Peters* • John Bailey *Lester Martin* • James Raglan *Inspector Parker* • Elsie Wagstaffe *Aunt Nora* ■ *Dir* Francis Searle • *Scr* Francis Searle, AR Rawlinson, Edward J Mason, from a radio serial by Edward J Mason

Celia ★★★★ 15
Drama   1988 · Ausl · Colour · 98mins

The innocence and dark horrors of childhood have rarely been better portrayed than in this bewitching, often disturbing Australian drama. Set in a dull suburban Melbourne of the fifties, Ann Turner's striking directorial debut focuses on a nine-year-old girl (a startlingly good performance by Rebecca Smart), whose confusion and resentment over adult behaviour sees her slip into a fantasy world, with tragic consequences. Turner beautifully captures not only the stuffy conservatism and paranoia of the period, but also the sheer wonder of growing up in what is, to a young child, a very strange world. ▭

Rebecca Smart *Celia Carmichael* • Nicholas Ede *Ray Carmichael* • Mary-Anne Fahey *Pat Carmichael* • Victoria Longley *Alice Tanner* • Alexander Hutchinson *Steve Tanner* ■ *Dir/Scr* Ann Turner

Celine and Julie Go Boating ★★★★★
Experimental supernatural drama
1974 · Fr · Colour · 193mins

Inspired by two Henry James stories and intended as a homage to Lewis Carroll and Jean Cocteau, this astonishing film alludes to so many different writers, artists and film-makers that it's impossible to begin listing them. Constantly blurring the line between fantasy and reality, Jacques Rivette dazzles us with his inventiveness as magician Juliet Berto takes librarian Dominique Labourier on a series of adventures around a mysterious town house, inhabited by the equally fantastic Bulle Ogier and Marie-France Pisier. In French with English subtitles.

Juliet Berto *Celine* • Dominique Labourier *Julie* • Bulle Ogier *Camille* • Marie-France Pisier *Sophie* • Barbet Schroeder *Olivier* • Philippe Clevenot *Guilou* • Nathalie Asnar *Madlyn* • Marie-Therese Saussure *Poupie* ■ *Dir* Jacques Rivette • *Scr* Eduardo de Gregorio, Juliet Berto, Dominique Labourier, Bulle Ogier, Marie-France Pisier, Jacques Rivette, from stories by Henry James

The Celluloid Closet ★★★★ 15
Documentary
1995 · US · Colour and BW · 101mins

How gay and lesbians have fared on the big screen is the subject of this hilarious and poignant documentary. Narrated by Lily Tomlin and featuring candid interviews with Gore Vidal, Susan Sarandon and Shirley MacLaine, to name just a few, this is both a history of homosexual images and a damning indictment of the cavalier way Hollywood has shaped views on sexuality. But mostly it's a feast for cinephiles with over a hundred clips from early Thomas Edison shorts to *Philadelphia*, assembled with wit, care and precision to illustrate a spicy and thought-provoking study.

Lily Tomlin *Narrator* ■ *Dir* Rob Epstein [Robert Epstein], Jeffrey Friedman • *Scr* Armistead Maupin, from a story by Rob Epstein, Jeffrey Friedman, Sharon Wood, Vito Russo

Celtic Pride ★★ 12
Sports comedy   1996 · US · Colour · 86mins

The subject matter (basketball) worked against this film getting a theatrical release over here, but *Celtic Pride* is still a winning sports comedy. Daniel Stern and Dan Ackroyd play fanatical fans of the Boston Celtics who kidnap the arrogant star of their arch rivals (Daman Wayons). It's expertly played by the three leads, and director Tom DeCerchio gets in some nice jibes about the antics of middle-aged armchair sports fans. Contains swearing. ▭

Damon Wayans *Lewis Scott* • Daniel Stern *Mike O'Hara* • Dan Aykroyd *Jimmy Flaherty* • Gail O'Grady *Carol* • Adam Hendershott *Tommy* • Paul Guilfoyle *Kevin O'Grady* ■ *Dir* Tom DeCerchio • *Scr* Judd Apatow, from a story by Colin Quinn, Judd Apatow

The Cement Garden ★★★★ 18
Drama   1992 · Ger/Fr/UK · Colour · 100mins

One of the few films based on Ian McEwan's psychologically complex novels which actually works, largely due to some outstanding acting and a script from director Andrew Birkin that sticks close to its source material. This disturbing story, adapted from McEwan's first novel, is about children and their reactions to death and loss, and it refuses to conform to any cosy notion of grief. As such, with its central theme about sexual desire and incest, it occasionally makes uncomfortable, intellectually challenging viewing. ▭

Andrew Robertson *Jack* • Charlotte Gainsbourg *Julie* • Sinead Cusack *Mother* • Alice Coulthard *Sue* • Ned Birkin *Tom* • Hanns Zischler *Father* • Jochen Horst *Derek* ■ *Dir* Andrew Birkin • *Scr* Andrew Birkin, from the novel by Ian McEwan

The Cemetery Club ★★★ 15
Comedy drama   1993 · US · Colour · 106mins

Former actor Bill Duke directs this gentle comedy drama, which scores highly by having three fine actresses – two of them Oscar-winners – top the bill. Ellen Burstyn, Diane Ladd and Olympia Dukakis play Pittsburgh widows who meet up, chat and help each other cope with their problems, while Danny Aiello, Christina Ricci and Wallace Shawn round out an attractive supporting cast. At times, however, Duke's film looks like the pilot for a TV series, while some viewers may feel it betrays its stage origins. ▭

Ellen Burstyn *Esther Moskowitz* • Olympia Dukakis *Doris Silverman* • Diane Ladd *Lucille Rubin* • Danny Aiello *Ben Katz* • Christina Ricci *Jessica* • Bernie Casey *John* • Wallace Shawn *Larry* ■ *Dir* Bill Duke • *Scr* Ivan Menchell, from the play by Ivan Menchell

Cemetery Man ★★★★ 18
Horror   1994 · It · Colour · 98mins

This is a highly acclaimed Italian horror masterpiece, dwelling on the more metaphysical elements of the genre. Graveyard undertaker Rupert Everett is seduced by beautiful zombie Anna Falchi and embarks on a personal crusade against the living. Beautifully directed by Michele Soavi with wit, style and emotional substance, Everett gives a bravura central performance in a unique original bursting with both gore and brains. Based on the novel *Dellamorte Dellamore* (the film's Italian title) by Tiziano Sclavi, Soavi's sophisticated shocker is a mordant delight. An Italian language film. ▭

Rupert Everett *Francesco Dellamorte* • François Hadji-Lazaro *Gnaghi* • Anna Falchi *She* • Stefano Masciarelli *Mayor* • Mickey

U = SUITABLE FOR ALL   **Uc** = SUITABLE FOR ALL, ESPECIALLY FOR YOUNG CHILDREN (VIDEO ONLY)   **PG** = PARENTAL GUIDANCE

Knox *Marshall Straniero* ■ *Dir* Michele Soavi • *Scr* Gianni Romoli, from the novel *Dellamorte Dellamore* by Tiziano Sclavi

Centennial Summer ★★★ U

Period musical 1946 · US · Colour · 102mins

A nostalgic period musical from Fox which seems to be emulating MGM's *Meet Me in St Louis*. Set in Philadelphia in 1876, where the Great Exposition is a cause for excitement, the film stars Jeanne Crain and Linda Darnell as sisters whose relationship suffers when they both take a fancy to dashing Frenchman Cornel Wilde. Veterans Dorothy Gish (sister of Lillian and a one-time silent star) and Walter Brennan play the girls' parents, but the real star of Otto Preminger's undemanding trifle is the music, composed by Jerome Kern shortly before his death.

Jeanne Crain *Julia* • Cornel Wilde *Philippe Lascalles* • Linda Darnell *Edith Rogers* • William Eythe *Benjamin Franklin Phelps* • Walter Brennan *Jesse Rogers* • Constance Bennett *Zenia Lascalles* • Dorothy Gish *Harriet Rogers* ■ *Dir* Otto Preminger • *Scr* Michael Kanin, from the novel by Albert E Idell

Central Airport ★ U

Adventure 1933 · US · BW · 74mins

This tedious airborne romance finds pilot Richard Barthelmess jilted by parachutist Sally Eilers when she marries his brother (Tom Brown) instead. Barthelmess would later strike gold with another flying drama – Howard Hawks's classic *Only Angels Have Wings* – but this one never gets off the ground. The only surprise is that director William Wellman was also in charge of that earlier flying epic, *Wings*. Blame the script, not to mention the papier-mâché planes.

Richard Barthelmess *Jim* • Tom Brown *Neil* • Sally Eilers *Jill* • Grant Mitchell *Mr Blaine* • James Murray *Eddie* ■ *Dir* William A Wellman • *Scr* Rian James, from a story by Jack Moffitt, James Seymour

Central Station ★★★★ 15

Drama 1998 · Bra/Fr/Sp/Jap · Colour · 110mins

This captivating Brazilian road movie picked up awards all around the world, as well as a deserved Oscar nomination for 69-year-old actress Fernanda Montenegro. Initially shown as selfish and uncaring, her character's gradual softening as she accompanies a young boy (Vinicius de Oliveira) on a quest to find his dad makes for compelling viewing. Director Walter Salles's filming of their journey of discovery stunningly captures an unglamorous land, seen from the perspective of two travellers whose final destination is far from certain. In Portuguese with English subtitles. Contains some swearing.

Fernanda Montenegro *Dora* • Marília Péra *Irene* • Vinicius de Oliveira *Josué* • Othon Bastos *César* ■ *Dir* Walter Salles • *Scr* João Emanuel Carneiro, Marcos Bernstein, from a idea by Walter Salles

Century ★★★ 15

Period drama 1993 · UK · Colour · 107mins

As we enter a new millennium, what lessons can be learnt from a previous society about to enter a new century? Not a lot, according to Stephen Poliakoff's absorbing look at a frantic culture in the midst of technological advancement and uncertainty about the future. TV heart-throb Clive Owen is the hot-headed medical researcher on the loose in late-Victorian London who exposes the dubious practices of eminent professor Charles Dance. Robert Stephens steals the sumptuously mounted show as Owen's eccentric Romanian father and brings a welcome touch of humour to what many will find a rather arch conceit. Contains some nudity. 🖵

Charles Dance *Professor Mandry* • Clive Owen *Paul Reisner* • Miranda Richardson *Clara* • Robert Stephens *Mr Reisner* • Joan Hickson *Mrs Whiteweather* • Lena Headey *Miriam* ■ *Dir/Scr* Stephen Poliakoff

La Cérémonie ★★★★ 15

Thriller 1995 · Fr · Colour · 107mins

Two of France's greatest current female stars, Sandrine Bonnaire and Isabelle Huppert, help make director Claude Chabrol's adaptation of British thriller writer Ruth Rendell's novel *A Judgement in Stone* an authentically chilling account of the way the French middle class brings ruin upon itself. Bonnaire is the new housekeeper, hired by a sweet-natured but condescending Breton family, whose relationship with envious postmistress Huppert results in a shocking finale. In French with English subtitles. Contains violence and swearing. 🖵

Sandrine Bonnaire *Sophie* • Isabelle Huppert *Jeanne* • Jacqueline Bisset *Catherine* • Jean-Pierre Cassel *Georges* • Virginie Ledoyen *Melinda* ■ *Dir* Claude Chabrol • *Scr* Claude Chabrol, Caroline Eliacheff, from the novel *A Judgement in Stone* by Ruth Rendell

The Ceremony ★★

Crime drama 1963 · US/Sp · BW · 107mins

Few actors were as chilling as Laurence Harvey, who also directed and produced this oddity in Spain. Harvey plays a bank robber, sentenced to death, whose 11th-hour escape is arranged by his brother disguised as a priest. Sarah Miles is the girl in the middle. This is a half-baked religious allegory, directed by Harvey as if he were Orson Welles in his *Mr Arkadin* period. Every scene screams "I am an Art Movie", and the result barely works as an oddball thriller.

Laurence Harvey *Sean McKenna* • Sarah Miles *Catherine* • Robert Walker Jr *Dominic* • John Ireland *Prison Warden* ■ *Dir* Laurence Harvey • *Scr* Ben Barzman, Alun Falconer, Laurence Harvey

Certain Fury ★★ 18

Action crime drama 1985 · US · Colour · 82mins

It's not often you get to watch two Oscar-winners making total prats of themselves, so sit back and enjoy this risible rubbish from director Stephen Gyllenhaal. Tatum O'Neal and songbird Irene Cara play two fugitives, handcuffed together and on the run after a violent court breakout. The film is obviously influenced by *The Defiant Ones*, but any chance of exploring interesting racial tensions between the women are sacrificed on the altar of a fast-moving plot. 🖵

Tatum O'Neal *Scarlet* • Irene Cara *Tracy* • Nicholas Campbell *Sniffer* • George Murdock *Lieutenant Speier* • Moses Gunn *Doctor Freeman* • Peter Fonda *Rodney* • Rodney Gage *Superman* ■ *Dir* Stephen Gyllenhaal • *Scr* Michael Jacobs

A Certain Smile ★★

Romantic drama 1958 · US · Colour · 104mins

Directed by Jean Negulesco with an eye for the visual possibilities of Paris and the French Riviera, this adaptation of Françoise Sagan's precocious bestseller is an otherwise limp and lacklustre affair. Christine Carere plays a student who gets involved with the glamorous, middle-aged Rossano Brazzi before returning to the more suitable Bradford Dillman; Joan Fontaine co-stars as Brazzi's betrayed wife. Johnny Mathis's performance of the title song is the only thing that lifts this adulterous excursion out of the ordinary.

Rossano Brazzi *Luc* • Joan Fontaine *Françoise Ferrand* • Christine Carere *Dominique* • Bradford Dillman *Bertrand* • Eduard Franz *M Vallon* ■ *Dir* Jean Negulesco • *Scr* Frances Goodrich, Albert Hackett, from the novel by Françoise Sagan

Cervantes ★★

Historical epic 1968 · Fr/It/Sp · Colour · 111mins

Horst Buchholz takes the title role in this dismal European co-production, which doesn't seem to bear much relation to the life of the famous Spanish writer. While on a secret mission from the Pope, Buchholz gets waylaid in a series of adventures involving the likes of Gina Lollobrigida, José Ferrer and Louis Jourdan.

Horst Buchholz *Miguel De Cervantes* • Gina Lollobrigida *Giulia* • José Ferrer *Hassan Bey* • Louis Jourdan *Cardinal Acquaviva* • Fernando Rey *King Philip II of Spain* ■ *Dir* Vincent Sherman • *Scr* David Karp, Enrique Llovet, Enrico Bomba, from the book by Bruno Frank

César ★★★★

Drama 1936 · Fr · BW · 125mins

The third and final film in writer Marcel Pagnol's sublime trilogy, which began with *Marius* in 1931 and continued with *Fanny* in 1932, is the only one of the three directed by Pagnol himself. It is 20 years later, and Marius (Pierre Fresnay) is working in a garage in Toulon. Fanny (Orane Demazis) tells her son Césariot (André Fouché) that Marius is his real father; with help from his grandfather, César (Raimu), the lovers are reunited. If Pagnol's direction is less expert than that of his predecessors, Alexander Korda and Marc Allégret, it's still a satisfying end to his humorous, sympathetic and acute portrait of Marseilles life. In French with English subtitles.

Raimu *César* • Orane Demazis *Fanny* • Pierre Fresnay *Marius* • Fernand Charpin *Panisse* • Milly Mathis *Aunt Claudine* • André Fouché *Césariot* • Maupi *Chauffeur* ■ *Dir* Marcel Pagnol • *Scr* Marcel Pagnol

César and Rosalie ★★★

Comedy 1972 · Fr · Colour · 105mins

Claude Sautet is a keen observer of the mores and susceptibilities of middle-aged, middle-class France, as this deft study of personal freedom and the pain involved in securing it proves. There's nothing particularly new about the romantic triangle formed by single mother Romy Schneider, wealthy lover Yves Montand and her old flame, Sami Frey. But thanks to a thoughtful script and plausible performances, this civilised, witty and ultimately moving drama is packed with the capricious twists that typify human nature. A French language film.

Yves Montand *César* • Romy Schneider *Rosalie* • Sami Frey *David* • Umberto Orsini *Antoine* ■ *Dir* Claude Sautet • *Scr* Claude Sautet, Jean-Loup Dabadie

C'est la Vie ★★★★ 12

Drama 1990 · Fr · Colour · 96mins

Set in the seaside resort of La Baule in 1958, this charming evocation of childhood summers concludes Diane Kurys's autobiographical trilogy, which began with *Diabolo Menthe* and continued with *Coup de Foudre*. Each little moment of mischief, amusement and affection is as fresh and colourful as a holiday snap, thus making the sudden intrusion of real life seem all the more shocking and sad. Julie Bataille and Candice Lefranc are splendid as the sisters by the sea, whether fooling with their cousins, teasing their nanny or responding with dismay to the news that their parents, Nathalie Baye and Richard Berry, are splitting up. In French with English subtitles. Contains brief nudity.

Nathalie Baye *Lena* • Richard Berry *Michel* • Zabou *Bella Mandel* • Jean-Pierre Bacri *Léon Mandel* • Julie Bataille *Frédérique* • Candice Lefranc *Sophie* ■ *Dir* Diane Kurys • *Scr* Diane Kurys, Alain Le Henry

Cha-Cha-Cha ★★★

Romantic comedy 1998 · Sp · Colour · 109mins

Four of Spain's hottest young stars headline this nineties variation on the *Pygmalion* theme. However, it's Eduardo Noriega who shines brightest as the doltish twentysomething who is given a real personality makeover by Madrid advertising executive Ana Alvarez. This is so he can lure her dance instructor friend (Maria Adanez) away from Jorge Sanz, the chauvinistic hunk she's lusted after since a drunken one-night stand. Antonio del Real's vibrant comedy entertains throughout but leaves little lasting impression. A Spanish language film.

Eduardo Noriega *Antonio* • Ana Alvarez *Lucia* • Maria Adanez *Maria* • Jorge Sanz *Pablo* ■ *Dir* Antonio del Real • *Scr* Antonio del Real, Fernando Leon, Carlos Asorey Brey

Chacun Cherche Son Chat ★★★★ 15

Romantic comedy 1996 · Fr · Colour · 90mins

Although comparisons with the work of Eric Rohmer are valid, Cédric Klapisch's urban comedy has sufficient wit and stylistic zest to stand on its own merits. As much about the changing face of Paris as the romantic fortunes of make-up artist Garance Clavel, this is something of a wild cat chase in terms of plot. But the search for missing moggy Gris Gris serves as an excellent excuse for some character study and conversations that are refreshingly authentic. Providing a sparkling slant on the familiar theme of love in the city, Klapisch draws vibrant performances from his cast. In French with English subtitles. Contains swearing and sex scenes.

Garance Clavel *Chloé* • Zinedine Soualem *Djamel* • Olivier Py *Michel* • Renée Lecalm *Madame Renée* • Simon Abkarian *Carlos* ■ *Dir/Scr* Cédric Klapisch

Chad Hanna ★★★ U

Period romantic drama
1940 · US · Colour · 88mins

Wonderful Technicolor and a marvellous feeling for life on the road in the upstate New York of the 1840s are the main assets here. Director Henry King displays a strong eye for Americana, and his film is full of offbeat episodes and oddball characters. The trouble is that nothing substantial ever really happens. Henry Fonda is well-cast as the country boy who becomes so infatuated with Dorothy Lamour's bareback rider that he joins the travelling circus where she performs. Linda Darnell also appears.

Henry Fonda *Chad Hanna* • Dorothy Lamour *Albany Yates* • Linda Darnell *Caroline* • Guy Kibbee *Huguenine* • Jane Darwell *Mrs Huguenine* • John Carradine *Bisbee* • Ted North *Fred Shepley* ■ *Dir* Henry King • *Scr* Nunnally Johnson, from the story *Red Wheels Rolling* by Walter D Edmonds

The Chain ★★ PG

Comedy　　1984 · UK · Colour · 92mins

Two giants of British television, writer Jack Rosenthal and director Jack Gold, use the *La Ronde* style of storytelling to depict that most British of insitutions: the housing chain. However, despite the presence of Denis Lawson, Nigel Hawthorne, Billie Whitelaw, Warren Mitchell and Leo McKern, the jokes fall rather flat. Nowadays, it's more interesting as a social record of the eighties than as a broad comedy.

Denis Lawson *Keith* • Maurice Denham *Grandpa* • Nigel Hawthorne *Mr Thorn* • Billie Whitelaw *Mrs Andreos* • Judy Parfitt *Deidre* • Leo McKern *Thomas* • Bernard Hill *Nick* • Warren Mitchell *Bamber* • Anna Massey *Betty* • David Troughton *Dudley* • Phyllis Logan *Alison* ■ *Dir* Jack Gold • *Scr* Jack Rosenthal

Chain Lightning ★★ U

Second World War drama
1950 · US · BW · 94mins

Even after such major movies as *The Big Sleep*, *Key Largo* and *The Treasure of the Sierra Madre*, Warner Bros still threw crumbs at Humphrey Bogart. This B-movie casts him as a fighter pilot, morbidly droning on about causing the death of his buddy (Richard Whorf) while testing an experimental safety device – and himself – in a new-fangled jet. The clichés are thick on the ground, but Bogart has a face you have to look at.

Humphrey Bogart *Matt Brennan* • Eleanor Parker *Jo Holloway* • Raymond Massey *Leland Willis* • Richard Whorf *Carl Troxall* • James

Brown (2) *Major Hinkle* ■ *Dir* Stuart Heisler • *Scr* Liam O'Brien, Vincent Evans, from a story by J Redmond Prior [Lester Cole]

Chain of Command ★★ 18

Action adventure thriller
1993 · US · Colour · 91mins

A cheerfully routine action thriller, executive-produced by Yoram Globus, one half of the infamous "Go-Go Boys" (the other half being Menahem Golan). Michael Dudikoff is an American secret agent who doesn't know who he can trust when he gets mixed up in a dodgy mission to a dangerous middle-eastern country. Definitely second-division stuff, though David Worth's film benefits from a typically no-nonsense performance from R Lee Ermey.

Michael Dudikoff *Merrill Ross* • Todd Curtis *Rawlings* • Keren Tishman *Maya* • R Lee Ermey *Benjamin Brewster* • Steve Greenstein *Ambassador Mosby* • Jack Adalist *CIA Director Linder* ■ *Dir* David Worth • *Scr* Christopher Applegate, Ben Johnson Handy

Chain of Desire ★ 18

Romantic drama
1992 · US · Colour · 102mins

An impressive cast – *The Last Seduction*'s Linda Fiorentino, Malcolm McDowell and *Crash* star Elias Koteas – can't conceal the lack of story or meaning in this film, which sets out to be some sort of Aids morality tale, but ends up as a series of tedious sexual encounters between a collection of pompous, unlikeable New Yorkers. Supposedly based on Max Ophüls's *La Ronde* (1950), Temistocles Lopez's drama is, at times, embarrassingly awful. You have been warned.

Malcolm McDowell *Hubert Bailey* • Linda Fiorentino *Alma D'Angeli* • Grace Zabriskie *Linda Baily* • Elias Koteas *Jesus* • Seymour Cassel *Mel* ■ *Dir/Scr* Temistocles Lopez

The Chain Reaction ★★★ 15

Thriller　　1980 · Ausl · Colour · 88mins

Boasting chase sequences by *Mad Max*'s George Miller, this hefty chunk of Australian exploitation knocks spots off similar big-budget Hollywood offerings. Director Ian Barry's smart use of both camera and sound effects transforms many of the action set pieces. Unfortunately, his delineation of character never rises above the comic book level, and there's a wasteful predictability about Steve Bisley and Arna Maria Winchester's bid to expose a leak at a nuclear plant. Great things were forecasted for Barry after this, but nine years were to pass before he directed the little-seen *Minnamurra*.

Steve Bisley *Larry* • Arna Maria Winchester *Carmel* • Ross Thompson *Heinrich* • Ralph Cotterill *Grey* • Hugh Keays-Byrne *Eagle* ■ *Dir/Scr* Ian Barry

Chain Reaction ★★★ 12

Action thriller　1996 · US · Colour · 102mins

Keanu Reeves as a scientist seeking to make cheap power out of water is a little hard to take. But it's when he and fellow researcher Rachel Weisz go on the run from mysterious saboteurs after cracking the formula that *The Fugitive* director Andrew Davis's

muddled suspense tale finally takes flight. With an unfocused script that's hazy on explanations, the film survives thanks to the pell-mell action that papers over the weak links in the convoluted plot. ◻ DVD

Keanu Reeves *Eddie Kasalivich* • Morgan Freeman *Paul Shannon* • Rachel Weisz *Lily Sinclair* • Fred Ward *FBI Agent Ford* • Kevin Dunn *FBI Agent Doyle* • Brian Cox *Lyman Earl Collier* • Joanna Cassidy *Maggie McDermott* • Chelcie Ross *Ed Rafferty* ■ *Dir* Andrew Davis • *Scr* Josh Friedman, JF Lawton, Michael Bortman, Arne L Schmidt, Rick Seaman

Chaindance ★★

Prison drama　1991 · US · Colour · 109mins

Michael Ironside is a premier league baddie, but with this quirky Canadian feature, which he also co-wrote and co-produced, he attempts to show there is more to his persona than just one-dimensional villains. He plays a convict roped into a radical rehabilitation programme in which prisoners are used to help at a hospital for the physically handicapped. With Brad Dourif as his reluctant patient and Rae Dawn Chong as a sympathetic social worker, the casting can't be faulted, but the over-earnest script makes the plot difficult to swallow. Contains swearing, violence and brief nudity.

Michael Ironside *JT Blake* • Rae Dawn Chong *Ilene* • Brad Dourif *Johnny Reynolds* • Bruce Glover *Casey* ■ *Dir* Allan A Goldstein • *Scr* Michael Ironside, Alan Aylward

Chained ★★★

Romantic drama　1934 · US · BW · 75mins

In this handsome romantic drama, Joan Crawford has to choose between shipping magnate Otto Kruger and playboy Clark Gable. The problem is, Crawford has already married Kruger and has several ocean liners in her name. What does Gable have that the older man doesn't? For stars like these – this was Gable and Crawford's fifth film together – this sort of thing was a breeze. Smartly written and stylishly directed, Clarence Brown's film motors along on star power and Crawford's show-stopping costumes.

Joan Crawford *Diane Lovering* • Clark Gable *Mike Bradley* • Otto Kruger *Richard Field* • Stuart Erwin *Johnny* • Una O'Connor *Amy* • Marjorie Gateson *Mrs Field* • Theresa Maxwell Conover *Secretary* • Lee Phelps *Bartender* ■ *Dir* Clarence Brown • *Scr* John Lee Mahin, from a story by Edgar Selwyn

Chained Heat ★★★ 18

Drama　1983 · US/W Ger · Colour · 93mins

This lip-smackingly good women-in-prison saga finds *Exorcist* star Linda Blair – topless for the first time! – learning the cell block ropes the hard way via degenerate guards, domineering inmates and the usual lesbian quota. Bolstered by a great B-movie cast – Stella Stevens, Sybil Danning, Tamara Dobson, Edy Williams – this sequel to *The Concrete Jungle* (1982) might arguably be the ultimate jail-and-jiggle trash-fest. John Vernon is an absolute hoot as the sleazy warden who videotapes desperate lags in his office hot-tub while feeding them cocaine. Contains swearing, sex scenes and violence. ◻

Linda Blair *Carol* • John Vernon *Warden Backman* • Sybil Danning *Ericka* • Tamara Dobson *Duchess* • Stella Stevens *Captain Taylor* • Sharon Hughes *Val* • Henry Silva *Lester* • Edy Williams ■ *Dir* Paul Nicholas • *Scr* Vincent Mongol, Paul Nicholas

Chains of Gold ★★ 15

Crime drama　1989 · US · Colour · 91mins

One of the low points of John Travolta's wilderness years, this weak crime drama was sold to cable TV after failing to secure a theatrical release. Travolta actually turns in a reasonable performance as a social worker who goes undercover to find a kid who's been abducted by a vicious drug gang. But the script (which Travolta had a go at polishing) veers wildly between the nasty and the sentimental, and is over-reliant on tough street language to cover up its deficiencies. Contains swearing, violence and drug abuse. ◻

John Travolta *Scott Barnes* • Marilu Henner *Jackie* • Joey Lawrence *Tommy Burke* • Bernie Casey *Sergeant Palco* • Ramon Franco *James* • Hector Elizondo *Lieutenant Ortega* ■ *Dir* Rod Holcomb • *Scr* John Petz, Linda Favila, Anson Downes, John Travolta

The Chairman ★★★

Spy thriller　1969 · UK · Colour · 101mins

Originally released in the UK as *The Most Dangerous Man in the World*, J Lee Thompson's effective countdown thriller uses the old comic-strip chestnut of a microchip in Gregory Peck's skull that's either a transmitter or a bomb detonator, depending upon the success of his assignment in Red China to track down a miraculous crop-growing formula. Laboured dashes of political sermonising aside, the *Mission Impossible*-style story is laced with enough outrageous twists and persistent suspense to grab full attention and deliver a gripping climax.

Gregory Peck *John Hathaway* • Anne Heywood *Kay Hanna* • Arthur Hill *Shelby* • Alan Dobie *Benson* • Conrad Yama *Chairman* • Zienia Merton *Ting Ling* • Ori Levy *Shertov* ■ *Dir* J Lee Thompson • *Scr* Ben Maddow, from the novel by Jay Richard Kennedy

Chairman of the Board ★★

Comedy　1998 · US · Colour · 95mins

Scott "Carrot Top" Thompson is something of a cult figure Stateside, but is virtually unheard of over here. He mines the same sort of manic hysteria put to much more profitable use by Jim Carrey and, like the latter, you'll either love him or loathe him. Alex Zamm's comedy finds him becoming the unlikely head of a giant corporation, much to the displeasure of Larry Miller (excellent as usual) and Raquel Welch. It's relentlessly juvenile, frequently tasteless – and perfect for undemanding teenagers.

Carrot Top *Edison* • Courtney Thorne-Smith *Natalie* • Larry Miller *Bradford* • Jack Warden *Armand* • Estelle Harris *Ms Krubavitch* • Raquel Welch *Grace Kosik* • M Emmet Walsh *Freemont* • Little Richard ■ *Dir* Alex Zamm • *Scr* Alex Zamm, Turi Meyer, Al Septien, from a story by Turi Meyer, Al Septien

Chalk ★

Sports drama　1996 · US · Colour · 145mins

An improvised drama from members of San Francisco's Tenderloin Action

Group (comprising addicts, down-and-outs and the homeless), marshalled into action by director Rob Nilsson and clearly modelled on the John Cassavetes school of street realism. Sometimes gritty, insightful and raw, this look at small-time pool hustlers, their ambitions and their complexes, is mostly amateur in presentation. The result is a slow-paced, experimental work in which the inexperience of everyone involved is on full view. The making of the movie – Nilsson trying to raise funds and keep his "actors" off drugs and alcohol long enough to get them on screen – is far more interesting than the film itself.

Kelvin Han Yee *TC* • Don Bajema *Dorian James* • Denise Concetta Cavaliere *Lois* • Johnnie Reese *Jones* • Edwin Johnson *Pop Watson* • Destiny Costa *Wanda* ■ *Dir* Rob Nilsson • *Scr* Rob Nilsson, Don Bajema

The Chalk Garden ★★★ U

Drama 1964 · UK · Colour · 106mins

Ronald Neame's adaptation of Enid Bagnold's play is nowhere near as glossy as producer Ross Hunter's Hollywood melodramas, and little effort is made to hide its stage origins. It's not merely a case of filmed theatre, however, as John Michael Hayes's screenplay shifts the emphasis away from Edith Evans's dotty grandmother and Deborah Kerr's mysterious governess, placing it instead on the precocious teenager played with typical bravado by Hayley Mills. With father John offering neat support as the family butler, this is a rather talkative acting showcase, while the Oscar-nominated Evans steals the limelight from the hesitant Kerr.

Deborah Kerr *Madrigal* • Hayley Mills *Laurel* • John Mills *Maitland* • Edith Evans *Mrs St Maugham* • Felix Aylmer *Judge McWhirrey* • Elizabeth Sellars *Olivia* • Lally Bowers *Anna* ■ *Dir* Ronald Neame • *Scr* John Michael Hayes, from the play by Enid Bagnold

The Challenge ★★★ PG

Adventure 1938 · UK · BW · 73mins

A remarkable mountaineering film about the scaling of the Matterhorn by Edward Whymper, here played by Robert Douglas (better remembered these days as a colourful Hollywood villain). The film was co-directed by the great climber and film-maker Luis Trenker, who also made a simultaneous German version called *Der Berg Ruft*, and who was helped with the English dialogue by his fellow director Milton Rosmer and a screenplay co-written by Michael Powell's partner-to-be, Emeric Pressburger. It may seem a little creaky today, but there's genuine tension in the Alpine sequences and a sense of joy and achievement that is quite rare in cinema. ▣

Robert Douglas *Edward Whymper* • Luis Trenker *Jean-Antoine Carrel* • Mary Clare *Carrel's mother* • Fred Groves *Favre* • Frank Birch *Rev Charles Hudson* • Joan Gardner *Felicitas* • Geoffrey Wardwell *Lord Francis Douglas* ■ *Dir* Milton Rosmer, Luis Trenker • *Scr* Patrick Kirwan, Milton Rosmer, from a story by Emeric Pressburger

The Challenge ★★

Crime drama 1960 · UK · BW · 95mins

Sometimes films are so mesmerisingly bad that they offer a diverse selection of delights to the viewer, though not all are intentional. This is one such movie, amazingly pairing Hollywood sexpot Jayne Mansfield and British classical actor Anthony Quayle in a crime thriller of murky intent and ludicrous result. Mansfield makes the least convincing criminal mastermind you'll ever clap eyes on, but Quayle is smitten with her all the same, and goes to jail to ensure the police don't capture the loot from a heist.

Jayne Mansfield *Billy Lacrosse* • Anthony Quayle *Jim Maxton* • Carl Mohner *Kristy* • Peter Reynolds *Buddy* ■ *Dir* John Gilling • *Scr* John Gilling, from his story

The Challenge ★★ 18

Thriller 1982 · US · Colour · 109mins

American boxer Scott Glenn helps Japanese descendants of revered samurai warriors reclaim their ancient heirlooms in this strange martial arts drama, co-written by John Sayles (one of the best genre scriptwriters in the business) and directed by John Frankenheimer with little of his renowned flair. The basic thrust of the piece sets honourable traditions against venal westernised capitalism, and shows how the sword has been replaced by the gun in modern Tokyo. The film is full of great kung-fu fighting and Sayles's trademark ironies, but it's far too slow for a thriller. ▣

Scott Glenn *Rick* • Toshiro Mifune *Yoshida* • Donna Kei Benz *Akiko* • Atsuo Nakamura *Hideo* • Miiko Taka *Keiko* ■ *Dir* John Frankenheimer • *Scr* John Sayles, Richard Maxwell, Ivan Moffatt

A Challenge for Robin Hood ★★ U

Adventure 1967 · UK · Colour · 95mins

Although it will always be best known for its horrors, Hammer had something of a reputation for swashbuckling in the sixties. Sadly, this adventure isn't half as much fun as Hammer's earlier Robin Hood outings. Barrie Ingham dons the Lincoln green to take on John Arnatt, here promoted to Sheriff of Nottingham after several seasons playing his scheming deputy in the fifties TV series. The action is staged with little imagination by director CM Pennington-Richards, but compensation comes in the ample form of James Hayter's Friar Tuck.

Barrie Ingham *Robin* • James Hayter *Friar Tuck* • Leon Greene *Little John* • Peter Blythe *Roger de Courtenay* • Gay Hamilton *Maid Marian* • Jenny Till *Lady Marian* • John Arnatt *Sheriff of Nottingham* ■ *Dir* CM Pennington-Richards • *Scr* Peter Bryan

Challenge to Be Free ★★ U

Adventure 1972 · US · Colour · 83mins

Released four years after it was completed, and also shown as *Mad Trapper of the Yukon*, this was the last of the nearly 50 features directed by Tay Garnett (although he did get a little assistance from experienced action specialist Ford Beebe). The Hollywood veteran also takes a cameo role as the lawman in hot pursuit of fur trapper Mike Mazurki across the Alaskan wastes. This is family entertainment of the tepid, worthy kind, although the 100 baying hounds should keep dog lovers happy. ▣

Mike Mazurki *Trapper* • Jimmy Kane *Old Tracks* • Fritz Ford *Sergeant* • Tay Garnett *Marshall McGee* • John McIntire *Narrator* ■ *Dir* Tay Garnett, Ford Beebe • *Scr* Chuck D Keen, Anne Bosworth, Tay Garnett

Challenge to Lassie ★★★ U

Drama 1949 · US · Colour · 75mins

This is a major character role for the movies' best-loved pooch, as the famed collie retreats to late-19th-century Edinburgh from the great American outdoors to play a faithful dog who keeps returning to a churchyard where her master is buried. Sound familiar? It's Disney's 1960 film *Greyfriars Bobby*, which was an uncredited remake of this 1949 MGM film, also featuring Donald Crisp, though in the later version Crisp starred as the cemetery keeper, whereas here he's Lassie's master. Lassie is utterly splendid in the lead, and the late forties Technicolor is ravishing.

Edmund Gwenn *John Traill* • Donald Crisp *"Jock" Gray* • Geraldine Brooks *Susan Brown* • Reginald Owen *Sergeant Davie* • Alan Webb *James Brown* • Ross Ford *William Traill* ■ *Dir* Richard Thorpe • *Scr* William Ludwig, from the novel *Greyfriars Bobby* by Eleanor Atkinson

The Chamber ★★ 15

Mystery thriller 1996 · US · Colour · 107mins

Gene Hackman gives a sensational performance in a bleak, static potboiler, based on the John Grisham bestseller. Hackman is the Ku Klux Klansman held responsible for racial murders in 1967, with 28 days left before his gas chamber execution. Did he act alone when he planted the bomb that killed two Jewish boys? That's for his duty-bound grandson Chris O'Donnell to ascertain when he grudgingly defends the white supremacist he hates. Director James Foley tries hard to make us care about the colourless characters, but interest remains on a consistent low throughout the very draggy proceedings. Contains some swearing and moderate violence. ▣

Chris O'Donnell *Adam Hall* • Gene Hackman *Sam Cayhall* • Faye Dunaway *Lee Bowen* • Robert Prosky *E Garner Goodman* • Raymond J Barry *Rollie Wedge* • Bo Jackson *Sergeant Packer* • Lela Rochon *Nora Stark* • Josef Sommer *Phelps Bowen* ■ • *Scr* William Goldman, Chris Reese, from the novel by John Grisham

Chamber of Horrors ★★★

Horror thriller 1966 · US · Colour · 97mins

Demented killer Patrick O'Neal chops off his own manacled hand to escape the hangman and terrorise 19th-century Baltimore with an array of detachable murder weapons in a great neglected shocker. Originally made as a TV series pilot, featuring Cesare Danova and Wilfrid Hyde White as crime-solving wax museum owners but considered too lurid to air, director Hy Averback's nifty nightmare had gimmicks galore for its cinema audience, with "Horror Horn" and "Fear Flasher" warnings of when to close your eyes to the terror. With a cast full of nostalgic surprises and O'Neal's marvellously malevolent turn, this is a textbook example of classic sixties American horror.

Cesare Danova *Anthony Draco* • Wilfrid Hyde White *Harold Blount* • Laura Devon *Marie Champlain* • Patrice Wymore *Vivian* • Suzy Parker *Barbara Dixon* • Tun Tun *Senor Pepe De Reyes* • Tony Curtis *Mr Julian* ■ *Dir* Hy Averback • *Scr* Stephen Kandel, from a story by Stephen Kandel, Ray Russell

The Chambermaid on the Titanic ★★★

Period romantic drama 1997 · Sp/Fr/It · Colour · 98mins

Set in the days when feature films were in their infancy, this dissertation on the art of storytelling is an unusually muted offering from the flamboyant Spanish director, Bigas Luna. Exploring the nature of truth and fiction, the tale of impoverished worker Olivier Martinez's nocturnal meeting with *Titanic* chambermaid Aitana Sanchez-Gijon is soon whipped up by constant retelling into an erotic epic that earns him the chance for theatrical fame. Whether depicting the daily grind at the Zola-esque foundry or the rapt faces as Martinez warms to his theme, this is an intoxicating and atmospheric fantasy. In French and English with subtitles.

Olivier Martinez *Horty* • Romane Bohringer *Zoe* • Aitana Sanchez-Gijon *Marie* • Didier Bezace *Simeon* • Aldo Maccione *Zeppe* • Jean-Marie Juan *Pascal* • Arno Chevrier *Al* • Marianne Groves *Bathilde* ■ *Dir* Bigas Luna • *Scr* Bigas Luna, Jean-Louis Benoit, Cuca Canals, from the novel *La Femme de Chambre du Titanic* by Didier Decoin

Chameleon ★★ 15

Crime thriller 1995 · US · Colour · 103mins

Anthony LaPaglia has a ball as a *Mission: Impossible*-style agent with a big make-up bag who adopts a bewildering number of disguises to nail crime boss Kevin Pollak who was responsible for the death of his family. The plot doesn't bear much scrutiny, but the leads deliver capable performances. Look out for *Seinfeld* regular Wayne Knight. ▣

Anthony LaPaglia *Willie Serling* • Kevin Pollak *Matt Gianni* • Melora Hardin *Jill Hallman* • Wayne Knight *Stuart Langston* ■ *Dir* Michael Pavone • *Scr* Michael Pavone, Dave Alan Johnson

Chameleon Street ★★★★

Biographical comedy drama 1989 · US · Colour · 98mins

A riveting, true-life account of the life of William Douglas Street, a black man from Detroit who imitated a *Time* reporter, an exchange student, a lawyer and a surgeon – without any qualifications whatsoever! Written, directed and starring Wendell B Harris Jr, this biographical comedy drama won raves on the festival circuit, but received only a nominal release. A "lost" film that deserves to be found.

Wendell B Harris Jr *William Douglas Street* • Angela Leslie *Gabrielle* • Amina Fakir *Tatiana* • Paula McGee • Mano Breckenridge *Neelish Ratnayaka* • Richard David Kiley Jr *Dr Hand* ■ *Dir/Scr* Wendell B Harris Jr

The Champ ★★★★
Melodrama 1931 · US · BW · 86mins

A divorced, washed-up boxer (Wallace Beery), now a heavy-drinking gambler, goes into training for a comeback accompanied by his adoring son (Jackie Cooper). MGM were a dab hand at tear-jerkers like this one, though the film's success owes much to Beery's performance and even more to young Cooper, who is disarmingly natural and precociously gifted. A massive hit in its day, it won Oscars for Beery and the story, and nominations for best picture and its distinguished director, King Vidor.

Wallace Beery *Champ* • Jackie Cooper *Dink* • Irene Rich *Linda* • Roscoe Ates *Sponge* • Edward Brophy *Tim* • Hale Hamilton *Tony* • Jesse Scott *Jonah* ■ *Dir* King Vidor • *Scr* Leonard Praskins, from a story by Frances Marion

The Champ ★★★ PG
Sports drama 1979 · US · Colour · 117mins

Director Franco Zeffirelli made his Hollywood debut with this rather routine remake of the 1931 tear-jerker. Jon Voight takes on the washed-up prizefighter role made famous by Wallace Beery, while Ricky Schroder, as the son Voight is determined to make a splashy comeback for, wrings the emotions so effectively he must have shares in Kleenex. Ex-wife Faye Dunaway returns to undermine Voight and son's growing understanding, yet even her unconvincing performance can't sabotage the weepie finale. ▭

Jon Voight *Billy Flynn* • Faye Dunaway *Annie* • Ricky Schroder [Rick Schroder] *TJ Flynn* • Jack Warden *Jackie* • Arthur Hill *Mike* • Strother Martin *Riley* • Joan Blondell *Dolly Kenyon* ■ *Dir* Franco Zeffirelli • *Scr* Walter Newman, from a story by Frances Marion

Champagne Charlie ★★★ PG
Comedy drama 1944 · UK · BW · 186mins

This period romp from Ealing Studios gave the great Tommy Trinder one of his best screen roles. As music-hall star George Leybourne, he is engaged in a contest with bellicose Stanley Holloway to secure "the most popular drinking song of the era" – the era in question being the 1860s, beautifully re-created and superbly photographed by Wilkie Cooper. Director Alberto Cavalcanti obviously loves the Victorian music hall, and has a fine eye for period detail, and the film is well cast, with Betty Warren and Jean Kent as the leading ladies. ▭

Tommy Trinder *George Leybourne* • Stanley Holloway *The Great Vance* • Betty Warren *Bessie Bellwood* • Jean Kent *Dolly Bellwood* • Austin Trevor *The Duke* • Peter De Greeff *Lord Petersfield* • Leslie Clarke *Fred Saunders* • Eddie Phillips *Tom Sayers* ■ *Dir* Alberto Cavalcanti • *Scr* Austin Melford, Angus MacPhail, John Dighton

Champagne for Caesar ★★★ U
Satire 1950 · US · BW · 99mins

One of the very earliest satires on Hollywood's major rival, television, this little-known film is still topical in these days of million-pound quiz shows. Ronald Colman, in one of his last roles, is the unemployed mastermind

who applies for a job at a soap company only to be snubbed by boss Vincent Price. In revenge, he enters a TV quiz show and proceeds to win a fortune, much to the chagrin of venal sponsor Price. Celeste Holm then poses as a nurse to try and sabotage Colman's winning run. Not quite as sharp or as funny as it might have been a decade later but nevertheless remarkably watchable, thanks to the clever casting of the leads.

Ronald Colman *Beauregard Bottomley* • Celeste Holm *Flame O'Neil* • Vincent Price *Burnbridge Waters* • Barbara Britton *Gwenn Bottomley* • Art Linkletter *Happy Hogan* ■ *Dir* Richard Whorf • *Scr* Hans Jacoby, Fred Brady Black

The Champagne Murders ★
Crime mystery 1966 · Fr · Colour · 98mins

A husband and wife (Anthony Perkins, Yvonne Furneaux), helped by Stéphane Audran, embark on an elaborate plan to convince playboy Maurice Ronet that he is a murderer. A deeply mediocre and offensive film from Claude Chabrol, going through career doldrums before rescuing his reputation with the stifling mastery of *The Butcher* three years later. With some neat contrivances and a wildly showy overhead final shot, this corked grotesquerie does have the possible makings of an unpleasant cult film. French dialogue dubbed into English.

Anthony Perkins *Christopher* • Maurice Ronet *Paul* • Stéphane Audran *Jacqueline* • Yvonne Furneaux *Christine* • Suzanne Lloyd *Evelyn* • Catherine Sola *Denise* ■ *Dir* Claude Chabrol • *Scr* Claude Brule, Derek Prouse, from a story by William Benjamin, Paul Gegauff

Champion ★★★★ PG
Drama 1949 · US · BW · 98mins

Kirk Douglas here gives one of the definitive performances of his career as ruthless boxer Midge Kelly, who will stop at almost nothing to become a success. Douglas repeatedly betrays his disabled brother (Arthur Kennedy), his watchful manager (Paul Stewart) and the women in his life (Marilyn Maxwell and Ruth Roman among them) right up until his fist-breaking comeuppance. It's a punishment producer Stanley Kramer must have wished he could have inflicted upon Douglas in real life after the star had a nose-job halfway through production, meaning nobody could lay a glove on him. Contains some moderate violence. ▭

Kirk Douglas *Midge Kelly* • Marilyn Maxwell *Grace Diamond* • Arthur Kennedy *Connie Kelly* • Paul Stewart *Tommy Haley* • Ruth Roman *Emma Bryce* • Lola Albright *Mrs Harris* ■ *Dir* Mark Robson • *Scr* Carl Foreman, from a story by Ring Lardner

Champions ★★★ PG
Biographical drama 1983 · UK · Colour · 109mins

Having always looked a bit on the wasted side, John Hurt was the perfect choice to play Bob Champion in this true story of a jockey who overcame cancer, an injured horse and the rest of the field to make a heroic comeback and win the Grand National. The film lacks psychological depth and risks going too far in avoiding the temptation

of portraying Champion as a saint. Yet, by combining the ingredients of a "disease of the week" movie with those of a *Boys' Own* story of sporting success against the odds, this tear-jerking tale certainly holds the attention. Contains swearing. ▭

John Hurt *Bob Champion* • Edward Woodward *Josh Gifford* • Ben Johnson *Burly Cocks* • Jan Francis *Jo Beswick* • Peter Barkworth *Nick Embiricos* • Ann Bell *Valda Embiricos* • Judy Parfitt *Dr Merrow* • Alison Steadman *Mary Hussey* • Kirstie Alley *Barbara* • Michael Byrne *Richard Hussey* ■ *Dir* John Irvin • *Scr* Evan Jones, from the book *Champion's Story* by Bob Champion, Jonathan Powell

A Champion's Fight ★★
Drama 1998 · US · Colour

This melodramatic TV weepie tells of a high school girl who defies her parents by falling in love with a boy they feel is beneath her, despite him being a star athlete. When he is stricken with cancer she sticks by his side, deepening the bond between them. Don't look for any big stars here; the only "name" is Adrienne Barbeau from *The Fog*.

Adrienne Barbeau *Nancy Muldenhower* • Beth Broderick *Patricia* • Scott Vickaryous *Luke* • Katie Harrod *Julie Ellis* ■ *Dir* James A Contner • *Scr* Kathryn Pratt, from the novel *Don't Die, My Love* by Lurlene McDaniel

Chan Is Missing ★★★ 15
Comedy 1982 · US · BW · 76mins

Debunking Charlie Chan stereotypes and faintly echoing *The Third Man*, this gently pulsating study of life in San Francisco's Chinatown was filmed for a mere $22,000. The search for "Chan", who owes cabbies Wood Moy and Marc Hayashi a small fortune, almost becomes an irrelevance as director Wayne Wang guides us through a community that is not only isolated from the rest of the country, but is also divided within itself by homeland political rivalries and cross-generational attitudes. Comic, intriguing and often almost anthropological, this was one of the first films to show what the American indie sector was capable of.

Wood Moy *Jo* • Marc Hayashi *Steve* • Laureen Chew *Amy* • Jud Y Nihei *Lawyer* • Peter Wang *Henry the cook* • Presco Tabios *Presco* • Frankie Alarcon *Frankie* ■ *Dir* Wayne Wang • *Scr* Wayne Wang, Isaac Cronin, Terrel Seltzer

Chance ★ 18
Crime drama 1990 · US · Colour · 81mins

Renegade cop Lawrence-Hilton Jacobs, who looks like a frightened animal staring into approaching headlights, becomes a kind of "Mild Harry" when his friend Dan Haggerty unwittingly repossesses a car holding diamonds from a recent robbery. There's so little story, the film frequently plays scenes unedited for time, even when it's something as mundane as Haggerty brushing his teeth. The ending leaves several unresolved problems for the heroes, though they seem as happy as the viewer that it's over. ▭

Lawrence-Hilton Jacobs *Detective Jon Chance* • Dan Haggerty *Zach, the repo man* • Roger Rodd *Kingsley* • Addison Randall • Charlie

Ganis *Alvin* • Pamela Dixon ■ *Dir* Charles T Kanganis, Addison Randall • *Scr* Joe Hart, Addison Randall, Lawrence-Hilton Jacobs

Chance of a Lifetime ★★ U
Comedy drama 1950 · UK · BW · 92mins

Co-written by director Bernard Miles and Walter Greenwood, author of the groundbreaking novel *Love on the Dole*, and played with conviction by a solid ensemble cast, this is a nostalgic look back to the days when people still genuinely believed in the co-operation of capital and labour. Regarded by some as a flight of fancy even on its original release, the story of a striking workforce that takes control of its factory seems more naive than ever. But there's more than a hint of truth behind many of the political platitudes and the finale has a pleasingly Capra-esque ring to it.

Basil Radford *Dickinson* • Niall MacGinnis *Baxter* • Bernard Miles *Stevens* • Julien Mitchell *Morris* • Kenneth More *Adam* • Patrick Troughton *Kettle* • Hattie Jacques *Alice* ■ *Dir* Bernard Miles, Alan Osbiston • *Scr* Bernard Miles, Walter Greenwood

Chance of a Lifetime ★★★ U
Romantic comedy 1991 · US · Colour · 93mins

A sweet romantic comedy about seizing every moment you have when you can, with *Golden Girls* star Betty White as the woman with only a few months to live who finds love during a holiday in Mexico. Leslie Nielsen is the lucky guy, and you'll also recognise TV regulars Ed Begley Jr and Elaine Stritch in this warm tale that resembles an episode of *The Love Boat*. ▭

Betty White *Evelyn Eglin* • Leslie Nielsen *Lloyd Dixon* • Ed Begley Jr *Darrel Eglin* • Michael Tucci *Randall* • William Windom *Dr Edelman* • Elaine Stritch *Sybil Sedgwick* • Orson Bean *Fred Novins* • Annabelle Gurwitch *Sherry* ■ *Dir* Jonathan Sanger • *Scr* Lynn Roth

Chance or Coincidence ★★★★ PG
Drama 1999 · Fr/Can · Colour · 116mins

A young widow on a global odyssey to all the sights her dead son would have loved to visit – polar bears in the Arctic, the divers of Acapulco, a Montreal hockey game – is the thrust of director Claude Lelouch's touching rumination on the vital role that chance and coincidence play in life. Yet it's only when her camcorder is stolen, and the sentimental images it contains strike a chord with its buyer, that Lelouch's unique romance begins to take flight. Superbly acted by Alessandra Martines, this is one of those movies where it's impossible to guess what's going to happen next. In French with English subtitles. Contains some coarse language. ▭

Alessandra Martines *Myriam Lini* • Pierre Arditi *Pierre Turi* • Marc Hollogne *Marc Deschamps* • Laurent Hilaire *Laurent* • Véronique Moreau *Catherine Desvilles* • Patrick Labbé *Michel Bonhomme* • Geoffrey Holder *Gerry* • Luigi Bonino *Mauro Lini* ■ *Dir/Scr* Claude Lelouch

Chances Are ★★★ **PG**

Romantic comedy
1989 · US · Colour · 103mins

The principle of reincarnation has provided fascinating material for film-makers over the years, but while this slightly sexy romantic comedy visits the same territory it doesn't reach the high plateau of such Oscar-winning delights as 1941's *Here Comes Mr Jordan*. Here, a dead husband returns to Earth in a new body, but with a partial memory of his previous life, and falls for the daughter he never knew he had. Cybill Shepherd, Robert Downey Jr and Ryan O'Neal give the idea their best shot, but Emile Ardolino's direction misses the target. Contains some swearing. ▥

Cybill Shepherd *Corinne Jeffries* • Robert Downey Jr *Alex Finch* • Ryan O'Neal *Philip Train* • Mary Stuart Masterson *Miranda Jeffries* • Christopher McDonald *Louie Jeffries* • Josef Sommer *Judge Fenwick* ■ *Dir* Emile Ardolino • *Scr* Perry Howze, Randy Howze

Chanel Solitaire ★★ **15**

Biographical drama
1981 · UK/Fr · Colour · 106mins

Rutger Hauer made his English language debut in this disappointing fantasy on the early life of Coco Chanel. Crediting her with little inspiration, Julian More's screenplay suggests she rose from rags to riches simply by recognising the moment and exploiting everyone she knew. However, Marie-France Pisier suggests something of the sorrowful isolation of an icon whose affairs were all doomed to failure, be they with Hauer and Timothy Dalton, or with lesbian Catherine Allégret.

Marie-France Pisier *Gabrielle "Coco" Chanel* • Timothy Dalton *Boy Capel* • Rutger Hauer *Etienne de Balsan* • Karen Black *Emilienne D'Alençon* • Catherine Allégret ■ *Dir* George Kaczender • *Scr* Julian More, from a novel by Claude Delay

Chang ★★★★

Silent documentary 1927 · US · BW · 69mins

Jungle fever had infected film-makers Merian C Cooper and Ernest B Schoedsack, even before they made *King Kong* in 1933, as this plot-driven documentary shows. Set in the Siamese jungle, it tells of Kru and his family as they fight for survival amid the indifferent forces of nature and rampaging wild animals, including a herd of elephants. ("Chang" is the Thai word for the beast.) Astonishing wildlife photography enlivens the narrative; this was the first jungle animal movie with a script.

Dir/Scr Merian C Cooper, Ernest B Schoedsack

Change of Habit ★ **PG**

Musical comedy drama
1969 · US · Colour · 88mins

A change of pace and style for Elvis Presley, here playing a doctor working in an ghetto whose three new helpers, unbeknown to him, are novice nuns. The talented Mary Tyler Moore co-stars, though she looks distinctly uncomfortable; she seemed much happier on the small screen the following year in her own smash hit series. Presley's film career was in free fall by this time, and the scripts and situations were becoming increasingly desperate. ▥

Elvis Presley *Dr John Carpenter* • Mary Tyler Moore *Sister Michelle* • Barbara McNair *Sister Irene* • Jane Elliot *Sister Barbara* • Leora Dana *Mother Joseph* • Edward Asner [Ed Asner] *Lieutenant Moretti* • Robert Emhardt *The banker* ■ *Dir* William A Graham • *Scr* James Lee, SS Schweitzer, Eric Bercovici, from a story by Richard Morris, John Joseph

Change of Heart ★★★ **U**

Musical 1943 · US · BW · 88mins

Songwriter John Carroll, burnt out and devoid of inspiration, teams up with Midwest girl Susan Hayward who obligingly ghosts his songs for him. A slender hook on which to hang a host of musical numbers and specialty acts, but in 88 minutes this production, directed by Albert S Rogell for Poverty Row studio Republic, does just that. Wisecracking Eve Arden is on hand in a supporting role, Dorothy Dandridge performs, while Count Basie appears with his orchestra. A modest, cheerfully amusing musical romance, which earned a best song Oscar nomination for Jule Styne and Harold Adamson.

John Carroll *Rick Farrell* • Susan Hayward *Jill Wright* • Gail Patrick *Toni Jarrett* • Eve Arden *Belinda Wright* • Melville Cooper *Bradley Cole* • Walter Catlett *J MacClellan Davis* • Mary Treen *Janie* • Tom Kennedy *Westinghouse* • Dorothy Dandridge ■ *Dir* Albert S Rogell • *Scr* Frank Gill Jr

Change of Heart ★★ **15**

Comedy drama 1993 · Can · Colour

Despite a Christmas setting and that dependable old plot device about a young girl searching for her long lost dad, this Canadian piece manages to keep the slushier elements of the tale at bay. Feisty Sarah Campbell promises her loser uncle (Jeremy Ratchford) that she'll pay off his debts if he helps her locate her missing father, leading the duo on a series of misadventures. The acting from the two largely unknown leads fizzes, and director Donald Shebib is careful to avoid the most groaning clichés. ▥

Sarah Campbell *Maggie Dolan* • Jeremy Ratchford *Felix* • Heath Lamberts *Axel* • Lenore Zann *Carmen* ■ *Dir* Donald Shebib • *Scr* Terence Heffernan

A Change of Place ★★

Romantic drama 1994 · US/Can/Ger · Colour

Since making her name with the lesbian love story *Desert Hearts*, director Donna Deitch has had to settle for a diet of TV movies. Set in a Paris fashion house, this melodrama makes up in style what it lacks in substance. Portraying twins is never easy, but Andrea Roth makes rather a meal of playing the bookish Kimberly, who trades places with model sister Dominique only to be suspected of leaking top-secret designs by whizkid Rick Springfield. Stephanie Beacham and Ian Richardson raise the tone, but once romance blossoms the suspense vanishes and schmaltz sets in.

Andrea Roth *Kimberly Jamison/Domenique* • Rick Springfield *Phillippe De Claremont* • Ian

Richardson *Duroche* • Stephanie Beacham *Marie* ■ *Dir* Donna Deitch • *Scr* Rosemary Anne Sisson

A Change of Seasons ★★★ **15**

Romantic drama 1980 · US · Colour · 97mins

When college professor Anthony Hopkins has an affair with student Bo Derek, his wife Shirley MacLaine retaliates by taking Michael Brandon to bed. In *Bob & Carol & Ted & Alice* fashion, they all take a holiday at a Vermont skiing resort just to show how broad-minded they are. Unfortunately, the leads are let down by a lacklustre script, co-written by *Love Story*'s Erich Segal, and the film rapidly runs out of steam. It's only the chirpiness of MacLaine and the professionalism of the actors that hold our interest. Contains swearing and nudity. ▥

Shirley MacLaine *Karen Evans* • Anthony Hopkins *Adam Evans* • Bo Derek *Lindsey Rutledge* • Michael Brandon *Pete Lachapelle* • Mary Beth Hurt *Kasey Evans* • Ed Winter [Edward Winter] *Steven Rutledge* • Paul Regina *Paul Dilisi* ■ *Dir* Richard Lang • *Scr* Erich Segal, Fred Segal, Ronni Kern, from a story by Martin Ransohoff, Erich Segal

The Changeling ★★★

Supernatural thriller
1980 · Can · Colour · 106mins

A satisfying twist on an old staple, the haunted house movie. George C Scott is a recently widowed composer who moves into an old house in Seattle (really Vancouver) run by the local historic society. Before long, the house starts croaking, juddering and generally behaving badly. With the help of local historian Trish Van Devere (Scott's then-wife), a century-old murder is discovered; there are further shocks in store, all neatly handled by Hungarian-born director Peter Medak, who sensibly refuses to let the special effects get the upper hand.

George C Scott *John Russell* • Trish Van Devere *Claire Norman* • Melvyn Douglas *Senator Joe Carmichael* • Jean Marsh *Joanna Russell* • Barry Morse *Dr Pemberton* • Bernard Behrens *Robert Lingstrom* ■ *Dir* Peter Medak • *Scr* William Gray, Adrian Morrall

Changes ★★ **PG**

Romantic drama 1991 · US · Colour · 91mins

Just in case you ever wanted to know what happened to Michael Nouri, who co-starred alongside Jennifer (*Flashdance*) Beals, here's your answer. He has now been relegated to the world of the TV movie, and here stars in the fluffiest example of that genre: the Danielle Steel novel adaptation. Joining him is Cheryl Ladd as a television reporter who falls for Nouri's widowed surgeon. There are all the twists, turns, highs, lows and heartbreaks you'd expect, but it's handled quite well and mercifully doesn't get as flowery as the book on which it is based. ▥

Cheryl Ladd *Melanie Adams* • Michael Nouri *Peter Hallam* • Christie Clark *Valerie Adams* • Renee O'Connor *Jessica Adams* • Christopher Gartin *Mark Hallam* • Ami Foster *Pam Hallam* • Joseph Gordon-Levitt *Matthew Hallam* ■ *Dir* Charles Jarrott • *Scr* Susan Nanus, from the novel by Danielle Steel

Changing Habits ★★

Romantic comedy drama
1997 · US · Colour · 95mins

Moira Kelly stars as a troubled young woman unable to have relationships with men thanks to her difficult upbringing with alcoholic father Christopher Lloyd. Retreating to a convent, Kelly begins a mural in the basement with materials shoplifted from her local art supplier (Dylan Walsh). A charming film from director Lynn Roth, with performances from the leads that compensate for the psychological baggage.

Moira Kelly *Soosh Teagarden* • Christopher Lloyd *Theo Teagarden* • Dylan Walsh *Felix Shepherd* • Shelley Duvall *Sister Agatha* • Bob Gunton *Bishop Creighton* • Eileen Brennan *Mother Superior* • Teri Garr *Connie* ■ *Dir* Lynn Roth • *Scr* Scott Davis Jones

Un Chant d'Amour ★★★★

Silent erotic drama 1950 · Fr · BW · 26mins

Jean Genet's only film is a completely silent, 26-minute "ciné-poem" containing many of the French novelist and playwright's themes and obsessions. Ex-thief Genet started writing in prison, and the setting of men alone in cells is a milieu he knew at first hand. Although the graphic scenes of masturbation and homosexual sex make this an intensely physical film, its lyrical evocation of passion and love raises it above the category of gay porn.

Dir/Scr Jean Genet

The Chant of Jimmie Blacksmith ★★★★ **18**

Drama 1978 · Ausl · Colour · 112mins

Not so much a chant by the half-Aborigine, played with conviction by Tommy Lewis, as a war cry of ferocious rebellion. The poignancy in one of director Fred Schepisi's most powerful movies is that Jimmie really believes he's a stakeholder in the new federation of Australian States announced at the turn of the century. The tragedy is that, discovering he's still of aborigine, and therefore inferior, status in white eyes, he goes on a murderous rampage. Contains violence and swearing. ▥

Tommy Lewis *Jimmie* • Freddy Reynolds *Mort* • Ray Barrett *Farrell* • Jack Thompson *Reverend Neville* • Angela Punch [Angela Punch McGregor] *Gilda Marshall* • Steve Dodds *Uncle Tabidgi* ■ *Dir* Fred Schepisi • *Scr* Fred Schepisi, from the novel by Thomas Keneally

Chaplin ★★★ **15**

Biographical drama
1992 · UK/US · Colour and BW · 138mins

A momentous and long-gestating personal project for director Richard Attenborough, this epic about Charlie Chaplin's early life suffers from its diffuseness, not aided by the device of having the older Chaplin dictate his tale to a diffident (and utterly fictitious) publisher, played by Anthony Hopkins. It's clearly the result of too many cooks, with William Boyd, Bryan Forbes and William Goldman among the writers who dipped into Chaplin's own autobiography and David Robinson's seminal biography for inspiration. Much of the film is extremely entertaining, and Oscar-nominated Robert Downey Jr is superb as the young Chaplin. Yet, overall, the depiction of a growing Hollywood is too rose-tinted, and the tragic tale of a misunderstood comic genius is reduced to a series of star-studded vignettes. Contains swearing and brief nudity. ▭

Robert Downey Jr *Charlie Chaplin* • Geraldine Chaplin *Hannah Chaplin* • Paul Rhys *Sydney Chaplin* • John Thaw *Fred Karno* • Moira Kelly *Hetty Kelly/Oona O'Neill* • Anthony Hopkins *George Hayden* • Dan Aykroyd *Mack Sennett* • Marisa Tomei *Mabel Normand* • Penelope Ann Miller *Edna Purviance* • Kevin Kline *Douglas Fairbanks* • Milla Jovovich *Mildred Harris* • Kevin Dunn *J Edgar Hoover* • Diane Lane *Paulette Goddard* • James Woods *Lawyer Scott* • David Duchovny *Rollie Totheroh* ■ *Dir* Richard Attenborough • *Scr* William Boyd, Bryan Forbes, William Goldman, from a story by Diana Hawkins, the biography *Chaplin: His Life And Art* by David Robinson and the autobiography by Charles Chaplin.

The Chapman Report ★★

Drama 1962 · US · Colour · 149mins

For "Chapman", read "Kinsey" in this glossy examination of four Los Angeles women with psychosexual difficulties: a bored housewife (the normally ebullient Shelley Winters); a nymphomaniac (the usually ice-cold Claire Bloom); a frigid widow (sexy Jane Fonda); and a romantic adulteress (coy Glynis Johns). George Cukor was the undisputed expert at handling actresses, but the distinguished veteran cannot dispel the impression that this is no more than a sleazy exploitation of early sixties permissiveness, masquerading as something more important.

Efrem Zimbalist Jr *Paul Radford* • Shelley Winters *Sarah Garnell* • Jane Fonda *Kathleen Barclay* • Claire Bloom *Naomi Shields* • Glynis Johns *Teresa Harnish* • Andrew Duggan *Dr George Chapman* ■ *Dir* George Cukor • *Scr* Wyatt Cooper, Don M Mankiewicz, from the novel by Irving Wallace

Chappaqua ★★ 15

Experimental biographical drama
1966 · US · Colour · 78mins

Forty years after his optical process enhanced Fritz Lang's *Metropolis*, Eugene Shuftan suffered the indignity of being fired from this trippy reverie by director Conrad Rooks. His replacement, Robert Frank, managed to produce some suitably hallucinatory cold turkey effects. Alas, nothing could save this autobiographical ramble, in which Rooks offers up blurred memories and confused visions of reality to the Parisian doctor (Jean-Louis Barrault) assigned to release him from his heroin addiction. With Allen Ginsberg and William S Burroughs adding some Beat cred and a score by Ravi Shankar, this is very much a product of its time. ▭

Conrad Rooks *Russel Harwick* • Jean-Louis Barrault *Doctor Benoit* • William S Burroughs *Opium Jones* • Allen Ginsberg *Messiah* • Ravi Shankar *Sun god* • Paula Pritchett *Water woman* ■ *Dir/Scr* Conrad Rooks

Chapter Two ★★ PG

Comedy drama 1979 · US · Colour · 121mins

Novelist James Caan suffers guilt over remarrying after the death of his first wife; his anxieties cause problems in

his second marriage. Adapted by Neil Simon from his semi-autobiographical Broadway play, the movie is heavy on wisecracks which defuse the potentially serious subject matter. Unfortunately, it's also heavy on talky and rather tedious argument. Caan is good, though, and Oscar-nominated Marsha Mason (the second Mrs Simon) is terrific. ▭

James Caan *George Schneider* • Marsha Mason *Jennie MacLaine* • Joseph Bologna *Leo Schneider* • Valerie Harper *Faye Medwick* • Alan Fudge *Lee Michaels* • Judy Farrell *Gwen Michaels* ■ *Dir* Robert Moore • *Scr* Neil Simon, from his play

Character ★★★★ 15

Epic period drama
1997 · Neth · Colour · 119mins

Adapted from Ferdinand Bordewijk's novel, a recognised classic of modern Dutch literature, Mike van Diem's Oscar-winning debut is demanding but hugely rewarding. Set in 1920s Rotterdam, it tells the story of a merciless bailiff (the ferociously austere Jan Decleir) and his twisted relationship with his illegitimate son (Fedja van Huêt). Victor Löw contributes a wonderfully eccentric cameo, and there is some handsomely dour photography and stylised art direction. In Dutch with English subtitles. Contains violence, some swearing and brief nudity. ▭

Jan Decleir *Dreverhaven* • Fedja Van Huêt *Jacob Katadreuffe* • Betty Schuurman *Joba Katadreuffe* • Tamar van den Dop *Lorna Te George* • Victor Löw *De Gankelaar* ■ *Dir* Mike Van Diem • *Scr* Mike van Diem, Laurens Geels, Ruud van Megen, from the novel *Karakter* by Ferdinand Bordewijk • *Cinematographer* Rogier Stoffers • *Art Director* Jelier & Schief

Charade ★★★★★ PG

Comedy thriller 1963 · US · Colour · 108mins

An absolutely wonderful comedy thriller from director Stanley Donen that out-Hitchcocks Hitchcock. With a "McGuffin" so clever you'll never guess, and a dream cast of Cary Grant and Audrey Hepburn on ravishingly Technicolored Parisian locations, what more could you possibly want in the way of movie entertainment? There's a clever plot that never lets up, a wondrously romantic score (by Henry Mancini), star-making turns from Walter Matthau and James Coburn, and set pieces that deserve classic status: Grant taking a shower fully-clothed; Audrey and Cary falling in love on a Paris river boat; and a one-handed villain in a roof-top cliffhanger. ▭

Cary Grant *Peter Joshua* • Audrey Hepburn *Regina "Reggie" Lambert* • Walter Matthau *Hamilton Bartholomew* • James Coburn *Tex Panthollow* • George Kennedy *Herman Scobie* • Ned Glass *Leopold Gideon* • Jacques Marin *Inspector Edouard Grandpierre* ■ *Dir* Stanley Donen • *Scr* Peter Stone, from the story *The Unsuspecting Wife* by Peter Stone, Marc Behm • *Costume Designer* Givenchy

The Charge at Feather River ★★★ U

Western 1953 · US · Colour · 95mins

A group of reprobates are rounded up and sent into Injun territory to rescue two white women in this marvellous western that anticipates the plot of

The Searchers. Unfortunately, it is seriously marred by the miscasting of handsome Guy Madison in the lead, a role that was intended for Gary Cooper. It was originally shown in 3-D, which explains why objects keep crashing towards the camera, notably the Indian lances in the charge and the tobacco juice spat into the audience by rugged Frank Lovejoy to keep a rattlesnake at bay. Even without its gimmick, this is a well-written and well-directed movie.

Guy Madison *Miles Archer* • Frank Lovejoy *Sergeant Baker* • Helen Westcott *Ann McKeever* • Vera Miles *Jennie McKeever* • Dick Wesson *Cullen* ■ *Dir* Gordon Douglas • *Scr* James R Webb

Charge of the Lancers ★ U

Period spy drama 1954 · US · Colour · 73mins

Paulette Goddard was an intelligent and vivacious actress whose cinema career had virtually come to an end by 1954. Reduced to starring in one of the cheap Technicolor potboilers churned out by the Sam Katzman unit at Columbia, she plays a gypsy who falls for a French captain (Jean-Pierre Aumont) and helps the English capture the Russian naval base at Sebastopol.

Paulette Goddard *Tanya* • Jean-Pierre Aumont *Captain Eric Evoir* • Richard Stapley *Major Bruce Lindsey* • Karin Booth *Maria Sand* ■ *Dir* William Castle • *Scr* Robert E Kent

The Charge of the Light Brigade ★★★★ PG

Historical war drama
1936 · US · BW · 110mins

A splendid early Errol Flynn vehicle that bears little relation to historical fact – but who cares? This wonderful swashbuckler from Warner Bros is set largely in India, but fetches up in the Crimea in time for a stunningly spectacular charge, punctuated with on-screen quotes from Tennyson, which was largely co-ordinated by second-unit director B Reeves ("Breezy") Eason. The great Michael Curtiz was in overall command, with Olivia de Havilland returning as Flynn's love interest a year after their screen partnership began with *Captain Blood*. The magnificent score was Max Steiner's first for Warners, and it provides the perfect accompaniment to this thunderingly good movie. ▭

Errol Flynn *Major Geoffrey Vickers* • Olivia de Havilland *Elsa Campbell* • Patric Knowles *Captain Perry Vickers* • Donald Crisp *Colonel Campbell* • Henry Stephenson *Sir Charles Macefield* • Nigel Bruce *Sir Benjamin Warrenton* • David Niven *Captain James Randall* • GP Huntley Jr *Major Jowett* ■ *Dir* Michael Curtiz • *Scr* Michel Jacoby, Rowland Leigh, from a story by Michael Jacoby

The Charge of the Light Brigade ★★★★★ PG

Historical drama
1968 · UK · Colour · 130mins

The charge of 1854, immortalised by Tennyson, is etched deep in our national psyche as a blunder of heroic proportions. Tony Richardson's film of the event was a failure on release, despite its *Sergeant Pepper*-like marketing. But it's a great, unsung masterpiece, filled with extraordinary set pieces and chillingly funny performances. It is a blistering satire

on England and those bickering, blithering aristocratic idiots who paid for their commissions and then picnicked as their men were mown down by Russian cannon. Richardson and his writer Charles Wood are less concerned with the "reason why" than with social context, a theme mirrored by Richard Williams's witty cartoon sequences. And the charge itself, brilliantly edited by Kevin Brownlow and Hugh Raggett, evokes the terrible carnage as pure chaos. ▭

Trevor Howard *Lord Cardigan* • Vanessa Redgrave *Clarissa Codrington* • David Hemmings *Captain Nolan* • John Gielgud *Lord Raglan* • Harry Andrews *Lord Lucan* • Jill Bennett *Mrs Duberly* • Peter Bowles *Paymaster Duberly* • Corin Redgrave *Featherstonhaugh* • Rachel Kempson *Mrs Codrington* ■ *Dir* Tony Richardson • *Scr* Charles Wood • *Cinematographer* David Watkin

Chariots of Fire ★★★★★ U

Sports drama 1981 · UK · Colour · 118mins

Unfairly dismissed by some as an empty exercise in cheap schmaltz, this has an old-fashioned innocence that celebrates the human spirit with a lot of careful detail. It's a powerful tale of two British athletes – one a contemplative Scottish missionary, the other an anxious Jewish student – aiming for glory in the 1924 Olympics, and it contains a compelling study of their characters and those of their competitors. Their experiences are drawn in thoughtfully by Hugh Hudson's direction and Colin Welland's Oscar-winning script. (It was Welland who exclaimed at the Oscar ceremony that "the British are coming!".) ▭

Ben Cross *Harold Abrahams* • Ian Charleson *Eric Liddell* • Nigel Havers *Lord Andrew Lindsay* • Nicholas Farrell *Aubrey Montague* • Ian Holm *Sam Mussabini* • John Gielgud *Master of Trinity* • Lindsay Anderson *Master of Caius* • Nigel Davenport *Lord Birkenhead* • Cheryl Campbell *Jennie Liddell* • Alice Krige *Sybil Gordon* • Dennis Christopher *Charles Paddock* • Brad Davis *Jackson Scholz* • Patrick Magee *Lord Cadogan* • Richard Griffiths *Head Porter, Caius College* • Ruby Wax *Bunty* ■ *Dir* Hugh Hudson • *Scr* Colin Welland • *Cinematographer* David Watkin • *Editor* Terry Rawlings • *Music* Vangelis • *Costume Designer* Milena Canonero

Charles & Diana: Unhappily Ever After ★

Drama 1992 · US · Colour · 92mins

This forgettable TV movie chronicles the marriage of the Prince and Princess of Wales, from their much-publicised fairy tale wedding in 1981 to their stormy, turbulent separation in 1992. Roger Rees and *Dynasty*'s Catherine Oxenberg star in a lifeless piece of trash that gives no new insights and reveals no new facts about the famous couple. Sensationalism at its worst.

Roger Rees *Prince Charles* • Catherine Oxenberg *Princess Diana* • Amanda Walker *Queen Elizabeth* • Tracy Brabin *Sarah Ferguson* • Benedict Taylor *Prince Andrew* ■ *Dir* John Power • *Scr* Nancy Sackett

Charley and the Angel ★★ U

Fantasy comedy 1973 · US · Colour · 90mins

A faltering Disney attempt to out-corn Frank Capra, this tolerable piece of

family fare mixes and mismatches plot devices from the 1946 film classic *It's a Wonderful Life* and Dickens's *A Christmas Carol*. Although Fred MacMurray does a nice line in hangdog expressions, he lacks the look of tousled desperation that made James Stewart's performance in Capra's original so heartrending, while Harry Morgan comes a long way behind Henry Travers in the role of the angel coaxing his charge into reassessing his contribution to life. 📺

Fred MacMurray *Charley Appleby* • Cloris Leachman *Nettie Appleby* • Harry Morgan *Angel* • Kurt Russell *Ray Ferris* • Kathleen Cody *Leonora Appleby* ■ *Dir* Vincent McVeety • *Scr* Roswell Rogers, from the novel *The Golden Evenings of Summer* by Will Stanton

Charley Moon ★★★ Ⓤ
Musical drama   1956 · UK · Colour · 90mins

This distinctly downbeat showbiz melodrama was co-written (with John Cresswell) by Leslie Bricusse, who went on to notch up ten Oscar nominations as a composer and songwriter. Here he paints a particularly lurid picture of life in the music halls, as Max Bygraves takes no prisoners on his way to the top before conscience finally triumphs over ambition. Offering fewer insights into the loneliness of the long-distance performer than, say, John Osborne's *The Entertainer*, the film nevertheless has a ring of authenticity.

Max Bygraves *Charley Moon* • Dennis Price *Harold Armytage* • Michael Medwin *Alf Higgins* • Florence Desmond *Mary Minton* • Shirley Eaton *Angel Dream* • Patricia Driscoll *Rose* ■ *Dir* Guy Hamilton • *Scr* Leslie Bricusse, John Cresswell, from the novel by Reginald Arkell

Charley Varrick ★★★★
Crime drama   1973 · US · Colour · 110mins

Walter Matthau looks as if he's having as much fun as we are in this delightful caper movie, about a small-time crook who lands himself in hot water when he mistakenly steals a small fortune belonging to the Mafia. Hit man Joe Don Baker is soon on his trail, but the cunning Matthau has a few tricks up his sleeve. Director Don Siegel directs the clever, exciting script with verve, and also contributes a brief cameo as a ping pong player. Unlike other caper movies of the period, it still seems invigorating.

Walter Matthau *Charley Varrick* • Joe Don Baker *Molly* • Felicia Farr *Sybil Fort* • Andrew Robinson *Harman Sullivan* • Sheree North *Jewell Everett* • John Vernon *Maynard Boyle* • Jacqueline Scott *Nadine Varrick* ■ *Dir* Don Siegel • *Scr* Howard Rodman, Dean Riesner, from the novel *The Looters* by John Reese

Charley's Aunt ★★★ Ⓤ
Comedy   1941 · US · BW · 81mins

Brandon Thomas's memorable creation is this time immortalised by the great Jack Benny, who always seemed strangely at home in drag. True, he's a little long in the tooth as an Oxford student, and, if it all seems a mite familiar, that's probably because this is one of several film versions. There's a super pace to this one, though, and a fabulous supporting cast, headed by the oh-so-elegant Kay Francis and a very young and lovely Anne Baxter.

Jack Benny *Babbs* • Kay Francis *Donna Lucia* • James Ellison *Jack Chesney* • Anne Baxter *Amy Spettigue* • Edmund Gwenn *Stephen Spettigue* • Reginald Owen *Redcliff* • Laird Cregar *Sir Francis Chesney* ■ *Dir* Archie Mayo • *Scr* George Seaton, from the play by Brandon Thomas

Charlie Bubbles ★★★
Drama   1967 · UK · Colour · 89mins

Albert Finney, an archetypally sixites British screen icon, directed this contemporary romantic drama, as well as playing the title role. In playwright Shelagh Delaney's screenplay, Charlie is a northern working-class lad made good – a popular theme of the time. A successful novelist, he's fed up with glitzy metropolitan values and decides to go in search of his roots. The women in his life are played by Liza Minnelli and Billie Whitelaw. Rich in resonances of the era.

Albert Finney *Charlie Bubbles* • Colin Blakely *Smokey Pickles* • Billie Whitelaw *Lottie Bubbles* • Liza Minnelli *Eliza* • Timothy Garland *Jack Bubbles* • Richard Pearson *Accountant* ■ *Dir* Albert Finney • *Scr* Shelagh Delaney

Charlie Chan and the Curse of the Dragon Queen ★★ Ⓟ🄶
Comedy   1981 · US · Colour · 91mins

This comedy is best viewed today as the film that introduced Michelle Pfeiffer to international audiences. It's an ill-advised attempt to resuscitate author Earl Derr Bigger's wily, politically incorrect Oriental detective, listlessly played by Peter Ustinov. Brian Keith, Lee Grant and Rachel Roberts throw away their dignity for the cash, but Richard Hatch, as Chan's half-Jewish, half-Chinese grandson, has some amusing moments. 📺

Peter Ustinov *Charlie Chan* • Angie Dickinson *Dragon Queen* • Lee Grant *Mrs Lupowitz* • Richard Hatch *Lee Chan Jr* • Brian Keith *Police Chief* • Roddy McDowall *Gillespie* • Rachel Roberts *Mrs Dangers* • Michelle Pfeiffer *Cordelia* • Paul Ryan *Masten* ■ *Dir* Clive Donner • *Scr* Stan Burns, David Axelrod, from a story by Jerry Sherlock, from characters created by Earl Derr Biggers

Charlie Chan at the Opera ★★★
Mystery   1936 · US · BW · 64mins

The famously inscrutable Chinese shamus, exquisitely played by Warner Oland, tackles an elaborate mystery in a prime puzzler from the solidly entertaining series. Boris Karloff plays the amnesiac baritone who escapes from a mental asylum and is blamed for the murder of his wife and her lover during a performance of *Carnival* (a fake opera composed especially for the film by Oscar Levant). Earl Derr Biggers's detective eventually figures out what's going on when he orders the opera to be played again. Karloff's singing voice may be dubbed, but his presence adds a formidable *frisson* to the usual suspenseful scenario.

Warner Oland *Charlie Chan* • Boris Karloff *Gravelle* • Keye Luke *Lee Chan* • Charlotte Henry *Mlle Kitty* • Margaret Irving *Mme Lilli Rochelle* • Thomas Beck *Phil Childers* • Gregory Gaye *Enrico Barelli* ■ *Dir* H Bruce

Humberstone • *Scr* Scott Darling, Charles S Belden, from a story by Bess Meredyth, from characters created by Earl Derr Biggers

Charlie Chan at the Olympics ★★ Ⓤ
Mystery   1937 · US · BW · 71mins

As if the presence of Hitler wasn't enough to blight the 1936 Berlin Games, the activities of a nest of spies nearly prevent Keye Luke from taking his place on the US swimming team. He's kidnapped when Warner Oland gets too close to discovering who is after the plans for a top secret autopilot mechanism. But the villains had not taken into consideration the debut appearance of Number Two Son (Layne Tom Jr), or Chan's unlikely alliance with the Nazi police.

Warner Oland *Charlie Chan* • Katherine DeMille *Yvonne Roland* • Pauline Moore *Betty Adams* • Allan Lane *Richard Masters* • Keye Luke *Lee Chan* • C Henry Gordon *Arthur Hughes* • John Eldredge *Cartwright* • Layne Tom Jr *Charlie Chan Jr* • Jonathan Hale *Hopkins* ■ *Dir* H Bruce Humberstone • *Scr* Robert Ellis, Helen Logan, from a story by Paul Burger, Earl Derr Biggers

Charlie Chan at Treasure Island ★★
Mystery   1939 · US · BW · 73mins

Treasure Island was the name of a popular fairground attraction in San Francisco, which is the only reason for the title of this entry in the long-running series. Sidney Toler is Chan, upset by a friend's suicide and looking into the activities of racketeering astrologers as a result. Regular Chan director Norman Foster keeps the story moving along pre-ordained lines.

Sidney Toler *Charlie Chan* • Cesar Romero *Fred Rhadini* • Pauline Moore *Eve Cairo* • Sen Yung *James Chan* • Douglas Fowley *Peter Lewis* • June Gale *Myra Rhadini* • Douglass Dumbrille *Thomas Gregory* ■ *Dir* Norman Foster • *Scr* John Larkin, from characters created by Earl Derr Biggers

Charlie Chan in Egypt ★★★
Mystery   1935 · US · BW · 73mins

This was the first of nine cases penned by Robert Ellis and Helen Logan, and it's easily one of the most exciting. At his inscrutable best, Warner Oland is called in by the managers of a French museum to investigate the rash of murders that follows the opening of a high priest's tomb. All that's missing from this creepy mystery is Boris Karloff swathed in bandages. However, there is the compensation of seeing a young Rita Hayworth, in her fourth credited appearance and still being billed as Rita Cansino.

Warner Oland *Charlie Chan* • Pat Paterson *Carol Arnold* • Thomas Beck *Tom Evans* • Rita Cansino [Rita Hayworth] *Nayda* • Jameson Thomas *Dr Anton Racine* • Frank Conroy *Professor John Thurston* ■ *Dir* Louis King • *Scr* Robert Ellis, Helen Logan, from characters created by Earl Derr Biggers

Charlie Chan in London ★★★
Mystery   1934 · US · BW · 79mins

Even though this was Swedish-born Warner Oland's sixth outing as Earl

Derr Biggers's Oriental detective, this is only our second chance to see him in action as, sadly, *Charlie Chan Carries On*, *Charlie Chan's Chance*, *Charlie Chan's Courage* and *Charlie Chan's Greatest Case* have all perished. A teasing mystery and a superb supporting cast make this one of the most enjoyable entries in the series, as Chan investigates a murder among the hunting, shooting and fishing set. Screenwriter Philip MacDonald's impression of English folk is a bit rum, but Ray Milland, EE Clive and Madge Bellamy admirably flesh out the caricatures.

Warner Oland *Charlie Chan* • Drue Leyton *Pamela Gray* • Douglas Walton *Paul Gray* • Alan Mowbray *Geoffrey Richmond* • Mona Barrie *Lady Mary Bristol* • Ray Milland *Neil Howard* • EE Clive *Detective Sergeant Thacker* • Madge Bellamy *Becky Fothergill* ■ *Dir* Eugene Forde • *Scr* Philip MacDonald, from characters created by Earl Derr Biggers

Charlie Chan in Paris ★★ Ⓤ
Mystery   1935 · US · BW · 71mins

Produced by Sol M Wurtzel, who later supervised 20th Century-Fox's other Oriental sleuth series, Mr Moto, the seventh case featuring Warner Oland is notable primarily for the introduction of Keye Luke as Lee Chan (otherwise known as "Number One Son"). Together they make short work of a gang of counterfeiters plaguing the City of Light with a batch of forged bonds. Toss in a little blackmail and murder and you have a sturdy thriller, briskly directed by Lewis Seiler.

Warner Oland *Charlie Chan* • Mary Brian *Yvette Lamartine* • Thomas Beck *Victor Descartes* • Erik Rhodes *Max Corday* • Keye Luke *Lee Chan* • Perry Ivins *Bedell* ■ *Dir* Lewis Seiler • *Scr* Edward T Lowe, Stuart Anthony, from a story by Philip MacDonald, from characters created by Earl Derr Biggers

Charlie Chan in Reno ★★★
Mystery   1939 · US · BW · 70 mins

Having handled several entries in Peter Lorre's Mr Moto series, director Norman Foster switched Oriental detectives for this brisk Fox programme filler. It was back projection all the way, as Sidney Toler (making only his second appearance as Earl Derr Biggers's sleuth) leaves Honolulu, in the company of "Number Two Son" Victor Sen Yung, to investigate why Hawaiian neighbour Pauline Moore is being framed for murder in the US divorce capital.

Sidney Toler *Charlie Chan* • Ricardo Cortez *Dr Ainsley* • Phyllis Brooks *Vivian Wells* • Slim Summerville *Sheriff Fletcher* • Kane Richmond *Curtis Whitman* • Victor Sen Yung *James Chan* • Pauline Moore *Mary Whitman* ■ *Dir* Norman Foster • *Scr* Frances Hyland, Albert Ray, Robert E Kent, from the story *Death Makes a Decree* by Philip Wylie and characters created by Earl Derr Biggers

Charlie Chan in Rio ★★
Mystery   1941 · US · BW · 61mins

Charlie Chan goes to Brazil for Sidney Toler's tenth outing in this long-running B-movie franchise. Director Harry Lachman exploits his exotic location to provide a lively musical background to this tale of double murder. Yet, in spite of featuring some of the series' most ingenious clues and, most

unusually, a brief burst of Mandarin (complete with subtitles), this is one of the least satisfying Chan mysteries.

Sidney Toler *Charlie Chan* • Mary Beth Hughes *Joan Reynolds* • Cobina Wright Jr *Grace Ellis* • Ted North *Carlos Dantas* • Victor Jory *Alfredo Marina* • Harold Huber *Chief Souto* • Victor Sen Yung *Jimmy Chan* ■ *Dir* Harry Lachman • *Scr* Samuel G Engel, Lester Ziffren, from characters created by Earl Derr Biggers

Charlie Chan in Shanghai
★★ U

Mystery   1935 · US · BW · 70mins

Swedish actor Warner Oland makes his ninth screen appearance as fabled Oriental sleuth Charlie Chan in this vintage tale of intrigue and murder. The suave Chinese detective is back on his home turf here, investigating an international opium ring. However, this is more of a children's picture than a smoky, sinister excursion, with "Number One Son" (Keye Luke) taking up a lot of screen time.

Warner Oland *Charlie Chan* • Irene Hervey *Diana Woodland* • Charles Locher [Jon Hall] *Philip Nash* • Russell Hicks *James Andrews* • Keye Luke *Lee Chan* • Halliwell Hobbes *Chief of Police* ■ *Dir* James Stone • *Scr* Edward T Lowe, Gerald Fairlie, from characters created by Earl Derr Biggers

Charlie Chan on Broadway
★★★

Mystery   1937 · US · BW · 68mins

An impressive cast was assembled for this above-average entry in the series. But was it newspaper tycoon J Edward Bromberg, ace reporter Donald Woods, nightclub boss Douglas Fowley or mobster Leon Ames who was responsible for the murder of the showgirl whose missing diary contains incriminating gangland details? One thing's for sure: "Number One Son" Keye Luke isn't the guilty party, but it still takes all of Warner Oland's Oriental ingenuity to convince the cops.

Warner Oland *Charlie Chan* • Keye Luke *Lee Chan* • Joan Marsh *Joan Wendall* • J Edward Bromberg *Murdock* • Douglas Fowley *John Burke* • Harold Huber *Insp Nelson* • Donald Woods *Speed Patten* ■ *Dir* Eugene Forde • *Scr* Charles Belden, Jerry Cady, from a story by Art Arthur, Robert Ellis, Helen Logan, from characters created by Earl Derr Biggers

Charlie, the Lonesome Cougar
★★ U

Adventure   1967 · US · Colour · 86mins

One of the last of the Disney studio's *True Life Adventures*, in which trick photography and cutesy narration makes wild animals seem almost human in their responses and social behaviour. Such anthropomorphism should have gone out with the stone age, but Uncle Walt entertained a whole generation of young moviegoers with the series until genuine nature documentaries on TV revealed how bogus the films were. In this effort, a cougar (mountain lion) called Charlie is reared from a cub by a forester in a lumber camp in Washington State. ▭

Ron Brown *Jess Bradley* • Brian Russell *Potlatch* • Linda Wallace *Jess's fiancée* • Jim Wilson *Farmer* • Clifford Peterson *Mill manager* • Lewis Sample *Chief engineer* ■ *Dir* Winston Hibler • *Scr* Jack Speirs, from a story by Jack Speirs, Winston Hibler

Charlie's Ghost Story
★

Supernatural comedy drama
1994 · US · Colour · 88mins

A lacklustre adaptation of a lesser-known Mark Twain story. Trenton Knight is the misunderstood son of Anthony Edwards, an archaeologist more comfortable with ancient artefacts than parenting. When Edwards discovers the remains of the Spanish explorer Coronado, his ghost ("Cheech" Marin) starts doling out fatherly advice to Knight while ensuring his bones get properly buried. Occasionally funny thanks to Marin's spiritual quips, the rest of the fine cast is wasted, while Edwards's direction shows no verve or imagination.

Anthony Edwards *Dave* • Richard "Cheech" Marin *Coronado* • Linda Fiorentino *Marta* • Trenton Knight *Charlie* • Charles Rocket *Van Leer* • JT Walsh *Darryl* • Daphne Zuniga *Penni* ■ *Dir* Anthony Edwards • *Scr* Lance W Dreesen, Clint Hutchison, from a short story by Mark Twain

Charlotte's Web
★★★ U

Animated musical
1973 · US · Colour · 94mins

Fans of such farmyard fables as *Babe* will love this charming animated adaptation of EB White's children's classic, one of the few features produced by celebrated cartoon team Hanna-Barbera. The critters are brought to life by some superb voice-overs as Charlotte the spider (Debbie Reynolds) joins with Templeton the rat (Paul Lynde) to save petrified porker Wilbur (Henry Gibson). The animation isn't up to Disney standard, and the Sherman brothers' songs are rather hit and miss. It's pleasing to look at, though, so a good time should be had by all. ▭

Debbie Reynolds *Charlotte* • Paul Lynde *Templeton* • Henry Gibson *Wilbur* • Rex Allen *Narrator* • Martha Scott *Mrs Arable* • Dave Madden *Old sheep* • Danny Bonaduce *Avery* • Don Messick *Geoffrey* • Herb Vigran *Lurvy* • Agnes Moorehead *The goose* ■ *Dir* Charles A Nichols, Iwao Takamoto • *Scr* Earl Hamner Jr, from the novel by EB White
.

Charly
★★★★ PG

Drama   1968 · US · Colour · 99mins

Cliff Robertson found himself cast as heroic types after he played the young John F Kennedy in *PT 109*, but the most rewarding role of his career came with this Oscar-winning portrayal of a mentally disabled man whose life is transformed by a brain operation. The scenes between Robertson and Claire Bloom are touching, and Algernon the mouse is unforgettable, so director Ralph Nelson can be forgiven for playing down some of the fascinating possibilities raised by Stirling Silliphant's script. ▭

Cliff Robertson *Charly Gordon* • Claire Bloom *Alice Kinian* • Leon Janney *Dr Richard Nemur* • Lilia Skala *Dr Anna Straus* • Dick Van Patten *Bert* • William Dwyer *Joey* ■ *Dir* Ralph Nelson • *Scr* Stirling Silliphant, from the short story and novel *Flowers for Algernon* by Daniel Keyes

Charro!
★ U

Western   1969 · US · Colour · 92mins

By this stage in his career, Elvis Presley must have been desperate to

get away from the fluffy nonsense of his musicals, but he should have chosen a far more convincing alternative than this bungled, "serious" western. The King struggles with his role as a supposedly hard-bitten gunfighter who fights to clear his name when he is set up by his old partners in crime, and the rest of the cast is not convincing either. ▭

Elvis Presley *Jess Wade* • Ina Balin *Tracy* • Barbara Werle *Sara Ramsey* • Lynn Kellogg *Marcie* • Victor French *Vince* • Solomon Sturges *Billy Roy* • James Sikking [James B Sikking] *Gunner* ■ *Dir* Charles Marquis Warren • *Scr* Charles Marquis Warren, from a story by Frederic Louis Fox

Charulata
★★★★ U

Period drama   1964 · Ind · BW · 118mins

This beautifully observed study of 19th-century domestic habits, also known as *The Lonely Wife*, won Satyajit Ray the best director prize at the Berlin Film Festival. Never has his debt to the great French film-maker Jean Renoir been more apparent than in this gently ironic tale from the pen of another key influence on Ray's style, Rabindranath Tagore. Mocking both male authority and the gentility of Victorian society, it also boasts a superb performance by Madhabi Mukherjee as the neglected Calcuttan wife who sees an affair with her husband's cousin as a way of boosting both her self-esteem and her writing ambitions. In Bengali with English subtitles.

Madhabi Mukherjee *Charulata* • Sailen Mukherjee *Bhupati Dutta* • Soumitra Chatterjee *Amal* • Shyamal Ghosal *Umapada* • Gitali Roy ■ *Dir* Satyajit Ray • *Scr* Satyajit Ray, from the story *Nastaneer* by Rabindranath Tagore

The Chase
★★★★

Film noir   1946 · US · BW · 85mins

Pretentious, bizarre and quite fascinating, this rarely shown psychological thriller stars Robert Cummings as the shell-shocked ex-soldier who becomes chauffeur to Steve Cochran's wealthy and sadistic gangster – a man whose favourite hobby is outrunning trains at level crossings. Michele Morgan plays his dissatisfied wife, while Peter Lorre is his bodyguard. Cleverly written by Philip Yordan from a novel by the outstanding crime writer Cornell Woolrich, with moody photography by Franz Planer, the result is one of the most dream-like *films noirs*.

Robert Cummings *Chuck* • Michèle Morgan *Lorna* • Peter Lorre *Gino* • Steve Cochran *Roman* • Lloyd Corrigan *Johnson* • Jack Holt *Davidson* ■ *Dir* Arthur Ripley • *Scr* Philip Yordan, from the novel *The Black Path of Fear* by Cornell Woolrich

The Chase
★★★★ 15

Drama   1966 · US · Colour · 127mins

Before he directed *Bonnie and Clyde*, Arthur Penn made this impressively cast and wondrously overcooked drama about a Texan sheriff who protects an escaped convict against a town that has run out of control. Marlon Brando has immense stature as the sheriff and clearly relishes the appalling beating he receives at the hands of the mob, while Robert Redford is

perfect as the angelic convict he protects. In one sense, Lillian Hellman's script is like an updated western; in another, it evokes the madness and violence that gripped America in the aftermath of the Kennedy assassination. Although Penn virtually disowned the picture after producer Sam Spiegel had it re-edited, it remains a genuinely disturbing evocation of that traumatic era. ▭

Marlon Brando *Sheriff Calder* • Jane Fonda *Anna Reeves* • Robert Redford *Bubber Reeves* • EG Marshall *Val Rogers* • Angie Dickinson *Ruby Calder* • Janice Rule *Emily Stewart* • Miriam Hopkins *Mrs Reeves* • Robert Duvall *Edwin Stewart* • James Fox *Jake Rogers* ■ *Dir* Arthur Penn • *Scr* Lillian Hellman, from the novel and play by Horton Foote

The Chase
★★★ 15

Drama based on a true story
1991 · US · Colour · 90mins

Veteran director Paul Wendkos made his name with a number of acclaimed low-budget features in the late fifties. But, after the relative disappointments of *The Mephisto Waltz* and *Special Delivery* in the seventies, Wendkos revived his career with a long string of TV movies. In this crime drama based on a true story, the cat-and-mouse antics rarely shy from the obvious, but Wendkos generates lively thrills from the ordinary material. Casey Siemaszko heads a cast that includes talk-show host Ricki Lake. ▭

Casey Siemaszko *Mark Taylor* • Ben Johnson *John Laurienti* • Robert Beltran *Mike Silva* • Barry Corbin *Bob Wallis* • Megan Follows *Gloria Whipple* • Ricki Lake *Tammie* ■ *Dir* Paul Wendkos • *Scr* Guerdon Trueblood

The Chase
★★ 15

Action adventure 1994 · US · Colour · 84mins

A dumb but amiable road movie, not to be confused with the rather more serious 1966 Marlon Brando vehicle of the same name. Here, Charlie Sheen is the loveable con who kidnaps millionaire's daughter Kristy Swanson, prompting a massive manhunt and a media frenzy. The two leads are seriously lightweight, but still spark off each other nicely, although the best performances come from supporting players Ray Wise and punk idol Henry Rollins, cast against type as a psychopathic policeman. Contains violence and swearing. ▭

Charlie Sheen *Jack Hammond* • Kristy Swanson *Natalie Voss* • Henry Rollins *Officer Dobbs* • Josh Mostel *Officer Figus* • Wayne Grace *Chief Boyle* • Rocky Carroll *Byron Wilder* ■ *Dir/Scr* Adam Rifkin

Chase a Crooked Shadow
★★★ U

Mystery thriller 1957 · UK · BW · 88mins

Coming off the back of *The Dam Busters*, *1984* and *Around the World in 80 Days*, director Michael Anderson was destined for a disappointment, but it is to his credit that this ludicrously contrived thriller not only holds the attention, but also actually manages to induce a short intake of breath at the totally unexpected denouement. Anne Baxter gives her best performance apart from *All about Eve* as a recuperating neurotic who is convinced

long-lost brother Richard Todd is after her diamonds.

Richard Todd *Ward* • Anne Baxter *Kimberley* • Herbert Lom *Vargas* • Alexander Knox *Chandler Brisson* • Faith Brook *Mrs Whitman* • Alan Tilvern *Carlos* ■ *Dir* Michael Anderson • *Scr* David D Osborn, Charles Sinclair • *Producer* Douglas Fairbanks Jr, Thomas Clyde

Chase Morran ★ 18

Science-fiction 1996 · US · Colour · 89mins

A cult cast – *The Evil Dead*'s Bruce Campbell, *Eraserhead*'s Jack Nance, *Blade Runner*'s Brion James – supply the sole points of interest in this by-the-numbers exploiter. Campbell plays a terrorist who takes over the small intergalactic settlement of Dome 4 and forces its residents to make bombs. Luckily, Chase Morran (Joseph Culp, son of Robert) is on hand to save the day. Contains violence, sexual references and swearing.

Bruce Campbell *Alex Windham* • Joseph Culp *Chase Morran* • Jocelyn Seagrave *Lily Moran* • Brion James *Chairman* • Jack Nance *Mellow* ■ *Dir* Gilbert Po • *Scr* Hesh Rephun

Chasers ★★ 15

Comedy 1994 · US · Colour · 96mins

Dennis Hopper, once the notorious film maverick, must have been keen to show that he could direct a movie with mainstream appeal. Here he certainly succeeds, but the result is a bland comedy, indistinguishable from all the other high concept projects that roll off the Hollywood production line. Tom Berenger and William McNamara are the bickering navy military policemen who are called in to transport a troublesome sailor to jail. The prisoner turns out to be Erika Eleniak, who then leads the straight-laced Berenger and his partner on a wild goose chase. It's an amiable enough road adventure, but it lacks the quirky edge one would expect Hopper to bring to the material. Contains swearing and nudity.

Tom Berenger *Rock Reilly* • William McNamara *Eddie Devane* • Erika Eleniak *Toni Johnson* • Crispin Glover *Howard Finster* • Dean Stockwell *Salesman Stig* • Gary Busey *Sergeant Vince Banger* • Seymour Cassel *Master Chief Bogg* ■ *Dir* Dennis Hopper • *Scr* Joe Batteer, John Rice, Dan Gilroy, from a story by Joe Batteer, John Rice

Chasing Amy ★★★★ 18

Romantic comedy
1996 · US · Colour · 108mins

Writer/director Kevin Smith comes up trumps with this cool, hilarious and sexy romantic comedy. New Jersey comic book writer Holden (Ben Affleck) falls for pal Alyssa (Joey Lauren Adams), despite the fact she's a lesbian. In addition to the chemistry between the two leads, *Chasing Amy* has so much more: an insightful and even heartbreaking script from Smith, hilarious support from Jason Lee as Affleck's sceptical pal, plus Jason Mewes and the director himself returning as regular characters Jay and Silent Bob. Watch out for a brief appearance from Matt Damon in what must be one of the hippest love stories of the nineties. Contains swearing and sexual references.

Ben Affleck *Holden* • Joey Lauren Adams *Alyssa* • Jason Lee *Banky* • Dwight Ewell

Hooper • Jason Mewes *Jay* • Ethan Suplee *Fan* • Scott Mosier *Collector* • Casey Affleck *Little Kid* • Guinevere Turner *Singer* • Matt Damon *Executive* • Kevin Smith *Silent Bob* ■ *Dir/Scr* Kevin Smith

Chasing Dreams ★★

Melodrama 1982 · Can · Colour · 94mins

Yet another dull story about a young lad's dream of playing college baseball is notable only for an early appearance from Kevin Costner. The actor would return to the subject nine years later in *Field of Dreams* – thankfully, to much greater effect.

David G Brown *Gavin Thompson* • John Fife Parks • Jim Shane *Mr Thompson* • Matthew Clark *Ben* • Kevin Costner *Ed* ■ *Dir* Sean Roche, Therese Conte • *Scr* David G Brown

Chasing the Deer ★★★ PG

Historical drama 1994 · UK · Colour · 90mins

Director Graham Holloway works wonders with a tiny budget for this Scottish labour of love, a gritty period piece about the events leading up to the ill-fated Battle of Culloden. The story focuses on a proud Highland family who unwittingly get drawn into – and are divided by – the Jacobite rebellion against the hated English. Money considerations means it doesn't have the epic sweep that is needed, but the talented cast (including Iain Cuthbertson, Brian Blessed and former Marillion singer Fish) more than make up for any budget deficiencies.

Brian Blessed *Major Elliot* • Iain Cuthbertson *Tullibardine* • Matthew Zajac *Alistair Campbell* • Fish *Angus Cameron* • Brian Donald *Old Campbell* • Sandy Welch *Old Cameron* • Peter Gordon *McKinnon* • Carolyn Konrad *Morag* ■ *Dir* Graham Holloway • *Scr* Jerome Vincent, Bob Carruthers, Steve Gillham, from an idea by Michele Ayson

Chastity ★★

Drama 1969 · US · Colour · 83mins

In an effort to change their hippy image and be more credible to the Woodstock generation, pop sensations Sonny and Cher produced this banal road movie. Written and scored by Sonny Bono, the film casts Cher as a teenage hitchhiker who gets involved in a robbery on the way to Mexico and discusses world problems while encountering prostitution and lesbianism. It's very sixties and all rather purposeless. Cher, making her solo acting debut, sings *Band of Thieves*, the fiasco may have ruined them financially, but the couple still named their daughter after it.

Cher *Chastity* • Barbara London *Diana Midnight* • Stephen Whittaker *Eddie* • Tom Nolan *Tommy* • Danny Zapien *Cab driver* • Elmer Valentine *1st truck driver* • Burke Rhind *Salesman* • Richard Armstrong *Husband* ■ *Dir* Alessio DePaola • *Scr* Sonny Bono

Le Château de Ma Mère ★★★★ U

Drama 1990 · Fr · Colour · 94mins

Easily surpassing *La Gloire de Mon Père*, this is as delightful a film as you could wish to see. The characters are old friends by now and in comparison with the boorish game hunting of the original, the encounter with a family of

fraudulent Bohemians and the duel with a grouchy watchman and his dog make for much more compelling viewing. Jean Rochefort is superb as the sham pseud, Robert Alazraki's photography of Provence is sublime and Yves Robert directs with a leisure that suggests long, hot summer days. In French with English subtitles.

Philippe Caubère *Joseph Pagnol* • Nathalie Roussel *Augustine Pagnol* • Didier Pain *Uncle Jules* • Thérèse Liotard *Aunt Rose* • Julien Ciamaca *Marcel* • Victorien Delamere *Paul* ■ *Dir* Yves Robert • *Scr* Jérôme Tonnerre, Yves Robert, from the story by Marcel Pagnol

Chato's Land ★★

Western 1972 · UK · Colour · 100mins

A trashily enjoyable western, flashily directed on a pittance budget by Michael Winner, with Charles Bronson as the eponymous half-breed slowly picking off the posse that is chasing him. Bronson – in a role not unlike his urban vigilante in *Death Wish* – is his usual craggy, monosyllabic self, while Jack Palance and James Whitmore complete a formidable trio of muscled ugliness. There are occasional hints that Winner and writer Gerald Wilson intended a story about racism, but mostly this is a spaghetti rip-off, filmed in Spain with a sharp eye for blood, sweat and death by rattlesnake.

Charles Bronson *Pardon Chato* • Jack Palance *Quincey Whitmore* • Richard Basehart *Nye Buell* • James Whitmore *Joshua Everette* • Simon Oakland *Jubal Hooker* • Ralph Waite *Elias Hooker* • Victor French *Martin Hall* ■ *Dir* Michael Winner • *Scr* Gerald Wilson

Chattahoochee ★★ 15

Biographical drama
1989 · US · Colour · 92mins

Korean War veteran Gary Oldman returns to his Southern home as a hero, goes on a shooting spree and ends up in a brutal insane asylum. The portrayal of his attempts to expose the nightmarish conditions in the fifties psychiatric facility owe as much to Hammer horror as documentary-style realism in director Mick Jackson's grim drama, which is straight-jacketed by mental illness clichés. Dennis Hopper and M Emmet Walsh play Oldman's fellow inmates, and Frances McDormand and Pamela Reed are his wife and sister.

Gary Oldman *Emmett Foley* • Dennis Hopper *Walker Benson* • Frances McDormand *Mae Foley* • Pamela Reed *Earlene* • Ned Beatty *Doctor Harwood* • M Emmet Walsh *Morris* • William De Acutis *Missy* • Lee Wilkof *Vernon* ■ *Dir* Mick Jackson • *Scr* James Hicks

Chattanooga Choo Choo ★★ PG

Comedy 1984 · US · Colour · 97mins

One of the many films which rely on the plot device of a conditional will. Here George Kennedy will only inherit his father's fortune if he can restore the famous Chattanooga express and get it to run to New York on time. Real-life gridiron star Joe Namath makes one of his rare big-screen appearances, and the cast also features Barbara Eden, the genie from TV's *I Dream of Jeannie*.

Barbara Eden *Maggie* • George Kennedy *Bert* • Melissa Sue Anderson *Jenny* • Joe Namath

Newt • Bridget Hanley *Estelle* • Christopher McDonald *Paul* ■ *Dir* Bruce Bilson • *Scr* Robert Mundy, Stephen Phillip Smith

Chatterbox ★★ U

Drama 1936 · US · BW · 68mins

A wholesome country girl from Vermont (Anne Shirley) has acting ambitions and makes for New York, where she gets her big break on Broadway in a play called *Virtue's Reward*. Things don't go quite to plan, however, leaving her to seek solace in the loving arms of a somewhat wooden Phillips Holmes. George Nichols Jr's direction is competent, Shirley's sweet and appealing, and the supporting cast includes Lucille Ball. For all its good intentions, though, the end result is vapid and uninspiring.

Anne Shirley *Jenny Yates* • Phillips Holmes *Philip Greene Jr* • Edward Ellis *Uriah Lowell* • Erik Rhodes *Archie Fisher* • Margaret Hamilton *Emily Tipton* • Lucille Ball *Lillian Temple* ■ *Dir* George Nichols Jr • *Scr* Sam Mintz, from a play by David Carb

Chatterbox ★ U

Comedy 1943 · US · BW · 76mins

There's much excitement when a popular radio personality (Joe E Brown) is signed to appear in a film. However, when he falls off a horse and is saved by his female co-star (Judy Canova), his image is badly dented. Needless to say, it's redeemed by the final fade. Joseph Santley directs this dismally unfunny display of ham acting by the two unattractive leads, set in the hurly-burly of a supposed film-making outfit.

Joe E Brown *Rex Vane* • Judy Canova *Judy Boggs* • John Hubbard *Sebastian Smart* • Rosemary Lane *Carol Forest* • Chester Clute *Wilfred Peckinpaugh* • Emmett Vogan *Roger Grant* ■ *Dir* Joseph Santley • *Scr* George Carleton Brown, Frank Gill Jr

Che! ★★ 15

Biographical drama
1969 · US · Colour · 91mins

Hollywood's take on the Cuban revolution, with Omar Sharif as Che Guevara and Jack Palance as Fidel Castro. Sharif looks oddly convincing – just like the poster every middle-class Marxist had over his bed – and the movie certainly celebrates Che's status as a revolutionary martyr and Robin Hood figure. As Castro, though, Palance is a rascal and a drunkard, a caricature of the man every patriotic American loves to hate. Sharif's contract included a "conscience clause" that allowed him to veto any scene he felt distorted the facts, but this is not a movie that's remotely believable. Richard Fleischer directs efficiently, as one would expect, on Puerto Rican locations.

Omar Sharif *Che Guevara* • Jack Palance *Fidel Castro* • Cesare Danova *Ramon Valdez* • Robert Loggia *Faustino Morales* • Woody Strode *Guillermo* • Barbara Luna *Anita Marquez* ■ *Dir* Richard Fleischer • *Scr* Michael Wilson, Sy Bartlett, from a story by David Karp, Sy Bartlett

The Cheap Detective ★★★

Film noir parody 1978 · US · Colour · 92mins

A Neil Simon-scripted spoof of Humphrey Bogart's classic *film noir* movies, directed by Robert Moore and with Peter Falk donning the raincoat as Lou Peckinpaugh. (Falk had previously played Bogart-like Sam Diamond in the same team's *Murder by Death* two years earlier.) As an idea, it quickly loses steam and one is left idly checking off the *Casablanca* references like a shopping list. Scatman Crothers is Tinker, asked to play *Jeepers Creepers* again, while Louise Fletcher and Fernando Lamas fill the shoes of Ingrid Bergman and Paul Henreid. There's also Ann-Margret as Mary Astor and John Houseman as Sydney Greenstreet from *The Maltese Falcon*. Fun for buffs, but a mite too detailed for the ordinary viewer.

Peter Falk *Lou Peckinpaugh* • Ann-Margret *Jezebel Dezire* • Eileen Brennan *Betty DeBoop* • Sid Caesar *Ezra Dezire* • Stockard Channing *Bess* • James Coco *Marcel* • Dom DeLuise *Pepe Damascus* • Louise Fletcher *Marlene DuChard* • John Houseman *Jasper Blubber* • Madeline Kahn *Mrs Montenegro* • Phil Silvers *Hoppy* • Marsha Mason *Georgia Merkle* ■ *Dir* Robert Moore • *Scr* Neil Simon

Cheaper by the Dozen ★★★ U

Comedy   1950 · US · Colour · 85mins

The success of *Meet Me in St Louis* and *Life with Father* led to a postwar hunger for turn-of-the-century nostalgia, and no studio managed to so regularly recapture those halcyon days as 20th Century-Fox, whose backlot was turned permanently into a standing period set. Here the Gilbreth family of 12 children, headed by the ineffable Clifton Webb and the incandescent Myrna Loy, raise a Technicolor ruckus and proved so popular that a follow-up (*Belles on Their Toes*) was immediately ordered.

Clifton Webb *Frank Bunker Gilbreth* • Jeanne Crain *Ann Gilbreth* • Myrna Loy *Mrs Lillian Gilbreth* • Betty Lynn *Libby Lancaster* • Edgar Buchanan *Dr Burton* • Barbara Bates *Ernestine* • Mildred Natwick *Mrs Mebane* • Sara Allgood *Mrs Monahan* ■ *Dir* Walter Lang • *Scr* Lamar Trotti, from the novel by Frank B Gilbreth Jr, Ernestine Gilbreth Carey

The Cheat ★★★

Silent melodrama   1915 · US · BW · 55mins

Directed by Cecil B DeMille, this melodrama caused a huge scandal in its day. Though its great age has blurred its quality and dramatic impact, it is interesting as an early example of lurid trash presented as high art. The plot concerns a society woman (Fannie Ward) who loses money that isn't hers on the stock market and borrows from a wealthy Oriental (Sessue Hayakawa) to pay her debts. When she refuses him her favours, he exacts a sadistic punishment, branding her as if she were cattle. Ward's anticipated career as a great tragedienne failed to materialise, but Hayakawa kept working until the sixties; he was Oscar-nominated for his performance in *The Bridge on the River Kwai*.

Fannie Ward *Edith Hardy* • James Neill *Jones* • Utaka Abe *Tori's valet* • Dana Ong *District attorney* • Hazel Childers *Mrs Reynolds* • Judge Arthur H William *Courtroom judge* • Sessue Hayakawa *Haka Arakau* • Jack Dean *Dick Hardy* ■ *Dir* Cecil B DeMille • *Scr* Hector Turnbull, Jeanie MacPherson

The Cheaters ★★★ U

Comedy   1945 · US · BW · 90mins

Thanks to the dizzy, spendthrift wife (Billie Burke) of a put-upon financier (Eugene Pallette in a characteristic role), a family of wealthy, upper-class eccentrics face ruin. A solution presents itself when a rich uncle leaves his fortune to an actress (Ona Munson) he never met. After a plethora of plot complications, the situation is sorted out with the help of an attractive, down-on-his-luck actor (Joseph Schildkraut giving an outstanding performance). Directed at an appropriate pace by Joseph Kane, the result is an enjoyable mélange of madcap comedy and sentimentality.

Joseph Schildkraut *Mr M* • Billie Burke *Mrs Pidgeon* • Eugene Pallette *Mr Pidgeon* • Ona Munson *Florrie* • Raymond Walburn *Willie* • Anne Gillis [Ann Gillis] *Angela* • Ruth Terry *Therese* ■ *Dir* Joseph Kane • *Scr* Frances Hyland, from a story by Frances Hyland, Albert Ray

The Check Is in the Mail ★★ 15

Comedy   1986 · US · Colour · 79mins

In what was his first starring role, Brian Dennehy plays a California pharmacist, an upstanding citizen married to the lovely Anne Archer. Everything goes pear-shaped when he accumulates massive gambling debts, so he reverts to a less materialistic age by ripping out the utilities, drawing water from a newly-dug well and growing his own food. Director Joan Darling cut her teeth on American TV sitcoms, and this might have been better had it been cut down to 30 minutes.

Brian Dennehy *Richard Jackson* • Anne Archer *Peggy Jackson* • Hallie Todd *Robin Jackson* • Chris Hebert *Danny Jackson* • Michael Bowen *Gary Jackson* • Nita Talbot *Mrs Rappaport* ■ *Dir* Joan Darling • *Scr* Robert Kaufman

Checkered Flag ★★

Sports drama   1990 · US · Colour · 91mins

James Bond director John Glen is the man behind the camera for this *Days of Thunder*-style tale about rivalry on the motor-racing circuit. It was the pilot for a TV series that never happened, probably because there are only so many stories you can create around a pair of arrogant drivers (William Campbell and Robert Estes), some grease monkeys and the groupies who hang around the track. Contains swearing, sex scenes and nudity.

William Campbell [Bill Campbell] *Tommy Traherne* • Robert Estes [Rob Estes] *Mike Reardon* • Amanda Wyss *Kris Traherne* • Carrie Hamilton *Alex Cross* • Adam Philipson *Sal Cippolina* • Leilani Sarelle *Jerri Simpson* • Robert Forester *Jack Cotton* ■ *Dir* John Glen • *Scr* EF Wallengren, Clayton Frohman

Checking Out ★ 15

Black comedy   1988 · UK · Colour · 90mins

Barely released to cinemas, this was another nail in the coffin of George Harrison's already troubled HandMade Films. Directed by David Leland and scripted by Joe Eszterhas, the talented writer of *Jagged Edge* and *Music Box*, the film stars Jeff Daniels as an advertising executive who becomes deeply neurotic after his colleague dies

of a heart attack. Searching for the meaning of life and the answer to the question "Why don't Italians have barbecues?", Daniels's odyssey isn't worth waiting for the answer: "Spaghetti falls through the grill." Contains swearing and nudity.

Jeff Daniels *Ray Macklin* • Melanie Mayron *Jenny Macklin* • Michael Tucker *Harry Lardner* • Kathleen York *Diana* • Ann Magnuson *Connie Hagen* • Allan Havey *Pat Hagen* • Jo Harvey Allen *Barbara* • Ian Wolfe *Mr D'Amato* ■ *Dir* David Leland • *Scr* Joe Eszterhas

Checkpoint ★★ U

Action adventure   1956 · UK · Colour · 85mins

Although they promise fast-paced action, fiction films about motor racing rarely get out of first gear. At least here there is the compensation of some nifty auto action (courtesy of cinematographer Ernest Stewart and editor Frederick Wilson) to pep up an otherwise pedestrian tale of industrial espionage, in which Stanley Baker attempts to poach some top secret car designs. Familiar faces crop up in virtually every role, but the most interesting is that of Robert Rietty (playing a humble frontier guard), the undisputed master of the voice-over.

Anthony Steel *Bill Fraser* • Odile Versois *Francesca* • Stanley Baker *O'Donovan* • James Robertson-Justice *Warren Ingram* • Maurice Denham *Ted Thornhill* • Michael Medwin *Ginger* • Paul Muller *Petersen* • Robert Rietty *Frontier guard* ■ *Dir* Ralph Thomas • *Scr* Robin Estridge

Checkpoint ★★★

Drama   1987 · US · Colour · 91mins

Set in the twilight days of the Carter presidency, this claustrophobic drama explores in microcosm the tensions that arose during the Iran hostage crisis. Written, produced, edited and directed by Parviz Sayyad, it suggests the freeze in US-Iranian relations was not solely the fault of the fundamentalist regime that overthrew the Shah. All shades of political opinion are expressed as Canadian border authorities detain a busload of students after they discover eight Iranians onboard. Mary Apick and Houshang Touzie stand out from an ensemble cast, while the film manages to personalise the diverse doctrines without confusing or alienating us.

Mary Apick *Firouzeh* • Houshang Touzie *Kazem* • Peter Spreague *Mike* • Mark Nichols *Bob* • Buck Kartalian *Frank* • Michael Zand *Farhad* • Mayeva Martin *Kate* • Ali Poutash *Hatam* ■ *Dir/Scr* Parviz Sayyad

Checkpoint ★★★★

War drama   1998 · Rus · Colour · 91mins

Following Sergei Bodrov's *Prisoner of the Mountains* into a Caucasus region that may or may not be Chechnya, Alexandr Rogozhkin's frontline drama is a tense and often bitterly humorous reminder of the futility of war. Fighting a campaign they care little about, an unruly Russian unit is dispatched to an isolated checkpoint as punishment for the needless death of a Muslim mother in a nearby village. Charting the troopers' uneasy accord with the locals, after they become the target of a woodland sniper, this dour battle of attrition benefits considerably from

both the relentlessly bleak imagery and the naturalistic ensemble playing. A Russian language film.

Andrei Krasko *Iliych* • Aleksander Ivanov *Boeing* • Zoya Buryak *Detective* • Aleksei Buldakov *General* • Roman Romantsov *Bones* ■ *Dir/Scr* Aleksandr Rogozhkin

Cheech & Chong's Next Movie ★★ 18

Comedy   1980 · US · Colour · 90mins

Tommy Chong made his directorial debut (he would go on to direct three more of the Cheech and Chong series) in this hit-and-miss follow-up to *Up in Smoke*, a massive cult hit around the world. The plotting this time around is even more episodic than before, but the subject matter and humour still seemed fresh and anarchic at the time. The result drifts along in an amiable, if somewhat hazy fashion.

Richard "Cheech" Marin *Cheech* • Thomas Chong [Tommy Chong] *Chong* • Evelyn Guerrero *Donna* • Betty Kennedy *Candy* • Sy Kramer *Mr Neatnik* • Rikki Marin *Gloria* • Michael Winslow *Welfare comedian* • Paul Reubens *Pee-wee Herman/Desk clerk* ■ *Dir* Thomas Chong [Tommy Chong] • *Scr* Thomas Chong, Richard "Cheech" Marin

Cheech & Chong's Nice Dreams ★★ 18

Comedy   1981 · US · Colour · 83mins

Number three in the series, and if you didn't appreciate the joke by now, you were never going to be won over. Stacy Keach returns from the original, Paul "Pee-Wee Herman" Reuben pops up, while the sharp-eyed will spot an early film appearance by Sandra Bernhard. There's even room for a cameo from sixties drug icon Timothy Leary, playing himself. Otherwise it's the usual sloppy mix of dope chat and slapstick from the two stars, "Cheech" Marin and Tommy Chong.

Tommy Chong *Chong* • Richard "Cheech" Marin *Cheech* • Stacy Keach *The Sarge* • Evelyn Guerrero *Donna* • Paul Reubens *Howie Hamburger* • Michael Masters *Willard "Animal" Bad* • Sandra Bernhard ■ *Dir* Thomas Chong [Tommy Chong] • *Scr* Thomas Chong, Richard "Cheech" Marin

Cheech & Chong's Still Smokin' ★ 18

Comedy   1983 · US · Colour · 86mins

As the medical authorities continue to tell us, smoking too much marijuana can be bad for your health. Sadly, the same applies to Cheech and Chong movies. While the duo can't be blamed for wanting to visit a cannabis mecca like Amsterdam, the resulting film is the weakest in the series: a lazy mixture of rambling sketches and concert footage.

Richard "Cheech" Marin *Cheech* • Thomas Chong [Tommy Chong] *Chong* • Carol Van Herwijnen *Hotel Manager* • Shireen Strooker *Assistant manager* ■ *Dir* Thomas Chong [Tommy Chong] • *Scr* Thomas Chong, Richard "Cheech" Marin

Cheech & Chong's The Corsican Brothers ★ 15

Comedy   1984 · US · Colour · 86mins

The stoner duo obviously enjoyed romping around in period dress in

Yellowbeard, judging from this unwise departure from their successful dopehead formula. Loosely based on the classic novel by Alexandre Dumas, with the duo mugging their way through a variety of increasingly unfunny roles, this dreadful comic caper makes Graham Chapman's laboured spoof seem positively subtle by comparison. 🎞

Richard "Cheech" Marin *Luis (Corsican brother)* • Thomas Chong [Tommy Chong] *Lucien (Corsican brother)* • Roy Dotrice *The Evil Fuckaire/Ye Olde Jailer* • Shelby Fiddis *1st Princess* • Rikki Marin *2nd Princess* ■ *Dir* Thomas Chong [Tommy Chong] • *Scr* Richard "Cheech" Marin, Thomas Chong

Cheech & Chong's Up in Smoke ★★★ 🔞
Comedy   1978 · US · Colour · 81mins

A good decade before the phrase was even coined, Richard "Cheech" Marin and Tommy Chong came up with what for some remains the ultimate "slacker" movie. Cheech and Chong originally existed on albums only, but they made a surprisingly successful transition to the big screen; the duo made six movies together, all essential viewing for students around the world. The first (and best) of all their films finds the genially stoned brothers looking to find the best grass in town. Stacy Keach has a ball as the deranged cop on their trail, while the car made of cannabis is a hoot. If you only watch one Cheech and Chong movie, make it this one. 🎞

Richard "Cheech" Marin *Pedro* • Thomas Chong [Tommy Chong] *Man* • Stacy Keach *Sergeant Stedenko* • Tom Skerritt *Strawberry* • Strother Martin *Arnold Stoner* ■ *Dir* Lou Adler • *Scr* Thomas Chong, Richard "Cheech" Marin

Cheer Boys Cheer ★★★ 🇺
Comedy   1939 · UK · BW · 83mins

A pleasing British comedy about two warring breweries: one mechanised, the other traditional. Tom Greenleaf (CV France) runs the good ale plant and makes the better brew; Edward Ironside (a bullying Edmund Gwenn) manages the other. In a subplot not a million miles from *Romeo and Juliet*, their offspring – lovely Nova Pilbeam (Greenleaf's daughter) and dapper Peter Coke (Ironside's son) – fall in love. Stir in a contrived shares sell-out, and the result is a pleasant film with a neat sting in its ale... sorry, tale.

Nova Pilbeam *Margaret Greenleaf* • Edmund Gwenn *Edward Ironside* • Jimmy O'Dea *Matt Boyle* • Moore Marriott *Geordie* • Graham Moffatt *Albert* • CV France *Tom Greenleaf* • Peter Coke *John Ironside* • Alexander Knox *Saunders* ■ *Dir* Walter Forde • *Scr* Roger MacDougall, Allan Mackinnon, from a story by Ian Dalrymple, Donald Bull

Cheer Up! ★★ 🇺
Musical   1936 · UK · BW · 68mins

The celebrated music hall and screen comedian Stanley Lupino (father of actress/director Ida) stars as a struggling writer/composer trying to get his show put on. While seeking backing from a millionaire, he is mistaken for one himself, saves a young actress (Sally Gray) from an unwelcome admirer and is plunged into a series of complications. Made by an

obscure director (Leo Mittler) with an equally unknown supporting cast, this low-budget musical comedy may be lively and energetic, but it's also simplistic and coarse-grained.

Stanley Lupino *Tom Denham* • Sally Gray *Sally Gray* • Roddy Hughes *Dick Dirk* • Gerald Barry *John Harman* • Kenneth Kove *Wilfred Harman* • Wyn Weaver *Mr Carter* • Marjorie Chard *Mrs Carter* ■ *Dir* Leo Mittler • *Scr* Michael Barringer, from a story by Stanley Lupino

Cheers for Miss Bishop ★★★ 🇺
Drama   1941 · US · BW · 94mins

After 50 years as a dedicated schoolteacher, Miss Bishop (Martha Scott) relives her life in flashback at a banquet in her honour. As the tale of her life unfolds, we learn why this attractive woman never married. Directed by Tay Garnett, this poignant, sentimental weepie co-stars William Gargan as the grocer who carries a hopeless torch for the teacher, while Donald Douglas and Sidney Blackmer play the two men she loved and lost.

Martha Scott *Ella Bishop* • William Gargan *Sam Peters* • Edmund Gwenn *President Corcoran* • Sterling Holloway *Chris Jensen* • Sidney Blackmer *John Stevens* • Mary Anderson *Amy Saunders* ■ *Dir* Tay Garnett • *Scr* Stephen Vincent Benet, Adelaide Heilbron, Sheridan Gibney, from the novel *Miss Bishop* by Bess Streeter Aldrich

Cheetah ★★★ 🇺
Adventure   1989 · US · Colour · 80mins

Fresh out of cute American baby animals, Disney decamped to Kenya for what amounts to a children's version of *Born Free*. It's an amiable adventure about two Californian youngsters teaming up with a Masai boy to raise an orphaned cheetah cub, but there are few surprises in the storyline. Where the film does pick up points, however, is in the splendid photography of the Kenyan bush, the fascinating glimpses of the Masai lifestyle and the unsentimental way in which the harsh realities of nature are explained. 🎞

Keith Coogan *Ted Johnson* • Lucy Deakins *Susan Johnson* • Collin Mothupi *Morogo* • Timothy Landfield *Earl Johnson* • Breon Gorman *Jean Johnson* • Ka Vundla *Kipoin* ■ *Dir* Jeff Blyth • *Scr* Erik Tarloff, John Cotter, Griff Du Rhone, from the book *The Cheetahs* by Alan Caillou

The Chelsea Girls ★★★★
Underground classic
1967 · US · BW and Colour · 210mins

This was the first Andy Warhol film to emerge from the underground and play at arthouses. The original version comprised two films projected side by side, with a combined running time of three-and-a-half hours. The version premiered in London in 1968, which still turns up occasionally, is one film lasting two hours. It consists of 12 virtually unedited takes in which such Warhol regulars as Nico, Ingrid Superstar and International Velvet improvise dialogue in rooms at New York's Chelsea Hotel. Many are boring or inaudible, but some of them are real shockers – like the "confession" scene in which "Pope" Ondine,

presumably off his head on some drug or other, becomes genuinely violent.

Angelica "Pepper" Davis • Ingrid Superstar • Albert René Ricard *Albert RenéRicard* • Mary Might [Mary Woronov] *Hanoi Hanna* • International Velvet [Susan Bottomly] • Brigit Polk • Ed Hood *Ed* • Patrick Flemming • Edie Sedgwick *Edie* • Arthur Loeb • Nico *Nico* ■ *Dir* Andy Warhol • *Scr* Andy Warhol, Ronald Tavel • *Music* The Velvet Underground

Chernobyl: the Final Warning ★★★ 🔞
Drama based on a true story
1991 · US · Colour · 94mins

This superior made-for-TV docudrama, a reconstruction of the events surrounding the Soviet nuclear disaster of 1986, is distinguished by an even-handed approach that shows sympathy for all those involved in this tragedy. Anthony Page gets fine performances from a cast that includes Jon Voight, Jason Robards and *One Foot in the Grave*'s Annette Crosbie. 🎞

Jon Voight *Dr Robert Gale* • Jason Robards [Jason Robards Jr] *Dr Armand Hammer* • Sammi Davis *Elena Mashenko* • Annette Crosbie *Dr Galena Petrovna* • Ian McDiarmid *Dr Vatisenko* ■ *Dir* Anthony Page • *Scr* Ernest Kinoy, from the book *Final Warning: The Legacy of Chernobyl* by Robert Peter Gale, Thomas Hauser

The Cherokee Kid ★★
Comedy western   1996 · US · Colour · 89mins

British audiences have resolutely failed to take American comedian Sinbad to their hearts, and much of his work ends up going straight to video over here. This half-hearted western spoof sank almost without trace, which is somewhat surprising given the quality of its cast. Sinbad plays the self-styled Cherokee Kid, who is seeking revenge on the man (James Coburn) who murdered his family. Burt Reynolds enjoys himself as a drunken former gunfighter who takes the dopey Sinbad under his wing. Contains some violence and strong language.

Sinbad *Isaiah Turner/The Cherokee Kid* • James Coburn *Cyrus Bloomington* • Gregory Hines *The Undertaker/Jedediah* • A Martinez *Cortina* • Burt Reynolds *Ottor Bob* ■ *Dir* Paris Barclay • *Scr* Denise DeClue, Tim Kazurinksy

Cherokee Strip ★★
Western   1940 · US · BW · 84mins

Richard Dix was no stranger to the Wild West, having earned an Oscar nomination for his role in the 1931 version of *Cimarron*, but he's rather looking his age in this unremarkable story about a square-jawed marshal taking on a gang of desperados. Lesley Selander, best known for his collaborations with Tim Holt and William "Hopalong Cassidy" Boyd, directs with undue fuss.

Richard Dix *Dave Morrell* • Florence Rice *Kate Cross* • Victor Jory *Coy Barrett* • Andy Clyde *Tex Crawford* • George E Stone *Abe Gabbert* • Morris Ankrum *Hawk* ■ *Dir* Lesley Selander • *Scr* Norman Houston, Bernard McConville, from a story by Bernard McConville

Cherry, Harry & Raquel ★★★ 🔞
Erotic drama   1969 · US · Colour · 72mins

A seminal trip down mammary lane for Russ Meyer, the "King Leer" of the American soft-core sexploitation industry. The plot has something to do with corrupt sheriff Harry (Charles Napier, a Meyer favourite) trying to keep the lid on his marijuana-smuggling scam when threatened with exposure by a rival Indian drugs runner. Punctuating the flimsy plot are sharply-edited bedroom scenes showing Harry, nurse Cherry and mob mistress Raquel in all manner of sexual situations. Witty and compact, this tried-and-tested combination of sex, violence and humour was co-scripted by famed author Tom Wolfe under the pseudonym Thomas J McGowan. Contains swearing, sexual situations and some violence. 🎞

Larissa Ely *Raquel* • Linda Ashton *Cherry* • Charles Napier *Harry* • Bert Santos *Enrique* • Franklin H Bolger *Mr Franklin* • Astrid Lillimor [Uschi Digard] *Soul* • Michele Grand *Millie* • John Milo *Apache* • Robert Aiken *Tom* • Russ Meyer ■ *Dir* Russ Meyer • *Scr* Russ Meyer, Thomas J McGowan [Tom Wolfe], from a story by Russ Meyer • *Producer* Russ Meyer

The Cherry Orchard ★★★ 🅿🅶
Drama   1998 · Gr/Cyp/Fr · Colour · 141mins

Anton Chekhov called his play a comedy, but there's nothing comic about this version from Greek director Michael Cacoyannis, which places the emphasis squarely on melancholy. Charlotte Rampling leaves an unhappy affair in Paris for a family estate inhabited by dissolute relatives. There, the only way to stave off bankruptcy is to have the orchard chopped down to make way for money-making new houses. Alan Bates plays Rampling's indecisive brother, Frances de la Tour is a deliciously mad governness, and it all looks stunning. The satire is missing, however, and the film is dour to the point of being lugubrious.

Charlotte Rampling *Lyubov Andreyevna (Ranevskaya)* • Alan Bates *Gaev (Leonid Andreyevich)* • Katrin Cartlidge *Varya (Varvara Mihailovna)* • Owen Teale *Lopahin (Yermolai Alexeyevich)* • Frances de la Tour *Charlotta* ■ *Dir* Michael Cacoyannis • *Scr* Michael Cacoyannis, from the play by Anton Chekhov

Cherry 2000 ★★ 🔞
Science-fiction thriller
1988 · US · Colour · 94mins

Melanie Griffith's career has certainly had its ups (*Working Girl*) and its downs (*The Bonfire of the Vanities*), and *Cherry 2000* falls firmly into the latter category. In this futuristic tale, set in the year 2017, sexual partners have been replaced by robot playmates. When his mechanical dream girl breaks down, Sam Treadwell (David Andrews) heads off into the desert for spare parts with expert scavenger E Johnson (Griffith).

Melanie Griffith *E Johnson* • David Andrews *Sam Treadwell* • Ben Johnson *Six Finger Jake* • Tim Thomerson *Lester* • Brion James *Stacy* • Pamela Gidley *Cherry 2000* • Harry Carey Jr *Snappy Tom* • Cameron Milzer *Ginger* ■ *Dir* Steve De Jarnatt • *Scr* Michael Almereyda, from a story by Lloyd Fonvielle

Chess Fever ★★★ U

Silent comedy 1925 · USSR · BW · 27mins

Co-directed by Nikolai Shpikovsky, this was the first film by the celebrated Soviet director Vsevolod Pudovkin to secure an international release. Attending an international tournament in Moscow, chess master José Capablanca had no idea he was being filmed for a comedy constructed by Pudovkin's teacher and the godfather of montage, Lev Kuleshov. However, there he is playing an unknowing part in reconciling chess fanatic Vladimir Fogel and fiancée Anna Zemtsova following a wedding day mix-up. Packed with incident (including a splendid kitten sequence) and cameos from directors Yuli Raizman and Yakov Protazanov, this is a fond tribute to an inspirational mentor. ▦

Vladimir Fogel *The Hero* • Anna Zemtsova *The Heroine* • José R Capablanca *Chess champion* ■ *Dir* Vsevolod I Pudovkin, Nikolai Shpikovsky • *Scr* Nikolai Shpikovsky

The Chess Player ★★★★ U

Silent period drama
1927 · Fr · BW and Tinted · 135mins

Although it boasts sumptuous production values, what most impresses about this period drama is the way in which director Raymond Bernard subtly uses silent imagery to convey exactly what all the characters are feeling. Hiding in a chess-playing automaton to avoid capture, Pierre Blanchar is surprisingly expressive as the Polish rebel who is delivered into the court of Catherine II (Marcelle Charles-Dullin). Banned by the Nazis in 1940, this exquisite film was restored 50 years later by archivist Kevin Brownlow from prints found in four different countries. ▦

Edith Jehanne *Sophie Novinska* • Pierre Blanchar *Boleslas Vorowski* • Pierre Batcheff *Prince Serge Oblomoff* • Charles Dullin *Baron von Kempelen* • Marcelle Charles-Dullin *Catherine II* ■ *Dir* Raymond Bernard • *Scr* Raymond Bernard, Jean-José Frappa, from the novel *Le Joueur d'Échecs* by Henri Dupuy-Mazuel

The Chess Players ★★★★ PG

Drama 1977 · Ind · Colour · 115mins

Largely dismissed for its precise symbolism and deliberate pacing, this is one of Satyajit Ray's most undervalued features. Exquisitely re-creating the opulence of Lucknow on the eve of the Indian Mutiny, this historical satire exposes both the ruthless ambition of the imperialists and the indolence of the local rulers. As the chess-playing noblemen who are as uninterested in their families as they are in affairs of state, Sanjeev Kumar and Saeed Jaffrey are deftly comic in their inability to equate their game with the power struggle going on around them, while Amjad Khan convinces as the aesthetically-minded maharajah. In Hindi with English subtitles. ▦

Sanjeev Kumar *Mirza* • Saeed Jaffrey *Mir* • Amjad Khan *Wajid Ali Shah* • Richard Attenborough *General Outram* • Shabana Azmi *Mirza's wife* • Farida Jalal *Mir's wife* ■ *Dir* Satyajit Ray • *Scr* Satyajit Ray, from a story by Munshi Premchand

Le Cheval d'Orgueil ★★★

Period drama 1980 · Fr · Colour · 118mins

French film-makers have often waxed lyrical about the transports of country living. Here Claude Chabrol, no stranger to the provinces, adopts an almost anthropological stance in chronicling the lives of a Breton family in the years preceding the Great War. Yet while he faithfully records the costumes and customs of the indomitable people celebrated in Pierre-Jakez Helias's book, he dilutes their socio-political problems by romanticising their poverty. The trio of actors playing "Petit-Pierre" down the years create a credible character. It's the environment that seems fake. In French with English subtitles.

Jacques Dufilho *Alain Le Goff* • Bernadette Le Saché *Anne-Marie Le Goff* • François Cluzet *Pierre-Alain Le Goff* • Ronan Hubert *Pierre-Jacques aged 7* • Arnel Hubert *Pierre-Jacques aged 17* ■ *Dir* Claude Chabrol • *Scr* Claude Chabrol, Daniel Boulanger, from the novel by Pierre-Jakez Helias

Cheyenne Autumn ★★★★ U

Epic western 1964 · US · Colour · 124mins

The last western made by the great John Ford is effectively an apology for the many wrongs done by Hollywood to the native American. The film maintains tremendous dignity in those sections actually dealing with the tragic resettlement of the Cheyenne by the US government, but is undermined by a tasteless would-be comic central section set in Dodge City. Still, here's Ford's beloved Monument Valley and a distinguished cast headed by the under-rated Richard Widmark in a story of genuine epic scale. ▦

Richard Widmark *Captain Thomas Archer* • Carroll Baker *Deborah Wright* • Karl Malden *Captain Oscar Wessels* • James Stewart *Wyatt Earp* • Edward G Robinson *Secretary of the Interior* • Sal Mineo *Red Shirt* • Dolores Del Rio *Spanish woman* • Ricardo Montalban *Little Wolf* ■ *Dir* John Ford • *Scr* James R Webb, from the novel by Mari Sandoz

The Cheyenne Social Club ★★★

Comedy western
1970 · US · Colour · 101mins

Gene Kelly was severely under-rated as a director in his post-MGM period, but his dry and lascivious wit was given full rein in several adult movies, notably *A Guide for the Married Man* and this tame western about a couple of cowboys who inherit a brothel. Since the pair are amiable Jimmy Stewart and Henry "Hank" Fonda, pals since the early thirties, there's a great deal of affectionate by-play between them. The photography (by western veteran William Clothier) looks good, and Shirley Jones is lively as ever, but some may be deterred by Kelly's rather smutty treatment of the subject matter. Contains some swearing and nudity.

James Stewart *John O'Hanlan* • Henry Fonda *Harley Sullivan* • Shirley Jones *Jenny* • Sue Ane Langdon *Opal Ann* • Elaine Devry *Pauline* • Robert Middleton *Barman* • Arch Johnson *Marshal Anderson* • Dabbs Greer *Willowby* ■ *Dir* Gene Kelly • *Scr* James Lee Barrett

Cheyenne Warrior ★★★

Western drama 1994 · US · Colour · 86mins

A pregnant widow and a badly wounded Cheyenne brave team up to survive after a Civil War massacre in a commendable western with an exceptional script. Kelly Preston isn't up to the acting demands made of her by director Mark Griffiths, but Pato Hoffman plays his native American role with a winning conviction well beyond the call of duty in this Roger Corman production. It's when the couple fall in love, and the differences in their respective cultures come into play, that this surprising sleeper takes flight towards a satisfying conclusion.

Kelly Preston *Rebecca Carver* • Pato Hoffmann *Hawk* • Bo Hopkins *Andrews* • Rick Dean *Kearney* • Clint Howard *Otto Nielsen* ■ *Dir* Mark Griffiths • *Scr* Michael B Druxman

Chicago Confidential ★★★

Crime drama 1957 · US · BW · 73mins

In one of those gangster exposés that flourished in the late fifties, the sincere and honest leader of a trade union is framed for murder by a gambling syndicate that wants to take over his organisation. Brian Keith, Beverly Garland and Elisha Cook Jr manage to hold the interest, while cowboy actor Dick Foran gets down from his horse to play the victimised union leader. It all feels rather predictable now, though.

Brian Keith *Jim Fremont* • Beverly Garland *Laura* • Dick Foran *Blane* • Beverly Tyler *Sylvia* • Elisha Cook Jr *Candymouth* • Paul Langton *Jake Parker* • Tony George *Duncan* ■ *Dir* Sidney Salkow • *Scr* Raymond T Marcus [Bernard Gordon], from the story by Hugh King (uncredited) and the book by Jack Lait, Lee Mortimer

Chicago Joe and the Showgirl ★★ 18

Wartime drama based on a true story
1989 · UK · Colour · 98mins

Bernard Rose, who made the rather tepid Beethoven biopic *Immortal Beloved*, had previously cast his directorial eye over another true story with this tale of an English showgirl (Emily Lloyd, daft and annoying) and an American GI (Kiefer Sutherland, over the top) who become lovers in wartime England and go on a crime and murder spree. However, because no one knows to this day why the pair actually committed the crimes, Rose and his scriptwriter David Yallop have to resort to clichés. Contains swearing. ▦

Kiefer Sutherland *Karl Hulten*/"Ricky Allen" • Emily Lloyd *Elizabeth Maud Jones*/"Georgina Grayson" • Patsy Kensit *Joyce Cook* • Keith Allen *Lenny Bexley* • Liz Fraser *Mrs Evans* ■ *Dir* Bernard Rose • *Scr* David Yallop

The Chicken Chronicles ★★ 18

Comedy 1977 · US · Colour · 90mins

Not a particular highpoint for Phil Silvers in the twilight of his career, though he still comes off best from this cheap teen comedy. Silvers aside, this is notable only for providing a very early film role for Steve Guttenberg, who plays a randy and confused adolescent trying to make sense of his

life. It's amusing, but tame compared to the likes of *American Pie*. ▦

Phil Silvers *Max Ober* • Ed Lauter *Mr Nastase* • Steve Guttenberg *David Kessler* • Lisa Reeves *Margaret Shaffer* • Meredith Baer *Tracy* • Branscombe Richmond *Mark* • Will Seltzer *Weinstein* ■ *Dir* Francis Simon • *Scr* Paul Diamond, from his novel

Chicken Every Sunday ★★

Comedy 1948 · US · BW · 94mins

A down-home slice of mom's apple pie served over the white picket fence with a side order of regulation family values. Dan Dailey stars as the husband who thinks he can reject honest hard work in favour of ill-judged scheming. As he is taught his life's lesson very slowly, we are left to wonder what a nice all-American "gal" like Celeste Holm is doing with him in the first place. Very dated.

Dan Dailey *Jim Hefferen* • Celeste Holm *Emily Hefferen* • Colleen Townsend *Rosemary Hefferen* • Alan Young *Geoffrey Lawson* • Natalie Wood *Ruth* ■ *Dir* George Seaton • *Scr* George Seaton, Valentine Davies, from the play by Julius J Epstein, Philip G Epstein, from a novel by Rosemary Taylor

Chicken Run ★★★★ U

Animated adventure
2000 · US/UK · Colour · 84mins

Four years in the making and easily the most ambitious project yet undertaken by the award-laden Aardman Animation unit, this feathered pastiche of such PoW classics as *The Great Escape* and *Stalag 17* is an awesome achievement by consummate film-makers. Rocky, a "lone free ranger" rooster, promises to help the hens in Mr and Mrs Tweedy's high-security egg farm find a way to freedom. The nods to classic film moments are funny and plentiful, the largely British voice cast (Julia Sawalha, Jane Horrocks, Miranda Richardson, Timothy Spall) lends moments of humour and pathos, and the set pieces are exhilarating in their ingenuity and comic élan. There are longueurs, many of which are prompted by the need to justify Mel Gibson's vocal presence as Rocky, but this is still a soaring flight of fancy.

Mel Gibson *Rocky* • Julia Sawalha *Ginger* • Imelda Staunton *Bunty* • Jane Horrocks *Babs* • Miranda Richardson *Mrs Tweedy* • Phil Daniels *Fetcher* • Timothy Spall *Nick* ■ *Dir* Nick Park, Peter Lord • *Scr* Karey Kirkpatrick, Jack Rosenthal, from a story by Nick Park, Peter Lord

Chief Crazy Horse ★★

Western 1955 · US · Colour · 86mins

Victor Mature is improbably cast as the great leader of the Sioux nation, but newcomers Ray Danton and Keith Larsen are on hand to add dignity, and veteran John Lund looks good in a cavalry outfit. There's no real thought or style on show here, and the target audience seems to have been a very young one. There is, however, poignancy in the fact that Mature's co-star is lovely Suzan Ball (Lucille's cousin), appearing after her leg was amputated in an operation for the cancer that was to take her life soon after this film was completed.

Victor Mature *Crazy Horse* • Suzan Ball *Black Shawl* • John Lund *Major Twist* • Ray Danton *Little Big Man* • Keith Larsen *Flying Hawk* • Paul Guilfoyle *Worm* • David Janssen *Lieutenant Cartwright* • Robert Warwick *Spotted Tail* ■ *Dir* George Sherman • *Scr* Franklin Coen, Gerald Drayson Adams, from a story by Gerald Drayson Adams

Un Chien Andalou ★★★★★ 15

Silent experimental classic
1928 · Fr · BW · 15mins

An eye-opener in more senses than one, this great surrealist masterpiece – co-written by Luis Buñuel and Salvador Dalí – still has the power to shock. Starting with an open razor (wielded by Buñuel) slicing a girl's eyeball, this short film goes on to clash lyrical images with violent ideas to show how love is held back by tradition. Not as meaningless as it seems, and as anti-clerical as Buñuel was to become in all his later films, it still has enormous intensity. ▭

Pierre Batcheff *Young man* • Simone Mareuil *Girl* • Luis Buñuel *Man with razor* • Salvador Dalí *Marist priest* • Jaime Miravilles *Seminarist* ■ *Dir* Luis Buñuel • *Scr* Luis Buñuel, Salvador Dalí

La Chienne ★★★★

Romantic drama   1931 · Fr · BW · 100mins

Unhappily married cashier Michel Simon becomes infatuated with prostitute Janie Marèze, and is callously exploited by her and her violent pimp Georges Flament. The clerk sets her up in an apartment, enjoys her every day and then obsessively paints her. This moral fable, in which the part-time artist inexorably slips down the criminal scale towards murder, was filmed by Jean Renoir on the streets of Montmartre – an influential break from the usual studio sets – and still makes for compelling viewing. Simon gives a superbly expressive performance, though in real life it was Marèze and Flament who became lovers. Shortly after filming was completed, they were involved in a car crash in which she was killed. The film was remade in Hollywood by Fritz Lang as *Scarlet Street*. In French with English subtitles.

Michel Simon *Maurice* • Janie Marèze *Lulu* • Georges Flament *André* ■ *Dir* Jean Renoir • *Scr* Jean Renoir, Andre Girard, from a novel by Georges de la Fouchardière

A Child for Satan ★★ 15

Horror   1991 · US · Colour · 83mins

Made as a pilot for a projected American TV series, this updated retelling of *Rosemary's Baby* never caught on. Marita Geraghty plays a pregnant woman who joins husband Peter Kowanko in his home town in New Mexico, but begins to worry that evil forces have designs on her baby. Old hands Anthony Zerbe and Shirley Knight take the acting honours, and there is a nice turn from Spalding Gray, but genuine shocks are few and far between. It's co-directed by Robert Lieberman, who helmed the alien abduction thriller *Fire in the Sky*. ▭

Marita Geraghty *Isabella Larson* • Shirley Knight *Rinda Larson* • Peter Kowanko [Pete Kowanko] *Garth Larson* • Anthony Zerbe *Lewis Larson* • Joseph Runningfox *Toby Coldcreek* • Janel Moloney *Janelle Lowry* • Spalding Gray

Hobart • Steven Gregory Tyler *Det Wetzel* • Phil Mead *Dr Bob* ■ *Dir* Robert Lieberman, John Schwartzman • *Scr* Joyce Eliason

Child in the House ★★★ U

Drama   1956 · UK · BW · 87mins

With her mother in hospital and her father (Stanley Baker) on the run, 11-year-old Mandy Miller is sent to live with her sniffy aunt Phyllis Calvert and rigid uncle Eric Portman. Her presence has an unexpected effect on all concerned. A modest British-made drama, directed by Cy Endfield (*Zulu*) and jam-packed with such stalwarts of the acting profession as Dora Bryan, Joan Hickson and Alfie Bass. Good for a tear or two, though Portman and Calvert are oddly cast.

Phyllis Calvert *Evelyn Acheson* • Eric Portman *Henry Acheson* • Stanley Baker *Stephen Lorimer* • Mandy Miller *Elizabeth Lorimer* • Dora Bryan *Cassie* • Joan Hickson *Cook* • Victor Maddern *Bert* • Alfie Bass *Ticket collector* ■ *Dir* C Raker Endfield [Cy Endfield] • *Scr* C Raker Endfield [Cy Endfield], from the novel by Janet McNeill

Child in the Night ★★ 15

Thriller   1990 · US · Colour · 91mins

Of all the young stars who've emerged in the nineties, Elijah Wood is arguably one of the most talented. Here he does well to convey something of the fear and confusion a child would feel as the only witness to his father's murder, especially when unsure whether to trust those closest to him, in this case his mother, grouchy grandfather and a kindly psychiatrist, played with typical skill by the under-rated JoBeth Williams. Anyone who enjoyed *The Client* will have little to complain about. ▭

JoBeth Williams *Dr Jackie Hollis* • Tom Skerritt *Detective Thurston T Bass* • Elijah Wood *Luke Winfield* • Darren McGavin *Os Winfield* • Season Hubley *Valerie Winfield* • Michael Pniewski *Bobby Palasek* • Tim Choate *Kurt Conrad* • Thom Bray *Harvey Rosen* ■ *Dir* Mike Robe • *Scr* Michael Petryni

A Child Is Missing ★★★ 12

Thriller   1995 · US · Colour · 83mins

Henry Winkler is cast against type in this above average TV-movie thriller, playing a hermit who comes to the assistance of a young boy whom a kidnapper has left buried in the woods only to find himself accused of the abduction. Winkler is surprisingly convincing as the recluse and there are fine turns from Dale Midkiff, Roma Downey and Richard A Dysart, while John Power keeps the action moving along at a brisk pace. ▭

Henry Winkler *Steven Moore* • Roma Downey *Samantha* • Dale Midkiff *Peter* • Alberta Watson *Graham* • Keegan Macintosh *Buddy* • Richard A Dysart [Richard Dysart] *Riley* • Hiro Kanagawa *Agent Kurosaka* ■ *Dir* John Power • *Scr* Wes Bishop

A Child Is Waiting ★★★

Drama   1962 · US · BW · 104mins

Originally broadcast live on American TV in 1957, this drama about mentally retarded children was to have been directed by Jack Clayton. After John Cassavetes shot it, producer Stanley Kramer fired him and edited it himself, turning what was reputedly a rather

tougher movie into a more slightly sentimental one that tub-thumps its message about the care for an autistic child, played by Bruce Ritchey. Burt Lancaster and Judy Garland play the child's psychologists and Gena Rowlands (Cassavetes's wife) and Steven Hill play the boy's parents.

Burt Lancaster *Dr Matthew Clark* • Judy Garland *Jean Hansen* • Gena Rowlands *Sophie Widdicombe* • Steven Hill *Ted Widdicombe* • Bruce Ritchey *Reuben Witticombe* • Gloria McGehee *Mattie* • Paul Stewart *Goodman* ■ *Dir* John Cassavetes • *Scr* Abby Mann, from his story

A Child Lost Forever ★★★ 15

Drama based on a true story
1992 · US · Colour · 90mins

An accomplished documentarist, Claudia Weill directed the features *Girlfriends* and *It's My Turn* before making her name with TV's *thirtysomething*. She shows here what can be done with a true-life TV movie if dramatic restraint is allowed to triumph over tabloid sensationalism. Steering clear of melodramatic excess, Beverly D'Angelo impresses as the mother determined to bring to book the woman who adopted her son 20 years earlier and is now suspected of his murder. Also known as *The Jerry Sherwood Story*, this is the kind of intelligent film that restores credence to the term "woman's picture". ▭

Beverly D'Angelo *Jerry Sherwood* • Will Patton *Frank Maxwell* • Annabella Price *Melinda Elledge* • Hank Stratton *Robert Jurgens* • Dana Ivey *Lois Jurgens* • Brent Jennings *Clayton Robinson* ■ *Dir* Claudia Weill • *Scr* Judith Parker, Stephanie Liss

Child of Divorce ★★★

Drama   1946 · US · BW · 62mins

A poignant B-movie, given strength and focus by Sharyn Moffet's performance as a little girl whose parents separate. The feature debut of Richard Fleischer, who went on to direct such fine films as *The Vikings*, *Compulsion* and *10 Rillington Place*, it's actually a remake of *Wednesday's Child* (1934), which was based on the Leopold Atlas play of the same name. Only an hour long, this is a good deal more touching than many a bigger film on the subject.

Sharyn Moffett *Bobby* • Regis Toomey *Ray* • Madge Meredith *Joan* • Walter Reed *Michael* • Una O'Connor *Nora* • Doris Merrick *Louise* ■ *Dir* Richard O Fleischer [Richard Fleischer] • *Scr* Lillie Hayward, from the play *Wednesday's Child* by Leopold Atlas

Child of Rage ★★ 15

Drama   1992 · US · Colour · 93mins

Set in Vancouver, this melodrama is yet further proof that there's nothing like a king-sized dollop of domestic misery to fill up those gaps in the TV schedule. Director Larry Peerce has such creditable features as *Goodbye, Columbus* and *The Incident* to his name, so it's hard to see what would have drawn him to this story in which a couple discover that their adopted daughter's violent tantrums are the result of abuse. ▭

Mel Harris *Jill Tyler* • Dwight Schultz *Rob Tyler* • Mariette Hartley *Dr Rosemary Myers* •

Ashley Peldon *Catherine* • Sam Gifaldi *Eric Krieger* ■ *Dir* Larry Peerce • *Scr* Phil Penningroth, Suzette Couture

A Child Too Many ★★★ PG

Drama based on a true story
1993 · US · Colour · 88mins

One of those TV movies that raises many questions, but doesn't give all the answers. *LA Law's* Michele Greene is the young married mother who agrees to carry a child for another couple who can't have any more children. It's hard enough for her to explain to her family why the new baby won't be coming home when it's born, and things get worse when she discovers she is carrying twins and the other parents only want one child and want to give the other up for adoption. Thought-provoking stuff, made without veering towards melodrama by Oscar-nominated documentary-maker Jorge Montesi.

Michele Greene *Patty Nowakowski* • Nancy Stafford *Sharon Davis* • Conor O'Farrell *Aaron Nowakowski* • Stephen Macht *Bill Davis* • Kevin McNulty *Daniel Hall* ■ *Dir* Jorge Montesi • *Scr* Jayne Martin

Childhood Sweetheart? ★★

Thriller   1997 · US · Colour

In her never-ending battle to shake the goody-goody image gained in *Little House on the Prairie*, Melissa Gilbert plays a potentially dangerous mystery woman in this barnstorming TV movie. Returning 17 years after she inexplicably vanished, she shocks her nearest and dearest with tales of solitary confinement and sexual abuse. But her former beau, Michael Reilly Burke, isn't convinced by her miraculous reappearance, especially when her father, Ronny Cox, dies in suspicious circumstances. Yet another variation on the *Return of Martin Guerre* theme, this is short on suspense, in spite of Gilbert's valiant attempt to bring some complexity to the humdrum proceedings.

Melissa Gilbert *Karen Carlson* • Michael Reilly Burke *Greg Davis* • Ed Lauter *Sheriff Bowman* • Leon Russom *Lieutenant Walker* • Barbara Babcock *Rose Carlson* • Ronny Cox *Warren Carlson* ■ *Dir* Marcus Cole • *Scr* Devra Maza

The Children ★★

Drama   1990 · UK/W Ger · Colour · 91mins

Previously filmed in 1929 as *The Marriage Playground*, Edith Wharton's novel is here respectfully adapted by playwright Timberlake Wertenbaker. Director Tony Palmer assembles an accomplished supporting cast around Ben Kingsley, who gives a typically sensitive performance as the Europe-based engineer whose plans to marry widow Kim Novak are waylaid by his growing obsession with Siri Neal. She's the eldest daughter of Joe Don Baker and Geraldine Chaplin, whose neglect of their sizeable brood prompts her to ask Kingsley to become their guardian. Though pictorially resplendent and played with precision, the film is still technically naive and dramatically unsatisfying.

Ben Kingsley *Martin Boyne* • Kim Novak *Rose Sellars* • Geraldine Chaplin *Joyce Wheater* • Joe Don Baker *Cliff Wheater* • Siri Neal *Judith* • Britt Ekland *Lady Wrench* • Donald Sinden

Lord Wrench • Karen Black *Sybil Lullmer* • Rupert Graves *Gerald Omerod* • Rosemary Leach *Miss Scope* • Terence Rigby *Duke of Mendip* • Robert Stevens *Dobree* ■ *Dir* Tony Palmer • *Scr* Timberlake Wertenbaker, from the novel by Edith Wharton

Children Galore ★★ U
Comedy 1954 · UK · BW · 60mins

In launching the famous Hammer horror cycle, Terence Fisher secured his place in history. However, this early comedy did nothing for his reputation even though, with its quaint country setting, it has a vaguely Ealing feel. By deciding to build a cottage for the family with the most grandchildren, squire Peter Evan Thomas sends the village of Tussock into turmoil, with neighbours jeopardising decades of friendship as the search for eligible grandfathers and cute kids intensifies. Fun in a very English sort of way, this programme-filler has the advantage of being short and to the point.

Eddie Byrne *Zacky Jones* • Marjorie Rhodes *Ada Jones* • June Thorburn *Milly Ark* • Peter Evan Thomas *Lord Redscarfe* • Marjorie Hume *Lady Redscarfe* • Lucy Griffiths *Miss Prescott* ■ *Dir* Terence Fisher • *Scr* John Bonnet, Emery Bonnet, Peter Plaskett

Children of a Lesser God ★★★★ 15
Romantic drama
1986 · US · Colour · 114mins

The story of a woman for whom life's challenge is the fact she cannot hear, this adaptation of Mark Medoff's poignant play picks up even more resonance in its understanding of the casual hurts we inflict upon the hearing-impaired. William Hurt is subtly complex as the speech therapist attracted to his pupil, but it's the first-time performance by deaf actress Marlee Matlin that brilliantly articulates both a character and a condition. She won an Oscar for this, and there's no question she deserved it. Contains swearing and nudity. ▣

William Hurt *James Leeds* • Marlee Matlin *Sarah Norman* • Piper Laurie *Mrs Norman* • Philip Bosco *Dr Curtis Franklin* • Allison Gompf *Lydia* • John F Cleary *Johnny* • Philip Holmes *Glen* • Georgia Ann Cline *Cheryl* • William D Byrd *Danny* • Frank Carter Jr *Tony* • John Limnidis *William* • Bob Hiltermann *Orin* ■ *Dir* Randa Haines • *Scr* Hesper Anderson, Mark Medoff, from the play by Mark Medoff

The Children of An Lac ★★★ U
Drama based on a true story
1980 · US · Colour · 92mins

Having established herself on stage, Ina Balin made only a moderate impression on Hollywood. However, she will never be forgotten for the courage she displayed during the Vietnam war, when she helped 400 children from the An Lac orphanage escape to safety as the battle for Saigon raged around them. Balin plays herself in this creditable re-creation, which owes as much to the spirit of Ingrid Bergman's *The Inn of the Sixth Happiness* as to hard facts. John Llewellyn Moxey directs deferentially, while Shirley Jones, as a Georgia housewife, and orphanage principal Beulah Quo provide solid support. ▣

Shirley Jones *Betty Tisdale* • Ina Balin • Beulah Quo *Madam Ngai* • Alan Fudge *Jerry King* • Lee Paul *Dr McKinney* • Ben Piazza *Dr Bensman* • Kieu Chinh *Thuy* • Vic Silayan *Dr Dan* • Robert "Toffy" Padua *Trong* ■ *Dir* John Llewellyn Moxey • *Scr* Blanche Hanalis, from a story by Ina Balin

Children of Chance ★★
Drama 1949 · UK · BW · 100mins

Set, and shot, on the isle of Ischia, this turgid melodrama stars the lovely Patricia Medina in a tale of a racketeer's ill-gotten gains being put to good use by a priest to fund an orphanage. Well intentioned, but a long way from the neorealist roots of director Luigi Zampa; indeed, the Italian version of the same tale, known as *Campane a Martello*, boasts a considerably expanded and raunchier story line.

Patricia Medina *Agostina* • Manning Whiley *Don Andrea* • Yvonne Mitchell *Australia* • Barbara Everest *Francesca* • Eliot Makeham *Vicar* • George Woodbridge *Butcher* • Frank Tickle *Mayor* • Eric Pohlmann *Sergeant* ■ *Dir* Luigi Zampa • *Scr* Piero Tellini, Michael Medwin, from a story by Piero Tellini

Children of Hannibal ★★★
Crime comedy 1998 · It · Colour · 89

Italian comedy doesn't always travel well, but this unconventional buddy movie has much to recommend it. Trading off their physical dissimilarity, unemployed Silvio Orlando and disillusioned executive Diego Abatantuono make an inspired team as they head to the photogenic southern region of Puglia with the proceeds of a bank robbery. In between experiments with camera speeds, framing techniques and transitional devices, director Davide Ferrario slips some gentle social comment into the engaging comedy, while also finding time to develop a sensitive gay subplot involving Abatantuono's cop lover (Flavio Insinna) and his daughter (Valentina Cervi). An Italian language film.

Diego Abatantuono *Tommaso* • Silvio Orlando *Domenico* • Valentina Cervi *Rita* • Ugo Conti *Ermes* • Flavio Insinna *Orfeo* ■ *Dir* Davide Ferrario • *Scr* Diego Abatantuono, Davide Ferrario, from a story by Diego Abatantuono, Davide Ferrario, Sergio Rubini

The Children of Heaven ★★★★
Comedy drama 1997 · Iran · Colour · 88mins

This delightful comedy from Majid Majidi, a key member of the younger generation of Iranian film-makers, proved something of a favourite on the festival circuit. Like *The White Balloon* and *The Apple*, it confirms the Iranian industry's genius for movies about children, with Mohammad Amir Naji and Mir Farrokh Hashemian wondrously natural as the impoverished siblings who try to disguise the loss of the latter's shoes by sharing a pair for school. With its deft comic shifts and bustling portrait of bazaar life, this enchants as much as it entertains. A Farsi language film.

Mohammad Amir Naji *Ali* • Mir Farrokh Hashemian *Zahra* • Bahareh Seddiqi • Nasifeh Jafar Mohammadi *Roya* • Fereshte Sarabandi *Ali's mother* • Kamal Mirkarimi *Principal* • Bezhad Rafi'im *Coach* ■ *Dir/Scr* Majid Majidi

The Children of Sanchez ★
Drama 1978 · US/Mex · Colour · 126mins

Miserably dull drama, adapted from Oscar Lewis's book, about a poor Mexican trying to keep his small army of offspring from starving. Anthony Quinn is as professional as ever as Jesus Sanchez, but the real interest lies in the role of Grandma, played by Dolores Del Rio. Trivia gatherers may like to know that she was silent movie star Ramon Navarro's second cousin, and that she retired shortly afterwards. Who can blame her after this debacle?

Anthony Quinn *Jesus Sanchez* • Lupita Ferrer *Consuelo* • Dolores Del Rio *Grandma* • Stathis Giallelis *Roberto* • Lucia Mendez *Marta* • Duncan Quinn *Manuel* • Katy Jurado *Chata* • Carmen Montejo *Aunt Guadalupe* ■ *Dir* Hall Bartlett • *Scr* Cesare Zavattini, Hall Bartlett, from the novel by Oscar Lewis

Children of the Bride ★
Comedy 1990 · US · Colour

Rue McClanahan – the man-hungry Blanche in TV's *The Golden Girls* – has no chance in this lacklustre comedy as a fiftysomething trying to get her children used to the idea that husband-to-be Patrick Duffy is their age. Had this been made by a director like Gregory La Cava or Alexander Hall in the thirties, it would have been a charming piece of fluff. Churned out by Jonathan Sanger as a TV schedule filler, it's an underscripted misfire.

Rue McClanahan *Margret Becker* • Kristy McNichol *Mary Becker* • Patrick Duffy *John* • Michael Hix • Jack Coleman *Dennis Becker* ■ *Dir* Jonathan Sanger • *Scr* Bart Baker

Children of the Corn ★ 18
Horror 1984 · US · Colour · 93mins

Adapted from a short story in Stephen King's *Night Shift* anthology, this is a pretty lame horror yarn padded to feature length with tepid special effects and ludicrous dialogue. Travellers Peter Horton and Linda Hamilton narrowly avoid being sacrificed to the "Corn God" in a rural Nebraska community, held in a grip of pagan terror by a 12-year-old preacher. Once past the atmospheric opening sequence – kids slaughtering their parents in a café – it's downhill all the way for this tacky nightmare. ▣

Peter Horton *Dr Burt Stanton* • Linda Hamilton *Vicky Baxter* • John Franklin *Isaac* • Courtney Gains *Malachai* • RG Armstrong *Diehl* • Robby Kiger *Job* • Annemarie McEvoy *Sarah* • John Philbin *Amos* • Julie Maddalena *Rachel* ■ *Dir* Fritz Kiersch • *Scr* George Goldsmith, from the short story by Stephen King

Children of the Corn II: the Final Sacrifice ★★ 18
Horror 1993 · US · Colour · 89mins

Tabloid journalists gather in Gatlin, Nebraska, to unravel the cause of the original massacre just as "He who walks behind the Rows" returns to manipulate the community's children into murdering again. Director David F Price's modestly mounted but enjoyably efficient slice of breezy horror is a quantum leap over the first film in terms of acting quality, homicidal set pieces and effective shock tactics. The endless nosebleed is a highlight. ▣

Terence Knox *John Garrett* • Paul Scherrer *Danny Garrett* • Ryan Bollman *Micah Balding* • Christie Clark *Lacey Hellerstar* • Rosalind Allen *Angela Casual* ■ *Dir* David F Price • *Scr* Al Katz, Gilbert Adler, from the short story *Children of the Corn* by Stephen King

Children of the Corn III: Urban Harvest ★★★ 18
Horror 1995 · US · Colour · 88mins

A refugee from the original corn cult of killer kids devises a plan to take their doctrine of dread to Chicago before going global. The enterprising second sequel to the Stephen King-based tale of terror is easily the best of the series, because director James Hickox (brother of horror veteran Anthony) knows how to use his low budget without sacrificing credibility or top-notch scares. ▣

Ron Melendez *Joshua* • Jim Metzler *William Porter* • Daniel Cerny *Eli* • Nancy Grahn *Alice* • Michael Ensign *Father Frank* ■ *Dir* James DR Hickox • *Scr* Dode B Levenson, from the short story *Children of the Corn* by Stephen King

Children of the Corn IV: the Gathering ★
Horror 1996 · US · Colour · 85mins

The unaccountably successful horror franchise limps on in this predictable retread. The last instalment saw the action relocated to Chicago, but this third sequel is set back in the familiar rural surroundings, where the children of a small town have been laid low with a mysterious illness that appears to be linked to a long-buried evil from the cornfields. Karen Black, overacting hysterically, is the only familiar face, while the effects are nothing to write home about. For completists only.

Karen Black *June Rhodes* • Naomi Watts *Grace Rhodes* • Samaria Graham *Mary Anne* • Brent Jennings *Donald Atkins* • Jamie Renee Smith *Margaret* ■ *Dir* Greg Spence • *Scr* Greg Spence, Stephen Berger, from the short story *Children of the Corn* by Stephen King

Children of the Damned ★★
Science-fiction thriller
1964 · UK · BW · 80mins

"Beware the eyes that paralyse!" In this less-than-thrilling sequel to *Village of the Damned*, six children of assorted nationalities with deadly extra-sensory powers escape from their respective London embassies. The alien kids demonstrate their lethal gifts against the armed forces who are trying to destroy them in the name of world security. However, despite a literate script (based on John Wyndham's novel *The Midwich Cuckoos*) and thoughtful direction by Anton M Leader, the film has nowhere to go and quickly runs out of steam.

Ian Hendry *Colonel Tom Lewellin* • Alan Badel *Dr David Neville* • Barbara Ferris *Susan Eliot* • Alfred Burke *Colin Webster* • Sheila Allen *Diana Looran* • Clive Powell *Paul* ■ *Dir* Anton M Leader • *Scr* John Briley, from the novel *The Midwich Cuckoos* by John Wyndham

Children of the Dark ★★ PG
Drama based on a true story
1994 · US · Colour · 93mins

Michelle Pfeiffer's ex-husband, Michael J Fox's wife and the head of an English acting dynasty co-star in this "disease

U = SUITABLE FOR ALL   Uc = SUITABLE FOR ALL, ESPECIALLY FOR YOUNG CHILDREN (VIDEO ONLY)   PG = PARENTAL GUIDANCE

of the week'' TV movie. Peter Horton and Tracy Pollan are the parents of daughters who have a potentially fatal intolerance to sunlight, while Roy Dotrice is the doctor trying to treat them. The performances are earnest, but lack the human touch that helps us identify with the characters. 🎬

Peter Horton *Jim Harrison* • Tracy Pollan *Kim Harrison* • Roy Dotrice *Dr Burnam* • Natalija Nogulich *Stanya Janecek* • Eric Pierpoint *Dr Tanner* ■ *Dir* Michael Switzer • *Scr* Jeff Andrus, Charles Wilkinson, Janet Brownell

The Children of the Marshland ★★★★ PG

Period comedy drama
1998 · Fr · Colour · 115mins

Fans of such arthouse classics as *Jean de Florette* will warm to this gentle portrait of rural France in the early thirties. A sort of Gallic *Last of the Summer Wine*, Jean Becker's comedy disappointingly skirts around its darker themes. However, there's plenty of nostalgic pleasure to be had from the adventures of shell-shocked soldier Jacques Gamblin, disgruntled peasant Jacques Villeret, world-weary millionaire Michel Serrault and timid bachelor André Dussollier. Complete with a cameo from Eric Cantona, this may be lightweight and sentimental, but it's also undeniably cinematic. In French with English subtitles.

Jacques Villeret *Riton* • Jacques Gamblin *Garris* • André Dussollier *Amedée* • Michel Serrault *Pépé* • Isabelle Carré *Marie* • Eric Cantona *Jo Sardi* • Suzanne Flon *Old Cri Cri* • Jacques Dufilho *The old man* ■ *Dir* Jean Becker • *Scr* Sébastien Japrisot, from the novel *Les Enfants du Marais* by Georges Montforez

Children of the Revolution ★★★★

Political comedy drama
1996 · Ausl · Colour · 102mins

This classy black comedy from Australia boasts the combined talents of Judy Davis, Sam Neill, Rachel Griffiths and Geoffrey Rush. Joan (Davis) is a die-hard Stalinist living in forties Oz. After writing weekly letters to the great man, she ends up at the 1952 Party Congress and subsequently beds him. Their son (Richard Roxburgh) grows up to become a political agitator who brings the Australian government into a state of crisis. Director Peter Duncan deftly mixes newsreel footage, montage sequences and musical comedy, with hysterical results.

Judy Davis *Joan Fraser* • Sam Neill *Nine* • Richard Roxburgh *Joe* • Rachel Griffiths *Anna* • F Murray Abraham *Stalin* • Russell Kiefel *Barry* • John Gaden *Dr Wilf Wilke* • Geoffrey Rush *Zachary Welch* ■ *Dir/Scr* Peter Duncan

The Children of Theatre Street ★★★ U

Documentary
1977 · US/USSR · Colour · 92mins

It needed to be a special assignment to lure the former Grace Kelly out of cinematic retirement, and Robert Dornhelm and Earle Mack's fly-on-the-wall study of the Kirov Ballet School is exactly that. While recalling such great names of the past as Nijinsky, Pavlova, Nureyev and Baryshnikov, this Oscar-nominated documentary is also

keen to concentrate on the stars of tomorrow as it follows three aspiring students through their stringent training. The reverential enthusiasm of Princess Grace's narration should fire the imagination of younger viewers, especially those already hooked on ballet's romantic elegance. In English and Russian with subtitles.

Princess Grace of Monaco [Grace Kelly] *Narrator* ■ *Dir* Robert Dornhelm, Earle Mack • *Scr* Beth Gutcheon (uncredited)

The Children's Hour ★★★

Drama 1961 · US · BW · 108mins

Retitled *The Loudest Whisper* in the UK, this screen remake of a notorious Lillian Hellman play is emphatically not for youngsters. Director William Wyler had filmed it before as *These Three* back in 1936 and, despite being shorn of its overt lesbian theme, the earlier version has considerably more power than this rather quiet and bloodless drama. Perhaps a few years on from 1961 the lesbian elements could have been properly dealt with, but here their muting harms the movie and both Audrey Hepburn and Shirley MacLaine fail to convince. James Garner, though, is very impressive, particularly in his weeping scene: many actors could not have done as well.

Audrey Hepburn *Karen Wright* • Shirley MacLaine *Martha Dobie* • James Garner *Dr Joe Cardin* • Miriam Hopkins *Lily Mortar* • Fay Bainter *Amelia Tilford* • Karen Balkin *Mary Tilford* • Veronica Cartwright *Rosalie* ■ *Dir* William Wyler • *Scr* John Michael Hayes, from the play by Lillian Hellman

A Child's Cry for Help ★★

Medical thriller 1994 · US · Colour · 110 mins

Pam Dawber continues her bid to break from the squeaky-clean image she forged in four years of the hit sitcom *Mork and Mindy* with this made-for-TV medical mystery. Could she really be trying to kill her eight-year-old child? Doctor Veronica Hamel thinks she is. Even Michael Crichton (the brains behind *Coma* and TV's *ER*) would have trouble resuscitating this terminally tedious plot, but keep an eye out for *Murder One*'s Daniel Benzali among the medics.

Veronica Hamel *Dr Paula Spencer* • Pam Dawber *Monica Shaw* • Daniel Benzali *Dr Everett Morris* • Lisa Jakub *Amanda Spencer* ■ *Dir* Sandor Stern • *Scr* Jan Jaffe Kahn, Sandor Stern, from a story by Jan Jaffe Kahn

Child's Play ★★★ U

Satirical comedy 1954 · UK · BW · 68mins

In this energetic British-made film, which plays upon the fifties' anxiety regarding nuclear science, the son of a scientist working at an atomic research plant invents radioactive popcorn. Margaret Thompson directs this quaintly backward look at the nuclear age, while Mona Washbourne heads a cast of otherwise unfamiliar names. Don Sharp, who wrote the original story, had a prolific career as director, screenwriter and occasional producer.

Mona Washbourne *Miss Goslett* • Peter Martyn *PC Parker* • Dorothy Alison *Margery Chappell* • Ingeborg Wells *Lea Blotz* • Carl Jaffe *Carl Blotz* • Ballard Berkeley *Dr*

Nightingale • Joan Young *Mrs Chizzler* ■ *Dir* Margaret Thompson • *Scr* Peter Blackmore, from a story by Don Sharp

Child's Play ★★

Drama 1972 · US · Colour · 99mins

Melodramatic nonsense from Sidney Lumet, set in a Roman Catholic boarding school for boys, where hateful teacher James Mason is being victimised and discredited by fellow master Robert Preston. Despite having a mother dying of cancer and a stockpile of pornographic pin-ups, Mason becomes an almost heroic figure when set against the bluff and blustering Preston. The latter won his role after Marlon Brando turned it down; Brando got the best of the deal.

James Mason *Jerome Malley* • Robert Preston *Joseph Dobbs* • Beau Bridges *Paul Reis* • Ronald Weyand *Father Mozian* • Charles White *Father Griffin* • David Rounds *Father Penny* • Kate Harrington *Mrs Carter* • Jamie Alexander Sheppard ■ *Dir* Sidney Lumet • *Scr* Leon Prochnik, from the play by Robert Marasco

Child's Play ★★★ 15

Horror 1988 · US · Colour · 83mins

Six-year old Alex Vincent's must-have ''Good Guy'' doll, Chucky, is possessed by the soul of dead serial killer Brad Dourif and goes on a wisecracking murder spree to get revenge on the cop (Chris Sarandon) who put him away. A steady stream of standard scares is dragged from a thinly-stretched, formula slasher plot, thanks to panache beyond the call of duty from director Tom Holland. Novelty value and great special effects made this dummy run a big hit. 🎬

Catherine Hicks *Karen Barclay* • Chris Sarandon *Mike Norris* • Alex Vincent *Andy Barclay* • Brad Dourif *Charles Lee Ray* • Dinah Manoff *Maggie Peterson* • Tommy Swerdlow *Jack Santos* • Jack Colvin *Dr Ardmore* • Neil Giuntoli *Eddie Caputo* ■ *Dir* Tom Holland • *Scr* Don Mancini, Tom Holland, John Lafia, from a story by Don Mancini

Child's Play 2 ★★ 15

Horror 1990 · US · Colour · 80mins

Chucky, the living ''Good Guy'' doll, returns to continue stalking his former owner (Alex Vincent) and terrorise his new foster parents (Jenny Agutter and Gerrit Graham). Still nobody believes the kid's possessed Action Man story – until two seconds before they're brutally murdered, of course – resulting in a predictable, mean-spirited rehash of the original concept. A few neat touches lighten the load: Chucky burying his replacement in the garden with a seaside spade, for example, or a *Shining*-inspired climax set in an eerie toy factory. However, director John Lafia was never able to disguise the fact that his derivative valley of the dolls is beyond all hope. 🎬

Alex Vincent *Andy Barclay* • Jenny Agutter *Joanne Simpson* • Gerrit Graham *Phil Simpson* • Christine Elise *Kyle* • Brad Dourif *Chucky* • Grace Zabriskie *Grace Poole* ■ *Dir* John Lafia • *Scr* Don Mancini

Child's Play 3 ★ 18

Horror 1991 · US · Colour · 85mins

Brought back to life when the ''Good Guy'' doll assembly line is reactivated,

Chucky – the plastic Terminator – traces his former owner (Justin Whalin, taking over from moppet Alex Vincent) to military school and starts decimating the student body. The bottom-of-the-barrel, slice-and-dice nonsense that follows embellishes the first sequel's sadistic streak and has an okay finale set on a carnival ride in an amusement park. Director Jack Bender's useless entry in the series is now infamous for being cited in the tabloid frenzy surrounding the Jamie Bulger murder case in Britain.

Justin Whalin *Andy Barclay* • Perrey Reeves *DeSilva* • Jeremy Sylvers *Tyler* • Travis Fine *Shelton* • Dean Jacobson *Whitehurst* • Brad Dourif *Chucky* • Peter Haskell *Sullivan* ■ *Dir* Jack Bender • *Scr* Don Mancini

Chill Factor ★★ 15

Comedy action thriller
1999 · US · Colour · mins

Whatever happened to Cuba Gooding Jr? Just three years after winning an Oscar for *Jerry Maguire*, he turns up in this bad rip-off of *Speed*. Store clerk Tom (Skeet Ulrich) hijacks the truck of ice cream delivery driver Arlo (Gooding Jr) in order to transport a secret chemical weapon that will annihilate everything for miles around if its temperature rises above 50 degrees. The star is totally wasted in this routine chase thriller.

Cuba Gooding Jr *Arlo* • Skeet Ulrich *Tim Mason* • Peter Firth *Captain Andrew Brynner* • David Paymer *Doctor Richard Long* • Hudson Leick *Vaughn* ■ *Dir* Hugh Johnson • *Scr* Drew Gitlin, Mike Cheda

Chiller ★★★ 15

Horror 1985 · US · Colour · 87mins

In this better-than-average TV movie from *Scream* director Wes Craven, Michael Beck is thawed out after being cryogenically frozen for ten years. Alas, a machine malfunction during his hibernation causes him to lose his soul and start acting in strange ways as he climbs the corporate ladder. A slim idea is elaborately carried off by Craven, who keeps the suspense mounting and makes great use of first-class make-up effects. A fun excursion into atmospheric horror that deliberately pays homage to the genre classics of the fifties. 🎬

Michael Beck *Miles Creighton* • Beatrice Straight *Marion Creighton* • Paul Sorvino *Rev Penny* • Jill Schoelen *Stacey* • Dick O'Neill *Clarence Beeson* • Laura Johnson *Leigh* ■ *Dir* Wes Craven • *Scr* JD Feigelson

Chilly Scenes of Winter ★★★

Drama 1979 · US · Colour · 98mins

Originally released as *Head over Heels*, this was something of a disappointment after Joan Micklin Silver's earlier directorial efforts, including *Hester Street* and *Between the Lines*. As a take on modern American love, it has a ring of authenticity. In its keenness to avoid any kind of romantic cliché, however, the story ends up having too little heart, and we're left with John Heard's memories of an idyllic past and his increasingly irritating entreaties to Mary Beth Hurt to give it another try. Ultimately, you want the couple to sort out their troubles to give the film a solid conclusion. Look out for Gloria Grahame as Heard's emotionally unbalanced mother.

John Heard *Charles* • Mary Beth Hurt *Laura* • Peter Riegert *Sam* • Kenneth McMillan *Pete* • Gloria Grahame *Clara* • Nora Heflin *Betty* • Jerry Hardin *Patterson* • Tarah Nutter *Susan* • Griffin Dunne *Dr Mark* • Dir Joan Micklin Silver • Scr Joan Micklin Silver, from the novel *Head over Heels* by Ann Beattie

The Chiltern Hundreds

★★★ **U**

Comedy   1949 · UK · BW · 84mins

Although John Paddy Carstairs directed several Norman Wisdom vehicles, this wry political satire is his most accomplished picture. Adapted by William Douglas Home from his own play, the film takes its title from the nominal office MPs take when they wish to resign. Recalling the gentle class comedies produced by Ealing in this period, the election battle between an earl's socialist son (David Tomlinson) and his true blue butler (Cecil Parker) is full of sly observations. Alas, we see too little of AE Matthews, who also starred in Home's stage sequel, *The Manor of Northshead*. That play, however, was never filmed.

Cecil Parker *Benjamin Beecham* • AE Matthews *Lord Lister* • David Tomlinson *Tony, Viscount Pym* • Lana Morris *Bessie Sykes* • Marjorie Fielding *Lady Lister* • Joyce Carey *Lady Caroline* • Tom Macauley *Jack Cleghorn* ■ Dir John Paddy Carstairs • Scr William Douglas Home, Patrick Kirwan, from the play by William Douglas Home

Chimes at Midnight ★★★ **U**

Historical comedy drama
1966 · Swi/Sp · BW · 115mins

Drawing his material from five Shakespeare plays, as well as Raphael Holinshed's chronicles, writer/ producer/director Orson Welles focuses on Falstaff's relationship with Prince Hal, later Henry V (Keith Baxter), who eventually deserts his rambunctious friend and mentor for kingly responsibility. This is a typical Wellesian venture, years in the making owing to its maker's characteristic difficulties with funding. The result is a technically uneven film that alternately irritates and dazzles. The realistic battle scenes are spectacular and Welles gives a towering performance as Falstaff, while the starry cast includes John Gielgud as Henry IV, Norman Rodway as Hotspur and Jeanne Moreau as Doll Tearsheet.

Orson Welles *Falstaff* • Keith Baxter *Prince Hal, later King Henry V* • John Gielgud *Henry IV* • Margaret Rutherford *Mistress Quickly* • Jeanne Moreau *Doll Tearsheet* • Norman Rodway *Henry Percy, "Hotspur"* • Marina Vlady *Kate Percy* • Fernando Rey *Worcester* • Ralph Richardson *Narrator* ■ Dir Orson Welles • Scr Orson Welles, from *The Chronicles of England* by Raphael Holinshed, from the plays by William Shakespeare

China ★★

Second World War drama
1943 · US · BW · 78mins

An American trader, in China to make money, changes his priorities after the bombing of Pearl Harbor and joins a band of Chinese guerrillas. Directed by

John Farrow, an expert manipulator of emotions, and starring Alan Ladd as the grimly determined hero who manages to blow up the Japanese forces almost singlehandedly, this patriotic wartime flag-waver feels laughably dated now. Loretta Young is on hand to supply the obligatory whiff of romance, while the Oriental supporting cast includes Philip Ahn.

Loretta Young *Carolyn Grant* • Alan Ladd *Mr Jones* • William Bendix *Johnny Sparrow* • Philip Ahn *Lin Cho* • Iris Wong *Kwan Su* • Victor Sen Yung *Lin Wei* • Marianne Quon *Tan Ying* • Jessie Tai Sing *Student* ■ Dir John Farrow • Scr Frank Butler, from the play *Fourth Brother* by Archibald Forbes

China Clipper ★★ **U**

Drama   1936 · US · BW · 89mins

Former pilot Pat O'Brien sacrifices friends and marriage for an obsession to start a trans-Pacific airline, flying from America to China. Pan Am gets a big screen credit for assistance, with the picture clearly intended as an advert for them, and the script is by Frank "Spig" Wead, an aviation hero later played by John Wayne in *The Wings of Eagles*. The wonky flying scenes and dime-novel melodramas on the ground don't help, though, and O'Brien isn't a natural screen hero.

Pat O'Brien *Dave Logan* • Beverly Roberts *Jean Logan* • Ross Alexander *Tom Collins* • Humphrey Bogart *Hap Stuart* • Marie Wilson *Sunny Avery* • Henry B Walthall *Dad Brunn* ■ Dir Raymond Enright [Ray Enright] • Scr Frank Wead

China Corsair ★★ **U**

Adventure   1951 · US · BW · 67mins

A bargain basement adventure in which various shady characters are after priceless antiques on an island off the coast of China. Our hero is Jon Hall, who specialised in such Hollywood exotica as *South of Pago Pago*, though here he's without his customary loincloth. Lisa Ferraday is the pretty heroine engaged to rascally Ron Randell, who uses her to get the jewels. Hall and Ferraday were teamed together the following year in *Last Train from Bombay*; she also cropped up in *Rancho Notorious* and *Death of a Scoundrel* before fading from sight.

Jon Hall *McMillen* • Lisa Ferraday *Tamara* • Ron Randell *Paul Lowell* • Douglas Kennedy *Frenchie* • Ernest Borgnine *Hu Chang* • John Dehner *Pedro* • Marya Marco *Lotus* ■ Dir Ray Nazarro • Scr Harold R Greene

China Cry ★★★

Historical drama
1990 · Tai/US · Colour · 101mins

China's cultural upheaval in the fifties meant no culture and a great deal of repression. This devotedly earnest retelling of a true story shows how a privileged girl witnessed some of Chairman Mao's atrocities before she escaped to Hong Kong, moving from there to the United States, where she has now settled. Julia Nickson Soul portrays the girl as more than just a passive spectator, but the film remains too aloof from a nation's anguish for it to be anything more than just a harrowing tale that's moderately well-told. Contains violence.

Julia Nickson-Soul *Sung Neng Yee* • Russell Wong *Lam Cheng Shen* • James Shigeta *Dr Sung* • France Nuyen *Mrs Sung* • Philip Tan *Colonel Cheng* • Elizabeth Sung *Interrogator* • Bennett Ohta *Labour camp doctor* • Daphne Cheung *Chung Shing* ■ Dir James F Collier • Scr James F Collier, from the book by Nora Lam [Sung Neng Yee], Irene Burke

China Doll ★★

Second World War romance
1958 · US · BW · 99mins

This out-and-out tearjerker marked the return of director Frank Borzage, Hollywood's most dedicated sentimentalist, after ten years in the McCarthyite wilderness. Alas, this tale of an American air force officer in China who marries his housekeeper is so overlaid with sugary sentimentality that it felt dated even in the fifties. Worth a look, though, for fans of its male star, Victor Mature.

Victor Mature *Cliff Brandon* • Li Li Hua *Shu-Jen* • Ward Bond *Father Cairns* • Bob Mathias *Phil Gates* • Johnny Desmond *Steve Hill* • Elaine Curtis *Alice Nichols* ■ Dir Frank Borzage • Scr Kitty Buhler, from the story *China Doll* by James Benson Nablo, Thomas F Kelly and the story *Time Is a Memory* by Kitty Buhler

China Gate ★★★

War drama   1957 · US · BW · 90mins

American soldier Gene Barry hooks up with his estranged Eurasian wife Angie Dickinson, a political activist, to lead a guerila assault on a Chinese ammunition dump in French-controlled Vietnam. The marital war between the couple, caught in a love-hate relationship, parallels the battle against the Reds in this tough-minded movie, produced, written and directed by Samuel Fuller. Lee Van Cleef plays the communist leader, and Nat King Cole does a good job as a veteran GI. He also croons the title song.

Gene Barry *Brock* • Angie Dickinson *Lucky Legs* • Nat King Cole *Goldie* • Paul Dubov *Captain Caumont* • Lee Van Cleef *Major Cham* • George Givot *Corporal Pigalle* • Gerald Milton *Private Andreades* ■ Dir/Scr Samuel Fuller

China Girl ★★

Second World War drama
1942 · US · BW · 95mins

An American news cameraman (George Montgomery), in Mandalay just before the attack on Pearl Harbor and carrying secret military information, is pursued by two traitorous army personnel (Victor McLaglen, Lynn Bari) in the pay of the Japanese. His life is further complicated when he falls in love with a beautiful, American-educated Chinese girl (Gene Tierney). Director Henry Hathaway injects as much tension as possible into this Oriental melodrama, helped by some good action sequences. The story is by one Melville Crossman, better known as Darryl F Zanuck.

Gene Tierney *Miss Young* • George Montgomery *Johnny Williams* • Lynn Bari *Captain Fifi* • Victor McLaglen *Major Bull Weed* • Alan Baxter *Chinese boy* • Sig Ruman *Jarubi* • Myron McCormick *Shorty* • Bobby Blake [Robert Blake] *Chinese boy* ■ Dir Henry Hathaway • Scr Ben Hecht, from a story by Melville Crossman [Darryl F Zanuck]

China Girl ★★★ **18**

Romantic drama 1987 · US · Colour · 86mins

Not the Henry Hathaway-directed wartime flagwaver, but Abel Ferrara's stylised reworking of Romeo and Juliet. Even when he's misfiring, Ferrara can never be accused of being dull, and he makes superb use here of both Little Italy and Chinatown as Richard Penebianco and Sari Chang find love across the criminal codes. Only marginally less energetic than Baz Luhrmann's high-voltage version, the film echoes the key theme of *The Godfather*: that, in ignoring family tradition, the younger generation risks losing everything. ▭

Richard Panebianco *Tony* • Sari Chang *Tye* • James Russo *Alby* • David Caruso *Mercury* ■ Dir Abel Ferrara • Scr Nicholas St John

The China Lake Murders

★★★ **15**

Crime thriller   1990 · US · Colour · 85mins

Don't be put off by the bland title of what is, in fact, a well-made, suspenseful thriller. A city cop who vacations every year in the small desert town of China Lake becomes the chief suspect in a serial murder inquiry run by the town sheriff. It's essentially a taut battle of wills between the cop and the sheriff, and both the leads (Michael Parks, Tom Skerritt) bring much weight to their roles. TV movie specialist Alan Metzger maintains the tension. ▭

Tom Skerritt *Sheriff Sam Brodie* • Michael Parks *Officer Donnelly* • Nancy Everhard *Cindy* • Lauren Tewes *Kitty* • Bill McKinney *Captain Ferry* • Lonny Chapman *Wallace* ■ Dir Alan Metzger • Scr ND Schreiner, Robert Harmon

China Moon ★★★ **18**

Romantic thriller 1994 · US · Colour · 95mins

Fine acting and a truly surprising climactic revelation are the main virtues of this *film noir* from John Bailey, whose brilliant work as cinematographer includes *Cat People*, *Silverado*, *Mishima* and *As Good As It Gets*. As you would expect, the photography is none too shabby as detective Ed Harris and abused wife Madeleine Stowe succumb to Florida passions. Although we've seen this story many times before, there are enough original touches (Harris is much smarter than your average *film noir* sucker) and tasty performances to sustain interest. ▭

Ed Harris *Kyle Bodine* • Madeleine Stowe *Rachel Munro* • Charles Dance *Rupert Munro* • Patricia Healy *Adele* • Benicio Del Toro *Lamar Dickey* • Tim Powell *Fraker* ■ Dir John Bailey • Scr Roy Carlson

China 9, Liberty 37 ★★★

Spaghetti western 1978 · It · Colour · 98mins

While not on the same par as his cult westerns *Ride in the Whirlwind* and *The Shooting*, director Monte Hellman's unusual mix of Sergio Leone and Sam Peckinpah (who has a bit part) is very interesting indeed. Gunslinger Fabio Testi is released from jail on condition he shoots rancher Warren Oates, enabling corrupt railroad barons to seize his land, However, once he meets Oates and falls for his sexually frustrated wife (Jenny Agutter),

U = SUITABLE FOR ALL • **Uc** = SUITABLE FOR ALL, ESPECIALLY FOR YOUNG CHILDREN (VIDEO ONLY) • **PG** = PARENTAL GUIDANCE

he finds the task difficult to accomplish. Gritty, violent and erotic, with a great score by Pino Donaggio.

Warren Oates *Matthew* • Fabio Testi *Clayton* • Jenny Agutter *Catherine* • Sam Peckinpah *Wilbur Olsen* • Isabel Mestres *Barbara* ▪ *Dir* Monte Hellman • *Scr* Gerald F Harvey, Douglas Venturelli

China O'Brien ★★ 18

Martial arts action thriller
1988 · US · Colour · 85mins

The breakthrough role – well, for the video market at least – for martial arts star Cynthia Rothrock, who provides a welcome antidote to the macho heroics of Chuck Norris et al. Here she plays a police officer who turns in her badge when she reluctantly uses her martial arts skills to kill a villain in self-defence. However, when she returns to her home town, her lethal abilities are once again called into use. Contains violence and swearing. ▭

Cynthia Rothrock *China O'Brien* • Richard Norton *Matt* • Keith Cooke *Dakota* • Patrick Adamson *Lickner* • David Blackwell *Sheriff O'Brien* • Nijel *Jonsey* • Steven Kerby *Summers* • Robert Tiller *Owens* ▪ *Dir* Robert Clouse • *Scr* Robert Clouse, from the story by Sandra Weintraub

China Seas ★★★★

Romantic adventure 1935 · US · BW · 86mins

The plot's tosh, the setting preposterous and the crew rip-roaring in this expensive Irving G Thalberg MGM action melodrama. But who cares when the cast is solid gold? Clark Gable's the captain, sailing south to Singapore; Wallace Beery's a mutinous pirate; Rosalind Russell's the captain's aristocratic former mistress; and, best of all, Jean Harlow's the prerequisite blonde floozy and another of Gable's ex-lovers. Add Robert Benchley and C Aubrey Smith to the brew, and this boat's got a cast movie fans would die for. Spendidly directed by the under-rated Tay Garnett, this is a major treat.

Clark Gable *Captain Alan Gaskell* • Jean Harlow *China Doll "Dolly Portland"* • Wallace Beery *Jamesy MacArdle* • Lewis Stone *Tom Davids* • Rosalind Russell *Sybil Barclay* • Dudley Digges *Dawson* • C Aubrey Smith *Sir Guy Wilmerding* • Robert Benchley *Charlie McCaleb* ▪ *Dir* Tay Garnett • *Scr* Jules Furthman, James Kevin McGuinness, from the novel by Crosbie Garstin

China Sky ★★

Second World War drama
1945 · US · BW · 78mins

RKO planned this adaptation of a novel by the once popular Pearl S Buck as a major starring vehicle for Claudette Colbert. But she took one look at the script and turned it down, leaving Ruth Warrick, Randolph Scott and Ellen Drew to co-star in what is a rather mundane romantic melodrama. Scott and Warrick play dedicated American doctors in a remote Chinese village threatened by Japanese forces; Drew is Scott's self-centred, jealous viper of a wife, while Anthony Quinn is the local guerrilla leader. The movie remains enjoyable precisely because it consists of heavily signposted clichés.

Randolph Scott *Thompson* • Ruth Warrick *Sara* • Ellen Drew *Louise* • Anthony Quinn *Chen Ta* • Carol Thurston *Siu Mei* • Richard

Loo *Col Yasuda* • "Ducky" Louie *"Little Goat"* • Philip Ahn *Dr Kim* ▪ *Dir* Ray Enright • *Scr* Brenda Weisberg, Joseph Hoffmann, from the novel by Pearl S Buck

The China Syndrome ★★★★ PG

Drama 1979 · US · Colour · 116mins

A genuinely chilling "what if..." thriller in which savvy foreman Jack Lemmon just prevents an atomic meltdown at a nuclear power station. The government tries to hush it up, but TV newswoman Jane Fonda (in one of her best performances) and radical cameraman Michael Douglas (who also produced) probe for the truth in a solidly exciting movie still packed with political relevance. The cautionary conclusions were given a great deal of credence by life imitating art when the Three Mile Island near-tragedy occurred a few weeks after the movie opened. Note the complete lack of background music – Douglas felt music would trivialise the events. ▭ **DVD**

Jane Fonda *Kimberly Wells* • Jack Lemmon *Jack Godell* • Michael Douglas *Richard Adams* • Scott Brady *Herman De Young* • James Hampton *Bill Gibson* • Peter Donat *Don Jacovich* • Wilford Brimley *Ted Spindler* ▪ *Dir* James Bridges • *Scr* Mike Gray, TS Cook, James Bridges

Chinatown ★★★★★ 15

Thriller 1974 · US · Colour · 125mins

Here's Jack Nicholson in his best-ever performance as private eye Jake Gittes, who pokes his nose rather too deeply into the lives of Faye Dunaway and her father, John Huston, a corrupt Los Angeles tycoon. Writer Robert Towne planned a trilogy about LA, and this first part, set in the thirties, deals with the city's water supply and how that source of life leads to death and profit. The script – the best original work since *Citizen Kane* – is brilliantly organised, though the ending was changed when Roman Polanski arrived as director. (Towne's story never got to Chinatown; Polanski insisted the climax was set there.) The result was acrimony behind the scenes, genius on the screen and a masterpiece that repays any number of viewings. Contains violence and swearing. ▭

Jack Nicholson *JJ Gittes* • Faye Dunaway *Evelyn Mulwray* • John Huston *Noah Cross* • Perry Lopez *Escobar* • John Hillerman *Yelburton* • Darrell Zwerling *Hollis Mulwray* • Diane Ladd *Ida Sessions* • Roy Jenson *Mulvihill* • Roman Polanski *Man with knife* ▪ *Dir* Roman Polanski • *Scr* Robert Towne • *Cinematographer* John A Alonzo • *Music* Jerry Goldsmith • *Art Director* Richard Sylbert, W Stewart Campbell • *Editor* Sam O'Steen • *Costume Designer* Anthea Sylbert

Chinese Box ★★★★

Romantic drama
1997 · Jap/Fr/US · Colour · 109mins

The brilliant Wayne Wang directs Jeremy Irons and Gong Li in a drama based around Hong Kong's return to China in 1997. Irons is a disgruntled journalist who discovers he has six months to live. Does he return to Britain or remain in Hong Kong, where he's fallen for bar girl Vivian (Li in her first English-speaking role)? As New Years Eve approaches, there's a strange ambiguity about what the

future holds. The allegory is clear: Irons represents the dying colonial past, while Li's boss (Michael Hui) is the future. A fascinating film, full of minute nuances that are enlightening about the human condition. In English and Mandarin with subtitles.

Gong Li *Vivian* • Jeremy Irons *John* • Rubén Blades *Jim* • Maggie Cheung *Jean* • Michael Hui *Chang* ▪ *Dir* Wayne Wang • *Scr* Jean-Claude Carriere, Larry Gross, from a story by Paul Theroux, Wayne Wang, Jean-Claude Carrière

Chinese Boxes ★★★ 15

Crime thriller
1984 · W Ger/UK · Colour · 83mins

Will Patton (*No Way Out*, *The Postman*) plays an American in West Berlin who lands in a world of trouble when the daughter of a US diplomat winds up dead in his bathroom. Robbie Coltrane and Gottfried John, who would both turn up a decade later in Pierce Brosnan's 007 debut *GoldenEye*, are just two of the shady characters Patton encounters in a complex thriller from former *Time Out* critic Christopher Petit that owes a considerable debt to the work of Wim Wenders. ▭

Will Patton *Lang Marsh* • Gottfried John *Zwemmer* • Adelheid Arndt *Sarah* • Robbie Coltrane *Harwood* • Beate Jensen *Donna* • Susanne Meierhofer *Eva* • Jonathan Kinsler *Alan* ▪ *Dir* Christopher Petit • *Scr* LM Kit Carson, Christopher Petit

The Chinese Connection ★★

Thriller 1988 · Fr · Colour · 85mins

France's colonial past provides the background for this thriller, set in the oriental quarter of Paris. Robin Renucci teams up with Marguerite Tran, the orphan he rescued during the fall of Saigon in 1975, to investigate a series of murders he's convinced stem from a feud between Chinese and Vietnamese gangsters. Solidly rooted in its environment, yet short on surprises, this holds the attention without being truly memorable. French dialogue dubbed into English.

Robin Renucci *Matthew* • Marguerite Tran *Jay* • Michael Piccoli *Batz* • Denys Hawthorne *Jason* • Luong Ham Chau *Sang* • Antoine Dulery *Bastien* • Claude Faraldo *Rinaldi* • JC Quinn *Mayotte* • Don Henderson *Malcolm* ▪ *Dir* Denys Granier-Deferre • *Scr* Denys Granier-Deferre, Yves Stavrides

A Chinese Ghost Story ★★★★ 15

Martial arts horror
1987 · HK · Colour · 91mins

This marvellous example of the ghost genre popular in Hong Kong and most Asian areas is a real treat that combines excellent martial art sequences with lavish fantasy scenes and slapstick. (The merging of comedy and horror, a relative rarity in the west, has long been a staple of this market.) The story concerns a tax collector who falls in love with a ghost and is drawn into a battle for her soul. But the plot is secondary to the haunting visuals and set pieces that make it a classic of its type. In Cantonese with English subtitles.

Leslie Cheung *Ning Tsai-Shen* • Wang Zuxian *Nieh Hsiao-Tsing* • Wu Ma *Yen Che-Hsia* ▪ *Dir* Ching Siu-Tung • *Scr* Ruan Jizhi

A Chinese Ghost Story II ★★ 12

Martial arts horror
1990 · HK · Colour · 97mins

Leslie Cheung returns, this time as the scholar Ling, rather than the first film's tax collector Ning, in a bristling sequel that is more of a monster movie than its fantastical predecessor. The story sticks closely to the winning "haunted house" formula of the original, and among the many terrors our heroes confront are a rapidly defrosting zombie and a vicious centipede. There's the odd moment of quiet comedy, but the mysticism of the first film is much missed. In Cantonese with English subtitles. Contains some moderate violence.

Leslie Cheung *Ling Choi Sin* • Jacky Cheung *Chi Chau, "Autumn"* • Michelle Reis *Yuet Chi, "Moon"* • Joey Wong *Ching Fung, "Windy"* • Wu Ma *Yin Chek Hsia, swordsman* ▪ *Dir* Ching Siu-Tung • *Scr* Tai-Mok Lau, Kei-To Lam, Yiu-Ming Leung

Chinese Roulette ★★★ 15

Drama 1976 · W Ger · Colour · 82mins

Icy in its satire, this is a cruelly manipulative and boldly unrealistic dissection of bourgeois foibles. Alexander Allerson and Margit Carstensen are tricked by their disabled daughter, Andrea Schober, into spending a weekend in the country with their respective lovers. Inevitably, this world of cheap deceptions and stylised poses is shattered as psychic shots give way to lethal lead during the eponymous truth game. Rainer Werner Fassbinder uses a roaming camera and reflective surfaces to expose their coldheartedness; alas, his cynical detachment leaves us appalled but unmoved. In German with English subtitles. Contains some swearing and sex scenes. ▭

Margit Carstensen *Ariane* • Ulli Lommel *Kolbe* • Anna Karina *Irene* • Alexander Allerson *Gerhard* • Andrea Schober *Angela* • Macha Meril *Traunitz* • Brigitte Mira *Kast* ▪ *Dir/Scr* Rainer Werner Fassbinder • *Cinematographer* Michael Ballhaus

La Chinoise ★★★★

Experimental political drama
1967 · Fr · Colour · 95mins

Marking Jean-Luc Godard's passage from mainstream maverick to militant outsider, this diatribe on Maoism and the possibility of western revolution was also his first collaboration with Jean-Pierre Gorin, with whom he would work until 1972 within the Dziga Vertov co-operative. With the ever-engaging Jean-Pierre Léaud leading a discussion as naive as it's impassioned, the film was accused of trivialising socialism, particularly through Godard's use of agitprop slogans, calligraphic gimmicks and poster imagery. Beneath the surface superficiality and glib wit, however, this was a radical and prescient political statement that represented a determined break from the tyranny of screen narrative. In French with English subtitles.

Anne Wiazemsky *Véronique* • Jean-Pierre Léaud *Guillaume* • Michel Semeniako *Henri* • Lex de Bruijn *Kirilov* • Juliet Berto *Yvonne* ▪ *Dir/Scr* Jean-Luc Godard

Chisum ★★ PG

Western 1970 · US · Colour · 106mins

A John Wayne movie, handsomely photographed by western veteran William H Clothier, that uses a fictional variation on the Lincoln County cattle war to tell the tale of the man who first hired Billy the Kid. The Duke is well served by director Andrew V McLaglen (son of Victor), Forrest Tucker makes an imposing villain, and the Dominic Frontiere score is above average. But the plot rambles, despite a fine supporting cast of home-on-the-range hombres such as Ben Johnson, Bruce Cabot and Richard Jaeckel. Contains some coarse language. ▣

John Wayne *John Chisum* • Forrest Tucker *Lawrence Murphy* • Christopher George *Dan Nodeen* • Ben Johnson *James Pepper* • Glenn Corbett *Pat Garrett* • Bruce Cabot *Sheriff Brady* • Richard Jaeckel *Jess Evans* ■ *Dir* Andrew V McLaglen • *Scr* Andrew J Fenady

Chitty Chitty Bang Bang ★★★ U

Musical fantasy 1968 · UK · Colour · 136mins

Producer Albert R "Cubby" Broccoli gave this children's story from the pen of Bond author Ian Fleming the big-budget treatment, and it nearly worked. With the combined talents of the teams from *Mary Poppins* and the Bond movies, this musical about a flying Edwardian motorcar should have been a box-office blockbuster. The fact that it wasn't is a mystery, given the expertise on board: writers Roald Dahl and Richard Maibaum; designer Ken Adam; musical star Dick Van Dyke; and songs from the Sherman brothers, including the unforgettable title tune. At two-and-a-half hours, it's probably too long but, if you're looking for something entertaining for the under tens, look no further. ▣ **DVD**

Dick Van Dyke *Caractacus Potts* • Sally Ann Howes *Truly Scrumptious* • Lionel Jeffries *Grandpa Potts* • Gert Frobe *Baron Bomburst* • Anna Quayle *Baroness Bomburst* • Benny Hill *Toymaker* • James Robertson-Justice *Lord Scrumptious* ■ *Dir* Ken Hughes • *Scr* Roald Dahl, Richard Maibaum, Ken Hughes, from the novel by Ian Fleming

Chocolat ★★★★ PG

Drama 1988 · Fr · Colour · 99mins

Set in the Cameroons, *Chocolat* is both a highly intelligent political allegory and a sensitive study of adult interaction and emotion, seen through the eyes of a child. In her directorial debut, Claire Denis makes exceptional use of the parched landscape and the isolation of district governor François Cluzet's quarters to intensify the relationship between his young daughter and a black servant. In this environment, the arrival of a party of plane crash survivors seems an even more portentous intrusion. Isaach de Bankolé is supremely dignified as the misused houseboy, while Cécile Ducasse is impish and vulnerable as his devoted little friend. In French with English subtitles. ▣

Isaach de Bankole *Protée* • Giulia Boschi *Aimée* • François Cluzet *Marc* • Jean-Claude Adelin *Luc* • Laurent Arnal *Machinard* • Kenneth Cranham *Boothby* • Jacques Denis

Delpich • Cécile Ducasse *France as a child* • Mireille Perrier *France* ■ *Dir* Claire Denis • *Scr* Claire Denis, Jean-Pol Fargeau

The Chocolate War ★★★ 15

Drama 1988 · US · Colour · 99mins

Working with Robert Cormier's novel, actor Keith Gordon made a creditable debut as writer/director with this brooding study of peer pressure gone mad. As the new boy who refuses the tradition of selling chocolates to boost school funds, Ilan Mitchell-Smith gives a stubborn rather than stoic performance, better at standing up to tyrannical headmaster John Glover than he is at resisting the ruthlessly persuasive methods of the Vigils, a senior elite charged with upholding Catholic principles. The world of the Vigils is, in reality, a breeding ground for sadistic control freaks. Making its points without undue insistence, this is as polished as it's provocative. ▣

John Glover *Brother Leon* • Ilan Mitchell-Smith *Jerry* • Wallace Langham *Archie* • Doug Hutchison *Obie* • Adam Baldwin *Carter* • Brent Fraser *Emille* • Bud Cort *Brother Jacques* ■ *Dir* Keith Gordon • *Scr* Keith Gordon, from the novel by Robert Cormier

Choice of Arms ★★★★

Crime drama 1981 · Fr · Colour · 135mins

Having moved on from the thuggish persona that helped establish his credentials, Gérard Depardieu was reluctant to commit to Alain Corneau's *policier*. However, he gives an imposing performance as an escapee on the run who, along with Michel Galabru, seeks sanctuary on the stud farm of retired gangster Yves Montand. Although the action is often ferocious, Corneau was determined to deglamorise violence by emphasising its finality. Though uncompromisingly staged and bleak in both tone and theme, this is superbly acted and touchingly concluded. In French with English subtitles.

Yves Montand *Noel* • Gérard Depardieu *Mickey* • Catherine Deneuve *Nicole* • Michel Galabru *Bonnardot* • Gérard Lanvin *Sarlat* • Marc Chapiteau *Savin* • Pierre Forget *Serge* • Christian Marquand *Jean* ■ *Dir* Alain Corneau • *Scr* Alain Corneau, Michel Grisolia

Choices ★★ 15

Drama 1986 · US · Colour · 89mins

A retired judge discovers that his unwed teenage daughter and his second wife are both pregnant. Each must decide whether they should have an abortion. George C Scott (*Patton*) and Jacqueline Bisset (*The Deep*) are the husband and wife, while *Little House on the Prairie* star Melissa Gilbert leaves Laura Ingalls behind to play a character faced with an adult decision. Try as they may, however, this cast can't save this tepid piece. ▣

George C Scott *Evan Granger* • Jacqueline Bisset *Marisa Granger* • Melissa Gilbert *Terry Granger* • Merwan Mehta *Joshua Granger* ■ *Dir* David Lowell Rich • *Scr* Judith Parker

Choices of the Heart: the Margaret Sanger Story ★★★ 15

Biography 1995 · Can · Colour · 88mins

A well-told story that confronts issues still being battled today. In 1914 New York, Margaret Sanger, a nurse and mother of three, is shocked by the alarming number of deaths caused by self-induced abortions among the city's impoverished women. She begins a campaign to establish "the right of women to make a choice about maternity". In doing so, she comes up against the powerful, puritanical Anthony Comstock, a government censor who's determined to stop her at all costs. Dana Delany gives a convincing performance as Sanger, while Rod Steiger plays Comstock with threatening vigour. Contains sexual references and an abortion scene. ▣

Dana Delany *Margaret Sanger* • Rod Steiger *Comstock* • Henry Czerny *Bill Sanger* • Jason Priestley *Narrator* ■ *Dir* Paul Shapiro • *Scr* Matt Dorff

The Choirboys ★ 18

Black comedy drama 1977 · US · Colour · 119mins

Influenced by the bitter aftertaste and moral quagmire of Vietnam, this tough, confused cop movie shows an LAPD squad's on- and off-duty behaviour. Supposedly a raunchy comedy, it's directed by Robert Aldrich with all the subtlety of a rampaging rhino, and the result is an extensive catalogue of bigoted attitudes that dismally fails to amuse. Joseph Wambaugh, who wrote the book on which this is based, successfully took legal action to have his name removed from the credits. Contains swearing. ▣

Charles Durning *"Spermwhale" Whalen* • Louis Gossett Jr *Calvin Motts* • Perry King *Baxter Slate* • Clyde Kusatsu *Francis Tanaguchi* • Tim McIntire *Roscoe Rules* • Randy Quaid *Dean Proust* • Don Stroud *Sam Lyles* • James Woods *Harold Bloomguard* • Burt Young *Sergeant Dominic Scuzzi* • Robert Webber *Deputy Chief Riggs* ■ *Dir* Robert Aldrich • *Scr* Christopher Knopf, from the novel by Joseph Wambaugh (uncredited)

C.H.O.M.P.S. ★★ PG

Comedy 1979 · US · Colour · 86mins

Based on a story by Joseph Barbera (of Hanna-Barbera cartoon fame), this film falls between two stools. It's a bit gritty for younger children and too simplistic for the pre-teens, so its mix of crime and comedy won't find many takers. The title refers to the Canine Home Protection System designed in the shape of a robotic dog by inventor Wesley Eure in a bid to save Conrad Bain's security company. The slapstick has the feel you'd expect of the man who'd helped create Tom and Jerry, but it's nothing for that cartoon's guard dog, Spike, to worry about. Contains some swearing. ▣

Wesley Eure *Brian Foster* • Valerie Bertinelli *Casey Norton* • Conrad Bain *Ralph Norton* • Chuck McCann *Brooks* • Red Buttons *Bracken* • Larry Bishop *Ken Sharp* • Hermoine Baddeley *Mrs Flower* ■ *Dir* Don Chaffey • *Scr* Dick Robbins, Duane Poole, Joseph Barbera, from a story by Joseph Barbera

Choose Me ★★★★ 15

Romantic comedy drama 1984 · US · Colour · 102mins

A languid psychological mosaic from writer/director Alan Rudolph, whose films resemble a slowed-down version of his mentor, Robert Altman's. In the neon-lit bar that is the focal point of this romantic comedy drama, the main characters are the bar's owner (Lesley Ann Warren) and a radio agony aunt (Geneviève Bujold). Both offer sex, but are frustrated until newcomer Mickey (Keith Carradine) becomes the man in their lives. Alan Rudolph's work is an acquired taste; once acquired, though, it's addictive. ■ **DVD**

Geneviève Bujold *Dr Nancy Love* • Keith Carradine *Mickey* • Lesley Ann Warren *Eve* • Patrick Bauchau *Zack Antoine* • Rae Dawn Chong *Pearl Antoine* • John Larroquette *Billy Ace* ■ *Dir/Scr* Alan Rudolph

Chopper Chicks in Zombietown ★ 15

Horror 1990 · US · Colour · 85mins

At no-budget film empire Troma, the film's title is usually more important than the content. This is no exception. On paper it sounds suitably wacky: an all-girl biker gang ride into a small town and face their toughest test when they confront a population of zombies. However, the direction is inept, the script and performances are awful, and it scores pretty low in the all important bad taste stakes as well. ▣

Jamie Rose *Dede* • Catherine Carlen *Rox* • Kristina Loggia *Jojo* • Martha Quinn *Mae Clutter* • Don Calfa *Ralph Willum* • Lycia Naff *TC* ■ *Dir/Scr* Dan Hoskins

Chori Chori ★★★★ U

Comedy 1956 · Ind · BW · 122mins

Having been the mainstay of RK Films for eight years, the most popular romantic teaming in the history of Indian cinema parted company after this reworking of the Frank Capra classic *It Happened One Night*. Stepping into the Claudette Colbert role of the heiress who defies her father and elopes to marry a heel, Nargis is suitably haughty. But it's only when she meets up on the road with journalist Raj Kapoor (who is every bit as impishly masculine as Clark Gable) that the picture catches light. A treat for fans and a fascinating insight into remakes, Bollywood style. A Hindi language film. ▣

Nargis *Baby* • Raj Kapoor *Suman* • Master Bhagwan • Johnny Walker • Mukri ■ *Dir* Anant Thakur • *Scr* Aga Jani Kashmiri

A Chorus Line ★★★ PG

Musical 1985 · US · Colour · 117mins

The highly successful Broadway show was so relentlessly theatrical that it was generally considered impossible to film. Richard Attenborough had already succeeded with a similar work, *Oh! What a Lovely War*, but *A Chorus Line* resisted him. The strength of the show remains, but, by incorporating flashbacks and, crucially, substituting songs and choreography, the original is undermined, not enhanced. Nevertheless, there is much of merit, especially Alyson Reed, touching as key dancer Cassie, and ex-*Dallas*

U = SUITABLE FOR ALL Uc = SUITABLE FOR ALL, ESPECIALLY FOR YOUNG CHILDREN (VIDEO ONLY) PG = PARENTAL GUIDANCE

regular Audrey Landers, who does well by one of the great show stoppers. Noteworthy, too, is the contribution of British editor John Bloom, while Michael Douglas puts in a sharp performance as the show's producer. Contains some swearing. ▣

Michael Douglas *Zach* • Alyson Reed *Cassie* • Terrence Mann *Larry* • Michael Blevins *Mark* • Yamil Borges *Morales* • Vicki Frederick *Sheila* • Audrey Landers *Val* • Jan Gan Boyd *Connie* • Sharon Brown *Kim* • Gregg Burge *Richie* • Cameron English *Paul* • Nicole Fosse *Kristine* ■ *Dir* Richard Attenborough • *Scr* Arnold Schulman, from the musical by Michael Bennett, Nicholas Dante, James Kirkwood

A Chorus of Disapproval ★ PG

Comedy   1988 · UK · Colour · 95mins

If you want to remove the comedy, pithy insights, energy and spirit from the work of stage maestro Alan Ayckbourn, your first choice of director should be Michael Winner. The very idea of Winner employing his customary sledgehammer to Ayckbourn's subtle drama is surreal in the extreme. And, as expected, the director lumbers his way through a text from which odd moments of social satire escape untouched, but more by good luck than design. He even manages to draw unflattering performances from several British notables (including Richard Briers, Sylvia Syms and Jeremy Irons), though Anthony Hopkins brings some force to his role as an amateur theatre director. Contains swearing. ▣

Anthony Hopkins *Dafydd Ap Llewellyn* • Jeremy Irons *Guy Jones* • Richard Briers *Ted Washbrook* • Gareth Hunt *Ian Hubbard* • Patsy Kensit *Linda Washbrook* • Alexandra Pigg *Bridget Baines* • Prunella Scales *Hannah Ap Llewellyn* • Jenny Seagrove *Fay Hubbard* • Lionel Jeffries *Jarvis Huntley-Pike* • Sylvia Syms *Rebecca Huntley-Pike* ■ *Dir* Michael Winner • *Scr* Alan Ayckbourn, Michael Winner, from the play by Alan Ayckbourn

The Chosen ★★★ PG

Drama   1981 · US · Colour · 103mins

Mannered or magnificent? Rod Steiger's performance as a Hassidic rabbi dominates the film, for good or bad. His son (Robby Benson) is venturing out of his restrictively religious range by becoming friends with the son of a Zionist scholar (Maximilian Schell). Set in New York at the time of the founding of Palestine, director Jeremy Paul Kagan conjures the time's fervent atmosphere, but it's Steiger's risk-all exhibition you'll remember. ▣

Maximilian Schell *Professor David Malter* • Rod Steiger *Reb Saunders* • Robby Benson *Danny Saunders* • Barry Miller *Reuven Malter* ■ *Dir* Jeremy Paul Kagan • *Scr* Edwin Gordon, from the novel by Chaim Potok

Christ Stopped at Eboli ★★★★ PG

Drama   1979 · It/Fr/W Ger · Colour · 213mins

Francesco Rosi's adaptation of Carlo Levi's memoir divided critics between those who felt it sentimentalised his opposition to the fascist regime, and those who reckoned the director's almost neorealist use of everyday characters and the rural landscape helped the film capture the spirit of its source. Surprisingly, for such a literate work, Rosi doesn't delve too deeply into the causes of Italy's lurch to the right. Thanks to a monumental performance from Gian Maria Volonté, however, he does succeed in conveying both the writer's fears for his country and his unswerving faith in the decency of its population. In Italian with English subtitles. ▣

Gian Maria Volonté *Carlo Levi* • Paolo Bonacelli *Don Luigi Magalone* • Alain Cuny *Baron Rotundo* • Lea Massari *Luisa Levi* • Irene Papas *Giulia* • François Simon *Don Traiella* ■ *Dir* Francesco Rosi • *Scr* Francesco Rosi, Tonino Guerra, Raffaele La Capria, from the memoirs *Cristo Si é Fermato a Eboli* by Carlo Levi

The Christian Licorice Store ★★★

Drama   1971 · US · Colour · 84mins

Now here's a weird thing. When did you last see a movie about a tennis champion who sells out to commercialism that boasts an acting role for Jean Renoir, one of the world's greatest directors? Add to this appearances by cult director Monte Hellman (*Two-Lane Blacktop*) and silent star Gilbert Roland, and you have a feast for buffs and a very arty, wacky piece of seventies indulgence. The tennis player who "goes Hollywood" is played by Beau Bridges, while Bond girl Maud Adams is the photographer who covers his life story.

Beau Bridges *Franklin Cane* • Maud Adams *Cynthia Vicstrom* • Gilbert Roland *Jonathan Carruthers* • Allan Arbus *Monroe* • Anne Randall *Texas girl* • Monte Hellman *Joseph* • Jean Renoir ■ *Dir* James Frawley • *Scr* Floyd Mutrux

Christiane F ★★★★ 18

Drama   1981 · W Ger · Colour · 120mins

Sending moral campaigners scrambling for their soapboxes and critics reaching for superlatives, this graphic depiction of the miseries of drug addiction is strewn with powerful images and provocative insights. Based on a bestselling book written by two reporters from *Der Stern*, the film traces one 13-year-old girl's descent into heroin dependency and prostitution. Newcomers Natja Brunckhorst and Thomas Haustein give agonisingly authentic performances, but director Uli Edel occasionally over-indulges himself, notably at the David Bowie concert. Sketchy in its sociology, but undeniably powerful in its impact. In German with English subtitles. ▣

Natja Brunckhorst *Christiane F* • Thomas Haustein *Detlef* • Jens Kuphal *Axel* • Jan Georg Effler *Bernd* • Christiane Reichelt *Babsi* • Daniela Jaeger *Kessi* • Kerstin Richter *Stella* • David Bowie ■ *Dir* Ulrich Edel [Uli Edel] • *Scr* Herman Weigel, from a non-fiction book by Kai Hermann, Horst Rieck

Christine ★★★ 18

Horror   1983 · US · Colour · 105mins

Adapted from the novel by Stephen King, this killer car chiller is the ultimate in auto eroticism. The idea that a 1958 Plymouth Fury can turn into a jealous mistress is a cracker and, through his ingenious use of close-ups and seductive angles, director John Carpenter turns Christine into the sassiest thing on four wheels. He also gets a likeable performance out of Keith Gordon, the geek who becomes a dude the moment he inserts the key in the ignition. Contains violence and swearing. ▣ *DVD*

Keith Gordon *Arnie Cunningham* • John Stockwell *Dennis Guilder* • Alexandra Paul *Leigh Cabot* • Robert Prosky *Will Darnell* • Harry Dean Stanton *Rudolph Junkins* • Christine Belford *Regina Cunningham* ■ *Dir* John Carpenter • *Scr* Bill Phillips, from the novel by Stephen King

The Christmas Box ★★

Seasonal drama   1995 · US · Colour

American TV networks love to show that anybody can learn the real meaning of Christmas, and this sentimental morality tale is a typical seasonal offering. Richard Thomas and his family move in to help elderly Maureen O'Hara and, after a few hiccups, settle down for a simply spiffing Christmas. It's good to see O'Hara back on the screen, but this is far too sentimental.

Richard Thomas *Richard Evans* • Maureen O'Hara *Mary Parkin* • Annette O'Toole *Keri Evans* • Kelsey Mulrooney *Jenna Evans* • Robert Curtis-Brown *George* • Michael Ensign *Mr Hoover* ■ *Dir* Marcus Cole • *Scr* Greg Taylor, from a novel by Richard Paul Evans

A Christmas Carol ★★★ U

Seasonal drama   1938 · US · BW · 69mins

Few would dispute the fact that Alastair Sim is the finest screen Scrooge, but Lionel Barrymore would have given him a hard act to follow. Sadly, disability forced him to withdraw from this typically polished MGM version of Charles Dickens's yuletide favourite. Reginald Owen is a good substitute, however, impressing particularly during the visitations of Marley and the other Christmas ghosts. Gene Lockhart is a mite too jolly for Bob Cratchit, but Terry Kilburn plays Tiny Tim without the traditional lashings of pathos. The hauntings might send the very young scurrying behind the settee. ▣

Reginald Owen *Ebenezer Scrooge* • Gene Lockhart *Bob Cratchit* • Kathleen Lockhart *Mrs Cratchit* • Terry Kilburn *Tiny Tim* • Barry MacKay *Fred* • Lynne Carver *Bess* ■ *Dir* Edwin L Marin • *Scr* Hugo Butler, from the story by Charles Dickens

A Christmas Carol ★★★ U

Seasonal drama   1984 · US · Colour · 96mins

George C Scott is in towering form in this handsome adaptation of Dickens's Yuletide favourite. Rather than settling for easy reformation, Scott's Scrooge gives the ghosts as good as he gets and has to be dragged away from ideals forged during a difficult youth. Unfortunately, the members of a stellar supporting cast lack Scott's rigour and turn in sentimental caricatures that dishonour both source and star. ▣

George C Scott *Ebenezer Scrooge* • Nigel Davenport *Silas Scrooge* • Frank Finlay *Marley's Ghost* • Angela Pleasence *Ghost of Christmas Past* • Roger Rees *Fred Holywell* • David Warner *Bob Cratchit* • Edward Woodward *Ghost of Christmas Present* ■ *Dir* Clive Donner • *Scr* Roger O Hirson, from the story by Charles Dickens

A Christmas Carol ★★ U

Animation   1985 · Ausl · Colour · 67mins

If you want your children to enjoy the delights of Dickens's ever-popular Yuletide tale without having to deal with the nightmares inspired by the three ghosts of Christmas, this Australian animation is just the thing. One of several Dicken's adaptations undertaken by Warwick Gilbert in the mid-eighties, this may not be cartooning of Disney calibre. Like *The Pickwick Papers* and *The Old Curiosity Shop*, however, it makes the story accessible to younger viewers without patronising them. ▣

Anne Haddy ■ *Dir* Warwick Gilbert

Christmas Every Day ★

Fantasy drama   1996 · US · Colour

A seasonal TV spin on *Groundhog Day*, but this fantasy drama isn't a patch on the brilliant Bill Murray comedy. Erik Von Detten plays the unhappy youngster whose Christmas wish comes true, but the result is a sickly concoction, lacking fun, charm and genuine warmth. Watching the lad improve at basketball, save his family's store and give toys to the needy provides a shallow festive experience. To be honest, once a year is more than enough for most.

Robert Hays *Henry Jackson* • Erik Von Detten *Billy Jackson* • Bess Armstrong *Molly Jackson* • Yvonne Zima *Sarah Jackson* • Robert Curtis-Brown *Uncle David* • Robin Riker *Aunt Carolyn* • Julia Whelan *Jacey Jackson* ■ *Dir* Larry Peerce • *Scr* Stephen Alix, Nancey Silvers, from a story by Stephen Alix

Christmas Holiday ★★★

Film noir   1944 · US · BW · 92mins

With that frothy title and a cast teaming Gene Kelly and Deanna Durbin, you could well expect a musical. However, apart from Deanna warbling (beautifully) *Spring Will Be a Little Late This Year*, this melodrama treads on the wilder shores of *film noir* in the hands of expert director Robert Siodmak and screenwriter Herman J Mankiewicz. A miscast Kelly never really convinces as a returned murderer, but Durbin is excellent in her only non-frivolous role. Gladys George (as a madam) and Gale Sondergaard (as a possessive mum) add to the film's overall mood of depravity.

Deanna Durbin *Jackie Lamont/Abigail Martin* • Gene Kelly *Robert Manette* • Richard Whorf *Simon Fenimore* • Dean Harens *Charles Mason* • Gladys George *Valerie de Merode* • Gale Sondergaard *Mrs Manette* • David Bruce *Gerald Tyler* ■ *Dir* Robert Siodmak • *Scr* Herman J Mankiewicz, from a story by W Somerset Maugham

Christmas in Connecticut ★★★

Comedy   1945 · US · BW · 101mins

A corny little piece, but enjoyable nonetheless. Barbara Stanwyck almost convinces as the oh-so-chic journalist whose column extols the virtues of home cooking and country living. As a promotional stunt, she is forced to look after a navy hero (Dennis Morgan) for Christmas – except, of course, she lives in the city, can't cook and has to rent a cottage in Connecticut. The idea

is sound enough, but it becomes awfully sentimental under Peter Godfrey's uninspired direction. Still, Sydney Greenstreet is splendid as Stanwyck's boss, and, although lacking in true wit, it's a good deal better than the 1992 TV remake.

Barbara Stanwyck *Elizabeth Lane* • Dennis Morgan *Jefferson Jones* • Sydney Greenstreet *Alexander Yardley* • Reginald Gardiner *John Sloan* • SZ Sakall *Felix Bassenak* • Robert Shayne *Dudley Beecham* • Una O'Connor *Norah* • Frank Jenks *Sinkewicz* • Joyce Compton *Mary Lee* ■ *Dir* Peter Godfrey • *Scr* Lionel Houser, Adele Commandini, from the story by Aileen Hamilton

Christmas in Connecticut
★★ U

Comedy   1992 · US · Colour · 89mins

Arnold Schwarzenegger opted for an unusual change of pace for his directorial debut, a remake of a sugary old Christmas favourite from 1945. Sadly, it needs some of the firepower that Schwarzenegger brings to his blockbuster action movies, for this is routine fare, updated with too little imagination for the nineties. Dyan Cannon, in the Barbara Stanwyck role, is entertaining and believable as the TV presenter who decides to take heroic ranger Kris Kristofferson into her home for Christmas as a publicity stunt, but Schwarzenegger has upped the saccharine content of the tale to unacceptable levels. Tony Curtis and Richard Roundtree work hard to make this digestible.

Dyan Cannon *Elizabeth Blane* • Kris Kristofferson *Jefferson Jones* • Tony Curtis *Alex Yardley* • Richard Roundtree *Mr Prescott* • Kelly Cinnante *Josie* • Gene Lythgow *Tyler* • Jimmy Workman *Kevin* ■ *Dir* Arnold Schwarzenegger • *Scr* Janet Brownell, from the 1945 film

Christmas in July
★★★ U

Comedy   1940 · US · BW · 67mins

Dick Powell stars as a young clerk who, mistakenly believing he's won $25,000 in a slogan-writing competition, goes on a manic spending spree. The second film from the uniquely inventive Preston Sturges is not in the same class as his first, *The Great McGinty*, or such subsequent classics as *The Lady Eve* and *Sullivan's Travels*. But it's beautifully played and peppered with brilliantly observed comedy cameos from a memorable supporting cast. A humane, funny and romantic romp.

Dick Powell *Jimmy MacDonald* • Ellen Drew *Betty Casey* • Raymond Walburn *Mr Maxford* • Alexander Carr *Mr Schindel* • William Demarest *Mr Bildocker* • Ernest Truex *Mr Baxter* • Franklin Pangborn *Announcer* ■ *Dir/ Scr* Preston Sturges

Christmas on Division Street
★★★ PG

Drama   1991 · US · Colour · 93mins

The Wonder Years star Fred Savage is the rich kid who gets to see the poorer side of life after he is befriended by vagrant Hume Cronyn in this well-played and well-meaning drama. Despite being intended as family entertainment, this tale does not soften the grim reality of life without hope as much as you'd expect. It is,

therefore, worth taking note that the underlying theme may be a bit too heavy for Savage's younger fans. ▭

Hume Cronyn *Cleveland Merriweather* • Fred Savage *Trevor Atwood* • Badja Djola *Scorpio* • Jim Byrnes *Benedetti* ■ *Dir* George Kaczender • *Scr* Barry Morrow

Christmas Present
★★★

Black comedy   1986 · It · Colour · 101mins

Italian director Pupi Avati is best known outside Italy for his observant, offbeat comedy *The Story of Boys and Girls*. However, there's a darker side to this decidedly non-festive offering. As the inveterate gambler who is lured into a card-playing Christmas by four people he considers to be his friends, Carlo Delle Piane gives a performance as subtle as a sharp's bluff. It's almost like watching a subtitled David Mamet play as the group round the table begin playing on each other's fears, while trying to hide their own weaknesses. An intriguing antidote to all that yuletide feel-good fare. In Italian with English subtitles.

Carlo Delle Piane *Santelia* • Diego Abatantuono *Franco* • Gianni Cavina *Ugo* • Alessandro Haber *Lele* • George Eastman *Stefano* ■ *Dir/Scr* Pupi Avati

A Christmas Romance ★★ U

Romantic drama
1994 · US/Can · Colour · 91mins

An unashamedly schmaltzy modern spin on the Scrooge theme starring the eternally squeaky clean Olivia Newton-John. She plays a struggling single mother who receives a most unwelcome Christmas present: an eviction notice delivered personally by hard-hearted bank executive Gregory Harrison. However, he's trapped by a sudden snowstorm and gradually unfrozen by Newton-John and her young daughters. It's heart-warming stuff, even if director Sheldon Larry puts in too much sugar. ▭

Olivia Newton-John *Julia Stonecypher* • Gregory Harrison *Brian Harding* • Chloe Lattanzi *Deenie Stonecypher* • Stephanie Sawyer *Emily Rose Stonecypher* ■ *Dir* Sheldon Larry • *Scr* Darrah Cloud, from the novel by Maggie Davis

The Christmas Stallion ★★

Drama   1992 · UK/US · Colour

Just how many Victorian children's stories are there that centre on poor little orphans who are forced to abandon everything they hold dear to go and live with grasping, uncaring relatives? This family TV film attempts to bring the formula up to date, by having teenager Sian Maclean face the prospect of losing her beloved stallion after her grandfather's farm is inherited by her ne'er-do-well uncle (Daniel J Travanti). Travanti gives it everything he's got, but, apart from nice shots of the horse in full gallop, there are no Christmas surprises here.

Daniel J Travanti *Alan Davies* • Lynette Davies *Nerys Jones* • Sian Maclean *Gwen Davies* • Patrick Loomer *Cliff* • Meredith Edwards *Sam* • Dafydd Hywel *Christopher Howard* ■ *Dir* Peter Edwards • *Scr* Paul Matthews

The Christmas Star ★★★ PG

Drama   1986 · US · Colour · 89mins

Written and directed by Alan Shapiro, this TV movie has Disney written all over it. Ed Asner stars as a prisoner on the run who disguises himself as Santa to recover the loot he has stashed in a department store. Guess what happens when he is spotted by a couple of quaintly chirpy kids? While youngsters can lose themselves in the "why can't it happen to me?" story, grown-ups can enjoy the performances of the supporting cast, including Fred Gwynne (Herman Munster himself) and the brassy Susan Tyrrell. ▭

Edward Asner [Ed Asner] *Horace McNickle* • René Auberjonois *Sumner* • Jim Metzler *Stuart Jameson* • Susan Tyrrell *Sara Jameson* • Karen Landry *Clara* • Alan North *Captain Whittaker* • Philip Bruns *Lucky* ■ *Dir* Alan Shapiro • *Scr* Alan Shapiro, from a story by Alan Shapiro, Jeffrey White, Carol Dysinger

A Christmas Story ★★★★ PG

Drama   1983 · US · Colour · 89mins

A much under-rated look at what it's like to be an avaricious child with Christmas approaching, this witty, insightful, hugely enjoyable movie is riven with glorious home truths and a merciful lack of saccharin surrounding a topic that generally reduces directors to lachrymose morons. Even more surprising is that it comes from Bob Clark, director of the smutty teen comedy *Porky's*. Peter Billingsley plays Ralphie, and his quest for juvenile justice and a Red Ryder BB gun is an enormous joy. ▭

Melinda Dillon *Mother* • Darren McGavin *Old Man* • Peter Billingsley *Ralphie* • Ian Petrella *Randy* • Scott Schwartz *Flick* • RD Robb *Schwartz* • Tedde Moore *Miss Shields* ■ *Dir* Bob Clark • *Scr* Jean Shepherd, Leigh Brown, Bob Clark, from the novel *In God We Trust, All Others Pay Cash* by Jean Shepherd

The Christmas Tree ★★ U

Drama   1969 · Fr/It · Colour · 107mins

This coy yuletide fare marks an unlikely departure for Terence Young, who directed three of the first four James Bond adventures. Young also scripted this heartfelt tale about a father's determination to make his son's last days as enjoyable as possible. Stricken with leukemia after a radioactive air accident, Brook Fuller is presented with gifts as different as a tractor and wolves stolen from a zoo, as William Holden and his old army pal Bourvil pander to his every whim. Nicely photographed by Henri Alekan, but Georges Auric's score only reinforces the gushing sentimentality which pervades the whole film.

William Holden (1) *Laurent* • Virna Lisi *Catherine* • Bourvil *Verdun* • Brook Fuller *Pascal* • Madeleine Damien *Marinette* • Friedrich Ledebur *Vernet* ■ *Dir/Scr* Terence Young

Christopher Columbus ★ U

Historical biography
1949 · UK · Colour · 105mins

If you thought Gérard Depardieu missed the mark in Ridley Scott's *1492: Conquest of Paradise*, wait till you set eyes on this turkey. Fredric March looks noble and the forties Technicolor is fabulous. Alas, the pace

is nonexistent and the action resembles little more than a series of wax tableaux sporting familiar faces. The scenes at the Spanish court are hysterically funny, though of course they're not meant to be; from then on, it's strictly dullsville. Needless to add, this joint Gainsborough/Rank production failed miserably in its attempt to crash the US market.

Fredric March *Christopher Columbus* • Florence Eldridge *Queen Isabella* • Francis L Sullivan *Francisco de Bobadilla* • Kathleen Ryan *Beatriz* • Derek Bond *Diego de Arana* • Nora Swinburne *Juana de Torres* • Abraham Sofaer *Luis de Santangel* • Linden Travers *Beatriz de Peraza* ■ *Dir* David MacDonald • *Scr* Sydney Box, Muriel Box, Cyril Roberts

Christopher Columbus: the Discovery
★★ PG

Historical adventure
1992 · US · Colour · 115mins

Not so much a milestone to mark the 500th anniversary of the discovery of America as a millstone round the neck of nearly everyone connected with it. George Corraface, as Columbus, bores for Spain and Rachel Ward's accent as Queen Isabella is almost as bizarre as Tom Selleck's wig. Marlon Brando, who as Torquemada resembles a tethered balloon, puts us on the rack of embarrassment for the waste of his talent. John Glen directs. Contains violence and brief nudity. ▭

George Corraface [Georges Corraface] *Christopher Columbus* • Marlon Brando *Torquemada* • Tom Selleck *King Ferdinand* • Rachel Ward *Queen Isabella* • Robert Davi *Martin Pinzon* • Catherine Zeta-Jones *Beatriz* • Oliver Cotton *Harana* • Benicio Del Toro *Alvaro* • Mathieu Carrière *King John* ■ *Dir* John Glen • *Scr* John Briley, Cary Bates, Mario Puzo, from a story by Mario Puzo

Christopher Strong ★★★

Romantic melodrama
1933 · US · BW · 77mins

Katharine Hepburn's sturdy performance and an abundance of intriguing ideas go some way to compensate for Dorothy Arzner's uneven direction of this romantic drama. Extremely advanced for its years, the film examines female independence and society's demands on women through the story of gutsy flier Hepburn and her affair with a married politician. In those days flying was almost exclusively a male domain, as was Hollywood itself, so this was a daring film for the time.

Katharine Hepburn *Lady Cynthia Darrington* • Colin Clive *Christopher Strong* • Billie Burke *Elaine Strong* • Helen Chandler *Monica Strong* ■ *Dir* Dorothy Arzner • *Scr* Zoe Akins, from the novel by Gilbert Frankau

Chronicle of a Death Foretold
★★★★ 15

Drama   1987 · It/Fr · Colour · 105mins

Sumptuously photographed by Pasqualino De Santis, this is a mesmerising (if occasionally sluggish) adaptation of Gabriel Garcia Marquez's novel of family honour, revenge and murder in a small Colombian town. Managing to create tension within a foregone conclusion, director Francesco Rosi deftly intercuts between flashbacks and

reminiscences, as doctor Gian Maria Volonté attempts to uncover the facts behind a 20-year-old crime. While Rupert Everett is overly languid as the wealthy suitor who abandons deflowered bride Ornella Muti, the other members of the cast provide the ring of authenticity you'd expect from Italy's finest latter-day realist. In Spanish with English subtitles. ▭

Rupert Everett *Bayardo San Roman* • Ornella Muti *Angela Vicario* • Gian Maria Volonté *Cristo Bedoia* • Irene Papas *Angela's mother* ■ *Dir* Francesco Rosi • *Scr* Francesco Rosi, Tonino Guerra, from the novel by Gabriel Garcia Marquez

Chronicle of a Love ★★★ PG
Drama   1950 · It · BW · 97mins

Departing from the neorealism of his postwar documentaries, Michelangelo Antonioni made his feature debut with this atypically conventional tale of suspicion and snobbery, adultery and guilt. Clearly, though, he is already employing those trademark long takes and making symbolic use of the physical environment to explore the recurrent themes of urban alienation, social displacement and the impermanence of relationships. Yet this reliance on inanimates for psychological revelation somewhat devalues the contribution of the cast, with Lucia Bosé only occasionally allowed the luxury of emotion as she and rekindled flame Massimo Girotti contemplate the murder of her tycoon husband. An Italian language film. ▭

Lucia Bosé *Paola* • Massimo Girotti *Guido* • Ferdinando Sarmi *Fontana* • Gino Rossi *Carloni* • Marika Rowsky *Joy* • Rosi Mirafiore *Barmaid* • Rubi d'Alma ■ *Dir* Michelangelo Antonioni • *Scr* Michelangelo Antonioni, Danièle D'Anza, Silvio Giovaninetti, Francesco Maselli, Piero Tellini

Chronicle of Anna Magdalena Bach   ★★★★
Experimental biographical drama
1968 · W Ger/It · BW · 93mins

Avant-garde director Jean-Marie Straub's second feature views the life and times of Johann Sebastian Bach – his conflicts with his patrons, his work as a composer, his relationships with his family – through the eyes of his second wife. Convincing in both its historical accuracy and musical authenticity (most of the roles are taken by professional musicians), this is an almost documentary account of instrumentalists at work during the 18th century, with Gustav Leonhardt playing Bach in both senses of the word. The chronicle is interspersed with concerts and landscape scenes, while the use of direct sound and long takes helps the images to supplement, rather than distract from the music. In German with English subtitles. ▭

Gustav Leonhardt *Johann Sebastian Bach* • Christiane Lang *Anna Magdalena Bach* • Paolo Carlini *Hölzel* • Ernst Castelli *Steger* • Hans-Peter Boye *Born* • Joachim Wolf *Rector* ■ *Dir* Jean-Marie Straub • *Scr* Jean-Marie Straub, Danièle Huillet • *Cinematographer* Ugo Piccone

Chronicle of the Burning Years   ★★★★
Political drama   1975 · Alg · Colour · 177mins

Throughout the period covered in this epic account of Algerian history (1939-54), the indigenous film industry was dominated by so-called "cinema mudjahad", or "freedom fighter cinema". It's ironic, therefore, that Mohammed Lakhdar-Hamina's Palme d'Or-winning film should belong to the tradition that succeeded it: "cinema djidid", or "new cinema". Couching a family drama in terms of a Hollywood melodrama and employing a diversity of symbolic character types, the film shows how the attempt to suppress cultural as well as political aspirations resulted in the politicisation of ordinary people and the FLN revolt against the colonial government. Imposing, but slightly impersonal. An Arabic language film.

Yorgo Voyagis *Achmed* • Mohammed Lakhdar-Hamina *Milhoud* • Cheik Nourredine *Friend* ■ *Dir* Mohammed Lakhdar-Hamina • *Scr* Mohammed Lakhdar-Hamina, Rachid Boujedra

Chu Chin Chow   ★★★ U
Musical fantasy   1934 · UK · BW · 103mins

This legendary and massively popular British stage musical by Oscar Asche, replete with its unimaginative Frederick Norton score, finally reached the screen with all its faults revealed. Nevertheless, George Robey's performance as Ali Baba is forever enshrined here, and there's some interesting period casting, with Anna May Wong as Zahrat the slave girl and villain Fritz Kortner as boss of the 40 thieves. The uninspired choreography is by ballet great Anton Dolin. This was part of a fashionable fixation during the thirties with all things Chinese, and invariably sinister and inscrutable characters seemed to populate British cinema at the time.

George Robey *Ali Baba* • Fritz Kortner *Abu Hassan* • Anna May Wong *Zahrat* • John Garrick *Nur-al-din* • Pearl Argyle *Marjanah* • Dennis Hoey *Rakham* ■ *Dir* Walter Forde • *Scr* Sidney Gilliat, L DuGarde Peach, Edward Knoblock, from the musical by Oscar Asche, Frederic Norton

Chu Chu and the Philly Flash
Romantic comedy   ★
1981 · US · Colour · 100mins

Silly title, silly film. Wonderful American comedian Carol Burnett proved she could cut it on the big screen in Robert Altman's *A Wedding* and has appeared in a number of interesting projects. Alas, *Chu Chu and the Philly Flash* marks a career low for both her and co-star Alan Arkin. The story concerns Flash (Arkin), a former baseball player now dabbling in petty crime who finds a briefcase containing stolen documents. When he tries to return the briefcase for a substantial reward, he gets involved in a number of far from comic situations.

Alan Arkin *Flash* • Carol Burnett *Emily* • Jack Warden *Commander* • Danny Aiello *Johnson* • Adam Arkin *Charlie* • Danny Glover *Morgan* • Sid Haig *Vince* ■ *Dir* David Lowell Rich • *Scr* Barbara Dana, from a story by Henry Barrow

Chubasco   ★★
Drama   1968 · US · Colour · 99mins

Produced by William Conrad, better known as TV detective Frank Cannon, this is an occasionally interesting melodrama based around the California fishing industry. Christopher Jones (*Ryan's Daughter*) and Susan Strasberg, who were married in real-life at the time, play lovers whose relationship is threatened by her father (Richard Egan). Hollywood legend Ann Sothern also appears.

Richard Egan *Sebastian* • Christopher Jones *Chubasco* • Susan Strasberg *Bunny* • Ann Sothern *Angela* • Simon Oakland *Laurindo* • Audrey Totter *Theresa* • Preston Foster *Nick* • Peter Whitney *Matt* ■ *Dir* Allen H Miner

Chubby Down Under and Other Sticky Regions ★★ 18
Comedy   1998 · UK · Colour · 81mins

Roy "Chubby" Brown made his name as a blue comic, but is known to millions not through TV – he's far too rude and politically incorrect for that – but through his best-selling videos. This is actually his second theatrical release: unlike the sci-fi romp *UFO*, however, this is essentially a big-budget version of his stage show. Most of the running time is devoted to his routines, filmed before adoring audiences in both Australia and Hong Kong. Guaranteed to offend virtually everybody, there are no half measures with Brown's brand of filthy humour. Contains swearing, coarse language and sexual references. ▭

Roy "Chubby" Brown ■ *Dir* Tom Poole • *Scr* Roy "Chubby" Brown

CHUD   ★ 18
Horror   1984 · US · Colour · 83mins

Thanks to toxic waste dumped in the Manhattan sewage system, tramps and derelicts have mutated into "Cannibalistic Humanoid Underground Dwellers". That's according to this lamentable urban horror movie, which is neither gory nor exciting enough to merit much attention. A photographer, the head of a soup kitchen and a police captain whose wife has fallen prey to the zombies join forces to get to the bottom of the cover-up. Ridiculous monsters, unappealing main characters and an inevitable twist ending only add insult to injury in this crass exploiter. ▭

John Heard *George Cooper* • Kim Greist *Lauren Daniels* • Daniel Stern *The Reverend* • Christopher Curry *Captain Bosch* • George Martin *Wilson* • John Ramsey *Commissioner* ■ *Dir* Douglas Cheek • *Scr* Parnell Hall

CHUD II: Bud the Chud   ★ 15
Horror comedy   1989 · US · Colour · 84mins

Sequel in name only to the 1984 turkey, which sees a bunch of teenagers steal a corpse from a government research facility, only for it to turn cannibalistic and run amok in a small town during Halloween. One look at the script, no doubt, prompted director David Irving to play this for broad laughs, but nobody saw the joke. A star-heavy supporting cast has fun with the zombie make-up, but it's only the odd gratuitous death that

keeps you from nodding off completely. ▭

Brian Robbins *Steve* • Bill Calvert *Kevin* • Tricia Leigh Fisher *Katie* • Gerrit Graham *Bud the Chud* • Robert Vaughn *Masters* ■ *Dir* David Irving • *Scr* M Kane Jeeves [Ed Naha]

Chuka   ★★
Western   1967 · US · Colour · 105mins

John Mills has left the employ of Queen Victoria's Fifth Lancers and now commands a fort besieged by excited Arapaho Indians. Inside the stockade are a number of thugs, among them Chuka (Rod Taylor), a gunfighter who used to be friendly with the Indians and is now even more friendly with Luciana Paluzzi. There is also surly scout James Whitmore, German sergeant Ernest Borgnine and the usual assortment of drunks, cowards and racists. Things pick up a bit when the Injuns arrive.

Rod Taylor *Chuka* • Ernest Borgnine *Sergeant Otto Hansbach* • John Mills *Colonel Stuart Valois* • Luciana Paluzzi *Veronica Kleitz* • James Whitmore *Trent* • Angela Dorian [Victoria Vetri] *Helena Chavez* • Louis Hayward *Major Benson* ■ *Dir* Gordon Douglas • *Scr* Richard Jessup, from a novel by Richard Jessup

A Chump at Oxford   ★★★ U
Comedy   1940 · US · BW · 62mins

Rewarded for foiling a bank robbery, Laurel and Hardy find themselves among the "dreaming spires" in this agreeable comedy. While the film reunites the boys with fabled producer Hal Roach, it also saddles them with third-rate director Alfred Goulding, who allows this loose collection of gags to ramble. Beside such stale situations as settling into the dean's lodgings, there are some classic moments, including the trek around the "haunted maze", Stan's glorious transformation into college hero Lord Paddington, and Ollie's demotion to the role of butler. Keep your eyes peeled for Peter Cushing as one of the students. ▭

Stan Laurel *Stan* • Oliver Hardy *Ollie* • James Finlayson *Baldy Vandevere* • Peter Cushing *Jones* ■ *Dir* Alfred Goulding • *Scr* Felix Adler, Harry Langdon, Charles Rogers

Chung King Express   ★★★★ 12
Romantic comedy
1994 · HK · Colour · 97mins

A film that Quentin Tarantino declared to be a masterpiece, and he's not far wrong, for director Wong Kar-Wai's exceptional control over the two disparate storylines is awe-inspiring. The first, shorter episode concerns a jilted cop's encounter with a blonde-wigged heroin trafficker, while the second focuses on a waitress's preoccupation with another cop, who doesn't appreciate her passion until it's too late. Established stars Tony Leung and Brigitte Lin are upstaged somewhat by newcomers Takeshi Kaneshiro and Faye Wong, but the performances as a whole are a joy. In Cantonese with English subtitles. ▭

Qingxia Lin [Brigitte Lin] *The drug dealer* • Takeshi Kaneshiro *He Qiwu, Cop 223* • Tony Chiu-Wai Leung [Tony Leung (1)] *Cop 663* • Faye Wong *Faye* • Valerie Chow *Air Hostess* ■ *Dir* Wong Kar-Wai • *Scr* Wong Kar-Wai

The Church ★★★ 18

Horror 1988 · It · Colour · 97mins

Originally slated to complete Dario Argento's *Demons* trilogy, this Gothic horror was turned over to Michele Soavi, with the co-scenarist taking a producing role. Opening with a medieval witch-hunt which results in a cathedral being built on the mass grave of some suspected Satanists, the story jumps forward in time to show bibliophile Tomas Arana and caretaker's daughter Asia Argento investigating the fiendish mechanical devices the architect installed to prevent malevolent spirits escaping into the world. Soavi's ingeniously designed film exerts a strong fascination, but the intriguing concept is wasted. An Italian language film.

Asia Argento *Lotte* • Thomas Arana [Tomas Arana] *Evald* • Feodor Chaliapin [Feodor Chaliapin Jr] *Bishop* • Hugh Quarshie *Father Gus* • Barbara Cupisti *Lisa* ■ *Dir* Michele Soavi • *Scr* Dario Argento, Franco Ferrini, Michele Soavi, from a story by Dario Argento, Franco Ferrini

Ciao, Federico! ★★★★ 15

Documentary 1970 · US/It · Colour · 57mins

One critic said Fellini's films ceased to be art when Fellini himself became a work of art. That self-aggrandisement is evident in this documentary about the Italian maestro, caught while directing his exotic Roman tale, *Satyricon*. The great man proves to be impossible to interview: an evasive, chronic liar and sly keeper of his own image. But he's such a marvellous raconteur, you can't help loving him and admiring Gideon Bachmann for colluding so graciously.

Dir Gideon Bachmann

El Cid ★★★★★ U

Epic historical adventure
1961 · US/It · Colour · 171mins

Although initially seen as an invincible weapon in the battle against television, the historical epic had earned itself a bad name with audiences, critics and studio executives alike by the time this lavish account of the life and times of Rodrigo Diaz de Bivar reached cinema screens. While not in the same class as *The Ten Commandments* or *Ben-Hur*, the film gave Charlton Heston another chance to carry the weight of a nation on his shoulders, this time as he takes on the Moors who invaded Spain in the 11th century. Director Anthony Mann avoids the history-lesson style that confounded many a blockbuster but, as well as he handles the feud between the Cid and his estranged wife (Sophia Loren) and the political intrigues at court, he is outdone by Yakima Canutt, the legendary stuntman and western villain who led the second unit responsible for the battle scenes.

Charlton Heston *Rodrigo Diaz de Bivar/El Cid* • Sophia Loren *Chimene* • John Fraser *King Alfonso* • Raf Vallone *Count Ordonez* • Genevieve Page *Queen Urraca* • Gary Raymond *King Sancho* • Herbert Lom *Ben Yussuf* • Massimo Serato *Fanez* • Douglas Wilmer *Moutamin* • Frank Thring *Al Kadir* • Hurd Hatfield *Count Arias* • Ralph Truman *King Ferdinand* • Andrew Cruickshank *Count Gomez* • Michael Hordern *Don Diego* ■ *Dir* Anthony Mann • *Scr* Philip Yordan, Fredric M

Frank, Ben Barzman (uncredited), from a story by Fredric M Frank • *Music* Miklos Rozsa • *Cinematographer* Robert Krasker

The Cider House Rules ★★★★★ 12

Drama 1999 · US · Colour · 125mins

The third John Irving novel to reach the screen (after *The World According to Garp* and *The Hotel New Hampshire*), this is a rich, evocative period piece that makes the most of its New England locations. Tobey Maguire (*Ride with the Devil*) plays Homer Wells, a foundling who, having spent all his young life at an orphanage run by Michael Caine's kindly abortionist, decides to seek new pastures. Alas, he find the codes he lives by of little use in the real world. Although drastically slimmed down from Irving's original (Homer's 15-year odyssey is reduced to a mere 15 months), Lasse Hallström's film has a simple integrity that fills every frame, while Caine won his second Oscar for his performance as the ether-addicted Dr Larch.

Tobey Maguire *Homer Wells* • Charlize Theron *Candy Kendall* • Delroy Lindo *Arthur Rose* • Paul Rudd *Wally Worthington* • Michael Caine *Dr Wilbur Larch* • Jane Alexander *Nurse Edna* • Kathy Baker *Nurse Angela* • Kate Nelligan *Olive Worthington* ■ *Dir* Lasse Hallström • *Scr* John Irving, from his novel

Cimarron ★★★

Epic western 1931 · US · BW · 131mins

Richard Dix, newspaper owner and maverick campaigner for human rights, is also a restless wanderer who disappears for long periods, leaving his indomitable wife Irene Dunne to carry on the paper and the fight for justice. Directed by Wesley Ruggles from a novel by Edna Ferber, this sprawling epic cost RKO the unprecedented sum of $1,433,000. The studio was rewarded with Oscars for best picture – the only western to get the award until *Dances with Wolves* six decades later – art direction and screenplay. There were also nominations for the director and both stars, though the film itself lost $500,000 at the Depression-hit box office. A little dated now, but otherwise excellent in all departments.

Richard Dix *Yancey Cravat* • Irene Dunne *Sabra Cravat* • Estelle Taylor *Dixie Lee* • Nance O'Neil *Felice Venable* • William Collier Jr *The Kid* ■ *Dir* Wesley Ruggles • *Scr* Howard Estabrook, from the novel by Edna Ferber • *Cinematographer* Edward Cronjager • *Art Director* Max Ree

Cimarron ★★★ U

Epic western 1960 · US · Colour · 147mins

A dignified and worthy remake of the classic 1931 version of Edna Ferber's novel about the Oklahoma Land Rush, this is, sadly, a misfire. It's the very least of *El Cid* director Anthony Mann's works, marred by MGM's insistence on studio filming when locations were imperative, and by a hopelessly inept and miscast Maria Schell in the key role of Sabra Cravet. Glenn Ford delivers a superb performance as Yancey Cravet, but the film remains little more than an insubstantial 19th-century melodrama.

Glenn Ford *Yancey Cravat* • Maria Schell *Sabra Cravat* • Anne Baxter *Dixie Lee* • Arthur

O'Connell *Tom Wyatt* • Russ Tamblyn *Cherokee Kid* • Mercedes McCambridge *Sarah Wyatt* ■ *Dir* Anthony Mann • *Scr* Arnold Schulman, from the novel by Edna Ferber

The Cincinnati Kid ★★★★ PG

Drama 1965 · US · Colour · 97mins

Intended as a *Hustler* for poker players, *The Cincinnati Kid* started out with Steve McQueen as the young hotshot and Spencer Tracy as his older, poker-faced adversary. Sam Peckinpah was the director and Paddy Chayefsky the screenwriter. Tracy was the first to go, being replaced by Edward G Robinson. Six days into shooting, Peckinpah was fired because he was working too slowly, though the press was told he shot a nude scene which wasn't in the script. Enter new writers and a new director, Norman Jewison. The result, considering the production's chequered history, is not at all bad, with nice supporting turns from Karl Malden and Ann-Margret, and the great duel at the poker table between McQueen and Robinson forming a tense climax.

Steve McQueen *Cincinnati Kid* • Edward G Robinson *Lancey Howard* • Ann-Margret *Melba* • Karl Malden *Shooter* • Tuesday Weld *Christian* • Joan Blondell *Lady Fingers* • Rip Torn *Slade* • Jack Weston *Pig* ■ *Dir* Norman Jewison • *Scr* Ring Lardner Jr, Terry Southern, from the novel by Richard Jessup

Cinderella ★★★★ U

Animated romance
1950 · US · Colour · 74mins

Industrial-strength Disney animation, with all the coy clichés of Charles Perrault's story reinforced, though not the sexual ones. There are some delightful singing mice, a sadistically erotic stepmother and a languidly cruel cat called Lucifer, voiced by June Foray. The songs are what give it an extra dimension, though: the Oscar-nominated *Bibbidi-Bobbidi-Boo*, sung by Verna Felton, and the winsome *A Dream Is a Wish Your Heart Makes*, performed by Ilene Woods.

Ilene Woods *Cinderella* • William Phipps *Prince Charming* • Eleanor Audley *Stepmother* • Verna Felton *Fairy Godmother* • James MacDonald *Jacques/Gus-Gus* • Rhoda Williams *Anastasia* ■ *Dir* Wilfred Jackson, Hamilton Luske, Clyde Geronimi • *Scr* William Peet, Ted Sears, Homer Brightman, Kenneth Anderson, Erdman Penner, Winston Hibler, Harry Reeves, Joe Rinaldi, from the story *Cinderella* by Charles Perrault

Cinderella Jones ★★ U

Musical comedy 1946 · US · BW · 83mins

Amiable but dated Warner Bros fable, shot during the war but held back so long that all wartime references had to be removed and some rather bland linking material filmed especially. The director of this trifle is, surprisingly, the great choreographer Busby Berkeley, making a return to the studio whose coffers he once helped fill with his splendidly outré dance creations. This is altogether a more modest piece, showcasing two Warners contract artistes in the leads. Both are talented, but the cinema-going public never really took to pert Joan Leslie or affable Robert Alda (Alan's dad).

Joan Leslie *Judy Jones* • Robert Alda *Tommy Coles* • SZ Sakall *Gabriel Popik* • Edward

Everett Horton *Keating* • Julie Bishop *Camille* • William Prince *Bart Williams* • Charles Dingle *Minland* • Ruth Donnelly *Cora Elliott* ■ *Dir* Busby Berkeley • *Scr* Charles Hoffman, from a story by Philip Wylie

Cinderella Liberty ★★★ 15

Drama 1973 · US · Colour · 111mins

Macho James Caan becomes hooked on Marsha Mason and the result is a blatantly manipulative urban fairy tale. The setting up of the schmaltzy floodgates is intriguing enough as Caan, a sailor in Seattle on the night-pass that gives its name to the movie, plays pool with hustling hooker Mason, with her body as his prize. After that, it becomes soggy with sentiment, though director Mark Rydell manages to give the ending a satisfyingly ironic twist. Contains swearing and brief nudity.

James Caan *John Baggs* • Marsha Mason *Maggie* • Kirk Calloway *Doug* • Eli Wallach *Lynn Forshay* • Allyn Ann McLerie *Miss Watkins* • Burt Young *Master-at-arms* • Bruno Kirby Jr [Bruno Kirby] *Alcott* • Dabney Coleman *Executive officer* ■ *Dir* Mark Rydell • *Scr* Darryl Ponicsan, from the novel by Darryl Ponicsan

Cinderfella ★★★ U

Comedy 1960 · US · Colour · 84mins

An amiable retelling of *Cinderella*, with Jerry Lewis cast as the put-upon stepson and winsome Anna Maria Alberghetti as a demure "Princess Charming". As producer, Lewis affords himself some notable set pieces, especially the entrance at the ball, zigzagging down a seemingly endless stairway to Count Basie's beat. Non-Lewis fans won't be converted, though, and may find the interminable goofing tiresome.

Jerry Lewis *Fella* • Judith Anderson *Wicked stepmother* • Ed Wynn *Fairy godfather* • Anna Maria Alberghetti *Princess Charmein* • Henry Silva *Maximilian* • Robert Hutton *Rupert* • Count Basie ■ *Dir/Scr* Frank Tashlin

Cinema Paradiso ★★★★★ PG

Drama 1988 · It/Fr · Colour · 117mins

Winner of the Oscar for best foreign language film, this is both an unashamedly sentimental "rite of passage" picture and a charming reminder of the lost art of cinema-going. The undoubted stars are projectionist Philippe Noiret and his adorable young assistant, Salvatore Cascio. Yet it's the patrons of the village cinema in Sicily who give the film its irresistible flavour, entering into the spirit of each and every movie, and treating the cinema as a part of life, not just an escape from it. After a lukewarm domestic response, co-writer/director Giuseppe Tornatore cut 32 minutes, but, with its exhilarating kiss montage, this remains a wonderfully nostalgic experience. In Italian and French with English subtitles. Contains swearing and nudity.

Philippe Noiret *Alfredo* • Jacques Perrin *Salvatore as an adult* • Salvatore Cascio *Toto (Salvatore as a child)* • Mario Leonardi *Salvatore as a teenager* • Agnese Nano *Elena* ■ *Dir* Giuseppe Tornatore • *Scr* Giuseppe Tornatore, Vanna Paoli

U = SUITABLE FOR ALL Uc = SUITABLE FOR ALL, ESPECIALLY FOR YOUNG CHILDREN (VIDEO ONLY) PG = PARENTAL GUIDANCE

Circle of Danger ★★★ U

Drama   1950 · UK · BW · 82mins

The clever plot here has Ray Milland investigating the death of his commando brother in the Second World War, only to find that things aren't quite what they seem to be. Unfortunately, despite the talented Jacques Tourneur in the director's chair and Alfred Hitchcock collaborator Joan Harrison as co-producer, the movie isn't quite what it seems to be either. Still, Tourneur does what he can with all those red herrings and makes the whole watchable enough.

Ray Milland *Clay Douglas* • Patricia Roc *Elspeth Graham* • Marius Goring *Sholto Lewis* • Hugh Sinclair *Hamish McArran* • Naunton Wayne *Reggie Sinclair* • Dora Bryan *Bubbles* ■ *Dir* Jacques Tourneur • *Scr* Philip MacDonald, from his novel *White Heather*

Circle of Deceit ★★

Drama   1981 · Fr/W Ger · Colour · 108mins

A West German journalist (Bruno Ganz), beset by marital woes, is on assignment in the Lebanon with his photographer (Jerzy Skolimowski). Once there, he gets caught up in events – among them an affair with Hanna Schygulla – that compromise both his professional and personal integrity and feed into his own crisis of conscience. A sobering but somewhat confused film from Germany's Volker Schlöndorff, who filmed it in the Lebanon during the dark days of the conflict and graphically depicts the scenes of chaos and human suffering. But this mix of the personal and the political is uneasy, and is compounded by a hero whose inadequacy and self-preoccupation render him deeply tiresome. A German language film.

Bruno Ganz *Georg Laschen* • Hanna Schygulla *Arianna Nassar* • Jerzy Skolimowski *Hoffmann* • Gila Von Weitershausen *Greta Laschen* • Jean Carmet *Rudnik* ■ *Dir* Volker Schlöndorff • *Scr* Volker Schlöndorff, Jean-Claude Carrière, Margarethe von Trotta, Kai Hermann, from the novel *Die Fälschung* by Nicolas Born

Circle of Deception ★★★

Second World War drama
1960 · UK · BW · 99mins

During the Second World War, a nervy and sensitive Canadian officer (Bradford Dillman) is made a fall guy by British intelligence, who drop him in Normandy with false information, confident he'll be captured by the Germans and crack under pressure. Well-directed by Jack Lee, with convincing performances from Dillman and a host of first-class English stage and TV actors such as Harry Andrews, Robert Stephens and Paul Rogers, this is a decent espionage drama that suffers mainly from the fact that we've been watching them for decades.

Suzy Parker *Lucy Bowen* • Bradford Dillman *Paul Raine* • Harry Andrews *Captain Rawson* • Paul Rogers *Major Spence* • John Welsh *Major Taylor* • Robert Stephens *Captain Stein* ■ *Dir* Jack Lee • *Scr* Nigel Balchin, Robert Musel, from the novel by Alec Waugh

Circle of Friends ★★★★ 15

Romantic drama
1995 · US/Ire · Colour · 98mins

As feature debuts go, they don't come much better than Minnie Driver's. She

not only holds together this amiable adaptation of Maeve Binchy's novel, but she positively lights up the screen as Benny, the country girl who has to abandon her Dublin education (and rugger star Chris O'Donnell) to work in the family shop and fight off the unwanted attentions of the wonderfully smarmy Alan Cumming. Colin Firth is overly mannered as the Protestant landlord, and Pat O'Connor slips in too many Emerald vistas, but the story is told with wit and charm. Contains swearing and sex scenes. ▭

Chris O'Donnell *Jack* • Minnie Driver *Benny* • Geraldine O'Rawe *Eve* • Saffron Burrows *Nan* • Alan Cumming *Sean* • Colin Firth *Simon Westward* • Aidan Gillen *Aidan* • Mick Lally *Dan Hogan* • Ciaran Hinds *Professor Flynn* ■ *Dir* Pat O'Connor • *Scr* Andrew Davies, from the novel by Maeve Binchy

Circle of Passion ★★★

Romantic drama
1996 · US/UK · Colour · 94mins

Writer/director Charles Finch takes a leading role as an unhappily married banker who has a fling with hat-maker Sandrine Bonnaire during a business trip to Paris. He has to decide where to hang *his* hat when he falls in love with her. Jane March plays the banker's less than amorous other half, and the emotion of her performance is a revelation after her rather flat performances in such films as *The Lover* and *The Color of Night*. Director Charles Finch cops a double paycheck by also playing the banker. In English and French with subtitles.

Sandrine Bonnaire *Katherine Beaufort* • Jane March *Amanda Murray* • James Fox *Arthur Trevane* • Charles Finch *Thomas Murray* • Jean Rochefort *Gerard Panier* • Julian Sands *Roderick* ■ *Dir/Scr* Charles Finch

Circle of Two ★

Drama   1980 · Can · Colour · 108mins

Sixteen-year-old student Tatum O'Neal goes to see a porno movie. Who should we spot in the audience but a haggard-looking Richard Burton! What follows is an inordinate amount of slush, with Burton urging O'Neal to become a writer and she urging him to resume his career as an artist. Naturally, he chooses to start by painting her in the nude. Burton received $750,000 for the role and delivered a bored performance that was hardly worth a single cent. The eagle-eyed may spot Tatum's dad, Ryan, in the porn movie audience.

Richard Burton *Ashley St Clair* • Tatum O'Neal *Sarah Norton* • Nuala Fitzgerald *Claudia Aldrich* • Robin Gammell *Mr Norton* • Patricia Collins *Mrs Norton* • Donann Cavin *Smitty* • Michael Wincott *Paul* • Kate Reid *Dr Emily Reid* ■ *Dir* Jules Dassin • *Scr* Thomas Hedley, from the story *A Lesson in Love* by Marie Terese Baird

Circle of Violence ★★

Drama   1986 · US · Colour · 100mins

Tuesday Weld, River Phoenix and Hollywood veteran Geraldine Fitzgerald star in this powerful TV movie that looks at three generations of the same family and how they cope with a crisis that threatens to tear them apart. Director David Greene maintains a steady pace before succumbing to

melodrama. The cast also includes Ellen Travolta, John's big sister.

Tuesday Weld *Georgia Benfield* • Geraldine Fitzgerald *Charlotte Kessling* • Peter Bonerz *Pete Benfield* • River Phoenix *Chris Benfield* • Philip Sterling *Jim McLane* • Zoaunne LeRoy *Florence McLane* • Ellen Travolta *Marion* ■ *Dir* David Greene • *Scr* William Wood

Circuit Breaker ★

Science-fiction thriller   1996 · US · Colour

Intergalactic repairman Corbin Bernsen and wife Lara Harris come across a broken-down spaceship in this cable TV movie, which is essentially *Dead Calm* in space. On board the craft is android Richard Grieco who, in time-honoured genre tradition, is planning to create a new breed of human. Slow-moving and predictable, this tepid thriller relies more on gratuitous sex and violence than anything of a science-fiction nature.

Lara Harris *Katrina Carver* • Richard Grieco *Adam* • Corbin Bernsen *Foster Carver* • Edie McClurg ■ *Dir/Scr* Victoria Muspratt

Circuitry Man ★★ 15

Science-fiction thriller
1990 · US · Colour · 88mins

Co-scripted by director Steven Lovy and his brother Robert, this is a futuristic patchwork made up of snippets from a range of sci-fi films, most notably *Blade Runner*, *Logan's Run* and *Mad Max*. More time spent at the typewriter and a little less playing with special effects might have resulted in a better and certainly more coherent movie. As it is, Dana Wheeler-Nicholson's flight from the villainous Lu Leonard, carrying a case full of pleasure-inducing computer chips, is little more than a string of clichés and pompous pronouncements. Our heroine's romance with android Jim Metzler and a scenery-chewing cameo from Dennis Christopher provide rare highlights. Contains swearing and violence. ▭

Jim Metzler *Danner* • Dana Wheeler-Nicholson *Lori* • Lu Leonard *Juice* • Vernon Wells *Plughead* • Barbara Alyn Woods *Yoyo* • Dennis Christopher *Leech* ■ *Dir* Steven Lovy • *Scr* Steven Lovy, Robert Lovy

Circumstances Unknown ★ 15

Crime thriller   1995 · Can · Colour · 87mins

Former Brat Packer Judd Nelson stars in this ludicrous TV movie as a greasy-haired psychopath so obsessed with the wife of an old friend (Isabel Glasser) that he commits a string of murders, including that of her husband. Suspecting foul play, Glasser sets out to find the killer, not realising he has been stalking her all along. The plot makes no sense and, aside from one twist, never surprises.

Judd Nelson *Paul Kinsey* • Isabel Glasser *Deena Reuschel* • William R Moses *Tim Reuschel* • Rhys Huber *John Reuschel* • Phillip MacKenzie *Martin Trayne* • William B Davis *Gene Reuschel* ■ *Dir* Robert Lewis • *Scr* Emily Shoemaker, Thomas Hood, from the novel by Jonellen Heckler

Circumstantial Evidence ★★★

Crime drama   1945 · US · BW · 67mins

A neat and unpretentious little 20th Century-Fox second feature about the fallibility of memory, in particular that of alleged eyewitnesses in a murder trial. The witnesses here see, or think they see, Michael O'Shea kill a grocer with whom he is fighting, resulting in his being accused of murder and subsequently convicted. That fine actor Lloyd Nolan brings his *Michael Shayne, Private Detective* persona to bear on this thoughtful plot, but O'Shea is a rather bland lead, making it hard to root for him. Nevertheless, John Larkin's direction is assured, and the moral uncertainties, predating the classic *12 Angry Men* by over a decade, make for compulsive viewing.

Michael O'Shea *Joe Reynolds* • Lloyd Nolan *Sam Lord* • Trudy Marshall *Agnes Hannon* • Billy Cummings *Pat* • Ruth Ford *Mrs Simms* • Reed Hadley *Prosecutor* • Roy Roberts *Marty Hannon* • Scotty Beckett *Freddy Hanlon* • Byron Foulger *Bolger* ■ *Dir* John Larkin • *Scr* Robert Metzler, Sam Ornitz, from a story by Nat Ferber, Sam Duncan

The Circus ★★★★ U

Silent comedy   1928 · US · BW · 71mins

Charles Chaplin's theme of despondent love all but overwhelms the brilliant slapstick set pieces (a chase through a hall of mirrors, being trapped in a lion's cage) when the Tramp, on the run from the police, joins the circus and falls for a bare-back rider (Merna Kennedy). Chaplin got a special award for acting, writing, directing and producing the film, but the best moments are the least self-conscious and hark back to his music hall origins (walking a tightrope with falling trousers and a clinging monkey, for example). Not the best Chaplin, but still pretty sensational. ▭

Charlie Chaplin *[Charles Chaplin] Tramp* • Allan Garcia *Circus proprietor* • Merna Kennedy *Girl* • Harry Crocker *Rex* • George Davis *Magician* • Stanley J Stanford *Head property man* • Henry Bergman *Old clown* ■ *Dir/Scr* Charles Chaplin

Circus ★ 18

Comedy thriller
1999 · UK/US · Colour · 95mins

Set in Brighton, this clueless British crime comedy in the Tarantino mould features a collection of unappealing crooks who repeatedly stab each other in the back and a ludicrous story that makes no sense whatsoever. Bad casting abounds: John Hannah is far too wimpy to convince as a tough, wily killer, while comedian Brian Conley is embarrassing as the least menacing crime lord in movie history. Quite what "Tiny" Lister's moronic henchman "Moose" (any resemblance to *Farewell My Lovely* is wishful thinking) and Eddie Izzard's bizarre singing bookie are doing here is anyone's guess.

John Hannah *Leo Garfield* • Famke Janssen *Lily Garfield* • Peter Stormare *Julius Harvey* • Eddie Izzard *Troy Cabrara* • Fred Ward *Elmo Somerset* • Brian Conley *Bruno Maitland* • "Tiny" Lister Jr *[Tom "Tiny" Lister Jr] George "Moose" Marley* ■ *Dir* Rob Walker • *Scr* David Logan

Circus Boys ★★★★ PG
Drama 1989 · Jap · BW · 101mins

One of the finest films to come out of Japan in years, this provides conclusive proof that cinema is much the poorer for the passing of black-and-white film. Yuichi Nagata's imagery has an austerity and clarity that few cinematographers could surpass, whether it's capturing the action in the big top, the disappointments behind the scenes or the deceptions of life on the open road. Director Kaizo Hayashi is similarly in total control of his art, conveying the passage of time with subtle symbolism and drawing a superb performance out of Hiroshi Mikami as the trapeze artist who turns to petty crime after a fall. In Japanese with English subtitles. ▣

Hiroshi Mikami *Jinta* • Moe Kamura *Omocha* • Xia Jian *Wataru* • Michiru Akiyoshi *Maria* • Yuki Asayama *Sayoko* • Sanshi Katsura *Samejima* ■ *Dir/Scr* Kaizo Hayashi

Circus Friends ★★ U
Drama 1956 · UK · BW · 64mins

Although it doesn't add up to much today, this little picture deserves its place in British screen history as the first project brought to completion by producer Peter Rogers and director Gerald Thomas, the godfathers of the *Carry On* series. It might seem an odd place for these bawdy merchants to get their start. However, there's a sentimental charm to this rural tale in which Alan Coleshill and Carol White rescue their pet pony from farmer Meredith Edwards after their penurious father, John Horsley, sells it to help pay his circus bills.

Alan Coleshill *Nicky* • Carol White *Nan* • David Tilley *Martin* • Pat Belcher *Beryl* • Meredith Edwards *Farmer Beasley* • John Horsley *Bert Marlow* • Sam Kydd *George* ■ *Dir* Gerald Thomas • *Scr* Peter Rogers

Circus of Fear ★★
Horror thriller 1967 · UK · Colour · 90mins

Christopher Lee wears a black woolly hood for nearly all of his scenes in this lame whodunit, based on the 1928 Edgar Wallace mystery *Again the Three Just Men*. He's the facially scarred lion tamer in Barberini's Circus, and one of the many suspects in a murder case investigated by Scotland Yard's Leo Genn. John Moxey's disappointing direction accents the cops-and-robbers elements over any marginal terror, but the stalwart efforts of the cast act as a safety net for the shaky plot.

Christopher Lee *Gregor* • Leo Genn *Inspector Elliott* • Anthony Newlands *Barberini* • Heinz Drache *Carl* • Eddi Arent *Eddie* • Klaus Kinski *Manfred* • Margaret Lee *Gina* • Suzy Kendall *Natasha* ■ *Dir* John Moxey [John Llewellyn Moxey] • *Scr* Peter Welbeck [Harry Alan Towers], from a story by Edgar Wallace

Circus of Horrors ★★★ 15
Horror thriller 1960 · UK · Colour · 87mins

Definitely a film to make your flesh creep, this nifty British horror is more in keeping with the gimmicky style of Roger Corman or William Castle than your average Hammer. Anton Diffring is perfectly cast as an incompetent plastic surgeon who takes refuge under Donald Pleasence's big top after

the knife slips once too often. Director Sidney Hayers makes superb use of the circus locale, dreaming up wonderfully grotesque ways of bumping off the outcasts that Diffring has remodelled, when they try to escape his barbarous regime. The atmospheric photography is by the incomparable Douglas Slocombe. ▣

Anton Diffring *Dr Schuler* • Erika Remberg *Elissa* • Yvonne Monlaur *Nicole* • Donald Pleasence *Vanet* • Jane Hylton *Angela* • Kenneth Griffith *Martin* • Conrad Phillips *Inspector Ames* • Jack Gwillim *Superintendent Andrews* ■ *Dir* Sidney Hayers • *Scr* George Baxt

The Cisco Kid ★★ PG
Comedy western 1994 · US · Colour · 91mins

Remember that wince-inducing, yet hugely popular TV show of the fifties, featuring Duncan Renaldo as Mexican adventurer Francisco "Cisco" Aguilar Solarez and Leo Carrillo as his sidekick, the wisecracking priest Pancho Rivera? Well, here they are again in the form of Jimmy Smits and "Cheech" Marin, who rush around fighting the occupying French army in mid-19th century Mexico. It's directed by Luis Valdez, best known for the Ritchie Valens biopic *La Bamba*. Contains some swearing. ▣

Jimmy Smits *The Cisco Kid* • Richard "Cheech" Marin *Pancho* • Sadie Frost *Dominique* • Bruce Payne *St Martin Dupre* • Ron Perlman *DeLacroix* • Tony Amendola *Washam* • Tim Tomerson *Lundquist* ■ *Dir* Luis Valdez • *Scr* Michael Kane, Luis Valdez, from a story by Michael Kane, from characters created by O Henry

The Cisco Kid and the Lady ★★★ U
Western 1939 · US · BW · 73mins

A deeply charming if fluffily slight outing for Cesar Romero as the Cisco Kid. The plot is a curious combination of boggling complexity and wafer-thin skimming: gold prospecting, abandoned babies, murder, weddings and funerals are all thrown helter-skelter into the tale and regurgitated as a delightful madcap romp. The supporting cast includes a veritable mishmash of the good Robert Barrat, the profoundly average Ward Bond and the simply dreadful George Montgomery. Overall good fun.

Cesar Romero *Cisco Kid* • Marjorie Weaver *Julie Lawson* • Chris-Pin Martin *Gordito* • George Montgomery *Tommy Bates* • Robert Barrat *Jim Harbison* • Virginia Field *Billie Graham* • Ward Bond *Walton* ■ *Dir* Herbert I Leeds • *Scr* Frances Hyland, from a story by Stanley Rauh, from characters created by O Henry

Cisco Pike ★★★
Crime drama 1971 · US · Colour · 94mins

In order to create a sense of the emptiness at the centre of seventies pop and drug culture, writer/director Bill L Norton decided here to dispense with any plot, with the result that his evocation of Los Angeles occasionally borders on the flabby. The film is awash with anti-establishment attitudes and creates an atmosphere that is still affecting, despite Norton's penchant for distracting showy touches. Kris Kristofferson, as the has-

been rock star, and Gene Hackman, as the corrupt cop, supply plenty of electricity. Contains swearing.

Kris Kristofferson *Cisco Pike* • Gene Hackman *Holland* • Karen Black *Sue* • Harry Dean Stanton *Jesse* • Viva *Merna* • Joy Bang *Lynn* • Roscoe Lee Browne *Music store owner* • Antonio Fargas *Buffalo* ■ *Dir/Scr* Bill L Norton

The Citadel ★★★★
Drama 1938 · US/UK · BW · 112mins

An idealistic young doctor (Robert Donat) battling the slum conditions of a Welsh mining village marries the local schoolteacher (Rosalind Russell) and moves to London, where he is corrupted by the moneyed ease of a society practice. Adapted from AJ Cronin's bestseller, this solid MGM drama makes for thoroughly satisfactory viewing. Donat – the handsome British star with the memorable speaking voice who died at 53 from chronic asthma – is perfectly cast, as are Ralph Richardson as his friend, Cecil Parker as a bungling surgeon and, in smaller roles, Rex Harrison, Emlyn Williams, Mary Clare and Francis L Sullivan.

Robert Donat *Andrew Manson* • Rosalind Russell *Christine Manson* • Ralph Richardson *Denny* • Rex Harrison *Dr Lawford* • Emlyn Williams *Owen* • Francis L Sullivan *Ben Chenkin* • Mary Clare *Mrs Orlando* • Cecil Parker *Charles Every* ■ *Dir* King Vidor • *Scr* Ian Dalrymple, Elizabeth Hill, Frank Wead, from the novel by AJ Cronin

The Citadel ★★★ PG
Comedy drama 1989 · Alg · Colour · 98mins

In seeking to expose what he sees as the iniquities of polygamy, Algerian director Mohamed Chouikh presents us with a stark portrait of life within a strict Muslim community. However, while he elicits sympathy for Khaled Barkat, the orphan adopted by decadent merchant Djillali Ain-Tedeles, and for the trio of wives the latter exploits, Chouikh fails to weave the characters into a satisfying dramatic whole, even after the boy falls for a married woman and his father plans to wed again. Unflinching in its depiction of rural patriarchy, this is still a courageous and haunting film. In Arabic with English subtitles.

Khaled Barkat *Kaddour* • Djillali Ain-Tedeles *Sidi* • Fettouma Ousliha *Helima* • Momo *Aissa* • Fatima Belhadj *Nedjama* ■ *Dir/Scr* Mohamed Chouikh

Citizen Cohn ★★★ 15
Biographical drama 1992 · US · Colour · 107mins

Roy Cohn's name will be unfamiliar to many in Britain, but the reasons for his infamy will be readily understandable after watching this scathing portrait. (Cohn destroyed countless lives as the sidekick of witch-hunting senator Joseph McCarthy.) The story unfolds in a series of flashbacks as Cohn (James Woods) lies dying of an Aids-related illness, the ruthlessly ambitious lawyer emerging as a person prepared to betray any principle for advancement. This so-called biography is more melodrama than history, but it's still powerful stuff. ▣

James Woods *Roy Cohn* • Lee Grant *Dora Cohn* • Josef Sommer *Al Cohn* • Joseph

Bologna *Walter Winchell* • Pat Hingle *J Edgar Hoover* • Joe Don Baker *Senator Joseph McCarthy* • Ed Flanders *Joseph Welch* ■ *Dir* Frank Pierson • *Scr* David Franzoni, from a book by Nicholas Von Hoffman

Citizen Kane ★★★★★ U
Classic drama 1941 · US · BW · 114mins

Acclaimed by critics and film-makers alike, *Citizen Kane* has topped *Sight and Sound*'s decennial "all-time top ten" since 1962. Not bad for the feature film debut of a 25-year-old, whose experience lay in theatre and radio (most of the actors in *Kane* were colleagues from his Mercury Theatre company), and who claimed his sole preparation was to watch John Ford's *Stagecoach* 40 times. In fact, Orson Welles considered a movie studio (his contract at the time was with RKO) to be the biggest train set a boy ever had. Unhindered by preconceptions, he proceeded to experiment with sound, camera angles and movement, and deep focus in a way few had even conceived of. Aided by cinematographer Gregg Toland, he brought visual drama to every shot, brilliantly disguising the picture's shoestring budget (it required a record 116 sets). In addition, Welles also turned in a magnificent performance as Charles Foster Kane, the press baron whose torrid life was so similar to that of William Randolph Hearst that the latter broke the film at the box office through negative publicity. Utterly unmissable. ▣ *DVD*

Orson Welles *Charles Foster Kane* • Joseph Cotten *Jedediah Leland* • Dorothy Comingore *Susan Alexander* • Everett Sloane *Mr Bernstein* • Ray Collins *Boss JW "Big Jim" Gettys* • George Coulouris *Walter Parks Thatcher* • Agnes Moorehead *Mrs Mary Kane* • Paul Stewart *Raymond, head butler* • Ruth Warrick *Emily Norton Kane* • Erskine Sanford *Herbert Carter* • William Alland *Jerry Thompson, chief reporter* • Fortunio Bonanova *Matisti* • Gus Schilling *Head waiter* ■ *Dir* Orson Welles • *Scr* Herman J Mankiewicz, Orson Welles • *Editor* Robert Wise, Mark Robson • *Art Director* Van Nest Polglase, Perry Ferguson • *Music* Bernard Herrmann • *Special Effects* Vernon L Walker

Citizen Ruth ★★★
Black comedy 1996 · US · Colour · 105mins

Laura Dern carries this issue-based film singlehandedly as the irredeemable Ruth Stoops: a homeless, pregnant drug-abuser who, while sniffing patio sealant, triggers a violent debate between pro-lifers and abortion rights campaigners. The range of characters includes Swoosie Kurtz and her lesbian lover Kelly Preston; elsewhere, Burt Reynolds's pro-lifer squares up against Tippi Hedren's pro-choice harpy. Clearly demonstrating the insanity that surrounds this issue in the US, director Alexander Payne manages to satirise as well as explain. The result is a brave and very black comedy which takes no prisoners.

Laura Dern *Ruth Stoops* • Swoosie Kurtz *Diane Sieglar* • Kurtwood Smith *Norm Stoney* • Mary Kay Place *Gail Stoney* • Kelly Preston *Rachel* • MC Gainey *Harlan* • Kenneth Mars *Dr Charlie Rollins* • Tippi Hedren *Jessica Weiss* • Burt Reynolds *Blaine Gibbons* • Diane Ladd *Ruth's mother* ■ *Dir* Alexander Payne • *Scr* Alexander Payne, Jim Taylor

U = SUITABLE FOR ALL Uc = SUITABLE FOR ALL, ESPECIALLY FOR YOUNG CHILDREN (VIDEO ONLY) PG = PARENTAL GUIDANCE

Citizen X ★★★ 18
Thriller   1995 · US · Colour · 98mins

The true story of the Soviet Union's most famous serial killer makes absorbing and fascinating viewing. Former schoolteacher Chikatilo (Jeffrey DeMunn) murders and mutilates 52 children over an eight-year period. Because of government corruption, backward police procedures and the fact the authorities couldn't admit to such western depravity polluting their culture, he is slow to be caught. Stephen Rea is subtly convincing as the forensic expert whose dogged persistence on the case causes him such personal grief, and Donald Sutherland won numerous awards as the military superior who backed his controversial hunches. ▣

Stephen Rea *Detective Viktor Burakov* • Donald Sutherland *Colonel Fetisov* • Max von Sydow *Dr Aleksandr Bukhanovsky* • Jeffrey DeMunn *Andre Chikatilo* • John Wood *Gorbunov* ■ *Dir* Chris Gerolmo • *Scr* Chris Gerolmo, from the non-fiction book *The Killer Department* by Robert Cullen

Citizens Band ★★★★
Comedy   1977 · US · Colour · 95mins

A highly amusing and raunchy comedy about CB radio enthusiasts (remember that craze?) in a small midwestern town, eavesdropping on one another with hilarious results. An excellent script, on-the-button performances from Paul Le Mat and Candy Clark, and a great soundtrack featuring Richie Havens and Joe Cocker brighten this charming slab of suburban American graffiti. An early effort from Jonathan Demme that more than hints at the excellence to come.

Paul LeMat *Blaine Lovejoy, Spider* • Candy Clark *Pam, Electra* • Ann Wedgeworth *Joyce Rissley, Dallas Angel* • Marcia Rodd *Connie Rissley, Portland Angel* • Charles Napier *Harold Rissley, Chrome Angel* • Roberts Blossom *Papa Thermodyne* • Bruce McGill *Dean Lovejoy, Blood* ■ *Dir* Jonathan Demme • *Scr* Paul Brickman

The City ★★★★ U
Documentary   1939 · US · BW · 43mins

Highly stylised in content, this ambitious, worthy and ultimately mesmerising socio-documentary was funded by the American Institute of Planners for the Roosevelt administration. Purporting to present the growth of an idealised city of the future and accompanied by an impressive Aaron Copland score, this 43-minute slice of social film-making by documentarists Ralph Steiner and Willard van Dyke today resembles extreme left-wing propaganda; indeed, it comes as no surprise to discover that commentator/actor Morris Carnovsky and writers Lewis Mumford and Pare Lorentz were subsequently blacklisted. The concept of a "new city" free from industrial grime and linked by interstate highways obviously was anathema to the less enlightened post-war US governments that followed FDR's, and the film was duly withdrawn.

Morris Carnovsky *Narrator* ■ *Dir* Ralph Steiner, Willard van Dyke • *Scr* Lewis Mumford, Pare Lorentz

City across the River ★★★
Drama   1949 · US · BW · 90mins

The exploits of a teenage gang in New York, focusing in particular on one member (Peter Fernandez) and demonstrating how a petty criminal, driven by circumstance, can become a killer. Directed by Maxwell Shane in tough, semi-documentary style, the movie grips with its pace and its graphic depiction of the harsh conditions of tenement life, but it doesn't say anything new. Stephen McNally is top-billed as a community councillor, Thelma Ritter is Fernandez's mother, and a very young Tony Curtis appears as a gang member.

Stephen McNally *Stan Albert* • Thelma Ritter *Mrs Cusack* • Peter Fernandez *Frank Cusack* • Luis Van Rooten *Joe Cusack* • Jeff Corey *Lt Macon* • Anthony Curtis [Tony Curtis] *Mitch* ■ *Dir* Maxwell Shane • *Scr* Dennis Cooper, Irving Schulman, Maxwell Shane, from the novel *The Amboy Dukes* by Irving Schulman

The City and the Dogs ★★★★
Drama   1985 · Peru · Colour · 133mins

Even though this was the novel that brought Mario Vargas Llosa to international attention, Francisco Lombardi, Peru's best-known film-maker, stripped the original non-linear story down to its bare essentials for this abrasive screen adaptation. Using the corruption and tyranny that existed within the country's military academies as a metaphor for the decay blighting Peruvian society as a whole, Lombardi occasionally errs on the side of sensationalism. Otherwise, though, he relates with persuasive realism the case of senior cadet Juan Manuel Ochoa, who kills a fellow clique member to cover up the exploitative activities tolerated by his superiors. In Spanish with English subtitles.

Pablo Serra *Poet* • Gustavo Bueno *Lieutenant Gamboa* • Juan Manuel Ochoa *Jaguar* • Luis Alvarez *Colonel* • Eduardo Adrianzen *Slave* ■ *Dir* Francisco José Lombardi • *Scr* Jose Watanabe, from the novel *The City and the Dogs* by Mario Vargas Llosa

City beneath the Sea ★★★ U
Adventure   1953 · US · Colour · 86mins

An underwater adventure romp with Robert Ryan and Anthony Quinn snarling at each other over hidden treasure. Love interest is provided by Mala Powers and Suzan Ball, Lucille Ball's lovely cousin, who would continue to act after her leg was amputated due to cancer, and who died tragically young in 1955. The director is Oscar "Budd" Boetticher, who would go on to make a superb series of westerns starring Randolph Scott in the late fifties.

Robert Ryan *Brad Carlton* • Mala Powers *Terry* • Anthony Quinn *Tony Bartlett* • Suzan Ball *Venita* • George Mathews *Captain Meade* • Karel Stepanek *Dwight Trevor* • Lalo Rios *Calypso* • Woody Strode *Djion* ■ *Dir* Budd Boetticher • *Scr* Jack Harvey, Ramon Romero, from the story *Port Royal - Ghost City beneath the Sea* by Harry E Riesberg

City beneath the Sea ★★ U
Science-fiction adventure
1971 · US · Colour · 89mins

Irwin Allen, Mr Disaster Movie himself, took a dive in this pilot for a TV series that was never made. It's easy to see why, as each crisis facing the vast submerged 21st-century metropolis of Pacifica had been done better in previous Allen shows. Asteroids on a collision course, sea monsters, internal dissension and bullion robberies are piled on in the desperate effort to build excitement. But the performances are wooden and the waterlogged effects absurd. ▣

Stuart Whitman *Admiral Michael Matthews* • Robert Wagner *Brett Matthews* • Rosemary Forsyth *Lia Holmes* • Robert Colbert *Commander Woody Patterson* • Susana Miranda *Elena* • Burr DeBenning *Dr Aguila* • Richard Basehart *President* • Joseph Cotten *Dr Ziegler* ■ *Dir* Irwin Allen • *Scr* John Meredyth Lucas, from a story by Irwin Allen

City Boy ★★
Period drama   1994 · US/Can · Colour

The reassuring presence of James Brolin adds some solidity to this made-for-TV family adventure. Set at the turn of the century, it follows the fortunes of a young boy who, while searching for his father, gets caught up in a battle to save a beautiful untouched piece of forest. It's a familiar enough story, ably directed by John Kent Harrison (who also served as co-writer) and enthusiastically played by a largely unknown cast. The striking locations are an added bonus.

James Brolin *Tom McLean* • Christian Campbell *Nick* • Wendel Meldrum *Olivia Pollard* • Sarah Chalke *Angelica McMurrich* • Christopher Bolton *Simon Wessner* ■ *Dir* John Kent Harrison • *Scr* John Kent Harrison, Coralee Elliott Testar, from the book *Freckles* by Gene Stratton Porter

City for Conquest ★★★★ PG
Melodrama   1940 · US · BW · 94mins

Director Anatole Litvak tells a tough tale as truck driver turned prize fighter James Cagney tries to protect his sensitive composer brother, superbly played by Arthur Kennedy in his adult movie debut. Check out future director Elia Kazan, here playing a hood, and watch Ann Sheridan interact with a young Anthony Quinn. The film is a worthy follow-up to Warner Bros' social dramas of the thirties, although these days a slightly sententious heaviness looms over the enterprise. ▣

James Cagney *Danny Kenny* • Ann Sheridan *Peggy Nash* • Frank Craven *"Old Timer"* • Donald Crisp *Scotty McPherson* • Arthur Kennedy *Eddie Kenny* • Elia Kazan *"Googi"* • Anthony Quinn *Murray Burns* ■ *Dir* Anatole Litvak • *Scr* John Wexley, from the novel by Aben Kandel

The City Girl ★★ 18
Drama   1984 · US · Colour · 81mins

The drama in Martha Coolidge's follow-up to *Valley Girl* derives from the opposing forces that pull struggling photographer Laura Harrington apart at the seams. Trying to assert her independence, she dumps her long-time partner to play the field. Things backfire badly when a pimp she is secretly snapping scares the living daylights out of her by trashing her apartment. Harrington impresses in this tale of a modern woman trying to survive in the big wide world. ▣

Laura Harrington *Anne* • Joe Mastroianni *Joey* • Carole McGill *Gracie* • Peter Riegert *Tim* • James Carrington *Steve* • Lawrence Phillips *The stripper* • Geraldine Baron *Monica* ■ *Dir* Martha Coolidge • *Scr* Judith Thompson, Leonard-John Gates, from a story by Martha Coolidge, John MacDonald

City Hall ★★★★ 15
Political drama   1996 · US · Colour · 106mins

This is reminiscent of one of those Warner Bros gangster films of the thirties, but director Harold Becker's update is even more violent and exciting. Al Pacino is the New York mayor, rabble-rousing as he plots a path to the White House, but finding himself thwarted in his political ambition by a *cause célèbre* when a child is killed in the crossfire between a cop and a drug dealer. His naive deputy, John Cusack, investigates the crime with the help of attorney Bridget Fonda, only to find the perpetrators are uncomfortably close to home. Not particularly original, but entertaining. Contains violence and swearing. ▣

Al Pacino *Mayor John Pappas* • John Cusack *Kevin Calhoun* • Bridget Fonda *Marybeth Cogan* • Danny Aiello *Frank Anselmo* • Martin Landau *Judge Walter Stern* • David Paymer *Abe Goodman* • Tony Franciosa [Anthony Franciosa] *Paul Zapatti* • Lindsay Duncan *Sydney Pappas* ■ *Dir* Harold Becker • *Scr* Ken Lipper, Paul Schrader, Nicholas Pileggi, Bo Goldman

City Heat ★★★ 15
Comedy thriller   1984 · US · Colour · 93mins

Clint Eastwood and Burt Reynolds were dream casting, but *City Heat* got off to a bad start. Originally called *Kansas City Jazz*, it had been written by Blake Edwards, who was to direct. But Eastwood and Edwards disliked each other from the first, so Edwards left and Richard Benjamin took over. Despite the on-set problems, the movie is a nostalgic sprint through Prohibition-era Kansas City, with Clint as a cop and Burt as a private eye who team up and clear the town of gangsters. Contains swearing and some violence. ▣

Clint Eastwood *Lieutenant Speer* • Burt Reynolds *Mike Murphy* • Jane Alexander *Addy* • Madeline Kahn *Caroline Howley* • Rip Torn *Primo Pitt* • Irene Cara *Ginny Lee* • Richard Roundtree *Dehl Swift* • Tony LoBianco *Leon Coll* ■ *Dir* Richard Benjamin • *Scr* Sam O Brown [Blake Edwards], Joseph C Stinson, from a story by Sam O Brown [Blake Edwards]

City Lights ★★★★★ U
Silent comedy romance
1931 · US · BW · 82mins

A consummate storyteller, Charles Chaplin could reduce his audience to fits of laughter and, without warning, plunge them to the depths of pathos. With this masterpiece, telling the story of a tramp and the blind flower girl (Virginia Cherrill) he falls in love with, Chaplin went against the incoming tide of talking pictures by using only music, sound effects, subtitles and his own inestimable pantomime skills. He told Sam Goldwyn: "If it's a failure, I believe it will strike a deeper blow than anything else that has ever happened to me in this life.'' It was, in fact, a resounding success. 📹

Charlie Chaplin [Charles Chaplin] *Tramp* • Virginia Cherrill *Blind girl* • Florence Lee *Her grandmother* • Harry Myers *Eccentric millionaire* • Allan Garcia *His butler* • Jean Harlow *Guest* ■ *Dir/Scr* Charles Chaplin • *Music* Charles Chaplin

City Limits ★★ 🔲

Science-fiction action adventure
1985 · US · Colour · 81mins

Set in a futuristic world where most adults have been eradicated by plague, this post-apocalyptic action adventure depicts a Los Angeles divided between two motorbike gangs – the DAs and the Clippers. Orphaned Lee (John Stockwell) comes to town to join the latter, only to uncover a plot to take control of the city by the sinister Sunya Corporation, whose chief is none other than Robby Benson! Rae Dawn Chong and Kim Cattrall co-star. 📹

Darrell Larson *Mick* • John Stockwell *Lee* • Kim Cattrall *Wickings* • Rae Dawn Chong *Yogi* • John Diehl *Whitey* • Danny De La Paz *Ray* • James Earl Jones *Albert* ■ *Dir* Aaron Lipstadt • *Scr* Don Opper, from a story by James Reigle, Aaron Lipstadt

City of Angels ★★★ 🔲

Fantasy drama 1998 · US · Colour · 109mins

A semi-remake of Wim Wenders's classic *Wings of Desire*, this Hollywood version has Nicolas Cage as an angel inhabiting Los Angeles who falls for heart surgeon Meg Ryan (yes, really). Will he give up his otherworldly delights so he can ''fall'' to earth and be with her? Will she realise he's not quite like other guys? And will they both drown in the slushy sentimentality of it all? Happily, not quite, thanks to a well-chosen soundtrack (Sarah McLachlan, Goo Goo Dolls, Alanis Morissette) and a winning – and moving – performance from Cage that will melt the hearts of his female fans. 📹 *DVD*

Nicolas Cage *Seth* • Meg Ryan *Dr Maggie Rice* • Dennis Franz *Nathaniel Messinger* • AndréBraugher *Cassiel* • Colm Feore *Jordan* ■ *Dir* Brad Silberling • *Scr* Dana Stevens

City of Fear ★★

Drama 1959 · US · BW · 74mins

Following their collaboration on *Murder by Contract*, action man Vince Edwards and director Irving Lerner reteamed for this tense little thriller that boasts photography by Lucien Ballard and a score by Jerry Goldsmith. Borrowing its ticking human time-bomb plot from *Panic in the Streets*, it follows Edwards as he tries to get rid of a canister that he thinks contains heroin, but is, in fact, loaded with a radioactive material. It's hardly heart-stopping stuff, and Edwards isn't the most gifted of actors, but it's not bad.

Vince Edwards *Vince Ryker* • Lyle Talbot *Chief Jensen* • John Archer *Lieutenant Mark Richards* • Steven Ritch *Dr Wallace* • Patricia Blair *June* • Joe Mell *Crown* ■ *Dir* Irving Lerner • *Scr* Steven Ritch, Robert Dillon

City of Fear ★

Spy drama 1965 · UK · BW · 75mins

Terry Moore had the reputation of being Hollywood's bad girl and is

perhaps better known these days for her string of front-page love affairs and her secret marriage to Howard Hughes. Her acting career was as good as over by the time she made this low-budget spy picture, in which she goes behind the Iron Curtain to help refugees escape from Hungary. Moore's uninterest, the by-the-numbers plot, Peter Bezencenet's lumpen direction and Paul Maxwell's shocking performance as a reporter who stumbles upon Moore's operation are four good reasons to steer clear.

Terry Moore *Suzan* • Albert Lieven *Paul* • Marisa Mell *Ilona* • Paul Maxwell *Mike Foster* • Pinkas Braun *Ferenc* • Maria Takacs *Marika* ■ *Dir* Peter Bezencenet • *Scr* Peter Welbeck [Harry Alan Towers], Max Bourne

City of Hope ★★★★★ 🔲

Drama 1991 · US · Colour · 124mins

A title ironic to the point of sarcasm, just as you'd expect from director John Sayles, the greatest of Hollywood independents. This film brilliantly reveals the conflicts and corruptions inherent within a New Jersey community from contractors' kickbacks to racism as fault-lines upon which the community is built. It's how these seeming abstractions affect people's lives that concerns Sayles and, while there's no central star to light up the dark places, the cast's ensemble acting is vivid enough for an epic that winds down to a desperately bleak finale. Hugely impressive. Contains some violence and swearing. 📹

Vincent Spano *Nick Rinaldi* • Joe Morton *Wynn* • Tony LoBianco *Joe Rinaldi* • Barbara Williams *Angela* • Stephen Mendillo *Yoyo* • Chris Cooper *Riggs* • Charlie Yanko *Stavros* • Jace Alexander *Bobby* • Angela Bassett *Reesha* ■ *Dir/Scr* John Sayles

City of Industry ★★ 🔲

Crime thriller 1996 · US · Colour · 92mins

This dour revenge thriller stars Harvey Keitel as a crook tracking down a cohort who got greedy after a lucrative robbery. The solid, if unexceptional performances from Keitel and Dorff (as the unscrupulous scumbag he pursues), combined with John Irvin's no-frills direction and a by-the-numbers plot (which sees almost every character beaten, killed or kidnapped) lend this the appearance of a tougher-than-average TV movie. Contains swearing and violence. 📹

Harvey Keitel *Roy Egan* • Stephen Dorff *Skip Kovich* • Timothy Hutton *Lee Egan* • Famke Janssen *Rachel Montana* • Wade Dominguez *Jorge Montana* • Michael Jai White *Odell Williams* • Reno Wilson *Keshaun Brown* • Elliott Gould *Gangster* ■ *Dir* John Irvin • *Scr* Ken Solarz

City of Joy ★★★ 🔲

Drama 1992 · Fr/UK · Colour · 129mins

A much derided movie on its release, Roland Joffé's overlong and occasionally muddled tale of life in a Calcutta slum actually has much to recommend it. Patrick Swayze turns in a credible performance as the dedicated if emotionally constipated doctor, and Pauline Collins is far from clichéd as the gutsy, confrontational nurse. Joffé brings the abject squalor of the overpopulated alleys to vibrant,

atmospheric life, and all concerned give it their best shot. Contains violence and swearing. 📹

Patrick Swayze *Max Lowe* • Pauline Collins *Joan Bethel* • Om Puri *Hasari Pal* • Shabana Azmi *Kamla Pal* • Art Malik *Ashoka* • Ayesha Dharker *Amrita Pal* • Santu Chowdhury *Shambu Pal* • Imran Badsah Khan *Manooj Pal* ■ *Dir* Roland Joffé • *Scr* Mark Medoff, from the novel by Dominique LaPierre

The City of Lost Children ★★★★ 🔲

Fantasy adventure
1995 · Fr/Sp/Ger · Colour · 107mins

Ron Perlman stars in this sinister fantasy adventure from French directors Jean-Pierre Jeunet and Marc Caro who, with their extraordinary *Delicatessen*, set new standards for dark fables. From its nightmare opening to the climactic battle, this surreal tale is an astonishing eye-opener as carnival strongman One (Perlman) leads the fight against the evil Krank (Daniel Emilfork), who steals children's dreams. If you think films can do nothing new, prepare to be surprised. In French with English subtitles. 📹

Ron Perlman *One* • Daniel Emilfork *Krank* • Judith Vittet *Miette* • Dominique Pinon *Clones/Diver/Stocle* • Jean-Claude Dreyfus *Marcello, the flea tamer* • Mireille Mossé *Mademoiselle Bismuth* ■ *Dir* Marc Caro, Jean-Pierre Jeunet • *Scr* Gilles Adrien, Jean-Pierre Jeunet, Marc Caro, Guillaume Laurant

A City of Sadness ★★★★ 🔲

Drama 1989 · Tai · Colour · 160mins

The winner of the Golden Lion at Venice, this epic of intimate details puts a human face on the momentous events that buffeted Taiwan between the Japanese surrender in 1945 and the arrival of Chiang Kai-Shek's Nationalists four years later. There's a sense of microcosm about the deteriorating widower's household, with one son working as a translator during the occupation, another a deaf mute fighting for independence, the third a petty gangster and the fourth a soldier presumed killed in action. Background knowledge is inessential, though, as Hou Hsiao-Hsien's subtle compositions and meticulous pacing draw the viewer into the heart of the drama. In Mandarin and Hokkien with English subtitles.

Tony Chiu-Wai Leung [Tony Leung (1)] *Lin Wen-Ching* • Xin Shufen *Hinomi* • Chen Sown-Yung *Lin Wen-Heung* • Kao Jai *Lin Wen-Leung* • Li Tienlu *Lin Ah-Lu* • Wu Yi-Fang *Hinoe* ■ *Dir* Hou Hsiao-Hsien • *Scr* Wu Nien-Jen, Chu Tien-Wen

The City of the Dead ★★★

Horror 1960 · UK · BW · 77mins

This cheap and chilling supernatural thriller reeks of atmospheric horror and benefits enormously from its stagebound sets and black-and-white photography. A young history student goes to a remote Massachusetts village to research black magic and falls prey to a reincarnated witch burned at the stake 250 years earlier. Professor Christopher Lee is part of the modern coven holding the hamlet in a grip of sacrificial terror.

Christopher Lee *Professor Driscoll* • Patricia Jessel *Elizabeth Selwyn/Mrs Newless* • Betta

St John *Patricia Russell* • Valentine Dyall *Jethrow Keane* • Dennis Lotis *Richard Barlow* • Venetia Stevenson *Nan Barlow* • Norman MacOwan *Reverend Russell* • Ann Beach *Lottie* ■ *Dir* John Moxey [John Llewellyn Moxey] • *Scr* George Baxt, from a story by Milton Subotsky

City of Women ★★★★ 🔲

Fantasy drama 1980 · It/Fr · Colour · 139mins

Intended as Federico Fellini's contribution to a collaboration with Ingmar Bergman entitled *Love Duet* and briefly touted as a Dustin Hoffman vehicle, this sexual variation on the Scrooge theme could only have been made by the director and star of 8½. Marcello Mastroianni returns as Fellini's alter ego to embark on a revelatory journey through a gynocentric hell. There's little wonder feminist commentators decried the picture, but this phantasmagoria of flesh also contains priceless moments of parody, autobiography and satire. In Italian with English subtitles. 📹

Marcello Mastroianni *Snaporaz* • Anna Prucnal *Elena* • Bernice Stegers *Woman on train* • Jole Silvani *Motorcyclist* • Donatella Damiani *Feminist on river skates* • Ettore Manni *Dr Katzone* ■ *Dir* Federico Fellini • *Scr* Federico Fellini, Bernardino Zapponi, Brunello Rondi

City on Fire ★★

Disaster movie 1979 · Can · Colour · 105mins

Just a year before *Airplane!* relaunched his career, Leslie Nielsen was still playing it straight in disaster movies, so this does at least provide some unintentional giggles. For the most part, though, it's minor league stuff, with a collection of vaguely familiar TV faces (Barry Newman, Susan Clark, James Franciscus) along with such movie legends as Henry Fonda and Ava Gardner almost being burned to a cinder after gasoline seeps into the city's sewer system.

Barry Newman *Frank Whitman* • Susan Clark *Diana Brockhurst-Lautrec* • Shelley Winters *Nurse Andrea Harper* • Leslie Nielsen *Mayor William Dudley* • James Franciscus *Jimbo* • Ava Gardner *Maggie Grayson* • Henry Fonda *Fire chief* ■ *Dir* Alvin Rakoff • *Scr* Jack Hill, David P Lewis, Celine La Freniere

City on Fire ★★★★ 🔲

Action thriller 1987 · HK · Colour · 100mins

In this violent Hong Kong thriller, the inspiration for Quentin Tarantino's *Reservoir Dogs*, Oriental superstar Chow Yun-Fat stars as an undercover cop who works his way into a gang planning a jewel heist. When it all goes wrong, the gang returns to its warehouse rendezvous, where the recriminations begin. Director Ringo Lam accelerates the violence with undoubted skill, though it lacks the poignancy that Tarantino was to inject into his groundbreaking crime drama. In Cantonese with English subtitles. Contains violence and nudity. 📹

Chow Yun-Fat *Ko Chow* • Lee Sau Yin [Danny Lee] *Ah Foo* • Sun Yueh *Inspector Lau* • Carrie Ng *Hung* ■ *Dir* Ringo Lam • *Scr* Tommy Sham, from a story by Ringo Lam

🔲 = SUITABLE FOR ALL 🔲c = SUITABLE FOR ALL, ESPECIALLY FOR YOUNG CHILDREN (VIDEO ONLY) **PG** = PARENTAL GUIDANCE

City Slickers ★★★★ 15

Comedy western
1991 · US · Colour · 109mins

Billy Crystal and chums Daniel Stern and Bruno Kirby are the city folk who get the chance to play at *Rawhide* in a winning comedy blockbuster that cleaned up at the box office. Seeking to stave off middle age, the trio join a motley group who have volunteered to drive cattle across the range under the eye of irascible old cowboy Jack Palance. Despite some worryingly sentimental moments of male bonding, this is an engaging, expertly played piece which gently pokes fun at both middle-aged angst and the Wild West. Palance won a best supporting actor Oscar for his performance, while director Ron Underwood proves to be as adept with the gags as he is with the large-scale set pieces. Contains swearing. ▦

Billy Crystal *Mitch Robbins* • Daniel Stern *Phil Berquist* • Bruno Kirby *Ed Furillo* • Patricia Wettig *Barbara Robbins* • Helen Slater *Bonnie Rayburn* • Jack Palance *Curly* • Noble Willingham *Clay Stone* • Tracey Walter *Cookie* ■ *Dir* Ron Underwood • *Scr* Lowell Ganz, Babaloo Mandel, from a story by Billy Crystal

City Slickers II: the Legend of Curly's Gold ★★ 12

Comedy western
1994 · US · Colour · 115mins

Producers always rush out sequels to sleepers (or surprise box-office hits), hoping to cash in while the audience is still in the right mood. Unfortunately, sleepers are by definition films no one initially had much confidence in, and film-makers often struggle to repeat the inexplicably successful formula. This is a case in point, as not even the usually reliable writing team of Lowell Ganz and Babaloo Mandel could give co-writer and star Billy Crystal the kind of verbal ammunition he thrives on. Jack Palance briefly reprises his Oscar-winning role, but a hit comedy needs more than cameos, cattle and scenery. Contains some swearing.

Billy Crystal *Mitch Robbins* • Daniel Stern *Phil Berquist* • Jon Lovitz *Glen Robbins* • Jack Palance *Duke/Curly Washburn* • Patricia Wettig *Barbara Robbins* • Pruitt Taylor Vince *Bud* • Bill McKinney *Matt* • Lindsay Crystal *Holly Robbins* • Beth Grant *Lois* ■ *Dir* Paul Weiland • *Scr* Billy Crystal, Lowell Ganz, Babaloo Mandel

City Streets ★★★

Crime melodrama 1931 · US · BW · 73mins

The story of a mobster's daughter (Sylvia Sidney), jailed for a crime she didn't commit, and her romance with a carnival worker (Gary Cooper), who finds himself in trouble as a result of their involvement. One of the key offerings of its period, the film introduced Sylvia Sidney, the brilliantly understated stage actress with the born-to-suffer face, and made her an instant star at Paramount. Although this gangster melodrama seems very dated now, the stars and Rouben Mamoulian's innovative, atmospheric direction provide much to enjoy.

Gary Cooper *The Kid* • Sylvia Sidney *Nan Cooley* • Paul Lukas *Big Fellow Maskal* • Guy Kibbee *Pop Cooley* • William Boyd *McCoy* •

Wynne Gibson *Agnes* • Betty Sinclair *Pansy* • Stanley Fields *Blackie* ■ *Dir* Rouben Mamoulian • *Scr* Max Marcin, Oliver HP Garrett, from a story by Dashiell Hammett

City That Never Sleeps ★★

Detective drama 1953 · US · BW · 90mins

Chicago cop Gig Young plans to quit the force, and his wife, for nightclub dancer Mala Powers. To finance his desertion, he accepts an offer from a crooked lawyer Edward Arnold to escort gangster William Talman to safety. But plans go awry when the latter turns violent... A moderately entertaining crime entry that gives an authentic picture of night-time police work in Chicago. For all that, it strains to fill its running time.

Gig Young *Johnny Kelly* • Mala Powers *Sally Connors* • William Talman *Hayes Stewart* • Edward Arnold *Penrod Biddel* • Chill Wills *Joe Chicago* • Marie Windsor *Lydia Biddel* • Paula Raymond *Kathy Kelly* • Otto Hulett *Sgt John Kelly Sr* ■ *Dir* John H Auer • *Scr* Steve Fisher

City under the Sea ★★★ U

Science-fiction adventure
1965 · UK · Colour · 83mins

Tenuously based on Edgar Allan Poe, with Jules Verne being the main uncredited inspiration, director Jacques Tourneur's final feature (Poe regular Roger Corman turned it down) is a fanciful mix of comedy adventure and submarine suspense. Vincent Price enjoyably camps it up as the immortal underwater leader of a Cornish contingent of smugglers-turned-gillmen, and the whole subterranean soufflé is highly watchable even if, sadly, it does slide from the poetic to the pathetic.

Vincent Price *Captain* • David Tomlinson *Harold* • Tab Hunter *Ben* • Susan Hart *Jill* • John Le Mesurier *Ives* • Henry Oscar *Mumford* • Derek Newark *Dan* ■ *Dir* Jacques Tourneur • *Scr* Charles Bennett, Louis M Heyward

A Civil Action ★★★ 15

Courtroom drama
1998 · US · Colour · 110mins

Legal drama based on a true story, starring John Travolta as an "ambulance chasing" attorney who takes on potentially lucrative cases so he can settle out of court and collect his cut. Writer/director Steven Zaillian proved his talent for bringing emotionally rich drama to the screen with his Oscar-winning script for *Schindler's List* and his excellent chess prodigy drama *Innocent Moves*, but this film isn't entirely credible (even if the events did actually happen). Travolta's miraculous metamorphosis from cynical manipulator to self-destructive righter of wrongs is hard to swallow, and even harder to empathise with. Classy performances all round though, with a brilliant turn from Robert Duvall as Travolta's level-headed legal opponent. Contains some swearing. ▦

John Travolta *Jan Schlichtmann* • Robert Duvall *Jerome Facher* • Tony Shalhoub *Kevin Conway* • William H Macy *James Gordon* • Zeljko Ivanek *Bill Crowley* • Bruce Norris *William Cheeseman* • John Lithgow *Judge Skinner* • Kathleen Quinlan *Anne Anderson* • James Gandolfini *Al Love* • Stephen Fry *Pinder* • Dan Hedaya *John Riley* • Sydney Pollack *Al*

Eustis • Kathy Bates *Judge* ■ *Dir* Steven Zaillian • *Scr* Steven Zaillian, from the novel by Jonathan Harr

Claire of the Moon ★ 18

Drama 1992 · US · Colour · 103mins

At an all-female writer's retreat in Oregon, straight-laced psychologist Karen Trumbo finds herself sexually attracted to her fun-loving roommate, Trisha Todd. But will either overcome their insecurities and accept their true feelings? Full of tedious talk, lesbian stereotypes and stilted acting, this amateurish gay love story is pure soap opera, loaded with lingering glances and bumper-sticker analysing. ▦

Trisha Todd *Claire Jabrowski* • Karen Trumbo *Dr Noel Benedict* • Craig Damen *Brian* • Faith McDevitt *Maggie* • Sheila Dickenson *BJ* • Caren Graham *Tara* • Melissa Mitchell *Adriennce* ■ *Dir/Scr* Nicole Conn

Claire's Knee ★★★★ PG

Comedy 1970 · Fr · Colour · 101mins

The fifth of Eric Rohmer's "Six Moral Tales", this is a hypnotic study of temptation, sumptuously shot by Nestor Almendros in the shimmering Annecy sunshine. Although events unfold from the viewpoint of diplomat Jean-Claude Brialy, the attention, as so often in Rohmer's films, is focused firmly on the emotions of young women, in this case, of the sisters (Laurence De Monaghan and Béatrice Romand) he has been encouraged to flirt with in a bid to experience passion before his forthcoming wedding. Typically, Rohmer allows the action to revolve around his characters' conversations, which are endlessly entertaining and provocative. In French with English subtitles. ▦

Jean-Claude Brialy *Jérôme* • Aurora Cornu *Aurora* • Béatrice Romand *Laura* • Laurence De Monaghan *Claire* • Michèle Montel *Madame Walter* • Gérard Falconetti *Gilles* ■ *Dir/Scr* Eric Rohmer • *Producer* Barbet Schroeder, Pierre Cottrell

The Clairvoyant ★★★

Drama 1934 · UK · BW · 80mins

Claude Rains was the unsung villain or patient victim of many a Hollywood melodrama. This underused British actor gets a crack at the lead in this creaky drama from director Maurice Elvey, in which he peddles fake predictions at a music hall until he suddenly starts hitting nails on the head. When his warnings about an impending tunnel disaster go unheeded, he finds himself the scapegoat for the hysteria that precipitated the tragedy. Rains is impressive throughout, whether faking on the stage, pleading to be taken seriously or explaining his friendship with Jane Baxter to wife Fay Wray.

Claude Rains *Maximus* • Fay Wray *Rene* • Jane Baxter *Christine* • Mary Clare *Mother* • Ben Field *Simon* • Athole Stewart *Lord Southwood* • Felix Aylmer *Counsel* • Donald Calthrop *Derelict* ■ *Dir* Maurice Elvey • *Scr* Charles Bennett, Bryan Edgar Wallace, from the novel by Ernst Lothar

Clambake ★ U

Musical 1967 · US · Colour · 95mins

Elvis Presley's 25th film – a reworking of *The Prince and the Pauper* – looks like it cost next to nothing, and probably did. Set in Miami, though Presley clearly never left Hollywood for his scenes, it features a perfunctory performance from the King, who actually has less screen time than his co-star Will Hutchins. The colour is garish, the back projection looks phoney and the songs – with the exception of *You Don't Know Me* – are below par. ▦

Elvis Presley *Scott Heyward* • Shelley Fabares *Dianne Carter* • Will Hutchins *Tom Wilson* • Bill Bixby *James Jamison III* • Gary Merrill *Sam Burton* • James Gregory *Duster Heyward* • Amanda Harley *Ellie* • Suzie Kaye *Sally* ■ *Dir* Arthur Nadel • *Scr* Arthur Browne Jr

The Clan of the Cave Bear ★★ 15

Fantasy drama 1986 · US · Colour · 93mins

One can applaud the quest for authenticity, but watching Raquel Welch dodging dinosaurs in *One Million Years BC* is really a lot more entertaining. Daryl Hannah is the strange blond prehistoric human who is taken in by a gang of grunting Neanderthals and proceeds to make her own small contribution to the evolution of the species. This boasts higher production values than its predecessor, and even a script by acclaimed film-maker John Sayles, but in the end it falls into the worthy but dull category. Contains violence. ▦

Daryl Hannah *Ayla* • Pamela Reed *Iza* • James Remar *Creb* • Thomas G Waites *Broud* • John Doolittle *Brun* • Curtis Armstrong *Goov* • Martin Doyle *Grod* • Adel C Hammoud *Vorn* ■ *Dir* Michael Chapman • *Scr* John Sayles, from the novel by Jean M Auel

Clancy Street Boys ★★ U

Comedy 1943 · US · BW · 65mins

This *East Side Kids* romp was originally filmed as *Grand Street Boys*. Leo Gorcey (as Muggs McGinnis, not yet the Bowery Boys wiseguy Slip Mahoney) gets the whole gang to pretend to be his relatives in order to fool uncle Noah Beery Sr. Connoisseurs of famous faces in drag should notice the bizarre rig-out here of pawky Huntz Hall, essaying a very funny routine as a female sibling.

Leo Gorcey *Muggs* • Huntz Hall *Glimpy* • Bobby Jordan *Danny* • Bennie Bartlett *Bennie* • Noah Beery Sr [Noah Beery] *Pete* • Amelita Ward *Judy* • Rick Vallin *George* • Martha Wentworth *Mrs McGinnis* • J Farrell MacDonald *Flanagan* ■ *Dir* William Beaudine • *Scr* Harvey Gates

The Clandestine Marriage ★★ 15

Period comedy drama
1999 · UK · Colour · 90mins

Though gamely directed by Christopher Miles, this 18th-century period piece is a mismatched mating of British talents. Nigel Hawthorne heads the cast as a drunken lord trying to get his family entwined with the nouveau riche, while Joan Collins puts her best bosoms forward as a domineering snob. Alas, they can't convince us there's much wit in the piece. The film's walking waxworks look is impeccable, but its theme of nobility migrating across class for money doesn't make us care about the outcome or the mercenary characters. It might have been different had there been someone to like, though audiences of the time no doubt found it hilarious. Contains sex scenes.

Nigel Hawthorne *Lord Ogleby* • Joan Collins *Mrs Heidelberg* • Timothy Spall *Sterling* • Tom Hollander *Sir John Ogleby* • Paul Nicholls *Lovewell* • Natasha Little *Fanny* • Cyril Shaps *Canton* ■ *Dir* Christopher Miles • *Scr* Trevor Bentham, from the play by George Coleman the Elder, David Garrick

Clara's Heart ★★★ 🔢
Melodrama 1988 · US · Colour · 108mins

Jamaican resort-hotel maid Clara (Whoopi Goldberg) gives comfort and wise counsel to a grieving couple (Kathleen Quinlan and Michael Ontkean) on vacation after the death of their baby. They then take her back with them to Baltimore to run their lives and that of their "rich kid" son (Neil Patrick Harris). Unashamedly old-fashioned and sentimental, this is a manipulative weepie-cum-feel good movie, expertly assembled by director Robert Mulligan from a script by Mark Medoff. Goldberg is on top form, and it's all against a background of glossy Freddie Francis photography and a Dave Grusin score. 🔲

Whoopi Goldberg *Clara Mayfield* • Michael Ontkean *Bill Hart* • Kathleen Quinlan *Leona Hart* • Neil Patrick Harris *David Hart* • Spalding Gray *Dr Peter Epstein* • Beverly Todd *Dora* • Hattie Winston *Blanche Loudon* ■ *Dir* Robert Mulligan • *Scr* Mark Medoff, from the novel by Joseph Olshan

Clarence, the Cross-Eyed Lion ★★★ 🆄
Adventure 1965 · US · Colour · 87mins

This pilot for the TV series *Daktari* makes for painless entertainment, but only hints at the superb blend of comedy and adventure that made the show such a big hit between 1966 and 1969. Marshall Thompson and Cheryl Miller play the heads of an Animal Behaviour Centre deep in the African jungle, going on to become TV regulars. Here, though, they are upstaged – not only by the wonderful Clarence, but also by movie veterans Richard Haydn and Betsy Drake. Action expert Andrew Marton fudges the quieter moments, but there is plenty to interest youngsters. 🔲

Marshall Thompson *Dr Marsh Tracy* • Betsy Drake *Julie Harper* • Cheryl Miller *Paula* • Richard Haydn *Rupert Rowbotham* • Alan Caillou *Carter* • Rockne Tarkington *Juma* ■ *Dir* Andrew Marton • *Scr* Alan Caillou, from a story by Art Arthur, Marshall Thompson

Clash by Night ★★★
Melodrama 1952 · US · BW · 104mins

Tough Barbara Stanwyck returns to her seaside hometown; she marries straight Paul Douglas, but hankers after wild fisherman Robert Ryan. The top-billed stars are of secondary interest today, however, as this movie features an early appearance by Marilyn Monroe, giving an intelligent and astoundingly sexy performance.

What is surprising is that this inexpensive RKO melodrama is from once revered émigré director Fritz Lang, who fails to disguise the inherent dullness of the original material or to mask the obvious studio backdrops and poor matching front projection. Watch it for Stanwyck and Ryan, and Monroe on the rise.

Barbara Stanwyck *Mae Doyle* • Paul Douglas *Jerry D'Amato* • Robert Ryan *Earl Pfeiffer* • Marilyn Monroe *Peggy* • J Carrol Naish *Uncle Vince* • Keith Andes *Joe Doyle* ■ *Dir* Fritz Lang • *Scr* Alfred Hayes, David Dortort, from the play by Clifford Odets

Clash by Night ★
Crime drama 1963 · UK · BW · 75mins

This British crime drama was released in the US as *Escape by Night* to avoid confusion with the 1952 Fritz Lang melodrama of the same name. The only interesting thing about this bargain-basement tale of escaped prisoners is the sight of Peter Sallis gleefully torching a barn that has already been doused in paraffin. Unsurprisingly, it was three years before Irish-born B-movie specialist Montgomery Tully directed another feature.

Terence Longden *Martin Lord* • Jennifer Jayne *Nita Lord* • Harry Fowler *Doug Roberts* • Peter Sallis *Victor Lush* • Alan Wheatley *Ronald Grey-Simmons* • Vanda Godsell *Mrs Grey-Simmons* ■ *Dir* Montgomery Tully • *Scr* Maurice J Wilson, Montgomery Tully, from the novel by Rupert Croft-Brooke

Clash of the Titans ★★★ 🔢
Fantasy adventure 1981 · US/UK · Colour · 117mins

A stodgy re-run of *Jason and the Argonauts*, with Perseus, Andromeda and assorted giant livestock going through their mythological paces. Harry Hamlin and Judi Bowker make anaemic heroes, Ray Harryhausen's stop-motion special effects are wobblesome and Laurence Olivier, dressed in a white bathrobe and a Santa Claus beard, overacts as Zeus. While fans of the genre may still find things to enjoy, professors of architecture will note that the ancient theatre used in the picture is of late-Roman design and, therefore, out of date by several centuries. Just like the movie itself. 🔲

Laurence Olivier *Zeus* • Harry Hamlin *Perseus* • Claire Bloom *Hera* • Maggie Smith *Thetis* • Ursula Andress *Aphrodite* • Judi Bowker *Andromeda* • Jack Gwillim *Poseidon* • Susan Fleetwood *Athena* • Pat Roach *Hephaestus* • Burgess Meredith *Ammon* • Sian Phillips *Cassiopeia* • Tim Pigott-Smith *Thallo* ■ *Dir* Desmond Davis • *Scr* Beverley Cross

Class ★★ 🔢
Comedy drama 1983 · US · Colour · 94mins

A typical sexual rites-of-passage movie, overlaid with dubious eighties concerns about making money and wearing the right designer clothes. There is something queasily tacky about the fragrant Jacqueline Bisset debagging her son's school friend in a glass-sided lift, and the rest of this distinctly self-satisfied movie is full of the kind of personal selfishness that takes you back to the decade of materialism. The characters lack any form of compassion or self-doubt, essential ingredients for a movie about teenage

sexual awakening. Contains violence and swearing. 🔲

Rob Lowe *Skip* • Andrew McCarthy *Jonathan* • Jacqueline Bisset *Ellen* • Cliff Robertson *Mr Burroughs* • Stuart Margolin *Balaban* • John Cusack *Roscoe* ■ *Dir* Lewis John Carlino • *Scr* Jim Kouf, David Greenwalt

Class Act ★ 🔢
Comedy 1992 · US · Colour · 93mins

There's trouble in the high school classroom when a tough street hood and an intellectual nerd swap identities. That's the premise behind this blunt comedy vehicle, built around the talents of one-time rap sensations Kid 'n' Play (Christopher Reid and Christopher Martin). The stars' winning personalities just about make this slight urban variation on *The Prince and the Pauper* bearable, despite the fact that the film suffers from in-joke fatigue and now looks as dated as break-dancing. 🔲

Christopher Reid *Duncan Pinderhughes* • Christopher Martin *Blade* • Andre Rosey Brown *Jail guard* • Meshach Taylor *Duncan's dad* • Mariann Aalda *Duncan's mum* ■ *Dir* Randall Miller • *Scr* John Semper, Cynthia Freidlob, from a story by Michael Swerdlick, Wayne Rice, Richard Brenne

Class Action ★★★ 🔢
Courtroom drama 1991 · US · Colour · 104mins

Proving that he has an instinct for populist drama with *Coronation Street*, and that he is no stranger to gritty authenticity in *7 Up* (the documentary about children whose lives he went on to update every seven years), British director Michael Apted combined both tendencies with real force in *Coal Miner's Daughter*. He continues in this vein with *Class Action*, where Gene Hackman and Mary Elizabeth Mastrantonio revel in grand dramatic gestures and the fine detail of character acting. They play dad-and-daughter lawyers – he's the concerned, scruffy liberal, she's the thrusting, power-suited achiever. The whiff of contrivance takes the edge off several scenes, but the powerful emotional centre galvanises two actors on top form. Contains swearing. 🔲

Gene Hackman *Jedediah Tucker Ward* • Mary Elizabeth Mastrantonio *Maggie Ward* • Joanna Merlin *Estelle Ward* • Colin Friels *Michael Grazier* • Jonathan Silverman *Brian* • Donald Moffat *Quinn* • Laurence Fishburne *Nick Holbrook* • Jan Rubes *Pavel* • Matt Clark *Judge Symes* ■ *Dir* Michael Apted • *Scr* Carolyn Shelby, Christopher Ames, Samantha Shad

Class of '44 ★★ 🔢
Drama 1973 · US · Colour · 90mins

It's graduation time at a Brooklyn high school, and three close friends must part; Benjie (Oliver Conant) goes off to war, while Oscy and Hermie (Jerry Houser and Gary Grimes) enrol in college. A recycled version of Robert Mulligan's hugely successful *Summer of '42*, using the same screenwriter (Herman Raucher), characters and lead actors. Raucher's narrative imagination has run out of steam, however, and director Paul Bogart is no Mulligan. Made with evocative attention to period detail and trading on the charm

of Grimes and his co-stars, it's OK – but not much more. 🔲

Gary Grimes *Hermie* • Jerry Houser *Oscy* • Oliver Conant *Benjie* • William Atherton *Fraternity President* • Sam Bottoms *Marty* • Deborah Winters *Julie* • Joe Ponazecki *Professor* • Murray Westgate *Principal* ■ *Dir* Paul Bogart • *Scr* Herman Raucher

Class of 1984 ★★ 🔞
Drama 1982 · Can · Colour · 93mins

This ultra-violent, ultra-cynical thriller built up something of a cult following: it was followed by two equally nasty sequels, and it continues to spawn bigger-budgeted imitators (*The Principal, The Substitute*). Perry King stars as the dedicated teacher who takes the law into his own hands to wrest control of his school back from psycho Timothy Van Patten and his chums, who are terrorising students and staff alike. The message may be unpalatable, but director Mark L Lester stages the set pieces with ruthless efficiency. Look out for an early appearance by Michael J Fox. 🔲

Perry King *Andy Norris* • Timothy Van Patten *Peter Stegman* • Merrie Lynn Ross *Diane Norris* • Roddy McDowall *Terry Corrigan* • Al Waxman *Detective Stawiski* • Lisa Langlois *Patsy* • David Gardner *Morganthau* • Michael J Fox *Arthur* ■ *Dir* Mark L Lester • *Scr* John Saxton, Mark L Lester, from a story by Tom Holland

Class of 1999 ★★ 🔞
Science-fiction 1990 · US · Colour · 91mins

This sequel to *Class of 1984* – directed, like the original, by Mark L Lester – presents the high school of the future as a violent battleground. It's so bad the teachers have been replaced by robots who can supposedly handle the psychopathic kids. Obviously the robots' programmers had never seen *Westworld*, and it's not long before the machines malfunction and things get hilariously ugly. Brutal and camp at the same time, this futuristic tale fails because Lester thinks he can insert some sort of message into the mayhem. 🔲

Malcolm McDowell *Dr Miles Langford* • Bradley Gregg *Cody Culp* • John P Ryan *Mr Hardin* • Pam Grier *Ms Connors* • Stacy Keach *Dr Bob Forrest* • Traci Lin *Christine Langford* ■ *Dir* Mark L Lester • *Scr* C Courtney Joyner, from a story by Mark L Lester

Class of 1999 II: The Substitute ★ 🔞
Science-fiction action adventure 1993 · US · Colour · 86mins

Cyborg substitute teacher Sasha Mitchell – the last of the A-77 series of battle droids – starts killing his high school students when they turn delinquent in a boring follow-up to the original video hit. Part *Blackboard Jungle*, part bloodthirsty war movie, this cynical sequel is a badly structured, sleazy shambles which incorporates footage from *Class of 1999* to beef up its running time. The high moral tone taken becomes even more of a joke once the vicious blood-letting begins in a film that plumbs the depths of unpleasantness. 🔲

Sasha Mitchell *John Bolen* • Nick Cassavetes *Emmett Grazer* • Caitlin Dulany *Jenna McKensie* • Jack Knight *Sheriff Tom Yost* ■ *Dir* Spiro Razatos • *Scr* Mark Sevi

The Class of Miss MacMichael ★★★ 15

Comedy drama   1978 · UK · Colour · 94mins

Loitering a long way behind *The Blackboard Jungle*, this chalkface bungle at least features two watchable, hyperactive performances by Glenda Jackson and Oliver Reed. At a special needs school, he's the headmaster who's a brute to the kids but a charmer with the parents, while she's a dedicated teacher whose caring integrity manages to break through student hostility. The loss of her stodgy boyfriend (Michael Murphy) seems a price well worth paying. There's more sexual permissiveness unleashed here than in other teenage dramas of the time but, when Jackson and Reed are absent, this doesn't make it any more watchable. Contains some swearing and violence. ▣

Glenda Jackson *Conor MacMichael* • Oliver Reed *Terence Sutton* • Michael Murphy *Martin* • Rosalind Cash *Una Ferrar* • John Standing *Fairbrother* • Riba Akabusi *Gaylord* • Phil Daniels *Stewart* • Patrick Murray *Boysie* • Sylvia O'Donnell *Marie* • Sharon Fussey *Belinda* ■ *Dir* Silvio Narizzano • *Scr* Judd Bernard, from the novel by Sandy Hutson

Class of Nuke 'Em High ★ 18

Science-fiction horror
1986 · US · Colour · 81mins

This typically bargain-basement production from Troma, the no-frills company who brought us the cult-ish *Toxic Avenger* movies, follows a bunch of high school kids who suffer radiation mutation from a local nuclear plant which makes the one in *The Simpsons* look like a model of health and safety. Yes, it's awfully acted, insanely scripted and cluelessly directed, but criticising a Troma movie is somewhat pointless, since they don't pretend to produce anything other than sick, silly entertainment for beered-up horror fans. Anybody else should steer clear. Two sequels followed. ▣

Janelle Brady *Chrissy* • Gilbert Brenton *Warren* • Robert Prichard *Spike* • RL Ryan *Mr Paley* • James Nugent Vernon *Eddie* • Brad Dunker *Gonzo* • Gary Schneider *Pete* ■ *Dir* Richard W Haines, Samuel Weil [Lloyd Kaufman] • *Scr* Richard W Haines, Mark Rudnitsky, Samuel Weil [Lloyd Kaufman], Stuart Strutin, from a story by Richard W Haines

Class Trip ★★★

Psychological thriller
1998 · Fr · Colour · 98mins

Imagination and reality become dangerously intertwined in this adaptation of Emmanuel Carrère's cult novel. Yet, in spite of a heroic performance from Clément Van Den Bergh as the outsider who spends a school holiday boasting that his father is a spy, this potentially gripping drama suffers from indifferent handling. Director Claude Miller makes effective use of the wintry light and the stunning snowscapes, but he too often resorts to obfuscation to disguise the holes in the screenplay. In French with English subtitles. Contains horror scenes.

Clément Van Den Bergh *Nicolas* • Lokman Nalcakan *Hodkann* • François Roy *The father* • Yves Verhoeven *Patrick* • Emmanuelle Béart *Miss Grimm* • Tina Sportolaro *The mother* • Yves Jacques *The visitor* ■ *Dir* Claude Miller, Claude Miller • *Scr* Claude Miller, Emmanuel Carrere, from a novel by Emmanuel Carrere • *Cinematographer* Guillaume Schiffman

Claudelle Inglish ★

Drama   1961 · US · BW · 96mins

Diane McBain stars as farm girl Claudelle, who goes to the bad with a succession of young men in this totally unengaging and unattractive melodrama. The supporting cast is uninspiring, with the exception of Arthur Kennedy as the girl's father, while director Gordon Douglas can do nothing to disguise producer Leonard Freeman's inept screenplay, based on a novel by Erskine Caldwell (of *Tobacco Road* fame).

Diane McBain *Claudelle Inglish* • Arthur Kennedy *Clyde Inglish* • Will Hutchins *Dennis Peasley* • Constance Ford *Jessie Inglish* • Claude Akins *ST Crawford* • Frank Overton *Harley Peasley* • Chad Everett *Linn Varner* ■ *Dir* Gordon Douglas • *Scr* Leonard Freeman, from the novel by Erskine Caldwell

Claudia ★★★★

Comedy drama   1943 · US · BW · 91mins

An enchanting film debut for Dorothy McGuire, who played the title role in Rose Franken's popular play on Broadway. Her performance as a young woman coming to terms with married life is the highlight of a film that's unusually frank for its time about domestic issues. Robert Young is perfectly cast as McGuire's husband and Ina Claire does well as her ailing mother. A less effective but equally well-acted sequel, *Claudia and David*, was released three years later, in which McGuire and Young are seen coping as worried parents.

Dorothy McGuire *Claudia* • Robert Young *David Naughton* • Ina Claire *Mrs Brown* • Reginald Gardiner *Jerry Seymour* • Olga Baclanova *Madame Daruska* • Jean Howard *Julie* ■ *Dir* Edmund Goulding • *Scr* Morrie Ryskind, from the play by Rose Franken

Claudia and David ★★★

Comedy drama   1946 · US · BW · 77mins

The follow-up to 1943's charming *Claudia*, continuing the ever-so-slight tale of the titular couple as they have a son and discover what really matters in life. Keeping sentiment at bay, Dorothy McGuire and her under-rated screen partner Robert Young turn in suitably enthusiastic performances. Effortlessly directed by talented Walter Lang, this lacks the then-daring plotline of its predecessor that showed the couple struggling to come to terms with marriage, but is extremely engaging nevertheless.

Dorothy McGuire *Claudia* • Robert Young *David* • Mary Astor *Elizabeth Van Doren* • John Sutton *Phil Dexter* • Gail Patrick *Julia Naughton* • Rose Hobart *Edith Dexter* • Harry Davenport *Dr Harry* • Florence Bates *Nancy Riddle* ■ *Dir* Walter Lang • *Scr* Rose Franken, William Brown Meloney, from the story by Rose Franken

Claudine ★★★

Drama   1974 · US · Colour · 92mins

The trials and tribulations of a single black mother, attempting to rear six children in an urban environment, and her relationship with her refuse collector boyfriend. Well directed by John Berry, this engaging drama is beautifully played by Diahann Carroll (who was nominated for a best actress Oscar), James Earl Jones and an excellent cast of youngsters. Devoid of the usual dose of drugs and crime, the film points up the problems of the working-class black community as they struggle to make something out of life.

Diahann Carroll *Claudine* • James Earl Jones *Roop* • Lawrence Hilton-Jacobs *Charles* • Tamu *Charlene* • David Kruger *Paul* • Yvette Curtis *Patrice* • Eric Jones *Francis* • Socorro Stephens *Lurlene* • Adam Wade *Owen* ■ *Dir* John Berry • *Scr* Tina Pine, Lester Pine

Clay Pigeons ★★★

Black comedy   1998 · US · Colour · 104mins

Double-double-cross and serial killing in Montana as Joaquin Phoenix, Janeane Garofalo and Vince Vaughn embark on a simultaneously entertaining and harrowing road trip in director David Dobkin's psychological comedy. Clay is a young man with a past who is befriended by a serial killer – and every woman Clay introduces him to seems to wind up dead. Bringing a unique and satirical edge to the weather-beaten sleazy crime genre, this Ridley Scott production features a great Golden Oldie soundtrack and cinematography evocative of early Gus Van Sant and Jim Jarmusch.

Joaquin Phoenix *Clay* • Vince Vaughn *Lester* • Janeane Garofalo *Agent Shelby* • Gregory Sporleder *Earl* • Georgina Cates *Amanda* • Scott Wilson *Sheriff Mooney* ■ *Dir* David Dobkin • *Scr* Matthew Healy • *Producer* Ridley Scott, Chris Zarpas • *Cinematographer* Eric Edwards

Clean and Sober ★★★ 15

Drama   1988 · US · Colour · 118mins

Although he made his name as a comic, Michael Keaton has always impressed in dramatic roles, particularly those with a darker tinge. This was his first real foray into straight territory, and he delivers a mesmerising performance as a cynical, bitter drug addict in rehab who slowly learns to face up to his responsibilities. There is able support from Kathy Baker and Morgan Freeman and, although the direction from *Moonlighting* creator Glenn Gordon Caron is too small-scale, there's no denying the film's power. ▣

Michael Keaton *Daryl Poynter* • Kathy Baker *Charlie Standers* • Morgan Freeman *Craig* • M Emmet Walsh *Richard Dirks* • Luca Bercovici *Lenny* • Tate Donovan *Donald Towle* • Henry Judd Baker *Xavier* • Claudia Christian *Iris* ■ *Dir* Glenn Gordon Caron • *Scr* Tod Carroll

Clean, Shaven ★★★★

Crime drama   1993 · US · Colour · 79mins

A schizophrenic searches for his daughter and falls under suspicion of being a child serial killer in director Lodge H Kerrigan's highly disturbing low-budget independent production. Peter Greene gives a haunting performance as the mentally disabled individual who hears voices and self-mutilates himself, while Kerrigan coldly points the finger at an uncaring society in this plea for tolerance. Not an easy film to watch by any means, but undeniably powerful nonetheless. Contains violence, swearing, sex scenes and nudity.

Peter Greene *Peter Winter* • Molly Castelloe *Melinda Frayne* • Megan Owen *Mrs Winter* • Jennifer MacDonald *Nicole Frayne* ■ *Dir/Scr* Lodge H Kerrigan

Clean Slate ★★★★ 12

Drama   1981 · Fr · Colour · 128mins

In transferring Jim Thompson's novel *Pop. 1280* from the American Deep South to equatorial Africa in 1938, Bertrand Tavernier passes comment on imperialism, appeasement and the corrupting nature of power, as well as exploring the psychology of a weak man pushed to his limits. For all the script's dark deliberations, however, the film's bite is provided by Philippe Noiret's dissemblingly shambolic performance as the scorned cop who abuses his position to cover up a murderous vendetta against everyone who's slighted him. In French with English subtitles.

Philippe Noiret *Lucien Cordier* • Isabelle Huppert *Rose* • Jean-Pierre Marielle *Le Peron/His brother* • Stéphane Audran *Huguette Cordier* • Eddy Mitchell *Nono* • Guy Marchand *Chavasson* ■ *Dir* Bertrand Tavernier • *Scr* Jean Aurenche, Bertrand Tavernier

Clean Slate ★★★ 12

Comedy   1994 · US · Colour · 102mins

Wayne's World star Dana Carvey is a detective with a rare form of amnesia in a mildly amusing comedy in the *Groundhog Day* mould. Every morning he wakes up with his memory wiped completely clean of the previous day's events – a particularly unfortunate occurrence seeing he's the key witness in a mob trial. Chuckles may be thin on the ground during Carvey's constant manic memory refreshment, but the endearingly dotty premise proves compulsive overall. ▣

Dana Carvey *Maurice Pogue* • Valeria Golino *Sarah/Beth* • James Earl Jones *Dolby* • Kevin Pollak *Rosenheim* • Michael Gambon *Cornell* • Michael Murphy *Dr Doover* • Jayne Brook *Paula* • Vyto Ruginis *Hendrix* • Olivia D'Abo *Judy* ■ *Dir* Mick Jackson • *Scr* Robert King

Clear and Present Danger ★★★ 12

Political thriller   1994 · US · Colour · 135mins

It's no wonder that three first-rank screenwriters were hired to adapt this sequel to *Patriot Games*, as there is so much plot in Tom Clancy's original novel that it's a minor miracle they squeezed it all into 135 minutes. It takes the picture some time to gather momentum, but, once the links between the Colombian drugs barons and some top US officials are established, it's action all the way, with Harrison Ford on commanding form for his second outing as CIA troubleshooter Jack Ryan. Contains some violence and swearing. ▣

Harrison Ford *Jack Ryan* • Willem Dafoe *Clark* • Anne Archer *Cathy Ryan* • Joaquin de Almeida *Felix Cortez* • Henry Czerny *Robert*

Ritter • Harris Yulin *James Cutter* • Donald Moffat *President Bennett* • Miguel Sandoval *Ernesto Escobedo* ■ *Dir* Phillip Noyce • *Scr* Donald Stewart, Steven Zaillian, John Milius, from the novel by Tom Clancy

Clearcut ★★★ 18

Fantasy thriller 1992 · Can · Colour · 97mins

Since *Dances with Wolves*, Graham Greene has been steadily building up an impressive body of work. As the volatile member of a band of Canadian Indians battling to keep a lumber company off their land, Greene gives a quietly imposing performance that suggests a deep commitment to the cause at issue. The film's subplot, about the corruption of the judicial system, is also handled with restraint, making the sudden outburst of violence even more shocking. Contains violence and swearing. ▣

Ron Lea *Peter Maguire* • Graham Greene *Arthur* • Rebecca Jenkins *Female reporter* • Michael Hogan *Bud Rickets* • Floyd Red Crow Westerman *Wilf Redwing* • Tia Smith *Polly* ■ *Dir* Richard Bugajski [Ryszard Bugajski] • *Scr* Rob Forsyth, from the novel *A Dream Like Mine* by MT Kelly

Cleo from 5 to 7 ★★★★★★

Drama 1961 · Fr · Colour and BW · 93mins

This remarkable feature typifies all that was good in French film-making during its celebrated New Wave. Writer/director Agnès Varda (one of the unsung stalwarts of the period) constantly introduces the unexpected into both the central story and its many diversions, cinematographer Jean Rabier's images of Paris are uncomplicated, and the performances are cleverly stylised. Beneath her cool exterior, Corinne Marchand as Cleo manages to convey a range of emotions, whether worrying about her medical tests, chatting with strangers or singing with Michel Legrand. In French with English subtitles.

Corinne Marchand *Cleo* • Antoine Bourseiller *Antoine* • Dorothée Blanck *Dorothee* • Michel Legrand *Bob, the pianist* • Dominique Davray *Angele* • José-Luis De Villalonga *The Lover* • Jean-Claude Brialy *Actor in comedy film* • Anna Karina *Actor in comedy film* • Eddie Constantine *Actor in comedy film* • Sami Frey *Actor in comedy film* • Danièle Delorme *Actor in comedy film* • Jean-Luc Godard *Actor in comedy film* • Yves Robert *Actor in comedy film* ■ *Dir/Scr* Agnès Varda

Cleopatra ★★★

Historical drama 1934 · US · BW · 99mins

Cecil B DeMille's film about Caesar, Anthony and Cleopatra isn't really a historical epic at all; it's a thirties sex comedy about two guys and a gal who also happen to rule the world. DeMille can't quite jump the major hurdle – that Cleopatra never two-timed Caesar – and thus ends up with two separate stories, but the movie has real charm, if little substance. Colbert is sexy and also captures Cleo's political shrewdness; the problem is that both Caesar (Warren William) and Anthony (Henry Wilcoxon) are such lummoxes.

Claudette Colbert *Cleopatra* • Warren William *Julius Caesar* • Henry Wilcoxon *Marc Anthony* • Gertrude Michael *Calpurnia* • Joseph Schildkraut *Herod* • Ian Keith *Octavian* • C Aubrey Smith *Enobarbus* • Ian Maclaren

Cassius • Arthur Hohl *Brutus* ■ *Dir* Cecil B DeMille • *Scr* Waldemar Young, Vincent Lawrence, Bartlett McCormick

Cleopatra ★★★ PG

Historical drama 1963 · US · Colour · 248mins

Taking inflation into account, *Cleopatra* remains the most expensive film ever made: around $40m at the time, roughly $250m in today's money. That's *Waterworld* plus *Die Hard*. So why did it cost so much? Well, starting production in wintry England with Peter Finch, Stephen Boyd and director Rouben Mamoulian didn't help matters. Cranking up again in Rome, this time with Joseph L Mankiewicz shooting by day and writing by night, Elizabeth Taylor's frequent illnesses gave the accountants nightmares, even if her on-set romance with Richard Burton was a publicist's dream. The spectacle is the thing; yet the film does manage to make some sense of an extraordinary moment in history, as Rome expanded from republic to empire. ▣

Elizabeth Taylor *Cleopatra* • Richard Burton *Mark Antony* • Rex Harrison *Julius Caesar* • Pamela Brown *High priestess* • George Cole *Flavius* • Hume Cronyn *Sosigenes* • Cesare Danova *Apollodorus* • Kenneth Haigh *Brutus* • Andrew Keir *Agrippa* • Martin Landau *Rufio* • Roddy McDowall *Octavian* ■ *Dir* Joseph L Mankiewicz • *Scr* Joseph L Mankiewicz, Ranald MacDougall, Sidney Buchman, from the works of Plutarch, Suetonius and Appian, and the novel *The Life and Times of Cleopatra* by Carlo Mario Franzero • *Costume Designer* Irene Sharaff, Vittorio Nino Novarese, Renie

Cleopatra Jones ★★ 15

Blaxploitation crime action 1973 · US · Colour · 84mins

After napalming opium fields in Turkey, statuesque narcotics agent Tamara Dobson returns to LA to confront Shelley Winters, lesbian queen of the drug underworld. Jack Starrett handles the action well, though clumsy martial arts and comic book theatrics conspire against his vigorous direction. Yet the meld of funky exuberance, urban angst and camp performances make this blaxploitation landmark a heady, bad-ass cocktail. ▣

Tamara Dobson *Cleopatra Jones* • Bernie Casey *Reuben* • Brenda Sykes *Tiffany* • Antonio Fargas *Doodlebug* • Bill McKinney *Officer Purdy* • Dan Frazer *Detective Crawford* • Stafford Morgan *Sergeant Kert* • Mike Warren [Michael Warren] *Andy* • Shelley Winters *Mommy* ■ *Dir* Jack Starrett • *Scr* Max Julien, from a story by Max Julien, Sheldon Keller

Cleopatra Jones and the Casino of Gold ★★ 15

Blaxploitation action drama 1975 · US/HK · Colour · 92mins

Super-foxy Tamara Dobson is sent to Hong Kong to free two CIA agents caught in the Chinatown underworld clutches of the evil Dragon Lady (Stella Stevens). The result is more glossy high camp and low-grade action, with the statuesque Dobson piling on the silver eye shadow and changing into increasingly outlandish outfits. Slick and outrageous fun. ▣

Tamara Dobson *Cleopatra Jones* • Stella Stevens *Dragon Lady* • Tanny *Mi Ling* •

Norman Fell *Stanley Nagel* • Albert Popwell *Matthew Johnson* • Caro Kenyatta *Melvin* ■ *Dir* Chuck Bail • *Scr* William Tennant, from characters created by Max Julien

Clerks ★★★★ 18

Comedy 1994 · US · BW · 88mins

Director Kevin Smith's prize-winning debut feature is a micro-budget, black-and-white marvel that focuses on a day in the life of a New Jersey convenience store. The double act of Brian O'Halloran and Jeff Anderson amuse, charm and offend as they lounge around discussing sex, videos, food prices, sex, *Star Wars* and sex. Their counter-culture diatribes are by turn screamingly funny and wincingly accurate, although those of a sensitive nature should be warned. Smith's direction is as delightful as it is often unreliable, with the surreal atmosphere resembling a Generation X treatment of *Are You Being Served?*. ▣

Brian O'Halloran *Dante Hicks* • Jeff Anderson *Randal* • Marilyn Ghigliotti *Veronica* • Lisa Spoonauer *Caitlin* • Jason Mewes *Jay* • Kevin Smith *Silent Bob* ■ *Dir/Scr* Kevin Smith

The Client ★★★★ 15

Thriller 1994 · US · Colour · 115mins

Lawyer Susan Sarandon takes on the case of her career when young Brad Renfro, who has inadvertently witnessed a mob-related suicide, asks her to represent him. She soon finds herself up against the full might of the legal establishment led by ambitious federal attorney Tommy Lee Jones while at the same time trying to protect her youthful client from vengeful Mafia hit man Anthony LaPaglia. Director Joel Schumacher isn't exactly noted for his subtlety, but he makes a pretty good go of producing a believable relationship between the stubborn but lonely Sarandon and the rebellious Renfro. He also makes excellent use of the Memphis locations and serves up some expertly staged action sequences. Contains violence and swearing. ▣ **DVD**

Susan Sarandon *Reggie Love* • Tommy Lee Jones *Roy Foltrigg* • Mary-Louise Parker *Dianne Sway* • Anthony LaPaglia *Barry Muldano* • JT Walsh *McThune* • Anthony Edwards *Clint Von Hooser* • Brad Renfro *Mark Sway* • Will Patton *Sergeant Hardy* ■ *Dir* Joel Schumacher • *Scr* Akiva Goldsman, Robert Getchell, from the novel by John Grisham

Cliffhanger ★★★★ 15

Action thriller 1993 · US Neth · Colour · 106mins

High adventure and vertigo blend with blood and bullets to make this tension-packed tall tale a spectacular avalanche of dizzying escapism. Sylvester Stallone is the rock-climbing "Rocky" clone who loses his nerve during the opening peak rescue and must find it again when a gang of desperate criminals crash-lands during a blizzard on his mountain manor. Nail-biting stunts and queasy photography are the true stars of this alpine *Die Hard*, directed with breathless energy by Renny Harlin. Contains swearing and violence. ▣

Sylvester Stallone *Gabe Walker* • John Lithgow *Qualen* • Michael Rooker *Hal Tucker* • Janine Turner *Jessie Deighan* • Rex Linn *Travers* •

Caroline Goodall *Kristel* • Leon *Kynette* • Craig Fairbrass *Delmar* • Paul Winfield *Walter Wright* ■ *Dir* Renny Harlin • *Scr* Michael France, Sylvester Stallone, from a story by Michael France, from an idea by John Long • *Cinematographer* Alex Thomson, Adam Dale

Clifford ★ PG

Comedy 1994 · US · Colour · 85mins

A desperately unfunny vehicle for Martin Short in which he plays a mischievous ten-year-year kid who acts like one of Joe Dante's gremlins. This isn't a body swap comedy à la *Vice Versa* or *Big* – Short actually *is* a kid, which has a certain novelty value for the first five minutes, until boredom at his antics sets in. All the face-pulling in the world can't convince us he isn't a grown-up acting like an idiot.

Martin Short *Clifford Daniels* • Charles Grodin *Martin Daniels* • Mary Steenburgen *Sarah Davis* • Dabney Coleman *Gerald Ellis* • Richard Kind *Julien Daniels* • Jennifer Savidge *Theodora Daniels* ■ *Dir* Paul Flaherty • *Scr* Jay Dee Rock, Bobby Von Hayes

Climbing High ★★ U

Comedy 1938 · UK · BW · 78mins

Although he won an Oscar for *Oliver!*, musicals weren't really Carol Reed's forte. However, he was fortunate to produce anything at all on this occasion, bearing in mind the tensions behind the scenes. Imported to play a bogus male model, American star Kent Taylor quit because of a delayed start, while Jessie Matthews disliked so many of the songs that they were dropped. It speaks volumes for Reed that the end result is not only watchable but rather entertaining, thanks, primarily, to Taylor's replacement, Michael Redgrave.

Jessie Matthews *Diana* • Michael Redgrave *Nicky Brooke* • Noel Madison *Gibson* • Alastair Sim *Max* • Margaret Vyner *Lady Constance* • Mary Clare *Lady Emily* • Francis L Sullivan *Madman* • Enid Stamp-Taylor *Winnie* ■ *Dir* Carol Reed • *Scr* Stephen Clarkson, from a story by Lesser Samuels, Marion Dix

Clive of India ★★★

Biographical drama 1935 · US · BW · 95mins

A very famous film of its day, this expensively produced but drearily directed epic offered the perfect role to the immaculately-spoken Ronald Colman: Robert Clive, one of Britain's great folk heroes. Colman is marvellous in the role, securing India for Britain at the cost of his own personal happiness, and it really doesn't matter at all that the real Clive lived a completely different life. Loretta Young looks lovely, and watch the battle scenes carefully: they all take place at night to save on budget.

Ronald Colman *Robert Clive* • Loretta Young *Margaret Maskelyne Clive* • Colin Clive *Captain Johnstone* • Francis Lister *Edmund Maskelyne* • Vernon Downing *Stringer* • Peter Shaw *Miller* • Neville Clark *Vincent* • Ian Wolfe *Kent* ■ *Dir* Richard Boleslawski • *Scr* WP Lipscomb, RJ Minney, from their play *Clive*

Cloak and Dagger ★★★ PG

Spy thriller 1946 · US · BW · 106mins

American nuclear research scientist Gary Cooper is seconded to the OSS and sent, in conditions of great danger, to learn the secrets of

Germany's atomic bomb programme. In hiding with the Resistance in war-torn, Nazi-occupied Italy, he is put in the care of violently anti-Fascist and embittered Lilli Palmer. A run-of-the-mill Second World War espionage story becomes gripping in the hands of director Fritz Lang, who injects it with nail-biting tension. Cooper is fine, while Palmer, making her American film debut, shows an admirable grasp of a complex character. ▣

Gary Cooper *Professor Alvah Jesper* • Lilli Palmer *Gina* • Robert Alda *Pinkie* • Vladimir Sokoloff *Dr Polda* • J Edward Bromberg *Trenk* • Marjorie Hoshelle *Ann Dawson* • Charles Marsh *Erich* ■ *Dir* Fritz Lang • *Scr* Albert Maltz, Ring Lardner Jr, from a story by Boris Ingster, John Larkin, from a non-fiction book by Corey Ford, Alastair MacBain

Cloak and Dagger ★★★ PG

Adventure thriller 1984 · US · Colour · 96mins

ET star Henry Thomas witnesses enemy agents trying to steal government secrets in director Richard Franklin's contrived update of the 1949 suspense classic, *The Window*. No one believes him apart from the evil spies themselves, so he goes on the run helped by imaginary superhero playmate Jack Flack (Dabney Coleman, who also plays the boy's father). Hitchcock disciple Franklin lurches from tongue-in-cheek humour to exciting espionage, but undercuts any palpable menace by unsuccessfully shuffling the two tones together. ▣

Henry Thomas *Davey Osborne* • Dabney Coleman *Jack Flack/Hal Osborne* • Michael Murphy *Rice* • Christina Nigra *Kim Gardener* • John McIntire *George MacCready* • Jeanette Nolan *Eunice MacCready* ■ *Dir* Richard Franklin • *Scr* Tom Holland

Cloak without Dagger ★★ U

Mystery 1955 · UK · BW · 68mins

Had this British B-movie been possessed of a sense of humour, it might have invited comparison with those breezy spy romps churned out by Hollywood a decade earlier. However, director Joseph Sterling spurns the screwball possibilities in the relationship between agent Philip Friend and ditzy girlfriend Mary Mackenzie, who reunite several years after her meddling caused him to bungle a Second World War mission. Consequently, what emerges is an uncomfortable mix of romance and mystery.

Philip Friend *Felix Gratton* • Mary Mackenzie *Kyra Gabaine* • Leslie Dwyer *Fred Borcombe* • Allan Cuthbertson *Colonel Packham* • John G Heller *Peppi Gilroudian* ■ *Dir* Joseph Sterling • *Scr* AR Rawlinson

The Clock ★★★★ U

Romantic drama 1945 · US · BW · 91mins

A charming MGM romance, containing a beguiling performance from the great Judy Garland, looking radiant and near her professional peak. She and soldier Robert Walker enjoy a brief encounter in New York, and director Vincente Minnelli cleverly makes the city the third character in the movie. There are also some minor players worthy of note: a drunken Keenan Wynn, a sympathetic James Gleason and a speechless Marshall Thompson.

Judy Garland *Alice Mayberry* • Robert Walker *Corporal Joe Allen* • James Gleason *Al Henry* • Keenan Wynn *Drunk* • Marshall Thompson *Bill* • Lucile Gleason *Mrs Al Henry* ■ *Dir* Vincente Minnelli • *Scr* Robert Nathan, Joseph Schrank, from a story by Paul Gallico, Pauline Gallico

Clockers ★★★★ 18

Crime thriller 1995 · US · Colour · 123mins

Based on Richard Price's complex novel about the drugs trade, Spike Lee's urban drama has cop Harvey Keitel investigating a killing. Low-level drug-dealer Mekhi Phifer is the prime suspect, though Phifer's brother Isaiah Washington has confessed to the crime. Not Lee's best work – some critics were distinctly cool about the stark imagery and idiosyncratic cinematography – but for once, at least, the director lets the story deliver the message, instead of imposing it from above. Contains violence and swearing. ▣

Harvey Keitel *Rocco Klein* • John Turturro *Larry Mazilli* • Delroy Lindo *Rodney* • Mekhi Phifer *Strike* • Isaiah Washington *Victor* • Keith David *Andre the Giant* • Pee Wee Love *Tyrone* • Regina Taylor *Iris Jeeter* • Tom Byrd [Thomas Jefferson Byrd] *Errol Barnes* • Sticky Fingaz *Scientific* ■ *Dir* Spike Lee • *Scr* Richard Price, Spike Lee, from the novel by Richard Price

Clockwatchers ★★ 15

Comedy drama 1997 · US · Colour · 92mins

In seeking to capture the ennui of office life, director Jill Sprecher succeeds all too well with a film as repetitive and monotonous as its subject. There is much potential in a cast headlined by Toni Collette, Parker Posey, Lisa Kudrow and Alanna Ubach, but they're merely required to do the dramatic equivalent of licking envelopes. As the quartet of temps whose friendship is tested by an outbreak of petty pilfering, they each have moments of inspiration. For the most part, however, they seem subdued by the banality of the script and the slow pace. Well observed but underwhelming. ▣ **DVD**

Toni Collette *Iris* • Parker Posey *Margaret* • Lisa Kudrow *Paula* • Alanna Ubach *Jane* • Helen FitzGerald *Cleo* • Stanley DeSantis *Art* • Jamie Kennedy *Eddie* ■ *Dir* Jill Sprecher • *Scr* Jill Sprecher, Karen Sprecher

Clockwise ★★★ PG

Comedy 1986 · UK · Colour · 91mins

John Cleese is a headmaster with a mania for punctuality who has to travel to Norwich for a conference. Unfortunately, he boards the wrong train, resulting in an increasingly frenzied cross-country dash with a schoolgirl and a former girlfriend in tow. Cleese finds it difficult to be unfunny, and he unravels here much as Basil Fawlty unravelled, from a manic starting point to a climax of epic proportions. Perhaps because of Cleese's background in TV comedy, the picture, written by Michael Frayn, is less a narrative than a series of sketches, plus some rather awkwardly placed propaganda about public and private education in that far-off land called Mrs Thatcher's Britain. ▣

John Cleese *Brian Stimpson* • Alison Steadman *Gwenda Stimpson* • Penelope Wilton *Pat* • Stephen Moore *Mr Jolly* • Sharon

Maiden *Laura* • Constance Chapman *Mrs Wheel* • Joan Hickson *Mrs Trellis* • Ann Way *Mrs Way* • Pat Keen *Mrs Wisely* • Geoffrey Hutchings *Mr Wisely* ■ *Dir* Christopher Morahan • *Scr* Michael Frayn

Clockwork Mice ★★★ 15

Drama 1994 · UK · Colour · 94mins

With its heart a little too determinedly on its sleeve, this is, nevertheless, an involving, amusing and, ultimately, rather sad film. There are echoes of *The Loneliness of the Long Distance Runner*, but director Vadim Jean skirts the harsher side of life in a special needs school to concentrate on the unlikely friendship between unruly Ruaidhri Conroy and Ian Hart, the novice teacher convinced he can make a difference. The staffroom romance makes for a pleasing diversion and there are expert cameos from John Alderton and James Bolam. Contains swearing and brief nudity. ▣

Ian Hart *Steve Drake* • Ruaidhri Conroy *Conrad James* • Catherine Russell *Polly* • Art Malik *Laney* • Claire Skinner *Fairy* • Nigel Planer *Parkey* • John Alderton *Swaney* • James Bolam *Wackey* • Lilly Edwards *Mrs Charlton* • Robin Soans *Millwright* ■ *Dir* Vadim Jean • *Scr* Rod Woodruff

A Clockwork Orange ★★★★★ 18

Futuristic drama 1971 · UK · Colour · 136mins

Stanley Kubrick's highly controversial – and still topical – dystopian fantasy is a landmark in the portrayal of screen sex and violence. Based on the Anthony Burgess novel, it follows the sadistic adventures, imprisonment and subsequent brainwashing of ''droog'' delinquent Alex (a frighteningly charismatic Malcolm McDowell) into a ''model'' citizen of the future. Kubrick makes a disturbing statement about morality in this classic of the science-fiction genre. Perfectly crafted, visually dazzling, often unpleasant to watch and superbly scored with synthesised classical music, this stands with Kubrick's other films as a chilling technical marvel. Essential viewing, even if the second, grittier and more realistic half does seem rather slow by contemporary standards.

Malcolm McDowell *Alex* • Patrick Magee *Mr Alexander* • Michael Bates *Chief Guard* • Warren Clarke *Dim* • John Clive *Stage Actor* • Adrienne Corri *Mrs Alexander* • Carl Duering *Dr Brodsky* • Paul Farrell *Tramp* • Miriam Karlin *Cat Lady* • Aubrey Morris *Deltoid* • Steven Berkoff *Constable* • David Prowse [Dave Prowse] *Julian* ■ *Dir* Stanley Kubrick • *Scr* Stanley Kubrick, from the novel by Anthony Burgess • *Cinematographer* John Alcott • *Editor* Bill Butler • *Production Designer* John Barry • *Music* Walter Carlos

Cloned ★★

Science-fiction drama 1997 · US · Colour

An intriguing sci-fi thriller, which unfortunately lacks a killer punch. Set in the near future, the under-rated Elizabeth Perkins plays a grieving mother still trying to come to terms with the death of her young boy. When she spots another youngster who is the spitting image of her dead child, she learns that her baby was cloned. Perkins is as good as ever, but this TV movie can't make up its mind whether

it's a chiller or a weepie. Contains some strong language and violence.

Elizabeth Perkins *Skye Weston* • Alan Rosenberg *Dr Wesley Kozak* • Bradley Whitford *Rick Weston* • Enrico Colantoni *Steve Rinker* • Scott Paulin *John Gryce* • Tina Lifford *Claire Barnes* • Hrothgar Mathews *Dr Richard Mason* ■ *Dir* Douglas Barr • *Scr* Carmen Culver, David Taylor, from a story by Perri Klass, Carmen Culver

Close Encounters of the Third Kind ★★★★★ PG

Science-fiction drama 1977 · US · Colour · 126mins

Remember the time when aliens were friendly? Here's the reverse of sci-fi smash hits *Independence Day* and *Men in Black*: a delightfully optimistic parable about secret government communications with a visiting spacecraft. Richard Dreyfuss plays the power worker who karmically gets caught up in all the UFO phenomena in a Steven Spielberg fantasy that's truly suspenseful and genuinely felt, rather than just sweet and sentimental. Awesome special effects (like the glittering mother ship) fuel a spiritually uplifting tale with a fabulous feel-good factor. Contains some swearing. ▣

Richard Dreyfuss *Roy Neary* • François Truffaut *Claude Lacombe* • Teri Garr *Ronnie Neary* • Melinda Dillon *Jillian Guiler* • Bob Balaban *David Laughlin* • J Patrick McNamara *Project leader* • Warren Kemmerling *Wild Bill* • Roberts Blossom *Farmer* ■ *Dir/Scr* Steven Spielberg • *Cinematographer* Vilmos Zsigmond • *Music* John Williams • *Production Designer* Joe Alves • *Art Director* Dan Lomino • *Set Designer* Phil Abramson • *Special Effects* Douglas Trumbull, Roy Arbogast, Gregory Jein, Matthew Yuricich, Richard Yuricich

Close My Eyes ★★★ 18

Drama 1991 · UK · Colour · 104mins

This overwrought, claustrophobic drama is playwright Stephen Poliakoff's best film. Saskia Reeves and Clive Owen are the siblings who are perhaps just a little too close for comfort, caught in an unusual, uncomfortable triangle with Reeves's husband Alan Rickman. Poliakoff, as both writer and director, handles the controversial subject matter with sensitivity, and he is rewarded with two heartrendingly intense performances from his two leads. However, the best playing comes from Rickman, obviously thankful that he doesn't have to ham things up, who delivers a witty yet melancholic performance. Contains swearing, sex scenes and nudity. ▣

Alan Rickman *Sinclair Bryant* • Clive Owen *Richard Gillespie* • Saskia Reeves *Natalie Gillespie* • Karl Johnson *Colin* • Lesley Sharp *Jessica* ■ *Dir/Scr* Stephen Poliakoff

Close to My Heart ★★★

Drama 1951 · US · BW · 90mins

The beautiful Gene Tierney and the dependable Ray Milland star as a couple in the process of adopting a baby from an orphanage, run by Fay Bainter. When they discover that the baby's father was a murderer, they nevertheless proceed with the adoption. Written and directed by William Keighley, this is a serviceable tale that combines drama with soap opera sentimentality and suggests environment is ultimately more important than heredity.

Ray Milland *Brad Sheridan* • Gene Tierney *Midge Sheridan* • Fay Bainter *Mrs Morrow* • Howard St John *EO Frost* • Mary Beth Hughes *Arlene* • Ann Morrison *Mrs Barker* • James Seay *Heilner* ■ *Dir* William Keighley • *Scr* James R Webb, from his story *A Baby for Midge* • *Cinematographer* Robert Burks • *Music* Max Steiner

Close-Up ★★★★ U
Experimental documentary drama
1989 · Iran · Colour · 93mins

Dazzling in its simple ingenuity, this fantasy on a true story is widely regarded as Abbas Kiarostami's masterpiece. The premise sounds complicated, with the action constantly cross-cutting between Hossain Sabzian's trial for impersonating celebrated Iranian director Moshen Makhmalbaf, and reconstructions of the way in which he duped a family into believing their son was to star in one of his films. However, such is Kiarostami's mastery of his material and his delicious sense of mischief in exploring the contrasts between art and life that everything slots into place with awesome precision. In Farsi with English subtitles. ▭

Hossain Sabzian • Mohsen Makhmalbaf • Abolfazl Ahankhah *Father* • Mehrdad Ahankhah *Son* • Manoochehr Ahankhah *Son* • Mahrokh Ahankhah *Daughter* • Nayer Mohseni Zonoozi *Daughter* • Abbas Kiarostami ■ *Dir/ Scr* Abbas Kiarostami

Closely Observed Trains ★★★★ 15
Second World War comedy drama
1966 · Cz · BW · 88mins

One of the key pictures of the Czech New Wave of the mid-sixties, this is a superbly controlled piece of cinema that deserved its Oscar for best foreign language film. Set during the Nazi occupation, the film follows the bungled efforts of a bashful young apprentice railway guard to lose his virginity, seduce the stationmaster's wife and commit suicide. After a variety of misadventures, he meets a beautiful resistance fighter who finally offers him the chance to prove himself. Employing a complex, episodic structure, Jiří Menzel – making his feature debut – seamlessly dovetails satire, romance, heroism and the horror of war to devastating tragicomic effect. In Czech with English subtitles. ▭

Vaclav Neckar *Milos Hrma* • Jitka Bendova *Masa* • Vladimir Valenta *Stationmaster* • Josef Somr *Hubicka* • Libuse Havelkova *Stationmaster's wife* ■ *Dir* Jiří Menzel • *Scr* Jiří Menzel, Bohumil Hrabal

The Closer ★★
Psychological drama
1990 · US · Colour · 87mins

Slow and ponderous drama about the head of a real estate development firm (Danny Aiello) who is looking to retire and find a replacement. Rather than promote an executive, he decides to look for a salesman like himself to take over the company. Aiello is fine as always, but the character he plays is so unlikeable (especially in the treatment of his family) that this flip side of the Willy Loman story isn't much fun to watch.

Danny Aiello *Chester Grant* • Michael Paré *Larry Freede* • Joe Cortese *John Mogen* • Justine Bateman *Jessica Grant* • Tim Quill *Chet Grant* • Rick Aiello *Billy Grant* • Diane Baker *Beatrice Grant* ■ *Dir* Dimitri Logothetis • *Scr* Robert Keats, Louis LaRusso Ii, from the play *The Wheelbarrow Closers* by Louis LaRusso II

Closer and Closer ★★
Thriller
1996 · Can · Colour

In real life, authors of novels about serial killers generally become so rich and famous that they need never have another original idea, but in the movies they are invariably stalked by psychopaths inspired to acts of insanity by the purple prose of their favourite writer. Here, bestselling scribe Kim Delaney can count herself doubly unfortunate: having been crippled by a maniac who read her first book, she then finds the same thing happening when she publishes a sequel. Free of plausibility, this TV movie is creepy enough if you're in the mood, but ludicrous if you're not.

Kim Delaney *Kate Sanders* • Bill MacDonald *Detective Whitley* • Jon Cubrt *Intruder* ■ *Dir* Fred Gerber • *Scr* Matt Dorff

The Closer You Get ★★★ 12
Comedy
2000 · Ire/UK · Colour · 92mins

Uberto Pasolini, producer of *The Full Monty*, strays into *Waking Ned* territory with this ribald piece of Oirish whimsy. Screenwriter William Ivory might have given the Blarney Stone an extra touch, but he's nevertheless concocted an amiable fable about the sexual frustrations of a small Donegal community, which would rather resort to Florida beach babes and Spanish trawlermen than see beneath the workaday façade of their neighbours. Ian Hart excels as the crotch-obsessed butcher, while Ewan Stewart impresses as a virginal mammy's boy.

Ian Hart *Kieran* • Sean McGinley *Ian* • Niamh Cusack *Kate* • Ruth McCabe *Mary* • Ewan Stewart *Pat* • Sean McDonagh *Sean* ■ *Dir* Aileen Ritchie • *Scr* William Ivory, from a story by Herbie Wave

Closet Land ★★★
Political drama
1991 · US · Colour · 95mins

Co-executive produced by Ron Howard, with guidance from Amnesty International, this intense drama stars Alan Rickman as an interrogator-cum-torturer and Madeleine Stowe as his victim, an author of children's stories who is accused of subversion. Using a single set – a gleaming, high-tech interrogation chamber – the drama is heavily allegorical: there are no names, no countries, just a universal symbol of oppression and a nod or two towards Franz Kafka. The sense of claustrophobia is overwhelming, and so are the performances, but Radha Bharadwaj's direction is perhaps better than her script. Contains swearing.

Madeleine Stowe *Woman* • Alan Rickman *Man* ■ *Dir/Scr* Radha Bharadwaj

The Cloud Capped Star ★★★★
Drama
1960 · Ind · BW · 134mins

A key figure in the Parallel Cinema movement, director Ritwik Ghatak combines social realism with stylised expressionism in this audacious melodrama, which also manages to evoke Bengali myth and the "selfless sister" pictures of the great Japanese director, Kenji Mizoguchi. Sacrificing her health and happiness to fulfil the ambitions of her siblings, Supriya Choudhury gives a performance of affecting determination and dignity. But while this first part of Ghatak's Calcutta trilogy was acclaimed for its political conviction and cinematic invention, the concluding instalments, *E Flat* (1961) and *The Golden Thread* (1962), caused such a furore that he was unable to work for a decade. In Bengali with English subtitles.

Supriya Choudhury *Nita* • Anil Chatterjee *Shankar* • Bijon Bhattacharya *Father* • Guita De *Mother* • Dwiju Bhawal *Montu, younger brother* • Niranjan Roy *Sanat* ■ *Dir* Ritwik Ghatak • *Scr* Ritwik Ghatak, from a story by Shaktipaka Rajguru

Cloud Dancer ★★
Drama
1980 · US · Colour · 91mins

Flying ace David Carradine thrills the crowd with his daredevil antics, but seems to have little time for his friends and family – until he helps drug-addicted pilot Joseph Bottoms kick his habit. Meanwhile, on the ground, Jennifer O'Neill fears for his safety. What he doesn't know is that she's just had his baby... Good aerial stunt work almost makes this bland melodrama worth watching.

David Carradine *Bradley Randolph* • Jennifer O'Neill *Helen St Clair* • Joseph Bottoms *Tom Loomis* • Albert Salmi *Ozzie Randolph* • Salome Jens *Jean Randolph* • Arnette Jens Zerbe *Edith Randolph* ■ *Dir* Barry Brown • *Scr* William Goodhart, from a story by William Goodhart, Barry Brown, Daniel Tamkus

Cloudburst ★★
Thriller
1951 · UK · BW · 83mins

The dynamic American stage and screen actor Robert Preston, yet to find stardom, is at the centre of this British-made thriller, directed by Francis Searle and co-starring Elizabeth Sellars. Preston is a code-cracking expert at the Foreign Office who uses the skills and contacts he accrued during the war to track down the hit-and-run criminals who killed his wife. The plot may strain credibility a little, but this bleak and violent potboiler is nevertheless quite involving.

Robert Preston *John Graham* • Elizabeth Sellars *Carol Graham* • Colin Tapley *Inspector Davis* • Sheila Burrell *Lorna* • Harold Lang *Mickie* • Mary Germaine *Peggy* ■ *Dir* Francis Searle • *Scr* Francis Searle, Leo Marks, from the play by Leo Marks

The Clouded Yellow ★★★ U
Crime drama
1950 · UK · BW · 111mins

A competent thriller from producer Betty Box, in which disgraced spy Trevor Howard finds himself involved with Jean Simmons and a case of murder after he becomes curator of a butterfly collection. As the cops close

in, the couple head for a boat to Mexico with special agent Kenneth More in hot pursuit. The plot has too few tricks up its sleeve to engross, but director Ralph Thomas teases it out effectively by making good use of such images as the unnerving display cabinets and the Liverpool waterfront.

Jean Simmons *Sophie Malraux* • Trevor Howard *David Somers* • Sonia Dresdel *Jess Fenton* • Barry Jones *Nicholas Fenton* • Maxwell Reed *Nick* • Kenneth More *Willy* • André Morell *Chubb* ■ *Dir* Ralph Thomas • *Scr* Eric Ambler, from a story by Janet Green • *Cinematographer* Geoffrey Unsworth

The Clown ★★
Drama
1952 · US · BW · 92mins

Red Skelton is now a forgotten clown, and this reworking of *The Champ* shows us why. He plays an alcoholic old vaudevillian, idolised by his son (Tim Considine), who dreams of making a comeback on television. Alas, he's flawed, and floored, by his own weak character. Some moments suggest what Skelton was capable of, but there aren't enough to rescue director Robert Z Leonard's mawkish melodrama from bathos. Roger Moore and Charles Bronson make early appearances in walk-on roles.

Red Skelton *Dodo Delwyn* • Tim Considine *Dink Delwyn* • Jane Greer *Paula Henderson* • Loring Smith *Goldie* • Fay Roope *Dr Strauss* • Philip Ober *Ralph Z Henderson* • Walter Reed *Joe Hoagley* ■ *Dir* Robert Z Leonard • *Scr* Martin Rackin, from a story by Frances Marion, Leonard Praskins

Clown at Midnight ★★
Horror
1998 · US/Can · Colour · 91mins

This is an uninspired reprise of the super Italian shocker *Stagefright*, itself heavily influenced by *The Phantom of the Opera*. A high school drama group is roped into cleaning out an old theatre for a grand re-opening in a few weeks' time. One of the kids (Sarah Lassez) is the daughter of a renowned opera singer who was brutally murdered in the theatre many years before by a clown-faced maniac. Pretty soon the same fate is befalling her schoolmates... There are hammy turns from Margot Kidder and Christopher Plummer, plus a sizeable body count. In these post-*Scream* days, though, it seems dreadfully dated.

Christopher Plummer *Mr Caruthers* • Margot Kidder *Ms Ellen Gibby* • James Duval *George* • Sarah Lassez *Kate* • Tatyana Ali *Monica* ■ *Dir* Jean Pellerin • *Scr* Kenneth J Hall

Clownhouse ★★ 15
Horror
1988 · US · Colour · 78mins

If viewers can somehow distance themselves from the behind-the-scenes scandal surrounding this movie (director Victor Salva molested one of his child actors), they will discover a genuinely spooky exercise in horror. In this incredibly atmospheric chiller, three escaped lunatics disguise themselves as clowns and terrorise three young brothers left home alone. The stalking sequences are nail-biting, though the lack of action makes things a little tedious. ▭

Nathan Forrest Winters *Casey* • Brian McHugh *Geoffrey* • Sam Rockwell *Randy* • Tree *Evil Cheezo* ■ *Dir/Scr* Victor Salva

U = SUITABLE FOR ALL   Uc = SUITABLE FOR ALL, ESPECIALLY FOR YOUNG CHILDREN (VIDEO ONLY)   PG = PARENTAL GUIDANCE

The Clowns ★★★★
Documentary
1970 · It/Fr/W Ger · Colour · 92mins

Italy's great ringmaster of the cinema returns to the source of his inspiration – the circus – and skilfully absorbs it into his own personal vision. Remembering the Rimini of his childhood when the circus came to town, Federico Fellini has stated: "My films owe an enormous amount to the circus. For me the clowns were always a traumatic visual experience, ambassadors of a vocation of a showman." Here, the maestro not only reveals their comedic craft by watching and talking to exponents of the profession. He also sends up the documentary-making process itself, years before *Spinal Tap* set the trend. In Italian with English subtitles.
Dir Federico Fellini • Scr Federico Fellini, Bernardino Zapponi • Music Nino Rota

The Club ★★★ 18
Drama   1980 · Ausl · Colour · 93mins

A bracing look behind the scenes at the personal and power politics involved in the running of an Australian Rules football club. It is based on an equally rumbustious stage play from David Williamson, who also wrote *Don's Party* – an earlier Australian film hit made by the same director, Bruce Beresford. This may not be as polished a film as Beresford's later success *Driving Miss Daisy*, but it makes up for what it might lack in finesse with rude energy and muscular acting. Contains swearing and brief nudity. ▭
Jack Thompson *Laurie Holden* • Graham Kennedy *Ted Parker* • Frank Wilson *Jock Riley* • Harold Hopkins *Danny Rowe* • John Howard (2) *Geoff Hayward* ■ Dir Bruce Beresford • Scr David Williamson, from his play

Club Paradise ★★ 15
Comedy   1986 · US · Colour · 91mins

Harold Ramis has matured into a fine comedy director – *Groundhog Day*, *Multiplicity* – but during the eighties he specialised in crass efforts like this early Robin Williams vehicle. Williams plays the host of a run-down Caribbean resort who has to cope with noisy American tourists and a brewing rebellion. The eclectic cast includes British actors Peter O'Toole and Twiggy, American comics Rick Moranis and Eugene Levy and reggae legend Jimmy Cliff, but the gags are about as sparse as the "luxury" facilities provided by the hotel. Even Williams's quick-fire routines fail to ignite many laughs. Contains swearing. ▭
Robin Williams *Jack Moniker* • Peter O'Toole *Governor Anthony Croyden Hayes* • Rick Moranis *Barry Nye* • Jimmy Cliff *Ernest Reed* • Twiggy *Phillipa Lloyd* • Adolph Caesar *Prime Minister Solomon Gundy* • Eugene Levy *Barry Steinberg* • Joanna Cassidy *Terry Hamlin* ■ Dir Harold Ramis • Scr Harold Ramis, Brian Doyle-Murray, from a story by Ed Roboto, Tom Leopold, Chris Miller, David Standish

Clubbed to Death ★★ 18
Romantic drama
1996 · Fr/Por/Neth · Colour · 84mins

Ever wonder what happened to Béatrice Dalle after *Betty Blue*? Well, she turns up here in a strange, dark and narrative-less film from director

Yolande Zauberman. Elodie Bouchez stars as a girl who falls asleep on a bus and awakes to find herself on the outskirts of Paris. Stumbling around, she ends up in a nightclub where she encounters Roschdy Zem. Few words are spoken in this pop video-style foray into Parisian rave culture; you'd probably be far better off going clubbing yourself. In French with English subtitles. Contains drug abuse, swearing and some violence. ▭
Elodie Bouchez *Lola Monnet* • Roschdy Zem *Emir Areski* • Béatrice Dalle *Saïda* • Richard Courcet *Ismael* ■ Dir Yolande Zauberman • Scr Yolande Zauberman, Noemie Lvovsky, Emmanuel Salinger, D Belloc

Clue ★★ PG
Comedy   1985 · US · Colour · 92mins

Based on the board game Clue (known as Cluedo in the UK), this is a perfect example of a gimmick movie. The plot (an amalgam of various Agatha Christie clichés) involves a number of guests invited to dinner at a spooky mansion, where they endure a murderous evening. Scripted and written by British sitcom stalwart Jonathan Lynn in his first Hollywood venture, this is a broad, somewhat camp comedy with a vulgar edge. It was originally released with three different endings, though there was only one version in the UK. ▭
Tim Curry *Wadsworth* • Madeline Kahn *Mrs White* • Christopher Lloyd *Professor Plum* • Eileen Brennan *Mrs Peacock* • Michael McKean *Mr Green* • Martin Mull *Colonel Mustard* • Lesley Ann Warren *Miss Scarlett* ■ Dir/Scr Jonathan Lynn

Clueless ★★★★ 12
Romantic comedy
1995 · US · Colour · 93mins

Would you believe a loose adaptation of Jane Austen's *Emma* plonked down squarely in *Beverly Hills 90210*? Well, that's the idea behind this screamingly funny satire-cum-parody, which perfectly captures the inanities of contemporary teen America. Alicia Silverstone is a delight as Cher, the chic but dippy blonde who's devoted to improving the love lives of her Rodeo Drive-shopping high-school girlfriends, even though she can't sort out her own. Silverstone indulges in the trials and tribulations of designer-label animosity and MTV promiscuity, while her lawyer father (Dan Hedaya) and intellectual stepbrother (Paul Rudd) look on in total bemusement. Like *Heathers* before it, director Amy Heckerling's smart satire sharpens its comedic scalpel on the manners and mores of self-centred fashion victims. Contains some swearing and substance abuse. ▭
Alicia Silverstone *Cher* • Stacey Dash *Dionne* • Paul Rudd *Josh* • Brittany Murphy *Tai* • Donald Adeosun Faison *Murray* • Elisa Donovan *Amber* • Wallace Shawn *Mr Hall* • Twink Caplan *Miss Geist* • Dan Hedaya *Mel* ■ Dir Amy Heckerling • Scr Amy Heckerling, from the novel *Emma* by Jane Austen

Cluny Brown ★★★
Romantic comedy   1946 · US · BW · 100mins

No longer quite what *Variety* called a "smasheroo", this somewhat outmoded satirical soufflé on British upper-class mores is nonetheless

diverting. A comedy romance from director Ernst Lubitsch, whose famous "touch" is still very much in evidence, it stars Jennifer Jones as a lady plumber doubling up as a maid for an English family who are all vague to the point of imbecility. Charles Boyer is a Czech writer who arrives in the household having fled the Nazis.
Jennifer Jones *Cluny Brown* • Charles Boyer *Adam Belinski* • Peter Lawford *Andrew Carmel* • Helen Walker *Betty Cream* • Reginald Gardiner *Hilary Ames* • Reginald Owen *Sir Henry Carmel* • C Aubrey Smith *Col Duff-Graham* ■ Dir Ernst Lubitsch • Scr Samuel Hoffenstein, Elizabeth Reinhardt, from the novel by Margery Sharp

Co-ed Call Girl ★★
Drama based on a true story
1996 · US · Colour · 90 mins

Tori Spelling plays the young student who gets mixed up in a classy prostitution ring overseen by TV-movie regular Susan Blakely. The wonderfully named Scott Plank, probably best known for his role in Michael Mann's *Heat* prototype *LA Takedown*, and veteran soap star Charles Grant are the only other familiar faces in the cast. The direction from Michael Ray Rhodes is depressingly formulaic. Contains some violence
Tori Spelling *Joanna* • Susan Blakely *Teri Halbert* • Scott Plank *Ron* • Carmen Argenziano *Henry Binder* • Jeri Lynn Ryan [Jeri Ryan] *Kimberly* • Barry Watson *Jack* ■ Dir Michael Ray Rhodes • Scr Allan Leicht

Coal Miner's Daughter ★★★★
Biography   1980 · US · Colour · 124mins

Sissy Spacek won a best actress Oscar for her heartfelt portrayal of country singer Loretta Lynn in this movie biopic from Michael Apted, the British director of *Stardust* and *Agatha* who went on to such Hollywood blockbusters as *Gorillas in the Mist*. Based on Lynn's autobiography, the film charts the singer's life from poverty in deepest Kentucky to her becoming the queen of country music. It's a fascinating, no-holds-barred adaptation that includes Loretta's battle with drugs, her rocky marriage and the death of friend Patsy Cline. Contains swearing and violence.
Sissy Spacek *Loretta Lynn* • Tommy Lee Jones *Doolittle Lynn* • Levon Helm *Ted Webb* • Phyllis Boyens *Clara Webb* • William Sanderson *Lee Dollarhide* • Beverly D'Angelo *Patsy Cline* ■ Dir Michael Apted • Scr Tom Rickman, from the autobiography by Loretta Lynn, George Vescey

Cobb ★★★★ 18
Biographical sports drama
1994 · US · Colour and BW · 122mins

This portrait of the sports hero as warped monster gives Tommy Lee Jones the chance to deliver a grandstand performance as Ty Cobb, the real-life baseball ace known as the "Georgia Peach". Soured by a lifetime of bigotry and bullying, Cobb is seen trying to camouflage past sins as he dictates his autobiography to a sports writer (Robert Wuhl). Director Ron Shelton, whose *Bull Durham* and *White Men Can't Jump* were jokey tales of disillusionment set in the sporting

world, redefines the life of an idol with honest savagery. Contains violence, swearing and nudity. ▭
Tommy Lee Jones *Ty Cobb* • Robert Wuhl *Al Stump* • Lolita Davidovich *Ramona* • Ned Bellamy *Ray* • Scott Burkholder *Jimmy* • Allan Malamud *Mud* ■ Dir Ron Shelton • Scr Ron Shelton, from the biography by Al Stump

Cobra ★★ 18
Detective action thriller
1986 · US · Colour · 83mins

"Crime is the disease and I'm the cure," claims cop Sylvester Stallone in a practically plotless mêlée of shooting and stabbing. The film tries to be Stallone's *Dirty Harry*, so it's unfortunate his idea of characterisation is mirror shades and a penchant for chewing matches. Although the relentless sequences of murder and mayhem are competently filmed by *Rambo: First Blood Part II* director George Pan Cosmatos, the film's unusually slender running time suggests any moments of tranquillity in the script must have been discarded somewhere along the way. Contains violence and some swearing. ▭ DVD
Sylvester Stallone *Marion "Cobra" Cobretti* • Brigitte Nielsen *Ingrid* • Reni Santoni *Gonzales* • Andrew Robinson *Detective Monte* • Lee Garlington *Nancy Stalk* ■ Dir George Pan Cosmatos • Scr Sylvester Stallone, from the novel *Fair Game* by Paula Gosling

Cobra Verde ★★ PG
Drama   1988 · W Ger · Colour · 99mins

Although again depicting the exploits of an obsessive outsider in an inhospitable environment, this is the least cohesive of the epic collaborations between Klaus Kinski and Werner Herzog. Filmed under typically arduous conditions in Ghana, the action follows the fortunes of an exiled Brazilian bandit whose attempts to revive the slave trade are dashed by the insane ruler of Dahomey. As ever, Herzog succeeds in anthropologically dissecting the civilisation under his gaze. However, his take on the evils of colonialism is uninspired. In German with English subtitles.
Klaus Kinski *Francisco Manoel da Silva* • Taparica *King Ampaw* • Jose Lewgoy *Don Octavio Coutinho* • Salvatore Basile *Captain Fraternidade* • Bossa Ahadee *Kwame II of Nsein* ■ Dir Werner Herzog • Scr Werner Herzog, from the novel *The Viceroy of Ouidah* by Bruce Chatwin

Cobra Woman ★★
Fantasy adventure
1944 · US · Colour · 70mins

High camp thrills aplenty in this richly dumb jungle melodrama about a bride-to-be kidnapped and taken to a mysterious island. There she discovers her evil twin sister is high priestess of a cobra-worshipping cult! Maria Montez, or "The Caribbean Cyclone" as she was better known, is something of a cult figure today, and her performance here as the dual protagonists is considered a career best. Alas, Robert Siodmak directs this bunkum with too straight a face.
Maria Montez *Tollea/Naja* • Jon Hall *Ramu* • Sabu *Kado* • Lon Chaney Jr *Hava* • Edgar Barrier *Martok* • Mary Nash *Queen* • Lois Collier *Veeda* • Samuel S Hinds *Father Paul* •

Moroni Olsen *MacDonald* ■ Dir Robert Siodmak • Scr Gene Lewis, Richard Brooks, from a story by W Scott Darling

The Cobweb ★★★★

Drama   1955 · US · Colour · 123mins

It's literally curtains for credibility as this wondrous tosh, one of the last of Hollywood's postwar psychiatric cycle, concerns the choosing of new drapes for the library of a psychiatric clinic, which causes as many problems for the staff as it does for the patients. The adaptation of William Gibson's novel becomes too wordy, but when you have the benefit of stars such as Richard Widmark, Lauren Bacall, Lillian Gish and Charles Boyer, who cares?

Richard Widmark *Dr Stewart McIver* • Lauren Bacall *Meg Faversen Rinehart* • Charles Boyer *Dr Douglas N Devanal* • Gloria Grahame *Karen McIver* • Lillian Gish *Victoria Inch* • John Kerr *Steven W Holte* • Susan Strasberg *Sue Brett* ■ Dir Vincente Minnelli • Scr John Paxton, from the novel by William Gibson

The Coca-Cola Kid ★★★ 15

Comedy   1985 · Ausl · Colour · 94mins

The political and sexual themes that Serbian director Dusan Makavejev explored in his earlier works are only quaintly challenging in this fizzy, off-beat comedy about corporate ideals. Eric Roberts is the Coca-Cola go-getter sent to Australia to test the market, where he comes into oddly engaging conflict with a wacky soft drinks manufacturer (Bill Kerr). The result is a laid-back, culture-clash whimsy full of incidental pleasures, the main one being Greta Scacchi burning up the screen as a sexy secretary.

Eric Roberts *Becker* • Greta Scacchi *Terri* • Bill Kerr *T George McDowell* • Max Gilles *Frank* • Kris McQuade *Juliana* • Tony Barry *Bushman* • Chris Haywood *Kim* ■ Dir Dusan Makavejev • Scr Frank Moorhouse, from his short stories

The Cock-Eyed World ★★★

Comedy musical   1929 · US · BW · 115mins

This early talkie from Raoul Walsh – who went on to be one of the best directors of such gangster movies as *White Heat* – is a rollicking adventure comedy about the further exploits of Sergeants Flagg and Quirt (Victor McLaglen and Edmund Lowe), the heroes of *What Price Glory?* (1926). Always trying to one-up each other, they unite with their fists in adversity. It holds the interest, though the narrative technique looks very dated.

Victor McLaglen *Sgt Flagg* • Edmund Lowe *Sgt Harry Quirt* • Lili Damita *Elenita* • Lelia Karnelly *Olga* • Bobby Burns *Connors* • Jean Bary *Fanny* ■ Dir Raoul Walsh • Scr Raoul Walsh, William K Wells, from a play by Maxwell Anderson, Laurence Stallings

The Cockeyed Cowboys of Calico County ★★

Comedy western   1970 · US · Colour · 99mins

Developed to exploit the likeability of gentle giant Dan Blocker (Hoss in the long-running western series *Bonanza*), this TV movie was impressive enough to be given a theatrical release. Blocker plays the local blacksmith of a western town who decides to move on when his bride-to-be jilts him. The townsfolk, reluctant to let him go, try

to hitch him up with someone else. A so-so script is enlivened by a first-rate cast that includes the always reliable Jim Backus (the voice of Mr Magoo) and the fine comedy actor Wally Cox.

Dan Blocker *Charley* • Nanette Fabray *Sadie* • Jim Backus *Staunch* • Wally Cox *Mr Bester* • Jack Elam *Kittrick* • Henry Jones *Hanson* • Stubby Kaye *Bartender* • Mickey Rooney *Indian Tom* • Noah Beery Jr *Eddie* ■ Dir Tony Leader • Scr Ranald MacDougall

The Cockleshell Heroes ★★★★ U

Second World War drama   1955 · UK · Colour · 93mins

A tremendously exciting war film, crisply directed in England by America's José Ferrer. With its impressive cast, including Trevor Howard, Ferrer himself, and the likes of Anthony Newley, this was a big hit at the time; so much so that it was reissued as the top half of a double bill with *From Here to Eternity*. This necessitated the optical blowing-up of the latter film into a widescreen format so that it wouldn't look shabby alongside this one!

José Ferrer *Major Stringer* • Trevor Howard *Captain Thompson* • Victor Maddern *Sergeant Craig* • Anthony Newley *Clarke* • David Lodge *Ruddock* • Peter Arne *Stevens* • Percy Herbert *Loman* • Graham Stewart *Booth* ■ Dir José Ferrer • Scr Bryan Forbes, Richard Maibaum, from a story by George Kent

Cocktail ★★ 15

Romantic drama   1988 · US · Colour · 99mins

Having turned fighter pilots and pool players into sex objects in *Top Gun* and *The Color of Money*, Tom Cruise did the same service for bartenders, learning the meaning of life by mixing drinks under the tutelage of Martini-mentor Bryan Brown. Cruise's technique is impressive; he juggles with bottles, jiggles his behind and makes his female customers drunk with desire. But then along comes Elisabeth Shue, who makes him re-assess his lifestyle. Perhaps the best one can say for this bland concoction mixed by agents and the studio executives is that every bartender in Hollywood wants to be Tom Cruise, and that suffices as an ironic subtext. Contains swearing and nudity.

Tom Cruise *Brian Flanagan* • Bryan Brown *Doug Coughlin* • Elisabeth Shue *Jordan Mooney* • Lisa Banes *Bonnie* • Laurence Luckinbill *Mr Mooney* • Kelly Lynch *Kerry Coughlin* • Gina Gershon *Coral* • Ron Dean *Uncle Pat* ■ Dir Roger Donaldson • Scr Heywood Gould, from his novel

The Cocoanuts ★★★ U

Comedy   1929 · US · BW · 95mins

With an energy that bursts through any attempts at sophistication, this is the first film the Marx brothers made for Paramount – indeed, for anyone. It's adapted – though you'd scarcely know it – from their Broadway stage hit, written by George S Kaufman and Irving Berlin. Groucho is the seedy manager of a Florida hotel, which has hot and cold running Harpo and Chico, besides jewel thieves and the matronly Margaret Dumont, a monument Groucho is always trying to climb or put down. Dated, but still fun.

Groucho Marx *Hammer* • Harpo Marx *Harpo* • Chico Marx *Chico* • Zeppo Marx *Jamison* • Mary Eaton *Polly* • Oscar Shaw *Bob* • Katherine Francis *Penelope* • Margaret Dumont *Mrs Potter* ■ Dir Robert Florey, Joseph Santley • Scr Morris Ryskind, from the play by George S Kaufman, Irving Berlin

Cocoon ★★★★ PG

Science-fiction fantasy   1985 · US · Colour · 111mins

Director Ron Howard hit the big time with this blockbuster about pensioners finding a new lease of life after stumbling across aliens on a rescue mission from another planet. What saves it from a complete wallow in sentimentality is the sharp and sassy playing of a distinguished cast of Hollywood legends – Oscar-winning Don Ameche, real-life husband and wife Jessica Tandy and Hume Cronyn, Wilford Brimley – all of whom easily steal the show from the bland but youthful Steve Guttenberg and Tahnee Welch. Howard handles the human drama and sci-fi with equal aplomb, though a dash of Victor Meldrew's cynicism would not have gone amiss. Contains swearing and brief nudity.

Steve Guttenberg *Jack Bonner* • Brian Dennehy *Walter* • Don Ameche *Art Selwyn* • Wilford Brimley *Ben Luckett* • Hume Cronyn *Joe Finley* • Jack Gilford *Bernie Lefkowitz* • Maureen Stapleton *Mary Luckett* • Jessica Tandy *Alma Finley* • Gwen Verdon *Bess McCarthy* • Herta Ware *Rose Lefkowitz* • Tahnee Welch *Kitty* • Barret Oliver *David* ■ Dir Ron Howard • Scr Tom Benedek, from a story by David Saperstein

Cocoon: the Return ★★ PG

Science-fiction comedy   1988 · US · Colour · 114mins

Straining far too hard to recapture the touching whimsy of Ron Howard's original film, director Daniel Petrie has succeeded only in producing a mawkish melodrama. Although the ever-dapper Don Ameche reprises his Oscar-winning role of Art Selwyn, there is much less of a spring in his step, and fellow old folks Wilford Brimley and Hume Cronyn are clearly equally uncomfortable with a script in which an emphasis on the joy of living has been overlaid with a glum resignation to the consolation prizes of old age. The performances remain endearing, however. Contains swearing.

Don Ameche *Art Selwyn* • Hume Cronyn *Joe Finley* • Wilford Brimley *Ben Luckett* • Courteney Cox *Sara* • Jack Gilford *Bernie Lefkowitz* • Steve Guttenberg *Jack Bonner* • Maureen Stapleton *Mary Luckett* • Elaine Stritch *Ruby* • Jessica Tandy *Alma Finley* • Gwen Verdon *Bess McCarthy* ■ Dir Daniel Petrie • Scr Stephen McPherson, from a story by Stephen McPherson, Elizabeth Bradley, from characters created by David Saperstein

Code Name: Dancer ★★ PG

Thriller   1987 · US · Colour · 90mins

Kate Capshaw, best known on screen as Willie Scott in *Indiana Jones and the Temple of Doom* and off it as Mrs Steven Spielberg, has never really attained the star status that her talent deserves. It certainly does nothing for her cause that, when she finally lands a starring role, it's in a film as humdrum as this one. Directed with little urgency by Buzz Kulick, this TV movie has Capshaw as a retired CIA

agent called back to Cuba for one last mission. There's a little romance tossed in, but the bid to rescue a stranded spy offers few surprises. Contains swearing and nudity.

Kate Capshaw *Annie* • Jeroen Krabbé *Malarin* • Gregory Sierra *Vic "the Dancer" Pena* • Valerie Mahaffey *Becky* • Cliff De Young *Paul Goodwin* • James Sloyan *Wardell* ■ Dir Buzz Kulik • Scr Carla Jean Wagner

Code Name: Emerald ★★ PG

Second World War thriller   1985 · US · Colour · 91mins

This is a polished piece of film-making. So polished, in fact, that any trace of originality or enterprise has been scrupulously wiped away. Surely the only excuse for making a Second World War espionage adventure in 1985 was to divulge the secrets of some hitherto hush-hush true-life operation. Not, as here, to take elements from any number of wartime thrillers and form them into yet another collage of double agents, decent Nazis, Gestapo sadists and sacrificial lambs engaged in a story of disinformation, torture and betrayal set in the weeks before D-Day. Contains mild swearing.

Ed Harris *Gus Lang* • Max von Sydow *Jurgen Brausch* • Horst Buchholz *Walter Hoffman* • Helmut Berger *Ernst Ritter* • Cyrielle Claire *Claire Jouvet* • Eric Stoltz *Andy Wheeler* • Patrick Stewart *Colonel Peters* • Graham Crowden *Sir Geoffrey Macklin* ■ Dir Jonathan Sanger • Scr Ronald Bass, from his novel *The Emerald Illusion*

Code Name: Wolverine ★★

Action drama   1996 · US · Colour

Frederick Forsyth's bestselling thrillers, rather surprisingly, haven't – with the honourable exception of *The Day of the Jackal* – enjoyed the same success on the screen. But this made-for-TV action drama, based on an original storyline by Forsyth, marks a new low. Antonio Sabato Jr is the former Navy SEAL who has to dust off his old combat training when his wife and son are kidnapped by drug-dealers after inadvertently picking up the wrong luggage. The setting is Italy but the direction, writing and performances are sadly far from exotic. Contains violence and swearing.

Antonio Sabato Jr *Harry Gordini* • Traci Lind *Monica Gordini* • Richard Brooks *John Baines* • Matthew Cox *Joey Gordini* • Danny Quinn *Adolfo James* • Urbano Barberini *Della Cortese* ■ Dir David Jackson • Scr Robert T Megginson, from a story by Frederick Forsyth

Code Name: Zebra ★

Action thriller   1986 · US · Colour · 96mins

Joe Tornatore, director of *Zebra Force*, the first of these outings, shows no more interest in characterisation or surprise than he did the first time around. As before, simple-minded characters spit out staccato dialogue beneath a roar of action that comes at you like a runaway train. Yet even the thrill of the chase can't paper over the sizeable cracks in the increasingly knotty plot (including two vendettas), which threatens to trip over itself.

Jim Mitchum [James Mitchum] *Frank Barnes* • Mike Lane *Carmine Longo* • Joe Donte Voce • Timmy Brown *Cougar* • Chuck Morrell *Lieutenant Dietrich* • Frank Sinatra Jr *Kozlo* •

Deanna Jurgens *Julie* • Lindsay Crosby *Police Sergeant* ■ *Dir* Joe Tornatore • *Scr* Robert Leon

Code of Silence ★★ 18

Action thriller   1985 · US · Colour · 96mins

The Fugitive director Andrew Davis made his name crafting efficient, no-frills action thrillers, and here, even with the rather wooden Chuck Norris in the lead, he still manages to generate a fair bit of mindless excitement. Norris is the maverick cop who gets caught up in a drug war. To make matters worse, he is not popular among his cop colleagues, supposedly because he breaks rank and speaks out against their corrupt practices, but probably because they find him incredibly boring. Nevertheless, there are some great action set pieces and a suitably destructive finale. Contains violence and swearing. ▭

Chuck Norris *Eddie Cusack* • Henry Silva *Luis Comacho* • Bert Remsen *Commander Kates* • Mike Genovese *Tony Luna* • Nathan Davis *Felix Scalese* • Ralph Foody *Cragie* • Allen Hamilton *Pirelli* ■ *Dir* Andrew Davis • *Scr* Michael Butler, Dennis Shryack, Mike Gray, from a story by Michael Butler, Dennis Shryack

Codename Wildgeese ★★ 15

Action adventure
1984 · UK/It · Colour · 88mins

Ridiculous European commando movie which bears absolutely no relation to the Richard Burton/Roger Moore action classic. What we get instead is a very sullen Lewis Collins leading a motley crew of mercenaries in a fight against an opium warlord in South East Asia. Plenty of explosions and car chases ensue, plus a fair quota of brutality; Lee Van Cleef and Ernest Borgnine seem to be in the cast purely to make up the numbers. Directed by Anthony Dawson (aka Antonio Margheriti), the film's working title was *Wild Geese 5*, despite the fact they'd never even been a *Wild Geese 3* or *4*. ▭

Lewis Collins *Wesley* • Lee Van Cleef *China* • Ernest Borgnine *Fletcher* • Klaus Kinski *Charlton* • Manfred Lehmann *Klein* • Mimsy Farmer *Kathy* • Thomas Danneberg *Arbib* • Frank Glaubrecht *Stone* • Wolfgang Pampel *Baldwin* ■ *Dir* Anthony Dawson [Antonio Margheriti] • *Scr* Michael Lester

Un Coeur en Hiver ★★★★ 15

Drama   1992 · Fr · Colour · 100mins

Few film-makers are capable of producing such incisive studies of intimate relationships as Claude Sautet, yet it was only with this intense picture that he first received the international acclaim he so richly deserved. This subtle and superbly crafted film is so naturalistic and touches on so many raw emotional nerves that, at times, it is almost unbearable to watch. Off-screen spouses Daniel Auteuil and Emmanuelle Béart are exceptional as the violin-maker and the musician whose fated attraction intrudes calamitously upon a world of order and beauty. The meticulous Béart actually learned to play the violin to make Ravel's ravishing music more realistic. In French with English subtitles.. ▭

Daniel Auteuil *Stéphane* • Emmanuelle Béart *Camille* • André Dussollier *Maxime* • Elisabeth Bourgine *Hélène* • Brigitte Catillon *Régine* ■ *Dir* Claude Sautet • *Scr* Claude Sautet, Jacques Fieschi, Jérôme Tonnerre

Coffy ★★★ 18

Blaxploitation action drama
1973 · US · Colour · 86mins

Nurse Pam Grier masquerades as a junkie to infiltrate a drug cartel and take revenge on the mob who turned her little sister into a catatonic addict. Jack Hill's extremely violent, blaxploitation classic made the halter-topped, Capri-panted Grier, in her first leading role, queen of the genre, while plenty of nudity and nasty blood-letting keep the high-energy action bubbling along. Thanks to strong roles like this, and awesome acting smarts to match them, Grier became a cult star. ▭

Pam Grier *Coffy* • Booker Bradshaw *Brunswick* • Robert DoQui *King George* • William Elliott *Carter* • Allan Arbus *Vitroni* • Sid Haig *Omar* • Barry Cahill *McHenry* ■ *Dir/Scr* Jack Hill

Cohen and Tate ★★ 18

Crime thriller   1988 · US · Colour · 82mins

Scoring a cult hit with *The Hitcher*, writer/director Eric Red sticks with the road movie format for this low-budget thriller about a boy who witnesses a gangland murder and gets kidnapped by a pair of professional hitmen, played by Roy Scheider and Adam Baldwin. High on humour and muscular doses of violence, the action is clumsily confined to the interior of a car, lending it a theatrical style which isn't helped by its concise time-scale. (The story unfolds over the course of one night.) Despite the best efforts of the always reliable Scheider, a lack of scope scuppers what could have been a real bottleneck of a film. ▭

Roy Scheider *Cohen* • Adam Baldwin *Tate* • Harley Cross *Travis Knight* • Cooper Huckabee *Jeff Knight* • Suzanne Savoy *Martha Knight* ■ *Dir/Scr* Eric Red

Coins in the Fountain ★★

Romantic comedy   1990 · US · Colour

Some would say that it's a sacrilege even to contemplate tinkering with the much-loved romantic comedy tale that many will be familiar with as *Three Coins in the Fountain*, and it must be said this made-for-TV update isn't really in the same league. However, it still makes for bright and breezy entertainment, with familiar TV faces Loni Anderson, Stefanie Kramer and Shanna Reed playing the trio of friends who find romance in Rome. There's a touch of the travelogue about the whole affair, but director Tony Wharmby ensures it bubbles along.

Loni Anderson *Leah Crawford* • Stefanie Kramer *Nikki Thomas* • Shanna Reed *Bonnie Mahaffey* • Anthony Newley *Alfred Bancroft* • Carl Weintraub *Joe Marino* • David Wilson *Phil Mahaffey* • John Sanderford *Mac Chambers* ■ *Dir* Tony Wharmby • *Scr* Lindsay Harrison

Cold Blood ★★ 18

Action thriller   1975 · W Ger · Colour · 75mins

Rutger Hauer made this obscure German thriller shortly before he began the collaboration with Paul Verhoeven that would transform his career. Still only a fledgling star, he relies on moody macho rather than character depth to see him through a bruising encounter that, for all its nastiness, has few surprises to offer. Hooking up with innocent Vera Tschechowa after swindling his employers, Hauer has to draw on all his ingenuity when they are taken hostage. Günter Vaessen's sloppy script depends entirely on platitudes, but Ralf Gregan's direction packs a visceral punch. German dialogue dubbed into English. ▭

Rutger Hauer *Blondi* • Vera Tschechowa *Corinna* • Horst Frank *Chef* • Walter Richter *Arthur* • Gunther Stoll *Stasi* • Erich Kleiber *Arzt* • Anna-Maria Asmus *Arztfrau* ■ *Dir* Ralf Gregan • *Scr* Günter Vaessen

Cold Comfort ★★★ U

Thriller   1989 · Can · Colour · 88mins

There are echoes of Stephen King's *Misery* in this chilling tale, but who's going to hear them out in the Canadian wilderness? A classic example of why you should never accept lifts from strangers, the story turns on the relationship that develops between teenager Margaret Langrick and the travelling salesman her father brings home as her birthday present. Maury Chaykin is splendidly malevolent as the deranged dad, while Paul Gross gives an astute performance as the lamb brought to the slaughter. Cleverly juxtaposing claustrophobic interiors and forbidding snowscapes, Vic Sarin directs with a sure hand, leaving events tantalisingly open-ended. Contains swearing and nudity.

Maury Chaykin *Floyd* • Paul Gross *Stephan* • Margaret Langrick *Dolores* ■ *Dir* Victor Sarin [Vic Sarin] • *Scr* Richard Beattie, L Elliott Simms, from a play by James Garrard

Cold Comfort Farm ★★★★ PG

Period comedy   1995 · UK · Colour · 98mins

Scripted by Malcolm Bradbury, John Schlesinger's film was originally intended for UK television, but ended up securing cinematic distribution in the US. Kate Beckinsale plays Flora Poste, an orphan in thirties England who is sent off to live with her distant rural relatives, the Starkadders. Instead of sinking into a deep depression, Flora sets about sorting out her mad kin (Eileen Atkins, Rufus Sewell, Ian McKellen). Based on the novel by Stella Gibbons, this dotty, very British comedy is a real treat. ▭

Eileen Atkins *Judith Starkadder* • Kate Beckinsale *Flora Poste* • Sheila Burrell *Ada Doom* • Stephen Fry *Mybug* • Freddie Jones *Adam Lambsbreath* • Joanna Lumley *Mrs Smiling* • Ian McKellen *Amos Starkadder* • Miriam Margolyes *Mrs Beetle* • Rufus Sewell *Seth* ■ *Dir* John Schlesinger • *Scr* Malcolm Bradbury, from the novel by Stella Gibbons

Cold Dog Soup ★★ 15

Comedy   1989 · US · Colour · 84mins

A sexually inexperienced young innocent, promised a close encounter by a tempting young lass if he agrees to bury her mother's dog, meets a disturbed cab driver who demands they form a team and sell the dog. Equally inexperienced (and it shows) is director Alan Metter, who has a clutch of good ideas about surreal black comedy, but seems unable to produce the right tone to put them across to his audience. As the two clowns trawl the city by night, looking for customers, Frank Whaley is reasonably funny as the youngster, while Randy Quaid, as the cabbie, squeezes some milage from one-note psychosis. ▭

Randy Quaid *Jack Cloud* • Frank Whaley *Michael Latchmer* • Christine Harnos *Sarah Hughes* • Sheree North *Mrs Hughes* • Nancy Kwan *Mme Chang* • Seymour Cassel *Jojo* ■ *Dir* Alan Metter • *Scr* Thomas Pope from a novel by Stephen Dobyns

Cold Feet ★★ 15

Comedy   1989 · US · Colour · 88mins

This bizarre tale of western eccentrics has the kind of brilliant but undisciplined cast (Keith Carradine, Sally Kirkland, Tom Waits) who wander off into method acting overdrive because there is no firm hand on the directorial tiller. Based on a script by Jim Harrison and the terribly hip Thomas McGuane and featuring a narrative that doesn't so much rove as list from side to side, this is a small cult hit which charmed some on its release while massively infuriating others. Contains violence and swearing. ▭

Keith Carradine *Monte* • Sally Kirkland *Maureen* • Tom Waits *Kenny* • Bill Pullman *Buck* • Rip Torn *Sheriff* • Kathleen York *Laura* • Jeff Bridges *Bartender* ■ *Dir* Robert Dornhelm • *Scr* Thomas McGuane, Jim Harrison

Cold Fever ★★★★ 15

Drama
1994 · Ice/Ger/Swi/US · Colour · 81mins

Considering its size, the Icelandic film industry produces films of a remarkably high quality, and Fridrik Thor Fridriksson's road movie is a case in point. In his bid to perform a traditional burial service for the geologist parents who died in Iceland seven years earlier, Japanese businessman Masatoshi Nagase encounters all manner of eccentric locals who make his odyssey a truly memorable experience. Fridriksson makes magnificent use of the island's snowy wastes and distinctive settlements, and only the contrived appearances of American "tourists" Lili Taylor and Fisher Stevens jar. Blending local myth and Wild West convention while gently mocking national stereotypes, this is a deadpan gem. In Japanese and Icelandic with English subtitles.

Masatoshi Nagase *Atsushi Hirata* • Lili Taylor *Jill* • Fisher Stevens *Jack* • Gisli Halldorsson *Siggi* • Laura Hughes [Laura Leigh Hughes] *Laura* • Seijun Suzuki *Hirata's Grandfather* • Hiromasa Shimada *Suzuki* • Mayayuki Sasaki *Higashino* ■ *Dir* Fridrik Thor Fridriksson • *Scr* Jim Stark, Fridrik Thor Fridriksson

Cold Front ★★★ 15

Spy thriller   1989 · US/Can · Colour · 89mins

A sturdy crime thriller which makes up for what it lacks in originality with two strong performances from Martin Sheen and Michael Ontkean (still best known as the sheriff in television's *Twin Peaks*). The pair play a US Drug Enforcement Agency officer and a plain-clothes Canadian Mountie respectively, who find themselves reluctantly teamed together when they get dragged into the world of espionage.

It's simple, undemanding stuff, and the violent mayhem is ably held together by director Paul Bnarbic. Contains swearing. 📺

Martin Sheen *John Hyde* • Michael Ontkean *Derek MacKenzie* • Kim Coates *Mantha* • Beverly D'Angelo *Amanda* • Yvan Ponton *Inspector Duchesne* ∎ *Dir* Paul Bnarbic • *Scr* Sean Allan, Stefan Arngrim

Cold Heart ★★ 18

Crime drama 1997 · US · Colour · 92mins

One of many inferior nineties crime stories inspired by *Reservoir Dogs*, and featuring Mr Orange, David Caruso, as a criminal seeking vengeance when his lover flees with the proceeds of their bungled diamond robbery. Kelly Lynch (playing a character called Jude Law!) is pretty good in her tough role, but Caruso's no Michael Madsen or Harvey Keitel – he just hasn't got the acting mettle to convince as a hard man. Contains swearing, nudity and violence. 📺

David Caruso *Ned Tash* • Kelly Lynch *Jude Law* • Stacey Dash *Bec Rosenberg* • Christopher Noth *T* • John Spencer *Uncle Mike* • Richard Kind *Nabbish* ∎ *Dir/Scr* John Ridley

Cold Heaven ★★★ 15

Psychological thriller
1992 · US · Colour · 102mins

Barely released to cinemas because the financing company ran into problems, this Nicolas Roeg mystery drama stars his wife, Theresa Russell, as a doctor's wife who starts an affair with another doctor only to discover her husband has been killed in a boating accident. What a coincidence! But then things start to get even more coincidental and decidedly weird. Based on a novel by Brian Moore, the picture never quite delivers the zingers it promises but the Mexican locations are splendid, and Russell is alluring and Will Patton plays a priest when things go all religious and metaphysical. 📺

Theresa Russell *Marie Davenport* • Mark Harmon *Alex Davenport* • James Russo *Daniel Corvin* • Will Patton *Father Niles* • Richard Bradford *Monsignor Cassidy* • Talia Shire *Sister Martha* • Julie Carmen *Anna Corvin* ∎ *Dir* Nicolas Roeg • *Scr* Allan Scott, from the novel by Brian Moore

Cold Justice ★ 15

Crime drama 1991 · UK · Colour · 101mins

Imagine an episode of *Cheers* with all the humour taken out. Then blame Dennis Waterman, who co-wrote, produced and stars as "priest" Father Jim, bringing further misery to a group of barflies in this ill-conceived drama. The misfits include Roger Daltrey as a former boxer dreaming of a comeback; unwed mother-to-be Bridget O'Connell; and Ralph Foody as the cynic who questions the priest's credentials. While their lives are falling apart, Father Jim is busy scamming them out of their money, inadvertently ripping off a local gangster in the process. Overlong and depressing. 📺

Roger Daltrey *Keith Gibson* • Dennis Waterman *Father Jim* • Ralph Foody *Ernie* • Ron Dean *Stan Lubinski* • Penelope Milford *Eileen* • Bert Rosario *Paquito* • Bridget O'Connell *Debbie* ∎ *Dir* Terry Green • *Scr* Terry Green, Trevor Preston, Dennis Waterman

Cold Light of Day ★★ 18

Biographical horror drama
1990 · UK · Colour · 76mins

Some of the facts in the case of mass murderer Dennis Nilsen are presented with grubby realism in this British counterpart to *Henry: Portrait of a Serial Killer*. The shoestring budget presumably accounts for a minimum of camera set-ups and poor sound, and the overall effect is so grim the film was barely released. Intercutting the 15 murders with the interrogation of the suspect is an old-fashioned device, but Bob Flag is horribly plausible as the milquetoast maniac. 📺

Bob Flag *Jordan March* • Geoffrey Greenhill *Inspector Simmons* • Martin Byrne-Quinn *Joe* • Andrew Edmans *Stephen* • Bill Merrow *Albert Green* ∎ *Dir/Scr* Fhiona Louise

The Cold Light of Day ★★ 18

Thriller 1995 · UK/Hol · Colour · 95mins

Detective Richard E Grant investigates the deaths of several young girls in a fair remake of the 1958 German classic *It Happened in Broad Daylight*. The dramatic crux of director Rudolph Van Den Berg's modernised thriller is how he sets a trap for the killer with a young child as bait. But he brings little of the flair or imagination of his neglected horror fantasy, *The Johnsons*, to this mundane police procedural. Contains swearing and some violence. 📺

Richard E Grant *Viktor Marek* • Heathcote Williams *Stephan Nuslauer* • Simon Cadell *Vladimir Kozant* • Lynsey Baxter *Milena* ∎ *Dir* Rudolf Van Den Berg • *Scr* Doug Magee

Cold River ★★ PG

Adventure 1982 · US · Colour · 90mins

Adapted from a novel by William Judson, this outdoor adventure will probably find its biggest audience among younger viewers. There's a Disney true-life feel to the action, which sees Suzanne Weber and Pat Petersen forced to fend for themselves after their father succumbs to a heart attack in the sub-zero temperatures of the Adirondack Mountains. However, as you'd expect of the kids of an expert guide, they've picked up the odd tip and make it back to civilisation without the intervention of any Lassie-style heroics. Cinematographer Bill Godsey supplies some spectacular views, but Fred G Sullivan's direction is a bit rough-and-ready. 📺

Suzanne Weber *Lizzy Allison* • Pat Petersen *Tim Hood* • Richard Jaeckel *Mike Allison* • Robert Earl Jones *The Trapper* ∎ *Dir* Fred G Sullivan • *Scr* Fred G Sullivan, from the novel *Winterkill* by William Judson

The Cold Room ★ 15

Supernatural thriller
1984 · UK/US · Colour · 94mins

Jeffrey Caine's ingenious novel focuses on the psychological stress placed on a modern-day college student when her trip behind the Berlin Wall lands her in mortal danger – from the Gestapo! Released on video as *The Prisoner*, this TV movie is directed by Basil Dearden's son, James. Unfortunately, he never has his material under control and, consequently, Amanda Pays looks just as dumbfounded by events as her

character. George Segal and Warren Clarke look as if they wish they'd read the script more carefully. 📺

George Segal *Hugh Martin* • Amanda Pays *Carla Martin/Christa Bruckner* • Renée Soutendijk *Lily* • Warren Clarke *Bruckner* • Anthony Higgins *Erich* ∎ *Dir* James Dearden • *Scr* James Dearden, from the novel by Jeffrey Caine

Cold Sassy Tree ★★★

Romantic drama 1989 · US · Colour

An above average made-for-TV movie starring the redoubtable Faye Dunaway in a role which is positively enhanced by her chronic overacting. She stars with the excellent Richard Widmark in this tale of a couple who outrage the sensibilities of a parochial one-horse town. Dunaway gives it her all, and is aided by a decent, thoughtful script and gentle, appropriate direction by Joan Tewkesbury. Based on the novel by Olive Ann Burns, this is a darn good yarn, well told.

Faye Dunaway *Love Simpson* • Richard Widmark *E Rucker Blakeslee* • Neil Patrick Harris *Will Tweedy* • Frances Fisher *Loma* • Lee Garlington *Mary Willis* • John Jackson [John M Jackson] *Hoyt* • Jay O Sanders *Clayton McAllister* • Jo Harvey Allen *Effie Belle Tate* ∎ *Dir* Joan Tewkesbury • *Scr* Joan Tewkesbury, from the novel by Olive Ann Burns

Cold Steel ★★ 18

Action drama 1987 · US · Colour · 86mins

An interesting cast of disparate acting talent isn't enough to save this standard action film from director Dorothy Ann Puzo, daughter of *Godfather* novelist Mario Puzo. Brad Davis is utterly wasted as an LA cop out to avenge the murder of his father by a disfigured former colleague. Lower down the billing is eighties pop icon Adam Ant, who actually turns in a surprisingly decent performance. Police show clichés abound, while car chases happen for the sheer sake of it. Worth catching only if you're curious to see a pre-*Basic Instinct* Sharon Stone. 📺

Brad Davis *Johnny Modine* • Sharon Stone *Kathy* • Adam Ant *Mick* • Jonathan Banks *Iceman* • Jay Acovone *Cookie* • Eddie Egan *Lieutenant Hill* • Sy Richardson *Rashid* ∎ *Dir* Dorothy Ann Puzo • *Scr* Michael Sonye, Moe Quigley, from a story by Lisa M Hansen, Dorothy Ann Puzo, Michael Sonye

The Cold Summer of 1953 ★★★

Political drama
1987 · USSR · Colour · 102mins

The films of Andrei Tarkovsky, John Ford and Akira Kurosawa provide the visual and thematic inspiration for this "Steppes western", which was one of the first *perestroika* features to criticise the gulag system openly. The Stalinist legacy is also called into question as a gang of criminals, released in the amnesty following his death, lay siege to a small Siberian town, which is delivered from its tyranny by escaped political prisoners Valeri Priyemykhov and Anatoli Papanov. Forcefully establishing the desolation of the landscape, director Alexandr Proshkin stages the violent action with a detachment in keeping

with the late dictator's regime. In Russian with English subtitles.

Valeri Priyemykhov *Kopalich* • Anatoli Papanov *Luzga* • Zoya Buryak • Viktor Stepanov ∎ *Dir* Alexandr Proshkin • *Scr* Edgar Dubrovski

Cold Sweat ★★ 15

Action thriller 1971 · Fr/It · Colour · 89mins

Stone-faced Charles Bronson takes time off from his busy urban vigilante schedule to head for the French Riviera, only to be forced into drug smuggling by crime boss James Mason. James Bond director Terence Young's overly familiar revenge tale is nominally taken from an early novel by veteran thriller writer Richard Matheson. It merely relies, once again, on turgid violence and Bronson's laid-back, tough-guy persona to drive a routine plot. Contains some mild swearing, and moderate violence, sex scenes and nudity. 📺

Charles Bronson *Joe Martin* • Liv Ullmann *Fabienne Martin* • James Mason *Ross* • Jill Ireland *Moira* • Michel Constantin *Whitey* ∎ *Dir* Terence Young • *Scr* Shimon Wincelberg, Albert Simonin, from the novel *Ride the Nightmare* by Richard Matheson

Cold Sweat ★★ 18

Supernatural thriller
1993 · US · Colour · 92mins

Not the 1971 Charles Bronson action vehicle, but a sex-and-slaying opus that has all the expected soft-core excesses of a Shannon Tweed vehicle. Naughty and naked as ever, Tweed plays the last target of hit man Ben Cross, who is planning to quit, having accidentally killed the innocent victim now haunting him. The seedy side of the story is depressingly familiar, but the ghostly subplot and the graveyard humour make it marginally more engaging than the average erotic thriller. Contains swearing, violence, sex scenes and nudity. 📺

Ben Cross *Mark Cahill* • Adam Baldwin *Mitch* • Shannon Tweed *Beth* • Dave Thomas (1) *Larry* • Henry Czerny *Sean* • Maria Del Mar *Joanne* • Lenore Zann *Ghost* ∎ *Dir* Gail Harvey • *Scr* Richard Beattie

Cold Turkey ★★

Satire 1969 · US · Colour · 101mins

A comedy about a town in Iowa whose population goes "cold turkey" when a tobacco company offers them $25 million to stop smoking for a month. The film marked the directing debut of comedy producer Norman Lear and very much reflects the time in which it was made. Dick Van Dyke – a huge star then, mainly on TV – plays the local priest; veteran comic Edward Everett Horton plays the cigarette tycoon; while stand-up comic Bob Newhart is the public relations whizkid who dreams up the idea and has to face the fact his company might lose the bet.

Dick Van Dyke *Rev Clayton Brooks* • Bob Newhart *Merwin Wren* • Vincent Gardenia *Mayor Wrappler* • Pippa Scott *Natalie Brooks* • Tom Poston *Edgar Stopworth* • Edward Everett Horton *Hiram C Grayson* • Jean Stapleton *Mrs Wrappler* • Barbara Cason *Letitia Hornsby* ∎ *Dir* Norman Lear • *Scr* Norman Lear, from a story by Norman Lear, William Price Fox Jr, from the novel *I'm Giving Them Up for Good* by Margaret Rau, Neil Rau

🅄 = SUITABLE FOR ALL   🅄c = SUITABLE FOR ALL, ESPECIALLY FOR YOUNG CHILDREN (VIDEO ONLY)   PG = PARENTAL GUIDANCE

A Cold Wind in August ★★★

Drama　　　　　　　　1961 · US · BW · 79mins

During an oppressively hot New York summer, a janitor's 17-year-old son (Scott Marlowe) is sent to fix the air conditioning of a much-married stripper (Lola Albright). The encounter leads to an affair and the shattering of the boy's illusions. A real shocker in its day, this tale of an older woman with a past seducing an innocent youngster still holds up thanks to Albright's superb performance, the all-round competence of first-time director Alexander Singer, and a convincing screenplay by Burton Wohl, adapted from his own novel. Low-budget but absorbing drama, with a cruel sting.

Lola Albright *Iris Hartford* • Scott Marlowe *Vito Perugino* • Herschel Bernardi *Juley Franz* • Joe De Santis *Papa Perugino* • Clark Gordon *Harry* • Janet Brandt *Shirley* ■ *Dir* Alexander Singer • *Scr* Burton Wohl, from his novel

Coldblooded ★★ 18

Crime comedy　　　1995 · US · Colour · 89mins

Jason Priestley became a teen idol overnight thanks to *Beverly Hills 90210*, but thus far his movie career has been something of a damp squib. Here he's cast as a nerdy Mafia bookie who gets promoted by his boss (Robert Loggia) to the rank of *Pulp Fiction*-style assassin, only to discover he has a natural talent for killing. This potentially novel spoof of hitman movies is smothered under a welter of unfunny gags and Priestley's charmless offensive, though Michael J Fox, who co-produced the film, turns in an amusing cameo. Contains violence and some swearing. ▭

Jason Priestley *Cosmo* • Kimberly Williams *Jasmine* • Peter Riegert *Steve* • Robert Loggia *Gordon* • Janeane Garofalo *Honey* • Josh Charles *Randy* • Michael J Fox *Tim Alexander* ■ *Dir/Scr* M Wallace Wolodarsky

The Colditz Story ★★★★ U

Second World War drama
1954 · UK · BW · 93mins

One of seemingly dozens of PoW dramas made in the mid-fifties, this one being set in the infamous German fortress of the title. The story about the daring escapes undertaken by the Allied prisoners has little time for the psychology of imprisonment, but the action is still well-played – tense at times, music-hall jolly at others. John Mills plays Pat Reid, on whose first-hand account the film is based, and Eric Portman, Ian Carmichael, Lionel Jeffries and Bryan Forbes are the other inmates of heroic hue. There were recent plans afoot to turn the Colditz site into a hotel, a scheme that understandably upset the surviving inmates and their descendants. ▭

John Mills *Pat Reid* • Eric Portman *Colonel Richmond* • Christopher Rhodes *Mac* • Lionel Jeffries *Harry* • Bryan Forbes *Jimmy* • Ian Carmichael *Robin* • Richard Wattis *Richard* ■ *Dir* Guy Hamilton • *Scr* Guy Hamilton, Ivan Foxwell, from the non-fiction book by PR Reid

La Collectionneuse ★★★★ 15

Drama　　　　　　　　1967 · Fr · Colour · 82mins

The third of Eric Rohmer's "Six Moral Tales", and the first of feature length.

Winner of the special jury prize at Berlin, it tells of the summer encounter between sexually liberated teenager Haydée Politoff, antique dealer Patrick Bauchau and his friend Daniel Pommereulle. Attracted and unnerved by Politoff's amorous exploits, they attempt to reform her without becoming part of her collection of lovers. As you would expect of Rohmer, there is plenty of amusing and insightful chat, as his young cast flirt and succumb, resist and reproach. In French with English subtitles.

Patrick Bauchau *Adrien* • Haydée Politoff *Haydée* • Daniel Pommereulle *Daniel* • Seymour Hertzberg [Eugene Archer] *Sam* • Mijanou Bardot *Carole* • Annik Morice *Carole's friend* ■ *Dir* Eric Rohmer • *Scr* Eric Rohmer, Patrick Bauchau, Haydée Politoff, Daniel Pommereulle

The Collector ★★★★ 15

Thriller　　　　1965 · US/UK · Colour · 114mins

A genuinely disturbing chunk of *Grand Guignol* about a maladjusted, butterfly-collecting young man who kidnaps an art student and keeps her in his cellar. Based on an equally disturbing and complex novel by John Fowles, this was in its day a fashionable shocker and X-certificated. Now it comes across as a fascinating period piece, featuring two quintessential sixties stars in possibly their best roles – painfully handsome Terence Stamp as the collector, and beautiful auburn-haired Samantha Eggar as the victim of his attentions. Kenneth More was also cast as Eggar's older lover, but his whole role was removed in the final edit. Contains some violence. ▭

Terence Stamp *Freddie Clegg* • Samantha Eggar *Miranda Grey* • Mona Washbourne *Aunt Annie* • Maurice Dallimore *Neighbour* • William Beckley *Crutchley* • Gordon Barclay *Clerk* ■ *Dir* William Wyler • *Scr* Stanley Mann, John Kohn, from the novel by John Fowles

Colleen ★★

Musical comedy　　　1936 · US · BW · 90mins

When eccentric millionaire Hugh Herbert puts gold-digger Joan Blondell in charge of his dress shop, his family is outraged. Complications ensue when his nephew, Dick Powell, brings Ruby Keeler in to take over. A feeble script and forgettable score make this a disappointing final outing for Powell and Keeler, paired for the sixth and last time in a Warner Bros musical. Alfred E Green directs, while the cast of stalwarts includes Jack Oakie. Alas, there's no Busby Berkeley on hand to save the enterprise with his explosively imaginative dance numbers.

Dick Powell *Donald Ames III* • Ruby Keeler *Colleen* • Jack Oakie *Joe Cork* • Joan Blondell *Minnie Hawkins* • Hugh Herbert *Cedric Ames* • Louise Fazenda *Alicia Ames* • Paul Draper *Paul* • Luis Alberni *Carlo* ■ *Dir* Alfred E Green • *Scr* Peter Milne, Frederick Hugh Herbert [F Hugh Herbert], Sig Herzig, from a story by Robert Lord • *Music director* Leo Forbstein [Leo F Forbstein]

College ★★★★★ U

Silent romantic comedy
1927 · US · BW · 66mins

Buster Keaton's running, jumping but rarely standing-still film is a story about his going to college and trying to transcend athletically his bookworm exterior to win the heart of student Anne Cornwall. She's surrounded by admiring jocks, but he's determined to flatten them in a decathlon of sports, though he gets it all wrong – knocking down hurdles, or being thrown by the hammer instead of the other way around. There's one spectacular sequence in which he apes a soda-jerk to disastrous effect, and the final pole-vault to rescue the girl is balletically brilliant. Genius at its most frenetic. ▭

Buster Keaton *Ronald* • Ann Cornwall *Mary Haines, the Girl* • Flora Bramley *Her Friend* • Harold Goodwin *Jeff Brown, a Rival* ■ *Dir* James W Horne • *Scr* Carl Harbaugh, Bryan Foy

College Swing ★★

Musical　　　　　1938 · US · BW · 82mins

Despite having three writers on the movie, including an uncredited Preston Sturges, and Raoul Walsh as director, this is little more than an excuse for a variety show. The silly plot, such as it is, has bird-brained Gracie Allen inheriting a college and hiring vaudevillians as professors. Allen does a few turns with husband George Burns, Martha Raye yells a number of songs, Bob Hope cracks corny jokes and Betty Grable shakes her legs. Former child star Jackie Coogan, who was married to Grable at the time, is also in the cast of this mildly entertaining movie.

George Burns *George Jonas* • Gracie Allen *Gracie Alden* • Martha Raye *Mabel* • Bob Hope *Bud Brady* • Edward Everett Horton *Hubert Dash* • Florence George *Ginna Ashburn* • Ben Blue *Ben Volt* • Betty Grable *Betty* • Jackie Coogan *Jackie* ■ *Dir* Raoul Walsh • *Scr* Walter DeLeon, Francis Martin, from a story by Ted Lesser

Collision Course ★★ 18

Comedy　　　　　1987 · US · Colour · 96mins

This thoroughly unremarkable variation on the Arnold Schwarzenegger vehicle *Red Heat* was shelved for three years after it was made, because of the lawsuit that followed the bankruptcy of its production company, DEG. It wasn't until 1992 that it was released on video in the US – something of an embarrassment for Jay Leno, who had just assumed the host's chair of that famous US chatfest *The Tonight Show*. As the detective teamed with visiting Japanese inspector Pat Morita, Leno reveals why this is his sole starring role to date. A major disappointment for director Lewis Teague following his success with *The Jewel of the Nile*. ▭

Noriyuki "Pat" Morita [Pat Morita] *Investigator Fujitsuka Natsuo* • Jay Leno *Detective Tony Costas* • Ernie Hudson *Shortcut* • Chris Sarandon *Philip Madras* • John Hancock *Lieutenant Ryerson* • Tom Noonan *Scully* • Al Waxman *Dingman* ■ *Dir* Lewis Teague • *Scr* Frank Darius Namei, Robert Resnikoff

Le Colonel Chabert ★★★ 12

Historical drama　1994 · Fr · Colour · 106mins

Having superbly photographed Gérard Depardieu in *Tous les Matins du Monde* and *Germinal*, and André Dussollier in *Un Coeur en Hiver*, Yves Angelo brought them together for his directorial debut. And they serve him well in this handsome adaptation of one of the novels making up Balzac's *Comédie Humaine*. Depardieu is typically bullish as the Napoleonic veteran returning ten years after his supposed death to discover his wife (Fanny Ardant) has remarried, taking his fortune with her. The war scenes are magnificent, the intrigue compelling and the sense of period faultless. However, Angelo occasionally gets so carried away by the grandeur and gravitas of the production that the pace drops to a crawl. In French with English subtitles.

Gérard Depardieu *Chabert* • Fanny Ardant *Countess Ferraud* • Fabrice Luchini *Derville* • André Dussollier *Count Ferraud* • Daniel Prévost *Boucard* • Olivier Saladin *Huré* ■ *Dir* Yves Angelo • *Scr* Jean Cosmos, Yves Angelo, Véronique Legrange, from the novel by Honoré de Balzac

Colonel Effingham's Raid ★★★ U

Comedy　　　　　1945 · US · BW · 70mins

Bluff Charles Coburn's 1943 supporting Oscar for *The More the Merrier* helped elevate him to lead status, and here he's well cast in this minor 20th Century-Fox rustic comedy drama about a returning army officer fighting a one-man battle to preserve his southern town's heritage. Coburn himself was from Savannah, Georgia, despite his gentrified British appearance, and well understood this particular character. He seldom played leads again, but was Oscar-nominated and top-billed for his subsequent movie, *The Green Years*.

Charles Coburn *Colonel Effingham* • Joan Bennett *Ella Sue Dozier* • William Eythe *Al* • Allyn Joslyn *Earl Hoats* • Elizabeth Patterson *Emma* ■ *Dir* Irving Pichel • *Scr* Kathryn Scola, from the novel by Barry Fleming

Colonel March Investigates ★

Crime mystery　　　1953 · UK · BW · 70mins

Boris Karloff runs a Scotland Yard division called the "Department of Queer Complaints", wears an eye-patch and carries a swordstick. These three short stories proving his investigative brilliance were actually glued together from Karloff's British TV show, *Colonel March of Scotland Yard*. Threadbare production values don't help this effort from Cy Endfield, the blacklisted, exiled director who went on to make *Zulu* in 1964.

Boris Karloff *Colonel March* • Ewan Roberts *Inspector Ames* • Richard Wattis *Cabot* • John Hewer *John Parrish* • Sheila Burrell *Joan Forsythe* • Joan Sims *Marjorie Dawson* ■ *Dir* Cyril Endfield [Cy Endfield] • *Scr* Leo Davis, from the TV series by Carter Dickson

Colonel Redl ★★★★ 15

Drama
1984 · Hun/W Ger/Aus · Colour · 143mins

Drawing on historical records and John Osborne's play *A Patriot for Me*, this is a compelling study of the decaying Austro-Hungarian empire and the social, racial and political tensions that eventually undermined it. Klaus Maria Brandauer excels as the railwayman's son whose casual facility for deceit and obsessive devotion to honour enable him to rise through the ranks of the Imperial Army until both his background and his bisexuality become an embarrassment to the establishment. Armin Mueller-Stahl's ruthless Franz Ferdinand is equally impressive, but it's the chilling way director István Szabó charts the complex web of events that makes this sumptuous picture so memorable. In German with English subtitles. Contains some violence, swearing, sex scenes and nudity. 🎞

Klaus Maria Brandauer *Alfred Redl* • Hans Christian Blech *Colonel von Roden* • Armin Mueller-Stahl *Archduke Franz Ferdinand* • Gudrun Landgrebe *Katalin Kubinyi* • Jan Niklas *Christoph Kubinyi* ■ *Dir* István Szabó • *Scr* István Szabó, Peter Dobai, from the play *A Patriot for Me* by John Osborne

The Colony ★ PG

Thriller   1995 · US · Colour · 89mins

Security expert John Ritter moves his family into "The Colony", an ultra-exclusive neighbourhood where crime and violence are non-existent. All is not as it seems in this Utopian community, however, as any non-conformity shown by the residents is dealt with in dark and sinister ways by boss man Hal Linden. This poorly executed TV movie variation on *The Stepford Wives* theme suffers from lightweight suspense and is not helped by Ritter, who's badly miscast. 🎞

John Ritter *Rick Knowlton* • Mary Page Keller *Leslie Knowlton* • Hal Linden *Philip Denig* • Marshall Teague *Doug Corwin* • Todd Jeffries *Mike Knowlton* ■ *Dir/Scr* Rob Hedden

Color Me Dead ★★

Crime thriller   1969 · Ausl · Colour · 97mins

An Australian movie that should be blushing with shame at its audacity in pinching its plot from *DOA* , Rudolph Maté's classic *film noir* from 1949, without identifying itself as a remake. An accountant is given a very slow-acting poison and tries to find out who has killed him, in advance of his death. This time around it's Tom Tryon as the victim.

Tom Tryon *Frank Bigelow* • Carolyn Jones *Paula Gibson* • Rick Jason *Bradley Taylor* • Patricia Connolly *Marla Rukubian* • Tony Ward *Halliday* ■ *Dir* Eddie Davis • *Scr* Russell Rouse, Clarence Greene

Color of a Brisk and Leaping Day ★★★

Period drama   1996 · US · BW · 85mins

Fight your way through the title and you will find an American indie production about a man who wants to rebuild and reopen the railroad that once ran through Yosemite national park. This majestic wilderness was made world famous by Ansel Adams's photographs; Christopher Münch's film mirrors Adams's imagery while the Chinese-American hero, played by Peter Alexander, sets about realising his obsession. Like the story itself the movie is a labour of love, set in the forties, incorporating archive footage and full of remarkable detail.

Peter Alexander *John Lee* • Jeri Arredondo *Nancy* • Henry Gibson *Robinson* • Michael Stipe *Skeeter* • David Chung *Mr Lee* • Diana Larkin *Wendy* ■ *Dir/Scr* Christopher Münch • *Cinematographer* Rob Sweeney

The Color of Destiny ★★★

Political drama   1986 · Bra · Colour · 104mins

Although this hard-hitting resistance drama is set in Rio, the focal point is actually Chile under the Pinochet dictatorship. By concentrating on the politicisation of teenager Guilherme Fontes, director Jorge Duran aims to show both the torment and the duty of the exile, while also depicting the human cost of militancy. Barely remembering the torture and murder of his brother, Fontes gives a thoughtful performance as he struggles to justify his obsession with girls and art once his cousin, Julia Lemmertz, persuades him to join a demonstration outside the Chilean embassy and reawakens his commitment to overthrowing the tyrannical regime. In Portuguese with English subtitles.

Guilherme Fontes *Paulo* • Norma Bengell *Laura* • Franklin Caicedo *Victor* • Julia Lemmertz *Patricia* • Andrea Beltrao *Helena* ■ *Dir* Jorge Duran • *Scr* Jorge Duran, Nelson Natotti, Jose Joffily, from a story by Jorge Duran

Color of Justice ★★★

Courtroom drama
1997 · US · Colour · 95 mins

Like most TV movies, this thoughtful examination of justice, media responsibility and racism from director Jeremy Kagan ultimately lacks real bite. However, the pedigree of the cast – including Bruce Davison, F Murray Abraham, Judd Hirsch and Gregory Hines – can't be faulted, and there's much to enjoy in their assured playing. The script is by Lionel Chetwynd, writer/director of Vietnam War drama *Hanoi Hilton*. Contains swearing.

Bruce Davison *Frank Gainer* • F Murray Abraham *Jim Sullivan* • Judd Hirsch *Sam Lind* • Gregory Hines *Reverend Walton* • Lisa Pelikan *Betty Gainer* • Saul Rubinek *Norm* ■ *Dir* Jeremy Kagan [Jeremy Paul Kagan] • *Scr* Lionel Chetwynd

The Color of Money ★★★★ 15

Drama   1986 · US · Colour · 114mins

Paul Newman reprised the role of "Fast Eddie" Felson, the pool shark he played in *The Hustler* (1961), and deservedly won the best actor Oscar. This time around, the ageing Felson takes on pushy pupil Vincent (Tom Cruise) and both learn a trick or two about life and each other as Felson prepares his prodigy for a national tournament in Atlantic City. The confrontational climax never quite convinces, but Richard Price's knockout script is one to treasure and director Martin Scorsese brings his hallmark visual style to bear on the production. Oscar-nominated Mary Elizabeth Mastrantonio puts in an accomplished performance as the naive Cruise's knowing girlfriend and look out, too, for Forest Whitaker in a supporting role as a young pool hustler. Contains swearing. 🎞 DVD

Paul Newman *"Fast Eddie" Felson* • Tom Cruise *Vincent Lauria* • Mary Elizabeth Mastrantonio *Carmen* • Helen Shaver *Janelle* • John Turturro *Julian* • Forest Whitaker *Amos* ■ *Dir* Martin Scorsese • *Scr* Richard Price, from the novel by Walter Tevis

Color of Night ★ 18

Erotic thriller   1994 · US · Colour · 117mins

Richard Rush was once a half-decent film-maker – take *Freebie and the Bean* or *The Stunt Man*, for example – but he came a cropper with this atrocity, which became notorious after some full-frontal shots of Bruce Willis were snipped by the censors. So even though we don't get the Full Brucey, we do get a lousy whodunit, in which every member of a therapy group goes out of their way to prove they're madder than the rest. This is so awful it can't be missed. Contains swearing, violence, sex scenes and nudity. 🎞

Bruce Willis *Dr Bill Capa* • Jane March *Rose* • Rubén Blades *Martinez* • Lesley Ann Warren *Sondra* • Scott Bakula *Dr Bob Moore* • Brad Dourif *Clark* • Lance Henriksen *Buck* • Kevin J O'Connor *Casey* • Andrew Lowery *Dale* ■ *Dir* Richard Rush • *Scr* Matthew Chapman, Billy Ray, from a story by Billy Ray

The Color Purple ★★★★ 15

Drama   1985 · US · Colour · 147mins

On this film's release, it was fashionable to castigate director Steven Spielberg for his somewhat glossy, sugar-coated version of Alice Walker's celebrated Pulitzer Prize-winning novel about a young black woman's struggle for self and racial identity. Yet this is actually an impressive, dignified attempt to transpose a radical and often difficult novel into mainstream entertainment with a message. Whoopi Goldberg is wonderful in the lead, Danny Glover and Margaret Avery are sublime, and watch out for Oprah Winfrey playing *very* out of character. Contains violence and swearing. 🎞 DVD

Whoopi Goldberg *Celie* • Danny Glover *Albert Johnson* • Margaret Avery *Shug Avery* • Oprah Winfrey *Sofia* • Willard Pugh *Harpo* • Akosua Busia *Nettie* • Desreta Jackson *Young Celie* • Adolph Caesar *Old Mister* • Rae Dawn Chong *Squeak* ■ *Dir* Steven Spielberg • *Scr* Menno Meyjes, from the novel by Alice Walker

Colorado Territory ★★★

Western   1949 · US · BW · 94mins

An exciting westernised remake of the Humphrey Bogart classic *High Sierra*, with an identical plot and the same director in Raoul Walsh. Walsh manages to create a superbly sweaty atmosphere, with Joel McCrea this time as the outlaw on the run, hiding out in the desert. The Ida Lupino and Joan Leslie roles are played here by Virginia Mayo and Dorothy Malone, and jolly sultry they are. The themes are adult and the tension is beautifully sustained; indeed, structurally, this version is better than its famous predecessor.

Joel McCrea *Wes McQueen* • Virginia Mayo *Colorado Carson* • Dorothy Malone *Julie Ann* • Henry Hull *Winslow* • John Archer *Reno Blake* • James Mitchell *Duke Harris* • Morris Ankrum *US marshal* • Basil Ruysdael *Dave Rickard* • Frank Puglia *Brother Tomas* ■ *Dir* Raoul Walsh • *Scr* John Twist, Edmund H North, from the novel by WR Burnett

Colors ★★★ 18

Crime drama   1988 · US · Colour · 126mins

With *Dragnet*-style gravity, this movie informs us of the 600 gangs, the 70,000 gang members and the 400

gang-related murders in LA County each year. Then cops Robert Duvall and Sean Penn take to the streets to apprehend the troublesome youths. Directed by Dennis Hopper with some urgency, the picture is tense, unpleasant (there is a literal grilling in a restaurant) and certainly seems authentic in its atmosphere and its obvious sympathy for both sides of the war. Duvall and Penn make a fine combination of old sage and high-octane rookie, but the film's grimness doesn't make for enjoyable viewing. Contains violence and swearing. 🎞

Sean Penn *Danny McGavin* • Robert Duvall *Bob Hodges* • Maria Conchita Alonso *Louisa Gomez* • Randy Brooks *Ron Delaney* • Don Cheadle *Rocket* ■ *Dir* Dennis Hopper • *Scr* Michael Schiffer, from a story by Michael Schiffer, Richard DiLello

The Colossus of New York ★

Science-fiction horror
1958 · US · BW · 71mins

When Otto Kruger stays late at the lab to transplant his brother's brain into a robot, he ends up with a combination of Frankenstein's monster and *The Wrong Trousers*. Man-made monsters are not noted for their gratitude, however, and instead of using his genius to save humanity, the big lad is soon biting chunks out of the Big Apple. The dialogue and effects are wretched, Kruger and Ross Martin are lifeless, while Eugène Lourié's direction is more leaden than the creature's footwear.

Ross Martin *Dr Jeremy Spensser* • Mala Powers *Anne Spensser* • Charles Herbert *Billy Spensser* • John Baragrey *Dr Henry Spensser* • Otto Kruger *Dr William Spensser* • Robert Hutton *Professor John Carrington* • Ed Wolff *Colossus* ■ *Dir* Eugène Lourié • *Scr* Thelma Schnee, from a story by Willis Goldbeck

The Colossus of Rhodes ★★★

Historical adventure
1961 · It/Fr/Sp · Colour · 127mins

Before he went on to make spaghetti westerns with such fierce artistry, and after several credits as screenwriter on historical epics, Sergio Leone made this spectacular adventure, his first credit as a director. The late Rory Calhoun stars as Athenian soldier Dario who joins a slave uprising against the Greek island's oppressive ruler. There are some explicit torture and battle scenes, and touches of Leone irony to lighten the rather lumpen load. It made 657 million lire at the Italian box office – enough to buy an awful lot of pasta.

Rory Calhoun *Dario* • Lea Massari *Diala* • Georges Marchal *Peliocles* • Conrado Sanmartin *Thar* • Angel Aranda *Koros* • Mabel Karr *Mirte* ■ *Dir* Sergio Leone • *Scr* Ennio De Concini, Sergio Leone, Cesare Seccia, Luciano Martino, Duccio Tessari, Age Gavioli, Carlo Gualtieri, Luciano Chittarini

Colossus: the Forbin Project ★★★

Science-fiction thriller
1969 · US · Colour · 99mins

The years have been kind to Joseph Sargent's thinking man's sci-fi entry, which imagines a time when one super computer has total control over all western defence systems. When it decides to link terminals with its Soviet counterpart in a bid for world domination, its human masters discover they can't switch the damn thing off. Cleverly playing up the thriller aspects of the story and cannily making the computer the film's central character, this well-acted and utterly persuasive shocker provides a cautionary warning regarding man's dependency on technology.

Eric Braeden *Dr Charles Forbin* • Susan Clark *Dr Cleo Markham* • Gordon Pinsent *The President* • William Schallert *Grauber* • Leonid Rostoff *1st Chairman* • Georg Stanford Brown *Fisher* • Tom Basham *Harrison* ■ *Dir* Joseph Sargent • *Scr* James Bridges, from the novel *Colossus* by DF Jones

The Colour of Pomegranates ★★★★★ Ⓤ
Lyrical biography　　1969 · USSR · Colour · 69mins

Ostensibly this is a fantasy on the life of the 18th-century Armenian poet Arutiun Sayadin, the carpet weaver's apprentice who rose to become first the court minstrel Sayat Nova ("the king of song"), and then an archbishop. Yet the sumptuous tableaux devised by director Sergei Paradjanov are only vaguely concerned with the depiction of actual events. Instead, they are a breathtaking amalgam of subversive symbols drawn from both religious iconography and nationalist folklore. Much of the meaning will be indecipherable to those without specialist knowledge, but you can still surrender yourself to the rhythm and beauty of this remarkable film, made in 1969 but not seen in the West until 1977. In Armenian with English subtitles. ▭

Sophico Chiaureli *[Sofiko Chiaureli] Young Poet/Poet's Love/Nun/Angel/Mime* • V Galestyan *Poet in the Cloister* • M Aleksanian *Poet as a Child* • G Gegechkori *Poet–as an Old Man* ■ *Dir/Scr* Sergei Paradjanov

Colt .45 ★★★ Ⓤ
Western　　1950 · US · Colour · 72mins

One of the most successful westerns in a great year for the genre (*Wagon Master, The Gunfighter* and *Broken Arrow* were also produced in 1950). Here craggy Randolph Scott is a gun salesman whose deadly wares are stolen by Zachary Scott and used in a series of hold-ups. Apart from a romantic interlude with Ruth Roman that's barely convincing in this context, it's a fast-moving, though conventional, western that benefits from the use of fifties Technicolor and the iconic charm of Randolph Scott, an often undervalued tall guy in the saddle.

Randolph Scott *Steve Farrell* • Ruth Roman *Beth Donovan* • Zachary Scott *Jason Brett* • Lloyd Bridges *Paul Donovan* • Alan Hale *Sheriff Harris* • Ian MacDonald *Miller* • Chief Thundercloud *Walking Bear* ■ *Dir* Edwin L Marin • *Scr* Thomas Blackburn, from his story

Column South ★★★ Ⓤ
Western　　1953 · US · Colour · 84mins

A beautifully photographed Universal western in which fresh-faced former war hero Audie Murphy plays a cavalry

officer sympathetic to the Indians, perceptively pointing out that helping the dispossessed native Americans would ultimately strengthen the Union. Don't worry, the politics don't get in the way of the well-staged action sequences. Director Frederick de Cordova was destined for a long and distinguished career in American television, most notably as producer of *The Johnny Carson Show.*

Audie Murphy *Lieutenant Jed Sayre* • Joan Evans *March Whitlock* • Robert Sterling *Captain Lee Whitlock* • Ray Collins *Brigadier General Storey* • Dennis Weaver *Menguito* ■ *Dir* Frederick De Cordova • *Scr* William Sackheim • *Cinematographer* Charles P Boyle

Coma ★★★★ ⓯
Thriller　　1977 · US · Colour · 108mins

Doctor Genevieve Bujold and sinister surgeon Richard Widmark clash memorably in this taut medical thriller, faithfully adapted from Robin Cook's bestseller by doctor-turned-novelist Michael Crichton. The *ER* creator also directs and expertly turns the suspense screws in the gripping way that has become his trademark. It's Crichton's assured sense of creepy paranoia that gives an extra edge to the hospital horrors.

Genevieve Bujold *Dr Susan Wheeler* • Michael Douglas *Dr Mark Bellows* • Elizabeth Ashley *Mrs Emerson* • Rip Torn *Dr George* • Richard Widmark *Dr George A Harris* • Lois Chiles *Nancy Greenly* • Harry Rhodes *Dr Morelind* • Tom Selleck *Sean Murphy* ■ *Dir* Michael Crichton • *Scr* Michael Crichton, from the novel by Robin Cook

Comanche ★★ Ⓤ
Western　　1956 · US · Colour · 87mins

This very routine western, allegedly based on fact, is made interesting by the fact that it introduced glamorous South American star Linda Cristal (who would go on to *The Alamo* and *Two Rode Together*) to an English-speaking audience. In the lead is the past-his-prime Dana Andrews, grim-faced and seemingly having trouble with his lines. Incidentally, the mint American pressing of this film's soundtrack, featuring the full-colour reproduction poster on its sleeve, is now a much sought-after collectors' item.

Dana Andrews *Read* • Kent Smith *Quanah Parker* • Linda Cristal *Margarita* • Nestor Paiva *Puffer* • Henry Brandon *Black Cloud* • John Litel *General Miles* • Reed Sherman *French* • Stacy Harris *Downey* • Lowell Gilmore *Ward* ■ *Dir* George Sherman • *Scr* Carl Krueger

Comanche Station ★★★★ ⓟⒼ
Western　　1960 · US · Colour · 70mins

The last in the fine series of westerns from director Budd Boetticher and co-producer/star Randolph Scott is a fine meditation on ageing, a companion piece thematically to John Ford's *The Searchers,* but arguably bleaker and more realistic. Supporting the craggy Scott is the well-cast Claude Akins as a flamboyant bounty hunter, and their final confrontation is especially effective. Notable too is Burt Kennedy's screenplay, which utilises the western's emotive iconography brilliantly. This was greatly under-rated and taken for granted on its original release. ▭

Randolph Scott *Jefferson Cody* • Nancy Gates *Mrs Lowe* • Claude Akins *Ben Lane* • Skip Homeier *Frank* • Richard Rust *Dobie* • Rand Brooks *Station man* • Dyke Johnson *Mr Lowe* ■ *Dir* Budd Boetticher • *Scr* Burt Kennedy

Comanche Territory ★★ Ⓤ
Western　　1950 · US · Colour · 75mins

American folk legend Jim Bowie (he of the knife fame) has been portrayed several times on the movie screen, perhaps most notably by Richard Widmark in *The Alamo* and Alan Ladd in *The Iron Mistress* (though Sterling Hayden in *The Last Command* comes a close third). This, alas, is one of the more lacklustre versions of Bowie's exploits. Macdonald Carey fails to convey any sense of destiny as he tries to stop lovely Maureen O'Hara and her evil brother Charles Drake from mining on Indian territory. O'Hara is as ravishing as ever, but this average western has little else to redeem it.

Maureen O'Hara *Katie* • Macdonald Carey *James Bowie* • Will Geer *Dan'l Seeger* • Charles Drake *Stacey Howard* • Pedro De Cordoba *Quisima* • Ian MacDonald *Walsh* • Rick Vallin *Pakanah* • Parley Baer *Boozer* ■ *Dir* George Sherman • *Scr* Oscar Brodney, Lewis Meltzer, from a story by Lewis Meltzer

The Comancheros ★★★★ ⓟⒼ
Western　　1961 · US · Colour · 102mins

A marvellous swan song for *Casablanca* director Michael Curtiz, who died after completing this film. Indeed, much of this handsome western was actually directed by star John Wayne himself, in tandem with second unit director Cliff Lyons. The scale is substantial, and Curtiz fills the screen with mucho action. The Duke is virtually the whole movie, but there's lively support from Stuart Whitman as gambler Paul Regret, catalyst for the whole shebang. The score is one of Elmer Bernstein's best and most elegiac, and there's a terrific star-building performance from Lee Marvin. A big hit in its day, this is the sort of sprawling horse opera that died, alas, with its star. ▭

John Wayne *Captain Jake Cutter* • Stuart Whitman *Paul Regret* • Ina Balin *Pilar* • Nehemiah Persoff *Graile* • Lee Marvin *Tully Crow* • Michael Ansara *Amelung* • Pat Wayne [Patrick Wayne] *Tobe* • Bruce Cabot *Major Henry* ■ *Dir* Michael Curtiz • *Scr* James Edward Grant, Clair Huffaker, from the novel by Paul I Wellman • *Cinematographer* William Clothier

Combat Academy ★ ⓟⒼ
Comedy　　1986 · US · Colour · 92mins

When George Clooney became the darling of Hollywood studios, it was inevitable that TV companies would start searching for early skeletons in the Clooney closet. This is by no means the worst – that accolade probably belongs to *Return of the Killer Tomatoes!* – but it is hardly an auspicious example of his early work. Keith Gordon, now a respected film director, is another familiar face in this substandard *Police Academy*-style affair about prank-loving students clashing with authority figures.

Robert Culp *General Woods* • Keith Gordon *Max Mendelsson* • Wally Ward *Perry Barnett* • George Clooney *Major Biff Woods* • Jamie Farr

Colonel Lawrence Frierick • John Ratzenberger *Mr Barnett* ■ *Dir* Neal Israel • *Scr* Paul W Shapiro

Combination Platter ★★★
Comedy drama　　1993 · US · Colour · 84mins

This directorial debut from 23-year-old Tony Chan is a quiet little film about a Chinese restaurant in Queens, NY, that successfully exposes the culture clash between the Chinese owners and their American clients. The film centres on Jeff Lau, an illegal immigrant seeking to remain in the US via marriage. Aided by his pal Kenneth Lu, he starts dating Colleen O'Brien, who's oblivious to his mercenary intentions. Remarkably good considering its $250,000 budget, this slice-of-life comedy drama really does make you care about Lau being hauled back to China.

Jeff Lau *Robert* • Colleen O'Brien *Claire* • Lester "Chit-Man" Chan *Sam* • Colin Mitchell *Benny* • Kenneth Lu *Andy* • Thomas K Hsiung *Mr Lee* ■ *Dir* Tony Chan • *Scr* Tony Chan, Edwin Baker

Come and Get It ★★ ⓟⒼ
Period drama　　1936 · US · BW · 95mins

This is the story of a humble young lumberjack (Edward Arnold) who becomes a wealthy and powerful tycoon. Sacrificing the woman he loves (Frances Farmer) to ambition along the way, he has to face the bitter disillusion of old age. Adapted from Edna Ferber's novel and co-directed by heavyweights William Wyler and Howard Hawks, this is a curate's egg of a period piece in which Arnold, Joel McCrea as his son, and Walter Brennan as his friend are terrific. Farmer in a dual role isn't, and the film itself, beautifully mounted, runs out of steam halfway through. ▭

Edward Arnold *Barney Glasgow* • Joel McCrea *Richard Glasgow* • Frances Farmer *Lotta Morgan/Lotta Bostrom* • Walter Brennan *Swan Bostrom* • Andrea Leeds *Evvie Glasgow* • Frank Shields *Tony Schwerke* ■ *Dir* Howard Hawks, William Wyler • *Scr* Jules Furthman, Jane Murfin, from the novel by Edna Ferber

Come and See ★★★ ⓯
Epic drama　　1985 · USSR · Colour and BW · 142mins

Set in Byelorussia in 1943, this worthy picture traces the harrowing experiences which turn green teenager Alexei Kravchenko into a hardened resistance fighter. Where Grigori Chukhrai's *Ballad of a Soldier* and Andrei Tarkovsky's *Ivan's Childhood* use stark monochrome images to emphasise the horror of war, Elem Klimov employs glossy colour images to create striking set pieces, skilfully staged to shock. However, the whole film suffers from a severe case of "Schindler Syndrome": the depiction of indefensible events to ensure the viewer unquestioningly accepts the director's vision. In Russian with English subtitles.

Alexei Kravchenko *Florya* • Olga Mironova *Glasha* • Liubomiras Laucevicius • Vladas Bagdonas ■ *Dir* Elem Klimov • *Scr* Elem Klimov, Ales Adamovich, from *The Khatyn Story_* and _*A Punitive Squad* by Ales Adamovich

Come Back, Little Sheba
★★★★

Domestic drama 1952 · US · BW · 98mins

Sheba is a little pooch and surrogate child that's gone missing; its owner, Lola (Shirley Booth), is desperate for its return. Her husband, meanwhile, a failed doctor, is so provoked by the cavortings of two virile student lodgers that he hits the bottle after a year on the wagon. Based on William Inge's Broadway hit, this is a classic slice of Americana, oscillating between comedy and tragedy and performed by actors who squeeze the text until not a drop of drama remains on the page. Daniel Mann directed the original play and changes very little here, though Sidney Blackmer – who played Doc Delaney on stage – is dropped in favour of Burt Lancaster. The show-stopper, though, is Booth, who won an Oscar for her screen debut.

Burt Lancaster *Doc Delaney* • Shirley Booth *Lola Delaney* • Terry Moore *Marie Buckholder* • Richard Jaeckel *Turk Fisher* • Philip Ober *Ed Anderson* • Lisa Golm *Mrs Goffman* • Walter Kelley *Bruce* ■ *Dir* Daniel Mann • *Scr* Ketti Frings, from the play by William Inge

Come Back to the Five and Dime, Jimmy Dean, Jimmy Dean
★★★★ 15

Drama 1982 · US · Colour · 109mins

Robert Altman drops his usual scattergun approach to direct a wholly focused adaptation of Ed Graczyk's play about a group of women who gather to commemorate the death of their beloved Jimmy Dean. Sandy Dennis, Cher and Karen Black are among the beautiful losers who are now slightly older and bitchier than they were when they originally formed the fan club. Altman brilliantly conveys their changes of mood via a wall mirror in what is altogether one of the better variations on a stage theme. ▭

Sandy Dennis *Mona* • Cher *Sissy* • Karen Black *Joanne* • Sudie Bond *Juanita* • Marta Heflin *Edna Louise* • Kathy Bates *Stella May* • Mark Patton *Joe Qualley* ■ *Dir* Robert Altman • *Scr* Ed Graczyk, from his play

Come Blow Your Horn
★★

Comedy 1963 · US · Colour · 111mins

The first in a long line of playwright Neil Simon's Broadway comedy successes to be filmed, this is not quite as funny on screen as it thinks it is. There's sterling work from Frank Sinatra as an unrepentant Jewish bachelor, but the problem lies in the over-acting of Lee J Cobb and the great Yiddish comedian Molly Picon as Frankie's parents. It's one of those incredibly glossy sixties productions from Paramount, and was Oscar-nominated for colour art direction, but all the dressing in Hollywood can't hide the lightweight, moralistic trifle that lies underneath.

Frank Sinatra *Alan Baker* • Lee J Cobb *Papa Baker* • Tony Bill *Buddy Baker* • Molly Picon *Mama Baker* • Barbara Rush *Connie* • Jill St John *Peggy* • Phyllis McGuire *Mrs Eckman* • Dan Blocker *Mr Eckman* • Joyce Nizzari *Snow* • Carole Wells *Eunice* ■ *Dir* Bud Yorkin • *Scr* Norman Lear, from the play by Neil Simon • *Producer* Norman Lear, Bud Yorkin • *Art Director* Hal Pereira, Roland Anderson

Come Die with Me
★★

Mystery 1994 · US · Colour

Following in the footsteps of Ralph Meeker, Stacy Keach and the detective's very own creator Mickey Spillane, Rob Estes assumes the mantle of Mike Hammer for this barely adequate TV-movie whodunit. The real interest for most viewers will not be in the solution to the case, but in the appearance of Pamela Anderson as Hammer's faithful assistant, Velda.

Rob Estes *Mike Hammer* • Pamela Anderson *Velda* • Randi Ingerman *Trinity Sinclair* • James Hong *Nathan* • Geoff Meed *Schlitz* • Darlanne Fluegel *Pat Chambers* ■ *Dir* Armand Mastroianni • *Scr* John Lau

Come Fill the Cup
★★★

Drama 1951 · US · BW · 110mins

A reporter loses his job as a result of his drinking problem but rehabilitates himself with the help of a reformed alcoholic friend and goes on to give similar assistance to his boss's son. Although this descends into the maudlin and improbable somewhere along the way, a strong cast and Gordon Douglas's gritty direction make for an attention-holding melodrama that also involves gangster elements. The always mesmerising James Cagney stars as the reporter, with James Gleason, Raymond Massey and an Oscar-nominated Gig Young.

James Cagney *Lew Marsh* • Phyllis Thaxter *Paula Copeland* • Raymond Massey *John Ives* • James Gleason *Charley Dolan* • Gig Young *Boyd Copeland* • Selena Royle *Dolly Copeland* ■ *Dir* Gordon Douglas • *Scr* Ivan Goff, Ben Roberts, from the novel by Harlan Ware

Come Fly with Me
★★ U

Comedy 1962 · US · Colour · 108mins

The romantic adventures and entanglements of three air hostesses (Dolores Hart, Pamela Tiffin, Lois Nettleton) make up this empty flimflam, more interesting as a glossy travelogue than a romantic comedy. Henry Levin directs the proceedings, with Karl Malden, Hugh O'Brian and the dishy German actor Karlheinz Böhm playing the male leads. The plotless waffle never becomes airborne, however – though watch out for Lois Maxwell, better known as Miss Moneypenny from the Bond films.

Dolores Hart *Donna Stuart* • Hugh O'Brian *First Officer Ray Winsley* • Karl Boehm [Karlheinz Böhm] *Baron Franz Von Elzingen* • Karl Malden *Walter Lucas* • Pamela Tiffin *Carol Brewster* • Lois Nettleton *Hilda Bergstrom* • Dawn Addams *Katie* • Richard Wattis *Oliver Garson* • Lois Maxwell *Gwen* ■ *Dir* Henry Levin • *Scr* William Roberts, from the novel *Girl on a Wing* by Bernard Glemser

Come Live with Me
★★★

Romantic comedy 1941 · US · BW · 86mins

Hedy Lamarr is the émigré who poor, starving writer James Stewart marries so she won't be thrown out of the country in this finely-mounted and intelligently-made MGM movie from Hollywood's golden era. Watch it for its star power alone, and marvel at how convincing and likeable the two leads are, as director Clarence Brown skilfully creates an atmosphere that allows you to care deeply about Lamarr's plight. The playing is exemplary, the mood sublime; this movie deserves to be better known.

James Stewart *Bill Smith* • Hedy Lamarr *Johnny Jones* • Ian Hunter *Barton Kendrick* • Verree Teasdale *Diana Kendrick* • Donald Meek *Joe Darsie* • Barton MacLane *Barney Grogan* • Edward Ashley *Arnold Stafford* ■ *Dir* Clarence Brown • *Scr* Patterson McNutt, from a story by Virginia Van Upp

Come Next Spring
★★★ U

Drama 1956 · US · Colour · 87mins

Long-absent Arkansas farmer Steve Cochran, cured of his drinking problems and restlessness, returns home to his understandably wary wife Ann Sheridan, his daughter Sherry Jackson, who lost the power of speech during one of his drinking bouts, and the son born after his departure. How he regains the love and respect of his family and the community forms the stuff of this rural tale. Directed by RG Springsteen, it's a whole lot better than it sounds, played with simple sincerity and mixing melodrama with an ultimately heartwarming outcome. Main support is from Walter Brennan as a sharecropper. ▭

Ann Sheridan *Bess Ballot* • Steve Cochran *Matt Ballot* • Walter Brennan *Jeff Storys* • Sherry Jackson *Annie* • Richard Eyer *Abraham* • Edgar Buchanan *Mr Canary* • Sonny Tufts *Leroy Hytower* ■ *Dir* RG Springsteen • *Scr* Montgomery Pittman

The Come On
★★

Romantic thriller 1956 · US · BW · 83mins

Anne Baxter, looking great but struggling against the odds with an unconvincing script and Russell Birdwell's uncertain direction, is the star of this less than compelling melodrama. She plays an unhappily married woman who tries to persuade honest fisherman Sterling Hayden to kill her husband after he falls for her on a Mexican beach. Although he refuses, the involvement leads to further plot complications and murder.

Anne Baxter *Rita Kendrick* • Sterling Hayden *Dave Arnold* • John Hoyt *Harley Kendrick* • Jesse White *JJ McGonigle* • Wally Cassell *Tony Margoli* • Alex Gerry *Chalmers* • Tyler McVey *Hogan* • Theodore Newton *Captain Getz* ■ *Dir* Russell Birdwell • *Scr* Warren Douglas, Whitman Chambers, from a novel by Whitman Chambers

Come On George
★★★ U

Comedy 1939 · UK · BW · 85mins

The remarkable thing about George Formby's film career is that he managed to make around 20 features, used a similar storyline in every single one, and nobody minded! He always played an eager beaver whom everyone thought was a dead loss apart from the girl whose smile inspired him to become a world-beater. Here, the object of his affections is Pat Kirkwood, and the sphere in which he gets to prove his previously unsuspected prowess is horse racing. There's the odd song and a few chuckles along the way as he tames a bucking bronco called Maneater. ▭

George Formby *George* • Pat Kirkwood *Ann Johnson* • Joss Ambler *Sir Charles Bailey* • Meriel Forbes *Monica Bailey* • Cyril Raymond *Jimmy Taylor* • George Hayes *Bannerman* ■ *Dir* Anthony Kimmins • *Scr* Anthony Kimmins, Leslie Arliss, Val Valentine

Come Out Fighting
★★

Comedy 1945 · US · BW · 62mins

This was the last of producer Sam Katzman's 22 *East Side Kids* B-movies; after this entry, star Leo Gorcey turned them into the *Bowery Boys*, under which moniker they made another 48 pictures. Considering the paltry plot – a police commissioner wants his nerdish son toughened up by the kids – you can see why Gorcey chose to rethink his position. The pace never lets up under veteran William "One Shot" Beaudine's direction, but the opportunities for clowning are non-existent. Gorcey and his sidekick Huntz Hall had much more fun in their next incarnation, and so did audiences.

Leo Gorcey *Muggs* • Huntz Hall *Glimpy* • Billy Benedict *Skinny* • Gabriel Dell *Pete* • June Carlson *Jane* • Amelita Ward *Rita* • Addison Richards *Mr Mitchell* • George Meeker *Henley* ■ *Dir* William Beaudine • *Scr* Earl Snell

Come See the Paradise
★★★ 15

Drama 1990 · US · Colour · 132mins

Fearful of offending potential patrons, Hollywood has largely steered clear of stories about the treatment of America's Japanese population during the Second World War. So it's disappointing that, when a film does finally tackle the subject, it opts for such a melodramatic approach. Never comfortable with the period or its implications, writer/director Alan Parker has an uphill struggle on his hands from the moment he decides to draw a comparison between the repression of the working classes and racial discrimination. However, he's on safer ground with his depiction of the romance between Dennis Quaid and Tamlyn Tomita, although he doesn't always succeed in keeping Quaid's exuberant style in check. Contains violence, swearing and nudity. ▭

Dennis Quaid *Jack McGurn* • Tamlyn Tomita *Lily Kawamura* • Sab Shimono *Mr Kawamura* • Shizuko Hoshi *Mrs Kawamura* • Stan Egi *Charlie Kawamura* • Ronald Yamamoto *Harry Kawamura* • Akemi Nishino *Dulcie Kawamura* ■ *Dir/Scr* Alan Parker

Come September
★★★

Romantic comedy 1961 · US · Colour · 113mins

When wealthy American businessman Rock Hudson visits his Italian villa in July, instead of September as usual, he discovers it is being run as a hotel in his absence. His major-domo (Walter Slezak), glamorous Gina Lollobrigida and young marrieds Bobby Darin and Sandra Dee (just married in real life, too) become involved in the comic confusions that follow. Directed with appropriate insouciance by Robert Mulligan and played with easy charm by Hudson, who had proved his comedy credentials in *Pillow Talk*, the result is an inconsequential but amusing movie that is typical of the style of early sixties Hollywood.

Rock Hudson *Robert Talbot* • Gina Lollobrigida *Lisa Fellini* • Sandra Dee *Sandy* • Bobby Darin *Tony* • Walter Slezak *Maurice* • Rossana Rory *Anna* ■ *Dir* Robert Mulligan • *Scr* Stanley Shapiro, Maurice Richlin

Come to the Stable ★★★ U

Comedy drama   1949 · US · BW · 94mins

Unless you have a positive aversion to nun movies, there's a great deal of pleasure to be had from watching Loretta Young and Celeste Holm as they arrive in the New England town of Bethlehem and set about their charitable work, initially aided by Elsa Lanchester as a bohemian artist. (All three actresses were Oscar-nominated for their work in this film.) Director Henry Koster handles the tale well, keeping it delightfully warm and sentimental without lapsing into schmaltz.

Loretta Young *Sister Margaret* • Celeste Holm *Sister Scolastica* • Hugh Marlowe *Robert Mason* • Thomas Gomez *Luigi Rossi* • Dorothy Patrick *Kitty* • Basil Ruysdael *Bishop* • Dooley Wilson *Anthony James* ■ *Dir* Henry Koster • *Scr* Oscar Millard, Sally Benson, from a story by Clare Boothe Luce

The Comeback ★ 18

Horror   1977 · UK · Colour · 96mins

Seventies crooner Jack Jones starring in a horror movie? That's about the scariest thing in this far-fetched gothic tale about an American singer recording a new album in an isolated English country manor full of dead bodies, including his ex-wife's. Director Pete Walker's heavy-handed crossbreed of rock and horror draws on numerous genre clichés, from *The Old Dark House* to *Psycho*. Alas, it offers up no decent chills of its own – only a catalogue of ever more gory murders and festering corpses. Contains violence and some swearing.

Jack Jones *Nick Cooper* • Pamela Stephenson *Linda Everett* • David Doyle *Webster Jones* • Bill Owen *Mr B* • Sheila Keith *Mrs B* • Holly Palance *Gail Cooper* ■ *Dir* Peter Walker • *Scr* Murray Smith

Comeback ★★★ 15

Romantic drama   1983 · US · Colour · 95mins

Also known as *Love Is Forever* and *Passion and Valour*, this drama is based on the true story of journalist John Everingham's rescue of his girlfriend from Laos following the Communist takeover. Landon gives a solid performance and is ably supported by Jürgen Prochnow and Edward Woodward. Yet controversy was caused by Moira Chen, better known as porn star Laura Gemser, being cast as the female lead.

Michael Landon *John Everingham* • Moira Chen [Laura Gemser] *Keo Sirisomphone* • Jürgen Prochnow *General Siegfried Kapler* • Edward Woodward *Derek McBracken* • Priscilla Presley *Sandy Redford* • David Leonard *Steve Hammond* • Gabriele Tinti *Georges* • Eric Miller *Frank Moseley* ■ *Dir/Scr* Hall Bartlett

The Comeback Trail ★★

Comedy   1972 · US · Colour · 76mins

A sad end to the career of Buster Crabbe, one of cinema's great action men and the US Olympic swimming star who delighted audiences as Flash Gordon and Buck Rogers. Here he plays Duke, an ageing B-movie actor coerced by a porno producer to appear in his latest movie. The movie was virtually completed in 1971 (the year Crabbe broke the world 400-metre freestyle record for the over-sixties), but it did not appear until 1982, when it crept onto US TV schedules. Trivia fans might like to know that Hugh Hefner and veteran comic Henry Youngman appear as themselves.

Chuck McCann *Enrico Kodac* • Buster Crabbe [Larry "Buster" Crabbe] *Duke Montana* • Robert Staats *E Eddie Eastman* • Ina Balin *Julie Thomas* • Jara Kahout *German producer* ■ *Dir* Harry Hurwitz • *Scr* Harry Hurwitz, from a story by Roy Frumkes, Robert J Winston, Harry Hurwitz

The Comedians ★★★ PG

Drama   1967 · Fr/US · Colour · 146mins

What a temptation it must have been for Elizabeth Taylor and Richard Burton to star in this Graham Greene adaptation of his own novel about the despairing turmoil of life in Haiti under the tyrannical Papa Doc Duvalier – a duet for two dramatic hands. Peter Glenville's leaden direction, however, generates little heat as Taylor, playing the wife of ambassador Peter Ustinov, has an affair with hotel owner Burton. Alec Guinness, as an arms dealer, makes the most profound contribution to an all-star cast; in the final confrontation with Burton, he even manages to upstage the great upstager.

Richard Burton *Brown* • Alec Guinness *Major Jones* • Elizabeth Taylor *Martha Pineda* • Peter Ustinov *Ambassador Pineda* • Paul Ford *Mr Smith* • Lillian Gish *Mrs Smith* • Georg Stanford Brown *Henri Philipot* • James Earl Jones *Dr Magiot* ■ *Dir* Peter Glenville • *Scr* Graham Greene, from his novel

The Comedy Man ★★★ 15

Comedy drama   1964 · UK · BW · 87mins

A struggling middle-aged rep actor, dreaming of the big break, finds fortune through a TV commercial, but walks away from the high life to pursue his career. Written by Peter Yeldham with a nice balance between irony and drama, and directed by Alvin Rakoff with an accurate eye for the dingy environments and brave bonhomie of unemployed actors, this modest British film boasts a superior cast. Kenneth More is the hero, Billie Whitelaw is the girl who loves him, while Cecil Parker plays a veteran actor whose career is washed up.

Kenneth More *Chick Byrd* • Cecil Parker *Rutherford* • Dennis Price *Tommy Morris* • Billie Whitelaw *Judy* • Norman Rossington *Theodore* • Angela Douglas *Fay* • Frank Finlay *Prout* • Edmund Purdom *Julian* ■ *Dir* Alvin Rakoff • *Scr* Peter Yeldham, from the novel by Douglas Hayes

The Comedy of Terrors ★★ 15

Horror comedy   1964 · US · Colour · 79mins

Undertakers Vincent Price and Peter Lorre (in one of his last films) drum up business by murdering potential customers in a lesser effort from Jacques Tourneur, director of such classics as *Cat People* and *Curse of the Demon*. Boris Karloff and Basil Rathbone complete a fearsome foursome who try hard to extract every ounce of humour from the regrettably dull script. Watching genre stars send up the horror clichés they themselves made famous is the only reason for watching this marginally interesting failure. Contains some violence.

Vincent Price *Waldo Trumbull* • Peter Lorre *Felix Gillie* • Boris Karloff *Amos Hinchley* • Basil Rathbone *John F Black* • Joe E Brown *Cemetery keeper* • Joyce Jameson *Amaryllis Trumbull* • Beverley Hills *Mrs Phipps* ■ *Dir* Jacques Tourneur • *Scr* Richard Matheson

Comes a Horseman ★★★ 15

Western   1978 · US · Colour · 113mins

Montana has never looked more beautiful than in this interesting but mightily flawed attempt at a Fordian western from Alan J Pakula. Despite some valiant performances from Jane Fonda as a hard-bitten ranch boss and Jason Robards as a land-grabbing cattle baron, the movie ultimately plods through its paces. Pakula makes the classic western directing mistake of hurling in a plethora of set pieces (stand-offs at the pass, saloon brawling et al) and attempts to hang the plot on these devices. Ford knew it was the other way round.

James Caan *Frank Athearn* • Jane Fonda *Ella Connors* • Jason Robards *Jason Robards Jr* • Jacob "JW" Ewing • George Grizzard *Neil Atkinson* • Richard Farnsworth *Dodger* • Jim Davis *Julie Blocker* • Mark Harmon *Billy Joe Meynert* ■ *Dir* Alan J Pakula • *Scr* Dennis Lynton Clark • *Cinematographer* Gordon Willis

Comfort and Joy ★★★★ PG

Comedy   1984 · UK · Colour · 100mins

We're in the eccentric territory of a Bill Forsyth movie when a Glaswegian radio station holds a pin-up contest, even though listeners cannot see the contestants. The story, which is full of such felicities, involves a local disc jockey (Bill Paterson) who has been abandoned by his partner (Eleanor David). His redemption comes about when he finds he's mediating in an ice-cream war between two branches of the "Scotia Nostra". Forsyth's film is too amiable to see any kind of menace in the terrorists, but as an urban fairy tale it works well and contains a few quirky surprises.

Bill Paterson *Alan "Dickie" Bird* • Eleanor David *Maddy* • CP Grogan [Clare Grogan] *Charlotte* • Alex Norton *Trevor* • Patrick Malahide *Colin* • Rikki Fulton *Hilary* • Roberto Bernardi *Mr McCool* • George Rossi *Bruno* • Peter Rossi *Paolo* ■ *Dir/Scr* Bill Forsyth

The Comfort of Strangers ★★ 18

Drama   1991 · It/UK · Colour · 100mins

The novels of Ian McEwan have proved irresistible to film-makers, but so far few have transferred to the screen with any degree of success. Like *The Cement Garden* and *The Innocent*, this brooding drama lacks both the elegance and the bite of McEwan's prose. Paul Schrader is one of American cinema's most literate directors, but his over-deliberate approach means this cat-and-mouse tale drips with pretension rather than significance. Christopher Walken seems uncomfortable in a role that should have been tailor-made for him, while Helen Mirren is reduced to onlooker status as he lures tourists Rupert Everett and Natasha Richardson into his Venetian flytrap.

Christopher Walken *Robert* • Natasha Richardson *Mary* • Rupert Everett *Colin* • Helen Mirren *Caroline* • Manfredi Aliquo *Concierge* ■ *Dir* Paul Schrader • *Scr* Harold Pinter, from the novel by Ian McEwan

The Comic ★★★★

Comedy   1969 · US · Colour · 95mins

An under-rated, little-seen tragicomedy about a silent film comic, magnificently played by Dick Van Dyke, who uses people and abuses himself in his struggle to get to the top. Written and directed by Carl Reiner (*All of Me, Oh, God!*), its Hollywood insights are many and brutal, while the acting is exceptional – Mickey Rooney is a standout. It only goes to show that comedy is no laughing matter.

Dick Van Dyke *Billy Bright* • Michele Lee *Mary Gibson* • Mickey Rooney *Cockeye* • Cornel Wilde *Frank Powers* • Nina Wayne *Sybil* • Pert Kelton *Mama* • Steve Allen • Barbara Heller *Ginger* • Ed Peck *Edwin C Englehardt* ■ *Dir* Carl Reiner • *Scr* Carl Reiner, Aaron Ruben

Comic Book Confidential ★★★ 15

Documentary   1988 · Can · Colour · 84mins

It's hard to know how to approach this documentary tracing the history of American comics from the forties onwards. The discussion by the country's leading cartoonists (including Marvel Comics' Stan Lee and the amazing Robert Crumb) of how the style and content of their work has changed is fascinating, and the comic books themselves are so irresistible that you find yourself longing to read them from cover to cover. But director Ron Mann presents his material in such a sloppy way that the energy and invention of the illustrations are frittered away and the attention soon begins to wander.

Dir/Scr Ron Mann

Coming Home ★★★★ 18

Drama   1978 · US · Colour · 122mins

High-powered, Oscar-winning performances by Jon Voight and Jane Fonda are the big attraction of this post-Vietnam melodrama. The film is set on the home front, and centres on the romance between an embittered paraplegic and a Marine captain's wife, working as a volunteer in a veteran's hospital. Bruce Dern is also topnotch as Fonda's husband. The screenplay – based on a story commissioned by Fonda, a highly vocal Vietnam War activist – skirts close to sentimentality, if not soap opera at points. But it too won an Oscar, and only a hard heart would remain unmoved. Contains swearing and sex scenes.

Jane Fonda *Sally Hyde* • Jon Voight *Luke Martin* • Bruce Dern *Captain Bob Hyde* • Robert Ginty *Sergeant Dink Mobley* • Penelope Milford *Viola Munson* • Robert Carradine *Billy Munson* • Charles Cyphers *Pee Wee* ■ *Dir* Hal Ashby • *Scr* Waldo Salt, Robert C Jones, from a story by Nancy Dowd

Coming to America ★★★ 15

Romantic comedy   1988 · US · Colour · 111mins

After strolling lazily through *The Golden Child* and *Beverly Hills Cop II*, Eddie Murphy teamed up once again with his

Trading Places director John Landis for a comedy that at least required him to do more than just chuckle. Murphy is the pampered African prince who rebels against his father (James Earl Jones) and comes to America, with sidekick Arsenio Hall in tow, to find a wife. Landis aims for a thirties-style feel for this comedy, but the script isn't as clever as it thinks it is, so it's left to Murphy to carry the picture. Contains swearing and nudity. ▭

Eddie Murphy *Prince Akeem/Clarence/Saul/Randy Watson* • Arsenio Hall *Semmi/Morris/Extremely ugly girl/Reverend Brown* • James Earl Jones *King Jaffe Joffer* • Shari Headley *Lisa McDowell* • Madge Sinclair *Queen Aoleon* • Calvin Lockhart *Colonel Izzi* • John Amos *Cleo McDowell* • Allison Dean *Patrice McDowell* • Eriq La Salle *Darryl Jenks* • Don Ameche *Mortimer Duke* • Ralph Bellamy *Randolph Duke* ■ *Dir* John Landis • *Scr* David Sheffield, Barry W Blaustein, from a story by Eddie Murphy

The Command ★★★ U
Western 1954 · US · Colour · 93mins

This now-forgotten western was important in its day for being the first Warner Bros film to be made in CinemaScope. It was also filmed, though never released, in 3-D, Warners understandably hedging their bets against the future. Because two versions were filmed simultaneously, involving twice as much work for a single fee, the cast is relatively undistinguished: the colourless but good-looking Guy Madison and Joan Weldon are the leads, but James Whitmore wins the acting honours. The action sequences, when they arrive, are spectacular. Contains violence.

Guy Madison *Capt MacClaw* • Joan Weldon *Martha* • James Whitmore *Sergeant Elliot* • Carl Benton Reid *Colonel Janeway* • Harvey Lembeck *Gottschalk* • Ray Teal *Dr Trent* • Bob Nichols *O'Hirons* • Don Shelton *Major Gibbs* ■ *Dir* David Butler • *Scr* Russell Hughes, Samuel Fuller, from the novel *Rear Guard* by James Warner Bellah

Command Decision ★★★★ U
Second World War drama
1948 · US · BW · 111mins

Now here's a plot: should the commander of American bomber squadrons in Britain send his crews deeper into Germany to try and destroy a factory making long-range aircraft, knowing full well that such forays effectively constitute suicide missions? The unlikely bearer of this harrowing moral dilemma is not, as might be expected, Gregory Peck, but the erstwhile King of Hollywood himself, Clark Gable, brilliantly anguished in a role given added resonance as a result of his own wartime flying experience on bombing missions. Under-rated director Sam Wood (*Goodbye, Mr Chips*, *Kings Row*) makes you forget that this was once a major Broadway theatrical hit, and a terrific cast, including Walter Pidgeon and Van Johnson, gives Gable superb back-up.

Clark Gable *Brig Gen KC "Casey" Dennis* • Walter Pidgeon *Major Gen Roland G Kane* • Van Johnson *Tech Sgt Immanuel T Evans* • Brian Donlevy *Brig Gen Clifton L Garnet* • Charles Bickford *Elmer Brockhurst* • John Hodiak *Col Edward R Martin* • Edward Arnold *Congressman Arthur Malcolm* • Cameron

Mitchell *Lt Ansel Goldberg* ■ *Dir* Sam Wood • *Scr* William R Laidlaw, George Froeschel, from the play by William Wister Haines

Command in Hell ★★ 15
Crime drama 1988 · US · Colour · 88mins

As TV movies go, this isn't bad, despite a run-of-the-mill plotline about a female police captain (the redoubtable Suzanne Pleshette) fighting a conspiracy of silence as she tries to find out who murdered one of her officers. Of course, the depiction of the inner-city precinct in which she works is inevitably sanitised for television, as is the language, but there's gritty support from Danny Aiello and Frank Converse, and actor-turned-director Georg Stanford Brown gets the most out of his material. ▭

Suzanne Pleshette *Captain Janet Hamilton* • Danny Aiello *Chief* • Jon Tenney *Todd Hansen* • Joe Morton *Ken Fraker* • Raymond Serra *Sergeant Sal Ruby* • Jon Polito *Brad Stakowski* ■ *Dir* Georg Stanford Brown • *Scr* Stephen Downing, Mark Rodgers

Command Performance ★ U
Musical 1937 · UK · BW · 83mins

Another of the feeble British vehicles that attempted to make a film star out of Arthur Tracy, popular on radio as "The Street Singer". This one has him playing an entertainer who, suffering from stage fright, takes up with a band of nomads and falls in love with a gypsy girl. An unconvincing tale, awash with sentimentality and treacly ballads, whose sole points of interest are Lilli Palmer and the splendid Finlay Currie (Magwitch in David Lean's *Great Expectations*). ▭

Arthur Tracy *Street Singer* • Lilli Palmer *Susan* • Mark Daly *Joe* • Rae Collett *Betty* • Finlay Currie *Manager* • Jack Melford *Reporter* • Stafford Hilliard *Sam* • Julian Vedey *Toni* ■ *Dir* Sinclair Hill • *Scr* George Pearson, Michael Hankinson, Sinclair Hill, from the play by C Stafford Dickens

Commandments ★★ 15
Comedy drama 1996 · US · Colour · 84mins

Losing his wife, his house and his job in a series of disasters, Seth Warner (Aidan Quinn) decides to test God by systematically breaking every one of his Ten Commandments, in the hope of receiving some sort of sign as to The Mighty One's plan. Naturally, he falls for his sister-in-law (Courteney Cox), which doesn't go down too well with her spouse (Anthony LaPaglia), but which kills two commandments with one stone, en route to the biggest one of them all: "Thou Shalt Not Kill." Perhaps commandment number 11 should be "Thou Shalt Not Waste Good Actors On Material Like This." Contains swearing, sexual references and some violence. ▭

Aidan Quinn *Seth Warner* • Courteney Cox *Rachel Luce* • Anthony LaPaglia *Harry Luce* • Shirl Bernheim *Sylvia* • Peter Jacobson *Banker* • Patrick Garner *Banker* • Marcia DeBonis *Receptionist* ■ *Dir/Scr* Daniel Taplitz

Commando ★★★ 18
Action adventure 1985 · US · Colour · 85mins

Arnold Schwarzenegger gets to play the good guy here, in his first movie after finding cult success with The

Terminator. Although he still looks a little awkward with dialogue, he makes for a spectacularly destructive hero, playing a former commando called back into action when his daughter is kidnapped by an old adversary. Dan Hedaya is an engaging chief villain, and there's a feisty turn from Rae Dawn Chong as Arnie's unwilling partner. Mark L Lester is a no-frills director, but his set pieces pack an explosive punch. Contains swearing and violence.

Arnold Schwarzenegger *Colonel John Matrix* • Rae Dawn Chong *Cindy* • Dan Hedaya *General Arius* • Vernon Wells *Bennett* • James Olson *General Kirby* • David Patrick Kelly *Sully* • Alyssa Milano *Jenny* • Bill Duke *Cooke* ■ *Dir* Mark L Lester • *Scr* Steven E de Souza, from a story by Joseph Loeb III, Matthew Weisman, Steven E de Souza

The Commandos Strike at Dawn ★★
Second World War drama
1942 · US · BW · 99mins

Paul Muni plays a Norwegian fisherman fighting Nazi tyranny alongside a team of British commandos. When his daughter is held hostage by the Nazis he escapes to England and leads a sabotage mission to Norway. Based on a yarn by *Hornblower* writer CS Forester and adapted by Irwin Shaw, it's a bit plodding for a flagwaver, getting bogged down with romance supplied by Anna Lee, but boasts an interesting cast, including silent screen legend Lillian Gish who hadn't made a film since 1933.

Paul Muni *Erik Toreson* • Anna Lee *Judith Bowen* • Lillian Gish *Mrs Bergesen* • Sir Cedric Hardwicke [Cedric Hardwicke] *Admiral Bowen* • Robert Coote *Robert Bowen* • Ray Collins *Bergesen* ■ *Dir* John Farrow • *Scr* Irwin Shaw, from a story by CS Forester

La Commare Secca ★★★
Crime drama 1962 · It · BW · 91

Bernardo Bertolucci's first feature was based on a five-page outline by Pier Paolo Pasolini, whom the young man had assisted on *Accattone* the previous year. But Bertolucci had less interest in the Roman proletariat than Pasolini, and the film, which follows an investigation into the murder of a prostitute seen from different perspectives, is merely an interesting cinematic exercise. In Italian with English subtitles.

Francesco Ruiu *Luciano Maialetti*, "Canticchia" • Giancarlo De Rosa *Nino* • Vincenzo Ciccora *Mayor* • Alvaro D'Ercole *Francolicchio* • Romano Labate *Pipito* ■ *Dir* Bernardo Bertolucci • *Scr* Bernardo Bertolucci, Sergio Citti, Pier Paolo Pasolini, from a story by Pier Paolo Pasolini

The Commissar ★★★★ PG
Drama 1967 · USSR · BW · 108mins

The winner of the Silver Bear at Berlin, 20 years after it was banned by the Kremlin, this allegory on the birth of the Soviet state is also one of the few films of the Communist era to deal with anti-Semitism and revolutionary womanhood. Consciously evoking the visual style of the great silent montagists, the story of Red Army commissar Nonna Mordyukova's stay with an impoverished Jewish family

during the last days of her pregnancy overflows with a tolerance and humanity utterly at odds with the Civil War raging outside. Director Alexander Askoldov's courageous stance meant he never worked again. In Russian with English subtitles.

Nonna Mordyukova *Clavdia Vavilova* • Rolan Bykov *Yefim* • Raisa Niedashkovskaya *Maria* • Vasily Shukshin *Commander* • Tina Nedashkovskaya • Pavlik Levin • Ludmilla Volinskaya ■ *Dir/Scr* Alexander Askoldov

The Commitments ★★★★ 15
Musical drama 1991 · UK · Colour · 112mins

The soundtrack album sold like hot cakes, it walked away with Bafta awards for best film, best direction and best adapted screenplay, and it should have made bigger stars of several of its cast than has actually been the case. Alan Parker's first feature on this side of the Atlantic since *Pink Floyd the Wall* nearly a decade earlier, this was also the film that brought the work of future Booker Prize-winning author Roddy Doyle to the attention of the chattering classes. Laced with Irish charm and blessed with some superb music sung with passion by Andrew Strong, Bronagh Gallagher, Angeline Ball and Maria Doyle, it's also very funny, especially the scenes of the band auditions held by the excellent Robert Arkins. Contains swearing. ▭

Robert Arkins *Jimmy Rabbitte* • Michael Aherne *Steven Clifford* • Angeline Ball *Imelda Quirke* • Maria Doyle [Maria Doyle Kennedy] *Natalie Murphy* • Dave Finnegan *Mickah Wallace* • Bronagh Gallagher *Bernie McGloughlin* • Felim Gormley *Dean Fay* • Glen Hansard *Outspan Foster* • Dick Massey *Billy Mooney* • Johnny Murphy *Joey "The Lips" Fagan* • Kenneth McCluskey *Derek Scully* • Andrew Strong *Deco Cuffe* ■ *Dir* Alan Parker • *Scr* Dick Clement, Ian La Frenais, Roddy Doyle, from the novel by Roddy Doyle

Common Law Cabin ★★★
Cult crime drama 1967 · US · Colour · 69mins

One of sexploitation director Russ Meyer's early breast-obsessed, mock morality melodramas that put him on the cult map. Using his familiar theme of sexually frustrated men and top-heavy women flung together in a weird setting and succumbing to temptation before paying the price for their illicit lust, this is the most existential item Meyer ever made. Stripper Babette Bardot (no relation) plays the "housekeeper" of a dilapidated inn in an out-of-the-way tourist spot where charter-boat customers "relax". Contains violence, swearing and nudity.

Babette Bardot • Jack Moran • Ken Swofford ■ *Dir* Russ Meyer • *Scr* Russ Meyer, Jack Moran, John E Moran

Common Threads: Stories from the Quilt ★★★★
Documentary 1989 · US · Colour · 75mins

An Oscar-winning documentary, narrated by Dustin Hoffman, highlighting the heartache and sorrow behind many of the embroidered panels that made up the Aids quilt laid out on the Mall in Washington DC at the height of the tragic epidemic. The personal stories of loss are often unbearably moving and have a sizeable

emotional impact as key social issues are raised and ill-informed perceptions are quashed. An important film in increasing awareness of a medical condition wrongly thought at the time to be just a gay problem.

Dustin Hoffman *Narrator* ■ *Dir* Robert Epstein, Jeffrey Friedman • *Scr* Jeffrey Friedman, Robert Epstein

Communion ★★ 15

Science-fiction thriller
1989 · US · Colour · 104mins

Was author Whitley Strieber abducted by aliens as outlined in his bestselling book *Communion*? Or was his close encounter and subsequent medical probing just a bizarre hallucination, or even a cynical marketing ploy as his detractors have claimed? You really won't be any the wiser after watching this ponderous, pompous and cost-cutting quasi-documentary, despite an enormous amount of conviction from Christopher Walken as the traumatised novelist. When it goes for cheap sci-fi scares, this earnest treatise is reasonable fun. But, compared to *The X Files*, it's old UFO news indeed. Contains violence and swearing. ▭

Christopher Walken *Whitley Strieber* • Lindsay Crouse *Anne Strieber* • Joel Carlson *Andrew Strieber* • Frances Sternhagen *Dr Janet Duffy* • Andreas Katsulas *Alex* • Terri Hanauer *Sara* • Basil Hoffman *Dr Friedman* • John Dennis Johnston *Fireman* • Dee Dee Rescher *Mrs Greenberg* ■ *Dir* Philippe Mora • *Scr* Whitley Strieber, from his book

Company Business ★★ 15

Comedy thriller 1991 · US · Colour · 94mins

For such a distinguished career, Gene Hackman still has an uncanny knack of making some poor film choices and, while this is a competent enough spy drama, it went straight to video in the UK. He plays a former CIA agent – shades of *Target*? – who is drawn back into the world of espionage for a spy swap involving Russian agent Mikhail Baryshnikov. Hackman more than covers for any deficiencies in the acting department from his co-star, however, it lacks the verve and imagination that writer/director Nicholas Meyer usually brings to his work. Contains some violence and swearing. ▭

Gene Hackman *Sam Boyd* • Mikhail Baryshnikov *Pyiotr Grushenko* • Kurtwood Smith *Elliot Jaffe* • Terry O'Quinn *Colonel Grissom* • Daniel Von Bargen *Mike Flinn* ■ *Dir/Scr* Nicholas Meyer

Company Limited ★★★★ U

Drama 1971 · Ind · BW · 113mins

Although he had a huge following abroad, the Bengali director Satyajit Ray was often accused by Indian critics of ignoring the subcontinent's myriad of social and political problems. This mild attack on the educated middle classes is the kind of film Frank Capra might have made, had he allowed his head to rule his heart. As the sales manager prepared to brook a little corruption to secure privilege, Barun Chanda is quite superb, whether showing off to his sceptical sister-in-law, or facing the realities of his situation during a company crisis.

Subtle, satirical and sharp as a tack. In Bengali with English subtitles.

Barun Chanda *Shyamal Chatterjee* • Sharmila Tagore *Tutul* • Parumita Chowdhary *Shyamal's sister-in-law* • Harindranath Chattopadhyaya *Sir Baren* ■ *Dir* Satyajit Ray • *Scr* Satyajit Ray, from the novel *Seemabaddha* by Sankar

Company of Killers ★★

Crime thriller 1970 · US · Colour · 86mins

Veterans Van Johnson and Ray Milland find themselves on opposite sides of the law in this thriller. Professional killer John Saxon loses the confidence of his boss and attracts the attention of police chief Johnson following a spell in hospital. Ordered to carry out a hit for ruthless businessman Milland, Saxon runs into a police trap. Using Denver locations instead of the familiar LA streets, this police drama aims to deliver gritty realism in its depiction of the way cops work, but eventually falls back on clichés.

Van Johnson *Sam Cahill* • Ray Milland *George DeSalles* • John Saxon *Dave Poohler* • Brian Kelly *Nick Andros* • Fritz Weaver *John Shankalien* • Clu Gulager *Frank Quinn* ■ *Dir* Jerry Thorpe • *Scr* E Jack Neuman

The Company of Strangers ★★★★ PG

Drama 1990 · Can · Colour · 100mins

The sisterhood of women is lovingly proclaimed by this Canadian movie in which non-actors play themselves in a fictitious situation: in this case, seven elderly women who are stranded in a remote farmhouse when their touring bus breaks down. Each woman's story illuminates the experience of being female and being human as the group waits to be picked up. Paced by director Cynthia Scott with patient care, it has a rare distinction for a recent movie – it actually likes people. ▭

Alice Diabo *Alice* • Constance Garneau *Constance* • Winifred Holden *Winnie* • Cissy Meddings *Cissy* • Mary Meigs *Mary* • Catherine Roche *Catherine* • Michelle Sweeney *Michelle* • Beth Webber *Beth* ■ *Dir* Cynthia Scott • *Scr* Gloria Demmers, Cynthia Scott, David Wilson, Sally Bochner

The Company of Wolves ★★★ 18

Supernatural fantasy
1984 · UK · Colour · 91mins

Dark variations on the *Little Red Riding Hood* theme are adeptly explored by *Crying Game* director Neil Jordan, co-writing with Angela Carter, in this arresting visual treat that at times resembles a pretentious Hammer horror. Dreams within dreams build up a psychological fright mosaic, as young Sarah Patterson goes through the broadest spectrum of emotions generally known as adolescence. Angela Lansbury is in super-eccentric form as an archetypal granny ready with "Once upon a time" werewolf fairy tales. Overall, a fine exercise in art design, lyrical mood and sinister allegory. Contains violence. ▭

Angela Lansbury *Grandmother* • David Warner *Father* • Sarah Patterson *Rosaleen* • Stephen Rea *Young groom* • Graham Crowden *Old priest* • Shane Johnstone *Amorous boy* • Brian Glover *Boy's father* • Susan Porrett *Boy's mother* ■ *Dir* Neil Jordan • *Scr* Angela

Carter, Neil Jordan, from the short stories by Angela Carter • *Cinematographer* Bryan Loftus • *Art Director* Anton Furst

The Company She Keeps ★★★

Drama 1950 · US · BW · 82mins

Notable for the screen debut of Jeff Bridges as a babe in arms, this is a suitably jaunty tale of an ex-con, played with convincing guile by Jane Greer, who dearly wishes to go straight but is not helped to that end when she falls for her parole officer's boyfriend. Greer is excellent, as is Dennis O'Keefe, and the two interact with just the right pinch of spice. A movie with a sizeable amount of charm inserted into its rather lame script.

Lizabeth Scott *Joan* • Jane Greer *Diane* • Dennis O'Keefe *Larry* • Fay Baker *Tilly* • John Hoyt *Judge Kendall* • James Bell *Mr Neeley* • Don Beddoe *Jamieson* • Bert Freed *Smitty* ■ *Dir* John Cromwell • *Scr* Ketti Frings

Les Compères ★★★★

Comedy drama 1983 · Fr · Colour · 92mins

Slickly scripted according to the rhythms of French stage farce, this was the second of three collaborations between director Francis Veber and actors Pierre Richard and Gérard Depardieu. As the journalist tricked into believing he is the father of teenage runaway Stephane Bierry, Depardieu essentially plays stooge to the manic-depressive Richard, who has been told the same fib by ex-girlfriend Anny Duperey. Less sentimental and more authentic than the Hollywood remake, *Fathers' Day*, this is also much sharper in its appreciation of the eternal juvenility of the average adult male. In French with English subtitles.

Pierre Richard *François Pignon* • Gérard Depardieu *Jean Lucas* • Anny Duperey *Christine Martin* • Michel Aumont *Paul Martin* • Stephane Bierry *Tristan Martin* • Roland Blanche *Jeannot* ■ *Dir/Scr* Francis Veber

The Competition ★★ 15

Romantic drama
1980 · US · Colour · 120mins

Does any actor visibly try harder than Richard Dreyfuss? In this romantic drama he plays a concert pianist, a sort of Richard Clayderman with pretensions, who duels over the ivories with a clearly besotted Amy Irving. Written and directed by Joel Oliansky, this is a clunky effort; Dreyfuss would have more success as a music teacher in 1995's *Mr Holland's Opus*, for which he was Oscar-nominated. Contains swearing. ▭

Richard Dreyfuss *Paul Dietrich* • Amy Irving *Heidi Schoonover* • Lee Remick *Greta Vandemann* • Sam Wanamaker *Erskine* • Joseph Cali *Jerry DiSalvo* • Ty Henderson *Michael Humphries* ■ *Dir* Joel Oliansky • *Scr* Joel Oliansky, from a story by William Sackheim, Joel Oliansky

The Compleat Beatles ★★★ PG

Music documentary
1982 · US · Colour and BW · 115mins

Beatles fans are not fond of this patchy American documentary about the Fab Four, but there is still much here to interest the casual viewer.

Director Patrick Montgomery, whose previous subject was Erich von Stroheim, does a thorough job with the early years and has tracked down Allan Williams ("the man who sold the Beatles") and Tony Sheridan (who used the Beatles as a backing band) among others. The film was made without the co-operation of the Beatles and their wives, and was superseded in 1995 by *The Beatles Anthology*. ▭

Malcolm McDowell *Narrator* ■ *Dir* Patrick Montgomery • *Scr* David Silver

Complex of Fear ★★★ 18

Thriller 1993 · US · Colour · 90mins

Chelsea Field lives in a creepy apartment block and feels threatened in this nifty little chiller. There are echoes of the Sharon Stone film *Sliver* in the plot, which focuses on a residential complex plagued by a series of vicious rapes. Field is a potential victim, Hart Bochner a resident rookie cop and the ever-reliable Joe Don Baker the investigating detective. The plotting is a mite predictable, but director Brian Grant still manages to summon up an air of claustrophobic suspense. Contains violence and swearing. ▭

Hart Bochner *Ray Dolan* • Chelsea Field *Michelle Dolan* • Joe Don Baker *Detective Frank Farrel* • Brett Cullen *Ed Wylie* • Farrah Forke *Vicki* • Ashley Gardner *Doreen Wylie* • Jordan Williams *Lee Harrison* ■ *Dir* Brian Grant • *Scr* Dyanne Asimow, Matt Dorff

Complicity ★ 18

Thriller 1999 · UK · Colour · 99mins

You'd be better off going back to Iain Banks's original novel than waste your time with this convoluted and unsatisfactory adaptation. Jonny Lee Miller stars as Banks's journalist anti-hero Cameron and, despite support from Brian Cox and Bill Paterson, he's endlessly bland. Director Gavin Millar seems all at sea with this Scotland-based tale, which involves sex, drugs and murderous atrocities. The excellent Keeley Hawes is wasted as Miller's married lover.

Jonny Lee Miller *Cameron* • Keeley Hawes *Yvonne* • Brian Cox *Detective Chief Inspector McDunn* • Paul Higgins *Andy Gould* • Jason Hetherington *William* • Rachael Stirling *Claire Gould* • Bill Paterson *Wallace Byatt* ■ *Dir* Gavin Millar • *Scr* Brian Elsley, from the novel by Iain Banks

Compromising Positions ★ 15

Comedy thriller 1985 · US · Colour · 94mins

Thelma and Louise star Susan Sarandon does her best with one of her few ropey roles in this uneven farce, about a woman who starts investigating the death of her dentist only to get caught up in a world of ex-mistresses and pornography. It's silly in the extreme, and Sarandon and her co-stars (Raul Julia, Joe Mantegna, Edward Herrmann) look distinctly uncomfortable. ▭

Susan Sarandon *Judith Singer* • Raul Julia *Lieutenant David Suarez* • Edward Herrmann *Bob Singer* • Judith Ivey *Nancy Miller* • Mary Beth Hurt *Peg Tuccio* • Joe Mantegna *Bruce Fleckstein* • Anne de Salvo *Phyllis Fleckstein* ■ *Dir* Frank Perry • *Scr* Susan Isaacs, from a novel by Susan Isaacs

Compulsion ★★★★
Crime drama   1959 · US · BW · 103mins

Bradford Dillman and Dean Stockwell, two wealthy, homosexual college students, murder a boy in cold blood to prove that the perfect crime is possible. Adapted from Meyer Levin's book and brilliantly directed by Richard Fleischer in semi-documentary style, this is a thinly veiled account of the notorious 1924 Leopold and Loeb case. Dillman's sneering psychopath is superb, as is Stockwell's more human, less confident Steiner, while Orson Welles's defending counsel, modelled on the famous Clarence Darrow who saved Leopold and Loeb from the chair, is a tour de force. ▭

Orson Welles _Jonathan Wilk_ • Dean Stockwell _Judd Steiner_ • Bradford Dillman _Artie Straus_ • EG Marshall _Horn_ • Diane Varsi _Ruth Evans_ • Martin Milner _Sid_ • Richard Anderson _Max_ ■ _Dir_ Richard Fleischer • _Scr_ Richard Murphy, from the novel by Meyer Levin

The Computer Wore Tennis Shoes ★★ Ⓤ
Comedy   1970 · US · Colour · 90mins

What might have been a nifty idea for a half-hour TV show is stretched to breaking point in this Disney comedy. The ever-willing Kurt Russell stars as the teenager who becomes a genius after a computer downloads its memory system into his brain. Suddenly, our hero is winning game shows and taking on Cesar Romero's stupendously inept crime ring. It's as engaging as it is predictable, although we could have done without the inevitable comic car chase. ▭

Cesar Romero _AJ Arno_ • Kurt Russell _Dexter_ • Joe Flynn _Dean Higgins_ • William Schallert _Professor Quigley_ • Alan Hewitt _Dean Collingsgood_ • Richard Bakalyan _Chillie Walsh_ ■ _Dir_ Robert Butler • _Scr_ Joseph L McEveety

The Computer Wore Tennis Shoes ★★ Ⓤ
Fantasy comedy   1995 · US · Colour · 86mins

Made 25 years after Kurt Russell starred in the original, this TV movie continues Disney's trend of updating its old hits for a new generation. Sure, the computer is a lot snazzier than the one Russell interfaced with, but Kirk Cameron has none of Russell's boyish charm. Once again, our hero makes a name for himself on the college quiz show circuit, but this time the focus falls on a jealous rival setting out to discredit the mega-byte brainbox. ▭

Kirk Cameron _Dexter Riley_ • Larry Miller _Dean Valentine_ • Jason Bernard _Professor Miles Quigley_ • Jeff Maynard _Gozin_ • Anne Marie Tremko _Sarah Matthews_ • Andrew Woodworth _Will_ • Mathew McCurley _Norwood_ • Dean Jones _Dean Carlson_ ■ _Dir_ Peyton Reed • _Scr_ Joseph L McEveety, Ryan Rowe

Comrade X ★★★ Ⓤ
Romantic comedy   1940 · US · BW · 89mins

Hedy Lamarr was seldom more glamorous than the Russian tram-driver who falls for hunky American journalist Clark Gable, the year after he played Rhett Butler in _Gone with the Wind_. You might expect more than just froth from master director King Vidor, but he was shrewd enough to know what wartime audiences wanted, and just let his two great stars get on with it. There was only ever one _Ninotchka_, though, and frankly, my dear, this lacks both the wit and style of its predecessor, despite sharing a writer in Walter Reisch and having a terrific hair-pulling fight between Lamarr and Russian secretary Natasha Lytess.

Clark Gable _McKinley B Thompson_ • Hedy Lamarr _Theodora_ • Oscar Homolka _Vasiliev_ • Felix Bressart _Vanya_ • Eve Arden _Jane Wilson_ • Sig Rumann [Sig Ruman] _Emil Von Hofer_ • Natasha Lytess _Olga_ • Vladimir Sokoloff _Michael Bastakoff_ ■ _Dir_ King Vidor • _Scr_ Ben Hecht, Charles Lederer, from a story by Walter Reisch

Comrades: a Lanternist's Account of the Tolpuddle Martyrs and What Became of Them ★★★★ ℙ𝔾
Historical drama   1986 · UK · Colour · 174mins

Despite the acclaim for his autobiographical trilogy, Bill Douglas struggled to finance this epic tribute to those pioneer trades unionists. Although set in Dorset in the 1830s, the story of the farm labourers who were deported to Australia for protesting against their harsh conditions and meagre wages had a contemporary resonance as, 150 years later, the Thatcher government sought to break union power. However, while Douglas is keen to highlight the continued existence of exploitation and social hypocrisy, the superb performances keep it rooted in its period. ▭

Robin Soans _George Loveless_ • William Gaminara _James Loveless_ • Stephen Bateman _Old Tom Stanfield_ • Philip Davis _Young Stanfield_ • Keith Allen _James Hammett_ • Alex Norton _Lanternist_ • James Fox _Norfolk_ • Michael Hordern _Mr Pitt_ • Vanessa Redgrave _Mrs Carlyle_ ■ _Dir/Scr_ Bill Douglas

The Comrades of Summer ★★★ ⑮
Sports comedy   1992 · US · Colour · 107mins

If John Candy can coach the Jamaican Olympic bobsleigh team in _Cool Runnings_, then what's to stop Joe Mantegna from teaching baseball to the Russians? Proving again what a versatile performer he is, Mantegna plays a Scrooge-like coach whose monetary motives for decamping to Moscow evaporate when he rediscovers a boyish enthusiasm for the game he had to quit through injury. Director Tommy Lee Wallace neatly combines slapstick with mild social comedy and, thankfully, prevents a romantic subplot involving Mantegna and Natalya Negoda from taking over. Contains swearing and sex scenes. ▭

Joe Mantegna _Sparky Smith_ • Natalya Negoda _Tanya_ • Michael Lerner _George_ • Eric Allan Kramer _Boris_ • Mark Rolston _Voronov_ • John Fleck _Milov_ • Ian Tracey _Andy_ ■ _Dir_ Tommy Lee Wallace • _Scr_ Robert Rodat

Con Air ★★★★ ⑱
Action thriller   1997 · US · Colour · 110mins

The middle movie of Nicolas Cage's 1996/7 triple-run of slick, successful action movies (between _The Rock_ and _Face/Off_) is a topnotch thrillathon for those who demand stylish destruction, quirky characterisations and a sly sense of fun. Cage is an ex-marine jailed for self-defence, whose release is interrupted by the aeroplane hijack of his ride home by a bunch of America's most dangerous felons. Cage's impossibly cool macho posturing is irresistible, as is John Malkovich's sneering, tongue-in-cheek turn as super-criminal Cyrus "the Virus" Grissom, while John Cusack, Ving Rhames and Steve Buscemi lend snappy support. A dynamic debut for British director Simon West, aided by Scott Rosenberg's entertaining script, which simply refuses to take itself seriously. ▭ **DVD**

Nicolas Cage _Cameron Poe_ • John Cusack _Vince Larkin_ • John Malkovich _Cyrus "the Virus"_ _Grissom_ • Steve Buscemi _Garland Greene_ • Nick Chinlund _Billy Bedlam_ • Rachel Ticotin _Sally Bishop_ • Colm Meaney _Duncan Malloy_ • Ving Rhames _Diamond Dog_ ■ _Dir_ Simon West • _Scr_ Scott Rosenberg

The Con Artists ★ ℙ𝔾
Comedy   1976 · It · Colour · 89mins

Having tackled both sword-and-sandal adventures and spaghetti westerns, versatile director Sergio Corbucci turned his attention to crime with this clumsily plotted caper. Alas, he lacked the lightness of touch to bring much life to this bovine variation on _The Sting_. Always prone to overplaying comedy, Anthony Quinn milks every gag as the escaped convict who teams up with the ambitious Adriano Celentano in a bid to dupe a scheming murderess out of her ill-gotten gains. Demonstrating a nice line in sultry villainy, Capucine is the only person to emerge with any credit. Italian dialogue dubbed into English. ▭

Anthony Quinn _Philippe Bang_ • Adriano Celentano _Felix_ • Capucine _Belle Duke_ • Corinne Cléry _Charlotte_ ■ _Dir_ Sergio Corbucci • _Scr_ Arnold Maury, Max D'Rita

Conagher ★★ ℙ𝔾
Western   1991 · US · Colour · 112mins

The prairie wouldn't have been so underpopulated if more people looked like the sexy husband-and-wife team of Sam Elliott and Katharine Ross, who star in this affecting romantic TV western based on the book by Louis L'Amour. Frontier widow Ross and her two children have to brave Indians, loneliness and hard times. But things look up when handsome cowboy Conagher (Elliott) rambles into her stagecoach station. Tired of ropin' and ridin', Elliott decides he finally might have found a reason to settle down. Reynoldo Villalobos, best known as a director of photography, brings his strong visual sense to the film's overall look and feel. ▭

Sam Elliott _Conn Conagher_ • Katharine Ross _Evie Teale_ • Barry Corbin _Charlie McCloud_ • Billy Green Bush _Jacob Teal_ • Ken Curtis _Seaborn Tay_ • Paul Koslo _Kiowa Staples_ • Gavan O'Herlihy _Kris Mahler_ • James Parks _Curly_ ■ _Dir_ Reynaldo Villalobos • _Scr_ Sam Elliott, Katharine Ross, Jeffrey M Meyer, from the novel by Louis L'Amour

Conan the Barbarian ★★★ ⑮
Fantasy action adventure   1982 · US · Colour · 125mins

Arnold Schwarzenegger may have ventured out in clothes since this movie, but here's how fans first remember him: bare and belted, a Nordic superman justified in his use of force to avenge his parents' deaths. Director John Milius quotes Nietzsche and ladles on the fantasy atmosphere with a Wagnerian flourish that's too heavyweight and humourless for its own good. The racist undertones, too, are most unwelcome, but the look of Conan's world is an astonishment to behold – rather like big Arnie himself. Contains violence, swearing and nudity. ▭

Arnold Schwarzenegger _Conan_ • James Earl Jones _Thulsa Doom_ • Max von Sydow _King Osric_ • Sandahl Bergman _Valeria_ • Ben Davidson _Rexor_ • Cassandra Gaviola _Witch_ • Gerry Lopez _Subotai_ • Mako _Wizard_ ■ _Dir_ John Milius • _Scr_ John Milius, Oliver Stone, from characters created by Robert E Howard

Conan the Destroyer ★★ ⑮
Fantasy action adventure   1984 · US · Colour · 96mins

Arnold Schwarzenegger returns to his breakthrough role as the mythical hero but the kitsch magic of the John Milius original is missing this time around. However, the requisite number of ugly villains, beautiful temptresses and doe-eyed heroines are present and correct, Schwarzenegger doesn't have to do too much acting and director Richard Fleischer keeps the often violent action flowing smoothly. Look out for Grace Jones as a lethal warrior. Contains violence. ▭

Arnold Schwarzenegger _Conan_ • Grace Jones _Zula_ • Wilt Chamberlain _Bombaara_ • Mako _Akjiro, the "Wizard"_ • Tracey Walter _Malak_ • Sarah Douglas _Queen Taramis_ • Olivia D'Abo _Princess Jehnna_ ■ _Dir_ Richard Fleischer • _Scr_ Stanley Mann, from a story by Roy Thomas, Gerry Conway, from characters created by Robert E Howard

The Concierge ★★ ℙ𝔾
Comedy   1993 · US · Colour · 91mins

Despite modest successes like _Doc Hollywood_ and _The Hard Way_, Michael J Fox's star has certainly lost some of its sparkle since the heady days of the _Back to the Future_ trilogy, and this uneven comedy did little to revitalise his career. He plays the smooth concierge who is desperate to open his own hotel, but to do that he needs the help of slimy millionaire Anthony Higgins, and Higgins's mistress (Gabrielle Anwar) happens to be the girl Fox loves. Director Barry Sonnenfeld seems strangely ill-at-ease with the material, and he is not helped by a script that swings from wild farce to slushy romance. ▭

Michael J Fox _Doug Ireland_ • Gabrielle Anwar _Andy Hart_ • Anthony Higgins _Christian Hanover_ • Michael Tucker _Mr Wegman_ • Bob Balaban _Mr Drinkwater_ • Isaac Mizrahi _Julian Russell_ • Patrick Breen _Gary Taubin_ • Udo Kier _Mr Himmelman_ ■ _Dir_ Barry Sonnenfeld • _Scr_ Mark Rosenthal, Lawrence Konner

The Concrete Jungle ★★ 18

Drama 1982 · US · Colour · 99mins

Credulous Tracy Bregman realises she's trusted her love-rat boyfriend (Peter Brown) too much after he has her busted for drug smuggling. From then on it's the kind of women's prison melodrama that was very popular around the time of *Chained Heat* (1983). It's directed by Tom DeSimone, whose idea of original film-making is to put warden Jill St John in spectacles to prove just how neurotic she is. Barbara Luna, however, is a stand-out as a hard-bitten veteran of the cell regime.

Jill St John *Warden Fletcher* • Tracy Bregman *Elizabeth Demming* • Barbara Luna *Cat* • June Barrett *Icy* • Peter Brown *Danny* • Aimee Eccles *Spider* • Sondra Currie *Katherine* ■ *Dir* Tom DeSimone • *Scr* Alan J Adler

Condemned ★★ U

Drama 1929 · US · BW · 82mins

Oscar history was made within the Best Actor category of 1930. Ronald Colman, George Arliss and Maurice Chevalier all received two separate nominations, but only Arliss emerged triumphant. Colman is great fun in *Bulldog Drummond*, but it's harder to fathom why he was nominated for this creaky early talkie about a prisoner who falls in love with the warden's wife (Ann Harding). Directed by Wesley Ruggles, it's a clumsy mix of action adventure, drippy romance and an exposé of the iniquities of the infamous Devil's Island. 🖵

Ronald Colman *Michel Oban* • Ann Harding *Mme Vidal* • Dudley Digges *Warden Jean Vidal* • Louis Wolheim *Jacques Duval* • William Elmer *Pierre* • William Vaughn *Vidal's orderly* ■ *Dir* Wesley Ruggles • *Scr* Sidney Howard

The Condemned of Altona ★★

Drama 1962 · Fr/It · BW · 113mins

Director Vittorio De Sica and screenwriter Cesare Zavattini were responsible for some of the masterworks of Italian neorealism. But they singularly failed with this forbidding melodrama about the effects of war guilt on one Hamburg family. The action crackles with an anti-German feeling that ruinously undermines the case made against the Gerlachs in particular and the nation in general. As the actress realising the enormity of the crimes of her new relations, Sophia Loren gives a brave performance. But it's dying tycoon Fredric March and his deranged son Maximilian Schell, who provide the power. An Italian language film.

Sophia Loren *Johanna* • Maximilian Schell *Franz* • Fredric March *Gerlach* • Robert Wagner *Werner* • Françoise Prévost *Leni* ■ *Dir* Vittorio De Sica • *Scr* Abby Mann, Cesare Zavattini, from the play *Les Sequestres* by Jean-Paul Sartre

Condemned Women ★★★

Prison drama 1938 · US · BW · 76mins

A thirties version of *Prisoner: Cell Block H*, minus the cardboard sets but heavy on the melodrama. There's no messing with these ladies of the slammer as they fight, eat, fight, sleep and fight again all the way to lights out, with surly Sally Eilers striking up a less than wholesome relationship with prison psychiatrist Louis Hayward. Nothing overly subtle here, but there are some cracking performances.

Sally Eilers *Linda Wilson* • Louis Hayward *Phillip Duncan* • Anne Shirley *Millie Anson* • Esther Dale *Matron Glover* • Lee Patrick *Big Annie* ■ *Dir* Lew Landers • *Scr* Lionel Houser

El Condor ★★

Western 1970 · US · Colour · 101mins

Director John Guillermin came unstuck with this western about a pair of mercenaries raiding a Mexican fort for its gold. The Spanish-shot movie wears on its sleeve all the gruesome Cohen trademarks that would be used to chilling effect in 1974's *It's Alive*, but contains none of the tongue-in-cheek humour that's often the salvation of the European western. As the protagonists, Lee Van Cleef and Jim Brown look good, but the constant brutality and slow pace make this very hard to enjoy. Contains violence, swearing and nudity.

Lee Van Cleef *Jaroo* • Jim Brown *Luke* • Patrick O'Neal *Chavez* • Mariana Hill [Marianna Hill] *Claudine* • Iron Eyes Cody *Santana* • Imogen Hassall *Dolores* • Elisha Cook Jr *Old convict* • Gustavo Rojo *Colonel Aguinaldo* ■ *Dir* John Guillermin • *Scr* Larry Cohen, Steven Carabatsos

Condorman ★ U

Comedy 1981 · US · Colour · 86mins

Disney, for all its ability to create animated magic, regularly churned out live-action pictures that would embarrass a camcorder enthusiast. This adaptation of Robert Sheckley's book, *The Game of X*, is worse than most. Michael Crawford managed to find time for this dismal comic-book comedy between his triumphs in *Some Mothers Do 'Ave 'Em* and *The Phantom of the Opera*. Surely both he and Oliver Reed (as the KGB agent trying to rescue cartoonist Crawford rescuing spy Barbara Carrera) could have found something better to do? 🖵

Michael Crawford *Woody* • Oliver Reed *Krokov* • Barbara Carrera *Natalia* • James Hampton *Harry* • Jean-Pierre Kalfon *Morovich* • Dana Elcar *Russ* • Vernon Dobtcheff *Russian agent* ■ *Dir* Charles Jarrott • *Scr* Marc Stirdivant, Glen Caron, Mickey Rose, from the novel *The Game of X* by Robert Sheckley

Conduct Unbecoming ★★ PG

Drama 1975 · UK · Colour · 102mins

Trevor Howard and Richard Attenborough almost redeem this dull, studio-bound drama set at the height of the British Raj. As the widow of the regimental hero, Susannah York accuses a newly arrived lieutenant of assaulting her, leading to his court martial, a lot of twitching moustaches and an exposure of Victorian moral hypocrisy. The plot seems a blatant rip-off of EM Forster's *A Passage to India*, and what on Earth is Stacy Keach doing as a British officer? 🖵

Michael York *Second Lieutenant Arthur Drake* • Richard Attenborough *Major Lionel Roach* • Trevor Howard *Colonel Benjamin Strang* • Stacy Keach *Captain Rupert Harper* • Christopher Plummer *Major Alastair* Wimbourne • Susannah York *Mrs Marjorie Scarlett* ■ *Dir* Michael Anderson • *Scr* Robert Enders, from the play by Barry England

The Conductor ★★★★

Musical drama 1980 · Pol · Colour · 110mins

After decades spent in the United States, a famous classical maestro (John Gielgud) returns to his birthplace in Poland as a guest conductor with the provincial town's struggling orchestra. Although in frail health and nearing the end of his life, he is able to inject new life into the musicians. Made by the great Andrzej Wajda, this poignant film is redolent with atmosphere and tension, but disappointingly hints at deeper significance without conveying much. Gielgud, however, is absolutely superb, despite being dubbed into Polish. In Polish with English subtitles.

John Gielgud *John Lasocki* • Krystyna Janda *Marta* • Andrzej Seweryn *Adam Pietryk* ■ *Dir* Andrzej Wajda • *Scr* Andrzej Kijowski

Cone of Silence ★★★

Drama 1960 · UK · BW · 76mins

An expertly made, taut British movie from *Scott of the Antarctic* director and former Hitchcock editor Charles Frend. It contains some fine heart-stopping moments, while Peter Cushing, George Sanders and character actor Bernard Lee give superb performances. Some of the technical details and hardware have inevitably dated in this aeronautical drama, but the striking black-and-white compositions and the beautifully paced editing by Max Benedict remain very impressive.

Michael Craig *Captain Hugh Dallas* • Peter Cushing *Captain Clive Judd* • Bernard Lee *Captain George Gort* • Elizabeth Seal *Charlotte Gort* • George Sanders *Sir Arnold Hobbes* • Andre Morrell *Captain Edward Manningham* • Gordon Jackson *Captain Bateson* ■ *Dir* Charles Frend • *Scr* Robert Westerby, from the novel by David Beaty • *Cinematographer* Arthur Grant

Coneheads ★★ PG

Comedy 1993 · US · Colour · 86mins

The American satirical series *Saturday Night Live* has spawned some blockbuster movies – *The Blues Brothers* and *Wayne's World*, for instance – but this Dan Aykroyd creation sank without trace. Aykroyd is reunited with old TV colleagues Jane Curtin and Laraine Newman for this dismal comedy about a family of aliens trying to get to grips with life on earth, but the characters are long past their sell-by date. Contains some swearing and sex scenes. 🖵

Dan Aykroyd *Beldar* • Jane Curtin *Prymaat* • Michael McKean *Seedling* • Michelle Burke *Connie* • David Spade *Turnbull* • Chris Farley *Ronnie* • Jason Alexander *Larry Farber* • Jon Lovitz *Dr Rudolf* • Phil Hartman *Marlax* • Laraine Newman *Laarta* • Ellen DeGeneres *Coach* ■ *Dir* Steve Barron • *Scr* Tom Davis, Dan Aykroyd, Bonnie Turner, Terry Turner

Coney Island ★★★ U

Musical comedy 1943 · US · Colour · 96mins

Here's pert Betty Grable at the peak of her wartime career, singing period songs like *Put Your Arms around Me, Honey* and *Cuddle Up a Little Closer* in gloriously garish, 20th Century-Fox Technicolor. It's a piece of tosh about saloon-keeper George Montgomery wanting to turn her into a big star, despite rival hotelier Cesar Romero, who wants her for himself. Familiar stuff, remade by Fox seven years later as *Wabash Avenue*, also with Grable. Nevertheless, this is vastly entertaining in its unsophisticated, mindless way, and it's absolutely typical Betty. 🖵

Betty Grable *Kate Farley* • George Montgomery *Eddie Johnson* • Cesar Romero *Joe Rocco* • Charles Winninger *Finnigan* • Phil Silvers *Frankie* ■ *Dir* Walter Lang • *Scr* George Seaton

Confession ★★★★

Melodrama 1937 · US · BW · 88mins

A splendid melodrama, told in flashback, starring the elegant Kay Francis as a singer who kills her seducer, pianist Basil Rathbone. (He'd taken a shine to her daughter, the swine!) This is a stunner, with design and camerawork very reminiscent of a classy German feature (it's based on a 1935 Pola Negri vehicle), while émigré director Joe May (born Joseph Mandel) pulls out all the stops and weaves a wonderfully flamboyant Hollywood tapestry. Strange to think he spent his final years running a restaurant in Los Angeles.

Kay Francis *Vera* • Ian Hunter *Leonide Kilrow* • Basil Rathbone *Michael Michailow* • Jane Bryan *Lisa* • Donald Crisp *Presiding judge* • Mary Maguire *Hildegard* • Dorothy Peterson *Mrs Koslov* ■ *Dir* Joe May • *Scr* Julius J Epstein, Margaret LaVino, Stanley Logan, from the film *Mazurka* by Hans Hameau • *Cinematographer* Sid Hickox • *Art Director* Anton Grot

Confession ★★ PG

Crime thriller 1955 · UK · BW · 86mins

The confidentiality of the confessional is a well-worn movie theme. It was best explored by Alfred Hitchcock in *I Confess* in 1953 and has reappeared as recently as 1994 in Antonia Bird's *Priest*. Here Ken Hughes finds nothing new to say about the subject: a priest hears a voice confess to murder and then finds his world collapsing around him as his vow of silence prevents him from passing on the information that will nail the killer. The film does, however, give viewers a rare chance to see Charlie Chaplin's son, Sydney, in a leading role. 🖵

Sydney Chaplin *Mike Nelson* • Audrey Dalton *Louise* • John Bentley *Inspector Kessler* • Peter Hammond *Alan* • John Welsh *Father Neil* • Jefferson Clifford *Pop* • Patrick Allen *Corey* • Pat McGrath *Williams* ■ *Dir* Ken Hughes • *Scr* Ken Hughes, from a play by Don Martin

The Confession ★★★

Political drama 1970 · Fr/It · Colour · 139mins

This *film à clef* is a thinly disguised account of the 1951 show trial in which Czech foreign minister Artur London and 13 other party officials were charged by the Communist regime with being American-backed, pro-Zionist spies. Clearly intent on demonstrating (after his right-wing exposé, *Z*) that extremism knows no boundaries, Costa-Gavras presents a grinding insight into Stalinist psychological brutality. Cast opposite

wife Simone Signoret, Yves Montand poignantly conveys the inner duel between ideology and terror that caused London to confess his ''crimes''. However, this works better as a portrait of a man under pressure than as a political argument. In French with English subtitles.

Yves Montand *''Gerard''/Artur London* • Simone Signoret *Lise* • Gabriele Ferzetti *Kohoutek* • Michel Vitold *Smola* • Jean Bouise *Boss* • Laszlo Szabo *Secret policeman* ■ *Dir* Costa-Gavras • *Scr* Jorge Semprun, from the non-fiction book *L'Aveu* by Lise London, Artur London

The Confession ★★
Courtroom drama
1999 · US · Colour · 104mins

A topnotch cast can't stop this well-meaning courtroom drama from toppling into uncomfortable melodrama. Alec Baldwin is the slick lawyer who finds his conscience pricked when he is hired to defend Ben Kingsley, who's accused of murdering the people he thinks are responsible for the accidental death of his son. The capable cast make the most of the emotionally-charged material, but it's too strident for its own good.

Alec Baldwin *Roy Bleakie* • Ben Kingsley *Harry Fertig* • Amy Irving *Sarah Fertig* • Ryan Marsini *Stevie Fertig* • Boyd Gaines *Liam Clarke* ■ *Dir* David Jones • *Scr* David Black, from the novel *Fertig* by Sol Yurick

The Confessional ★★★★
Thriller
1995 · Can/UK/Fr · Colour and BW · 104mins

The filming in the fifties of Hitchcock's *I Confess*, the Quebec-based thriller about the sanctity of a priest's confessional, provides the background to this intricate story of an adopted brother seeking his real father. It marks the film directorial debut of Robert Lepage, a noted Canadian theatre director whose style is as compulsive as it is sumptuous. The story seesaws between 1989, and the hunt for paternal identity, and 1952, when Hitchcock (played by Ron Burrage) arrives in Quebec and blames his assistant (Kristin Scott Thomas) for letting the Catholic Church make too many cuts in his film. Lepage pays visual homages to the Master in the modern story of a rent boy's anguish, but it becomes too tricksy. Worth seeing, though, for its display of dazzling, if complicated, talent at work. In English and French with subtitles.

Lothaire Bluteau *Pierre Lamontagne* • Patrick Goyette *Marc Lamontagne* • Jean-Louis Millette *Raymond Massicotte* • Kristin Scott Thomas *Hitchcock's secretary* • Ron Burrage *Alfred Hitchcock* • Richard Fréchette *Andrè* • François Papineau *Lamontagne* • Anne-Marie Cadieux *Manon* ■ *Dir/Scr* Robert Lepage

Confessions from a Holiday Camp ★ 18
Sex comedy
1977 · UK · Colour · 84mins

Coming between the *Carry Ons* and *The Adventures of...* series, the *Confessions* films relied on a blend of saucy humour and ''What the Butler Saw''-style smut. This was the fourth and last of these cheap but cheerful comedies, with Robin Askwith returning as an over-sexed entertainments

officer at a camp run by an ex-prison officer. Irish director Norman Cohen, who handled three of the quartet (Val Guest made the original *Confessions of a Window Cleaner*), also made the movie versions of *Till Death Us Do Part* and *Dad's Army*. Contains swearing and nudity.

Robin Askwith *Timothy Lea* • Anthony Booth *Sidney Noggett* • Doris Hare *Mum* • Bill Maynard *Dad* • Sheila White *Rosie* • Colin Crompton *Roughage* • Liz Frazer *Mrs Whitemonk* • Linda Hayden *Brigitte* ■ *Dir* Norman Cohen • *Scr* Christopher Wood, from a novel by Timothy Lea [Christopher Wood]

Confessions of a Driving Instructor ★ 18
Sex comedy
1976 · UK · Colour · 85mins

The third in the series of smutty comedies based on the novels of Timothy Lea is something of an embarrassment to all concerned. The story about the rivalry between two driving schools never gets out of first gear and the mix of *doubles entendres* and soft-core gropings can only be described as abysmal. Robin Askwith mugs like a trouper, but it's sad that accomplished comedy actresses Irene Handl and Liz Fraser signed up for rubbish like this. Contains swearing and nudity.

Robin Askwith *Timothy Lea* • Anthony Booth *Sidney Noggett* • Windsor Davies *Mr Truscott* • Sheila White *Rosie* • Doris Hare *Mum* • Bill Maynard *Dad* • Liz Fraser *Mrs Chalmers* • Irene Handl *Miss Slenderparts* • George Layton *Tony Bender* ■ *Dir* Norman Cohen • *Scr* Christopher Wood, from a novel by Timothy Lea [Christopher Wood]

Confessions of a Hit Man ★★ 15
Crime drama
1994 · US · Colour · 92mins

Ambitious but ultimately dreary take on the lot of a hired assassin. James Remar is the killer who, on what could be his last assignment, tries to make peace with his victims' loved ones and others who have crossed his path over the years. Remar does well in a weightier role than he usually gets, but it is far too talky and the existential air fails to convince. Contains swearing and violence.

James Remar *Bruno Sarrano* • Michael Wright *Charley* • Emily Longstreth *Corine* ■ *Dir* Larry Leahy • *Scr* Tony Cinciripini, Larry Leahy

Confessions of a Lady Cop ★★ PG
Thriller
1988 · US · Colour · 93mins

In this follow-up to the *Police Story* series of eighties crime dramas, Karen Black plays vice squad officer Evelyn Carter, the ''lady cop'' of the title, who has to cope with the suicide of a close friend and former colleague while dealing with day-to-day life at the precinct (murders, shoot-outs and the like). Frank Sinatra Jr (son of Old Blue Eyes) provides some interest as a pimp, but all in all it's not a patch on even the worst episodes of *Cagney and Lacey* or *NYPD Blue*.

Karen Black *Evelyn Carter* • Don Murray *Sergeant Jack Leland* • James Whitmore Jr *Sergeant Jeff Allen* • David Cadiente *Paul*

Urbano • Donald May *George Merrick* • A Martinez *Julio Mendez* • Frank Sinatra Jr *Pimp* ■ *Dir* Lee H Katzin • *Scr* Mark Rodgers

Confessions of a Married Man ★★★ PG
Drama
1983 · US · Colour · 89mins

The dark heart of America's picket-fence provinces has given many films a shot of ready drama. Here, the appearance of mid-American, middle-aged perfection is wiped away to reveal a complex family unit comprising a frustrated husband, a wife who exists to serve him, a son dwarfed by his successful father and a daughter who has just become engaged. The uneasy undercurrents in this troubled household provide much of the plot's cement, although the ideas are sometimes awkwardly expressed where they should emerge smoothly through character development.

Robert Conrad *Walter Price* • Jennifer Warren *Pat Price* • Mary Crosby *Ellen Price* • Ann Dusenberry *Jennifer* • Lance Guest *Arthur Price* • John Shepherd *Tom* • Bettye Ackerman *Interviewer* ■ *Dir/Scr* Steven Gethers

Confessions of a Nazi Spy ★★★ U
Spy drama
1939 · US · BW · 110mins

Warner Bros declared war on Germany long before America itself and this documentary-style spy drama, showing G-men searching out Nazis rallying undercover in America, is one of its most blatant pieces of propaganda. Paul Lukas and Edward G Robinson blend into the woodwork well enough, but there's a whole casting directory of scar-faced villains to make you wonder how they ever got through immigration. What was topical for the time has inevitably dated, but director Anatole Litvak can still chill us with his depiction of the crawling swastika.

Edward G Robinson *Ed Renard* • Francis Lederer *Schneider* • George Sanders *Schlager* • Paul Lukas *Dr Kassel* • Henry O'Neill *Da Kellogg* • Lya Lys *Erika Wolff* • Grace Stafford *Mrs Schneider* ■ *Dir* Anatole Litvak • *Scr* Milton Krims, John Wexley, from a story by Milton Krims, John Wexley, from the article *Storm over America* by Leon G Turrou

Confessions of a Pop Performer ★ 18
Sex comedy
1975 · UK · Colour · 86mins

Robin Askwith abandons his window-cleaning round to help organise a tour for a band of no-hopers and finds himself knee-deep in groupies. (The finale at the Palladium has to be seen to be believed.) Askwith struggles manfully with a dismal script and comes off much better than the Prime Minister's father-in-law, Anthony Booth. Among the other familiar faces are Doris Hare and Benny Hill's longtime accomplice, Bob Todd. Contains swearing, sex scenes and nudity.

Robin Askwith *Timothy Lea* • Anthony Booth *Sidney Noggett* • Bill Maynard *Mr Lea* • Doris Hare *Mrs Lea* • Sheila White *Rosie* • Bob Todd *Mr Barnwell* • Jill Gascoine *Mrs Barnwell* • Peter Cleall *Nutter Normington* ■ *Dir* Norman Cohen • *Scr* Christopher Wood, from a novel by Timothy Lea [Christopher Wood]

Confessions of a Serial Killer ★★★★
Crime drama
1987 · US · Colour · 80mins

Savage yet brilliant, this minor masterpiece will inevitably be compared to the similar *Henry: Portrait of a Serial Killer*, made around the same time. In police custody, serial killer Daniel Ray Hawkins (extremely well-played by Robert A Burns) begins a series of confessions about his life and crimes. The flaw in this narrative device (we know Hawkins will eventually be caught) is outweighed by the movie's virtues, which include gritty location shooting that lends a kind of *cinéma vérité* feel to the proceedings.

Robert A Burns *Daniel Ray Hawkins* • Dennis Hill *Moon Lawton* • Berkley Garrett *Sheriff Will Gaines* • Sidney Brammer *Molly* • Dee Dee Norton *Monica* ■ *Dir/Scr* Mark Blair

Confessions of a Trick Baby ★★ 18
Black comedy thriller
1999 · US · Colour · 97mins

The second film (after *Freeway*) in Matthew Bright's proposed trilogy of radically reworked fairytales is so over-the-top, it's halfway down the other side. In this outrageous spin on *Hansel and Gretel*, Natasha Lyonne and Maria Celedonio play damaged teens who break out of detention and strike out on a murderous road trip to Mexico for a climactic confrontation with transvestite nun Vincent Gallo. Skilfully directed in the style of the sexploitation films it so obviously spoofs, this is a picture many people will loathe, though it could earn cult status with those who appreciate its tongue-in-cheek extravagance.

Natasha Lyonne *''White Girl''* • Maria Celedonio *Cyclona* • Vincent Gallo *Sister Gomez* ■ *Dir/Scr* Matthew Bright

Confessions of a Window Cleaner ★ 18
Sex comedy
1974 · UK · Colour · 90mins

The first of the four saucy comedies adapted from the bestselling novels of Timothy Lea. In addition to introducing us to Robin Askwith and his shiftless brother-in-law (played by Tony Blair's father-in-law, Anthony Booth), the film also wastes some of Britain's finest comic talent, with Richard Wattis, John Le Mesurier, Joan Hickson and Dandy Nichols among those vainly trying to wring a laugh out of the smutty situations and limp jokes. Contains swearing, sex scenes and nudity.

Robin Askwith *Timothy Lea* • Anthony Booth *Sidney Noggett* • Sheila White *Rosie Noggett* • Dandy Nichols *Mrs Lea* • Bill Maynard *Mr Lea* • Linda Hayden *Elizabeth Radlett* • John Le Mesurier *Inspector Radlett* • Joan Hickson *Mrs Radlett* ■ *Dir* Val Guest • *Scr* Christopher Wood, Val Guest, from a novel by Timothy Lea [Christopher Wood]

The Confessions of Pastor Burg ★★★
Drama
1992 · Swi · Colour · 100mins

The Lutheran strain that runs through much Germanic and Scandinavian melodrama resurfaces in this Swiss tale of revenge and recrimination. Evoking the films of Ingmar Bergman,

director Jean-Jacques Lagrange gives the Swede's chamber-drama intensity an Alpine airing as he explores the damage that holier-than-thou attitudes can wreak. Gradually shedding his dour persona, Frédéric Van Den Driessche dominates proceedings as the newly arrived pastor who discovers the joys and pangs of love after he plots to expose the hypocrisy of wealthy farmer Jean-Marc Bory by luring his beloved daughter (Vanessa Larre) into sin. In French with English subtitles.

Frédéric Van Den Driessche *Pasteur Jean Burg* • Jean-Marc Bory *Samuel Mottier* • Vanessa Larre *Geneviève* • Jean-Claude Drouot *Paul Henchoz* • Pierre Forget *Pasteur Bouvier* ■ *Dir* Jean-Jacques Lagrange • *Scr* Jean-Louis Roncoroni, Jean-Jacques Lagrange, from the novel by Jacques Chessex

Confessions: Two Faces of Evil ★★ 15

Mystery mystery based on a true story 1994 · US · Colour · 88mins

This TV murder mystery takes such a giddy delight in capturing the facts that it leaves out the drama. The ambiguity of the situation, where a successful student and a small-time criminal both confess to the murder of a policeman when only one of them can be guilty, should have provided the cornerstone of the suspense. Instead, this episodic plodder gets bogged down in boring explanation that's relieved only by the giant presence and vocal thunder of James Earl Jones as the lawyer who defends the student. [video]

Jason Bateman *William Mothershed* • James Wilder *Robert Berndt* • James Earl Jones *Charles Lloyd* • Arye Gross *Jay Jaffe* • William Converse-Roberts *DA John Watson* • Melinda Dillon *Carol Mothershed* ■ *Dir* Gilbert Cates • *Scr* Gy Waldron

Confidence ★★★★ U

Drama 1979 · Hun · Colour · 117mins

Although the underlying theme of this intense drama is the mutual confidence civilisation needs to survive, István Szabó is, for once, less concerned with the momentous events of history than the simple interaction of individuals. Forced to pose as a married couple during the Nazi occupation of Budapest, Ildiko Bansagi and Peter Andorai progress from fear and superstition to implicit trust and passion as they realise their interdependence. While the film frequently ventures outside, it's the claustrophobic exchanges that give it a power and truth that owes as much to Szabó and cinematographer Lajos Koltai as to the superlative leads. in Hungarian with English subtitles.

Ildiko Bansagi *Kata* • Peter Andorai *Janos* • O Gombik *Old woman* • Karoly Csaki *Old man* ■ *Dir* István Szabó • *Scr* István Szabó, from a story by Erika Szanto, István Szábo

Confidential ★★★

Crime drama 1935 · US · BW · 67mins

A terse, zappy little poverty row gangster movie from prolific director Edward L Cahn, here still making halfway decent flicks. This features G-man Donald Cook infiltrating the Mob, getting the hots for sexy Evalyn Knapp and tangling with nasty sadist J Carrol Naish. It moves along at a fine rate of knots like a good programmer should, and doesn't outstay its welcome, a lesson many contemporary movie-makers could learn. Watch out especially for Warren Hymer as a heavily Brooklyn-accented dumb hood.

Donald Cook *Dave Elliot* • Evalyn Knapp *Maxine* • Warren Hymer *Midget* • J Carrol Naish *Lefty* • Herbert Rawlinson *JW Keaton* • Theodore von Eltz *Walsh* • Morgan Wallace *Van Cleve* ■ *Dir* Edward L Cahn • *Scr* Weilyn Totman, Olive Cooper, from a story by John Rathmell, Scott Darling

Confidential ★ 18

Crime drama 1986 · Can · Colour · 87mins

No one has a good word to say about this Canadian thriller, and we're not about to buck the trend. Shooting with a minuscule budget and on a tight schedule, writer/director Bruce Pittman has come up with a *film noir* homage that really does look as if it was made with next to nothing in next to no time. You'd have thought there must be something of interest in a story in which a journalist and then a private detective go missing while investigating a 30-year-old axe murder. But you'd be wrong! Contains violence, swearing and nudity. [video]

Neil Munro *Hugh Jameson* • August Schellenberg *Charles Ripley* • Chapelle Jaffe *Amelia* • Tom Butler *Edmund Eislin* • Antony Parr [Anthony Parr] *Rufus* • Doris Petrie *Mrs McAlister* • Kay Hawtrey *Doris* ■ *Dir/Scr* Bruce Pittman

Confidential Agent ★★

Thriller 1945 · US · BW · 117mins

A Warner Bros version of a novel by Graham Greene about a former Spanish musician who gives up his career to fight the Fascists and goes to Britain to stop the English selling coal to Franco's troops. Charles Boyer makes an engaging hero, but the Hollywood England takes some swallowing. Villains Peter Lorre and Katina Paxinou do their best to stop Boyer, but Lauren Bacall fails to convince as a British coal baron's daughter. Direction was unwisely entrusted to Herman Shumlin, whose previous experience lay mainly in the New York theatre. This movie isn't uneventful, though, just uninvolving.

Charles Boyer *Denard* • Lauren Bacall *Rose Cullen* • Victor Francen *Licata* • Wanda Hendrix *Else* • George Coulouris *Captain Currie* • Peter Lorre *Contreras* • Katina Paxinou *Mrs Melandey* • John Warburton *Neil Forbes* ■ *Dir* Herman Shumlin • *Scr* Robert Buckner, from the novel by Graham Greene

Confidential Report ★★★ PG

Film noir 1955 · Sp/Fr · BW · 93mins

Also known as *Mr Arkadin*, this fascinating picture is a fearful mess that betrays, all too clearly, the financial and production problems with which Orson Welles had to contend. As in *Citizen Kane*, the subject is a mysterious, all-powerful man, but this time around the approach is one of self-parody and self-indulgence. Welles filmed it in his beloved place of exile, Spain, with a fancy cast and fanciful camera angles. The producers – quite a shady bunch of characters – took the movie, cut it and withheld it from American release for ten years. [video]

Orson Welles *Gregory Arkadin* • Paola Mori *Raina Arkadin* • Robert Arden *Guy Van Stratten* • Akim Tamiroff *Jakob Zouk* • Michael Redgrave *Burgomil Trebitsch* • Patricia Medina *Mily* • Mischa Auer *Professor* • Katina Paxinou *Sophie* ■ *Dir* Orson Welles • *Scr* Orson Welles, from his novel

Confidentially Connie ★★ U

Comedy 1953 · US · BW · 71mins

Unsuitable for vegetarians, this vapid comedy involves a professor of poetry (Van Johnson, if you can believe it) who is so underpaid he can't afford to buy meat for his pregnant wife (Janet Leigh). Gene Lockhart is the hungry dean who dines out on teachers angling for promotion, while Louis Calhern steals the picture as the flamboyant Texas rancher who puts steak back on the table. The film, directed by veteran Edward Buzzell, is commendably brief.

Van Johnson *Joe Bedloe* • Janet Leigh *Connie Bedloe* • Louis Calhern *Opie Bedloe* • Walter Slezak *Emil Spangenberg* • Gene Lockhart *Dean Magruder* • Hayden Rorke *Simmons* • Robert Burton *Dr Willis Shoop* ■ *Dir* Edward Buzzell • *Scr* Max Shulman, from a story by Herman Wouk, Max Shulman

Confidentially Yours ★★★

Comedy mystery thriller 1983 · Fr · BW · 111mins

As he did with *Tirez sur le Pianiste* and *The Bride Wore Black*, François Truffaut took an American pulp novel (*The Long Saturday Night* by Charles Williams) as the basis for this rather self-regarding, mildly amusing comedy thriller. Shot in black and white by Nestor Almendros in an attempt to capture the style of the forties *film noir*, it tells of a real estate agent (Jean-Louis Trintignant) who, accused of the murder of his wife and her lover, goes into hiding while his secretary (Fanny Ardant) tries to prove his innocence. Ardant, Truffaut's real-life lover, has since proved to be one of France's most versatile actresses. In French with English subtitles.

Fanny Ardant *Barbara Becker* • Jean-Louis Trintignant *Julien Vercel* • Philippe Laudenbach *M Clement* • Caroline Sihol *Marie-Christine Vercel* • Xavier Saint-Macary *Bertrand Fabre* • Jean-Pierre Kalfon *Massoulier* ■ *Dir* François Truffaut • *Scr* François Truffaut, Suzanne Schiffman, Jean Aurel, from the novel *The Long Saturday Night* by Charles Williams

Confirm or Deny ★★★

Second World War drama 1941 · US · BW · 73mins

A top-flight cast who know their way around a Second World War spy thriller and a decent script (from a story co-written by Samuel Fuller) make this a cut above the ordinary blitzkrieg saga. The Ministry of Disinformation plotline gets a trifle convoluted in the middle, but the movie is saved from disappearing under its own self-importance by the effective playing of Don Ameche and Joan Bennett. The jittery, knife-edge atmosphere of a war-torn world is neatly fleshed out by director Archie Mayo.

Don Ameche *Mitch* • Joan Bennett *Jennifer Carson* • Roddy McDowall *Albert Perkins* • John Loder *Captain Channing* • Raymond Walburn *H Cyrus Sturtevant* • Arthur Shields *Jeff* • Eric Blore *Mr Hobbs* • Helene Reynolds *Dorothy* • Claude Allister [Claud Allister] *Williams* ■ *Dir* Archie Mayo • *Scr* Jo Swerling, from a story by Henry Wales, Samuel Fuller

Conflagration ★★★★

Tragedy 1958 · Jap · BW · 96mins

Adapted from Yukio Mishima's novel, *The Temple of the Golden Pavilion*, which was itself based on actual events, Kon Ichikawa's painstaking study of disillusion and misguided devotion has often been accused of being a clinical, desolate enterprise, obsessed with textured imagery and surface symbolism. However, Raizo Ichikawa poignantly conveys the pain experienced by the student priest, whose dismay at what he sees as the desecration of his temple prompts him to preserve its beauty and integrity by destroying it. Strikingly photographed by Kazuo Miyagawa (who also shot that other flashback masterpiece, *Rashomon*), this is a rigidly formal but unforgettable picture. In Japanese with English subtitles.

Raizo Ichikawa *Mizoguchi* • Tatsuya Nakadai • Ganjiro Nakamura *Tayama* • Yoko Uraji • Michiyo Aratama • Tamao Nakamura ■ *Dir* Kon Ichikawa • *Scr* Natto Wada, Keiji Hasebe, Kon Ichikawa, from the novel *The Temple of the Golden Pavillion* by Yukio Mishima

Conflict ★★★ PG

Thriller 1945 · US · BW · 81mins

From a great period in *film noir*, this is a slightly substandard Warner Bros melodrama, despite a story co-written by Robert Siodmak (*Phantom Lady*, *The Killers*). It is held together by Humphrey Bogart, who occasionally looks as though he'd rather be somewhere else, even when he's plotting to do away with his wife in order to marry her sister. Psychologist and friend of the family Sydney Greenstreet proffers a discourse on the perils of marriage; then the audience is thrown a did-he-or-didn't-he plot. The censor was pretty tough in those days, but the mood's still dark and tense, even if the conclusion is obvious. [video]

Humphrey Bogart *Richard Mason* • Alexis Smith *Evelyn Turner* • Sydney Greenstreet *Dr Mark Hamilton* • Rose Hobart *Katherine Mason* • Charles Drake *Professor Norman Holdsworth* • Grant Mitchell *Dr Grant* • Patrick O'Moore *Detective Lieutenant Egan* • Ann Shoemaker *Nora Grant* • Frank Wilcox *Robert Freston* ■ *Dir* Curtis Bernhardt • *Scr* Arthur T Horman, Dwight Taylor, from a story by Robert Siodmak, Alfred Neumann

Conflict of Interest ★★ 18

Detective action 1992 · US · Colour · 84mins

A grim made-for-cable thriller which is just about worth a look for its above-average cast. Judd Nelson is the larger-than-life club owner who goes head to head with idealistic detective Christopher McDonald. First-time director Gary Davis lays on the standard exploitation clichés with relish, though the end result is indistinguishable from hundreds of other sleazy crime dramas. [video]

Christopher McDonald *Mickey Flannery* • Judd Nelson *Gideon* • Alyssa Milano *Eve* • Gregory Alan Harris *Jason Flannery* ■ *Dir* Gary Davis • *Scr* Gregory Miller, Michael Angeli

Conflict of Wings ★★ U

Comedy 1953 · UK · Colour · 85mins

The borrowings come thick and fast in this sentimental rural drama. The most obvious source is the wartime allegory *Tawny Pipit*, with more than a hint of *The Titfield Thunderbolt* and *Passport to Pimlico*. But, while it never lives up to its illustrious ancestry, this is still a pleasing little picture, with the Norfolk Broads looking lovely in Arthur Grant and Martin Curtis's washed-out colour photography. The folklore behind the tale is charming, there are a couple of tear-jerking moments and a rousing rally-round finale, which, like so much else in this Group Three production, has that Ealing ring.

John Gregson *Bill Morris* • Muriel Pavlow *Sally* • Kieron Moore *Squadron Leader Parsons* • Niall MacGinnis *Harry Tilney* • Harry Fowler *Buster* • Guy Middleton *Adjutant* • Sheila Sweet *Fanny Bates* • Campbell Singer *Flight Sergeant Campbell* ■ *Dir* John Eldridge • *Scr* Don Sharp, John Pudney, from the novel by Don Sharp

The Conformist ★★★★★ 18

Drama 1969 · It/Fr · Colour · 113mins

Bernardo Bertolucci's adaptation of Alberto Moravia's novel examines the link between sexual and political repression in order to assess the impact of Italy's authoritarian past on its deeply divided present. Aided by the luscious fluidity of Vittorio Storaro's cinematography, Bertolucci perfectly captures the false sense of well-being exuded by Mussolini's regime, while Jean-Louis Trintignant is superb as the assassin paralysed by the contradictions of his life and times. A former victim of child abuse, his desperate desire to belong forces him into a loveless marriage and a slavish allegiance to the party. Trintignant is ably supported by Stefania Sandrelli and Dominique Sanda in this masterful blend of Freud and fascism. In Italian with English subtitles.

Jean-Louis Trintignant *Marcello Clerici* • Stefania Sandrelli *Giulia* • Gastone Moschin *Manganiello* • Enzo Tarascio *Quadri* • Pierre Clementi *Lino Seminara* • Dominique Sanda *Anna Quadri* • Christian Alegny *Raoul* ■ *Dir* Bernardo Bertolucci • *Scr* Bernardo Bertolucci, from a novel by Alberto Moravia

Congo ★★ 12

Adventure 1995 · US · Colour · 103mins

Michael Crichton's novel, on which this adventure is based, tried to do for gorillas what his *Jurassic Park* did for dinosaurs. But, under Frank Marshall's bland direction, this trek-through-the-jungle adventure is a disappointingly old-fashioned affair that lacks any sense of wonder. The plot, combining a lost civilisation, a highly intelligent gorilla that's been taught communication skills and venal scientists after diamonds for a laser gun, is a lacklustre *Boys' Own* no-brainer, and the movie scrapes the bottom of the fantasy barrel in terms of credibility, dire acting and clichéd special effects. Contains swearing. ▭

Dylan Walsh *Peter Elliot* • Laura Linney *Dr Karen Ross* • Ernie Hudson *Monroe Kelly* • Tim Curry *Herkermer Homolka* • Grant Heslov *Richard* • Joe Don Baker *RB Travis* • Mary

Ellen Trainor *Moira* • Stuart Pankin *Boyd* ■ *Dir* Frank Marshall • *Scr* John Patrick Shanley, from the novel by Michael Crichton

Congo Crossing ★★

Crime drama 1956 · US · Colour · 85mins

Here's a B-western with a gimmick – it's set in an obscure jungle backwater in central Africa where outlaws congregate, safe from arrest. Into this tropical enclave of vice comes Virginia Mayo, on the run from a murder rap, and hero George Nader, who works for the Belgian government and is surveying the land to confirm whether it falls within the jurisdiction of the colonial government. Peter Lorre represents the forces of law and order, such as they are, and Rex Ingram plays the local doctor. Filmed in the crocodile-infested wilds of the Universal backlot, it serves up honest hokum and Mayo modelling a lot of neat safari outfits.

Virginia Mayo *Louise Whitman* • George Nader *David Carr* • Peter Lorre *Colonel Arragas* • Michael Pate *Bart O'Connell* • Rex Ingram *Dr Gorman* • Tonio Selwart *Carl Rittner* • Kathryn Givney *Amelia Abbott* • Tudor Owen *Emile Zorfus* • Raymond Bailey *Peter Mannering* ■ *Dir* Joseph Pevney • *Scr* Richard Alan Simmons, from a story by Houston Branch

Congo Maisie ★★★

Comedy 1940 · US · BW · 70mins

Stuck for a plot to follow their first successful "Maisie" feature, MGM shamelessly reworked their 1932 Clark Gable/Jean Harlow hit *Red Dust* as a programme filler. Vivacious Ann Sothern stars as Wilson Collison's brassy Brooklyn chorus girl Maisie Ravier, in one of the better of the popular series that eventually ran to ten features. Here Maisie finds herself in a heavily back-projected Africa (left over from old *Tarzan* movies), helping doctor John Carroll avoid marauding natives. Director Henry Potter keeps the mayhem bubbling nicely.

Ann Sothern *Maisie Ravier* • John Carroll *Dr Michael Shane* • Rita Johnson *Kay McWade* • Shepperd Strudwick *Dr McWade* • JM Kerrigan *Captain Finch* • EE Clive *Horace Snell* ■ *Dir* Henry Potter • *Scr* Mary C McCall Jr, from the book *Congo Landing* by Wilson Collison

Congress Dances ★★★

Musical 1931 · Ger · BW · 92mins

In Vienna for the 1814 Congress, Tsar Alexander of Russia (Willy Fritsch) falls for a shop assistant (Lillian Harvey) rather than the countess (Lil Dagover) put his way by the devious Prince Metternich (Conrad Veidt). Delicately directed by Erik Charell from a soufflé-light script, this early German musical largely ignores the political implications of the setting. Filmed in three different versions – English, French and German, with Henri Garat replacing Fritsch for the French market – its charm has faded with time, though its lightweight approach and opulent settings proved hugely influential throughout the decade.

Lillian Harvey [Lilian Harvey] *Christel Weinzinger* • Conrad Veidt *Prince Metternich* • Lil Dagover *The Countess* • Willy Fritsch *Tsar Alexander of Russia/Uralsky* • Gibb McLaughlin *Bibikoff, the Czar's adjutant* ■ *Dir* Erik Charell • *Scr* Norman Falk, Robert Liebmann

A Connecticut Yankee ★★★

Comedy 1931 · US · BW · 95mins

Will Rogers stars in this comedy of a man who dreams that he is back in the middle ages, where he brings his foreign influence to bear on the manners and morals of King Arthur's court. Mark Twain's classic satirical fantasy had been the basis of a 1921 silent, and would resurface in 1949 as a Bing Crosby musical. This version, directed by David Butler with Maureen O'Sullivan, Myrna Loy, Frank Albertson and William Farnum in support, is witty and agreeable, yet somewhat dated.

Will Rogers *Hank* • William Farnum *King Arthur* • Myrna Loy *Queen Morgan Le Fay* • Maureen O'Sullivan *Alisande* • Frank Albertson *Clarence* • Mitchell Harris *Merlin* ■ *Dir* David Butler • *Scr* William Conselman, Owen Davis, from the novel *A Connecticut Yankee in King Arthur's Court* by Mark Twain

A Connecticut Yankee in King Arthur's Court ★★★ U

Musical 1949 · US · Colour · 102mins

Bing Crosby stars in this musical adaptation of Mark Twain's fantasy about a 20th-century American who dreams himself back to medieval times. Arriving at Camelot, he is regarded as something of a wizard at King Arthur's court. The film substitutes broad comedy for wit, and the musical numbers – with the exception of *Busy Doing Nothing* – are pretty forgettable. The Technicolor production is eye-catchingly lavish, though, as is romantic interest Rhonda Fleming. Crosby is in good voice, while Tay Garnett directs with spirit. ▭

Bing Crosby *Hank Martin* • William Bendix *Sir Sagramore* • Rhonda Fleming *Sandy* • Cedric Hardwicke *King Arthur* • Murvyn Vye *Merlin* • Henry Wilcoxon *Sir Lancelot* • Richard Webb *Sir Galahad* ■ *Dir* Tay Garnett • *Scr* Edmund Beloin, from the novel by Mark Twain

A Connecticut Yankee in King Arthur's Court ★

Fantasy adventure 1989 · US · Colour

No, this is not Bing Crosby crooning in tights, but an excuse to try out a ten-year-old *Cosby Show* co-star in a feature, with distinctly patchy results. It's a hastily thrown-together TV hotch-potch of lame jokes and schmaltzy sentiment, as the MTV generation fails to get to grips with Arthurian England. You can see the joins in this sloppily pasted script at a hundred paces, with the only redeeming feature a certain *joie de vivre* which fights its way through against the odds.

Keshia Knight Pulliam *Karen Jones* • Michael Gross *King Arthur* • Whip Hubley *Sir Lancelot* • Emma Samms *Queen Guenevere* • Bryce Hamnet *Clarence* • Jean Marsh *Morgana* ■ *Dir* Mel Damski • *Scr* Paul Zindel, from the novel by Mark Twain

Connecting Rooms ★★

Romantic drama 1969 · UK · Colour · 103mins

A slightly bonkers drama about a schoolteacher (Michael Redgrave) on the run from child abuse charges and near to suicide, and a female cellist (Bette Davis) who claims to be a solo artist but is in fact a street busker. Together they share rooms in a shabby

Bayswater B&B run by Kay Walsh. It's all very thirties, except for the "Swinging London" appendages of pop stars and a general air of kookiness. While Redgrave seems perfectly at home amongst the mustiness and sexual torment, Davis is very weird as the self-confessed "old bag".

Bette Davis *Wanda Fleming* • Michael Redgrave *James Wallraven* • Alexis Kanner *Mickey* • Kay Walsh *Mrs Brent* • Gabrielle Drake *Jean* ■ *Dir* Franklin Gollings • *Scr* Franklin Gollings, from the play *The Cellist* by Marion Hart

The Connection ★★★

Drama 1961 · US · BW · 111mins

The debut feature of the influential alternative film-maker Shirley Clarke is shot in documentary style, largely within the confines of one room, and framed as a film-within-a-film. This early example of independent film-making charts a day in the life of a group of Manhattan junkies as they sit around, waiting for their fix. Matter-of-fact, gritty stuff with excellent acting from unknowns; though there are no narrative frills, the movie is not without incident, some of it quite shocking. Shot on a shoestring budget, it pulls no punches, and few films have dealt with drug addiction as realistically.

Warren Finnerty *Leach* • Garry Goodrow *Ernie* • William Redfield *Jim Dunn* • Jerome Raphael *Solly* • James Anderson *Sam* • Carl Lee *Cowboy* • Barbara Winchester *Sister Salvation* ■ *Dir* Shirley Clarke • *Scr* Jack Gelber, from his play

The Conqueror ★★

Action adventure 1956 · US · Colour · 109mins

This splendid hokum is rendered ludicrous today by the casting of John Wayne as Genghis Khan, but it doesn't deserve its reputation as one of the worst movies ever made. Splendidly directed by former crooner Dick Powell, it is best viewed dubbed into any foreign language as the dialogue is silly beyond belief. Susan Hayward is Wayne's woman, and their exchanges show what canny casting this was by producer Howard Hughes in one of the last epics he made at his ailing RKO studios.

John Wayne *Temujin* • Susan Hayward *Bortai* • Pedro Armendariz *Jamuga* • Agnes Moorehead *Hunlun* • Thomas Gomez *Wang Kahn* • John Hoyt *Shaman* • William Conrad *Kasar* • Ted DeCorsia *Kumlek* • Lee Van Cleef *Chepei* ■ *Dir* Dick Powell • *Scr* Oscar Millard

Conquest ★★★★ U

Historical romantic drama 1937 · US · BW · 115mins

"Sire, you stand in the sun." says Greta Garbo's Marie to Charles Boyer's Napoleon, perhaps aware for once of finding herself playing opposite a suitably talented co-star. Garbo, as you would expect, is simply superb (when was she ever not?) as Bonaparte's Polish mistress, and the Great Lover himself makes an endearingly vulnerable Napoleon in this finely mounted MGM production. Clarence Brown – surely a film craftsman who deserves more appreciation – shows why he was Garbo's favourite director, enhancing her striking features and

U = SUITABLE FOR ALL Uc = SUITABLE FOR ALL, ESPECIALLY FOR YOUNG CHILDREN (VIDEO ONLY) PG = PARENTAL GUIDANCE

presenting her as a warm and tender woman fit for the Emperor of France.

Greta Garbo *Marie Walewska* • Charles Boyer *Napoleon* • Reginald Owen *Talleyrand* • Alan Marshal *Captain D'Ornano* • Henry Stephenson *Count Walewska* • Leif Erikson *Paul Lachinski* • Dame May Whitty *Laetitia Bonaparte* • C Henry Gordon *Prince Poniatowski* • *Dir* Clarence Brown • *Scr* Samuel Hoffenstein, Salka Viertel, SN Behrman, from a play by Helen Jerome, from the novel *Pani Walewska* by Waclaw Gasiorowski

The Conquest of Everest ★★★★ U

Documentary 1953 · UK · Colour · 74mins

Ever since Herbert G Ponting recorded Captain Scott's ill-fated bid to reach the South Pole, the movie camera has been accompanying heroic ventures. Shot in even more arduous conditions, this is a remarkable account of the expedition that saw Edmund Hillary and Sherpa Tensing become the first to reach the peak of the world's highest mountain. It's a pity the camera couldn't make the final ascent, but the various stages of the climb, with their attendant difficulties and dangers, make gripping viewing thanks to some inspired editing, Louis MacNeice's literate commentary and Arthur Benjamin's rousing score.

Meredith Edwards *Narrator* • *Dir* George Lowe • *Scr* Louis MacNeice • *Editor* Adrian de Potier

Conquest of Space ★★★ U

Science-fiction drama
1955 · US · Colour · 77mins

Paramount slashed the budget and added soap-opera bubbles to George Pal's sequel to *Destination Moon*, hastening the end of the producer's relationship with the studio. With the accent more on science than on fiction, *Conquest of Space* aims to offer an accurate reflection of what a trip to Mars would be like technically, and how it would affect the crew psychologically. Despite an out-of-sync religious tone and the sight of snow falling on the red planet when the astronauts land on Christmas Day, the reverential approach still manages to evoke a sense of wonder.

Walter Brooke *Samuel Merritt* • Eric Fleming *Barney Merritt* • Mickey Shaughnessy *Mahoney* • Phil Foster *Siegle* • William Redfield *Cooper* • William Hopper *Fenton* • Benson Fong *Imoto* • Ross Martin *Fodor* • *Dir* Byron Haskin • *Scr* Philip Yordan, Barre Lyndon, George Worthingtonyates, from the book *The Mars Project* by Chesley Bonestell, Willy Ley

Conquest of the Air ★★ U

Documentary drama
1936 · UK/US · BW · 70mins

This was to be the first instalment of an ambitious trilogy on the development of land, sea and air transport planned by producer Alexander Korda as part of his assault on the American market. However, this untidy collage of history lesson and dramatic reconstruction was an age in production and looked no better in the screening room. Zoltan Korda shared the directorial credit with several others, which can't have helped the

continuity. Disney did it better in *Victory through Air Power*.

Frederick Culley *Roger Bacon* • Franklin Dyall *Jerome de Ascoli* • Alan Wheatley *Borelli* • Hay Petrie *Tiberius Cavallo* • John Abbott *Derozier* • Laurence Olivier *Vincent Lunardi* • Bryan Powley *Sir George Cayley* • Henry Victor *Otto Lilienthal* • John Trumbull *Von Zeppelin* • *Dir* Zoltan Korda, Alexander Esway, Alexander Shaw, John Monk Saunders • *Scr* Hugh Gray, Peter Bezencenet, from stories by John Monk Saunders, Antoine de St Exupery

Conquest of the Planet of the Apes ★★★ 15

Science-fiction adventure
1972 · US · Colour · 83mins

The fourth film in the sci-fi saga illustrates how the ape revolt happened in the first place. Caesar, played by series regular Roddy McDowall, gains the power of speech, forms enslaved fellow simians into guerrilla groups and leads them against the evil human race who have adopted them as household pets. Gritty direction from J Lee Thompson and plenty of fun philosophising, complete with intriguing moral lessons and neat ape/man role reversals, make this episode a compelling outing into futuristic monkey business. Contains violence.

Roddy McDowall *Caesar* • Don Murray *Breck* • Ricardo Montalban *Armando* • Natalie Trundy *Lisa* • Hari Rhodes *MacDonald* • Severn Darden *Kolp* • Lou Wagner *Busboy* • John Randolph *Commission chairman* • *Dir* J Lee Thompson • *Scr* Paul Dehn, from characters created by Pierre Boulle

Conquest of the South Pole ★★★ 12

Drama 1989 · UK · Colour · 95mins

Manfred Karge's allegorical fantasy was a huge hit for the Traverse Theatre in Edinburgh, so it's fitting that the film version should be shot in and around the now-defunct docks of the Scottish capital. Though hampered by an ultra-low budget, debutant director Gilles MacKinnon exploits the visual potential of this story of a group of unemployed youths who ward off despair by re-creating Amundsen's journey to the South Pole in their own back yard. The central device remains an inherently theatrical conceit, but screenwriter Gareth Wardell deftly embroils us in the characters' lunatic quest, while the march up Arthur's Seat makes an uplifting climax.

Stevan Rimkus *Sloopianek* • Ewen Bremner *Penguin* • Leonard O'Malley *Butcher* • Laura Girling *Louise* • Gordon Cameron *Brown* • Alastair Galbraith *Frankieboy* • Julie-Kate Oliver *Rosie* • *Dir* Gillies MacKinnon • *Scr* Gareth Wardell, from the play by Manfred Karge

Conrack ★★

Drama 1974 · US · Colour · 106mins

Jon Voight stars as liberal teacher Pat Conroy, who fetches up on one of South Carolina's barrier islands and a class of kids who can't read or write. Martin Ritt's movie is often sentimental and hectoring, ramming home the contrast between Voight's comfy, secure rebellion against the Vietnam War and the utter destitution and backwardness of his pupils. He gives them Beethoven, swimming

lessons, nature trips and poetry; they give him grateful smiles until he's fired by Hume Cronyn. Based on Conroy's autobiographical book *The Water Is Wide*, the film oozes sincerity yet somehow seems totally phoney.

Jon Voight *Pat Conroy* • Paul Winfield *Mad Billy* • Madge Sinclair *Mrs Scott* • Tina Andrews *Mary* • Antonio Fargas *Quickfellow* • Ruth Attaway *Edna* • James O'Rear *Little Man* • Hume Cronyn *Skeffington* • *Dir* Martin Ritt • *Scr* Irving Ravetch, Harriet Frank Jr, from the book *The Water Is Wide* by Pat Conroy

Consenting Adults ★★★ 15

Psychological thriller
1992 · US · Colour · 94mins

Kevin Kline and Mary Elizabeth Mastrantonio are the ordinary husband and wife whose lives are turned upside down when a couple-from-hell move in next door and get them involved in wife-swapping and murder. Extremely plodding action from *All the President's Men* director Alan J Pakula and a rather wooden Kline slow things down somewhat, but the day is saved by a mesmerising performance from Kevin Spacey as the creepy neighbour. Contains violence, swearing and nudity.

Kevin Kline *Richard Parker* • Mary Elizabeth Mastrantonio *Priscilla Parker* • Kevin Spacey *Eddy Otis* • Rebecca Miller *Kay Otis* • Forest Whitaker *David Duttonville* • EG Marshall *George Gordon* • *Dir* Alan J Pakula • *Scr* Matthew Chapman

Consolation Marriage ★★★

Comedy drama 1931 · US · BW · 82mins

Irene Dunne and Pat O'Brien, both on the rebound, meet and marry for solace and companionship. They carve out a decent life for themselves and have a child, but their equilibrium is threatened when their former flames (Lester Vail and Myrna Loy) re-appear. This was one of the first of the "woman's weepie" roles that Dunne was to make her own, though director Paul H Sloane offers a satisfying measure of charm and humour to balance the sentimentality.

Irene Dunne *Mary Brown Porter* • Pat O'Brien *Steve Porter* • John Halliday *Jeff* • Myrna Loy *Elaine Brandon* • Lester Vail *Aubrey* • Matt Moore *Colonel* • Pauline Stevens *Baby* • *Dir* Paul Sloane [Paul H Sloane] • *Scr* Humphrey Pearson, from a story by William Cunningham

Conspiracy ★★ 15

Political thriller 1989 · UK · Colour · 86mins

James Wilby is the defence secretary who has a sexual secret in his past which could damage his political career, so measures are taken in a covert operation to prevent the story getting out. Unfortunately, neither Wilby nor his co-star, Kate Hardie, have the presence required to carry such a drama, and comparisons with the more famous *Scandal* are inevitable. Moreover, with so many government indiscretions hitting the headlines these days, our response to Wilby's secret is likely to be "so what?"

James Wilby • Kate Hardie • Glyn Houston • *Dir/Scr* Christopher Barnard

Conspiracy in Teheran ★ U

Spy drama 1947 · UK · BW · 87mins

The story of this shambolic British thriller is encapsulated in its American title, *The Plot to Kill Roosevelt*. It is 1943 and plans are afoot for the Allied invasion of Europe. Churchill, Stalin and Roosevelt meet in the Iranian capital to agree strategy, but not everyone present is keen for the conference to succeed and journalist Derek Farr discovers a conspiracy in the nick of time. Farr is as bland as ever and takes an age to put together pieces larger than a three-year-old's jigsaw puzzle.

Derek Farr *Pemberton Grant* • Marta Labarr *Natalie Trubetzin* • Manning Whiley *Paul Sherek* • John Slater *Major Sobieski* • John Warwick *Major McIntyre* • Pamela Stirling *Hali* • *Dir* William Freshman • *Scr* Akos Tolnay, William Freshman

The Conspiracy of Fear ★ 18

Action thriller 1996 · Can · Colour · 101mins

A mysterious package left to Andrew Lowery when his father dies in an explosion becomes much sought-after by a bunch of heavies. This implausible thriller generates little suspense and wastes the talents of Christopher Plummer and Geraint Wyn Davies, the latter playing a remorseless killer. Inevitably, director John Eyres's reliance on close-ups of walking shoes to create tension becomes an overused and laughable device.

Geraint Wyn Davies *Straker* • Andrew Lowery *Chris King* • Leslie Hope *Jimmy* • Rino Romano *Zelmo* • David Nerman *Wolfe* • Alan Jordan *Mr King* • Christopher Plummer *Wakeman* • Philip Akin *Patterson* • *Dir* John Eyres • *Scr* Roy Sallows

Conspiracy of Hearts ★★★★ U

Second World War drama
1960 · UK · BW · 112mins

A moving and under-rated tale about nuns helping Jewish children escape the Nazis in war-torn Italy, made with sincerity and feeling by the director of the *Doctor* series, Ralph Thomas, himself a Jew. The movie boasts an immensely talented cast, headed by the luminous Lilli Palmer as the mother superior, with Sylvia Syms and Yvonne Mitchell as caring nuns and David Kossoff as a rabbi. This thoughtful casting lends the film resonance, and it's far better than its potentially mawkish plot combination of children and nuns would suggest.

Lilli Palmer *Mother Katherine* • Sylvia Syms *Sister Mitya* • Ronald Lewis *Major Spoletti* • Albert Lieven *Colonel Horsten* • Yvonne Mitchell *Sister Gerta* • *Dir* Ralph Thomas • *Scr* Robert Presnell Jr, from material by Dale Pitt (front for Adrian Scott)

Conspiracy of Love ★★

Drama 1987 · US · Colour

One from the "cute kiddie" period of Drew Barrymore's career, before rehab and her re-invention as a teen sexpot. She acquits herself well in this solid but formulaic TV weepie, which details an "only in America" custody battle involving Barrymore and her devoted grandfather, played by veteran Robert

Young. Noel Black milks the material for maximum sentiment and tear-jerker fans won't be disappointed.

Robert Young *Grandpa Joe* • Drew Barrymore *Jody Wykowski* • Elizabeth Wilson *Lillie Wykowski* • Mitchell Laurance *Jack* • John Fujioka *Mr Nakamura* • Alan Fawcett *Joe Wykowski* • Glynnis O'Connor *Marcia* ■ *Dir* Noel Black • *Scr* Barry Morrow

Conspiracy Theory ★★★ 🅸🅱

Romantic comedy thriller
1997 · US · Colour · 129mins

Mel Gibson is a neurotic New York cabbie consumed by wild conspiracy theories and their implications in director Richard Donner's uneven romantic comedy thriller. It's the newsletter he produces that suddenly intensifies interest in him from ominous parties like creepy Patrick Stewart, who may work for the CIA. But that's only the half of it, because when he turns to Justice Department attorney Julia Roberts for help, the main *Manchurian Candidate*-like plot kicks off. While Donner glosses over the improbabilities with his usual considerable style and bravura, and Gibson and Roberts make an engaging team, the uneasy combination of light laughs and unsavoury darkness eventually conspires against it. Contains some violence. 📺 *DVD*

Mel Gibson *Jerry Fletcher* • Julia Roberts *Alice Sutton* • Patrick Stewart *Dr Jonas* • Cylk Cozart *Agent Lowry* • Stephen Kahan *Wilson* • Terry Alexander *Flip* • Alex McArthur *Cynic* ■ *Dir* Richard Donner • *Scr* Brian Helgeland

Conspirator ★ 🆄

Spy drama   1949 · UK · BW · 86mins

A dire, anti-communist tract that fitted in with Hollywood's post-war paranoia but is transposed to Britain where Guards Officer Robert Taylor seems to be passing military secrets to the Russians. He's also married to Elizabeth Taylor, which makes matters even worse, because he's ordered to kill her; if he doesn't, he has to kill himself. Mr Taylor gives his usual impersonation of a plank of wood, while the young Miss Taylor looks gorgeous but seems lost.

Robert Taylor (1) *Maj Michael Curragh* • Elizabeth Taylor *Melinda Greyton* • Robert Flemyng *Capt Hugh Ladholme* • Harold Warrender *Col Hammerbrook* • Honor Blackman *Joyce* • Marjorie Fielding *Aunt Jessica* • Thora Hird *Broaders* • Wilfrid Hyde White *Lord Pennistone* ■ *Dir* Victor Saville • *Scr* Sally Benson, Gerard Fairlie, from a novel by Humphrey Slater

The Conspirators ★★

Spy drama   1944 · US · BW · 101mins

Is this an unofficial sequel to *Casablanca*? Resistance fighter Paul Henreid is finally in Lisbon after escaping from Holland, hunted by the Nazis but finding shelter with Sydney Greenstreet, Peter Lorre and exotic Hedy Lamarr who are all resistance underground members. However, Greenstreet suspects a traitor is in their midst after an obvious frame-up. The cast are like the furniture in your grandmother's living room – familiar, snug, a bit moth-eaten. But they more than compensate for the formulaic plotting and the patriotic slogans that

pass for a script, and for the unusually lethargic direction by Jean Negulesco.

Hedy Lamarr *Irene* • Paul Henreid *Vincent* • Sydney Greenstreet *Quintanilla* • Peter Lorre *Bernazsky* • Victor Francen *Von Mohr* • Joseph Calleia *Capt Pereira* • Carol Thurston *Rosa* • Vladimir Sokoloff *Miguel* • George Macready *The Con Man* ■ *Dir* Jean Negulesco • *Scr* Vladimir Pozner, Leo Rosten, from a novel by Frederic Prokosch

Conspirators of Pleasure

★★★★ 🅸🆁

Experimental fantasy comedy
1996 · Cz Rep/Swi/UK · Colour · 82mins

Focusing on the antics of some lonely Prague neighbours, Jan Svankmajer's darkly subversive satire explores everything from de Sade and Freud to the nature of political freedom, the influence of the media and the possibility of happiness in a world primed to prevent it. From the man making papier-mâché chickens out of porn mags and umbrellas to the woman with a bagful of breadcrumbs, the gallery of eccentrics is both sinister and sympathetic; the performances are all the more remarkable considering each fantasy is acted out in silence. Exhilarating, unnerving and, even without the trademark animation, very Svankmajer. A Czech language film. Contains some nudity and violence. 📺

Petr Meissel *Mr Peony* • Gabriela Wilhelmova *Mrs Loubalova* • Barbara Hrzanova *Mrs Malkova the postmistress* • Anna Wetlinska *Mrs Beltinska the newscaster* • Jiri Labus *Mr Kula the news vendor* • Pavel Novy *Mr Beltinska the police commissioner* ■ *Dir/Scr* Jan Svankmajer

Constance ★★★★ 🅸🅱

Drama   1984 · NZ · Colour · 98mins

The debuting Donogh Rees is outstanding in this inspired exploration of the relationship between the Hollywood "woman's picture" and real life in forties Auckland. Tempering the nostalgia evoked by his knowing visuals, director Bruce Morrison makes Rees's disastrous attempt to behave like a movie heroine truly excruciating. Yet he also succeeds in exposing the hypocrisies of the rising middle classes, with their self-aggrandising charity work and fraudulent morality. Although the dialogue is occasionally too self-conscious, the references to the films of Garbo, Dietrich, Davis and Crawford are splendidly staged, making their ironic commentary on the hapless Constance's existence all the more prescient. 📺

Donogh Rees *Constance Elsworthy* • Shane Briant *Simon Malyon* • Judie Douglass *Sylvia Elsworthy* • Martin Vaughan *Alexander Elsworthy* • Donald MacDonald *John Munroe* • Mark Wignall *Richard Lewis* • Graham Harvey *Errol Barr* ■ *Dir* Bruce Morrison • *Scr* Jonathan Hardy, Bruce Morrison

The Constant Husband ★★★★ 🆄

Comedy   1955 · UK · Colour · 88mins

Rex Harrison is superbly cast as an amnesiac philanderer in this jolly romp from British film-makers Frank Launder and Sidney Gilliat. Indeed, it is said that Harrison's performance secured him the role of Henry Higgins in the

Broadway production of *My Fair Lady*. Giving Harrison a run for his money are Kay Kendall (whom he later married), Margaret Leighton and French actress Nicole Maurey. The fifties Technicolor photography gives the film a very pleasant period sheen, while the witty screenplay by Gilliat and Val Valentine ensures this comedy is a delight.

Rex Harrison *Charles Hathaway* • Margaret Leighton *Miss Chesterman* • Kay Kendall *Monica* • Cecil Parker *Llewellyn* • Nicole Maurey *Lola* • George Cole *Luigi Sopranelli* • Raymond Huntley *JF Hassett* ■ *Dir* Sidney Gilliat • *Scr* Sidney Gilliat, Val Valentine • *Cinematographer* Ted Scaife

The Constant Nymph ★

Silent drama   1928 · UK · BW

This British-made silent version of the best-selling twenties novel by Margaret Kennedy and a hit West End play (by Kennedy and Basil Dean) is the first of three screen adaptations. It's by far the least successful, despite the presence of matinée idol Ivor Novello in the starring role as a composer struggling for inspiration and inadvertently breaking the heart of a schoolgirl (Mabel Poulton), who remains in love with him into her adulthood. Neither the screenplay nor the direction capture the essence of this poignant tale. Over-long and under-characterised, it's of little interest now.

Mary Clare *Linda Sanger* • Ivor Novello *Lewis Dodd* • Mabel Poulton *Tessa Sanger* • Benita Hume *Antonia Sanger* • Dorothy Boyd *Pauline Sanger* ■ *Dir* Adrian Brunel • *Scr* Margaret Kennedy, Basil Dean, Alma Reville, from the play by Margaret Kennedy, Basil Dean, from the novel by Margaret Kennedy

The Constant Nymph ★★★

Drama   1933 · UK · BW · 97mins

After the ineptitude of the 1928 silent version of the hit play by Basil Dean and Margaret Kennedy (based on her popular novel), eminent theatre director Dean made this first sound version, starring Brian Aherne as the composer struggling for inspiration and Victoria Hopper as the young girl whose constant love provides it, only for events to end in tragedy. A fragile piece, delicately if somewhat sedately played, it's probably too delicate for present-day audiences, but remains a stylish and poignant offering from the British cinema of the time.

Victoria Hopper *Tess Sanger* • Brian Aherne *Lewis Dodd* • Leonora Corbett *Florence* • Lyn Harding *Albert Sanger* • Mary Clare *Linda Sanger* • Jane Baxter *Antonia Sanger* ■ *Dir* Basil Dean • *Scr* Margaret Kennedy, Basil Dean, Dorothy Farnum, from the play by Margaret Kennedy, Basil Dean, from the novel by Margaret Kennedy • *Producer* Michael Balcon

The Constant Nymph ★★★

Drama   1943 · US · BW · 111mins

Already filmed twice in Britain (as a silent in 1928 and again in 1933), this Warner Bros version of Margaret Kennedy's popular 1924 novel and stage success (written with Basil Dean) is sensitively directed, for maximum emotional impact, by Edmund Goulding. Charles Boyer stars as the composer loved by schoolgirl Joan Fontaine (Oscar-nominated), whose constancy accompanies him into

adulthood. Interminably slow to get going, it nevertheless succeeds in tugging the heartstrings and it boasts a terrific supporting cast, which includes Alexis Smith, Charles Coburn, Dame May Whitty and Peter Lorre.

Charles Boyer *Lewis Dodd* • Joan Fontaine *Tessa Sanger* • Alexis Smith *Florence Creighton* • Charles Coburn *Charles Creighton* • Brenda Marshall *Toni Sanger* • Dame May Whitty *Lady Longborough* • Peter Lorre *Bercovi, Fritz* • Joyce Reynolds *Paula Sanger* ■ *Dir* Edmund Goulding • *Scr* Kathryn Scola, from the play by Margaret Kennedy, Basil Dean, from the novel by Margaret Kennedy

Consuming Passions ★★ 🅸🅱

Comedy   1988 · UK/US · Colour · 94mins

Based on a play by Michael Palin and Terry Jones, of Monty Python fame, Giles Foster's comedy is not exactly a masterpiece. The premise involves a floundering chocolate factory whose fortunes improve dramatically when three workers are accidentally knocked into a mixing vat. Suddenly the nation starts clamouring for their "special" chocolate with its mystery ingredient. Vanessa Redgrave delivers a strange performance as a litigating widow, while Jonathan Pryce seems to have developed an obsession with the word "yah". Sit down with a bar of Dairy Milk instead. 📺

Vanessa Redgrave *Mrs Garza* • Jonathan Pryce *Mr Farris* • Tyler Butterworth *Ian Littleton* • Freddie Jones *Graham Chumley* • Sammi Davis *Felicity* • Prunella Scales *Ethel* • Thora Hird *Mrs Gordon* • William Rushton *Big Teddy* ■ *Dir* Giles Foster • *Scr* Paul D Zimmerman, Andrew Davies, from the play *Secrets* by Michael Palin, Terry Jones

Contact ★★★ 🅿🅶

Science-fiction drama
1997 · US · Colour · 143mins

A rather over-zealous take on new-age spirituality mars this otherwise impressive adaption of Carl Sagan's bestselling novel. Jodie Foster is the dedicated watcher of the stars who becomes the unlikely recipient of a message from extraterrestrials explaining how humble humans can build a spacecraft and go to meet them. Matthew McConaughey is the religious adviser battling for her soul, while Tom Skerritt and James Woods play her ambitious bosses; along with the always reliable Foster, they deliver excellent performances. The digital effects are stunning, and director Robert Zemeckis is at home with the action sequences; if only he had stuck to the sci-fi. 📺 *DVD*

Jodie Foster *Dr Eleanor "Ellie" Arroway* • Matthew McConaughey *Palmer Joss* • Tom Skerritt *Dr David Drumlin* • Angela Bassett *Rachel Constantine* • John Hurt *SR Hadden* • David Morse *Theodore "Ted" Arroway* • Rob Lowe *Richard Rank* • William Fichtner *Kent* • James Woods *Michael Kitz* ■ *Dir* Robert Zemeckis • *Scr* James V Hart, Michael Goldenberg, from a story by Ann Druyan, Carl Sagan, from the novel by Carl Sagan

Contagious ★ 🅸🅱

Thriller   1997 · US · Colour · 86mins

This derivative and hokey thriller stars *Bionic Woman* and TV-movie veteran Lindsey Wagner in this poor man's version of *Outback*. A drug smuggler becomes ill after arriving by air from

Peru and, having been diagnosed with cholera, dies. Fearing a virulent epidemic of the highly contagious disease, a concerned doctor (Wagner), teams up with narcotics detective Elizabeth Pena to locate all those who might be infected. Together they race against time to find the source of the contagion. ▣

Lindsay Wagner *Hannah* • Elizabeth Pena *Lou* • Tom Wopat *Sam* • Ken Pogue *George Ryburn* • Brendan Fletcher *Brian* ■ *Dir* Joe Napolitano • *Scr* Sandy Kroopf

Contes Immoraux ★★★ 🔞
Erotic drama   1974 · Fr · Colour · 98mins

Using a visual style so sumptuous it's almost tactile, this collection of *Immoral Tales* is as much an exercise in artistic pastiche as erotic iconography. A different sexual taboo is tackled in each episode: the loss of virginity in *The Tide*; masturbation in *Thérèse, the Philosopher*; lesbianism in *Erzsebet Bathory*; and incest in *Lucrezia Borgia*. Yet director Walerian Borowczyk seems more interested in staging stylised tableaux than exploring either society's response to or the emotional make-up of his characters. In French with English subtitles. ▣

Lise Danvers *Julie* • Fabrice Luchini *André* • Charlotte Alexandra *Thérèse* • Paloma Picasso *Erzsebet Bathory* • Pascale Christophe *Istvan* • Florence Bellamy *Lucrezia Borgia* • Lorenzo Berinizi *Casar Borgia* ■ *Dir* Walerian Borowczyk • *Scr* Walerian Borowczyk, from the story *La Marée* by André Pieyre De Mandiargues

Continental Divide ★★★ 🅿🅶
Romantic comedy
1981 · US · Colour · 98mins

Although John Belushi will probably be only remembered for his gross clowning in the likes of *National Lampoon's Animal House* and *The Blues Brothers*, this under-rated romantic comedy demonstrated that he clearly possessed subtler gifts than that. In a not entirely successful attempt to re-create the golden age of Tracy and Hepburn, Belushi plays a slobbish, urbanised journalist who falls in and out of love with nature scientist Blair Brown. The leads work surprisingly well together and, although the pacing and tone is a little uneasy, the film is eminently watchable. ▣

John Belushi *Ernie Souchak* • Blair Brown *Nell Porter* • Allen Goorwitz [Allen Garfield] *Howard* • Carlin Glynn *Sylvia* • Tony Ganios *Possum* • Val Avery *Yablonowitz* • Bill Henderson *Train conductor* • Liam Russell *Deke* ■ *Dir* Michael Apted • *Scr* Lawrence Kasdan

Contraband ★★★ 🅿🅶
Spy thriller   1940 · UK · BW · 85mins

Directed by Michael Powell from a story by Emeric Pressburger, this is a neat wartime espionage thriller that depicts a London crawling with spies, rather in the manner of Alfred Hitchcock's *Sabotage* and *The Man Who Knew Too Much*. Powell makes brilliant use of the blackouts and includes one cheeky sequence when hundreds of unwanted plaster casts of Neville Chamberlain get shot to pieces. This would have been Deborah Kerr's first feature film, but all her scenes were left on the cutting room floor. ▣

Conrad Veidt *Captain Andersen* • Valerie Hobson *Mrs Sorensen* • Hay Petrie *Axel Skold/Erik Skold* • Esmond Knight *Mr Pidgeon* • Raymond Lovell *Van Dyne* ■ *Dir* Michael Powell • *Scr* Michael Powell, Brock Williams, from a story by Emeric Pressburger

Contraband Spain ★★ 🆄
Mystery   1955 · UK · Colour · 82mins

The same year he landed the lead in TV's *Robin Hood*, Richard Greene headlined this mediocre thriller as an American agent intent on rounding up a gang of smugglers operating out of Barcelona. Clearly aiming for a Graham Greene sort of entertainment, writer/ director Lawrence Huntington is hampered more by the paucity of his imagination than the meagreness of his resources. However, the acting is disappointing considering the calibre of the cast.

Richard Greene *Lee Scott* • Anouk Aimée *Elena Vargas* • Michael Denison *Ricky Metcalfe* • Jose Nieto *Pierre* • John Warwick *Bryan* • Philip Saville *Martin Scott* • Alfonso Estella *Marcos* • GH Mulcaster *Colonel Ingleby* ■ *Dir/Scr* Lawrence Huntington

The Contract ★★★
Drama   1980 · Pol · Colour · 111mins

A Warsaw doctor arranges the civil marriage of his son (Tadeusz Lomnicki) but his young wife refuses to go through with the subsequent church service. Nevertheless, her father-in-law goes ahead with the wedding reception, where sex, alcohol and family divisions crash the party. This is filmmaker Krzysztof Zanussi at his most straightforward, making an ironic, sometimes funny film that examines a wealthy strata of Polish society on the brink of its collapse. Interesting and entertaining, it contains a multitude of different languages, including English, and a standout performance by Leslie Caron as a kleptomaniac ballerina. In Polish, French, English, German and Swedish with subtitles.

Maja Komorowska *Dorota* • Tadeusz Lomnicki *Adam* • Magda Jaroszówna *Lilka* • Krzysztof Kolberger *Piotr* • Nina Andrycz *Olga* • Zofia Mrozowska *Maria* • Beata Tyszkiewicz *Nina* • Janusz Gajos *Boleslaw* • Leslie Caron *Penelope Wilson* ■ *Dir/Scr* Krzysztof Zanussi

Conundrum ★★★
Thriller   1995 · US · Colour · 97mins

The presence of Michael Biehn lifts this otherwise formulaic police thriller out of the ordinary. He plays a cop who, along with partner Marg Helgenberger, finds himself being hunted by a mysterious hit man, seemingly hired by the vengeful mobster who blames them for the death of his son. However, the case turns out to be more convoluted than it first appeared. The two leads work well together, there's an interesting enough support cast (Ron White, Peter MacNeill) and director Douglas Barr stages the action sequences with maximum efficiency. Contains swearing, violence and sex scenes.

Marg Helgenberger *Rose Ekberg* • Michael Biehn *Stash Horak* • Arthur Eng *Joey Tam* • Ron White • Peter MacNeill • Dan Lett ■ *Dir/Scr* Douglas Barr

The Convent ★★
Mystery drama
1995 · Fr/Por · Colour · 90mins

The legend of Faust is cloaked in the conventions of the Gothic novel in this intriguing, if baffling curio from Portuguese maestro Manoel de Oliveira. Strewing the action with casual literary references, the veteran director prompts us to muse on the nature of good and evil and the seductive power of truth and beauty as he lures us into the cavernous convent of Arrabida. John Malkovich is the scholar seeking to prove that Shakespeare was a Hispanic Jew, but for once he is outshone by Luis Miguel Cintra as the sinister guardian who tempts the professor with intellectual immortality in order to seduce his wife (Catherine Deneuve). In English, French and Portuguese with subtitles.

Catherine Deneuve *Helene* • John Malkovich *Michael Padovic* • Luis Miguel Cintra *Baltar* • Leonor Silveira *Piedade* • Duarte D'Almeida *Baltazar* ■ *Dir* Manoel de Oliveira • *Scr* Manoel de Oliveira, from a idea by Agustina Bessa-Luis

The Conversation ★★★★★ 🔞
Crime drama   1974 · US · Colour · 108mins

A small masterpiece from Francis Ford Coppola, who is superbly served by Gene Hackman playing a lonely surveillance expert tracking the movements and voices of Frederic Forrest and Cindy Williams, only to find that marital infidelity could be part of a murder plot. Coppola tweaks the idea to surreal effect, while editor Walter Murch orchestrates eavesdropping into a uniquely baffling wall of sound. Two years after Coppola's *The Godfather*, it's an intensely fascinating study of a man betrayed by what he thought was omnipotence. ▣

Gene Hackman *Harry Caul* • John Cazale *Stan* • Allen Garfield *"Bernie" Moran* • Frederic Forrest *Mark* • Cindy Williams *Ann* • Michael Higgins *Paul* • Elizabeth MacRae *Meredith* • Teri Garr *Amy* • Harrison Ford *Martin Stett* • Mark Wheeler *Receptionist* • Robert Shields *Mime* • Phoebe Alexander *Lurleen* ■ *Dir/Scr* Francis Ford Coppola • *Sound* Walter Murch, Arthur Rochester

Conversation Piece ★★★
Drama   1974 · It/Fr · Colour · 121mins

Luchino Visconti, having suffered a major stroke that confined him to a wheelchair, concocted this story about an ageing, homosexual professor who lives surrounded by art and books. Cut off from the real world both physically and intellectually, he finds his ivory tower invaded when a countess and her jet-setting brood rent the apartment upstairs. All the usual Visconti themes – the collision of cultures, the clash between old and new, the imminence of death – are covered in his customary opulent fashion. The film reunited the director with his *Leopard* star, Burt Lancaster.

Burt Lancaster *Professor* • Helmut Berger *Konrad Hubel* • Claudia Marsani *Lietta Brumonti* • Silvana Mangano *Bianca Brumonti* • Stefano Patrizi *Stefano* • Elvira Cortese *Erminia* • Claudia Cardinale *Professor's wife* ■ *Dir* Luchino Visconti • *Scr* Suso Cecchi D'Amico, Luchino Visconti, from a story by Enrico Medioli

Convict Cowboy ★★★ 🔞
Prison drama   1995 · US · Colour · 94mins

After a long, barren period in the eighties, John Voight has been popping up all over the place of late in films such as *Heat*, *Mission: Impossible* and *Anaconda*. This made-for-cable prison drama is one of his lesser-known movies, but he gives a typically gritty performance. Voight is the ex-rodeo champion now serving life for murder, who reluctantly takes a youthful convict (Kyle Chandler) under his protective wing, sparking off a conflict with drugs dealer Stephen McHattie. Director Rod Holcomb delivers an unusual spin on the jailbird genre and is rewarded with outstanding work from the strong cast. Contains swearing and violence. ▣

Jon Voight *Ry Weston* • Kyle Chandler *Clay Treyton* • Marcia Gay Harden *Maggie Sinclair* • Ben Gazzara *Warden Ferguson* • Glenn Plummer *Jimmy Latrell* • Stephen McHattie *Jagges Neff* • Brent Woolsey *Cody Stavert* ■ *Dir* Rod Holcomb • *Scr* Rick Way, Jim Lindsay

Convict 99 ★★ 🆄
Comedy   1938 · UK · BW · 84mins

Who else but Will Hay could apply for the headship of a school only to find himself appointed a prison governor and then get mistaken for the most dangerous inmate? Sadly, the film loses its way once Hay assumes power and introduces a regime so liberal that the lags proceed to take over. The great man is somewhat below par in this muddled and overlong comedy, while regular stooges Moore Marriott and Graham Moffat are disappointingly sidelined by a subplot involving Googie Withers posing as a prison-reforming countess whose embezzling leads to an unfunny slapstick finale. ▣

Will Hay *Benjamin Twist* • Moore Marriott *Jerry the Mole* • Graham Moffatt *Albert* • Googie Withers *Lottie* • Garry Marsh *Johnson* • Peter Gawthorne *Sir Cyril Wagstaffe* • Basil Radford *Governor* ■ *Dir* Marcel Varnel • *Scr* Marriott Edgar, Val Guest, Jack Davies, Ralph Smart, from a story by Cyril Campion

Convict 762 ★ 🔞
Science-fiction   1997 · US · Colour · 91mins

When a spaceship full of women conveniently crash-lands on a prison planet, they discover just two inhabitants left alive: a guard and Convict 762, the man responsible for massacring the entire prison population. The only problem is that *both* men claim to be the warden. Directed by Luca Bercovici, this inexplicably bad sci-fi movie would have been a waste of talent, if only there had been some talent involved in the first place. Contains violence, nudity and some swearing. ▣

Frank Zagarino *Vigo* • Billy Drago *Mannix* • Shannon Sturges *Nile* • Michole White *Austin* • Tawny Ellis *Reno* • Shae D'Lyn *Sheridan* • Charlie Spradling *Helena* • Merle Kennedy *Lincoln* ■ *Dir* Luca Bercovici • *Scr* J Reifel

Convicted ★★
Prison drama   1950 · US · BW · 90mins

Jailed for manslaughter after killing a man in a bar-room brawl, Glenn Ford becomes romantically entangled with Dorothy Malone, the daughter of governor Broderick Crawford. Ford's situation worsens, however, when he sees convict Millard Mitchell kill another inmate. Although strongly cast, well played and competently directed by Henry Levin, this prison melodrama is so monumentally routine that it quickly becomes predictable.

Glenn Ford *Joe Hufford* • Broderick Crawford *George Knowland* • Millard Mitchell *Malloby* • Dorothy Malone *Kay Knowland* • Carl Benton Reid *Capt Douglas* • Frank Faylen *Ponti* ■ *Dir* Henry Levin • *Scr* William Bowers, Fred Niblo Jr, Seton I Miller, from the play *The Criminal Code* by Martin Flavin

Convicted ★★★ **15**

Drama based on a true story
1986 · US · Colour · 90mins

What would the American teleplay industry do without sensational courtroom drama? This true-life story stars Lindsay Wagner, the unofficial queen of the TV movie, as a postman's wife determined to clear her husband's name after he is convicted of rape. You, the jury, are asked to decide whether this is yet another case of injustice or a fair verdict, and, in all honesty, it's hardly the most taxing of decisions. But director David Lowell Rich sows enough seeds of doubt and arouses sufficient indignation to hold the attention. Wagner crusades with typical conviction, while John Larroquette impresses as the man in the dock. ▦

Lindsay Wagner *Martha Forbes* • John Larroquette *Douglas Forbes* • Carroll O'Connor *Lewis May* • Gary Grubbs *Tom Cowan* • Jenny Lewis *Shelley Forbes* ■ *Dir* David Lowell Rich • *Scr* Jonathan B Rintels Jr

The Conviction of Kitty Dodds ★ **15**

Drama   1993 · US · Colour · 92mins

A bland "issue of the week" TV movie in which abused Veronica Hamel (*Hill Street Blues*) escapes from jail, gets recaptured and then tries to get her sentence reduced. Veering between mild exploitation and soap opera dramatics with no firm basis in either camp, the true story it's based on must surely have been far more interesting than what's on view in this histrionic melodrama. ▦

Veronica Hamel *Kitty Dodds* • Kevin Dobson *Chuck Hayes* • Mark Rolston *Charlie Dodds* • Keith Coulouris *Rodney Blackwell* • Neva Howell *Millie* • Johnetta Shearer *Indie* ■ *Dir* Michael Tuchner • *Scr* Doug Magee

Convicts ★★★

Period drama   1991 · US · Colour · 92mins

There's a major theme here – the dying days of the Old South – but it's compressed by playwright/screenwriter Horton Foote into almost allegorical terms. Robert Duvall acts his socks off as the senile plantation owner who fights in the Civil War and then hires black convicts to work the place, thus preserving slavery. It's this shadowy history that is recalled by Lukas Haas in the film's rather peculiar dramatic structure. Duvall's portrayal of senility makes the film worth seeing; the actor won his Oscar for another Foote work, *Tender Mercies*.

Robert Duvall *Soll Gautier* • Lukas Haas *Horace Robedaux* • Starletta DuPois *Martha Johnson* • James Earl Jones *Ben Johnson* •

Carlin Glynn *Asa* • Gary Swanson *Billy* • Mel Winkler *Jackson* ■ *Dir* Peter Masterson • *Scr* Horton Foote, from a play by Horton Foote

Convicts Four ★★

Prison drama   1962 · US · BW · 105mins

Also known as *Reprieve*, this dour prison drama takes a turn for the better when a convict is granted a stay of execution and takes up painting, a pastime which changes his uncaring character and leads to his eventual rehabilitation. Millard Kaufman's film is well-meaning and sincere, while Ben Gazzara, Vincent Price and Rod Stieger deliver strong performances. After a while, though, it becomes a bit dull.

Ben Gazzara *John Resko* • Stuart Whitman *Principal Keeper* • Ray Walston *Iggy* • Vincent Price *Carl Carmer* • Rod Steiger *Tiptoes* • Broderick Crawford *Warden* • Dodie Stevens *Resko's sister* • Sammy Davis Jr *Wino* ■ *Dir* Millard Kaufman • *Scr* Millard Kaufman, from the non-fiction book *Reprieve* by John Resko

Convoy ★★★ **PG**

Second World War drama
1940 · UK · BW · 85mins

A convoy of ships, led by captain Clive Brook, is intercepted in the North Sea by a German battleship. Its firepower destroys Brook's cruiser and kills the first officer (John Clements), who had been the lover of the skipper's wife. A taut, realistic and emotionally involving British flag-waver, well directed by the highly regarded Pen Tennyson, tragically killed in 1941 before he could fulfil his potential. Among the large supporting cast you can spot Michael Wilding, John Laurie and Stewart Granger; on the distaff side, there's Judy Campbell and Penelope Dudley-Ward.

Clive Brook *Captain Armitage* • John Clements *Lieutenant Crawford* • Edward Chapman *Captain Eckersley* • Judy Campbell *Lucy Armitage* • Edward Rigby *Mr Mathews* • Charles Williams *Shorty Howard* • Allan Jeayes *Commander Blount* • John Laurie *Gates* • Stewart Granger *Sutton* • Michael Wilding *Dot* • Penelope Dudley-Ward *Mabel* ■ *Dir* Pen Tennyson • *Scr* Pen Tennyson, Patrick Kirwan

Convoy ★★★ **15**

Comedy adventure
1978 · US · Colour · 105mins

Forget about the inanities of *Smokey and the Bandit*: this film remains the epitome of trucking movies. Kris Kristofferson is the heroic driver who thumbs his nose at authority and collects a disparate group of truckers in an epic journey across the US, which sees him cross the roadblocks of sheriff Ernest Borgnine. It's pretty lightweight fare for director Sam Peckinpah, but he builds an unstoppable momentum that makes you forget about the weak performances from Kristofferson and Ali MacGraw. The appalling title song by CW McCall, which is actually the source of the movie, was a massive hit at the time. ▦

Kris Kristofferson *Martin Penwald, "Rubber Duck"* • Ali MacGraw *Melissa* • Ernest Borgnine *Lyle Wallace, "Dirty"* • Burt Young *Bobby, "Pig Pen"* • Madge Sinclair *"Widow Woman"* ■ *Dir* Sam Peckinpah • *Scr* BWL Norton, from a song by CW McCall

Les Convoyeurs Attendent ★★★★ **15**

Comedy drama
1999 · Bel/Fr/Swi · BW · 93mins

Having impressed as the serial killer in *Man Bites Dog*, Benoît Poelvoorde surpasses himself in this bizarre black comedy from Belgium. As the ambulance-chasing photojournalist bullying his son to break the world door-opening record in order to win a car in a millennial contest, he combines tough love, class consciousness and repressed self-loathing to create a truly unique character whose muddled motives almost excuse his eccentric excesses. Yet the austere lyricism of Philippe Guilbert's monocrome landscapes, combined with director Benoît Mariage's astute mix of melodrama and macabre humour, also give this often disconcerting picture a real sense of social relevance. In French with English subtitles.

Benoît Poelvoorde *Roger* • Morgane Simon *Luise* • Bouli Lanners *Coach* • Dominique Baeyens *Mother* • Philippe Grand'Henry *Felix* • Jean-François Devigne *Michel* • Lisa LaCroix *Jocelyne* ■ *Dir* Benôt Mariage • *Scr* Benôt Mariage, Emmanuelle Bada, Jean-Luc Seigle

Coogan's Bluff ★★★ **15**

Crime drama   1968 · US · Colour · 90mins

Clint Eastwood still wore a cowboy hat in his first attempt to move from the western landscape into the contemporary urban setting, but under Don Siegel's taut direction he carried off the switch successfully. In many ways the forerunner of *Dirty Harry*, Eastwood's laconic Arizona sheriff tracking down a murderer in Manhattan was his first character to get upset by big city sleaze and escalating crime. A stylish and gritty action thriller which set the seal on Eastwood's screen persona for decades to come. ▦

Clint Eastwood *Walt Coogan* • Lee J Cobb *Sheriff McElroy* • Susan Clark *Julie* • Tisha Sterling *Linny Raven* • Don Stroud *Ringerman* • Betty Field *Mrs Ringerman* • Tom Tully *Sheriff McCrea* • Melodie Johnson *Millie* ■ *Dir* Don Siegel • *Scr* Herman Miller, Dean Reisner, Howard Rodman, from a story by Herman Miller

The Cook, the Thief, His Wife and Her Lover ★★★★ **18**

Black comedy drama
1989 · UK/Fr · Colour · 118mins

Avant-garde director Peter Greenaway's most accessible film to date is a truly elegant, shocking and transfixing experience. A Jacobean drama in contemporary clothing, this savage indictment of greed, power and control in today's wannabe society finds Helen Mirren memorably strutting her stuff in another risky, and risqué, performance, while manic Michael Gambon portrays evil personified. Memorably scored by Michael Nyman, Greenaway's stunning "designer dream" is sick, sexy and rude in about equal provocative proportions and totally unforgettable. Contains violence, swearing, sex scenes and nudity. ▦

Richard Bohringer *Richard Borst, the Cook* • Michael Gambon *Albert Spica, the Thief* • Helen Mirren *Georgina Spica, the Wife* • Alan

Howard *Michael, the Lover* • Tim Roth *Mitchel* • Gary Olsen *Spangler* • Liz Smith *Grace* • Alex Kingston *Adele* • Ian Dury *Terry Fitch* ■ *Dir/Scr* Peter Greenaway • *Cinematographer* Sacha Vierny • *Costume Designer* Jean-Paul Gaultier

Cookie ★★ **15**

Crime comedy   1989 · US · Colour · 89mins

Emily Lloyd is the mobster's daughter trying to keep dad out of trouble in this uneven comedy. Unfortunately, despite talents like Lloyd, Peter Falk and co-writer Nora Ephron being on board, director Susan Seidelman has still managed to make a bland, unfunny mess of a movie whose behind-the-scenes stories (Falk allegedly slapped Lloyd, who annoyed him, during a scene when he was supposed to fake it) are much more interesting than what's going on in front of the camera. Contains violence and swearing. ▦

Peter Falk *Dominick "Dino" Capisco* • Dianne Wiest *Lenore* • Emily Lloyd *Carmella "Cookie" Voltecki* • Michael V Gazzo *Carmine Taratino* • Brenda Vaccaro *Bunny* • Adrian Pasdar *Vito* • Lionel Stander *Enzo Della Testa* • Jerry Lewis *Arnold Ross* ■ *Dir* Susan Seidelman • *Scr* Nora Ephron, Alice Arlen

Cookie's Fortune ★★★ **12**

Comedy drama   1999 · US · Colour · 117mins

Director Robert Altman has a bizarre collection of hits and misses in his *oeuvre*, which ranges from the brilliance of *The Player* and *Short Cuts* to the mishmash of *Prêt-à-Porter*. *Cookie's Fortune* falls somewhere in the middle. This ensemble piece finds Glenn Close and Julianne Moore hamming it up as two sisters trying to cover up the "disgraceful" suicide of ageing relative Cookie, while simultaneously attempting to inherit her worldly goods. Cookie's more worthy heirs, rebel Liv Tyler and long standing handyman Charles S Dutton, cotton on to their strange shenanigans and, in an atmosphere of Deep South crawfish and jazz, justice is done. Contains some mild sex scenes.

Glenn Close *Camille* • Julianne Moore *Cora Duvall* • Liv Tyler *Emma Duvall* • Chris O'Donnell *Jason Brown* • Charles S Dutton *Willis Richland* • Patricia Neal *Jewel Mae "Cookie" Orcutt* • Ned Beatty *Lester Boyle* ■ *Dir* Robert Altman • *Scr* Anne Rapp

The Cool and the Crazy ★★★

Drama   1958 · US · BW · 78mins

Take a walk on the jive side with this cheap and cheerful juvenile delinquent classic starring James Dean wannabe Scott Marlowe. It's all here: seedy pushers, flaming car crashes, wild ones "hooked on smoke", service station hold-ups and rebels without a cause resorting to violence to feed their addictions. By teen exploitation standards of the era, however, this high school dope exposé is remarkably well-acted, fast-paced and realistic. Despite descending into hilariously moral *Reefer Madness* territory, they don't come any better than this.

Scott Marlowe *Bennie Saul* • Gigi Perreau *Amy* • Dick Bakalyan [Richard Bakalyan] *Jackie Barzan* • Dick Jones [Dickie Jones] *Stu Summerville* • Shelby Storck *Lt Sloan* ■ *Dir* William Witney • *Scr* Richard C Sarafian

U = SUITABLE FOR ALL   **Uc** = SUITABLE FOR ALL, ESPECIALLY FOR YOUNG CHILDREN (VIDEO ONLY)   **PG** = PARENTAL GUIDANCE

The Cool and the Crazy
★★ 18

Drama   1994 · US · Colour · 81mins

Alicia Silverstone is the big name draw
n this oddly subdued entry in one of a
series of B-movie remakes. She plays
a young bride, married to nice but dull
Jared Leto, who finds herself drawn
into a dangerous affair with bad boy
Matthew Flint. There's plenty of scope
for melodramatic excess here, but
Ralph Bakshi's direction is surprisingly
pedestrian and it lacks the knowing
humour of others in the series.
Nevertheless, Silverstone is as
watchable as ever and the rest of the
cast give it their all. Contains violence,
swearing and nudity. ▭

Alicia Silverstone *Roslyn* • Jared Leto *Michael*
• Jennifer Blanc *Joannie* • Matthew Flint *Joey*
• Bradford Tatum *Frankie* • Christine Harnos
Lorraine ■ *Dir/Scr* Ralph Bakshi

Cool as Ice
★★ PG

Drama   1991 · US · Colour · 87mins

Just what is it that makes singers
think they can act? Here rapper Vanilla
Ice (remember him?) proves that he
hasn't mastered the thespian art, as
he tries and fails to translate his
musical persona to the screen. Ice
rides into town with his posse like *The
Wild One*, and he's soon romancing
the kind of girl whose daddy wouldn't
approve of anyone, let alone someone
like Ice who's got hair that resembles
a bleached hedgehog. Still, the
music's catchy, and that's the most
important thing if you take *Cool as Ice*
at face value as the feature-length pop
video it is. Contains mild swearing. ▭

Vanilla Ice *Johnny Van Owen* • Kristin Minter
Kathy • Michael Gross *Gordon Winslow* •
Sydney Lassick *Roscoe McCallister* • Dody
Goodman *Mae McCallister* • Naomi Campbell
Singer at first club ■ *Dir* David Kellogg • *Scr*
David Stenn

Cool Blue
★ 15

Romantic comedy
1988 · US · Colour · 86mins

An early film role for Woody Harrelson,
better known at the time for playing
dumb barman Woody Boyd in the long-
running sitcom *Cheers*. Here he plays
an aspiring painter who loves, then
loses a girl (Ely Pouget). Realising his
life won't be the same without her, he
decides to track her down. A straight-
to-video cheapie, notable only for
featuring an uncredited cameo from
Sean Penn. ▭

Woody Harrelson *Dustin* • Ely Pouget
Christiane • Gloria LeRoy *Ida* • Hank Azaria
Buzz • Sean Penn *Phil the plumber* ■ *Dir/Scr*
Richard Shepard, Mark Mullin

A Cool, Dry Place
★★★ 15

Drama   1998 · US · Colour · 95mins

Not many people saw this vastly under-
rated drama about a single father who
puts his career as a high-powered
lawyer on hold to raise his five-year-old
son in a small town. Vince Vaughn is
awe-inspiring in the lead, and the rest
of the cast, which includes Joey Lauren
Adams (*Chasing Amy*) as his new
girlfriend and Monica Potter as his ex-
wife, is also terrific. *A Cool, Dry Place*
may not be as showy as some
dramas, but it has heart. ▭

Vince Vaughn *Russell Durrell* • Monica Potter
Kate • Joey Lauren Adams *Beth* • Devon
Sawa *Noah* • Bobby Moat *Calvin Durrell* ■ *Dir*
John N Smith • *Scr* Matthew McDuffie, from
the novel *Dance Real Slow* by Michael Grant
Jaffe

Cool Hand Luke
★★★★ 15

Prison drama   1967 · US · Colour · 121mins

One of the key American films of the
sixties, a subtle blend acknowledging
the needs of the individual and
respecting a freedom of spirit that
chimed perfectly with the "Summer of
Love" in which it was released.
Basically an old-fashioned chain-gang
movie – not much had changed at
Warner Bros since the days of Paul
Muni's *I Am a Fugitive from a Chain
Gang* – except that this time the tale is
told in stunning Technicolor. Paul
Newman is superb in the Muni role,
and both the prologue and the egg-
eating scene have become screen
classics. The religious symbolism does
get a little tiresome, but the movie is
clearly the career high point of director
Stuart Rosenberg. An immense
pleasure to watch, and a real credit to
Jack Lemmon's production company.
The film was also influential in the
massive popularity of Raybans! ▭

Paul Newman *Luke Jackson* • George
Kennedy *Dragline* • JD Cannon *Society Red* •
Lou Antonio *Koko* • Robert Drivas *Loudmouth
Steve* • Strother Martin *Captain* • Jo Van Fleet
Arletta • Clifton James *Carr* • Dennis Hopper
Babalugats ■ *Dir* Stuart Rosenberg • *Scr*
Donn Pearce, Frank R Pierson, from a novel by
Donn Pearce • *Cinematographer* Conrad Hall

Cool Runnings
★★★★ PG

Sports comedy based on a true story
1993 · US · Colour · 94mins

If someone had invented the story of a
Jamaican bobsleigh team entering the
Olympics, they'd have been laughed
out of the room. But, as the story is
true and Disney knows how to produce
feel-good material better than most,
what results is a hugely entertaining
comedy guaranteed to have you
cheering on the underdogs. Michael
Ritchie co-wrote the story on which the
film is based, no doubt drawing on his
directorial experiences of winter sports
Downhill Racer and sporting no-hopers
Bad News Bears. Admittedly, it's a
little predictable at times, but the
eager performances of John Candy and
his charges carry the day. Contains
some mild swearing. ▭ **DVD**

Leon *Derice Bannock* • Doug E Doug *Sanka
Coffie* • Rawle D Lewis *Junior Bevil* • Malik
Yoba *Yul Brenner* • John Candy *Irving Blitzer* •
Raymond J Barry *Kurt Hemphill* • Peter
Outerbridge *Josef Grool* • Paul Coeur *Roger* ■
Dir Jon Turteltaub • *Scr* Michael Goldberg,
Tommy Swerdlow, Lynn Siefert, from a story
by Lynn Siefert, Michael Ritchie

The Cool Surface
★★★ 18

Thriller   1993 · US · Colour · 88mins

This erotic thriller enjoyed a successful
life on video, particularly when it was
discovered that Teri Hatcher, the star
of TV's *The New Adventures of
Superman*, takes her clothes off with
some enthusiasm. That said, this
stylish and faintly disturbing drama is
much classier than most "skeletons in
the closet" features. Robert Patrick is
the shy writer who finds reality and
fiction becoming dangerously mixed
when he gets involved with his
beautiful neighbour (Hatcher). ▭

Robert Patrick *Jarvis Scott* • Teri Hatcher *Dani
Payson* • Matt McCoy *Chazz Stone* • Ian
Buchanan *Terrence* ■ *Dir/Scr* Erik Anjou

The Cool World
★★★★

Drama   1963 · US · BW · 105mins

A semi-underground movie and a near-
classic, *The Cool World* depicts the
lives of street gangs in the black
ghetto of Harlem. Director Shirley
Clarke had been born into affluent Park
Avenue society and seemed destined
to be a choreographer before she
started making movies. Her first
feature, *The Connection*, dealt frankly
with heroin addiction, and this, her
second, has the same documentary
style and poetic rawness. Using non-
professional actors, it shows life as it
is lived (and lost) on the streets, with
jazz and compassion but without
condescension. It premiered to acclaim
at the Venice Film Festival and became
an international arthouse hit.

Hampton Clanton *Duke* • Carl Lee *Priest* •
Yolanda Rodriguez *Luanee* • Clarence Williams
III *Blood* • Marilyn Cox *Miss Dewpoint* •
Georgia Burke *Grandma* • Gloria Foster *Mrs
Custis* • Bostic Felton *Rod* ■ *Dir* Shirley
Clarke • *Scr* Shirley Clarke, Carl Lee, from the
play by Robert Rossen, Warren Miller, from
the novel by Warren Miller

Cool World
★★ 15

Part-animated comedy fantasy
1992 · US · Colour · 97mins

Director Ralph Bakshi looked set to
produce an adult version of *Who
Framed Roger Rabbit* with this mix of
animation and live action, but
somewhere down the line it ran out of
steam. Gabriel Byrne is the creator of
the comic *Cool World*, who discovers
that his fictional creation – *femme
fatale* Holli Would (voiced by Kim
Basinger) – actually exists.She wants
to be real; all that stands in her way is
Brad Pitt, the human detective of the
cartoon world. Although Bakshi has
come up with some stunning animated
characters, they are not always
seamlessly integrated with their live-
action counterparts, and the cast
hardly looks comfortable with the
confusing, unfunny script. Contains
some violence and swearing. ▭

Kim Basinger *Holli Would* • Gabriel Byrne *Jack
Deebs* • Brad Pitt *Detective Frank Harris* •
Michele Abrams *Jennifer Malley* • Janni Brenn-
Lowen *Mom Harris* • William Frankfather *Cop*
• Carrie Hamilton *Comic bookstore cashier* •
Greg Collins *Cop* • Murray Podwal *Store
patron* ■ *Dir* Ralph Bakshi • *Scr* Mark Victor,
Michael Grais, Larry Gross, from a story by
Ralph Bakshi, Frank Mancuso Jr • *Animation*
Bruce Woodside

Coopersmith: Sweet Scent of Murder
★ 15

Mystery   1992 · US · Colour · 80mins

Just how many more unconventional
lawmen do American programme
planners think we can take? Grant
Show has the misfortune to star in this
risible TV movie as a motorcycling
insurance investigator who peels off
the leathers to probe the supposedly
accidental death of a racing driver's
wife. It was made as a pilot for a
prospective TV series that never
materialised. You deserve a medal if
you sit through this misfiring thriller
that is more predictable than night
following day. ▭

Grant Show *CD Coopersmith* • Colleen Coffey
Allison Grey • Clark Johnson *Sergeant Mike
Delaney* • James McDonnell *Jennings
Whitehurst* • Nicolas Surovy *Jesse Wilder* ■
Dir Peter Crane • *Scr* Peter S Fischer

Cooperstown
★★★★

Sports drama   1993 · US · Colour

Even if your usual reaction to the word
"sport" is to reach for the remote,
think twice with this superior TV movie.
You don't need to know much about
baseball to enjoy the performances of
Alan Arkin and Graham Greene in this
wisecracking comedy drama about
memory, friendship and regret. Having
never forgiven recently deceased
catcher Greene for the play that cost
their team a big game, Arkin's
forgotten pitcher sets out for the
Cooperstown Hall of Fame to set the
record straight. Beautifully written by
playwright Lee Blessing, the banter
between Arkin and Greene – whose
ghost accompanies Arkin on his
journey – is as sharp as it's priceless.

Alan Arkin *Harry Willette* • Ed Begley Jr *Dave
Cormeer* • Josh Charles *Jody* • Paul Dooley
Sid Wiggins • Graham Greene *Raymond
Maracle* • Charles Haid *Little Eddie McVee* ■
Dir Charles Haid • *Scr* Lee Blessing

Le Cop
★★★★ 18

Comedy   1985 · Fr · Colour · 102mins

The wonderful Philippe Noiret is the
French equivalent to Walter Matthau or
an over-lunched great dane. Here he
stars as a Parisian cop, René, who
lives with a tart in Montmartre, bets on
the gee-gees, readily accepts bribes
and buys lavish meals with the ill-
gotten gains. More smalltime crook
than cop, in fact, especially when he
inducts his straightlaced rookie partner
(Thierry Lhermitte) into the joys of
crime. Whenever Hollywood turns its
attention to police corruption they
make *Serpico* or *Prince of the City*; in
France it's a cause for comedy, a
shrug, a deep drag on a Gauloise and
c'est la vie! Noiret makes this skate
along the moral edge, a balancing act
to marvel at. In French with English
subtitles. ▭

Philippe Noiret *René* • Thierry Lhermitte
François • Régine *Simone* • Grace De Capitani
Natacha • Julien Guiomar *Bloret* • Pierre Frag
Pierrot • Claude Brosset *Inspector Vidal* •
Albert Simono *Inspector LeBlanc* ■ *Dir* Claude
Zidi • *Scr* Claude Zidi, Didier Kaminka

Cop
★★★★ 18

Crime thriller   1988 · US · Colour · 105mins

A dazzling, dangerous performance
from James Woods lifts what could
otherwise have been another variation
on the *Dirty Harry* theme into a
different league altogether. Woods
plays an obsessive homicide detective,
bordering on the psychotic, who
becomes convinced there is a serial
killer on the loose in Los Angeles. The
only common link appears to be
feminist book shop manager Lesley
Ann Warren. Director James B Harris
fails to capture the twisted sickness of
James Ellroy's source novel, but more

than compensates by cranking up the tension to unbearable levels. Woods is simply mesmerising, and there's fine support from Charles Durning and Charles Haid as a twisted policeman. Contains swearing, violence and sex scenes.

James Woods *Lloyd Hopkins* • Lesley Ann Warren *Kathleen McCarthy* • Charles Durning *Dutch Pelz* • Charles Haid *Whitey Haines* • Raymond J Barry *Fred Gaffney* • Randi Brooks *Joanie Pratt* • Steven Lambert *Bobby Franco* • Christopher Wynne *Jack Gibbs* ■ *Dir* James B Harris • *Scr* James B Harris, from the novel *Blood on the Moon* by James Ellroy

Le Cop II ★★★ 15

Comedy drama 1989 · Fr · Colour · 102mins

Claude Zidi's *Le Cop* was a huge hit in France and nabbed the nation's top film award, the César. A sequel was therefore inevitable, requiring Philippe Noiret and Thierry Lhermitte to reprise their roles as the dirty cop and his idealistic young apprentice. The story revolves around the latter's decision to go straight – an appalling prospect for his partner, who takes bribes and drugs race horses. Once again the low-life of Paris is beautifully observed, and there is a classic scene in a bank vault. However, the portrait of a police force riddled with corruption makes the whole experience rather depressing. In French with English subtitles.

Philippe Noiret *René* • Thierry Lhermitte *François* • Guy Marchand *Felix Brisson* • Line Renaud *Simone* • Grace De Capitani *Natacha* • Michel Aumont *Commissioner Bloret* • Jean-Pierre Castaldi *Guy Portal* • Jean-Claude Brialy *Banker* ■ *Dir* Claude Zidi • *Scr* Claude Zidi, Simon Michael, Didier Kaminka

Cop and a Half ★ PG

Comedy thriller 1993 · US · Colour · 88mins

This feeble comedy thriller is the perfect yardstick for measuring just how far Burt Reynolds had fallen from grace since his peak in the seventies. It wastes the talents of a star normally at ease with such frivolity, and the efforts of the rest of the cast are sunk by a heavy script and ponderous direction from former *Happy Days* star Henry Winkler. It was the TV comedy series *Evening Shade* that called a halt to Reynold's demise (he won an Emmy for his performance), and his fortunes improved further following the box-office success of *Boogie Nights*. Contains some mild swearing and violence.

Burt Reynolds *Nick McKenna* • Norman D Golden II *Devon Butler* • Ruby Dee *Rachel* • Holland Taylor *Captain Rubio* • Ray Sharkey *Fountain* • Sammy Hernandez *Raymond* • Frank Sivero *Chu* • Rocky Giordani *Quintero* ■ *Dir* Henry Winkler • *Scr* Arne Olsen

Cop au Vin ★★★★ 15

Drama 1984 · Fr · Colour · 104mins

There's usually a slap-up meal in every Chabrol movie, so how typical of him to name one after a cornerstone of French cuisine, *Poulet au Vinaigre*, but the English title is even wittier. The story involves a contentious property deal, a clutch of corpses, a postman and his crippled mother, played by Stéphane Audran. Yet the movie is dominated by Jean Poiret, who arrives halfway through as an out-of-town detective with a nose for a suspect and the stomach for a big dinner. As ever, the combination of Chabrol's mordant tone and a certain technical flair produces a delectable dish. A sequel, *Inspector Lavardin* followed in 1986, with Poiret reprising his role. In French with English subtitles.

Jean Poiret *Inspector Lavardin* • Stéphane Audran *Mme Cuno* • Michel Bouquet *Hubert Lavoisier* • Jean Topart *Philippe Morasseau* • Lucas Belvaux *Louis Cuno* • Pauline Lafont *Henriette Uriel* ■ *Dir* Claude Chabrol • *Scr* Dominique Roulet, Claude Chabrol, from the novel *Une Mort en Trop* by Dominique Roulet

A Cop for the Killing ★★ 15

Thriller based on a true story 1990 · US · Colour · 88mins

This police thriller rarely rises above cliché, despite managing to provide a fine balance between action thrills and character portrayals. One of a series of cop outings by director Dick Lowry, it does, however, capture the ebb and flow of police routine as the film probes the murder of an undercover narcotics cop and the effect this has on the morale of his colleagues. In this fact-based tale, some authentic scenes manage to emerge from the generally mediocre material.

James Farentino *Ray Wiltern* • Charles Haid *Tommy Quinn* • Steven Weber *Matthew Fisher* • Susan Walters *Julie Tobias* • Harold Sylvester *Art Regan* • Dan Lauria *Kadazian* • Jane Daly *Barbara* • Clyde Kusatsu *Matsumo* ■ *Dir* Dick Lowry • *Scr* Philip Rosenberg

Cop Land ★★★★ 18

Police drama 1997 · US · Colour · 110mins

A real change of pace for Sylvester Stallone in a touching role as an out-of-shape New Jersey cop with a hearing disability and zero self-esteem, who uncovers police corruption among his major league police friends. Stallone gives it his all (including a dramatic weight gain for the role) and is easily the match of the terrific cast, which includes Robert De Niro, Harvey Keitel and a really nasty Ray Loitta. Writer/director James Mangold's urban western succumbs to a few clumsy contrivances, but the quality of acting and an inspired climactic twist are recommendation enough. Contains swearing, violence and some nudity. DVD

Sylvester Stallone *Sheriff Freddy Heflin* • Robert De Niro *Moe Tilden* • Harvey Keitel *Ray Donlan* • Ray Liotta *Gary Figgis* • Peter Berg *Joey Randone* • Janeane Garofalo *Deputy Cindy Betts* • Robert Patrick *Jack Rucker* • Michael Rapaport *Murray Babitch* • Annabella Sciorra *Liz Randone* • Cathy Moriarty *Rose Donlan* ■ *Dir/Scr* James Mangold

Copacabana ★ U

Musical comedy 1947 · US · BW · 91mins

No, not the Barry Manilow musical that enjoyed a brief spell in London's West End, but a staggeringly unscintillating pairing of two stars whose careers were all behind them: the great Groucho Marx, here shorn of his siblings and reduced to wearing a *real* moustache, and none other than Carmen Miranda, who has difficulty accommodating her usual headgear on this cheapie's pathetic budget. Director Alfred E Green does what he can in the circumstances. Unless you're a die-hard fan of the two stars, however, this turkey's a non-starter.

Groucho Marx *Lionel Q Devereaux* • Carmen Miranda *Carmen Novarro/Fifi* • Steve Cochran *Steve Hunt* • Gloria Jean *Anne* • Ralph Sanford *Liggett* • Andy Russell *Andy Russell* ■ *Dir* Alfred E Green • *Scr* Laslo Vadnay, Alan Boretz, Howard Harris, Sydney P Zelinka, from a story by Laslo Vadnay

Copacabana ★★★ U

Musical romance 1985 · US · Colour · 95mins

In a TV movie inspired by Barry Manilow's pop hit, the man himself plays an aspiring composer who falls in love with a comely dancer (Annette O'Toole) at the famous Copacabana nightclub in New York City. The owner of a nightclub in Havana is intent on making her a star, forcing the lovers to part – but not before they belt out a few pleasing tunes. Manilow is charming, O'Toole has talent to spare, and the result is a good, old-fashioned romp. Manilow later used the song as the basis for a West End musical.

Barry Manilow *Tony Starr* • Annette O'Toole *Lola Lamar* • Joseph Bologna *Rico Castelli* • Estelle Getty *Bella Stern* • James Callahan *Dennis Riley* • Andra Akers *Pamela Devereaux* ■ *Dir* Waris Hussein • *Scr* James Lipton, from the song by Barry Manilow, Bruce Sussman, Jack Feldman

Copper Canyon ★★★

Western 1950 · US · Colour · 83mins

Forties beauty Hedy Lamarr had just made something of a comeback in the blockbuster *Samson and Delilah* when Paramount put her in this intriguing western, set just after the Civil War and directed by John Farrow (Mia's father). The script is by Jonathan Latimer, better known for *noir*-ish thrillers like *The Big Clock*, also directed by Farrow. Beautiful colour photography by Oscar-winning Charles Lang enhances the action, while Ray Milland is well cast as a Confederate officer working undercover to foil crooks out to exploit festering north-south antagonisms.

Ray Milland *Johnny Carter* • Hedy Lamarr *Lisa Roselle* • Macdonald Carey *Lane Travis* • Mona Freeman *Caroline Desmond* • Harry Carey Jr *Lt Ord* • Frank Faylen *Mullins* ■ *Dir* John Farrow • *Scr* Jonathan Latimer, from a story by Richard English

Cops and Robbers ★★★

Crime drama 1973 · US · Colour · 88mins

This rattling crime caper is taken at such a lick by director Aram Avakian that you don't notice the inconsistencies and contrivances in the plot. Cliff Gorman and Joseph Bologna give winning performances as a couple of New York cops who use a parade for returning astronauts as cover for an audacious Wall Street raid. The heist is a doddle, however, compared to laundering the loot through the Mafia. The frantic action is given extra zip by the splendid score, composed by Michel Legrand with a little help from Ennio Morricone.

Cliff Gorman *Tom* • Joseph Bologna *Joe* • Dick Ward [Richard Ward] *Paul Jones* • Shepperd Strudwick *Eastpoole* • Ellen Holly *Mrs Wells* • John Ryan [John Ryan] *Patsy O'Neill* • Nino Ruggeri *Mr Joe* • Gayle Gorman *Mary* ■ *Dir* Aram Avakian • *Scr* Donald E Westlake, from his novel

Cops and Robbersons ★★ PG

Comedy 1994 · US · Colour · 88mins

Jack Palance's Oscar-winning turn in *City Slickers* opened up the possibility of a new and unlikely comedy career for the veteran actor. Apart from this straight-to-video effort, though, it never materialised. Basically, it's one of those efforts where most of the creative energy seems to have gone into dreaming up the snappy concept, in this case *Stakeout* meets *National Lampoon's Vacation*. Palance is the grouchy cop on surveillance duty, who is forced to move in with dysfunctional suburbanites the Robbersons, headed up by TV cop show fan Chevy Chase. Chase, in amiable buffoon mode, makes a nice foil for Palance and there are creditable supporting turns from Robert Davi and Dianne Wiest, but director Michael Ritchie's heart doesn't appear to be in the project. Contains swearing and nudity.

Chevy Chase *Norman Robberson* • Jack Palance *Jack Stone* • Dianne Wiest *Helen Robberson* • Robert Davi *Osborn* • David Barry Gray *Tony Moore* • Jason James Richter *Kevin Robberson* • Fay Masterson *Cindy Robberson* ■ *Dir* Michael Ritchie • *Scr* Bernie Somers

The Cops Are Robbers ★★★ 15

Crime drama based on a true story 1990 · US · Colour · 94mins

City police corruption (their rural cousins are presumed to be as white as a picket fence) has provided Hollywood with crime drama for years. Sidney Lumet's *Serpico* and *Prince of the City* are classy examples of the genre. Though not in that league, *The Cops Are Robbers* neatly avoids cliché, helped by strong performances from Ed Asner and Ray Sharkey. Given his humanitarian politics off-screen, Asner's acceptance of a role dealing with justice is no surprise. Contains violence, swearing and drug abuse.

Ray Sharkey *Captain Gerry Clemente* • Edward Asner [Ed Asner] *Superintendent Jake Quinn* • George Kennedy *Commissioner Dan Kirkland* • Robert F Lyons *Benny Brown* • James Keach *Frank Moran* • Steve Railsback *Jimmy Donnelly* ■ *Dir* Paul Wendkos • *Scr* Bill Bleich [William Bleich], from the book by Gerald W Clemente, Kevin Stevens

The Copter Kids ★★ U

Drama 1976 · UK · Colour · 56mins

Proving that the Children's Film Foundation wasn't the only source of kid-friendly films in the seventies, this breezy mini-feature doubtless kept audiences amused in the dying days of the Saturday matinée. But the tale of a gang who team up with a helicopter crew to confound some cattle rustlers won't have quite the same appeal for the youngsters of today, who are so rarely challenged to use their imagination by the special effects that litter their beloved blockbusters. Producer/director Ronnie Spencer handles the action sequences adequately enough, but, with the exception of Sophie Ward, he struggles to animate the cast.

Derek Fowlds *Captain Peters* • Sophie Neville *Liz Peters* • Sophie Ward *Jill Peters* • Jonathan Scott-Taylor *Bill Peters* • Paul

Chambers *David Owen* • Kate Dorning *Gwen Owen* • Robert Twitcher *Bob Evans* ■ *Dir* Ronnie Spencer • *Scr* Patricia Latham

Copycat ★★★★ 18
Thriller 1995 · US · Colour · 117mins

In this inventive, stylish and gripping thriller, tough detective Holly Hunter teams up with agoraphobic criminal psychologist Sigourney Weaver in the hunt for a serial killer duplicating the crimes of his most notorious predecessors. Thanks to director Jon Amiel's imaginative direction – the bathroom-set climax is a crackerjack shocker – a super-smart script and the two leads attacking their roles with gusto, this mimic murder mystery is one of the best crafted chillers in the *Se7en* tradition. Contains swearing and violence 🎞 **DVD**

Sigourney Weaver *Helen Hudson* • Holly Hunter *MJ Monahan* • Dermot Mulroney *Ruben Goetz* • William McNamara *Peter Foley* • Harry Connick Jr *Daryll Lee Cullum* • Will Patton *Nicoletti* • John Rothman *Andy* • Shannon O'Hurley *Susan Schiffer* ■ *Dir* Jon Amiel • *Scr* Ann Biderman, David Madsen

Coquette ★★★
Melodrama 1929 · US · BW · 75mins

Back in the silent era, Mary Pickford's little-girl mannerisms earned her the title of "The World's Sweetheart". This was her first talkie, in which she plays a Southern belle whose flirtation with handsome beau Johnny Mack Brown gets her into big trouble. Pickford won an Oscar for the film, though it was really in recognition of her previous work; the public weren't quite ready to see her as a Deep South damsel.

Mary Pickford *Norma Besant* • Johnny Mack Brown *Michael Jeffery* • Matt Moore *Stanley Wentworth* • John St Polis *Dr John Besant* ■ *Dir* Sam Taylor • *Scr* Sam Taylor, John Grey, Allen McNeil, from the play by George Abbott, Anne P Bridges

Corky ★ U
Drama 1972 · US · Colour · 88mins

A grease monkey from the Deep South (Robert Blake), more in love with his car than his long-suffering wife (Charlotte Rampling), becomes insanely jealous when she gets a job, believing she is having an affair. There's a fight here and a car chase there, but the opportunity for a gripping drama is lost somewhere in the middle. Bruce Geller was so incensed at the way his central character was treated that he had his screenwriting credit removed, though he was still billed as producer.

Robert Blake *Corky* • Charlotte Rampling *Corky's wife* • Patrick O'Neal *Randy* • Christopher Connelly *Billy* • Pamela Payton-Wright *Rhonda* • Ben Johnson *Boland* • Laurence Luckinbill *Wayne* • Paul Stevens *Tobin Hayes* ■ *Dir* Leonard Horn • *Scr* Eugene Price, Bruce Geller (uncredited)

The Corn Is Green ★★★
Period drama 1945 · US · BW · 113mins

Bette Davis stars as legendary spinster schoolteacher Lilly Moffat in a very Warner Bros version of Emlyn Williams's distinguished play. Unfortunately, this film seriously betrays its theatrical origins, not just in

its hokey plot about Davis trying to send her star pupil (John Dall, far too callow) to Oxford, but also in its relentlessly phoney Hollywood studio/ Welsh village setting. Nevertheless, Davis is mighty fine and the supporting cast is excellent, particularly Nigel Bruce as the local squire. In 1979, Katharine Hepburn starred in a made-for-TV version shot on actual Welsh locations that was actually a far superior telling of the tale.

Bette Davis *Lilly Moffat* • John Dall *Morgan Evans* • Joan Lorring *Bessie Watty* • Nigel Bruce *Squire* • Rhys Williams *Mr Jones* • Rosalind Ivan *Mrs Watty* • Mildred Dunnock *Miss Ronberry* • Arthur Shields *Will Davis* ■ *Dir* Irving Rapper • *Scr* Casey Robinson, Frank Cavett, from the play by Emlyn Williams

The Corn Is Green ★★★
Drama 1979 · US · Colour

Emlyn Williams's play had been filmed in 1945, with 37-year-old Bette Davis as Miss Moffat, the dedicated spinster schoolteacher in a bleak Welsh mining village who helps a young miner (John Dall) gain a scholarship to Oxford. This version, made for TV, stars 72-year-old Katharine Hepburn, with Ian Saynor as the lad. Too old for the role, and with her incipient Parkinson's disease already evident, Hepburn nonetheless conveys the character's passionate idealism, and is compulsively watchable. The film marked the last of the star's ten collaborations with director George Cukor (by then aged 80), who directs with competence, and benefits from the authentic locations in Wales on which Hepburn insisted.

Katharine Hepburn *Lilly Moffat* • Ian Saynor *Morgan Evans* • Bill Fraser *Squire* • Patricia Hayes *Mrs Watty* • Anna Massey *Miss Ronberry* • Artro Morris *John Goronwy Jones* • Dorothea Phillips *Sarah Pugh* • Toyah Willcox *Bessie Watty* ■ *Dir* George Cukor • *Scr* Ivan Davis, from the play by Emlyn Williams

Cornered ★★★ U
Crime drama 1945 · US · BW · 62mins

This is a pleasant little toughie, not quite a thriller and a shade too bright for a *film noir*, and directed with consummate skill by up-and-coming Edward Dmytryk. Powell here continued to erase all memories of his Busby Berkeley days at Warners as he delivers a high-octane performance, chasing down his wife's murderer in Second World War Argentina, in a Buenos Aires peopled with veteran character actors like Walter Slezak and Morris Carnovsky. The women (Micheline Cheirel, Nina Vale) are a shade uninteresting, but Powell's tough demeanour more than compensates.

Dick Powell *Gerard* • Walter Slezak *Incza* • Micheline Cheirel *Madame Jarnac* • Nina Vale *Senora Camargo* • Edgar Barrier *DuBois* • Morris Carnovsky *Santana* • Steven Geray *Senor Camargo* • Jack La Rue [Jack LaRue] *Diego* ■ *Dir* Edward Dmytryk • *Scr* John Paxton, from a story by John Wexley, from a title by Ben Hecht

Corridors of Blood ★★★ 15
Horror drama 1962 · UK · BW · 82mins

Compassionate surgeon Boris Karloff, seeking to perfect an experimental anaesthetic in 19th-century London, gets involved with two loathsome

graverobbers (Christopher Lee and Francis de Wolff) who force him to sign false death certificates. Boasting beautiful black-and-white photography, this robust horror yarn is a great combination of gas-lit melodrama, pseudo-historic science and body-snatcher gruesomeness. Director Robert Day's picture is reminiscent of Hogarth and marked the first time Karloff and Lee worked together. 🎞

Boris Karloff *Dr Bolton* • Betta St John *Susan* • Christopher Lee *Resurrection Joe* • Finlay Currie *Supt Matheson* • Adrienne Corri *Rachel* ■ *Dir* Robert Day • *Scr* Jean Scott Rogers • *Cinematographer* Geoffrey Faithfull

Corrina, Corrina ★★★ U
Romantic drama 1994 · US · Colour · 110mins

Forget the casting here of Ray Liotta, better known nowadays for his psychotic roles. Here he's merely the lone parental contrivance that enables housekeeper Whoopi Goldberg to get to grips with Tina Majorino, a sad little seven-year-old who has stopped speaking since the death of her mother. These two make one of the most appealing double acts of recent years and it's a shame that the conventions of romantic comedy end up dictating the direction in which their relationship develops. As the action is set in 1959, there are some barbed comments about interracial love affairs and the obstacles educated black women had to overcome to fulfil their potential. 🎞

Whoopi Goldberg *Corrina Washington* • Ray Liotta *Manny Singer* • Tina Majorino *Molly Singer* • Wendy Crewson *Jenny Davis* • Larry Miller *Sid* • Erica Yohn *Grandma Eva* • Jenifer Lewis *Jevina* • Joan Cusack *Jonesy* • Harold Sylvester *Frank* • Don Ameche *Grandpa Harry* ■ *Dir/Scr* Jessie Nelson

The Corruptor ★★ 18
Crime action 1999 · US · Colour · 109mins

With muscle man Mark Wahlberg and cool Hong Kong star Chow Yun-Fat on board, you'd expect this tale of police corruption, Chinese gangs and murder in New York's Chinatown to be action-packed from start to finish. Instead, this is a surprisingly plodding and confusing thriller that's low on interesting set pieces. James Foley's direction is surprisingly uninspired and, while both stars have charisma to spare, they're bogged down by the unnecessarily convoluted plot. Contains violence.

Chow Yun-Fat *Nick Chen* • Mark Wahlberg *Danny Wallace* • Ric Young *Henry Lee* • Paul Ben-Victor *Schabacker* • Andrew Pang *Willy Ung* • Byron Mann *Bobby Vu* • Elizabeth Lindsey *Louise Deng* • Brian Cox *Sean Wallace* ■ *Dir* James Foley • *Scr* Robert Pucci

The Corsican Brothers ★★★ U
Swashbuckling adventure 1941 · US · BW · 95mins

Douglas Fairbanks Jr summons up some of the swashbuckling bravado associated with his father in this adaptation of the Alexandre Dumas story from producer Edward Small, who had already made films of *The Man in the Iron Mask* and *The Count of Monte Cristo*. Fairbanks got the dual role of

separated Siamese twins, Mario and Lucien – one rich, the other poor – who reunite to seek out those who killed their relatives. It dawdles in places, Akim Tamiroff is more laughable than villainous and it lacks a proper heroine. Yet Fairbanks is worth watching, if only for his imitation of his father's mannerisms. 🎞

Douglas Fairbanks Jr *Mario Franchi/Lucien Franchi* • Ruth Warrick *Isabelle* • Akim Tamiroff *Colorra* • HB Warner *Dr Paoli* • Henry Wilcoxon *Count Franchi* • J Carrol Naish *Lorenzo* ■ *Dir* Gregory Ratoff • *Scr* George Bruce, from the novel by Alexandre Dumas

Corvette K-225 ★★ U
Second World War drama 1943 · US · BW · 98mins

This wartime flag-waver is an unabashed tribute to the crews of the Corvettes, the nimble craft that escorted freighters across the Atlantic, taking on the U-boats that preyed on them. Randolph Scott is the skipper who falls in love with Ella Raines, whose brother is on Scott's ship and whose other brother has already been killed in action. Below decks, Robert Mitchum takes a minor role in one of the 18 movies he made in 1943.

Randolph Scott *Lt Cmdr MacClain* • James Brown (2) *Paul Cartwright* • Ella Raines *Joyce Cartwright* • Barry Fitzgerald *Stooky O'Meara* • Andy Devine *Walsh* • Walter Sande *Evans* • Richard Lane *Admiral* • James Flavin *Gardner* • Robert Mitchum *Shepard* ■ *Dir* Richard Rosson • *Scr* John Rhodes Sturdy

Corvette Summer ★★★
Comedy adventure drama 1978 · US · Colour · 104mins

The directing debut of Matthew Robbins, co-writer (with Hal Barwood) of Steven Spielberg's *The Sugarland Express*, is a youth movie very much in the mould of *American Graffiti*. Mark Hamill, then fresh from the original *Star Wars*, stars as a young man who spends most of his time fondling, stroking and polishing the love of his life: a restored and customised Chevrolet Corvette. When the car is stolen, Hamill goes looking for it with the help of trainee prostitute Annie Potts. Robbins's directing career proved to be fairly undistinguished after this promising first feature.

Mark Hamill *Kent Dantley* • Annie Potts *Vanessa* • Eugene Roche *Ed McGrath* • Kim Milford *Wayne Lowry* • Richard McKenzie *Principal* • William Bryant *Police PR* • Philip Bruns *Gil* ■ *Dir* Matthew Robbins • *Scr* Hal Barwood, Matthew Robbins

Cosa Nostra: the Last Word ★★ 18
Crime drama 1995 · US · Colour · 90mins

The Mafia and the movie business collided to glorious effect in *Get Shorty*, and this intriguing, if flawed, crime drama covers much the same ground. Timothy Hutton is the cynical journalist who has made his name exposing Mafia activities. To help out his shady chum Joe Pantoliano, he travels to Hollywood to convert his columns into a gangster movie. However, when he falls for troubled stripper Michelle Burke, he is faced with an awkward moral dilemma. It's a much more cerebral affair than *Shorty*, but the fabulous cast ensures it is always watchable. Contains swearing, violence and nudity. **DVD**

Timothy Hutton *Martin* • Joe Pantoliano *Doc* • Michelle Burke *Sara* • Chazz Palminteri *Ricky* • Tony Goldwyn *Stan* • Cybill Shepherd *Kiki Taylor* • Roma Downey *Roxy* • Joe Cortese *Jimmy* • Jimmy Smits *Actor* • Richard Dreyfuss *Larry* ■ *Dir/Scr* Tony Spiridakis

Cosh Boy ★★★
Crime drama 1952 · UK · BW · 72mins

Packed with incidents that scandalised the middle-class moralists who read sensationalist tabloids behind drawn curtains, Lewis Gilbert's film purported to be a realistic portrait of juvenile delinquency. It may have seemed daring at the time, but four decades on this overwrought study of alienation and rebellion seems very tame and stands only as a testament to an innocent age when people were more easily shocked. James Kenney is the most gentle thug ever to terrorise the streets of London, but Joan Collins comes closer to life as the nice girl doomed to a life of misery.

James Kenney *Roy Walsh* • Joan Collins *Rene Collins* • Betty Ann Davies *Elsie Walsh* • Robert Ayres *Bob Stevens* • Hermione Baddeley *Mrs Collins* • Hermione Gingold *Queenie* • Nancy Roberts *Gran Walsh* • Stanley Escane *Pete* ■ *Dir* Lewis Gilbert • *Scr* Lewis Gilbert, Vernon Harris, from the play *Master Crook* by Bruce Walker

Cosi ★★★
Comedy 1996 · Ausl · Colour · 100mins

A typically broad Australian comedy about a slacker named Lewis (Ben Mendelsohn) who takes a job as dramatic director at an insane asylum. One of the inmates is obsessed with staging the Mozart opera *Cosi Fan Tutte*, which Lewis directs against all the odds and the wishes of the asylum's administrators. Mark Joffe's film is quite funny most of the way through, but it veers into cheap sentimentality towards the end.

Ben Mendelsohn *Lewis* • Barry Otto *Roy* • Toni Collette *Julie* • Aden Young *Nick* • Rachel Griffiths *Lucy* • Pamela Rabe *Ruth* • Colin Friels *Errol* ■ *Dir* Mark Joffe • *Scr* Louis Nowra, from his play

The Cosmic Man ★ **U**
Science-fiction 1959 · US · BW · 69mins

John Carradine is the mysterious creature from another planet who arrives on earth in a huge weightless globe. His presence unleashes a debate between the military authorities who want to blow him up, and the scientific establishment who want to keep him alive. This dismal science-fiction programme-filler is mercifully short in length and equally short of action and ideas. In these days of special effects blockbusters and advanced scientific knowledge, it's deader than a Dodo. ▭

Bruce Bennett *Dr Karl Sorenson* • John Carradine *Cosmic man* • Angela Greene *Kathy Grant* • Paul Langton *Colonel Mathews* • Scotty Morrow *Ken Grant* • Lyn Osborn *Sergeant Gray* • Walter Maslow *Dr Richie* ■ *Dir* Herbert Greene • *Scr* Arthur C Pierce

The Cossacks ★ **U**
Historical drama 1959 · It/Fr · Colour · 113mins

Edmund Purdom was a sort of downmarket Tony Curtis who went to Hollywood before eventually settling for Italian rubbish like this and a British TV series called *Sword of Freedom*. Purdom was rarely without a sword, a dirk or a smirk, but he kept a straight face for this costume epic set in Imperial Russia, despite moments that surpass Monty Python for silliness. Italian dialogue dubbed into English.

Edmund Purdom *Shamil* • John Drew Barrymore *Giamal* • Georgia Moll [Giorgia Moll] *Tatiana* • Pierre Brice *Boris* • Elena Zareschi *Patimat* ■ *Dir* Giorgio Rivalta, Victor Tourjansky • *Scr* Victor Tourjansky

Cottage to Let ★★★ **U**
Second World War thriller 1941 · UK · BW · 86mins

The American release title *Bombsight Stolen* is a clue to what Alfred Hitchcock would call the "McGuffin" (or plot device) that drives this lively wartime propaganda piece from director Anthony Asquith. The story of a Nazi kidnap plot set in the wilds of Scotland is pretty much par for the course, but what sets this picture apart is the truly extraordinary cast. Michael Wilding and John Mills have to settle for supporting roles behind Leslie Banks and Alastair Sim, but stealing everyone's thunder is debutant George Cole (a protégé of Sim's) as the cockney evacuee who becomes a hero.

Leslie Banks *John Barrington* • Alastair Sim *Charles Dimble* • John Mills *Lieutenant George Perrey* • Jeanne de Casalis *Mrs Barrington* • Carla Lehmann *Helen Barrington* • George Cole *Ronald Mittsby* • Michael Wilding *Alan Trentley* ■ *Dir* Anthony Asquith • *Scr* Anatole de Grunwald, JOC Orton, from the play by Geoffrey Kerr

The Cotton Club ★★★ **15**
Period drama 1984 · US · Colour · 123mins

Those of you who think that Richard Gere only has room for Buddhism, models and the odd good film may not know that he can also play the cornet. This big news is the only point of interest in a performance which seems to veer on the edge of a hypnotic trance. Still, in this tale of music and the mob in toe-tappin' Harlem, the blame must lie with director Francis Coppola who, in expending his energy on the visual clout and the showbiz scenes (some of which are fab), underdirects his actors and forgets about plot. Nevertheless, Bob Hoskins as the club owner and Fred Gwynne as his henchman certainly make their mark, while the Duke Ellington soundtrack is sheer creative bliss. Contains swearing. ▭

Richard Gere *Dixie Dwyer* • Gregory Hines *Sandman Williams* • Diane Lane *Vera Cicero* • Bob Hoskins *Owney Madden* • Lonette McKee *Lila Rose Oliver* • James Remar *Dutch Schultz* • Nicolas Cage *Vincent Dwyer* • Allen Garfield *Abbadabba Berman* • Fred Gwynne *Frenchy Demange* • Gwen Verdon *Tish Dwyer* ■ *Dir* Francis Coppola [Francis Ford Coppola] • *Scr* William Kennedy, Francis Ford Coppola, from a story by William Kennedy, Francis Ford Coppola, Mario Puzo, from a pictorial history by James Haskins

Cotton Comes to Harlem ★★★★
Comedy thriller 1970 · US · Colour · 96mins

Although a respected actor and civil rights activist, Ossie Davis put much more than his reputation on the line when he directed this abrasive crime comedy on the streets of Harlem. Residents and militant campaigners alike were appalled that he should choose to further the cause with such a seemingly flippant picture. But the script (adapted by Davis and Arnold Perl from the novel by Chester Himes) gives Raymond St Jacques plenty of scope to make social statements as he and Godfrey Cambridge investigate preacher Calvin Lockhart's dodgy pan-African association. A huge commercial success, this rousing movie opened the door for other black film-makers.

Godfrey Cambridge *Grave Digger Jones* • Raymond St Jacques *Coffin Ed Johnson* • Redd Foxx *Uncle Bud* • Cleavon Little *Lo Boy* ■ *Dir* Ossie Davis • *Scr* Ossie Davis, Arnold Perl, from a novel by Chester Himes

Cotton Mary ★★ **15**
Period drama 1999 · UK · Colour · 123mins

This handsomely mounted study of the socio-racial rifts that divided India in the years after Independence proves once again that, while Ismail Merchant is a producer of exemplary taste, his approach to direction lacks finesse and stifles potentially interesting ideas with ponderous performances and rarified aestheticism. He's not helped here by co-director Madhur Jaffrey, whose snobbish Anglo-Indian nurse overwhelms a drama already awash with unsympathetic characters, notably Greta Scacchi as an Englishwoman with post-natal depression and James Wilby as her adulterous husband. Reducing peripheral personae to caricatures, the film disappointingly shies away from its political themes.

Greta Scacchi *Lily MacIntosh* • Madhur Jaffrey *Cotton Mary* • James Wilby *John MacIntosh* • Sarah Badel *Mrs Evans* • Riju Bajaj *Mugs* • Gerson Da Cunha *Doctor Correa* • Joanna David *Mrs Smythe* • Neena Gupta *Blossom* ■ *Dir* Ismail Merchant, Madhur Jaffrey • *Scr* Alexandra Viets

Cotton Queen ★★ **U**
Comedy 1937 · UK · BW · 84mins

Long regarded as a mere journeyman, German-born director Bernard Vorhaus has enjoyed something of a renaissance of late. This was the last film he made in this country before relocating to Hollywood, although it's hard to see why the studio executives would have been impressed by this underfunded production, a creaky comedy in which mill owner's daughter Mary Lawson goes snooping in a rival's factory and falls for his son.

Will Fyffe *Bob Todcastle* • Stanley Holloway *Sam Owen* • Mary Lawson *Joan* • Helen Haye *Margaret Owen* • Jimmy Hanley *Johnny Owen* • Gibson Gowland *Jailor* ■ *Dir* Bernard Vorhaus • *Scr* Louis Golding, Scott Pembroke, from a story by Syd Courtnenay, Barry Peake

The Couch Trip ★★★ **15**
Comedy 1988 · US · Colour · 93mins

Perhaps director Michael Ritchie, who made the chilling *Downhill Racer* with

Robert Redford, took his cue for this loose comic ramble from his father, a professor of psychology. In this often too slack offering, Ritchie is thankfully well served by the infectious comic nonsense of Dan Aykroyd, as a mental patient who carries out a nifty scam and becomes a celebrity therapist in LA. It is Aykroyd's wild, high-flying invention that turns this skinny offering into a one-man party at which the star has the most fun. Even Walter Matthau, wheeled on to be typically lugubrious and crusty, is dull by comparison. Contains swearing. ▭

Dan Aykroyd *John W Burns Jr* • Walter Matthau *Donald Becker* • Charles Grodin *Dr George Maitlin* • Donna Dixon *Dr Laura Rollins* • Richard Romanus *Harvey Michaels* • Mary Gross *Vera Maitlin* • Chevy Chase *Condom father* ■ *Dir* Michael Ritchie • *Scr* Steven Kampmann, Will Porter, Sean Stein, from a novel by Ken Kolb

Counsellor-at-Law ★★★
Drama 1933 · US · BW · 77mins

Adapted by Elmer Rice from his own successful Broadway play, and impeccably directed by William Wyler, the movie details the professional and personal crises that beset a brilliant, self-made Jewish lawyer (John Barrymore) whose future is affected by the surfacing of a past indiscretion. In the role created on stage by Jewish actor Paul Muni, who apparently refused the screen role for fear of being typecast, Barrymore gives a compelling performance, with excellent support from Doris Kenyon as his unsympathetic gentile wife and Bebe Daniels as the secretary who loves him. Solid, substantial drama.

John Barrymore *George Simon* • Bebe Daniels *Regina Gordon* • Doris Kenyon *Cora Simon* • Onslow Stevens *John P Tedesco* • Isabel Jewell *Bessie Green* • Melvyn Douglas *Roy Darwin* • Thelma Todd *Lillian La Rue* • Marvin Kline *Weinberg* • John Qualen *Breitstein* ■ *Dir* William Wyler • *Scr* Elmer Rice, from his play

Count Dracula ★★ **12**
Horror 1970 · Sp/It/W Ger/UK · Colour · 96mins

Fed up by Hammer playing fast and loose with the famous vampire figure, Christopher Lee joined forces with Spanish schlock-meister Jess (Jesus) Franco to make the most faithful adaptation ever of Bram Stoker's 1897 novel. The end result falls way short of those good intentions thanks to an even lower budget than Hammer standards, numerous script inconsistencies, camera shadows in full view and Franco's usual deadly direction. However, Lee comes closest to Stoker's physical approximation of the evil bloodsucker (an old man whose white hair turns darker after each transfusion), and some of the early sequences (the grief-stricken mother crying at the castle gate, Dracula reminiscing about battling Turks in the 15th Century) are extremely faithful to the book. Contains some violence. ▭

Christopher Lee *Dracula* • Herbert Lom *Van Helsing* • Klaus Kinski *Renfield* • Soledad Miranda *Lucy Westenra* • Maria Rohm *Mina Harker* • Fred Williams *Jonathan Harker* • Jack Taylor *Quincy Morris* • Paul Muller *Dr Seward* ■ *Dir* Jesus Franco • *Scr* Jesus Franco,

August Finochi, Harry Alan Towers, Carlo Fadda, Milo G Cuccia, Dietmar Behnke, from the novel *Dracula* by Bram Stoker

Count Five and Die ★★★

Second World War spy drama
1957 · UK · BW · 91mins

When plans to peddle false information to the Nazis about the whereabouts of the forthcoming D-Day invasion begin to come unstuck, British intelligence officer Nigel Patrick is made alert to the possibility of their being a traitor in his team. The obvious suspect is glamorous new radio operator Annemarie Düringer, with whom Patrick's second-in-command (Jeffrey Hunter) is in love. Though covering familiar territory that's well past its sell-by date, this efficient British Second World War spy drama is nonetheless suspenseful and entertaining.

Jeffrey Hunter *Ranson* • Nigel Patrick *Howard* • Anne-Marie Düringer [Annemarie Düringer] *Rolande* • David Kossoff *Mulder* • Claude Kingston *Willem* • Philip Bond *Piet* • Rolf Lefebvre *Faber* • Larry Burns *Martins* • Arthur Gross *Jan* ■ *Dir* Victor Vicas • *Scr* Jack Seddon, David Pursall

The Count of Monte Cristo ★★★

Period adventure   1934 · US · BW · 113mins

This is still regarded as the best of the many versions of Alexandre Dumas's tale, though that doesn't say much for all the others. Bear in mind, too, that this was made in 1934 and will seem slow and creaky by modern standards. Robert Donat plays the hero, Edmond Dantes, rotting in jail and plotting revenge on the people who put him there. Donat was a singularly reluctant star: whisked from England to Hollywood, he made the film and promptly headed home to make *The 39 Steps* for Alfred Hitchcock.

Robert Donat *Edmond Dantes* • Elissa Landi *Mercedes* • Louis Calhern *Raymond de Villefort Jr* • Sidney Blackmer *Mondego* • Raymond Walburn *Danglars* • OP Heggie *Abbe Foria* • William Farnum *Captain Leclere* ■ *Dir* Rowland V Lee • *Scr* Philip Dunne, Dan Totheroh, Rowland V Lee, from the novel by Alexandre Dumas

The Count of Monte Cristo ★★★ U

Historical adventure
1974 · UK · Colour · 98mins

A lavish adaptation of the classic Alexandre Dumas tale about the disguised nobleman who exacts revenge on those who had him imprisoned. Director David Greene struggles with the more static jail sequences, but once the action switches to Paris he makes the most of the plush settings and the period costumes to bring the picture to life. Richard Chamberlain is a sturdy Edmond Dantes and Louis Jourdan (who played the lead in the 1961 French version) does well as De Villefort. But nearly spoiling everything is Tony Curtis who, as the villainous Mondego, confuses behaving like a star with acting. 🎞

Richard Chamberlain *Edmond Dantes* • Tony Curtis *Mondego* • Trevor Howard *Abbe Faria* • Louis Jourdan *De Villefort* • Donald Pleasence

Danglars • Kate Nelligan *Mercedes* ■ *Dir* David Greene • *Scr* Sidney Carroll, from the novel by Alexandre Dumas

The Count of the Old Town ★★★

Comedy   1935 · Swe · BW · 84mins

This film marked Ingrid Bergman's screen debut, although she is pretty much a peripheral character in a freewheeling tour around Stockholm's bohemian quarter. Valdemar Dahlquist topped the bill as the leader of a group of amiable wastrels who spend much of the picture carousing and careering around the town to keep out of the clutches of the local constabulary. Playing a maid in one of their watering holes, Bergman also has some love scenes with Edvin Adolphson, but contemporary critics paid more attention to her puppy fat than her acting. In Swedish with English subtitles.

Valdemar Dahlquist *The Count* • Sigurd Wallen *The Gherkin* • Eric Abrahamsson *Borstis* • Weyler Hildebrand *Detective Goransson* • Artur Cederborgh *Engstrom* • Ingrid Bergman *Elsa Edlund* ■ *Dir* Edvin Adolphson, Sigurd Wallen • *Scr* Arthur Natorp, Siegfried Fischer

Count the Hours ★★

Crime drama   1953 · US · BW · 76mins

When an itinerant farm worker is sentenced to death for murder, his wife and a lawyer, who shows more than a passing interest in her, battle to prove his innocence and bring the true culprit to book. MacDonald Carey, Teresa Wright, John Craven and Dolores Moran (as Carey's rich fiancée) star in an efficient directorial exercise for Don Siegel, who employs a terrific pace to make bricks from straw and maintain the tension in what is essentially no more than a so-so programme-filler.

Macdonald Carey *Doug Madison* • Teresa Wright *Ellen Braden* • John Craven *George Braden* • Dolores Moran *Paula Mitchener* • Edgar Barrier *Gillespie* • Jack Elam *Max Verne* ■ *Dir* Don Siegel • *Scr* Doane R Hoag, Karen De Wolf, from a story by Doane R Hoag

Count Three and Pray ★★★

Drama   1955 · US · Colour · 102mins

Not to be confused with the similarly titled *Count Five and Die* (1958), this grim, bucolic period drama marked the screen debut of Broadway and TV actress Joanne Woodward, soon-to-be Mrs Paul Newman, as a tough-minded orphan gal caught up in the mayhem caused by new preacher in town Van Heflin, a pastor with a past. Notable today for its early use of CinemaScope, the movie benefits from fine acting from Heflin and Woodward, and a noteworthy typecast villain in Raymond Burr.

Van Heflin *Luke Fargo* • Joanne Woodward *Lissy* • Phil Carey [Philip Carey] *Albert Loomis* • Raymond Burr *Yancey Huggins* • Allison Hayes *Georgina Decrais* • Myron Healey *Floyd Miller* ■ *Dir* George Sherman • *Scr* Herb Meadow

Count Yorga, Vampire ★★★

Horror   1970 · US · Colour · 89mins

Robert Quarry entered the "Horror Hall of Fame" thanks to his convincing turn

here as an amoral Californian bloodsucker in this low-budget grossout, blending crude horror with macabre wit. Originally planning to make a sex film (hence the inclusion of numerous soft-core starlets as vampire brides in the cast), director Bob Kelljan saw the light when *Night of the Living Dead* mopped up at the box office. So in came the ashen-faced undead feasting on cat's intestines, plus other moments of shock sleaze.

Robert Quarry *Count Yorga* • Roger Perry *Dr Hayes* • Michael Murphy *Paul* • Michael Macready *Michael* • Donna Anders *Donna* • Judith Lang *Erica* ■ *Dir/Scr* Bob Kelljan

Count Your Blessings ★★ U

Comedy   1959 · US · Colour · 102mins

As fatuous as its title, this soft-focus MGM confection has one of those plots that everyone hates: a loathsome child brings together an estranged couple, in this case hard-working Deborah Kerr and perpetually wooden Rossano Brazzi. Director Jean Negulesco proves yet again that, in the words of noted critic Andrew Sarris, his career falls into two clear halves: before CinemaScope, with tight movies such as *The Mask of Dimitrios* and *Johnny Belinda*, and after Scope, with soggy romances like *Three Coins in the Fountain* and this one. Not even Maurice Chevalier can help.

Deborah Kerr *Grace Allingham* • Rossano Brazzi *Charles-Edouard de Valhubert* • Maurice Chevalier *Duc de St Cloud* • Martin Stephens *Sigismond* • Tom Helmore *Hugh Palgrave* ■ *Dir* Jean Negulesco • *Scr* Karl Tunberg, from the novel *The Blessing* by Nancy Mitford

Countdown ★★★★ U

Drama   1968 · US · Colour · 97mins

A fascinating early work from Robert Altman about the planning of a mission to the Moon and its effect on the lives of those involved. There are early signs of what would become Altman trademarks (the large cast; the cool, documentary air) and he coaxes fine, naturalistic performances from James Caan and Robert Duvall (later to be reunited in *The Godfather*) as the two astronauts, only one of whom will go on the mission. 🎞

James Caan *Lee Stegler* • Joanna Moore *Mickey Stegler* • Robert Duvall *Chiz* • Barbara Baxley *Jean* • Charles Aidman *Gus* • Steve Ihnat *Ross Llewellyn* • Michael Murphy *Rick* ■ *Dir* Robert Altman • *Scr* Loring Mandel, from the novel *The Pilgram Project* by Hank Searls

Countdown ★★ 18

Action thriller   1996 · US · Colour · 86mins

A cheap and not particularly cheerful spin on the barmy bomber theme popularised by *Speed*. An almost unrecognisable Lori Petty, brunette rather than her usual blonde, is the hard-nosed FBI agent on the trail of someone who seems intent on blowing up university lecturers. When she captures her girlfriend, the bomber turns his attention to the agents themselves. The only other well-known face in the cast, James LeGros, sleepwalks through his role as a police lieutenant, and director Keoni Waxman fails to hide the deficiencies in both plot and budget. 🎞

Lori Petty *Sara Davis* • Jason London *Chris Murdoch* • James LeGros *Lieutenant* ■ *Dir/Scr* Keoni Waxman

The Counterfeit Contessa ★★★ U

Romantic comedy
1994 · US · Colour · 87mins

In American sitcoms such as *The Naked Truth*, Téa Leoni has usually been cast as the wealthy Wasp. In this slight but amiable romantic comedy, though, she plays a working-class Brooklyn girl who dreams of finding romance with the rich and sophisticated set that frequent the upmarket deli where she works. Her dreams look set to come true when she is mistaken for an Italian aristocrat at a fashion show, but her charade soon leads to complications. Leoni is better than the material on offer, and she shines above a largely anonymous cast, among whom DW Moffett and Holland Taylor are probably the best-known. 🎞

Téa Leoni *Gina Nardino* • David Beecroft *Sinclair Gresham* • DW Moffett *Dawson Gresham* • Holland Taylor *Wallace* • Susan Walters *Palmer* • Willem Keane *Vinnie Nardino* • Nikki DeBoer [Nicole deBoer] *Helena Everett* ■ *Dir* Ron Lagomarsino • *Scr* Scott Davis Jones, Christine Burrill, Randi Johnson, from a story by Christine Burrill, Randi Johnson

The Counterfeit Traitor ★★★

Second World War spy drama
1962 · US · Colour · 140mins

Adapted from Alexander Klein's book about the true-life exploits of a Swedish undercover agent, this is a slickly-made espionage story, but with too few moments of nail-biting tension to justify its excessive running time. As the oil importer posing as a Nazi sympathiser, William Holden hurtles across northern Europe with some conviction, and is well supported in his endeavours by the likes of Lilli Palmer, Eva Dahlbeck and Klaus Kinski. But while writer/director George Seaton makes glossy use of his locations and keeps the dialogue terse and credible, he too often dawdles when the action demands a bit of dash.

William Holden (1) *Eric Erickson* • Lilli Palmer *Marianne Mollendorf* • Hugh Griffith *Collins* • Ernst Schroder *Baron Von Oldenbourg* • Eva Dahlbeck *Ingrid Erickson* • Ulf Palme *Max Gumpel* • Carl Raddatz *Otto Holtz* ■ *Dir* George Seaton • *Scr* George Seaton, from a book by Alexander Klein

The Counterfeiters ★★

Crime thriller   1948 · US · BW · 73mins

Sam Newfield was such a prolific B-movie director that he occasionally used the pseudonyms Sherman Scott or Peter Stewart to cover up just how many sub-standard programme fillers he actually churned out. This "Peter Stewart" effort is slightly above his usual average, and he might have been better advised to release it under his own name. Playing against type, John Sutton is the Scotland Yard flatfoot on the trail of Hugh Beaumont's funny money gang. Considering he had just come off the back of a series of classic horror Bs, it's a shame to see Lon Chaney Jr wasted in an undemanding supporting turn.

John Sutton *Jeff MacAllister* • Doris Merrick *Margo* • Hugh Beaumont *Philip Drake* • Lon Chaney Jr *Louie* • George O'Hanlon *Frankie* • Douglas Blackley *Tony* • Herbert Rawlinson *Norman Talbott* ■ *Dir* Peter Stewart [Sam Newfield] • *Scr* Fred Myton, Barbara Worth, from a story by Maurice H Conn

Counterforce ★★ 15

Action adventure 1987 · US · Colour · 90mins

A pretty dire action thriller, with faintly embarrassing turns from a group of older stars who really should have known better. The "counterforce" of the title consists of a mismatched bag of mercenaries hired to protect a nice Arabian leader. The likes of George Kennedy, Louis Jourdan, Isaac Hayes and Robert Forster give this utterly predictable venture a marquee value that it never deserves. ▦

Jorge Rivero *Harris* • George Kennedy *Vince Colby* • Andrew Stevens *Nash* • Isaac Hayes *Ballard* • Louis Jourdan *Kassar* • Kevin Bernhardt *Sutherland* • Robert Forster *The dictator* ■ *Dir* J Anthony Loma • *Scr* Douglas Borton, Carlos Vassalo

Counterpoint ★★

Second World War drama
1967 · US · Colour · 106mins

This film offers a rare chance to see Charlton Heston in an evening suit instead of biblical robes or a Roman toga. He plays an American conductor who, along with his 70-strong orchestra, is captured by the Germans in Belgium during the Battle of the Bulge. Nazi general Maximilian Schell has orders to shoot all prisoners, but will spare the lives of the musicians if they play a concert. The Los Angeles Philharmonic Orchestra pulls out all the stops for the musical extracts, which are by far the most convincing moments in an otherwise implausible story. Contains some swearing.

Charlton Heston *Lionel Evans* • Maximilian Schell *General Schiller* • Kathryn Hays *Annabelle Rice* • Leslie Nielsen *Victor Rice* • Anton Diffring *Colonel Arndt* • Linden Chiles *Lieutenant Long* ■ *Dir* Ralph Nelson • *Scr* Joel Oliansky, James Lee, from the novel *The General* by Alan Sillitoe

Counterspy ★★ U

Comedy thriller 1953 · UK · BW · 68mins

Typical "quota quickie" about a ring of spies who use an innocuous nursing home as their hideout. Some topicality is given to the otherwise threadbare plot – the spies are after plans for jet engines, and there's a chase through one of London's newest tourist attractions, the Festival Gardens on the South Bank. B-movie regular Dermot Walsh gets duped into espionage, Hermoine Baddeley camps it up as a clairvoyant, and Alexander Gauge is the villain.

Dermot Walsh *Manning* • Hazel Court *Clare Manning* • Hermoine Baddeley *Del Mar* • Alexander Gauge *Smith* • James Vivian *Larry* • Archie Duncan *Jim* • Frederick Schrecker *Plattnauer* • Hugh Latimer *Barlow* • Bill Travers *Rex* • Beryl Baxter *Girl* ■ *Dir* Vernon Sewell • *Scr* Gary Elmes, Michael Lefevre

Countess Dracula ★★★ 18

Horror 1970 · UK · Colour · 89mins

In order to masquerade as her own daughter, an ageing countess begins bathing in the blood of virgins to restore her youth. The first lady of British horror movies, Ingrid Pitt, excels in this colourful hokum, which gives a new meaning to the word bloodbath. She is ably supported by Nigel Green as the faithful retainer who procures her victims, Sandor Eles as her dashing love interest, and a host of Hammer stalwarts as the typically irate villagers. Based on the legend of notorious Hungarian countess Elizabeth Bathory, the film atones for its lack of terror with a brittle atmosphere of regret and decay. ▦

Ingrid Pitt *Countess Elisabeth Nadasdy* • Nigel Green *Captain Dobi* • Sandor Eles *Imre Toth* • Maurice Denham *Master Fabio* • Lesley-Anne Down *Ilona* • Patience Collier *Julia* ■ *Dir* Peter Sasdy • *Scr* Jeremy Paul, from a story by Alexander Paal, Peter Sasdy, Gabriel Ronay

A Countess from Hong Kong ★★

Romantic comedy
1967 · UK · Colour · 122mins

To misjudge Sophia Loren and Marlon Brando so completely in this clumsy romantic comedy requires an enormous lapse of judgement. And Charles Chaplin, as director, sadly disappointed fans eagerly awaiting his first film in ten years. The result is hugely embarrassing, with Brando surly instead of suave as the diplomat who finds Loren, as the Russian émigrée aristocrat, stowed away in his cabin. Tippi Hedren, though, as Brando's wife – his diplomatic baggage, as she says – injects a touch of pleasant irony when she appears near the end.

Marlon Brando *Ogden Mears* • Sophia Loren *Natascha* • Sydney Chaplin *Harvey Crothers* • Tippi Hedren *Martha* • Patrick Cargill *Hudson* • Margaret Rutherford *Miss Gaulswallow* • Michael Medwin *John Felix* • Oliver Johnston *Clark* ■ *Dir/Scr* Charles Chaplin

The Countess of Monte Cristo ★★

Musical 1948 · US · BW · 79mins

The last screen appearance of charming blonde-haired, blue-eyed Norwegian Olympic ice-skating champion Sonja Henie, who made several highly successful films in the late thirties and early forties when her competitive days were over. Sadly, this is not one of them. The one-joke plot has Henie and Olga San Juan as Norwegian barmaids posing as a countess and her maid at a luxury hotel, where the witless proceedings are enlivened by three songs from San Juan and six skating turns from Henie. Romance is provided by the star's off-screen skating partner, Michael Kirby.

Sonja Henie *Karen Kirsten* • Olga San Juan *Jenny Johnsen* • Michael Kirby *Paul von Cram* • Dorothy Hart *Peg Manning* • Arthur Treacher *Managing director* ■ *Dir* Frederick De Cordova • *Scr* William Bowers, from the film by Walter Reisch

Country ★★★ PG

Drama 1984 · US · Colour · 105mins

Iowa farmers Jessica Lange and Sam Shepard survive a twister, but face foreclosure and bankruptcy when the US government demands the full and immediate return on a huge loan. Very much a personal project for Lange (she also served as co-producer), this social drama may beat its "big message" drum a little too loudly, but it also provides a convincing portrait of how harsh country life was during the Depression. It was the second on-screen pairing (after *Frances*) of real-life partners Shepard and Lange, the latter winning an Oscar nomination for her down-to-earth performance. ▦

Jessica Lange *Jewell Ivy* • Sam Shepard *Gil Ivy* • Wilford Brimley *Otis* • Matt Clark *Tom McMullen* • Therese Graham *Marlene Ivy* • Levi L Knebel *Carlisle Ivy* • Jim Haynie *Arlon Brewer* • Sandra Seacat *Louise Brewer* ■ *Dir* Richard Pearce • *Scr* William D Wittliff

Country Dance ★★★

Drama 1970 · UK · Colour · 112mins

In *Country Dance* Peter O'Toole is ideally cast as – wait for it – Sir Charles Henry Arbuthnot Pinkerton Ferguson, a dipsomaniac Scots aristocrat who once canoodled with his sister in the barn and has been besotted by her ever since. But the sister, Susannah York, is now married to Michael Craig. Incest as a theme has always been a risky business and this accordingly bombed at the box-office, perhaps because this title – it was originally *Brotherly Love* – threatened clogs and bagpipes. But director J Lee Thompson does what he can with the material, while O'Toole is just inches away from the funny farm.

Peter O'Toole *Sir Charles Ferguson* • Susannah York *Hilary Dow* • Michael Craig *Douglas Dow* • Harry Andrews *Brigadier Crieff* • Cyril Cusack *Dr Maitland* • Judy Cornwell *Rosie* • Brian Blessed *Jock Baird* • Robert Urquhart *Auctioneer* ■ *Dir* J Lee Thompson • *Scr* James Kennaway

The Country Doctor ★★

Drama 1936 · US · BW · 93mins

Jean Hersholt, who arguably played more doctors than any other Hollywood actor, is his usual solid, sympathetic self in this backwoods drama set in Canada, which involves a diphtheria outbreak, the fight to build a hospital and the birth of quintuplets to one of the doctor's patients. Inspired by the famous Dionne quintuplets, this version features real newsreel footage and the quins themselves playing their fictional counterparts. Folksy, worthy and old-fashioned, this historical slice of exploitative nostalgia was directed by Henry King.

Jean Hersholt *Dr John Luke* • June Lang *Mary MacKenzie* • George "Slim" Summerville [Slim Summerville] *Constable Jim Ogden* • Michael Whalen *Tony Luke* • Dorothy Peterson *Nurse Katherine Kennedy* • Robert Barrat *MacKenzie* • Jane Darwell *Mrs Graham* ■ *Dir* Henry King • *Scr* Sonya Levien, from a story by Charles E Blake

The Country Girl ★★★

Drama 1954 · US · BW · 104mins

Grace Kelly won a Best Actress Oscar for putting on glasses and looking after alcoholic hubby Bing Crosby in this version of Clifford Odets's turgid play, which also won director George Seaton an Academy Award for his screenplay. William Holden plays the theatre director keen to cast Crosby who becomes embroiled with Grace. With hindsight, and the demise of all three principles, the film has an extra piquancy, provided the viewer knows that in real life Kelly was romantically involved with both Crosby and Holden. Crosby is excellent, and Grace isn't far behind, but many felt the Oscar should have gone to Judy Garland for *A Star Is Born*. Groucho Marx called it "the greatest robbery since Brink's".

Bing Crosby *Frank Elgin* • Grace Kelly *Georgie Elgin* • William Holden (1) *Bernie Dodd* • Anthony Ross *Phil Cook* • Gene Reynolds *Larry* • Eddie Ryder *Ed* ■ *Dir* George Seaton • *Scr* George Seaton, from the play by Clifford Odets

The Country Girls ★★★ PG

Period drama 1983 · UK · Colour · 102mins

Most rite of passage pictures focus on teenage lads, so it makes a refreshing change to follow a couple of girls discovering the pleasures and pitfalls of life. Adapted from the novel by Edna O'Brien, this engaging account of growing up in fifties Ireland takes us along the familiar route from convent school to the big city. However, director Desmond Davis succeeds in presenting each little act of rebellion and stolen moment of innocent passion as something exhilaratingly new. Maeve Germaine and Jill Doyle seem to burst through the screen, but it's the corrosive charm of Sam Neill which lingers in the memory. ▦

Sam Neill *Mr Gentleman* • Maeve Germaine *Kate* • Jill Doyle *Baba Brennan* • Britta Smith *Lil* • John Olohan *Hickey* • Patricia Martin *Martha* • Des Nealon *Mr Brennan* • John Kavanagh *James* ■ *Dir* Desmond Davis • *Scr* Edna O'Brien, from the novel by Edna O'Brien

Country Life ★★★★ 12

Period drama 1994 · Ausl · Colour · 112mins

A drawn-out but absorbing take on Chekhov's *Uncle Vanya*, adapted by writer/director Michael Blakemore and transplanted to post-First World War Australia. A failed writer (Blakemore himself) returns to a New South Wales sheep farm with new wife Greta Scacchi, who becomes the object of desire of drunken doctor Sam Neill and nervy landowner John Hargreaves. Neatly capturing the inherent comedy in people's everyday successes and failures, the film's vein of melancholy sets off that humour to real effect. ▦

Sam Neill *Dr Max Askey* • Greta Scacchi *Deborah Voysey* • Kerry Fox *Sally Voysey* • John Hargreaves *Jack Dickens* • Michael Blakemore *Alexander Voysey* • Googie Withers *Hannah* • Patricia Kennedy *Maud Dickens* ■ *Dir* Michael Blakemore • *Scr* Michael Blakemore, from the play *Uncle Vanya* by Anton Chekhov

County Hospital ★★ U

Comedy 1932 · US · BW · 18mins

Who else but Stan Laurel would visit someone in traction and offer them hard-boiled eggs and nuts? Unfortunately, that's about as funny as this two-reeler gets. There are a couple of good moments as Ollie's plastered

leg heads ceilingward. But once they head home, the action lapses back to the earliest days of silent slapstick as Stan careers through the streets causing all manner of vehicular chaos. Adding insult to unoriginality, director James Parrott stages the entire episode against a barely disguised back projection. Proof that even geniuses can have an off day. 🎞

Stan Laurel *Stan* • Oliver Hardy *Ollie* • William Austin *Englishman* • Baldwin Cooke *Orderly* • Billy Gilbert *Doctor* • Belle Hare *Nurse* • Frank Holliday *Hospital visitor* • Lilyan Irene *Nurse* ▪ *Dir* James Parrott • *Scr* HM Walker

Coupe de Ville ★★★ 🔞

Comedy drama   1990 · US · Colour · 93mins

This could have simply been just another road movie. Or alternatively, just another sixties film and an excuse to put classic tunes on the soundtrack. Fortunately it is neither. It's funny, endearing and very unlike director Joe Roth's earlier attempts (*Streets of Gold* and *Revenge of the Nerds II*). Three estranged brothers are ordered by their father, Alan Arkin, to drive across America with a car for their mother's 50th birthday. Cue much argument and a particularly memorable scene where they all dispute the significance of hit *Louie, Louie*. Ultimately status quo is found, just as their father intended. With decent comic gags punctuating throughout, it's slight but entertaining fare. 🎞

Patrick Dempsey *Bobby Libner* • Arye Gross *Buddy Libner* • Daniel Stern *Marvin Libner* • Annabeth Gish *Tammy* • Rita Taggart *Betty Libner* • Joseph Bologna *Uncle Phil* • Alan Arkin *Fred Libner* • James Gammon *Doc Sturgeon* ▪ *Dir* Joe Roth • *Scr* Mike Binder

Courage ★★★ 🔞

Drama based on a true story
1986 · US · Colour · 134mins

This is a stylish showcase for the still-stunning Sophia Loren, cleverly cast as a mother from the Queens district of New York, who ends up working for the US Drug Enforcement Agency when her son becomes a cocaine addict. Propagandist and forthright, this grim TV movie is based on a *New York* magazine article entitled "Mother Courage", and is well made by sometime feature director Jeremy Paul Kagan. The only trouble lies in actually believing Loren who, though dressed drably, still manages to look like the glamorous film star she is. Still, there's terrific support from Billy Dee Williams, Dan Hedaya and, particularly, Hector Elizondo. Contains violence, swearing and drug abuse. 🎞

Sophia Loren *Marianna Miraldo* • Billy Dee Williams *Bobby Jay* • Hector Elizondo *Nick Miraldo* • Val Avery *Pete Solto* • Ron Rifkin *Eppy Lucido* • Jose Perez *Jose Morales* • Mary McDonnell *Gabriella Estrada* • Dan Hedaya *John Fosh* ▪ *Dir* Jeremy Paul Kagan • *Scr* E Jack Neuman, from the article *Mother Courage* in *New York*, *magazine*

Courage Mountain ★★ 🔞

Adventure drama
1989 · US/Fr · Colour · 94mins

Continuing Johanna Sypri's much-loved story about a joy-bringing Swiss mountain girl, this lovingly staged but impossibly contrived adventure will doubtless appeal to adolescent females. It's they who will revel in Juliette Caton's pluck as she first confounds the villains at Leslie Caron's exclusive Italian school, then leads her classmates to safety across the Alps when the First World War encroaches on their patch. However, while they will acknowledge the precision of Christopher Leitch's directorial pitch, more discriminating types will wince at everything from the dialogue and music to Charlie Sheen's mortified performance as Peter the goatherd.

Juliette Caton *Heidi* • Charlie Sheen *Peter* • Leslie Caron *Jane Hillary* • Yorgo Voyagis *Signor Bonelli* • Laura Betti *Signora Bonelli* • Jan Rubes *Grandfather* • Joanna Clarke *Ursula* • Nicola Stapleton *Ilsa* ▪ *Dir* Christopher Leitch • *Scr* Weaver Webb, from a story by Fred Brogger, Mark Brogger, from characters created by Johanna Spyri

Courage of Black Beauty ★ 🔞

Drama   1957 · US · Colour · 79mins

In this belated attempt by independent producer Edward L Alperson to follow up his 1946 production of *Black Beauty*, the English setting of Anna Sewell's original novel is dropped in favour of California's San Fernando valley. Otherwise, though, it's the same old tale. A difficult youngster, played by John Crawford, bonds with a colt that he raises and names Black Beauty. Problems arise, however, when the animal shows signs of a vicious nature and is seriously injured. A big yawn, deficient in almost every area.

John Crawford *Bobby Adams* • Mimi Gibson *Lily Rowden* • John Bryant *Sam Adams* • Diane Brewster *Ann Rowden* • J Pat O'Malley *Mike Green* • Russell Johnson *Ben Farraday* ▪ *Dir* Harold Shuster • *Scr* Steve Fisher, from the novel *Black Beauty* by Anna Sewell

Courage of Lassie ★★★ 🔞

Drama   1946 · US · Colour · 92mins

The title of this moving tale of wartime doggie heroism is misleading, as Lassie actually plays a collie called Bill. Humans on board include the lovely young Elizabeth Taylor (from *Lassie Come Home*) and the always likeable Frank Morgan. Tom Drake is also effective as the "boy next door", but the real star – apart from the mutt – is the sumptuous Technicolor. The plot owes more than a little to canine classics like *Owd Bob* and *Greyfriars Bobby*, and while there's only so much you can do with a dog, it should be said that the last long pan is a remarkable feat of animal acting.

Elizabeth Taylor *Kathie Merrick* • Frank Morgan *Harry MacBain* • Tom Drake *Sgt Smitty* • Selena Royle *Mrs Merrick* • Harry Davenport *Judge Payson* • George Cleveland *Old Man* ▪ *Dir* Fred M Wilcox • *Scr* Lionel Houser

Courage under Fire ★★★ 🔞

War drama   1996 · US · Colour · 111mins

Once you recover your senses after finding little Meg Ryan in the thick of the Gulf War, *Courage under Fire* turns into a big, self-important war movie that looks good, sounds noble but rings rather hollow. Ryan is a pilot due to get a posthumous medal for bravery, but has there been a cover-up of the real events? This is a *Rashomon* for the nineties, with war hero Denzel Washington searching for the truth and, naturally, a *Washington Post* reporter sniffing around as well. The subject matter, the strong performances from Washington and Scott Glenn, and stylish direction from Edward Zwick – who directed Washington in *Glory* – combine to make the movie seem more incisive than it really is. Contains violence and some swearing. 🎞 **DVD**

Denzel Washington *Nat Serling* • Meg Ryan *Karen Walden* • Lou Diamond Phillips *Monfriez* • Michael Moriarty *General Hershberg* • Matt Damon *Ilario* • Bronson Pinchot *Bruno* • Seth Gilliam *Altemeyer* • Regina Taylor *Meredith Serling* • Scott Glenn *Tony Gartner* ▪ *Dir* Edward Zwick • *Scr* Patrick Sheane Duncan

The Courier ★★ 🔞

Detective thriller
1987 · UK/Ire · Colour · 81mins

An Irish thriller with nothing to do with the Troubles? That in itself is something of a rarity. Alas, that's the only whiff of originality in this story of a motorbike messenger (Padraig O'Loingsigh) who becomes embroiled in a drugs ring. Gabriel Byrne is the chief villain, while Ian Bannen and some other distinguished Irish actors also put in appearances. Elvis Costello wrote the score under his real name, Declan McManus. 🎞

Gabriel Byrne *Val* • Ian Bannen *McGuigan* • Cait O'Riordan *Colette* • Kevin Doyle *Joe* • Padraig O'Loingsigh *Mark* • Mary Ryan *Carol* • Patrick Bergin *Christy* ▪ *Dir* Joe Lee, Frank Deasy • *Scr* Frank Deasy

Cours du Soir ★★★ 🔞

Comedy   1967 · Fr · Colour · 27mins

Taking the form of an evening class and shot on the set of *Playtime*, this may not be Jacques Tati's most innovative film, but it provides an invaluable record of the vaudeville sketches with which he made his name. Starting with a demonstration of smoking styles, Tati trots out his famous tennis, fishing and horse-riding techniques, as well as a brief reprise of his beloved postman routine. But you only have to look at how badly his besuited students cope with the simple slapstick task of tripping on a step to realise how deceptively easy Tati makes each mime appear. In French with English subtitles.

Jacques Tati ▪ *Dir* Nicolas Ribowski • *Scr* Jacques Tati

The Court Jester ★★★★ 🔞

Comedy   1956 · US · Colour · 96mins

This medieval spoof, produced, written and directed by the formidable team of Norman Panama and Melvin Frank, gave Danny Kaye one of his finest roles, as the meek and mild valet who saves a kingdom from its tyrannical ruler. It's worth watching alone for the classic "vessel-with-the-pestle" routine that is one of the funniest devices Kaye ever employed. Basil Rathbone cuts an elegant figure of villainy, while Glynis Johns, Cecil Parker and Angela Lansbury get almost as many laughs as Kaye by playing it straight. As much horseplay as swordplay and, altogether, a witty delight. 🎞

Danny Kaye *Hawkins* • Glynis Johns *Maid Jean* • Basil Rathbone *Sir Ravenhurst* • Angela Lansbury *Princess Gwendolyn* • Cecil Parker *King Roderick* • Mildred Natwick *Griselda* • Robert Middleton *Sir Griswold* ▪ *Dir/Scr* Norman Panama, Melvin Frank

The Court-Martial of Billy Mitchell ★★★★ 🔞

Courtroom drama based on a true story
1955 · US · Colour · 100mins

Because of the technicalities, this is a real-life trial only a lawyer could love. Yet it's given enormous impact by director Otto Preminger and his Oscar-nominated writers, Milton Sperling and Emmet Lavery. The film is based on events in 1925, when US Army executive Mitchell (played by Gary Cooper) dared to question bureaucracy and argue for a separate Air Force. He also predicted that America and Japan would one day go to war, years before Pearl Harbour. Cooper's languid sincerity makes its mark, but it's Rod Steiger, arriving late on the scene as a venomous prosecutor, who gets all the best lines. 🎞

Gary Cooper *General Billy Mitchell* • Rod Steiger *Major Allan Guillion* • Charles Bickford *General Guthrie* • Ralph Bellamy *Congressman Frank Reid* • Elizabeth Montgomery *Margaret Lansdowne* • Jack Lord *Commander Zachary Lansdowne* • Peter Graves (1) *Captain Elliott* • Darren McGavin *Russ Peters* ▪ *Dir* Otto Preminger • *Scr* Milton Sperling, Emmet Lavery, from their story

The Court-Martial of Jackie Robinson ★★★

Drama based on a true story
1990 · US · Colour · 100 mins

A TV movie about Jackie Robinson, who went on to become the first black player in big-time baseball and a full-blown national hero, which homes in on an incident early in his life when he endured bigotry as a GI. André Braugher supplies ample energy as Robinson while Bruce Dern stands out in an impressive supporting cast that also includes Ruby Dee, who played Robinson's wife in 1950's *The Jackie Robinson Story*, and who returns here as his mum. Director Larry Peerce cleverly avoids any self-conscious analysing of issues, thereby maintaining the power of the piece.

AndréBraugher *Jackie Robinson* • Ruby Dee *Mallie Robinson* • Stan Shaw *Joe Louis* • Daniel Stern *William Cline* • Bruce Dern *Ed Higgins* • Kasi Lemmons *Rachel Robinson* ▪ *Dir* Larry Peerce • *Scr* L Travis Clark, Steve Duncan, Clayton Frohman, Dennis Lynton Clark, from a story by Dennis Lynton Clark

The Courtneys of Curzon Street ★★★ 🔞

Period drama   1947 · UK · BW · 120mins

Although it now seems twee, it's easy to see why this class-divide drama would have been so popular in postwar Britain. With an egalitarian theme and plenty of period gaiety to distract from the austerity of the time, this box-office smash perfectly demonstrates director Herbert Wilcox's ability to gauge public taste. However, Wilcox's master stroke was the teaming of his wife Anna Neagle and Michael Wilding. This was the second of their six collaborations, with Wilding's aristocrat shocking

Victorian society by falling for Neagle's spirited maid. Spanning the 19th century, it boasts the corniest of twists, but somehow it works.

Anna Neagle *Catherine O'Halloran* • Michael Wilding *Sir Edward Courtney* • Gladys Young *Lady Courtney* • Michael Medwin *Edward Courtney* • Coral Browne *Valerie* • Daphne Slater *Cynthia* • Jack Watling *Teddy Courtney* ■ *Dir* Herbert Wilcox • *Scr* Nicholas Phipps, from a story by Florence Tranter

The Courtship of Andy Hardy ★★ U

Comedy drama 1942 · US · BW · 94mins

The Andy Hardy series clocked up a dozen episodes with this offering which gave all-American families role models and reassurance while father was away fighting the war. In this story, Judge Hardy (Lewis Stone, as usual) uses his son Mickey Rooney to help a married couple reconcile themselves to their tearaway daughter. Oh, and Andy gets caught stealing a car. Life is so complicated in sunny Carvel.

Mickey Rooney *Andy Hardy* • Lewis Stone *Judge James K Hardy* • Donna Reed *Melodie Nesbitt* • Fay Holden *Mrs Emily Hardy* • Cecilia Parker *Marian Hardy* • Ann Rutherford *Polly Benedict* • William Lundigan *Jeff Willis* • Sara Haden *Aunt Milly* ■ *Dir* George B Seitz • *Scr* Agnes Christine Johnston, from characters created by Aurania Rouverol

The Courtship of Eddie's Father ★★★★ U

Comedy drama 1963 · US · Colour · 118mins

This absolutely charming and unfairly neglected film is directed by Vincente Minnelli, beautifully filmed by veteran cinematographer Milton Krasner, and features a simply swell performance from the excellent Glenn Ford. Former child star turned hot director Ron Howard (*Ransom*, *Apollo 13*) keeps sentimentality at bay as the six-year-old Eddie, as do those dynamic dames Stella Stevens and Shirley Jones; there's also a terrific cameo from Dick Van Dyke's under-rated brother, Jerry. This is a warm-hearted treat, far superior to the TV series it spawned.

Glenn Ford *Tom Corbett* • Ronny Howard [Ron Howard] *Eddie Corbett* • Shirley Jones *Elizabeth Marten* • Dina Merrill *Rita Behrens* • Stella Stevens *Dollye Daly* • Roberta Sherwood *Mrs Livingston* • Jerry Van Dyke *Norman Jones* ■ *Dir* Vincente Minnelli • *Scr* John Gay, from a novel by Mark Toby

The Courtyard ★★★

Thriller 1995 · US · Colour · 103mins

Andrew McCarthy has worked long and hard to lose his lightweight teen image and turns in a suitably bewildered performance in this above-average, sexy thriller. He plays a Los Angeles architect who becomes involved in a murder investigation that takes an unexpected turn when he falls for *femme fatale* Mädchen Amick. There's a nice chemistry between the two leads and a rock solid supporting cast, which includes Richard "Cheech" Marin and Vincent Schiavelli, while director Fred Walton navigates the intriguing plot with flair. Contains swearing, violence and nudity.

Andrew McCarthy *Jonathan Hoffman* • Mädchen Amick *Lauren* • David Packer *Jack Morgan* • Bonnie Bartlett *Cathleen Fitzgerald* •

Vincent Schiavelli *Ivan* • Richard "Cheech" Marin *Detective Steiner* ■ *Dir* Fred Walton • *Scr* Wendy Biller, Christopher Hawthorne

Cousin Bette ★★★ 15

Period drama 1997 · US/UK · Colour · 104mins

This version of Balzac's novel has Jessica Lange in the title role, plotting revenge on her family who have virtually abandoned her while lavishing everything on her cousin Adeline. While its story of social upheaval is mirrored by the political chaos of the French Revolution, the picture suffers rather from international casting and other compromises brought on by trans-Atlantic financing. But Lange gives a wonderful portrait of malice, while Elisabeth Shue has fun as a flirtatious stage actress. Contains nudity, sex scenes and some swearing and violence. ▣

Jessica Lange *Bette Fisher* • Elisabeth Shue *Jenny Cadine* • Geraldine Chaplin *Adeline Hulot* • Bob Hoskins *Mayor Cesar Crevel* • Hugh Laurie *Baron Hector Hulot* • Laura Fraser *Mariette* • Toby Stephens *Victorin Hulot* • Kelly Macdonald *Hortense Hulot* ■ *Dir* Des McAnuff • *Scr* Lynn Siefert, Susan Tarr, from the novel by Honoré de Balzac

Cousin Bobby ★★★ PG

Documentary 1992 · US · Colour · 70mins

Jonathan Demme directs this absolutely fascinating documentary about his cousin Robert Castle, an Episcopalian priest in Harlem. The Oscar-winning director follows the outspoken radical activist as he goes about his daily ministering and builds up a riveting portrait of the man, his life and the dedicated work he does among his adoring flock. The use of race riot footage is heavy-handed, but otherwise this is a nicely crafted valentine from one proud relative to another.

Dir Jonathan Demme

Cousin, Cousine ★★★ 12

Comedy 1975 · Fr · Colour · 91mins

The problem with accessible arthouse movies is that they often feel empty. That's certainly the case in this gentle satire on middle-class mores, which was so successful in the States that it was remade as *Cousins*. Fondly mocking the morality of his characters, Jean-Charles Tacchella refuses to rip into them as Buñuel would have done, choosing instead to make the romance between wronged wife Marie-Christine Barrault (who was Oscar-nominated for her performance) and Victor Lanoux seem rather sweet. Consequently, the philandering Guy Marchand and testy Marie-France Pisier carry the brunt of Tacchella's opprobrium merely for being human. In French with English subtitles. ▣

Marie-Christine Barrault *Marthe* • Victor Lanoux *Ludovic* • Marie-France Pisier *Karine* • Guy Marchand *Pascal* • Ginette Garcin *Biju* • Sybil Maas *Diane* • Jean Herbert *Sacy* ■ *Dir* Jean-Charles Tacchella • *Scr* Jean-Charles Tacchella, Danièle Thompson

Les Cousins ★★★★

Drama 1959 · Fr · BW · 109mins

Winner of the Golden Bear at the 1959 Berlin Film Festival, this is an intriguing variation on the "town mouse and country mouse" theme which cynically asserts that just desserts are simply pie in the sky. Gérard Blain skilfully charts the descent from wide-eyed wonder to self-pitying despair as the student from the sticks who slaves at the Sorbonne, only to fail his exams and lose his girlfriend to his indolent but ultimately successful cousin (Jean-Claude Brialy). Parisian Claude Chabrol presents his home town with evident enthusiasm, though the scenes of student excess have dated badly. In French with English subtitles.

Gérard Blain *Charles* • Jean-Claude Brialy *Paul* • Juliette Mayniel *Florence* • Claude Cerval *Clovis* • Genevieve Cluny *Genevieve* • Michèle Meritz *Yvonne* • Corrado Guarducci *Italian Count* • Guy Decomble *Librarian* ■ *Dir* Claude Chabrol • *Scr* Claude Chabrol, Paul Gegauff

Cousins ★★★ 15

Romantic comedy 1989 · US · Colour · 108mins

A remake of the French film *Cousin, Cousine*, this is a glossy romance featuring Isabella Rossellini and Ted Danson as relatives-by-marriage who find themselves falling in love during a succession of family gatherings. He's married to ice-cold Sean Young, who in turn is having an affair with Rossellini's hubby, William Petersen. Danson, trying to break away from his role as Sam in *Cheers*, gives one of his most likeable movie performances, while Young manages to steal the show by playing the role of bitchy cheating wife to the max. Intermittently funny, but still a slight disappointment from director Joel Schumacher. ▣

Ted Danson *Larry Kozinski* • Isabella Rossellini *Maria Hardy* • Sean Young *Tish Kozinski* • William Petersen *Tom Hardy* • Lloyd Bridges *Vince Kozinski* • Norma Aleandro *Edie Costello* • Keith Coogan *Mitch Kozinski* ■ *Dir* Joel Schumacher • *Scr* Stephen Metcalfe, from the film *Cousin, Cousine* by Jean-Charles Tacchella, Danièle Thompson

A Covenant with Death ★★

Courtroom drama 1967 · US · Colour · 96mins

A potentially interesting and original idea (an innocent man convicted of murder kills the hangman, and is then found not guilty of the first offence) is poorly handled by director Lamont Johnson, who ironically became regarded as a promising feature director on the strength of this film. Former television star George Maharis (*Route 66*) simply can't convey the moral quandary and angst the role demands, but there is marvellous support from Laura Devon, Earl Holliman, Katy Jurado and Sidney Blackmer, not to mention Gene Hackman in an early feature film role. Contains violent scenes.

George Maharis *Ben Lewis* • Laura Devon *Rosemary* • Katy Jurado *Eulalia* • Earl Holliman *Bryan Talbot* • O'Connell *Judge Hochstadter* • Sidney Blackmer *Colonel Oates* • Gene Hackman *Harmsworth* • John Anderson *Dietrich* ■ *Dir* Lamont Johnson • *Scr* Larry B Marcus, Saul Levitt, from a novel by Stephen Becker

Cover Girl ★★★★ U

Musical romantic comedy 1944 · US · Colour · 102mins

Not just a Technicolor treat featuring a ravishing Rita Hayworth and a score by Jerome Kern that includes *Long Ago and Far Away*, this was a milestone in the history of the glossy film musical. Columbia borrowed the young Gene Kelly from MGM and gave him free rein with his own sections of the movie. Kelly flexed his cinematic muscles here, knocking down soundstage walls to create a continuous street scene for himself, Hayworth and Phil Silvers to dance through without any need for cuts, and using trick photography to dance with himself in the "alter ego" routine. He returned to MGM a master of his craft, and left this charming legacy. It's a little dated, a little overlong and a little corny, but a treat nonetheless. ▣

Rita Hayworth *Rusty Parker/Maribelle Hicks* • Gene Kelly *Danny McGuire* • Phil Silvers *Genius* • Lee Bowman *Noel Wheaton* • Jinx Falkenburg *Jinx* • Leslie Brooks *Maurine Martin* • Eve Arden *Cornelia Jackson* • Otto Kruger *John Coudair* • Jess Barker *John Coudair as a young man* • Anita Colby *Anita* ■ *Dir* Charles Vidor • *Scr* Virginia Van Upp, Marion Parsonnet, Paul Gangelin, from a story by Erwin Gelsey • *Cinematographer* Rudolph Maté, Allen M Davey • *Music Director* MW Stoloff [Morris Stoloff] • *Orchestration* Carmen Dragon • *Art Director* Lionel Banks, Gary Odell • *Set Designer* Fay Babcock

Cover Girl Killer ★★★

Crime drama 1959 · UK · BW · 61mins

Apart from a handful of low-budget movies, writer/director Terry Bishop spent much of his career in TV, which would appear to have been the British cinema's loss if this clipped little thriller is anything to go by. If the dialogue strikes a false note every now and then, Bishop succeeds in re-creating a world of tawdry glamour that is a far cry from the glitz of today's supermodels as a serial killer targets a magazine's pin-ups. Bishop also sustains the suspense throughout, and you're never quite sure who's going to walk into the trap laid by the publisher to catch the killer. *Steptoe and Son* fans will be interested in the presence of a young Harry H Corbett in the cast.

Harry H Corbett *The man* • Felicity Young *June Rawson* • Spencer Teakle *John Mason* • Victor Brooks *Inspector Brunner* • Tony Doonan *Sergeant* • Bernadette Milne *Gloria* • Christina Gregg *Joy* • Charles Lloyd Pack *Captain Adams* ■ *Dir/Scr* Terry Bishop

The Cover Girl Murders ★★ 15

Mystery 1993 · US · Colour · 83mins

Murder-mystery fluff, made for cable and notable only for the fact that it brought the original Six Million Dollar Man, Lee Majors, back to the screen. The plot involves a killer stalking a group of models stranded on an isolated island, but it's mainly an excuse for some tame shots of girls in swimsuits. Majors's return to the limelight is largely undistinguished, and co-star Jennifer O'Neill looks equally uncomfortable with the hackneyed script and insipid direction. Contains some violence. ▣

U = SUITABLE FOR ALL Uc = SUITABLE FOR ALL, ESPECIALLY FOR YOUNG CHILDREN (VIDEO ONLY) PG = PARENTAL GUIDANCE

Lee Majors *Rex Kingman* • Jennifer O'Neill *Kate Branigan* • Adrian Paul *Patrice Dufour* • Beverly Johnson *Mikela Dawn* • Vanessa Angel *Rachel Branigan* • Arthur Taxier *Martin Haas* • Bobbie Phillips *Hedi Barnett* ■ *Dir* James A Contner • *Scr* Douglas Barr, Bernard Maybeck, from a story by Brian Taggert

The Covered Wagon ★★★★★

Silent western   1923 · US · BW · 98mins

Shot on a lavish scale in Utah and Nevada, this was the first truly epic western and one of the biggest-grossing silent movies ever made. It also created the imprint for countless movies and TV series with its story of pioneers facing redskins and ruffians on the wagon trail westwards. Directed by James Cruze – with, it's said, John Ford as his assistant – the film's many highlights include a buffalo hunt and a dramatic river crossing, though the vapid romance between J Warren Kerrigan and Lois Wilson tends to diminish the storyline. With terrific camerawork from Karl Brown, it set the standard for all future westerns.

Lois Wilson *Molly Wingate* • J Warren Kerrigan *Will Banion* • Ernest Torrence *Jackson* • Charles Ogle *Mr Wingate* • Ethel Wales *Mrs Wingate* • Alan Hale *Sam Woodhull* • Tully Marshall *Bridger* • Guy Oliver *Kit Carson* ■ *Dir* James Cruze • *Scr* Jack Cunningham

Cover-Up ★★ 18

Action thriller   1991 · US/Is · Colour · 87mins

Dolph Lundgren plays a journalist assigned to cover a raid on a military base in Israel. The official reports say the terrorists merely attacked the base, but Dolph soon discovers that a secret chemical weapon may have been the real target. What could have been an engaging thriller spends too much time catching up with Lundgren's previous acquaintances, and things get bogged down quickly. Louis Gossett Jr is on hand to inject some urgency, but it's too little, too late. ▭

Dolph Lundgren *Mike Anderson* • Louis Gossett Jr *Jackson* • John Finn *Colonel Jeff Cooper* • Lisa Berkley *Susan Clifford* ■ *Dir* Manny Coto • *Scr* William Tannen

Cowboy ★★★ U

Western   1958 · US · Colour · 91mins

A grim and gripping western, reuniting star and director from the previous year's *3:10 to Yuma*, taciturn Glenn Ford and talented Delmer Daves. This is the story of a young tenderfoot (the excellent Jack Lemmon) and his relationship with tough trail boss Ford. The atmosphere here is thoroughly authentic: listen to Ford's acute description of the intelligence of a cowboy's horse. The lady along for the ride is Marlon Brando's then-wife, the sultry Anna Kashfi, and the Technicolor photography is particularly sharp. ▭

Glenn Ford *Tom Reece* • Jack Lemmon *Frank Harris* • Anna Kashfi *Maria Vidal* • Brian Donlevy *Doc Bender* • Dick York *Charlie* • Victor Manuel Mendoza *Mendoza* • Richard Jaeckel *Paul Curtis* ■ *Dir* Delmer Daves • *Scr* Edmund H North, from the non-fiction book *My Reminiscences as a Cowboy* by Frank Harris • *Cinematographer* Charles Lawton Jr

The Cowboy and the Lady ★★★ U

Comedy   1938 · US · BW · 87mins

This film started life as what today would be called a high-concept idea, with producer Samuel Goldwyn teaming up former mountain cowboy of few words Gary Cooper and aristocratic Merle Oberon. So far, so good, but what about a plot? The slight story Goldwyn came up with is actually encapsulated by the catchpenny title, but to compensate he had the good sense to hire some of the period's cleverest writers. The screen never ignites, but Merle and Coop make a handsome couple. ▭

Gary Cooper *Stretch* • Merle Oberon *Mary Smith* • Patsy Kelly *Katie Callahan* • Walter Brennan *Sugar* • Fuzzy Knight *Buzz* • Mabel Todd *Elly* • Henry Kolker *Mr Smith* • Harry Davenport *Uncle Hannibal Smith* • Emma Dunn *Ma Hawkins* ■ *Dir* HC Potter • *Scr* SN Behrman, Sonya Levien, from a story by Leo McCarey, Frank R Adams

The Cowboy Way ★★ 12

Comedy western
1994 · US · Colour · 102mins

Woody Harrelson, with a gleeful disregard for restraint, whoops and hollers his way through the picture, as he and rodeo partner Kiefer Sutherland stalk the Big Apple in search of their Mexican buddy's kidnapped daughter. In Harrelson's defence, he does at least try to make something out of Bill Wittliff's hugely derivative script. There's also a neat turn from Ernie Hudson as a cowboy crazy cop, but as a whole it's all rather coarse and clumsy. Contains some swearing. ▭

Woody Harrelson *Pepper* • Kiefer Sutherland *Sonny* • Dylan McDermott *Stark* • Ernie Hudson *Officer Sam Shaw* • Cara Buono *Teresa* • Marg Helgenberger *Margarette* • Tomas Milian *Huerta* • Luis Guzman *Chango* ■ *Dir* Gregg Champion • *Scr* Bill Wittliff, from a story by Bill Wittliff, Rob Thomson

The Cowboys ★★ PG

Western   1972 · US · Colour · 121mins

The first thing any audience should be told about this western is that its star, Big John Wayne, is killed off as a trigger for later events, and the titular cowboys are literally that, a group of 11 young cowhands forced to grow up quickly in the shadow of the Duke's demise. Morose, awkwardly paced and overlong, this rites-of-passage saga just doesn't work, owing to a cumbersome structure and a nauseating pro-violence, revenge-is-good message. Bruce Dern and Slim Pickens are good to watch, and Roscoe Lee Browne and Colleen Dewhurst add thespian dignity, but the movie isn't worthy of Wayne. ▭ **DVD**

John Wayne *Wil Andersen* • Roscoe Lee Browne *Jebediah Nightlinger* • Bruce Dern *Long Hair* • Colleen Dewhurst *Kate* • Slim Pickens *Anse* • Lonny Chapman *Preacher* ■ *Dir* Mark Rydell • *Scr* Irving Ravetch, Harriett Frank Jr, William Dale Jennings, from the novel by William Dale Jennings

Coyote ★★

Experimental erotic drama
1992 · Can · Colour · 95mins

Marking the debut of Mitsou, the controversial pop singer who took

Canada by storm, this is a moody love story that ends up being consumed more by pretension than passion. Director Richard Ciupka manages some striking shots of a rundown suburb littered with the debris of depressed industry, but he is less successful in making us care what happens between aspiring film-maker Patrick Labbé and Mitsou, a waif whose troubled childhood continues to haunt her. The girl-power image on which Mitsou's celebrity is based rather works against her character, but she looks great in what is essentially a glorified video. Contains violence, swearing, sex scenes and nudity. ▭

Mitsou *Louise Coyote* • Patrick Labbé *Chomi* • Thierry Magnier • Claude Legault • Francois Massicotte ■ *Dir* Richard Ciupka • *Scr* Michel Michaud, Richard Sadler, Louise Anne Bouchard, Richard Ciupka

Crack House ★ 18

Crime drama   1989 · US · Colour · 86mins

In 50 years, this movie will be rediscovered and appreciated in the same way that *Reefer Madness* is now. Like that camp classic, this movie is an anti-drug pamphlet dressed up in exploitation clothing, though it's considerably more violent and sexually explicit. Drug lord Jim Brown has everyone in his LA neighborhood on drugs except for one teenage Hispanic couple. When the boy ends up in jail, she is alone long enough to get sucked into the world of crack and be used and abused like all the other female cast members. Funny at times, *Crack House* needs time to reach its full laugh potential. ▭

Jim Brown *Steadman* • Richard Roundtree *Lieutenant Johnson* • Anthony Geary *Dockett* • Angel Tompkins *Mother* • Cheryl Kay *Melissa* • Gregg Gomez Thomsen *Rick Morales* ■ *Dir* Michael Fischa • *Scr* Blake Schaeffer, from a story by Jack Silverman

Crack in the Mirror ★★★

Crime drama   1960 · US · BW · 96mins

A working-class woman of a certain age (Juliette Greco) murders her construction worker husband (Orson Welles) with the help of her virile young lover (Bradford Dillman). The couple are brought to trial, where she is defended by an ambitious young lawyer (Dillman again), who is having an affair with the wife (Greco) of the young man's elderly counsel (Welles)... An ingenious idea, directed with pace and style by Richard Fleischer, and with excellent performance from the dual role-playing principals. The message is simplistic and obvious, however, and all six characters are cold, heartless and unsympathetic.

Orson Welles *Hagolin/Lamoriciere* • Juliette Greco *Exponine/Florence* • Bradford Dillman *Larnier/Claud* • Alexander Knox *President* • Catherine Lacey *Mother Superior* • William Lucas *Kerstner* • Maurice Teynac *Doctor* ■ *Dir* Richard Fleischer • *Scr* Mark Canfield [Darryl F Zanuck], from the novel *Drama in the Mirror* by Marcel Haedrich

Crack in the World ★★★ U

Science-fiction thriller
1965 · US · Colour · 95mins

Scientists attempt to harness the inner energy of the earth and get it all wrong in this moderate sci-fi thriller. Director

Andrew Marton knows how to milk this kind of thing, and no one looks more worried about the end of the world than tight-lipped Dana Andrews, who had to deal with a similar scale of problem in *The Satan Bug* the same year. Among the cast, Alexander Knox brings a touch of class to the proceedings, while Janette Scott and Kieron Moore reprise their double act from *The Day of the Triffids*. The effects just about pass muster, though they may look familiar to fans of other movies in the genre.

Dana Andrews *Dr Stephen Sorensen* • Janette Scott *Maggie Sorensen* • Kieron Moore *Ted Rampion* • Alexander Knox *Sir Charles Eggerston* • Peter Damon *Masefield* • Gary Lasdun *Markov* ■ *Dir* Andrew Marton • *Scr* Jon Manchip White, Julian Halevy [Julian Zimet], from a story by Jon Manchip White

Crack-Up ★★ U

Spy drama   1936 · US · BW · 70mins

A very routine programme-filler, made far livelier than it has any right to be by the solid acting of an adept supporting cast. Brian Donlevy (the future Professor Quatermass) is Ace Martin, a test pilot bribed to steal the design plans of a revolutionary new war plane. Peter Lorre, always watchable even in below-par formula espionage material like this, is the airport's dumb, bugle-blowing mascot who's really a double agent with his bug-eyes on the same blueprints.

Peter Lorre *Colonel Gimpy* • Brian Donlevy *Ace Martin* • Helen Wood *Ruth Franklin* • Ralph Morgan *John Fleming* • Thomas Beck *Joe Randall* • Kay Linaker *Mrs Fleming* • Lester Matthews *Sidney Grant* ■ *Dir* Malcolm St Clair • *Scr* Charles Kenyon, Sam Mintz, from a story by John Goodrich

Crack-Up ★★

Thriller   1946 · US · BW · 93mins

When art lecturer and curator Pat O'Brien tumbles to the forgeries originating from an international consortium of villains, strange things begin happening and he suffers, or appears to suffer, a nervous breakdown. This is an unusual role for O'Brien who stars alongside Claire Trevor, as his loyal girlfriend, and classy Herbert Marshall as a Scotland Yard investigator posing as an art expert. Directed with real flair by Irving Reis, the movie gets off to a terrific start but promises more than it delivers, due in part to a screenplay that becomes progressively more confused as it goes along.

Pat O'Brien *George Steele* • Claire Trevor *Terry* • Herbert Marshall *Traybin* • Ray Collins *Dr Lowell* • Wallace Ford *Cochrane* • Dean Harens *Reynolds* • Damian O'Flynn *Stevenson* • Erskine Sanford *Barton* • Mary Ware *Mary* ■ *Dir* Irving Reis • *Scr* John Paxton, Ben Bengal, Ray Spencer, from the short story *Madman's Holiday* by Fredric Brown

The Cracker Factory ★★★★

Drama   1979 · US/UK · Colour · 100mins

Natalie Wood excels in this made-for-TV movie, imbuing this distinguished drama with both class and dignity as a depressed suburban housewife committed to care after a failed suicide bid. Wood is exceptionally good, and there's a marvellous supporting cast on hand in this prestige production, made with help from EMI Television (a British company). Watch for Vivian Blaine, who played Adelaide in the screen version of *Guys and Dolls*, plus Juliet Mills and a pre-*Cheers* appearance from Shelley Long. The men are negligible, but doctor Perry King is suitably sympathetic.

Natalie Wood *Cassie Barrett* • Perry King *Dr Edwin Alexander* • Peter Haskell *Charlie Barrett* • Shelley Long *Clara* • Vivian Blaine *Helen* • Marian Mercer *Eleanor* • Juliet Mills *Tinkerbell* • John Harkins *Father Dunhill* ■ *Dir* Burt Brinckerhoff • *Scr* Richard A Shapiro, from the novel by Joyce Rebeta-Burditt

Crackerjack ★★ U

Comedy drama   1938 · UK · BW · 76mins

Not the children's TV show, but a vehicle for Tom Walls, well-loved star of the Aldwych farces during the twenties. He plays burglar Jack Drake, a sort of "Robbing Hood" who lifts from the rich to help the poor. His success makes other local crooks jealous, and thereby hangs this awfully thin tale, enlivened only by the youthful presence of the lovely Lilli Palmer as co-star. It takes a long time to get up to speed, and today seems very dated indeed. Still, in its time, this average British film did Gainsborough's reputation as a production house no end of good. 🎞

Tom Walls *Jack Drake* • Lilli Palmer *Baroness von Haltse* • Noel Madison *Sculpie* • Edmond Breon [Edmund Breon] *Tony Davenport* • Leon M Lion *Hambro Golding* • Charles Heslop *Burge* • Ethel Griffies *Annie* • HG Stoker *Inspector Benting* ■ *Dir* Albert de Courville • *Scr* AR Rawlinson, Michael Pertwee, Basil Mason, from a novel by WB Ferguson

Crackerjack ★★ 18

Action crime   1994 · Can · Colour · 96mins

The setting of this Canadian *Die Hard* – in and around a mountain resort – promises a change of scenery and some variety in the action, and at times it reaches these goals. The pacing is static and clunky, however, and the special effects are remarkably poor, even for a straight-to-video movie. Thomas Ian Griffith makes an unsympathetic hero, despite the film taking time to explain his traumatic past, and Christopher Plummer isn't much better. One wonders if he's really supporting his country's cinema so much, when he usually appears in low-budget quickies like this. 🎞

Thomas Ian Griffith *Jack Wild* • Christopher Plummer *Ivan Getz* • Nastassja Kinski *KC* ■ *Dir* Michael Mazo • *Scr* Jonas Quastel, Michael Bafaro

Crackers ★★ 15

Comedy   1984 · US · Colour · 87mins

Directed by Louis Malle, the award-winning French film-maker who gave us *Pretty Baby, Atlantic City* and *Damage*, this off-beat American comedy caper is actually a remake of the 1956 Italian movie, *Big Deal on Madonna Street*. Donald Sutherland is an unemployed security guard who plots to crack the safe in Jack Warden's San Francisco pawn shop with his group of misfits. Like the plot itself, this is a botched job, neither as funny or as tense as intended. That said, it is full of whimsy

and weird performances, and features Sean Penn in an early role. 🎞

Donald Sutherland *Weslake* • Jack Warden *Garvey* • Sean Penn *Dillard* • Wallace Shawn *Turtle* • Larry Riley *Boardwalk* • Trinidad Silva *Ramon* • Christine Baranski *Maxine* ■ *Dir* Louis Malle • *Scr* Jeffrey Fiskin, from the film *Big Deal on Madonna Street* by Suso Cecchi D'Amico, Mario Monicelli, Agenore Incrocci, Furio Scarpelli

The Cracksman ★★ U

Comedy   1963 · UK · Colour · 107mins

This is far and away Charlie Drake's finest hour on the big screen. Sadly, that's not saying much. He also co-scripted this distinctly average crime comedy, in which he plays a trusting locksmith whose devotion to duty lands him in jail. A muddle of slapstick and pathos, the film is ridiculously overlong and needlessly opulent. 🎞

Charlie Drake *Ernest Wright* • George Sanders *The Guv'nor* • Dennis Price *Grantley* • Nyree Dawn Porter *Muriel* • Eddie Byrne *Domino* • Finlay Currie *Feathers* • Percy Herbert *Nosher* ■ *Dir* Peter Graham Scott • *Scr* Lew Schwartz, Mike Watts, Charlie Drake

Cradle of Conspiracy ★★ 15

Drama based on a true story
1994 · US · Colour · 87mins

Danica McKellar, Fred Savage's long-running love interest in the TV series *The Wonder Years*, tackles a slightly more grown-up role for this air-brushed TV-movie look at the seamier side of American life. She plays a naive teenager who runs away with the drifter whose child she is carrying and then discovers that he wants to sell the baby on the black market. It's a lurid enough tale and the playing is competent enough, but the script gives them little in the way of grit or passion. Contains some violence and swearing. 🎞

Danica McKellar *Kristin Guthrie* • Dee Wallace Stone *Suzanne Guthrie* • Carmen Argenziano *Jack Guthrie* • Kurt Deutsch *Kenny* • Geoffrey Thorne *Gary Pritchard* ■ *Dir* Gabrielle Beaumont • *Scr* Jayne Martin

Cradle Will Rock ★★★ 15

Drama   1999 · US · Colour · 134mins

Set during the anti-communist witch-hunts of the thirties, this dense and rather gruelling political drama focuses on the efforts of a bunch of New York theatre folk, including Orson Welles, to stage a left-wing play. When the powers that be block the project, all involved decide the show must go on. Actor turned director Tim Robbins marshals the material with skill, convincingly evoking the vibrancy of both place and period. Yet he over-eggs the pudding by cramming in too many intertwined storylines and characters – some historical, some fictional. John Cusack, Susan Sarandon and Emily Watson head the cast, though the star turn comes from Bill Murray as a paranoid ventriloquist.

Hank Azaria *Marc Blitzstein* • Rubén Blades *Diego Rivera* • Joan Cusack *Hazel Huffman* • John Cusack *Nelson Rockefeller* • Cary Elwes *John Houseman* • Philip Baker Hall *Gray Mathers* • Cherry Jones *Hallie Flanagan* • Angus MacFadyen *Orson Welles* • Bill Murray *Tommy Crickshaw* • Vanessa Redgrave *Countess LaGrange* • Susan Sarandon

Margherita Sarfatti* • John Turturro *Aldo Silvano* • Emily Watson *Olive Stanton* ■ *Dir/Scr* Tim Robbins

The Craft ★★★ 15

Supernatural horror thriller
1996 · US · Colour · 100mins

A quartet of wannabe witches find that sorcery is a real help when it comes to relationship problems and dealing with their various physical and emotional worries. Until one of them seeks real power, that is. This engaging teen version of *The Witches of Eastwick* skilfully mixes a brew of plausible characters, neat visual effects and a few genuinely creepy moments. The attractive cast of stars-to-be (including *Scream*'s Neve Campbell and Skeet Ulrich) coupled with the film's glossy visual style lift this above your average genre fare, as does a smarter-than-expected script that puts a sinister spin on female bonding. The full-on sorcery showdown belongs in another movie, though. 📀 *DVD*

Robin Tunney *Sarah* • Fairuza Balk *Nancy* • Neve Campbell *Bonnie* • Rachel True *Rochelle* • Skeet Ulrich *Chris* • Christine Taylor *Laura Lizzie* • Breckin Meyer *Mitt* • Nathaniel Marston *Trey* • Cliff De Young *Mr Bailey* ■ *Dir* Andrew Fleming • *Scr* Peter Filardi, Andrew Fleming, from a story by Peter Filardi

Craig's Wife ★★

Drama   1936 · US · BW · 74mins

This was the movie that turned actress Rosalind Russell into a fully fledged box-office name: a turgid tale about a housewife who cares more for material things than for her husband. (Since he's played by boring John Boles, who can blame her?) Over-rated cult director Dorothy Arzner, a former editor and scriptwriter, tries to add hidden depths to the source material, an intractable play by Grace Kelly's uncle, George.

Rosalind Russell *Harriet Craig* • John Boles *Walter Craig* • Billie Burke *Mrs Frazier* • Jane Darwell *Mrs Harold* • Dorothy Wilson *Ethel Landreth* • Alma Kruger *Miss Austen* ■ *Dir* Dorothy Arzner • *Scr* Mary C McCall Jr, from the play by George Kelly

The Cranes Are Flying ★★★★ U

Romantic drama   1957 · USSR · BW · 91mins

One of the first Soviet films made after a political "thaw" which seemed to herald a new artistic freedom in the country's cinema, this prize-winning love story, directed by Mikhail Kalatozov, concerns a young hospital worker (Tatyana Samoilova) who contracts a loveless marriage following reports that her soldier fiancé has been killed. An unpretentious and poetic movie about love and the Second World War that benefits from some majestic camerawork and a sensitive performance by Samoilova. The film received the Palme d'Or at Cannes in 1958; international recognition and admiration followed.

Tatyana Samoilova *Veronica* • Alexei Batalov *Boris* • Vasili Merkuriev *Byodor Ivanovich* • Aleksandr Shvorin [A Shvorin] *Mark* • S Kharitonova *Irina* ■ *Dir* Mikhail Kalatozov • *Scr* Victor Rosov, from a play by Victor Rosov • *Cinematographer* Sergei Urusevsky

Crash! ★

Horror   1977 · US · Colour · 89mins

An early low-budget wreck from director Charles Band, the king of seventies schlock and future video horror maverick. Sue Lyon brings home a supernatural relic whose spirit possesses anything with wheels, including the family auto. When her crippled husband (José Ferrer) tries to kill her, the demonic vehicle tries to kill him in return. An undeniably strange mix of infidelity, sorcery and garage mechanics, made solely to cash in on Universal's heavily hyped *The Car*, this mediocre effort would be funny were it not so confusing.

José Ferrer *Marc Denne* • John Carradine *Dr Edwards* • Sue Lyon *Kim Denne* • John Ericson *Greg* • Leslie Parrish *Kathy* ■ *Dir* Charles Band • *Scr* Marc Marais

Crash ★★★★★ 18

Drama   1996 · Can · Colour · 96mins

How the giving and receiving of love, and the sexual act that usually communicates those primal feelings, will evolve and transform in our increasingly technological world, is the core of director David Cronenberg's controversial masterpiece, based on JG Ballard's cult novel. Set among a group of urban sophisticates so morally exhausted they need to invent perversions to keep what sensuality they have left alive, the film turns car accidents into sado-masochistic turn-ons, while bodily injury becomes a science-fiction metaphor for how we must reshape our eroded humanity to exist in the high-tech future. In no way pornographic or exploitative, and containing the most astonishing performance from Deborah Unger, Cronenberg's uncompromising, daring and intellectual wake-up call is potent, adult food for thought and a landmark nineties fantasy. Contains swearing, sex scenes and violence. 🎞 📀 *DVD*

James Spader *James Ballard* • Holly Hunter *Dr Helen Remington* • Elias Koteas *Vaughan* • Deborah Kara Unger *Catherine Ballard* • Rosanna Arquette *Gabrielle* • Peter MacNeil [Peter MacNeill] *Colin Seagrave* ■ *Dir* David Cronenberg • *Scr* David Cronenberg, from the novel by JG Ballard

Crash Dive ★★ U

Second World War adventure
1943 · US · Colour · 105mins

It seems there was nothing more important over at 20th Century-Fox post-Pearl Harbor than whether handsome Tyrone Power or rugged Dana Andrews would land up with pretty Anne Baxter. Since this was Ty's last movie before his own Second World War service, and since he's also top-billed, you've probably guessed the result. But stick with this (it's dull in patches) to witness Hollywood propaganda at its most blatant. The special effects actually managed to win an Oscar (Fred Sersen for visuals, Roger Heman for sound).

Tyrone Power *Lieutenant Ward Stewart* • Anne Baxter *Jean Hewlett* • Dana Andrews *Lieutenant Commander Dewey Connors* • James Gleason *McDonnell* • Dame May Whitty *Grandmother* ■ *Dir* Archie Mayo • *Scr* Jo Swerling, from a story by WR Burnett

U = SUITABLE FOR ALL   Uc = SUITABLE FOR ALL, ESPECIALLY FOR YOUNG CHILDREN (VIDEO ONLY)   PG = PARENTAL GUIDANCE

Crash Dive ★★ 15
Action thriller 1996 · US · Colour · 86mins

Cut-price cash-in that shamelessly plunders the plots of *Under Siege* and *Crimson Tide*, though the end result is not unentertaining. Michael Dudikoff is the special agent who becomes America's last hope when a gang of crazed terrorists hijack a nuclear submarine and threaten to turn its arsenal on Washington. Frederic Forrest provides a bit of class, while the claustrophobic direction is by Andrew Stevens, better known for such erotic thrillers as *Illicit Dreams* and *A Woman Scorned*. ▭

Michael Dudikoff *James Carter* • Frederic Forrest *Admiral Pendelton* • Reiner Schone *Richter* • Jay Acovone *Murphy* • Catherine Bell *Lisa Stark* • Brittain Marcus *Tommy* • Michael Cavanaugh *Captain Lange* ■ *Dir* Andrew Stevens • *Scr* William C Martell

Crash Landing ★ U
Disaster drama 1958 · US · BW · 76mins

This low-budget drama about a passenger airplane that develops engine trouble mid-Atlantic and is forced to ditch in the ocean has troubles of its own holding the audience's attention. There is the usual varied assortment of characters, with flashbacks to their lives on terra firma merely dissipating any tension that might have been built up over the impending splashdown. Gary Merrill is the captain, while Nancy Davis plays his wife; she quit acting after this film to concentrate on life as Mrs Ronald Reagan. There are no surprises at the climax, either, in one of the last films directed by B-specialist Fred F Sears.

Gary Merrill *Steve Williams* • Nancy Reagan [Nancy Davis] *Helen Williams* • Irene Hervey *Bernice Willouby* • Roger Smith *John Smithback* • Bek Nelson *Nancy Arthur* • Jewell Lain *Ann Thatcher* • Sheridan Comerate *Howard Whitney* • Richard Newton *Jed Sutton* ■ *Dir* Fred F Sears • *Scr* Fred Freiberger

Crash: the Mystery of Flight 1501 ★★★
Drama 1990 · US · Colour · 120mins

A nearly-but-not-quite fascinating American TV movie, starring ex-Charlie's Angel Cheryl Ladd and centring on the crash of a plane that goes down with no clear explanation. The in-flight scenes avoid most of the clichés of the airplane disaster genre, but the attempt to solve the mystery of the film's title gets a spot mired in the excessive detail provided about the life of one of the crash's two survivors. Philip Saville made a better and very different film the previous year called *Fellow Traveller*, but this is perfectly respectable fare.

Cheryl Ladd *Diane Halstead* • Jeffrey DeMunn *Scott Cody* • Doug Sheehan *Greg Halstead* • Frederick Coffin *Goddard* • Peter Jurasik *Stanton* • Jim Metzler *Zolman* • Jeff McCarthy *Harmon* • Moira Walley *Pamela Hayes* ■ *Dir* Philip Saville • *Scr* E Arthur Kean

Crashout ★★★ 15
Crime drama 1955 · US · BW · 84mins

This tough crime drama follows six escaped convicts as they spend three days holed up in a cave before going after buried loot. The usual fall-outs

and double crosses steadily reduce their number, but telling characterisations and clever plot developments maintain the interest. The strong cast of character actors includes William Bendix as the sadistic leader and Arthur Kennedy as an embittered thief, while Gloria Talbott registers sharply as a woman passenger on a train. All credit to the usually undistinguished director and co-writer, Lewis R Foster, who has the benefit of some terrific black-and-white photography by Russell Metty. ▭

William Bendix *Van Duff* • Arthur Kennedy *Joe Quinn* • Luther Adler *Pete Mendoza* • William Talman *Swanee Remsen* • Gene Evans *Monk Collins* • Marshall Thompson *Billy Lang* • Beverly Michaels *Alice Mosher* • Gloria Talbott *Girl on train* ■ *Dir* Lewis R Foster • *Scr* Lewis R Foster, Hal E Chester

The Crater Lake Monster ★
Science-fiction 1977 · US · Colour · 85mins

Though the title suggests a story about a rampaging beast, the movie is actually more concerned with two cretins who live around the lake, getting into endless bouts of comic chatter and slapstick situations. Occasionally we get a few seconds of stop-motion dinosaur mayhem (by David Allen), but it's not up to Ray Harryhausen standard. This account of a meteorite thawing a frozen dinosaur egg at the bottom of a lake is so slow and shoddy, it makes some of the worst fifties monster movies look like masterpieces.

Richard Cardella *Sherriff Steve Hanson* • Glen Roberts *Arnie Chabot* • Mark Siegel *Mitch Kowalski* • Kacey Cobb *Susan Patterson* ■ *Dir* William R Stromberg • *Scr* William R Stromberg, Richard Cardella

Craze ★
Horror 1973 · UK · Colour · 95mins

Jack Palance gives his eye-rolling all as a mad antique collector who plans to increase his wealth by sacrificing London dolly birds to his favourite African idol. Trashy, endless rubbish from producer Herman Cohen, with an amazingly eclectic cast including Diana Dors, Dame Edith Evans, Trevor Howard and Hugh Griffith, this infernal nonsense even defeats veteran horror director Freddie Francis, a past master at disguising junk with style and atmosphere. A waste of everyone's time – including yours, should you be foolish enough to watch it.

Jack Palance *Neal Mottram* • Diana Dors *Dolly Newman* • Julie Ege *Helena* • Edith Evans *Aunt Louise* • Trevor Howard *Superintendent Bellamy* • Suzy Kendall *Sally* • Michael Jayston *Detective Sergeant Wall* • Hugh Griffith *Solicitor* ■ *Dir* Freddie Francis • *Scr* Aben Kandel, Herman Cohen, from the novel *Infernal Idol* by Henry Seymour

The Crazies ★★★ 18
Horror science-fiction 1973 · US · Colour · 102mins

A commendable, if unsuccessful attempt by director George A Romero to repeat the success of his revolutionary horror classic *Night of the Living Dead*. This time around, panic and paranoia prevail when an army plane carrying a bio-chemical virus crashes in Pennsylvania and turns the locals into killers. Consistently shifting

points-of-view keep involvement to a minimum and greatly undercut the suspense, despite the sudden acts of shocking violence and some effective gore moments. ▭

Lane Carroll *Judy* • WG McMillan *David* • Harold Wayne Jones *Clank* • Lloyd Hollar *Col Pockem* • Richard Liberty *Artie* • Lynn Lowry *Kathie* • Richard France *Dr Watts* ■ *Dir* George A Romero • *Scr* George A Romero, from a story by Paul McCollough

Crazy from the Heart ★★★★ PG
Romantic comedy 1991 · US · Colour · 90mins

The consistently under-rated Christine Lahti gives a glorious performance as a schoolteacher who falls for janitor Rubén Blades, causing all sorts of ructions in her small town. Lahti's real-life husband Thomas Schlamme directs with a sure, delicate touch that lifts this potentially ordinary story, revealing considerable character insight. The pace is nigh on perfect, the leading actors are believable and the charge generated between them keeps the audience guessing to the very end. Contains some swearing. ▭

Christine Lahti *Charlotte Bain* • Rubén Blades *Ernesto Ontiveros* • William Russ *Coach Dewey Whitcomb* • Louise Latham *Mae Esther Bain* • Tommy Muniz *Tomas Ontiveros* ■ *Dir* Thomas Schlamme • *Scr* Linda Vorhees

Crazy in Alabama ★★★ 12
Comedy drama 1999 · US · Colour · 108mins

Antonio Banderas makes an accomplished directorial debut with an engaging mix of quirky comedy and civil rights drama that gives his partner, Melanie Griffith, her best role in years. While downtrodden housewife Lucille (Griffith) heads for Hollywood with her husband's head in a hatbox, her young nephew Peejoe (Lucas Black) becomes a key witness in the murder of a black protester. Screenwriter Mark Childress, adapting his own novel, strives to draw parallels between Lucille's quest for liberation and the broader issue of racial equality. While the contrasts don't stick, it's still fun to watch pros like Robert Wagner and Rod Steiger shine in supporting roles. ▭ *DVD*

Melanie Griffith *Lucille* • David Morse *Dove* • Lucas Black *Peejoe* • Cathy Moriarty *Earlene* • Meat Loaf Aday [Meat Loaf] *Sheriff John Doggett* • Rod Steiger *Judge Mead* • Robert Wagner *Harry Hall* • Elizabeth Perkins *Joan Blake* ■ *Dir* Antonio Banderas • *Scr* Mark Childress, from his novel

Crazy in Love ★★★ PG
Romantic drama 1992 · US · Colour · 89mins

Here's one for those who usually give TV movies a miss. Fresh from the success of *Rambling Rose*, director Martha Coolidge conjured up another winning drama in which she once again gets the balance between comedy and sentiment just about right. Adapted from Luanne Rice's bestseller, this is the sort of frothy romance Hollywood made to order before someone mislaid the formula. Holly Hunter and her one-time flatmate Frances McDormand give lovely performances as two island dwellers trapped by convention and insecurity. Yet the film belongs to

Gena Rowlands who, as usual, makes acting look so easy. ▭

Holly Hunter *Georgie Symonds* • Gena Rowlands *Honora* • Frances McDormand *Clare* • Bill Pullman *Nick Symonds* • Julian Sands *Mark Constable* • Herta Ware *Pem* • Joanne Baron *Mona Tuchman* • Diane Robin *Jean Snizort* ■ *Dir* Martha Coolidge • *Scr* Gerald Ayres, from the novel by Luanne Rice

Crazy Mama ★★★
Crime road movie 1975 · US · Colour · 79mins

This rough-hewn road movie from director Jonathan Demme (*The Silence of the Lambs*) tracks three generations of women, plus their partners, on a lunatic trans-American crime spree. Cloris Leachman, Ann Sothern, Jim Backus and Stuart Whitman head the eclectic cast of an upbeat celebration of fifties Americana that stems from Demme's so-called "exploitation" period. Worth seeing as an indication of where a top talent learns his trade.

Cloris Leachman *Melba* • Stuart Whitman *Jim Bob* • Ann Sothern *Sheba* • Jim Backus *Mr Albertson* • Donny Most *Shawn* • Linda Purl *Cheryl* • Bryan England *Snake* • Dennis Quaid ■ *Dir* Jonathan Demme • *Scr* Robert Thom, from a story by Frances Doel

Crazy Moon ★★★★ 15
Comedy drama 1986 · Can · Colour · 85mins

This comic tale originally went by the rather hideous name of *Huggers*, but don't let either title put you off: this sweet, if somewhat clichéd romance has a lot to recommend it. Kiefer Sutherland is moving as the wealthy high-school outsider who falls for a deaf girl (Vanessa Vaughan) and encounters opposition from family and peers. Judging from Allan Eastman's film, Sutherland has clearly inherited a considerable amount of talent from his father, Donald – though in subsequent movies (*The Vanishing*, *Flatliners*) it was not always so evident. ▭

Kiefer Sutherland *Brooks* • Peter Spence *Cleveland* • Vanessa Vaughan *Anne* • Ken Pogue *Alec* • Eve Napier *Mimi* • Harry Hill *Dr Bruno* ■ *Dir* Allan Eastman • *Scr* Tom Berry, Stefan Wodoslawsky

Crazy People ★★ 15
Comedy 1990 · US · Colour · 87mins

An embarrassingly bungled comedy which started life with the best of intentions (to satirise the glossy excesses of the advertising industry) but which slipped heavily on its own banana skin. Dudley Moore, hamming it up with relish, is the ad man who is thrown into a luxury sanatorium after he launches a campaign of slogans which tell the truth. He meets, amongst others, kooky Daryl Hannah in a vast array of frayed cardigans. This is a variation on the old chestnut "we lock up the sane", but it is so ineptly handled that it veers on the offensive. Contains swearing. ▭

Dudley Moore *Emory Leeson* • Daryl Hannah *Kathy Burgess* • Paul Reiser *Stephen Bachman* • JT Walsh *Charles F Drucker* • Bill Smitrovich *Bruce* • Alan North *Judge* • David Paymer *George* • Mercedes Ruehl *Dr Liz Baylor* ■ *Dir* Tony Bill • *Scr* Mitch Markowitz

Crazy Times ★★

Drama   1981 · US · Colour · 91mins

The corridors of television are littered with pilots for unoptioned series. Even though this tough take on *Happy Days* boasted the young Ray Liotta, David Caruso and Michael Paré in the leads, the schedulers still weren't convinced. There is little wrong with director Lee Philips's re-creation of the sights and sounds around New York's Rockaway Beach, circa 1955. So it must have been the fact that audiences had tired of rock 'n' roll nostalgia by the time this TV movie aired. The plot follows the boys as they rumble with greased street gang The Deacons while trying to get to first base with clotheshorses Talia Balsam and Annette McCarthy.

Ray Liotta *Wizard* • David Caruso *Bobby* • Michael Paré *Harry* • Talia Balsam *Eva* • Annette McCarthy *Carol* • Sandra Giles *Esther* • Ernie Hudson *Jazzman* • John Aprea *Ralph* ■ *Dir* Lee Philips • *Scr* George Reeves

The Crazy World of Laurel and Hardy ★★★ U

Compilation   1964 · US · BW · 81mins

Robert Youngson was the master of the comedy compilation and his tributes to Stan and Ollie are vastly superior to this so-so selection from producer Jay Ward. While it's possible to overlook the slapdash treatment of their slapstick silents and the haphazard ordering of the talkie clips, it's hard to forgive the fact that the gags have been so pared down that all that remains is a fistful of punchlines. The boys are always welcome, but Garry Moore's smart-aleck commentary is an unwanted intrusion.

Stan Laurel *Stan* • Oliver Hardy *Ollie* • James Finlayson *James Finlayson* • Jean Harlow *Jean Harlow* • Garry Moore *Narrator* ■ *Dir* Garry Moore • *Scr* Bill Scott

Creator ★★ 15

Romantic comedy drama
1985 · US · Colour · 103mins

Based on Jeremy Leven's novel, this jumbled comedy drama involves a Nobel Prize-winning scientist turned college professor who tries to resurrect his long-dead wife via cloning. Peter O'Toole brings his customary God-like grandeur to the lead role, complemented by the young, amiable supporting cast that includes Mariel Hemingway, Virginia Madsen and Vincent Spano. The film's chief handicap is an excess of soap opera-style plot strands: the intervention of O'Toole's scientist rival (David Ogden Stiers), a pair of budding romances and an incurable illness. ▥

Peter O'Toole *Dr Harry Wolper* • Mariel Hemingway *Meli* • Vincent Spano *Boris* • Virginia Madsen *Barbara Spencer* • David Ogden Stiers *Sid Kuhlenbeck* • John Dehner *Paul* • Karen Kopins *Lucy Wolper* • Kenneth Tigar *Pavlo* ■ *Dir* Ivan Passer • *Scr* Jeremy Leven, from his novel

Creature from the Black Lagoon ★★★★ PG

Horror   1954 · US · BW · 75mins

It's horribly dated, the acting's lousy, the 3-D effects are worthless and the monster is a man in a rubber suit. Yet *Creature from the Black Lagoon*

remains one of the all-time classic monster movies. The by-the-numbers plot – explorers encounter a half-man, half-fish that has the hots for Julia Adams – is enlivened by director Jack Arnold's atmospheric use of the Florida Everglades locations and a sympathetic portrait of the "Gill-Man". (Champion swimmer Ricou Browning was picked for the role because he could hold his breath for four minutes at a time.) The underwater sequences are particularly memorable, while the scene where Adams swims alone with the creature watching from below plays upon all our fears of what may lurk beneath the sea. A massive hit in its day, the Gill-Man justly entered the horror hall of fame alongside Universal's other great monsters, Dracula and Frankenstein. Avoid the two turgid sequels that followed. ▥

Richard Carlson *David Reed* • Julia Adams [Julie Adams] *Kay Lawrence* • Richard Denning *Mark Williams* • Antonio Moreno *Carl Maia* • Nestor Paiva *Lucas* • Whit Bissell *Edwin Thompson* • Ben Chapman *Gill-Man* • Ricou Browning *Gill-Man (underwater sequences only)* ■ *Dir* Jack Arnold • *Scr* Harry Essex, Arthur Ross, from a story by Maurice Zimm

Creature with the Atom Brain ★

Science-fiction crime horror
1955 · US · BW · 69mins

"He comes from beyond the grave!" hailed the poster, and you'll feel like crawling into one after watching this laboured hokum. Here a suitably bonkers Richard Denning uses atomic energy to create zombie-like robots as instruments of his tortured revenge. Curt Siodmak, who wrote the classic *I Walked with a Zombie* in 1943, really seems to be slumming it here. However, the real surprise is how a film combining gangsters, zombies and Nazis could turn out to be such a monotonous watch.

Richard Denning *Dr Chet Walker* • Angela Stevens *Joyce Walker* • S John Launer *Captain Dave Harris* • Michael Granger *Frank Buchanan* • Gregory Gaye *Professor Steigg* ■ *Dir* Edward L Cahn • *Scr* Curt Siodmak

Creatures the World Forgot ★★ 18

Horror   1971 · UK · Colour · 91mins

Hammer's fourth exotic excursion back to One Million Years BC skips monster dinosaurs and special effects to concentrate on sexy cavewomen. Buxom Julie Ege is the daughter of a tribal chief given to the leader of a rival clan, in a thin story that's just an excuse for the former Miss Norway to slip into a revealing wardrobe of leather bikinis and skimpy furs. Some may find this enough, though director Don Chaffey does try hard to keep his Jurassic lark on the side of seriousness. Contains nudity. ▥

Julie Ege *Nala* • Brian O'Shaughnessy *Mak* • Tony Bonner *Toomak* • Robert John *Rool* • Marcia Fox *Dumb girl* • Rosalie Crutchley *Old crone* • Don Leonard *Old leader* • Beverley Blake *Young lover* • Ken Hare *Fair leader* ■ *Dir* Don Chaffey • *Scr* Carreras

The Creeping Flesh ★★★ 15

Horror   1972 · UK · Colour · 88mins

Scientist Peter Cushing discovers a giant skeleton in Borneo, which grows flesh when touched by water, in this over-complicated Victorian morality fable given a classy Hammer-style sheen by director Freddie Francis. Don't try to make sense of it: just enjoy the gloomily disturbing dark tone and some neat shocks provided by the prehistoric perambulating bones. Co-star Christopher Lee is bloodcurdling as an envious brother, while Cushing's sympathetic performance ranks with his best screen work. ▥

Christopher Lee *James Hildern* • Peter Cushing *Emmanuel Hildern* • Lorna Heilbron *Penelope* • George Benson *Waterlow* • Kenneth J Warren *Lenny* • Duncan Lamont *Inspector* • Harry Locke *Barman* • Hedger Wallace *Dr Perry* • Michael Ripper *Carter* ■ *Dir* Freddie Francis • *Scr* Peter Spenceley, Jonathon Rumbold

Creepshow ★★★ 15

Horror   1982 · US · Colour · 115mins

Night of the Living Dead director George A Romero and top terror writer Stephen King neatly capture the ironic spirit of those forbidden fifties horror comics in a lively anthology of ghoulishly funny fear tales. Zombie fathers, green space fungus, caged ancient creatures and the walking dead adroitly come alive from the pages of a comic book thrown away by a concerned parent. The creepiest tale is a "man versus nature" allegory about a paranoid millionaire and millions of cockroaches. Anyone with an insect phobia, beware! Stylishly scary stuff. Contains swearing and violence. ▥

Hal Holbrook *Henry* • Adrienne Barbeau *Wilma* • Fritz Weaver *Dexter* • Leslie Nielsen *Richard* • EG Marshall *Upson* • Ed Harris *Hank* • Ted Danson *Harry* • Stephen King *Jordy* ■ *Dir* George A Romero • *Scr* Stephen King

Creepshow 2 ★ 18

Horror   1987 · US · Colour · 85mins

Penny-dreadful in every respect, this three-part anthology is one of the worst vehicles off the Stephen King production line. A comic-crazed kid opens the latest issue of *Creepshow* and delves into tales concerning a murderous cigar store Indian, a killer oil slick and a zombie hitchhiker. If the sight of four students menaced by a plastic bin liner doesn't reduce you to helpless laughter, then former glamour queen Dorothy Lamour acting more wooden than her Indian mannequin will. Scripted by George Romero with a distinct lack of originality, and directed by Michael Gornick with awesome predictability, this slapdash dud is devoid of any imagination. ▥

Tom Savini *The Creep* • Domenick John *Boy Billy* • Dan Kamin *Old Chief Wood'nhead* • George Kennedy *Ray Spruce* • Dorothy Lamour *Martha Spruce* • Frank S Salsedo [Frank Salsedo] *Ben Whitemoon* • Paul Satterfield *Deke* ■ *Dir* Michael Gornick • *Scr* George A Romero, from stories by Stephen King

Crescendo ★★★

Horror   1970 · UK · Colour · 95mins

This "mini-Hitchcock" thriller from Hammer Films borrows as much from *Psycho* as it does from the studio's

own series of early sixties whodunits (*Paranoiac*, for example). Touted as a new departure for the "House of Horror", this demented tale of dead composers, lunatic twins and drug-addicted cripples merely adds sex and discreet nudity to the tried-and-tested shocker formula. If you can swallow Stefanie Powers as a PhD music student, this one's for you. Look out for Jane Lapotaire in her movie debut.

Stefanie Powers *Susan* • James Olson *Georges* • Margaretta Scott *Danielle* • Jane Lapotaire *Lillianne* • Joss Ackland *Carter* • Kirsten Betts *Catherine* ■ *Dir* Alan Gibson • *Scr* Jimmy Sangster, Alfred Shaughnessy

Le Cri du Coeur ★★★

Drama
1994 · Fr/Burkina Faso · Colour · 86mins

Burkina Faso's Idrissa Ouedraogo is among the best known sub-Saharan film-makers, with *Yaaba* and *Tilä* garnering international acclaim. His seventh feature follows 11-year-old Moctar and his mother as they leave their village in Mali to join his father in Paris, where he has recently bought a garage. However, hopes that Moctar will one day study medicine are jeopardised after he suffers a series of nightmares about a wild hyena. Measured, thoughtful and earnestly played, this is not Ouedraogo's best work, but the insights into the lives of Africans in urban exile are fascinating. In French with English subtitles.

Richard Bohringer *Paulo* • Said Diarra *Moctar* • FélicitéWouassi *Saffi* • Alex Descas *Ibrahim Sow* • Clementine Celarié *Deborah* ■ *Dir* Idrissa Ouedraogo • *Scr* Idrissa Ouedraogo, Robert Gardner, Jacques Akchoti

Cria Cuervos ★★★

Drama   1975 · Sp · Colour · 109mins

Although it became something of a totem of post-Franco optimism, this elliptical chronicle of a young woman's tormented inner life is really about the passivity of a population disenfranchised by fascism and the guilt it would have to endure before Spain's painful memories could be assuaged. As the child who believes she has power over death after witnessing the demise of her father, Ana Torrent superbly conveys that mix of terror and innocence that is unique to childhood. However, Carlos Saura muddles matters by having Geraldine Chaplin play both Ana's mother and Ana as an adult. In Spanish with English subtitles.

Geraldine Chaplin *Ana as an adult/Maria* • Ana Torrent *Ana* • Conchita Perez *Irene* • Maite Sanchez *Juana* • Monica Randall *Paulina* ■ *Dir/Scr* Carlos Saura

Cries and Whispers ★★★★★

Drama   1972 · Swe · Colour · 90mins

Focusing on the failure of love and the agony of loss, this is one of Ingmar Bergman's finest achievements. Combining memories, fantasies and moments of intense family drama, this harrowing study of pain, passion, sisterhood and death brought Bergman a hat-trick of Oscar nominations, although it was Sven Nykvist who won the award for his luscious cinematography. However, it's the stunning art direction of Marik Vos that

U = SUITABLE FOR ALL   Uc = SUITABLE FOR ALL, ESPECIALLY FOR YOUNG CHILDREN (VIDEO ONLY)   PG = PARENTAL GUIDANCE

provides this disturbing chamber drama with its unforgettable manor house setting and its mesmerising red colour scheme. Harriet Andersson, Ingrid Thulin and Liv Ullmann dominate proceedings as the well-heeled sisters, but Kari Sylwan is every bit as impressive as the peasant maid. In Swedish with English subtitles. Contains emotional scenes of death and self-mutilation.

Ingrid Thulin *Karin* • Liv Ullmann *Maria* • Harriet Andersson *Agnes* • Kari Sylwan *Anna* • Erland Josephson *Doctor* • George Arlin *Karin's husband* • Henning Moritzen *Joakin* ■ *Dir/Scr* Ingmar Bergman

Crime and Passion ★

Comedy drama
1976 · US/W Ger · Colour · 92mins

Shady investment banker Omar Sharif convinces his mistress/secretary Karen Black to marry tycoon Bernhard Wicki, to whom he's heavily in debt. The plan goes awry, however, and Wicki swears vengeance. Sharif and Black do their utmost to make the daft plot of this slight comedy drama fly, but it's an uphill battle, especially as they have no really suspenseful or amusing moments to back them up.

Omar Sharif *Andre* • Karen Black *Susan* • Joseph Bottoms *Larry* • Bernhard Wicki *Rolf* ■ *Dir* Ivan Passer • *Scr* Jesse Lasky Jr, Pat Silver, from the novel *An Ace Up Your Sleeve* by James Hadley Chase

Crime and Punishment ★★★★

Crime drama
1935 · Fr · BW · 110mins

In a year that saw the release of two film versions of Dostoyevsky's classic tale of guilt and pursuit, two actors had varying degrees of success in the principal role. While Peter Lorre enhanced his reputation in Josef von Sternberg's Hollywood rendition, Pierre Blanchar walked away with the best actor prize at Venice for his portrayal of Raskolnikov, the angst-ridden student whose killing of a pawnbroker brings the relentless police inspector Porphyre (Harry Baur) down on his head. Blanchar is matched all the way by the brilliant Baur, but this is as much a triumph of art direction as it is of acting, with the doom-laden sets superbly capturing the poverty and despair that make Raskolnikov the most sympathetic of murderers. In French with English subtitles.

Harry Baur *Porphyre* • Pierre Blanchar *Raskolnikov* • Madeleine Ozeray *Sonia* • Marcelle Geniat *Madame Raskolnikov* • Lucienne Lemarchand *Dounia* • Alexandre Rignault *Raxoumikhine* ■ *Dir* Pierre Chenal • *Scr* Marcel Ayme, Pierre Chenal, Christian Stengal, Wladimir Strijewski, from the novel by Feodor Dostoyevsky • *Art Director* Eugène Lourié

Crime and Punishment ★★★

Psychological drama 1935 · US · BW · 87mins

A minor Josef von Sternberg to be sure, but no less fascinating for that. Made on a relatively low budget at Columbia, this dark, semi-expressionist version of the Dostoyevsky classic is pared to the bone; like the novel, it's virtually a two-hander. Peter Lorre extends his childlike *M* persona as

Raskolnikov, while Edward Arnold makes a very American Porfiry. The women, however, are deeply interesting: the pawnbroker murdered by Lorre is played by Mrs Patrick Campbell in one of her rare film roles, while Marian Marsh's streetwalker is made up to resemble von Sternberg's great protégé, Marlene Dietrich.

Edward Arnold *Inspector Porfiry* • Peter Lorre *Raskolnikov* • Marian Marsh *Sonya* • Tala Birell *Antonya* • Elisabeth Risdon *Mrs Raskolnikov* • Robert Allen *Dmitri* • Douglass Dumbrille *Grilov* • Mrs Patrick Campbell *Pawnbroker* ■ *Dir* Josef von Sternberg • *Scr* SK Lauren, Joseph Anthony, from the novel by Feodor Dostoyevsky

Crime and Punishment, USA ★★★

Crime drama
1959 · US · BW · 80mins

A genuine curio from American independent director Denis Sanders, who won an Oscar for his brilliant short *A Time out of War* and is now best remembered for his superb but untypical rockumentary, *Elvis: That's the Way It Is*. This update of Dostoyevsky's novel stars a debuting George Hamilton as the young law student, Robert, giving an impressive performance that is totally at odds with his later "celebrity" status. Providing solidly unglamorous and gritty support are Frank Silvera and Mary Murphy.

George Hamilton *Robert* • Mary Murphy *Sally* • Frank Silvera *Porter* • Marian Seldes *Debbie* • John Harding *Swanson* • Wayne Heffley *Rafe* • Toni Merrill *Mrs Cole* • Lew Brown *Samuels* ■ *Dir* Denis Sanders • *Scr* Walter Newman, from the novel by Feodor Dostoyevsky

Crime and Punishment ★★★

Crime drama
1983 · Fin · Colour · 93mins

This was the remarkably assured feature debut of Finnish director Aki Kaurismäki, who was soon recognised as one of the brightest new talents of European cinema. He has made something of a speciality of updating literary classics (*Hamlet Goes Business* and *La Vie de Bohème* are more recent examples), but this reworking of Dostoyevsky's harrowing novel is perhaps his most audacious. Markku Toikka stars as Rahikainen, a suitably dissolute-looking latter-day Raskolnikov, whose descent into crime is laid firmly at the door of eighties Finnish society. Not content with examining the dehumanising effects of Helsinki life, Kaurismäki aims a sharp eye at the nature of modern policing. In Finnish with English subtitles.

Markku Toikka *Rahikainen* • Aino Seppo • Esko Nikkari • Hannu Lauri • Olli Tuominen ■ *Dir* Aki Kaurismäki • *Scr* Aki Kaurismaki, Paul Pentti, from the novel by Feodor Dostoyevsky

Crime Broker ★★ 18

Thriller
1993 · Ausl · Colour · 99mins

Jacqueline Bisset stars in this Australian thriller, which, thanks to its implausible twists, never manages to convince. Bisset plays a judge who uses the criminal contacts she makes at work to turn lawbreaker in her spare time. Bisset forges an unusual partnership with visiting Japanese criminologist Masaya Kato, who also seems unsure of which side of the law

he is meant to be on. Despite the fascinating premise, director Ian Barry never grasps the comic potential of the idea and the uncertain performances don't help. Contains violence, sex scenes and nudity. ▭

Jacqueline Bisset *Holly Soames* • Masaya Kato *Jin Okazaki* • John Bach *Frank McPhee* • Sally Warwick *Belinda* • Justin Lewis *Josh* ■ *Dir* Ian Barry • *Scr* Tony Morphett

Le Crime de Monsieur Lange ★★★★ PG

Black comedy
1935 · Fr · BW · 80mins

This black comedy belongs to the optimistic phase of French film-making in the thirties known as "poetic realism". Reflecting director Jean Renoir's enthusiasm for the new government of the left-wing Popular Front, it shows how the workers successfully take over a pulp publishing house on the reported death of its exploitative owner. Jules Berry, as the brutal boss, and René Lefèvre, as the writer whose "Arizona Jim" westerns revive the company's fortunes, are exceptional. However, the film's greatness rests on Renoir's masterly use of deep focus photography, which brings vibrant life to every corner of the magnificent studio set. In French with English subtitles. ▭

René Lefèvre *Lange* • Jules Berry *Batala* • Florelle *Valentine* • Nadia Sibirskaïa *Estelle* • Sylvia Bataille *Edith* • Henri Guisol *Meunier* • Maurice Baquet *Charles* • Marcel Levesque *Concierge* ■ *Dir* Jean Renoir • *Scr* Jacques Prévert, Jean Renoir, Jean Castanier, from a story by Jean Castanier • *Cinematographer* Jean Bachelet

Crime in the Streets ★★★★

Crime drama
1956 · US · BW · 90mins

A terrific early Don Siegel movie, a quintessential fifties teen angst flick that contains the trademark intensity of writer Reginald Rose. Like Rose's *12 Angry Men*, released the following year, this film started life as a television play in the heyday of US TV drama. John Cassavetes may seem a little old for the teenage lead (he played the role on TV), but Sal Mineo and future director Mark Rydell are superb as his grisly sidekicks. These juvenile delinquents may try your patience as people, but they certainly demand attention in this razor-sharp depiction of street violence. Top-billed James Whitmore plays the awkward role of sympathetic settlement worker with great skill.

James Whitmore *Ben Wagner* • John Cassavetes *Frankie Dane* • Sal Mineo *Baby Gioia* • Mark Rydell *Lou Macklin* • Denise Alexander *Maria Gioia* • Malcolm Atterbury *Mr McAllister* • Peter Votrian *Richie Dane* • Virginia Gregg *Mrs Dane* ■ *Dir* Don Siegel • *Scr* Reginald Rose, from his TV play

Crime Lords ★★ 18

Crime thriller
1991 · US · Colour · 91mins

Two loser cops find themselves alone against the largest crime syndicate in the world in this overlong buddy film. Director and star Wayne Crawford probably saw it as an excuse to take a vacation in Hong Kong, because somehow the policemen make their way to the Chinese city despite being

suspended from the force. Some interesting locales, but otherwise wholly unremarkable. ▭

Wayne Crawford *Elmo Lagrange* • Martin Hewitt *Peter Russo* • Susan Byun *Monahan* • James Hong *Ling* ■ *Dir* Wayne Crawford • *Scr* Rand Ravich, Gregory Small

Crime of Passion ★★★★

Film noir
1957 · US · BW · 85mins

In a role tailor-made for her, Barbara Stanwyck stars as the wife of decent cop Sterling Hayden. Ruthlessly ambitious for her husband, she sleeps with about-to-retire police chief Raymond Burr. When he names somebody else as his successor, however, the enraged Stanwyck pulls a gun on him. A skilful suspense drama in the *film noir* mould, this is well directed by Gerd Oswald and played for all its worth by both the principals and the supporting cast, which includes Royal Dano as Hayden's work rival and Fay Wray as Burr's ailing wife.

Barbara Stanwyck *Kathy Ferguson* • Sterling Hayden *Bill Doyle* • Raymond Burr *Inspector Tony Pope* • Fay Wray *Alice Pope* • Royal Dano *Captain Alidos* • Virginia Grey *Sara* ■ *Dir* Gerd Oswald • *Scr* Jo Eisinger

Crime of the Century ★★★★ 15

Drama based on a true story
1996 · US · Colour · 110mins

This interesting if rather downbeat movie focuses on the 1932 Lindbergh baby kidnapping and the German immigrant, Bruno Richard Hauptmann, who was arrested for the crime. Based on Ludovic Kennedy's book, the film stars *The Crying Game's* Stephen Rea as the unfortunate Hauptmann, while Isabella Rossellini plays Hauptmann's wife Anna, who stood by him when he was accused of the crime that shocked America and for which the authorities desperately needed a culprit. Gripping stuff, but don't expect all the ends to be tied up by the final credits. ▭

Stephen Rea *Bruno Richard Hauptmann* • Isabella Rossellini *Anna Hauptmann* • JT Walsh *Colonel Norman Schwarzkopf Sr* • Michael Moriarty *Governor Harold Hoffman* • Allen Garfield *Lieutenant James Finn* ■ *Dir* Mark Rydell • *Scr* William Nicholson, from the non-fiction book *The Airman and the Carpenter* by Ludovic Kennedy

Crime on the Hill ★★

Crime drama
1933 · UK · BW · 68mins

When a member of the landed gentry is murdered, his estate is expected to go to his niece Sally Blane. But then Phyllis Dare reveals that she and the victim were secretly married. Local vicar Lewis Casson and his friend, doctor Nigel Playfair, decide to investigate further, with the finger of suspicion pointing at Blane's fiancé Anthony Bushell. Creaky, sub-Agatha Christie murder mystery, directed by Bernard Vorhaus and set in an idyllic rural England.

Sally Blane *Sylvia Kennett* • Nigel Playfair *Dr Moody* • Lewis Casson *Rev Michael Gray* • Anthony Bushell *Tony Fields* • Phyllis Dare *Claire Winslow* • Judy Kelly *Alice Green* ■ *Dir* Bernard Vorhaus • *Scr* Michael Hankinson, Vera Allinson, EM Delafield, Bernard Vorhaus, from a play by Jack de Leon, Jack Celestin

Crime Story ★★★ 18

Martial arts action adventure
1993 · HK · Colour · 102mins

Although Jackie Chan's new Hollywood fans know him chiefly for such light-hearted romps as *Rush Hour*, when he was in Hong Kong he didn't shy away from harder-edged material. This is a prime example: an action-packed thriller, based loosely on the real-life epidemic of kidnapping that once plagued the colony. Chan, in a serious role playing a cop hunting for a missing businessman, keeps the comic mugging down to bearable levels, but still comes up trumps in some dazzling martial arts action, less fancy but more realistic than some of his later films. In Cantonese with English subtitles. ▭

Jackie Chan *Inspector Eddie Chan* • Kent Cheng *Inspector Hung* • Lo Ka-Ying *Wong Yat-Fei* ■ *Dir* Kirk Wong • *Scr* Cheun Tin-nam, Chan Man-keung, Cheung Tsi-sing, Chan Tak-sam

The City Is Dark ★★★

Film noir
1954 · US · BW · 73mins

Ex-con Gene Nelson on parole in Los Angeles attempts to go straight with the support of his wife Phyllis Kirk, but soon finds himself up against hostile forces. Nelson, better known for dancing up a storm in such musicals as *Lullaby of Broadway* and *Oklahoma!*, is excellent; so is Sterling Hayden as a vengeful and sadistic cop. Solid and pacey, Andre De Toth's movie takes a gritty look at police methods, the criminal world and the difficulties crooks face when they try to escape their former lives.

Sterling Hayden *Detective Sergeant Sims* • Gene Nelson *Steve Lacey* • Phyllis Kirk *Ellen* • Ted De Corsia *"Doc" Penny* • Charles Buchinsky [Charles Bronson] *Ben Hastings* • Jay Novello *Dr Otto Hessler* • James Bell *Daniel O'Keefe* ■ *Dir* Andre De Toth • *Scr* Crane Wilbur, Bernard Gordon, Richard Wormser, from the story *Criminals Mark* by John Hawkins, Ward Hawkins

Crime without Passion ★★★

Crime drama
1934 · US · BW · 67mins

So successful was the writing partnership of Ben Hecht and Charles MacArthur – the creators of *The Front Page* – that Paramount gave them carte blanche to produce, direct and write this tale about a celebrated lawyer who murders his mistress when he falls for another woman. There's a nice twist in store, though. A silky smooth Claude Rains unravels most effectively, while the girl is played by Margo, whose real name was Maria Marguerita Guadalupe Teresa Estela Bolado Castilla y O'Donnell. It's smart, gripping and doesn't hang about.

Claude Rains *Lee Gentry* • Margo *Carmen Brown* • Whitney Bourne *Katy Costello* • Stanley Ridges *Eddie White* • Paula Trueman *Buster Malloy* • Leslie Adams *O'Brien* • Greta Granstedt *Della* • Esther Dale *Miss Keeley* ■ *Dir/Scr* Ben Hecht, Charles MacArthur

Crimes and Misdemeanors ★★★★★ 15

Comedy drama   1989 · US · Colour · 99mins

Woody Allen is the finest practitioner of screen comedy since the collapse of the studio system. He is more than capable, however, of tackling weightier topics in the manner of his idol, Ingmar Bergman. In one of his most ambitious films, Allen attempts to combine his archetypal wisecracking style with his more serious moral preoccupations, and the result is a compelling piece of cinema that is as troubling as it is hilarious. The excellent Martin Landau plays an eminent eye surgeon whose lover (Anjelica Huston) threatens to expose his private and professional indiscretions to his loyal wife (Claire Bloom). Allen, as a documentary film-maker, is also at war with himself, although he has a convenient scapegoat for his failures in his brother-in-law (Alan Alda), a TV sitcom director with a gleeful lack of taste and a talent for seducing women. The notion that crimes go unpunished while misdemeanours have life-shattering repercussions is hardly original, but this is still a challenging and sophisticated picture that few other American directors could have carried off with such aplomb. Contains some swearing. ▭

Martin Landau *Judah Rosenthal* • Mia Farrow *Halley Reed* • Alan Alda *Lester* • Woody Allen *Clifford Stern* • Anjelica Huston *Dolores Paley* • Claire Bloom *Miriam Rosenthal* • Joanna Gleason *Wendy Stern* • Sam Waterston *Ben* ■ *Dir/Scr* Woody Allen

Crimes at the Dark House ★★★

Crime melodrama   1939 · UK · BW · 69mins

Tod Slaughter was one of the first cult stars of British cinema. Even at the height of his popularity, his rolling-eye acting style was the last thing in prime ham, yet the barnstorming melodramas in which he appeared make for marvellous entertainment and deserve their place in the hallowed halls of turkeydom. Who cares if this reworking of Wilkie Collins's classic *The Woman in White* creaks so loudly you can scarcely hear the dialogue? It's a rattling good yarn, played with amateur theatrical gusto.

Tod Slaughter *Sir Percival Glyde* • Hilary Eaves *Marian Fairlie* • Sylvia Marriott *Laura Fairlie* • Hay Petrie *Dr Fosco* • Geoffrey Wardwell *Paul Hartwright* • David Horne *Mr Fairlie* • Margaret Yarde *Mrs Bullen* ■ *Dir* George King • *Scr* Edward Dryhurst, Frederick Hayward, HF Maltby, from the novel *The Woman in White* by Wilkie Collins

Crimes of Passion ★★ 18

Drama   1984 · US · Colour · 102mins

Ken Russell deserves some credit for attempting this pitch-black satire on sexual fantasy, puritanism and hypocrisy, but his execution leaves much to be desired. The stylistic contrast between the nonchalant naturalism of Kathleen Turner's daytime existence and the lurid sensationalism of her nightly excursions as hooker China Blue works quite well. But there is nothing erotic about China's encounters with naive client John Laughlin or unnerving about her brushes with Anthony Perkins's sweatily repressed preacher. For all her efforts, Turner can't quite atone for either the wild excesses of Perkins or the peekaboo preoccupations of her director. Contains violence, swearing, sex scenes and nudity. ▭

Kathleen Turner *Joanna Crane Tees/China Blue* • Anthony Perkins *Reverend Peter Shayne* • John Laughlin *Bobby Grady* • Annie Potts *Amy Grady* • Bruce Davison *Donny Hopper* • Norman Burton *Lou Bateman* • James Crittenden *Tom Marshall* • Peggy Feury *Adrian* ■ *Dir* Ken Russell • *Scr* Barry Sandler

Crimes of Passion: One Hot Summer Night ★

Thriller   1998 · US · Colour

A bright executive soon regrets her hasty marriage when her new husband falls off the wagon and becomes an abusive alcoholic. She finds comfort in the arms of her lawyer, but the thoughts of all concerned soon turn to murder. Notable only for featuring the first acting appearance of Christopher Darden, prosecutor in the OJ Simpson trial, this tired TV thriller feels like an extended episode of a generic law and order TV show.

Erika Eleniak *Kelly Brooks* • Brian Wimmer *Richard Linski* • Barry Bostwick *Art Brooks* • Christopher Darden *Earl Mingus* ■ *Dir* James A Contner • *Scr* Michael O'Hara

Crimes of Silence ★★ 15

Drama based on a true story
1996 · US · Colour · 88mins

Michele Greene stars in this drama based on a true story about a happily married woman who is surprised to discover that she has just become pregnant, despite the fact that husband William R Moses is infertile and she has been scrupulously faithful. Greene is terrified by the thought that she has been raped and is blocking the shock of the memory, but the finger of suspicion points towards smooth dentist Joe Penny. It's histrionic stuff but always watchable, and director James A Contner generates a fair bit of suspense. Contains some mild swearing and violent scenes. ▭

Michele Greene *Connie Loftis* • William R Moses *Tom* • Joe Penny *Dr Roger Nolten* • Theresa Saldana *District Attorney Doris Cantore* • Lynda Carter *Susan Saroyan* ■ *Dir* James A Contner • *Scr* Michael O'Hara

The Crimes of Stephen Hawke ★★★

Period melodrama   1936 · UK · BW · 69mins

Tod Slaughter throws himself with gusto into a gloriously over-the-top performance as a monstrous Regency supervillain, rolling the worst of Jack the Ripper, Frankenstein's monster and Jekyll and Hyde into one. Outwardly a kind-at-heart moneylender, he has, in fact, gained his wealth by murder, viciously snapping the spines of his victims. The only outlet for his humanity is his adopted daughter. A joyously hammy melodrama, mingling chills with laughs.

Tod Slaughter *Stephen Hawke* • Marjorie Taylor *Julia Hawke* • Eric Portman *Matthew Trimble* • Gerald Barry *Miles Archer* • Ben Soutten *Nathaniel* • DJ Williams *Joshua*

Trimble • Charles Penrose *Sir Franklyn* • Norman Pierce *Landlord* ■ *Dir* George King • *Scr* HF Maltby, from a story by Jack Celestin

Crimes of the Future ★★

Science-fiction horror
1970 · Can · BW · 63mins

Canadian cult director David Cronenberg's second underground feature – a companion piece to his debut *Stereo* (1969) – deals with deadly cosmetics wiping out the female race, and how the male population sublimate their sexual desires by becoming paedophiles. All the diverse themes Cronenberg subsequently expands on in his later works are here in seminal form, but the film is rather a pretentious, eccentric and over-stylised black satire. The soundtrack, a mix of disembodied marine-life sounds and techno-babble, doesn't help matters.

Ronald Mlodzik *Adrian Tripod* • Jon Lidolt • Tania Zolty • Jack Messinger • William Haslam ■ *Dir/Scr* David Cronenberg

Crimes of the Heart ★★★★ 15

Comedy drama   1986 · US · Colour · 100mins

Beth Henley, adapting her own Pulitzer Prize-winning play, serves up three meaty parts for a trio of Hollywood's leading actresses – Jessica Lange, Diane Keaton and Sissy Spacek – and they certainly make the most of it. The story is pretty slight – three sisters are reunited after one of them is released from prison – and the stage origins are very apparent. However, all three actresses deliver stunning performances (though Spacek was the only one of the trio to receive an Oscar nomination), and the result is a warm, rewarding tragicomedy. Sam Shepard is among the supporting cast, but the film belongs to the ladies. Contains swearing. ▭

Diane Keaton *Lenny Magrath* • Jessica Lange *Meg Magrath* • Sissy Spacek *Babe Magrath* • Sam Shepard *Doc Porter* • Tess Harper *Chick Boyle* • David Carpenter *Barnette Lloyd* • Hurd Hatfield *Old Grandaddy* • Beeson Carroll *Zackery Botrelle* ■ *Dir* Bruce Beresford • *Scr* Beth Henley, from her play

Crimetime ★★ 18

Crime drama
1996 · UK/US/Ger · Colour · 113mins

George Sluizer has a fine idea to explore, but his uncertain handling ensures that what should have been a pertinent and deeply disturbing treatise on the media's presentation of violence becomes unintentionally and grotesquely comic. At no stage does he appear to have control over the performances of Pete Postlethwaite and Stephen Baldwin as, respectively, a serial killer and the actor who plays him on a TV crime reconstruction show. Badly botched, but not unwatchable. Contains sex scenes, swearing and some violence. ▭

Stephen Baldwin *Bobby Mahon* • Pete Postlethwaite *Sidney* • Sadie Frost *Val* • Geraldine Chaplin *Thelma* • Karen Black *Millicent Hargreave* • James Faulkner *Crowley* • Philip Davis *Simon* • Marianne Faithfull *Club singer* ■ *Dir* George Sluizer • *Scr* Brendan Somers

Crimewave ★★★ PG
Crime comedy 1985 · US · Colour · 82mins

Opening with a car filled with nuns speeding through Detroit and ending with an extended chase sequence, this never slows down enough in between to pick up our interest, even though it wants to take us for a ride. It's a slapstick attempt at *film noir* by director Sam Raimi, who also co-wrote the script with Joel and Ethan Coen. The end result, however, is too simplistic, and its story of a security-systems installer caught between a couple of hit men is rather patronising. There are some splendidly eccentric moments but, with character names such as Faron Crush and Arthur Coddish, it's all too obviously an in-joke that excludes the rest of us. ▣
Louise Lasser *Helene Trend* • Reed Birney *Vic Ajax* • Paul L Smith [Paul Smith] *Faron Crush* • Brion James *Arthur Coddish* • Sheree J Wilson *Nancy* • Edward R Pressman *Ernest Trend* • Bruce Campbell *Renaldo "The Heel"* • Antonio Fargas *Blind man* • Wiley Harker *Governor* ■ *Dir* Sam Raimi • *Scr* Joel Coen, Ethan Coen, Sam Raimi

The Criminal ★★★ PG
Prison drama 1960 · UK · BW · 93mins

A steely crime thriller, scripted by Alun Owen from a story by Jimmy Sangster, that unflinchingly explores the cut-throat nature of urban crime and the cold realities of prison life. Stanley Baker is outstanding as the tough villain whose contempt for authority of any sort makes him a target for both monstrous prison officer Patrick Magee and racketeer Sam Wanamaker after he refuses to disclose the whereabouts of the loot snatched during a racecourse heist. Returning to his key theme of the relentless crushing of the individual spirit, director Joseph Losey punctuates the simmering tension with eruptions of violence that still shock today. ▣
Stanley Baker *Johnny Bannion* • Sam Wanamaker *Mike Carter* • Grégoire Aslan *Frank Saffron* • Margit Saad *Suzanne* • Jill Bennett *Maggie* • Rupert Davies *Mr Edwards* ■ *Dir* Joseph Losey • *Scr* Alun Owen, from a story by Jimmy Sangster

The Criminal ★★★
Mystery drama 1999 · UK · Colour · 98mins

Eddie Izzard foregoes comedy in this contemporary *film noir*, which marks Julian Simpson's directorial debut. The opening sequence, in which J (as opposed to Kafka's equally victimized K) is lured into a one-night stand, is quite mesmerising. Yet from the moment he wakes to find himself up to his neck in conspiracy, the action follows an all-too-familiar route to its convoluted conclusion. Simpson's mistrust of the system is couched in unimaginatively hushed threats, though Steven Mackintosh admirably conveys the everyman's terror at finding his head above the parapet. The best moments, however, are provided by cops Bernard Hill and Holly Aird.
Steven Mackintosh *J* • Bernard Hill *Walker* • Holly Aird *Rebecca White* • Eddie Izzard *Peter Hume* • Natasha Little *Sarah* • Yvan Attal *Mason* • Barry Stearn *Noble* • Justin Shevlin *Barker* ■ *Dir/Scr* Julian Simpson

Criminal Behaviour ★ PG
Thriller 1992 · US · Colour · 88mins

One of Farrah Fawcett's many unrewarding career choices, this so-so TV movie finds her playing a lawyer who has to seek police protection after she is targeted by a killer. It's a slim tale with nothing to distinguish it from numerous other thrillers, and both Fawcett and co-star A Martinez sleepwalk through their performances, obviously realising the script wasn't worth the time or effort. ▣
Farrah Fawcett *Jessie Lee Stubbs* • A Martinez *Pike Grenada* • Dakin Matthews *Albee Ferguson* • John Hancock *Lt Wills* • Cliff De Young *Darrel Smathers* • Angela Paton *Adelaide* ■ *Dir* Michael Miller • *Scr* Wendell Mayes, from the novel *The Ferguson Affair* by Ross MacDonald

The Criminal Code ★★★
Prison drama 1930 · US · BW · 98mins

This was the film that elevated Boris Karloff to stardom and led to his portrayal of Frankenstein's monster. He'd played Ned Galloway on stage and the role was enlarged for this movie. Master draughtsman director Howard Hawks doesn't allow the theatrical origins to show, although the tragic ending has disappeared as Karloff now snarls: "That kid don't take no rap from me." Cell life is well evoked, and the film convinces as long as you believe warden Walter Huston would hire his daughter's lover, trusted convict Phillips Holmes, to be his personal driver! Stylistically, though, it creaks in places.
Walter Huston *Warden Brady* • Phillips Holmes *Robert Graham* • Constance Cummings *Mary Brady* • Boris Karloff *Ned Galloway* • Mary Doran *Gertrude Williams* • DeWitt Jennings *Gleason* • John Sheehan *McManus* • Otto Hoffman *Fales* ■ *Dir* Howard Hawks • *Scr* Fred Niblo Jr, Seton I Miller, from the play by Martin Flavin

Criminal Court ★★
Crime drama 1946 · US · BW · 62mins

Tom Conway is a defence lawyer with political ambitions, and nightclub singer Martha O'Driscoll is his fiancée. Conway, however, has accidentally killed someone, and O'Driscoll is blamed for it because she found the body. Conway defends her in court, finds time to get married *and* elected as district attorney. All this in about an hour's running time – and there's still time for a few songs! Director Robert Wise knocked this out at RKO in about a fortnight and manages to pack in quite a lot of style and tension.
Tom Conway *Steve Barnes* • Martha O'Driscoll *Georgia Gale* • June Clayworth *Joan Mason* • Robert Armstrong *Vic Wright* • Addison Richards *District Attorney Gordon* • Pat Gleason *Joe West* • Steve Brodie *Frankie* ■ *Dir* Robert Wise • *Scr* Lawrence Kimble, from a story by Earl Felton

Criminal Hearts ★★★
Erotic thriller 1995 · US · Colour · 92mins

More of a quirky road movie than an erotic thriller, this speeds along rather pleasantly. Hitchhiker Kevin Dillon is the crook on the run who gets Amy Locane mixed up in all sorts of shenanigans when she gives him a lift. The two leads hit it off perfectly and

they are well supported by M Emmet Walsh and Morgan Fairchild. Writer/director David Payne doesn't let the pace slacken for a moment and shows a nice line in sardonic humour. Contains some swearing and violence.
Kevin Dillon *Rafe* • Amy Locane *Keli* • Morgan Fairchild *DA* • M Emmet Walsh *Martin* ■ *Dir* David Payne [Dave Payne] • *Scr* David Payne

Criminal Intent ★★ 18
Crime drama 1998 · US · Colour · 99mins

An intriguing idea is given an all-too-predictable treatment in this adaptation of Edna Buchanan's potboiler, *Nobody Lives Forever*. The rivalry between a cop's girlfriend and his female partner could have been the basis for an intelligent drama, but screenwriter Camilla Carr can't resist playing up the sensationalist side of the story. This is undistinguished stuff, but it could have been even worse in the hands of a director less experienced than Paul Wendkos. ▣
Greg Evigan *Rick Barrish* • Brenda Bakke *Laurel Trevelyn* • Alexandra Powers *Dusty Dustin* • Kevin Dobson *Lieutenant Jim Ransom* ■ *Dir* Paul Wendkos • *Scr* Camilla Carr, from the novel *Nobody Lives Forever* by Edna Buchanan

Criminal Justice ★★★ 15
Crime drama 1990 · US · Colour · 86mins

This undiscovered little gem from American television is powered along by a fine performance from Forest Whitaker, who has since made the transition to director with such films as *Waiting to Exhale* and *Hope Floats*. Here he plays a former criminal who finds himself in the sights of a determined young district attorney (Jennifer Grey). The leads are backed by the now familiar likes of Rosie Perez and Anthony LaPaglia, and director Andy Wolk avoids most of the usual melodramatic clichés. Contains some swearing. ▣
Forest Whitaker *Jesse Williams* • Jennifer Grey *Liz Carter* • Rosie Perez *Denise Moore* • Anthony LaPaglia *David Ringel* • Tony Todd *Detective Riley* • Saundra McClain *Loretta Charles* ■ *Dir/Scr* Andy Wolk

Criminal Law ★★ 18
Thriller 1988 · US · Colour · 109mins

British actor Gary Oldman's first major Hollywood movie sees him in one of his oh-so-rare good guy roles. He's a defence attorney who gets suspected rapist/murderer Kevin Bacon off, only to later discover that's he's guilty. What does he do? Despite director Martin Campbell's efficiency at creating tension, this starts off as fairly implausible and gets sillier as it goes on. The stars add class, but ultimately this is little more than a TV-movie script sprinkled with a light dusting of cinematic gloss. ▣
Gary Oldman *Ben Chase* • Kevin Bacon *Martin Thiel* • Tess Harper *Detective Stillwell* • Karen Young *Ellen Faulkner* • Joe Don Baker *Detective Mesel* • Ron Lea *Gary Hull* • Karen Woolridge *Claudia Curwen* ■ *Dir* Martin Campbell • *Scr* Mark Kasdan

Criminal Lawyer ★★★
Crime drama 1937 · US · BW · 71mins

Lee Tracy stars as a lawyer whose successful ascent up the power ladder comes to a halt when he confesses to his criminal associations. He brings gangland supremo Eduardo Ciannelli down with him, winning the heart of Margot Grahame in the process. Christy Cabanne directs this programme-filler from RKO, drawing first-class performances from his cast – in particular Tracy – to make for a tight and absorbing addition to the popular legal-political genre.
Lee Tracy *Brandon* • Margot Grahame *Madge Carter* • Eduardo Ciannelli *Larkin* • Erik Rhodes *Bandini* • Betty Lawford *Molly Walker* • Frank M Thomas *William Walker* • Wilfred Lucas *Brandon's assistant* ■ *Dir* Christy Cabanne • *Scr* GV Atwater, Thomas Lennon, from a story by Louis Stevens

The Criminal Life of Archibaldo de la Cruz ★★★
Comedy crime drama
1955 · Mex · BW · 72mins

Loosely based on Rudolfo Usigli's fact-based story, this was Luis Buñuel's response to his first return to Europe in almost a decade. His target was the kind of seemingly solid citizen who maintains the iniquitous status quo while proclaiming moral superiority. Buñuel shoots away his pedestal by portraying him as an inhibited transvestite whose childhood experience of death inspires a spree of fetishistic murder attempts. Employing a naturalism that makes Ernesto Alonso's imagined crimes all the more grotesquely amusing, Buñuel also manages to parody his own obsessions in this audacious but essentially flawed black comedy. In Spanish with English subtitles.
Ernesto Alonso *Archibaldo de la Cruz* • Miroslava Lavinia • Rita Macedo *Patricia* • Ariadna Welter *Carlota* • Rodolfo Landa *Alejandro* • Andrea Palma *Cervantes* ■ *Dir* Luis Buñuel • *Scr* Luis Buñuel, Eduardo Ugarte Pages, from a story by Rodolfo Usigli

The Criminal Mind ★★ 15
Action crime drama
1995 · US · Colour · 92mins

Up-and-coming DA Frank Rossi discovers one day that he's the younger brother to mob boss Ben Cross. They were separated after the murders of their parents: Rossi grew up as a sheltered, educated young man, while Cross was forced to work his way up through the ranks of the Mafia that killed his father. Once reunited the sibling rivalry kicks in, and Rossi must decide whether his newfound feelings of familial loyalty outweigh his lifetime as a reputable citizen. The result is a film so bad that you may find yourself engrossed before you realise it. ▣
Ben Cross *Carlo Augustine* • Frank Rossi *Nick August* • Tahnee Welch *Gabrielle* • Lance Henriksen *Winslow* ■ *Dir* Joseph Vittorie • *Scr* Sam A Scribner

Criminal Passion ★★ 15
Psychological thriller
1995 · US · Colour · 89mins

With the press reporting an alarming increase in the number of stalkings, this TV movie takes a rather melodramatic look at the torment endured by victims and their families. Teenager Brooke Langton is the object of college tutor Jere Burns's unwanted affections here. As the obsessive stalker, Burns is made to look evil rather than disturbed and the methods to which anxious mother Joanna Cassidy ultimately resorts are incredibly extreme. Regrettably, this thriller trivialises an important issue. Contains violence and swearing. ▢

Joanna Cassidy *Martha Knowlton* • Jere Burns *Stephen Primes* • Brooke Langton *Beth Knowlton* • Dennis Burkley *Danny Zerbo* ■ Dir Reza Badiyi • Scr Priscilla English

The Crimson Curtain ★★★★
Period romance
1952 · Fr · BW · 43mins

Novelist and film critic Alexandre Astruc, renowned for coining the phrase *camera-stylo*, wrote that cinema should be "a means of writing as supple and as subtle as that of written language". Practising what he preaches in this, his debut film as a director, he unfolds the tale of a young officer's illicit, silent and nocturnal affair with the daughter of the household where he's billeted. Stylish and unusual, the narrative takes the place of the dialogue, with the camera and mute presence of the actors conveying the drama. This jewel of a short feature, which demonstrates that, for movies, less can sometimes be more, stars Jean-Claude Pascal and the ravishingly lovely Anouk Aimée. With English narration.

Jean-Claude Pascal *The officer* • Anouk Aimée *Albertine* • Madeleine Garcia *Her mother* • Jim Gérald *Her father* ■ Dir Alexandre Astruc • Scr Alexandre Astruc, from the short story *Le Rideau Cramoisi* by Barbey d'Aurevilly

The Crimson Kimono ★★★
Crime drama
1959 · US · BW · 81mins

An oddly poignant excursion into maverick American independent director Sam Fuller's underworld. Two detectives in the Little Tokyo district of Los Angeles fall for the same woman who's involved in their investigation into a stripper's murder. Characters range from the hard-boiled to the plain mushy, but Fuller's energetic methods stir up a sympathy not normally present in his other movies. This may be low-key and sometimes banal, but it's still a stylish work that could not have been tailored by anyone else.

Victoria Shaw *Christine Downs* • Glenn Corbett *Detective Sergeant Charlie Bancroft* • James Shigeta *Detective Joe Kojaku* • Anna Lee *Mac* ■ Dir/Scr Samuel Fuller

The Crimson Pirate
★★★★ U
Swashbuckling adventure
1952 · US · Colour · 104mins

A gorgeous swashbuckler, with Burt Lancaster and his diminutive former circus colleague Nick Cravat swinging through the rigging with sharpened blades clamped between their perfect teeth. Encouraged by the success of *The Flame and the Arrow*, Lancaster and his partner Harold Hecht persuaded Warner Bros to agree to a big budget, and shooting got underway on European locations without a finished script. But most of the praise goes to Lancaster, who designed the terrific action sequences and puts in a mesmerising star turn. As supporting actor Christopher Lee said: "I don't think I've ever seen a better co-ordinated man. He moved remarkably well, immensely strong and fearless.

Burt Lancaster *Vallo* • Nick Cravat *Ojo* • Eva Bartok *Consuelo* • Torin Thatcher *Humble Bellows* • James Hayter *Prudence* • Leslie Bradley *Baron Gruda* • Margot Graham *Bianca* • Christopher Lee *Attache* ■ Dir Robert Siodmak • Scr Roland Kibbee

Crisis ★★
Melodrama
1950 · US · BW · 95mins

Cary Grant, the smooth embodiment of American decency in scores of Hollywood productions, strolls through this misfiring melodrama as a brain surgeon forced to perform a dangerous operation on a South American dictator. Ideas concerning repression and freedom are rather too obviously put forward in Richard Brooks's flawed directorial debut, but he went on to the rather more subtle *The Blackboard Jungle* and *Cat on a Hot Tin Roof*.

Cary Grant *Dr Eugene Norland Ferguson* • JoséFerrer *Raoul Farrago* • Paula Raymond *Helen Ferguson* • Signe Hasso *Senora Isabel Farrago* • Ramon Novarro *Colonel Adragon* • Gilbert Roland *Gonzales* ■ Dir Richard Brooks • Scr Richard Brooks, from the story *The Doubters* by George Tabori

Criss Cross ★★★★
Film noir
1949 · US · BW · 87mins

This classic *film noir* reunites Burt Lancaster with Robert Siodmak, who directed *The Killers*, and the alluring Yvonne De Carlo, his co-star in *Brute Force*. Lancaster plays a decent armoured car guard who starts courting his ex-wife, De Carlo, now engaged to rich mafioso Dan Duryea. Lancaster is trapped into robbing his own firm, leading to much double-crossing and murder. Having all the *noir* trappings one needs – fateful flashbacks, a drab urban setting, doom-laden Miklos Rozsa music – this also contains a lot of sexual energy, a thrillingly shot robbery and Tony Curtis, making a brief appearance as a pretty gigolo who dances with De Carlo.

Burt Lancaster *Steve Thompson* • Yvonne De Carlo *Anna* • Dan Duryea *Slim* • Stephen McNally *Ramirez* • Richard Long *Slade Thompson* • James Curtis [Tony Curtis] *Gigolo* ■ Dir Robert Siodmak • Scr Daniel Fuchs, from the novel by Don Tracy

CrissCross ★★ 15
Drama
1992 · US · Colour · 96mins

After all the acclaim for *A World Apart*, former cinematographer Chris Menges came horribly unstuck with this, his second stab at directing. While he admirably captures the sights and sounds of Key West in the late sixties, he fails to inject any life into an all-too-predictable tale of a waitress who turns to stripping to support her son after they're abandoned by her Vietnam-scarred husband. Goldie Hawn is hopelessly miscast as the mother, while the subplot, in which young David Arnott tries to turn the tables on some drug smugglers, is ludicrously contrived. Contains violence, swearing and nudity. ▢

Goldie Hawn *Tracy Cross* • Arliss Howard *Joe* • James Gammon *Emmett* • David Arnott *Chris Cross* • Keith Carradine *John Cross* • JC Quinn *Jetty* • Steve Buscemi *Louis* • Paul Calderon *Blacky* ■ Dir Chris Menges • Scr Scott Sommer, from his novella

Crimson Tide ★★★★ 15
Action thriller
1995 · US · Colour · 116mins

This gung-ho blockbuster from the *Top Gun* team, director Tony Scott and producers Don Simpson and Jerry Bruckheimer, dusts off the time-honoured Russian menace with a script that turns post-Cold War cartwheels to explain an impending Armageddon. An American nuclear submarine, the USS *Alabama*, is ordered to make a pre-emptive strike on Russian "ultra-nationalist" rebels who have taken over a missile base, then receives a second, incomplete, radio message suggesting they hold off the attack. The submarine's captain, Gene Hackman, is determined to remedy the explosive situation using his nuclear capability, whatever the consequences. However, his mutinous executive officer (Denzel Washington) stands between him and the horribly alluring Doomsday button. Propelled at full throttle by fast pacing and a palpable friction between the two leads, the underwater action is further fuelled by a slick score from Hans Zimmer. Contains violence and swearing. ▶ DVD

Denzel Washington *Lieutenant Commander Ron Hunter* • Gene Hackman *Captain Ramsey* • George Dzundza *Cob* • Viggo Mortensen *Lieutenant Peter Ince* • Matt Craven *Lieutenant Roy Zimmer* • James Gandolfini *Lieutenant Bobby Dougherty* ■ Dir Tony Scott • Scr Michael Schiffer, from a story by Michael Schiffer, Richard P Henrick

La Crise ★★★★ 15
Comedy
1992 · Fr · Colour · 91mins

Awarded a César for its screenplay, Coline Serreau's study of social exclusion continues her search to find genuine emotion beneath the masculine veneer of invulnerability. Sacked for being too good at his job and shocked by the infidelity of both his wife and his mother, bourgeois Parisian Vincent Lindon finds his glib idealism repeatedly shattered by the realities of modern life. Solace comes via an unlikely friendship with orphan Patrick Timsit. A dark satire with a distinctly Voltairean morality about it, the film's exposure of class snobbery and liberal hypocrisy eventually gives way to sentimentality. The performances, however, are first-rate. In French with English subtitles. ▢

Vincent Lindon *Victor* • Patrick Timsit *Michou* • Zabou *Isabelle* • Maria Pacôme *Victor's mother* • Yves Robert *Victor's father* • Annick Alane *Mamie* • Valerie Alane *Thérèse* • Gilles Privat *Laurent* ■ Dir/Scr Coline Serreau

Critical Care ★★★
Medical drama
1997 · US · Colour · 109mins

A comedy drama about medical ethics, directed by Sidney Lumet and starring James Spader, Kyra Sedgwick and *Prime Suspect*'s Helen Mirren. Spader is on top form as young resident doctor Werner Ernst, supervising a man on life support and attempting to assist his two daughters, who fundamentally disagree on the choice of treatment. One (Kyra Sedgwick) wants to pull the plug; the other (Margo Martindale) wants to maintain a state of vegetative survival as long as possible. The hospital, meanwhile, is content to keep the patient alive as long as his insurance money swells their coffers. Not quite *ER*, this is still an enjoyable mix of moral dilemmas, sexual manipulation and sutures.

James Spader *Dr Werner Ernst* • Kyra Sedgwick *Felicia Potter* • Helen Mirren *Stella* • Anne Bancroft *Nun* • Albert Brooks *Dr Butz* • Margo Martindale *Connie Potter* • Wallace Shawn *Furnaceman* ■ Dir Sidney Lumet • Scr Steven S Schwartz, from the novel by Richard Dooling

Critical Choices ★★ 15
Drama
1996 · US · Colour · 85mins

Betty Buckley, Diana Scarwid and Pamela Reed co-star in this thought-provoking and controversial TV movie. Wisconsin abortion clinic doctor Buckley tries to proceed with her work while demonstrations rage outside. Among the protesters are two very different women: a pro-choice activist and a religious mother of four who strongly opposes abortion. Claudia Weill directs this tense social drama, which aims to give equal prominence to both sides of a difficult issue. Contains some swearing and violence. ▢

Betty Buckley *Dr Margaret Ludlow* • Pamela Reed *Arlene Dickens* • Diana Scarwid *Diana Johnson* • Brian Kerwin *Bobby Ray Flood* ■ Dir Claudia Weill • Scr Susan Cuscuna, Robin L Green, Mitchell Burgess

Critical Condition ★ 15
Comedy
1987 · US · Colour · 93mins

Director Michael Apted, whose eclectic CV includes *Gorillas in the Mist* and *Coal Miner's Daughter*, must have been having a bad day when he agreed to direct this unamusing star vehicle for Richard Pryor. Pryor, an influential comedian during the seventies and early eighties, plays a hustler who feigns insanity to stay out of prison and, after a series of ludicrous misadventures, ends up running the mental institution into which he has been committed. Yes, it's that ridiculous. Contains swearing. ▢

Richard Pryor *Eddie* • Joe Mantegna *Chambers* • Rubén Blades *Louis* • Rachel Ticotin *Rachel* • Bob Dishy *Dr Foster* • Sylvia Miles *Maggie* • Joe Dallesandro *Stucky* • Randall "Tex" Cobb *Box* ■ Dir Michael Apted • Scr Denis Hamill, John Hamill, from a story by Alan Swyer

Critic's Choice ★★★
Comedy
1963 · US · Colour · 99mins

This started life as a Broadway in-joke as to whether theatre critic Walter Kerr should review his wife Jean's play, but became diluted en route to the movies

and fetched up as a vehicle for Bob Hope and Lucille Ball, reuniting after their hits with *Fancy Pants* and *The Facts of Life*. It's not very funny, though director Don Weis – who was responsible for *I Love Melvin* and some of the better episodes of *M*A*S*H* – paints a sharp picture of the waspish New York theatre milieu. Nice turns, too, from Marilyn Maxwell and Rip Torn.

Bob Hope *Parker Ballantine* • Lucille Ball *Angela Ballantine* • Marilyn Maxwell *Ivy London* • Rip Torn *Dion Kapakos* • Jessie Royce Landis *Charlotte Orr* • John Dehner *SP Champlain* ■ *Dir* Don Weis • *Scr* Jack Sher, from the play by Ira Levin

Critters ★★★ 15
Horror comedy   1986 · US · Colour · 82mins

Stephen Herek, later to hit the jackpot with *Bill and Ted's Excellent Adventure*, directs a cheeky smash-and-grab raid on *Gremlins* and comes up with a crude but entertaining horror comedy. The "critters" of the title are a race of nasty hedgehog-like alien creatures who invade a small American town and proceed to wreak havoc until two intergalactic bounty hunters arrive to save the day. The cast, which includes Dee Wallace Stone, M Emmet Walsh and a young Billy Zane, remains stoically straight-faced throughout, the creatures nab the best lines (in subtitles), and Herek keeps his tongue stuck firmly in his cheek. Contains violence and swearing.

Dee Wallace Stone *Helen Brown* • M Emmet Walsh *Harv* • Billy Green Bush *Jay Brown* • Scott Grimes *Brad Brown* • Nadine Van Der Velde *April Brown* • Don Opper *Charlie McFadden* • Terrence Mann *Johnny Steele* • Billy Zane *Steve Elliot* ■ *Dir* Stephen Herek • *Scr* Stephen Herek, Dominic Muir

Critters 2: the Main Course ★★ 15
Horror   1988 · US · Colour · 82mins

Critters was cheap but hugely entertaining junk food, an affectionate cash-in on *Gremlins*. Quite how it manage to spawn so many sequels beggars belief, but this at least sticks pretty close to the original and manages to hold on to much of the cast. Scott Grimes is once again pressed into action when he discovers that two of the evil space scum have survived and are now a family, while Don Opper and Terrence Mann beam in from outer space to help the doubting townfolk. Director Mick Garris adeptly mixes the gags with the gore, but it doesn't quite satisfy the appetite as much as the first course.

Scott Grimes *Brad Brown* • Liane Curtis *Megan Morgan* • Don Opper *Charlie McFadden* • Barry Corbin *Harv* • Tom Hodges *Wesley* • Sam Anderson *Mr Morgan* • Lindsay Parker *Cindy Morgan* • Terrence Mann *Ug* ■ *Dir* Mick Garris • *Scr* DT Twohy, Mick Garris

Critters 3 ★★ 15
Horror comedy   1991 · US · Colour · 81mins

This largely forgotten entry in a largely forgettable B-movie franchise has received a new lease of life thanks to the presence of one Leonardo DiCaprio in the cast. The *Titanic* hero reveals little star potential in this cheap and cheerful caper, which finds the man-

eating space critters hitting the city for the first time and laying siege to a tenement building. There are a few good gags, but it lacks the anarchic inspiration of *Gremlins*. Contains violence and swearing.

Aimee Brooks *Annie* • John Calvin *Clifford* • Katherine Cortez *Marcia* • Leonardo DiCaprio *Josh* • Geoffrey Blake *Frank* • Don Opper *Charlie McFadden* • William Dennis Hunt *Briggs* ■ *Dir* Kristine Peterson • *Scr* David J Schow

Critters 4 ★★★ 15
Horror comedy   1992 · US · Colour · 90mins

The *Critters* series has provided a few skeletons in the closet for now famous stars. Part three offered an early role for Leonardo DiCaprio, and part four – actually shot back to back with number three – features Angela Bassett, later to find fame and acclaim in the Tina Turner biopic *What's Love Got To Do with It*. This one's set in outer space, allowing for some gags at the expense of bigger-budgeted sci-fi fare. Contains swearing and violence.

Don Keith Opper [Don Opper] *Charlie McFadden* • Angela Bassett *Fran* • Brad Dourif *Al Bert* • Paul Whitthorne *Ethan* • Terrence Mann *Ug/Counselor Tetra* ■ *Dir* Rupert Harvey • *Scr* Joseph Lyle, David J Schow

"Crocodile" Dundee ★★★★ 15
Comedy adventure
1986 · Ausl/US · Colour · 92mins

The first, and best, of the tales about the Australian outback's living legend, who can wrestle crocodiles with bare hands and subdue ladies with naked charisma. Paul Hogan took his lager-commercial he-man into the big time, and the big city, and the result is as agreeable as if it were Tarzan coping in a concrete jungle. Director Peter Faiman's languid pace gives us time to appreciate this particular Wizard from Oz as he survives sophisticates' taunts and outwits street villains. A pity Hogan couldn't keep the momentum going for later movies, but for this, at least, he created a totally likeable superhero. Contains swearing.

Paul Hogan *Michael J "Crocodile" Dundee* • Linda Kozlowski *Sue Charlton* • John Meillon *Walter Reilly* • David Gulpilil *Neville Bell* • Mark Blum *Richard Mason* • Michael Lombard *Sam Charlton* • Ritchie Singer *Con* ■ *Dir* Peter Faiman • *Scr* Paul Hogan, Ken Shadie, John Cornell, from a story by Paul Hogan

"Crocodile" Dundee II ★★★ PG
Comedy   1988 · US/Ausl · Colour · 106mins

Having scored the biggest, non-Hollywood box-office hit in US history, Paul Hogan could be forgiven for reprising the role of Mick "Crocodile" Dundee. Less excusable, however, is the misguided attempt to blend the inspired comedy of the original with the kind of rescue adventure that was old hat in the long-gone days of the film serial. But Hogan is as amiable as before and there are funny moments, mostly in his outback approach to urban life, as well as in the attitudes of the Aborigines and bushwhackers towards the city slickers who have kidnapped Mick's journalist girlfriend, played again by Hogan's real-life wife

Linda Kozlowski. Contains violence and swearing.

Paul Hogan *Michael J "Crocodile" Dundee* • Linda Kozlowski *Sue Charlton* • John Meillon *Walter Reilly* • Ernie Dingo *Charlie* • Steve Rackman *Donk* • Gerry Skilton *Nugget* • Gus Mercurio *Frank* • Jim Holt *Erskine* ■ *Dir* John Cornell • *Scr* Paul Hogan, Brett Hogan

Cromwell ★★★★ PG
Historical drama
1970 · UK · Colour · 133mins

Richard Harris's warts-and-all Oliver Cromwell and Alec Guinness's unyielding Charles I make this a historical double act well worth catching. They bring past politics to vivid life and put pay to the idea that right and grace were on the side of royalist Cavaliers as opposed to the Puritan Roundheads. The usually undervalued writer/director Ken Hughes was given an enormous budget for a British film at the time, and the result is a long-winded but compulsive epic with some mighty battles mightily well-staged.

Richard Harris *Oliver Cromwell* • Alec Guinness *King Charles I* • Robert Morley *Earl of Manchester* • Dorothy Tutin *Queen Henrietta Maria* • Frank Finlay *John Carter* • Timothy Dalton *Prince Rupert* • Patrick Wymark *Earl of Stafford* • Patrick Magee *Hugh Peters* • Nigel Stock *Sir Edward Hyde* ■ *Dir* Ken Hughes • *Scr* Ken Hughes, Ronald Harwood • *Cinematographer* Geoffrey Unsworth

Cronos ★★★★ 18
Horror   1992 · Mex · Colour · 88mins

A compelling, complex and wonderfully atmospheric film from Mexican director Guillermo del Toro that is as much about religion and the nature of cinema as it is a horror story. Although thematically profound, stately in pace and largely devoid of the kind of blood-letting beloved of schlock fans, this is still a highly effective chiller. Federico Luppi gives a performance of great wit and dignity as the antiques dealer who becomes enslaved by the Cronos device, a mysterious mechanical insect that forces its victims into acts of vampirism. In English and Spanish with subtitles. Contains violence and swearing.

Federico Luppi *Jesus Gris* • Ron Perlman *Angel de la Guardia* • Claudio Brook *Dieter de la Guardia* • Margarita Isabel *Mercedes Gris* ■ *Dir/Scr* Guillermo Del Toro

Crooked Hearts ★★★ 15
Drama   1991 · US · Colour · 107mins

A thoughtful low-budget "relationships" movie that disappeared swiftly on release but was revived some time later by dint of word of mouth. Peter Coyote, an excellent actor whom the industry rarely knows what to do with, is solid in a pivotal role as an unfaithful patriarch causing ripples in the family pond. There are many strands to this intelligent, well-paced film that evolve delicately on screen, aided by strong performances from Jennifer Jason Leigh and Vincent D'Onofrio. Contains swearing, sex scenes and nudity.

Peter Berg *Tom* • Vincent D'Onofrio *Charley* • Jennifer Jason Leigh *Marriet* • Noah Wyle *Ask* • Peter Coyote *Edward* • Cindy Pickett *Jill* •

Juliette Lewis *Cassie* ■ *Dir* Michael Bortman • *Scr* Michael Bortman, from the novel by Robert Boswell

The Crooked Road ★★
Thriller   1964 · UK/Yug · BW · 94mins

This thriller is a story of Balkan intrigue starring Robert Ryan as a US reporter investigating a corrupt dictator. Stewart Granger plays the dictator, the Duke of Orgagna, with his tongue in his cheek, but the sad script, derived from a Morris West novel, lets the cast down badly. It was filmed in Yugoslavia, which President Tito was then promoting as the next Almeria. Contains some coarse language.

Robert Ryan *Richard Ashley* • Stewart Granger *Duke of Orgagna* • Nadia Gray *Cosima* • Marius Goring *Harlequin* • George Coulouris *Carlos* • Catherine Woodville *Elena* • Robert Rietty *Police chief* ■ *Dir* Don Chaffey • *Scr* Jay Garrison, Don Chaffey, from the novel *The Big Story* by Morris L West

The Crooked Sky ★★ U
Crime thriller   1957 · US · BW · 76mins

Based on a story co-written by stalwart B-director Maclean Rogers, this crime quickie is notable primarily because it was scripted by Norman Hudis, who went on to become a key scribe in both the *Carry On* and *Man from UNCLE* series. Once again the lead role is taken by an American actor down on his luck, with Wayne Morris as a detective flown over to help Scotland Yard smash an international counterfeit ring. Morris turns in a no-nonsense performance, but is easily upstaged by that master of menace, Anton Diffring.

Wayne Morris *Mike Conklin* • Karin Booth *Sandra Hastings* • Anton Diffring *Fraser* • Bruce Seton *Mac* • Sheldon Lawrence *Bill* • Collette Barthrop *Penny* • Frank Hawkins *Robson* • Murray Kash *Lewis* ■ *Dir* Henry Cass • *Scr* Norman Hudis, from a story by Lance Z Hargreaves, Maclean Rogers

Crooklyn ★★★ 12
Comedy drama   1994 · US · Colour · 109mins

An African-American family living in seventies Brooklyn struggles to recover from the racial turmoil of the sixties in Spike Lee's semi-autobiographical tale, inspired by his youth. Alfre Woodard and Delroy Lindo are excellent as the middle-class Carmichaels, whose household is a reflection of the outside tensions tearing at the fabric of society. While not as confrontational as Lee's other films, *Crooklyn* still suffers slightly from the director's choppy narrative style. That said, this nostalgic look at an important period in the race relations controversy is a sure and mature work.

Alfre Woodard *Carolyn Carmichael* • Delroy Lindo *Woody Carmichael* • David Patrick Kelly *Tony Eyes* • Zelda Harris *Troy Carmichael* • Spike Lee *Snuffy* • Vondie Curtis-Hall *Uncle Brown* ■ *Dir* Spike Lee • *Scr* from a story by Joie Susannah Lee, Spike Lee, Joie Susannah Lee, Cinqué Lee

Crooks and Coronets ★★ U
Comedy crime thriller
1969 · UK · Colour · 104mins

An old-style English caper comedy, with the likes of Edith Evans, Hattie Jacques and Harry H Corbett

improbably joined by Hollywood heavies Telly Savalas and Warren Oates. This strange casting gives the film a certain interest, not to mention eccentricity, as the cast are involved in a plot to rob a British stately home of its silver and art treasures. Dame Edith owns the stately pile and does her doddery old dowager act to perfection, but the overall tone is far too frantic and full of those terribly dated, Swinging Sixties fads and fashions.

Telly Savalas *Herbie Hassler* • Edith Evans *Lady Sophie Fitzmore* • Warren Oates *Marty Miller* • Cesar Romero *Nick Marco* • Harry H Corbett *Frank Finley* • Nicky Henson *Lord Fitzmore* • Hattie Jacques *Mabel* • Arthur Mullard *Perce* ■ *Dir/Scr* Jim O'Connolly

Crooks Anonymous ★★ U

Comedy   1962 · UK · BW · 83mins

Playing a stripper was hardly the most auspicious start to Julie Christie's career, but she manages to cover herself in some glory in this amiable, if unremarkable comedy. It's an amusing but limited idea: what else would the members of a villains' self-help group do but put their individual expertise to collective misuse? Stanley Baxter and Leslie Phillips run through their usual party tricks, while those crafty comic sidekicks Wilfrid Hyde White, James Robertson-Justice and Robertson Hare steal scenes at will. Ken Annakin and much of his cast would reunite for the marginally better *The Fast Lady* in the same year. ▣

Leslie Phillips *Dandy Forsdyke* • Stanley Baxter *RS Widdowes* • Wilfrid Hyde White *Montague* • Julie Christie *Babette* • James Robertson-Justice *Sir Harvey Russelrod* • Michael Medwin *Ronnie* • Pauline Jameson *Prunella* • Robertson Hare *Grimsdale* ■ *Dir* Ken Annakin • *Scr* Jack Davies, Henry Blyth

Crooks in Cloisters ★★★ U

Comedy   1963 · UK · Colour · 98mins

Anything but a pseudo-*Carry On*, this cosy comedy is much more a product of the post-Ealing school and a close relation of bungled crime comedies like *Too Many Crooks*. The emphasis is firmly on character as Ronald Fraser and his gang lie low in a monastery to throw the cops off their trail. (Do you think the writers of *Nuns on the Run* and *Sister Act* might have seen this?) Bernard Cribbins is in fine fettle as one of Fraser's gormless colleagues and Barbara Windsor (rejoicing under the name Brother Bikini) is funnier than the *Carry Ons* ever allowed her to be.

Ronald Fraser *Walt* • Barbara Windsor *Bikini* • Grégoire Aslan *Lorenzo* • Bernard Cribbins *Squirts* • Davy Kaye *Specs* • Melvyn Hayes *Willy* • Wilfrid Brambell *Phineas* • Joseph O'Connor *Father Septimus* • Corin Redgrave *Brother Lucius* • Francesca Annis *June* ■ *Dir* Jeremy Summers • *Scr* TJ Morrison, Mike Watts, from a story by Mike Watts

Crooks' Tour ★★ U

Spy comedy   1940 · UK · BW · 81mins

Basil Radford and Naunton Wayne reprise the Charters and Caldicott characters first seen in Alfred Hitchcock's *The Lady Vanishes* in this slight comic flagwaver, adapted from a radio serial produced by that film's screenwriters, Frank Launder and Sidney Gilliat. Once again it's espionage all the way for the cricket-

mad duo, who this time around are mistaken for Nazi spies in Baghdad. Director John Baxter was better known for realistic social treatises than vaudeville, but he maintains a jaunty pace throughout.

Basil Radford *Charters* • Naunton Wayne *Caldicott* • Greta Gynt *La Palermo* • Abraham Sofaer *Ali* • Charles Oliver *Sheik* • Gordon McLeod *Rossenger* ■ *Dir* John Baxter • *Scr* John Watt, Max Kester

Cross Creek ★★ U

Biographical drama
1983 · US · Colour · 115mins

Beautifully filmed by John A Alonzo, this autobiographical drama suggests how Marjorie Kinnan Rawlings might have got the inspiration for her sentimental classic, *The Yearling*. Yet in devoting so much of his energy to capturing the atmosphere of the Florida backwoods in the late twenties, director Martin Ritt leaves little room for anything other than loosely connected vignettes. As the would-be author who abandons the security of New York to learn her craft, Mary Steenburgen is passively doe-eyed, and not even her encounters with bullish Rip Torn shake her serenity. Peter Coyote and Steenburgen's then-husband, Malcolm McDowell, fare no better in support. ▣

Mary Steenburgen *Marjorie Kinnan Rawlings* • Rip Torn *Marsh Turner* • Peter Coyote *Norton Baskin* • Dana Hill *Ellie Turner* • Alfre Woodard *Geechee* • Malcolm McDowell *Maxwell Perkins* ■ *Dir* Martin Ritt • *Scr* Dalene Young, from the memoirs by Marjorie Kinnan Rawlings

Cross My Heart ★★★ 18

Comedy   1987 · US · Colour · 86mins

This thoroughly amiable and under-rated romantic comedy makes up for what it lacks in wit with charming central performances. Intended as a vehicle for Martin Short, the picture is stolen out from under him by Annette O'Toole, who surely deserves to be a bigger star than she is. Barriers and pretences predictably come tumbling down as newly sacked Short and single mum O'Toole stumble through a date, while the contrived ending is a disappointing fudge. However, there are some nice observations and a couple of cute moments. ▣

Martin Short *David* • Annette O'Toole *Kathy* • Paul Reiser *Bruce* • Joanna Kerns *Nancy* • Jessica Puscas *Jessica* • Lee Arenberg *Parking attendant* ■ *Dir* Armyan Bernstein • *Scr* Armyan Bernstein, Gail Parent

Cross My Heart ★★★★ PG

Comedy drama   1990 · Fr · Colour · 104mins

This charming French pre-teen comedy is a hybrid of François Truffaut's *Small Change* and Ian McEwan's *The Cement Garden*. Sylvain Copans is hugely impressive as the 12-year-old whose friends rally round to keep his mother's death a secret so that the authorities can't pack him off to an orphanage. The ingenious methods to which they resort to deflect suspicion have both an innocence and a black comedic edge that makes this such a treat for both the young and those who might have forgotten how troubling and invigorating childhood can be. Steven Spielberg was reported to have bought

the rights for a Hollywood remake. In French with English subtitles.

Sylvain Copans *Martin* • Nicolas Parodi *Jérôme* • Cécilia Rouaud *Marianne* • Delphine Gouttman *Hélène* • Olivier Montiège *Antoine* • Lucie Blossier *Claire* • Kaldi El Hadj *Dédé* ■ *Dir/Scr* Jacques Fansten

Cross of Iron ★★★★ 18

Second World War drama
1977 · UK/W Ger · Colour · 126mins

Director Sam Peckinpah's switch from westerns such as *The Wild Bunch* to another kind of savagery — Germans in retreat on the Russian Front during the Second World War — helped make this as graphic an anti-war film as anything since *All Quiet on the Western Front*. In this adaptation of a book by Willi Heinrich, James Coburn is the disillusioned sergeant, sickened by slaughter and the double dealings of officers like Maximilian Schell. There's little room for women in Peckinpah's exercise in macho ideals, though an encounter with girl guerrillas shows them exacting revenge with dreadful results. Bloody action, elegantly choreographed to chilling effect. Contains violence, some swearing and sex scenes. ▣

James Coburn *Steiner* • Maximilian Schell *Stransky* • James Mason *Brandt* • David Warner *Kiesel* • Klaus Lowitsch [Klaus Löwitsch] *Kruger* • Vadim Glowna *Kern* • Roger Fritz *Triebig* ■ *Dir* Sam Peckinpah • *Scr* Herbert Asmodi, Julius J Epstein, from the book by Willi Heinrich

The Cross of Lorraine ★★★

Second World War drama
1943 · US · BW · 90mins

A sincere and well-made wartime tribute to the French Resistance, telling the story of a group of PoWs held in a Nazi concentration camp. Yet, despite MGM's topnotch production values and a fine cast, it is difficult to accept the likes of Gene Kelly, Cedric Hardwicke and Peter Lorre in such a grim drama; only dashing Jean Pierre Aumont and nasty Hume Cronyn really convince. As a piece of propaganda, though, the movie did its job well.

Jean-Pierre Aumont *Paul* • Gene Kelly *Victor* • Sir Cedric Hardwicke [Cedric Hardwicke] *Father Sebastian* • Richard Whorf *François* • Joseph Calleia *Rodriguez* • Peter Lorre *Sergeant Berger* • Hume Cronyn *Duval* • Billy Roy *Louis* ■ *Dir* Tay Garnett • *Scr* Michael Kanin, Ring Lardner Jr, Alexander Esway, Robert D Andrews, from a story by Lilo Damert, Robert Aisner, from the book *A Thousand Shall Fall* by Hans Habe

Crosscut ★★ 18

Crime drama   1995 · US · Colour · 94mins

This daft but likeable mobster thriller finds gangster Costas Mandylor hiding out from a rival gang at a remote logging camp and finding out, to paraphrase Monty Python, that being a lumberjack is OK. However, it is not long before his past catches up with him. The casting is fairly B-list, but the forest locations are attractive and some of the action set-ups are striking. Contains swearing, violence and some sex scenes. ▣

Costas Mandylor *Martin Niconi* • Megan Gallagher *Anna Hennessey* • Casey Sander

Max Dodger • Allen Cutler *Jeff Hennessey* ■ *Dir* Paul Raimondi • *Scr* Paul Raimondi, Scott Phillips, David Masiel

Crossed Swords ★★ U

Swashbuckling adventure
1954 · It/US · Colour · 83mins

One of the films Errol Flynn made in Europe during his flight from debts and marriage in America. It's a swashbuckler — of course — with an obviously dyspeptic-looking Flynn strutting his stuff in a tinpot dukedom called Sidonia, which has decreed bachelorhood to be illegal. Of the dozens of women on offer it's Gina Lollobrigida, playing the duke's daughter, who lays down the law at Flynn's feet, threatening to put an end to his "wandering". Ace British cameraman Jack Cardiff shot it during an extended period in Italy which also included credits on *The Barefoot Contessa* and *War and Peace*.

Errol Flynn *Renzo* • Gina Lollobrigida *Francesca* • Cesare Danova *Raniero* • Nadia Gray *Fulvia* • Paola Mori *Tomasina* • Roldano Lupi *Pavoncello* • Alberto Rabagliati *Gennarelli* • Silvio Bagolini *Buio* ■ *Dir* Milton Krims, Vittorio Vassarotti • *Scr* Milton Krims

Crossfire ★★★★ PG

Film noir   1947 · US · BW · 82mins

A terrific and neatly compressed thriller about four GIs, just back from the Second World War, and a murder in a hotel room. Richard Brooks's original novel made the victim a homosexual, but in the movie he's a Jew — at the time, not only a safer choice as far as censorship was concerned, but also more resonant in the aftermath of the war and considering Hollywood's own racial mix. The GIs are Robert Ryan, Steve Brodie, George Cooper and William Phipps; Robert Young is the investigating detective; Sam Levene is the victim, and Gloria Grahame is his girlfriend. Directed by Edward Dmytryk and produced by Adrian Scott (both of whom were later blacklisted in the communist witch-hunt), it's an impressive and gripping film, superbly performed. ▣

Robert Young *Finlay* • Robert Mitchum *Keeley* • Robert Ryan *Montgomery* • Gloria Grahame *Ginny* • Paul Kelly *Man* • Sam Levene *Joseph Samuels* • Jacqueline White *Mary Mitchell* • Steve Brodie *Floyd* • George Cooper *Mitchell* • William Phipps *Leroy* ■ *Dir* Edward Dmytryk • *Scr* John Paxton, from the novel *The Brick Foxhole* by Richard Brooks

Crossfire ★★

Drama based on a true story
1989 · Is · Colour · 90mins

Having made his name as a documentary director, Gideon Ganani turned to two of Israel's most accomplished film-makers to help with his feature debut: producer Marek Rosenbaum and screenwriter Benny Barbash. Unfortunately, this promising trio came up with a film that, while benefiting from Ganani's location expertise, betrays his inexperience as a storyteller. Set in Tel Aviv and based on actual events, this Romeo and Juliet story makes a plea for greater understanding between the country's Arab and Jewish populations. The end result, though, is heavy going. In Hebrew with English subtitles.

U = SUITABLE FOR ALL   Uc = SUITABLE FOR ALL, ESPECIALLY FOR YOUNG CHILDREN (VIDEO ONLY)   PG = PARENTAL GUIDANCE

Dan Turgeman *George Chury* • Sharon Brandon-Hacohen *Miriam Ziedman* • Daniel Friedman *Israel* • Milad Matar *Pierre* • Peter Sinai *Shraga* ■ *Dir* Gideon Ganani • *Scr* Benny Barbash, from a story by Gideon Ganani, Hanan Peled

Crossing Delancey ★★★★ PG
Romantic comedy
1988 · US · Colour · 92mins

Adapted by Susan Sandler from her own play, this charismatic comedy about thirtysomething New Yorkers proves that love is not only blind, but also has a poor sense of smell. Peter Riegert makes the unlikeliest romantic hero as the pickle maker who tries to convince pretentious bookseller Amy Irving that they are made for one another, in spite of her interest in hack novelist Jeroen Krabbé. Lovingly capturing the sights and sounds of the Jewish neighbourhood situated south of Delancey Street, director Joan Micklin Silver never allows emotion to descend into sentiment. ▣

Amy Irving *Isabelle Grossman* • Peter Riegert *Sam Posner* • Jeroen Krabbé *Anton Maes* • Reizl Bozyk *Bubbie Kantor* • Sylvia Miles *Hannah Mandelbaum* ■ *Dir* Joan Micklin Silver • *Scr* Susan Sandler, from her play

The Crossing Guard
★★★★ 15
Drama
1995 · US · Colour · 106mins

Sean Penn is not only a talented character actor, but an accomplished writer/director as well. His forceful drama features one of Jack Nicholson's least showy roles, as the father of a drink-driving victim who vows to kill the man responsible (David Morse). What follows is not a plot-heavy revenge thriller, but a poignant and believable study of a tragedy that has sucked the life out of its tormented protagonists. A slow-burning pace, fine performances and an intelligent script makes this drama feel painfully real. Most of all, we genuinely care about the outcome. ▣

Jack Nicholson *Freddy Gale* • David Morse *John Booth* • Anjelica Huston *Mary* • Robin Wright [Robin Wright Penn] *JoJo* • Piper Laurie *Helen Booth* • Priscilla Barnes *Verna* • Robbie Robertson *Roger* ■ *Dir/Scr* Sean Penn

Crossing the Bridge   ★★ 15
Drama thriller   1992 · US · Colour · 99mins

The lives of three best friends are changed irrevocably when they decide to traffic drugs across the Canadian border in a get-rich quick scheme. An average rites-of-passage drama set to the music of Elton John, Jimi Hendrix and Jackson Browne among others, this film suffers from the fact that the soundtrack is often more interesting than the movie itself. However, it does feature Stephen Baldwin and David Schwimmer in early roles.

Josh Charles *Mort Golden* • Jason Gedrick *Tim Reese* • Stephen Baldwin *Danny Morgan* • Cheryl Pollak *Carol Brockton* • Rita Taggart *Kate Golden* • Hy Anzell *Manny Goldfarb* • David Schwimmer *John Henderson* ■ *Dir/Scr* Mike Binder

Crossover Dreams   ★★
Musical drama   1985 · US · Colour · 86mins

With the resurgent popularity of salsa, you might think a movie on the subject would be a good idea. Here's a film that will soon disabuse you of that notion. Rubén Blades stars as the Latino expert whose career appears on the ascendant. Yet his cockiness costs him the friends he needs when his latest record fails. Despite a great soundtrack, Leon Ichaso's effort is formulaic and trite. Blades has charisma and presence, though, and used this vehicle to cross over himself into mainstream Hollywood.

Rubén Blades *Rudy Veloz* • Shawn Elliot *Orlando* • Tom Signorelli *Lou Rose* • Elizabeth Pena *Liz Garcia* • Frank Robles *Ray Soto* • Joel Diamond *Neil Silver* • Virgilio Marti *Cheo Babalu* • Amanda Barber *Radio DJ* ■ *Dir* Leon Ichaso • *Scr* Leon Ichaso, Manuel Arce, Rubén Blades, from a story by Kenny Vance, Leon Ichaso, Manuel Arce

Crossplot   ★★
Spy drama   1969 · UK · Colour · 96mins

Roger Moore wasn't James Bond when he made this, just a TV star with some time to kill between *The Saint* and *The Persuaders*. Not a million miles from Hitchcock's *North by Northwest*, and set in swinging London, the plot has Moore as an advertising executive looking for the ideal girl for a campaign, who just happens to be mixed up with a sinister political organisation. *Variety* rightly condemned the film's listlessness, though they lacked prescience by saying "Moore is not wholly convincing as a man of action." Tell that to M... and you can, as Bernard Lee is also in the cast.

Roger Moore *Gary Fenn* • Martha Hyer *Jo Grinling* • Claudie Lange *Marla Kogash* • Alexis Kanner *Tarquin* • Francis Matthews *Ruddock* • Bernard Lee *Chilmore* ■ *Dir* Alvin Rakoff • *Scr* Leigh Vance, John Kruse, from a story by Leigh Vance

Crossroads   ★★
Mystery   1942 · US · BW · 83mins

A Hollywood remake of a 1938 French film called *Carrefour* (not to be confused with Renoir's *La Nuit de Carrefour* of the same year), with William Powell as an amnesiac diplomat in Paris who becomes the target of blackmailers. He is then accused of being a wanted criminal in court and, because of his amnesia, cannot prove otherwise. Filmed on a studio backlot version of Paris, its chief virtues are in the cast: Hedy Lamarr as Powell's wife, Basil Rathbone as his blackmailer and Claire Trevor as a nightclub singer.

William Powell *David Talbot* • Hedy Lamarr *Lucienne Talbot* • Claire Trevor *Michelle Allaine* • Basil Rathbone *Henri Sarrow* • Felix Bressart *Dr André Tessier* • Margaret Wycherly *Mme Pelletier* • Reginald Owen *Concierge* ■ *Dir* Jack Conway • *Scr* Gus Trosper

Crossroads   ★★ 15
Road movie   1986 · US · Colour · 94mins

Based on the myth that blues legend Robert Johnson sold his soul to the Devil, this is essentially a musical version of *The Karate Kid*. Instead of "Pat" Morita as the sage imparting wisdom to fresh-faced Ralph Macchio,

we have Joe Seneca as an old compadre of Johnson's who persuades the young guitarist to take him home to Mississippi. Only Seneca's yarns and Ry Cooder's lazy score make the trek tolerable, though it's infinitely more entertaining than the ludicrous finale, in which Macchio trades riffs with Frank Zappa's old axeman, Steve Vai. Director Walter Hill (*48 HRS*) was clearly on an off day. ▣

Ralph Macchio *Eugene Martone* • Joe Seneca *Willie Brown* • Jami Gertz *Frances* • Robert Judd *Scratch* • Joe Morton *Scratch's assistant* • Steve Vai *Jack Butler* ■ *Dir* Walter Hill • *Scr* John Fusco

Crossworlds   ★★★ 15
Science-fiction adventure
1996 · US · Colour · 87mins

Cheap and cliché-ridden it may be, but this *Stargate* meets *Star Wars* hybrid is an enjoyably unpretentious fantasy romp. All-American Josh Charles learns from a mysterious stranger that the crystal around his neck is the key to a trans-dimensional portal where time and space have no meaning. In this crossworld, where everyone is wild-hued and moves in slow motion, he teams up with Ben Kenobi clone Rutger Hauer in a battle for survival against megalomaniac Stuart Wilson, who not only has designs on the universe but also killed Charles's father years earlier. If you can get over the slow start, this will be an entertaining experience. ▣

Rutger Hauer *AT* • Josh Charles *Joe Talbot* • Stuart Wilson *Ferris* • Andrea Roth *Laura* • Perry Anzilotti *Rebo* ■ *Dir* Krishna Rao • *Scr* Krishna Rao, Raman Rao

Croupier   ★★★
Thriller   1998 · Fr/Ger/UK · Colour · 91mins

Director Mike Hodges's account of double-dealing in a London casino is fascinating in its detail, but the improbable romantic backdrop given to the story by scriptwriter Paul Mayersberg does films no favours. South African émigré Jack (Clive Owen) is a straight-as-an-arrow croupier who's in emotional hock to his buccaneering father (Nicholas Ball) and is writing a book about his experiences, which include affairs with girl croupier Kate Hardie and gambler Alex Kingston. His ex-policewoman girlfriend (Gina McKee) has had enough of both his infatuation with his life story and the hours he keeps. Owen's poker-faced acting doesn't involve us, while the double strands of the story never properly intertwine. But there are moments here that prove Hodges is still a film-maker to be reckoned with.

Clive Owen *Jack Manfred* • Alex Kingston *Jani de Villiers* • Kate Hardie *Bella* • Nicholas Ball *Jack's father* • Gina McKee *Marion* ■ *Dir* Mike Hodges • *Scr* Paul Mayersberg

The Crow   ★★★★ 18
Action fantasy   1994 · US · Colour · 101mins

A dark, surreal version of James O'Barr's eighties cult comic book. Brandon Lee (son of Bruce) plays a rock musician returning from the grave to take revenge on the notorious street gang who murdered him and his fiancée. It's a stunningly designed fantasy with *Grand Guignol* gloominess

at a jolting premium. The comic-book origins may be too obvious at times, but the dynamic action scenes and the bravura kinetic style of director Alex Proyas mean it always grips and thoroughly entertains. A masterpiece compared to its lousy sequel, this dark fable about life after death was given a poignant spin when Lee was tragically killed during an on-set stunt accident. Contains violence, swearing, drug abuse and brief nudity. ▣ **DVD**

Brandon Lee *Eric Draven* • Michael Wincott *Top Dollar* • Rochelle Davis *Sarah* • Ernie Hudson *Albrecht* • David Patrick Kelly *T Bird* • Angel David *Skank* ■ *Dir* Alex Proyas • *Scr* David J Schow, John Shirley, from the comic book by James O'Barr • *Cinematographer* Dariusz Wolski • *Art Director* Simon Murton

The Crow: City of Angels
★ 18
Action fantasy horror
1996 · US · Colour · 90mins

Vincent Perez replaces the late Brandon Lee as a murder victim resurrected from the dead to confront his killers in this shameless rehash of the darkly uncompromising original. Lacking the tragic resonance and strong performances of its Hammer-styled predecessor, director Tim Pope's sequel, again based on James O'Barr's cult Gothic comic strip, plays like an extended pop video and quickly becomes a rock-blasting, S&M-posturing endurance test. Ponderous, dull and mechanical, the only thing worth crowing about here is Iggy Pop's feisty performance. Contains swearing, sex scenes and violence. ▣ **DVD**

Vincent Perez *Ashe* • Mia Kirshner *Sarah* • Richard Brooks *Judah* • Iggy Pop *Curve* • Thuy Trang *Kali* • Ian Dury *Noah* • Thomas Jane *Nemo* • Vincent Castellanos *Spider Monkey* ■ *Dir* Tim Pope • *Scr* David S Goyer, from the comic book by James O'Barr

The Crowd   ★★★★★
Silent drama   1928 · US · BW · 104mins

An ambitious young man in a dead-end job meets a girl on a blind date, whom he later marries. Then the setbacks begin. Director King Vidor uses real locations to great effect, displays a wonderful eye for telling detail and draws a superlative performance from James Murray, who had been plucked from a crowd of extras. (Tragically, though, he was unable to cope with stardom.) Eleanor Boardman, who was married to Vidor at the time, is also touching as the hero's young wife. The film's bold use of the moving camera still amazes, and its depiction of regimented office life and the palliative power of mass laughter were later referenced by such eminent directors as Billy Wilder (in *The Apartment*) and Preston Sturges (in *Sullivan's Travels*).

Eleanor Boardman *Mary* • James Murray *John* • Bert Roach *Bert* • Estelle Clark *Jane* • Daniel G Tomlinson *Jim* • Dell Henderson *Dick* ■ *Dir* King Vidor • *Scr* King Vidor, John VA Weaver, Harry Behn, Joe Farnham [Joseph Farnham] (titles), from a story by King Vidor • *Cinematographer* Henry Sharp

The Crowd Roars   ★★★
Drama   1932 · US · BW · 84mins

This dated motor-racing melodrama is redeemed by a knock-out performance from a cocky James Cagney, acting away on all cylinders despite the rather obvious back projection and model shots. The film has all the fast-paced style Warner Bros fans expect, speedy dialogue and a batch of regulars (Joan Blondell, Frank McHugh) in the cast. However, it's a far cry from Howard Hawks's best work (the director was reunited with Cagney three years later, to far better effect, in the superb *Ceiling Zero*), and those studio racetrack shots really let it down. The same shots were used in the 1939 remake, *Indianapolis Speedway*.

James Cagney *Joe Greer* • Joan Blondell *Anne* • Eric Linden *Eddie Greer* • Ann Dvorak *Lee* • Guy Kibbee *Dad Greer* • Frank McHugh *Spud Connors* • Regis Toomey *Dick Wilbur* • William Arnold *Bill Arnold* ■ *Dir* Howard Hawks • *Scr* John Bright, Niven Busch, Kubec Glasmon

The Crowd Roars ★★
Sports drama   1938 · US · BW · 90mins

As part of MGM's strategy to give him a tougher image that would appeal to a male audience, Robert Taylor here plays a boxer who is soured on life after he accidentally kills an opponent. Becoming a pawn of Edward Arnold's racketeer, he falls in love with the man's daughter (Maureen O'Sullivan). Frank Morgan does one of his tipsy turns as Taylor's alcoholic father, while Richard Thorpe directs competently. Alas, the film lacks any real punch. Mickey Rooney starred in a 1947 remake, *Killer McCoy*.

Robert Taylor (1) *Tommy McCoy* • Edward Arnold *Jim Cain* • Frank Morgan *Brian McCoy* • Maureen O'Sullivan *Sheila Carson* • William Gargan *Johnny Martin* • Lionel Stander "Happy" *Lane* • Jane Wyman *Vivian* • Nat Pendleton "Pug" *Walsh* ■ *Dir* Richard Thorpe • *Scr* Thomas Lennon, George Bruce, George Oppenheimer, from a story by George Bruce

The Crowded Sky ★★★
Drama   1960 · US · Colour · 105mins

Progenitor of the group jeopardy movie, with a pre-*Airport* collection of second-string movie stars slightly past their prime, this typically glossy Warner Bros melodrama has a look that virtually enshrines its year. The plot is satisfyingly and classically simple – an airliner and a navy jet are on a collision course – and the whole is skilfully directed by former Universal craftsman Joseph Pevney, whose previous work includes *Man of a Thousand Faces* and *Away All Boats*. Film fans will enjoy watching the cast go through their paces: John Kerr (*South Pacific*), Troy Donahue (*A Summer Place*), Patsy Kelly and the luscious Rhonda Fleming. A camp treat, maybe, but a treat nonetheless.

Dana Andrews *Dick Barnett* • Rhonda Fleming *Cheryl Heath* • Efrem Zimbalist Jr *Dale Heath* • John Kerr *Mike* • Anne Francis *Kitty Foster* • Keenan Wynn *Nick Hyland* • Troy Donahue *McVey* • Patsy Kelly *Gertrude* ■ *Dir* Joseph Pevney • *Scr* Charles Schnee, from the novel by Hank Searls

Crowned and Dangerous ★★[12]
Crime thriller   1997 · US · Colour · 85mins

You'll want to add this over-the-top murder mystery to your list of guilty pleasures. Jill Clayburgh (*An Unmarried*

Woman) stars as the pushy mother of a Californian beauty contestant (played by *Baywatch* babe Yasmine Bleeth). When her daughter's main rival is found dead, it looks as if mom may have gone too far. While it won't win any prizes, this dryly amusing TV movie is a rollicking good time and campy fun. Contains some swearing, sexual reference and violence. ▭

Yasmine Bleeth *Danielle* • Jill Clayburgh *Kathy* • Cassidy Rae *Shauna Langley* • Gates McFadden *Patrice* • Troy Evans *Wallace* • Lily Knight *Meyers* ■ *Dir* Christopher Leitch • *Scr* Alan Hines, Carey W Hayes, Chad Hayes

Crows and Sparrows ★★★★
Political drama   1949 · Chi · BW · 113mins

Already established as one of China's finest film-makers with *Spring River Flows East* (1947), Zheng Junli had to change his political tune for a paean to Maoist ideology that confirmed his status within the communist film industry. There are similarities in this tale of tenement folk to Jean Renoir's Popular Front picture, *Le Crime de Monsieur Lange*, as various residents struggle to stay the right side of their avaricious landlord while also trying to pick a path through the minefield of political affiliations. Legendary actresses Wu Yin and Shangguan Yunzhu are outstanding, as is Sun Daolin as the timid schoolteacher. In Mandarin with English subtitles.

Zhao Dan *Little Broadcast* • Wu Yin *Mrs Xiao* • Wei Heling *Mr Kong* • Sun Daolin *Teacher Hua* • Shangguan Yunzhu *Mrs Hua* • Li Tianji *Mr Hou* ■ *Dir* Zheng Junli • *Scr* Baichen Chen, Lingu Wang, Tao Xu, Dan Zhao, Junli Zheng, Fu Shen

The Crucible ★★★★[12]
Historical drama   1996 · US · Colour · 118mins

This is a powerful, vivid filming of Arthur Miller's emotionally raw tale of suspected witchcraft in 17th century Massachusetts – the author and screenwriter's veiled attack on the McCarthy communist trials of the fifties. Director Nicholas Hytner (*The Madness of King George*) brilliantly captures both a believable period flavour and the stifling atmosphere of fear and suspicion in Salem. Daniel Day-Lewis is characteristically intense as the married man caught in the middle, but the real fireworks come from Winona Ryder, as the wicked young girl whose manipulative behaviour is the story's catalyst, and Paul Scofield's commanding presence as the trial's judge. The film's final third is absolutely electrifying. ▭

Daniel Day-Lewis *John Proctor* • Winona Ryder *Abigail Williams* • Paul Scofield *Judge Danforth* • Joan Allen *Elizabeth Proctor* • Bruce Davison *Reverend Parris* • Rob Campbell *Reverend Hale* • Jeffrey Jones *Thomas Putnam* • Peter Vaughan *Giles Corey* ■ *Dir* Nicholas Hytner • *Scr* Arthur Miller, from a play by Arthur Miller

Crucible of Terror ★[18]
Horror   1971 · UK · Colour · 85mins

Former Radio One disc jockey Mike Raven turned actor to appear in this kooky *House of Wax* variant. He shouldn't have given up his day job! Woodenly playing an insane sculptor, Raven covers the dead bodies of his

murder victims in bronze after being possessed by an evil spirit. Longer on talk than terror, the stilted direction and ridiculous dialogue doom any attempt at thrills or suspense. Contains violence and nudity. ▭

Mike Raven *Victor Clare* • Mary Maude *Millie* • James Bolam *John Davies* • Ronald Lacey *Michael* • Betty Alberge *Dorothy* • John Arnatt *Bill* • Beth Morris *Jane Clare* ■ *Dir* Ted Hooker • *Scr* Ted Hooker, Tom Parkinson

The Crucifer of Blood ★★
Mystery   1991 · US · Colour · 103 mins

A fairly standard Sherlock Holmes mystery concerning sinister pacts, Indian treasures and killer pygmies. Charlton Heston is not very convincing as the Baker Street sleuth in this bland affair directed by his son Fraser. Other lead performances by Richard Johnson (Dr Watson) and Simon Callow (Inspector Lestrade) take up the slack, but its uninspired TV-movie sheen is apparent from the outset. Still, Conan Doyle completists will want to catch it.

Charlton Heston *Sherlock Holmes* • Richard Johnson *Dr Watson* • Susannah Harker *Irene St Claire* • John Castle *Neville St Claire* • Clive Wood *Jonathan Small* • Simon Callow *Inspector Lestrade* • Edward Fox *Alistair Ross* ■ *Dir* Fraser C Heston • *Scr* Fraser C Heston, from a play by Paul Giovanni, from the novel *The Sign of Four* by Sir Arthur Conan Doyle

The Crucified Lovers ★★★★
Romantic period drama   1954 · Jap · BW · 101mins

Originally written as a piece for marionettes by the 16th-century playwright Monzaemon Chikamatsu and subsequently adapted for the kabuki stage, this tale of doomed defiance has been filmed with a painterly yet wholly cinematic realism by the master Japanese director, Kenji Mizoguchi. Subtly depicting passion without any physical contact between merchant's wife Kyoko Kagawa and besotted clerk Kazuo Hasegawa, he retains the human element of the story in spite of his unceasing attention to period detail. He also makes expert use of the landscape (sublimely photographed by Kazuo Miyagawa) to contrast their innocent devotion with the brutality of shogunate society. In Japanese with English subtitles.

Kazuo Hasegawa *Mohei* • Kyoko Kagawa *Osan* • Yoko Minamida *Otama* • Eitaro Shindo *Ishun* • Chieko Naniwa *Oko* • Ichiro Sugai *Gembei* ■ *Dir* Kenji Mizoguchi • *Scr* Yoshikata Yoda, Matsutaro Kawaguchi, from the play *The Legend of the Grand Scroll Makers* by Monzaemon Chikamatsu

Cruel Intentions ★★★[15]
Drama   1999 · US · Colour · 94mins

Dangerous Liaisons for the under-20s is the basic premise of this sexed-up, revved-up teen picture. Spring chickens Sarah Michelle Gellar and Ryan Phillippe star as the contemporary Merteuil and Valmont, machinating round New York and laying their bet as to whether or not Phillippe can bed Reese Witherspoon. You can understand why director Roger Kumble saw the classic novel as an apt metaphor for burgeoning teenage sexuality and exploration, but the crucial distinction is that Merteuil and Valmont, when played by middle-aged,

have the motive of bitter life experience to fuel their dangerous games. With peaches 'n' cream teens at its centre, the same plot seems to reverberate with unprovoked spite. The depth gone, this is simply a fluffy entertaining rompette, far surpassed by Frears's earlier adaptation of the tale. ▭ *DVD*

Sarah Michelle Gellar *Kathryn Merteuil* • Ryan Phillippe *Sebastian Valmont* • Reese Witherspoon *Annette Hargrove* • Selma Blair *Cecile Caldwell* • Louise Fletcher *Helen Rosemond* • Joshua Jackson *Blaine Tuttle* ■ *Dir* Roger Kumble • *Scr* Roger Kumble, from the novel *Les Liasions Dangereuses* by Choderlos de Laclos

The Cruel Sea ★★★★[PG]
Second World War drama   1953 · UK · BW · 120mins

Charles Frend's *San Demetrio London* was one of the finest naval combat films made anywhere during the Second World War. Here, Frend's insight into the conditions endured and the emotions experienced by embattled sailors of all ranks is very much to the fore in a stirring adaptation (by Eric Ambler) of Nicholas Monsarrat's bestselling novel. Produced by Leslie Norman (father of Barry), this is a prime example of the docudramatic style that, spurning the gung-ho heroics of Hollywood, characterised the best British war films. The selfless playing of Jack Hawkins and his crew reinforces the sense of realism. ▭

Jack Hawkins *Ericson* • Donald Sinden *Lockhart* • John Stratton *Ferraby* • Denholm Elliott *Morrell* • Stanley Baker *Bennett* • Virginia McKenna *Julie Hallam* • Glyn Houston *Phillips* • Alec McCowen *Tonbridge* ■ *Dir* Charles Frend • *Scr* Eric Ambler, from the novel by Nicholas Monsarrat

The Cruise ★★★
Documentary   1998 · US · BW · 76mins

For all its technical limitations, this is a quizzically admiring and highly entertaining portrait of New York tour guide and street poet, Timothy "Speed" Levitch. Vivacious, brash and disarmingly persuasive, Levitch has an opinion on everything and is never shy to express it – at length. However, while director Bennett Miller is always prepared to let this nonconformist motormouth go into overdrive, he leaves unanswered too many questions about his background and his impact on the people he encounters. He also wastes the chance to explore Levitch's stomping ground in grainy video monochrome by resorting too often to tight close-up.

Dir Bennett Miller

Cruise Missile ★★
Spy thriller   1978 · W Ger/It/Sp · Colour

A proposed peace conference is under threat from terrorists, so American agent Peter Graves teams up with his Russian counterpart (Curt Jurgens) to thwart them. A negligible programmer which, if nothing else, at least answered the question of who would take over the necessary role of all-purpose villain once the Cold War thawed out. Gaunt horror veteran John Carradine pops up in a supporting role.

Peter Graves (1) *Alec* • Curt Jurgens *Baron* • John Carradine *Nikolajeff* • Michael Dante *Konstantin* ■ *Dir* Leslie H Martinson • *Scr* Clark Reynolds, Elio Romano

Cruising ★★ 18

Detective thriller
1980 · US · Colour · 100mins

William Friedkin's typically intense thriller finds Al Pacino overacting alarmingly as the clear-eyed New York cop who leathers up and enters the gay, sado-masochistic underworld in order to track down a psychopath. Inevitably, his hormones get very confused. Drawing criticism from gay groups in America and Britain – as it was almost calculated to do – it pushes to the limit what is acceptable in a mainstream studio picture. However, while the savagery of the murders and the explicitness of the sexual practices on display are initially unsettling, they soon become numbing and, ultimately, yawn-inducing. ▭

Al Pacino *Steve Burns* • Paul Sorvino *Captain Edelson* • Karen Allen *Nancy* • Richard Cox *Stuart Richards* • Don Scardino *Ted Bailey* ■ *Dir* William Friedkin • *Scr* William Friedkin, from a novel by Gerald Walker

Crumb ★★★★ 18

Documentary 1995 · US · Colour · 120mins

Robert Crumb became a hero of the American underground in the mid-sixties for such cartoon strips as *Fritz the Cat* and *Keep on Truckin'*. Yet, as Terry Zwigoff's documentary opens, the cult cartoonist was packing his bags to settle in France and abandon not just a legion of fans, but also the various feminist groups who denounced him for the sexism of his work and the chauvinism of his private life. This is anything but hagiography, with Crumb coming across as a highly resistible character, while his brothers Charles and Maxon prove every bit as fascinating. This is an often shocking, sometimes horrifying portrait of an artist and his world. ▭

Dir Terry Zwigoff

The Crusades ★★

Historical drama 1935 · US · BW · 123mins

Another episode in *The History of the World* by Cecil B DeMille. This time Cecil tackles the Crusades, following Richard I and the Christians as they set forth from Europe to attack Saladin's Muslim hordes. Mixed up in this is Loretta Young, Richard's lady love, whom he agrees to marry in exchange for food and horses; he absents himself from their wedding, sending his sword in his place. This was a box-office disaster, though the siege of Jerusalem is as juicy as one expects from this legendary director.

Loretta Young *Berengaria* • Henry Wilcoxon *Richard* • Ian Keith *Saladin* • Katherine DeMille *Alice* • C Aubrey Smith *The Hermit* • Joseph Schildkraut *Conrad of Montferrat* ■ *Dir* Cecil B DeMille • *Scr* Harold Lamb, Waldemar Young, Dudley Nichols, from the non-fiction book *The Crusade: Iron Men and Saints* by Harold Lamb

Crush ★★★ 18

Drama 1992 · NZ · Colour · 92mins

Alison Maclean makes an arresting feature debut with this dark treatise on sexual ambiguity, power games and identity crises. Metaphors abound as the mercenary Marcia Gay Harden exploits literary critic Donogh Rees's incapacity to move in on author William Zappa and his impressionable daughter, Caitlin Bossley. The bubbling mud of New Zealand's top tourist site Rotorua symbolises the seething emotions underlying the increasingly sinister events, while Harden's ruthless opportunism represents the threat of American cultural imperialism. All themes aside, though, this erotic psychological thriller eventually boils over into melodrama. ▭

Marcia Gay Harden *Lane* • Donogh Rees *Christina* • Caitlin Bossley *Angela* • William Zappa *Colin* • Pete Smith *Horse* • Jon Brazier *Arthur* ■ *Dir* Alison Maclean • *Scr* Alison Maclean, Anne Kennedy

The Crush ★★★ 15

Thriller 1993 · US · Colour · 85mins

Fatal Attraction meets *Lolita* in this daft, shamelessly derivative thriller. Alicia Silverstone, making her film debut, is the precocious 14-year-old whose flirtation with Cary Elwes's journalist becomes a campaign of terror when he rejects her overtures in favour of a grown-up woman. The dangerously obsessed teen's progress from scratching his car to ruining his life plays up her under-age sexuality, leading to some nastily unnerving fun. Silverstone's psychotic performance displays undeniable star quality. ▭

Cary Elwes *Nick Eliot* • Alicia Silverstone *Darian* • Jennifer Rubin *Amy* • Kurtwood Smith *Cliff Forrester* • Gwynyth Walsh *Liv Forrester* ■ *Dir/Scr* Alan Shapiro

Crush Proof ★★★ 18

Drama 1998 · UK/Ire/Ger · Colour · 93mins

A million miles from the cosy Barrytown backstreets of Roddy Doyle, director Paul Tickell's bruising Dublin-set debut is an inner-city western, complete with horses, posses and mobile phones. No sooner out of jail than straight back into trouble, Darren Healy gives a defiant performance as the teenage outlaw to whom life keeps happening with a vengeance. Although reasons for his plight are touched upon, this is anything but a message movie. Instead, it's a frenetic frontier tale, with the unexpectedly quiet passages being every bit as effective as the shocking set pieces – an accidental lynching and a rustling riot among them. Contains violence, swearing and sex scenes.

Darren Healy *Neal* • Viviana Verveen *Nuala* • Jeff O'Toole *Liam* • Mark Dunne *Sean* • Michael McElhatton *Detective Sergeant Hogan* ■ *Dir* Paul Tickell • *Scr* James Mathers, from a story by John Edwards, James Mathers

Crusoe ★★★ 15

Period adventure 1988 · US · Colour · 90mins

Daniel Defoe's classic allegory gets another makeover, this time with Aidan Quinn as the shipwrecked hero. His Robinson Crusoe is a slave trader whose moral failings are reversed first by his pet dog, then by an escaped slave whom he saves, and finally by a cannibal. Directed by Caleb Deschanel, better known as a cameraman, and superbly shot in the Seychelles, it's a generally impressive achievement that pushes its message home without undue force. Luis Buñuel's 1952 version of the story remains the benchmark, though. ▭

Aidan Quinn *Crusoe* • Ade Sapara *The Warrior* • Elvis Payne *Runaway Slave* • Richard Sharp *Colcol* • Colin Bruce *Clerk* • Jimmy Nail *Tarik* • Timothy Spall *Reverend Milne* • Warren Clarke *Captain Lee* ■ *Dir* Caleb Deschanel • *Scr* Walon Green, Christopher Logue, from the novel *The Life and Adventures of Robinson Crusoe* by Daniel Defoe

Cry-Baby ★★★ 15

Musical parody 1989 · US · Colour · 81mins

John Waters's hilarious send-up of *Grease* and *Jailhouse Rock* revolves around juvenile delinquent Johnny Depp having the hots for square Amy Locane. A superb soundtrack mixes real throbbing golden oldies with wonderful rock 'n' roll parodies, and the usual hip cast (including Iggy Pop and porn queen Traci Lords) pushes the vivid cartoon caricatures as close to the edge as possible. The nostalgic delights in Waters's reform school drool are often more subtle than his other period offering, *Hairspray*, but it's still a polished debunking of pop culture from the "Pope of Trash". Contains swearing.

Johnny Depp *Wade "Cry-Baby" Walker* • Amy Locane *Allison Vernon-Williams* • Susan Tyrrell *Ramona* • Polly Bergen *Mrs Vernon-Williams* • Iggy Pop *Belvedere* • Ricki Lake *Pepper* • Traci Lords *Wanda* ■ *Dir/Scr* John Waters

The Cry Baby Killer ★★

Crime drama 1958 · US · BW · 61mins

Jack Nicholson's first big break – and his last for some time – was gaining the title role in this low-budget contribution to the juvenile delinquency cycle of the time. Nicholson makes his film debut as the frightened teenager who shoots two bullies and barricades himself in a storeroom with hostages. The siege that follows – with police, parents and friends trying to make the essentially decent youngster surrender – is well handled by director Jus Addiss, but Nicholson's part is too underwritten for him to make much of it. The script was mainly by actor Leo Gordon, seen as a vicious onlooker.

Harry Lauter *Porter* • Jack Nicholson *Jimmy* • Carolyn Mitchell *Carole* • Brett Halsey *Manny* • Lynn Cartwright *Julie* • Ralph Reed *Joey* • John Shay *Gannon* • Barbara Knudson *Mrs Maxton* ■ *Dir* Jus Addiss • *Scr* Melvin Levy, Leo Gordon, from a story by Leo Gordon

Cry Danger ★★★

Crime drama 1951 · US · BW · 79mins

A former child actor and film editor, Robert Parrish made an impressive directorial debut with this tough thriller starring one-time crooner Dick Powell as an ex-convict on a quest to free a pal still in jail. The film is set in the ghetto area of Los Angeles, to allow Powell to hole up in a seedy trailer camp to stake out said friend's wife (played by Rhonda Fleming). Hot on atmosphere (provided by legendary cameraman and Robert Aldrich favourite Joseph Biroc) and tight on suspense, this was an auspicious debut from a still very interesting and under-rated director.

Dick Powell *Rocky Malloy* • Rhonda Fleming *Nancy* • Richard Erdman *Delong* • William Conrad *Castro* • Regis Toomey *Cobb* • Jean Porter *Darlene* • Jay Adler *Williams* ■ *Dir* Robert Parrish • *Scr* William Bowers, from a story by Jerome Cady

Cry for Happy ★

Romantic comedy 1961 · US · Colour · 110mins

A quartet of American navy photographers, on leave in Japan during the Korean War, become romantically entangled with four geisha girls who are attempting to found an orphanage. Starring Glenn Ford and Donald O'Connor, George Marshall's movie is a predictable, witless and desperately unfunny attempt at romantic comedy, while the portrayal of the girls (one of whom is played by Miyoshi Umeki, who won an Oscar for *Sayonara*) is deeply patronising.

Glenn Ford *Andy Cyphers* • Donald O'Connor *Murray Prince* • Miiko Taka *Chiyoko* • James Shigeta *Suzuki* • Miyoshi Umeki *Harue* • Michi Kobi *Hanakichi* • Howard St John *Admiral Bennett* ■ *Dir* George Marshall • *Scr* Irving Brecher, from the novel by George Campbell

A Cry for Help: the Tracey Thurman Story ★★★ 18

Drama based on a true story 1989 · US · Colour · 90mins

A fact-based drama about a woman whose husband physically abuses her at every opportunity, even when she's pregnant. When he takes a knife to her, she ends up in hospital and finally in court, where her legal action and crusading lawyer affect a change in Connecticut state law which impels the police to respond immediately to all reports of domestic violence. This is a fascinating tale of courage, although in TV movie form it is rather reduced to melodrama in socially responsible wrapping. Contains violent scenes. ▭

Nancy McKeon *Tracey Thurman* • Dale Midkiff *Buck* • Bruce Weitz *Burton Weinstein* • Graham Jarvis *Officer Danziger* • Yvette Heyden *Judy Bentley* • Terri Hanauer *Cheryl* ■ *Dir* Robert Markowitz • *Scr* Beth Sullivan

Cry for Me Billy ★★

Western 1972 · US · Colour · 87mins

Long in post-production and never properly released, this post-hippy western is not entirely without interest. Cliff Potts plays an alienated gunfighter who rescues an Indian girl after being appalled at the white man's treatment of the native American. When she's raped, he sets out on a violent quest for revenge. Despite having the excellent Harry Dean Stanton in support, director William A Graham can't really bring off this excursion into Anthony Mann or John Sturges territory.

Cliff Potts *Billy* • Oaxchitl *Indian girl* • Harry Dean Stanton *Luke Todd* • Don Wilbanks *Sergeant* • Woodrow Chambliss *Prospector* • Roy Jenson *Blacksmith* ■ *Dir* William A Graham • *Scr* David Markson

Cry Freedom ★★★★ PG

Biographical drama
1987 · UK · Colour · 151mins

An ambitious, worthy attempt by Richard Attenborough to re-create the success of *Gandhi* with another epic biographical portrait, this time of the doomed South African civil rights leader Steve Biko. Attenborough is well served by the charismatic playing of Denzel Washington as the black activist and Kevin Kline as the liberal newspaper editor Donald Woods, whose political conscience is awakened by Biko. The early scenes, in which the comfortably middle class Woods gradually has his eyes opened to the true horrors of the apartheid system, are sharply observed, and the finale focusing on the Soweto riots carries a powerful emotional punch. The film loses its way a little when the attention switches to the plight of the Woods family, but their final attempts at flight are genuinely suspenseful. Contains mild swearing.

Kevin Kline *Donald Woods* • Denzel Washington *Steve Biko* • Wendy Woods • John Hargreaves *Bruce* • Alec McCowen *Acting High Commissioner* • Kevin McNally *Ken* • Zakes Mokae *Father Kani* • Ian Richardson *State prosecutor* • Josette Simon *Dr Ramphele* • John Thaw *Kruger* • Timothy West *Captain de Wet* • Miles Anderson *Lemick* ■ *Dir* Richard Attenborough • *Scr* John Briley, from the non-fiction books *Biko* and *Asking for Trouble* by Donald Woods

A Cry from the Streets ★★★ U

Drama   1957 · UK · BW · 100mins

A dogmatic social worker (Barbara Murray), who deals with underprivileged children, enlists the help of Max Bygraves as an assistant. It is he who saves the day when a child whose mother commits suicide goes on the run with the kids of a murderer – and a gun. Neither as melodramatic as it sounds, nor all doom and gloom, this is a decent attempt at realism, directed in quasi-documentary style by Lewis Gilbert. In a huge cast, the children take top honours.

Max Bygraves *Bill Lowther* • Barbara Murray *Ann Farrow* • Colin Petersen *Georgie* • Dana Wilson *Barbie* • Kathleen Harrison *Mrs Farrer* • Mona Washbourne *Mrs Daniels* ■ *Dir* Lewis Gilbert • *Scr* Vernon Harris, from the novel *The Friend in Need* by Elizabeth Coxhead

Cry Havoc ★★★

Second World War melodrama
1943 · US · BW · 97mins

An interesting, accomplished cast does the *Tenko* routine as the likes of Joan Blondell and Ann Sothern pitch up on the island of Bataan during the height of Second World War hostilities. The material originated on the stage, and it shows in the movie's enclosed, claustrophobic look. However, despite the rather hackneyed dialogue and abundance of realistic make-up, this is a stirring, emotive tale which packs a major punch.

Margaret Sullavan *Lieutenant Smith* • Ann Sothern *Pat* • Joan Blondell *Grace* • Fay Bainter *Captain Marsh* • Marsha Hunt *Flo Norris* • Ella Raines *Connie* • Frances Gifford *Helen* • Diana Lewis *Nydia* ■ *Dir* Richard Thorpe • *Scr* Paul Osborne, from the play *Proof Thro' the Night* by Allen R Kenward

A Cry in the Dark ★★★★ 15

Drama based on a true story
1988 · US/Ausl · Colour · 116mins

An absolutely riveting and at times harrowing telling of the bizarre real-life story of Lindy Chamberlain, who claimed her baby was killed by a dingo at Ayers Rock in 1980. The movie covers a huge amount of ground: Aboriginal myths, the Chamberlains' Seventh Day Adventism, the media circus and the way the case challenged the legal system and obsessed Australians for years. Meryl Streep gives probably her best performance: a portrait of a tough, humourless woman who eventually earns our sympathy and pity. Sam Neill as her morose preacher husband is equally impressive. The material could have made for a dreadfully insincere TV movie, but Fred Schepisi's direction is clear-headed and unsensational. Contains swearing.

Meryl Streep *Lindy Chamberlain* • Sam Neill *Michael Chamberlain* • Bruce Myles *Barker* • Charles Tingwell *Justice Muirhead* • Nick Tate *Charlwood* • Neil Fitzpatrick *Phillips* • Maurie Fields *Barritt* ■ *Dir* Fred Schepisi • *Scr* Robert Caswell, Fred Schepisi, from the non-fiction book *Evil Angels* by John Bryson

A Cry in the Night ★

Crime drama   1956 · US · BW · 75mins

Alan Ladd's Jaguar company made this rather sordid melodrama, with Ladd himself delivering the brief narration. It's all the fault of the parents: young Natalie Wood can't stand being at home with her domineering policeman father (Edmond O'Brien), and Raymond Burr's middle-aged Peeping Tom has been messed up by a possessive mother. The trouble starts when Burr, spying on Wood and boyfriend Richard Anderson in Lover's Lane, knocks him out and kidnaps her. There's never any doubt how it will end.

Edmond O'Brien *Taggart* • Brian Donlevy *Bates* • Natalie Wood *Liz* • Raymond Burr *Loftus* • Richard Anderson *Owen* • Irene Hervey *Helen* • Carol Veazie *Mrs Loftus* • Mary Lawrence *Madge* • Alan Ladd *Narrator* ■ *Dir* Frank Tuttle • *Scr* David Dortort, from the novel *All Through the Night* by Whit Masterson

A Cry in the Wild ★★

Adventure thriller 1990 · US · Colour · 81mins

Those looking for tips on parenting skills need look no futher than Pamela Sue Martin. Seeing her son off on a trip to visit his father, this paragon of American motherhood presents the boy with a hatchet and entrusts him to the care of Ned Beatty's alcoholic pilot. The plane crash-lands in the Canadian wilderness, and the boy (Jaried Rushton) is able to learn some valuable life lessons as he builds a shelter, starts fires and competes with racoons and bears for food. With no other humans around, this is not a *Lord of the Flies* style meditation on man's baser instincts. Still, the hatchet comes in handy.

Jared Rushton *Brian* • Pamela Sue Martin *Brian's mother* • Stephen Meadows *Brian's father* • Ned Beatty *Pilot* ■ *Dir* Mark Griffiths • *Scr* Gary Paulsen, Catherine Cryan, from the novel *Hatchet* by Gary Paulsen

Cry in the Wild: the Taking of Peggy Ann ★★ 15

Drama based on a true story
1991 · US · Colour · 91mins

Looking a little older than in his *Starsky and Hutch* days, David Soul stars in this true-life TV movie as the officer in charge of Pennsylvania's biggest-ever police operation. Set in 1966, the film follows the hunt for Peggy Ann Bradnick, the 17-year-old kidnapped by an eccentric recluse known as Bicycle Pete. The interest doesn't lie in the search, but in the peculiar relationship that develops between the victim and her abductor, adequately played by Megan Follows and David Morse. Yet another example of the adage that news headlines rarely make good movie entertainment. Contains violence and swearing.

David Morse *Bicycle Pete* • David Soul *Terry Anderson* • Megan Follows *Peggy Ann Bradnick* • Dion Anderson *Tom Reugg* • Tom Atkins *Joe Jamieson* • Jack Kehler *Eugene Bradnick* • Taylor Fry *Carol Jean Bradnick* ■ *Dir* Charles Correll • *Scr* Durrell Royce Crays

Cry of the Banshee ★★ 15

Horror   1970 · UK · Colour · 83mins

The last period horror Vincent Price ever made finds the flamboyant villain back on *Witchfinder General* territory as an obsessed 16th-century witch-hunting magistrate hounded by demonic forces. Veteran actress Elisabeth Bergner (her name was misspelt on the original credits) plays the witch who unleashes werewolf-in-disguise Patrick Mower on the hedonistic patriarch. Director Gordon Hessler's lightweight chiller is a rather coy affair that's neither sexy nor spooky enough, giving Price few moments to shine and failing to create a palpable sense of haunting evil. Contains violence and nudity.

Vincent Price *Lord Edward Whitman* • Elisabeth Bergner *Oona* • Essy Persson *Lady Patricia* • Hugh Griffith *Mickey* • Patrick Mower *Roderick* • Hilary Dwyer *Maureen* • Carl Rigg *Harry* ■ *Dir* Gordon Hessler • *Scr* Tim Kelly, Christopher Wicking, from a story by Tim Kelly

Cry of the City ★★★★

Film noir   1948 · US · BW · 95mins

One of the toughest and most uncompromising examples from that great period of 20th Century-Fox *film noir*, an emotive and exciting study of the relationship between one-time boyhood pals, gangster Richard Conte and cop Victor Mature. Richard Murphy's screenplay is adult and clever, and expressionist émigré director Robert Siodmak knows exactly how to paint this particular ultra-urban picture. The female casting is particularly quirky: watch for Hope Emerson's censor-baiting masseuse, and super support work from Shelley Winters and Debra Paget. For those who have been unable to take Mature seriously as an actor, this ranks with his best work.

Victor Mature *Lieutenant Candella* • Richard Conte *Martin Rome* • Fred Clark *Lieutenant Collins* • Shelley Winters *Brenda* • Betty Garde *Mrs Pruett* • Berry Kroeger *Niles* • Tommy Cook *Tony* • Debra Paget *Teena Riconti* • Hope Emerson *Rose Given* • Roland Winters

Ledbetter ■ *Dir* Robert Siodmak • *Scr* Richard Murphy, from the novel *The Chair for Martin Rome* by Henry Edward Helseth

Cry of the Hunted ★★★

Drama   1953 · US · BW · 78mins

Italian heart-throb Vittorio Gassman is an escaped convict being pursued through the boggy Louisiana bayous by officer Barry Sullivan. The few scenes with Polly Bergen – playing Sullivan's wife – were added later in an attempt to attract the female audience. But this is really a suspenseful chase movie, shot on authentically swampy locations by Joseph H Lewis. What's good about the movie is the amount of material pressed into 78 minutes: the internal politics at the jail and the deals struck with prisoners are all made clear as the chase gets underway.

Vittorio Gassman *Jory* • Barry Sullivan *Lt Tunner* • Polly Bergen *Janet Tunner* • William Conrad *Goodwin* • Mary Zavian *Ella* • Robert Burton *Warden Keeley* • Harry Shannon *Sheriff Brown* • Jonathan Cott *Deputy Davis* ■ *Dir* Joseph H Lewis • *Scr* Jack Leonard, from the story by Jack Leonard, Marion Wolfe

Cry of the Innocent ★★★

Thriller   1980 · US · Colour · 93mins

Dashing Rod Taylor – best known for *The Birds* and *The Time Machine* – plays a grieving widower whose wife and daughter are killed in a plane crash near their Irish holiday home. However, the crash may not have been an accident... This made-for-TV thriller zips along at a fair old pace against the lush Irish scenery, and is played, directed and scripted with enough flair to suggest it could have done some smart business on the big screen.

Rod Taylor *Steve Donigan* • Joanna Pettet *Cynthia Donigan/Candia Leighton* • Cyril Cusack *Tom Moloney* • Nigel Davenport *Gray Harrison Hunt* • Jim Norton *Jasper Tooms* ■ *Dir* Michael O'Herlihy • *Scr* Sidney Michaels, from a story by Frederick Forsyth

Cry Terror ★★★★

Crime thriller   1958 · US · BW · 96mins

Low budget meets high suspense in this adroit thriller from writer/director Andrew L Stone, in which TV repairman James Mason, his wife Inger Stevens and his daughter Terry Ann Ross are held hostage by Rod Steiger, Angie Dickinson and Jack Klugman, who are plotting an extortion coup. Inventively contrived and executed, the action grips as it accelerates.

James Mason *Jim Molner* • Rod Steiger *Paul Hoplin* • Inger Stevens *Joan Molner* • Neville Brand *Steve* • Angie Dickinson *Kelly* • Kenneth Tobey *Frank Cole* • Jack Klugman *Vince* • Jack Kruschen *Charles Pope* • Terry Ann Ross *Pat Molner* ■ *Dir/Scr* Andrew L Stone

Cry, the Beloved Country ★★★★ PG

Drama   1951 · UK · BW · 99mins

Made in those grievous days of apartheid in South Africa, this adaptation of Alan Paton's stirring bestseller – with Canada Lee as the country minister looking for a lost son in Johannesburg – so obviously had its heart in the right place that it was hard

U = SUITABLE FOR ALL   Uc = SUITABLE FOR ALL, ESPECIALLY FOR YOUNG CHILDREN (VIDEO ONLY)   PG = PARENTAL GUIDANCE

to criticise. It still is, even in the post-apartheid era, because Zoltan Korda's direction, though naive, has a passionate directness that is timeless. One of the acting delights is Sidney Poitier as a young preacher who forgives all, but forgets nothing. ▭

Canada Lee *Stephen Kumalo* • Charles Carson *James Jarvis* • Sidney Poitier *Reverend Maimangu* • Joyce Carey *Margaret Jarvis* • Edric Connor *John Kumalo* • Geoffrey Keen *Father Vincent* ■ *Dir* Zoltan Korda • *Scr* Alan Paton, John Howard Lawson (uncredited), from the novel by Alan Paton

Cry, the Beloved Country ★★★★
Period drama   1995 • SAfr • Colour • 111mins

A powerful adaptation of Alan Paton's forties-set racial drama (previously filmed by Zoltan Korda in 1951) about the converging journey undergone by a black minister in rural South Africa and his white landowner neighbour. The first major feature to be shot in South Africa since the abolition of apartheid, Darrell James Roodt's film gains much emotional resonance from the gentle, softly-spoken sincerity of James Earl Jones as the pastor, devastated by the dreadful fates that have befallen his family in Johannesburg. Even if it occasionally feels a little manipulative (John Barry's score, for example), it is hard not to be affected by the film's uncompromising conclusion. ▭

Richard Harris *James Jarvis* • James Earl Jones *Reverend Stephen Kumalo* • Charles S Dutton *John Kumalo* • Vusi Kunene *Father Msimangu* • Leleti Khumalo *Katie* • Ian Roberts *Evans* • Dambisa Kente *Gertrude Kumalo* ■ *Dir* Darrell James Roodt • *Scr* Ronald Harwood, from the novel by Alan Paton

Cry Vengeance ★★★
Crime drama   1954 • US • BW • 81mins

Mark Stevens, the handsome if rather bland leading man of Fox pictures of the forties, took on a tougher image in the fifties. In this gripping crime drama, the first of five films he directed, Stevens plays a former detective who, after three years in prison, seeks revenge on the man he thinks framed him for a crime he didn't commit. A pulsating score and rapid editing helps give the film a lively pace, though the plot is somewhat convoluted and contrived.

Mark Stevens *Vic Barron* • Martha Hyer *Peggy Harding* • Skip Homeier *Roxey* • Joan Vohs *Lily Arnold* • Douglas Kennedy *Tino Morelli* • Don Haggerty *Lt Ryan* ■ *Dir* Mark Stevens • *Scr* Warren Douglas, George Bricker • *Editor* Elmo Veron • *Music* Paul Dunlap

Cry Wolf ★★ PG
Mystery   1947 • US • BW • 80mins

Screen icons Barbara Stanwyck and Errol Flynn were both past their box-office prime when they teamed up for this dour Warner Bros drama. When her husband kicks the bucket, Stanwyck returns to the old estate to find Flynn up to no good in the west wing. All very Charlotte Brontë, and very little fun thanks to Peter Godfrey's turgid direction. There's always pleasure to be gained from watching real movie stars go through their paces, but this *Old Dark House* tale is worthy of neither. ▭

Errol Flynn *Mark Caldwell* • Barbara Stanwyck *Sandra Marshall* • Richard Basehart *James Demarest* • Geraldine Brooks *Julie Demarest* • Jerome Cowan *Senator Caldwell* • John Ridgely *Jackson Laidell* • Patricia White *Angela* ■ *Dir* Peter Godfrey • *Scr* Catherine Turney, from the novel by Marjorie Carleton

Crying Freeman ★★★ 18
Action drama
1995 • Fr/Jap/Can/US • Colour • 97mins

Hong Kong-style action meets James Bond in a beautifully crafted adaptation of the cult Japanese comic strip. Enigmatic Mark Dacascos is the latest in a long line of human killing machines programmed by the Sons of the Dragon Society to respond to hypnotic signals. Because he sheds a tear after each contract killing, he earns the nickname "Crying Freeman". How he keeps his identity a secret fuels a cranked-up plot packed with inventive explosions, balletic gunplay, hyperkinetic stunts and forbidden love. A visually arresting slant on the usual comic book capers. Contains sex scenes, swearing and violence. ▭

Mark Dacascos *Yo Hinomura/Freeman* • Julie Condra *Emu O'Hara* • Rae Dawn Chong *Detective Forge* • Byron Mann *Koh* • Mako *Shudo Shimizaki* • Tcheky Karyo *Detective Netah* ■ *Dir* Christophe Gans • *Scr* Christophe Gans, Thierry Cazals, from the comic book by Kazuo Koike, Ryoichi Ikegami

The Crying Game ★★★★ 18
Drama   1992 • UK • Colour • 107mins

Virtually ignored on its release, this offbeat tale went on to become a monster hit in America and even earned an Oscar for best original screenplay for writer/director Neil Jordan. It's a beguiling, eccentric blend of romantic drama and political thriller, and at its centre is a charismatic performance from Stephen Rea. He plays an IRA terrorist who flees to London after the botched kidnapping of a British soldier, played somewhat unconvincingly by Forest Whitaker. Ridden with guilt he locates the dead man's former lover (an extraordinary performance from Jaye Davidson that was deservedly rewarded with an Oscar nomination) and finds himself falling in love. After a series of Hollywood flops, this marked a major return to form for Jordan. Contains violence, swearing and nudity. ▭

Stephen Rea *Fergus* • Miranda Richardson *Jude* • Jaye Davidson *Dil* • Forest Whitaker *Jody* • Adrian Dunbar *Maguire* • Breffini McKenna *Tinker* • Jim Broadbent *Col* • Tony Slattery *Deveroux* • Shar Campbell *Bar performer* • David Crionelly *Security man* ■ *Dir/Scr* Neil Jordan

The Crystal Ball ★★ U
Comedy   1943 • US • BW • 81mins

When gorgeous Texan Paulette Goddard fails to win a beauty contest, she takes up fake fortune-telling to earn a buck and gets involved with a bunch of swindlers. All ends happily when her shenanigans lead to Ray Milland, the man of her dreams. An innocuous, slightly fantastical, but reasonably diverting comedy with a slapstick finale, this is nicely played and directed with the right touch of irreverence by Elliott Nugent. Character

actors Cecil Kellaway, William Bendix and Ernest Truex keep things lively.

Ray Milland *Brad Cavanaugh* • Paulette Goddard *Toni Gerard* • Gladys George *Mme Zenobia* • Virginia Field *Jo Ainsley* • Cecil Kellaway *Pop Tibbets* • William Bendix *Biff Carter* • Mary Field *Foster* • Ernest Truex *Mr Martin* ■ *Dir* Elliott Nugent • *Scr* Virginia Van Upp, from a story by Steven Vas

Crystal Heart ★★ 15
Melodrama   1987 • US • Colour • 102mins

Mawkish, over-earnest drama which rather misguidedly mixes music with a "disease of the week" scenario. Former centrefold Tawny Kitaen is the aspiring rock star who becomes infatuated with Lee Curreri, a young man suffering from an immune deficiency that keeps him literally sealed off from the rest of the world. It's an interesting concept, but the two leads are terribly bland, and the supporting players are largely anonymous. The lashings of sentiment are also hard to digest. Contains swearing and nudity. ▭

Lee Curreri *Christopher Newley* • Tawny Kitaen *Alley Daniels* • Lloyd Bochner *Frank Newley* • May Heatherly *Diana Newley* • Simon Andreu *Jean-Claude* • Marina Saura *Justine* ■ *Dir* Gil Bettman • *Scr* Linda Shayne, from a story by Alberto Vazquez-Figueroa

Crystalstone ★★★ PG
Adventure   1988 • Sp/UK • Colour • 94mins

An imaginative fantasy that captures the innocence and determination of a young brother and sister who, threatened with separation after their mother's death, run off. During their travels, they meet an odd old man who tells them a tale of an Aztec relic. This adventure, made for and about children in the Disney live-action tradition, is beautifully balanced and successfully conveys the emotional insecurity of childhood. ▭

Kamlesh Gupta *Pablo* • Laura Jane Goodwin *Maria* • Frank Grimes *Captain* • Edward Kelsey *Hook* • Sydney Bromley *Old man* • Terence Bayler *Policeman* • Patricia Conti *Filomena* ■ *Dir/Scr* Antonio Pelaez

Cuba ★★★★ 12
Adventure   1979 • US • Colour • 117mins

Hugely under-rated drama with Sean Connery as the British security adviser who washes up in Cuba at the time of the revolution. Naturally, he's been hired by the losing side and his growing doubts are set beside his love for a woman he first met in 1942, in Casablanca. This keys in one aspect of this bracing satire – the idea of the loner haunted by his past, wondering if he's chosen the wrong side, suspicious of commitment. If there's a lot of Bogart's Rick in Connery, there's also a lot of Graham Greene guilt and Hemingway machismo. Somehow Connery contains it all: it's a great performance. Sub-plots spin off and there is a wealth of secondary characters as director Richard Lester weaves this fascinating tale about a country where romance, revolution and bombs co-exist. ▭

Sean Connery *Robert Dapes* • Brooke Adams *Alexandra Pulido* • Jack Weston *Gutman* • Hector Elizondo *Ramirez* • Denholm Elliott

Skinner • Martin Balsam *General Bello* • Chris Sarandon *Juan Pulido* ■ *Dir* Richard Lester • *Scr* Charles Wood

Cuba Crossing ★★
Spy drama   1980 • US • Colour • 90mins

In addition to *Cuba Crossing*, this little item has had at least four other titles at various times: *Key West Crossing*, which hinted at the main location; *The Mercenaries*, which pointed to the theme; *Assignment: Kill Castro*, which told of the story; and *Sweet Violent Tony*, which referred to the hero. Stuart Whitman plays a loner who runs a bar in the Florida Keys and thinks of bumping off the bearded, cigar-chomping one, while Robert Vaughn is his usual smooth and creepy self.

Stuart Whitman *Captain Tony Terracino* • Robert Vaughn *Hudd* • Woody Strode *Titi* • Sybil Danning *Veronica* • Raymond St Jacques *Bell* • Caren Kaye *Tracy* • Mary Lou Gassen *Maria* ■ *Dir/Scr* Chuck Workman

Cube ★★★★ 15
Science-fiction thriller
1997 • Can • Colour • 86mins

Six strangers wake up to find themselves in a 14ft by 14ft cube. When they try to get out of their prison, they find they are snared in a seemingly endless maze of interlocking cubicles armed with lethal booby traps. How did they get there? Why have they been incarcerated? Director Vincenzo Natali's extraordinary Canadian debut feature takes a unique idea and milks its potential to the maximum with dark panache and visual dexterity. Genuinely creepy and gory, with the discernible influence of David Cronenberg, this science-fiction horror puzzler is awash with bold ideas and unsettling tension. Contains swearing and violence. ▭ *DVD*

Nicole deBoer *Leaven* • Nicky Guadagni *Holloway* • David Hewlett *Worth* • Andrew Miller *Kazan* • Julian Richings *Alderson* • Wayne Robson *Rennes* • Maurice Dean Wint *Quentin* ■ *Dir* Vincenzo Natali • *Scr* Vincenzo Natali, André Bijelic, Graeme Manson

A Cuckoo in the Nest ★★★
Comedy   1933 • UK • BW • 87mins

Ben Travers's farces have dated badly on screen, though they still play perfectly well in their various current theatre versions. So the main pleasure in watching this stagey British talkie lies in its preservation of the original Aldwych company interpretation, as directed by chief *farceur* Tom Walls. Walls co-stars with Ralph Lynn in a slight but appealing saga, which concludes splendidly with a confused husband (Lynn) discovered without his trousers on by his in-laws (Walls and Grace Edwin) in a hotel bedroom with a lady (Yvonne Arnaud) who is not his wife! The most durable member of the cast is the still very funny Robertson Hare ("Oh, Calamity!") as a parson on a visit.

Tom Walls *Major Bone* • Ralph Lynn *Peter Wyckham* • Yvonne Arnaud *Marguerite Hickett* • Robertson Hare *Reverend Sloley-Jones* • Mary Brough *Mrs Spoker* • Veronica Rose *Barbara Wyckham* • Gordon James *Noony* ■ *Dir* Tom Walls • *Scr* Ben Travers, AR Rawlinson, from the play by Ben Travers

Cujo ★★ 🔞

Horror   1983 · US · Colour · 89mins

Add another title to the list of Stephen King movie adaptations that fail to ignite the screen. A rabid St Bernard traps spirited Dee Wallace and her son (Danny Pintauro) in a Ford Pinto and terrorises them for days in director Lewis Teague's predictable shocker, which sports a half-baked script and an altered, upbeat ending. The car siege should be a harrowing ordeal, but Teague barks up the wrong tree by focusing earlier on Pintauro's fear of the dark and subsequent phobic attacks. The suspense becomes laughably static, despite all the visual trickery thrown in to generate an interest that manifestly fails to materialise. *Cujo* is a dog! Contains swearing and violence. 📼

Dee Wallace [Dee Wallace Stone] *Donna Trenton* • Christopher Stone *Steve Kemp* • Danny Pintauro *Tad Trenton* • Daniel Hugh-Kelly *Vic Trenton* • Ed Lauter *Joe Camber* ■ *Dir* Lewis Teague • *Scr* Don Carlos Dunaway, Lauren Currier, from the novel by Stephen King

Cul-de-Sac ★★★ 15

Psychological chiller
1966 · UK · BW · 100mins

From neurosis to psychosis: that's where the unholy goings-on in a Holy Island castle lead in Roman Polanski's surreal, macabre thriller. Reclusive Donald Pleasence, striving to keep his young wife Françoise Dorléac cloistered for himself, is emotionally invaded by the arrival of gangsters Lionel Stander and Jack MacGowran. Fetishes abound in this, the most Buñuelian of all Polanski's work, but weird slapstick comedy often undermines the serious kinkiness. An acquired taste. 📼

Donald Pleasence *George* • Françoise Dorléac *Teresa* • Lionel Stander *Richard* • Jack MacGowran *Albert* • Iain Quarrier *Christopher* • Geoffrey Sumner *Christopher's father* • Renee Houston *Christopher's mother* • William Franklyn *Cecil* • Trevor Delaney *Nicholas* ■ *Dir* Roman Polanski • *Scr* Gérard Brach, Roman Polanski

The Culpepper Cattle Co ★★★★

Western   1972 · US · Colour · 92mins

A grim rites-of-passage western, superbly directed by Dick Richards, whose subsequent career failed to live up to this early promise. *Summer of 42's* Gary Grimes is the 16-year-old who sets out on a cattle drive alongside authentic western types such as Luke Askew and Bo Hopkins. There are also superb performances from Clint Eastwood regular Geoffrey Lewis and Billy "Green" Bush as the hardy trail boss. The extreme violence (tame by today's standards) earned it an X certificate in the UK.

Gary Grimes *Ben Mockridge* • Billy "Green" Bush [Billy Green Bush] *Frank Culpepper* • Luke Askew *Luke* • Bo Hopkins *Dixie Brick* • Geoffrey Lewis *Russ* • Wayne Sutherlin *Missoula* • Charles Martin Smith *Tim Slater* ■ *Dir* Dick Richards • *Scr* Eric Bercovici, Gregory Prentiss, from a story by Dick Richards

Cult of the Cobra ★★

Horror thriller   1955 · US · BW · 79mins

This is one of those inexplicable cases of a humdrum potboiler achieving cult recognition in later life. Thematically a distant cousin of *Cat People*, but with none of that film's atmosphere and moody tension, this is a war movie with a difference, in that American GIs face death, not from Nazi bullets, but an ancient curse. When a group of overly curious soldiers enter an Indian temple during a secret ceremony, they're followed home by an exotic serpent woman who starts bumping them off one by one. Francis D Lyon's direction is uninvolving, but his film is saved by solid performances and imaginative camerawork. Watch out for David Janssen in a minor role.

Faith Domergue *Lisa* • Richard Long *Paul Able* • Marshall Thompson *Tom Markel* • Kathleen Hughes *Julia* • Jack Kelly *Carl Turner* • Walter Coy *Inspector* • Myrna Hansen *Marian* • David Janssen *Rico Nardi* ■ *Dir* Francis D Lyon • *Scr* Jerry Davis, Cecil Maiden, Richard Collins, from a story by Jerry Davis

Cult Rescue ★★ 12

Drama   1994 · US · Colour · 87mins

TV-movie regular Joan Van Ark is suitably agonised in this predictable stroll through American real-life crime files. She plays a housewife suffering from depression who goes to therapist Tom Kurlander for help, only to find herself brainwashed into the beliefs of his "consciousness centre", and an acceptance of his group's financial demands. The performances are adequate, but the plotting and direction are strictly routine. 📼

Joan Van Ark *Nora McGill* • Stephen Macht *Harry McGill* • Tom Kurlander *Dr Alan Ter Horst* ■ *Dir* Chuck Bowman

The Cup ★★★★ 🅟🅖

Comedy   1999 · Bhu/Ausl · Colour · 94mins

Directed by Khyentse Norbu, one of the most revered incarnate lamas in the Tibetan Buddhist hierarchy, this is Bhutan's first ever feature film. Played exclusively by non-professionals, it follows mischievous novice monk Jamyang Lodro in his bid to watch his hero Ronaldo play for Brazil in the 1998 World Cup final. Using shadow puppetry and satellite TV to highlight the need for tradition and progress to co-exist, this charmingly humorous tale also celebrates the exuberance of youth and the sagacity of the elderly, as Jamyang finds an unlikely ally in his venerable abbot. Beautifully shot in glowing colours, this is simply inspirational cinema. In Hindi and Tibetan with English subtitles.

Jamyang Lodro *Orgyen* • Orgyen Tobgyal *Geko* • Neten Chokling *Lodo* ■ *Dir/Scr* Khyentse Norbu • *Cinematographer* Paul Warren

Cup Final ★★★★ 15

Drama   1991 · Is · Colour · 104mins

It's good to see this thoughtful and accomplished piece of film-making finally reaching the wider audience it deserves. Set against the political complexities of the Middle East, this simple tale of war, humanity and football explores the relationship that develops between a Jewish soldier and his Arab jailer during the 1982 World Cup finals. The scenes depicting the Israeli invasion of Lebanon are rather tentatively handled, but director Eran Riklis is on much surer ground with the interaction between the two men, whose loathing turns to respect as the tournament progresses. In Arabic and Hebrew with English subtitles. 📼

Moshe Ivgi *Cohen* • Muhamad Bacri [Muhamad Bakri] *Ziad* • Salim Dau *Mussa* • Basam Zuamut *Abu Eyash* • Yussef Abu Warda *George* • Suheil Haddad *Omar* ■ *Dir* Eran Riklis • *Scr* Eyal Halfon, from an idea by Eran Riklis

Cupid ★★ 15

Thriller   1997 · US · Colour · 91mins

Although he has been behind such high-profile releases as *Deep Cover* and *Videodrome*, producer Pierre David has a nice little sideline in efficient but mechanical straight-to-video thrillers. This one has *Gremlins* star Zach Galligan as a wealthy but twisted writer hooked on the Cupid legend, who believes that somewhere out there is his ideal woman. The problem is that when they fail to live up to his expectations, he bumps them off. There's a little bit of suspense here, but Doug Campbell's direction is pedestrian and the performances are unconvincing. Contains some swearing and violence. 📼

Zach Galligan *Eric Rhodes* • Ashley Lauren [Ashley Laurence] *Jennifer Taylor* • Mary Crosby *Dana Rhodes* • Michael Bowen *Mike Logan* • Joseph Kell *Richard Minor* • Michael Fairman *Carl* ■ *Dir* Doug Campbell • *Scr* David Benullo

Curacao ★★ 15

Spy thriller   1993 · US · Colour · 88mins

George C Scott and Alexei Sayle are the only familiar faces in this spy thriller, set on the same Caribbean island in the Netherland Antilles that gave its name to a certain orange-flavoured liqueur. But genre fans may be familiar with star William Petersen (*Manhunter*, *To Live and Die in LA*), while Scott's fifth wife, Trish Van Devere, also appears in the cast. 📼

George C Scott *Cornelius Wettering* • William Petersen *Stephen Guerin* • Alexei Sayle *Seemuller* • Trish Van Devere *Rose* ■ *Dir* Carl Schultz • *Scr* James David Buchanan

Curdled ★★ 🔞

Black comedy thriller
1995 · US · Colour · 85mins

This comedy thriller began life as a short film that inspired part of Quentin Tarantino's *Pulp Fiction*. He then turned executive producer to help director and co-writer Reb Braddock expand the original into a full-length movie. Itinerant cleaning maid Angela Jones discovers the identity of a serial killer from the debris left behind in his flat, but has difficulty proving it. The result has some neat touches, but it might have been better had it kept to its original duration. William Baldwin and Bruce Ramsay co-star. Contains swearing and violence. 📼

Angela Jones *Gabriela* • William Baldwin *Paul Guell* • Bruce Ramsay *Eduardo* • Lois Chiles *Katrina Brandt* • Barry Corbin *Lodger* • Mel Gorham *Elena* ■ *Dir* Reb Braddock • *Scr* John Maass, Reb Braddock

The Cure ★★★★★ 🅤

Silent comedy   1917 · US · BW · 23mins

Charles Chaplin's 1917 short is a ruthlessly comic and inventive frolic. When Charlie goes to stay at a spa for recovering alcoholics, gallons of liquor get dumped into the resort's water and change everyone into hyperactive lunatics. Our hero falls for Edna Purviance, as usual, and comes up against the massive Eric Campbell. This early masterpiece contains some remarkable comedy routines that Chaplin later said were derived from his days in music hall. 📼

Charles Chaplin *Alcoholic gentleman at spa* • Edna Purviance *Fellow guest at spa* • Eric Campbell *Man with gout* • John Rand *Male Nurse* • Albert Austin *Male Nurse* • Frank J Coleman *Proprietor* • James T Kelley *Ancient Bell Boy* ■ *Dir/Scr* Charles Chaplin

The Cure ★★★ 12

Drama   1995 · US · Colour · 94mins

A thoughtful drama dealing with the friendship between two boys, one of whom has contracted Aids from a blood transfusion. Directed by actor Peter Horton, this small, insightful movie deals with big issues and benefits enormously from a talented cast. Tough kid Brad Renfro and the poorly Joseph Mazzello are first-rate, skilfully supported by Annabella Sciorra as Mazzello's mother and Bruce Davison as his doctor. Although the boys' later odyssey for a cure to Mazzello's condition does hamper credibility, the young stars make their deepening relationship both believable and affecting. 📼

Joseph Mazzello *Dexter* • Brad Renfro *Erik* • Diana Scarwid *Gail* • Bruce Davison *Dr Stevens* • Annabella Sciorra *Linda* • Aeryk Egan *Tyler* • Delphine French *Tyler's girlfriend* • Andrew Broder *Tyler's buddy* ■ *Dir* Peter Horton • *Scr* Robert Kuhn

Curiosity Kills ★★ 15

Thriller   1990 · US · Colour · 82mins

C Thomas Howell's career, which probably peaked with *The Hitcher*, continued its descent with this mediocre thriller about a young man who is convinced his neighbour's death was murder, not the suicide police claim. Joining him for the predictable twists and turns of the plot are Rae Dawn Chong and *The Lawnmower Man's* Jeff Fahey, both of whom look like they would rather be somewhere else (preferably in a better movie). Watch out for *Friends* star Courteney Cox in a supporting role. Contains swearing and violence. 📼

C Thomas Howell *Cat Thomas* • Rae Dawn Chong *Jane Conlan* • Courteney Cox *Gwen Hartwick* • Jeff Fahey *Manus* • Larry Dobkin [Lawrence Dobkin] *Harry Van Beek* • Louis A Rivera *Falco* ■ *Dir* Colin Bucksey • *Scr* Joe Batteer, John Rice, Frank de Palma, Terry Borst

Curious Dr Humpp ★★★

Cult erotic science-fiction drama
1967 · Arg · BW · 85mins

This real oddity is one of the most bizarre mixes of sex, horror and sci-fi ever made. Forget the story about a voyeuristic mad scientist giving kidnapped girls aphrodisiacs; it's the fusion of paranoid fantasy, horrific

morality play and soft-core banality that makes this Argentinian movie such a gob-smacker. Striking imagery, misshapen monsters, black-faced mutants, a talking brain from Italy and creatures playing weird musical instruments in foggy courtyards surrounded by zombies make this black-and-white drama curiously unforgettable. Spanish dialogue dubbed into English.

Ricardo Bauleo *Gloria Prat* • Aldo Barbero • Susan Beltrán • Justin Martin • Michel Angel • Mary Albano • Al Bugatti ■ *Dir* Emilio Vieyra • *Scr* Emilio Vieyra, Raul Zorrilla

Curly Sue ★ ★ PG
Comedy   1991 · US · Colour · 97mins

John Hughes – who directed such hits as *The Breakfast Club* and *Ferris Bueller's Day Off* and produced the phenomenally successful *Home Alone* trilogy – unexpectedly misses the target somewhat with this too-sickly comedy about a young girl and her con artist travelling companion (James Belushi) who attempt to take Chicago lawyer Kelly Lynch for a ride. Belushi is always highly watchable, but even he can't make up for the cutesy performance of Alisan Porter in the title role. One for younger viewers who may enjoy seeing a little girl getting everything she ever wanted, but not one for parents, who may find that concept rather worrying. Contains some swearing. ▭

James Belushi *Bill Dancer* • Kelly Lynch *Grey Ellison* • Alisan Porter *Curly Sue* • John Getz *Walker McCormick* • Fred Dalton Thompson *Bernard Oxbar* ■ *Dir/Scr* John Hughes

Curly Top ★ ★ ★ U
Musical   1935 · US · BW · 76mins

Shirley Temple at her exquisite best: a dimpled, ringleted moppet playing Cupid to her sister Rochelle Hudson and handsome John Boles, who adopts Temple and Hudson from an orphanage. This kind of movie made Temple a top movie star across the world and saved her studio, 20th Century-Fox, from bankruptcy. If you've never seen Temple and wonder what all the fuss was about, she's as good as she ever was here, revealing a talent and a surety of poise that's positively frightening in one so young. If the plot seems familiar, it's a reworking of that old stand-by *Daddy Long Legs*, given a new twist.

Shirley Temple *Elizabeth Blair* • John Boles *Edward Morgan* • Rochelle Hudson *Mary Blair* • Jane Darwell *Mrs Denham* • Rafaela Ottiano *Mrs Higgins* • Esther Dale *Aunt Genevieve Graham* • Etienne Girardo *Mr Wyckoff* • Maurice Murphy *Jimmie Rogers* ■ *Dir* Irving Cummings • *Scr* Patterson McNutt, Arthur Beckhard, from a story by Jean Webster

The Curse ★ ★ ★ 18
Horror   1987 · US · Colour · 82mins

Take method actor turned director David Keith, put him together with Italian rip-off producer Ovidio G Assonitis, and the result is very grisly food for thought. In this loose adaptation of the HP Lovecraft tale *The Colour Out of Space* (already filmed as *Monster of Terror* with Boris Karloff), a glowing meteor crash lands near the Tennessee farm of redneck Claude

Akins, mutating his produce and livestock before affecting the local community. Keith raises the social issue stakes when Akins becomes a religious fanatic who blinkers his eyes to the poisoned environment. There's a lot going on in this cynical chiller, though it's severely undercut once the film degenerates into formula zombie territory. Nevertheless, against all the odds, Keith sustains a palpable sense of apocalyptic doom. ▭

Wil Wheaton *Zachary Hayes* • Claude Akins *Nathan Hayes* • Malcolm Danare *Cyrus* • Cooper Huckabee *Dr Alan Forbes* • John Schneider *Carl Willis* • Amy Wheaton *Alice Hayes* ■ *Dir* David Keith • *Scr* David Chaskin, from the story *The Colour Out of Space* by HP Lovecraft

Curse II: The Bite ★ ★ 18
Horror thriller   1989 · US/It/Jap · Colour · 93mins

Although it has absolutely nothing to do with *The Curse* (1987), opportunist Italian producer Ovidio G Assonitis tacked on the title to this insanely stupid snake spectacular. Jill Schoelen and boyfriend J Eddie Peck are driving through a nuclear testing ground in Arizona when a radioactive rattler bites Peck on the arm. The mutated venom mixes with his DNA and turns his arm into a snake. With daft glove-puppet special effects defusing the gore factor, this entertaining trash features better-than-average performances from a cast who can barely keep a straight face amid the mayhem.

Jill Schoelen *Lisa* • J Eddie Peck *Clark* • Jamie Farr *Harry* • Savina Gersak *Iris* • Bo Svenson *Sheriff* • Marianne Muellerleile *Big Flo* ■ *Dir* Fred Goodwin [Federico Prosperi] • *Scr* Fred Goodwin, Susan Zelouf

Curse III: Blood Sacrifice ★ 18
Horror   1991 · US · Colour · 87mins

Completely unrelated to the previous two *Curse* movies, this catchpenny chiller (originally titled *Panga*) is set in early fifties East Africa and concerns a plantation owner's pregnant wife (Jenilee Harrison) interrupting a witch doctor's black magic ceremony. For her sin, she is earmarked as sacrificial victim to a rubber monster. Christopher Lee lends gravity to the poorly shot production, which relies heavily on false scares, unconvincing gore and topless natives. ▭

Christopher Lee *Doctor Pearson* • Jenilee Harrison *Elizabeth Armstrong* • Henry Cele *Mletch* • Andre Jacobs *Geoff Armstrong* • Zoe Randall *Anthea Steed* ■ *Dir* Sean Barton • *Scr* John Hunt, Sean Barton, from a story by Richard Haddon Haines

Curse IV: The Ultimate Sacrifice ★ 18
Horror   1993 · US · Colour · 84mins

Originally titled *Catacombs*, this is yet another instalment in the otherwise unconnected *Curse* series. A new father superior (Jeremy West) and a young monk losing his faith (Timothy Van Patten) and a visiting Catholic schoolteacher (Laura Schaefer) join forces to fight a revived medieval demon imprisoned in a dark cell of an Italian church. Ho-hum horror featuring

limited special effects, crucifixions and satanic possessions. ▭

Ian Abercrombie *Father Orsint* • Timothy Van Patten *Father John Durham* • Laura Schaefer *Elizabeth Magrino* • Jeremy West *Father Marinus* ■ *Dir* David Schmoeller • *Scr* Giovanni Dimarco, R Barker Price

The Curse of Frankenstein ★ ★ ★ ★ 15
Horror   1957 · UK · Colour · 79mins

This was the classic that single-handedly revived traditional British Gothic and firmly placed the "Hammer House of Horror" on the global gore map. Peter Cushing is the demented Baron who yearns to resurrect the dead, while Christopher Lee plays the hideous creature who proves his mad theories correct. With its gruesome atmosphere, unflinching direction and outstanding design, this phenomenally successful film was the first colour version of Mary Shelley's gallows fairy tale, setting a standard Hammer found it hard to live up to. ▭

Peter Cushing *Baron Victor Frankenstein* • Christopher Lee *The Creature* • Hazel Court *Elizabeth* • Robert Urquhart *Paul Krempe* • Valerie Gaunt *Justine* • Noel Hood *Aunt Sophia* ■ *Dir* Terence Fisher • *Scr* Jimmy Sangster, from the novel *Frankenstein* by Mary Shelley • *Art Director* Bernard Robinson

The Curse of the Cat People ★ ★ ★ ★ U
Horror fantasy   1944 · US · BW · 66mins

Producer Val Lewton originally wanted to call this picture *Aimée and Her Friend*, but RKO executives were so determined to cash in on Lewton's 1942 success, *Cat People*, that he was persuaded to change the title. Inspired by a Robert Louis Stevenson short story, it is more a study of child psychology than a horror film, but the brooding lighting, the all-pervading sense of menace and the occasional shock make for tense viewing. Simone Simon, the star of *Cat People*, is again superb as Irena, the cursed panther-woman who inspires pity rather than fear. Co-directed by Robert Wise, who was responsible for *The Sound of Music*, this is one of the most charming chillers ever made. ▭

Simone Simon *Irena* • Kent Smith *Oliver Reed* • Jane Randolph *Alice Reed* • Ann Carter *Amy* • Elizabeth Russell *Barbara* • Julia Dean *Julia Farren* • Eve March *Miss Callahan* • Erford Gage *Captain of the guard* ■ *Dir* Robert Wise, Gunther von Fritsch • *Scr* DeWitt Bodeen • *Cinematographer* Nicholas Musuraca

Curse of the Crimson Altar ★ ★
Horror   1968 · UK · Colour · 87mins

There are sacrifices galore, of course, as you'd expect from a title like this, but none was as great as that made by Boris Karloff, starring in a film with such a lacklustre script about devil worship in an old dark house. Not that Karloff cared much about quality, as he was enjoying the pleasure of being back in England, having taken a flat near Lord's in order to be close to his adored cricket. Christopher Lee co-stars. Contains brief nudity. ▭

Boris Karloff *Professor Marsh* • Christopher Lee *JD Morley* • Mark Eden *Robert Manning* •

Virginia Wetherell *Eve* • Barbara Steele *Lavinia* • Rupert Davies *Vicar* • Michael Gough *Elder* • Rosemarie Reede *Esther* ■ *Dir* Vernon Sewell • *Scr* Mervyn Haisman, Henry Lincoln

Curse of the Fly ★ ★
Horror   1965 · UK · BW · 86mins

Brian Donlevy takes over from Vincent Price as the mad doctor experimenting with teleportation through the fourth dimension in this average second sequel to monster hit *The Fly*. Unfortunately, he still can't get the matter transmissions right, and the mutant results of his labours are locked in a closet, ready to scare his son's unbalanced wife (Carole Gray). Journeyman director Don Sharp's talent for shock effects gets lost amid the stiff acting, slow pacing and cheap production values, but the odd moment of eerie atmosphere does surface.

Brian Donlevy *Henri Delambre* • George Baker *Martin Delambre* • Carole Gray *Patricia Stanley* • Yvette Rees *Wan* • Bert Kwouk *Tai* • Michael Graham *Albert Delambre* • Jeremy Wilkin *Inspector Ronet* ■ *Dir* Don Sharp • *Scr* Harry Spalding, from characters created by George Langelaan

The Curse of the Living Corpse ★
Horror   1964 · US · BW · 83mins

A millionaire vows to murder all his spiteful relatives if he is buried alive. When he is, a hooded maniac starts assassinating everyone in nasty ways. A drab attempt to emulate Roger Corman's Edgar Allan Poe adaptations, this laughably bad early gore movie from writer/producer/director Del Tenney has little to recommend it, besides the fact that it features Roy Scheider's film debut.

Helen Warren *Abigail Sinclair* • Roy Scheider *Philip Sinclair* • Margot Hartman *Vivian Sinclair* • Robert Milli *Bruce Sinclair* • Hugh Franklin *James Benson* ■ *Dir/Scr* Del Tenney

The Curse of the Mummy's Tomb ★ ★ 15
Horror   1964 · UK · Colour · 76mins

After moderate success with *The Mummy* (1959), Hammer made several more films featuring the bandaged monster, though all lacked inspiration. In this, the second, there's the customary tomb opening, followed by the customary resurrection of its occupant. The mummy, played by forgotten bit player Dickie Owen, takes an unconscionably long time to go on his customary killing spree, though when it comes it does produce a few tense moments. There's also quite a nasty amputation scene. ▭

Terence Morgan *Adam Beauchamp* • Ronald Howard *John Bray* • Fred Clark *Alexander King* • Jeanne Roland *Annette Dubois* • John Paul *Inspector Mackenzie* • Jack Gwillim *Sir Giles* • George Pastell *Hashmi Bey* • Dickie Owen *Mummy* ■ *Dir* Michael Carreras • *Scr* Henry Younger [Michael Carreras]

The Curse of the Pink Panther ★ ★ PG
Comedy mystery   1983 · UK · Colour · 105mins

Without Peter Sellers, this eighth instalment in the comedy series produces negligible humour. The search for the amiable but idiotic Inspector Clouseau wavers when the inspector's vindictive boss (Herbert Lom) programmes the computer to select the world's worst detective for the job. A bumbling Ted Wass is chosen and sets about interviewing characters from previous movies, among them David Niven, Capucine and Robert Wagner. This was Niven's last film, more's the pity. 🖵

David Niven *Sir Charles Litton* • Ted Wass *Clifton Sleigh* • Rich Little *Sir Charles Litton* (voice) • Robert Wagner *George Litton* • Herbert Lom *Dreyfus* • Joanna Lumley *Chandra* • Capucine *Lady Litton* • Robert Loggia *Bruno* • Harvey Korman *Professor Balls* • Burt Kwouk *Cato* • Leslie Ash *Juleta Shane* • Roger Moore *Jacques Clouseau* ■ Dir Blake Edwards • Scr Blake Edwards, Geoffrey Edwards

Curse of the Starving Class ★★

Drama 1994 · US · Colour · 95mins

The American Dream turns sour in this impressively acted but strangely uninvolving adaptation by Bruce Beresford (better known as a director) of Sam Shepard's 1977 play. It's all very Eugene O'Neill-ish, with James Woods as the patriarch whose boozing has led to a family and a farm on the edge of destruction. Wife Kathy Bates dreams of Paris, Woods has nightmares about Vietnam while their children are a heap of crossed wires.

James Woods *Weston Tate* • Kathy Bates *Ella Tate* • Henry Thomas *Wesley Tate* • Kristin Fiorella *Emma Tate* • Louis Gossett Jr *Ellis* • Randy Quaid *Taylor* • James Fitzpatrick *Emerson* • Joel Anderson *Slater* ■ Dir J Michael McClary • Scr Bruce Beresford, from the play by Sam Shepard

The Curse of the Werewolf
★★ 12

Horror 1961 · UK · Colour · 87mins

Hammer's stab at the werewolf legend may look tame compared to later computerised transformations, but this was shocking stuff in its day, and much horrid imagery was censored. Today the scenes with villagers muttering in the inn look like parody, and everything is so brightly lit there's not much atmosphere. There's also a long prologue that has little to do with the story of poor, cursed Leon (Oliver Reed), who goes on a killing spree every full moon. When Reed does appear, however, he gives a riveting performance. 🖵

Oliver Reed *Leon* • Clifford Evans *Alfredo* • Yvonne Romain *Servant girl* • Catherine Feller *Cristina* • Anthony Dawson *Marques Siniestro* • Josephine Llewellyn *Marquesa* • Richard Wordsworth *Beggar* ■ Dir Terence Fisher • Scr John Elder [Anthony Hinds], from the novel *The Werewolf of Paris* by Guy Endore

The Curse of the Wraydons
★★

Crime melodrama 1946 · UK · BW · 99mins

There was a time when Tod Slaughter was considered the scariest actor alive. It's hard to imagine that now, judging from his ultra-stagey performance in this dull adaptation of Maurice Sandoz's Victorian play *Springheeled Jack, the Terror of London*, which freely embroiders on the

19th-century legend of a leaping prowler. Larger-than-life Slaughter is always fun to watch, though, slicing the ham thick as a mad inventor who commits murder with a diabolical gizmo. A quaint diversion, then, best viewed as an entertaining period piece rather than a full-blooded chiller.

Tod Slaughter *Philip Wraydon* • Bruce Seton *Captain Jack Clayton* • Gabriel Toyne *Lieutenant Payne* • Andrew Laurence *George Heeningham* • Lorraine Clews *Helen Sedgefield* • Pearl Cameron *Rose Wraydon* ■ Dir Victor M Gover • Scr Michael Barringer, from the play *Springheeled Jack, the Terror of London* by Maurice Sandoz

Curtain Call ★★ U

Supernatural comedy
1998 · US · Colour · 95mins

Between his Oscar-winning performances in *Hannah and Her Sisters* and *The Cider House Rules*, Michael Caine made a few clunkers, not least this *Ghost*-like comedy from *Bullitt* director Peter Yates. James Spader moves into a New York apartment, unaware that his new home already has two tenants: the quarreling ghosts of two former Broadway stars, Caine and Maggie Smith. When they realise new flatmate is having girlfriend troubles, the pair (whom only Stevenson can see and hear) decide to meddle, with supposedly hilarious results. Despite all-out efforts from the heavyweight cast, this is never more than mildly amusing.

James Spader *Stevenson Lowe* • Michael Caine *Max Gale* • Sam Shepard *Senator Will Dodge* • Buck Henry *Charles Van Allsburg* • Polly Walker *Julia Winston* • Maggie Smith *Lilly Marlowe* • Frank Whaley *Brett* • Valerie Perrine *Monica* ■ Dir Peter Yates • Scr Todd Alcott, from a story by Andrew S Karsch

Curtain Up ★★★ U

Comedy 1952 · UK · BW · 78mins

There's a nice irony in the fact that a film about a play in which the author refuses to sacrifice a single word of her text has been loosely adapted from the original stage show. Margaret Rutherford is in fine fettle as the persistent playwright, while Robert Morley gives a performance of polished petulance as the director of the down-at-heel stock company who insists on wholesale changes. Considerably better than *A Chorus of Disapproval*, this amusing dig at showbiz preciousness whiles away the time most agreeably. 🖵

Robert Morley *Harry* • Margaret Rutherford *Catherine* • Olive Sloane *Maud* • Joan Rice *Avis* • Charlotte Mitchell *Daphne* • Kay Kendall *Sandra* • Liam Gaffney *Norwood* • Margaret Avery *Mary* ■ Dir Ralph Smart • Scr Michael Pertwee, Jack Davies, from the play *On Monday Next* by Philip King

Custer of the West ★★★ U

Western 1968 · US/Sp · Colour · 134mins

Intended as an epic of Cinerama spectacle, this became a miscasting mistake. British star Robert Shaw, as the Indian-bashing general, is at odds with both accent and character, and the great *film noir* director Robert Siodmak (*Phantom Lady, The Killers*) doesn't tell his story straight because of widescreen gimmickry. There are some fine battle sequences, though,

and Custer's "Last Stand" makes a poignant finale, while Robert Ryan, as an army deserter, brands the screen with white-hot style. 🖵 📀**DVD**

Robert Shaw *General George Custer* • Mary Ure *Elizabeth Custer* • Jeffrey Hunter *Lieutenant Benteen* • Ty Hardin *Major Marcus Reno* • Robert Ryan *Sergeant Mulligan* • Charles Stalnaker *Lieutenant Howells* • Robert Hall *Sergeant Buckley* ■ Dir Robert Siodmak • Scr Bernard Gordon, Julian Halevy [Julian Zimet]

The Custodian ★★★ 15

Crime thriller 1993 · Ausl · Colour · 105mins

It's hard to believe but Anthony LaPaglia, who has proved his tough American credentials in programmes as diverse as *The Client* and the TV series *Murder One*, is in fact an Australian. With an impeccable Oz accent in place, he adds an extra layer of class to an already impressive corruption thriller, as a Machiavellian cop playing the internal affairs department and his ruthless, bent colleagues off against each other. Part of the film's appeal is that you're never quite sure which side LaPaglia is on, and some of the credit for that must go writer/director John Dingwall's intelligent script. The supporting performances are first rate, too, in particular Hugo Weaving (the baddie from *The Matrix*) and Barry Otto as the hapless corruption investigator. 🖵

Anthony LaPaglia *Quinlan* • Hugo Weaving *Church* • Barry Otto *Ferguson* • Kelly Dingwall *Reynolds* • Essie Davis *Jilly* • Bill Hunter *Managing director* • Skye Wansey *Claire* ■ Dir/Scr John Dingwall

A Cut Above ★★★ 15

Comedy drama 1989 · US · Colour · 105mins

Released in the States as *Gross Anatomy*, this lightweight *ER*-style frolic focuses on a group of young students getting to grips with grown-up medicine. Matthew Modine is the charismatic underachiever who refuses to play the competitive games set by harsh tutor Christine Lahti; Daphne Zuniga supplies the romantic interest and Zakes Mokae pops up as a wise old doctor. Director Thom Eberhardt does his best, but the script – co-written by Ron Nyswaner, who would later go on to pen *Philadelphia* – uneasily mixes slapstick with sentimentality. Contains swearing. 🖵

Matthew Modine *Joe Slovak* • Daphne Zuniga *Laurie Rorbach* • Christine Lahti *Dr Rachel Woodruff* • Todd Field *David Schreiner* • John Scott Clough *Miles Reed* • Alice Carter *Kim McCauley* • Zakes Mokae *Dr Banumbra* ■ Dir Thom Eberhardt • Scr Ron Nyswaner, Mark Spragg, Ron Nyswaner, Mark Spragg, from a story by Howard Rosenman, Alan Jay Glueckman, Stanley Isaacs, Mark Spragg

Cutter's Way ★★★★ 15

Crime drama 1981 · US · Colour · 104mins

An overwrought thriller that's a study in moral responsibility. Disabled Vietnam veteran Cutter (John Heard) teams up with his gigolo friend Bone (Jeff Bridges) in a bid to expose tycoon Stephen Elliott as the murderer of a hitchhiker. Cutter and Bone are seriously unlikeable characters, yet Czech émigré director Ivan Passer and writer Jeffrey Alan Fiskin make us see light in these hearts of darkness. The

original title, *Cutter and Bone*, was changed because the studio thought it sounded too much like surgery. Contains swearing. 🖵

Jeff Bridges *Richard Bone* • John Heard *Alex Cutter* • Lisa Eichhorn *Maureen "Mo" Cutter* • Ann Dusenberry *Valerie Duran* • Stephen Elliott *JJ Cord* • Arthur Rosenberg *George Swanson* • Nina Van Pallandt *Woman in hotel* ■ Dir Ivan Passer • Scr Jeffrey Alan Fiskin, from the novel *Cutter and Bone* by Newton Thornburg

CutThroat Island ★★ PG

Action adventure
1995 · US · Colour · 117mins

Renny Harlin's pirate picture has all the ingredients to shiver the timbers and it also boasts the best treasure map ever seen on screen, yet it has gone down in history as one of the biggest box-office disasters of recent times. Geena Davis and Matthew Modine swagger with suitable bravado, but their performances are sunk by the predictability of the action. The storm, the sea battle, the sword fights and the romance all work like clockwork, so there's little suspense to transform familiar spectacle into edge-of-the-seat excitement. Polished entertainment, but with a little more imagination it could have been exhilarating. Contains violence and mild swearing. 🖵

Geena Davis *Morgan Adams* • Matthew Modine *William Shaw* • Frank Langella *Captain Dawg Brown* • Maury Chaykin *John Reed* • Patrick Malahide *Ainslee* • Stan Shaw *Glasspoole* • Rex Linn *Mr Blair* • Paul Dillon *Snelgrave* ■ Dir Renny Harlin • Scr Robert King, Marc Norman, from a story by Michael Frost Beckner, James Gorman, Bruce A Evans, Raynold Gideon

Cutting Class ★★ 18

Comedy horror 1989 · US · Colour · 87mins

Notable only for featuring a very early performance from Brad Pitt, *Cutting Class* is for shlock horror fans only. In this tale of a teenage slasher carving up his high school, Jill Schloelen stars as an all-American cutie who has school jock Pitt for a boyfriend. When pupils start mysteriously dying, blame automatically falls on nutcase Donovan Leitch. But then Schloelen starts noticing Pitt isn't all he seems... The *Scream* series shoots bare like this out of the water, while lines like "I am a murderer. Not as prestigious as a lawyer or a doctor, but the hours are good!" will have you reaching for the remote. 🖵

Donovan Leitch *Brian Woods* • Jill Schloelen *Paula Carson* • Brad Pitt *Dwight Ingalls* • Roddy McDowall *Dr Dante* • Martin Mull *William Carson III* ■ Dir Rospo Pallenberg • Scr Steve Slavkin

The Cutting Edge ★★★ PG

Romantic sports drama
1992 · US · Colour · 97mins

An amiable romantic drama with DB Sweeney as the macho ice hockey player who is paired with snooty ice-skating hopeful Moira Kelly in a bid to win gold at the Olympics. Sweeney and Kelly spark off each other nicely and they are ably supported by the likes of Terry O'Quinn and Roy Dotrice. The skating scenes are splendidly staged, and director Paul Michael Glaser only

U = SUITABLE FOR ALL **Uc** = SUITABLE FOR ALL, ESPECIALLY FOR YOUNG CHILDREN (VIDEO ONLY) **PG** = PARENTAL GUIDANCE

loses his footing during the *Rocky*-style histrionics at the end. [TV]

DB Sweeney *Doug Dorsey* • Moira Kelly *Kate Moseley* • Roy Dotrice *Anton Pamchenko* • Terry O'Quinn *Jack Moseley* • Dwier Brown *Hale* • Chris Benson *Walter Dorsey* • Kevin Peeks *Brian* ■ *Dir* Paul M Glaser [Paul Michael Glaser] • *Scr* Tony Gilroy

Cutting It Short ★★★
Comedy   1980 · Cz · Colour · 98mins

Although a prize-winner at Venice, this chronicle of the early married life of screenwriter Bohumil Hrabal's parents ranks among Jiří Menzel's least trenchant satires on the Czech establishment. Effortlessly blending small-town period detail with whimsical character comedy, it charts brewery manager Jiri Schmitzer's attempts to curb the progressive inclinations of his beautiful, liberated wife (Magda Vasaryova) and the antics of his eccentric brother (Jaromir Hanzlik). However, Menzel also manages to poke gentle fun at the pompous liggers who exploit all the privileges of sitting on the brewery board without doing any of the work. Charmingly played and filmed, but rather lacking in bite.

Jiri Schmitzer *Francin* • Magda Vasaryova *Marja* • Jaromir Hanzlik *Pepin* • Rudolf Hrusinsky *Dr Gruntorad* • Oldrich Vlach *Ruzicka* • Frantisek Rehak *Vejvoda* • Petr Cepek • Oldrich Vizner *Barber* ■ *Dir* Jiri Menzel • *Scr* Jiri Menzel, Bohumil Hrabal

Cyber-Tracker ★★ 18
Action science-fiction thriller
1994 · US · Colour · 90mins

Don "The Dragon" Wilson looks uncomfortable in the suit and tie he's forced to wear while playing a Secret Service agent and loyal servant of a future American government. But it looks like he's about to be made obsolete by the new "robotic justice" programme, which hunts down escaped criminals and carries out their executions in public. Of course, there's an evil conspiracy behind it all; once Wilson finds out the truth, he must escape the robots himself. Die-hard sci-fi fans might enjoy this generic action thriller. [TV]

Don "The Dragon" Wilson *Eric Phillips* • Joseph Ruskin *J Craig Round* ■ *Dir* Richard Pepin • *Scr* Jacobsen Hart

Cyborg ★★★ 18
Science-fiction adventure
1989 · US · Colour · 79mins

Mad Max meets *Escape from New York* in director Albert Pyun's cheap and cheerful science-fiction adventure where all the characters are named after electric guitars (Fender, Rickenbacker). Jean-Claude Van Damme is a futuristic mercenary hired to escort a cyborg carrying the antidote to a deadly plague that has almost wiped out mankind in the 21st century. On the journey they fall foul of the Flesh Pirates, torturers, flashbacks and crucifixion as genre master Pyun piles on the trash, panache and gratuitous violence with cut-price style. [TV] **DVD**

Jean-Claude Van Damme *Gibson Rickenbacker* • Deborah Richter *Nady Simmons* • Vincent Klyn *Fender Tremolo* • Alex Daniels *Marshall*

Strat • Dayle Haddon *Pearl Prophet* • Blaise Loong *Furman Vox* • Rolf Muller *Brick Bardo* ■ *Dir* Albert Pyun • *Scr* Kitty Chalmers

Cyborg 2: Glass Shadow ★★★ 18
Science-fiction adventure
1993 · US · Colour · 95mins

A martial-arts-fighting cyborg (Angelina Jolie) is created by a sinister US corporation to destroy a Japanese rival in an action-packed futuristic adventure with a fun cast. Hero Elias Koteas falls for the sexy humanoid, and together they fight drug-addicted bounty hunter Billy Drago and mercenary storm troopers sent out by evil president Allen Garfield to foil their insidious plan. Writer/director Michael Schroeder keeps everything bubbling along neatly in this *Blade Runner*-inspired violent fantasy, which has flashbacks to the Jean-Claude Van Damme original. [TV]

Elias Koteas *Colson "Colt" Ricks* • Angelina Jolie *Casella "Cash" Reese* • Billy Drago *Danny Bench* • Jack Palance *Mercy* • Allen Garfield *Martin Dunn* ■ *Dir* Michael Schroeder • *Scr* Ron Yanover, Mark Gelman, Michael Schroeder, from a story by Ron Yanover, Mark Gelman

Cyborg 3: The Recycler ★★★ 18
Science-fiction   1994 · US · Colour · 87mins

With a more thought-provoking script and better delineated characters than before, director Michael Schroeder climbs aboard the *Cyborg* franchise once more to even greater effect. Here, the apocalyptic landscape becomes the stomping ground for despicable "recycler" (bounty hunter) Richard Lynch who preys on the comfort of benevolent humanoids. Scientist Zach Galligan and reproductive replicant Khrystyne Haje are caught up in the battle between blood-thirsty mankind and innocent robots for the right to procreate. As compelling as the bleak scenario is, it's veteran bad guy Lynch you'll remember as he takes magnetic evil to a superb new level of villainy. [TV]

Zach Galligan *Evans* • Malcolm McDowell *Lord Talon* • Michael Bailey Smith *Donovan* • Rebecca Ferratti *Elexia* • Khrystyne Haje *Cash* • Andrew Bryniarski *Jocko* • Richard Lynch *Llewellyn* ■ *Dir* Michael Schroeder • *Scr* Barry Victor, Troy Bolotnick

Cyborg Cop ★ 18
Science-fiction action
1993 · US · Colour · 92mins

In a plot that seems ripped off from director Sam Firstenberg's earlier *American Ninja 2* (1987), David Bradley heads off to a Caribbean island in search of his missing brother. There he uncovers a secret organisation run by John Rhys-Davies that kidnaps innocent people and converts them into killer cyborgs. Seemingly filmed in abandoned buildings or vacant lots, this is a cheesy *Terminator* rip-off with unexceptional action scenes. The only reason it spawned a sequel is that both films were filmed back to back. [TV]

David Bradley (2) *Jack Ryan* • John Rhys-Davies *Kessel* • Alonna Shaw *Cathy* • Todd

Jensen *Phillip* • Rufus Swart *Cyborg* • Ron Smerczak *Callan* • Anthony Fridjohn *Hogan* ■ *Dir* Sam Firstenberg • *Scr* Greg Latter

Cyborg Cop II ★ 18
Science-fiction   1994 · US · Colour · 93mins

RoboCop David Bradley returns to track down psycho serial killer Morgan Hunter, who tricks prison authorities into making him a cyborg in a lazy rip-off of all the far better half-man/half-machine fantasy adventures around. Because Bradley is etched as chauvinistically arrogant and no less sadistic than his criminal prey, there's no tension generated or character empathy elicited in a below-par sequel totally lacking in logic. [TV]

David Bradley (2) *Jack Ryan* • Morgan Hunter *Starkraven* • Jill Pierce *Liz McDowell* ■ *Dir* Sam Firstenberg • *Scr* Jon Stevens, from a story by Sam Firstenberg

Cyclo ★★★★★ 18
Drama   1995 · Fr/Viet · Colour · 123mins

In total contrast to the elegiac *Scent of Green Papaya*, this is a quite stunning achievement from Vietnamese director Tran Anh Hung. Tackling such complex themes as paternity, mother-child affinity and spiritual twinship, it is also an uncompromising portrait of life on the streets of Ho Chi Minh City. Le Van Loc is sensational as the teenage pedicab driver who falls in with gangster-pimp Tony Leung when his cycle is stolen. The camerawork is exceptional, with long, energetic takes arranged alongside slow, poetic images. Bold and brave, determined and disturbing, this is film-making of the highest order. [TV] In Vietnamese with English subtitles. [TV]

Le Van Loc *The Cyclo* • Tony Chiu-Wai Leung [Tony Leung (1)] *The Poet* • Tran Nu Yen-Khe *The Sister* • Nguyen Nhu Quynh *The Madam* ■ *Dir* Tran Anh Hung • *Scr* Tran Anh Hung, Nguyen Trung Bing

The Cyclops ★
Science-fiction   1957 · US · BW · 75mins

Director Bert I Gordon had an unhealthy fixation with giants: most of his output revolved around them, from colossal men to mutant ants. Even by Gordon's low standards, however, this is a seriously dumb film. Gloria Talbott plays a woman searching for her fiancé, who goes missing after his plane crashes in a radiation-polluted area. He subsequently turns up as a 50ft tall, one-eyed mutant. Guess the wedding's off, then. Bargain basement tosh that relies too heavily on a risible array of special effects, including giant spiders, lizards and rodents.

James Craig *Russ Bradford* • Gloria Talbott *Susan Winter* • Lon Chaney Jr *Martin Melville* • Tom Drake *Lee Brand* • Duncan "Dean" Parkin *Bruce Barton/The Cyclops* • Vincente Padula [Vincent Padula] *The Governor* ■ *Dir/Scr* Bert I Gordon

Cynara ★★ PG
Melodrama   1932 · US · BW · 74mins

Based on a Broadway play, which Sam Goldwyn tended to buy in job lots, *Cynara*'s title came from a poem by Ernest Dowson: "I have always been faithful to thee, Cynara, in my fashion". Goldwyn's publicity

department then reminded audiences that *Cynara* was pronounced "SIN-ara". Directed by King Vidor, it's a story of marital infidelity, with Ronald Colman's London barrister betraying his wife, Kay Francis, by falling for shopgirl Phyllis Barry. It's a tragedy, though the real drama was on the set, when Colman's dislike of the role led to press reports of his drunkenness. Colman sued Goldwyn for $1 million, dropped the case and brazenly announced his retirement. The movie bombed. [TV]

Ronald Colman *Jim Warlock* • Kay Francis *Clemency Warlock* • Phyllis Barry *Doris Lea* • Henry Stephenson *John Tring* • Viva Tattersall *Milly Miles* • Florine McKinney *Garla* ■ *Dir* King Vidor • *Scr* Frances Marion, Lynn Starling, from the play by HM Harwood, Robert Gore-Brown, from the novel *An Imperfect Lover* by Robert Gore-Brown

Cynthia ★★ U
Comedy drama   1947 · US · BW · 98mins

Fifteen-year-old Elizabeth Taylor, already blossoming into sensuous young womanhood, is the eponymous heroine of this light domestic drama, directed by the expert Robert Z Leonard. It's the facile but reasonably involving tale of an adolescent girl fighting to loosen the controlling bonds of an over-protective mother (Mary Astor) and be allowed to go on her first date (with Jimmy Lydon). The young star is both appealing and convincing, and receives able support from Astor, George Murphy, SZ "Cuddles" Sakall and Gene Lockhart.

Elizabeth Taylor *Cynthia Bishop* • George Murphy *Larry Bishop* • SZ Sakall *Prof Rosenkrantz* • Mary Astor *Louise Bishop* • Gene Lockhart *Dr Fred I Jannings* • Spring Byington *Carrie Jannings* • Jimmy Lydon [James Lydon] *Ricky Latham* • Scotty Beckett *Will Parker* ■ *Dir* Robert Z Leonard • *Scr* Charles Kaufman, Harold Buchman, from the play *The Rich, Full Life* by Vina Delmar

Cyrano de Bergerac ★★★ U
Period drama   1950 · US · BW · 112mins

Edmond Rostand's famous classic about the French army officer whose oversized nose prevents him declaring his love for the beautiful Roxane. Instead he woos her with poetic love letters on behalf of his young friend, Christian. This faithful, respectful screen translation stars José Ferrer as a dignified, moving Cyrano, a part he had played on Broadway and which here won him an Oscar for best actor. Michael Gordon directs in journeyman fashion, while William Prince and Mala Powers are adequate as the young lovers. It's interesting to compare it with the rambunctious version made in 1980 starring Gérard Depardieu, or Steve Martin's semi-comical modernisation, *Roxanne* (1987). [TV]

José Ferrer *Cyrano* • Mala Powers *Roxane* • William Prince *Christian* • Morris Carnovsky *Le Bret* • Ralph Clanton *de Guiche* • Lloyd Corrigan *Ragueneau* • Virginia Farmer *Duenna* • Edgar Barrier *Cardinal* ■ *Dir* Michael Gordon • *Scr* Carl Foreman, from the play by Edmond Rostand

Cyrano de Bergerac ★★★★★ U

Romantic drama 1990 · Fr · Colour · 137mins

Subtitles too often distract viewers from vital action, but they are a necessary evil and far preferable to dubbing voices. It makes something of a change, therefore, to acclaim the subtitles as a major selling point for a film. Novelist Anthony Burgess provided the English translation for this sumptuous adaptation of Edmond Rostand's classic play by director Jean-Paul Rappeneau, and audiences are treated to both exquisite poetry and an exceptional performance from Gérard Depardieu. He thoroughly merited his best actor prize at Cannes for the passion and wit he shows here. Also worthy of mention are cinematographer Pierre Lhomme, art director Ezio Frigerio and Michèle Burke, who made that magnificent nose. In French with English subtitles. ▭

Gérard Depardieu *Cyrano de Bergerac* • Anne Brochet *Roxane* • Vincent Perez *Christian de Neuvillette* • Jacques Weber *Comte de Guiche* • Roland Bertin *Ragueneau* • Philippe Morier-Genoud *Le Bret* • Pierre Maguelon *Carbon de Castel-Jaloux* • Josiane Stoleru *Duenna* • Anatole Delalande *Child* ■ *Dir* Jean-Paul Rappeneau • *Scr* Jean-Claude Carriere, Jean-Paul Rappeneau, from the play by Edmond Rostand

D2: the Mighty Ducks ★★ U

Sports comedy 1994 · US · Colour · 102mins

The original *Mighty Ducks* was a bit of a surprise package given that ice hockey is probably only marginally more popular than baseball in this country. However, it has gone on to spawn a couple of equally inoffensive if bland sequels, of which this is probably the best. Emilio Estevez is once again the coach of the ragbag misfits, leading them to the Goodwill Games only to get seduced by the trappings of fame. Sam Weisman's direction is surprise-free and, he stages the actual ice hockey games with some flair. ▭

Emilio Estevez *Gordon Bombay* • Kathryn Erbe *Michele* • Michael Tucker *Tibbles* • Jan Rubes *Jan* • Carsten Norgaard *Wolf* ■ *Dir* Sam Weisman • *Scr* Steven Brill

D3: the Mighty Ducks ★★ PG

Comedy 1996 · US · Colour · 99mins

Original star Emilio Estevez makes a brief appearance in this third instalment in the successful but unremarkable franchise about the junior hockey team. (His coaching boots are filled instead by Jeffrey Nordling.) In Robert Lieberman's contribution to the series, the Mighty Ducks – slightly more grown-up this time around – are bonafide champs, but they still find it difficult to adapt at their snooty new school. Joss Ackland turns up in another cartoonish villain role but even fans of the first two films will notice the law of diminishing returns kicking in. ▭

Emilio Estevez *Gordon Bombay* • Jeffrey Nordling *Coach Orion* • David Selby *Dean Buckley* • Heidi Kling *Casey* • Joshua Jackson *Charlie* • Joss Ackland *Hans* ■ *Dir* Robert Lieberman • *Scr* Steven Brill, from a story by Kenneth Johnson, Jim Burnstein, from characters created by Steven Brill

DC Cab ★★ 15

Comedy 1983 · US · Colour · 99mins

Made just before Joel Schumacher's break-through bratpack hit *St Elmo's Fire*, this uneasy mix of blue collar laughs and drama focuses on the battle between two rival groups orf cabbies. The interesting cast includes Gary Busey, the *A-Team*'s Mr T and future satirical chat show host Bill Maher, but it's unremarkable stuff and is only interesting as a career marker for fans of Schumacher.

Max Gail *Harold* • Adam Baldwin *Albert* • Mr T *Samson* • Charlie Barnett *Tyrone* • Gary Busey *Dell* • DeWayne Jessie *Bongo* • Gloria Gifford *Miss Floyd* • Marsha Warfield *Ophelia* • Irene Cara ■ *Dir* Joel Schumacher • *Scr* Joel Schumacher, from a story by Topper Carew, from a story by Joel Schumacher

D-Day the Sixth of June ★★★ PG

Second World War romance 1956 · US · Colour · 101mins

A stirring and well-played romantic drama set at the time of the Normandy landings in 1944 that is unusual for a film made in the fifties in that it shows the personal problems of officers actually encroaching on their work. Robert Taylor stars as the American serviceman who recalls his affair with Dana Wynter, while her fiancé Richard Todd was fighting in Africa. Aside from the familiar "us-and-them" scenario and the "stiff-upper-lip" heroics of the D-Day invasion, the many pluses of this movie include some fine acting and spectacular action sequences. ▭

Robert Taylor (1) *Brad Parker* • Richard Todd *John Wynter* • Dana Wynter *Valerie* • Edmond O'Brien *Colonel Timmer* • John Williams *Brigadier Russell* • Jerry Paris *Raymond Boyce* • Robert Gist *Dan Stenick* • Richard Stapley *David Archer* • Ross Elliott *Major Mills* • Alex Finlayson *Colonel Harkens* ■ *Dir* Henry Koster by Lionel Shapiro

DNA ★★★ 15

Science-fiction thriller 1996 · US · Colour · 93mins

Mark Dacascos is one of the more interesting and charismatic action heroes to have emerged in recent years. He remains best known for the flawed live-action *manga* feature *Crying Freeman*, but his talent is also well deployed in this otherwise formulaic thriller. He plays a doctor who is reluctantly coerced into tracking down mad scientist Jürgen Prochnow, who left him for dead years ago and has now regenerated an ancient, possibly alien, killing machine. Director William Mesa, who designed the stunning visual effects for *The Fugitive*, cheerfully splices together elements of *Jurassic Park* and *Predator* into an entertaining low-budget thriller. Contains violence and swearing. ▭

Mark Dacascos *Ash Mattley* • Jürgen Prochnow *Dr Carl Wessinger* • Robin McKee *Claire Sommers* • Roger Aaron Brown *Loren Azenfeld* • John H Brennan *Halton* ■ *Dir* William Mesa • *Scr* Nick Davis

DOA ★★★ PG

Film noir 1949 · US · BW · 83mins

This may not be the best *film noir* of the immediate postwar period, but it's one of the most unusual – how many people get to hunt for their own murderer? Edmond O'Brien responds to that unenviable challenge with grim determination in this slow-burning thriller that perhaps takes a mite too long to catch light. But once the scene is set, director Rudolph Maté takes us on a tortuous journey through the less salubrious parts of Los Angeles. Moodily shot by Ernest Laszlo and with a cracking score by Dimitri Tiomkin, it stands up well to 1988 Dennis Quaid remake. ▭

Edmond O'Brien *Frank Bigelow* • Pamela Britton *Paul Gibson* • Luther Adler *Majak* • Beverly Campbell *Miss Foster* • Lynn Baggett *Mrs Philips* • William Ching *Halliday* • Henry Hart *Stanley Philips* • Neville Brand *Chester* ■ *Dir* Rudolph Maté • *Scr* Russell Rouse, Clarence Green

DOA ★★★ 18

Music documentary 1980 · US · Colour · 89mins

A chaotic rockumentary detailing punk music's assault on comfortable America, set against the bleak backdrop of British daily life that spawned the movement. Extensive coverage of the Sex Pistols' US tour combines with rare footage of X-Ray Spex, Generation X, Sham 69 and the Rich Kids, plus a harrowing interview with a spaced-out Sid Vicious and Nancy Spungen, to give an overview of why punk scared the establishment so much. As a film, it's a complete shambles with some shining moments of frenzied energy and excitement. In other words, the perfect record of its subject matter. ▭

Dir Lech Kowalski

DOA ★★★★ 15

Crime thriller 1988 · US · Colour · 93mins

Dennis Quaid's gripping performance is just one reason why this smart and snappy retread of the 1949 *film noir* is ripe for reappraisal. Beginning with the now famous exchange: "I wanna report a murder." "Whose?" "Mine!", directors Rocky Morton and Annabel Jankel (of *Max Headroom* fame) give their psycho thriller a smashing visual flash. It may be MTV imagery, but it works. Particularly impressive is the gimmick allying Quaid's deteriorating health to the colour draining out of the film, ending up in monochrome. A terrific touch in a thoroughly enjoyable remake. Contains violence and swearing. ▭

Dennis Quaid *Dexter Cornell* • Meg Ryan *Sydney Fuller* • Charlotte Rampling *Mrs Fitzwaring* • Daniel Stern *Hal Petersham* • Jane Kaczmarek *Gail Cornell* • Christopher Neame *Bernard* • Robin Johnson *Cookie Fitzwaring* • Rob Knepper [Robert Knepper] *Nicholas Lang* • Brion James *Detective Ulmer* ■ *Dir* Rocky Morton, Annabel Jankel • *Scr* Charles Edward Pogue, from a story by Charles Edward Pogue, Clarence Greene, Russell Rouse • *Cinematographer* Yuri Neyman

Da ★★★ PG

Fantasy comedy drama 1988 · US · Colour · 97mins

Irish-American writer Martin Sheen returns to Ireland for the funeral of his father (Barnard Hughes). However, no sooner is Sheen back on the old sod than the old sod materialises by his elbow, only too keen to reminisce about the old days, good and bad. Adapted by Hugh Leonard from his own play, the film's theatrical roots are all too visible. Nevertheless, this is an unashamed heartstring-tugger that manages to be both funny and touching. Leonard has a cameo as a pallbearer. ▭

Barnard Hughes *Da* • Martin Sheen *Charlie* • William Hickey *Drumm* • Doreen Hepburn *Mother* • Karl Hayden *Young Charlie* • Hugh O'Conor *Boy Charlie* • Ingrid Craigie *Polly* • Joan O'Hara *Mrs Prynne* ■ *Dir* Matt Clark • *Scr* Hugh Leonard, from his play and from his novel *Home before Night*

U = SUITABLE FOR ALL   **Uc** = SUITABLE FOR ALL, ESPECIALLY FOR YOUNG CHILDREN (VIDEO ONLY)   **PG** = PARENTAL GUIDANCE

Dad ★★ PG

Drama　1989 · US · Colour · 112mins

Adapted from William Wharton's novel by director Gary David Goldberg, *Dad* tries to provoke and uplift, but ends up being nothing more than an utterly false and manipulative melodrama. This is a shame because it starts well, yet from the moment Jack Lemmon falls ill, the film falls apart. His sudden rejuvenation is more in keeping with the fantasy of *Cocoon* than a serious study of parent-child relationships, although his performance is not without its merits and just about atones for the wild overplaying of Ted Danson as his son and the sloppy turn of Ethan Hawke as his grandson. 📼

Jack Lemmon *Jake Tremont* • Ted Danson *John Tremont* • Olympia Dukakis *Bette Tremont* • Kathy Baker *Annie* • Kevin Spacey *Mario* • Ethan Hawke *Billy Tremont* • Zakes Mokae *Dr Chad* • JT Walsh *Dr Santana* • Peter Michael Goetz *Dr Ethridge* ■ *Dir* Gary David Goldberg • *Scr* Gary David Goldberg, from the novel *Dad* by William Wharton

Dad Savage ★★ 18

Crime thriller　1997 · UK · Colour · 99mins

A downright strange British stab at a *Reservoir Dogs*-style robbery aftermath, told in jumping snippets of flashback and set in Norfolk. Patrick Stewart is entirely unconvincing as the titular loving flower grower who has a hidden "pension fund" accrued from various illegal activities. His gang members' desire for the loot leads to murder, double-cross and all the other clichés of the genre. Alternately boring and confusing, this has the graphic violence you might expect, but without the usual visual style, narrative sophistication or snappy dialogue necessary to pull this Tarantino impression off. Contains violence and swearing. 📼

Patrick Stewart *Dad Savage* • Kevin McKidd *H* • Helen McCrory *Chris* • Joseph McFadden *Bob* • Marc Warren *Vic* • Jake Wood *Sav* ■ *Dir* Betsan Morris Evans • *Scr* Steven Williams

Daddy ★★★ 15

Drama　1987 · US · Colour · 92mins

Even though you sometimes feel you're being given a stern lecture on youthful stupidity, this is, by and large, a considered film which manages to be dramatically successful without swamping the raw, real experience of two kids. Dermot Mulroney and Patricia Arquette play high school pupils who are forced to wrestle with the adult world when she becomes pregnant and his career plans hit the buffers. The leads cover both arrogance and insecurity in rangy performances that regularly catch fire, and the result is a highly perceptive movie that doesn't shy away from its subject. 📼

Dermot Mulroney *Bobby Burnette* • Patricia Arquette *Stacey Holder* • John Karlen *Mike Burnette* • Tess Harper *Ann Burnette* • JJ Cohen *Dewey* • Trey Adams *Chris Burnette* • Danny Aiello *Coach Jacobs* • Darren Dalton *Sparks* ■ *Dir/Scr* John Herzfeld

Daddy ★★ PG

Romantic drama　1991 · US · Colour · 91mins

One of the more enjoyable (and less schmaltzy) adaptations of a Danielle Steel romantic novel, with *Dallas* star Patrick Duffy trying to cope after his wife, Kate Mulgrew (of *Star Trek: Voyager* fame), leaves him and their children. Of course, this being a Mills and Boon-style affair, there is romance on the horizon in the form of Wonder Woman Lynda Carter. Contains coarse language. 📼

Patrick Duffy *Oliver Watson* • Lynda Carter *Charlotte Sampson* • Kate Mulgrew *Sarah Watson* • John Anderson *George Watson* • Ben Affleck *Benjamin Watson* ■ *Dir* Michael Miller • *Scr* L Virginia Browne, from the novel by Danielle Steel

Daddy Long Legs ★★★★

Silent comedy drama　1919 · US · BW · 85

In pigtails rather than her customary curls, 27-year-old Mary Pickford plays the rebellious youngster who leads a revolt against the prison-like conditions in her orphanage. There is much honest emotion along with the humour (Mary getting drunk, for example), while Marshall Neilan shows why he was her favourite director. (He also appears as a prospective suitor.) The girl's rich benefactor, the mysterious Daddy Long Legs, would register more importantly in later versions of the story, most notably the 1955 musical with Leslie Caron and Fred Astaire.

Mary Pickford *"Judy" Abbott* • Milla Davenport *Mrs Lippert* • Wesley Barry *Her pal* • Marshall Neilan *Jimmie McBride* ■ *Dir* Marshall Neilan • *Scr* Agnes Christine Johnston, from the novel and play by Jean Webster

Daddy Long Legs ★★★ U

Comedy drama　1931 · US · BW · 80mins

Mary Pickford's silent First National hit, based on Jean Webster's popular novel of letters, metamorphosed into one of 20th Century-Fox's hardy perennials, but this tale of a secret guardian falling for his young ward needed to be handled with extreme care on the grounds of taste. In this version, pretty Janet Gaynor, though a shade too old for the part, makes a charming foundling, Warner Baxter is a handsomely sturdy patron of at least a convincing age, and the whole story of their May-December relationship is deeply satisfying.

Janet Gaynor *Judy Abbott* • Warner Baxter *Jervis Pendleton* • Una Merkel *Sally McBride* • John Arledge *Jimmy McBride* • Claude Gillingwater Sr [Claude Gillingwater] *Riggs* • Kathlyn Williams *Mrs Pendleton* ■ *Dir* Alfred Santell • *Scr* Sonya Levien, SN Behrman, from the novel and play by Jean Webster

Daddy Long Legs ★★★★ U

Romantic musical comedy　1955 · US · Colour · 121mins

The fourth screen version of Jean Webster's novel, this time with a perfectly cast Fred Astaire, who literally glides his way through the tissue-thin plot about an orphan falling for her playboy benefactor. This could be tasteless, bearing in mind the vast age gap, but since it's a musical and the delightful Leslie Caron is the girl – well, in the words of the movie's Oscar-nominated song by Johnny Mercer, *Something's Gotta Give*. Interestingly, this was released when rock 'n' roll was at its peak, and features the great Astaire doing the Sluefoot. (Watch Astaire's face: he's not joking.) A charming, old-fashioned musical with Fred Clark, Thelma Ritter and Terry Moore providing excellent support. 📼

Fred Astaire *Jervis Pendleton* • Leslie Caron *Julie* • Terry Moore *Linda* • Thelma Ritter *Miss Pritchard* • Fred Clark *Griggs* ■ *Dir* Jean Negulesco • *Scr* Phoebe Ephron, Henry Ephron, from the novel and play by Jean Webster • *Music/Lyrics* Johnny Mercer

Daddy-O ★

Musical drama　1959 · US · Colour · 70mins

Here's an early embarrassment in the career of composer John Williams: a cheap and awful slice of teen schlock, its catchpenny title derived from then-contemporary slang. The negligible plot follows truck driver Dick Contino as he fights hoodlums and smashes a drugs ring, all the while singing forgettable tunes to Sandra Giles, who could give most movie vamps serious lessons in pouting. This was already out of date by the time it was made.

Dick Contino *Phil Sandifer* • Sandra Giles *Jana Ryan* • Bruno VeSota *Sidney Chillas* • Gloria Victor *Marcia* • Ron McNeil *Duke* ■ *Dir* Lou Place • *Scr* David Moessinger

Daddy's Dyin'... Who's Got the Will? ★★★ 15

Comedy drama　1990 · US · Colour · 92mins

Every now and then a director has to concede defeat and admit that a play with crackling dialogue and eccentric characters can get by without cinematic flourishes. Jack Fisk makes all the right choices in this adaptation of Del Shores's hit play and the result is an often hilarious comedy of dysfunctional family life. Beau Bridges has rarely been better as a white trash loudmouth, bullying his chalk-and-cheese sisters, who are played to perfection by Amy Wright, Tess Harper and Beverly D'Angelo (who comes close to stealing the picture with hippy boyfriend Judge Reinhold). Contains swearing and drug abuse. 📼

Beau Bridges *Orville Turnover* • Beverly D'Angelo *Evalita Turnover* • Tess Harper *Sara Lee* • Judge Reinhold *Harmony* • Amy Wright *Lurlene* • Patrika Darbo *Marlene Turnover* • Bert Remsen *Buford Turnover* • Molly McClure *Mama Wheelis* • Keith Carradine *Clarence* • Newell Alexander *Sid Cranford* ■ *Dir* Jack Fisk • *Scr* Del Shores, from his play

Daddy's Gone A-Hunting ★★ 12

Thriller　1969 · US · Colour · 12mins

Having picked up a trick or two as both editor and director for ace horror producer Val Lewton, you would have expected Mark Robson to have made a better fist of this San Francisco-based chiller. The thrills he concentrates on, however, are those of a sexual, rather than a suspenseful, nature and consequently the action is nowhere near as tense as it should be. Still, there are a couple of black comic touches, notably having a kidnapped baby transported in a dog basket, and Scott Hylands is convincingly deranged as he seeks revenge on Carol White for the abortion she kept secret from him. Contains mild swearing.

Carol White *Cathy Palmer* • Scott Hylands *Kenneth Daly* • Paul Burke *Jack Byrnes* • Mala Powers *Meg Stone* • Rachel Ames *Dr Parkington's nurse* • Barry Cahill *FBI Agent Crosley* • James Sikking [James B Sikking] *FBI Agent Menchell* ■ *Dir* Mark Robson • *Scr* Lorenzo Semple Jr, Larry Cohen

Dad's Army ★★★ U

Comedy　1971 · UK · Colour · 90mins

Totalling 64 episodes and two Christmas specials during its nine-year run, *Dad's Army* remains one of the best loved of all British comedy series. As with so many other TV spin-offs, the producers couldn't resist the temptation of tinkering with the winning formula, and here we are treated to a Nazi invasion of Walmington-on-Sea that is somewhat at odds with the cosy incompetence that made the series so irresistible. Nevertheless, it's still great fun and it's always a pleasure to see such gifted character actors at work.

Arthur Lowe *Captain Mainwaring* • John Le Mesurier *Sergeant Wilson* • Clive Dunn *Corporal Jones* • John Laurie *Private Frazer* • James Beck *Private Walker* • Arnold Ridley *Private Godfrey* • Ian Lavender *Private Pike* • Liz Fraser *Mrs Pike* • Bernard Archard *General Fuller* • Derek Newark *RSM* • Bill Pertwee *Hodges* • Frank Williams *Vicar* • Edward Sinclair *Verger* • Anthony Sager *Police sergeant* • Pat Coombs *Mrs Hall* ■ *Dir* Norman Cohen • *Scr* Jimmy Perry, David Croft, from their TV series

Daens ★★★★ 15

Drama　1992 · Bel/Fr/Neth · Colour · 132mins

An Oscar-nominated journey through the life and hard times of a 19th-century Catholic priest in Flanders, who took on a political role in order to speak up for the downtrodden mill workers in the textile town of Aalst. The struggle between Father Adolf Daens and the establishment is spelled out in simple, didactic fashion. But the growling performance of Jan Decleir, as Daens, and a narrative anger that threatens immediate revolution both help to accelerate the drama into something to savour. In Flemish with English subtitles. 📼

Jan Decleir *Adolf Daens* • Gérard Desarthe *Charles Woeste* • Antje De Boeck *Nette Scholliers* • Michael Pas *Jan De Meeter* ■ *Dir* Stijn Coninx • *Scr* François Chevallier, Stijn Coninx, from the novel *Pieter Daens* by Louis Paul Boon

Daffy Duck's Movie: Fantastic Island ★★★ U

Animation　1983 · US · Colour · 74mins

Directed by the legendary Friz Freleng and with voices by the great Mel Blanc, this is yet another collection of old Warner Bros cartoons combined and released under a new title. It's a veritable Who's Who of Looney Tunes/Merrie Melodie favourites, with Sylvester and Tweety, Yosemite Sam (as a pirate), Foghorn Leghorn, Pepe LePew and Speedy Gonzales all putting in an appearance. However, there's the odd classic tucked away here, notably *Mutiny on the Bunny*, starring the irrepressible Bugs himself. 📼

Mel Blanc • June Foray • Les Tremayne ■ *Dir* Friz Freleng • *Scr* John Dunn, David Detiege, Friz Freleng

Daffy Duck's Quackbusters
★★★ U

Animated compilation
1988 · US · Colour · 75mins

Disney is the undoubted master of the animated feature, but when it comes to the five-minute cartoon, however, Warner Bros clearly has the edge. The best thing about compilation films like this one is that each component is a classic in its own right. In this neat spoof of *Ghostbusters*, Daffy, Bugs Bunny and Porky Pig join forces to rid the world of spooks. Younger viewers might not get all the subtle references to classic horror films, but *The Night of the Living Duck* and *The Duxorcist* are hilarious. ▣

Mel Blanc • Roy Firestone • BJ Ward ■ *Dir* Greg Ford, Terry Lennon

Daisies
★★★★ 15

Comedy　1966 · Cz · Colour · 72mins

The two most significant female artists of the Czech New Wave collaborated on this anarchic assault on materialism. In addition to designing the stylised visuals, Ester Krumbachová co-wrote the screenplay with director Vera Chytilová, whose husband, Jaroslav Kucera, served as cinematographer. Employing collage, superimposition, symbolic *mise en scène* and prismatic distortion, they concoct a surrealist fantasy of the banality and conformity of Czech society as two girls, both named Marie, dupe several boorish males before indulging in an orgy of gleeful destruction. It now looks its age, but the authorities were sufficiently piqued to limit Chytilová to only one film in the ensuing decade. In Czech with English subtitles. ▣

Jitka Cerhová *Marie I* • Ivana Karbonová *Marie II* ■ *Dir* Vera Chytilová • *Scr* Vera Chytilová, Ester Krumbachová

Daisy Kenyon
★★★★

Romantic melodrama
1947 · US · BW · 98mins

Beginning with *Laura*, director Otto Preminger served up a dark and sinister series of movies throughout the forties, today labelled *film noir* but then just called thrillers. They're really melodramas at heart, served up with all the seaminess the censors and 20th Century-Fox would allow, and hold up well today as a consistently fine body of work. Here, Joan Crawford is Daisy, torn between Fox's quintessential leading men Dana Andrews and Henry Fonda. There's also a surprisingly daring (for its day) subplot about child abuse and a guest appearance from John Garfield.

Joan Crawford *Daisy Kenyon* • Dana Andrews *Dan O'Mara* • Henry Fonda *Peter* • Ruth Warrick *Lucile O'Mara* • Martha Stewart *Mary Angelus* • Peggy Ann Garner *Rosamund* • John Garfield *Man in restaurant* ■ *Dir* Otto Preminger • *Scr* David Hertz, from the novel by Elizabeth Janeway

Daisy Miller
★★★ U

Drama　1974 · US · Colour · 87mins

One of the key theme of Henry James's writings was the clash between American and European culture. So it's fascinating to watch a story in which surface actions are almost irrelevant being related by a director steeped in the storytelling traditions of John Ford and Howard Hawks. Peter Bogdanovich captures the styles, the manners and the atmosphere of late 19th-century Italy, but never comes close to conveying the inner life of the characters, which is precisely what interested James. The director was criticised for casting then-girlfriend Cybill Shepherd in the title role, and the film marked the beginning of his critical and commercial decline. ▣

Cybill Shepherd *Annie P "Daisy" Miller* • Barry Brown *Frederick Winterbourne* • Cloris Leachman *Mrs Ezra B Miller* • Mildred Natwick *Mrs Costello* • Eileen Brennan *Mrs Walker* • Duilio Del Prete *Mr Giovanelli* • James McMurtry *Randolph C Miller* • Nicholas Jones *Charles* ■ *Dir* Peter Bogdanovich • *Scr* Frederic Raphael, from the novel by Henry James

Dakota
★★★ PG

Western　1945 · US · BW · 81mins

Big John Wayne found himself trapped between two major war movies, working out his Republic contract in a western directed by a studio hack, which despite a strong support cast, is fairly typical of that minor studio's output. Even the female lead is played by Vera Hruba Ralston, wife of the studio head. Ironically, *Dakota*'s original story was by left-winger Carl Foreman, later blacklisted by those who shared Wayne's right-wing views. Wayne rides to the rescue of farmers whose valuable land is targeted by crooks, but his heart doesn't seem to be in it. ▣

John Wayne *John Devlin* • Vera Hruba Ralston [Vera Ralston] *Sandy* • Walter Brennan *Captain Bounce* • Ward Bond *Jim Bender* • Ona Munson *"Jersey" Thomas* • Hugo Haas *Marko Poli* ■ *Dir* Joseph Kane • *Scr* Lawrence Hazard, Howard Estabrook, from a story by Carl Foreman

Dakota
★★ U

Drama　1987 · US · Colour · 91mins

After the success of *La Bamba*, Lou Diamond Phillips's next screen outing was a marked change of pace. He plays a teenager on the run, with all the usual adolescent hang-ups, who gets to grips with his life while working on a Texas ranch. Phillips smoulders away effectively enough and there are good supporting turns from a largely unknown cast, while Fred Holmes, who would team up again with Phillips for 1990's *Harley*, handles the directorial chores with some skill. Contains swearing and violence. ▣

Lou Diamond Phillips *Dakota* • Eli Cummins *Walt* • Dee Dee Norton *Molly* ■ *Dir* Fred Holmes • *Scr* Darryl Kuntz, Sara Lynn Kuntz

Dakota Incident
★ U

Western　1956 · US · Colour · 88mins

A dire western, this has an adequate cast – headed by Dale Robertson and Linda Darnell – hamstrung by pretentious dialogue and fuzzy characterisations. After interminable scenes in town setting up these boring characters, they set off on the stage to be attacked by Indians, but this only leads to more excessive gabbing after the group takes cover in a dry waterhole. It's a particular relief when Ward Bond's foolish windbag of a senator discovers that his sympathy for the Indians is not reciprocated.

Dale Robertson *John Banner* • Linda Darnell *Amy Clarke* • John Lund *Carter Hamilton* • Ward Bond *Senator Blakely* ■ *Dir* Lewis R Foster • *Scr* Frederick Louis Fox

Daleks – Invasion Earth 2150 AD
★★★ U

Science-fiction adventure
1966 · UK · Colour · 83mins

The second feature starring Peter Cushing as Doctor Who has the BBC's world famous Time Lord aiding human survivors in their future guerrilla war against the diabolical Daleks. *Independence Day* it's not, but director Gordon Flemyng keeps the colourful action moving swiftly along to cheap and cheerful effect. Youngsters will love it, while adults will want to E-X-T-E-R-M-I-N-A-T-E Bernard Cribbins, who provides comic relief as the bumbling bobby. Yet, through all the mindless mayhem roll the ever-impressive Daleks, truly one of science fiction's greatest alien creations.

Peter Cushing *Doctor Who* • Bernard Cribbins *Tom Campbell* • Ray Brooks *David* • Jill Curzon *Louise* • Roberta Tovey *Susan* • Andrew Keir *Wyler* • Godfrey Quigley *Dortmun* ■ *Dir* Gordon Flemyng • *Scr* Milton Subotsky

Dallas
★★★ PG

Western　1950 · US · Colour · 90mins

Before his Oscar-winning role in *High Noon*, Gary Cooper's career was heading for the doldrums. Ageing and thought to be past his prime, he had become hard to cast, and in general his vehicles had become unworthy of their star. In this very average Warner Bros Technicolor western, Coop has little to do as a former Confederate officer seeking revenge by pretending to be a lawman, and looks uncomfortable doing it, and by the time this movie was made the epic town-taming western was heading for its final showdown. ▣

Gary Cooper *Blayde "Reb" Hollister* • Ruth Roman *Tonia Robles* • Steve Cochran *Bryant Marlow* • Raymond Massey *Will Marlow* • Barbara Payton *Flo* • Leif Erickson *Martin Weatherby* • Antonio Moreno *Felipe* • Jerome Cowan *Matt Coulter* • Reed Hadley *Wild Bill Hickok* ■ *Dir* Stuart Heisler • *Scr* John Twist, from his story

Dallas Doll
★★ 18

Comedy drama　1994 · US · Colour · 100mins

Having scored a cult hit with her feature debut *Celia*, and made a fair stab at costume drama with the little-seen *Hammers over the Anvil*, Australian director Ann Turner came seriously unstuck with this comedy drama, an unacknowledged reworking of Pier Paolo Pasolini's 1968 classic *Theorem*. Sandra Bernhard stars as a golf guru who disrupts the ridiculously ordinary life of an average middle-class Sydney family by raising their expectations of life and fulfilling their sexual fantasies. Bernhard has none of the mystery and charm Terence Stamp brought to *Theorem* and is never allowed to go into her customary overdrive. Compensation comes in a delicious performance by Victoria Longley as the liberated mum. ▣

Sandra Bernhard *Dallas Adair* • Victoria Longley *Rosalind* • Frank Gallacher *Stephen* • Jake Blundell *Charlie* • Rose Byrne *Rastus* • Jonathan Leahy *Eddy* • Douglas Hedge *Mayor Tonkin* • Melissa Thomas *Margaret* • Elaine Lee *Mrs Winthrop* • Alethea McGrath *Aunt Mary* • John Frawley *Mr Fellowes* • Roy Billing *Dave Harry* ■ *Dir/Scr* Ann Turner

Dallas: JR Returns
★★ PG

Drama　1996 · US · Colour · 90mins

This entertaining reunion of our old favourites has Texas bad boy JR Ewing (Larry Hagman) returning to Southfork after five years in Paris to regain control of the family oil business. He's still scheming to cheat longtime rival Cliff Barnes (Ken Kercheval), brother Bobby (Patrick Duffy) and ex-wife Sue Ellen (Linda Gray), yet the story isn't half as much fun as seeing the cast members reprising their familiar roles. One of TV's most popular shows, *Dallas* lasted more than 13 years. ▣

Larry Hagman *JR Ewing* • Linda Gray *Sue Ellen Ewing* • Patrick Duffy *Bobby Ewing* • Ken Kercheval *Cliff Barnes* • George Kennedy *Carter McKay* • Omri Katz *John Ross Ewing III* ■ *Dir* Leonard Katzman • *Scr* Leonard Katzman, Arthur Bernard Lewis, from a story by Arthur Bernard Lewis, from characters created by David Jacobs

Dallas: War of the Ewings
★★ PG

Drama　1998 · US · Colour · 82mins

Back by popular demand, this second *Dallas* reunion movie brings back the familiar Southfork gang for another round of cheatin', lyin' and lovin'. JR, now chief of Weststar Oil, manipulates anyone who gets in his way as he pursues his quest to regain control of Ewing Oil, which is being run by his brother, Bobby, and his ex-wife, Sue Ellen. After all these years, beleaguered JR refuses to give up, and you gotta love him for it. The familiar cast may be greyer and older, but they still leave fans wanting more. ▣

Larry Hagman *JR Ewing* • Patrick Duffy *Bobby Ewing* • Linda Gray *Sue Ellen Ewing* • Michelle Johnson *Jennifer Jantzen* • Steve Kanaly *Ray Krebbs* • George Kennedy *Carter McKay* • Tracy Scoggins *Anita Smithfield* • *Scr* Arthur Bernard Lewis, Julie Sayres, from a story by Arthur Bernard Lewis, from characters created by David Jacobs

The Daltons Ride Again
★★

Western　1945 · US · BW · 72mins

Five years after *When the Daltons Rode*, here they are again in a virtual remake. This time, though, it's a resolutely B-grade cast taking over from Randolph Scott and co, with the four outlaw brothers played here by Alan Curtis, Kent Taylor, Lon Chaney Jr and Noah Beery Jr. The quartet wreak havoc, just as they did in the earlier film, throughout Kansas before the all-action climactic bank raid. Efficient enough entertainment which was shot in just 16 days by director Ray Taylor.

Alan Curtis *Emmett Dalton* • Kent Taylor *Bob Dalton* • Lon Chaney Jr *Grat Dalton* • Noah Beery Jr *Ben Dalton* • Martha O'Driscoll *Mary* • Jess Barker *Jeff* • Thomas Gomez *McKenna* ■ *Dir* Ray Taylor • *Scr* Roy Chanslor, Paul Gangelin, Henry Blankfort

U = SUITABLE FOR ALL　Uc = SUITABLE FOR ALL, ESPECIALLY FOR YOUNG CHILDREN (VIDEO ONLY)　PG = PARENTAL GUIDANCE

Dalva ★★★
Drama   1996 · US · Colour

A starry tale about a woman's attempts to find her roots, which nevertheless can't quite shake off its soapy mini-series feel. Farrah Fawcett, in serious actress mode, is the woman whose incestuous affair with her half brother sparks off a crisis of identity and a life-long search for inner happiness. Unfortunately, this TV movie is as hokey as it sounds, although director Ken Cameron's melodramatic flashes and the excellent supporting cast mean it is always very watchable. Contains some violence.

Farrah Fawcett *Dalva Northridge* • Rod Steiger *Grandfather* • Powers Boothe *Sam* • Peter Coyote *Michael* ■ *Dir* Ken Cameron

The Dam Busters ★★★★★ U
Classic Second World War drama
1954 · UK · BW · 119mins

Michael Anderson's film is truly compelling viewing, standing among the best British movies about the Second World War. Indeed, thanks to its potent blend of scientific suspense and aerial action accompanied by that stirring soundtrack, it has convinced generations of movie-watchers that the bouncing bomb raid on the dams of the Ruhr valley was a major turning point in the war rather than a risky venture that the brass hats considered something of a sideshow. Michael Redgrave puts a pinch too much bumbling boffin into his Barnes Wallis, but Richard Todd was never better as Wing Commander Guy Gibson.

Richard Todd *Wing Commander Guy Gibson* • Michael Redgrave *Dr Barnes N Wallis* • Ursula Jeans *Mrs Wallis* • Basil Sydney *Sir Arthur Harris* • Patrick Barr *Captain Joseph Summers* • Ernest Clark *AVM Ralph Cochrane* • Derek Farr *Group Captain Whitworth* • Charles Carson *Doctor* • Stanley Van Beers *Sir David Pye* • Colin Tapley *Dr WH Glanville* • John Fraser *Flight Lieutenant Hopgood* • George Baker *Flight Lieutenant Maltby* • Robert Shaw *Flight Sergeant Pulford* ■ *Dir* Michael Anderson • *Scr* RC Sherriff, from the non-fiction book *The Dam Busters* by Paul Brickhill, from the story *Enemy Coast Ahead* by Wing Commander Guy Gibson

Damage ★★★ 18
Erotic drama 1992 · UK/Fr · Colour · 105mins

Louis Malle, directing his first English-language film since his return from America to France, employs an almost leisurely (but always exact) camera to highlight the emotional centre of this traumatic tale. Taken from Josephine Hart's bestseller by scriptwriter David Hare, the explosion of emotion is muted by moments of implausibility, caused by some widely varying acting styles. Whereas Miranda Richardson crumbles believably as the spurned wife, Juliette Binoche, as the object of an MP's lust, simply pouts seductively, while Jeremy Irons, as the politician, spends too much time behaving like a startled rabbit. Contains swearing, sex scenes and nudity.

Jeremy Irons *Stephen Fleming* • Juliette Binoche *Anna Barton* • Miranda Richardson *Ingrid Fleming* • Rupert Graves *Martyn Fleming* • Leslie Caron *Elizabeth Prideaux* • Ian Bannen *Edward Lloyd* • Gemma Clarke *Sally Fleming* • Peter Stormare *Peter* • Julian Fellowes *Donald Lindsay* ■ *Dir* Louis Malle • *Scr* David Hare, from the novel by Josephine Hart

Dames ★★★
Musical comedy 1934 · US · BW · 91mins

This is a super Warner Bros Depression-era musical, with wonderfully kaleidoscopic choreography from maestro Busby Berkeley. The dialogue is as witty as ever, but the blackmail-cum-putting on a show storyline is contrived, and the whole lacks the dazzle of stablemates *42nd Street* and the first two Berkeley *Gold Diggers*. No matter: the production numbers are sensational, and the cast, featuring witty Joan Blondell and wacky ZaSu Pitts, is compulsively watchable.

Joan Blondell *Mabel Anderson* • Dick Powell *Jimmy Higgens* • Ruby Keeler *Barbara Hemingway* • ZaSu Pitts *Mathilda Hemingway* • Hugh Herbert *Ezra Ounce* • Guy Kibbee *Horace* • Arthur Vinton *Bulger* • Phil Regan *Johnny Harris* • Busby Berkeley *Choreography* ■ *Dir* Ray Enright • *Scr* Delmer Daves, from a story by Robert Lord, Delmer Daves

Les Dames du Bois de Boulogne ★★★★★ PG
Second World War drama
1946 · Fr · BW · 81mins

Robert Bresson's second feature, his last to use professional actors and be filmed in a studio, takes an anecdote from Diderot's *Jacques le Fataliste* and moves it to a 20th-century setting. When a man tells his girlfriend that he no longer loves her, she wreaks revenge by arranging a meeting between him and an ex-prostitute, only revealing her history after they marry. Jean Cocteau's screenplay brilliantly dissects the fable's ethical issues, while the director's natural austerity enhances the dramatic tension. In French with English subtitles.

Paul Bernard *Jean* • Maria Casarès *Hélène* • Elina Labourdette *Agnès* • Lucienne Bogaert *Agnès's mother* • Jean Marchat *Jacques* ■ *Dir* Robert Bresson • *Scr* Robert Bresson, Jean Cocteau, from the novel *Jacques le Fataliste et Son Maître* by Denis Diderot

Damien – Omen II ★★★ 18
Horror 1978 · US · Colour · 102mins

The Antichrist becomes an adolescent evil-doer in this watered-down version of the Satanic saga, which relies too openly on the same shock suspense tricks that made *The Omen* (1976) such a great success. Damien reads the Book of Revelations and discovers all about his true past. Lightning refuses to strike twice, mainly because of over-familiarity with the chilling concept, and Don Taylor's banal direction. William Holden and Lee Grant handle their roles as Damien's foster parents with considerable skill, and their apocalyptic finale is the high point of a missed opportunity.

William Holden (1) *Richard Thorn* • Lee Grant *Ann Thorn* • Jonathan Scott-Taylor *Damien Thorn* • Robert Foxworth *Paul Buher* • Nicholas Pryor *Charles Warren* • Lew Ayres *Bill Atherton* • Sylvia Sidney *Aunt Marion* • Lance Henriksen *Sergeant Neff* ■ *Dir* Don Taylor • *Scr* Stanley Mann, Michael Hodges

Damn Citizen ★★
Crime drama 1958 · US · BW · 88mins

Keith Andes plays the Second World War hero brought in to fight the corruption endemic in his native Louisiana. Filmed in and around New Orleans, Robert Gordon's picture has a documentary feel. Andes is not the most interesting of actors, however, and the screenplay (an early work by Stirling Silliphant) follows a rather straightforward, predictable and episodic course.

Keith Andes *Colonel Francis C Grevemberg* • Maggie Hayes *Dorothy Grevemberg* • Gene Evans *Major Al Arthur* • Lynn Bari *Pat Noble* • Jeffrey Stone *Paul Musso* • Edward Platt *Joseph Kosta* • Ann Robinson *Cleo* • Sam Buffington *DeButts* ■ *Dir* Robert Gordon • *Scr* Stirling Silliphant

Damn the Defiant! ★★★
Historical adventure
1962 · UK · Colour · 100mins

An entertaining seafaring adventure from skilled director Lewis Gilbert, who virtually told the same tale (albeit set in a different war) in *Sink the Bismarck!* This richly coloured adventure benefits immensely from the experienced playing of Dirk Bogarde, Alec Guinness and an underused Anthony Quayle, all of whom are clearly enjoying themselves as they swash buckles in the Napoleonic wars. It's hard to keep your eyes off the young Bogarde, who's absolutely splendid as a demented martinet. Contains some violence.

Alec Guinness *Captain Crawford* • Dirk Bogarde *Lieutenant Scott-Padget* • Anthony Quayle *Vizard* • Tom Bell *Evans* • Maurice Denham *Surgeon Goss* • Walter Fitzgerald *Admiral Jackson* • Victor Maddern *Dawlish* • Murray Melvin *Wagstaffe* • Nigel Stock *Senior Midshipman Kilpatrick* • Richard Carpenter *Lieutenant Ponsonby* ■ *Dir* Lewis Gilbert • *Scr* Nigel Kneale, Edmund H North, from the novel *Mutiny* by Frank Tilsley

Damn Yankees ★★★ U
Musical 1958 · US · Colour · 105mins

After the success of *The Pajama Game*, Broadway's George Abbott and Hollywood's Stanley Donen teamed up again for this second show by the same writing team. Despite this talent, this time round the show didn't quite transfer, despite a supporting cast comprised entirely of the stage cast, and the retention of the original Bob Fosse choreography (plus Mr Fosse himself for one number). The problem lies with Tab Hunter in the difficult leading role: to put it mildly, he lacks pizzazz. There's still a lot of fun to be gleaned, though: Gwen Verdon (Mrs Fosse) is a knockout as Lola, and Ray Walston is arguably the definitive movie Devil, Mr Applegate.

Tab Hunter *Joe Hardy* • Gwen Verdon *Lola* • Ray Walston *Applegate* • Russ Brown *Van Buren* • Shannon Bolin *Meg Boyd* • Nathaniel Frey *Smokey* • Jimmie Komack *Rocky* • Rae Allen *Gloria* • Robert Shafer *Joe Boyd* • Jean Stapleton *Sister* • Albert Linville *Vernon* • Bob Fosse *Mambo dancer* ■ *Dir* George Abbott, Stanley Donen • *Scr* George Abbott, from the play *Damn Yankees* by Douglas Wallop, George Abbott, from the novel *The Year The Yankees Lost the Pennant* by Douglas Wallop

Damnation ★★★
Drama 1988 · Hun · BW · 114mins

Long after Gabor Medvigy's meandering monochrome images have faded, the unrelenting bleakness of Bela Tarr's study of an all-encompassing obsession will linger in the mind. Whether it's the sight of outcast Miklos B Szekely peering through the rain to watch his married lover (Vali Kerekes) singing at the Titanic Bar or the shocking finale, in which he prowls through a pack of scavenging dogs, the film exercises a compulsion that is never diminished by its pessimism. This intense picture could almost be called an apocalyptic *noir*. In Hungarian with English subtitles..

Miklos B Szekely *Karrer* • Vali Kerekes *The singer* ■ *Dir* Bela Tarr • *Scr* Bela Tarr, Laszlo Krasznahorkai

Damnation Alley ★ PG
Science-fiction drama
1977 · US · Colour · 87mins

An utterly pedestrian adaptation of Roger Zelazny's much-admired novel, this science-fiction epic takes place after a nuclear holocaust and features psychedelic visual effects that are really quite awful. Five survivors cross America in a futuristic tank driven by George Peppard, looking for others after receiving mystery radio signals. Lacklustre acting, tedious exposition and laughable rubber monsters damn this forgettable, regrettable misfire.

Jan-Michael Vincent *Tanner* • George Peppard *Denton* • Dominique Sanda *Janice* • Paul Winfield *Keegan* • Jackie Earle Haley *Billy* ■ *Dir* Jack Smight • *Scr* Alan Sharp, Lukas Heller, from the novel by Roger Zelazny

The Damned ★★
Science-fiction 1961 · UK · BW · 94mins

A downbeat financial disaster from Hammer, this clearly reflects the troubled shoot, the creative differences between director Joseph Losey and the cost-conscious House of Horror, and the delayed release in butchered form. While on holiday in Weymouth, and after being mugged by biker gang leader Oliver Reed, American boat owner Macdonald Carey stumbles on a secret government programme in which radioactive children are being schooled to repopulate the planet after a nuclear war. The plot never really fuses to create the powerful Orwellian fable the film was once acclaimed as.

Macdonald Carey *Simon Wells* • Shirley Anne Field *Joan* • Viveca Lindfors *Freya Nelson, sculptress* • Alexander Knox *Bernard, scientist* • Oliver Reed *King* • Walter Gotell *Maj Holland* • Brian Oulton *Mr Dingle* • Kenneth Cope *Sid* ■ *Dir* Joseph Losey • *Scr* Evan Jones, from the novel *The Children of Light* by HL Lawrence

The Damned ★★★★ 18
Drama 1969 · It/W Ger · Colour · 146mins

Luchino Visconti's grand-operatic account views the rise of Fascism in the thirties through an upper-class household (clearly based on the Krupps) as they murder and blackmail each other for the ownership of an armaments factory. Helmut Berger is the son who sleeps with his mother

(Ingrid Thulin); Dirk Bogarde, as the mother's lover, looks bemused by all these unloosed deviations; and the whole is decked out in what amounts to Nazi chic. Although ponderous, this is still a remarkable work – if not of art, then definitely of artifice. Italian dialogue dubbed into English.. ▣

Dirk Bogarde *Friedrich Bruckmann* • Ingrid Thulin *Baroness Sophie von Essenbeck* • Helmut Griem *Aschenbach* • Helmut Berger *Martin von Essenbeck* • Charlotte Rampling *Elisabeth Thallman* ◼ *Dir* Luchino Visconti • *Scr* Luchino Visconti, Nicola Badalucco, Enrico Medioli • *Cinematographer* Pasqualino de Santis, Armando Nannuzzi

The Damned Don't Cry ★★★
Crime drama   1950 · US · BW · 100mins

A splendidly titled but resolutely low-rent Joan Crawford vehicle. It's a steamy crime drama that's almost a follow-up to the previous year's *Flamingo Road*, but without the controlling hand of director Michael Curtiz to rein in Crawford's excesses. Here, Vincent Sherman exercises no such restraints, and Crawford chews the scenery and her men as only she can. She is as splendid as ever, but the males (colourless David Brian, mean Steve Cochran, bland Kent Smith) are rather a let-down.

Joan Crawford *Ethel Whitehead* • David Brian *George Castleman* • Steve Cochran *Nick Prenta* • Kent Smith *Martin Blackford* • Hugh Sanders *Grady* • Selena Royle *Patricia Longworth* ◼ *Dir* Vincent Sherman • *Scr* Harold Medford, Jerome Weidman, from a story by Gertrude Walker

Damned in the USA ★★
Documentary   1991 · UK · Colour · 68mins

Originally produced for Channel Four, this documentary on censorship and arts funding in the States hit the headlines when conservative activist Reverend Donald Wildmon sued director Paul Yule for $8m. He also tried to have the film impounded for misrepresenting his attack on the National Endowment for the Arts's sponsorship of what he considered sacrilegious and pornographic work. Focusing primarily on the reaction to a controversial Robert Mapplethorpe exhibition, Yule undermines his arguments by relying on Jimmy Tingle's cheap-shot stand-up routine to mock opinions with which he does not agree.

Dir Paul Yule

Damned River ★ 18
Action adventure   1989 · US · Colour · 91mins

A crude exploitation effort directed by Michael Schroeder, who once worked for Paul Bartel and made his directing debut with the mordantly funny *Out of the Dark*, in which Bartel himself starred. This second effort isn't up to par, though, being a virtual rip-off of *Deliverance* about a bunch of young Americans shooting the rapids in Zimbabwe. Their guide (Stephen Shellen) turns out to be a real psycho: a former soldier who starts picking off the chaps and brutally rapes the solitary girl. ▣

Stephen Shellen *Ray* • Lisa Aliff *Anne* • John Terlesky *Carl* • Marc Poppel *Luke* • Bradford

Bancroft *Jerry* • Louis Van Niekerk *Von Hoenigen* ◼ *Dir* Michael Schroeder, John Crowther • *Scr* Bayard Johnson

A Damsel in Distress ★★★ U
Comedy musical   1937 · US · BW · 96mins

Adapted by PG Wodehouse from a play that was based on his own novel, this was Fred Astaire's second film without Ginger Rogers. But he's in sparkling form as a dance star attempting to trip the light fantastic with aristocratic Joan Fontaine. Hermes Pan's choreography won an Oscar, but every step is pure Astaire, and Fontaine (who was better known as a dramatic actress) never misses a beat. Playing themselves, George Burns and Gracie Allen show why they are so fondly remembered. And if that's not enough, there is a clutch of eminently hummable Gershwin songs. ▣

Fred Astaire *Jerry Halliday* • George Burns *George Burns* • Gracie Allen *Gracie Allen* • Joan Fontaine *Lady Alyce Marshmorton* • Reginald Gardiner *Keggs* • Ray Noble *Reggie* • Constance Collier *Lady Caroline Marshmorton* • Montagu Love *Lord John Marshmorton* ◼ *Dir* George Stevens • *Scr* PG Wodehouse, SK Lauren, Ernest Pagano, from a play by PG Wodehouse, Ian Hay, from a novel by PG Wodehouse

Dan Candy's Law ★★★
Historical western   1973 · Can · Colour · 90mins

This is based on the true story of a Cree Indian fugitive who evaded the Canadian Mounties for more than a year. The plot may not be up to much, but honours go to Donald Sutherland as Dan Candy, the rangy, tall-tale-telling Mountie who always gets his man. It's most interesting as a chance to see how conflict between white police officers and native American Indians was dealt with back in the seventies and for Claude Fournier's stunning photography, evoking the brutality of the rugged Canadian landscape.

Donald Sutherland *Sgt Dan Candy* • Kevin McCarthy *Sgt Malcolm Grant* • Chief Dan George *Sounding Sky* • Gordon Tootoosis *Almighty Voice* ◼ *Dir* Claude Fournier • *Scr* George Malko

Dance Academy ★★ PG
Dance drama   1988 · US/It · Colour · 101mins

An American-Italian co-production that borrows shamelessly from *Fame* and countless other musicals, in which a staid institution is shaken to its foundations by a new style that the kids love and the teachers simply don't understand. Here, it's a few funky jazz steps from Tony Dean Fields that divide a ballet school that is on its uppers and needs that magical something to revive its fortunes. The school principal is Julie Newmar, TV's Catwoman, whose name inspired the drag comedy *To Wong Foo, Thanks for Everything, Julie Newmar*. ▣

Tony Dean Fields [Tony Fields] *Moon* • Galyn Gorg *Jana* • Scott Grossman *Tommy* • Eliska Krupka *Patrizia* • Steve La Chance *Vince* • Paula Nichols *Paula* • Julie Newmar *Miss McKenzie* ◼ *Dir* Ted Mather • *Scr* Ted Mather, from his story

Dance, Fools, Dance ★★★
Crime drama   1931 · US · BW · 81mins

Joan Crawford – young, bright-eyed and light years away from the monster image for which she is more familiar – stars in this Depression-era drama as the spoilt daughter of a stockbroker who loses everything when the market crashes. Left with nothing, Joan becomes a cub reporter and goes undercover to investigate bootlegging gangster Clark Gable. Tightly directed by Harry Beaumont, this is a compact, suspenseful and entertaining film that makes some telling points about the idle rich. It also has a leggy Crawford dancing up a storm.

Joan Crawford *Bonnie Jordan* • Lester Vail *Bob Townsend* • Cliff Edwards *Bert Scranton* • William Bakewell *Rodney Jordan* • William Holden (2) *Stanley Jordan* • Clark Gable *Jake Luva* • Earle Foxe *Wally Baxter* ◼ *Dir* Harry Beaumont • *Scr* Aurania Rouverol, Richard Schayer, from a story by Aurania Rouverol

Dance, Girl, Dance ★★
Musical   1940 · US · BW · 89mins

Lucille Ball and Maureen O'Hara are ambitious chorus girls in Maria Ouspenskaya's dance troupe in this musical about the life, loves, trials and tribulations of showbiz folk. While O'Hara aspires to being a classical ballerina, Ball is happy to become a successful stripper. Both are in love with Louis Hayward. Pioneering female director Dorothy Arzner, who took over at short notice after filming commenced, does her best with an inadequate script and a miscast O'Hara; she manages to bring the film to life from time to time – usually when Ball is on screen. ▣

Lucille Ball *Bubbles* • Maureen O'Hara *Judy* • Louis Hayward *Jimmy Harris* • Ralph Bellamy *Steve Adams* • Virginia Field *Elinor Harris* • Maria Ouspenskaya *Madame Basilova* • Mary Carlisle *Sally* • Katherine Alexander *Miss Olmstead* • Edward Brophy *Dwarfie* ◼ *Dir* Dorothy Arzner • *Scr* Tess Slesinger, Frank Davis, from a story by Vicki Baum

The Dance Goes On ★★
Drama   1990 · Can · Colour · 110mins

A drama that's something of a family affair, with its young star, Matthew James Almond, being the son of writer/director Paul Almond and his ex-wife Geneviève Bujold, who has a supporting role here. Almond Jr plays a cynical city slicker who plans to flog the family farm to fund his flashy lifestyle. However, his return to his roots brings an reunion with his estranged father (James Keach) and you can guess what happens next. This mildewed situation is taken at a snail's pace by Almond Sr and played with such agonising sincerity that you've lost patience before a voice is raised in anger. At least rural Quebec looks beautiful.

James Keach *James Smith* • Matthew James Almond *Rick Smith* • Cary Lawrence *Molly Mackenzie* • Geneviève Bujold ◼ *Dir/Scr* Paul Almond

Dance Hall ★★
Drama   1950 · UK · BW · 80mins

Several of Ealing's biggest talents collaborated on this downbeat drama,

which fully captures the sense of austerity that pervaded postwar Britain. With Alexander Mackendrick among the screenwriters, Douglas Slocombe behind the camera, Seth Holt at the editing desk and Michael Balcon producing, one can't question the film's pedigree. However, director Charles Crichton settles for too many caricatures in this story of four women who assert the independence they gained doing war work. The performances are utterly credible, though Donald Houston is excessively boorish towards new wife Natasha Parry.

Donald Houston *Phil* • Bonar Colleano *Alec* • Petula Clark *Georgie Wilson* • Natasha Parry *Eve* • Jane Hylton *Mary* • Diana Dors *Carol* • Gladys Henson *Mrs Wilson* • Sydney Tafler *Manager* • Douglas Barr *Peter* • Kay Kendall *Doreen* • Eunice Gayson *Mona* • Dandy Nichols *Mrs Crabtree* ◼ *Dir* Charles Crichton • *Scr* EVH Emmett, Diana Morgan, Alexander Mackendrick

Dance Little Lady ★★ U
Drama   1954 · UK · Colour · 87mins

Terence Morgan made something of a habit of being horrid to little Mandy Miller on screen in the mid-fifties. He was her pig-headed father in *Mandy*, the moving Ealing drama about deafness, and here he is the unscrupulous stage father who is determined to see her name in lights. The dance sequences are fine, but the poor production values ruin the look of the film.

Terence Morgan *Mack Gordon* • Mai Zetterling *Nina Gordon* • Guy Rolfe *Dr John Ransome* • Mandy Miller *Jill Gordon* • Eunice Gayson *Adele* • Reginald Beckwith *Poldi* • Ina De La Haye *Madame Bayanova* • Harold Lang *Mr Bridson* • Richard O'Sullivan *Peter* • Jane Aird *Mary* ◼ *Dir* Val Guest • *Scr* Val Guest, Doreen Montgomery, from a story by R Howard Alexander, Alfred Dunning

Dance Me Outside ★★★
Drama   1994 · US/Can · Colour · 84mins

Thankfully avoiding the cinematic clichés of the past about Native Americans, this movie examines their lives in a contemporary context with seriousness and wit. Ryan Rajendra Black and Adam Beach are the young men on a Canadian reservation constantly diverted from fulfilling their ambitions by booze and drugs, while the racist killer of a dance-hall girl gets off with a light sentence, angering the community. The mix of quirky humour and sententious drama doesn't always blend, but this look at a nation within a nation still has considerable power. Contains violence and swearing.

Ryan Rajendra Black *Silas Crow* • Adam Beach *Frank Fencepost* • Jennifer Podemski *Sadie Maracle* • Michael Greyeyes *Gooch* • Lisa Lacroix [Lisa LaCroix] *Illiana* • Kevin Hicks *Robert McVay* • Rose Marie Trudeau *Ma Crow* ◼ *Dir* Bruce McDonald • *Scr* Bruce McDonald, Don McKellar, John Frizzell, from the novel by WP Kinsella

The Dance of Death ★★
Drama   1969 · UK · Colour · 148mins

One of Sir Laurence Olivier's last stage performances is captured on film in this static version of the National Theatre production of August Strindberg's classic play. Cantankerous

sea captain Olivier and wife Geraldine McEwan continuously bicker on their island home and turn what's left of their marriage into a war zone. As a record of Olivier's mesmerising stagecraft, it's a must. As a film, though, it's a torpid bore, with the camera placed in one position throughout the angst-ridden action and little accompanying style beyond the stage directions.

Laurence Olivier *Edgar* • Geraldine McEwan *Alice* • Robert Lang *Kurt* • Janina Faye *Judith* • Malcolm Reynolds *Allan* • Carolyn Jones *Jenny* • Maggie Riley *Kristin* ■ *Dir* David Giles • *Scr* CD Locock, from the play by August Strindberg

Dance of the Wind ★★★ 🆄

Drama
1997 · UK/Ger/Ind/Fr/Neth · Colour · 82mins
Celebrating the oral tradition of Indian classical music and stressing the need for ancient art to survive the passage of time, Rajan Khosa's debut feature is a simple, but affecting, delight. In a film that rings with echoes and duets. Besides showing the teeming streets of Delhi, there's a much reduced socio-political element to the story of a singer (Kitu Gidwani) who rediscovers the voice (provided by Shweta Zaveri) she lost on the death of her mother and mentor through her relationship with divine urchin Roshan Bano. In Hindi with English subtitles. 📼

Kitu Gidwani *Pallavi Sehgel* • Bhaveen Gossain *Ranmal* • BC Sanyal *Munir Baba* • Roshan Bano *Tara* ■ *Dir* Rajan Khosa • *Scr* Robin Mukherjee, Rajan Khosa

Dance with a Stranger
★★★★ 🔢

Biographical drama
1984 · UK · Colour · 97mins
See how good an actress Miranda Richardson always was, despite only recently being internationally acclaimed in *Damage* and *Tom and Viv*. She's incandescent as Soho nightclub hostess Ruth Ellis, the last woman to be hanged in Britain, in this absorbing, brutal account of the infamous 1955 murder case. Sticking closely to the facts about why she shot her aristocratic lover, racing driver David Blakely (Rupert Everett), this film from *Donnie Brasco* and *Four Weddings and a Funeral* director Mike Newell has a great sense of period and strikes the exact balance between fascination and luridness. Contains violence, swearing, sex scenes and nudity. 📼

Miranda Richardson *Ruth Ellis* • Rupert Everett *David Blakely* • Ian Holm *Desmond Cussen* • Matthew Carroll *Andy* • Tom Chadbon *Anthony Findlater* • Jane Bertish *Carole Findlater* • David Troughton *Cliff Davis* • Paul Mooney *Clive Gunnel* • Stratford Johns *Morrie Conley* • Joanne Whalley *Christine* • Susan Kyd *Barbara* • Lesley Manville *Maryanne* ■ *Dir* Mike Newell • *Scr* Shelagh Delaney

Dance with Me ★★ 🅿🅶

Romantic drama
1998 · US · Colour · 126mins
Think *Strictly Ballroom* with a mambo beat and you'll easily figure out the entire plot of this easy on the eye (and even easier on the brain) dance drama from director Randa Haines. Chayanne plays Cuban youngster Rafael, who gets a job as a handyman at a

Houston dance studio working for a man (Kris Kristofferson) he believes to be his father. There he meets Vanessa L Williams, and it's not long before the two of them are steaming up the dance floor with their stunningly choreographed Latin numbers. Forget the clichéd plot and performances and just enjoy those salsa dance moves.

Vanessa L Williams *Ruby* • Chayanne *Rafael* • Kris Kristofferson *John* • Joan Plowright *Bea* • Jane Krakowski *Patricia* • Beth Grant *Lovejoy* ■ *Dir* Randa Haines • *Scr* Daryl Matthews • *Choreographer* Daryl Matthews, Liz Curtis

Dance with Me Henry ★★ 🆄

Comedy
1956 · US · BW · 80mins
This was Bud Abbott and Lou Costello's last film together, and it's obvious that their comic partnership had reached the end of its tether. Here Lou plays the owner of an amusement park who becomes involved in Bud's gambling debts. When a district attorney is murdered, Lou finds he's being pursued by the police *and* the mob. The boys strive hard to make it work, and the strain shows.

Lou Costello *Lou Henry* • Bud Abbott *Bud Flick* • Gigi Perreau *Shelley* ■ *Dir* Charles Barton • *Scr* Devery Freeman, from a story by William Kozlenko, Leslie Kardos

Dancehall Queen ★★ 🔢

Musical dance drama
1996 · Jam · Colour · 96mins
Knowing patois is a useful skill when it comes to understanding this Jamaican street film. Audrey Reid stars as a single mother, struggling to survive by selling drinks outside popular dance halls, while predatory men are after her 15-year-old daughter. Adopting a mystery persona, Reid starts wowing in the dance halls. The soundtrack is as atmospheric as walking through the Notting Hill Carnival, but the sudden shift from Reid's extremely grim life into comedy doesn't quite hang together. 📼 *DVD*

Audrey Reid *Marcia* • Carl Davis *Uncle Larry* • Paul Campbell *Priest* • Pauline Stone-Myrie *Mrs Gordon* ■ *Dir* Don Letts, Rick Elgood • *Scr* Suzanne Fenn, Don Letts, Ed Wallace, from an idea by Don Letts, Ed Wallace

Dancers ★★ 🅿🅶

Drama
1987 · US · Colour · 94mins
The infamous raunchy ballet movie with the flowing blond locks of Mikhail Baryshnikov tumbling over both the stage and boudoir. One is left marvelling at where he gets his energy from, in this torrid tale of a dance company and its various intrigues. Director Herbert Ross's version of a dance soap works moderately well on a light, inconsequential level, with Julie Kent making a bright debut as the latest ingénue to get Baryshnikov's tights in a twist. Despite all that, the dancing throughout is a marvellous treat. Contains mild swearing. 📼

Mikhail Baryshnikov *Anton (Tony)* • Alessandra Ferri *Francesca* • Leslie Browne *Nadine* • Thomas Rall *[Tommy Rall]* *Patrick* • Lynn Seymour *Muriel* • Victor Barbee *Wade* • Julie Kent *Lisa* ■ *Dir* Herbert Ross • *Scr* Sarah Kernochan

Dances with Wolves
★★★★ 🔢

Epic western 1990 · US · Colour · 172mins
Kevin Costner's directorial debut, the first western to win the best picture Oscar for 60 years, is a heartfelt attempt to create a frontier epic and to atone for Hollywood's shameful depiction of native American life. Costner himself plays the depressed, battle weary Union officer John Dunbar, a Civil War hero who, given the choice, opts for a remote posting in South Dakota to see the frontier before it disappears. After befriending the Sioux Indians he decides to join them, and marries Stands with a Fist (Mary McDonnell), a white woman also adopted by the tribe. Although the film is three hours long, Costner directs his pet project with a clear passion for the subject, and in so doing proves that epic westerns can still work if their heart is in the right place, the characters are real, and the cinematography is stunning. Some Sioux dialogue with English subtitles. Contains violence and brief nudity. 📼

Kevin Costner *Lieutenant John Dunbar/Dances with Wolves* • Mary McDonnell *Stands with a Fist* • Graham Greene *Kicking Bird* • Rodney A Grant *Wind in His Hair* • Floyd Red Crow Westerman *Chief Ten Bears* • Tantoo Cardinal *Black Shawl* • Robert Pastorelli *Timmons* • Charles Rocket *Lieutenant Elgin* • Maury Chaykin *Major Fambrough* ■ *Dir* Kevin Costner • *Scr* Michael Blake, from the novel by Michael Blake • *Cinematographer* Dean Semler

Dancin' thru the Dark
★★★ 🔢

Comedy drama 1989 · UK · Colour · 91mins
Between staging the musical hits *Me and My Girl* and *Crazy for You* in the West End and on Broadway, director Mike Ockrent took a minor Willy Russell play and turned it into a reasonably pleasant screen diversion. On the eve of Claire Hackett and Con O'Neill's wedding, both her hen party and his stag "do" end up at the same nightclub. Cue an avalanche of Scouse home truths and tart comedy, especially when it's revealed the bride's ex-boyfriend is in the house band. Although the script lacks Russell's trademark bite and wit, Ockrent gets good enough performances from the lead actors to make it worthwhile. 📼

Claire Hackett *Linda* • Con O'Neill *Peter* • Colin Welland *Manager* • Willy Russell *Sourface* • Julia Deakin *Bernadette* • Angela Clarke *Maureen* • Sandy Hendrickse *Carol* • Louise Duprey *Frances* • Simon O'Brien *Kav* • Conrad Nelson *Dave* • Mark Womack *Eddie* • Andrew Naylor *Billy* • Peter Watts *Robbie* ■ *Dir* Mike Ockrent • *Scr* Willy Russell, from his play *Stags and Hens*

Dancing at Lughnasa
★★★ 🅿🅶

Drama 1998 · UK/Ire · Colour · 91mins
Director Pat O'Connor, who made the enjoyably romantic Irish drama *Circle of Friends*, stumbles a little with this rather meandering adaptation of Brian Friel's acclaimed play about five unmarried sisters living in rural Ireland in the thirties. Meryl Streep is Kate, the eldest; the household also

includes young Michael, the son of Kate's youngest sister Catherine McCormack. Into this secluded world comes their elder brother Michael Gambon, a missionary in Africa who has been seduced by "heathen" ways, and Rhys Ifans, Christina's Welsh ex-lover and the father of her child. However, O'Connor spends too much time dwelling on the beautiful Irish countryside for the pace ever to move above a slow crawl. That said, the cast all perform superbly. Contains some swearing. 📼

Meryl Streep *Kate Mundy* • Michael Gambon *Father Jack Mundy* • Catherine McCormack *Christina Mundy* • Kathy Burke *Maggie Mundy* • Sophie Thompson *Rose Mundy* • Brid Brennan *Agnes Mundy* • Rhys Ifans *Gerry Evans* • Darrell Johnston *Michael Mundy* • Lorcan Cranitch *Danny Bradley* ■ *Dir* Pat O'Connor • *Scr* Frank McGuinness, from the play by Brian Friel

Dancing Co-Ed ★★

Musical comedy 1939 · US · BW · 82mins
The co-ed of the title is 19-year-old Lana Turner, at the gateway to major stardom at MGM, playing a college student with show biz ambitions who triumphs in both classroom and theatre. Flimsy nonsense, but one which serves its purpose as a star vehicle for the "sweater girl", directed by S Sylvan Simon and supported by Richard Carlson, Leon Errol, Ann Rutherford and bandleader Artie Shaw who soon became the first of Turners's seven husbands.

Lana Turner *Patty Marlow* • Richard Carlson *Pug Braddock* • Artie Shaw • Ann Rutherford *Eve* • Lee Bowman *Freddie Tobin* • Leon Errol *Sam "Pops" Marlow* • Roscoe Karns *Joe Drews* • Monty Woolley *Prof Lange* • Thurston Hall *HW Workman* ■ *Dir* S Sylvan Simon • *Scr* Albert Mannheimer, from a story by Albert Treynor

Dancing in the Dark ★★★ 🆄

Musical comedy 1949 · US · Colour · 89mins
Former vaudeville star George Jessel forged a later career as producer of musicals at 20th Century-Fox, of which this is set in the Fox studio itself (glamorous, and also cheap). Debonair William Powell is most welcome as a former star, now down on his luck and working as a talent scout, who discovers pert Betsy Drake in a plot twist that will have you hollering "enough!". But the real joke for insiders is Adolphe Menjou's uncanny impersonation of Fox boss Darryl F Zanuck. This is a pleasing time-waster, not quite as garish as Fox's usual run of musicals of the period.

William Powell *Emery Slide* • Mark Stevens *Bill Davis* • Betsy Drake *Julie* • Adolphe Menjou *Grossman* • Randy Stuart *Rosalie* • Lloyd Corrigan *Barker* • Hope Emerson *Mrs Schlaghammer* ■ *Dir* Irving Reis • *Scr* Mary C McCall Jr, Marion Turk, Jay Dratler, from the musical *Bandwagon* by George S Kaufman, Howard Dietz, Arthur Schwartz

Dancing in the Dark ★★★ 🔢

Drama 1986 · Can · Colour · 98mins
The mundane existence of a middle-class housewife begins to take its toll on her sanity in this dour Canadian drama. Recalled through confessions to a psychiatrist in flashback, Martha

Henry's 20-year marriage to Neil Munro seems like a life sentence, as each meal and chore is greeted with the same self-centred boorishness. Lifting mannerisms from Jack Lemmon in full midlife crisis, Munro certainly comes across as thoughtless, but he has none of the maliciousness that drives nosey neighbour Carole Galloway to destroy their far from happy home.

Martha Henry *Edna* • Neil Munro *Harry* • Rosemary Dunsmore *Nurse* • Richard Monette *Doctor* • Elena Kudaba *Edna's roommate* • Brenda Bazinet *Susan* ■ *Dir* Leon Marr • *Scr* Leon Marr, from the novel by Joan Barfoot

Dancing in the Dark ★★ 15
Drama based on a true story
1995 · US · Colour · 87mins

Not the 1949 William Powell musical, but a TV movie that gives Victoria Principal the chance to suffer in ways that Joan Crawford could only have dreamed of. Here Principal is committed to an asylum by her husband, who refuses to believe that she is being sexually harassed by his father. Robert Vaughn is loathsome as the lecherous in-law, but there's little else to recommend this. Contains some moderate violence.

Victoria Principal *Anna Forbes* • Robert Vaughn *Dennis Forbes* • Nicholas Campbell *Mark Forbes* • Kenneth Welsh *Dr Bell* • Geraint Wyn Davies *Dr Lambert* ■ *Dir* Bill Corcoran • *Scr* David Seidler, Jacqueline Feather

Dancing Lady ★★★
Musical
1933 · US · BW · 92mins

This vintage MGM musical melodrama teams two of the great sex symbols of their day, Joan Crawford and Clark Gable; they were real-life lovers off screen, and it shows. The *ménage à trois* is aptly completed by suave Franchot Tone, a future Mr Joan Crawford. There's more to this backstage story than the smouldering leads, however. Fred Astaire makes his movie debut, playing himself and bringing some dignity to the ridiculously tasteless production number, *Let's Go Bavarian.*

Joan Crawford *Janie Barlow* • Clark Gable *Patch Gallagher* • Franchot Tone *Tod Newton* • Fred Astaire • Nelson Eddy • May Robson *Dolly Todhunter* • Winnie Lightner *Rosette Henrietta La Rue* • Robert Benchley *Ward King* ■ *Dir* Robert Z Leonard • *Scr* Allen Rivkin, PJ Wolfson, from the novel by James Warner Bellah

The Dancing Masters ★★ PG
Comedy
1943 · US · BW · 63mins

One of the decidedly non-vintage films that Laurel and Hardy made for 20th Century-Fox in the forties. Considerably below their best, they play struggling dance school patrons, whose client Trudy Marshall is in love with would-be inventor Robert Bailey. The boys stage some madcap schemes in a bid to raise money for Bailey, but the drippy lovers are given far too much screen time. Not even the presence of Groucho Marx's inspired sparring partner Margaret Dumont, and Robert Mitchum in a bit part can enliven the proceedings.

Stan Laurel *Stan* • Oliver Hardy *Ollie* • Trudy Marshall *Mary Harlan* • Robert Bailey *Grant Lawrence* • Matt Briggs *Wentworth Harlan* •

Margaret Dumont *Mrs Harlan* • Bob Mitchum [Robert Mitchum] *Mickey* ■ *Dir* Malcolm St Clair • *Scr* W Scott Darling, from a story by George Bricker

Dancing with Crime ★★
Crime drama
1946 · UK · BW · 82mins

Real-life newly-weds Richard Attenborough and Sheila Sim co-star in this stark crime quickie, which also marks the feature debut of Dirk Bogarde as a bobby on the beat. Attenborough, who played a teenage Scarface in his next venture, *Brighton Rock*, is here cast as a cabby who becomes the scourge of black marketeers when he investigates the suspicious death of an army pal (Bill Owen). With Sim going undercover at the local dance hall, the film will evoke memories of Saturday nights gone by.

Richard Attenborough *Ted* • Sheila Sim *Joy* • Barry K Barnes *Paul* • Garry Marsh *Sergeant Murray* • John Warwick *Inspector Carter* • Judy Kelly *Toni* • Barry Jones *Gregory* • Bill Owen *Dave* • Diana Dors *Hostess* • Dirk Bogarde *Policeman* ■ *Dir* John Paddy Carstairs • *Scr* Brock Williams, Peter Fraser

Dancing with Danger ★★ 15
Thriller
1994 · US · Colour · 87mins

A tame and tepid TV-movie reworking the well-trodden "did she/didn't she" formula. Ed Marinaro, still best remembered for his role in *Hill Street Blues*, plays a private eye hired to track down the missing Cheryl Ladd, who turns up working as a dancer in a seedy club. The pair fall in love, even though her acquaintances have a habit of expiring suddenly. Director Stuart Cooper delivers little in the way of suspense, and the two leads turn in bland performances.

Cheryl Ladd *Mary Dannon* • Ed Marinaro *Derek Lidor* • Miguel Sandoval *Boris Chowder* ■ *Dir* Stuart Cooper • *Scr* Elisa Bell

The Dancing Years ★★ U
Musical drama
1949 · UK · Colour · 98mins

A love affair between a young composer (Dennis Price) and a star of the musical stage (Giselle Preville) falters through a misunderstanding which leads her to leave him and marry a prince (Anthony Nicholls). Directed by Harold French, this screen transfer of a musical by Ivor Novello is outmoded, sickly sweet and devoid of what charm the original stage show offered. The debonair Price is hardly a natural for the genre, but the film does offer plenty of Novello's melodies.

Dennis Price *Rudi Kleiber* • Giselle Preville *Maria Zeitler* • Patricia Dainton *Grete* • Anthony Nicholls *Prince Reinaldt* ■ *Dir* Harold French • *Scr* Warwick Ward, Jack Whittingham, from an operetta by Ivor Novello

Dandin ★★★★
Comedy
1988 · Fr · Colour · 116mins

Based on Molière's comedy *Georges Dandin*, this rumbustious tale of greed, suspicion and debasement is a lesser-known example of the playwright's genius for exposing the complexities and absurdities of human nature. Roger Planchon keeps this cruellest of comedies racing along, drawing an excellent performance from Claude Brasseur as the peasant who suffers

an endless round of humiliations after he takes a wife to improve his social standing. He is ably supported by Zabou as his spouse, and Daniel Gélin as the father-in-law who is the chief architect of his misery. In French with English subtitles.

Claude Brasseur *Georges Dandin* • Zabou *Angélique* • Daniel Gélin *M de Sotenville* • Nelly Bourgeaud *Mme de Sotenville* ■ *Dir* Roger Planchon • *Scr* Roger Planchon, from the play *Georges Dandin* by Molière

A Dandy in Aspic ★★
Spy drama
1968 · UK · Colour · 100mins

The spy cycle of the sixties produced a handful of serious espionage dramas, one of which is this unsuccessful, two-dimensional adaptation of Derek Marlowe's complex novel. Laurence Harvey is dull as the double agent assigned by British Intelligence to kill himself. Bodies pile up so fast, it becomes almost impossible to know who is doing what to whom. It cannot have helped that director Anthony Mann died during production; the film was completed by Harvey. It's still of interest, however, for its London and west Berlin locations.

Laurence Harvey *Alexander Eberlin* • Tom Courtenay *Gatiss* • Mia Farrow *Caroline* • Lionel Stander *Sobakevich* • Harry Andrews *Intelligence Chief Fraser* • Peter Cook *Prentiss* • Per Oscarsson *Pavel* • Barbara Murray *Heather Vogler* • Richard O'Sullivan *Nevil* ■ *Dir* Anthony Mann, Laurence Harvey • *Scr* Derek Marlowe, from his novel

Danger by My Side ★
Crime thriller
1962 · UK · BW · 63mins

This is a very poor example of a British B-movie and rarely will an hour feel so much like an eternity. All the usual excuses can be trotted out in its defence, but this is a lousy film whichever way you cut it. The hit-and-run murder, the sleazy nightclub scenes, the heist and the motor-launch finale are all executed with the minimum of imagination as a woman takes a job in a strip club to prove its owner killed her brother.

Anthony Oliver *Inspector Willoughby* • Maureen Connell *Lynne* • Alan Tilvern *Venning* • Bill Nagy *Sam Warren* • Sonya Cordeau *Francine Dumont* ■ *Dir* Charles Saunders • *Scr* Ronald C Liles, Aubrey Cash

Danger: Diabolik ★★★
Crime comedy
1967 · It/Fr · Colour · 98mins

Based on a cult comic strip, this mix of fantasy and madcap criminality is directed with mischievous glee by horror specialist Mario Bava. Utilising stylised sets and encouraging his multi-national cast to camp it up something rotten, Bava arrives at a *Barbarella*-style romp, a comparison that is reinforced by the presence of John Phillip Law as the master criminal who curries favour with the populace by destroying Italy's tax records. The finale, with its radioactive gold shower, is justifiably famous, and the press conference given by pompous minister Terry-Thomas, under the influence of laughing gas, is riotously funny.

John Phillip Law *Diabolik* • Marisa Mell *Eva Kant* • Michel Piccoli *Inspector Ginko* • Adolfo Celi *Ralph Valmont* • Terry-Thomas *Minister of Finance* ■ *Dir* Mario Bava • *Scr* Mario Bava,

Dino Maiuri, Brian Degas, Tudor Gates, from a story by Angela Giussani, Luciana Giussani, Dino Maiuri, Adriano Baracco

Danger Island ★★
Science-fiction thriller
1992 · US · Colour · 100mins

Tommy Lee Wallace – best known as the director of schlock horrors such as *Fright Night Part 2* and *Halloween III: Season of the Witch* – here directs a TV-movie disaster adventure in which the hapless protagonists not only have to survive a plane crash, but must also fight a deadly virus prevalent on the tropical island where they end up. Worth watching just to see Richard Beymer, who starred as Tony in *West Side Story* over 30 years before, hamming it up.

Richard Beymer *Ben* • June Lockhart *Kate* • Gary Graham *Rick* • Lisa Banes *Diana* • Kathy Ireland *Laura* • Nikki Cox *Ariel* • Maria Celedonio *Melissa* • Christopher Pettiet *Brian* ■ *Dir* Tommy Lee Wallace • *Scr* William Bleich

Danger Lights ★★
Comedy drama
1930 · US · BW · 87mins

Beefy Louis Wolheim and dapper Robert Armstrong lock in conflict over Jean Arthur, against a background of problems in running a railway. A mélange of romance, melodrama and macho tension, directed by George B Seitz, this otherwise mediocre movie is of interest in that it saw the short-lived launch (by RKO) of a new "wide stereoscopic" process. The technique, and Karl Struss's cinematography, does add a dimension of depth to the proceedings, but the huge costs involved, including special projection equipment, made this the first and last time the experiment was attempted.

Louis Wolheim *Dan Thorn* • Robert Armstrong *Larry Doyle* • Jean Arthur *Mary Ryan* • Hugh Herbert *Professor* • Frank Sheridan *Ed Ryan* ■ *Dir* George B Seitz • *Scr* James Ashmore Creelman, Hugh Herbert

Danger – Love at Work ★★★
Comedy
1937 · US · BW · 81mins

The Viennese-born Otto Preminger had only directed one film in Germany when he was given a contract at 20th Century-Fox. This enjoyable screwball comedy was the second picture he made for the studio. The inconsequential plot involves Jack Haley as a lawyer sent to a small town to buy up a piece of property owned by an eccentric family. But it is the cast that makes the movie: Mary Boland at her most scatterbrained, pert Ann Sothern, fussy Edward Everett Horton and demented John Carradine.

Ann Sothern *Toni Pemberton* • Jack Haley *Henry MacMorrow* • Mary Boland *Mrs Alice Pemberton* • Edward Everett Horton *Howard Rogers* • John Carradine *Herbert Pemberton* • Walter Catlett *Uncle Alan* ■ *Dir* Otto Preminger • *Scr* James Edward Grant, Ben Markson, from a story by James Edward Grant

The Danger of Love ★★
Drama based on a true story
1992 · US · Colour · 94mins

A good cast is left high and dry by a ponderous script in this disappointing true-lifer from director Joyce Chopra.

U = SUITABLE FOR ALL, **Uc** = SUITABLE FOR ALL, ESPECIALLY FOR YOUNG CHILDREN (VIDEO ONLY) **PG** = PARENTAL GUIDANCE

Jenny Robertson gives it all she's got as Carolyn Warmus, the seemingly ordinary woman who became the talk of New York's Westchester County when she was accused of murdering her lover's wife. Joseph Bologna sleepwalks through the picture as the cop who apprehended her and Joe Penny makes little impression as the man she loves.

Joe Penny *Michael Carlin* • Jenny Robertson *Carolyn Warmus* • Joseph Bologna *Detective John Pollina* • Deborah Benson *Mary Ann Carlin* • Richard Lewis *Edward Sanders* • Fairuza Balk *Lisa Carlin* ■ *Dir* Joyce Chopra • *Scr* Ara Watson, Sam Blackwell

Danger Patrol ★★ U
Adventure   1937 · US · BW · 59mins

Sixteen years before Henri-Georges Clouzot's classic, *The Wages of Fear*, there came this RKO second feature on the same subject – the foolhardy men who transport dangerous nitroglycerin to oil fields to quench fires. Artistically, however, they are aeons apart. Because of the pedestrian direction by the prolific journeyman Lew Landers, the potentially explosive material fails to catch alight. However, it's good to see veteran character actor Harry Carey in a leading role. He is a driver who is opposed to his daughter (pretty Sally Eilers) marrying a man in the same dangerous profession.

Sally Eilers *Cathie Street* • John Beal *Dan Loring* • Harry Carey *Sam "Easy" Street* • Frank M Thomas *Rocky Sanders* • Edward Gargan *Gabby Donovan* ■ *Dir* Lew Landers • *Scr* Sy Bartlett, from a story by Helen Vreeland, Hilda Vincent

Danger Route ★
Spy thriller   1967 · UK · Colour · 92mins

This is a sloppily constructed spy thriller that aims for the gloss, levity and excitement of a Bond movie and misses by a mile. Always an inconsistent director, Seth Holt goes off on so many tangents that the central plot – about agent Richard Johnson's mission to kill a Soviet scientist before he can pass secrets to the Americans – is completely obscured. Johnson looks the part during the action sequences, but neither he nor a splendid but woefully wasted supporting cast can do much with Meade Roberts's dismal dialogue.

Richard Johnson *Jonas Wilde* • Carol Lynley *Jocelyn* • Barbara Bouchet *Mari* • Sylvia Syms *Barbara Canning* • Gordon Jackson *Stern* • Harry Andrews *Canning* • Diana Dors *Rhoda Gooderich* • Maurice Denham *Peter Ravenspur* • Sam Wanamaker *Lucinda* ■ *Dir* Seth Holt • *Scr* Meade Roberts, from the novel *The Eliminator* by Andrew York

Danger Within ★★★ U
Second World War drama
1958 · UK · BW · 96mins

Anyone who has seen Billy Wilder's PoW camp classic *Stalag 17* will find this workmanlike British imitation somewhat predictable. Co-written by Bryan Forbes, the story has a whodunit element that is cleverly and wittily plotted, but prisoners and guards alike are cardboard cutouts and it takes some competent character acting to make them even half credible. Richard Attenborough and Bernard Lee come

off best, while Richard Todd trots out all his gruff officer mannerisms, Michael Wilding smarms to order and Dennis Price reprises the fruity theatrical he played in *Charley Moon*. Director Don Chaffey sustains the suspense with unfussy ease. ▭

Richard Todd *Lt Col David Baird* • Bernard Lee *Lt Col Huxley* • Michael Wilding *Maj Charles Marquand* • Richard Attenborough *Capt Bunter Phillips* • Dennis Price *Capt Rupert Callender* • Donald Houston *Capt Roger Byford* • Michael Caine ■ *Dir* Don Chaffey • *Scr* Bryan Forbes, Frank Harvey, from the novel by Michael Gilbert

Danger Zone ★★ 18
Action adventure   1996 · US · Colour · 88mins

Billy Zane (who also co-produces) plays a mine inspector in a small African state, duped into carrying the can for a catastrophic spillage of lethal toxic waste supplied by CIA agent and former buddy Robert Downey Jr. Or is the plot thicker than it seems? The action rattles along nicely and the two leads are charismatic, but the ecological message grates and the starry cast struggles to lift this fairly routine straight-to-video action adventure. Contains violence. ▭

Billy Zane *Rick Morgan* • Robert Downey Jr *Jim Scott* • Ron Silver *Dupont* • Cary-Hiroyuki Tagawa *Chang* • Lisa Collins *Dr Kim Woods* ■ *Dir* Allan Eastman • *Scr* Jeff Albert

Dangerous ★★★★ PG
Melodrama   1935 · US · BW · 75mins

Bette Davis won her first Oscar (the second was for *Jezebel*) for this fine melodrama about an alcoholic star, although at the time it was felt that the Academy Award was a compensatory one for Davis not winning the previous year as the spiteful Mildred in *Of Human Bondage*. Seen today, Davis's performance here is truly magnificent and splendidly overblown, with all those mannerisms well under control as Warner Bros veteran director Alfred E Green (better known for, surprisingly, *The Jolson Story*) hands the movie to her on a platter. If you've never seen this treat, don't miss it. ▭

Bette Davis *Joyce Heath* • Franchot Tone *Don Bellows* • Margaret Lindsay *Gail Armitage* • Alison Skipworth *Mrs Williams* • John Eldredge *Gordon Heath* • Dick Foran *Teddy* • Pierre Watkin *George Sheffield* ■ *Dir* Alfred E Green • *Scr* Laird Doyle

Dangerous Affair ★★ 15
Thriller   1995 · US · Colour · 92mins

It's a teleplay rule of thumb that if a beautiful, but lonely, career woman meets Mr Right, he'll barely be able to close his cupboard door for all the skeletons. Unfortunately, Gregory Harrison's dark secrets are all too familiar and director Alan Metzger has to resort to the cheapest of trick endings to bale out his mediocre melodrama. Connie Selleca, one of the new generation of small-screen queens, gets to demonstrate her line in imperilled expressions, as she comes to realise that Harrison is, in fact, a psychotic stalker. ▭

Connie Selleca *Sharon Blake* • Gregory Harrison *Robert Kenzer* • Christopher Meloni *Tommy Moretti* • Rosalind Cash *Dr Robertson* ■ *Dir* Alan Metzger • *Scr* Alan Rosen

Dangerous Affection ★ PG
Thriller   1987 · US · Colour · 90mins

Jimmy Smits has largely failed to make an impression in films despite his success in TV series such as *LA Law* and *NYPD Blue*. Here he stars with Judith Light (as a pregnant woman whose husband wants a divorce) in a thriller that's a *Witness* rip-off with a few ill-advised laughs thrown in. ▭

Judith Light *Cathy Proctor* • Jimmy Smits *Detective Braden* • Rhea Perlman *Claudia* • Billy Sullivan [Billy L Sullivan] *Sam* • Bill Dore *Dr Jacobs* ■ *Dir* Larry Elikann • *Scr* Susan Rice, Annabel Davis-Goff

Dangerous Afternoon ★★ U
Crime drama   1961 · UK · BW · 61mins

Former editor Charles Saunders turned out a series of unexceptional movies after taking to directing, including this negligible crime drama. The story – about an escaped convict whose refuge for former women prisoners is threatened by a blackmailer – began life on stage, and Saunders does little to open out Gerald Anstruther's long-forgotten play. Neither Howard Pays nor Ruth Dunning look comfortable before the camera and it's theatre stalwart Nora Nicholson who stands out.

Ruth Dunning *Miss Frost* • Nora Nicholson *Mrs Sprule* • Joanna Dunham *Freda* • Howard Pays *Jack Loring* • May Hallatt *Miss Burge* ■ *Dir* Charles Saunders • *Scr* Brandon Fleming, from a play by Gerald Anstruther

Dangerous Corner ★
Mystery melodrama   1934 · US · BW · 66mins

The only reason for sticking with this – and it's a long wait – is the double ending retained from JB Priestley's play, which RKO Radio bought after it was even more of a success on Broadway than it had been in London. Starring Virginia Bruce, Conrad Nagel and Melvyn Douglas, this abridged screen version makes heavy weather of an after-dinner discussion between a publisher and friends about the apparent suicide of one of their group and the disappearance of valuable bonds. Skeletons cascade from closets, but director Phil Rosen's handling of the drama is dreary.

Melvyn Douglas *Charles* • Conrad Nagel *Robert* • Virginia Bruce *Olwen* • Erin O'Brien-Moore *Freda* • Ian Keith *Martin* • Betty Furness *Betty* ■ *Dir* Phil Rosen • *Scr* Anne Morrison Chapin, Madeleine Ruthven, from the play by JB Priestley

Dangerous Desire ★★ 18
Drama   1993 · US · Colour · 91mins

A daft moggy-mutation thriller that's closer to *Top Cat* than *Cat People*. Former teenage heart-throb Richard Grieco plays a dying man who gets a new lease of life when his lover Maryam D'Abo pumps some feline hormones into him. Unfortunately, this transforms him into a playful psychopath. It's a nice idea, but director Paul Donovan botches things badly and only succeeds in raising

laughs, not scares. He's not helped by the uninspiring performances of the two leads. Contains swearing, violence, sex scenes and nudity. ▭

Richard Grieco *Tom* • Natalie Radford *Imogen* • Maryam D'Abo *Dr Jackie Eddington* • Serge Houde *Dr Pace* • David McLeod *Myron* • Ben Ratner [Benjamin Ratner] *Fred* • Christine Lippa *Randy* • Brenda Crichlow *Darryl* ■ *Dir/Scr* Paul Donovan

Dangerous Exile ★★★ PG
Swashbuckling adventure
1957 · UK · Colour · 97mins

Stylishly shot in Wales by Geoffrey Unsworth and featuring a rousing score by Georges Auric, this historical adventure makes up for its cumbersome plot with some slick swashbuckling and an unrelenting pace. Louis Jourdan proves surprisingly fleet-of-foot as the aristocrat who smuggles the son of Louis XVI across the channel to prevent the rabid revolutionaries from getting their egalitarian mitts on him. This kind of romp wasn't really Irish director Brian Desmond Hurst's strong suit, but he keeps the action rattling along, getting decent turns out of Keith Michell and Martita Hunt in the process.

Louis Jourdan *Duc de Beauvais* • Belinda Lee *Virginia Traill* • Keith Michell *Colonel St Gerard* • Richard O'Sullivan *Louis* • Martita Hunt *Aunt Fell* • Finlay Currie *Mr Patient* • Anne Heywood *Glynis* ■ *Dir* Brian Desmond Hurst • *Scr* Robin Estridge, Patrick Kirwan, from the novel *A King Reluctant* by Vaughan Wilkins

Dangerous Female ★★★★
Crime drama   1931 · US · BW · 80mins

Here's a discovery: the first film version of *The Maltese Falcon*, retitled for release in Britain and subsequent TV screenings to avoid confusion with John Huston's 1941 Humphrey Bogart classic. There's another version as well, called *Satan Met a Lady*, released in 1936, in which the legendary falcon became a ram's horn. This early Warners melodrama is faithful to the great Dashiell Hammett novel, and Ricardo Cortez is a much more womanising Sam Spade than Bogey. Bebe Daniels makes a very fetching client, and the supporting cast is almost the equal of Huston's.

Bebe Daniels *Ruth Wonderly* • Ricardo Cortez *Sam Spade* • Dudley Digges *Kaspar Gutman* • Una Merkel *Effie Perine* • Robert Elliott *Detective Dundy* • J Farrell MacDonald *Polhouse* ■ *Dir* Roy Del Ruth • *Scr* Maude Fulton, Lucien Hubbard, Brown Holmes, Dashiell Hammett, from the novel *The Maltese Falcon* by Dashiell Hammett

Dangerous Game ★ 18
Drama   1993 · US · Colour · 104mins

Abel Ferrara aims to give us an unadorned insight into the film-making process and show how on-set tensions can often result in great art. Instead, he came up with a pretentious folly, in which an over-indulged cast bandy expletives and gorge themselves in an orgy of grandiloquence and gesturing. Harvey Keitel has his moments as a director whose stars' (Madonna and James Russo) on- and off-screen feuds become increasingly indistinguishable. A best-forgotten aberration. Contains violence, swearing, sex scenes, drug abuse and nudity. ▭

Madonna *Sarah Jennings* • Harvey Keitel *Eddie Israel* • James Russo *Francis Burns* • Nancy Ferrara *Madlyn Israel* • Reilly Murphy *Tommy* • Victor Argo *Director of photography* • Leonard Thomas *Prop guy* • Christina Fulton *Blonde* ■ *Dir* Abel Ferrara • *Scr* Abel Ferrara, Nicholas St John

Dangerous Ground ★★🔞

Crime thriller   1996 · US · Colour and BW · 91mins

Well-meaning but severely botched study of crime in post-Apartheid Johannesburg. Sex, drugs and corruption in the new South Africa is an interesting concept, but the potentially fascinating political undercurrents are as irrelevant as they are in Arnold Schwarzenegger's Soviet "shoot 'em up" *Red Heat*. Other than the visual appeal of real locations like the glitzy Sun City, Darrell James Roodt's film suffers from unconvincing characters (particularly Elizabeth Hurley as a junkie stripper), over-ripe dialogue and ineffectual stabs at social comment. 📼

Ice Cube *Vusi* • Elizabeth Hurley *Karin* • Thokozani Nkosi *Young Vusi* • Ron Smerczac [Ron Smerczak] *Interrogation policeman* • Wilson Dunster *Heavy policeman* • Ving Rhames *Muki* ■ *Dir* Darrell James Roodt • *Scr* Greg Latter, Darrell James Roodt

Dangerous Heart ★★★🔞

Thriller   1994 · US · Colour · 89mins

If you think that virtue triumphant is a lost cause, here's a thriller that proves otherwise. Made with some flamboyant and intriguing twists and turns by young director Michael Scott, it gets yet more mileage out of the theme of the opportunist romancing a bereft woman for money and then falling in love. In this case, it's a drug baron wooing the widow of the corrupt cop he killed. This is not an original idea, but it's well enough executed and, in the end, quite satisfying. Contains some swearing. 📼

Timothy Daly *Angel Perno* • Lauren Holly *Carol* • Alice Carter *Mai* • Joe Pantoliano *Barclay* • Jeffrey Nordling *Lee* • Robert P Lieb *Uncle Ed* ■ *Dir* Michael Scott • *Scr* Patrick Cirillo

Dangerous Indiscretion ★★🔞

Thriller   1994 · US · Colour · 77mins

A quality cast and an intriguing psychological edge just about lift this straight-to-video erotic thriller out of the routine. *The Hitcher* star C Thomas Howell is the advertising executive who ends up having an affair with mysterious Joan Severance, only to fall foul of her insanely possessive husband, Malcolm McDowell, who then sets about destroying Howell's life. McDowell hams it up for all it's worth as the barmy businessman, while director Richard Kletter tries his best to avoid the usual clichés. Contains swearing, violence and brief nudity. 📼

C Thomas Howell *Jim Lomax* • Malcolm McDowell *Roger Everett* • Joan Severance *Caroline Everett* • Wendy Abbott *Receptionist* • Alex Doduk *Matthew* ■ *Dir* Richard Kletter • *Scr* Richard Kletter, Jack Tarpon, from a story by Jack Tarpon

Dangerous Intentions ★★🔞

Drama based on a true story   1995 · US · Colour · 92mins

Queen of the true-life TV movie Donna Mills plays another tormented character in this routine outing. She is the battered wife of nasty Corbin Bernsen who eventually summons up the courage to leave him, only to discover that he has no intention of allowing her to break up the family. Indistinguishable from hundreds of other true story weepies. Contains violence and mild swearing. 📼

Donna Mills *Beth Williamson* • Corbin Bernsen *Tim Williamson* • Robin Givens *Kaye* • Allison Hossack *Terri* • Sheila Larken *Nancy Boyle* • Ken Pogue *Andrew Madden* • Anna Ferguson *Alice Madden* ■ *Dir* Michael Toshiyuki Uno • *Scr* David J Hill

Dangerous Liaisons ★★★★🔞

Period drama   1988 · US · Colour · 114mins

Stephen Frears's richly textured production of the scandalous 18th-century "sex as power-play" novel is a handsome homage to the idea that women lose out in a man's world even where they at first appear to be in control. The extraordinary performances of Glenn Close, as the vindictive Marquise de Merteuil, and Michelle Pfeiffer, as the pure wife despoiled by the slimy Valmont (John Malkovich) on a wager, help make this chilling depiction of an era's corruption totally believable. Malkovich, though, seems ill-cast, with all the sleaze but none of the necessary seduction in his portrayal. Despite that, a treat for eye and mind. Contains sex scenes and nudity. 📼 **DVD**

Glenn Close *Marquise de Merteuil* • John Malkovich *Vicomte de Valmont* • Michelle Pfeiffer *Madame de Tourvel* • Swoosie Kurtz *Madame de Volanges* • Keanu Reeves *Chevalier Dancény* • Mildred Natwick *Madame de Rosemonde* • Uma Thurman *Cécile de Volanges* • Peter Capaldi *Azolan* • Joe Sheridan *Georges* ■ *Dir* Stephen Frears • *Scr* Christopher Hampton, from his play *Les Liaisons Dangereuses*, from the novel by Choderlos de Laclos • *Production Designer* Stuart Craig • *Set Designer* Gerard James • *Costume Designer* James Acheson

Dangerous Minds ★★★🔞

Drama based on a true story   1995 · US · Colour · 94mins

With an entire romantic subplot involving Andy Garcia ending up on the cutting-room floor, this schoolroom drama may have gained a singularity of purpose, but it definitely lost a much-needed release from the intensity of the classroom crusade. Although not a convincing ex-Marine, Michelle Pfeiffer gives a solid performance as she tries to give her deprived students some sort of chance in life. Screenwriter Ronald Bass pushes his luck linking Bob Dylan and Dylan Thomas, and the results-by-reward policy will have many teachers up in arms. Contains swearing and some violence. 📼 **DVD**

Michelle Pfeiffer *Louanne Johnson* • George Dzundza *Hal Griffith* • Courtney B Vance *Mr George Grandey* • Robin Bartlett *Ms Carla Nichols* • Bruklin Harris *Callie Roberts* • Renoly Santiago *Raul Sanchero* ■ *Dir* John N

Smith • *Scr* Ronald Bass, Elaine May (uncredited), from the book *My Posse Don't Do Homework* by LouAnne Johnson

Dangerous Mission ★🔘

Crime thriller   1954 · US · Colour · 74mins

Originally filmed in 3-D, this is widely acknowledged as one of the worst films made during the great stereoscopic experiment of the early fifties. Victor Mature gives one of his most convincing impressions of a cardboard cut-out as a New York lawman who treks into Montana's Glacier National Park to prevent hoodlum Vincent Price from rubbing out Piper Laurie, the runaway witness to a gangland shooting. Directed by Louis King with little sense of adventure, the 3-D set pieces that were supposed to wow audiences – an avalanche, a forest fire and a cable car episode – now look very flat indeed.

Victor Mature *Matt Hallett* • Piper Laurie *Louise Graham* • William Bendix *Joe Parker* • Vincent Price *Paul Adams* • Betta St John *Mary Tiller* ■ *Dir* Louis King • *Scr* Horace McCoy, WR Burnett, Charles Bennett, from a story by Horace McCoy, James Edmiston

Dangerous Money ★

Mystery   1946 · US · BW · 65mins

Sidney Toler rang up his 21st and penultimate appearance as Earl Derr Biggers's Oriental sleuth Charlie Chan. The slim plot has the duo trying to figure out who bumped off a government agent. Although he was known as one of the "B-Hive's" most efficient editors, Terry Morse was no great shakes as a director. With its caricatured suspects and stock whodunit situations, Miriam Kissinger's script would, however, have defeated even Hitchcock.

Sidney Toler *Charlie Chan* • Gloria Warren *Rona Simmonds* • Victor Sen Yung *Jimmy Chan* • Rick Vallin *Tao Erickson* • Joseph Crehan *Capt Black* • Willie Best *Chattanooga* ■ *Dir* Terry Morse • *Scr* Miriam Kissinger, from characters created by Earl Derr Biggers

Dangerous Moonlight ★★★🔘

Second World War drama   1941 · UK · BW · 97mins

This is the wartime movie remembered for its Richard Addinsell score, which introduced to the world the massively popular (and ultra-corny) *Warsaw Concerto*, as irredeemably romantic pianist Anton Walbrook never stops playing it. The impossibly lovely Sally Gray is the American journalist Walbrook marries and who helps the musician recover his memory after a brush with a German bomber. However, it's awfully dull and not particularly well directed, but it's such potent tosh, why quibble?

Anton Walbrook *Stefan Radetzky* • Sally Gray *Carole Peters* • Derrick de Marney *Mike Carroll* • Keneth Kent *De Guise* • Percy Parsons *Bill Peters* ■ *Dir* Brian Desmond Hurst • *Scr* Shaun Terence Young, Brian Desmond Hurst, Rodney Ackland, from a story by Shaun Terence Young

Dangerous Moves ★★★🅿🅶

Drama   1984 · Swi · Colour · 100mins

Richard Dembo's directorial debut may have landed the best foreign film Oscar, but it scarcely ranks among the worthiest winners of the award. Somewhat labouring the strategic comparisons, he uses the World Chess Championship in Geneva as a metaphor for the Cold War. Ailing Soviet Grand Master Michel Piccoli (in imperious form) enjoins battle with Alexandre Arbatt, a Russian who defected to the west. While there's a sly wit underlying the suspense, what stands out is the way ruthless cunning impinges on the cerebral jousting, notably the Kremlin's release of Arbatt's unstable wife Liv Ullmann in a bid to distract him. In French with English subtitles.

Michel Piccoli *Akiva Liebskind* • Alexandre Arbatt *Pavius Fromm* • Leslie Caron *Henia* • Liv Ullmann *Marina* • Daniel Olbrychski *Tac-Tac* • Michel Aumont *Kerossian* ■ *Dir/Scr* Richard Dembo

Dangerous Passion ★★🔞

Crime drama   1990 · US · Colour · 91mins

Carl Weathers (Apollo Creed from the *Rocky* films) stars in this hackneyed romantic thriller about a naive security man who becomes the pawn of a dangerous gangster. When he falls in love with the mobster's abused wife, they are forced to fight their way to freedom. Sure it's shlocky, and the characters are paper-thin. But it's all good fun in a stylish TV movie that culminates in a rock 'em, sock 'em finale.

Billy Dee Williams *Lou* • Lonette McKee *Meg* • Carl Weathers *Kyle Weston* • Elpidia Carrillo *Angela* • Michael Beach *Steve* • L Scott Caldwell *Ruby* ■ *Dir* Michael Miller • *Scr* Brian Taggert, from an idea by Andrew Hill

A Dangerous Profession★★

Crime drama   1949 · US · BW · 79mins

A fast-moving, comfortably familiar and thoroughly forgettable crime programme-filler, in which ex-cop George Raft, now a partner in a bail bond company with Pat O'Brien, decides to investigate the mysterious death of a suspect (Bill Williams) he has bailed out. Could his interest in the dead man's pretty widow (Ella Raines) have anything to do with his determination to solve the crime? Director Ted Tetzlaff efficiently disguises the uninspiring and occasionally woolly content with an overlay of pace.

George Raft *Kane* • Pat O'Brien *Farley* • Ella Raines *Lucy* • Bill Williams *Brackett* • Jim Backus *Ferrone* • Roland Winters *McKay* • Betty Underwood *Elaine* ■ *Dir* Ted Tetzlaff • *Scr* Martin Rackin, Warren Duff

A Dangerous Summer ★★🔞

Thriller   1981 · Ausl · Colour · 85mins

Tom Skerritt, James Mason and Wendy Hughes star in this little-seen Australian adventure, directed by Quentin Masters (*The Stud*). American businessman Skerritt discovers that his high hopes for a mountain resort could go up in smoke in this fiery thriller set in the week before Christmas – the height of summer

Down Under. Exciting bush fire sequences help to leaven the somewhat stolid plot. 📼

Tom Skerritt *Howard Anderson* • Ian Gilmour *Steve Adams* • James Mason *George Engels* • Wendy Hughes *Sophie McCann* ■ *Dir* Quentin Masters • *Scr* Quentin Masters, David Ambrose

Dangerous Touch ★★ 18

Erotic thriller 1994 · US · Colour · 97mins

Lou Diamond Phillips plays a sinister outsider who initially charms sex therapist Kate Vernon, then ensnares her in a twisting murder plot. Phillips casts himself well against type and it gets pretty steamy at times, but the script soon runs off the rails and the result is an all-too-average erotic thriller. Contains swearing, violence, sex scenes and nudity. 📼

Lou Diamond Phillips *Mick Burroughs* • Kate Vernon *Amanda Grace* • Berlinda Tolbert *Sasha Taylor* • Max Gail *Jasper Stone* • Robert Prentiss *Charlie* • Mitch Pileggi *Vince* • Monique Parent *Nicole* ■ *Dir* Lou Diamond Phillips • *Scr* Kurt Voss, Lou Diamond Phillips

Dangerous Waters ★★

Adventure 1999 · US · Colour

Rafting used to be such a wonderful sport. Now, however, it's a mecca for maniacs and psycho killers, at least as far as this clichéd TV-movie thriller is concerned. A single mother takes her son and daughter white-water rafting, and her new boyfriend comes along for the ride. What they don't know is that he plans to use the trip to locate some lost stolen money. Connie Sellecca is a Meryl Streep wannabe, but Matt McCoy is no Kevin Bacon in this blatant rip-off of *The River Wild*.

Connie Sellecca *Sarah Slavin* • Matt McCoy *Bob Brown* ■ *Dir/Scr* Catherine Cyran

Dangerous When Wet
★★★ U

Musical comedy 1953 · US · Colour · 95mins

An utterly meaningless (but smart) title for one of Esther Williams's most amiable musical comedies, in which she and her whole health-nut family are persuaded to swim the English Channel. There's a super live/animated sequence featuring Tom and Jerry, and a marvellous moment when the film stops for a number by Barbara Whiting, playing Esther's peppy younger sister. Williams married her leading man in this movie in reality, and became Mrs Fernando Lamas.

Esther Williams *Katy* • Fernando Lamas *André Lanet* • Jack Carson *Windy Webbe* • Charlotte Greenwood *Ma Higgins* • Denise Darcel *Gigi Mignon* • William Demarest *Pa Higgins* • Donna Corcoran *Junior Higgins* • Barbara Whiting *Suzie Higgins* ■ *Dir* Charles Walters • *Scr* Dorothy Kingsley

A Dangerous Woman
★★★ 18

Thriller 1993 · US · Colour · 97mins

This slow-burning drama about "care in the community" issues is directed with sensitivity by Stephen Gyllenhaal and given greater depth than the Hollywood norm by the script, written by his wife Naomi Foner. Debra Winger is an emotionally disturbed woman trying to

come to terms with life in small-town America. A chain of events involving her aunt Barbara Hershey, handyman Gabriel Byrne and sleazy David Strathairn pushes the child-like Winger to the edge of psychosis. The result is a slightly mannered, yet highly affecting case history about how a socially inept individual deals with love and responsibility. 📼

Debra Winger *Martha Horgan* • Barbara Hershey *Frances Beecham* • Gabriel Byrne *Colin Mackey* • David Strathairn *Getso* • Chloe Webb *Birdie* • John Terry *Steve Bell* ■ *Dir* Stephen Gyllenhaal • *Scr* Naomi Foner, from a novel by Mary McGarry Morris

Dangerous Years ★★★

Crime 1947 · US · BW · 62mins

Marilyn Monroe has an early role in this interesting little movie that broached the subject of teenage delinquency, a growing problem in the postwar years. Former "Dead End Kid" William (Billy) Halop is a disoriented youth, raised in an orphanage, who turns to crime and is ultimately tried for murder. Ann E Todd, an accomplished and popular child actress of the time, added the "E" to her name to avoid confusion with British star Ann Todd.

Billy Halop *Danny Jones* • Ann E Todd *Doris Martin* • Jerome Cowan *Weston* • Anabel Shaw *Connie Burns* • Richard Gaines *Edgar Burns* • Scotty Beckett *Willy Miller* • Marilyn Monroe *Evie* ■ *Dir* Arthur Pierson • *Scr* Arnold Belgard

Dangerously Close ★★ 18

Crime thriller 1986 · US · Colour · 90mins

What begins as an intriguing suspense movie, about student vigilantes who take their self-appointed enforcement policies too far, degenerates into a sloppy thriller once the bodies of low-income pupils start piling up. John Stockwell, who also co-wrote the poorly conceived script, stars as the leader of "The Sentinels", a bunch of neo-Nazi bully boys who patrol their affluent high school rooting out "undesirables". The young cast, which includes future Bond girl Carey Lowell and Michelle Pfeiffer's sister Dedee, are improbably good-looking, and Albert Pyun directs with consummate anonymity. 📼

John Stockwell *Randy McDevitt* • J Eddie Peck *Donny Lennox* • Carey Lowell *Julie* • Bradford Bancroft *Krooger Raines* • Don Michael Paul *Ripper* • Thom Mathews *Brian Rigletti* • Jerry Dinome *Lang Bridges* • Madison Mason *Corrigan* • Dedee Pfeiffer *Nikki* ■ *Dir* Albert Pyun • *Scr* Scott Fields, John Stockwell, Marty Ross, from a story by Marty Ross

Dangerously They Live ★★★

Second World War spy drama
1942 · US · BW · 76mins

A Warner Bros wartime melodrama mixing spies and medicine, starring the great John Garfield (*The Postman Always Rings Twice*), miscast as a doctor caught up with a kidnapped Allied secret agent, fetchingly played by Nancy Coleman. Tosh, of course, and Garfield is wasted in a routine role, but it helped wake up American audiences to the fact that there was a war on. Writer Marion Parsonnet is better known for *Gilda*, which also features similar Nazi stuff. Watch the hospital scenes involving amnesia treatment:

Parsonnet clearly hasn't done his medical homework!

John Garfield *Dr Michael Lewis* • Nancy Coleman *Jane* • Raymond Massey *Dr Ingersoll* • Moroni Olsen *Mr Goodwin* • Esther Dale *Dawson* • Lee Patrick *Nurse Johnson* • John Ridgely *John* ■ *Dir* Robert Florey • *Scr* Marion Parsonnet, from his story

Daniel ★★ 15

Drama 1983 · US · Colour · 129mins

EL Doctorow's adaptation of his own novel about the famous Rosenberg spying case becomes a worthy, terribly talkie drama that might just have caught fire had it had a stronger, starrier cast. Timothy Hutton plays a student who investigates the events that led to the execution of both his parents in the fifties. Both were convicted of selling atomic secrets to the Russians and, as Hutton's work proceeds, flashbacks take us through a 20-year period of war, Cold War and general paranoia. Often vague and muddled, it's filled with psychobabble, since Hutton's mission is all to do with his sister's suicide.

Timothy Hutton *Daniel Isaacson* • Mandy Patinkin *Paul Isaacson* • Lindsay Crouse *Rochelle* • Edward Asner [Ed Asner] *Jacob Ascher* • Ellen Barkin *Phyllis Isaacson* • Julie Bovasso *Frieda Stein* • Tovah Feldshuh *Linda Mindish* • Joseph Leon *Selig Mindish* • Amanda Plummer *Susan Isaacson* ■ *Dir* Sidney Lumet • *Scr* El Doctorow, from his novel *The Book of Daniel*

Daniel and the Devil ★★

Fantasy drama 1941 · US · BW

Variously known as *All That Money Can Buy* and *The Devil and Daniel Webster*, this features a fine musical score that rightly won an Academy Award for composer Bernard Herrmann (*Citizen Kane*, *Psycho*). Would that the rest of the movie were as good. New England farmer James Craig (wholly inadequate and utterly charmless) sells his soul to scene-stealing, wicked Walter Huston's Mr Scratch. Lawyer Daniel Webster, portrayed by Edward Arnold, is hijacked into the story to plead Craig's case. This is a rigidly humourless and prosaic telling of an old, old story. It has many admirers, but, truth to tell, it hasn't really worn very well.

Edward Arnold *Daniel Webster* • Walter Huston *Mr Scratch* • James Craig *Jabez Stone* • Jane Darwell *Ma Stone* • Simone Simon *Belle* • Gene Lockhart *Squire Slossum* • John Qualen *Miser Stevens* ■ *Dir* William Dieterle • *Scr* Dan Totheroh, from the story *The Devil and Daniel Webster* by Stephen Vincent Benet

Daniel Boone, Trail Blazer
★★ PG

Adventure 1957 · US · Colour · 72mins

This lively action film from Poverty Row studio Republic has its own little place in movie history as the final picture shot in Hollywood using two-colour stock (modern films are three-colour). Bruce Bennett, who made his name as Tarzan in the mid-thirties, stars as the legendary frontiersman guiding a wagon train from North Carolina to Kentucky (actually Mexico, because it was cheaper to film there). Lon Chaney Jr is on form as his lumbering sidekick, but the performances merit a better script. 📼

Bruce Bennett *Daniel Boone* • Lon Chaney Jr *Blackfish* • Damian O'Flynn *Andy Callaway* • Jacqueline Evans *Rebecca Boone* • Nancy Rodman *Susannah Boone* • Freddy Fernandez *Israel Boone* • Carol Kelly *Jemima Boone* • Eduardo Noriega *Squire Boone* ■ *Dir* Albert C Gannaway, Ismael Rodriguez • *Scr* Tom Hubbard, John Patrick

Danielle Steel's A Perfect Stranger ★★ 12

Romantic drama 1994 · US · Colour · 87mins

From the moment you see the author's name in the title, you know what to expect of this glitzy melodrama. Luxury, deception and no little passion are all to the fore here as ambitious attorney Robert Urich finds himself falling for Stacy Haiduk, the trophy wife of terminally ill millionaire Darren McGavin. Under the unsubtle direction of Michael Miller, the members of the cast give it their all. But this TV movie is strictly for soap fans and Steel readers only. 📼

Robert Urich *Alex Hale* • Stacy Haiduk *Raphaella Phillips* • Marion Ross *Charlotte Brandon* • Darren McGavin *John Henry Phillips* • Susan Sullivan *Kaye* • Holly Marie Combs *Amanda* ■ *Scr* Jan Worthington, from the novel by Danielle Steel

Danielle Steel's Mixed Blessings ★★ 12

Romantic drama 1995 · US · Colour · 86mins

Three couples deal with pregnancy, adoption and infertility in this weepie based on the Danielle Steel romantic novel. The plot is predictable, but the TV-based cast gives its all, and there are top-notch performances from ex-*Happy Days* star Scott Baio, *St Elsewhere's* Bruce Greenwood and *Baywatch's* Alexandra Paul. Meanwhile, director Bethany Rooney makes sure every moment is a three-hankie one. 📼

Gabrielle Carteris *Diana Douglas* • Bruce Greenwood *Andy Douglas* • Scott Baio *Charlie Winwood* • Julie Condra *Barbie Winwood* • Alexandra Paul *Beth* • Bess Armstrong *Pilar Coleman* • James Naughton *Brad Coleman* • Bruce Weitz *Dr Alex Johnson* ■ *Dir* Bethany Rooney • *Scr* L Virginia Browne, Rebecca Soladay, from the novel by Danielle Steel

Danielle Steel's No Greater Love ★★ PG

Romantic drama 1996 · US · Colour · 86mins

This frothy melodramatic confection, takes in cataclysmic world news (the sinking of the *Titanic*) and reduces it to a facile excuse for showing us yet another of Steel's strong, brave and well turned-out women battling the odds. The cast has been wheeled out on castors, including Simon MacCorkindale, and it runs through its hand-wringing paces as if the script is being relayed by hidden short-wave radio. 📼

Kelly Rutherford *Edwina Winfield* • Chris Sarandon *Sam Horowitz* • Nicholas Campbell *Stone* • Daniel Hugh-Kelly *Ben Jones* • Simon MacCorkindale *Patrick Kelly* • Michael Landes *George Winfield* • Gina Philips *Alexis Winfield* ■ *Dir* Richard Heffron [Richard T Heffron] • *Scr* Carmen Culver from the novel by Danielle Steel

Danielle Steel's Once in a Lifetime ★★ PG

Romantic drama 1994 · US · Colour · 87mins

Get out those hankies this is one of the weepier movie adaptations of a Danielle Steel novel. Lindsay Wagner, ex-Bionic Woman and queen of the TV movie, plays Daphne Fields, an author reluctant to love again after her husband and daughter are killed in a fire. On top of all this, her young son is deaf; there's no prize for guessing who rescues our heroine from all – this TV-movie king Barry Bostwick. ▣

Lindsay Wagner *Daphne Fields* • Barry Bostwick *Dr Matthew Dane* • Duncan Regehr *Justin* • Amy Aquino *Barbara* • Rex Smith *Jeffrey Fields* ■ *Dir* Michael Miller • *Scr* Syrie Astrahan James, from the novel by Danielle Steel

Danielle Steel's Remembrance ★★ PG

Romantic drama 1996 · US · Colour · 87mins

Eva LaRue may not be in the same league as Joan Crawford and Barbara Stanwyck, but she suffers nobly as the Italian wife of an American army officer frozen out of the family by hellish mother-in-law Angie Dickinson. Directed with exemplary overstatement by Bethany Rooney, this is undemanding escapism of the tear-jerking kind. ▣

Angie Dickinson *Margaret Fullerton* • Eva LaRue *Serena Fullerton* • Jeffrey Nordling *Brad Fullerton* • James Calvert *Teddy Fullerton* ■ *Dir* Bethany Rooney • *Scr* David Ambrose, from the novel by Danielle Steel

Danielle Steel's Secrets ★★ 15

Romantic drama 1992 · US · Colour · 89mins

Scandals, love affairs and skeletons-in-the-closet as suffered by Tinseltown's rich and famous. Christopher Plummer is the TV producer who experiences a few steamy moments of his own, while the cast on his show including Stephanie Beacham as the star, Linda Purl as the daytime soap queen and Ben Browder as the hot new hunk spends more time jumping in and out of bed than it does filming the series. Silly, over-the-top, and, if you watch for too long, scarily addictive. ▣

Christopher Plummer *Mel Wexler* • Stephanie Beacham *Sabina Quarles* • Linda Purl *Jane Adams* • Gary Collins *Zack Taylor* • Ben Browder *Bill Warwick* • Josie Bissett *Gaby Smith* • John Bennett Perry *Dan Adams* ■ *Dir* Peter Hunt • *Scr* William Bast, Paul Huson, from the novel by Danielle Steel

Danielle Steel's Star ★★ 15

Romantic melodrama
1993 · US · Colour · 92mins

Beverly Hills 90210 star Jennie Garth plays a rising young star of the entertainment world who has put her personal tragedies behind her, but remains haunted by her first love Craig Bierko. Director Michael Miller, who made the cult prisoner-on-the-run drama *Jackson County Jail* revels in the melodramatic clichés, and the result is an undemanding slice of romantic tosh. ▣

Jennie Garth *Crystal Wyatt* • Craig Bierko *Spencer Hill* • Ted Wass *Ernie* • Terry Farrell

Elizabeth ■ *Dir* Michael Miller • *Scr* Claire Labine, Danielle Steel, from the novel by Danielle Steel

Danielle Steel's Vanished ★★ PG

Romantic drama 1995 · US · Colour · 86mins

George Hamilton reveals that beneath the tan there beats the heart of a heel in this TV movie based on another novel by the queen of popular fiction. Refusing to forgive ex-wife Lisa Rinna for the death of their son, Hamilton jets to the States to kidnap Alex D Linz (clearly defenceless in his pre-*Home Alone III* infancy), the little moppet she's since had with new beau Robert Hays. Director George Kaczender works overtime to make us believe in this melodramatic tosh and its cardboard characters. ▣

Lisa Rinna *Marielle Delauney* • George Hamilton *Malcolm Patterson* • Robert Hays *John Taylor* • Maurice Godin *Charles Delauney* • Daniela Akerblom *Brigitte* • Alex D Linz *Teddy* ■ *Dir* George Kaczender • *Scr* Kathleen Rowell, from the novel by Danielle Steel

Danny Boy ★ U

Drama 1941 · UK · BW · 79mins

What on earth was someone of Ann Todd's stature doing in a piece of sentimental nonsense like this? Admittedly, she was returning to films after a two-year absence, but she is woefully miscast as a singer hitting the road to find her estranged husband and son, who have become buskers. Things must have been at a pretty low ebb for anyone to have emerged from watching this slipshod entertainment with a spring in their step.

Ann Todd *Jane Kay* • Wilfrid Lawson *Jack Newton* • John Warwick *Nick Carter* • Grant Tyler *Danny* • David Farrar *Harold Martin* ■ *Dir* Oswald Mitchell • *Scr* Vera Allinson

Danny, the Champion of the World ★★★ U

Comedy drama 1989 · UK · Colour · 94mins

Solid family entertainment based on Roald Dahl's popular novel. Jeremy Irons and his real son Samuel play a happy single-parent family in the fifties who go head to head with obnoxious squire Robbie Coltrane over poaching and ownership of land. Samuel saves the day in a well-observed comedy drama in the Ealing style, with fleshed-out characterisations provided by a great supporting cast. ▣

Jeremy Irons *William Smith* • Samuel Irons *Danny Smith* • Cyril Cusack *Dr Spencer* • Robbie Coltrane *Victor Hazell* • Lionel Jeffries *Mr Snoddy* • Ronald Pickup *Captain Lancaster* • Jimmy Nail *Rabbetts* • William Armstrong *Springer* • Michael Hordern *Lord Claybury* • Jean Marsh *Miss Hunter* ■ *Dir* Gavin Millar • *Scr* John Goldsmith, from the novel by Roald Dahl

Dante's Inferno ★★★

Drama 1935 · US · BW · 89mins

As the title implies, there is an absolutely super vision of hell, replete with nudity, in this early Fox feature. Most of the screen time, however, is taken up with a Spencer Tracy–Claire Trevor romance; the two Broadway actors acquit themselves well, assuring themselves of future

Hollywood success. Tracy's bombast suits his role as a carnival barker owner who gets too big for his boots, and watch closely for a young dancer called Rita Cansino, before she altered her hairline and changed her surname to Hayworth. The film shows its age, though, so viewers should be tolerant.

Spencer Tracy *Jim Carter* • Claire Trevor *Betty McWade* • Henry B Walthall *Pop McWade* • Scotty Beckett *Sonny* • Alan Dinehart *Jonesy* • Rita Cansino [Rita Hayworth] *Speciality dancer* ■ *Dir* Harry Lachman • *Scr* Philip Klein, Robert Yost, from a story by Cyrus Wood, adapted by Edmund Goulding

Dante's Peak ★★★ 12

Disaster action adventure
1997 · US · Colour · 103mins

Pierce Brosnan's vulcanologist sees the warning signs for major lava problems in the small mountainside town but no one will believe him, in a typically FX-orientated nineties disaster flick. Like the same year's larger-scale *Volcano*, this has some corking digital magma and a lot of cardboard in its path. Director Roger Donaldson handles things in the same way he did in *Species*, papering over dialogue and character deficiencies with some exciting set-pieces, as buildings crumble and roads receive a molten overcoat. Brosnan and romantic interest Linda Hamilton offer serviceable performances, but they're battling against more than just the elements. ▣ DVD

Pierce Brosnan *Harry Dalton* • Linda Hamilton *Rachel Wando* • Jamie Renee Smith *Lauren Wando* • Jeremy Foley *Graham Wando* • Elizabeth Hoffman *Ruth* ■ *Dir* Roger Donaldson • *Scr* Leslie Bohem

Danton ★★★★ PG

Historical drama
1982 · Fr/Pol · Colour · 130mins

With Agnieszka Holland among the scriptwriting team and the great Polish director Andrzej Wajda behind the camera, it's easy to read (despite denials at the time, and the fact that it's based on a 1931 play) this passionate account of the political ambushing of one of the key figures of the French Revolution as an allegorical study of the Solidarity movement. Gérard Depardieu gives arguably the finest performance of his career as the corrupt but committed man of the people, impressing both with his public oratory and his bitter ideological feuds with Wojciech Pszoniak's Robespierre. Although Wajda's free with the facts, he captures the fervour and fury of the period superbly. In French with English subtitles. Contains violence and brief nudity. ▣

Gérard Depardieu *Georges Danton* • Wojciech Pszoniak *Maximilien Robespierre* • Patrice Chéreau *Camille Desmoulins* • Angela Winkler *Lucile Desmoulins* ■ *Dir* Andrzej Wajda • *Scr* Jean-Claude Carrière, Andrzej Wajda, Agnieszka Holland, Boleslaw Michalek, Jacek Gasiorowski, from the play *The Danton Affair* by Stanisława Przybyszewska

Danzón ★★★ PG

Drama 1991 · Mex · Colour · 101mins

The danzón is a type of Latin American dance that recalls with wistful good humour the heartbreaks and missed opportunities of the performer. This

sedate Mexican melodrama takes its cue from the gentle rhythms of such song-and-dance routines, as telephonist Maria Rojo is tempted by the attentions of a younger man in the course of her search for her missing dancing partner. Directed by Maria Novaro, the film lacks focus, with the digs at the conservatism of Mexican society too sly to provoke, and the routines, while hypnotic, no substitute for a more substantial plot. In Spanish with English subtitles. ▣

Maria Rojo *Julia* • Carmen Salinas *Doña Ti* • Blanca Guerra *La Colorada* • Tito Vasconcelos *Susy* • Victor Carpintiero *Rubén* • Margarita Isabel *Silvia* • Cheli Godinez *Tere* ■ *Dir* Maria Novaro • *Scr* Beatriz Novaro, Maria Novaro

Darby O'Gill and the Little People ★★★ U

Fantasy 1959 · US · Colour · 86mins

Although Walt Disney himself, on the film's release, personally thanked King Brian of Knocknasheega (played by Jimmy O'Dea) for his assistance in completing this slice of whimsy, the entire picture was shot in Hollywood. Tall-tale teller extraordinaire Albert Sharpe does a deal with the leprechauns (led by King Brian) to ensure daughter Janet Munro's happiness with the Sean Connery. Although Connery looks a little uneasy at having to sing, the performances are largely fine. But this is all about special effects, ranging from the mischievous imps on horseback to the terrifying arrival of the ghostly Costa Bower or Death Coach. ▣

Albert Sharpe *Darby O'Gill* • Jimmy O'Dea *King Brian* • Janet Munro *Katie* • Sean Connery *Michael McBride* • Kieron Moore *Pony Sugrue* • Estelle Winwood *Sheelah* • Walter Fitzgerald *Lord Fitzpatrick* ■ *Dir* Robert Stevenson • *Scr* Lawrence E Watkin, from the Darby O'Gill stories by HT Kavanagh

Darby's Rangers ★★

Second World War drama
1958 · US · BW · 105mins

This overlong, routine, dreary-looking drama follows American commandos in front-line action in north Africa and Italy during the Second World War. Charlton Heston signed up for the lead, but Jack L Warner apparently welched on the deal; so veteran director William A Wellman had to settle for young TV stars James Garner and Edd Byrnes and European newcomer Etchika Choureau, none of whom make much of an impression.

James Garner *Major William Darby* • Etchika Choureau *Angelina De Lotta* • Jack Warden *Master Sergeant Saul Rosen* • Edward Byrnes [Edd Byrnes] *Lieutenant Arnold Dittman* • Venetia Stevenson *Peggy McTavish* • Torin Thatcher *Sergeant McTavish* • Peter Brown *Rollo Burns* • Joan Elan *Wendy Hollister* • Stuart Whitman *Hank Bishop* ■ *Dir* William A Wellman • *Scr* Guy Trosper, from a book by Major James Altieri

Dare to Love ★★ 12

Drama based on a true story
1995 · US · Colour · 89mins

Director Armand Mastroianni began his career in the lower budget end of the horror genre (*Cameron's Closet*, *He Knows You're Alone*) but these days is more likely to be found making TV-movie fare like this tearjerker, based on a true story. Former *LA Law* star Jill Eikenberry plays a mother bravely trying to cope with her schizophrenic daughter Josie Bissett, who is traumatised following the death of her brother. The talented cast provides solid performances, but it's really only one for true-story fans.

Josie Bissett *Jessica Wells* • Jason Gedrick *Patrick Sherman* • Jill Eikenberry *Alicia Wells* • James B Sikking *Ron Wells* • Chad Lowe *Stephen Wells* • Terry Loughlin *Dr Anderson* ■ *Dir* Armand Mastroianni • *Scr* Sara Flanagan, Rama Laurie Stagner

The Daring Dobermans ★★
Crime caper 1973 · US · Colour · 90mins

The Doberman Gang had a group of thieves training some Doberman dogs to commit the perfect bank robbery. In this follow-up, the Dobermans are being trained by a new group of criminal masterminds, but their plans could be thwarted after a young boy, who loves the dogs, tries to set them free. Simple stuff for kids, this is most impressive for the clever use of the dogs, especially taking into account the film was made before the use of computer animation could make a pet do just about anything.

Charles Knox Robinson • Tim Considine • David Moses • Claudio Martinez • Joan Caulfield • *Dir* Byron Ross Chudnow • *Scr* Alan Alch, Jack Kaplan

Daring Game ★★ **U**
Action adventure
1968 · US · Colour · 100mins

A *Mission Impossible*-style adventure with Lloyd Bridges liberating a professor and his daughter from the clutches of a Latin American dictator. This mission, shot in Florida, involves skydiving as well as scuba diving. The director, Laslo Benedek, had his finest moment in the early fifties with *Death of a Salesman* and *The Wild One* but here he's just a journeyman controlled by producer Ivan Tors who had a wildlife park called Africa, USA.

Lloyd Bridges *Vic Powers* • Nico Minardos *Ricardo Balboa* • Michael Ansara *President Eduardo Delgado* • Joan Blackman *Kathryn Carlyle* • Shepperd Strudwick *Dr Carlyle* • Alex Montoya *General Tovrea* • Irene Dailey *Mrs Carlyle* ■ *Dir* Laslo Benedek • *Scr* Andy White, from a story by Andy White, Art Arthur

The Dark ★★ **15**
Science-fiction horror
1979 · US · Colour · 86mins

Started by director Tobe Hooper as a fully-fledged horror, then completed by John "Bud" Cardos when something more *Alien*-inspired was required – no wonder the end result is a confusing mix of supernatural slasher and intergalactic monster movie. A seven-ft alien in blue jeans stalks Los Angeles, ripping the heads off its victims and mutilating them with laser vision. Author William Devane, TV reporter Cathy Lee Crosby and cop Richard Jaeckel set out to track it down. The murders themselves have minimal impact thanks to Cardos's unimaginative restraint. ▭

William Devane *Ray Warner* • Cathy Lee Crosby *Zoe Owens* • Richard Jaeckel *Detective*

Mooney* • Warren Kemmerling *Captain Speer* • Biff Elliot *Bresler* ■ *Dir* John "Bud" Cardos • *Scr* Stanford Whitmore

The Dark ★★ **18**
Horror 1994 · Can · Colour · 87mins

Scientist Stephen McHattie battles crazed cop Brion James over the fate of a prehistoric carnivorous rodent living below a Canadian graveyard. Tongue-in-cheek humour and slick suspense create enjoyable fluff in this silly but fun horror tale. Monster point-of-view shots heighten the tension in a well-produced quickie, which also features an early appearance by *Scream* star Neve Campbell. ▭

Stephen McHattie *Hunter* • Cynthia Belliveau *Tracy* • Jaimz Woolvett *Ed* • Dennis O'Connor *Jake* • Neve Campbell *Jesse* • Brion James *Buckner* ■ *Scr* Robert Cooper

Dark Alibi ★
Mystery 1946 · US · BW · 61mins

The first eight entries in the Charlie Chan series after it transferred from Fox to Monogram were bashed out by journeyman writer George Callahan and the strain was readily evident by his swansong, in which as much emphasis is placed on humour as on the clues. Sidney Toler investigates who is responsible for leaving fake fingerprints at the scenes of crimes to implicate innocent people, but he receives little assistance from Phil Karlson's slapdash direction.

Sidney Toler *Charlie Chan* • Mantan Moreland *Birmingham* • Ben Carter *Carter* • Benson Fong *Tommy Chan* • Teala Loring *June* ■ *Dir* Phil Karlson • *Scr* George Callahan, from characters created by Earl Derr Biggers

The Dark Angel ★★★ **U**
Romantic drama 1935 · US · BW · 101mins

One of the great four-hankie melodramas, this is the talkie remake of a famous Guy Bolton play originally filmed in 1925 with Ronald Colman and Vilma Banky. Here Merle Oberon gives an Oscar-nominated performance as Kitty Vane, loved by upright Herbert Marshall and war-blinded Fredric March, a love buffeted by fate in a series of plot complications. This is an expertly crafted "woman's picture" in which Oberon, shorn of her trademark fashionable hairstyles and expensive wardrobes, is a revelation. The creaky theatrical origins seep through now and then, but acerbic co-scriptwriter Lillian Hellman manages to keep bathos at bay, and the result is a mighty fine wallow. ▭

Fredric March *Alan Trent* • Merle Oberon *Kitty Vane* • Herbert Marshall *Gerald Shannon* • Janet Beecher *Mrs Shannon* • John Halliday *Sir George Barton* • Henrietta Crosman *Granny Vane* ■ *Dir* Sidney Franklin • *Scr* Lillian Hellman, Mordaunt Shairp, from the play by Guy Bolton

Dark Angel ★★★ **18**
Science-fiction thriller
1989 · US · Colour · 87mins

Dolph Lundgren gives his best performance to date as a Houston detective on the trail of an intergalactic drug dealer in this smartly scripted and crisply directed science-fiction spin on the buddy cop movie. The alien pusher

has come to Earth to obtain a substance produced within the human body that is much sought after as a narcotic on his planet. Owing debts to *Predator*, *Alien Nation* and *Miami Vice*, the stock ingredients are all well proportioned in a cracking yarn that's exciting to watch thanks to the extra twists added by Baxley. Brian Benben scores as Lundgren's by-the-book FBI sidekick, while the inventive alien weaponry provides graphic thrills. ▭

Dolph Lundgren *Jack Caine* • Brian Benben *Laurence Smith* • Betsy Brantley *Diane Pollon* • Matthias Hues *Talec* • David Ackroyd *Switzer* • Jim Haynie *Captain Malone* ■ *Dir* Craig R Baxley • *Scr* Jonathan Tydor, Leonard Maas Jr

Dark Angel ★★
Thriller 1996 · US · Colour

Director Robert Iscove is currently riding high on the back of recent release *She's All That*. However, his earlier work was mainly restricted to proficient but routine TV movies such as this rather dull cop thriller. Hard-working Eric Roberts is a new detective on the block who seems to have uncomfortably close ties to the serial killer he's meant to be tracking down. Contains swearing and violence.

Eric Roberts *Walter D'Arcangelo* • Ashley Crow *Anna St Cyr* • Linden Ashby *Detective Harry Foley* • Paul Calderon *Lieutenant Vance Pickett* • Gina Torres *Lamayne* ■ *Dir* Robert Iscove • *Scr* John Romanco, from a story by Randall Wallace, John Romano

The Dark at the Top of the Stairs ★★
Drama 1960 · US · Colour · 123mins

The William Inge play on which this memoir of life in twenties Oklahoma is based won the Pulitzer Prize. Unfortunately, whatever merit the original might have had as a theatrical experience has been dissipated here by Delbert Mann's reverential approach to its themes of sexual awakening, family discord, class snobbery and anti-Semitism. The main problem for modern audiences is the fact that many of its attitudes have become so outdated that they are likely to breach even the most flexible code of political correctness.

Robert Preston *Rubin Flood* • Dorothy McGuire *Cora Flood* • Eve Arden *Lottie* • Angela Lansbury *Mavis Pruitt* • Shirley Knight *Reenie Flood* • Lee Kinsolving *Sammy Golden* ■ *Dir* Delbert Mann • *Scr* Irving Ravetch, Harriet Frank Jr, from the play by William Inge

The Dark Avenger ★★★ **U**
Swashbuckling drama
1955 · US/UK · Colour · 84mins

Before he stiffened up into arthritic gestures that passed for acting, Errol Flynn made this final parry-and-lunge costumed swashbuckler. Its story – about an English prince fighting off Peter Finch and his unmerry French conspirators and safeguarding Joanne Dru in the process – is no history lesson, but tuition on how to get away with Flynn's kind of daredevilry. It's a small-scale epic that does his roistering reputation no discredit, for he was, indeed, a class act.

Errol Flynn *Prince Edward* • Joanne Dru *Lady Joan Holland* • Peter Finch *Count de Ville* • Yvonne Furneaux *Marie* • Patrick Holt *Sir Ellys*

• Michael Hordern *King Edward III* • Moultrie Kelsall *Sir Bruce* • Robert Urquhart *Sir Philip* ■ *Dir* Henry Levin • *Scr* Daniel B Ullman, Phil Park (uncredited)

The Dark Backward ★★ **15**
Comedy fantasy 1991 · US · Colour · 99mins

Writer/director Adam Rifkin has scripted a number of idiosyncratic movies (*Small Soldiers*, *Mousehunt*), but this early entry in his oeuvre is really off the wall. Judd Nelson is a garbage collector who dreams of becoming a stand-up comic, but who only succeeds in getting noticed when a third arm starts to grow out of his back. An eclectic cast and the extraordinary premise failed to make this the cult hit it seemed destined to be, but you have to give it an "A" for effort. ▭

Judd Nelson *Marty Malt* • Bill Paxton *Gus* • Wayne Newton *Jackie Chrome* • Lara Flynn Boyle *Rosarita* • James Caan *Dr Scurvy* • Rob Lowe *Dirk Delta* • King Moody *Twinkee Doodle* • Claudia Christian *Kitty* • Adam Rifkin *Rufus Bing* ■ *Dir/Scr* Adam Rifkin

Dark City ★★★
Mystery drama 1950 · US · BW · 97mins

Don DeFore loses all the company cash in a rigged poker game, then hangs himself. It's a fabulous *noir* opening, but director William Dieterle fails to maintain the tight suspense as Charlton Heston, here making his feature debut, is stalked by DeFore's psychotic brother. That said, it's a typically well-crafted Paramount production, and Lizabeth Scott smoulders seductively. Heston's character, a cynical outsider, is far removed from the epic heroics with which he was later associated, yet it's easy to see why he became a superstar after this brooding debut.

Charlton Heston *Danny Haley* • Lizabeth Scott *Fran* • Don DeFore *Arthur Winant* • Jack Webb *Augie* • Ed Begley *Barney* • Henry Morgan [Harry Morgan] *Soldier* ■ *Dir* William Dieterle • *Scr* Larry Marcus, John Meredyth Lucas, from a story by Larry Marcus

Dark City ★★★
Political thriller
1990 · UK/Zim · Colour · 98mins

Following the lead of Oliver Schmitz's crime drama *Mapantsula*, this taut thriller manages to say more about life in South Africa under apartheid than numerous more overtly political tracts. The immediate presumption that black people must be guilty of a township crime, the brutality of the security forces and the bias of the legal system are all exposed in Chris Curling's hard-hitting film. Reinforcing these abuses is the struggle of seven suspects to prove they are innocent of the murder of a prominent councillor, which may or may not be bound up with a burglary at the mayor's house.

Sello Maake Ka-Ncube *Victor Mtetwa* • Vusi Dibakwane *Edison* • Thapelo Mafokeng *Mayor Seko* • Ernest Ndlovu *Reverend Bricks* • Moses Mphahlele *Oscar* • Pierre Knoesen *Major Fisher* • Charles Pillai *Reddy* ■ *Dir* Chris Curling • *Scr* David Lan

Dark City　★★★★ 15

Science-fiction fantasy mystery
1998 · US · Colour · 96mins

Director Alex Proyas lends a potent gothic atmosphere to this dreamlike *film noir* fantasy about a race of mysterious bald figures who continually reconfigure a surreal, gloomy city and its inhabitants as some sort of weird experiment. As with *The Crow*, Proyas employs every striking camera angle in his visual vocabulary, breathing dread into the overhanging *Batman*-style architecture. The effects are impressively realised, too, as buildings stretch and widen before our eyes. Although overshadowed by the film's visual flair, the eclectic cast – including Rufus Sewell, Kiefer Sutherland, William Hurt and Ian Richardson – adds a splash of colour to the shadowy surroundings. 🔲 **DVD**

Rufus Sewell *John Murdoch* • Kiefer Sutherland *Dr Daniel Schreber* • Jennifer Connelly *Emma Murdoch* • Richard O'Brien *Mr Hand* • Ian Richardson *Mr Book* • Colin Friels *Walenski* • Mitchell Butel *Husselbeck* • Frank Gallacher *Stromboli* • Melissa George *May* • William Hurt *Inspector Frank Bumstead* ■ Dir Alex Proyas • Scr Alex Proyas, Lem Dobbs, David S Goyer, from a story by Alex Proyas • Cinematographer Dariusz Wolski

Dark Command　★★ U

Western　　　　　　1940 · US · BW · 89mins

After John Wayne's success opposite Claire Trevor in *Stagecoach*, his home studio, Republic, promoted him from B-westerns to this big budget effort which re-teamed him with Trevor. Wayne is the simple cowpoke who successfully runs for marshal to impress his girl and, as a result, Walter Pidgeon (the better qualified candidate) turns to a life of crime. Raoul Walsh was imported to direct and the film lurches between static dialogue scenes and bursts of action. There's a celebrated stunt, arranged by Yakima Canutt, in which four men ride a wagon and team off a bluff into water 50 feet below. 🔲

John Wayne *Bob Seton* • Claire Trevor *Mary McCloud* • Walter Pidgeon *William Cantrell* • Roy Rogers *Fletch McCloud* • George "Gabby" Hayes *Doc Grunch* • Porter Hall *Angus McCloud* ■ Dir Raoul Walsh • Scr Grover Jones, Lionel Hauser, F Hugh Herbert, from the novel by WR Burnett

The Dark Corner　★★★

Film noir　　　　　1946 · US · BW · 99mins

Although relatively unknown, this is a rattlingly good and cleverly plotted *film noir*, skilfully directed by Henry Hathaway. It's marred only by too-obvious studio sets and a bland leading man in Mark Stevens, who's not quite tough enough as the private eye framed by his former partner. Still, there's a nicely etched performance from, of all people, Lucille Ball (in her pre-*I Love Lucy* days) as a hard-boiled secretary, and welcome character work from art dealer Clifton Webb and thug William Bendix. Constance Collier also has a notable cameo, and the crisp black-and-white photography is typical of 20th Century-Fox films of the period.

Mark Stevens *Bradford Galt* • Lucille Ball *Kathleen* • Clifton Webb *Hardy Cathcart* • William Bendix *White Suit* • Kurt Kreuger *Tony Jardine* • Cathy Downs *Mari Cathcart* • Reed

Hadley *Lt Frank Reeves* • Constance Collier *Mrs Kingsley* ■ Dir Henry Hathaway • Scr Jay Dratler, Bernard Schoenfeld, from a short story by Leo Rosten • Cinematographer Joseph MacDonald

The Dark Crystal　★★★★ PG

Fantasy adventure
1982 · UK · Colour · 87mins

Few film-makers feel at home in the realms of fantasy, but Jim Henson had an affinity with the magical. Although *The Dark Crystal* emerged from the darker side of his imagination, it's still a mesmerising picture that will enchant older children and adults alike. The story is a basic slice of sword and sorcery, following Jen and Kira as they attempt to restore a splinter of a crystal that will free the "Mystics" from the tyranny of the "Skeksis". However, there is a liberal sprinkling of Muppet-style humour to enliven the adventure, and, with the exception of the "Gelflings", the creatures are inspired. 🔲 **DVD**

Stephen Garlick *Jen* • Billie Whitelaw *Aughra* • Lisa Maxwell *Kira* • Barry Dennen *Chamberlain* • Michael Kilgarriff *General* • Percy Edwards *Fizzgig* ■ Dir Jim Henson, Frank Oz • Scr David Odell, from a story by Jim Henson

Dark Eyes　★★ PG

Romantic comedy
1987 · It · Colour · 112mins

In addition to winning the best actor prize at Cannes, Marcello Mastroianni landed an Oscar nomination for his bravura performance in this self-conscious amalgamation of four Chekhov short stories. Directing with a fine eye for period detail, Nikita Mikhalkov robs the action of its social and psychological subtlety by calling for grandiloquent gestures and stereotypical characterisations, which turn delicate situations into potboiler set pieces. As an ageing playboy, the ever astute Mastroianni is able to give a shaded performance. Wife Silvia Mangano, mistress Marthe Keller and the elusive Elena Sofonova aren't give the same chance to shine. In Italian with English subtitles. 🔲

Marcello Mastroianni *Romano* • Silvana Mangano *Elisa* • Marthe Keller *Tina* • Elena Sofonova *Anna* • Pina Cei *Elisa's mother* ■ Dir Nikita Mikhalkov • Scr Alexander Adabashian, Nikita Mikhalkov, Suso Cecchi D'Amico, from the short stories *Anna around the Neck*, *The Lady with the Little Dog*, *My Wife*, *The Name-Day Party* by Anton Chekhov

Dark Eyes of London　★★★

Horror　　　　　1939 · UK · BW · 75mins

In one of the most effective examples of screen *Grand Guignol*, Bela Lugosi is at his evil best as the director of an insurance company who kills his clients so he can collect on their policies. Disguised as the kindly old proprietor of a home for the blind, he carries out his nefarious swindles with the assistance of a hideous giant. Based on an Edgar Wallace novel, this British-made shocker, directed by Walter Summers, is both bleak and remarkably scary for the time.

Bela Lugosi *Dr Orloff* • Hugh Williams *Inspector Holt* • Greta Gynt *Diana Stuart* • Edmond Ryan [Edmon Ryan] *Lt O'Reilly* • Wilfrid Walter *Jake, the Monster* • Alexander

Field *Grogan* ■ Dir Walter Summers • Scr Patrick Kirwan, Walter Summers, John Argyle, from a novel by Edgar Wallace

The Dark Half　★★★ 18

Horror　　　1991 · US · Colour · 116mins

Cult zombie director George A Romero liberally sprays the scare freshener in his adaptation of Stephen King's popular horror novel. Timothy Hutton does his finest work in years as best-selling writer Thad Beaumont, whose emerging supernatural side manifests itself in the form of a brutal serial killer and starts stalking his New England family home. Romero makes the premise both plausible and frightening by using slasher genre conventions in unique ways. Alas, he blows the suspenseful build-up with a ridiculously overblown ending. Up to this point, though, it's compelling stuff. 🔲

Timothy Hutton *Thad Beaumont* • Michael Rooker *Sheriff Alan Pangborn* • Amy Madigan *Liz Beaumont* • Julie Harris *Reggie Delesseps* • Robert Joy *Fred Clawson* • Rutanya Alda *Miriam Cowley* • Chelsea Field *Annie Pangborn* ■ Dir George A Romero • Scr George A Romero, from the novel by Stephen King

Dark Harbor　★★

Thriller　　1998 · US · Colour · 88mins

Polly Walker and Alan Rickman star in this average, straight-to-video thriller, directed by Adam Coleman Howard. They play a squabbling couple, struggling through a storm to reach the ferry that will take them to their island home. Their arguments accelerate when they stop to check on a body they spot by the side of the road. However, their problems *really* begin when they pick up the battered boy (Norman Reedus)... Walker and Rickman are fine as the icy marrieds. For all that, this is one of those films that just doesn't hang together.

Alan Rickman *David Weinberg* • Polly Walker *Alexis Chandler Weinberg* • Norman Reedus *Young man* ■ Dir Adam Coleman Howard • Scr Adam Coleman Howard, Justin Lazard

Dark Horse　★★ 15

Drama　　　1992 · US · Colour · 70mins

After her mother dies, teenager Ari Meyers goes out of her way to get into trouble to get some attention from her workaholic dad played by Ed Begley Jr. Ordered to do community service at a local horse ranch, she learns to love horses with the help of ranch owner Mimi Rogers. The kid's a brat, Rogers is sleepwalking, and who told Ed Begley Jr he could act? There's a twist towards the end, but only lovers of weepy drama will make it that far. 🔲

Mimi Rogers *Dr Susan Hadley* • Ed Begley Jr *Jack Mills* • Ari Meyers *Allison Mills* • Samantha Eggar *Mrs Curtis* • Tab Hunter *Perkins* • Chad Smith *Clint* ■ Dir David Hemmings • Scr JE MacLean, from a story by Tab Hunter

Dark Intruder　★★★

Horror　　　1965 · US · BW · 58mins

Murders occurring in turn-of-the-century San Francisco are traced back to Sumerian devil creatures in this pilot for a horror series. (The show, to be called *Black Cloak*, never materialised, so the pilot

was given a theatrical release.) Superior make-up effects and a nifty HP Lovecraft-style atmosphere add power to the supernatural shocks, while future *Naked Gun* star Leslie Nielsen proves once again what a loss he was to straight melodrama. An above-average effort for all concerned.

Leslie Nielsen *Brett Kingsford* • Gilbert Green *Harvey Misbach* • Charles Bolender *Nikola* • Mark Richman [Peter Mark Richman] *Robert Vandenburg* • Judi Meredith *Evelyn Lang* • Werner Klemperer *Prof Malaki* ■ Dir Harvey Hart • Scr Barre Lyndon

Dark Journey　★★★ U

First World War spy drama
1937 · UK · BW · 80mins

Vivien Leigh runs a Stockholm dress shop during the First World War. In reality, though, she's a double agent working for the Allies. Complications ensue when she becomes emotionally involved with a German baron (the silkily threatening Conrad Veidt) who cottons on to the truth. Producer Alexander Korda brought out all the big guns for this spy drama: Victor Saville directs, Georges Périnal and Harry Stradling provide some beautiful photography, while Richard Addinsell supplies the score. Meticulously wrought tosh.

Conrad Veidt *Baron Karl Von Marwitz* • Vivien Leigh *Madeleine Goddard* • Joan Gardner *Lupita* • Anthony Bushell *Bob Carter* • Ursula Jeans *Gertrude* • Margery Pickard *Colette* • Eliot Makeham *Anatole* • Austin Trevor *Dr Muller* ■ Dir Victor Saville • Scr Arthur Wimperis, from a story by Lajos Biro

The Dark Light　★

Crime thriller　1951 · UK · BW · 66mins

Imagine *Shallow Grave* shot in a lighthouse with a cast of no-hopers and the budget of a public information film, and you'll have some idea of what this dismal Hammer offering is like. "Quota quickie" veteran Vernon Sewell gets matters off to a promising start as a desperate gang of bank robbers are rescued from the stormy sea by a lighthouse crew. By tossing away the dramatic possibilities of the claustrophobic setting, however, he is unable to sustain the tension as the crew begin scheming to keep the swag for themselves.

Albert Lieven *Mark* • David Greene *Johnny* • Norman MacOwan *Rigby* • Martin Benson *Luigi* • Catherine Blake *Linda* • Jack Stewart *Matt* ■ Dir/Scr Vernon Sewell

The Dark Mirror　★★★★ PG

Psychological mystery
1946 · US · BW · 81mins

Directed by Robert Siodmak , this is a near-classic thriller with Lew Ayres as a psychologist trying to discover which twin sister is a killer. Nunnally Johnson's script springs few real surprises, raiding the textbooks of Freud who was the John Grisham of the day (everybody took Freud to the pool at the Beverly Hills Hotel). Siodmak, who also made *The Spiral Staircase*, pulls out all the melodramatic stops with low-key lighting and weird camera angles. Dimitri Tiomkin's music, meanwhile, heaves like an ocean in a bad mood, and, as the two sisters, Olivia de

　　　U = SUITABLE FOR ALL　　Uc = SUITABLE FOR ALL, ESPECIALLY FOR YOUNG CHILDREN (VIDEO ONLY)　　PG = PARENTAL GUIDANCE

Havilland seems to be saying, "Bette Davis, eat your heart out." 🖵

Olivia de Havilland *Terry Collins/Ruth Collins* • Lew Ayres *Dr Scott Elliott* • Thomas Mitchell *Detective Stevenson* • Richard Long *Rusty* • Charles Evans *District Attorney Girard* ■ *Dir* Robert Siodmak • *Scr* Nunnally Johnson, from the novel by Vladimir Pozner • *Cinematographer* Milton Krasner

Dark of the Sun ★★ 15

Adventure   1967 · UK · Colour · 96mins

A tough colonial adventure, based on a Wilbur Smith novel that follows Rod Taylor and Jim Brown as they become entangled in the civil war in the Congo in 1960. Taylor is the man of no principle, until the script's sermonising gets to him, while Brown, as his buddy, plays the Congo native with a conscience. Kenneth More has a brief role as a drunken doctor and Yvette Mimieux is a French refugee and Taylor's love interest. Directed on location by Jack Cardiff, a former ace cameraman, the film's schoolboy heroics sit awkwardly beside its political rhetoric, but action fans will enjoy the all-stops-out finale. Contains some violence and swearing. 🖵

Rod Taylor *Captain Bruce Curry* • Yvette Mimieux *Claire* • Jim Brown *Sergeant Ruffo* • Kenneth More *Dr Wreid* • Peter Carsten *Henlein* • Olivier Despax *Surrier* ■ *Dir* Jack Cardiff • *Scr* Quentin Werty, Adrian Spies, from the novel by Wilbur A Smith

Dark Passage ★★ 15

Film noir thriller   1947 · US · BW · 106mins

Escaped convict Humphrey Bogart changes his appearance with plastic surgery and hides out with artist Lauren Bacall while he attempts to prove he is innocent of his wife's murder. The third Bogart–Bacall outing, written and directed by Delmer Daves and featuring an excellent supporting performance from Tom D'Andrea and an over-the-top one by Agnes Moorehead, is slick and efficient, yet disappointing. The first 40 minutes or so are ingeniously photographed from Bogart's subjective point of view, tantalisingly keeping us waiting for the star's appearance. Otherwise, though, the movie is a plodding affair. 🖵

Humphrey Bogart *Vincent Parry* • Lauren Bacall *Irene Jansen* • Bruce Bennett *Bob* • Agnes Moorehead *Madge Rapf* • Tom D'Andrea *Sam* • Clifton Young *Baker* ■ *Dir* Delmer Daves • *Scr* Delmer Daves, from the novel *Dark Passage* by David Goodis

The Dark Past ★★★ PG

Crime drama   1948 · US · BW · 71mins

A moody remake of 1939's *Blind Alley*, the melodrama about a demented thug holding the local psychologist hostage while the latter tries to talk the convict into reasoning out why he turned bad. It always was a good plot, and here skilled director Rudolph Maté brings light and shade (quite literally; he was a distinguished former cameraman, most notably on the silent classic *The Passion of Joan of Arc*) to bear on this once trail-blazing subject. A crew cut and highly strung William Holden makes a brave stab at the killer, but Lee J Cobb brings real Method intensity to the understanding

psychiatrist, played in the earlier version by Ralph Bellamy. 🖵

William Holden (1) *Al Walker* • Nina Foch *Betty* • Lee J Cobb *Dr Andrew Collins* • Adele Jergens *Laura Stevens* • Stephen Dunne *Owen Talbot* • Lois Maxwell *Ruth Collins* • Berry Kroeger *Mike* • Steven Geray *Professor Fred Linder* • Wilton Graff *Frank Stevens* • Robert Osterloh *Pete* ■ *Dir* Rudolph Maté • *Scr* Philip MacDonald, Michael Blankfort, Albert Duffy, Malvin Wald, Oscar Saul, from the play *Blind Alley* by James Warwick

Dark Places ★★

Horror   1973 · UK · Colour · 90mins

Asylum administrator Robert Hardy inherits a supposedly haunted mansion where some grisly deaths occurred and a great deal of money is hidden. Psychiatrist Christopher Lee and his sister, Joan Collins, plot to cheat him out of his estate, despite the murderous spiritual presence of its previous owner. Leaden sub-Hammer horror, directed with little flair by veteran Don Sharp and containing inert performances across the board.

Christopher Lee *Dr Mandeville* • Joan Collins *Sarah* • Robert Hardy *Edward/Andrew* • Herbert Lom *Prescott* • Jane Birkin *Alta* • Carleton Hobbs *Old Marr* ■ *Dir* Don Sharp • *Scr* Ed Brennan, Joseph Van Winkle

Dark Planet ★★ 15

Science-fiction   1997 · US · Colour · 92mins

"Dark" is an appropriate word for this cheap science-fiction effort, in which the lighting is so bad it's hard to determine what's happening. On a deep space mission, Michael York and Harley Jane Kozak represent two sides at war on Earth who have called a truce in order to find the eponymous planet, which may provide sanctuary for the survivors of their dying world. Slow and shabby, the film still generates interest thanks to decent performances from most of the cast, while the characters are more developed than usual. Contains some swearing, violence and sexual references. 🖵

Paul Mercurio *Anson Hawke* • Harley Jane Kozak *Commander Brendan* • Michael York *Commander Winter* • Maria Ford *Salera* • Ed O'Ross *Byron* ■ *Dir* Albert Magnoli • *Scr* SO Lee, J Reifel

The Dark Road ★★

Drama   1948 · UK · BW · 74mins

This was Alfred Goulding's first feature after directing Laurel and Hardy in *A Chump at Oxford* in 1940. With his background in comedies, he struggles with this grim tale tracing the life and crimes of a surly borstal boy. To his credit, he achieves a certain cheap realism and catches the argot of postwar criminality. But neither Charles Stuart, as the delinquent who drifts from petty larceny to jewel robbery, nor Joyce Linden, as the girl he exploits, are up to the task.

Charles Stuart *Sidney Robertson* • Joyce Linden *Ann* ■ *Dir* Alfred Goulding

Dark Secrets ★★★

Comedy thriller   1995 · US · Colour · 83mins

The horror comedy *A Bucket of Blood* is one of Roger Corman's best-loved B movies, thanks largely to its sly script

that pokes fun at the beatnik scene of the fifties. Corman is behind this remake as well, as co-executive producer, and its satirical jibes at the trendy nineties art scene are equally spot on. Anthony Michael Hall is perfectly cast as the nerdy artist whose use of corpses in his work brings him a new audience. Justine Bateman is the more recognisable face, but look out too for cult icons Paul Bartel and Mink Stole. Contains violence and nudity.

Anthony Michael Hall *Walter Paisley* • Justine Bateman *Carla* • Shadoe Stevens *Maxwell Brock* • Sam Lloyd *Leonard Desantis* • Jesse D Goins *Art* • Kin Shriner *Lou* • Paul Bartel *Older man* • Mink Stole *Older woman* ■ *Dir* Michael James McDonald • *Scr* Brendan Broderick, Charles B Griffith

The Dark Side of the Heart ★★★

Romance   1992 · Arg/Can · Colour · 127mins

Eliseo Subiela confirms his reputation as Argentina's most ambitious auteur with this literate study of lust, death, poetry and the true value of money. Weary of his art, Dario Grandinetti writes only when he needs cash, and then only accepts commissions from a lovesick chef. His unworldliness stands in stark contrast to the work ethic of prostitute Sandra Bellesteros, yet together they enjoy a passionate relationship. With the dialogue containing lengthy passages of verse, this could easily have become precious, yet Subiela shrewdly uses sentiment and sensuality to retain the film's humanity. In Spanish with English subtitles.

Dario Grandinetti *Oliverio* • Sandra Ballesteros *Ana* • Nacha Guevara *Muerte* • AndréMelançon *Erik* ■ *Dir/Scr* Eliseo Subiela

Dark Star ★★★★

Science-fiction   1974 · US · Colour · 82mins

In director John Carpenter's impressive feature debut, hippie spacemen fight boredom on a 20-year mission to seek out and destroy unstable planets. Produced as a film project at the University of Southern California for just $60,000, this sly parody begins as a satire on *2001: a Space Odyssey*. However, it quickly moves into original territory as the cabin-fevered crew cope with a vicious alien stowaway, a nagging computer and a thermo-nuclear device that's all set to explode. Witty, profound and cleverly scored by Carpenter with a selection of electronic country and western tunes, this cult favourite was co-written and cast member Dan O'Bannon, who later worked on *Alien*.

Brian Narelle *Doolittle* • Andreijah Pahich *Talby* • Carl Duniholm *Boiler* • Dan O'Bannon *Pinback* • Joe Sanders *Powell* ■ *Dir* John Carpenter • *Scr* John Carpenter, Dan O'Bannon

Dark Summer ★★ 12

Drama   1994 · UK · Colour · 70mins

As the familiar Scouse skyline recedes, to be replaced by sobering images of urban decay, there's a glimmer that Charles Teton's debut feature is going to deal with the real Liverpool, rather than the melodramatised *Brookside* version. But the social implications of

the relationship between black labourer Steve Ako and Joeline Garnier-Joel, his white boss's daughter, are soon forgotten, as Ako embarks on a boxing career that will cost him everything. Director Teton's advertising background is proclaimed in almost every self-consciously grubby shot. His grasp of pacing and plot is less assured, while the performances are more willing than able.

Steve Ako *Abraham Wilson* • Joeline Garnier-Joel *Jess Shepherd* • Bernie Deasy *Amateur coach* • Chris Darwin *Alan Shepherd* • Dermott Mulholland ■ *Dir* Charles Teton • *Scr* Charles Teton, with additional material from Bernie Deasy, Steve Cheers, Bernd Lubke

Dark Tide ★★ 18

Erotic thriller   1993 · US · Colour · 89mins

In the Philippines, Brigitte Bako joins her husband Chris Sarandon at his business, which happens to be capturing poisonous sea snakes. Her presence causes studly Richard Tyson to arrange an "accident". Everyone in this movie seems to realise it's nothing more than junk, which makes it kind of fun – but you may wonder how the many sea snakes manage to hiss under water. 🖵

Brigitte Bako *Andi* • Chris Sarandon *Tim* • Richard Tyson *Dak* ■ *Dir* Luca Bercovici • *Scr* Robert L Levy, Sam Bernard

Dark Tower ★ 18

Supernatural horror thriller
1989 · US · Colour · 91mins

Oscar Wilde's Lady Bracknell would have summed up Michael Moriarty's career thus: "To make one dire horror movie may be regarded as a misfortune; to make two, nay three, looks like carelessness." On probation from *A Return to Salem's Lot* and *It's Alive III*, Moriarty plays an investigator called in when a supernatural force starts bumping off people in a skyscraper. Filmed in Barcelona, this appalling mix of *Omen*-style operatic deaths and *Poltergeist* scares ran into production problems, and Hammer horror veteran Freddie Francis was replaced as director. The cast weren't so lucky, though. 🖵

Michael Moriarty *Dennis Randall* • Jenny Agutter *Carolyn Page* • Carol Lynley *Tilly Ambrose* • Theodore Bikel *Dr Max Gold* • Anne Lockhart *Elaine* • Kevin McCarthy *Sergie* ■ *Dir* Freddie Francis • *Scr* Robert J Avrech, Ken Wiederhorn, Ken Blackwell, from a story by Robert J Avrech

Dark Victory ★★★★ PG

Melodrama   1939 · US · BW · 100mins

Possibly the best terminal illness movie prior to *Love Story*, and easily surpassing that tear-jerker in style, this Bette Davis vehicle boasts one of her best performances as heiress Judith Traherne, tragically stricken with a brain tumour. The condition means that she will go blind before dying, and so paves the way for a death scene so memorably heart-rending (aided by a knockout Max Steiner score which the star loathed) that it took Davis to the number one female movie star slot in the US. All of those classy Warner Bros production values are well in evidence, hiding the fact that this is really a load of old codswallop.

Humphrey Bogart performs as though he knows he's been miscast.

Bette Davis *Judith Traherne* • George Brent *Dr Frederick Steele* • Humphrey Bogart *Michael O'Leary* • Geraldine Fitzgerald *Ann King* • Ronald Reagan *Alec Hamin* • Henry Travers *Dr Parsons* • Cora Witherspoon *Carrie Spottswood* • Virginia Brissac *Martha* ■ *Dir* Edmund Goulding • *Scr* Casey Robinson, from the play by George Emerson Brewer Jr, Bertram Bloch

Dark Waters ★★ U

Drama 1944 · US · BW · 85mins

Merle Oberon lends her exotic allure to this Andre De Toth-directed melodrama set in the Louisiana bayou. Oberon plays an heiress, traumatised by the shipping accident in which her parents died, while Thomas Mitchell plays the malcontent who, sensing her incipient madness, hopes to push her over the edge and collect the money. Franchot Tone is the kindly medic who also takes a fancy to his patient. It's another variation on *Gaslight*, juicily acted when the script allows, with some good moments.

Merle Oberon *Leslie Calvin* • Franchot Tone *Dr George Grover* • Thomas Mitchell *Mr Sydney* • Fay Bainter *Aunt Emily* • John Qualen *Uncle Norbert* • Elisha Cook Jr *Cleeve* • Rex Ingram *Pearson Jackson* ■ *Dir* Andre De Toth • *Scr* Joan Harrison, Marian Cockrell, Arthur Horman, from the novel Frank Cockrell, Marian Cockrell

Dark Waters ★★ 18

Horror 1993 · Rus/Ukr · Colour · 93mins

A tepid chiller relating the quest of British girl Louise Salter to discover the secrets of a mysterious sect on a Russian island that's somehow linked to her late father. Zombie nuns and malevolent forces spring into action in this beautifully photographed but pretentious horror, strangely bereft of the jolts and gore that are the usual currency of the genre. A good attempt by director Mariano Baino to wed classic Italian fantasy imagery within a dreamy, atmospheric landscape, but the ultimate result is an awkwardly weird wash-out. Russian dialogue dubbed into English.

Louise Salter *Elizabeth* • Venera Simmons • Maria Kapnist ■ *Dir* Mariano Baino • *Scr* Mariano Baino, Andrew Bark

The Dark Wind ★★★ 15

Crime mystery 1991 · US · Colour · 106mins

Rookie native American cop Lou Diamond Phillips tracks down a group of murderous drug dealers operating on the Navajo reservations in this intermittently fascinating adaptation of Tony Hillerman's novel. Despite much artistic licence taken with the book's characters, director Errol Morris makes superb use of the magnificent Arizona and New Mexico locations and gives this unusual thriller an intensely brooding atmosphere. Although Indian leaders objected to the ancient rites depicted, they're an intriguing aspect which sets the film apart from other similarly-styled cop adventures.

Lou Diamond Phillips *Officer Jim Chee* • Fred Ward *Lieutenant Joe Leaphorn* • Gary Farmer *Sheriff Albert "Cowboy" Dashee* • John Karlen *Jake West* • Lance Baker *Mr Archer* • Gary

Basaraba *Larry* ■ *Dir* Errol Morris • *Scr* Eric Bergren, Neal Jimenez, Mark Horowitz, from the novel by Tony Hillerman

Darkbreed ★★★ 18

Science-fiction horror 1996 · US · Colour · 91mins

Jack Scalia wages a one-man war against an alien invasion force in a mindlessly enjoyable blend of *The X-Files*, *The Invaders* and *The A-Team*. The former astronaut learns Earth is about to be taken over by the dark breed, a deadly race of parasites, so he embarks on a mission to destroy a canister containing their eggs. Wall-to-wall violence, action and mayhem ensue in a cliché-ridden plot which contains the odd flash of impressive special effects. Reliable B-movie action man Scalia gives this thriller a touch of extra class. Contains violence, and some swearing.

Jack Scalia *Nicholas Saxon* • Donna W Scott *Deborah* • Jonathan Banks *Joseph Shay* • Robin Curtis *Marian* ■ *Dir* Richard Pepin • *Scr* Richard Preston Jr

The Darker Side of Terror ★ 15

Horror 1979 · US · Colour · 91mins

Research scientist Robert Forster doesn't get the important job he was angling for, so he clones himself to prove he was right for the appointment. Unfortunately, his trouble-making duplicate sets his sights on seducing his creator's wife (Adrienne Barbeau). A deranged TV movie with little to offer in the thrill or surprise departments, though there is plenty to scoff at in disbelief. Director Gus Trikonis, responsible for the far better *Nashville Girl* and *The Evil*, was once married to Goldie Hawn.

Robert Forster *Prof Paul Corwin/Clone* • Adrienne Barbeau *Margaret* • Ray Milland *Prof Meredith* • John Lehne *Lt Merholz* • David Sheiner *Prof Hillstrom* ■ *Dir* Gus Trikonis • *Scr* John Herman Shaner, Al Ramrus

Darker than Amber ★★

Crime thriller 1970 · US · Colour · 97mins

Here's thriller writer John D MacDonald's thick-ear detective Travis McGee in his only cinematic outing, (though a series was mooted) incarnated by likeable Rod Taylor, and glossily filmed on exotic Caribbean and Miami locations. Director Robert Clouse proved to have a talent for globetrotting violence, as shown here, fetching up eventually in Hong Kong as director of Bruce Lee's *Enter the Dragon*, and Jackie Chan and Cynthia Rothrock vehicles. Watch for Jane Russell's penultimate screen appearance.

Rod Taylor *Travis McGee* • Suzy Kendall *Vangie/Merrimay* • Theodore Bikel *Meyer* • Jane Russell *Alabama Tiger* • James Booth *Burk* ■ *Dir* Robert Clouse • *Scr* Ed Waters, from the novel by John D MacDonald

The Darkest Light ★★ 12

Drama 1999 · UK · Colour · 93mins

This post-millennial downer outlines the never-ending misfortunes of Stephen Dillane and Kerry Fox's Yorkshire family. It's only when their daughter (Keri Arnold) and her Indian

schoolmate think they've seen a vision of the Virgin Mary on the moors that Beaufoy's contemplation on the true meaning of faith gathers momentum.,The film is well acted, with both the Christian and Hindu religions used in interesting conceptual ways – especially with regard to what's supposed to be an uplifting ending. The subject matter is so depressing, however, that even those with patience to wallow in abject misery will find it a long haul. Contains swearing.

Keri Arnold *Catherine* • Stephen Dillane *Tom* • Kerry Fox *Sue* • Kavita Sungha *Uma* • Jason Walton *Matthew* • Nisha K Nayar *Nisha* • Nicholas Hope *Father Mark* ■ *Dir* Simon Beaufoy, Bille Eltringham • *Scr* Simon Beaufoy

Darklands ★★★ 18

Horror thriller 1996 · UK · Colour · 86mins

Although it's a virtual rip-off of *The Wicker Man*, this shocker is an impressively dark and reasonably frightening tale of pagan ritual and human sacrifice. Journalist Craig Fairbrass investigates a series of killings in south Wales and learns, too late, that he has a terrifying part to play in blood-soaked rites aimed at regenerating an ancient religion. While *Eastenders* star Fairbrass lacks the range to milk his part for every shaded nuance – Julian Richards's feature debut proves the spirit of Hammer lives on. Contains swearing, nudity and violence.

Craig Fairbrass *Frazer Truick* • Rowena King *Rachel Morris* • Jon Finch *David Keller* • David Duffy *Carver* • Roger Nott *Dennis Cox* • Richard Lynch *Salvy* • Nicola Branson *Becky* ■ *Dir/Scr* Julian Richards

Darkman ★★★★ 18

Fantasy horror 1990 · US · Colour · 91mins

Independent director Sam Raimi's first studio movie is a splashy amalgam of *The Phantom of the Opera* and *Doctor X*, with a perfectly cast Liam Neeson donning synthetic flesh masks to take revenge on the mob who disfigured him. Pathos and tragedy are always lurking beneath the horrific surface of the *Evil Dead* creator's take on classic thirties *Grand Guignol*, given a nifty nineties spin by exaggerated camera moves and psychedelic visuals. A tasty buffet of gothic moodiness, startling make-up effects and expressionistic artifice, this is Raimi on vibrant virtuoso form. Contains swearing and violence. **DVD**

Liam Neeson *Peyton Westlake/Darkman* • Frances McDormand *Julie Hastings* • Colin Friels *Louis Strack Jr* • Larry Drake *Robert G Durant* • Nelson Mashita *Yakitito* • Jessie Lawrence Ferguson *Eddie Black* • Rafael H Robledo *Rudy Guzman* • Danny Hicks *Skip* • Theodore Raimi *Rick* ■ *Dir* Sam Raimi • *Scr* Chuck Pfarrer, Sam Raimi, Ivan Raimi, Daniel Goldin, Joshua Goldin, from a story by Sam Raimi • *Cinematographer* Bill Pope

Darkman II – the Return of Durant ★★★ 18

Fantasy horror 1995 · US · Colour · 88mins

This direct-to-video sequel is equally as dynamic and fast-paced as its predecessor, thanks to director Bradford May taking more than a few leaves out of the Sam Raimi style book. Arnold Vosloo takes over from

Liam Neeson as the synthetic mask-wearing Dr Peyton Westlake.The formula is still forties pulp fiction with a twist of black comedy and some superior special effects, but it all works like a charm for an effective reprise. *Darkman III: Die Darkman Die* followed in 1996.

Arnold Vosloo *Dr Peyton Westlake/Darkman* • Larry Drake *Robert G Durant* • Renee O'Connor *Laurie Brinkman* • Kim Delaney *Jill Randall* • Lawrence Dane *Dr Alfred Hathaway* • Jesse Collins *Dr David Brinkman* • David Ferry *Eddie* ■ *Dir* Bradford May • *Scr* Steve McKay, from a story by Robert Eisele, from characters created by Sam Raimi,

Darkness before Dawn ★★★ 15

Drama based on a true story 1992 · US · Colour · 92mins

Stephen Lang – probably best-known for playing the gay leader in *Last Exit to Brooklyn* – portrays a recovering drug addict, who finds inspiration in the strength of a woman (Meredith Baxter of *Family Ties* fame) working at the clinic that is treating him. Until, that is, he discovers that her troubles are worse than his. Not a load of laughs in this TV movie, but sufficient dramatic interest. Contains drug abuse.

Meredith Baxter *Mary Ann Thompson* • Stephen Lang *Guy Grand* ■ *Dir* John Patterson • *Scr* Karen Hall

Darkness Falls ★ 15

Psychological thriller 1998 · UK · Colour · 88mins

Sherilyn Fenn's career hasn't exactly thrived since *Twin Peaks*, so one can understand her taking any old role. However, what *Nil by Mouth* star Ray Winstone is doing in a drama that's not only poorly directed but also so badly acted it makes the cast of *Crossroads* look like Royal Shakespeare Company players is anybody's guess. Winstone plays John, a man teetering on the edge of insanity following a car crash which has left his pregnant wife in a coma. Tricking his way into the Isle of Man home of obnoxious businessman Tim Dutton and his neglected wife (Fenn), Winstone holds them at gunpoint. There are some daft subplots involving clunkingly awful roles for Oliver Tobias and Anita Dobson, but long before those two natural familiar TV faces turn up you'll have left the cinema in disgust. Contains swearing.

Sherilyn Fenn *Sally Driscoll* • Ray Winstone *John Barrett* • Tim Dutton *Mark Driscoll* • Anita Dobson *Mrs Hayter* • Bryan Pringle *Clive Hayter* • Robin McCaffrey *Jane Barrett* • Michael Praed *Hit man* • Oliver Tobias *Simpson* ■ *Dir* Gerry Lively • *Scr* John Howlett, from the play *Dangerous Obsession* by NJ Crisp

Darkness in Tallinn ★★★★ 15

Crime thriller 1993 · Fin/Est · BW and Colour · 95mins

If you can excuse the transition from monochrome to colour and Ilkka Jarvilaturi's determination to include every conceivable directorial flourish, then you're in for a treat with this Estonian heist movie. As the power-

station worker persuaded by his pregnant wife to assist in the theft of the national treasury on its return from safe-keeping in Paris, Ivo Uukkivi gives a wonderfully bemused performance that gains a harder edge as the blood begins to flow. But this isn't just a quirky film noir. It's also a fascinating portrait of a long-oppressed country still not sure of its fate despite regaining independence. Produced with backing from the United States and Sweden. In Estonian and Russian with English subtitles..
▣

Ivo Uukkivi *Toivo* • Milena Gulbe *Maria* • Monika Mager *Terje* • Enn Klooren *Mihhail "Misha"* • Vaino Laes *Andres* ■ *Dir* Ilkka Jarvilaturi • *Scr* Paul Kolsby

Darling ★★★★ 15
Drama   1965 · UK · BW · 121mins

At every turn of his Oscar-winning script, Frederic Raphael invites us to admire just how clever he's been in dissecting the shallowness of celebrity and the gullibility of the public. Yet no matter how much we want to resist falling under the spell of such a self-congratulatory piece of work, there's no denying that this is both an astute snapshot of a moment in time and a wicked insight into the national character that still has relevance today. Julie Christie thoroughly merited her Oscar as the immoral starlet hellbent on fame and Dirk Bogarde is equally splendid. ▣

Laurence Harvey *Miles Brand* • Dirk Bogarde *Robert Gold* • Julie Christie *Diana Scott* • Roland Curram *Malcolm* • José-Luis De Villalonga *Cesare* • Alex Scott *Sean Martin* ■ *Dir* John Schlesinger • *Scr* Frederic Raphael, from a story by Frederic Raphael, John Schlesinger, Joseph Janni

Darling, How Could You! ★★
Comedy   1951 · US · BW · 95mins

This adaptation based on Gloria Swanson's follow-up to *Sunset Boulevard*. When she refused to test for the role, however, it was given to Joan Fontaine. Quickly shot using the Washington Square sets left over from *The Heiress*, this tale of an imaginative daughter who erroneously thinks her mother is having an affair is not one of director Mitchell Leisen's better efforts. Despite some very funny lines, the pace is too lethargic, while the playing is more cute than charming.

Joan Fontaine *Alice Grey* • John Lund *Dr Robert Grey* • Mona Freeman *Amy* • Peter Hanson *Dr Steve Clark* • David Stollery *Cosmo* • Virginia Farmer *Fanny* ■ *Dir* Mitchell Leisen • *Scr* Dodie Smith, Lesser Samuels, from the play *Alice-Sit-by-the-Fire* by JM Barrie

Darling Lili ★★★ U
Spy drama   1970 · US · Colour · 135mins

An under-rated and utterly charming valentine from director Blake Edwards to his wife, Julie Andrews, who takes the lead role of a Mata Hari-type figure in this lengthy First World War charade. The star is marvellously supported by dashing air ace Rock Hudson and British satirist Lance Percival in his best film role. The film was shot by *Red River* cinematographer Russell Harlan, and also boasts some marvellous aerial dogfight sequences.

It does take itself rather too seriously at times, though, and non-Andrews fans should avoid it.

Julie Andrews *Lili Smith* • Rock Hudson *Major William Larrabee* • Jeremy Kemp *Kurt von Ruger* • Lance Percival *TC* • Michael Witney *Youngblood Carson* • Jacques Marin *Major Duvalle* • André Maranne *Lt Liggett* • Gloria Paul *Suzette* • Bernard Kay *Bedford* • Doreen Keogh *Emma* ■ *Dir* Blake Edwards • *Scr* Blake Edwards, William Peter Blatty

D'Artagnan's Daughter ★★★ 15
Period adventure   1994 · Fr · Colour · 124mins

Costume adventures might not be what we expect from Bertrand Tavernier, but his enthusiasm for this spirited romp is evident in the pace and panache of his direction. Inevitably building on Richard Lester's musketeers trilogy, Tavernier also draws on the playful tone of such Gérard Philipe adventures as *Fanfan la Tulipe*, as Sophie Marceau leaves her convent to coax father Philippe Noiret out of retirement in order to save Louis XIV's throne. With Sami Frey and Charlotte Kady providing disdainful villainy, this is huge fun, but prone to longueurs and incongruous slapstick. In French with English subtitles. Contains violence and nudity. ▣

Sophie Marceau *Eloise* • Philippe Noiret *D'Artagnan* • Claude Rich *Duke of Crassac* • Sami Frey *Aramis* • Jean-Luc Bideau *Athos* • Raoul Billerey *Porthos* • Charlotte Kady *Scarlet woman* • Nils Tavernier *Quentin* ■ *Dir* Bertrand Tavernier • *Scr* Michel Leviant

The Darwin Adventure ★★ U
Biography   1972 · UK · Colour · 90mins

A biopic about Charles Darwin, whose voyages to South America and the Galapagos Islands aboard HMS *Beagle* fuelled his theory of natural selection, a theory that shocked the religious establishment of the Victorian world. In a subject far more suited to the television drama or mini-series, this is a sketchy effort that convinces us of Darwin's importance but turns his romantic life into soap opera. Ian Richardson, meanwhile, plays the *Beagle*'s skipper as a fanatical Captain Nemo, who argues with Darwin simply so the audience can understand the issues.

Nicholas Clay *Charles Darwin* • Susan Macready *Emma Wedgewood* • Ian Richardson *Captain Fitzroy* • Robert Flemyng *Professor Henslow* ■ *Dir* Jack Couffer • *Scr* William Fairchild, from a story by Jack Couffer, Max Bella

DARYL ★★★ PG
Science-fiction drama
1985 · US · Colour · 95mins

Although highly derivative of *ET*, *WarGames* and more, this New Age fairy tale is a charming, lightweight diversion about a Florida couple whose lives are transformed after fostering a young boy suffering from what they believe to be amnesia. When they learn DARYL actually stands for Data Analysing Robot Youth Lifeform, the real drama unfolds as they fight to stop his termination by Pentagon intelligence agents. Well acted and well written, considering it has such a formula sci-fi plot, director Simon

Wincer's popcorn picture with heart echoes his later success with *Free Willy*. Perfect family viewing. ▣

Mary Beth Hurt *Joyce Richardson* • Michael McKean *Andy Richardson* • Barret Oliver *Daryl* • Colleen Camp *Elaine Fox* • Kathryn Walker *Ellen Lamb* • Josef Sommer *Dr Jeffrey Stewart* ■ *Dir* Simon Wincer • *Scr* David Ambrose, Allan Scott, Jeffrey Ellis

A Date with a Lonely Girl ★★
Comedy drama   1971 · US · Colour · 89mins

Despite boasting Herbert Ross (*The Turning Point*, *Steel Magnolias*) as the director and a screenplay by producer Peter Hyams (who directed the Schwarznegger film *End of Days*), this is a bit of a disappointment. It's a flabby tale of a naive country girl seeking happiness – and not finding it – in Chicago. The lovely Candice Bergen is in the lead, with James Caan playing one of her lovers. This is also known as *TR Baskin*.

Candice Bergen *TR Baskin* • Peter Boyle *Jack Mitchell* • James Caan *Larry Moore* • Marcia Rodd *Dayle* • Erin O'Reilly *Kathy* • Howard Platt *Arthur* • William Wise *Gary* ■ *Dir* Herbert Ross • *Scr* Peter Hyams

A Date with Judy ★★★ U
Musical comedy 1948 · US · Colour · 113mins

An utterly charming musical from MGM's greatest period, though it may be a little overlong and twee for today's tastes. Sweet Jane Powell plays the title role, but Richard Thorpe's film also gives the young and oh-so-beautiful Elizabeth Taylor a chance to shine. Wallace Beery is top-billed, but he was near the end of this life and Technicolor wasn't kind to him. Still, at least he gets to perform with Carmen Miranda. The song *It's a Most Unusual Day* was a huge hit.

Wallace Beery *Melvin R Foster* • Jane Powell *Judy Foster* • Elizabeth Taylor *Carol Pringle* • Carmen Miranda *Rosita Conchellas* • Xavier Cugat *Cugat* • Robert Stack *Stephen Andrews* ■ *Dir* Richard Thorpe • *Scr* Dorothy Cooper, Dorothy Kingsley, Aleen Leslie

A Date with the Falcon ★★
Crime drama   1941 · US · BW · 63mins

This was the second film in the 16-episode *Falcon* series, with which RKO followed their *Saint* movies. (Leslie Charteris sued the studio because of the unmistakable similarities between the characters.). Here the suave investigator (George Sanders) and his nervy sidekick (Allen Jenkins) get involved in the case of a kidnapped scientist. Typical of the plethora of "gentleman sleuth" second features popular in the thirties and forties, it's of little interest now, though Sanders is always a pleasure to watch. He got bored with the Falcon after the first three films and handed the role over to his real-life brother, Tom Conway.

George Sanders *Falcon* • Wendy Barrie *Helen Reed* • James Gleason *O'Hara* • Allen Jenkins *Goldy* • Mona Maris *Rita Mara* • Victor Kilian *Max* ■ *Dir* Irving Reis • *Scr* Lynn Root, Frank Fenton, from the character created by Michael Arlen

Date with an Angel ★★ PG
Fantasy comedy romance
1987 · US · Colour · 100mins

Musician Michael E Knight saves a beautiful angel (Emmanuelle Béart) from drowning in a swimming pool. He then starts wondering if he should go ahead with his marriage to Phoebe Cates, the daughter of a cosmetics tycoon (David Dukes) who tries to make Béart his new cover girl. As wet as the nearly-drowned angel's wings, this otherworldly tosh marked an inauspicious American debut for French actress Béart after the success of *Manon des Sources*. ▣

Michael E Knight *Jim Sanders* • Phoebe Cates *Patty Winston* • Emmanuelle Béart *Angel* • David Dukes *Ed Winston* • Phil Brock *George* • Albert Macklin *Don* • Peter Kowanko [Pete Kowanko] *Rex* ■ *Dir/Scr* Tom McLoughlin

Daughter of Darkness ★★
Crime drama   1948 · UK · BW · 91mins

This brooding, violent melodrama concerns an Irish servant girl (Siobhan McKenna) who is not only a nymphomaniac, but also a psychopathic killer given to murdering her admirers. Directed by Lance Comfort, this British offering is an opportunity to see McKenna, one of the most compelling of Irish stage actresses, portraying a maniac with full-blooded commitment. The picture has little else to recommend it, though the young Honor Blackman can be spotted along with Maxwell Reed, George Thorpe and Barry Morse.

Anne Crawford *Bess Stanforth* • Maxwell Reed *Dan* • Siobhan McKenna *Emily Beaudine* • George Thorpe *Mr Tallent* • Barry Morse *Robert Stanforth* • Liam Redmond *Father Cocoran* • Honor Blackman *Julie Tallent* ■ *Dir* Lance Comfort • *Scr* Max Catto, from his play *They Walk Alone*

Daughter of Darkness ★★ 18
Horror   1990 · US · Colour · 89mins

Was Mia Sara's long-lost father Dracula? No such luck, in this rather uninspired TV movie from *Re-Animator* director Stuart Gordon. Instead, dad turns out to be kindly vampire Anthony Perkins, giving another off-the-wall performance, who bids to save her from a cult of bloodsuckers. Lacking the full-bodied grossness of Gordon's HP Lovecraft-based sagas, this film has the director relying on pacing and atmosphere for tension. But the irrational script scuppers any attempt at cohesion. Nice Romanian locations and a few good special effects may please the less particular. Contains violence. ▣

Mia Sara *Cathy Stevens* • Robert Reynolds *Grigore Petrescu* • Anthony Perkins *Anton Crainic* • Jack Coleman *Jack Devlin* • Dezso Garas *Max* • Erika Bodnar *Nicole* ■ *Dir* Stuart Gordon • *Scr* Andrew Laskos

Daughter of Dr Jekyll ★
Horror   1957 · US · BW · 69mins

Dr Jekyll doesn't actually appear in this unusual take on the gothic classic. Instead, the film tells of his less well-known daughter, who, upon landing in England to claim her father's inheritance, is blamed for a series of grisly murders. The result is a

hotchpotch of vampire, werewolf and Jekyll-and-Hyde elements, all searching in vain for a coherent storyline. Shot not at a studio but in an authentic crumbling mansion in the suburbs of Hollywood, this is a masterclass of abysmal acting.

John Agar *George Hastings* • Gloria Talbott *Janet Smith* • Arthur Shields *Dr Lomas* • John Dierkes *Jacob* • Martha Wentworth *Mrs Merchant* ■ *Dir* Edgar G Ulmer • *Scr* Jack Pollexfen

The Daughter of Rosie O'Grady ★★★ U

Musical comedy 1950 · US · Colour · 103mins

An unpretentious, charming Warner Bros period musical (Betty Grable had appeared in Fox's *Sweet Rosie O'Grady* in 1943) with an attractive cast, headed by June Haver, a former Fox blonde who married Fred MacMurray and whose talent and appeal tend to be forgotten nowadays. Debonair singer Gordon MacRae and talented dancer Gene Nelson provide solid support, but look out for that young teenager: it's Debbie Reynolds, making her movie musical debut.

June Haver *Patricia O'Grady* • Gordon MacRae *Tony Pastor* • James Barton *Dennis O'Grady* • Debbie Reynolds *Maureen O'Grady* • SZ "Cuddles" Sakall [SZ Sakall] *Miklos Teretzky* • Gene Nelson *Doug Martin* • Sean McClory *James Moore* • Marsha Jones *Katie O'Grady* ■ *Dir* David Butler • *Scr* Jack Rose, Melville Shavelson, Peter Milne, from a story by Jack Rose, Melville Shavelson • *Music Director* Ray Heindorf

Daughter of the Nile ★★★ PG

Drama 1987 · Tai · Colour · 83mins

The least typical entry in Hou Hsiao-hsien's filmography, this Taipei tale of family in-fighting and social frustration dazzles with its urban iconography – the neon signs, the designer clothes, the blaring pop music and the Japanese time-travel comic books that keep schoolgirl Yang Lin sane, as she tries to tend house, hold down a fast-food job and prevent her cop father and gangster brother from tearing each other apart. But Hou's assured sense of composition and rhythm remains unchanged, as he blends wit with warmth in exploring both the complex web of relationships and the ambitions that drive his superbly realised characters. In Mandarin and Hokkien with English subtitles.

Yang Lin *Lin Hsiao-yang* • Kao Jai *Lin Hsiao-fang* • Yang Fan *Ah-sang* ■ *Dir* Hou Hsiao-Hsien • *Scr* Zhu Tianwen

Daughters Courageous ★★★

Drama 1939 · US · BW · 106mins

Wandering Claude Rains returns to his cosy home town just in time to stop wife Fay Bainter marrying Donald Crisp and to deal with daughter Priscilla Lane's engagement to John Garfield. Put over with fluent ease, this sentimental and lightweight movie is almost as charming as its blockbusting predecessor, *Four Daughters*, which had made an instant star of Warner Bros newcomer Garfield the previous year. Rushing to capitalise on that

success, the studio recycled the formula, re-employing the same director (Michael Curtiz) and cast.

Claude Rains *Jim Masters* • John Garfield *Gabriel Lopez* • Jeffrey Lynn *Johnny Heming* • Fay Bainter *Nan Masters* • Donald Crisp *Sam Sloane* • May Robson *Penny* • Frank McHugh *George* • Dick Foran *Eddie Moore* • George Humbert *Manuel Lopez* • Berton Churchill *Judge Hornsby* • Priscilla Lane *Buff Masters* • Rosemary Lane *Tinka Masters* • Lola Lane *Linda Masters* ■ *Dir* Michael Curtiz • *Scr* Julius J Epstein, Philip C Epstein, from the play *Fly Away Home* by Irving White, Dorothy Bennett

Daughters of Darkness ★★★★ 18

Horror 1970 · Bel/Fr/W Ger · Colour · 95mins

The legend of Elizabeth Bathory (who Hammer lionised in *Countess Dracula*) provides the inspiration for this lyrically erotic, arthouse shocker, expertly directed by the Belgian Harry Kümel. Delphine Seyrig is the well-preserved *haute couture* vampire who insinuates her evil self on an unsuspecting honeymoon couple at a luxurious seaside hotel in Ostend. Before long the husband is sadistically killed by the immortal beauty and his wife becomes Bathory's lesbian lover. Explicitly sexual and violent, the haunting atmosphere, Seyrig's brilliant performance and the always striking imagery make this European chiller a stunning masterwork. A French language film. ▭

Delphine Seyrig *Countess Bathory* • Daniele Ouimet *Valerie* • John Karlen *Stefan Chiltern* • Andrea Rau *Ilona Harczy* ■ *Dir* Harry Kümel • *Scr* Harry Kümel, Pierre Drouot, JJ Amiel • *Cinematographer* Van Der Enden

Daughters of Satan ★

Horror 1972 · US · Colour

A bottom-of-the-barrel horror, notable only for putting future *Magnum PI* star Tom Selleck on the road to fame. He's an art collector in Manila whose wife buys a painting of three witches being burned at the stake and gradually becomes possessed by the one she resembles. Terrible dialogue and soap-opera dramatics undo any attempt to chill the bone.

Tom Selleck *James Robertson* • Barra Grant *Chris Robertson* • Tani Phelps Guthrie [Tani Guthrie] *Kitty Duarte* • Vic Silayan *Dr Dangal* ■ *Dir* Hollingsworth Morse • *Scr* John C Higgins, from a story by John Bushelman

Daughters of the Dust ★★★★ PG

Experimental period drama 1991 · US · Colour · 107mins

Completed over several years, Julie Dash's low-budget feature debut is a poetic tribute to African culture, the oral tradition and the spirit of the Gullah people, who owe their descent to the freed slaves who settled on the islands off the coasts of South Carolina and Georgia. Set in 1902, the film uses a gathering that precedes the mainland odyssey of five women to explore questions of race, sex and family as well as nationality and exile. It's the imagery that most impresses, though, with the naturally-lit colours given a sense of history remembered

by Dash's stylised use of slow motion. ▭

Adisa Anderson *Eli Peazant* • Cheryl Lynn Bruce *Viola* • Cora Lee Day *Nana Peazant* • Kaycee Moore *Haagar* • Alva Rogers *Eula Peazant* • Bahni Turpin *Iona Peazant* • Trula Hoosier *Trula* ■ *Dir/Scr* Julie Dash

Dave ★★★★ 15

Political comedy 1993 · US · Colour · 105mins

Director Ivan Reitman isn't known for his subtlety, but there is nothing crass about this delightful, gentle satire on the Washington political scene. Part-time presidential impersonator Kevin Kline is called into the White House when the real president suffers a stroke. However, he soon begins to get a taste for the job, much to the horror of shifty White House aide Frank Langella. Kline is excellent as both the naive stand-in and the ruthless president, while Sigourney Weaver is fine as the bitter First Lady who begins to see her "husband" in a new light. Look out for Oliver Stone, playing himself, trying to convince a disbelieving chat-show host that there is another White House conspiracy afoot. ▭ **DVD**

Kevin Kline *Dave Kovic/President Bill Mitchell* • Sigourney Weaver *Ellen Mitchell* • Frank Langella *Bob Alexander* • Kevin Dunn *Alan Reed* • Ving Rhames *Duane Stevenson* • Ben Kingsley *Vice-President Nance* • Charles Grodin *Murray Blum* • Faith Prince *Alice* ■ *Dir* Ivan Reitman • *Scr* Gary Ross

David ★★★★ U

Drama 1979 · W Ger · Colour · 125mins

One of the most powerful films ever made about the Holocaust, this adaptation of Joel Konig's fact-based book isn't primarily about courage or heroic charity. Instead, it's a harrowing study of the gnawing terror that was part of everyday life for Jews living under the Nazi tyranny. Director Peter Lilienthal refuses to sentimentalise the humanity of the decent few, or reduce the endless round of concealment and escape to mere action set pieces. With Mario Fischel's determination born out of fear as the hunted teenager and Walter Taub outstanding as his Rabbi father, this thoroughly merited its Golden Bear at Berlin. In German with English subtitles.

Walter Taub *Rabbi Singer* • Irena Vrkljan *Wife* • Eva Mattes *Toni* • Mario Fischel *David* ■ *Dir* Peter Lilienthal • *Scr* Jurek Becker, Ulla Ziemann, Peter Lilienthal, from the novel by Joel Konig

David and Bathsheba ★★

Biblical drama 1951 · US · Colour · 115mins

Gregory Peck is the King of Israel, who spots Susan Hayward's red-headed Bathsheba going about her ablutions and is instantly smitten, subsequently incurring the wrath of God and having to atone for his sins. More of a plodding, pompous moral debate than an epic, Henry King's movie eschews a lot of the DeMille-style orgies and battles one would expect. There is, however, a cleverly staged flashback to David's famous fight with Goliath. Peck manages to exude nobility and Hayward is ravishing, in a Kansas farmgirl sort of way.

Gregory Peck *David* • Susan Hayward *Bathsheba* • Raymond Massey *Nathan* • Kieron Moore *Uriah* • James Robertson-Justice *Abishai* • Jayne Meadows *Michal* ■ *Dir* Henry King • *Scr* Philip Dunne

David and Lisa ★★★

Drama based on a true story 1962 · US · BW · 93mins

David and Lisa are mental patients. He's autistic, obsessively tidy, hates being touched and has a recurrent nightmare about cutting people's heads off with the hands of a clock. She's a schizophrenic who talks only in childish, gobbledegook rhymes, or else doesn't talk at all. One the one hand, this seems like a typical slice of American psychobabble about misunderstood kids. The acting, however, raises the story to an entirely different level. The performances of Keir Dullea and Janet Margolin are totally sincere and deeply touching as they are drawn together, rather like Adam and Eve searching for that first innocent touch of hands.

Keir Dullea *David* • Janet Margolin *Lisa* • Howard Da Silva *Dr Swinford* • Neva Patterson *Mrs Clemens* • Clifton James *John* • Richard McMurray *Mr Clemens* • Nancy Nutter *Maureen* ■ *Dir* Frank Perry • *Scr* Eleanor Perry, from a non-fiction book by Dr Theodore Isaac Rubin

David and Lisa ★★★ PG

Drama 1998 · US · Colour · 86mins

This is a well-meaning TV remake of the 1962 indie, but what was innovative back then now feels very dated and similar to countless other dysfunctional teen movies. At a boarding school for emotionally disturbed adolescents, a hostile loner who detests being touched falls in love with a child-like girl who only speaks in rhyme. With the help of a sensitive psychiatrist, the two damaged teenagers learn trust, faith and happiness. Sidney Poitier gives a sympathetic performance as the caring doctor; Lukas Haas turns in a fine portrayal as the troubled David; while Brittany Murphy is engaging as the fragile object of his love. Slow-paced at times, but moving. Contains some violence and swearing. ▭

Sidney Poitier *Dr Jack Miller* • Lukas Haas *David* • Brittany Murphy *Lisa* • Debi Mazar *Maggie* • Allison Janney *Alix* • Kim Murphy *Natalie* ■ *Dir* Lloyd Kramer • *Scr* Eleanor Perry, Lloyd Kramer, Theodore Isaac Rubin

David and the Magic Pearl ★★

Animated adventure 1990 · Pol · Colour · 75mins

Poland was once a world leader in animation, but, sadly, the cartoon sector was among the major casualties when the state-sponsored film industry collapsed with communism. Yet Wieslaw Zieba managed to complete this green fantasy, which, rather curiously, focuses on a boy from Chicago who joins a mysterious group of "spacers" in a search for a pearl that can not only grant them wisdom, but can also help prevent the destruction of the jungle. This will interest those looking for cartoons

without that saccharine commercial coating.
Dir Wieslaw Zieba

David Copperfield ★★★★★

Classic drama   1935 · US · BW · 124mins
An immaculately cast and designed David O Selznick production for MGM that remains the definitive version of Charles Dickens's vaguely autobiographical classic. While Basil Rathbone is Mr Murdstone to a T, and there couldn't possibly be any other Aunt Betsey Trotwood but Edna May Oliver, the real casting coups are Lennox Pawle's career-defining, perfect Mr Dick, and Roland Young's ubiquitous Uriah Heep. If the great WC Fields makes Micawber a star turn, it's no bad thing, and both Freddie Bartholomew and Frank Lawton as the young and the grown-up David, respectively, could not be bettered. This film is a richly entertaining reminder of what Hollywood, and especially MGM, did best. ▭

WC Fields *Mr Micawber* • Lionel Barrymore *Dan Peggotty* • Freddie Bartholomew *David as a child* • Maureen O'Sullivan *Dora* • Madge Evans *Agnes* • Edna May Oliver *Aunt Betsey* • Lewis Stone *Mr Wickfield* • Frank Lawton *David as a man* • Elizabeth Allan *Mrs Copperfield* • Roland Young *Uriah Heep* • Basil Rathbone *Mr Murdstone* • Elsa Lanchester *Clickett* • Jean Cadell *Mrs Micawber* • Jessie Ralph *Nurse Peggotty* • Lennox Pawle *Mr Dick* ■ *Dir* George Cukor • *Scr* Howard Estabrook, Hugh Walpole, from the novel by Charles Dickens • *Cinematographer* Oliver T Marsh • *Editor* Robert J Kern

David Copperfield ★★★ U

Drama 1969 · UK/US/Mex · Colour · 117mins
Charles Dickens's ever-popular novel suffers from a clumsy flashback structure that not only interrupts the flow of the picaresque narrative, but also prevents the action from gaining any pace. There are compensations, however, not least being the opportunity to revel in the performances of a superlative British cast. In partnership with Richard Attenborough, the Emmy-nominated Laurence Olivier is particularly impressive as Mr Creakle, but Ralph Richardson fails to exorcise the memory of WC Fields as Micawber, while Robin Phillips is singularly charmless in the title role. It's handsome enough for a TV-movie, but lacks style.
Robin Phillips *David Copperfield* • Susan Hampshire *Agnes Wickfield* • Edith Evans *Betsey Trotwood* • Michael Redgrave *Mr Peggotty* • Ralph Richardson *Mr Micawber* • Wendy Hiller *Mrs Micawber* • Corin Redgrave *Steerforth* • Pamela Franklin *Dora Spenlow* • Ron Moody *Uriah Heep* • Laurence Olivier *Mr Creakle* • Richard Attenborough *Mr Tungay* • Anna Massey *Jane Murdstone* • Cyril Cusack *Barkis* • Sinead Cusack *Emily* ■ *Dir* Delbert Mann • *Scr* Jack Pulman, from the novel by Charles Dickens

David Copperfield ★ U

Animated adventure
1993 · UK · Colour · 90mins
Who on earth had the unfathomable idea of turning David Copperfield into a mouse who is sent to work in a cheese factory by his cruel stepfather?

That's the silly notion behind this cartoon adaptation of Charles Dickens's masterpiece. Leading a band of orphans against the notorious Cheese Police, Julian Lennon valiantly attempts to strike the right note, as do fellow voiceover artists Michael York, Kelly LeBrock and Sheena Easton. ▭
Julian Lennon *David Copperfield* • Michael York *Murdstone* • Sheena Easton *Agnes* • Howie Mandel *Mealy* • Kelly LeBrock *Clara* ■ *Dir* Don Arioli • *Scr* Judith Reeves-Stevens, Garfield Reeves-Stevens, from the novel by Charles Dickens

David Holzman's Diary ★★

Satire   1968 · US · BW · 74mins
Considered daring and experimental in its day, Jim McBride's directorial debut is a *ciné-vérité* counterculture classic that now looks dull and pretentious. LM Kit Carson (future scriptwriter of *Running on Empty* and Karen Black's husband) plays film-maker Holzman, who decides to record his own life for a couple of weeks and, in the self-obsessed process, loses his girlfriend. There are some interesting moments – for example, the speeded-up montage of what Holzman watches on television one evening – plus the sort of avant-garde imagery that would soon enter the mainstream, such as the angst-ridden rants to camera. But, overall, this sixties curio is a self-indulgent exercise from a director who would only come into his own in the eighties with *Breathless* and *The Big Easy*.
LM Kit Carson *David Holzman* • Eileen Dietz *Penny Wohl* • Louise Levine *Sandra* • Lorenzo Mans *Pepe* ■ *Dir* Jim McBride • *Scr* LM Kit Carson, Jim McBride

David: the David Rothenberg Story ★★ 15

Drama based on a true story
1988 · US/UK · Colour · 94mins
The makers of TV movies have hardly any qualms about sensationalising real-life horror and exploiting emotional trauma. This is one of the most painful examples, in which an estranged father, played by John Glover, sets fire to his six-year-old son Matthew Lawrence who, disfigured, has to come to terms with his life and the suffering of his mother Bernadette Peters. The admirable performances do transcend the opportunism of the idea. ▭
Bernadette Peters *Marie Rothenberg* • Matthew Lawrence *David Rothenberg* • John Glover *Charles Rothenberg* • George Grizzard *Dr Achauer* • Dan Lauria *John Cirillo* • Christopher Allport *Terry Branum* • Georgann Johnson *Loraine Levy* ■ *Dir* John Erman • *Scr* Stephanie Liss, from the book *David* by Marie Rothenberg, Mel White

David's Mother ★★★ PG

Drama   1994 · US · Colour · 92mins
Everyone knows Kirstie Alley's comic credentials are pretty sound, following TV success in *Cheers* and a handful of *Look Who's Talking* hits at the cinema. But she proves herself a more than capable dramatic actress in this sensitive TV movie, as a mother who devotes her life to the care of her autistic son. Alley won an Emmy for her performance, as did Michael Goorjian, who plays David as a teenager. The script presents genuine

situations and emotions without resorting to platitudes or easy sentiment, and gives the powerhouse cast, including Stockard Channing, Sam Waterston and Chris Sarandon, plenty to get its teeth into. ▭
Kirstie Alley *Sally Goodson* • Sam Waterston *John* • Stockard Channing *Bea* • Michael Goorjian *David aged 17* • Chris Sarandon *Phillip* • Phylicia Rashad *Gladys* • Steve Ivany *David aged 59* • *Dir* Robert Allan Ackerman • *Scr* Bob Randall, from the play by Walt Lloyd

Davy Crockett and the River Pirates ★★ U

Adventure   1956 · US · Colour · 86mins
Davy Crockett was a phenomenon of the fifties. Originally intended only for Disney's US TV shows, the noble buckskin-clad frontiersman swept the world after Uncle Walt strung some episodes together and released them in cinemas. This was the second theatrical outing, a feast of fun that falls clearly into two halves. The more enjoyable first part pits Crockett (Fess Parker) against self-styled "King of the River", splendidly hammed by Jeff York, while the second half deals with Indian confrontations. ▭
Fess Parker *Davy Crockett* • Buddy Ebsen *George Russel* • Jeff York *Mike Fink* • Kenneth Tobey *Jocko* • Clem Evans *Cap'n Cobb* • Irving Ashkenazy *Moose* • Mort Mills *Sam Mason* ■ *Dir* Norman Foster • *Scr* Norman Foster, Tom Blackburn

Davy Crockett, King of the Wild Frontier ★★ U

Biographical action adventure
1955 · US · Colour · 88mins
The first of two cinema features, both adapted from a TV series produced by the Disney studio, about the legendary backwoodsman who became a congressman and died at the Alamo. Crockett is one of America's most bizarre, contradictory and elusive historical personages, but this movie simply prints the legend. Fess Parker, a jovial, athletic type, plays Crockett and successfully turned the coonskin hat into the fashion accessory most demanded by children in the mid-fifties, plus there's that hit theme song to hum along with as well. ▭
Fess Parker *Davy Crockett* • Buddy Ebsen *George Russel* • Basil Ruysdael *Andrew Jackson* • Hans Conried *Thimblerig* • William Bakewell *Tobias Norton* • Kenneth Tobey *Colonel Jim Bowie* • Pat Hogan *Chief Red Stick* • Helene Stanley *Polly Crockett* ■ *Dir* Norman Foster • *Scr* Tom Blackburn

Dawn! ★★★ U

Biographical drama
1979 · Ausl · Colour · 111mins
Dawn Fraser is the only swimmer in Olympic history to win the same event at three consecutive games, taking the 100 metres freestyle gold at Melbourne, Rome and Tokyo. She also set 27 world records, making her one of the most remarkable swimmers of all time. Avoiding the usual sports biopic formula of running through the list of achievements by means of a few phoney action sequences, director Ken Hannam explores the strain such success exerts and the flatness of life away from the roar of the crowd.

Bronwyn Mackay-Payne is magnificent in the title role.
Bronwyn Mackay-Payne *Dawn* • Tom Richards *Harry* • John Diedrich *Gary* • Bunney Brooke *Mum* • Ron Haddrick *Pop* ■ *Dir* Ken Hannam • *Scr* Joy Cavill

Dawn at Socorro ★★

Western   1954 · US · Colour · 80mins
One of the last western co-features in rich Technicolor, before Eastman Colour took over, and jolly splendid it looks, too, with glistening saloon interiors and bright location exteriors. But veteran director George Sherman brings his usual lack of style to bear and fails to get the best out of the sexually-charged co-starring of rugged Rory Calhoun and fiery Piper Laurie, both of whom are excellent in what is basically a routine plot.
Rory Calhoun *Brett Wade* • Piper Laurie *Rannah Hayes* • David Brian *Dick Braden* • Kathleen Hughes *Clare* • Alex Nicol *Jimmy Rapp* • Edgar Buchanan *Sheriff Cauthen* • Lee Van Cleef *Earl Ferris* ■ *Dir* George Sherman • *Scr* George Zuckerman • *Cinematographer* Carl Guthrie

Dawn of the Dead ★★★★ 18

Horror   1979 · US · Colour · 139mins
The *Citizen Kane* of gore. Some see George A Romero's astoundingly violent sequel to his classic *Night of the Living Dead* as a satirical attack on American consumerism and blind materialistic values, as it continues the premise of the reawakened dead stalking the living with cannibal intent through a shopping mall. Others see it as the greatest zombie fantasy of all time. Cynical, devastating and relentless, Romero's gruelling masterpiece about the American Dream turning into a terrifying nightmare is an ideal blend of black comedy and harrowing carnage. Contains swearing and violence. ▭
DVD
David Emge *Stephen* • Ken Foree *Peter* • Scott Reiniger *Roger* • Gaylen Ross *Francine* • David Crawford *Dr Foster* • David Early *Mr Berman* • George A Romero *TV director* ■ *Dir/Scr* George A Romero • *Music* Dario Argento and the Goblins

Dawn of the Mummy ★ 18

Horror   1981 · US · Colour · 86mins
The bright arc lights used for a photo shoot in an Egyptian tomb revive the ancient pharaoh and his slave army in this dispiriting mix of Hammer horror and extreme zombie violence. Completely vapid, with ham acting and shameless mugging galore, this brainless B-movie can only be recommended to splatter addicts. ▭
Brenda King • Barry Sattels • George Peck • John Salvo • Joan Levy • Diane Beatty ■ *Dir* Frank Agrama [Farouk Agrama] • *Scr* Daria Price, Ronald Dobrin, Frank Agrama, from a story by Ronald Dobrin, Daria Price

The Dawn Patrol ★★

First World War drama
1930 · US · BW · 105mins
This famous flying picture was Howard Hawks's first talkie but he ran into problems with Howard Hughes, producer/director of the rival *Hell's Angels*. Hughes tried to prevent the

Hawks movie from going into production, even suing writer John Monk Saunders. The story concerns a squadron of British flyers stoically running near-suicidal bombing raids over Germany during the First World War. Hawks later made far better flying pictures – *Only Angels Have Wings* and *Air Force* – but this one seems hampered by the primitive talkie technology, the artificiality of the dialogue and the performances which are as wooden as the rickety planes.

Richard Barthelmess *Dick Courtney* • Douglas Fairbanks Jr *Douglas Scott* • Neil Hamilton *Major Brand* • William Janney *Gordon Scott* • James Finlayson *Field Sergeant* ■ *Dir* Howard Hawks • *Scr* Howard Hawks, Dan Totheroh, Seton I Miller, from the story *The Flight Commander* by John Monk Saunders • *Music* Leo F Forbstein

The Dawn Patrol ★★★★ U
First World War melodrama
1938 · US · BW · 98mins

A marvellously unsentimental First World War melodrama, this remake of an earlier Howard Hawks classic movie is actually better cast (Errol Flynn, David Niven and Basil Rathbone all on top form) and better directed (by *Grand Hotel's* Edmund Goulding) than the earlier hit, though it still incorporates library material and action sequences from the former movie. There is a very real sense of the passion and futility of war in the gripping screenplay, and a genuine conveyance of horror among comrades and grace under pressure, with neither romance nor women to interfere. This is a very fine film indeed, a tribute to a great studio (Warner Bros) at its height. ▣

Errol Flynn *Captain Courtney* • David Niven *Lieutenant Scott* • Basil Rathbone *Major Brand* • Donald Crisp *Phipps* • Melville Cooper *Sergeant Watkins* • Barry Fitzgerald *Music* • Carl Esmond *Von Mueller* • Peter Willes *Hollister* • Morton Lowater *Ronny Scott* • Michael Brooke *Squires* • James Burke *Flaherty* • Stuart Hall *Bentham* ■ *Dir* Edmund Goulding • *Scr* Seton I Miller, Dan Totheroh, from the story *The Flight Commander* by John Monk Saunders

Dawn: Portrait of a Teenage Runaway ★ 15
Drama
1976 · US · Colour · 93mins

Eve Plumb – Jan Brady in *The Brady Bunch* – takes the title role in this irresponsible TV movie that takes the problem of young runaways and turns it into a sordid and sensationalist melodrama. In exploring the reasons why teenagers are drawn into prostitution, scriptwriter Dalene Young virtually ignores the social issues and pays undue attention to life on the Hollywood Boulevard beat. Tasteless trash. Contains violence. ▣

Eve Plumb *Dawn Wetherby* • Leigh McCloskey *Alexander* • Lynn Carlin *Dawn's mother* ■ *Dir* Randal Kleiser • *Scr* Dalene Young

The Dawn Rider ★★ U
Western
1935 · US · BW · 53mins

An uninspiring John Wayne programme filler, from that period when he was trapped in Lone Star westerns, between *The Big Trail* in 1930 and his resurrection in *Stagecoach* nine years later. The Duke is chasing his father's

murderer, who turns out to be Denny Meadows, who later changed his name to Dennis Moore and propped up many a B-movie. Cinematographer Archie Stout ended his career with Wayne, working on some of the Duke's more famous Warner Bros movies, including the 3-D *Hondo* and the CinemaScope *The High and the Mighty*, but his work here is purely functional. ▣

John Wayne *John Mason* • Marion Burns *Alice* • Yakima Canutt *Barkeeper* • Reed Howes *Ben* • Denny Meadows [Dennis Moore] *Rudd* • Bert Dillard *Buck* • Jack Jones *Black* ■ *Dir* RN Bradbury [Robert N Bradbury] • *Scr* RN Bradbury, from a story by Lloyd Nosler

The Dawning ★★★★ PG
Period drama
1988 · UK · Colour · 93mins

Now the wife of David Mamet, Rebecca Pidgeon made her debut in this striking film about pre-Partition Ireland. Pidgeon, stifled by living with aunt Jean Simmons and disabled grandfather Trevor Howard (in his last role), falls in love with bumbling city boy Hugh Grant. When she meets an enigmatic stranger (Anthony Hopkins), however, suddenly her world begins to turn on its head. Avoiding heavy-handedness or didacticism, director Robert Knights cleverly depicts the rise of the Irish Republican Army through Pidgeon's own progression from naive teenager to adult woman. ▣

Anthony Hopkins *Major Angus Barry/Cassius* • Rebecca Pidgeon *Nancy Gulliver* • Jean Simmons *Aunt Mary* • Trevor Howard *Grandfather* • Tara MacGowran *Maeve* • Hugh Grant *Harry* • Ronnie Masterson *Bridie* ■ *Dir* Robert Knights • *Scr* Moira Williams, from the novel *The Old Jest* by Jennifer Johnston

The Day After ★★★ 12
Drama
1983 · US · Colour · 115mins

The effect of nuclear war and its aftermath on several Kansas families makes for a mild diversion in this lavish TV movie directed by Nicholas Meyer. The impact of the twin explosions, subsequent radiation poisoning, looting and firing squads, is lessened due to network-imposed soft-pedalling of the true horrors. But the keen eye kept on the more personally-felt traumas of the grim situation gives a better than average focus as the apocalypse victims try to rebuild society. The A-list cast, including Steve Guttenberg, John Lithgow and Jason Robards, rise to the often heavy-handed occasion. ▣

Jason Robards [Jason Robards Jr] *Dr Russell Oakes* • JoBeth Williams *Nancy Bauer* • Steve Guttenberg *Stephen Klein* • John Cullum *Jim Dahlberg* • John Lithgow *Joe Huxley* • Bibi Besch *Eve Dahlberg* • Lori Lethin *Denise Dahlberg* • Amy Madigan *Alison Ransom* ■ *Dir* Nicholas Meyer • *Scr* Edward Hume

A Day at the Races ★★★★ U
Comedy
1937 · US · BW · 104mins

The Marx Brothers' second film for MGM was hidebound by the decision to overload the mayhem with mediocre musical interludes that the studio bigwigs believed would give the picture more class. The inconsistent support playing similarly saps much of the action's energy, with the soppy wooings of Allan Jones and Maureen

O'Sullivan undoing the sterling work of the wonderful Margaret Dumont. As ever, the trio's own performances are splendid, with the "Tootsie frootsie ice cream" sketch standing as the best of the Chico-Groucho wordplay routines. ▣

Groucho Marx *Dr Hugo Z Hackenbush* • Chico Marx *Tony* • Harpo Marx *Stuffy* • Allan Jones *Gil* • Maureen O'Sullivan *Judy* • Margaret Dumont *Mrs Upjohn* ■ *Dir* Sam Wood • *Scr* Robert Pirosh, George Seaton, George Oppenheimer, from a story by Robert Pirosh, George Seaton

Day for Night ★★★★★ PG
Drama
1973 · Fr · Colour · 110mins

The winner of the best foreign film Oscar, this is an exhilarating celebration of the movie-making process. Everything that could possibly go wrong on François Truffaut's film-within-the-film, *Meet Pamela*, does so in spades. Yet Truffaut's character battles on in the search for meaningful art. Regular collaborator Jean-Pierre Léaud is on cracking form as the actor who falls passionately in love with leading lady Jacqueline Bisset, who spoofs her own image to perfection. There are also lovely supporting turns from Valentina Cortese and Nathalie Baye, while novelist Graham Greene (billed as Henry Graham) pops up in a cameo that was something of a practical joke at Truffaut's expense. In French with English subtitles. ▣

François Truffaut *Ferrand* • Jacqueline Bisset *Julie* • Jean-Pierre Léaud *Alphonse* • Valentina Cortese *Severine* • Jean-Pierre Aumont *Alexandre* • Jean Champion *Bertrand* • Dani *Lilianne* • Alexandra Stewart *Stacey* • Bernard Menez *Bernard* • Nike Arrighi *Odile* • Nathalie Baye *Assistant* • Bernard Menez *Bernard* ■ *Dir* François Truffaut • *Scr* François Truffaut, Suzanne Schiffman, Jean-Louis Richard

A Day for Thanks on Waltons Mountain ★★
Drama
1982 · US · Colour

The Waltons bade their farewells in this lacklustre TV movie that has all the signs of being a tale too far. There's still plenty of incident to keep die-hard fans guessing will Jason become a composer; can Erin really leave the mountain; will Jim-Bob get to be his own boss? Yet things can never really be the same again, what with Robert Wightman now playing John-Boy and Olivia being kept off-screen altogether in a hospital bed in the town. However, Ralph Waite and Ellen Corby bring some sort of continuity and the good old kindred spirit is still hugely appealing.

Ralph Waite *John Walton* • Jon Walmsley *Jason Walton* • Judy Norton-Taylor *Mary Ellen Walton* • Eric Scott *Ben Walton* • David W Harper *Jim-Bob Walton* • Kami Cotler *Elizabeth Walton* • Robert Wightman *John-Boy Walton* • Ellen Corby *Grandma Walton* ■ *Dir* Harry Harris • *Scr* Kathleen Hite

A Day in October ★★★ 15
Second World War drama
1991 · US/Den · Colour · 96mins

Such was Denmark's antipathy to the invading Nazis and its sense of indivisible nationhood that only a relatively small percentage of its Jewish population was consigned to concentration camps. Although based

on actual events, this melodrama opts against exploring the reasons for this courageous stance, preferring instead to concentrate on the heroism of a single family whose protection of a wounded partisan led to the mass exodus of Danish Jews to Sweden. Kenneth Madsen's uplifting film is given additional power by the understated performances of DB Sweeney and Daniel Benzali. ▣

DB Sweeney *Niels Jensen* • Kelly Wolf *Sara Kublitz* • Tovah Feldshuh *Emma Kublitz* • Daniel Benzali *Solomon Kublitz* • Ole Lemmeke *Larson* • Kim Romer *Arne* ■ *Dir* Kenneth Madsen • *Scr* Damian F Slattery

A Day in the Death of Joe Egg ★★★★
Black comedy drama
1971 · UK · Colour · 108mins

The fate of a child with cerebral palsy might not appear suitable material for a black comedy. Yet Peter Nichols's adaptation of his own hit play is less concerned with euthanasia than with the very human emotions being experienced by the girl's angst-ridden parents. Faced with constant shifts in tone, director Peter Medak manages to prevent the action from becoming either tasteless or sentimental, thanks, largely, to the exceptional performances of Alan Bates and Janet Suzman. Free of the Brechtian devices that characterised the stage version, this is a provocative look at people under pressure and the transience of love. Contains swearing and nudity.

Alan Bates *Brian* • Janet Suzman *Sheila* • Peter Bowles *Freddie* • Sheila Gish *Pam* • Joan Hickson *Grace* • Elizabeth Robillard *Jo* • Murray Melvin *Doctor* ■ *Dir* Peter Medak • *Scr* Peter Nichols, from his play

The Day Lincoln Was Shot ★★★
Historical drama
1998 · US · Colour · 95mins

The basic facts are well-known, but director John Gray digs a bit deeper and comes up with a very modern political thriller. His made-for-TV film also features audacious against-type casting, with Lance Henriksen surprisingly convincing as the war-weary Lincoln, and *Northern Exposure's* Rob Morrow believably psychotic as John Wilkes Booth. Gray deftly switches between his protagonists as they move closer to their fateful rendezvous.

Rob Morrow *John Wilkes Booth* • Lance Henriksen *Abraham Lincoln* • Donna Murphy *Mary Todd Lincoln* • Jean Louisa Kelly *Lucy Halle* • Wil Wheaton *Robert Lincoln* ■ *Dir* John Gray • *Scr* John Gray, Tim Metcalfe, from the non-fiction book by Jim Bishop

Day of Atonement ★★ 18
Thriller
1993 · Fr/It · Colour · 96mins

France's answer to *The Godfather*, this long-winded gangster movie is the sequel to director Alexandre Arcady's 1982 hit, *La Grand Pardon*, which also starred French heavy Roger Hanin. The first film dealt mainly with the internecine war conducted by Franco-Algerian Jewish gangsters; this sequel changes only in location: the film was shot mainly in Miami, allowing Christopher Walken to play a drug

U = SUITABLE FOR ALL   Uc = SUITABLE FOR ALL, ESPECIALLY FOR YOUNG CHILDREN (VIDEO ONLY)   PG = PARENTAL GUIDANCE

baron and the son of a former Nazi who fled to Chile. 📺

Roger Hanin *Raymond Bettoun* • Richard Berry *Maurice Bettoun* • Jennifer Beals *Joyce Feranti* • Jill Clayburgh *Sally White* • Gérard Darmon *Roland Bettoun* • Christopher Walken *Pasco Meisner* ■ *Dir* Alexandre Arcady • *Scr* Alexandre Arcady, Daniel Saint-Hamont

A Day of Fury ★★

Western   1956 · US · Colour · 77mins

A moody little western, very much of its time, with rebel Dale Robertson finding himself outside civic convention in a conservative frontier town. It has its moments, but Robertson is both too bland and too old for the role, and the direction is very average. Former stuntman Jock Mahoney registers well in a serious role, and TV western aficionados will relish watching *The Range Rider's* Mahoney paired with *Tales of Wells Fargo's* Robertson. Fifties' starlet Mara Corday is the girl.

Dale Robertson *Jagade* • Mara Corday *Sharman Fulton* • Jock Mahoney *Marshal Allan Burnett* • Carl Benton Reid *Judge John J McLean* ■ *Dir* Harmon Jones • *Scr* James Edmiston, Oscar Brodney, from a story by James Edmiston

Day of the Animals ★★★ 15

Horror   1977 · US · Colour · 92mins

One of the best movies made by horror hack William Girdler, who died in a tragic helicopter accident just as he was about to hit the big time with *The Manitou*. Ecological erosion of the ozone layer causes wild creatures to attack a group of Californian mountain hikers in this creditable effort. Bears, wolves, vultures, snakes, dogs and rats (in a truly amazing forest ranger attack) all get in on the menacing act that's beautifully photographed and directed for lively shock value and welcome chuckles between the carnage. 📺

Christopher George *Steve Buckner* • Leslie Nielsen *Paul Jensen* • Lynda Day George *Terry Marsh* • Richard Jaeckel *Taylor MacGregor* • Michael Ansara *Daniel Santee* ■ *Dir* William Girdler • *Scr* William Norton, Eleanor Norton, from a story by Edward E Montoro

Day of the Bad Man ★★

Western   1958 · US · Colour · 82mins

A routine Universal western, enhanced by the majestic photography of Irving Glassberg that gives the small tale a certain grandeur. Ageing Fred MacMurray stars as a judge who's trying to maintain law and order until the hour arrives when a condemned outlaw goes to the gallows. Director Harry Keller pays far too much attention to MacMurray's grim features, but there is the compensation of some irresistible western stalwarts in the cast; oh, and there's a romance, too, between MacMurray and Joan Weldon.

Fred MacMurray *Judge Jim Scott* • Joan Weldon *Myra Owens* • John Ericson *Sheriff Barney Wiley* • Robert Middleton *Charlie Hayes* • Marie Windsor *Cora Johnson* • Edgar Buchanan *Sam Wyckoff* • Skip Homeier *Howard Hayes* • Lee Van Cleef *Jake Hayes* ■ *Dir* Harry Keller • *Scr* Lawrence Roman, from a story by John M Cunningham

The Day of the Beast ★★★★ 18

Black comedy   1995 · Sp/It · Colour · 99mins

Spanish director Alex de la Iglesia's highly engaging continental smash hit is a wicked parody of doom prophecy movies like *The Omen* and *The Devil Rides Out*, with a dash of *Die Hard* thrown in. This scintillating and original spoof effortlessly mixes the sinister with the absurd, as three very unusual wise men search for the birth place of the Antichrist in Madrid on Christmas Eve. A screwball horror that's packed with demons, demises and diverting detail, it's as much a serious indictment of the way the media distorts reality as it is a clever genre satire. In Spanish with English subtitles. Contains violence, swearing and nudity. 📺

Alex Angulo *Angel Berriartua* • Armando De Razza *Ennio Lombardi* • Santiago Segura *Jose Maria* • Terele Pavez *Rosario* • Nathalie Sesena *Mina* • Jaime Blanch *Toyota 1* • Maria Grazia Cucinotta *Susana* ■ *Dir* Alex de la Iglesia • *Scr* Alex de la Iglesia, Jorge Guerricaechevarria

Day of the Dead ★★★★ 18

Horror   1985 · US · Colour · 100mins

George A Romero ends his *Living Dead* trilogy in the most sophisticated, disturbing and horrifying way possible. Scientists in an underground missile base try to find ways of domesticating and controlling the cannibalistic zombie hordes so they can be re-integrated into society. The result is a lean, mean and shocking sequel whose gore is so realistic, it's like being trapped in a morgue for 100 minutes. Investing the living, rotting corpses with touching humanism (they shave and listen to personal stereos) is a stroke of genius on Romero's part, and one that makes his unnervingly bleak world vision both an intellectual and terrifying shock to the system. 📺 **DVD**

Lori Cardille *Sarah* • Terry Alexander *John* • Joseph Pilato *Captain Rhodes* • Jarlath Conroy *McDermott* • Antone DiLeo Jr *Miguel* • Richard Liberty *Dr Logan* • Howard Sherman *Bub* ■ *Dir/Scr* George A Romero

The Day of the Dolphin ★★ PG

Drama   1973 · US · Colour · 100mins

George C Scott takes on one of the biggest challenges of his career by conducting meaningful conversations with dolphins. He even teaches his pet dolphin endearments like "Fa" and "Pa". But this isn't a Flipperish, Disney-pic. Indeed, things get decidedly bleak when it's revealed that Scott's dolphins are destined to be used as sentient torpedoes in a plot to assassinate the President aboard his yacht. Georges Delerue's score is a high point. 📺

George C Scott *Dr Jake Terrell* • Trish Van Devere *Maggie Terrell* • Paul Sorvino *Mahoney* • Fritz Weaver *Harold DeMilo* • Jon Korkes *David* • Edward Herrmann *Mike* • Leslie Charleson *Maryanne* ■ *Dir* Mike Nichols • *Scr* Buck Henry, from a novel by Robert Merle

Day of the Evil Gun ★★ PG

Western   1968 · US · Colour · 89mins

Originally planned as a TV movie, this western starts out as an unofficial and wholly competent remake of *The Searchers*. Glenn Ford and Arthur Kennedy bond surprisingly well as they survive all manner of perils in a bid to rescue Ford's family from the Apache, and there's solid support from the under-rated Dean Jagger as an untrustworthy Indian trader. But then the action takes an unexpected and rather improbable turn, which, while exciting enough, has nothing to do with the rest of the story and rather spoils the film. Shame about the title, too. Contains violence. 📺

Glenn Ford *Lorn Warfield* • Arthur Kennedy *Owen Forbes* • Dean Jagger *Jimmy Noble* • John Anderson *Captain Jefferson Addis* • Paul Fix *Sheriff Kelso* • Nico Minardos *Deleon* • Dean Stanton [Harry Dean Stanton] *Sergeant Parker* ■ *Dir* Jerry Thorpe • *Scr* Charles Marquis Warren, Eric Bercovici, from the novel by Charles Marquis Warren

The Day of the Jackal ★★★★ 15

Thriller   1973 · UK/Fr · Colour · 136mins

A magnificent script from Kenneth Ross and a masterly central performance from Edward Fox form the backbone of this big-screen version of Frederick Forsyth's best-selling novel, but it's Fred Zinnemann's matchless direction that makes it such compelling viewing. The pacing of the picture is superb, a methodical accumulation of detail that is as fastidious as Fox's preparation for his mission to assassinate General de Gaulle. Although the action crisscrosses Europe, there's no postcard prettiness, just a sure grasp of the atmosphere of each place before getting down to the business of the scene. An object lesson in suspense. Contains mild swearing and brief nudity. 📺

Edward Fox *The Jackal* • Michael Lonsdale [Michel Lonsdale] *Claude Lebel* • Alan Badel *Minister* • Tony Britton *Inspector Thomas* • Adrien Cayla-Legrand *President* • Cyril Cusack *Gunsmith* • Donald Sinden *Mallinson* • Derek Jacobi *Caron* • Eric Porter *Colonel Rodin* • Delphine Seyrig *Colette de Montpelier* • Timothy West *Berthier* ■ *Dir* Fred Zinnemann • *Scr* Kenneth Ross, from the novel by Frederick Forsyth

The Day of the Locust ★★★★

Drama   1975 · US · Colour · 143mins

This chronicle of Hollywood losers, eaten up by ambition but possessing no talent, gets lavish coverage from British director John Schlesinger. Karen Black stars as a would-be starlet, the daughter of drunken vaudevillian Burgess Meredith, who takes Donald Sutherland for a ride and almost snares sketch artist William Atherton as well. Adapted from Nathanael West's famous novel about early Tinseltown, the film sprawls too indulgently but remains enormously watchable throughout. Contains some nudity and swearing.

Donald Sutherland *Homer Simpson* • Karen Black *Faye Greener* • Burgess Meredith *Harry Greener* • William Atherton *Tod Hackett* •

Geraldine Page *Big Sister* ■ *Dir* John Schlesinger • *Scr* Waldo Salt, from the novel by Nathanael West

Day of the Outlaw ★★★

Western   1959 · US · BW · 92mins

A fine bleak winter western from veteran director Andre De Toth, who manages to emphasise every nuance of rage in anti-McCarthyite screenwriter Philip Yordan's bitter isolationist allegory. Rugged Robert Ryan is the rancher who finally makes a stand against Burl Ives's gang of renegade cutthroats. The snow-covered landscape (beautifully photographed in stark black and white by Russell Harlan) makes the tale seem even bleaker, with the climactic gunfight in a blizzard quite remarkable. Fifties' starlet Tina Louise does well as the female lead.

Robert Ryan *Blaise Starrett* • Burl Ives *Jack Bruhn* • Tina Louise *Helen Crane* • Alan Marshal *Hal Crane* • Nehemiah Persoff *Dan* • Venetia Stevenson *Ernine* • Donald Elson *Vic* ■ *Dir* Andre De Toth • *Scr* Philip Yordan

The Day of the Triffids ★★★ 15

Science-fiction horror
1962 · UK · Colour · 94mins

A meteor shower blinds all but a few Earthlings, leaving society at the mercy of carnivorous plants from outer space in this rather disappointing version of John Wyndham's classic sci-fi novel. While the Triffids themselves are efficiently bizarre and menacing, Steve Sekely's barely competent direction hardly provides the sinister spores with a shining showcase. That was left to Freddie Francis, director of the lighthouse scenes added later in a bravura effort to beef up the chills and thrills. 📺

Howard Keel *Bill Masen* • Janette Scott *Karen Goodwin* • Nicole Maurey *Christine Durrant* • Kieron Moore *Tom Goodwin* • Mervyn Johns *Mr Coker* • Alison Leggatt *Miss Coker* ■ *Dir* Steve Sekely • *Scr* Philip Yordan, from the novel by John Wyndham

Day of the Wolves ★★

Crime drama   1973 · US · Colour · 95mins

A thoughtful B-picture thriller, this has former sheriff Richard Egan battling against a weird conspiracy by a mysterious gang who want to cut off his home town for three days to prepare for the "ultimate heist". Martha Hyer, in one of her final screen appearances, is Egan's reward for his courage. The director is Ferde Grofe Jr, and there's a touch of science-fiction to spice up the tension.

Richard Egan *Pete Anderson* • Rick Jason *Number Four* • Martha Hyer *Mrs Anderson* • Jan Murray *Uncle Murray* ■ *Dir/Scr* Ferde Grofe Jr

Day of Wrath ★★★★★ PG

Drama   1943 · Den · BW · 92mins

Put to the stake for witchcraft, Anna Svierkier places a curse on the pastor (Thorkild Roose) who condemned her. Disaster and death are then visited upon Roose and his family, beginning with his discovery that his wife Lisbeth Movin is having an affair with a younger man (Preben Lerdoff Rye).

Made by Denmark's great genius of the cinema, Carl Theodor Dreyer (his first film since *Vampyr* a decade earlier), this is a coldly uncompromising vision of human frailty, stupidity, bigotry and cruelty, made all the more horrifying by the startling beauty of its images. Not an easy experience, but a rewarding one. In Danish with English subtitles. Contains some nudity. ▨

Thorkild Roose *Absalon Pedersson* • Lisbeth Movin *Anne, his wife* • Sigrid Neiiendam *Meret, his mother* • Preben Lerdorff Rye *Martin, son by his first marriage* ■ *Dir* Carl Theodor Dreyer • *Scr* Carl Dreyer, Poul Knudsen, Mogens Skot-Hansen, from the novel *Vredens Dag* by Wiers Jenssens

A Day on the Grand Canal with the Emperor of China ★★★

Documentary   1988 · US · Colour · 46mins

Rejoicing under the alternative title *Surface Is Illusion but So Is Depth*, this is a predictably lucid yet surprisingly entertaining treatise on the rigidity of western artistic traditions. Illustrating his thesis by contrasting a 72-ft long scroll by the 17th-century Chinese painter Wang Hui with a Venetian cityscape by Canaletto, David Hockney demonstrates how much more imaginatively the Oriental artist has used perspective and iconography than his High Renaissance counterpart. With Philip Haas freeing the camera to rove around the sights witnessed by the Emperor on his progress, this can be classed alongside the artistic documentaries of Luciano Emmer.

Dir Philip Haas • *Scr* David Hockney

Day One ★★★★

Second World War drama
1989 · US · Colour · 141mins

The spectre of nuclear warfare is made real and immediate in this TV movie based on the true story of the Second World War Manhattan Project's race to build the first atomic bomb, and the struggle of the scientists and government leaders to cope with its implications. David W Rintels's taut script, veteran Joseph Sargent's insightful direction and a splendid cast, including Brian Dennehy, Hal Holbrook and *LA Law*'s Michael Tucker and Richard Dysart, make this Emmy-winning production gleam with the feeling of living history. Moving, frightening and richly rewarding.

John McMartin *Dr Arthur Compton* • Brian Dennehy *General Leslie Groves* • Richard Dysart *President Harry S Truman* • Michael Tucker *Leo Szilard* • Hume Cronyn *James F Byrnes* • Hal Holbrook *General George Marshall* ■ *Dir* Joseph Sargent • *Scr* David W Rintels, from the book *Day One: Before Hiroshima and After* by Peter Wyden

The Day the Earth Caught Fire ★★★

Science-fiction drama
1961 · UK · BW · 98mins

Atomic explosions at the two poles put the planet on a collision course with the Sun in this bleak British doomsday vision. With the emphasis on the reactions of some London journalists to the impending catastrophe rather than elaborate special effects, this

tautly intelligent sci-fi thriller hits all the right buttons, helped by a script full of fatalistic quips and apocalyptic cynicism. Engrossing, with a memorable fade-out on two possible newspaper headlines.

Leo McKern *Bill Maguire* • Janet Munro *Jeannie* • Edward Judd *Peter Stenning* • Michael Goodliffe *Night editor* • Bernard Braden *News editor* • Reginald Beckwith *Harry* • Gene Anderson *May* • Arthur Christiansen *Editor* • Austin Trevor *Sir John Kelly* • Renée Asherson *Angela* • Michael Caine *Policeman* ■ *Dir* Val Guest • *Scr* Val Guest, Wolf Mankowitz

The Day the Earth Stood Still ★★★★★ Ⓤ

Classic science-fiction drama
1951 · US · BW · 88mins

Coming just four months after Christian Nyby and Howard Hawks had unleashed *The Thing from Another World* upon a petrified Cold War public, director Robert Wise's sci-fi classic was a welcome sign of hope that we might not be going up in flames after all. From Bernard Herrmann's otherworldly score to Lyle Wheeler and Addison Hehr's deceptively simple designs, *The Day the Earth Stood Still* has had an incalculable influence on big screen science-fiction. For all its philosophical solemnity and heavy-handed religious symbolism, Edmund H North's script deftly pokes fun at the Red-baiters who had done so much to foster the nuclear scare, while his notion that children accept without question what grown-ups are too cynical to see has continued to resurface throughout the blockbuster era, notably in those Spielberg landmarks *Close Encounters of the Third Kind* and *ET*. ▨

Michael Rennie *Klaatu* • Patricia Neal *Helen Benson* • Hugh Marlowe *Tom Stevens* • Sam Jaffe *Dr Barnhardt* • Billy Gray *Bobby Benson* • Frances Bavier *Mrs Barley* • Lock Martin *Gort* ■ *Dir* Robert Wise • *Scr* Edmund H North, from the short story *Farewell to the Master* by Harry Bates

The Day the Fish Came Out ★★

Satire   1967 · UK/Gr · Colour · 109mins

Michael Cacoyannis's follow-up to his highly acclaimed *Zorba the Greek* couldn't have been more different, or more of a disappointment: a ham-fisted satire that falls prisoner to the modish mood of its time. Tom Courtenay and Colin Blakely play Nato airmen whose plane, carrying a pair of H-bombs and a doomsday weapon, ditches in the sea near a Greek island. Cacoyannis, who not only directs but also wrote the screenplay, struggles to integrate the clashing styles of farce and realism into any coherent whole. Amid all the fake psychedelia, you can spot a fresh-faced Candice Bergen and a pre-*Saint* Ian Ogilvy.

Tom Courtenay *Navigator* • Sam Wanamaker *Elias* • Colin Blakely *Pilot* • Candice Bergen *Electra* • Ian Ogilvy *Peter* ■ *Dir/Scr* Michael Cacoyannis

The Day the Loving Stopped ★★ Ⓟ⒢

Drama   1981 · US · Colour · 95mins

Veteran director Daniel Mann showed he was easily able to deal with emotionally tricky subjects in films such as *Come Back, Little Sheba* and *I'll Cry Tomorrow*, but this made-for-TV movie shows no signs of his obvious talent. Its story of youngsters left bereft by divorce covers old ground and becomes trapped in a minefield of sentimentality, into which the film steps with careless abandon. Despite the performances of Dennis Weaver and Valerie Harper (and a young Ally Sheedy), clichés cloud issues that should touch our hearts, not our cynicism. ▨

Dennis Weaver *Aaron Danner* • Valerie Harper *Norma Danner* • Dominique Dunne *Judy Danner* • Sam Groom *Bryan Forma* • Ally Sheedy *Debbie Danner* ■ *Dir* Daniel Mann • *Scr* Liz Coe

The Day the Sun Turned Cold ★★★★ ⒓

Drama based on a true story
1994 · HK · Colour · 100mins

Taken as a political allegory or an Oedipal melodrama, Yim Ho's award-winning film is both troubling and compelling. It scarcely matters whether Si Ching Gao Wa (a powerful Mongolian actress who also starred in the director's 1984 breakthrough, *Homecoming*) actually killed her husband. What is so intriguing is why her son (Tao Chung Wa) would betray her to the authorities, and why he would wait a decade before doing so. Based on true events and told in a measured, unsettlingly realistic manner, this provocative picture will linger long in the mind. In Mandarin with English subtitles.

Si Ching Gao Wa *Pu Fengying, the mother* • Tao Chung Wa *Guan Jian, the son* • Ma Jingwu *Guan Shichang, the father* ■ *Dir* Yim Ho • *Scr* Yim Ho, Wang Xing Dong

The Day the World Ended ★★

Science-fiction   1956 · US · BW · 81mins

The first science-fiction film from cult director Roger Corman has seven survivors of a nuclear war fighting off atomic radiation mutants from their mountain retreat. Not much else happens in this cheesy yet ludicrously entertaining fright flick, which transposes the Garden of Eden myth into an uncertain future. The ads at the time promised "a new high in naked shrieking terror", but the only shrieks to be heard now will be ones of laughter at the three-eyed, four-armed monster suits.

Richard Denning *Rick* • Lori Nelson *Louise* • Adele Jergens *Ruby* • Touch Connors [Mike Connors] *Tony* • Paul Birch *Maddison* ■ *Dir* Roger Corman • *Scr* Lou Rusoff, from his story

The Day They Gave Babies Away ★★ Ⓤ

Period drama   1957 · US · Colour · 102mins

A rather curious account of the hardships and tragedies faced by a mid-19th-century Scottish immigrant family in the American backwoods.

Based on the experiences of scriptwriters Dale and Katherine Eunson's ancestors, it stars the unlikely pairing of Britain's Glynis Johns and the hunky, pre-*High Chaparral* Cameron Mitchell. The result is little more than a plodding seasonal tear-jerker, but, despite the weak characterisation and mediocre direction (by Allen Reisner), it's good to see the famously husky-voiced Johns as a doughty pioneer wife.

Glynis Johns *Mamie Eunson* • Cameron Mitchell *Robert Eunson* • Rex Thompson *Robbie Eunson* • Patty McCormack *Annabelle Eunson* ■ *Dir* Allen Reisner • *Scr* Dale Eunson, Katherine Eunson

The Day They Robbed the Bank of England ★★★

Crime caper   1960 · UK · BW · 85mins

In 1901, Irish nationalists plot to rob the Old Lady of Threadneedle Street of its gold bullion, taking it through the sewers and down the River Thames. Both a heist thriller and a sophisticated political drama, the film was co-scripted by Howard Clewes (who would later write *The Avengers* TV series) and Richard Maibaum (who later wrote the Bond movies). Director John Guillermin makes the most of the planning and features some clever use of locations, but most eyes will be on Peter O'Toole as the young security guard Fitch. David Lean saw his performance and cast him in *Lawrence of Arabia*.

Aldo Ray *Norgate* • Elizabeth Sellars *Iris Muldoon* • Hugh Griffith *O'Shea* • Peter O'Toole *Fitch* • Kieron Moore *Walsh* • Albert Sharpe *Tosher* • John Le Mesurier *Green* • Joseph Tomelty *Cohoun* ■ *Dir* John Guillermin • *Scr* Howard Clewes, Richard Maibaum, from the novel by John Brophy

The Day Time Ended ★

Science-fiction
1980 · US/Sp · Colour · 80mins

The Day Time Ended can't end soon enough! Jim Davis's family moves into a solar-powered desert home, only to find they're slap-bang in the middle of a time vortex that lures visiting aliens to warn them about Earth's imminent destruction. A nonsensical blend of cardboard special effects, this crudely assembled affair is directed by low-budget genius John "Bud" Cardos with little of the knowing jauntiness or exploitation smarts that exemplifies his best work (*Kingdom of the Spiders*, *The Dark*).

Jim Davis *Grant* • Christopher Mitchum *Richard* • Dorothy Malone *Ana* • Marcy Lafferty *Beth* • Scott Kolden *Steve* • Natasha Ryan *Jenny* ■ *Dir* John "Bud" Cardos • *Scr* Wayne Schmidt, J Larry Carroll, David Schmoeller, from a story by Steve Neill

A Day to Remember ★★ Ⓤ

Drama   1953 · UK · BW · 91mins

This mix of poignant drama and postcard comedy follows Cockney darts captain Stanley Holloway as he leads his team on a day trip to Boulogne. A host of familiar faces, including Thora Hird and Bill Owen, take caricature cameos. However, the stories that linger longest in the mind are those owing least to contrivance: notably widower James Hayter's return to his

Ⓤ = SUITABLE FOR ALL   Ⓤ⒞ = SUITABLE FOR ALL, ESPECIALLY FOR YOUNG CHILDREN (VIDEO ONLY)   Ⓟ⒢ = PARENTAL GUIDANCE

honeymoon hotel, and ex-soldier Donald Sinden's reunion with Odile Versois, the beauty he'd known as a child during the war.

Stanley Holloway *Charley Porter* • Donald Sinden *Jim Carver* • Joan Rice *Vera Mitchell* • Odile Versois *Martine Berthier* • James Hayter *Fred Collins* • Harry Fowler *Stan Harvey* • Edward Chapman *Mr Robinson* • Peter Jones *Percy Goodall* • Bill Owen *Shorty Sharpe* • Meredith Edwards *Bert Tripp* • George Coulouris *Captain* • Vernon Gray *Marvin* • Thora Hird *Mrs Trott* • Theodore Bikel *Henri Dubot* ■ *Dir* Ralph Thomas • *Scr* Robin Estridge, from the novel *The Hand and the Flower* by Jerrard Tickell

The Day Will Dawn ★★★ U

Second World War romance
1942 · UK · BW · 98mins

Markedly less restrained than many other British tales of wartime resistance, this well-meaning flagwaver is still far more effective than the majority of have-a-go Hollywood movies on the same theme. The story of a British journalist liaising with the Norwegian underground to help destroy a German U-boat base is merely par for the course. What sets this apart is a remarkable cast of British stalwarts, not one of whom puts a foot wrong. Special mention should be made, however, of Deborah Kerr, who lends quiet courage to an unrewarding romantic part, and Francis L Sullivan, who makes a most malevolent Nazi.

Ralph Richardson *Lockwood* • Deborah Kerr *Kari Alstead* • Hugh Williams *Colin Metcalfe* • Griffith Manes *Inspector Gunter* • Francis L Sullivan *Wettau* • Roland Culver *Naval Attaché* • Niall MacGinnis *Olaf* • Finlay Currie *Alstead* ■ *Dir* Harold French • *Scr* Terence Rattigan, Anatole de Grunwald, Patrick Kirwan, from a story by Frank Owen

Daybreak ★★

Period romance   1931 · US · BW · 72mins

Ramon Novarro stars as a handsome Austrian guardsman who falls in love with the appealing Helen Chandler in this period romance. Although the film is elegantly and sensitively directed by Frenchman Jacques Feyder, with a supporting cast that includes the redoubtable C Aubrey Smith, it failed to appeal to the public then and is unlikely to do so now.

Ramon Novarro *Willi* • Helen Chandler *Laura* • Jean Hersholt *Herr Schnabel* • C Aubrey Smith *Gen von Hartz* ■ *Dir* Jacques Feyder • *Scr* Ruth Cummings, Cyril Hume, Zelda Sears, from the play by Arthur Schnitzler

Daybreak ★★ PG

Crime drama   1946 · US · BW · 77mins

At the time, the producers Muriel and Sydney Box complained that their British melodrama – a follow-up to *The Seventh Veil* directed by Compton Bennett – had been held up by censorship and ruined by cuts. It is hard to see how it could have worked, even in its entirety, as Eric Portman portrays an unemployed hangman seeking revenge on the Swedish lover (Maxwell Reed) of his wife (Ann Todd). Despite the title, the film throws no light on character or situation. In fact, at times, despite Portman's usual magnetism, the result is quite laughable. 🖳

Eric Portman *Eddie* • Ann Todd *Frankie* • Maxwell Reed *Olaf* • Edward Rigby *Bill Shackle* • Bill Owen *Ron* • Jane Hylton *Doris* • Eliot Makeham *Mr Bigley* • Margaret Withers *Mrs Bigley* • John Turnbull *Superintendent* • Maurice Denham *Inspector* ■ *Dir* Compton Bennett • *Scr* Muriel Box, Sydney Box, from a play by Monckton Hoffe

Daybreak ★★ 18

Science-fiction drama
1993 · US · Colour · 87mins

Set in a crumbling New York, this provocative parable is based on Alan Browne's off-Broadway success, *Beirut*. An Aids-like epidemic has persuaded the government to keep the afflicted in quarantine centres that are tantamount to concentration camps. Cuba Gooding Jr and Moira Kelly are among the rebels opposing the vigilantes who mercilessly round up suspects. The commitment of the cast can't be faulted and writer/director Stephen Tolkin ensures the action never lets up. Unfortunately, both his symbolism and his plea for increased toleration are regrettably heavy-handed. 🖳

Cuba Gooding Jr *Torch* • Martha Plimpton *Lauri* • Moira Kelly *Blue* • Omar Epps *Hunter* ■ *Dir* Stephen Tolkin • *Scr* Stephen Tolkin, from the play *Beirut* by Alan Browne

Daydream Believer ★★ 15

Romantic comedy
1991 · Ausl · Colour · 81mins

This Australian movie is a curious mix of screwball comedy and bodice-ripping romance. Beginning with unpleasant scenes of child abuse, Kathy Mueller's film suddenly lurches forward in time to find the child in question has grown into the understandably timid Miranda Otto, whose tactic in times of stress is to imagine she's a horse. There is some heavy-handed satire at the expense of wealthy businessman Martin Kemp and a last-minute rescue worthy of a silent melodrama, but it's far from clear who the film is aimed at or what it's trying to achieve. Contains swearing, violence and nudity. 🖳

Miranda Otto *Nell* • Martin Kemp *Digby* • Anne Looby *Margot* • Alister Smart *Ron* • Gia Carides *Wendy* • Bruce Venables *Stu* ■ *Dir* Kathy Mueller • *Scr* Saturday Rosenberg

Daydreams ★★★★★

Silent comedy   1922 · US · BW · 17mins

Whether he's being pursued by an army of policemen on to a ferry, or walking round and round a ship's paddle-wheel like a hamster, Buster Keaton is just trying to prove his love for Renée Adorée (best known for MGM's war epic *The Big Parade*). He wants to show her he can get – and keep – a job in the city. But since the jobs include working as a street-sweeper and as a nurse in a pet hospital, it takes a lot of persuasion. An early Keaton three-reeler, this manages to insert elements of surreality into even the humdrum. 🖳

Buster Keaton *The young man* • Renée Adorée *The girl* • Joe Keaton *The girl's father* • Edward F Cline [Edward Cline] ■ *Dir* Buster Keaton • *Scr* Buster Keaton, Edward F Cline

Daylight ★★★ 12

Disaster action adventure
1996 · US · Colour · 109mins

An involving tale of New York tunnel survivors searching for a way out. Director Rob Cohen's classy contribution to the nineties' disaster movie resurgence is less reliant on visual effects expertise than most, and Sylvester Stallone displays more vulnerability than expected as the determined leader of an escape party. Cohen's orchestration of the formula check-list (including the early, eye-popping tunnel destruction and a blatant underwater steal from *The Poseidon Adventure*) is slick and impressive. Not a genre classic, but *Daylight* does provide enough solid action entertainment to offset its overly familiar mechanics. 🖳 *DVD*

Sylvester Stallone *Kit Latura* • Amy Brenneman *Madelyne Thompson* • Viggo Mortensen *Roy Nord* • Dan Hedaya *Frank Kraft* • Jay O Sanders *Steven Crighton* • Karen Young *Sarah Crighton* • Claire Bloom *Eleanor Trilling* • Sage Stallone *Vincent* ■ *Dir* Rob Cohen • *Scr* Leslie Bohem

Daylight Robbery ★★ U

Drama   1964 · UK · BW · 57mins

In the same year that he co-starred with The Beatles in *A Hard Day's Night*, Norman Rossington found himself up to his neck in trouble in this lively production from the Children's Film Foundation. The focus of the action falls on a kid quartet that gets locked overnight in a department store and thwarts the knockabout efforts of a gang of incompetent crooks. However, it's the supporting cast that now commands most attention, with Gordon Jackson and Ronald Fraser all imparting their expertise. Michael Truman directs without much invention.

Trudy Moors *Trudy* • Janet Hannington *Janet* • Kirk Martin *Kirk* • Darryl Read *Darryl* • Douglas Robinson *Gangster* • John Trenaman *Gangster* • Gordon Jackson • Ronald Fraser ■ *Dir* Michael Truman • *Scr* Dermot Quinn, from a story by Frank Wells

The Days ★★★

Drama   1993 · Chi · BW · 75mins

Wang Xiaoshuai's subtle drama looks at a couple of Beijing art tutors whose common bonds can't save their ailing relationship, especially when professional success passes from one to the other. Dipping into images of modern China for added emphasis, *The Days* elegantly employs style, music and an unfussy narrative to comment on the duo, the choice of black and white over colour simply reinforcing the lyrical beauty. The writer/director found it impossible to secure state approval and distribution and was blacklisted as a result; his film has yet to be seen in China. In Mandarin with English subtitles.

Yu Hong *Chun* • Liu Xiaodong *Dong* • Wang Xiaoshuai *Narrator* ■ *Dir* Wang Xiaoshuai • *Scr* Wang Xiaoshuai

Days and Nights in the Forest ★★★★

Drama   1969 · Ind · BW · 115mins

Satyajit Ray was personally encouraged in his early film career by the great French director Jean Renoir, and his influence is clearly evident in this Bengali reworking of the classic featurette *Une Partie de Campagne*. Seeking to escape from the stress of Calcutta, four friends travel to the forest, where their encounters and misadventures cause them to take stock of their lives. Supremely capturing the warmth and glow of a summer's day and taking sly shots at the bourgeois mentality, Ray draws inspired performances from the leading quartet, whose escapades make for irresistible viewing. In Bengali with English subtitles.

Soumitra Chatterjee *Ashim* • Subhendu Chatterjee *Sanjoy* • Samit Bhanja *Harinath* • Robi Ghosh *Sekhar* ■ *Dir* Satyajit Ray • *Scr* Satyajit Ray, from the novel by Suil Ganguly

Days of Being Wild ★★★★ 12

Drama   1990 · HK · Colour · 90mins

This stylish, intricately structured drama not only harks back to the sixties, but also explores the fears attending Hong Kong's handover to China. Leslie Cheung excels as a rebel with the cause of tracing his Filipino mother, callously leaving the broken hearts of waitress Maggie Cheung and showgirl Carina Lau in his wake. Two years in production, and strikingly shot by Christopher Doyle, Wong Kar-wai's second feature was such a flop at the domestic box-office that a sequel was abandoned (hence the incomprehensibility of Tony Leung's late-arriving character). However, internationally, it confirmed Wong's reputation as a rising art-house star. In Cantonese with English subtitles. 🖳

Leslie Cheung *Yuddy* • Maggie Cheung *Su Lizhen* • Tony Chiu-Wai Leung [Tony Leung (1)] *Smirk* • Carina Lau *Fung-Ying* ■ *Dir* Wong Kar-Wai • *Scr* Wong Kar-Wai

Days of Glory ★★

Second World War romantic drama
1944 · US · BW · 85mins

After discovering his taste for the stage at Berkeley University, Gregory Peck headed for Broadway where he was spotted by David O Selznick, and eventually made his Hollywood debut in *Days of Glory*. Peck plays a Russian patriot fighting the Nazi invaders in this wartime flagwaver. Designed to show how friendly Uncle Sam was with Uncle Joe Stalin, it's never more than a B-picture, efficiently directed by Jacques Tourneur and co-starring Tamara Toumanova, a prima ballerina who grandly resisted Hollywood's efforts to turn her into a star.

Gregory Peck *Vladimir* • Tamara Toumanova *Nina* • Alan Reed *Sasha* • Maria Palmer *Yelena* • Lowell Gilmore *Semyon* • Hugo Haas *Fedor* ■ *Dir* Jacques Tourneur • *Scr* Casey Robinson, from a story by Melchior Lengyel

Days of Heaven ★★★★ PG

Drama   1978 · US · Colour · 88mins

This truly extraordinary visual treat from director Terrence Malick and

Oscar-winning cinematographer Nestor Almendros was not a great commercial success, but has inspired film and particularly commercial directors for over a decade. Malick, who has only made two other films (*Badlands* and *The Thin Red Line*), takes a couple of disenfranchised labourers, Richard Gere and Brooke Adams, and Gere's little sister Linda Manz, and sets them down in the golden vastness of the Texas wheatfields. A tragedy-strewn love triangle develops between Gere, Adams and their employer, Sam Shepard, though Malick steps back from the narrative to give us a curiously disembodied elegy on poverty and freedom. One to luxuriate in as an accomplished cinematic exercise, rather than engage with as an involving tale. Contains violence, swearing and brief nudity. 🎬

Richard Gere *Bill* • Brooke Adams *Abby* • Sam Shepard *Farmer* • Linda Manz *Linda* • Robert Wilke [Robert J Wilke] *Farm foreman* • Jackie Shultis *Linda's friend* • Stuart Margolin *Mill foreman* ■ *Dir/Scr* Terrence Malick

Days of Thrills and Laughter ★★★ U

Compilation   1961 · US · BW · 89mins

Film purists balk at these Robert Youngson compilations (this was his third) but they did achieve a cinema release, and as a result became, for many, an introduction to the wonderful world of silent cinema. At the time, it was difficult, or more accurately, impossible to see pre-sound movies in anywhere near decent copies with proper projection. This is a fine selection (albeit with added commentary by Jay Jackson, music and a little juggling with projection speeds) and includes the work of such geniuses as Charlie Chaplin, Harry Langdon, Laurel and Hardy, Douglas Fairbanks (Sr, of course!) and queen of the serials, Pearl White. For those who have never seen them, especially children, this is a good introduction and will fuel the desire to view more from this fabulous period when the movies were young. 🎬

Jay Jackson *Narrator* ■ *Dir/Scr* Robert Youngson

Days of Thunder ★★★ 15

Sports drama   1990 · US · Colour · 102mins

The master of the flashy, trashy action picture, Britain's very own Tony Scott, sought to recapture the glories of *Top Gun* in this reunion with Tom Cruise, which resulted in Cruise's marital union with co-star Nicole Kidman. Motor sports movies have a lousy track record at the box office and this cliché-ridden stock car action movie was a costly flop. Reworking many of the themes in Howard Hawks's *The Crowd Roars*, Robert Towne's script must have looked a sure-fire winner, and there's little wrong with Scott's zippy race sequences or Robert Duvall's performance as Cruise's manager. Contains swearing. 🎬

Tom Cruise *Cole Trickle* • Robert Duvall *Harry Hogge* • Nicole Kidman *Dr Claire Lewicki* • Randy Quaid *Tim Daland* • Cary Elwes *Russ Wheeler* • Michael Rooker *Rowdy Burns* • Fred Dalton Thompson *Big John* • John C Reilly

Buck Bretherton • JC Quinn *Waddell* ■ *Dir* Tony Scott • *Scr* Robert Towne, from a story by Robert Towne, Tom Cruise

Days of Wine and Roses ★★★★

Drama   1962 · US · BW · 117mins

Those who know Jack Lemmon only as one half of *The Odd Couple*, or as a Grumpy Old Man, should stand well clear: he's in heart-rending dramatic mode as an advertising executive, driven to drink by his work and taking wife Lee Remick along for the alcoholic ride. Adapted by JP Miller from his own TV play, the film is directed by Blake Edwards with a poignancy you don't expect, and acted by Lemmon and Remick with a force that remains memorable long after viewing. 🎬

Jack Lemmon *Joe Clay* • Lee Remick *Kirsten Arnesen* • Charles Bickford *Ellis Arnesen* • Jack Klugman *Jim Hungerford* • Alan Hewitt *Leland* • Tom Palmer *Ballefoy* ■ *Dir* Blake Edwards • *Scr* JP Miller, from his television play

A Day's Pleasure ★★★★ U

Silent comedy drama
1919 · US · BW · 18mins

In this Charlie Chaplin two-reeler, the comedy is condensed into a chaotic family outing on the river, where sea-sickness afflicts every passenger on a crowded cruiser. Edna Purviance is along for the ride, while Jackie Coogan makes his first appearance with Chaplin; he would later co-star with the great man in *The Kid* (1921). 🎬

Charles Chaplin *Father* • Edna Purviance *Mother* • Tom Wilson *Cop* • Sydney Chaplin [Syd Chaplin] *Father* • Jackie Coogan *Boy* ■ *Dir/Scr* Charles Chaplin

Dayton's Devils ★★ U

Adventure drama
1968 · US · Colour · 100mins

Fifties action hunk Rory Calhoun, Leslie Nielsen (in his screen heavy days) and other unsocial types launch a daring raid on a military base and steal a $1.5 million payroll. Taking every cliché out of the heist movie manual, it's *The Dirty Dozen* meets *Rififi*, with a lot of screen time devoted to the planning of the robbery. There's a chase after that, followed by those other key ingredients of the genre – the sudden twist and the ironic ending. A late-night no-brainer.

Leslie Nielsen *Frank Dayton* • Rory Calhoun *Mike Page* • Lainie Kazan *Leda Martell* • Hans Gudegast [Eric Braeden] *Max Eckhart* • Barry Sadler *Barney Barry* • Pat Renella *Claude Sadi* • Georg Stanford Brown *Theon Gibson* ■ *Dir* Jack Shea • *Scr* Fred De Gorter, from a story by Fred De Gorter

The Daytrippers ★★★★ 15

Comedy   1998 · US · Colour · 83mins

All of the mother-in-law-from-hell jibes that comedians used to make are on display in this sparky story about relationships among a family of oddballs. Led by dominating mother Anne Meara, the clan drives to the city to track down the husband (Stanley Tucci) whom Hope Davis thinks has been unfaithful. Davis is fairly sane about the whole issue, which is more than can be said about the rest of the

family, with Meara being the wackiest of the lot, taking her son-in-law's alleged infidelity as a personal affront. Writer/director Greg Mottola has contrived some great one-liners, but his one flaw is that the mother-in-law is almost too obnoxious for comfort. Contains swearing. 🎬

Hope Davis *Eliza* • Stanley Tucci *Louis D'Amico* • Parker Posey *Jo Malone* • Liev Schreiber *Carl* • Anne Meara *Rita Malone* • Pat McNamara *Jim Malone* • Campbell Scott *Eddie* ■ *Dir/Scr* Greg Mottola

Dazed and Confused ★★★★ 18

Comedy drama   1993 · US · Colour · 97mins

Some of Hollywood's hottest young talent cut their teeth on this ultra-hip movie, among them Matthew McConaughey and Milla Jovovich. But it's Jason London and Rory Cochrane who carry this freewheeling story, as a couple of high school wasters on the last day of the summer term. After giving voice to the disconnected youth of Austin, Texas, in his highly influential debut feature, *Slacker*, director Richard Linklater here employs a pseudo-documentary style to expose teenage life in the raw, with all the attendant angst, arrogance, aggression and amorousness. This honest and incisive portrait of the way we were is both funny and scary and ranks among the very best rock 'n' roll high school movies. Contains swearing and drug abuse. 🎬

Jason London *Randy "Pink" Floyd* • Sasha Jenson *Don Dawson* • Rory Cochrane *Slater* • Wiley Wiggins *Mitch Kramer* • Michelle Burke *Jodi Kramer* • Shawn Andrews *Pickford* • Anthony Rapp *Tony* • Adam Goldberg *Mike* • Christin Hinojosa *Sabrina* • Milla Jovovich *Michelle* • Matthew McConaughey *Wooderson* • Ben Affleck *O'Bannion* ■ *Dir/Scr* Richard Linklater

De Sade ★★

Biographical drama
1969 · US/W Ger · Colour · 107mins

Smearing jam on nipples is about as torrid as it gets in this ridiculous biography of the Marquis de Sade and his sexually adventurous exploits. Begun by director Cy Endfield and completed by Roger Corman (uncredited), it's a beautiful-looking muddle of historical fact and hysterical fiction, with tame debauchery, fuzzy fantasy and soft-core orgies punctuating the hopelessly contrived flow. Keir Dullea does his best to whip up enthusiasm for the marquis, but the Eurotrash supporting cast (the film was shot in Berlin) and John Huston's embarrassing turn as de Sade's cruel father places this squarely in the "interesting flop" category.

Keir Dullea *Marquis de Sade* • Senta Berger *Anne de Montreuil* • Lilli Palmer *Mme de Montreuil* • John Huston *Abbé de Sade* • Anna Massey *Renée de Montreuil* • Ute Levka *Rose Keller* ■ *Dir* Cy Endfield • *Scr* Richard Matheson, Peter Berg

The Dead ★★★★ U

Drama   1987 · US/UK · Colour · 79mins

Warm, nostalgic and intimate, John Huston's swansong is a beautifully judged adaptation of the finest story contained within James Joyce's *The*

Dubliners. Long resident in Ireland, Huston captures the national character with a deft economy that few film-makers could hope to emulate. But it's the quality of the ensemble acting that makes this such a memorable and moving experience. Anjelica Huston is superb as Gretta Conroy, with the speech in which she describes her lost love possibly the high spot of her career. Donal McCann also impresses as her regretful husband, while Donal Donnelly is outstanding as the tiddly Freddy Malins. 🎬

Anjelica Huston *Gretta Conroy* • Donal McCann *Gabriel Conroy* • Rachael Dowling *Lily* • Cathleen Delany *Aunt Julia Morkan* • Helena Carroll *Aunt Kate Morkan* • Ingrid Craigie *Mary Jane* • Dan O'Herlihy *Mr Browne* • Frank Patterson *Bartell D'Arcy* • Donal Donnelly *Freddy Malins* ■ *Dir* John Huston • *Scr* Tony Huston, from the short story by James Joyce

Dead Again ★★★ 15

Thriller   1991 · US · Colour and BW · 103mins

The present is tense because the past is imperfect in Kenneth Branagh's determinedly old-fashioned thriller in the Hitchcock tradition. He's a cynical LA private detective hired to research the background of amnesiac mystery woman Emma Thompson, who's obsessed by scissors and tormented by nightmares from someone else's life. An enjoyably overdone, stylish mix of *film noir* trivia and eccentric plotting, director Branagh's darkly delicious reincarnation parody will keep you guessing right up until the deliriously OTT finale. Contains swearing. 🎬

Kenneth Branagh *Mike Church/Roman Strauss* • Emma Thompson *Grace/Margaret Strauss* • Derek Jacobi *Franklyn Madson* • Andy Garcia *Gray Baker* • Wayne Knight *"Piccolo" Pete* • Hanna Schygulla *Inge* • Campbell Scott *Doug* • Gregor Hesse *Frankie* ■ *Dir* Kenneth Branagh • *Scr* Scott Frank

Dead Ahead ★ 15

Action thriller   1996 · US · Colour · 88mins

Mediocre, contrived thriller with next to no thrills. With the help of her teenage daughter, a mother desperately tracks the gang of bank robbers who have taken her young son hostage. Armed only with her deadly bow and arrow, she eventually hunts them down. Stephanie Zimbalist plays the avenging supermom in this routine family-in-peril TV drama. Aim your remote at a different target.

Stephanie Zimbalist *Maura Loch* • Peter Onorati *Frank Cacey* • Sarah Chalke *Heather Loch* • Tom Butler *Brian Loch* • Brendan Fletcher *Douglas Loch* • John Tench *Anthony* ■ *Dir* Stuart Cooper • *Scr* David Alexander

Dead Air ★★ 12

Psychological thriller
1994 · US · Colour · 86mins

Anyone who's seen *Play Misty for Me* or *Talk Radio* will know that being a late-shift DJ in America is just asking for trouble. So we shouldn't be too surprised when Gregory Hines starts getting weird phone calls from a woman who claims to have framed him for the murder of his girlfriend. Luckily, Hines has a sympathetic psychology student up his sleeve and the game is soon afoot. It's not that long ago that great things were predicted for talented actor/dancer Hines, but they didn't

U = SUITABLE FOR ALL   Uc = SUITABLE FOR ALL, ESPECIALLY FOR YOUNG CHILDREN (VIDEO ONLY)   PG = PARENTAL GUIDANCE

nclude run-of-the-mill thrillers like this. Contains some violence. 📺

Gregory Hines *Mark Jannek* • Debrah Farentino *Karen/Laura* • Laura Harrington *Susan Nichols* • Gloria Reuben *Judy* • Beau Starr *Lt Gagglis* • John Hawkes *Morton* ■ *Dir* Fred Walton • *Scr* David Amann

The Dead and the Deadly ★★★★ 18

Supernatural comedy drama
1983 · HK · Colour · 97mins

Rightly considered one of the best supernatural comedies ever made in Hong Kong, this mix of kung fu, Chinese spiritualism and knockabout fun makes a point that the producers of *Godzilla* should have taken to heart - that size really doesn't matter. Diminutive Wu Ma (who also directs) is killed while attempting an inheritance swindle, and his ghost takes over the body of hulking martial-arts superstar Samo Kam-Bo Hung. It takes Cherry Cho-Hung Chung's battle with some supernatural powers, however, to put things right. Played for laughs rather than thrills, Ma's film has a seductively mystic feel that considerably enhances its appeal. In Cantonese and Mandarin with English subtitles.

Samo Kam-Bo Hung [Sammo Hung] • Cherry Cho-Hung Chung [Cherie Chung] ■ *Dir* Wu Ma • *Scr* Samo Kam-Bo Hung [Sammo Hung], Barry Ping-Yiu Wong

Dead Badge ★★★ 18

Crime thriller 1995 · US · Colour · 89mins

Clichés abound in this police drama about a cop (Brian Wimmer) investigating the death of a fellow officer and finding himself up to his eyes in corruption. Sounds completely missable. doesn't it? However, thanks to the gritty feel and some strong performances from a top-notch cast (including M Emmet Walsh, *Homicide*'s Yaphet Kotto and James B Sikking from *Hill Street Blues*), this is a well-paced and quite interesting tale. 📺

Brian Wimmer *Dan Sampson* • M Emmet Walsh *Sgt Miller* • James B Sikking *Wheeler/Feld* • Yaphet Kotto *Capt Hunt* • Marta DuBois *Billie Torres* • Olympia Dukakis *Dr Doris Ric* ■ *Dir/Scr* Douglas Barr

Dead-Bang ★★★ 18

Detective action thriller
1989 · US · Colour · 101mins

Don Johnson stars in this thriller as a cop with the usual hang-ups – divorced, kids, workaholic, hot temper, tendency to kill people. In other words: Clint's syndrome. On the trail of a cop killer, he winds up in Nowhere, Oklahoma, home of white supremacists who plan the overthrow of the US government. Director John Frankenheimer pumps this up nicely, orchestrating some clever twists, cleanly-shot action and some very quirky characterisation, notably Bob Balaban as Johnson's bookish buddy. And whereas Eastwood has sometimes threatened to spit on people, Johnson promises a full Technicolor yawn to get the information he wants.

Don Johnson *Jerry Beck* • Bob Balaban *Elliot Webly* • William Forsythe *Arthur Kressler* • Penelope Ann Miller *Linda* • Frank Military

Bobby Burns • Tate Donovan *John Burns* • Antoni Stutz *Ray* • Mickey Jones *Sleepy* ■ *Dir* John Frankenheimer • *Scr* Robert Foster

Dead Beat ★★★

Crime thriller 1994 · US · Colour · 92mins

A serial killer chiller, set in New Mexico in 1965, with Bruce Ramsay playing an Elvis-fixated psychopath whose band of disciples include little lost rich girl Natasha Gregson Wagner and snivelling acolyte Balthazar Getty. Adam Dubov's directorial debut was co-produced by the actor Christopher Lambert, while the casting of Natalie Wood's daughter and Jean-Paul Getty's great-grandson adds a certain frisson to the proceedings. It's often been suggested that Charles Manson was "inspired" by the real-life case on which the film is based.

Bruce Ramsay *Kit* • Balthazar Getty *Rudy* • Natasha Gregson Wagner *Kirsten* • Meredith Salenger *Donna* • Deborah Harry *Mrs Kurtz* • Sara Gilbert *Martha* • Max Perlich *Jimmie* • Alex Cox *English teacher* ■ *Dir* Adam Dubov • *Scr* Adam Dubov, Janice Shapiro

Dead before Dawn ★★ 15

Thriller 1993 · US · Colour · 93mins

Cheryl Ladd is generally acceptable in movies that don't require her to provide her characters with much emotional or psychological depth. In a made-for-TV film that cries out for an actress with a greater range, she's merely adequate as the wife threatened by her murderous husband and forced to seek assistance from the FBI. However, director Charles Correll manages to come up with the odd suspenseful and atmospheric scene. Contains some swearing. 📺

Cheryl Ladd *Linda Edelman* • Jameson Parker *Robert Edelman* • GW Bailey *Masterson* • Keone Young *James Young* • Kim Coates *Zack* • Matt Clark *John DeSilva* • Hope Lange *Virginia DeSilva* ■ *Dir* Charles Correll • *Scr* John Ireland, from a story by Ricky Blackwood

Dead by Dawn ★★

Erotic thriller 1998 · US · Colour · 91mins

If there was a lifetime achievement Oscar for disrobing, Shannon Tweed would be among the frontrunners to win the award. The queen of erotic thrillers is in familiar steamy territory here, as she and husband Bill Ferrell discover that there is a murderous downside to Hollywood hedonism. This is supposedly an upright fable about the dangers of debauchery, but of course director James Salisbury and his enthusiastic cast seem to relish its every salacious moment. Contains swearing, violence and sex scenes.

Shannon Tweed *Wendy Marsh* • Bill Ferrell *Tim Marsh* • Ted Prior *Don White* • Jodie Fisher ■ *Dir* James Salisbury

Dead Calm ★★★★ 15

Thriller 1988 · Ausl · Colour · 96mins

Australian actress Nicole Kidman and director Phillip Noyce were catapulted into the Hollywood frontline by this scary revel without a pause. An ingenious psychological thriller in the grand Hitchcock tradition, the dead simple premise revolves around two boats, two men, one woman and a dog. But, once Noyce expertly turns

the high anxiety screws up to fever pitch, you'll be screaming with delicious panic in the sweaty palm of his sure hand. The best watertight shocker since *Jaws*. Dead fab. Contains swearing, violence and nudity. 📺 **DVD**

Sam Neill *John Ingram* • Nicole Kidman *Rae Ingram* • Billy Zane *Hughie Warriner* • Rod Mullinar *Russell Bellows* • Joshua Tilden *Danny* ■ *Dir* Phillip Noyce • *Scr* Terry Hayes, from the novel by Charles Williams

The Dead Can't Lie ★★★ 15

Supernatural thriller
1988 · US · Colour · 93mins

Playboy Colin Bruce is being pursued by his dead wife, the immaculately groomed Virginia Madsen, and hires hard-boiled private eye Tommy Lee Jones to give her back the jewels that she was buried with, in order to be left alone. Needless to add, the detective falls for the ghost, and they cruise the city at night. This is a real one-off, directed by Lloyd Fonvielle, a writer on such diverse movies as *The Lords of Discipline* and *Good Morning, Babylon*. There's a bewhiskered Frederic Forrest as a Russian Orthodox priest and some smart dialogue about Lillian Gish, but it's probably too pretentious for some tastes, and Fonvielle never managed anything so original again. Contains swearing and brief nudity. 📺

Tommy Lee Jones *Eddie Martel Mallard* • Virginia Madsen *Rachel Carlyle* • Colin Bruce *Charlie Rand* • Kevin Jarre *Tim* • Denise Stephenson *Debbie* • Frederic Forrest *Father George* ■ *Dir/Scr* Lloyd Fonvielle

Dead Cert ★★

Sports drama 1974 · UK · Colour · 99mins

Co-adapted from Dick Francis's runaway bestseller by Channel 4's own racing pundit, Lord Oaksey, this tale of death and doping on the eve of the Grand National is a desperate stab for a box-office hit by director Tony Richardson. Some writers can only live on the page, and the authentic atmosphere of stableyards, enclosures and racecourses that characterises Francis's thrillers has been missed by a lot more than a short head. Hardly an impenetrable mystery, but it passes the time.

Judi Dench *Laura Davidson* • Michael Williams *Sandy* • Scott Antony *Alan* • Ian Hogg *Bill Davidson* • Nina Thomas *Penny* • Mark Dignam *Clifford Tudor* • Julian Glover *Lodge* ■ *Dir* Tony Richardson • *Scr* Tony Richardson, John Oaksey, from the novel by Dick Francis

Dead Cold ★★ 18

Thriller 1996 · US · Colour · 87mins

This daft but enjoyable suspense thriller has British actress Lysette Anthony and Chris Mulkey (*Twin Peaks*) as a couple who decide to have a second honeymoon at a remote mountain cabin. (Haven't you watched enough of these films to know that is never a good idea?) Of course, their smoochy idyll is not very idyllic for long, as a homicidal maniac appears and kills poor Mulkey by throwing him into a ravine. As things descend into complete and utter ludicrousness in the second half, this becomes campily enjoyable. Contains swearing, violence and some sex scenes. 📺

Lysette Anthony *Alicia* • Chris Mulkey *Eric* • Peter Dobson *Kale* • Alina Thompson *Sarah* • Michael Champion *Bill Butler* ■ *Dir* Kurt Anderson • *Scr* Richard Brandes, from a story by Kurt Anderson, Richard Brandes

The Dead Don't Die ★★

Horror 1975 · US · Colour · 90mins

Robert Bloch (*Psycho*) wrote this peculiar TV movie as an homage to the pulp thrillers of the thirties, and B-horror veteran Curtis Harrington roped in an all-star cast to play up its knowingly camp nostalgia. In Depression-hit Chicago, George Hamilton uncovers a plot by mad scientist Ray Milland to create an army of zombies and take over the world. Shot entirely at night, and using the surreal atmosphere inherent in the Republic serial format, Harrington's reliance on overstated acting and overheated melodrama turns all the disparate elements into a sinister, heady cocktail, almost by default.

George Hamilton *Don Drake* • Ray Milland *Jim Moss* • Linda Cristal *Vera Lavalle* • Joan Blondell *Levenia Hatcher* • Ralph Meeker *Lieutenant Reardon* • James McEachin *Frankie Specht* • Reggie Nalder *Perdido* ■ *Dir* Curtis Harrington • *Scr* Robert Bloch

The Dead Don't Dream ★★

Western 1947 · US · BW · 62mins

The splendid title can't disguise the fact that this is a rather routine Hopalong Cassidy programme filler, actually the penultimate of that series's amazing 66 entries. Although the series was drawing to its cinematic end, a whole new, and largely children's, audience discovered Hoppy on television re-runs and advertising promotions, and silver-haired William Boyd became popular all over again. This episode is more of a thriller than a western, but none the worse for that.

William Boyd *Hopalong Cassidy* • Andy Clyde *California Carlson* • Rand Brooks *Lucky Jenkins* • John Parrish *Jeff Potter* • Leonard Penn *Earl Wesson* • Mary Tucker *Mary Benton* ■ *Dir* George Archainbaud • *Scr* Francis Rosenwald, from characters created by Clarence E Mulford

Dead End ★★★★ PG

Crime drama 1937 · US · BW · 87mins

A marvellously evocative, albeit resolutely studio-bound, version of Sidney Kingsley's fine play, brilliantly directed by William Wyler from an adaptation by Lillian Hellman. Unfortunately it was "cleaned-up" by its producer Samuel Goldwyn, who couldn't believe that "dead end" meant exactly that. As a consequence, the streets and gutters of production designer Richard Day's magnificent set are a little too clean, a little too well lit. Nevertheless, this is a fine work with brilliant performances, particularly from Sylvia Sidney and then new face Humphrey Bogart. Though Joel McCrea is a shade too bland as the worthy hero, the youngsters in the movie went on to their own series success, initially as the Dead End Kids and, eventually, as the Bowery Boys. 📺

Sylvia Sidney *Drina* • Joel McCrea *Dave* • Humphrey Bogart *Baby Face Martin* • Wendy Barrie *Kay* • Claire Trevor *Francie* • Allen Jenkins *Hunk* • Marjorie Main *Mrs Martin* • Billy Halop *Tommy* • Huntz Hall *Dippy* • Bobby

Jordan *Angel* • Gabriel Dell *TB* • Bernard Punsley *Milty* • Charles Peck *Philip Griswold* • Leo Gorcey *Spit* ■ *Dir* William Wyler • *Scr* Lillian Hellman, from the play by Sidney Kingsley • *Cinematographer* Gregg Toland

Dead End Kids ★★★

Experimental documentary drama
1986 · US · Colour and BW · 87mins

Adapted from the off-Broadway play, *Dead End Kids: a Story of Nuclear Power*, this blend of eyewitness testimonies, scholarly articles and interviews attempts to put a satirical spin on the history of the nuclear industry. Lacking the cutting edge of that similarly cynical scrapbook, *The Atomic Café*, JoAnne Akalaitis's production is so in thrall of the text, it's as if the camera is bolted down. However, the performances of the self-effacing ensemble (most of whom take dual roles) are excellent, and there are cameo roles for David Byrne and Philip Glass, who composed the score.

Ellen McElduff *Television host/Army Stenographer/Schoolteacher* • Ruth Maleczech *Marie Curie* • George Bartenieff *Faust/Gen Groves* • David Brisbin *Nightclub comic/Gen Farrell* ■ *Dir* JoAnne Akalaitis • *Scr* JoAnne Akalaitis, from her play • *Music* David Byrne, Philip Glass

Dead Funny ★★★

Comedy mystery
1995 · US/UK · Colour · 91mins

At the start of this comedy, Andrew McCarthy lies on the kitchen table, impaled by a samurai sword and completely dead. When his girlfriend (Elizabeth Pena) comes home and discovers him, she opens a bottle of champagne and calls a friend over. That's when the flashbacks begin, showing how McCarthy's practical joker reached such a pretty pass. The slightly nerdy McCarthy is well-cast here, and Pena – always an attractive actress to watch – makes her Manhattan museum employee a very wacky character. The film's charms are perhaps too slight to make it memorable, however.

Elizabeth Pena *Vivian Saunders* • Andrew McCarthy *Reggie Barker* • Paige Turco *Louise* • Blanche Baker *Barbara* • Allison Janney *Jennifer* • Adelle Lutz *Mari* • Lisa Jane Persky *Sarah* ■ *Dir* John Feldman • *Scr* John Feldman, Cindy Oswin

Dead Heart ★★ 18

Detective thriller
1996 · Ausl · Colour · 101mins

When it comes to depicting the Aborigines on screen, the infringement of tribal rights seems to be the only topic producers consider worth tackling. Consequently, what we have here is another thriller in which the clash of progress and tradition results in a murder, which is investigated by a well-intentioned white cop. Bryan Brown (who also co-produces) uncovers evidence of bootlegging, adultery and black magic with grim determination. The use made by director/writer Nicholas Parsons of the scorching red desert around the village of Wala Wala gives the film both the feel of an outback western and a strong sense of mystery. Contains swearing, violence and some nudity. 📺

Bryan Brown *Ray Lorkin* • Ernie Dingo *David* • Angie Milliken *Kate* • Aaron Pedersen *Tony* • Lewis Fitz-Gerald *Les* • John Jarratt *Charlie* ■ *Dir/Scr* Nicholas Parsons

Dead Heat ★★★ 18

Comedy horror   1988 · US · Colour · 80mins

Just when you thought nothing original could be made of the buddy-cop genre, along comes Mark Goldblatt's outlandish horror-gore comedy. Treat Williams, who never quite hit the big time that his looks and easy charm perhaps merited, and Joe Piscopo star as LA cops who uncover a scheme by batty old Vincent Price (woefully misused in a cameo role) to resuscitate the dead. In a movie that's imaginative and disgusting in equal measure, a butcher shop full of meat comes alive to do battle with the heroes, while Williams himself hilariously turns into a zombie and has 12 hours to solve the case before decomposition sets in. 📺

Treat Williams *Roger Mortis* • Joe Piscopo *Doug Bigelow* • Darren McGavin *Dr Ernest McNab* • Lindsay Frost *Randi James* • Vincent Price *Arthur P Loudermilk* • Clare Kirkconnell *Rebecca Smythers* • Keye Luke *Mr Thule* ■ *Dir* Mark Goldblatt • *Scr* Terry Black

Dead Heat on a Merry-Go-Round ★★ PG

Crime caper   1966 · US · Colour · 102mins

There's little to distinguish this crime caper from others of its ilk, though it does give Harrison Ford fans the opportunity to see their hero make his big-screen debut. Few could carry off the wisecracking tough guy act better than James Coburn, but even he seems to be going through the motions here as he robs the bank at Los Angeles airport during the arrival of the Russian premier. As with all *Rififi* rip-offs, the action gets bogged down in its own cleverness, while writer/director Bernard Girard simply doesn't have the nous to sustain either momentum or interest. 📺

James Coburn *Eli Kotch* • Camilla Sparv *Inger Knudson* • Aldo Ray *Eddie Hart* • Nina Wayne *Frieda Schmid* • Robert Webber *Milo Stewart* • Rose Marie *Margaret Kirby* • Todd Armstrong *Alfred Morgan* • Harrison Ford *Bellhop* ■ *Dir/Scr* Bernard Girard

Dead Husbands ★★★ 15

Black comedy   1998 · US · Colour · 86mins

What seems like a sleazy tale of marital revenge is actually quite a cheeky romp, thanks to a witty script and brisk performances by TV favourite John Ritter and former soap star Nicollette Sheridan. The social-climbing wife of a doctor turned author is not happy when her husband decides to quit writing and return to his small-town practice. Faced with having to leave New York, she finds a permanent solution to her woes when she joins a secret circle of scheming socialites who kill each other's boorish spouses. Contains some swearing and comic violence. 📺

John Ritter *Dr Carter Elson* • Nicollette Sheridan *Alexandra Elson* • Sonja Smits *Sheila Feinstein* • Amy Yasbeck *Betty Lansing* • Sherry Miller *Nicole Allison* • Bill MacDonald

Detective ■ *Dir* Paul Shapiro • *Scr* Lindsay Harrison, from the book *The Last Man on the List* by Bob Randall, adapted by Warren Taylor

Dead in the Water ★★ 15

Mystery   1991 · US · Colour · 86mins

So this is what Teri Hatcher was doing before she won the role of Lois in *The New Adventures of Superman*. It's a run-of-the-mill, *film noir*-style thriller, with Bryan Brown as the lawyer who decides to murder his wealthy wife and live happily ever after with his secretary. Needless to say his plans go awry. Nothing new, then, but both Hatcher and Brown are pleasing to the eye, and the time passes quickly enough. 📺

Bryan Brown *Charlie Deegan* • Teri Hatcher *Laura Stewart* • Anne DeSalvo *Olivia Deegan* • Veronica Cartwright *Victoria Haines* • Seymour Cassel *Lieutenant Frank Vaness* • Anna Thomson [Anna Levine] *Edie Myers* • Pruitt Taylor Vince *Lou Recsetti* ■ *Dir* Bill Condon • *Scr* Eleanor E Gaver, Robert Seidenberg, Walter Klenhard, from the novel *Web of Murder* by Harry Whittington

Dead Innocent ★★ 15

Thriller   1996 · Can · Colour · 91mins

Although she's been in films for 35 years, Geneviève Bujold has never quite received the acclaim due to her. Perhaps she's been too loyal to her native Canadian film industry, for there's nothing in this contrived thriller to test an actress of her ability. Returning home to find her maid murdered and her daughter kidnapped, lawyer Bujold is ordered to commit suicide by someone following her every move through a network of video cameras. The plot is convoluted rather than ingenious, and Sara Botsford's direction fails to exploit the claustrophobic possibilities of a script that settles for easy options. Contains swearing and violence. 📺

Geneviève Bujold *Suzanne St Laurent* • Nancy Beatty *Donna Swift* • Graham Greene *Mike* • Emily Hampshire *Nicole* • Jonathan Scarfe *Jimmy* ■ *Dir* Sara Botsford • *Scr* Delores Payne, Mort Pattigo

Dead Letter Office ★★★

Drama   1998 · Ausl · Colour · 95mins

John Ruane's surreal, often lyrical drama is both sad and uplifting. Set in an office for undeliverable mail that is under threat of mechanisation, this tale of damaged people and indefatigable hope turns on the unlikely relationship between new employee, Mirando Otto (who still writes to her long-absent father) and her Chilean boss George DelHoyo, who was driven from his homeland because of his political views. With a quaint sub-plot involving a directionless homing pigeon, this precisely paced drama has both power and poignancy. In English and Spanish with subtitles. Contains some swearing.

George DelHoyo *Frank Lopez* • Miranda Otto *Alice* • Nicholas Bell *Kevin* • Georgina Naidu *Mary* • Syd Brisbane *Peter* • Barry Otto *Gerald Urquhart* • Vanessa Steele *Carmen* ■ *Dir* John Ruane • *Scr* Deborah Cox

Dead Man ★★★ 18

Western   1995 · US/Ger · BW · 116mins

Johnny Depp stars as William Blake – not the poet – but a mundane clerk, who arrives in the shoot-'em-up Wild West town of Machine to take a job as an accountant only to find the position has been filled. Things go from bad to worse when he accidentally kills a man and is pursued as a gunslinger. Independent director Jim Jarmusch's black-and-white take on the cowboy movie is as bizarre and deadpan as his usual work, but it's enlivened by appearances from the likes of John Hurt and, briefly, Robert Mitchum. Contains swearing and brief nudity. 📺

Johnny Depp *William Blake* • Crispin Glover *Train fireman* • Gibby Haines *Man with gun in alley* • George Duckworth *Man at end of street* • Richard Boes *Man with wrench* • John Hurt *John Scholfield* • John North *Mr Olafsen* • Robert Mitchum *John Dickinson* • Mili Avital *Thel Russell* • Peter Schrum *Drunk* • Gabriel Byrne *Charlie Dickinson* • Lance Henriksen *Cole Wilson* • Gary Farmer *Nobody* • Iggy Pop *Salvatore "Sally" Jenko* ■ *Dir/Scr* Jim Jarmusch

Dead Man on Campus ★★ 15

Comedy   1998 · US · Colour · 90mins

Pitched at a young teen audience, this has Tom Everett Scott and Mark-Paul Gosselaar on the verge of being kicked out of school because of low grades. When they discover a clause in the school constitution saying they will get automatic A's if a roommate commits suicide, they set about finding a suitably depressed person to share with – a task that turns out to be more difficult than they imagined. It's amiably played, but Alan Cohn's direction lacks bite. Contains swearing and sexual references. 📺

Tom Everett Scott *Josh* • Mark-Paul Gosselaar *Cooper* • Poppy Montgomery *Rachel* • Lochlyn Munro *Cliff* • Randy Pearlstein *Buckley* • Corey Page *Matt* • Alyson Hannigan *Lucy* • Dave Ruby *Zeke* ■ *Dir* Alan Cohn • *Scr* Michael Traeger, Mike White, from a story by Adam Larson Broder, Anthony Abrams

Dead Man Walking ★★★★ 15

Prison drama   1995 · US · Colour · 127mins

Sean Penn gives a chilling and mesmerising portrayal of sociopathy, as Matthew Poncelet, a white trash multiple killer on death row with no sense of remorse. His sparring partner is Susan Sarandon, in an Oscar-winning performance as Sister Helen Prejean, the real-life nun who became Poncelet's spiritual adviser during his final countdown, and whose book about the experience was the inspiration for the film. Sarandon's nun is a sort of social worker with faith, whose sexually charged chats with Penn, and her meetings with his family and the families of his victims, take us into the heart of the debate about capital punishment. Director Tim Robbins's refusal to make a clear judgement on the issue is frustrating, some may say perverse. Is he taking a deliberately ambiguous stance, or can't he make his own mind up? Contains violence, swearing and brief nudity. 📺
DVD

🅄 = SUITABLE FOR ALL   🅄c = SUITABLE FOR ALL, ESPECIALLY FOR YOUNG CHILDREN (VIDEO ONLY)   PG = PARENTAL GUIDANCE

Susan Sarandon *Sister Helen Prejean* • Sean Penn *Matthew Poncelet* • Robert Prosky *Hilton Barber* • Raymond J Barry *Earl Delacroix* • R Lee Ermey *Clyde Percy* • Celia Weston *Mary Beth Percy* • Lois Smith *Helen's mother* ■ *Dir* Tim Robbins • *Scr* Tim Robbins, from the book by Sister Helen Prejean

Dead Man's Curve ★★★★ 15

Black comedy thriller
1997 · US · Colour · 86mins

This twisted comedy thriller becomes addictive viewing, thanks to the completely bonkers and mesmerising performance from young actor Matthew Lillard (*Love's Labour's Lost*). Three roommates (Lillard, Michael Vartan and Randall Batinkoff) learn that their college has an unspoken rule that, should a student commit suicide, the students sharing their room are automatically awarded perfect grades for the rest of the academic year because they have had to suffer such a trauma. So, it's not long before Vartan and Lillard have offed their best pal and – in true *Shallow Grave* style – this is only the beginning of double-crossing, back-stabbing and murder on campus. Written and directed with a wicked gleam in his eye by Dan Rosen. Contains swearing, sex scenes, sexual references and some violence.

Matthew Lillard *Tim* • Michael Vartan *Chris* • Randall Batinkoff *Rand* • Keri Russell *Emma* • Tamara Craig Thomas *Natalie* • Anthony Griffith *Detective Schipper* • Bo Dietl *Detective Amato* ■ *Dir/Scr* Dan Rosen

Dead Man's Evidence ★★ U

Spy drama
1962 · UK · BW · 67mins

This provides a sobering insight into how the rest of the British film industry was handling espionage thrillers while Terence Young was making *Dr No*. With his heyday as TV's William Tell already behind him, Conrad Phillips stars as a spy sent to investigate when the body of a defector is washed up on an Irish beach. Francis Searle's direction is as perfunctory as Arthur La Bern and Gordon Wellesley's script.

Conrad Phillips *David Baxter* • Jane Griffiths *Linda Howard* • Veronica Hurst *Gay Clifford* ■ *Dir* Francis Searle • *Scr* Arthur La Bern, Gordon Wellesley, from a story by Arthur La Bern

Dead Man's Float ★★

Crime adventure
1980 · Ausl · Colour · 75mins

Bill Hunter may be the only familiar face in this children's adventure, but his young co-stars turn in spirited performances as they abandon their obsession with surfing to prevent drug smugglers from operating on their beach. Working from a novel by Roger Carr (who also wrote the screenplay), director Peter Sharp sets the scene with broad strokes, making the villains suitably doltish in spite of their dark trade. However, it's in the depiction of the kids that the film scores.

Sally Boyden *Anne* • Greg Rowe *Johnny* • Jacqui Gordon *Sue* • Rick Ireland *Pete* • Bill Hunter *Eddie Bell* • Sue Jones *Shirley Bell* • John Heywood *Captain Collins* • Gus Mercurio *Mr Dobraski* ■ *Dir* Peter Sharp • *Scr* Roger Carr, from his novel

Dead Man's Folly ★★★ PG

Murder mystery 1986 · US · Colour · 89mins

While not perhaps one of Agatha Christie's best mysteries, this slick TV movie will still keep you guessing whodunit right to the end. As the fastidious Belgian detective Hercule Poirot, Peter Ustinov is invited to organise a murder hunt for a village fête only to find himself confronted with the real thing. In a case where nearly everybody is a thoroughly nasty piece of work, there is plenty of scope for the solid support cast to ham it up, with veterans Constance Cummings and Jean Stapleton showing the others how it should be done. 🖵

Peter Ustinov *Hercule Poirot* • Jean Stapleton *Mrs Oliver* • Constance Cummings *Mrs Folliat* • Tim Pigott-Smith *Sir George Stubbs* • Jonathan Cecil *Hastings* • Kenneth Cranham *Inspector Bland* • Susan Wooldridge *Miss Brewis* • Christopher Guard *Alec Legge* • Jeff Yagher *Eddie South* ■ *Dir* Clive Donner • *Scr* Rod Browning, from the novel by Agatha Christie

Dead Man's Island ★★ PG

Mystery thriller 1996 · US · Colour · 84mins

A splendid cast of has-beens and might-have-beens enjoy themselves by delivering deliciously ripe performances in this entirely predictable TV mystery thriller. Barbara Eden is the journalist who gets caught up in a devilish murder plot on a luxurious, isolated island retreat, while William Shatner, Morgan Fairchild and Traci Lords are among the familiar faces hamming it up for all it's worth. 🖵

Barbara Eden *Henrie O* • William Shatner *Chase Prescott* • Morgan Fairchild *Valerie St Vincent* • Traci Lords *Miranda Prescott* • Jameson Parker *Lyle Stedman* • Roddy McDowall *Trevor Dunaway* • Christopher Atkins *Roger Prescott* ■ *Dir* Peter Hunt • *Scr* Peter S Fischer, from the novel by Carolyn G Hart

Dead Men Can't Dance ★★

War action adventure
1997 · US · Colour · 97mins

They can't act, either, and the same can be said for the cast of this war drama about the first women to be accepted into the ranks of the US Rangers. Borrowing heavily from *Full Metal Jacket*, director Stephen M Anderson charts the progress of a group of women through the Rangers training programme; we then see them in action in the demilitarised zone outside North Korea. Somewhere along the line, Michael Biehn's group of CIA covert operatives get in on the act. Some good action scenes, but nothing to keep you on the edge of your seat.

Michael Biehn *Hart* • Kathleen York *Victoria Elliot* • Adrian Paul *Shooter* • R Lee Ermey *Pullman T Fowler* • Shawnee Smith *Sgt Addie Cooper* • Joel McKinnon Miller *Bearclaw* • John Carroll Lynch *Sgt Plonder* • Grace Zabriskie *Brigadier General Burke* ■ *Dir* Stephen M Anderson [Steve Anderson] • *Scr* Bill Kerby, Mark Sevi, Paul Sinor

Dead Men Don't Die ★ PG

Black comedy 1991 · US · Colour · 94mins

Elliott Gould, whose career seemed to peak in the mid-seventies, here stars in a dire comedy about a newsreader who is shot dead and then brought back to life by his voodoo-chanting cleaning lady. It's completely silly, with Gould lumbering from one pratfall to another, looking uncomfortable throughout. Well worth avoiding. Contains violence and swearing. 🖵

Elliott Gould *Barry Barron* • Melissa Anderson [Melissa Sue Anderson] *Dulcie Niles* • Mark Moses *Jordan Penrose* ■ *Dir/Scr* Malcolm Marmorstein

Dead Men Don't Wear Plaid ★★★★ PG

Detective spoof 1982 · US · BW · 84mins

The box-office hits came later, but Steve Martin's early collaborations with director and co-writer Carl Reiner from *The Jerk* to *All of Me* still rank among his best. This ingenious spoof finds Martin as a hard-boiled private eye with a dangerous phobia about cleaning women who gets involved in a supremely silly story involving a cheese professor and sinister Nazis. However, this provides the slenderest of excuses for Martin to be spliced into an array of classic movies and swap dumb dialogue with stars such as Bette Davis, Burt Lancaster, Barbara Stanwyck, Ray Milland and the like in some of their most famous roles. There are some wonderful moments for film buffs, Martin is on inspired form and Rachel Ward is a revelation in a rare comic role. Look out, too, for Reiner himself. Contains swearing. 🖵

Steve Martin *Rigby Reardon* • Rachel Ward *Juliet Forrest* • Carl Reiner *Field Marshal Von Kluck* • Reni Santoni *Carlos Rodriguez* • George Gaynes *Dr Forrest* ■ *Dir* Carl Reiner • *Scr* George Gipe, Carl Reiner, Steve Martin

Dead of Night ★★★★★ PG

Portmanteau horror 1945 · UK · BW · 98mins

Ealing will for ever be associated with its celebrated comedies, but this chilling quintet deserves to be considered among the studio's finest achievements. Including stories penned by HG Wells and EF Benson, *Dead of Night* illustrates how ghost stories should be filmed. Alberto Cavalcanti's "The Ventriloquist's Dummy" episode has lost none of its shocking power, thanks largely to Michael Redgrave's astonishing performance, which ranks among the best of his career. There's also much to raise the hair on the back of the neck in Robert Hamer's "The Haunted Mirror", while the linking story involving architect Mervyn Johns brings the whole thing to a nightmarish conclusion. 🖵

Mervyn Johns *Walter Craig* • Roland Culver *Eliot Foley* • Mary Merrall *Mrs Foley* • Anthony Baird *Hugh Grainger* • Judy Kelly *Joyce Grainger* • Sally Ann Howes *Sally O'Hara* • Michael Allen *Jimmy Watson* • Googie Withers *Joan Courtland* • Ralph Michael *Peter Courtland* • Michael Redgrave *Maxwell Frere* ■ *Dir* Alberto Cavalcanti, Basil Dearden, Robert Hamer, Charles Crichton • *Scr* John Baines, Angus MacPhail, TEB Clarke, from stories by HG Wells, EF Benson, Baines, MacPhail

Dead of Winter ★★★ 15

Thriller 1987 · US · Colour · 96mins

It's slightly disconcerting to see Arthur Penn, the highly distinctive director of *Bonnie and Clyde* and *Alice's Restaurant*, switching to formula. That said, it's a pleasure to see a film where suspense is sustained by craft rather than through wham-bam action or gore. Taking his cue from the 1945 film *My Name Is Julia Ross*, Penn allows Mary Steenburgen to relish no less than three roles, while Roddy McDowall is an unnerving study in controlled evil as the assistant to Jan Rubes's eccentric doctor. 🖵

Mary Steenburgen *Katie McGovern/Julie Rose/Evelyn* • Roddy McDowall *Thomas* • Jan Rubes *Dr Joseph Lewis* • William Russ *Rod Sweeney* • Mark Malone *Roland McGovern* • Ken Pogue *Officer Mullavy* ■ *Dir* Arthur Penn • *Scr* Marc Shmuger, Mark Malone

Dead On ★ 18

Erotic thriller 1993 · US · Colour · 87mins

This shameless rip-off of *Strangers on a Train* even invokes the name of the Hitchcock classic. A pilot (Matt McCoy), unhappily married to frigid Tracy Scoggins, enters a murder pact with a relative stranger (Shari Shattuck), with whom he's having an affair. They agree he'll murder her abusive husband and she will off his controlling spouse. It doesn't take much to see the inevitable twist coming, but McCoy's character is as dumb as a post and he doesn't catch on until the bitter end. 🖵

Matt McCoy *Ted Beaumont* • Shari Shattuck *Erin* • David Ackroyd *Dexter Davenport* • Thomas Wagner *Det Maldonado* • Tracy Scoggins *Marla* ■ *Dir* Ralph Hemecker • *Scr* April Wayne

Dead on Sight ★★

Crime thriller 1994 · US · Colour · 90mins

A college professor who lectures on serial killers is obsessively tracking down the killer of his wife with the help of one of his students, herself haunted by a terrifying childhood episode. There are more psychological hang-ups here than in Dr Freud's casebook, and they manifest themselves in visions, dreams and flashbacks. Jennifer Beals plays the traumatised student, with Daniel Baldwin as the troubled professor, although neither is helped by Ruben Preuss's too-flashy direction. For fans of the unpredictable and the improbable. Contains swearing and violence.

Jennifer Beals *Rebecca* • Daniel Baldwin *Caleb O'Dell* • William H Macy *Stephen Meeker* • Kurtwood Smith *Tommy* • Eleanor Comegys *Stephanie* ■ *Dir* Ruben Preuss • *Scr* Lewis Green

Dead on the Money ★★

Thriller 1991 · US · Colour · 92mins

Never eat at a place called "Mom's". Never play cards with a man called "Doc". And never trust a film that keeps changing its title such as this American made-for-TV thriller, which has at various points also gone by such names as *The Scream* and *The End of Tragedy*. Corbin Bernsen does well enough as the suave charmer who draws a lovely actress (Bernsen's real-life wife Amanda Pays) into a scheme of revenge. Yet the film ultimately lacks the class of *LA Law*, the TV series for which Bernsen is better known. Contains some swearing.

Corbin Bernsen *Carter Matthews* • Amanda Pays *Jennifer Ashford* • John Glover *Russell Blake* • Allan Rich *Director* • Eleanor Parker *Catherine Blake* • Kevin McCarthy *Waverly Blake* • Sheree North *Mrs Roach* ■ *Dir* Mark Cullingham • *Scr* Gavin Lambert, from the novella *The End of Tragedy* by Rachel Ingalls

Dead Pigeon on Beethoven Street ★★ 15

Detective mystery
1972 · W Ger · Colour · 86mins

Near the end of a long working career veteran maverick director Samuel Fuller managed to put together this turgid hotchpotch of half-baked ideas, funded by German television and filmed entirely in Germany. Hard to tell if this is genuine tongue-in-cheek spy stuff or just inept movie storytelling, but Fuller's fans seem eager to accord Sam the benefit of the doubt. There's no excusing the wooden performances from Columbia contractee Glenn Corbett or Christa Lang (Mrs S Fuller) in the leading roles, though. But it's nice to see Anton Diffring flex his acting muscles. ■

Glenn Corbett *Sandy* • Christa Lang *Christa* • Sieghardt Rupp *Kessin* • Anton Diffring *Mensur* • Alex D'Arcy *Novka* • Anthony Chinn *Fong* ■ *Dir/Scr* Samuel Fuller

Dead Poets Society ★★★★ PG

Drama
1989 · US · Colour · 123mins

Peter Weir's lyricism may sometimes seem out of place in modern Hollywood, but there is no denying that this warm, touching tale struck a chord with audiences around the world. Robin Williams is the unconventional teacher at a stuffy boys' school in late-fifties America, who awakens a love of poetry and writing among a disparate group of troubled adolescents headed by Robert Sean Leonard and Ethan Hawke. However, the individualism he fosters eventually leads to tragedy. The two young leads turn in subtle performances; and, if Tom Schulman's Oscar-winning screenplay does lurch occasionally into mawkish melodrama, it's lusciously photographed and genuinely moving. ■ *DVD*

Robin Williams *John Keating* • Robert Sean Leonard *Neil Perry* • Ethan Hawke *Todd Anderson* • Josh Charles *Knox Overstreet* • Gale Hansen *Charlie Dalton* • Dylan Kussman *Richard Cameron* • Allelon Ruggiero *Steven Meeks* • James Waterston *Gerard Pitts* • Norman Lloyd *Mr Nolan* • Kurtwood Smith *Mr Perry* ■ *Dir* Peter Weir • *Scr* Tom Schulman • Cinematographer John Seale

The Dead Pool ★★ 18

Crime thriller
1988 · US · Colour · 87mins

"Dirty" Harry Callahan's fifth outing finds the San Francisco detective looking decidedly ropey around the edges. Clint Eastwood goes through his iconic paces and directs the film in all but name; the actual credit, however, goes to Buddy Van Horn, Clint's stuntman. It's a flaccid, silly and extremely sadistic tale involving a demented movie fan who bumps off minor celebrities, with Liam Neeson co-starring as a British horror film director. The result is a B-thriller without much style and even less

substance. Contains violence and swearing. ■

Clint Eastwood *Inspector Harry Callahan* • Patricia Clarkson *Samantha Walker* • Evan C Kim [Evan Kim] *Al Quan* • Liam Neeson *Peter Swan* • David Hunt *Harlan Rook* ■ *Dir* Buddy Van Horn • *Scr* Steve Sharon, from a story by Steve Sharon, Durk Pearson, Sandy Shaw, from the character created by Harry Julian Fink, RM Fink

Dead Presidents ★★★ 18

Crime drama
1995 · US · Colour · 114mins

In the Hughes Brothers' brutal seventies drama, Bronx boy Larenz Tate returns from a tour of Vietnam to find his urban life just as screwed-up as the war. Armed robbery seems the only solution. It's interesting to see the "coming home" story told from a black perspective, and there are some stunning sequences. (The heist finale is a knockout.) However, the film's tone is so grim, and the characters so superficial, that it never quite sucks you in. Great period detail and a superb soundtrack of soul classics, though. Contains swearing, violence and sex scenes. ■ *DVD*

Larenz Tate *Anthony Curtis* • Keith David *Kirby* • Chris Tucker *Skip* • Freddy Rodriguez *Jose* • Rose Jackson *Juanita Benson* • N'Bushe Wright *Delilah Benson* • Alvaletah Guess *Mrs Benson* • James Pickens Jr *Mr Curtis* ■ *Dir* Albert Hughes, Allen Hughes • *Scr* Michael Henry Brown, from a story by Albert Hughes, Allen Hughes, Michael Henry Brown, from the story *Specialist No 4 Haywood T "The Kid" Kirkland* by Wallace Terry

Dead Reckoning ★★★ U

Film noir
1947 · US · BW · 96mins

A hardboiled thriller starring Humphrey Bogart, with sultry Lizabeth Scott as the duplicitous dame. The plot's very ordinary – war veteran Bogart trying to find out who killed his buddy – but the dialogue is as sharp as a razor: in one scene, Bogie confides of chanteuse Scott, "Maybe she was all right, and maybe Christmas comes in July." Watch out for America's greatest King Lear, Morris Carnovsky, in one of his last roles before he was blacklisted during the McCarthy witch-hunt, here playing a villainous nightclub owner. With this talent at his disposal, director John Cromwell steps back and just lets his cast get on with it. ■

Humphrey Bogart *Rip Murdock* • Lizabeth Scott *Coral Chandler* • Morris Carnovsky *Martinelli* • Charles Cane *Lt Kincaid* • William Prince *Johnny Drake* • Marvin Miller *Krause* • Wallace Ford *McGee* • James Bell *Father Logan* ■ *Dir* John Cromwell • *Scr* Oliver HP Garrett, Steve Fisher, Allen Rivkin (adaptation), from an unpublished story by Gerald Adams, Sidney Biddell

Dead Reckoning ★★ 18

Thriller
1990 · US · Colour · 90mins

Don't get your hopes up, because this isn't the tense 1947 Humphrey Bogart *film noir*. In fact, it is a less-than-inspired TV movie starring Cliff Robertson as a rich husband targeted for murder by his wife and her lover during a sailing trip. Director Robert Lewis contrives to miss every cue for suspense and Robertson's career really must have run aground if the one-time Oscar-winner was forced to

come on board a leaky tub like this. Contains violence. ■

Cliff Robertson *Dr Daniel Barnard* • Susan Blakely *Alex Barnard* • Rick Springfield *Kyle Rath* • Linda Darlow *Chi-Chi* • Michael Macrae *Sheriff Cline* • Jano Frandsen *Senator Killian* ■ *Dir* Robert Lewis • *Scr* Neill D Hicks, Andie McCuaig, from an unproduced • *Scr* by Robert Lewis, Les Green

Dead Ringer ★★★ PG

Melodrama
1964 · US · BW · 111mins

Not to be confused with David Cronenberg's misogynistic *Dead Ringers*, this is a late Bette Davis vehicle in which she stars as twins. Under the gritty direction of her *Now, Voyager* co-star Paul Henreid she's in post-Baby Jane mode, as one sister kills the other and takes her place in the mansion on the hill. It's good to see sixties' stalwarts like Peter Lawford and Karl Malden with something to get their teeth into. ■

Bette Davis *Margaret/Edith* • Karl Malden *Sergeant Jim Hobbson* • Peter Lawford *Tony Collins* • Philip Carey *Sergeant Ben Hoag* • Jean Hagen *Dede* • George Macready *Paul Harrison* • Estelle Winwood *Matriarch* ■ *Dir* Paul Henreid • *Scr* Albert Beich, Oscar Millard, from the story *La Otra* by Rian James

Dead Ringers ★★★★ 18

Psychological thriller
1988 · Can · Colour · 110mins

A finely wrought urban horror tale, inspired by the true story of identical twin gynaecologists who were found dead on New York's Upper East Side in 1975. Here, with the setting transposed to Toronto, Jeremy Irons expertly plays both Beverly and Elliot Mantle, and Geneviève Bujold is the internationally famous, infertile actress who, quite literally, can't choose between them. Director David Cronenberg is better known, perhaps, for his more overt horror subjects, notably his 1986 remake of *The Fly*, but here he demonstrates a uniquely distressing and subtle talent, and the result is enough to put you off visiting fertility clinics for ever. Contains swearing. ■ *DVD*

Jeremy Irons *Beverly/Elliot Mantle* • Geneviève Bujold *Claire Niveau* • Heidi Von Palleske *Dr Cary Weiler* • Barbara Gordon *Danuta* • Shirley Douglas *Laura* • Stephen Lack *Anders Wolleck* • Nick Nichols *Leo* • Lynne Cormack *Arlene* ■ *Dir* David Cronenberg • *Scr* David Cronenberg, Norman Snider, from the book *Twins* by Bari Wood, Jack Geasland

Dead Run ★★ U

Spy comedy
1967 · Fr/W Ger/It · Colour · 96mins

A tongue-in-cheek spy thriller with CIA agent Peter Lawford and the Mafia both chasing a petty thief who has inadvertently run off with an attaché case containing top, top secret papers. In fact, the papers are just our old friend the McGuffin, since the movie is really all about Lawford's smarmy womanising and gentle spoofing from French director Christian-Jaque. It's set in Berlin and Vienna and the high point is the scene in which the characters converge on the Ferris wheel in Vienna for a jokey replay of *The Third Man*. French dialogue dubbed into English.

Georges Geret *Carlos* • Peter Lawford *Dain* • Ira von Furstenberg *Suzanne* • Maria Grazia

Buccella *Anna* • Horst Frank *Manganne* • Werner Peters *Bardieff* • Jean Tissier *Adelgate* ■ *Dir* Christian-Jaque • *Scr* Michel Levine, Christian-Jaque, Pascal Jardin, Dany Tyber, from the novel by Robert Scheckley

Dead Run ★★★

Thriller
1991 · US · Colour · 95mins

The dry Texas heat almost chokes this TV movie, in the best possible sense, providing a telling metaphor for the agitated spirit of taciturn farmer Robert Urich, who's hiding a troubled past. Yet the picture also manages to thrill as it follows a rich city wife (Markie Post) on her flight from a murderous husband towards Urich's controlled, silent world. That the stars successfully manage to abandon their usual squeaky-clean images is an imaginative plus.

Robert Urich *Joe Fortier* • Markie Post *Sharon Dancey* • Michael Beck *Jimmy Lee Dancey* • James Gammon *Sheriff Harv Bitterman* ■ *Dir* Vincent McEveety • *Scr* Peter S Fischer

Dead Silence ★★ 15

Thriller
1991 · US · Colour · 88mins

This TV-movie thriller is worth watching if only to see whether some of the old family talent has rubbed off on leads Renee Estevez (daughter of Martin Sheen and sister of Charlie Sheen and Emilio Estevez) and Carrie Mitchum (granddaughter of Robert); their co-star Lisanne Falk isn't related to Peter. This is one of those truth-will-out stories, in which the trio vows to keep mum after they accidentally kill a vagrant during a wild holiday. Director Peter O'Fallon unfolds events quite neatly and the young women acquit themselves adequately enough, but ultimately there's too little suspense and no surprises. ■

Renée Estevez *Zanna Young* • Carrie Mitchum *Sunnie Haines* • Lisanne Falk *Joan Reducci* • Steven Brill *Tommy* • Claudette Nevins *Mrs Stillman* • Tim Russ *Deputy Ryan* • Beau Starr *Detective Barton* ■ *Dir* Peter O'Fallon • *Scr* J David Miles, Bob Bibb [Robert Bibb], from a story by Lewis Goldstein, from a story by Ernest Holzman

Dead Silence ★★★ 15

Thriller
1996 · US · Colour · 95mins

James Garner shows he has lost none of his easy-going charisma in this absorbing, if somewhat awkward, thriller. It starts with almost true-story earnestness as three convicts, led by Kim Coates, hijack a bus-load of deaf students and their hearing-impaired teacher (Marlee Matlin); Garner, a wise old FBI hostage negotiator, sits back to play the waiting game. The impressive playing of the cast (there are also strong supporting turns from Lolita Davidovitch and Charles Martin Smith) lifts this above the average and, although the pay-off twist is rather obvious, it still makes for engaging viewing. Contains swearing, sexual references and some violence. ■

James Garner *John Potter* • Kim Coates *Theodore Handy* • Marlee Matlin *Melanie Charrol* • Lolita Davidovich *Sharon Foster* • Charles Martin Smith *Roland W Marks* ■ *Dir* Daniel Petrie Jr • *Scr* Donald Stewart, from the novel by Jeffrey Deaver

Dead Solid Perfect ★★ 15
Sports comedy drama
1988 · US · Colour · 92mins

A small but well-told tale of the unsung heroes of the golfing world. Randy Quaid is the resolutely second-division player who still dreams of his day of glory on the links. Adapted by Dan Jenkins from his successful book, this made-for-cable feature displays a real affection for the sport, yet is not afraid to show the unglamorous side of the golfing circuit.

Randy Quaid Kenny Lee • Jack Warden Bad Hair Wimberly • Kathryn Harrold Beverly T Lee • Larry Riley Spec • Corinne Bohrer Janie Rimmer • Brett Cullen Donny Smithern • DeLane Matthews Katie Beth Smithern ■ Dir Bobby Roth • Scr Bobby Roth, Dan Jenkins, from the book by Dan Jenkins

Dead Women in Lingerie ★★
Mystery thriller 1990 · US · Colour · 89 mins

Great title, shame about the film. In his feeble spoof on the gumshoe genre, John Romo plays a bloodshot private eye who finds it more and more difficult to disentangle himself from a murder case. This kind of Chandleresque lampoon requires a cool nerve and steady hand, but Erica Fox's lame thriller is much too frenetic to make any kind of satirical impact.

John Romo Nick • Maura Tierney Molly Field • Jerry Orbach Bartoli • Maria Strova Carmen • Dennis Christopher Lapin • Jeanne Sal Bing • David S Cameron Lt North ■ Dir Erica Fox • Scr Erica Fox, John Romo

Dead Wrong ★★ 15
Romantic adventure
1983 · Can · Colour · 93mins

An air of leaden predictability hangs over this tale, in which romance and crime combine in true B-movie style. Perhaps the action might have been more credible had it not been Britt Ekland playing the feisty Mountie agent who helps impoverished fisherman Winston Rekert fight off the Columbian mafiosi who have commandeered his boat for a drug run. Her derring-do has a distinct Charlie's Angels feel to it, as she takes on all comers without a hair falling out of place.

Britt Ekland Priscilla "Penny" Lancaster • Winston Rekert Sean Phelan • Dale Wilson Mike Brady • Jackson Davies Inspector Fred Foster • Alex Daikun Stringer • Leon Bibb Bahama Jones • Annie Kidder Didi ■ Dir Len Kowalewich • Scr Ron Graham

The Dead Zone ★★★ 18
Horror 1983 · US · Colour · 103mins

An engrossing yet strangely unembellished filming of Stephen King's bestseller by director David Cronenberg, with teacher Christopher Walken waking up from a coma to find he has acquired the ability to foresee the future. As his value to society increases, his life crumbles, especially when he envisions the horrifying truth of mankind's destiny under the possible control of evil politician Martin Sheen. While it has none of Cronenberg's usual bracing style and is quite abrupt in parts, it does carry a surprisingly thoughtful and moving charge at times, with Walken, Sheen

and Brooke Adams giving topnotch performances. Contains violence, swearing and brief nudity.

Christopher Walken Johnny Smith • Brooke Adams Sarah Bracknell • Tom Skerritt Sheriff George Bannerman • Herbert Lom Dr Sam Weizak • Anthony Zerbe Roger Stuart • Colleen Dewhurst Henrietta Dodd • Martin Sheen Greg Stillson ■ Dir David Cronenberg • Scr Jeffrey Boam, from the novel by Stephen King

Deadbolt ★★ 15
Thriller 1992 · US · Colour · 89mins

This is an uninspired yet incredibly nasty reworking of the terrible-tenant theme explored in much superior films like Pacific Heights and Single White Female. Divorced medical student Justine Bateman is the apartment owner who finds romance with hunky lodger Adam Baldwin, only to discover that he's not only one clause short of a lease, but also probably responsible for the death of her ex-husband. Director Douglas Jackson builds the suspense neatly enough, but the action (including some pretty shocking violence) doggedly follows its all-too-predictable course.

Justine Bateman Marty • Adam Baldwin Alec • Chris Mulkey Jordan • Michele Scarabelli Theresa • Cyndi Pass Diana • Isabelle Truchon Linda ■ Dir Douglas Jackson • Scr Mara Trafficante, Frank Rehwaldt

Deadfall ★
Crime thriller 1968 · UK · Colour · 126mins

This insufferably pretentious twaddle from writer/director Bryan Forbes masquerades as a heist movie, as Michael Caine teams up with husband-and-wife Eric Portman and Giovanna Ralli for an audacious robbery. But the plot also involves repressed desire and clumsily signposted homosexuality, as well as Ralli's convoluted Nazi heritage. The excessive Freudian psychodrama comes complete with a song from Shirley Bassey and some luscious guitar music over the robbery itself. Sadly, the film is far too convinced of its own superiority to provide any workaday thrills, and also fatally lacks a sense of humour.

Michael Caine Henry Clarke • Giovanna Ralli Fe Moreau • Eric Portman Richard Moreau • Nanette Newman Girl • David Buck Salinas • Carlos Pierre Antonio • Leonard Rossiter Fillmore ■ Dir Bryan Forbes • Scr Bryan Forbes, from the novel by Desmond Cory • Music John Barry

Deadfall ★★ 18
Crime thriller 1993 · US · Colour · 94mins

Deadfall is half-homage, half send-up of film noir, with James Coburn and Michael Biehn as father-and-son conmen. When son accidentally kills father early on, it instigates an incredibly complicated plot. Generally regarded as a misfire, it's worth a look for its peculiar pedigree: director Christopher Coppola is Francis's nephew and he casts his own brothers, Nicolas Cage and Marc Coppola, his aunt Talia Shire, plus Peter Fonda and Charlie Sheen.

Michael Biehn Joe Donan • James Coburn Mike Donan • Nicolas Cage Eddie • Sarah Trigger Diane • Charlie Sheen Steve • Talia Shire Sam • Angus Scrimm Dr Lyme • Peter

Fonda Pete • Marc Coppola Bob ■ Dir Christopher Coppola • Scr Christopher Coppola, Nick Vallelonga

Deadhead Miles ★★
Comedy road movie
1972 · US · Colour · 93mins

After making the sublime cult movie The Unholy Rollers, director Vernon Zimmerman tried to match it with this offbeat road movie about a long-distance trucker and the wacky people he meets en route. Despite an inspired and often hilarious script by Terrence Malick, and Alan Arkin acting his socks off, the end result is a meandering muddle that remained unreleased for over ten years. Eminently watchable and absolutely terrible by turns; look out for director John Milius as a trooper and cameos from Hollywood legends George Raft and Ida Lupino.

Alan Arkin Cooper • Paul Benedict Tramp • Hector Elizondo Bad character • Oliver Clark Durazno • Charles Durning Red ball rider • Lawrence Wolf Pineapple • Barnard Hughes Old man • William Duell Auto parts salesman • Loretta Swit Woman with glass eye • John Milius 2nd state trooper • Ida Lupino She • George Raft ■ Dir Vernon Zimmerman • Scr Terrence Malick

Deadlier than the Male ★
Action drama 1966 · UK · Colour · 100mins

James Bond, who made his first screen appearance four years earlier, might have got away with this unpleasant mix of sex and sadism, but fascist-minded "Bulldog" Drummond (Richard Johnson) just isn't nonchalant enough to make it palatable. He's in hot pursuit of Nigel Green's lady killers (Elke Sommer and Sylva Koscina), who wipe out opposition to his takeover bids. Director Ralph Thomas made the likeable Doctor movies, but there's not much to like about this.

Richard Johnson Hugh "Bulldog" Drummond • Elke Sommer Irma Eckman • Sylva Koscina Penelope • Nigel Green Carl Petersen • Suzanna Leigh Grace ■ Dir Ralph Thomas • Scr Jimmy Sangster, David Osborn, Liz Charles-Williams, from a story by Jimmy Sangster, from the novels by Sapper [HC McNeile]

Deadline at Dawn ★★
Mystery 1946 · US · BW · 83mins

This was the only movie directed by the Group Theater of New York's influential left-winger Harold Clurman, and dismayingly pretentious it is, too, despite a sterling performance from Susan Hayward as a dancer trying to clear a sailor (the undercast Bill Williams) of murder. Based on a noir-ish thriller by Cornell Woolrich (Rear Window), written under the pseudonym William Irish, the picture has a screenplay by Clifford Odets, who knew the theatre milieu well. Clurman turned out to be an inept director in this medium, failing to make much of the opportunities to hand. What could have been a major film noir thus becomes a half-hearted film gris.

Susan Hayward June Goff • Paul Lukas Gus • Bill Williams Alex Winkley • Joseph Calleia Bartelli • Osa Massen Helen Robinson • Lola Lane Edna Bartelli • Jerome Cowan Lester Brady • Marvin Miller Sleepy Parsons ■ Dir Harold Clurman • Scr Clifford Odets, from a novel by William Irish [Cornell Woolrich]

Deadline – USA ★★★
Crime drama 1952 · US · BW · 86mins

A clever but improbable tale, with Humphrey Bogart lending his formidable presence to the role of a hard-boiled newspaper editor trying to persuade proprietor Ethel Barrymore not to sell the Pulitzer Prize-winning journal The Day, while he simultaneously confronts the mob and argues before the bench over the obligations of the press to its readers. It's an interesting subject, but dully filmed, too early in Blackboard Jungle writer/director Richard Brooks's career for him to have learned how to do the story justice. Actually filmed in the offices of the New York Daily News, it was, not surprisingly, just called Deadline in the UK.

Humphrey Bogart Ed Hutcheson • Ethel Barrymore Mrs Garrison • Kim Hunter Nora • Ed Begley Frank Allen • Warren Stevens Burrows • Paul Stewart Thompson • Martin Gabel Rienzi • Joseph De Santis [Joe De Santis] Schmidt ■ Dir/Scr Richard Brooks

Deadly ★★ 15
Thriller 1991 · Ausl · Colour · 101mins

Presenting a stark view of life among Australia's Aboriginal population, this thriller from director Esben Storm misses many of the chances it had to both excite and enlighten. The script teasingly suggests that many of the country's ingrained attitudes derive from the macho image of the Aussie male, but Storm shies away from this point to concentrate on a clichéd examination of racism. Similarly, the story of a cop given one last chance after he accidentally kills a girl on a drugs bust falls flat because there's nothing mysterious about the case he takes on in the outback. Ultimately more frustrating than fulfilling.

Jerome Ehlers Tony Bourke • Frank Gallacher Mick Thornton • Lydia Miller Daphne • John Moore Eddie • Caz Lederman Irene • Bill Hunter Bar owner ■ Dir Esben Storm • Scr Esben Storm, Ranald Allan

Deadly Advice ★ 15
Black comedy 1993 · UK · Colour · 86mins

You'd think an Arsenic and Old Lace-style sitcom from Mandie Fletcher, the director of two TV series of Blackadder, would be a bit of a giggle, especially with Absolutely Fabulous regular Jane Horrocks as its star. Sadly, this dreary farce is low on laughs as the spirits of infamous British murderers such as Dr Crippen dole out advice to henpecked Horrocks on how best to kill her domineering mother, Brenda Fricker. John Mills's portrayal of Jack the Ripper as a music-hall comedian hits the right degree of tastelessness, but the rest of this semi-detached suburban shocker misses by miles.

Jane Horrocks Jodie Greenwood • Brenda Fricker Iris Greenwood • Imelda Staunton Beth Greenwood • Jonathan Pryce Dr Ted Philips • Edward Woodward Major Herbert Armstrong • Billie Whitelaw Kate Webster • Hywel Bennett Dr Crippen • Jonathan Hyde George Joseph Smith • John Mills Jack the Ripper • Ian Abbey Bunny • Eleanor Bron Judge ■ Dir Mandie Fletcher • Scr Glenn Chandler

The Deadly Affair ★★★★

Spy drama · 1966 · UK · Colour · 106mins

James Mason worked regularly with Sidney Lumet on both stage and television, but this gripping adaptation of John le Carré's novel *Call for the Dead* was their first film collaboration. Mason gives a studied performance as the intelligence officer investigating the suspicious suicide of a diplomat, with the ever-dependable Harry Andrews also on bristling form as a no-nonsense copper. Director Lumet expertly weaves Mason's deplorable domestic situation into the equation, coaxing an unsympathetic portrayal from Harriet Andersson as Mason's promiscuous wife. But his other big-name imports, Simone Signoret and Maximilian Schell, are less inspired.

James Mason *Charles Dobbs* • Simone Signoret *Elsa Fennan* • Maximilian Schell *Dieter Frey* • Harriet Andersson *Ann Dobbs* • Harry Andrews *Inspector Mendel* • Kenneth Haigh *Bill Appleby* • Lynn Redgrave *Virgin* • Roy Kinnear *Adam Scarr* ■ *Dir* Sidney Lumet • *Scr* Paul Dehn, from the novel *Call for the Dead* by John le Carré

The Deadly Bees ★

Horror · 1967 · UK · Colour · 83mins

Suzanna Leigh is the pop singer who visits a remote island to recover from exhaustion. There she meets an insane beekeeper who breeds a strain of mutant bee that attacks a certain scent. This is one of the worst films Oscar-winning cinematographer-turned-director Freddie Francis ever made for Hammer rivals Amicus. More a routine whodunnit than a horror film, this is a lacklustre plod through obvious red herrings and banal dialogue.

Suzanna Leigh *Vicki Robbins* • Frank Finlay *Manfred* • Guy Doleman *Hargrove* • Catherine Finn *Mrs Hargrove* • John Harvey *Thompson* • Michael Ripper *Hawkins* • Anthony Bailey *Compere* • Tim Barrett *Harcourt* ■ *Dir* Freddie Francis • *Scr* Robert Bloch, Anthony Marriott, from the novel *A Taste of Honey* by HF Heard

Deadly Blessing ★★★ 18

Horror · 1981 · US · Colour · 97mins

This early nerve-jangler from horrormeister Wes Craven turns an everyday woman-in-peril terror tale into an epic of vindictive evil. In the rural serenity of eastern Pennsylvania, young widow Maren Jensen is persecuted by a religious cult led by Ernest Borgnine backed up by demonic forces that not even Sharon Stone, in her second movie role, can withstand. Snake-haters should beware of one shock scene, but fans of the genre should stay with it as the whole engenders a chilling despair that makes the ending all the more scary. Contains violence, swearing and nudity. ▭

Ernest Borgnine *Isaiah* • Maren Jensen *Martha* • Susan Buckner *Vicky* • Sharon Stone *Lana* • Jeff East *John Schmidt* • Lisa Hartman *Faith* • Lois Nettleton *Louisa* • Coleen Riley *Melissa* ■ *Dir* Wes Craven • *Scr* Wes Craven, Glenn M Benest, Matthew Barr

A Deadly Business ★★★

Drama based on a true story
1986 · US · Colour · 96mins

Alan Arkin stars as real-life ex-con Harold Kaufman, who has to decide between loyalty to his employer, waste-disposal boss Armand Assante, and his civic duty when he discovers that Assante and his criminal associates are making money through the dumping of toxic chemicals. The use of authentic locations in New Jersey plus the gritty performances lift this a notch or two above the average made-for-TV opus. Contains violence.

Alan Arkin *Harold Kaufman* • Armand Assante *Charles Macaluso* • Michael Learned *Ann* • Jon Polito *Vitola* • Raymond Serra *Di Nardi* ■ *Dir* John Korty • *Scr* Al Ramrus

Deadly Care ★ 15

Medical drama based on a true story
1987 · US · Colour · 90mins

Originally called *One Way Out*, this TV movie is based on the true story of a critical care nurse in a Phoenix cardiac unit who succumbs to drink and drugs in an attempt to relieve the pressure of her job. Under David Anspaugh's direction, Cheryl Ladd turns in a melodramatic performance as she manages to hide her addiction. From its pompous pre-credits disclaimer to its predictable ending, this is overwrought and overplayed, trivialising a very real problem with its sensationalist approach. ▭

Cheryl Ladd *Anne Halloran* • Jason Miller *Dr Miles Keefer* • Jennifer Salt *Carol Arbiter* • Belinda Balaski *Terry* • Joe Dorsey *Kevin Halloran* • Richard Evans *Jim* ■ *Dir* David Anspaugh • *Scr* Lane Slate

The Deadly Companions ★★★

Western · 1961 · US · Colour · 93mins

After cutting his teeth on TV shows like *Gunsmoke* and *The Rifleman*, Sam Peckinpah made his debut as a movie director with this often gripping psychological western, which concentrates on the interaction of its quartet of key characters before it bursts into violent life on the streets of a ghost town. As the rose among three thorns, Maureen O'Hara is excellent, but it's the posturing between gunmen Brian Keith, Chill Wills and Steve Cochran that holds the attention. The direction is tentative at times, but AS Fleischman's script, from his own novel, is solid as a rock.

Maureen O'Hara *Kit* • Brian Keith *Yellowleg* • Steve Cochran *Billy* • Chill Wills *Turk* • Strother Martin *Parson* • Will Wright *Doctor* • Jim O'Hara *Cal* ■ *Dir* Sam Peckinpah • *Scr* AS Fleischman, from his novel

Deadly Current ★★ 15

Action thriller · 1996 · Can · Colour · 89mins

Two of straight-to-video's finest, Gary Busey and Jeff Fahey, team up for this sly thriller that sensibly doesn't take itself too seriously while still delivering the goods on the action front. This time Fahey is the good-guy policeman who is conveniently visiting a dam when it is taken over by a gang of terrorists, led by Busey, who intend holding a city's water supply to ransom. It's a poor man's *Die Hard*, but enjoyable enough. ▭

Jeff Fahey *David Chase* • Kim Coates *Montessi* • Carrie-Anne Moss *Melissa Wilkins* • Gary Busey *Mr Turner* ■ *Dir* John Bradshaw • *Scr* Tony Johnston

Deadly Family Secrets ★★

Drama · 1995 · US · Colour

A host of familiar small-screen faces props up this otherwise far-fetched TV thriller. Loni Anderson is the career woman back in her home town whose planned family reunion turns into a nightmare when she witnesses her brother-in-law (Greg Evigan) murder a woman. There's a reliable supporting turn from Barry Corbin, but there's little imagination on show in either the writing or directing departments.

Loni Anderson *Martha* • Gigi Rice *Linda* • Greg Evigan *Eddie* • Barry Corbin *Potter* • William Converse Roberts *Brooke Akins* • Anjanette Comer *Hilda Potter* ■ *Dir* Richard T Heffron • *Scr* Brian Taggert, from the novel *Vinegar Hill* by Franklin Coen

Deadly Force ★ 18

Crime drama · 1983 · US · Colour · 95mins

Wings Hauser, who gave a great performance as a psychotic pimp in the previous year's *Vice Squad*, reunites with the makers of that film, with disappointing results. Hauser plays a half-crazy ex-cop who's so obnoxious, we are actually pleased when his former colleagues harass him as he pounds the streets of LA looking for a serial killer. Despite violence, swearing and a sweaty Hauser taking his clothes off, it looks and plays suspiciously like a TV production. ▭

Wings Hauser *Stoney Cooper* • Joyce Ingalls *Eddie Cooper* • Paul Shenar *Joshua Adams* • Al Ruscio *Sam Goodwin* • Arlen Dean Snyder *Ashley Maynard* • Lincoln Kilpatrick *Otto Hoxley* ■ *Dir* Paul Aaron • *Scr* Ken Barnett, Barry Schneider, Robert Vincent O'Neil

Deadly Friend ★★ 18

Horror · 1986 · US · Colour · 86mins

In this daft horror yarn from *Nightmare on Elm Street* director Wes Craven, Matthew Laborteaux is the teen genius whose robot is destroyed shortly before his girlfriend is killed. Naturally, he decides to plant the robot's brain into his girl's head – but things don't go as planned. The plot bears a remarkable resemblance to the cult shocker *Re-Animator*, made the year before. Despite this, *Deadly Friend* is still an enjoyable, if unscary piece of entertainment. ▭

Matthew Laborteaux *Paul* • Kristy Swanson *Samantha* • Anne Twomey *Jeannie Conway* • Michael Sharrett *Tom* • Richard Marcus *Harry* • Anne Ramsey *Elvira Williams* • Russ Marin *Dr Johanson* • Andrew Roperto *Carl Denton* ■ *Dir* Wes Craven • *Scr* Bruce Joel Rubin, from the novel *Friend* by Diana Henstell

Deadly Game ★★

Drama · 1982 · W Ger · Colour · 87mins

Hungarian director Karoly Makk is known for his sympathetic portraits of individuals in emotional turmoil. So why venture to Germany for this routine thriller about a game warden caught up for the second time in a murderous *ménage à trois* with the mistress of the estate on which he works? Stunning mountain scenery is the wrong location for a *film noir* as it's virtually impossible to create the characteristic intensity and menace in such wide open spaces. Barbara Sukowa is fine as the *femme fatale*, but Helmut Berger fails to convey the warden's conflict between ambition, lust and conscience. German dialogue dubbed into English.

Helmut Berger *Boris* • Mel Ferrer *Stephan* • Barbara Sukowa *Daniela* • Karin Baal *Anna* • Josef Kroner [Jozef Kroner] *Marek* • Gisela Hahn *Angela* ■ *Dir* Karoly Makk • *Scr* Karster Peters

The Deadly Game ★★★ PG

Drama · 1986 · US · Colour · 107mins

That superb character actor John Lithgow is here given the chance to get his teeth into a decent leading role in co-writer/director Marshall Brickman's wry drama, which is also known as *The Manhattan Project*. Lithgow is entirely persuasive as the nuclear physicist slowly emerging from the protective cocoon of his intellect and beginning to understand the ramifications of his work when his girlfriend's teenage son enters a homemade bomb in a science fair. The moral is rather hammered home in the later stages, but there is plenty of clever chat and an ingeniously comic heist to prevent the weighty topic from becoming too heavy. ▭

John Lithgow *John Mathewson* • Christopher Collet *Paul Stephens* • Cynthia Nixon *Jenny Anderman* • Jill Eikenberry *Elizabeth Stephens* • John Mahoney *Lieutenant Colonel Conroy* ■ *Dir* Marshall Brickman • *Scr* Marshall Brickman, Thomas Baum

Deadly Harvest ★★

Drama · 1972 · US · Colour

Shot against the scorching splendour of California's Napa Valley, this is a tense adaptation of Geoffrey Household's acclaimed novel, *Watcher in the Shadows*. Richard Boone stars as a defector from the Eastern Bloc who, having started afresh as a vineyard owner, is hunted down by a murderous enemy from his past. Boone doesn't have the range to make the transition from respected outsider to frightened man convincing, but Michael O'Herlihy directs at such a ferocious lick we're too busy trying to keep up with the tortuous plot to notice any deficiencies in the acting.

Richard Boone *Anton Solca* • Patty Duke *Jenny* • Michael Constantine *Stefan* • Jack Kruschen *Vartamian* • Murray Hamilton *Sheriff Bill Jessup* • Fred Carson *McAndrews/George Anson* • Jack DeMave *Franklin* • Bill McKeever *Charley* ■ *Dir* Michael O'Herlihy • *Scr* Dan Ullman, from the novel *Watcher in the Shadows* by Geoffrey Household

Deadly Hero ★★★ 18

Crime thriller · 1976 · US · Colour · 97mins

A taut, complex thriller in which Diahn Williams is first assaulted by James Earl Jones and then tormented by the cop (Don Murray) who saves her. This is a real Hitchcockian conceit – one twist deserves another as Williams experiences the full frying pan and fire proverb. Jones is truly scary, Murray creepily effective and note the screen debut of Treat Williams, who was once tipped to be the new Pacino. ▭

Don Murray *Ed Lacy* • Diahn Williams *Sally Deveraux* • James Earl Jones *Rabbit* • Lilia Skala *Mrs Broderick* • George S Irving *Reilly* • Treat Williams *Billings* • Charles Siebert *Baker* ■ *Dir* Ivan Nagy • *Scr* George Wislocki

U = SUITABLE FOR ALL Uc = SUITABLE FOR ALL, ESPECIALLY FOR YOUNG CHILDREN (VIDEO ONLY) PG = PARENTAL GUIDANCE

Deadly Identity ★★★ 15

Mystery thriller 1991 · US · Colour · 86mins

Czech director Ivan Passer's career in Hollywood has never really clicked, and, apart from the superb crime drama *Cutter's Way*, he has struggled with some very routine material. After the awful comedy *Creator*, this made-for-cable mystery thriller marks something of a return to form, and he brings a neat, stylish touch to the story. Mark Harmon and Mimi Rogers are attractive leads, and there is reliable support from M Emmet Walsh. Released on video in the UK as *Basic Deception* and also known as *Fourth Story*. Contains brief nudity.

Mark Harmon *David Shepherd* • Mimi Rogers *Valerie McCoughlin* • Paul Gleason *Lt Hank Petkavich* • Michael Boatman *Sergeant Teal* • Cliff De Young *Darryl McCoughlin* • M Emmet Walsh *Harry* • Eric Menyuk *Detective Babbitt* ■ *Dir* Ivan Passer • *Scr* Andrew Guerdat

Deadly Illusion ★★ 15

Action crime thriller
1987 · US · Colour · 86mins

Also known as *Love You to Death*, this thriller was written and co-directed by Larry Cohen, acclaimed creator of exuberant and full-blooded horror films. This might explain why there are some exotic touches of humour in this generic story of a private detective (Billy Dee Williams from *The Empire Strikes Back*) who battles to clear his name after he is framed for murder. Morgan Fairchild co-stars.

Billy Dee Williams *Hamberger* • Vanity *Rina* • Morgan Fairchild *Jane/Sharon* • John Beck *Alex Burton* • Joe Cortese *Detective Lefferts* • Michael Wilding [Michael Wilding Jr] *Costillion* • Dennis Hallahan *Fake Burton* • Allison Woodward *Nancy Costillion* ■ *Dir* William Tannen, Larry Cohen • *Scr* Larry Cohen

Deadly Innocents ★★ 18

Psychological thriller
1988 · US · Colour · 93mins

A rather daft psychological thriller with an interesting cast that includes Mary Crosby (daughter of Bing) and Andrew Stevens (son of Stella). A schizophrenic woman (Crosby) with murder on her mind escapes from a mental institution and befriends an innocent and naive girl (Amanda Wyss). Unfortunately, Crosby is better at playing rich bitch (she was Kristin in *Dallas*) than a character with depth, but there are still some moments of tension. Contains brief nudity.

Mary Crosby *Beth/Cathy* • Amanda Wyss *Andy/Angela* • Andrew Stevens *Bob Appling* • Bonnie Hellman *Pee Wee* • John Anderson *Gus* • Gerald Bangs *Sheriff* ■ *Dir* John D Patterson [John Patterson] • *Scr* Hugh Parks, Joseph Tankersley

Deadly Intentions... Again? ★★★ 15

Thriller based on a true story
1991 · US · Colour · 92mins

The odd title is deliberately resonant, since this is a TV-movie sequel to a popular mini-series that starred *The Terminator*'s Michael Biehn as Dr Charles Raynor, jailed for plotting his first wife's murder. Here, Raynor is played by *LA Law*'s Harry Hamlin, who, somewhat bizarrely, actually watches Biehn as himself in the first movie shades of Larry Parks as Al Jolson meeting Larry Parks as Parks in 1949's *Jolson Sings Again*. Still, this is watchable enough, distinguished by contributions from Eileen Brennan and Fairuza Balk.

Joanna Kerns *Sally Raynor* • Harry Hamlin *Charles Raynor* • Eileen Brennan *Charlotte Raynor* • Conchata Ferrell *Joan Walter* • Kevin McNulty *Dr Uttley* • Fairuza Balk *Stacey* ■ *Dir* James Steven Sadwith • *Scr* William Wood

Deadly Invasion ★★

Thriller 1995 · US · Colour · 75mins

"Killer bees" seem to be the most durable entomological threat in the annals of movie horror. We've all had those panic attacks when trapped in a room with one of the little buzzers, so why can't film-makers duplicate that scare factor with any success? Bee movies always turn out to be such disappointingly laughable B-movies, and here's another yellow-and-black-striped menace that merely manages to while away the time.

Robert Hays *Chad Ingram* • Nancy Stafford *Karen Ingram* • Gina Philips *Tracy Ingram* • Gregory Gordon *Kevin Ingram* • Whitney Danielle Porter *Lucy Ingram* • Ryan Phillippe *Tom Redman* • Dennis Christopher *Beauchamp* ■ *Dir* Rockne S O'Bannon • *Scr* Steven Rae, William Bast, from a story by Matthew Williams

Deadly Justice ★★ 15

Crime thriller 1995 · US · Colour · 87mins

Also known as *A Killer among Us*, this entry in the Jack Reed series of TV movies features burly Brian Dennehy as the veteran Chicago lawman. Dennehy also directed and co-scripted this brisk police procedural, in which the murder attempt on a young woman has ramifications closer to home after our hero uncovers a den of corruption at City Hall. Dennehy is an imposing presence and his partnership with Charles S Dutton is bruisingly effective. But, as most of Reed's previous cases had also led to brushes with scheming civic officials, the plot seems somewhat stale.

Brian Dennehy *Jack Reed* • Charles S Dutton *Lieutenant Charles Silvera* • Susan Ruttan *Arlene Reed* • Suki Kaiser *Sara Landry* • Justin Louis *Michael Quinn* • Michael Talbott *Eddie Dirkson* • CCH Pounder *Mrs Harris* ■ *Dir* Brian Dennehy • *Scr* Brian Dennehy, Bill Phillips

The Deadly Mantis ★★

Science-fiction thriller
1957 · US · BW · 78mins

The dawning of the atomic age gave rise to an invasion of big bug movies, but this perfunctorily-directed, would-be sci-fi epic from Nathan Juran isn't in the same league as *Them!* or *Tarantula*. Still, there's something cathartic about watching a giant praying mantis, awoken from its arctic slumber by nuclear testing, laying waste to tourist attractions in New York and Washington DC. The obligatory love story featuring Craig Stevens, then famous as television's Peter Gunn, critically shifts focus from some good effects sequences.

Craig Stevens *Colonel Joe Parkman* • William Hopper *Dr Ned Jackson* • Alix Talton *Marge* Blaine • Donald Randolph *General Mark Ford* ■ *Dir* Nathan Juran • *Scr* Martin Berkeley, from a story by William Alland

Deadly Messages ★★

Thriller 1985 · US · Colour

Dempsey and Makepeace's Michael Brandon – surely the sexiest actor never to have a career in Hollywood – here stars in a daft TV-movie chiller alongside Kathleen Beller (*Dynasty*). The latter plays a young woman with a patchy memory who starts getting weird messages on an old Ouija board. Naturally, there's a killer on her trail as well. Brandon tries to keep a straight face as Beller's perplexed lover, but you know things are going downhill when the plot twist relies on a relative the heroine has blotted out of her memory. Perhaps Brandon should blot this silly tale out of his, too.

Kathleen Beller *Laura Daniels* • Michael Brandon *Michael Krasnick* • Dennis Franz *Detective Max Lucas* • Scott Paulin *Roger Kelton* ■ *Dir* Jack Bender • *Scr* Bill Bleich

Deadly Nightshade ★★ PG

Crime drama 1953 · UK · BW · 58mins

In spite of its penury, this typical fifties British crime quickie – about an escaped convict who unwittingly assumes the identity of a spy – is curiously engaging. Although director John Gilling throws in a few Cornish coastal views, he's mostly confined to unconvincing sets, though the cheapskate look only adds to the charm.

Emrys Jones *Robert Matthews/John Barlow* • Zena Marshall *Ann Farrington* • John Horsley *Inspector Clements* • Joan Hickson *Mrs Fenton* • Hector Ross *Canning* ■ *Dir* John Gilling • *Scr* Lawrence Huntington

Deadly Past ★★

Thriller 1995 · US · Colour

Dedee Pfeiffer, along with the likes of Don Swayze, Joey Travolta, Frank Stallone and countless other less famous siblings of big stars, has found herself a nice little niche in straight-to-video fare (as well as her regular supporting slot in the *Cybill* TV series), and this is a fairly standard example. It's an erotic thriller that mixes in the usual elements of *femmes fatales*, dupes, murder conspiracies and a liberal smattering of sex, but Tibor Takacs's direction is strictly routine. Contains swearing, sex scenes, nudity and violence.

Carol Alt *Saundra* • Dedee Pfeiffer *Kirsten* • Ron Marquette *Luke* • Vinnie Curto *Nick* • Mark Dacascos *Leo* ■ *Dir* Tibor Takacs • *Scr* Steven Iyama

Deadly Pursuit ★★ 15

Action thriller 1988 · US · Colour · 105mins

A solid thriller, but it treads too much familiar ground to stand out from the pack. Once again Sidney Poitier finds himself as a lawman saddled with a mismatched partner, this time played by Tom Berenger, who gives him as much trouble as the bad guy. The fact that Berenger's girlfriend Kirstie Alley is directly in danger from the crazed killer comes as no surprise, either. The performances are pretty good, considering the uninspiring material, and British director Roger Spottiswoode makes the most of the great outdoors and stages a couple of pulsating action sequences. Contains swearing and violence.

Sidney Poitier *Warren Stantin* • Tom Berenger *Jonathan Knox* • Kirstie Alley *Sarah* • Clancy Brown *Steve* • Richard Masur *Norman* ■ *Dir* Roger Spottiswoode • *Scr* Harv Zimmel, Michael Burton, Daniel Petrie Jr, from a story by Harv Zimmel

Deadly Pursuits ★★

Thriller 1996 · US · Colour

A bland made-for-TV thriller, directed with little flair by Felix Enriquez Alcala, who isn't helped by the insipid performances of his cast. *Melrose Place*'s Patrick Muldoon and *Beverly Hills 90210* star Tori Spelling team up to play a student and an ex-waitress who set out to investigate the mysterious deaths of Muldoon's mother and sister. Despite a neat turn from stand-up comic-turned-serious actor Richard Belzer, of *Homicide* fame, this is very average fare.

Tori Spelling *Meredith* • Patrick Muldoon *Tim Faulkner* • Richard Belzer *Mariano* • Reginald VelJohnson *Ed Conroy* ■ *Dir* Felix Enriquez Alcala • *Scr* Michael Ahnemann

Deadly Relations ★★ 15

Crime drama 1993 · US · Colour · 87mins

Back in 1993, this made-for-TV thriller slipped by virtually unnoticed. However, the fact that it was an early vehicle for both future Oscar-winner Gwyneth Paltrow and *Friends* star Matthew Perry marks it out as an intriguing curiosity. Director Bill Condon has also gone on to better things with the critically acclaimed *Gods and Monsters*. TV favourite Robert Urich takes the lead role, playing a monstrous dad who gets his family mixed up in a dangerous insurance scam.

Robert Urich *Leonard J Fagot* • Shelley Fabares *Shirley Fagot* • Gwyneth Paltrow *Carol Fagot Holland* • Tony Higgins *Mike Holland* • Georgia Emelin *Joanne Fagot Westerfield* • Matthew Perry *George Westerfield* ■ *Dir* Bill Condon • *Scr* Dennis Nemec, from the book *Deadly Relations: A True Story of Murder in a Suburban Family* by Carol Donohue, Shirley Hall

Deadly Reunion ★★ PG

Detective action drama
1994 · US · Colour · 87mins

An unremarkable feature-length tale from Chuck Norris's *Walker: Texas Ranger* TV series, this nevertheless gives some rare screen time to a distinguished posse of western character actors. The plot finds the tough unorthodox cops, led by Norris, on the trail of a group of killers aiming to stage another high profile Dallas political assassination. Complicating matters are a group of ex-rangers, including familiar elder statesman Stuart Whitman. It's competent enough – although age hasn't made Norris's acting any less one-note.

Chuck Norris *Cordell Walker* • Sheree J Wilson *Alex Cahill* • Noble Willingham *CD Parker* • Stuart Whitman ■ *Dir* Michael Preece • *Scr* Donald G Thompson

Deadly Rivals ★ 18

Crime thriller   1992 · US · Colour · 88mins

A cast of C-list actors do their best to make some sense of this overly complex thriller, but ultimately you come away wondering what has happened, and why. Andrew Stevens, Margaux Hemingway and Joseph Bologna are the ''stars'' battling with static dialogue and a dull plot, set in the world of jewel-smuggling and corporate espionage. Halfway through this attempt at gripping adventure, you'll either have nodded off or turned over. 📺

Andrew Stevens *Dr Kevin Fitzgerald* • Francesco Quinn *Bunny Wedman* • Joseph Bologna *Anthony Canberra* • Richard Roundtree *Agent Daniel Peterson* • Margaux Hemingway *Agent Linda Howerton* ■ *Dir* James Dodson • *Scr* Redge Mahaffey

A Deadly Silence ★★ 15

Drama based on a true story
1989 · US · Colour · 90mins

This grisly true tale of small-town secrets and murder is rather mishandled by director John Patterson, who falls into the trap of elbowing drama for detail. He is so keen not to sensationalise that he presents us with a dull series of facts. As a result, star Bruce Weitz, the scruffy, grumbling cop in *Hill Street Blues*, and Mike Farrell, Alan Alda's partner-in-wit from *M*A*S*H*, are both cast adrift. Contains some violence. 📺

Bruce Weitz *Detective James McCready* • Heather Fairfield *Cheryl Pierson* • Charles Haid *Jim Pierson* • Sally Struthers *Marilyn Adams* • Mike Farrell *Paul Gianelli* • Richard Portnow *Ed Jablonski* ■ *Dir* John Patterson • *Scr* Jennifer Miller, from the book by Dena Kleiman

Deadly Sins ★★

Psychological thriller
1996 · US · Colour · 98mins

Alyssa Milano, of *Melrose Place* fame, stars in this TV-movie chiller that also goes under the name of *The Sisterhood*. As the least likely private eye you'll ever see, she goes undercover at a Catholic girls' college, where missing students have been found dead. Milano delves deep into the darkest recesses of the dormitories to uncover some clues for her deputy sheriff sidekick, David Keith. For all its gothic trappings, this is a pale imitation of the ultimate schoolgirl slasher, Dario Argento's *Suspiria*. Contains violence, sex scenes and nudity.

David Keith *Jack Gates* • Alyssa Milano *Cristina Herrera* • Terry David Mulligan *Doc* • Corrie Clark *Beth* ■ *Dir* Michael Robison • *Scr* Malcolm Barbour, John Langley

Deadly Spygames ★

Spy thriller   1989 · US · Colour · 86mins

Apparently James Bond hasn't managed to eliminate all those maniacs who are bent on world domination and destruction, leaving us with the wafer-thin premise for this film. At least Jack M Sell's movie has an intriguing cast, as Troy Donahue and Tippi Hedren battle to prevent a nuclear war by destroying a Cuban radar station. Dramatic interest stems from the fact that they're former lovers, but viewers will probably be

trying to work out the last time one of these sixties stars got wind of a decent script.

Troy Donahue *Python* • Jack M Sell *Banner* • Tippi Hedren *Chastity* • Adrianne Richmond *Jacqueline* ■ *Dir* Jack M Sell • *Scr* Jack M Sell, Adrianne Richmond

Deadly Surveillance ★★ 15

Crime drama   1991 · Can · Colour · 88mins

Directed by Paul Ziller for Canadian cable TV, this would-be erotic thriller falls short in both the erotic and the thriller departments. The usually dependable Michael Ironside is out of sorts here as a cop ordered to stake out the home of his partner's girlfriend (Susan Almgren), who knows more about a series of drug-related murders than she's letting on. Not even a cameo from David Carradine can pep up the action, which all too quickly abandons the mystery for some buddy bonding between Ironside and his partner Christopher Bondy. 📺

Michael Ironside *Fender* • Christopher Bondy *Nickels* • Susan Almgren *Rachel* • David Carradine *Lieutenant* ■ *Dir* Paul Ziller • *Scr* Paul Ziller, Hal Salwen

Deadly Takeover ★★ 18

Action adventure   1996 · US · Colour · 90mins

This is one of the better rip-offs of *Die Hard*, with good production values and acceptable action sequences making up for a fairly predictable script. Ron Silver leads a terrorist group into Israel and invades a chemical laboratory, intent on stealing a new biological weapon. US Embassy guard Jeff Speakman happens to be in the building when the bullets start flying, so he takes it upon himself to save the day and rescue the chief scientist (Rochelle Swanson). Viewers who don't mind seeing the same basic story for the umpteenth time will find it entertaining. 📺

Jeff Speakman *Dutton Hatfield* • Ron Silver *Colonel Baron* • Rochelle Swanson *Dr Allie Levin* • Kevin Jones *Hopper* ■ *Dir* Rick Avery • *Scr* Charles Morris Jr, Harel Goldstein

The Deadly Trackers ★★★ 15

Western   1973 · US · Colour · 100mins

Richard Harris stars as a peace-loving sheriff who becomes a vengeance-seeking animal after his wife and son are killed by Rod Taylor and his vile gang. Rated PG in America but given an X certificate on its release in Britain, the picture has an intense physicality as Harris undergoes his usual sado-masochistic, Brando-esque voyage of self-denial, self-discovery and self-parody. Samuel Fuller began the film in Spain, but the footage was scrapped and the film was restarted in Mexico with Barry Shear as director. To save money, Warner Bros stuck the music score for *The Wild Bunch* on it. A fascinating, trashy rag-bag of a movie. 📺

Richard Harris *Kilpatrick* • Rod Taylor *Brand* • Al Lettieri *Gutierrez* • Neville Brand *Choo Choo* • William Smith *Schoolboy* • Paul Benjamin *Jacob* • Pedro Armendariz Jr *Blacksmith* ■ *Dir* Barry Shear • *Scr* Lukas Heller, from the story *Riata* by Samuel Fuller

The Deadly Trap ★

Psychological spy thriller
1971 · Fr/It · Colour · 97mins

Neorealist French director René Clément was well past his prime when he tackled this lacklustre thriller, a hotchpotch of soap-opera dramatics, murder and espionage. Faye Dunaway and Frank Langella try to give the sub-Hitchcock plot an edge, but the leisurely pace and colour-supplement locations do little to inspire any tension or suspension of disbelief.

Faye Dunaway *Jill Hallard* • Frank Langella *Philip Hallard* • Barbara Parkins *Cynthia* • Michèle Lourié *Kathy* • Patrick Vincent *Patrick* ■ *Dir* René Clément • *Scr* Sidney Buchman, Eleanor Perry, from the novel *The Children Are Gone* by Arthur Cavanaugh, adapted by Daniel Boulanger, René Clément

Deadly Vows ★★ 15

Drama based on a true story
1994 · US · Colour · 93mins

In this TV movie, Gerald McRaney is the trucker whose delusions of grandeur prompt him to enter into a bigamous marriage and then conspire with his new bride to murder his first wife. McRaney is suitably unhinged, but writer Philip Rosenberg fails to fully flesh out the other characters, so that Peggy Lipton and Josie Bissett are left with nothing to do but react to their husband's perverse and, ultimately, deadly fantasies. Former cinematographer Alan Metzger provides competent but uninspired direction. Contains violence and swearing. 📺

Gerald McRaney *Tom Weston* • Peggy Lipton *Nancy Weston* • Josie Bissett *Bobbi Gilbert* ■ *Dir* Alan Metzger • *Scr* Philip Rosenberg

Deadly Web ★★

Thriller   1995 · US · Colour

The theme of computers and e-mail may be bang up to date but there is nothing else to lift this variation on the ''woman in peril'' story above the banal. Gigi Rice plays a divorcee who discovers a seedier and more dangerous side to the internet when she finds herself stalked across cyberspace by a psycho. There is no shortage of suspects – ex-husband Ted McGinley, colleague Raphael Sbarge, security consultant Ed Marinaro – but director Jorge Montesi won't surprise many when he reveals the guilty party in this TV movie. Contains violence.

Gigi Rice *Terri Lawrence* • Andrew Lawrence *Spence Lawrence* • Ed Marinaro *Fred Jones* • Robin Quivers *Lee Aaron* • Ted McGinley *Peter Lawrence* • John Wesley Shipp *Doctor Todd Stanton* • Raphael Sbarge *Barry Fox* ■ *Dir* Jorge Montesi • *Scr* Alan Ormsby

Deadly Whispers ★★ 15

Thriller   1995 · US · Colour · 90mins

Based on a novel by Ted Schwarz, this TV movie deals with the increasingly familiar phenomenon of a loved one at a police press conference becoming the prime suspect in the subsequent murder investigation. Here it's Tony Danza who vows to apprehend his daughter's killer only for the evidence to begin stacking up against him. Yet it's Pamela Reed who turns in the strongest performance as the wife caught between love for her husband and a desire to know the truth.

Director Bill L Norton allows the clues to seep into the speculation with some skill, but the melodramatic tone is pretty unrelenting. 📺

Tony Danza *Tom Acton* • Pamela Reed *Carol Acton* • Ving Rhames *Detective Jackson* • Heather Tom *Kathy Acton* • Sean Haberle *Jim* ■ *Dir* Bill Norton [Bill L Norton] • *Scr* Dennis Turner, from the novel by Ted Schwarz

Deal of the Century ★★ 15

Satirical black comedy
1983 · US · Colour · 94mins

Given the talent on show, this brackish political satire has to go down as a major disappointment. Chevy Chase, Sigourney Weaver and Gregory Hines are the trio who luck into the weapons deal of century, only to find things go horribly wrong. The performances are likeable enough, but the screenplay by Paul Brickman (who scripted *Risky Business*) lacks focus and William Friedkin's direction never strikes the right tone. 📺

Chevy Chase *Eddie Muntz* • Sigourney Weaver *Mrs De Voto* • Gregory Hines *Ray Kasternak* • Vince Edwards *Frank Stryker* • William Marquez *General Cordosa* ■ *Dir* William Friedkin • *Scr* Paul Brickman

Dealers ★★★ 15

Drama   1989 · UK · Colour · 87mins

This somewhat impoverished imitation of *Wall Street* would have been a much better movie had it stuck to the clinical, cynical depiction of life in the City rather than veering off into the realms of predictable thrillerdom. Rebecca De Mornay and Paul McGann might be the headliners, but there's nothing new about the way their love-hate relationship shifts once they start pulling in the big bucks. Derrick O'Connor, on the other hand, gives a compelling performance as the former whizz-kid hooked on the devil's dandruff. Dated perhaps, but still a sobering reminder of the unattractive side of the yuppie mentality. 📺 *DVD*

Paul McGann *Daniel Pascoe* • Rebecca De Mornay *Anna Schuman* • Derrick O'Connor *Robby Barrell* • John Castle *Frank Mallory* • Paul Guilfoyle *Lee Peters* • Rosalind Bennett *Bonnie* • Adrian Dunbar *Lennox Mayhew* • Nicholas Hewetson *Jamie Dunbar* • Sara Sugarman *Elana* • Dikran Tulaine *Wolfgang* • Douglas Hodge *Patrick Skill* ■ *Dir* Colin Bucksey • *Scr* Andrew MacLear

Dealing: or the Berkeley-to-Boston Forty-Brick Lost-Bag Blues ★★

Comedy   1971 · US · Colour · 88mins

In the ranking of stupid titles, this must come near the top. It's one of those ''youth movies'', made in the wake of *Easy Rider* by Paul Williams, whose previous effort was the 1970 political drama *The Revolutionary*. The aforementioned bricks are made of marijuana and ferried between the two college campuses on opposite coasts of America. One of the oddest relics of the counterculture, it co-stars Barbara Hershey and John Lithgow (making his screen debut) and is based on a novel by ''Michael Douglas'' – in fact, a pseudonym for Michael Crichton.

Barbara Hershey *Susan* • Robert F Lyons *Peter* • Charles Durning *Murphy* • Joy Bang *Sandra* • John Lithgow *John* • Ellen Barber

nnie • Gene Borkan *Musty* ■ Dir Paul
Williams • Scr Paul Williams, David Odell,
om a novel by Michael Douglas [Michael
Crichton]

Dear America: Letters Home from Vietnam
★★★★ PG

Documentary
1987 · US · Colour and BW · 82mins

Rarely has the horror of the Vietnam
war been brought home with such
immediacy and power. Director Bill
Couturie ploughed through thousands
of missives for this highly personal
history, appositely and soberingly
illustrated by footage gleaned from the
archives of NBC and the Department of
Defense, much of it previously unseen.
Read with selfless sincerity and
dramatic simplicity by the likes of
Robert De Niro, Sean Penn, Michael J
Fox and Kathleen Turner, the letters
heartrendingly demonstrate how the
naive optimism turned into grim
disenchantment of senseless slaughter
and humiliating defeat. ▣

Dir Bill Couturie • Scr from the non-fiction
book *Dear America: Letters Home from
Vietnam* by Bernard Edelman

Dear Brigitte
★★★ U

Comedy
1966 · US · Colour · 100mins

Directed by Henry Koster, veteran of
light-hearted family entertainment, this
incident-packed comedy stars James
Stewart and Glynis Johns and features
a charming cameo from Brigitte Bardot,
playing herself. Pro-arts professor
Stewart has an eight-year-old son (Billy
Mumy) who, much to his father's
annoyance, is revealed to be a
mathematical genius. The boy also
writes love letters to Bardot and
dreams of going to France to meet
her... Lots of twists and turns ensue,
with Stewart and Johns giving typically
expert performances.

James Stewart *Robert Leaf* • Fabian *Kenneth*
■ Glynis Johns *Vina* • Cindy Carol *Pandora* •
Billy Mumy [Bill Mumy] *Erasmus* • John
Williams *Upjohn* • Ed Wynn *Captain* • Brigitte
Bardot ■ Dir Henry Koster • Scr Hal Kanter,
from the novel *Erasmus with Freckles* by John
Haase

Dear Diary
★★★★★ 15

Biographical comedy drama
1994 · It/Fr · Colour · 100mins

Nanni Moretti is the maverick genius of
modern Italian cinema. Here he
abandons the formulas of traditional
film-making and embarks upon a
personal journey that takes him to a
movie theatre, the site of Pier Paolo
Pasolini's murder, the Aeolian Islands
and his own doctor's surgery. The side
swipes at Roman architecture, *Henry:
Portrait of a Serial Killer*, teenagers,
television and the Italian health service
are as sharp as they are quirky. Each
section of this three-part pseudo-
documentary contains a memorable
moment, whether it's Moretti's
encounter with Jennifer Beals or the
relaying of soap-opera plotlines across
Stromboli. Unhurried, unusual and
unmissable. In Italian and French with
English subtitles. ▣

Nanni Moretti *Italian film* • Giovanna Bozzolo *Actor in
Italian film* • Sebastiano Nardone *Actor in*

Italian film • Antonio Petrocelli *Actor in Italian
film* • Giulio Base *Car driver* • Jennifer Beals
■ Dir/Scr Nanni Moretti

Dear God
★★ PG

Comedy
1996 · US · Colour · 107mins

Comedian Greg Kinnear – who was
nominated for an Oscar for his work in
As Good As It Gets – got his first
leading role in this slight little comedy
about a petty criminal, made to work
for the post office, who takes it upon
himself to read and reply to the many
letters written to God. Cute, inoffensive
stuff, perfect for a rainy afternoon and
enlivened by Kinnear's enjoyable
performance. Laurie Metcalf (Jackie in
the TV series *Roseanne*) and Hector
Elizondo (*Pretty Woman, Chicago Hope*)
offer strong support. ▣

Greg Kinnear *Tom Turner* • Laurie Metcalf
Rebecca Frazen • Maria Pitillo *Gloria McKinney*
• Tim Conway *Herman Dooly* • Hector Elizondo
Vladek Vidov • Jon Seda *Handsome* • Roscoe
Lee Browne *Idris Abraham* • Anna Maria
Horsford *Lucille* • Rue McClanahan *Mom
Turner* ■ Dir Garry Marshall • Scr Warren
Leight, Ed Kaplan

Dear Heart
★★★★

Romantic comedy
1964 · US · BW · 96mins

Forlorn small-town postmistress
Geraldine Page – in New York for a
post office convention – causes trouble
when she falls for delegate Glenn Ford,
who's betrothed to, but not enamoured
of, widow Angela Lansbury. Written by
Tad Mosel, a great name from early
American TV, it's properly sentimental
without being mawkish, while Page,
clutching isolation to herself as
steadfastly as a security blanket, is
touchingly true as a middle-aged
woman teetering on the edge of the
eccentricity. It's a film that gives loners
and losers a chance in the same way
that 1955's *Marty* did. Not surprising,
as Delbert Mann directed both.

Glenn Ford *Harry Monk* • Geraldine Page *Evie
Jackson* • Michael Anderson Jr *Patrick* •
Barbara Nichols *June* • Patricia Barry *Mitchell*
• Charles Drake *Frank Taylor* • Angela
Lansbury *Phyllis* ■ Dir Delbert Mann • Scr Tad
Mosel, from his story *The Out-Of-Towners*

Dear John
★★★

Romance
1964 · Swe · BW · 110mins

Nominated for a best foreign film
Oscar, this was Lars Magnus
Lindgren's fourth feature. Yet for all its
success, he would make only three
more films. Easily as lyrical a study of
summer love as *Elvira Madigan*, but
lacking its tragic period lushness, it
has sea captain Jarl Kulle's romance
with waitress Christina Schollin skilfully
interspersed with flashbacks detailing
their pre-stories – he was abandoned
by his wife and she was so hurt by the
man who left her pregnant that she is
now suspicious of Kulle's eager
intentions. Sensitively photographed by
Rune Ericson and watchfully played. In
Swedish with English subtitles.

Jarl Kulle *John* • Christina Schollin *Anita* •
Helena Nilsson *Helene* • Morgan Anderson
Raymond ■ Dir Lars Magnus Lindgren • Scr
Lars Magnus Lindgren, from the novel by Olle
Lansberg

Dear Murderer
★★ PG

Crime thriller
1947 · UK · BW · 90mins

When a wealthy London businessman
(Eric Portman) learns his wife (Greta
Gynt) has had an affair during his
absence, he murders the man. When
he discovers she has a new lover
(Maxwell Reed), he frames him for the
crime... A nifty but thoroughly
unpleasant British thriller, in which the
protagonists are so vile we can only
rejoice when they get their
comeuppance. Dennis Price and Jack
Warner offer support; the stolid
direction is by Arthur Crabtree. ▣

Eric Portman *Lee Warren* • Greta Gynt *Vivien
Warren* • Dennis Price *Richard Fenton* • Jack
Warner *Inspector Pembury* • Maxwell Reed
Jimmy Martin ■ Dir Arthur Crabtree • Scr
Muriel Box, Sydney Box, Peter Rogers, from
the play *Dear Murderer* by St John L Clowes

Dear Ruth
★★★

Comedy
1947 · US · BW · 95mins

William Holden co-stars with
Paramount's briefly popular Joan
Caulfield in this adaptation of Norman
Krasna's hit Broadway play about a
pen-pal relationship with a difference.
Mayhem ensues as a result of a
recalcitrant, precocious and idealistic
schoolgirl (bouncy Mona Freeman)
corresponding with a soldier on active
duty, using elder sister Caulfield's
name. Director William D Russell deftly
controls the polished cast and
increasingly manic plot of this
endearing and delightful comedy from
a gentler age. Top acting honours go
to veteran Edward Arnold as the head
of his all-female family.

Joan Caulfield *Ruth Wilkins* • William Holden
(1) *Lt William Seacroft* • Edward Arnold *Judge
Harry Wilkins* • Mary Philips *Edith Wilkins* •
Mona Freeman *Miriam Wilkins* • Billy De Wolfe
Albert Kummer ■ Dir William D Russell • Scr
Arthur Sheekman, from the play by Norman
Krasna

Dear Sarah
★★★

Drama based on a true story
1990 · Ire · Colour

Guiseppe Conlon, the father of Gerry
and one of the "Maguire Seven" jailed
following an IRA pub bombing in
Guildford, will be forever associated
with actor Pete Postlethwaite, who
played Conlon in Jim Sheridan's *In the
Name of the Father* with a great deal
of subtle power. That film's passion for
justice also courses through this TV
movie, which was, in fact, made three
years earlier. More focused on the
personal than the political (though the
latter always shines through), the film
is shaped around the letters Conlon
wrote to his wife, Sarah, while in jail,
and offers an insight into his
frustrating, anxious world.

Stella McCusker *Sarah Conlon* • Barry
McGovern *Guiseppe Conlon* • Patrick F Rocks
Gerard Conlon • Simon Chandler *Alastair
Logan* • Bronagh Gallagher *Anne Conlon* •
Eileen Pollock *Mary Kelly* ■ Dir Frank
Cvitanovich • Scr Tom McGurk

Dear Wife
★★ U

Comedy
1949 · US · BW · 88mins

Marx Brothers scriptwriter Arthur
Sheekman and Broadway playwright N
Richard Nash, basing their screenplay
on Norman Krasna's original

characters, delivered this sequel to the
successful comedy *Dear Ruth* (1947),
directed by Richard Haydn with the
same leading players. The plot finds
William Holden married to Joan
Caulfield and running against his
father-in-law Edward Arnold for the
state senate, while her former suitor
Billy De Wolfe continues to hanker
after her, and her younger sister Mona
Freeman continues on her socially
conscious way. Freeman almost steals
the show from the more seasoned
players.

William Holden (1) *Bill Seacroft* • Joan
Caulfield *Ruth Seacroft* • Billy De Wolfe *Albert
Kummer* • Mona Freeman *Miriam Wilkins* •
Edward Arnold *Judge Wilkins* ■ Dir Richard
Haydn • Scr Arthur Sheekman, N Richard
Nash, from characters created by Norman
Krasna

Dearly Devoted
★★ 18

Psychological thriller
1998 · US · Colour · 88mins

A depressingly ordinary psycho thriller,
despite the presence of Rose
McGowan, one of the more interesting
actresses around (check out the little
seen *Doom Generation* and *Lewis &
Clarke & George*). In the over-cooked
tradition of *Fatal Attraction*, McGowan
plays a demented student who
develops unhealthily obsessive
crushes on her teachers. After the
mysterious death of her parents, she's
sent to a new school where she finds
a new object of affection, the rather
dull Alex McArthur, whose girlfriend is
out of town. McGowan shines, but both
the plotting and direction are
unimaginative Contains violence,
swearing and sex scenes. ▣

Rose McGowan *Debbie Strand* • Alex McArthur
Peter Rinaldi • Phil Morris *Detective Joe
Rosales* • Robert Silver *Detective Phil Archer* •
Peg Shirley *Fiona* • Julia Nickson [Julia
Nickson-Soul] *Anna Nakashi* ■ Dir Steve
Cohen • Scr Michael Michaud, Kelly Carlin-
McCall, Robert McCall, Steve Cohen, from a
story by Richard Brandes, Kurt Anderson

Death and the Maiden
★★★★ 18

Drama
1994 · UK/US/Fr · Colour · 99mins

Adapted for the screen by Rafael
Yglesias and Ariel Dorfman from
Dorfman's play, this is an anguished
tour de force, in which a traumatised
woman turns her living room into a
court to try the neighbour she believes
raped and tortured her during a
previous fascist dictatorship.
Outstandingly played by Sigourney
Weaver and Ben Kingsley (as her
possible tormentor), the effective
three-hander succeeds because of a
dreadful electricity sparking between
the two leads, while Stuart Wilson, as
her husband, tries not to get burned.
Director Roman Polanski keeps it all
as claustrophobic as a coffin and it is
one of the most notable of his more
recent movies. Contains violence,
swearing and nudity. ▣

Sigourney Weaver *Paulina Escobar* • Ben
Kingsley *Dr Roberto Miranda* • Stuart Wilson
Gerardo Escobar • Krystia Mova *Dr Miranda's
wife* • Rodolphe Vega *Dr Miranda's son* ■ Dir
Roman Polanski • Scr Rafael Yglesias, Ariel
Dorfman, from the play by Ariel Dorfman

Death at Love House ★ 🔟🔳

Horror 1976 · US · Colour · 70mins

Scriptwriter Robert Wagner and his wife, Kate Jackson, move into the mansion of deceased thirties movie star Lorna Love to research her life for a screenplay. The problem is that Wagner's father once had an affair with the wanton glamour queen, causing her spirit to arise from a glass tomb and take revenge. A dire TV movie with billowing curtains and half-glimpsed ghosts standing in for shock atmosphere; the inclusion of Hollywood legends Joan Blondell, Sylvia Sidney and Dorothy Lamour brings nothing to the torpid terror table.

Robert Wagner *Joel* • Kate Jackson *Donna* • Sylvia Sidney *Clara Josephs* • Mariana Hill [Marianna Hill] *Lorna Love* • Joan Blondell *Marcella* • John Carradine *Conan Carroll* • Dorothy Lamour *Denise Christian* • Bill Macy *Oscar* ■ *Dir* EW Swackhamer • *Scr* Jim Barnett

Death Becomes Her
★★★★ 🔳

Black comedy 1992 · US · Colour · 99mins

See Meryl Streep and Goldie Hawn as you've never seen them before, enlivening this special-effects laden, extremely dark comedy from Robert Zemeckis. Superbitch actress Streep and ex-heavyweight novelist Hawn are the present and former loves of plastic surgeon-turned-mortician Bruce Willis, whose talents can't compete with witch Isabella Rossellini's devilish gift of eternal youth. Zemeckis's under-rehearsed direction is at odds with a savagely delicious script and inspired casting: both leading ladies are superbly acerbic as they try to outwit and outbitch each other, while Willis is a pleasant surprise as the put-upon hubby in this quirky but most enjoyable oddity. Contains swearing and some nudity. 🖵 *DVD*

Meryl Streep *Madeline Ashton* • Bruce Willis *Ernest Menville* • Goldie Hawn *Helen Sharp* • Isabella Rossellini *Lisle Von Rhuman* • Ian Ogilvy *Chagall* • Adam Storke *Dakota* • Nancy Fish *Rose* ■ *Dir* Robert Zemeckis • *Scr* Martin Donovan, David Koepp

Death before Dishonor ★ 🔟🔳

Action adventure 1987 · US · Colour · 89mins

Rambo rides again in this rather second-rate thriller, with Fred Dryer (a former American sportsman better known for his role in the TV series *Hunter*) as the Stallone-like hero, a marine with a short fuse hunting the Middle Eastern terrorists who've kidnapped his pal, colonel Brian Keith. There are some nasty moments, and there's little redeeming humour in this gung-ho, jingoistic gobbledegook. Contains violence and swearing.; 🖵

Fred Dryer *Sergeant Jack Burns* • Joey Gian *Ramirez* • Sasha Mitchell *Ruggieri* • Peter Parros *James* • Brian Keith *Colonel Halloran* • Paul Winfield *Ambassador* • Joanna Pacula *Elli* ■ *Dir* Terry J Leonard • *Scr* John Gatliff, Lawrence Kubik, from their story

Death Benefit ★★★ 🔢

Crime drama based on a true story
1996 · US · Colour · 85mins

From the producers of the mulitple Emmy-winning *Autobiography of Miss*

Jane Pittman, this probing crime drama tells the real-life story of Kentucky tax attorney Steven Keeney, who becomes obsessed with proving that a young woman's fall from a California cliff was not accidental, but linked somehow to the elderly couple with whom she was staying. Peter Horton (*thirtysomething*) and Carrie Snodgress (an Academy award nominee for *Diary of a Mad Housewife*) are both knockouts in this eminently watchable tale of obsession, guilt and intelligence. 🖵

Peter Horton *Steven Keeney* • Carrie Snodgress *Virginia McGinnis* • Wendy Makkena *Wynn Burkholder* • Penny Johnson *Sylvia Guzman* • Elizabeth Ruscio *LouAnne Wilkens* ■ *Dir* Mark Piznarski • *Scr* Phillip Rosenberg, from the novel by David Heilbroner

Death by Hanging ★★★★

Black comedy based on a true story
1968 · Jap · BW · 117mins

If Akira Kurosawa was Japan's most American director, then Nagisa Oshima is its most European. The influence of Brecht, Buñuel, Godard and Dusan Makavejev can all be felt in this stylised account of a true story, which typifies Oshima's combative approach to both film-making and politics. Charged with the murder and rape of two girls, a first-generation Korean student (Yun-Do Yun) survives the noose but loses his memory. So his jailers subject him to a macabre and increasingly menacing reconstruction of his alleged crimes. A scathing denunciation of capital punishment and Japan's almost institutionalised hatred of the Korean community. In Japanese with English subtitles.

Yun-Do Yun *R* • Kei Sato *Head of execution ground* • Fumio Watanabe *Education officer* • Toshiro Ishido *Chaplain* • Masao Adachi *Security officer* • Mutsuhiro Toura *Doctor* • Nagisa Oshima *Narrator* ■ *Dir* Nagisa Oshima • *Scr* Tsutomu Tamura, Mamoru Sasaki, Michinori Fukao, Nagisa Oshima

Death Collector ★★★ 🔳

Crime drama 1976 · US · Colour · 88mins

An under-rated thriller in which young Joe Cortese gets a job as a debt collector and gets caught up in the Mafia lifestyle, with suitably violent consequences. Although considered nothing more than a *Mean Streets* clone at the time, in retrospect director Ralph DeVito's gritty drama foreshadows many of the themes Martin Scorsese would later explore in *GoodFellas* and *Casino*. (Look out for Joe Pesci, the star of those two movies, in one of his earliest roles.) Great goon dialogue and quirky details set this apart from other gangster fables. 🖵

Joe Cortese *Jerry Bolanti* • Lou Criscuolo *Anthony Iadavia* • Joe Pesci *Joey* • Bobby Alto *Serge* • Frank Vincent *Bernie Feldshuh* • Keith Davis *Marley* • Jack Ramage *Herb Greene* • Anne Johns *Paula* • Bob D'Andrea *Neil* ■ *Dir/Scr* Ralph DeVito

Death Dreams ★★ 🔳

Supernatural thriller
1991 · US · Colour · 94mins

Christopher Reeve didn't have a lot of luck with the roles he chose after hanging up his *Superman* tights, and this routine, made-for-TV supernatural thriller gives him too little to work with.

He plays a businessman whose wife begins to be haunted by ghostly voices following the mysterious death of her daughter from a previous marriage. What scares there are here tend to be strictly run-of-the-mill. 🖵

Christopher Reeve *George Westfield* • Marg Helgenberger *Crista Westfield* • Fionnula Flanagan *Dr Neuberger* • Taylor Fry *Jennie Westfield* • George Dickerson *Dr Drake* ■ *Dir* Martin Donovan • *Scr* Robert Glass, from the novel by William Katz

Death Drums along the River ★★ 🔳🔳

Crime mystery 1963 · UK · Colour · 79mins

British veteran director Lawrence Huntington fetched up in South Africa in the days when it wasn't politically kosher to do so, to deliver this strangely appealing update of the hoary old Edgar Wallace imperialist saga *Sanders of the River*. Memorably filmed in 1935 with Paul Robeson and Leslie Banks under its original title, this time the film features Richard Todd attempting to resuscitate his career by playing the police inspector. Produced by Harry Alan Towers, this would-be epic was, somewhat surprisingly, co-scripted by Nicolas Roeg a decade before he directed his masterpiece *Don't Look Now.* 🖵

Richard Todd *Inspector Harry Sanders* • Marianne Koch *Dr Inge Jung* • Vivi Bach *Marlene* • Walter Rilla *Dr Schneider* • Jeremy Lloyd *Hamilton* ■ *Dir* Lawrence Huntington • *Scr* Harry Alan Towers, Nicolas Roeg, Kevin Kavanagh, Lawrence Huntington, from the novel *Sanders of the River* by Edgar Wallace

Death Game ★★

Thriller 1976 · US · Colour · 86mins

San Francisco architect Seymour Cassel lets two hitchhikers, Sondra Locke and Colleen Camp, into his house where they proceed to seduce, bind and torture him and, after drowning a delivery boy in a fish tank, finally threaten him with castration and execution. This is an unnerving psychodrama, with sleazy sex and compelling depravity oozing from every exploitative frame. A prime example of seventies post-Manson paranoia, only the ridiculous twist ending lets this sublimely degenerate shocker down.

Sondra Locke *Jackson* • Colleen Camp *Donna* • Seymour Cassel *George Manning* • Beth Brickell *Karen Manning* • Michael Kalmansohn *Delivery boy* • Ruth Warshawsky *Mrs Grossman* ■ *Dir* Peter S Traynor • *Scr* Anthony Overman, Michael Ronald Ross

Death Hunt ★★ 🔟🔳

Thriller based on a true story
1981 · US · Colour · 96mins

Charles Bronson gets up to his old macho tricks in a violent adventure that trades on his *Death Wish* persona. He's a trapper in the Canadian Rockies who gets wrongly accused of murder and goes on the run, pursued by Mountie Lee Marvin. Director Peter Hunt does a decent job of shaping the borderline exploitation thrills into a highly watchable form, and the crisp photography helps enormously. Animal lovers, take note: beware the very graphic dog fight. 🖵

Charles Bronson *Albert Johnson* • Lee Marvin *Sergeant Millen* • Angie Dickinson *Vanessa*

McBride • Andrew Stevens *Alvin Adams* • Carl Weathers *Sundog* • William Sanderson *Ned Warren* • Jon Cedar *Hawkins* ■ *Dir* Peter Hunt • *Scr* Michael Grais, Mark Victor • *Cinematographer* James Devis

Death in a French Garden
★★★★ 🔟🔳

Thriller 1985 · Fr · Colour · 97mins

Eternally teasing and dripping with style, this is that rare blend of form and content that engages both the eye and the mind. Through elliptical editing and arch manipulation of his characters, director Michel Deville leaves us as baffled as his hero, a young guitar teacher played by Christophe Malavoy. Not only does he discover his affair with his pupil's mother (Nicole Garcia) is being filmed; he also learns he's being stalked by the gay assassin who's been hired to kill his employer (Michel Piccoli). The ambiguity and elegance may not be to all tastes, but the performances, especially Piccoli's, are excellent. In French with English subtitles. 🖵

Michel Piccoli *Graham Tombsthay* • Nicole Garcia *Julia Tombsthay* • Anémone *Edwige Ledieu* • Christophe Malavoy *David Aurphet* • Richard Bohringer *Daniel Forest* ■ *Dir* Michel Deville • *Scr* Michel Deville, Rosalinde Damamme, from the novel *Sur la Terre comme au Ciel* by René Belletto

Death in Brunswick
★★★★ 🔳

Black comedy 1990 · Ausl · Colour · 103mins

Now here is the Sam Neill you won't have seen before. He's on cracking form as a cook in a sleazy restaurant in the Brunswick area of Melbourne, who hopes that an affair with waitress Zoe Carides will help him escape his domineering mother. But the only bodily contact he gets is with the corpse of his Turkish colleague in this black comedy that works best during the restaurant scenes as the dialogue fizzes and the racial mix bubbles. Marking the directorial debut of John Ruane, this was one of the key films in the brief "New Urban Cinema" boom of the early nineties. Contains violence, swearing and nudity. 🖵

Sam Neill *Carl Fitzgerald* • Zoe Carides *Sophie Papafagos* • John Clarke *Dave* • Yvonne Lawley *Mrs Fitzgerald* • Nico Lathouris *Mustafa* • Nicholas Papademetriou *Yanni Voulgaris* ■ *Dir* John Ruane • *Scr* John Ruane, Boyd Oxlade, from the novel by Boyd Oxlade

Death in Small Doses ★★ 🔳

Courtroom drama based on a true story
1995 · US · Colour · 91mins

Directed by Sondra Locke, this TV movie is based on a true story in which landscape gardener Richard Thomas (still best known as John Boy Walton) is charged with poisoning his wife Glynnis O'Connor by lacing her vitamin pills with arsenic. However, all is not as it seems and we are treated to one of those courtroom dramas where a watertight case proves to have more holes in it than a Gruyère cheese. It's hardly a breath-bater, but there's a solid performance by the under-rated Tess Harper as the assistant DA. 🖵

Richard Thomas *Richard Lyon* • Tess Harper *Assistant DA Jerri Sims* • Glynnis O'Connor *Nancy Lyon* • Gary Frank *Bill Dillard Jr* ■ *Dir* Sondra Locke • *Scr* Scott Swanton

Death in the Garden ★★★
Thriller 1956 · Fr/Mex · Colour · 95mins

Devised to exploit the success of *The Wages of Fear*, this jungle western was originally to be scripted by Jean Genet as a vehicle for Yves Montand. Luis Buñuel accepted the directorial reins with reluctance, yet he manages to explore his key themes of bourgeois avarice, religious hypocrisy and sexual repression while following a motley crew as it escapes across hostile terrain after a South American uprising. The perils encountered are drearily generic, but Buñuel still transforms this gloriously photographed Eden into a gruellingly perilous place. In French with English subtitles.

Simone Signoret *Djin* • Georges Marchal *Chark* • Michel Piccoli *Father Lisardi* • Michèle Girardon *Maria* ■ *Dir* Luis Buñuel • *Scr* Luis Buñuel, Luis Alcoriza, Raymond Queneau, Gabriel Arout, from a story by José-André Lacour • *Cinematographer* Jorge Stahl

Death in the Shadows ★★★ 15
Drama based on a true story
1998 · US · Colour · 90mins

Believe it or not, *The Fugitive* – about an innocent doctor wrongly accused of murder – was actually based on a real story. In this true-life tale, however, events have moved on and are now seen through the eyes of the physician's grown-up son. Peter Strauss plays the brilliant but arrogant surgeon Sam Sheppard, while Henry Czerney is his son, who starts digging into his father's case with the help of a local lawyer. It's an intriguing spin on a now-familiar tale, and essential viewing for fans of either the TV series or the blockbuster feature film.

Peter Strauss *Dr Sam Sheppard* • Henry Czerny *Sam "Chip" Reese Sheppard* • Lindsay Frost *Marilyn Sheppard* ■ *Dir* Peter Levin • *Scr* Adam Greenman, from the non-fiction book *Memory of Justice: the True Story of the Sam Sheppard Murder Case* by Cynthia L Cooper, Sam Reese Sheppard

Death in the Sun ★
Action adventure
1975 · W Ger/SAfr · Colour · 95mins

Trevor Howard and Christopher Lee put in fine cameo performances in an otherwise amateur exploitation thriller shot in Zimbabwe (the former Rhodesia) with a stupid script, inept direction and mediocre photography. In an East African British colony under threat from a Mau-Mau style uprising, farmer Howard's daughter is graphically raped by an albino native (Horst Frank in a totally unconvincing coat of whitewash). Virtually unwatchable, it marks a reunion appearance for *Cockleshell Heroes* stars Howard and Lee.

Christopher Lee *Bill* • James Faulkner *Terrick* • Trevor Howard *Johannes* • Horst Frank *Whispering Death* • Sybil Danning *Sally* • Sascha Hehn *Peter* • Sam Williams *Katchemu* ■ *Dir* Jürgen Goslar • *Scr* Scot Finch, from the novel *Whispering Death* by Daniel Carney

Death in Venice ★★★★★ 15
Drama 1971 · It/Fr · Colour · 125mins

Former matinée idols Dirk Bogarde and Silvana Mangano increased their standing with art-house audiences after this sumptuous reworking of Thomas Mann's novella. Bogarde's composer (he was an author in the original) arrives in Venice amid rumours of a cholera epidemic, troubled that he can no longer experience emotion, but the sight of Mangano's teenage son, Bjorn Andresen, stirs long dormant feelings. A master of colour composition, Luchino Visconti has created a haunting work that is as operatic as it is cinematic. It is perhaps too sedate in places, but Pasquale De Santis's shimmering photography more than compensates.

Dirk Bogarde *Gustav von Aschenbach* • Bjorn Andresen *Tadzio* • Silvana Mangano *Tadzio's mother* • Marisa Berenson *Frau von Aschenbach* • Mark Burns *Alfred* ■ *Dir* Luchino Visconti • *Scr* Luchino Visconti, Nicola Badalucco, from the novella by Thomas Mann • *Cinematographer* Pasqualino de Santis • *Art Director* Ferdinando Scarfiotti • *Costume Designer* Piero Tosi

Death Japanese Style ★★★★ 18
Black comedy
1984 · Jap · Colour and BW · 123mins

The high cost of dying in Japan is shrewdly, albeit sometimes crudely, satirised by director Juzo Itami, whose deconstruction of a three-day wake for a bad-tempered elder by his daughter and son-in-law is as wild as it is witty. Seemingly inspired by his own experiences, Itami establishes the samurai-slash style of film-making railing at a society that has lost touch with its traditions – a style he was to reinforce with his subsequent, better-known comedy *Tampopo*. In Japanese with English subtitles.

Tsutomu Yamazaki *Wabisuke Inoue* • Nobuko Miyamoto *Chizuko Amamiya* • Kin Sugai *Kikue Amamiya* • Shuji Otaki *Shokichi Amamiya* • Ichiro Zaitsu *Satomi* ■ *Dir/Scr* Juzo Itami

The Death Kiss ★★★
Mystery 1933 · US · BW and Tinted · 74mins

Despite the title, and the fact that it stars Bela Lugosi, director Edwin L Marin's pot-boiler is an old-fashioned Hollywood thriller in every sense. The *Dracula* star plays the manager of Tinseltown's Tiffany Studios where a murder is committed on the set of a new production. Two of his *Dracula* cast join him – David Manners and Edward Van Sloan (playing the director) – as he tries to solve the creaky whodunit. While no great shakes in the mystery department, this is an intriguing behind-the-scenes look at the motion picture mechanics of the era. For Lugosi fans this is a flawed but fascinating artefact from the vintage horror star's golden period.

David Manners *Franklyn Drew* • Adrienne Ames *Marcia Lane* • Bela Lugosi *Joseph Steiner* • John Wray *Detective Lieut Sheehan* • Vince Barnett *Officer Gulliver* • Alexander Carr *Leon A Grossmith* • Edward Van Sloan *Tom Avery* ■ *Dir* Edwin L Marin • *Scr* Gordon Kahn, Barry Barringer, Joe Traub, from the novel by Madelon St Denis

Death Line ★★★★ 18
Horror 1972 · UK · Colour · 83mins

Reactionary cop Donald Pleasence investigates mysterious disappearances in the London Underground and makes the startling discovery that a colony of cannibals has existed in the creepy tunnels since a Victorian cave-in disaster. Strong stuff in its day, Gary Sherman never directed a better movie than this grisly chiller, which provides dark scares while presenting an effective commentary on violence. An under-rated slice of British horror, this manages to be eerie, touching, melancholic and imaginative to a degree rarely seen in the genre. Highly recommended.

Donald Pleasence *Inspector Colquhoun* • Christopher Lee *Stratton-Villiers* • Norman Rossington *Detective Rogers* • David Ladd *Alex Campbell* • Sharon Gurney *Patricia Wilson* ■ *Dir* Gary Sherman • *Scr* Ceri Jones, from the story *Death Line* by Gary Sherman

Death Machine ★★★ 18
Science-fiction horror
1994 · UK · Colour · 111mins

Cheerfully lifting from the likes of *The Terminator*, *Alien* and *Die Hard*, homegrown director Stephen Norrington fashions a distinctly un-British but hugely entertaining techno-thriller. Set in the near future, the story pits high-tech weapons firm executive Ely Pouget and a gang of terrorists against barmy scientist Brad Dourif and his bone-crunching killing machine in a deserted office building. There's little in the way of character development, but former effects man Norrington never lets the pace slacken for a minute and designs some ingenious action sequences.

Brad Dourif *Jack Dante* • Ely Pouget *Hayden Cale* • William Hootkins *John Carpenter* • John Sharian *Sam Raimi* • Martin McDougall *Yutani* • Richard Brake *Scott Ridley* • Andreas Wisniewski *Weyland* • Rachel Weisz *AN Other personnel manager* ■ *Dir/Scr* Stephen Norrington

Death Match ★★ 18
Martial arts action
1994 · US · Colour · 89mins

This is another bloody, brutal and ultimately rather boring variation on the no-rules fighting formula, a popular little video genre in the nineties. Ian Jacklin is the former martial-arts champion who gets dragged back into the ring when he goes searching for a missing friend. The fight scenes are OK, but Jacklin is hardly the most charismatic of leads and the rest of the cast is forgettable. Contains nudity and sexual situations.

Martin Kove *Paul Landis* • Matthias Hues *Mark Vanik* • Ian Jacklin *John Larson* ■ *Dir* Joe Coppoletta • *Scr* Curtis Gleaves, Bob Wyatt, Steve Tymon, from a story by Curtis Gleaves

Death of a Bureaucrat ★★★★
Black comedy 1966 · Cub · BW · 84mins

Twenty years after he made his first short, Tomás Gutiérrez Alea achieved international acclaim with this deliciously macabre comedy. Produced

for the state-run ICAIC, it reveals an unexpected tolerance on the part of the Castro regime, as the satire at its expense is both funny and far from flattering. Frustrated at every turn by red tape, Salvador Wood has to resort to graverobbing to retrieve the union card his recently widowed aunt requires for her pension. Shot through with a Buñuelian strain of humour, Alea's approach also owes a good deal to silent slapstick and the anti-establishment ethos of contemporary Czech cinema. In Spanish with English subtitles.

Salvador Wood *Nephew* • Silvia Planas *Aunt* • Manuel Estanillo *Bureaucrat* • Gaspar De Santelices *Nephew's boss* ■ *Dir* Tomás Gutiérrez Alea • *Scr* Alfredo Del Cueto, Ramón Suárez, Tomás Gutiérrez Alea

Death of a Cheerleader ★★★ 12
Mystery drama 1994 · US · Colour · 87mins

This isn't in the same league as the witty Holly Hunter film *The Positively True Adventures of the Alleged Texas Cheerleader-Murdering Mom*, but still provides a gripping portrait of high-school politics, US-style. *Beverly Hills 90210*'s Tori Spelling is the high-school queen who delights in tormenting the school's geeks, including bright-but-plain Kellie Martin. When Spelling turns up dead, it quickly becomes apparent a worm has turned. Director William A Graham sympathetically chronicles the complex, and often unbearable, pressures of adolescent life. Contains drug abuse.

Kellie Martin *Angela Delvecchio* • Tori Spelling *Stacy Lockwood* • Valerie Harper *Mrs Delvecchio* • Terry O'Quinn *Ed Saxe* • James Avery *Agent Gilwood* • Andy Romano *Mr Delvecchio* • Margaret Langrick *Jill Anderson* ■ *Dir* William A Graham • *Scr* Dan Bronson, from a story by Dan Bronson, Randall Sullivan, from an article by Randall Sullivan

Death of a Gunfighter ★★★
Western 1969 · US · Colour · 94mins

A fine, grim western bearing all the hallmarks of its uncredited director, the great Don Siegel, who took over from Robert Totten after Totten fell out with star Richard Widmark. The credit was given to that alias agreed by the Directors Guild, one Allen Smithee (this was, in fact, the first feature to bear the name). Widmark is once again compulsively watchable as a former gunman-turned-marshal while Lena Horne is brilliantly cast as his woman. This may be too downbeat and slow for many tastes, but it's always interesting, and the casting of Widmark and Horne makes it quite a collector's item.

Richard Widmark *Marshal Frank Patch* • Lena Horne *Claire Quintana* • Carroll O'Connor *Lester Locke* • David Opatoshu *Edward Rosenbloom* • Kent Smith *Andrew Oxley* ■ *Dir* Allen Smithee [Robert Totten], Allen Smithee [Don Siegel] • *Scr* Joseph Calvelli, from the novel by Lewis B Patten

Death of a Salesman ★★★★
Drama 1951 · US · BW · 111mins

This powerful and generally faithful film version of Arthur Miller's hit Broadway

12 15 18 = PASSED FOR PEOPLE OF THESE AGES AND OVER ▭ = RELEASED ON VIDEO **DVD** = RELEASED ON DVD

play – the tragedy of a mediocre individual trying to understand his life of failure – replaced the original stage star, Lee J Cobb, with screen veteran Fredric March. Sad for Cobb when some other members of the stage production – Mildred Dunnock as the wife, Cameron Mitchell as one of his two sons – were retained, but March is superb as the despairing salesman and gained an Oscar nomination. (He lost to Humphrey Bogart in The African Queen.) The theatrical transitions to flashbacks might have been avoided, but this is highly commendable work by director Laslo Benedek.

Fredric March *Willy Loman* • Mildred Dunnock *Linda Loman* • Kevin McCarthy *Biff* • Cameron Mitchell *Happy* • Howard Smith *Charley* • Royal Beal *Ben* ■ *Dir* Laslo Benedek • *Scr* Stanley Roberts, from the play by Arthur Miller

Death of a Salesman
★★★ PG

Drama   1985 · US · Colour · 130mins

Dustin Hoffman re-creates his Broadway role as Willy Loman, the ageing commercial traveller trapped in his vision of the go-getting American Dream, in director Volker Schlöndorffs fascinating version of Arthur Miller's Pulitzer Prize-winning play. Hoffman starts at the top of his voice and continues in the same vein, as if still playing to the back row, though Kate Reid, as Loman's long-suffering wife, and Stephen Lang and Emmy Award-winning John Malkovich as their sons, give more subtle performances. Those searching for the definitive film of the play should check out the 1952 version. ▭

Dustin Hoffman *Willy Loman* • Kate Reid *Linda Loman* • John Malkovich *Biff Loman* • Stephen Lang *Happy Loman* • Charles Durning *Charley* • Louis Zorich *Ben* ■ *Dir* Volker Schlöndorff • *Scr* Arthur Miller, adapted from the original Broadway production staged by Michael Rudman

Death of a Schoolboy
★★★ PG

Biographical drama
1990 · Aust · Colour · 89mins

Austrian director Peter Patzak's film about the assassination of Archduke Franz Ferdinand in Sarajevo was full of possibilities. The spark that ignited the ''tinderbox of Europe'' was provided by Gavrilo Princip, a member of the Black Hand freedom fighters, but this biopic gives us too few insights into either the tense political situation in the summer of 1914 or the convictions that drove the boy to murder. It's handsomely mounted and the performances have an earnestness that atones for their stiltedness, but it's too ponderous to really engross. Some German dialogue dubbed into English. ▭

Reuben Pillsbury *Gavrilo* • Christopher Chaplin *Trifco* • Robert Munic *Cabri* • Sinolicka Trpkova *Sophia* • Hans Michael Rehberg *School director* • Philippe Léotard *Dr Levin* • Alexis Arquette *Milan* • Alan Cox *Anarchist* ■ *Dir* Peter Patzak • *Scr* David Anthony, Peter Patzak, from the book by Hans Konig

Death of a Scoundrel   ★★

Crime drama   1956 · US · BW · 119mins

This *film à clef* on the life of Serge Rubenstein is something of a family affair, with George Sanders getting the chance to betray real-life brother Tom Conway and seduce then wife Zsa Zsa Gabor. Overlong and repetitive, the action follows Sanders as he treads the familiar path from stony-broke immigrant to spendthrift playboy. A welter of second division stars are caught up in an endless round of knavery, theft and death, which would be quite intolerable without the debonair Sanders at full throttle.

George Sanders *Clementi Sabourin* • Yvonne De Carlo *Bridget Kelly* • Zsa Zsa Gabor *Mrs Ryan* • Victor Jory *Leonard Wilson* • Nancy Gates *Stephanie North* • John Hoyt *Mr O'Hara* • Coleen Gray *Mrs Van Renassalear* • Lisa Ferraday *Zina Monte* • Tom Conway *Gerry Monte* ■ *Dir/Scr* Charles Martin

Death of a Soldier   ★★ 18

War drama based on a true story
1985 · Aust · Colour · 92mins

This wartime drama is something of a departure for French-born, Australian-raised film-maker Philippe Mora. Although there are some expressionistic touches, the action is much less stylised than in his earlier documentaries. Rugged performances from James Coburn and Bill Hunter convey some of the tensions that arise between the US Army and the authorities Down Under during the hunt for a GI (Reb Brown) suspected of strangling several Melbourne women. However, the shift in attitude towards the soldier's crimes is much less satisfactory, as Mora seeks to score some political points by questioning the justice of US military law. Contains violence, swearing and nudity. ▭

James Coburn *Major Patrick Danneberg* • Reb Brown *Edward J Leonski* • Bill Hunter *Detective Sergeant Adams* • Maurie Fields *Detective Sergeant Martin* • Belinda Davey *Margot Saunders* • Max Fairchild *Major William Fricks* • Jon Sidney *General MacArthur* ■ *Dir* Philippe Mora • *Scr* William Nagle

Death of an Angel   ★

Crime drama   1951 · UK · BW · 64mins

When Jane Baxter, the wife of a country doctor is murdered, suspicion falls on her husband Patrick Barr, his new young assistant Raymond Young, his daughter Julie Somers and the local bank manager Russell Waters. Whodunit? That would be telling. Suffice to say suspense is minimal in this British murder mystery, directed at a snail's pace by Charles Saunders and lasting just over an hour.

Jane Baxter *Mary Welling* • Patrick Barr *Robert Welling* • Julie Somers *Judy Welling* • Jean Lodge *Ann Marlow* • Raymond Young *Chris Boswell* • Russell Waters *Walter Grannage* • Russell Napier *Superintendent Walshaw* • Katie Johnson *Sarah Oddy* ■ *Dir* Charles Saunders • *Scr* Reginald Long, from the play This Is Mary's Chair by Frank King

Death of an Angel   ★★★

Drama   1985 · US · Colour · 92mins

Cult indoctrination and its attendant psychological problems are snapped into sharp focus in this psychological thriller. Bonnie Bedelia goes to Mexico

to wrest her impressionable daughter, Pamela Ludwig, from the evil clutches of a religious sect and its charismatic leader, Nick Mancuso. The superior cast and intelligent treatment of religious power-plays elevate this thriller above the norm, despite some fantasy elements dissipating the stark reality of the premise.

Bonnie Bedelia *Grace* • Nick Mancuso *Father Angel* • Pamela Ludwig *Vera* • Alex Colon *Robles* ■ *Dir/Scr* Petru Popescu

The Death of Mario Ricci
★★★

Mystery romance
1983 · Fr/Swi · Colour · 101m

A Swiss investigative journalist comes to a remote mountain village to interview an expert on famine. The man appears to be on the edge of a nervous breakdown, which is somehow connected with the mystery surrounding the death of Mario Ricci, an Italian immigrant worker. Brilliantly assembled by Swiss director Claude Goretta, with a central performance by Gian Maria Volonté that deservedly won him the best actor award at Cannes, the film is redolent with atmosphere, tension and visual flair. However, the maze of false leads, secondary plots and philosophising makes it a little disappointing. In French with English subtitles.

Gian Maria Volonté *Bernard Fontana* • Magali Noël *Solange* • Heinz Bennent *Henri Kremer* • Mimsy Farmer *Cathy Burns* • Jean-Michel Dupuis *Didier Meylan* ■ *Dir* Claude Goretta • *Scr* Claude Goretta, Georges Haldas

The Death of the Incredible Hulk   ★★ PG

Action adventure   1990 · US · Colour · 94mins

One of a number of TV movie spin-offs from the wearisome series, this has Bill Bixby still searching for a way of ridding himself of the alter ego who ruins all his clothes. Here he finds a sympathetic scientist (Phillip Sterling) to help reverse the genetic process only to find himself the target of evil terrorists out to build the perfect soldier. Green-dyed Lou Ferrigno once again gets a chance to ripple his muscles but the playing and the direction is as bland as usual. One for people who like reading the final chapter of a book first. ▭

Bill Bixby *Dr David Banner* • Lou Ferrigno *The Hulk* • Carla Ferrigno *Bank clerk* • Elizabeth Gracen *Jasmin* • Philip Sterling *Dr Ronald Pratt* • Barbara Tarbuck *Amy Pratt* ■ *Dir* Bill Bixby • *Scr* Gerald DiPego, from the comic strip The Incredible Hulk by Stan Lee

Death on the Nile   ★★★ PG

Murder mystery   1978 · UK · Colour · 133mins

The biggest mystery here is how director John Guillermin managed to take a splendid Agatha Christie novel, some stunning scenery and a stellar cast and produce such a disappointing film. Setting the scene and establishing the characters is a vital part of any whodunit, but the only thing fatal about the first half of this picture is its pace. Peter Ustinov clearly enjoys his first outing as the fastidious Belgian super-sleuth Hercule Poirot and there's some delicious overplaying by Maggie Smith and Angela Lansbury.

Yet David Niven and Bette Davis are wasted, and George Kennedy and Lois Chiles are simply dreadful. ▭

Peter Ustinov *Hercule Poirot* • Jane Birkin *Louise Bourget* • Lois Chiles *Linnet Ridgeway* • Bette Davis *Mrs Van Schuyler* • Mia Farrow *Jacqueline de Bellefort* • Jon Finch *Mr Ferguson* • Olivia Hussey *Rosalie Otterbourne* • IS Johar *Manager of the Karnak* • George Kennedy *Andrew Pennington* • Angela Lansbury *Mrs Salome Otterbourne* • Simon MacCorkindale *Simon Doyle* • David Niven *Colonel Race* • Maggie Smith *Miss Bowers* • Jack Warden *Dr Bessner* • Harry Andrews *Barnstaple* • Sam Wanamaker *Rockford* ■ *Dir* John Guillermin • *Scr* Anthony Shaffer, from the novel by Agatha Christie

Death on the Set   ★

Crime mystery   1935 · UK · BW · 72mins

A year after Reginald Denham treated us to Death at Broadcasting House, the crime scene shifted from the BBC to a British film set for this creaky thriller. Based on a deservedly forgotten novel by Victor MacClure, this barnstorming balóney stars Henry Kendall as both an American gangster and his movie-directing lookalike. Blackmail leads to murder, with Kendall-the-gangster trying to pin the dirty deed on leading lady Jeanne Stuart. Leslie S Hiscott's direction is not only blissfully free of suspense, but it also fails to exploit the unique atmosphere of the film studio.

Henry Kendall *Cayley Morden/Charlie Marsh* • Jeanne Stuart *Lady Blanche* • Eve Gray *Laura Lane* • Lewis Shaw *Jimmy Frayle* • Garry Marsh *Inspector Burford* • Wally Patch *Sergeant Crowther* • Alfred Wellesley *Studio manager* • Rita Helsham *Constance Lyon* ■ *Dir* Leslie S Hiscott *[Leslie Hiscott]* • *Scr* Michael Barringer, from the novel by Victor MacClure

Death Race   ★★★ PG

Second World War drama
1973 · US · Colour · 69mins

During the Second World War, the crew of a US fighter plane grounded in the North African desert is relentlessly hunted down by a Nazi tank. Well played by Lloyd Bridges and Roy Thinnes, this attention-grabbing TV movie dwells more on the psychological aspects of warfare than the formula action side. The claustrophobic power struggle is expertly conveyed, while the sting in the tale is effectively spellbinding. ▭

Lloyd Bridges *General Beimler* • Roy Thinnes *Arnold McMillan* • Eric Braeden *Sgt Stoeffer* • Doug McClure *Lt Del Culpepper* • Dennis Rucker *Lt Voelke* • Christopher Cary *British Radioman* • Brendon Boone *Private Huffman* • Ivor Barry *Major Barry* • Dennis Dugan *Private Becker* • William Beckley *British airman* • Eric Micklewood *British officer* ■ *Dir* David Lowell Rich • *Scr* Charles Kuenstle

Death Race 2000   ★★★★ 18

Futuristic action   1975 · US · Colour · 76mins

An ultra-violent, action-packed satire set in the future showing the fascist American government sponsoring a nationally-televised road race where drivers score points for ramming pedestrians. The event is staged to pacify the ravenous public's lust for blood and stop them from getting involved with revolutionaries determined to overthrow the President.

U = SUITABLE FOR ALL   Uc = SUITABLE FOR ALL, ESPECIALLY FOR YOUNG CHILDREN (VIDEO ONLY)   PG = PARENTAL GUIDANCE

Although very graphic and bloody, light-hearted direction by Paul Bartel keeps the subversive demolition derby on an amusing track while making strong points about US political apathy and sports obsessions. The drivers are all cartoon caricatures – David Carradine is a bionic Frankenstein, Sylvester Stallone is Machine Gun Joe Viterbo – and this Roger Corman production is a lot more entertaining than its more serious and expensive contemporary, *Rollerball*. ▨

David Carradine *Frankenstein* • Simone Griffeth *Annie* • Sylvester Stallone *Machine Gun Joe Viterbo* • Mary Woronov *Calamity Jane* • Roberta Collins *Mathilda the Hun* • Martin Kove *Nero the Hero* • Louisa Moritz *Myra* • Don Steele *Junior Bruce* ■ *Dir* Paul Bartel • *Scr* Robert Thom, Charles B Griffith, from a story by Ib Melchior

Death Ride to Osaka
★★★ 18

Crime drama based on a true story
1983 · US · Colour · 93mins

Jennifer Jason Leigh answers an advertisement for American nightclub singers to entertain in Japan. It's only when she gets there that she finds out she's expected to front for a prostitution ring run by the Yakuza. Extra steamy footage was added for the video release of this hard-hitting TV movie, which features a powerful performance from the future star of *Single White Female* and *eXistenZ*. The film is based on something that actually happened to the girlfriend of actor Tom Allard. ▨

Jennifer Jason Leigh *Carol Heath* • Thomas Byrd *Don Potter* • Mako *Takejiro* • Carolyn Seymour *Katje Mori* • Ann Jillian *Marilyn Henderson* • Richard Narita *Shiro* • Soon-Teck Oh *Hatanaka* • Philip Charles MacKenzie *Cavanaugh* • Yvonne McCord *Susanne* • Leslie Wing *Lisa* ■ *Dir* Jonathan Kaplan • *Scr* Carole Raschella, Michael Raschella

Death Rides a Horse ★★ 15

Spaghetti western
1969 · It · Colour · 110mins

An overlong but spirited spaghetti western that confidently uses the tried and tested clichés of the genre: the greenhorn gunfighter joining forces with a master marksman; the baddies turned upstanding leaders of the community; and the duellist with an empty gun. John Phillip Law is the youth searching for his parents' murderers, the same people Lee Van Cleef is hunting after they put him in jail. Together they take on their foes, now occupying important positions in society. With stylish direction by Giulio Petroni and a neat twist in the tale, this is an efficient and effective horse opera. Italian dialogue dubbed into English. ▨

Lee Van Cleef *Ryan* • John Phillip Law *Bill* • Luigi Pistilli *Wolcott* ■ *Dir* Giulio Petroni • *Scr* Luciano Vincenzoni

The Death Squad ★ 15

Crime drama 1974 · US · Colour · 70mins

This below-average thriller finds detective Robert Forster investigating the murders of recently reprieved criminals. He soon discovers that the killings are the work of a vigilante group of cops who are fed up with

criminals being treated leniently by the courts. Though there's nothing to get excited about, the film does feature an early performance from Michelle Phillips of the Mamas and the Papas; she later became a regular on *Knots Landing*. ▨

Melvyn Douglas *Capt Earl Kreski* • Robert Forster *Eric Benoit* • Michelle Phillips *Joyce Kreski* • Claude Akins *Connie* • Kenneth Tobey *Hartman* • George Murdock *Vern Acker* ■ *Dir* Harry Falk • *Scr* James David Buchanan [James D Buchanan], Robert Austin

Death Takes a Holiday ★★★

Fantasy romance 1934 · US · BW · 79mins

A witty and sophisticated Paramount fable with a clever, though wordy, screenplay co-penned by Maxwell Anderson and based on an Alberto Casella play. It stars Fredric March as a very urbane grim reaper visiting Earth to learn how he is perceived and discover why humans are so scared of him. He takes the form of a handsome prince, only to fall in love during a palazzo house party. Director Mitchell Leisen keeps this bubbling along at a very healthy 79 minutes, which really makes you wonder how the 1998 remake *Meet Joe Black* clocked in at a grim three hours. ▨

Fredric March *Prince Sirk* • Evelyn Venable *Grazia* • Sir Guy Standing [Guy Standing] *Duke Lambert* • Katherine Alexander *Alda* • Gail Patrick *Rhoda* • Helen Westley *Stephanie* • Kathleen Howard *Princess Maria* • Kent Taylot *Corrado* ■ *Dir* Mitchell Leisen • *Scr* Maxwell Anderson, Gladys Lehman, Walter Ferris, from the play by Alberto Casella

Death Train ★★ 18

Action thriller
1993 · UK/Cro/US · Colour · 90mins

In what seems like a vague remake of Alistair MacLean's script for his western *Breakheart Pass*, this very minor TV movie transplants events to the post-Cold War Eastern bloc. Renegade Russian general Christopher Lee is exporting nuclear weapons to Iraq to start a revolution and Patrick Stewart is head of the UN army task force deciding to call in drunken ex-SAS officer Pierce Brosnan to head the mission. Cue the ripe dialogue, very tepid thrills and typical low-rent action in a would-be tough thriller. The stellar cast doesn't help much. Contains swearing and violence. ▨

Pierce Brosnan *Mike Graham* • Patrick Stewart *Malcolm Philpott* • Alexandra Paul *Sabrina Carver* • Ted Levine *Alex Tierney* • Christopher Lee *General Benin* • John Abineri *Leitzig* • Nic D'Avirro *Rodenko* • Clarke Peters *Whitlock* • Andreas Sportelli *Kolchinsky* • Ron Berglas *Roger Flint* • Lorrie Marlow *Yolanda* ■ *Dir* David S Jackson [David Jackson] • *Scr* David S Jackson, from the novel by Alistair MacLean

Death Valley ★★ 18

Crime thriller 1982 · US · Colour · 84mins

Low-grade "stalk and slash" movie, focusing on a young boy visiting his mother in Arizona who unwittingly becomes the target of a psychopath. Director Dick Richards succeeds in creating a low quota of suspense, even blowing a potentially explosive scene where the child is concealed in the back seat of the murderer's car. (Think what Hitchcock would have done with that!) Richards allows the

predictable plot to be further hampered by inferior acting, notably from young Peter Billingsley, one of those irksome brats Hollywood breed so well. By the film's end, you're rooting for the killer to bump him off as quickly and painfully as possible. ▨

Paul LeMat *Mike* • Catherine Hicks *Sally* • Stephen McHattie *Hal* • Wilford Brimley *Sheriff* • Peter Billingsley *Billy* • Edward Herrmann *Paul* • Jack O'Leary *Earl* • Mary Steelsmith *Babysitter* ■ *Dir* Dick Richards • *Scr* Richard Rothstein

Death Vengeance ★★★ 18

Action crime drama
1982 · US · Colour · 91mins

Charles Bronson has a lot to answer for, having created a whole sub-genre of vigilante movies. As *Death Wish* rip-offs go, though, Lewis Teague's film is fairly close to the cream of the crop. Tom Skerritt is excellent as a Philadelphia shopkeeper who organises a vigilante group to crack down on local deviants, becoming a media celebrity by default. The pace is lively, as befits the director of trash classic *Alligator*. However, Teague tries to have his cake and eat it, denouncing violent retribution on the one hand while succumbing to crowd-pleasing mayhem on the other. Shot through with conviction, this is a solid slice of right-wing movie making. ▨

Tom Skerritt *John D'Angelo* • Patti LuPone *Lisa D'Angelo* • Michael Sarrazin *Vince Morelli* • Yaphet Kotto *Ivanhoe Washington* • David Rasche *Michael Taylor* • Donna DeVarona *Sara Rogers* • Gina DeAngelis *Vera D'Angelo* • Jonathan Adam Sherman *Danny D'Angelo* ■ *Dir* Lewis Teague • *Scr* Tom Hedley, David Zelag Goodman

Death Warrant ★★★ 18

Action thriller
1990 · US/Can · Colour · 85mins

Even for a Jean-Claude Van Damme movie, this is an excessively violent, if clinically efficient exercise in body pulverizing. Van Damme stars as a maverick Royal Canadian Mountie (yes, you *did* read that correctly!), sent to a prison where there's been a series of grisly unsolved murders. There he comes face to face with an old foe: the psychopathic "Sandman", played with zealous enthusiasm by Patrick Kilpatrick. To some extent this marked a career breakthrough for Van Damme, who got to play not just a kickboxer, but – hey! – an *undercover* kickboxer. Deran Sarafian's direction is brutal and moronic, while the script, such as it is, seems merely an excuse to get Van Damme into situations where he has to kickbox himself out. Fans of the "Muscles from Brussels" won't be disappointed, though. ▨

Jean-Claude Van Damme *Louis Burke* • Cynthia Gibb *Amanda Beckett* • Robert Guillaume *Hawkins* • George Dickerson *Tom Vogler* • Art LaFleur *Sergeant DeGraf* • Patrick Kilpatrick *Naylor, "The Sandman"* ■ *Dir* Deran Sarafian • *Scr* David S Goyer

Death Wish ★★★ 18

Crime thriller 1974 · US · Colour · 93mins

This is the highly controversial sleaze epic that finally made Charles Bronson a star in America, and set a regrettable trend for trashy and ultra-violent vigilante thrillers. Bronson

mechanically plays liberal architect Paul Kersey, who takes matters into his own hands after his wife is killed and his daughter is raped by a Manhattan gang (led by Jeff Goldblum in his film debut). Director Michael Winner's blood-lusting shocker is as intense and upsetting as it is morally reprehensible, but it remains the foremost in its revenge field, especially when compared to its dismal sequels. ▨

Charles Bronson *Paul Kersey* • Hope Lange *Joanna Kersey* • Vincent Gardenia *Frank Ochoa* • Steven Keats *Jack Toby* • William Redfield *Sam Kreutzer* • Stuart Margolin *Aimes Jainchill* • Jeff Goldblum *Mugger* ■ *Dir* Michael Winner • *Scr* Wendell Mayes, from the novel by Brian Garfield

Death Wish II ★ 18

Crime thriller 1981 · US · Colour · 85mins

Charles Bronson takes his lone vigilante act to Los Angeles in this crudely exploitative, belated first sequel to Michael Winner's trend-setting trash thriller. Beginning as it means to go on with the rape and murder of Bronson's Spanish maid, it would be offensive if it weren't so laughably over the top. Even his comatose daughter from the first marginally original outing ends up impaled on railings after being raped again in another horrendous example of Winner not knowing when to stop piling on the excess. Contains swearing, violence and nudity. ▨

Charles Bronson *Paul Kersey* • Jill Ireland *Geri Nichols* • Vincent Gardenia *Frank Ochoa* • JD Cannon *New York DA* • Anthony Franciosa *LA Police Commissioner* • Ben Frank *Lieutenant Mankiewicz* • Robin Sherwood *Carol Kersey* ■ *Dir* Michael Winner • *Scr* David Engelbach, from characters created by Brian Garfield

Death Wish 3 ★ 18

Crime thriller 1985 · US · Colour · 86mins

With any remaining shred of political subtlety erased by the appallingly exploitative *Death Wish II*, director Michael Winner continues his freelance vigilante saga in ludicrously over-the-top mode. This time a pack of punks and gay Hell's Angels terrorises a Manhattan apartment block. Because the impotent police do nothing as usual except bust Paul Kersey (the ever-laconic Charles Bronson) by mistake, the rebel with neighbourly applause resumes his gun-toting/grenade-launching ways to dispense the kind of justice this type of broadly-etched ghetto scum understand. Ridiculous and revolting. ▨

Charles Bronson *Paul Kersey* • Deborah Raffin *Kathryn Davis* • Ed Lauter *Richard Striker* • Martin Balsam *Bennett* • Gavan O'Herlihy *Fraker* • Kirk Taylor *Giggler* • Alex Winter *Hermosa* ■ *Dir* Michael Winner • *Scr* Don Jakoby, Michael Edmonds, from characters created by Brian Garfield

Death Wish 4: the Crackdown ★ 18

Crime thriller 1987 · US · Colour · 94mins

Crusading vigilante architect Charles Bronson cleans up three crack-dealing LA syndicates after one causes the death of his girlfriend's (Kay Lenz) daughter in this shoddily staged sequel. J Lee Thompson takes over the directing ropes from Michael Winner and incredibly does an even lousier job marshalling the brain-damaged plot, inane dialogue and abruptly senseless violence. Awful. 📺

Charles Bronson *Paul Kersey* • Kay Lenz *Karen Sheldon* • John P Ryan *Nathan White* • Perry Lopez *Ed Zacharias* • Soon-Teck Oh *Detective Nozaki* • George Dickerson *Detective Reiner* • Jesse Dabson *Randy Viscovich* • Dana Barron *Erica Sheldon* ■ *Dir* J Lee Thompson • *Scr* Gail Morgan Hickman, from characters created by Brian Garfield

Death Wish V: the Face of Death ★ 18

Crime thriller   1994 · US · Colour · 91mins

Charles Bronson's one-man crusade against low-lifes continues when his girlfriend, fashion designer Lesley-Anne Down, is slaughtered by her mobster ex-lover Michael Parks. Absolute dross, with transvestite henchmen and acid attacks barely livening up the formulaic violence. Bronson was 72 when he starred in this sequel and both the man and the creaking concept are showing their age. 📺

Charles Bronson *Paul Kersey* • Lesley-Anne Down *Olivia Regent* • Eric Lancaster *Chelsea Regent* • Michael Parks *Tommy O'Shea* • Saul Rubinek *Brian Hoyle* ■ *Dir* Allan A Goldstein • *Scr* Stephen Peters, from characters created by Brian Garfield

Deathmask ★

Crime drama   1984 · US · Colour · 103mins

Tasteless, plotless thriller in which a medical examiner investigates the murder of a young boy in an attempt to ease the guilt of not being able to save his own daughter from her untimely death. Directed by Richard Friedman and starring Farley Granger of *Strangers on a Train* fame, this is nasty stuff that never amounts to much. Watch *Quincy* instead.

Farley Granger *Doug Andrews* • Lee Bryant *Jane Andrews* • John McCurry *Jim O'Brien* • Arch Johnson *Dr Riordan* • Barbara Bingham *Suzy Andrews* • Danny Aiello *Captain Mike Gress* ■ *Dir* Richard Friedman • *Scr* Jeffrey Goldenberg, Richard Friedman

Deathsport ★★

Science-fiction   1978 · US · Colour · 82mins

Ranger guides David Carradine and Claudia Jennings battle the evil Statesmen, futuristic Hell's Angels who ride cycles called Death Machines, in a banal reworking of *Death Race 2000*. It's set in the post-apocalyptic year 3000, and mixes cheap *Star Wars* tricks and cannibal mutants into the vehicular violence. There's lots of fiery crashes and gory comedy, but little sense in a movie shot separately by directors Henry Suso and Allan Arkush and then literally stuck together. It shows! Jennings was *Playboy* playmate of the year in 1970, and died in a car accident less than a year after this film was completed.

David Carradine *Kaz Oshay* • Claudia Jennings *Deneer* • Richard Lynch *Ankar Moor* • William Smithers *Doctor Karl* • David McLean *Lord Zirpola* • Jesse Vint *Polna* ■ *Dir* Henry Suso, Allan Arkush • *Scr* Henry Suso, Donald Steward, from a story by Frances Doel

Deathtrap ★★ PG

Thriller   1982 · US · Colour · 111mins

The play by Ira Levin (*Rosemary's Baby*, *A Kiss before Dying*) was a particularly clever piece of stagecraft that, like *Sleuth*, was heavily dependent on the theatre itself to make its tricks work. No matter how well director Sidney Lumet manages to disguise the theatricality, and despite hard work by leads Michael Caine and Christopher Reeve, the basic plot devices sink the project cinematically. However, Dyan Cannon is splendid, and Irene Worth puts in a rare movie appearance. It may work for some, but it's really very silly and quite unpleasant in tone and character, with some desperately gratuitous, vulgar moments. Contains some swearing. 📺

Michael Caine *Sidney Bruhl* • Christopher Reeve *Clifford Anderson* • Dyan Cannon *Myra Elizabeth Maxwell Bruhl* • Irene Worth *Helga Ten Dorp* • Henry Jones *Porter Milgrim* ■ *Dir* Sidney Lumet • *Scr* Jay Presson Allen, from the play by Ira Levin

Deathwatch ★★★ 15

Science-fiction satire
1980 · Fr/W Ger · Colour · 124mins

Inspired by a novel by David Compton, this futuristic discourse on the intrusiveness of television is much bleaker and censorious than either Didier Grousset's *Kamikaze* or *The Truman Show*. With Glasgow providing the desolate backdrop, this shows how easy it is to commit acts of psychological trespass, as Harvey Keitel uses a miniature camera implanted in his skull to record the final days of the terminally ill Romy Schneider for unscrupulous Harry Dean Stanton's TV show. Had the focus remained on the docu-soap mentality, this might have packed more of a punch, but director Betrand Tavernier's humanism deflects his purpose. 📺

Romy Schneider *Katherine Mortenhoe* • Harvey Keitel *Roddy* • Harry Dean Stanton *Vincent Ferriman* • Thérèse Liotard *Tracey* • Max von Sydow *Gerald Mortenhoe* ■ *Dir* Bertrand Tavernier • *Scr* Bertrand Tavernier, David Rayfiel, from the novel *The Continuous Katherine Mortenhoe* (*The Unsleeping Eye*) by David Compton

The Debt Collector ★★★★ 18

Drama   1999 · UK · Colour · 105mins

As hard-hitting as a kick in the stomach, this gritty Scottish drama is outstanding on all fronts. First-time director Anthony Neilson has crafted a visceral and cathartic tale with virtuoso skill, combining tragedy on a Shakespearean scale with vibrant colour and superb camera control. Billy Connolly stars as a reformed ex-con and now successful sculptor whose violent past comes back to haunt him in the shape of his arresting officer, Ken Stott. Stott takes it upon himself to deal Connolly true retribution for his crimes, and in the process both they and their families suffer severe repercussions. With a simple enough synopsis in the revenge tragedy vein, Neilson's film manages to exist in a class of its own owing to incredible performances from Francesca Annis, Annette Crosbie, Connolly and Stott and the formidable talent of this new

director. Contains violence, sexual threat and swearing. 📺 *DVD*

Billy Connolly *Nickie Dryden* • Ken Stott *Gary Keltie* • Francesca Annis *Val Dryden* • Iain Robertson *Flipper* • Annette Crosbie *Lana* • Alastair Galbraith *Colquhoun* ■ *Dir/Scr* Anthony Neilson • *Music* Adrian Johnston • *Cinematographer* Dick Pope

Decadence ★★ 18

Comedy   1993 · UK/Ger · Colour · 113mins

Steven Berkoff's in-your-face style of theatre has its admirers, even if his talents lie more in self-promotion than performance. Alas, this pretentious film version of his own play is a virtual textbook on how not to make the transition from stage to screen. Berkoff, who both directs and stars alongside Joan Collins, can't bear to excise a single rhyming couplet, resulting in interminable monologues interspersed with bouts of lame slapstick, plus bizarre cameos from the likes of Christopher Biggins and Michael Winner. The leads play dual roles from different ends of the social spectrum, but plot comes a poor second to the author's laboured satire on the privileged classes. 📺

Steven Berkoff *Steve/Les/Helen's "Couturier"* • Joan Collins *Helen/Sybil* • Christopher Biggins *Entourage* • Michael Winner *Entourage* • Marc Sinden *Entourage* ■ *Dir* Steven Berkoff • *Scr* Steven Berkoff, from his play

The Decameron ★★★★ 18

Period drama
1970 · It/Fr/W Ger · Colour · 106mins

This was the first film in Pier Paolo Pasolini's trilogy based on famous medieval story cycles. (*The Canterbury Tales* and *Arabian Nights* followed.) The director himself plays Giotto, seen working on a fresco; around him revolve eight of Boccaccio's bawdy tales of sexual deception, which involve lascivious nuns, a false saint and three brothers who kill their sister's lover. Untrammelled by any Freudian or religious guilt, the episodic movie captures much of the spirit of the original, while Pasolini chose many ordinary Neapolitans to populate his re-creation of teeming 14th-century Naples. In Italian with English subtitles. 📺

Franco Citti *Ciappelletto* • Ninetto Davoli *Andreuccio of Perugia* • Angela Luce *Peronella* • Patrizia Capparelli *Alibech* • Jovan Jovanovic *Rustico* • Gianni Rizzo *Head friar* • Pier Paolo Pasolini *Giotto* ■ *Dir* Pier Paolo Pasolini • *Scr* Pier Paolo Pasolini, from the stories by Giovanni Boccaccio • *Cinematographer* Tonino Delli Colli

Decameron Nights ★★★

Period adventure   1953 · UK · Colour · 93mins

Suave Louis Jourdan plays both yarnspinner Boccaccio and the leads in a trio of stories, framed by a device whereby he and Joan Fontaine flee 14th-century Florence to escape the plague, holing up in her villa. Unsurprisingly, Fontaine co-stars in the three tales as well. The result is diverting and mildly risqué tosh, beautifully photographed in rich Technicolor by talented cameraman Guy Green. Director Hugo Fregonese knows how to get the most out of this kind of flamboyant material; he also has an eye for the ladies, who include

British lovelies Joan Collins and Mara Lane. Producer Mike Frankovich's wife Binnie Barnes also has a featured role, and fans of music hall shouldn't overlook a rare performance from George and Bert Bernard.

Joan Fontaine *Fiametta/Ginevra/Isabella/Bartolomea* • Louis Jourdan *Boccaccio/Paganino/Giulio/Bertrando* • Binnie Barnes *Contessa/Old witch/Nerina* • Godfrey Tearle *Ricciardo/Bernabo* • Joan Collins *Pampinea/Maria* • Mara Lane *Girl in villa* • George Bernard *Messenger* • Bert Bernard *Messenger* ■ *Dir* Hugo Fregonese • *Scr* George Oppenheimer, from the stories by Giovanni Boccaccio

Deceived ★★★ 15

Psychological thriller
1991 · US · Colour · 103mins

Goldie Hawn takes a break from her usually frothy comedies for this flawed but mildly diverting thriller. Hawn is happily married to John Heard, only to discover after his accidental death that she knew very little about him. Despite her best efforts, Hawn lacks credibility in the pivotal role, so it's left to the ever-excellent Heard to make the most of what is, sadly, one of his rare leading roles. Damian Harris, son of actor Richard Harris, generates some suspense as director, but the climax is just plain silly. Contains swearing, and some violence. 📺 *DVD*

Goldie Hawn *Adrienne Saunders* • John Heard *Jack Saunders* • Ashley Peldon *Mary Saunders* • Robin Bartlett *Charlotte* • Tom Irwin *Harvey Schwartz* • Amy Wright *Evelyn Wade* • Jan Rubes *Tomasz Kestler* • Kate Reid *Rosalie* ■ *Dir* Damian Harris • *Scr* Mary Agnes Donoghue, Derek Saunders, from a story by Mary Agnes Donoghue

Deceived by Trust ★★ 12

Drama based on a true story
1995 · US · Colour · 85mins

This is formulaic fare, although it will be a must for all true-story devotees. Stephanie Kramer is a trusty social worker who goes into battle against the educational establishment when a respected high school principal (Michael Gross) is accused of sexually assaulting a student. Director Chuck Bowman specialises in these sort of sensationalist true stories and builds the action here to a suitably melodramatic climax. Contains violence.

Stephanie Kramer *Sarah Collins* • Michael Gross *Gordon Powell* • Shannon Fill *Cindy Webster* ■ *Dir* Chuck Bowman • *Scr* Dan Levine

The Deceivers ★★ 15

Drama   1988 · UK · Colour · 98mins

In the absence of regular partner James Ivory, producer Ismail Merchant has managed to miss both the rousing adventure and the intriguing ideas contained in John Masters's novel of cultism and culture clash. Part of the problem lies with director Nicholas Meyer, who is unsure whether to opt for mini-series glossiness or schlock goriness as a secret cult is linked to a spate of murders that disturb the peace of 1820s India. But the weight of blame must fall on the performers, with usually dependable stalwarts like Saeed Jaffrey and Shashi Kapoor every bit as inanimate as the current 007,

Pierce Brosnan, who looks neither shaken nor stirred throughout.

Pierce Brosnan *William Savage* • Saeed Jaffrey *Hussein* • Shashi Kapoor *Chandra Singh* • Helen Michell *Sarah Wilson* • Keith Michell *Colonel Wilson* • David Robb *George Angelsmith* • Tariq Yunus *Feringea* ■ *Dir* Nicholas Meyer • *Scr* Michael Hirst, from the novel by John Masters

December ★★ PG

Second World War drama
1991 · US · Colour · 87mins

The month in question is December 1941; the subject is the "day of infamy", as FDR famously described the Japanese attack on Pearl Harbor. That event has been used as the basis for several movies, but this one rings the changes by focusing on five high school seniors deciding whether to enlist, be drafted or register as conscientious objectors. The cast, led by Balthazar Getty as a gung-ho teenager too young to join up, strike their poses and argue their cases somewhat in the manner of *Dead Poets Society*.

Balthazar Getty *Allister Gibbs* • Jason London *Russell Littlejohn* • Brian Krause *Tim Mitchell* • Wil Wheaton *Kipp Gibbs* • Chris Young *Stuart Brayton* • Robert Miller *Headmaster Thurston* • Ann Hartfield *Mrs Langley* • Soren Bailey *Billy Wade* ■ *Dir/Scr* Gabe Torres

December Bride ★★★ PG

Period drama
1990 · UK · Colour · 84mins

On the surface yet another tale of undisclosed paternity from the Emerald Isle, this is, in fact, a careful and sincere study of the social, political and religious problems that have divided the Irish people throughout the 20th century. Saskia Reeves impresses as the maid whose simultaneous affairs with brothers Donal McCann and Ciaran Hinds scandalise the God-fearing members of an isolated farming community. But what elevates this film, adapted from Sam Hanna Bell's novel, above the average melodrama is French cinematographer Bruno de Keyzer's brooding views of the austere Northern Ireland coastline and director Thaddeus O'Sullivan's adroit avoidance of sensationalism.

Saskia Reeves *Sarah* • Donal McCann *Hamilton Echlin* • Ciaran Hinds *Frank Echlin* • Patrick Malahide *Sorleyson* • Brenda Bruce *Martha* • Michael McKnight *Fergus* • Dervla Kirwan *Young Martha* • Peter Capaldi *Young Sorleyson* ■ *Dir* Thaddeus O'Sullivan • *Scr* David Rudkin, from the novel by Sam Hanna Bell

Deception ★★★★ PG

Crime drama
1946 · US · BW · 107mins

It's music, music, music as the great film composer Eric Wolfgang Korngold (*The Adventures of Robin Hood*, *The Sea Hawk*) receives as much of a showcase here as does star Bette Davis, who plays a pianist whose patron is suave composer/conductor Claude Rains. This is splendid stuff, brilliantly orchestrated in both senses as Bette lies to her husband, refugee cellist Paul Henreid, about her former relationship with Rains. Rains gets the best lines, and delivers them quite superbly, but Davis is at her best in what was to be one of her last great

melodramas for Warner Bros. This joins *Humoresque* and *The Seventh Veil* as one of the great "concerto" movies.

Bette Davis *Christine Radcliffe* • Paul Henreid *Karel Novak* • Claude Rains *Alexander Hollenius* • John Abbott *Bertram Gribble* • Benson Fong *Manservant* ■ *Dir* Irving Rapper • *Scr* John Collier, Joseph Than, from the play *Jealousy (Monsieur Lamberthier)* by Louis Verneuil

Deception ★★★ 15

Thriller
2000 · US · Colour · mins

A lukewarm thriller that benefits greatly from a few fun plot twists and a colourful cast. Ben Affleck is an ex-con who assumes the identity of his dead cellmate in order to hook up with the guy's gorgeous pen-pal girlfriend (Charlize Theron). They share a few passionate moments before her nasty brother, sleazy Gary Sinise, coerces Affleck into robbing a casino. Sinise plays his role with just the right touch of menace and humour, but Affleck is out of his league as an action hero. John Frankenheimer's workmanlike direction robs this promising movie of any distinctive personality.

Ben Affleck *Rudy Duncan* • Charlize Theron *Ashley* • Gary Sinise *Gabriel* • Clarence Williams III *Merlin* • Dennis Farina *Jack Bangs* • James Frain *Nick* • Donal Logue *Pug* ■ *Dir* John Frankenheimer • *Scr* Ehren Kruger

Deceptions ★★ 18

Thriller
1990 · US · Colour · 100mins

LA Law's Harry Hamlin is a cop investigating a murder who ends up falling in love with the prime suspect (Hamlin's former real-life wife Nicollette Sheridan). Hamlin, who won female hearts with his clean-cut looks and business suits on TV, here spends most of the movie unshaven and in a rather unsightly shirt that's sure to turn off even his most devoted fans – if they haven't already been turned off by the hackneyed plot. Contains swearing, sex scenes and nudity.

Harry Hamlin *Nick Gentry* • Nicollette Sheridan *Adrienne Erickson* • Robert Davi *Jack "Harley" Kessler* • Marshall Colt *Douglas Erickson* ■ *Dir* Ruben Preuss • *Scr* Richard Taylor, from a story by Ken Denbow

Decision at Sundown ★★ U

Western
1957 · US · Colour · 77mins

Western star Randolph Scott hit a winning streak when he teamed up with director Budd Boetticher and writer Burt Kennedy on such gems as *The Tall T* and *Comanche Station*. Scott and Boetticher made this one; unfortunately, Kennedy wasn't involved. It's visually less impressive, set in town rather than out in the wide open spaces, while the plot – which revolves around Randy's personal feud with local bigwig John Carroll – is rather verbose.

Randolph Scott *Bart Allison* • John Carroll *Tate Kimbrough* • Karen Steele *Lucy Summerton* • Valerie French *Ruby James* • Noah Beery Jr *Sam* • John Archer *Dr Storrow* • Andrew Duggan *Sheriff Swede Hansen* ■ *Dir* Budd Boetticher • *Scr* Charles Lang, from a story by Vernon L Fluharty

Decision before Dawn ★★★

Spy drama
1951 · US · BW · 119mins

This is a long and distinctly sombre spy drama, with Oskar Werner playing a German PoW who agrees to spy against his own people, apparently motivated by the belief that he can help shorten the war and save lives. The Americans train him and send him back home loaded up with espionage tricks, giving rise to a moral conundrum: is he a traitor, a hero or simply a martyr-in-waiting? The most impressive aspect of the film is the location shooting in a bombed-out postwar Germany. It received a best picture Oscar nomination, the second in a row for Soviet émigré director Anatole Litvak.

Richard Basehart *Lt Rennick* • Gary Merrill *Colonel Devlin* • Oskar Werner *Happy* • Hildegarde Neff *Hilde* • Dominique Blanchar *Monique* • OE Hasse *Oberst Von Ecker* • Wilfried Seyfert [Wilfried Seyferth] *SS Man Scholtz* • Hans Christian Blech *Tiger* ■ *Dir* Anatole Litvak • *Scr* Peter Viertel, from the novel *Call It Treason* by George Howe • *Cinematographer* Frank Planer

The Decks Ran Red ★

Crime
1958 · US · BW · 84mins

James Mason plays the captain of a rusty old freighter whose crew unscrupulous deckhand Broderick Crawford is planning to murder so he can scuttle the ship and claim the salvage money. Mason, however, foils the plan with a little help from the cook's wife (beautiful Dorothy Dandridge), Director Andrew Stone specialised in preposterous suspense movies, shot mainly on location, and he maintains the tension here. Alas, the film is sunk by Stone's banal dialogue, while the cast are all at sea.

James Mason *Capt Edwin Rumill* • Dorothy Dandridge *Mahia* • Broderick Crawford *Henry Scott* • Stuart Whitman *Leroy Martin* • Katherine Bard *Joan Rumill* • Jack Kruschen *Alex Cole* • John Gallaudet *"Bull" Pringle* ■ *Dir* Andrew Stone [Andrew L Stone] • *Scr* Andrew Stone

Decline and Fall... of a Birdwatcher ★

Satire
1968 · UK · Colour · 123mins

Three years after Tony Richardson failed to breathe cinematic life into Evelyn Waugh's novel *The Loved One*, ex-documentary director John Krish had a stab at Waugh's partly autobiographical 1928 work, *Decline and Fall*, which ranks among the most spectacular literary debuts of the century. It was a vainglorious attempt, as the joys of this hilarious comedy of upper-class manners lie solely on the page; neither Krish nor his trio of scriptwriters have the satirical wit or irreverent verve to translate them to the screen. Their cause isn't helped by Robin Phillips's ghastly performance as Paul Pennyfeather.

Robin Phillips *Paul Pennyfeather* • Donald Wolfit *Dr Fagan* • Genevieve Page *Margot Beste-Chetwynde* • Robert Harris *Prendergast* • Leo McKern *Captain Grimes* • Colin Blakely *Philbrick* • Rodney Bewes *Arthur Potts* • Donald Sinden *Prison governor* ■ *Dir* John Krish • *Scr* Ivan Foxwell, Alan Hackney, Hugh Whitemore, from the novel *Decline and Fall* by Evelyn Waugh

The Decline of the American Empire ★★★★ 18

Comedy drama
1986 · Can · Colour · 97mins

Nominated for a best foreign film Oscar, this sophisticated satire on the sexual mores of a group of ageing intellectuals is superbly structured and paced by the Québecois director, Denys Arcand. Having shown us the quartet of history tutors and their four female friends separately expressing their forthright views on physical pleasure, he then brings them together for a dinner party at which bourgeois discretion is soon forgotten amid the seepage of guilty secrets. As revealing as the bristling dialogue, flashbacks seamlessly punctuate the action to shade in personal and political details about the characters, whose very imperfection makes them fascinating. In French with English subtitles.

Pierre Curzi *Pierre* • Rémy Girard *Remy* • Yves Jacques *Claude* • Daniel Briere *Alain* • Dominique Michel *Dominique* • Louise Portal *Diane* • Dorothée Berryman *Louise* • Genevieve Rioux *Danielle* • Gabriel Arcand *Mario* ■ *Dir/Scr* Denys Arcand

The Decline of Western Civilization ★★★★

Music documentary
1980 · US · Colour · 100mins

Penelope Spheeris's cult documentary takes an unflinching and non-judgemental look at the Los Angeles punk scene at the fag end of the seventies. She blends live performances from anonymous bands such as Circle Jerks, Black Flag and Fear (who were a particular favourite of John Belushi) with revealing contributions from managers, fans and the group members themselves. While most use the camera as a mirror for their preening, some are surprisingly articulate about their lifestyle – the downside of which is illustrated in the interview with Darby Crash, lead singer of the Germs, who ended up on a mortuary slab before the film was even released. This is the first in a trilogy of rock documentaries made by Spheeris that, viewed today, seem like valuable cultural documents.

Dir/Scr Penelope Spheeris

The Decline of Western Civilization Part II: the Metal Years ★★★ 18

Music documentary
1988 · US · Colour · 88mins

A great companion piece to *This Is Spinal Tap*, Penelope Spheeris's documentary follow-up to her revealing record of the Los Angeles punk scene at the end of the seventies exposes the less than blemish-free world of Heavy Metal music. MTV-style concert footage is mixed with unplugged, warts-and-all interviews with the likes of Kiss, Ozzy Osbourne and Alice Cooper; Guns N Roses declined to appear. Unsurprisingly, common themes broached are groupies, booze and drugs: Steve Tyler of Aerosmith freely admits "millions went up my nose". Utterly compelling, insightful and often hilarious.

Dir Penelope Spheeris

The Decline of Western Civilization Part III ★★★

Music documentary
1997 · US · Colour · 89mins

Searing final chapter in Penelope Spheeris's trilogy of music documentaries, focusing this time not on the rock personalities themselves, but on the disenfranchised Hollywood waifs who make up the dwindling audience of Los Angeles's contemporary punk/metal scene. Grimmer in tone than its two predecessors, this wounded film maps out a generation of no-hopers with a bleak vision of the future. Despite Spheeris's exploitative interview techniques, this deservedly won the Freedom of Expression award at Robert Redford's Sundance film festival.

Dir Penelope Spheeris

Deconstructing Harry ★★★★ 🔞

Comedy drama 1997 · US · Colour · 91mins

Woody Allen's tumultuous private life seems to spill sourly into this brilliant bad-taste story about a novelist, Harry Block (Allen), whose friends and relatives are used as thinly-disguised characters in his books, despite screams of protest from those he exploits (Judy Davis and Kirstie Alley among them). But they can't hate him more than he hates himself, as a fantasy sequence with the Devil (Billy Crystal) makes plain. Block is suffering from a lack of inspiration for his latest book and is as out of focus with life as actor Robin Williams is – literally – out of focus in one of the film's funniest ideas. Rarely has Allen's use of a movie as a psychiatrist's couch been quite so evident. Contains swearing, sex scenes and sexual references. 🖂

Caroline Aaron *Doris* • Woody Allen *Harry Block* • Kirstie Alley *Joan* • Bob Balaban *Richard* • Richard Benjamin *Ken* • Eric Bogosian *Burt* • Billy Crystal *Larry* • Judy Davis *Lucy* • Hazelle Goodman *Cookie* • Mariel Hemingway *Beth Kramer* • Amy Irving *Jane* • Julie Kavner *Grace* • Julia Louis-Dreyfus *Leslie* • Demi Moore *Helen* • Elisabeth Shue *Fay* • Stanley Tucci *Paul Epstein* • Robin Williams *Mel* ■ *Dir/Scr* Woody Allen

Decoration Day ★★★ 🅿🅶

Drama 1990 · US · Colour · 94mins

James Garner here swaps the wisecracking persona he is normally associated with in TV series like *The Rockford Files* for something a lot more serious, playing a retired and recently widowed judge who finds the strength to carry on when he hears from a childhood friend left disillusioned by war service. It's a moving, if rather slow story, but Garner is always worth watching, and he is ably supported by a cast that includes Bill Cobbs and Ruby Dee. 🖂

James Garner *Judge Albert Sidney Finch* • Bill Cobbs *Gaspard "Gee" Penniwell* • Judith Ivey *Terry Novis* • Ruby Dee *Rowena* • Jo Anderson *Loreen Wendell* • Norm Skaggs *Billy Wendell* • Laurence Fishburne *Michael Waring* ■ *Dir* Robert Markowitz • *Scr* Robert W Lenski, from the novella by John William Corrington

Decoy ★ 🔞

Action adventure 1995 · US · Colour · 92mins

Violent, clumsily-made action romp that somehow managed to sign two sci-fi genre favourites: Peter Weller (*RoboCop*) and Robert Patrick, the indestructible T-1000 from *Terminator 2*. Both play heavies hired to protect a millionaire's daughter, played by the beautiful Charlotte Lewis, from the clutches of would-be kidnappers. Director Victor Rambaldi, whose one and only film this was, stages a mind-numbing collection of bloody shootouts in which, predictably, no one hits anything. Low-grade, brain-rotting video fodder? 🖂

Peter Weller *Baxter* • Robert Patrick *Travis* • Charlotte Lewis *Katya* • Peter Breck *Wellington* • Darlene Vogel *Diana* • Scott Hylands *Jenner* ■ *Dir* Victor Rambaldi • *Scr* Robert Sarno

Dee Snider's Strangeland ★

Horror thriller 1998 · US · Colour · 91mins

Yes, *that* Dee Snider – the bizarre former lead singer of Twisted Sister. If you remember the band, you'll have some idea of what's on offer here: sleaze and nastiness galore, with a bit of tasteless humour thrown in. The story, such as it is, involves a man who uses the internet to lure people into his clutches, whereupon he subjects them to 18-certificate tortures. However, what will really make you shiver is the thought that some movie producer gave Snider (who both writes and stars) and director John Pieplow the money to make this poorly realised film in the first place.

Dee Snider *Captain Howdy/Carleton Hendricks* • Elizabeth Pena *Toni Gage* • Brett Harrelson *Steve Christian* • Kevin Gage *Detective Mike Gage* • Amy Smart *Angela* • Robert Englund *Jackson Roth* • Linda Cardellini *Genevieve Gage* ■ *Dir* John Pieplow • *Scr* Dee Snider

The Deep ★★★ 🔞

Adventure 1977 · US · Colour · 119mins

Jacqueline Bisset in a wet T-shirt, Donna Summer's titular disco hit and *Jaws* author Peter Benchley co-scripting from his own novel were enough to make this soggy sea saga of rival divers after shipwrecked drugs a major box-office hit in the summer of 1977. With 40 per cent of his action taking place underwater in creepy depths, director Peter Yates doesn't have to do much to keep tension on an even keel, and the mean moray eel sequence is a real shocker when it arrives. But slick photography aside, the silly script and two-dimensional characterisations from Nick Nolte, Robert Shaw and Louis Gossett succeed in sinking plausibility every time reality threatens to surface. Contains violence, swearing and brief nudity. 🖂 **DVD**

Robert Shaw *Romer Treece* • Jacqueline Bisset *Gail Berke* • Nick Nolte *David Sanders* • Louis Gossett [Louis Gossett Jr] *Henri Cloche* • Eli Wallach *Adam Coffin* • Robert Tessier *Kevin* • Earl Maynard *Ronald* ■ *Dir* Peter Yates • *Scr* Peter Benchley, Tracey Keenan Wynn, from the novel by Peter Benchley

The Deep Blue Sea ★★★

Drama 1955 · UK · Colour · 98mins

Hester (Vivien Leigh), a beautiful, middle-aged woman, has left her husband, a judge, and the comfort of her home to live in drab digs and continue an affair with Freddie (Kenneth More), an attractive younger man. An ex-RAF pilot, Freddie is unable to adjust to post-war life, taking refuge in memories of wartime camaraderie and drinking heavily. He is also losing interest in Hester, which leads her to a suicidal crisis. Terence Rattigan's famous and oft-revived play is a sharply observed and emotionally searing period piece. All the more pity, then, that the film fails to capture the emotion of the original and is visually sub-standard.

Vivien Leigh *Hester* • Kenneth More *Freddie Page* • Eric Portman *Miller* • Emlyn Williams *Sir William Collyer* • Moira Lister *Dawn Maxwell* • Alec McCowen *Ken Thompson* • Dandy Nichols *Mrs Elton* • Arthur Hill *Jackie Jackson* • Miriam Karlin *Katya* • Sidney James *Man in street* ■ *Dir* Anatole Litvak • *Scr* Terence Rattigan, from his play

Deep Blue Sea ★★★ 15

Science-fiction action thriller
1999 · US · Colour · 90mins

The disaster movie genre meets *Jaws* in director Renny Harlin's popcorn screamer about three genetically mutated, brainy sharks stalking the marooned members of an underwater research facility. Despite a waterlogged script, this remains afloat through sheer nerve, technical prowess and some truly spectacular shock moments involving computer special effects. Saffron Burrows's wet-suit strip is the hilarious high point in this dumbed-down shark lark. Contains horror and swearing. 🖂 **DVD**

Saffron Burrows *Dr Susan McAlester* • Thomas Jane *Carter Blake* • LL Cool J *Preacher Dudley* • Jacqueline McKenzie *Janice Higgins* • Michael Rapaport *Tom "Scog" Scoggins* • Stellan Skarsgård *Jim Whitlock* • Samuel L Jackson *Russell Franklin* ■ *Dir* Renny Harlin • *Scr* Duncan Kennedy, Donna Powers, Wayne Powers

Deep Cover ★★★★ 🔞

Crime drama 1992 · US · Colour · 103mins

One of the most under-rated cop thrillers of the nineties, this is an exhilarating and intelligent examination of blurred lines between those who break the law and those who enforce it. A suitably intense Laurence (still being billed as Larry) Fishburne is the undercover detective who sets out to unravel a major drugs ring by forming a curious alliance with shady, neurotic lawyer Jeff Goldblum. It's their relationship that forms the heart of the movie and both deliver superb performances, particularly Goldblum as the middle-class boy fatally addicted to the glamour of crime. However, director Bill Duke doesn't stint on the action sequences and delivers some stunningly choreographed slices of screen mayhem. 🖂

Larry Fishburne [Laurence Fishburne] *John Q Hull* • Jeff Goldblum *David Jason* • Victoria Dillard *Betty McCutcheon* • Charles Martin Smith *Carver* • Sydney Lassick *Gopher* ■ *Dir* Bill Duke • *Scr* Henry Bean, Michael Tolkin

Deep Crimson ★★★ 🔞

Crime romance
1996 · Mex/Fr/Sp · Colour · 109mins

Dedicated to Leonard Kastle, who covered the same true-life case in *The Honeymoon Killers*, this Mexican melodrama is notable for both the genuine passion of its grotesque protagonists and the muted savagery of their crimes. Posing as brother and sister, corpulent nurse Regina Orozco and temperamental gigolo Daniel Gimenez Cacho prey on lonely heart widows with an insouciance that is hideous in its pitilessness. Arturo Ripstein cleverly uses period kitsch to reinforce their twisted motivation. He hurries the ending, though, as the couple tire of the chase and meet their fate. In Spanish with English subtitles. Contains violence, swearing and sex scenes. 🖂

Daniel Gimenez Cacho *Nicolas Estrella* • Regina Orozco *Coral Fabre* • Marisa Paredes *Irene Gallardo* • Veronica Merchant *Rebeca Sampedro* • Julieta Egurrola *Juanita Norton* • Rosa Furman *Mrs Silberman* ■ *Dir* Arturo Ripstein • *Scr* Paz Alicia Garciadiego

Deep End ★★★★

Drama 1970 · US/W Ger · Colour · 91mins

This is one of the strangest movies to come out of the Swinging Sixties. Directed by Polish émigré Jerzy Skolimowski, it's set in the grottily dank Chelsea public baths. John Moulder-Brown – a callow, haunted-looking 15-year-old – and Jane Asher are the employees, who swap changing rooms so he can please the ladies (including bosomy football fanatic Diana Dors) and she can pleasure the gents. The pool provides the film's central metaphor and some bizarre, shocking things happen in it – such as the search for Asher's engagement ring diamond in bagfuls of snow, melting in the empty pool. 🖂

Jane Asher *Susan* • John Moulder-Brown *Mike* • Karl Michael Vogler *Swimming instructor* • Christopher Sandford *Fiance* • Diana Dors *Lady client* ■ *Dir* Jerzy Skolimowski • *Scr* Jerzy Skolimowski, Jerzy Gruza, Boleslaw Sulik

The Deep End of the Ocean ★★ 12

Drama 1999 · US · Colour · 103mins

Michelle Pfeiffer is the mother whose life is turned upside down after her toddler son goes missing, never, it seems, to be seen again. How she and her family (including older son Jonathan Jackson and husband Treat Williams) cope or, more to the point, *don't* cope is really the stuff of TV movies, and there's little here to raise this above that status. Even the presence of Whoopi Goldberg as the cop in charge of the case adds little interest. The costume and make-up departments have done their best to make Pfeiffer look dowdy, but no amount of dressing-down can hide the fact that this is an A-list star giving a classy performance in a merely average weepie. Contains swearing. 🖂

Michelle Pfeiffer *Beth Cappadora* • Treat Williams *Pat Cappadora* • Jonathan Jackson *Vincent Cappadora aged 16* • John Kapelos *George Karras* • Ryan Merriman *Sam* •

🅤 = SUITABLE FOR ALL   🆄🅲 = SUITABLE FOR ALL, ESPECIALLY FOR YOUNG CHILDREN (VIDEO ONLY)   🅿🅶 = PARENTAL GUIDANCE

Whoopi Goldberg *Candy Bliss* ■ *Dir* Ulu Grosbard • *Scr* Stephen Schiff, from the novel by Jacquelyn Mitchard

Deep Family Secrets ★★★
Thriller based on a true story
1997 · US · Colour

Another juicy slice of ''stranger-than-fiction'' TV fodder, which at least boasts a starrier cast than normal. Richard Crenna and Angie Dickinson play a seemingly ordinary married couple who have a graveyard's worth of skeletons in their cupboard. When Dickinson goes missing, daughter Molly Gross uncovers even a web of deceit, adultery and perhaps even murder. The ludicrously melodramatic storyline is utterly compulsive. Contains swearing.

Richard Crenna *Clay Chadway* • Angie Dickinson *Renee Chadway* • Molly Gross *JoAnne Chadway* • Christie Lynn Smith *Lisa* • Meg Foster *Ellen* • Craig Wasson *Jack Winters* ■ *Dir* Arthur Allan Seidelman • *Scr* Nevin Schreiner, David Madsen, Dena Kleiman, from a story by Nevin Schreiner

Deep Impact ★★★★ 12
Science-fiction drama
1998 · US · Colour · 116mins

A huge comet is on a collision course with Earth in *ER* director Mimi Leder's science-fiction disaster movie, which gains a certain amount of credibility by highlighting the human side of the impending catastrophe. The frightening scenario focuses on TV reporter Téa Leoni, who uncovers the story after teenage stargazer Elijah Wood discovers the wayward mass, and on astronaut Robert Duvall as he and his young colleagues try to destroy the threat in space. Using her trademark documentary-style realism and frenzied camerawork, Leder adds gripping immediacy to this loose remake of Rudolph Maté's 1951 movie *When Worlds Collide*, capping it all with a spectacular trail of epic destruction. Contains swearing. 📼

Robert Duvall *Spurgeon Tanner* • Téa Leoni *Jenny Lerner* • Elijah Wood *Leo Biederman* • Vanessa Redgrave *Robin Lerner* • Maximilian Schell *Jason Lerner* • Morgan Freeman *President Tom Beck* • James Cromwell *Alan Rittenhouse* ■ *Dir* Mimi Leder • *Scr* Michael Tolkin, Bruce Joel Rubin

Deep in My Heart ★★★ U
Musical biography
1954 · US · Colour · 126mins

Under-rated in its day, this is the fictionalised biopic of composer Sigmund Romberg, of *The Student Prince* and *Desert Song* fame, featuring a cast of MGM contract stars performing magnificently. Most of it was directed by Stanley Donen, though ace choreographers Robert Alton and Jack Donohue helped out, and the whole is held together by the bravura performance of José Ferrer as Romberg. Good fun all round, and quite moving too. 📼

JoséFerrer *Sigmund Romberg* • Merle Oberon *Dorothy Donnelly* • Helen Traubel *Anna Mueller* • Doe Avedon *Lillian Romberg* • Walter Pidgeon *JJ Shubert* • Paul Henreid *Florenz Ziegfeld* • Tamara Toumanova *Gaby Deslys* • Paul Stewart *Bert Towsend* • Rosemary Clooney • Gene Kelly • Fred Kelly • Jane Powell • Vic Damone • Ann Miller • Cyd

Charisse • Howard Keel • Tony Martin ■ *Dir* Stanley Donen • *Scr* Leonard Spigelgass, from the biography by Elliott Arnold

Deep Red ★ 18
Science-fiction thriller
1994 · US · Colour · 121mins

A weak science-fiction thriller about a girl whose blood is contaminated and her ageing process halted thanks to an alien close encounter. It's up to bland private eye Michael Biehn and his estranged wife Joanna Pacula to protect her from being kidnapped and used in weird experiments by shape-shifting evil doctor John de Lancie, who sends killer milkmen to trace her. As daft as it sounds, and cliché-ridden to the humdrum hilt. Contains violence. 📼

Michael Biehn *Joe Keyes* • Joanna Pacula *Monica Quik* • Steven Williams *Eldon James* • Lisa Collins *Mrs Helen Rickman* • Tobin Bell *Warren Rickman* • Lindsey Haun *Gracie Rickman* • John de Lancie *Thomas Newmeyer* • John Kapelos *Mack Waters* ■ *Dir* Craig R Baxley • *Scr* D Brent Mote

Deep Rising ★★ 15
Science-fiction action
1997 · US · Colour · 101mins

Tremors meets *Titanic* in a dopey sea-monster movie from director Stephen Sommers, who went to direct *The Mummy*. In this tepid horror tale, a high-tech pleasure cruiser on its maiden voyage is overrun by modern-day pirates, then attacked by a multi-tentacled, Hydra-like creature. The film navigates an ocean of hilarious monster-movie clichés and derivative special-effects sequences, while Treat Williams does a poor Kurt Russell impression and Famke Janssen (of *Goldeneye* fame) lets her wet T-shirt do the acting. A gruesome fantasy, *Deep Rising* is sadly all at sea in terms of coherence and any vestige of credibility. Contains violence and swearing. 📼 **DVD**

Treat Williams *John Finnegan* • Famke Janssen *Trillian* • Anthony Heald *Simon Canton* • Kevin J O'Connor *Joey Pantucci* • Wes Studi *Hanover* • Derrick O'Connor *Captain* • Jason Flemyng *Mulligan* • Cliff Curtis *Mamooli* ■ *Dir/Scr* Stephen Sommers

The Deep Six ★★ U
Second World War drama
1958 · US · Colour · 108mins

When Alan Ladd turned producer/star through his Jaguar company just after his career peaked with *Shane*, he stuck to formula film-making with old cronies. *The Deep Six* is a wartime drama set on a cruiser in the Pacific, the main complication being whether Ladd's Quaker beliefs will get in the way of his duties as the ship's gunnery officer. The issue is never properly resolved, but the film is slickly made and quite watchable, with strong supporting performances from William Bendix and Keenan Wynn.

Alan Ladd *Alec Austen* • Dianne Foster *Susan Cahill* • William Bendix *Frenchy Shapiro* • Keenan Wynn *Lt Cdr Edge* • James Whitmore *Cdr Meredith* • Efrem Zimbalist Jr *Lt Blanchard* • Jeanette Nolan *Mrs Austen* ■ *Dir* Rudolph Maté • *Scr* John Twist, Harry Brown, Martin Rackin, from the novel by Martin Dibner

Deep Sleep ★★
Drama
1990 · Can · Colour · 90mins

Stuart Margolin's career has been rather patchy, and this Canadian thriller did not bring about a significant revival in his fortunes. Megan Follows co-stars in this hackneyed hokum about a troubled teen who begins to recall the events surrounding her father's unexplained death as her trauma-induced amnesia slowly lifts. Making her big screen debut, writer/director Patricia Gruben has produced a plot that is overladen with unimaginative nightmare sequences and decidedly short on surprises. Contains swearing.

Megan Follows *Shelley McBride* • Stuart Margolin *Bob Bolden* • Patricia Collins *Barbara McBride* • David Hewlett *Terry McBride* • Damon D'Oliveira *Angel* • Deanne Henry *Dr Cole* ■ *Dir/Scr* Patricia Gruben

Deep Throat ★★★
Erotic comedy   1972 · US · Colour · 73mins

The most infamous, commercially successful and influential hardcore movie ever produced made Linda Lovelace an overnight sensation and director Gerard Damiano the leading light of fashionable ''porno chic''. Groundbreaking because it made watching porn acceptable, the film itself is badly made and full of stupid humour and dull stretches. It's important to note that Lovelace is not a sexual object being used by male abusers, but a take-charge, independent woman pursuing pleasure for her own needs.

Linda Lovelace • Harry Reems • Dolly Sharp • Carol Connors • William Love • Ted Street ■ *Dir/Scr* Gerard Damiano

Deep Valley ★★★
Drama   1947 · US · BW · 103mins

This is one of director Jean Negulesco's better movies, with Ida Lupino as a parent-dominated farm girl who shelters a convict (played by Dane Clark) after he escapes from a chain gang. Clark's scenes with Lupino are extremely touching, in a screenplay which boasts added dialogue by William Faulkner. There's a fine Max Steiner score, and a special bonus comes from some attractive location shooting, brought about by the lucky fact that a studio strike prevented the use of the Warners backlot.

Ida Lupino *Libby* • Dane Clark *Barry* • Wayne Morris *Barker* • Fay Bainter *Mrs Saul* • Henry Hull *Mr Saul* • Willard Robertson *Sheriff* • Rory Mallinson *Foreman* • Jack Mower *Supervisor* ■ *Dir* Jean Negulesco • *Scr* Salka Viertel, Stephen Morehouse Avery, from the novel by Dan Totheroh

DeepStar Six ★ 15
Science-fiction horror
1989 · US · Colour · 94mins

An experimental underwater colony disturbs a prehistoric sea creature in this shallow combination of *Alien* and *Jaws*. Directed by Sean S Cunningham, the originator of the *Friday the 13th* series, this soggy farrago sinks fast in an ocean of technical mumbo jumbo, murky model work and outrageously bad acting. The rubber monster looks like a giant, cross-eyed lobster, while

Cunningham is completely out of his depth in his attempts to scare up tides of terror from an unfathomable and laughable script. ■

Taurean Blacque *Laidlaw* • Nancy Everhard *Joyce Collins* • Greg Evigan *McBride* • Miguel Ferrer *Snyder* • Nia Peeples *Scarpelli* • Matt McCoy *Richardson* • Cindy Pickett *Diane Norris* • Marius Weyers *Van Gelder* ■ *Dir* Sean S Cunningham • *Scr* Lewis Abernathy, Geof Miller, from a story by Lewis Abernathy

The Deer Hunter ★★★★★ 18
Drama   1978 · US · Colour · 182mins

Michael Cimino's multi-Oscar winner was the first major movie about the Vietnam War and it remains one of the finest and most controversial, notably for the harrowing sequence in wich American PoWs are forced by their Vietcong captors to play Russian roulette, a compelling if historically dubious metaphor for the war. Running for three hours, it begins, *Godfather*-style, with a long wedding party at which a group of Russian emigrant steelworkers get drunk and then hunt deer before boarding their plane for the heart of darkness. Starring Robert De Niro, Christopher Walken, John Savage and John Cazale, this is a modern version of Second World War drama *The Best Years of Our Lives*, showing how men and America itself cope with the horrors of war and its aftermath. With its mournful guitar theme, this intense drama lingers long in the memory and elevated Cimino to the front rank of American directors. But his next film was the notorious flop *Heaven's Gate*, and he has only worked occasionally since. Contains violence and swearing.

Robert De Niro *Michael Vronsky* • John Cazale *Stan, ''Stosh''* • John Savage *Steven* • Christopher Walken *Nick* • Meryl Streep *Linda* • George Dzundza *John* • Chuck Aspegren *Axel* • Shirley Stoler *Steven's mother* ■ *Dir* Michael Cimino • *Scr* Deric Washburn, from a story by Michael Cimino, Deric Washburn, Louis Garfinkle, Quinn K Redeker • *Cinematographer* Vilmos Zsigmond • *Editor* Peter Zinner • *Music* Stanley Myers

The Deerslayer ★★ U
Historical adventure
1957 · US · Colour · 76mins

An adaptation of James Fenimore Cooper's classic adventure, with Lex Barker as the hunter who teams up with his Mohican blood brother, Chingachgook (Carlos Rivas), to rescue a trapper and his two daughters from nasty Indians. A dead duck as far as suspense is concerned, back projection and indoor sets make Kurt Neumann's film seem as artificial as the acting. One of the daughters is played by Rita Moreno, who would later win an Oscar for *West Side Story*.

Lex Barker *The Deerslayer* • Rita Moreno *Hetty* • Forrest Tucker *Harry Marsh* • Cathy O'Donnell *Judith* • Jay C Flippen *Old Tom Hutter* • Carlos Rivas *Chingachgook* • John Halloran *Old warrior* ■ *Dir* Kurt Neumann • *Scr* Carroll Young, Kurt Neumann, from the novel by James Fenimore Cooper

Def by Temptation ★★ 18
Horror   1990 · US · Colour · 94mins

A hip-hop, skip and a jump away from the generic blaxploitation of the seventies, this initially stylish, erotic and funny mix of *Abby* and *House Party* loses momentum as it wends its way through over-familiar territory. Producer, director and writer James Bond III (really!) also stars as a redneck divinity student, in New York for a final fling before entering the ministry. However, he soon falls prey to Cynthia Bond, an ancient demon who cruises uptown singles bars for victims and sees destroying his faith as the ultimate feather in her cap. Daft special effects and formula blood-letting is jazzed up with perverse sexual twists, adroit acting and a great soundtrack.

James Bond III *Joel* • Cynthia Bond *Temptress* • Kadeem Hardison *K* • Bill Nunn *Dougy* • Minnie Gentry *Grandma* • Samuel L Jackson *Minister Garth* • Melba Moore *Madam Sonya* ■ *Dir/Scr* James Bond III • *Cinematographer* Ernest R Dickerson

Def-Con 4 ★★★ 15

Action adventure 1984 · US · Colour · 83mins

This post-apocalyptic action film doesn't have the budget to provide too many futuristic thrills, yet what it lacks in hardware trappings it more than makes up for in imaginative staging. While radiation-ravaged America is overrun by as many ideas lifted from better science-fiction entries (*WarGames*, *The Terminator*) as it is with sadistic punks and militant cannibals, this low-rent *Mad Max* remains a watchable enough potboiler before it degenerates into a routine cat-and-mouse chase.

Lenore Zann *JJ* • Maury Chaykin *Vinny* • Kate Lynch *Jordan* • Kevin King *Gideon Hayes* • John Walsch *Walker* • Tim Choate *Howe* • Jeff Pustil *Lacey* ■ *Dir/Scr* Paul Donovan

Def Jam's How to Be a Player ★★ 18

Sex comedy 1997 · US · Colour · 89mins

Wearing its politically incorrect badges with some pride – although the guys get their comeuppance in the end – this breezy sex comedy is still a lot of fun. MTV host and comic Bill Bellamy is the wonderfully conceited stud who takes time out to show his chums how to be a player – that is, how to keep all sorts of girls happy while still remaining in a long-term relationship. However, he has not reckoned on his sister (Natalie Desselle), who thinks it's time that this particular player got a red card. Subtlety doesn't come into it, but Lionel C Martin's energetic direction ensures it never flags. Contains swearing, sex scenes and sexual references.

Bill Bellamy *Drayton Jackson* • Natalie Desselle *Jenny Jackson* • Lark Voorhies *Lisa* • Mari Morrow *Katrina* • Pierre Edwards *David* • Jermaine "Big Hugg" Hopkins [Jermaine Hopkins] *Kilo* ■ *Dir* Lionel C Martin • *Scr* Mark Brown, Demetria Johnson, from a story by Mark Brown

The Defector ★★

Spy drama 1966 · W Ger/Fr · Colour · 68mins

Sadly, this muddled European spy drama was the last film of the great Montgomery Clift, here looking tired and displaying little of the talent that illuminated *From Here to Eternity* and *A Place in the Sun*. This is a hackneyed Cold War drama, which was heavily truncated for its British release. Clift's loyal friend Roddy McDowall was on board to guide him through his barbiturate and alcohol-induced haze, and ends up giving the better performance. Brigitte Bardot's producer Raoul Lévy here directs ineptly, though there's a cameo from famed French director Jean-Luc Godard.

Montgomery Clift *Professor James Bower* • Hardy Kruger *Peter Heinzman* • Roddy McDowall *CIA Agent Adams* • Macha Meril *Frieda Hoffman* • Christine Delaroche *Ingrid* • David Opatoshu *Orlovsky* • Hannes Messemer *Dr Saltzer* • Jean-Luc Godard *Orlovsky's friend* ■ *Dir* Raoul Lévy • *Scr* Robert Guenette, Lewis Gannet, Peter Francke, Raoul Lévy, from the novel *The Spy* by Paul Thomas

Defence of the Realm ★★★★ PG

Thriller 1985 · UK · Colour · 91mins

The role of the sozzled veteran reporter who for once finds himself involved in a meaningful story is brought wonderfully to life by Denholm Elliott, here trying to clear the name of an opposition MP forced to resign after a sex scandal. Gabriel Byrne, as Elliott's ambitious young colleague, is less effective, but the film has plenty of tension and co-star Greta Scacchi proves a worthy accomplice. An unsettling movie that claims that *all* governments are up to no good. Contains mild swearing. DVD

Gabriel Byrne *Nick Mullen* • Greta Scacchi *Nina Beckman* • Denholm Elliott *Vernon Bayliss* • Ian Bannen *Dennis Markham* • Fulton Mackay *Victor Kingsbrook* • Bill Paterson *Jack Macleod* • David Calder *Harry Champion* • Robbie Coltrane *Leo McAskey* ■ *Dir* David Drury • *Scr* Martin Stellman

Defending Your Life ★★ PG

Comedy drama 1991 · US · Colour · 106mins

Director/star Albert Brooks here takes a ham-fisted run at judgement after demise, one of the most abused movie concepts since the glorious *A Matter of Life and Death*, with heaven portrayed as a large shopping mall complete with shuttle trucks and revolving doors. This is not Mr Brooks bumping into Van Gogh looking miserable or Abraham Lincoln looking wise, but rather the "ordinary Joe" version of the tale. Brooks's ensuing "trial" for entry through the non-pearly gates is an example of movie-making at its most tedious, and not even Meryl Streep in her heyday can enliven events. Contains some swearing.

Albert Brooks *Daniel Miller* • Meryl Streep *Julia* • Rip Torn *Bob Diamond* • Lee Grant *Lena Foster* • Buck Henry *Dick Stanley* ■ *Dir/Scr* Albert Brooks

Defenseless ★★★ 18

Thriller 1991 · US · Colour · 99mins

An intriguing thriller with a classy cast, headed by Barbara Hershey as a lawyer who is drawn into a murderous conspiracy when her former lover and client (JT Walsh) is found dead. With Sam Shepard, Mary Beth Hurt and Sheree North offering strong support, the playing can't be faulted, while director Martin Campbell (who later hit paydirt with *GoldenEye* and *The Mask of Zorro*) skilfully sustains the suspense throughout. Contains violence, swearing and brief nudity.

Barbara Hershey *TK Katwuller* • Sam Shepard *George Beutel* • Mary Beth Hurt *Ellie Seldes* • JT Walsh *Steven Seldes* • Kellie Overbey *Janna Seldes* • Jay O Sanders *Bull Dozer* ■ *Dir* Martin Campbell • *Scr* James Hicks, from the story by Jeff Burkhart, James Hicks

Defiance ★★★ 15

Action drama 1979 · US · Colour · 102mins

Jan Michael Vincent is pitted against a vicious New York street gang in this weirdly engaging, if violent combination of vintage *Boys Town* melodrama, serial western and 1979's *The Warriors*. No prizes for guessing who tames who, though. The old-fashioned "man against the world" plot gains extra interest from the strong supporting cast, which includes Art Carney, Danny Aiello and Theresa Saldana, gritty dialogue and John Flynn's atmospheric direction. Contains violence and swearing.

Jan-Michael Vincent *Tommy Gamble* • Theresa Saldana *Marsha Bernstein* • Fernando Lopez *"Kid"* • Danny Aiello *Carmine* • Art Carney *Abe* • Santos Morales *Paolo* • Rudy Ramos *Angel Cruz* ■ *Dir* John Flynn • *Scr* Thomas Michael Donnelly, from a story by Thomas Michael Donnelly, Mark Tulin

The Defiant ★★★

Drama 1972 · US · Colour · 88mins

Based on a story by Brazilian author Jorge Amado, this is the heartfelt story of a gang of orphans who steal food in order to survive. Also known as *The Wild Pack* and *The Sandpit Generals*, Hall Bartlett's drama won the Grand Prize at the Moscow Film Festival, presumably because of the optimistic comradeship the film engenders. Its attitudes come across as dated and quaint, but it's still worth a look.

Kent Lane *Bullet* • Tisha Sterling *Dora* • John Rubinstein *Professor* • Alejandro Rey *Father Jose Pedro* • Butch Patrick *No Legs* ■ *Dir* Hall Bartlett • *Scr* Hall Bartlett, from the story *Capitaes da Areira* by Jorge Amado

The Defiant Ones ★★★★ U

Prison drama 1958 · US · BW · 96mins

A superb cinematic strike for racial equality, as black Southerner Sidney Poitier and bigot Tony Curtis find themselves shackled together in their escape to freedom from a chain gang. Curtis finally shed his "pretty boy" image with this one and Poitier leapt to instant stardom. It's still powerful today, and is one of under-rated producer/director Stanley Kramer's finest liberal humanitarian movies. Interestingly, the Oscar-winning story and screenplay were co-written by blacklisted actor Nedrick Young, writing under the pseudonym Nathan E Douglas, an indication of Kramer's faith and courage at the time.

Tony Curtis *John "Joker" Jackson* • Sidney Poitier *Noah Cullen* • Theodore Bikel *Sheriff Max Muller* • Charles McGraw *Captain Frank Gibbons* • Lon Chaney Jr *Big Sam* • King Donovan *Solly* • Claude Akins *Mac* ■ *Dir* Stanley Kramer • *Scr* Nathan E Douglas [Nedrick Young], Harold Jacob Smith

The Defiant Ones ★★★ PG

Crime drama 1986 · US · Colour · 90mins

A solid remake of Stanley Kramer's 1958 racial drama, with Robert Urich and Carl Weathers in the roles originally created by Tony Curtis and Sidney Poitier. As a story about black and white, the plot offers few grey areas, dealing with two escaped criminals shackled to each other and to each other's prejudices. In 1958, Kramer's picture anticipated the civil rights movement, yet it hectored its audience constantly; the remake lacks the original's power, but is still gripping. The screenplay is by James Lee Barrett, who wrote the ultra-right wing *The Green Berets*.

Robert Urich *Johnny "Joker" Johnson* • Carl Weathers *Cullen Monroe* • Barry Corbin *Floyd Carpenter* • Ed Lauter *Sheriff Leroy Doyle* • William Sanderson *Mason* • Charles Bartlett *Jeffcoat* • Wil Wheaton *Clyde* ■ *Dir* David Lowell Rich • *Scr* James Lee Barrett, from the 1958 film

Déjà Vu ★ 15

Supernatural thriller 1984 · UK · Colour · 90mins

An apt title for a movie sporting the age-old soul transference plot, but with nothing tweaked to make it unique or remotely interesting. The ghost of a prima ballerina is upsetting writer Nigel Terry and his wife, Jaclyn Smith. When tarot card reader Shelley Winters regresses Terry back to the thirties, it turns out that he was a choreographer in love with the dancer, and that Smith is her reincarnation. Hokey and unconvincing stuff, based on Trevor Meldal-Johnson's novel *Always*.

Jaclyn Smith *Maggie Rogers/Brooke Ashley* • Nigel Terry *Gregory Thomas/Michael Richardson* • Claire Bloom *Eleanor Harvey* • Shelley Winters *Olga Nabokov* • Richard Kay *William Tanner in 1935* • Frank Gatliff *William Tanner in 1984* • Michael Ladkin *Willmer* ■ *Dir* Anthony Richmond [Tonino Ricci] • *Scr* Ezra D Rappaport, Anthony Richmond [Tonino Ricci], Arnold Schmidt, Joane A Gil, from the novel *Always* by Trevor Meldal-Johnson

Déjà Vu ★★ 15

Romance 1997 · US/UK · Colour · 117mins

Starting as a short story in 1974, Henry Jaglom's study of love perhaps owes more to his own sudden bliss than to his success in shaping some recalcitrant material into a screenplay. Since he met and married Victoria Foyt, Jaglom admits to toning down the autobiographical content of his films, sadly depriving them of the idiosyncracies that made them so fascinating. This is clearly a love letter to Foyt, with Stephen Dillane taking the Jaglom part of the man whose world is turned upside down by a chance encounter with a woman he feels he's known forever. Contains swearing.

Stephen Dillane *Sean Elias* • Victoria Foyt *Dana Howard* • Vanessa Redgrave *Skelly* • Glynis Barber *Claire Stoner* • Michael Brandon *Alex* • Vernon Dobtcheff *Konstantine* ■ *Dir* Henry Jaglom • *Scr* Henry Jaglom, Victoria Foyt

Delayed Action ★★

Crime drama 1954 · UK · BW · 60mins

Melancholic author Robert Ayres has a change of heart after accepting a notorious gang's offer of a tidy nest egg if he takes responsibility for their crimes before topping himself. Quitting features after 21 years of unbroken mediocrity, John Harlow shows a sure sense of pace and atmosphere that would serve him well in television.

368

U = SUITABLE FOR ALL Uc = SUITABLE FOR ALL, ESPECIALLY FOR YOUNG CHILDREN (VIDEO ONLY) PG = PARENTAL GUIDANCE

Robert Ayres *Ned Ellison* • Alan Wheatley *Mark Cruden* • June Thorburn *Ann Curlew* • Michael Kelly *Lobb* • Bruce Seton *Sellers* ■ *Dir* John Harlow • *Scr* Geoffrey Orme

A Delicate Balance ★★★

Drama 1973 · US/UK · Colour · 133mins

Despite an extraordinary cast, this version of Edward Albee's Pulitzer Prize-winning play – directed by Tony Richardson for TV's American Film Theatre – is a stiff narrative about a neurotic Connecticut family that goes to war with itself and its friends. Katharine Hepburn, Paul Scofield, Lee Remick, Joseph Cotten and Betsy Blair pull out the dramatic stops, but the result remains defiantly stagebound.

Katharine Hepburn *Agnes* • Paul Scofield *Tobias* • Lee Remick *Julia* • Kate Reid *Claire* • Joseph Cotten *Harry* • Betsy Blair *Edna* ■ *Dir* Tony Richardson • *Scr* Edward Albee, from his play

The Delicate Delinquent ★★★U

Comedy 1957 · US · BW · 103mins

Although mooted as a Dean Martin and Jerry Lewis vehicle, the strain was beginning to show in *Pardners* (1956). So Lewis went solo for the first time, with Darren McGavin in the cop role earmarked for Martin. As the titular "teenager", Lewis's mix of schmaltz and slapstick ensured he maintained his public popularity. Today both subject and title have lost their resonance, but in the days of *The Blackboard Jungle* these antics passed for satire. It marked the beginning of "Le Roi du Crazy's" long career as one of America's finest (and most critically despised) comic geniuses.

Jerry Lewis *Sidney Pythias* • Darren McGavin *Mike Damon* • Martha Hyer *Martha Henshaw* • Robert Ivers *Monk* • Horace McMahon *Captain Riley* • Richard Bakalyan *Artie* • Joseph Corey *Harry* • Mary Webster *Patricia* ■ *Dir/Scr* Don McGuire

Delicatessen ★★★★15

Black comedy fantasy
1990 · Fr · Colour · 95mins

Jean-Pierre Jeunet and Marc Caro made their feature debut with this gloriously surreal comedy. Rarely can a film have had so many disparate influences. In addition to the visual inspiration of French comic books and the eccentricity of Heath Robinson, there are references to the poetic realism of Marcel Carné and René Clair, as well as the darker visions of David Lynch and Terry Gilliam. The gallery of grotesques gathered at butcher Jean-Claude Dreyfus's tenement participate in some of the funniest set pieces of recent years, most notably the deliriously unerotic sex scene and Sylvie Laguna's preposterous suicide attempts. In French with English subtitles. Contains violence and nudity. ▭

Dominique Pinon *Louison* • Marie-Laure Dougnac *Julie Clapet* • Jean-Claude Dreyfus *The Butcher* • Karin Viard *Mademoiselle Plusse* • Ticky Holgado *Monsieur Tapioca* • Anne-Marie Pisani *Madame Tapioca* • Jacques Mathou *Roger Cube* • Rufus *Robert Cube* • Jean-François Perrier *Monsieur Interligator* • Sylvie Laguna *Madame Interligator* ■ *Dir/Scr* Jean-Pierre Jeunet, Marc Caro

The Delinquents ★

Drama 1957 · US · BW · 71mins

Robert Altman's first feature, directed in his beloved home town of Kansas City, is a fascinating, if cheesy relic of its era. Tom Laughlin plays a good boy who gets mixed up in a street gang with his girlfriend (Rosemary Howard), whose parents think she is not old enough to go steady. Julia Lee sings *The Dirty Rock Boogie* – and sadly, that's as good as it gets.

Tom Laughlin *Scotty* • Peter Miller *Cholly* • Richard Bakalyan *Eddy* • Rosemary Howard *Janice* • Helene Hawley *Mrs White* • Leonard Belove *Mr White* • Lotus Corelli *Mrs Wilson* • James Lantz *Mr Wilson* • Christine Altman *Sissy* ■ *Dir/Scr* Robert Altman

The Delinquents ★★15

Romantic drama
1989 · Ausl · Colour · 100mins

At the height of her soap opera/pop singer fame, *Neighbours* star Kylie Minogue made her feature film debut in this OK tale of teenage torment set in fifties Australia. Minogue and Charlie Schlatter co-star as the misunderstood young lovers ignoring adult condemnation in director Chris Thomson's tear-jerker, based on the novel by Criena Rohan, tennis player Pat Cash's aunt. ▭

Kylie Minogue *Lola Lovell* • Charlie Schlatter *Brownie Hansen* • Desiree Smith *Mavis* • Todd Boyce *Lyle* • Angela Punch McGregor *Mrs Lovell* • Lynette Curran *Mrs Hansen* ■ *Dir* Chris Thomson • *Scr* Mac Gudgeon, Clayton Frohman, Dorothy Hewitt, from a novel by Criena Rohan

Delirious ★★PG

Comedy 1991 · US · Colour · 91mins

Soap opera scriptwriter John Candy is knocked unconscious, wakes up inside his own fictional TV serial *Beyond Our Dreams*, and watches in comic horror as his own romantic plotlines backfire. Written by former James Bond screenwriter Tom Mankiewicz, this tediously strained fiasco hinges on lovelorn Candy's magical ability to manipulate lathered events by typing them out seconds before they happen. A game cast – including *Dynasty* star Emma Samms – is wasted in a painfully unfunny *Walter Mitty* meets *Soapdish* affair.

John Candy *Jack Gable* • Emma Samms *Rachel Hedison/Laura* • Mariel Hemingway *Janet Dubois/Louise* • Raymond Burr *Carter Hedison* • Dylan Baker *Blake Hedison* • Charles Rocket *Ty Hedison* • David Rasche *Dr Paul Kirkland/Dennis* • Jerry Orbach *Lou Sherwood* ■ *Dir* Tom Mankiewicz • *Scr* Fred Freeman, Lawrence J Cohen

Deliver Them from Evil: the Taking of Alta View ★★15

Thriller based on a true story
1992 · US · Colour · 89mins

Released on video as *Under Pressure*, this TV movie is based on the real-life siege that took place at the Alta View maternity hospital in Salt Lake City. Harry Hamlin stars as Richard Worthington, the devoutly religious father of eight who, armed with guns and a bomb, held a ward hostage for 18 hours in protest at his wife's sterilisation. The "pro-life" issue has recently taken a violent turn in

America, and this film tries to maintain a balance between both sides of the argument. Timely and pertinent it may be, but it makes for dull viewing. ▭

Harry Hamlin *Richard Worthington* • Teri Garr *Susan Woolley* • Terry O'Quinn *Sergeant Don Bell* • Gary Frank *Dr Garrick* • Joycelyn O'Brien *Barbara* • Georgia Emelin *Cristan Downey* ■ *Dir* Peter Levin • *Scr* John Miglis

Deliver Us from Evil ★★18

Action drama 1973 · US · Colour · 92mins

This routine TV movie charts a predictable course through a clichéd script. Five men hiking in the mountains discover an injured "skyjacker" who has parachuted from a plane with $600,000. After they kill him in a fit of malicious greed, they start fighting among each other over how best to divide up the money. Initial interest in their motivations and behaviour soon wanes as the B-movie cast (which includes George Kennedy and *Airwolf* star Jan-Michael Vincent) go through the expected motions.

George Kennedy *Walter "Cowboy" McAdams* • Jan-Michael Vincent *Nick Fleming* • Bradford Dillman *Steven Dennis* • Charles Aidman *Arnold Fleming* • Jack Weston *Al Zabrocki* ■ *Dir* Boris Sagal • *Scr* Jack B Sowards

Deliverance ★★★★★18

Thriller 1972 · US · Colour · 104mins

John Boorman's provocative, violent and compelling thriller takes American poet James Dickey's novel to giddy heights of suspenseful stress, and proves that Burt Reynolds can act. Central to the success of Boorman's culture-clash nightmare, and what makes it resonate with such a rare intensity, is the powerful theme of red-blooded masculinity under hostile threat. Expertly capturing the majesty of the Appalachian scenery, plus the enigma of its "duelling banjo" mountain dwellers, the film delivers in superlative spades. Contains swearing and violence. **DVD**

Jon Voight *Ed Gentry* • Burt Reynolds *Lewis Medlock* • Ned Beatty *Bobby Trippe* • Ronny Cox *Drew Ballinger* • Bill McKinney *Mountain man* • Herbert "Cowboy" Coward *Toothless man* • James Dickey *Sheriff Bullard* ■ *Dir* John Boorman • *Scr* James Dickey, from his novel • *Cinematographer* Vilmos Zsigmond • *Editor* Tom Priestley

Della ★★

Drama 1965 · US · BW

Joan Crawford's once-glittering career was in terminal decline by the time this dreary, second-rate TV movie was made, despite her memorable performance alongside Bette Davis in *What Ever Happened to Baby Jane?* just a few years before. In an attempt to capture the *film noir* style that had made her name, Crawford plays a mother who keeps her beautiful daughter prisoner in a vast mansion. Sadly, despite the promising premise, the end result is a boring and predictable mess, only saved from total failure by Crawford's valiant attempt to rise above the material.

Joan Crawford *Della Chappel* • Paul Burke *Bernard "Barney" Stafford* • Diane Baker *Jenny Chappel* • Charles Bickford *Hugh Stafford* • Richard Carlson *David Stafford* ■ *Dir* Robert Gist • *Scr* Richard Allen Simmons

The Delta Factor ★

Adventure 1970 · US · Colour · 91mins

Mickey Spillane himself backed this adaptation of one of his lesser-known novels, but Christopher George is a poor man's James Bond as an adventurer recruited by the CIA to head an undercover mission. Stingy on the action, this would-be international drama is more confusing than intriguing, while a ridiculous subplot about an imprisoned scientist seems tacked-on by director Tay Garnett as an excuse to have a bloody jailbreak. This was the last professional assignment for veteran film-maker Raoul Walsh, who receives a co-writing credit.

Christopher George *Morgan* • Yvette Mimieux *Kim Stacy* • Diane McBain *Lisa Gordot* • Ralph Taeger *Art Keefer* • Yvonne De Carlo *Valerie* • Sherri Spillane *Rosa* ■ *Dir* Tay Garnett • *Scr* Tay Garnett, Raoul Walsh, from the novel by Mickey Spillane

Delta Fever ★15

Drama 1988 · US · Colour · 90mins

Watching this straight-to-video teen action movie, you get some idea of how low Martin Landau's career had sunk before he made the remarkable comeback that started with successive Oscar nominations for *Tucker: the Man and His Dream* and *Crimes and Misdemeanors*, and culminated in an Academy Award for his portrayal of Bela Lugosi in *Ed Wood*. This is not only a bad film, but it is also a shocking advertisement for water-skiing and American family values, as a young man's parents and girlfriend try to blunt his competitive spirit and get him to accept his responsibilities. Contains violence. ▭

Tom Eplin *Nick Ramsey* • Leif Garrett *Lance Stanford* • Katherine Kelly Lang *Jillian Downey* • Martin Landau *William "Bud" Ramsey* • Denver Pyle *Walt Downey* • Wendie Jo Sperber *Claire* • Will Bledsoe *Bryce* ■ *Dir* William Webb • *Scr* Reed Steiner, from a story by Tom Eplin

The Delta Force ★★18

Action adventure
1986 · US · Colour · 123mins

Middle-eastern terrorists menace a planeload of Hollywood has-beens in an exploitative, revisionist version of the actual 1985 skyjacking of a TWA flight in Athens. The surprisingly accurate first half supplies some swift-paced tension before low-rent action hero Chuck Norris arrives on the scene, riding a rocket-armed motorcycle and destroying all credibility along with the baddies. Despite the abrupt change from jet-powered realism to cartoon wish-fulfilment, the constant catalogue of cheap thrills keeps boredom at bay. ▭

Chuck Norris *Major Scott McCoy* • Lee Marvin *Colonel Nick Alexander* • Martin Balsam *Ben Kaplan* • Joey Bishop *Harry Goldman* • Robert Forster *Abdul* • Lainie Kazan *Sylvia Goldman* • George Kennedy *Father O'Malley* • Hanna Schygulla *Ingrid* • Susan Strasberg *Debra Levine* • Bo Svenson *Captain Campbell* • Robert Vaughn *General Woolbridge* • Shelley Winters *Edie Kaplan* ■ *Dir* Menahem Golan • *Scr* Menahem Golan, James Bruner

Delta Force 2 ★ 18

Action adventure
1990 · US · Colour · 105mins

Clumsy sequel to a film that itself was something of a shambles. At least the original had Lee Marvin heading the cast; here we're left with just stone-face Chuck Norris, whose neck muscles do most of the acting here. Where the original explored the theme of political terrorism (albeit with all the subtlety of a Vinnie Jones tackle), the follow-up has Norris leading his anonymous bull-necked marines against the drug cartels of Colombia. The movie is dedicated to the five people who died in a helicopter crash during shooting in the Philippines; sadly, it's not much of an epitaph. ▣

Chuck Norris *Colonel Scott McCoy* • Billy Drago *Ramon Cota* • John P Ryan *General Taylor* • Richard Jaeckel *John Page* • Begona Plaza *Quinquina* • Paul Perri *Major Bobby Chavez* • Hector Mercado *Miguel* • Mark Margolis *General Olmedo* ■ *Dir* Aaron Norris • *Scr* Lee Reynolds, from characters created by James Bruner, Menahem Golan

Delta of Venus ★★ 18

Erotic drama 1995 · Fr/US · Colour · 97mins

Soft-core king Zalman King is only interested in the salacious element in Anaïs Nin's oeuvre, so the result here is a beautifully packaged but stunningly dull tale set in forties Paris, punctuated by pop promo-style sex scenes. Audie England plays the ambitious writer who discovers a profitable sideline in writing rude stories. The performers look good but struggle to bring even a touch of credibility to their roles. Contains swearing, sex scenes, drug abuse and nudity. ▣

Audie England *Elena* • Costas Mandylor *Lawrence* • Eric Da Silva *Marcel* • Marek Vasut *Luc* • Emma Louise Moore *Ariel* ■ *Dir* Zalman King • *Scr* Elisa Rothstein, Patricia Louisiana Knop, from the novel by Anaïs Nin

Delta Pi ★ 18

Comedy 1985 · US · Colour · 84mins

Possibly the only feature-length film ever devoted to the noble sport of mud wrestling, this sploshed on to the UK market as *Mugsy's Girls*. The plot focuses on a group of female students who take to the mucky ring in a bid to save their sorority. Among those getting dirty are Laura Branigan, a one-hit American rock wonder in the late eighties and – more mind-bogglingly – veteran Oscar-winning actress Ruth Gordon. Unspeakably bad. ▣

Ruth Gordon *Mugsy* • Eddie Deezen *Lane* • James Marcel *Shawn* • Steve Brodie *Jack Enoff* • Laura Branigan *Monica* ■ *Dir/Scr* Kevin Brodie

Delusion ★★★

Thriller 1991 · US · Colour · 88mins

A little-seen but engaging thriller that provides a new twist on the "yuppie in peril" genre, with Jim Metzler getting caught up with a hit man and a showgirl on the road. The cast is largely unfamiliar, with the exception of the always reliable Jerry Orbach – best known as Martin Landau's hoodlum brother in *Crimes and Misdemeanors* – but Carl Colpaert directs the

proceedings with panache. Contains swearing, violence and nudity.

Jim Metzler *George O'Brien* • Jennifer Rubin *Patti* • Kyle Secor *Chevy* • Jerry Orbach *Larry* • Robert Costanzo *Myron Sales* • Tracey Walter *Bus ticket cashier* • Barbara Alyn Woods *Julie* • Barbra Horan *Carly* ■ *Dir* Carl Colpaert • *Scr* Kurt Voss, Carl Colpaert

Delusions of Grandeur ★★★

Period comedy 1971 · Fr · Colour

Gérard Oury – never the subtlest of film-makers – casts restraint aside in this bawdy lampoon, based on Victor Hugo's play *Ruy Blas*. Such excess won't suit all devotees of costume drama, but it's pitched perfectly for Louis de Funès. Best known here for the *Gendarme of St Tropez* series, the actor gleefully overplays every scene as the jilted noble seeking revenge on the King of Spain by arranging for his wife to commit adultery with valet Yves Montand, who bears a striking resemblance to the monarch's cousin. Beautifully shot by Henri Decae and lavishly designed by Georges Wakhevitch, this is still something of an acquired taste. French dialogue dubbed into English.

Yves Montand *Blaze* • Louis de Funès *Salluste* • Alberto de Mendoza *King* • Karin Schubert *Queen* • Gabriele Tinti *Cesar* • Alice Sapritch *Dona Juna* • Don Jaime De Mora *Priego* ■ *Dir* Gérard Oury • *Scr* Gerard Oury, Marcel Jullian, Daniele Thompson, from the play *Ruy Blas* by Victor Hugo

Dementia 13 ★★ 15

Horror 1963 · US · BW · 74mins

A series of axe murders marks the anniversary of a little girl's drowning at an eerie Irish castle. This is a passable horror whodunit, directed by Francis Ford Coppola, aged 24, on a $22,000 budget. The future seeping light of Hollywood convinced Ireland's prestigious Abbey Players to appear for minimum wages, begged William Campbell and Patrick Magee to star and used the same sets as the Roger Corman production he was assisting on. Those sets give an atmospheric patina to proceedings, despite numerous continuity errors and poor production values. A seminal minor classic with many recognisable traits soon to emerge in the master film-maker's blockbusters. ▣

William Campbell *Richard Haloran* • Luana Anders *Louise Haloran* • Bart Patton *Billy Haloran* • Mary Mitchell *Kane* • Patrick Magee *Justin Caleb* • Eithne Dunn *Lady Haloran* • Peter Read *John Haloran* • Karl Schanzer *Simon* ■ *Dir/Scr* Francis Ford Coppola

Demetrius and the Gladiators ★★★ PG

Epic 1954 · US · Colour · 96mins

In this sequel to *The Robe*, Victor Mature – the custodian of Christ's bloodstained piece of homespun – tries to keep it from falling into the clutches of Caligula. Forced to become a gladiator, Mature's antics in the arena arouse the passion of Messalina (Susan Hayward), the wife of limping, stuttering Claudius, and antagonise Caligula, played by the scene-stealing and deliriously camp Jay Robinson. The result is a juicy excursion into ancient Rome which thankfully lacks the

oppressive religiosity of the first film. ▣

Victor Mature *Demetrius* • Susan Hayward *Messalina* • Michael Rennie *Peter* • Debra Paget *Lucia* • Anne Bancroft *Paula* • Jay Robinson *Caligula* • Barry Jones *Claudius* • Ernest Borgnine *Strabo* ■ *Dir* Delmer Daves • *Scr* Philip Dunne, from characters created by Lloyd C Douglas

The Demi-Paradise ★★★ U

Drama 1943 · UK · BW · 114mins

A wartime propaganda piece from director Anthony Asquith. Heavily accented Russian visitor Laurence Olivier comes to England and finds a country stuffed to the brim with national stereotypes. In his wisdom, however, he manages to see beyond the peculiarities and peccadillos and, after falling in love with lovely Penelope Dudley-Ward, appreciates England for what it really is. This being wartime, and him being the inventor of a new type of ship's propeller, it's all jolly timely and actually quite charming. The finale, though, is as daft as a brush.

Laurence Olivier *Ivan Dimitrevitch Kouzenetsoff* • Penelope Dudley Ward *Ann Tisdall* • Marjorie Fielding *Mrs Tisdall* • Margaret Rutherford *Rowena Ventnor* • Felix Aylmer *Mr Runalow* • Edie Martin *Aunt Winnie* • Joyce Grenfell *Mrs Pawson* • Wilfrid Hyde White *Waiter* ■ *Dir* Anthony Asquith • *Scr* Anatole de Grunwald

Demobbed ★ U

Comedy 1944 · UK · BW · 95mins

This civvy street comedy is fast, furious and totally unfunny. Despite their music hall experience, neither Nat Jackley nor famed female impersonator Norman Evans had appeared in features before. Their greenness causes them both to pitch to the back of the gallery, thus emphasising the lack of wit in a screenplay which sees them join a top secret scientific company after the war. Irredeemable tosh, with a midway variety show that only makes things worse.

Nat Jackley *Nat* • Norman Evans *Norman* • Dan Young *Dan* • Betty Jumel *Betty* • Tony Dalton *Billy Brown* • Jimmy Plant *Graham* • Anne Firth *Norma Deane* ■ *Dir* John E Blakeley • *Scr* Roney Parsons, Anthony Toner, from a story by Julius Cantor, Max Zorlini

The Democratic Terrorist ★★★

Action thriller 1992 · Ger/Swe · Colour · 96mins

Swedish actor Stellan Skarsgård has become an international star thanks to his excellent performances in films like *Breaking the Waves* and *Good Will Hunting*. Earlier in his career he was known throughout northern Europe for complex characterisations such as the secret agent in this tense thriller. Taken from the novel by Jan Guillou, the story intriguingly sets the Baader-Meinhof terrorist group on a mission to destroy European unity. But the real excitement comes from the fact that Skarsgård's infatuation with Katja Flint convinces his superiors that he's defected, thus making him a target for both sides. Briskly directed by Per Berglund, this is essentially low-budget Bond, but none the worse for that. In Swedish, Norwegian and German with

English subtitles. Contains violence, swearing and nudity.

Stellan Skarsgård *Captain Carl Hamilton* • Katja Flint *Monika* • Karl Heinz Maslo *Werner* • Heikko Deutschmann *Martin* • Burkhard Dreist *Horst* • Ulrich Tukur *Siegfried Maak* ■ *Dir* Per Berglund • *Scr* Hans Iverberg, from the novel by Jan Guillou

Demolition Man ★★★★ 15

Science-fiction thriller 1993 · US · Colour · 110mins

This comes pretty close to being Sylvester Stallone's best picture: a pretension-free, futuristic thriller in which he wisely keeps his tongue stuck firmly in his cheek. Stallone is a tough cop whose unconventional methods land him in a cryogenic prison. Decades later, he is defrosted to hunt down an old sparring partner, the spectacularly psychopathic Wesley Snipes, who has escaped from his deep frozen state and is creating havoc in the now crime-free Los Angeles (renamed San Angeles). The writers have a lot of fun sending up modern-day political correctness in this caring vision of the future, and director Marco Brambilla delivers the goods when it comes to the all-important action set pieces. Contains swearing and violence. ▣ DVD

Sylvester Stallone *John Spartan* • Wesley Snipes *Simon Phoenix* • Sandra Bullock *Lenina Huxley* • Nigel Hawthorne *Dr Raymond Cocteau* • Benjamin Bratt *Alfredo Garcia* • Bob Gunton *Chief George Earle* • Glenn Shadix *Associate Bob* • Denis Leary *Edgar Friendly* ■ *Dir* Marco Brambilla • *Scr* Daniel Waters, Robert Reneau, Peter M Lenkov, from a story by Peter M Lenkov, Robert Reneau

The Demolitionist ★★ 18

Science-fiction thriller 1995 · US · Colour · 85mins

Former *Baywatch* babe Nicole Eggert plays an undercover police officer who undergoes a futuristic blood transplant after she's slain by villain Richard Grieco and is transformed into an enhanced human fighting machine. Clad in a masked bodysuit, she wreaks vengeance on Grieco's gang as director Robert Kurtzman laboriously piles on the intermittently funny in-jokes. Contains swearing, violence and nudity. ▣

Nicole Eggert *Alyssa Lloyd* • Richard Grieco *Mad Dog* • Bruce Abbott *Professor Jack Crowley* • Susan Tyrrell *Mayor Grimbaum* • Peter Jason *Police Chief Higgins* ■ *Dir* Robert Kurtzman • *Scr* Brian DiMuccio, Dino Vindeni

Demon Seed ★★★★ 15

Science-fiction chiller 1977 · US · Colour · 90mins

This literate sci-fi take on *Rosemary's Baby*, based on a Dean R Koontz novel, is as weird, provocative and compelling as you would expect from Donald Cammell, the co-director of *Performance*. Julie Christie is dazzling as the victim of a power-crazed computer that decides it's greater than its genius creator and malfunctions to conceive a child. A claustrophobic cautionary tale that shrouds its incredible special effects in a powerful hallucinatory atmosphere, with Robert Vaughn providing the creepily compelling voice of the machine. Contains violence and nudity. ▣

Julie Christie *Dr Susan Harris* • Fritz Weaver *Dr Alex Harris* • Gerrit Graham *Walter Gabler* • Berry Kroeger *Petrosian* • Lisa Lu *Dr Soon Yen* • Larry J Blake [Larry Blake] *Cameron* • John O'Leary *Royce* • Robert Vaughn *Proteus* ■ *Dir* Donald Cammell • *Scr* Robert Jaffe, Roger O Hirson, from the novel by Dean R Koontz

Demons of the Mind ★★★ 18

Psychological drama
1971 · UK · Colour · 84mins

As the seventies dawned, Hammer tried different avenues of horror to survive the chilling competition. This cod-Freudian nightmare was an experiment by director Peter Sykes to foster the artier side of the genre by delving deep into the psychological roots of the madness afflicting a troubled aristocratic family and the dark reasons why the baron keeps his children locked up in his Bavarian castle. Acted with a conviction way beyond the call of duty by Robert Hardy, Shane Briant, Gillian Hills and ex-Manfred Mann singer Paul Jones, it's ambitious, difficult, often intelligent stuff. Contains swearing. ▦

Paul Jones *Carl Richter* • Patrick Magee *Dr Falkenberg* • Yvonne Mitchell *Aunt Hilda* • Robert Hardy *Baron Frederic Zorn* • Gillian Hills *Elizabeth Zorn* • Michael Hordern *Priest* ■ *Dir* Peter Sykes • *Scr* Christopher Wicking, from a story by Frank Godwin, Christopher Wicking

Demonstone ★

Action horror 1989 · Ausl · Colour · 92mins

Tough major R Lee Ermey teams up with ex-marine Jan-Michael Vincent to solve a series of grisly murders in Manila in a movie that's more action adventure than horror film. Political intrigue, machine gun battles and car crashes take precedence over the limited special effects, which involve such old-fashioned tricks as glowing eyes and images turning negative.

R Lee Ermey *Major Joe Haines* • Jan-Michael Vincent *Andrew Buck* • Nancy Everhard *Sharon Gale* • Pat Skipper *Tony McKee* • Peter Brown *Admiral* • Joonee Gamboa *Senator Belfardo/ Chief pirate* • Rolando Tinio *Professor Olmeda* ■ *Dir* Andrew Prowse • *Scr* John Trayne, David Phillips, Frederick Bailey

Denial ★

Psychological drama
1991 · US · Colour · 103mins

A straight-to-video muddle that has Robin Wright Penn remembering a hot-blooded romance with Jason Patric which she abandoned for the easy life. Directed by Erin Dignam, who would work with Wright Penn five years later on *Loved*, this psychological drama is confused and confusing; ennui ensues, not enigma. The excellent cast does its best, but the actors seem as clueless as we are.

Robin Wright [Robin Wright Penn] *Loon* • Rae Dawn Chong *Julie* • Jason Patric *Michael* • Barry Primus *Jay* ■ *Dir/Scr* Erin Dignam

Denise Calls Up ★★★ 15

Romantic comedy
1995 · US · Colour · 79mins

People fall in love without holding hands; women have babies without a mate; and friends stay close for years without ever seeing each other. Writer/ director Hal Salwen's sophisticated

cautionary fable is bound to strike a communication chord with those who feel technology has a lot to answer for when it comes to modern relationships. This perceptive and consistently funny look at lifestyles today shows a small group of workaholic New Yorkers conducting their lives over the telephone to such an extent that they have forgotten how to interact on a human level. Call-waiting, answer machines and the internet are the villains of this highly unusual, painfully true and stimulating party-line diversion. ▦

Tim Daly [Timothy Daly] *Frank Oliver* • Caroleen Feeney *Barbara* • Dan Gunther *Martin Wiener* • Dana Wheeler-Nicholson *Gale* • Liev Schreiber *Jerry* • Aida Turturro *Linda* • Alanna Ubach *Denise* ■ *Dir/Scr* Hal Salwen

Dennis ★★★ PG

Comedy 1993 · US · Colour · 91mins

Directed by Nick Castle, who played the murderous Shape in *Halloween*, this adaptation of Hank Ketcham's comic strip was released as *Dennis the Menace* in the USA, but shortened simply to *Dennis* in this country to avoid confusion with *The Beano*'s tousle-haired terror. Often very funny, but just as often painfully poor, the film was co-written and produced by John Hughes, who seems to have cobbled it together from ideas left over from *Home Alone*. Mason Gamble just gets by as the mischievous imp; Walter Matthau, however, is brilliant as his long-suffering victim, Mr Wilson. Contains some violence. ▦

Walter Matthau *Mr Wilson* • Mason Gamble *Dennis Mitchell* • Joan Plowright *Martha Wilson* • Christopher Lloyd *Switchblade Sam* • Lea Thompson *Alice Mitchell* • Robert Stanton *Henry Mitchell* • Amy Sakasitz *Margaret Wade* • Kellen Hathaway *Joey* • Paul Winfield *Chief of Police* • Natasha Lyonne *Polly* ■ *Dir* Nick Castle • *Scr* John Hughes, from characters created by Hank Ketcham

Dennis Strikes Again ★★★ U

Comedy 1998 · US · Colour · 71mins

How the likes of Don Rickles and Betty White got roped into this treacly kids' comedy is a mystery, but there they are, appearing as Dennis's neigbours, Mr and Mrs Wilson. If the first five minutes – featuring a menagerie of escaped animals and Rickles's wagon ride down a flight of stairs half-naked – don't send you off screaming, then perhaps you'll actually enjoy the subsequent appearance of George Kennedy as Dennis's grandfather. The child actors play their cartoon counterparts with varying degrees of success, but for adults, watching Rickles provides most of the fun. Warning: this contains the comedic stylings of Carrot Top. ▦

Justin Cooper *Dennis Mitchell* • Don Rickles *Mr Wilson* • George Kennedy *Grandpa* • Brian Doyle-Murray *Professor* • Carrot Top *Sylvester* • Betty White *Mrs Wilson* • Dwier Brown *George Mitchell* • Heidi Swedberg *Alice Mitchell* • George Wendt *Cop* ■ *Dir* Charles T Kanganis • *Scr* Tim McCanlies, from a story by Tim McCanlies, Jeff Schechter, from characters created by Hank Ketcham

The Dentist ★★★★ U

Comedy 1932 · US · BW · 20mins

Based on a sketch first performed in the Earl Carroll Vanities, this marked WC Fields's debut for slapstick supremo, Mack Sennett. Having forbidden his daughter to marry the ice man and endured golfing hell, Fields is next tormented by a bearded patient and Elise Cavanna's stubborn tooth. (The shots in which she throws her legs around his waist to assist his merciless assault with the dental pliers were excised for TV screenings until the seventies.) The film established the Fields persona that would serve him to the end of his career. ▦

WC Fields *Dentist* • Babe Kane *Daughter* • Arnold Gray *Arthur the iceman* • Dorothy Granger *Patient (Miss Peppitone)* • Elise Cavanna *Patient (Miss Mason)* ■ *Dir* Leslie Pearce • *Scr* WC Fields

The Dentist ★★★ 18

Horror 1996 · US · Colour · 88mins

A gory oral scare-fest from director Brian Yuzna, the producer of *Re-Animator*. Corbin Bernsen is the Beverly Hills dentist who goes murderously crazy when his professional and private lives stop conforming to his impossibly high standards. As paranoia sets in, he fights the moral decay contaminating his world with the sharp tools of his trade. The dental torture that follows is both grisly and hilariously funny and slyly sent up by Bernsen, though *The Dentist II* is even better. Contains violence. ▦

Corbin Bernsen *Dr Feinstone* • Linda Hoffman *Brooke* • Molly Hagan *Jessica* • Ken Foree *Detective Gibbs* • Virginya Keehne *Sarah* • Patty Toy *Karen* • Jan Hoag *Candy* • Christa Sauls *April Reign* • Tony Noakes *Detectice Sunshine* • Earl Boen *Marvin Goldblum* • Michael Stadvec *Matt* ■ *Dir* Brian Yuzna • *Scr* Stuart Gordon, Dennis Paoli, Charles Finch

The Dentist II ★★★★ 18

Thriller 1998 · US · Colour · 93mins

The tagline "You know the drill" sums it all up rather nicely. But if you don't, here's a résumé. The original *Dentist* was one of the funniest and nastiest horrors in years and sent blackboard-scraping chills up the spine. The good news is that Brian Yuzna's sequel is just as black, just as gruesome and will convince another generation of fans to put the annual dental check-up on hold. Corbin Bernsen is back as the psychotic gum mutilator, resuming practice after escaping from an asylum. However, those old problems of decay, plus the arrival of nosey parkers, soon has him spitting – and spilling – blood. Contains violence, nudity and some swearing. ▦

Corbin Bernsen *Dr Lawrence Caine* • Linda Hoffman *Brooke Sullivan* • Jillian McWhirter *Jamie Devers* • Susanne Wright *Bev Trotter* • Wendy Robie *Bernice* • Clint Howard *Mr Toothache* ■ *Dir* Brian Yuzna • *Scr* Richard Dana Smith, from characters created by Stuart Gordon, Dennis Paoli, Charles Finch

Dentist in the Chair ★★ U

Comedy 1960 · UK · BW · 75mins

Bob Monkhouse co-wrote and stars in this unremarkable little comedy, which will only have viewers in fits if they

have been subjected to laughing gas. If the flimsy plot about stolen instruments at a dental training school isn't bad enough, the ghastly gags will set your teeth on edge. Numbing the pain, however, are the rollicking performances of Monkhouse and Kenneth Connor, and typically sound comic support from Eric Barker. ▦

Bob Monkhouse *David Cookson* • Peggy Cummins *Peggy Travers* • Kenneth Connor *Sam Field* • Eric Barker *The Dean* • Ronnie Stevens *Brian Dexter* • Vincent Ball *Michaels* ■ *Dir* Don Chaffey • *Scr* Val Guest, Bob Monkhouse, George Wadmore, from the novel by Matthew Finch

Dentist on the Job ★ PG

Comedy 1961 · UK · BW · 84mins

A year after cutting his teeth on *Dentist in the Chair*, Bob Monkhouse returned in this disappointing sequel with a script that's so full of cavities you'll soon be wincing with pain and crying out for laughing gas. Newly qualified Monkhouse beams his way through a series of gags that could easily have been extracted from *Doctor in the House* author Richard Gordon's reject file. No film that numbers Charles Hawtrey, Kenneth Connor, Eric Barker and Richard Wattis among its cast should be totally ignored, but there is a temptation to keep yelling the American title – *Get On with It* – at the screen. ▦

Bob Monkhouse *David Cookson* • Kenneth Connor *Sam Field* • Ronnie Stevens *Brian Dexter* • Shirley Eaton *Jill Venner* • Eric Barker *Colonel JJ Proudfoot/Dean* • Richard Wattis *Macreedy* • Reginald Beckwith *Duff* • Charles Hawtrey *Pharmacist* • Graham Stark *Man* ■ *Dir* CM Pennington-Richards • *Scr* Hazel Adair, Hugh Woodhouse, Bob Monkhouse

Deranged ★★★ 18

Horror 1974 · US · Colour · 82mins

Based on the abhorrent real-life crimes of cannibal killer Ed Gein, who inspired *Psycho* and *The Texas Chain Saw Massacre*, this ghoulish shocker was disowned by its producer for being too repellently realistic. Roberts Blossom plays a sexually repressed mummy's boy who preserves the old dear's corpse and murders people to keep her company. Blossom gives a stand-out central performance, managing the near-impossible feat of making a sympathetic character out of a psychopathic killer. Contains violence and some swearing. ▦

Roberts Blossom *Ezra Cobb* • Cosette Lee *Ma Cobb* • Robert Warner *Harlan Kootz* • Marcia Diamond *Jenny Kootz* • Robert McHeady *Sheriff* • Marian Waldman *Maureen Selby* • Jack Mather *Drunk* ■ *Dir* Jeff Gillen, Alan Ormsby • *Scr* Alan Ormsby

Derby ★★

Drama 1995 · US · Colour

Having spent much of his acting career in the sand and surf of *Baywatch*, David Charvet obviously fancied a break from anything remotely nautical. Here he remains in California, but the setting is a ranch rather than the beach. There he comes to the aid of his childhood sweetheart, Joanne Vannicola, the reluctant new boss of a family estate. To save the homestead, she must gamble everything on the Kentucky Derby. It looks nice but the plotting in this TV movie is strictly routine, as is the direction of Bob Clark.

Joanne Vannicola *Katie Woods* • David Charvet *Cass Sundstrom* • Len Cariou *Henry Woods* • Darren McGavin *Lester Corbett* • Dean McDermott *Eric McDowell* • Felton Perry *Jessup* ■ Dir Bob Clark • Scr Charles Rath, Joseph Pipher, Heather Conkie, from a story by Charles Rath, Joseph Pipher

Derby Day ★★★ U
Drama   1952 · UK · BW · 81mins

An engaging, absorbing look at the various flotsam and jetsam that pit themselves against the Fates at Epsom Downs on Derby Day. This is the early fifties, when the British class system was firmly rooted and unassailable, and director Herbert Wilcox nicely milks its rituals and nuances at a great cultural event. The portmanteau cast effortlessly goes through its paces with the likes of Googie Withers, Michael Wilding and Wilcox's wife Anna Neagle traversing familiar territory with aplomb and confidence. We have been here many times before, but it's still fun. ▣

Anna Neagle *Lady Helen Forbes* • Michael Wilding *David Scott* • Googie Withers *Betty Molloy* • John McCallum *Tommy Dillon* • Peter Graves (2) *Gerald Berkeley* • Suzanne Cloutier *Michele Jolivet* • Gordon Harker *Joe Jenkins* • Gladys Henson *Gladys* ■ Dir Herbert Wilcox • Scr Monckton Hoffe, John Baines, Alan Melville, from a story by Arthur Austie

Dersu Uzala ★★★ U
Period adventure
1975 · USSR/Jap · Colour · 134mins

Anxious to appear open to cultural exchange, the Soviet Union gave Japanese maestro Akira Kurosawa untold roubles and all of Siberia's wilderness to play with for this eco-epic. It's a vast tone poem, set at the turn of the century when an expedition, led by Arseniev, set out to map the icy wastes. And that's it, really: a collection of episodes showing man's attempts to come to terms with nature at its toughest. There are some great moments, and Maxim Munzuk has undoubted charisma as Uzala, but there are also long periods when the camera just stares meaningfully at nothing and you expect David Attenborough's soft voice any moment. In Russian with English subtitles. ▣

Maxim Munzuk *Dersu Uzala* • Yuri Solomin *Captain Arseniev* • A Pyatkov *Olentiev* • V Kremena *Turtygin* • S Chokmorov *Chang-Bao* • S Danilchenko *Anna* ■ Dir Akira Kurosawa • Scr Akira Kurosawa, Yuri Nagibin, from the novel by Vladimir Arseniev

Descending Angel ★★★ 15
Thriller   1990 · US · Colour · 94mins

There are echoes of Costa-Gavras's *Music Box* in this worthy made-for-cable drama. George C Scott plays a seemingly respectable East European immigrant who is outed as a Nazi collaborator by his future son-in-law, Eric Roberts. The playing by the entire cast, which also includes Diane Lane and Jan Rubes, is faultless, and, although Jeremy Paul Kagan's direction is a little too static at times, this still makes for compelling viewing. ▣

Eric Roberts *Michael Rossi* • Diane Lane *Irina Stroia* • George C Scott *Florian Stroia* • Jan Rubes *Bishop Dancu* • Elsa Raven *Vera* • Mark Margolis *Jacob Bercovici* • Ken Jenkins *Sam Murray* ■ Dir Jeremy Paul Kagan • Scr Robert Siegel, Grace Woodard, Alan Sharp, from a story by Grace Woodard, Robert Siegel

Descent into Hell ★★★
Crime thriller   1986 · Fr · Colour · 90mins

Adapted from a novel by David Goodis, whose pulp classic *Down There* was the inspiration for François Truffaut's *Tirez sur le Pianiste*, this is a tidy enough *film noir*. Unfortunately, it lacks both the hard-boiled edge and star credibility that would raise it above the average. Claude Brasseur is sufficiently world-weary as the alcoholic author who accidentally kills a petty thief while vacationing in Haiti. But Sophie Marceau, as the trophy wife who helps conceal his crime, is short on *femme fatality*. Consequently, the interest lies in such peripheral characters as Marie Dubois and Sidiki Bakaba, whose dealings with the guilty couple becoming increasingly sinister. French dialogue dubbed into English.

Claude Brasseur *Alan Kolber* • Sophie Marceau *Lola Kolber* • Sidiki Bakaba *Theophile Bijou* • Hyppolyte Girardot *Philippe Devignat* • Gérard Rinaldi *Elvis* • Marie Dubois *Lucette Beulemans* • Betsy Blair *Mrs Burns* ■ Dir Francis Girod • Scr Francis Girod, Jean-Loup Dabadic, from the novel *The Wounded and the Slain* by David Goodis

Desert Bloom ★★★★ PG
Drama   1985 · US · Colour · 101mins

In this period piece director Eugene Corr splendidly captures the simmering, underlying tensions and almost childlike incredulity of a fifties America heralding in the nuclear age. The bigger scares of the Bomb are used to add colour to an enclosed tale of dysfunctional family life, wonderfully played by Jon Voight as the drunken stepfather of young Annabeth Gish and Ellen Barkin as her sexy aunt. Corr takes an age to establish his characters and plot, but once up and running there isn't a more atmospheric film about pre-Kennedy America. Contains some swearing. ▣

Annabeth Gish *Rose* • Jon Voight *Jack* • JoBeth Williams *Lily* • Ellen Barkin *Starr* • Jay Underwood *Robin* • Desiree Joseph *Dee Ann* • Dusty Balcerzak *Barbara Jo* • Allen Garfield *Mr Mosol* • Tressi Loria *Shelly* ■ Dir Eugene Corr • Scr Eugene Corr, from a story by Linda Remy, Eugene Corr

Desert Blue ★★★
Comedy drama   1998 · US · Colour · 90mins

A small-town teen movie starring the up-and-coming Brendan Sexton III, Christina Ricci and Ben Affleck's brother Casey. Two travellers, father John Heard and daughter Kate Hudson, get trapped in a rural backwater after a chemical truck spillage. Their encounters with the town's restless youth expose personal prejudices and result in an unlikely romance between snobbish Hudson and bad boy Blue (Sexton). Director Morgan J Freeman should not be confused with the celebrated star of *The Shawshank Redemption*.

Brendan Sexton III *Blue Baxter* • Kate Hudson *Skye* • John Heard *Father* • Christina Ricci *Ely*

• Casey Affleck *Pete* • Sara Gilbert *Sandy* • Ethan Suplee *Cale* • Michael Ironside *Agent Bellows* ■ Dir/Scr Morgan J Freeman

The Desert Fox ★★★ PG
Second World War action drama
1951 · US · BW · 84mins

Twentieth Century-Fox here casts James Mason – an actor memorable for playing charming villains – as Field Marshal Erwin Rommel, who was known as a professional soldier rather than a Nazi sadist. Filmed not in North Africa but Borrego Springs, California, Henry Hathaway's film begins as a wartime adventure, then turns into a study of disenchantment as Rommel, beaten by Montgomery's 8th Army, returns to Germany and joins the plot against Hitler. There's a good supporting cast, notably Jessica Tandy as Frau Rommel and Luther Adler as Hitler, and Hathaway directs with solid assurance. ▣

James Mason *Erwin Rommel* • Cedric Hardwicke *Dr Karl Strolin* • Jessica Tandy *Frau Rommel* • Luther Adler *Hitler* • Everett Sloane *General Burgdorf* • Leo G Carroll *Field Marshal Von Rundstedt* • George Macready *General Fritz Bayerlein* ■ Dir Henry Hathaway • Scr Nunnally Johnson, from the biography by Desmond Young

Desert Fury ★★★
Drama   1947 · US · Colour · 96mins

Lizabeth Scott runs away from school and heads home to Nevada where her mom, Mary Astor, runs a gambling house and where the men get very steamed up indeed. There's widowed gambler John Hodiak, his henchman Wendell Corey and the most virile cop west of the Pecos, Burt Lancaster, in his third screen outing. It's really a western in modern dress, a display of macho posturing that's ridiculous and gripping at the same time, with the husky Scott relishing her role as a Salome-style seductress.

John Hodiak *Eddie Bendix* • Lizabeth Scott *Paula Haller* • Burt Lancaster *Tom Hanson* • Wendell Corey *Johnny Ryan* • Mary Astor *Fritzie Haller* • Kristine Miller *Claire Lindquist* • William Harrigan *Judge Berle Lindquist* • James Flavin *Pat Johnson* ■ Dir Lewis Allen • Scr Robert Rossen, from the novel *Desert Town* by Ramona Stewart

Desert Hearts ★★★★★ 18
Drama   1985 · US · Colour · 87mins

One of the very few truly risk-taking movies to come out of the mid-eighties, this tale of lesbian love in Reno was a deserved critical success at the time. Based on Jane Rule's novel, Natalie Cooper's intriguing, intelligent screenplay gives great roles to Helen Shaver and Patricia Charbonneau, and the resulting juxtaposition – of a disillusioned older woman falling for a younger, freer spirit – works a treat. What scenes of carnal knowledge there are – for this is a film about relationships and prejudice – are deftly handled without either sensationalism or coy fudging. This is one of those seminal pictures that show what Hollywood can do when it casts fear aside. ▣

Helen Shaver *Vivian Bell* • Patricia Charbonneau *Cay Rivvers* • Audra Lindley *Frances Parker* • Andra Akers *Silver Dale* •

Dean Butler *Darrell* • Gwen Welles *Gwen* ■ Dir Donna Deitch • Scr Natalie Cooper, from the novel *Desert of the Heart* by Jane Rule

Desert Legion ★★ U
Swashbuckling adventure
1953 · US · Colour · 85mins

Alan Ladd stars in this B-grade swashbuckler, a rehash of *Beau Geste* and *Gunga Din* with a bit of *The Man Who Would Be King* thrown in for good measure. Ladd plays a soldier in the Foreign Legion who survives an ambush and is nursed back to health by the alluring Arlene Dahl. Dahl lives in a hidden city called Madara, and enlists Ladd to help keep it from the clutches of villain Richard Conte. Comic relief comes from Ladd's buddy, Akim Tamiroff.

Alan Ladd *Paul Lartel* • Richard Conte *Crito/Calif* • Arlene Dahl *Morjana* • Akim Tamiroff *Private Plevko* • Leon Askin *Major Vasil* • Oscar Beregi *Khalil* • Anthony Caruso *Lieutenant Messaoud* • Don Blackman *Kumbaba* ■ Dir Joseph Pevney • Scr Irving Wallace, Lewis Meltzer, from the novel *The Demon Caravan* by George Arthur Surdez

Desert Mice ★★ U
Second World War comedy
1959 · UK · BW · 83mins

The feeble title pun on "Desert Rats" (the nickname given to the British troops who fought against Rommel in North Africa) rather sets the tone for this overlookable comedy from director Michael Relph. Full of predictable characters, humdrum incidents and gags that would have lowered the morale of even the most battle-hardened tommy, it accompanies an Ensa concert party on its tour of army camps. Sid James, Dora Bryan and Irene Handl prove again to be reliable troupers, but Alfred Marks lacks the range and presence to carry the lead.

Alfred Marks *Major Poskett* • Sidney James *Bert Bennett* • Dora Bryan *Gay* • Dick Bentley *Gavin O'Toole* • Reginald Beckwith *Fred* • Irene Handl *Miss Patch* • Liz Fraser *Edie* ■ Dir Michael Relph • Scr David Climie

Desert Passage ★
Western   1952 · US · BW · 62mins

After 12 years of grinding out nearly 50 B-westerns for RKO Radio with occasional (and sometimes memorable) appearances in bigger pictures, Tim Holt turned in his saddle and – save some fleeting later appearances – retired from the big screen. Far from ending the series on a high note, this one cuts back on action and atmosphere with a minimum number of extras and most of the scenes located indoors at a hostelry. The story is lively enough, though, with Holt and sidekick Richard Martin driving a stagecoach carrying loot coveted by various parties.

Tim Holt *Tim* • Joan Dixon *Emily* • Walter Reed *Carver* • Richard Martin *Chito Rafferty* • Dorothy Patrick *Rosa* • John Dehner *Bronson* ■ Dir Lesley Selander • Scr Norman Houston

The Desert Rats ★★★ U
Second World War action drama
1953 · US · BW · 84mins

A rather aloof desert-stormer, meant as a follow-up to *The Desert Fox*, and again boasting James Mason as Field

Marshal Rommel, this time ordering the Battle of Tobruk against Allied forces that include Richard Burton commanding Aussie troops. Burton has his own problems with his cowardly old schoolteacher turned volunteer Robert Newton, but still manages to bring down Rommel's forces. The German maestro should have known better; in Allied flag-wavers like this, he never stood a chance. ▭

Richard Burton *Captain MacRoberts* • Robert Newton *Bartlett* • Robert Douglas *General* • Torin Thatcher *Barney* • Chips Rafferty *Smith* • Charles Tingwell *Lieutenant Carstairs* • James Mason *Rommel* • Charles Davis *Pete* ■ *Dir* Robert Wise • *Scr* Richard Murphy

The Desert Song ★★

Musical 1929 · US · BW and Colour · 125mins

An early sound version of the Sigmund Romberg operetta about a seemingly wimpish Briton who, as the mysterious "Red Shadow", leads a revolt against villainous Arabs. Remade in 1944 and 1953, this rendition is worth seeing, not for its competence, but for its unintentional laughs. John Boles sings adequately, despite his stiff upper lip, while Carlotta King has a certain winsome banality as the girl who despises him at first.

John Boles *The Red Shadow* • Carlotta King *Margot* • Louise Fazenda *Susan* • Johnny Arthur *Benny Kidd* • Edward Martindel *Gen Birbeau* • Jack Pratt *Pasha* • Myrna Loy *Azuri* ■ *Dir* Roy Del Ruth • *Scr* Harvey Gates, from the operetta by Sigmund Romberg, Otto Harbach, Lawrence Schwab, Frank Mandel, Oscar Hammerstein II

The Desert Song ★★★ U

Musical 1944 · US · Colour · 94mins

The second of three screen versions of the operetta about the romantic, heroic leader of a band of Riffs in North Africa who fight off their evil oppressors. This version was given contemporary relevance by having the villains as Nazis and the hero (Dennis Morgan) an American in disguise who, with his band of men, sabotages the building of a railway track. Directed by Robert Florey, this romantic nonsense can't miss for fans of Romberg's lush and rousing melodies, which include *One Alone* and *The Riff Song*.

Dennis Morgan *Paul Hudson* • Irene Manning *Margot* • Bruce Cabot *Col Fontaine* • Victor Francen *Caid Yousseff* • Lynne Overman *Johnny Walsh* • Gene Lockhart *Pere FanFan* • Faye Emerson *Hajy* • Marcel Dalio *Tarbouch* ■ *Dir* Robert Florey • *Scr* Robert Buckner, from the operetta by Sigmund Romberg, Otto Harbach, Lawrence Schwab, Frank Mandel, Oscar Hammerstein II

The Desert Song ★★ U

Musical 1953 · US · Colour · 105mins

This handsomely mounted Warner Bros remake of Sigmund Romberg's popular operetta is easy enough on the eye, and easier still on the ear. But the good-looking Gordon MacRae is miscast as the young American anthropologist doubling by night as El Khobar, avenger of the desert Riffs. Still, Kathryn Grayson sings *One Alone* as if her life depended on it, and Raymond Massey is perfect as the cruel and villainous sheik. ▭

Kathryn Grayson *Margot* • Gordon MacRae *Paul Bonnard/El Khobar* • Steve Cochran *Captain Fontaine* • Raymond Massey *Yousseff* • Dick Wesson *Benjy Kidd* • Allyn McLerie [Allyn Ann McLerie] *Azuri* • Ray Collins *General Birabeau* ■ *Dir* Bruce Humberstone [H Bruce Humberstone] • *Scr* Roland Kibbee, from the operetta by Sigmund Romberg, Otto Harbach, Lawrence Schwab, Frank Mandel, Oscar Hammerstein II

The Desert Trail ★★ U

Western 1935 · US · BW · 54mins

Trapped at Monogram Studios and contracted to a seemingly relentless series of B-westerns, John Wayne managed to hone his persona and learn screencraft in routine films like this one. Director Cullin Lewis (Lewis Collins) does what he can with the desperately average "mistaken identity" plot, but there's not much to work with, despite Eddy Chandler's sterling work as Wayne's comic sidekick, Kansas Charlie. The script is by Lindsley Parsons, who went on to become a prolific producer. ▭

John Wayne *John Scott* • Mary Kornman *Anne* • Paul Fix *Jim* • Eddy Chandler *Kansas Charlie* • Carmen Laroux *Juanita* • Lafe McKee *Sheriff Barker* • Al Ferguson *Pete* ■ *Dir* Cullin Lewis [Lewis Collins] • *Scr* Lindsley Parsons

The Deserter ★★ 15

Western 1971 · It/Yug · Colour · 94mins

A lot of familiar western faces are in this cavalry versus Indians epic – Chuck Connors, Woody Strode, Slim Pickens and the Duke's son, Patrick Wayne, but since this is a Euro-western, shot in Yugoslavia, there are also several swarthy Italians, plus Yugoslavian heart-throb Bekim Fehmiu in the title role. Hollywood director Burt Kennedy – noted for maintaining a sharp pace and no messing about – somehow talked John Huston into a cameo appearance as the general setting up a special unit with the aim of wiping out the hostiles. ▭

Bekim Fehmiu *Captain Victor Kaleb* • John Huston *General Miles* • Richard Crenna *Major Wade Brown* • Chuck Connors *Reynolds* • Ricardo Montalban *Natachai* • Ian Bannen *Crawford* • Brandon de Wilde *Ferguson* • Slim Pickens *Tattinger* • Albert Salmi *Schmidt* • Woody Strode *Jackson* • Patrick Wayne *Bill Robinson* ■ *Dir* Burt Kennedy • *Scr* Clair Huffaker, from a story by Stuart J Byrne, William H James

Design for Living ★★★

Romantic comedy drama 1933 · US · BW · 86mins

A famous Noël Coward play becomes a minor work in the canon of the great Ernst Lubitsch. His usually witty visual style is seemingly cramped by having to rely too much on the master's witticisms, as translated into movietalk by ace scenarist Ben Hecht. Of course, in this famous *ménage à trois* tale, Gary Cooper and Fredric March are super fun. But why on earth are they both in such a dither over the self-regarding Miriam Hopkins? Edward Everett Horton saves this show single-handed as Max Plunkett, the stuffed shirt Hopkins eventually marries.

Fredric March *Tom Chambers* • Gary Cooper *George Curtis* • Miriam Hopkins *Gilda Farrell* • Edward Everett Horton *Max Plunkett* • Franklin Pangborn *Mr Douglas* • Isabel Jewell *Lisping*

Stenographer • Harry Dunkinson *Mr Egelbauer* • Helena Phillips *Mrs Egelbauer* ■ *Dir* Ernst Lubitsch • *Scr* Ben Hecht, from the play by Noël Coward

Design for Scandal ★★★ U

Romantic comedy 1941 · US · BW · 84mins

The last movie the fabulous Rosalind Russell made under her MGM contract is a deft romantic comedy based on a clever idea: ace newshound Walter Pidgeon is sent out to dish some dirt on squeaky-clean judge Russell, and falls for her. Screenwriter Lionel Houser provides some sparkling repartee, and director Norman Taurog keeps the froth moving along at a brisk pace. Mix in those glossy MGM production values and you have a very watchable time-filler, which is exactly what it was designed to be.

Rosalind Russell *Judge Cornelia Porter* • Walter Pidgeon *Jeff Sherman* • Edward Arnold *Judson M Blair* • Lee Bowman *Walter Caldwell* • Jean Rogers *Dotty* • Donald Meek *Mr Wade* • Guy Kibbee *Judge Graham* ■ *Dir* Norman Taurog • *Scr* Lionel Houser

The Designated Mourner ★★

Drama 1997 · UK · Colour · 94mins

Anyone familiar with Wallace Shawn's earlier screenwriting effort *My Dinner with Andre* (which he co-scripted with theatre director Andre Gregory) will know what to expect from this chat-fest: a lament on the passing of high art in an age of middlebrow mediocrity. Set in an unnamed country on the edge of revolution, the action centres around the discussions between shiftless intellectual Mike Nichols, his wife Miranda Richardson, and her poet father, David De Keyser. Focusing on the dialogue – the actors address the camera instead of each other – rather than seeking ways to open out Shawn's stage play, director David Hare slams the door shut on all but the cognoscenti. Contains swearing.

Mike Nichols *Jack* • Miranda Richardson *Judy* • David De Keyser *Howard* ■ *Dir* David Hare • *Scr* Wallace Shawn, from his play

Designing Woman ★★★★ U

Romantic comedy 1957 · US · Colour · 117mins

This has a nicely punning title, plus a witty Oscar-winning screenplay by George Wells that seems to have missed its decade, despite having sophisticated and assured comedy direction from MGM ace Vincente Minnelli. With its plot about a fashion designer and crusading sports columnist getting married, it's reminiscent of a Spencer Tracy/Katharine Hepburn comedy. Lauren Bacall gives good value, as does Dolores Gray as a girl from the past; only Gregory Peck lacks the lightness of touch required. The original idea was suggested by MGM's great costume designer, Helen Rose.

Gregory Peck *Mike Hagen* • Lauren Bacall *Marilla Hagen* • Dolores Gray *Lori Shannon* • Sam Levene *Ned Hammerstein* • Tom Helmore *Zachary Wilde* • Mickey Shaughnessy *Maxie Stulz* • Jesse White *Charlie Arneg* ■ *Dir* Vincente Minnelli • *Scr* George Wells, from an idea by Helen Rose

Desire ★★★★

Romantic comedy 1936 · US · BW · 95mins

To evade detection at the Spanish border, a glamorous lady jewel thief hides the pearls she stole in Paris by dropping them into the pocket of an unsuspecting American motor car designer. In the course of her manoeuvrings to retrieve them, she falls in love with him. Marlene Dietrich and Gary Cooper star in this scintillating romantic comedy, produced by Ernst Lubitsch and full of the "Lubitsch touch". While it's not quite *Trouble in Paradise*, the screenplay and performances inhabit the same sophisticated territory.

Marlene Dietrich *Madeleine de Beaupré* • Gary Cooper *Tom Bradley* • John Halliday *Margoli, Carlos* • William Frawley *Mr Gibson* • Ernest Cossart *Aristide Duval* • Akim Tamiroff *Police Official* • Alan Mowbray *Dr Edouard Pauquet* ■ *Dir* Frank Borzage • *Scr* Edward Justus Mayer, Waldemar Young, Samuel Hoffenstein, from the play *Die Schönen Tage von Aranjuez* by Hans Szekely, RA Stemmle

Desire & Hell at Sunset Motel ★★★ 15

Comedy thriller 1991 · US · Colour · 95mins

Fifties nostalgia meets oddball *film noir* when bombshell Sherilyn Fenn and her toy salesman husband (Whip Hubley) shack up in a dingy motel on the way to Disneyland. The deliberately convoluted plot involves Hubley hiring David Hewlett to spy on Fenn and her new lover, while the latter (David Johansen) plots to kill her spouse. Corkscrew twists abound, but for all its attempts to be wacky, erotic and offbeat, Alan Castle's crafty nightmare comedy remains little more than an interesting diversion. ▭

Sherilyn Fenn *Bridey DeSoto* • Whip Hubley *Chester DeSoto* • David Hewlett *Deadpan Winchester* • David Johansen *Auggie March* • Paul Bartel *Manager* • Kenneth Tobey *Captain Holiday* • Parker Whitman *Boss* • Shannon Sturges *Louella* ■ *Dir/Scr* Alan Castle

Desire in the Dust ★★

Drama 1960 · US · BW · 102mins

This tale of lust, death and madness in the Deep South generates much heat but little light. Directed by William F Claxton and shot in black-and-white CinemaScope by Lucien Ballard, this good-looking film involves an ex-convict (Ken Scott) who, having taken a manslaughter rap for his lover (Martha Hyer), returns home to put the cat among the pigeons. These include Hyer's father (Raymond Burr), a political bigwig with lofty ambitions, and her mother (Joan Bennett), who has gone insane. Decently enough acted, but no match for *The Long Hot Summer* and other films of that ilk.

Raymond Burr *Colonel Ben Marquand* • Martha Hyer *Melinda Marquand* • Joan Bennett *Mrs Marquand* • Ken Scott *Lonnie Wilson* • Brett Halsey *Dr Ned Thomas* • Edward Binns *Luke Connett* ■ *Dir* William F Claxton • *Scr* Charles Lang, from the novel by Harry Whittington

Desire Me ★★

Drama 1947 · US · BW · 90mins

The first MGM film to be released with no director credit is pretty silly, but it's no worse and a good deal glossier than most Hollywood pap. Greer Garson is told by buddy Richard Hart that hubby Robert Mitchum was killed in the war; naturally, he wasn't. The director who took his name off the film was George Cukor, and both Mervyn LeRoy and Jack Conway allegedly directed bits. Not that bad, and a real curio for collectors.

Greer Garson *Marise Aubert* • Robert Mitchum *Paul Aubert* • Richard Hart *Jean Renaud* • Morris Ankrum *Martin* • George Zucco *Father Donnard* • Cecil Humphreys *Dr Andre Leclair* • David Hoffman *Postman* • Florence Bates *Mrs Lannie, "Joo-Lou"* ■ • Scr Marguerite Roberts, Zoe Akins

Desire under the Elms ★★
Drama   1958 · US · BW · 113mins

Gloomy Eugene O'Neill drama about New Englander Burl Ives's hot young wife (a virtually incomprehensible Sophia Loren) falling for his son (an overtly sensitive Anthony Perkins). This is overblown melodrama, pure and simple, but director Delbert Mann (*Marty*) opts for realism, despite the fact that Daniel Fapp's crystal-clear (and Oscar-nominated) VistaVision photography reveals every phoney set and emotion for what it is. Irwin Shaw's screenplay is no improvement on O'Neill's play, though the adult themes brought the film an "X" certificate on its British release.

Sophia Loren *Anna Cabot* • Anthony Perkins *Eben Cabot* • Burl Ives *Ephraim Cabot* • Frank Overton *Simeon Cabot* • Pernell Roberts *Peter Cabot* • Rebecca Welles *Lucinda* • Jean Willes *Florence* ■ • Dir Delbert Mann • Scr Irwin Shaw, from the play by Eugene O'Neill

Desiree ★★★ U
Historical romance
1954 · US · Colour · 105mins

Marlon Brando as Napoleon may seem like ideal casting – indeed, the "Great Mumbler" looks and sounds splendid – but it's clear from his sleepwalking performance that the star himself regarded this as a chore. In fact, it was, being Fox boss Darryl F Zanuck's settlement for Brando walking off *The Egyptian*. Nevertheless, there is a splendid coronation sequence and some elegant costumes, plus a lovely Josephine played by Merle Oberon. The title role went to the lovely Jean Simmons; she and Brando would do much better work together the following year in *Guys and Dolls*. 🎞

Marlon Brando *Napoleon Bonaparte* • Jean Simmons *Desiree Clary* • Merle Oberon *Josephine* • Michael Rennie *Bernadotte* • Cameron Mitchell *Joseph Bonaparte* • Elizabeth Sellars *Julie* • Charlotte Austin *Paulette* • Cathleen Nesbitt *Madame Bonaparte* • Evelyn Varden *Marie* ■ • Dir Henry Koster • Scr Daniel Taradash, from the novel by Annemarie Selinko • Costume Designer André Hubert, Charles Le Maire

Desk Set ★★★★ U
Romantic comedy
1957 · US · Colour · 103mins

The wit of the original title was lost in the UK when it was released as *His Other Woman*. But the sparkle in this penultimate pairing of the great Spencer Tracy and the wonderful Katharine Hepburn still endures, even if the slight plot in which Tracy plays

an efficiency expert hired to automate Hepburn's office seems stretched. Watching their on-screen clash from the sidelines are splendid comic players Gig Young and Joan Blondell, and director Walter Lang sensibly lets the stars get on with it. Tracy and Hepburn, in colour for the first time, are as watchable as ever.

Spencer Tracy *Richard Sumner* • Katharine Hepburn *Bunny Watson* • Gig Young *Mike Cutler* • Joan Blondell *Peg Costello* • Dina Merrill *Sylvia* • Sue Randall *Ruthie* • Neva Patterson *Miss Warringer* ■ • Dir Walter Lang • Scr Phoebe Ephron, Henry Ephron, from the play by William Marchant

Despair ★★★ 15
Drama   1978 · W Ger · Colour · 114mins

A whiff of *Satan's Brew* pervades Rainer Werner Fassbinder's dark drama of dual identity and the desire for death. However, there's none of the grubbiness of that showy experiment in this tale, set in pre-Nazi Germany, which – as you would expect of a screenplay adapted by Tom Stoppard from a novel by Vladimir Nabokov – has an ingenuity to match its erudition. Warning of the perils of confusing life with art, Fassbinder uses Dirk Bogarde's failed bid to pass himself off as a murdered tramp to explore the inevitability of fascism and the indolence of the individual. 🎞

Dirk Bogarde *Hermann Herman* • Andrea Ferreol *Lydia Herman* • Volker Spengler *Ardalion* • Klaus Löwitsch *Felix Weber* • Alexander Allerson *Mayer* • Bernhard Wicki *Orlovius* • Peter Kern *Muller* ■ • Dir Rainer Werner Fassbinder • Scr Tom Stoppard, from a novel by Vladimir Nabokov

Desperado ★★ 15
Western   1987 · US · Colour · 91mins

After dozens of assignments as an editor during the fifties, Virgil W Vogel made his name as a director with that priceless turkey, *The Mole People*. Three decades on, he was still editing and directing, albeit TV movies like this laboured reworking of *Shane*. Even a script by cult novelist Elmore Leonard can do nothing to enliven a story that has its roots in the old Eagles song. The cast is much more interesting, with soul singer Gladys Knight joining up with such dependables as Robert Vaughn, Yaphet Kotto and David Warner. Contains swearing. 🎞

Alex McArthur *Duell McCall* • David Warner *Johnny Ballard* • Yaphet Kotto *Bede* • Robert Vaughn *Sheriff Whaley* • Pernell Roberts *Marshal Dancey* • Gladys Knight *Mona Lisa* • Stephen Davies *Calvin* ■ • Dir Virgil W Vogel • Scr Elmore Leonard

Desperado ★★★★ 18
Action adventure
1995 · US · Colour · 100mins

The quirky no-budget charm of *El Mariachi* may have gone, but director Robert Rodriguez clearly revels in the chance to splash out with the backing of a studio to remake his modest debut feature. Antonio Banderas assumes the mantle of the mysterious guitar-playing stranger who arrives south of the border seeking vengeance against an evil drugs baron and keeps his tongue wedged firmly in cheek as he carries out his acrobatic slaughter of hordes of bad guys. Add to that a

smouldering early appearance from Salma Hayek, sharp cameos from Quentin Tarantino and Steve Buscemi and a rootsy rocking soundtrack from Los Lobos and the result is a 100 minutes of joyfully mindless mayhem. Contains swearing, sex scenes and violence. 🎞 DVD

Antonio Banderas *El Mariachi* • Salma Hayek *Carolina* • Joaquim de Almeida *Bucho* • Richard "Cheech" Marin *Short Bartender* • Steve Buscemi • Quentin Tarantino *Pick-up Guy* ■ • Dir/Scr Robert Rodriguez • Editor Robert Rodriguez

The Desperadoes ★★ U
Western   1943 · US · Colour · 86mins

Historically important as Columbia's first feature in Technicolor, this large-scale western has the dubious benefits of some rather garish art direction and some strangely-lit night sequences. The star teaming of Randolph Scott and Glenn Ford makes this routinely plotted tale very watchable, though neither had fully developed their screen persona: Scott isn't quite taciturn enough, and Ford is still very much the juvenile in a role that calls for more maturity.

Randolph Scott *Sheriff Steve Upton* • Glenn Ford *Cheyenne Rogers* • Claire Trevor *The Countess* • Evelyn Keyes *Allison McLeod* • Edgar Buchanan *Uncle Willie McLeod* • Guinn Williams *Nitro Rankin* • Raymond Walburn *Judge Cameron* • Porter Hall *Banker Stanton* ■ • Dir Charles Vidor • Scr Robert Carson, from a story by Max Brand

The Desperados ★★ 15
Western   1969 · US/Spa · Colour · 86mins

Jack Palance – clearly off his rocker and loving every minute – plays a parson who takes his three boys off on an orgy of rape and pillage after the American Civil War. Oldest son Vince Edwards leaves Dad and settles in Texas; six years later, they meet again. Shot in Spain for financial reasons, Henry Levin's film is pretty shoddy in all departments. On the plus side, you have George Maharis of *Route 66* fame, Neville Brand and Sylvia Syms putting in appearances. 🎞

Jack Palance *Parson Josiah Galt* • Vince Edwards *David Galt/David Whitaker* • George Maharis *Jacob Galt* • Neville Brand *Sheriff Kilpatrick* • Sylvia Syms *Laura* • Christian Roberts *Adam Galt* • Kate O'Mara *Adah* ■ • Dir Henry Levin • Scr Walter Brough, from a story by Clarke Reynolds

Desperate ★★★★
Film noir   1947 · US · BW · 71mins

Director Anthony Mann made a knockout series of B-thrillers in the forties that were notable for their cracking pace and economic use of sets and lighting. In today's climate these are called *films noirs*, an expression that would have been unknown at the time. Steve Brodie plays an honest trucker who is forced to flee the mob after he gets caught up in a warehouse caper and the killing of a cop. The movie is one virtually continuous flight and has a terrific twist at the end. Mann went on to direct a marvellous series of features with James Stewart – plus, of course, *El Cid*.

Steve Brodie *Steve Randall* • Audrey Long *Anne Randall* • Raymond Burr *Walt Radak* • Douglas Fowley *Pete* • William Challee *Reynolds* • Jason Robards *Ferrari* • Freddie Steele *Shorty* ■ • Dir Anthony Mann • Scr Harry Essex, Martin Rackin, from a story by Dorothy Atlas, Anthony Mann

Desperate Characters ★★★
Drama   1971 · US · Colour · 87mins

Shirley MacLaine heads a cast of little-known screen actors in a nightmare glimpse into the horrors of Manhattan life, as perceived, written and directed by Broadway playwright Frank D Gilroy. Covering 48 hours in the life of MacLaine and her husband (Kenneth Mars), there's no conventional narrative, just a series of incidents that reflect the breakdown of urban life and the struggle to live with it. We've seen it all before, and the movie is rather downbeat. Yet it's beautifully constructed, acutely observed and well-served by an excellent team of actors.

Shirley MacLaine *Sophie* • Kenneth Mars *Otto* • Gerald S O'Loughlin *Charlie* • Sada Thompson *Claire* • Jack Somack *Leon* • Chris Gampel *Mike* • Mary Ellen Hokanson *Flo* • Robert Bauer *Young man* • Carol Kane *Young girl* ■ • Dir Frank D Gilroy • Scr Frank D Gilroy, from the novel by Paula Fox

Desperate for Love ★★
Drama   1989 · US · Colour · 93mins

Aside from a typically charismatic performance from a pre-stardom Christian Slater, this is routine TV fodder. Slater and Brian Bloom are the two school friends who get locked in a tragic love triangle with Tammy Lauren. The young leads are well supported by a cast which includes Veronica Cartwright (the nosey neighbour in *The Witches of Eastwick*) and Arthur Rosenberg, and it's competently directed by Michael Tuchner. Alas, the idea never really catches fire.

Christian Slater *Cliff Petrie* • Tammy Lauren *Lily Becker* • Brian Bloom *Alex Cutler* • Veronica Cartwright *Betty Petrie* • Scott Paulin *Merl Becker* • Arthur Rosenberg *Buck Cameron* • Amy O'Neill *Cindy* • Lulee Fisher *Sue Becker* ■ • Dir Michael Tuchner • Scr Judith Paige Mitchell

The Desperate Hours ★★★★
Thriller   1955 · US · BW · 112mins

Superbly directed by William Wyler, this searing adaptation of author Joseph Hayes's Broadway hit features the last great villainous performance of Humphrey Bogart, playing an escaped convict holding Fredric March and his family hostage in their own house. The location becomes unbearably claustrophobic as March summons up hidden strengths to protect his loved ones from a criminal who has no redeeming humanitarian features. This was the first movie to be filmed in black-and-white VistaVision ("motion picture high fidelity"), and the depth of field and overall quality of Lee Garmes's photography is superb.

Humphrey Bogart *Glenn* • Fredric March *Dan Hilliard* • Arthur Kennedy *Jesse Bard* • Martha Scott *Eleanor Hilliard* • Dewey Martin *Hal* • Gig Young *Chuck* • Mary Murphy *Cindy* • Richard Eyer *Ralphie* ■ • Dir William Wyler • Scr Joseph Hayes, from his novel and play

U = SUITABLE FOR ALL   Uc = SUITABLE FOR ALL, ESPECIALLY FOR YOUNG CHILDREN (VIDEO ONLY)   PG = PARENTAL GUIDANCE

Desperate Hours ★★★ 15

Thriller 1990 · US · Colour · 100mins

Michael Cimino's combustible thriller stars Mickey Rourke as the psychotic gangster who invades the suburban home of Anthony Hopkins and Mimi Rogers. Cimino breaks free of the story's stage origins (there are some vivid scenes in the Colorado wilderness) and updates William Wyler's 1955 version by having Hopkins's marriage on the verge of collapse. The director of *The Deer Hunter* and *Heaven's Gate* takes things over the brink, and the result bristles with drama and visual spectacle. Contains violence and swearing.

Mickey Rourke *Michael Bosworth* • Anthony Hopkins *Tim Cornell* • Mimi Rogers *Nora Cornell* • Lindsay Crouse *Chandler* • Kelly Lynch *Nancy Breyers* • Elias Koteas *Wally Bosworth* • Mike Nussbaum *Mr Nelson* • David Morse *Albert* ■ *Dir* Michael Cimino • *Scr* Lawrence Konner, Mark Rosenthal, Joseph Hayes, from the film, novel and play by Joseph Hayes • *Cinematographer* Douglas Milsome

Desperate Journey ★★★ PG

Second World War adventure
1942 · US · BW · 103mins

Superstar Errol Flynn was medically unfit for military service, but fought the Second World War memorably on screen in a series of Warner Bros action adventures, invariably directed with great pace by Raoul Walsh. Here, Flynn and four other RAF recruits crash-land in Germany and attempt to make their way back to England in *Boys' Own* fashion. "Now for Australia and a crack at the Japs!" says our Errol, though another memorable line – "They know but one command – attack!" – was deleted after previews. (Flynn was embroiled in a rape scandal at the time.)

Errol Flynn *Flight Lieutenant Terrence Forbes* • Ronald Reagan *Flying Officer Johnny Hammond* • Raymond Massey *Major Otto Baumeister* • Nancy Coleman *Kaethe Brahms* • Alan Hale *Flight Sergeant Kirk Edwards* • Arthur Kennedy *Flying Officer Jed Forrest* • Sig Rumann [Sig Ruman] *Preuss* ■ *Dir* Raoul Walsh • *Scr* Arthur T Horman, from his story *Forced Landing*

Desperate Justice ★★★ PG

Drama 1993 · US · Colour · 88mins

Lesley Ann Warren has rarely been allowed to display her broad talent on screen. Aside from a charismatically blunt role in *Victor/Victoria* (which scooped her an Oscar nomination), she has more often been at the centre of efficient yet mundane offerings. Certainly, her charm in Disney family fare of the sixties could not have prepared us for this surprisingly hard-edged outing, in which she plays a mother so distraught over her daughter's assault that she shoots the suspected attacker. Warren gets excellent support from the likes of Bruce Davison, Shirley Knight and Annette O'Toole, while director Armand Mastroianni is admirably unsentimental in his approach to a difficult subject.

Lesley Ann Warren *Carol Sanders* • Bruce Davison *Bill Sanders* • Missy Crider *Jill Sanders* • Allison Mack *Wendy Sanders* •

Annette O'Toole *Ellen Wells* • David Byron Frank Warden • Shirley Knight *Bess Warden* ■ *Dir* Armand Mastroianni • *Scr* John Robert Bensink, from the novel by Richard Speight

Desperate Living ★★★★ 18

Satirical melodrama
1977 · US · Colour · 90mins

John Waters followed his two works of "accidental art" – *Pink Flamingos* and *Female Trouble* – with this lurid ensemble melodrama. Peggy Gravel (Mink Stole) is a highly-strung, bourgeois housewife whose quest for self-realisation and liberation leads her to a fascistic royal kingdom ruled by the very pink and vulgar Queen Carlotta (Edith Massey). The villagers are commanded to walk and dress backwards, while sex changes, rabies and auto-castration all work their magic into the plot. A woman's picture *par excellence*, the film may look cheap and cluttered, but it comes with a poignant ending that is endearingly apocalyptic.

Mink Stole *Peggy Gravel* • Edith Massey *Queen Carlotta* • Liz Renay *Muffy St Jacques* • Susan Lowe *Mole McHenry* • Mary Vivian Pearce *Princess Coo-Coo* • Jean Hill *Grizelda Brown* • Brook Blake *Bosley Gravel Jr* • Cookie Mueller *Flipper* ■ *Dir/Scr* John Waters

Desperate Measures ★★

Thriller 1995 · Ger/US · Colour · 90mins

This rather tasteless thriller chronicles the attempt of a childless American couple to kidnap the baby of the German nanny they had hired in the middle of what turned out to be a phantom pregnancy. After so many sinister childminders down the years, the fact that Nicolette Krebitz is the endangered party gives this straight-to-video offering some sort of curiosity value. For all the leering malevolence of Matt McCoy and Marita Geraghty, however, director Nikolai Müllerschön fails to generate a sense of menace.

Nicolette Krebitz *Anna Richter* • Matt McCoy *Derek Mitchelson* • Marita Geraghty *Carla Mitchelson* • Marco Leonardi *Eddie Sanchez* • Paul Winfield *William Stone* • Carroll Baker *Elaine Mitchelson* ■ *Dir* Nikolai Müllerschön • *Scr* Jennifer Grusskopf

Desperate Measures ★★ 15

Thriller 1998 · US · Colour · 96mins

A good premise, a great cast and an excellent director (Barbet Schroeder) amounts to very little in a dumb thriller that rapidly goes downhill. In order to save his ill son, cop Andy Garcia needs the rare bone marrow of the very unhinged Michael Keaton. Initially an intriguing variant on *The Silence of the Lambs*, this disappointingly develops into an implausible action thriller as the overacting Keaton runs amok in a hospital and Garcia begins to regret his decision. So idiotic at times you wonder if anybody actually read the script before signing on.

Michael Keaton *Peter McCabe* • Andy Garcia *Frank Connor* • Brian Cox *Captain Jeremiah Cassidy* • Marcia Gay Harden *Dr Samantha Hawkins* • Erik King *Nate Oliver* • Efrain Figueroa *Vargus* • Joseph Cross *Matthew Conner* • Janel Maloney *Sarah Davis* ■ *Dir* Barbet Schroeder • *Scr* David Klass

Desperate Moment ★★★ U

Mystery thriller 1953 · UK · BW · 88mins

This was one of several films in which handsome young Dirk Bogarde played a fugitive on the run, prior to consolidating his popularity and stardom with the following year's *Doctor in the House*. The meaningless title conceals a ludicrous plot in which Bogarde, believing girlfriend Mai Zetterling is dead, confesses to a murder he did not commit. When he discovers she is still alive, they go off to catch the real villain. Director Compton Bennett (*The Seventh Veil*) fails to get a grip on the narrative, and who could blame him? Luckily, the stars make it entertaining enough that you don't really care what's going on.

Dirk Bogarde *Simon von Halder* • Mai Zetterling *Anna de Burgh* • Philip Friend *Robert Sawyer* • Albert Lieven *Paul* • Frederick Wendhousen *Grote* • Carl Jaffe *Becker* • Gerard Heinz *Bones* • Andre Mikhelson *Inspector* ■ *Dir* Compton Bennett • *Scr* Patrick Kirwan, George H Brown, from the novel by Martha Albrand

Desperate Remedies ★★★ 18

Period drama 1993 · NZ · Colour · 89mins

The liaisons are more dangerous, the ladies more wicked and the obsessions even more magnificent in this extraordinary historical (not to say hysterical) soap opera from New Zealand. Fabulously stylised sets, amazing design and deafening opera music accompany this gaudy Brontë-esque tale about the fall of high society draper Jennifer Ward-Lealand when she hires a penniless immigrant to marry her opium-addicted sister. John Waters camp meets Pedro Almodóvar's kitsch imagery in this little gem, co-directed by Stewart Main and Peter Wells. Contains violence, swearing, drug abuse and nudity.

Jennifer Ward-Lealand *Dorothea Brook* • Kevin Smith *Lawrence Hayes* • Lisa Chappell *Anne Cooper* • Cliff Curtis *Fraser* • Michael Hurst *William Poyser* • Kiri Mills *Rose* ■ *Dir/Scr* Stewart Main, Peter Wells • *Production Designer* Michael Kane • *Set Designer* Shane Radford

Desperate Rescue ★★

Thriller 1993 · US · Colour · 100mins

Shades of the Sally Field weepie *Not without My Daughter* echo through this routine thriller. Cast against type, Mariel Hemingway plays a distraught American mother who takes extreme measures when her Jordanian ex-husband kidnaps their daughter. Hemingway is competent in the lead role, although James Russo steals most of his scenes. The action is handled blandly but efficiently by TV movie veteran Richard Colla.

Mariel Hemingway *Cathy Mahone* • Jeff Kober *JD Roberts* • James Russo *Feeney* • Clancy Brown *Dave Chattelaar* • Lindsey Haun *Lauren Mahone* • Andrew Masset *Ali* ■ *Dir* Richard Colla [Richard A Colla] • *Scr* Guerdon Trueblood

Desperate Search ★★★

Adventure drama 1952 · US · BW · 71mins

One of those co-features turned out by MGM that were often much better than

the main picture. This is a tight little drama, beautifully directed by Joseph H Lewis, a former film editor who became the cult director of such terrific films as *Gun Crazy* and *The Big Combo*. The always under-rated Howard Keel, a major star over this period, said that this unheralded little black-and-white movie was his personal favourite among his films, and he and Jane Greer are exceptionally fine as the parents of two children who are missing after a plane crash.

Howard Keel *Vince Heldon* • Jane Greer *Julie Heldon* • Patricia Medina *Nora Stead* • Keenan Wynn *Brandy* • Robert Burton *Wayne* • Lee Aaker *Don* • Linda Lowell *Janet* ■ *Dir* Joseph Lewis [Joseph H Lewis] • *Scr* Walter Doniger, from the novel by Arthur Mayse

The Desperate Trail ★★

Western 1995 · US · Colour · 93mins

A somewhat confused western, this can't seem to make up its mind whether it's a comedy romp or a more serious revenge tale. It doesn't help that its young stars – Linda Fiorentino, Craig Sheffer, Frank Whaley – are less than convincing in western garb, playing a mismatched trio thrown into a life of crime. However, Sam Elliott, as the vengeful lawman on their trail, provides some much needed, gritty authenticity. Contains violence, swearing, nudity and sexual situations.

Sam Elliott *Marshall Bill Speakes* • Craig Sheffer *Jack Cooper* • Linda Fiorentino *Sarah O'Rourke* • Frank Whaley *Walter Cooper* • John Furlong *Zeb Hollister* • Robin Westphal *Mamie Hollister* ■ *Dir* PJ Pesce • *Scr* PJ Pesce, Tom Abrams

Desperately Seeking Susan ★★★★ 15

Comedy thriller 1985 · US · Colour · 99mins

A delightful and funny movie, most notable for the fact that Madonna is actually very good in it. She's the free-living, wildly dressed Susan who trades messages with her lover in the *New York Times*, while Rosanna Arquette is Roberta, the bored housewife who follows the ads until a bump on the head leads her to believe she actually is Susan. What makes this movie so enjoyable are the performances of the two lead women, both of whom turn out to be tough and desirable at the same time. They are ably supported by Mark Blum as Roberta's moronic husband and Aidan Quinn as the man even the strongest woman could not resist being rescued by. Utterly charming. Contains swearing.

Rosanna Arquette *Roberta Glass* • Madonna *Susan* • Aidan Quinn *Dez* • Mark Blum *Gary Glass* • Robert Joy *Jim* • Laurie Metcalf *Leslie Glass* • Will Patton *Wayne Nolan* • Steven Wright *Larry Stillman* • John Turturro *Ray* ■ *Dir* Susan Seidelman • *Scr* Leora Barish

Destination: America ★★ PG

Crime drama 1987 · US · Colour · 94mins

It's hard to see how this barnstorming melodrama could have been more far-fetched. The feud between the rebellious Bruce Greenwood and his grandiose father, Rip Torn, would have sufficed, but there's also a maniacal trucker who resorts to theft and kidnap to get back at his feisty wife, Corinne

Bohrer, plus a murder thrown in for good measure. Director Corey Allen struggles to keep the plot in check and only the bullish Torn emerges with his reputation intact from this TV movie. 🖵

Bruce Greenwood *Corbet St James V* • Corinne Bohrer *Tricia* • Rip Torn *Corbet St James IV* • Robert Newman *David St James* • Alan Autry *Larry Leathergood* • Joe Pantoliano *Lieutenant Mike Amico* ■ *Dir* Corey Allen • *Scr* Patrick Hasburgh

Destination Gobi ★★ U
Second World War drama
1953 · US · Colour · 89mins

A US Navy contingent sent to observe weather conditions in the Gobi desert join forces with the Mongol hordes to fight the Japanese. Richard Widmark delivers his usual no-nonsense performance in this load of old nonsense, which claims to be a true story. Robert Wise, later the director of *The Sound of Music* and *The Sand Pebbles*, keeps the desert scenery shifting while the story, which even finds time for romance between a marine and a Mongol maiden, remains fairly static.

Richard Widmark *CPO Sam McHale* • Don Taylor *Jenkins* • Casey Adams [Max Showalter] *Walter Landers* • Murvyn Vye *Kengtu* • Darryl Hickman *Wilbur Cohen* • Martin Milner *Elwood Halsey* ■ *Dir* Robert Wise • *Scr* Everett Freeman, from a story by Edmund G Love

Destination Moon ★★★ U
Science-fiction
1950 · US · Colour · 91mins

Intended to be the first realistic film about space exploration, producer George Pal's fun effort was beaten into cinemas by the exploitation quickie *Rocketship X-M*. But that didn't have an animated lecture on the principles of space travel hosted by Woody Woodpecker! Co-scripted by science fiction great Robert A Heinlein, the pedestrian tale of man's first lunar landing has dated badly. Yet the enthralling look, taken straight from the pulp fiction illustrations of the day, is enchanting and colourful and the special effects (which won an Oscar) are impressive for the era. 🖵

Warner Anderson *Dr Charles Cargraves* • John Archer *Jim Barnes* • Tom Powers *Gen Thayer* • Dick Wesson *Joe Sweeney* • Erin O'Brien-Moore *Emily Cargraves* ■ *Dir* Irving Pichel • *Scr* Rip van Ronkel, Robert A Heinlein, James O'Hanlon • *Special Effects* Lee Zavitz • *Cartoon Sequence* Walter Lantz • *Production Designer* Ernst Fegte

Destination Murder ★★
Thriller
1950 · US · BW · 72mins

Stanley Clements had played young thug roles in some decent movies (notably *Going My Way*). Married to Oscar-winning actress Gloria Grahame, he never managed to turn his teenage toughness into adult charm. This is an average Clements B-movie, of interest only to collectors, though Joyce MacKenzie makes a pert co-star. Clements wound up his career supporting the Bowery Boys and died an alcoholic recluse, but he left behind an enduring image of petty toughness.

Joyce MacKenzie *Laura Mansfield* • Stanley Clements *Jackie Wales* • Hurd Hatfield *Stretch*

Norton • Albert Dekker *Armitage* • Myrna Dell *Alice Wentworth* • James Flavin *Lt Brewster* ■ *Dir* Edward L Cahn • *Scr* Don Martin

Destination Tokyo ★★★ U
Second World War drama
1943 · US · BW · 129mins

"Here is a film," said *Variety* at the time, "whose hero is the Stars and Stripes; the performers are merely symbols of that heroism." And flag-wavers rarely come as patriotic as this: more than two hours with Cary Grant and John Garfield as they steer their submarine towards Tokyo. Their mission is to land a meteorologist secretly in Japan to tell an aircraft carrier's bombers when the weather will be clear enough for an attack. Getting there is the real story as the sub runs the underwater gauntlet of depth charges and the usual on-board mishaps. Grant, as the captain, does his best in a cardboard role, though Garfield does better as the womaniser with no women around. 🖵

Cary Grant *Captain Cassidy* • John Garfield *Wolf* • Alan Hale *Cookie* • John Ridgely *Reserve* • Dane Clark *Tin Can* • Warner Anderson *Executive* • William Prince *Pills* • Robert Hutton *Tommy* • Tom Tully *Mike* ■ *Dir* Delmer Daves • *Scr* Albert Maltz, from a story by Steve Fisher

Destiny ★★★★
Silent fantasy drama
1921 · Ger · BW · 79mins

Luis Buñuel once claimed that *Destiny* "opened my eyes to the poetic expressiveness of the cinema". This dark and mystical allegory was Fritz Lang's first notable critical success, and it remains impressive for its range of mood, the mastery of its visual composition, its extravagant settings and its special effects. Written by Lang with Thea von Harbou (whom he married in 1924), it's the story of a wife (Lil Dagover) who begs Death to spare her husband's life.

Lil Dagover *Fiancée/Zobeide/Fiametta/Tiao Tsien* • Walter Janssen *Fiancé/European/Liang* • Bernhard Goetzke *Death/El Mot/Archer* • Rudolf Klein-Rogge *Girolamo* • Lewis Brody *The Moor* ■ *Dir* Fritz Lang • *Scr* Fritz Lang, Thea von Harbou

Destiny of a Man ★★★★
Drama
1959 · USSR · BW · 102mins

Having left his wife and children to fight on the Front during the Second World War, Sergei Bondarchuk is taken prisoner by the Nazis and sent to a concentration camp. He escapes and returns home to find that his family is dead. A powerfully realistic and much acclaimed Russian film, this marks the directing debut of the legendary actor Bondarchuk. He gives a searing portrayal of an ordinary man's despair and courage, and he captures all too graphically the horror of the war as experienced by the Russians. Winner of the best film award at the first Moscow Film Festival, this is heavyweight stuff, lifted by a message of hope at the end. Russian dialogue dubbed into English.

Sergei Bondarchuk *Andrei Sokolov* • Zinaida Kirienko *Irina* • Pavlik Boriskin *Vanyushka* • Pavel Volkov *Ivan Timofeyevich* • Yuri Averin

Myuller ■ *Dir* Sergei Bondarchuk • *Scr* Yuri Lukin, Fyodor Shakhmagonov, from a novel by Mikhail Sholokhov

Destiny Turns on the Radio ★ 15
Comedy fantasy 1995 · US · Colour · 98mins

Self-consciously quirky comedy with a clumsy dollop of mysticism dumped on top. Dylan McDermott stars as an escaped convict returning to Las Vegas to reclaim his stolen cash; Nancy Travis plays his singer ex-girlfriend. Both give charmless performances, while Quentin Tarantino's embarrassing turn as supernatural stalker Johnny (the supposedly hip embodiment of destiny), could be the worst acting work by a director ever. There are few things more excruciating than a film that honestly believes itself to be offbeat, cool and clever. This one fails on every level 🖵

James LeGros *Thoreau* • Dylan McDermott *Julian* • Quentin Tarantino *Johnny Destiny* • Nancy Travis *Lucille* • James Belushi *Tuerto* • Janet Carroll *Escabel* ■ *Dir* Jack Baran • *Scr* Robert Ramsey, Matthew Stone

Destroy All Monsters ★★★ PG
Science-fiction fantasy
1968 · Jap · Colour · 85mins

Alien Kilaaks unleash Toho Studios' entire repertory company of rubber-suited, scaly behemoths to raze a selection of capital cities in this, the ultimate Japanese monster movie. Godzilla attacks New York, Mothra invades Peking and Rodan obliterates Moscow, while Wenda, Baragon and Spigas, the mega-spider from *Son of Godzilla*, all make appearances. Even three-headed Ghidrah shows up for this mighty marathon, which features a zany comic-strip plot, hilariously wooden acting, atrocious dubbing and special effects miniatures that make *Thunderbirds* look like *Terminator 2*. What are you waiting for? Set the video immediately! Japanese dialogue dubbed into English. 🖵

Akira Kubo *Flight Captain* • Jun Tazaki *Dr Yoshido* • Yoshio Tsuchiya *Dr Otani* • Kyoko Ai *Queen of the Kilaaks* ■ *Dir* Ishiro Honda [Inoshiro Honda] • *Scr* Kaoru Mabuchi, Ishiro Honda

Destroyer ★★
Action thriller 1988 · US · Colour · 94mins

Former football player Lyle Alzado plays Ivan Moser, a vicious serial killer on his way to the electric chair who vanishes mysteriously during a sudden prison riot. Eighteen months later, a film crew headed by Anthony Perkins arrives at the abandoned prison to shoot a women-in-prison movie. When the crew start disappearing... Perkins displays a flair for light comedy as the B-director who takes his craft very seriously, while Alzado has definite screen presence. None of the other actors show the least bit of enthusiasm, however, and most of the predictable proceedings are made up of endless scenes of people shuffling down hallways before their inevitable slashing.

Anthony Perkins *Director Edwards* • Lyle Alzado *Ivan Moser* • Deborah Foreman *Susan Malone* • Clayton Rohner *David Harris* • Jim

Turner *Rewire* • Lannie Garrett *Sharon Fox* • Tobias Andersen *Russell* ■ *Dir* Robert Kirk • *Scr* Peter Garrity, Rex Hauck

Destry ★★★
Western 1954 · US · Colour · 94mins

Good fun, especially for fans of baby-faced Audie Murphy and lovers of Universal westerns of the fifties, until you realise this is a remake of the superb James Stewart/Marlene Dietrich film *Destry Rides Again*, itself a reworking of an early Tom Mix classic. It isn't up to those distinguished predecessors, and shouldn't really be judged against them as it was made for a whole new generation of film-goers. Murphy is ideally cast, but blonde sexpot Mari Blanchard just ain't Dietrich.

Audie Murphy *Tom Destry* • Mari Blanchard *Brandy* • Lyle Bettger *Decker* • Lori Nelson *Martha Phillips* • Thomas Mitchell *Rags Barnaby* • Edgar Buchanan *Mayor Hirim Sellers* • Wallace Ford *Doc Curtis* ■ *Dir* George Marshall • *Scr* Edmund H North, DD Beauchamp, from a story by Felix Jackson, from the novel *Destry Rides Again* by Max Brand

Destry Rides Again ★★★★★
Comedy western 1939 · US · BW · 94mins

Remembered today for its rollicking good humour and the fabulous Marlene Dietrich performing *See What the Boys in the Back Room Will Have*, this is one of those comedy westerns that has a universal appeal. Lanky and loveable James Stewart is Tom Destry, who manages to clean up the lawless town of Bottle Neck by using a slow drawl rather than a quick draw. Chief villain is scowling, snide Brian Donlevy, and there's marvellous character support from Mischa Auer, Charles Winninger and Allen Jenkins. Dietrich, cast against type, and Stewart, in his first western lead, strike sparks off one another (and in real life, too!), and the cat-fight between Dietrich and Una Merkel has never been bettered. Director George Marshall keeps well back, and some may find his style rather flat, but he created a comedy classic.

Marlene Dietrich *Frenchy* • James Stewart *Tom Destry* • Mischa Auer *Boris Callahan* • Charles Winninger *"Wash" Dimsdale* • Brian Donlevy *Kent* • Allen Jenkins *Gyp Watson* • Warren Hymer *Bugs Watson* • Billy Gilbert *Loupgeron* • Una Merkel *Lily Belle Callahan* ■ *Dir* George Marshall • *Scr* Felix Jackson, Henry Meyers, Gertrude Purcell, from the novel by Max Brand

The Detective ★★★ 15
Crime drama 1968 · US · Colour · 109mins

Cynical New York police detective Joe Leland (Frank Sinatra) is called upon to solve a case involving the brutal murder of a gay man. What follows is a hard-hitting, well-paced drama that takes swipes at slipshod policing and corruption in City Hall and features one of Sinatra's best performances. Lee Remick and Jacqueline Bisset also star, while Robert Duvall pops up in a small early role. Sadly, the film's attitude towards homosexuality and sex – considered daring back in 1968 – now gives it a dated air. 🖵

Frank Sinatra *Joe Leland* • Lee Remick *Karen Leland* • Ralph Meeker *Curran* • Jack Klugman

Dave Schoenstein • Jacqueline Bisset *Norma MacIver* • Horace McMahon *Farrell* • Lloyd Bochner *Dr Roberts* • William Windom *Colin MacIver* • Robert Duvall *Nestor* • Sugar Ray Robinson *Kelly* ■ *Dir* Gordon Douglas • *Scr* Abby Mann, from the novel by Roderick Thorp

Detective ★★★ 15

Detective thriller 1985 · Fr · Colour · 93mins

It's rare that one of French director Jean-Luc Godard's movies actually aims to entertain but *Detective* does, being a jokey movie about detective movies in which various characters try to solve a murder committed in a once-luxury Paris hotel two years earlier. The plot sprouts myriad subplots and Godard dedicates the picture to Clint Eastwood, John Cassavetes and cult forties director Edgar G Ulmer because, well, why not? Newish things Nathalie Baye and Johnny Hallyday pleased the contemporary audience, while New Wave icons like Claude Brasseur and Jean-Pierre Léaud bring nostalgia to the party. In French with English subtitles.

Claude Brasseur *Emile Chenal* • Nathalie Baye *Francoise Chenal* • Johnny Hallyday *Jim Fox-Warner* • Laurent Terzieff *Detective William Prospero* • Jean-Pierre Léaud *Nephew* • Alain Cuny *Old Mafioso* • Stephane Ferrara *Tiger Jones* • Emmanuelle Seigner *Grace Kelly, miancée* • Julie Delpy *Wise young girl* ■ *Dir* Jean-Luc Godard • *Scr* Alain Sarde, Philippe Setbon, Anne-Marie Mieville, Jean-Luc Godard

Detective Sadie and Son ★★

Detective comedy 1987 · US · Colour

Debbie Reynolds is one of the last actresses you would expect to see playing an unconventional cop with a nose for clues and a liking for the rough stuff. But that's exactly what's on offer in this fast-moving crime TV film, in which she is teamed with her lackadaisical son on the case that will make or break her already chequered career. After seeing Debbie play vigilante you can just about swallow anything, and thanks to British director John Llewellyn Moxey her pursuit of a subway killer is often entertaining.

Debbie Reynolds *Sadie Rothman* • Brian McNamara *Nolie Rothman* • Sam Wanamaker *Marty* • Cynthia Dale *Paula* • David Ferry *Captain Ruggles* ■ *Dir* John Llewellyn Moxey • *Scr* Carl Kleinschmitt

Detective Story ★★★★

Crime drama 1951 · US · BW · 117mins

Sidney Kingsley's smash-hit play about the ugliness of life as seen from the squad room of a drab police station loses none of its claustrophic intensity on screen under William Wyler's resourceful direction. Kirk Douglas is memorable as the cop who despises weakness and wrongdoing, only to find that his intolerance is his undoing. Lee Grant and Joseph Wiseman were imported from the Broadway production for their showy parts of simple-minded shoplifter and dope-addicted three-time loser. But many others are equally good, including William Bendix (fellow cop), Eleanor Parker (Douglas's wife) and George Macready (despicable abortionist). Only the wet young lovers (Cathy O'Donnell and Craig Hill) are a pain, but at least the Hollywood censors permitted abortion to be retained as an issue.

Kirk Douglas *Det James McLeod* • Eleanor Parker *Mary McLeod* • William Bendix *Det Lou Brody* • Lee Grant *Shoplifter* • Bert Freed *Det Dakis* • Frank Faylen *Det Gallagher* • Horace McMahon *Lt Monaghan* • Craig Hill *Arthur Kindred* • George Macready *Karl Schneider* • Joseph Wiseman *Charley Gennini* • Cathy O'Donnell *Susan Carmichael* ■ *Dir* William Wyler • *Scr* Philip Yordan, Robert Wyler, from the play by Sidney Kingsley

Detour ★★★★ U

Road movie thriller 1945 · US · BW · 65mins

A remarkably pacey and stylish B-movie thriller that's now rightly recognised as a minor classic. It's a fitting tribute to skilled director Edgar G Ulmer, who made this hard-boiled little gem in just six days. Lead Tom Neal's lack of acting ability actually helps the stark tale of a hitchhiker buffeted by fate, and the remarkable Ann Savage creates the kind of *femme fatale* you wouldn't want to meet in the dark. The clever use of night shooting and a score seemingly made up from Chopin's out-takes enhance the grimy tale which, despite its ultimately weak resolution, is a deeply satisfying example of what enthusiasts today refer to as *film noir*. Ulmer would have laughed at the term.

Tom Neal *Al Roberts* • Ann Savage *Vera* • Claudia Drake *Sue* • Edmund MacDonald *Charles Haskell Jr* • Tim Ryan *Diner proprietor* • Esther Howard *Hedy* • Roger Clark *Dillon* ■ *Dir* Edgar G Ulmer • *Scr* Martin Goldsmith

Detour ★

Crime thriller 1992 · US · Colour · 89mins

A deeply obscure, no-budget thriller with more than a touch of the Ed Woods about it. Seemingly a remake of a well-respected 1945 thriller from Edgar G Ulmer that starred Tom Neal, this one stars, er, Tom Neal Jr as the hitchhiker who gets caught up with *femme fatales*. Topping up the oddness quotient is Susanna Foster, who was groomed for stardom alongside Judy Garland and made a string of movies in the late thirties and forties. She then vanished completely from sight, popping up here over four decades later. Clearly, the story behind the film is a lot more interesting than the film itself.

Tom Neal Jr *Al Roberts* • Lea Lavish *Vera* • Erin McGrane *Sue Harvey* • Duke Howze *Charles Haskell* • Susanna Foster *Evvy* • Brad Bittiker *Cowboy* ■ *Dir* Wade Williams III • *Scr* Roger Hull, Wade Williams III, from the film by Martin Goldsmith

Detroit 9000 ★★ 18

Blaxploitation crime thriller 1973 · US · Colour · 102mins

A crudely photographed and relentlessly violent cops-and-robbers thriller, blaxploitation style. Jewel thieves make off with $400,000 of loot from attendees at a black congressman's fundraiser in Detroit, the murder capital of the world. Two cops – one black, the other white – are assigned to the case, which plonks the usual clichés (pimps, thugs, hookers and racial hatreds) into a mediocre mix of police procedural and crime drama. The title is police code for "officer needs assistance".

Alex Rocco *Lieutenant Danny Bassett* • Hari Rhodes *Sergeant Jesse Williams* • Vonetta McGee *Roby Harris* • Ella Edwards *Helen* • Scatman Crothers *Reverend Markham* ■ *Dir* Arthur Marks • *Scr* Orville Hampton, from a story by Arthur Marks, Orville Hampton

Detroit Rock City ★★★ 15

Comedy 1999 · US · Colour · 94mins

High school and the seventies have always been popular topics in Hollywood. In *Detroit Rock City* they meet head on, with a bit of road movie and country mouse comedy thrown in for good measure. With only the soundtrack to nail down the period, there's a universality about the adventures of four lads bunking off to Motown for a KISS concert. Virginities, anxieties and parent problems are laid to rest as manliness is exerted, toilets explode and disco gets trashed, but the inevitabilities are given nostalgic bravura by the pace and idiosyncrasy of *Mousehunt* scribe Adam Rifkin's direction. Contains swearing and sexual references.

Edward Furlong *Hawk* • Giuseppe Andrews *Lex* • James DeBello *Trip* • Sam Huntington *Jeremiah "Jam" Bruce* • Gene Simmons • Paul Stanley • Shannon Tweed *Amanda Finch* ■ *Dir* Adam Rifkin • *Scr* Carl V Dupré • *Producer* Gene Simmons, Barry Levine, Kathleen Haase

Deuce Bigalow: Male Gigolo ★★ 15

Comedy 1999 · US · Colour · 88mins

A taste-free comedy that will either have you laughing like a drain or looking for the nearest exit. Pitched low and hitting even lower, Mike Mitchell's movie is the latest addition to a mainstream "smut glut" spawned by the success of *There's Something about Mary* and *American Pie*. Rob Schneider plays an idiot aquarist who, while fish-sitting for a male escort, gets hooked into servicing a clientele of his own. His customers embrace every conceivable physical and mental imperfection, from Tourette syndrome to missing limbs.

Rob Schneider *Deuce Bigalow* • Arija Bareikis *Kate* • William Forsythe *Detective Chuck Fowler* • Eddie Griffin *TJ* • Oded Fehr *Antoine LeConte* • Gail O'Grady *Claire* • Richard Riehle *Bob Bigalow* ■ *Dir* Mike Mitchell • *Scr* Harris Goldberg, Rob Schneider

Le Deuxième Souffle ★★★

Crime thriller 1966 · Fr · BW · 149mins

From the opening homage to *A Man Escaped*, the influence of Robert Bresson can be felt throughout this intense investigation into that old cliché about honour among thieves. Yet this *noir*-ish mix of poetic realism and police procedural also bears the indelible imprint of Jean-Pierre Melville, even though the thrilling mountain heist is less typical of his precise style than the cat-and-mouse confrontation between escaped gangster Lino Ventura and circumspect detective Paul Meurisse. With fine support from the likes of Raymond Pellegrin, this proved a useful warm-up for Melville's next project, *Le Samouraï*. In French with English subtitles.

Lino Ventura *Gustave Minda* • Paul Meurisse *Inspector Blot* • Raymond Pellegrin *Paul Ricci* • Christine Fabrega *Manouche* • Pierre Zimmer *Orloff* • Marcel Bozzuffi *Ricci* ■ *Dir* Jean-Pierre Melville • *Scr* Jean-Pierre Melville, José Giovanni, from a novel by José Giovanni

Devi ★★★★ PG

Drama 1960 · Ind · BW · 100mins

Examining religious fanaticism, Satyajit Ray's first film after the completion of the Apu trilogy was briefly banned for being disrespectful towards the goddess Kali. But this is as much a study of rural superstition and the passing of a traditional way of life as a calculated assault on the Hindu faith. Exceptionally played, if occasionally melodramatic, it also explores the position of women in Indian society, as Chhabi Biswas destroys his 17-year-old daughter-in-law (Sharmila Tagore) after becoming convinced she is a divine reincarnation. Departing from his customarily rigorous realism, Ray enhances his powerful story with some hauntingly stylised imagery. In Bengali with English subtitles.

Soumitra Chatterjee *Umaprasad* • Sharmila Tagore *Doyamoyee* • Karuna Bannerjee *Harasundari* • Chhabi Biswas *Kalikinkar Roy* ■ *Dir/Scr* Satyajit Ray

The Devil and Max Devlin ★★ PG

Comedy 1981 · US · Colour · 91mins

In spite of Bill Cosby's wicked turn as the Devil, this mawkish "rat repents" tale has none of the uplifting charm that Disney clearly believed it possessed. Elliott Gould plays Max Devlin, a venal sinner who is offered the chance of salvation if he can lure three innocents into perdition. The hell sequences are easily the most inspired here; the remainder takes in the sights and sounds of Hollywood as Gould grants wishes to the gullible in return for their souls. The result is short on laughs, but awash with sentiment.

Elliott Gould *Max Devlin* • Bill Cosby *Barney Satin* • Susan Anspach *Penny Hart* • Adam Rich *Toby Hart* • Julie Budd *Stella Summers* • David Knell *Nerve Nordlinger* • Sonny Shroyer *Big Billy* • Charles Shamata [Chuck Shamata] *Jerry* ■ *Dir* Steven Hilliard Stern • *Scr* Mary Rodgers, from a story by Mary Rodgers, Jimmy Sangster

The Devil and Miss Jones ★★★ U

Comedy 1941 · US · BW · 92mins

Jean Arthur's smart, sassy brittleness can brighten up any comedy – including this one, which has a touch of Frank Capra in its bogus courting of socialist issues. Arthur plays a shopgirl who suddenly comes face to face with the big boss, zillionaire Charles Coburn, when he decides to get a taste of real life by posing as a shop assistant himself. It has its moments, but what it really needs is a proper leading man. Instead it has Robert Cummings, whose main interest is forming a union. Arthur's husband, Frank Ross, was the producer.

Jean Arthur *Mary Jones* • Robert Cummings *Joe* • Charles Coburn *John P Merrick* • Edmund Gwenn *Hooper* • Spring Byington *Elizabeth* • SZ Sakall *George* • William Demarest *First detective* • Walter Kingsford *Allison* • Montagu Love *Harrison* ■ *Dir* Sam Wood • *Scr* Norman Krasna

Devil and the Deep ★★

Drama   1932 · US · BW · 72mins

Submarine commander Charles Laughton is consumed with jealousy every time anybody so much as glances in the direction of his glamorous wife (Tallulah Bankhead). When he discovers she has formed a more-than-friendly alliance with Gary Cooper, Laughton takes extreme measures that backfire on him. Directed by Marion Gering (who was a man, by the way) and boasting an appearance by newcomer Cary Grant, this melodrama contrives to be both overheated and undernourished. Laughton, however, has a wonderful time in his first American film.

Tallulah Bankhead *Diana Sturm* • Gary Cooper *Lt Sempter* • Charles Laughton *Cmdr Charles Sturm* • Cary Grant *Lt Jaeckel* • Paul Porcasi *Hassan* • Juliette Compton *Mrs Planet* ■ *Dir* Marion Gering • *Scr* Benn W Levy, from a story by Harry Hervey, from the novel *Sirènes et Tritons, le Roman Du Sous-marin* by Maurice Larrouy

The Devil and the Nun ★★★★

Supernatural drama based on a true story
1960 · Pol · BW · 105mins

The winner of the Special Jury prize at Cannes, this intensely disturbing drama is based on the same occurrences at the French convent of Loudun that inspired Ken Russell's *The Devils*. While certainly a stylised representation, director Jerzy Kawalerowicz's version exhibits considerably more restraint in depicting the demonic possession of Ursuline superior Lucyna Winnicka, whose lusts not only consume the other sisters, but also drive devout exorcist Mieczyslaw Voit to murder in a bid to win her favour. This outward study of good and evil also contains veiled references to Poland's postwar political situation. In Polish with English subtitles.

Lucyna Winnicka *Mother Joan of the Angels* • Mieczyslaw Voit *Father Jozef Suryn/Rabbi* • Anna Ciepielewska *Sister Malgorzata* • Maria Chwalibóg *Awdosia* • Kazimierz Fabisiak *Father Brym* ■ *Dir* Jerzy Kawalerowicz • *Scr* Tadeusz Konwicki, Jerzy Kawalerowicz, from a story by Jaroslaw Iwaszkiewicz

The Devil at Four o'Clock ★★★ PG

Disaster adventure
1961 · US · Colour · 121mins

Director Mervyn LeRoy always enjoyed an exotic location, and this overlong Pacific island-set hokum was probably more fun to make than it is to watch. Our advice is to park your brains and enjoy old-fashioned Hollywood as it lurches into the sixties, exploding volcano and all. Cast as an agnostic convict, Frank Sinatra gets a chance to act with his idol Spencer Tracy, who never turned down an opportunity to play a priest, his original calling. Even though it constantly tries your patience, this adventure remains compulsively viewable because of the sheer star power on display. 〔CD〕

Spencer Tracy *Father Matthew Doonan* • Frank Sinatra *Harry* • Kerwin Mathews *Father Joseph Perreau* • Jean-Pierre Aumont *Jacques* • Grégoire Aslan *Marcel* • Alexander Scourby

---

Governor • Barbara Luna *Camille* • Cathy Lewis *Matron* ■ *Dir* Mervyn LeRoy • *Scr* Liam O'Brien, from the novel by Max Catto

Devil Bat ★★

Crime horror   1940 · US · BW · 68mins

One of the better-known films from Bela Lugosi's sad years on Poverty Row. In this tedious and predictable shocker, the *Dracula* star is in his other customary role, playing a mad scientist who takes revenge on his enemies by setting his giant killer bats on them. Although he is laughably hammy, fans rate his performance better than those he would later give for Monogram. The rest of the cast, including Dave O'Brien from *Reefer Madness* (1936), are adequate, but the bat effects are amateurish.

Bela Lugosi *Dr Paul Carruthers* • Suzanne Kaaren *Mary Heath* • Dave O'Brien *Johnny Layton* • Guy Usher *Henry Morton* • Yolande Mallott *Maxine* • Donald Kerr *One Shot Maguire* • Edward Mortimer *Martin Heath* ■ *Dir* Jean Yarbrough • *Scr* John Thomas Neville, from a story by George Bricker

The Devil Commands ★★★

Horror   1941 · US · BW · 61mins

Boris Karloff grabs the attention in one of the weirdest movies he made, playing an unhinged scientist trying to communicate with the dead (specifically, his late wife) via a brainwave recording contraption and stolen corpses. Vastly under-rated, time has been kind to director Edward Dmytryk's macabre miniature. Today, the quaint surrealist touches of wired-up bodies in diving suits give it a strangely quirky atmosphere, while Anne Revere's evil spiritualist adds further chills in a must-see for Karloff collectors.

Boris Karloff *Dr Julian Blair* • Richard Fiske *Dr Richard Sayles* • Amanda Duff *Anne Blair* • Anne Revere *Mrs Walters* • Ralph Penney *Karl* • Dorothy Adams *Mrs Marcy* ■ *Dir* Edward Dmytryk • *Scr* Robert D Andrews, Milton Gunzberg, from the novel *The Edge of Running Water* by William Sloane

Devil Dogs of the Air ★★

Drama   1935 · US · BW · 86mins

This is a very average piece of Marine Flying Corps hokum, with James Cagney and Pat O'Brien striking sparks off each other and air sequences that are a combination of back projection and library shots. It moves fast and looks good, but relies too much on the personalities of its stars. For Cagney fans only.

James Cagney *Thomas Jefferson "Tommy" O'Toole* • Pat O'Brien *Lt Bill Brannigan* • Margaret Lindsay *Betty Roberts* • Frank McHugh *Crash Kelly* • Helen Lowell *Ma Roberts* ■ *Dir* Lloyd Bacon • *Scr* Malcolm Stuart Boylan, Earl Baldwin

The Devil-Doll ★★★

Horror   1936 · US · BW · 77mins

The sight of Lionel Barrymore in drag adds a note of merriment to this engagingly bizarre tale of terror, which was the penultimate movie from director Tod Browning, Hollywood's first master of the macabre. Barrymore plays a wrongly convicted criminal who escapes from prison and poses as a sweet old dollmaker, exacting his

---

revenge by using a serum that shrinks people to Barbie size. The scares may be dated, but the miniaturised special effects, relying on oversized props, are still enthralling, and the offbeat fantasy atmosphere is highly unusual.

Lionel Barrymore *Paul Lavond, "Madame Mandelip"* • Maureen O'Sullivan *Lorraine Lavond* • Frank Lawton *Toto* • Robert Greig *Emil Coulvet* • Lucy Beaumont *Madame Lavond* • Henry B Walthall *Marcel* ■ *Dir* Tod Browning • *Scr* Garret Fort, Guy Endore, Erich von Stroheim, from a story by Tod Browning, from the novel *Burn, Witch, Burn!* by Abraham Merritt

Devil Doll ★★ 15

Horror   1964 · UK · BW · 76mins

Not Tod Browning's 1936 chiller, but a cheap British shocker that owes more than a little to the classic ventriloquist episode in *Dead of Night*. Surprisingly highly regarded in some quarters, this low budget exploitation movie features Bryant Halliday as the Great Vorelli, who has the knack of transferring souls into his ventriloquist's dummy. Canadian William Sylvester is the good guy, and Yvonne Romain is the leading lady. 〔CD〕

Bryant Halliday *The Great Vorelli* • William Sylvester *Mark English* • Yvonne Romain *Marianne* • Sandra Dorne *Vorelli's assistant* • Karel Stepanek *Dr Heller* • Francis De Wolff *Dr Keisling* • Nora Nicholson *Aunt Eva* • Philip Ray *Uncle Walter* ■ *Dir* Lindsay Shonteff • *Scr* George Barclay, Lance Z Hargreaves, from a story by Frederick E Smith

Devil in a Blue Dress ★★★★ 15

Crime thriller   1995 · US · Colour · 97mins

After his brilliant thriller *One False Move*, director Carl Franklin makes all the right moves with this *film noir*. It's a supremely stylish thriller that has Denzel Washington as a man with time on his hands who's hired to find a politician's girlfriend (Jennifer Beals), and in the process is framed for murder. The film has a timberyard full of sawn-off dialogue and enough high-voltage tension to work an electric chair. Contains violence, swearing, sex scenes and nudity. 〔CD〕 **DVD**

Denzel Washington *Ezekial "Easy" Rawlins* • Tom Sizemore *Dewitt Albright* • Jennifer Beals *Daphne Monet* • Don Cheadle *Mouse* • Maury Chaykin *Matthew Terell* • Terry Kinney *Todd Carter* • Mel Winkler *Joppy* • Albert Hall *Odell* • Lisa Nicole Carson *Coretta James* ■ *Dir* Carl Franklin • *Scr* Carl Franklin, from the novel by Walter Mosley

Devil in the Flesh ★★★

Romance   1946 · Fr · BW · 77mins

Based on Raymond Radiguet's semi-autobiographical novel and set during the last months of the First World War, this once controversial love story stars Micheline Presle as a young wife who embarks on an affair with a 17-year-old schoolboy (Gérard Philipe) while her husband is fighting at the Front. Directed by the Claude Autant-Lara, who was no stranger to controversy himself, the film sparked outrage in certain quarters for its uncritically sympathetic portrayal of lovers betraying a soldier away at war. Viewed now, it can be seen as a richly romantic and sensuous tale, supported

---

by two touching lead performances. A French language film.

Micheline Presle *Marthe Grangier* • Gérard Philipe *François Jaubert* • Jean Debucourt *Mons Jaubert* • Denise Grey *Mme Grangier* • Pierre Palau [Palau] *Mons Marin* • Jean Varas *Jacques Lacombe* • Jeanne Perez *Mme Marin* ■ *Dir* Claude Autant-Lara • *Scr* Jean Aurenche, Pierre Bost, from the novel *Le Diable au Corps* by Raymond Radiguet

The Devil Is a Sissy ★★

Drama   1936 · US · BW · 91mins

Three New York schoolboys – rich kid Freddie Bartholomew, whose parents are in the middle of a divorce, ordinary middle-class Jackie Cooper, and slum child Mickey Rooney – team up and get into trouble. Deftly directed by WS Van Dyke, this was designed to showcase three members of MGM's impressive roster of juvenile actors. Cooper was already an established star, Bartholomew was on the way up and Rooney was the least-known – though he would become the biggest name and most enduring talent of the three. They are the reason for watching an otherwise run-of-the-mill movie.

Freddie Bartholomew *Claude* • Jackie Cooper *"Buck" Murphy* • Mickey Rooney *"Gig" Stevens* • Ian Hunter *Jay Pierce* • Peggy Conklin *Rose* • Katherine Alexander *Hilda Pierce* • Gene Lockhart *Mr Murphy* ■ *Dir* WS Van Dyke • *Scr* John Lee Mahin, Richard Schayer, from a story by Rowland Brown

The Devil Is a Woman ★★★★★

Romantic drama   1935 · US · BW · 79mins

The film that archivist John Kobal described as "a shower of diamonds" and the one that Marlene Dietrich felt best captured her beauty was the final of seven vehicles engineered for her by director Josef von Sternberg, the "Leonardo of the lenses".In it she plays Concha Perez, a seductress who, during carnival week in the south of Spain, finds her two most devoted infatuees in a duel for her attentions. A triumph of lighting, make-up and design, *The Devil Is a Woman* is high camp stylisation of an unusually luxuriant kind, relentlessly amusing but not remotely silly. Even bemused viewers will delight at Dietrich's sublimely ridiculous costumes as well as some of Hollywood's most awe-inspiring imagery. The unobtainable object of desire has never been more sumptuously captured.

Marlene Dietrich *Concha Perez* • Lionel Atwill *Don Pasqual* • Edward Everett Horton *Don Paquito* • Alison Skipworth *Señora Perez* • Cesar Romero *Antonio Galvan* • Don Alvarado *Morenito* • Tempe Pigott *Tuerta* • Paco Moreno *Secretary* ■ *Dir* Josef von Sternberg • *Scr* John Dos Passos, SK Winston, from the novel and play *La Femme et le Pantin (The Woman and the Puppet)* by Pierre Louys • *Cinematographer* Josef von Sternberg, Lucien Ballard • *Costume Designer* Travis Banton • *Art Director* Josef von Sternberg, Hans Dreier

The Devil Makes Three ★★ U

Drama   1952 · US · BW · 90mins

An effective thriller, filmed in Bavaria, that enabled MGM to satisfy the "I must do non-musicals" clause in Gene Kelly's contract and use up their post-

U = SUITABLE FOR ALL   **Uc** = SUITABLE FOR ALL, ESPECIALLY FOR YOUNG CHILDREN (VIDEO ONLY)   **PG** = PARENTAL GUIDANCE

war frozen Deutschmarks. Andrew Marton directs with verve but little regard for pace; he also fails to stop a miscast Kelly mugging as a counterintelligence officer who returns to Munich to find the German family who saved his life during the war. Pier Angeli, whose sincerity and talent enhanced every movie in which she appeared, brightens up the grim proceedings, while Richard Egan brings some grit to the action. After a while, though, you really couldn't care less about the black market plot.

Gene Kelly *Capt Jeff Eliot* • Pier Angeli *Wilhelmina Lehrt* • Richard Rober *Col James Terry* • Richard Egan *Lt Parker* • Claus Clausen *Heisemann* • Wilfried Seyferth *Hansig* ▪ *Dir* Andrew Marton • *Scr* Jerry Davis, from the story by Lawrence Bachmann

Devil on Horseback ★★ U

Drama   1954 · UK · BW · 93mins

The young son of a miner becomes a successful jockey, but his cruel tendency to flog the horses has disastrous consequences. Juvenile star Jeremy Spenser is the focus of this British film, directed by Cyril Frankel. Well acted by a cast that features husband-and-wife team Googie Withers and John McCallum, along with Liam Redmond and Sam Kydd as jockeys, it's strong on atmosphere and story. Sadly, the film suffers from lack of pace, disappointing racing sequences and an overdose of sentimentality.

Googie Withers *Mrs Jane Cadell* • John McCallum *Charles Roberts* • Jeremy Spenser *Moppy Parfitt* • Meredith Edwards *Ted Fellowes* • Liam Redmond *"Scarlett" O'Hara* • Sam Kydd *Darky* • Malcolm Knight *Squib* ▪ *Dir* Cyril Frankel • *Scr* Neil Paterson, Montagu Slater, from a story by James Curtis

The Devil, Probably ★★ 18

Drama   1977 · Fr · Colour · 91mins

Although it won a prestigious award at Berlin, Robert Bresson's most earnest film is also his least engaging. In having 20-year-old student Antoine Monnier pay a junkie to stage his "suicide" in Père Lachaise (the Parisian cemetery containing many national luminaries), Bresson is clearly lamenting the death of individualism in an indifferent world. However, he is unable to find a suitable motive for the crime. Militant ecologist Henri de Maublanc blames society's ills on pollution and famine, but others seek political, spiritual, cultural and psychological causes. Each case is cogently argued, but the debate never fires the intellect. In French with English subtitles. ▭

Antoine Monnier *Charles* • Tina Irissari *Alberte* • Henri de Maublanc *Michel* • Laelita Carcano *Edwige* • Regis Hanrion *Dr Mime* • Nicolas Deguy *Valentin* • Geoffroy Gaussen *Bookseller* ▪ *Dir/Scr* Robert Bresson

The Devil Rides Out ★★★ 15

Horror   1968 · UK · Colour · 91mins

As a Satanic spectacular, this is the business, even if, for once in a Hammer horror, Christopher Lee is on the side of virtue. Director Terence Fisher searches for credibility in Dennis Wheatley's trashy tale of the Duc de Richleau (Lee) trying to save Patrick Mower's soul from the clutches of

Charles Gray, a rotted limb of Satan. Whatever cynical giggles this might cause are soon flattened by the deadpan approach, some seriously orgiastic production numbers and a scary script from the ever-reliable Richard Matheson that's guaranteed to get your goose bumps rising. ▭

Christopher Lee *Duc De Richleau* • Charles Gray *Mocata* • Nike Arrighi *Tanith* • Leon Greene *Rex* • Patrick Mower *Simon* • Gwen Ffrangcon-Davies *Countess* • Sarah Lawson *Marie* • Paul Eddington *Richard* ▪ *Dir* Terence Fisher • *Scr* Richard Matheson, from the novel by Dennis Wheatley

The Devil's General ★★★

War drama   1955 · W Ger · BW · 96mins

Featuring an award-winning performance from Curt Jurgens and based on a play by Carl Zuckmayer, this West German-made drama was inspired by the life of Ernst Udets, the highest-ranking German air ace to have survived the Great War, who took his own life just prior to the Second World War because of his disgust with Hitler. In Helmut Käutner's version, Jurgens is General Harras of the Luftwaffe, a loyal patriot and officer, driven to extremes by his abhorrence of the Nazi regime. The stalwart German actor is excellent and the movie is well made and engrossing. In German with English subtitles.

Curt Jurgens *General Harras* • Victor de Kowa *Schmidt-Lausitz* • Karl John *Oderbruch* • Eva-Ingeborg Scholz *Fräulein Mohrungen* • Marianne Koch *Dorothea Geiss* • Albert Lieven *Oberst Eilers* ▪ *Dir* Helmut Käutner • *Scr* Georg Hurdalek, Helmut Käutner, from a play by Carl Zuckmayer

The Devil-Ship Pirates ★★★ PG

Historical swashbuckling drama
1964 · UK · Colour · 82mins

Christopher Lee received top-billing for the first time in this agreeable Hammer excursion into swashbuckling costume drama. He's the Spanish Captain Robeles, looting the English coast during the Armada era, who hits on a daring plan to save his crew when his ship runs aground – seal off the area and convince the locals Spain has conquered England. Does it work? You won't get bored finding out, especially as Hammer delivers its usual topnotch production values and Lee indulges in some splendid sword fighting. ▭

Christopher Lee *Captain Robeles* • Andrew Keir *Tom* • John Cairney *Harry* • Duncan Lamont *Bosun* • Michael Ripper *Pepe* • Ernest Clark *Sir Basil* • Barry Warren *Manuel* ▪ *Dir* Don Sharp • *Scr* Jimmy Sangster

The Devil Thumbs a Ride ★★★

Thriller   1947 · US · BW · 62mins

Short and sharp, writer/director Felix Feist's low-budget gem features a no-nonsense performance from Lawrence Tierney, 44 years before his memorable turn as crime boss Joe Cabot in Quentin Tarantino's *Reservoir Dogs*. Here he plays a hitchhiker, picked up by innocent motorist Ted North, who soon reveals himself to be an amoral killer. Tierney's electrifying presence overcomes the talky script

and lifts this rarely seen thriller to the status of minor classic.

Lawrence Tierney *Steve* • Ted North *Jimmy* • Nan Leslie *Carol* • Betty Lawford *Agnes* • Andrew Tombes *Joe Brayden* • Harry Shannon *Owens* • Glenn Vernon *Jack* • Marian Carr *Diane* ▪ *Dir* Felix Feist • *Scr* Felix Feist, from the novel by Robert C DuSoe

The Devil to Pay ★★★ U

Comedy   1930 · US · BW · 69mins

Ronald Colman's dashing good looks made him a star in the silent era, but what really consolidated his appeal and catapulted him to the ranks of the all-time movie greats was the coming of sound. It revealed an elegant speaking voice that, when gently softened for the American market, became every male's ideal. This early talkie creaks a bit now, but clearly confirms Colman's magnetic screen presence, despite the primitive recording techniques. Colman co-stars with two luminous ladies near the start of their illustrious careers: Loretta Young and Myrna Loy. A real curio that's well worth watching. ▭

Ronald Colman *Willie Leeland* • Loretta Young *Dorothy Hope* • Florence Britton *Susan Leeland* • Frederick Kerr *Lord Leeland* • David Torrence *Mr Hope* • Mary Forbes *Mrs Hope* • Paul Cavanagh *Grand Duke Paul* • Myrna Loy *Mary Carlyle* ▪ *Dir* George Fitzmaurice • *Scr* Benjamin Glazer, Frederick Lonsdale, from a play by Frederick Lonsdale

The Devils ★★★★ 18

Historical drama
1971 · UK · Colour · 106mins

Ken Russell's adaptation of Aldous Huxley's *The Devils of Loudun* is repulsive, hysterical, disturbing, overwhelming, stunning, compelling and fascinating. For once, Russell's surreal hallucinogenic style matches his frenzied material and, while condemned as being anti-religious, this is in fact a highly moral tale of absolute faith. In one of the most controversial and censored films of all time, Oliver Reed gives his best ever performance as the 17th-century French priest destroyed by political manipulators, and Vanessa Redgrave is almost as good as a humpbacked nun; Derek Jarman's sets are nearly a match for them both, however. Contains violence, swearing, sex scenes, drug abuse and nudity. ▭

Oliver Reed *Father Urbain Grandier* • Vanessa Redgrave *Sister Jeanne* • Dudley Sutton *Baron de Laubardemont* • Max Adrian *Ibert* • Gemma Jones *Madeleine* • Murray Melvin *Mignon* • Michael Gothard *Father Barre* • Georgina Hale *Philippe* ▪ *Dir* Ken Russell • *Scr* Ken Russell, from the play by John Whiting, from the novel *The Devils of Loudun* by Aldous Huxley

The Devil's Advocate ★★ PG

Drama   1977 · W Ger · Colour · 104mins

Based on the bestselling novel by Morris West, who also wrote the script, this moral fable stars John Mills as a terminally ill Catholic priest who comes to Rome in 1958 to decide if a man executed 14 years earlier deserves canonisation. The story that follows is strangely uninvolving, due mainly to having English actors play Italian characters. Tackling the persecution of the Jews as well as homosexuality within the priesthood, Guy Green's

movie is also overloaded with would-be significance. ▭

John Mills *Monsignor Blaise Meredith* • Stéphane Audran *Contessa* • Jason Miller *Dr Meyer* • Paola Pitagora *Nina* • Leigh Lawson *Nerone* • Timothy West *Anselmo* • Patrick Mower *Il Lupo* • Raf Vallone *Aurelio* • Daniel Massey *Black* ▪ *Dir* Guy Green • *Scr* Morris West, from his novel

The Devil's Advocate ★★ 18

Supernatural thriller
1997 · US · Colour · 137mins

You can see how the writer pitched this project: *The Exorcist* meets John Grisham, with Keanu Reeves in the Linda Blair role. Reeves is a hotshot lawyer from Florida, lured to a New York law firm by Al Pacino who is, in fact, Lucifer himself. Like *Wall Street*, it's a tale about a man who sells his soul to the Devil while his wife, Charlize Theron, goes into a fit of jealous rage. There isn't a single scene that's believable, but the whole concoction, right down to the *Ghostbusters* finale, is mindlessly enjoyable and directed by Taylor Hackford (aka Mr Helen Mirren) with po-faced urgency. Contains swearing, violence and sex scenes. ▭

Keanu Reeves *Kevin Lomax* • Al Pacino *John Milton* • Charlize Theron *Mary Ann Lomax* • Jeffrey Jones *Eddie Barzoon* • Judith Ivey *Mrs Lomax* • Connie Nielsen *Christabella* • Craig T Nelson *Alexander Cullen* • Don King ▪ *Dir* Taylor Hackford • *Scr* Jonathan Lemkin, Tony Gilroy, Andrew Neiderman

The Devil's Arithmetic ★★★

Second World War fantasy drama
1999 · US · Colour · 95mins

A modern teenager, Kirsten Dunst, who only grudgingly accepts the Jewish faith, finds herself swept into the life of a Nazi death camp prisoner when she is asked to "open the front door" at a Seder feast. There, like a refugee Dorothy in *The Wizard of Oz*, she experiences all the Holocaust horrors first hand and learns to understand why traditions are so important to her people. Gritty and raw, if sometimes over-preachy, this historical semi-fantasy packs a potent punch.

Kirsten Dunst *Hannah Stern* • Brittany Murphy *Rivkah* • Paul Freeman *Rabbi* • Mimi Rogers *Lenore Stern* • Louise Fletcher *Aunt Eva* • Nitzan Sharron *Ariel* • Shelly Skandrani *Leah* ▪ *Dir* Donna Deitch • *Scr* Robert J Avrech, from the novel by Jane Yolen

Devil's Bait ★★ U

Drama   1959 · UK · BW · 58mins

A baker doesn't get on very well with his wife. When he discovers rats on his premises, he hires a rat-catcher who is totally blotto and mixes the cyanide in one of the baker's baking tins. Ah, we think in a Hitchcockian way, now the baker will serve his wife a suspect scone and she'll pass away. Or maybe she'll do *him* in. But no: all that happens is that a couple of picnickers are sold some poisoned bread and the police are called in to find them. This takes the sting out of the tale, but the cast, including Gordon Jackson, make this "quota quickie" pass very quickly.

Geoffrey Keen *Joe Frisby* • Jane Hylton *Ellen Frisby* • Gordon Jackson *Det Sgt Malcolm* • Dermot Kelly *Mr Love* • Eileen Moore *Barbara*

• Molly Urquhart *Mrs Tanner* • Rupert Davies *Landlord* ■ *Dir* Peter Graham Scott • *Scr* Peter Johnston, Diana K Watson

The Devil's Bed ★★

Drama   1994 · US · Colour

New Zealander Sam Pillsbury took the helm for this steamy TV potboiler in which the romantic rivalry between two brothers disturbs the calm of the midwestern countryside. Joe Lando and Adrian Pasdar star as the feuding siblings, with Nicollette Sheridan as the returning prodigal tearing them apart. Piper Laurie and Richard Roundtree lend a certain dignity to the proceedings, but there's little here that hasn't been done better before.

Nicollette Sheridan *Rowena Eklund* • Adrian Pasdar *Jude Snow* • Joe Lando *Sonny Snow* • Piper Laurie *Ellis Snow* • Richard Roundtree *Dunc* • Brandon Smith *Bobby* • Eleese Lester *Kerry* • Laura Poe *Josie Lee* ■ *Dir* Sam Pillsbury • *Scr* Joyce Eliason

The Devil's Brigade ★★

Second World War adventure
1968 · US · Colour · 131mins

A blatant rip-off of Robert Aldrich's *The Dirty Dozen*, albeit based on truth, with William Holden ordered to train a bunch of thugs to fight the Nazis in the Norwegian mountains. The usual stock character tensions break out and the action scenes are only routinely directed by Andrew V MacLaglen. The normally exuberant Holden seems becalmed by the surrounding cheerlessness, though the picture did reunite him with his real-life friend Cliff Robertson.

William Holden (1) *Lt Col Robert T Frederick* • Cliff Robertson *Major Alan Crown* • Vince Edwards *Major Cliff Bricker* • Michael Rennie *Lt Gen Mark Clark* • Dana Andrews *Brig Gen Walter Naylor* • Andrew Prine *Theodore Ransom* • Claude Akins *Rocky Rockman* • Richard Jaeckel *Greco* ■ *Dir* Andrew V McLaglen • *Scr* William Roberts, from the book by Robert H Adleman, Col George Walton

Devil's Canyon ★★

Western   1953 · US · Colour · 89mins

Originally filmed in 3-D, this RKO western is actually more of a thriller, as psychotic killer Stephen McNally attempts to wreak revenge on fellow inmate Dale Robertson, a former US marshal serving ten years for his involvement in a fatal shoot-out. Virginia Mayo helps McNally escape from jail, but no prizes for guessing who she ends up with. The period realism of the Arizona Territorial Prison setting makes this an unusual time-passer, and South Dakota-born director Alfred Werker had a way with westerns. It's all a bit grim, though, and a stronger cast would have helped.

Dale Robertson *Billy Reynolds* • Virginia Mayo *Abby Nixon* • Stephen McNally *Jesse Gorman* • Arthur Hunnicutt *Frank Taggert* • Robert Keith *Steve Morgan* • Jay C Flippen *Captain Wells* ■ *Dir* Alfred Werker • *Scr* Frederick Hazlitt Brennan, Harry Essex, from a story by Bennett R Cohen, Norton S Parker • *Cinematographer* Nicholas Musuraca

Devil's Child ★★ 18

Supernatural thriller
1997 · US · Colour · 87mins

In this proficient, if unremarkable variation on *Rosemary's Baby*, *NYPD Blue* star Kim Delaney plays a wealthy woman who meets the man of her dreams. In fact, she's so happy she initially fails to spot that he has ''666'' tattooed on his forehead. Delaney shrieks convincingly enough in all the right places, although Matthew Lillard steals the show. Bobby Roth's direction is competent, though he doesn't generate nearly enough frights. Contains swearing and violence. ▭

Kim Delaney *Nikki DeMarco* • Thomas Gibson *Alexander Cole* • Colleen Flynn *Ruby* • Matthew Lillard *Tim* • Grace Zabriskie *Rose DeMarco* • Christopher John Fields *Father Darcy* • Larry Holden *Todd Gilman* • Paul Bartel *Dr Zimmerman* • Tracey Walter *Ezra Hersch* ■ *Dir* Bobby Roth • *Scr* Pablo F Fenjves, from a story by Laurence Minkoff, Pablo F Fenjves

The Devil's Disciple ★★ U

Historical comedy drama
1959 · US/UK · BW · 83mins

Burt Lancaster took a shine to George Bernard Shaw's comedy of mistaken identity, set during the American War of Independence. So he lured his buddy Kirk Douglas and Laurence Olivier into co-starring with him and hired Alexander Mackendrick to direct. Mackendrick later quit and was replaced by Guy Hamilton. Like so many Shavian adaptations, it sits on the screen like a lump of stodge, the stilted dialogue slowing up the action. Lancaster plays a preacher; Douglas the good-for-nothing who gets mistaken for him. Olivier, as a British general, plays to the gallery, delighting Douglas so much he cast him in *Spartacus*.

Burt Lancaster *Anthony Anderson* • Kirk Douglas *Richard Dudgeon* • Laurence Olivier *General Burgoyne* • Janette Scott *Judith Anderson* • Eva Le Gallienne *Mrs Dudgeon* • Harry Andrews *Major Swindon* ■ *Dir* Guy Hamilton • *Scr* John Dighton, Roland Kibbee, from the play by George Bernard Shaw

Devil's Doorway ★★★ U

Western   1950 · US · BW · 84mins

Robert Taylor gives one of his best performances as the Shoshone Indian who fights with distinction in the Civil War but is deprived of his valuable Wyoming spread by racists taking advantage of new homesteading laws. The contrived introduction of an inexperienced female lawyer to argue his case does little to lighten the mood of stark hopelessness in Guy Trosper's screenplay. Well acted by Paula Raymond and Louis Calhern as the bigoted rival lawyer who stirs up most of the trouble, this is a visually powerful film thanks to the keen eye of director Anthony Mann and his cameraman John Alton.

Robert Taylor (1) *Lance Poole* • Louis Calhern *Verne Coolan* • Paula Raymond *Orrie Masters* • Marshall Thompson *Rod MacDougall* • James Mitchell *Red Rock* • Edgar Buchanan *Zeke Carmody* • Rhys Williams *Scotty MacDougall* • Spring Byington *Mrs Masters* ■ *Dir* Anthony Mann • *Scr* Guy Trosper

The Devil's Eye ★★ PG

Comedy   1960 · Swe · BW · 83mins

Based on Oluf Bang's Danish radio play, *Don Juan Returns*, this is one of Ingmar Bergman's poorest pictures. From the moment Gunnar Bjornstrand appears to introduce the methodology, the heavy hand of theatricality rests heavily on both the staging and the performances. Jarl Kulle injects a little verve as the playboy released from Hell to seduce parson's daughter Bibi Andersson, thus removing the sty her purity has caused in the devil's eye. Alas, a mixture of on-set tension and Bergman's sheer exhaustion after completing *The Virgin Spring* meant this laboured comedy was almost predestined to fail. In Swedish with English subtitles. ▭

Jarl Kulle *Don Juan* • Bibi Andersson *Britt-Marie* • Axel Duberg *Jonas, her fiancé* • Nils Poppe *Pastor, her father* • Gertrud Fridh *Pastor's wife* • Sture Lagerwall *Pablo* • Stig Jarrel *Satan* • Gunnar Björnstrand *Actor* ■ *Dir* Ingmar Bergman • *Scr* Ingmar Bergman, from the play *Don Juan Returns* by Oluf Bang

Devil's Food ★★

Comedy drama   1996 · US · Colour

Screenwriter Henry Olek dips into the murky waters of body fascism for this mildly amusing TV movie, directed by George Kaczender. But, instead of revisiting a tired old Faustian theme, Olek might have had more joy satirising the world of local TV stations. What we get is a female empowerment comedy, in which television celebrity Suzanne Somers makes a deal with the devilish Dabney Coleman to lose both her soul and the pounds that are hampering her career.

Suzanne Somers *Sally McCormick* • Dabney Coleman *Seymour Kecker* • William Katt *Andrew Burns* • Charles R Frank *Charles Leyden* • Shannon Lawson *Dori Vogel* ■ *Dir* George Kaczender • *Scr* Henry Olek

The Devil's Hairpin ★★

Sports drama   1957 · US · Colour · 83mins

In his second film as director, Cornel Wilde plays a washed-up racing champ who runs a bar and has a drunken girlfriend (Jean Wallace, the star's real-life wife). Goaded into making a comeback, Wilde has to fight his inner demons, which stem from the time when he almost killed his brother. (It was this that estranged him from his mother, played by Mary Astor.) It's a corny story, but petrol-heads should enjoy the racing footage and the sight of some lovely fifties cars.

Cornel Wilde *Nick Jargin* • Jean Wallace *Kelly* • Arthur Franz *Rhinegold* • Mary Astor *Mrs Jargin* • Paul Fix *Doc* • Larry Pennell *Johnny* ■ *Dir* Cornel Wilde • *Scr* James Edmiston, Cornel Wilde, from the novel *The Fastest Man on Earth* by James Edmiston

The Devil's Holiday ★★★

Drama   1930 · US · BW · 80mins

A young manicurist (Nancy Carroll) on the make is rescued from amorality and transformed by the strength of a young man's love. A morality play for its time that has little bearing on life now, this nonetheless remains a tender love story and is sensitively directed by Edmund Goulding, who also wrote it. The film boasts a genuinely affecting performance by Carroll, who narrowly lost the 1929/30 best actress Oscar to Norma Shearer. Phillips Holmes co-stars convincingly as her noble-spirited suitor and James Kirkwood, Paul Lukas and ZaSu Pitts feature in support.

Nancy Carroll *Hallie Hobart* • Phillips Holmes *David Stone* • James Kirkwood *Mark Stone* • Hobart Bosworth *Ezra Stone* • Ned Sparks *Charlie Thorne* • Morgan Farley *Monkey McConnell* • Jed Prouty *Kent Carr* • Paul Lukas *Dr Reynolds* ■ *Dir* Edmund Goulding • *Scr* Edmund Goulding, from his story

The Devil's in Love ★★

Medical drama   1933 · US · BW · 70mins

A morose-looking Victor Jory (a late replacement for Warner Baxter) stars as the French army doctor falsely accused of murder who runs off to help the poor in Africa. There he falls in love with missionary's niece Loretta Young, here at her most exquisitely beautiful. The contrived and predictable storyline remains watchable thanks to intelligent, lively direction from Wilhelm (later William) Dieterle and a surprise appearance from Bela Lugosi as a military prosecutor.

Victor Jory *Lt Andre Morand/Paul Vernay* • Loretta Young *Margot LeSesne* • Vivienne Osborne *Rena* • David Manners *Jean* • C Henry Gordon *Capt Radak* • Herbert Mundin *Bimpy* • Emil Chautard [Emile Chautard] *Father Carmion* • J Carrol Naish *Salazar* • Bela Lugosi *Military prosecutor* ■ *Dir* Wilhelm Dieterle [William Dieterle] • *Scr* Howard Estabrook, from a story by Harry Hervey

Devil's Island ★★

Drama   1940 · US · BW · 65mins

After treating a wounded political revolutionary, respected brain surgeon Boris Karloff is unjustly sentenced to ten years imprisonment on the notorious Devil's Island. There he must survive barbaric conditions and preserve his humanity in the shadow of the guillotine. Condemned by the French government on its first outing, the film was heavily censored and re-released a year later. Karloff's convincing performance holds director William Clemens's reasonable adventure/exposé together.

Boris Karloff *Dr Charles Gaudet* • Nedda Harrigan *Mme Lucien* • James Stephenson *Colonel Armand* • Adia Kuznetzoff *Pierre* • Rolla Gourvitch *Colette* • Will Stanton *Bobo* • Edward Keane *Dr Duval* • Robert Warwick *Demontre* • Pedro De Cordoba *Marcal* ■ *Dir* William Clemens • *Scr* Kenneth Garnet, Don Ryan, from the story *The Return of Doctor X* by Anthony Coldeway, Raymond Schrock

Devil's Island ★★★ 15

Drama
1996 · Ice/Ger/Nor/Den · Colour · 103mins

Set in the immediate postwar era, this cocked snook at American imperialism is not so self-satisfied as to ignore the very real problems caused by Iceland's cultural, as well as geographical, isolation. A product of the Reykjavik slums, Baddi (Baltasar Kormákur) can almost be excused for his arrogance on returning from visiting his runaway mother in the States. However, our sympathy remains with his put-upon brother, Danni (Sveinn Geirsson), whose hopes are left as bereft as the

U = SUITABLE FOR ALL   Uc = SUITABLE FOR ALL, ESPECIALLY FOR YOUNG CHILDREN (VIDEO ONLY)   PG = PARENTAL GUIDANCE

abandoned barracks in which his family now lives. Eccentric but engaging, this energetic, episodic picture is directed with wit and insight by Fridrik Thor Fridriksson. In English and Icelandic with subtitles. Contains swearing and some violence.

Baltasar Kormákur *Baddi Tomasson* • Gisli Halldórsson *Tommi Tomasson* • Sigurveig Jónsdóttir *Karolina Tomasson* • Halldóra Geirhardsdóttir *Dolli* • Sveinn Geirsson *Danni Tomasson* • Gudmundur Ólafsson *Grettir* ■ *Dir* Fridrik Thor Fridriksson • *Scr* Einar Kárason

The Devil's Kiss   ★
Erotic drama   1971 · Sp · Colour

While never on a par with his compatriots Jesus Franco and Jacinto Molina, Jorge (credited as Georges) Gigo managed to keep busy during the seventies as a director of erotic horror flicks. However, those salubrious offerings can't hold a candle to this abysmal reworking of the Frankenstein story. The voluptuous Silvia Solar stars as a demented scientist who, with the aid of a diminutive sidekick, creates a slave male who has a problem with subservience. Spanish dialogue dubbed into English. Contains violence, sex scenes and nudity.

Silvia Solar *Clair Grandier* • Olivier Mathot *Prof. Gambler* • Jose Nieto *Duc de Haussemont* • Evelyne Scott *Loretta* • Daniel Martin *Richard* • Maria Silva *Susan* • Ronnie Harp *Le Nain* ■ *Dir* Georges Gigo [Jorge Gigo] • *Scr* Georges Gigo [Jorge Gigo]

Devils of Darkness   ★★ 15
Horror   1964 · UK · Colour · 84mins

The first British vampire movie to use a contemporary setting finds undead Count Sinistre posing as an artist in Brittany. There he heads a cult of devil worshippers who indulge in orgies with exotic snake dancers and sacrifice innocent tourists on their graveyard crypt altar. Little sense of terror, or even atmosphere, is raised in this undistinguished, stilted dud from cameraman turned director Lance Comfort, despite an intriguing attempt to combine witchcraft and reincarnation with the more standard elements of vampirism.

William Sylvester *Paul Baxter* • Hubert Noel *Count Sinistre/Armond du Moliere* • Tracy Reed *Karen* • Carole Gray *Tania* • Diana Decker *Madeline Braun* • Rona Anderson *Anne Forest* • Peter Illing *Inspector Malin* ■ *Dir* Lance Comfort • *Scr* Lyn Fairhurst

The Devil's Own   ★★ 15
Thriller   1997 · US · Colour · 106mins

Bedevilled by its own production problems (constant script changes, disenchanted Brad Pitt wanting to quit, changes in the political situation while shooting), it's hardly surprising that director Alan J Pakula's IRA thriller is a fudged disappointment. Harrison Ford is the New York cop who takes Irish émigré Pitt into his home without realising he's a wanted terrorist on a missile-buying mission for the Republican cause. The tepid tension is supposed to emerge from Pitt taking to Ford's family and establishing an emotional bond with the father figure he never had, but it not being enough to deflect him from his single-minded purpose. Both dramatically and

politically incorrect. Contains swearing and some violence. ▭ **DVD**

Harrison Ford *Tom O'Meara* • Brad Pitt *Frankie McGuire, "Rory Devaney"* • Margaret Colin *Sheila O'Meara* • Rubén Blades *Edwin "Eddie" Diaz* • Treat Williams *Billy Burke* • George Hearn *Peter Fitzsimmons* • Mitchell Ryan *Chief Jim Kelly* • Natascha McElhone *Megan Doherty* • David O'Hara *Martin MacDuff* ■ *Dir* Alan J Pakula • *Scr* David Aaron Cohen, Vincent Patrick, Kevin Jarre

The Devil's Playground   ★★ U
Western   1946 · US · BW · 65mins

This was the first of 12 Hopalong Cassidy features to be produced by their star, silver-haired William Boyd. Boyd ensured his character operated according to a rigid ethical code, unusual considering that Hopalong dressed entirely in black, the clothing usually worn by the western villain, and rode a lone range. Here, though, he's accompanied by sidekick Andy Clyde, and, of course, his trusty steed Topper. An excellent example of a series western, and a fine introduction to Clarence E Mulford's gentleman cowboy.

William Boyd *Hopalong Cassidy* • Andy Clyde *California Carlson* • Rand Brooks *Lucky Jenkins* • Elaine Riley *Mrs Evans* • Robert Elliott *Judge Morton* • Joseph J Greene *Sheriff* ■ *Dir* George Archainbaud • *Scr* Doris Schroeder, from a story by Ted Wilson, from characters created by Clarence E Mulford

The Devil's Playground   ★★★ 15
Drama   1976 · Ausl · Colour · 94mins

A nicely structured, if a tad po-faced look at the awkward sexual awakenings of boys at a Roman Catholic boarding school, made by Australian writer/director Fred Schepisi and based on his childhood experiences. This is always a fertile ground for film-makers like Schepisi who deal in emotions rather than direct action, and his intelligent screenplay gives the little-known Australian cast a chance to indulge in a great deal of entertaining breast-beating. But he doesn't take us any deeper into the issue than a legion of others before him.

Arthur Dignam *Brother Francine* • Nick Tate *Brother Victor* • Simon Burke *Tom Allen* • Charles McCallum *Brother Sebastian* • John Frawley *Brother Celian* • Jonathan Hardy *Brother Arnold* • Gerry Duggan *Father Hanrahan* ■ *Dir/Scr* Fred Schepisi

The Devil's Rain   ★★★
Horror   1975 · US/Mex · Colour · 85mins

A colourful, if confusing Satanic shocker with coven leader Ernest Borgnine searching for an ancient book that will enable him to deliver a fresh batch of souls to the prince of darkness. Worth persevering through the muddled set-up for the effects-laden climax where most of the cast members are reduced to screaming, oozing slime. Also notable for the sight of *Star Trek*'s William Shatner tied naked to a sacrificial altar, and a brief appearance from John Travolta.

Ernest Borgnine *Jonathan Corbis* • Eddie Albert *Dr Richards* • Ida Lupino *Mrs Preston* • William Shatner *Mark Preston* • Keenan Wynn

Sheriff Owens • Tom Skerritt *Tom Preston* • Joan Prather *Julie Preston* • John Travolta *Danny* ■ *Dir* Robert Fuest • *Scr* Gabe Essoe, James Ashton, Gerald Hopman

The Devil's Wanton   ★★★
Drama   1949 · Swe · BW · 72mins

Based on his own script, Ingmar Bergman's first important film contains many of his later philosophical preoccupations, particularly his view of a Godless, loveless universe. Over-ambitious, though interesting in the light of its creator's entire oeuvre, it tells of a director and writer who become embroiled in the wretched life of a suicidal prostitute. Made very cheaply and using sets from another movie, it made no profit but enhanced Bergman's reputation in Sweden. However, he had to wait six years for *Smiles of a Summer's Night* to make his name internationally. In Swedish with English subtitles.

Doris Svedlund *Birgitta-Carolina Soderberg* • Birger Malmsten *Thomas* • Eva Henning *Sofi* • Hasse Ekman *Martin Grande* • Stig Olin *Peter* • Irma Christenson *Linnea* • Anders Henrikson *Paul* ■ *Dir/Scr* Ingmar Bergman

Devlin   ★★ 18
Thriller   1992 · US · Colour · 105mins

Based on the novel by Roderick Thorp (*Die Hard*), this derivative fugitive yarn is a case of more style than substance. Bryan Brown stars as a tough New York cop who finds himself on the run from the mob and the police when he is framed for the murder of his brother-in-law, a respected city politician. Roma Downey gives a strong performance as Brown's faithful girlfriend, but the gritty urban locations and sharp camerawork can't save this convoluted story.

Bryan Brown *Frank Devlin* • Roma Downey *Eileen O'Malley* • Lloyd Bridges *Bill Brennan* • Whip Hubley *Sam Lord* • Lawrence Dane *Art Wolfe* • Lisa Eichhorn *Anita Brennan* ■ *Dir* Rick Rosenthal • *Scr* David Taylor, from the novel by Roderick Thorp • *Cinematographer* Neil Roach

Devotion   ★★★ U
Biographical drama 1946 · US · BW · 106mins

Writers are notoriously difficult to portray on film: since writing is an intellectual concept and cinema a visual medium, how does one convey what makes a writer write? Director Curtis Bernhardt doesn't bother with such ramifications, though. Olivia de Havilland and Ida Lupino play Charlotte and Emily Brontë, both of whom lust after Paul Henried, while Arthur Kennedy is excellent as the alcoholic Bramwell. This syrupy, romanticised saga could really be about anybody, but it's still a splendid period melodrama.

Ida Lupino *Emily Brontë* • Olivia de Havilland *Charlotte Brontë* • Nancy Coleman *Anne Brontë* • Paul Henreid *Nicholls* • Sydney Greenstreet *Thackeray* • Arthur Kennedy *Branwell Brontë* • Dame May Whitty *Lady Thornton* ■ *Dir* Curtis Bernhardt • *Scr* Keith Winter, from a story by Theodore Reeves

El Diablo   ★★ 15
Comedy western   1990 · US · Colour · 103mins

ER's Anthony Edwards swaps his scalpel for cowboy duds in this gentle comic western, co-written by horror-meisters John Carpenter and Tommy Lee Wallace (with Bill Phillips). Edwards is the geeky 19th-century schoolteacher who gets the chance to live out his cowboy fantasies when one of his students is kidnapped by a Mexican bandit. There's little in the way of originality, but the dependable cast has a fine old time. ▭

Anthony Edwards *Billy Ray* • Louis Gossett Jr *Van Leek* • John Glover *Preacher* ■ *Dir* Peter Markle • *Scr* Tommy Lee Wallace, John Carpenter, Bill Phillips

Diabolically Yours   ★★★
Psychological thriller 1967 · Fr · Colour · 93mins

Diabolically dubbed, more like. This excellent Gallic thriller, the last film made by master director Julien Duvivier (*Pépé le Moko*), was distributed worldwide in a version that saddled handsome Alain Delon and sexy Senta Berger with bland American accents, a poor decision that seriously affects the credibility of their characters. Not that it really matters, for this is one of those glossy French thrillers where the goodies are good-looking, the baddies are slimy and all the plot twists unravel by the end. Jolly entertaining it is, too, though perhaps it's best to remember the redoubtable Duvivier by his earlier works. French dialogue dubbed into English.

Alain Delon *Pierre* • Senta Berger *Christiane* • Sergio Fantoni *Freddie* • Peter Mosbacher *Kim* ■ *Dir* Julien Duvivier • *Scr* Julien Duvivier, Paul Gégauff, from the novel by Louis Thomas

Diabolique   ★★ 18
Thriller   1996 · US · Colour · 102mins

If ever a film didn't need or deserve a Hollywood remake, it's Henri-Georges Clouzot's superb, twist-packed 1954 suspense thriller *Les Diaboliques*, about a corpse who refuses to stay dead. Director Jeremiah Chechik hasn't got the foggiest idea how to create atmosphere, relying instead on melodramatic performances and the odd thunderstorm. Nothing seems to have any purpose; from Isabelle Adjani's wholly unnecessary early flesh exposure, to swapping the original's male detective to Kathy Bates's breast cancer sufferer. Sharon Stone is suitably icy and Chazz Palminteri loathsome as the violent husband, but they deserve better than this. ▭

Sharon Stone *Nicole Horner* • Isabelle Adjani *Mia Baran* • Chazz Palminteri *Guy Baran* • Kathy Bates *Shirley Vogel* • Spalding Gray *Simon Veatch* • Shirley Knight *Edie Danziger* • Allen Garfield *Leo Kaztman* • Adam Hann-Byrd *Erik Pretzer* ■ *Dir* Jeremiah Chechik • *Scr* Don Roos, from the film *Les Diaboliques* by Henri-Georges Clouzot, from the novel *Celle Qui N'Etait Plus* by Pierre Boileau, Thomas Narcejac

Les Diaboliques   ★★★★★ 15
Thriller   1954 · Fr · BW · 116mins

When a sadistic headmaster's wife and mistress plot together to kill him – and then find his body is missing – the result is a brilliantly nasty thriller from Henri-Georges Clouzot. Paul Meurisse is the headmaster, Simone Signoret the mistress and Vera Clouzot the wife, while the climax is one of cinema's most diabolical scenes. The film has a graveyard gloom to match the school's oppressive atmosphere of neglect and despair, while the final shot marvellously suggests unpleasantness to come. A masterpiece in its own terrifying way. In French with English subtitles. ▦

Simone Signoret *Nicole* • Vera Clouzot *Christina* • Paul Meurisse *Michel* • Charles Vanel *Fichet* • Pierre Larquey *Drain* • Michel Serrault *Raymond* ■ *Dir* Henri-Georges Clouzot • *Scr* Henri-Georges Clouzot, Jérôme Géromini, Frédéric Grendel, René Masson, from the novel *Celle Qui N'Etait Plus* by Pierre Boileau, Thomas Narcejac • *Cinematographer* Armand Thirard

Diabolo Menthe ★★★★ 12

Romance   1977 · Fr · Colour · 96mins

Director Diane Kurys also wrote the script for this highly-rated French film, an insightful portrayal of early adolescence that was extensively based on her own experiences. The film follows a rebellious schoolgirl through her spell at a stuffy French lycée. It's a rollercoaster ride whose ups and downs encompass sadistic teachers and first periods, parental divorce and first love. Kurys would later draw on other life experiences for such films as *Cocktail Molotov* and *C'est la Vie*, but this is widely regarded as the best of her bunch. In French with English subtitles. Contains some sexual references. ▦

Eléonore Klarwein *Anne Weber* • Odile Michel *Frederique Weber* • Anouk Ferjac *Madame Weber* • Coralie Clément *Perrine Jacquet* • Marie Véronique Maurin *Muriel Cazau* • Valérie Stand *Martine Dubreuil* ■ *Dir/Scr* Diane Kurys

Diagnosis: Murder ★★

Crime thriller   1974 · UK · Colour · 90mins

Psychiatrist Christopher Lee is suspected of murdering his wife after she disappears. The twist is that he was planning to murder her anyway so he could be with his mistress. This tepid made-for-television thriller received a brief theatrical release thanks to its star cast, which includes Jon Finch, Judy Geeson and Tony Beckley. A stoic performance from Lee and a few whodunit wrinkles along the way make it of passing interest.

Jon Finch *Inspector Lomax* • Judy Geeson *Helen* • Christopher Lee *Dr Stephen Hayward* • Tony Beckley *Sergeant Green* • Dilys Hamlett *Julia Hayward* • Jane Merrow *Mary Dawson* • Colin Jeavons *Bob Dawson* ■ *Dir* Sidney Hayers • *Scr* Philip Levene

Dial M for Murder ★★★ PG

Thriller   1954 · US · Colour · 100mins

Alfred Hitchcock only took on this version of Frederick Knott's play to fulfil his Warners contract, and such was his lack of interest in the project that he claimed he could have phoned in his direction and that the action wouldn't have been any less interesting if he had staged it in a phone box. It's true to say that many of the set pieces literally fall flat, as they were originally composed for presentation in 3-D, but as Ray Milland plots to bump off wife Grace Kelly there are plenty of deft touches that loudly proclaim "genius at work". Milland's sinister sophistication catches the eye, but Kelly's subtly shaded suffering is superb. ▦

Ray Milland *Tony Wendice* • Grace Kelly *Margot Wendice* • Robert Cummings *Mark Halliday* • John Williams *Chief Inspector Hubbard* • Anthony Dawson *Captain Lesgate* • Patrick Allen *Pearson* • George Leigh *William* • George Alderson *Detective* • Robin Hughes *Police sergeant* ■ *Dir* Alfred Hitchcock • *Scr* Frederick Knott, from his play

Diamond Head ★★★

Melodrama   1962 · US · Colour · 106mins

Charlton Heston plays a powerful landowner with ambitions to be Hawaii's senator. When his sister (Yvette Mimieux) plans to marry a Polynesian (James Darren in heavy make-up), Heston does everything he can to prevent it – despite having a Hawaiian mistress who's pregnant with his child. This isn't the Hawaii of grass skirts, ukeleles, hula-hula and aloha. Instead it's the exotic setting for a no-holds-barred melodrama, with Heston simmering impressively like the Diamond Head volcano of the title. One may laugh, one may snigger, but one is never bored by this self-important piece of tosh.

Charlton Heston *Richard Howland* • Yvette Mimieux *Sloan Howland* • George Chakiris *Dr Dean Kahana* • France Nuyen *Mei Chen* • James Darren *Paul Kahana* • Aline MacMahon *Kapiolani Kahana* ■ *Dir* Guy Green • *Scr* Marguerite Roberts

The Diamond Queen ★★ U

Historical adventure
1953 · US · Colour · 76mins

A swashbuckler about a French adventurer (Fernando Lamas) who goes to India in search of a jewel fit for the crown of Louis XIV. There he finds a big, fat, sparkly diamond attached to Maya, queen of Nepal (Arlene Dahl), who is herself attached to the Great Mogul, a jealous cove played by Sheldon Leonard. As usual with these essays in exotica, there's a lot of silly dialogue, lavish costumes, lascivious dance routines and the odd man-eating tiger prowling the Burbank backlot. Lamas and Dahl married shortly after the film was completed. ▦

Fernando Lamas *Jean Tavernier* • Arlene Dahl *Maya* • Gilbert Roland *Baron Paul de Cabannes* • Sheldon Leonard *Great Mogul* • Jay Novello *Gujar* • Michael Ansara *Jumla* • Richard Hale *Gabriel Tavernier* • Sujata *Hindu Dancer* • Asoka *Hindu Dancer* ■ *Dir* John Brahm • *Scr* Otto Englander, from his story

Diamond Skulls ★★★ 18

Drama   1989 · UK · Colour · 83mins

In its own quiet way, Gabriel Byrne's CV is one of the most impressive in modern cinema. Here he opts for a picture that might not have rung too many box-office bells, but which has a couple of interesting ideas and offers him a chance to extend his already considerable range of characters. In a rare venture into fictional films, documentary specialist Nick Broomfield only scratches the surface of his themes of class responsibility and dangerous obsession. Yet he maintains the dramatic tension more than adequately and coaxes knowing performances from Byrne and veteran co-stars Michael Hordern and Ian Carmichael. Contains violence, swearing and sex scenes. ▦

Gabriel Byrne *Lord Hugo Buckton* • Amanda Donohoe *Ginny Buckton* • Douglas Hodge *Jamie* • Sadie Frost *Rebecca* • Matthew Marsh *Raul* • Michael Hordern *Lord Crewne* • Judy Parfitt *Lady Crewne* • Ralph Brown *Jack* • Ian Carmichael *Exeter* ■ *Dir* Nick Broomfield • *Scr* Tim Rose Price, from an idea by Nick Broomfield, Tim Rose Price

Diamonds ★ PG

Crime drama   1975 · US/Is · Colour · 103mins

A heist picture with Robert Shaw in a dual role as two brothers: one a jewel thief, the other a security expert. This sort of set-up is both technically cumbersome and rather tiresome, and the film does not disappoint on either count, being very tedious and shoddily made. Shaw was a big name at the time – he had just starred in *The Sting* and *Jaws*, both massive hits – so what attracted him to this rubbish is anyone's guess. Shelley Winters contributes an excruciating cameo as a widow on holiday in Israel, which was where the film was made. ▦

Robert Shaw *Charles/Earl Hodgson* • Richard Roundtree *Archie* • Barbara Seagull [Barbara Hershey] *Sally* • Shelley Winters *Zelda Shapiro* • Shai K Ophir *Moshe* • Gadi Yageel *Gaby* • Joseph Shiloah [Joseph Shiloach] *Mustafa* ■ *Dir* Menahem Golan • *Scr* Menaham Golan, David Paulsen, from a story by Menahem Golan

Diamonds ★★

Comedy drama
1999 · US/Ger · Colour · 91mins

To see Kirk Douglas slowed by both his own physical disability and a bland script is sad indeed. The 83-year-old actor plays a man who, like himself, is suffering from the aftereffects of a stroke. His son (Dan Aykroyd) wants him to go into a home, but Dad, who used to be a boxer, wants to stay independent. Deciding to pick up the gems he was once paid to throw a fight, Douglas, his son and grandson (Corbin Allred) drive to Reno. There they visit a bothel whose madame (Lauren Bacall) takes the oldster into her bed. The dialogue is tedious and the ideas are more ancient than Douglas himself; surely he deserves better than this.

Kirk Douglas *Harry* • Lauren Bacall *Sin-Dee* • Dan Aykroyd *Lance* • Corbin Allred *Michael* • Jenny McCarthy *Sugar* • Kurt Fuller *Moses* • Mariah O'Brien *Tiffany* • John Landis *Gambler* ■ *Dir* John Asher [John Mallory Asher] • *Scr* Allan Aaron Katz

Diamonds Are Forever ★★ PG

Spy adventure 1971 · UK · Colour · 114mins

After *You Only Live Twice*, Sean Connery said "never again". After George Lazenby's sole effort in *On Her Majesty's Secret Service*, however, Connery was lured back for a fee of $1 million, which he donated to the Scottish International Educational Trust. One of the weakest Bonds, its plot about diamond smuggling develops rather tiresomely, while Connery simply goes through the motions. The Las Vegas sequences have some dash, and Bruce Glover and Porter Smith make an intriguing double-act as gay hit men Wint and Kidd. ▦

Sean Connery *James Bond* • Jill St John *Tiffany Case* • Charles Gray *Blofeld* • Lana Wood *Plenty O'Toole* • Jimmy Dean *Willard Whyte* • Bruce Cabot *Saxby* • Putter Smith *Mr Kidd* • Bruce Glover *Mr Wint* • Norman Burton *Felix Leiter* • Joseph Furst *Dr Metz* • Bernard Lee *"M"* • Desmond Llewelyn *"Q"* • Leonard Barr *Shady Tree* • Lois Maxwell *Miss Moneypenny* ■ *Dir* Guy Hamilton • *Scr* Richard Maibaum, Tom Mankiewicz, from the novel by Ian Fleming

Diamonds for Breakfast ★★ U

Crime caper   1968 · UK · Colour · 102mins

Coming off Visconti's *The Stranger*, Marcello Mastroianni clearly felt the need for an easier assignment, and he sleepwalks through this dotty crime caper that, like so many sixties co-productions, sought to reproduce the suave heroism of the Bond movies. He plays a shop-owner who is fourth in line to the Russian throne. Debutant director Christopher Morahan failed to invest much fun or excitement into this tale of an impoverished nobleman's bid to swipe the Romanov gems with the help of seven sexy assistants.

Marcello Mastroianni *"Nicky"*, *Grand Duke Nicholas* • Rita Tushingham *Bridget* • Elaine Taylor *Victoria* • Maggie Blye *Honey* • Francesca Tu [Francisca Tu] *Jeanne* • Warren Mitchell *Popov* ■ *Dir* Christopher Morahan • *Scr* Pierre Rouve, NF Simpson, Ronald Harwood

Diamonds in the Rough ★★ U

Crime comedy   1996 · US · Colour · 19mins

There's so much plot packed into this breakneck crime comedy that it's hard to keep track of just who is duping whom. Jim Gray and David Richard star as a couple of delivery drivers who find themselves up to their necks in gangsters, crooked cops and jealous hairdressers after they're tricked into a diamond robbery by receptionist Michelle Verhunce. The ensuing mayhem is taken at a ferocious clip by writer/director Serge Rodnunsky.

Jim Gray *Erick* • David Richard *Ralph* • Michelle Verhunce *Gina* • Gina La Piana *Maria* • Jonathan Lutz *Detective Michaels* ■ *Dir/Scr* Serge Rodnunsky

Diamonds on Wheels ★★ U

Action adventure
1973 · UK/US · Colour · 81mins

This generally robust children's thriller, one of Disney's British productions, centres on a 24-hour car rally. Three teenagers (one of whom is Peter Firth) enter the race, unaware of stolen diamonds hidden in their car. The villains (Barry Jackson and Dudley Sutton) give chase. Unfortunately the film runs out of steam when it leaves the racetrack and a slapstick sequence in a warehouse brings everything to a rather tired conclusion. Director Jerome Courtland was a juvenile lead in Hollywood in the forties. ▦

Peter Firth *Robert Stewart* • Dudley Sutton *Finch* • Andrew McCulloch *Billy* • Cynthia Lund *Susan Stewart* • Derek Newark *Mercer* • George Sewell *Henry* • Spencer Banks *Charlie Todd* • Barry Jackson *Wheeler* ■ *Dir* Jerome Courtland • *Scr* William Robert Yates, from the novel *Nightmare Rally* by Pierre Castex

Diana & Me ★★

Romantic comedy
1997 · Ausl · Colour · 97mins

Toni Collette plays a frumpy Australian innocent whose name, Diana Spencer, wins her a trip to London. There her determined efforts to meet her namesake lead to much crossing of paths, serial misadventures with paparazzi photographer Dominic West and her obligatory transformation from geek to chic. Written and produced before the Princess of Wales's death, this cheerful romantic comedy reeks of bad taste, despite the addition of an opening scene that turns the rest of the movie into a flashback.

Toni Collette *Diana Spencer* • Dominic West *Rob Naylor* • Malcolm Kennard *Mark Fraser* • Victoria Eagger *Carol* • John Simm *Neil* • Serena Gordon *Lady Sarah Myers-Booth* • Roger Barclay *Richard* • Tom Hillier *Neville* • Jerry Hall • Bob Geldof • Kylie Minogue ■ *Dir* David Parker • *Scr* Matt Ford, from a screenplay by Elizabeth Coleman

Diane ★★ U

Historical romance
1955 · US · Colour · 110mins

"Sweater girl" Lana Turner is in period costume as Diane de Poitier, the love consultant to French king Pedro Armendariz who nevertheless falls for the king's son, Roger Moore. Stuffed to the frills with Hollywood detail, this lavish production does benefit from its majestic score by the great Miklos Rozsa. The dialogue, however, betrays none of the usual wit and grace of its writer, Christopher Isherwood, whose work inspired *Cabaret* and who was one of that famous group of English writers in the thirties that included WH Auden and Stephen Spender.

Lana Turner *Diane* • Roger Moore *Prince Henri* • Pedro Armendariz *Francis I* • Marisa Pavan *Catherine de Medici* • Cedric Hardwicke *Ruggieri* • Torin Thatcher *Count de Breze* • Taina Elg *Alys* ■ *Dir* David Miller • *Scr* Christopher Isherwood, from the novel *Diane de Poitier* by John Erskine

Diary for My Children ★★★★ PG

Political biographical drama
1982 · Hun · BW · 106mins

Winner of the special jury prize at Cannes, this is the first part of Marta Mészáros's superb *Diary* trilogy. Based on her own experiences in Budapest after her family returned from exile in the Soviet Union, the film gives such a precise portrait of a nation coming to terms with the strictures of communism that it was not shown in the west until 1984. Although time and place are established with great skill, the direction is curiously dispassionate for an autobiography. However, the performances of Zsuzsa Czinkoczi, Anna Polony and Jan Nowicki ensure we are drawn into the drama. In Hungarian with English subtitles.

Zsuzsa Czinkoczi *Juli* • Anna Polony *Magda* • Jan Nowicki *Janos* • Tamas Toth *Janos's son* • Mari Szemes *Grandmother* • Pal Zolnay *Grandfather* ■ *Dir/Scr* Marta Mészáros

Diary for My Father and Mother ★★★

Political biographical drama
1990 · Hun · Colour and BW · 110mins

The concluding part of director Marta Mészáros's autobiographical trilogy, which began with *Diary for My Children* and continued with *Diary for My Loves*. Tracing the course and consequences of the 1956 uprising in Hungary, the film is more focused on historical events than its predecessors. So, while those familiar with the central characters (played with courage and conviction by Zsuzsa Czinkoczi and Jan Nowicki) will have an advantage, the action should still be comprehensible to new viewers. Mészáros spins her complex web of shifting loyalties, dubious motives and personal crises with great skill. In Hungarian with English subtitles.

Zsuzsa Czinkoczi *Juli* • Jan Nowicki *Janos* • Mari Torocsik *Vera* • Ildiko Bansagi *Ildi* • Anna Polony *Magda* • Lajos Balazsovits • Jolan Jaszai • Irina Kouberskaya ■ *Dir* Marta Mészáros • *Scr* Marta Mészáros, Eva Pataki

Diary for My Loves ★★★★ PG

Political biographical drama
1987 · Hun · Colour and BW · 130mins

The sequel to *Diary for My Children* takes events from the death of Stalin to the 1956 Hungarian uprising. Again, Marta Mészáros humanises this momentous period by focusing on Zsuzsa Czinkoczi, the 18-year-old girl whose determination to use her Moscow film scholarship to trace her imprisoned father results in a relationship with activist Jan Nowicki. Acted with integrity and consistently probing the psychological depths of its characters, this is a highly personal yet acutely political film that takes its history from hearts and streets rather than books and Party dictates. In Hungarian with English subtitles.

Zsuzsa Czinkoczi *Juli* • Anna Polony *Magda* • Jan Nowicki *Janos* • Pal Zolnay *Grandfather* • Mari Szemes *Grandmother* • Irina Kouberskaya *Anna Pavlova* • Adel Kovats *Natacha* ■ *Dir* Marta Mészáros • *Scr* Marta Mészáros, Eva Pataki

Diary of a Chambermaid ★★★

Drama
1946 · US · BW · 86mins

Although ostensibly a vehicle for Paulette Goddard, penned and co-produced by her then-husband, Burgess Meredith, this is also a bold attempt by Jean Renoir to make a comedy of domestic manners in the style of his own *La Règle du Jeu*, within the strictures of the Hollywood system. But his intentions are undermined by the inconsistent playing of a seemingly well-chosen cast. Eugene Lourie's sets are also overly intrusive. Yet Meredith's adaptation of Octave Mirbeau's novel and Renoir's direction are not without merit.

Paulette Goddard *Celestine* • Burgess Meredith *Capt Mauger* • Hurd Hatfield *Georges* • Francis Lederer *Joseph* • Judith

Anderson *Mme Lanlaire* • Florence Bates *Rose* • Irene Ryan *Louise* ■ *Dir* Jean Renoir • *Scr* Burgess Meredith, from the novel by Octave Mirbeau

The Diary of a Chambermaid ★★★★ 15

Drama
1964 · Fr/It · BW · 93mins

Shifting the action from the turn of the century to 1928, Luis Buñuel's reworking of Octave Mirbeau's novel is far more savage than Jean Renoir's 1946 version. Exploring his pet themes of sexual frustration, political repression and religious hypocrisy, Buñuel scathingly reveals the fascist tendencies of the French bourgeoisie, while simultaneously presenting a hilarious gallery of grotesques for us to laugh at. Unlike her predecessor, the frantic Paulette Goddard, Jeanne Moreau plays Célestine as a cooly calculating customer, while Michel Piccoli's rakish husband and Georges Géret's bigoted gamekeeper are both suitably loathsome. A mercilessly bitter film, undeservedly overshadowed by the director's other masterpieces. A French language film. ▭

Jeanne Moreau *Célestine* • Georges Géret *Joseph* • Michel Piccoli *M Monteil* • Françoise Lugagne *Mme Monteil* • Daniel Ivernel *Capitaine Mauger* • Jean Ozenne *M Rabour* • Jean-Claude Carrière *Curé* ■ *Dir* Luis Buñuel • *Scr* Luis Buñuel, Jean-Claude Carrière, from the novel by Octave Mirbeau

Diary of a Country Priest ★★★★★ U

Drama
1950 · Fr · BW · 114mins

One of the most influential films ever made, this sublime masterpiece shows how an adaptation can remain faithful to its source while still being wholly cinematic. Building atmosphere, character and content through the gradual accumulation of detail, director Robert Bresson minutely captures the agony, humility and despair suffered by a dying priest who feels he has failed in his mission to increase the holiness of his flock. Claude Laydu, whose first film this was, is utterly convincing in the lead role, and the result is an almost spiritual experience. Although Bresson was forced by his distributors to cut 40 minutes, this is nonetheless a glorious example of the power that cinema can attain. In French with English subtitles.

Claude Laydu *Priest of Ambricourt* • Jean Riveyre *Count* • André Guibert *Priest of Torcy* • Nicole Ladmiral *Chantal* • Martine Lemaire *Seraphita* • Nicole Maurey *Louise* • Marie-Monique Arkell *Countess* • Antoine Balpêtré *Doctor Delbende* ■ *Dir* Robert Bresson • *Scr* Robert Bresson, from the novel by Georges Bernanos • *Cinematographer* Léonce-Henri Burel

Diary of a Hit Man ★★ 18

Crime thriller
1992 · US · Colour · 86mins

This ambitious but gloomy existential thriller never really shakes off its stage origins (Kenneth Pressman adapted his own play) despite an impressive cast. Forest Whitaker plays a world-weary assassin who has an attack of conscience when he is hired to kill Sherilyn Fenn and her Aids-afflicted child. The performances, including cameos from Seymour Cassel, Sharon

Stone and James Belushi, are impressively low-key, but it's just a little too talky and static for its own good. ▭

Forest Whitaker *Dekker* • Sherilyn Fenn *Jain* • Sharon Stone *Kiki* • Seymour Cassel *Koenig* • James Belushi *Shandy* • Lewis Smith *Zidzyk* ■ *Dir* Roy London • *Scr* Kenneth Pressman, from his play *Insider's Price*

Diary of a Lost Girl ★★★★★ PG

Silent drama
1929 · Ger · BW · 74mins

It took German director GW Pabst to recognise the unique qualities of Louise Brooks, ill-used by Hollywood. Having made the exquisite bob-haired actress into an enduring icon with *Pandora's Box*, charting the decline and fall of the amoral Lulu, *Diary of a Lost Girl* followed immediately. This time Brooks's heroine descends into degradation as an innocent victim of circumstance, suffering harsh and painful cruelties at the hands of a social order dominated by sex, money and hypocrisy. Massacred by the censors, apparently almost half the film was excised before its release, but what remains is an absorbing masterpiece of silent cinema. ▭

Louise Brooks *Thymiane Henning* • Josef Rovensky *Robert Henning* • Fritz Rasp *Meinert* • Edith Meinhard *Erika* • Vera Pawlowa *Aunt Frieda* • André Roanne *Count Osdorff* • Arnold Korff *Elder Count Osdorff* • Andrews Engelmann *Director of reform school* ■ *Dir* GW Pabst • *Scr* Rudolf Leonhardt, from the novel *Das Tagebuch einer Verlorenen* by Margarethe Boehme

Diary of a Mad Housewife ★★★★

Drama
1970 · US · Colour · 94mins

An acerbic, witty and perceptive peek at the world of American housewife Carrie Snodgress, married to ineffable snob Richard Benjamin and locked into an affair with suave author Frank Langella. Snodgress was never this good again (she was nominated for an Oscar for her performance), soon descending into sex and drugs and rock 'n' roll (she was married to rock legend Neil Young). Benjamin virtually repeated his smarmy performance in *Marriage of a Young Stockbroker* the following year.

Richard Benjamin *Jonathan Balser* • Frank Langella *George Prager* • Carrie Snodgress *Tina Balser* • Lorraine Cullen *Sylvie Balser* • Frannie Michel *Liz Balser* • Lee Addoms *Mrs Prinz* ■ *Dir* Frank Perry • *Scr* Eleanor Perry, from the novel by Sue Kaufman

Diary of a Madman ★★

Horror
1963 · US · Colour · 96mins

Nineteenth-century French magistrate Vincent Price inherits an invisible evil spirit when he accidentally kills a condemned murderer in prison. This entity, the "Horla", then forces him to slash to death Nancy Kovack, the opportunistic model who has been posing for his amateur sculptures. Then he discovers the Horla responds unfavourably to fire. Standard horror fare, with a neat period atmosphere and Price having another shuddery field day in a tailor-made histrionic role.

Vincent Price *Simon Cordier* • Nancy Kovack *Odette* • Chris Warfield *Paul* • Elaine Devry

Jeanne • Stephen Roberts *Rennedon* • Lewis Martin *Priest* • Ian Wolfe *Pierre* • Edward Colmans *Andre* • Mary Adams *Louise* ■ *Dir* Reginald Le Borg • *Scr* Robert E Kent, from the story *La Horla* by Guy de Maupassant

Diary of a Serial Killer ★ 18

Thriller 1997 · US · Colour · 88mins

While investigating transvestite nightlife, a struggling freelance writer stumbles across a serial killer in action. But rather than report the crime to the driven detective in charge of the case, he strikes up a bizarre deal to document the killer's motives and handiwork. A promising concept is ruined by the soap opera approach taken by director Alan Jacobs and the miscast lead actors. Contains swearing and violence.

Gary Busey *Nelson Keece* • Michael Madsen *Haynes* • Arnold Vosloo *Stefan* • Julia Campbell *Juliette* • Reno Wilson *Larou* ■ *Dir* Alan Jacobs • *Scr* Jennifer Badham-Stewart, Christopher Koefoed

The Diary of Anne Frank ★★★★★ U

Biographical drama 1959 · US · BW · 176mins

Marvellous screen version, based on a successful Broadway adaptation, of one of the most moving stories to emerge from the tragedy of the Second World War, about a Jewish girl forced to hide from the Nazis in occupied Amsterdam. It's beautifully directed by George Stevens in claustrophobic black-and-white CinemaScope, and superbly cast, with doe-eyed Millie Perkins near-perfect as Anne, the role that made Susan Strasberg a star on stage. Shelley Winters garnered a best supporting Oscar, and Academy Awards also rightly went to the camerawork and art direction. This film was seriously under-rated on its release, and is by no means as well-known as it should be.

Millie Perkins *Anne Frank* • Joseph Schildkraut *Otto Frank* • Shelley Winters *Mrs Van Daan* • Ed Wynn *Mr Dussell* • Richard Beymer *Peter Van Daan* • Gusti Huber *Mrs Frank* • Lou Jacobi *Mr Van Daan* • Diane Baker *Margot Frank* ■ *Dir* George Stevens • *Scr* Frances Goodrich, Albert Hackett, from their play, from the diary by Anne Frank • *Cinematographer* William C Mellor • *Art Director* Lyle Wheeler, George W Davis • *Music* Alfred Newman

The Diary of Anne Frank ★★★

Drama based on a true story
1980 · US · Colour · 100mins

In 1959, George Stevens's adaptation of Anne Frank's celebrated diary drew eight Oscar nominations, with Shelley Winters winning a statuette for best supporting actress. Doris Roberts steps into her shoes for this TV-movie remake and turns in a creditable performance, as does Melissa Gilbert in the title role previously played by Millie Perkins. Director Boris Sagal sensibly retained the services of Frances Goodrich and Albert Hackett, who wrote the prize-winning Broadway version of the tale, but the young cast still needed to be handled with care and he was fortunate in having experienced veterans such as Maximilian Schell and Joan Plowright to coax them along.

Melissa Gilbert *Anne Frank* • Maximilian Schell *Otto Frank* • Joan Plowright *Edith Frank* • James Coco *Mr Van Daan* • Doris Roberts *Mrs Van Daan* • Clive Revill *Mr Dussel* • Scott Jacoby *Peter Van Daan* • Melora Marshall *Margot Frank* ■ *Dir* Boris Sagal • *Scr* Frances Goodrich, Albert Hackett, from their play, from the diary by Anne Frank

The Diary of Lady M ★★ 18

Drama
1992 · Swi/Bel/Sp/Fr · Colour · 112mins

Resuming low-budget film-making after a couple of high-profile ventures, Swiss director Alain Tanner reunites with *Flame in My Heart* star Myriam Mézières for what is clearly a vanity project. As the tempestuous leader of an all-girl cabaret act, Mézières is not afraid to flaunt herself as she seduces both Catalan artist Juanjo Puigcorbé and his black wife, Félicité Wouassi. With so much soft-focus sex and so many scenes of Mézières writhing with her pen as she commits her *pensées* to paper, this feels more like a porn flick than the work of a major arthouse talent. Stylish, but wincingly trite. French dialogue with English subtitles.

Myriam Mézières *M* • Juanjo Puigcorbé *Diego* • FélicitéWouassi *Nuria* • Nanou • Marie Peyrucq-Yamou • Gladys Gambie ■ *Dir* Alain Tanner • *Scr* Myriam Mézières

The Diary of Major Thompson ★★★ U

Comedy 1955 · Fr · BW · 87mins

The last outing for Hollywood writer/ director Preston Sturges, who by the time he made this in France seemed more interested in running restaurants than making films. Britain's debonair Jack Buchanan, at the end of his career, still sparkles and is remarkably well-cast. There's much to enjoy in this semi-sophisticated farce with a genuinely Gallic air, faithfully based on author Pierre Daninos's very popular book. But be warned: the crude dubbing mars the American version, saddling such French stars as the delectable Martine Carol and the funny Noël-Noël with extremely unfortunate voice talents. A French language film.

Jack Buchanan *Major Thompson* • Martine Carol *Martine* • Noël-Noël *Taupin* ■ *Dir* Preston Sturges • *Scr* Preston Sturges, from the novel *Les Carnets du Major Thompson* by Pierre Daninos

Dick ★★★

Comedy 1999 · US · Colour · 94mins

Clueless meets *All the President's Men* in this comedy, which stars Kirsten Dunst and Michelle Williams as two dim teens who stumble into the Watergate break-in and soon find themselves working as presidential dogwalkers for "Tricky Dick". It playfully tweaks at the Watergate myths, with the girls becoming fixtures in the Nixon White House and eventually serving as "Deep Throat" for vain, bumbling reporters Woodward and Bernstein. Dunst and Williams are a pleasure to watch; the latter's taped confession of her crush on the president is a high point, as is Dan Hedaya as a foul-mouthed Nixon.

Kirsten Dunst *Betsy Jobs* • Michelle Williams *Arlene Lorenzo* • Dan Hedaya *President Richard M Nixon* • Dave Foley *Bob Haldeman* • Harry Shearer *G Gordon Liddy* • Ana Gasteyer *Rosemary Woods* • Will Ferrell *Bob Woodward* • Bruce McCulloch *Carl Bernstein* • Teri Garr *Helen Lorenzo* ■ *Dir* Andrew Fleming • *Scr* Andrew Fleming, Sheryl Longin

Dick Tracy ★★ PG

Crime drama 1945 · US · BW · 58mins

Cartoonist Chester Gould's square-jawed detective had a remarkable career that culminated when Warren Beatty played him in the 1990 all-star extravaganza. This was the first Dick Tracy feature, though the sleuth had previously appeared in four superb serials, incarnated by the appropriately rugged Ralph Byrd. This flick isn't terribly good; the detective is played by Morgan Conway, who completed two features before public demand had him replaced with – you've guessed it – Byrd. Jane Greer and Mike Mazurki add some clout, but the whole is more cheap than cheerful.

Morgan Conway *Dick Tracy* • Anne Jeffreys *Tess Trueheart* • Mike Mazurki *Splitface* • Jane Greer *Judith Owens* • Lyle Latell *Pat Patton* • Joseph Crehan *Chief Brandon* • Mickey Kuhn *Tracy Jr* • Trevor Bardette *Professor Starling* • Morgan Wallace *Steven Owens* • Milton Parsons *Deathridge* ■ *Dir* William Berke • *Scr* Eric Taylor, from the comic strip by Chester Gould

Dick Tracy ★★★★ PG

Detective adventure
1990 · US · Colour · 100mins

A strange yet successful departure for Warren Beatty, who nurtured this marvellous-looking rendition of the forties comic strip for several years and through many rewrites. Beatty takes the title role as the laconic and almost monosyllabic detective surrounded by villains of a more colourful hue, such as Al Pacino as Big Boy. The film was received with faint but reverential praise at the time, though Beatty fails to inject the enterprise with any great depth or warmth. A near-perfect example of how to bring florid characters off the page and on to the screen. Contains some mild swearing and comic-book violence. DVD

Warren Beatty *Dick Tracy* • Madonna *Breathless Mahoney* • Al Pacino *Big Boy Caprice* • Glenne Headly *Tess Trueheart* • Charlie Korsmo *Kid* • Mandy Patinkin *88 Keys* • Charles Durning *Chief Brandon* • Paul Sorvino *Lips Manlis* • William Forsythe *Flattop* • Dustin Hoffman *Mumbles* • James Caan *Spaldoni* • Kathy Bates *Mrs Green* • Dick Van Dyke *Da Fletcher* • Estelle Parsons *Mrs Trueheart* • Jim Wilkey *Stooge* ■ *Dir* Warren Beatty • *Scr* Jim Cash, Jack Epps Jr, from the comic strip by Chester Gould • *Cinematographer* Vittoria Storaro • *Art Director* Richard Sylbert, Rick Simpson

Dick Tracy Meets Gruesome ★★ PG

Crime drama 1947 · US · BW · 62mins

A rare instance of one of those weirdly named cartoon creations sharing title billing with our hero, and rightly so, since Gruesome is played by none other than the great Boris Karloff, top-billed over many cinema-goers' favourite Dick Tracy, Ralph Byrd. This was the last Tracy movie until Warren Beatty donned the fedora four decades later, and the plot's a hoot: Karloff uses deep-freeze gas to hold people in place while he commits bank robberies.

Boris Karloff *Gruesome* • Ralph Byrd *Dick Tracy* • Anne Gwynne *Tess Trueheart* • Edward Ashley *LE Thal* • June Clayworth *Dr IM Learned* • Lyle Latell *Pat Patton* • Tony Barrett *Melody* • Skelton Knaggs *X-Ray* • Jim Nolan *Dan Sterne* • Joseph Crehan *Chief Brandon* ■ *Dir* John Rawlins • *Scr* Robertson White, Eric Taylor, from a story by William H Graffis, Robert E Kent, from the comic strip by Chester Gould

Dick Tracy vs Cueball ★★ PG

Crime drama 1946 · US · BW · 59mins

The second of RKO's Dick Tracy B movies, with the detective portrayed by the vapid Morgan Conway; Ralph Byrd, who had played the role more convincingly for Republic, would return to the part in the last two RKO films. This is an apprentice work for director Gordon M Douglas, better known for *Them!* and *The Detective* among others, and he keeps the pace up well. Sadly, the production values are shoddy.

Morgan Conway *Dick Tracy* • Anne Jeffreys *Tess Trueheart* • Lyle Latell *Pat Patton* • Rita Corday *Mona Clyde* • Ian Keith *Vitamin Flintheart* • Dick Wessel *Cueball* • Douglas Walton *Priceless* • Esther Howard *Filthy Flora* • Joseph Crehan *Chief Brandon* ■ *Dir* Gordon M Douglas [Gordon Douglas] • *Scr* Dane Lussier, Robert E Kent, from a story by Luci Ward, from the comic strip by Chester Gould

Dick Tracy's Dilemma ★★ PG

Crime drama 1947 · US · BW · 57mins

In the penultimate feature in the RKO series, the studio at last realised the wisdom of casting Ralph Byrd as Chester Gould's comic-strip detective. Byrd, who had previously played Tracy in four Republic serials, seemed born to play the role, and audiences warmed to him. Here he's surrounded by RKO contract players like Jack Lambert and Ian Keith in a quickie that fairly zips through its running time. Though unadventurous in its B-movie plotting, it's a perfectly respectable addition to the series.

Ralph Byrd *Dick Tracy* • Kay Christopher *Tess Trueheart* • Lyle Latell *Pat Patton* • Jack Lambert *The Claw* • Ian Keith *Vitamin Flintheart* • Bernadene Hayes *Longshot Lillie* ■ *Dir* John Rawlins • *Scr* Robert Stephen Brode, from the comic strip by Chester Gould

Dick Turpin – Highwayman ★★ U

Period drama 1956 · UK · Colour · 26mins

There may not be a lot to detain the casual viewer in this brisk tale of highway robbery, which sees Philip Friend stealing the golden dowry of Diane Hart, only for a mutual attraction to develop between them. However, David Paltenghi's slickly directed short is significant in that it launched Hammer Films' very own widescreen process, Hammerscope, which would be used on such prestige projects as *The Abominable Snowman* (1957).

Philip Friend *Dick Turpin* • Diane Hart *Liz* • Allan Cuthbertson *Redgrove* • Gabrielle May *Genevieve* • Hal Osmond *Mac* • Raymond Rollett *Hawkins* • Norman Mitchell *Rooks* ■ *Dir* David Paltenghi • *Scr* Joel Murcott

384
U = SUITABLE FOR ALL Uc = SUITABLE FOR ALL, ESPECIALLY FOR YOUNG CHILDREN (VIDEO ONLY) PG = PARENTAL GUIDANCE

The Dictator ★★

Period romance 1935 · UK/Ger · BW · 87mins

Among the most expensive pictures then produced in Britain, this costume drama had prestige written all over it. Co-sponsored by the German Toeplitz studio, it boasted lavish sets by the Russian designer André Andreyev and sumptuous cinematography by Franz Planer. It even had a fascinating story to tell, as Denmark's 18th-century ruler Charles VII is deposed by his wife, Caroline Mathilde, and a German doctor who falls in love with her on a medical visit. But under the direction of Victor Saville, the action is suffocated by too much pomp and circumstance, while the dashing Clive Brook as the doctor and the stately Madeleine Carroll as the queen are reduced to one-dimensional cyphers.

Clive Brook *Struensee* • Madeleine Carroll *Queen Caroline* • Emlyn Williams *King Charles VII* • Alfred Drayton *Brandt* • Nicholas Hannen *Goldberg* • Helen Haye *Queen Mother Juliana* ■ *Dir* Victor Saville • *Scr* Benn Levy, Hans Wilhelm, HG Lustig, Michael Logan, from a story by HG Lustig, Michael Logan

Did You Hear the One about the Traveling Saleslady? ★ U

Comedy 1968 · US · Colour · 96mins

A showcase for the larger-than-life comedy monster Phyllis Diller, here playing a travelling saleslady who roams the west peddling player pianos. Her career is derailed when she arrives in a small town and her Pianola throws a fit. Local inventor Bob Denver claims he can fix her instrument, but instead embroils her in a number of farcical situations. A charmless offering.

Phyllis Diller *Agatha Knabenshu* • Bob Denver *Bertram Webb* • Joe Flynn *Shelton* • Eileen Wesson *Jeanine* • Jeanette Nolan *Ma Webb* • Paul Reed *Pa Webb* • Bob Hastings *Lyle* • David Hartman *Constable* ■ *Dir* Don Weis • *Scr* John Fenton Murray, from a story by Jim Fritzell, Everett Greenbaum

Didier ★★★

Fantasy sports comedy
1997 · Fr · Colour · 105mins

A bizarre but funny and offbeat French comedy from actor/director Alain Chabat. Costa (Jean-Pierre Bacri) discovers his friend's pet pooch has miraculously turned into a man (Chabat). Capitalising on the canine's capability with balls, Costa hires the man/dog out as a top footballer. Managing to weave into this farcical tale the odd poignant comment on racial tolerance, this is a darn sight better than your average "straight" sports movie, while Chabat is quite remarkable in the title role. A French language film.

Alain Chabat *Didier* • Jean-Pierre Bacri *Costa* • Isabelle Gelinas *Maria* • Caroline Cellier *Annabelle* • Lionel Abelanski • Jean-Marie Frin • Michel Bompoil ■ *Dir/Scr* Alain Chabat

Die! Die! My Darling ★★★

Horror thriller 1964 · UK · Colour · 96mins

For its first suspense thriller in colour, Hammer turned to specialist genre screenwriter Richard (*The Incredible Shrinking Man*) Matheson and asked Tallulah Bankhead to star as a *Baby Jane*-inspired mad matron. Despite being intoxicated throughout the entire shoot, the legendary Broadway diva produced a venomous characterisation of terrifying intensity as the religious fanatic keeping her dead son's fiancée (Stefanie Powers) a prisoner in her rambling mansion. (It was her last screen performance.) Donald Sutherland plays Bankhead's imbecile handyman in one of Hammer's best stabs at the *Psycho*-style chiller.

Tallulah Bankhead *Mrs Trefoile* • Stefanie Powers *Pat Carroll* • Peter Vaughan *Harry* • Maurice Kaufman *Alan Glentower* • Yootha Joyce *Anna* • Donald Sutherland *Joseph* • Robert Dorning *Ormsby* ■ *Dir* Silvio Narizzano • *Scr* Richard Matheson, from the novel *Nightmare* by Anne Blaisdell

Die Hard ★★★★★ 18

Action thriller 1988 · US · Colour · 126mins

Quite simply one of the best action thrillers ever made. Forget the two inferior sequels: director John McTiernan redefined the meaning of suspense when he placed one-man army Bruce Willis in a skyscraper under terrorist control and then had the supercop engaging in one dynamite, eyeball-grazing stunt after another. Willis cemented his sardonic tough-guy image with this hugely popular success, while Alan Rickman brought new dimensions to evil as the German mastermind behind the sinister plot. One of those rare films that just keeps getting better on repeated viewings. Contains violence, swearing, drug abuse and nudity. [video] *DVD*

Bruce Willis *John McClane* • Alan Rickman *Hans Gruber* • Bonnie Bedelia *Holly Gennaro McClane* • Reginald VelJohnson *Sergeant Al Powell* • Paul Gleason *Dwayne T Robinson* • De'Voreaux White *Argyle* • William Atherton *Thornburg* • Hart Bochner *Harry Ellis* • James Shigeta *Takagi* • Alexander Godunov *Karl* ■ *Dir* John McTiernan • *Scr* Jeb Stuart, Steven E de Souza, from the novel *Nothing Lasts Forever* by Roderick Thorp

Die Hard 2: Die Harder ★★★★ 18

Action thriller 1990 · US · Colour · 118mins

Bruce Willis wonders aloud how it could happen to him again, but dons the white singlet anyway for another hugely entertaining slice of action hokum. Director Renny Harlin makes no attempt to re-create the intriguing battle of wits in the original between Alan Rickman and Willis, and instead cheerfully piles on the increasingly grander explosions and set pieces. This time around Willis uncovers a terrorist plot on the ground and in the air as he waits for his wife to fly in to a snowbound Washington airport. Bonnie Bedelia is once again Willis's jinxed wife, while Reginald Veljohnson and William Atherton reprise their roles from the original. Contains swearing, violence and brief nudity. [video] *DVD*

Bruce Willis *John McClane* • Bonnie Bedelia *Holly McClane* • William Atherton *Dick Thornberg* • Reginald VelJohnson *Al Powell* • Franco Nero *General Ramon Esperanza* • William Sadler *Colonel Stuart* • John Amos *Captain Grant* • Dennis Franz *Carmine Lorenzo* • Art Evans *Barnes* ■ *Dir* Renny Harlin • *Scr* Steven E de Souza, Doug Richardson, from the novel *58 Minutes* by Walter Wager

Die Hard with a Vengeance ★★★★ 15

Action thriller 1995 · US · Colour · 122mins

Mad bomber Jeremy Irons keeps Bruce Willis and Samuel L Jackson on their mettle in this third instalment of the *Die Hard* series, with a set of Simple Simon tasks that give a high-speed 20th-century labours-of-Hercules twist to the plot. Whether solving riddles and mathematical puzzles or hurtling along crowded pavements in a taxi cab, Jackson and Willis make a testy duo, trading quips and insults at a pace that matches the breathless action. Returning to the fray after missing the first sequel, John McTiernan directs with a gleeful disregard for narrative logic, especially in the closing stages. Cracking entertainment, though. [video] *DVD*

Bruce Willis *John McClane* • Jeremy Irons *Simon/Peter Gruber* • Samuel L Jackson *Zeus Craver* • Graham Greene *Joe Lambert* • Colleen Camp *Connie Kowalski* • Larry Bryggman *Arthur Cobb* • Anthony Peck *Ricky Walsh* • Nick Wyman *Targo* ■ *Dir* John McTiernan • *Scr* Jonathan Hensleigh, from characters created by Roderick Thorp

Die, Monster, Die! ★★ 15

Horror 1965 · US/UK · Colour · 74mins

Supposedly, but barely, based on the HP Lovecraft story *The Colour out of Space*, former Roger Corman art director Daniel Haller's feature debut is a creditable genre effort in spite of itself. American scientist Nick Adams turns up at a remote village to visit his fiancée Suzan Farmer and her crippled father Boris Karloff only to find that a recently crash-landed meteorite is causing strange mutations. Haller is instinctively adept at getting the most atmospheric chills from the visual components of his terror tale, rather than from the muddled script and weak acting. [video]

Boris Karloff *Nahum Witley* • Nick Adams *Stephen Reinhart* • Freda Jackson *Letitia Witley* • Suzan Farmer *Susan Witley* ■ *Dir* Daniel Haller • *Scr* Jerry Sohl, from the novel *The Colour out of Space* by HP Lovecraft

Die Screaming Marianne ★★

Horror thriller 1970 · UK · Colour · 100mins

Cheaply-made, sensational suspense thriller, filmed during a transitional period that took British director Pete Walker from skin flicks to cult horror films. The plot involves a variety of shady characters trying to force dancer Marianne (Susan George) to reveal the number of a Swiss bank account. Although crudely done by today's standards, some sequences, notably the one in which Marianne's husband (Barry Evans) gradually realises two policemen are bogus, have a certain noteworthy flair. The film was shot in and around Walker's holiday retreat in the Algarve, which adds to the appeal.

Susan George *Marianne* • Barry Evans *Eli Frome* • Christopher Sandford *Sebastian Smith* • Judy Huxtable *Hildegarde* • Leo Genn *Judge* • Kenneth Hendel *Rodriguez* • Anthony Sharp *Registrar* • Martin Wyldeck *Policeman* ■ *Dir* Peter Walker • *Scr* Murray Smith

Die Watching ★★★ 18

Thriller 1993 · US · Colour · 81mins

B-movie king Tim Thomerson is underused here as the detective in charge of a serial murder investigation; somehow we're supposed to believe that Christopher Atkins can carry the film as the antisocial serial murderer. Atkins' character makes erotic videos and occasionally strangles the women who star in them. The police start to suspect him about the same time he falls in love with a local artist. Trashy but titillating, with some hilariously absurd fright effects, it's probably not at the top of Atkins' resume. [video]

Christopher Atkins *Michael Terrence* • Vali Ashton *Nola Carlisle* • Tim Thomerson *Detective Lewis* • Carlos Palomino *Detective Barry* • Mike Jacobs Jr *Adam Parker* ■ *Dir* Charles Davis • *Scr* Kenneth J Hall

Different for Girls ★★★ 15

Comedy drama 1996 · UK · Colour · 92mins

What's Rupert Graves to do? His best mate (Steven Mackintosh) has had a sex change since they last met, and now he's finding himself attracted to her. That's the dilemma in director Richard Spence's decidedly offbeat romantic comedy. What follows is sometimes awkward, sometimes emotionally remote but, because of Graves and Mackintosh's fine acting, always watchable. Thanks to the perceptive dialogue and barbed humour, what could have been a yawn-inducing slice of political correctness turns into a heart-warming tale of sexual confusion and love against the odds. Contains violence, swearing and nudity. [video]

Steven Mackintosh *Kim Foyle* • Rupert Graves *Paul Prentice* • Miriam Margolyes *Pamela* • Saskia Reeves *Jean Payne* • Charlotte Coleman *Alison* • Neil Dudgeon *Neil Payne* ■ *Dir* Richard Spence • *Scr* Tony Marchant

A Different Kind of Christmas ★★

Seasonal drama 1996 · US · Colour

Also known as *Santa and Me*, this is yet another reworking of the old Scrooge formula. Although she's so far failed to find her niche on the big screen, Shelley Long remains a more than capable comic actress and she fully enters into the spirit in this TV movie as the crotchety lawyer who suddenly finds her life turned upside down by pesky part-time Santa Bruce Kirby. This feel-good fare is every bit as sickly sweet as you'd expect it to be.

Shelley Long *Elizabeth Gates* • Bruce Kirby *Santa Claus/Robert George* • Barry Bostwick *Frank Mallory* • Nathan Lawrence *Tommy Gates* • Michael E Knight *Alan Schaeffer* ■ *Dir* Tom McLoughlin • *Scr* Bart Baker

A Different Story ★★ 15

Drama 1978 · US · Colour · 103mins

A ridiculously dated melodrama about homosexual Perry King marrying lesbian Meg Foster to avoid deportation and how they unexpectedly fall in love with each other. Director Paul Aaron's homophobic soap opera-style treatment reinforces every old-fashioned cliché about the ability of gay closet cases to "go straight" and advocates what a fine goal that is. Hopelessly naive when it isn't being insulting, and well acted beyond the call of duty, this isn't a different story, just a simplistic one. ▣

Perry King *Albert* • Meg Foster *Stella* • Valerie Curtin *Phyllis* • Peter Donat *Sills* • Richard Bull *Mr Cooke* • Barbara Collentine *Mrs Cooke* • Guerin Barry *Ned* • Doug Higgins *Roger* ■ *Dir* Paul Aaron • *Scr* Henry Olek

Digby, the Biggest Dog in the World ★★ U

Comedy fantasy 1973 · UK · Colour · 88mins

While Peter Sellers was a natural before a movie camera, his fellow Goons never really found a screen niche. Spike Milligan, for example, looks singularly lost in this kiddie comedy about a nosey pooch who guzzles down a sample of miracle plant food, Project X, and just keeps growing. Even the versatile Jim Dale struggles to make a go of Michael Pertwee's script, which is essentially a one-gag shaggy dog story. Younger viewers will doubtless enjoy the sight of a king-size sheepdog, but older children and grown-ups will probably be put off by the ropey special effects.

Jim Dale *Jeff Eldon* • Spike Milligan *Dr Harz* • Angela Douglas *Janine* • John Bluthal *Jerry* • Norman Rossington *Tom* • Milo O'Shea *Dr Jameson* • Richard Beaumont *Billy White* • Dinsdale Landen *Colonel Masters* • Garfield Morgan *Rogerson* • Victor Spinetti *Professor Ribart* ■ *Dir* Joseph McGrath • *Scr* Michael Pertwee, from a story by Charles Isaacs, from the book *Hazel* by Ted Key

Digging to China ★★ PG

Drama 1998 · US · Colour · 94mins

Evan Rachel Wood is Harriet, a ten-year-old girl unhappy at home with her drunk mother (Cathy Moriarty) and sister (Mary Stuart Masterson). Diving into an imaginary world, she finds companionship and empathy with mentally disabled Kevin Bacon. Together they make plans to dig to China... Far too sentimental and similar in theme to the more successful *Lawn Dogs*, actor Timothy Hutton's directorial debut features scenes between Bacon and Wood that lean towards the unbearable. ▣

Kevin Bacon *Ricky Schroth* • Mary Stuart Masterson *Gwen Frankovitz* • Cathy Moriarty *Mrs Frankovitz* • Evan Rachel Wood *Harriet Frankovitz* • Marian Seldes *Leah Schroth* ■ *Dir* Timothy Hutton • *Scr* Karen Janszen

Digital Man ★★ 15

Science-fiction 1994 · US · Colour · 91mins

A cyborg soldier is assigned to take out a band of high-tech terrorists and ends up with the launch codes to 250 missile silos. As his megalomania increases, he holds the world to ransom in director Phillip J Roth's science-fiction opus, which boasts good special effects and super weaponry but little sense of structure. When things explode and spacecraft fly, Roth's futuristic one-man-army tale passes muster. When the action grinds to a halt, however, so does the dumb story. ▣

Ed Lauter *General Roberts* • Ken Olandt *Sergeant Anders* • Matthias Hues *Digital Man* • Paul Gleason *Dr Parker* • Adam Baldwin

Captain West • Sherman Augustus *Jackson* • Don Swayze *Billy* ■ *Dir* Phillip J Roth • *Scr* Ken Melamed, Paul J Robbins

Dil Se... ★★★ 12

Romantic musical drama 1998 · Ind · Colour · 157mins

Proving that mainstream Indian cinema doesn't necessarily have to be dressed up in Bollywood razzmatazz, this stylish melodrama uses a doomed romance to analyse the subcontinent's political heritage. Director Mani Rathnam may utilise songs to explore his characters' emotions, but he refuses to allow the escapist elements to dominate the story of radio journalist Shahrukh Khan's obsession with provincial girl Manisha Koirala who, unbeknown to him, is a key figure in a terrorist plot to disrupt a parade marking 50 years of independence. Filmed in Delhi and the northern regions, this is a provocative study of a land of drastic contrasts. In Hindi with English subtitles. Contains some violence. ▣

Shahrukh Khan *Amar* • Manisha Koirala *Meghna* • Preity Zinta ■ *Dir* Mani Rathnam • *Scr* Mani Ratnam, Sujatha, Tigmanshu Dhulia, from a story by Mani Ratnam

Dilemma ★

Drama 1962 · UK · BW · 67mins

What would you do if you came home and found your wife missing and a dead body in the bath? Bury the corpse beneath the floorboards? Surely not. Then again, if you were the returning wife, would you condone your husband's actions and spend the rest of your life confined to the house for fear of discovery? Well, this is the situation in which Peter Halliday and Ingrid Hafner find themselves in this risible slice of everyday life. No wonder British B-movies of the sixties had such an awful reputation.

Peter Halliday *Harry Barnes* • Ingrid Hafner *Jean Barnes* • Patricia Burke *Mrs Jones* • Patrick Jordan *Inspector Murray* • Joan Heath *Mrs Barnes* • Robert Dean *Doctor* ■ *Dir* Peter Maxwell • *Scr* Pip Baker, Jane Baker

Dillinger ★★★ PG

Crime drama 1945 · US · BW · 66mins

This is an extraordinarily effective Monogram B-movie, very successful in its day and still playing theatrically over 20 years later in a double-bill with the 1959 film, *Al Capone*. Budget limitations are obvious, but a tough, tight, Oscar-nominated screenplay by Phil Yordan more than compensates. The persuasive direction is by the eclectic Max Nosseck, whose career stretches from shooting cheap movies in Yiddish on Long Island to making the first nudist feature, the infamous *Garden of Eden*. Lawrence Tierney, Scott Brady's brother, wields a tight lip as public enemy number one John Dillinger. The story was remade in 1973 with Warren Oates. ▣

Lawrence Tierney *Dillinger* • Anne Jeffreys *Helen* • Edmund Lowe *Specs* • Eduardo Ciannelli *Murph* • Marc Lawrence *Doc* • Elisha Cook Jr *Kirk* • Ralph Lewis *Tony* • Ludwig Stossel *Otto* ■ *Dir* Max Nosseck • *Scr* Leon Charles, Phil Yordan

Dillinger ★★★★ 18

Thriller 1973 · US · Colour · 106mins

A bullet-laced biography of gangster John Dillinger, who blazed his way to notoriety during the thirties and was the first man to be tagged public enemy number one. Warren Oates gives a wonderfully slimy performance as the rat-like Dillinger, who's pursued across America by Ben Johnson as FBI man Melvin Purvis. The movie was a coup for debut director John Milius, who saw every project as a work-out for his own views on contemporary myth; he went on to co-write *Apocalypse Now* and *Geronimo: an American Legend*. Putting down Bonnie and Clyde as two-bit psychopaths, this hoodlum history is small-scale but devastating all the same. Contains violence and swearing. ▣

Warren Oates *John Dillinger* • Ben Johnson *Melvin Purvis* • Michelle Phillips *Billie Frechette* • Cloris Leachman *Anna Sage* • Harry Dean Stanton *Homer Van Meter* • Geoffrey Lewis *Harry Pierpont* • John Ryan [John P Ryan] *Charles Mackley* • Richard Dreyfuss *George "Baby Face" Nelson* • Steve Kanaly *Lester "Pretty Boy" Floyd* ■ *Dir/Scr* John Milius

Dillinger ★★★ 15

Crime drama 1991 · US · Colour · 91mins

The story of John Dillinger, one of America's most notorious gangsters, has been told on the screen almost as many times as that of Al Capone. Here is one of the most recent versions of the tale, a TV movie starring Mark Harmon, who played the similarly notorious serial killer Ted Bundy in the 1986 TV movie *The Deliberate Stranger*. Harmon manages to be suitably sinister in this interesting film, which also features Sherilyn Fenn and Patricia Arquette. Contains violence and some swearing. ▣

Mark Harmon *John Dillinger* • Will Patton *Melvin Purvis* • Vince Edwards *J Edgar Hoover* • Sherilyn Fenn *Billie Frechette* • Patricia Arquette *Polly Hamilton* ■ *Dir* Rupert Wainwright • *Scr* Paul F Edwards

Dillinger and Capone ★★★

Period crime drama 1995 · US · Colour · 95mins

What could have been a run-of-the-mill gangster picture is given a boost by an interesting and intriguing plot. In 1934, criminal John Dillinger was gunned down by the Feds outside the Biograph Theater in Chicago. In this film, though, it's not Dillinger who gets killed but his brother, and the FBI are unaware of their error. A few years later, Al Capone, who knows the former bank robber's secret, holds John Dillinger's family hostage to get him to recover money Capone has stashed in a Chicago hotel. The film moves briskly along, in part thanks to Jon Purdy's strong direction, but mainly due to the talents of his cast. Martin Sheen hits all the right notes as Dillinger, while F Murray Abraham is surprisingly effective as Capone. Fascinating stuff for fans of the genre. ▣

Martin Sheen *John Dillinger* • F Murray Abraham *Al Capone* • Catherine Hicks *Abigail Dalton* • Michael Oliver *Sam Dalton* • Don Stroud *George* • Anthony Crivello *Lou Gazzo* • Stephen Davies *Cecil* • Clint Howard *Bobo* ■ *Dir* Jon Purdy • *Scr* Michael B Druxman

Dim Sum: a Little Bit of Heart ★★★★ U

Comedy 1985 · US · Colour · 87mins

Delicate but deceptively spicy, this delicious film shows just how easy it is to appear selfless while acting purely out of self-interest. Taking his stylistic cue from Yasujiro Ozu, director Wayne Wang allows the story to develop in its own time and space while drawing us into the world of San Francisco's Chinese community. This enables us to appreciate more fully the emotional games being played out by the elderly Mrs Tam (Kim Chew), her westernised daughter (Laureen Chew) and her roguish uncle (Victor Wong), all of whom dissemble in their relationships to avoid making difficult decisions.

Laureen Chew *Geraldine Tam* • Kim Chew *Mrs Tam* • Victor Wong *Uncle Tam* • Ida FO Chung *Auntie Mary* • Cora Miao *Julia* • John Nishio *Richard* • Amy Hill *Amy Tam* • Keith Choy *Kevin Tam* ■ *Dir* Wayne Wang • *Scr* Terrel Seltzer, from an idea by Terrel Seltzer, Laureen Chew, Wayne Wang

Dimples ★★★ U

Musical drama 1936 · US · BW · 78mins

One of Shirley Temple's biggest hits and, if you've never seen the ring-curled little charmer who became the world's biggest box-office draw, this is as good an introduction as any. There's no doubt that young Shirley had a tremendous instinctive talent, something that her detractors are impervious to. Here she sings (and swings) *Oh Mister Man up in the Moon* and *Hey, What Did the Bluebird Say?* with great aplomb, and plays dialogue scenes with screen grandad Frank Morgan like the seasoned trouper she is. Some may disagree, but, frankly, as a well-meaning kiddie in mid-19th century New York, she's irresistible.

Shirley Temple *Sylvia Dolores Appleby, "Dimples"* • Frank Morgan *Professor Eustace Appleby* • Helen Westley *Mrs Caroline Drew* • Robert Kent *Allen Drew* • Delma Byron *Betty Loring* • Astrid Allwyn *Cleo Marsh* • Stepin Fetchit *Cicero* ■ *Dir* William A Seiter • *Scr* Arthur Sheekman, Nat Perrin, from an idea by Nunnally Johnson

Diner ★★★★ 15

Comedy drama 1982 · US · Colour · 105mins

This debut feature from Barry Levinson remains among his finest work: a gentle, warm-hearted look back at a group of young men in fifties Baltimore. Episodic in structure, this sympathetic portrait of young people on the threshold of adulthood also happens to be rather funny. In addition, Levinson shows a remarkable eye for talent; at the time most of the performers were far from being household names; how much would it cost nowadays to bring Steve Guttenberg, Mickey Rourke, Ellen Barkin, Kevin Bacon, Daniel Stern and Paul Reiser together for one movie? Contains swearing. ▣

Steve Guttenberg *Eddie* • Mickey Rourke *Boogie* • Ellen Barkin *Beth* • Kevin Bacon *Fenwick* • Daniel Stern *Shrevie* • Timothy Daly *Billy* • Paul Reiser *Modell* • Kathryn Dowling *Barbara* ■ *Dir/Scr* Barry Levinson

Le Dîner de Cons ★★★★ 15

Comedy   1998 · Fr · Colour · 79mins

Despite frequently betraying its stage origins, writer/director Francis Veber's splutteringly funny farce – a box-office hit in France – is a model of snowball comedy. From the moment publisher Thierry Lhermitte agrees to exhibit matchstick model-maker Jacques Villeret at one of his clique's "idiot dinners", his idyllic existence begins to fall apart as this balding bundle of good intentions dismantles his deceptions with devastating artlessness. Lhermitte is admirably selfless as the despicable straight man, but Villeret has fashioned a masterly creation: a buffoonish descendant of Stan Laurel, Inspector Clouseau and Norman Wisdom whose every word and gesture has catastrophic consequences. In French with English subtitles.

Jacques Villeret *François Pignon* • Thierry Lhermitte *Pierre Brochant* • Francis Huster *Leblanc* • Alexandra Vandernoot *Christine* • Daniel Prévost *Cheval* • Catherine Frot *Marlène* • Edgar Givry *Cordier* • Christian Pereira *Sorbier* ■ *Dir* Francis Veber • *Scr* Francis Veber, from his play

Dingo ★★

Drama   1991 · Ausl/Fr · Colour · 108mins

Miles Davis and Michel Legrand are the true stars here for producing a jazz score that, for all its geniality, this Australian drama scarcely deserves. Directing with little of the imagination he would demonstrate on his follow-up feature, *Bad Boy Bubby*, Rolf De Heer attempts to impart a fantastical element to this middling meditation on dreams and destiny, in which a chance meeting with a legendary trumpeter transforms the life of a Poona Flats wannabe. Colin Friels impresses as he strives to fulfil his ambition, but – unlike Dexter Gordon in *'Round Midnight* – co-star Davis gives a disappointingly one-note performance.

Colin Friels *John "Dingo" Anderson* • Miles Davis *Billy Cross* • Helen Buday *Jane Anderson* • Joe Petruzzi *Peter* • Bernadette Lafont *Angie Cross* • Steve Shaw *Archie* • Helen Doig *Ruth* • Daniel Scott *Young John* ■ *Dir* Rolf De Heer • *Scr* Marc Rosenberg

Dinner at Eight ★★★★ PG

Comedy drama   1933 · US · BW · 106mins

A sumptuously produced (by David O Selznick) all-star MGM extravaganza, based on the witty George S Kaufman/Edna Ferber Broadway success, but with an even smarter screenplay by Frances Marion, Herman J Mankiewicz and the mordant Donald Ogden Stewart. In the distinguished company of Marie Dressler, Wallace Beery and a couple of Barrymores, blonde bombshell Jean Harlow really shines, and affords Dressler the opportunity for one of cinema's greatest ever last lines. Director George Cukor proved himself highly skilled at handling this kind of super-production; in its day, this was a popular and critical hit. Well worth tuning in for, especially if you've never seen Harlow.

Marie Dressler *Carlotta Vance* • John Barrymore *Larry Renault* • Wallace Beery *Dan Packard* • Jean Harlow *Kitty Packard* • Lionel Barrymore *Oliver Jordan* • Lee Tracy *Max Kane* • Edmund Lowe *Dr Wayne Talbot* • Billie Burke

Mrs Oliver Jordan • Madge Evans *Paula Jordan* • Jean Hersholt *Joe Stengel* ■ *Dir* George Cukor • *Scr* Frances Marion, Herman J Mankiewicz, Donald Ogden Stewart, from the play by George S Kaufman, Edna Ferber

Dinner at Eight ★★★ 15

Comedy drama   1989 · US · Colour · 93mins

Lauren Bacall, Marsha Mason and Harry Hamlin head a prestige cast in this updated TV remake of George Cukor's classic 1933 comedy of New York social manners, itself based on the Broadway hit by George S Kaufman and Edna Ferber. The writing and direction may lack the sparkle of the Cukor version, but Bacall turns on the style as acid-tongued pulp novelist Carlotta Vance, and the story surrounding various guests limbering up for a high-society dinner party offers sufficient human interest to hold the attention. ⸬

Lauren Bacall *Carlotta Vance* • Marsha Mason *Millicent Jordan* • Charles Durning *Dan Packard* • Ellen Greene *Kitty Packard* • Harry Hamlin *Larry Renault* • John Mahoney *Oliver Jordan* • Stacy Edwards *Paula Jordan* ■ *Dir* Ron Lagomarsino • *Scr* Tom Griffin, from the 1933 film, from the play by George S Kaufman, Edna Ferber • *Executive Producer* Shelley Duvall

Dinner at the Ritz ★★ U

Romantic thriller   1937 · UK · BW · 80mins

Despite the utterly enchanting presence of French actress Annabella (the future Mrs Tyrone Power), this British thriller suffers from slack pacing and a hackneyed plot. Annabella plays the daughter of a murdered banker who comes to London to find the men responsible, with a little help from David Niven's government agent. There's little such likeable players as Paul Lukas and Francis L Sullivan can do but go through the motions, although there are a few surprises en route. A period artifact now, this was once considered the epitome of chic.

David Niven *Paul de Brack* • Annabella *Ranie Racine* • Paul Lukas *Philip de Beaufort* • Romney Brent *Jimmy Raine* • Francis L Sullivan *Brogard* • Stewart Rome *Racine* ■ *Dir* Harold D Schuster [Harold Schuster] • *Scr* Roland Pertwee, from a story by Roland Pertwee, Romney Brent

Dino ★★

Drama   1957 · US · BW · 94mins

From the era of *The Blackboard Jungle*, when juvenile delinquency was all the rage, comes this predictably moral story of a teenager (Sal Mineo) who has a hard time in reform school and an even harder time trying to stay straight outside. Adapted by Reginald Rose from his TV play, it has the many of the same concerns he revealed in *12 Angry Men*. Nowadays, though, it looks rather dated and subdued.

Sal Mineo *Dino* • Brian Keith *Sheridan* • Susan Kohner *Shirley* • Frank Faylen *Mandel* • Joe De Santis *Mr Minetta* • Penny Santon *Mrs Minetta* • Pat DeSimone *Tony* • Richard Bakalyan *Chuck* ■ *Dir* Thomas Carr • *Scr* Reginald Rose, from his play

Dinosaur ★★★★ PG

Animated adventure
2000 · US · Colour · 82mins

Disney's most ambitious movie to date (48 animators spent more than three million hours making 70,000 CD-Roms of information that make up the computer-generated animation) is also a return to form after a run of less-than-vintage animated features (*Hercules*, *Tarzan*). While the story isn't exactly Kafka – abandoned baby dinosaur is raised by lemurs until they have to flee during a fiery meteor storm and join other dinosaurs on a treacherous trek to a new land – the animation and characterisations are superb, especially the extraordinary details of the prehistoric creatures' skin and fur. DB Sweeney and Julianna Margulies give life to their characters – the orphaned Aladar and Neera, the dino-babe he meets in his adventures – and there is great vocal support from a cast that includes Ossie Davis, Alfre Woodard and – best of all – Joan Plowright and Della Reese as two ageing and crabby old dinosaurs.

DB Sweeney *Aladar* • Alfre Woodard *Plio* • Ossie Davis *Yar* • Samuel E Wright *Kron* • Julianna Margulies *Neera* • Joan Plowright *Baylene* • Della Reese *Eema* ■ *Dir* Eric Leighton, Ralph Zondag • *Scr* John Harrison, Robert Nelson Jacobs, from a screenplay by Walon Green, from a story by Thom Enriquez, John Harrison, Robert Nelson Jacobs, Ralph Zondag • *Music* James Newton Howard

Dinosaurus! ★★

Fantasy   1960 · US · Colour · 82mins

Jurassic Park this ain't! A caveman, a friendly brontosaurus and a nasty T-Rex are disturbed from their slumber on a tropical island by construction workers in one of the funniest monster movies ever made. Best described as a prehistoric take on the Three Stooges' brand of comedy (see the Neanderthal man have "comical" problems with modern appliances; see the T-Rex fight a steam shovel), viewers will shake their heads in dismay at the cheap mindlessness. Still, lousy special effects and worse acting make it hilariously compulsive viewing.

Ward Ramsey *Bart Thompson* • Paul Lukather *Chuck* • Kristina Hanson *Betty Piper* • Alan Roberts *Julio* • Gregg Martell *Prehistoric man* • Fred Engelberg *Mike Hacker* ■ *Dir* Irvin S Yeaworth Jr • *Scr* Jean Yeaworth, Dan E Weisburd, from an idea by Jack H Harris

Diplomatic Courier ★★★ U

Spy drama   1952 · US · BW · 97mins

A rattlingly good 20th Century-Fox Cold War thriller, shot on actual European locations, with Tyrone Power's blandness offset by his female co-stars: Soviet agent Hildegarde Neff and American tourist Patricia Neal. Look out too for Karl Malden, Lee Marvin and Charles Bronson on their respective paths to stardom. The source for the clever screenplay is from a novel by Peter Cheyney and, with hindsight, the "secret agenda" plot seems chillingly appropriate. Under-rated and well worth a look.

Tyrone Power *Mike Kells* • Patricia Neal *Joan Ross* • Stephen McNally *Colonel Cagle* • Hildegarde Neff *Janine* • Karl Malden *Ernie* • James Millican *Sam Carew* • Stefan Schnabel

Platov ■ *Dir* Henry Hathaway • *Scr* Casey Robinson, Liam O'Brien, from the novel *Sinister Errand* by Peter Cheyney

Diplomatic Immunity ★ 18

Action thriller   1991 · US · Colour · 90mins

A plodding revenge film that, had it been made in the eighties for the big screen (and with a much bigger budget), would have probably starred Steven Seagal. Instead, it is TV star Bruce Boxleitner who gets to kick some bad guy's butt. His daughter is murdered, but her killer is set free because he has diplomatic immunity. Happily, dad is an ex-marine, so he thinks nothing of hopping on a plane and pursuing said baddie to Paraguay. From then on, talking gives way to grunting and punching. ⸬

Bruce Boxleitner *Cole Hickel* • Billy Drago *Cowboy* • Tom Breznahan *Klaus Hermann* • Christopher Neame *Stefan Noll* • Fabiana Udenio *Teresa Escobal* • Matthias Hues *Gephardt* • Meg Foster *Gerta Hermann* • Robert Forster *Stonebridge* ■ *Dir* Peter Maris • *Scr* Randall Frakes, Richard Donn, Jim Trombetta, from the novel *The Stalker* by Theodore Taylor

Dirigible ★★★

Adventure   1931 · US · BW · 104mins

Made some years before his sentimental association with small-town America transformed him into a Hollywood great, *Dirigible* reminds us that Frank Capra also worked in other genres. Two navy pilots experiment with airships, one of which crashes in the Antarctic, resulting in a three-way tug of war between the fame-seeking pilot, his dissatisfied wife and a colleague who covets her. Capra knows how to build and sustain action, but he is less sure with the tortured mush of romance that, at times, sets the film in cement.

Jack Holt *Jack Bradon* • Ralph Graves *Frisky Pierce* • Fay Wray *Helen* • Hobart Bosworth *Rondelle* • Roscoe Karns *Sock McGuire* • Harold Goodwin *Hansen* • Clarence Muse *Clarence* ■ *Dir* Frank Capra • *Scr* Jo Swerling, Dorothy Howell, from a story by Lieutenant Commander Frank W Weed

El Dirigible ★★

Drama   1994 · Urug · BW and Colour · 80mins

Inspired by the suicide of Baltasar Brum, the nation's youngest president, this broad comedy was only the second feature to be completed in Uruguay since the fifties. Unfortunately, director Pablo Dotta fritters away a potentially interesting subject by indulging a penchant for elliptical construction that muddles proceedings rather than imbuing them with a sense of mystery. As the journalist trying to recover a stolen video interview with a reclusive author who witnessed Brum's demise, Laura Schneider gives a spirited performance, as does Gonzalo Cardoza as the kid who steals her camcorder. In Spanish with English subtitles.

Laura Schneider *The Frenchwoman* • Marcello Buquet *Translator* • Ricardo Espalter *Police detective* • Eduardo Miglionico • Gonzalo Cardozo *Snotty* ■ *Dir/Scr* Pablo Dotta

The Dirt Bike Kid ★★★ PG

Fantasy comedy 1986 · US · Colour · 86mins

Fans of the *Herbie* movies should enjoy this similar tale of a boy with a bike that has a mind of its own. Peter Billingsley is the young teen in question, and he seems to have fun playing a character who is continually getting into the sorts of trouble only his wonder bike can get him out of. Not exactly memorable, but amusing nonetheless. ▣

Peter Billingsley *Jack Simmons* • Stuart Pankin *Mr Hodgkins* • Anne Bloom *Janet Simmons* • Patrick Collins *Mike* • Sage Parker *Miss Clavell* • Chad Sheets *Bo* • Gavin Allen *Max* • Danny Breen *Flaherty* ▪ *Dir* Hoite C Caston • *Scr* David Brandes, Lewis Colick, from a story by J Halloran [Julie Corman]

Dirty Dancing ★★★★ 15

Romantic drama 1987 · US · Colour · 95mins

The ultimate feel-good movie, which works a curious charismatic magic and catapulted the then-unknown Patrick Swayze to stardom. Intended as a low-budget filler, this sentimental but never cloying tale of sexual awakening at a Jewish holiday camp in 1963 became a much-loved blockbuster and kick-started major industry careers for its production team. The casting is perfect, with ex-dancer Swayze as the sexy dancing coach and Jennifer Grey as the feisty teenager, and their relationship never strikes a false note. But what really makes the film unmissable is the fabulous dancing which, despite being highly erotic, is never tacky. Contains swearing. ▣

Jennifer Grey *Frances "Baby" Houseman* • Patrick Swayze *Johnny Castle* • Jerry Orbach *Dr Jake Houseman* • Cynthia Rhodes *Penny Johnson* • Jack Weston *Max Kellerman* • Jane Brucker *Lisa Houseman* • Kelly Bishop *Marjorie Houseman* • Lonny Price *Neil Kellerman* • Max Cantor *Robbie Gould* ▪ *Dir* Emile Ardolino • *Scr* Eleanor Bergstein • *Choreographer* Kenny Ortega, Miranda John Pritchett

Dirty Dingus Magee ★★ PG

Comedy western 1970 · US · Colour · 86mins

Frank Sinatra plays a literally lousy outlaw in this vulgar, gross and bawdy comedy western, but he only succeeds in looking anachronistically stupid. There's a nice cast of old western reliables like Jack Elam and Harry Carey Jr on hand to keep director Burt Kennedy's film watchable, plus a gem of a performance from the under-rated Lois Nettleton as a sexually schoolteacher. However, George Kennedy is too heavyweight a presence to co-star in fluff like this, while James Garner would have been a far more suitable lead. ▣

Frank Sinatra *Dingus Magee* • George Kennedy *Hoke* • Anne Jackson *Belle* • Lois Nettleton *Prudence* • Jack Elam *John Wesley Hardin* • Michele Carey *Anna* • John Dehner *General* • Harry Carey Jr *Stuart* ▪ *Dir* Burt Kennedy • *Scr* Frank Waldman, Tom Waldman, Joseph Heller, from the novel *The Ballad of Dingus Magee* by David Markson

The Dirty Dozen ★★★★ 15

Second World War adventure 1967 · US/UK · Colour · 143mins

One of the smash hits of its year, this action-packed war movie is violent and amoral and fans would say all the better for it. Whatever your tastes, there's no denying director Robert Aldrich's consummate skill with such material or the powerhouse impact of the starry all-male cast headed by Lee Marvin, both factors that have helped maintain the film's popularity. The violence is in fact mild by today's standards, but it nevertheless leaves a nasty taste in the mouth as a group of sociopaths are released from jail on a suicide mission to murder Nazis, and the movie rightly earned its original ''X'' certificate. John Poyner won the best sound effects Oscar for his superb soundtrack. ▣

Lee Marvin *Major Reisman* • Ernest Borgnine *General Worden* • Charles Bronson *Joseph Wladislaw* • Jim Brown *Robert Jefferson* • John Cassavetes *Victor Franko* • Richard Jaeckel *Sergeant Bowren* • George Kennedy *Major Max Armbruster* • Trini Lopez *Pedro Jiminez* • Ralph Meeker *Captain Stuart Kinder* • Robert Ryan *Colonel Everett Dasher-breed* • Telly Savalas *Archer Maggott* • Donald Sutherland *Vernon Pinkley* • Clint Walker *Samson Posey* • Robert Webber *Colonel Denton* ▪ *Dir* Robert Aldrich • *Scr* Lukas Heller, Nunnally Johnson, from the novel by EM Nathanson

The Dirty Dozen: the Deadly Mission ★★ 15

Second World War adventure 1987 · US · Colour · 90mins

Having given the world the original *Dirty Dozen* in 1967, MGM probably felt it had the right to send the boys back into battle, after the survivors (plus nine) had appeared in the NBC TV movie *The Dirty Dozen: the Next Mission*. Sadly, MGM's own TV movie was even more ill-advised (although, apparently, insufficiently deadly, as the 12 would not be laid to rest until *The Fatal Mission* in 1988). Telly Savalas (in a new role after dying 20 years earlier) returns alongside the ever-present Ernest Borgnine in a bid to rescue six scientists unwillingly working in a nerve gas factory. ▣

Telly Savalas *Major Wright* • Ernest Borgnine *General Worden* • Randall "Tex" Cobb *"Swede"* • Vince Edwards *Sergeant Holt* • Gary Graham *Stern* • Wolf Kahler *SS Colonel Krieger* • Thom Mathews *Kelly* • Emmanuelle Messignac *Marie Verlaine* • James Van Patten *Ronnie Webber* • Vincent Van Patten *David Webber* • Bo Svenson *Maurice Fontenac* ▪ *Dir* Lee H Katzin • *Scr* Mark Rodgers

The Dirty Dozen: the Fatal Mission ★★ PG

Second World War adventure 1988 · US · Colour · 90mins

Who's doing the dirty on the dozen in this tepid TV movie? Unfortunately, Lee H Katzin's action sequel is utterly predictable. Ordered to foil a plot that will give the Nazis a gateway to the Middle East, Ernest Borgnine and Telly Savalas select a new batch of recruits, which includes such second division TV celebrities as Erik Estrada, Jeff Conaway and Heather Thomas (the first woman to make the team). The plot rapidly descends into a series of murders on the Orient Express as Borgnine and Savalas try to discover which of the team is a traitor. ▣

Telly Savalas *Major Wright* • Ernest Borgnine *General Worden* • Hunt Block *Joe Stern* • Matthew Burton *General Karl Richter* • Jeff Conaway *Sergeant Holt* • Alex Cord *Dravko Demchuk* • Erik Estrada *Carmine D'Agostino* • Ernie Hudson *Joe Hamilton* • James Carroll Jordan *Lonnie Wilson* • Ray Mancini *Tom Ricketts* • John Matuszak *Fred Collins* • Natalia Nogulich [Natalija Nogulich] *Yelena Petrovic* • Heather Thomas *Lieutenant Carol Campbell* ▪ *Dir* Lee H Katzin • *Scr* Mark Rodgers

The Dirty Dozen: the Next Mission ★★ PG

Second World War adventure 1985 · US · Colour · 91mins

It was unwise to attempt to recapture the glory of Robert Aldrich's cynical 1967 Second World War action hit, even though a few of the original cast did manage to show up. Lee Marvin is once again the hard-as-nails officer offering convicts the chance of an early parole and a likely early grave on a suicide mission behind enemy lines, in this case to assassinate a Nazi general. Ernest Borgnine and Richard Jaeckel also survive from the earlier film, but the presence of Larry Wilcox, of *CHiPs* fame, is an indication of the drab, TV feel of the movie. ▣

Lee Marvin *Major Reisman* • Ernest Borgnine *General Worden* • Ken Wahl *Anthony Valentine* • Larry Wilcox *Tommy Wells* • Sonny Landham *Sam Sixkiller* • Richard Jaeckel *MP Sergeant Bowren* • Ricco Ross *Arlen Driggers* • Wolf Kahler *Colonel Sepp Dietrich* ▪ *Dir* Andrew V McLaglen • *Scr* Michael Kane, from the film by Nunnally Johnson, Lukas Heller, from the novel by EM Nathanson

The Dirty Game ★★

Portmanteau spy drama 1965 · Fr/It/W Ger · BW · 91mins

This deglamorising spy compendium is patchy in the extreme. The first section has Vittorio Gassman going undercover in Rome to kidnap a jet fuel specialist; the second involves rival detachments of frogmen doing battle beneath the Gulf of Aden. Sit tight during the sub-standard James Bondism of the opening two episodes, for the Le Carré-esque conclusion affords Henry Fonda the opportunity to demonstrate what a superb actor he is – even though he utters no more than a couple of lines of dialogue.

Henry Fonda *Kourlov* • Robert Ryan *General Bruce* • Vittorio Gassman *Perego* • Annie Girardot *Nanette* • Bourvil *Laland* • Robert Hossein *Dupont* • Peter Van Eyck *Berlin CIA head Petchatkin* • Maria Grazia Buccella *Natalia* ▪ *Dir* Terence Young, Christian-Jaque, Carlo Lizzani, Werner Klinger • *Scr* Jo Eisinger, Jacques Remy, Christian-Jacque, Ennio De Concini, from a screenplay by Philippe Bouvard

Dirty Hands ★★

Crime drama 1976 · Fr/It/W Ger · Colour · 120mins

This is one melodrama that Rod Steiger wanted to wash his hands of. In a faintly risible plot, he's the husband whose wife (Romy Schneider) and her lover (Paolo Giusti) conspire to murder for money. Director Claude Chabrol was nearly as bored with the idea as audiences (he played poker while making the film). Nevertheless, he manages to create some genuinely creepy moments, while Steiger puts together a professional performance. A French language film.

Rod Steiger *Louis Wormser* • Romy Schneider *Julie Wormser* • Paolo Giusti *Jeff Marle* • Jean Rochefort *Lawyer legal* • François Maistre *Inspector Lamy* • Pierre Santini *Inspector Villon* • François Perrot *Georges Thorent* • Hans Christian Blech *Judge* ▪ *Dir* Claude Chabrol • *Scr* Claude Chabrol, from the novel *Damned Innocents* by Richard Neely

Dirty Harry ★★★★★ 18

Crime thriller 1971 · US · Colour · 98mins

Movie history might have run differently had Frank Sinatra not injured his hand, causing him to relinquish the role of renegade cop ''Dirty'' Harry Callahan to Clint Eastwood. This is the first, and best, outing for Eastwood's San Francisco police inspector, in which he tramples on the American Constitution to bring gibbering psychopath Andrew Robinson to justice. A masterpiece of action movie-making, directed by Don Siegel with his usual toughness and crisp efficiency, and acted by Clint with the characteristic hard-boiled traits that are now part of his screen persona and cinema folklore. Making good use of Golden Gate locations, and armed with a darkly cynical and smart script, this original generates an excitement that none of the four sequels could match. Contains violence, swearing and brief nudity. ▣ **DVD**

Clint Eastwood *Harry Callahan* • Harry Guardino *Lieutenant Bressler* • Reni Santoni *Chico* • John Vernon *Mayor* • Andrew Robinson *Killer* • John Larch *Chief* • John Mitchum *DeGeorgio* • Mae Mercer *Mrs Russell* ▪ *Dir* Don Siegel • *Scr* Harry Julian Fink, Rita M Fink, Dean Riesner, from a story by Harry Julian Fink, Rita M Fink • *Cinematographer* Bruce Surtees

Dirty Little Billy ★★★★

Western 1972 · US · Colour · 92mins

Rarely has a myth been so muddied as that of Billy the Kid in this early revisionist western, in which the lad is seen before notoriety gave him outlaw celebrity. Director Stan Dragoti's often surreal visuals mesmerise, with Coffeyville, Kansas seen as a slop-bucket community from which Billy is only too happy to escape. The fictionalised antihero of the Wild West is played here by Michael J Pollard as a mentally challenged eccentric, which tends to subtract some sympathy from his situation. This is probably nearer the truth of the period than the legend, which is why John Ford would have hated it. Contains swearing.

Michael J Pollard *Billy Bonney* • Lee Purcell *Berle* • Richard Evans *Goldie Evans* • Charles Aidman *Ben Antrim* • Dran Hamilton *Catherine McCarty* • Willard Sage *Henry McCarty* • Josip Elic *Jawbone* • Mills Watson *Ed* ▪ *Dir* Stan Dragoti • *Scr* Stan Dragoti, Charles Moss • *Cinematographer* Ralph Woolsey

Dirty Little Secret ★★ 15

Crime drama 1998 · US · Colour · 88mins

This melodrama is a hotchpotch of crimes mixed together to create an unlikely stew. Mary Page Keller plays the wife of a small-town sheriff (Jack Wagner) who finds herself living a nightmare. Their adopted son is kidnapped and held for a $100,000 ransom by a pair of petty criminals, one of whom turns out to be the child's biological mother. The motive for the kidnapping reveals a sordid tale

U = SUITABLE FOR ALL   **Uc** = SUITABLE FOR ALL, ESPECIALLY FOR YOUNG CHILDREN (VIDEO ONLY)   **PG** = PARENTAL GUIDANCE

nvolving her husband and the young woman, played by Tracey Gold. An over-the-top, silly thriller that makes you wonder if anyone in TV movieland ever checks up on their intended before they get married. Contains some violence and swearing. 🎬

Tracey Gold *Sarah* • Jack Wagner *Jack* • Mary Page Keller *Ellie* • Ian Tracey *Ray* • Michael Suchanek *Charlie* • Ben Cardinal *Chuck* ■ *Dir/Scr* Rob Fresco

Dirty Mary Crazy Larry ★★ 15

Action adventure 1974 · US · Colour · 88mins
Peter Fonda steals $150,000 from a supermarket, buys a souped-up car and hits the road with Susan George and Adam Roarke, with cop Vic Morrow in pursuit. Still trading on his *Easy Rider* image, Fonda drifts through what rapidly becomes a demolition derby with pit stops for disputes over Ms George's sexual favours. As one would expect, the cars crash and career spectacularly and the California scenery is often eye-catching, but this road movie pales beside *Two-Lane Blacktop* and *Vanishing Point*. 🎬

Peter Fonda *Larry* • Susan George *Mary* • Adam Roarke *Deke* • Vic Morrow *Franklin* • Kenneth Tobey *Donohue* • Roddy McDowall *Stanton* ■ *Dir* John Hough • *Scr* Leigh Chapman, Antonio Santean, Richard Unekis

Dirty Money ★★★

Crime thriller 1972 · Fr · Colour · 98mins
Jean-Pierre Melville wound down his incalculably influential career with this return to his favourite stomping ground, the *film noir*. This may not be his most innovative work, but the duel between cop Alain Delon and drug-smuggling bank robber Richard Crenna does contain some of his most audacious set pieces, in particular the transfer of a consignment of heroin from a speeding train to a waiting helicopter. The narrative gets a little messy in places as Melville experiments with elliptical editing and shifting time frames. Delon is typically laconic, however, while Catherine Deneuve delivers a virtually silent performance as his mistress. French dialogue dubbed into English. 🎬

Alain Delon *Coleman* • Catherine Deneuve *Cathy* • Richard Crenna *Simon* • Ricardo Cucciolla *Paul* • Michael Conrad *Costa* • André Pousse *Albouis* • Paul Crauchet *Morand* ■ *Dir/Scr* Jean-Pierre Melville

Dirty Rotten Scoundrels ★★★ PG

Comedy 1988 · US · Colour · 105mins
A proficient remake of the old David Niven/Marlon Brando caper movie *Bedtime Story* that attempts to cruise by on star power alone. Michael Caine is the veteran con man eking out a comfortable living on the Riviera, who takes brash American Steve Martin under his wing. However, the pair fall out when they compete to take rich heiress Glenne Headly to the cleaners. Caine more than holds his own against the manic Martin and, while the script holds few surprises, the south of France looks great and director Frank Oz ensures the action slips along

smoothly. Harmless, frothy fun. Contains swearing. 🎬

Michael Caine *Lawrence Jamieson* • Steve Martin *Freddy Benson* • Glenne Headly *Janet Colgate* • Anton Rodgers *Inspector André* • Barbara Harris *Fanny Eubanks* • Ian McDiarmid *Arthur* • Dana Ivey *Mrs Reed* ■ *Dir* Frank Oz • *Scr* Dale Launer, Stanley Shapiro, Paul Henning

Dirty Weekend ★★ 18

Thriller 1992 · UK · Colour · 96mins
Directed by Michael Winner, this was released to a crescendo of controversy concerning its gross violence. Regarded as a sort of *Death Wish* in a skirt, it is definitely Winner's best effort in recent years – though that's not saying much. Lia Williams plays Bella, a much-abused young woman who is egged on by a Brighton clairvoyant to take her revenge on all men. She takes the advice very much to heart, using the knife he gives her to gruesome effect. The film received six minutes of cuts when released on video in the UK. Contains violence, sex scenes and swearing. 🎬

Lia Williams *Bella* • Ian Richardson *Nimrod* • David McCallum *Reggie* • Rufus Sewell *Tim* • Miriam Kelly *Marion* • Sylvia Syms *Mrs Crosby* • Shaughan Seymour *Charles* • Christopher Adamson *Serial Killer* • Sean Pertwee ■ *Dir* Michael Winner • *Scr* Michael Winner, from the novel by Helen Zahavi

Dirty Work ★★★ 12

Comedy 1998 · US · Colour · 78mins
Saturday Night Live has proved to be a valuable creative pool for Hollywood, even if for every *Wayne's World* and *Blues Brothers* there's been a *Coneheads* or a *Night at the Roxbury*. On first glance, this vehicle for Norm MacDonald falls into the latter category. It is a lot smarter than that, however, and, despite losing its nerve by the end, it is for the most part a crudely nasty treat. MacDonald and Artie Lange play a couple of losers who discover their vocation in life: being paid to play humiliating pranks on behalf of wronged victims. Chevy Chase pops up as a cheerfully amoral surgeon, and there's a nicely grumpy turn from Jack Warden. Contains some swearing, violence and sexual references. 🎬

Norm MacDonald *Mitch* • Artie Lange *Sam* • Christopher McDonald *Travis Cole* • Traylor Howard *Kathy* • Chevy Chase *Dr Farthing* • Don Rickles *Hamilton* • Jack Warden *Pops* • Chris Farley • Adam Sandler ■ • *Scr* Fred Wolf, Norm Macdonald, Frank Sebastiano

The Disappearance ★★★ 15

Crime drama 1977 · Can/UK · Colour · 87mins
Few titles have proved as prophetic, for this elegantly-mounted mystery promptly vanished from screens as quickly as it arrived. A shame, for there is much to admire in this tale of a hitman, played by a suitably haunting Donald Sutherland, pondering the disappearance of his wife while planning his next job. Beautifully shot on location in icy Canada, a symbol of the assassin's frozen emotions, the British supporting cast shine, notably David Warner, John Hurt and Virginia McKenna. Only Stuart Cooper's somewhat arty approach to Paul

Mayersberg's admittedly confusing script lets the side down. 🎬

Donald Sutherland *Jay* • Francine Racette *Celandine* • David Hemmings *Edward* • Virginia McKenna *Catherine* • Christopher Plummer *Deverell* • John Hurt *Atkinson* • David Warner *Burbank* ■ *Dir* Stuart Cooper • *Scr* Paul Mayersberg, from the novel *Echoes of Celandine* by Derek Marlowe • *Cinematographer* John Alcott

The Disappearance of Aimee ★★★★

Mystery drama 1976 · US · Colour · 110mins
Based on a true story, this fascinating TV movie involves the disappearance of evangelist Aimee Semple McPherson (played by Faye Dunaway) in 1926. When she returned, Aimee claimed she had been abducted. Her mother, however, believed she had run off to have an affair, and the events became a national scandal. The story is handled in a gripping manner by director Anthony Harvey (*The Lion in Winter*), but it's the performances which keep you pinned to your seat.

Faye Dunaway *Sister Aimee McPherson* • Bette Davis *Minnie Kennedy* • James Sloyan *District Attorney Asa Keyes* • James Woods *Assistant DA Joseph Ryan* • John Lehne *Captain Cline* • Lelia Goldoni *Emma Shaffer* ■ *Dir* Anthony Harvey • *Scr* John McGreevey

The Disappearance of Finbar ★★★ 15

Drama 1996 · Ire/UK/Swe/Fr · Colour · 104mins
The title refers to the vanishing act of a failed young Irish footballer from his home on a Dublin housing estate. Initially a mournful study of the repercussions of Finbar's departure, the film takes on an altogether more humorous tone when his best friend embarks on a Scandinavian odyssey to seek some answers. Griffin's journey provides a few oddly appealing moments and, although the film possesses the strange look of two different movies spliced together, the curious clash of tones and cultures is not without charm. Contains swearing and a sex scene.

Luke Griffin *Danny Quinn* • Jonathan Rhys-Meyers *Finbar Flynn* • Sean McGinley *Detective Roche* • Fanny Risberg *Abbi* • Marie Mullen *Ellen Quinn* • Lorraine Pilkington *Katie Dunnigan* • Sean Lawlor *Michael Flynn* ■ *Dir* Sue Clayton • *Scr* Sue Clayton, Dermot Bolger, from the novel *The Disappearance of Rory Brophy* by Carl Lombard

The Disappearance of Garcia Lorca ★★

Mystery thriller 1997 · US/Fr · Colour · 142mins
After a teenage encounter with Spanish writer Federico García Lorca (Andy Garcia), Esai Morales grows up determined to return to Spain and uncover the truth behind the great man's disappearance and untimely death. His amateur murder investigation suggests that, while a dead poet can be a national hero, a live one can be a national threat. Based on the speculations of author Ian Gibson, this is an interesting study of Lorca and the Spanish civil war, though not a wholly successful one.

Andy Garcia *Federico Garcia Lorca* • Esai Morales *Ricardo* • Edward James Olmos *Roberto Lozano* • Jeroen Krabbé *Colonel Aguirre* • Giancarlo Giannini *Taxi* • Miguel Ferrer *Centeno* • Marcela Walerstein *Maria Eugenia* • Eusebio Lazaro *Vicente Fernandez* ■ *Dir* Marcos Zurinaga • *Scr* Marcos Zurinaga, Juan Antonio Ramos, Neil Cohen, from the non-fiction books by Ian Gibson

The Disappearance of Kevin Johnson ★★★ 15

Mystery thriller 1995 · US/UK · Colour · 101mins
A whodunit thriller set in the movie world featuring Pierce Brosnan, Dudley Moore and James Coburn playing themselves. Filmed in mock-documentary style and unfolding like a real-life piece of investigative journalism, the twists and turns come thick and fast, with the suspense increasing as the surprise ending veers into view. Fascinating, original and hugely entertaining. Contains swearing and sexual references. 🎬

Pierce Brosnan • James Coburn • Dudley Moore • Alexander Folk *Police Detective* • Carl Sundstrom *Security Guard* • Bridget Baiss *Gayle Hamilton* • Ian Ogilvy *Gary* • Charlotte Brosnan *Amy* ■ *Dir/Scr* Francis Megahy

The Disappearance of Vonnie ★★★

Drama based on a true story 1994 · US · Colour · 91mins
The mere mention of the name Ann Jillian should tip you off that we are in true-life TV movie land here. But this story about a woman's determination to explain her sister's sudden disappearance is above the usual standard. Looking typically angst-ridden, Jillian begins to fire on all cylinders as she uncovers more and more unsavoury details about her brother-in-law and discovers the lengths to which the police will go to protect one of their own. Graeme Campbell directs with assurance and restraint, while Joe Penny provides some cynical villainy.

Ann Jillian *Corrine Kaczmarek* • Joe Penny *Ron Rickman* • Graham Beckel *Ken Brodhagen* • Robert Wisden *Randy Winkler* • Kim Zimmer *Vonnie Rickman* • Alicia Witt *Jennine* • Garry Chalk *Andy Kaczmarek* ■ *Dir* Graeme Campbell • *Scr* Ellen Weston

Disaster at Silo 7 ★★ PG

Drama based on a true story 1988 · US · Colour · 92mins
This *China Syndrome*-style drama takes its cue from a real-life, narrowly averted disaster, though much of the potential energy in this tale, of an Air Force technician racing against the clock to prevent an explosion, is snuffed out by an insistence on endless technical detail. (After a while, it feels like we're being given a lesson in heavy engineering.) Ill-defined characters and bland dialogue don't help in a TV movie that appears to have been written by the sort of person who believes that the joy of driving an E-type Jag can be captured simply by reading the manual. 🎬

Michael O'Keefe *Sergeant Mike Fitzgerald* • Patricia Charbonneau *Kathy Fitzgerald* • Dennis Weaver *Sheriff Ben Harlen* • Perry King

Major Hicks • Joe Spano *Sergeant Swofford* • Peter Boyle *General Sanger* ■ *Dir* Larry Elikann • *Scr* Douglas Lloyd McIntosh

Disaster at Valdez ★★★

Drama documentary   1992 · US/UK · Colour

This compelling investigative drama is based on a real-life tragedy that had far-reaching implications because of its devastation to the environment. In 1989, oil tanker *Exxon Valdez* ran aground, spilling 11 million gallons of oil into Alaska's Prince William Sound. Made for TV, the film shows corporate, state and government officials fighting with each other, creating bureaucratic quagmires that lead to crucial delays in the clean-up. The result is the worst environmental catastrophe in US history. A smart, credible docudrama based on extensive research, news footage and interviews, this was filmed in Alaska and Vancouver and stars John Heard, Christopher Lloyd (*Back to the Future*) and Rip Torn (an Emmy winner for *The Larry Sanders Show*).

Christopher Lloyd *Frank Iarossi* • John Heard *Dan Lawn* • Rip Torn *Yost* • Michael Murphy *Bill Reilly* • Ron Frazier *Cornett* • Paul Guilfoyle *McCall* • Bob Gunton *Dietrich* • Mark Metcalf *Kelso* ■ *Dir* Paul Seed • *Scr* Michael Baker

Disaster on the Coastliner

★★★ U

Thriller   1979 · US · Colour · 91mins

A reasonable disaster movie, with a fair quota of stars and an occasionally nail-biting plot about trains on a collision course. As usual in this genre, numerous subplots intermesh with varying degrees of success. William Shatner scarcely convinces as a con man, but Lloyd Bridges and Raymond Burr play the sort of roles they do so well. Richard C Sarafian directs at breakneck speed. 🎬

Lloyd Bridges *Al Mitchell* • Raymond Burr *Estes Hill* • Robert Fuller *Matt Leigh* • Pat Hingle *John Marsh* • EG Marshall *Roy Snyder* • Yvette Mimieux *Paula Harvey* • William Shatner *Stuart Peters* ■ *Dir* Richard C Sarafian • *Scr* David E Ambrose

Disclosure ★★ 18

Thriller   1994 · US · Colour · 122mins

Michael Douglas is caught in that *Fatal Attraction*/*Basic Instinct* trap again, this time with Demi Moore as a former lover who is promoted above him in a smart, intense computer corporation. When Moore seeks to rekindle their passion, the now-married Douglas has second thoughts at a vital moment, and the much-miffed Moore accuses him of sexual harassment. Then the legal eagles descend. Based on a bestselling novel by Michael Crichton and directed by Barry Levinson, this is a self-important and unintentionally funny thriller about corporate power and sexual equality. Moore models some slinky lingerie and Douglas soaks his collars in sweat, though the emphasis on computer gizmos and cyber-babble encourages a verdict of virtual rubbish. Contains swearing and sex scenes. 🎬 **DVD**

Michael Douglas *Tom Sanders* • Demi Moore *Meredith Johnson* • Donald Sutherland *Bob Garvin* • Roma Maffia *Catherine Alvarez* • Caroline Goodall *Susan Hendler* • Dennis Miller *Mark Lewyn* • Rosemary Forsyth

Stephanie Kaplan • Dylan Baker *Philip Blackbum* • Nicholas Sadler *Don Cherry* ■ *Dir* Barry Levinson • *Scr* Paul Attanasio, from the novel by Michael Crichton

The Discreet Charm of the Bourgeoisie ★★★★★ 15

Comedy drama   1972 · Fr · Colour · 97mins

Brilliantly interweaving a sequence of disrupted dinners, three diversionary tales and a quartet of awakenings that alert us to the fact we have been sharing a dream, this sharply satirical and teasingly structured picture is one of Luis Buñuel's finest achievements as both film-maker and social commentator. At once a delightful comedy and a clinical assault on the bastions and behaviour of the bourgeoisie, it touches on all the director's favourite themes: sexual repression, religious hypocrisy and patriarchal paranoia. The playing is exceptional, though Fernando Rey, Delphine Seyrig and Michel Piccoli merit special mention. In French with English subtitles. 🎬

Fernando Rey *Ambassador* • Delphine Seyrig *Mme Simone Thévenot* • Stéphane Audran *Mme Alice Sénéchal* • Bulle Ogier *Florence* • Jean-Pierre Cassel *M Sénéchal* • Paul Frankeur *M Thévenot* • Julien Bertheau *Bishop Dufour* • Claude Piéplu *Colonel* • Michel Piccoli *Home Secretary* ■ *Dir* Luis Buñuel • *Scr* Luis Buñuel, Jean-Claude Carrière

Disha ★★★

Drama   1990 · Ind · Colour · 130mins

Of Russian-Marathi extraction and mostly raised in Australia, Sai Paranjpye was best known for bourgeois satires and children's plays before she tackled this naturalistic town-and-country tale. Firmly rooting the characters in their environment, she makes evocative use of Bombay's teeming textile quarter as Nana Patekar and Raghuvir Yadav arrive in the city, seeking work after their farms are parched by drought. But the most compelling drama takes place back home, where Patekar's wife (Shabana Azmi) falls for the boss of a thriving factory, and Yadav's brother (Om Puri) goes divining to save his homestead. In Hindi with English subtitles.

Shabana Azmi *Nana Patekar Vasant* • Raghuvir Yadav *Soma* • Om Puri • Nilu Phule • Rajshree Sawant ■ *Dir/Scr* Sai Paranjpye

Dishonored ★★★★★

First World War spy drama
1931 · US · BW · 91mins

An erotic dream doubling as a First World War espionage drama, this was the third of director Josef von Sternberg's celebrated collaborations with Marlene Dietrich, and casts the latter as "Agent X-27" and Victor McLaglen as her rival and sexual plaything, "Agent H-14". Rivalling Garbo's *Mata Hari*, which was released the same year, it was a huge box-office hit, luring audiences with its promise of sex and spying. As the sultry spy doomed by her predatory nature, Dietrich is radiant and poised in a performance that is at once controlled and all over the place, the result of von Sternberg's customary exactitude.

Marlene Dietrich *Magda/X-27* • Victor McLaglen *Lt Kranau* • Lew Cody *Col Kovrin* •

Gustav von Seyffertitz *Head of Austrian Secret Service* • Barry Norton *Young lieutenant* • Warner Oland *Gen von Hindau* • Davison Clark *Court martial officer* ■ *Dir* Josef von Sternberg • *Scr* Josef von Sternberg, Daniel N Rubin • *Cinematographer* Lee Garmes

Dishonored Lady ★★

Crime   1947 · US · BW · 85mins

Produced by Hedy Lamarr herself, this screen version of a Broadway hit finds her playing a neurotic magazine editor who goes off the rails and attempts to kill herself by driving her car into a garden wall. Luckily for her, said wall belongs to a psychiatrist! Alas, her shady past catches up with her and she's accused of murder. The wordy script (by Edmund H North, who later won an Oscar for *Patton*) and Robert Stevenson's pedestrian direction are drawbacks, but Lamarr does reasonably well in a role that Bette Davis or Joan Crawford would have turned into a six-course dinner.

Hedy Lamarr *Madeleine Damien* • Dennis O'Keefe *Dr David Cousins* • John Loder *Felix Courtland* • William Lundigan *Jack Garet* • Morris Carnovsky *Dr Caleb* • Paul Cavanagh *Victor Kranish* • Douglass Dumbrille *District attorney* ■ *Dir* Robert Stevenson • *Scr* Edmund H North, from the play by Edward Sheldon, Margaret Ayer Barnes

Disorderlies ★ PG

Comedy   1987 · US · Colour · 82mins

With a combined weight of half a ton – and that's without the obligatory gold teeth and chains – it was hard to ignore rappers the Fat Boys during the mid-eighties. However, their attempt to break into the movies is unlikely to stand the test of time. This Three Stooges-influenced screwball comedy sees the boys coming to the aid of millionaire Ralph Bellamy, who's about to be murdered by an evil nephew. Bellamy's career survived this turkey unscathed – he went on to collect an honorary Oscar – but the Fat Boys' bumbling soon wears thin. 🎬

Damon Wimbley *Kool Rock* • Darren Robinson *Buffy* • Mark Morales *Markie* • Ralph Bellamy *Albert Dennison* • Tony Plana *Miguel* • Anthony Geary *Winslow Lowry* • Marco Rodriguez *Luis Montana* • Troy Beyer *Carla* ■ *Dir* Michael Schultz • *Scr* Mark Feldberg, Mitchell Klebanoff

The Disorderly Orderly

★★★ U

Comedy   1964 · US · Colour · 89mins

Jerry Lewis's comic genius is very much a matter of taste. In France he's virtually canonised; elsewhere, though, he has admirers and detractors in equal parts. This is exactly the type of movie that tends to infuriate both parties. It's very, very funny, with a wonderful climactic chase and a particularly hysterical moment where Lewis has sympathy pains with the choleric Alice Pearce. However, the film also contains some of the most melancholy and cloying sentiment in the whole of Lewis's oeuvre. For once, director Frank Tashlin seems unable to control Jerry, which is not necessarily a bad thing, and the sight gags are tremendous.

Jerry Lewis *Jerome Littlefield* • Glenda Farrell *Dr Jean Howard* • Everett Sloane *Mr Tuffington* •

• Karen Sharpe *Julie Blair* • Kathleen Freeman *Maggie Higgins* • Del Moore *Dr Davenport* • Susan Oliver *Susan Andrews* • Alice Pearce *Talkative patient* • Jack E Leonard *Fat Jack* ■ *Dir* Frank Tashlin • *Scr* Frank Tashlin, from a story by Norm Liebmann, Ed Haas

Disorganized Crime ★★ 15

Crime comedy   1989 · US · Colour · 97mins

A weedy, shambolic crime caper, notable for the early appearances of some emerging minor stars – Corbin Bernsen and Lou Diamond Phillips. In what could have been a jolly roller-coaster ride, a group of criminals mooch about expectantly as they wait for the mastermind behind their latest heist to show up, but the movie deteriorates all too swiftly. Still, the assembled actors fight gamely with the lousy script, managing to create the occasional flicker of interest. Contains violence and swearing. 🎬

Hoyt Axton *Sheriff Henault* • Corbin Bernsen *Frank Salazar* • Rubén Blades *Carlos Barrios* • Fred Gwynne *Max Green* • Ed O'Neill *George Denver* • Lou Diamond Phillips *Ray Forgy* ■ *Dir/Scr* Jim Kouf

A Dispatch from Reuters

★★★ U

Biography   1940 · US · BW · 98mins

In the last of its series of high-minded historical biographies, Warner Bros squeezes a surprising amount of tense drama out of the story of Julius Reuter, whose passion for spreading the news goes from pigeon post to establishing his famous impartial wire service. Relishing a peaceful character part for once, Edward G Robinson is eminently watchable as Reuter, while director William Dieterle, teamed with ace cameraman James Wong Howe, gives the film pace and visual distinction.

Edward G Robinson *Julius Reuter* • Edna Best *Ida Magnus* • Albert Basserman *Franz Geller* • Gene Lockhart *Bauer* • Otto Kruger *Dr Magnus* • Nigel Bruce *Sir Randolph Persham* ■ *Dir* William Dieterle • *Scr* Milton Krims

Disraeli ★★

Biographical drama   1929 · US · BW · 90mins

Stolid biopic of the prime minister and Victorian novelist starring the monocled George Arliss, who had previously played Dizzy in a silent movie of 1921, as well as a play that toured the world for years. The real Mrs Arliss, Florence, gets to play Mrs Disraeli as well, so that must have been nice. On the political front, it's the race to purchase the Suez Canal in front of the Russians that commands the PM's attention, but on the domestic front it's romantic matchmaking. A legend has come down to us about an American tourist who said in Westminster Abbey: "My, what a lovely statue of George Arliss."

George Arliss *Disraeli* • Joan Bennett *Lady Clarissa Pevensey* • Florence Arliss *Lady Mary Beaconfield* • Anthony Bushell *Charles, Lord Deeford* • David Torrence *Sir Michael, Lord Probert* ■ *Dir* Alfred E Green • *Scr* Julien Josephson, from the play by Louis Napoleon Parker

U = SUITABLE FOR ALL   Uc = SUITABLE FOR ALL, ESPECIALLY FOR YOUNG CHILDREN (VIDEO ONLY)   PG = PARENTAL GUIDANCE

Distance ★★

Drama 1975 · US · Colour · 94mins

This rarely-seen independent movie capably chronicles the trials and tribulations of two Army couples during the fifties. Though watchable enough, the film is most notable for an early lead performance from James Woods who, even 25 years ago, was starting to develop the edgy, electrifying acting style that he'd later bring to such films as *Salvador*, *Against All Odds* and *The Boost* . Bibi Besch is the mother of actress Samantha Mathis.

Paul Benjamin *Elwood* • Eija Pokkinen *Greta* • James Woods *Larry* • Bibi Besch *Joanne* ■ *Dir* Anthony Lover • *Scr* Jay Castle

Distant Drums ★★**U**

Adventure 1951 · US · Colour · 99mins

Set in Florida, this Warner Bros movie is technically not a western, despite dealing with Red Indian Seminoles on the warpath against an expeditionary force in 1840. The supporting cast, led by Mari Aldon, is way below par, so the whole thing is held together by the sheer star power of Cooper. If it all seems a little familiar, that's because this is actually a reworking of an earlier success by the same director, the controversial Second World War drama, *Objective, Burma!*.

Gary Cooper *Captain Quincy Wyatt* • Mari Aldon *Judy Beckett* • Richard Webb *Richard Tufts* • Ray Teal *Private Mohair* • Arthur Hunnicutt *Monk* • Robert Barrat *General Zachary Taylor* • Clancy Cooper *Sergeant Shane* ■ *Dir* Raoul Walsh • *Scr* Niven Busch, Martin Rackin, from a story by Niven Busch

Distant Harmony ★★

Music documentary
1987 · US · Colour · 85mins

Seeing that *From Mao to Mozart: Isaac Stern in China* won the Oscar for best documentary, it's easy to see why DeWitt Sage was tempted to record Luciano Pavarotti's 1986 visit to the Forbidden City. Where Stern placed himself at the service of budding Chinese musicians, however, Pavarotti is content to be treated like a celebrity. Sage follows the legendary tenor at a respectable distance, capturing the inevitable culture clashes with a wry detachment. Once he reaches the Great Hall and the focus shifts firmly to music, though, you can almost forgive him for everything.

Dir DeWitt Sage

Distant Justice ★★**18**

Thriller 1992 · Jap/US · Colour · 87mins

A routine title for a routine thriller about a committed police chief who throws away the rulebook to help a pal track down the man who killed his wife and kidnapped his kid. The result is less than arresting, though Hollywood veteran George Kennedy turns in a better performance than the material merits. David Carradine co-stars. 🖿

Bunta Sugawara *Rio Yuki* • David Carradine *Joe Foley* • George Kennedy *Tom Bradfield* • Yoko Nogiwa *Hiroko* • Eric Lutes *Charlie Givens* • Sakura Sugawara *Sakura* ■ *Dir* Toru Murakawa • *Scr* Toshiyuki Tabe

Distant Thunder ★★★★

Drama 1973 · Ind · Colour · 101mins

Winner of the Golden Bear for best movie at the Berlin film festival, this harrowing drama, set during the famine that ravaged Bengal in the early forties, is one of Satyajit Ray's most politically committed films. Yet it retains the humanism and concern for character that makes his work so compelling and rewarding. While the railings at the caste system and government corruption make for powerful viewing, it's the slow realisation of a Brahmin and his wife that people matter more than rigid rules that makes this an unmissable experience. Soumitra Chatterjee and Babita are superb in the leads, bringing intimacy and humanity to a monumental and tragic tale. In Bengali with English subtitles.

Soumitra Chatterjee *Gangacharan* • Babita *Ananga* • Sandhya Roy *Chutki* • Ramesh Mukherjee *Biswas* • Chitra Bannerjee • Govinda Chakravarty • Noni Ganguly • Seli Pal • Suchita Roy ■ *Dir/Scr* Satyajit Ray

Distant Thunder ★★★**18**

Drama 1988 · Can/US · Colour · 109mins

Not to be confused with Satyajit Ray's prize-winning Indian film of the same name, this more recent and less acclaimed Canadian/US effort casts the admirable John Lithgow as a traumatised Vietnam vet who has abandoned society for life in the wilds. Karate Kid Ralph Macchio plays the teenage son he deserted as a toddler. Thanks mainly to Lithgow, who doesn't know how to give a bad performance, this occasionally violent film holds the attention, despite struggling at times to keep its maudlin elements in check. Contains swearing. 🖿

John Lithgow *Mark Lambert* • Ralph Macchio *Jack Lambert* • Kerrie Keane *Char* • Reb Brown *Harvey Nitz* • Janet Margolin *Barbara Lambert* • Denis Arndt *Larry* • Jamey Sheridan *Moss* • Tom Bower *Louis* ■ *Dir* Rick Rosenthal • *Scr* Robert Stitzel, from a story by Robert Stitzel, Deedee Wehle

A Distant Trumpet ★★★★

Western 1964 · US · Colour · 117mins

The last film from veteran director Raoul Walsh, who was deemed too old to be insured at the time this was made – Jack Warner himself (the last surviving Warner brother) posted the bond for his old associate. The result is impressive: a handsome, intelligent cavalry western, superbly scored by Max Steiner and ravishingly shot by western old-hand William Clothier. Walsh makes partial reparation to the hordes of Indians slaughtered in previous westerns by using subtitles in an attempt to preserve their dignity, and the complex military themes are well handled. What lets this fine movie down, though, is the casting. Newlyweds Troy Donahue and Suzanne Pleshette are just too sixties in hairstyle and attitude to convince us they belong in Walsh's Old West. Some native American dialogue with English subtitles.

Troy Donahue *Second Lt Matthew Hazard* • Suzanne Pleshette *Kitty Mainwaring* • Diane McBain *Laura Greenleaf* • James Gregory *General Alexander Quait* • William Reynolds *Lt*

Mainwaring • Claude Akins *Seely Jones* ■ *Dir* Raoul Walsh • *Scr* John Twist, Richard Fielder, Albert Beich, from the novel by Paul Horgan

Distant Voices, Still Lives ★★★★**15**

Drama 1988 · UK · Colour · 80mins

British cinema has no reputation whatever for musicals. Yet never has song been used so poignantly as in Terence Davies's painful, yet curiously fond recollection of postwar Liverpool. The popular tunes that punctuate the ritualistic round of family gatherings and boozer sing-songs jarringly counterpoint the irrational violence perpetrated by Pete Postlethwaite's short-fused father. Unflinchingly depicting both the beatings and their consequences, Davies brings a bruising realism to the stylised series of vignettes, which adeptly avoid the patronising tone that jaundices so many portraits of working-class life. The director followed this haunting film with the even more remarkable *The Long Day Closes*. 🖿

Freda Dowie *Mother* • Pete Postlethwaite *Father* • Angela Walsh *Eileen* • Dean Williams *Tony* • Lorraine Ashbourne *Maisie* • Marie Jelliman *Jingles* • Sally Davies *Eileen as a child* • Nathan Walsh *Tony as a child* • Susan Flanagan *Maisie as a child* • Michael Starke *Dave* ■ *Dir/Scr* Terence Davies

The Distinguished Gentleman ★★★**15**

Comedy 1992 · US · Colour · 107mins

After a semi-successful attempt at a more sophisticated style in *Boomerang*, Eddie Murphy seems happier in this return to familiar territory, playing a smooth talking grifter who sets his sights on the ultimate con – politics. However, on his election as a senator, he quickly learns that the biggest villains are in Washington. Director Jonathan Lynn, of *Yes, Minister* fame, is a lot gentler on the American political scene than he was with our own. But there are some neat satirical jibes and he gives free rein to Murphy, who delivers his most relaxed performance in years. Contains swearing and nudity. 🖿

Eddie Murphy *Thomas Jefferson Johnson* • Lane Smith *Dick Dodge* • Sheryl Lee Ralph *Miss Loretta* • Joe Don Baker *Olaf Andersen* • Kevin McCarthy *Terry Corrigan* • Charles S Dutton *Elijah Hawkins* • Noble Willingham *Zeke Bridges* • James Garner *Jeff Johnson* ■ *Dir* Jonathan Lynn • *Scr* Marty Kaplan, from a story by Marty Kaplan, Jonathan Reynolds

Distortions ★★★**18**

Thriller 1987 · US · Colour · 94mins

Ever wonder what happened to Piper Laurie in between *The Hustler* and *Twin Peaks*? Apparently she was in training for her role in David Lynch's weird but wonderful TV series, appearing in Armand Mastroianni's almost equally bizarre thriller. Olivia Hussey's husband meets a violent end following an encounter with a gigolo. Presented with his charred remains, his widow starts to experience disturbing hallucinations under the malign influence of Margot (Laurie), who is holding her captive. Not well-known, but worth seeking out for lovers of suspense. 🖿

Olivia Hussey *Amy* • Piper Laurie *Margot* • Steve Railsback *Scott* • Rita Gam *Mildred* • June Chadwick • Terence Knox ■ *Dir* Armand Mastroianni • *Scr* John F Goff

Disturbed ★★**18**

Psychological horror thriller
1990 · US · Colour · 93mins

The asylum has become almost as popular a location for horror films as the gothic mansion or spooky cemetery, but none have been played more for laughs than this low-budget thriller from director Charles Winkler, son of *Rocky* producer Irvin. A blond Malcolm McDowell stars as a psychiatrist who probably needs more treatment than the whole ward of stereotypical nuts he treats, especially when a patient he murdered returns to haunt him. McDowell's broad brush strokes are in tune with Winkler's demented camerawork. 🖿

Malcolm McDowell *Dr Derek Russell* • Geoffrey Lewis *Michael* • Priscilla Pointer *Nurse Francine* • Pamela Gidley *Sandy Ramirez* • Irwin Keyes *Pat Tuel* • Clint Howard *Brian* ■ *Dir* Charles Winkler • *Scr* Charles Winkler, Emerson Bixby

Disturbing Behaviour ★★**15**

Thriller 1998 · US · Colour · 80mins

Bad kids in a small town are turning good after undergoing experimental psychological treatment in this tepid teen variation on *The Stepford Wives*. Trouble is, they turn homicidal when sexually aroused, and it seems high school student James Marsden is the only one to notice. Director David Nutter brings some of his trademark *X Files* moodiness to the material, but he can't seem to decide what sort of film he's making. A statement about individuality versus conformity? Or just another run-of-the-mill slash-fest? Hopes that this might turn out to be a smart, paranoid conspiracy thriller are slowly dashed. Contains swearing. **DVD**

Bruce Greenwood *Dr Caldicott* • Katie Holmes *Rachel Wagner* • William Sadler *Dorian Newberry* • Nick Stahl *Gavin Strick* • Steve Railsback *Officer Cox* • James Marsden *Steve Clark* • Tobias Mehler *Andy Effkin* ■ *Dir* David Nutter • *Scr* Scott Rosenberg

Diva ★★★★**15**

Crime drama 1981 · Fr · Colour · 112mins

Considered one of the masterpieces of *cinéma du look* (the name given to French films of the eighties in which style took precedence over content), *Diva* marked the directorial debut of Jean-Jacques Beineix. It's a dazzling job, brimful with bravura camera movements and ultra-chic images. The tale of two tapes (one a bootlegged recording of an opera star, the other incriminating evidence against a police inspector) rather gets lost as Beineix experiments with styles ranging from the Feuillade serials of the early years of the last century to the New Wave of the fifties and sixties. Yet this remains compelling viewing, if only for the amazing performance of Dominique Pinon (*Delicatessen*). In French with English subtitles. Contains violence, swearing and nudity. 🖿

Frédéric Andrei *Jules* • Wilhelmenia Wiggins Fernandez *Cynthia Hawkins* • Richard Bohringer *Gorodish* • Thuy An Luu *Alba* •

Jacques Fabbri *Inspector Jean Saporta* • Dominique Pinon *Le Curé* • Jean-Jacques Moreau *Krantz* ■ *Dir* Jean-Jacques Beineix • *Scr* Jean-Jacques Beineix, Jean Van Hamme, from the novel by Delacorta • *Cinematographer* Philippe Rousselot

The Dive ★ 15
Thriller 1989 · Nor/UK · Colour · 92mins

It may be one of Norway's biggest box-office successes, but this pedestrian deep sea action thriller really only merits "nul point". A dangerous rescue operation is launched when a group of divers is trapped underwater, but the formulaic plot poses a far bigger threat to the proceedings than the treacherous ocean currents. Nicely shot in shimmering dark hues, but hopeless in the suspense and empathy departments. ▣

Michael Kitchen *Bricks* • Frank Grimes *Dobs* • Bjorn Sundquist *Gunnar* • Marika Lagercrantz *Ann* • Sverre Anker Ousdal *Captain* • Nils Ole Oftebro *Akselsen* ■ *Dir* Tristan De Vere Cole • *Scr* Leidulv Risan, Carlos Wigan

Dive Bomber ★★★ PG
Wartime drama 1941 · US · Colour · 126mins

A wonderful flying drama, with the likes of Errol Flynn and Fred MacMurray in fine fettle for a *Boys' Own* treat directed by Michael Curtiz, a year before he made *Casablanca*. Ostensibly a piece of serious research into pilot blackout, it gives all concerned a roaring excuse to slap each other about in friendly fashion in a flurry of patched leather elbows. If your idea of a good film is the wind in your hair and aerial thrills and spills, this is the perfect movie. ▣

Errol Flynn *Lieutenant Doug Lee* • Fred MacMurray *Commander Joe Blake* • Ralph Bellamy *Dr Lance Rogers* • Alexis Smith *Linda Fisher* • Regis Toomey *Tim Griffin* • Robert Armstrong *Art Lyons* • Allen Jenkins *Lucky Dice* ■ *Dir* Michael Curtiz • *Scr* Frank Wead, Robert Buckner, from the story *Beyond the Blue Sky* by Frank Wead

Divided by Hate ★★ PG
Drama based on a true story
1997 · US · Colour · 88mins

Tom Skerritt both directs and stars in this family drama in which an unemployed farmer's wife turns to a local prayer meeting for solace. What she finds is not redemption, but a rapidly growing hate group who lure the downtrodden into their cult with promises of eternal salvation. Her husband sees through their façade, but not before his wife has taken their children and run off with the group to live in their compound. Skerritt does an admirable turn as the charismatic cult leader, as does Andrea Roth as the gripped wife. Yet good intentions and a social conscience don't justify the convoluted narrative, which disintegrates into melodrama by the end. ▣

Dylan Walsh *Louis Gibbs* • Andrea Roth *Carol Gibbs* • Jim Beaver *Danny Leland* • Tom Skerritt *Steve Riordan* • Michael Ruud *Harlan Sorenson* • Kyle Hansen *Billy Gibbs* ■ *Dir* Tom Skerritt • *Scr* Leonard Gross, from a story by Dennis O'Flaherty, Leonard Gross

The Divided Heart ★★ U
Drama 1954 · UK · BW · 89mins

This British melodrama would be dismissed as sentimental tosh if it wasn't based on a true story that hit the headlines in the mid-forties. Drawing on the actual records of the case, director Charles Crichton uses a series of artful flashbacks to pad out the courtroom battle at the centre of the action, as biological mother Yvonne Mitchell fights Cornell Borchers for custody of the child Borchers adopted as a war orphan. Crichton lays on the pathos so thickly that the emotional drama never really tugs at our heartstrings.

Cornell Borchers *Inga* • Yvonne Mitchell *Sonja* • Armin Dahlen *Franz* • Alexander Knox *Chief Justice* • Geoffrey Keen *Marks* • Michel Ray *Toni* • Martin Keller • Liam Redmond *First Justice* • Eddie Byrne *Second Justice* ■ *Dir* Charles Crichton • *Scr* Jack Whittingham, Richard Hughes

The Divine Comedy ★★
Psychological drama
1992 · Por · Colour · 140mins

Winner of the special jury prize at Venice, this densely symbolic tract has little in common with Dante's medieval masterpiece, even though it shares such themes as faith and truth, sin and delusion. Veteran Portuguese director Manoel de Oliveira also scripted this portrait of an asylum where every patient believes themselves to be a character from the Bible or, in the case of Maria de Medeiros and Miguel Guilherme, from *Crime and Punishment*. Indeed, the ideas of Dostoyevsky and Nietzsche are referenced as often as the scriptures in a wordy picture that is rarely enlightening or engrossing. In Portuguese with English subtitles.

Maria de Medeiros *Sonya* • Miguel Guilherme *Raskolnikov* • Luis Miguel Cintra *The prophet* • Mario Viegas *The philosopher* • Leonor Silveira *Eve* • Diogo Doria *Ivan* • Paulo Matos *Jesus* • Carlos Gomes *Adam* • Ruy Furtado *The director* ■ *Dir/Scr* Manoel de Oliveira

The Divine Lady ★★★
Silent historical drama 1928 · US · BW

Director Frank Lloyd won an early Oscar for this story of Emma, Lady Hamilton, Nelson's mistress and one of the most notorious women in English history. Corinne Griffith has a generous sweep of personality as Emma, though her performance pales in comparison with Vivien Leigh's in *That Hamilton Woman* (1941). The historical detail is taken very much for granted, and the film's appeal at the time was mainly due to its novelty.

Corinne Griffith *Emma, Lady Hamilton* • Victor Varconi *Lord Nelson* • HB Warner *Sir William Hamilton* • Ian Keith *Greville* • William Conklin *Romney* • Marie Dressler *Mrs Hart* ■ *Dir* Frank Lloyd • *Scr* Harry Carr (titles), Edwin Justus Mayer (titles), Forrest Halsey, from the novel *The Divine Lady: a Romance of Nelson and Emma Hamilton* by E Barrington

Divine Madness ★★★ 15
Concert movie 1980 · US · Colour · 82mins

Shot over four days using up to 20 cameras, Michael Ritchie's record of Bette Midler's shows at the Pasadena Civic Auditorium broke the mould for concert films in terms of look and technique. Backed by the Harlettes, Bette blazes through songs and comic routines with the kind of unfettered energy that is sometimes the undoing of her feature work. Midler has an amazing range as a singer, but there's nothing particularly new in her interpretations, unlike her mix of stand-up and sketches that are as varied as her outlandish costumes. There's little sense of "being there", however, and ultimately the exercise seems rather clinical. Contains swearing. ▣

Dir Michael Ritchie • *Scr* Jerry Blatt, Bette Midler, Bruce Vilanch

The Divine Woman
Silent romantic drama 1928 · US · BW

A long-lost treat for Greta Garbo fans, this film is now one of the American Film Institute's "most wanted" movies. The divine Greta starts out as a Breton peasant girl and ends up taking Paris – and lover Lars Hanson – by storm. Directed by by Garbo's great mentor, Victor Seastrom.

Greta Garbo *Marianne* • Lars Hanson *Lucien* • Lowell Sherman *Legrand* • Polly Moran *Mme Pigonier* • Dorothy Cumming *Mme Zizi Rouck* • John Mack Brown [Johnny Mack Brown] *Jean Lery* • Cesare Gravina *Gigi* • Paulette Duval *Paulette* ■ *Dir* Victor Seastrom [Victor Sjöström] • *Scr* Dorothy Farnum, John Colton (titles), from the play *Starlight* by Gladys Unger

The Diviners ★★★
Period drama 1992 · Can · Colour · 117mins

A respectful and suitably epic tale of Canadian life, based on a controversial but much-loved novel from Margaret Laurence. *Videodrome's* Sonja Smits takes centre stage as Morag Gunn, a country girl who went on to become an acclaimed writer but who remained haunted by a troubled family life. Smits is excellent and she is well supported by a largely unfamiliar cast, while director Anne Wheeler and cinematographer Rene Ohashi work hard to avoid the bland visual design usually associated with TV movies.

Sonja Smits *Morag Gunn* • Tom Jackson *Jules Tonnerre* • Wayne Robson *Christie Logan* • Nicola Cavendish *Ella Gerson* • Jennifer Podemski *Pique Gunn Tonnerre* • Don Francks *Royland* • Geordie Johnson *Brooke Skelton* ■ *Dir* Anne Wheeler • *Scr* Linda Svendsen, from the novel by Margaret Laurence

Divorce American Style ★★★
Satirical comedy
1967 · US · Colour · 109mins

This sophisticated, brilliantly cast comedy is compulsive viewing. The title, taken from the 1961 Italian original, masks a witty tale of contemporary mores in which separating spouses Dick Van Dyke and Debbie Reynolds take a baleful look at the effects of divorce on their friends. Jason Robards is brilliant as a man so crippled by alimony payments he's desperate to pair off ex-wife Jean Simmons, while Debbie's ex-MGM stablemate Van Johnson makes even a used car salesman seem boyishly beguiling. Director Bud Yorkin know the material backwards, although some may find it an acquired taste.

Dick Van Dyke *Richard Harmon* • Debbie Reynolds *Barbara Harmon* • Jason Robards [Jason Robards Jr] *Nelson Downes* • Jean Simmons *Nancy Downes* • Van Johnson *Al Yearling* • Joe Flynn *Lionel Blandsforth* • Shelley Berman *David Grieff* ■ *Dir* Bud Yorkin • *Scr* Norman Lear, from a story by Robert Kaufman

Divorce – Italian Style ★★★★
Black comedy 1961 · It · BW · 103mins

It's not often that a foreign language film takes a mainstream Oscar, so the success of Pietro Germi and his fellow screenwriters suggests this wicked black comedy is doubly special. For all the ingenuity of the script, though, it's Marcello Mastroianni (who added an Oscar nomination to his Golden Globe and Bafta victories) that makes these sinister Sicilian shenanigans so memorable. He plays the lovesick husband who opts to kill his shrewish wife (Daniella Rocca) rather than divorce her; in Italy, that's the easier option! Mastroianni expertly combines deadpan suavity with impeccable comic timing, while Germi directs with flair. An Italian language film.

Marcello Mastroianni *Ferdinando Cefalu* • Daniela Rocca *Rosalie Cefalu* • Stefania Sandrelli *Angela* • Leopoldo Trieste *Carmelo Patane* • Odoardo Spadaro *Don Gaetano* ■ *Dir* Pietro Germi • *Scr* Pietro Germi, Ennio DeConcini, Alfredo Giannetti

The Divorce of Lady X ★★★ U
Comedy 1938 · UK · Colour · 87mins

Producer Alexander Korda used marvellous early three-strip Technicolor to give this piece of screwball whimsy a special lustre. The film starred his wife-to-be Merle Oberon, who plays a partygoer trapped in a London hotel by one of those fogs so beloved of Americans. The Technicolor works, but Oberon doesn't: comedy clearly wasn't her forte, and she fared much better when paired again with her co-star here, Laurence Olivier, in *Wuthering Heights* the following year. Olivier does little more than pout, so the acting honours are stolen by Ralph Richardson and Binnie Barnes. The film's quite amusing, though, in its daffy way. ▣

Merle Oberon *Leslie Steele* • Laurence Olivier *Logan* • Binnie Barnes *Lady Mere* • Ralph Richardson *Lord Mere* • Morton Selten *Lord Steele* • JH Roberts *Slade* • Gertrude Musgrove *Saunders* • Gus McNaughton *Waiter* • Eileen Peele *Mrs Johnson* ■ *Dir* Tim Whelan • *Scr* Ian Dalrymple, Arthur Wimperis, Lajos Biró, Robert Sherwood, from the play *Counsel's Opinion* by Gilbert Wakefield, adapted by Lajos Biró

Divorce Wars ★★★★
Drama 1982 · US · Colour

This cleverly scripted and insightful domestic drama about a divorce lawyer who can't solve the problems within his own marriage is co-written and directed by the talented Donald Wrye, whose work includes the Jack Lemmon version of *The Entertainer*. As the high-powered attorney, Tom Selleck proves yet again what a personable actor he is, and he's well teamed here with Jane Curtin. This made-for-TV drama is also worth catching for the last screen

U = SUITABLE FOR ALL   Uc = SUITABLE FOR ALL, ESPECIALLY FOR YOUNG CHILDREN (VIDEO ONLY)   PG = PARENTAL GUIDANCE

appearance of Joan Bennett, whose film career began in 1916 and includes such highlights as *Little Women* and *Father of the Bride*.

Tom Selleck *Jack Kaiser* • Jane Curtin *Vickey Kaiser* • Candy Azzara *Sylvia Bemous* • Joan Bennett *Adele Burgess* • Maggie Cooper *Leslie Fields* • Charles Haid *Fred Bemous* ■ *Dir* Donald Wrye • *Scr* Donald Wrye, Linda Elstad, from a story by Linda Elstad

The Divorcee ★★★
Romantic drama   1930 · US · BW · 83mins

Norma Shearer won her best actress Academy Award for the spunky, sexy performance on display here. This may surprise viewers who only recall her as the grand queen of the lot in her later roles at a prestige-conscious MGM run by her husband, Irving Thalberg. In fact, this movie was based on a novel so racy that the author published it anonymously, and much of that substance (though not the actual plot) is on screen in those halcyon pre-Code days. Shearer plays a woman having an affair with a man loved by another woman. It all looks a bit creaky now, and who'd want to end up with stodgy square-jawed Chester Morris anyhow?

Norma Shearer *Jerry* • Chester Morris *Ted* • Conrad Nagel *Paul* • Robert Montgomery *Don* • Florence Eldridge *Helen* • Helene Millard *Mary* • Robert Elliott *Bill* • Mary Doran *Janice* ■ *Dir* Robert Z Leonard • *Scr* Nick Grinde, Zelda Sears, John Meehan, from the novel *Ex-Wife* by Ursula Parrott

Divorcing Jack ★★★ 15
Comedy thriller
1998 · UK/Fr · Colour · 105mins

David Thewlis, like Pete Postelthwaite, is an ugly mug who's turned himself into a star character actor. He utterly dominates this chase thriller set in Northern Ireland, in which he plays a drunken, foul-mouthed reporter whose life is in ruins. Robert Lindsay co-stars as a politician who threatens to solve all of Ulster's troubles. Like a grubby, gutter-level *North by Northwest*, the picture barely stops for breath, while Thewlis, with his grotty wardrobe, filthy hair and pathetic face fur, is a refreshingly different action hero. Contains swearing, violence and sex scenes. ▭

David Thewlis *Dan Starkey* • Rachel Griffiths *Lee Cooper* • Robert Lindsay *Michael Brinn* • Jason Isaacs *"Cow Pat" Keegan* • Laura Fraser *Margaret* • Richard Gant *Charles Parker* • Laine Megaw *Patricia Starkey* • Kitty Aldridge *Agnes Brinn* • Bronagh Gallagher *Taxi driver* ■ *Dir* David Caffrey • *Scr* Colin Bateman, from his novel

Dixie ★★★ U
Musical biographical drama
1943 · US · Colour · 89mins

A big hit in its day, this Bing Crosby vehicle purports to be the biography of Daniel Decatur Emmett, the man who wrote the South's most famous marching song. With its corny sentiment and minstrel shows, it's rather difficult, especially if you don't warm to Bing. (The continual series of jokes concerning Crosby's carelessness with his pipe are both tasteless and tiresome in the extreme.) But there's a notable screen debut from comedian Billy de Wolfe, and the forties Technicolor is simply

sumptuous. Not to be confused with the superior *Mississippi*, which paired Bing with WC Fields.

Bing Crosby *Dan Emmett* • Dorothy Lamour *Millie Cook* • Billie de Wolfe *Mr Bones* • Marjorie Reynolds *Jean Mason* • Lynne Overman *Mr Whitlock* • Eddie Foy Jr *Mr Felham* • Raymond Walburn *Mr Cook* • Grant Mitchell *Mr Mason* ■ *Dir* A Edward Sutherland • *Scr* Darrell Ware, Claude Binyon, from the story by William Rankin

Dixie Dynamite ★
Crime action   1976 · US · Colour · 88mins

This "good ol' boy" nonsense from director Lee Frost is punishment for the eyes, while the soundtrack, which includes songs by Duane Eddy, gives the ears a bashing too. Sam Peckinpah stalwart Warren Oates stars as a motorcycle racer enlisted by two sisters to exact revenge upon the trigger-happy sheriff who killed their moonshiner father. Exuberant action and risible dialogue add up to a none-too-heady brew which fails to rise above the average.

Warren Oates *Mack* • Christopher George *Sheriff Phil Marsh* • Jane Anne Johnstone *Dixie* • Kathy McHaley *Patsy* ■ *Dir* Lee Frost • *Scr* Lee Frost, Wes Bishop

Django ★★★★ 18
Spaghetti western
1966 · It/Sp · Colour · 86mins

Switching effortlessly from the gritty realism of the mud-splattered streets to the stylised violence of the machine-gun shoot-outs, this superior spaghetti western from Sergio Corbucci owes as much to the Japanese samurai film as it does to the Hollywood horse opera. Franco Nero stars as the avenging angel who uses the armoury he keeps in a coffin to settle the feud between Mexican general Angel Alvarez and Civil War veteran Jose Bodalo and his red-hooded horsemen. Packed with floggings, ambushes and robberies, with a little mud-wrestling and ear-eating for good measure, this is not one for the faint-hearted. Italian dialogue dubbed into English. ▭

Franco Nero *Django* • Loredana Nusciak *Maria* • Jose Bodalo *Major Jackson* • Angel Alvarez *General Hugo Rodrigues* ■ *Dir* Sergio Corbucci • *Scr* Sergio Corbucci, Bruno Corbucci, Franco Rossetti, Jose G Maesso

Django against Sartana ★★
Spaghetti western 1970 · It · Colour · 89mins

Sergio Leone's "The Man with No Name" may be the most famous spaghetti western icon, but the 30-plus *Django* movies truly represent the foundation of the genre. In one of the last gasps in the series, the bounty hunter joins forces with another hero in decline – Sartana, the star of his own Italian western series – who he blames for the lynching of his brother. Sartana is innocent, however, so together they go after the real villains. Director Pasquale Squitieri (billed as William Redford) has fun blurring the links between the two mythic characters, making them virtually indistinguishable from each other despite their differing backgrounds. In the end, though, it remains a routine shoot 'em up. Italian dialogue dubbed into English.

Giorgio Ardisson [George Ardisson] *Django* • Tony Kendall *Sartana* • José Torres *Philip Singer* • John Alvar *Steve* ■ *Dir* William Redford [Pasquale Squitieri] • *Scr* William Redford [Pasquale Squitieri]

Django Kill ★★★
Spaghetti western
1967 · It/Sp · Colour · 101mins

Giulio Questi began his career as an assistant to Federico Fellini, which might explain why this surreal film feels like a spaghetti *Satyricon*. Tomas Milian takes on the role of the avenging gunslinger made famous by Franco Nero, finding a unique solution to a feud over a stolen gold shipment. But the plot is almost irrelevant in what is considered by many to be the most violent western ever made. The action includes a human barbecue and a death by liquid gold; yet, providing a bizarre balance to the brutality, there's a melodramatic band of outlaws and a parrot who's a gunfight aficionado. Italian dialogue dubbed into English.

Tomas Milian *Django* • Piero Lulli *Oaks* • Milo Quesada *Tembler* • Paco Sanz *Hagerman* • Roberto Camardiel *Sorro* • Marilu Tolo *Flory* • Raymond Lovelock *Evan* • Patrizia Valturri *Lizabeth* ■ *Dir* Giulio Questi • *Scr* Giulio Questi, Franco Arcalli

Django the Bastard ★★★ 12
Western   1970 · It · Colour · 94mins

Directed by Sergio Garrone and scripted by Antonio de Teffe (who often used the pseudonym Anthony Steffen), this is among the best films in this seminal spaghetti series. De Teffe also stars as the Civil War veteran who takes revenge on the Confederate officers who slaughtered his comrades. Stately, stylish and prone to sudden eruptions of violence (most notably the massacre of a band of Mexican desperados), this Wild West ghost story was clearly an influence on Clint Eastwood's *High Plains Drifter*. Italian dialogue dubbed into English. ▭

Antonio de Teffe *Django* • Rada Rassimov *Alethea* • Paolo Gozlino *Rod Murdoch* • Lu Kanante *Luke Murdoch* ■ *Dir* Sergio Garrone • *Scr* Anthony de Teffe, Sergio Garrone

Do Not Disturb ★★★
Comedy   1965 · US · Colour · 101mins

By the time this movie was made, the sixties were swinging and sunny Doris Day had developed a chic and slightly risqué image, promoted by her producer/husband Martin Melcher. Melcher encouraged her towards projects like this one, in which she and screen husband Rod Taylor suspect each other of varying infidelities abroad. The problem is that both Day and Taylor deserve much better; indeed, they went on to show what a good partnership they could be the following year in *The Glass Bottom Boat*. Taylor was capable in his prime of enlivening mediocre material, and here he proves a worthy successor to Rock Hudson as a foil for Day. Five movies after this, Doris Day would prematurely retire from the big screen, her husband's early death leaving her insolvent and forcing her to work in television.

Doris Day *Janet Harper* • Rod Taylor *Mike Harper* • Hermione Baddeley *Vanessa*

Courtwright • Sergio Fantoni *Paul Bellasi* • Reginald Gardiner *Simmons* • Maura McGiveny *Claire Hackett* • Aram Katcher *Culkos* • Leon Askin *Langsdorf* ■ *Dir* Ralph Levy • *Scr* Milt Rosen, Richard Breen, from the play *Some Other Love* by William Fairchild

Do Not Fold, Spindle or Mutilate ★★★
Thriller   1971 · US · Colour · 73mins

Four elderly ladies who want a little fun in their lives fill in a dating agency questionnaire and wait for the men to call. The title may be lousy but it's a neat idea, and vintage movie fans will enjoy seeing the seasoned cast having a whale of a time. Helen Hayes and Mildred Natwick, who co-starred in the TV series *The Snoop Sisters*, here appear alongside the legendary Myrna Loy and Sylvia Sidney, the archetypal gangster's moll of the thirties. It's a pity, though, that the only male lead they could find was Vince Edwards.

Helen Hayes *Sophie Curtis* • Myrna Loy *Evelyn Tryon* • Mildred Natwick *Shelby Saunders* • Sylvia Sidney *Elizabeth Gibson* • Vince Edwards *Mal Weston* • John Beradino *Lt Hallum* • Larry D Mann *Sergeant Lutz* ■ *Dir* Ted Post • *Scr* John DF Black, from the novel by Doris Miles Disney

Do the Right Thing ★★★★ 18
Drama   1989 · US · Colour · 114mins

Spike Lee's fierce racial drama remains his most assured and controversial film to date, and time hasn't diminished any of its power. It concentrates on one sweltering day in New York where simmering racial tensions are about to explode: the focal point becomes a pizza parlour run by Danny Aiello, who refuses to replace his old Italian photographs with pictures of black heroes. Lee himself is excellent as Aiello's delivery boy, but the playing of the ensemble cast is exemplary and, although there are a dozen different storylines, Lee effortlessly meshes them together without losing sight of his central theme. Add to that Ernest Dickerson's bright, vibrant cinematography and the superb soundtrack, and the result is an exhilarating, passionate and often very funny modern classic. Contains swearing. ▭

Danny Aiello *Sal* • Spike Lee *Mookie* • John Turturro *Pino* • Richard Edson *Vito* • Ossie Davis *Da Mayor* • Ruby Dee *Mother Sister* • Giancarlo Esposito *Buggin' Out* • Bill Nunn *Radio Raheem* • Rosie Perez *Tina* • John Savage *Clifton* • Sam Jackson [Samuel L Jackson] *Mister Señor Love Daddy* ■ *Dir/Scr* Spike Lee

Do You Love Me? ★★★ U
Musical   1946 · US · Colour · 90mins

A charming 20th Century-Fox musical, resplendent in forties Technicolor, the better to show off Maureen O'Hara's flowing red tresses. She's a college dean, as if you care, and she's loved by band vocalist Dick Haymes, fresh from *State Fair*, who proves yet again that he was one of the greatest ever singers of slow-tempo ballads. Harry James, one of the biggest band stars of the period, also appears, while Reginald Gardiner provides the laughs.

Maureen O'Hara *Katherine Hilliard* • Dick Haymes *Jimmy Hale* • Harry James *Barry*

Clayton • Reginald Gardiner *Herbert Benham* • Richard Gaines *Ralph Wainwright* • Stanley Prager *Dilly* • BS Pully *Taxi driver* • Chick Chandler *Earl Williams* • Alma Kruger *Mrs Crackleton* ■ *Dir* Gregory Ratoff • *Scr* Robert Ellis, Helen Logan, Dorothy Bennett, from a story by Bert Granet

Do You Remember Love
★★★★ 🅿🅶

Drama 1985 · US · Colour · 92mins

Joanne Woodward won an Emmy for her role in this made-for-TV movie about how the family of a middle-aged college professor copes when she contracts Alzheimer's. Scriptwriter Vickie Patik also walked away with an award for her moving script, which pulls no punches and steers clear of melodrama, However, most plaudits should go to director Jeff Bleckner and the cast, which also includes *LA Law's* Susan Ruttan and Ron Rifkin (*The Negotiator, LA Confidential*). 🖵

Joanne Woodward *Barbara Wyatt-Hollis* • Richard Kiley *George Hollis* • Geraldine Fitzgerald *Lorraine Wyatt* • Jim Metzler *Tom Hollis* • Jordan Charney *Marvin Langdon* • Ron Rifkin *Gerry Kaplan* • Susan Ruttan *Julie Myers* ■ *Dir* Jeff Bleckner • *Scr* Vickie Patik

The Doberman Gang ★★★

Crime caper 1972 · US · Colour · 86mins

A low-budget comedy about a gang of bungling bank robbers who come up with the idea of training a pack of dogs to do the job for them. They even name the pooches after legendary gangsters: Dillinger, Bonnie and Clyde and so on. The canines pull off the caper to plan, but are less keen on handing over the dough. It's not Shakespeare, but once you've bought the premise it has its moments. Two sequels followed.

Byron Mabe *Eddie Newton* • Hal Reed *Barney Greer* • Julie Parrish *June* • Simmy Bow *Sammy* • Jojo D'Amore *Jojo* • John Tull *Pet shop owner* • Jay Paxton *Bank manager* • Diane Prior *Sandy* ■ *Dir* Byron Ross Chudnow • *Scr* Louis Garfinkle, Frank Ray Perilli

Dobermann ★★★★ 🔞

Crime thriller 1997 · Fr · Colour · 98mins

Wildly stylish, tongue-in-cheek cops and robbers tale bursting with dazzling technical trickery, explosive action scenes and deranged performances, particularly from Tcheky Karyo as the scariest cop who ever lived. Energetic and bloody, Jan Kounen's comic-strip concoction has a fairly simplistic plot, but slick, sexy camerawork and editing, plus super-cool criminal posturing from Vincent Cassel and Monica Bellucci (who co-starred in the gem *L'Appartement*) give the film a dynamic edge over the majority of recent foreign language thrillers. If you can stomach the extreme violence, *Dobermann* is a heart-pumping, high-speed chase through the more commercial district of French cinema. In French with English subtitles. Contains violence, sex scenes and drug abuse. 🖵

Vincent Cassel *Yann LePentrec, "Le Dob"* • Monica Bellucci *Nathalie, "Nat la gitane"* • Tcheky Karyo *Chief Inspector Sauveur Christini* • Antoine Basler *Jean-Claude Ayache, "Mosquito"* • Dominique Bettenfeld *Elie Frossard, "Padre"* ■ *Dir* Jan Kounen • *Scr* Jan Kounen, Joël Houssin, from the novels by Joël Houssin

Doc ★★★★ 15

Western 1971 · US · Colour · 91mins

A flawed but fascinating account of the famous gunfight at the OK Corral with Stacey Keach as Doc Holliday, Faye Dunaway as his girlfriend Katie Elder, and Harris Yulin especially impressive as the political opportunist Wyatt Earp. The shoot-out, when it comes, is impressively handled by director Frank Perry, who successfully avoids mimicking previous versions, notably Ford's *My Darling Clementine* and John Sturges's two films on the same subject. Shorn of many of the familiar trappings, this account may disappoint traditional western fans, but its focus on Holliday's disenchantment seems to be a little parable about the moral bankruptcy of Nixon's America. 🖵

Stacey Keach *Doc Holliday* • Faye Dunaway *Kate Elder* • Harris Yulin *Wyatt Earp* • Mike Witney [Michael Witney] *Ike Clanton* • Denver John Collins *Kid* ■ *Dir* Frank Perry • *Scr* Pete Hamill

Doc Hollywood ★★★ 15

Romantic comedy
1991 · US · Colour · 98mins

A mildly diverting, folksy comedy, in which Michael J Fox plays an ambitious California-bound intern who finds himself press-ganged into becoming a doctor in a small South Carolina community. Revelling in local idiosyncrasies, director Michael Caton-Jones gives the film a lovely golden glow and produces a Capra-like hymn to the small town. There are fine performances from Fox and a talented supporting cast, which includes Julie Warner, Woody Harrelson, Bridget Fonda and Barnard Hughes; look out, too, for a neat cameo from George Hamilton near the end. Contains swearing and nudity. 🖵

Michael J Fox *Dr Benjamin Stone* • Julie Warner *Lou* • Barnard Hughes *Dr Hogue* • Woody Harrelson *Henry "Hank" Gordon* • David Ogden Stiers *Nick Nicholson* • Frances Sternhagen *Lillian* • George Hamilton *Dr Halberstrom* • Bridget Fonda *Nancy Lee* • Mel Winkler *Melvin* ■ *Dir* Michael Caton-Jones • *Scr* Jeffrey Price, Peter S Seaman, Daniel Pyne, from the novel *What?...Dead Again* by Neil B Shulman

Doc Savage: the Man of Bronze ★★ 🅿🅶

Fantasy adventure
1975 · US · Colour · 96mins

George Pal was a legendary figure in the worlds of sci-fi and fantasy, but his swan-song film as a producer is not the best way to remember him. The story is taken from the ever-popular Doc Savage books of the thirties, with television's Tarzan, Ron Ely, in the title role. Despite director Michael Anderson's admirable attempts to insert some knowing humour, however, it remains a rather tame and routine adventure. 🖵

Ron Ely *Doc Savage* • Paul Gleason *Long Tom* • Bill Lucking [William Lucking] *Renny* • Michael Miller *Monk* • Eldon Quick *Johnny* • Darrell Zwerling *Ham* • Paul Wexler *Captain Seas* • Janice Heiden *Andriana* ■ *Dir* Michael Anderson • *Scr* George Pal, Joe Morhaim, from the novel by Kenneth Robeson

The Docks of New York
★★★★

Silent drama 1928 · US · BW · 60mins

Josef von Sternberg's movie flopped in America, mainly because it was previewed the same week as the first talkie, *The Jazz Singer*. A singular case of bad timing. Over the years, though, the picture has been rediscovered as a highly effective melodrama about a ship's stoker who saves a streetwalker from suicide, marries her and then takes the blame when she's accused of murder. The film's romantic fatalism is compelling, and von Sternberg creates some stunning imagery out of his low-life settings.

George Bancroft *Bill Roberts* • Betty Compson *Sadie* • Olga Baclanova *Lou* • Clyde Cook "*Sugar*" *Steve* • Mitchell Lewis *Third Engineer* • Gustav von Seyffertitz "*Hymn Book*" *Harry* • Guy Oliver *The Crimp* • May Foster *Mrs Crimp* ■ *Dir* Josef von Sternberg • *Scr* Jules Furthman • *Cinematographer* Harold Rosson

Docks of New York ★★

Crime comedy drama
1945 · US · BW · 61mins

This is not the masterful 1928 Josef von Sternberg classic, but one of the last gasps of the *East Side Kids*, made shortly before star Leo Gorcey picked up the franchise and continued the series (successfully) as *The Bowery Boys*. It's the same mixture as usual, involving some mayhem around stolen jewellery, while Huntz Hall's mugging over-compensates for the absence of series regulars Gabriel Dell and Bobby Jordan, both off working for Uncle Sam. Movie buffs should note that the Carlyle Blackwell Jr who appears here is *not* the infamous fashion critic "Mr Blackwell", as has been claimed.

Leo Gorcey *Muggs McGinnis* • Huntz Hall *Glimpy* • Billy Benedict *Skinny* • Bud Gorman *Danny* • Mende Koenig *Sam* • Gloria Pope *Saundra* • Carlyle Blackwell Jr *Marty* • George Meeker *Naclet* • Betty Blythe *Mrs Darcy* ■ *Dir* Wallace Fox • *Scr* Harvey Gates

Docteur Petiot ★★★★ 15

Biographical drama
1990 · Fr · Colour and BW · 97mins

While most people are now familiar with the Holocaust heroics of Raoul Wallenberg and Oskar Schindler, the hideous crimes of Marcel Petiot have largely gone unrecorded. Based on a true story, this chilling film recounts the career of one of France's most notorious serial killers, who conned Jews into believing he could smuggle them to Argentina before murdering them and incinerating their bodies. Michel Serrault is quite superb, whether reassuring loved ones or hurtling round the darkened streets, with his cape billowing like a vampire. Christian de Chalonge's flamboyant direction exploits every cinematic trick in the book to create an authentic and genuinely horrific atmosphere. In French with English subtitles. 🖵

Michel Serrault *Docteur Petiot* • Pierre Romans *Ivan Drezner* • Zbigniew Horoks *Nathan Guzik* • Bérangère Bonvoisin *Georgette Petiot* • Aurore Prieto *Madame Guzik* ■ *Dir* Christian de Chalonge • *Scr* Dominique Garnier, Christian de Chalonge

The Docks of New York
★★★★

Drama 1991 · US · Colour · 117mins

William Hurt goes from being a glib, egotistical doctor to a cancer patient in his own hospital, becoming a thoroughly decent chap in the process. What could so easily have been an empty exercise in Hollywood schmaltz is given life by a probing script and first-class acting in a film that places moral issues under the microscope – a rare enough event in Hollywood. Hurt makes no concessions to star likeability and proves just as credible once he begins to soften up, while Elizabeth Perkins, excellent as Tom Hanks's girlfriend in *Big*, gives a performance of equal richness and strength as the fellow patient who pushes him beyond his ego. 🖵

William Hurt *Dr Jack McKee* • Christine Lahti *Anne McKee* • Elizabeth Perkins *June* • Mandy Patinkin *Murray* • Adam Arkin *Eli* • Charlie Korsmo *Nicky* • Wendy Crewson *Dr Leslie Abbott* ■ *Dir* Randa Haines • *Scr* Robert Caswell, from the memoirs *A Taste of My Own Medicine* by Ed Rosenbaum

The Doctor and the Devils
★★★ 15

Historical crime drama
1985 · UK · Colour · 88mins

A rather earnest resurrection of the Burke and Hare bodysnatchers tale, pitched more as a dark moral fable than a horror film. Based on a script written by Dylan Thomas in the forties (unproduced because of censor problems), producer Mel Brooks got veteran Hammer horror director/cinematographer Freddie Francis to rework it. The result is high on period detail, often uncomfortably so, but low on *Grand Guignol* chills, although Timothy Dalton, Jonathan Pryce and Stephen Rea give it the necessary touch of evil. Contains violence, swearing, nudity and sex scenes. 🖵

Timothy Dalton *Dr Thomas Rock* • Jonathan Pryce *Robert Fallon* • Twiggy *Jenny Bailey* • Julian Sands *Dr Murray* • Stephen Rea *Timothy Broom* • Phyllis Logan *Elizabeth Rock* ■ *Dir* Freddie Francis • *Scr* Ronald Harwood, from a screenplay by Dylan Thomas

The Doctor and the Girl ★★

Medical drama 1949 · US · BW · 97mins

MGM, the studio that brought us the *Dr Kildare* series, returned to the hospital for Glenn Ford's first picture with the studio. Under the competent direction of Curtis Bernhardt, Ford plays an idealistic medic who eschews the rewards of becoming a specialist in order to help the underprivileged. The girl? Take your pick between patients Janet Leigh and Gloria De Haven, though Nancy Davis – the future Mrs Ronald Reagan – is in it too.

Glenn Ford *Dr Michael Corday* • Charles Coburn *Dr John Corday* • Gloria De Haven [Gloria DeHaven] *Fabienne Corday* • Janet Leigh *Evelyn Heldon* • Bruce Bennett *Dr Alfred Norton* • Nancy Davis *Mariette* ■ *Dir* Curtis Bernhardt • *Scr* Theodore Reeves, from the novel *Bodies and Souls* by Maxence van der Meersch

🅤 = SUITABLE FOR ALL   🅤🅒 = SUITABLE FOR ALL, ESPECIALLY FOR YOUNG CHILDREN (VIDEO ONLY)   🅿🅶 = PARENTAL GUIDANCE

Doctor at Large ★★★ U

Comedy   1957 · UK · Colour · 94mins

In this third entry in the series inspired by the novels of Richard Gordon, Dirk Bogarde, as accident-prone houseman Simon Sparrow, once again escapes the confines of St Swithin's in order to explore pastures new, in this case a country practice where virtually nothing goes right. But it's only once he's back under the beady gaze of James Robertson-Justice that the film comes to life, although even then the romantic interludes with Muriel Pavlow slow down the proceedings. Amiable enough, but everyone is just a touch off colour, and the film shows signs of the terminal decline that would set in after Bogarde quit the series.

Dirk Bogarde *Simon Sparrow* • Muriel Pavlow *Joy* • Donald Sinden *Benskin* • James Robertson-Justice *Sir Lancelot Spratt* • Shirley Eaton *Nan* • Derek Farr *Dr Potter-Shine* • Michael Medwin *Bingham* • Lionel Jeffries *Dr Hackett* ■ *Dir* Ralph Thomas • *Scr* Nicholas Phipps, Richard Gordon, from the novel by Richard Gordon

Doctor at Sea ★★ PG

Comedy   1955 · UK · Colour · 89mins

Do not adjust your set: that really *is* Brigitte Bardot! Appearing in her first British film and still a year away from taking world cinema by storm in *And God Created Woman*, she provides Dirk Bogarde with a welcome distraction from the miserable seasickness he experiences away from the terra firma of St Swithin's. Despite the lively rapport between the stars, however, the second of Rank's popular series is short on truly comic incident, and the shipboard location is limiting. As cantankerous as ever, James Robertson-Justice is another survivor from *Doctor in the House*, although here he plays the ship's captain rather than Sir Lancelot Spratt.

Dirk Bogarde *Simon Sparrow* • Brigitte Bardot *Helene Colbert* • Brenda de Banzie *Muriel Mallet* • James Robertson-Justice *Captain Hogg* • Maurice Denham *Easter* • Michael Medwin *Trail* • Hubert Gregg *Archer* ■ *Dir* Ralph Thomas • *Scr* Nicholas Phipps, Richard Gordon, Jack Davies, from the novel by Richard Gordon

Doctor Blood's Coffin ★★

Horror   1960 · UK · Colour · 92mins

Before he launched his mainstream career with *The Ipcress File* and *Lady Sings the Blues*, director Sidney J Furie cut his teeth on such British programme fillers as this cheap and cheerful *Frankenstein*-flavoured tale. Doctor Kieron Moore experiments in bringing the dead back to life while his fetching nurse (Hazel Court) screams a lot amid the lurid, Hammer Horror-style glossiness. Enhanced by its Cornish tin-mine setting, Furie's cardboard suspense shocker is hardly a classic. It's great fun, though, and Moore is impressive as the madman torn between science and evil.

Kieron Moore *Doctor Peter Blood* • Hazel Court *Linda Parker* • Ian Hunter *Doctor Robert Blood* • Fred Johnson *Mr Morton* • Kenneth J Warren *Sergeant Cook* • Andy Alston *Beale* • Paul Stockman *Steve Parker* • John Ronane *Hanson* • Gerald C Lawson *Sweeting* ■ *Dir* Sidney J Furie • *Scr* Jerry Juran, James Kelly, Peter Miller, from a story by Jerry Juran

Dr Broadway ★★

Crime comedy drama   1942 · US · BW · 68mins

Anthony Mann's first feature film is a tight little thriller revolving around a Times Square medic who finds himself becoming a detective in a murder mystery. The second-league cast is headed by the competent Macdonald Carey and Jean Phillips, usually Ginger Rogers's stand-in. Various Broadway characters people the plot, there is some good location work and Mann keeps the action moving smartly. It's the sort of B-picture the director would soon become an expert in.

Macdonald Carey *Dr Timothy "Doc" Kane* • Jean Phillips *Connie Madigan* • J Carrol Naish *Jack Venner* • Richard Lane *Patrick Doyle* • Edward Ciannelli [Eduardo Ciannelli] *Vic Telli* • Joan Woodbury *Margie Dove* • Arthur Loft *Captain Mahoney* • Warren Hymer *Maxie the goat* ■ *Dir* Anthony Mann • *Scr* Art Arthur, from the short story by Borden Chase

Dr Bull ★★★ U

Drama   1933 · US · BW · 79mins

The folksy wisdom and whimsical humour of Will Rogers seem hopelessly old-fashioned today, but in the first third of this century he was one of the biggest stars in the States. The first of his three collaborations with that master of Americana, John Ford, sees Rogers playing a small-town GP making light of his limited resources and the suspicions of would-be patients, including Andy Devine, Louise Dresser and Rochelle Hudson. Ford, who was a sucker for this brand of homespun philosophising, loved the film, although modern audiences will probably find it somewhat twee.

Will Rogers *Dr Bull* • Vera Allen *Janet Cardmaker* • Marian Nixon *May Tripping* • Howard Lally *Joe Tripping* • Berton Churchill *Herbert Banning* • Louise Dresser *Mrs Banning* • Andy Devine *Larry Ward* • Rochelle Hudson *Virginia Banning* ■ *Dir* John Ford • *Scr* Paul Green, Jane Storm, from the novel *The Last Adam* by James Gould Cozzens

Dr Crippen ★★ PG

Historical crime drama   1962 · UK · BW · 94mins

Considering the notoriously sordid subject matter, director Robert Lynn's true crime case history should have been a far more riveting affair than this so-so account. But you can't blame Donald Pleasence, at his sinister best playing the monstrous doctor who murders his persecuting wife in order to elope with his typist lover. Told in flashback as Crippen stands trial as much for his lack of Edwardian morals as homicide, there's a distinct lack of insight into either area to warrant too much attention. Straightforward and to the point, yet remote and uninvolving precisely because of that deliberately austere quasi-documentary stance.

Donald Pleasence *Dr Hawley Harvey Crippen* • Coral Browne *Belle Crippen* • Samantha Eggar *Ethel Le Neve* • James Robertson-Justice *Captain Kendall* • Geoffrey Toone *Mr Tobin* • Oliver Johnston *Lord Chief Justice* ■ *Dir* Robert Lynn • *Scr* Leigh Vance

Dr Cyclops ★★★

Science-fiction thriller   1940 · US · Colour · 78mins

Ernest B Schoedsack, co-director of the original *King Kong*, returns to the fantasy genre with this wonderfully weird tale of a mad scientist (Albert Dekker) who miniaturises explorers in his Amazon jungle laboratory. Borrowing ideas from *Kong* special effects man Willis O'Brien, Schoedsack crafts a well-mounted science-fiction thriller, the first of its kind in vivid Technicolor. The standard plot now looks hackneyed, and the cueball-headed Dekker is stereotypically crazy. However, the impressive array of oversize props make this a lot of fun.

Albert Dekker *Dr Thorkel* • Janice Logan *Dr Mary Mitchell* • Thomas Coley *Bill Stockton* • Charles Halton *Dr Bulfinch* • Victor Kilian *Steve Baker* • Frank Yaconelli *Pedro* • Bill Wilkerson *Silent Indian* • Allen Fox *Cab driver* • Paul Fix *Dr Mendoza* • Frank Reicher *Prof Kendall* ■ *Dir* Ernest B Schoedsack • *Scr* Tom Kilpatrick • *Special Effects* Farciot Edouard

Doctor Detroit ★★ 15

Comedy   1983 · US · Colour · 86mins

Featuring Dan Aykroyd in his first leading role after the death of his partner John Belushi, this comedy is only a partial success. The plot, which finds Aykroyd's mild-mannered college teacher getting mixed up with some hookers, gives him full rein to showcase all of his comic talents, and he is particularly good as a ludicrously OTT pimp. However, he is let down by a loose script and crude direction by Michael Pressman.

Dan Aykroyd *Clifford Skridlow* • Howard Hesseman *Smooth Walker* • TK Carter *Diavolo Washington* • Donna Dixon *Monica McNeil* • Lynn Whitfield *Thelma Cleland* • Lydia Lei *Jasmine Wu* • Fran Drescher *Karen Blittstein* • Kate Murtagh *Mom* ■ *Dir* Michael Pressman • *Scr* Carl Gottlieb, Robert Boris, Bruce Jay Friedman, from the novel *Detroit Abe* by Bruce Jay Friedman

Doctor Dolittle ★★★ U

Musical fantasy adventure   1967 · US · Colour · 138mins

Children will revel in this infamous musical comedy based on Hugh Lofting's stories, but this was a costly disaster in its day which almost killed off 20th Century-Fox. Its longevity belies a thumpingly leaden affair, in which Rex Harrison is squeakily embarrassing as the dotty doc. There are some good tunes, including the Oscar-winning *Talk to the Animals*, and the special effects also won an Academy Award, but overall it is rather a bore. To adults, that is; children find it entertaining enough.

Rex Harrison *Doctor John Dolittle* • Anthony Newley *Matthew Mugg* • Peter Bull *General Bellowes* • William Dix *Tommy Stubbins* • Portia Nelson *Sarah Dolittle* • Samantha Eggar *Emma Fairfax* • Richard Attenborough *Albert Blossom* ■ *Dir* Richard Fleischer • *Scr* Leslie Bricusse, from the stories by Hugh Lofting • *Music/Lyrics* Leslie Bricusse

Doctor Dolittle ★★ PG

Comedy   1998 · US · Colour · 81mins

After the success of *The Nutty Professor*, Eddie Murphy completed the transformation from foul-mouthed, fast-talking comic to all-round family entertainer with *Doctor Dolittle*, the UK's second highest grossing film in 1998 (after *Titanic*). Murphy plays a doctor whose life is turned upside down when his old childhood gift – the ability to "talk to the animals" – returns. That's the cue for lots of juvenile gags from a host of guest voices (Garry Shandling, Albert Brooks, Ellen DeGeneres), while the likes of Ossie Davis and Oliver Platt look on bemused. Contains some swearing and sexual references.

Eddie Murphy *Dr John Dolittle* • Ossie Davis *Archer Dolittle* • Oliver Platt *Dr Mark Weller* • Peter Boyle *Calloway* • Richard Schiff *Dr Gene Reiss* • Kristen Wilson *Lisa* • Jeffrey Tambor *Dr Fish* • Kyla Pratt *Maya* ■ *Dir* Betty Thomas • *Scr* Nat Mauldin, Larry Levin, Hugh Lofting

Dr Ehrlich's Magic Bullet ★★★

Biography   1940 · US · BW · 102mins

Edward G Robinson plays the German doctor who discovered a cure for syphilis – not celibacy but the drug Salvarsan – and won a Nobel Prize in 1908. A tricky subject for a Warner Bros biopic in 1940, but everything is done in the most tasteful manner. The original story by Norman Burnside was thoroughly rewritten with the help of John Huston and Heinz Herald, cutting out all the romantic twaddle to concentrate on Ehrlich peering through a microscope. It's absorbing viewing, and Robinson later regarded it as his finest performance.

Edward G Robinson *Dr Paul Ehrlich* • Ruth Gordon *Mrs Ehrlich* • Otto Kruger *Dr Emil von Behring* • Donald Crisp *Minister Althoff* • Maria Ouspenskaya *Franziska Speyer* • Montagu Love *Professor Hartmann* • Sig Rumann [Sig Ruman] *Dr Hans Wolfert* ■ *Dir* William Dieterle • *Scr* John Huston, Heinz Herald, Norman Burnside, from a story by Norman Burnside

Doctor Faustus ★★★ PG

Drama   1967 · UK · Colour · 88mins

Christopher Marlowe's play, about the man who sold his soul to the devil, was a favourite of Richard Burton's, who may have looked at Faust and seen himself, the great stage actor who willingly sold out to Hollywood and celebrity. Casting himself as Faust and his wife Elizabeth Taylor as Helen of Troy, Burton put the play on at Oxford and then used all his box-office clout to produce and co-direct this screen version. To his credit, Burton took with him his co-director and the Oxford cast, though the result is more a fascinating record of the stage production – Burton's reading of Marlowe's verse is magnificent – than a fully realised film.

Richard Burton *Doctor Faustus* • Elizabeth Taylor *Helen of Troy* • Andreas Teuber *Mephistopheles* • Ian Marter *Emperor* • Elizabeth O'Donovan *Empress* • David McIntosh *Lucifer* • Jeremy Eccles *Beelzebub* • Ram Chopra *Valdes* • Richard Carwardine *Cornelius* ■ *Dir* Richard Burton, Nevill Coghill • *Scr* Nevill Coghill, from the play by Christopher Marlowe

Doctor Françoise Gailland
★★★

Drama 1975 · Fr · Colour · 100mins

Jean-Louis Bertucelli has the happy knack of coaxing award-winning portrayals from his leading ladies, which might explain why Annie Girardot won a César (the French equivalent of an Oscar) for her performance in this three-hankie weepie. Also known as *No Time for Breakfast*, the film sticks pretty closely to the classic "women's picture" formula of the careerist whose professional ambitions are compromised by events in her personal life. Girardot skilfully captures first the anger, then the courage of the eponymous cancer victim, while Jean-Pierre Cassel and Isabelle Huppert offer selfless support. French dialogue dubbed into English.

Annie Girardot *Françoise Gailland* • Jean-Pierre Cassel *Daniel Letessier* • François Périer *Gérard Gailland* • Isabelle Huppert *Elisabeth Gailland* • William Coryn *Julien Gailland* ■ *Dir* Jean-Louis Bertucelli • *Scr* André G Brunelin, Jean-Louis Bertucelli, from the novel *Un Cri* by Noelle Loriot

Dr Giggles
★ **18**

Horror 1992 · US · Colour · 91mins

Heard the one about the kid sent mad by his father's surgical obsessions, who escapes from an asylum years later and turns up in his home town to wreak vengeance? Of course you have. This ultra-derivative slasher is simply a medical *Halloween* and what appeared to be one of the last gasps of old-school splatter until the genre's resurgence with the *Scream* movies. There isn't one iota of originality on display in this comatose collection of "Dr Kill-Dare" cliché casualties. Call for first aid! Contains swearing and violence.

Larry Drake *Evan Rendell* • Holly Marie Combs *Jennifer Campbell* • Glenn Quinn *Max Anderson* • Cliff De Young *Tom Campbell* • Richard Bradford *Officer Hank Magruder* • Keith Diamond *Officer Joe Reitz* • Michelle Johnson *Tamara* ■ *Dir* Manny Coto • *Scr* Manny Coto, Graeme Whifler

Dr Gillespie's Criminal Case
★★★

Medical drama 1943 · US · BW · 88mins

With James Craven stepping into the shoes vacated by Phil Brown, this entry in MGM's popular medical series continues the plotline started in *Calling Dr Gillespie*. Upset by former fiancée Donna Reed's romance with sergeant Michael Duane, Craven's homicidal maniac reduces Blair General to chaos, and the venerable senior surgeon is forced to call on junior doctors Van Johnson and Keye Luke for assistance. Although Lionel Barrymore turns in another performance of crusty geniality, the film is more notable for boosting Johnson's ascent up the fame ladder, and for keeping neophyte star Margaret O'Brien in the public eye.

Lionel Barrymore *Dr Leonard Gillespie* • Van Johnson *Dr Randall Adams* • Donna Reed *Marcia Bradburn* • Keye Luke *Dr Lee Wong How* • James Craven *Roy Todwell* • Nat Pendleton *Joe Wayman* • Alma Kruger *Molly Byrd* • Margaret O'Brien *Margaret* • Walter Kingsford *Dr Walter Carew* • Nell Craig *Nurse*

Parker • Michael Duane *Sergeant Orisin* ■ *Dir* Willis Goldbeck • *Scr* Martin Berkeley, Harry Ruskin, Lawrence P Bachmann, from characters created by Max Brand

Dr Gillespie's New Assistant
★★★

Medical drama 1942 · US · BW · 87mins

Bereft of Dr Kildare, MGM entrusted new director Willis Goldbeck with the task of resuscitating its long-running medical series by contriving a contest to find a personable assistant to crotchety surgeon Lionel Barrymore. In setting three interns each a tricky case to diagnose, the studio sought to showcase star-in-waiting Van Johnson, while Goldbeck aimed to add a touch of topicality by having Keye Luke decamp partway through to join the Chinese nationalist army.

Lionel Barrymore *Dr Leonard Gillespie* • Van Johnson *Dr Randall Adams* • Susan Peters *Mrs Howard Young* • Richard Quine *Dr Dennis Lindsey* • Keye Luke *Dr Lee Wong How* • Nat Pendleton *Joe Wayman* • Alma Kruger *Molly Byrd* • Horace McNally [Stephen McNally] *Howard Young* • Nell Craig *Nurse Parker* ■ *Dir* Willis Goldbeck • *Scr* Martin Berkeley, Harry Ruskin, Lawrence P Bachmann, from characters created by Max Brand

Dr Goldfoot and the Bikini Machine
★★ **PG**

Comedy 1965 · US · Colour · 84mins

Very much a product of the Swinging Sixties, this slice of tosh combines several of the elements that made AIP films so popular at the drive-ins. Vincent Price plays the eponymous doctor, who creates female robots so they can marry rich men and line his coffers. Susan Hart plays the female lead, and Frankie Avalon and Dwayne Hickman are also along for the ride. Even Annette Funicello drops in! It's all a little too daft, though, while the humour is positively leaden. ▣

Vincent Price *Dr Goldfoot* • Frankie Avalon *Craig Gamble* • Dwayne Hickman *Todd Armstrong* • Susan Hart *Diane* • Jack Mullaney *Igor* • Fred Clark *DJ Pevney* ■ *Dir* Norman Taurog • *Scr* Elwood Ullman, Robert Kaufman, from a story by James Hartford

Dr Goldfoot and the Girl Bombs
★★

Comedy 1966 · US/It · Colour · 85mins

Only in the mid-sixties could you have got away with a film like this! Thanks to cult Italian horror director Mario Bava, this sequel to *Dr Goldfoot and the Bikini Machine* piles on the style, but rather loses out in the fun stakes. Still, Vincent Price is his usual hammy self as Dr Goldfoot, who gets backing from China to start a war between the Americans and the Soviets using sexy robot girls with bombs implanted in their navels. (As the advertising went: "Don't touch – she's a booby bomb!") Teen idol Fabian plays the spy out to foil the dastardly plan, while Italian comics Franco and Ciccio – arguably cinema's worst-ever comedy double act – have supporting roles. Makes *Austin Powers* look like *The Third Man*.

Vincent Price *Dr Goldfoot* • Fabian *Bill Dexter* • Franco Franchi *Franco* • Ciccio Ingrassia *Ciccio* • Laura Antonelli *Rosanna* ■ *Dir* Mario

Bava • *Scr* Louis M Heyward, Castellano Pipolo, Robert Kaufman, from a story by James Hartford

Dr Heckyl & Mr Hype
★★

Comedy 1980 · US · Colour · 97mins

Oliver Reed tackles the title role in a clumsy comedy that mixes the Jekyll and Hyde idea with elements of *The Nutty Professor*. Reed is engagingly grotesque – bulbous nose, mangy skin, the works – as a scientist who overdoses on an experimental diet formula and transforms into a dashing playboy with a predilection for killing. Reed enters into the rollicking spirit of the piece, but director Charles B Griffith, whose career began on such Roger Corman movies as *Little Shop of Horrors*, ruins the amusing idea with laboured dialogue and stilted slapstick.

Oliver Reed *Dr Heckyl/Mr Hype* • Sunny Johnson *Coral Careen* • Maia Danziger *Miss Finebum* • Virgil Frye *Lieutenant Mack Druck "Il Topo"* • Mel Welles *Dr Hinkle* • Kedrick Wolfe *Dr Lew Hoo* • Jackie Coogan *Sergeant Fleacollar* ■ *Dir/Scr* Charles B Griffith

Doctor in Clover
★★ **PG**

Comedy 1966 · UK · Colour · 96mins

The penultimate entry in the seven-film series based on the comic novels of Richard Gordon is possibly the least strong in terms of incident, but there are some pleasing performances to ensure it avoids the bottom slot. Demonstrating once again his flair for the debonair, Leslie Phillips just about makes the whole thing worthwhile, but even he struggles with the anaemic story in which a romance with a physiotherapist and a new wonder drug complicate his already hectic love life. Surely it took more than this to tickle the nation's funny bones? ▣

Leslie Phillips *Dr Gaston Grimsdyke* • James Robertson-Justice *Sir Lancelot Spratt* • Shirley Anne Field *Nurse Bancroft* • John Fraser *Dr Miles Grimsdyke* • Joan Sims *Matron Sweet* • Fenella Fielding *Tatiana Rubikov* ■ *Dir* Ralph Thomas • *Scr* Jack Davies, from the novel by Richard Gordon

Doctor in Distress
★★ **PG**

Comedy 1963 · UK · Colour · 98mins

What a cast! What a letdown! After a one-film absence, Dirk Bogarde reluctantly returned to the role of Simon Sparrow in this muddled comedy and immediately announced he'd never step inside St Swithin's again. Faced with a script that reads like a medical school rag mag, the cast plods through the picture as though under anaesthetic. James Robertson-Justice has the most fun as the lovesick Lancelot Spratt and Leo McKern as a film producer flirting with starlet Jill Adams takes an accurate pot shot at movie moguls. But Bogarde looks bored, and Samantha Eggar is required to do nothing more than provide the glamour. ▣

Dirk Bogarde *Dr Simon Sparrow* • Samantha Eggar *Delia* • James Robertson-Justice *Sir Lancelot Spratt* • Mylene Demongeot *Sonja* • Donald Houston *Major French* • Barbara Murray *Iris* • Dennis Price *Blacker* • Peter Butterworth *Ambulance driver* • Leo McKern *Heilbronn* ■ *Dir* Ralph Thomas • *Scr* Nicholas Phipps, Ronald Scott Thorn, from characters created by Richard Gordon

Doctor in Love
★★ **PG**

Comedy 1960 · UK · Colour · 92mins

Once more taken from the Richard Gordon novels, Ralph Thomas's box-office hit is even more episodic than others in the long-running series and comes over now as a thin excuse for a series of risqué encounters and double entendres. Leslie Phillips is impeccable as a philandering doctor finding the country air conducive to consultancies of the canoodling kind, and James Robertson-Justice, Joan Sims, Liz Fraser and Irene Handl are as solid as ever. The film fails, however, because of Michael Craig, who is not only no Dirk Bogarde, but also no comedian. ▣

Michael Craig *Dr Richard Hare* • Virginia Maskell *Dr Nicola Barrington* • Leslie Phillips *Dr Tony Burke* • James Robertson-Justice *Sir Lancelot Spratt* • Carole Lesley *Kitten Strudwick* • Liz Fraser *Leonora* • Joan Sims *Dawn* • Nicholas Parsons *Dr Hinxman* • Irene Handl *Professor MacRitchie* ■ *Dir* Ralph Thomas • *Scr* Nicholas Phipps, from characters created by Richard Gordon

Doctor in the House
★★★★ **U**

Comedy 1954 · UK · Colour · 87mins

Produced by Betty Box, directed by Ralph Thomas and adapted by Ronald Wilkins, Nicholas Phipps and Richard Gordon from Gordon's own bestselling novel, this film launched the popular St Swithin's series and made a matinée idol out of Dirk Bogarde. Following a class of students through their training, it delights in the dark side of hospital humour, with the medical misadventures providing much better entertainment than the romantic interludes. Kenneth More, Donald Sinden and Donald Houston are on top form as the duffers doing retakes, while Bogarde oozes charm and quiet comic flair. But stealing all their thunder is James Robertson-Justice as the dictatorial Sir Lancelot Spratt. ▣

Dirk Bogarde *Simon Sparrow* • Muriel Pavlow *Joy* • Kenneth More *Grimsdyke* • Donald Sinden *Benskin* • Kay Kendall *Isobel* • James Robertson-Justice *Sir Lancelot Spratt* • Donald Houston *Taffy* • Suzanne Cloutier *Stella* ■ *Dir* Ralph Thomas • *Scr* Nicholas Phipps, from the novel by Richard Gordon

Doctor in Trouble
★★ **PG**

Comedy 1970 · UK · Colour · 86mins

The seventh and last movie to be culled from Richard Gordon's bestselling series was based on a book called *Doctor on Toast*, which would have been a pretty apt title for this innocently smutty film, as it feels as if it has been warmed up from the left-overs of *Doctor at Sea*. Director Ralph Thomas seems at a loss for inspiration here, and any enjoyment there is comes from the bullish performance of Leslie Phillips as the medic turned steward onboard a luxury liner. Contains brief nudity. ▣

Leslie Phillips *Dr Burke* • Harry Secombe *Llewellyn Wendover* • James Robertson-Justice *Sir Lancelot Spratt* • Angela Scoular *Ophelia O'Brien* • Irene Handl *Mrs Dailey* • Robert Morley *Captain George Spratt* • Freddie Jones *Master-at-Arms* • Joan Sims *Russian captain* • John Le Mesurier *Purser* • Simon Dee *Basil*

U = SUITABLE FOR ALL   **Uc** = SUITABLE FOR ALL, ESPECIALLY FOR YOUNG CHILDREN (VIDEO ONLY)   **PG** = PARENTAL GUIDANCE

Beauchamp • Graham Chapman *Roddy* ■ *Dir* Ralph Thomas • *Scr* Jack Davies, from the novel *Doctor on Toast* by Richard Gordon

Dr Jekyll and Mr Hyde ★★

Silent horror 1920 · US · Tinted · 63mins

Based on Thomas Russell Sullivan's Victorian stage adaptation and steeped in the attitudes of that era, this is generally considered to be the best silent version of Robert Louis Stevenson's classic story. It's hopelessly dated by modern standards, though, while John Barrymore slices the ham far too thickly. His Jekyll isn't the villain of the piece so much as his girlfriend's father, played by Brandon Hurst. It's Hurst who suggests idealist Jekyll experiments with the good and evil sides of human nature, and he's also the one who deliberately leads him into temptation with silent goddess Nita Naldi. The initial transformation is nothing more than Barrymore twisting his face into an evil grimace, but a nightmare vision of a monstrous spider with Hyde's face still carries a potent charge.

John Barrymore *Dr Henry Jekyll/Mr Edward Hyde* • Martha Mansfield *Millicent Carew* • Nita Naldi *Gina* • Brandon Hurst *Sir George Carew* • Charles Lane (2) *Dr Richard Lanyon* • Louis Wolheim *Music hall proprietor* ■ *Dir* John S Robertson • *Scr* Clara S Beranger, from the novel *The Strange Case of Dr Jekyll and Mr Hyde* by Robert Louis Stevenson

Dr Jekyll and Mr Hyde ★★★★ 12

Horror 1932 · US · BW · 91mins

Robert Louis Stevenson's oft-told split personality tale receives its most stylish, erotic and exciting treatment under Rouben Mamoulian's sure direction. While Fredric March deservedly won the best actor Oscar shared with Wallace Beery in *The Champ* for his tormented performance (coupled with the impressive single-take transformation scenes), equally remarkable is the smouldering sensuality of Miriam Hopkins as the object of his evil attentions. The most enduring adaptation of this Faustian moral fable. [video]

Fredric March *Dr Henry Jekyll/Mr Hyde* • Miriam Hopkins *Ivy Pearson* • Rose Hobart *Muriel Carew* • Holmes Herbert *Dr Lanyon* • Halliwell Hobbes *Brigadier General Carew* • Edgar Norton *Poole* • Arnold Lucy *Utterson* • Colonel McDonnell *Hobson* • Tempe Pigott *Mrs Hawkins* ■ *Dir* Rouben Mamoulian • *Scr* Samuel Hoffenstein, Percy Heath, from the novel *The Strange Case of Dr Jekyll and Mr Hyde* by Robert Louis Stevenson • *Cinematographer* Karl Struss

Dr Jekyll and Mr Hyde ★★★

Horror 1941 · US · BW · 126mins

Director Victor Fleming's first film after *Gone with the Wind* was this lavish MGM treatment of Robert Louis Stevenson's classic cautionary tale. With the accent on the bad doctor's emotional turmoil rendered in complex Freudian terms to little dramatic effect rather than the horror of the situation, it's a poor, if at times scary relation to the superior 1932 version, which starred Fredric March. Spencer Tracy adds scant shading to either side of his split personality, despite an impressive and sinister transformation montage. Worth seeing for the luminescent Ingrid Bergman.

Spencer Tracy *Dr Harry Jekyll/Mr Hyde* • Ingrid Bergman *Ivy Peterson* • Lana Turner *Beatrix Emery* • Donald Crisp *Sir Charles Emery* • Ian Hunter *Dr John Lanyon* • Barton MacLane *Sam Higgins* • C Aubrey Smith *The bishop* • Peter Godfrey *Poole* ■ *Dir* Victor Fleming • *Scr* John Lee Mahin, from the novel *The Strange Case Of Dr Jekyll and Mr Hyde* by Robert Louis Stevenson

Dr Jekyll and Ms Hyde ★ 12

Comedy 1995 · US · Colour · 86mins

This dire, unfunny and completely unnecessary comic twist on Robert Louis Stevenson's classic tale stars Tim Daly as Jekyll's descendant, a gormless fellow who has the unhappy knack of turning into trampy vamp Helen Hyde (Sean Young). Neither funny nor frightening, the only really scary thing in the movie is Young's bad acting. As you would expect, this lamentable affair ended up in bargain video bins everywhere. Contains swearing and nudity. [video]

Sean Young *Helen Hyde* • Tim Daly [Timothy Daly] *Dr Richard Jacks* • Lysette Anthony *Sarah Carver* • Stephen Tobolowsky *Oliver Mintz* • Harvey Fierstein *Yves DuBois* • Thea Vidale *Valerie* • Jeremy Piven *Pete Walston* • Polly Bergen *Mrs Unterveldt* ■ *Dir* David F Price • *Scr* Tim John, Oliver Butcher, William Davies, William Osborne, from a story by David Price, from the novel *The Strange Case of Dr Jekyll and Mr Hyde* by Robert Louis Stevenson

Dr Jekyll and Sister Hyde ★★★ 18

Horror 1971 · UK · Colour · 93mins

Written by Brian Clemens (longtime writer and producer of the *Avengers* TV series), this bizarre bisexual take on the split personality classic even includes the grave robbers Burke and Hare and a Jack the Ripper subplot. While not quite living up to its initial hype – "the transformation of a man into a woman will take place before your very eyes," warned the ads – it's still mid-range Hammer horror with extra heat supplied by solid Ralph Bates and Martine Beswick as the good and evil flip sides. Contains some violence. [video]

Ralph Bates *Dr Jekyll* • Martine Beswick *Sister Hyde* • Gerald Sim *Professor Robertson* • Lewis Fiander *Howard* • Dorothy Alison *Mrs Spencer* • Neil Wilson *Older policeman* • Ivor Dean *Burke* • Paul Whitsun-Jones *Sergeant Danvers* • Philip Madoc *Byker* • Tony Calvin *Hare* • Susan Brodrick *Susan* ■ *Dir* Roy Ward Baker • *Scr* Brian Clemens, from the novel *The Strange Case of Dr Jekyll and Mr Hyde* by Robert Louis Stevenson

Dr Kildare Goes Home ★★★ U

Medical drama 1940 · US · BW · 78mins

The fifth entry in MGM's popular hospital series is one of the few to move the action away from Blair General. Lew Ayres is impeccable as the idealistic young medic, who this time around sacrifices his chances of promotion by going off to help his country doctor father set up a clinic. Lionel Barrymore's wheelchair-bound Dr Gillespie is less visible than usual, his father-figure presence replaced by veteran character actor Samuel S Hinds, here playing Kildare's real father. Harold S Bucquet directs; Laraine Day and Gene Lockhart co-star.

Lew Ayres *Dr James Kildare* • Lionel Barrymore *Dr Leonard Gillespie* • Laraine Day *Mary Lamont* • Samuel S Hinds *Dr Stephen Kildare* • Gene Lockhart *George Winslow* • John Shelton *Dr Davidson* • Nat Pendleton *Wayman* ■ *Dir* Harold S Bucquet • *Scr* Harry Ruskin, Goldbeck Willis, from a story by Max Brand, Goldbeck Willis

Dr Kildare's Crisis ★★★

Medical drama 1940 · US · BW · 74mins

The "crisis" in the sixth movie in the long-running medic series is one that personally affects young Dr James Kildare (Lew Ayres): his future brother-in-law may be suffering from epilepsy, a disease which could run in the family. Unusually for this B-movie series, the unfortunate patient is played by Robert Young, a star from MGM's A-company. Otherwise the regulars are in place, including Laraine Day as Kildare's fiancée, Lionel Barrymore, of course, and director Harold S Bucquet.

Lew Ayres *Dr James Kildare* • Robert Young *Douglas Lamont* • Lionel Barrymore *Dr Leonard Gillespie* • Laraine Day *Mary Lamont* • Emma Dunn *Mrs Martha Kildaire* • Nat Pendleton *Joe Wayman* • Bobs Watson *Tommy* ■ *Dir* Harold S Bucquet • *Scr* Harry Ruskin, Willis Goldbeck, from a story by Max Brand, Willis Goldbeck

Dr Kildare's Strange Case ★★★

Medical drama 1940 · US · BW · 76mins

An even bigger hit than the previous three pictures in the Dr Kildare series, this one concerns the use of electric shock therapy to cure a mental patient. The medical techniques might be somewhat dated, but the ethical questions remain valid in this snappy entry. Lew Ayres is again the perfect foil for Lionel Barrymore's irascible Dr Gillespie, who is bossed about in turn by Alma Kruger's Nurse Molly Byrd. Broad comedy is once again provided by Nat Pendleton as the simple-minded ambulance driver.

Lew Ayres *Dr James Kildare* • Lionel Barrymore *Dr Leonard Gillespie* • Laraine Day *Mary Lamont* • Shepperd Strudwick *Dr Gregory Lane* • Samuel S Hinds *Dr Stephen Kildare* • Emma Dunn *Martha Kildare* • Alma Kruger *Molly Byrd* • Nat Pendleton *Wayman* • *Dir* Harold S Bucquet • *Scr* Harry Ruskin, Willis Goldbeck, from a story by Max Brand, Willis Goldbeck

Dr Kildare's Victory ★★★

Medical drama 1941 · US · BW · 92mins

His fiancée having been killed off in the previous movie, *Dr Kildare's Wedding Day*, the eponymous medic seeks solace by falling for socialite patient Ann Ayars. This was the only picture in the 15-film series directed by WS Van Dyke, although the style differs not a jot from the others. It was released just before the news broke of Lew Ayres's conscientious objection to the war, which led him to be dropped by MGM after nine appearances as Dr Kildare. Blair General functioned without him for a further six titles.

Lew Ayres *Dr James Kildare* • Lionel Barrymore *Dr Leonard Gillespie* • Robert Sterling *Dr Roger Winthrop* • Ann Ayars *Edith "Cookie" Charles* • Jean Rogers *Annabelle Kirke* • Alma Kruger *Molly Byrd* • Walter Kingsford *Dr Walter Carew* • Nell Craig *Nurse Parker* ■ *Dir* Major WS Van Dyke II [WS Van Dyke] • *Scr* Harry Ruskin, Willis Goldbeck, from a story by Joseph Harrington, from characters created by Max Brand

Dr Kildare's Wedding Day ★★★

Medical drama 1941 · US · BW · 82mins

Laraine Day was gaining a large following as Mary Lamont, the dedicated nurse and fiancée of Dr Kildare (Lew Ayres), when MGM, who had been grooming her for bigger pictures, decided to have her killed by a truck. The elegant and attractive brunette, who had featured in eight Kildare episodes, was never again able to find a distinctive screen image. Up-and-coming comic Red Skelton provides some comic relief in this ironically titled and somewhat gloomy episode, while Swedish actor Nils Asther, a former Garbo co-star, plays an orchestra conductor in one of the three subplots.

Lew Ayres *Dr James Kildare* • Lionel Barrymore *Dr Leonard Gillespie* • Laraine Day *Mary Lamont* • Red Skelton *Vernon Briggs* • Fay Holden *Mrs Bartlett* • Walter Kingsford *Dr Walter Carew* • Samuel S Hinds *Dr Stephen Kildare* • Nils Asther *Constanzo Labardi* ■ *Dir* Harold S Bucquet • *Scr* Willis Goldbeck, Harry Ruskin, from a story by Ormond Ruthven, Lawrence P Bachmann, from characters created by Max Brand

Dr M ★★ 18

Horror thriller
1989 · W Ger/It/Fr · Colour · 111mins

Claude Chabrol is one of the most unpredictable directors in world cinema, and even his failures make for more interesting and compelling viewing than the latest bland Hollywood sequel. *Dr M* is a case in point. Set in a futuristic Berlin, the action centres on the evil schemes of Alan Bates, a media mogul who has obviously been modelled on Fritz Lang's hypnotising hoodlum Dr Mabuse. Chabrol also seems to be heading towards Lang's *Metropolis* territory, but he takes a wrong turning en route and ends up in a low budget version of Gotham City. The story is jumbled and the acting unrestrained, but it's worth a look. Contains violence and swearing. [video]

Alan Bates *Dr Marsfeldt* • Jennifer Beals *Sonja Vogler* • Jan Niklas *Klaus Hartmann* • Hanns Zischler *Moser* • Benoît Régent *Stieglitz* • William Berger *Penck* • Alexander Radszun *Engler* ■ *Dir* Claude Chabrol • *Scr* Sollace Mitchell, from a story by Thomas Bauermeister, from the novel *Dr Mabuse, der Spieler* by Norbert Jacques

Dr Mabuse, the Gambler ★★★★

Silent crime thriller 1922 · Ger · BW

Director Fritz Lang's famous anti-totalitarianism silent allegory about a mad professor (Rudolf Klein-Rogge who starred in Lang's *Metropolis*) trying to take over the world could be hard work for today's television audiences. Despite being superbly designed, the plots-within-plots, characters in disguises and weird coincidental plot twists might prove childish and tiresome to some. Many, though, will attest to Lang's wit and cleverness at putting one over on the future Nazis by satirising the ideas of fascism. This was originally shown in two halves; the first is the more entertaining.

Rudolf Klein-Rogge *Dr Mabuse* • Alfred Abel *Graf Told* • Aud Egede Nissen *Cara Carozza* • Gertrude Welcker *Graefin Told* • Paul Richter *Edgar Hull* • Bernhard Goetzke *von Wenk* • Hans Adalbert von Schlettow *Georg* • Georg John *Pesch* ■ *Dir* Fritz Lang • *Scr* Fritz Lang, Thea von Harbou, from the novel *Dr Mabuse, der Spieler* by Norbert Jacques

Dr Morelle – the Case of the Missing Heiress ★

Detective drama 1949 · UK · BW · 73mins

The first (and last) of an intended series based on a popular radio detective, this undistinguished B-feature murder mystery is typical of the early postwar output of Hammer before it discovered horror. Directed by Godfrey Grayson, it stars Valentine Dyall as Doctor Morelle, the sleuth who solves the murder of a heiress by standard Sherlock Holmes-style means of disguise, interrogation and deduction. Dyall has considerable presence but it's not enough to surmount the implausible plot. Roy Plomley, long-time host of *Desert Island Discs*, was one of the writers.

Valentine Dyall *Dr Morelle* • Julia Lang *Miss Frayle* • Philip Leaver *Samuel Kimber* • Jean Lodge *Cynthia Mason* • Peter Drury *Peter* ■ *Dir* Godfrey Grayson • *Scr* Ambrose Grayson, Roy Plomley, from a radio series by Ernest Dudley and a play by Wilfred Burr

Dr No ★★★★★ PG

Spy adventure 1962 · UK · Colour · 105mins

The James Bond series started in great style with this cleverly conceived dose of sheer escapism which, unlike later episodes, remained true to the essence of Ian Fleming's super-spy novels. Director Terence Young set the 007 standard with terrific action sequences, highly exotic atmosphere and witty humour, while Sean Connery is just perfect as the dashing, debonair and ruthless secret agent with a licence to kill. There was also the sex, of course, and bikini-clad Ursula Andress couldn't have asked for a better star-making entrance. It's understandable why this caused so much excitement: it was entirely different from anything else. Released the same day as the first Beatles single, *Dr No* announced the death of social realism movies like *Saturday Night and Sunday Morning*. It said: "welcome to the sixties." 🎬 **DVD**

Sean Connery *James Bond* • Ursula Andress *Honey* • Joseph Wiseman *Dr No* • Jack Lord *Felix Leiter* • Bernard Lee *"M"* • Anthony Dawson *Professor Dent* • John Kitzmiller *Quarrel* • Zena Marshall *Miss Taro* • Eunice Gayson *Sylvia* • Lois Maxwell *Miss Moneypenny* • Lester Prendergast *Puss Feller* • Reggie Carter *Jones* • Peter Burton *Major Boothroyd* ■ *Dir* Terence Young • *Scr* Richard Maibaum, Johanna Harwood, Berkely Mather, from the novel by Ian Fleming

Dr Phibes Rises Again ★★★ 15

Horror 1972 · UK · Colour · 84mins

Vincent Price returns as the ingenious doctor, now in Egypt searching for the elixir of life, but continuing to outwit enemies with macabre murders, each grislier and funnier than the last. While it's not as splendid as *The Abominable Dr Phibes*, this sequel is mounted with lavish care by Robert Fuest, director of several classic episodes of *The Avengers*, and still scores high in the squirm and chuckle departments, mainly thanks to Price's perfect timing and grandiose camp relish. 🎬

Vincent Price *Dr Anton Phibes* • Robert Quarry *Biederbeck* • Valli Kemp *Vulnavia* • Hugh Griffith *Ambrose* • John Thaw *Shavers* • Keith Buckley *Stuart* • Lewis Fiander *Baker* ■ *Dir* Robert Fuest • *Scr* Robert Fuest, Robert Blees, from characters created by James Whiton, William Goldstein

Doctor Rhythm ★★ U

Musical comedy 1938 · US · BW · 81mins

On the surface, this is a vapid, well below-average Bing Crosby flick. Connoisseurs should note, however, that the wondrous Beatrice Lillie co-stars as one Lorelei Dodge-Blodgett and performs her famous stage and record sketch, *Two Dozen Double Damask Dinner Napkins*. In addition, Crosby gets to croon *This Is My Night to Dream* and *My Heart Is Taking Lessons*. The silly plot, based on a story by O Henry, has Crosby as a doctor pretending to be a cop to stop Lillie's niece marrying a fortune-hunter.

Bing Crosby *Bill Remsen* • Mary Carlisle *Judy* • Beatrice Lillie *Lorelei Dodge-Blodgett* • Andy Devine *O'Roon* • Laura Hope Crews *Mrs Twombling* ■ *Dir* Frank Tuttle • *Scr* Jo Swerling, Richard Connell, from the story *The Badge of Policeman O'Roon* by O Henry

Dr Socrates ★★★★

Crime drama 1935 · US · BW · 71mins

Paul Muni was the Marlon Brando of the thirties, in technique if not in looks. His method of character establishment from the inside out earned him starring roles in many worthy biographies, so this was a welcome change of pace: a gangster thriller in which he plays the small-town doctor who is forced to treat wounded mobsters. There's wonderfully brisk direction by William Dieterle and a blustering performance by Barton MacLane as the gang leader nearly, but not quite, upstaging Muni.

Paul Muni *Dr Caldwell* • Ann Dvorak *Josephine Gray* • Barton MacLane *Red Bastian* • Raymond Brown *Ben Suggs* • Ralph Remley *Bill Payne* • Hal K Dawson *Mel Towne* ■ *Dir* William Dieterle • *Scr* Robert Lord, Mary C McCall Jr, from a story by WR Burnett

Dr Strangelove, or How I Learned to Stop Worrying and Love the Bomb ★★★★★ PG

Satirical comedy 1963 · UK · BW · 90mins

Is this the way the world ends, not with a bang but a simper? The late Stanley Kubrick's ferocious Cold War satire makes us smile through gritted teeth as unhinged general Sterling

Hayden sends a squadron of nuclear bombers to attack Russia and trigger an apocalypse-laden doomsday machine. Peter Sellers's trio of performances (bemused airman, confused president and defused US Nazi adviser, re-armed by the prospect of world annihilation) spirals from gentle humour to surreal horror. The scenes in which Hayden raves about "bodily fluids" and Pentagon general George C Scott rants about statistical deaths were obviously inspired by Sellers's genius. Kubrick's unsparing disgust with our warlike instincts has never been so obvious nor so grimly comic. Contains swearing. 🎬 **DVD**

Peter Sellers *Group Captain Lionel Mandrake/President Merkin Muffley/Dr Strangelove* • George C Scott *General "Buck" Turgidson* • Sterling Hayden *General Jack D Ripper* • Keenan Wynn *Colonel "Bat" Guano* • Slim Pickens *Major TJ "King" Kong* • Peter Bull *Ambassador de Sadesky* • Tracy Reed *Miss Scott* • James Earl Jones *Lieutenant Lothar Zogg* ■ *Dir* Stanley Kubrick • *Scr* Stanley Kubrick, Terry Southern, Peter George, from the novel *Red Alert* by Peter George • *Cinematographer* Gilbert Taylor • *Art Director* Ken Adam • *Editor* Anthony Harvey

Dr Syn ★★★

Adventure 1937 · UK · BW · 81mins

George Arliss retired from movies after starring in this sprightly 19th-century smuggling adventure. By day the respected vicar of Dymchurch, Arliss uses the cover of darkness to masquerade as the ruthless Dr Syn, daredevil brigand and scourge of the Kent coast. Defying his 69 years and reputation for stuffiness, Arliss gives a rousing performance, turning from meek goodness into sneering evil with a melodramatic flourish worthy of Tod Slaughter. Roy William Neill, who made many of the Basil Rathbone *Sherlock Holmes* mysteries, directs with atmospheric efficiency.

George Arliss *Dr Syn* • John Loder *Denis Cobtree* • Margaret Lockwood *Imogene* • Roy Emerton *Captain Howard Collyer* • Graham Moffatt *Jerry Jerk* • Frederick Burtwell *Rash* • George Merritt *Mipps* ■ *Dir* Roy William Neill • *Scr* Roger Burford, Michael Hogan, from the novel by Russell Thorndike

Dr Syn, Alias the Scarecrow ★★★ U

Adventure 1963 · US · Colour · 97mins

Patrick McGoohan sails through this Disney frolic as the kindly vicar of Dymchurch by day who becomes the notorious smuggler Dr Syn by night. George Cole, Michael Hordern, Kay Walsh and a host of other stalwarts add to the quaint Georgian atmosphere, augmented by some nice photography (by Paul Beeson) of authentic Kentish locations. It's all very tame, of course, but kids should enjoy its slick piratical flavour. Made for American TV, the film was originally shown in three episodes as *The Scarecrow of Romney Marsh* but was released theatrically overseas.

Patrick McGoohan *Dr Syn* • George Cole *Mr Mipps* • Michael Hordern *Squire Banks* • Tony Britton *Bates* • Geoffrey Keen *General Pugh* • Eric Flynn *Philip Brackenbury* • Kay Walsh *Mrs Waggett* ■ *Dir* James Neilson • *Scr* Robert Westerby, from the novel *Christopher Syn* by Russell Thorndike, William Buchanan

Dr Terror's House of Horrors ★★★

Horror 1964 · UK · Colour · 97mins

Vampires, werewolves, crawling hands, voodoo curses and creeping vines – they're all present and enjoyably correct in the first, and best, fun fright anthology from the Amicus horror factory, Hammer's only real sixties' rival. Peter Cushing is the tarot card reader telling five men on a train (including Christopher Lee, Donald Sutherland and Roy Castle) their grim fortunes. Veteran horror director Freddie Francis delivers a fair quota of entertaining shocks with his trademark visual flair, and it's a joy to see DJ turned actor Alan Freeman at the mercy of that peculiar writhing plant.

Peter Cushing *Dr Schreck* • Neil McCallum *Jim Dawson* • Alan Freeman *Bill Rogers* • Roy Castle *Biff Bailey* • Christopher Lee *Franklyn Marsh* • Donald Sutherland *Bob Carroll* • Max Adrian *Dr Blake* • Edward Underdown *Tod* ■ *Dir* Freddie Francis • *Scr* Milton Subotsky

Dr Who and the Daleks ★★★ U

Science-fiction adventure 1965 · UK · Colour · 82mins

The first big-screen outing for the BBC's ever-popular sci-fi TV series has Peter Cushing playing the time-travelling Doctor with amiable seriousness as he pits his wits against those mobile knobbly tin cans forever shrieking "Exterminate". Lacking the bite and inventiveness that set the landmark series apart, this spin-off unwisely injects humour into its sparse scenario. However, despite the many faults, it's still a slick slice of enjoyable mayhem generating loads of fun for the uninitiated and die-hard fans alike.

Peter Cushing *Dr Who* • Roy Castle *Ian* • Jennie Linden *Barbara* • Roberta Tovey *Susan* • Barrie Ingham *Alydon* • Michael Coles *Ganatus* • Geoffrey Toone *Temmosus* • Mark Peterson *Elydon* ■ *Dir* Gordon Flemyng • *Scr* Milton Subotsky, from the BBC TV series by Sydney Newman, from the characters created by Terry Nation

Doctor X ★★★

Horror 1932 · US · Colour · 76mins

A weird mix of effective horror, creaky haunted house clichés and dated comic relief, the latter single-handedly disrupting the sombre mood created by director Michael Curtiz as police hunt for the "Full Moon Killer" among a group of eccentric medics. Considered a classic mainly for the scary "synthetic flesh" sequence, the film's more tiresome moments are masked by energetic lead performances: Preston Foster's cannibalistic monster and *King Kong's* Fay Wray, screaming away again as mysterious Lionel Atwill's daughter.

Lionel Atwill *Doctor Xavier* • Lee Tracy *Lee* • Fay Wray *Joan* • Preston Foster *Dr Wells* • Arthur Edmund Carewe *Dr Rowitz* • John Wray *Dr Haines* • Harry Beresford *Dr Duke* ■ *Dir* Michael Curtiz • *Scr* Robert Tasker, Earl Baldwin, from a play by Howard W Comstock, Allen C Miller

U = SUITABLE FOR ALL Uc = SUITABLE FOR ALL, ESPECIALLY FOR YOUNG CHILDREN (VIDEO ONLY) PG = PARENTAL GUIDANCE

Doctor Zhivago ★★★★★ 15

Romantic epic 1965 · US · Colour · 193mins

Nominated for ten Oscars (and winning a respectable five), David Lean's adaptation of Boris Pasternak's classic novel has all the sweep and stateliness one expects of this most meticulous of directors. He sets his scene superbly – thanks largely to the brilliant designs for both the plush and the poverty-ridden quarters of Moscow, and to Freddie Young's atmospheric cinematography – and tells this epic story with a grasp of period and a concern for character that is often masterly. The performances are rather uneven, but Omar Sharif is outstanding in the lead and Tom Courtenay and Julie Christie bring great humanity to the tragedy. ▭

Omar Sharif *Yuri Zhivago* • Julie Christie *Lara* • Geraldine Chaplin *Tonya* • Rod Steiger *Komarovsky* • Alec Guinness *Yevgraf* • Tom Courtenay *Pasha/Strelnikov* • Ralph Richardson *Alexander* • Siobhan McKenna *Anna* • Rita Tushingham *Girl* • Bernard Kay *Bolshevik* • Klaus Kinski *Kostoyed* ■ *Dir* David Lean • *Scr* Robert Bolt, from the novel by Boris Pasternak

The Doctor's Dilemma ★★ U

Comedy 1958 · UK · Colour · 99mins

Anthony Asquith was something of an expert at bringing celebrated stage plays to the screen, yet he fails to breathe life into this fast-fading satire on the foibles of Harley Street. Self-obsessed artist Dirk Bogarde improves the worse his tuberculosis becomes, but Leslie Caron never captures the stubborn devotion that inspires her fight to save him, while Alastair Sim, Robert Morley and Felix Aylmer are equally disappointing as her medical adversaries. George Bernard Shaw's comedy might have been scalpel-sharp back in 1903, but the foundation of the National Health Service rather blunted its edge.

Leslie Caron *Mrs Jennifer Dubedat* • Dirk Bogarde *Louis Dubedat* • Alastair Sim *Cutler Walpole* • Robert Morley *Sir Ralph Bloomfield-Bonington* • John Robinson *Sir Colenso Ridgeon* • Felix Aylmer *Sir Patrick Cullen* • Peter Sallis *Picture gallery secretary* ■ *Dir* Anthony Asquith • *Scr* Anatole de Grunwald, from the play by George Bernard Shaw

Doctor's Orders ★★ U

Comedy 1934 · UK · BW · 69mins

No less than five writers had a hand in the script for this tale of a medical student (John Mills) whose romantic plans are complicated when his father, travelling medicine man Bill Blake, is revealed to be a carnival confidence trickster. The result is a flimsy, music hall-style comedy which gives the then-popular Leslie Fuller plenty of opportunities to deliver his trademark bombast as the quack whose heart turns out to be in the right place.

Leslie Fuller *Bill Blake* • John Mills *Ronnie Blake* • Marguerite Allan *Gwen Summerfield* • Mary Jerrold *Mary Blake* • Ronald Shiner *Miggs* • Georgie Harris *Duffin* • Felix Aylmer *Sir Daniel Summerfield* • William Kendall *Jackson* ■ *Dir* Norman Lee • *Scr* Clifford Grey, RP Weston, Bert Lee, from a story by Clifford Grey, Syd Courtenay, Lola Harvey

Doctors' Wives ★★★ 18

Medical drama 1970 · US · Colour · 97mins

Based on the principle that "if you can't beat 'em, join 'em", this attempts to be a super-sudsy soap opera like the ones TV was using to gnaw away at cinema attendances. Like *Peyton Place*, it's built around a community going through the usual rituals (neurosis, adultery, murder), though the acting is considerably classier: a young Gene Hackman, Dyan Cannon, Rachel Roberts and Carroll O'Connor. Distinguished screenwriter Daniel Taradash (*Rancho Notorious*) does not distinguish himself. ▭

Dyan Cannon *Lorrie Dellman* • Richard Crenna *Pete Brennan* • Gene Hackman *Dave Randolph* • Carroll O'Connor *Joe Gray* • Rachel Roberts *Della Randolph* • Janice Rule *Amy Brennan* • Diana Sands *Helen Straughn* • Ralph Bellamy *Jake Porter* ■ *Dir* George Schaefer • *Scr* Daniel Taradash, from the novel by Frank G Slaughter

Dodes'ka-Den ★★★★

Fantasy drama 1970 · Jap · Colour · 139mins

After a five-year break (during which time he bailed on *Tora! Tora! Tora!*), Akira Kurosawa returned to make his first film in colour. Adapted from a collection of short stories by Shugoro Yamamoto, this affecting study of the hopes, fears and bitter realities of a group of slum dwellers originally ran for 244 minutes. Sensitively played and demonstrating an instinctive genius for colour, the gently paced mix of fantasy and melodrama typifies Kurosawa's essential humanity. Despite receiving an Oscar nomination for best foreign film, however, it was dismissed by the critics. Soon afterwards, the director attempted suicide. In Japanese with English subtitles.

Yoshitaka Zushi *Rokkuchan* • Kin Sugai *Rokkuchan's mother* • Junzaburo Ban *Yukichi Shima* • Kiyoko Tange *Mrs Shima* • Hisashi Igawa *Masuo Masuda* • Hideko Okiyama *Masuda's wife* ■ *Dir* Akira Kurosawa • *Scr* Akira Kurosawa, Hideo Oguni, Shinobu Hashimoto, from a short story collection by Shugoro Yamamoto

Dodge City ★★★★ PG

Western 1939 · US · Colour · 99mins

Errol Flynn stars as one Wade Hatton, who rides into Dodge, sees that "knavery is rampant" (as *Variety* described it in 1939) and sets about cleaning up the town with military precision. Why Warner Bros couldn't come clean and call him Wyatt Earp is a mystery. It's knockabout stuff, exuberantly directed in lush, early Technicolor by Michael Curtiz, and is in sharp contrast to John Ford's later *My Darling Clementine* as well as more recent, revisionist trawls through the Earp legend. Flynn is in swashbuckling Robin Hood/Captain Blood mode and Olivia de Havilland, as usual, is the woman in his life. ▭

Errol Flynn *Wade Hatton* • Olivia de Havilland *Abbie Irving* • Ann Sheridan *Ruby Gilman* • Bruce Cabot *Jeff Surrett* • Frank McHugh *Joe Clemens* • Alan Hale *Rusty Hart* • John Litel *Matt Cole* • Henry Travers *Dr Irving* ■ *Dir* Michael Curtiz • *Scr* Robert Buckner

Dodsworth ★★★★ PG

Drama 1936 · US · BW · 96mins

William Wyler's masterly film of Sinclair Lewis's novel, with Walter Huston, Ruth Chatterton, Mary Astor and David Niven giving wonderful performances. It's a full-blown romance with a darker edge, gleamingly shot and nominated for seven Oscars, winning one for art direction. Producer Sam Goldwyn was offered the book for $20,000 and turned it down, thinking it would make a lousy movie. Sidney Howard subsequently adapted it into a Broadway hit starring Huston and Fay Bainter, and Goldwyn ended up buying the screen rights for $165,000. "I don't understand," said Howard. "Two years ago you could have had it for $20,000." Goldwyn replied, "I don't care. This way I buy a successful play. Before it was just a novel." ▭

Walter Huston *Sam Dodsworth* • Ruth Chatterton *Fran Dodsworth* • Paul Lukas *Arnold Iselin* • Mary Astor *Edith Cortright* • David Niven *Lockert* • Gregory Gaye *Kurt von Obersdorf* • Maria Ouspenskaya *Baroness von Obersdorf* • Odette Myrtil *Madame de Penable* ■ *Dir* William Wyler • *Scr* Sidney Howard, from his play, from the novel by Sinclair Lewis • *Art Director* Richard Day

The Dog and the Diamonds ★★

Drama 1953 · UK · BW · 55mins

Although the Children's Film Foundation is now dismissed with mocking nostalgia, the unit often commanded the services of some highly influential people. This tale of a gang that appropriates the garden of an abandoned manor for a pet zoo was directed by Ralph Thomas just before he launched the famous *Doctor* series, while producer Peter Rogers would shortly embark on the *Carry Ons* with Ralph's brother, Gerald. There's much fun to be had in watching the kids confound the jewel thieves who are using the house to hide their stash, but it's of a dated, innocent kind.

Kathleen Harrison *Mrs Fossett* • George Coulouris *Forbes* • Geoffrey Sumner *Mr Gayford* • Brian Oulton *Mr Plumpton* • Michael McGuire *Jimmy* • Robert Sandford *Peter* • Robert Scroggins *Ginger* ■ *Dir* Ralph Thomas • *Scr* Patricia Latham, from the story by Mary Cathcart Borer

Dog Day Afternoon ★★★★ 15

Crime drama 1975 · US · Colour · 119mins

A film about a bank robbery, the proceeds of which are needed to pay for a sex-change operation. Weird but apparently true; well, this is New York. From this material, Sidney Lumet creates a marvellous patchwork of a movie, cutting between the inept but passionate bank robbers (Al Pacino and John Cazale, both fresh from *The Godfather Part II*) whose bungled heist turns into a hostage situation, the corpulent cop leading the police siege (Charles Durning) and the mob that gathers outside the bank. It's an insane circus and you know that something, or someone, is going to blow a gasket. Pacino's performance (which earned him a fourth Oscar nomination) is a multi-layered display and the whole picture seems infected by his jitters. Contains violence and swearing. ▭ **DVD**

Al Pacino *Sonny Wortzik* • John Cazale *Sal* • Charles Durning *Moretti* • Chris Sarandon *Leon Shermer* • Sully Boyar *Mulvaney* • Penelope Allen *Sylvia* • James Broderick *Sheldon* • Carol Kane *Jenny* • Beulah Garrick *Margaret* ■ *Dir* Sidney Lumet • *Scr* Frank Pierson, from an article by BF Kluge, Thomas Moore • *Cinematographer* Victor J Kemper

A Dog of Flanders ★★ U

Drama 1959 · US · Colour · 96mins

Based on Ouida's novel which was twice filmed as a silent, this lachrymose children's picture epitomises Hollywood's vision of family entertainment in the late fifties. However, while youngsters will delight in the restoration of the abandoned pup, they may find the gentle adventures of his young master rather hard going. Following a couple of outings with his father, Alan, David Ladd went solo here as the orphan who is raised first by his milkman grandfather (Donald Crisp), and then by kindly artist Theodore Bikel. Otto Heller's shots of the Flanders plain are picturesque, but the action is often just as flat.

David Ladd *Nello* • Donald Crisp *Daas* • Theodore Bikel *Piet* • Max Croiset *Mr Cogez* • Monique Ahrens *Corrie* • Siobhan Taylor *Alois* ■ *Dir* James B Clark • *Scr* Ted Sherderman, from the novel by Ouida

Dog Park ★★

Romantic comedy 1998 · Can · Colour · 91mins

It's a well-known fact that the best way to meet people is by walking the dog, and Bruce McCulloch's film is built around just such a premise. Luke Wilson stars as a recently dumped bloke who gets the hots for Natasha Henstridge in the park; sadly, she only has eyes for her dog. Meanwhile, Wilson's angst at being chucked by Kathleen Robertson is affecting their dog. Fluffy fare that should appeal to those sympathetic to the needs of our four-legged friends.

Natasha Henstridge *Lorna* • Luke Wilson *Andy* • Kathleen Robertson *Cheryl* • Janeane Garofalo *Jeri* • Bruce McCulloch *Jeff* • Kristin Lehman *Keiran* • Amie Carey *Rachel* • Gordon Currie *Trevor* ■ *Dir/Scr* Bruce McCulloch

Dog Star Man ★★★★

Experimental silent drama 1964 · US · Colour and BW · 78mins

The most famous work produced by avant-gardist Stan Brakhage is a masterpiece of superimpositional editing that recalls the pioneering work of Dziga Vertov. Following a prelude, the four parts of the piece (approximating the seasons) trace the stages of human life from cradle to grave, while also frequently alluding to the evolution of artistic endeavour. Utterly devoid of narrative, this dazzling, silent collage of frantic camera movements, boldly coloured fragments and poetic diversions is impossible to appreciate in a single viewing. Brakhage later unravelled the multiple imagery for a 270-minute exposition entitled *The Art of Vision*.

Stan Brakhage ■ *Dir/Scr* Stan Brakhage

The Dog Who Stopped the War ★★★ U

Drama   1984 · Can · Colour · 86mins

Clint Eastwood fans might just spot hints of his *A Fistful of Dollars* peeping through this story about a snowball fight that escalates into a neighbourhood war. Director André Melançon coaxes spirited performances from his young cast, with Cédric Jourde doing well as the cunning peace envoy, but, as you might expect, it's the handsome hound that steals every scene. The glorious photography adds to the enjoyment. French dialogue dubbed into English. ▭

Cédric Jourde *Luke* • Julien Elie *Mark* • Maripierre Arseneau-d'Anou *Sophie* • Duc Minh Vu *Warren* • Luc Boucher *Johnny* • Gilbert Monette *George* ■ *Dir* André Melançon • *Scr* Danyèle Patenaude • *Cinematographer* François Protat

Dogboys ★★★

Prison drama   1998 · US · Colour · 92mins

The New Adventures of Superman star Dean Cain gets to wear his underpants on the inside in this oddish prison movie caper, distinguished by an unusually eclectic cast. The "dogboys" of the title are inmates who are used to "train" the guard dogs at a brutal high security prison; Cain is the latest recruit who begins to suspect there are even murkier goings-on at the facility. Cain enjoys himself in a grittier-than-usual role, but Bryan Brown grabs the acting honours as the deranged warden and Tia Carrere brings some much needed (if vaguely implausible) glamour to the affair as the Assistant DA suspicious of conditions at the prison. Ken Russell fans will not necessarily recognise any of his trademark excesses, but he still directed this made-for-TV fare. Contains swearing and violence.

Bryan Brown *Captain Brown* • Dean Cain *Julian Taylor* • Tia Carrere *Assistant DA Jennifer Dern* • Ken James *Warden Wakefield* • Sean McCann *Pappy* • Richard Chevolleau *Willy B* ■ *Dir* Ken Russell • *Scr* Rob Stork, David Taylor, from a story by Rob Stork, Dennis Kleinman, Hugh Martin

Dogfight ★★★★ 15

Romantic drama   1991 · US · Colour · 89mins

Barely seen on its original release, this poignant drama only emphasises what cinema lost with the death of River Phoenix. Most young actors could have carried off the role of the rookie marine who squires sensitive peacenik Lili Taylor to a pre-Vietnam "ugly date" party. But few would have brought such truth to a story so dependent on genuine emotion. Taylor is equally impressive, swallowing her hurt to discover what lies beneath an exterior necessarily toughened by boot camp. Directed by Nancy Savoca with an impeccable grasp of the mood of Kennedy's America, this is a must for more than just Phoenix fans. ▭

River Phoenix *Birdlace* • Lili Taylor *Rose* • Richard Panebianco *Berzin* • Anthony Clark *Oakie* • Mitchell Whitfield *Benjamin* • Holly Near *Rose Snr* • EG Daily [Elizabeth Daily] *Marcie* ■ *Dir* Nancy Savoca • *Scr* Bob Comfort

Dogma ★★★★ 15

Religious satire   1999 · US · Colour · 122mins

Writer/director Kevin Smith – who made the wonderful *Clerks* and *Chasing Amy* and the slightly less wonderful *Mallrats* – here tackles the subject of religion with a wickedly humorous touch that unsurprisingly offended some Catholic groups when the film was released in the US. Matt Damon and Ben Affleck star as two fallen angels who discover there is a loophole which will allow them back into heaven, obliterating the earth in the process. Non-believer Linda Fiorentino is called upon to stop them, with the help of two guardians (recurring characters Jay and Silent Bob, played by Jason Mewes and Smith himself). While the film does not work on every level, Smith has once again delivered a unique script and some terrifically funny performances from a cast which includes Salma Hayek and Alanis Morissette. ▭

Ben Affleck *Bartleby* • George Carlin *Cardinal Glick* • Matt Damon *Loki* • Linda Fiorentino *Bethany* • Salma Hayek *Serendipity* • Jason Lee *Azrael* • Jason Mewes *Jay* • Alan Rickman *Metatron* • Chris Rock *Rufus* • Bud Cort *John Doe Jersey* • Alanis Morissette *God* • Kevin Smith *Silent Bob* • Janeane Garofalo *Clinic girl* ■ *Dir/Scr* Kevin Smith

Dogpound Shuffle ★★★

Comedy drama 1974 · Can · Colour · 100mins

So often a scene-stealing character actor, Ron Moody gets a rare crack at a lead in this amiable piece of family entertainment. As the onetime vaudevillian desperate to raise $30 to get his beloved pet out of the dog pound, he demonstrates some of the soft-shoe style that made him such a hit as Fagin in *Oliver!* There's also some unselfish support from David Soul, who calls on his experiences as a pop singer for his tuneful turn as the washed-up prizefighter who becomes Moody's song-and-dance partner.

Ron Moody *Steps* • David Soul *Pritt* • Pamela McMyler *Pound lady* • Ray Strickland *Mr Lester Jr* • Raymond Sutton *Pound Attendant* ■ *Dir/Scr* Jeffrey Bloom

Dogs ★

Horror   1976 · US · Colour · 89mins

Where Alfred Hitchcock managed to sustain audience belief that our feathered friends had begun attacking humans in *The Birds*, this low-budget howler fails to convince with its tale of a pack of killer hounds on the loose in an isolated college campus. Ex-Man from UNCLE David McCallum struggles gamely as a biology professor whose students end up as Winalot chunks. The Hitchcock connection resurfaces in a pastiche of the *Psycho* shower scene, with one of the canine stars in the Anthony Perkins role. If movies were dogs, this would be a shih-tzu.

David McCallum *Harlan Thompson* • George Wyner *Michael Fitzgerald* • Eric Server *Jimmy Goodmann* • Sandra McCabe *Caroline Donoghue* • Sterling Swanson *Dr Martin Koppelman* • Holly Harris *Mrs Koppelman* ■ *Dir* Burt Brinckerhoff • *Scr* O'Brian Tomalin

A Dog's Best Friend ★★

Children's drama   1960 · US · BW · 70mins

There are shades of Rin Tin Tin in this tale of a wounded German Shepherd who befriends an emotionally scarred orphan struggling to acclimatise to adoption. Making his screen debut, young Roger Mobley turns in a creditable display of simmering resentment, which quickly deflects into terror once he realises his new pal has witnessed a murder and that the killer is now on their trail. Director Edward L Cahn demonstrates both the B-movie sensibility honed over 30 years on Poverty Row and a keen grasp of what keeps kids on the edge of their seats.

Bill Williams *Wes Thurman* • Marcia Henderson *Millie Thurman* • Roger Mobley *Pip Wheeler* • Charles Cooper *Bill Beamer* • Dean Stanton [Harry Dean Stanton] *Roy Janney* • Roy Engel *Sheriff Dan Murdock* ■ *Dir* Edward L Cahn • *Scr* Orville H Hampton

Dogs in Space ★★★★ 18

Drama   1986 · Ausl · Colour · 104mins

This appealingly quirky snapshot of punk life Down Under in the late seventies marked the film debut of the INXS singer Michael Hutchence, who plays a heroin-taking wannabe rock star. The film focuses on struggling band Dogs in Space, led by Hutchence, plus their friends and hangers-on as they drift from party to gig to, er, another party. However, hanging over their idyllic lifestyle is the spectre of drugs and the fact that, one day, the real world is going to catch up with them. The soundtrack, which mixes Aussie punk with Iggy Pop and Brian Eno, is superb, while the direction – from pop promo man Richard Lowenstein – is surprisingly unflashy. ▭

Michael Hutchence *Sam* • Saskia Post *Anna* • Nique Needles *Tim* • Deanna Bond *Girl* • Tony Helou *Luchio* • Chris Haywood *Chainsaw man* • Peter Walsh *Anthony* • Laura Swanson *Clare* ■ *Dir/Scr* Richard Lowenstein

The Dogs of War ★★ 15

Action drama   1980 · UK · Colour · 113mins

Unleashed upon the big screen from Frederick Forsyth's thriller, these hounds unfortunately have been muzzled and boast all too few snarls. Christopher Walken is the disillusioned mercenary caught up in a dastardly plot to take over a West African state, but any possible thrills are quickly overpowered by too much explanation. John Irvin's direction of the macho passions on display is both predictable and unfocused; all Tom Berenger and Colin Blakely seem to do is grimace a lot. Set in Graham Greene territory, the tale needs that author's emotional urgency to give it the purpose it lacks. Contains violence and swearing. ▭

Christopher Walken *Jamie Shannon* • Tom Berenger *Drew* • Colin Blakely *North* • Hugh Millais *Endean* • Paul Freeman *Derek* • JoBeth Williams *Jessie* • Ed Dish *Jessie* • Jean-François DeVore, George Malko, from the novel by Frederick Forsyth

Dogtanian – the Movie ★★ U

Animated adventure 1989 · Sp · Colour · 93mins

Directed by Luis Ballester, this full-length version of the popular Spanish cartoon series sticks closely to the familiar Dumas story. Like most other animated spin-offs, however, characters who are comfortable companions for 20 minutes become insufferable after an hour. A brash, yappy pup not unlike Scooby Doo's nephew, Scrappy, Dogtanian is the least likeable of the Muskehounds, and we don't get nearly enough of the foxy Cardinal Richelieu as he plots an alliance with England. ▭

Dir Luis Ballester • *Scr* from characters created by Claudio Biem Boyd, from the novel *The Three Musketeers* by Alexandre Dumas

Dogwatch ★★ 18

Crime action   1997 · US · Colour · 95mins

Sam Elliott and Paul Sorvino star in a hard-hitting crime thriller about a tough San Francisco cop who discovers his late partner wasn't exactly whiter than white. Having killed the man he thinks is responsible for his friend's death, detective Charlie Falon (Elliott) and his new partner (Esai Morales) become entangled in two murder investigations. Like a cross between *The Bad Lieutenant* and *The Big Easy*, John Langley's drama has all the seediness of the former but, alas, none of the humour of the latter. Contains swearing and violence. ▭

Sam Elliott *Charlie Falon* • Esai Morales *Murrow* • Paul Sorvino *Delgoti* • Dan Lauria *Halloway* • Richard Gilliland *Orlanski* • Mimi Graven *Sally* ■ *Dir* John Langley • *Scr* Martin Zurla, from a story by Dan Lauria, Martin Zurla

Doin' Time on Planet Earth ★★ 15

Comedy   1988 · US · Colour · 79mins

Ryan Richmond (Nicholas Strouse) is a teenager who, in the course of his search for a date for his brother's wedding, comes to believe he is an alien from outer space. Candice Azzara and Adam West are two other potential aliens who believe Ryan holds the information that will lead them all home. It all has something to do with the wedding being on a blue moon and in Ryan's father's revolving restaurant. A supposed comedy that's too complicated to be funny. ▭

Nicholas Strouse *Ryan Richmond* • Matt Adler *Dan Forrester* • Andrea Thompson *Lisa Winston* • Martha Scott *Virginia Camalier* • Adam West *Charles Pinsky* • Hugh Gillin *Fred Richmond* • Timothy Patrick Murphy *Jeff Richmond* • Candice Azzara [Candy Azzara] *Edna Pinsky* ■ *Dir* Charles Matthau • *Scr* Darren Star, from a story by Andrew Licht, Jeffrey A Mueller, Darren Star

Doing Time for Patsy Cline ★★★

Comedy road movie 1997 · Ausl · Colour · 93mins

Miranda Otto teams up with real-life paramour Richard Roxburgh in a genial Aussie road movie with a country and western twang. Matt Day (*Muriel's Wedding*) is a young innocent off to seek fame and fortune in Nashville. En route he hooks up with drug-dealing rogue Roxburgh and his redheaded girlfriend (Otto), who harbours her own dreams of stardom. Things go pear-shaped when the trio get busted by the police, while writer/director Chris Kennedy throws in a tragic illness for good measure. Attractively played by the three leads, the end result has a rich vein of self-mocking humour that leavens the rather heavy-handed stab at third-act pathos.

Matt Day *Ralph* • Richard Roxburgh *Boyd* • Miranda Otto *Patsy* • Gus Mercurio *Tyrone* • Tony Barry *Dwayne* • Kiri Paramore *Ken* ■ *Dir/Scr* Chris Kennedy

La Dolce Vita ★★★★★ 15

Classic drama 1960 · It · BW · 167mins

Winner of the Palme d'Or at Cannes, this sprawling, scathing satire on the decadence of contemporary Italy and the hypocrisy of the Catholic Church confirmed Federico Fellini's reputation for flamboyant, controversial imagery. Marcello Mastroianni is outstanding as the journalist who, by day, jostles with the paparazzi in the hunt for movie stars, miraculous visitations and flying statues of Christ. By night, he indulges his passion for intellectual pretension and the indolent delights of the jet set. A dire warning that Italy was still politically and socially prone to the false promises of fascism, this almost Dantesque odyssey so drained its Oscar-nominated director, he did not make another feature for three years. In Italian with English subtitles. [VIDEO]

Marcello Mastroianni *Marcello Rubini* • Anita Ekberg *Sylvia* • Anouk Aimée *Maddalena* • Yvonne Furneaux *Emma* • Magali Noel *Fanny* • Alain Cuny *Steiner* • Nadia Gray *Nadia* • Lex Barker *Robert* • Annibale Ninchi *Marcello's father* ■ *Dir* Federico Fellini • *Scr* Federico Fellini, Ennio Flaiano, Tullio Pinelli, Brunello Rondi, from a story by Federico Fellini, Ennio Flaiano, Tullio Pinelli

Dollar ★★★

Comedy 1938 · Swe · BW · 88mins

Having found stardom in romantic melodramas, Ingrid Bergman took a bit of a risk making this frantic comedy. As usual, though, she carried it off with an ease and grace that made her one of the finest actresses in cinema history. What with illicit romances, false suspicions, gambling debts, stock market crashes, secret pacts and mysterious illnesses, the plot concocted by co-writer/director Gustaf Molander takes credibility to its elastic limit – but when did farce start resembling life? Bergman excels as the neglected wife whose act of kindness inspires marital and financial chaos, but the neurotic Tutta Rolf and the prudish Elsa Burnett aren't bad either. In Swedish with English subtitles.

Georg Rydeberg *Kurt Balzar* • Ingrid Bergman *Julia Balzar* • Kotti Chave *Louis Brenner* • Tutta Rolf *Sussi Brenner* • Hakan Westergren *Ludvig von Bathwyhl* • Birgit Tengroth *Katja* • Elsa Burnett *Mary Jonstone* • Edvin Adolphson *Dr Jonsson* ■ *Dir* Gustaf Molander • *Scr* Stina Bergman, Gustaf Molander, from the play by Hjalmar Bergman

Dollar for the Dead ★★ PG

Western 1998 · US · Colour · 94mins

Commendable but flawed attempt to re-create the spaghetti western style of Sergio Leone, right down to shooting on the same Spanish sets the great man used in the sixties. Director Gene Quintano also recalls John Woo in the two-fisted action and non-stop gunplay that feature throughout. Emilio Estevez (no stranger to the Wild West after *Young Guns* and its sequel) comes to the aid of a crippled Civil War veteran, and the pair hitch up to re-assemble a treasure map embossed on four leather holsters. Out to stop them are "The Regulators" and a renegade troop of US cavalry. [VIDEO]

Emilio Estevez *The Cowboy* • William Forsythe *Dooley* • Howie Long *Reager* • Joaquim DeAlmeida *Friar Ramon* • Jonathan Banks *Skinner* • Ed Lauter *Colby* • Lance Kinsey *Tracker* • Jordi Mollà *Federal Captain* ■ *Dir/Scr* Gene Quintano

Dollar Mambo ★★★

Musical drama 1993 · Pan · Colour · 80mins

Re-enacting actual events, this mix of dance and mime completes the trilogy that began with *Barocco* and *Latino Bar* and proves that the musical is a suitable vehicle for political comment. Once more, Mexican director Paul Leduc employs a diversity of dance styles as the American invasion of Panama brings a halt to the lively entertainment at a downtown cabaret, where comics, magicians and showgirls provide the exploited workers with an escape from their toils. The shift in tone, once the gas-masked soldiers violate the bar and drive a dancer to suicide, is deeply disturbing. In Spanish with English subtitles.

Roberto Sosa • Dolores Pedro • Javier Molina • Kandido Uranga ■ *Dir* Paul Leduc • *Scr* Paul Leduc, Jaime Aviles, Jose Jaquin Blanco, Hector Ortego, Juan Tovar

The Dollmaker ★★★★ PG

Drama 1984 · US · Colour · 137mins

This was Jane Fonda's first venture into small-screen movies, and she won an Emmy for her performance. After her husband lands a key wartime job in Detroit, Gertie Nevels's only escape from the trials of raising five children away from their Kentucky home comes from carving wooden dolls. Fonda reveals an intensity which has often been missing in the latter part of her career, although it helps that she's working with superior material. Susan Cooper and Hume Cronyn's adaptation of Harriette Arnow's novel is directed with a sure sense of time and place by Daniel Petrie. [VIDEO]

Jane Fonda *Gertie Nevels* • Levon Helm *Clovis Nevels* • Geraldine Page *Mrs Kendrick* • Amanda Plummer *Marnie Childers* • Susan Kingsley *Sophronie* • Ann Hearn *Max* • Robert Swan *Victor* • Nikki Creswell *Cassie Nevels* • David Dawson *Amos Nevels* ■ *Dir* Daniel Petrie • *Scr* Susan Cooper, Hume Cronyn, from the novel by Harriette Arnow

Dolls ★★ 18

Comedy horror 1987 · US · Colour · 74mins

A novel variation on the eighties "stalk and slash" movie, replacing the usual lone killer with knife-wielding mannequins. Director Stuart Gordon carved out something of a niche for himself as a gore fiend with such films as *Re-Animator*, but this film – about a disparate group of travellers holed up in a spooky mansion inhabited by an ageing couple who make homicidal puppets – is fairly restrained and has a good, perverse sense of humour. There's also a degree of moralising: the dolls administer rough justice only to those who deserve it. You'll never look at your little sister's doll the same way again. [VIDEO]

Ian Patrick Williams *David Bower* • Carolyn Purdy-Gordon *Rosemary Bower* • Carrie Lorraine *Judy Bower* • Guy Rolfe *Gabriel Hartwicke* • Hilary Mason *Hilary Hartwicke* • Bunty Bailey *Isabel Prange* • Cassie Stuart *Enid Tilley* • Stephen Lee *Ralph Morris* ■ *Dir* Stuart Gordon • *Scr* Ed Naha

A Doll's House ★★★

Drama 1973 · US · Colour · 85mins

Derived from the 1971 Broadway production directed by Patrick Garland, this version of Ibsen's classic play about the way marriage straitjackets women stars Claire Bloom as Nora, the flirtatious child-wife who gradually takes on an independence of spirit which resounds like the final slam of the symbolic door. She has some fine support by Anthony Hopkins and Ralph Richardson, though the result is a bit too earnest.

Claire Bloom *Nora Helmer* • Anthony Hopkins *Torvald Helmer* • Ralph Richardson *Dr Rank* • Denholm Elliott *Krogstad* • Anna Massey *Kristine Linde* • Edith Evans *Anne-Marie* ■ *Dir* Patrick Garland • *Scr* Christopher Hampton, from the play by Henrik Ibsen

A Doll's House ★★★★ PG

Drama 1973 · UK · Colour · 102mins

This adaptation (by playwright David Mercer) of Ibsen's play appeared the same time as the other 1973 version. Directed by Joseph Losey, however, it's the more cinematic, with its use of location (Norway) and camerawork (a mobile witness of events). Jane Fonda as Nora speaks up a little too blatantly for early women's liberation, but David Warner and Trevor Howard sustain Ibsen's then-revolutionary arguments with a care and subtlety which carries the play's message across time. [VIDEO]

Jane Fonda *Nora* • David Warner *Torvald* • Trevor Howard *Dr Rank* • Delphine Seyrig *Kristine Linde* • Edward Fox *Krogstad* • Anna Wing *Anne-Marie* ■ *Dir* Joseph Losey • *Scr* David Mercer, from the play by Henrik Ibsen

The Dolly Sisters ★★★

Musical biography
1945 · US · Colour · 113mins

Produced by vaudeville legend George Jessel, this zesty biopic of Hungarian singing sensations Jenny and Rosie Dolly was tailor-made for the talents of Betty Grable and June Haver. The story follows a predictable route as the girls bid farewell to cuddly uncle SZ Sakall to make it big the world over and romance John Payne and Frank Latimore respectively. Blending period and newly penned tunes (including the Oscar-nominated *I Can't Begin to Tell You*), this colourful turn-of-the-century romp became one of 20th Century-Fox's most profitable musicals.

Betty Grable *Jenny* • June Haver *Rosie* • John Payne *Harry Fox* • SZ Sakall *Uncle Latsie* • Reginald Gardiner *Duke* • Frank Latimore *Irving Netcher* ■ *Dir* Irving Cummings • *Scr* John Larkin, Marian Spitzer

Dolores Claiborne ★★★★ 18

Mystery drama 1995 · US · Colour · 126mins

Kathy Bates strikes again. The actress, who won an Oscar for her performance in Stephen King's *Misery*, here stars in another King adaptation, this time as Dolores, accused of killing her employer and friend (Judy Parfitt) and finding it hard to convince returned daughter Jennifer Jason Leigh of her innocence. There are magnificent portrayals all round, especially from Christopher Plummer as a retired and vengeful cop, but it's always Bates's film. She can't help but steal every scene she's in. Contains violence and swearing. [VIDEO]

Kathy Bates *Dolores Claiborne* • Jennifer Jason Leigh *Selena St George* • Judy Parfitt *Vera Donovan* • Christopher Plummer *Detective John Mackey* • David Strathairn *Joe St George* • Eric Bogosian *Peter* • John C Reilly *Constable Frank Stamshaw* ■ *Dir* Taylor Hackford • *Scr* Tony Gilroy, from the novel by Stephen King

Dominick and Eugene ★★★ 15

Drama 1988 · US · Colour · 104mins

Have the Kleenex handy when you watch this heart-rending tale of brotherly love, originally known here as *Nicky and Gino*. In a welcome change from his more usual villainous roles, Ray Liotta is a bright medical student devoted to his mentally disabled twin, Tom Hulce. But, if Liotta pursues his glittering career, who will look after his brother? Overly sentimental perhaps, but grippingly compassionate and superbly played by the two leads. Contains some violence and swearing. [VIDEO]

Tom Hulce *Dominick "Nicky" Luciano* • Ray Liotta *Eugene "Gino" Luciano* • Jamie Lee Curtis *Jennifer Reston* • Todd Graff *Larry "Snake" Higgins* • Bill Cobbs *Jesse Johnson* • David Strathairn *Martin Chernak* ■ *Dir* Robert M Young • *Scr* Alvin Sargent, Corey Blechman, from a story by Danny Porfirio

Dominique ★★

Thriller 1978 · UK · Colour · 99mins

This daft thriller – about a husband who drives his crippled wife mad and then has to cope with her ghostly presence after she dies – is a variation on the old haunted house routine that offers few surprises and a lot of padding. The cast, however, is surprisingly good, with the perpetually perplexed Cliff Robertson and the lovely Jean Simmons joined by Jenny Agutter, Simon Ward, Michael Jayston, Flora Robson, Ron Moody and Judy Geeson. An expert at action movies, director Michael Anderson comes over all arty here and denies us the jolts the story promises.

Cliff Robertson *David Ballard* • Jean Simmons *Dominique Ballard* • Jenny Agutter *Ann Ballard* • Simon Ward *Tony Calvert* • Ron Moody *Doctor Rogers* • Judy Geeson *Marjorie Craven* • Michael Jayston *Arnold Craven* • Flora Robson *Mrs Davis* • David Tomlinson *Solicitor* • Jack Warner *George* ■ *Dir* Michael Anderson • *Scr* Edward Abraham, Valerie Abraham

12 15 18 = PASSED FOR PEOPLE OF THESE AGES AND OVER [VIDEO] = RELEASED ON VIDEO DVD = RELEASED ON DVD
401

The Domino Principle ★★

Political thriller 1977 · US · Colour · 101mins

This feeble thriller – also known as *The Domino Killings* – has Gene Hackman as an expert marksman sprung from prison by an unnamed government agency and assigned to shoot an international bigwig. Adam Kennedy adapts his own novel, while director Stanley Kramer assembles a first-rate cast that includes Richard Widmark, Mickey Rooney, Edward Albert, Eli Wallach and lovely Candice Bergen. The result, however, is a third-rate intrigue that is neither deep nor complex – just obscure.

Gene Hackman *Roy Tucker* • Candice Bergen *Ellie* • Richard Widmark *Tagge* • Mickey Rooney *Spiventa* • Edward Albert *Ross Pine* • Eli Wallach *General Tom Reser* • Ken Swofford *Warden Ditcher* ■ Dir Stanley Kramer • Scr Adam Kennedy, from his novel

Don Giovanni ★★★

Opera 1979 · Fr/It/W Ger · Colour · 184mins

Joseph Losey spent much time in France towards the end of his career, and it was there that he made this labour of love. Mozart's opera tells of a libertine who is offered redemption by the father of one of his conquests; it has been filmed many times, though never as sumptuously as this. Beautiful scenery and voices make this ideal for those who love opera but can't afford Covent Garden prices. In Italian with English subtitles.

Ruggero Raimondi *Don Giovanni* • John Macurdy *The Commander* • Edda Moser *Donna Anna* • Kiri Te Kanawa *Donna Elvira* • Kenneth Riegel *Don Ottavio* • José Van Dam *Leporello* • Teresa Berganza *Zerlina* • Malcolm King *Masetto* ■ Dir Joseph Losey • Scr Patricia Losey, Joseph Losey, Frantz Salieri, from the opera *Don Giovanni* by Wolfgang Amadeus Mozart, Lorenzo Da Ponte

The Don Is Dead ★★ 18

Crime drama 1973 · US · Colour · 108mins

In this hastily produced rip-off of *The Godfather*, Anthony Quinn is the Mafia boss while Robert Forster (long before his career-reviving performance in *Jackie Brown*) is the hothead who precipitates a gang war. It might have passed muster as a mobster pic had it been released before Francis Ford Coppola's Oscar-winning epic, but coming after it only emphasises the film's failings. Director Richard Fleischer is no slouch when it comes to action sequences, however, and the climactic raid on the enemy HQ is particularly impressive.

Anthony Quinn *Don Angelo* • Frederic Forrest *Tony* • Robert Forster *Frank* • Al Lettieri *Vince* • Angel Tomkins *Ruby* • Charles Cioffi *Orlando* ■ Dir Richard Fleischer • Scr Marvin H Albert, from his novel, adapted by Michael Philip Butler, Christopher Trumbo

Don Juan ★★★★

Silent romantic drama
1926 · US · BW · 93mins

Historically important, this was Warner Bros's (and indeed Hollywood's) first synchronised sound movie. No dialogue or songs – they would come the following year with *The Jazz Singer* – the film has a synchronised score and some pointed (though shamefully non-synchronised) sound effects. Yet this would have been a spectacular success with or without sound, the title role being tailor-made for the great John Barrymore, who clearly revels in the part. The beautiful young Mary Astor reforms the Don, while Estelle Taylor makes a super Lucretia Borgia. The expensive production is exceptionally well directed by Alan Crosland, who would also direct that Jolson milestone.

John Barrymore *Don Juan* • Mary Astor *Adriana Della Varnese* • Willard Louis *Perdillo* • Estelle Taylor *Lucretia Borgia* • Helene Costello *Rena, Adriana's maid* • Myrna Loy *Maria, Lucretia's maid* • Jane Winton *Beatrice* • John Roche *Leandro* • Warner Oland *Caesar Borgia* ■ Dir Alan Crosland • Scr Bess Meredyth, from the poem by Lord Byron • Art Design Ben Carré

Don Juan DeMarco ★★★★ 15

Romantic drama 1995 · US · Colour · 93mins

Lunatics take over the asylum again in an enchanting feel-good fable showcasing a masked Johnny Depp as the world's greatest lover on the verge of suicide. As a burnt-out shrink, Marlon Brando must prick the cod Casanova's fantasy bubble in therapy sessions, where his exaggerated Mexican past and hopelessly romantic conquests are revealed in mythic flashback, or have him committed. Instead, through Depp's grandiose, poetic delusions, Brando re-examines the importance of passion in his own marriage to Faye Dunaway. A scintillating lyrical tone and magical realism make director Jeremy Leven's film a wonderfully funny, touching odyssey through a red-hot landscape of Latin rhythms, swooning senoritas and duelling Zorros. Contains swearing and nudity.

Marlon Brando *Jack Mickler* • Johnny Depp *Don Juan DeMarco* • Faye Dunaway *Marilyn Mickler* • Geraldine Pailhas *Dona Ana* • Bob Dishy *Dr Paul Showalter* • Rachel Ticotin *Dona Inez* • Talisa Soto *Dona Julia* ■ Dir Jeremy Leven • Scr Jeremy Leven, from a character created by Lord Byron

Don Juan 73, or If Don Juan Were a Woman ★★ 18

Drama 1973 · Fr/It · Colour · 89mins

Brigitte Bardot still looks stunning at 39, but her films were not getting much better; this was one of the last she made before vanishing from show business altogether. Roger Vadim's film centres on three traumatic affairs involving the same libertine woman, who affirms her personality through her conquests. Notorious for a lesbian bed scene between Bardot and British actress Jane Birkin, this marked the first time the French superstar had ever appeared full-frontal before cameras. A glorious piece of salacious soft core posing as art. French dialogue dubbed into English.

Brigitte Bardot *Jeanne* • Jane Birkin *Clara* • Maurice Ronet *Pierre* • Mathieu Carrière *Paul* • Robert Hossein *Prevost* • Jane Birkin *Leporella* • Robert Walker Jr *Young Spaniard* ■ Dir Roger Vadim • Scr Jean Cau, Roger Vadim, Jean-Pierre Petrolacci

Don Q, Son of Zorro ★★★

Silent swashbuckling adventure
1925 · US · BW · 111mins

If you liked Antonio Banderas and Anthony Hopkins as Zorro, here's a version they made much, much earlier with the original swashbuckling hero, Douglas Fairbanks, playing both father and son. In fact, Fairbanks had already played the swish swordsmith in *The Mark of Zorro* in 1921, but this time round he had more money and Mary Astor as his co-star. While due allowance should be made for the histrionic acting, this remains a key Fairbanks adventure, with spectacular sets and rousing action.

Douglas Fairbanks *Don Cesar de Vega/Zorro* • Mary Astor *Dolores de Muro* • Donald Crisp *Don Sebastian* • Stella de Lanti *The Queen* • Warner Oland *Archduke Paul of Austria* • Jean Hersholt *Don Fabrique* • Albert MacQuarrie *Col Matsado* • Lottie Pickford Forrest *Lola* ■ Dir Donald Crisp • Scr Jack Cunningham • Art Director Edward M Langley

Don Quixote ★★★ U

Musical drama 1933 · UK/Fr · BW · 78mins

Cervantes's epic novel had already been adapted nine times before the exiled GW Pabst shot this rather stilted version with the great Russian vocalist Feodor Chaliapin. The supporting cast depended on the language you spoke: George Robey played the English Sancho Panza, while Dorville was his French counterpart. But what matters is Chaliapin, who occasionally exceeds his thespian limitations to produce moments of real pathos, most notably as he tilts at the famous windmills. Pabst is ill-served by song composer Jacques Ibert, but Nikolas Farkas's cinematography is sublime.

Feodor Chaliapin *Don Quixote* • George Robey *Sancho Panza* • Sidney Fox *The Niece* • Miles Mander *The Duke* • Oscar Asche *Police Captain* • Dannio *Carrasco* • Emily Fitzroy *Sancho's wife* • Frank Stanmore *Priest* ■ Dir GW Pabst • Scr Paul Morand, Alexandre Arnoux, from the novel *Don Quixote de la Mancha* by Miguel de Cervantes

Don Quixote ★★★★★ U

Drama 1957 · USSR · Colour · 106mins

Having already played Alexander Nevsky and Ivan the Terrible for Eisenstein, Nikolai Cherkassov confirmed his status as one of Soviet cinema's finest actors by playing Cervantes's eccentric knight. With the Crimea standing in for the Spanish plains, the film achieves a picaresque sweep through Grigori Kozintsev's majestic use of widescreen colour. Assuredly staging such classic episodes as the encounter with the windmills, he wisely prevents the finale from becoming too maudlin. Yet it's the delightful performances that sustain the novel's wit and warmth, with Cherkassov expertly conveying Quixote's delusional pride and naive idealism, and Yuri Tolubeyev bringing a earthy loyalty to Sancho Panza.. Russian dialogue dubbed into English.

Nikolai Cherkassov *Don Quixote* • Yuri Tolubeyev *Sancho Panza* • T Agamirova *Altisidora* • V Freindlich *Duke* • L Vertinskaya *Duchess* • G Vitsin *Carrasco* • L Kasyanova *Aldonsa* ■ Dir Grigori Kozintsev • Scr Yevgeni Shvarts, from the novel *Don Quixote de la Mancha* by Miguel de Cervantes

Don Quixote ★★★ U

Dance 1973 · Ausl · Colour · 111mins

Co-directed by Robert Helpmann and Rudolf Nureyev, this film of Marius Petipa's light-hearted romantic ballet doesn't have much to do with tilting windmills. Instead it deals with a barber (Nureyev) who woos and wins his sweetheart with the aid of Helpmann's misguided knight and Sancho Panza (Ray Powell). Cinematographer Geoffrey Unsworth uses overhead shots to capture the full scale of the action; as a result, you feel as if you're in the frame instead of just watching it.

Robert Helpmann *Don Quixote* • Ray Powell *Sancho Panza* • Rudolf Nureyev *Basilio* • Francis Croese *Lorenzo* • Lucette Aldous *Kitri* • Colin Peasley *Gamache* • Marilyn Rowe *Street dancer* • Kelvin Coe *Espada* ■ Dir Rudolf Nureyev, Robert Helpmann • Choreographer Marius Petipa, Rudolf Nureyev

Dona Flor and Her Two Husbands ★★ 18

Romantic comedy
1977 · Bra · Colour · 104mins

This raunchy reworking of Noël Coward's *Blithe Spirit* wants to be a smart and sexy satire. But it's little more than an upmarket "pornochanchada", the sort of soft-core comedy that dominates Brazilian film-making. There are some flashes of intelligence in the way Sonia Braga exploits the security offered by living with second husband Mauro Mendonca, while also accepting vigorous advances from her ex-husband's ghost (Jose Wilker). But there are many more flashes of Braga herself in the frantic bedroom scenes that pepper Bruno Barreto's adaptation of Jorge Amado's novel. Sally Field starred in a witless American remake entitled *Kiss Me Goodbye*. A Portuguese language film.

Sonia Braga *Dona Flor* • José Wilker *Vadinho* • Mauro Mendonca *Teodoro* • Dinorah Brillanti *Rozilda* • Nelson Xavier *Mirandao* • Arthur Costa Filho *Carlinhos* ■ Dir Bruno Barreto • Scr Bruno Barreto, from the novel *Doña Flor e Seus Dois Maridos* by Jorge Amado

Dona Herlinda and Her Son ★★★★ 15

Comedy 1986 · Mex · Colour · 89mins

This gay comedy from Mexican director Jaime Humberto Hermosillo has much in common with *The Wedding Banquet*, which it comfortably predates. However, the humour in Ang Lee's film is much less acerbic than in this low-budget satire of sexual manners, as doctor Marco Antonio Trevino marries to placate his matchmaking mother, Guadalupe Del Toro, while cohabiting with his music student lover, Arturo Meza. Mocking machismo, romance, sexual duplicity and social snobbery, the picture benefits from some adroit playing and a sharp script based on Hermosillo's own experiences as a homosexual in an unsympathetic society. In Spanish with English subtitles.

Guadalupe Del Toro *Dona Herlinda* • Arturo Meza *Ramon* • Marco Antonio Trevino *Rodolfo* • Leticia Lupersio *Olga* • Angelica Guerrero *Ramon's mother* • Donato Castaneda *Ramon's father* • Guillermina Alba *Billy* ■ Dir/ Scr Jaime Humberto Hermosillo

U = SUITABLE FOR ALL Uc = SUITABLE FOR ALL, ESPECIALLY FOR YOUNG CHILDREN (VIDEO ONLY) PG = PARENTAL GUIDANCE

Donato and Daughter ★★ 15
Police drama 1993 · US · Colour · 89mins

It always feels with Charles Bronson that, if he cracked even a single smile, it would be as if another actor had arrived on screen by mistake. Just when it seemed he'd put to rest his dour features and action-man antics with *Death Wish 4: the Crackdown*, back he comes in this TV thriller as the familiar righteous avenger, this time in the guise of a cop. Or rather, one of two cops, a dad-and-daughter team who set out on the trail of a serial killer and become closer in the process. Sentiment in the midst of thuggery – what a treat. Contains swearing and violence. 📺

Charles Bronson *Mike Donato* • Dana Delany *Dina Donato* • Xander Berkeley *Russ Lawrence* • Louis Giambalvo *Hugh Halliday* • Jenette Goldstein *Judy McCartney* • Marc Alaimo *Detective Petsky* • Tom Verica *Bobby Keegan* ■ *Dir* Rod Holcomb • *Scr* Robert Roy Pool, from a novel by Jack Early

Donnie Brasco ★★★★ 18
Crime drama 1997 · US · Colour · 121mins

In this seventies-set crime drama, Al Pacino stars as a sleazeball who inducts young Brasco, played by Johnny Depp, into the codes and ''family'' values of organised crime. In fact, Brasco is an FBI undercover agent whose job threatens his marriage to Anne Heche as well as his life. In a way, it's a curious reversal of Pacino's earlier role in *Serpico*, in which his character went undercover. Directed by Mike Newell – a change of pace from *Four Weddings and a Funeral* – it's pitched midway between the epic *Godfather* and the flash *GoodFellas*, and develops nicely as Depp finds himself becoming rather fond of his monstrous mentor. The period setting – a world of tacky shirts, fur collars and plastic lawns – is also beautifully evoked. Contains swearing, violence and a sex scene. 📺 **DVD**

Al Pacino *Lefty Ruggiero* • Johnny Depp *Joe Pistone, ''Donnie Brasco''* • Michael Madsen *Sonny Black* • Bruno Kirby *Nicky* • James Russo *Paulie* • Anne Heche *Maggie Pistone* • Zeljko Ivanek *Tim Curley* • Gerry Becker *Dean Blandford* ■ *Dir* Mike Newell • *Scr* Paul Attanasio, from a non-fiction book by Joseph D Pistone, Richard Woodley

Donor ★★ 15
Medical thriller 1990 · US · Colour · 88mins

With vital plot components transplanted from *Coma* and *Malice*, this TV movie will have you rushing to your video collection on the off-chance you have some episodes of *Casualty* or *ER* to watch again instead. *Little House on the Prairie* star Melissa Gilbert-Brinkman plays the new doc on the block, who discovers that the person responsible for a spate of hospital killings is also conducting sinister experiments into halting the ageing process. It's a shame to see that excellent Australian actress Wendy Hughes wasting her time in this kind of malarkey. 📺

Melissa Gilbert-Brinkman [Melissa Gilbert] *Dr Kristine Lipton* • Jack Scalia *Dr Eugene Kesselman* • Wendy Hughes *Dr Farrell* • Gregory Sierra *Hector Aliosa* • Gale Mayron *Melody* • Marc Lawrence *Ben Beliot* ■ *Dir* Larry Shaw • *Scr* Michael Braverman

The Donor ★★
Medical thriller 1994 · US · Colour · 94mins

Jeff Wincott is one of many who have attempted to follow in the Hollywood footsteps of Jean-Claude Van Damme and failed. His English is better and so is his acting, but he isn't exactly pin-up material. In this flawed but intriguing thriller, he gets the opportunity to flex something other than his muscles playing a stuntman who, discovering that he has been the victim of some smash-and-grab organ surgery, sets out to uncover the conspiracy. The story stretches credibility, but director Damian Lee powers the action along in robust fashion. Contains swearing, violence and sex scenes.

Jeff Wincott *Billy Castle* • Michelle Johnson *Dr Lucy Flynn* • Gordon Thomson *Dr Jonathan Cross* ■ *Dir* Damian Lee • *Scr* Neal Dobrofsky, Tippi Dobrofsky

Donovan's Brain ★★★
Science-fiction 1953 · US · BW · 83mins

Directed with unnerving seriousness by MGM journeyman Felix Feist, this is the most faithful and easily the best adaptation of Curt Siodmak's fiendish novel. The tale of doctor Lew Ayres's struggle with the maniacal powers of a dead industrialist's transplanted brain is given chilling credibility by the extraordinary range of expressions Ayres assumes whenever he's gripped by the millionaire's insane desire to destroy his family and former associates. Gene Evans and Nancy Davis (Ronald Reagan's future first lady) are on hand to provide effectively uncomprehending support.

Lew Ayres *Dr Patrick J Corey* • Gene Evans *Dr Frank Schratt* • Nancy Davis *Janice Cory* • Steve Brodie *Herbie Yocum* • Lisa K Howard *Chloe Donovan* • Tom Powers *Advisor* ■ *Dir* Felix Feist • *Scr* Felix Feist, from the novel by Curt Siodmak

Donovan's Reef ★★★ U
Comedy drama 1963 · US · Colour · 108mins

Ramshackle but immensely enjoyable South Sea island romp, the last teaming of the great director John Ford and his friend and star, John Wayne. Elizabeth Allen co-stars as the prim Bostonian whose presence on a Pacific island disturbs the ''drinking and brawling'' lifestyle of the Duke and his crony, Lee Marvin. There's a seasonal touch involving Dorothy Lamour and a children's Christmas, though the best thing here is really the Technicolor photography by veteran William Clothier.

John Wayne *''Guns'' Donovan* • Lee Marvin *''Boats'' Gilhooley* • Jack Warden *''Doc'' Dedham* • Elizabeth Allen *Amelia Dedham* • Cesar Romero *Andre de Lage* • Dorothy Lamour *Fleur* • Jacqueline Malouf *Lelani* • Mike Mazurki *Sergeant Menkowicz* ■ *Dir* John Ford • *Scr* Frank Nugent, James Edward Grant, from a story by Edmund Beloin, from material by James Michener (uncredited)

Don's Party ★★★★ 18
Black comedy 1976 · Ausl · Colour · 86mins

Set on election night, 1969, this savage black comedy lifts the lid off suburban Australia and exposes all the prejudice and resentment simmering underneath. Adapted by David

Williamson from his own play, the dialogue crackles with offensive opinions and lacerating insults as the 11 guests throw off their ill-fitting gentility and let rip at one another as the beer flows and the results come in. Bruce Beresford paces the descent into uncivil war to perfection, while the cast are uniformly excellent in turning grotesque caricatures into credible specimens of boorish humanity. Look out for then-prime minister, John Gorton, in a cameo. 📺

Ray Barrett *Mal* • Claire Binney *Susan* • Pat Bishop *Jenny* • Graeme Blundell *Simon* • John Hargreaves *Don Henderson* • Harold Hopkins *Cooley* • John Gorton ■ *Dir* Bruce Beresford • *Scr* David Williamson, from his play

Don't Be a Menace to South Central while Drinking Your Juice in the Hood ★
Comedy 1996 · US · Colour · 88mins

It's a great title, and there's no denying that the ghetto drama genre is ripe for send-up. However, the fact that this didn't even make it to video in Britain is an indication of how dire it is. The spoofery is lazy, the plotting ramshackle. Not even the presence of what appears to be the entire Wayans family (Marlon, Shawn, Keenen Ivory and Craig) can save this sorry mess.

Shawn Wayans *Ashtray* • Marlon Wayans *Loc Dog* • Tracey Cherelle Jones *Dashiki* • Chris Spencer *Preach* • Suli McCullough *Crazy Legs* • Helen Martin *Grandma* • Isaiah Barnes *Doo Rag* • Lahmard Tate *Ashtray's father* • Keenen Ivory Wayans *Mailman* • Craig Wayans *First thug* ■ *Dir* Paris Barclay • *Scr* Shawn Wayans, Marlon Wayans, Phil Beauman

Don't Bother to Knock ★★★ PG
Thriller 1952 · US · BW · 76mins

Marilyn Monroe was just a year away from stardom when she made this hysterical melodrama, which finds her trading twitches with that master of mannered mania, Richard Widmark. As the suicidal babysitter confronted by Widmark's leering hotel guest, Monroe occasionally looks close to the edge. Alas, Daniel Taradash's adaptation of Charlotte Armstrong's novel lacks both the psychological depth and the necessary suspense to distract us from the stilted acting and Roy Baker's laboured direction. As Widmark's chanteuse lover, Anne Bancroft impresses in her feature debut – but it's the cast-against-type Monroe who catches the eye.

Richard Widmark *Jed Towers* • Marilyn Monroe *Nell* • Anne Bancroft *Lyn Leslie* • Donna Corcoran *Bunny* • Jeanne Cagney *Rochelle* • Lurene Tuttle *Ruth Jones* • Elisha Cook Jr *Eddie* • Jim Backus *Peter Jones* ■ *Dir* Roy Baker [Roy Ward Baker] • *Scr* Daniel Taradash, from the novel by Charlotte Armstrong

Don't Bother to Knock ★★ PG
Comedy 1961 · UK · Colour · 84mins

Frederic Raphael was among the writers who adapted Clifford Hanley's novel *Love from Everybody* for the screen, yet not even his eloquence could enliven a leaden romp that starts

out smug and ends up tasteless. Considering he also produced the project, Richard Todd looks distinctly uncomfortable as the philandering travel agent who discovers, to girlfriend June Thorburn's horror, that all his European flirtations have arrived at his Edinburgh home at once. With sharper one-liners and pacier direction, this tacky tale could have been a reasonably entertaining bedroom farce, and thanks to Geoffrey Unsworth and Anne V Coates respectively, it has better photography and editing than it deserves. 📺

Richard Todd *Bill Ferguson* • Nicole Maurey *Lucille* • Elke Sommer *Ingrid* • June Thorburn *Stella* • Rik Battaglia *Giulio* • Judith Anderson *Maggie* • Dawn Beret *Harry* • Scott Finch *Perry* • Eleanor Summerfield *Mother* • John Le Mesurier *Father* • Warren Mitchell *Waiter* ■ *Dir* Cyril Frankel • *Scr* Denis Cannan, Frederick Gotfurt, Frederic Raphael, from the novel *Love from Everybody* by Clifford Hanley

Don't Cry, It's Only Thunder ★★★
War drama 1982 · US · Colour · 108mins

Based on a true story, this Vietnam drama looks at a topic that few war movies examine. Dennis Christopher is outstanding as an initially selfish army medic who is saddled with the responsibility of helping nuns take care of war orphans. The movie shows us the human cost of armed conflict, not just by examining its helpless victims, but also by making Christopher and his fellow soldiers evolve and grow over time. However, the subplot involving Christopher's relationship with doctor Susan Saint James feels unfinished.

Dennis Christopher *Brian* • Susan Saint James *Katherine* • Lisa Lu *Sister Marie* • Thu Thuy *Sister Hoa* • Mai Thi Lien *Anh* • Truong Minh Hai *Duc* • Robert Englund *Tripper* • James Whitmore Jr *Major Flaherty* ■ *Dir* Peter Werner • *Scr* Paul Hensler

Don't Drink the Water ★★
Comedy 1969 · US · Colour · 98mins

Woody Allen's sharp and angry stage play is bloated to portly buffoonry to suit comic actor Jackie Gleason, with Allen's words rewritten for the screen by RS Allen and Harvey Bullock. Gleason stars as a Jewish caterer who is forced to take refuge in the American embassy in Vulgaria. He's suspected of spying by East European officials when he takes some snaps at the airport, and then tries to flee the fictional Iron Curtain country. The film went unreleased in the UK, which meant the British were one up on everyone else.

Jackie Gleason *Walter Hollander* • Estelle Parsons *Marion Hollander* • Ted Bessell *Axel Magee* • Joan Delaney *Susan Hollander* • Michael Constantine *Krojack* • Howard St John *Ambassador Magee* • Danny Meehan *Kilroy* • Richard Libertini *Father Drobney* ■ *Dir* Howard Morris • *Scr* RS Allen, Harvey Bullock, from the play by Woody Allen

Don't Drink the Water ★★★
Comedy 1994 · US · Colour

Woody Allen conceived the original play about Americans abroad and all things foreign when he was in Paris filming *What's New, Pussycat?*. It was performed on Broadway in 1966 with

Lou Jacobi in the leading role, and in 1969 it was made for TV with Jackie Gleason as the caterer accused of spying in an East European hell-hole. Allen always had a soft spot for the play, perhaps because he had based the main role on his own father. As he disliked Gleason's performance, he welcomed the chance to direct this remake for TV, casting himself and several of his friends.

Woody Allen *Walter Hollander* • Michael J Fox *Axel Magee* • Julie Kavner *Marion Hollander* • Mayim Bialik *Susan Hollander* • Dom DeLuise *Father Drobney* • Josef Sommer *Ambassador Magee* • Edward Herrmann *Mr Kilroy* • Austin Pendleton *Chef Oscar* ■ *Dir* Woody Allen • *Scr* Woody Allen, from his play

Don't Ever Leave Me ★ ★ U
Comedy   1949 · UK · BW · 80mins

Petula Clark is on typically ebullient form in this unconvincing adaptation of Anthony Armstrong's novel, *The Wide Guy*. Pet plays the spoiled daughter of a star actress who is kidnapped by a wily old crook, only to fall for his grandson and refuse to go home. Jimmy Hanley simply has to look fetching in the latter role, but as the older man veteran character actor Edward Rigby relishes the chance to display a little Dickensian devilment. Ex-cinematographer Arthur Crabtree was more comfortable with exotic period pieces, and his direction fails to hit a consistent tone. ▣

Petula Clark *Sheila Farlaine* • Jimmy Hanley *Jack Denton* • Hugh Sinclair *Michael Farlaine* • Linden Travers *Mary Lamont* • Anthony Newley *Jimmy Knowles* ■ *Dir* Arthur Crabtree • *Scr* Robert Westerby, from the novel *The Wide Guy* by Anthony Armstrong

Don't Forget You're Going to Die   ★★★★
Drama   1995 · Fr · Colour · 118mins

This uncompromising study of a life cut short by Aids-related illness earned a certain notoriety for its terrifyingly realistic depiction of drug use and sexual oblivion. Frequently compared to that Romantic icon Lord Byron, lead character Xavier Beauvois's art historian accidentally becomes HIV-positive at the hands of a careless doctor. Yet it's his friendship with Roschdy Zem's trafficker that casts a chilling pall of despair and self-destruction over affairs, which refuses to lift even as Beauvois experiences happiness during his brief affair with student Chiara Mastroianni. In French with English subtitles.

Xavier Beauvois *Benoît* • Chiara Mastroianni *Claudia* • Roschdy Zem *Omar* • Bulle Ogier *Benoît's mother* • Emmanuel Salinger *Military doctor* • Jean-Louis Richard *Benoît's father* • Jean Douchet *Jean-Paul* ■ *Dir* Xavier Beauvois • *Scr* Xavier Beauvois, Anne-Marie Sauzeau, Emmanuel Salinger, Zoubir Tligui

Don't Get Me Started   ★
Comedy drama
1994 · UK/Ger · Colour · 76mins

Re-edited after its disastrous Cannes showing under its original title *Psychotherapy*, Arthur Ellis's feature debut comes as a major disappointment following such acclaimed shorts as *A Turnip Head's Guide to Alan Parker*. Caught between

sinister satire and symbolic *film noir*, Ellis gives too little direction to a cast which is consequently unable to strike a consistent tone. Trevor Eve is particularly exposed as the happily married man whose pent-up frustration, brought on by quitting smoking, is indicative of a murderous past.

Trevor Eve *Jack Lane* • Steven Waddington *Jerry Hoff* • Marion Bailey *Gill Lane* • Ralph Brown *Larry Swift* • Marcia Warren *Pauline Lewis* ■ *Dir/Scr* Arthur Ellis

Don't Give Up the Ship   ★★★ U
Comedy   1959 · US · BW · 88mins

Very, very funny Jerry Lewis vehicle from the period when Lewis had just split with Dean Martin and was still trying to establish his solo style. The wonderful wacky plot involves Jerry and sidekick Mickey Shaughnessy looking for a naval battleship that Lewis commanded during the Second World War and is now lost. (Don't ask!) Veteran director Norman Taurog knows better than to get in the way. Classy rich girl Dina Merrill turns in a mighty cute performance that makes you regret that she semi-retired from the screen in 1989 in order to run RKO Pictures with her husband, Ted Hartley.

Jerry Lewis *John Paul Steckler* • Dina Merrill *Ensign Benson* • Diana Spencer *Prudence Trabert* • Mickey Shaughnessy *Stan Wychinski* • Robert Middleton *Admiral Bludde* • Gale Gordon *Congressman Mandeville* • Mabel Albertson *Mrs Trabert* ■ *Dir* Norman Taurog • *Scr* Herbert Baker, Edmund Beloin, Henry Garson, from a story by Ellis Kadison

Don't Go Breaking My Heart   ★★ PG
Romantic comedy
1999 · UK · Colour · 90mins

Silly, harmless British fluff about the romantic entanglements of widowed plant expert Jenny Seagrove, whose suitors include big-hearted sports therapist Anthony Edwards and devious dentist Charles Dance. They're both perfect, but the script is frustratingly daft, depending upon a ludicrous twist that has Dance utilising his hypnotist training to win Seagrove's affections. Although the climactic race is nicely handled and Edwards and Seagrove make a cute couple, the sitcom-level humour and unlikely contrivances render the film obvious and uninspired. Contains some swearing and sexual references. ▣

Anthony Edwards *Tony* • Jenny Seagrove *Suzanne* • Charles Dance *Frank* • Jane Leeves *Juliet* • Tom Conti *Doctor Fiedler* • Linford Christie • Ben Reynolds *Ben* ■ *Dir* Willi Patterson • *Scr* Geoff Morrow

Don't Go in the House   ★ 18
Horror   1979 · US · Colour · 75mins

Offensive and simple-minded, this movie's only point of interest is the anti-feminist slant it shares with many late seventies and early eighties horror movies. Dan Grimaldi turns psycho when his mother suddenly dies. She repeatedly burned his arms on the stove as a child, so continuing the family tradition, he gets a flamethrower and burns to death women foolish enough to enter his home. The body count isn't very high, leaving most of

the movie devoted to pointless sequences involving dreams and Grimaldi wandering around. Extremely poor photography and bad lighting make it even more of an ordeal. ▣

Dan Grimaldi *Donny Kohler* • Charlie Bonet *Ben* • Bill Ricci *Vito* • Robert Osth *Bobby Tuttle* • Dennis Hunt *Locker room worker* • John Hedberg *Locker room worker* • Ruth Dardick *Mrs Kohler* • Johanna Brushay *Kathy Jordan* ■ *Dir* Joseph Ellison • *Scr* Joseph Ellison, Ellen Hammill, Joseph Masefield

Don't Go Near the Water   ★★★ U
Comedy   1957 · US · Colour · 106mins

Patchy but always amiable and sometimes hilarious, this slapstick comedy deals with the problems faced by a naval public relations unit on a South Pacific island in attempting to promote a wholesome image of the service with little or no experience of ever having been at sea. Glenn Ford and Gia Scala are top-billed, but the standouts are Fred Clark, on top form as the irascible commanding officer, and burly Mickey Shaughnessy as a most unfortunate choice of sailor to thrust into the spotlight.

Glenn Ford *Lieutenant Max Siegel* • Gia Scala *Melora* • Earl Holliman *Adam Garrett* • Anne Francis *Lieutenant Alice Tomlen* • Keenan Wynn *Gordon Ripwell* • Fred Clark *Lieutenant Commander Clinton Nash* • Russ Tamblyn *Ensign Tyson* ■ *Dir* Charles Walters • *Scr* Dorothy Kingsley, George Wells, from the novel by William Brinkley

Don't Just Lie There, Say Something!   ★ PG
Comedy   1973 · UK · Colour · 87mins

The Whitehall farces may have delighted London theatre-goers from the fifties to the seventies, but they have never worked on the screen. This film reduces the precise timing of the double entendres, the bedroom entrances and exits and the dropped-trouser misunderstandings to the level of clumsy contrivance, which not even the slickest of players can redeem. Few *farceurs* are as practised as Leslie Phillips and Brian Rix, but they are powerless to save this slipshod story, in which MPs find themselves caught up in a sex scandal and a free-love campaign during the passage of an anti-pornography bill. ▣

Leslie Phillips *Sir William* • Brian Rix *Barry Ovis* • Joanna Lumley *Miss Parkyn* • Joan Sims *Birdie* • Derek Royle *Wilfred Potts* • Peter Bland *Inspector Ruff* • Katy Manning *Damina* ■ *Dir* Bob Kellett • *Scr* Michael Pertwee, from his play

Don't Just Stand There   ★★★
Comedy drama   1968 · US · Colour · 99mins

This clever comedy is given added appeal by the pairing of the extremely likeable Robert Wagner and Mary Tyler Moore. The two join forces to search for novelist Glynis Johns, who has only managed to pen the first half of her new book. Harvey Korman pops up en route to great effect, and director Ron Winston papers over the holes in the script by keeping the pace at fever pitch. Glossy production values, period Technicolor and Techniscope lensing lend this artifact a quaint charm.

Robert Wagner *Lawrence Colby* • Mary Tyler Moore *Martine Randall* • Glynis Johns *Sabine Manning* • Barbara Rhoades *Kendall Flanagan* • Harvey Korman *Merriman Dudley* • Vincent Beck *Painter* • Joseph Perry *Jean-Jacques* ■ *Dir* Ron Winston • *Scr* Charles Williams, from his novel *The Wrong Venus*

Don't Knock the Rock   ★★ U
Musical   1956 · US · BW · 84mins

Quickie producer Sam Katzman's follow-up to the enormously successful *Rock around the Clock* also features the airwave-shattering Bill Haley and the Comets. There's great period value in this movie: kiss-curled Haley and his great line-up playing numbers like *Hook, Line and Sinker*, and the fabulous Little Richard at his peak performing *Long Tall Sally* and *Tutti Frutti*. But it lacks the innocence of its predecessor and looks as if it was thrown together in a hurry.

Bill Haley • Little Richard • Alan Dale *Arnie Haines* • Alan Freed • The Treniers • Patricia Hardy *Francine MacLaine* • Fay Baker *Arlene MacLaine* • Jana Lund *Sunny Everett* ■ *Dir* Fred F Sears • *Scr* Robert E Kent, James B Gordon

Don't Look Back   ★★★★
Music documentary   1967 · US · BW · 95mins

Fans of Bob Dylan will need no encouragement to watch this brilliantly filmed record of his British tour in 1965, the year of *Subterranean Homesick Blues*. But film enthusiasts should also note that this is also a fine example of the craft of director/cameraman DA Pennebaker, one of the masters of *cinéma vérité*. Pennebaker just followed Dylan around, picking up truthful insights along the way, including revelatory moments with Joan Baez, Alan Price and, particularly, Dylan's manager Albert Grossman. The end result, edited down from over 20 hours of material, is a telling portrait of a unique performer at the height of his powers.

Dir DA Pennebaker

Don't Look Back   ★★★ 18
Thriller   1995 · US · Colour · 87mins

A low-key but finely acted crime drama, with junkie muso Eric Stoltz stumbling upon a fortune in drugs money and high tailing it back to his sleepy home town. While he cautiously re-establishes bonds with his childhood chums, drugs dealer Billy Bob Thornton (who also had a hand in the script) is on the trail of his missing money. The eclectic cast, which includes Annabeth Gish, John Corbett and country star Dwight Yoakam, all produce credible performances, while the direction from Geoff Murphy (best known for the sequels to *Young Guns* and *Under Siege*) is admirably understated. ▣

Eric Stoltz *Jesse Parish* • John Corbett *Morgan* • Josh Hamilton *Steve* • Annabeth Gish *Michelle* • Amanda Plummer *Bridget* • Billy Bob Thornton *Marshall* • Dwight Yoakam *Skipper* ■ *Dir* Geoff Murphy • *Scr* Billy Bob Thornton, Tom Epperson, from the story by Tom Epperson, Peter Gilman

Don't Look Down ★★
Horror thriller · 1998 · US · Colour · 86mins

Despite the presence of *Scream* director Wes Craven as co-executive producer, this TV movie struggles to make an impression. After her sister falls off a cliff in a freak accident, Megan Ward joins a controversial support group to overcome her fear of heights. When the members of the group start getting killed one by one, the weak terror begins. Has the ghost of Ward's sister returned to wreak vengeance? It's just about worth sitting through the incessant spooky whisperings and half-baked dreamy horror to find out. Not so much a classy *Vertigo* riff as a throwback to such sixties Hammer whodunits as *Nightmare* and *Paranoiac*.

Megan Ward *Carla Engel* • Billy Burke *Mark Engel* • Terry Kinney *Dr Paul Sadowski* • Angela Moore *Jocelyn* • William McDonald *Ben* • Kate Robbins *Hallie* • Aaron Smolinski *Zak* ■ *Dir* Larry Shaw • *Scr* Gregory Goodell • *Executive Producer* Wes Craven

Don't Look Now ★★★★★ 18
Supernatural thriller
1973 · UK/It · Colour · 105mins

A fiercely erotic scene of love-making between Donald Sutherland and Julie Christie forms the sensual core of this supernatural chiller, which offers a time-distorted vision of terror set in wintertime Venice, portrayed here as a hostile city of brooding silences and fog-shrouded canals. After the death of their small daughter, church restorer Sutherland and wife Christie take their grief with them to Italy, where the spectral presence of their child draws them into a labyrinth of cryptic signs and doom-laden portents. Adapted from a Daphne du Maurier short story, this is director Nicolas Roeg's masterpiece; the fear-drenched mood of alienation is sustained right up until the final shot. Contains violence, swearing, a sex scene and nudity. ▣

Donald Sutherland *John Baxter* • Julie Christie *Laura Baxter* • Hilary Mason *Heather* • Clelia Matania *Wendy* • Massimo Serato *Bishop Barbarrigo* • Renato Scarpa *Inspector Longhi* • David Tree *Anthony Babbage* ■ *Dir* Nicolas Roeg • *Scr* Allan Scott, Chris Bryant, from a short story by Daphne du Maurier • *Cinematographer* Anthony Richmond • *Editor* Graeme Clifford • *Music* Pino Donaggio

Don't Look Now... We're Being Shot At ★★
Second World War comedy
1966 · Fr · Colour · 130mins

It would be hard to better the credits for this frantic French farce. Shot by Jean Renoir's nephew, Claude, and with a score by France's finest film composer, Georges Auric, it is directed with gleeful assurance by Gérard Oury, a former member of the world-famous Comédie-Française. The stars are our own Terry-Thomas, the gently comedic Bourvil and practised farceur Louis De Funès, perhaps best known here for the *Gendarme of St Tropez* series. Why, then, does this story of an RAF pilot sheltered from the incompetent Nazis by the Resistance manage to be less funny than *'Allo, 'Allo*? French dialogue dubbed into English.

Terry-Thomas *Reginald* • Bourvil *Augustin Bouvet* • Louis De Funès *Stanislas Lefort* • Claudio Brook *Peter Cunningham* • Marie Dubois *Juliette* • Benno Sterzenbach *Col Achbach* • Colette Brosset *Madame Germaine* ■ *Dir* Gérard Oury • *Scr* Gérard Oury, Georges Tabet, André Tabet • *Cinematographer* Claude Renoir • *Music* Georges Auric

Don't Make Waves ★★★
Comedy · 1967 · US · Colour · 97mins

Good-natured satire on Californian lifestyles from Ealing expatriate Alexander Mackendrick, better known for *Whisky Galore!* and *Sweet Smell of Success*. Tony Curtis gives a clever performance as a tourist who gets a job selling swimming pools. However, the real revelation is the witty comic playing of Sharon Tate, tragically murdered by the Manson "family" two years later. The wacky plot is taken from Ira Wallach's novel *Muscle Beach*, while the Byrds provide the title song for a film that's nostalgically rooted in the early days of psychedelia.

Tony Curtis *Carlo Cofield* • Claudia Cardinale *Laura Califatti* • Sharon Tate *Malibu* • Robert Webber *Rod Prescott* • Joanna Barnes *Diane Prescott* • David Draper *Harry Hollard* • Mort Sahl *Sam Lingonberry* • Edgar Bergen *Madame Lavinia* • Ann Elder *Millie Gunder* ■ *Dir* Alexander Mackendrick • *Scr* Ira Wallach, George Kirgo, Maurice Richlin, from the novel *Muscle Beach* by Ira Wallach

Don't Move, Die and Rise Again ★★★★ 12
Period drama · 1989 · USSR · BW · 102mins

Winner of the Camera d'Or at Cannes for the best debut feature, this is a bleak study of the way Japanese PoWs were treated by their Soviet captors in the Stalinist era of the mid-forties. Faithfully re-creating the ghastly conditions in which everyone lived and worked in a remote mining town, director Vitaly Kanevsky is keen to point out that the Russian miners were as much in captivity as the prisoners, and they wouldn't be able to go home once hostilities ended. The presence of two children, playing happily amid the degradation, only reinforces Kanevsky's depressing but well-made point. Sobering and provocative. In Russian with English subtitles.

Dinara Drukarova *Galiia* • Pavel Nazarov *Valerka* • Elena Popova *Nina* • Valery Ivchenko • Vyacheslav Bambushek • Vadim Ermolaev ■ *Dir/Scr* Vitaly Kanevsky

Don't Raise the Bridge, Lower the River ★★ U
Comedy · 1968 · UK · Colour · 95mins

Jerry Lewis is quite hopelessly adrift and desperately unfunny in an awkward UK adaptation of humorist Max Wilk's novel. It's ham-fistedly directed by former actor Jerry Paris, and concerns Lewis's plans to steal a high-speed oil drill and peddle the plans to oil-rich Arabs. The Brits acquit themselves well, particularly co-star Terry-Thomas, while Patricia Routledge registers strongly as a lascivious Girl Guide leader. Yet both pace and tone are uncertain, and Lewis's performance is embarrassingly undirected. ▣

Jerry Lewis *George Lester* • Terry-Thomas *H William Homer* • Jacqueline Pearce *Pamela Lester* • Bernard Cribbins *Fred Davies* •

Patricia Routledge *Lucille Beatty* • Nicholas Parsons *Dudley Heath* • Michael Bates *Dr Spink* • Colin Gordon *Mr Hartford* ■ *Dir* Jerry Paris • *Scr* Max Wilk, from his novel

Don't Take It to Heart ★★★ U
Comedy · 1944 · UK · BW · 86mins

Written and directed by Jeffrey Dell, this haunted house comedy is a triumph of eccentricity over substance. It was made during wartime, but only the British could find propaganda value in a film in which the aristocracy triumphs over the beastly nouveaux riches thanks to an alliance between a ghost and a lawyer. Although Richard Greene and Patricia Medina are the leads, it's the supporting cast that takes the acting honours, with Alfred Drayton eminently hissable as the tycoon trying to land Brefni O'Rorke's stately pile at a knockdown price.

Richard Greene *Peter Hayward* • David Horne *Sir Henry Wade* • Patricia Medina *Lady Mary* • Alfred Drayton *Mr Pike* • Joan Hickson *Mrs Pike* • Richard Bird *Ghost Arthur* • Wylie Watson *Harry Bucket* • Brefni O'Rorke *Lord Chaundyt* ■ *Dir/Scr* Jeffrey Dell

Don't Talk to Strange Men ★★
Thriller · 1962 · UK · BW · 65mins

A worthy little feature with a social message that's more interesting now for its depiction of early sixties Britain. But director Pat Jackson's thriller still has relevance today. Christina Gregg is the young girl in trouble after disobeying the instruction of the title, while Gillian Lind and Cyril Raymond (the husband in *Brief Encounter*) are her very middle-class parents. Watch for Dandy Nichols in support.

Christina Gregg *Jean Painter* • Janina Faye *Ann Painter* • Conrad Phillips *Ron* • Dandy Nichols *Molly* • Cyril Raymond *Mr Painter* • Gillian Lind *Mrs Painter* • Gwen Nelson *Mrs Mason* ■ *Dir* Pat Jackson • *Scr* Gwen Cherrell

Don't Talk to Strangers ★★★ 12
Thriller · 1994 · US · Colour · 89mins

With Pierce Brosnan now established as James Bond, it's easy to forget that just a few years ago he could be found in run-of-the-mill TV movies like this one. Reprising the kind of too-good-to-be-true character he played in *Mrs Doubtfire*, Brosnan is about to sweep Shanna Reed and her son off to a new life in California when the nine-year-old is kidnapped. Suspicion falls on Reed's ex-husband, Terry O'Quinn, a cop putting up a bitter custody battle. But it couldn't be that simple – could it? The plot hardly stands close scrutiny, but there are enough twists to keep you guessing.

Shanna Reed *Jane Bonner* • Pierce Brosnan *Patrick Brody* • Terry O'Quinn *Bonner* • Keegan Macintosh *Eric Bonner* • Michael MacRae *Detective Sandstrum* • Roger R Cross *Detective Barrett* • Alan Robertson *Bobby Carkin* ■ *Dir* Robert Lewis • *Scr* Neill D Hicks, Jon George, Nevin Schreiner

Don't Tell Her It's Me ★★ 15
Romantic comedy
1990 · US · Colour · 97mins

Gus (Steve Guttenberg) is a cartoonist with Hodgkin's disease whose recent dose of chemotherapy has left him bald, bloated and with little hope of finding a girlfriend. So Gus's sister (Shelley Long) decides to help by transforming him into a grizzled Kiwi biker. Soon Gus is being pursued by Emily (Jami Gertz), a girl attracted to the wrong sort of guy, though complications ensue when she finds out the truth. A rather clumsy comedy from director Malcolm Mowbray, who had earlier demonstrated such a deft touch with *A Private Function*. ▣

Shelley Long *Lizzie Potts* • Steve Guttenberg *Gus Kubicek* • Jami Gertz *Emily Pear* • Kyle MacLachlan *Trout* • Kevin Scannell *Mitchell Potts* • Mädchen Amick *Mandy* ■ *Dir* Malcolm Mowbray • *Scr* Sarah Bird, from her novel *The Boyfriend School*

Don't Tell Mom the Babysitter's Dead ★★ 15
Comedy · 1991 · US · Colour · 100mins

The children of the Crandell family are forced to fend for themselves when their elderly and decidedly crotchety babysitter drops dead while their mother is on holiday in Australia. This reasonably engaging comedy fantasy from Stephen Herek, director of *Bill and Ted's Excellent Adventure*, veers uneasily from slightly adult comedy to farcical teenage wish-fulfilment. Nevertheless, it manages to remain remarkably good-humoured throughout such awkward shifts in tone. Many will consider Christina Applegate's charms a good enough substitute for the lack of any really fast and furious fun. Contains swearing. ▣

Christina Applegate *Sue Ellen "Swell" Crandell* • Joanna Cassidy *Rose Lindsey* • John Getz *Gus Brandon* • Josh Charles *Bryan* • Keith Coogan *Kenny Crandell* • Concetta Tomei *Mom Crandell* • David Duchovny *Bruce* • Kimmy Robertson *Cathy* ■ *Dir* Stephen Herek • *Scr* Neil Landau, Tara Ison

Don't Touch My Daughter ★ 15
Crime thriller · 1991 · US · Colour · 90mins

Dallas's Victoria Principal stars in a highly-charged story of a single mother who takes the law into her own hands when the legal system fails to deal appropriately with the man who abducted her 11-year-old daughter. Based on the book *Nightmare* by Marjorie Dorner, this TV movie has it's share of suspenseful moments, with enough twists and turns to keep you guessing. It's a well-told story that could happen in real life. Paul Sorvino gives a good performance as a world-weary but sympathetic detective. ▣

Victoria Principal *Linda Hemmings* • Jonathan Banks *Edward Ryter* • Paul Sorvino *Lieutenant Jake Willman* • Danielle Harris *Dana Hemmings* • Christopher Wynne *Officer Haggerty* • Christine Healy *Susan Fisher* • Gregg Henry *Hal Lawrence* ■ *Dir* John Pasquin • *Scr* John Robert Bensink, Rick Husky, from the novel *Nightmare* by Marjorie Dorner

The Doolins of Oklahoma
★ U

Western　　　　　　1949 · US · BW · 89mins

Meet the Doolin gang: not in the same league as the James boys or the Daltons, but a lively bunch of bank robbers nonetheless. Their leader is played by Randolph Scott, who decides to turn over a new leaf, marry a deacon's daughter (Virginia Huston) and take up farming, only to find his past won't leave him alone. This is no great shakes as a western, despite echoes of the 1939 Tyrone Power hit *Jesse James*, yet it's briskly directed by Gordon Douglas.

Randolph Scott *Bill Doolin* • George Macready *Sam Hughes* • Louise Allbritton *Rose of Cimarron* • John Ireland *Bitter Creek* • Virginia Huston *Elaine Burton* • Charles Kemper *Arkansas* • Noah Beery Jr *Little Bill* • Dona Drake *Cattle Annie* ■ *Dir* Gordon Douglas • *Scr* Kenneth Gamet

Doom Asylum
★

Horror　　　　　1987 · US · Colour · 78mins

It's six movies for the price of one as A lovesick zombie terrorises and murders a female rock band with autopsy tools in an abandoned mental asylum. This is a feeble fright farce, tricked out with endless slow-motion sex fantasies and puzzling pans to a TV screen, which shows five extended clips of the best scenes from British horror icon Tod Slaughter's thirties and forties *Grand Guignol* movies. Obviously the running time needed beefing up and anything resembling terror was included in this ludicrous hotchpotch.

Patty Mullen *Judy/Kiki* • Ruth Collins *Tina* • Kristin Davis *Jane* • William Hay *Mike* • Kenny L Price *Dennis* ■ *Dir* Richard Friedman • *Scr* Rick Marx, from the story by Richard Friedman, Steven Menkin, Rick Marx

The Doom Generation
★★★ 18

Road movie　1995 · US/Fr · Colour · 80mins

Gregg Araki succeeds triumphantly in both shocking the prudish and exhibiting his technical mastery in what he describes as his first heterosexual outing. Recalling such murderous road movies as *Natural Born Killers*, this is a self-satisfied affair that too often thinks a cinematic in-joke or a cheap shot at middle American mores is more important than expanding the characters of teenage lovers Rose McGowan and James Duval and their maniacal mentor, Johnathon Schaech. Araki glamorises the sex as much as the violence, but the sight of a shopkeeper's severed head continuing to scream after it lands will be most people's abiding memory. ▭

James Duval *Jordan White* • Rose McGowan *Amy Blue* • Johnathon Schaech *Xavier Red, "X"* • Cress Williams *Peanut* • Skinny Puppy *Gang of goons* • Dustin Nguyen *Quickiemart clerk* • Margaret Cho *Clerk's wife* • Lauren Tewes *TV anchorwoman* • Christopher Knight (2) *TV anchorman* ■ *Dir/Scr* Gregg Araki

The Doomsday Flight　★★★

Thriller　　　　1966 · US · Colour · 97mins

Only the fifth TV movie to be released in the United States, this chillingly authentic hijack thriller had to be withdrawn by Universal after it inspired a copycat extortion bid. Scripted by *Twilight Zone* creator Rod Serling, it is a clear forerunner of *Speed*, in that embittered Edmond O'Brien has planted a bomb aboard an internal flight that's primed to go off if the plane dips beneath 5,000 feet. With *Hawaii Five-O* star Jack Lord as the agent sent to deal with the crisis and a nerve-jangling soundtrack from *Mission: Impossible* and *Starsky and Hutch* composer Lalo Schifrin, this is an entertaining roller-coaster ride.

Jack Lord *Special agent Frank Thompson* • Edmond O'Brien *The Man* • Van Johnson *Captain Anderson* • Katharine Crawford *Jean* • John Saxon *George Ducette* • Michael Sarrazin *Army corporal* • Ed Asner *Feldman* ■ *Dir* William A Graham • *Scr* Rod Serling

Doomsday Gun
★★★ 15

Spy thriller based on a true story
1994 · US · Colour · 106mins

Saddam Hussein's supergun, that lethal gizmo designed to shoot nerve-gas rockets from Iraq to Israel, caused one of the biggest controversies in recent British political history. The parts came from a British company – so did the government know about it? Hard questions were asked, men were wrongly convicted and heads rolled. This TV drama, made for HBO in America, casts Frank Langella as Gerald Bull, the designer of the supergun who was later murdered. Alan Arkin, Kevin Spacey, Michael Kitchen and James Fox also feature in the extremely impressive cast. Contains swearing. ▭

Frank Langella *Gerald Bull* • Alan Arkin *Yossi* • Kevin Spacey *Price* • Michael Kitchen *Chris* • Francesca Annis *Sophie* • Zia Mohyeddin *Hashim* • Tony Goldwyn *Duvall* • James Fox *Whittington* ■ *Dir* Robert Young • *Scr* Walter Bernstein, Lionel Chetwynd

Doomsday Rock
★★

Science-fiction thriller　1997 · US · Colour

Although it's not exactly *Deep Impact* on a shoestring, this TV movie shows all too clearly just what a difference a budget makes. Australian Brian Trenchard-Smith has always had a sure touch with action subjects and builds up a fair head of steam here, as astrologer William Devane and his daughter Connie Sellecca occupy a nuclear silo in a bid to alert the world to the danger from an approaching giant comet. However, whereas *Deep Impact* director Mimi Leder could throw in a few computer-generated set pieces to sustain the tension, Trenchard-Smith has to rely on ominous sounding jargon and heated confrontations.

Connie Sellecca *Katherine Sorenson* • Ed Marinaro *Richard Chase* • William Devane *Dr Carl Sorenson* • Marsha Warfield *Lisa Dillon* • Jessica Walter *Secretary of Defense McGregor* ■ *Dir* Brian Trenchard-Smith • *Scr* David Bourla, Michael Norell

Doomwatch
★★

Mystery thriller　1972 · UK · Colour · 91mins

As a spin-off from a modish ecological BBC TV series, this crash-landed unhappily in the swamp of horror instead of on the firmer ground of science fact or fiction. John Paul, Ian Bannen and Judy Geeson look suitably intense as an investigation is mounted into the effects of a sunken oil tanker on the inhabitants of an island off the Cornish coast only to discover something nastily mutated in the biological woodshed. Risibly alarmist, but the environmental dangers it pinpoints are only too topical.

Ian Bannen *Dr Del Shaw* • Judy Geeson *Victoria Brown* • John Paul *Dr Quist* • Simon Oates *Dr Ridge* • George Sanders *Admiral* • Percy Herbert *Hartwell* • Geoffrey Keen *Sir Henry Layton* • Joseph O'Conor *Vicar* ■ *Dir* Peter Sasdy • *Scr* Clive Exton, from the TV series by Kit Pedler, Gerry Davis

Door-to-Door Maniac
★

Crime action　　1961 · US · BW · 75mins

Country-and-western singer Johnny Cash does himself few favours by appearing in this turgid and trashy thriller as a guitar-toting thug who extorts money from a bank president while holding his wife for ransom. Cash sings two songs: the extraordinary *I've Come to Kill* and *Five Minutes to Live*. The latter doubled as the movie's original title; the film was re-released as *Door-to-Door Maniac* with an additional rape scene. Future *Happy Days* star and *Apollo 13* director Ron Howard also makes an appearance.

Johnny Cash *Johnny Cabot* • Donald Woods *Ken Wilson* • Cay Forrester *Nancy Wilson* • Pamela Mason *Ellen* • Midge Ware *Doris* • Vic Tayback *Fred* • Ronnie Howard [Ron Howard] *Bobby* • Merle Travis *Max* ■ *Dir* Bill Karn • *Scr* MK Forrester, Robert L Joseph, from a story by Palmer Thompson

The Doors
★★★ 18

Musical biography
1991 · US · Colour · 134mins

Although the title would have you believe that this is a biopic of the entire band, we learn next to nothing about Ray Manzarek, John Densmore or Robby Krieger, as the emphasis is so firmly on the Doors' charismatic, enigmatic frontman, Jim Morrison. Unfortunately, co-writer/director Oliver Stone is so preoccupied with exploring the native American influences on Morrison's music and re-creating the sights and sounds of the sixties that we discover precious little about Morrison either. Val Kilmer does, however, pull off a remarkable impression of the vocalist, though he's more convincing on stage than he is in his drunken, drug-fuelled reveries. Contains swearing, sex scenes, drug abuse and nudity. ▭

Val Kilmer *Jim Morrison* • Meg Ryan *Pamela Courson* • Kyle MacLachlan *Ray Manzarek* • Kevin Dillon *John Densmore* • Frank Whaley *Robby Krieger* • Billy Idol *Cat* • Dennis Burkley *Dog* • Josh Evans *Bill Siddons* • Michael Madsen *Tom Baker* • Kathleen Quinlan *Patricia Kennealy* ■ *Dir* Oliver Stone • *Scr* Oliver Stone, J Randall Johnson, Randy Johnson, Ralph Thomas, from the non-fiction book *Riders on the Storm* by John Densmore

Doorway to Hell
★★★

Crime melodrama　1931 · US · BW · 78mins

The chief of a bootlegging outfit decides to retire and hands over his racketeering interests to another. But he finds himself embroiled in the underworld again after his wife leaves him and his young brother is killed by his former rivals. Oscar-nominated for its story and directed with tough brio by Archie Mayo for Warner Bros, the studio that put the gangster movie on the map, the film stars clean-cut, good-looking Lew Ayres (the future Dr Kildare) as the troubled gangster, and a youthful James Cagney as the man who takes over his empire. Solid genre stuff, despite pulling its punches.

Lewis Ayres [Lew Ayres] *Louis Ricarno* • Dorothy Mathews *Doris* • Leon Janney *Jackie Lamarr* • Robert Elliott *Capt O'Grady* • James Cagney *Steve Mileway* • Jerry Mandy *Joe* • Noel Madison *Rocco* ■ *Dir* Archie Mayo • *Scr* George Rosener, from the story *A Handful of Clouds* by Rowland Brown

Doppelganger
★★ 18

Horror　　　1993 · US · Colour · 100mins

Three years before becoming one of the first victims of the *Scream* franchise, Drew Barrymore was the star of her own hokey slasher flick, playing a young woman terrorised by an evil alter ego who's killing off her family in New York. Moving out to Los Angeles, Drew begins an affair with her new roommate. But is it her or her doppelgänger that he's fallen in love with? This intriguing premise is stifled by Avi Nesher's predictable and at times crass direction, allowing this psychosexual horror thriller to flounder towards its wholly disappointing conclusion. Little wonder it bypassed cinemas and went straight to video, though Drew shines. ▭

Drew Barrymore *Holly Gooding* • George Newbern *Patrick Highsmith* • Dennis Christopher *Dr Heller* • Sally Kellerman *Sister Jan* • Leslie Hope *Elizabeth* • George Maharis *Wallace* ■ *Dir/Scr* Avi Nesher

Dot and Keeto
★★ U

Part-animated adventure
1986 · Ausl · Colour · 70mins

Director/producer Yoram Gross hit pay dirt in Australia with this series of animated features. Here writer John Palmer borrows from Lewis Carroll as likeable little Dot eats a magic root, becomes ever littler and gets menaced by bigger creatures such as spiders and ants. It's all right, though – she's befriended and looked after by Butterwalk the caterpillar and, yup, Keeto the mosquito. The result is some harmless, charming, moral stuff for children of all ages, especially under-tens who won't worry too much about the simplistic animation and nonexistent lip-synchronisation. There's some clever intercutting of real insects in with the cartoon stuff as well. ▭

Robyn Moore *Dot* • Keith Scott *Keeto* ■ *Dir* Yoram Gross • *Scr* John Palmer, from a character created by Ethel Pedley

Dot and the Bunny
★★ Uc

Part-animated adventure
1983 · Ausl · Colour · 78mins

The third in Yoram Gross's series about the little girl who can talk to animals is the usual conservation-conscious mix of live action and animation. Befriending an eager bunny in her search for an elusive kangaroo, Dot meets various indigenous beasts, including a koala and an emu, all of whom are originally shown in wildlife footage before turning into colourful

U = SUITABLE FOR ALL　　Uc = SUITABLE FOR ALL, ESPECIALLY FOR YOUNG CHILDREN (VIDEO ONLY)　　PG = PARENTAL GUIDANCE

artoon critters who provide Dot with
lues for her quest. Leavening the
environmental message with music
and gentle comedy, Gross aims the
action squarely at younger viewers,
although grown-ups will appreciate the
subtle underlying humour. ▭

Robyn Moore *Dot* • Drew Forsythe • Barbara
Frawley • Ron Haddrick • Anne Haddy • Ross
Higgins ■ *Dir* Yoram Gross • *Scr* John Palmer,
from a story by Yoram Gross, from a character
created by Ethel Pedley

Dot and the Kangaroo ★★ Uc

Part-animated adventure
1976 · Ausl · Colour · 71mins

Based on the children's character
created by Ethel Pedley, this is the first
of Yoram Gross's series of live-action/
animation films about the little red-
headed girl who can talk to animals.
There isn't much to get excited about
in the story, in which Dot gets lost in
the Australian bush and is helped out
by a kindly kangaroo, and the songs
will hardly set toes a-tapping, but the
blend of cartoon characters and real
wildlife footage is neatly done. ▭

Robyn Moore *Dot* ■ *Dir* Yoram Gross • *Scr*
Yoram Gross, John Palmer, from a character
created by Ethel Pedley

Dot and the Koala ★★★ U

Part-animated adventure
1985 · Ausl · Colour · 67mins

Dot first learned how to talk to the
animals in *Dot and the Kangaroo*
(1976). Nearly a decade on, Yoram
Gross's engaging blend of wildlife
footage and colourful animation shows
signs of strain, but the idea of
teaching children how thoughtless
humans can damage the environment
is still a laudable one. This story,
about a plan to clear the bush to make
way for a dam, makes its point
effectively, while the combination of
live-action backgrounds and cartoon
characters gives the film a 3-D effect
that holds the attention. ▭

Robyn Moore *Dot* • Keith Scott ■ *Dir* Yoram
Gross • *Scr* Yoram Gross, Greg Flynn, from a
character created by Ethel Pedley

Dot and the Smugglers ★★ U

Part-animated adventure
1987 · Ausl · Colour · 55mins

This is easily the weakest of Yoram
Gross's series of part-animated films
about the Doctor Dolittle-style redhead
and her adventures among the flora
and fauna of Australia. Once again the
technical side cannot be faulted, and
the conservation message is as strong
as ever, with Dot tackling a gang of
smugglers intent on stealing animals
from their natural habitats. The cute
quotient is way too high, though, and
much of the impact is lost in the
sentiment. ▭

Robyn Moore *Dot* • Keith Scott ■ *Dir* Yoram
Gross • *Scr* Greg Flynn, from a character
created by Ethel Pedley

Dot and the Whale ★★★

Part-animated adventure
1985 · Ausl · Colour · 75mins

One of a long-running series of
Australian children's adventure movies,
which cast cartoon characters against

live action backgrounds in the style of
Who Framed Roger Rabbit in a
concerted effort to target the
kindergarten set. In this outing, the
plucky and resourceful young Dot joins
forces with a dolphin called Nelson to
save a stranded young whale called Tonga,
while at the same time seeing off a
variety of villains and ne'er-do-wells
like some pre-pubescent female
version of James Bond. Ripping stuff.

Robyn Moore *Dot* • Keith Scott ■ *Dir* Yoram
Gross • *Scr* John Palmer, from a character
created by Ethel Pedley

Double Blast ★★

Martial arts action adventure
1994 · US · Colour · 89mins

Offering junior-league martial arts
mayhem, this bustles along engagingly
enough. Crystal Summer and Lorne
Berfield are the plucky young crime-
fighters who come to the aid of an
academic (a somewhat unlikely Linda
Blair), while ace kick-boxer Dale Cook
provides some lethal support. There's
plenty of kung fu biffing, though it's
tame stuff that won't upset the young
audiences this movie is aimed at.

Linda Blair *Professor Claudia Whyle* • Dale
"Apollo" Cook *Greg* • Ron Hall *Blade* • Lorne
Berfield *Jimmy* • Crystal Summer *Lisa* • Joe
Estevez *Nadir* • Robert Z'Dar *Goose* • Chuck
Williams *Bogus* ■ *Dir* Tim Spring • *Scr* Paul
Joseph Gulino, Paul Wolansky

Double Bunk ★★

Comedy 1961 · UK · BW · 94mins

There's more pleasure to be had from
spotting the support cast than from
following the stars in some vintage
British movies, and this under-directed
comedy about honeymooners racing
their houseboat is no exception. The
nominal lead is Ian Carmichael,
displaying his usual Hugh Grant-like
dottiness. But he had lost his ability to
carry a picture by this point, and lovely
though Thora Hird's daughter Janette
Scott may be, she's no great shakes
as an actress. Thankfully there's a
veritable treasure trove of eccentrics
here, including Sidney James, Naunton
Wayne, Irene Handl, Miles Malleson
and Noel Purcell – not to mention old
smoothie himself, Dennis Price.

Ian Carmichael *Jack Goddard* • Janette Scott
Peggy Deeley • Liz Fraser *Sandra* • Sidney
James *Sid Randall* • Dennis Price *Leonard
Watson* • Reginald Beckwith *Alfred Harper* •
Irene Handl *Mrs Harper* • Noel Purcell
O'Malley • Miles Malleson *Reverend Thomas*
■ *Dir/Scr* CM Pennington-Richards

Double Cross ★★ U

Spy drama 1955 · UK · BW · 71mins

This adaptation of Kern Bennett's spy
thriller, *The Queer Fish*, benefits from
its Cornish locations and director
Anthony Squire's tight use of the
cramped conditions onboard a cross-
channel fishing boat. Otherwise, it's B-
business as usual, as salmon poacher
Donald Houston realises mysterious
passengers Anton Diffring and Delphi
Lawrence have tricked him into ferrying
Cold War secrets. Fay Compton and
William Hartnell provide serviceable
support, and there's a taste of things
to come for inspector Raymond
Francis, who would headline the TV
crime series *No Hiding Place*.

Donald Houston *Albert Pascoe* • Fay Compton
Alice Pascoe • Anton Diffring *Dmitri Krassin* •
Delphi Lawrence *Anna Krassin* • Allan
Cuthbertson *Clifford* • William Hartnell
Whiteway • Frank Lawton *Chief Constable* •
Raymond Francis *Inspector Harris* ■ *Dir*
Anthony Squire • *Scr* Anthony Squire, Kern
Bennett, from the novel *The Queer Fish* by
Kern Bennett

Double Cross ★★★ 18

Erotic thriller 1994 · Can · Colour · 87mins

It's billed as an erotic thriller, but the
classy cast and an enjoyably cynical
script lift this straight-to-video offering
way above the average. Patrick Bergin
is the small-town video dealer with a
Wall Street past who falls for beautiful
femme fatale Kelly Preston, only to find
himself caught up in murder and
subterfuge. The leads generate a fair
bit of steam in the bedroom and there
are good performances from Jennifer
Tilly and Kevin Tighe, while Michael
Keusch's capable direction more than
makes up for the odd credibility gaps
in the plotting. Contains swearing,
violence, nudity and sex scenes. ▭

Patrick Bergin *Jack Conealy* • Jennifer Tilly
Melissa • Kelly Preston *Vera Blanchard* • Matt
Craven *Bernard March* • Kevin Tighe *Brian
Cody* • Philip Hayes *Nimitz* ■ *Dir* Michael
Keusch • *Scr* Henry C Clarke

Double Crossbones ★★★ U

Satire 1951 · US · Colour · 75mins

This smashing Donald O'Connor
vehicle uses all of Universal's pirate-
ship sets and costumes in a jolly tale
of an apprentice shopkeeper who is
mistaken for a famous buccaneer. Alan
Napier makes a splendid Captain Kidd,
and Hope Emerson is a fearsome Ann
Bonney. However, the real pleasure is
the sumptuous Technicolor, which
makes the whole shebang seem rather
better than it is. (Despite O'Connor's
valiant attempts, Oscar Brodney's
script isn't up to much.) Fans of
Yankee Buccaneer and *Against All
Flags* will have fun recognising props,
while the narration is by Jeff Chandler,
swashbuckling star of *Yankee Pasha*.

Donald O'Connor *Davy Crandell* • Helena
Carter *Lady Sylvia Copeland* • Will Geer *Tom
Botts* • John Emery *Governor Elden* • Hope
Emerson *Mistress Ann Bonney* • Charles
McGraw *Capt Ben Wickett* • Alan Napier *Capt
Kidd* • Jeff Chandler *Narrator* ■ *Dir* Charles T
Barton [Charles Barton] • *Scr* Oscar Brodney

Double Crossed ★★ 15

Crime drama based on a true story
1991 · US · Colour · 105mins

Dennis Hopper gives a bravura
performance as Barry Seal, a
flamboyant former airline pilot who
smuggles drugs into the US for the
Medellín drug cartel. After he is
arrested by the DEA, he turns
informant and helps set up his old
bosses in Miami and Colombia.
Unfortunately, the protagonist is
despicable and, despite Hopper's star
power, viewers will have little sympathy
for his plight and forced redemption.
The overall effect is unsatisfying;
indeed, it's the viewer who might end
up feeling double-crossed. ▭

Dennis Hopper *Barry Seal* • Robert Carradine
Booker • Adrienne Barbeau *Debbie Seal* • GW
Bailey *Emille Camp* ■ *Dir* Roger Young • *Scr*
Roger Young, Alex Lasker, from their story

Double Dare ★★★

Comedy thriller 1981 · Fr · BW · 100mins

Miou-Miou and Gérard Lanvin, who first
worked together in *café-théâtre*, are
here reunited by veteran director
Georges Lautner for this sprightly
comedy thriller. Written by Jean-Marie
Poire, who broke box-office records in
1993 with his time-travel farce, *Les
Visiteurs*, it's a frothy tale that has
Lanvin steal a judge's robes to escape
his trial, only for Miou-Miou to insist he
accompanies her to Nice and solve a
murder mystery. There's plenty of
spark between the leads, Michel
Galabru provides typically flustered
support, and screen legend Renée
Saint-Cyr (the director's mother)
contributes a neat cameo. French
dialogue dubbed into English.

Miou-Miou *Julie Boucher* • Gérard Lanvin
Gerard Louvier • Renée Saint-Cyr *Madame
Bertillon* • Julien Guiomar *Raymond* • Michel
Galabru *Bailiff* ■ *Dir* Georges Lautner • *Scr*
Jean-Marie Poire

Double Deal ★★

Romantic crime drama
1981 · Ausl · Colour · 90mins

This self-consciously smart-aleck
thriller sat on the shelf for three years,
and it's easy to see why. With double
the characters but half the surprises of
Anthony Shaffer's *Sleuth*, Brian
Kavanagh tries desperately to deceive
us as bored fashion model Angela
Punch McGregor and criminal biker
Warwick Comber play an increasingly
far-fetched game of cat and mouse
with her tycoon husband (Louis
Jourdan) and his secretary (Diana
Craig). Such is the banality of the
scams and the resistibility of the
protagonists, however, that the final
revelations fail to produce the admiring
gasps the director seeks.

Louis Jourdan *Peter Sterling* • Angela Punch
McGregor *Christina Sterling* • Diane Craig *June
Stevens* • Warwick Comber *Young man* •
Peter Cummins *Detective Mills* • Bruce
Spence *Doug Mitchell* • June Jago *Mrs
Coolidge* ■ *Dir/Scr* Brian Kavanagh

Double Deception ★★

Crime thriller 1993 · US · Colour · 96mins

It's hard to fathom who is double-
crossing whom in this trashy TV movie,
which features the usual cast of
stereotypical characters. These include:
an ex-cop private eye (James Russo),
naturally enough living in southern
California; his friend Anita, an ex-call
girl turned estate agent (Sally
Kirkland); and a tough yet decent
policeman (Burt Young). And,
predictably, there's a *femme fatale*
who's looking for someone. The script
is uninspired, while the mystery has so
many twists and turns it's hard to
keep up. Both previously Oscar-
nominated, Kirkland and Young are
past their best.

James Russo *Jon Kane* • Burt Young *Zimmer*
• Sally Kirkland *Anita Cortez* • Alice Krige
Pamela Sparrow • Luis Guzman *Ronald
Sharkey* • Lewis Van Bergen *Mark Sawyers* •
Brad Sullivan *CT* • Jack Carter *Matty* ■ *Dir*
Jan Egleson • *Scr* Richard Rothstein

Double, Double Toil and Trouble ★★

Comedy   1993 · US · Colour · 89mins

The hurly-burly starts, of course, at Halloween, when twin sisters Lynn and Kelly encounter a dwarf clown and realise that their aunt is a witch. The reason for all these jolly japes is the impending sale of the twins' beloved home in Vancouver, a location that allows for the inclusion of some beautiful scenery. Mary-Kate and Ashley Olsen play the twins with just about enough charm, while Cloris Leachman – an Oscar-winner for *The Last Picture Show* – turns up the eccentricity as the mad auntie.

Ashley Olsen *Lynn Farmer* • Mary-Kate Olsen *Kelly Farmer* • Cloris Leachman *Aunt Agatha/ Aunt Sophia* • Meshach Taylor *Mr N Nofziger* • Phil Fondacaro *Oscar* • Wayne Robson *Gravedigger* • Eric McCormack *Don Farmer* ■ *Dir* Stuart Margolin • *Scr* Jurgen Wolff

Double Dragon ★★ 12

Martial arts adventure
1994 · US · Colour · 91mins

In the ravaged, flooded Los Angeles of 2007, Jimmy and Billy (Mark Dacascos and Scott Wolf) are streetwise youths who come upon one half of an ancient Chinese talisman, which gives awesome power to whoever possesses both halves. Unfortunately, the other portion is owned by unscrupulous gang boss Koga Shuko (Robert Patrick) and his phalanx of gigantic henchmen. Naturally, he's out to reunite the "Double Dragon" and take over the world. A few nifty ideas include cars that run on any old garbage lying around, though it appears kickboxing will still be the preferred method of self-defence in 2007. Decent effects and a wisecracking screenplay lift James Yukich's movie above the usual futuristic fare. ▭

Robert Patrick *Koga Shuko* • Mark Dacascos *Jimmy Lee* • Scott Wolf *Billy Lee* • Kristina Malandro Wagner *Linda Lash* • Julia Nickson [Julia Nickson-Soul] *Sartori Imada* • Alyssa Milano *Marian Delario* ■ *Dir* James Yukich • *Scr* Michael Davis, Peter Gould, from a story by Neal Shusterman, Paul Dini

Double Dynamite ★★ U

Comedy   1951 · US · BW · 77mins

Thanks to a favour from a bookie (Nestor Paiva), a decent young bank clerk (Frank Sinatra) wins a fortune on a race. When $75,000 goes missing from the bank, however, the clerk's fiancée (Jane Russell) and unconventional waiter friend (Groucho Marx) are convinced he stole his new-found wealth. Apart from an occasional laugh supplied by Groucho, this is a thin and dismally unfunny comedy that does nothing for anybody, especially the audience. It's directed by Irving Cummings for the eccentric Howard Hughes. He withheld release for three years while publicising it on the strength of Russell's breasts, rather as he had done with *The Outlaw*. This time the ploy failed. ▭

Jane Russell *Mildred "Mibs" Goodhug* • Groucho Marx *Emil J Keck* • Frank Sinatra *Johnny Dalton* • Don McGuire *Bob Pulsifer Jr* • Howard Freeman *RB Pulsifer Sr* • Harry Hayden *JL McKissack* • Nestor Paiva *"Hot Horse" Harris* • Lou Nova *Max* ■ *Dir* Irving

Cummings • *Scr* Melville Shavelson, Harry Crane, from a story by Leo Rosten, from a character created by Mannie Manheim

Double Edge ★★

Action thriller   1992 · US · Colour · 85mins

Daytime soap star Susan Lucci plays both an FBI agent and the cold-blooded killer she is trying to catch in this rather preposterous thriller. Although the pacing is fast and the action well handled, there are too many plot twists that defy belief, so the experienced cast (including Robert Urich and Robert Prosky) has its work cut out trying to make the film seem remotely realistic.

Susan Lucci *Maggie/Carmen* • Robert Urich *Harry Carter* • Robert Prosky *Father* • Paul Freeman *Ferese* ■ *Dir* Stephen Stafford • *Scr* Joe Reb Moffly, Otis Jones

Double Edge ★★

Political drama   1992 · Is · Colour · 86mins

Assigned to Israel for three weeks, intrepid reporter Faye Milano (Faye Dunaway) finds herself drawn to both sides in the Arab/Israeli conflict. But when she writes about a family of Palestinian resistance fighters, the story gets her into trouble both politically and emotionally. Dunaway isn't at her most charismatic here, but the film is interesting enough and the ending has a nice punch.

Faye Dunaway *Faye Milano* • Amos Kollek *David* • Muhamad Bacri [Muhamad Bakri] *Mustafa Shafik* • Makram Khouri *Ahmed Shafik* • Michael Schneider *Max* • Shmuel Shiloh *Moshe* • Anat Atzmon *Censor* ■ *Dir/ Scr* Amos Kollek

Double Exposure ★ U

Detective thriller   1954 · UK · BW · 63mins

John Bentley, who later became the lacklustre hero of low-budget action movies and played Hugh Mortimer in the long-running TV soap opera *Crossroads*, turns up here in an entirely missable British B-movie. Director John Gilling, who went on to make several Hammer horrors, tries to bring some mystery and tension to the story of a private eye investigating the apparent suicide of an advertising executive's wife. However, the cardboard sets, static performances and his own perfunctory script end up defeating him.

John Bentley *Pete Fleming* • Rona Anderson *Barbara Leyland* • Garry Marsh *Daniel Beaumont* • Alexander Gauge *Denis Clayton* • Maxine Goldner *Ingeborg Wells* • John Horsley *Lamport* • Rick Rydon *Trixon* • Frank Forsyth *Inspector Grayle* ■ *Dir* John Gilling • *Scr* John Gilling, from a story by John Roddick

Double Exposure ★★ 18

Mystery crime thriller
1993 · US · Colour · 92mins

Ron Perlman, star of TV's *Beauty and the Beast*, plays a detective hired by nasty Ian Buchanan to find out whether his wife (Jennifer Gatti) is unfaithful. When Gatti is found dead, her husband looks responsible. But is he really the culprit? Yes, it's double-crossing lovers time – only with a more predictable plot and outcome than usual. There are some nice performances, though, most notably from the gruff Perlman, ex-*Falcon Crest* star William R Moses

and Dedee Pfeiffer, sister of Michelle. ▭

Ron Perlman *Mac McClure* • Ian Buchanan *Roger Putnam* • Jennifer Gatti *Maria* • William R Moses *Det Joiner* • Dedee Pfeiffer *Linda* ■ *Dir* Claudia Hoover • *Scr* Christine Colfer, Bridget Hoffman, Claudia Hoover

Double Impact ★★★ 18

Action thriller   1991 · US · Colour · 105mins

Yet to convincingly handle one role, Jean-Claude Van Damme was a tad ambitious to take on two in this otherwise straightforward action thriller. In a performance that adds a new meaning to the term identical twins, Van Damme is equally equable as the two brothers – one good, one a bit of a rogue – who are reunited to avenge the death of their parents. However, there's plenty of biffing, kicking and explosions for those who like that sort of thing, plus reliable support from Geoffrey Lewis, father of Juliette. Contains swearing, violence, drug abuse and nudity. ▭

Jean-Claude Van Damme *Chad Wagner/Alex Wagner* • Geoffrey Lewis *Frank Avery* • Alan Scarfe *Nigel Griffith* • Alonna Shaw *Danielle Wilde* • Cory Everson *Kara* • Philip Yan Kin Chan [Philip Chan] *Raymond Zhang* • Bolo Yeung *Moon* ■ *Dir* Sheldon Lettich • *Scr* Sheldon Lettich, Jean-Claude Van Damme, from a story by Sheldon Lettich, Jean-Claude Van Damme, Steve Meerson, Peter Krikes

Double Indemnity ★★★★★

Classic film noir   1944 · US · BW · 107mins

Billy Wilder's classic thriller, with its crackling screenplay co-written by Raymond Chandler, is one of the best-loved examples of *film noir* ever made. Based on a short story by James M Cain (author of *The Postman Always Rings Twice*), it follows definitive *femme fatale* Barbara Stanwyck as she seduces insurance salesman Fred MacMurray into murdering – then feigning the accidental death of – her husband Tom Powers, before claiming the premium on the latter's life. However, dogged insurance investigator Edward G Robinson smells a rat and suspects Stanwyck of murder. Wilder was nominated for an Oscar, as was John F Seitz's cinematography and Miklos Rozsa's atmospheric score, while in the best actress category Stanwyck lost out to Ingrid Bergman for *Gaslight*.

Barbara Stanwyck *Phyllis Dietrichson* • Fred MacMurray *Walter Neff* • Edward G Robinson *Barton Keyes* • Porter Hall *Mr Jackson* • Jean Heather *Lola Dietrichson* • Byron Barr *Nino Zachette* • Tom Powers *Mr Dietrichson* • Richard Gaines *Mr Norton* ■ *Dir* Billy Wilder • *Scr* Billy Wilder, Raymond Chandler, from the short story *Three of a Kind* by James M Cain

Double Jeopardy ★★★ 18

Drama   1992 · US · Colour · 99mins

Rachel Ward is perfectly cast as the sexy *femme fatale* who tempts married Bruce Boxleitner away from his family and gets him involved in a murder in this made-for-cable thriller. Although this movie does pale slightly in comparison with *The Last Seduction* and *LA Confidential*, it does benefit from the topnotch performances of its cast – which includes Sela Ward as Boxleitner's lawyer wife and Sally Kirkland – and the taut direction of

Lawrence Schiller, still best known for the award-winning *The Executioner's Song.* ▭

Bruce Boxleitner *Jack Hart* • Rachel Ward *Lisa Burns* • Sela Ward *Karen Hart* • Sally Kirkland *Detective Camden* • Whitney Porter [Whitney Danielle Porter] *Sascha* ■ *Dir* Lawrence Schiller • *Scr* Craig Tepper, Monte Stettin, from a story by Craig Tepper

Double Jeopardy ★★★ 15

Action thriller
1999 · US/Ger · Colour · 105mins

This unintentionally funny thriller was a big hit in the US, where women lined up to see wronged wife Ashley Judd get her own back on her evil, cheating partner. Judd and hubby set off on a romantic sailing trip, only for her to wake up surrounded by coastguards with her spouse missing and pools of blood all over the boat. Sent to prison for his murder, she discovers he faked his own death and has run off with their child and her best friend. So, released on parole, she decides to get back what's hers and give her husband the punishment he deserves, inspired by a loophole in the law that says she can't be tried for his murder twice. Judd gives a believable performance, but Tommy Lee Jones gives a sub-*Fugitive* turn as the federal officer on her trail. Completely preposterous, of course, but perfect if you want to see a sister really doing it for herself.

Tommy Lee Jones *Travis Lehman* • Ashley Judd *Libby Parsons* • Bruce Greenwood *Nick Parsons* • Annabeth Gish *Angie* • Benjamin Weir *Matty aged 4* ■ *Dir* Bruce Beresford • *Scr* David Weisberg, Douglas S Cook

A Double Life ★★★ PG

Crime drama   1947 · US · BW · 99mins

The popular and debonair Ronald Colman won his only Oscar for his performance in this overtly theatrical melodrama. Written by Ruth Gordon and Garson Kanin, it tells the story of a psychopathic actor who identifies with his stage roles in real life. The problem is, he's about to play Othello! Colman makes an unlikely moor, but he manages to convince with the help of George Cukor's adroit direction and a brilliant, Oscar-winning score by the great Miklos Rozsa. The story, though, remains resolutely silly at heart, while Colman only gets to rehearse killing his Desdemona (played by Swedish actress Signe Hasso). ▭

Ronald Colman *Anthony John* • Signe Hasso *Brita* • Edmond O'Brien *Bill Friend* • Shelley Winters *Pat Kroll* • Ray Collins *Victor Donlan* • Philip Loeb *Max Lasker* • Millard Mitchell *Al Cooley* ■ *Dir* George Cukor • *Scr* Ruth Gordon, Garson Kanin, from the play *Othello* by William Shakespeare

The Double Life of Véronique ★★★★ 15

Drama   1991 · Fr/Pol · Colour · 93mins

A slight but nonetheless mesmerising tale from Polish director Krzysztof Kieslowski, this disappointed some critics on its release after the scope, depth and insight of his monumental *Ten Commandments*. However, this is also a work of great intelligence, with its discussion of the fragility of humanity, the perils of ambition and the possibility that we may all have a

U = SUITABLE FOR ALL   Uc = SUITABLE FOR ALL, ESPECIALLY FOR YOUNG CHILDREN (VIDEO ONLY)   PG = PARENTAL GUIDANCE

spiritual twin somewhere in the world, as troubling and provocative as anything broached in his earlier work. Irène Jacob won the best actress prize at Cannes for her subtle dual performance. In Polish and French with English subtitles. Contains nudity. ▣

Irène Jacob Weronika/Véronique • Philippe Volter Alexandre Fabbri • Halina Gryglaszewska Aunt • Kalina Jedrusik Gaudy woman • Aleksander Bardini Orchestra conductor • Wladyslaw Kowalski Weronika's father ■ Dir Krzysztof Kieslowski • Scr Krzysztof Kieslowski, Krzysztof Piesiewicz

The Double McGuffin ★★ PG

Mystery 1979 · US · Colour · 93mins

Despite the presence of screen heavies Ernest Borgnine and George Kennedy, this is a children's film about a plot to kill a middle-eastern head of state, played with mind-boggling implausibility by blonde German actress Elke Sommer. Also involved are a bunch of wholesome American kids who try and avert the assassination. The setting is a real bonus – Charleston in South Carolina, America's most beautiful city. There is an introduction from an uncredited Orson Welles, who explains what a McGuffin is. ▣

Ernest Borgnine Firat • George Kennedy Chief Talasek • Elke Sommer Prime Minister Kura • Ed "Too Tall" Jones First assassin • Lyle Alzado Second assassin • Rod Browning Moras • Orson Welles Narrator ■ Dir Joe Camp • Scr Joe Camp, from a story by Richard Baker, Joe Camp

The Double Man ★★ PG

Spy thriller 1967 · UK · Colour · 100mins

A spy flick from a time when audiences were conditioned to expect a double agent around every corner. A miscast Yul Brynner plays two characters, one American and one German, and makes both of these tight-lipped agents equally dull. The real surprise is that this Swiss-located Elstree-based murk is directed by the redoubtable Franklin J Schaffner, best remembered for Patton and The War Lord. Goes to show that, no matter how talented a director is, if it's not in the script it'll never be on the screen. Nice actors, such as Lloyd Nolan, Moira Lister, Clive Revill and David Bauer, do what they can to help, and cameraman Denys Coop at least ensures the movie looks fetching. ▣

Yul Brynner Dan Slater/Kalmar • Britt Ekland Gina • Clive Revill Frank Wheatley • Anton Diffring Col Berthold • Moira Lister Mrs Carrington • Lloyd Nolan Edwards • David Bauer Miller ■ Dir Franklin J Schaffner • Scr Henry S Maxfield

Double Nickels ★

Action drama 1977 · US · Colour · 89mins

Shots of fast cars stand in for a credible plot in this story of a highway patrolman (played by director and co-writer Jack Vanek) who repossesses cars on the side. The problems start when his boss (a pre-Minder George Cole) has him stealing vehicles instead of reclaiming them. A clumsy, amateurish series of car chases ensues in a film that quickly grinds to a halt.

Jack Vacek Smokey • Ed Abrams Ed • Patrice Schubert Jordan • George Cole George • Heidi Schubert Tami ■ Dir Jack Vacek • Scr Jack Vacek, Patrice Schubert, Jack Vacek

The Double O Kid ★★ 15

Action spy comedy 1992 · US · Colour · 89mins

In this unappealing and unimaginative vehicle for teenage idol Corey Haim, he plays an apprentice secret agent who puts his elders to shame by uncovering a devious terrorist plot. There's a solid enough roster of supporting players (John Rhys-Davies, Wallace Shawn, Karen Black), but Haim's smug mugging will only be appreciated by his die-hard fans. ▣

Corey Haim Lance Elliot • Brigitte Nielsen Rhonda • Nicole Eggert Melinda • Wallace Shawn Cashpot • Basil Hoffman Trout • John Rhys-Davies • Karen Black ■ Dir Duncan McLachlan • Scr Duncan McLachlan, Andrea Buck, from a story by Steven Paul, Stuart Paul

Double Platinum ★★ PG

Musical drama 1999 · US · Colour · 86mins

Eighteen number-one hits make Diana Ross the most successful female recording artist of all time. Her movie career pales in comparison, although she did receive an Oscar nod for Lady Sings the Blues in 1972. Here she stars with teen sensation Brandy (I Still Know What You Did Last Summer), a pretender to her crown. Ross is Olivia, a struggling lounge singer who abandons daughter Kayla (Brandy) to pursue her showbiz dream. Flash forward 18 years, and Olivia is now a massive star to whom Kayla – ignorant of her origins and just embarking on her own warbling career – goes to for advice. Fans will enjoy the tunes, but the creaking melodrama is less attractive. ▣ **DVD**

Diana Ross Olivia King • Brandy Norwood [Brandy] Kayla Harris • Christine Ebersole Peggy • Allen Payne Ric Ortega • Brian Stokes Mitchell Adam Harris • Roger Rees Marc Reckler • Samantha Brown Royana ■ Dir Robert Allan Ackerman • Scr Nina Shengold

Double Suspicion ★★ 18

Thriller 1993 · US/Can · Colour · 91mins

Also known as Breaking Point, this generic crime thriller is only notable for giving a rare leading role to Gary Busey, better known for his villainous turns in such high-octane action romps as Lethal Weapon, Under Siege and Drop Zone. Busey plays Dwight Meadows, an ex-cop who comes out of retirement to track down a serial killer known as "The Surgeon". Kim Cattrall (Sex and the City) co-stars.

Gary Busey Dwight Meadows • Kim Cattrall Allison Meadows • Darlanne Fluegel Dana Preston/Molly Carpenter • Jeff Griggs Greg Pike • Blu Mankuma Mary Lockhart • Leam Blackwood Arthur ■ Dir Paul Ziller • Scr Michael Berlin, Eric Estrin

Double Take ★★ 18

Crime thriller 1997 · US · Colour · 82mins

Craig Sheffer plays a successful author who witnesses a murder. His testimony puts the gunman away, but a few days later he spots the imprisoned man's twin on the street. With the help of the accused man's wife (Brigitte Bako), Sheffer discovers there is much more

going on here than a case of mistaken identity. This thriller is slow and not very exciting. Writers Ed and Ralph Rugoff throw in every plot twist they can think of. Unfortunately, none of them make any sense whatsoever. ▣

Craig Sheffer • Costas Mandylor • Brigitte Bako ■ Dir Mark L Lester • Scr Ed Rugoff, Ralph Rugoff

Double Tap ★★★ 18

Action crime thriller 1997 · US · Colour · 86mins

The words "gritty drama" and "Heather Locklear" are not often found in the same sentence, but they could be combined to describe this hard-nosed thriller. Locklear plays an undercover agent assigned to track down a lethal assassin whose trademark is the "double tap" – two bullets to the head. However, all his victims seem to be drugs barons. Is he, in fact, one of the good guys? Locklear is surprisingly convincing, Stephen Rea is his usual lugubrious self and there's a solid cast of supporting players. Director Greg Yaitanes delivers the requisite gunplay, but also displays a quirky eye for detail. Contains swearing, violence and sex scenes. ▣

Stephen Rea Cypher • Heather Locklear Katherine • Peter Greene Nash • Mykel T Williamson Hamilton • Kevin Gage Burke • Robert LaSardo Rodriguez • Richard Edson Fischer ■ Dir Greg Yaitanes • Scr Erik Saltzgaber, Alfred Gough, Miles Millar

Double Team ★★ 18

Action adventure 1997 · US · Colour · 89mins

Jean-Claude Van Damme continues to work with Hong Kong's finest directors (Hard Target and Maximum Risk were the Hollywood debuts of compatriots John Woo and Ringo Lam) to very little effect. Here Tsui Hark, probably best-known as the producer of the A Better Tomorrow series, supplies a hyper-realistic surface sheen and loads of slow-motion violence, but gets no closer to drawing out a convincing performance from the Belgian star. To make matters worse, Tsui also has to cope with another non-actor, in the shape of basketball legend Dennis Rodman. His ludicrous hair and clothes do at least deflect attention from his unfunny performance as a mysterious gun-runner, who helps Van Damme track down master criminal Mickey Rourke. Contains violence, and some swearing. ▣ **DVD**

Jean-Claude Van Damme Jack Quinn • Dennis Rodman Yaz • Mickey Rourke Stavros • Paul Freeman Goldsmythe • Natacha Lindinger Kath • Valeria Cavalli Dr Maria Trifioli ■ Dir Tsui Hark • Scr Don Jakoby, Paul Mones, from a story by Don Jakoby

Double Threat ★

Erotic thriller 1992 · US · Colour · 96mins

Sally Kirkland plays Monica Martel, an ageing actress who reluctantly agrees to have a body double come in for her sex scenes. Unfortunately, her boyfriend and co-star (Andrew Stevens) takes a shine to the stand-in, and a twisted tale of lust, jealousy and revenge ensues. Kirkland should have hired an acting double, as the movie

has all the melodrama of a daytime soap and is just as predictable.

Sally Kirkland Monica Martel • Andrew Stevens Eric Cline • Anthony Franciosa Crocker Scott • Sherrie Rose Lisa Shane • Richard Lynch Fenich • Chick Vennera Stephen Ross ■ Dir/Scr David A Prior

Double Trouble ★ U

Musical drama 1967 · US · Colour · 91mins

Arguably the worst of the stream of pap movies the great Elvis Presley found himself trapped in by dint of manager Col Tom Parker's wheeling and dealing, this substandard frolic is actually set in a nonexistent England (filmed on a badly designed MGM set in Culver City) in a pathetic nod to the shift in musical culture at the time. Elvis sings one decent rock number, Long-Legged Girl (with the Short Dress on), but this is truly lame-brained nonsense, even in Panavision. Matters are not helped by the casting of Annette Day, an English girl who happened to be in Hollywood at the time. Also found on these cheapskate sets are the likes of Australian Chips Rafferty, urbane John Williams and loveable Norman Rossington, the only actor to co-star with both Elvis and the Beatles (in A Hard Day's Night).

Elvis Presley Guy Lambert • Annette Day Jill Conway • John Williams Gerald Waverly • Yvonne Romain Claire Dunham • The Wiere Brothers Wiere Brothers • Chips Rafferty Archie Brown • Norman Rossington Arthur Babcock ■ Dir Norman Taurog • Scr Jo Heims, from a story by Marc Brandel

Double Trouble ★ 18

Action comedy 1992 · US · Colour · 83mins

The Barbarian Brothers (David and Peter Paul) usually have a lot of fun in their movies, but here they seem sullen and subdued, even during their requisite comic banter. A sloppy cop is forced to team up with his twin, a high-class thief, to bust a diamond operation helmed by Roddy McDowall. Though it's designed as a comedy with some action elements, there is always a feeling of hostility in the background and the savage killings sour what laughter the film provokes. ▣

Peter Paul Peter Jade • David Paul David Jade • Roddy McDowall Chamberlain • Adrienne-Joi Johnson [AJ Johnson] Danitra • Collin Bernsen Whitney Regan • David Carradine Mr C • Bill Mumy Bob • James Doohan Chief O'Brien • Troy Donahue Leonard Stewart ■ Dir John Paragon • Scr Jeffrey Kerns, Kurt Wimmer, from a story by Chuck Osborne, Kurt Wimmer

Double Wedding ★★★ U

Comedy 1937 · US · BW · 86mins

This wonderfully wacky farce stars William Powell as an eccentric artist and Myrna Loy as a bossy designer, bent on forcing her feisty, movie-mad sister (Florence Rice) to marry conservative John Beal. At the time, several reviewers thought this frolic too European in tone – hardly surprising, since it's loosely based on Ferenc Molnar's play, Great Love. A silly cavil really, since the whole purpose of these beautifully produced MGM comedies was simply to entertain, which this one most certainly does.

William Powell Charlie Lodge • Myrna Loy Margit Agnew • Florence Rice Irene Agnew

John Beal *Waldo Beaver* • Jessie Ralph *Mrs Kensington Bly* • Edgar Kennedy *Spike* • Sidney Toler *Keough* ■ *Dir* Richard Thorpe • *Scr* Jo Swerling, Waldo Salt, from the play *Great Love* by Ferenc Molnar

Double X: the Name of the Game ★ 15

Crime drama   1991 · UK · Colour · 93mins

Some people never learn. Even in the darkest days of the low-budget crime drama, few films plumbed the depths reached by this atrocity. Returning to the screen after a long absence, Norman Wisdom does his best to convince as a petty crook trying to keep his daughter out of the clutches of a criminal gang. But such is the awfulness of director Shani S Grewal's dialogue that Wisdom raises more laughs than he used to get in his sentimental comedies. Bernard Hill fares slightly better behind the Irish brogue of his limping thug, but the action (complete with obligatory American import, William Katt) is dated. Contains violence and swearing. ▦

SImon Ward *Edward Ross* • William Katt *Michael Cooper* • Norman Wisdom *Arthur Clutton* • Bernard Hill *Iggy Smith* • Gemma Craven *Jenny Eskridge* • Leon Herbert *Ollie* • Derren Nesbitt *Minister* ■ *Dir* Shani S Grewal • *Scr* Shani S Grewal, from the short story *Vengeance* by David Fleming

Dougal and the Blue Cat ★★★ U

Animated adventure
1970 · Fr · Colour · 78mins

Did you know that Dougal was called Pollux in the original French version of *The Magic Roundabout*? In this awesomely weird feature spin-off, the cynical shaggy dog is the only creature who can prevent the devious double act of Buxton the Cat and Madame Blue from stealing Zebedee's moustache and taking control of the Magic Garden. Directed with typically surreal inventiveness by Serge Danot, this zany adventure is made all the more hilarious by the crackling dialogue penned and delivered by Eric Thompson, father of the Oscar-winning Emma. ▦

Eric Thompson *Narrator/Dougal/Zebedee/Florence/Dylan/Buxton* • Fenella Fielding *Madame Blue* ■ *Dir* Serge Danot, Eric Thompson • *Scr* Serge Danot, Jacques Josselin, Eric Thompson

Doughboys ★★

First World War comedy
1930 · US · BW · 80mins

For a comic genius who made his reputation in the silent era with such classics as *Sherlock Junior* and *The General*, this tale of a rich man joining the army by mistake was quite a risk for Buster Keaton. (It was his first talkie.) Based on Keaton's own experiences in the First World War, Edward Sedgwick's film works reasonably well, though sound was never Buster's natural medium.

Buster Keaton *Elmer* • Sally Eilers *Mary* • Cliff Edwards *Nescopeck* • Edward Brophy *Sgt Brophy* • Victor Potel *Svendenburg* • Arnold Korff *Gustave* • Frank Mayo *Capt Scott* ■ *Dir*

Edward Sedgwick • *Scr* Al Boasberg, Sidney Lazarus, Richard Schayer, from a story by Al Boasberg, Sidney Lazarus

The Doughgirls ★★★

Wartime comedy   1944 · US · BW · 101mins

This bowdlerised screen version of Joseph A Fields's Broadway hit about the wartime housing shortage in Washington DC is still very funny, but it's a long way behind other movies on the same subject (*The More the Merrier*, for example). Warner Bros contract players get a chance to shine in this ensemble comedy, particularly Ann Sheridan, Alexis Smith and Jane Wyman (then married to Ronald Reagan). Once again, however, the priceless Eve Arden – here playing a Russian – effortlessly walks away with every scene she's in. Look out for Craig Stevens, star of the fifties TV series *Peter Gunn*.

Jack Carson *Arthur Halstead* • Jane Wyman *Vivian Halstead* • John Ridgely *Julian Cadman* • Ann Sheridan *Edna Stokes* • Charles Ruggles *Slade* • Alexis Smith *Nan* • Craig Stevens *Tom* • Eve Arden *Natalia* ■ *Dir* James V Kern • *Scr* James V Kern, Sam Hellman, from a play by Joseph A Fields

Doug's 1st Movie ★★★ U

Animated adventure
1999 · US · Colour · 77mins

As an introduction to wider audiences for a much-loved American children's TV character, this full-length Disney animation has to establish an oddball cuteness that is already well-known in the States. It does a fairly successful job, with a tale hinging on a now-familiar eco-message. A squidgy, pollution-induced monster (named after *Moby Dick* writer Herman Melville) is found by high school student Doug Funnie and his friend Skeeter in a lake owned by wicked tycoon Bill Bluff. The cautionary conclusion will be understood by the three- to eight-year-olds at which it's aimed, and they'll probably have an enjoyable time getting there.

Thomas McHugh *Doug Funnie/Lincoln* • Fred Newman *Skeeter/Mr Dink/Porkchop/Ned* • Chris Phillips *Roger Klotz/Boomer/Larry/Mr Chiminy* • Constance Shulman *Patti Mayonnaise* • Frank Welker *Herman Melville* ■ *Dir* Maurice Joyce • *Scr* Ken Scarborough

Le Doulos ★★★

Crime drama   1962 · Fr · BW · 108mins

Jean-Pierre Melville's flawed but fascinating crime thriller – a tribute to the classic American gangster movies of the thirties and forties – casts Jean-Paul Belmondo as an underworld figure and police informer for whom treachery is a religion. First he helps an ex-con plan a heist; then he betrays him. Then he plans the man's escape from prison. Oh, and he kills his girlfriend, too. Look out for the famous nine-minute take in the policeman's office: Melville insisted the camera crew wore black and donned face masks to eliminate the risk of reflection in the windows and mirrors. In French with English subtitles.

Jean-Paul Belmondo *Silien* • Serge Reggiani *Maurice* • Monique Hennessy *Therese* • RenéLefèvre *Gilbert* • Jean Desailly *Inspector*

• Michel Piccoli *Leader* • Carl Studer *Kern* ■ *Dir* Jean-Pierre Melville • *Scr* Jean-Pierre Melville, from the novel by Pierre Lesou

The Dove ★★★ PG

Biographical adventure
1974 · US/UK · Colour · 99mins

Gregory Peck produced this beautifully shot family film, based on a true story, in which a 16-year-old boy comes of age during a five-year solo circumnavigation of the globe in a small boat. Part travelogue, part round-the-world adventure, the film makes you yearn for the days when not every city, beach and seaside town was over-developed, and features accomplished performances from a young Joseph Bottoms as the intrepid sailor, Deborah Raffin and Dabney Coleman. Charles Jarrott lovingly directs. ▦

Joseph Bottoms *Robin Lee Graham* • Deborah Raffin *Patti Ratteree* • John McLiam *Lyle Graham* • Dabney Coleman *Charles Huntley* • John Anderson *Mike Turk* • Colby Chester *Tom Barkley* • Ivor Barry *Kenniston* ■ *Dir* Charles Jarrott • *Scr* Peter Beagle, Adam Kennedy, from the non-fiction book by Robin Lee Graham, Derek Gill

Down among the Z-Men ★ U

Comedy   1952 · UK · BW · 67mins

Although Peter Sellers, Harry Secombe and Spike Milligan co-starred in *Penny Points to Paradise* (1951), this was the only time all four founders of *The Goon Show* appeared together on celluloid. However, Michael Bentine's turn as a mad professor is just one of many space-fillers in this dismal army romp. Gone is the zany humour that made the radio show essential listening and, in its place, comes crude slapstick and obvious observation. Veteran director Maclean Rogers fails to disguise either the cheapness of the production or the bankruptcy of the plot, which is held together with interminable numbers from the camp radio programme. ▦

Harry Secombe *Harry Jones* • Carole Carr *Carole Gayley* • Peter Sellers *Major Bloodnock* • Michael Bentine *Professor Osrick Purehart* • Spike Milligan *Private Eccles* ■ *Dir* Maclean Rogers • *Scr* Jimmy Grafton, France Charles

Down and Dirty ★★★ 15

Comedy   1976 · It · Colour · 111mins

Ettore Scola was named best director at Cannes for this raucous comedy, which exploits the conventions of neorealism to mock its sentimental attitude to poverty. Set in a crumbling shanty town on the outskirts of Rome, the film introduces us to a gallery of grotesques, none more revolting than Nino Manfredi's one-eyed patriarch, whose vulgarity and greed eventually bring out the darker side of his desperate relations. Although graphic in his depiction of their squalor, Scola refuses to portray the poor as innocent victims of an invidious system. Yet he also refrains from cruelty in satirising their low expectations and boorish behaviour. In Italian with English subtitles. ▦

Nino Manfredi *Giacinto* ■ *Dir* Ettore Scola • *Scr* Ruggero Maccari, Ettore Scola

Down and Out in Beverly Hills ★★★ 15

Comedy   1986 · US · Colour · 99min

This was phenomenally successful at the box office and provided Nick Nolte with a choice comic role. But there is something a shade too frantic and nervy about the film's pace and the performances of Bette Midler and Richard Dreyfuss, as the *nouveau riche* Beverly Hills couple who find themselves giving house room to Nolte's hobo. Some very funny set pieces, usually involving the family dog, and the occasional unerring spotlight on snobbery make it a movie worth watching, but it is not a patch on the classic French original *Boudu Saved from Drowning*. Contains some swearing and nudity. ▦

Nick Nolte *Jerry Baskin* • Bette Midler *Barbara Whiteman* • Richard Dreyfuss *Dave Whiteman* • Little Richard *Orvis Goodnight* • Tracy Nelson *Jenny Whiteman* • Elizabeth Pena *Carmen* • Evan Richards *Max Whiteman* • Donald F Muhich *Dr Von Zimmer* ■ *Dir* Paul Mazursky • *Scr* Paul Mazursky, Leon Capetanos, from the film *Boudu, Saved from Drowning* by Jean Renoir, from the play by René Fauchois

Down Argentine Way ★★★ U

Musical   1940 · US · Colour · 88mins

When this movie was first shown in cinemas, Argentina was as alien to American movie audiences as Mars, and the kind of Latin music presented here by Carmen Miranda was tremendously exciting. It's important to bear that in mind as you watch this witless farrago set in an Argentina that never gets off the 20th Century-Fox backlot (though Miranda's numbers were filmed in New York where she was starring on Broadway). Betty Grable became a star after replacing an indisposed Alice Faye, and Miranda became a sensation. The forties Technicolor is nice, but the supporting cast leaves a lot to be desired.

Don Ameche *Ricardo Quintana* • Betty Grable *Glenda Crawford* • Carmen Miranda • Charlotte Greenwood *Binnie Crawford* • J Carrol Naish *Casiano* • Henry Stephenson *Don Diego Quintana* • Katharine Aldridge *Helen Carson* ■ *Dir* Irving Cummings • *Scr* Darrell Ware, Karl Tunberg, from a story by Rian James, Ralph Spence

Down by Law ★★★★ 15

Comedy   1986 · US · BW · 102mins

Jim Jarmusch's uneven but stylish *comédie noire* is an astute mixture of prison picture, road movie and downbeat screwball. Posturing hard men Tom Waits and John Lurie find themselves sharing a cell after they are framed for transporting a corpse and corrupting a minor respectively. Their petty feuding is interrupted by chatty new cellmate Roberto Benigni, who soon devises an escape plan. As the excellent soundtrack testifies, Waits and Lurie are more effectively paired as songwriters than performers, but they offer solid support to the brilliant Benigni, whose pidgin prattling is a joy. Contains swearing. ▦

Tom Waits *Zack* • John Lurie *Jack Romano* • Roberto Benigni *Roberto* • Nicoletta Braschi *Nicoletta* • Ellen Barkin *Laurette* • Billie Neal *Bobbie* ■ *Dir/Scr* Jim Jarmusch

Down Came a Blackbird ★★★

Drama   1995 · US · Colour · 113mins

This surprisingly gritty made-for-TV drama is notable for being Raul Julia's last film. Julia, the well-loved *Addams Family* star, plays a professor with a shady past who is among the patients in a private clinic for victims of torture, while Laura Dern is the journalist whose research draws her to the clinic. As painful memories are brought to the surface, the strong script brings raw performances from the cast, which also includes Vanessa Redgrave. Director Jonathan Sanger invests the film with a power and political passion rarely seen in American TV drama.

Laura Dern *Helen McNulty* • Raul Julia *Tomas Ramirez* • Vanessa Redgrave *Anna Lenke* • Jay O Sanders *Jan Telbeck* • Cliff Gorman ■ *Dir* Jonathan Sanger • *Scr* Kevin Droney

Down in the Delta ★★★

Drama   1997 · US · Colour · 111mins

Any film with the wonderful Alfre Woodard is worth catching, so don't miss this moving drama directed by the poet Maya Angelou. Woodard is the Chicago mother packed off with her children to a Mississippi backwater to escape the perils of the inner city streets. While Angelou loads on the family values theme a little thickly in places, this is nonetheless an enjoyable and heartrending picture, given extra weight by some classy performances from Loretta Devine, Esther Rolle and Wesley Snipes.

Alfre Woodard *Loretta* • Al Freeman Jr *Earl* • Mary Alice *Rosa Lynn* • Esther Rolle *Annie* • Loretta Devine *Zenia* • Wesley Snipes *Will* • Mpho Koaha *Thomas* • Kulani Hassen *Tracy* ■ *Dir* Maya Angelou • *Scr* Myron Goble

Down Mexico Way ★★ U

Western   1941 · US · BW · 79mins

A popular Gene Autry feature, this western has a little more action than most, plus a fair amount of well-known songs. These include not just the title number but also *South of the Border*, *Maria Elena* and *Roll Out the Barrel* (*Beer Barrel Polka*). Maybe that's why Joseph Santley, better known for musicals than westerns, was hired to direct. The plot's nothing about Autry chasing some con men who are posing as movie-makers, but the strong supporting cast includes veteran character actors Paul Fix and Sidney Blackmer, plus television's future *Cisco Kid*, Duncan Renaldo.

Gene Autry *Gene* • Smiley Burnette *Frog* • Fay McKenzie *Maria Elena* • Harold Huber *Pancho Grande* • Sidney Blackmer *Gibson* • Joe Sawyer *Allen* • Andrew Tombes *Mayor Tubbs* • Murray Alper *Flood* • Paul Fix *Davis* • Duncan Renaldo *Juan* ■ *Dir* Joseph Santley • *Scr* Olive Cooper, Albert Duffy, from the story by Stuart McGowan, Dorrell McGowan

Down Periscope ★★ 12

Comedy   1996 · US · Colour · 88mins

Frasier's Kelsey Grammer has tried to make it big on the cinema screen, with the same lack of success as his *Cheers* companion Shelley Long. Here it's partly owing to the been-there, seen-that feel of the plot. Grammer is a useless submarine commander who

will be kicked out of the navy unless he can train a hapless crew in an old boiler of a sub how to outmanoeuvre the entire fleet. Director David S Ward has done this type of slapstick so many times before (*Major League*, *King Ralph*) that he's run out of ideas. Grammer is as funny as he is on TV, however, and there are amusing turns from Harry Dean Stanton, Bruce Dern, William H Macy and Rip Torn. Contains some swearing. ▭

Kelsey Grammer *Lt Commander Thomas Dodge* • Lauren Holly *Lt Emily Lake* • Rob Schneider *Executive Officer Martin Pascal* • Harry Dean Stanton *Howard* • Bruce Dern *Admiral Yancy Graham* • William H Macy *Captain Knox* • Ken Hudson Campbell *Buckman* • Toby Huss *Nitro* • Rip Torn *Admiral Winslow* ■ *Dir* David S Ward • *Scr* Hugh Wilson, Eliot Wald, Andrew Kurtzman, from a story by Hugh Wilson

Down the Long Hills ★★★ U

Adventure   1987 · US · Colour · 85mins

Bruce Boxleitner co-stars in this western about two kids who are the sole survivors following an Indian attack on their wagon train. With their striking red horse, the pair have to make their way through the wilderness of Utah, coming up against the elements, horse thieves and – of course – a grizzly bear. This fun, old-style adventure also stars the gruff-voiced Bo Hopkins, best known for his roles in *American Graffitti* and *More American Graffiti* and his appearances in the eighties TV soap *Dynasty*. ▭

Bruce Boxleitner *Scott Collins* • Bo Hopkins *Jud* • Michael Wren *Cal* • Don Shanks *Ashawakie* • Ed Bruce *Bregman* • Buck Taylor *Grey* • Thomas Wilson Brown *Hardy Collins* ■ *Dir* Burt Kennedy • *Scr* Jon Povare, Ruth Povare, from a novel by Louis L'Amour

Down Three Dark Streets ★★★ U

Detective crime drama
1954 · US · BW · 85mins

When an FBI agent dies, a colleague takes on his caseload and finds himself caught up in three different crimes involving car theft, a gangster on the run and an extortion racket. Broderick Crawford stars as the investigator, while Martha Hyer makes an excellent gangster's moll. Ruth Roman and Marisa Pavan also appear, as a widow under threat and a blind girl respectively. In the best tradition of gritty, low-key crime thrillers, Arnold Laven's movie keeps the suspense going all the way to the final fade.

Broderick Crawford *Ripley* • Ruth Roman *Kate Martel* • Martha Hyer *Connie Anderson* • Marisa Pavan *Julie Angelino* • Casey Adams [Max Showalter] *Dave Millson* • Kenneth Tobey *Zack Stewart* • Gene Reynolds *Vince Angelino* • William Johnstone *Frank Pace* ■ *Dir* Arnold Laven • *Scr* Bernard C Schoenfeld, The Gordons [Gordon Gordon, Margaret Gordon], from their novel *Case File FBI*

Down to Earth ★★★ U

Musical fantasy   1947 · US · Colour · 96mins

Along the same lines as the following year's *One Touch of Venus*, and incorporating a couple of characters directly from 1941's *Here Comes Mr Jordan*, this Columbia musical boasts two significant assets: Rita Hayworth and Technicolor. Some may find this

whimsy about the goddess of dance (Hayworth) landing on Earth to help Larry Parks jazz up a musical show tiresome in the extreme. But there's pleasure to be had from watching dancer Marc Platt, while Hayworth is in nearly every scene. ▭

Rita Hayworth *Terpsichore/Kitty Pendleton* • Larry Parks *Danny Miller* • Marc Platt *Eddie Marin* • Roland Culver *Mr Jordan* • James Gleason *Max Corkle* • Edward Everett Horton *Messenger 7013* • Adele Jergens *Georgia Evans* • George Macready *Joe Mannion* ■ *Dir* Alexander Hall • *Scr* Edwin Blum, Don Hartman, from the characters created by Harry Segall in his play *Heaven Can Wait*

Down to the Sea in Ships ★★★ U

Adventure   1949 · US · BW · 120mins

Henry Hathaway was one of the great action directors of Hollywood's golden age and he keeps this rousing whaling adventure firmly on course. Lionel Barrymore is his cantankerous self as a 19th-century Massachusetts seafarer whose grandson (Dean Stockwell) is torn between the old methods of the family firm and the modern techniques of first mate Richard Widmark. Though not a topic to attract the more ecologically aware actors of today's Hollywood, there is still plenty of passion in the exchanges between Widmark and Barrymore, and Hathaway makes the most of the set pieces, such as the iceberg wreck. The real highlight, however, is the playing of such stalwarts as Cecil Kellaway, Gene Lockhart and Harry Davenport.

Richard Widmark *Dan Lunceford* • Lionel Barrymore *Captain Bering Joy* • Dean Stockwell *Jed Joy* • Cecil Kellaway *Slush Tubbs* • Gene Lockhart *Andrew Bush* • Berry Kroeger *Manchester* • John McIntire *Thatch* • Henry Morgan [Harry Morgan] *Britton* • Harry Davenport *Mr Harris* ■ *Dir* Henry Hathaway • *Scr* John Lee Mahin, Sy Bartlett, from a story by Sy Bartlett, from the film by John LE Pell

Down to You ★★ 12

Romantic comedy
2000 · US · Colour · 92mins

A teenage romance with delusions of grandeur about the relationship between two New York college kids, from starting out to falling out to starting over. Freddie Prinze Jr and Julia Stiles make attractive leads, but Kris Isacsson's film is marred by irritating voice-overs, asides to camera and crackerbarrel philosophising about life and love. The production values are high, and there's a fine supporting performance from Henry Winkler as Prinze Jr's TV chef dad. But the picture would have benefited from a less smart-aleck approach.

Freddie Prinze Jr *Al Connelly* • Julia Stiles *Imogen* • Shawn Hatosy *Eddie Hicks* • Selma Blair *Cyrus* • Zak Orth *Monk Jablonski* • Ashton Kutcher *Jim Morrison* • Rosario Dawson *Lana* • Henry Winkler *Chef Ray* ■ *Dir/Scr* Kris Isacsson

Down Twisted ★ 15

Crime caper   1987 · US · Colour · 84mins

Hack director Albert Pyun strikes again with this international robbery caper, in which a wealthy art collector hires some thieves to steal the ancient symbol of a small country. Naturally, the thieves pull a double cross. The

cinematography is unusually competent for Pyun, but the ham-fisted editing and terrible acting let the side down. Look out for *Friends* star Courteney Cox as a waitress. ▭

Carey Lowell *Maxine* • Charles Rocket *Reno* • Trudi Dochtermann *Michelle* • Thom Mathews *Damalas* • Norbert Weisser *Deltoid* • Linda Kerridge *Soames* • Courteney Cox *Tarah* ■ *Dir* Albert Pyun • *Scr* Gene O'Neill, Noreen Tobin, from a story by Albert Pyun

The Downfall of Osen ★★★

Drama   1935 · Jap · BW · 78mins

Kenji Mizoguchi made 55 films between 1922 and 1935, of which only six have survived. However, while the director dismissed many of the pictures completed in this period, this moving drama is not only predicative of his recurrent themes, but also demonstrates considerable technical innovation. Employing Japanese, Hollywood and Expressionist tropes, the story of servant girl Isuzu Yamada's bid to help Daijiro Natsukawa enter medical school by becoming a prostitute echoes the sacrifice of Mizoguchi's own geisha sister. Yet it's the stylised realism and the inventive use of flashbacks that gives the film its historical value. A Japanese language film.

Isuzu Yamada *Osen* • Daijiro Natsukawa *Sokichi Hata* • Mitsusaburo Ramon *Ukiki* • Shin Shibata *Kumazawa* • Genichi Fujii *Matsuda* • Mitsuru Tojo *Kanya* • Junichi Kitamura *Sakazuki no Keishiro* ■ *Dir* Kenji Mizoguchi • *Scr* Tatsunosuke Takashima, from the short story *Baishoku Kamonanban* by Kyoka Izumi • *Cinematographer* Shigeto Miki [Minoru Miki]

Downhill Racer ★★★★ PG

Action drama   1969 · US · Colour · 101mins

This is a real Hollywood rarity. A simple plot means that characters and ideas can breathe, while the star (Robert Redford) goes against the grain of his perceived screen persona. The thrilling skiing scenes thus exist to reveal the shallow psychology and deep-freeze arrogance of a small-town skier (Redford) thrust into the limelight of the Olympics. Director Michael Ritchie sustains his sharp attack on the consequences of winning and the temptations of fame all the way through to the dramatic climax. Gene Hackman co-stars as Redford's tough-talking coach. ▭

Robert Redford *David Chappellet* • Gene Hackman *Eugene Claire* • Camilla Sparv *Carole Stahl* • Joe Jay Jalbert *Tommy Erb* • Timothy Kirk *DK Bryan* • Dabney Coleman *Mayo* • Jim McMullan *Johnny Creech* ■ *Dir* Michael Ritchie • *Scr* James Salter, from the novel *The Downhill Racers* by Oakley Hall

Downpayment on Murder ★★ 15

Crime drama based on a true story
1987 · US · Colour · 95mins

Based on a real story, this TV movie has domestic violence as its central theme. Connie Sellecca gives a poignant performance as the abused wife of a financially distressed real-estate man (Ben Gazzara). After deciding she can no longer tolerate her husband's behaviour, she finally musters the courage to take her children and move out. Furious at her actions, her husband hires a cold-blooded hit man to kill her. Gazzara is superb as the murderous husband, while Sellecca is appealing as the long-suffering housewife. ▣

Ben Gazzara *Harry Cardell* • Connie Sellecca *Karen Cardell* • David Morse *Detective Jackson* • Jonathan Banks *Detective McKenzie* • GW Bailey *Kyle* ■ *Dir* Waris Hussein • *Scr* Barry Schneider, Bill Driskill

Downtime ★ 15
Romantic thriller 1997 · UK/Fr · Colour · 86mins

Two people from totally different backgrounds fall in love while trapped in a dangerously derelict lift in a Newcastle high rise. Even dafter than it sounds, this ludicrous fiasco switches between low-rent suspense (the dodgy elevator sequences) and glib, socially aware drama (teenage thugs terrorising the neighbourhood) with absolutely no rhyme, reason or logic. No one acts sensibly in Bharat Nalluri's dumb mix of *Die Hard* and Barbara Cartland, while the hostage crisis finale defies belief. This is British film-making at its nadir. Contains swearing and some violence. ▣

Paul McGann *Rob* • Susan Lynch *Chrissy* • Tom Georgeson *Jimmy* • David Roper *Mike* • Denise Bryson *Jan* • Adam Johnston *Jake* • David Horsefield *Kevin* • Stephen Graham *Jacko* ■ *Dir* Bharat Nalluri • *Scr* Caspar Berry

Downtown ★★★ 18
Action comedy 1990 · US · Colour · 91mins

Great things were predicted for Anthony Edwards after he scored as "Goose" in *Top Gun*. That he has achieved them on TV in *ER* and not on the big screen could be owing to a string of mediocre films, though this buddy cop movie is far from his worst. Comedy specialist Richard Benjamin, who gave us *Mermaids* and *Made in America*, is perhaps not the best director for a tough crime picture and there's nothing new or profound about his slant on white liberalism versus black realism. Yet Edwards and co-star Forest Whitaker are at least committed to giving their characters some depth. Contains swearing and violence. ▣

Anthony Edwards *Alex Kearney* • Forest Whitaker *Dennis Curren* • Penelope Ann Miller *Lori Mitchell* • Joe Pantoliano *White* • David Clennon *Jerome Sweet* • Art Evans *Henry Coleman* • Kimberly Scott *Christine Curren* ■ *Dir* Richard Benjamin • *Scr* Nat Mauldin

Dr Caligari ★★★
Horror comedy 1989 · US · Colour · 80mins

Under the pseudonym "Rinse Dream", Stephen Sayadian directed *Cafe Flesh* (1982), an influential slice of expressionism porn. This, his only mainstream film to date, is Sayadian's similarly styled version of *The Cabinet of Dr Caligari* (1919), with Caligari played by a woman (model Madeleine Reynal) who presides over bizarre experiments at her sanatorium. Sick humour, stupid dialogue and emetic effects will repel most viewers, but lovers of the truly outré should seek out this amazing product of a warped imagination. The supporting cast includes several players with substantial horror pedigrees, among

them Fox Harris; this was one of several movies released after the actor's death in 1988.

Madeleine Reynal *Dr Caligari* • Fox Harris *Dr Avol* • Laura Albert *Mrs Van Houten* • Jennifer Balgobin *Ramona Lodger* • John Durbin *Gus Pratt* • Gene Zerna *Les Van Houten* • David Parry *Dr Lodger* ■ *Dir* Stephen Sayadian • *Scr* Jerry Stahl, Stephen Sayadian

Dracula ★★★★ PG
Classic horror 1931 · US · BW · 71mins

One of the most famous horror movies ever made, director Tod Browning's seminal classic is, by today's standards, rather talky, stagebound and bloodless. Most of its important chills occur off-screen, too. But it remains the most subtly romantic and highly atmospheric rendition of Bram Stoker's tale of the Transylvanian count's parasitic trip to London, with Browning orchestrating the opening scenes to macabre perfection. Bela Lugosi's star turn (he'd been in the stage version since 1927) is an impressive film debut. ▣

Bela Lugosi *Count Dracula* • Helen Chandler *Mina Seward* • David Manners *Jonathan Harker* • Dwight Frye *Renfield* • Edward Van Sloan *Dr Van Helsing* • Herbert Bunston *Dr Seward* • Frances Dade *Lucy Weston* • Charles Gerrard *Martin* ■ *Dir* Tod Browning • *Scr* Garrett Fort, from the novel by Bram Stoker and the play by Hamilton Deane, John Balderston • *Cinematographer* Karl Freund • *Art Director* Charles D Hall • *Make-up* Jack Pierce

Dracula ★★★★★ 15
Classic horror 1958 · UK · Colour · 77mins

Bram Stoker's terrifying vampire creation becomes a modern classic in the adept hands of the House of Hammer. The film was epoch-making in its impact, due to the fabulous Gothic atmosphere, Terence Fisher's stylish direction and the fact that the undead tale was shot in vivd, gory colour for the first time. Christopher Lee's interpretation of Dracula is astonishingly fresh, heroic and powerful, while Peter Cushing makes an ideal Van Helsing. The latter's climactic battle with his blood-sucking nemesis is justly acclaimed as a magic movie moment in the history and development of the horror genre. ▣

Peter Cushing *Van Helsing* • Michael Gough *Arthur Holmwood* • Melissa Stribling *Mina Holmwood* • Christopher Lee *Count Dracula* • Carol Marsh *Lucy* • John Van Eyssen *Jonathan Harker* • Miles Malleson *Marx, the undertaker* ■ *Dir* Terence Fisher • *Scr* Jimmy Sangster, from the novel by Bram Stoker

Dracula ★★★ 15
Horror 1974 · US · Colour · 93mins

Originally made for American television by director Dan Curtis, this adaption of the Bram Stoker classic was given a theatrical release overseas, albeit in a pared-down version. Jack Palance gives one of his better performances as a sympathetic, Byronic Dracula, a Transylvanian count motivated by love as much as bloodlust. Veteran screenwriter Richard Matheson scripts this under-rated and well-appointed adaptation, which offers refreshing new slants on the usual undead clichés. Nigel Davenport supplies a dynamic reading of Van Helsing and Fiona Lewis

makes a voluptuous Lucy, in an effort that's sure to delight serious Stoker buffs. ▣

Jack Palance *Count Dracula* • Simon Ward *Arthur Holmwood* • Nigel Davenport *Dr Van Helsing* • Pamela Brown *Mrs Westerna* • Fiona Lewis *Lucy Westerna* • Penelope Horner *Mina Murray* • Murray Brown *Jonathan Harker* ■ *Dir* Dan Curtis • *Scr* Richard Matheson, from the novel by Bram Stoker

Dracula ★★★★ 15
Horror 1979 · US · Colour · 104mins

Like the 1931 version of Bram Stoker's tale, this streamlined remake is based on the hoary twenties stage play, with the emphasis less on the supernatural horror and more on the Transylvanian count's seduction techniques. Frank Langella, fresh from the hit Broadway version, turns on the sensuality to great effect in director John Badham's stylishly atmospheric retread, with Laurence Olivier passionately histrionic as his nemesis, Van Helsing. While it's crafted as mainstream melodrama, there are enough chills to satisfy a more hardened horror crowd. ▣

Frank Langella *Dracula* • Laurence Olivier *Van Helsing* • Donald Pleasence *Seward* • Kate Nelligan *Lucy* • Trevor Eve *Harker* • Jan Francis *Mina* • Janine Duvitski *Annie* • Tony Haygarth *Renfield* • Teddy Turner *Swales* ■ *Dir* John Badham • *Scr* WD Richter, from the play by Hamilton Deane, John Balderston, from the novel by Bram Stoker

Dracula AD 1972 ★★ 18
Horror 1972 · UK · Colour · 91mins

For the sixth entry in their enduring *Dracula* series, Hammer relocated the count to swinging Chelsea, where he's holed up in a deconsecrated King's Road church and putting the bite on hippie layabouts. Derided at the time as a monumental misjudgement on the House of Horror's part, this slice of bell-bottomed phoniness can now be enjoyed as a camp period piece. Despite the mod trappings, Christopher Lee and Peter Cushing are as convincing as ever in their familiar roles, and director Alan Gibson keeps things moving at a fine pace. ▣

Christopher Lee *Count Dracula* • Peter Cushing *Professor Van Helsing* • Stephanie Beacham *Jessica* • Christopher Neame *Johnny* • Michael Coles *Inspector* • Marsha A Hunt *Gaynor* • Caroline Munro *Laura* ■ *Dir* Alan Gibson • *Scr* Don Houghton, from the characters created by Bram Stoker

Dracula: Dead and Loving It ★★ PG
Comedy horror 1995 · US · Colour · 86mins

Mel Brooks's run of cinematic disappointments continues with this woeful spoof on vampire movies. Leslie Nielsen is dreadfully miscast as the count. However most of the blame must be levelled at director Brooks and his co-writers, who not only show no understanding of the genre they're sending up but who also seem to have forgotten how to actually write a remotely funny gag. What makes it doubly depressing is that Brooks's other excursion into horror satire, *Young Frankenstein*, remains one of his best films. ▣

Leslie Nielsen *Dracula* • Peter MacNicol *Renfield* • Steven Weber *Jonathan Harker* • Amy Yasbeck *Mina* • Lysette Anthony *Lucy* • Harvey Korman *Dr Seward* • Mel Brooks *Professor Van Helsing* • Mark Blankfield *Martin* ■ *Dir* Mel Brooks • *Scr* Mel Brooks, Rudy De Luca, Steve Haberman, from a story by Rudy De Luca, Steve Haberman, from the characters created by Bram Stoker

Dracula Has Risen from the Grave ★★★ 15
Horror 1968 · UK · Colour · 88mins

A weak priest provides the blood that revives the evil Count Dracula and becomes his servant in a typical dose of vampire flesh-creeping from the Hammer House of Horror. A minor triumph of style over content, the third sequel to Hammer's 1958 classic succeeds by virtue of Freddie Francis's adventurous direction and his ability to extract religious irony from the formulaic script. Moody red filters are used to enhance the sanguinary motifs, while the ever-reliable Christopher Lee evokes the customary chills and supernatural menace. Dracula not dying after being gorily staked by an atheist is this iconoclastic pictures's most striking – if ludicrous – scene. ▣

Christopher Lee *Count Dracula* • Rupert Davies *Monsignor* • Veronica Carlson *Maria* • Barbara Ewing *Zena* • Barry Andrews *Paul* • Ewan Hooper *Priest* • Michael Ripper *Max* • Marion Mathie *Anna* ■ *Dir* Freddie Francis • *Scr* John Elder [Anthony Hinds], from the characters created by Bram Stoker

Dracula – Prince of Darkness ★★★★ 15
Horror 1965 · UK · Colour · 86mins

Two English couples dare to go travelling through the Carpathian mountains in one of the best in the Hammer Dracula series. Veteran horror director Terence Fisher brings out the innate sexuality in the tightly plotted story and Christopher Lee is awesome as the dreaded count, despite having no dialogue. The gruesome sequence where the infamous bloodsucker is resurrected in a perverse religious ritual still retains its shock value, with scream queen Barbara Shelley's demise just as memorable. Andrew Keir is no real substitute for Peter Cushing (glimpsed in the prologue lifted from the studio's 1958 *Dracula* blockbuster), but in every other respect this is a text-book example of top-grade ghoulish horror. ▣

Christopher Lee *Count Dracula* • Barbara Shelley *Helen Kent* • Andrew Keir *Father Sandor* • Francis Matthews *Charles Kent* • Suzan Farmer *Diana Kent* • Charles Tingwell *Alan Kent* • Thorley Walters *Ludwig* • Walter Brown *Brother Mark* ■ *Dir* Terence Fisher • *Scr* John Sansom, from the characters created by Bram Stoker

Dracula, Prisoner of Frankenstein ★
Horror 1972 · Sp · Colour · 86mins

Spanish hack director Jesus Franco intended to make a parody of horror myths, but clearly doesn't have the talent or the budget to pull off such a cartoonish conceit. This sorry spectacle has Dr Frankenstein (a slumming Dennis Price) reviving

U = SUITABLE FOR ALL Uc = SUITABLE FOR ALL, ESPECIALLY FOR YOUNG CHILDREN (VIDEO ONLY) PG = PARENTAL GUIDANCE

Dracula (Franco regular Howard Vernon) with a nightclub singer's blood, so that he can use his vampire acolytes to conquer the world. Lousy make-up, shoddy special effects and practically no dialogue degrade the Transylvanian count and good doctor's names. Shot on location in Spain and Portugal, the film should really have been shot at dawn. Spanish dialogue dubbed into English.

Dennis Price *Dr Frankenstein* • Howard Vernon *Dracula* • Alberto Dalbes • Genevieve Deloir ■ *Dir/Scr* Jesus Franco

Dracula vs Frankenstein ★

Horror   1970 · US · Colour · 90mins

Director Al Adamson surely ranks alongside Ed Wood as one of the genre's true incompetents. This is arguably his crowning glory – a hilarious mix of bad music, teenage dopeheads, beach parties and unconvincing monsters. Horror veterans J Carrol Naish and Lon Chaney Jr (who both never made another film) look thoroughly embarrassed, while the plot is a complete shambles. Hardly surprising, since the movie started life as a biker film before being turned into a monster free-for-all. A must for all bad movie lovers.

J Carrol Naish *Dr Frankenstein* • Lon Chaney Jr *Groton, the Mad Zombie* • Regina Carrol *Judith* • John Bloom *The Monster* • Anthony Eisley *Mike Howard* • Russ Tamblyn *Rico* • Jim Davis *Sgt Martin* • Zandor Vorkov *Count Dracula* ■ *Dir* Al Adamson • *Scr* William Pugsley, Samuel M Sherman

Dracula's Daughter ★★★ PG

Horror   1936 · US · BW · 68mins

Edward Van Sloan's Von Helsing returns to face the undead once more in the neglected sequel to the 1931 *Dracula*, based on Bram Stoker's *Dracula's Guest*. As Countess Marya Zaleska, Gloria Holden became the first female vampire star, unforgettably stalking the streets looking for a cure for her nocturnal agitations. In another first for the genre, she looks for young model Marguerite Churchill with more than blood-sucking in mind. Moody and beautifully shot, this is saturated with an atmosphere of bleak hopelessness.

Otto Kruger *Dr Jeffrey Garth* • Gloria Holden *Countess Marya Zaleska* • Marguerite Churchill *Janet Blake* • Irving Pichel *Sandor* • Edward Van Sloan *Dr Von Helsing* • Nan Grey *Lili* • Hedda Hopper *Lady Esme Hammond* ■ *Dir* Lambert Hillyer • *Scr* Garrett Fort, from a story by John Balderston, Oliver Jeffries [David O Selznick], from the short story *Dracula's Guest* by Bram Stoker • *Cinematographer* George Robinson

Dracula's Widow ★ 18

Horror   1988 · US · Colour · 81mins

Emmanuelle star Sylvia Kristel makes a poor and remarkably unsexy vampire in an anaemic addition to the undead genre from director Christopher Coppola, Francis Ford's nephew. As "the true wife of Dracula", Kristel arrives in Hollywood and takes up residence in a wax museum, whose owner (Lenny Von Dohlen) she enslaves. Transforming into an ugly monster and a laughably mechanical

bat, Kristel slaughters a devil cult and seeks out a descendant of her husband's nemesis, Von Helsing. Done with little wit, style or imagination, this gore bore is a pathetic wash-out.

Sylvia Kristel *Vanessa* • Josef Sommer *Lieutenant Lannon* • Lenny Von Dohlen *Raymond Everett* • Marc Coppola *Brad* • Stefan Schnabel *Von Helsing* • Rachel Jones *Jenny* ■ *Dir* Christopher Coppola • *Scr* Kathryn Ann Thomas, Christopher Coppola

Drag ★★

Comedy   1929 · US · BW · 118mins

Richard Barthelmess, the publisher of a local Vermont newspaper, marries Alice Day, despite his attraction to socialite Lila Lee. His wife is inseparable from her parents, however, which causes friction in their relationship. Directed by Frank Lloyd (*Cavalcade*, *Mutiny on the Bounty*), this unexceptional romantic comedy is a good example of its type, with a plot typical of both the period and the genre.

Richard Barthelmess *David Carroll* • Lucien Littlefield *Pa Parker* • Alice Day *Allie Parker* • Katherine Ward *Ma Parker* • Tom Dugan *Charlie Parker* • Lila Lee *Dot* ■ *Dir* Frank Lloyd • *Scr* Bradley King, Gene Towne, from the novel by William Dudley Pelley

The Dragnet ★★★★

Silent crime drama   1928 · US · BW

A marvellous crime drama, directed at a cracking pace by Josef von Sternberg, this features superb performances from George Bancroft, as a cruelly duped chief of detectives, and lovely Evelyn Brent, who leaves slimy gang boss William Powell for the dogged Bancroft. Based on an Oliver HP Garrett tale, the terse screenplay was partly the work of two men who would help shape the style of Hollywood storytelling over the next few decades – Jules Furthman (*Shanghai Express*, *The Big Sleep*) and Herman J Mankiewicz (*Citizen Kane*). The superb camerawork is by the great Harold Rosson (*On the Town*, *Singin' in the Rain*).

George Bancroft *Two-Gun Nolan* • Evelyn Brent *The Magpie* • William Powell *Dapper Frank Trent* • Fred Kohler *"Gabby" Steve* • Francis McDonald *Sniper Dawson* • Leslie Fenton *Shakespeare* ■ *Dir* Josef von Sternberg • *Scr* Jules Furthman, Charles Furthman, Herman J Mankiewicz (titles), from the story *Nightstick* by Oliver HP Garrett • *Editor* Helen Lewis

Dragnet ★★★ PG

Police drama   1954 · US · Colour · 88mins

This spin-off from the famous American radio and TV series finds Jack Webb directing himself as Sergeant Joe Friday of the LAPD. The main problem with TV spin-offs is what works at 30 minutes doesn't always work at three times the length. This is certainly true of *Dragnet*, with its emphasis on police procedure making it look like a "How to Be a Detective" recruitment film. Nevertheless, it offers a nostalgic look at the days before *Dirty Harry* and *The French Connection* came along. Webb directed another version for TV in 1969.

Jack Webb *Sergeant Joe Friday* • Ben Alexander *Officer Frank Smith* • Richard Boone *Captain Hamilton* • Ann Robinson *Grace*

Downey • Stacy Harris *Max Troy* • Virginia Gregg *Ethel Marie Starkie* • Victor Perrin *Adolph Alexander* • Georgia Ellis *Belle Davitt* ■ *Dir* Jack Webb • *Scr* Richard L Breen

Dragnet ★★ PG

Spoof police drama   1987 · US · Colour · 101mins

It's a trawl through the comic depths for this parody of Jack Webb's fifties TV series. Dan Aykroyd is the deadpan nephew of Webb's Sergeant Joe Friday, lumbered with an amoral, dishevelled partner in Tom Hanks and battling with porn king Dabney Coleman and satanist Christopher Plummer. A virgin sacrifice is the least of it and, as far as laughs are concerned, the most of it, despite the talents of Aykroyd and Hanks and the efforts of director Tom Mankiewicz, who made his name as a scriptwriter on three Bond movies in the early seventies. Contains swearing.

Dan Aykroyd *Det Sgt Joe Friday* • Tom Hanks *Pep Streebek* • Christopher Plummer *Rev Jonathan Whirley* • Harry Morgan *Captain Bill Gannon* • Alexandra Paul *Connie Swail* • Jack O'Halloran *Emil Muzz* • Dabney Coleman *Jerry Caesar* • Bruce Gray *Mayor Parvin* ■ *Dir* Tom Mankiewicz • *Scr* Dan Aykroyd, Alan Zweibel, Tom Mankiewicz

Dragon Seed ★★

War drama   1944 · US · BW · 147mins

This MGM version of life in China during the 1937 Japanese invasion couldn't have been more wierdly cast if they'd put all the studio contract players' names in a hat and just shaken them out. But if you can believe a slant-eyed, Bryn Mawr-accented Katharine Hepburn, you'll probably accept her extended family of Walter Huston, Akim Tamiroff and Aline MacMahon – though Henry Travers, Turhan Bey, Hurd Hatfield (his movie debut) and Agnes Moorehead are all very difficult to take seriously as Chinese. The last credit of MGM's great contract director Jack Conway, this is one of Hollywood's most misconceived movies. And boy, is it long!

Katharine Hepburn *Jade* • Walter Huston *Ling Tan* • Aline MacMahon *Mrs Ling Tan* • Akim Tamiroff *Wu Lien* • Turhan Bey *Lao Er* • Hurd Hatfield *Lao San* • Frances Rafferty *Orchid* • Agnes Moorehead *3rd cousin's wife* • Lionel Barrymore *Narrator* ■ *Dir* Jack Conway, Harold S Bucquet • *Scr* Marguerite Roberts, Jane Murfin, from the novel by Peal S Buck • *Producer* Pandro S Berman

Dragon: the Bruce Lee Story ★★★★ 15

Biography   1993 · US · Colour · 119mins

Adapted from the book by Lee's wife, Linda Lee Cadwell (played in the film by Lauren Holly), this is a curious mix of traditional Hollywood biography and Hong Kong ghost story. Jason Scott Lee (no relation) captures Bruce's exuberance and finesse with considerable skill, particularly impressing in the scenes re-created from such films as *Fists of Fury* and *Enter the Dragon*. Directed with panache by Rob Cohen, the rags-to-riches tale, which sees Lee rise from street kid to martial-arts master, is pretty standard stuff. Yet what's so fascinating is the insight into the

private torment that the film suggests led to Lee's death. Contains swearing, violence and sex scenes. DVD

Jason Scott Lee *Bruce Lee* • Lauren Holly *Linda Lee* • Robert Wagner *Bill Krieger* • Michael Learned *Vivian Emery* • Nancy Kwan *Gussie Yang* • Ric Young *Bruce's father* • Wang Luoyong *Yip man* • Sterling Macer *Jerome Sprout* ■ *Dir* Rob Cohen • *Scr* Edward Khmara, John Raffo, Rob Cohen, from the non-fiction book *Bruce Lee: The Man Only I Knew* by Linda Lee Cadwell

Dragonard ★ 18

Period drama   1987 · US · Colour · 85mins

Part bodice ripper, part slave drama, this 18th-century tale is a tough movie to figure out. On a British island in the Carribean, the governor is killed the same night his daughter seduces a slave. The slave is accused of murder; when he can't be found, new governor Shanks (Oliver Reed, even more over-the-top than usual) begins torturing the island's black population. Every now and then a rape scene is thrown in, just to make this disgusting display more intolerable.

Oliver Reed *Captain Shanks* • Eartha Kitt *Naomi* • Annabel Schofield *Honore* • Claudia Udy *Arabella* • Patrick Warburton *Richard Abdee* • Drummond Marais *Pierre* • Dennis Folbigge *Governor* ■ *Dir* Gérard Kikoine • *Scr* Peter Welbeck [Harry Alan Towers], Rick Marx, from a novel by Rupert Gilchrist

DragonHeart ★★★ PG

Fantasy adventure   1996 · US · Colour · 98mins

Over the years, Sean Connery has played a Turkish warrior, an Irish cop, a Russian submarine commander and 007 – all with the same Scottish accent. Here he lends his distinctive burr to Draco, a 10th-century dragon who joins forces with an itinerant knight (Dennis Quaid). The result is a likeable, if a tad over-eager mix of derring-do and special effects, which has everything from wicked kings and poetic monks to romantic encounters and revolting peasants. Quaid gives a rousing performance, while Pete Postlethwaite is charmingly awkward as the religious wayfarer with a penchant for rhyming couplets. As the dastardly despot, however, David Thewlis belongs in a pantomime. DVD

Dennis Quaid *Bowen* • David Thewlis *Einon* • Pete Postlethwaite *Gilbert* • Dina Meyer *Kara* • Jason Isaacs *Felton* • Brian Thompson *Brok* • Sean Connery *Draco* • Lee Oakes *Young Einon* • Julie Christie *Aislinn* • John Gielgud *King Arthur* ■ *Dir* Rob Cohen • *Scr* Charles Edward Pogue, from a story by Patrick Read Johnson, Charles Edward Pogue

Dragonslayer ★★★ PG

Fantasy adventure   1981 · US · Colour · 104mins

The early eighties brought a rash of fantasy adventures, ranging from the camp fun of *Conan the Barbarian* to such dire examples as *The Sword and the Sorcerer*. This film, which follows a magician's assistant on his quest to kill a dragon, is aimed more at a family audience, though it's not without its violent moments, and it benefits from a good cast that includes Ralph Richardson and John Hallam. The effects aren't bad either. Contains violence.

Peter MacNicol *Galen* • Caitlin Clarke *Valerian* • Ralph Richardson *Ulrich* • John Hallam *Tyrian* • Peter Eyre *Casiodorus* • Albert Salmi *Greil* • Chloe Salaman *Princess Elspeth* • Roger Kemp *Horsrik* ■ *Dir* Matthew Robbins • *Scr* Hal Barwood, Matthew Robbins

Dragonworld ★★ U

Fantasy   1994 · US · Colour · 82mins

Although executive producer Charles Band remains a cult horror icon for bringing such cult classics as *Re-Animator* and *Trancers* to the screen, the nineties found him delving rather bizarrely into the children's market. Although the setting looks suspiciously like the eastern European castle Band used for his more adult horrors, this is a charming if slight tale of a young boy's friendship with a gentle baby dragon, which is threatened by a ruthless Scottish developer. The effects aren't up too much, but it is a curiously innocent affair, and John Woodvine and Andrew Keir (*Rob Roy*) add a bit of class.

Sam Mackenzie *John McGowan* • Brittney Powell *Beth Armstrong* • John Calvin *Bob Armstrong* • Courtland Mead *Young Johnny McGowan* • Lila Kaye *Mrs Cosgrove* • John Woodvine *Lester MacIntyre* • Andrew Keir *Angus McGowan* ■ *Dir* Ted Nicolaou • *Scr* Suzanne Glazener Naha, Ted Nicolaou, from a story by Charles Band

Dragonworld: the Legend Continues ★★

Fantasy   1997 · US · Colour

Andrew Keir reprises his role as the kindly Scotsman versed in the lore of ancient magic in this sword-and-sorcery TV sequel to 1994's *Dragonworld*. When he is struck down by the dastardly dark knight McClain, who plans to use the blood of Yowler, the world's last dragon, to bring about a reign of terror and tyranny, it's up to Keir's grandson, played by Drake Bell, to try and save the day. While it's less imaginative than the original, its passable effects and classic good-versus-evil showdown should keep pre-teens amused.

Andrew Keir *Angus* • Tina Martin *Mrs Cosgrove* • Judith Paris *Mrs Churchill* • Richard Trask *Yowler* • Drake Bell *Johnny* ■ *Dir/Scr* Ted Nicolaou

Dragonwyck ★★

Gothic melodrama   1946 · US · BW · 102mins

This preposterous old tosh, a sort of Manderley-on-the-Hudson, marked distinguished film-maker Joseph L Mankiewicz's directorial debut. He does well by the material, but the casting leaves a lot to be desired. Top-billed Gene Tierney is a lovely governess, but Vincent Price hams quite extraordinarily as a sadistic master of the estate, while Glenn Langan is truly hopeless as the local doctor. Of course, there's a great deal of pleasure to be had from watching these ludicrous performances on phoney sets, but you can't escape the feeling that it was originally meant to be taken seriously.

Gene Tierney *Miranda Wells* • Walter Huston *Ephraim Wells* • Vincent Price *Nicholas Van Ryn* • Glenn Langan *Dr Jeff Turner* • Anne Revere *Abigail Wells* • Spring Byington *Magda* ■ *Dir* Joseph L Mankiewicz • *Scr* Joseph L Mankiewicz, from the novel by Anya Seton

Dragoon Wells Massacre ★★ PG

Western   1957 · US · Colour · 82mins

This brisk, good-looking western that benefits greatly from CinemaScope and the camerawork of William Clothier, who also shot *The Alamo* and *Cheyenne Autumn*. The plot is routine, but Barry Sullivan and *High Noon's* Katy Jurado make the most of their roles. He's a killer, she's a hooker; they are forced to join together to protect themselves from marauding Apaches. Co-stars Dennis O'Keefe and Mona Freeman, both well past their prime, are less than interesting.

Barry Sullivan *Link Ferris* • Dennis O'Keefe *Captain Matt Riordan* • Mona Freeman *Ann Bradley* • Katy Jurado *Mara Fay* • Jack Elam *Tioga* • Sebastian Cabot *Jonah* • Casey Adams [Max Showalter] *Phillip Scott* • Trevor Bardette *Marshal Bill Haney* ■ *Dir* Harold Schuster • *Scr* Warren Douglas, from a story by Oliver Drake

Dragstrip Girl ★

Drama   1957 · US · BW · 69mins

Only the smouldering presence of fifties cult sexpot Fay Spain in the title role makes this AIP cheapie at all watchable. Spain showed better form in higher-budgeted movies such as *Al Capone* (opposite Rod Steiger) and *God's Little Acre* (supporting Robert Ryan and Aldo Ray), but she did not achieve lasting fame. Here she transcends the material in this banal teen flick about hot-rod racing.

Fay Spain *Louise Blake* • Steven Terrell *Jim Donaldson* • John Ashley *Fred Armstrong* • Tommy Ivo *Rick Camden* • Frank Gorshin *Tommy* • Judy Bamber *Rhoda, the blonde* ■ *Dir* Edward L Cahn • *Scr* Lou Rusoff

Dragstrip Girl ★★ 15

Drama   1994 · US · Colour · 79mins

One of the weaker entries in the series of films made under *The Young and the Reckless* banner, this would struggle to gain a parking space at a drive-in. Natasha Gregson Wagner, stepdaughter of Robert Wagner and daughter of Natalie Wood, is the nice young Roman Catholic girl who falls for bad boy Mark Dacascos, who divides his time between drag racing and car theft. Throw in a disabled younger brother and a prostitute with a heart of gold (former porn star Traci Lords), and all the elements of a ripe teen melodrama are present and correct. However, Mary Lambert's direction is plodding, there is precious little racing action and it lacks the knowing humour of others in the series. Contains swearing and sex scenes.

Mark Dacascos *Johnny Ramirez* • Natasha Gregson Wagner *Laura Bickford* • Raymond Cruz *Doogie* • Augusto Cesar Sandino *Anthony* • Traci Lords *Blanche* • Frederick Coffin *Mr Bickford* • Carolyn Mignini *Mrs Bickford* ■ *Dir* Mary Lambert • *Scr* Jerome Gary

Dramatic School ★★★ U

Drama   1938 · US · BW · 80mins

Luise Rainer, a fragile and hard-to-cast talent, made precious few movies after her back-to-back best actress Oscars for *The Great Ziegfeld* (1936) and *The Good Earth* (1937). In all of them, however, she was superb. In this MGM drama reminiscent of the popular *Stage Door*, a big hit for RKO, her co-stars are the up-and-coming Lana Turner and the lovely Paulette Goddard – but it's Rainer's movie through and through. Look out for such future notables as Ann Rutherford and Dick Haymes.

Luise Rainer *Louise* • Paulette Goddard *Nana* • Lana Turner *Mado* • Alan Marshal *Andre D'Abbencourt* • Anthony Allan [John Hubbard] *Fleury* • Henry Stephenson *Pasquel Sr* • Genevieve Tobin *Gina Bertier* • Gale Sondergaard *Madame Charlot* • Ann Rutherford *Yvonne* • Margaret Dumont *Teacher* • Dick Haymes *Student* ■ *Dir* Robert B Sinclair • *Scr* Ernst Vadja, Mary C McCall Jr, from the play *School of Drama* by Hans Szekely, Zoltan Egyed

Drango ★★ U

Western drama   1957 · US · Colour · 92mins

Jeff Chandler is Drango, a Union officer who faces considerable hostility when he takes charge of a small town in Georgia in the aftermath of the Civil War. The issues are poorly developed, and writer/producer Hall Bartlett rather awkwardly shares the direction with Jules Bricken. But Joanne Dru and Julie London make forceful leading ladies, and there's a surprising but effective appearance from British actor Ronald Howard as a vicious, revenge-seeking Southerner.

Jeff Chandler *Drango* • John Lupton *Marc* • Joanne Dru *Kate* • Morris Ankrum *Calder* • Julie London *Shelby* • Donald Crisp *Allen* • Ronald Howard *Clay* ■ *Dir* Hall Bartlett, Jules Bricken • *Scr* Hall Bartlett

The Draughtsman's Contract ★★★★★ 15

Period drama   1982 · UK · Colour · 103mins

As an introduction to a unique personal vision, director Peter Greenaway's first commercially released feature film is a calling card of dazzling virtuosity. A 17th-century draughtsman (Anthony Higgins) is hired to make 12 drawings of a country estate, and is paid in sexual favours by the landowner's wife and daughter (Janet Suzman and Anne Louise Lambert). The possibility of his drawings being an artistic witness to murder is deftly, tantalisingly displayed and his ultimate downfall from arrogant posturing is a lesson in class-distinction, only to be expected from the aristocratic world he's tried to enter. Clever, witty and with obsessively minimalist music by Michael Nyman to reinforce the remarkable visuals, this has the growing momentum of a ground-breaking debut.

Anthony Higgins *Mr Neville* • Janet Suzman *Mrs Herbert* • Anne Louise Lambert *Mrs Talmann* • Neil Cunningham *Mr Noyes* • Hugh Fraser *Mr Talmann* • Dave Hill *Mr Herbert* ■ *Dir/Scr* Peter Greenaway

Draw! ★★ 15

Western   1984 · US · Colour · 93mins

One of the first movies made directly for cable TV with big stars, this is a decidedly substandard western, despite the ever-dynamic screen presences of veterans Kirk Douglas and James Coburn. Alas, here they are undirected, overacting and stretching thin material to breaking point. Douglas and Coburn play an aged outlaw and an alcoholic lawman respectively who line up for one last shootout. The casting might have actually worked better with the roles reversed.

Kirk Douglas *Harry H Holland* • James Coburn *Sam Starret* • Alexandra Bastedo *Bess* • Graham Jarvis *Wally Blodgett* • Derek McGrath *Reggie Bell* • Jason Michas *Moses* • Len Birman *Ephraim* • Maurice Brand *Mr Gibson* ■ *Dir* Steven Hilliard Stern • *Scr* Stanley Mann

Dream a Little Dream ★ 15

Comedy drama   1989 · US · Colour · 110mins

Yet another body-swap movie with nothing new to offer. Here Jason Robards ends up in the body of spotty 16-year-old Corey Feldman after the latter crashes into his meditation session on a bicycle. The problem is that Feldman is utterly incapable of acting like an elderly man in a youngster's body, thus defeating the entire premise of the film. Robards, Piper Laurie and Harry Dean Stanton must still be hanging their heads in shame. (What were they thinking?) For some unknown reason, a sequel followed six years later.

Corey Feldman *Bobby Keller* • Corey Haim *Dinger* • Jason Robards *Jason Robards Jr]* • Coleman Ettinger • Piper Laurie *Gena Ettinger* • Harry Dean Stanton *Ike Baker* • Meredith Salenger *Lainie Diamond* ■ *Dir* Marc Rocco • *Scr* Daniel Jay Franklin, Marc Rocco, DE Eisenberg, from a story by Daniel Jay Franklin

Dream Breakers ★★ 15

Drama   1989 · US · Colour · 90mins

This undistinguished drama of family conflict flounders on a plot lacking imagination. *Twin Peaks* star Kyle MacLachlan does his utmost to lift this story of a Harvard graduate (DW Moffett) who finds himself in conflict with his younger brother, a priest (MacLachlan) when he takes a job with his father's business rival. Robert Loggia (the private eye in *Jagged Edge* and the toy company boss in *Big*), is the most watchable member of the cast. It's a shame that this could not have been a better showcase for his talents.

Robert Loggia *Joseph O'Connor* • Kyle MacLachlan *Father Bobby O'Connor* • DW Moffett *Mark O'Connor* • Charles Cioffi *John Sloan* • Laila Robins *Phoebe* • John McIntire *Cardinal Angelo* ■ *Dir* Stuart Miller • *Scr* Stuart Millar, Victor Levin

Dream Date ★

Comedy   1989 · US · Colour · 96mins

Tempestt Bledsoe (*The Cosby Show*) is the teenager going on her first date, only to be spied on by her overprotective father in a mindless teen movie, which lacks both originality and entertainment value. Director Anson Williams should know better – after all, he did appear as "Potsie" in *Happy Days*, one of the best teenage comedy series made for US TV.

Tempestt Bledsoe *Dani Fairview* • Clifton Davis *Bill Fairview* • Anne-Marie Johnson *Donna Thompson* • Kadeem Hardison *Jim*

Parker • Michelle Thomas *Sally Palmer* • Howard French *Mike* • Michael Prokopuk *TJ* ■ *Dir* Anson Williams • *Scr* Peter Crabbe, from a story by Mark C Miller

Dream Demon ★★ 18
Fantasy thriller 1988 · UK · Colour · 85mins

This tragic British answer to Freddy Krueger – ''A Nightmare on Sloane Street'' – is about as scary as a trip to Harvey Nichols. Jemma Redgrave is the upper-class socialite hunted by the press and suffering dream premonitions after her friends dying. Directed by Harley Cokliss, this plummy Wes Craven photocopy teeters between the ridiculous (champagne for elevenses!), the bewildering (Jimmy Nail and Timothy Spall as vicious tabloid journalists) and the irritating (Kathleen Wilhoite as the heroine's kooky best friend). A pointless terror exercise with awful performances that kill the lame premise of Hooray Henry horror stone dead. ▭

Jemma Redgrave *Diana Markham* • Kathleen Wilhoite *Jenny Hoffman* • Timothy Spall *Peck* • Jimmy Nail *Paul* • Mark Greenstreet *Oliver* • Susan Fleetwood *Deborah* • Annabelle Lanyon *Little Jenny* • Nickolas Grace *Jenny's father* ■ *Dir* Harley Cokliss • *Scr* Harley Cokliss, Christopher Wicking

Dream Flights ★★★
Drama 1983 · USSR · Colour · 90mins

Although he regularly collaborated with Andrei Tarkovsky, Oleg Yankovsky gives his most electrifying performance in this finely judged tragicomedy from Roman Balayan. As a 40-year-old charmer with an underdeveloped sense of responsibility, he is forced to re-evaluate his priorities when his adulterous private life and directionless career begin to collapse around him. The result is a fascinating study of Soviet socio-sexual mores, with the response of Yankovsky's comrades to his antics being almost as revealing as his infuriatingly attractive mix of idiocy and iconoclasm, which eventually gives way to a painful vulnerability and deep-seated misery. In Russian with English subtitles.

Oleg Yankovsky *Sergei Makarov* • Liudmila Gurchenko *Larisa* • Oleg Tabakov *Nikolai ''Kolya'' Pavlovich* • Liudmila Ivanova *Nina Sergeyevna* • Liudmila Zorina *Natasha Makarov* • Elena Kostina *Alisa* • Oleg Menshikov *Alisa's friend* ■ *Dir* Roman Balayan • *Scr* Viktor Merezhko

Dream for an Insomniac ★★★ 15
Romantic comedy
1996 · US · BW and Colour · 83mins

Ione Skye is the sleep-disordered romantic who, with best friend Jennifer Aniston, is determined to make it big in Hollywood. But her life gets complicated by the arrival of hunky kindred spirit MacKenzie Astin, who has a girlfriend. She moves to LA, sure that he will dump the girl and follow her. Filmed in a mixture of black and white and colour, this has enough good lines to keep you smiling and the young cast members deliver attractive performances. Contains some swearing and sexual references. ▭

Ione Skye *Frankie* • Jennifer Aniston *Allison* • MacKenzie Astin *David Schrader* • Michael

Landes *Rob* • Robert Kelker-Kelly *Trent* • Seymour Cassel *Uncle Leo* • Sean San Jose Blackman *Juice* • Michael Sterk *B J* • Leslie Stevens *Molly* ■ *Dir/Scr* Tiffanie DeBartolo

Dream Girl ★★
Comedy 1948 · US · BW · 85mins

Elmer Rice's Broadway satire, a vehicle for his wife Betty Field, is turned into a fun-fest for Paramount's reigning laff queen Betty Hutton. She hams every line and milks every gag as a daydreamer who imagines she's an understudy to an opera star or a broken-hearted whore. Hutton was immensely popular in the forties, and two films later was perfectly cast as Annie Oakley, but as a distaff version of *The Secret Life of Walter Mitty* this just doesn't cut it. It's sad to find Mitchell Leisen (*The Lady in the Dark*) helming this lowbrow romp.

Betty Hutton *Georgina Allerton* • Macdonald Carey *Clark Redfield* • Patric Knowles *Jim Lucas* • Virginia Field *Miriam Allerton Lucas* • Walter Abel *George Allerton* • Peggy Wood *Lucy Allerton* • Carolyn Butler *Claire* • Lowell Gilmore *George Hand* ■ *Dir* Mitchell Leisen • *Scr* Arthur Sheekman, from the play by Elmer Rice • *Music* Victor Young

The Dream Life of Angels ★★★★ 18
Drama 1998 · Fr · Colour · 108mins

Elodie Bouchez and Natacha Régnier shared the best actress prize at Cannes for their work in Erick Zonca's painfully realistic debut. Bouchez particularly impresses as the optimistic drifter whose creativity and resourcefulness see her through the daily crises that consistently floor her cynical new friend, who has become morbidly dependent on a doomed love affair with a rich man. Although prone to disconcerting moments of melodrama, this is still a provocative study of the dislocation and isolation experienced by so many seeking their niche in the world. Moreover, there's a hint of Michelangelo Antonioni in the way Zonca combines unsentimental social comment with subtle characterisation and an assured sense of place. In French with English subtitles. Contains sex scenes. ▭

Elodie Bouchez *Isa* • Natacha Régnier *Marie* • Grégoire Colin *Chriss* • Patrick Mercado *Charly* • Jo Prestia *Fredo* • Francine Massenhave *Attendant* • Zivko Niklevski *Yugoslav patron* ■ *Dir* Erick Zonca • *Scr* Erick Zonca, Roger Bohbot, Virginie Wagon, Pierre Schoeller, Frederic Carpentier, Pierre Chosson, Jean-Daniel Magnin

Dream Lover ★ 15
Psychological thriller
1986 · US · Colour · 99mins

This dreadful mess of a movie purports to explore the repercussions of extensive ''dream therapy'' on a young girl desperate to rid herself of a recurring nightmare. A highly professional cast does its best to pick its way through a minefield of psychobabble and histrionics. Directed by Alan J Pakula with a leaden hand and somnambulistic air, this is one movie without any redeeming features whatsoever. Contains violence, swearing and nudity. ▭

Kristy McNichol *Kathy Gardner* • Ben Masters *Michael Hansen* • Paul Shenar *Ben Gardner* • Justin Deas *Kevin McCann* • John McMartin *Martin* • Gayle Hunnicutt *Claire* ■ *Dir* Alan J Pakula • *Scr* Jon Boorstin

Dream Lover ★★ 18
Thriller 1993 · US · Colour · 99mins

Successful architect James Spader meets the woman of his dreams (*Twin Peaks* star Mädchen Amick) and, after a whirlwind romance, they get married. But slowly (very slowly!) he begins to wonder about her real motives in director Nicholas Kazan's low-key suspense thriller. While Kazan has fun setting up the stock situations and spinning plot threads off in surprising directions, this lethargically paced drama comes off as part *Suspicion*, part *Body Heat* – without the stylish flair of either. Spader and Amick do their best with the half-baked material, but it's only mildly interesting at best, despite the neat twist ending. Contains violence, swearing, sex scenes and nudity. ▭

James Spader *Ray Reardon* • Mädchen Amick *Lena Reardon* • Bess Armstrong *Elaine* • Fredrick Lehne [Fredric Lehne] *Larry* • Larry Miller *Norman* • Kathleen York *Martha* • Kate Williamson *Mrs Sneeder* ■ *Dir/Scr* Nicholas Kazan

The Dream Machine ★★ PG
Action comedy 1990 · US · Colour · 82mins

One of those rarities – a Corey Haim movie without a starring role for his chum Corey Feldman. Not that it marks any great improvement in quality, with Haim reprising his cheeky charmer persona to outwit bumbling grown-ups. Here he plays a student who rather implausibly is presented with the car of his dreams, only to discover that the previous owner is dead in the boot and that the killer wants the body back. With a cast of unknowns, this rests on the leading man's charisma. If you're not a fan now, this won't win you over. Contains violence and swearing. ▭

Corey Haim *Barry Davis* • Evan Richards *Meese* • Jeremy Slate *Mr Chamberlain* • Susan Seaforth Hayes *Margo Chamberlain* • Randall England *Lance* • Susan Kent *Jean Davis* • James MacKrell *Claude Davis* ■ *Dir* Lyman Dayton • *Scr* Eric Hendershot

Dream Man ★ 18
Erotic thriller 1995 · US · Colour · 90mins

Faced with career doldrums or typecasting, performers are liable to make the most ill-advised choices in their bid to break the mould. That's exactly what Patsy Kensit did with this far-fetched crime flick, in which she plays a detective who allows love to cloud her usually unerring psychic powers. Brat Packer Andrew McCarthy, who has struggled to find his niche since the eighties, co-stars as the playboy the amorous Kensit hopes didn't kill his wife. Miscast and even more badly scripted, this TV movie was injected with a little raunch and violence in a bid to lure a late-night audience. Contains violence, swearing and some sex scenes. ▭

Patsy Kensit *Kris Anderson* • Andrew McCarthy • Bruce Greenwood • Denise Crosby • Armin Shimerman ■ *Dir* René Bonnière • *Scr* Michael Alexander Miller

A Dream of Kings ★★★
Drama 1969 · US · Colour · 110mins

Anthony Quinn transfers his ''Zorba the Greek'' persona to urban Chicago in this powerful portrayal of a Graeco-American paterfamilias. It's a neglected, marvellous, warm-hearted movie that works brilliantly – unless, of course, you're one of the many who has developed an aversion to Quinn's salt-of-the-earth, all-purpose ethnic mensch. Here he's exceptionally fine as the gambler-philosopher trying to raise the money to send his dying son to Greece, in a faithful dramatisation of Harry Mark Petrakis's novel. Irene Papas is well cast as Quinn's wife, but tragic beauty Inger Stevens steals the film as the young widow Quinn has an affair with. It's a beautifully observed movie, excellently directed by Daniel Mann, and it wears its emotional heart on its sleeve.

Anthony Quinn *Matsoukas* • Irene Papas *Caliope* • Inger Stevens *Anna* • Sam Levene *Cicero* • Val Avery *Fatsas* • Tamara Daykarhanova *Mother-in-law* • Peter Mamakos *Falconis* • Alan Reed Sr [Alan Reed] *Fig King* • Radames Pera *Stavros* ■ *Dir* Daniel Mann • *Scr* Harry Mark Petrakis, Ian Hunter, from the novel by Harry Mark Petrakis

A Dream of Passion ★ 18
Drama 1978 · Gr · Colour · 101mins

A thick pall of pretension hangs over this rancid cocktail of Greek myth and arthouse angst. Who director Jules Dassin hoped to fool with this artifice is anyone's guess, but he clearly saw it as a worthy showcase for the tub-thumping talents of his wife, Melina Mercouri. She gnaws her way through the scenery with a voracious appetite as the Greek actress who sees Ellen Burstyn's murderous American mother as the perfect publicity ruse for her new production of *Medea*. So far so ghastly. But once the women begin to merge emotionally *à la* Ingmar Bergman's *Persona*, the entire edifice comes tumbling down. An English/Greek language film. ▭

Melina Mercouri *Maya* • Ellen Burstyn *Brenda* • Andreas Voutsinas *Kostas* • Despo Diamantidou *Maria* • Dimitris Papamichael *Dimitris/Jason* • Yannis Voglis *Edward* ■ *Dir* Jules Dassin • *Scr* Jules Dassin, from the play *Medea* by Euripides

Dream Street ★★
Silent drama 1921 · US · BW · 102mins

A heavily melodramatic outing from the great silent movie maestro DW Griffith, who actually wrote his own pseudonymous screenplay for this sub-*Broken Blossoms* tale. It's inspired by two *Limehouse Nights* short stories by *Blossoms* author Thomas Burke. The result is uncomfortably racist and shows few signs of Griffith's undoubted picture-making genius, as dancer Carol Dempster inadequately serves as an obsessive sex object, whose very existence causes death, mayhem and destruction. Dempster referred to only as Gypsy Fair, is placed on a cinematic pedestal, all the Chinese are wily and there's some rather unacceptable blacking-up comedy. Overlong and stilted it may be, but it's not without a certain watchability.

Carol Dempster *Gypsy Fair* • Ralph Graves James "Spike" McFadden • Charles Emmett Mack *Billy McFadden* • Edward Peil [Edward Peil Sr] *Swan Way* • WJ Ferguson *Gypsy's father* • Porter Strong *Samuel Jones* ■ *Dir* DW Griffith • *Scr* Roy Sinclair [DW Griffith], from the short stories *Gina of the Chinatown* and *The Sign of the Lamp* by Thomas Burke

The Dream Team ★★★★ 15

Comedy 1989 · US · Colour · 107mins

This light-hearted spin on *One Flew over the Cuckoo's Nest* has a group of inmates from a psychiatric hospital slipping the leash while on a day trip to New York. For Michael Keaton, in the year he became a superstar in *Batman*, the role offered the chance to return to what he does best – the silver-tongued, loveable rogue. He also benefits from a gallery of accomplished supporting players, most notably an anally retentive Christopher Lloyd and Peter Boyle as the reformed advertising executive with a Christ complex. Director Howard Zieff makes an occasional attempt at seriousness, but, for the most part, keeps the laughs flowing smoothly. Contains swearing, violence and brief nudity. 🖵

Michael Keaton *Billy Caulfield* • Christopher Lloyd *Henry Sikorsky* • Peter Boyle *Jack McDermott* • Stephen Furst *Albert Ianuzzi* • Dennis Boutsikaris *Dr Weitzman* • Lorraine Bracco *Riley* • Milo O'Shea *Dr Newald* • Philip Bosco *O'Malley* ■ *Dir* Howard Zieff • *Scr* Jon Connolly, David Loucka

Dream Wife ★★ U

Comedy 1953 · US · BW · 98mins

Cary Grant and Deborah Kerr dull? Well, they certainly are in this feeble slapstick concoction, a rare excursion into directing from screenwriter Sidney Sheldon. Grant's engaged to Kerr but falls for dusky Betta St John, who has been trained to please men. Other worthies wasted in this nonsense are Walter Pidgeon, Gloria Holden and Steve Forrest. Grant and Kerr teamed up again to far better effect in *An Affair to Remember*, but Sidney Sheldon made an even more wretched film (*The Buster Keaton Story*) before becoming a novelist.

Cary Grant *Clemson Reade* • Deborah Kerr *Effie* • Walter Pidgeon *Walter McBride* • Betta St John *Tarji* • Eduard Franz *Khan* • Buddy Baer *Vizier* • Les Tremayne *Ken Landwell* • Gloria Holden *Mrs Landwell* • Steve Forrest *Louis* ■ *Dir* Sidney Sheldon • *Scr* Sidney Sheldon, Herbert Baker, Alfred Lewis Levitt, from a story by Alfred Lewis Levitt

Dream with the Fishes ★★★ 18

Black comedy drama
1996 · US · Colour · 92mins

Darkly melancholic, but also charmingly offbeat, Finn Taylor's directorial debut offers a moving study of loss and obsession. *Scream* star David Arquette, who also co-produced, plays a grieving, voyeuristic loner who gradually comes out of his shell when he gets mixed up with the dying Brad Hunt. Hunt is determined to live his final days to the full – which, in his case, means nude bowling, nude bank robbery and giving LSD to traffic policemen. All the performances are first-rate, and Taylor's vision is both

quirky and lyrical. Contains swearing, nudity and some violence. 🖵

David Arquette *Terry* • Brad Hunt *Nick* • Cathy Moriarty *Aunt Elise* • Kathryn Erbe *Liz* • Patrick McGaw *Don* • JE Freeman *Joe, Nick's father* • Timi Prulhiere *Michelle* • Anita Barone *Mary* ■ *Dir* Finn Taylor • *Scr* Finn Taylor, from a story by Jeffrey Brown, Finn Taylor

Dreamboat ★★★ U

Satirical comedy 1952 · US · BW · 83mins

This very funny satire on the early days of television was made when TV was a novelty newcomer and not yet a threat to cinemas. Ginger Rogers is delightful as a silent-movie queen who revives her popularity by presenting her old movies on TV, greatly annoying her former co-star Clifton Webb, now ensconced in "the groves of Academe". It was particularly topical in its day, as back then MGM was still holding out against showing its classics on TV and the best bits are the re-creations of the silent movies. Rogers and Webb are particularly fetching as their younger selves, while Elsa Lanchester is a joy as Webb's lustful superior.

Clifton Webb *Thornton Sayre* • Ginger Rogers *Gloria* • Anne Francis *Carol Sayre* • Jeffrey Hunter *Bill Ainslee* • Elsa Lanchester *Dr Coffey* • Fred Clark *Sam Levitt* • Paul Harvey *Harrington* ■ *Dir* Claude Binyon • *Scr* Claude Binyon, from a story by John D Weaver

Dreamchild ★★★ PG

Fantasy drama 1985 · UK · Colour · 94mins

A fascinating and imaginative, if seriously flawed exploration of the real-life person on whom the Reverend Charles Dodgson (aka Lewis Carroll) allegedly based his fictional character Alice. Coral Browne gives a deeply layered performance as the 80-year-old Alice Hargreaves, traumatised by her recollections of the famous relationship, while Dennis Potter's screenplay is typically taut and riveting. As sound as Potter is on main narrative, however, his approach to subplot is almost surreal. There are more red herrings here than in the North Sea, and Browne has a love interest that is rather unnecessary. A veritable curate's egg of a movie. 🖵

Coral Browne *Mrs Alice Hargreaves* • Ian Holm *Reverend Charles Dodgson* • Peter Gallagher *Jack Dolan* • Caris Corfman *Sally Mackeson* • Nicola Cowper *Lucy* • Jane Asher *Mrs Liddell* ■ *Dir* Gavin Millar • *Scr* Dennis Potter

Dreamer ★ PG

Drama 1979 · US · Colour · 86mins

One-dimensional actor Tim Matheson gets to show off his lack of acting skills once again in a sporting drama set around the heady world of bowling. One can only assume that the title of this yawnsome movie could also be used to describe director Noel Nosseck, who must have been in a comatose state when he decided this would make good entertainment. Contains swearing. 🖵

Tim Matheson *Dreamer* • Susan Blakely *Karen* • Jack Warden *Harry* • Richard B Shull *Taylor* • Barbara Stuart *Angie* • Owen Bush *Fan* • Marya Small *Elaine* ■ *Dir* Noel Nosseck • *Scr* James Proctor, Larry Bishoff

Dreaming ★★ U

Comedy 1944 · UK · BW · 78mins

Comedians Bud Flanagan and Chesney Allen from the Crazy Gang star in this gently naive comedy produced by Britain's Ealing Studios. It's about a soldier who gets a knock on his head and drifts into a dream world. The dreams feature appearances from music hall turns such as xylophonist Teddy Brown and violinist Alfredo Campoli, plus cameos from famous jockeys ordon Richards and Dick Francis (before he became a bestselling novelist) in an attempt to comfort wartime audiences.

Bud Flanagan [Dennis O'Keefe] *Bud* • Chesney Allen *Ches* • Hazel Court *Wren/Avalah/Miss Grey* • Dick Francis *Sir Charles Paddock* • Philip Wade *Dr Goebbels* • Gerry Wilmott *United States General* • Peter Bernard *American soldier* • Ian MacLean *General* • Gordon Richards ■ *Dir* John Baxter • *Scr* Bud Flanagan [Dennis O'Keefe], Reginald Purdell

Dreaming of Joseph Lees ★★ 12

Drama 1998 · US/UK · Colour · 88mins

Filmed on the Isle of Man, standing in for fifties Somerset, this rural melodrama is heavy going, despite some glowingly worthy performances. Eva (Samantha Morton) falls in love with geologist Joseph Lees (Rupert Graves), her cousin; when he takes off, she marries pig farmer Lee Ross. Then Lees returns, re-igniting passions that burn as fiercely as a barn fire. Eric Styles's direction is overwrought, while Catherine Linstrum's script is declamatory and stagey. Contains some violence, and sexual references. 🖵

Samantha Morton *Eva Babbins* • Rupert Graves *Joseph Lees* • Lee Ross *Harry Flite* • Miriam Margolyes *Signora Caldoni* • Frank Finlay *Eva's father* • Holly Aird *Maria Flite, Harry's sister* • Nicholas Woodeson *Mr Dian* ■ *Dir* Eric Styles • *Scr* Catherine Linstrum

Dreams ★★★

Drama 1955 · Swe · BW · 86mins

Sophisticated fashion photographer Susanne (Eva Dahlbeck) and jaunty model Doris (Harriet Andersson) go to Gothenberg where the former attempts to revive an affair with a married man (Ulf Palme), and the latter has a flirtation with a rich, retired diplomat (Gunnar Bjornstrand). The gap between illusion and reality in this film, written and directed by Ingmar Bergman, is reflected in the literal translation of the original Swedish title, *Women's Dreams*, while the casting of the lead actresses mirrors the shifting moods of the piece, alternately light-hearted and sombre. A Swedish language film.

Harriet Andersson *Doris* • Eva Dahlbeck *Susanne* • Gunnar Bjornstrand *The consul* • Ulf Palme *Henrik Lobelius* • Inga Landgre *Marta Lobelius* • Sven Lindberg *Palle* • Naima Wifstrand *Mrs Aren* • Benkt-Ake Benktsson *Magnus* ■ *Dir/Scr* Ingmar Bergman

Dreams of Gold: the Mel Fisher Story ★★★

Drama based on a true story
1986 · US · Colour · 95mins

A dramatisation of Mel Fisher's obsessive 17-year search for a

treasure-laden 17th-century galleon off the Florida coast, which threatened his family unity and led to a battle through the courts. This tale of doggedness and derring-do is yet another obvious metaphor for the pursuit of the American dream and, though inevitably episodic, it is handled with quiet efficiency. Cliff Robertson, a lobster trapper in his youth, looks particularly at home at sea, while Loretta Swit fits the bill as his wife.

Cliff Robertson *Mel Fisher* • Loretta Swit *Deo Fisher* • Ed O'Ross *Trooper Hudley* • Scott Paulin *Don Kincaid* • Jennifer Runyon *Angel Fisher* • Judi Evans *Penelope Cabot* • Bruce Toms *Kane Fisher* • Kerry Remsen *Taffi Fisher* • Jonathan Hogan *David Horan* ■ *Dir* James Goldstone • *Scr* Stanford Whitmore

Dreamscape ★★ 15

Science-fiction 1984 · US · Colour · 94mins

Psychic Dennis Quaid enters the American president's guilt-plagued nuclear nightmares to save him from a paranormal assassin in a workmanlike fantasy thriller directed (and co-written) by Joseph Ruben (director of *Sleeping with the Enemy*). The perfectly cast actors fly as high as they can with the intriguing concept, but the script is mediocre and lacks any real excitement. The real pleasure of this efficient piece of film-making comes from the dream sequences that punctuate the political thriller framework. These include a dose of sex comedy, a post-holocaust vision, an erotic interlude and, best of all, a no-holds-barred "Snake Man" nightmare. 🖵

Dennis Quaid *Alex Gardner* • Max von Sydow *Dr Paul Novotny* • Christopher Plummer *Bob Blair* • Eddie Albert *President* • Kate Capshaw *Dr Jane Devries* • David Patrick Kelly *Tommy Ray Glatman* • George Wendt *Charlie Prince* ■ *Dir* Joseph Ruben • *Scr* Joseph Ruben, David Loughery, Chuck Russell, from a story by David Loughery

Dressed to Kill ★★ U

Crime mystery 1946 · US · BW · 71mins

Basil Rathbone's final film as Sherlock Holmes, released in Britain as *Sherlock Holmes and the Secret Code*, is a muddled affair in which a trio of music boxes bought by an inmate at Dartmoor prison conceals a set of engraving plates stolen from the Bank of England. As the chief villain, Patricia Morison is no Moriarty. However, there is a notable contribution from Nigel Bruce, in his regular role as Dr Watson, which lightens the dour atmosphere. 🖵

Basil Rathbone *Sherlock Holmes* • Nigel Bruce *Dr Watson* • Patricia Morison *Hilda Courtney* • Edmond Breon [Edmund Breon] *Gilbert Emery* • Frederick Worlock *Colonel Cavanaugh* • Carl Harbord *Inspector Hopkins* ■ *Dir* Roy William Neill • *Scr* Leonard Lee, Frank Gruber, from a story by Sir Arthur Conan Doyle

Dressed to Kill ★★★★ 18

Thriller 1980 · US · Colour · 100mins

Brian De Palma does his witty Hitchcock imitation again and adds his own trademark layers of macabre black comedy and visual ingenuity to the *Psycho*-influenced proceedings. After sex-starved housewife Angie Dickinson is murdered with a razor in a lift, her son Keith Gordon and prostitute Nancy

U = SUITABLE FOR ALL   Uc = SUITABLE FOR ALL, ESPECIALLY FOR YOUNG CHILDREN (VIDEO ONLY)   PG = PARENTAL GUIDANCE

Allen (then the director's wife) join forces to track down the killer. An eyebrow-raising performance from Michael Caine keeps this clever shocker moving along nicely, as De Palma's brilliant sleight-of-hand direction pulls out all the suspense stops, providing some unforgettable jolts. Contains swearing, violence, sex scenes and nudity. ▭

Michael Caine *Dr Robert Elliott* • Angie Dickinson *Kate Miller* • Nancy Allen *Liz Blake* • Keith Gordon *Peter Miller* • Dennis Franz *Detective Marino* • David Margulies *Dr Levy* ■ *Dir/Scr* Brian De Palma • *Editor* Jerry Greenberg • *Music* Pino Donaggio

The Dresser ★★★★ PG
Drama 1983 · UK · Colour · 113mins

The inspiration for Ronald Harwood's play came from his own experiences as Sir Donald Wolfit's dresser in the fifties. Wolfit was an actor/manager of enormous girth and even greater eccentricity. To play the Wolfit character, Albert Finney also borrowed from Laurence Olivier and Charles Laughton, creating a vivid composite of a man who had "flashes of greatness". Getting Finney into his costumes is Tom Courtenay, giving another splendid performance: small-scaled, seedy, obsequious. Acting is the subject and the reason to watch – both Finney and Courtenay were rightly nominated for Oscars. Contains swearing. ▭

Albert Finney *Sir* • Tom Courtenay *Norman* • Edward Fox *Oxenby* • Zena Walker *Her Ladyship* • Eileen Atkins *Madge* • Michael Gough *Frank Carrington* • Cathryn Harrison *Irene* • Betty Marsden *Violet Manning* • Sheila Reid *Lydia Gibson* ■ *Dir* Peter Yates • *Scr* Ronald Harwood, from his play

The Dressmaker ★★★★ 15
Drama 1988 · UK · Colour · 91mins

It is 1944, and Joan Plowright defends Merseyside against the Germans. (No wonder they lost.) This is an excellent example of what the British do best: a large sprinkling of honourable thespians acting their utility socks off; and adaptation of a novel by Beryl Bainbridge, written with great skill and flair by the always interesting John McGrath; and lots of moody shots of Liverpool under fire. Courage, fear, repression and sex with GIs are all mixed into this glorious, tautly acted vehicle. It can all seem a trifle claustrophobic at times, with the proscenium arch just out of view, but this is a minor quibble in a masterly movie. ▭

Joan Plowright *Nellie* • Billie Whitelaw *Margo* • Jane Horrocks *Rita* • Peter Postlethwaite *[Pete Postlethwaite] Jack* • Tim Ransom *Wesley* • Rosemary Martin *Mrs Manders* • Pippa Hinchley *Valerie* • Tony Haygarth *Mr Manders* • Michael James-Reed *Chuck* ■ *Dir* Jim O'Brien • *Scr* John McGrath, from the novel by Beryl Bainbridge

Dreyfus ★★ U
Historical drama 1931 · UK · BW · 96mins

An extremely worthy British reworking of a notable German success, this makes a deliberate shifting of emphasis, since the Dreyfus case was not only a staggering miscarriage of justice but also a national manifestation of anti-Jewish feeling.

The famous case tells of a Jew in the French general staff who is framed for treason and sent to Devil's Island. Later movie versions of the tale – most notably *The Life of Emile Zola* and the under-rated *I Accuse!* – may be more accessible, but there's no doubting this film's sincerity.

Cedric Hardwicke *Alfred Dreyfus* • Charles Carson *Col Picquart* • George Merritt *Emile Zola* • Sam Livesey *Labori* • Beatrix Thompson *Lucie Dreyfus* • Garry Marsh *Major Esterhazy* ■ *Dir* FW Kraemer, Milton Rosmer

The Drifter ★★
Thriller 1988 · US · Colour · 90mins

What at first appears like another spin on the *Play Misty for Me* formula turns into quite a satisfying, low-budget thriller. A pre-*NYPD Blue* Kim Delaney stars as a fashion designer whose one-night stand with a mysterious hitchhiker (Miles O'Keeffe) turns into a nightmare when he won't leave her alone. Director Larry Brand, who also makes an appearance as a cop, does a reasonably effective job within the narrow parameters he's forced to work and Delaney makes a totally believable heroine.

Kim Delaney *Julia* • Timothy Bottoms *Arthur* • Al Shannon *Kriger* • Miles O'Keeffe *Trey* • Anna Gray Garduno *Matty* • Loren Haines *Willie Monroe* ■ *Dir/Scr* Larry Brand • *Executive Producer* Roger Corman

Drifting Clouds ★★★★ PG
Romance 1996 · Fin/Ger/Fr · Colour · 92mins

Aki Kaurismäki considers this urban morality tale as a mix of *Bicycle Thieves* and *It's a Wonderful Life*. Yet the bright colours and ironic soundtrack make it a Helsinki version of *The Umbrellas of Cherbourg*, as waitress Kati Outinen and her ex-tram driver husband Kari Väänänen unite to overcome the humiliations of poverty and menial employment. Minutely observed, perfectly paced and beautifully underplayed by the director's stock company, this is an affectionate portrait of real people surviving slings and arrows with a decency and determination that few film-makers consider worth putting on screen. In Finnish with English subtitles. ▭

Kati Outinen *Ilona Koponen* • Kari Väänänen *Lauri Koponen* • Elina Salo *Mrs Sjoholm* • Sakari Kuosmanen *Melartin* • Markku Peltola *Lajunen* ■ *Dir/Scr* Aki Kaurismäki

Driftwood ★★★ U
Drama 1946 · US · BW · 84mins

A charmingly bucolic tale about likeable doctor Walter Brennan, who looks after an orphan waif who's never before strayed from the backwoods. She's winsomely played by nine-year-old Natalie Wood. Though some may feel Wood's performance a tad calculated, she shows all the early glimmerings of that bright shining talent that rightly made her a major star of the fifties and sixties. Veteran director Allan Dwan wisely keeps the sentimentality reined in. There's also fine work from Ruth Warrick and stalwarts Dean Jagger and Charlotte Greenwood among the supporting cast. A class act for Republic studios. ▭

Ruth Warrick *Susan* • Walter Brennan *Murph* • Dean Jagger *Dr Steve Webster* • Charlotte Greenwood *Mathilda* • Natalie Wood *Jenny* • Margaret Hamilton *Essie Keenan* ■ *Dir* Allan Dwan • *Scr* Mary Loos, Richard Sale

Driftwood ★ 18
Drama 1996 · Ire/UK · Colour · 100mins

While clearly aiming for something as disturbing and profound as *Woman of the Dunes*, Ronan O'Leary's film comes across as an unintentional parody of *Misery*. Alone on a windswept island, Anne Brochet gets to roll her eyes as the seemingly normal sculptress who helps amnesiac castaway James Spader. Her kindness is gradually replaced by ritualistic mannerisms and, finally, violent hysteria as her new lover threatens to return to civilisation. With Spader offering no more than typically distracted hesitancy, the burden of dramatic impetus falls on Brochet, who responds with a display of desperate theatricality. Sexist and derivative.

James Spader *The Man* • Anne Brochet *Sarah* • Barry McGovern *McTavish* • Anna Massey *Mother* • Aiden Grenell *Father* • Kevin McHugh *Motorcycle driver* ■ *Dir* Ronan O'Leary • *Scr* Richard MN Waring, Ronan O'Leary

The Driller Killer ★★ 18
Horror 1979 · US · Colour · 94mins

Abel Ferrara's notorious contribution to Do-It-Yourself serial slaying is actually an amateurish, arthouse affair that hardly deserves the "video nasty" label it received at the hands of the British tabloids in the early eighties. A disturbed artist is continually thwarted in his career. Noisy neighbours are his first targets as he enforces his own brand of peace and quiet with his Black and Decker. From there his madness accelerates. When it was finally released on video in the UK in 1999, it had an extra six-and-a-half minutes of footage not seen before. There were 54 seconds cut, and some of the more gratuitous scenes of violence were toned down via optical editing. Contains swearing, violence and sex scenes. ▭ *DVD*

Jimmy Laine [Abel Ferrara] *Reno* • Carolyn Marz *Carol* • Baybi Day *Pamela* • Harry Schultz *Dalton Briggs* • Alan Wynroth *Landlord* • Maria Helhoski *Nun* • James O'Hara *Man in church* ■ *Dir* Abel Ferrara • *Scr* Nicholas St John

Drinking Crude ★★
Drama 1997 · Ire · Colour · 85mins

Irish writer/director Owen McPolin made his feature debut with this dour drama that tries to turn the cleaning of a vast storage tank into a nail-biting experience. Having severed links with his rural roots, Andrew Scott's stay in London is cut short when he accepts James Quarton's offer of work back home. There's a hidden agenda, however, and Scott is soon up to his neck in much more than crude oil. Exploring the limited options open to Ireland's youth and the poverty and traditionalism of its isolated country communities, this makes for unusual but hardly compelling viewing.

Andrew Scott *Paul Kelliher* • James Quarton *Al Russell* • Eva Birthistle • Harry O'Callaghan • Colin J Farrell • Sarah Pilkington • Natalie Stringer ■ *Dir/Scr* Owen McPolin

Drive ★★★ 18
Martial arts thriller 1997 · US · Colour · 99mins

Mark Dacascos stars in this outrageously violent martial arts adventure with vaguely sci-fi overtones. Taking unemployed songwriter Kadeem Hardison hostage, superhuman fighter Dacascos goes on the run and fights endless acrobatic villains for no reason whatsoever. Forget the story – it's the endless parade of Jackie Chan-style stunts, hardcore gore and bizarre humour, superbly woven together by director Steve Wang, that matter in this turbo-charged *Lethal Weapon* clone. Wang was responsible for *Mighty Morphin Power Rangers: the Movie*, so he's on familiar territory here. Contains swearing and violence. ▭

Mark Dacascos *Toby Wong* • Kadeem Hardison *Malik Brody* • John Pyper-Ferguson *Vic Madison* • Brittany Murphy *Deliverance Bodine* • Tracey Walter *Hedgehog* • James Shigeta *Mr Lau* • Masaya Kato *Advanced model* • Dom Magwili *Mr Chow* ■ *Dir* Steve Wang • *Scr* Scott Phillips

Drive a Crooked Road ★★★
Crime drama 1954 · US · BW · 82mins

A prime example of a Hollywood B-melodrama, this was originally shown in the UK as the support to *Father Brown*. Director Richard Quine's first thriller (he made the excellent *Pushover* the same year), this tautly paced Columbia action tale reminds us of what a talented film-maker he was and how under-rated he is today. The style may be a little drawn-out for contemporary tastes, and star Mickey Rooney's tendency to chew the scenery has not worn well. But Dianne Foster is an attractive foil, and familiar faces Kevin McCarthy and Jack Kelly add the appropriate grit in supporting roles.

Mickey Rooney *Eddie Shannon* • Dianne Foster *Barbara Mathews* • Kevin McCarthy *Steve Norris* • Jack Kelly *Harold Baker* • Harry Landers *Ralph* • Jerry Paris *Phil* • Paul Picerni *Carl* • Dick Crockett *Don* ■ *Dir* Richard Quine • *Scr* Blake Edwards, Richard Quine (adaptation), from a story by James Benson Nablo

Drive, He Said ★★★
Drama 1971 · US · Colour · 90mins

In the mid-sixties Jack Nicholson took a shine to Jeremy Larner's novel, which fused basketball (one of Nicholson's obsessions) with the activities of campus radicals during the escalation of the Vietnam War. Five years later, and two years after *Easy Rider*, Nicholson had become a star but realised he couldn't play a basketball star. So he turned director and delivered this funky piece, which has lofty ambitions but never quite comes together. It is, however, a far greater achievement than radical rivals *The Strawberry Statement* and *Zabriskie Point*, and there's a fascinating cast, including Nicholson's friends Robert Towne, Karen Black and Bruce Dern.

William Tepper *Hector* • Karen Black *Olive* • Michael Margotta *Gabriel* • Bruce Dern *Bullion* • Robert Towne *Richard* • Henry Jaglom

Conrad ■ *Dir* Jack Nicholson • *Scr* Jack Nicholson, Jeremy Larner, from the novel by Jeremy Larner

Drive Me Crazy ★★★ 12
Romantic comedy 1999 · US · Colour · 91mins
Made specifically for teenage girls (it stars *Sabrina the Teenage Witch's* Melissa Joan Hart and has a title song by Britney Spears), this is a slight but sweet romantic comedy that doesn't break any new ground yet features some nice performances. Hart plays Nicole, a high school senior who is looking for a date to take her to the prom. When the school jock directs his attentions elsewhere, she only has a few days to find a suitable replacement. So she sets her sights on the brooding boy next door (Adrian Grenier), though he needs a major makeover before she'll consider going out with him. You can guess the rest, but it's cutely done and sure to entertain under-18s everywhere.
Melissa Joan Hart *Nicole Maris* • Adrian Grenier *Chase Hammond* • Stephen Collins *Mr Maris* • Mark Metcalf *Mr Rope* • William Converse-Roberts *Mr Hammond* • Faye Grant *Mrs Maris* • Susan May Pratt *Alicia* • Kris Park *Ray Neeley* ■ *Dir* John Schultz • *Scr* Rob Thomas, from the novel *How I Created My Perfect Dream Date* by Todd Strasser

The Driver ★★★★ 15
Crime thriller 1978 · US · Colour · 86mins
The story of a getaway driver who has no life outside his work is pared down to its absolute existential essentials in Walter Hill's terrific thriller. Critics thought that the writer/director was paying tribute to Jean-Pierre Melville's 1967 classic *Le Samouraï*, though he denied he'd ever seen it. However, Ryan O'Neal wears the same trenchcoat as Alain Delon; he also has the same cool demeanour and ruthless tunnel vision. The car chases are amazing, but it's O'Neal's calm you remember, together with its ultimate unravelling, as Isabelle Adjani and cop Bruce Dern get under his skin. ▭
Ryan O'Neal *The Driver* • Bruce Dern *The Detective* • Isabelle Adjani *The Player* • Ronee Blakley *The Connection* • Matt Clark *Red plainclothes man* • Felice Orlandi *Gold plainclothes man* • Joseph Walsh *Glasses* • Rudy Ramos *Teeth* ■ *Dir/Scr* Walter Hill

The Driver's Seat ★ 15
Drama 1975 · It · Colour · 93mins
"It's not sex I want," says Elizabeth Taylor at the outset of this obscure melodrama, "but death." She also says she has used up all her supply of happiness, a line that one of her biographers pounced upon, claiming the movie was deeply personal. Based on a novel by Muriel Spark, it's a doom-laden affair, acted with such seriousness it rates as a camp send-up of Antonioni's meditations on urban alienation. Taylor, who wanders around Rome just as Jeanne Moreau wandered around Milan in *La Notte*, is simply playing herself as a cultural icon; and Andy Warhol, connoisseur of fleeting fame, makes an appropriately fleeting appearance. Ian Bannen is one of Taylor's casual lovers; and Mona Washbourne plays her somewhat mysterious companion. ▭

Elizabeth Taylor *Lise* • Ian Bannen *Richard* • Guido Mannari *Carlo* • Mona Washbourne *Mrs Fiedke* • Maxence Mailfort *Bill* • Andy Warhol ■ *Dir* Giuseppe Patroni-Griffi • *Scr* Raffaele La Capria, Giuseppe Patroni-Griffi, from the novel by Muriel Spark

Driving Academy ★ PG
Comedy 1988 · US · Colour · 94mins
The success of the *Police Academy* movies spawned numerous substandard copies, including the Rebecca De Mornay flop *Feds*. However, none is more interminable than this attempt at hilarity centred around the pratfalls of a group of youngsters at a driving school. The cast of unknowns (you may just recognise *Family Ties's* Tina Yothers) fails to help matters in what could be one of the least funny comedies ever committed to celluloid. ▭
Jackée *Edna Savage* • Charles Robinson *Larry Pearle* • Harvey Korman *Abner Fraser* • Dick Butkus *Smilin' Ed Konner* • Edie McClurg *Mrs Beth Crawford* • Ray Walston *Wendell Paulson* • Tina Yothers *Alice Santini* ■ *Dir Oz Scott* • *Scr* William A Schwartz, Alan Glueckman, Jeff Cohn

Driving Force ★★ 15
Science-fiction adventure 1988 · Ausl · Colour · 90mins
Wouldn't it be nice, just once, if, after an apocalyptic nuclear disaster, the Earth was ruled by ruthless, neatly dressed accountants and clerks rather than the leather-clad bikers who inevitably run riot? This is another substandard excursion into *Mad Max* territory, with Sam Jones as the moody hero fighting off the bad guys led by fellow straight-to-video star Don Swayze (Patrick's brother). The performances are nondescript; the requisite explosions are loud but staged with little originality or flair. Contains violence, swearing and nudity. ▭
Sam Jones • Catherine Bach • Emma Samms • Angel Cook • Don Swayze ■ *Dir* Andrew Prowse • *Scr* Patrick Edgeworth

Driving Me Crazy ★★ PG
Comedy 1991 · US · Colour · 103mins
Released in the States as *Dutch*, this was the first sign that teenpic wunderkind John Hughes was beginning to run out of ideas. This story of a sulky kid travelling through America for Thanksgiving in the company of his mother's beau may well strike you as familiar – think *Planes, Trains and Automobiles*, also penned by Hughes. Long on contrivance and short on comedy, this film will soon drive you crazy too, as Ethan Randall's tantrums and Ed O'Neill's corny Joe Public mannerisms erode your patience. A touch more of JoBeth Williams might have helped. Contains swearing. ▭
Ed O'Neill *Dutch Dooley* • Ethan Randall [Ethan Embry] *Doyle Standish* • JoBeth Williams *Natalie Standish* • Ari Meyers *Brock* • Christopher McDonald *Reed Standish* • EG Daily [Elizabeth Daily] *Halley* ■ *Dir* Peter Faiman • *Scr* John Hughes

Driving Miss Daisy ★★★★ U
Drama 1989 · US · Colour · 94mins
This is a small, unassuming movie that went up against the big guns of Hollywood and emerged with a best picture Oscar and a hefty profit. Based on the 1987 one-act play by Alfred Uhry, it charts the deepening relationship between an elderly widow and her black chauffeur in Atlanta. Miss Daisy (Oscar-winner Jessica Tandy), is an independent former schoolteacher with a will of iron, until she crashes her new car and cannot get insurance on another. So her son (Dan Aykroyd, in a non-comic role) arranges a chauffeur (Morgan Freeman). Although Miss Daisy is Jewish and regards herself as without racial prejudice, Hoke must gradually win acceptance and put up with her tirades from the back of the gleaming Hudson. The story covers the years from 1948 until 1973 – a period of racial strife and the civil rights movement – attaining the status of allegory in the process. ▭ *DVD*
Jessica Tandy *Miss Daisy Werthan* • Morgan Freeman *Hoke Colburn* • Dan Aykroyd *Boolie Werthan* • Patti LuPone *Florine Werthan* • Esther Rolle *Idella* • Joann Havrilla *Miss McClatchey* • William Hall Jr *Oscar* • Alvin M Sugarman *Dr Weil* ■ *Dir* Bruce Beresford • *Scr* Alfred Uhry, from his play

Drôle de Drame ★★★★
Period black comedy 1937 · Fr · BW · 84mins
Set in Edwardian London, this witty and anarchic farce was the second of director Marcel Carné's seven collaborations with screenwriter Jacques Prévert; they went on to make the classic *Les Enfants du Paradis* in 1945. Played to perfection by a superb cast, the film involves a mystery writer (Michel Simon) accused by a visiting bishop (Louis Jouvet) of murdering his wife (Françoise Rosay). Jean-Louis Barrault appears as an animal-lover who kills butchers. In French with English subtitles.
Louis Jouvet *Archibald Soper, Bishop of Bedford* • Françoise Rosay *Margaret Molyneux* • Michel Simon *Irwin Molyneux/Felix Chapel* • Jean-Louis Barrault *William Kramps* • Jean-Pierre Aumont *The milkman* • Nadine Vogel *Eva* • Pierre Alcover *Detective* • Henri Guisol *Reporter* ■ *Dir* Marcel Carné • *Scr* Jacques Prévert, from a story by J Storer-Clouston

Drop Dead Darling ★★★
Comedy 1966 · UK · Colour · 100mins
British director Ken Hughes is an unsung British talent, responsible for, among other films, *The Trials of Oscar Wilde* and *Chitty Chitty Bang Bang*. This handsome Shepperton-shot farce, released in the USA as *Arrivederci, Baby!*, offers a bravura role to the terrific Tony Curtis, as a charming Bluebeard, and some plum lines and opportunities for grimacing to the irascible Lionel Jeffries. Tastelessness abounds, but for once it's deliberate, and the Panavision and Technicolor photography is extremely glossy.
Tony Curtis *Nick Johnson* • Zsa Zsa Gabor *Gigi* • Rosanna Schiaffino *Francesca* • Lionel Jeffries *Parker* • Nancy Kwan *Baby* • Fenella Fielding *Fenella* • Anna Quayle *Aunt Miriam* • Warren Mitchell *Count de Rienzi/Maximilian* • Mischa Auer *Romeo* ■ *Dir* Ken Hughes • *Scr* Ken Hughes, from a story by Ken Hughes,

Ronald Harwood, suggested by the novel *The Careful Man* by Richard Deming • Cinematographer Denys Coup

Drop Dead Fred ★★ 15
Fantasy comedy 1991 · US · Colour · 94mins
A high-energy performance by Rik Mayall in the title role is the chief interest in this largely uninteresting and unfunny comedy. It's the story of a grown woman (Phoebe Cates) who is revisited by the imaginary friend of her childhood (Mayall), on a mission to cheer her up at a bad time. A nice idea falls between all available stools and ends up as a mess on the floor. It's particularly irritating if you've seen the much better *Harvey*. Contains swearing. ▭
Phoebe Cates *Elizabeth Cronin* • Rik Mayall *Drop Dead Fred* • Marsha Mason *Polly* • Tim Matheson *Charles Cronin* • Bridget Fonda *Annabella* • Carrie Fisher *Janie* • Keith Charles *Murray* • Ashley Peldon *Young Elizabeth* • Daniel Gerroll *Nigel* ■ *Dir* Ate De Jong • *Scr* Carlos Davis, Anthony Fingleton, from a story by Elizabeth Livingston

Drop Dead Gorgeous ★★★★ 15
Black comedy 1999 · US · Colour · 94mins
A pseudo-documentary and highly sophisticated black comedy, *Drop Dead Gorgeous* traces a small-town beauty pageant from the auditions to the glitz and glamour of the finals. Kirsten Dunst, a sweet girl from a trailer-trash background, is pitted against spoilt little rich bitch Denise Richards. Meanwhile, someone in town is knocking off their competition. Ellen Barkin and Kirstie Alley are both excellent as the girls' cat-fighting moms, and overall this is a refreshing and ironic take on suburban American life. Director Michael Patrick Jann has succeeded in making an accessible and intelligent independent film in the same vein as *Fargo*. It's much more interesting than your average Hollywood fare. Contains swearing and sexual references. ▭ *DVD*
Kirstie Alley *Gladys Leeman* • Ellen Barkin *Annette Atkins* • Kirsten Dunst *Amber Atkins* • Denise Richards *Becky Leeman* • Allison Janney *Loretta* • Will Sasso *Hank Vilmes* • Mindy Sterling *Iris Clark* • Sam McMurray *Lester Leeman* • Adam West ■ *Dir* Michael Patrick Jann • *Scr* Lona Williams

DROP Squad ★★ 15
Satirical drama 1994 · US · Colour · 83mins
Although the title makes the film sound like a *Delta Force*-style action picture, the "drop" in the title stands for "Deprogramming and Restoration of Pride". It's the name of a group that attempts to persuade African-Americans that they have "sold out" their culture. From Spike Lee's production company, it's marred by a tone that is a too tad strident. The plot concerns advertising exec Eriq La Salle (*ER*) proving a tough nut to crack, while the group's leader finds himself facing a moral dilemma. Not necessarily as balanced as the controversial subject matter demands, but well performed. ▭
Eriq La Salle *Bruford Jamison Jr* • Vondie Curtis-Hall *Rocky* • Ving Rhames *Garvey* • Leonard Thomas *XB* • Michael Ralph *Trevor*

Billy Williams *Huey* • Eric A Payne [Eric Payne] *Stokeley* • Vanessa Williams *Mali* ■ Dir David Johnson • Scr Butch Robinson, David Taylor

Drop Zone ★★★ 15
Thriller 1994 · US · Colour · 101mins

You go for years without seeing a movie about skydiving and then suddenly, like buses, two of them come along at the same time – this and the Charlie Sheen vehicle *Terminal Velocity*. This is the pick of the pair: an exhilarating ride, directed by action specialist John Badham with his usual flair and eye for spectacular set pieces. Wesley Snipes exudes charisma as the US marshal who sets out to hunt down the parachuting crooks whose airborne antics cost Snipes's brother his life. Gary Busey delivers another entertainingly villainous performance, while Yancy Butler is equally good as Snipes's reluctant partner. Contains swearing and violence. ▣

Wesley Snipes *Pete Nessip* • Gary Busey *Ty Moncrief* • Yancy Butler *Jessie Crossman* • Michael Jeter *Earl Leedy* • Corin Nemec *Selkirk* • Kyle Secor *Swoop* • Luca Bercovici *Jagger* • Malcolm-Jamal Warner *Terry Nessip* ■ Dir John Badham • Scr Peter Barsocchini, John Bishop, from a story by Tony Griffin

Drowning by Numbers ★★★★ 18
Drama 1988 · UK · Colour · 113mins

In one of writer/director Peter Greenaway's darkest comedies, three generations of womenfolk, all named Cissie Colpitts, drown their menfolk with the acquiescence of the local coroner, Madgett (Bernard Hill). Joan Plowright, Juliet Stevenson and Joely Richardson are delightfully lethal as the scheming trio, while Greenaway indulges his obsessions with word games, lists and the ache of mortality. Michael Nyman's score builds momentum, even though there isn't any, and the whole is luminous and lurid in equal measure. ▣

Bernard Hill *Madgett* • Joan Plowright *Cissie Colpitts 1* • Juliet Stevenson *Cissie Colpitts 2* • Joely Richardson *Cissie Colpitts 3* • Jason Edwards *Smut* • Bryan Pringle *Jake* • Trevor Cooper *Hardy* • David Morrissey *Bellamy* ■ Dir/Scr Peter Greenaway

Drowning Mona ★★
Black comedy 2000 · US · Colour · 95mins

This lame comedy starts out in a promising fashion by having Bette Midler killed during the opening credits. Alas, it quickly goes downhill. Police chief Danny DeVito is dealing with a much bigger mystery than discovering who offed Midler, the most hated resident of Verplanck, NY: he has to find someone who *didn't* want her dead. Nick Gomez's movie desperately wants to be a quirky black farce, but ends up more like an episode of *White Trash Family Feud*. You want to be amused by these characters, but they're just too stupid to be funny.

Danny DeVito *Chief Wyatt Rash* • Bette Midler *Mona Dearly* • Neve Campbell *Ellen Rash* • Jamie Lee Curtis *Rona Mace* • Casey Affleck *Bobby Calzone* • William Fichtner *Phil Dearly* ■ Dir Nick Gomez • Scr Peter Steinfeld

The Drowning Pool ★★★ 12
Mystery thriller 1975 · US · Colour · 103mins

Paul Newman's second outing as novelist Ross MacDonald's private detective Lew Harper (after 1966's *The Moving Target*), sees him plunging into a swamp of Deep South greed and murder when he's called to oil baroness Joanne Woodward's bayou home to investigate a blackmail plot against her. The title refers to a hydrotherapy bath in an abandoned mental home, which is typical of the oddball eccentricity of the film and its characters – of whom Murray Hamilton's oil tycoon is a stand-out. It's a pity that Stuart Rosenberg's direction is so forthright when the impenetrable plot needed a more bizarre approach to keep us interested. ▣

Paul Newman *Lew Harper* • Joanne Woodward *Iris Devereaux* • Anthony Franciosa *Chief Broussard* • Murray Hamilton *JJ Kilbourne* • Gail Strickland *Mavis Kilbourne* • Melanie Griffith *Schuyler Devereaux* • Linda Haynes *Gretchen* • Richard Jaeckel *Lieutenant Franks* ■ Dir Stuart Rosenberg • Scr Tracy Keenan Wynn, Lorenzo Semple Jr, Walter Hill, from the novel by Ross MacDonald

Drugstore Cowboy ★★★★ 18
Drama 1989 · US · Colour · 97mins

A provocative and downbeat look at the sordid life of a "family" of four junkies who rob pharmacies to support their habits, set in the early seventies in Portland, Oregon. Director Gus Van Sant casts his usual quirky eye over the fascinating proceedings and brings an extraordinary visual style to this credible, nonjudgemental portrayal of addiction, which is based on an unpublished semi-autobiographical novel by prisoner James Fogle. Matt Dillon gives a compelling performance; *The Naked Lunch* author William S Burroughs appears in a cameo as a priest turned dope fiend. There's a good oldies soundtrack, too. Contains violence, swearing and drug abuse. ▣

Matt Dillon *Bob Hughes* • Kelly Lynch *Dianne Hughes* • James Remar *Gentry* • James LeGros *Rick* • Heather Graham *Nadine* • Beah Richards *Drug counsellor* • Grace Zabriskie *Bob's mother* • Max Perlich *David* • William S Burroughs *Tom the priest* • Eric Hull *Druggist* ■ Dir Gus Van Sant • Scr Gus Van Sant, Daniel Yost, from a novel by James Fogle

The Drum ★★★★ U
Adventure 1938 · UK · Colour · 89mins

AEW Mason, author of *The Four Feathers*, wrote this story especially for producer Alexander Korda as a vehicle for the talented 14-year-old star of *Elephant Boy*, Sabu. The youngster delivers a truly beguiling performance as Prince Azim, forced from his inheritance by his uncle, the irredeemably swinish villain Raymond Massey. It's ravishingly photographed in three-strip Technicolor (by Georges Perinal, Robert Krasker, Osmond Borrodaile, Christopher Challis and Geoffrey Unsworth – talk about an A team!). This is a stirring reminder of what British cinema was once about, telling a tale of the courageous struggle between right and wrong with an unerring sense of patriotism. ▣

Sabu *Prince Azim* • Raymond Massey *Prince Ghul* • Valerie Hobson *Mrs Carruthers* • Roger

Livesey *Captain Carruthers* • Desmond Tester *Bill Holder* • Martin Walker *Herrick* • David Tree *Lieutenant Escott* • Francis L Sullivan *Governor* ■ Dir Zoltan Korda • Scr Arthur Wimperis, Patric Kirwan, Hugh Gray, Lajos Biró (adaptation), from the novel by AEW Mason

Drum ★ 18
Drama 1976 · US · Colour · 99mins

While *Mandingo* walked the tightrope between exploitation and gothic melodrama, this wretched sequel has no pretensions at all. It's a real cheapo, with Warren Oates as a slave breeder and Yaphet Kotto as one of his purchases. Things get seriously bogged down in a plot about interbreeding, before Kotto turns into Spartacus and instigates a very bloody slave revolt. ▣

Warren Oates *Hammond Maxwell* • Ken Norton *Drum* • Isela Vega *Marianna* • Pam Grier *Regine* • Yaphet Kotto *Blaise* • John Colicos *DeMarigny* • Fiona Lewis *Augusta Chauvet* ■ Dir Steve Carver • Scr Norman Wexler, from the novel by Kyle Onstott

Drum Beat ★★★ U
Western 1954 · US · Colour · 107mins

Alan Ladd brings an end to the Indian Wars in this fact-based western, which gave Charles Bronson his first starring role. Writer/director Delmer Daves toiled away in the public record office in order to be as impartial as possible in his account of the 1869 Modoc uprising. The script has an intelligence that matches his earlier *Broken Arrow*, one of the first Hollywood features to see the Wild West from the native American perspective. The upstanding Ladd is upstaged by the young Bronson as Modoc brave Captain Jack, while J Peverell Marley's views of the Oregon/California landscape are stunning.

Alan Ladd *Johnny MacKay* • Charles Bronson *Captain Jack* • Audrey Dalton *Nancy Meek* • Marisa Pavan *Toby* • Robert Keith *Bill Satterwhite* • Rodolfo Acosta *Scarface Charlie* • Warner Anderson *General Canby* • Elisha Cook Jr *Crackel* ■ Dir/Scr Delmer Daves

Drums across the River ★★ PG
Western 1954 · US · Colour · 74mins

This very average Audie Murphy western is somewhat redeemed by nice fifties Technicolor and a very short running time. The plot – about how deceitful whites stole gold from the native Americans – deserves a better treatment, but the baby-faced Murphy, a former war hero, makes a sympathetic leading man. There's good work, too, from snarling villain Lyle Bettger, grizzled Walter Brennan as Audie's dad, and especially Hugh O'Brian, here beginning to show signs of star quality. Elsewhere, Lisa Gaye and Mara Corday are splendid period wenches. ▣

Audie Murphy *Gary Brannon* • Lisa Gaye *Jennie Marlowe* • Lyle Bettger *Frank Walker* • Walter Brennan *Sam Brannon* • Mara Corday *Sue* • Hugh O'Brian *Morgan* • Jay Silverheels *Taos* • Regis Toomey *Sheriff Beal* ■ Dir Nathan Juran • Scr John K Butler, Lawrence Roman, from a story by John K Butler

Drums along the Mohawk ★★★★
Western 1939 · US · Colour · 103mins

One of the most beautiful and distinguished achievements of early colour, this fine movie tends to be overlooked among the other highlights of Hollywood's *annus mirabilis*, 1939. This is effectively a pre-western, dealing with Indian raids among the early settlers during the American War of Independence. It contains a rather disturbing anti-British bias, not for the first time from ace director John Ford, himself of Irish stock. Taken as a romantic action adventure, though, it rattles along. Claudette Colbert seems a little too well groomed for the frontier, but Henry Fonda seems perfectly at home and is a constant pleasure to watch.

Claudette Colbert *Lana "Magdelena" Martin* • Henry Fonda *Gilbert Martin* • Edna May Oliver *Mrs Sarah McKlennar* • Eddie Collins *Christian Reall* • John Carradine *Caldwell* • Dorris Bowdon *Mary Reall* • Jessie Ralph *Mrs Weaver* ■ Dir John Ford • Scr Lamar Trotti, Sonya Levien, from a novel by Walter D Edmonds • Cinematographer Bert Glennon, Ray Rennahan • Art Director Richard Day, Mark-Lee Kirk

Drunken Angel ★★★★ PG
Drama 1948 · Jap · BW · 93mins

Drunken Angel is notable as the first major screen appearance of Toshiro Mifune, whom director Akira Kurosawa would cast in virtually every one of his subsequent films. Later films such as *Rashomon* and *The Seven Samurai* made Mifune a star, but in this early work he plays a volatile gangster who has a bullet removed by a drunken doctor. When the doctor, played by another Kurosawa favourite, Takashi Shimura, also discovers that Mifune is suffering from tuberculosis, he is inexorably drawn into his patient's underworld of crime and violence. Part realist drama, part gangster movie, this is a gripping story that also casts an observant eye over the evolving postwar Japanese society. In Japanese with English subtitles. ▣

Toshiro Mifune *Matsunaga* • Takashi Shimura *Dr Sanada* • Reisaburo Yamamoto *Okada* • Michiyo Kogure *Nanse* • Chiefko Nakakita *Miyo* • Noriko Sengoku *Gin* • Choko Lida *Old Maid Servant* ■ Dir Akira Kurosawa • Scr Keinosuke Uegusa, Akira Kurosawa

Drunken Master ★★★★ 15
Martial arts action comedy
1978 · HK · Colour · 106mins

This was the film that saw Jackie Chan crowned as the clown prince of kung fu. As the legendary folk hero, Wong Fei-Hung, who is forced to suffer the humiliations of uncle Yuen Hsiao Tian's pitiless training programme, Chan frequently illustrates why he's so often acclaimed as Hong Kong's answer to Buster Keaton. But not everything is as gloriously knockabout as the final fight with the eight immortals and the roadside encounter with assassin Huang Cheng Li is particularly brutal. Two sequels were released in 1994 – and yes, that is Bond girl Michelle Yeoh as Jackie's aunt. A Cantonese language film. ▣

Jackie Chan *Wong Fei-Hung* • Yuen Hsiao Tian [Simon Yuen] *Sam Seed* • Huang Cheng Li [Hwang Jang Lee] *Thunderfoot* • Michelle Yeoh ■ *Dir* Yuen Woo-Ping • *Scr* Hsiao Lung, Ng See Yuen

Drunken Master II ★★ 🄵🄸

Martial arts action comedy
1994 · HK · Colour · 101mins

During Jackie Chan's deserved rise to mainstream American acceptance, he has left us a legacy of sometimes daft, sometimes awful, but always enjoyable, Hong Kong movies. This is a typical example. Forget the artefact smuggling plot (the writer obviously did), it's the action that counts. A fight aboard a train and a bout with an axe-wielding gang are stand-outs. Star and director clashed during filming; Chan subsequently took over the reins himself. As with all of his movies, stay to the end to catch the outtakes that play with the closing credits, usually showing stunts that backfired. A Cantonese language film.

Jackie Chan *Wong Fei-Hung* • Anita Mui *Madam Wong* • Ti Lung *Wong Kei-Ying* • Felix Wong *Master Tsan* • Lau Kar-leung *Fu Min-Chi* ■ *Dir* Liu Chia-liang [Lau Kar-Leung], Jackie Chan • *Scr* Yun Kai-Chi

Drunks ★★

Drama
1995 · US · Colour · 90mins

Determinedly theatrical, Gary Lennon's adaptation of his own play *Blackout* is a studied example of characters that don't go beyond the stereotype. Every attendee at this Manhattan Alcoholics Anonymous meeting has a specific function to perform, even if this precludes any sort of genuine interchange. Faye Dunaway exists to suffer maternally; Calista Flockhart appears waiflike; comic relief is provided by Spalding Gray; while self-recrimination is the onerous duty of Howard Rollins. Every speech is stuffed with sociological insight, each incident is ingeniously revelatory. Operating on a shoestring, Peter Cohn works hard, but never drags his material above the schematic.

Richard Lewis *Jim* • Faye Dunaway *Becky* • Dianne Wiest *Rachel* • Amanda Plummer *Shelley* • Howard E Rollins Jr *Joseph* • Liza Harris *Melanie* • Liam Ahern *Billy* • Parker Posey *Debbie* • Lisa Gay Hamilton *Brenda* • Calista Flockhart *Helen* • Spalding Gray *Louis* ■ *Dir* Peter Cohn • *Scr* Gary Lennon, from his play *Blackout*

Dry Cleaning ★★

Black comedy 1997 · Fr/Sp · Colour · 97mins

Unsure whether to be a comedy of sexual manners or a bawdy farce, this study of the repressed desires that simmer beneath even the most respectable bourgeois exteriors ends up more amusing than outrageous. Miou-Miou and Charles Berling give sporting performances as the staid marrieds whose fascination with bisexual drag artist Stanislas Merhar prompts them to offer him a job in their dry-cleaning shop. Director Anne Fontaine's dissection of the *ménage à trois's* domestic arrangements is swift and precise, but the shifting bedroom alliances are contrived. A French language film.

Miou-Miou *Nicole Kunstler* • Charles Berling *Jean-Marie Kunstler* • Stanislas Merhar *Loic* •

Mathilde Seigner *Marylin* • Nanou Meister *Yvette* • Noe Pflieger *Pierre* • Michel Bompoil *Robert* • Christopher King *Steve* ■ *Dir* Anne Fontaine • *Scr* Gilles Taurand, Anne Fontaine

Dry Rot ★★ 🄴

Comedy 1956 · UK · BW · 85mins

Making his debut in 1913, Maurice Elvey was one of the longest-serving of all British directors, claiming to have shot over 300 films. This was his penultimate picture and, in keeping with many of the comedies that occupied his twilight years, it's not very good. Adapted by John Chapman from his own hit West End play, this tale of crooked bookies plods along more slowly than a doped horse. Thankfully, those expert *farceurs* Ronald Shiner, Brian Rix and Sid James give polished performances.

Ronald Shiner *Alf Tubbs* • Brian Rix *Fred Phipps* • Peggy Mount *Sgt Fire* • Lee Patterson *Danby* • Sidney James *Flash Harry* • Christian Duvaleix *Polignac* • Joan Sims *Beth* • Heather Sears *Susan* ■ *Dir* Maurice Elvey • *Scr* John Chapman, from his play

A Dry White Season ★★★ 🄸🄵

Drama 1989 · US · Colour · 102mins

Marlon Brando's sporadic screen appearances over the last ten years or so have veered between the lightweight *Don Juan DeMarco* to the downright embarrassing *The Island of Dr Moreau*. However, this worthy drama saw him deliver one of his most passionate performances in a long time, even if it is in a supporting role. Donald Sutherland stars as the ordinary white South African who is gradually awakened to the injustices of the repressive apartheid regime; Brando is the liberal lawyer who helps him challenge the establishment. The star-studded support cast also includes Susan Sarandon, Zakes Mokae, Jürgen Prochnow and Janet Suzman, while director Euzhan Palcy succeeds in producing a compelling and disturbing portrait of the brutality in pre-Mandela South Africa. Contains violence and swearing. 🖵

Donald Sutherland *Ben du Toit* • Janet Suzman *Susan du Toit* • Zakes Mokae *Stanley Makhaya* • Jürgen Prochnow *Captain Stolz* • Susan Sarandon *Melanie Bruwer* • Marlon Brando *Ian McKenzie* • Winston Ntshona *Gordon Ngubene* • Thoko Ntshinga *Emily* ■ *Dir* Euzhan Palcy • *Scr* Euzhan Palcy, Colin Welland, from the novel by André Brink

DuBarry Was a Lady ★★★

Musical comedy 1943 · US · Colour · 96mins

Cole Porter's risqué musical play was a hit on Broadway in 1939, but arrived on the screen four years later as a bowdlerised Red Skelton/Lucille Ball vehicle. Lucy, MGM's resident chirpy redhead, never looked lovelier than here, and newcomer Gene Kelly learned from this film never to look down at his feet again while dancing. It's an amiable romp, officially credited to director Roy Del Ruth, though the choreography is by Charles Walters, who began a distinguished career (*Easter Parade, High Society*) with this movie. Here he does full Hollywood justice to one of Porter's most beautiful songs, *Do I Love You?*.

Lucille Ball *May Daly/Madame DuBarry* • Red Skelton *Louis Blore/King Louis* • Gene Kelly *Alec Howe/Black Arrow* • Douglass Dumbrille *Willie/Duc De Rigor* • Rags Ragland *Charlie/Dauphin* • Donald Meek *Mr Jones/Duc De Choiseul* • George Givot *Cheezy/De Roqueford* • Zero Mostel *Rami the Swami/Cagliostro* ■ *Dir* Roy Del Ruth • *Scr* Irving Brecher, Nancy Hamilton, Wilkie Mahoney, Albert Mannheimer, Jack McGowan, Charles Sherman, Mary C McCall, from a play by BG De Sylva, Herbert Fields • *Music* Cole Porter

Dublin Nightmare ★★ 🄴

Murder mystery 1958 · UK · BW · 63mins

A Canadian photographer in Dublin discovers that his "dead" wartime friend is really an IRA leader. Sounds familiar? It should: this is a totally shameless B-movie rip-off of *The Third Man*, with Dublin substituted for Vienna and the IRA taking the place of penicillin. Canny producers Jon Penington and David Eady obviously knew what they were up to and, since the film went out under the Rank imprimatur, they clearly managed to get away with it. Editor John Pomeroy directs effectively, while William Sylvester and Marla Landi are perfectly adequate stand-ins for Joseph Cotten and Alida Valli. Did anyone notice the similarity at the time?

William Sylvester *John Kevin* • Marla Landi *Anna* • Richard Leech *Steven Lawlor* • William Sherwood *Edward Dillon* • Harry Hutchinson *"Vulture"* • Helen Lindsay *Mary O'Callaghan* • Jack Cunningham *Inspector O'Connor* ■ *Dir* John Pomeroy • *Scr* John Tully

The Duchess and the Dirtwater Fox ★★★ 🄿🄶

Comedy western 1976 · US · Colour · 99mins

There's an idea here that works for half the movie and then becomes extremely irritating. George Segal and Goldie Hawn co-star as a gambler and a dance hall girl thrown together in adversity who pull off a few judicious scams. They fight, they make up, they swindle each other, he tells an awful lot of old Jewish jokes and we laugh – but not for long. Segal often seems to think that all he has to do is stand around and wink at the camera a few times and that will suffice. Occasionally, with a good script, this can work, but that's exactly what's missing here. Hawn, meanwhile, remains an overrated actress for some, and this movie will do nothing to change their opinion. 🖵

George Segal *Charlie Malloy* • Goldie Hawn *Amanda Quaid* • Conrad Janis *Gladstone* • Thayer David *Widdicombe* • Jennifer Lee *Trollop* • Roy Jenson *Bloodworth* • Pat Ast *Dance hall girl* • Sid Gould *Rabbi* ■ *Dir* Melvin Frank • *Scr* Barry Sandler, Jack Rose, Melvin Frank, from a story by Barry Sandler

Duck Soup ★★★★★ 🄴

Comedy 1933 · US · BW · 65mins

The Marx Brothers reached peaks of anarchic brilliance in this comedy masterpiece, which burst upon audiences four years after their primitive debut in *The Cocoanuts*. Groucho, Chico, Harpo and the uncharismatic Zeppo are all entangled in a runaway satire that finds Groucho as a Ruritanian leader going to war because he's paid a month's advance rent on the battlefield. What helps

make *Duck Soup* the funniest Marx Brothers' picture – besides the absence of the romantic interludes which dogged later outings – are the exchanges between Groucho and Margaret Dumont's stately matriarch, plus a stunningly surreal mirror sequence. Classic quips, classy delivery. 🖵

Groucho Marx *Rufus T Firefly* • Chico Marx *Chicolini* • Harpo Marx *Brownie* • Zeppo Marx *Bob Rolland* • Raquel Torres *Vera Marcal* • Louis Calhern *Ambassador Trentino* • Margaret Dumont *Mrs Teasdale* • Verna Hillie *Secretary* • Leonid Kinskey *Agitator* ■ *Dir* Leo McCarey • *Scr* Burt Kalmar, Harry Ruby, Arthur Sheekman, Nat Perrin

Duck Tales: the Movie – Treasure of the Lost Lamp ★★★ 🄴

Animated adventure
1990 · US · Colour · 70mins

There won't be many takers over the age of six for this animated adventure that launched Disney's *Movietoons* series. Something akin to *Raiders of the Lost Duck*, the film sends Scrooge McDuck and the ever-troublesome Huey, Duey and Louie in search of a genie's lamp before it falls into the evil clutches of Merlock. Alan Young (who once chatted to Mr Ed, the talking horse) voices Uncle Scrooge, while Christopher Lloyd brings some menace to the villain. It all feels a touch rough-and-ready, but younger children may enjoy it. 🖵

Alan Young *Scrooge McDuck* • Terence McGovern *Launchpad McQuack* • Russi Taylor *Huey/Duey/Louie/Webby* • Richard Libertini *Dijon* • Christopher Lloyd *Merlock* • June Foray *Mrs Featherby* • Chuck McCann *Duckworth* ■ *Dir* Bob Hathcock • *Scr* Alan Burnett

Dudes ★★★ 🄸🄵

Comedy 1987 · US · Colour · 86mins

Penelope Spheeris made her name chronicling the punk scene, but is now better known for mainstream comedies like *Wayne's World*. In this transitional film, Jon Cryer and Daniel Roebuck play New York punks hunting the renegade biker gang, led by Lee Ving, who murdered their buddy Flea (later to find fame as a member of the Red Hot Chili Peppers). The western elements are clumsily crafted on to the tale, but it's still an enjoyable offbeat ride. 🖵

Jon Cryer *Grant* • Daniel Roebuck *Biscuit* • Flea *Milo* • Lee Ving *Missoula* • Billy Ray Sharkey *Blix* • Glenn Withrow *Wes* • Michael Melvin *Logan* • Axxel G Reese *Red* ■ *Dir* Penelope Spheeris • *Scr* Randall Jahnson

Dudley Do-Right ★★ 🄿🄶

Comedy 1999 · US · Colour · mins

Brendan Fraser, who scored a surprise hit in 1997 with *George of the Jungle*, brings another of Jay Ward's cartoon favourites to life, though with considerably less success. Director Hugh Wilson (*Police Academy*) seems to be aiming for an affectionate live-action tribute to the likes of Dastardly and Muttley as the likeably dumb mountie of the title (Fraser) does battle with his nemesis, Snidely Whiplash (Alfred Molina), who has created a fake gold rush in Canada. The actors, who include Sarah Jessica Parker and Eric Idle, enthusiastically enter in the spirit of tomfoolery, but there's far too much reliance on slapdash slapstick.

Brendan Fraser *Dudley Do-Right* • Sarah Jessica Parker *Nell Fenwick* • Alfred Molina *Snidely Whiplash* • Alex Rocco *The Chief* • Eric Idle *The Prospector* • Robert Prosky *Inspector Fenwick* ■ *Dir* Hugh Wilson • *Scr* Hugh Wilson, from characters created by Jay Ward

Duel ★★★★★ PG

Thriller   1971 · US · Colour · 85mins

Dennis Weaver leaves his pleasant house on a routine business trip. When he gets to the highway, a rusting, smoke-belching rust-bucket of an oil tanker proceeds to chase him, taunt him and run him off the road. Filmed in a mere 16 days, mainly on the scenic Highway 14, north of Los Angeles, this celebrated TV movie was the making of 23-year-old Steven Spielberg's career. You can read as much or as little as you like into Richard Matheson's story. Is it a parable about urban alienation and the treachery of machines, or nothing more than a brilliant use of modest resources that keeps you on the edge of your seat, even after repeated viewings? It's both of these, and a whole lot more. 🎞

Dennis Weaver *David Mann* • Jacqueline Scott *Mrs Mann* • Eddie Firestone *Cafe owner* • Lou Frizzell *Bus driver* • Gene Dynarski *Man in cafe* • Lucille Benson *Lady at Snakarama* ■ *Dir* Steven Spielberg • *Scr* Richard Matheson, from a story by Richard Matheson

Duel at Diablo ★★★ 15

Western   1966 · US · Colour · 100mins

Co-producer/director Ralph Nelson's well-intentioned attempt to liberalise the western explores racist themes using an international cast. Unfortunately, it doesn't quite succeed, partly because the eclectic casting (including Swedish Bibi Andersson and British Bill Travers) gets in the way of the authenticity. There is plenty of action, however, and a considerable amount of violence, as a cavalry troop escorts a wagon train of explosives out west, beset by Indians and internal racial conflict. Sidney Poitier looks ill at ease, but a grim and quietly snarling James Garner makes one wish he'd played more straight western roles before launching into a series of western satires.

James Garner *Jess Remsberg* • Sidney Poitier *Toller* • Bill Travers *Lieutenant McAllister, "Scotty"* • Bibi Andersson *Ellen Grange* • Dennis Weaver *Willard Grange* • William Redfield *Sergeant Ferguson* • John Hoyt *Chata* ■ *Dir* Ralph Nelson • *Scr* Marvin H Albert, Michael M Grilikhes, from the novel *Apache Rising* by Marvin H Albert

The Duel at Silver Creek ★★ U

Western   1952 · US · Colour · 73mins

A minor and utterly unremarkable Audie Murphy western that somewhat surprisingly bears the name of ace *Dirty Harry* director Don Siegel. Unfortunately, it's absolutely devoid of the personal style Siegel brought to such low-budget films as *Invasion of the Body Snatchers* and *Riot in Cell Block 11*. Murphy and Siegel fans won't want to miss it, of course, and

the supporting cast of Faith Domergue, Stephen McNally and a pre-stardom Lee Marvin also makes it watchable. But these days not even young cowboy fans will get much from this very ordinary western. 🎞

Audie Murphy *Silver Kid* • Faith Domergue *Opal Lacey* • Stephen McNally *Lightning Tyrone* • Susan Cabot *Dusty Fargo* • Gerald Mohr *Rod Lacey* • Eugene Iglesias *Johnny Sombrero* • Lee Marvin *Tinhorn Burgess* • Walter Sande *Pete Fargo* ■ *Dir* Don Siegel • *Scr* Gerald Adams, Joseph Hoffman, from a story by Gerald Adams

Duel in the Jungle ★★★ PG

Adventure   1954 · UK · Colour · 97mins

This immensely entertaining, if a little simplistic, action adventure is a real tribute to its producer, Marcel Hellman. The Technicolor photography, shot on location in Rhodesia by Erwin Hillier, is thrilling, and the film reunites the co-stars of *State Fair* (1945), Dana Andrews and Jeanne Crain. David Farrar steals the acting thunder as the villain, while Hollywood veteran George Marshall keeps the tension taut. Alas, English assistant director Tony Kelly lost his life during the shoot, and no amount of derring-do can compensate for such a tragedy. 🎞

Dana Andrews *Scott Walters* • Jeanne Crain *Marian Taylor* • David Farrar *Perry Henderson/Arthur Henderson* • Patrick Barr *Superintendent Roberts* • George Coulouris *Captain Malburn* • Charles Goldner *Martell* • Wilfrid Hyde White *Pitt* • Mary Merrall *Mrs Henderson* ■ *Dir* George Marshall • *Scr* Sam Marx, TJ Morrison, from a story by SK Kennedy

Duel in the Sun ★★★★ PG

Western melodrama
1946 · US · Colour · 129mins

Producer David O Selznick intended this costly production to be the equal of his *Gone with the Wind*. What he ended up with was a lurid, sex-sodden western which, in its day, managed to offend church leaders and censorship boards alike. (Unsurprisingly, it became a mammoth box-office hit.) Jennifer Jones is half-breed Pearl Chavez and Gregory Peck is lewd Lewt McCanles – roles which must surely embarrass them both as they watch themselves today, cocooned in their Los Angeles haciendas. The infamous finale is simultaneously ludicrous and stunning, as Jones and Peck, both dying, orgasmically crawl towards each other as the desert sun blazes down. It was this that led audiences to refer to the movie as *Lust in the Dust*. 🎞

Jennifer Jones *Pearl Chavez* • Gregory Peck *Lewt McCanles* • Joseph Cotten *Jesse McCanles* • Lionel Barrymore *Senator McCanles* • Lillian Gish *Laura Belle McCanles* • Walter Huston *Sin Killer* • Butterfly McQueen *Vashti* • Herbert Marshall *Scott Chavez* • Charles Bickford *Sam Pierce* • Orson Welles *Narrator* ■ *Dir* King Vidor, Josef von Sternberg • *Scr* David O Selznick, Oliver HP Garrett, from the novel by Niven Busch • *Producer* David O Selznick • *Cinematographer* Lee Garmes, Harold Rosson, Ray Rennahan • *Art Director* James Basevi

Duel of Champions ★★ PG

Historical drama
1961 · It/Sp · Colour · 85mins

Having learned a few tricks while serving as an assistant director on *Ben-Hur*, Ferdinando Baldi (assisted by Terence Young) embarked on his own Roman adventure, albeit with a lower budget and a second-string cast. Already looking ill, Alan Ladd clearly feels uncomfortable in his period costume and delivers his lines with the conviction of a man who'd rather be somewhere else. However, this sword-and-sandal romp, in which Rome and Alba decide to let two teams of three brothers fight the final battle of their protracted war, did give him the chance to co-star with daughter Alana. Italian dialogue dubbed into English. 🎞

Alan Ladd *Horatio* • Franco Bettoja *Marcia* • Franco Fabrizi *Curiazio* • Robert Keith *King of Rome* • Jacques Sernas *King of Alba* • Andrea Aureli *King of Alba* • Mino Doro *Caio* • Alana Ladd *Scilla* ■ *Dir* Ferdinando Baldi, Terence Young • *Scr* Carlo Lizzani, Ennio De Concini, Giuliano Montaldo, from a story by Luciano Vincenzoni

Duel of Hearts ★★★

Romantic adventure
1990 · UK/US · Colour · 95mins

Fans of Barbara Cartland and all things utterly unbelievable will love to wallow in this made-for-TV adaptation of Cartland's novel *Duel of Love*. Alison Doody, whose career never took off after her role in *Indiana Jones and the Last Crusade*, squeezes into tight corsets to help her one true love who, unfortunately, is accused of murder. Whoever said the course of love runs smooth? Extremely silly stuff, which should be enjoyed with a pile of tissues, a box of chocolates and a complete lack of cynicism.

Alison Doody *Lady Caroline Faye* • Michael York *Gervase Warlingham* • Benedict Taylor *Lord Vane Brecon* • Geraldine Chaplin *Mrs Miller* • Billie Whitelaw *Dorcas* • Suzanna Hamilton *Harriet Wantage* ■ *Dir* John Hough • *Scr* Terence Freely, from the novel *Duel of Love* by Barbara Cartland

Duel of the Titans ★★★ U

Historical adventure
1961 · It · Colour · 105mins

Two of the finest exponents of the spaghetti western join forces on this superior sword-and-sandal offering. Sergio Corbucci called the shots, while Sergio Leone was among the septet of screenwriters. There's also an impressive double act in front of the camera, with ex-Mr Universe Steve Reeves teaming with onetime Tarzan Gordon Scott as the founders of Rome, Romulus and Remus. Even the supporting cast is better than average, with Virna Lisi providing the glamour and Massimo Girotti the gravitas. Italian dialogue dubbed into English.

Steve Reeves *Romulus* • Gordon Scott *Remus* • Virna Lisi *Julia* • Massimo Girotti *Tazio* • Jacques Sernas *Curzio* ■ *Dir* Sergio Corbucci • *Scr* Sergio Corbucci, Sergio Leone, Luciano Martino, Sergio Prosperi, Franco Rossetti, Ennio De Concini, Duccio Tessari

The Duellists ★★★★ PG

Historical drama 1977 · UK · Colour · 95mins

Set against the heavyweight hostilities of the Napoleonic Wars, the small-time conflict of hussars Harvey Keitel and Keith Carradine – challenging each other over the years to a series of duels – might seem ludicrously beside the point. But Keitel's manic man of honour is a character whose chilling fixation says something about the wider conflict and humankind's need to struggle. This was director Ridley Scott's first feature after graduating from commercials, and it comes across as a coldly brilliant portrait of obsession. 🎞

Keith Carradine *Armand d'Hubert* • Harvey Keitel *Gabriel Feraud* • Albert Finney *Fouché* • Edward Fox *Colonel* • Cristina Raines *Adèle* • Robert Stephens *General Treillard* • Tom Conti *Dr Jacquin* • Diana Quick *Laura* ■ *Dir* Ridley Scott • *Scr* Gerald Vaughan-Hughes, from the novella *The Duel* by Joseph Conrad

Duet for One ★★★★ 15

Drama   1986 · UK · Colour · 102mins

Julie Andrews gives a moving, unsentimental performance as a concert violinist whose life is shattered, in slow motion, by the onset of multiple sclerosis. Saccharine music aside, director Andrei Konchalovsky ensures the story – which echoes the real-life experience of cellist Jacqueline du Pré – has real conviction, with Alan Bates movingly surly as Julie's composer husband and Max von Sydow disagreeably callous as the death-fearing psychotherapist. It's Andrews, however, who makes this film version of Tom Kempinski's acclaimed play memorable.

Julie Andrews *Stephanie Anderson* • Alan Bates *David Cornwallis* • Max von Sydow *Dr Louis Feldman* • Rupert Everett *Constantine Kassanis* • Margaret Courtenay *Sonia Randvich* • Cathryn Harrison *Penny Smallwood* ■ *Dir* Andrei Konchalovsky • *Scr* Tom Kempinski, Jeremy Lipp, Andrei Konchalovsky, from the play by Tom Kempinski

Duffy ★★

Crime caper   1968 · UK · Colour · 101mins

Portraitist Donald Cammell broke into films as the co-author of a slipshod heist caper that would have you believe its anarchic chaos is really ultra-chic comedy. Compounding the script's lack of focus is director Robert Parrish's preoccupation with flashy visuals and the Mediterranean locations, which leaves his cast floundering. James Coburn is particularly bemused as the hippy drifter hired by half-brothers James Fox and John Alderton to rob their mean-spirited millionaire father, James Mason. Fox, meanwhile, turns in a wildly mannered performance that's almost as eccentric as his fashion sense.

James Coburn *Duffy* • James Mason *Calvert* • James Fox *Stefane* • Susannah York *Segolene* • John Alderton *Anthony* • Barry Shawzin *Bakirgian* • Carl Duering *Bonivet* ■ *Dir* Robert Parrish • *Scr* Donald Cammell, Harry Joe Brown Jr, from a story by Donald Cammell, Harry Joe Brown Jr, Pierre De La Salle

Duffy's Tavern ★ U
Musical comedy 1945 · US · BW · 97mins

This revue-style aberration from a distinguished studio (Paramount) hangs dozens of embarrassed-looking contract stars performing second-rate songs and sketches on to a paper-thin excuse for a plot. They are supposedly putting on a benefit show for innkeeper Ed Gardner (whose popular radio show of the same title gave rise to the idea) and record company exec Victor Moore. A smidgen of romance is introduced between Barry Sullivan and Marjorie Reynolds, while such luminaries as Bing Crosby, Betty Hutton, Paulette Goddard, Dorothy Lamour, Eddie Bracken, Veronica Lake and Alan Ladd supply the acts.

Bing Crosby • Betty Hutton • Paulette Goddard • Alan Ladd • Dorothy Lamour • Eddie Bracken • Veronica Lake • Ed Gardner *Archie* • Victor Moore *Michael O'Malley* • Barry Sullivan *Danny Murphy* • Marjorie Reynolds *Peggy O'Malley* • Brian Donlevy • Sonny Tufts ■ *Dir* Hal Walker • *Scr* Melvin Frank, Norman Panama, Abe S Burrows, Barney Dean, George White, Eddie Davis, Matt Brooks, from characters created by Ed Gardner

The Duke of West Point ★★ U
Drama 1938 · US · BW · 109mins

Minor South African star Louis Hayward was as bland a leading man as they came. He made this feature between playing the Saint and the Man in the Iron Mask, in what could be considered the peak of his career. Co-star Joan Fontaine makes a charming ingénue, three years before tremulously winning an Oscar for Alfred Hitchcock's *Suspicion*. However, the real star of the movie is America's military academy West Point, whose governors recognised the recruitment value of such films as *Ten Gentlemen from West Point*, *West Point Story* and John Ford's *The Long Gray Line*.

Louis Hayward *Steven Early* • Joan Fontaine *Ann Porter* • Tom Brown *Sonny Drew* • Richard Carlson *Jack West* • Alan Curtis *Cadet Strong* • Donald Barry *Cadet Grady* • Gaylord Pendleton *[Steve Pendleton] Cadet Rains* • Charles D Brown *Doc Porter* • Jed Prouty *Mr Drew* ■ *Dir* Alfred E Green • *Scr* George Bruce

The Duke Wore Jeans ★★ U
Musical 1958 · UK · BW · 89mins

Where movies are concerned, a single Tommy Steele is usually one too many, but two are more than flesh and blood can bear. Here he plays a likely lad who helps a charmless lookalike noble to escape being married off to feisty princess June Laverick. The "trading places" plot is one of the venerable old chestnuts of drama and the jerry-built sets and fifth-rate pop songs that adorn this tosh considerably scuff the sheen. Gerald Thomas and Peter Rogers made cheapskate part of the *Carry On* appeal, but here it simply seems tatty.

Tommy Steele *Tony Whitecliffe/Tommy Hudson* • June Laverick *Princess Maria* • Michael Medwin *Cooper* • Eric Pohlmann *Bastini* • Alan Wheatley *King of Ritallia* • Mary Kerridge *Queen* • Ambrosine Philpotts *Duchess* • Clive Morton *Lord Whitecliffe* ■ *Dir* Gerald Thomas • *Scr* Norman Hudis, from a story by Lionel Bart, Michael Pratt

Dukes of Hazzard Reunion ★★
Action adventure 1997 · US · Colour

Over 300 Dodge Chargers bit the dust between 1979 and 1985 as Luke and Bo Duke rattled through 147 harum-scarum adventures in the TV series. But the "General Lee" looks in mint condition for this TV movie, which reunited Tom Wopat and John Schneider with their kissin' cousin, Catherine Bach. Sadly, Sorrel Booke's death meant they were denied the chance to lock fenders one last time with Boss Hogg, but Mama Max's attempt to build a theme park in the middle of Hazzard County's swamp keeps them occupied. As you'd expect with Lewis Teague in charge, the action is fast and furious, and the freewheeling spirit of the original series still shines through.

John Schneider *Bo Duke* • Tom Wopat *Luke Duke* • Catherine Bach *Daisy Duke* • Denver Pyle *Uncle Jesse* • James Best *Sheriff Rosco Coltrane* • Sonny Shroyer *Enos Strate* ■ *Dir* Lewis Teague • *Scr* Gy Waldron

Dulcima ★★
Drama 1971 · UK · Colour · 97mins

British film-makers are so obsessed with urban decay that rural life is often overlooked. This adaptation of HE Bates's story may be overly ripe, but at least it attempts to redress the balance. John Mills gives a rambunctious performance as the Gloucestershire farmer who risks losing his carefully stashed wealth when he falls in lust with gold-digging Carol White. Writer/director Frank Nesbitt indulges in a little crude comedy, and Mills can't quite manage to avoid caricature. By the time White seduces gamekeeper Stuart Wilson, however, the tone has descended to the level of penny-dreadful melodrama.

Carol White *Dulcima Gaskin* • John Mills *Mr Parker* • Stuart Wilson *Gamekeeper* • Bernard Lee *Mr Gaskin* • Sheila Raynor *Mrs Gaskin* • Dudley Foster *Symes* • Cyril Cross *Harris* • Neil Wilson *Auctioneer* ■ *Dir* Frank Nesbitt • *Scr* Frank Nesbitt, from a story by HE Bates

Dumb and Dumber ★★★★ 12
Comedy 1994 · US · Colour · 106mins

With Jim Carrey, there are no half measures. So you'll either love this as one of his finest moments or loathe it as a perfect example of mind-numbing Hollywood cinema. But even the harshest critic will find it hard to suppress a couple of chuckles during this cheerfully moronic mix of slapstick, sight gags and toilet humour. Carrey and Jeff Daniels play two of the world's stupidest people who set off on a chaotic road trip when they attempt to return Lauren Holly's missing briefcase. Disengage the brain and enjoy. Contains violence and nudity. **DVD**

Jim Carrey *Lloyd Christmas* • Jeff Daniels *Harry Dunne* • Lauren Holly *Mary Swanson* • Mike Starr *Joe Mentalino* • Karen Duffy *JP Shay* • Charles Rocket *Nicholas Andre* • Victoria Rowell *Athletic beauty* • Teri Garr *Helen Swanson* ■ *Dir* Peter Farrelly • *Scr* Peter Farrelly, Bennett Yellin, Bobby Farrelly

Dumbo ★★★★★ U
Classic animation 1941 · US · Colour · 60mins

Although directed by Ben Sharpsteen, every frame of this story from the Disney studio of the outcast elephant with huge ears was personally approved by Uncle Walt himself. The film won an Oscar for its score, but it's songs such as *When I See an Elephant Fly* and *Baby of Mine* (from the heartbreaking mother-child reunion) that linger in the memory. On the animation side, the highlight is the parade of pink elephants after Dumbo and Timothy Mouse get tipsy. Made for a fraction of the cost of previous Disney animations, this may be one of the studio's shortest features, but it's also among the best. **DVD**

Edward Brophy *Timothy Mouse* • Herman Bing *Ringmaster* • Verna Felton *Elephant* • Sterling Holloway *Stork* • Cliff Edwards *Jim Crow* ■ *Dir* Ben Sharpsteen • *Scr* Joe Grant, Dick Huemer, from a book by Helen Aberson, Harold Pearl • *Music/Lyrics* Frank Churchill, Oliver Wallace, Ned Washington

Dune ★★★★ 15
Science-fiction drama 1984 · US · Colour · 130mins

Frank Herbert's mammoth cult novel, about the competition between two warring families for control of a barren planet renowned for its mind-expanding spice, is converted by director David Lynch into a dense, swirling mass of religious symbolism and mysticism. Under-rated on its release and unjustly criticised for a lack of narrative drive, this is a film that definitely deserves revisiting. Lynch was, reportedly, unhappy with the final cut, but his film is visually stunning, and many of the scenes are among the most memorable and original, of the genre. Kyle MacLachlan (in his film debut) stars as the "messiah" alongside an amazing cast that includes Sean Young, Francesca Annis, Sting, Patrick Stewart and Kenneth McMillan (as the decaying, bloated Baron Harkonnen, perhaps the most repellent villian ever created). Contains violence and swearing. **DVD**

Kyle MacLachlan *Paul Atreides* • Francesca Annis *Lady Jessica* • Brad Dourif *Piter De Vries* • José Ferrer *Padishah Emperor Shaddam IV* • Linda Hunt *Shadout Mapes* • Freddie Jones *Thufir Hawat* • Richard Jordan *Duncan Idaho* • Virginia Madsen *Princess Irulan* • Silvana Mangano *Reverend Mother Ramallo* • Kenneth McMillan *Baron Vladimir Harkonnen* • Patrick Stewart *Gurney Halleck* • Sting *Feyd Rautha* • Dean Stockwell *Dr Wellington Yueh* • Max von Sydow *Dr Kynes* • Sean Young *Chani* ■ *Dir* David Lynch • *Scr* David Lynch, from the novel by Frank Herbert

Dunkirk ★★★ PG
Second World War drama 1958 · UK · BW · 129mins

Produced by Michael Balcon, this Ealing reconstruction of the evacuation of Dunkirk is impressive in its scale and authenticity, but slightly disappointing in its writing and execution. John Mills, Richard Attenborough and Bernard Lee scarcely have to act as their respective parts – a corporal lost on the beaches, a snivelling stay-at-home and a cynical reporter – are so cleverly tailor-made. Director Leslie Norman handles the manoeuvres with skill and does well to maintain the docu-dramatic feel, in spite of some shoddy dialogue, but his approach is too reverential. ▣

John Mills *Binns* • Bernard Lee *Charles Foreman* • Richard Attenborough *Holden* • Robert Urquhart *Mike* • Ray Jackson *Barlow* • Meredith Edwards *Dave Bellman* • Anthony Nicholls *Military spokesman* • Michael Shillo *Jouvet* ■ *Dir* Leslie Norman • *Scr* David Divine, WP Lipscomb, from the novel *The Big Pick-Up* by Elleston Trevor and the play *Dunkirk* by Lt Col Ewen Butler, Maj JS Bradford

Dunston Checks In ★★★ PG
Comedy 1996 · Can · Colour · 84mins

Early Tarzan films led the way, with the ape-man's own furry jungle swinger, Cheetah. Now there's Dunston, an orang-utan acting as the unwilling sidekick to a snooty English peer (Rupert Everett) who wants to use him to burgle New York's Majestic Hotel. It's amiable tosh, but Dunston's antics are as delightfully appealing as Faye Dunaway's rudely ruthless proprietor is unattractive. ▣

Jason Alexander *Robert Grant* • Faye Dunaway *Mrs Dubrow* • Eric Lloyd *Kyle Grant* • Rupert Everett *Lord Rutledge* • Graham Sack *Brian* • Paul Reubens *La Farge* • Glenn Shadix *Lionel Spalding* • Nathan Davis *Victor* ■ *Dir* Ken Kwapis • *Scr* John Hopkins, Bruce Graham, from a story by John Hopkins

The Dunwich Horror ★★ 18
Horror 1970 · US · Colour · 84mins

Lovers of HP Lovecraft's stories had to wait until *Re-Animator* to see full justice done to his full-blooded *Necronomicon* tales. Back in the sixties, fans made do with fun fiascos from the Roger Corman scrap heap. In this comic caper, a hopelessly miscast Sandra Dee – the squeaky-clean starlet immortalised by a *Grease* song – plays a student who is the drugged victim of a fertility rite, set up by the hammy Dean Stockwell in his bid to restore ancient powers of evil. A psychedelic howler. Contains violence. ▣

Sandra Dee *Nancy Walker* • Dean Stockwell *Wilbur Whateley* • Ed Begley *Dr Henry Armitage* • Sam Jaffe *Old Whateley* • Donna Baccala *Elizabeth Hamilton* • Joanne Moore Jordan *Lavinia* • Talia Coppola [Talia Shire] *Cora* ■ *Dir* Daniel Haller • *Scr* Curtis Lee Hanson, Henry Rosenbaum, Ronald Silkosky, from the story by HP Lovecraft

Dupetta ★★★ PG
Drama 1952 · Pak · BW · 143mins

At times possessed of the brooding pathos that was a staple of the more maudlin Boris Karloff movies, this cautionary tale takes an age to spring the hardly startling revelation that love is blind. Noor Jehan is striking as the endlessly suffering woman whose inability to recognise her disfigured husband compounds her woes. Although the monochrome suits the mood of the story, the lack of colour detracts from the song and dance routines which, in keeping with the masala musical tradition, tell us more about the thoughts and emotions of the characters than their actions. In Urdu with English subtitles. ▣

Noor Jehan • Ajay Kumar Sudhir ■ *Dir* S Fazli

Dust ★★★ 18

Drama   1985 · Fr/Bel · Colour · 85mins

Adapted from JM Coetzee's novel *In the Heart of the Country*, this brooding South African drama gives Trevor Howard the opportunity to explore a fully rounded character after years of formulaic cameos. As the boorish farmer who seduces the wife of his black foreman, he chillingly conveys the arrogance of supremacy and the lust of isolation. Yet it's Jane Birkin, as the daughter who becomes increasingly jealous of her father's new flame, who provides both the film's emotional core and its shocking resolution. Directed with extreme care by Marion Hänsel, this is stern stuff that's never as dry as its title.

Jane Birkin *Magda* • Trevor Howard *Father* • John Matshikiza *Hendrik* • Nadine Uwampa *Klein anna* • Lourdes Christina Sayo Momoboko *Old Anna* • René Diaz *Jacob* • Tom Vrebos *Piet* ■ *Dir* Marion Hänsel • *Scr* Marion Hänsel, from the novel *In the Heart of the Country* by JM Coetzee

Dust Be My Destiny ★★

Crime drama   1939 · US · BW · 88mins

One of those Warner Bros "torn from today's headlines" crime movies, this routine melodrama is redeemed by the ever-excellent John Garfield. He's ideally cast as an innocent on the run, fleeing a murder rap. In jail, he falls for Priscilla Lane, the work-farm boss's stepdaughter, while newspaper editor Alan Hale takes an interest in his case. The story's more than a mite overfamiliar, but there's sterling acting from a cast of Warners regulars, including John Litel, Stanley Ridges and Moroni Olsen, and director Lewis Seiler doesn't get in the way. A little more originality all round wouldn't have gone amiss, though.

John Garfield *Joe Bell* • Priscilla Lane *Mabel* • Alan Hale *Mike Leonard* • Frank McHugh *Caruthers* • Billy Halop *Hank* • Bobby Jordan *Jimmy* • Charley Grapewin *Pop* • Henry Armetta *Nick* ■ *Dir* Lewis Seiler • *Scr* Robert Rossen, from a novel by Jerome Odlum

Dust Devil ★★★★ 18

Horror thriller   1992 · UK · Colour · 103mins

Richard Stanley's surreal serial killer horror thriller is a landmark British film of the nineties. Combining African tribal myths with spaghetti western folklore, the *Hardware* director's highly personal magical mystery tour through sweeping Namibian vistas is an embarrassment of cinematic riches. It's a hallucinogenic eye-popper, a political allegory – accent on the gory – that bursts with atmospheric moodiness. Robert Burke is a forbidding presence as "The Hitcher from Hell", spinning an illusory web of dream-like terror around his suicidal victims. Once seen, never forgotten. Contains violence, swearing, sex scenes and nudity. ▭

Robert Burke *Dust Devil/"Hitch"* • Chelsea Field *Wendy Robinson* • Zakes Mokae *Ben Mukuron* • John Matshikiza *Joe Niemand* • Rufus Swart *Mark Robinson* • William Hootkins *Captain Cornelius Beyman* • Marianne Sägebrecht *Dr Leidzinger* ■ *Dir/Scr* Richard Stanley

Dust in the Wind ★★★ 15

Romantic drama
1987 · Tai · Colour · 109mins

While not Hou Hsiao-Hsien's most ambitious picture, this bittersweet tale of country mice finding love in the big city, only to drift apart when patriotic duty calls, is full of human foibles and shrewd observations. As the teenagers leaving their mining village to complete their studies in Taipei, Wang Ching-Won and Xin Shufen have an honesty that reinforces the film's social realism, while the director's command of their environment, be it the rundown cinema where they live, the rugged coastline or the forbidding mountainscapes, is impeccable. For all the implied criticisms of Taiwan and China, however, it's a fairly noncommittal picture. In Hokkien and Mandarin with English subtitles.

Wang Ching-Won *Wan* • Xin Shufen *Huen* • Che'en Shu-Fang *Huen's mother* • Li Tienlu *Grandpa* ■ *Dir* Hou Hsiao-Hsien • *Scr* Wu Nien-Jen, Chu Tien-Wen

Dust of Life ★★★

Drama   1994 · Fr/Alg/HK · Colour · 87mins

Based on a book by Duyen Ahn, this grinding study of institutionalised brutality and indomitable hope provides telling insights into a neglected aspect of the Vietnam War. Despised for being the son of an African-American, Daniel Guyant is sent to a labour camp on the Cambodian border. Although he eventually makes an almost suicidal bid for freedom, director Rachid Bouhareb is more concerned with depicting the harsh conditions inside the compound and the way Guyant responds to them. Uncompromisingly photographed and played with courage and conviction, this is a worthy tribute to quiet heroism in the face of near-genocidal racism. In French with English subtitles.

Daniel Guyant *Son* • Gilles Chitlaphone *Bob* • Leon Outtrabady *Shrimp* • Jehan Pages *Little Hai* • Lam Siu Lin *Greaser* • Yann Roussel *Steel Muscles* • William Low *Commander* ■ *Dir* Rachid Bouchareb • *Scr* Rachid Bouchareb, Bernard Gesbert, from the novel *La Colline de Fanta* by Duyen Ahn

Dusty ★★★

Drama   1982 · Ausl · Colour · 90mins

Bill Kerr made his name on radio as one of Tony Hancock's sidekicks. But, in later years, his grizzled features suited him for roles in a number of Australian outdoor dramas. Here he plays a bushman turned shepherd who trains an abandoned wild hound (Dusty) into a champion sheepdog. Director John Richardson lovingly captures the tasks of the farm and the unique relationship between man and dog, thus making the hunt for Dusty (who has retained his predatory instincts) all the more heart-rending. Kerr is superb as the outsider whose loyalties lie with the wilds.

Bill Kerr *Tom* • Noel Trevarthen *Harry* • Carol Burns *Clara* • John Stanton *Railey Jordan* ■ *Dir* John Richardson • *Scr* Sonia Borg, from a novel by Frank Dalby Davison

Dusty Ermine ★★

Crime drama   1936 · UK · BW · 85mins

Although the British title sounds as if this should be a "silly ass" comedy with Tom Wells and Ralph Lynn, the American alternative, *Hideout in the Alps*, leaves you in no doubt as to what's really on offer. Adapted from the play by Neil Grant, this is far from the best film made by the recently rediscovered director Bernard Vorhaus. However, detective Anthony Bushell's pursuit of criminal peer Ronald Squire is not without its moments of tension and droll humour. Jane Baxter provides the glamour, but the real interest lies in the supporting performances of Felix Aylmer and Margaret Rutherford.

Jane Baxter *Linda Kent* • Anthony Bushell *Inspector Forsyth* • Ronald Squire *Jim Kent* • Margaret Rutherford *Miss Butterby* • Davina Craig *Goldie* • Athole Stewart *Mr Kent* • Felix Aylmer *Assistant commissoner* ■ *Dir* Bernard Vorhaus • *Scr* L du Garde Peach, Michael Hankinson, Arthur Macrae, Paul Hervey Fox, H Fowler Mear, from the play by Neil Grant

Dutchman ★★

Drama   1966 · UK · BW · 54mins

Ostensibly, this lean screen version of LeRoi Jones's controversial play shows how sadistic white woman Shirley Knight persecutes and eventually assaults black man Al Freeman Jr on the New York subway. But while there are multiple layers of socio-political symbolism beneath the surface, the action is so slow and portentous you soon tire of searching for them. Having edited several significant British features, Anthony Harvey made his directorial debut with this 54-minute film. He earned an Oscar nomination for his first feature, *The Lion in Winter*.

Shirley Knight *Lula* • Al Freeman Jr *Clay* • Frank Lieberman *Subway Rider* • Robert Calvert *Subway Rider* • Howard Bennett *Subway Rider* • Sandy McDonald *Subway Rider* • Denis Peters *Subway Rider* ■ *Dir* Anthony Harvey • *Scr* Anthony Harvey, from the play *Dutchman* by LeRoi Jones

Duty Free Marriage ★★★

Romantic drama
1980 · Hun/Fin · Colour · 100mins

While gently mocking the national characteristics of its principals, this Finnish-Hungarian co-production also had the more serious purpose of attacking the 1981 immigration laws that forbade Hungarians who married outside the country from returning home within five years. Pausing for some acerbic asides on generational and town-and-country politics, János Zsombolyai seamlessly segues from comedy into drama as Mari Kiss's marriage of convenience to Tom Wentzel's Finnish bachelor takes a turn for the worse once they realise its impact on his family and her friends. Direct, disarming and delightful. In Hungarian with English subtitles.

Mari Kiss *Mari* • Tom Wentzel *Pekka* • Cecilia Esztergályos *Ili* • Agi Margittay *Agi* ■ *Dir* János Zsombolyai • *Scr* János Zsombolyai, Akos Kertesz, from a story by János Zsombolyai

D'Ye Ken John Peel? ★★

Drama   1934 · UK · BW · 84mins

Released in the States as *Captain Moonlight*, this is a crusty old melodrama in the Tod Slaughter tradition. Chewing the scenery with a delicious lack of restraint, Leslie Perrins plays the dastardly rogue whose idea of payment for an outstanding debt is to marry the debtor's daughter. But fear not for Winifred Shotter: riding to the rescue is Waterloo veteran John Garrick, who knows a thing or two about delivering damsels from distress. This is anything but a lost classic, but there is the chance to see Stanley Holloway as Sam Small, the character he adopted for many of his famous monologues.

John Garrick *Major John Peel* • Winifred Shotter *Lucy Merrall* • Stanley Holloway *Sam Small* • John Stuart *Captain Moonlight* • Leslie Perrins *Mr Craven* • Mary Lawson *Toinette* ■ *Dir* Henry Edwards • *Scr* H Fowler Mear, from a story by Charles Cullum

Dying of Laughter ★★★

Black comedy   1999 · Sp · Colour · 105mins

After nearly coming off the rails with *Perdita Durango*, maverick director Alex de la Iglesia returns to the realms of pitch-black comedy with this macabre tale of a comedy double act whose success disguises a pathological rivalry. Superb performances from the dashingly witty El Gran Wyoming and his put-upon stooge, Santiago Segura, are the key to this scathing memoir of Spanish light entertainment during two decades of almost ceaseless socio-political upheaval. Yet the romantic feuds, drug-induced separations and explosive reunions would be nothing without the knowing kitsch of the decor and the irreverence of the direction. In Spanish with English subtitles.

Santiago Segura *Nino* • El Gran Wyoming *Bruno* • Alex Angulo *Julian* • Carla Hidalgo *Laura* • Eduardo Gomez *El Pobre Tino* ■ *Dir* Alex de la Iglesia • *Scr* Alex de la Iglesia, Jorge Guerricaechevarria

Dying to Belong ★★

Thriller   1997 · US · Colour

The characters quite literally die to belong, in this rather po-faced TV-movie attempt to show up the darker side of fraternity high jinks. Here, the girls show they can be just as nasty as their male counterparts, as a young student attempts to find out what really happened to her best friend during sorority week. It's a worthy attempt, but the unknown cast and formless direction do little to hammer home the message. *Sorority Babes in the Slimeball Bowl-o-Rama* covered the same territory and was a lot more fun. Contains violence.

Hilary Swank *Lisa Connors* • Mark-Paul Gosselaar *Steve Tyler* • Sarah Chalke *Drea* • Jenna Von Oy *Shelby* • Laurel Holloman ■ *Dir* William A Graham • *Scr* Ron McGee

Dying to Live ★ PG

Fantasy drama   1999 · US · Colour · 85mins

Jonathan Frakes (*Star Trek: The Next Generation*) beams down for this pale imitation of *Ghost*. After his girlfriend tragically drowns on prom night, a high-school athlete begins receiving unsettling signals, seemingly from the deceased girl, that a jealous female friend played a role in her "accidental" death. Soon we learn that the teenage girl's guardian angel (Frakes) is helping to avenge her death before she moves on to eternal life. Dull, rambling and hokey, you'll find better performances at your local puppet show. 🎦

Jonathan Frakes *Angel* • Gabriel Mann *Matthew* • Hayley DuMond *Rachel Linden* • Linda Cardellini *Leslie* • Shannon Elizabeth *Vanessa* • Brian Poth *Evan* ■ *Dir* Rob Hedden • *Scr* Victor Bumbalo, Rob Hedden, from a story by Victor Bumbalo

Dying to Love You ★★ 15

Thriller based on a true story
1993 · US · Colour · 90mins

If Tim Matheson had watched *Sea of Love*, he would have known that dynamic sexpots who answer lonely hearts ads are going to lead to trouble rather than the altar. Tracy Pollan proves to be just such a *femme fatale* in this unremarkable TV movie, also known as *Lethal White Female*, that yet again purports to be based on a true story. Director Robert Iscove is pushing his luck stretching this thriller to an hour-and-a-half because, once we've discovered Pollan's shady past (not to mention her assortment of identity cards), it doesn't take Mystic Meg to foresee the outcome. Contains some violence and sex scenes.

Tim Matheson *Roger Paulson* • Tracy Pollan *Elaine/Lisa Ann Rohn* • Christine Ebersole *Cheryl New* • Lee Garlington *Rita* • Frances Lee McCain *Sue Graham* • Alan Blumenfeld *Max* • Jordan Bond *Matt Paulson* ■ *Dir* Robert Iscove • *Scr* John Miglis

Dying Young ★★ 15

Romantic drama
1991 · US · Colour · 106mins

Cruel though it may be, Joel Schumacher's lamentable tear-jerker leaves one wishing that the terminally sick rich lad at the centre of this interminable nonsense had died even younger (or at least before the cameras arrived). Campbell Scott tries hard in a thankless role, made all the more difficult by the fact that Schumacher only has eyes for Julia Roberts as the blowzy girl from the wrong side of the tracks who answers Scott's advert for a carer. A crass crossbreed of *Love Story* and *Pretty Woman*, this is a must-see, if only to discover how low Hollywood can stoop. Contains swearing and nudity. 🎦

Julia Roberts *Hilary O'Neil* • Campbell Scott *Victor Geddes* • Vincent D'Onofrio *Gordon* • Colleen Dewhurst *Estelle Whittier* • David Selby *Richard Geddes* • Ellen Burstyn *Mrs O'Neil* • Dion Anderson *Cappy* • Daniel Beer *Danny* ■ *Dir* Joel Schumacher • *Scr* Richard Friedenberg, from the novel by Marti Leimbach

Dynamite ★★★ U

Drama
1929 · US · BW · 69mins

The first talkie from producer/director Cecil B DeMille, one of the few directors (along with Hitchcock and Spielberg) whose name was always instantly recognised by the public, largely because his invariably epic productions promised a great deal of sex and glamour. This is very typical of DeMille, with a love triangle involving a condemned murderer (Charles Bickford), a giddy socialite (Kay Johnson) and a noble hero (Conrad Nagel), all thrown together in a mammoth mine disaster. The cave-in is spectacular, the costumes are

splendid and the bathrooms are lavish. Watch for a very young Joel McCrea as Marco the Sheik, plus a song, *How Am I to Know?*, penned by Dorothy Parker.

Conrad Nagel *Roger Towne* • Kay Johnson *Cynthia Crothers* • Charles Bickford *Hagon Derk* • Julia Faye *Marcia Towne* • Muriel McCormac *Katie Derk* • Tyler Brooke *Life of the Party* • Joel McCrea *Marco the Sheik* ■ *Dir* Cecil B DeMille • *Scr* Jeanie Macpherson, John Howard Lawson, Gladys Unger, from a story by Jeanie Macpherson

Dynamite Chicken ★★ 18

Satirical documentary
1971 · US · Colour · 75mins

Only the sixties could have given birth to a concept like this: a "multi-media mosaic" of American pop culture that incorporates rock footage, animation, newsreels and nudity. By turns offensive and enlightening, there are all too brief glimpses of such 20th-century icons as Jimi Hendrix, John and Yoko, the Velvet Underground and Lenny Bruce, and far too many shots of hippies doing what hippies did back then. A pre-fame Richard Pryor provides ironic comedy links. Even for curiosity seekers it's a real mixed bag, but any film that features a stripping nun can't be all bad. 🎦

Joan Baez • Richard Pryor • Ron Carey • Marshall Efron • Lisa Ryan • Paul Krasner • Leonard Cohen • John Lennon • Ondine *Ondine* • Andy Warhol ■ *Dir/Scr* Ernest Pintoff

E' Lollipop ★★ U

Drama
1975 · SAfr · Colour · 92mins

Young Muntu Ndebele finds himself cast adrift in Harlem after an airport mix-up sees him separated from José Ferrer, the priest escorting him from South Africa. He's only here in America to cheer up his buddy, fellow orphan Norman Knox, who is recovering from emergency surgery. Asserting that racial tolerance could become a reality if only we adopted the innocence of children, this well-meaning melodrama might have preached more forcibly had it not resorted so readily to sentimentality. Writer/director Ashley Lazarus coaxes admirable performances from his young leads, but their naturalism is corrupted by the contrivances of the plot.

José Ferrer *Father Alberto* • Karen Valentine *Carol Anne* • Bess Finney *Sister Marguerita* • Muntu Ndebele *Tsepo* • Norman Knox *Jannie* • Bingo Mbonjeni *Cash general* • Simon Sabela *Rakwaba* ■ *Dir* Ashley Lazarus • *Scr* Ashley Lazarus, from a story by Andre Pieterse

ET the Extra-Terrestrial ★★★★★ U

Classic science-fiction adventure
1982 · US · Colour · 109mins

Steven Spielberg's ode to aliens could also be seen as a tribute to all the loners of the world, as little ET, abandoned by his pot-bellied extra-terrestrial pals, has to cope on earth until they can come back and rescue him. Luckily, he's befriended by an equally lonely little boy named Elliott, played by Henry Thomas, who proceeds to teach his alien chum how to talk, dress up in women's clothes and guzzle beer. A delightful adventure in which Spielberg manages not only to entertain young children, but also to reach out to the child in all of us. Contains some mild swearing. 🎦

Henry Thomas *Elliott* • Dee Wallace [Dee Wallace Stone] *Mary* • Peter Coyote *Keys* • Robert MacNaughton *Michael* • Drew Barrymore *Gertie* • KC Martel *Greg* • Sean Frye *Steve* • Tom Howell *Tyler* • Erika Eleniak *Pretty girl* ■ *Dir* Steven Spielberg • *Scr* Melissa Mathison • *Cinematographer* Allen Daviau • *Music* John Williams • *Special Effects* Carlo Rambaldi

Each Dawn I Die ★★★ PG

Prison drama
1939 · US · BW · 87mins

What's lacking in credibility is made up for in ferocious energy here, as James Cagney portrays a framed campaigning reporter who is sent to prison and brutalised into throwing in his lot with a crime boss. Sombre undercurrents run below the routine melodrama, with the reporter believing he's been betrayed by both life and by fellow convict George Raft. Cagney gives it all

he's got, including a panic attack in solitary confinement that prefigures his outburst in *White Heat*. 🎦

James Cagney *Frank Ross* • George Raft "Hood" *Stacey* • Jane Bryan *Joyce Conover* • George Bancroft *Warden John Armstrong* • Stanley Ridges *Meuller* • Alan Baxter *Polecat Carlisle* ■ *Dir* William Keighley • *Scr* Norman Reilly Raine, Warren Duff, Charles Perry, from the novel by Jerome Odlum

The Eagle ★★★★ U

Silent adventure
1925 · US · BW · 70mins

A film of enormous curiosity value because Rudolph Valentino's penultimate surge before he died shows — in his smouldering-eyed, he-man presence — just what his attraction was to those women who formed a cult after his death. As a modern-day Robin Hood – the Black Eagle – Valentino makes a sinewy play for Vilma Banky, while being ironically observed by Czarina Louise Dresser, who puts herself about as much as the hero. Much parodied since its release, it still has the charisma to compel – and that's because of Valentino. His star quality was so great he really only needed one to tango.

Rudolph Valentino *Vladimir Dubrovsky* • Vilma Banky *Mascha Troekouroff* • Louise Dresser *Czarina* • Albert Conti *Kuschka* • James Marcus *Kyrilla Troekouroff* • George Nichols *Judge* • Carrie Clark Ward *Aunt Aurelia* ■ *Dir* Clarence Brown • *Scr* Hans Kräly

The Eagle and the Hawk ★★★★

War drama
1933 · US · BW · 63mins

Mordant and very bitter "lost generation" First World War tale, based on a story by aviation specialist John Monk Saunders (Fay Wray's husband) and with a quite superb cast to do it justice. You couldn't wish for better than Fredric March as the disaffected leader of a British flying squadron, Cary Grant as his truculent air gunner, Jack Oakie as his best mate and Carole Lombard as March's London society doll. Reissue prints give Mitchell Leisen his due as assistant director, but first time out the credit went to Stuart Walker alone.

Fredric March *Jeremiah Young* • Cary Grant *Henry Crocker* • Jack Oakie *Mike Richards* • Carole Lombard *Beautiful lady* • Sir Guy Standing [Guy Standing] *Major Dunham* • Forrester Harvey *Hogan* • Kenneth Howell *John Stevens* ■ *Dir* Stuart Walker, Mitchell Leisen • *Scr* Bogart Rogers, Seton I Miller, from the story by John Monk Saunders

The Eagle Has Landed ★★★ 15

Second World War adventure
1976 · US · Colour · 117mins

This far-fetched wartime thriller, from Jack Higgins's novel, has German colonel Michael Caine as the unlikely leader of a task force infiltrating an English village in 1943 with the aim of kidnapping prime minister Winston Churchill. Even more unlikely is English-hating Donald Sutherland's Irish accent allied with Jenny Agutter's cut-glass tones. As a lurking party, the Germans aren't very convincing, but director John Sturges puts some hefty action into the untidy package, while Donald Pleasence's impersonation of Heinrich

Himmler is totally credible. Unlike the film. Contains mild swearing. DVD

Michael Caine *Colonel Kurt Steiner* • Donald Sutherland *Liam Devlin* • Robert Duvall *Colonel Max Radl* • Jenny Agutter *Molly Prior* • Donald Pleasence *Heinrich Himmler* • Anthony Quayle *Admiral Wilhelm Canaris* • Jean Marsh *Joanna Grey* • John Standing *Father Philip Verecker* • Judy Geeson *Pamela Verecker* ■ *Dir* John Sturges • *Scr* Tom Mankiewicz, from the novel by Jack Higgins

Eagle in a Cage ★★★★

Historical drama 1971 · UK · Colour · 102mins

Napoleon's frustrating last years in exile on the tiny, remote island of St Helena make for a compelling drama. Seizing one of the best roles of his career, Kenneth Haigh is superb as the unbowed Bonaparte, and he's beautifully supported by John Gielgud, Ralph Richardson and Billie Whitelaw. Producer/screenwriter Millard Lampell had already nursed this project into an Emmy award-winning TV production starring Trevor Howard in 1965, and his bitter personal experience of exile, as a blacklisted writer during the McCarthy era, resonates throughout.

John Gielgud *Lord Sissal* • Ralph Richardson *Sir Hudson Lowe* • Billie Whitelaw *Madame Bertrand* • Kenneth Haigh *Napoleon Bonaparte* • Moses Gunn *General Gourgaud* • Ferdy Mayne *Count Bertrand* • Lee Montague *Cipriani* • Georgina Hale *Betty Balcombe* ■ *Dir* Fielder Cook • *Scr* Millard Lampell

Eagle with Two Heads ★★★

Drama 1948 · Fr · BW · 94mins

Jean Cocteau's film of his play, *L'Aigle à Deux Têtes*, with Jean Marais – the hero of Cocteau's *Orphée* and star of the stage version – as a 19th-century anarchist who falls in love with the king's widow when he plans to assassinate her. The fact that he's also a dead ringer for the deceased king complicates matters, as do the plans of the queen's enemies. Less of an achievement than Cocteau's better-known movies – such as *Blood of a Poet* (1930) – this has an exuberant romanticism that's hard to resist. In French with English subtitles.

Edwige Feuillère *The Queen* • Jean Marais *Stanislas* • Sylvia Monfort *Edith de Berg* • Jean Debucourt *Felix de Willenstein* • Jacques Varennes *Count de Foehn* • Abdallah *Tony* ■ *Dir* Jean Cocteau • *Scr* Jean Cocteau, from his play *L'Aigle à Deux Têtes*

Eagle's Wing ★★★ PG

Western 1978 · UK · Colour · 99mins

An interesting western that has become something of a cult film. British director Anthony Harvey's strange, myth-laden movie pits two deeply troubled men against each other in a spiritual and material battle for the prize of a white stallion named Eagle's Wing. As, respectively, cowboy and native American Indian, Martin Sheen and Sam Waterston are both superb in their playing of traditional enemies who recognise in each other the same desire to acquit themselves bravely in the critical eyes of their communities. The movie loses a certain momentum as Harvey piles subplot upon subplot, but otherwise this intelligent western is a treat. [video]

Martin Sheen *Pike* • Sam Waterston *White Bull* • Harvey Keitel *Henry* • Stéphane Audran *Widow* • Caroline Langrishe *Judith* • John Castle *Priest* • Jorge Luke *Red Sky* • Jose Carlos Ruis *Lame Wolf* • Manuel Ojeda *Miguel* ■ *Dir* Anthony Harvey • *Scr* John Briley, from a story by Michael Syson

The Ear ★★★★

Political thriller 1969 · Cz · BW · 93mins

This is one of the films "banned forever" by the Czech government in 1969, which finally emerged to great acclaim following the Velvet Revolution 20 years later. Directed with awesome control by Karel Kachyna, *The Ear* is a blistering combination of political allegory and domestic drama. Radoslav Brzobohaty is the epitome of paranoia as the minor official who arrives home from a blood-letting party function convinced that he is next in line for dismissal and arrest. His feuds with wife Jirina Bohdalova as they strip the house of incriminating evidence are excruciating in their bitterness. In Czech with English subtitles.

Jirina Bohdalova *Anna* • Radoslav Brzobohaty *Ludvik* • Gustav Opocensky *Conrade* • Miloslav Holub [Miroslav Holub] *General* • Lubor Tokos *Minister* ■ *Dir* Karel Kachyna • *Scr* Karel Kachyna, Jan Prochazka, from a story by Jan Prochazka

Earl Carroll Vanities ★★ U

Musical 1945 · US · BW · 91mins

Princess Drina (Constance Moore) comes to New York to try and raise some money for her impoverished country. Desperate situations call for desperate measures, and she finds herself starring on Broadway in one of Earl Carroll's musical extravaganzas and receiving the romantic attentions of Dennis O'Keefe. Directed by Joseph Santley and offering some lively production numbers, as well as the always welcome presence of Eve Arden in the supporting cast, this is, nonetheless, a candidate for the most idiotic musical of all time award.

Dennis O'Keefe *Danny Baldwin* • Constance Moore *Drina* • Eve Arden *Tex Donnelly* • Otto Kruger *Earl Carroll* • Alan Mowbray *Grand Duke Paul* • Stephanie Bachelor *Claire Elliott* ■ *Dir* Joseph Santley • *Scr* Frank Gill Jr, from a story by Cortland Fitzsimmons

The Earl of Chicago ★★

Comedy drama 1940 · US · BW · 87mins

Robert Montgomery is "Silky" Kilmount, a Chicago gangster who inherits a title – and a castle! Accompanied by crooked lawyer Edward Arnold, he visits a very backlot England where he encounters butler Edmund Gwenn and solicitor Reginald Owen. Produced by the distinguished Victor Saville, who should have known better, and directed by MGM hack Richard Thorpe, who does what he can, this wasn't amusing then and sorely tries the patience now.

Robert Montgomery *"Silky" Kilmount* • Edward Arnold *"Doc" Ramsey* • Reginald Owen *Gervase Gonwell* • Edmund Gwenn *Munsey* • EE Clive *Redwood* • Norma Varden *Maureen Kilmount* • Halliwell Hobbes *Lord Chancellor* ■ *Dir* Richard Thorpe • *Scr* Lesser Samuels, from a story by Charles de Grandcourt, Gene Fowler, Brock Williams

Early Autumn ★★★★★

Drama 1961 · Jap · Colour · 103mins

Yasujiro Ozu's penultimate film shows a deep concern for the everyday life of his middle-class characters through the somewhat melancholy story of an elderly widower who, much to the dismay of his three daughters, decides to resume a relationship with his former mistress. The film is understandably presented from the viewpoint of a Japanese family, but the relationships are universal. Ozu uses delicate colour and shoots in long scenes with his camera at a constant height to reveal both the inner truth and outer manifestation of life, which he depicts with rigorous perception. In Japanese with English subtitles.

Ganjiro Nakamura *Manbei Kohayagawa* • Setsuko Hara *Akiko Kohayagawa* • Yoko Tsukasa *Noriko Kohayagawa* • Michiyo Aratama *Fumiko Kohayagawa* • Yumi Shirakawa *Takako* ■ *Dir* Yasujiro Ozu • *Scr* Kogo Noda, Yasujiro Ozu

The Early Bird ★★ U

Comedy 1965 · UK · Colour · 93mins

Well past his movie sell-by date, Norman Wisdom is powerless to prevent this dreary dairy comedy from turning sour. The satirical jibes at large-scale automation are nowhere near sharp enough, while the tribute to Britain's fast-fading family firms is too twee. As co-scriptwriter, Wisdom must shoulder much of the blame himself, as regular straight men Jerry Desmonde and Edward Chapman are as solid as rocks and longtime director Robert Asher gives his star plenty of leeway to milk every maudlin moment to the full. Hardly the most distinguished picture in which to make one's colour debut. [video]

Norman Wisdom *Norman Pitkin* • Edward Chapman *Mr Grimsdale* • Jerry Desmonde *Hunter* • Paddie O'Neil *Mrs Hoskins* • Bryan Pringle *Austin* • Richard Vernon *Sir Roger* • John Le Mesurier *Colonel Foster* ■ *Dir* Robert Asher • *Scr* Jack Davies, Norman Wisdom, Eddie Leslie, Henry Blyth

Early Frost ★ 18

Crime thriller 1981 · Aus · Colour · 86mins

Not the award-winning Aidan Quinn Aids drama of (nearly) the same name, but a weak Australian thriller about a private detective who finds a corpse while working on a divorce case and suspects murder, even though a verdict of accidental death is recorded. The paranoia inherent in the situation is unfortunately underplayed, while the ham-fisted actors (who have no doubt been kicked off a few Aussie soaps in their time) give no indication that they know what they are doing. [video]

Guy Doleman *Mike Hayes* • Diana McLean *Val Meadows* • Jon Blake *Peter Meadows* • Janet Kingsbury *Peg Prentice* • Kit Taylor *Paul Sloane* ■ *Dir/Scr* Terry O'Connor

An Early Frost ★★★★ 15

Drama 1985 · US · Colour · 96mins

One of the first dramas on TV to tackle the subject of Aids, this is a poignant and powerful movie about a son who has to tell his parents he is both homosexual and has an Aids-related disease. Aidan Quinn gives a moving performance as the son, while Gena Rowlands and Ben Gazzara are superb as his mum and dad. Subsequent movies on the subject, such as the Tom Hanks Oscar-winner *Philadelphia*, have lapsed into sentimentality, but director John Erman successfully manages to keep the schmaltz in check and produce a touching and effective film. [video]

Aidan Quinn *Michael Pierson* • Gena Rowlands *Katherine Pierson* • Ben Gazzara *Nick Pierson* • Sylvia Sidney *Beatrice McKenna* • DW Moffett *Peter Hilton* • John Glover *Victor Dimato* • Sydney Walsh *Susan Maracek* ■ *Dir* John Erman • *Scr* Ron Cowen, Daniel Lipman, from a story by Sherman Yellen

Early Spring ★★★★

Drama 1956 · Jap · BW · 144mins

Stylistically and thematically, the postwar films of Yasujiro Ozu are very much alike – even their titles (*Late Spring*, *Early Summer*, *Late Autumn*) are confusingly similar – yet each one is a gem. In this mature work, young clerk Sugiyama (Ryo Ikebe) finds temporary respite from the boredom of his job and his marriage in a brief affair with the firm's flirt. The characteristically slight plot, involving a modern Japanese couple, unravels slowly with great formal beauty, economy, lucidity and humour. The outdoor scenes are limited to brief glimpses or to pauses in the action. In Japanese with English subtitles.

Chikage Awashima *Masako* • Ryo Ikebe *Sugiyama* • Keiko Kishi *"Goldfish"* • Chishu Ryu *Onodera* • So Yamamura *Kawai* • Haruko Sugimura *Masako's mother* • Kuniko Miyake *Sakae* • Eijiro Tono *Hattori* ■ *Dir* Yasujiro Ozu • *Scr* Yasujiro Ozu, Kogo Noda

Early Summer ★★★★

Drama 1951 · Jap · BW · 150mins

Few could manipulate screen space and time better than director Yasujiro Ozu. Precious little appears to happen in these two-and-a-half hours, yet they seem to fly by as the director's deceptively inobtrusive style draws you ever more deeply into the lives of Setsuko Hara and her family. As the devoted daughter who suddenly refuses to accept her ageing parents' choice of husband, Hara gives a wonderfully nuanced performance of quiet determination and dignity. But it's the way in which Ozu slowly accumulates detail and gently forces the characters to reveal themselves that makes this simple human drama so compelling. In Japanese with English subtitles..

Setsuko Hara *Noriko* • Chishu Ryu *Koichi* • Kuniko Miyake *Fumiko* • Chikage Awashima *Aya Tamura* • Chieko Higashiyama *Shige* • Zen Murase *Minoru* • Ichiro Sugai *Shukichi* • Haruko Sugimura *Tami Yabe* ■ *Dir* Yasujiro Ozu • *Scr* Yasujiro Ozu, Kogo Noda

Earth ★★★★★ U

Silent drama 1930 · USSR · BW · 83mins

Among the most moving films ever made, director Alexander Dovzhenko's hymn of praise to his native Ukraine comes as close as any silent picture to achieving cinematic poetry. Paced to match the gentle rhythms of nature, the story of the feud between a family of wealthy kulaks and some idealistic

collective farmers has a pronounced political purpose. But it's primarily a celebration of the unending cycle of birth, love and death, hence the funeral of the murdered village chairman ending with a life-giving shower of summer rain. Combining lyrical beauty with simple truth, this is a masterpiece with a soul. A Russian language film. ▭

Stepan Shkurat *Opanas Trubenko* • Semyon Savshenko *Vasil Trubenko* • Pyotr Masokha *Khoma Belokon* • Mikola Nademski *Grandfather Semion Trubenko* • Nikolai Mikhailov *Father Gerasim* • Yelena Maksimova *Natalka* ■ *Dir/Scr* Alexander Dovzhenko

Earth ★★★ 🄵

Political romantic drama
1998 · Ind · Colour · 105mins

Following the lesbian love story *Fire*, Deepa Mehta continues her controversial "elements" trilogy with this disturbing depiction of Muslims, Hindus and Sikhs literally tearing each other apart. Considering the complexity of the political situation in late-forties India, Mehta admirably delineates the different rivalries, though it's only when independence is declared and Lahore erupts into sickening violence that the extent of these enmities becomes apparent. The plot is provocative and relevant, and the acting, particularly from Nandita Das, is committed. Dramatically, it's something of a disappointment. In English and Hindi with subtitles. Contains some swearing.

Maaia [Maia Sethna] *Lenny Sethna* • Nandita Das *Shanta (Lenny's ayah)* • Aamir Khan *Dil Nawaz (Ice Candy man)* • Rahul Khanna *Hasan (Masseur)* • Kulbhushan Kharbanda *Imam Din* • Kitu Gidwani *Bunty Sethna* ■ *Dir* Deepa Mehta • *Scr* Deepa Mehta

Earth Angel ★★★ 🄿🄶

Fantasy comedy 1991 · US · Colour · 90mins

The most fun you can have with this TV movie is to make a list of the films it has pillaged for its plot. Just to get you started, we'll give you *Back to the Future* and *The Curse of the Cat People*, but there are many more. Cathy Podewell is pleasing enough as the student sent back to Earth to sort out the complications that have arisen in the 30 years since she cheated on her boyfriend with the class swot. Mark Hamill and Roddy McDowall are among the guest stars. ▭

Cathy Podewell *Angela* • Erik Estrada *Duke* • Cindy Williams *Judith* • Mark Hamill *Wayne Stein* • Roddy McDowall *Mr Tatum* • Rainbow Harvest *Cindy* • Brian Krause *Mike* ■ *Dir* Joe Napolitano • *Scr* Nina Shengold

Earth Girls Are Easy ★★★★ 🄿🄶

Musical satire 1988 · US · Colour · 100mins

Three randy aliens crash-land in LA and are given a guided tour through Planet Hollywood's craziness by two beautician Valley Girls in an enormously entertaining musical comedy. Geena Davis and Julie Brown, an American cult singer/comedian whose songs inspired this "Martian Beach Party", are terrific in a poppet of a popcorn movie full of bitchy one-liners and frothy fantasy. There's no attempt at a reality check in this

hairsprayed *Lost in Space*, just breezy glitz, garish glamour and *Grease*-type songs in a contemporary trash setting. Fab. ▭

Geena Davis *Valerie Dale* • Jeff Goldblum *Mac* • Jim Carrey *Wiploc* • Damon Wayans *Zebo* • Julie Brown *Candy Pink* • Charles Rocket *Ted* • Michael McKean *Woody* • Larry Linville *Dr Bob* ■ *Dir* Julien Temple • *Scr* Julie Brown, Charlie Coffey, Terrence E McNally

Earth II ★★ 🅄

Science-fiction 1971 · US · Colour · 93mins

This TV pilot was another attempt by American networks to cash in on the success of *Star Trek* – with mixed results. Gary Lockwood (*2001*) and Anthony Franciosa lead the 2,000 inhabitants of the *Earth II* space station, situated between the Earth and the Moon, and declared an independent country. Peace is threatened when an atomic bomb is activated against the station. Predictable space opera with superior special effects but little else to engage the mind. No Mr Spock either. ▭

Gary Lockwood *David Seville* • Scott Hylands *Jim Capa* • Hari Rhodes *Loren Huxley* • Tony Franciosa [Anthony Franciosa] *Frank Karger* • Mariette Hartley *Lisa Karger* • Gary Merrill *Walter Dietrich* • Inga Swenson *Ilyana Kovalefskii* ■ *Dir* Tom Gries • *Scr* William Read Woodfield, Allan Balter

Earth vs the Flying Saucers ★★ 🅄

Science-fiction fantasy 1956 · US · BW · 79mins

Commendable only for special effects genius Ray Harryhausen's flying saucers trashing Washington DC's landmarks, this routine potboiler lifts most of its plot from HG Wells's *The War of the Worlds* but does little else with its *Mars Attacks!* scenario. Hero scientist Hugh Marlowe, back in the nation's capital after surviving *The Day the Earth Stood Still*, slows down the plodding story even further by embarking on a sluggish romantic interlude with Joan Taylor. It just goes to show how little has changed in 30 years: modern blockbusters are all special effects and little story too. For serial Harryhausen freaks only. ▭

Hugh Marlowe *Dr Russell A Marvin* • Joan Taylor *Carol Marvin* • Donald Curtis *Major Huglin* • Morris Ankrum *General Hanley* • John Zaremba *Professor Kanter* • Tom Browne Henry [Thomas Browne Henry] *Admiral Enright* • Grandon Rhodes *General Edmunds* • Larry Blake *Motorcycle officer* ■ *Dir* Fred F Sears • *Scr* George Worthing Yates, Raymond T Marcus [Bernard Gordon], from a story by Curt Siodmak, from the article *Flying Saucers from Outer Space* by Major Donald E Keyhoe

Earth vs the Spider ★

Science-fiction horror 1958 · US · BW · 72mins

A high-school biology teacher finds a "dead" giant spider and puts it in the gym. But when the local rock 'n' roll band starts practising for the prom, the mutation wakes up and rampages around town sucking the vital fluids from terrified teenagers. It sounds like trashy fun, and it is for about five minutes. But cult schlock director Bert I Gordon gets wound up in a tangled web of his own once the dreadful

special effects and awful performances lose their camp lustre.

Edward Kemmer *Mr Kingman* • June Kenny *Carol Flynn* • Gene Persson *Mike Simpson* • Gene Roth *Sheriff Cagle* • Hal Torey *Mr Simpson* • June Jocelyn *Mrs Flynn* ■ *Dir* Bert I Gordon • *Scr* Laszlo Gorog

Earthbound ★

Science-fiction drama 1981 · US · Colour · 94mins

Pandemonium breaks out in the town of Gold Rush when a disabled spaceship lands in its midst and the humanoid cargo seeks out grandfather Burl Ives for help. Evil government agent Joseph Campanella is convinced the aliens are anything but benevolent in this tiresome retread of science-fiction clichés without an iota of style.

Burl Ives *Ned Anderson* • Christopher Connelly *Zef* • Meredith MacRae *Lara* • Joseph Campanella *Conrad* • Todd Porter *Tommy* • Marc Gilpin *Dalem* • Elissa Leeds *Teva* ■ *Dir* James L Conway • *Scr* Michael Fisher

The Earthling ★★ 🄿🄶

Adventure drama 1980 · Ausl · Colour · 96mins

Terminally-ill William Holden gives recently orphaned Ricky Schroder a crash course in life and survival techniques in the Australian outback. Any hopes that this might vaguely resemble Nicolas Roeg's classic *Walkabout* are soon dashed once the sentimental tone becomes evident; there is also an inordinate number of shots featuring cuddly koalas and loping kangaroos. Originally set in America but transferred Down Under, it's not quite a children's film, while most adults will find it hard to stick with. Holden has an undeniable craggy charm, though Schroder isn't as cute as he could have been. ▭

William Holden (1) *Patrick Foley* • Ricky Schroder [Rick Schroder] *Shawn Daley* • Jack Thompson *Ross Daley* • Olivia Hamnett *Bettina Daley* • Alwyn Kurts *Christian Neilson* • Redmond Phillips *Bobby Burns* • Willie Fennell *RC* ■ *Dir* Peter Collinson • *Scr* Lanny Cotler

Earthly Possessions ★★

Drama 1999 · US · Colour · 105mins

A trip to the local bank goes horribly wrong for preacher's wife Charlotte Emery (Susan Sarandon) when she's taken hostage by robber Jake Simms Jr (Stephen Dorff). Far from playing the victim, Sarandon manages to help Dorff escape and get his pregnant girlfriend (Elisabeth Moss) out of a home for unwed mothers. Sarandon does a great line in bored housewives (see *Anywhere but Here*), but her talents are smothered by James Lapine's mediocre TV movie.

Susan Sarandon *Charlotte Emery* • Stephen Dorff *Jake Simms Jr* • Jay O Sanders *Zack Emery* • Elisabeth Moss *Mindy* • Phoebe Lapine *Cheerleader No 1* • Anna Menken *Cheerleader No 2* ■ *Dir* James Lapine • *Scr* Steven Rogers, from the novel by Anne Tyler

Earthquake ★★★★ 🄿🄶

Disaster movie 1974 · US · Colour · 116mins

Highly enjoyable hokum about "the big one" finally hitting Los Angeles, as usual in disaster movies at the worst

possible moment for the cast. The first hour builds up the tension with tremor suspense before the entire city is razed spectacularly to the ground; the dam-busting sequence has since inspired a Universal theme park favourite. Mark Robson's star-packed extravaganza deservedly won a special achievement Oscar for best visual effects. (Did making us believe Ava Gardner was Lorne Greene's daughter come under that category, too?) Registers an eight on the entertainment Richter scale. ▭

Charlton Heston *Stuart Graff* • Ava Gardner *Remy Graff* • George Kennedy *Lew Slade* • Lorne Greene *Sam Royce* • Geneviève Bujold *Denise Marshall* • Richard Roundtree *Miles Quade* • Marjoe Gortner *Jody* • Barry Sullivan *Dr Stockle* • Lloyd Nolan *Dr Vance* • Victoria Principal *Rosa* • Walter Matuschanskavasky [Walter Matthau] *Drunk* ■ *Dir* Mark Robson • *Scr* George Fox, Mario Puzo

East Is East ★★★ 🄵

Comedy 1999 · UK · Colour · 92mins

Films about Asian integration in Britain have tended to be both serious (*My Son the Fanatic*) and marginalised (*My Beautiful Laundrette*). *East Is East* breaks the mould: it's a thoroughly accessible comedy which, like the BBC's *Goodness Gracious Me*, doesn't take itself too seriously. A Pakistani dad, now married to an English woman, is desperate that his four sons buckle under and accept arranged marriages. But the boys, heady with sixties teenage freedom and feeling "British" as opposed to "Asian", are resistant. Family wrangling ensues. Funny, charming and refreshing, this is a great little film, the key word being "little". It's not especially cinematic and feels televisual – though you could say the same about *The Full Monty*. 🄳🅅🄳

Om Puri *George Khan* • Linda Bassett *Ella Khan* • Jordan Routledge *Sajid Khan* • Archie Panjabi *Meenah Khan* • Emil Marwa *Maneer Khan* • Chris Bisson *Saleem Khan* • Jimi Mistry *Tariq Khan* ■ *Dir* Damien O'Donnell • *Scr* Ayub Khan-Din, from his play

East LA ★★ 🄵

Crime drama 1989 · US · Colour · 121mins

Cliché-ridden, low-budget thriller with a largely Mexican cast and some spurious nods to mythicism. Lawrence Hilton-Jacobs is the best-known face in the largely unknown cast, while writer Raymond Martino would go on to the heights of making vehicles for *Playboy* star Anna Nicole Smith.

Tony Bravo *Aurelo* • Kamar Reyes *Paulo Santees* • William Smith *Mr Martel* • Lawrence Hilton-Jacobs *Chesare* ■ *Dir* Addison Randall • *Scr* Addison Randall, Raymond Martino

East Lynne ★★★★

Melodrama 1931 · US · BW · 102mins

One of the greatest Victorian melodramas becomes a surprisingly credible movie in the skilled hands of director Frank Lloyd (*Cavalcade*, *Mutiny on the Bounty*), who has assembled an immaculate cast to bring conviction to a story that is, quite frankly, twaddle. Ann Harding is both beautiful and touching as the fallen woman struggling to regain her child, while

Clive Brook and Conrad Nagel are both sturdy and excellent. Fox spared no expense on the war scenes, and art director Joseph Urban's European re-creations on the backlot would be used and recognised again and again.

Ann Harding *Lady Isabella* • Clive Brook *Captain Levinson* • Conrad Nagel *Robert Carlyle* • Cecilia Loftus *Cornelia Carlyle* • Beryl Mercer *Joyce* • OP Heggie *Earl of Mount Severn* ■ *Dir* Frank Lloyd • *Scr* Bradley King, Tom Barry, from the novel by Mrs Henry Wood

East of Eden ★★★★ PG

Drama 1955 · US · Colour · 112mins

John Steinbeck's sprawling, wordy novel becomes a sprawling, wordy movie about two brothers vying for their father's love. It's Cain and Abel territory and the Biblical parallels are rammed home by Elia Kazan's heavy-handed direction and Paul Osborn's turgid script. The film has dated badly, but it's still worth seeing, for one main reason: James Dean's screen debut. Kazan was set on casting Marlon Brando, but when he met Dean – ''a heap of twisted legs and denim rags, looking resentful for no particular reason'' – he saw the potential. 🖭

James Dean *Cal Trask* • Julie Harris *Abra* • Raymond Massey *Adam Trask* • Jo Van Fleet *Kate Trask* • Burl Ives *Sheriff* • Richard Davalos *Aron Trask* • Albert Dekker *Will* • Lois Smith *Ann* • Harold Gordon *Albrecht* ■ *Dir* Elia Kazan • *Scr* Paul Osborn, from the novel by John Steinbeck

East of Elephant Rock ★★

Drama 1976 · UK · Colour · 92mins

When Bette Davis gunned down her lover in a jealous rage in *The Letter* and pleaded with husband Herbert Marshall that it was self-defence, it was plain we were in for some gripping melodrama. When Judi Bowker does it here, there's an inescapable feeling that what is about to follow is going to be highly embarrassing. Don Boyd's film is carried along by the momentum of a cracking story, thanks to a structure that bears more than a passing resemblance to *The Letter* and an urge to see just how much lower it can descend. The Sri Lankan countryside, however, looks amazing. Contains some nudity.

John Hurt *Nash* • Jeremy Kemp *Harry Rawlins* • Judi Bowker *Eve Proudfoot* • Christopher Cazenove *Robert Proudfoot* • Anton Rodgers *Mackintosh* ■ *Dir* Don Boyd • *Scr* Don Boyd, from a story by Richard Boyle, James Atherton

East of Piccadilly ★★

Crime drama 1940 · UK · BW · 78mins

Adapted from a novel by Gordon Beckles, this sordid murder mystery was an unusual offering to place before a country at war. Director Harold Huth paints a fascinating portrait of Soho in the late thirties, but his handling of the whodunit is much less assured. Red herrings abound as reporter Judy Campbell and crime writer Sebastian Shaw debate whether a waiter, an actor or a Soviet spy is responsible for a series of murders with a silk stocking. Perhaps the most notable feature of this negligible thriller is that it was photographed by Claude Friese-Greene, son of British movie pioneer William.

Judy Campbell *Penny Sutton* • Sebastian Shaw *Tamsie Green* • Niall MacGinnis *Joe* • Henry Edwards *Inspector* • George Pughe *Oscar Juloff* • Martita Hunt *Ma* ■ *Dir* Harold Huth • *Scr* J Lee Thompson, Lesley Storym, from the novel by Gordon Beckles

East of Sumatra ★★ U

Action adventure 1953 · US · Colour · 81mins

A thinly disguised western, set in the Pacific, with Jeff Chandler in the John Wayne role as macho American mining engineer Duke Mullane. Thanks to his boss (John Sutton) he soon falls foul of the island's ruler Anthony Quinn, whose alluring native fiancée, is played by actress Suzan Ball. Quinn and Ball also worked together on *City beneath the Sea* but the latter died tragically in 1955 of bone cancer.

Jeff Chandler *Duke Mullane* • Marilyn Maxwell *Lory Hale* • Anthony Quinn *Kiang* • Suzan Ball *Minyora* • John Sutton *Daniel Catlin* • Jay C Flippen *Mac* • Scatman Crothers *Baltimore* ■ *Dir* Budd Boetticher • *Scr* Frank Gill Jr, Jack Natteford (adaptation), from a story by Louis L'Amour

East Side of Heaven ★★★ U

Musical comedy 1939 · US · BW · 87mins

Dripping in sentimentality, but nonetheless sweet-natured, this comedy marks the debut of 10-month-old Baby Sandy, a girl here cast as a boy (who would know!) who went on to become the star of her own series of movies. In this one, though, she is the excuse for star Bing Crosby to croon a handful of songs as a singing cab driver, saddled with the care of an abandoned baby. The always delightful Joan Blondell co-stars, along with Mischa Auer as Crosby's buddy.

Bing Crosby *Denny Martin* • Joan Blondell *Mary Wilson* • Mischa Auer *Nicky* • Irene Hervey *Mona* • Jerome Cowan *Claudius De Wolfe* • Robert Kent *Cyrus Barrett Jr* • C Aubrey Smith *Cyrus Barrett Sr* ■ *Dir* David Butler • *Scr* William Conselman, from a story by David Butler, Herbert Polesie

East Side, West Side ★★

Drama 1949 · US · BW · 107mins

A rather overcooked melodrama, with James Mason married to Barbara Stanwyck, but unable to resist playing away with Ava Gardner. Stanwyck, meanwhile, does her best to be all saintly and forgive him, while war veteran Van Heflin offers her all the comfort he can muster. Smoothly performed by the appealing cast and smothered in Miklos Rozsa's syrupy music, this is an old-time soap opera, which Mason, in his memoirs, described as ''lamentable''.

Barbara Stanwyck *Jessie Bourne* • James Mason *Brandon Bourne* • Van Heflin *Mark Dwyer* • Ava Gardner *Isabel Lorrison* • Cyd Charisse *Rosa Senta* • Nancy Davis *Helen Lee* • Gale Sondergaard *Nora Kernan* • William Conrad *Lieutenant Jacobi* ■ *Dir* Mervyn LeRoy • *Scr* Isobel Lennart, from the novel by Marcia Davenport

Easter Parade ★★★★ U

Classic musical 1948 · US · Colour · 98mins

Originally intended as a re-teaming of Judy Garland and Gene Kelly under Vincente Minnelli's direction after *The Pirate*, this turned out to be one of MGM's great seasonal delights, as producer Arthur Freed coaxed Fred Astaire out of retirement when Kelly broke his ankle, and entrusted the direction to the brilliant craftsman Charles Walters. The result was simply wonderful. Aided by terrific Irving Berlin songs and radiant Technicolor design – all browns and greens – Astaire, Garland and Walters made an all-time classic, with Fred and Judy particularly outstanding in the perennial favourite *A Couple of Swells*. The screenplay is witty, co-star Ann Miller dances up a storm, and this is the one opportunity to enjoy the talents of Astaire and Garland on screen together.

Judy Garland *Hannah Brown* • Fred Astaire *Don Hewes* • Peter Lawford *Jonathan Harrow III* • Ann Miller *Nadine Hale* • Jules Munshin *François* • Clinton Sundberg *Mike, the bartender* • Jeni Legon *Essie* ■ *Dir* Charles Walters • *Scr* Frances Goodrich, Albert Hackett, Sidney Sheldon, Guy Bolton, from a story by Frances Goodrich, Albert Hackett • *Cinematographer* Harry Stradling • *Art Director* Cedric Gibbons, Jack Martin Smith • *Music/Lyrics* Irving Berlin

Easy Come, Easy Go ★★ U

Musical 1967 · US · Colour · 90mins

One of the weakest of Elvis Presley's later Paramount vehicles, this is almost as embarrassing for audiences as it clearly is for Elvis himself, dealing both with stupid and intractable material about finding lost treasure, and demeaning songs like ''Yoga Is as Yoga Does''. The humour is feeble and invariably tasteless (anti-beatnik jokes in the sixties?) and it's tough to watch Elsa Lanchester used as a figure of fun. The garish Technicolor just about makes this watchable. 🖭

Elvis Presley *Ted Jackson* • Dodie Marshall *Jo Symington* • Elsa Lanchester *Madame Neherina* • Pat Priest *Dina Bishop* • Pat Harrington *Judd Whitman* • Skip Ward *Gil Carey* • Sandy Kenyon *Lt Schwartz* • Frank McHugh *Captain Jack* ■ *Dir* John Rich • *Scr* Allan Weiss, Anthony Lawrence

The Easy Life ★★★★

Drama 1962 · It · BW · 105mins

Writer/director Dino Risi established himself as one of the most scathing critics of Italian complacency during the economic boom of the late fifties. He was at his sharpest with this tragicomic two-hander, in which cynical waster Vittorio Gassman sets about corrupting idealistic student Jean-Louis Trintignant. Exploiting the beauty of the Riviera to highlight the indolence of its residents, Risi gets the most out of his exceptional cast during Trintignant's meeting with Gassman's daughter, Catherine Spaak. In Italian with English subtitles..

Vittorio Gassman *Bruno Cortona* • Jean-Louis Trintignant *Roberto Mariani* • Catherine Spaak *Lilly, Bruno's daughter* • Luciana Angiolillo *Bruno's wife* • Linda Sini *Aunt Lidia* • Corrado Olmi *Alfredo* ■ *Dir* Dino Risi • *Scr* Dino Risi, Ettore Scola, Ruggero Maccari

Easy Living ★★★★

Comedy 1937 · US · BW · 87mins

A smashing slapstick comedy, due mainly to the cracking script by Preston Sturges. The story is simple: a fur coat thrown out of a window gets simple stenographer Jean Arthur mistaken for a millionaire's mistress, leading to all sorts of misunderstandings. As with her films for director Frank Capra, Arthur shows what a gifted comedian she was, coping beautifully with the wisecracks and pratfalls Sturges provides. Edward Arnold and Ray Milland also give spot-on performances, and there's a spectacular update on the old custard pie fight set in a New York automat.

Jean Arthur *Mary Smith* • Edward Arnold *JB Ball* • Ray Milland *John Ball Jr* • Luis Alberni *Mr Louis Louis* • Mary Nash *Mrs Ball* • Franklin Pangborn *Van Buren* • William Demarest *Wallace Whistling* ■ *Dir* Mitchell Leisen • *Scr* Preston Sturges

Easy Living ★★★ PG

Romantic drama 1949 · US · BW · 76mins

Based on an Irwin Shaw story, this tale of a retiring football player worried about his pension is smart, sassy and very satisfying. Victor Mature is cleverly cast as the New York Chiefs' ex-star halfback, and he gets terrific support from Lizabeth Scott as his overspending spouse and Lucille Ball as the team secretary who has the hots for him. Talented director Jacques Tourneur makes this work far better than anyone has a right to expect, Charles Schnee provides some zippy dialogue, and even Sonny Tufts turns in a good performance as the man who beats Mature to a prized coaching job. 🖭

Victor Mature *Pete Wilson* • Lucille Ball *Anne* • Lizabeth Scott *Liza Wilson* • Sonny Tufts *Tim McCarr* • Lloyd Nolan *Lenahan* • Paul Stewart *Argus* • Jack Paar *''Scoop'' Spooner* • Donnell Jeff *Penny McCarr* ■ *Dir* Jacques Tourneur • *Scr* Charles Schnee, from the story *Education of the Heart* by Irwin Shaw

Easy Money ★★ U

Portmanteau comedy drama 1948 · UK · BW · 89mins

This portmanteau picture is based on a play by Arnold Ridley (Private Godfrey in TV's *Dad's Army*), about four characters who dream of winning the pools. In the era of postwar austerity, thousands lived in hope of a windfall, but, as these four stories show, money is no guarantee of contentment. Frankly, none of the tales is particularly original and the ones involving crooked Dennis Price and meek Mervyn Johns are decidedly ropey. But Edward Rigby's generosity towards his beloved band and the arguments that divide Jack Warner's family are rather neatly played. 🖭

Jack Warner *Phillip Stafford* • Marjorie Fielding *Ruth Stafford* • Yvonne Owen *Carol Stafford* • Jack Watling *Dennis Stafford* • Petula Clark *Jackie Stafford* • Mabel Constanduros *Grandma* • Mervyn Johns *Herbert Atkins* • Joan Young *Agnes Atkins* • Dennis Price *Joe Henry* • Bill Owen *Mr Lee* ■ *Dir* Bernard Knowles • *Scr* Muriel Box, Sydney Box, from the play by Arnold Ridley

Easy Money ★★ 15

Comedy 1983 · US · Colour · 95mins

The quickfire vulgarity of Rodney Dangerfield isn't to everyone's taste, but even doubters will find it difficult to stifle the odd chuckle at this cheerfully crude comedy. The plot bears more than a passing resemblance to *Brewster's Millions*: slob-about-town Dangerfield has a year to clean up his act or face forfeiting millions from an inheritance. Joe Pesci scores in an early comic outing, and look out for Jennifer Jason Leigh in a small supporting role.

Rodney Dangerfield *Monty* • Joe Pesci *Nicky* • Geraldine Fitzgerald *Mrs Monahan* • Candy Azzara *Rose* • Taylor Negron *Julio* • Val Avery *Louie* • Jeffrey Jones *Clive* • Tom Ewell *Scrappleton* • Jennifer Jason Leigh *Allison* ■ *Dir* James Signorelli • *Scr* Rodney Dangerfield, Michael Endler, PJ O'Rourke, Dennis Blair

Easy Prey ★★ 15
Thriller   1986 · US · Colour · 90mins

Gerald McRaney is usually associated with likeable Texans, but here he is surprisingly effective as a serial killer preying on young innocents. Shawnee Smith is the teenager who is promised a modelling career but finds herself McRaney's prisoner as the FBI begins a nationwide manhunt. Sandor Stern's direction is distinctly pedestrian and the constraints of the TV-movie format rob the film of much of its impact. McRaney's chilling performance always commands attention, though. ▣

Gerald McRaney *Christopher Wilder* • Shawnee Smith *Tina Marie Risico* • Sean McCann *Paul Worthy* • Susan Hogan *Carol Risico* • Kate Lynch *Fran Altman* • Barry Flatman *Wells* • Neil Clifford *Blake* ■ *Dir* Sandor Stern • *Scr* John Carlen

Easy Rider ★★★★★ 18
Cult road movie   1969 · US · Colour · 91mins

As laid-back as the machines straddled by Dennis Hopper and Peter Fonda in their search for "the real America", and as hip as a whole drop-out generation, this magical mystery tour of the US has a casual conviction that outstrips Hopper's own on-the-run direction to touch a mythic nerve. Jack Nicholson's boozy lawyer successfully articulates the yearning of the alienated young. That the film ends in sullen and sudden death raises it to the power of allegory, and its success proved there was an audience and a need that the box-office pundits didn't even know existed. The studios tried desperately to repeat its low-budget magic, but couldn't. It just didn't equate with the usual Hollywood formula; it had created its own. Contains sex scenes, drug abuse and brief nudity. **DVD**

Peter Fonda *Wyatt/"Captain America"* • Dennis Hopper *Billy* • Jack Nicholson *George Hanson* • Phil Spector *Connection* • Antonio Mendoza *Jesus* • Warren Finnerty *Rancher* • Tita Colorado *Rancher's wife* • Robert Walker Jr *Jack* • Keith Green *Sheriff* • Toni Basil *Mary* • Karen Black *Karen* ■ *Dir* Dennis Hopper • *Scr* Dennis Hopper, Peter Fonda, Terry Southern • *Cinematographer* Laszlo Kovacs

Easy to Love ★★
Romantic comedy   1934 · US · BW · 62mins

The stylishness of the playing keeps this mildly sophisticated, if rather old-fashioned marital comedy alive now as it did on its release. Adolphe Menjou and pert blonde Genevieve Tobin star as a married couple whose relationship founders when she finds him romancing a glamorous brunette and retaliates by claiming to be having an affair herself. A running time of little over an hour is advantageous to the one-idea plot; so is a polished cast

that includes Mary Astor, Edward Everett Horton, Hugh Herbert and Guy Kibbee.

Genevieve Tobin *Carol Townsend* • Adolphe Menjou *John Townsend* • Mary Astor *Charlotte Hopkins* • Edward Everett Horton *Eric Schulte* • Patricia Ellis *Janet Townsend* • Guy Kibbee *Justice of the Peace* • Hugh Herbert *Detective John McTavish* ■ *Dir* William Keighley • *Scr* Carl Erickson, Manuel Seff, David Boehm (adaptation, from the play *As Good as News* by Thompson Buchanan)

Easy to Love ★★★ U
Musical   1953 · US · Colour · 95mins

There's not too much plot and few memorable songs (except for the Cole Porter title classic), but stunning Esther Williams needs no such help. This MGM musical is a perfectly constructed vehicle for the swimming star whose bossy, no-nonsense screen personality is well suited to this Florida-set satire on advertising. The canny direction is by the talented Charles Walters, but lovers of high camp will cherish ace choreographer Busby Berkeley's contribution to the water ballets, stacking bodies upon water-skis with perfect symmetry. Co-stars Van Johnson and Tony Martin glide through the movie without too much strain, and watch out for a pre-*Baby Doll* Carroll Baker in an early scene.

Esther Williams *Julie Hallerton* • Van Johnson *Ray Lloyd* • Tony Martin *Barry Gordon* • John Bromfield *Hank* • Edna Skinner *Nancy Parmel* • King Donovan *Ben* • Paul Bryar *Mr Barnes* • Carroll Baker *Clarice* ■ *Dir* Charles Walters • *Scr* Laslo Vadnay, William Roberts, from a story by Laslo Vadnay

Easy to Wed ★★★
Musical   1946 · US · Colour · 110mins

Although it lacked the star power of the original, MGM could have no complaints about the performances in this remake of its 1936 screwball classic, *Libeled Lady*. Keenan Wynn is no substitute for Spencer Tracy, but he barks admirably as the editor who sends reporter Van Johnson to charm heiress Esther Williams out of a suit against their paper. The leads can't match the chemistry of William Powell and Myrna Loy, but they still look good together, while Lucille Ball, in one of her breakthrough roles, is every bit as sparky as Jean Harlow.

Van Johnson *Bill Stevens Chandler* • Esther Williams *Connie Allenbury* • Lucille Ball *Gladys Benton* • Keenan Wynn *Warren Haggerty* • Cecil Kellaway *JB Allenbury* • June Lockhart *Babs Norvell* ■ *Dir* Edward Buzzell • *Scr* Dorothy Kingsley, from the film *Libeled Lady* by Maurine Watkins, Howard Emmett Rodgers, George Oppenheimer

Easy Virtue ★★★
Silent drama   1927 · UK · BW · 79mins

An early Alfred Hitchcock film which sees him still developing his distinctive style. This is an adaptation of Nöel Coward's play about a charming divorcee (Isabel Jeans) with a scandal in her past, who marries into a staid provincial family with predictable results. It's well scripted by Eliot Stannard, and manages to capture the essence of the play even without Coward's witty dialogue. In one of the best scenes, when the hero is

proposing to the heroine over the telephone, Hitch cuts away from them and cleverly shows only the reactions on the face of the telephone operator.

Isabel Jeans *Larita Filton* • Robin Irvine *John Whittaker* • Franklin Dyall *Mr Filton* • Enid Stamp-Taylor *Sarah* • Violet Farebrother *Mrs Whittaker* • Darcia Deane *Marion Whittaker* ■ *Dir* Alfred Hitchcock • *Scr* Eliot Stannard, from the play by Nöel Coward

Easy Wheels ★ 15
Action adventure comedy
1989 · US · Colour · 90mins

The battle of the sexes meets the biker movie in this action comedy from director David O'Malley, who went on to write *Fatal Instinct*. She-Wolf (Eileen Davidson) and Bruce (Paul LeMat) are the rival gang leaders whose clashes lead the girls to take increasingly desperate measures. Davidson's plan to subjugate the male population involves kidnapping girl babies and turning them over to wolves to toughen them up. If you're looking for sophisticated comedy and trenchant social comment, you're looking in the wrong place. For sheer daftness, though, this takes some beating. ▣

Paul LeMat *Bruce* • Eileen Davidson *She-Wolf* • Marjorie Bransfield *Wendy* • Jon Menick *Professor* • Barry Livingston *Reporter* • George Plimpton • Ted Raimi ■ *Dir* David O'Malley • *Scr* David O'Malley, Ivan Raimi

Eat a Bowl of Tea ★★★ 15
Comedy drama   1989 · US · Colour · 98mins

In his early films, Wayne Wang was more interested in the behaviour of his characters in specific cultural and social situations than he was in exploring their motives and emotions. While this made his work intriguing, it often lacked depth. Here the period atmosphere enhances a story about Chinese immigrants in postwar America, but again, beneath the layers of detail and quirky characterisation, there is scant substance. We learn little about how Chinese women adapted to their new surroundings, or how this enclosed community fitted into society as a whole. As a result, this engaging film is ultimately unsatisfying. In English and Mandarin with subtitles. ▣

Victor Wong *Wah Gay* • Russell Wong *Ben Loy* • Cora Miao *Mei Oi* • Eric Chi Wai Tsang *Ah Song* • Lau Siu-Ming *Lee Gong* • Wu Ming Yu *Mei Oi's mother* • Hui Funi *Ben Loy's mother* ■ *Dir* Wayne Wang • *Scr* Judith Rascoe, from the novel by Louis Chu

Eat and Run ★★★ 15
Science-fiction comedy
1986 · US · Colour · 80mins

This spoof on the "creature features" of the fifties, those sci-fi cheapies which went for the bizarre with an earnestness that now seems camp, revolves around a king-sized alien whose favourite discovery on earth turns out to be Italian food. Devouring an Italian sausage maker helps his appetite on its way, though it soon brings Irish cop Mickey McSorely (Ron Silver) on his trail. Certain humorous interludes are just too slack to hit home, but Silver, a much underused actor, acquits himself well at the centre of this amiable nonsense. ▣

Ron Silver *Mickey McSorely* • Sharon Schlarth *Judge Cheryl Cohen* • RL Ryan *Murray Creature* • John F Fleming *Police captain* • Derek Murcott *Sorely McSorely* • Robert Silver *Pusher* • Mimi Cecchini *Grandmother* • Tony Moundroukas *Zepoli kid* ■ *Dir* Christopher Hart • *Scr* Stan Hart, Christopher Hart

Eat Drink Man Woman ★★★★ PG
Comedy drama   1994 · Tai · Colour · 119mins

Of the seven features made so far by Taiwanese director Ang Lee, two have already won the Golden Bear at the Berlin film festival. Yet this is far superior to either *The Wedding Banquet* or *Sense and Sensibility*. Although the prime influence on Lee's stately style and several of the film's themes is the Japanese genius Yasujiro Ozu, there is more than a hint of Woody Allen in this complex ensemble comedy, as the action flits between the problems facing each member of master chef Lung Sihung's family. The performances are light and believable, the dialogue full of wit and wisdom. And as for the food... In Mandarin with English subtitles. ▣

Lung Sihung *Mr Chu* • Wang Yu-wen *Jia-ning* • Wu Chien-lien *Jia-chien* • Yang Kuei-Mai *Jia-jen* • Sylvia Chang *Jin-rong* • Winston Chao *Li Kai* • Chen Chao-jung *Guo Lun* ■ *Dir* Ang Lee • *Scr* Ang Lee, Wang Hui-ling, James Schamus

Eat My Dust! ★
Comedy action adventure
1976 · US · Colour · 88mins

Charles B Griffith, the prolific writer of Roger Corman's best movies, turned director with this inept car crash comedy starring the famous Howard family of Ron, father Rance and brother Clint. Nothing more than a patchy excuse to destroy automobiles, trucks, boats and buildings on the cheap in a frantic demolition derby, while dumb cops and grease monkey Ron Howard's romantic interest look on in bemusement. A crashing bore.

Ron Howard *Hoover Niebold* • Chrissie Norris *Darlene* • Warren Kemmerling *Sheriff Harry Niebold* • Dave Madden *Big Bubba Jones* • Rance Howard *Deputy Clark* • Clint Howard *Georgie* ■ *Dir/Scr* Charles B Griffith

Eat the Peach ★★★ PG
Comedy drama   1986 · Ire · Colour · 91mins

Armed with a true story, a tight budget and a video of the Elvis Presley vehicle *Roustabout*, director Peter Ormrod comes up with an engaging film whose main fault is its determination to be offbeat. As the jobless duo who set out to build a "Wall of Death", Stephen Brennan and Eamon Morrissey have a likeable loopiness that stops just short of being eccentrically "Oirish", though the rascally side to their characters is perhaps overdone. Memorable moments include the sight of Brennan's small daughter tricycling around the lower wall, though there's a lot of dull stuff in between. ▣

Eamon Morrissey *Arthur* • Stephen Brennan *Vinnie Galvin* • Catherine Byrne *Nora Galvin* • Niall Toibin *Boots* • Joe Lynch *Boss Murtagh* • Tony Doyle *Sean Murtagh* • Takashi Kawahara *Bunzo* • Victoria Armstrong *Vicky Galvin* ■ *Dir* Peter Ormrod • *Scr* Peter Ormrod, John Kelleher, from an idea by Peter Ormrod

U = SUITABLE FOR ALL   Uc = SUITABLE FOR ALL, ESPECIALLY FOR YOUNG CHILDREN (VIDEO ONLY)   PG = PARENTAL GUIDANCE

Eat the Rich ★★ 15
Comedy 1987 · UK · Colour · 84mins

When a waiter loses his job at trendy London restaurant Bastards, he plots with a band of revolutionaries to put its customers on the menu. Peter Richardson's film is more of a student prank than a subversive satire in the tradition of Buñuel's The Exterminating Angel or Lindsay Anderson's if.... Of the main performers, Nosher Powell is memorable as a Home Secretary who behaves like a Kray brother. However, the movie's main fascination lies in its extraordinary array of cameos, from Paul McCartney and Bill Wyman to Koo Stark and French and Saunders.

Lanah Pellay Alex • Nosher Powell Nosher • Fiona Richmond Fiona • Ronald Allen Commander Fortune • Lemmy Spider • Robbie Coltrane Jeremy • Kathy Burke Kathy • Miles Copeland Derek • Adrian Edmondson Charles • Dawn French Debbie Draws • Jools Holland "Sun" Reporter • Rik Mayall Micky • Shane McGowan Terrorist • Nigel Planer DHSS manager • Miranda Richardson DHSS blonde • Jennifer Saunders Lady Caroline • Sandy Shaw Edgeley's girlfriend • Koo Stark Hazel • Ruby Wax Bibi de Coutts • Bill Wyman Toilet victim • Paul McCartney ■ Dir Peter Richardson • Scr Peter Richens, Peter Richardson

Eaten Alive ★★ 18
Horror thriller 1976 · US · Colour · 81mins

Tobe Hooper's little-seen and undervalued follow-up to his seminal Texas Chain Saw Massacre is a heavily stylised tale that incorporates the shock value of the EC horror comics of the fifties. Neville Brand stars as the psychopathic proprietor of a rundown hotel who feeds guests to his pet crocodile. While the film is perhaps guilty of perpetuating the myth that all backwoods yokels are a couple of strings short of a banjo, the goofy plot and impressive production design win the day. Watch out for Robert Englund as a nauseous redneck. 🖵

Neville Brand Judd • Mel Ferrer Harvey Wood • Carolyn Jones Miss Hattie • Marilyn Burns Faye • William Finley Roy • Stuart Whitman Sheriff Martin • Robert Englund Buck ■ Dir Tobe Hooper • Scr Alvin L Fast, Mardi Rustam, Kim Henkel

Eating ★★★
Comedy drama 1990 · US · Colour · 110mins

As the only male presence at this women-only feast, director Henry Jaglom somewhat outstays his welcome. A group of women talk about food and life at a birthday party, yet, fascinating though the interchanges and revelations are, they don't merit 110 minutes. The performances, however, are sparkling, with birthday girls Mary Crosby (30), Lisa Richards (40) and Marlena Giovi (50) revelling in a script exploring the ways in which women view food as both a comfort and a scourge. This is very much an ensemble piece, but mouthy Frances Bergen, mousy Daphna Kastner and bitchy bulimic Gwen Welles do stand out.

Lisa Richards Helene • Mary Crosby Kate • Marlena Giovi Sadie • Gwen Welles Sophie • Nelly Alard Martine • Frances Bergen Mrs Williams • Daphna Kastner Jennifer •

Elizabeth Kemp Nancy • Rachelle Carson Cathy • Toni Basil Jackie • Marina Gregory Lydia ■ Dir/Scr Henry Jaglom

Eating Raoul ★★★★ 18
Black comedy 1982 · US · Colour · 79mins

Paul and Mary Bland (brilliantly portrayed by director Paul Bartel and actress Mary Woronov) finance their dream restaurant by advertising for wealthy swingers and killing them off during sex for their cash. Handyman Raoul (Robert Beltran of Star Trek: Voyager fame) muscles in on the action by selling the bodies to a dog food factory. A cute black comedy, hilariously sending up California culture and executed with sadistic glee by all concerned, including Buck Henry and Ed Begley Jr. Bartel turned his cult sleeper into an off-Broadway musical in 1992. 🖵

Paul Bartel Paul Bland • Mary Woronov Mary Bland • Robert Beltran Raoul • Susana Saiger Doris the Dominatrix • Ed Begley Jr Hippy • Dan Barrows Bobbie R • Richard Blackburn James • Ralph Brannen Paco • Buck Henry Mr Leech ■ Dir Paul Bartel • Scr Paul Bartel, Richard Blackburn

L'Eau Froide ★★★★
Drama 1994 · Fr · Colour · 92mins

This is a frank yet tender insight into troubled adolescence from director Olivier Assayas. Virginie Ledoyen (who also stars in Assayas's Late August, Early September) gives a heartrending performance as the mentally fragile product of a broken home who goes on the run with short-fused Parisian schoolboy Cyprien Fouquet after her father puts her in an institution. Shot with energy and authenticity, yet without condescension, the film not only captures the anxiety of youth, but also the feel of the early seventies. In French with English subtitles.

Virginie Ledoyen Christine • Cyprien Fouquet Gilles • Laszlo Szabo Gilles's father • Jean-Pierre Darroussin Inspector • Dominique Faysse Christine's mother • Smail Mekki Mourad • Jackie Berroyer Christine's father ■ Dir/Scr Olivier Assayas

Ebbie ★★★ U
Fantasy drama 1995 · Can · Colour · 89mins

A Christmas Carol gets a makeover in this radical rethink of Dickens's classic tale. Susan Lucci takes the title role as the tunnel-visioned head of an exclusive department store who gets her comeuppance at the hands of the most stylish Christmas spirits you'll ever see. The script is a tad too clever at times, but there are some astute comments on our consumerist times that make you wonder just how far we've come since the bleak midwinters of the Victorian era.

Susan Lucci Elizabeth Ebbie Scrooge • Wendy Crewson Roberta Crachit Smith • Taran Noah Smith Tiny Tim Crachit • Ron Lea Paul Taylor • Molly Parker Francine • Lorena Gale Rita ■ Dir George Kaczender • Scr Paul Redford, Ed Redlich, from the story A Christmas Carol by Charles Dickens

Ebbtide ★★ 18
Erotic thriller 1994 · Ausl · Colour · 89mins

Former LA Law star Harry Hamlin finds himself back in legal territory, in this

steamy Australian thriller that went straight to video here. Hamlin plays a jaded lawyer who discovers a conscience when he gets mixed up with environmentalists, political corruption and shady land deals in a throwback to acclaimed Australian thrillers such as Phillip Noyce's Heatwave. There is able support from Judy McIntosh and John Waters, but in the end it's let down by slack plotting. Contains violence, swearing, nudity and sex scenes.

Harry Hamlin Jeff Warren • Judy McIntosh Ellen Fielding • Susan Lyons Alison • John Waters Michael Suresch • John Gregg Chalmers • Frankie J Holden Ernie Miller ■ Dir Craig Lahiff • Scr Robert Ellis, Peter Goldsworthy, from a story by Craig Lahiff, Helen Leake, Warwick Hind

Ebenezer ★★
Western drama 1998 · Can · Colour · 94mins

Dickens gets a western makeover, as his classic A Christmas Carol is relocated to the American West of the 1870s. When cowboy Rick Schroder (NYPD Blue) is swindled out of his land by the town's miserly card shark, Ebenezer Scrooge, he challenges the old skinflint to a gunfight at high noon on Christmas Day. But a haunting, ghost-filled Christmas Eve shows Scrooge the error of his ways and sets him on the path towards redemption. Jack Palance has lots of fun with his scenery chewing turn as nasty Scrooge. A little generosity of spirit will forgive the weak spots in this oft-told tale.

Jack Palance Ebenezer/Future Scrooge • Rick Schroder Sam Benson • Amy Locane Erica • Albert Schultz Bob Cratchit • Daryl Shuttleworth Fred ■ Dir Ken Jubenvill • Scr Donald Martin, from the story A Christmas Carol by Charles Dickens

Ebirah, Horror of the Deep ★★ U
Horror 1966 · Jap · Colour · 83mins

Or Godzilla versus the Sea Monster, as it was known everywhere else. In his sixth screen outing, the king of the monsters and his one-time arch enemy, Mothra, hiss and make up to battle the evil giant lobster Ebirah, being used as a p(r)awn by the nasty Red Bamboo gang seeking world domination. Typical Japanese monster fare featuring cardboard mayhem, laughable special effects and failed comedy sees Godzilla play football. Total trash? Naturally. Absolutely unmissable? Of course. Japanese dialogue dubbed into English. 🖵

Akira Takarada • Toru Watanabe • Hideo Sunazuka • Kumi Mizuno • Jun Tazaki ■ Dir Jun Fukuda • Scr Shinichi Sekizawa

Echo of Diana ★★ U
Spy drama 1963 · UK · BW · 61mins

A low-budget spy drama from those long forgotten B-movie specialists Butchers Film Service. The newshound leads (making a refreshing change from the usual fading Hollywood stars) are two Australian performers, Vincent Ball and Betty McDowall, whose noses for a story begin to twitch when a mysterious death puts them on the track of one of the most alfresco covert operations you are ever likely to

clap eyes on. Director Ernest Morris does well to sustain it for an hour.

Vincent Ball Bill Vernon • Betty McDowall Joan Scott • Geoffrey Toone Colonel Justin • Clare Owen Pam Jennings • Peter Illing Kovali ■ Dir Ernest Morris • Scr Reginald Hearne

The Echo of Thunder ★★
Drama 1998 · US · Colour · 98mins

Set against the glorious backdrop of the Australian outback, this family drama plays like any other TV movie. Father Jamey Sheridan is shocked to hear that his ex-wife has died, and is even more surprised when his daughter (Lauren Hewett) arrives to join the family. Dad is determined to help her fit in, but he's pitted against his testy new wife (Judy Davis) and school bully Jamie Croft. An all-too-familiar tune plays out adequately enough, but Simon Wincer's film has nothing new to say.

Judy Davis Gladwyn Ritchie • Jamey Sheridan Larry Ritchie • Lauren Hewett Lara Ritchie • Bill Hunter Cooper • Ernie Dingo Neil • Michael Caton Bill Gadrey • Emily Jane Browning Opal Ritchie • Jamie Croft Gowd ■ Dir Simon Wincer • Scr H Haden Yelin, from the novel Thunderwith by Libby Hathorn

Echo Park ★★★★ 15
Comedy drama 1985 · Aus/US · Colour · 84mins

This story of a trio of losers – Susan Dey as the aspiring actress reduced to working in a sleazy bar, Tom Hulce as a song-writing pizza boy and Michael Bowen body-building himself up to disappointment – has moments of real truth and affection from its director Robert Dornhelm. As a study in human relationships it doesn't exactly resound with insight, but it almost – but not quite – reminds us of Jules et Jim, another tale of a ménage à trois. 🖵

Tom Hulce Jonathan • Susan Dey May • Michael Bowen August • Christopher Walker Henry Greer • Shirley Jo Finney Gloria • Heinrich Schweiger August's father • Richard "Cheech" Marin Syd • John Paragon Hugo ■ Dir Robert Dornhelm • Scr Michael Ventura

Echoes ★★ 15
Fantasy thriller 1983 · US · Colour · 85mins

Despite the efforts of director Arthur Allan Seidelman and an intriguing Freudian premise, this psychological thriller fails to live up to its promise. Art student Richard Alfieri keeps dreaming that his twin brother – who died before birth – is determined to kill him and take over his body. Girlfriend Nathalie Nell mops his fevered brow, while oldsters Gale Sondergaard, Mercedes McCambridge and Ruth Roman offer fine support. Alas, the idea doesn't connect as it should, and it becomes rather melodramatic. 🖵

Richard Alfieri Michael Durant/Dream Michael • Nathalie Nell Christine • Mercedes McCambridge Lillian Gerben • Ruth Roman Michael's mother • Gale Sondergaard Mrs Edmunds • Mike Kellin Sid Berman ■ Dir Arthur Allan Seidelman • Scr Richard J Anthony

Echoes of a Summer ★
Drama 1976 · US/Can · Colour · 99mins

Jodie Foster assaults the tear ducts by playing a 12-year-old with a terminal heart condition. Facing certain death with startling courage, she makes life a little easier for her parents, played by Lois Nettleton and Richard Harris. Foster, who looks more like a boy than a girl in some scenes, is an odd blend of natural talent and applied emotion, although her love affair with childhood sweetheart Brad Savage is unspeakably yucky.

Richard Harris *Eugene Striden* • Lois Nettleton *Ruth Striden* • Geraldine Fitzgerald *Sara* • William Windom *Doctor Hallett* • Brad Savage *Phillip Anding* • Jodie Foster *Deirdre Striden* ■ *Dir* Don Taylor • *Scr* Robert L Joseph

Eclipse ★★★★ PG
Romantic drama 1962 · Fr/It · BW · 123mins

The winner of the Special Jury Prize at Cannes in 1962, this troubling, stylised film completed director Michelangelo Antonioni's "alienation trilogy". As in *L'Avventura* and *La Notte*, Monica Vitti is at the centre of events, here ending a passionless affair with the bookish Francisco Rabal to indulge in a fling with her mother's stockbroker, Alain Delon. Returning to his recurrent themes of the desensitising impact of urban life and the hopelessness of love, Antonioni presents his bleakest portrait of the modern age, with the famous seven-minute, 58-shot montage of cold, impersonal buildings symbolising the city's final victory over its inhabitants. In Italian with English subtitles. ▣

Monica Vitti *Vittoria* • Alain Delon *Piero* • Lilla Brignone *Vittoria's mother* • Francisco Rabal *Riccardo* • Louis Seignier *Ercoli* • Rossana Rory *Anita* • Mirella Ricciardi *Marta* ■ *Dir* Michelangelo Antonioni • *Scr* Michelangelo Antonioni, Tonino Guerra, Elio Bartoloni, Ottiero Ottieri

Ecoute Voir... ★★★
Crime drama 1978 · Fr · Colour · 125mins

Argentinian director Hugo Santiago is renowned for his rather strange political commentaries, and this film is no exception. The gracious Catherine Deneuve stars as a private detective hired to investigate and expose a sinister cult. Her trail leads to a mansion house in the middle of nowhere, where the group is attempting to interrupt radio waves with subliminal propaganda. Atmospheric and stylishly shot, the film's moodiness is compounded by a great soundtrack. In French with English subtitles.

Catherine Deneuve *Claude Alphand* • Sami Frey *Arnaud* • Anne Parillaud *Chole* • Florence Delay *Flora* • Antoine Vitez *Sect man* • Didier Haudepin *Secretary* ■ *Dir* Hugo Santiago • *Scr* Hugo Santiago, Claude Ollier

Ecstasy ★★★★
Drama 1933 · Cz · BW · 68mins

It's difficult to separate this Czech film from the furore it created at the time; it was banned outright in Germany and cut to ribbons by the rest of the world. However, it was imported into the USA and shown privately all over Hollywood, where its star – the young Heidi Kiesler – would be imported and renamed Hedy Lamarr, becoming one of Tinseltown's loveliest love goddesses. The reason is a famous sequence where Hedy is swimming in

the nude; her horse runs off with her clothes, so she runs starkers through the woods. In another famous sequence, she discovers and demonstrates sexual pleasure in extreme close-up. Director Gustav Machaty creates a wondrous mood, and the overall (uncut) movie is one of cinema's great sensual masterpieces. In Czech with English subtitles.

Hedy Kiesler [Hedy Lamarr] *Eva* • Jaromir Rogoz *Emile* • Aribert Mog *Adam* • Leopold Kramer *Eva's father* ■ *Dir* Gustav Machaty • *Scr* Gustav Machaty, Franz Horky, Vitezslav Nezval, Jacques A Koerpel

Ed ★ PG
Sports comedy 1996 · US · Colour · 90mins

The graduation of the cast of TV's *Friends* to the big screen hasn't been entirely successful, although this lamentable vehicle for Matt LeBlanc easily remains the worst. Even the struggling actor LeBlanc plays in the hit series would surely have passed on this dim-witted family comedy, in which the star effectively plays second fiddle to a monkey. The Ed of the title is the chimpanzee mascot of a struggling baseball team who, naturally, becomes the star of the team and helps the human lead out of his pitching slump. The ape gets the best lines – and all he does is grunt and shreik. Avoid. ▣

Matt LeBlanc *Cooper* • Jayne Brook *Lydia* • Jack Warden *Chubb* • Gene Ross *Red* • Paul Hewitt *Bucky* • Sage Allen *Cooper's mother* • Stan Ivar *Cooper's mather* ■ *Dir* Bill Couturie • *Scr* David Mickey Evans, from a story by Janus Cercone, Ken Richards

Ed McBain's 87th Precinct ★★★
Crime drama 1995 · US · Colour · 95mins

Ed McBain has long been a staple of American crime fiction and, despite its TV roots, this film does full justice to his streetwise sense of realism. Randy Quaid is perfectly cast as the cynical veteran detective who teams up with the younger Alex McArthur to track down the killer of a star athlete. The two leads are backed up with scene-stealing turns from Ving Rhames (*Pulp Fiction*) and Ron Perkins. Director Bruce Paltrow admirably keeps the tension on the boil.

Randy Quaid *Steve Carella* • Alex McArthur *Bert Kling* • Deanne Bray *Teddy* • Ving Rhames *Brown* • Eddie Jones *Lieutenant Byrnes* • Alan Blumenfeld *Ollie Weeks* • Ron Perkins *Meyer* ■ *Dir* Bruce Paltrow • *Scr* Dan Levine, Mike Krohn, from the novel *Lightning* by Ed McBain [Evan Hunter]

Ed McBain's 87th Precinct: Ice ★★★
Crime drama 1996 · US · Colour

Horror specialist Larry Cohen is perhaps the last person you would expect to adapt one of Ed McBain's hard-boiled crime novels for TV. But he makes a decent job of this snappy police thriller, in which four cops check out the seemingly unconnected murders of a chorus dancer, a drug dealer, a pimp and a diamond merchant. Joe Pantoliano and Dale Midkiff turn in uncomplicated performances, but it's the assured manner in which the pieces are put

together by director Bradford May that makes this so satisfying.

Dale Midkiff *Detective Steve Carella* • Joe Pantoliano *Detective Meyer* • Paul Johansson *Detective Bert Kling* • Andrea Parker *Detective Eileen Burke* • Michael Gross *Lieutenant Byrnes* • Andrea Ferrell *Teddy Carella* ■ *Dir* Bradford May • *Scr* Larry Cohen, from the novel by Ed McBain [Evan Hunter]

Ed McBain's 87th Precinct: Heatwave ★★
Crime drama 1997 · US · Colour · 94mins

This third instalment in the series of TV movies based on the novels of Ed McBain is pretty much summed up by its title, which sets the meteorological scene for a nasty affair involving the rape of a policewoman during a stakeout. McBain is, of course, the pseudonym of Evan Hunter, but this is a far cry from Hunter's work for Alfred Hitchcock, even though he shares a writing credit with the usually dependable Larry Cohen.

Dale Midkiff *Detective Steve Carella* • Michael Gross *Lieutenant Peter Byrnes* • Erika Eleniak *Detective Eileen Burke* • Paul Johansson *Detective Bert Kling* • Paul Ben-Victor *Detective Meyer* • Marc Gomes *Detective Arthur Brown* ■ *Dir* Douglas Barr • *Scr* Larry Cohen, from characters created by Ed McBain [Evan Hunter]

Ed Wood ★★★★★ 15
Biographical drama 1994 · US · BW · 121mins

Only one of cinema's finest directors could have so lovingly crafted this homage to one of its worst. Tim Burton's wonderful celebration of awful art, and the fascination it continues to exert, traces the weird career of Edward D Wood Jr from his autobiographical exploitation quickie *Glen or Glenda*, in which he cast himself as an anguished cross-dresser, to his "masterpiece", the truly terrible *Plan 9 from Outer Space*. Johnny Depp is amazing as director Wood in Burton's black-and-white evocation of fifties life in Grade Z-land, and Martin Landau deservedly won an Oscar for his uncanny impersonation of Wood's low-rent inspiration, Bela Lugosi. The re-creation of Wood's unashamedly anti-aesthetic productions is astonishing. ▣

Johnny Depp *Ed Wood* • Martin Landau *Bela Lugosi* • Sarah Jessica Parker *Dolores Fuller* • Patricia Arquette *Kathy O'Hara* • Jeffrey Jones *Criswell* • GD Spradlin *Reverend Lemon* • Vincent D'Onofrio *Orson Welles* • Bill Murray *John "Bunny" Breckinridge* • Mike Starr *Georgie Weiss* ■ *Dir* Tim Burton • *Scr* Scott Alexander, Larry Karaszewski, from the book *Nightmare of Ecstasy* by Rudolph Grey

Eddie ★★★ 12
Comedy drama 1996 · US · Colour · 96mins

This sports comedy has a couple of new twists on the old "against the odds" storyline. The first is that the newly appointed basketball coach is both an obsessive fan and a woman (motormouth Whoopi Goldberg). Moreover, this is no lower-division team that needs licking into shape, but the legendary New York Knicks (not the actual team, by the way, but a side comprising various real-life hoop heroes). Not bad of its kind, with Goldberg taking no nonsense from the

NBA stars, and there are also some stimulating slam-dunk sequences. However, if you don't have a penchant for the star or sport, steer clear. ▣

Whoopi Goldberg *Edwina "Eddie" Franklin* • Frank Langella *Wild Bill Burgess* • Dennis Farina *Coach Bailey* • Richard Jenkins *Assistant Coach Zimmer* • Lisa Ann Walter *Claudine* • John Benjamin Hickey *Joe Nader* • Troy Beyer *Beth Hastings* ■ *Dir* Steve Rash • *Scr* John Connolly, David Loucka, Eric Champnela, Keith Mitchell, Steve Zacharias, Jeff Buhai, from a story by John Connolly, David Loucka, Steve Zacharias, Jeff Buhai

Eddie and the Cruisers ★★ PG
Drama 1983 · US · Colour · 91mins

Intriguing, if not completely successful spin on the rock movie, which also provided an early platform for two actors on the verge of stardom. Tom Berenger plays a musician who, along with journalist Ellen Barkin, sets out to uncover the mystery behind the demise of his band Eddie and the Cruisers, the archetypal one-hit wonders who fell apart when the lead singer abruptly vanished. With a supporting cast which includes Joe Pantoliano, it is never dull and director Martin Davidson manages to sidestep some of the more obvious rock clichés. However, it begins to fall apart near the end and, sadly, the music isn't very memorable. ▣

Tom Berenger *Frank Ridgeway* • Michael Paré *Eddie Wilson* • Joe Pantoliano *"Doc" Robbins* • Matthew Laurance *Sal Amato* • Helen Schneider *Joann Carlino* • David Wilson *Kenny Hopkins* • Michael "Tunes" Antunes *Wendell Newton* • Ellen Barkin *Maggie Foley* ■ *Dir* Martin Davidson • *Scr* Martin Davidson, Arlene Davidson, from a novel by PF Kluge

Eddie and the Cruisers II: Eddie Lives! ★★ PG
Drama 1989 · US/Can · Colour · 99mins

The 1983 original was a massive video hit, so this belated, cliché-ridden sequel brings Eddie (Michael Paré) back from the dead – or at least back from the blue-collar identity he's been hiding behind since his supposed fatal accident. Once again, Eddie's music has become popular and his cynical record company smells a money-making cash-in. Can he return to the career he loves without compromising his principles? Sadly, the music machinations don't ring true and, unless they're fans of eighties soft rock, most people would advise Eddie not to give up his day job. ▣

Michael Paré *Eddie Wilson/Joe West* • Marina Orsini *Diane* • Bernie Coulson *Rick* • Matthew Laurance *Sal* • Michael Rhoades *Dave Pagent* • Larry King • Bo Diddley • Martha Quinn *Music video hostess* ■ *Dir* Jean-Claude Lord • *Scr* Charles Zev Cohen, Rick Doehring, from characters created by PF Kluge

The Eddie Cantor Story ★★ U
Biographical musical 1953 · US · Colour · 116mins

The tale of how Israel Iskowitz, a poor Jewish boy from the Lower East Side of New York, became the rich and famous Hollywood star Eddie Cantor, has all the usual rags-to-riches ingredients and successfully invokes the atmosphere of vaudeville where

U = SUITABLE FOR ALL   Uc = SUITABLE FOR ALL, ESPECIALLY FOR YOUNG CHILDREN (VIDEO ONLY)   PG = PARENTAL GUIDANCE

Eddie started out as an entertainer. A number of his best songs (*If You Knew Susie*, *Making Whoopee*) are included, too, but the lack of a star personality, allied to a weak script, makes for a dreary and unengaging showbiz biopic.

Keefe Brasselle *Eddie Cantor* • Marilyn Erskine *Ida* • Aline MacMahon *Grandma Esther* • Arthur Franz *Harry Harris* • Alex Gerry *David Tobias* • Greta Granstedt *Rachel Tobias* • Gerald Mohr *Rocky* • William Forrest *Ziegfeld* ■ *Dir* Alfred E Green • *Scr* Sidney Skolsky, Ted Sherdeman, Jerome Weidman, from a story by Sidney Skolsky

Eddie Macon's Run ★★ 15

Action   1983 · US · Colour · 90mins

This uncomfortable late Kirk Douglas flick gives second billing to John Schneider, one of the stars of *The Dukes of Hazzard*. Like that TV show, this is little more than a prolonged celluloid chase, with a fair amount of crashes and smashes. Kirk shouldn't have been doing this kind of stuff at this stage of his career, but director Jeff Kanew also persuaded him to co-star with an ailing Burt Lancaster in *Tough Guys* next – which, like this, also failed to hit the mark. Big John Goodman makes his movie bow here.

Kirk Douglas *Marzack* • John Schneider *Eddie Macon* • Lee Purcell *Jilly Buck* • Leah Ayres *Chris* • Lisa Dunsheath *Kay Potts* • Tom Noonan *Daryl Potts* • John Goodman *Hebert* ■ *Dir* Jeff Kanew • *Scr* Jeff Kanew, from the novel by James McLendon

Eddie Murphy Raw ★★ 18

Comedy   1987 · US · Colour · 86mins

Overlong and poorly shot concert film of Eddie Murphy's one-man show. He may be a phenomenon as a movie star, but his stand-up routine leaves much to be desired – a foul-mouthed concoction trading on racial and sexual stereotypes that effortlessly offends majority tastes. Murphy's frenetic energy and virtual non-stop delivery is impressive, though, and his comic imitation of Bill Cosby is inspired. Directed by *Hollywood Shuffle*'s Robert Townsend, this is for die-hard Murphy fans only. Watch out for an uproarious fictional prologue set in a sixties Murphy household.

Eddie Murphy • Tatyana Ali *Singing child* • Billie Allen *Eddie's aunt* • Clebert Ford *Uncle Lester* • Geri Gibson *Second card player* • Samuel L Jackson *Eddie's uncle* ■ *Dir* Robert Townsend • *Scr* Eddie Murphy, Keenen Ivory Wayans

The Eddy Duchin Story ★★★★ U

Biographical drama
1956 · US · Colour · 117mins

A deeply satisfying weepie about the New York society pianist struck down by leukaemia in his prime. Though the actual illness isn't named, the scenes in which Duchin, sympathetically portrayed by a mature Tyrone Power, takes leave of his son (Rex Thompson from *The King and I*) are unbearably moving. This is a film strong on romance, and Power's relationship with the lovely Kim Novak is superbly orchestrated by director George Sidney against exquisite New York locations in autumnal colours to the backing of

Rodgers and Hart's evergreen *Manhattan*. Sidney, who also directed *Anchors Aweigh*, *Show Boat* and *Annie Get Your Gun*, knows a thing or three about musicals, while the actual piano-playing is cleverly done by Carmen Cavallero, who mimics and updates Duchin's style.

Tyrone Power *Eddy Duchin* • Kim Novak *Marjorie Oelrichs* • Victoria Shaw *Chiquita* • James Whitmore *Lou Sherwood* • Rex Thompson *Peter Duchin as a boy* • Shepperd Strudwick *Mr Wadsworth* • Frieda Inescort *Mrs Wadsworth* • Gloria Holden *Mrs Duchin* • Gregory Gaye *Philip* ■ *Dir* George Sidney • *Scr* Samuel Taylor, from a story by Leo Katcher

Eden Valley ★★★ 15

Drama   1994 · UK · Colour · 40mins

A slow, lyrical, almost impressionistic effort by the Amber Films collective, featuring famous harness racing family the Laidlers, who also starred in Amber's much acclaimed *Seacoal*. You either find these working-class denizens of the North East fascinating, or you don't. Most of us uneasily straddle the two camps, one of which says that the work of Amber and its ilk is vital in keeping alive the drama and tension of dying ways of life, while the other says it is like watching paint dry, complete with impenetrable accents.

Brian Hogg *Hoggy* • Darren Bell *Billy* • Mike Elliott *Danker* • Jimmy Killeen *Probation officer* • Wayne Buck *Young lad* • Kevin Buck *Young lad* ■ *Dir/Scr* Richard Grassick, Ellen Hare, Sirkka Liisa Konttinen, Murray Martin, Pat McCarthy, Lorna Powell, Pete Roberts

The Edge ★★★★ 15

Action adventure
1997 · US · Colour · 112mins

The title refers to the margin between primitive and civilised behaviour – and between Anthony Hopkins and Alec Baldwin – amid the Alaskan wilderness. Hopkins, the billionaire who believes fashion photographer Baldwin is after his wife (Elle Macpherson), finds himself stranded with the would-be adulterer when their small plane crashes. From then on it's a crash-course in survival – with Hopkins coming out tops in terms of savage crafts – while being pursued by a vast man-eating bear. David Mamet's city-bred dialogue is visually developed by the awesome camerawork of director Lee Tamahori.

Anthony Hopkins *Charles Morse* • Alec Baldwin *Robert Green* • Elle Macpherson *Mickey Morse* • Harold Perrineau *Stephen* • LQ Jones *Styles* • Kathleen Wilhoite *Ginny* ■ *Dir* Lee Tamahori • *Scr* David Mamet

Edge of Darkness ★★★ PG

Second World War drama
1943 · US · BW · 114mins

An impressively grim Warner Bros war movie about the Norwegian Resistance, with a stellar cast headed up by unlikely Scandinavians Errol Flynn, Ann Sheridan and Walter Huston. Flynn acquits himself well, and the film is expertly directed by veteran Lewis Milestone (*All Quiet on the Western Front*) and superbly photographed by Sid Hickox. There's also fine support work, most notably from Morris Carnovsky as an old schoolmaster pitting his wits against Helmut Dantine's Nazi commandant

and from Charles Dingle as a Nazi sympathiser. Stirring stuff, that was overtly propagandist when it was made and is still pretty potent today. ▭

Errol Flynn *Gunnar Brogge* • Ann Sheridan *Karen Stensgard* • Walter Huston *Dr Martin Stensgard* • Nancy Coleman *Katja* • Helmut Dantine *Captain Koenig* • Judith Anderson *Gerd Bjarnesen* • Ruth Gordon *Anna Stensgard* • John Beal *Johann Stensgard* • Morris Carnovsky *Sixtus Andresen* ■ *Dir* Lewis Milestone • *Scr* Robert Rossen, from the novel by William Woods

Edge of Deception ★★

Mystery   1994 · US · Colour · 100mins

A second-rate *film noir*, with all the obligatory *femmes fatales* and tortuous conspiracies, but none of the style associated with the genre. Stephen Shellen plays a womanising detective who becomes obsessed with his beautiful neighbour, Jennifer Rubin. But when he tries to intervene in Rubin's violent marriage, he finds himself up to his neck in an intrigue which may or may not involve nosey journalist Mariel Hemingway. There are a couple of nifty twists, but George Mihalka's direction is strictly bargain basement. Contains violence, swearing, sex scenes and nudity.

Mariel Hemingway *Joan Braden* • Stephen Shellen *Nick Gentry* • Jennifer Rubin *Irene Stadler* • Wally Dalton *Detective Rains* • Vladimir Kulich *Allan Stadler* • Ken Roberts *Captain Harrelson* ■ *Dir* George Mihalka • *Scr* Miguel Tejada-Flores, from a story by Miguel Tejada-Flores, Simon Abbott, from characters created by Ken Denbow

Edge of Doom ★★ PG

Drama   1950 · US · BW · 93mins

Produced by Samuel Goldwyn and written by Philip Yordan, this is one of those "street punk" dramas that John Garfield used to swallow whole. Unfortunately, all Farley Granger can manage in the way of torment are a few scowls and sulks as he tries to prevent kindly priest Dana Andrews from discovering that he's guilty of murdering the cleric who denied his mother a decent funeral. Bearing in mind he was coming off the back of *Champion* and *Home of the Brave*, Mark Robson's inconsistent direction is all the more disappointing. ▭

Dana Andrews *Father Roth* • Farley Granger *Martin Lynn* • Joan Evans *Rita Conroy* • Robert Keith *Det Mandel* • Paul Stewart *Craig* • Mala Powers *Julie* ■ *Dir* Mark Robson • *Scr* Philip Yordan, from a novel by Leo Brady

Edge of Eternity ★★★ U

Western   1959 · US · Colour · 79mins

A moderately exciting modern-day western, with lawman Cornel Wilde pursuing murderer Mickey Shaughnessy towards the Grand Canyon and a cable-car climax. The overall effect is marred only by some cheap back projection that jars against the footage of the real thing. *Dirty Harry* director Don Siegel does wonders with the low budget and his short schedule, but even he can't get a performance out of Victoria Shaw.

Cornel Wilde *Les Martin* • Victoria Shaw *Janice Kendon* • Mickey Shaughnessy *Scotty O'Brien* • Edgar Buchanan *Sheriff Edwards* • Rian Garrick *Bob Kendon* • Jack Elam *Bill Ward* ■ *Dir* Donald Siegel [Don Siegel] • *Scr*

Knut Swenson [Marion Hargrove], Richard Collins, from a story by Ben Markson, Knut Swenson [Marion Hargrove]

Edge of Sanity ★ 18

Psychological horror
1989 · UK · Colour · 84mins

Yet another variant on the shopworn Jekyll-and-Hyde theme, unpleasant in tone but enlivened by the stellar presence of Anthony Perkins. This time around, the Jekyll figure turns into a cocaine-snorting killer after experiments with a new drug backfire. Perkins, giving the most outrageous performance of his career, dwells more on the psychological change in his character than the physical one. No ghoulish make-up here, then; just a look that makes him come across like a hungover Iggy Pop. Director Gérard Kikoine learnt his trade making French porno movies, which just about sums it up. ▭

Anthony Perkins *Dr Henry Jekyll/Mr Jack Hyde* • Glynis Barber *Elisabeth Jekyll* • David Lodge *Gabriel Underwood* • Sarah Maur-Thorp *Susannah* • Ben Cole *Johnny* • Ray Jewers *Newcomen* ■ *Dir* Gérard Kikoine • *Scr* JP Felix, Ron Raley, from the novel *Dr Jekyll and Mr Hyde* by Robert Louis Stevenson

Edge of the City ★★★

Drama   1957 · US · BW · 85mins

A dated and hectoring liberal drama, originally a TV play called *A Man Is Ten Feet Tall*, about the destructive friendship between the unstable John Cassavetes and hard-working labourer Sidney Poitier. Owing much to *On the Waterfront*, released three years earlier, the picture also followed teen dramas such as *Rebel without a Cause* and *The Blackboard Jungle* by taking delinquency out of the classroom and into the world of work. Despite its sledgehammer script and direction, it can still be enjoyed for the acting and the realistic location photography.

John Cassavetes *Axel North* • Sidney Poitier *Tommy Tyler* • Jack Warden *Charles Malik* • Kathleen Maguire *Ellen Wilson* • Ruby Dee *Lucy Tyler* • Robert Simon *Mr Nordmann* • Ruth White *Mrs Nordmann* ■ *Dir* Martin Ritt • *Scr* Robert Alan Aurthur, from his TV play *A Man Is Ten Feet Tall*

The Edge of the Horizon ★★★

Drama   1993 · Fr/Por · Colour · 91mins

Portugal is the poor relation of European cinema; until recently, even its greatest film-maker, Manoel de Oliveira, struggled to find financial backing. Director Fernando Lopes accepted French funding for this atmospheric *film noir*, which stars Claude Brasseur as a pathologist whose life is transformed when he begins to delve into the criminal past of a corpse that appears to be his younger self. Full of neat touches, this is as much an exercise in style as it is a thriller, with Lopes bathing Lisbon's backstreets in shadow to keep us as much in the dark as Brasseur himself. In Portuguese with English subtitles.

Claude Brasseur *Spino* • Andrea Ferreol *Francesca* • Ana Padrao *Prostitute* • Antonio Valero *Alvaro* ■ *Dir* Fernando Lopes • *Scr* Christopher Frank, Jean Nachbaur, from the novel *Il Filo dell'Orizzonte* by Antonio Tabucchi

The Edge of the World
★★★★

Drama   1937 · UK · BW · 80mins

Made by Michael Powell, arguably the British cinema's most profoundly creative director, this is a fictional account of the harsh lives led by a dwindling community high on the cliffs above the cruel and majestic sea off the Scottish mainland. Filmed on the island of Foula, whose real-life inhabitants play the village people, it stars Niall MacGinnis, John Laurie, Finlay Currie and Belle Chrystal, all superb. But it is the landscape, and the spirit of a way of life being slowly but inevitably eroded, that dominate this poignant, elegiac tale of life, love and death. A leisurely film in semi-documentary style, its images of people and place weave a haunting spell – stay with it. In 1978, Powell returned to the isle and shot a prologue and epilogue to the film, retitling the new version *Return to the Edge of the World*.

John Laurie *Peter Manson* • Belle Chrystal *Ruth Manson* • Niall MacGinnis *Andrew Gray* • Finlay Currie *James Gray* • Eric Berry *Robbie Manson* • Michael Powell *Yachtsman* ■ *Dir/Scr* Michael Powell

Edie & Pen
★★★

Romantic comedy drama
1996 · US · Colour · 98mins

Oscar nominees Stockard Channing (*Six Degrees of Separation*) and Jennifer Tilly (*Bullets over Broadway*) join forces for this hilarious romantic comedy. They play two very different women, in Reno for quickie divorces, who find they have more in common than they could ever have imagined. Scott Glenn, Randy Travis and Stuart Wilson provide the beef in a film written and produced by Victoria Tennant, the English actress better known as Steve Martin's ex-wife.

Stockard Channing *Pen* • Jennifer Tilly *Edie* • Scott Glenn *Harry* • Stuart Wilson *Victor* • Randy Travis *Pony Cobb* • Martin Mull *Johnnie Sparkle* • Chris Sarandon *Max* • Louise Fletcher *Judge* • Beverly D'Angelo *Barlady* ■ *Dir* Matthew Irmas • *Scr* Victoria Tennant

Edison, the Man
★★★ U

Biography   1940 · US · BW · 106mins

In a movie that contains almost as much sentimental invention as the practical kind, Thomas Alva Edison emerges as the sort of against-all-odds, American pioneer that Hollywood loves. Despite the sanitisation, Spencer Tracy offers a convincing study of the inventor, stubbornly fighting trials and tribulations and constructing the light bulb in a radiant sequence as exciting as any thriller. Clarence Brown's sequel to Mickey Rooney's *Young Tom Edison* takes itself much more seriously; interestingly, MGM produced both features in the same year.

Spencer Tracy *Thomas Alva Edison* • Rita Johnson *Mary Stilwell* • Lynne Overman *Bunt Cavatt* • Charles Coburn *General Powell* • Gene Lockhart *Mr Taggart* • Henry Travers *Ben Els* • Felix Bressart *Michael Somon* ■ *Dir* Clarence Brown • *Scr* Talbot Jennings, Bradbury Foote, from a story by Dore Schary, Bradbury Foote

Edith and Marcel
★★ PG

Biographical romantic drama
1983 · Fr · Colour · 140mins

When Patrick Dewaere killed himself early in the production, Marcel Cerdan Jr stepped up from technical adviser to play his famous boxing father in this account of his love affair with "the little sparrow", Edith Piaf. If Claude Lelouch had captured just a modicum of the passion the couple generated, this might have been a compelling picture. But he spends too much time on an irrelevant subplot involving a bibliophile and a prisoner of war. Lethargic, pretentious and wasteful. In French with English subtitles.

Evelyne Bouix *Edith Piaf/Margot de Villedieu* • Jacques Villeret *Jacques Barbier* • Francis Huster *Francis Roman* • Jean-Claude Brialy *Loulou Barrier* • Jean Bouise *Lucien Roupp* • Marcel Cerdan Jr *Marcel Cerdan* • Charles Aznavour ■ *Dir/Scr* Claude Lelouch

Ed's Next Move
★★★

Romantic comedy
1996 · US · Colour · 88mins

An engaging comedy about a Wisconsin nerd, Matt Ross (the Ed in question), going to the Big Apple and falling for musician Lee (Callie Thorne). Complications ensue when it transpires Lee is involved with someone else. Fortunately, Ed's worldly wise roommate Ray is on hand to take him to diners and pump him with advice about women. Writer/director John Walsh makes an impressive debut with this low-budget feature. Romantic comedy is one of the toughest genres to crack; this one just about makes the grade.

Matt Ross *Eddie Brodsky* • Callie Thorne *Lee Nicol* • Kevin Carroll *Ray Obregon* • Ramsey Faragallah *Dr Banarjee* • Nina Sheveleva *Elenka* ■ *Dir/Scr* John Walsh

EDtv
★★★ 12

Comedy   1999 · US · Colour · 118mins

Small-town video store assistant Matthew McConaughey agrees to be filmed 24 hours a day by a camera crew for a ratings-hungry cable network. But the novelty soon wears off when his regular-guy persona makes him nationally famous, disrupting his entire existence. Comparisons to *The Truman Show* are inevitable but misplaced, as director Ron Howard's soft-centred rumination on the excesses of television is more concerned with "feel-good" laughs and formulaic romantic complications than hard-edged satire. McConaughey delivers the homespun messages with winning aplomb, Ellen DeGeneres steals every scene as his TV producer, and Elizabeth Hurley ensures her role as the wannabe "It Girl" hitching her career wagon to Ed's rising star, pays maximum dividends. 🖵 **DVD**

Matthew McConaughey *Ed Pekurny* • Ellen DeGeneres *Cynthia Topping* • Jenna Elfman *Shari* • Woody Harrelson *Ray Pekurny* • Sally Kirkland *Jeanette* • Martin Landau *Al* • Rob Reiner *Whitaker* • Dennis Hopper *Hank* • Elizabeth Hurley *Jill* • Michael Moore (2) *Panel member* • Clint Howard *Ken* ■ *Dir* Ron Howard • *Scr* Lowell Ganz, Babaloo Mandel, from the film *Louis XIX: Roi des Ondes* by Emile Gaudreault, Sylvie Bouchard

Educating Rita
★★★★ 15

Comedy drama   1983 · UK · Colour · 106mins

A joy from start to finish, largely thanks to Willy Russell's crisp adaptation of his successful stage play and the lead players' divine suitability for the roles. Julie Walters is great as the sassy and streetwise heroine, eager for higher learning but smart enough to spot Michael Caine's foibles at a hundred paces, and Caine is given one of his best ever roles as the drink-sodden, cynical lecturer. Some felt that Walters's portrayal patronised bright, working-class girls, but she brings genuine warmth to the part. Contains swearing. 🖵 **DVD**

Michael Caine *Dr Frank Bryant* • Julie Walters *Rita "Susan" White* • Michael Williams *Brian* • Maureen Lipman *Trish* • Jeananne Crowley *Julia* • Malcolm Douglas *Denny* • Godfrey Quigley *Rita's father* ■ *Dir* Lewis Gilbert • *Scr* Willy Russell, from his play

The Education of Little Tree
★★

Drama   1997 · US/Can · Colour · 115mins

Quiet, thoroughly tasteful account of a part-Cherokee boy (Joseph Ashton) struggling to come to terms with the white man's world when he goes to live with his grandparents in thirties America. James Cromwell adds suitable moral authority to a moving tale which is occasionally a touch too reverential. Based on the novel by Forrest Carter, which was originally regarded as autobiographical before the author was revealed as a former white supremacist.

Joseph Ashton *Little Tree* • James Cromwell *Granpa* • Tantoo Cardinal *Granma* • Leni Parker *Martha* • Rebecca Dewey *Dolly* • William Rowat *Henry* • Robert Daviau *Ralph* • Graham Greene *Willow John* ■ *Dir* Richard Friedenberg • *Scr* Richard Friedenberg, from the novel by Forrest Carter

Edward, My Son
★★

Drama   1949 · US/UK · BW · 112mins

This British MGM feature was clearly intended as a prestige production, fielding two major stars and a grade-A director, but the whole enterprise reeks of theatricality. The fault lies with the gimmick-ridden play on which it was based; co-written by actor Robert Morley as a vehicle for himself, it traced an ailing marriage and deliberately refrained from showing the eponymous Edward on stage. The film, which awkwardly preserves the same convention, features Hollywood import Spencer Tracy, uncomfortable as the despotic dad, and Deborah Kerr, unconvincing as his alcoholic missus. It's a bleak piece, and director George Cukor seems at a loss depicting the English class system. However, he's well served by his indigenous actors in a film that remains an honourable and intriguing failure.

Spencer Tracy *Arnold Boult* • Deborah Kerr *Evelyn Boult* • Ian Hunter *Dr Larry Woodhope* • Leueen MacGrath *Eileen Perrin* • James Donald *Bronton* • Mervyn Johns *Harry Simpkin* • Harriette Johns *Phyllis Mayden* • Felix Aylmer *Mr Hanray* • Walter Fitzgerald *Mr Kedner* ■ *Dir* George Cukor • *Scr* Donald Ogden Stewart, from the play by Robert Morley, Noel Langley

Edward Scissorhands
★★★★★ PG

Fantasy   1990 · US · Colour · 100mins

Tim Burton's bewitchingly oddball "Beauty and the Beast" fairy tale is a superlative masterpiece and one of the best fantasy films ever made. It matches the spellbinding work of Hans Christian Andersen in terms of haunting power, exquisite charm and dark romance, with Johnny Depp's sensitive rendition of Vincent Price's "Punkenstein" creation also a major revelation. Humanoid Edward being unable to touch the things he loves because of his razor fingers is potent symbolism of the highest order, and the finale, assisted by Danny Elfman's gloriously magical score, packs an unforgettable emotional wallop. 🖵

Johnny Depp *Edward Scissorhands* • Winona Ryder *Kim Boggs* • Dianne Wiest *Peg Boggs* • Anthony Michael Hall *Jim* • Kathy Baker *Joyce Monroe* • Vincent Price *Inventor* • Alan Arkin *Bill Boggs* ■ *Dir* Tim Burton • *Scr* Caroline Thompson, from a story by Caroline Thompson, Tim Burton • *Cinematographer* Stefan Czapsky • *Art Director* Bo Welch

Edward II
★★ 18

Historical drama   1991 · UK · Colour · 86mins

Director Derek Jarman's adaptation of Christopher Marlowe's play of court favouritism and lethal power games behind the throne is both a challenging and off-putting experience. Telling the admittedly compelling story of Britain's only acknowledged homosexual monarch, whose preference for his male lover rather than Queen Isabella led to a civil war, Jarman turns the grim 16th-century drama into a typically radical and confrontational polemic about the evils of homophobia. Stylishly staged in modern dress, with the gay activist group Act Up playing Edward's supporters, Steven Waddington is a handsome, if tiresome Edward, while Tilda Swinton makes the best impression as his cruelly-rejected queen. 🖵

Steven Waddington *Edward II* • Tilda Swinton *Isabella* • Andrew Tiernan *Gaveston* • Nigel Terry *Mortimer* • Dudley Sutton *Bishop of Winchester* • Kevin Collins *Lightborn* • John Lynch *Spencer* • Jerome Flynn *Kent* ■ *Dir* Derek Jarman • *Scr* Derek Jarman, Stephen McBride, Ken Butler, from the play by Christopher Marlowe

The Eel
★★★ 18

Drama   1997 · Jap · Colour · 111mins

The joint winner of the 1997 Palme d'Or (it tied with Abbas Kiarostami's *Taste of Cherry*), this is a curious, sometimes powerful tale of one man's isolated existence, interlaced with fantasy, farce and a fish. Some will be touched by director Shohei Imamura's story of a reformed wife-killer whose only real friend is his pet eel. Others will be mystified by the near-silent central character, the dreamlike moments and a bizarre comedy subplot involving unidentified flying objects. At times gentle and poignant, at others shockingly brutal (the early murder scene especially), *The Eel* is striking, but difficult to get to grips with. In Japanese with English subtitles. Contains violent scenes and swearing. 🖵

U = SUITABLE FOR ALL   Uc = SUITABLE FOR ALL, ESPECIALLY FOR YOUNG CHILDREN (VIDEO ONLY)   PG = PARENTAL GUIDANCE

Koji Yakusho *Takuro Yamashita* • Misa Shimizu *Keiko Hattori* • Fujio Tsuneta *Jiro Nakajima* • Mitsuko Baisho *Misako Nakajima* ■ *Dir* Shohei Imamura • *Scr* Motofumi Tomikawa, Shohei Imamura, Daisuke Tengan, from the novel *Sparkles in the Darkness* by Akira Yoshimura.

The Effect of Gamma Rays on Man-in-the-Moon Marigolds ★★

Drama　　1972 · US · Colour · 100mins

Although it won him a Pulitzer Prize, Paul Zindel's play feels like a clumsy pastiche of Tennessee Williams. So while it's possible to see why Paul Newman might be drawn to a film of the project, it's hard to see what he felt he could bring to the story of an unkempt widow struggling to raise her chalk-and-cheese daughters, given the spluttering machismo of his refusal to explore its deeper emotional resonances. Clearly the chance of working with his wife Joanne Woodward and daughter Nell Potts was an incentive, but his stagey direction leaves them straining for the effects he is reluctant to broach.

Joanne Woodward *Beatrice* • Nell Potts *Matilda* • Roberta Wallach *Ruth* • Judith Lowry *Nanny* • Richard Venture *Floyd* • Estelle Omens *Floyd's wife* • Carolyn Coates *Granny's daughter* • Will Hare *Junk man* • Jess Osuna *Sonny* ■ *Dir* Paul Newman • *Scr* Alvin Sargent, from the play by Paul Zindel.

Effi Briest ★★★★ U

Period drama　1974 · W Ger · BW · 134mins

Teenager Effi (Hanna Schygulla) is forced into an unsuitable marriage in Fassbinder's adaptation of Theodor Fontane's classic 19th-century novel. A lonely existence drives Effi to infidelity, and her husband's later discovery of the affair has tragic consequences. Despite an increasingly tempestuous professional relationship with Schygulla, Fassbinder has created a stylised but truly literary film. Using elegant monochrome photography and with mirrors reflecting the artifice of Effi's world, the director treats the original text with awed reverence. In German with English subtitles. 🎞

Hanna Schygulla *Effi Briest* • Wolfgang Schenck *Baron Geert von Instetten* • Ulli Lommel *Major Crampas* • Lilo Pempeit *Frau Briest* • Herbert Steinmetz *Herr Briest* • Hark Bohm *Gieshuebler* ■ *Dir* Rainer Werner Fassbinder • *Scr* Rainer Werner Fassbinder, from the novel by Theodor Fontane

The Egg and I ★★★ U

Comedy　　1947 · US · BW · 107mins

This massively popular film version of Betty MacDonald's autobiographical bestseller follows a couple of city slickers who buy a clapped-out old farmhouse and renovate it. Claudette Colbert is delightful as the newly-wed who discovers on her wedding night that her husband, attractively played by a wry Fred MacMurray, wants to be a chicken farmer. Producer/director/ screenwriter Chester Erskine perhaps keeps events on too even a keel, but it still makes for a very pleasant, if undramatic, whole. The picture also marks the first appearance of Ma and Pa Kettle (Marjorie Main and Percy

Kilbride), who were later given their own series by Universal.

Claudette Colbert *Betty* • Fred MacMurray *Bob* • Marjorie Main *Ma Kettle* • Percy Kilbride *Pa Kettle* • Louise Allbritton *Harriet Putnam* • Richard Long *Tom Kettle* • Billy House *Billy* ■ *Dir* Chester Erskine • *Scr* Chester Erskine, Fred F Finklehoffe, from the autobiography by Betty MacDonald.

Egghead's Robot ★★ U

Science-fiction adventure
1970 · UK · Colour · 56mins

These days, Hollywood seems to have cornered the market in children's movies, spelling the end of amiable romps like this one from the Children's Film Foundation. A young Keith Chegwin stars as the son of inventor Richard Wattis, who borrows a lookalike robot to do his chores and get him out of all manner of scrapes. However, even with Roy Kinnear pantomiming as a park keeper, this will seem painfully twee to today's pre-teen sophisticates.

Keith Chegwin *Egghead Wentworth* • Jeffrey Chegwin *Eric* • Kathryn Dawe *Elspeth* • Roy Kinnear *Park keeper* • Richard Wattis *Paul Wentworth* • Patricia Routledge *Mrs Wentworth* ■ *Dir* Milo Lewis • *Scr* Leif Saxon

The Egyptian ★★

Historical epic　1954 · US · Colour · 138mins

Even an old pro like director Michael Curtiz has difficulty in jollying-up this solemn, overlong historical epic about the search for God in ancient Egypt. Casting the dishy but wooden Edmund Purdom in the leading role of Sinuhe doesn't help matters, and neither does hunky Victor Mature as Horemheb – though Jean Simmons and Peter Ustinov seem to take things with a huge pinch of salt. The excellent music is a singular collaboration between Alfred Newman and Bernard Herrmann, while Leon Shamroy's colour CinemaScope photography was nominated for an Oscar. The less said about the script, the better.

Edmund Purdom *Sinuhe* • Jean Simmons *Merit* • Victor Mature *Horemheb* • Peter Ustinov *Kaptah* • Gene Tierney *Baketamon* • Michael Wilding *Akhnaton* ■ *Dir* Michael Curtiz • *Scr* Philip Dunne, Casey Robinson, from the novel by Mika Waltari

The Eiger Sanction ★★ 15

Spy thriller　　1975 · US · Colour · 113mins

Conceived as a Bond-style adventure, this story of an ex-spy mountaineer and art collector was rejected by Paul Newman. Clint Eastwood picked it up and turned it into a critical and box-office failure, arguably the weakest of the films he has directed himself. As Jonathan Hemlock, Eastwood agrees to climb the Eiger and eliminate an agent in return for preferential tax status. It often looks spectacular, but the thin plotting and weak dialogue seriously let the film down. 🎞

Clint Eastwood *Jonathan Hemlock* • George Kennedy *Ben Bowman* • Vonetta McGee *Jemima Brown* • Jack Cassidy *Miles Mellough* • Heidi Bruhl *Mrs Montaigne* • Thayer David *Dragon* • Reiner Schoene *Freytag* • Michael Grimm *Meyer* ■ *Dir* Clint Eastwood • *Scr* Hal Dresner, Warren B Murphy, Rod Whitaker, from the novel by Trevanian

8½ ★★★★★ 15

Drama　　1963 · It · BW · 137mins

Having made six features and three short films, director Federico Fellini reckoned that this mesmerising insight into the creative process took his tally of movies to eight-and-a-half. The winner of the best foreign language film Oscar, this is a complex, painfully honest study of a man in a personal and professional crisis. After *La Dolce Vita*, Fellini was faced with the problem of repeating his success and this soul-searching film, with its mix of daydreams, memories, nightmares and frustrating confrontations, is a fantasy chronicle of his attempts to sustain his reputation as a cinematic genius. As the tormented film-maker, the exceptional Marcello Mastroianni is superbly supported by Anouk Aimée and Claudia Cardinale. In Italian with English subtitles.

Marcello Mastroianni *Guido Anselmi* • Claudia Cardinale *Claudia* • Anouk Aimée *Luisa Anselmi* • Sandra Milo *Carla* • Rossella Falk *Rossella* • Barbara Steele *Gloria Morin* • Mario Pisu *Mezzabotta* • Guido Alberti *Producer* ■ *Dir* Federico Fellini • *Scr* Federico Fellini, Tullio Pinelli, Ennio Flajano, Brunello Rondi, from a story by Federico Fellini, Ennio Flajano • *Music* Nino Rota • *Costume Designer* Piero Gherardi

8½ Women ★★ 15

Comedy drama
1999 · Neth/UK/Lux/Ger · Colour · 120mins

Intended as a tribute to Federico Fellini, Peter Greenaway's misfiring comedy has none of the acidity or acuity of either *8½* or *City of Women*. Less visually audacious than *The Pillow Book*, it seeks to explore man's tendency to idealise women. However, such is Greenaway's preoccupation with referencing cultural history that he fails to capitalise on the themes and relationships that arise when widowed businessman John Standing and son Matthew Delamere open their doors to various disaffected women. While trivialising the talents of such actresses as Toni Collette and Polly Walker, this is less misogynist than angrier critics would have you believe. Yet it's still unworthy of its auteur.

John Standing *Philip Emmenthal* • Matthew Delamere *Storey Emmenthal* • Vivian Wu *Kito* • Shizuka Inoh *Simato* • Barbara Sarafian *Clothilde* • Kirina Mano *Mio* • Toni Collette *Griselda* • Amanda Plummer *Beryl* • Polly Walker *Palmira* ■ *Dir/Scr* Peter Greenaway

Eight Days a Week ★★★

Comedy　　1996 · US · Colour · 92mins

Having worked on a short film featuring Steven Spielberg and George Lucas, writer/director Michael Davis made his feature debut with this coming-of-age comedy. The story focuses on Joshua Schaefer's passion for his neighbour Keri Russell and the romantic vigil (inspired by the wooing methods of his ancestors) with which he hopes to win her heart. More a crash course in suburban living than a guide to successful courting, this often wincingly accurate insight into confused male adolescence may not be the ultimate teen pic, but it's far from being the worst.

Joshua Schaefer *Peter* • Keri Russell *Erica* • RD Robb *Matt* • Mark Taylor *Peter's father* •

Marcia Shapiro *Peter's mother* • Johnny Green *Nick* • Buck Kartallan *Nonno* • Catherine Hicks *Ms Lewis* ■ *Dir/Scr* Michael Davis

8 Heads in a Duffel Bag ★ 15

Black comedy　1997 · US · Colour · 94mins

Tom Schulman makes his directorial debut with a lame comedy that doesn't have enough laughs to sustain its hour-and-a-half running time. Joe Pesci plays a mob hitman whose bag of heads gets mixed up with one belonging to a medical student. The expected complications ensue, but Pesci and most of the supporting cast simply mug their way through the "hilarious" proceedings. Only David Spade escapes with any degree of dignity. 🎞 **DVD**

Joe Pesci *Tommy Spinelli* • Andy Comeau *Charlie* • Kristy Swanson *Laurie Bennett* • Todd Louiso *Steve* • George Hamilton *Dick Bennett* • Dyan Cannon *Annette Bennett* • David Spade *Ernie* • Anthony Mangano *Rico* ■ *Dir/Scr* Tom Schulman

800 Leagues down the Amazon ★★

Historical adventure
1993 · US/Mex · Colour · 88mins

Executive produced by Roger Corman, this unprepossessing costume adventure was directed by Luis Llosa, who returned to the Amazon in 1997 for the laugh-a-minute monster movie *Anaconda*. Barry Bostwick stars as a wealthy plantation owner escorting his daughter, Daphne Zuniga, to her wedding. However, they reckoned without the perils of the river and the schemes of bounty hunter Adam Baldwin. Corman has never been one to throw money at a production, but a bigger budget would have done nothing to improve the long-winded script. Contains some violence.

Daphne Zuniga *Minha* • Barry Bostwick *Garral* • Adam Baldwin *Koja* • Tom Verica *Monoel* • EE Ross *Frolgoso* ■ *Dir* Luis Llosa • *Scr* Laura Schiff, Jackson Barr, from the novel by Jules Verne

Eight Is Enough: a Family Reunion ★★

Comedy drama　1987 · US · Colour · 100mins

Hollywood is never on safer or more commercial turf than when giving a big hug to cosy family life. This feature-length instalment of an early seventies American TV series, *Eight Is Enough*, which homed in on the joys, insecurities and trivia of Dick Van Patten's large family, is certainly safe, and undoubtedly cashed in on the TV show's popularity. Starting out with the events surrounding Van Patten's 50th birthday, the film veers between real emotional depth and schmaltz, but there's some fun mixed in with the rather obvious drama.

Dick Van Patten *Tom Bradford* • Mary Frann *Abby Bradford* • Adam Rich *Nicholas* • Lani O'Grady *Mary* • Susan Richardson *Susan* • Willie Aames *Tommy* • Connie Needham *Elizabeth* • Grant Goodeve *David* ■ *Dir* Harry Harris • *Scr* Gwen Bagni-Dubov [Gwen Bagni], from the TV series

Eight Men Out ★★★ 15

Drama   1988 · US · Colour · 114mins

John Cusack and Charlie Sheen star in a low-key and serious exposé of corruption in the American baseball game when, in 1919, the Chicago White Sox threw the World Series. When the truth became known, it was quickly dubbed the Black Sox Scandal. Written and directed by John Sayles, the picture details the social and economic stresses of the time that led the players into the clutches of hustlers and organised crime. It's a sad and compelling piece that is totally convincing and doesn't require a knowledge of baseball. Sayles himself plays sports writer Ring Lardner, whose screenwriter son was one of the original "Hollywood Ten" – a group blacklisted in 1948 during the communist witch-hunt in the film industry. ▢

John Cusack *Buck Weaver* • Charlie Sheen *Hap Felsch* • John Mahoney *Kid Gleason* • DB Sweeney *"Shoeless" Joe Jackson* • Clifton James *Charles Comiskey* • Eliot Asinof *Heydler* • David Strathairn *Eddie Cicotte* • John Sayles *Ring Lardner* ■ *Dir* John Sayles • *Scr* John Sayles, from the novel by Eliot Asinof

8mm ★★ 18

Mystery thriller
1999 · US/Ger · Colour · 118mins

Snuff movies get a gratuitously sleazy work-out under Joel Schumacher's ham-fisted direction in this disappointing and depressing thriller. Honourable private detective Nicolas Cage is hired by a wealthy widow to uncover the identity of a teenage girl, who the widow believes has been murdered in a reel of pornographic film found among her late husband's belongings. The trail leads a surprisingly bland Cage through LA's hardcore underworld to overacting on a grand scale by pornographer Peter Stormare and an assortment of unconvincing sex scenarios, before he learns the "shocking" truth. The movie does have one saving grace in Joaquin Phoenix's jaded sex-shop assistant, who guides Cage through the S&M scene. Contains violence, swearing and sex scenes. ▢ **DVD**

Nicolas Cage *Tom Welles* • Joaquin Phoenix *Max California* • James Gandolfini *Eddie Poole* • Peter Stormare *Dino Velvet* • Anthony Heald *Longdale* • Chris Bauer *Machine* • Catherine Keener *Amy Welles* ■ *Dir* Joel Schumacher • *Scr* Andrew Kevin Walker

8 Million Ways to Die ★★★ 18

Crime thriller   1986 · US · Colour · 110mins

Oliver Stone wrote the original script of this urban thriller, intending to direct it himself. But financial problems led to a delay and, when Hal Ashby was brought in to direct, Robert Towne rewrote the script under a pseudonym. Stone disowns it, Ashby was reportedly fired near the end of production and few people ever saw it. The title comes from the population of Los Angeles County; the story comes from eight million other cop pictures. On the credit side, there are some vivid locations and a decent cast: Jeff Bridges as the cop with a drink problem, Rosanna Arquette as the

mobster's moll and Andy Garcia as a drug dealer. ▢

Jeff Bridges *Matthew Scudder* • Rosanna Arquette *Sarah* • Alexandra Paul *Sunny* • Randy Brooks *Chance* • Andy Garcia *Angel Maldonado* • Lisa Sloan *Linda Scudder* ■ *Dir* Hal Ashby • *Scr* Oliver Stone, David Lee Henry, Robert Towne (uncredited), from the novel by Lawrence Block

Eight O'Clock Walk ★★ PG

Drama   1953 · UK · BW · 83mins

Having faced the rope in *London Belongs to Me*, Richard Attenborough finds himself on trial for his life again in this lukewarm legal drama. Typically with courtroom pictures, there's too much chat and not enough action, although father-and-son barristers Ian Hunter and Derek Farr enjoy a few jousts before the verdict is returned. The problem is that, no matter how damning the evidence, you never believe for a second that cabby Attenborough is guilty of murder and, consequently, the picture is devoid of any suspense. The jury discussions and the street gossip never ring true, either. ▢

Richard Attenborough *Tom Manning* • Derek Farr *Peter Tanner* • Cathy O'Donnell *Jill Manning* • Ian Hunter *Geoffrey Tanner* • Maurice Denham *Horace Clifford* • Bruce Seton *DCI* • Harry Welchman *Justice Harrington* • Kynaston Reeves *Mr Munro* ■ *Dir* Lance Comfort • *Scr* Katherine Strueby, Guy Morgan, from a story by Jack Roffey, Gordon Harbord

Eight on the Lam ★★ U

Comedy   1967 · US · Colour · 107mins

There was safety in numbers for Bob Hope at this stage of a career that wasn't just flagging but seemed at half-mast. A few years after *The Seven Little Foys* this came along, with Bob as a nervous bank clerk accused of embezzlement who goes on the run with his seven children. Not even the acerbic wit of Phyllis Diller can cut through the bland sentimentality.

Bob Hope *Henry Dimsdale* • Phyllis Diller *Golda* • Jonathan Winters *Jasper Lynch* • Shirley Eaton *Ellie Barton* • Jill St John *Monica* • Stacey Maxwell *Linda* • Kevin Brody *Steve* ■ *Dir* George Marshall • *Scr* Albert E Lewin, Burt Styler, Bob Fisher, Arthur Marx, from a story by Bob Fisher, Arthur Marx

8 Seconds ★★ PG

Biographical drama
1994 · US · Colour · 100mins

As anyone familiar with *Rocky* will know, John G Avildsen tends to romanticise sport rather than tell it as it is. Bareback riding has never looked so easy as in this biopic of Lane Frost, whose brief career saw him become one of America's youngest ever rodeo champions. Such is the predictability of the bucking sequences that it's almost a relief to be plunged into Lane's marital misery and his search for the popularity he craves to compensate for his father's disapproval. Luke Perry, still best-known for *Beverly Hills 90210*, and Cynthia Geary are well matched as the ill-fated Frosts, but the action is just too tame to thrill. ▢

Luke Perry *Lane Frost* • Stephen Baldwin *Tuff Hedeman* • Cynthia Geary *Kellie Frost* • James

Rebhorn *Clyde Frost* • Red Mitchell *Cody Lambert* • Carrie Snodgress *Elsie Frost* ■ *Dir* John G Avildsen • *Scr* Monte Merrick

18 Again! ★★ PG

Comedy   1988 · US · Colour · 95mins

George Burns did the majority of his best work on stage, radio and TV with his wife Gracie Allen. However, most viewers will remember him as a mischievous old man in films like *The Sunshine Boys* and *Oh, God!* Either of these would better have shown off the talents of the veteran trouper, who died shortly after his 100th birthday, as he's given little screen time in this non-starting "body swap" comedy that crept in at the end of the cycle that began with *Big* and *Vice Versa.*

George Burns *Jack Watson* • Charlie Schlatter *David Watson* • Tony Roberts *Arnold* • Anita Morris *Madelyn* • Miriam Flynn *Betty* • Jennifer Runyon *Robin* • Red Buttons *Charlie* • George DiCenzo *Coach* ■ *Dir* Paul Flaherty • *Scr* Josh Goldstein, Jonathan Prince

1871 ★★ 15

Period romantic drama
1989 · UK · Colour · 100mins

Ken McMullen's drama, set during the time of the Paris Commune, focuses on actors from Ramborde's Theatre. Severine (Ana Padrao) is the actress with the complicated love life, caught between John Lynch and Roshan Seth during this turbulent period of French history. Directed with awkward solemnity by McMullen, the actors give of their all, but that turns out to be not much. The supporting cast includes Mike Leigh regular Timothy Spall.

Ana Padrao *Severine* • John Lynch *O'Brien* • Roshan Seth *Lord Grafton* • Jack Klaff *Cluseret* • Timothy Spall *Ramborde* • Maria de Medeiros *Maria* • Jacqueline Dankworth *Street singer* • Ian McNeice *Prince of Wales* • Dominique Pinon *Napoleon III* • Med Hondo *Karl Marx* ■ *Dir* Ken McMullen • *Scr* Terry James, James Leahy, Ken McMullen

1860 ★★★

Historical political drama
1933 · It · BW · 75mins

Alessandro Blasetti was one of the major directors of the Italian cinema of the thirties, and was a direct influence on Luchino Visconti. Describing the events surrounding the battle of Calatafimi in May 1860 when the Sicilians rose up and defeated the troops of the King of Naples, the film avoids many of the rhetorical postures of the other historical epics made in Fascist Italy at the time. The use of non-professional actors, actual landscapes and regional dialects makes it a precursor of neorealism. The main difference is that the film presents the peasants as part of the historical process and not as individual victims. An Italian language film.

Aida Bellia *Gesuzza* • Giuseppe Gullino *Carmeliddu* ■ *Dir/Scr* Alessandro Blasetti

The Eighteenth Angel ★★ 15

Horror   1997 · US · Colour · 84mins

Soon after the unexplained death of his wife, Christopher McDonald accompanies his daughter, Rachael Leigh Cook, on a modelling assignment to Italy. There she

becomes the target of a mysterious sect of priests preparing for the return of Satan. More Bible-based horror from David Seltzer, writer of *The Omen*, who clearly should get out a bit more if these sloppy seconds are anything to go by. Some reasonable chills register along the way, despite the film's obvious contrivances, but the overly clichéd ending is a bust. ▢

Christopher McDonald *Hugh Stanton* • Rachael Leigh Cook *Lucy Stanton* • Stanley Tucci *Todd Stanton* • Wendy Crewson *Norah Stanton* • Maximilian Schell *Father Simeon* ■ *Dir* William Bindley • *Scr* David Seltzer

The Eighth Day ★★★ PG

Drama   1996 · Bel · Colour · 112mins

Sentimental, life-affirming movie from Belgium, dealing with the friendship between a corporate businessman who loathes his existence, and a man with Down's syndrome who embraces life. Daniel Auteuil and Pascal Duquenne (who shared the best actor prize at Cannes) are both excellent, and their *Rain Man*-style relationship has some profoundly touching moments. However, director Jaco Van Dormael (*Toto the Hero*) strives a little too hard for profundity, decorating the film with poetic images of nature and taking Auteuil's life-changing experience to rather extreme levels. His screenplay also imbues Duquenne with an uncomfortably Christ-like significance. In French with English subtitles. ▢

Daniel Auteuil *Harry* • Pascal Duquenne *Georges* • Miou-Miou *Julie* • Isabelle Sadoyan *Georges's mother* • Henri Garcin *Company director* • Michele Maes *Nathalie* • Laszlo Harmati *Luis Mariano* • Helene Roussel *Julie's mother* ■ *Dir/Scr* Jaco Van Dormael

84 Charing Cross Road ★★★★ U

Biographical drama
1986 · UK · Colour · 95mins

Adapted from Helene Hanff's bestselling account of her dealings with the staff of a London bookshop, this is an absolute delight. Building his film around the letters exchanged between Hanff and manager Frank Doel, director David Jones manages to create utterly credible characters, convey something of the beauty of books and make some telling comparisons between the gloomy reserve of postwar Britain and the effervescence of Cold War America. However, what makes this gentle drama so compelling are the performances of Anne Bancroft and Anthony Hopkins, who ingeniously fashion a romance between two people who never met. ▢

Anne Bancroft *Helene Hanff* • Anthony Hopkins *Frank Doel* • Judi Dench *Nora Doel* • Jean De Baer *Maxine Bellamy* • Maurice Denham *George Martin* • Eleanor David *Cecily Farr* • Mercedes Ruehl *Kay* • Daniel Gerroll *Brian* • Wendy Morgan *Megan Wells* ■ *Dir* David Jones • *Scr* Hugh Whitemore, from the book by Helene Hanff

84 Charlie Mopic ★★★ 18

War drama   1989 · US · Colour · 90mins

Tired of films about the Vietnam conflict? Try this as an eye-opener with a viewpoint that neither waves flags nor wastes blame, as it follows a two-

U = SUITABLE FOR ALL   Uc = SUITABLE FOR ALL, ESPECIALLY FOR YOUNG CHILDREN (VIDEO ONLY)   PG = PARENTAL GUIDANCE

man documentary film crew accompanying a platoon "to record procedures peculiar to the combat situation". Such is the skill of writer/director Patrick Duncan that it all comes across as reality. The constant slang, though, is a barbed barrier to our understanding, while the continual hand-held camera becomes too unsettling for comfort. But then comfort was not what Vietnam was all about. Contains swearing. ▭

Jonathan Emerson *LT* • Nicholas Cascone *Easy* • Jason Tomlins *Pretty Boy* • Christopher Burgard *Hammer* • Glenn Morshower *Cracker* • Richard Brooks *OD* • Byron Thomas *Mopic* ■ *Dir/Scr* Patrick Duncan

Eighty Steps to Jonah ★★

Drama   1969 · US · Colour · 107mins

Vegas vocalist Wayne Newton turns up in this sentimental tale of an innocent man on the run who poses as a handyman in a children's summer camp for the blind. The set-up is a cinema staple from Edward G Robinson in *Brother Orchid* through to *Nuns on the Run*, but unlike, say, *Sister Act*, the treatment of the story stays just a shade this side of saccharine. Several familiar faces, such as Mickey Rooney, turn up in small roles. British jazz pianist George Shearing, himself born blind, provides the score.

Wayne Newton *Mark Jonah Winters* • Jo Van Fleet *Nonna* • Keenan Wynn *Barney Glover* • Diana Ewing *Tracy* • Slim Pickens *Scott* • RG Armstrong *Mackray* • Brandon Cruz *Little Joe* • Erin Moran *Kim* • Mickey Rooney *Wilfred Bashford* • Sal Mineo *Jerry Taggart* ■ *Dir* Gerd Oswald • *Scr* Frederic Louis Fox, from a story by Gerd Oswald, Frederic Louis Fox • *Music* George Shearing

80,000 Suspects ★★

Drama   1963 · UK · BW · 116mins

Movies about epidemics seem to have everything going for them – a bit of cod science, millions being threatened by malevolent micro-organisms and a race against time involving the daredevil doctor and the unsuspecting carrier. It worked brilliantly in 1950's *Panic in the Streets*, but it doesn't come off in this innocuous offering from Rank. As in Wolfgang Petersen's 1995 thriller *Outbreak*, more emphasis is placed on repairing the hero's marriage than on preventing disaster, which should add a human dimension to the tale, but here totally deprives the picture of any suspense.

Claire Bloom *Julie Monks* • Richard Johnson *Steven Monks* • Yolande Donlan *Ruth Preston* • Cyril Cusack *Father Maguire* • Michael Goodliffe *Clifford Preston* • Mervyn Johns *Buckridge* • Kay Walsh *Matron* • Norman Bird *Mr Davis* • Basil Dignam *Medical officer* ■ *Dir* Val Guest • *Scr* Val Guest, from the novel *The Pillars of Midnight* by Elleston Trevor

83 Hours till Dawn ★★★★

Drama based on a true story
1990 · US · Colour · 97mins

A premature-burial chiller based on alarming fact and, for a TV movie, scripted (Gale Patrick Hickman and OR Keyes) and directed (Donald Wrye) well enough to send a whole flock of goose-pimples squawking. Peter Strauss abandons his more usual heroic roles to become as nasty a villain as ever entombed the daughter (Samantha

Mathis) of a rich businessman (Robert Urich) with just enough air to last until his ransom demands run out. Contains some swearing.

Peter Strauss *Wayne Stracton* • Robert Urich *Bradley Burdock* • Samantha Mathis *Julie Burdock* • Shannon Wilcox *Janet Burdock* • Paul Winfield *Dr Dantley* • Elizabeth Gracen *Maria Ranfield* • Kevin Kilner *Bobby Dankworth* • Cameron Bancroft *David Burdock* ■ *Dir* Donald Wrye • *Scr* Gale Patrick Hickman, OR Keyes, from the non-fiction book by Barbara Jane Mackle, Gene Miller

Ek Hi Rasta ★★★ U

Drama   1956 · Ind · BW · 153mins

Baldev Raj Chopra was already one of India's most influential film critics when he turned director in 1951. This was one of the first features made for his own production company BR Films, which was renowned for tackling key social issues within the context of commercial pictures. With a title meaning "The Only Way", this is ostensibly an old-fashioned melodrama about revenge, murder and thwarted passion, with a villain straight out of a penny-dreadful. Yet it is also a heartfelt protest about the Hindu custom preventing the remarriage of widows. In Hindi and Urdu with English subtitles. ▭

Ashok Kumar • Sunil Dutt • Meena Kumari • Daisy Irani • Jeevan ■ *Dir* BR Chopra

El ★★★★

Black comedy drama
1952 · Mex · BW · 100mins

Exploring Luis Buñuel's perennial themes of sexual terror, religious hypocrisy and bourgeois indolence, this seething melodrama was based on Mercedes Pinto's autobiographical novel. Buñuel also drew inspiration from his insanely jealous brother-in-law and his own emotional conflicts (to the extent of personally donning the monk's habit as his deranged protagonist staggers along a monastery path). Amazingly, the film was poorly received on its Mexican release, but the tale of 40-year-old Catholic virgin Arturo De Cordova's descent into paranoia after marrying the much younger Delia Garces is a probing study of moral and psychological collapse, stuffed with moments of inspired surrealism. A Spanish language film.

Arturo De Cordova *Francisco* • Delia Garces *Gloria* • Luis Beristain *Raoul* • Aurora Walker *Mother* ■ *Dir* Luis Buñuel • *Scr* Luis Buñuel, Luis Alcoriza, from the novel *Pensamientos* by Mercedes Pinto

El Dorado ★★★★★ PG

Western   1967 · US · Colour · 121mins

"Ride, boldly ride..." sings George Alexander over the Remington-styled western paintings that accompany the titles to this elegiac masterwork, a fabulously entertaining tale from ace director Howard Hawks. John Wayne is gunfighter Cole Thornton, a flawed hero whose actions lead to the suicide of a boy (Johnny Crawford) in a superbly staged preface to the plot, and whose resulting wounds dictate the pace and outcome of the movie. More than a match for the Duke is the great Robert Mitchum, in one of his best screen

roles as alcoholic sheriff JP Harrah. This film suffered by comparison to Hawks's earlier western masterpiece *Rio Bravo* when it came out. Now, reassessed on its own merits, *El Dorado* proves to be one of the most pleasurable of all Hollywood movies, and a magnificent screen meditation on ageing. ▭

John Wayne *Cole Thornton* • Robert Mitchum *JP Harrah* • James Caan *Mississippi* • Charlene Holt *Maudie* • Michele Carey *Joey MacDonald* • Arthur Hunnicutt *Bull Harris* • RG Armstrong *Kevin MacDonald* • Edward Asner [Ed Asner] *Bart Jason* • Johnny Crawford *Luke MacDonald* ■ *Dir* Howard Hawks • *Scr* Leigh Brackett, from the novel *The Stars in Their Courses* by Harry Brown

El Dorado ★★★ 15

Adventure   1988 · Sp/Fr · Colour · 122mins

Director Carlos Saura's re-creation of the doomed 1560 expedition to find the fabled New World land of El Dorado is historically accurate, earnestly played and magnificently photographed by Teo Escamilla. But it never comes close to topping the achievement of *Aguirre, Wrath of God*, Werner Herzog's remarkable account of the same story made 16 years earlier. Omero Antonutti gives it everything he's got, but he simply cannot erase the memory of Klaus Kinski's exceptional performance as the deranged Aguirre. However, Saura does succeed in conveying the mix of greed and reckless folly that inspired the conquistadors to risk all in the pursuit of wealth and power. In Spanish with English subtitles. Contains violence.

Omero Antonutti *Lope de Aguirre* • Eusebio Poncela *Fernando de Guzman* • Lambert Wilson *Pedro de Ursua* • Gabriela Roel *Dona Ines* • Jose Sancho *Juan de la Bandera* • Feodor Atkine *Montoya* • Patxi Bisquert *Pedrarias* ■ *Dir/Scr* Carlos Saura

Election ★★★★ 15

Comedy   1999 · US · Colour · 99mins

Topping the league table of recent high-school movies, this is the rightful heir to the John Hughes youth-antics tradition. The casting of Matthew Broderick (familiar to many as determined truant Ferris Bueller) as a devoted teacher trying to prevent manipulative overachiever Reese Witherspoon from becoming student president is inspired. Director/co-writer Alexander Payne is repaid by his star with a performance of sincere, if muddled idealism. Pitted against jock Chris Klein and his lesbian sister (Jessica Campbell making a revelatory debut), Witherspoon's blend of corruption and compassion slyly satirises contemporary American politics, while George Washington Carver High serves as a microcosm of *fin-de-siècle* society. Astute, offbeat and uproarious. ▭

Matthew Broderick *Jim McAllister* • Reese Witherspoon *Tracy Flick* • Chris Klein *Paul Metzler* • Phil Reeves *Walt Hendricks* • Mark Harelik *Dave Novotny* • Delaney Driscoll *Linda Novotny* • Molly Hagan *Diane McAllister* • Jessica Campbell *Tammy Metzler* ■ *Dir* Alexander Payne • *Scr* Alexander Payne, Jim Taylor, from the novel by Tom Perrotta

Electra ★★ 18

Erotic thriller   1995 · US · Colour · 86mins

Possibly the wackiest of Shannon Tweed's considerable canon of erotic thrillers, this is an absolutely barmy mix of soft-core porn and sci-fi silliness. Tweed plays a frustrated widow whose stepson holds the key to a sexually transmittable formula for creating the master race. It's all utter tosh, of course, although in the company of charisma-free unknowns such as Joe Tab and Sten Eirik, Tweed positively shines – even when she's got her clothes on. ▭

Shannon Tweed *Lorna Duncan/Electra* • Joe Tab *Billy Duncan* • Sten Eirik *Marcus Roach* • Katie Griffin *Mary Anne Parker* • Lara Daans *Karen* ■ *Dir* Julian Grant • *Scr* Lou Aguilar, Damian Lee

Electra Glide in Blue ★★★★ 18

Crime drama   1973 · US · Colour · 108mins

One of the great cult movies, this abrasive mix of black comedy and satire made a one-hit wonder of its director, record producer James William Guercio. Robert Blake (who'd made his name as Little Beaver in numerous *Red Ryder* B-movies) gives one of the performances of his career as a diminutive motorcycle cop who justifies his tough-guy act by claiming to be the exact same height as Alan Ladd. After some of the most graphic violence then seen on screen, the ending is something of a cop-out. But it's always good to see such stalwarts as Elisha Cook and Royal Dano, and Conrad Hall's photography is outstanding. ▭

Robert Blake *John Wintergreen* • Billy Green Bush *Zipper Davis* • Mitchell Ryan *Harve Poole* • Jeannine Riley *Jolene* • Elisha Cook [Elisha Cook Jr] *Willie* • Royal Dano *Coroner* ■ *Dir* James William Guercio • *Scr* Robert Boris, Michael Butler, from a story by Robert Boris, Rupert Hitzig

Electric Dreams ★ PG

Romance   1984 · US/UK · Colour · 92mins

Daft romantic comedy on the "computers are alive" theme. Lenny Von Dohlen plays Miles, a geeky architect whose new computer comes to life when champagne is spilt over it. Both owner and computer then fall for the girl next door (Virginia Madsen). Shot by director Steve Barron in the style of a pop promo, *Electric Dreams* starts brightly enough but ultimately disintegrates. It hardly helps matters that the lead character (voiced by Bud Cort) is nothing more than a household appliance. ▭

Lenny Von Dohlen *Miles* • Virginia Madsen *Madeline* • Maxwell Caulfield *Bill* • Bud Cort *Edgar* • Don Fellows *Ryley* • Alan Polonsky *Frank* • Wendy Miller *Computer clerk* • Harry Rabinowitz *Conductor* • Miriam Margolyes *Ticket girl* • Koo Stark *Soap opera girl* ■ *Dir* Steve Barron • *Scr* Rusty Lemorande

The Electric Horseman ★★★ PG

Comedy western
1979 · US · Colour · 120mins

Despite its title and the sparks-flying relationship between Robert Redford and Jane Fonda, this early eco-warning tale about mindless consumerism carries too little charge. When Redford, a down-on-his-luck rodeo rider, saves a thoroughbred horse from corporate greed, it all becomes excessively preachy under Sydney Pollack's heavy direction: he doesn't seem able to film a sunset without silhouetting people against it. It means well, but moral fables need more subtlety. ▭

Robert Redford *Sonny Steele* • Jane Fonda *Hallie Martin* • Valerie Perrine *Charlotta* • Willie Nelson *Wendell* • John Saxon *Hunt Sears* • Nicholas Coster [Nicolas Coster] *Fitzgerald* • Allan Arbus *Danny* • Wilford Brimley *Farmer* ■ *Dir* Sydney Pollack • *Scr* Robert Garland, from a screenplay by Robert Garland, Paul Gaer, from a story by Shelly Burton

Electric Moon ★★ 15
Satirical drama 1992 · UK · Colour · 102mins

There's a distinct Ealing feel to this wry satire on themed holidays, which are seemingly designed to reinforce patronising perceptions of an idealised past. But there are also acerbic asides on India's colonial legacy and its predilection for bureaucratic pettifogging. Exacting revenge for decades of subcontinental stereotyping, director Pradip Krishen reduces the western tourists to hideous stereotypes. Yet he takes such a time doing so that the film fails to gain any momentum until rulebook martinet Naseeruddin Shah and duplicitous lodge manager Roshan Seth begin to feud over the latter's bogus safari operation. Knowingly played, but haphazard in its execution.

Roshan Seth *Ranveer* • Naseeruddin Shah *Rambuhj Goswami* • Leela Naidu *Socks/Sukanya* • Gerson Da Cunha *Bubbles/Raja* Ran Bikram Singh • Raghubir Yadav [Raghuvir Yadav] *Boltoo* ■ *Dir* Pradip Krishen • *Scr* Arundhati Roy

Elektra ★★
Drama 1962 · Gr · BW · 113mins

This is the first entry in Michael Cacoyannis's Euripides trilogy, which he completed with *The Trojan Women* (1971) and *Iphigenia* (1976). It may have garnered international critical acclaim (including a gong at Cannes) but, for all the spartan beauty of the Mycenae locations, Cacoyannis's fussy use of tight close-ups and jarring flashbacks too often hold the action to ransom. Irene Papas's brooding histrionics in the title role are also detrimental. Yet this durable drama retains its fascination, as Elektra and her brother Orestes seek revenge on their adulterous mother, Clytemnestra, for the death of their father. In Greek with English subtitles.

Irene Papas *Elektra* • Aleka Katselli *Clytemnestra* • Yannis Fertis *Orestes* • Theano Ioannidou *Chorus leader* • Notis Peryalis *Electra's husband* • Takis Emmanuel *Pylades* • Phoebus Rhazis *Aegisthus* ■ *Dir* Michael Cacoyannis • *Scr* Michael Cacoyannis, from the play by Euripides

The Element of Crime ★★★★ 15
Fantasy crime mystery 1984 · Den · Colour · 103mins

Shrouded in post-apocalyptic sepia, Lars von Trier's debut feature is a

ragbag of visual allusions to everything from German Expressionism and Hollywood *noir* to the self-reflexivity of the *Nouvelle Vague* and the grim poetry of Andrei Tarkovsky. Yet shamus Michael Elphick's quest to unmask the mathematically minded serial perpetrator of the "Lotto murders" still makes for compelling viewing. With Esmond Knight leading a first-rate cast, this was rightly hailed as the work of a master-in-waiting.

Michael Elphick *Fisher* • Esmond Knight *Osborne* • Me Me Lai *Kim* • Jerold Wells *Police Chief Kramer* • Ahmed El Shenawi *Therapist* • Astrid Henning-Jensen *Osborne's housekeeper* • Janos Hersko *Coroner* • Stig Larsson *Coroner's assistant* • Lars von Trier *Schmuck of Ages* ■ *Dir* Lars von Trier • *Scr* Lars von Trier, Niels Vørsel

An Element of Truth ★★ 12
Thriller 1995 · US · Colour · 91mins

TV movie queen Donna Mills aims for a slightly more risqué role here, although she still looks as squeaky clean as ever. In this soufflé-light caper thriller she plays a beautiful con artist who runs into trouble when she sets up her latest scam in a smart financial investment company. There's a good supporting cast (Peter Riegert, Cliff De Young) and the direction from Larry Peerce, perhaps best known for the ill-fated John Belushi biopic *Wired*, is competent enough. Contains swearing and sex scenes. ▭

Donna Mills *Vanessa* • Peter Riegert *Sidney* • Perrey Reeves *Maizie* • Brock Peters *Alex* • Cliff De Young *Norm* • Harriet Sansom *Anne* • Robin Thomas *Peter* ■ *Dir* Larry Peerce • *Scr* Douglas Stefen Borghi

Elementary School ★★★
Comedy 1991 · Cz · Colour · 100mins

Four years after taking numerous prizes for his student film, *Oil Gobblers*, Jan Sverak made his feature debut with this powerful drama. Written by and starring Sverak's father, Zdenek, this largely autobiographical story focuses on life in Prague during the all-too-brief interlude between liberation from the Nazis and subjugation by the Communists. In addition to Zdenek and the leading Czech actor Rudolf Hrusinsky, the cast also includes legendary film-makers Jiri Menzel and Karel Kachyna in cameo roles. The film was nominated for an Oscar, but the Sveraks were to go one better with the enchanting *Kolya*, which won the 1996 Academy Award for best foreign language film. In Czech with English subtitles.

Jan Triska *Igor Hnizdo* • Zdenek Sverak *Soucek* • Libuse Safrankova *Mrs Soucek* • Rudolf Hrusinsky *Schoolmaster* • Daniela Kolarova *Miss Maxova* • Vaclav Jakoubek *Eda* ■ *Dir* Jan Sverak • *Scr* Zdenek Sverak

Elena et les Hommes ★★★ U
Romantic drama 1956 · Fr/Ital · Colour · 62mins

This deceptively lightweight period piece from writer/director Jean Renoir provides a glistening showcase for Ingrid Bergman. She plays a beautiful royal in Paris at the end of the 19th century looking for a wealthy meal ticket who gradually learns about the

true meaning of love. As with *French Cancan*, filmed the year before, Renoir's main concern is evoking the colour and gaiety of the time. The result is an enchanting romantic fable. In French with English subtitles.

Ingrid Bergman *Elena* • Mel Ferrer *Henri de Chevincourt* • Jean Marais *Rollan* • Jean Richard *Hector* • Magali Noel *Lolotte* • Juliette Greco *Miarka* • Pierre Bertin *Martin-Michaud* • Jean Castanier *Isnard* ■ *Dir/Scr* Jean Renoir

Eleni ★★★ PG
Biographical drama 1985 · US · Colour · 110mins

What was uplifting on the page comes out flatly on film, in this re-creation of Nicholas Gage's book about his real-life search for the executioners of his peasant mother, who sacrificed herself to save her children from the communist faction that took over her Greek village. Although Kate Nelligan, as Eleni, gives a poignant performance in flashback, it's the search for truth by John Malkovich (as Gage) that holds what little tension there is. ▭

Kate Nelligan *Eleni Gatzoyiannis* • John Malkovich *Nicholas Gage* • Linda Hunt *Katina* • Oliver Cotton *Katis* • Ronald Pickup *Spiro Skevis* • Glenne Headly *Joan* • Alfred Molina *Young Christos* ■ *Dir* Peter Yates • *Scr* Steve Tesich, from the book by Nicholas Gage

Elenya ★★★ PG
Second World War drama 1992 · UK · Colour · 78mins

This Second World War tale, about a young woman of Italian descent living with her aunt in the Welsh countryside, feels dispiritingly familiar. Pascale Delafouge Jones superbly plays the ostracised girl, while Klaus Behrendt is utterly believable as the German pilot she befriends after he crashes in the woods. It's all skilfully portrayed and consummately photographed, yet one cannot shake off the lingering feeling that Hayley Mills might bound in at any moment. So much talent on display – a pity it's not put to better use. ▭

Margaret John *Old Elenya* • Pascale Delafouge Jones *Young Elenya* • Seiriol Tomos *Glyn* • Sue Jones-Davies *Maggie* • Iago Wynn Jones *Sidney* • Llio Millward *Schoolteacher* • Klaus Behrendt *Franz* ■ *Dir/Scr* Steve Gough

The Elephant and the Bicycle ★★★
Drama 1995 · Cub · Colour · 81mins

Cuban director Juan Carlos Tabio is best known for the wonderfully inventive comedy *Plaff!* and the Oscar-nominated gay classic *Strawberry and Chocolate*, which he directed with Tomas Gutierrez Alea. In keeping with the worldwide celebrations to mark the centenary of cinema, this film recalls the glorious silent days when movies were presented by travelling showmen and Douglas Fairbanks was the king of the swashbucklers. Cleverly contrasting the action of Fairbanks's stirring version of *Robin Hood* with events in Cuba on the eve of the Machado coup, the film has its share of quirky characters, but it rather lacks pace. In Spanish with English subtitles.

Luis Alberto Garcia *Isleño* • Lilian Vega *Marina* • Daisy Granados • Raul Pomares • Adolfo Llaurado • Marta Farre ■ *Dir* Juan Carlos Tabio • *Scr* Eliseo Alberto Diego

Elephant Boy ★★ U
Adventure 1937 · UK · BW · 78mins

In 1936, the British-based movie mogul Alexander Korda dispatched the famed documentarist Robert Flaherty to India to make a version of Rudyard Kipling's *Toomai of the Elephants*. Flaherty discovered Sabu, who was a 12-year-old stable boy to a maharajah, and cast him in the leading role; he then shot some 50 hours of footage and returned to England with fine images but no story. Korda then put his brother Zoltan to work to patch things together. The result, predictably, is a bit of a mess, but it retains its exoticism. Sabu became an overnight sensation and was typecast until his early death in 1963. ▭

Sabu *Toomai* • Walter Hudd *Petersen* • Allan Jeayes *Machua Appa* • WE Holloway *Father* • Bruce Gordon *Rham Lahl* • DJ Williams *Hunter* • Wilfrid Hyde White *Commissioner* • Iravatha *Kala Nag* ■ *Dir* Robert Flaherty, Zoltan Korda • *Scr* John Collier, Akos Tolnay, Marcia de Silva, from the novel *Toomai of the Elephants* by Rudyard Kipling

An Elephant Called Slowly ★★
Adventure 1969 · UK · Colour · 87mins

Director James Hill tries to do for elephants what he did for lions in *Born Free* (1966), though with rather less success. The wildlife story again involves Virginia McKenna and Bill Travers, this time trying to protect three orphaned baby elephants. In the process they rub shoulders with the real-life Adamsons, the couple they played in the earlier film. Alas, the film failed to please audiences. ▭

Virginia McKenna *Ginny* • Bill Travers *Bill* • Vinay Inambar *Mr Mophagee* • Joab Collins *Henry* • Ali Twaha *Mutiso* ■ *Dir* James Hill • *Scr* Bill Travers, James Hill

Elephant Juice ★★ 18
Comedy drama 1999 · US/UK · Colour · 90mins

Pitched as a penetrating look at the relationship merry-go-round in modern-day London, this arch comedy drama is a shallow and banal bust. In her British film debut, French star Emmanuelle Béart plays a city whiz kid whose engagement to handsome artist Daniel LaPaine causes her close circle of friends to re-evaluate their own lives as they all approach the dangerous age of 30. Secret affairs, crises of conscience and a suicide attempt lead to a ho-hum happy ending in a mundane soap opera from writer Amy Jenkins and director Sam Miller.

Emmanuelle Béart *Jules* • Sean Gallagher *Billy* • Daniel LaPaine *Will* • Mark Strong *Frank* • Daniela Nardini *Daphne* • Kimberly Williams *Dodie* • Lennie James *Graham* • Lee Williams *George* ■ *Dir* Sam Miller • *Scr* Amy Jenkins, from an idea by Amy Jenkins, Sam Miller

The Elephant Man ★★★★ PG
Biographical drama 1980 · US · BW · 118mins

Probably the closest director David Lynch has got to the mainstream – outside of the disastrous *Dune* – this stylish, poignant drama is based on the true story of the horrifically disfigured John Merrick (a superb, unrecognisable John Hurt) who battled

U = SUITABLE FOR ALL   Uc = SUITABLE FOR ALL, ESPECIALLY FOR YOUNG CHILDREN (VIDEO ONLY)   PG = PARENTAL GUIDANCE

he prejudices of Victorian society. Full marks, too, for Freddie Francis's striking black-and-white photography and the excellent playing from a top-drawer cast (Anthony Hopkins, Anne Bancroft, John Gielgud). Made, surprisingly, by comic Mel Brooks's production company. ▭

John Hurt *John Merrick* • Anthony Hopkins *Frederick Treves* • Anne Bancroft *Mrs Madge Kendal* • John Gielgud *Carr Gomm* • Wendy Hiller *Motherhead* • Freddie Jones *Bytes* • Michael Elphick *Night porter* • Hannah Gordon *Mrs Treves* ■ *Dir* David Lynch • *Scr* Christopher de Vore, Eric Bergren, David Lynch, from the non-fiction books *The Elephant Man: A Study In Human Dignity* by Ashley Montagu and *The Elephant Man and Other Reminiscences* by Sir Frederick Treves • *Make-up* Christopher Tucker

Elephant Walk ★★★ U

Drama   1954 · US · Colour · 102mins

Peter Finch marries Elizabeth Taylor and takes her back to Ceylon where his tea plantation has been established right in the path of commuting pachyderms. But domestic squabbles, an outbreak of typhoid and the promised elephant stampede do not prevent our heroes from producing a good, strong, freshly-brewed cuppa in this sold Imperial melodrama. In shots of the early car journey from the airport the eagle-eyed may spot Vivien Leigh, who was originally cast as Finch's wife. But Leigh's illness in Ceylon led to complications, and she then suffered a nervous breakdown.

Elizabeth Taylor *Ruth Wiley* • Dana Andrews *Dick Carver* • Peter Finch *John Wiley* • Abraham Sofaer *Appuhamy* • Abner Biberman *Dr Pereira* • Noel Drayton *Planter Atkinson* • Rosalind Ivan *Mrs Lakin* ■ *Dir* William Dieterle • *Scr* John Lee Mahin, from the novel by Robert Standish

11 Harrowhouse ★★

Crime comedy 1974 · UK · Colour · 108mins

This overeager comedy foolhardily attempts to send up a style of film-making that was already parodic – the heist caper. Only the bullish playing saves the day, as Aram Avakian's direction is so slipshod that the enterprise has descended into low farce long before the extended chase finale. Hard though Charles Grodin and Candice Bergen try as the ingenious vacuuming jewel thieves, they're totally outclassed by a venerable supporting cast that includes a deliciously embittered James Mason, a gloriously sniffy John Gielgud and an unashamedly barnstorming Trevor Howard. Fun but forgettable.

Charles Grodin *Chesser* • Candice Bergen *Maren* • John Gielgud *Meecham* • Trevor Howard *Clyde Massey* • James Mason *Watts* • Peter Vaughan *Coglin* • Helen Cherry *Lady Bolding* • Jack Watson *Miller* • Jack Watling *Fitzmaurice* ■ *Dir* Aram Avakian • *Scr* Jeffrey Bloom, Charles Grodin, from the novel *11 Harrowhouse Street* by Gerald A Browne

Elisa ★★ 15

Drama   1994 · Fr · Colour · 110mins

As he proved with *One Deadly Summer*, Jean Becker is a master at combining the commercial with the psychological. He is also clearly fascinated by the way in which disturbed teenage girls resolve their problems. Like Isabelle Adjani in the earlier film, Vanessa Paradis uses her wiles to right a past wrong, though her pin-up looks prevent her from carrying off the part of a tough little hussy – a sizeable drawback considering she's on screen for much of the film. Unfortunately, the same cannot be said of the underused Gérard Depardieu. In French with English subtitles. ▭

Vanessa Paradis *Marie* • Gérard Depardieu *Jacques Lébovitch* • Clothilde Courau [Clotilde Courau] *Solange* • Sekkou Sall *Ahmed* • Florence Thomassin *Elisa* • Michel Bouquet *Samuel* • Philippe Léotard *Smoker* ■ *Dir* Jean Becker • *Scr* Jean Becker, Fabrice Carazo

Elizabeth ★★★★ 15

Historical drama
1998 · UK · Colour · 118mins

This Elizabethan political thriller charting the turbulent life and times of the self-proclaimed "Virgin Queen" is given a vivid contemporary focus by Indian director Shekhar Kapur's keen visual eye. A far cry from the usual "frock opera", this sumptuous biography is a thoughtful and dramatic triumph, with Australian actress Cate Blanchett revelatory as the strong-willed monarch who nimbly transforms from naive girlhood to true majesty, assisted by Sir Francis Walsingham (*Shine's* Geoffrey Rush). Richard Attenborough, Joseph Fiennes and ex-footballer Eric Cantona flesh out an interesting cast. School history lessons were never this good! Contains violence and sex scenes. ▭ **DVD**

Cate Blanchett *Elizabeth I* • Geoffrey Rush *Sir Francis Walsingham* • Richard Attenborough *Sir William Cecil* • John Gielgud *The Pope* • Fanny Ardant *Mary of Guise* • Terence Rigby *Bishop Gardiner* • Christopher Eccleston *Duke of Norfolk* • Amanda Ryan *Lettice Howard* • Kathy Burke *Queen Mary Tudor* • Joseph Fiennes *Robert Dudley, Earl of Leicester* • Wayne Sleep *Dance tutor* • Angus Deayton *Waad, Chancellor of the Exchequer* • Eric Cantona *Monsieur de Foix* ■ *Dir* Shekhar Kapur • *Scr* Michael Hirst

Ellen Foster ★★

Drama   1997 · US · Colour · 120mins

Child actress Jena Malone (*Contact*) plays the title role in this family drama. After her mother dies, Malone is systematically abused by her father (Ted Levine) and taken into care. This initiates a long-winded process where she goes from grandmother to aunts to foster homes, getting on with precisely nobody. Malone is intensely watchable, however, and makes Ellen both interesting and empathetic. Director John Erman manages the material without descending into whimsy.

Julie Harris *Leonora* • Jena Malone *Ellen Foster* • Ted Levine *Bill* • Glynnis O'Connor *Charlotte* • Debra Monk *Nadine* • Barbara Garrick *Betsy* • Kimberly Brown [Kimberly J Brown] *Dora* • Allison Jones *Starletta* • Kate Burton *Abigail* ■ *Dir* John Erman • *Scr* Maria Nation, William Hanley, from the novel by Kaye Gibbons

Ellery Queen Master Detective ★★

Crime mystery 1940 · US · BW · 67mins

Ellery Queen, one of the most successful fictional detectives of all time, didn't have much luck with his movie incarnations, eventually finding his natural home as a TV series sleuth, played by both George Nader and Jim Hutton, among others. Ellery Queen was, in fact, a pseudonym used by the detective's creators, Frederic Dannay and Manfred Bennington Lee, who must have been appalled if they ever saw this series entry, where Queen is portrayed by an embarrassed Ralph Bellamy as a comic bumbling dolt. Bellamy only played Queen on four occasions, leaving the role to William Gargan in 1942, but the damage was done.

Ralph Bellamy *Ellery Queen* • Margaret Lindsay *Nikki Porter* • Charley Grapewin *Inspector Queen* • James Burke *Sergeant Velie* • Michael Whalen *Dr James Rogers* • Marsha Hunt *Barbara Braun* • Fred Niblo *John Braun* ■ *Dir* Kurt Neumann • *Scr* Eric Taylor, from a story by Ellery Queen [Frederic Dannay, Manfred Bennington Lee]

Ellie ★ 15

Comedy   1984 · US · Colour · 85mins

A soft-core sex comedy, somewhat dignified by the presence of Shelley Winters, but mainly a pretext for *Penthouse* pet Sheila Kennedy to pose in any number of designer underwear outfits – and sometimes less. The latter has more curves than a mountain road as a virginal country girl, besieged by Winters's three sons after her wheelchair-bound father is murdered. Kennedy swears vengeance, a campaign that almost always involves taking off her clothes, and starts bumping off the sons. ▭

Sheila Kennedy *Ellie* • Shelley Winters *Cora* • Edward Albert *Tom* • Pat Paulsen *Sheriff* • George Gobel *Preacher* ■ *Dir* Peter Wittman • *Scr* Glenn Allen Smith

The Elm-Chanted Forest ★★ U

Animated fantasy 1986 · US · Colour · 90mins

A young artist finds he can talk to the animals and paint magic pictures each time he falls asleep beneath an enchanted elm, deep in Fantasy Forest. He soon needs to put his powers to good use in order to ward off the Spine Tinglers, an army of living spears and axes under the command of the evil Emperor Spine. Awash with psychedelic and religious imagery, this curious cartoon feature blithely treads a fine line between imaginative fantasy and hippy hogwash.

Dir Milan Blazekovic • *Scr* Fred P Sharkey

Elmer Gantry ★★★★★ PG

Drama   1960 · US · Colour · 140mins

Seldom does the cinema see such a perfect match of star and role as here, with Burt Lancaster as author Sinclair Lewis's con man who finds evangelism as easy to sell as vacuum cleaners. Lancaster rightly won the best actor Oscar for the finest performance of his career; the film also picked up Oscars for director Richard Brooks's screenplay and Shirley Jones's supporting turn as vengeful prostitute Lulu Bains. Also brilliantly cast is Jean Simmons as Sister Sharon Falconer, whose sincerity, like Gantry's, is never questioned. John Alton's colour photography is superb, but it's Brooks's handling of the key scenes that makes this film a Hollywood classic. ▭

Burt Lancaster *Elmer Gantry* • Jean Simmons *Sister Sharon Falconer* • Arthur Kennedy *Jim Lefferts* • Shirley Jones *Lulu Bains* • Dean Jagger *William L Morgan* • Patti Page *Sister Rachel* • Edward Andrews *George Babbitt* • John McIntyre *Rev Pengilly* • Joe Maross *Pete* ■ *Dir* Richard Brooks • *Scr* Richard Brooks, from the novel by Sinclair Lewis

Elmore Leonard's Gold Coast ★★★ 18

Crime mystery 1997 · US · Colour · 104mins

Although this has the name Elmore Leonard on it, *Get Shorty* or *Jackie Brown* it isn't. But this crime mystery from the savvy pen of the bestselling author is unusually intelligent and well-acted for a cable television production. David Caruso plays a dolphin trainer, small-time crook and all-round nice guy who protects wealthy Mafia widow Marg Helgenberger from a condition in her late husband's will that pretty much rules out her ever being involved with a man again. Jeff Kober is the scary psycho-baddie hired to implement the clause. Solid entertainment with great dialogue, great twists and a truly surprising ending. Contains violence, sex scenes and swearing. ▭

Marg Helgenberger *Karen DiCilia* • David Caruso *Maguire* • Jeff Kober *Roland Crowe* • Barry Primus *Ed Grossi* • Wanda DeJesus *Vivian Arzola* • Richard Bradford *Frank DiCilia* ■ *Dir* Peter Weller • *Scr* Harley Peyton, from the novel by Elmore Leonard

The Elusive Pimpernel ★★ U

Period comedy adventure
1950 · UK · Colour · 104mins

This version of Baroness Orczy's *The Scarlet Pimpernel* is one of Michael Powell and Emeric Pressburger's lesser efforts; Powell had at one stage wanted the project to be a musical and called what he ended up with "a terrible mess". This is a little harsh, though, since the film is not without its moments of colour and excitement. David Niven is as suave as ever in the title role of the jaunty Englishman who, beneath his carefree exterior, dedicates himself to the task of saving French aristocrats from the revolutionary guillotine. ▭

David Niven *Sir Percy Blakeney* • Margaret Leighton *Marguerite Blakeney* • Jack Hawkins *Prince of Wales* • Cyril Cusack *Chauvelin* • Robert Coote *Sir Andrew Ffoulkes* • Edmond Audran *Armand St Juste* • Danielle Godet *Suzanne de Tournai* ■ *Dir* Michael Powell, Emeric Pressburger • *Scr* Michael Powell, Emeric Pressburger, from the novel *The Scarlet Pimpernel* by Baroness Orczy

Elves ★ 18

Science-fiction horror
1989 · US · Colour · 89mins

The credits indicate the town of Colorado Springs lent a generous hand to this videotaped backyard production, though its perverse nature makes one ask why. The budget seems to have been almost entirely spent on star Dan Haggerty, possibly explaining why there is only one stiff animatronic elf, despite the plural title. Haggerty plays a small-town department store Santa investigating his predecessor's castration, with plenty of Nazis, incest,

rape, drugs, and other questionable elements thrown in. ▣

Dan Haggerty • Deanna Lund • Julie Austin • Borah Silver ■ *Dir* Jeffrey Mandel • *Scr* Mike Griffin, Bruce Taylor, Jeff Mandel

Elvira Madigan ★★★ PG

Romantic drama
1967 · Swe · Colour · 85mins

Previously filmed in 1943 by Ake Ohberg, this true tale of doomed love and flouted convention will either have you sobbing uncontrollably or wincing at its overt sentimentality. Although the narrative suggests a Bergmanesque monochrome gloom, director Bo Widerberg shoots the illicit romance between a tightrope artist and a married soldier in hazy pastels, thus enhancing both the picturesque delights of the Swedish countryside and the innocent beauty of Pia Degermark, who won the best actress prize at Cannes for her performance. If only there'd been more discussion of 19th-century attitudes towards illicit sexuality, and less of Mozart's cloying *Piano Concerto No 21*. In Swedish with English subtitles. ▣

Pia Degermark *Elvira* • Thommy Berggren *Sixten* • Lennart Malmer *Friend* • Nina Widerberg *Girl* • Cleo Jensen *Cook* ■ *Dir* Bo Widerberg • *Scr* Bo Widerberg, from the song *Visan om den Sköna Konstberiderskan Elvira Madigans Kälek och Grymma Död* by Johan Lindström Saxon

Elvira, Mistress of the Dark ★ 15

Comedy
1988 · US · Colour · 91mins

A distinctly American phenomenon, Elvira (real name Cassandra Peterson) is a camp vampette, an amalgam of Morticia Addams and Dolly Parton, who hosts horror movie nights on television. Graduating to her own feature movie, Peterson is cast as, well, a television horror movie host who inherits a haunted house. Horror buffs may get a kick out of the numerous references to the genre, but the rest of us will be bored by the predictable plot and unimpressed with the shoddy effects. Director James Signorelli seems unable to draw his camera away from his star's ample bosom for more than five minutes. ▣

Cassandra Peterson *Elvira* • W Morgan Sheppard [Morgan Sheppard] *Vincent Talbot* • Daniel Greene *Bob Redding* • Susan Kellermann *Aunt* • Jeff Conaway *Travis* • Edie McClurg *Chastity Pariah* • Kurt Fuller *Mr Glotter* • Pat Crawford Brown *Mrs Meeker* • Lee McLaughlin *Earl Hooter* ■ *Dir* James Signorelli • *Scr* Sam Egan, John Paragon, Cassandra Peterson

Elvis and the Colonel: the Untold Story ★★★ PG

Biographical drama
1993 · US · Colour · 88mins

Elvis Presley TV movies are virtually an industry on their own, with John Carpenter's 1979 biopic starring Kurt Russell remaining the quality yardstick. This is a good deal better than the likes of *Elvis and Me* (1988) or *Elvis and the Beauty Queen* (1981). It contains a blistering performance from Beau Bridges as Colonel Tom Parker, the man who ruthlessly masterminded Presley's rise to world stardom. Rob

Youngblood as Presley narrates the tale from the afterlife, while the excellent Scott Wilson plays Elvis's dad Vernon. ▣

Beau Bridges *Colonel Tom Parker* • Rob Youngblood *Elvis Presley* • Scott Wilson *Vernon Presley* • Dan Shor *Jass* • Micole Mercurio *Gladys* • Ben Slack *Oscar Davis* ■ *Dir* William A Graham • *Scr* Phil Penningroth, from a story by Frank Furino

Elvis! Elvis! ★★★

Drama 1977 · Swe · Colour · 101mins

Although the King made 33 films himself, most of them unworthy of his immense talent, he has since been posthumously immortalised in such diverse works as Tony Scott's *True Romance* and Jim Jarmusch's *Mystery Train*. This charming Swedish picture therefore forms part of an eclectic sub-genre: the non-Elvis Elvis movie. It's a domestic drama, based on a series of stories about a real boy whose mother was so obsessed with Elvis she saddled her son with his moniker. Fictionalised here, the seven-year-old hero proves, unsurprisingly, to be more understanding of the world outside than his immature mother. Leisurely directed by Kay Pollak, this sweet film offers the chance to view some early cinematography from Mikael Salomon, best known for his stunning work on *Backdraft* and *The Abyss*. In Swedish with English subtitles.

Lele Dorazio *Elvis* • Lena-Pia Bernhardsson *Elvis's mother* • Fred Gunnarsson *Elvis's father* • Elisaveta *Elvis's grandmother* • Allan Edwall *Elvis's grandfather* ■ *Dir* Kay Pollak • *Scr* Kay Pollak, Maria Gripe, from a novel by Maria Gripe

Elvis on Tour ★★★ PG

Music documentary
1972 · US · Colour · 89mins

Essential viewing for Elvis fans as the King goes on stage, but the raw energy of his fifties performances and songs are long gone. The directors this time are Pierre Adidge and Robert Abel, who had filmed the Joe Cocker/Leon Russell tour as *Mad Dogs and Englishmen*. The then-fashionable multiscreen technique here becomes tiresome: the King only needs one screen to himself. Nevertheless, the material is mesmerising for fans, and there's also a skilfully assembled trawl through Elvis's earlier life for non-devotees. Interesting to note that a youngster in the cutting rooms graduated from a similiar role on the multiscreen *Woodstock*: an assistant film editor named Martin Scorsese. ▣

Dir Pierre Adidge, Robert Abel

Elvis: That's the Way It Is ★★★ U

Music documentary
1970 · US · Colour · 103mins

A magnificent record of the King's return to live performances, stunningly filmed in Las Vegas. More than just a documentary, this is a carefully-crafted Metro special, filmed in Panavision by the great cameraman Lucien Ballard (*The Wild Bunch*) under the canny direction of Denis Sanders. The film is shot through with Presley's delicious sense of self-mockery, but the real pleasure comes from watching one of

the greatest performers of the 20th century doing what he does best. Preserved here are great performances of such standards as *Suspicious Minds*, *You've Lost That Lovin' Feeling* and the electric *I Just Can't Help Believing*. Forget the 30-odd Hollywood movies that preceded this – here's the real thing. ▣

Dir Denis Sanders

Elvis – the Movie ★★★ U

Biographical drama
1979 · US · Colour · 119mins

John Carpenter's made-for-TV version of the Elvis Presley saga, which was sadly truncated on its cinema release in the UK, is a detailed and truthful account of one of the most potent myths of modern popular culture. Kurt Russell, though no lookalike, makes a fine job of playing Presley – as a child actor, he played alongside the King in a scene in *It Happened at the World's Fair* – while Shelley Winters is particularly moving as Elvis's tragic mother, Gladys. For those who don't know the story, this is a worthwhile introduction – a biopic made with respect and affection.

Kurt Russell *Elvis Presley* • Shelley Winters *Gladys Presley* • Bing Russell *Vernon Presley* • Robert Gray *Red West* • Season Hubley *Priscilla Presley* • Pat Hingle *Colonel Tom Parker* • Abi Young *Natalie Wood* ■ *Dir* John Carpenter • *Scr* Anthony Lawrence

Elvjs & Merilijn ★★★

Drama 1998 · It · Colour · 93mins

Although Armando Manni's directorial debut isn't without humour, the tragedy of the Balkans always impinges on the story of Goran Navojec and Edyta Olszowka, the winners of a *Stars in Their Eyes*-type contest, who see their prize trip to Italy as the start of something big. But the Bulgarian Elvis and the Romanian Marilyn Monroe are soon confronted with the realities of the region, with the suicide of Yugoslav colonel Toni Bertorelli taking the sheen off Olszowka's dayglow dreams. The descent into porn and the mood of the ending are badly mismanaged, but the leads do enough to retain our sympathy. In Italian, Romanian, Bulgarian, Serbo-Croatian and French with English subtitles.

Edyta Olszowka *Ileana/Merilijn* • Goran Navojec *Nicolaj/Elvjs* • Giorgio Faletti *Gino* • Toni Bertorelli *Colonel* • Julietta Koleva *Eva Petrova* • Sasa Vulicevic *Goran* • Margaretha Von Kraus *Ileana's mother* • Mariana Jichich *Nicolaj's wife* ■ *Dir* Armando Manni • *Scr* Armando Manni, Massimo Torre, from their story

Embassy ★★

Spy drama 1972 · UK · Colour · 89mins

Few actors can look more quietly harassed than Max von Sydow and, as the Soviet defector coming in from the cold to the protective warmth of the US embassy in Beirut, he looks even more disturbed than usual. He has good reason for alarm, as KGB agent Chuck Connors is out to get him and there's an awful lot of over-emphatic dialogue to get through, a task that overwhelms most of the cast. Occasional flashes of action do make for moderate

excitement, but that's not really enough to save this mediocre effort.

Richard Roundtree *Shannon* • Chuck Connors *Kesten* • Marie-José Nat *Laure* • Ray Milland *Ambassador* • Broderick Crawford *Dunninger* • Max von Sydow *Gorenko* • David Bauer *Kadish* ■ *Dir* Gordon Hessler • *Scr* William Fairchild, from a novel by Stephen Coulter

Embassy ★★

Thriller 1985 · US · Colour · 104mins

A pilot for a projected TV series that was never made, this stars Nick Mancuso as the overworked, always dependable assistant ambassador at the US embassy in Rome. This makes for some pleasant travelogue material (characters tend to drive or walk by the Colosseum) and a seemingly endless parade of supporting mini-stars like Eli Wallach and Sam Wanamaker.

Nick Mancuso *Harry Brackett* • Mimi Rogers *Nancy Russell* • Richard Masur *Dennis Thorne* • Kim Darby *Sue Davidson* • Eli Wallach *Joe Varga* • Sam Wanamaker *Ambassador Ingram* • George Grizzard *Senator Tunnard* • Richard Gilliland *Ted Davidson* • Blanche Baker *Megan Hillyer* ■ *Dir* Robert Michael Lewis [Robert Lewis] • *Scr* John McGreevey

Embrace of the Vampire ★ 18

Erotic horror 1994 · US · Colour · 88mins

Virginal Alyssa Milano falls under vampire Martin Kemp's spell in the days leading up to her 18th birthday, after which she must choose between a mortal existence or immortality with her undead lover. Poorly scripted with inane dialogue and virtually no plot, the whole reason for this contrived fantasy's existence is to show Milano's nude body at every available opportunity. That aside, there's nothing else worth watching in an aimless and sleep-inducing production. ▣

Alyssa Milano *Charlotte* • Jennifer Tilly *Marika* • Martin Kemp *Vampire* • Harrison Pruett *Chris* • Charlotte Lewis *Sarah* • Jordan Ladd *Eliza* ■ *Dir* Anne Goursaud • *Scr* Nicole Coady, Halle Eaton, Rick Bitzelberger

Embryo ★★ 15

Science-fiction drama
1976 · US · Colour · 103mins

Frankenstein rides again in director Ralph Nelson's stylish but pointless seventies update. Rock Hudson gives one of his worst performances as the scientist who invents a hormone enabling foetuses to grow rapidly to maturity outside the womb. When he develops gorgeous Barbara Carrera, she turns into a homicidal maniac looking for the formula to stop her accelerated ageing. Embarrassing dialogue – Rock teaching his artificial creation about sex and mathematics! – and nauseating special effects will further test the patience. ▣

Dir Ralph Nelson • *Scr* Anita Doohan, Jack W Thomas

The Emerald Forest ★★★ 15

Drama 1985 · UK · Colour · 108mins

Following the trail of Mowgli and Tarzan, director John Boorman teaches us a conservation lesson, with his son Charley as the boy kidnapped in the jungles of the Amazon. Found by engineer-father Powers Boothe, the

wild child ponders whether a return to civilisation is worth it, while dad wonders if his dam-building is of any value. Such weighty matters are unbalanced by Charley's awkward acting and an over-earnest approach, though the film's appeal is strengthened by Philippe Rousselot's breathtakingly beautiful photography which lives up to the title by making the jungle glisten with menace. ▭

Powers Boothe *Bill Markham* • Charley Boorman *Tommy* • Meg Foster *Jean Markham* • Estee Chandler *Heather* • Dira Paes *Kachiri* • William Rodriquez *Young Tommy* • Eduardo Conde *Uwe Werner* • Rui Polonah *Wanadi* ■ *Dir* John Boorman • *Scr* Rospo Pallenberg

Emergency ★★ U
Drama　　　　　1962 · UK · BW · 64mins

Francis Searle's anaemic little movie re-creates the agony of an estranged couple and their young daughter who is in desperate need of a blood donor. Glyn Houston is the earnest Scotland Yard flatfoot looking for likely candidates – a traitor, a football player and a fugitive murderer all make an appearance – while the parents Zena Walker and Dermot Walsh look suitably in need of tranquillisers. Things get quite dramatic before the hour and the budget is up, in this remake of Lewis Gilbert's *Emergency Call* (1952).

Glyn Houston *Inspector Harris* • Zena Walker *Joan Bell* • Dermot Walsh *John Bell* • Colin Tapley *Dr Lloyd* • Garard Green *Professor Graham* • Anthony Dawes *Sergeant Phillips* • Edward Ogden *Tommy Day* • Helen Forrest *Mrs Day* ■ *Dir* Francis Searle • *Scr* Don Nicholl, James O'Connolly, from a story by Lewis Gilbert, Vernon Harris

Emergency! ★★★
Medical drama　　　　1971 · US · Colour

Hands up those who remember the seventies American TV show *Emergency!* about a team of Los Angeles paramedics always at the beck and call of the fire department. Well, this is the pilot that launched the series, which was something of a cross between *London's Burning* and *ER.* Jack Webb, who had been the brains behind *Dragnet* and *Adam-12*, directs with his usual style, drawing naturalistic performances from doctors Robert Fuller and Bobby Troup and nurse Julie London.

Robert Fuller *Dr Kelly Brackett* • Julie London *Nurse Dixie McCall* • Bobby Troup *Dr Joe Early* • Randolph Mantooth *John Gage* • Kevin Tighe *Roy DeSoto* • Martin Milner *Officer Pete Malloy* ■ *Dir* Jack Webb • *Scr* Harold Jack Bloom, Robert A Cinader

Emergency Call ★★ U
Medical drama　　1952 · UK · BW · 90mins

Doesn't this sound awful? A small child with a rare blood type needs a transfusion to pull through a critical operation, and the only donors available are a boxer at a career crossroads, a black sailor with attitude and a killer on the run. It says much for director Lewis Gilbert that he was able to take this cliché-ridden mishmash and mould it into a mildly diverting and well-edited drama. Holding it all together are Anthony Steel as the chief surgeon and Jack

Warner as the copper in pursuit of the potential life-savers.

Jack Warner *Inspector Lane* • Anthony Steel *Dr Carter* • Joy Shelton *Laura Bishop* • Sidney James *Danny Marks* • Freddie Mills *Tim Mahoney* • Earl Cameron *George Robinson* • John Robinson *Dr Braithwaite* • Thora Hird *Mrs Cornelius* • Eric Pohlmann *Flash Harry* • Sydney Tafler *Brett* ■ *Dir* Lewis Gilbert • *Scr* Lewis Gilbert, Vernon Harris

The Emigrants ★★★
Historical epic 1971 · Swe · Colour · 150mins

Not content with co-scripting and directing this cross-continental epic, Oscar nominated for best picture in 1972, Jan Troell also shot and edited the imposing imagery that so powerfully conveys the pain of leaving Sweden forever and the enormity of the challenge awaiting farmer Max von Sydow and his wife Liv Ullmann on the plains of Minnesota. Though grindingly slow, it's impossible not to be moved by the dangers and hardships they face en route to their new home. Swedish dialogue dubbed into English.

Max von Sydow *Karl Oskar* • Liv Ullmann *Kristina* • Eddie Axberg *Robert* • Pierre Lindstedt *Arvid* • Allan Edwall *Danjel* • Monica Zeterlund *Ulrika* • Hans Alfredson *Jonas Petter* • Aina Alfredsson *Marta* ■ *Dir* Jan Troell • *Scr* Bengt Forslund, Jan Troell, from the novels by Vilhelm Moberg

Emil and the Detectives ★★ U

Crime comedy adventure
1964 · US · Colour · 92mins

This Disney version of Erich Kästner's ever-popular novel is not a patch on Gerhard Lamprecht's 1931 German original. There's a Children's Film Foundation feel to the story of a boy who stumbles across a master criminal's plan to rob Berlin's richest bank. Walter Slezak proved himself to be one of Hollywood's most loathsome villains in films like *Lifeboat*, but here he plays the Baron with an unnecessarily pantomimic brio. However, most under-tens will be too busy identifying with the heroic Bryan Russell to notice. ▭

Walter Slezak *Baron* • Bryan Russell *Emil* • Roger Mobley *Gustav* • Heinz Schubert *Grundeis* • Peter Ehrlich *Muller* • Cindy Cassell *Pony* • Elsa Wagner *Nana* ■ *Dir* Peter Tewksbury • *Scr* AJ Carothers, from the novel *Emil und die Detektiven* by Erich Kästner

Emily's Ghost ★★
Period drama　　　1992 · UK · Colour

Emily is a young girl with a desperate desire to emulate her grandfather and become a doctor – not an easy ambition to fulfil in Edwardian England. This, combined with some ghostly visitations, causes tension within the family. The result is a cute family drama that should keep younger viewers entertained, but anyone older will probably be disappointed by the amateurish effects and predictable storyline. Nice direction from Colin Finbow, though, who also directed *Survivors* and *The Gingerbread House.*

Anna Jones *Emily* • Martin Jarvis *Papa* • Anna Massey *Miss Rabstock* • Ron Moody *Dawson* • Rosalind Ayres *Mama* • Patsy Byrne *Mrs Crabtree* • Peter Bayliss *Reverend* • Emily Howes *Ghost girl* ■ *Dir/Scr* Colin Finbow

Eminent Domain ★★ 15
Political thriller
1991 · Can/Fr/Is · Colour · 106mins

Donald Sutherland is the Politburo official who finds himself out in the cold in this Kafkaesque thriller, set in pre-Solidarity Poland. More sinisterly, Sutherland can't find anyone to explain his sudden loss of power and status. Anne Archer and Bernard Hepton co-star in a film that has its intriguing aspects, but whose confusions and complexities may be a bit of a "trial" for some viewers.

Donald Sutherland *Josef Borski* • Anne Archer *Mira* • Bernard Hepton *Slovak* • Jodhi May *Ewa* • Paul Freeman *Ben* • Anthony Bate *Kowal* • Pip Torrens *Anton* • Françoise Michaud *Nicole* • Yves Beneyton *Roger* • Denys Fouqueray *Dr Marwicz* ■ *Dir* John Irvin • *Scr* Andrzej Krakowski, Richard Greggson, from a story by Andrzej Krakowski

Emma ★★★
Melodrama　　　　1932 · US · BW · 71mins

Not Gwyneth Paltrow as Jane Austen's heroine, but a marvellous showcase for MGM superstar Marie Dressler, here cast as a long-suffering servant condemned to watch the family she has tended turn against her in her unuseful old age. In other hands this could be a recipe for gibbering bathos, but the great Dressler convinces with every single movement and gesture. (She was rightly nominated for an Academy Award.) Jean Hersholt is also excellent as the man of the house, and there's fine support from youngsters Richard Cromwell and Myrna Loy. The short running time mitigates greatly for the film.

Marie Dressler *Emma Thatcher* • Richard Cromwell *Ronnie Smith* • Jean Hersholt *Mr Smith* • Myrna Loy *Isabelle* • John Miljan *District attorney* ■ *Dir* Clarence Brown • *Scr* Leonard Praskins, Zelda Sears

Emma ★★★★ U
Period romantic comedy
1996 · UK/US · Colour · 116mins

Before she became Shakespeare's love object, Anglophile Oscar-winner Gwyneth Paltrow made her mark as the quintessential Jane Austen heroine. In writer/director Douglas McGrath's confident period romance, Paltrow stars as the strong-willed matchmaker who entangles her friend (Toni Collette) in hopeless passion while trying to uncover the identity of her own true soulmate. Laced with wit, style and a host of fine supporting performances (Jeremy Northam, Alan Cumming, Juliet Stevenson), this bright and breezy drama weaves its magic, with Paltrow at its charming centre. ▭ **DVD**

Gwyneth Paltrow *Emma* • Toni Collette *Harriet* • Alan Cumming *Mr Elton* • Jeremy Northam *Mr Knightley* • Ewan McGregor *Frank Churchill* • Greta Scacchi *Mrs Weston* • Juliet Stevenson *Mrs Elton* • Polly Walker *Jane Fairfax* • Sophie Thompson *Miss Bates* • Phyllida Law *Mrs Bates* • James Cosmo *Mr Weston* • Denys Hawthorne *Mr Woodhouse* ■ *Dir* Douglas McGrath • *Scr* Douglas McGrath, from the novel by Jane Austen

Emmanuelle ★★ 18
Erotic drama　　　1974 · Fr · Colour · 89mins

Possibly the best-known porn film in the world, this made Sylvia Kristel an

international star and spawned countless imitations. So is it any good? Well, put it this way, it's light years ahead of the films showcased by Dirk Diggler in *Boogie Nights*. It's artfully shot by director Just Jaeckin, the Thailand locations are occasionally stunning and Kristel disrobes with some elegance. However, acting is far from her strong suit, and the dialogue and story, about the sexual awakening of a young woman, is pretty banal. Still, if you are going to watch one porn film… French dialogue dubbed into English. ▭

Sylvia Kristel *Emmanuelle* • Alain Cuny *Mario* • Daniel Sarky *Jean* • Jeanne Colletin *Ariane* • Marika Green *Bee* • Christine Boisson *Marie-Ange* ■ *Dir* Just Jaeckin • *Scr* Jean-Louis Richard, from the book by Emmanuelle Arsan

Emmanuelle 2 ★★ 18
Erotic drama　　　1978 · Fr · Colour · 87mins

This sequel came four years after Just Jaeckin's titillating original had made Sylvia Kristel a star. The scene shifts from Bangkok to Hong Kong and then Bali – not that you'd notice, however, as most of the action takes place in soft-focus close-up. Credit must be given to the Dutch actress for managing to invest the endless round of sexual encounters with a modicum of eroticism. But it's clear that director Francis Giacobetti was not interested in either the psychological aspects of Kristel's wanderlust or in the acting ability of her co-stars. French dialogue dubbed into English. ▭

Sylvia Kristel *Emmanuelle* • Umberto Orsini *Jean* • Catherine Rivet *Anna-Maria* • Frédéric Lagache *Christopher* • Caroline Laurence *Ingrid* • Florence Lafuma *Laura* ■ *Dir* Francis Giacobetti • *Scr* Bob Elia, Francis Giacobetti

Emma's War ★★ PG
Drama　　　　　1985 · Ausl · Colour · 92mins

This wartime rites of passage picture is notable only for the fact that it was one of Lee Remick's last features before her tragic death from cancer at just 55. Struggling to find depth in a film in which image takes precedence over content, she plays a lonely, drunken mother who drags her daughters away from their blissful boarding school existence and deposits them in a rundown outback town where very little ever happens. Tom Cowan's photography neatly suggests the contrasting atmosphere of the two places, but the patchwork screenplay flits between episodes with no discernible dramatic focus. ▭

Lee Remick *Anne Grange* • Miranda Otto *Emma Grange* • Bridey Lee *Laurel Grange* • Terence Donovan *Frank Grange* • Mark Lee *John Davidson* • Pat Evison *Miss Arnott* • Donal Gibson *Hank* • Grigor Taylor *Dr Friedlander* • Noeline Brown *Mrs Mortimer* • Rebel Russell *Miss Gunz* ■ *Dir* Clytie Jessop • *Scr* Peter Smalley, Clytie Jessop

The Emperor and the Assassin ★★★ 12
Historical drama
1999 · Chi/Jap/Fr · Colour · 161mins

Despite four attempts at reworking this five-chaptered historical epic, Chen Kaige has again succumbed to the pictorialism that blighted *Temptress Moon* (1996). Embroidering the fragmentary facts known about Ying Zheng's unification of China in the late third century BC, Chen concocts a story of such complexity and specialised significance that it's difficult not only to keep track of events, but also to invest much emotional energy in the central characters. Gong Li is elegant but detached as the royal mistress whose bellicose schemes backfire when the man she hires to stage an enemy assassination attempt proves to be dangerously unstable. In Mandarin with English subtitles.

Gong Li *Lady Zhao* • Zhang Fengyi *Jing Ke* • Li Xuejian *Ying Zheng, King of Qin* • Wang Zhiwen *Marquis Changxin* ■ *Dir* Chen Kaige • *Scr* Wang Peigong, Chen Kaige

The Emperor Jones ★★
Drama   1933 · US · BW · 81mins

The commanding presence and glorious voice of Paul Robeson dominate this screen version of Eugene O'Neill's play; indeed, it's an indication of his stature that he was given the lead at a time when few black actors starred in Hollywood movies. Scriptwriter DuBose Heyward (who later wrote the libretto and lyrics for *Porgy and Bess*) opens out the play to include Jones's earlier life as an opportunistic railroad porter before following him to the West Indies, where he becomes the tyrannical ruler of a remote isle. Despite a wealth of incident, though, the pacing is stilted and Dudley Murphy's film fails to capture the powerful aura of fatalism that marked the original.

Paul Robeson *Brutus Jones* • Dudley Digges *Smithers* • Frank Wilson *Jeff* • Fredi Washington *Undine* • Ruby Elzy *Dolly* • George Haymid Stamper *Lem* • Jackie Mayble *Marcella* • Blueboy O'Connor *Treasurer* ■ *Dir* Dudley Murphy • *Scr* DuBose Heyward, from the play by Eugene O'Neill

Emperor of the North ★★★★☑
Action adventure
1973 · US · Colour · 120mins

Director Robert Aldrich's addictively tough outing about a railway guard (Ernest Borgnine) who is proud of the fact that no tramp, especially not Lee Marvin, rides his train for free. Aldrich's direction comes at the viewer like an express train and, typically fusing darkness with wit, creates a symbolic tale of the Depression, even if the drifter in this film is rather absurdly elevated to hero status. His train does screech to a halt now and again with rather more chat than action, but there is enough pulsating drama and compelling background detail to keep you glued. ▣

Lee Marvin *A No 1* • Ernest Borgnine *Shack* • Keith Carradine *Cigaret* • Charles Tyner *Cracker* • Malcolm Atterbury *Hogger* • Simon Oakland *Policeman* • Harry Caesar *Coaly* ■ *Dir* Robert Aldrich • *Scr* Christopher Knopf

The Emperor Waltz ★★★
Musical comedy 1948 · US · Colour · 107mins

Legend has it that this is Billy Wilder's worst movie, though it does have its delectably barmy moments. Set in the Austrian Tyrol, it stars Bing Crosby and his pet pooch, Buttons, peddling

gramophones to the European nobility. Crosby falls for a countess, Joan Fontaine, while Buttons falls for a poodle. It's a fable about American enterprise and a lament for a Europe buried beneath the ruins of war. Paramount delayed releasing it for two years but, for collectors of kitsch, this all-yodelling musical comedy is essential viewing.

Bing Crosby *Virgil Smith* • Joan Fontaine *Johanna Franziska Von Stolzenberg* • Roland Culver *Baron Holenia* • Richard Haydn *Emperor Franz Josef* • Lucile Watson *Princess Bitotska* • Sig Rumann [Sig Ruman] *Dr Zwieback* ■ *Dir* Billy Wilder • *Scr* Charles Brackett, Billy Wilder

The Emperor's Candlesticks ★★★☑
Romantic spy drama 1937 · US · BW · 88mins

In the early 1900s, rival spies Baron Wolensky (William Powell) and Countess Olga (Luise Rainer) make the mistake of hiding their vital documents in a pair of candlesticks. This leads the stylish pair on a chase round Europe during which – of course – they fall in love. Lavishly mounted, acted as if the hokum were serious, and well directed by George Fitzmaurice, this is a charming, elegant and romantic tale of impeccably dressed and well-connected spies, adapted from a novel by Baroness Orczy, creator of *The Scarlet Pimpernel*.

William Powell *Baron Stephan Wolensky* • Luise Rainer *Countess Olga Mironova* • Frank Morgan *Col Baron Suroff* • Maureen O'Sullivan *Maria* • Henry Stephenson *Prince Johann* • Robert Young *Grand Duke Peter* • Douglas Dumbrille [Douglass Dumbrille] *Korum* • Bernadene Hayes *Mitzi* ■ *Dir* George Fitzmaurice • *Scr* Monckton Hoffe, Harold Goldman, from a novel by Baroness Orczy

The Emperor's New Clothes ★★☑
Musical fantasy 1987 · US · Colour · 80mins

Simple but pleasant enough fare for children, this musical reworking of the old folk tale features veteran comedian Sid Caesar as the pompous monarch being conned by tailor Robert Morse, whose bespoke clothes are so "fine and delicate" they're invisible. Director David Irving plays it all with an obvious turn, but it's bound to reach its young audience. ▣

Sid Caesar *The Emperor* • Robert Morse *Henry* • Jason Carter *Nicholas* • Lysette Anthony *Gilda* • Clive Revill *Prime Minister* • Julian Joy-Chagrin [Julian Chagrin] *Duke* • Eli Gorenstein *Sergeant* ■ *Dir* David Irving • *Scr* Anna Mathias, Len Talan, David Irving, from the fairy tale by Hans Christian Andersen

The Emperor's Shadow ★★★★
Historical epic 1996 · HK · Colour · 123mins

A tragedy of epic proportions, this is, nevertheless, a very human story in which love is destroyed by the misuse of power. Wen Jiang gives a towering performance as Ying Zheng, the emperor who united China in the second century BC and whose dictatorial treatment of his childhood friend Gao Jianli results in the death of his own daughter. You Ge is also impressive as Gao, the enslaved musician whose acts of defiance

topple the imperial edifice. But it's the way in which Xiaowen Zhou combines sweeping scale with intimate detail that gives the film both its power and its subtle contemporary subtext. In Cantonese with English subtitles.

Jiang Wen *Ying Zheng* • Ge You *Gao Jianli* • Xu Qing *Ying Yueyang* ■ *Dir* Zhou Xiaowen • *Scr* Lu Wei

Empire City ★★☑
Thriller   1991 · US · Colour · 78mins

Underachieving American action man Michael Paré sleepwalks through a wannabe *film noir* that is nothing more than a patchwork of police thriller clichés loosely strung together. How many times have we seen macho cops saddled with partners they neither want nor need? In this instance, Paré is paired with Mary Mara, who proves to be more than a match for him as they bicker their way through an investigation of murder in high places. Contains violence and swearing. ▣

Michael Paré *Joe Andre* • Mary Mara *Nancy Krause* • Beau Starr *Lieutenant Bob Conway* • Peter Frechette *Graham MacGowan* • Ron Vawter *Lieutenant Spinell* • Kelly Carnahan *Robin Christopher* ■ *Dir/Scr* Mark Rosner

Empire of the Ants ★★
Science-fiction drama
1977 · US · Colour · 84mins

Supposedly based on a story by HG Wells, this tacky tale of tepid terror is just another poverty-row, giant-insect tale from schlock director Bert I Gordon, more famous now for featuring a pre-*Dynasty* Joan Collins up to her designer khakis in mud fighting off laughably phoney mutant ants. She's the head swindler of a housing development consortium on a resort island where radiation waste has been dumped. In between the slipshod special effects, the actors bicker a lot while trying to escape the boring menace.

Joan Collins *Marilyn Fryser* • Robert Lansing *Dan Stokely* • John David Carson *Joe Morrison* • Albert Salmi *Sheriff Art Kincade* • Jacqueline Scott *Margaret Ellis* • Pamela Shoop *Coreen Bradford* • Robert Pine *Larry Graham* • Edward Power *Charlie Pearson* ■ *Dir* Bert I Gordon • *Scr* Jack Turley, from a story by Bert I Gordon, from a story by HG Wells

Empire of the Sun ★★★☑
Second World War drama
1987 · US · Colour · 146mins

Now considered a trial run for the more moving, horrifying and involving *Schindler's List*, Steven Spielberg's drama set in China during the Second World War is a glossy and rather tame affair, based on JG Ballard's semi-autobiographical novel. Bland Christian Bale plays 11-year-old Jim, who is separated from his family in Shanghai and ends up in a Japanese internment camp. As you'd expect from Spielberg, the film has its fair share of heroic moments and scenes that depict the horror of war through the eyes of a child. However, despite the presence of such talents as John Malkovich, Miranda Richardson and Nigel Havers, this never depicts the true effects of armed conflict. Contains swearing. ▣

Christian Bale *Jim Graham* • John Malkovich *Basie* • Miranda Richardson *Mrs Victor* • Nigel

Havers *Dr Rawlins* • Joe Pantoliano *Frank Demerest* • Leslie Phillips *Maxton* • Robert Stephens *Mr Lockwood* • Burt Kwouk *Mr Chen* • Paul McGann *Lieutenant Price* ■ *Dir* Steven Spielberg • *Scr* Tom Stoppard, from the novel by JG Ballard

Empire Records ★★★☑
Comedy drama 1995 · US · Colour · 86mins

This likeable, if faintly preposterous teen flick is set around one day in the life of Empire Records, a small independent music store, run by Anthony LaPaglia, which is about to be taken over by a record giant. Liv Tyler looks suitably winsome but is overshadowed by co-stars Renee Zellweger and Rory Cochrane, while Maxwell Caulfield enjoys himself as a spoilt rock idol. Director Allan Moyle, who made the excellent *Pump Up the Volume*, demonstrates a keen understanding of adolescent angst, though the film as a whole has a distinctly old-fashioned feel. ▣

Anthony LaPaglia *Joe* • Rory Cochrane *Lucas* • Johnny Whitworth *A J* • Liv Tyler *Corey* • Renee Zellweger *Gina* • Robin Tunney *Debra* • Ethan Randall [Ethan Embry] *Mark* • Maxwell Caulfield *Rex* • Debi Mazar *Jane* ■ *Dir* Allan Moyle • *Scr* Carol Heikkinen

The Empire Strikes Back ★★★★★☑
Science-fiction epic
1980 · US · Colour · 124mins

In the second part of George Lucas's first *Star Wars* trilogy, Darth Vader sends Imperial troops to crush the rebels on the ice planet Hoth, while Luke Skywalker searches out Jedi master Yoda for further instruction in the mysterious ways of "the Force". Irvin Kershner takes over the directing reins and splendidly continues the space saga, darkening the imagery of Lucas's vibrant, futuristic fairy tale and deepening its narrative with provocative plot strands. The much-loved characters are developed in intriguing ways, events take place all over the universe, and there's a cynical, harder edge that lifts this sequel above the serial roots of its predecessor. Kershner's imaginative supervision of Lucas's brainchild gives it a truly epic dimension, adding a mature, philosophical aspect to the brilliant special effects. ▣

Mark Hamill *Luke Skywalker* • Harrison Ford *Han Solo* • Carrie Fisher *Princess Leia* • Billy Dee Williams *Lando Calrissian* • Anthony Daniels *C-3PO* • David Prowse [Dave Prowse] *Darth Vader* • Peter Mayhew *Chewbacca* • Kenny Baker (1) *R2-D2* • Frank Oz *Yoda* • Alec Guinness *Ben Kenobi* ■ *Dir* Irvin Kershner • *Scr* Leigh Brackett, Lawrence Kasdan, from a story by George Lucas • *Music* John Williams • *Art Director* Norman Reynold

The Empty Beach ★★★☑
Crime drama   1985 · Ausl · Colour · 86mins

Bryan Brown takes a walk on the seamy side of Sydney and Bondi in this violent Australian *film noir* about a hard-boiled gumshoe, with more than a touch of Chandler's Philip Marlowe in him, who is hired by a wealthy widow to solve the mystery of her hubby's disappearance. This was one of the last films Brown made in Oz before following his compatriot Mel Gibson to Hollywood. Sadly, he's not enjoyed the

U = SUITABLE FOR ALL   **U꜀** = SUITABLE FOR ALL, ESPECIALLY FOR YOUNG CHILDREN (VIDEO ONLY)   **PG** = PARENTAL GUIDANCE

same success as the Oscar-winning Gibson. This may not be the most original film, but it rates as a perfectly acceptable Australian take on a familiar genre. Contains swearing. 📼

Bryan Brown *Cliff Hardy* • Anna Maria Monticelli *Anne Winter* • Ray Barrett *MacLeary* • John Wood *Parker* • Nick Tate *Brian Hennebery* • Belinda Giblin *Marion Singer* ■ *Dir* Chris Thomson • *Scr* Keith Dewhurst, from the novel by Peter Corris

The Empty Canvas ★

Drama   1963 · Fr/It · BW · 104mins

When Bette Davis met Damiano Damiani, the Italian cult director clearly lost. In one of her strangest roles, the bitch goddess does her utmost to save her artist son, Horst Buchholz, from his obsessive love for model Catherine Spaak. Davis is all at sea in an avant-garde melodrama, based on an Alberto Moravia novel, where her determination to stay in front of sixties cameras, no matter what the cost to her reputation, is her only steely motivation. A weird and sad viewing experience. Some dialogue dubbed into English.

Bette Davis *Dino's mother* • Horst Buchholz *Dino* • Catherine Spaak *Cecilia* • Isa Miranda *Cecilia's mother* • Lea Padovani *Balestrieri's widow* • Daniela Rocca *Rita* • Georges Wilson *Cecilia's father* • Leonida Repaci *Balestrieri* ■ *Dir* Damiano Damiani • *Scr* Damiano Damiani, Tonino Guerra, Ugo Liberatore, from the novel *La Noia* by Alberto Moravia

Empty Cradle ★★★ 15

Drama based on a true story
1993 · US · Colour · 87mins

Although formulaic, American true story TV movies do occasionally offer the chance for well-known TV faces to be cast against type. This is one such example, with Kate Jackson being less than angelic as a nurse who steals a newborn baby and then tries to convince the authorities that the child died during the birth. *ER's* Eriq La Salle and Lori Loughlin deliver capable supporting turns and the sensationalist subject matter makes for gripping viewing. 📼

Kate Jackson *Rita Donahue* • Lori Loughlin *Jane Morgan* • Eriq La Salle *Detective Knoll* • David Lansbury *Bob Morgan* • Jonah Blechman *Patrick Donahue* • Karmin Murcelo *Nurse Ramsey* • Peter Crook *Dr Evans* ■ *Dir* Paul Schneider • *Scr* Rebecca Soladay

The Empty Table ★★★★ PG

Drama   1985 · Jap · Colour · 141mins

A modest, tradition-minded Japanese family suddenly realise that their son is a terrorist and that they will be stigmatised because of his actions. Set in the seventies, when the much-feared Japanese Red Army were committing outrages across the world, this Masaki Kobayashi picture is slow to unfold yet presents the world of the terrorist and his family with unusual insight, taking a real event – a televised police raid on the terrorists' mountain training centre in 1970 – as its starting point. It was the last film directed by Kobayashi, perhaps best known for the ghost story *Kwaidan*. In Japanese with English subtitles.

Tatsuya Nakadai *Nobuyuki Kidoji* • Mayumi Ogawa *Yukimo Kidoji* • Kie Nakai *Tamae Kidoji* • Kiichi Nakai *Otohiko Kidoji* • Takayuki

Takemoto *Osamu Kidoji* • Shima Iwashita *Kiwa Nakahara* • Mikijiro Hira *Kawabe's lawyer* ■ *Dir* Masaki Kobayashi • *Scr* Masaki Kobayashi, from a story by Fumiko Enchi

Enchanted April ★★ U

Romantic drama   1991 · UK · Colour · 89mins

Genteel to the point of tedium, this British period piece relies on its four female stars – Oscar-nominated Joan Plowright, Miranda Richardson, Josie Lawrence and Polly Walker – who play four women bonding on an Italian holiday while waiting for their male partners. The women are worth the wait, but otherwise this has all the careful, itemised hallmarks of a made-for-TV movie. Director Mike Newell went on to make the box-office hit *Four Weddings and a Funeral.* 📼

Miranda Richardson *Rose Arbuthnot* • Josie Lawrence *Lotty Wilkins* • Polly Walker *Lady Caroline Dester* • Joan Plowright *Mrs Fisher* • Alfred Molina *Mellersh Wilkins* • Michael Kitchen *George Briggs* • Jim Broadbent *Frederick Arbuthnot* • Davide Manuli *Beppo* ■ *Dir* Mike Newell • *Scr* Peter Barnes, from the novel by Elizabeth von Arnim

The Enchanted Cottage ★★★★ U

Romance   1945 · US · BW · 92mins

One of the great romances of the cinema, this tale of two society misfits depends very heavily on a serious suspension of disbelief from its audience. Writer Arthur Pinero referred to the original as a fable, and was very aware of its low credibility factor. But the First World War update works superbly, and director John Cromwell achieves a perfect tone. Of course, it's a Hollywood movie, so leads Dorothy McGuire and Robert Young aren't disfigured or plain enough. However, the cinema works its magic: give your heart to it, rather than your mind, and you'll love it.

Dorothy McGuire *Laura* • Robert Young *Oliver* • Herbert Marshall *Hillgrove* • Mildred Natwick *Abigail Minnett* • Spring Byington *Violet Price* • Hillary Brooke *Beatrice* • Richard Gaines *Frederick* • Alec Englander *Danny* • Mary Worth *Mrs Stanton* ■ *Dir* John Cromwell • *Scr* DeWitt Bodeen, Herman J Mankiewicz, from the play by Sir Arthur Wing Pinero

Enchantment ★★★ U

Romantic drama   1948 · US · BW · 96mins

Films following events in an English stately home have long held an attraction for American audiences. This one has the unusual distinction of being told by the ancestral pile itself. Based on a novel by Rumer Godden, it was advertised by RKO as "just about the most wonderful love story ever filmed". Of course it's nothing of the sort. However, David Niven gives a good account of himself as the hot-blooded lover in the first story and the wise old head in the second. 📼

David Niven *General Sir Roland Dane* • Teresa Wright *Lark Ingoldsby* • Evelyn Keyes *Grizel Dane* • Farley Granger *Pilot Pax Masterson* • Jayne Meadows *Selina Dane* • Leo G Carroll *Proutie* • Philip Friend *Pilot Dane* ■ *Dir* Irving Reis • *Scr* John Patrick, from the novel *Take Three Tenses* by Rumer Godden

Encore ★★★

Portmanteau drama   1951 · UK · BW · 88mins

Without ever really exerting a grip, this portmanteau picture, based on the stories of W Somerset Maugham, is a diverting collection of passable vignettes. The direction of Pat Jackson, Anthony Pelissier and Harold French is pedestrian, but the performances of a fine cast of British stalwarts save the day. Nigel Patrick and Roland Culver give a polished demonstration of comic timing in "The Ant and the Grasshopper", while Glynis Johns and Terence Morgan struggle valiantly to find the pathos in "Gigolo and Gigolette". Best of all, however, is Kay Walsh, chattering interminably in "Winter Cruise".

Nigel Patrick *Tom Ramsey* • Roland Culver *George Ramsey* • Alison Leggatt *Freda Ramsey* • Kay Walsh *Miss Reid* • Noel Purcell *Captain* • Ronald Squire *Doctor* • Glynis Johns *Stella Cotman* • Terence Morgan *Syd Cotman* ■ *Dir* Harold French, Pat Jackson, Anthony Pelissier • *Scr* T EB Clarke, Arthur Macrae, Eric Ambler, from the short stories *The Ant and the Grasshopper* , *Gigolo and Gigolette* and *Winter Cruise* by W Somerset Maugham

Encounter at Raven's Gate ★★★★ 15

Science-fiction thriller
1988 · Ausl · Colour · 85mins

This stand-out Australian science-fiction thriller involves a paroled ex-convict, his brother, the brother's bored wife and the strange phenomena that occur at Raven's Gate farm – perhaps the work of visiting evil aliens. Director Rolf De Heer allows the viewer's imagination to go into overdrive thanks to creepy photography and evocative use of sound – both of which create more edge-of-seat menace than using cheap UFO effects or rubber monsters. Tense, engrossing and packed with unusual incident (the sky raining dead birds), this atmospheric gem is a fine example of low-budget success. 📼

Steven Vidler *Eddie Cleary* • Celine Griffin *Rachel Cleary* • Ritchie Singer *Richard* • Vincent Gil *Felix Skinner* • Saturday Rosenberg *Annie* • Terry Camilleri *Dr Hemmings* ■ *Dir* Rolf De Heer • *Scr* Marc Rosenberg, Rolf De Heer, James Michael Vernon

The End ★ 15

Comedy   1978 · US · Colour · 96mins

Burt Reynolds directed himself in this tasteless mishmash so, presumably, Jerry Belson's script must have meant something to him. It means nothing to us, however, as a bearded Reynolds discovers he's medically doomed and starts to square his conscience with a life that has been totally selfish. Hamming is the order of the dying day – with Dom DeLuise coming a close second to the star – so that when the title announces itself, it's with a feeling of huge relief. 📼

Burt Reynolds *Wendell Sonny Lawson* • Dom DeLuise *Marlon Borunki* • Sally Field *Mary Ellen* • Strother Martin *Dr Waldo Kling* • David Steinberg *Marty Lieberman* • Joanne Woodward *Jessica* • Norman Fell *Dr Samuel Krugman* • Myrna Loy *Maureen Lawson* ■ *Dir* Burt Reynolds • *Scr* Jerry Belson

End of Days ★★★ 18

Supernatural action thriller
1999 · US · Colour · 122mins

This millennium's end action movie is a calculated but fairly enjoyable attempt to a) give Arnold Schwarzenegger a less indestructible, more human side, and b) cash in on the revitalised horror genre. While Arnie's amateurish emoting never rings true in the role of a run-down, suicidal, alcoholic ex-cop, the "Devil searching for his bride" story provides some decent popcorn entertainment. Gabriel Byrne, meanwhile, rises above the clumsily structured and wholly derivative script to give an attention-grabbing performance as a very laid-back Prince of Darkness. (The scene in which he seductively bribes Arnold with the chance of a new start is a cracker.) It should have been sharper and scarier, but the final half-hour delivers the demonic goods. 📼

Arnold Schwarzenegger *Jericho Cane* • Gabriel Byrne *The Man* • Kevin Pollak *Chicago* • Robin Tunney *Christine York* • CCH Pounder *Detective Marge Francis* • Rod Steiger *Father Kovak* • Miriam Margolyes *Mabel* ■ *Dir* Peter Hyams • *Scr* Andrew W Marlowe

The End of Innocence ★★

Drama   1990 · US · Colour · 102mins

Actress Dyan Cannon writes, directs and stars in this drama about one woman's disappointments and setbacks. Evidently Cannon – who gets to scream, rant and wave her legs around for a good proportion of the film – saw this as an opportunity to flex her creative muscle. For the viewer, though, it's a rather depressing and relentless tale, made even more so by the final appearance of Rebecca Schaeffer (playing Cannon's character at a younger age), who was tragically murdered at the age of 21.

Dyan Cannon *Stephanie Lewis* • John Heard *Dean* • George Coe *Dad* • Lola Mason *Mom* • Rebecca Schaeffer *Stephanie at 18* • Stephen Meadows *Michael* • Michael Madsen *Earl* ■ *Dir/Scr* Dyan Cannon

The End of St Petersburg ★★★★

Silent political drama
1927 · USSR · BW · 110mins

Commissioned as part of the tenth anniversary celebrations of the Russian Revolution, the film was shot by the great Russian director Vsevolod Pudovkin at the same time and place (Leningrad) as Sergei Eisenstein's more famous *October* (1928). Both films dealt with subjects such as the storming of the Winter Palace and the triumph of the Bolsheviks, but Pudovkin's film was shown two months before *October* and was the more popular version. The events were witnessed through the eyes of a central character (an uneducated peasant boy), someone with whom audiences could identify. Not as dazzling technically as *October*, it has some marvellous montage sequences and much emotional appeal.

AP Chistyakov *Worker* • Vera Baranovskaya *His wife* • Ivan Chuvelov *Ivan, a peasant* • V Chuvelov *Friend from the village* • A Gromov *Revolutionary* ■ *Dir* Vsevolod I Pudovkin • *Scr*

Nathan Zarkhi, from the poem *The Bronze Horseman* by Vsevolod I Pudovkin, from the novel *St Petersburg* by Andrey Biely

The End of the Affair
★★★★ **PG**

Wartime romantic drama
1955 · UK · BW · 101mins

Graham Greene's mystical, semi-autobiographical novel of doomed romance is convincingly brought to life by director Edward Dmytryk and contains a trio of powerful star performances from Deborah Kerr, John Mills and the outstanding Peter Cushing. Only miscast lead Van Johnson fails to achieve the requisite Catholic angst, which is certainly suggested but not really explored by Stephen Murray as the all-important priest. Dmytryk's London locations are deeply affecting, and it's interesting to note that Neil Jordan, director of the Ralph Fiennes remake, professed not to know of the existence of this fine earlier version, and then, when shown it, disliked it for its phoneyness. ▥

Deborah Kerr *Sarah Miles* • Van Johnson *Maurice Bendrix* • John Mills *Albert Parkis* • Peter Cushing *Henry Miles* • Michael Goodliffe *Smythe* • Stephen Murray *Father Crompton* ■ *Dir* Edward Dmytryk • *Scr* Lenore Coffee, from the novel by Graham Greene

The End of the Affair
★★★★ **18**

Wartime romantic drama
1999 · US/UK · Colour · 101mins

Graham Greene's literary style was always consciously cinematic, but he has been singularly ill-served by those translating his novels to the screen. However, Neil Jordan has made a laudable attempt at conveying the characters' inner lives in this second filming of Greene's most autobiographical fiction. With a Catholicism more redolent of Evelyn Waugh, the story of doomed adultery between writer Bendrix (Ralph Fiennes) and married Sarah (Julianne Moore) has a delicious sense of stolen joy. Then an air raid prompts a spiritual crisis for Sarah and a difficult choice. With Ian Hart outstanding as the detective hired by the jealous Fiennes, and Stephen Rea no less impressive as Sarah's stuffy husband, this is an admirable study of adult emotion. Contains sex scenes.

Ralph Fiennes *Maurice Bendrix* • Julianne Moore *Sarah Miles* • Stephen Rea *Henry Miles* • Ian Hart *Mr Parkis* • Jason Isaacs *Father Smythe* • James Bolam *Mr Savage* ■ *Dir* Neil Jordan, *Scr* Neil Jordan, from the novel by Graham Greene

The End of the Day ★★★★

Drama
1939 · Fr · BW · 93mins

The least penetrating of the poetic realist allegories on the ruinous decadence of prewar France, this is still a superbly realised and desperately sad film. Director Julien Duvivier creates a tangible atmosphere of melancholy pride in which this exceptional cast essay the various retired actors who have lost their very identities after years of playing roles on and off the stage. Each performance is a gem, from failed classicist Victor Francen's attempts to

insinuate himself into Madeleine Ozeray's affections, to the fury of ladies' man Louis Jouvet. But, as ever, it's Michel Simon, as a lifelong understudy, who steals the show. In French with English subtitles.

Arquillieres [Alexandre C Arquillière] *Monsieur Lucien* • Michel Simon *Cabrissade* • Victor Francen *Gilles Marny* • Louis Jouvet *Raphaël Saint-Clair* • Madeleine Ozeray *Jeannette* • Gabrielle Dorziat *Madame Chabert* • Sylvie *Madame Tusini* ■ *Dir* Julien Duvivier • *Scr* Charles Spaak, Julien Duvivier

End of the Game ★★★

Mystery drama
1976 · W Ger/It · Colour · 106mins

It's role reversal time, with actor Maximilian Schell taking the director's chair, and director Martin Ritt (*Hud*, *Hombre*) making a rare foray in front of the cameras. Ritt neatly plays a dying police commissioner who makes one last attempt to catch the master criminal he's been hunting for the last 30 years. Jon Voight, Robert Shaw and Donald Sutherland (in a cameo role) are the better-known acting names in a complicated but rewarding Euro-thriller.

Jon Voight *Walter Tschantz* • Jacqueline Bisset *Anna Crawley* • Martin Ritt *Hans Barlach* • Robert Shaw *Richard Gastman* • Helmut Qualtinger *Von Schwendi* • Gabriele Ferzetti *Dr Lutz* • Rita Calderoni *Nadine* • Friedrich Dürrenmatt *Friedrich* • Donald Sutherland *Corpse* ■ *Dir* Maximilian Schell • *Scr* Friedrich Dürrenmatt, Bo Goldmann, Maximilian Schell, from the novel *The Judge and His Hangman* by Friedrich Dürrenmatt

The End of the Golden Weather ★★★ **PG**

Drama
1992 · NZ · Colour · 98mins

A rare chance to see this cult oddity from New Zealand, which may be too eccentric for some. Director Ian Mune and playwright Bruce Mason adapted Mason's one-man show about the imaginary world of a 12-year-old boy (Stephen Fulford). The gaggle of grotesques on parade lacks a single redeeming feature; meanwhile, the age gap between the adolescent boy and his father widens to a predictable chasm. Unlike the curate's egg, this family drama really is good in parts. Contains some swearing. ▥

Stephen Fulford *Geoff* • Stephen Papps *Firpo* • Paul Gittins *Dad* • Gabrielle Hammond *Mum* • David Taylor *Ted* • Alexandra Marshall *Molly* ■ *Dir* Ian Mune • *Scr* Ian Mune, Bruce Mason, from the play by Bruce Mason

End of the Line ★★★ **PG**

Drama
1987 · US · Colour · 103mins

It's man versus the system time again in a warm and touching drama about tradition and doing the right thing. Shocked when they hear the news that their freight depot is about to be closed down, railway workers Wilford Brimley and Levon Helm steal a locomotive and head to corporate headquarters in Chicago to make their feelings known to the chairman, Henderson Forsyth. Beautifully played by the down-home lead duo, they don't come more graceful than this. ▥

Wilford Brimley *Will Haney* • Levon Helm *Leo Pickett* • Mary Steenburgen *Rose Pickett* • Barbara Barrie *Jean Haney* • Henderson Forsythe *Thomas Clinton* • Bob Balaban

Warren Gerber • Kevin Bacon *Everett* • Holly Hunter *Charlotte* ■ *Dir* Jay Russell • *Scr* Jay Russell, John Wohlbruck

The End of the River ★★ **U**

Drama
1947 · UK · BW · 79mins

A curio, produced by Michael Powell and Emeric Pressburger and directed by Derek Twist, who had edited Powell's 1937 semi-documentary about Shetland islanders, *The Edge of the World*. The all-purpose exotic Sabu, who also appeared in Powell and Pressburger's *Black Narcissus*, here plays Manoel, forced to leave his jungle home for the corrupt and dirty city and finding himself on trial for murder. Despite a good cast and the Brazilian locations, the results are both confusing and disappointing. ▥

Sabu *Manoel* • Bibi Ferreira *Teresa* • Esmond Knight *Dantos* • Robert Douglas *Mr Jones* • Antoinette Cellier *Conceicao* • Torin Thatcher *Lisboa* • Orlando Martins *Harrigan* • Raymond Lovell *Colonel Porpino* • James Hayter *Chico* ■ *Dir* Derek Twist • *Scr* Wolfgang Wilhelm, from the novel *Death of a Common Man* by Desmond Holdridge

End of the Road ★

Drama
1970 · US · Colour · 110mins

One day, a visiting alien may alight upon a can of film containing this movie. After ten minutes, he'll switch it off and say to his alien comrade, "Fancy a beer, mate?" For few movies are as boringly awful as this one. Co-written by sixties satirist Terry Southern (the man who put the laughs into *Dr Strangelove* and the yawns into *The Magic Christian*), it's a counterculture affair with psychedelic trips, mental illness and a graphic message about abortion. Everyone looks stoned out of their minds and tends to cavort about naked.

Stacy Keach *Jake Horner* • Harris Yulin *Joe Morgan* • Dorothy Tristan *Rennie Morgan* • James Earl Jones *Doctor D* • Grayson Hall *Peggie Rankin* • Ray Brock *Sniperman/Mrs Dockey* • James Coco *School man* • Oliver Clark *Dog man* ■ *Dir* Aram Avakian • *Scr* Dennis McGuire, Terry Southern, Aram Avakian, from a novel by John Barth

End of the World ★

Science-fiction
1977 · US · Colour · 86mins

Space invaders use a Californian convent as a base of operations in their plot to blow up the Earth because mankind is polluting the universe. Christopher Lee lends a modicum of dignity to the incredibly tacky proceedings as a Catholic priest and his extra-terrestrial double who is controlling the murderous alien nuns. Tedious junk with a has-been cast, including Sue Lyon (*Lolita*).

Christopher Lee *Father Pergado/Zindar* • Sue Lyon *Sylvia Boran* • Kirk Scott *Professor Andrew Boran* • Dean Jagger *Ray Collins* • Lew Ayres *Beckerman* • Macdonald Carey *John Davis* • Liz Ross *Sister Patrizia* ■ *Dir* John Hayes • *Scr* Frank Ray Perilli

The End of Violence ★★ **15**

Thriller 1997 · US/Ger/Fr · Colour · 116mins

As a mysterious figure (Gabriel Byrne) uses surveillance cameras to keep watch over the city, a Hollywood producer (Bill Pullman), who's become rich thanks to the public's thirst for

blood, is kidnapped by inept gangsters. Escaping, he goes undercover and finds kindness on the streets; his wife (Andie MacDowell), meanwhile, tries to find him. The result is an uneasy mix of Fritz Lang determinism and Frank Capra optimism, but, in the hands of director Wim Wenders, it makes for a very watchable and oddly poignant film. Contains swearing. ▥

Bill Pullman *Mike* • Andie MacDowell *Paige* • Gabriel Byrne *Ray* • Loren Dean *Doc* • Traci Lind *Cat* • Rosalind Chao *Claire* • K Todd Freeman *Six* • Chris Douridas *Technician* ■ *Dir* Wim Wenders • *Scr* Nicholas Klein, from a story by Wim Wenders, Nicholas Klein

Endangered Species
★★★ **15**

Drama based on a true story
1982 · US · Colour · 92mins

A burnt-out New York cop moves west to investigate a series of cattle mutilations in director Alan Rudolph's offbeat thriller, based on a true-life incident. Is it the work of aliens performing surgical experiments as UFO fanatics speculate? Or does the answer lie with a covert germ warfare research programme? Local sheriff JoBeth Williams teams up with hard-nosed Robert Urich to expose the conspiracy in a suspense mystery with an edgy difference. ▥

Robert Urich *Ruben Castle* • JoBeth Williams *Harriet Purdue* • Paul Dooley *Joe Hiatt* • Hoyt Axton *Ben Morgan* • Peter Coyote *Steele* • Marin Kanter *MacKenzie Castle* • Gailard Sartain *Mayor* • Dan Hedaya *Peck* • Harry Carey Jr *Dr Emmer* ■ *Dir* Alan Rudolph • *Scr* Alan Rudolph, John Binder, from a story by Judson Klinger, Richard Woods

Endless Love ★★ **15**

Romantic drama
1981 · US · Colour · 110mins

Vaguely interesting for causing controversy at the time, this tacky tale of illicit teenage romance hasn't aged particularly well. Martin Hewitt and Brooke Shields are the mismatched youngsters who fall in love, much to the disapproval of the latter's father (Don Murray). Director Franco Zeffirelli brings a modicum of class and style to the affair, but not enough to overcome the cloying sentimentality on show. Hewitt fares better than Shields in the lead role but, ultimately, it was another teenager who made the most of this break: Tom Cruise, here making his feature debut. ▥

Brooke Shields *Jade Butterfield* • Martin Hewitt *David Axelrod* • Tom Cruise *Billy* • Shirley Knight *Anne Butterfield* • Don Murray *Hugh Butterfield* • Richard Kiley *Arthur Axelrod* • Beatrice Straight *Rose Axelrod* • James Spader *Keith* • Ian Ziering *Sammy* ■ *Dir* Franco Zeffirelli • *Scr* Judith Rascoe, from the novel by Scott Spencer

Endless Night ★★★ **15**

Psychological thriller
1971 · UK · Colour · 95mins

A torrid sex scene shatters the carefully established suspense in this dark thriller – hardly the kind of thing you'd expect from an Agatha Christie mystery. But then, this is not a typical offering from the queen of crime. Country manors might have been *de rigueur* for Christie, but gypsy curses

were much more unusual. Comedy specialist Sidney Gilliat had proved with *Green for Danger* (1946) that he was capable of handling whodunits, and he keeps you guessing here as American heiress Hayley Mills becomes convinced that not even husband Hywel Bennett and best friend Britt Ekland can protect her from a malevolent menace. ▭

Hayley Mills *Ellie* • Hywel Bennett *Michael* • Britt Ekland *Greta* • George Sanders *Lippincott* • Per Oscarsson *Santonix* • Peter Bowles *Reuben* • Lois Maxwell *Cora* • Aubrey Richards *Philpott* ■ *Dir* Sidney Gilliat • *Scr* Sidney Gilliat, from the novel by Agatha Christie

The Endless Summer ★★★
Documentary   1966 · US · Colour · 91mins

Two surfers, Mike Hynson and Robert August, travel the world in search of the "perfect wave" in this classic surfing documentary put together by film-maker Bruce Brown. Capturing the subculture at the precise time it was having the most profound influence on popular music and Californian lifestyles, the duo visit the virgin beaches of Africa, Australia, New Zealand, Tahiti and Hawaii for time-elapsed sunsets and fabulous shots of them riding wild surf. Groovy music by the Sandals, a five-piece surfing outfit, accompany the beautiful images and Brown's hip surfer-speak is a history lesson in itself.

Bruce Brown *Narrator* ■ *Dir/Scr* Bruce Brown

The Endless Summer II ★★
Documentary   1994 · US · Colour · 107mins

Twenty-eight years on, the search for the "perfect wave" continues with tanned and toned beach boys Pat O'Connell and Robert "Wingnut" Weaver being followed around the world by all-round film-maker Bruce Brown. This time it's Alaska, Bali, Fiji, France and Java getting the photographic picture postcard treatment. Fans of the original will be equally impressed by this stunningly-shot document, despite Brown's narration being slightly more pretentious and irritating.

Dir Bruce Brown • *Scr* Bruce Brown, Dana Brown

Endurance ★★★ U
Sports documentary drama
1998 · US/UK/Ger · Colour · 94mins

Bud Greenspan may have supervised the Atlanta Olympic sequences, but this portrait of the veteran Ethiopian distance runner, Haile Gebrselassie, is very much the work of ethnographer Leslie Woodhead. The athlete's young nephew, Yonas Zergaw, plays him in a series of dramatic reconstructions showing how he ran 12 miles every day to the school nearest his home village of Asela and then relocated to Addis Ababa in the hope of emulating his 10,000-metre hero, Miruts Yifter ("The Shifter"). With Haile's sister, Shawanness, playing their mother, and his wife Alem Tellahun as herself, this is a stirring study of raw ambition and awesome dedication. An English/Amharic language film.

Haile Gebrselassie *Gebrselassie* • Gebrselassie Bekele • Alem Tellahun • Yonas Zergaw *Young Haile*

Gebrselassie • Shawanness Gebrselassie *Haile's mother* • Tedesse Haile *Haile's father* ■ *Dir* Leslie Woodhead, Bud Greenspan • *Scr* Leslie Woodhead

Enemies, a Love Story
★★★★ 15
Comedy drama   1989 · US · Colour · 114mins

A wonderfully lyrical and multi-layered ensemble piece, about the painful, tangled relationships of a group of Jewish immigrants in postwar New York. The acting is simply sublime, particularly from Lena Olin as a disturbed but passionate Holocaust survivor and Ron Silver as her emotionally repressed, egocentric lover. Director Paul Mazursky has fashioned a deeply moving, thought-provoking movie which, despite suffering marginally from insufficient light and shade, manages to challenge the mind while stirring the heart. ▭

Anjelica Huston *Tamara* • Ron Silver *Herman Broder* • Lena Olin *Masha* • Margaret Sophie Stein *Yadwiga* • Judith Malina *Masha's mother* • Alan King *Rabbi Lembeck* • Rita Karin *Mrs Schreier* ■ *Dir* Paul Mazursky • *Scr* Roger L Simon, Paul Mazursky, from the novel by Isaac Bashevis Singer

The Enemy Below ★★★★ PG
Second World War drama
1957 · US · Colour · 93mins

Here's the very best submarine movie of its kind: a stunning drama about a Second World War German U-boat and the US destroyer that's stalking it, whose captains only meet in the final reel. As the respective naval skippers, Curt Jurgens and, particularly, Robert Mitchum turn in fine performances. The special effects won an Oscar, but it is the direction by former crooner Dick Powell that is really remarkable. There's superb use of CinemaScope, the ideal format for submarines, and Powell's taut handling of the action makes this one of his finest movie achievements. ▭

Robert Mitchum *Captain Murrell* • Curt Jurgens *Von Stolberg* • Al Hedison [David Hedison] *Lieutenant Ware* • Theodore Bikel *Schwaffer* • Russell Collins *Doctor* • Kurt Kreuger *Von Holem* • Frank Albertson *Chief Petty Officer Crain* ■ *Dir* Dick Powell • *Scr* Wendell Mayes, from the novel by DA Rayner

Enemy Mine ★★★★ 15
Science-fiction fantasy
1985 · US · Colour · 89mins

Star Wars meets *Love Thy Neighbour* as Earthman Dennis Quaid and lizard-like alien Louis Gossett Jr (virtually unrecognisable under very impressive scaly make-up) crash-land on an unknown planet and learn that co-operation equals survival. Director Wolfgang Petersen makes this racial tolerance plea in outer space disguise a satisfying blend of action spills and emotional thrills. It touches both the brain and heart, remaining true to its pulp science-fiction roots while never being anything less than engrossing entertainment. Contains some violence and swearing. ▭

Dennis Quaid *Willis Davidge* • Louis Gossett Jr *Jeriba Shigan* • Brion James *Stubbs* • Richard Marcus *Arnold* • Carolyn McCormick *Morse* • Bumper Robinson *Zammis* • Jim

Mapp *Old Drac* • Lance Kerwin *Wooster* ■ *Dir* Wolfgang Petersen • *Scr* Edward Khmara, from a story by Barry Longyear

An Enemy of the People
★★★ U
Period drama   1977 · US · Colour · 106mins

Action hero Steve McQueen peers through a thicket of beard to take on a much-coveted role as the doctor whose warning that the local spa is polluted leads to antagonism from the small town's inhabitants. The theme of the prophet in his own country was to carry through to *Jaws*, and George Schaefer's direction is as worthy as McQueen's performance. But Charles Durning's counterbalance to the doctor's righteous indignation shows us what real acting is, and how dull McQueen seems in comparison. ▭

Steve McQueen *Dr Thomas Stockmann* • Charles Durning *Peter Stockmann* • Bibi Andersson *Catherine Stockmann* • Eric Christmas *Morten Kiil* • Michael Cristofer *Hovstad* • Richard A Dysart [Richard Dysart] *Aslaksen* • Michael Higgins *Billing* • Richard Bradford *Captain Forster* ■ *Dir* George Schaefer • *Scr* Alexander Jacobs, from the play by Henrik Ibsen, Arthur Miller (adaptation)

An Enemy of the People
★★ U
Drama   1989 · Ind · Colour · 95mins

In many ways this adaptation of Ibsen's play (also released as *Ganashatru*) was a courageous enterprise, as director Satyajit Ray was returning to work after a four-year hiatus following a heart attack and was forbidden to shoot on location by his doctors. However, while we can forgive the studio-bound feel and can applaud Ray's attempt to expose the corruption and superstition that blight Indian society, it's hard to ignore the fact that this is a dull film made almost interminable by the impossibly earnest performance of Soumitra Chatterjee as the doctor trying to close a temple following the contamination of its water supply. In Bengali with English subtitles. ▭

Soumitra Chatterjee *Dr Ashok Gupta* • Ruma Guha-Thakurta *Maya Gupta* • Dhritiman Chatterjee *Nichit Gupta* • Mamata Shankar *Ranu Gupta* • Dipankar Dey *Haridas Bagchi* • Subhendu Chatterjee *Biresh* ■ *Dir* Satyajit Ray • *Scr* Satyajit Ray, from the play by Henrik Ibsen

Enemy of the State
★★★★ 15
Spy thriller   1998 · US · Colour · 128mins

Expert direction by Tony Scott and a winning central performance by Will Smith give this cracking high-tech thriller extra edge and appeal. When an incriminating tape revealing the murder of congressman Jason Robards accidentally ends up in Smith's possession, he finds himself relentlessly pursued by corrupt Jon Voight and his posse of electronic trackers, who use spy satellites, transmitters and all manner of undercover gizmos to trace him. *The Fugitive* meets *The Conversation* in a dynamically exciting action adventure that's both intriguing and scarily thought-provoking. Contains swearing. ▭ **DVD**

Will Smith *Robert Clayton Dean* • Gene Hackman *Brill* • Jon Voight *Reynolds* • Lisa Bonet *Rachel Banks* • Regina King *Carla Dean* • Ian Hart *Bingham* • Jason Lee *Zavitz* • Gabriel Byrne *"Brill"* • Jason Robards Jr *Hammersly* • Tom Sizemore *Pintero* ■ *Dir* Tony Scott • *Scr* David Marconi

Enemy Territory ★★ 18
Action   1987 · US · Colour · 85mins

An exercise in urban terror that was perhaps inspired by *The Most Dangerous Game*. Gary Frank is an insurance agent whose job takes him into a dangerous part of the city. He and telephone man Ray Parker Jr (composer of *Ghostbusters*) are quickly targeted by a particularly vicious street gang, and spend the rest of the movie hiding and trying to get out of the building. The better parts of the movie are those that don't take themselves completely seriously, including Jan-Michael Vincent as a paranoid ex-soldier who has converted his apartment into a bunker. ▭

Gary Frank *Barry* • Ray Parker Jr *Jackson* • Jan-Michael Vincent *Parker* • Frances Foster *Elva Briggs* • Tony Todd *The count* • Stacey Dash *Toni Briggs* • Deon Richmond *Chet* • Tiger Haynes *Barton* ■ *Dir* Peter Manoogian • *Scr* Stuart M Kaminsky, Bobby Liddell, from a story by Stuart M Kaminsky

The Enemy Within ★★★ 12
Thriller   1994 · US · Colour · 86mins

Would anyone dare to challenge the authority of Uncle Sam and overthrow an elected US government? That's the intriguing premise behind this efficient remake of the 1964 Burt Lancaster/Kirk Douglas film *Seven Days in May*. By TV movie standards, a strong cast has been assembled here, led by Forest Whitaker and Sam Waterston, and the performances are professional enough. But it lacks the raw power that Lancaster and Douglas brought to the original and director Jonathan Darby's handling of the suspense fails to match John Frankenheimer's. ▭

Forest Whitaker *Colonel Mac Casey* • Sam Waterston *President William Foster* • Dana Delany *Chief of Staff Betsy Corcoran* • Jason Robards [Jason Robards Jr] *General Lloyd* • Josef Sommer *Secretary of Defense Potter* • George Dzundza *Jake* ■ *Dir* Jonathan Darby • *Scr* Ron Bass [Ronald Bass], Darryl Ponicsan, from the film *Seven Days in May* by Rod Serling, from the novel *Seven Days in May* by Fletcher Knebel, Charles Waldo Bailey

L'Enfance Nue ★★★
Drama   1968 · Fr · Colour · 83mins

Co-produced by François Truffaut this is a remarkable first feature from director Maurice Pialat, especially since the participants are not professional actors. This sensitive yet unsentimental tale focuses on a ten-year-old boy who is abandoned by his mother. Handed over to the social services, he is treated with dispassion and becomes a teenage nightmare when placed with foster parents. This extremely well-observed docudrama takes all perspectives into account, while the relationship the child develops with his aged grandmother, Marie Marc, is particularly touching. In French with English subtitles.

Michel Terrazon *François* • Linda Gutemberg *Simone* • Raoul Billerey *Roby* • Pierette

Deplanque *Josette* • Marie-Louise Thierry *Mme Minguet* • Rene Thierry *M Minguet* • Henri Puff *Raoul* • Marie Marc *Meme* • Maurice Coussoneau *Letillon* ■ *Dir/Scr* Maurice Pialat

L'Enfant Sauvage ★★★★ U

Period drama based on a true story
1970 · Fr · BW · 84mins

This is a historical drama that eschews costume finery in favour of philosophical debate. The film tackles such complex notions as natural law, the supremacy of society, the right to resist injustice and the conflict between scientific research and emotional subjectivity, but it is also a very human tale. Set in 1798, it relates the true story of Victor (Jean-Pierre Cargol), the forest foundling who is introduced to the basics of civilisation by Dr Jean Itard (Truffaut). Making pleasing use of antiquated cinematic devices and actual journal extracts, this has a documentary feel that not only makes it more authentic, but also more fascinating. In French with English subtitles.

Jean-Pierre Cargol *Victor, the boy* • Paul Villé *Rémy* • François Truffaut *Dr Jean Itard* • Françoise Seigner *Madame Guérin* • Claude Miller *Monsieur Lemeri* • Annie Miller *Madame Lemeri* ■ *Dir* François Truffaut • *Scr* François Truffaut, Jean Gruault, from the non-fiction book *Mémoire et Rapport sur Victor de L'Aveyron* by Jean-Marc Gaspard Itard

Les Enfants de Lumière ★★★★★

Compilation
1995 · Fr · BW and Colour · 102mins

Several fictional features and personal memoirs were commissioned to commemorate the centenary of cinema, but few celebrate film's unique ability to entertain, move, provoke or reminisce with such charm and intelligence as this superb French compilation. Divided thematically, this priceless collection of greatest clips features a *Who's Who* of French film, with Gérard Philipe and Jean Marais rubbing shoulders with the great Jean Gabin and Jean-Louis Barrault, and Arletty, Michèle Morgan and Simone Signoret competing for the soft-focus spotlight. The brainchild of top producer Jacques Perrin, it also has the benefit of a spine-tingling score from Michel Legrand. In English and French with subtitles.

Anthony Valentine *Narrator* ■ *Dir* Andre Asseo, Pierre Billard, Alain Corneau, Claude Miller, Claude Sautet

Les Enfants du Paradis ★★★★★ PG

Classic drama   1945 · Fr · BW · 181mins

The most courageous and elegant act of defiance in cinema history, this beautiful tale of Parisian popular theatre in the early 19th century was shot under the very noses of the Gestapo towards the end of the Second World War. Determined to premiere the picture in a liberated France, director Marcel Carné tolerated all manner of delays, including the absence of cast members sent on missions for the Resistance. On the surface, the film is a tale of unrequited love, but it is in fact a tribute to the indomitable spirit of Free France, as

personified by Garance, the legendary actress who resists all attempts to possess her. The message was tarnished slightly by postwar revelations that Arletty (who played Garance) had taken Nazi lovers. In French with English subtitles.

Arletty *Garance* • Jean-Louis Barrault *Baptiste Debureau* • Pierre Brasseur *Frédérick Lemaître* • Marcel Herrand *Lacenaire* • Pierre Renoir *Jéricho, the old clothes man* • Maria Casarès *Natalie* • Etienne Decroux *Anselme Debureau* ■ *Dir* Marcel Carné • *Scr* Jacques Prévert, Marcel Carné, from an idea by Jacques Prévert, Marcel Carné • *Art Director* Alexandre Trauner, Léon Barsacq, Raymond Gabutti

Les Enfants Terribles ★★★★

Drama   1949 · Fr · BW · 107mins

Budgetary restraint goes a long way to explaining the effectiveness of this adaptation of Jean Cocteau's 1929 novel. By shooting much of the action in his own apartment and on the stage of the Théâtre Pigalle, director Jean-Pierre Melville was able to reproduce the simmering claustrophobia that makes the obsessive relationship between brother and sister Edouard Dermit and Nicole Stéphane so intense. Although Cocteau narrates and directed the seaside scene, the film's erotic tension and visual poetry are down to Melville's finesse, which ensures that the tale is troubling tragicomedy instead of melodramatic high camp. In French with English subtitles.

Nicole Stéphane *Elisabeth* • Edouard Dermit *Paul* • Jacques Bernard *Gerad* • Renée Cosima *Dargelos/Agathe* • Roger Gaillard *Gerard's Uncle* • Melvyn Martin *Michael* • Jean Cocteau *Narrator* ■ *Dir* Jean-Pierre Melville • *Scr* Jean Cocteau, Jean-Pierre Melville, from the novel by Jean Cocteau

L'Enfer ★★★ 15

Thriller   1994 · Fr · Colour · 98mins

L'Enfer, or *Hell*, began in 1964 as a movie starring Romy Schneider and Serge Reggiani and directed by Henri-Georges Clouzot (*The Wages of Fear* and *Les Diaboliques*). Shortly after shooting started, Reggiani quit through illness; then Clouzot himself was felled by a heart attack. Only after Clouzot's death in 1977 did the project pass to Claude Chabrol. It's a story about pathological jealousy, acted to the hilt by the sensuous and possibly two-timing Emmanuelle Béart, whose character is married to seething hotel owner François Cluzet. Things get seriously out of control, tipping the picture quickly into the realm of black comedy. Not one of Chabrol's best, but still good fun. A French language film. 🎬

Emmanuelle Béart *Nelly* • François Cluzet *Paul* • Nathalie Cardone *Marylin* • André Wilms *Doctor Arnoux* • Marc Lavoine *Martineau* • Christiane Minazzoli *Madame Vernon* • Dora Doll *Madame Chabert* • Mario David *Duhamel* ■ *Dir* Claude Chabrol • *Scr* Henri-Georges Clouzot, José-André Lacour

The Enforcer ★★ 18

Crime thriller   1976 · US · Colour · 92mins

The third of the five *Dirty Harry* pictures and the point at which the series went into an irretrievable tailspin. Clint

Eastwood returns as Harry Callahan, but the identikit collection of corrupt cops and crazed killers confronting him is hardly a match for his unique talents. In this tiresome, violent tale of kidnapping, San Francisco becomes a shooting gallery in which the characters are set up simply to be shot down. Only Harry's new partner (played with spirit by Tyne Daly) has any depth, but this intriguing relationship is wasted in a welter of sexist one-liners. Contains violence, swearing and nudity. 🎬

Clint Eastwood *Harry Callahan* • Tyne Daly *Kate Moore* • Bradford Dillman *Captain McKay* • Harry Guardino *Lieutenant Bressler* • Bookwalter DeVeren *Bobby Maxwell* • John Mitchum *DiGeorgio* • John Crawford *Mayor* ■ *Dir* James Fargo • *Scr* Stirling Silliphant, Dean Reisner, from characters created by Harry Julian Fink, RM Fink

England Made Me ★★★★

Drama   1973 · UK · Colour · 100mins

Graham Greene's least-known novel was the inspiration behind this under-rated film which, like *Cabaret* the year before, offers a fascinating glimpse of pre-Second World War Germany. Michael York plays a sponging Englishman whose dealings with Peter Finch's sinister financier almost lead him to become incestuously involved with his own sister (Hildegard Neil). The potential for atmosphere is vividly explored by director Peter Duffell.

Peter Finch *Erich Krogh* • Michael York *Anthony Farrant* • Hildegard Neil *Kate Farrant* • Michael Hordern *F Minty* • Joss Ackland *Hiller* • Tessa Wyatt *Liz Davidge* • Michael Sheard *Fromm* • William Baskiville *[Bill Baskiville] Stein* ■ *Dir* Peter Duffell • *Scr* Peter Duffell, Desmond Cory, from the novel by Graham Greene

The English Patient ★★★★★ 15

Second World War romantic drama
1996 · US · Colour · 155mins

Plaudits rained on this sublime adaptation of Michael Ondaatje's difficult novel, which leaps between the past, set against the sweeping backdrop of the Sahara, and the present in an Italy ravaged by the Second World War. Ralph Fiennes stars as the mortally-wounded pilot mentally reliving his adulterous affair with Kristin Scott Thomas. The burgeoning love affair between his nurse, Juliette Binoche, and a soldier, Naveen Andrews, instils hope after so much tragedy. Oscars aside, Anthony Minghella's film divided audiences into two factions: those who were moved, and those who were not. 🎬 **DVD**

Ralph Fiennes *Almásy* • Juliette Binoche *Hana* • Willem Dafoe *Caravaggio* • Kristin Scott Thomas *Katharine Clifton* • Naveen Andrews *Kip* • Colin Firth *Geoffrey Clifton* • Julian Wadham *Madox* • Kevin Whately *Hardy* ■ *Dir* Anthony Minghella • *Scr* Anthony Minghella, from the novel by Michael Ondaatje

English without Tears ★★

Romantic comedy   1944 · UK · BW · 88mins

Five years after screenwriters Terence Rattigan and Anatole de Grunwald and cinematographer Bernard Knowles collaborated on the witty comedy of manners *French without Tears*, they reunited for this less perceptive, but

still amusing, satire on the leisured classes at war. While the romance between wealthy ATS girl Penelope Ward and butler Michael Wilding had its social significance, the attack on the League of Nations (which had failed to prevent the Second World War) would have struck the loudest chord with contemporary audiences.

Michael Wilding *Tom Gilbey* • Lilli Palmer *Brigid Knudsen* • Penelope Ward *Joan Heseltine* • Claude Dauphin *Jean de Freyeinet* • Roland Culver *Sir Cosmo Brandon* • Peggy Cummins *Bobby Heseltine* • Margaret Rutherford *Lady Christabel Beauclerk* ■ *Dir* Harold French • *Scr* Terence Rattigan, Anatole de Grunwald

The Englishman Who Went up a Hill, but Came down a Mountain ★★★ PG

Romantic comedy
1995 · UK · Colour · 95mins

Hugh Grant returned to the persona he does best – mildly bumbling, nice Englishness – for this engaging slice of whimsy, which harks back (a little optimistically, it must be said) to the Ealing comedies of old. Grant plays a cartographer who is called upon to rule on whether a Welsh village's beloved landmark is a hill or a mountain; the canny locals are determined it's the latter and proceed to run rings around the hapless Grant. The plot is about as a slight as the slope in question, but the talented playing of the cast (Tara FitzGerald, Colm Meaney, Ian Hart) makes it a modest treat. 🎬

Hugh Grant *Reginald Anson* • Tara FitzGerald *Betty of Cardiff* • Colm Meaney *Morgan the Goat* • Ian Hart *Johnny Shellshocked* • Kenneth Griffith *Reverend Jones* • Ian McNeice *George Garrad* • Robert Blythe *Ivor the Grocer* • Robert Pugh *Williams the Petroleum* ■ *Dir* Christopher Monger • *Scr* Christopher Monger, from a story by Ifor David Monger, Ivor Monger

Enigma ★★

Thriller   1982 · UK/Fr · Colour · 122mins

Director Jeannot Szwarc is a real movie buff, yet of his efforts only *Somewhere in Time* shows real quality. Others – *Santa Claus* or *Supergirl*, for example – are well-made without being inspiring. Similarly, this Cold War thriller is neither one thing nor another, and seems to have suffered some post-production rethinking plot-wise. A classy cast pretend they know what's going on as the KGB try to kill five dissidents in the west, only to find their way barred, not by James Bond, but unlikely CIA agent Martin Sheen. The title of this Anglo-French co-production is rather apt.

Martin Sheen *Alex Holbeck* • Brigitte Fossey *Karen* • Sam Neill *Dimitri Vasilkov* • Derek Jacobi *Kurt Limmer* • Michel Lonsdale *Bodley* • Frank Finlay *Canarsky* • David Baxt *Melton* • Kevin McNally *Bruno* ■ *Dir* Jeannot Szwarc • *Scr* John Briley, from the novel *Enigma Sacrifice* by Michael Barak

The Enigma of Kaspar Hauser ★★★★ PG

Historical drama
1974 · W Ger · Colour · 110mins

The Nuremberg of the 1820s is here seen through the eyes of Kaspar Hauser, the real-life child genius who

was dumped in the town square after a lifetime of beatings and sensory deprivation. Werner Herzog's fact-based drama, though ostensibly the tale of one man's response to civilisation, is really a study of landscape, and more a film about awakening than socio-political values. Yet it's easy to sneer at the smug bourgeois attitudes of the townsfolk and be captivated by Bruno S's eager expression as he drinks in sights and sounds like a greedy, excited child. In German with English subtitles. 🎞

Bruno S *Kaspar* • Brigitte Mira *Kathe, the servant* • Willy Semmelrogge *Circus director* • Hans Musaus *Unknown man* • Michael Kroecher *Lord Stanhope* • Henry van Lyck *Captain* ■ *Dir/Scr* Werner Herzog

L'Ennui ★★★ 18
Erotic comedy drama
1998 · Fr · Colour · 122mins
Director Cédric Kahn eschews the pleasure principle to explore the lust for power that underpins so many modern relationships. However, with its repeated acts of perfunctory sex and the slow descent into manic envy by an intellectually moribund academic, this adaptation of Alberto Moravia's novel might have made for heavy going, were it not for the outstanding performances of Charles Berling and Sophie Guillemin. As the physically unremarkable, socially inept teenager blithely fuelling her lover's neurosis, the debuting Guillemin is a revelation, while Berling's midlife misery is agonisingly persuasive. In French with English subtitles.

Charles Berling *Martin* • Sophie Guillemin *Cécilia* • Arielle Dombasle *Sophie* • Robert Kramer *Leopold Meyers* • Alice Grey *Cécilia's mother* • Maurice Antoni *Cécilia's father* ■ *Dir* Cédric Kahn • *Scr* Cédric Kahn, Laurence Ferreira Barbosa, Gilles Taurand, from the novel *La Noia* by Alberto Moravia

Enormous Changes at the Last Minute ★★★
Drama 1983 · US · Colour · 98mins
Also known as *Trumps*, this is a collection of three dramas (two filmed in 1982 and one back in 1978) based on the stories of Grace Paley. While the trio don't completely work together, this is nonetheless an interesting group of stories about women living in New York and their relationships with their families and the men in their lives. The impressive cast includes David Strathairn, Ellen Barkin and Kevin Bacon, while writer John Sayles went on to direct *Eight Men Out*.

Maria Tucci *Alexandra* • Ellen Barkin *Virginia* • Lynn Milgrim *Faith* • Sudie Bond *Mrs Raftery* • Kevin Bacon *Dennis* • Didi Velez *Blanca* • David Strathairn *Jerry* • Jeffrey DeMunn *Ricardo* ■ *Dir* Mirra Bank, Ellen Hovde, Muffie Meyer • *Scr* John Sayles, Susan Rice, from stories by Grace Paley

Ensign Pulver ★★
Comedy drama 1964 · US · Colour · 104mins
Mister Roberts had been an overwhelming triumph on stage and screen. So, spurred on by the fact that Jack Lemmon had won an Oscar as Ensign Pulver, Warner Bros decided to push out the boat once more. Robert Walker Jr tries valiantly to recapture the impishness of the wheeler-dealer Pulver, but (like the rest of the cast) he never emerges from the shadow of his illustrious predecessor. The shipboard comedy is infantile, and director Joshua Logan gives the island sequences a daytime soap feel.

Robert Walker Jr *Ensign Pulver* • Burl Ives *Captain* • Walter Matthau *Doc* • Tommy Sands *Bruno* • Millie Perkins *Scotty* • Kay Medford *Head nurse* • Larry Hagman *Billings* • Gerald S O'Loughlin *Lasueur* • Sal Papa *Gabrowski* • Jack Nicholson *Dolan* ■ *Dir* Joshua Logan • *Scr* Joshua Logan, Peter S Feibleman, from characters created by Joshua Logan, Thomas Heggen

Enter Arsene Lupin ★★
Crime 1944 · US · BW · 71mins
Hungarian exile and one-time cinematographer Charles Korvin made his acting debut here as writer Maurice Leblanc's notorious gentleman thief. But for once, purloining gems and avoiding the clutches of inspector J Carrol Naish are nowhere near as important as stealing the heart of Ella Raines. Sloppily scripted by Bertram Millhauser and directed with little suspense by Ford Beebe, the film's biggest crime is wasting a supporting cast that includes Gale Sondergaard and Miles Mander, both of whom were seen to much better advantage in Universal's *Sherlock Holmes* series.

Charles Korvin *Arsene Lupin* • Ella Raines *Stacie* • J Carrol Naish *Ganimard* • George Dolenz *Dubose* • Gale Sondergaard *Bessie Seagrave* • Miles Mander *Charles Seagrave* • Leyland Hodgson *Constable Ryder* ■ *Dir* Ford Beebe • *Scr* Bertram Millhauser, from characters created by Maurice Leblanc

Enter Laughing ★★★★ U
Comedy 1967 · US · Colour · 110mins
...and exit giggling at director Carl Reiner's adaptation of the play based on his early career experiences. Reni Santoni is the young man who defies mother Shelley Winters and decides to become a professional actor. He goes through the usual rituals of acceptance before realising his dream. Very astute and witty stuff, with José Ferrer's turn as a pompous producer worth the price of admission alone.

Reni Santoni *David Kolowitz* • José Ferrer *Mr Marlowe* • Shelley Winters *Mrs Kolowitz* • Elaine May *Angela* • Jack Gilford *Mr Foreman* • Janet Margolin *Wanda* • David Opatoshu *Mr Kolowitz* • Michael J Pollard *Marvin* ■ *Dir* Carl Reiner • *Scr* Joseph Stein, Carl Reiner, from the play by Joseph Stein, from the novel by Carl Reiner

Enter Madame! ★★
Musical comedy drama 1933 · US · BW · 81mins
The wealthy husband (Cary Grant) of a tantrum-throwing opera star (Elissa Landi), constantly surrounded by an entourage of peculiar characters, has to cope with playing second fiddle to both her career and her cohorts. This film version of a 1920 Broadway hit comedy fails to survive the transfer to another medium or the passage of time. The coolly lovely and ladylike Landi (her singing dubbed by Nina Koshetz) was hardly the ideal choice for this extrovert role, but Grant exudes his usual easy charm, and director Elliott Nugent does his best to disguise the inadequacies of the piece with pace.

Elissa Landi *Lisa Della Robbia* • Cary Grant *Gerald Fitzgerald* • Lynne Overman *Mr Farnum* • Sharon Lynne *Flora Preston* • Michelette Burani *Bice* • Paul Porcasi *Archimede* • Adrian Rosley *Doctor* • Cecilia Parker *Aline Chalmers* ■ *Dir* Elliott Nugent, • *Scr* Charles Brackett, Gladys Lehman, from the play by Gilda Varesi Archibald, Dorothea Donn-Byrne

Enter the Dragon ★★★★ 18
Martial arts action
1973 · US · Colour · 96mins
Bruce Lee, "the Fred Astaire of martial arts", is at his balletic, brilliant best in this kung fu classic that, tragically, proved to be his last completed film. When his sister commits suicide rather than succumb to the henchmen of a ruthless master criminal, Lee leaves the Shaolin temple where he teaches kung fu and spiritual discipline to become a James Bond-style secret agent. When he arrives at an island fortress to take part in a notoriously brutal martial arts tournament, he finds himself having to smash an opium ring and a white slavery racket, as well as fight for his own life. Director Robert Clouse produces a series of fast, furious, intricate and athletic fight scenes that, in the opinion of many aficionados, have yet to be bettered. 🎞 **DVD**

Bruce Lee *Lee* • John Saxon *Roper* • Jim Kelly *Williams* • Kien Shih *Han* • Bob Wall *Oharra* • Ahna Capri *Tania* • Angela Mao Ying *Su-Lin* • Betty Chung *Mei Ling* ■ *Dir* Robert Clouse • *Scr* Michael Allin

Enter the Ninja ★★★ 18
Martial arts action
1981 · US · Colour · 91mins
After the kung fu mania of the early seventies cooled off – following the unfortunate death of martial arts superstar Bruce Lee – came a spate of movies relishing the silent but lethal killing machine that is the Japanese ninja. An evil Philipino crime baron (Christopher George) is intimidating a farmer into giving him his precious land. But he reckons without visiting friend and ninja Franco Nero who makes short shrift of various henchmen until he is forced into a real ninja-style showdown with all the trimmings laid on by far-eastern superstar Sho Kosugi. 🎞

Franco Nero *Cole* • Susan George *Mary-Ann Landers* • Sho Kosugi *Hasegawa* • Alex Courtney *Frank Landers* • Will Hare *Dollars* • Zachi Noy *The "Hook"* • Dale Ishimoto *Komori* • Christopher George *Charles Venarius* ■ *Dir* Menahem Golan • *Scr* Dick Desmond

The Entertainer ★★★ PG
Drama 1960 · UK · BW · 99mins
John Osborne's follow-up to his ground-breaking *Look Back in Anger*, brought Laurence Olivier to the world of kitchen-sink drama. Olivier gives a stunning performance as music-hall has-been Archie Rice, a seedy vaudeville artist who brings misery to all who know him. It was a personal triumph for Olivier on stage but, in enshrining the legendary actor's performance on celluloid, director Tony Richardson laid bare Olivier's technique. The result was too mannered and flopped at the box office, yet now can be viewed as an enduring record of that great stage production. It also boasts screen debuts from two future stars, Alan Bates and Albert Finney. Olivier married co-star Joan Plowright (who plays his protective daughter Jean) the following year. 🎞

Laurence Olivier *Archie Rice* • Brenda de Banzie *Phoebe Rice* • Joan Plowright *Jean* • Roger Livesey *Billy* • Alan Bates *Frank* • Daniel Massey *Graham* • Albert Finney *Mick Rice* • Miriam Karlin *Soubrette* • Shirley Anne Field *Tina* • Thora Hird *Mrs Lapford* ■ *Dir* Tony Richardson • *Scr* John Osborne, Nigel Kneale, from the play by John Osborne

The Entertainer ★★★
Drama 1975 · US/Ausl · Colour · 106mins
Jack Lemmon boldly goes where few actors would dare to go – into the sleazy footsteps of Laurence Olivier as on-the-skids music hall comedian, Archie Rice. John Osborne's play, written for Olivier, is switched from Britain to the US and from the Suez Crisis to 1944. Married Archie's young *femme fatale* this time is Bambi (Annette O'Toole), whose rich father could back a musical to revive Archie's fortunes, but it doesn't work out. Directed by Donald Wrye, this is a pointless remake that has none of the social savagery of Osborne's original. Jack Lemmon contributes a fascinating reading of Archie, but the question remains: why bother?

Jack Lemmon *Archie Rice* • Ray Bolger *Billy Rice* • Sada Thompson *Phoebe Rice* • Tyne Daly *Jean* • Michael Cristofer *Frank* • Annette O'Toole *Bambi* • Mitchell Ryan *Mr Pasko* ■ *Dir* Donald Wrye • *Scr* Elliott Baker, from the play by John Osborne

Entertaining Angels: the Dorothy Day Story ★★★ 12
Period biographical drama
1996 · US · Colour · 106mins
Moira Kelly (*Chaplin*) stars as Dorothy Day in this moving and well-played family film set during the Depression era. Day was a radical journalist who later became a Catholic and devoted her life to looking after the poor. While younger viewers will learn about helping others and older viewers will feel uplifted, film buffs should also tune in for the cast, which includes Martin Sheen and a pre-*Austin Powers* Heather Graham. 🎞

Moira Kelly *Dorothy Day* • Martin Sheen *Peter Maurin* • Lenny Von Dohlen *Forster* • Heather Graham *Maggie* • Paul Lieber *Mike Gold* • Geoffrey Blake *Floyd Dell* • James Lancaster *Eugene O'Neill* • Boyd Kestner *Lionel Moise* ■ *Dir* Michael Ray Rhodes • *Scr* John Wells

Entertaining Mr Sloane ★★★ 15
Black comedy 1969 · UK · Colour · 89mins
The quintessential black comedy from Joe Orton, in which a brother and sister vie for the sexual favours of a muscle-bound stud, is brought to the screen with some panache by director Douglas Hickox. Clive Exton's semi-faithful script attempts to widen the play's rather enclosed feel, but Orton is essentially a playwright who belongs on a small stage with one chintz sofa. The cast is superb, particularly Beryl

Reid as Kath and Harry Andrews as her homosexual sibling. 🔲

Beryl Reid *Kath* • Peter McEnery *Mr Sloane* • Harry Andrews *Ed* • Alan Webb *Kemp* ■ *Dir* Douglas Hickox • *Scr* Clive Exton, from the play by Joe Orton

The Entity ★★★ 18
Horror   1981 · US · Colour · 119mins

Barbara Hershey is being repeatedly raped by an invisible evil spirit. But is the widowed mother under consistent demonic assault, or is it all in her subconscious? Director Sidney J Furie's above-average supernatural thriller has a literate script by genre writer Frank De Felitta from his own novel. Horror aficionados may be disappointed by the lack of *Exorcist*-style special effects, but a tense, fearful atmosphere is maintained precisely because of this creative choice. Hershey adds her own special magic to a complex chiller. Contains violence and swearing. 🔲

Barbara Hershey *Carla Moran* • Ron Silver *Phil Schneidermann* • David Labiosa *Billy* • George Coe *Dr Weber* • Margaret Blye [Maggie Blye] *Cindy Nash* • Jacqueline Brookes *Dr Cooley* • Richard Brestoff *Gene Kraft* ■ *Dir* Sidney J Furie • *Scr* Frank DeFelitta, from his novel

Entrapment ★★ 12
Romantic thriller
1999 · US · Colour · 108mins

Few 68-year-old actors would turn down a chance to enjoy old-fashioned heist high jinks with the beautiful Catherine Zeta-Jones. But surely Sean Connery must have had his doubts about whether co-starring with an actress of Zeta-Jones's calibre would make the romantic undertones plausible. They aren't, but in a film where logic, intelligence and charm take a back-seat to the leading lady's tight trousers, that isn't particularly surprising. The robbery scenes are mechanical yet effective, but what's shocking is the absence of the merest whiff of screen chemistry and the fact that somebody thought it would be a smart move to play the whole thing completely straight. 🔲 *DVD*

Sean Connery *Robert "Mac" MacDougal* • Catherine Zeta-Jones *Virginia "Gin" Baker* • Ving Rhames *Thibadeaux* • Will Patton *Hector Cruz* • Maury Chaykin *Conrad Greene* • Kevin McNally *Haas* • Terry O'Neill *Quinn* • Madhav Sharma *Security chief* ■ *Dir* Jon Amiel • *Scr* Ronald Bass, William Broyles Jr, from a story by Ronald Bass, Michael Hertzberg

Entre Nous ★★★ 15
Romantic drama 1983 · Fr · Colour · 110mins

Diane Kurys's absorbing third feature stars Miou-Miou as a former art student and Isabelle Huppert as a Jewish refugee, both bored with their lives and on the verge of walking out on their husbands and children. Taking the separation of her own parents as her starting point, Kurys offers a frank and convincing story that's set in a superbly evoked Lyons in the early fifties. The two fine female leads are matched by Guy Marchand as Huppert's husband, also a Jewish refugee whose only crime is his innate goodness. A French language film.

Miou-Miou *Madeleine* • Isabelle Huppert *Lena* • Guy Marchand *Michel* • Jean-Pierre Bacri

---

Costa • Robin Renucci *Raymond* • Patrick Bauchau *Carlier* • Jacques Alric *Monsieur Vernier* • Jacqueline Doyen *Madame Vernier* ■ *Dir* Diane Kurys • *Scr* Diane Kurys, from the book by Olivier Cohen, Diane Kurys

Equinox ★★★★ 15
Drama   1992 · US · Colour · 105mins

Alan Rudolph is one of the most eclectic directors currently working in American cinema. This latter-day fairy tale offers the part of a lifetime to Matthew Modine as chalk-and-cheese twins: one a violent gangster who longs to settle down, the other a tongue-tied geek besotted with an equally bashful Lara Flynn Boyle. Boyle finally emerges from the shadow of Donna, her character in *Twin Peaks*, with this exquisite portrayal of painful shyness. As you'd expect from Rudolph, the dialogue is intelligent and provocative, and he handles his excellent cast with great finesse. 🔲

Matthew Modine *Henry Petosa/Freddy Ace* • Lara Flynn Boyle *Beverly Franks* • Fred Ward *Mr Paris* • Tyra Ferrell *Sonya Kirk* • Marisa Tomei *Rosie Rivers* • Kevin J O'Connor *Russell Franks* • Lori Singer *Sharon Ace* • M Emmet Walsh *Pete Petosa* • Tate Donovan *Richie Nunn* ■ *Dir/Scr* Alan Rudolph

Equinox Flower ★★★★
Drama   1958 · Jap · Colour · 118mins

A film of parallel plotlines and elliptical shifts, this ranks among Yasujiro Ozu's most playful pictures, as well as being his first in colour. Exposing the ironic duality of the subservient "salaryman" who insists on being master in his own household, Ozu uses this two-act satire to espouse the emancipation of women and the emergence of youth. As the father dumbfounded by his daughter's decision to refuse an arranged liaison, Shin Saburi gives a fine display of stubborn impotence in the face of the quiet determination of the headstrong Ineko Arima and his prudent wife, Kinuyo Tanaka. A Japanese language film.

Shin Saburi *Watara Hirayama* • Kinuyo Tanaka *Kiyoko Hirayama* • Ineko Arima *Setsuko Hirayama* • Miyuki Kuwano *Hisako Hirayama* ■ *Dir* Yasujiro Ozu • *Scr* Kogo Noda, Yasujiro Ozu, from a novel by Ton Satomi

Equus ★★★ 15
Psychological drama
1977 · US · Colour · 132mins

Peter Shaffer's powerful play – about a boy whose repressed emotions lead him to blind six horses – was so acclaimed that it was inevitable it would become a film. However, this is very much a theatrical piece, and the set pieces that work so well on stage lose much of their impact on screen. For example, the long speeches delivered by psychiatrist Richard Burton hold theatre audiences spellbound, but here seem as flatly staged as a party political broadcast. Peter Firth is clearly in awe of Burton, and Sidney Lumet has too much respect for the text. 🔲

Richard Burton *Martin Dysart* • Peter Firth *Alan Strang* • Colin Blakely *Frank Strang* • Joan Plowright *Dora Strang* • Harry Andrews *Harry Dalton* • Eileen Atkins *Hesther Saloman* • Jenny Agutter *Jill Mason* • Kate Reid *Margaret Dysart* ■ *Dir* Sidney Lumet • *Scr* Peter Shaffer, from his play

---

Eraser ★★ 15
Action thriller   1996 · US · Colour · 106mins

Arnold Schwarzenegger is the "eraser" of the title – a federal marshal for the witness protection programme who protects witnesses by wiping out their identities (which usually involves him blowing up some building or other). Of course, for the purposes of this action movie, things don't go to plan, and he and damsel-in-distress Vanessa Williams have to dodge bullets, explosions and quips before our hero can save the day. A disappointing adventure, *Eraser* lacks the nonstop gung-ho action and entertainment we've come to expect from a Schwarzenegger movie. Contains violent scenes and swearing. 🔲 *DVD*

Arnold Schwarzenegger *US Marshal John Kruger* • James Caan *Deguerin* • Vanessa Williams [Vanessa L Williams] *Lee* • James Coburn *Beller* • Robert Pastorelli *Johnny C* • James Cromwell *Donahue* • Danny Nucci *Monroe* • Andy Romano *Harper* ■ *Dir* Charles Russell [Chuck Russell] • *Scr* Tony Puryear, Walon Green, from a story by Michael S Chernuchin, Tony Puryear, Walon Green

Eraserhead ★★★★ 18
Cult fantasy drama   1976 · US · BW · 85mins

Filmed over a five-year period, this is the legendary cult movie that put director David Lynch on the morbid mystery map. Lynch's surreal study in urban alienation, retarded sexuality and parental nightmare is a relentless assault on the senses (maternal ones especially) that recalls Luis Buñuel's groundbreaking *Un Chien Andalou* in its powerful graphic imagery and non-linear monochrome narrative. Consistently creepy, arcane and unsettling, many will find Lynch's intense mood piece increasingly uncomfortable to watch. 🔲

John Nance [Jack Nance] *Henry Spencer* • Charlotte Stewart *Mary* • Allen Joseph *Bill* • Jeanne Bates *Mary's mother* • Judith Anna Roberts *Beautiful girl across the hall* • Laurel Near *Lady in the radiator* • V Phipps-Wilson *Landlady* • Jack Fisk *Man in the planet* • Jean Lange *Grandmother* ■ *Dir/Scr* David Lynch

Erendira ★★★ 18
Drama
1982 · Mex/Fr/W Ger · Colour · 96mins

Laced with magical realism and black comedy, this sinister fable is based on stories by Gabriel Garcia Marquez. For once, Irene Papas's tempestuous gesturing is totally in keeping with the tone of the piece, as director Ruy Guerra exploits stylised designs and surreal locations to chronicle the bizarre events that ensue when Papas delivers granddaughter Claudia Ohana into prostitution to atone for the incineration of her house. With Ohana's recurrent visions and the sudden prosperity of everyone she encounters adding mysticism to the proceedings, *Erendira* is both troubling and entertaining. In Spanish with English subtitles.

Claudia Ohana *Erendira* • Irene Papas *Grandmother* • Oliver Wehe *Ulysses* • Michel Lonsdale *Senator* ■ *Dir* Ruy Guerra • *Scr* Gabriel Garcia Marquez, from his works

---

Eric ★★
Drama based on a true story
1975 · US · Colour · 100mins

Terminal disease time, with John Savage (who went on to star in *The Deer Hunter* three years later) as the athletic leukaemia sufferer who won't give in. Mark Hamill (who was soon to play Luke Skywalker in *Star Wars*) is one of his mates, but the main acting interest is in Patricia Neal, who plays Eric's mother. She suffered a series of strokes in the sixties, yet forced herself to act again – a story told in *The Patricia Neal Story* starring Glenda Jackson. Neal's presence gives this true-life story an extra dimension, but it's still the usual formula.

John Savage *Eric* • Patricia Neal *Doris* • Claude Akins *Sydney* • Sian Barbara Allen *Mary Lou* • Mark Hamill *Mark* • Eileen McDonough *Lisa* • Nehemiah Persoff *Dr Duchsenes* ■ *Dir* James Goldstone • *Scr* Nigel McKeand, Carol Evan McKeand, from the book by Doris Lund

Erik the Viking ★★ 15
Comedy adventure
1989 · UK · Colour · 89mins

The individual Pythons have come up with some classics over the years, but for every *Personal Services* and *A Fish Called Wanda* there is also a *Yellowbeard* and the likes of this sadly wanting Nordic spoof. Tim Robbins would probably prefer to forget his role as a sort of "New Man" Viking who seeks to put an end to such traditional activities as raping and looting. Despite the presence of John Cleese and writer/director Terry Jones in a top-flight British cast (which also includes Anthony Sher, Imogen Stubbs and John Gordon Sinclair), you can't escape the feeling that this was a lot more fun to make than it is to watch. Contains swearing.

Tim Robbins *Erik* • Mickey Rooney *Erik's grandfather* • Eartha Kitt *Freya* • Imogen Stubbs *Princess Aud* • John Cleese *Halfdan the Black* • Gary Cady *Keitel Blacksmith* • Antony Sher *Loki* • John Gordon-Sinclair *Ivar the Boneless* • Samantha Bond *Helga* • Tim McInnerny *Sven the Berserk* • Terry Jones *King Arnulf* ■ *Dir/Scr* Terry Jones

Erin Brockovich ★★★★ 15
Biographical drama
2000 · US · Colour · 131mins

It might resemble a standard "issue of the week" TV movie, but this drama's ace in the hole is Julia Roberts, who earns every cent of her $20 million salary as the spirited heroine. A twice-divorced mother of three, Erin lands a job in the office of small-time lawyer Albert Finney, where she stumbles across some misplaced medical records while filing real estate documents. Intrigued, she investigates, eventually uncovering evidence that a power company has wrecked the health of a local community with contaminated water. Based on a true story, Soderbergh's emotionally-rich drama is compulsive viewing, thanks to Roberts's throat-grabbing performance, Finney's loveable turn as a minor-league attorney well out of his depth and a perfectly pitched script by Susannah Grant. Contains swearing.

Julia Roberts *Erin Brockovich* • Albert Finney *Ed Masry* • Aaron Eckhart *George* • Marg

---

elgenberger *Donna Jensen* • Cherry Jones
amela Duncan • Peter Coyote *Kurt Potter* •
rin Brockovich-Ellis *Waitress* ■ *Dir* Steven
oderbergh • *Scr* Susannah Grant

Ermo ★★★★ 12

atirical drama
1994 · Chi/HK · Colour · 95mins

hinese cinema has occasionally been
enounced for lacking a sense of
umour, but no such accusations
ould be levelled at this sly satire
bout the impact socio-economic
eforms made at the centre of
overnment actually have on the
opulation as a whole. In the world
habited by a humble noodle-seller
uch as Ermo (a feisty portrayal by
lia), a job in the town and a large
elevision set are much-envied status
ymbols worth risking nearly all for.
Director Zhou Xiaowen superbly
aptures the industrious bustle of the
own, and the poverty and petty
ivalries of the countryside. In
Mandarin with English subtitles.
lia *Ermo* • Liu Peiqi *Xiazi, "Blind"* • Ge Zhijun
Village chief, Ermo's husband • Zhang Haiyan
Xiazi's wife • Yan Zhenguo *Huzi, Ermo's son*
■ *Dir* Zhou Xiaowen • *Scr* Lang Yun, from the
ovella by Xu Baoqi

Ernest Goes to Africa ★ PG

omedy adventure
1997 · US · Colour · 89mins

One of the most spectacularly unfunny
ilm franchises limps on, with Jim
Varney reprising his dim-witted loser
ole for the umpteenth time. This
nstalment finds the incompetent
handyman mixed up with diamond
smugglers and travelling to the wilds to
escue his girlfriend (Linda Kash). Even
small children are likely to find this too
nfantile. ▭
Jim Varney *Ernest* • Linda Kash *Renee* •
Jamie Bartlett *Thompson* ■ *Dir/Scr* John R
Cherry III

Ernest Goes to Camp ★ PG

Comedy　　　　　　1987 · US · Colour · 88mins

The appeal of American comedy star
Jim Varney remains bewildering to
British audiences, but he must have
something going for him if the movie
output of his Ernest P Worrell character
is anything to go by. This is the one
that launched the whole sorry saga,
with gormless Ernest (Varney) causing
havoc at a summer camp. The
charmless mugging of the star grates,
while the unappetising combination of
childish slapstick and cornball
sentimentality will only appeal to the
youngest viewers. ▭
Jim Varney *Ernest P Worrell* • Victoria Racimo
Nurse St Cloud • John Vernon *Sherman
Krader* • Iron Eyes Cody *Old Indian Chief* •
Lyle Alzado *Bronk Stinson* ■ *Dir* John R Cherry
III • *Scr* John Cherry III, Coke Sams

Ernest Goes to Jail ★★★ PG

Comedy　　　　　　1990 · US · Colour · 77mins

Jim Varney reprises his "mad as a
rat" routine as Ernest P Worrell, this
time finding himself holed up in jail
while an Ernest lookalike runs amok,
sullying his already dubious reputation.
Fans of Ernest come in two distinct
categories: children under 14 who wish
to suspend their brains for 90

minutes, and those who were never in
the habit of exercising their brains in
the first place. But, for whatever
reason, young children do adore the
man and will enjoy this typical tale as
much as the others. ▭
Jim Varney *Ernest P Worrell/Felix Nash/Auntie
Nelda* • Gailard Sartain *Chuck* • Bill Byrge
Bobby • Barbara Bush *Charlotte Sparrow* •
Barry Scott *Rubin Bartlett* • Randall "Tex"
Cobb *Lyle* • Dan Leegant *Oscar Pendlesmythe*
• Charles Napier *Warden* ■ *Dir* John Cherry
[John R Cherry III] • *Scr* Charlie Cohen

Ernest Goes to School ★ PG

Comedy　　　　　　1994 · US · Colour · 85mins

Jim Varney's unloveable creation
Ernest P Worrell gets a dose of
learning in yet another instalment in
this dim saga. Forced to return to the
classroom to finish his high school
diploma, the lowly janitor is
transformed into an intellectual with
the help of two mad scientists.
However, it's not long before the whole
school is plunged into chaos. Even by
the low standards of the franchise,
this is feeble stuff. ▭
Jim Varney *Ernest P Worrell* • Linda Kash
Gerta • Bill Byrge *Bobby* • Jason Michas
Donald • Sarah Chalk [Sarah Chalke] *Maisy* ■
Dir/Scr Coke Sams

Ernest in the Army ★ PG

Comedy　　　　　　1998 · US · Colour · 84mins

Another year, another *Ernest*
adventure. Who is watching this stuff?
To make matters worse, this one's
even more sentimental than ever. Here
Ernest (Jim Varney) joins the army and
comes to the aid of a troubled village,
where he takes a fatherless kid under
his wing. Moronically played and
witlessly scripted, this is a laughter-
free zone. ▭
Jim Varney *Ernest P Worrell* • Hayley Tyson
Cindy Swanson • David Muller *Colonel Gullet* •
Jeffrey Pillars *General Rodney Allen* ■ *Dir* John
Cherry [John R Cherry III] • *Scr* Jeff Pillars

Ernest Rides Again ★ PG

Comedy　　　　　　1993 · US · Colour · 89mins

Jim Varney must be a real glutton for
punishment. He returns yet again as
Ernest P Worrell in this silly children's
comedy that falls so far short of funny
it's pitiful. Only in an Ernest film would
a nutty professor claim that the crown
jewels were hidden inside a cannon
from the American War of
Independence and be proved correct!
And so the slapstick begins, with
Ernest competing against spies and
crooked antiques dealers to seize the
royal sparklers. Varney was acting
"stoopid" long before *Dumb and
Dumber*, but he's too well-meaning to
be a real no-brainer. ▭
Jim Varney *Ernest P Worrell* • Ron K James
Abner Melon • Linda Kash *Nan Melon* • Tom
Butler *Dr Glencliff* ■ *Dir* John Cherry [John R
Cherry III] • *Scr* John Cherry [John R Cherry III],
William M Akers

Ernest Saves Christmas ★★★ U

Fantasy　　　　　　1988 · US · Colour · 87mins

Ernest is a character from American TV
commercials who suddenly popped up
in the eighties to brief but heady
celluloid success. Designed here very

firmly to celebrate all things festive,
this tale has the frenetic Jim Varney
(as cab driver Ernest P Worrell) helping
Santa Claus look for his successor.
Everyone thinks Santa's a white-
bearded old nuisance – apart from Mr
Varney, of course – and, lots of jolly
adventures later, all is successfully
resolved. The kids will love it. ▭
Jim Varney *Ernest P Worrell* • Douglas Seale
Santa • Oliver Clark *Joe Carruthers* • Noëlle
Parker *Harmony* • Robert Lesser *Marty* •
Gailard Sartain *Chuck* ■ *Dir* John Cherry [John
R Cherry III] • *Scr* B Kline, Ed Turner, from a
story by Ed Turner

Ernest Scared Stupid ★★ PG

Comedy horror　　1991 · US · Colour · 88mins

The success of the *Scream* films
proves there's life in the old haunted
house yet. However, this entry in the
long-running *Ernest* series harks back
to the days when Laurel and Hardy or
Abbott and Costello could spook each
other with a white sheet. Jim Varney
returns as the doltish Ernest P Worrell,
accidentally waking up a troll he then
has to stop making off with the town's
children. The slapstick style should
raise a few giggles, but subtle it ain't.
▭
Jim Varney *Ernest P Worrell* • Eartha Kitt *Old
Lady Hackmore* • John Cadenhead *Tom Tulip*
• Bill Byrge *Bobby Tulip* • Austin Nagler *Kenny
Trantor* • Shay Astar *Elizabeth* • Jonas Moscartolo
Trantor • Richard Woolf *Matt* ■ *Dir* John
Cherry [John R Cherry III] • *Scr* Charles Gale,
Coke Sams, from a story by Coke Sams, John
Cherry [John R Cherry III]

Eroica ★★★

Portmanteau wartime drama
1958 · Pol · BW · 82mins

True to the ironic intent of its subtitle,
this portmanteau of wartime tales was
A Heroic Symphony in Two Movements.
The first story, *Scherzo alla Polacca*,
focuses on a cowardly black-marketeer
who blunders into the ranks of the
Polish underground and becomes the
voice of sanity in a mad world.
Ostinato Lugubre centres on a group of
concentration camp inmates who
sustain their morale by believing one
of their number has escaped.
Released at a time when all Iron
Curtain combat films were made purely
for propaganda purposes, Andrzej
Munk's sly feature stimulated
audiences and infuriated the
authorities. Tragically, he would only
complete a handful more films before
his death in a car crash in 1961. In
Polish with English subtitles.
Edward Dziewonski *Dzidzius* • Barbara
Polomska *Zosia* • Leon Niemczyk *Lt Kolya* •
Ignacy Machowski *Major* • Jozef Nowak
Kurzawa • Roman Klosowski *Szpakowski* •
Bogumil Kobiela *Dabecki* ■ *Dir* Andrzej Munk
• *Scr* Jerzy Stefan Stawinski

Erotic Tales ★

Erotic drama　　1994 · Ger · Colour · 170mins

Six directors, including Ken Russell,
Bob Rafelson and Susan Seidelman,
waste their time and talent telling sexy
stories, each with unexpected endings.
More silly than erotic, each tale is
serviceable at best and has little
sexual content or nudity to warrant
even the description soft-core. Mira
Sorvino's "The Dutch Master" episode
is more in the vein of a *Night Gallery*

segment, while Cynda Williams's comic
scenario completely misses the point
of the exercise. There's nothing for
anyone to get excited about here.
Arliss Howard *Bruce Lomann* • Cynda Williams
Davida Urked • Mira Sorvino *Teresa* • John
Turturro *Kim* • Hetty Baynes *Mrs Kirsch* •
Richard Barboza *Leroy* • Gosia Dobrowolska
Sarah • Anu Arya Aggarwal ■ *Dir* Bob
Rafelson, Susan Seidelman, Ken Russell,
Melvin Van Peebles, Paul Cox, Mani Kaul •
Scr Bob Rafelson, Jonathan Brett, Susan
Seidelman, Ken Russell, Melvin Van Peebles,
Paul Cox, Barry Dickins, Margot Wiburd

Erotique ★★ 18

Erotic comedy drama
1994 · US/Ger · Colour · 83mins

Despite the intriguing concept – three
women directors from the independent
film sector offer up a trio of erotic
tales from the female perspective –
this has to go down as a noble failure.
In *Let's Talk about Sex* Lizzie Borden
provides a dry examination of an
actress who won't compromise her
ideals, even though she works for a
phone sex company, while Monika
Treut offers up a stylish but uneven
tale about a wealthy lesbian, her
bisexual lover and a dumb hunk in
Taboo Parlor. The pick of the three,
though, is *Wonton Soup* from Clara
Law, who delivers some much-needed
laughs with a refreshing romp about a
confused man trying to impress his
partner with his knowledge of ancient
Asian sex texts. ▭
Kamala Lopez-Dawson *Rosie* • Bryan Cranston
Dr Robert Stern • Ron Orbach *Nikki* • Priscilla
Barnes *Claire* • Camilla Soeberg *Julia* •
Michael Carr *Victor* • Marianne Sägebrecht
Hilde • Tim Lounibos *Adrian* • Hayley Man *Ann*
• Choi Hark-kin *Uncle* ■ *Dir* Lizzie Borden,
Monika Treut, Clara Law • *Scr* Lizzie Borden
(from her story), Susie Bright, Monika Treut,
Eddie Ling-Ching Fong

The Errand Boy ★★★ U

Comedy　　　　　　1961 · US · BW · 92mins

One of the highlight movies in the
career of comic genius Jerry Lewis. He
co-wrote, produced, directed and
starred in this extremely funny satire of
movie-making, filmed with great
affection in his home studio
Paramount. Lewis has cast the film
brilliantly, with veterans like Brian
Donlevy and the great Sig Ruman
providing the perfect foil for the
madcap comedian. If you don't care for
him at all, you won't be converted. But
if you only know Jerry Lewis from *The
King of Comedy*, then this is the film to
see to fully understand the resonances
of his recent appearances. ▭
Jerry Lewis *Morty S Tashman* • Brian Donlevy
TP • Howard McNear *Dexter Sneak* • Dick
Wesson *The AD* • Pat Dahl *Miss Carson* • Sig
Ruman *Baron Elston Carteblanche* ■ *Dir* Jerry
Lewis • *Scr* Jerry Lewis, Bill Richmond

Erreur de jeunesse ★★★

Drama　　　　　1989 · Fr · BW and Colour · 91mins

Stylishly and evocatively photographed
in black and white, this lyrical study of
loneliness presents a view of Paris
that is rarely depicted on screen – that
of the alienating city, in which even the
people living on the same staircase
know nothing about each other.
Disorientated after an auto accident,
poet Francis Frappat is taken under

the wing of his landlady, Muni, who tries to match him with sensitive neighbour, Géraldine Danon. With Irène Jacob featuring in minor support, this almost plotless drama is heavy going in places. But the performances are sincere and Radovan Tadic's direction imaginative. A French language film.

Francis Frappat *Antoine* • Muni *Thérèse* • Géraldine Danon *Françoise* • Patrick Bauchau *Paul* • Didier Flamand *Patrick* • Irène Jacob ■ *Dir/Scr* Radovan Tadic

Eruption ★★ 15
Political action adventure
1997 · US · Colour · 92mins

Producer Roger Corman's typically no-frills but surprisingly intelligent variation on the volcano disaster movie, is actually sharper than the big-budget turkeys it seeks to emulate (*Volcano*, *Dante's Peak*). Cyril O'Reilly plays a journalist, caught up in a power struggle in a South American country, who learns that an even more dangerous eruption is on its way. F Murray Abraham hams it up as the evil dictator, while writer/director Gwyneth Gibby works wonders with a limited budget. ⬚

F Murray Abraham *President Mendoza* • Cyril O'Reilly *Sam* ■ *Dir* Gwyneth Gibby • *Scr* Gwyneth Gibby, Christopher Wood

Escapade ★★
Period romance
1935 · US · BW · 87mins

A somewhat stale comedy which marked the Hollywood debut of Luise Rainer, promoted as the "New Garbo". Taking a part turned down by Myrna Loy, Rainer plays a naive young girl who falls under the spell of Viennese womaniser William Powell. Set in the 1900s, it's fluffy enough but lacks the lightness that German director Ernst Lubitsch brought to similar material. In original release prints, Powell steps out of character and introduces the audience to Miss Rainer, promising a great career ahead of her. Three years later she'd won two Oscars; in another two years she was all but forgotten.

William Powell *Fritz Heideneck* • Luise Rainer *Leopoldine Major* • Frank Morgan *Karl Harrandt* • Virginia Bruce *Gerta Keller* • Reginald Owen *Paul Harrandt* • Mady Christians *Anita Keller* • Laura Hope Crews *Countess Feldon* ■ *Dir* Robert Z Leonard • *Scr* Herman J Mankiewicz, from the film *Maskerade* by Walter Reisch

Escapade in Japan ★★★ U
Adventure
1957 · US · Colour · 92mins

One of the last few feature films made by RKO Radio, this is an attractively produced heart-warmer, filmed on Japanese locations in Technirama and sumptuous Technicolor. Teresa Wright, past her prime, and Cameron Mitchell, in a rare leading role, are the worried grown-ups in what is really a *Boys' Own* adventure, geared for the whole family and cleverly directed for maximum schmaltz by veteran Arthur Lubin. The boys are good, but take a closer look at that rangy serviceman, the one called Dumbo. It's Clint Eastwood, two movies before *Rawhide*.

Teresa Wright *Mary Saunders* • Cameron Mitchell *Dick Saunders* • Jon Provost *Tony Saunders* • Roger Nakagawa *Hiko* • Kuniko

Miyake *Michiko* • Susumu Fujita *Kei Tanaka* • Clint Eastwood *Dumbo* ■ *Dir* Arthur Lubin • *Scr* Winston Miller

The Escape ★★★
Silent drama
1914 · US · BW

A long-lost title from the great innovator DW Griffith's massive motion picture output, based on a stage melodrama about a tenement family from New York's East Side. Fred Turner is the father, while Mae Marsh and Blanche Sweet play his daughters. The former falls in with gangster "Bull" McGee (Donald Crisp), a wrong 'un if ever there was one, though the latter has a chance to get out of the ghetto when she falls for handsome Owen Moore. Sentimental tosh was dear to Griffith's heart, and his genius made it possible for him to transcend such material on occasion.

Donald Crisp *"Bull" McGee* • Fred Turner *Jim Joyce* • Robert Harron *Larry Joyce* • Blanche Sweet *Mae Joyce* • Mae Marsh *Jennie Joyce* • Owen Moore *Dr Von Eiden* • Ralph Lewis *Senator* • Tammany Young *McGee's henchman* ■ *Dir* DW Griffith • *Scr* DW Griffith, from the play by Paul Armstrong

Escape ★★
Drama
1930 · UK · BW · 70mins

Impresario Basil Dean, who had taken only tentative steps into silent cinema, broke into talkies with this tale of a fugitive on Dartmoor. Unfortunately, his inexperience with both the camera and the primitive sound technology further compound the staginess of his own adaptation of John Galsworthy's tedious play. Sir Gerald Du Maurier also struggles, often failing to rein in an effusiveness designed to hit the back of the stalls. The supporting cast boasts some of the biggest names in British theatre, but the episodic structure and the cluttered staging leave them all looking amateurish.

Gerald Du Maurier *Captain Matt Denant* • Edna Best *Shingled lady* • Gordon Harker *Convict* • Horace Hodges *Gentleman* • Madeleine Carroll *Dora* • Mabel Poulton *Girl of the town* • Lewis Casson *Farmer* ■ *Dir* Basil Dean • *Scr* Basil Dean, John Galsworthy, from the play by John Galsworthy

Escape ★★ U
Second World War drama
1940 · US · BW · 103mins

Robert Taylor stars as an American travelling to Germany in a desperate bid to rescue his mother (Russian actress Alla Nazimova) from a Nazi concentration camp. He's helped by countess Norma Shearer, a German-American whose lover is the dastardly Conrad Veidt, a Nazi general. All very starry and, alas, all very phoney. The novel on which this vaguely enjoyable tosh is based was a bestseller by a certain Ethel Vance, a pseudonym dreamed up by the publishers as a means of protecting the real writer from reprisals from Nazi supporters.

Norma Shearer *Countess Von Treck* • Robert Taylor (1) *Mark Preysing* • Conrad Veidt *Gen Kurt Von Kolb* • Alla Nazimova *Emmy Ritter* • Felix Bressart *Fritz Keller* • Albert Bassermann [Albert Basserman] *Dr Arthur Henning* • Philip Dorn *Dr Ditten* ■ *Dir* Mervyn LeRoy • *Scr* Arch Oboler, Marguerite Roberts, from a novel by Ethel Vance

Escape ★★★
Drama based on a true story
1980 · US · Colour

Based on a true story, this TV movie stars Timothy Bottoms as Dwight Worker, an American citizen caught at Mexico City airport with a concealed package of cocaine. Incarcerated without trial in the notorious Lecumberri Prison, he is brutally beaten by guards but eventually stages a daring breakout. Fans of *Midnight Express* may find the plot a tad familiar, but Bottoms (*The Last Picture Show*) is as dependable as ever.

Timothy Bottoms *Dwight Worker* • Kay Lenz *Barbara Chilcoate* • Colleen Dewhurst *Lily Levinson* • Miguel Angel Suarez *Fernando Gardner-Pasquel* • Sandra Alexander *Gabrielle* ■ *Dir* Robert Michael Lewis [Robert Lewis] • *Scr* Michael Zagor, from an autobiography by Dwight Worker, Barbara Worker

The Escape ★★ 18
Romantic action thriller
1997 · Can · Colour · 87mins

Patrick Dempsey has another stab at losing his cute teen image, with largely forgettable results. He plays an innocent man wrongly sent to prison who, having escaped from jail, forms an unlikely relationship with the beautiful young woman (Brigitte Bako) he rescues from a car crash. Essentially a two-hander, Stuart Gillard's drama sympathetically sketches the awkward affair between the two leads. Despite this, the whole project never really grips or convinces. Contains swearing, violence and a sex scene. ⬚

Patrick Dempsey *Charles Jacob Clayton* • Brigitte Bako *Sarah* • Colm Feore *Hickman* • Vincent Gale *Newby* • John Aylward *Sheriff* • Nathaniel Deveaux *Moses* ■ *Dir* Stuart Gillard • *Scr* Scott Busby

The Escape Artist ★★ PG
Drama
1982 · US · Colour · 89mins

Ryan O'Neal's son Griffin holds his own in this mishmash of vaudeville and small town corruption. Bragging that he will escape a prison sentence within an hour cues a flashback for O'Neal about his childhood in theatre. Exploited by his aunt and uncle, who perform "the best escape act since Houdini" he hones his skills and escapes, lifting the wallet of the vindictive son of the local major, Raul Julia. Julia then sends his goons to threaten the boy. This is a mess of a film and far too formulaic – despite cinematographer turned director Caleb Deschanel's visual skill. ⬚

Griffin O'Neal *Danny Masters* • Raul Julia *Stu Quinones* • Teri Garr *Arlene* • Gabriel Dell *Uncle Burke* • Desi Arnaz *Mayor Quinones* • John P Ryan *Vernon* • Elizabeth Daily *Sandra* • M Emmet Walsh *Fritz* • Jackie Coogan *Magic shop owner* ■ *Dir* Caleb Deschanel • *Scr* Melissa Mathison, Stephen Zito, from the novel by David Wagoner

Escape by Night ★★
Crime drama
1953 · UK · BW · 78mins

Something of an improvement on the usual hokum churned out by low-budget expert John Gilling, this drama lacks any of the menace or desperation with which it would have been saturated by even the most

pedestrian Hollywood B-movie director. Yet Sid James gives a solid performance as the vice boss on the run who holds a journalist hostage, and he is well supported by Bonar Colleano as the crusading reporter after an exclusive. Letting the side down, however, is Andrew Ray, whose "little boy lost" act is utterly phoney.

Bonar Colleano *Tom Buchan* • Andrew Ray *Joey Weston* • Sidney James *Gino Rossini* • Ted Ray *Mr Weston* • Simone Silva *Rosetta Mantania* • Patrick Barr *Inspector Frampton* ■ *Dir/Scr* John Gilling

Escape Clause ★★ 1
Thriller
1996 · US · Colour · 95min

Smoothly engineered, straight-to-video thriller that will keep you guessing right to the end. Andrew McCarthy plays a smug insurance executive who is stunned when a mystery man tells him he has been hired to kill both him and his wife. However, when his spouse and the "killer" turn up dead, it is McCarthy who finds himself in the frame. The star does his patented bewildered innocent act, while Paul Sorvino provides menacing support. Contains violence, swearing and sex scenes. ⬚

Andrew McCarthy *Richard Ramsay* • Paul Sorvino *Lieutenant Gil Farrand* • Connie Britton *Leslie Bullard* • Kate McNeil *Sarah Ramsay* • Stan Egi *Abe Shinoda* ■ *Dir* Brian Trenchard-Smith • *Scr* Danilo Bach

Escape from Alcatraz ★★★★ 15
Prison drama based on a true story
1979 · US · Colour · 107mins

Don Siegel did much to establish his reputation with *Riot in Cell Block 11* in 1954. He went back behind bars for this tough and compelling reconstruction of the only successful escape from San Francisco's notorious island prison in its 29-year history. Driven stir crazy by the strictures of warden Patrick McGoohan's regime and the brutality of his fellow inmates, Clint Eastwood plans an ingenious bid for freedom with Fred Ward and Jack Thibeau. Blessed with expert performances, Siegel shoots the preparations with an attention to detail that exerts as strong a grip as the events of the escape itself. ⬚

Clint Eastwood *Frank Morris* • Patrick McGoohan *Warden* • Roberts Blossom *Chester "Doc" Dalton* • Jack Thibeau *Clarence Anglin* • Fred Ward *John Anglin* • Paul Benjamin *English* • Larry Hankin *Charley Butts* ■ *Dir* Don Siegel • *Scr* Richard Tuggle, from the book by J Campbell Bruce

Escape from Bogen County ★★
Thriller
1977 · US · Colour · 100mins

Hackneyed drama about a woman who tries to escape the clutches of her powerful husband, and the officer who decides to help her after he has been sent to bring her back. This has all been done a million times before, and with a cast headed by Jaclyn Smith, you know exactly what you are going to get. Very predictable but, thanks to co-stars Pat Hingle and Fred Willard, almost watchable.

Jaclyn Smith *Maggie Bowman* • Mitchell Ryan *Ambler Bowman* • Michael Parks *Jack Kern* •

U = SUITABLE FOR ALL Uc = SUITABLE FOR ALL, ESPECIALLY FOR YOUNG CHILDREN (VIDEO ONLY) PG = PARENTAL GUIDANCE

Henry Gibson *Abe Rand* • Pat Hingle *Judge Henry Martin* • Philip Abbott *Harry Webb* • Julie Mannix *Emily Martin* • John Quade *Sheriff Mason* • Fred Willard *Pearson* ■ *Dir* Steven Hilliard Stern • *Scr* Judith Parker

Escape from Fort Bravo ★★★ PG

Western 1953 · US · Colour · 94mins

Intended for 3-D (hence the kicking the dead rattlesnake into the audience shot) but ultimately shown flat, this otherwise impressive early John Sturges western suffers from the use of obvious studio exteriors in many key sequences. On location, though, in the dust of the desert as Mescalero Indians menace the escapees, the use of landscape is mighty fine, especially in a sequence featuring the best use of arrows since Olivier's *Henry V*. Union captain William Holden is suitably rugged, lovely Eleanor Parker is deceptively charming, and honourable Confederate leader John Forsythe reminds you of what a boring movie actor he was before his hair turned blue in TV's *Dynasty*. ▭

William Holden (1) *Captain Roper* • Eleanor Parker *Carla Forester* • John Forsythe *Captain John Marsh* • William Demarest *Campbell* • William Campbell *Cabot Young* • Polly Bergen *Alice Owens* • Richard Anderson *Lieutenant Beecher* • Carl Benton Reid *Colonel Owens* ■ *Dir* John Sturges • *Scr* Frank Fenton, from a story by Michael Pate, Phillip Rock

Escape from LA ★★ 15

Science-fiction action 1996 · US · Colour · 96mins

In John Carpenter's shambolic, big-budget sequel to his superior *Escape from New York*, Kurt Russell returns as mucho-macho hero Snake Plissken, who this time around is blackmailed into scouring the City of Angels for a doomsday device stolen by the president's daughter. Apart from the witty, face-lifted zombie section, this inept, unexciting and routine rehash lacks the sharp black comedy of the original *Escape*. Lacklustre special effects don't either. A major disappointment from the usually reliable genre maestro. ▭

Kurt Russell *Snake Plissken* • AJ Langer *Utopia* • Steve Buscemi *"Map to the Stars" Eddie* • George Corraface [Georges Corraface] *Cuervo Jones* • Stacy Keach *Malloy* • Michelle Forbes *Brazen* • Pam Grier *Hershe* • Jeff Imada *Saigon Shadow* • Cliff Robertson *President* • Valeria Golino *Taslima* • Peter Fonda *Pipeline* ■ *Dir* John Carpenter • *Scr* John Carpenter, Debra Hill, Kurt Russell, from characters created by John Carpenter, Nick Castle

Escape from New York ★★★ 15

Science-fiction adventure 1981 · US · Colour · 94mins

Sullen Kurt Russell impersonates Clint Eastwood in director John Carpenter's tough futuristic western, which never surpasses or fulfils the ingenuity of its premise – Manhattan Island as a maximum security prison where the president has crashed his plane. Closely resembling *Assault on Precinct 13* in tone and plot dynamics, it's certainly Carpenter's slickest looking film, with the presence of Lee Van Cleef reinforcing its Sergio Leone

associations. However, despite a marvellous night-time scene-setting beginning, the escapism that really counts is strictly routine. ▭ **DVD**

Kurt Russell *Snake Plissken* • Lee Van Cleef *Bob Hauk* • Donald Pleasence *President* • Isaac Hayes *Duke of New York* • Adrienne Barbeau *Maggie* • Harry Dean Stanton *"Brain"* • Ernest Borgnine *Cabby* ■ *Dir* John Carpenter • *Scr* John Carpenter, Nick Castle

Escape from Terror ★★★ 15

Drama based on a true story 1995 · US · Colour · 87mins

A better-than-average TV movie which works mainly because it is more outrageous than fiction. Maria Pitillo plays a naive country girl who becomes romantically involved with her charming boss (Adam Storke). But she soon discovers that, underneath, he is an absolute monster. When her child is put at risk, she begins plotting her escape. The two leads are watchable enough, and there's sterling work from co-stars Brad Dourif and Cindy Williams. ▭

Adam Storke *Paul Stamper* • Maria Pitillo *Teresa Walden Stamper* • Brad Dourif *Sheriff Bill Douglas* • Tony Becker *Chris Butler* • Cindy Williams *Wanda Walden* • Phillip A Luna *Martinez* • Annette Marin *Agent Hynde* ■ *Dir* Michael Scott • *Scr* Camilla Carr, Walter Klenhard, from a story by Camilla Carr

Escape from the Dark ★★★ U

Period drama 1976 · UK · Colour · 99mins

Perhaps better known by its US title, *The Littlest Horse Thieves*, this Disney period piece provided Alastair Sim with his last screen role. There are echoes of the unreformed Scrooge in his performance as Lord Harrogate, the Edwardian mine owner who is as unmoved by the plight of some discarded pit ponies as he is by the conditions in which many of his Emdale tenants live and work. Director Charles Jarrott makes the most of the Yorkshire scenery, but the most exciting scenes take place underground as the three scamps who rescue the ponies use them to save some trapped miners. ▭

Alastair Sim *Lord Harrogate* • Peter Barkworth *Richard Sandman* • Maurice Colbourne *Luke Armstrong* • Susan Tebbs *Violet Armstrong* • Geraldine McEwan *Miss Coutts* • Prunella Scales *Mrs Sandman* ■ *Dir* Charles Jarrott • *Scr* Rosemary Anne Sisson, from a story by Rosemary Anne Sisson, Burt Kennedy

Escape from the Planet of the Apes ★★★★ PG

Science-fiction adventure drama 1971 · US · Colour · 93mins

The third of the popular movie series sees Roddy McDowall and Kim Hunter land in present-day California after surviving the catastrophe that ended *Beneath the Planet of the Apes*. This is very much a film of two halves, the first being an amusing collection of observations on modern life, as seen through the eyes of the more advanced apes. The second half, however, is much darker, with the arrogant and fearful humans being driven to unspeakable cruelty to protect their future. An intelligent script, capable

direction and solid performances add up to a fine film. ▭

Roddy McDowall *Cornelius* • Kim Hunter *Zira* • Bradford Dillman *Dr Lewis Dixon* • Natalie Trundy *Dr Stephanie Branton* • Eric Braeden *Dr Otto Hasslein* • William Windom *The President* • Sal Mineo *Milo* • Albert Salmi *E-1* • Jason Evers *E-2* • John Randolph *Chairman* ■ *Dir* Don Taylor • *Scr* Paul Dehn, from characters created by Pierre Boulle

Escape from Zahrain ★★ U

Action thriller 1962 · US · Colour · 93mins

Well upholstered but ultimately mundane would-be thriller set in what used to be called the Middle East powder keg. Yul Brynner leads a motley crew across the Panavisioned desert to find guest star James Mason. Such worthies as Sal Mineo and Jack Warden are along for the (underscripted) ride, but veteran director Ronald Neame shows little sense of dramatic pacing despite the handsome location photography by Ellsworth Fredericks.

Yul Brynner *Sharif* • Sal Mineo *Ahmed* • Madlyn Rhue *Laila* • Jack Warden *Huston* • James Mason *Johnson* ■ *Dir* Ronald Neame • *Scr* Robin Estridge, from a novel by Michael Barrett • *Cinematographer* Ellsworth Fredericks

Escape: Human Cargo ★★★

Thriller based on a true story 1998 · US · Colour · 107mins

Treat Williams's everyman persona makes him a good choice to play the central role in this TV movie about American businessman John McDonald, who found himself unable to leave Saudi Arabia because of the influence of a disreputable sheik. After all legal avenues are exhausted, he hatches a wild idea to escape from the country. It takes time for the story to get moving, with almost half the movie gone before McDonald finds himself in serious trouble. After that, though, it's compelling stuff.

Treat Williams *John McDonald* • Stephen Lang *Dennis* • Lawrence Dane *Pinder* • Sasson Gabai *Suliman* ■ *Dir* Simon Wincer • *Scr* William Mickelberry, Dan Vining, from the book *Flight from Dhahran* by John McDonald, Clyde Burleson

Escape Me Never ★★★

Drama 1935 · UK · BW · 101mins

The smash-hit play was especially written by Margaret Kennedy to exploit the considerable abilities of star Elisabeth Bergner. this unsurprising film version, directed by Bergman's husband Paul Czinner, is virtually a transcript of the show, even down to the same male smoothie leads (Hugh Sinclair and Griffith Jones). The tale is pure tosh, involving unwed mother Bergner going nuts over no-good cad composer Sinclair. But it does reveal Bergner's range, and you'll be surprised at how charming, delightful, sexy and talented the lady is.

Elisabeth Bergner *Gemma Jones* • Hugh Sinclair *Sebastian Sanger* • Griffith Jones *Caryl Sanger* • Penelope Dudley-Ward *Fenella McClean* • Irene Vanbrugh *Mrs McClean* • Leon Quartermaine *Mr McClean* ■ *Dir* Paul Czinner • *Scr* Carl Zuckmayer, Robert J Cullen, from the play by Margaret Kennedy

Escape Me Never ★★

Melodrama 1947 · US · BW · 103mins

Idiotically cast remake of the old Elisabeth Bergner vehicle, with Ida Lupino as the Bergnerian waif (you're no waif, Ida!) and Errol Flynn as the caddish composer she falls for. Only skilled Eleanor Parker really convinces as Flynn's fling after he marries Ida. British expatriate director Peter Godfrey does what he can with this stale tosh, though the Erich Wolfgang Korngold score does go some way to mitigate the silliness. Watch for the great Albert Basserman in his last American screen role as Professor Heinrich.

Errol Flynn *Sebastian Dubrok* • Ida Lupino *Gemma Smith* • Eleanor Parker *Fenella MacLean* • Gig Young *Caryl Dubrok* • Reginald Denny *Ivor MacLean* • Isobel Elsom *Mrs MacLean* • Albert Basserman *Professor Heinrich* • Ludwig Stossel *Mr Steinach* ■ *Dir* Peter Godfrey • *Scr* Thomas Williamson, from the novel *The Fool of the Family* and the play *Escape Me Never* by Margaret Kennedy

Escape of the Amethyst ★★★ U

War drama based on a true story 1956 · UK · BW · 112mins

This adventure plays like a low-budget rehearsal for Robert Wise's 1966 epic *The Sand Pebbles*. It's a fact-based yarn about a British warship, HMS *Amethyst*, which sails up the Yangtse in 1949 intending to relieve the British Embassy at Nanking. Instead, it comes under massive bombardment from Chinese communists, who blockade the river and trap the ship. Made less than ten years after Mao's revolution, one shouldn't expect an analysis of Chinese politics. What we get is standard British heroics from a crew commanded by Richard Todd, courtesy of an Eric Ambler script, efficiently handled by Michael Anderson.

Richard Todd *Lieutenant Commander Kerans* • William Hartnell *Leading Seaman Frank* • Akim Tamiroff *Colonel Peng* • Keye Luke *Captain Kuo Tai* • Donald Houston *Lieutenant Weston* • Robert Urquhart *Flight Lieutenant Fearnley* • Sophie Stewart *Charlotte Dunlap* • James Kenney *Lieutenant Hett* ■ *Dir* Michael Anderson • *Scr* Eric Ambler, from the non-fiction book by Laurence Earl

Escape Route ★★ U

Spy thriller 1952 · UK · BW · 79mins

George Raft gives a fair impression of a man who has had his arms welded to his sides in this dismissable quickie thriller. One of the handful of films Raft made in Europe after his Hollywood fortunes dipped, it's a lightweight affair in which he plays a FBI agent called in to discover who is smuggling scientists to the east. The villain's identity is painfully obvious, as is the distaste with which undercover operative Sally Gray smooches her ageing co-star.

George Raft *Steve Rossi* • Sally Gray *Joan Miller* • Clifford Evans *Michael Grand* • Reginald Tate *Colonel Wilkes* • Patricia Laffan *Miss Brooks* • Frederick Piper *Inspector Reid* • Roddy Hughes *Porter* • John Warwick *Brice* ■ *Dir* Seymour Friedman, Peter Graham Scott • *Scr* John V Baines, Nicholas Phipps

Escape to Athena ★★ PG

Second World War adventure
1979 · UK · Colour · 114mins

Despite the best efforts and intentions of mogul Lew Grade, most of his film-producing legacy is, regrettably, a pile of old tosh. This is a prime example: a slight plot combining an ancient treasure caper with a Second World War escape adventure, stretching to around two hours and incorporating (and wasting) the talents of such diverse names as David Niven, Elliott Gould, Claudia Cardinale and Sonny Bono. And they aren't even the leads! If you can bear to watch a movie starring Roger Moore and Telly Savalas, all well and good. 🎞

Roger Moore *Major Otto Hecht* • Telly Savalas *Zeno* • David Niven *Professor Blake* • Claudia Cardinale *Eleana* • Stefanie Powers *Dottie Del Mar* • Richard Roundtree *Nat Judson* • Sonny Bono *Bruno Rotelli* • Elliott Gould *Charlie Dane* • William Holden (1) *Prisoner* ■ *Dir* George Pan Cosmatos • *Scr* Richard S Lochte, Edward Anhalt, from a story by Richard S Lochte, George Pan Cosmatos

Escape to Burma ★★

Adventure   1955 · US · Colour · 83mins

One of the last films to be directed by veteran Allan Dwan, this trite melodrama contributed to the decline of RKO, along with a clutch of similar movies. Barbara Stanwyck and Robert Ryan, who were so good together in the same studio's *Clash by Night*, are wasted here as lovers in the jungle whose tryst is disturbed by David Farrar when he tries to arrest Ryan for murder. There's a last-minute twist, but you'll be numb with boredom before then. 🎞

Barbara Stanwyck *Gwen Moore* • Robert Ryan *Jim Brecan* • David Farrar *Cardigan* • Murvyn Vye *Makesh* • Lisa Montelli *Andora* • Robert Warwick *Sawbwa* ■ *Dir* Allan Dwan • *Scr* Talbot Jennings, Hobart Donavan, from the story *Bow Tamely to Me* by Kenneth Perkins

Escape to Nowhere ★★

Supernatural thriller
1996 · US · Colour · 83mins

A surprisingly grisly supernatural thriller, given the presence of such bland television faces as Greg Evigan and Alexandra Paul. They play an American couple who settle in Ireland with their young daughter (Briana Evigan) only to find themselves up to their necks in black magic. There are obvious nods to *The Wicker Man* and, while it isn't the same league as that cult classic, the Irish settings make for a refreshing change of scenery. Contains violence.

Greg Evigan *Will South* • Alexandra Paul *Maura South* • Briana Evigan *Aubrey South* ■ *Dir* Scott Levy • *Scr* Brendan Broderick

Escape to Victory ★★★ PG

Second World War drama
1981 · US · Colour · 111mins

Can you imagine what this corny prisoner-of-war picture would have been like if producer Freddie Fields had not secured the services of Michael Caine, Sylvester Stallone, Max von Sydow and a squad of international footballing legends? It's pretty obvious that director John Huston didn't quite know what to make of it all, but his sure

touch and Pele's football choreography turn this into a rousing romp, made all the more enjoyable by the shocking performances of the players. Escapist entertainment in every sense. 🎞

Sylvester Stallone *Robert Hatch* • Michael Caine *John Colby* • Pele *Luis Fernandez* • Bobby Moore *Terry Brady* • Osvaldo Ardiles *Carlos Rey* • Paul Van Himst *Michel Fileu* • Kazimierz Deyna *Paul Wolchek* • Hallvar Thoresen *Gunnar Hilsson* • Mike Summerbee *Sid Harmor* • Co Prins *Pieter Van Beck* • Russell Osman *Doug Clure* • John Wark *Arthur Hayes* • Soren Linsted *Erik Borge* • Kevin O'Calloghan *Tony Lewis* • Max von Sydow *Major Karl Von Steiner* • Daniel Massey *Colonel Waldron* • Tim Pigott-Smith *Rose* ■ *Dir* John Huston • *Scr* Evan Jones, Yabo Yablonsky, from a story by Yabo Yablonsky, Djordje Milicevic, Jeff Maguire

Escape to Witch Mountain ★★★★ U

Science-fiction drama
1975 · US · Colour · 90mins

With actors such as Ray Milland, Eddie Albert and Donald Pleasence treating this Disney children's movie as seriously as any other adult-themed movie they might tackle, the result, with a well-written narrative by Robert Malcolm Young, succeeds in being speedy, scary and sentimental all at once. The two clairvoyant youngsters soon seem to get accustomed to being pursued, and Milland is oozingly malevolent as the villain who wants to use their powers for his own nefarious ends. Bette Davis was to loom alarmingly in the follow-up movie *Return from Witch Mountain*, but this has plenty of thrills to be going on with for grown-ups as well as children. 🎞

Kim Richards *Tia Malone* • Ike Eisenmann *Tony Malone* • Ray Milland *Aristotle Bolt* • Eddie Albert *Jason O'Day* • Donald Pleasence *Lucas Deranian* • Walter Barnes *Sheriff Purdy* ■ *Dir* John Hough • *Scr* Robert Malcolm Young, from the novel by Alexander Key

Escape to Witch Mountain ★★

Drama   1995 · US · Colour · 87mins

John Hough's 1975 adaptation of Alexander Key's exciting children's novel was a hard act to follow. But Disney has made a fair fist of this TV-movie remake, executive produced by Les Mayfield (who directed the 1994 version of *Miracle on 34th Street*). Robert Vaughn replaces Ray Milland as the evil millionaire seeking to exploit the mystical powers of orphaned twins Elisabeth Moss and Erik Von Detten. Brad Dourif, Henry Gibson and Vincent Schiavelli are among the solid supporting cast.

Robert Vaughn *Edward Bolt* • Elisabeth Moss *Anna* • Erik Von Detten *Danny* • Lynne Moody *Lindsay Brown* • Perrey Reeves *Zoe Moon* • Lauren Tom *Claudia Ford* • Vincent Schiavelli *Waldo Fudd* • Henry Gibson *Professor Ravetch* • Brad Dourif *Luther* ■ *Dir* Peter Rader • *Scr* Peter Rader, from the film by Robert Malcolm Young, from the novel by Alexander Key

Escapement ★★

Mystery thriller   1958 · UK · BW · 77mins

Also known under the more lurid title of *The Electronic Monster* this underwhelming British thriller has Rod Cameron investigating an actor's death at a clinic specialising in electronic

hypnosis. Barely mesmerising, it was one of those zero-budget British movies that gave refuge to B-picture stars from Hollywood, in this case Mary Murphy and former Fred MacMurray stand-in, Cameron.

Rod Cameron *Keenan* • Mary Murphy *Ruth* • Meredith Edwards *Dr Maxwell* • Peter Illing *Zekon* • Kay Callard *Laura Maxwell* • Carl Jaffe *Dr Erich Hoff* ■ *Dir* Montgomery Tully • *Scr* Charles Eric Maine, J MacLaren-Ross, from the novel by Charles Eric Maine

The Escapist ★★

Action adventure 1983 · US · Colour · 87mins

One of those belting movies that contains such an overdose of wacky plotlines you can only sit and gawp. Bill Shirk wants to be the greatest escapologist in the world, so director Eddie Beverly Jr has him buried alive, stuck underwater and making the acquaintance of several deadly animals. All phobics are thus well catered for in this substandard action adventure, in which great flurries of melodramatic activity paper over absolutely nothing of substance.

Bill Shirk *Shirk* • Milbourne Christopher *Weiss* • Peter Lupus *Sharky* • Dick the Bruiser *Bruiser* • Gary Todd *Doug Meyers* • Terri Mann *Polly* • Cynthia Johns *Stormy* ■ *Dir* Eddie Beverly Jr • *Scr* Stephen Meyers

Escort West ★★★ U

Western   1959 · US · BW · 76mins

Produced by John Wayne's brother, Robert E Morrison, this was too modest a venture to interest the big man himself. So Victor Mature takes the lead as the ex-Confederate soldier heading west with his young daughter. Along the way he picks up two sisters (Elaine Stewart and Faith Domergue) and their wounded servant (Rex Ingram), all survivors of an Indian attack. Co-scripted by actor Leo Gordon, who also takes a supporting role, this is a cut above the average thanks to an eventful narrative and well-developed characters.

Victor Mature *Ben Lassiter* • Elaine Stewart *Beth Drury* • Faith Domergue *Martha Drury* • Reba Waters *Abbey Lassiter* • Noah Beery Jr *Jamison* • Leo Gordon *Vogel* • Rex Ingram *Nelson* • John Hubbard *Lieutenant Weeks* • Harry Carey Jr *Travis* • Slim Pickens *Wheeler* ■ *Dir* Francis D Lyon • *Scr* Leo Gordon, Fred Hartsook, from a story by Steven Hayes

Eskiya ★★★★ 15

Drama   1996 · Tur · Colour · 127mins

Turkey's biggest ever box-office hit, this astute drama exploits Hollywood convention to produce a film few in America would have the wit to make. Yavuz Turgul turns Istanbul into a hostile wilderness as Kurdish bandit Sener Sen returns from 35 years in jail to take his revenge on the friend who not only betrayed him, but also stole his girl. Rambling and brimming over with life, this is an engrossing mix of social comment, unassuming heroism, wry humour and shameless sentiment, with the relationship between the bandit and a brash street rogue symbolising what young and old can learn from each other. In Turkish with English subtitles.

Sener Sen *Baran* • Ugur Yucel *Cumali* • Sermin Sen *Keje* • Yasim Salkim *Emel* ■ *Dir/ Scr* Yavuz Turgul

Espionage ★★★ U

Adventure drama   1937 · US · BW · 66mins

Suave Edmund Lowe and romantic Madge Evans (a former child star) make a sophisticated pair as rival reporters tracking down arms tycoon Paul Lukas on the Orient Express. Adapted from Walter Hackett's play, it manages to be as slick and fast-paced as the train on which most of the action takes place. The following year, Lukas played another villain on a train in Hitchcock's *The Lady Vanishes*. The director Kurt Neumann, who made mostly second features, is best known for *The Fly* (1958).

Edmund Lowe *Kenneth* • Madge Evans *Patricia* • Paul Lukas *Kronsky* • Ketti Gallian *Sonia* • Richard ''Skeets'' Gallagher *Brown* • Frank Reicher *Von Cram* • Billy Gilbert *Turk* • Robert Graves *Duval* ■ *Dir* Kurt Neumann • *Scr* Manuel Seff, Leonard Lee, Ainsworth Morgan, from a play by Walter Hackett

Essex Boys ★★★ 18

Crime drama based on a true story
1999 · UK · Colour · 102mins

This slick British crime thriller breaks no new ground and tries too hard to be tough. Yet interest is sustained by taut pacing, a nicely murky plot and spirited performances from Alex Kingston, Tom Wilkinson, Charlie Creed-Miles and a scenery-chewing Sean Bean. The story centres on a young minicab driver who is hired by a hard man fresh out of prison. The youth finds himself in the firing line when a major drug deal prompts a power struggle among rival elements of the Essex criminal fraternity. Contains violence, swearing, drug abuse and sex scenes.

Sean Bean *Jason Locke* • Alex Kingston *Lisa Locke* • Charlie Creed-Miles *Billy Reynolds* • Tom Wilkinson *John Dyke* • Larry Lamb *Peter Chase* • Terence Rigby *Henry Hobbs* • Billy Murray *Perry Elley* • Amelia Lowdell *Nicole* ■ *Dir* Terry Winsor • *Scr* Jeff Pope, Terry Winsor

Est-Ouest ★★★

Period romantic drama
1999 · Fr/Rus/Sp/Bul · Colour · 120mins

Improving on *Indochine*'s balancing act between psychological realism and visual lyricism, Régis Wargnier's Oscar-nominated period piece not only sheds light on a little-known episode in Soviet history, but also provides plenty of satisfyingly dramatic incident. The teaming of Oleg Menshikov and Sandrine Bonnaire is crucial, as they provide the emotional core of this stark exposé of the conditions that greet a White Russian exile and his French wife on accepting Stalin's duplicitous postwar amnesty. However, the secondary characters are also well delineated, particularly Catherine Deneuve's touring stage diva, who provides the increasingly desperate Bonnaire with the opportunity to escape. In French and Russian with English subtitles.

Sandrine Bonnaire *Marie* • Catherine Deneuve *Gabrielle Develay* • Oleg Menshikov *Alexei Golovin* • Sergei Bodrov Jr *Sasha* • Ruben Tapiero *Seryozha aged 7* • Erwan Baynaud *Seryozha aged 14* • Grigori Manukov *Pirogov* •

U = SUITABLE FOR ALL   Uc = SUITABLE FOR ALL, ESPECIALLY FOR YOUNG CHILDREN (VIDEO ONLY)   PG = PARENTAL GUIDANCE

Tatyana Dogilova *Olga* ■ *Dir* Régis Wargnier • *Scr* Régis Wargnier, Sergei Bodrov, Rustam bragimbekov, Louis Gardel

Esther and the King ★

Biblical drama
1960 · US/It · Colour · 109mins

Biblical stuff and nonsense, with Joan Collins marrying the Persian king to stop the oppression of the Jews and save the throne from various plots and assassins. Shot in Italy like so many Hollywood epics, it veers between the laughable and the plodding, and you'd never guess that Hollywood action maestro Raoul Walsh directed it. Occasionally there's a striking image, courtesy of cameraman Mario Bava, who directed the Italian language version of the film, and who later made several highly regarded movies about mythical musclemen like Hercules.

Joan Collins *Esther* • Richard Egan *King Ahasuerus* • Denis O'Dea *Mordecai* • Sergio Fantoni *Haman* • Rick Battaglia [Rik Battaglia] *Simon* • Renato Baldini *Klydrathes* ■ *Dir* Raoul Walsh • *Scr* Raoul Walsh, Michael Elkins

Esther Waters ★★ U

Period melodrama 1948 · UK · BW · 105mins

George Moore's source novel was strongly influenced by the naturalism of Emile Zola, but there is little of the earthiness of the original in this tawdry adaptation, which rapidly plunges between the two stools of heritage production and sensationalist melodrama. Dirk Bogarde is suitably scurrilous as a rascally footman, but the action slows fatally when he is off screen, with Esther (Kathleen Ryan) facing all her trials (single motherhood, the workhouse and Bogarde's drinking) with sulkiness rather than dignity and determination.

Kathleen Ryan *Esther Waters* • Dirk Bogarde *William Latch* • Cyril Cusack *Fred Parsons* • Ivor Barnard *Randal* • Fay Compton *Mrs Barfield* • Margaret Diamond *Sarah Tucker* • Morland Graham *Ketley* ■ *Dir* Ian Dalrymple, Peter Proud • *Scr* Michael Gordon, William Rose, from a novel by George Moore

Eternal Love ★★★ PG

Romantic drama 1943 · Fr · BW · 107mins

The subject of endless debates about whether this updating of the legend of Tristan and Isolde had pro-Nazi sympathies, this is also a film that leaves one wondering how much better it might have been had screenwriter Jean Cocteau also directed instead of the more literal Jean Delannoy. Permanently on set, Cocteau clearly influenced the fairy-tale setting, the dreamy atmosphere and the rather bloodless acting of doomed lovers Jean Marais and Madeleine Solonge. Yet he seems to have done little to dissuade Delannoy from his more laboured attempts at ethereal beauty and high tragedy. The result is pompous, perhaps, but undeniably arresting and affecting. In French with English subtitles. ▭

Madeleine Sologne *Nathalie* • Jean Marais *Patrice* • Yvonne de Bray *Gertrude* • Jane Marken *Anne* • Jean Murat *Marc* • Pierre Piéral *Achille* • Roland Toutain *Lionel* ■ *Dir* Jean Delannoy • *Scr* Jean Cocteau

Eternally Yours ★★★

Romantic drama 1939 · US · BW · 99mins

Lightweight but endearing romance from an era when Hollywood really knew how to cook this recipe properly, featuring the lovely Loretta Young involved with magician David Niven in a vicissitude-strewn marriage. Director Tay Garnett brings his aerial knowledge to bear on some scenes, but seems generally content to let the movie coast along on the charms of the leading players. This is no bad thing, though a few more touches of wit in the script wouldn't have gone amiss.

David Niven *Tony Halstead* • Loretta Young *Anita Halstead* • Broderick Crawford *Don Barnes* • Hugh Herbert *Benton* • Billie Burke *Aunt Abby* • C Aubrey Smith *Bishop Hubert Peabody* • ZaSu Pitts *Carrie Bingham* • Eve Arden *Gloria* ■ *Dir* Tay Garnett • *Scr* Gene Towne, Graham Baker, John Meehan

Eternity ★★ 18

Fantasy drama 1990 · US · Colour · 121mins

Jon Voight battles it out with Armand Assante in medieval times, losing his beloved Eileen Davidson in the process. Then the temporal rug is pulled out from under events and moved to the present-day where Voight is a do-gooder at odds with Assante, a right-wing tycoon. Voight wrote the screenplay with the director, Steven Paul, and his mother, Dorothy Koster Paul, and their view of what-goes-around-comes-around reincarnation is a mixture of half-baked metaphysics and a labour of love. It comes across, though, as just laboured. ▭

Jon Voight *James/Edward* • Armand Assante *Sean/Roni* • Eileen Davidson *Valerie/Dahlia* • Wilford Brimley *Eric/King* • Kaye Ballard *Selma/Sabrina* • Steven Keats *Harold/Tax collector* • Lainie Kazan *Bernice/Mother* ■ *Dir* Steven Paul • *Scr* Jon Voight, Steven Paul, Dorothy Koster Paul

Eternity and a Day ★★★ PG

Drama 1998 · Gr/Fr/It/Ger · Colour · 132mins

Winner of the Palme d'Or at Cannes, this searching meditation on memory and mortality follows dying writer Bruno Ganz around Salonika as he seeks to atone for a life of self-obsession by helping a young Albanian refugee. Switching lyrically between a sunlit past filled with missed opportunities and the murky moodiness of the poet's directionless present, director Theo Angelopoulos is somewhat overdeliberate in both its pacing and symbolism. For all its epic scope, its stately assessment of significant cultural and political themes, and its sublime camera movements, this typically intense odyssey is never as provocative as Angelopoulos's impressive 1995 film, *Ulysses' Gaze*. In Greek with English subtitles.

Bruno Ganz *Alexandre* • Isabelle Renaud *Anna* • Fabrizio Bentivoglio *The Poet* • Despina Bebedeli *Mother* • Achileas Skevis *The Child* • Vassilis Seimenis *Son-in-law* ■ *Dir* Theo Angelopoulos • *Scr* Theo Angelopoulos, Petros Markaris, Tonino Guerra, Giorgio Silvagni

Ethan Frome ★★★

Period drama 1993 · US/UK · Colour · 107mins

This adaptation of an Edith Wharton novel couldn't be more different from

Martin Scorsese's sumptuous version of the American writer's *The Age of Innocence*. Whereas Scorsese cloaked the tragic tale of his movie with dazzling sets and costumes, this is a much bleaker, darker affair, and almost as rewarding. Liam Neeson is the proud farmer trapped in a cold marriage with Joan Allen who finds love in the shape of her cousin, Patricia Arquette. The three leads bring resonance to the doom-laden story and, although it can be heavy going at times, it remains a moving experience.

Liam Neeson *Ethan Frome* • Patricia Arquette *Mattie Silver* • Joan Allen *Zeena Frome* • Tate Donovan *Reverend Smith* • Katharine Houghton *Ruth Hale* • Stephen Mendillo *Ned Hale* • Deborah Ayer *Young Ruth* • Jay Goede *Denis Eady* ■ *Dir* John Madden • *Scr* Richard Nelson, from the novel by Edith Wharton

Eureka ★★ 18

Drama 1982 · UK · Colour · 123mins

Gene Hackman would be given an extract from the Bible every night to get him in the mood for the following day's shooting, but it made director Nicolas Roeg's weird self-indulgence no clearer. Hackman plays a gold prospector who strikes it rich but not lucky; instead he becomes paranoid, especially when his daughter (Theresa Russell) marries a fortune-hunter. Villainous Joe Pesci settles it all in a welter of slaughter which solves most problems, but not Roeg's awful storytelling – which is so oblique as to be out of sight. Contains violence. ▭

Gene Hackman *Jack McCann* • Theresa Russell *Tracy* • Rutger Hauer *Claude Maillot Van Horn* • Jane Lapotaire *Helen McCann* • Mickey Rourke *Aurelio D'Amato* • Ed Lauter *Charles Perkins* • Joe Pesci *Mayakofsky* • Helena Kallianiotes *Frieda* • Corin Redgrave *Worsley* ■ *Dir* Nicolas Roeg • *Scr* Paul Mayersberg, from the novel *Who Killed Sir Harry Oakes?* by Marshall Houts

Eureka Stockade ★★ U

Adventure 1949 · UK · BW · 101mins

After the success of Harry Watt's *The Overlanders* in 1946, Ealing Studios established a branch at the abandoned Pagewood Studios in Sydney, where Watt made this follow-up. It's the story of the clashes between police and miners during the Australian gold rush of the 1850s after the government tried to restrict the miners' freedom of movement. Chips Rafferty, the star of *The Overlanders*, plays the sharpest thorn in the authorities' side, but despite the obvious research and the efforts at authenticity, it's a stodgy film that hasn't worn the years well.

Chips Rafferty *Peter Lalor* • Jane Barrett *Alicia Dunne* • Jack Lambert *Commissioner Rede* • Peter Illing *Raffaello* • Gordon Jackson *Tom Kennedy* • Ralph Truman *Gov Hotham* • Sydney Loder *Vern* • John Fernside *Sly grog seller* ■ *Dir* Harry Watt • *Scr* Harry Watt, Walter Greenwood, from a story by Harry Watt

Europa ★★★★ 15

Political thriller 1991 · Den · Colour and BW · 107mins

Anything but universally admired, Lars von Trier's mesmerising study of a defeated nation is a bold and imaginative attempt to fuse Kafkaesque paranoia with a mix of visual styles as diverse as those of

Ingmar Bergman and Carol Reed. Max von Sydow's opening narration came in for the most criticism; yet, when combined with hypnotic shots of a maze of railway tracks, it manages to create an atmosphere of uncertainty that pervades the rest of the picture. Jean-Marc Barr gives a suitably wide-eyed performance as the American sleeping-car conductor caught between the occupying Allies, Nazi partisans and the railway company in postwar Germany. In English and German with subtitles. Contains violence. ▭

Jean-Marc Barr *Leopold Kessler* • Barbara Sukowa *Katharina Hartmann* • Udo Kier *Lawrence Hartmann* • Ernst-Hugo Jaregard *Uncle Kessler* • Erik Merk *Pater* • Jorgen Reenberg *Max Hartmann* • Henning Jensen *Siggy* • Eddie Constantine *Colonel Harris* • Max von Sydow *Narrator* ■ *Dir* Lars von Trier • *Scr* Lars von Trier, Niels Vorsel

Europa, Europa ★★★★ 15

Second World War drama 1991 · Fr/Ger · Colour · 107mins

This extraordinary story proves once again that truth is stranger than fiction. Marco Hofschneider is hugely impressive as Salomon Perel, the Jewish teenager who fled to Soviet-occupied Poland to escape the Nazi tyranny, only to become accepted as a loyal Aryan after he was captured by the advancing Germans. Agonisingly hiding the physical clues to his extraction, he becomes a hero of the Hitler Youth and even manages to romance rabid anti-Semite Julie Delpy. Holland's wonderfully understated direction allows the cruel ironies to bite harder and she makes chilling use of the paraphernalia of totalitarianism. In German with English subtitles. Contains nudity. ▭

Marco Hofschneider *Young Salomon Perel* • Julie Delpy *Leni* • André Wilms *Robert* • Salomon Perel *Old Salomon Perel* • Ashley Wanninger *Gerd* • René Hofschneider *Isaak Perel* • Piotr Kozlowski *David Perel* ■ *Dir* Agnieszka Holland • *Scr* Agnieszka Holland, from the memoirs by Salomon Perel

Europa '51 ★★★

Drama 1952 · It · BW · 118mins

Probably the best of the four spiritual melodramas Ingrid Bergman made with her husband Roberto Rossellini, it gave the Swedish star more of a chance to show her beauty and range than the others. Bergman plays a superficial American society woman living in Rome who believes she is the cause of her young son's suicide. She seeks salvation by tending the poor and the sick, much to the incomprehension of her bourgeois husband (Alexander Knox). Giulietta Masina, in one of her rare non-Fellini roles, plays a factory girl whom Bergman rescues. Naive though some of the film is, Rossellini's unfussy direction creates a genuine feeling of spirituality. In Italian with English subtitles.

Ingrid Bergman *Irene Girard* • Alexander Knox *George Girard* • Ettore Giannini *Andrea* • Giulietta Masina *Passerotto* • Sandro Franchina *Michele* • Teresa Pellati *Ines* ■ *Dir* Roberto Rossellini • *Scr* Roberto Rossellini, Sandro De Leo, Mario Pannunzio, Ivo Perilli, Brunello Rondi, Diego Fabbri, Donald Ogden Stewart (English dialogue)

The Europeans ★★★★ U

Period drama 1979 · UK · Colour · 90mins

Made before he discovered EM Forster, James Ivory came closer than anyone to translating the near-unfilmable Henry James to the screen with this beautifully-judged drama. Aided, as ever, by the impeccable production values of Ismail Merchant and the intelligent writing of Ruth Prawer Jhabvala, Ivory's take on cross-continental snobbery is deliciously played by an immaculate, if unfamiliar cast. Returning to 1850s Boston, Lee Remick expertly keeps the lid on a performance that begged extravagance, thus ensuring that her gold-digging countess remains sympathetic for all her schemes and jibes. Elegant, witty and highly literate.

Lee Remick *Eugenia* • Robin Ellis *Robert Acton* • Wesley Addy *Mr Wentworth* • Tim Choate *Clifford Wentworth* • Lisa Eichhorn *Gertrude Wentworth* • Nancy New *Charlotte Wentworth* • Kristin Griffith *Lizzie Acton* ■ *Dir* James Ivory • *Scr* Ruth Prawer Jhabvala, from the novel by Henry James

Eva ★★★★ 15

Drama 1962 · Fr/It · BW · 104mins

This simmering study of obsession provides Jeanne Moreau with one of the meatiest roles of her career. As the ruthless opportunist exploiting the weakness of successful novelist Stanley Baker, she presents in many ways the darker side of Catherine, the character she played the previous year in François Truffaut's *Jules et Jim* – a perfect woman whose middle name is trouble. It's as if *Blow Up* director Michelangelo Antonioni had decided to make a *film noir*, as director Joseph Losey turns Venice into a city of lost souls, over which hangs the sour odour of lust and greed. ▭

Jeanne Moreau *Eva* • Stanley Baker *Tyvian* • Virna Lisi *Francesca* • Giorgio Albertazzi *Braneo Maloni* • James Villiers *Arthur McCormick* • Riccardo Garrone *Michele* • Lisa Gastoni *The redhead* • Checco Rissone *Pieri* ■ *Dir* Joseph Losey • *Scr* Hugo Butler, Evan Jones, from the novel by James Hadley Chase

Eve of Destruction ★ 18

Science-fiction thriller 1991 · US · Colour · 95mins

This female version of *The Terminator* features an eye-catching performance from Dutch star Renée Soutendijk as a scientist who creates a cyborg in her own image, which then runs amok with a thermonuclear bomb in its womb. Gregory Hines plays the cop tracking her down, while Duncan Gibbins directs with some verve. However, the interesting premise of a robotic doppelgänger acting out its maker's sexual fantasies and fears isn't sufficiently explored amid the obligatory explosions and fifth-rate effects. ▭

Gregory Hines *Jim McQuade* • Renée Soutendijk *Dr Eve Simmons/Eve VIII* • Michael Greene *General Curtis* • Kurt Fuller *Schneider* • John M Jackson *Peter Arnold* • Loren Haynes *Steve the robot* ■ *Dir* Duncan Gibbins • *Scr* Duncan Gibbins, Yale Udoff

The Eve of St Mark ★★★

Second World War drama 1944 · US · BW · 96mins

Maxwell Anderson's flag-waving Broadway play was a key wartime work, written in a form of blank verse and extremely emotive for an audience with sons and relatives at war immediately after Pearl Harbor. To its credit, the movie doesn't greatly expand the piece, although it does expurgate some of the original dialogue. The barrack room scenes in particular convey the heartfelt feelings of the time, despite serious undercasting owing to the fact that 20th Century-Fox's top leading men were themselves in the forces. Michael O'Shea effectively repeats his Broadway role, while Vincent Price shines as a poetry-speaking Southerner. Anne Baxter, however, is wasted as the romantic interest.

Anne Baxter *Janet Feller* • William Eythe *Private Quizz West* • Michael O'Shea *Private Thomas Mulveray* • Vincent Price *Private Francis Marion* • Ruth Nelson *Nell West* • Ray Collins *Deckman West* • Stanley Prager *Private Glinka* • Henry Morgan *Private Shevlin* ■ *Dir* John M Stahl • *Scr* George Seaton, from the play by Maxwell Anderson

Evel Knievel ★★

Biography 1971 · US · Colour · 88mins

George Hamilton stars as the famed daredevil motorcyclist, reflecting on major events that have shaped his life in this mildly diverting and insightful film biography of one of the great cultural figures of the seventies. The script, co-written by *Apocalypse Now* scribe John Milius, is guilty of too much cod philosophising, but Marvin J Chomsky's film is redeemed by some truly wonderful stock footage of Knievel in action. This is not to be confused with *Viva Kneivel!*, which appeared six years later and featured the great man playing himself.

George Hamilton *Evel Knievel* • Sue Lyon *Linda* • Bert Freed *Doc Kincaid* • Rod Cameron *Charlie Kresson* • Dub Taylor *Turquoise Smith* ■ *Dir* Marvin J Chomsky • *Scr* Alan Caillou, John Milius

Evelyn Prentice ★★★

Mystery melodrama 1934 · US · BW · 78mins

Star power makes this overheated soap opera of infidelity, murder and courtroom revelations seem better than it is. William Powell and Myrna Loy were teamed for the third time in this tale of a lawyer, suspected of philandering by his wife, who promptly gets involved with a blackmailing gigolo. The plot convolutions stretch credibility to breaking point, but the film is saved by its cast. The Powell–Loy chemistry was a proven plus, Rosalind Russell makes her screen debut as a client of Powell's, and Una Merkel sparkles as Loy's perceptive best friend.

William Powell *John Prentice* • Myrna Loy *Evelyn Prentice* • Una Merkel *Amy Drexel* • Rosalind Russell *Nancy Harrison* • Isabel Jewell *Judith Wilson* • Harvey Stephens *Lawrence Kennard* • Edward Brophy *Eddie Delaney* ■ *Dir* William K Howard • *Scr* Lenore Coffee, from the novel by WE Woodward

Even Cowgirls Get the Blues ★★ 15

Comedy adventure 1993 · US · Colour · 92mins

Uma Thurman just can't pick 'em, if the big-screen travesty *The Avengers* was anything to go by. Here she's lumbered with the role of Sissy Hankshaw, a fashion model who, with abnormally long thumbs, takes to hitchhiking and ends up at a ranch inhabited by lesbian cowgirls. Adapted from a bizarre novel by Tom Robbins, complete with character names such as Bonanza Jellybean and the Chink, it's a belated flower-power idea that's decidedly below par. An embarrassment to watch. ▭

Uma Thurman *Sissy Hankshaw* • John Hurt *The Countess* • Rain Phoenix *Bonanza Jellybean* • Noriyuki "Pat" Morita [Pat Morita] *The Chink* • Keanu Reeves *Julian Gitchie* • Lorraine Bracco *Delores Del Ruby* • Angie Dickinson *Miss Adrian* • Sean Young *Marie Barth* • Crispin Glover *Howard Barth* • Roseanne Arnold [Roseanne] *Madame Zoe* ■ *Dir* Gus Van Sant • *Scr* Gus Van Sant, from the novel by Tom Robbins

The Evening Star ★★★ 15

Drama 1996 · US · Colour · 123mins

A disappointing but nonetheless interesting sequel to *Terms of Endearment*, which picks up over a decade after the original. Shirley MacLaine returns as eccentric matriarch Aurora, now of pensionable age but just as feisty as she wars with her late daughter Emma's children (including a does-she-ever-get-any-older Juliette Lewis) and equally spiky best friend (Miranda Richardson). Despite a brief cameo from *Endearment* Oscar-winner Jack Nicholson, this *Evening Star* never truly sparkles, largely due to a lacklustre script. But it does manage to touch the heart and, by the end, lives up to the description "weepie". Contains some swearing and sex scenes. ▭

Shirley MacLaine *Aurora Greenway* • Bill Paxton *Jerry Bruckner* • Juliette Lewis *Melanie Horton* • Miranda Richardson *Patsy Carpenter* • Ben Johnson *Arthur Cotton* • Scott Wolf *Bruce* • George Newbern *Tommy Horton* • Jack Nicholson *Garret Breedlove* ■ *Dir* Robert Harling • *Scr* Robert Harling, from the novel by Larry McMurtry

Evensong ★★★ U

Musical drama 1934 · UK · BW · 81mins

Evelyn Laye plays an Irish opera singer pursued by the likes of handsome Archduke Carl Esmond who eventually expires while listening to one of her own recordings. Some may find this Beverly Nichols-derived saga poignant; others will think it unbearably silly and slow. However, Fritz Kortner makes a powerful contribution as the impresario Kober, and if you peer hard enough you'll spot Alec Guinness in a small role. It's impossible not to enjoy a film that contains dialogue like "My cousin has been assassinated at Sarajevo – God only knows what this is going to lead to!" ▭

Evelyn Laye *Irela* • Fritz Kortner *Kober* • Alice Delysia *Mme Valmond* • Carl Esmond *Archduke Theodore* • Emlyn Williams *George Murray* • Muriel Aked *Tremlowe* • Patrick O'Moore *Bob McNeil* • Alec Guinness *Soldier* ■ *Dir* Victor Saville • *Scr* Edward Knoblock,

Dorothy Farnum, from the play by Edward Knoblock, Beverley Nichols, from the novel by Beverley Nichols

Event Horizon ★★★ 18

Science-fiction horror 1997 · US/UK · Colour · 91mins

A messy (in more ways than one) but enjoyable slice of space splatter from British director Paul Anderson. The *Event Horizon* of the title is an experimental spacecraft which has been missing for years but has just been located. A rescue team, led by Laurence Fishburne, is sent to retrieve it, but it soon becomes apparent that it's in the grip of a malevolent force. Fishburne, Sam Neill, Joely Richardson and Sean Pertwee bring some class to the determinedly B-movie dialogue, and Anderson delivers some nasty sequences that will please horror fans. Contains swearing and disturbing scenes. ▭

Laurence Fishburne *Miller* • Sam Neill *Weir* • Kathleen Quinlan *Peters* • Joely Richardson *Starck* • Richard T Jones *Cooper* • Jason Isaacs *DJ* • Sean Pertwee *Smith* ■ *Dir* Paul Anderson • *Scr* Philip Eisner

Ever After ★★★★ PG

Romantic fantasy 1998 · US · Colour · 116mins

As Baz Luhrmann did with *William Shakespeare's Romeo + Juliet*, director Andy Tennant brings new freshness and vitality to the Cinderella story in a delightful reworking that treats the legend as if it were hard historical fact. All the pantomime sorcery and comical sidekicks have been jettisoned, and the result allows the romance between feisty servant girl Drew Barrymore and Dougray Scott's handsome prince to shine even brighter. Anjelica Huston re-interprets the evil stepmother role with deft assurance, and Leonardo da Vinci makes a surprising fairy godmother figure. A handsomely mounted epic with lots of glamour and a fabulous grand ball. ▭

Drew Barrymore *Danielle* • Anjelica Huston *Baroness Rodmilla* • Dougray Scott *Prince Henry* • Patrick Godfrey *Leonardo da Vinci* • Megan Dodds *Marguerite* • Melanie Lynskey *Jacqueline* • Timothy West *King Francis* • Judy Parfitt *Queen Marie* ■ *Dir* Andy Tennant • *Scr* Andy Tennant, Susannah Grant, Rick Parks, from the story *Cinderella* by Charles Perrault

Ever in My Heart ★★

Drama 1933 · US · BW · 70mins

This far-fetched weepie presents Barbara Stanwyck as an upper-crust New Englander defiantly marrying a good German who's forced by anti-Hun fervour to return home during the First World War. They meet again: she as a frontline canteen worker, he as a German spy… Ever-reliable Stanwyck gives it all she's got and almost manages to draw some warmth from Otto Kruger as the love of her life, but the brief running time and cursory direction of Archie Mayo deprive it of any real impact.

Barbara Stanwyck *Mary Archer* • Otto Kruger *Hugo Wilbrandt* • Ralph Bellamy *Jeff* • Ruth Donnelly *Lizzie* • Laura Hope Crews *Grandma Archer* • Frank Albertson *Sam* • Ronnie Crosby

U = SUITABLE FOR ALL Uc = SUITABLE FOR ALL, ESPECIALLY FOR YOUNG CHILDREN (VIDEO ONLY) PG = PARENTAL GUIDANCE

Teddy • Clara Blandick *Anna* ■ *Dir* Archie Mayo • *Scr* Bertram Milhauser, from a story by Beulah Marie Dix, Bertram Milhauser

Evergreen ★★★ U
Musical 1934 · UK · BW · 89mins

Unquestionably British musical star Jessie Matthews's most popular movie, a Michael Balcon-produced trifle directed by Victor Saville about a girl posing as her own music-hall star mum, a situation which naturally evokes complications when romance arrives. Jessie is quite lovely, sumptuously photographed by Glen MacWilliams, and given to wearing endearing see-through gowns. The score is one of her best; not just Rodgers and Hart's *Dancing on the Ceiling*, but also *Over My Shoulder* and *A Little Springtime in Your Heart*. ▭

Jessie Matthews *Harriet Green* • Sonnie Hale *Leslie Benn* • Betty Balfour *Maudie* • Barry MacKay *Tommy Thompson* • Ivor MacLaren *Marquis of Staines* • Hartley Power *Treadwell* • Patrick Ludlow *Lord Shropshire* • Betty Shale *Mrs Hawkes* ■ *Dir* Victor Saville • *Scr* Emlyn Williams, Marjorie Gaffney, from the play by Benn W Levy

Eversmile, New Jersey ★★ PG
Road movie 1989 · Arg/UK · Colour · 87mins

This Anglo-Argentine production must rank as one of the most unusual entries on the CV of star Daniel Day-Lewis. He plays a bike-riding dentist preaching the gospel of good dental hygiene with missionary zeal in the most far-flung parts of Argentina. The film's quirkiness is initially rather appealing, but the tooth, the whole tooth and nothing but the tooth is that it rapidly palls. ▭

Daniel Day-Lewis *Fergus O'Connell* • Mirjana Jokovic *Estela* • Gabriela Acher *Celeste* • Ignacio Quiros *The "Boss"* • Boy Olmi *Radio announcer* • Alberto Benegas *Sheriff* • Ruben Patagonia *Butler* • Matias Puelles *Child* • Eduardo Santoro *Party guest* ■ *Dir* Carlos Sorin • *Scr* Jorge Goldenberg, Roberto Sheuer, Carlos Sorin

Every Breath ★★ 18
Erotic thriller 1993 · US · Colour · 84mins

Above average, straight-to-video thriller which places more emphasis on suspense than steamy thrills. Judd Nelson plays an out-of-work actor who gets caught up in a bizarre love triangle with the beautiful Joanna Pacula and her rich husband, Patrick Bauchau. You can see the plot twists coming a mile off, but it's put together with some style, and Bauchau steals every scene he's in. ▭

Judd Nelson *Jimmy* • Joanna Pacula *Lauren* • Patrick Bauchau *Richard* • Willie Garson *Bob* • Rebeca Arthur *Mimi* • John Pyper Ferguson *Hal* • Cynthia Brimhall *Kris* • Kathleen Beaton *Kim* ■ *Dir* Steve Bing • *Scr* Andrew Fleming, Steve Bing, Judd Nelson

Every Day's a Holiday ★★★
Comedy 1937 · US · BW · 78mins

Deprived of her salty dialogue by the censors, there's little Mae West can do but sing and flounce, but she still does it better than anybody else. In this substandard vehicle, she's a delight, disguised as a French singer

to escape New York detective Edmund Lowe because she sold Herman Bing the Brooklyn Bridge. Lloyd Nolan plays Lowe's crooked boss and there's a rare glimpse of Louis Armstrong for good measure.

Mae West *Peaches O'Day* • Edmund Lowe *Captain Jim McCarey* • Charles Butterworth *Larmadou Graves* • Charles Winninger *Von Reighle Van Pelter Van Doon* • Walter Catlett *Nifty Bailey* • Lloyd Nolan *Honest John Quade* • Louis Armstrong • Herman Bing *Fritz Krausmeyer* ■ *Dir* A Edward Sutherland • *Scr* Mae West

Every Day's a Holiday ★★ U
Musical comedy 1964 · UK · Colour · 93mins

Released two years before he achieved international success with *Born Free*, director James Hill's attempt to take the Swinging Sixties to the seaside is often laughably bad. John Leyton is the nominal star of this talent show farrago, although the musical headliners are Freddie and the Dreamers, who were desperately trying to match the movie achievements of the Beatles in *A Hard Day's Night*. However, no film with cinematography by Nicolas Roeg can be dismissed out of hand, and Ron Moody and Liz Fraser provide accomplished comic support.

Freddie and the Dreamers *The Chefs* • John Leyton *Gerry Pullman* • Mike Sarne [Michael Sarne] *Timothy Gilbin* • Ron Moody *Professor Bastinado* • Liz Fraser *Miss Slightly* • Grazina Frame *Christina Barrington de Witt* • Susan Baker *Susan* ■ *Dir* James Hill • *Scr* Anthony Marriott, Jeri Matos, James Hill, from the story by Anthony Marriott

Every Girl Should Be Married ★★ U
Romantic comedy 1948 · US · BW · 81mins

A lightweight movie in one of the greatest Hollywood careers ever, that of Cary Grant, who used his considerable sway to cast his future wife Betsy Drake in the female lead. It's not only the title that renders this unworthy vehicle desperately old-fashioned in today's post-feminist world; there's also a rather unpalatable plotline about a paediatrician (Grant) and a department store clerk (Drake) who wants to get married at all costs. The other man is suave Franchot Tone, trying heroically to make something out of a nothing part. ▭

Cary Grant *Dr Madison Brown* • Betsy Drake *Anabel Sims* • Franchot Tone *Roger Sanford* • Diana Lynn *Julie Hudson* • Alan Mowbray *Mr Spitzer* • Elisabeth Risdon *Mary Nolan* ■ *Dir* Don Hartman • *Scr* Stephen Morehouse Avery, Don Hartman, from a story by Eleanor Harris

Every Home Should Have One ★ 15
Comedy 1970 · UK · Colour · 89mins

This dismal comedy was co-scripted by Marty Feldman, Barry Took and Denis Norden. It boasts a topnotch comic cast including Penelope Keith, Patrick Cargill and Dinsdale Landen. But their efforts are totally overshadowed by a shambolic, leering performance from Feldman, making only his second screen appearance, as a mad advertising executive who devises a series of steamy commercials for a brand of frozen porridge. Contains

swearing, sex scenes and brief nudity. ▭

Marty Feldman *Teddy* • Shelley Berman *Nat Kaplan* • Judy Cornwell *Liz* • Julie Ege *Inga Giltenberg* • Patrick Cargill *Wallace Trufitt MP* • Jack Watson *McLaughlin* • Patience Collier *Mrs Levin* • Penelope Keith *Lotte von Gelbstein* • Dinsdale Landen *Reverend Mellish* ■ *Dir* Jim Clark • *Scr* Marty Feldman, Barry Took, Denis Norden, from a story by Milton Shulman, Herman Kretzmer

Every Little Crook and Nanny ★★★
Comedy 1972 · US · Colour · 92mins

A glorious piece of self-guying from Victor Mature illuminates this hit-and-miss mob comedy, though we don't spend nearly enough time in his company. Instead we get Lynn Redgrave, mugging for all she's worth, as a nanny who abducts the son of a Mafia godfather (guess who?). If only Cy Howard had written himself a better script; he might not have had to direct with such frenetic energy. He might even have had time to rein in those arch hams, John Astin and Dom DeLuise. But it's worth waiting for the odd sightings of Mature, whose knowing performance compares favourably with the fading film star he played in *After the Fox*.

Lynn Redgrave *Miss Poole, Nanny* • Victor Mature *Carmine Ganucci* • Paul Sand *Benny Napkins* • Maggie Blye *Stella* • Austin Pendleton *Luther* • John Astin *Garbugli* • Dom DeLuise *Azzecca* • Louise Sorel *Marie* • Phillip Graves *Lewis Ganucci* ■ *Dir* Cy Howard • *Scr* Cy Howard, Jonathan Axelrod, Robert Klane, from a novel by Ed McBain [Evan Hunter]

Every Picture Tells a Story ★★ PG
Biographical drama 1984 · UK · Colour · 82mins

Director James Scott recalls the troubled adolescence that helped shape his father William's sensibilities in this portrait of the artist as a young man. Scripted by Shane Connaughton, who co-wrote *My Left Foot*, it begins as an unsentimental study of working-class life in Scotland and Northern Ireland in the early twenties. Phyllis Logan is typically assured as William's mother, and the trio playing the growing boy all do well. Once Alex Norton (who plays Scott senior) departs the scene, however, the action starts to falter in this visually impressive but dramatically flawed film.

Phyllis Logan *Agnes Scott* • Alex Norton *William Scott Sr* • Leonard O'Malley *William aged 15-18* • John Docherty *William aged 11-14* • Mark Airlie *William aged 5-8* • Natasha Richardson *Miss Bridle* ■ *Dir* James Scott • *Scr* Shane Connaughton

Every Sunday ★★★ U
Musical 1936 · US · BW · 10mins

This enchanting 10-minute featurette is a historic document designed by MGM as a screen test for young contractees Judy Garland and Deanna Durbin. They play a pair of teenage friends who save a Sunday afternoon park orchestra from closure by taking to the bandstand to modernise the repertoire, singing a song each and a duet. MGM ended up retaining Garland, while Durbin went off to Universal, where her

string of hits saved the studio from bankruptcy. A must for fans of either star.

Judy Garland *Judy* • Deanna Durbin *Edna* ■ *Dir* Felix E Feist [Felix Feist] • *Scr* Mauri Grashin

Every Time We Say Goodbye ★★ 15
Romantic drama 1986 · US/Isr · Colour · 93mins

After a string of comedy successes – *Splash*, *Bachelor Party* and *Volunteers* – Tom Hanks took his first crack at something weightier in this modest romantic drama. He plays a Second World War pilot stationed near Jerusalem who falls for a local Jewish girl (Cristina Marsillach), much to the anger of her family. Hanks looks a little uncomfortable in the lead role and there are hardly any familiar faces in the supporting cast. However, director Moshe Mizrahi pulls most of the right emotional strings and the presence of Hanks makes it an intriguing curiosity. ▭

Tom Hanks *David* • Cristina Marsillach *Sarah* • Benedict Taylor *Peter* • Anat Atzmon *Victoria* • Gila Almagor *Lea* • Moni Moshanov *Nessin* ■ *Dir* Moshe Mizrahi • *Scr* Moshe Mizrahi, Rachel Fabien, Leah Appet, from a story by Moshe Mizrahi

Every Which Way but Loose ★★★ 15
Comedy drama 1978 · US · Colour · 109mins

Clint Eastwood cruises through this coarse comedy as a travelling prizefighter whose best buddy is a beer-swilling, lowlife orang-utan named Clyde. There are plenty of lively scenes to keep fans satisfied (with some bare-knuckle fight sequences that squeamish viewers may find disturbing), and Eastwood just about manages to avoid being made a monkey of by his scene-stealing co-star. His romantic hankerings after country singer Sondra Locke don't add much to the brew, though. It did such good box-office that Eastwood was tempted back into a feeble sequel, *Any Which Way You Can*. Contains swearing and brief nudity. ▭

Clint Eastwood *Philo Beddoe* • Sondra Locke *Lynn Halsey-Taylor* • Geoffrey Lewis *Orville* • Ruth Gordon *Ma* • Beverly D'Angelo *Echo* • Walter Barnes *Tank Murdock* • Sam Gilman *Fat man's friend* ■ *Dir* James Fargo • *Scr* Jeremy Joe Kronsberg

Every Woman's Dream ★★ 15
Drama 1996 · NZ/US · Colour · 91mins

In this true crime TV movie Jeff Fahey (*The Lawnmower Man*) plays charming, manipulative bigamist Mitch Parker. With a wife already in Los Angeles, he then meets and marries another woman living in Florida (*Sex and the City*'s Kim Cattrall). When his second wife finally exposes his duplicitous behaviour, Mitch's charm turns to rage. Actor William H Macy (*Fargo*), penned this smart script with co-writer Martin Davidson. Unfortunately director Steven Schachter gets mired in psychological claptrap after the brisk first hour, leaving you with a pretty predictable woman-in-jeopardy melodrama. 🖵

Jeff Fahey *Mitch Parker* • Kim Cattrall *Liz* • DeLane Matthews *Candy* • Walter Addison *Mr Wells* • Judith McConnell *Mrs Wells* • Felicia Bell *Jodee* • Debra Eisenstadt *Cynthia* • Paul Linke *Guy* • Jay Saussey *Samant* ■ *Dir* Steven Schachter • *Scr* Martin Davidson, Steven Schachter, William H Macy, from the novel *Deadly Pretender* by Karen Kingsbury

Everybody Does It ★★★ Ⓤ

Comedy   1949 · US · BW · 97mins

This very funny remake of *Wife, Husband and Friend* sensibly retains Nunnally Johnson's clever script almost word for word, but is far better cast than that 1939 Loretta Young vehicle. Celeste Holm is simply terrific as a woman who wants to sing opera but can't, while Paul Douglas is no less fine as her husband, who *can* sing opera but doesn't! Elsewhere Linda Darnell is lovely as the local neighbourhood diva. This trifle is lightly directed by *Grand Hotel* veteran Edmund Goulding, and is consistantly amusing throughout.

Paul Douglas *Leonard Borland* • Linda Darnell *Cecil Carver* • Celeste Holm *Doris Borland* • Charles Coburn *Major Blair* • Millard Mitchell *Mike Craig* • Lucile Watson *Mrs Blair* • John Hoyt *Wilkins* • Leon Belasco *Hugo* ■ *Dir* Edmund Goulding • *Scr* Nunnally Johnson, from a story by James M Cain

Everybody Sing ★★★ Ⓤ

Musical   1938 · US · BW · 91mins

Best-known today as a sparkling young Judy Garland flick, this was actually one of those "crazy family" movies so popular in the thirties. Judy is the second daughter, to lovely Lynne Carver, of Reginald Owen and actress Billie Burke, who puts on a show with cook Fanny Brice and top-billed Allen Jones. Judy sings five numbers, all especially arranged for her by her mentor, the great Roger Edens, and reveals that magnificent talent that only a year later would make her an international star in *The Wizard of Oz*, a film that also features Owen and Burke. Good fun.

Judy Garland *Judy Bellaire* • Allan Jones *Ricky Saboni* • Fanny Brice *Olga Chekaloff* • Reginald Owen *Hillary Bellaire* • Billie Burke *Diana Bellaire* • Reginald Gardner *Jerrold Hope* • Lynne Carver *Sylvia Bellaire* • Monty Woolley *John Fleming* ■ *Dir* Edwin L Marin • *Scr* Florence Ryerson, Edgar Allan Woolf, James Gruen, from their story • *Music Director* Roger Edens

Everybody Wins ★ ⑮

Mystery drama   1990 · UK · Colour · 92mins

If you want to see the vast gulf that exists between the stage and the screen, look no further than *Everybody Wins*, which proves that, while Arthur Miller is a great playwright, he can't write a decent screenplay. It's a sort of thriller, really, with Nick Nolte as a widowed private eye hired and then seduced by mysterious Debra Winger, who wants him to open up an old murder case. Not only are Winger's motives obscure, but she is also given reams of dialogue to declaim and some utterly unplayable scenes to wade through. Winger is a great actress, but here she's handed a poisoned chalice. 🖵

Debra Winger *Angela Crispini* • Nick Nolte *Tom O'Toole* • Will Patton *Jerry* • Jack Warden *Judge Harry Murdoch* • Judith Ivey *Connie* • Frank Converse *Charlie Haggerty* • Kathleen Wilhoite *Amy* • Frank Military *Felix* ■ *Dir* Karel Reisz • *Scr* Arthur Miller

Everybody's All-American ★★★ ⑮

Drama   1988 · US · Colour · 121mins

Dennis Quaid plays a legendary American football star in this saga of sporting success and failure that begins in the Eisenhower era of flash cars, material plenty and patriotism. Quaid marries a local beauty queen (Jessica Lange), and the film charts 25 turbulent years in their lives. Directed by *An Officer and a Gentleman's* Taylor Hackford, the picture comes across as *Born on the Fourth of July* meets *Bull Durham* meets any TV soap you care to name. It's over-plotted, though Lange's performance, as always, lifts the essentially lightweight material. 🖵

Dennis Quaid *Gavin Grey* • Jessica Lange *Babs Rogers Grey* • Timothy Hutton *Donnie "Cake"* • John Goodman *Ed Lawrence* • Carl Lumbly *Narvel Blue* • Raymond Baker [Ray Baker] *Bolling Kiely* • Savannah Smith Boucher *Darlene Kiely* • Patricia Clarkson *Leslie Stone* ■ *Dir* Taylor Hackford • *Scr* Tom Rickman, from the novel by Frank Deford

Everybody's Baby: the Rescue of Jessica McClure ★★★ ⑫

Drama based on a true story
1989 · US · Colour · 90mins

A strong, highly experienced TV-movie cast here re-enacts the true story of a Texas toddler who plunged into a disused well. Though the ensuing nail-biting rescue attempt created world headlines, it has to be said that this is not a complicated tale and the ending is never in doubt from scene one. But, given those limitations, writer David Eyre Jr does a fine job of holding our interest until the thankfully robust finale, which makes the *999* TV series look like a boy scout first aid course. 🖵

Beau Bridges *Richard Czeh* • Roxana Zal *Cissy McClure* • Pat Hingle *James Roberts* • Patty Duke *Carolyn Henry* • Will Oldham *Chip McClure* ■ *Dir* Mel Damski • *Scr* David Eyre Jr

Everybody's Fine ★★★ ⑫

Drama   1990 · It/Fr · Colour · 120mins

Marcello Mastroianni has a ball as an elderly father of five who travels all over Italy to visit his now grown-up clan and gets some shocks when he discovers his children haven't quite turned out as he expected. There's a welcome appearance by Michèle Morgan as a Rimini widow, but this is predominantly a showcase for the delightful Mastroianni, who makes the most of the opportunity. Director/co-writer Giuseppe Tornatore, who made the Oscar-winning *Cinema Paradiso*, finds room for sentimentality in an otherwise cynical tale. In Italian with English subtitles. 🖵

Marcello Mastroianni *Matteo Scuro* • Michèle Morgan *Woman on train* • Marino Cenna *Canio* • Roberto Nobile *Guglielmo* • Valeria Cavalli *Tosca* • Norma Martelli *Norma* ■ *Dir*

Giuseppe Tornatore • *Scr* Giuseppe Tornatore, Tonino Guerra, Massimo De Rita, from a story by Giuseppe Tornatore

Everyone Says I Love You ★★★★ ⑫

Musical comedy 1996 · US · Colour · 96mins

Woody Allen's musical dares to be different – nobody can sing. A comedy of frustrated emotions, everyone's yearning power is at full stretch as Woody tries to woo and win Julia Roberts, ex-wife Goldie Hawn takes charge of an ex-convict and Drew Barrymore is absorbed by teenage angst. Characters launch into standard songs at the drop of a crotchet – and there's a wonderful dance on the banks of the Seine – but they just can't vocalise to any credible extent. The result, though, is strangely endearing and endearingly strange. 🖵

Woody Allen *Joe* • Alan Alda *Bob* • Goldie Hawn *Steffi* • Drew Barrymore *Skylar* • Edward Norton *Holden* • Natasha Lyonne *DJ* • Gaby Hoffmann *Lane* • Natalie Portman *Lauren* • Lukas Haas *Scott* • Julia Roberts *Von* • Tim Roth *Charles Ferry* ■ *Dir/Scr* Woody Allen

Everything I Have Is Yours ★★★ Ⓤ

Musical   1952 · US · Colour · 91mins

Sumptuously Technicolored starring vehicle for the marvellous MGM dance team of Marge and Gower Champion, who shot to fame together in the smash hit *Show Boat* the previous year. Unfortunately, all the MGM gloss in the world can't help this frankly tasteless tale of a pregnant Marge wondering if partner Gower is faithful. There are, though, some knockout dance numbers along the way, including Marge's solo *Derry Down Dilly*, and some nice glamour moments from Monica Lewis and Elaine Stewart.

Marge Champion *Pamela Hubbard* • Gower Champion *Chuck Hubbard* • Dennis O'Keefe *Alec Tackabury* • Monica Lewis *Sybil Meriden* • Dean Miller *Monty Dunston* • Eduard Franz *Phil Meisner* • Elaine Stewart *Showgirl* ■ *Dir* Robert Z Leonard • *Scr* George Wells

Everything That Rises ★★★★ ⑫

Western drama 1998 · US · Colour · 90mins

A heart-warming and uplifting look at the harsh struggles faced by contemporary American farmers. Dennis Quaid and Mare Winningham are the credible heroes of this gritty neo-western who face the challenges and seemingly insurmountable obstacles placed before them, including their son's disability and bank loan problems, with vim, vigour and personal sacrifice. Beautifully acted, this realistic drama makes for refreshing, thought-provoking and compelling viewing. 🖵

Dennis Quaid *Jim Clay* • Mare Winningham *Kyle Clay* • Harve Presnell *Garth* • Meat Loaf *Red* • Ryan Merriman *Nathan Clay* • Bruce McGill *Alan Jamison* • Denise Durham *Red's wife* ■ *Dir* Dennis Quaid • *Scr* Mark Spragg

Everything You Always Wanted to Know about Sex (But Were Afraid to Ask) ★★★ ⑱

Comedy   1972 · US · Colour · 84mins

Woody Allen's third outing as actor/writer/director, made in the days when his films were largely an excuse to string together a relentless series of gags, is one of his least satisfying pictures. But this seven-story sex-manual parody does have its redeeming features. The razor-sharp Michelangelo Antonioni spoof and Lou Jacobi's ill-timed experiment in cross-dressing are neatly done, but Gene Wilder's affair with a sheep is rather woolly and the "What's My Perversion?" panel game quickly runs out of steam. The less said about the dismal sex clinic and chastity belt sequences the better. The best is left to last, as Woody and his fellow sperms prepare to parachute to unknown glory. 📀

Woody Allen *Victor/Fabrizio/Fool/Sperm* • John Carradine *Doctor Bernardo* • Lou Jacobi *Sam* • Louise Lasser *Gina* • Anthony Quayle *King* • Tony Randall *Operator* • Lynn Redgrave *Queen* • Burt Reynolds *Switchboard* • Gene Wilder *Doctor Ross* ■ *Dir* Woody Allen • *Scr* Woody Allen, from a non-fiction book by Dr David Reuben

Eve's Bayou ★★★★ ⑮

Drama   1997 · US · Colour and BW · 104mins

"The summer I killed my father I was ten years old," begins this remarkable study in Louisiana history, the highly promising debut of director Kasi Lemmons. The hero/antihero is Doctor Batiste (Samuel L Jackson), a revered local physician, whose love for his daughters – Eve and Cisely – is nearly as great as his love for the women he visits for his work. Domestic tensions mount, but recollections play false in this Tennessee Williams-style story in which atmosphere, as well as drama, is all. Contains swearing. 🖵

Samuel L Jackson *Louis Batiste* • Lynn Whitfield *Roz Batiste* • Debbi Morgan *Mozelle Batiste Delacroix* • Vondie Curtis-Hall *Julian Grayraven* • Branford Marsalis *Harry Delacroix* • Lisa Nicole Carson *Matty Mereaux* • Meagan Good *Cisely Batiste* • Jurnee Smollett *Eve Batiste* ■ *Dir/Scr* Kasi Lemmons

The Evictors ★★ ⑱

Horror   1979 · US · Colour · 88mins

This uneven mix of *Old Dark House* chills and *Texas Chain Saw Massacre* shock tactics plays on the fears of all new home owners: that their dream house may be hiding a terrible past. When city newly-weds rent a lonely farm in an isolated village in Arizona, the locals view them with distrust, while it appears the previous owners are refusing to stay buried. Director Charles B Pierce generates a convincing sense of place and community amid the requisite splatter, and the final twist is just good enough to catch you off guard. Ultimately, though, this isn't strong enough to escape being a rehash of all-too-familiar elements. 🖵

Vic Morrow *Jake Rudd* • Michael Parks *Ben Watkins* • Jessica Harper *Ruth Watkins* • Sue Ane Langdon *Olie Gibson* • Dennis Fimple *Bumford* • Bill Thurman *Preacher Higgins* •

Jimmy Clem *Buckner* • Harry Thomasson *Wheeler* ■ *Dir* Charles B Pierce • *Scr* Charles B Pierce, Paul Fisk, Garry Rusoff

Evidence of Blood ★★★ 15

Mystery thriller 1998 · US · Colour · 104mins
David Strathairn and Mary McDonnell, a memorable pairing in John Sayles's Oscar-nominated *Passion Fish*, are reunited for this fine made-for-TV thriller set in the Deep South. Award-winning writer Strathairn returns to his home town and finds himself involved in a 40-year-old murder case for which a local man was sent to the electric chair. Director Andrew Mondshein sets a leisurely pace and the film works all the better for it. ▣

David Strathairn *Jackson Kinley* • Mary McDonnell *Dora Overton* • Sean McCann *Theodore Warfield* • Chris Wiggins *Horace Talbott* • Jackie Burroughs *Granny Dollar* ■ *Dir* Andrew Mondshein • *Scr* Dalene Young, from a novel by Thomas H Cook

Evidence of Love ★★★★ 18

Crime drama based on a true story
1990 · US · Colour · 90mins
Shocking crimes that jolt respectable American communities have provided movie fodder for years. Joining a long list is this true tale about a supposedly kindly, decent, devout Texas housewife who beat her best friend to death with an axe. The build-up and backdrop to this grim event are filtered through the trial with tremendous insight and a hefty dramatic punch by director Stephen Gyllenhaal. It is, however, Barbara Hershey's far-reaching, soulful performance you'll remember. ▣

Barbara Hershey *Candy Morrison* • Brian Dennehy *Ed Reivers* • John Terry *Stan Blankenship* • Richard Gilliland *Dale Morrison* • Lee Garlington *Peggy Blankenship* • Hal Holbrook *Dr Beardsley* • Matthew Posey *Norman Billings* ■ *Dir* Stephen Gyllenhaal • *Scr* Cynthia Cidre, from the non-fiction book by John Bloom, Jim Atkinson

The Evil ★★

Horror 1978 · US · Colour · 89mins
Joanna Pettet and Richard Crenna want to convert an old mansion into a drug rehabilitation centre. Problem is it's packed with poltergeists, and when Crenna unleashes a hostile force in the cellar, their existence turns into a shutter-banging, corpse-finding nightmare. Victor Buono turns up at the entertaining climax in a white suit and horns as the Devil in this low-rent version of *The Haunting*. Shoddy special effects undercut most of the horror in this rather routine outing.

Richard Crenna *CJ* • Joanna Pettet *Caroline* • Andrew Prine *Raymond* • Cassie Yates *Mary* • Lynne Moody *Felicia* • Victor Buono *The Devil* ■ *Dir* Gus Trikonis • *Scr* Donald G Thompson

The Evil Dead ★★★★ 18

Horror 1983 · US · Colour · 79mins
Director Sam Raimi burst on the horror scene (endorsed by none other than fan Stephen King) with this crude cult favourite, short on story but long on excessive gore and innovative camera work. An evil force tries to destroy four friends on vacation in a backwoods cabin when they discover an ancient Sumerian Book of the Dead and begin

reciting it. Cue all manner of vicious zombies, giggling ghouls and hideous demons to go overboard on the blood-splattering, pus-spurting attack – and the only way to kill them is to hack them to pieces. Watch the body parts and viscera fly! Contains strong langauge and scenes of violence. ▣

Bruce Campbell *Ash* • Ellen Sandweiss *Cheryl* • Betsy Baker *Linda* • Hal Delrich *Scott* • Sarah York *Shelly* ■ *Dir/Scr* Sam Raimi

Evil Dead II ★★★ 18

Horror comedy 1987 · US · Colour · 80mins
Director Sam Raimi's thrill-packed heaven for gore-hounds starts with an embellished recap of the original film before spinning off into another possession tale, with hopeless hero Ash (Bruce Campbell) again trying to repel a nasty demonic onslaught. Flashy special effects, hysterical scare tactics and Three Stooges-style farce combine with Raimi's trademark dizzying camera angles and manic wit for a breathless roller-coaster ride through twisted genre conventions. Campbell mugs shamelessly, clearly having a ball outdoing each preceding scene in comic thrust and haphazard horror, with hilarious gross-out results. An example: Ash's scuttling severed hand is held down by a copy of *A Farewell to Arms*. ▣ **DVD**

Bruce Campbell *Ash* • Sarah Berry *Annie* • Dan Hicks [Danny Hicks] *Jake* • Kassie Wesley *Bobby Joe* • Theodore Raimi *Possessed Henrietta* • Denise Bixler *Linda* • Richard Domeier *Ed* • John Peaks *Professor Raymond Knowby* • Lou Hancock *Henrietta* ■ *Dir* Sam Raimi • *Scr* Sam Raimi, Scott Spiegel

Evil Ed ★ 18

Horror comedy 1995 · Swe · Colour · 89mins
A young film editor is hired to censor the gruesome bits out of horror series titled *Loose Limbs*. He begins to lose his mind and turns into a murderer in this low-budget genre comedy from Sweden. Packed with fake gore, unfunny gags and dreadful acting, insulting lip-service is paid to the argument that screen violence leads to violent behaviour, which looks decidedly hollow in context. Compared to *The Evil Dead*, it's an unmemorable bust. Contains violence. ▣

Johan Rudeback *Edward Svensson* • Olof Rhodin *Sam Campbell* • Gert Fylking *Nurse* • Per Loftberg *Nick* • Cecelia Ljung *Barbara* ■ *Dir* Anders Jacobsson • *Scr* Anders Jacobsson, Goran Lundstrom

Evil Has a Face ★ 15

Thriller 1996 · US · Colour · 89mins
Sean Young is a talented young female sketch artist who uses her enviable abilities to track down an evil child molester in this standard police procedural movie. The case she takes is near her hometown, close to scenes from her own childhood traumas, and the sketch she produces from an abducted girl is that of her own stepfather. This offers little suspense, few surprises and relatively little action amongst its yawningly clichéd characterisations. ▣

Sean Young *Gwen* • William R Moses *Tom* • Brighton Hertford *Bria* • Joe Guzaldo *Radachek*

• Chelcie Ross *McGarrell* • Kate Buddeke *Ellen* • Suzanne Petri *Phyliss* • Dick Cusack *Lester* ■ *Dir/Scr* Rob Fresco

Evil in Clear River ★★ PG

Drama based on a true story
1988 · US · Colour · 93mins
Worthy but stodgy drama, featuring that icon of TV movies, Lindsay Wagner. She plays a mother in a small town in Canada who discovers that her hockey-loving son has fallen under the influence of anti-Semitic teacher Randy Quaid. The two leads turn in credible performances, and the supporting performances are equally good, but they are all let down by an over-melodramatic script. ▣

Lindsay Wagner *Kate McKinnon* • Randy Quaid *Pete Suvak* • Thomas Wilson Brown *Mark McKinnon* • Michael Flynn *Glen McKinnon* • Stephanie Dees *Heather McKinnon* ■ *Dir* Karen Arthur • *Scr* William Schmidt

Evil of Frankenstein ★★

Horror 1964 · UK · Colour · 86mins
The third of Hammer's *Frankenstein* sequels and the least interesting of all – although, because it was made for Universal, it's the only one that could use their copyrighted Boris Karloff monster look. Peter Cushing lends his usual conviction to the mad doctor part, this time bringing his brain-damaged creation back to life with the help of a mesmerist. But the crooked Zoltan (Peter Woodthorpe) hypnotises the monster into carrying out his vengeful crimes. Lumbering direction by Freddie Francis matches the gait of New Zealand wrestler Kiwi Kingston as the infamous bolted one.

Peter Cushing *Baron Frankenstein* • Peter Woodthorpe *Zoltan* • Sandor Eles *Hans* • Kiwi Kingston *Creature* • Duncan Lamont *Chief of Police* • Katy Wild *Beggar girl* ■ *Dir* Freddie Francis • *Scr* John Elder

Evil Spirits ★★

Mystery horror 1991 · US · Colour · 95mins
Psycho undergoes a sex change, as batty landlady Karen Black is apparently bumping off her low-life boarders and banking their social security cheques, while psychically conversing with her husband's wheelchair-bound, mummified corpse. Supposedly a gory black comedy, the only laughs to be had are unintentional ones, although the above-average celebrity horror cast, including Hammer starlet Martine Beswick, plus the odd atmospheric gothic image, will hold the interest of genre enthusiasts.

Karen Black *Mrs Purdy* • Michael Berryman *Mr Balzac* • Arte Johnson *Lester Potts* • Virginia Mayo *Mrs Wilson* • Martine Beswick *Vanya* • Bert Remsen *Mr Wilson* • Mikel Angel *Willie* ■ *Dir* Gary Graver • *Scr* Mikel Angel

The Evil That Men Do ★ 18

Action thriller 1984 · US · Colour · 85mins
With its numerous beatings and rapes, this repellent film surely ranks as Charles Bronson's most depraved picture – quite a feat! Ol' stone eyes stars as a professional hit man coaxed out of retirement to deal with a torturer working in an oppressed South American country. Action veteran J Lee Thompson gets an adequate

performance from the big man, but suffers from muddled ethics – by taking the moral high ground, the film is guilty of revelling in the scenes of torture it supposedly decries. Besides, Bronson is getting way too old for this kind of thing. Contains violence. ▣

Charles Bronson *Holland* • Theresa Saldana *Rhiana Hidalgo* • Joseph Maher *Dr Clement Molloch* • José Ferrer *Dr Hector Lomelin* • Rene Enriquez *Max Ortiz* • John Glover *Briggs* • Raymond St Jacques *Randolph* • Antoinette Bower *Claire* ■ *Dir* J Lee Thompson • *Scr* David Lee Henry, John Crowther, from the novel by Lance R Hill

The Evil Trap ★★★

Thriller 1975 · Fr · Colour
Yves Boisset had several run-ins with the censor for the decidedly left-wing content of his grittily realistic *policiers*. However, suspense is more to the fore in this adaptation of Jean-Patrick Manchette's crime novel, *O Dingos, O Châteaux*, as governess Marlène Jobert searches for her young charge before she's framed for his murder by kidnapper Tomas Milian. Jobert courageously exhibits the emotional fragility of a woman fresh out of a clinic, and Milian is a study in malevolence. But Thomas Waintrop is outstanding as the brattish tycoon's nephew who barely deserves rescuing. French dialogue dubbed into English.

Marlène Jobert *Julie* • Tomas Milian *Thompson* • Thomas Waintrop *Thomas* • Michael Lonsdale [Michel Lonsdale] *Mostri* ■ *Dir* Yves Boisset • *Scr* Yves Boisset, from the novel *O Dingos, O Châteaux* by Jean-Patrick Manchette

Evil under the Sun ★★★ PG

Murder mystery 1982 · UK · Colour · 111mins
This is a typically polished whodunit, which sees Peter Ustinov make his second appearance as the fussy Belgian detective Hercule Poirot. You won't use up too many little grey cells figuring out who is responsible for the murder of actress Diana Rigg, but there's enormous pleasure to be had from sitting through the picture while waiting to be proved right. The stellar cast clearly enjoys itself, with Maggie Smith in fine fettle as the hotel manageress. Majorca looks hot, but it would have been nice if the producers had retained the original Cornish setting. ▣

Peter Ustinov *Hercule Poirot* • Colin Blakely *Sir Horace Blatt* • Jane Birkin *Christine Redfern* • Nicholas Clay *Patrick Redfern* • Maggie Smith *Daphne Castle* • Roddy McDowall *Rex Brewster* • Sylvia Miles *Myra Gardener* • James Mason *Odell Gardener* • Denis Quilley *Kenneth Marshall* • Diana Rigg *Arlena Marshall* ■ *Dir* Guy Hamilton • *Scr* Anthony Shaffer, from the novel by Agatha Christie

Evita ★★★ PG

Musical biography
1996 · US · Colour · 134mins
Madonna's most successful foray into movies, taken from one of the most successful musicals of recent years, casts her as the woman who became mother-figure to her country through marriage to fascist dictator Juan Peron (Jonathan Pryce). Director Alan Parker eschews explanatory dialogue to link the music, resulting in a curiously airless and enigmatic piece which

never involves us in the traumas of Evita or Argentina. Antonio Banderas, meanwhile, co-stars as the Everyman revolutionary whose appearance and reappearance in Evita's life is never fully explained. Probably better to have seen the original first; then you'll know why Evita sings *Don't Cry for Me Argentina*. ▦ **DVD**

Madonna *Eva Peron* • Antonio Banderas *Che* • Jonathan Pryce *Juan Peron* • Jimmy Nail *Agustin Magaldi* • Victoria Sus *Dona Juana* • Julian Littman *Brother Juan* • Olga Merediz *Blanca* • Laura Pallas *Elisa* • Andrea Corr *Peron's mistress* ■ *Dir* Alan Parker • *Scr* Alan Parker, Oliver Stone, from the musical by Andrew Lloyd Webber, Tim Rice

Evolver ★★ 🔢

Thriller 1994 · US · Colour · 87mins

A scrapped military project is turned into a virtual reality game named "Evolver" in director Mark Rosman's cheap TV movie. Ethan Randall plays the top laser tag champion in America who gets the chance to play it internationally, only to end up fighting for survival. A predictable science-fiction potboiler from one-time genre hopeful Rosman, director of *The House on Sorority Row*. ▦

Ethan Randall [Ethan Embry] *Kyle Baxter* • John DeLancie *Russell Bennett* • Cindy Pickett *Melanie Baxter* • Paul Dooley *Jerry Briggs* • Cassidy Rae *Jamie Saunders* • William H Macy *Computer* ■ *Dir* Mark Rosman • *Scr* Mark Rosman, Manny Coto

The Ex ★★★ 🔢

Erotic thriller 1996 · US · Colour · 83mins

The *Fatal Attraction* premise – bonkers man/woman obsessively pursues reluctant partner – is now a staple of the straight-to-video market. This is one of the better examples, even though it is still a slightly sordid slice of exploitation. Yancy Butler is the deranged ex-wife of architect Nick Mancuso who wheedles her way back into his life by befriending his new wife, Suzy Amis. Butler is suitably over the top as the woman scorned, while the no-frills direction ensures the action never flags. ▦

Nick Mancuso *David Kenyon* • Suzy Amis *Molly Kenyon* • Yancy Butler *Deidre Kenyon* • Hamish Tildseley *Michael Kenyon* • Babs Chula *Doctor Lillian Jonas* • John Novak *Miles Endicott* ■ *Dir* Mark L Lester • *Scr* Larry Cohen, from a novel by John Lutz

Ex-Lady ★

Drama 1933 · US · BW · 67mins

Inexplicably making a retreat of *Illicit*, in which Warners had starred another rising queen of melodrama, Barbara Stanwyck, only two years earlier, the studio gave Bette Davis her first "official" starring role, that of a woman with startlingly progressive attitudes to sex and marriage that moderate when love enters her life. Davis described the result as a shaming "piece of junk", critics and audiences agreed, and her official leading lady status was delayed for a year or two.

Bette Davis *Helen Bauer* • Gene Raymond *Don Peterson* • Frank McHugh *Hugo Van Hugh* • Monroe Owsley *Nick Malvyn* • Claire Dodd

Iris Van Hugh • Kay Strozzi *Peggy Smith* ■ *Dir* Robert Florey • *Scr* David Boehm, from the story by Edith Fitzgerald, Robert Riskin

The Ex-Mrs Bradford ★★★

Comedy mystery 1936 · US · BW · 81mins

A fast-moving screwball farce, delightfully teaming a post-*Thin Man* William Powell with the lovely Jean Arthur. The sophisticated Powell is a surgeon this time, investigating a murder in which a black widow spider was the weapon. It's all good, clean fun, really, with a marvellous supporting cast of RKO regulars, notably cop James Gleason and wonderful Eric Blore, typecast as a butler. It's not directed too well, but it's always a pleasure to view such endearing stars.

William Powell *Dr Bradford* • Jean Arthur *Paula Bradford* • James Gleason *Inspector Corrigan* • Eric Blore *Stokes* • Robert Armstrong *Nick Martel* • Lila Lee *Miss Prentiss* • Grant Mitchell *Mr Summers* ■ *Dir* Stephen Roberts • *Scr* Anthony Veiller, from a story by James Edward Grant

Excalibur ★★★★ 🔢

Action fantasy
1981 · UK/US · Colour · 134mins

Director John Boorman's vivid and passionate telling of the Arthurian legend is a thoroughly convincing visualisation of the Knights of the Round Table myth within Dark Ages history. Masterfully intermingling fable and magic with a gritty reality, Boorman explores the cosmic duality of good versus evil, paganism versus Christianity, mighty Merlin versus malevolent Morgana, with eccentric élan. The search for the Holy Grail and the final battle are simply stunning sequences, and, while the dizzying pace leaves scant time for proper characterisation, Nicol Williamson, Nigel Terry and Helen Mirren make their mark. Contains some violence and brief nudity. ▦ **DVD**

Nigel Terry *King Arthur* • Helen Mirren *Morgana* • Nicol Williamson *Merlin* • Nicholas Clay *Lancelot* • Cherie Lunghi *Guenevere* • Paul Geoffrey *Perceval* • Robert Addie *Mordred* • Gabriel Byrne *Uther Pendragon* • Liam Neeson *Gawain* • Corin Redgrave *Duke of Cornwall* • Patrick Stewart *Leondegrance* ■ *Dir* John Boorman • *Scr* Rospo Pallenberg, John Boorman, from the medieval prose romance *Le Morte d'Arthur* by Thomas Malory

Exception to the Rule ★★ 🔢

Thriller 1996 · US · Colour · 99mins

With *Sex and the City*, Liverpool-born Kim Cattrall finally found a vehicle worthy of her under-rated talents. But she has to make do with a generic *femme fatale* role in this thriller-by-numbers. Reeking of corrupt carnality, she upstages Sean Young as she lures her husband first into bed and then into a dubious diamond transaction. Never one to fade into the background, Young bites back tenaciously, but whether Eric McCormack's adulterous sap is worth fighting for is open to debate. With William Devane lending a touch of class, this predictable hokum is at least better acted than most erotic pulp. ▦

Kim Cattrall *Carla Rainer* • Sean Young *Angela Bayer* • Eric McCormack *Timothy Bayer* •

William Devane *Lawrence Kellerman* • Stephen Mendel ■ *Dir* David Winning • *Scr* Shuki Levy, Shell Danielson

Excess Baggage ★ 🔢

Romance 1997 · US · Colour · 96mins

Oh dear. In the first film from her production company First Kiss, Alicia Silverstone stars as an annoying, spoiled brat who fakes her own kidnapping by locking herself in the trunk of her car. She then gets snatched for real when thief Benicio Del Toro steals it in this dire comedy adventure from *Demolition Man* director Marco Brambilla. Lacking in laughs, romance and action, the film plods along painfully, with only the reliable Christopher Walken injecting any entertaining moments. A bad misstep for Silverstone who, while superb in the hilarious *Clueless*, is simply grating here. ▦ **DVD**

Alicia Silverstone *Emily* • Benicio Del Toro *Vincent* • Christopher Walken *Ray* • Jack Thompson *Alexander* • Harry Connick Jr *Greg* • Nicholas Turturro *Stick* • Michael Bowen *Gus* • Robert Wisden *Detective Sims* ■ *Dir* Marco Brambilla • *Scr* Max D Adams, Dick Clement, Ian La Frenais, from a story by Max D Adams

Excessive Force ★★★ 🔢

Thriller 1993 · US · Colour · 82mins

Thomas Ian Griffith has always stood out from the ranks of action heroes as someone who can act a bit. He's never really crossed over into the mainstream but his thrillers usually deliver the goods, and this is no exception. He's helped by an outstanding supporting cast that includes James Earl Jones, Lance Henriksen, Tony Todd and Burt Young. The latter plays a gangster who murders Griffith's police colleagues in revenge for a drugs bust, prompting our moody hero to take the law into his own hands. ▦

Thomas Ian Griffith *Terry McCain* • Lance Henriksen *Devlin* • Burt Young *Sal DiMarco* • James Earl Jones *Jake* • Charlotte Lewis *Anita Gilmour* • Tom Hodges *Dylan* • Tony Todd *Frankie Hawkins* • Randy Popplewell *Tony* ■ *Dir* Jon Hess • *Scr* Eric Rhodes

Exclusive ★★ 🔢

Thriller 1992 · US · Colour · 87mins

Suzanne Somers is always going to struggle to lose the dippy blonde tag she gained in the sitcom *Three's Company*, and, try as she might, she is not particularly convincing here as an ace journalist. Taking a break from her anchorwoman's job, Somers sets out to uncover the mystery behind the death of seven people in a nightclub. Ed Begley Jr and Michael Nouri offer solid support for the star, but the direction and script are strictly routine. ▦

Suzanne Somers *Marcy Singer* • Michael Nouri *Reed Pierce* • Ed Begley Jr *Allen* • Joe Cortese *Oliver* • Scott Bryce *Chandler* • Kelly Rowan *Sunny* • Jerry Adler *Mort* • James Pickens Jr *Jonathan Heglin* • Eric Poppick *Jeffrey Fein* ■ *Dir* Alan Metzger • *Scr* Bill Wells, Mimi Rothman Schapiro

The Execution ★★ 🔢

Thriller 1985 · US · Colour · 89mins

A rather tasteless drama about a group of women in LA, all survivors of the Birkenau Nazi concentration camp, who discover one of their tormentors making a living in the same city as a successful restaurant owner. Loretta Swit, Jessica Walter, Barbara Barrie, Sandy Dennis and Valerie Harper are the women with bad European accents who decide to exact revenge in what is essentially an exploitative TV copy of *The Odessa File*. ▦

Loretta Swit *Marysia Walenka* • Valerie Harper *Hannah Epstein* • Jessica Walter *Gertrude Simon* • Sandy Dennis *Elsa Spahn* • Barbara Barrie *Sophie Langbein* • Rip Torn *Walter Grossman/Wilheim Gehbert* • Martin E Brooks *Martin Renner* ■ *Dir* Paul Wendkos • *Scr* William Wood, Oliver Crawford, from the novel by Oliver Crawford

The Execution of Raymond Graham ★★

Prison drama 1985 · US · Colour · 104mins

Daniel Petrie (*Cocoon: The Return*) directs this TV drama about the last hours of a man's life before he is executed. Originally shown as a live broadcast on US television, this film suffers in comparison to superior dramas on the same subject like *The Executioner's Song* and *Dead Man Walking*. Jeff Fahey is the condemned man but more interesting is the supporting cast which includes George Dzundza (*Basic Instinct*), Morgan Freeman as the prison warden and Josef Sommer (*Witness*).

Jeff Fahey *Raymond Graham* • Graham Beckel *Vic Graham* • Laurie Metcalf *Carol Graham* • Kate Reid *Mrs Graham* • Josef Sommer *Jim Neal* • Lois Smith *Mary Neal* • Philip Sterling *Max Adler* • Morgan Freeman *Warden Pratt* • George Dzundza *Chaplain* ■ *Dir* Daniel Petrie • *Scr* Mal Frohman

The Executioner ★★ 🔢

Spy drama 1970 · UK · Colour · 105mins

This convoluted spy drama finds George Peppard playing a British secret agent uncovering treachery within his department and collusion within the CIA. It's sad to think Peppard was cast because it was thought he might boost the film's chances at the American box office, and he does look rather lost amid a cast of English stalwarts (Joan Collins, Nigel Patrick, George Baker) and the inevitable Oscar Homolka as a communist defector. Director Sam Wanamaker seems far more interested in scoring points about the British class system than concentrating on plot logic and suspense. ▦

George Peppard *John Shay* • Joan Collins *Sarah Booth* • Judy Geeson *Polly Bendel* • Oscar Homolka *Racovsky* • Charles Gray *Vaughan Jones* • Nigel Patrick *Colonel Scott* • George Baker *Philip Crawford* ■ *Dir* Sam Wanamaker • *Scr* Jack Pulman, from a story by Gordon McDonell

The Executioner of Venice ★★★

Historical swashbuckling adventure
1963 · It · Colour · 90mins

Director Luigi Capuano is often referred to as the Italian Michael Curtiz

because he specialised in highly colourful, continental costume epics, always managing to give even the most predictable plots a high energy lift. Here's one of his best: a smooth spectacle about pirate bands operating in the Adriatic, in which hero Lex Barker (who made his name playing Tarzan) is torn between duty and romance with Venetian vixen Sandra Panaro. An effervescent swashbuckler laced with modest suspense. Italian dialogue dubbed into English.

Lex Barker *Sandrigo* • Sandra Panaro [Alessandra Panaro] *Leonora* • Mario Petri *Guarnieri* • Guy Madison *Rodrigo Zeno* ■ *Dir* Luigi Capuano • *Scr* Luigi Capuano, Arpad De Riso

Executive Action ★★★★ PG

Political thriller 1973 · US · Colour · 86mins

Unshown on TV for many years, this drama about the Kennedy assassination in Dallas makes for absolutely riveting viewing. It shows how a shadowy group of businessmen and military leaders (including Robert Ryan and Burt Lancaster) plots to kill JFK, who has "gone soft on communism and the blacks". Brilliantly organised, the film describes how the shooters plan their kill as well as the search for a fall guy, Lee Harvey Oswald. It's as tense as *The Day of the Jackal*, only this time the question is not how does he fail, but how do they get away with it? 🎞

Burt Lancaster *Farrington* • Robert Ryan *Foster* • Will Geer *Ferguson* • Gilbert Green *Paulitz* • John Anderson *Halliday* • Paul Carr *Gunman Chris* • Colby Chester *Tim* • Ed Lauter *Operation chief, team A* ■ *Dir* David Miller • *Scr* Dalton Trumbo, from a story by Donald Freed, Mark Lane

Executive Decision ★★★ 15

Action thriller 1996 · US · Colour · 127mins

Producer Joel Silver is no mug at the action game (*Lethal Weapon* and the *Die Hard* series), and, though no match for his best work, this competent thriller is entertaining enough. Director Stuart Baird makes good use of the thrills and spills, diverting attention from the far-fetched plot in which David Suchet's gang of Arab terrorists is headed towards the US in a hijacked jumbo jet with enough stolen Russian nerve gas to kill millions of Americans. Steven Seagal and the deceptively urbane Kurt Russell share top billing as part of an elite team that sets out in a stealth bomber (Hollywood's favourite prop of the nineties) to try and defuse the situation. Enjoyably mindless fun. 🎞 *DVD*

Kurt Russell *David Grant* • Steven Seagal *Lieutenant Colonel Austin Travis* • Halle Berry *Jean* • John Leguizamo *Rat* • Oliver Platt *Cahill* • Joe Morton *Cappy* • David Suchet *Nagi Hassan* • BD Wong *Louie* ■ *Dir* Stuart Baird • *Scr* Jim Thomas, John Thomas

Executive Power ★★

Political thriller 1998 · US · Colour · 115mins

The real-life scandals of the Clinton era are probably more compelling than events in this slow-moving potboiler. In a plot obviously inspired by the suicide of one of Bill Clinton's friends, Vince Foster, disillusioned ex-Secret Service

agent Nick finds himself investigating the mysterious death of a presidential adviser. What makes this movie so frustrating is that a character's motivation at any given time is apparently dictated solely by what is needed to keep the action going.

Craig Sheffer *Nick* • John Heard *Walker* • William Atherton *President Fields* • Joanna Cassidy *First Lady* • Denise Crosby *Christine Rolands* ■ *Dir/Scr* David Corley

Executive Suite ★★★★ U

Drama 1954 · US · BW · 104mins

Cameron Hawley's novel about a boardroom battle for power seemed an unlikely subject for a glossy MGM movie. However, in the hands of editor turned director Robert Wise (*West Side Story* and *The Sound of Music*) this gritty drama is riveting, helped by an all-star cast, and not at all hindered by MGM's insistence on the advertising campaign "It's sweet, sweet, sweet!", just in case anyone thought the title was pronounced "executive suit". William Holden heads the corporate suits, and there's particularly strong support from Fredric March, Nina Foch and Walter Pidgeon. But what dignifies the whole proceedings is, uniquely for Hollywood, the absence of a music score.

William Holden (1) *McDonald Walling* • June Allyson *Mary Blemond Walling* • Barbara Stanwyck *Julia O Tredway* • Fredric March *Loren Phineas Shaw* • Walter Pidgeon *Frederick Y Alderson* • Shelley Winters *Eva Bardeman* • Paul Douglas *Josiah Walter Dudley* • Louis Calhern *George Nyle Caswell* • Nina Foch *Erica Martin* ■ *Dir* Robert Wise • *Scr* Ernest Lehman, from the novel by Cameron Hawley

Executive Target ★★★ 18

Action thriller 1997 · US · Colour · 91mins

Essentially a series of increasingly spectacular car chases, this cheap and cheerful action thriller makes for entertainingly stupid viewing. Michael Madsen stars as the stunt driver who's sprung from prison by a shady organisation to help kidnap the president (Roy Scheider) when he's visiting Los Angeles. Keith David is splendidly over-the-top as the chief villain, while director Joseph Merhi just can't wait to smash up more vehicles. Great fun. Contains violence, swearing and nudity. 🎞

Michael Madsen *Nick James* • Roy Scheider *President Carlson* • Keith David *Lamar Quentin* • Angie Everhart *Lacey* • Dayton Callie *Bela* ■ *Dir* Joseph Merhi • *Scr* Jacobsen Hart, Dayton Callie

The Exile ★★ U

Drama 1947 · US · BW · 91mins

Douglas Fairbanks Jr not only stars as the exiled Charles II; he also wrote the script and produced the picture. So what we see is evidence of a star's clout rather than his talent, since it's a poorly written piece of historical flummery that gives Fairbanks a number of women to romance while hiding from Cromwell's agents in Europe. As one would expect from director Max Ophüls, it contains some sensuous camerawork. Original prints were in sepia tones.

Douglas Fairbanks Jr *Charles Stuart* • Maria Montez *The Countess* • Paula Croset [Rita Corday] *Katie* • Henry Daniell *Colonel Ingram* • Nigel Bruce *Sir Edward Hyde* • Robert Coote *Pinner* • Otto Waldis *Jan* • Eldon Gorst *Seymour* ■ *Dir* Max Ophüls • *Scr* Douglas Fairbanks Jr, from the novel *His Majesty, the King* by Cosmo Hamilton

eXistenZ ★★★★★ 15

Futuristic drama 1999 · Can/UK · Colour · 96mins

David Cronenberg's futuristic thriller confidently expands on the themes of *Videodrome* for another of his typical "body horror" shockers. Jennifer Jason Leigh invents a game system — "eXistenZ" – that taps so deeply into users' fears and desires that it blurs the boundaries between escapism and reality. Security guard Jude Law is drawn into playing the game with its creator as he attempts to find out who is behind an assassination attempt on her life. Nothing is what it seems in Cronenberg's phantasmagoric world where games consoles are inserted directly into the spinal column, gristle guns fire human teeth instead of bullets and two-headed reptiles roam the wilds. Fiendishly clever and brilliantly audacious. Contains violence and swearing.

Jennifer Jason Leigh *Allegra Geller* • Jude Law *Ted Pikul* • Ian Holm *Kiri Vinokur* • Don McKellar *Yevgeny Nourish* • Callum Keith Rennie *Hugo Carlaw* • Sarah Polley *Merle* • Christopher Eccleston *Levi* • Willem Dafoe *Gas* ■ *Dir/Scr* David Cronenberg • *Cinematographer* Peter Suschitzky

Exit in Red ★ 18

Erotic mystery drama 1996 · US · Colour · 94mins

The *Wild Orchid* pair of Mickey Rourke and Carre Otis are reunited for this would-be erotic thriller. This time around, though, there's barely enough steam to fog up a pocket mirror. Rourke is the psychiatrist with a past trying to set up a new life with lawyer Otis who gets involved in a complex murder plot when he meets sexy Annabel Schofield. It's sloppily acted and directed, while the few sex scenes have a tacked-on feel about them. 🎞

Mickey Rourke *Ed Altman* • Anthony Michael Hall *Nick* • Carre Otis *Kate* • Annabel Schofield *Ally* • Johnny Venocur *Cop* • Robert F Lyons *Detective Vollers* ■ *Dir* Yurek Bogayevicz • *Scr* David Womark

Exit to Eden ★ 18

Erotic comedy 1994 · US · Colour · 109mins

Based on a novel by Anne Rice, author of *Interview with the Vampire*, this unfunny sex comedy is only worth catching if you're sure you can stomach the sight of Dan Aykroyd in bondage gear. Aykroyd and Rosie O'Donnell play a pair of investigators going "undercover" at an S&M resort run by Dana Delany, while *Strictly Ballroom* star Paul Mercurio wanders around in something resembling a nappy. A career low for *Pretty Woman* director Garry Marshall and just about everyone else involved. 🎞

Dana Delany *Lisa Emerson* • Paul Mercurio *Elliot Slater* • Rosie O'Donnell *Sheila* • Dan Aykroyd *Fred* • Hector Elizondo *Martin Halifax*

• Stuart Wilson *Omar* • Iman *Nina* ■ *Dir* Garry Marshall • *Scr* Deborah Amelon, Bob Brunner, from the novel by Anne Rice

Exodus ★★★★ PG

Epic drama 1960 · US · Colour · 199mins

Leon Uris's bestseller gets the Preminger treatment in this accomplished, epic retelling of events leading to the birth of Israel in 1948. With a script by former blacklistee Dalton Trumbo, this is a gritty, forthright and marvellously cinematic experience, if a long one. Some critics weren't happy about the all-star cast and sentiment, though it's hard to imagine better casting than Paul Newman as Haganah leader Ari Ben Canaan or Eva Marie Saint as nurse Kitty Fremont. Sal Mineo was nominated for best supporting actor as freedom fighter Dov Landau, but the Oscar went to Ernest Gold's marvellously grandiose music, which has achieved classic status. 🎞

Paul Newman *Ari Ben Canaan* • Eva Marie Saint *Kitty Fremont* • Gen Sutherland • Peter Lawford *Maj Caldwell* • Lee J Cobb *Barak Ben Canaan* • Sal Mineo *Dov Landau* • John Derek *Taha* • Hugh Griffith *Mandria* • Gregory Ratoff *Lakavitch* ■ *Dir* Otto Preminger • *Scr* Dalton Trumbo, from the novel by Leon Uris

The Exorcist ★★★★★ 18

Horror 1973 · US · Colour · 116mins

The most talked-about and reviled horror movie of all time. It's an influential (and Oscar-winning) adaptation by William Peter Blatty of his own bestselling novel about the demonic possession of an actress's young daughter (played by Linda Blair) in Washington DC. Unbelievably scary when it first came out, its overall impact has been lessened by time and repeated genre duplication. But the macabre, obscene demonstrations of the Devil still retain their power to startle and nauseate. Aside from the graphic and revolutionary special effects, director William Friedkin dwells on the allegorical religious subtleties for a richly satisfying fright workout. Max von Sydow and Ellen Burstyn also rise to the landmark occasion to provide a torrent of terror. Contains swearing, sexual references and violence. 🎞 *DVD*

Ellen Burstyn *Mrs MacNeil* • Max von Sydow *Father Merrin* • Lee J Cobb *Lieutenant Kinderman* • Kitty Winn *Sharon* • Jack MacGowran *Burke Dennings* • Jason Miller *Father Karras* • Linda Blair *Regan MacNeil* • Reverend William O'Malley *Father Dyer* ■ *Dir* William Friedkin • *Scr* William Peter Blatty, from his novel • *Cinematographer* Owen Roizman • *Art Director* Bill Malley • *Make-up* Dick Smith • *Sound* Robert Knudsen, Chris Newman

Exorcist II: The Heretic ★★★ 18

Horror 1977 · US · Colour · 112mins

The jury is still out on this critical and financial disaster, tampered with by the studio after audiences cracked up at the devilish finale. The focus here is on the quest of Father Richard Burton to quell the demon still present within Linda Blair, now in therapy to combat recurring nightmares. Yes, Burton overplays the doom-laden script. And, yes, all the African mumbo jumbo is bewildering. But director John Boorman deliberately accents the weighty mythological angles to create a film as complex and intellectual as it is visceral, and his daring approach is well overdue for reappraisal. 🖥

Linda Blair *Regan MacNeil* • Richard Burton *Father Lamont* • Louise Fletcher *Dr Gene Tuskin* • Max von Sydow *Father Merrin* • Kitty Winn *Sharon* • Paul Henreid *The Cardinal* • James Earl Jones *Older Kokumo* • Ned Beatty *Edwards* • *Dir* John Boorman • *Scr* William Goodhart, from characters created by William Peter Blatty

The Exorcist III ★★★ 🔞

Horror 1990 · US · Colour · 105mins

The Exorcist is a tough act to follow but director William Peter Blatty's official sequel to his original story, based on his book *Legion*, is more an intellectual suspense chiller drawn from the cerebral creaks and shadows of the mind. Lieutenant Kinderman (George C Scott replacing Lee J Cobb from the original terror classic) investigates a series of sacrilegious murders by the Gemini Killer, who may be a servant of the Devil. Relying heavily on static shots, elongated close-ups and academic dialogue (not tacky gore theatrics) to convey the real horror of life, sin and unbelief, Blatty's high-class bible-bash is full of unexpected surprises, quirkiness and one absolutely frightening moment of pure shock. 🖥

George C Scott *Lieutenant William Kinderman* • Ed Flanders *Father Dyer* • Brad Dourif *The Gemini Killer* • Jason Miller *Patient X* • Nicol Williamson *Father Morning* • Nancy Fish *Nurse Allerton* • Samuel L Jackson *Dream blind man* ■ *Dir* William Peter Blatty • *Scr* William Peter Blatty, from his novel *Legion*

Exotica ★★★★ 🔞

Drama 1994 · Can · Colour · 103mins

Prying behind the façade of the respectable is director Atom Egoyan's stock-in-trade. In this pulsating study of need, isolation and fantasy, he effortlessly slips between past and present to create a myriad of plot strands that he finally ties together with a mastery few can match. The scenes within the strip club of the title drip with erotic tension, reinforced by the sinister DJing of Elias Koteas, the seductive dancing of Mia Kirshner and the disturbing willingness of auditor Bruce Greenwood to succumb to her charms. Add in a smuggling operation centred on a pet shop and you have a truly provocative movie. Contains swearing, sex scenes and nudity. 🖥

Bruce Greenwood *Francis* • Mia Kirshner *Christina* • Elias Koteas *Eric* • Don McKellar *Thomas* • Arsinée Khanjian *Zoe* • David Hemblen *Inspector* • Sarah Polley *Tracey* • Victor Garber *Harold* • *Dir/Scr* Atom Egoyan

Expect No Mercy ★ 🔞

Science-fiction action
1995 · Can · Colour · 90mins

Wolf Larson plays Warbeck, the kind of megalomaniac who sports long blond hair and runs one of those high-tech labs/fight schools. Of course, no one running such places is ever up to any good, so it falls to Federal agents Billy Blanks and Jalal Merhi to go undercover and save the day. When

not involved in countless fight sequences, Blanks completely relies on his undeniable screen presence, while Merhi's strong accent makes him sound goofy. The attempt to portray virtual reality and high-tech on a small budget make the movie come across as one big eyesore. 🖥

Billy Blanks *Justin Vanier* • Wolf Larson *Warbeck* • Laurie Holden *Vicki* • Jalal Merhi *Eric* • Brett Halsey *Bromfield* ■ *Dir* Zale Dalen • *Scr* J Stephen Maunder

Experiment in Terror ★★★

Thriller 1962 · US · BW · 123mins

An unlikely offering from Blake Edwards, a director better known for his comedies. Teaming up here with Lee Remick – the star of his drama about alcoholism, *Days of Wine and Roses* – Edwards goes berserk with his camera, which goes everywhere, searching for a bug's-eye view and then a bird's, making the audience rather dizzy if not very scared. Problem is, this isn't a horror movie but an overlong glossy B-movie thriller, about a bank cashier (Remick) forced to embezzle $100,000 by a killer.

Glenn Ford *John Ripley* • Lee Remick *Kelly Sherwood* • Stefanie Powers *Toby* • Roy Poole *Brad* • Ned Glass *Popcorn* • Anita Loo *Lisa* • Patricia Huston *Nancy* • Ross Martin *Red Lynch* • Clifton James *Captain Moreno* ■ *Dir* Blake Edwards • *Scr* Gordon Gordon, Mildred Gordon, from their novel *Operation Terror*

Experiment Perilous ★★★

Melodrama 1944 · US · BW · 91mins

A clever but wordy suspenser, expertly directed by talented Jacques Tourneur in the wake of the similar *Gaslight*. This time it's insane husband Paul Lukas and glamorous wife Hedy Lamarr who are embroiled in a psychological battle of wits. George Brent plays the psychiatrist trying to rescue Lamarr, while Albert Dekker and Carl Esmond are also along for the ride.

Hedy Lamarr *Allida Bedereaux* • George Brent *Dr Huntington Bailey* • Paul Lukas *Nick Bedereaux* • Albert Dekker *Claghorne* • Carl Esmond *Maitland* • Olive Blakeney *Cissie* ■ *Dir* Jacques Tourneur • *Scr* Warren Duff, from the novel by Margaret Carpenter

The Expert ★★ 🔞

Action adventure 1994 · US · Colour · 94mins

Cult favourite Larry Cohen had a hand in the script, so this is a notch above the usual straight-to-video fodder. Jeff Speakman plays a police instructor seeking to avenge himself on the serial killer (Michael Shaner) who murdered his sister and is now on Death Row. To get to him, Speakman must break into prison. Shaner, though, is already planning to escape. Speakman's unflashy fighting style is impressive, the set pieces are nicely choreographed and Shaner makes for a creepy villain. 🖥

Jeff Speakman *John Lomax* • Michael Shaner *Martin Kagan* • Wolfgang Bodison *Dan Mason* • Alex Datcher *Dr Alice Barnes* • James Brolin *Warden Munsey* • Jim Varney ■ *Dir* Rick Avery • *Scr* Larry Cohen, Max Allan Collins, from a story by Jill Gatsby

The Experts ★★ 🔞

Spy comedy 1989 · US · Colour · 89mins

John Travolta spent a long time in the wilderness before Quentin Tarantino rejuvenated his career in *Pulp Fiction*, and this is an excellent example of the drivel he was making. This part screwball comedy, part Cold War satire stars Travolta, Arye Gross and Travolta's now-wife Kelly Preston in a tale of slick city types inveigled into aiding the dreaded "Ruskies" in their secret project to replicate American suburbia. Quite why the KGB should waste its valuable time on such futility is never sufficiently explained. 🖥

John Travolta *Travis* • Kelly Preston *Bonnie* • Arye Gross *Wendell* • Deborah Foreman *Jill* • James Keach *Yuri* • Charles Martin Smith *Cameron Smith* ■ *Dir* Dave Thomas (1) • *Scr* Nick Thile, Steven Greene, Eric Alter, from a story by Steven Greene, Eric Alter

Explorers ★★★ 🔞

Science-fiction adventure
1985 · US · Colour · 104mins

This is a minor entry in the Joe Dante canon, but an amusing family yarn all the same. A pre-fame Ethan Hawke and River Phoenix team up with Jason Presson as a trio of kids who build their own spacecraft and set off on the adventure of a lifetime. The youngsters are uniformly excellent, Mary Kay Place and Dante regular Dick Miller stand out among the grown-ups, and the tone is refreshingly unpatronising and unsentimental. Kids will love it, while adults will enjoy spotting the in-jokes Dante could not resist including. 🖥

Ethan Hawke *Ben Crandall* • River Phoenix *Wolfgang Müller* • Jason Presson *Darren Woods* • Amanda Peterson *Lori Swenson* • Dick Miller *Charlie Drake* • James Cromwell *Mr Müller* • Dana Ivey *Mrs Müller* • Leslie Rickert *Neek* • Mary Kay Place *Mrs Crandall* ■ *Dir* Joe Dante • *Scr* Eric Luke

The Explosive Generation ★★

Drama 1961 · US · BW · 89mins

Teen-angst movie about high school students who support their teacher (William Shatner) when he gets fired for teaching them about the birds and the bees. It seems that the students' parents can't talk to their kids about anything, and are shocked by the frankness of the discussion in the classroom. One of literally scores of movies Hollywood made at the time about teenage delinquency, shot on a slender budget by debutant director Buzz Kulik, a graduate of live TV.

William Shatner *Peter Gifford* • Patty McCormack *Janet Sommers* • Lee Kinsolving *Dan Carlyle* • Billy Gray *Bobby Herman Jr* • Steve Dunne *Bobby Herman Sr* • Arch Johnson *Mr Sommers* • Virginia Field *Mrs Sommers* • Beau Bridges *Mark* ■ *Dir* Buzz Kulik • *Scr* Joseph Landon

Exposed ★★ 🔞

Drama 1983 · US · Colour · 95mins

Before *Reservoir Dogs* star Harvey Keitel became cool he appeared in this tepid thriller as a terrorist who crosses paths with jet-set model Nastassja Kinski when she's not romancing violinist Rudolf Nureyev. Kinski has travelled to the big city to become a

concert pianist. Supposedly sexy and arty, *Exposed* is actually neither. 🖥

Nastassia Kinski [Nastassja Kinski] *Elizabeth Carlson* • Rudolf Nureyev *Daniel Jelline* • Harvey Keitel *Rivas* • Ian McShane *Greg Miller* • Bibi Andersson *Margaret* • Ron Randell *Curt* • Pierre Clementi *Vic* • Dov Gottesfeld *Marcel* • James Russo *Nick* ■ *Dir/Scr* James Toback

Expresso Bongo ★★★★ 🅿🅶

Musical 1959 · UK · BW · 101mins

This isn't only a fascinating snapshot of Soho in the skiffle and coffee bar era, but it's also one of the best musicals ever produced in this country. Oozing the easy charm and shiftless opportunism that had just served him so well in *Room at the Top*, Laurence Harvey is perfectly cast as the talent agent hoping to get rich quick through rookie rocker Cliff Richard, who, for all his raw appeal, is also very religious. Val Guest captures the fads and fashions of the late fifties, but it's Wolf Mankowitz's crackling script that gives the film its authenticity. 🖥

Laurence Harvey *Johnny Jackson* • Sylvia Syms *Maisie King* • Yolande Donlan *Dixie Collins* • Cliff Richard *Bongo Herbert* • Meier Tzelniker *Mayer* • Ambrosine Philpotts *Lady Rosemary* • Eric Pohlmann *Leon* ■ *Dir* Val Guest • *Scr* Wolf Mankowitz, from a play by Julian More, Wolf Mankowitz

Exquisite Tenderness ★★★ 🔞

Medical horror drama
1995 · US/Ger/Can · Colour · 95mins

Side effects from pituitary gland experiments turn former doctor Sean Haberle into a slobbering maniac in this crackpot chiller from director Carl Schenkel. A ghoulish and garish exercise in retro-slasher nostalgia, Schenkel's Hitch-cocktail of nightmare imagery, tasteless violence and lip-smacking gore is both terribly enjoyable and enjoyably terrible. Luckily, Haberle sews up hospital administrator Charles Dance's mouth so no one has to endure his terrible American accent for too long! Extra kicks are supplied by dazzling camerawork and creepy twists, all crammed into an entertaining, if overwrought spectacular. 🖥 **DVD**

Isabel Glasser *Dr Theresa McCann* • James Remar *Dr Benjamin Hendricks* • Sean Haberle *Dr Julian Matar* • Charles Dance *Dr Ed Mittlesbay* • Peter Boyle *Lieutenant Daryl McEllwaine* • Malcolm McDowell *Dr Roger Stein* • Charles Bailey-Gates *Sgt Ross* • Gregory West *Tommy Beaton* ■ *Dir* Carl Schenkel • *Scr* Patrick Cirillo, from a screenplay by Bernard Sloane

The Exterminating Angel ★★★★ 12

Satirical drama 1962 · Mex · BW · 89mins

Following his merciless attack on Catholicism in *Viridiana*, Luis Buñuel turned his attention to another of his favourite targets, the middle classes, in this searing condemnation of convention and outmoded morality. Clearly revealing his surrealist roots, this blackly comic film ingeniously uses a nightmare dinner party to make the terrifying assertion that the bourgeois lifestyle is every bit as hideous and limiting as any concentration camp regime. Brilliantly played by a cast

🅤 = SUITABLE FOR ALL   🅤🅒 = SUITABLE FOR ALL, ESPECIALLY FOR YOUNG CHILDREN (VIDEO ONLY)   🅿🅶 = PARENTAL GUIDANCE

including regulars Silvia Pinal and Claudio Brook, this is one of Buñuel's most pessimistic films, and its chilling ending will leave you dumbstruck. In Spanish with English subtitles. ▣

Silvia Pinal *Letitia* • Jacqueline Andere *Alicia Roc* • Jose Baviera *Leandro* • Augusto Benedico *Doctor* • Luis Beristain *Cristian Ugalde* • Antonio Bravo *Russell* • Claudio Brook *Julio, majordomo* • Cesar Del Campo *Colonel* • Rosa Elena Durgel *Silvia* ■ *Dir* Luis Buñuel • *Scr* Luis Buñuel, Luis Alcoriza, from the play *Los Naufragos de la Calle de la Providencia* by José Bergamin

The Exterminator ★★ 18

Crime drama   1980 · US · Colour · 94mins

For a straightforward tale of violent revenge, *The Exterminator* is a surprisingly influential film in straight-to-video circles. Avenging Vietnam vet Robert Ginty was henceforth known as Robert ''Exterminator'' Ginty, and became quite a draw in his own right. The genre kicks off here with Ginty on the trail of the murderous gang that beat up his comrade. He rapidly finds himself using his brutal combat skills to tackle the CIA, the cops and various crime families who all seem to be after his blood. Christopher George plays the head villain and Samantha Eggar provides the glamour. ◦

Christopher George *Detective James Dalton* • Samantha Eggar *Dr Megan Stewart* • Robert Ginty *John Eastland* • Steve James *Michael Jefferson* • Tony DiBenedetto *Chicken Pimp* • Dick Boccelli *Gino Pontivini* • Patrick Farrelly *CIA Agent Shaw* • Michele Harrell *Maria Jefferson* ■ *Dir/Scr* James Glickenhaus

Exterminator 2 ★★ 18

Crime thriller   1980 · US · Colour · 83mins

Unimaginatively titled sequel set in sleazy New York street crime circles. Robert Ginty, star of the original, is once again on the violent revenge trail, this time because some very bad people indeed, led by a mysterious master criminal, have been picking on his girlfriend – first seriously wounding her and then committing murder. Blaxploitation star Mario Van Peebles and a young John Turturro turn up in supporting roles. ▣

Robert Ginty *Johnny Eastland* • Mario Van Peebles *X* • Deborah Geffner *Caroline* • Frankie Faison *Be Gee* • Scott Randolph *Eyes* • Reggie Rock Bythewood *Spider* • Bruce Smolanoff *Red Rat* • John Turturro *1st guy* ■ *Dir/Scr* Mark Buntzman, William Sachs

The Extra Day ★★ U

Portmanteau drama
1956 · UK · Colour · 83mins

Had this portmanteau picture been shot in Italy or France in the same period, the five short stories about the mundane lives of some movie extras would have been made with *bona fide* bit players rather than with a cast comprising a second division Hollywood star, a faded French siren and umpteen ubiquitous British character actors. With Richard Basehart and Simone Simon unable to shake off the star lustre, Sid James comes closest to convincing us he's a real human being, but the trite tales and the bogus behind-the-scenes atmosphere render this merely a disappointing curio.

Richard Basehart *Joe Blake* • Simone Simon *Michele Blanchard* • George Baker *Steven Marlow* • Josephine Griffin *Toni Howard* • Colin Gordon *Sir George Howard* • Laurence Naismith *Kurt Vorn* • Charles Victor *Bert* • Sidney James *Barney West* • Joan Hickson *Mrs West* ■ *Dir/Scr* William Fairchild

Extralarge: Moving Target ★★

Detective drama
1990 · It/US · Colour · 88mins

Best known for his partnership with Terence Hill in spaghetti westerns and comedy action films, Bud Spencer (real name Carlo Pedersoli) here finds himself pounding a Florida beat with former *Miami Vice* star Philip Michael Thomas. As private eyes in possession of a nuclear secret wanted by both desperate assassins and crooked CIA agents, it doesn't take a genius to work out that much tyre tread will be lost before it's all quiet on the waterfront. It's lively, but it doesn't have that *Vice*-like grip. This was the first in a series of seven *Extralarge* made-for-TV movies.

Bud Spencer *Jack ''Extralarge'' Costello* • Philip Michael Thomas *Dumas* • Juan Fernandez *Rashid* • Vivian Ruiz *Mrs Martinez* • Lou Bedford *Sam* • Jackie Davis *Harry* ■ *Dir/Scr* Enzo G Castellari

The Extraordinary Seaman ★★

Second World War comedy
1969 · US · Colour · 80mins

David Niven was going through a rough patch at this point in his career and with this movie he hit a positive thicket. Alan Alda, Mickey Rooney and Jack Carter, on the run from the Japanese, find a natty Niven living on a beached ship in the Philippines. Faye Dunaway joins the crew, which is consolation for nobody but her agent, as action director John Frankenheimer just can't get to grips with this alleged comedy. Niven, however, handles it all with his customary aplomb.

David Niven *Lieutenant Commander Finchhaven* • Faye Dunaway *Jennifer Winslow* • Alan Alda *Lieutenant JG Morton Krim* • Mickey Rooney *Cook 3rd Class W WJ Oglethorpe* • Jack Carter *Gunner's Mate Orville Toole* • Juano Hernandez *Ali Shar* • Manu Tupou *Seaman 1st Class Lightfoot Star* • Barry Kelley *Admiral Barnwell* ■ *Dir* John Frankenheimer • *Scr* Phillip Rock, Hal Dresner, from a story by Phillip Rock

Extreme Close-Up ★★

Drama   1973 · US · Colour · 80mins

Television reporter James McMullan, working on a series about invasion of privacy, gets sucked into the kind of sexual voyeurism he's seeking to expose when he spies on a woman in the block opposite him. Although the script by *Jurassic Park's* Michael Crichton cleverly plays with *Rear Window* and *Peeping Tom* motifs, Jeannot Szwarc's direction can't elevate the material from superficial, seedy exploitation. Serious issues such as guilt and accountability are barely touched on.

James McMullan [Jim McMullan] *John Norman* • Kate Woodville *Sally Norman* • James A Watson Jr *Cameraman* ■ *Dir* Jeannot Szwarc • *Scr* Michael Crichton

Extreme Close-Up ★★

Drama   1990 · US · Colour · 93mins

Morgan Weisser plays a troubled teen who attempts to get to grips with the loss of his mother by making home movies of his own life in this intriguing, if flawed drama directed by former *thirtysomething* star Peter Horton. Weisser gives a captivating performance, and he is well served by a classy supporting cast that includes Craig T Nelson and Blair Brown. Look out, too, for Samantha Mathis in an early role.

Craig T Nelson *Philip* • Morgan Weisser *David Toll* • Samantha Mathis *Laura* • Blair Brown *Margaret* ■ *Dir* Peter Horton • *Scr* Marshall Herskovitz, Edward Zwick

Extreme Measures ★★★ 15

Mystery thriller
1996 · US/UK · Colour · 113mins

An extremely silly but enjoyable medical thriller in the style of *Coma*, with Hugh Grant as a doctor uncovering dastardly deeds involving homeless patients at a big city hospital. Grant – too wooden to ever be convincing – is out-acted and outclassed at every turn by co-star Gene Hackman, who chews up the scenery and spits it out as the revered surgeon who is Grant's number one suspect. Director Michael Apted's film contains no surprises, but it does have a few laughs thanks to Grant and Hackman (unintentionally and intentionally, respectively). ▣ **DVD**

Hugh Grant *Dr Guy Luthan* • Gene Hackman *Dr Lawrence Myrick* • Sarah Jessica Parker *Jodie Trammel* • David Morse *Frank Hare* • Bill Nunn *Detective Burke* • John Toles-Bey *Bobby* • Paul Guilfoyle *Dr Jeffery Manko* • David Cronenberg *Hospital lawyer* ■ *Dir* Michael Apted • *Scr* Tony Gilroy, from the novel by Michael Palmer

Extreme Prejudice ★★★ 18

Action thriller   1987 · US · Colour · 100mins

Director Walter Hill, initially revered for his unravelling of the male psyche and his lyrical expression of violence (à la Sam Peckinpah), has in recent years simply settled for violent action. Even though he is clearly in awe of Peckinpah's *The Wild Bunch*, he does poke wry fun here at the central clichéd conflict between two old pals who each end up on opposite sides of the law. Hill is also aided by two actors who exude tough-guy behaviour with ease: Nick Nolte as the Texas Ranger and Powers Boothe as the chum-turned-drug lord. Contains violence, swearing, sex scenes, drug abuse and nudity. ▣

Nick Nolte *Jack Benteen* • Powers Boothe *Cash Bailey* • Michael Ironside *Major Paul Hackett* • Maria Conchita Alonso *Sarita Cisneros* • Rip Torn *Sheriff Hank Pearson* • Clancy Brown *Sergeant McRose* • Matt Mulhern *Sergeant Coker* • William Forsythe *Sergeant Atwater* ■ *Dir* Walter Hill • *Scr* Deric Washburn, Harry Kleiner, from a story by John Milius, Fred Rexer

Extremities ★★ 18

Drama   1986 · US · Colour · 84mins

Is *Extremities* controversial or exploitative? There's a large helping of both as Farrah Fawcett escapes a would-be rapist (James Russo) only for

him to return and terrorise her. The surprise comes when she turns the tables on him, but this leads to a relentless catalogue of brutality that never truly tackles the sensitive subject at hand. Robert M Young's interpretation of William Mastrosimone's play can't hide its theatrical origins, and only succeeds in offending the audience as Fawcett's character is humiliated and tortured while we helplessly – and voyeuristically – look on. ▣

Farrah Fawcett *Marjorie* • James Russo *Joe* • Diana Scarwid *Terry* • Alfre Woodard *Patricia* • Sandy Martin *Officer Sudow* • Eddie Velez *1st officer* ■ *Dir* Robert M Young • *Scr* William Mastrosimone, from his play

An Eye for an Eye ★★

Western   1966 · US · Colour · 91mins

Talion (Robert Lansing) sets out to find the gang who murdered his wife and child. Teaming up with younger bounty hunter Pat Wayne (son of the Duke), they get badly shot up when they find nasty Slim Pickens and his cronies. Lansing is shot through his gun hand and Wayne is blinded, but don't count them out: they combine talents, with Lansing telling Wayne where to point and when to shoot! This plot twist gives this western a certain novelty value and makes the biblical title doubly allusive – but otherwise it's poorly acted and sluggishly directed.

Robert Lansing *Talion* • Pat Wayne [Patrick Wayne] *Benny* • Slim Pickens *Ike Slant* • Gloria Talbott *Bri Quince* • Paul Fix *Quince* • Strother Martin *Trumbull* • Henry Wills *Charles* • Jerry Gatlin *Jonas* • Clint Howard *Jo-Hi* ■ *Dir* Michael Moore (1) • *Scr* Bing Russell, Sumner Williams

An Eye for an Eye ★★ 18

Martial arts action thriller
1981 · US · Colour · 99mins

When this was made, Chuck Norris just about ruled supreme in the martial arts stakes, and, though he was no Bruce Lee, this is a serviceable enough vehicle for his talents. He is his usual monosyllabic self as the former cop who launches a destructive private war against the Triads after the death of his partner. Quite what Christopher Lee is doing here is anybody's guess, but there are enough fights and set pieces to keep genre fans contented. ▣

Chuck Norris *Sean Kane* • Christopher Lee *Morgan Canfield* • Richard Roundtree *Capt Stevens* • Matt Clark *Tom McCoy* • Mako *James Chan* • Maggie Cooper *Heather Sullivan* • Rosalind Chao *Linda Chan* ■ *Dir* Steve Carver • *Scr* William Gray, James Bruner, from a story by James Bruner

Eye for an Eye ★★★ 18

Thriller   1995 · US · Colour · 97mins

The casting of Sally Field as a gun-toting vigilante and Kiefer Sutherland as an out-and-out baddie gives novelty value to this revenge thriller from director John Schlesinger. Field plays an ordinary woman who is catapulted into a world of terror when her daughter is raped and murdered. Forensic evidence points to Sutherland, but when he escapes jail on a legal technicality Field sets out to exact her own form of justice. Field is perhaps a touch too mumsy to convince totally in her role, though

Sutherland clearly relishes the opportunity to play a lowlife killer. Contains some violence and swearing. ▣

Sally Field *Karen McCann* • Ed Harris *Mack McCann* • Olivia Burnette *Julie McCann* • Alexandra Kyle *Megan McCann* • Kiefer Sutherland *Robert Doob* • Joe Mantegna *Detective Sergeant Denillo* • Beverly D'Angelo *Dolly Green* • Darrell Larson *Peter Green* ▪ *Dir* John Schlesinger • *Scr* Amanda Silver, Rick Jaffa, from the novel by Erika Holzer

Eye of God ★★★ 15

Drama   1997 · US · Colour · 82mins

This labyrinthine tale of passion, violence and religious fanaticism in small-town America is held together by a simmering performance from Kevin Anderson, who leaves jail to marry Martha Plimpton, the burger waitress who's been writing to him during his sentence for assault. But cutting across this uneasy romance is sheriff Hal Holbrook's attempt to coax the truth from terrified teenager Nick Stahl, found dazed and bloodied. Director Tim Blake Nelson plays fast and loose with the narrative structure, but it's worth staying the course, if only for the sinister restraint of Anderson's born-again zeal. ▣

Martha Plimpton *Ainsley Dupree* • Kevin Anderson *Jack Stillings* • Hal Holbrook *Sheriff Sam Rogers* • Nick Stahl *Tom Spencer* • Margo Martindale *Dorothy* • Mary Kay Place *Claire Spencer* • Richard Jenkins *Willard Sprague* ▪ *Dir/Scr* Tim Blake Nelson

Eye of the Beholder ★★ 18

Thriller
1999 · Can/UK/US/Ausl · Colour · 109mins

A stodgy combination of ersatz James Bond and sub-Hitchcock thriller, director Stephan Elliott's psychological love story is a dismally daft adaptation of Marc Behm's novel. Secret service agent Ewan McGregor is assigned to follow serial killer Ashley Judd. However, because the seductive assassin reminds him of his long-lost daughter, he darts all over the world obsessively spying on her, even committing suicide himself to ensure she isn't apprehended. Unable to navigate such deep and emotionally complex waters, Elliott's farcical potboiler paints itself into far too many ludicrous corners, while McGregor does little with a thankless role he clearly isn't old enough to play.

Ashley Judd *Joanna* • Ewan McGregor *The Eye* • Jason Priestley *Gary* • kd lang *Hilary* ▪ *Dir* Stephan Elliott • *Scr* Stephan Elliott, from the novel by Marc Behm

Eye of the Cat ★★★

Thriller   1969 · US · Colour · 100mins

Riddled with laughable lines and so many plot potholes that the story forever teeters on the brink of collapse, it's hard to believe that this rickety chiller was penned by Joseph Stefano, the man who wrote the screenplay for *Psycho*. What keeps you watching are the performances of the three leads, who play it with earnest conviction. Eleanor Parker particularly enjoys herself as the disabled *grande dame*, whose house full of cats (led by Tullia, the menacing moggy mastermind) thwarts the gold-digging

ambitions of nephew Michael Sarrazin and his accomplice, Gayle Hunnicutt.

Michael Sarrazin *Wylie* • Gayle Hunnicutt *Kassia* • Eleanor Parker *Aunt Danny* • Tim Henry *Luke* • Laurence Naismith *Dr Mills* • Jennifer Leak *Poor Dear* • Linden Chiles *Bendetto* • Mark Herron *Bellemondo* ▪ *Dir* David Lowell Rich • *Scr* Joseph Stefano

Eye of the Devil ★

Horror   1968 · UK · BW · 95mins

Controversial in its day, and extensively cut for American release, director J Lee Thompson's daft British occult thriller concerns a French nobleman sacrificing himself to the grape gods to improve the vintage of his faltering vineyard. David Niven and Deborah Kerr add considerable authority to the silly premise largely wasting the talents of Donald Pleasence, Flora Robson and Edward Mulhare. Warlock David Hemmings and witch Sharon Tate have their moments turning a toad into a dove and hypnotising the locals.

Deborah Kerr *Catherine de Montfaucon* • David Niven *Philippe de Montfaucon* • Donald Pleasence *Pere Dominic* • Edward Mulhare *Jean-Claude Ibert* • Flora Robson *Countess Estell* • Emlyn Williams *Alain de Montfaucon* • David Hemmings *Christian de Caray* • Sharon Tate *Odile* • John Le Mesurier *Dr Monnet* ▪ *Dir* J Lee Thompson • *Scr* Robin Estridge, Dennis Murphy, from the novel *Day of the Arrow* by Philip Loraine

Eye of the Needle ★★★ 15

Second World War spy thriller
1981 · UK · Colour · 108mins

Before he became the favourite literary figure-about-town of Tony Blair's Labour Party, Ken Follett was just a humble thriller writer. This is a film version of his novel about a lethal Nazi agent who has somehow managed to infiltrate the lower reaches of, er, British Rail during the war. This might seem an unglamorous base of operations from which to subvert the Allied war effort, but Donald Sutherland as the Nazi keeps the suspenseful story of murder, romance and intrigue on the right track. ▣

Donald Sutherland *Henry Faber* • Kate Nelligan *Lucy Rose* • Ian Bannen *Percy Godliman* • Christopher Cazenove *David Rose* • Faith Brook *Lucy's mother* • Barbara Ewing *Mrs Garden* • David Hayman *Canter* ▪ *Dir* Richard Marquand • *Scr* Stanley Mann, from the novel by Ken Follett

Eye of the Stalker ★★★

Thriller   1995 · US · Colour

What seems like an exploitative idea reeking of sensationalism becomes an involving drama in this TV movie, another in the *Moment of Truth* original series of docudramas dealing with teen problems. Brooke Langton is an Arizona college student who is relentlessly stalked by an older man (Jere Burns), but the legal system and his shrewd manipulations hamper her mother Joanna Cassidy (who happens to be a judge) and the police. Burns's realistic portrayal of the chilling predator makes this one to watch, as does Reza Badiyi's direction.

Joanna Cassidy *Judge Martha Knowlton* • Jere Burns *Stephen Primes* • Dennis Burkley *Danny*

Zerbo • Brooke Langton *Beth Knowlton* • Lucinda Jenney *Liz Knowlton* • ▪ *Dir* Reza Badiyi • *Scr* Priscilla English

Eye of the Storm ★★

Psychological crime thriller
1991 · Ger/US · Colour · 98mins

More a character study than a straight horror film, this teenage *Psycho* fails to capitalise on its flashy build-up and only really comes alive at the end. After their parents' murder, two brothers take over the family's remote desert motel. However, things go pear-shaped when drunken Dennis Hopper and his trashy young wife, played by *Twin Peaks* star Lara Flynn Boyle, arrive. Director Yuri Zeltser keeps us pondering as to which of the boys will emerge as the Norman Bates-style nutter. Unsurprisingly, this went straight to video in the States. Contains violence, drug abuse and swearing.

Craig Sheffer *Ray* • Bradley Gregg *Steven* • Lara Flynn Boyle *Sandra Gladstone* • Leon Rippy *Sheriff* • Dennis Hopper *Marvin Gladstone* ▪ *Dir* Yuri Zeltser • *Scr* Yuri Zeltser, Michael Stewart

Eye of the Stranger ★★ 15

Action mystery   1993 · US · Colour · 96mins

Writer/director/actor David Heavener casts himself in the Clint Eastwood role as the nameless stranger who wanders into a small town. Corrupt mayor Baines (Martin Landau) seems to be calling all the shots, but the stranger sets about bringing him and his cronies to justice for an unsolved murder. Many fights and meaningful shots of the stranger's boots follow. Inept and cliché-ridden, the film offers few surprises beyond the opportunity to see a couple of actors' siblings go through their paces – Joe Estevez (Martin Sheen's brother) and Don Swayze (Patrick's brother) are in the supporting cast. ▣

David Heavener *Stranger* • Martin Landau *Mayor Howard Baines* • Sally Kirkland *Lori* • Don Swayze *Rudy* • Stella Stevens *Doc* • Sy Richardson *Jeb* • Joe Estevez *Sheriff* • John Pleshette *Joe* • Thomas F Duffy *Ballack* ▪ *Dir/Scr* David Heavener

Eye of the Tiger ★★ 18

Thriller   1986 · US · Colour · 87mins

Framed for a crime he didn't commit, Vietnam veteran Gary Busey goes home after his release from jail to take vengeance on the real culprits, biker drug-dealers led by William Smith. Wire decapitations, dynamite stuck in people's orifices and Busey's RV customised with cannons are the various methods of dispatch in this violent and unpleasant thriller. And yes, the *Rocky III* theme song is used on the soundtrack. Contains violence and swearing. ▣

Gary Busey *Buck Matthews* • Yaphet Kotto *JB Deveraux* • Seymour Cassel *Sheriff* • Bert Remsen *Father Healey* • Jorge Gil *Jamie* • William Smith *Blade* • Kimberlin Ann Brown *Dawn* • Denise Galik *Christie* ▪ *Dir* Richard C Sarafian • *Scr* Michael Montgomery

Eye on the Sparrow ★★★ PG

Drama based on a true story
1987 · US · Colour · 95mins

So many true-life TV movies descend into maudlin melodrama that it's something of a relief to come across one that tackles its topic with dignity and intelligence. Director John Korty had already explored the theme of blind people determined to live full and active lives in *Second Sight: a Love Story*, and he proves just as sensitive here, as a sightless couple seeks to adopt a child in the face of petty bureaucracy. Mare Winningham and Keith Carradine underplay their blindness while still turning in powerful performances, but the key factor in the movie's success is Barbara Turner's restrained screenplay. ▣

Mare Winningham *Ethel Hollars* • Keith Carradine *Jim Lee* • Joy Carlin *Mrs Grissom* • Anne Lawder *Mrs Lee* • Winifred Mann *Mrs Magnuson* • Conchata Ferrell *Mary* ▪ *Dir* John Korty • *Scr* Barbara Turner

Eyes in the Night ★★★

Crime drama   1942 · US · BW · 79mins

A superior MGM thriller that's a bit too polished to be a *film noir*, starring avuncular character actor Edward Arnold as blind detective Duncan Maclain. It's one of those formula movies offered to gifted new directorial talent, in this case the young Fred Zinnemann (*High Noon*, *A Man for All Seasons*), one of whose earliest films this was. The nominal star is graceful Ann Harding, but perky Donna Reed shows she has real star quality. Arnold, often relegated to unsympathetic roles, elicits genuine empathy as he helps out Harding and Reed, but the real star of this movie is a scene-stealing pooch called Friday!

Edward Arnold *Captain Duncan Maclain* • Ann Harding *Norma Lawry* • Donna Reed *Barbara Lawry* • Allen Jenkins *Marty* • John Emery *Paul Gerente* • Horace McNally [Stephen McNally] *Gabriel Hoffman* • Katherine Emery *Cheli Scott* ▪ *Dir* Fred Zinnemann • *Scr* Guy Trosper, Howard Emmett Rogers, from the novel *Odor of Violets* by Baynard Kendrick

Eyes of a Stranger ★ 18

Horror   1980 · US · Colour · 79mins

The multi-talented and versatile Jennifer Jason Leigh here plays the blind and deaf sister of TV anchorwoman Lauren Tewes. During the Miami summer, serial killer Stanley Herbert (John DiSanti) has been raping and murdering local women. Tewes discovers the killer just happens to be her next-door neighbour, and attempts to prove his guilt before he comes after her and the defenceless Leigh. An archetypal horror from director Ken Wiederhorn, this does women no favours on the victimisation front, despite the spunky efforts of *The Love Boat*'s Tewes.

Lauren Tewes *Jane* • Jennifer Jason Leigh *Tracy* • John DiSanti *Stanley Herbert* • Peter DuPre *David* • Gwen Lewis *Debbie* • Kitty Lunn *Annette* ▪ *Dir* Ken Wiederhorn • *Scr* Mark Jackson, Eric L Bloom

U = SUITABLE FOR ALL   Uc = SUITABLE FOR ALL, ESPECIALLY FOR YOUNG CHILDREN (VIDEO ONLY)   PG = PARENTAL GUIDANCE

Eyes of an Angel ★★
Adventure crime drama
1991 · US · Colour · 91mins

John Travolta stars as single parent Bobby, struggling to bring up his daughter (Ellie Raab). Only released on the coat-tails of its star's post-*Pulp Fiction* comeback, this violent story follows Raab as she nurses a mobster's injured Doberman back to health, not realising that her involvement with the pooch will have her and Travolta fleeing Chicago. The dog, of course, makes an implausible road trip of its own to find its nice new mistress, with Mafia heavies in hot pursuit. It really is no surprise to learn Robert Harmon's movie failed to find a distributor for four years.

John Travolta *Bobby* • Ellie Raab *The Girl* • Tito Larriva *Cissy* • Richard Edson *Goon* • Vincent Guastaferro *Goon* • Jeffrey DeMunn *Georgie* • Jacqueline Pulliam *Gloria* ■ *Dir* Robert Harmon • *Scr* Robert Stitzel

The Eyes of Charles Sand ★★
Horror
1972 · US · Colour · 75mins

Peter Haskell inherits the ability to see visions beyond the grave in this TV-movie pilot for a series that never materialised. Using his precognition talents and clairvoyance, Haskell helps a girl solve her brother's alleged murder in the old family mansion. The by-the-numbers plot is lifted by sure-handed direction and some atmospheric moments, but there aren't enough of those to stop boredom setting in. Composer Henry Mancini sued the producers for lifting his score from *Wait until Dark* as background music.

Peter Haskell *Charles Sand* • Barbara Rush *Kathryn Winslow* • Sharon Farrell *Emily Parkhurst* • Bradford Dillman *Jeffrey Winslow* • Adam West *Dr Paul Scott* • Joan Bennett *Aunt Alexandria* • Ivor Francis *Dr Sam Ballard* ■ *Dir* Reza S Badiyi [Reza Badiyi] • *Scr* Henry Farrell, Stanford Whitmore, from a story by Henry Farrell

Eyes of Laura Mars ★★★ 15
Psychological thriller
1978 · US · Colour · 99mins

Designed as a vehicle for Barbra Streisand (she sings the theme song), this movie ended up starring Faye Dunaway as the glamorous photographer who develops a psychic link with a killer and witnesses his gruesome murders while they are being committed. Co-written by John Carpenter, it's a standard slasher melodrama given a glitzy face-lift and, because Dunaway blends sex with sadism in her chic layouts (her gallery photos were actually taken by Helmut Newton), there's a great deal of pop analysis on exploitative images. Decently done, though surface gloss always wins out over deeper psychological substance. ▣ *DVD*

Faye Dunaway *Laura Mars* • Tommy Lee Jones *Detective John Neville* • Brad Dourif *Tommy Ludlow* • René Auberjonois *Donald Phelps* • Raul Julia *Michael Reisler* • Frank Adonis *Sal Volpe* • Michael Tucker *Bert* • Lisa Taylor *Michele* ■ *Dir* Irvin Kershner • *Scr* John Carpenter, David Zelag Goodman

Eyes of the Spider ★★★
Crime thriller
1999 · Jap · Colour · 83mins

Shot along with *Serpent's Path* in a phenomenal four-week burst of creativity, this is a somewhat disappointing conclusion to the adventures of callously cool opportunist Niijima (Sho Aikawa). Ordered by crime boss Ren Osugi to eliminate an old friend (Dankan), Aikawa presents a knowing variation on the Takeshi Kitano type of hoodlum – part eccentric, part homicidal time bomb – while director Kiyoshi Kurosawa typically laces the story with offbeat characters and disconcerting details. However, the shift from Seijun Suzuki-style Yakuza comedy to psychological thriller lacks conviction. A Japanese language film.

Sho Aikawa *Niijima* • Ren Osugi • Shun Sugata • Susumu Terajima • Dankan ■ *Dir* Kiyoshi Kurosawa • *Scr* Yoichi Nishiyama, Kiyoshi Kurosawa

Eyes Wide Shut ★★★ 18
Psychological drama
1999 · US/UK · Colour · 152mins

Full of trademark themes and characteristic compositions, Stanley Kubrick's final film is also his most fascinatingly flawed. With its style often resembling seventies European arthouse movies, it lacks the morbidity to pass as a Buñuelian satire, while it is far too stately and serious to succeed as a commercial enterprise. Tom Cruise – as the doctor recklessly seeking a means of avenging his wife's fantasised infidelity – is too controlled for his character's fraught nocturnal adventures to be plausible. Nicole Kidman as his wife is less visible, though she simmers with the potential for erotic danger. Despite expectations, this is a disappointingly conservative conclusion to a career spent pushing back cinematic boundaries. ▣ *DVD*

Tom Cruise *Dr William Harford* • Nicole Kidman *Alice Harford* • Sydney Pollack *Victor Ziegler* • Marie Richardson *Marion Nathanson* • Rade Sherbedgia *Milich* • Todd Field *Nick Nightingale* • Vinessa Shaw *Domino* • Alan Cumming *Desk clerk* ■ *Dir* Stanley Kubrick • *Scr* Stanley Kubrick, Frederic Raphael, from the novella *Traumnovelle* by Arthur Schnitzler

Eyes without a Face ★★★★★ 18
Horror
1959 · Fr/It · BW · 86mins

This is one of the most haunting horror films ever made. Director Georges Franju made his name with a series of inspired documentary shorts, and it's the realism of his approach that makes his "poetic fantasy" so unnerving. There's nothing of the hammy Hollywood mad scientist in Pierre Brasseur, as he and assistant Alida Valli resort to murder in order to rebuild the face of his daughter, Edith Scob. Franju's control of atmosphere is masterly, Eugen Schüfftan's photography is outstanding, and Auguste Capelier deserves a mention for designing Scob's unforgettable mask. In French with English subtitles. Contains violence. ▣

Pierre Brasseur *Professor Génessier* • Alida Valli *Louise* • Edith Scob *Christiane* • François Guérin *Jacques* • Juliette Mayniel *Edna Gruber*

■ *Dir* Georges Franju • *Scr* Jean Redon, Georges Franju, Jean Redon, Claude Sautet, Pierre Boileau, Thomas Narcejac, from the novel *Les Yeux sans Visage* by Jean Redon • *Music* Maurice Jarre

Eyewitness ★★★
Crime drama
1956 · UK · BW · 82mins

Donald Sinden, a rather bland leading man on both stage and screen before this was made, successfully attempts a rather different character role, conveying all the ruthlessness of the heartless killer as he tries to rub out the witness to a crime. He is effectively supported by Muriel Pavlow (as his would-be victim), Belinda Lee, Michael Craig and Nigel Stock, while director Muriel Box unfurls the suspense with a good sense of timing.

Donald Sinden *Wade* • Muriel Pavlow *Lucy Church* • Belinda Lee *Penny* • Michael Craig *Jay Church* • Nigel Stock *Barney* • Susan Beaumont *Probationer nurse* • David Knight *Mike* ■ *Dir* Muriel Box • *Scr* Janet Green

Eyewitness ★★ 15
Thriller
1970 · UK · Colour · 87mins

Why did a playwright of the calibre of Ronald Harwood bother himself with this adaptation of Mark Hebden's minor "cry wolf" thriller? It's hardly original stuff, and the threadbare plot leaves players a lot more experienced than Mark Lester looking forlorn. Fresh from his success in the title role of *Oliver!*, Lester is wincingly wide-eyed as the fanciful child whose account of a murder is disbelieved by all and sundry. But he's not helped by second-time director John Hough, who is obviously still too obsessed with "meaningful" angles and camera trickery to concern himself with the pivotal performance. ▣

Mark Lester (1) *Timothy, "Ziggy"* • Lionel Jeffries *Colonel* • Susan George *Pippa* • Tony Bonner *Tom* • Jeremy Kemp *Galleria* • Peter Vaughan *Paul* • Peter Bowles *Victor* • Betty Marsden *Madame Robiac* • Anthony Stamboulish *Tacherie* ■ *Dir* John Hough • *Scr* Ronald Harwood, from the novel by Mark Hebden

Eyewitness ★★★ 15
Thriller
1981 · US · Colour · 97mins

Shy night janitor William Hurt foolishly pretends to know something about a murder at his building in order to get close to TV newswoman Sigourney Weaver. Peter Yates's Hitchcockian cocktail of New York paranoia and fairy-tale romance reteamed Yates with screenwriter Steve Tesich after their surprise success *Breaking Away*. While not as effective as that previous outing, Yates deftly moves his classy cast through one mind-bending plot contortion after another to fashion a slick, enjoyable and under-rated thriller. The film may be more familiar by its British title, *The Janitor*. ▣

William Hurt *Daryll Deever* • Sigourney Weaver *Tony Sokolow* • Christopher Plummer *Joseph* • James Woods *Aldo* • Irene Worth *Mrs Sokolow* • Kenneth McMillan *Mr Deever* • Pamela Reed *Linda* • Morgan Freeman *Lieutenant Black* ■ *Dir* Peter Yates • *Scr* Steve Tesich

The FBI Story ★★★★ PG
Crime drama
1959 · US · Colour · 142mins

Virtually a potted history of America's Federal Bureau of Investigation under its now notorious head, J Edgar Hoover, a very long recruitment poster on celluloid, directed by *Little Caesar's* Mervyn LeRoy and given tremendous credibility and heart by the late, great James Stewart. The device of telling the story through the eyes and exploits of one agent, who takes on everyone from the Klan to the mob to the Nazi secret service, verges on the unlikely, but is colourfully told against the backdrop of Stewart's domestic life. Who else could have conveyed such high-minded, sincere idealism against a background of such violence? Vera Miles is impressive as his wife, and there's a marvellous supporting cast, most notably the ever-excellent Murray Hamilton as Stewart's buddy. Interestingly, the bestselling book on which the film was based was a factual history of the organisation. ▣

James Stewart *Chip Hardesty* • Vera Miles *Lucy Hardesty* • Murray Hamilton *Sam Crandall* • Larry Pennell *George Crandall* • Nick Adams *John Graham* • Diane Jergens *Jennie, as an adult* • Jean Willes *Anna Sage* • Joyce Taylor *Anne, as an adult* ■ *Dir* Mervyn LeRoy • *Scr* Richard L Breen, John Twist, from the book by Don Whitehead

FDR: the Last Year ★★★
Biographical drama
1980 · US · Colour · 100mins

Jason Robards stars in this reverential account of Franklin Delano Roosevelt's hectic final months, as he plays down a chronic heart condition to run for a fourth term as president, help co-ordinate the D-Day landings and plan for the postwar world with Churchill and Stalin at Yalta. The film really comes to life during the election battle, although the scenes with his super-efficient wife Eleanor (played by Eileen Heckart) and sympathetic mistress Lucy Rutherford (Kim Hunter) are also revealing. The speeches to camera, in which White House figures explain their roles in FDR's life, don't quite come off, but Robards and Heckart give solid impersonations.

Jason Robards [Jason Robards Jr] *President Franklin Delano Roosevelt* • Eileen Heckart *Eleanor Roosevelt* • Edward Binns *General "Pa" Watson* • Augusta Dabney *Grace Tully* • Larry Gates *Admiral Leahy* • Michael Gross *Dr Howard Bruenn* • Kim Hunter *Lucy Rutherford* • James Karen *Admiral McIntire* • Nehemiah Persoff *Josef Stalin* ■ *Dir* Anthony Page • *Scr* Stanley R Greenberg, from the book *FDR's Last Year* by Jim Bishop

F for Fake ★★★ PG

Documentary
1973 · Fr/Iran/W Ger · Colour · 84mins

Much of this sly treatise on deception was shot by François Reichenbach for a TV documentary on art forger supreme, Elmyr de Hory. When news broke that his biographer, Clifford Irving, had also faked his life of Howard Hughes, Orson Welles jumped at the chance to use Reichenbach's footage and added to it sequences of prestidigitation, confessional pieces on his own chicanery, a marvellously convoluted story about Oja Kodar and some Picasso paintings. Welles opens the film by promising to tell the absolute truth for one hour. It has the feel of a personal project for the great director, but given its nature, who knows? ▣

Oja Kodar *The Girl* • Orson Welles • Joseph Cotten *The Guest* ■ *Dir* Orson Welles • *Scr* from a original by Clifford Irving

FM ★★

Music drama   1977 · US · Colour · 104mins

It tells you something when a soundtrack album ends up being more popular than the film it's taken from. Such was the case for cinematographer-turned-director John A Alonzo's debut feature, a sketch-driven take on life at a progressive rock station in seventies Los Angeles. Michael Brandon stars as a DJ determined to keep commercialism at bay, who leads a revolt when the playlist becomes too damn square for his liking. Amiable enough and significantly bolstered by concert appearances from Tom Petty and Linda Ronstadt, skirmishes during filming between the two strands of creative talent, film and music, over which influence should dominate the movie, resulted in a deeply flawed product.

Michael Brandon *Jeff Dugan* • Eileen Brennan *Mother* • Alex Karras *Doc Holiday* • Cleavon Little *Prince* • Martin Mull *Eric Swan* • Cassie Yates *Laura Coe* • Norman Lloyd *Carl Billings* • James Keach *Lieutenant Reach* • Linda Ronstadt • Jimmy Buffett • Tom Petty ■ *Dir* John A Alonzo • *Scr* Ezra Sacks

FP1 ★★

Science-fiction drama
1932 · UK/Ger · BW · 74mins

An early instance of trilingual film-making, this sci-fi melodrama was a German venture with different casts for the German, French and English versions under one director, Karl Hartl. The best scenes show planes using the huge floating aerodrome in the middle of the Atlantic Ocean that serves as a stopping point for flights between Europe and America. The shorter British version stars Conrad Veidt as the aviator and inventor who saves the base from a sabotage attempt. Like modern "Europuddings", it met with mixed success.

Conrad Veidt *Maj Ellisen* • Leslie Fenton *Capt Droste* • Jill Esmond *Claire* • George Merritt *Lubin* • Donald Calthrop *Photographer* • Warwick Ward *1st Officer* • Philip Manning *Doctor* • Nicholas Hannen *Matthias* ■ *Dir* Karl Hartl • *Scr* Walter Reisch, Kurt Siodmak, Robert Stevenson, Peter Macfarlane, from a story by Walter Reisch, Kurt Siodmak

FTA ★★

Political documentary
1972 · US · Colour · 97mins

The makers of this documentary claimed the title stood for "Free the Army" or even, bearing in mind the project's collaborative nature, "Free Theatre Associates". But few doubted what the "F" signified, in light of Jane Fonda's well-publicised stance against the Vietnam War. She insisted that the shows were staged as a feminist response to the girlie entertainment being offered to the troops by the likes of Bob Hope, but the army saw only anti-war propaganda and kept the troupe off its bases. Seen now, the many songs and sketches recorded by Francine Parker are committed, but lacking in bite.

Jane Fonda • Donald Sutherland • Pamela Donegan • Len Chandler • Rita Martinson • Holly Near ■ *Dir* Francine Parker • *Scr* Michael Alaimo, Pamela Donegan, Jane Fonda, Robin Menken, Holly Near, Donald Sutherland, Dalton Trumbo

FTW ★★★ 18

Crime thriller   1994 · US · Colour · 97mins

The initials stand for Frank T Wells, the rodeo rider played by Mickey Rourke. After serving ten years for manslaughter, Wells is determined to revive his rodeo career and gets drawn into an affair with Lori Singer, who pays for his career on the proceeds of bank robberies. It's a sort of *Bronco and Clyde*, a peculiar mix, populated by assorted low-lifes and shot amid the spectacular scenery of Montana. Reminiscent of Peckinpah's *Junior Bonner* and the Kirk Douglas picture, *Lonely Are the Brave*, it offers Rourke his best role for years. Contains swearing and sex scenes. ▣

Mickey Rourke *Frank T Wells* • Lori Singer *Scarlett Stuart* • Brion James *Sheriff Rudy Morgan* • Peter Berg *Clem* ■ *Dir* Michael Karbelnikoff • *Scr* Mari Kornhauser, from a story by Sir Eddie Cook

F/X ★★★★ 15

Thriller   1985 · US · Colour · 103mins

A political paranoia-cum-quasi-horror thriller that's compulsively watchable because it's set in the intriguing world of special effects. Bryan Brown is the ace film technician hired by the US government to stage the fake assassination of a mobster-turned-informant. But the assignment takes a number of violent twists ending with Brown on the run, armed only with his bag of tricks to expose the corruption in high places. For action fans and gore hounds, *F/X* is nimble, fast-paced and fun. Contains violence and swearing. ▣

Bryan Brown *Rollie Tyler* • Brian Dennehy *Leo McCarthy* • Diane Venora *Ellen* • Cliff De Young *Lipton* • Mason Adams *Colonel Mason* • Jerry Orbach *Nicholas DeFranco* • Joe Grifasi *Mickey* ■ *Dir* Robert Mandel • *Scr* Robert T Megginson, Gregory Fleeman

F/X2: the Deadly Art of Illusion ★★★ 15

Crime thriller   1991 · US · Colour · 103mins

Bryan Brown returns as the special effects whiz in this sequel, which, while lacking the fresh ingenuity of the original, remains a sly, entertaining thriller. This time Brown gets mixed up with crooked law enforcement officers, among others, but again runs rings around the crooks with the use of his incredible skills. Brian Dennehy once more provides solid support, while the under-rated Richard Franklin (who made the excellent first *Psycho* sequel) directs with some style and an appropriate light touch. Contains violence, swearing and nudity. ▣

Bryan Brown *Rollie Tyler* • Brian Dennehy *Leo McCarthy* • Rachel Ticotin *Kim Brandon* • Joanna Gleason *Liz Kennedy* • Philip Bosco *Ray Silak* • Kevin J O'Connor *Matt Neely* ■ *Dir* Richard Franklin • *Scr* Bill Condon, from characters created by Robert T Megginson, Gregory Freeman

The Fabulous Baker Boys ★★★★ 15

Romantic drama
1989 · US · Colour · 108mins

A sophisticated salute to family, romance, friends and disillusionment, Steve Kloves's sweetly directed comedy drama is pure bliss from start to finish. Real brothers Jeff and Beau Bridges play the cocktail lounge piano players of the title whose volatile relationship explodes when they employ sultry torch singer Michelle Pfeiffer to revitalise their tired act. As the film smoothly zeroes in on many universal truths along its delightful way, the fabulous Bridges boys' faultless timing and expert underplaying allows Pfeiffer to shine radiantly. You won't forget her sizzling rendition of *Makin' Whoopee* while draped over a grand piano in a hurry, either. Contains swearing. ▣ *DVD*

Jeff Bridges *Jack Baker* • Michelle Pfeiffer *Susie Diamond* • Beau Bridges *Frank Baker* • Ellie Raab *Nina* • Jennifer Tilly *Monica Moran* • Xander Berkeley *Lloyd* • Dakin Matthews *Charlie* • Gregory Itzin *Vince Nancy* • Wendy Girard *Donna Baker* ■ *Dir/Scr* Steve Kloves

The Fabulous Dorseys ★★ U

Biographical musical
1947 · US · BW · 83mins

Warring bandleaders Tommy and Jimmy Dorsey were stolid and ageing when they played themselves in this rather lacklustre biopic, which is best enjoyed simply as a visual record of the music. *Green Eyes*, *Marie* and a load of hits are included, and there's a solid jam session involving Art Tatum and Charlie Barnet, but the story-telling is homogenised and perfunctory and the Dorsey Brothers themselves are no actors. Perhaps the most telling fact about the Dorseys is that they were prepared to portray themselves on screen constantly battling with each other and that it took the death of their father to bring them together. These days we would probably call their relationship dysfunctional. ▣

Tommy Dorsey • Jimmy Dorsey • Janet Blair *Jane Howard* • Paul Whiteman • William Lundigan *Bob Burton* • Sara Allgood *Mrs Dorsey* • Arthur Shields *Mr Dorsey* • James Flavin *Gorman* ■ *Dir* Alfred E Green • *Scr* Richard English, Art Arthur, Curtis Kenyon

The Face ★★★

Fantasy drama   1958 · Swe · BW · 107mins

Winner of the special jury prize at Venice, Ingmar Bergman's Gothic drama has been described as a comedy without jokes and a horror film without chills. Focusing on the artist's value to society and exploring such themes as illusion, faith, science and truth, this has the feel of a man trying too hard to repeat the success of the previous year's masterpieces *The Seventh Seal* and *Wild Strawberries*. Max von Sydow gives a bravura performance as the 19th-century mesmerist Vogler and Gunnar Fischer's photography creates the right mood of uncertainty, but, for all the director's sleights of hand, there's no magic. In Swedish with English subtitles.

Max von Sydow *Vogler* • Ingrid Thulin *Manda* • Gunnar Björnstrand *Dr Vergerus* • Naima Wifstrand *Grandmother* • Bengt Ekerot *Spegel* • Bibi Andersson *Sara* • Gertrud Fridh *Ottilia* • Lars Ekborg *Simson* • Erland Josephson *Egerman* ■ *Dir/Scr* Ingmar Bergman • *Cinematographer* Gunnar Fischer

The Face ★★ 15

Drama   1996 · US · Colour · 89mins

Baywatch babe Yasmine Bleeth swaps the sand and surf for another world of escapist fantasy in this hokey but fun drama. She plays a shy, disfigured woman who ends up in prison after being set-up by smooth womaniser James Wilder. While serving her sentence she is given a new look by a plastic surgeon that changes her life for ever. The performances are lacklustre – Robin Givens is particularly unconvincing as Bleeth's prison chum – but director Jack Bender makes the action so fast and furious you can overlook the daft plot. ▣

Yasmine Bleeth *Emily Gilmore* • James Wilder *Alec Dalton* • Robin Givens *Claudia* ■ *Dir* Jack Bender • *Scr* Duane Poole

Face ★★★ 18

Crime thriller   1997 · UK · Colour · 101mins

Robert Carlyle who became a star in the space of two movies and a TV series (*Trainspotting*, *The Full Monty*, *Hamish Macbeth*) is seen here in modern-day preparation for his highwayman role in *Plunkett and MacLeane*. He plays a thief seeking a traitor in his gang following a bungled robbery. Apart from the gimmick of having the villains all wearing yellow overalls, the film is simple-mindedly clichéd and as predictable as a calendar. Still, there are terrific performances from Carlyle, Ray Winstone, Peter Vaughan and Sue Johnston, plus the novelty of Blur frontman and singer Damon Albarn in an acting role, while director Antonia Bird shows that screen violence is not just a game that boys can play. Contains violence and swearing. ▣

Robert Carlyle *Ray* • Ray Winstone *Dave* • Steven Waddington *Stevie* • Philip Davis *Julian* • Damon Albarn *Jason* • Lena Headey *Connie* • Peter Vaughan *Sonny* • Sue Johnston *Alice* • Kit Jackson *Uniformed Officer* ■ *Dir* Antonia Bird • *Scr* Ronan Bennett

U = SUITABLE FOR ALL   Uc = SUITABLE FOR ALL, ESPECIALLY FOR YOUNG CHILDREN (VIDEO ONLY)   PG = PARENTAL GUIDANCE

The Face at the Window ★★
Crime melodrama   1939 · UK · BW · 66mins

Arguably barnstormer Tod Slaughter's best performance (surely no one ever called it acting?) was in this third version of a Parisian *Petit Guignol* about a revived presumed-dead body, revealing our hero and his mad brother to be serious bank robbers. Slaughter follows in the murky footsteps of predecessors C Aubrey Smith and Raymond Massey in the earlier versions, and chews a good deal more scenery than either. Director George King keeps the length down to just over an hour, but sometimes the pace is, dare we suggest, funereal.

Tod Slaughter *Chevalier Del Gardo* • Marjorie Taylor *Cecile De Brisson* • John Warwick *Lucien Cortier* • Leonard Henry *Gaston* • Aubrey Mallalieu *De Brisson* ■ *Dir* George King • *Scr* AR Rawlinson, Randall Faye, from the play by F Brooke Warren

The Face behind the Mask
★★★★
Horror   1941 · US · BW · 68mins

Peter Lorre is ideally cast in this low-budget gem, as the watchmaker disfigured in a fire who turns to crime and romances a blind girl with tragic results. A truly haunting expressionist B-movie garnished with gruesome poetry, Robert Florey's subtle direction turns a stock horror situation on its head and gives threatening tension to the simmering, sinister undercurrent. Florey directed Lorre once more in *The Beast with Five Fingers*, but neither reached the same powerful heights again as in this magical mood piece.

Peter Lorre *Janos Szabo* • Evelyn Keyes *Helen Williams* • Don Beddoe *Jim O'Hara* • George E Stone *Dinky* • John Tyrell *Watts* • Stanley Brown *Harry* • Al Seymour *Benson* • James Seay *Jeff* • Warren Ashe *Johnson* ■ *Dir* Robert Florey • *Scr* Allen Vincent, Paul Jarrico, from a story by Arthur Levinson, from a radio play by Thomas Edward O'Connell

Face Down ★★★
Thriller   1996 · US · Colour · 96mins

A suitably hard-boiled thriller that gets by on an intelligent script and a classy cast, even though it was made for the small screen. In time-honoured fashion, Joe Mantegna plays a seedy private eye who falls under the spell of Kelli Maroney and soon finds himself up to his neck in corpses and deceit. As usual, Mantegna doesn't disappoint as the troubled hero, and he is well backed by a talented supporting cast that includes Peter Riegert and Adam Ant as a shady art gallery owner. Contains violence and swearing.

Joe Mantegna *Bob Signorelli* • Peter Riegert *Lt Cooper* • Kelli Maroney *Merre* • Adam Ant *Derek Fry* ■ *Dir/Scr* Thom Eberhardt

A Face in the Crowd ★★★★
Satirical drama   1957 · US · BW · 125mins

Andy Griffith gives the performance of his career as "Lonesome" Rhodes, the small-town philosopher who is discovered by a TV producer (Patricia Neal) and rocketed to fame, fortune and corruption. Director Elia Kazan and writer Budd Schulberg had previously collaborated on *On the Waterfront*, both winning Oscars. Although less

celebrated, this film remains topical in our media-obsessed times. Watch out for Lee Remick in her first film. ▭

Andy Griffith *"Lonesome" Rhodes* • Patricia Neal *Marcia Jeffries* • Anthony Franciosa *Joey Kiely* • Walter Matthau *Mel Miller* • Lee Remick *Betty Lou Fleckum* • Percy Waram *Colonel Hollister* • Rod Brasfield *Beanie* • Charles Irving *Mr Luffler* ■ *Dir* Elia Kazan • *Scr* Budd Schulberg, from his short story *The Arkansas Traveler* • *Art Director* Richard Sylbert, Paul Sylbert

A Face in the Rain ★★
Second World War drama
1963 · US · BW · 80mins

Third-rung war movie with Rory Calhoun as an American agent dropped behind enemy lines in Italy where the wife of the local resistance leader is having an affair with a Gestapo officer. That's terribly inconvenient for Calhoun who's trapped in their apartment. Apart from its notably ironic climax, the movie offers a decent assortment of thrills, some genuine tension and a nicely orchestrated chase across the rooftops. Playing the treacherous wife is Italo-British beauty Marina Berti who appeared in *Quo Vadis* and *Ben-Hur*. Director Irvin Kershner is probably better remembered for *The Empire Strikes Back*.

Rory Calhoun *Rand* • Marina Berti *Anna* • Niall MacGinnis *Klaus* • Massimo Giuliani *Paolo* • Danny Ryais *Peter Zander* ■ *Dir* Irvin Kershner • *Scr* Hugo Butler, Jean Rouverol, from a story by Guy Elmes

Face of a Fugitive ★★★ Ⓤ
Western   1959 · US · Colour · 80mins

An intriguing minor western, cleverly expanded from Peter Dawson's 1956 short story *Long Gone* and particularly well directed by Paul Wendkos, who made a number of highly regarded low-budget films around this period before basing his career in television. Star Fred MacMurray is a shade too old and staid for his role as a bank robber trying to shake off his past and settle down in a new town (and, besides, his toupee never really convinces), but watch out for then-newcomer James Coburn taking over the screen every time he appears. This is much admired by French critics.

Fred MacMurray *Jim Larson/Ray Kincaid* • Lin McCarthy *Mark Riley* • Dorothy Green *Ellen Bailey* • Alan Baxter *Reed Williams* • Myrna Fahey *Janet* • James Coburn *Purdy* • Francis De Sales *Allison* ■ *Dir* Paul Wendkos • *Scr* David T Chantler, Daniel B Ullman, from the story *Long Gone* by Peter Dawson

Face of a Stranger ★★
Romantic drama   1978 · US · Colour · 97mins

Also known as *The Promise*, this is an archetypal weepie about a woman (Kathleen Quinlan) who is disfigured in a car accident and accepts money for her reconstructive surgery from her fiancé's mother. The condition for this generosity is that she must move away and never see him again. It's predictable stuff, but Stephen Collins gives a nice turn as the lover Quinlan will, of course, cross paths with again (if true love has anything to do with it) and Beatrice Straight has fun as the mother from hell.

Tracey Gold *Darcy Palmer* • Perry King *Russell Polk* • Shawnee Smith *Jeanelle Polk* • Don

Kathleen Quinlan *Nancy/Marie* • Stephen Collins *Michael Hillyard* • Beatrice Straight *Marion Hillyard* • Laurence Luckinbill *Dr Gregson* • William Prince *George Calloway* • Michael O'Hare *Ben Avery* ■ *Dir* Gilbert Cates • *Scr* Garry Michael White, from a story by Fred Weintraub, Paul Heller

Face of a Stranger ★★★
Drama based on a true story
1991 · US · Colour · 97mins

Best known as the director of the cult TV series *thirtysomething*, Claudia Weill is an under-rated film-maker, so it's no surprise that she was able to elicit a fine performance here from Gena Rowlands as a wealthy woman forced to face harsh financial reality after she is suddenly widowed. But it takes a director of considerable ability to coax such a nuanced performance out of the usually one-paced Tyne Daly, whose bag lady is both sharp-tongued and sympathetic. The film also provided Rowlands with the opportunity to be reunited with Seymour Cassel, her co-star in several films made by her husband, John Cassavetes, before his death in 1989.

Gena Rowlands *Pat Foster* • Tyne Daly *Dollie Madison* • Cynthia Nixon *Tina* • Kevin Tighe *Richard Foster* • Rae Allen *Ruthie* • Seymour Cassel *Ralph* • Elizabeth Franz *Becky Brown* ■ *Dir* Claudia Weill • *Scr* Marsha Norman, from an article by Mary Stuart

The Face of Another ★★★★
Drama   1966 · Jap · BW · 121mins

A compelling treatise on identity and the correlation between physique and personality, this was Hiroshi Teshigahara's first feature since *Woman of the Dunes*, which was also adapted from a novel by Kobo Abe. Shades of Franju's *Eyes without a Face* fall upon the action, as Tatsuya Nakadai dons a mask to disguise the hideous disfigurement incurred in an industrial accident. But, is it the mask that prompts him to discard his wife on a spurious charge of adultery, or the same desperate feelings of alienation that drive scarred Miki Irie to commit incest with her devoted brother? Disturbing, but absorbing. In Japanese with English subtitles.

Machiko Kyo *Mrs Okuyama* • Tatsuya Nakadai *Mr Okuyama* • Mikijiro Hira • Miki Irie ■ *Dir* Hiroshi Teshigahara • *Scr* Kobo Abe, from the novel *Tanin No Kao* by Kobo Abe

Face of Evil ★★★
Thriller   1996 · US · Colour · 90mins

This is a solidly constructed, well-played, occasionally gruesome thriller, but there's nowhere near enough material to merit the running time. This fact is doubly disappointing given the lively start, as scheming artist Tracey Gold resorts to murder and deception to help further her career. Gold, who appeared as a teenager in several eighties TV-movie dramas, relishes playing such a hateful character and is admirably backed by Shawnee Smith and Perry King. If only Mary Lambert's meandering direction had not taken much of the sting out of the plot. Contains violence and swearing.

Harvey Quinn • Brigitta Dau *Sabrina* • Simi Mehta *Zoe* • Nicole Prescott *Marney* ■ *Dir* Mary Lambert • *Scr* Gregory Goodell

The Face of Fear   ★★★★
Drama   1971 · US · Colour · 75mins

You'll have some idea of the quality of this TV movie when you learn it was executive produced by Quinn Martin, the man responsible for such gems as *The Untouchables*, *The Fugitive* and *The Streets of San Francisco*. Based on EV Cummingham's novel, *Sally*, it stars Elizabeth Ashley as the leukemia-stricken Iowa teacher who hires a hitman to spare her the agonies of a slow death – only to discover she isn't fatally ill! Ashley seems genuinely terrified, but the acting honours go to Ricardo Montalban and Jack Warden as the cops racing against time to find her unknown assassin.

Ricardo Montalban *Sgt Frank Ortega* • Jack Warden *Lt George Coye* • Elizabeth Ashley *Sally Dillman* • Dane Clark *Tamworth* • Roy Poole *Glenn Kennedy* • Charles Dierkop *Patsy Fain* • Burr DeBenning *Fennington* • Regis J Cordic *Dr Landsteiner* ■ *Dir* George McCowan • *Scr* Edward Hume, from the novel *Sally* by EV Cummingham

The Face of Fear ★★ ⓯
Thriller   1990 · US · Colour · 89mins

Co-adapted by Dean R Koontz from his own novel, this unexceptional effort splices together two suspense favourites; the serial killer and the average guy who summons up extraordinary powers to try to save the day. Too episodic by half, and not always given the right pacey touch by director Farhad Mann, this does sport the odd engaging twist, even if its premise the hero is a mountaineer who survives an ever-so-handy fall, picking up immense psychic abilities in the process is a little far-fetched. ▭

Lee Horsley *Graham Harris* • Pam Dawber *Connie Weaver* • Kevin Conroy *Frank Bollinger* • Bob Balaban *Detective Ira Preduski* • William Sadler *Anthony Prine* • Donna Theodore *Edna Mowry* • David A Kimball *Blond Man* ■ *Dir* Farhad Mann • *Scr* Dean R Koontz, Alan Jay Glueckman, from the novel by Dean R Koontz

Face of Fire ★★
Drama   1959 · US/UK · BW · 80mins

This obscure film of some ambition founders in trying to expand a short story by the eminent Stephen Crane into a feature-length drama. In turn-of-the-century New England, James Whitmore plays a much-loved handyman who becomes hideously disfigured after saving a small boy from a fire and finds people can no longer stand him. Curiously, this was made in Sweden under the direction of Albert Band, with a largely Hollywood cast that includes Cameron Mitchell and Royal Dano. The latter's memorable appearance in that much superior Crane adaptation, *The Red Badge of Courage*, only serves to underline this film's shortcomings.

Cameron Mitchell *Ned Trescott* • James Whitmore *Monk Johnson* • Bettye Ackerman *Grace Trescott* • Miko Oscard *Jimmie Trescott* • Royal Dano *Jake Winter* • Robert Simon *The Judge* • Richard Erdman *Al Williams* ■ *Dir* Albert Band • *Scr* Louis Garfinkle, from the story *The Monster* by Stephen Crane

The Face of Fu Manchu ★★★ PG

Horror   1965 · UK · Colour · 92mins

The first and best of Christopher Lee's portrayals of mystery writer Sax Rohmer's insidious East-Asian arch villain. Here he plans to conquer the world with a poison gas invented by a German professor held prisoner in his secret HQ under the Thames – very handy for those Chinese water tortures. Propelled by an eerie opening, this atmospheric comic strip fantasy is skilfully assembled, and Nigel Green is superb as Fu Manchu's Scotland Yard nemesis, Nayland Smith.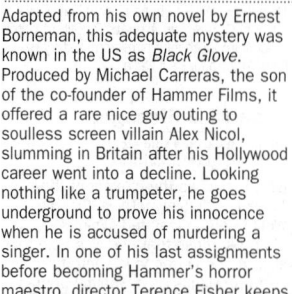

Christopher Lee *Fu Manchu* • Nigel Green *Nayland Smith* • James Robertson-Justice *Sir Charles Fortesque* • Howard Marion-Crawford *Dr Walter Petrie* • Tsai Chin *Lin Tang* • Joachim Fuchsberger *Carl Jansen* • Karin Dor *Maria* • Walter Rilla *Professor Muller* ■ *Dir* Don Sharp • *Scr* Harry Alan Towers, from characters created by Sax Rohmer

Face/Off ★★★★ 18

Action thriller   1997 · US · Colour · 133mins

Nicolas Cage has lost his face and now he wants it back. Problem is, it's attached to John Travolta whose own face has been stitched on to Cage. Hard to swallow? Not if you treat this movie as the popcorn entertainment it's intended to be. Cage is Castor Troy, a terrorist, who, having planted a bomb somewhere in LA, is put into a coma by his FBI agent nemesis, Sean Archer (Travolta). This is when the plastic surgery comes in – it is the only way to dupe Troy's cohorts into revealing the bomb's location. There's a clever story here, especially when Cage begins to revive Travolta's stale marriage to Joan Allen, but director John Woo partially wrecks what could have been a great movie with some overblown action sequences. Contains swearing, violence and sexual references. ▭ *DVD*

John Travolta *Sean Archer* • Nicolas Cage *Castor Troy* • Joan Allen *Eve Archer* • Alessandro Nivola *Pollux Troy* • Gina Gershon *Sasha Hassler* • Dominique Swain *Jamie Archer* • Nick Cassavetes *Dietrich Hassler* • Harve Presnell *Lazzaro* ■ *Dir* John Woo • *Scr* Mike Werb, Michael Colleary

Face on the Milk Carton ★★

Drama   1995 · US · Colour

In the US, pictures of missing children are placed on milk cartons, a practice that remarkably delivers results. This TV movie poses a fascinating question: what would you do if you learnt, from such a picture, that you were, in fact, a missing child? Kellie Martin stars as the confused, worried teenager, Edward Herrmann/Jill Clayburgh and Richard Masur/Sharon Lawrence are her possible parents. TV-movie veteran Waris Hussein doesn't make the most of the intriguing premise.

Kellie Martin *Janie Jessmon* • Jill Clayburgh *Miranda Jessmon* • Sharon Lawrence *Sada Sands* • Edward Herrmann *Frank Jessmon* • Johnny Green *Reeve Shields* • Richard Masur *Jonathan Sands* ■ *Dir* Waris Hussein • *Scr* Nancy Isaak, from the book *The Face on the Milk Carton/Whatever Happened to Janie* by Caroline B Cooney

Face the Music ★★

Crime drama   1954 · UK · BW · 84mins

Adapted from his own novel by Ernest Borneman, this adequate mystery was known in the US as *Black Glove*. Produced by Michael Carreras, the son of the co-founder of Hammer Films, it offered a rare nice guy outing to soulless screen villain Alex Nicol, slumming in Britain after his Hollywood career went into a decline. Looking nothing like a trumpeter, he goes underground to prove his innocence when he is accused of murdering a singer. In one of his last assignments before becoming Hammer's horror maestro, director Terence Fisher keeps the clues coming without ever managing to intrigue.

Alex Nicol *James Bradley* • Eleanor Summerfield *Barbara Quigley* • John Salew *Max Marguiles* • Paul Carpenter *Johnny Sutherland* • Geoffrey Keen *Maurice Green* ■ *Dir* Terence Fisher • *Scr* Ernest Borneman, from his novel

Face the Music ★★

Romance   1992 · Fr · Colour · 93mins

Molly Ringwald and Patrick Dempsey both enjoyed considerable success as teen stars, but they've endured some pretty lean years since, and this decidedly hackneyed contrivance would have been considered old hat in the silent era. The two leads play a once-successful songwriting team who have since separated and now barely exchange Christmas cards. You don't need a diploma in creative writing to work out what happens when they reunite to work on a movie score, even though Dempsey is now dating Lysette Anthony. Cornball rather than screwball, with Ringwald hitting more right notes than Dempsey.

Molly Ringwald *Lisa Hollis* • Patrick Dempsey *Charlie Hunter* • Lysette Anthony *Julie* ■ *Dir* Carol Wiseman • *Scr* Randee Russell

Face to Face ★★ U

Portmanteau drama   1952 · US · BW · 89mins

Inspired by portmanteau movies, such as *Dead of Night* and *Forever and a Day*, which glued several short stories together, a young millionaire named Huntington Hartford somehow persuaded RKO to revive the format. John Brahm's section is a version of Joseph Conrad's *The Secret Sharer*, with James Mason hiding a murder suspect on his ship. Bretaigne Windust's film is *The Bride Comes to Yellow Sky*, based on a Stephen Crane story, with Robert Preston as a Texan sheriff whose fiancée is threatened by a long-time adversary. The fiancée is played by Marjorie Steele, who was married to Hartford. Both stories are effectively told on dime budgets, and audiences stayed away in droves.

James Mason *Captain* • Gene Lockhart *Capt Archbold* • Michael Pate *Swimmer* • Albert Sharpe *1st Mate* • Robert Preston *Sheriff* • Marjorie Steele *Bride* • Minor Watson *Bad man* • Dan Seymour *Drummer* • James Agee *Prisoner* ■ *Dir* John Brahm, Bretaigne Windust • *Scr* Aeneas MacKenzie, James Agee, from the short story *The Secret Sharer* by Joseph Conrad, from the short story *The Bride Comes to Yellow Sky* by Stephen Crane

Face to Face ★★★ 15

Western   1967 · It/Sp · Colour · 90mins

An Italian/Spanish co-production, this is less a spaghetti western than a political parable raking over the coals of each country's fascist past. Gian Maria Volonté gives a highly persuasive performance as a college professor who discovers a talent for banditry when sent to recover his health at a small western town. But the subtext is too often thrust to the fore, with the result that the exploits of the prof and his gang virtually become an irrelevance as writer/director Sergio Sollima sermonises on the misuse of power and the rule of fear. Ennio Morricone contributes a typically poignant score. Italian dialogue dubbed into English. ▭

Gian Maria Volonté *Brad Fletcher* • Tomas Milian *Solomon "Beauregard"Bennett* • William Berger *Charles Siringo* • Jolanda Modio *Marie* • Carole Andre *Cattle Annie* • Gianni Rizzo *Williams* ■ *Dir/Scr* Sergio Sollima • *Music* Ennio Morricone

Face to Face ★★

Drama   1976 · Swe · Colour · 135mins

Originally presented as a four-part TV series, this intense, hugely personal drama suffers fatally from its drastic truncation. After a string of successes, Ingmar Bergman allows introspection to get the better of him with this tiresome study of suppressed trauma, which is so riddled with familiar images and themes it often feels like a bad homage by a slavish acolyte. Fortunately, while Bergman loses himself in unresolved homosexual subplots and stylised dream sequences, Liv Ullmann turns in a compelling performance as the psychiatrist whose breakdown finally enables her to come to terms with her troubled adolescence. In Swedish with English subtitles.

Liv Ullmann *Dr Jenny Isaksson* • Erland Josephson *Dr Tomas Jacobi* • Gunnar Björnstrand *Grandfather* • Aino Taube-Henrikson [Aino Taube] *Grandmother* • Kari Sylwan *Maria* • Sif Raud *Elizabeth Wankel* • Sven Lindberg *Dr Erik Isaksson* • Tore Segelcke *The lady* ■ *Dir/Scr* Ingmar Bergman

Face to Face ★★

Romantic comedy   1990 · US · Colour · 93mins

Elizabeth Montgomery (TV's *Bewitched*) is a scientist on an archeological dig in Africa who crosses swords with grumpy miner Robert Foxworth in this lightweight romantic comedy. The basic plot is nearly as old as some of the fossils Montgomery is digging up, but the stars are charming enough and director Lou Antonio (who also co-stars) moves things along unfussily.

Elizabeth Montgomery *Diana Firestone* • Robert Foxworth *Tobias Williams* • Lou Antonio *Dr Calvin Finch* • Ronald Lacey *Dr Brinkman* • Lydia Kigada *Miriam Sioki* • Richard Ngati *Enjoro* ■ *Dir* Lou Antonio • *Scr* John Sweet

Face Value ★★★ 15

Thriller based on a true story   1991 · US · Colour · 91mins

The flipside of the modelling business is revealed in this surprisingly forceful drama, based on a true story. Cheryl Pollak plays a naive young girl, newly arrived in New York, who looks set for a big career in modelling, only to fall foul of obsessive make-up man Kirk Baltz, with tragic results. Telling the story in flashback, writer/director John Gray succeeds in making some hard-hitting points on the nature of fame and harassment, and coaxes good performances from his young cast. ▭

Cheryl Pollak *Marla Hanson* • Dale Midkiff *Eric Warner* • Kirk Baltz *Steve Roth* • Jennifer Van Dyke *Lyn* • Jack Blessing *Agent* • Stephen Tobolowsky *Attorney Crain* • Juanita Jennings *Elaine* ■ *Dir/Scr* John Gray

Faces ★★★★ 15

Drama   1968 · US · BW · 124mins

A challenging, gritty example of sixties New American cinema from John Cassavetes, that combines Method acting with the cinematic techniques of the French New Wave. The marriage of Californian liberals John Marley and Lynn Carlin is on the rocks and after yet another row he storms out to spend the night with prostitute Gena Rowlands, while she finds solace in the arms of disco-dancing hippy Seymour Cassel. The picture originally lasted six hours and there are still places where some judicious cutting would not go amiss. But the improvised performances are exceptional, with Marley and Rowlands every bit as impressive as the Oscar-nominated Carlin and Cassel. Cassavetes's screenplay also received a nomination. ▭

John Marley *Richard Forst* • Gena Rowlands *Jeannie Rapp* • Lynn Carlin *Maria Forst* • Fred Draper *Freddie* • Seymour Cassel *Chet* • Val Avery *McCarthy* • Dorothy Gulliver *Florence* • Joanne Moore *Jordan Louise* • Darlene Conley *Billy Mae* ■ *Dir/Scr* John Cassavetes

Faces in the Dark ★★

Thriller   1960 · UK · BW · 84mins

Adapted from the novel by Pierre Boileau and Thomas Narcejac (the writers of *The Woman Who Was No More*, on which *Les Diaboliques* was based) this tale of blindness and rage should have been a real nail-biter. Sadly, ex-documentary director David Eady simply doesn't have the thriller instinct and throws away countless opportunities to make the tension unbearable. You feel far more concern for gutsy heroines such as Audrey Hepburn in *Wait until Dark* and Mia Farrow in *Blind Terror* than you do for mild-mannered John Gregson, the blind person under threat here.

John Gregson *Richard Hammond* • Mai Zetterling *Christiane Hammond* • Michael Denison *David Merton* • John Ireland *Max Hammond* • Tony Wright *Clem* • Nanette Newman *Janet* • Valerie Taylor *Miss Hopkins* ■ *Dir* David Eady • *Scr* Ephraim Kogan, John Tully, from the novel by Pierre Boileau, Thomas Narcejac

Faces of Children ★★★

Silent drama   1925 · Swi/Fr · BW · 114mins

Having experimented with Expressionism in his early career, Belgian-born director Jacques Feyder refined the poetic realist style that he had pioneered in *Crainquebille* in this sentimental tale of motherly love. But not even a director with his visual gifts could completely eradicate the

U = SUITABLE FOR ALL   Uc = SUITABLE FOR ALL, ESPECIALLY FOR YOUNG CHILDREN (VIDEO ONLY)   PG = PARENTAL GUIDANCE

melodramatic miming endemic in silent acting. Consequently, the performances work against the stylised authenticity of the sets, although the story itself is more than a little contrived. Child star Jean Forest is the pick of the cast, as the boy who expresses his resentment at his father's remarriage by tormenting his new stepsister, Arlette Peyran.

Jean Forest *Jean Amsler* • Rachel Devirys *Jeanne Dutois* • Victor Vina *Pierre Amsler* • Arlette Peyran *Arlette Dutois* • Pierrette Houyez *Pierrette Amsler* • Henri Duval *Canon Taillier* • Suzy Vernon *Jean's mother* ■ *Dir* Jacques Feyder • *Scr* Jacques Feyder, Françoise Rosay

The Facts of Life ★★★
Comedy 1960 · US · BW · 103mins

A comedy that's well worth watching for its pairing of two of the screen's greatest clowns (though both Bob Hope and Lucille Ball play virtually straight parts here) as a pair of married – but not to each other– lovers desperately trying to consummate their affair, and being thwarted at every turn. Naughty rather than raunchy, it was deemed suitable as a saucy dish to present to the Queen at that year's Royal Film Performance. Bob and Lucy were wackier in *Fancy Pants* and *Critic's Choice*, but it's their engaging teamwork in this little flick that you'll remember with affection.

Bob Hope *Larry Gilbert* • Lucille Ball *Kitty Weaver* • Ruth Hussey *Mary Gilbert* • Don DeFore *Jack Weaver* • Louis Nye *Charles Busbee* • Philip Ober *Doc Mason* • Marianne Stewart *Connie Mason* • Peter Leeds *Thompson* • Hollis Irving *Myrtle Busbee* ■ *Dir* Melvin Frank • *Scr* Norman Panama, Melvin Frank • *Costume Designer* Edith Head

The Faculty ★★★ 15
Science-fiction horror thriller
1998 · US · Colour · 99mins

Scream writer Kevin Williamson teams up with *From Dusk till Dawn* director Robert Rodriguez for an enjoyable reworking of alien invasion movies, bolstered by Williamson's patented in-jokes and genre subversions. Considerably less subtle than the fifties films that inspired it, *The Faculty* succeeds through assured performances from the teenage cast, zippy direction and the writer's refusal to take even the most tense moments seriously. Along the way, there's humorous homage paid to sci-fi related novels, TV and films. Despite a disappointing reliance on digital effects in the final third, this is classy, extraterrestrial entertainment. Contains swearing and violence. 📺 **DVD**

Jordana Brewster *Delilah* • Clea DuVall *Stokely* • Laura Harris *Marybeth* • Josh Hartnett *Zeke* • Shawn Hatosy *Stan* • Salma Hayek *Nurse Harper* • Famke Janssen *Miss Burke* • Piper Laurie *Mrs Olson* • Robert Patrick *Coach Willis* • Elijah Wood *Casey* ■ *Dir* Robert Rodriguez • *Scr* Kevin Williamson, from a story by David Wechter, Bruce Kimmel

Fade to Black ★★★ 18
Horror 1980 · US · Colour · 97mins

A homage to Hollywood's golden age, but with a difference! When a movie fanatic's loser lifestyle tips him over the edge into insanity, he embarks on a killing spree disguised as his favourite film characters, such as

Dracula and the Mummy. Vernon Zimmerman turns in an intelligent and imaginative movie, with plenty of cinematic references and in-jokes to enjoy, including one of the best ever send-ups of the *Psycho* shower scene, but an excess of violence leaves a bitter aftertaste. Dennis Christopher's carefully judged central performance is made ridiculous by turning him into just another slasher killer. Still, this is one of the darkest teenage-angst movies of the decade. And look out for Mickey Rourke in an early film role. 📺

Dennis Christopher *Eric* • Linda Kerridge *Marilyn* • Tim Thomerson *Dr Moriarty* • Morgan Paull *Gary* • Hennen Chambers *Bart* • Marya Small *Doreen* • Mickey Rourke *Richie* ■ *Dir/ Scr* Vernon Zimmerman

Fade to Black ★ 15
Thriller 1993 · US · Colour · 81mins

In this plodding, thin *Rear Window* imitation, Timothy Busfield (*thirtysomething*) plays a social anthropologist college professor, who uses the excuse of researching human behavior to act as a Peeping Tom. While on the job, he inadvertently films what he thinks might be a homicide, but is unable to convince the police when they can't find a body. Sound familiar? Despite the presence of television's favourite vixen, Heather Locklear, as the killer's quarry, overly familiar elements, poor direction and dull performances will have you fading off to sleep. 📺

Timothy Busfield *Del Calvin* • Heather Locklear *Victoria Kilburn* • Cloris Leachman *Ruth Weinstaub* • Michael Beck *Nic Braith* • Louis Giambalvo *Detective Miflin* ■ *Dir* John McPherson • *Scr* Douglas Barr

Fahrenheit 451 ★★★
Science-fiction drama
1966 · UK · Colour · 112mins

One of François Truffaut's lesser efforts, the only film he directed in English is full of unfulfilled promise. Syd Cain's futuristic sets cleverly convey the menace and desperation of a society in which books are banned and burned. Cyril Cusack's fire chief is hugely resistible as he unquestioningly performs his duty and Julie Christie superbly judges the contrasts in her dual role. But Oskar Werner who starred in Truffaut's *Jules et Jim* seems to have lost the plot and as he's its driving force, this is a major stumbling block.

Oskar Werner *Montag* • Julie Christie *Linda/ Clarisse* • Cyril Cusack *Captain* • Anton Diffring *Fabian* • Jeremy Spenser *Man with apple* • Alex Scott *Henry Brulard* ■ *Dir* François Truffaut • *Scr* François Truffaut, Jean-Louis Richard, David Rudkin, Helen Scott, from the novel by Ray Bradbury • *Cinematographer* Nicolas Roeg

Fail-Safe ★★★★ PG
Drama 1964 · US · BW · 107mins

Dr Strangelove by any other name! This suspense movie follows the same flight path as *Strangelove* – in fact, there was an aborted charge of literary plagiarism – as a squadron of US planes, loaded with nuclear bombs, accidentally sets off to devastate Moscow and cannot be halted from its doomsday mission. Director Sidney

Lumet builds the tension from neurotic jitters (Larry Hagman as presidential interpreter) through to psychotic jeopardy (Walter Matthau's anti-Soviet professor urging the Armageddon sanction) when fail-safe devices fail and American president Henry Fonda has to warn his Soviet counterpart that the world is heading into nightmare. By telling it straight, the idea loses a certain satirical edge, but gains a hint of reality. Anyway, it's a warning we can't hear too often: that machines should never be the masters of men. 📺

Henry Fonda *The President* • Walter Matthau *Groeteschele* • Frank Overton *General Bogan* • Dan O'Herlihy *General Black* • Fritz Weaver *Colonel Cascio* • Larry Hagman *Buck* • Edward Binns *Colonel Grady* • William Hansen *Secretary Swenson* ■ *Dir* Sidney Lumet • *Scr* Walter Bernstein, from the novel by Eugene Burdick, Harvey Wheeler

Fair Game ★★ 15
Action drama 1995 · US · Colour · 86mins

T-shirt clad Cindy Crawford gets chased by baddies and falls into the water a lot. Err, that's about it. The supermodel wanted to be taken seriously as an actress but she doesn't get much chance to show what she can do in this, her big Hollywood debut. If you can believe Crawford is a high-powered lawyer then you will probably just about swallow the nonsensical story about Russian villains who are convinced the former Mrs Gere has some valuable information about their American operation. William Baldwin simply looks bored as the cop who comes to her aid. Some enjoyably destructive set pieces aside, the only fun to be had is savouring Steven Berkoff's barmy performance. Contains swearing, violence and nudity. 📺

William Baldwin *Detective Max Kirkpatrick* • Cindy Crawford *Kate McQueen* • Steven Berkoff *Kazak* • Christopher McDonald *Lieutenant Mayerson* • Miguel Sandoval *Juantorena* ■ *Dir* Andrew Sipes • *Scr* Charlie Fletcher, from the novel by Paula Gosling

Fair Warning ★★
Western 1937 · US · BW · 68mins

One of those 20th Century-Fox programme fillers made swiftly and cheaply, invariably on existing sets, intended as little more than support for the main feature, and undeniably fascinating to view today. This western features John Howard Payne, before he discarded his middle name to become one of Fox's handsome if a little dull leading men of the forties. He plays Jim Preston, a swimming instructor involved in murder. Top-billed, however, is the excellent J Edward Bromberg, whose career would be tragically cut short by the communist witch-hunt (he was blacklisted and died in London in 1951 at the age of 48).

J Edward Bromberg *Matthew Jericho* • Betty Furness *Kay Farnham* • John Howard Payne [John Payne] *Jim Preston* • Victor Kilian *Sam* • Billy Burrud *Malcolm Berkhardt* • Gavin Muir *Herbert Willett* • Gloria Roy *Grace Hamilton* • Andrew Tombes *JC Farnham* ■ *Dir* Norman Foster • *Scr* Norman Foster, from a story by Philip Wylie

Fair Wind to Java ★★★ PG
Adventure 1953 · US · Colour · 87mins

Fred MacMurray stars as a seafaring skipper in this rip-roaring adventure, racing against time and pirate Robert Douglas to recover a hoard of diamonds before Krakatoa erupts, and romancing Vera Ralston along the way. Unfortunately, the film is spoiled by its cheap studio backdrops and hopeless effects – you'll fall about laughing when the volcano blows. Still, there's much to enjoy, including Victor McLaglen as a drunken sailor. 📺

Fred MacMurray *Captain Boll* • Vera Ralston *Kim Kim* • Robert Douglas *Pulo Besar/St Ebenezer* • Victor McLaglen *O'Brien* • John Russell *Flint* • Buddy Baer *Kung* • Claude Jarman Jr *Chess* • Grant Withers *Jason Blue* ■ *Dir* Joseph Kane • *Scr* Richard Tregaskis, from the novel by Garland Roark

Fairy Tale for Seventeen Year Olds ★★★
Drama 1986 · Viet · BW · 77mins

Vietnamese films were shot in black and white until the mid-1980s, but few directors turned such budgetary constraint to such striking advantage as Xuan Son Nguyen in this touching home-front drama. Making particularly effective use of moonlight and reflective surfaces, the director brings a dreamlike quality to the tale of the teenager whose impression of the bitterly fought civil war is romanticised by her love for a handsome soldier at the front. However, he also depicts, all too realistically, the quiet heroism of those left behind as they endure the unbearable pain of waiting and hoping. A Vietnamese language film.

Vy Le • Tranh Hahn • Tu Thanh ■ *Dir* Nguyen Xuan Son • *Scr* Trinh Thanh Nha

FairyTale: a True Story ★★★★ U
Historical drama 1997 · US · Colour · 93mins

Charles Sturridge (*Brideshead Revisited*) lyrically directs this family tale, based on the true story of two young girls who, in 1917, produced photographs of a group of winged, fairy-like creatures they had taken at the bottom of their garden. The story follows the controversy which surrounded the photographs – were they real or were they faked? Could it be a trick of the light, or proof that fairies exist? – as luminaries such as Sir Arthur Conan Doyle (Peter O'Toole) and Harry Houdini (Harvey Keitel) debated the authenticity of the pictures. It's beautifully filmed, with nice special effects by Tim Webber, and Sturridge infuses the film with a sense of wonder and romanticism that contrasts with the more sombre backdrop of the First World War. 📺

Florence Hoath *Elsie Wright* • Elizabeth Earl *Frances Griffiths* • Paul McGann *Arthur Wright* • Phoebe Nicholls *Polly Wright* • Bill Nighy *Edward Gardner* • Bob Peck *Harry Briggs* • Harvey Keitel *Harry Houdini* • Peter O'Toole *Sir Arthur Conan Doyle* • Mel Gibson *Frances' father* ■ *Dir* Charles Sturridge • *Scr* Ernie Contreras, from a story by Ernie Contreras, Albert Ash, Tom McLoughlin

Faithful ★

Comedy   1996 · US · Colour · 91mins

Actor/scriptwriter Chazz Palminteri isn't so lucky with this adaptation of his stage play as he was with *A Bronx Tale*. In director Paul Mazursky's hands, Palminteri's three-hander turns into bland fare, showing little insight and featuring Cher in one of her worst performances. She plays the wife of Ryan O'Neal, who has hired hit man Palminteri to kill her on their 20th wedding anniversary. But unwittingly he becomes their marital therapist instead, in Mazursky's depressingly flat, entertainment-free zone.

Cher *Margaret O'Donnell* • Chazz Palminteri *Tony* • Ryan O'Neal *Jack O'Donnell* • Paul Mazursky *Dr Susskind* • Amber Smith *Debbie* • Elisa Leonetti *Maria* ■ *Dir* Paul Mazursky • *Scr* Chazz Palminteri

The Falcon and the Co-Eds ★★

Crime mystery   1943 · US · BW · 68mins

Logic was never the byword of this RKO series, but utter confusion reigns in this entry. Tom Conway investigates the death of a professor at a girls' school. Screenwriters Ardel Wray and Gerard Geraghty are pretty adept at bumping off suspects, but the motives are so obscure that repeated viewing of Conway's accusatory summation only reveals additional loose ends and inconsistencies. No wonder William Clemens directed at such a lick. However, with a staffroom full of sinister eccentrics and a student body combining the sultry and the hysterical, this breezy mystery is never less than entertaining.

Tom Conway *Tom Lawrence/The Falcon* • Jean Brooks *Vicky Gaines* • Rita Corday *Marguerita Serena* • Amelita Ward *Jane Harris* • Isabel Jewell *Mary Phoebus* • George Givot *Dr Anatole Graelich* • Cliff Clark *Timothy Donovan* • Ed Gargan [Edward Gargan] *Bates* ■ *Dir* William Clemens • *Scr* Ardel Wray, Gerald Geraghty, from the story by Ardel Wray, from the character created by Michael Arlen

The Falcon and the Snowman ★★★ 15

Spy drama based on a true story
1985 · US · Colour · 125mins

A convoluted spy thriller, with Timothy Hutton as a college dropout who obtains US secrets and, with his drug-addicted buddy Sean Penn, passes them on to the Soviet embassy in Mexico. Purportedly based on fact, the movie is about the motives for treason and the loss of moral purpose in America, underlined by some heavy-handed flashbacks to Vietnam, the Kennedys, Martin Luther King and even John Lennon. Directed with customary visual flair by John Schlesinger, from a screenplay by Steven Zaillian, who later wrote the film script for *Schindler's List*, it's undeniably gripping, if a little long and unfocused. Contains violence and swearing. 🎬

Timothy Hutton *Christopher Boyce* • Sean Penn *Daulton Lee* • Pat Hingle *Mr Boyce* • Richard Dysart *Dr Lee* • Lori Singer *Lana* • David Suchet *Alex* • Dorian Harewood *Gene* • Priscilla Pointer *Mrs Lee* ■ *Dir* John Schlesinger • *Scr* Steven Zaillian, from the book by Robert Lindsey

The Falcon in Danger ★★

Crime mystery   1943 · US · BW · 70mins

When $100,00 in securities go missing and two corpses show up, who else could the man to solve the mystery be but that debonair detective, Tom Conway? The sixth entry in RKO's B-movie series is far from being the most suspenseful. Indeed, apart from the opening sequence, in which an empty plane crashes at an airport and a couple of assassination attempts take place, the mystery is often forced to take a backseat to the Falcon's romance with Amelita Ward. Don't even bother looking for clues as the script, for all its red herrings and sudden revelations, isn't that subtle.

Tom Conway *The Falcon* • Jean Brooks *Iris* • Elaine Shepard *Nancy* • Amelita Ward *Bonnie* • Cliff Clark *Donovan* • Ed Gargan [Edward Gargan] *Bates* • Clarence Klob *Palmer* • Felix Basch *Morley* • Richard Davies *Ken* ■ *Dir* William Clemens • *Scr* Fred Nibilo Jr, Craig Rice, from the character created by Michael Arlen

The Falcon in Hollywood ★★

Crime mystery   1944 · US · BW · 67mins

Hooray for Hollywood, because without the trip around RKO's back lot and visits to such landmarks as the Hollywood Bowl, this whodunit would have been over in two reels. The vacationing Tom Conway clearly revels in being surrounded by beautiful starlets as he tries to discover who killed the acting ex of a costume designer on the eve of her wedding to a hot-shot director. But, apart from the sneak peeks behind the scenes, this is a ploddingly predictable thriller, with so many suspects bumped off it doesn't take a genius to find the culprit among the survivors.

Tom Conway *Tom Lawrence/The Falcon* • Barbara Hale *Peggy Callahan* • Veda Ann Borg *Billie* • Jean Brooks *Roxanna* • Rita Corday *Lilli D'Allio* • John Abbott *Martin Dwyer* • Sheldon Leonard *Louie* ■ *Dir* Gordon Douglas • *Scr* Gerald Geraghty, from the character created by Michael Arlen

The Falcon in Mexico ★★

Crime mystery   1944 · US · BW · 70mins

According to Hollywood legend, the location footage used in this puzzling series entry was borrowed from Orson Welles's infamously scuppered documentary, *It's All True*. Certainly, the Mexican vistas add to the appeal of this typically brusque mystery, in which Tom Conway allies with artist's daughter Martha MacVicar to discover how her long-dead father could have painted a portrait of Cecilia Callejo. With a trio of murders, a couple of unnecessary musical interludes and one near miss, this is certainly a busy picture and not even William Berke's undistinguished direction can detract from the entertainment.

Tom Conway *Tom Lawrence/The Falcon* • Mona Maris *Raquel* • Martha MacVicar *Barbara Wade* • Nestor Paiva *Manuel Romero* • Mary Currier *Paula Dudley* • Cecilia Callejo *Dolores Ybarra* ■ *Dir* William Berke • *Scr* Gerald Geraghty, George Worthing Yates, from the character created by Michael Arlen

The Falcon in San Francisco ★★★

Crime mystery   1945 · US · BW · 65mins

Made immediately before his breakthrough picture, *My Name Is Julia Ross*, Joseph H Lewis's sole entry in RKO's long-running crime series is undoubtedly the most stylish. For example, note the way he uses locations for atmosphere and not window-dressing. It's also the funniest, with Tom Conway's doltish sidekick Edward Brophy spending as much time searching for a wife to ease his tax burden as he does looking for clues to solve the case. A murder on a train sparks this lively adventure, in which the Falcon plays nursemaid to orphaned Sharyn Moffett while trying to clear Rita Corday of involvement with a gang of silk smugglers.

Tom Conway *Tom Lawrence/The Falcon* • Rita Corday *Joan Marshall* • Edward S Brophy [Edward Brophy] *Goldie Locke* • Sharyn Moffett *Annie Marshall* • Fay Helm *Doreen Temple* ■ *Dir* Joseph H Lewis • *Scr* Robert Kent, Ben Markson, from a story by Robert Kent, from the character created by Michael Arlen

The Falcon Out West ★★

Crime mystery   1944 · US · BW · 64mins

In his fifth outing as supersleuth Tom Lawrence, Tom Conway found himself in sagebrush country after millionaire Lyle Talbot collapses inexplicably on a New York dance floor. A trip to his ranch in Texas, in the unwelcome company of inspector Cliff Clark and his doltish sidekick Don Douglas, reveals the culprit, but not before Conway has survived two attempts on his life and evaded a kidnapper armed with rattlesnake poison. Although Barbara Hale provides some testy Texan support, this is not one of the series' best entries, with the script coasting along on such western clichés as ambushes and stagecoach chases.

Tom Conway *The Falcon* • Barbara Hale *Marion* • Don Douglas *Hayden* • Carole Gallagher *Vanessa* • Joan Barclay *Mrs Irwin* • Cliff Clark *Inspector Donovan* • Ed Gargan [Edward Gargan] *Bates* • Minor Watson *Caldwell* ■ *Dir* William Clemens • *Scr* Billy Jones, Morton Grant, from the character created by Michael Arlen

The Falcon Strikes Back ★★★

Crime mystery   1943 · US · BW · 65mins

One of the finest slapstick stooges since the silent era, Edgar Kennedy revealed there was more to his screen persona than the famous "slow burn" in this slickly staged mystery. He steals the show here as a malevolent puppeteer caught up in the same war bond scam for which the police want to question our dapper hero, The Falcon (Tom Conway), after he is found unconscious alongside a very dead bank manager. Dashing off the playful dialogue with typical aplomb, Conway seems to relish the prospect of trapping swindler Rita Corday's killer. Clearly, the superior direction of Edward Dmytryk suited him in this, his first solo outing as the crime fighter.

Tom Conway *The Falcon* • Harriet Hilliard *Gwynne Gregory* • Jane Randolph *Marcia Brooks* • Edgar Kennedy *Smiley Dugan* • Cliff

Edwards *Goldie* • Rita Corday *Mia Bruger* • Erford Gage *Rickey Davis* ■ *Dir* Edward Dmytryk • *Scr* Edward Dein, Gerald Geraghty, from a story by Stuart Palmer, from the character created by Michael Arlen

The Falcon Takes Over ★★★

Crime mystery   1942 · US · BW · 63mins

Raymond Chandler's *Farewell, My Lovely* was the inspiration for George Sanders's penultimate outing as Michael Arlen's suave sleuth. An escaped convict, a priceless necklace and a clever imposter are the plot strands that Irving Reis weaves together at breakneck speed. But it's to his credit that Chandler's classic tale retains its intrigue, as chauffeur Allen Jenkins and inspector James Gleason gamely attempt to hang onto Sanders's coat-tails as he seeks to reunite the vengeful Ward Bond with his duplicitous girlfriend. With the Falcon making a dashing stand-in for Chandler's hero Philip Marlowe, this is easily the best entry in RKO's ever-enjoyable series.

George Sanders *The Falcon* • Lynn Bari *Ann Riordan* • Allen Jenkins *Goldie Locke* • James Gleason *Inspector Mike O'Hara* • Helen Gilbert *Diana Kenyon* • Ward Bond *Moose Malloy* • Ed Gargan [Edward Gargan] *Bates* ■ *Dir* Irving Reis • *Scr* Lynn Root, Frank Fenton, from the character created by Michael Arlen and the novel *Farewell, My Lovely* by Raymond Chandler

The Falcon's Adventure ★★

Crime mystery   1946 · US · BW · 61mins

Considering the uninspiring job he did on *The Falcon in Mexico*, it's rather surprising that RKO executives gave William Berke a second entry in this ever-lively series. It turned out to be the troubleshooter's final assignment for the studio, however, as Tom Conway cancels his vacation to keep both Madge Meredith and a formula for synthetic industrial diamonds out of the hands of the villains who have framed him for her father's murder. Bearing more than a passing resemblance to *A Date with the Falcon*, this disappointing swansong is enlivened only by the comic mugging of Edward S Brophy as the Falcon's sidekick, Goldie.

Tom Conway *The Falcon* • Madge Meredith *Luisa Braganza* • Edward S Brophy [Edward Brophy] *Goldie* • Robert Warwick *Sutton* • Myrna Dell *Doris* • Steve Brodie *Benny* • Ian Wolfe *Denison* • Carol Forman *Helen* ■ *Dir* William Berke • *Scr* Aubrey Wisberg, Robert Kent, from the character created by Michael Arlen

The Falcon's Alibi ★★

Crime mystery   1946 · US · BW · 62mins

One of the weakest entries in the series, this tale of jewel theft and murders leaves you doubting Tom Conway's powers of detection, as the culprit is evident almost from their first appearance. A waiter, a hotel guest and sassy band singer Jane Greer have all bitten the dust and Conway has even endured a stint in the slammer before he finally twigs who's responsible for the theft of Esther Howard's pearls, which he was supposed to protect. Vince Barnett stooges admirably, and there's pretty support from suspected secretary Rita

Corday, but the only memorable performance comes from Elisha Cook Jr as a sinister radio disc jockey.

Tom Conway *The Falcon* • Rita Corday *Joan* • Vince Barnett *Goldie* • Jane Greer *Lola* • Elisha Cook Jr *Nick* • Emory Parnell *Metcalf* • Al Bridge *Inspector Blake* • Esther Howard *Mrs Peabody* ■ *Dir* Ray McCarey • *Scr* Paul Yawitz, from a story by Dane Lussior, Manny Seff, from the character created by Michael Arlen

The Falcon's Brother ★★

Crime mystery 1942 · US · BW · 62mins

George Sanders handed over the reins of RKO's popular B-franchise to his brother Tom Conway during this disappointing thriller. The war rears its ugly head for the only time in the series, as Conway arrives in South America in time to help Sanders track down the Fifth Columnists who are using a fashion magazine to disseminate information about an assassination attempt on a prominent politician. Directed with brisk efficiency, but little imagination, by Stanley Logan, the entire enterprise feels like a gimmicky way of letting Sanders out of a role he thought was becoming a caricature, while offering a little flagwaving patriotism in the process. Conway, handed the role, went on to star as the Falcon a further nine times.

George Sanders *Gay Lawrence* • Tom Conway *Tom Lawrence* • Jane Randolph *Marcie Brooks* • Don Barclay *Lefty* • Cliff Clark *Inspector Timothy Donovan* ■ *Dir* Stanley Logan • *Scr* Stuart Palmer, Craig Rice, from the character created by Michael Arlen

Fall ★★ 18

Romantic drama 1997 · US · Colour · 86mins

Directed by, written by and starring Eric Schaeffer this is a romantic drama with a refreshingly realistic edge. Despite the totally obvious premise – Schaeffer meets model Amanda De Cadenet, they have steamy sex and then part, as she's married – it moves from semi-soft-porn style rot to become an interesting drama about how the two of them can genuinely remain friends. De Cadenet is watchable and Schaeffer handles his role and a sharp script with skill. Contains swearing and sex scenes. ▭

Eric Schaeffer *Michael Shiver* • Amanda De Cadenet *Sarah Easton* • Rudolph Martin *Philippe* • Francie Swift *Robin* • Lisa Vidal *Sally* ■ *Dir/Scr* Eric Schaeffer

Fall from Grace ★★★ PG

Drama based on a true story
1990 · US · Colour · 91mins

Hilariously bad but hugely enjoyable dramatisation of the adventures of TV evangelists Jim and Tammy Faye Bakker (she was the one wearing enough make-up to stock a chain of chemists). Bernadette Peters tries her best to portray Tammy as more than just a caricature for greed, but Kevin Spacey (an Oscar winner for *The Usual Suspects*) fares less well as the unlikeable, unbelievable and almost unwatchable Jim. Filmed in the style of *National Enquirer* magazine (cheap and tacky with very little fact thrown in), this is one of those movies that falls under the category "so bad it's actually quite good". ▭

Kevin Spacey *Jim Bakker* • Bernadette Peters *Tammy Faye Bakker* • Beth Grant *Paulene* • Travis Swords *Patrick Stone* • Richard Herd *Richard Dortch* • Richard Paul *Jerry Falwell* • Jon Lindstrom *Brian Dunlap* ■ *Dir* Karen Arthur • *Scr* Ken Trevey

Fall into Darkness ★★ 15

Mystery thriller 1996 · US · Colour · 87mins

The execution is pretty routine, but there is more intrigue than usual in this made-for-TV thriller. Tatyana Ali a regular on TV's *The Fresh Prince of Bel-Air* plays a brilliant music student who falls victim to a young socialite's plan to avenge her brother's death. The playing of Ali and her co-star Jonathan Brandis (*Seaquest DSV*) is bland, but there are enough twists and turns in the plot to keep the viewer guessing virtually to the end. Contains swearing and violence. ▭

Tatyana M Ali [Tatyana Ali] *Sharon McKay* • Jonathan Brandis *Chad Lear* • Charlotte Ross *Ann Price* • Sean Murray *Jerry Price* • Paul Scherrer *Paul Lear* ■ *Dir* Mark Sobel • *Scr* JB White, from the novel by Christopher Pike

The Fall of Babylon ★★★

Silent historical epic 1919 · US · BW · 82mins

Seventy years before Spielberg and Cameron started tampering with their earlier films and re-releasing them in longer versions, DW Griffith was recycling a section from his 1916 epic *Intolerance*. That film, which contained four separate stories, virtually bankrupted Griffith, and audiences found it far too much to swallow in one gulp. So Griffith took out the juiciest story, about a mountain girl who loves Belshazzar and protects him against the evil high priest of Bel, added some new scenes and released the "new" film in 1919. There's lashings of sex and violence, and that staggering set filled with elephant statues and thousands of swirling, semi-naked extras. The penalty is Griffith's overlay of moral indignation, which says, "This movie is bad for you but thanks for buying a ticket."

Tully Marshall *The High Priest of Bel* • Constance Talmadge *The Mountain girl* • Elmer Clifton *The Rhapsode* • Alfred Paget *Prince Belshazzar* • Carl Stockdale *Nabonidus, King of Babylonia* • Seena Owen *Attarea, favorite of Belshazzar* ■ *Dir/Scr* DW Griffith • *Cinematographer* GW Bitzer [Billy Bitzer]

The Fall of the House of Usher ★★★★ 15

Horror 1960 · US · Colour · 75mins

The huge success of this elegant tale of foreboding horror, based on an Edgar Allan Poe story of substance (unlike some later knock-offs), cemented director Roger Corman's artistic style and developed Vincent Price's "Master of the Macabre" persona. Price is superb as the white-haired, hypersensitive recluse Roderick Usher who buries his sister alive because of a demented obsession with his ancestors. Lavishly produced, visually gorgeous and still scary after all these years. ▭

Vincent Price *Roderick Usher* • Mark Damon *Philip Winthrop* • Myrna Fahey *Madeline Usher* • Harry Ellerbe *Bristol* ■ *Dir* Roger Corman •

Scr Richard Matheson, from the story by Edgar Allan Poe • *Cinematographer* Floyd Crosby

The Fall of the Roman Empire ★★★★ U

Historical epic 1964 · US · Colour · 172mins

Producer Samuel Bronston's legacy of six European-shot epics looks more cherishable as the years pass, and leaves one aching to see them once more in their full cinematic glory. Even on TV, though, they tend to impress, thanks to fine casting, superb art direction and majestic scoring. This is no exception that's excellent chariot action and a wonderful, if brief, performance by Alec Guinness as Marcus Aurelius. Sophia Loren has seldom looked lovelier, and the screenplay with its nods to Gibbon is resolutely intelligent. The distinguished support cast ensures that the long movie never palls, and director Anthony Mann supplies his usual finesse. ▭

Sophia Loren *Lucilla* • Stephen Boyd *Livius* • Alec Guinness *Marcus Aurelius* • Christopher Plummer *Commodus* • James Mason *Timonides* • Omar Sharif *Sohamus* • Anthony Quayle *Verulus* • John Ireland *Ballomar* • Mel Ferrer *Cleander* • Eric Porter *Julianus* ■ *Dir* Anthony Mann • *Scr* Ben Barzman, Basilio Franchina, Philip Yordan • *Cinematographer* Robert Krasker • *Music* Dmitri Tiomkin

Fall Time ★★ 18

Crime thriller 1994 · US · Colour · 84mins

Mickey Rourke's career decline continued with this daft, muddled crime thriller. He and Stephen Baldwin (wildly over the top) play two vicious bank robbers who kidnap a trio of prank-loving teenagers who they mistakenly believe are planning to rob a bank they have already targeted. Despite the credible playing of the adolescents (notably future *Scream* star David Arquette), in director Paul Warner's hands the film lurches clumsily from one unlikely situation to the next. Contains violence and swearing. ▭

Mickey Rourke *Florence* • Stephen Baldwin *Leon* • Sheryl Lee *Patty* • Sammy Kershaw *Officer Donny* • Jason London *Tim* • David Arquette *David* ■ *Dir* Paul Warner, Paul Warner • *Scr* Steven Alden, Paul Skemp

Fallen ★★★ 15

Supernatural thriller
1998 · US · Colour · 119mins

This is a convoluted, *Omen*-esque chiller from the director of *Primal Fear*. Denzel Washington gives a strong central performance as a Manhattan homicide detective pursuing a supernatural serial killer. Some initial intrigue over the genesis of the ancient god initiating the prophesied apocalypse, and a fitfully-scary atmosphere, make up for the loose-ended, pretentiously unresolved script by producer Nicholas Kazan. While the best sequence has the evil spirit transferred by simple touch around police headquarters, it's the shock *Revelations*-inspired climax that makes the biggest impression for being so outrageously daft. Contains swearing and violence. ▭ *DVD*

Denzel Washington *John Hobbes* • John Goodman *Jonesy* • Donald Sutherland

Lieutenant Stanton • Embeth Davidtz *Gretta Milano* • James Gandolfini *Lou* • Elias Koteas *Edgar Reese* • Gabriel Casseus *Art* ■ *Dir* Gregory Hoblit • *Scr* Nicholas Kazan

Fallen Angel ★★★★

Film noir 1945 · US · BW · 94mins

This terrific Fox *film noir* was directed by Otto Preminger in the wake of his classic *Laura*. Slightly softened by the casting of a non-musical Alice Faye, who was ill at ease in a leading role, it is greatly enhanced by the presence of Dana Andrews and Linda Darnell. They're a nervy opportunist and sexy paramour respectively in a knockout plot involving Andrews's wish to quit respectable Faye for bad girl Darnell, when, shall we say, certain events cause him to change plan. Watch Andrews – his quizzical, deadpan features always seemed more alert for Preminger than under any other director in his long career.

Alice Faye *June Mills* • Dana Andrews *Eric Stanton* • Linda Darnell *Stella* • Charles Bickford *Mark Judd* • Anne Revere *Clara Mills* • Bruce Cabot *Dave Atkins* • John Carradine *Professor Madley* • Percy Kilbride *Pop* ■ *Dir* Otto Preminger • *Scr* Harry Kleiner, from the novel by Marty Holland

Fallen Angel ★★★ 15

Drama 1981 · US · Colour · 91mins

A made-for-TV drama about a 13-year-old girl who runs away from home and straight into the arms of a pornographer, who persuades her and other children to pose for pictures. Reminiscent of Paul Schrader's 1979 film *Hardcore*, which starred George C Scott, its controversial subject matter earned the movie huge ratings on American TV as well as an Emmy nomination. The film stars Melinda Dillon as the girl's mother, Richard Masur as the pornographer and Dana Hill as the unfortunate youngster. ▭

Melinda Dillon *Sherry Phillips* • Richard Masur *Howard Nichols* • Dana Hill *Jennifer Phillips* • Ronny Cox *Frank Dawson* • David Hayward *Dennis* ■ *Dir* Robert Michael Lewis [Robert Lewis] • *Scr* Lew Hunter

Fallen Angels ★★★★ 15

Comedy drama 1995 · HK · Colour · 96mins

Asian film-maker Wong Kar-Wai always offers skewed and original views of a seemingly familiar world, accompanied by weirdly inappropriate pop music. Following on from *Chung King Express*, the director takes his peripatetic camera on a vivid trip through the neon-soaked nightlife of Hong Kong as hitman Leon Lai comes into contact with three other frustrated lost souls. The multi-layered, overlapping story blends riveting philosophical musings on missed opportunities, the impermanence of memory and the inevitability of loneliness, brilliantly serving it all up in a *Pulp Fiction*-style wrapper. *Fallen Angels* may be an acquired taste, but it's always sneakily enigmatic, stylish and compelling. In Cantonese with English subtitles.

Li Ming [Leon Lai] *Wong Chi-Ming* • Jin Chengwu [Takashi Kaneshiro] *He Zhiwu* • Yang Caili [Charlie Young] *Cherry* • Li Jiaxin [Michelle Reis] *Agent* • Mo Wenwei [Karen Mok] *Blondie* ■ *Dir* Wang Jiawei [Wong Kar-Wai] • *Scr* Jiawei Wang [Wong Kar-Wai]

The Fallen Idol ★★★★
Thriller 1948 · UK · BW · 94mins

While working as a film critic in the thirties, Graham Greene had first noticed Carol Reed's developing directorial talent. Adapted from Greene's short story *The Basement Room*, this was the first of their three collaborations as writer and director, and what a minor masterpiece it is. Bobby Henrey gives an exceptional performance as the ambassador's son whose attempts to help the butler he idolises only land the latter in hot water with the police after the suspicious death of the butler's wife. Credit is also due to Ralph Richardson and Michèle Morgan for allowing the boy to steal every scene in the interest of suspense.

Ralph Richardson *Baines* • Michèle Morgan *Julie* • Bobby Henrey *Felipe* • Sonia Dresdel *Mrs Baines* • Denis O'Dea *Inspector Crowe* • Walter Fitzgerald *Dr Fenton* • Dandy Nichols *Mrs Patterson* • Bernard Lee *Detective Hart* • Jack Hawkins *Detective Lake* ■ *Dir* Carol Reed • *Scr* Graham Greene, Lesley Storm, William Templeton, from the short story *The Basement Room* by Graham Greene

The Fallen Sparrow ★★★ PG
Spy drama 1943 · US · BW · 93mins

Based on Dorothy B Hughes's bestseller, there's a strong feeling here of a left-leaning plot that's been knobbled by the studio. Tough guy John Garfield returns from the hell of an internment camp in the Spanish Civil War only to find he's being chased by Nazi agents in the US. Strong femme Maureen O'Hara is on hand to help, but this *noir*-ish material needs a tighter hand on the tiller than studio hack Richard Wallace, no matter how sympathetic he may be to the material. Broadway's *Kiss Me Kate* star-to-be Patricia Morison is the other woman, and "heavy" would be too kind a description for Walter Slezak's Dr Skaas. The Roy Webb music score was Oscar-nominated.

John Garfield *Kit* • Maureen O'Hara *Toni Donne* • Walter Slezak *Dr Skaas* • Patricia Morison *Barby Taviton* • Martha O'Driscoll *Whitney Hamilton* • Bruce Edwards *Ab Parker* ■ *Dir* Richard Wallace • *Scr* Warren Duff, from the novel by Dorothy B Hughes

Falling Down ★★★★★ 18
Action thriller 1992 · US/Fr · Colour · 107mins

Made from a script rejected by every major Hollywood studio, this is a storming portrait of inner-city life in America. That stateside critics were virtually unanimous in condemning it as a dangerous and irresponsible fantasy says more about the insecurities of the world's sole remaining superpower than it does about the merits of Joel Schumacher's bold, believable and darkly funny film. As the headlines never cease to remind us, the idea that an ordinary Joe can snap and go on a shooting spree is depressingly feasible, as Michael Douglas's superb performance makes plain. This is courageous, mature film-making that simply has to be seen. Contains swearing and violence. ■ *DVD*

Michael Douglas *D-Fens, William Foster* • Robert Duvall *Prendergast* • Barbara Hershey

Beth • Rachel Ticotin *Sandra* • Tuesday Weld *Mrs Prendergast* • Frederic Forrest *Surplus store owner* • Lois Smith *D-Fens's Mother* • Joey Hope Singer *Adele* ■ *Dir* Joel Schumacher • *Scr* Ebbe Roe Smith

Falling for You ★★ 15
Mystery thriller 1995 · US · Colour · 92mins

Beverly Hills 90210 alumnus Jenny Garth gets another chance to dump her empty-headed blonde image in this able, if unsurprising, made-for-TV thriller. She plays a woman who miraculously survives being thrown out of window by a serial killer but suffers partial amnesia, meaning she is unable to identify her attacker. It's good to see Billy Dee Williams back on screen, but Garth is only marginally convincing in the lead and the direction from Eric Till is thoroughly routine. Contains violence and swearing. ▭

Jennie Garth *Meg Crane* • Currie Graham *Detective Tim Colton* • Costas Mandylor *Paul Blankenship/Eric* • Billy Dee Williams *Lieutenant Frank Lazaro* ■ *Dir* Eric Till • *Scr* Tim Kring, Paul Eric Myers, from the play *Last Tag* by Mitch Giannunzio

Falling from Grace ★★ 15
Drama 1992 · US · Colour · 96mins

Rock star John Mellencamp made his directorial debut with this tale of a country singer who discovers he has few fans in his home town. Larry McMurtry wrote the screenplay, but this is closer to *Texasville* than it is to *The Last Picture Show*, with such clichéd characters as a brutal father, an envious brother and an embittered old flame moping around this dead-end part of Indiana. The storyline is unlikely in the extreme, but as a portrait of the Midwest in decline and the delusions that attend celebrity, it's astute and accomplished. Mellencamp's acting is adequate, but Kay Lenz is excellent as his mouthy ex.

John Mellencamp *Bud Parks* • Mariel Hemingway *Alice Parks* • Claude Akins *Speck Parks* • Dub Taylor *Grandpa Parks* • Kay Lenz *PJ Parks* • Larry Crane *Ramey Parks* • Kate Noonan *Linda* ■ *Dir* John Mellencamp • *Scr* Larry McMurtry

Falling in Love ★★★ PG
Romantic drama 1984 · US · Colour · 101mins

Robert De Niro and Meryl Streep are such dramatic heavyweights it's difficult to see them as ordinary people involved in a typical affair. Yet this light romance – a cooler version of *Brief Encounter* – succeeds thanks to their subtle performances, which brilliantly adjust to the artificial pace of a dangerous liaison as architect Frank and graphic artist Molly, separately married Manhattan commuters, make daily contact that becomes mutual obsession. Ulu Grosbard's rather stilted direction is a hindrance, but De Niro and Streep, reunited for the first and only time to date after the award-winning success of *The Deer Hunter*, more than compensate. ▭

Meryl Streep *Molly Gilmore* • Robert De Niro *Frank Raftis* • Harvey Keitel *Ed Lasky* • Jane Kaczmarek *Ann Raftis* • George Martin *John Trainer* • David Clennon *Brian Gilmore* • Dianne Wiest *Isabelle* ■ *Dir* Ulu Grosbard • *Scr* Michael Christofer

Falling in Love Again ★★★ 15
Romantic comedy 1980 · US · Colour · 98mins

Elliott Gould is perfectly cast as the New Yorker in mid-life crisis, remembering the girl he loved and won when they were both much younger. Unfortunately, his wife (Susannah York) couldn't make a success of their married life. For all its spot-on observations, this comedy drama is introspective and narcissistic. Some of the dialogue was written by York herself; her younger self is played by Michelle Pfeiffer with an inner glow that suggested stardom was ahead. ▭

Elliott Gould *Harry Lewis* • Susannah York *Sue Lewis* • Michelle Pfeiffer *Sue Wellington* • Kaye Ballard *Mrs Lewis* • Stuart Paul *Pompadour/Young Harry* • Robert Hackman *Mr Lewis* • Steven Paul *Stan the Con* • Todd Helper *Alan Childs* ■ *Dir* Steven Paul • *Scr* Steven Paul, Ted Allan, Susannah York, from a story by Hank Paul, Steven Paul

False Identity ★★ 15
Thriller 1990 · US · Colour · 94mins

James Keach directs his brother Stacy (still best known from TV's *Mike Hammer*) in this suspense thriller about a man who returns home after nearly 20 years in prison, unable to remember much of his past. Keach is terrific as the disturbed ex-con and is given impressive support from Geneviève Bujold (*Coma*) and Veronica Cartwright (*Alien*), but this is eventually spoiled by a badly fitting finale. Shame, because otherwise this is a well-played and interesting drama. ▭

Stacy Keach *Harlan Errickson/Ben Driscoll* • Geneviève Bujold *Rachel Roux* • Tobin Bell *Marshall Errickson* • Veronica Cartwright *Vera Errickson* • Mimi Maynard *Audrey* • Mike Champion [Michael Champion] *Luther* ■ *Dir* James Keach • *Scr* Sandra K Bailey

False Paradise ★★ U
Western 1948 · US · BW · 59mins

One of the last of the Hopalong Cassidy series, this standard western potboiler has William Boyd (who by this time was his own producer and about to transfer to TV) outshooting the usual villains and coming out with the heroine on his arm. Andy Clyde is in attendance in his usual sidekick role as California Carlson; so is regular director George Archainbaud, who was also one of Gene Autry's preferred megaphone men.

William Boyd *Hopalong Cassidy* • Andy Clyde *California Carlson* • Rand Brooks *Lucky Jenkins* ■ *Dir* George Archainbaud • *Scr* Doris Schroeder, Harrison Jacobs

False Pretense ★★
Police thriller 1997 · Can · Colour · 93mins

Straight-to-video star Eric Roberts breezes through this dull, seen-it-all-before thriller, that also features his real-life wife (and frequent co-star) Eliza. In a typically mannered performance, he plays a detective who finds himself one of the suspects when his ex-wife takes a tumble from a tall building. As well as trying to clear his name, he also has to patch up his relationship with son Jacob Tierney.

Made for cable, it's low on suspense and ultimately one for Roberts's diehard fans only. Contains violence, swearing, substance abuse and nudity.

Eric Roberts *Henry Smovinsky* • Jacob Tierney *Adam Compton* • Eliza Roberts *Maggie Furness* • Frank Schorpion *Dennis* • Lynne Adams *Sally* ■ *Dir* Doug Jackson [Douglas Jackson] • *Scr* Karl Schiffman

False Witness ★★ 18
Crime drama 1989 · US · Colour · 94mins

The brutal attack on a swinging talk-show host, who practises the free love by night that she preaches by day, horrifies New Orleans. But assistant district attorney Lynne Jacobi (played by *The Cosby Show's* Phylicia Rashad) and her colleague and lover Bobby Jones (Philip Michael Thomas in the year *Miami Vice* ended) are soon on the trail of the culprit. However, the closer they get to the attacker, the further they grow apart from one another. While the material sounds daring, the pace is humdrum and the execution dull. Contains violence. ▭

Phylicia Rashad *Lynne Jacobi* • Philip Michael Thomas *Bobby Jones* • Teri Austin *Sandra Lee Dawson* • George Grizzard *Lynne's Boss* • Robin Mattson ■ *Dir* Arthur Allan Seidelman • *Scr* Bill Driskill, from a book by Dorothy Uhnak

Falsely Accused ★★★ PG
Drama 1993 · US · Colour · 90mins

Lisa Hartman Black rushes to hospital with her new-born baby gasping for breath, but the efforts of medical staff are tragically to little effect and the child dies. The doctor's diagnosis is that the baby had been poisoned with the chemicals found in anti-freeze, and Hartman Black is imprisoned pending her trial for murder. Then the plot really gets into gear – Hartman Black discovers she's pregnant, and the new arrival is put into a foster home, but despite that also becomes ill with symptoms of anti-freeze poisoning. A gut-churner, as contrived as they come yet irritatingly addictive, with Cloris Leachman in a supporting role. Contains swearing. ▭

Lisa Hartman Black *Laurie Samuels* • Christopher Meloni *Ray Samuels* • Cloris Leachman *Mrs Samuels* • David Ogden Stiers *Gerald Orr* • Gwynyth Walsh *Jenine* • James Staley *Myron Ogelsby* ■ *Dir* Noel Nosseck • *Scr* James Duff

Fame ★★★ 15
Musical drama 1980 · US · Colour · 128mins

A timely reminder of what *Evita* director Alan Parker can do with a song-and-dance routine. It might not be as much fun as *Bugsy Malone* and the songs aren't a patch on those in *The Commitments*, but this is a thoroughly entertaining look at life in New York's High School for the Performing Arts (and, more to the point, it's miles better than the TV series that followed). Interestingly enough, none of the cast in a film all about making it big has gone on to become a movie star. Contains swearing, drug abuse and nudity. ▭

Eddie Barth *Angelo* • Irene Cara *Coco Hernandez* • Lee Curreri *Bruno Martelli* • Laura Dean *Lisa Monroe* • Antonia Franceschi *Hilary Van Doren* • Boyd Gaines *Michael* • Albert Hague *Shorofsky* • Tresa Hughes

U = SUITABLE FOR ALL   Uc = SUITABLE FOR ALL, ESPECIALLY FOR YOUNG CHILDREN (VIDEO ONLY)   PG = PARENTAL GUIDANCE

Naomi Finsecker • Gene Anthony Ray *Leroy Johnson* • Debbie Allen *Lydia* ■ *Dir* Alan Parker • *Scr* Christopher Gore

Fame Is the Spur ★★★

Drama 1947 · UK · BW · 115mins

Labour's first prime minister, Ramsay MacDonald, was supposedly the inspiration for Howard Spring's bestseller, which is the source for director Roy Boulting's political drama. Yet Nigel Balchin's screenplay owes more to melodramatic contrivance than to historical fact, as Michael Redgrave rises from the north country slums to high office by waving his grandfather's trusty sword during his rabble-rousing speeches, and exploiting friends and foes alike. It's a powerhouse performance, with his gradual shedding of heartfelt beliefs as vanity replaces commitment having a chillingly convincing ring. But such is Redgrave's dominance that there's little room for other characters to develop or for any cogent social agenda.

Michael Redgrave *Hamer Radshaw* • Rosamund John *Ann Radshaw* • Bernard Miles *Tom Hanaway* • Hugh Burden *Arnold Ryerson* • Jean Shepherd *Mrs Radshaw* • Guy Verney *Grandpa* ■ *Dir* Roy Boulting • *Scr* Nigel Balchin, from a book by Howard Spring

The Family ★★★★

Drama 1987 · It/Fr · Colour · 130mins

Faint stirrings of David Lean's *This Happy Breed* ring round this intimate chronicle of 20th-century Italy. Without once leaving the symbolically decorated apartment of an upper-middle-class Roman family, this increasingly static conversation piece explores 80 years of national and domestic trauma through the eyes of one man and his quarrelsome kinsmen. Leading an ensemble cast of uniform excellence, Vittorio Gassman laments his decision to marry Stefania Sandrelli instead of her sister, Fanny Ardant, while director Ettore Scola shifts effortlessly between melodrama and comedy, as he combines personal memories and common experiences to pass insightful comments on the national character. In Italian with English subtitles.

Vittorio Gassman *Carlo/Carlo's grandfather* • Fanny Ardant *Adriana* • Stefania Sandrelli *Beatrice* • Andrea Occhipinti *Carlo, as a young man* • Jo Champa *Adriana, as a young woman* ■ *Dir* Ettore Scola • *Scr* Ruggero Maccari, Furio Scarpelli, Ettore Scola

A Family Affair ★★

Comedy 1937 · US · BW · 68mins

Worthy of a modest footnote in cinema history as being the first in the long-running Andy Hardy series – 15 films in all. Mickey Rooney plays the small-town American teen whose father is the local judge – the role played here by Lionel Barrymore, later inherited by Lewis Stone. Rooney falls for a girl, while his dad has work-related problems. As per the series which followed, it's a hymn to all things American, land of the free and, it seems, of the cute and precocious.

Lionel Barrymore *Judge Hardy* • Mickey Rooney *Andy Hardy* • Cecilia Parker *Marian Hardy* • Eric Linden *Wayne Trenton* • Charley Grapewin *Frank Redmond* • Spring Byington

Mrs Hardy • Julie Haydon *Joan Hardy* ■ *Dir* George B Seitz • *Scr* Kay Van Riper, from the play *Skidding* by Aurania Rouverol

Family Album ★★

Romantic comedy 1994 · Sp · Colour · 92mins

Having previously directed several shorts, Marta Balletbò-Coll made her feature debut with this lesbian love story, which took a mere 14 days to shoot. She also stars as the Barcelona tour guide who uses all her powers of persuasion to prevent bisexual seismologist, Desi del Valle, from terminating their hesitant romance and taking a job abroad. As with so many low-budget projects, it's a highly talkative affair, with Balletbò-Coll declaiming at length about past lovers and the video monologue she's preparing for a San Francisco theatre troupe. Eager and amiable, but short on substance and style.

Desi del Valle *Montserrat Ehrzman-Rosas* • Marta Balletbò-Coll *Anna Giralt-Romaguera* • Montserrat Gausachs *Marta L Puig* • Emili Remolins Casas *Man at the computer* • Josep Maria Brugues *Jordi* ■ *Dir* Marta Balletbò-Coll • *Scr* Marta Balletbò-Coll, Ana Simon Cerezo

Family Business ★★★ 15

Comedy drama 1989 · US · Colour · 108mins

The line-up is mouthwatering (Sean Connery, Dustin Hoffman and Matthew Broderick, plus director Sidney Lumet), but the result is something of a disappointment. Connery is the irascible, old-school thief and Hoffman his bitter son who is now desperately trying to go straight. However, he is reluctantly drawn back into a life of crime when he learns that his own son (Broderick) is about to go to work with grandpa in the family business. The scenes between the three leads are superb, but the trio is poorly served by an ill-focused script and surprisingly sluggish direction from the usually reliable Lumet. Contains swearing and violence. ▭

Sean Connery *Jessie McMullen* • Dustin Hoffman *Vito McMullen* • Matthew Broderick *Adam McMullen* • Rosana Desoto *Elaine McMullen* • Janet Carroll *Margie* • Victoria Jackson *Christine* • Bill McCutcheon *Doheny* • Deborah Rush *Michele Dempsey* ■ *Dir* Sidney Lumet • *Scr* Vincent Patrick, from his book

A Family Divided ★★

Drama 1995 · US · Colour · 96mins

Based on Judith Henry Wall's novel *Mother Love*, this is melodrama with a capital M. However, no film with Faye Dunaway in the cast can be dismissed out of hand, and she comes up with a performance of Joan Crawford-like suffering as the mother who not only learns that her son has been involved in a vicious gang rape, but also that her husband intends to cover the boy's tracks. Stephen Collins and Cameron Bancroft put their backs into it, but Dunaway dominates every scene, turning a mediocre movie into something worth looking at.

Faye Dunaway *Karen Billingsly* • Cameron Bancroft *Chad Billingsly* • Stephen Collins *Roger Billingsly* • Judson Mills ■ *Dir* Donald Wrye • *Scr* Philip Rosenberg, from a novel by Judith Henry Wall

Family Flight ★★

Adventure drama 1972 · US · Colour · 73mins

Director Marvin J Chomsky, better known for his action films, made this TV movie about a feuding family who agree to bury their differences after their flight to Mexico crashes into the inhospitable wilderness of Baja, California. Perhaps it might have been more exciting if the family's fate had at any time been in doubt. But with parents Rod Taylor and Dina Merrill setting a good example to children Kristoffer Tabori and Janet Margolin, it's clear that the hostility between them is only temporary, and so the sentimental manner of their reconciliation is more tiresome than heart-warming.

Rod Taylor *Jason Carlyle* • Dina Merrill *Florence Carlyle* • Kristoffer Tabori *David Carlyle* • Janet Margolin *Carol Rutledge* • Gene Nelson *Aircraft Carrier Captain* • Richard Roat *Officer of the Deck* ■ *Dir* Marvin J Chomsky • *Scr* Guerdon S Trueblood

The Family Jewels ★ U

Comedy 1965 · US · Colour · 99mins

After the split with comedy partner Dean Martin, the unique talents of Jerry Lewis made him one of those performers you just couldn't ignore. The French, in particular, seem to find him irresistible. But the man who influenced Jim Carrey and Adam Sandler began at one point to overreach himself and this movie is a sorry reminder of that period. Here, Lewis plays seven roles as potential guardians of precocious little Donna Butterworth, heiress to a fortune. He also directed this clumsy, mawkish and unfunny load of old tripe. Better to remember the sheer inventive comic genius of *The Nutty Professor* or *The Ladies' Man* instead.

Jerry Lewis *Willard Woodward/Everett Peyton/ James Peyton/Eddie Peyton/Julius Peyton/ "Bugs" Peyton/Skylock Peyton* • Sebastian Cabot *Dr Matson* • Donna Butterworth *Donna Peyton* • Jay Adler *Attorney* ■ *Dir* Jerry Lewis • *Scr* Jerry Lewis, Bill Richmond

Family Life ★★★

Drama 1971 · UK · Colour · 107mins

Adapted by David Mercer from his TV play *In Two Minds*, this is a harrowing study of mental illness and the methods of treating it. Making only his third feature, director Ken Loach was already employing the uncompromisingly realistic style that has since become his trademark and some of the scenes in which teenager Sandy Ratcliff is subjected to electroconvulsive therapy are among the most traumatic of his career. Rarely has family life been presented in such a gloomy light, and Bill Dean and Grace Cave deserve much credit for depicting such thoroughly detestable parents. Over-manipulative, maybe, but still deeply disturbing. Contains violence and swearing.

Sandy Ratcliff *Janice Baildon* • Bill Dean *Mr Baildon* • Grace Cave *Mrs Baildon* • Malcolm Tierney *Tim* • Hilary Martyn *Barbara Baildon* • Michael Riddall *Dr Donaldson* • Alan MacNaughtan *Mr Carswell* • Johnny Gee *Man in garden* ■ *Dir* Ken Loach • *Scr* David Mercer, from his play *In Two Minds*

Family of Cops ★★ 15

Crime drama 1995 · Can · Colour · 86mins

The title has huge comic possibilities: imagine arguments over who does the washing up ending in shoot-outs and multiple arrests. Sadly, this is a straight-faced, rather dreary thriller about a family of cops who get mixed up in skulduggery and murder. Charles Bronson (on stone-faced auto-pilot) is the patriarch who rallies the family when his youngest daughter (Angela Featherstone) is charged with the murder of a wealthy businessman. Despite a stellar supporting cast (Lesley-Anne Down, Daniel Baldwin, Simon MacCorkindale), it's an uninspired affair and the direction from the usually reliable Ted Kotcheff (*First Blood*) is pedestrian. Contains violence. ▭

Charles Bronson *Police Commander Paul Fein* • Angela Featherstone *Jackie* • Simon MacCorkindale *Adam Novacek* • Daniel Baldwin *Ben* • Sebastian Spence *Eddie* • Lesley-Anne Down *Anna Novacek* ■ *Dir* Ted Kotcheff • *Scr* Joel Blasberg

A Family of Strangers ★★ PG

Drama based on a true story 1993 · US/Can · Colour · 89mins

Star Trek's William Shatner goes terrestrial in one of those TV movies in which passions are as entangled as the plotlines. In this case, a young woman finds out she's adopted and must trace her natural parents because, on the basis of her family's medical history, she may need a life-saving operation. Shrewdly grabbing its audience's attention by matching matters medical and emotional, it stars Melissa Gilbert and Patty Duke. Shatner is the token male, but keep an eye out for *NYPD Blue*'s Gordon Clapp. Contains swearing and some violence.

Melissa Gilbert *Julie* • Patty Duke *Beth* • William Shatner *Earl* • Martha Gibson *Sue* • Gordon Clapp *Del* • Chuck Shamata *Tim* ■ *Dir* Larry Sheldon • *Scr* Anna Sandor, from the book *Jody* by Jerry Hulse

Family Plan ★ PG

Comedy 1997 · US · Colour · 92mins

Leslie Nielsen has persisted with the spoofery that relaunched his career, with patchy results. With this turkey, however, he hits a new low. After the death of an old friend, the bungling Nielson finds himself in charge of a crumbling summer camp for orphans; Judge Reinhold is the slimy businessman out to convert the property into a holiday resort. Tiny youngsters will probably get a giggle out of the gormless slapstick, but most grown-ups will be secretly praying that Jason from *Friday the 13th* shows up. Sadly, he never arrives. Contains mild swearing.

Leslie Nielsen *Harry Haber* • Judge Reinhold *Jeffrey Shayes* • Eddie Bowz *Matt Nolan* • Emily Procter *Julie Rubins* ■ *Dir* Fred Gerber • *Scr* Paul Bernbaum

Family Plot ★★★★ PG

Thriller 1976 · US · Colour · 115mins

Fifty years after he made what he regarded as his directorial debut, Alfred Hitchcock signed off with this gently twisting thriller in the mould of such playful pictures as *The Lady Vanishes* and *North by Northwest*. Hitchcock coaxes along a deliciously contrived plot that sets kidnappers William Devane and Karen Black on a collision course with fake medium Barbara Harris and her partner Bruce Dern as they search for a missing heir. The performances are perfect, and it is to Hollywood's shame that it has not made better use of such gifted players since. ▣

Karen Black *Fran* • Bruce Dern *Lumley* • Barbara Harris *Blanche* • William Devane *Adamson* • Ed Lauter *Maloney* • Cathleen Nesbitt *Julia Rainbird* • Katherine Helmond *Mrs Maloney* • Warren J Kemmerling [Warren Kemmerling] *Grandison* ■ *Dir* Alfred Hitchcock • *Scr* Ernest Lehman, from the book *The Rainbird Pattern* by Victor Canning

Family Prayers ★★PG

Drama 1991 · US · Colour · 104mins

Released two years after its completion, producer Scott Rosenfelt's directorial debut brims over with credible detail about growing up Jewish in the late sixties. By contrast, Steve Ginsberg's screenplay solves too many of its problems by recourse to nostalgia and sentimentality. Unknown Tzvi Ratner-Stauber makes a good impression as the sheltered teenager suddenly confronted with both the endless bickering of his promise-breaking, gambling father (Joe Mantegna) and his end-of-tether mother (Anne Archer), and the harsh facts of life that he learns from Paul Reiser, the tutor preparing him for his bar mitzvah.

Joe Mantegna *Martin Jacobs* • Anne Archer *Rita Jacobs* • Paul Reiser *Dan Linder* • Patti LuPone *Aunt Nan* • Tzvi Ratner-Stauber *Andrew Jacobs* • Allen Garfield *Cantor* ■ *Dir* Scott Rosenfelt • *Scr* Steve Ginsberg

Family Rescue ★★★ 15

Drama 1997 · US · Colour · 87mins

George C Scott makes this made-for-TV weepie just a little special. He plays a crusty old miner who is left bringing up baby when his no-good daughter (Ally Sheedy) does a runner. Fifteen years later, the now grown-up Rachel Leigh Cook finds herself caught up in a nasty custody battle between Scott and her errant dad. It's a slushy formulaic tale, but the terrific performances – particularly those from Cook, who more than holds her own against her famous co-stars – ensures it is always watchable. ▣

George C Scott *Clayton Harris* • Rachael Leigh Cook *Emma Baker* • Don Diamont *Ray Wilcox* • Ally Sheedy *Angie Baker* • Trent McDevitt *Gary O'Leary* • Stan Kelly *Gilford Crowell* ■ *Dir* Graeme Campbell • *Scr* Linda Taddeo

Family Reunion ★★★

Drama 1981 · US · Colour · 174mins

Bette Davis showboats shamelessly in this TV movie, in which she co-stars with her own grandson, J Ashley Hyman. Although it gets off to a mawkish start, as teacher Davis is summarily dismissed after 50 years of loyal service, the action begins to pick up after she sets off to visit her family in the company of a neighbour's kid (Hyman). The tension crackles as

Davis re-meets relatives she's clearly not missed for an instant, and it's a shame that screenwriter Allan Sloane felt the need for a contrived New England land subplot when a more defined character study might have been more explosive.

Bette Davis *Elizabeth Winfield* • J Ashley Hyman *Richard Cooper* • David Huddleston *Senator Chester Winfield* • John Shea *James Cookman* • Roy Dotrice *Luther Frye* • David Rounds *Grover Winfield* • Kathryn Walker *Louisa King* ■ *Dir* Fielder Cook • *Scr* Allan Sloane, from the article *How America Lives* in *Ladies Home Journal* by Joe Spartan, from a story by Allan Sloane

The Family Rico ★★

Crime drama 1972 · US · Colour · 73mins

Previously filmed under its original title of *The Brothers Rico*, Georges Simenon's novella gets a satisfactory make-over in this stylish TV movie. Although it suffers slightly from an opening salvo of Method posturing, the action settles down once Ben Gazzara grows into the role of the one-time mobster who is faced with losing his new-found wealth and respectability in order to save his chiselling brothers from the "family". Although less hard-nosed or atmospheric than its predecessor, this is still an involving study of divided loyalty, with strong support from Sal Mineo and Jo Van Fleet as members of Gazzara's family.

Ben Gazzara *Eddie Rico* • Jack Carter *McGee* • Dane Clark *Boston Phil* • Leif Erickson *Mike Lamont* • James Farentino *Gino Rico* • John Marley *Sid Kubik* • Sal Mineo *Nick Rico* • Jo Van Fleet *Mama Rico* ■ *Dir* Paul Wendkos • *Scr* David Karp, from the novel *The Brothers Rico* by Georges Simenon

Family Sins ★★ 15

Drama 1987 · US · Colour · 93mins

Nearly 15 years after he made *Bloodsport*, director Jerrold Freedman returns to the theme of a sports mad father grooming his son for stardom in this overheated TV movie. This time, however, there's a second son who can't tell the difference between a football and an ice-hockey puck and it's this relationship that holds centre stage. James Farentino gets to rant a good deal as the disgusted father, while Jill Eikenberry (*LA Law*) tries to referee as his wife. If a continuous stream of verbose confrontations is your idea of good drama, then you're in for a ball. ▣

James Farentino *Gordon Williams* • Jill Eikenberry *Kate Williams* • Andrew Bednarski *Keith* • Mimi Kuzyk *Sara Burke* • Brent Spiner *Mcmahon* • Michael Durrell *Hamilton* ■ *Dir* Jerrold Freedman • *Scr* George Rubino

A Family Thing ★★ 15

Comedy drama 1996 · US · Colour · 104mins

A charming if somewhat flimsy vehicle for two of Hollywood's finest actors, Robert Duvall and James Earl Jones, both relishing a rare chance to take centre stage. Duvall's a good ole boy from Clinton territory (Arkansas) who is astonished to discover on his mother's death that his real mum was a black servant. He then reluctantly sets out to meet his half-brother, city cop Jones. The accomplished sparring of the two grumpy old men overcomes the deficiencies in plot and an odd strain

of sentimentality in a script co-written by Billy Bob Thornton, best known for his Oscar-winning *Sling Blade*, from the same year. Contains swearing and brief violence. ▣

Robert Duvall *Earl Pilcher, Jr* • James Earl Jones *Roy Murdoch* • Michael Beach *Virgil* • Irma P Hall *Aunt T* • Grace Zabriskie *Ruby* • Regina Taylor *Ann* • Mary Jackson *Carrie* ■ *Dir* Richard Pearce • *Scr* Tom Epperson, Billy Bob Thornton

Family Viewing ★★★★ 18

Satirical drama 1987 · Can · Colour · 86mins

Two years before the much-vaunted *sex, lies, and videotape*, Atom Egoyan made inspired use of camcorder footage in this remarkable satire on dysfunctional nuclear family life. Delving into the darkest corners of society, Egoyan emerges with a story about a quiet teenager Van (Aidan Tierney) who finds refuge with his institutionalised grandmother away from the sexual obsessions of his seemingly respectable father and stepmother. Exploring themes that recur in all his films, this is a sly, sharp and often touching picture.

David Hemblen *Stan* • Aidan Tierney *Van* • Gabrielle Rose *Sandra* • Arsinée Khanjian *Aline* • Selma Keklikian *Armen* • Jeanne Sabourin *Aline's Mother* • Rose Sarkisyan *Van's Mother* ■ *Dir/Scr* Atom Egoyan

The Family Way ★★★★ 15

Comedy drama 1966 · UK · Colour · 110mins

Considered somewhat risqué in its day, this gentle comedy can now be seen as a fond portrait of an era when sex was still taboo. Complete with a score by Paul McCartney, it recounts the experience of so many sixties' newlyweds who had to share a house with their in-laws for much of the early part of their married lives. Hywel Bennett is bang on form as the husband so wound up by cohabitation that he is unable to consummate his marriage to the equally impressive Hayley Mills. But it's her real-life dad, John Mills, who steals the show with a splendid study in working-class cantankerousness.

Hayley Mills *Jenny Piper* • Hywel Bennett *Arthur Fitton* • John Mills *Ezra Fitton* • Marjorie Rhodes *Lucy Fitton* • Avril Angers *Liz Piper* • John Comer *Leslie Piper* • Wilfred Pickles *Uncle Fred* • Barry Foster *Joe Thompson* ■ *Dir* Roy Boulting • *Scr* Bill Naughton, Roy Boulting, Jeffrey Dell, from the play *All in Good Time* by Bill Naughton • *Music* Paul McCartney

The Famous Sword ★★★

Drama 1945 · Jap · BW · 66mins

Keen to keep working, but reluctant to shoot the kind of propaganda demanded by the government, Kenji Mizoguchi spent the Second World War making historical dramas. This was his last solo wartime project and scrupulously avoids any overtly political message. Instead, it serves up a tale of daughterly determination and loyal devotion, in which apprentice swordmaker Shotaro Hanayagi seeks the assistance of master craftsman Eijiro Yanagi in making the weapon that will enable Isuzu Yamada to avenge her murdered father. While nowhere near as impressive as his

work either side of the war, this is anything but anodyne entertainment. In Japanese with English subtitles.

Shotaro Hanayagi *Kiyone Sakurai* • Isuzu Yamada *Sasae Onoda* • Ichijiro Oya *Kozaemon Onoda* • Eijiro Yanagi *Kiyohide Yamatonokami* • Kan Ishii *Kiyotsugu* ■ *Dir* Kenji Mizoguchi • *Scr* Matsutaro Kawaguchi, from a story by Masamune Yotsuya • *Cinematographer* Shigeto Miki [Minoru Miki], Haruo Takeno

The Fan ★★

Drama 1949 · US · BW · 79mins

This is director Otto Preminger's rather dull, abridged version of one of the wittiest plays ever written, Oscar Wilde's *Lady Windermere's Fan*. Unfortunately you'd only guess it from the names of the characters, for all wit has vanished in the heavy-handed directorial style. Preminger, who took over from Ernst Lubitsch on *That Lady in Ermine*, lacked the latter's lightness of touch (Lubitsch had directed the 1925 silent version of Wilde's play). Although the screenplay was co-authored by famed wit Dorothy Parker, this is an updated and desecrated version of the plot. Jeanne Crain and Richard Greene are particularly colourless Windermeres, George Sanders is a dull Lord Darlington, and, in her last movie, the lovely Madeleine Carroll a wan Mrs Erlynne.

Jeanne Crain *Lady Windermere* • Madeleine Carroll *Mrs Erlynne* • George Sanders *Lord Darlington* • Richard Greene *Lord Windermere* • Martita Hunt *Duchess of Berwick* ■ *Dir* Otto Preminger • *Scr* Walter Reisch, Dorothy Parker, Ross Evans, from the play *Lady Windermere's Fan* by Oscar Wilde

The Fan ★★★ 18

Thriller 1981 · US · Colour · 90mins

Fans of charismatic old-timers will enjoy this thriller about a glamorous stage star (Lauren Bacall) pursued by a psychotic stalker (Michael Biehn). The excellent James Garner appears as Bacall's ex-husband, and Maureen Stapleton plays her secretary. But it's Bacall's picture, and she has no problems convincing us she's a star. (Edward Bianchi's movie was released just as his leading lady was enjoying a huge hit on Broadway with *Woman of the Year*.) ▣

Lauren Bacall *Sally Ross* • James Garner *Jake Berman* • Maureen Stapleton *Belle Goldman* • Hector Elizondo *Ralph Andrews* • Michael Biehn *Douglas Breen* • Anna Maria Horsford *Emily Stolz* • Kurt Johnson *David Branum* ■ *Dir* Edward Bianchi • *Scr* Priscilla Chapman, John Hartwell, from the novel by Bob Randall

The Fan ★★ 15

Thriller 1996 · US · Colour · 111mins

Look who's stalking! Robert De Niro is the psycho fan from hell and the object of his obsession is baseball star Wesley Snipes. It's when the San Francisco Giant team member hits a losing streak that the pitiful loser moves into action with fatal consequences. Despite being directed by Tony Scott with his trademark flash and dash, his sometimes over-vigorous use of mannered camera angles does nothing for this implausible plot that's short of both suspense and surprise. Scott's ace card is De Niro putting on his *Taxi Driver* act to good effect once

U = SUITABLE FOR ALL   **Uc** = SUITABLE FOR ALL, ESPECIALLY FOR YOUNG CHILDREN (VIDEO ONLY)   **PG** = PARENTAL GUIDANCE

more. Although the edgy persona is familiar, it's all this vulgar exploitation essay has to offer. 🖵 **DVD**

Robert De Niro *Gil Renard* • Wesley Snipes *Bobby Rayburn* • Ellen Barkin *Jewel Stern* • John Leguizamo *Manny* • Benicio Del Toro *Juan Primo* • Patti D'Arbanville-Quinn *Ellen Renard* ■ *Dir* Tony Scott • *Scr* Phoef Sutton, from the story by Peter Abrahams

Fanci's Persuasion ★★★

Surreal comedy fantasy
1994 · US · Colour · 80mins

Something of a hit on the gay and lesbian festival circuit, Charles Herman-Wurmfeld's directorial debut is a modern fairy tale that sets out to prove that "love is a many-gendered thing". As Fanci prepares for her marriage to her girlfriend, the whole of San Francisco falls under a magical spell that forces people to reveal their true sexual identity and forsake their stubborn prejudices. In keeping with such lesbian films as *I've Heard the Mermaids Singing* and *Go Fish*, the tone is decidedly romantic, although the fantasy elements make it more of a companion piece to the excellent gay comedy *Jeffrey*.

Jessica Patton *Fanci* • Justin Bond *Irene Wiesenthal* • Robert Coffman *Irving Wiesenthal* • Boa *Loretta* • Alyssa Wendt ■ *Dir* Charles Herman-Wurmfeld • *Scr* Charles Herman-Wurmfeld, Caroline Juliet Libresco

Fancy Pants ★★★ U

Musical comedy 1950 · US · Colour · 92mins

A riotous teaming of Bob Hope and Lucille Ball in yet another reworking of *Ruggles of Red Gap*. This finds Hope out West again, after his success as *The Paleface*. There's even a song hit, though *Home Cookin'* is no *Buttons and Bows*. Hope makes not the slightest attempt to "buttle" in the English manner, but Ball is excellent as rootin' tootin' tomboy heiress, Agatha Floud. Director George Marshall (*Destry Rides Again*) simply indulges them. Bob and Lucy would team up twice more, in the more serious comedies *The Facts of Life* and *Critic's Choice*.

Bob Hope *Humphrey* • Lucille Ball *Agatha Floud* • Bruce Cabot *Cart Belknap* • Jack Kirkwood *Mike Floud* • Lea Penman *Effie Floud* • Hugh French *George Van-Basingwell* ■ *Dir* George Marshall • *Scr* Edmund Hartman, Robert O'Brien, from the story *Ruggles of Red Gap* by Harry Leon Wilson

Fandango ★★★ 15

Comedy drama 1985 · US · Colour · 86mins

Not only the first film to give an indication of Kevin Costner's star power, but also a crucial point in his career, as the director here, Kevin Reynolds, became a firm friend and went on to make *Robin Hood: Prince of Thieves* and *Waterworld* with him. This gently quirky rites-of-passage comedy drama began life as a student project for Reynolds, and follows five college friends in the early seventies who set off on one last adolescent adventure before entering adulthood. Costner shines as the anarchic unofficial leader of the group, but he is more than matched by Judd Nelson, who turns in a powerful, mature performance. Contains swearing and brief nudity. 🖵

Kevin Costner *Gardner Barnes* • Judd Nelson *Phil Hicks* • Sam Robards *Kenneth Waggener* • Chuck Bush *Dorman* • Brian Cesak *Lester* • Elizabeth Daily *Judy* ■ *Dir* Kevin Reynolds • *Scr* Kevin Reynolds, from his short film

Fanfan la Tulipe ★★★★

Satirical historical romance
1951 · Fr · BW · 94mins

Following *La Chartreuse de Parme* (1948) and *Souvenirs Perdus* (1950), actor Gérard Philipe and director Christian-Jaque bade each other a fond farewell with this glorious spoof on the Hollywood swashbuckler. Beautifully designed, and filmed with a real feel for both the period trappings and the energetic action by cinematographer Christian Matras, the plot is fabulously preposterous, as Philipe confounds bandits and the Austrian army to win the heart of princess Sylvie Pelayo. With a sparkling script, a dashing lead and solid support from the likes of Gina Lollobrigida as Fanfan's mentor, it's no wonder Christian-Jaque won the best director prize at Cannes. In French with English subtitles.

Gérard Philipe *Fanfan La Tulipe* • Gina Lollobrigida *Adeline* • Noël Roquevert *Fier-a-Bras* • Olivier Hussenot *Tranche Montagne* • Marcel Herrand *Louis XV* • Jean-Marc Tennberg *Lebel* • Jean Paredes *Captain De La Houlette* ■ *Dir* Christian-Jaque • *Scr* Christian-Jaque, Rene Wheeler, from a story by Rene Wheeler, Rene Fallet

Fanny ★★★★

Drama 1932 · Fr · BW · 126mins

Coming between *Marius* and *César*, the central segment of writer Marcel Pagnol's Marseilles trilogy is easily the best directed. However, not even Marc Allégret could get much of a performance out of Orane Demazis, Pagnol's wife at the time. The rest of the cast are impeccable, though, with Raimu outstanding as the wily bar owner who persuades seafaring son Pierre Fresnay to abandon all claim to the child who has now found a father in widowed sailmaker, Fernand Charpin. The perfectly observed ambience and subtly shaded characters make this a joy to behold, with little flashes of warm humour illuminating the knotty family drama. In French with English subtitles.

Orane Demazis *Fanny* • Raimu *César* • Fernand Charpin *Panisse* • Pierre Fresnay *Marius* • Alida Rouffe *Honorine* • Robert Vattier *Mr Brun* ■ *Dir* Marc Allégret • *Scr* Marcel Pagnol, from his play, from his books *Marseilles Trilogy*

Fanny ★★

Drama 1961 · US · Colour · 133mins

Stripped of its songs, Joshua Logan's reworking of his own 1954 Broadway production might have the striking Technicolor photography of Jack Cardiff in its corner, but it is utterly devoid of the local colour that made the 1932 adaptation of Marcel Pagnol's *Marseilles* trilogy so enchanting. Charles Boyer is slyly charming as the waterfront bar owner who competes with sailmaker Maurice Chevalier for the affections of waif Leslie Caron, after lover Horst Buchholz leaves her pregnant. Cardiff and Boyer were well worth their Oscar nominations, but it's

harder to see why this tacky melodrama merited a best picture nod.

Leslie Caron *Fanny* • Maurice Chevalier *Panisse* • Charles Boyer *César* • Horst Buchholz *Marius* • Baccaloni [Salvatore Baccaloni] *Escartifique* • Lionel Jeffries *M Brun* • Raymond Bussires *Admiral* • Victor Francen *Louis Panisse* ■ *Dir* Joshua Logan • *Scr* Julius J Epstein, from a play by SN Behrman, Joshua Logan, from the play by Marcel Pagnol, from the books *Marseilles Trilogy* by Marcel Pagnol

Fanny and Alexander
★★★★★ 15

Period drama
1982 · Swe/Fr/W Ger · Colour · 300mins

The warmth, humour and compassion of this wonderful turn-of-the-century family saga make it one of the most accessible movies ever made by Sweden's greatest director, Ingmar Bergman. The story, which covers two years in the life of a well-to-do household as seen through the eyes of a small boy, is rendered all the more fascinating by the autobiographical elements that Bergman has included and by Sven Nykvist's Oscar-winning photography. The film takes us on a magical mystery tour of the child's encounters with his oppressive, puritanical father, his God-fearing mother and his loving family in an atmosphere that is both cosy and scary. The result is an unmissable experience from a master film-maker. In Swedish with English subtitles. 🖵

Pernilla Allwin *Fanny Ekdahl* • Bertil Guve *Alexander Ekdahl* • Gunn Wallgren *Grandmother Helena Ekdahl* • Börje Ahlstedt *Professor Carl Ekdahl* • Christina Schollin *Lydia Ekdahl* • Allan Edwall *Oscar Ekdahl* • Ewa Fröling *Emilie Ekdahl* • Mona Malm *Alma Ekdahl* • Pernilla Wallgren [Pernilla August] *Maj* • Anna Bergman *Hanna Schwarz* • Lena Olin *Rosa* • *Dir/Scr* Ingmar Bergman • *Cinematographer* Sven Nykvist

Fanny & Elvis ★★ 15

Romantic comedy
1999 · UK/Fr · Colour · 107mins

Since making her mark with TV's *Band of Gold*, writer Kay Mellor has shown a decidedly soft centre with her film work. Following the maudlin *Girls' Night*, which she wrote, she makes her directorial debut with this soppy second-chance romance, in which a budding Barbara Cartland finds millennial love with a much-married car dealer. Were it not for the knowing performances of Kerry Fox and Ray Winstone, the stodginess of Mellor's staging and the laziness of her script would be all the more apparent. However, from the screaming match that marks their first encounter to the umpteenth breakdown in communication, they just about keep things bubbling. Contains swearing and sex scenes. 🖵 **DVD**

Kerry Fox *Kate* • Ray Winstone *Dave* • Ben Daniels *Andrew* • David Morrissey *Rob* • Jennifer Saunders *Roanna* • Colin Salmon *Alan* • Gaynor Faye *Samantha* • William Ash *Rick* ■ *Dir/Scr* Kay Mellor

Fanny by Gaslight ★★★ PG

Period drama 1944 · UK · BW · 102mins

A Gainsborough picture that's more luridly Hogarthian than usual, (it was adapted from a controversial Michael

Sadleir novel), and, director Anthony Asquith's film, despite being visually sanitised, doesn't hesitate in drawing attention to the sleazier corners of Victorian society. Phyllis Calvert is the politician's illegitimate daughter about to become bawdyhouse baggage, while James Mason and Stewart Granger swagger in appropriate fashion. It seems innocent now, but it caused quite a fuss in its day. My dear! How low can décolletage get? 🖵

Phyllis Calvert *Fanny* • James Mason *Lord Manderstoke* • Stewart Granger *Harry Somerford* • Wilfrid Lawson *Chunks* • Jean Kent *Lucy* • Margaretta Scott *Alicia* • Nora Swinburne *Mrs Hopwood* • Cathleen Nesbitt *Kate Somerford* ■ *Dir* Anthony Asquith • *Scr* Doreen Montgomery, Aimee Stuart, from a novel by Michael Sadleir

Fanny Hill: Memoirs of a Woman of Pleasure ★

Period erotic melodrama
1964 · US/W Ger · BW · 104mins

Hilariously hyped at the time as a "female *Tom Jones*", this is notorious flesh merchant Russ Meyer's brush with the classics. In this case Meyer characteristically exploits John Cleland's bawdy 18th-century novel about a young woman who finds herself working in a brothel, but his direction lacks any style or discernible talent. By his standards this is fairly innocuous stuff, but while the bare flesh quota is low, the schoolboy smuttiness remains. Veteran actress Miriam Hopkins, who in her prime worked with Ernst Lubitsch and Bette Davis, looks understandably embarrassed to be there. This is amateurish drivel that fails as comedy, titillation or historical fiction.

Miriam Hopkins *Mrs Maude Brown* • Leticia Roman *Fanny Hill* • Walter Giller *Hemingway* • Alex D'Arcy *The Admiral* • Helmut Weiss *Mr Dinklespieler* • Chris Howland *Mr Norbert* • Ulli Lommel *Charles* • Cara Garnett *Phoebe* ■ *Dir* Russ Meyer • *Scr* Robert Hill, from the novel *Fanny Hill; or, Memoirs of a Woman of Pleasure* by John Cleland

Fantasia ★★★★★ U

Animation 1940 · US · Colour · 114mins

A tremendous leap into the light, which won a special Oscar for Walt Disney and conductor Leopold Stokowski, and a mighty innovation in feature-length cartoons as a concert of classical music is made visually articulate – from Bach to Stravinsky to Tchaikovsky. Beethoven's *Pastoral* gets the kitsch treatment with cute mythology, and Mussorgsky's *Night on Bald Mountain* is a *danse macabre* of opened graves and broom-riding witches. Mickey Mouse even appears as Dukas's *Sorcerer's Apprentice*. Most successful are Bach abstractions, while the dying dinosaurs of Stravinsky's *Rite Of Spring* is a massive decimation of reptiles – and affirmation for life. A high-voltage masterpiece which showed what could be achieved with a marriage of the technical (multiplane cameras, stereo sound) and the creative. 🖵

Deems Taylor • Leopold Stokowski conducting the Philadelphia Symphony Orchestra *Leopold Stokowski* ■ *Dir* Samuel Armstrong, James Algar, Bill Roberts, Paul Satterfield, Hamilton Luske, Jim Handley, Ford Beebe, Norman Ferguson, Wilfred Jackson

Fantasia 2000 ★★★ U

Animation   1999 · US · Colour · 75mins

The first release of the 21st century, and the only animated feature to be made in the giant IMAX format, Disney's long-awaited follow-up to the 1940 classic *Fantasia* is something of a disappointment. For while the spectacle is impressive, the artistic content is regrettably lacklustre. An ecological theme informs the visuals for Beethoven's *Fifth Symphony*, Respighi's *Pines of Rome* and Stravinsky's *Firebird Suite*; the same applies to Donald Duck's adventure aboard Noah's ark, enacted to the accompaniment of Elgar's *Pomp and Circumstance*. Shostakovich's *Piano Concerto No 2* provides the inspiration for Hans Christian Andersen's *The Steadfast Tin Soldier*, while Mickey Mouse returns for a underwhelming digital remastering of *The Sorcerer's Apprentice*. The flamingo who yo-yos to Saint-Saëns's *Carnival of the Animals* impresses, as does a bustling New York portmanteau tale, drawn in the style of Al Hirschfeld and set to Gershwin's *Rhapsody in Blue* – though the latter is tainted with glaring political incorrectness. More of a one-off than the future of animation, but worth catching for the experience.

James Levine *James Levine conducting the Chicago Symphony Orchestra* • Steve Martin • James Levine ∎ *Dir* Pixote Hunt, Hendel Butoy, Eric Goldberg, James Algar, Francis Glebas, Paul Brizzi, Gaetan Brizzi, Don Hahn

Fantastic Planet ★★★★ PG

Science-fiction fantasy animation
1973 · Fr/Cz · Colour · 69mins

A remarkable animated French/Czech science-fiction fantasy conceived by Roland Topor and René Laloux, depicting the odd happenings on planet Yagam. There, humans, called Oms, are pets of the giant Draags, and numerous allegorical references are imaginatively drawn as a war breaks out between the two factions. A fascinating fable utilising impressive organic design, surreal composition and stunning visuals, this Cannes award-winner is highly intriguing and compulsive viewing. French dialogue dubbed into English. ▭

Barry Bostwick • Marvin Miller • Olan Soule • Cynthia Alder • Nora Heflin • Hal Smith • Mark Gruner • Monika Ramirez • Janet Waldo ∎ *Dir* René Laloux • *Scr* René Laloux, from the book *Oms en Serie* by Stefan Wul

Fantastic Voyage ★★★★ U

Science-fiction adventure
1966 · US · Colour · 96mins

Shrunken doctors in a mini-sub journeying through the body of a dying Czech scientist to perform interior brain surgery provide the plot for this wonderfully ludicrous sixties classic. An interesting cast includes secret agent Stephen Boyd, Raquel Welch in a tight diving suit and Donald Pleasence in danger from rampaging white corpuscles. Deft execution by director Richard Fleischer and tremendous special effects for the time ensure an imaginative guided tour through the bloodstream to witness the wonders of the heart, lungs and other assorted organs along with the requisite doses of sex, suspense and sabotage. ▭

Stephen Boyd *Grant* • Raquel Welch *Cora Peterson* • Donald Pleasence *Dr Michaels* • Edmond O'Brien *General Carter* • Arthur O'Connell *Colonel Donald Reid* • William Redfield *Captain Bill Owens* • Arthur Kennedy *Dr Duval* • Jean Del Val *Jan Benes* ∎ *Dir* Richard Fleischer • *Scr* Harry Kleiner, David Duncan, from the novel by Otto Klement, Jay Lewis Bixby • *Art Director* Jack Martin Smith, Dale Hennesy • *Cinematographer* Ernest Laszlo

Far and Away ★★ 15

Period romantic drama
1992 · US · Colour · 134mins

Tom Cruise's long-held ambition to discover his Irish ancestry led to this curious, frothy 19th-century period piece, in which he somewhat unbelievably earns his living as a bare knuckle fighter, while his co-star and real-life wife Nicole Kidman flounces around, tossing acres of pre-Raphaelite curls. Directed with predictable gloss and visual panache by Ron Howard, and with a soundtrack featuring the stirring strains of Irish singer Enya, this is a movie that bounces along pleasingly enough on a sea of ripped petticoats, horse whips and rotten teeth, yet has the depth of one of Cruise's mock punches. All is vapid, pretty, stereotypical and rather lame. Contains some violence, swearing and brief nudity. ▭ *DVD*

Tom Cruise *Joseph Donelly* • Nicole Kidman *Shannon Christie* • Thomas Gibson *Stephen* • Robert Prosky *Daniel Christie* • Barbara Babcock *Nora Christie* • Cyril Cusack *Danty Duff* • Colm Meaney *Kelly* • Eileen Pollock *Molly Kay* • Michelle Johnson *Grace* ∎ *Dir* Ron Howard • *Scr* Bob Dolman, from a story by Ron Howard, Bob Dolman

The Far Country ★★★ U

Western   1955 · US · Colour · 96mins

The collaboration between star James Stewart and director Anthony Mann formed one of the highlights of postwar American cinema, and includes such pleasurable masterworks as *The Glenn Miller Story* and *Winchester '73*. This is a beautifully made western, set way up north in snowy gold rush territory. Stewart's character is unusual for a movie hero of this period: he's basically self-absorbed, a ruthless loner, a contrast to the remarkably affable villain, played with relish by John McIntire. This concept of character reversal doesn't quite come off, but director Mann's striking use of landscape and the intense and satisfying fury of the action sequences more than compensate.

James Stewart *Jeff Webster* • Ruth Roman *Ronda Castle* • Corinne Calvet *Renee Vallon* • Walter Brennan *Ben Tatem* • John McIntire *Mr Gannon* • Jay C Flippen *Rube* • Henry Morgan [Harry Morgan] *Ketchum* • Jack Elam *Newberry* ∎ *Dir* Anthony Mann • *Scr* Borden Chase

Far East ★

Action drama   1982 · Ausl · Colour · 107mins

Director John Duigan (*Flirting*, *Sirens*) bit off more than he could chew with this excursion into the thriller genre. Clearly he aimed to explore the nature of post-colonial rule and the iniquities of expatriate opulence within a *Casablanca*-like framework. Unfortunately the romance between Koala Klub boss Bryan Brown and married good-time-gal Helen Morse is so devoid of passion that you never begin to care what happens to them. When Morse's journalist husband (John Bell) gets into trouble it falls to his love rival to help him out, but it's hard to see why he would bother. Derivative, disappointing and dull.

Bryan Brown *Morgan Keefe* • Helen Morse *Jo Reeves* • John Bell *Peter Reeves* • Raina McKeon *Rosita Constanza* • Henry Duval *Rudolf DeCruz* ∎ *Dir/Scr* John Duigan

Far from Home ★★ 18

Horror thriller   1989 · US · Colour · 85mins

Drew Barrymore kicked off her Lolita phase (*Poison Ivy* was the highpoint) with this rather undistinguished straight-to-video thriller. While on a cross-country trip, Matt Frewer and daughter Barrymore are forced to take refuge in a run-down trailer park when their vehicle breaks down. Pretty soon the teenage hormones are working overtime, and there is a killer on the loose. Barrymore shows that she possessed the talent to make the transition from child to grown-up star, although the way director Meiert Avis lingers over her is a little distasteful. There is solid support from Frewer, Richard Masur and Dick Miller. ▭

Matt Frewer *Charlie Cross* • Drew Barrymore *Joleen Cross* • Richard Masur *Duckett* • Karen Austin *Louise* • Susan Tyrrell *Agnes Reed* • Anthony Rapp *Pinky Sears* • Jennifer Tilly *Amy* ∎ *Dir* Meiert Avis • *Scr* Tommy Lee Wallace, from a story by Theodore Gershuny

Far from Home: the Adventures of Yellow Dog ★★★ U

Adventure   1994 · US · Colour · 77mins

Ever since Rin Tin Tin, movie mutts have been rescuing helpless humans. Thankfully, the sentiment that crept in during the Lassie era is absent from this adventure, in which a golden labrador sticks by his teenage master, Jesse Bradford, after their boat capsizes in the wilds of British Columbia. Some of the survival methods might prove too strong for youngsters (although many will revel in the insect eating), but there is enough exciting action to keep them amused. Mimi Rogers and Bruce Davison are fine as the pursuing parents, although we spend a little too much time in their company. ▭

Mimi Rogers *Katherine McCormick* • Bruce Davison *John McCormick* • Jesse Bradford *Angus McCormick* • Tom Bower *John Gale* • Joel Palmer *Silas McCormick* • Josh Wannamaker *David Finlay* • Margot Finley *Sara* ∎ *Dir/Scr* Phillip Borsos

Far from the Madding Crowd ★★★ U

Period romantic drama
1967 · UK · Colour · 155mins

Helped by the shimmering photography of Nicolas Roeg (who went on to become a leading director) and hindered by a straitjacket of a script by Frederic Raphael, this laudable, lengthy adaptation of Thomas Hardy's classic novel might have benefited from a less respectful treatment. Departing from the contemporary scene for the first time, director John Schlesinger fails to impose his own personality on the proceedings and, consequently, he never challenges his cast to explore their characters. Julie Christie narrowly misses the spirit of Bathsheba, and, while Terence Stamp looks suitably soldierly, he just doesn't convince as one of the three suitors besotted with Christie. The same could be said of his rivals, Alan Bates and Peter Finch. Contains some strong language and sexual references. ▭

Julie Christie *Bathsheba Everdene* • Terence Stamp *Sergeant Troy* • Peter Finch *William Boldwood* • Alan Bates *Gabriel Oak* • Fiona Walker *Liddy* • Prunella Ransome *Fanny Robin* • Alison Leggatt *Mrs Hurst* ∎ *Dir* John Schlesinger • *Scr* Frederic Raphael, from the novel by Thomas Hardy

Far from Vietnam ★★★

Experimental political documentary
1967 · Fr · BW and Colour · 120mins

For all the rhetoric spouted in this passionate protest against American involvement in Vietnam, it's the dreadful simplicity of the combat footage that has the most powerful effect. The opening sequence, for example, which juxtaposes US preparations for an air raid and the terrified response it evokes in Hanoi, makes for chilling viewing over 30 years on. There's undoubted socio-artistic integrity in Jean-Luc Godard's emotive confession and Alain Resnais's assessment of the war's morality, while the film is edited with supreme propagandist skill by Chris Marker. Far more revealing, however, are the American TV clips exposing the extent to which the nation was divided by the conflict. In French and English with subtitles.

Dir Alain Resnais, William Klein, Joris Ivens, Agnès Varda, Claude Lelouch, Jean-Luc Godard • *Editor* Chris Marker

The Far Frontier ★★ U

Western   1949 · US · Colour · 68mins

Routine Roy Rogers fodder, given a little more glitz than usual for being filmed in the cheap colour process Trucolor, and notable for being the last time sidekick Andy Devine rode with the (self-styled) King of the Cowboys. The plot's not without interest either, dealing as it does with illegal wetbacks, outlaws smuggled back into the US from Mexico. Of course, Roy still has time to woo Gail Davis (long before she became TV's Annie Oakley), sing along with The Riders of the Purple Sage, and ride Trigger into the sunset. Watch out for the Lone Ranger-to-be Clayton Moore in a small role.

Roy Rogers • Gail Davis *Susan Hathaway* • Andy Devine *Judge Cookie Bullfleacher* • Francis Ford *Alf Sharper* • Roy Barcroft *Bart Carroll* • Clayton Moore *Tom Sharper* • Robert Strange *Willis Newcomb* • Holly Bane *Rocco* ∎ *Dir* William Witney • *Scr* Sloan Nibley

The Far Horizons ★★ U

Historical adventure
1955 · US · Colour · 107mins

Canoes replace horses in this American frontier saga which takes dramatic liberties with the real-life expedition of Lewis and Clark up the Missouri river into the Northwest.

U = SUITABLE FOR ALL   Uc = SUITABLE FOR ALL, ESPECIALLY FOR YOUNG CHILDREN (VIDEO ONLY)   PG = PARENTAL GUIDANCE

Dangerous rapids, tall cliffs and hostile Indians enliven a journey that goes on far too long but is often spectacularly beautiful to behold. Veteran Fred MacMurray is the stern-jawed Lewis while newer star Charlton Heston plays the virile Clark who forgets the girl back home (Barbara Hale) when he runs into Donna Reed's Indian maiden.
Fred MacMurray *Meriwether Lewis* • Charlton Heston *William Clark* • Donna Reed *Sacajawea* • Barbara Hale *Julia Hancock* • William Demarest *Sergeant Gass* • Alan Reed *Charboneau* • Eduardo Noriega *Cameahwait* ■ *Dir* Rudolph Maté • *Scr* Winston Miller, Edmund H North, from the novel *Sacajawea of the Shoshones* by Della Gould Emmons

Far North ★★ 15
Drama　　　1988 · US · Colour · 84mins
Playwright Sam Shepard's feature film debut as director, starring his real-life partner Jessica Lange. Despite the fact that Lange is arguably the most accomplished movie actress of her generation, this still manages to be a major head-banging exercise in dragging Freudian clichés through the farm dust of Minnesota. The cast is impeccable – Tess Harper, Charles Durning, Patricia Arquette – but Shepard's tediously tangled script and lumpen direction badly let it down. Don't give up the day job, Sam. Contains swearing.
Jessica Lange *Kate* • Charles Durning *Bertrum* • Tess Harper *Rita* • Donald Moffat *Uncle Dane* • Ann Wedgeworth *Amy* • Patricia Arquette *Jilly* • Nina Draxten *Gramma* • Pearl Fuller *Older Nurse* ■ *Dir/Scr* Sam Shepard

A Far Off Place ★★ PG
Adventure　　1993 · US · Colour · 102mins
Although it boasts some stunning photography, this is a disappointingly Disneyfied adaptation of Laurens van der Post's novels *A Far Off Place* and *A Story like the Wind*. As a highly acclaimed cinematographer, debuting director Mikael Salomon clearly knows where to place his camera. Yet, in dumbing down the ecological themes for his adolescent audience, he inadvertently patronises Sarel Bok, the Kalahari bush guide who leads imperilled teens Reese Witherspoon and Ethan Randall across the desert and out of the clutches of evil ivory hunter Jack Thompson. Inspired by the best of intentions, but clumsy and old-fashioned. Contains violence.
Reese Witherspoon *Nonnie Parker* • Ethan Randall [Ethan Embry] *Harry Winslow* • Jack Thompson *John Ricketts* • Maximilian Schell *Colonel Mopani Theron* • Sarel Bok *Xhabbo* • Robert Burke *Paul Parker* • Patricia Kalember *Elizabeth Parker* • Daniel Gerroll *John Winslow* ■ *Dir* Mikael Salomon • *Scr* Robert Caswell, Jonathan Hensleigh, Sally Robinson, from the books *A Story like the Wind* and *A Far Off Place* by Laurens van der Post

Faraway, So Close ★★★ 15
Fantasy drama
1993 · Ger · BW and Colour · 138mins
Wim Wenders's sequel to the fabulous *Wings of Desire* is as visually beautiful and sweet-natured as the original. Fallen angel Bruno Ganz now runs a pizza restaurant, which makes his ghostly pal Otto Sander want a slice of mortality for himself. Unfortunately, he ends up working for an illegal arms

dealer (Horst Buchholz). Wenders's mix of recent German history with weighty metaphysical concerns again uses stark black and white to depict the angels' viewpoint, and indulges the director's favourite pastime of sending up American genre conventions. It's overlong and a bit daft – but when was the last time you saw Peter Falk, Lou Reed and Mikhail Gorbachev in the same movie? In English and German with subtitles.
Otto Sander *Cassiel* • Peter Falk • Horst Buchholz *Tony Baker* • Nastassja Kinski *Raphaela* • Heinz Ruhmann *Konrad* • Bruno Ganz *Damiel* • Solveig Dommartin *Marion* • Rüdiger Vogler *Phillip Winter* • Lou Reed • Willem Dafoe *Emit Flesti* • Mikhail Gorbachev ■ *Dir* Wim Wenders • *Scr* Wim Wenders, Ulrich Zieger, Richard Reitinger, from a story by Wim Wenders

Farewell Miss Freedom ★★★
Drama based on a true story
1988 · US · Colour · 89mins
A sensitive and interesting drama based on *Miss 4th of July, Goodbye*, Christopher G Janus's account of his family's experiences as Greek immigrants in America. Beginning in 1917 as Chris Sarandon tries to build a new life in West Virginia for his family, it focuses on the experiences of his teenage daughter and the problems with the Ku Klux Klan that ensue when she becomes friends with a black neighbour (Louis Gossett Jr). The lead actors are all convincing and are competently supported by the rest of the cast, which includes Chynna Phillips (formerly of the pop group Wilson Phillips).
Roxana Zal *Niki Janus* • Chris Sarandon *George Janus* • Chantal Contouri *Olympia Janus* • Chynna Phillips *Alma* • Louis Gossett Jr *Big John Creed* • Mitchell Anderson *Henderson Kerr* ■ *Scr* George Miller (1) • *Scr* Kathy McCormick, from the novel *Miss 4th of July, Goodbye* by Christopher G Janus

Farewell My Concubine ★★★★★ 15
Epic drama　　1993 · Chi · Colour · 150mins
Banned for a time in China, Oscar nominated and joint winner of the Palme d'Or at Cannes in 1993 with Jane Campion's *The Piano*, Chen Kaige's fifth feature sweeps impressively across 50 years of Chinese history to trace the shifting relationship between Peking opera singers Zhang Fengyi and Leslie Cheung. A reluctance to explore, with any depth, the character Cheng's gay love for his friend Duan and a rather prosaic presentation of the political events that rocked China after 1925 are the only quibbles one can have with this majestic and often riveting piece of film-making. Both men give remarkable performances, as does the beguiling Gong Li as Duan's put-upon wife. In Mandarin with English subtitles.
Leslie Cheung *Douzi/Cheng Dieyi (young man)* • Zhang Fengyi *Shitou/Duan Xiaolou (young man)* • Gong Li *Juxian* • Lu Qi *Guan Jifa* • Ying Da *Na Kun* • Ge You *Master Yuan* • Li Chun *Xiao Si (teenager)* • Lei Han *Xiao Si (adult)* • Ma Mingwei *Douzi (child)* • Yin Zhi *Douzi (teenager)* • Fei Yang *Shitou (child)* • Zhao Hailong *Shitou (teenager)* ■ *Dir* Chen Kaige • *Scr* Lillian Lee, Lu Wei

Farewell My Lovely ★★★★★ PG
Classic film noir　1945 · US · BW · 91mins
Also known by its American title *Murder, My Sweet*, this terrific adaptation of the Raymond Chandler novel was the movie that established former crooner Dick Powell's new hard-boiled image. He out-Bogies Bogart playing the impoverished private eye Philip Marlowe, caught up in two tough and nasty cases that eventually dovetail into one. Quintessential *film noir*, this is superbly directed by Edward Dmytryk, with an economic use of voice-over that now stands as a skiful example of the device. Mike Mazurki is a perfect Moose Malloy, but it's Claire Trevor as Velma that you'll remember. Parts of the plot were used previously in *The Falcon Takes Over*, and the film was later remade with Robert Mitchum as Marlowe, but this tight black-and-white masterpiece is as good as it gets. 🖭 **DVD**
Dick Powell *Philip Marlowe* • Claire Trevor *Mrs Grayle* • Anne Shirley *Ann Grayle* • Otto Kruger *Jules Amthor* • Mike Mazurki "*Moose*" *Malloy* • Douglas Walton *Marriott* • Miles Mander *Mr Grayle* ■ *Dir* Edward Dmytryk • *Scr* John Paxton, from the novel by Raymond Chandler

Farewell, My Lovely ★★★★ 15
Detective drama　1975 · US · Colour · 91mins
This is a richly atmospheric and affectionate tribute to Raymond Chandler and forties *film noir*, with Robert Mitchum as Philip Marlowe. It's amazing that Mitchum came so late to the role as he seems born to play it. The corrupt mess of Los Angeles hangs on those rumpled eyelids as he gives a mesmeric performance of world-weariness. Also impressive is Charlotte Rampling as the alluring Velma, who gives Mitchum a smile that, he says, he can feel in his hip pocket. Old hands like John Ireland and Sylvia Miles add layers of nostalgia, and look out, too, for Sylvester Stallone, just a year before *Rocky* shot him to world stardom. The director is Dick Richards, who chose to make this rather than *Jaws*. 🖭
Robert Mitchum *Philip Marlowe* • Charlotte Rampling *Mrs Velma Grayle* • John Ireland *Lieutenant Nulty* • Sylvia Miles *Mrs Jessie Florian* • Jack O'Halloran *Moose Malloy* • Harry Dean Stanton *Billy Rolfe* • Sylvester Stallone *Kelly/Jonnie* ■ *Dir* Dick Richards • *Scr* David Zelag Goodman, from the novel by Raymond Chandler

A Farewell to Arms ★★★ PG
Classic First World War romance
1932 · US · BW · 75mins
Time has not been terribly kind to this adaptation of Ernest Hemingway's First World War love story about an English nurse and an American ambulance driver. But, in 1932, Helen Hayes and Gary Cooper (accompanied by Wagner on the soundtrack) created tidal waves of tears in movie theatres. Still worth seeing for those classically romantic performances and for the Oscar-winning photography by Charles Lang. There was a 1957 remake with Rock Hudson and Jennifer Jones, and Richard Attenborough's film, *In Love*

and War, deals with the real-life story behind Hemingway's novel. 🖭
Gary Cooper *Lieutenant Frederic Henry* • Helen Hayes *Catherine Barkley* • Adolphe Menjou *Major Rinaldi* • Mary Philips *Helen Ferguson* • Jack LaRue *Priest* • Blanche Frederici *Head nurse* • Henry Armetta *Bonello* ■ *Dir* Frank Borzage • *Scr* Benjamin Glazer, Oliver HP Garret, from the novel by Ernest Hemingway

A Farewell to Arms ★★★ 15
First World War romantic drama
1957 · US · Colour · 146mins
Ambulance driver Rock Hudson is wounded in Italy during the First World War and, while recovering from his injuries, falls in love with nurse Jennifer Jones. The voluptuous Jones was married to the film's producer, David O Selznick, who not only wanted to pay adoring tribute to his wife's beauty, but also sought to repeat the huge success of his earlier blockbuster *Gone with the Wind*. As a result, this adaptation of Ernest Hemingway's autobiographical novel is just as overblown and compulsively enjoyable (even with its disturbing depiction of war) as the other epic Selznick made with Jones, *Duel in the Sun*. 🖭
Rock Hudson *Lt Frederic Henry* • Jennifer Jones *Catherine Barkley* • Vittorio De Sica *Major Alessandro Rinaldi* • Kurt Kasznar *Bonello* • Mercedes McCambridge *Miss Van Campen* • Oscar Homolka *Dr Emerich* ■ *Dir* Charles Vidor • *Scr* Ben Hecht, from the novel by Ernest Hemingway

Farewell to the King ★★ PG
Second World War adventure
1988 · US · Colour · 112mins
Here's a weird tale, a sort of *Apocalypse Now* of the Second World War, as captain Nigel Havers (poorly cast) treks into Borneo's heart of darkness and discovers jungle "King" Nick Nolte, who's gone native to the strains of Basil Poledouris's score. Unsurprisingly, this militaristic nonsense is written and directed by John Milius, co-screenwriter of *Apocalypse Now*, who completely fails to uncover any significant resonance in his own material, as he did so superbly with *The Wind and the Lion*. Here, alas, he succeeds only in delivering one of the great clunkers of the eighties, a would-be epic which helped to sink Vestron, the company that made it. Contains some violence and swearing. 🖭
Nick Nolte *Learoyd* • Nigel Havers *Captain Fairbourne* • Frank McRae *Sergeant Tenga* • James Fox *Colonel Ferguson* • Marilyn Tokuda *Yoo* • Marius Weyers *Conklin* ■ *Dir* John Milius • *Scr* John Milius, from the book *L'Adieu au Roi* by Pierre Shoendoerffer

Fargo ★★★★★ 18
Black comedy thriller
1995 · US · Colour · 93mins
The Coen brothers (director/writer Joel, producer/writer Ethan) are on top form with a quirky, unconventional, comedy-tinged crime thriller set in snowy Minnesota. That's where amateur kidnappers Steve Buscemi and Peter Stormare leave a trail of dead bodies that is investigated, with rare instinct and understanding, by heavily pregnant police chief Frances McDormand (who won an Oscar for her performance). Supposedly inspired by a true story,

the Coens neatly subvert thriller clichés for their own surreal and philosophical ends, while retaining the genre's old-fashioned virtues and screw-tightening tension. While sweet-natured mirth is combined with deliciously twisted malice, and gory horror merges with offbeat humour, the whole is set against an extraordinary winter wonderland backdrop. A modern masterpiece. ▣ **DVD**

Frances McDormand *Marge Gunderson* • Steve Buscemi *Carl Showalter* • Peter Stormare *Gaear Grimsrud* • William H Macy *Jerry Lundegaard* • Harve Presnell *Wade Gustafson* • Kristin Rudrüd *Jean Lundegaard* • Tony Denman *Scotty Lundegaard* • Kurt Schweickhardt *Car salesman* ∎ *Dir* Joel Coen • *Scr* Ethan Coen, Joel Coen • *Producer* Ethan Coen • *Cinematographer* Roger Deakins

Farinelli il Castrato
★★★★ **15**

Historical drama
1994 · Bel/Fr/It · Colour · 106mins

Not since *Amadeus* has a film made classical music so popular as this bizarre take on the musical past. Stéfano Dionisi stars as castrated singer Farinelli, one of a select band of tonal high-fliers, whose emasculated voice can drive an audience of women wild with lust, and who is forever feuding with his more virile brother and arguing with the composer Handel. In the film, Farinelli's reedy resonance is the digital result of combining counter-tenor with soprano. Passionless vocals, maybe, but this is an emotion-charged story. In French and Italian with English subtitles. Contains sex scenes.

Stefano Dionisi *Farinelli/Carlo Broschi* • Enrico Lo Verso *Riccardo Broschi* • Elsa Zylberstein *Alexandra* • Caroline Cellier *Margaret Hunter* • Marianne Basler *Countess Mauer* • Jacques Boudet *Philip V* • Graham Valentine *The Prince of Wales* • Jeroen Krabbé *Handel* ∎ *Dir* Gérard Corbiau • *Scr* Andrée Corbiau, from a screenplay (unproduced) by Andrée Corbiau, Gérard Corbiau which they adapted with Marcel Beaulieu

The Farm: Angola, USA
★★★

Documentary 1996 · US · Colour · 90mins

The Shawshank Redemption superbly captured the bleakness of prison life – but this is the real McCoy. This acclaimed documentary focuses on Angola Prison, a facility that is home for 5,000 convicts facing life sentences, the majority of whom will never seen the outside world again. It's essentially a day in the life of a number of the prisoners, with co-director Wilbert Rideau sympathetically listening to the sobering, thoughtful insights of the felons as they desperately cling to the remote hope of one day leaving the facility.

Bernard Addison *Narrator* ∎ *Dir* Jonathan Stack, Liz Garbus, Wilbert Rideau

The Farmer Takes a Wife
★★★ **U**

Romantic drama 1935 · US · Colour · 93mins

Henry Fonda made his movie debut in this charming romance set along the Erie Canal in the 1850s, and created a screen persona that would endure for five decades. Determined, caring and

trustworthy, he was virtually the American ideal, and perfectly suited for such future roles as Tom Joad in *The Grapes of Wrath* and Abraham Lincoln in *Young Mr Lincoln*. The top-billed star is Janet Gaynor, who was immensely popular at the time, though nearing the end of her career. She and Fonda are well matched under the direction of Victor Fleming (*Gone with the Wind*, *The Wizard of Oz*) who, refreshingly, elects to shoot mainly in the open, away from studio backdrops. Twentieth Century-Fox, never a studio to waste a good property, dusted this off as a Betty Grable vehicle in 1953, but Dale Robertson was no substitute for Fonda.

Janet Gaynor *Molly Larkins* • Henry Fonda *Dan Harrow* • Charles Bickford *Jotham Klore* • Slim Summerville *Fortune Friendly* • Andy Devine *Elmer Otway* • Roger Imhof *Sam Weaver* • Siegfried Rumann [Sig Ruman] *Blacksmith* ∎ *Dir* Victor Fleming • *Scr* Edwin Burke, from the play by Frank B Elser, Marc Connelly, from the novel *Rome Haul* by Walter D Edmonds

The Farmer Takes a Wife
★★ **U**

Musical 1953 · US · Colour · 80mins

This is an ill-advised musical remake of the 1935 period romance. Dale Robertson steps into Henry Fonda's shoes as the 19th-century land-lover who signs on to a barge on the Erie Canal to raise the money to buy a farm. But he lacks the naiveté of the young Fonda, while brassy Betty Grable has none of the wide-eyed idealism that made Janet Gaynor so persuasive as the barge cook who comes to share his dream. Harold Arlen and Dorothy Fields's blaring songs, Arthur E Arling's garish photography and director Henry Levin's idea of cosy nostalgia don't help much either.

Betty Grable *Molly* • Dale Robertson *Daniel Harrow* • Thelma Ritter *Lucy Cashdollar* • John Carroll *Jotham Klore* • Eddie Foy Jr *Fortune Friendly* • Charlotte Austin *Pearl* ∎ *Dir* Henry Levin • *Scr* Walter Bullock, Sally Benson, Joseph Fields, from the play by Frank B Elser, Marc Connelly, from the novel *Rome Haul* by Walter D Edmonds • *Music* Cyril Mockridge • *Music/Lyrics* Harold Arlen, Dorothy Fields

The Farmer's Daughter
★★★ **U**

Comedy drama 1946 · US · BW · 96mins

Loretta Young picked up her best actress Oscar for this strangely accented, but utterly charming, performance as Katrin Holstrom, a fictionalised Swede who comes to Washington as a lady's maid and ends up running for Congress opposing the man she loves. Holstrom's really an RKO mouthpiece for producer Dore Schary's Hollywood-liberal political views, but the original play *Hulda, Daughter of Parliament* was, amazingly, a hit in Finland. Eventually Schary took over MGM from the ousted reactionary Louis B Mayer, and Young became one of the brightest names in the early days of television. ▣

Loretta Young *Katrin Holstrom* • Joseph Cotten *Glenn Morley* • Ethel Barrymore *Mrs Morley* • Charles Bickford *Clancy* • Rose Hobart *Virginia* • Rhys Williams *Adolph* ∎ *Dir* HC Potter • *Scr* Allen Rivkin, Laura Kerr, from the play *Hulda, Daughter of Parliament* by Juhni Tervataa

Fascination
★★ **18**

Erotic horror 1979 · Fr · Colour · 78mins

More nonsensical soft-core horror trash from French hack director Jean Rollin. It's a turn-of-the-century fairy tale combining ritual slaughter, cannibal orgies and exploitation gore. A hunky thief comes between two lesbian vampires. It's better than some of Rollin's yawn-inducing efforts like *Sex and the Vampire* or *Requiem for a Vampire*, thanks to halfway-decent acting from a cast including top European hardcore star Brigitte Lahaie. However, it's still a slow-moving bore thanks to Rollin's camera dwelling on the visual properties of naked bodies, fabrics and furnishings above the thin plot. In French with English subtitles. ▣

Franca Mai *Elisabeth* • Brigitte Lahaie *Eva* ∎ *Dir/Scr* Jean Rollin

Fashions of 1934
★★★

Musical comedy 1934 · US · BW · 78mins

A *Prêt-à-Porter* for the thirties? Not really, but it's actually a lot more fun than Robert Altman's nineties take on *haute couture*. Smooth charmer William Powell and glamorous assistant Bette Davis play the visiting Americans who succeed in running rings around the snooty, fashion-conscious inhabitants of Paris. Director William Dieterle spares no expense in invoking a dizzying world of elegant artifice, and there's sharp playing from the two leads.

William Powell *Sherwood Nash* • Bette Davis *Lynn Mason* • Frank McHugh *Snap* • Verree Teasdale *Grand Duchess Alix* • Reginald Owen *Oscar Baroque* • Henry O'Neill *Duryea* • Philip Reed *Jimmy* • Hugh Herbert *Joe Ward* ∎ *Dir* William Dieterle • *Scr* F Hugh Herbert, Gene Markey, Kathryn Scola, Carl Erickson, from a story by Harry Collins, Warren Duff

Fast and Furious
★★

Comedy mystery 1939 · US · BW · 73mins

This was the last of three features written for MGM by the clever and witty Harry Kurnitz, and starred suave Franchot Tone and sexy Ann Sothern as rare book dealers Joel and Garda Sloane. The series was MGM's attempt to emulate the success of their popular *Thin Man* detective series, also featuring a married couple. This particular episode proved a training ground for Busby Berkeley, best known for his groundbreaking flamboyant choreography, who had left his home studio Warner Bros to establish himself as a "serious" director over at MGM. Despite the sparseness of the budget, it was a competent enough effort, allowing Berkeley to prove to Metro that he could take charge of whole features and not just musical segments.

Franchot Tone *Joel Sloane* • Ann Sothern *Garda Sloane* • Ruth Hussey *Lily Cole* • Lee Bowman *Mike Stevens* • Allyn Joslyn *Ted Bentley* • John Miljan *Erie Bartell* ∎ *Dir* Busby Berkeley • *Scr* Harry Kurnitz

Fast and Loose
★★

Comedy 1930 · US · BW · 70mins

Miriam Hopkins was to become one of the brightest stars of the thirties, but few would have guessed from her

screen debut in this comedic misfire. Despite a script co-written by Preston Sturges, the story is a conventional rich-girl-falls-for-poor-boy affair, based on a play *The Best People* by David Gray and Avery Hopwood. Carole Lombard, in the smaller role of a chorus girl who reforms Hopkins's playboy brother, comes off better, though Fred C Newmeyer's stilted direction favours no one. The great Ernst Lubitsch was to direct Hopkins in her next film, *The Smiling Lieutenant*, a project more worthy of her talent.

Miriam Hopkins *Marion Lenox* • Carole Lombard *Alice O'Neil* • Frank Morgan *Bronson Lenox* • Charles Starrett *Henry Morgan* • Henry Wadsworth *Bertie Lenox* • Winifred Harris *Carrie Lenox* • Herbert Yost *George Grafton* ∎ *Dir* Fred C Newmeyer • *Scr* Doris Anderson, Jack Kirkland, Preston Sturges, from the play *The Best People* by David Gray, Avery Hopwood

Fast and Loose
★★

Comedy mystery 1939 · US · BW · 79mins

The sequel to *Fast Company*, which starred Melvyn Douglas and Florence Rice as married sleuths, this one stars Robert Montgomery trying to discover what's happened to a collection of manuscripts which vanish from a library, and Rosalind Russell as his wife who complicates the situation. An undemanding piece of fluff, with the stars on good form. MGM made a further film, *Fast and Furious*, before abandoning the format which was a rip-off of *The Thin Man* series.

Robert Montgomery *Joel Sloane* • Rosalind Russell *Garda Sloane* • Reginald Owen *Vincent Charlton* • Ralph Morgan *Nicholas Torrent* • Etienne Girardot *Christopher Oates* • Alan Dinehart *David Hilliard* ∎ *Dir* Edwin L Marin • *Scr* Harry Kurnitz

Fast Break
★★★

Comedy 1979 · US · Colour · 107mins

One of the first attempts to duplicate the "worst – insert activity – team in the world whipped into shape by dedicated coach" formula that originated from *The Bad News Bears*, is one of the best. Basketball is the sport this time, with Gabe Kaplan playing the New York coach hired by a small college to produce a winning team, doing so by recruiting a number of eccentric players. Instead of concentrating on the usual story clichés, the movie is content to focus on the players, who are not just funny, but surprisingly well-rounded characters. There's also some great basketball action, with even the predictable final game fun to watch.

Gabe Kaplan *David Greene* • Harold Sylvester *DC* • Mike Warren [Michael Warren] *Preacher* • Bernard King *Hustler* • Reb Brown *Bull* • Mavis Washington *Swish* • Bert Remsen *Bo Winnegar* ∎ *Dir* Jack Smight • *Scr* Sandy Stern [Sandor Stern], from a story by Marc Kaplan

Fast Charlie: the Moonbeam Rider
★★ **PG**

Action adventure 1978 · US · Colour · 94mins

This is an adequate action drama laced with barbed comedy about a disenchanted First World War soldier (David Carradine) who deserts his unit to enter the first transcontinental cross-country motorcycle race. He hires his war buddies, whom he had let down in an attack, to help. Authentic production design, and credible support from Brenda Vaccaro as his faithful groupie, add class to another B-movie from the Roger Corman production conveyor belt. ▣

David Carradine *Charlie Swattle* • Brenda Vaccaro *Grace Wolf* • LQ Jones *Floyd Bevins* • RG Armstrong *Al Barber* • Terry Kiser *Lester Neal* • Jesse Vint *Calvin Hawk* ■ *Dir* Steve Carver • *Scr* Michael Gleason, from the story by Ed Spielman, Howard Friedlander

Fast Company ★★

Comedy mystery 1938 · US · BW · 73mins

Melvyn Douglas and Florence Rice star as amateur detectives who specialise in finding stolen and bogus books but find themselves also caught up in a murder. The background of book auctions has some interest and Douglas is always an exceptionally smooth performer, though Rice never had the star appeal MGM initially thought she had. It was the first in a three-part series about married detectives – *Fast and Loose* and *Fast and Furious* followed.

Melvyn Douglas *Joel Sloane* • Florence Rice *Garda Sloane* • Claire Dodd *Julia Thorne* • Shepperd Strudwick *Ned Morgan* • Louis Calhern *Elias Z Bannerman* • Nat Pendleton *Paul Torison* • Douglass Dumbrille *Arnold Stamper* ■ *Dir* Edward Buzzell • *Scr* Marco Page, Harold Tarshis, from a story by Marco Page, Harry Kurnitz

Fast Food ★★★ PG

Comedy 1989 · US · Colour · 88mins

Anything goes in the burger wars – including spiking the sauce with an aphrodisiac. Students and scam artists, Clark Brandon and Randal Patrick, take on ruthless burger king Jim Varney whose expansion plans threaten their friend Samantha's gas station. This good-natured comedy – a little reminiscent of an Ealing film – boasts some decent jokes and an eccentric cast that includes Melanie Griffith's half-sister, Tracy, Michael J Pollard from *Bonnie and Clyde* and ex-porn star Traci Lords. ▣

Clark Brandon *Auggie* • Randal Patrick *Drew* • Tracy Griffith *Samantha* • Michael J Pollard *Bud* • Lanny Horn *Calvin* • Jim Varney *Wrangler Bob Bundy* • Blake Clark *EG McCormick* • Traci Lords *Dixie Love* ■ *Dir* Michael A Simpson • *Scr* Randal Patrick, Clark Brandon, Lanny Horn, from a story by Scott B Sowers, Jim Bastille

Fast Food ★ 18

Comedy drama 1998 · UK · Colour · 95mins

Stewart Sugg proclaimed his directorial debut would ditch the clichés of British cinema and combine the "sparkle and bite" of American indie cinema with a European angle. Alas, all he's managed to do is dish up an overcooked, indigestible mess that borrows indiscriminately from *A Clockwork Orange*, *Blue Velvet* and diverse Scorsese and Tarantino pictures. Of the five friends reunited after decades of disappointment, only Douglas Henshall comes remotely close to giving a performance as he tries to save blind hooker Emily Woof from her safe-blowing mates and her

savage pimp. A new low for the homegrown crime movie. ▣

Douglas Henshall *Benny* • Emily Woof *Letitia/Claudia* • Miles Anderson *Dwayne* • Gerard Butler *Jacko* • Danny Midwinter *Bisto* • Sean Hughes ■ *Dir/Scr* Stewart Sugg

Fast Getaway ★★ 15

Action adventure 1991 · US · Colour · 82mins

A lazy comedy thriller which did reasonable business on the UK video market, thanks mainly to the presence of teenage idol Corey Haim as a youngster who follows his dad (Leo Rossi) into the family business of robbing banks. Problems arise when father and son fall out with fellow gang member (Cynthia Rothrock). There are a smattering of good car chases, but laughs are few and far between, while martial arts star Rothrock is as wooden as ever. A largely redundant sequel followed in 1994. ▣

Corey Haim *Nelson Potter* • Cynthia Rothrock *Lilly* • Leo Rossi *Sam Potter* • Marcia Strassman *Lorraine* • Ken Lerner *Tony* ■ *Dir* Spiro Razatos • *Scr* James Dixon

The Fast Lady ★★★

Comedy 1963 · UK · Colour · 95mins

Despite driving up too many B roads, this story of a civil servant (Stanley Baxter), his car (a Bentley) and the girl on whom he dotes (Julie Christie) has such a degree of fresh-faced innocence that you appreciate the film's charm rather than notice the rambling plot. This Rank movie is tackled with relish by the cast: Christie is simpering and decent, Baxter is spot-on with his "gormless comic" style and James Robertson-Justice booms throughout.

James Robertson-Justice *Charles Chingford* • Leslie Phillips *Freddy Fox* • Stanley Baxter *Murdoch Troon* • Kathleen Harrison *Mrs Staggers* • Julie Christie *Claire Chingford* • Dick Emery *Shingler* ■ *Dir* Ken Annakin • *Scr* Jack Davies, Helen Blyth, from a story by Howard Keble

Fast Money ★★ 18

Action crime romance 1995 · US · Colour · 88mins

This rehash of the old thief-and-innocent-bystander-together-on-the-run formula is no great shakes, but it passes the time well enough. The twist comes with the sexes being reversed: Yancy Butler plays Francesca, a car thief with a liking for luxury vehicles, who is on the run after causing a major accident. Along for the ride is Jack (Matt McCoy) an unassuming reporter minding his business on a mundane assignment. They're brought together by a suitcase full of $2.7 million of mob money. The action sequences are fine but the main attraction here is the chemistry between the actors. The two stars give their characters an intense yet believable relationship – both in and out of the bedroom – that constantly changes between hot and cold. Contains swearing and violence. ▣

Yancy Butler *Francesca* • Matt McCoy *Jack* • John Ashton *Lt Diego* • Trevor Goddard *Regy* • Jacob Witkin *Stewart* • Patrika Darbo *Teebou* ■ *Dir/Scr* Alexander Wright

Fast Times at Ridgemont High ★★★★ 18

Comedy 1982 · US · Colour · 85mins

The success of *Animal House* spawned a spate of dreadful teen sex comedies best typified by the crass *Porky's* series. However, Amy Heckerling's insightful, sympathetic and still very funny foray into high school life was a stunning exception. Thoughtfully adapted by Cameron (*Jerry Maguire*) Crowe from his own novel, on the surface it's just another episodic story of high school students trying to lose their virginity – except this also chronicles serious issues such as teenage pregnancy along with the usual hi-jinks. It also boasts a quite astonishing cast of then unknowns: Jennifer Jason Leigh, Phoebe Cates, Judge Reinhold, Forest Whitaker, Eric Stoltz, Anthony Edwards and, best of all, Sean Penn as a permanently stoned surfer, the template for everybody from Bill and Ted to Beavis and Butthead. ▣

Sean Penn *Jeff Spicoli* • Jennifer Jason Leigh *Stacy Hamilton* • Judge Reinhold *Brad Hamilton* • Robert Romanus *Mike Damone* • Brian Backer *Mark Ratner* • Phoebe Cates *Linda Barrett* • Forest Whitaker *Charles Jefferson* • Eric Stoltz *Stoner Bud* • Anthony Edwards *Stoner Bud* ■ *Dir* Amy Heckerling • *Scr* Cameron Crowe, from his novel

Fast-Walking ★★ 18

Comedy drama 1982 · US · Colour · 111mins

This prison drama has James Woods in a typically amoral role as a guard who becomes involved in a plot to assassinate black activist Robert Hooks. There are some good performances from Tim McIntire, M Emmet Walsh and the ever-reliable Woods, but these accomplished actors can't hide the fact that this is a rather nasty and unpleasant film that leaves a bad taste in the mouth. Contains swearing. ▣

James Woods *Miniver* • Kay Lenz *Moke* • Tim McIntire *Wasco* • Robert Hooks *Galliot* • M Emmet Walsh *Sergeant Sanger* • Susan Tyrrell *Evie* • Charles Weldon *Jackson* ■ *Dir* James B Harris • *Scr* James B Harris, from the novel *The Rap* by Ernest Brawley

Faster, Pussycat! Kill! Kill! ★★★★ 18

Action comedy drama 1965 · US · BW · 83mins

Three go-go dancers, led by incomparable *femme fatale* Tura Satana, go on a wild crime spree in California in soft-core sexpert Russ Meyer's cult favourite. After indulging in kidnapping, theft, murder and wanton exposure of their seemingly limitless cleavages, the crazy-for-kicks chicks take the Battle of the Sexes to the extreme, involving some hapless males in a violently perverse cat-and-mouse game. Along with *Beyond the Valley of the Dolls*, this double-entendre parade through the seamier side of the Swinging Sixties is the definitive Meyer movie. A grotesque gala of deranged perfection guaranteed to keep you on the edge of disbelief. Contains violence and sex scenes. ▣

Tura Satana *Varla* • Haji *Rosie* • Lori Williams *Billie* • Susan Bernard [Sue Bernard] *Linda* •

Stuart Lancaster *Old Man* • Paul Trinka *Kirk* • Dennis Busch *"Boy"* ■ *Dir* Russ Meyer • *Scr* Jack Moran, from a story by Russ Meyer

The Fastest Gun Alive ★★★ U

Western 1956 · US · BW · 85mins

This is a neglected gem. Glenn Ford, following his success in *The Blackboard Jungle* with another fine performance, is trying to live down his father's gunslinging past by working as a town storekeeper, when Broderick Crawford's venal Vinnie Harold blasts in, exposing Ford and taunting him with his father's name. It's taut stuff, cleverly co-scripted by Frank D Gilroy, who had written the original television play from which this was drawn. Russ Tamblyn has some knockabout moments at a barn dance, and Jeanne Crain is earnest and pretty as the pleading wife, but this is Ford's movie, an under-rated western deserving of your full attention. ▣

Glenn Ford *George Temple* • Jeanne Crain *Dora Temple* • Broderick Crawford *Vinnie Harold* • Russ Tamblyn *Eric Doolittle* • Allyn Joslyn *Harvey Maxwell* • Leif Erickson *Lou Glover* • Noah Beery Jr *Dink Wells* ■ *Dir* Russell Rouse • *Scr* Frank D Gilroy, Russell Rouse, Frank D Gilroy

Fat City ★★★★

Sports drama 1972 · US · Colour · 96mins

Strip away the sleaziness of the setting and you have that old Hollywood standby *A Star Is Born*, recycled into a boxing picture. Stacy Keach (in a role offered first to Marlon Brando) is the boxer on the slide and Jeff Bridges is the one on the rise; theirs is a troubled relationship. John Huston, who directed wearing an oxygen mask owing to acute emphysema, shot the picture on skid row in Stockton, California, and aimed for a grimly realistic, but not seedy, look. "There's a big difference between photographing a hovel so it looks like a hovel and doing it so it looks like bad photography," he said. The result is a minor classic, necessarily brutal but with humanity and an underlying optimism. Contains violence and swearing.

Stacy Keach *Billy Tully* • Jeff Bridges *Ernie Munger* • Susan Tyrrell *Oma* • Candy Clark *Faye* • Nicholas Colasanto *Ruben* • Art Aragon *Babe* • Curtis Cokes *Earl* • Sixto Rodriguez *Lucero* • Billy Walker *Wes* ■ *Dir* John Huston • *Scr* Leonard Gardner, from his novel • *Cinematographer* Conrad Hall

Fatal Affair ★★

Thriller 1998 · Can · Colour · 94mins

Ever since Glenn Close put a bunny on the boil, it's been a racing certainty that any film with "fatal" in the title will be about some deranged, grievance-harbouring crank with murder in mind. This Canadian thriller is no exception, with Jay Underwood seeking to take out his twisted revenge on C Thomas Howell, the family-oriented juror who once dated the wife Underwood is now on trial for killing. When photographs of the victim are shown to the jury, Howell's reaction alerts Underwood to the possibility of a link with the murdered woman. Marc S Grenier does what he can to freshen

up the cliché-ridden script, but it's a thankless task. Contains violence, swearing and sex scenes.
C Thomas Howell *Mack Maddox* • Maxim Roy *Laura Maddox* • Jay Underwood *Ezra Tyler* • Mark Camacho *Walt Rosenbaum* • Louis DiBianco *Detective Deleone* ■ *Dir* Marc S Grenier • *Scr* Michael Rauch

Fatal Attraction ★★★★ 18
Thriller 1987 · US · Colour · 114mins

The movie which, among other things, helped create a new genre: the psychotic female from hell (see *Basic Instinct*, *The Hand That Rocks the Cradle* and *The Crush* for prime examples). Glenn Close is the obsessed woman driven to extreme lengths when she discovers that Michael Douglas is not going to leave his wife (Anne Archer) for her. Close is excellent in a thankless role, while Douglas established himself as the troubled icon of middle-class America, the ordinary man who would later find himself getting out of his depth in the likes of *Falling Down* and *Disclosure*. The movie's message (it's alright to have an affair as long as it's not with a nutcase) is more than a little dubious, but there is no denying its slick power and director Adrian Lyne milks the tension for all it's worth. However, he had to reshoot the movie's climax after test audiences gave the thumbs down to his first ending. Lyne later got the chance to reinstate the original ending with his director's cut. Contains violence, swearing, sex scenes and nudity. ▭
Michael Douglas *Dan Gallagher* • Glenn Close *Alex Forrest* • Anne Archer *Beth Gallagher* • Ellen Hamilton Latzen *Ellen Gallagher* • Stuart Pankin *Jimmy* • Ellen Foley *Hildy* • Fred Gwynne *Arthur* • Meg Mundy *Joan Rogerson* ■ *Dir* Adrian Lyne • *Scr* James Dearden

Fatal Beauty ★★ 18
Comedy thriller 1987 · US · Colour · 99mins

Tom Holland, who directed comic horror movies such as *Fright Night* and *Child's Play*, loses his humorous touch with this lukewarm vehicle for Whoopi Goldberg, which aspires to being the female equivalent of Eddie Murphy's *Beverly Hills Cop*. Goldberg stars as Rita Rizzoli, a tough narcotics cop on the trail of some drug-dealing bad guys. This gives Whoopi an excuse to totter around in ill-advised prostitute disguise, while Cheech Marin, Rubén Blades and Sam Elliott (as Goldberg's love interest) try their best to pretend they're in a movie worth sitting through until the end. Contains swearing. ▭
Whoopi Goldberg *Rita Rizzoli* • Sam Elliott *Mike Marshak* • Rubén Blades *Carl Jimenez* • Harris Yulin *Conrad Kroll* • Brad Dourif *Leo Nova* • Cheech Marin *[Richard "Cheech" Marin] Bartender* ■ *Dir* Tom Holland • *Scr* Hilary Henkin, Dean Riesner

Fatal Bond ★★
Thriller 1991 · Ausl · Colour · 89mins

The *Exorcist* spoof *Repossessed* aside, Linda Blair rarely breaks out of straight-to-video mode these days, and even a change of continents here fails to provide a remedy. In this seedy, supposedly erotic, Australian-set thriller, Blair is the bored suburbanite who falls for smouldering drifter

Jerome Ehlers, who may or may not be a psychopathic killer. The Australian locations are a pleasant change, but the storyline is far-fetched and director Vincent Monton never gets to grips with the material. Contains swearing, violence and nudity.
Linda Blair *Leonie Stevens* • Jerome Ehlers *Joe Martinez* • Stephen Leeder *Anthony Boon* • Donal Gibson *Rocky Bargetta* • Caz Lederman *Detective Chenko* • Joe Bugner *Miller* • Roger Ward *Greaves* ■ *Dir* Vincent Monton • *Scr* Phillip Avalon

Fatal Deception: Mrs Lee Harvey Oswald ★★★ PG
Biographical drama
1993 · US · Colour · 87mins

Anyone who still thinks Helena Bonham Carter is nothing more than an Edwardian clothes horse should make a date with this fascinating TV movie. She is hugely impressive as Marina Oswald, the wife of the man who (conspiracy theories aside) shot President Kennedy in Dallas in November 1963. While it can't compete in terms of scope and complexity with Oliver Stone's *JFK*, Robert Dornhelm's film still manages to come up with some persuasive information, as Marina attempts to uncover the truth about her husband's tangled past. Robert Picardo, Frank Whaley and Russian star Ingeborga Dapkunaite stand out in the strong supporting cast. ▭
Helena Bonham Carter *Marina Oswald* • Frank Whaley *Lee Harvey Oswald* • Robert Picardo *George Demorenschildt* • Brandon Smith *Kenneth Porter* • Lisa Renee Wilson *Rachel Porter* ■ *Dir* Robert Dornhelm • *Scr* Steve Bello

Fatal Instinct ★★★ 15
Comedy thriller 1993 · US · Colour · 86mins

Panned on its original release, this spoof thriller boasts some slick gags and several knowing performances. The problem is, it's often far too clever for its own good. Veteran director Carl Reiner has got the look and feel of latter-day *films noirs* off to a T, and sets about such movies as *Fatal Attraction*, *Basic Instinct*, *Body Heat* and *Sleeping with the Enemy* with evident relish. He's well served by Armand Assante as a cop who doubles as a lawyer for the people he arrests, Kate Nelligan as his blatantly adulterous wife, and Sherilyn Fenn and Sean Young as his *femmes fatales*. Contains swearing and sex scenes. ▭
Armand Assante *Ned Ravine* • Sherilyn Fenn *Laura* • Kate Nelligan *Lana Ravine* • Sean Young *Lola Cain* • Christopher McDonald *Frank Kelbo* • James Remar *Max Shady* ■ *Dir* Carl Reiner • *Scr* David O'Malley

Fatal Lady ★★
Murder mystery 1936 · US · BW · 75mins

Walter Pidgeon returned to Hollywood from the Broadway stage (he didn't want to be known as just a singing star) to play opposite Mary Ellis in this ill-conceived attempt to turn the leading lady of stage musicals into a movie name. She plays an opera star suspected of murder, but the title of this hackneyed backstage drama proved sadly prophetic for Ellis, whose

casting as a prima donna seemed both appropriate and unsympathetic. The film was a box-office disaster and producer Walter Wanger, who had placed Pidgeon under contract, immediately dropped him. Seen today, the film is not without period interest, but it's easy to see why it did nothing to enhance the careers of its stars. Pidgeon went on to a successful career at MGM as a contract player, but Mary Ellis's screen stardom was effectively over.
Mary Ellis *Marion Stuart/Marla Delasano/Malevo* • Walter Pidgeon *David Roberts* • Ruth Donnelly *Melba York* • Norman Foster *Phillip Roberts* • Guy Bates Post *Feodor Glinka* • John Halliday *Romero Fontes* ■ *Dir* Edward Ludwig • *Scr* Samuel Ornitz, Horice McCoy, from a story by Harry Segall

Fatal Love ★★★ 15
Drama based on a true story
1992 · US · Colour · 93mins

Based on the true story of Alison Gertz, a white upper-middle-class girl who has only a handful of sexual partners prior to discovering she's HIV-positive, this hard-hitting drama features a compellingly strong performance from Molly Ringwald, an actress whose career started with a bang in the early eighties in all those Brat-Pack movies, but who subsequently struggled to find good adult roles. The problem here is not the usual "drowning in a sea of tears" scenario, but the rather overt and simplistic way that the movie suggests there are "nice girls" like Gertz who don't deserve Aids and the "other sort" who somehow do. ▭
Molly Ringwald *Alison Gertz* • Lee Grant *Carol Gertz* • Perry King *Mark* • Martin Landau *Jerry Gertz* • Roxana Zal *Tracy* • Kim Myers *Lindy* • Peter Spears *Peter* ■ *Dir* Tom McLoughlin • *Scr* Deborah Joy Levine

Fatal Mission ★★
War drama 1990 · US · Colour · 84mins

"Nothin's guaranteed in the 'Nam", or so declares American "black" operations agent Andrews (Peter Fonda) at the beginning of this movie. What is guaranteed is that you will have flashbacks to *Hell in the Pacific* about halfway through. Andrews assassinates a Communist leader, and while trying to escape, is taken prisoner by a Chinese agent, played by Tia Carrere. Together they find out that everyone's against them, and they have to rely on each other to survive. Who says that movies have lost their moral lessons?
Peter Fonda *Ken Andrews* • Tia Carrere *Mai Chong* • Mako Trang • Ted Markland *CIA Man* • Jim Mitchum *[James Mitchum] Captain Bauer* • Felind Obach *NVA Sergeant Tuong* • Joonee Gamboa *NVA Captain Hao* • Joe Mari *Vietnam general* ■ *Dir* George Rowe • *Scr* Anthony Gentile, John Gentile, George Rowe, Chosei Funahara, Peter Fonda, from a story by Erlinda Quiaoit Rowe

Fatal Vows ★★ 15
Thriller 1994 · US · Colour · 91mins

Unwitting Cynthia Gibb marries psychopath John Stamos and then, when she sees his true murderous colours, desperately tries to escape from his clutches. A sort of low rent version of *The Stepfather* which still

manages to provoke a few screams thanks to the story being based on true facts and an excellent performance by Stamos. Otherwise it's more of the same in the *Fatal Attraction* mould. Contains some violence and coarse language. ▭
Cynthia Gibb *Alexandra* • John Stamos *Nick Pagan* • Ben Gazzara *Papa* • Sean McCann *Shapiro* ■ *Dir* John Power • *Scr* Danielle Hill

Fate Is the Hunter ★★★
Mystery drama 1964 · US · BW · 106mins

Glenn Ford leads the investigation into an air crash for which his friend, pilot Rod Taylor, is thought to be responsible. Flashbacks show us what might have happened, until Ford and sole survivor Suzanne Pleshette restage the flight to solve the mystery. A lot of interesting detail and a surprising cast – Dorothy Malone, Nancy Kwan, Jane Russell playing herself as a forties singer – make this quite watchable, though Ford is fairly glum throughout.
Glenn Ford *McBane* • Nancy Kwan *Sally Fraser* • Rod Taylor *Capt Jack Savage* • Suzanne Pleshette *Martha Webster* • Jane Russell ■ *Dir* Ralph Nelson • *Scr* Harold Medford, from the novel by Ernest K Gann

Father ★★★
Drama 1990 · Ausl · Colour · 106mins

The father is Max von Sydow, a German living in Melbourne with his daughter (Carol Drinkwater), son-in-law and two grandchildren. A nice, happy family, until grandad is suddenly charged with committing wartime atrocities and is put on trial. While not in the same league as Costa-Gavras's *Music Box*, which starred Armin Mueller-Stahl and Jessica Lange, *Father* is nevertheless a gripping drama, superbly played by von Sydow. The film explores the themes of guilt and the nature of truth with skill, even drawing parallels with the son-in-law's experiences in Vietnam. Contains swearing and nudity.
Max von Sydow *Joe Mueller* • Carol Drinkwater *Anne Winton* • Julia Blake *Iya Zetnick* • Steve Jacobs *Bobby Winton* • Simone Robertson *Rebecca Winton* • Kahli Sneddon *Amy Winton* • Nicholas Bell *Paul Jamieson* ■ *Dir* John Power • *Scr* Tony Cavanaugh, Graham Hartley

Father and Scout ★★ U
Comedy 1994 · US · Colour · 90mins

Bob Saget is soon out of his depth as a non-athletic dad who's dragged along on a "Dad & Lad" camping trip with his ten-year-old son (Brian Bonsall). There is plenty of broad comedy here, as the reluctant Saget displays his ineptitude in a variety of activities and embarrasses the kid. Of course, as the weekend comes to an end, both father and son have learned those all-important life lessons. With enough twists and turns along the way to make it interesting, this fun TV movie is good family entertainment. ▭
Bob Saget *Spenser Paley* • Brian Bonsall *Michael Paley* • Troy Evans *Scoutmaster* • Stuart Pankin *Aaron* • David Graf *Chet* • Heidi Swedberg *Donna Paley* ■ *Dir* Richard Michaels • *Scr* Sheldon Bull, Hoyt Hilsman

U = SUITABLE FOR ALL   **Uc** = SUITABLE FOR ALL, ESPECIALLY FOR YOUNG CHILDREN (VIDEO ONLY)   **PG** = PARENTAL GUIDANCE

Father Brown ★★★★ U
Comedy thriller 1954 · UK · BW · 93mins
Although occasionally overdoing the unworldliness, Alec Guinness brings GK Chesterton's sermonising sleuth to rich and vigorous life in this hugely enjoyable comedy thriller from director Robert Hamer, who also made Guinness's classic comedy *Kind Hearts and Coronets*. Fans of the original stories might be a tad aggrieved by the slight shift of period and the marked reduction in religious undertone, but the case of St Augustine's Cross is nevertheless packed with incident and intrigue. Peter Finch is languidly villainous as the dastardly criminal Flambeau and Joan Greenwood huskily seductive as the devout Lady Warren, but it's Cecil Parker's bishop and Ernest Thesiger's doddering librarian who stay longest in the memory.

Alec Guinness *Father Brown* • Joan Greenwood *Lady Warren* • Peter Finch *Flambeau* • Cecil Parker *Bishop* • Bernard Lee *Inspector Valentine* • Sidney James *Parkinson* • Gérard Oury *Inspector Dubois* • Ernest Thesiger *Vicomte* ■ *Dir* Robert Hamer • *Scr* Thelma Schnee, Maurice Rapf, Robert Hamer, from the characters created by GK Chesterton

Father Came Too ★★
Comedy 1963 · UK · Colour · 92mins
Stanley Baxter, Leslie Phillips and James Robertson-Justice teamed up twice for Rank in the early sixties. But following 1962's *The Fast Lady*, this was a disappointing outing, considering that it had all the makings of being an amusing inversion of the old mother-in-law joke. Robertson-Justice stars as the father-in-law from hell who shatters the bliss of newlyweds Baxter and Sally Smith with his tactless intrusions and incessant hectoring. Such is his dominance of the action that there simply aren't enough gags to go around, leaving Phillips and Ronnie Barker twiddling their thumbs on the periphery.

James Robertson-Justice *Sir Beverley Grant* • Leslie Phillips *Roddy Chipfield* • Stanley Baxter *Dexter Munro* • Sally Smith *Juliet Munro* • Ronnie Barker *Josh* • James Villiers *Benzil Bulstrode* ■ *Dir* Peter Graham Scott • *Scr* Jack Davies, Henry Blyth

The Father Clements Story ★★★
Drama based on a true story
1987 · US · Colour · 100mins
Movie priests have been coming to the rescue of delinquents since the days of Spencer Tracy and *Boys Town*. But truth is nearly always stranger than fiction, as this engrossing TV movie proves. As the Chicago cleric whose ''One Church One Child'' crusade prompted him to adopt a teenage boy, Louis Gossett Jr gives an upstanding performance, distinctly at odds with his *An Officer and a Gentleman* tough-guy image. Also playing against type is Carroll O'Connor, best known as TV's Archie Bunker, here playing a conservative cardinal. The portrait of street life has been somewhat sanitised for small-screen viewing, but there's still enough here to provoke.

Louis Gossett Jr *Father George Clements* • Malcolm-Jamal Warner *Joey* • Carroll O'Connor

Cardinal Cody • Ron McClarty *O'Hare* • Leon Robinson [*Leon*] *Ice* • Rosetta Le Noire *Mrs Clements* • Glenn Plummer *Daryl* ■ *Dir* Edwin Sherin • *Scr* Arthur Heinemann, Ted Tally, from a story by Ted Tally

Father Dear Father ★★ U
Comedy 1972 · UK · Colour · 94mins
First shown in 1968, this enduring sitcom ran for some 40 episodes in all (although Patrick Cargill made another seven in a series shown exclusively in Australia). As with most film versions of popular TV shows, this lacks the cosy comic consistency of the original, even though it retains most of the cast and was directed by the series producer William G Stewart, now the frontman of Channel 4's quiz show *Fifteen to One*. Guest stars Beryl Reid, Donald Sinden and Richard O'Sullivan are given too little to do as novelist Cargill's marriage to his agent is jeopardised by his trouble-prone daughters. ▭

Patrick Cargill *Patrick Glover* • Natasha Pyne *Anna* • Ann Holloway *Karen* • Noel Dyson *Nanny* • Beryl Reid *Mrs Stoppard* • Donald Sinden *Philip* • Richard O'Sullivan *Richard* • Jack Watling *Bill Mossman* ■ *Dir* William G Stewart • *Scr* Johnnie Mortimer, from the TV series by Johnnie Mortimer, Brian Cooke

Father Goose ★★★ U
Comedy drama 1964 · US · Colour · 116mins
Cary Grant stars as a boozy beach bum caught up in Second World War heroics involving a gaggle of schoolgirls and their teacher, Leslie Caron. Grant is terrific, as ever, and his air of discomfort certainly helps the plot, but you have to wonder if a comedy about the Japanese invasion of the Pacific is actually a good idea. The Hollywood Academy thought so, and writers Peter Stone and Frank Tarloff won an Oscar for their screenplay. Also along for the ride are gruff Trevor Howard and, somewhat surprisingly in an acting role, the British grandfather of rock 'n' roll television, *Oh Boy!*'s Jack Good. ▭

Cary Grant *Walter Eckland* • Leslie Caron *Catharine Freneau* • Trevor Howard *Frank Houghton* • Stephanie Berrington *Elizabeth* • Jennifer Berrington *Harriet* • Jack Good *Stebbings* ■ *Dir* Ralph Nelson • *Scr* Frank Tarloff, Peter Stone, from the story *A Place of Dragons* by SH Barnett

Father Hood ★★ PG
Crime comedy 1993 · US · Colour · 91mins
An early low point in Patrick Swayze's career decline, this dislikeable family comedy is really only for diehard *Dirty Dancing* fans. Swayze is the supposedly loveable rogue who sets off on the adventure of a lifetime with his two young kids who have been languishing in horrid foster care. The tone veers unevenly between naturalistic drama and simple-minded slapstick, and not even a talented supporting cast (Halle Berry, Diane Ladd, Michael Ironside) can rescue this sinking ship. Contains some violence and swearing. ▭

Patrick Swayze *Jack Charles* • Halle Berry *Kathleen Mercer* • Sabrina Lloyd *Kelly Charles* • Brian Bonsall *Eddie Charles* • Michael Ironside *Jerry* • Diane Ladd *Rita* ■ *Dir* Darrell James Roodt • *Scr* Scott Spencer

Father of the Bride ★★★★ U
Comedy 1950 · US · BW · 88mins
Forget the Steve Martin/Diane Keaton 1991 remake, here's the timeless MGM original, based on Edward Streeter's bestseller, as Spencer Tracy and Joan Bennett give their daughter a smashing send-off. And since she's the lovely Elizabeth Taylor, who wouldn't? Director Vincente Minnelli keeps up a sprightly pace and gets the most out of Frances Goodrich and Albert Hackett's witty screenplay, handing the best lines on a platter to Tracy, who has seldom been better than here in the title role. His gnarled face is peerless when confronted with so much frustration, and his retelling of the events leading up to the debris that was once his home is a joy. This film was so successful that it inspired a sequel, *Father's Little Dividend*. ▭

Spencer Tracy *Stanley T Banks* • Joan Bennett *Ellie Banks* • Elizabeth Taylor *Kay Banks* • Don Taylor *Buckley Dunstan* • Billie Burke *Doris Dunstan* • Leo G Carroll *Mr Massoula* • Moroni Olsen *Herbert Dunstan* • Melville Cooper *Mr Tringle* ■ *Dir* Vincente Minnelli • *Scr* Albert Hackett, Francis Goodrich, from the novel by Edward Streeter

Father of the Bride ★★★ PG
Comedy 1991 · US · Colour · 100mins
The original 1950 marriage-go-round starring Spencer Tracy is given an amiable nineties work-out by the *Baby Boom* and *Private Benjamin* husband-and-wife team of Charles Shyer and Nancy Meyers. Steve Martin shines as usual playing the Tracy role of the anxious parent who can't find a single thing to like about his daughter's perfect fiancé, while continually counting the ceremony costs. Watch for his Tom Jones impersonation: it's a scream! Diane Keaton gives him sparkling back-up as the uncomplaining wife, but it's Martin Short who steals the entire movie as the camp wedding organiser. ▭ **DVD**

Steve Martin *George Banks* • Diane Keaton *Nina Banks* • Kimberley Williams *Annie Banks* • Kieran Culkin *Matty Banks* • George Newbern *Bryan MacKenzie* • Martin Short *Franck Eggelhoffer* • BD Wong *Howard Weinstein* ■ *Dir* Charles Shyer • *Scr* Nancy Meyers, Charles Shyer, from the film by Frances Goodrich, Albert Hackett, from the novel by Edward Streeter

Father of the Bride Part II ★★ PG
Comedy 1995 · US · Colour · 101mins
Far weaker in all departments than the heart-warming original 1991 film (itself a remake of the 1950 Spencer Tracy/ Elizabeth Taylor classic), this loose version of 1951's *Father's Little Dividend* is full of false emotion, lame humour and pointless details (the mystifying return of Martin Short's camp interior decorator for one). Steve Martin's peaceful life is upset this time by the simultaneous pregnancies of both his wife (Diane Keaton) and his new-married daughter (Kimberly Williams). Although flashes of Martin's comic genius occasionally shine through the syrupy script, the verbal comedy on offer is dim-witted and unfocused. ▭ **DVD**

Steve Martin *George Banks* • Diane Keaton *Nina Banks* • Martin Short *Franck Eggelhoffer* • Kimberley Williams *Annie Banks-MacKenzie* • George Newbern *Bryan MacKenzie* • Kieran Culkin *Matty Banks* • BD Wong *Howard Weinstein* ■ *Dir* Charles Shyer • *Scr* Nancy Meyers, Charles Shyer, from the film *Father's Little Dividend* by Albert Hackett, Frances Goodrich, from the characters created by Edward Streeter

Father, Son and the Mistress ★★
Comedy 1992 · US · Colour · 90mins
A contemporary comedy that fails to exploit its promising premise and doesn't deserve its distinguished cast. Jack Lemmon stars as a quirky millionaire who decides to bankrupt himself for the fun of starting over, while Talia Shire, best known for her roles in *The Godfather* and the *Rocky* movies, and for being Francis Ford Coppola's sister, plays the pampered wife whom he wants to teach a lesson. Lemmon can't give a bad performance, but this TV movie must rank as one of his least distinguished films. Contains swearing.

Jack Lemmon *Aram Katourian* • Talia Shire *Millie Katourian* • Jonathan Silverman *Michael* • Madeline Kahn *Billie* • Joanna Gleason *Irene* • George Wyner *Harry* • Dakin Matthews *Lenny* ■ *Dir* Jay Sandrich • *Scr* Stan Daniels

Father to Be ★★★
Comedy drama 1979 · Swe · Colour · 107mins
Those who sat through the Hugh Grant comedy *Nine Months* may have had enough of expectant father movies to last a lifetime. This Swedish film takes a different slant on the subject, as directed by Lasse Hallström, (of *ABBA the Movie* and *My Life as a Dog* fame). In the film's defence, it can be said that, through the use of live-action and animated daydreams, it does manage to be occasionally amusing before it goes off at a post-natal tangent. The big plus is Magnus Harenstam as the diligent father-to-be. In Swedish with English subtitles.

Magnus Harenstam *Bosse* • Anki Liden *Lena* • Micha Gabay *Bosse's pal* • Ulf Brunnberg *Bjorn* ■ *Dir/Scr* Lasse Hallström

Father Was a Fullback ★★
Comedy 1949 · US · BW · 78mins
One of those post-*Life with Father* movies, where the mother actually runs the household and the father manages to preserve his dignity and the illusion of being boss in his own home. Here, Maureen O'Hara rules the roost while Fred MacMurray buckles down on the gridiron as the football coach to a losing college team. Their extended family includes a very young Natalie Wood, a charming Betty Lynn, an irascible Thelma Ritter and crooner Rudy Vallee. Pleasant lightweight fare.

Fred MacMurray *George Cooper* • Maureen O'Hara *Elizabeth Cooper* • Betty Lynn *Connie Cooper* • Rudy Vallee *Mr Jessop* • Thelma Ritter *Geraldine* • Natalie Wood *Ellen Cooper* ■ *Dir* John M Stahl • *Scr* Aleen Leslie, Casey Robinson, Mary Loos, Richard Sale, from a play by Clifford Goldsmith

Fatherland ★★★ 15
Political drama
1986 · UK/Ger · Colour · 104mins

To borrow a footballing cliché, this is a film of two halves. The opening section is classic Ken Loach, even though the setting might be unfamiliar. Making his screen debut, Gerulf Pannach is suitably despondent as the liberated East German folk singer whose creativity dries up after he exchanges the political restrictions of the Communist bloc for the capitalist demands of his new American record label. But the fascinating case study of clashing cultures is disappointingly sacrificed for a thriller subplot, as Pannach goes in search of his missing father in England. An intense, intelligent drama, but ultimately an unfocused one. In German and English with subtitles. ▢

Gerulf Pannach *Drittemann* • Fabienne Babe *Emma* • Cristine Rose *Lucy* • Sigfrit Steiner *James Dryden* • Robert Dietl *Lawyer* • Heike Schrotter *Marita* • Stephan Samuel *Max* ■ *Dir* Ken Loach • *Scr* Trevor Griffiths

Fatherland ★★★ 15
Political thriller 1994 · US · Colour · 106mins

Fans of Robert Harris's bestseller were unanimous in denouncing this made-for-cable movie as a pale shadow of the page-turning original. But they would say that, wouldn't they? The audacious plot (which turns on the premise that Hitler is still in power 20 years after winning the war) remains as compelling as ever and its startling ingenuity atones for the occasional dip in tempo. Rutger Hauer and Miranda Richardson race against time to expose the Holocaust with admirable conviction, but it's Jean Marsh who steals the show with a disturbing cameo as a fanatical Nazi actress. It's not the book, but it's not bad, either. Contains violence and swearing. ▢

Rutger Hauer *Xavier March* • Miranda Richardson *Charlie Maguire* • Michael Kitchen *Max Jaeger* • Jean Marsh *Anna Von Hagen* • Peter Vaughan *Nebe* ■ *Dir* Christopher Menaul • *Scr* Stanley Weiser, Ron Hutchinson, from the novel by Robert Harris

Fathers and Sons ★★ 18
Melodrama 1992 · US · Colour · 95mins

Jeff Goldblum tries to make a go of this rather embarrassing project, to little avail. Max Fish (Goldblum) is a struggling alcoholic who tries to bond with his increasingly alienated teenage son, Ed (Rory Cochrane), a boy who is fascinated by dolphins and drugs in equal measure. Written and directed by Paul Mones, this is supposed to be a sensitive portrait of men trying to find themselves, but suffers from an overdose of sentimentality. ▢

Jeff Goldblum *Max Fish* • Rory Cochrane *Ed Fish* • Mitchell Marchand *Smiley* • Famke Janssen *Kyle* • Natasha Gregson Wagner *Lisa* • Ellen Greene *Judy* • Samuel L Jackson *Marshall* • Joie Lee *Lois* • Rosanna Arquette *Miss Athena* ■ *Dir/Scr* Paul Mones

A Father's Betrayal ★★★ 15
Drama 1997 · US · Colour · 87mins

Brian Dennehy both directs and stars in this high-quality, made-for-TV drama. He plays Ed Brannigan, a ruthless attorney slowly rebuilding his relationship with his estranged son (Reed Diamond). All that changes, however, when a friend of his son's (Alice Krige) accuses his father of raping her. Dennehy is in commanding form and his direction is equally dependable. He also draws good performances from a talented cast that includes Lynn Redgrave. Contains some violence.

Brian Dennehy *Ed Brannigan Sr* • Lynn Redgrave *Monica Brannigan* • Reed Diamond *Ed Brannigan Jr* • Alice Krige *Rebecca Daly* ■ *Dir* Brian Dennehy • *Scr* Joe Cacaci

Fathers' Day ★ 12
Comedy 1997 · US · Colour · 95mins

A surprisingly unfunny comedy (based on the French movie *Les Compères*) starring Billy Crystal and Robin Williams as two men who are both told by Nastassja Kinski that they are the father of her wayward missing teenage son, in an attempt to get them to help her find him. From the director of *Ghostbusters*, Ivan Reitman, this had the potential to be hilarious, but instead falls alarmingly flat thanks to a weak and jokeless script, which even the combined comedic talents of Williams and Crystal can't perk up. Disappointing. ▢

Robin Williams *Dale Putley* • Billy Crystal *Jack Lawrence* • Julia Louis-Dreyfus *Carrie Lawrence* • Nastassja Kinski *Collette Andrews* • Charlie Hofheimer *Scott Andrews* ■ *Dir* Ivan Reitman • *Scr* Lowell Ganz, Babaloo Mandel, from the film *Les Compères* by Francis Veber

Father's Doing Fine ★★★ U
Comedy 1952 · UK · Colour · 83mins

A certain bourgeois self-satisfaction permeates this superficial situation comedy, which is based on Noel Langley's stage farce *Little Lambs Eat Ivy*. However, such is the precision of Henry Cass's direction and the exuberance of the performances that it's difficult not to be sucked into this frantic world of scatterbrained daughters, disastrous share deals and crooked butlers. Seemingly a door can't open without a fresh crisis breezing in, but Heather Thatcher's ennobled widow takes it all in her stride, unlike Richard Attenborough's nerve-jangled father-to-be. The pace disguises the fact that the humour has dated somewhat, but there's rarely a dull moment.

Richard Attenborough *Dougall* • Heather Thatcher *Lady Buckering* • Noel Purcell *Shaughnessy* • George Thorpe *Dr Drew* • Diane Hart *Doreen* • Susan Stephen *Bicky* • Mary Germaine *Gerda* • Virginia McKenna *Catherine* • Sidney James *Taxi driver* ■ *Dir* Henry Cass • *Scr* Anne Burnaby, from the play *Little Lambs Eat Ivy* by Noel Langley

Father's Little Dividend ★★★ U
Comedy 1951 · US · BW · 81mins

Director Vincente Minnelli was reunited with Spencer Tracy, Joan Bennett, Elizabeth Taylor and Don Taylor for this sequel to their 1950 smash hit *Father of the Bride*. The dividend, of course, is a grandchild, which leads Tracy into dialogue of the "coochy, coochy, coo" variety. Minnelli shot the film in a remarkably rapid 22 days while the sets for the final ballet in *An American in Paris* were being constructed. The original was remade with Steve Martin and Diane Keaton in 1991, itself followed by a sequel based on the same premise. ▢

Spencer Tracy *Stanley Banks* • Joan Bennett *Ellie Banks* • Elizabeth Taylor *Kay Dunstan* • Don Taylor *Buckley Dunstan* • Billie Burke *Doris Dunstan* • Moroni Olsen *Herbert Dunstan* ■ *Dir* Vincente Minnelli • *Scr* Frances Goodrich, Albert Hackett, from the characters created by Edward Streeter

A Father's Revenge ★★ 15
Thriller 1987 · US · Colour · 92mins

Brian Dennehy can bring life to the most routine script and it's his presence that lifts this otherwise ordinary thriller. Frustrated at the lack of action taken by the authorities when his daughter is held hostage by terrorists, Dennehy decides to take the law into his own hands and recruits professional help to rescue her. There's solid enough support from Joanna Cassidy, Ron Silver and British actor Anthony Valentine, but sadly the script and the direction lack real punch. Contains some violence. ▢

Brian Dennehy *Paul Hobart* • Joanna Cassidy *Barbara Hobart* • Helen Patton *Karen Hobart* • Anthony Valentine *Peter Vickers* • Ron Silver *Max Greenwald* • Christopher M Ohrt *Wolfgang Becker* • Angus McInnes [Angus MacInnes] *Bud Patterson* ■ *Dir* John Herzfeld • *Scr* Mel Frohman, from a story by Mel Frohman, Tom Schulman

Fathom ★★★ U
Spoof spy adventure
1967 · UK · Colour · 100mins

Fresh from the success of their 1966 big-screen version of *Batman*, writer Lorenzo Semple Jr and director Leslie H Martinson came up with this sprightly spoof, which combines the frenetic pace of a crime caper with the flashiness of a Bond movie. Shifting from the search for a lost H-bomb trigger to a race for a priceless statuette, the plot is almost an irrelevance as agents Raquel Welch and Tony Franciosa hurtle around the Mediterranean in the company of such British stalwarts as Richard Briers and Ronald Fraser. Revelling in the sunny locations and the shenanigans, Welch gives one of her best performances in an often disappointing career.

Raquel Welch *Fathom Harvill* • Tony Franciosa [Anthony Franciosa] *Peter Merriweather* • Ronald Fraser *Douglas Campbell* • Greta Chi *Jo-May Soon* • Richard Briers *Timothy* ■ *Dir* Leslie H Martinson • *Scr* Lorenzo Semple Jr, from the novel by Larry Forrester

Fatso ★★
Comedy 1979 · US · Colour · 93mins

Anne Bancroft is such an attractively classy actress you'd expect her debut as feature director to be the same. Sadly, not. Following the death of an obese cousin, Dominick DiNapoli (Dom DeLuise) is trying to lose weight, hoping both to stay alive and impress Antoinette (Bancroft). The results are mawkish and crude, with enough jokes about excrement to fill a bucket. Bancroft should have known better, though she contributes a performance, to contrast with that of DeLuise, that is as elegant as the rest of the movie should have been.

Dom DeLuise *Dominick DiNapoli* • Anne Bancroft *Antoinette* • Ron Carey *Frankie* • Candice Azzara [Candy Azzara] *Lydia* • Michael Lombard *Charlie* ■ *Dir/Scr* Anne Bancroft

Faust ★★★★★
Classic silent fantasy
1926 · Ger · BW · 116mins

Adapted from Goethe, Marlowe and folklore, this is as much a masterpiece of design as a triumph for the director and his international cast. Inspired by the paintings of Caspar David Friedrich, Robert Herlth and Walter Röhrig brought all their Expressionist expertise to sculpting light, smoke and steam into the malevolent atmosphere that FW Murnau required for Faust's epic duel with Mephistopheles. Emil Jannings makes an imposing demon, Swedish star Gösta Ekman unassumingly transforms from decrepitude to youth and the untried Camilla Horn is suitably pure as the misused Marguerite (a role that was rejected by the great Lillian Gish).

Gösta Ekman (1) *Faust* • Emil Jannings *Mephistopheles* • Camilla Horn *Marguerite* • Frida Richard *Marguerite's mother* • Wilhelm Dieterle [Wilhelm Dieterle] *Valentin, Marguerite's brother* • Yvette Guilbert *Marthe Schwerdtlein, Marguerite's aunt* • Eric Barclay *Duke of Parma* • Hanna Ralph *Duchess of Parma* ■ *Dir* Friedrich W Murnau [FW Murnau] • *Scr* Hans Kyser, from the play *The Tragical History of Doctor Faustus* by Christopher Marlowe, from the writings *Faust: eine Tragödie* by Johann Wolfgang von Goethe • *Cinematographer* Carl Hoffman

Faust ★★★★★ 12
Animated drama
1994 · UK/Cz Rep/Fr · Colour · 92mins

Jan Svankmajer is the undisputed king of the puppet film, equally at ease with marionettes, claymation and stop-motion animation. His version of *Alice's Adventures in Wonderland* put a dark, disturbing slant on a much-loved fantasy, and here he succeeds in adding a chilling new dimension to the legend of *Faust*. Largely set inside a timelessly magical theatre in modern-day Prague, the mind-bending action is littered with surreal images, satirical asides and serious messages. Petr Cepek gives a remarkable performance, like Bob Hoskins in *Who Framed Roger Rabbit*, never once betraying the fact that his co-stars are inanimates. Beautiful, troubling, unmissable. ▢

Petr Cepek *Faust* • Andrew Sachs ■ *Dir/Scr* Jan Svankmajer

Fausto ★★ 15
Comedy drama 1992 · Fr · Colour · 78mins

In spite of an ebullient performance from Jean Yanne as a kindly, hunchbacked tailor, this fashion fantasy is as flimsy and improbable as the grass suits that make orphan Ken Higelin the toast of the catwalks. Set in 1965, this wry tale captures the eccentricity of the sixties quite well. But Higelin's rags-to-riches odyssey is devoid of conflict, and relies over-heavily on the talents of Higelin's corpulent pal, François Hauteserre, and his lusty relationship with garage owner's daughter, Florence Darel.

Optimistic, if naive, Rémy Duchemin's amiable debut will make you smile, but leave you feeling untouched. In French with English subtitles.

Jean Yanne *Mietek* • Ken Higelin *Fausto* • Florence Darel *Tonie* • François Hautesserre *Raymond* • Maurice Bénichou *Lucien* • Bruce Myers *Roger* • Marianne Groves *Myriam* ■ *Dir* Rémy Duchemin • *Scr* Richard Morgiève, Rémy Duchemin, from the novel by Richard Morgiève

The Favor ★★ 15
Romantic comedy
1994 · US · Colour · 93mins

The main point of interest in this misguided romantic comedy is the appearance of Brad Pitt, before he established himself as one of Hollywood's leading pin-ups. The starring role goes to Harley Jane Kozak, who gets involved in all sorts of entanglements when she sets up best friend Elizabeth McGovern with old flame Ken Wahl. The supporting cast, which includes Bill Pullman and Larry Miller, can't be faulted, but the script is short on decent gags and Donald Petrie's direction is clumsy. Contains swearing. 🖭

Harley Jane Kozak *Kathy* • Elizabeth McGovern *Emily* • Bill Pullman *Peter* • Brad Pitt *Elliott* • Larry Miller *Joe Dubin* • Ken Wahl *Tom Andrews* • Ginger Orsi *Gina* • Leigh Ann Orsi *Hannah* ■ *Dir* Donald Petrie • *Scr* Sara Parriot, Josann McGibbon

The Favour, the Watch and the Very Big Fish ★★ 15
Comedy 1991 · Fr/UK · Colour · 84mins

In this would-be surreal comedy, Bob Hoskins plays a photographer of religious tableaux involved with Natasha Richardson, who does orgiastic voice-overs for porn movies. When her ex-boyfriend (Jeff Goldblum) is released from jail, he agrees to pose for Hoskins as Christ, but the problems start when he tries to work miracles. Director Ben Lewin has a leaden approach to this Loony Toon-style farce, whose title whets the appetite. The execution, however, leaves a lot to be desired. 🖭

Bob Hoskins *Louis Aubinard* • Jeff Goldblum *Pianist* • Natasha Richardson *Sybil* • Michel Blanc *Norbert* • Jacques Villeret *Charles* • Angela Pleasence *Elizabeth* • Jean-Pierre Cassel *Zalman* ■ *Dir* Ben Lewin • *Scr* Ben Lewin, from the short story *Rue Saint-Sulpice* by Marcel Aymé

Fazil ★★
Silent romantic drama
1928 · US · BW · 88mins

Rudolph Valentino in *Son of the Sheik* inspired a flurry of exotic imitations, including this dated melodrama from the Fox studio, directed by Howard Hawks – his sixth silent movie. It features Charles Farrell (who became a star opposite Janet Gaynor in the classic *Seventh Heaven*) as a petulant Arab prince who meets a pretty Parisienne, played by Norwegian actress Greta Nissen, and whisks her off to marriage and Mecca. However her liberated European ways clash with Arab tradition and his visits to his harem. Apparently this was quite sexy for its time, but is now only of interest as an early piece from a great American director.

Charles Farrell *Prince Fazil* • Greta Nissen *Fabienne* • Mae Busch *Helene Debreuze* • Vadim Uraneff *Ahmed* • Tyler Brooke *Jacques Debreuze* • Eddie Sturgis *Rice* • Josephine Borio *Aicha* • John Boles *John Clavering* • John T Murray *Gondolier* ■ *Dir* Howard Hawks • *Scr* Seton I Miller, Philip Klein (adaptation), from the play *L'Insoumise* by Pierre Frondaie

Fear ★★★
Drama 1954 · It/W Ger · BW · 91mins

A German industrialist's wife, who had an affair while her husband was in a POW camp during the Second World War, finds herself blackmailed by her former lover's mistress. Ingrid Bergman stars in this German-Italian co-production, which marks the last of the six films she made with her writer/director husband, Roberto Rossellini, during her exile from Hollywood. A combination of psychological thriller and marital drama, the film, based on Stefan Zweig's *Der Angst*, is a rather lumbering affair but, thanks to the presence of the star, and the style of the director, it holds one's interest. In German with English subtitles.

Ingrid Bergman *Irene Wagner* • Mathias Wieman *Professor Albert Wagner* • Renate Mannhart *Joanna Schultze* • Kurt Kreuger *Heinz Baumann* • Elise Aulinger *Martha* ■ *Dir* Roberto Rossellini • *Scr* Roberto Rossellini, Sergio Amidei, Franz Graf Treuberg, from the novel *Der Angst* by Stefan Zweig

Fear ★★ 18
Crime action adventure
1988 · US · Colour · 91mins

Yet another therapy session for America on the Vietnam couch, it's just a shame the rest of us have to suffer. This one follows a tiresomely predictable course as a family are held hostage in their isolated cabin by a gang of escaped cons, one of whom is played by Frank Stallone, brother of the more famous Sly. Fellow con Robert Factor turns out to be a pscho, but luckily dad (Cliff De Young) shares his Vietnam background and fights back thanks to various ingenious booby traps. Debut director Robert A Ferretti does his best with a restrictive budget but, like the war itself, this is a lost cause. 🖭

Cliff De Young *Don Haden* • Kay Lenz *Sharon Haden* • Robert Factor *Jack Gracie* • Scott Schwartz *Brian Haden* • Geri Betzler *Jennifer Haden* • Frank Stallone *Robert Armitage* ■ *Dir* Robert A Ferretti • *Scr* Rick Scarry, Kathryn Connell, from a story by Robert A Ferretti

Fear ★★★ 18
Thriller 1990 · US · Colour · 90mins

This unusual thriller was originally made for cinema release, but, having failed to find a distributor, was premiered on American cable TV. Breaking with her girl-next-door image, ex-Brat Packer Ally Sheedy shows an unexpected steely side as a novelist who finds material for her bestsellers by using psychic powers to get inside the minds of serial killers. There's little in the way of mystery, but there's plenty of unnerving action as Sheedy pits her wits against a mind-reading murderer intent on adding her to his list of victims. Solid support comes from Lauren Hutton and John Agar, Shirley Temple's first husband. Contains violence and nudity. 🖭

Ally Sheedy *Cayce Bridges* • Lauren Hutton *Jessica Moreau* • Michael O'Keefe *Jack Hays* • Stan Shaw *Thomas Weber* • Dina Merrill *Catherine Tarr* • Dean Goodman *William Tarr* ■ *Dir/Scr* Rockne S O'Bannon

The Fear ★ 18
Horror 1995 · US · Colour · 101mins

A group of students are taken on an experimental "Coming to Terms with Fear" weekend only to find themselves being bumped off by Morty, the killer wooden mannequin, and confessor figure of sad student psychologist Eddie Bowz. A perfunctory attempt at *Elm Street*-style slasher horror with a paucity of imagination that, like the vengeful Morty himself, is in dire need of a further polish. For no discernible reason whatsoever, director Wes Craven makes a cameo appearance as Dr Arnold. 🖭

Eddie Bowz *Richard* • Leland Hayward *Vance* • Erick Weiss *Morty* • Vince Edwards *Uncle Pete* • Ann Turkel *Leslie* • Heather Medway *Ashley* • Darin Heames *Troy* • Wes Craven *Dr Arnold* ■ *Dir* Vincent Robert • *Scr* Ron Ford, from a story by Ron Ford, Greg H Sims

Fear ★★★ 18
Psychological thriller
1996 · US · Colour · 92mins

Would you trust Mark Wahlberg with your 16-year-old daughter? Of course you wouldn't! But when the Walker family first meet her latest date, they think he's a saint with a great body. Alas, he soon turns into the "Boyfriend from Hell" in director James Foley's tautly constructed, albeit predictable thriller. The plot may be contrived, and the mould seems familiar after *Single White Female* and *Fatal Attraction*. Yet Foley adds a few more complexities than usual, while an excellent cast (including William Petersen as the concerned father) brings credibility to the relationships in crisis. 🖭

Mark Wahlberg *David McCall* • Reese Witherspoon *Nicole Walker* • William Petersen *Steve Walker* • Amy Brenneman *Laura Walker* • Alyssa Milano *Margo Masse* ■ *Dir* James Foley • *Scr* Christopher Crowe

Fear and Desire ★
War drama 1953 · US · BW · 68mins

Stanley Kubrick believed his first feature – about a platoon of soldiers in an unspecified war fighting behind enemy lines – was "a serious effort, ineptly done", so he tried to suppress it. He was right to do so; for, despite some striking imagery, what wrecks the movie – made with money borrowed from relatives – are the uniformly terrible performances and the atrocious dialogue. The script, written by Kubrick and poet Howard O Sackler, includes a scene in which a girl is tied to a tree and lectured about the morality of war. But any chance to see an early work from one of the world's greatest film-makers should not be missed.

Frank Silvera *Mac* • Kenneth Harp *Lt Corby* • Virginia Leith *The Girl* • Paul Mazursky *Sidney* • Steve Coit *Fletcher* ■ *Dir* Stanley Kubrick • *Scr* Howard O Sackler, Stanley Kubrick

Fear and Loathing in Las Vegas ★★★ 18
Road movie 1998 · US · Colour · 118mins

Already a novel with a life of its own, this was perhaps a foolhardy venture, even for maverick director Terry Gilliam (who replaced Alex Cox in pre-production). Hunter S Thompson's distinctive prose proves unmalleable and, although Johnny Depp brings an eccentric energy to the role of gonzo journalist Raoul Duke, this brave film presents only the faintest impression of the book's vibrancy. Less a road movie than a tale of two "trippies", it admirably resists the temptation to go morph crazy. The pace is too fast to allow the audience to clamber on board, however, so one can only watch in bemused admiration as it zooms past. Contains drug abuse and swearing. 🖭

Johnny Depp *Raoul Duke* • Benicio Del Toro *Dr Gonzo* • Tobey Maguire *Hitchiker* • Ellen Barkin *North Star waitress* • Gary Busey *Highway patrolman* • Christina Ricci *Lucy* • Mark Harmon *Magazine reporter* • Cameron Diaz *Blonde TV reporter* • Lyle Lovett *Road person* ■ *Dir* Terry Gilliam • *Scr* Terry Gilliam, Tony Grisoni, Tod Davies, Alex Cox, from the novel by Hunter S Thompson

Fear, Anxiety, and Depression ★★
Comedy 1989 · US · Colour · 85mins

Those familiar with Todd Solondz's *Welcome to the Dollhouse* and *Happiness* won't be entirely surprised by the title of this earlier effort. The themes explored with so successfully in the later films are all bubbling away under the surface of this sober romance. Solondz plays Ira, the Woody Allen-esque hero on the unblinking lookout for love but finding only ugliness and disappointment in his choice of partner. This film suffers from an overdose of wackiness and is too forced to be entirely believable but look out for an early performance from Stanley Tucci (*Big Night*).

Todd Solondz *Ira Ellis* • Max Cantor *Jack* • Alexandra Gersten *Janice* • Jane Hamper *Junk* • Stanley Tucci *Donny* ■ *Dir/Scr* Todd Solondz

Fear City ★★★ 18
Crime drama 1984 · US · Colour · 91mins

Melanie Griffith makes an early appearance in this vivid, exploitatitive shocker from director Abel Ferrara (*The Bad Lieutenant*). The future star of *Working Girl* plays a stripper in mid-town Manhattan, helping out talent agent Tom Berenger just as a homicidal maniac is going about slaughtering professional striptease artists. Scenes of both straight and gay sex, not to mention the multiple murders, have a raw and visceral impact, and Ferrara turns up the heat with such expertise you rather wish he wouldn't. 🖭

Tom Berenger *Matt Rossi* • Billy Dee Williams *Al Wheeler* • Jack Scalia *Nicky Piacenza* • Melanie Griffith *Loretta* • Rossano Brazzi *Carmine* • Rae Dawn Chong *Leila* • Joe Santos *Frank* • Michael V Gazzo *Mike* ■ *Dir* Abel Ferrara • *Scr* Nicholas St John

Fear Eats the Soul
★★★★ 15

Romantic drama
1973 · W Ger · Colour · 89mins

Inspired by Douglas Sirk's *All That Heaven Allows* (1955), Rainer Werner Fassbinder's affecting film uses an unconventional love story to attack the prejudices inherent in German society in the early seventies. As the widowed cleaner and the Moroccan mechanic whose cross-cultural, age-gap romance is frowned upon by their family and friends, Brigitte Mira and El Hedi Ben Salem are so convincing it's easy to forget they are merely playing roles. Fassbinder also impresses as Mira's loathsome son-in-law, but it's the deceptive simplicity of his direction that elevates this incisive drama above the more popular period pieces of his later career. In German with English subtitles. ▭

Brigitte Mira *Emmi* ● El Hedi Ben Salem *Ali* ● Barbara Valentin *Barbara* ● Irm Hermann *Krista* ● Peter Gauhe *Bruno* ● Karl Scheydt *Albert* ● Rainer Werner Fassbinder *Eugen* ■ *Dir/Scr* Rainer Werner Fassbinder

Fear in the Night
★★★★

Film noir
1947 · US · BW · 72mins

This is the sort of B-movie that used to be called a "sleeper". A highly original thriller with a literally nightmarish quality, it is based on a book by *noir* specialist Cornell Woolrich (*Rear Window*), and the requisite *noir* elements of paranoia and uncertainty are evident in this tale of a man whose horrific dream seems to have truly taken place. The film's grip is maintained from the haunting opening, set in a room composed entirely of mirrored doors, and Jack Greenhalgh's stylised photography enhances the moody narrative. The hero is a suitably anguished DeForest Kelley, who would achieve fame many years later as Dr "Bones" McCoy in *Star Trek*. Director Maxwell Shane made the same story again, as *Nightmare*, in 1956.

Paul Kelly *Cliff Herlihy* ● DeForest Kelley *Vince Grayson* ● Ann Doran *Lil Herlihy* ● Kay Scott *Betty Winters* ● Robert Emmett Keane *Lewis* ● Jeff York *Torrence* ● Charles Victor *Capt Warner* ■ *Dir* Maxwell Shane ● *Scr* Maxwell Shane, from the short story *Nightmare* by William Irish [Cornell Woolrich]

Fear in the Night
★★★ 15

Drama
1972 · UK · Colour · 91mins

Recalling both *Les Diaboliques* and *Taste of Fear* – a 1961 Hammer horror, which was penned by this film's director Jimmy Sangster – this school chiller gets off to a cracking start with an eerie title sequence that concludes with a genuine shock. Peter Cushing, complete with an artificial arm and a genius for appearing when least expected, is on creepy form as a demented headmaster who plays sound effects records to re-create the atmosphere of his fire-damaged school. Judy Geeson is admirably ill at ease, while Ralph Bates and Joan Collins whip up some truly malevolent passion. More fun than frightening. Contains violence and swearing. ▭

Peter Cushing *Michael Carmichael* ● Joan Collins *Molly Carmichael* ● Ralph Bates *Robert* Heller ● Judy Geeson *Peggy Heller* ● James Cossins *Doctor* ■ *Dir* Jimmy Sangster ● *Scr* Jimmy Sangster, Michael Syson

Fear Is the Key
★★★ 15

Action thriller   1972 · UK · Colour · 100mins

A satisfying action thriller, based on an Alistair MacLean novel, with Barry Newman pursuing stolen jewels as well as vengeance for his wife and child who died aboard a hijacked plane. An excitingly staged car chase gets things off to a cracking start and Newman makes a convincingly hyped-up hero. It also marks the screen debut of Ben Kingsley, who was offered nothing else until *Gandhi* nearly ten years later. ▭

Barry Newman *John Talbot* ● Suzy Kendall *Sarah Ruthven* ● John Vernon *Vyland* ● Dolph Sweet *Jablonski* ● Ben Kingsley *Royale* ● Ray McAnally *Ruthven* ● Peter Marinker *Larry* ■ *Dir* Michael Tuchner ● *Scr* Robert Carrington, from the novel by Alistair MacLean

Fear No Evil
★★ 18

Supernatural horror
1980 · US · Colour · 94mins

In director Frank LaLoggia's ambitious feature debut, Lucifer is reincarnated as an American high school student who does battle with two archangels in disguise. The acting is on the amateurish side, and the story (based on the Book of Revelations) loses its way in some aimless subplots. Yet this is still a strangely affecting vision of low-budget armageddon whose punk rock soundtrack (The Ramones, Talking Heads, The Sex Pistols) is skilfully augmented by an elaborate symphonic score co-written by David Spear and LaLoggia. The latter went on to direct *Lady in White* (1988), an equally bizarre horror oddity. ▭

Stefan Arngrim *Andrew* ● Elizabeth Hoffman *Mikhail/Margaret Buchanan* ● Frank Birney *Father Daly* ● Kathleen Rowe McAllen *Gabrielle/Hulie* ● Daniel Eden *Tony* ● Jack Holland *Rafael/Father Damon* ● Barry Cooper *Mr Williams* ■ *Dir/Scr* Frank LaLoggia

Fear of a Black Hat ★★★ 15

Spoof documentary
1992 · US · Colour · 81mins

Sampling freely from Rob Reiner's cult heavy metal comedy, this music-biz spoof could have been retitled "This Is Spinal Rap". Although it treads warily in places, the script scores countless direct hits as it follows the career of the rapping trio NWH (Niggaz with Hats). The blurred line between commercial success and social protest, the ludicrous press conference generalisations and the intrigues among the entourage are all keenly observed. Even the band members' names are spot on – Tone-Def, Tasty Taste and Ice Cold. But the music can't hold a candle to the cod anthems of the mighty *Tap*. Contains sex scenes, swearing and nudity. ▭

Mark Christopher Lawrence *Tone Def* ● Larry B Scott *Tasty Taste* ● Rusty Cundieff *Ice Cold* ● Kasi Lemmons *Nina Blackburn* ● Howie Gold *Guy Friesh* ● G Smokey Campbell *First backstage manager* ■ *Dir/Scr* Rusty Cundieff

Fear of Fear
★★★★

Psychological drama
1976 · W Ger · Colour · 88mins

Comfortable conformity is cited as the first sign of madness in this little-known film from Rainer Werner Fassbinder, originally made for television. Shot with a measured intensity, Margit Carstensen's slow decline into misery is charted with the apprehensive potency of a thriller. Will she commit suicide like her dishevelled neighbour? Or will she reconcile herself to her bourgeois ordinariness and resume her life without recourse to adulterous affairs or chemical solace? Refusing to provide any easy solutions, this makes for challenging viewing, but its pull is irresistible.

Margit Carstensen *Margot* ● Ulrich Faulhaber *Kurt* ● Brigitte Mira *Mother* ● Irm Hermann *Lore* ● Armin Meier *Karli* ● Adrian Hoven *Dr Merck* ● Kurt Raab *Herr Bauer* ● Ingrid Caven *Edda* ● Lilo Pempeit *Mrs Schall* ■ *Dir* Rainer Werner Fassbinder ● *Scr* Rainer Werner Fassbinder, from a idea by Asta Scheib ● *Cinematographer* Jürgen Jüges, Ulrich Prinz

Fear on Trial
★★★★

Drama based on a true story
1975 · US · Colour · 100mins

One of the best TV movies, telling the tragic true story of television personality John Henry Faulk, who fell victim to the McCarthyite blacklist in the fifties and, with his career ruined, decided to sue for libel. William Devane gives a moving performance as Faulk and George C Scott is magnificent as his lawyer Louis Nizer. This riveting saga is expertly told by director Lamont Johnson and writer David W Rintels, working from Faulk's autobiography. TV producers David Susskind and Mark Goodson play themselves, and Bruce Geller, the creator of TV series *Mission: Impossible*, plays his real-life father, the presiding judge in the case. It's a subject seldom touched on by TV since many still working in the medium have no cause to be proud of their pasts.

George C Scott *Louis Nizer* ● William Devane *John Henry Faulk* ● Dorothy Tristan *Laura Faulk* ● William Redfield *Stan Hopp* ● Bruce Geller *Judge Abraham N Geller* ● David Susskind ● Mark Goodson ■ *Dir* Lamont Johnson ● *Scr* David W Rintels, from an autobiography by John Henry Faulk

Fear Stalk
★★ 18

Thriller   1989 · US · Colour · 92mins

Jill Clayburgh, received two Oscar nominations in the late seventies for *An Unmarried Woman* and *Starting Over*, yet her career never quite lived up to that early promise. In this made-for-TV movie she adds much-needed class to the story of a TV producer in peril from a stranger who starts to take over her life. In every other department, this is a conventional but moderately entertaining thriller. ▭

Jill Clayburgh *Alexandra "Ally" Maynard* ● Stephen Macht *Tom Hagar* ● Lynne Thigpen *Barbara Ivanello* ● Sandy McPeak *Det Richard Danning* ● Sada Thompson *Pearl* ● Mary Ellen Trainor *Jennifer* ● Lorna Luft *Doris* ■ *Dir* Larry Shaw ● *Scr* Ellen Weston

Fear Strikes Out
★★★★

Biographical sports drama
1957 · US · BW · 102mins

Director Robert Mulligan's feature film debut is a harrowing and intense biopic of Boston Red Sox baseball star Jim Piersall, superbly portrayed by Anthony Perkins, whose later mannerisms are held well in check as he movingly conveys Piersall's breakdown. Karl Malden has a tendency to over-emote but under Mulligan's direction, he gives a fine performance as the over-ambitious father, whose behaviour had such a devastating impact on his son. This is a touching and tragic tale, beautifully photographed in stunning black-and-white VistaVision by Haskell Boggs, and featuring a fine early score from Elmer Bernstein. This first movie from the director/producer partnership of Robert Mulligan and Alan J Pakula would be responsible for a series of remarkable movies (including *To Kill a Mockingbird*) before Pakula himself moved into directing.

Anthony Perkins *Jimmy Piersall* ● Karl Malden *John Piersall* ● Norma Moore *Mary Teevan* ● Adam Williams *Dr Brown* ● Perry Wilson *Mrs John Piersall* ● Peter Votrian *Jimmy Piersall as a boy* ● Dennis McMullen *Phil* ■ *Dir* Robert Mulligan ● *Scr* Ted Berkman, Raphael Blau, from the autobiography by James A Piersall, Albert S Hirshberg

Fearless
★★★ 15

Drama   1993 · US · Colour · 116mins

Containing sequences of astonishing power, this is an intense drama about the pain of loss and the stress of surviving a near-death experience. Director Peter Weir has spent his career studying people trapped in unfamiliar environments, but here plane-crash survivor Jeff Bridges is a stranger to his own self. Unfortunately, the film struggles to live up to its breathtaking opening, and neither the heartrending scenes between Bridges and Oscar-nominated fellow survivor Rosie Perez nor his exchanges with incomprehending wife Isabella Rossellini are quite as compelling. Still, it remains a painful reminder of just how fragile life really is. Contains violence and swearing. ▭

Jeff Bridges *Max Klein* ● Isabella Rossellini *Laura Klein* ● Rosie Perez *Carla Rodrigo* ● Tom Hulce *Brillstein* ● Dir Bill Perlman ● Benicio Del Toro *Manny Rodrigo* ● Deirdre O'Connell *Nan Gordon* ● John de Lancie *Jeff Gordon* ■ *Dir* Peter Weir ● *Scr* Rafael Yglesias, from his novel

The Fearless Vampire Killers
★★★★ 12

Horror comedy   1967 · US · Colour · 103mins

Want to know where *Interview with the Vampire* found most of its best ideas? Look no further than Roman Polanski's lyrical exploration of undead myths, poised on the knife edge of Hammer nightmare and *Carry On* farce, that's eerie, funny, scary and brilliantly baroque. Polanski's astoundingly beautiful tour de force features two genre firsts – a Jewish vampire unaffected by the crucifix and a gay vampire – plus his ill-fated wife-to-be Sharon Tate in her best role. Worth seeing for the breathtaking ballroom mirror sequence alone. ▭

Jack MacGowran *Professor Abronsius* • Roman Polanski *Alfred* • Alfie Bass *Shagal* • Jessie Robins *Mrs Shagal* • Sharon Tate *Sarah Shagal* • Ferdy Mayne *Count Von Krolock* • Iain Quarrier *Herbert Von Krolock* • Terry Downes *Koukol* ■ *Dir* Roman Polanski • *Scr* Gerald Brach, Roman Polanski

The Fearmakers ★

Political drama 1958 · US · BW · 84mins

This preposterous right-wing melodrama has Dana Andrews returning to his Washington-based public relations firm only to find that his partner has mysteriously disappeared. The agency has been taken over by communists, whose agenda includes rigging opinion polls and promoting an end to the Cold War. The film's xenophobia extends to pointing out that a French architect's design makes the Pentagon vulnerable to aerial attack, while the statue of Abe Lincoln beams approvingly on the triumph of 100 per cent Americanism. It's a demeaning assignment for a talented director, Jacques Tourneur, who had previously collaborated with Dana Andrews on *Night of the Demon.*

Dana Andrews *Alan Eaton* • Dick Foran *Jim McGinnis* • Mel Tormé *Barney Bond* • Marilee Earle *Lorraine Dennis* • Veda Ann Borg *Vivian Loder* • Kelly Thordsen *Harold Loder* ■ *Dir* Jacques Tourneur • *Scr* Elliot West, Chris Appley, from a novel by Darwin L Teilhet

A Feast at Midnight ★★ PG

Comedy 1995 · UK · Colour · 106mins

Recalling the golden age of children's heroes Bunter and Jennings, this is a nostalgic fantasy on the cruelty and cameraderie of public school life. Unfortunately, the style adopted by director Justin Hardy harks back to another bygone era, that of the Children's Film Foundation. Stereotypes abound as Freddie Findlay attempts to win over the bullies by starting the secret "Scoffers Society"; its aim is to sample culinary delights denied them by the strict health food regime imposed by headmaster Robert Hardy. Completing this familiar rites of passage recipe is a little romance; Findlay dotes on Lisa Faulkner's character, daughter of stern Latin master Christopher Lee. [VIDEO]

Freddie Findlay *Magnus* • Aled Roberts *Goof* • Andrew Lusher *Tava* • Christopher Lee *Longfellow (Raptor)* • Robert Hardy *Headmaster* • Sam West [Samuel West] *Chef* • Lisa Faulkner *Miss Charlotte* • Edward Fox *Magnus's father* ■ *Dir* Justin Hardy • *Scr* Justin Hardy, Yoshi Nishio

Feast of July ★★ 15

Romantic period drama
1995 · UK · Colour · 111mins

The title promises a feast, but this melancholy story set in 1890s England offers slim pickings. Embeth Davidtz plays a young woman deserted by her lover (Greg Wise) who is taken in by a rural family, headed by Tom Bell. There she befriends his three sons and, when two of them go to war, falls for the youngest – simple-minded Con (Ben Chaplin) – with whom she enjoys limited happiness. Christopher Menaul directs this Merchant-Ivory production, adapted from the novel by HE Bates, with an inappropriate emphasis on melodramatic flourishes. [VIDEO]

Embeth Davidtz *Bella Ford* • Tom Bell *Ben Wainwright* • Gemma Jones *Mrs Wainwright* • James Purefoy *Jedd Wainwright* • Ben Chaplin *Con* • Kenneth Anderson *Matty Wainwright* • Greg Wise *Arch Wilson* ■ *Dir* Christopher Menaul • *Scr* Christopher Neame, from the novel by HE Bates

Federal Hill ★★★

Drama 1994 · US · BW · 100mins

BOYZ N the Hood Italian-style, as a gang of Rhode Island punks struggle to make sense of their lives as they hurtle down a drug-fuelled, self-destructive path. Nicholas Turturro (John's younger brother) stars as a jewel thief who specialises in random violence with his gang. Independent film-maker Michael Corrente's cutting edge black-and-white effort infuses the *Mean Streets* genre with a new raw, raucous and insightful energy helped enormously by a powerhouse performance from Turturro as a screwed-up psycho thief.

Nicholas Turturro *Ralph* • Anthony DeSando *Nicky* • Libby Langdon *Wendy* • Michael Raynor *Frank* • Jason Andrews *Bobby* • Robert Turano *Joey* ■ *Dir/Scr* Michael Corrente

Fedora ★★★★ PG

Drama 1978 · W Ger/Fr · Colour · 108mins

This is director Billy Wilder's bittersweet tale about a fabled, Garbo-esque star of the thirties who appears to have the secret of youth and lives in seclusion in Corfu. William Holden, the hero of Wilder's *Sunset Boulevard*, is the independent producer who worms his way into Fedora's secret and tries to coax her out of retirement. Yes, there are flaws and some unintentional laughs – Michael York as a living screen legend? – but this is also a richly comic, deeply melancholy movie, enriched by Wilder's long perspective on the picture business. It is both Holden and Wilder who explain their career problems: "the kids with beards have taken over," meaning Francis Ford Coppola and George Lucas. And when Henry Fonda pops up to present Fedora with an Oscar and says, "Hello, I'm Henry Fonda," movie fans everywhere will dissolve in tears. [VIDEO]

William Holden (1) *Barry Detweiler* • Marthe Keller *Fedora* • José Ferrer *Dr Vando* • Hildegarde Neff *Countess Sobryanski* • Frances Sternhagen *Miss Balfour* • Michael York • Henry Fonda ■ *Dir* Billy Wilder • *Scr* Billy Wilder, I AL Diamond, from the novel *Crowned Heads* by Thomas Tryon

Feds ★★ 15

Comedy 1988 · US · Colour · 79mins

Rebecca De Mornay who went on to give a searching, scorching performance in *The Hand That Rocks the Cradle* had already made an unimpressive living playing anaemic, pretty blondes. In the light of that success, *Feds* is one film she'll be happy to forget. As one of two female students who are aspiring FBI agents, she encounters male prejudice on a grand scale. All comic efforts in this direction seem to delight in the obvious, yet De Mornay herself has the right, light touch. Contains violence and swearing. [VIDEO]

Rebecca De Mornay *Ellie Dewitt* • Mary Gross *Janis Zuckerman* • Ken Marshall *Brent Sheppard* • Fred Dalton Thompson *Bill Belecki* • Larry Cedar *Howard Butz* • James Luisi *Sperry* • Raymond Singer *Hupperman* ■ *Dir* Dan Goldberg • *Scr* Len Blum, Dan Goldberg

A Feel for Murder ★★★ 18

Psychological thriller
1995 · US · Colour · 90mins

Also known as *Sketch Artist II: Hands That See*, this TV-movie sequel sees Jeff Fahey return as one of those bods who produce the artist's impressions for the police that you see on the news and that usually bear little resemblance to the actual suspect. In this case accuracy doesn't matter, because rape victim Courteney Cox (of *Friends* fame) is blind and this makes bringing the culprit to justice all the more tricky. An improvement on the first film in regard to plot, if not in terms of casting, as the support team here is no substitute for the presence of Sean Young and Drew Barrymore in the original. Contains swearing, violence and nudity. [VIDEO]

Jeff Fahey *Jack Whitfield* • Courteney Cox *Emmy* • Michael Nicolosi *Rothko* • Jonathan Silverman *Glenn O'Conner* • Michael Beach *George* • Scott Burkholder *Zia* ■ *Dir* Jack Sholder • *Scr* Michael Angeli

Feeling Minnesota ★★ 18

Romantic comedy drama
1996 · US · Colour · 94mins

A quirky, low-budget comedy drama, with Cameron Diaz as the bride who ditches her husband-to-be (Vincent D'Onofrio) on her wedding day to run off with his estranged, wayward brother (Keanu Reeves), only to have her fiancé and an assortment of heavies come after them. Amusingly odd rather than hilariously funny – and with a liberal splattering of violence and bad language – this has its moments, but is perhaps of most appeal to fans of the two leads. Contains swearing, violence and sex scenes. [VIDEO]

Keanu Reeves *Jjaks* • Vincent D'Onofrio *Sam* • Cameron Diaz *Freddie* • Delroy Lindo *Red* • Courtney Love *Rhonda, the waitress* • Tuesday Weld *Nora* • Dan Aykroyd *Ben* • Levon Helm *Bible Salesman* ■ *Dir/Scr* Steven Baigelman

Feet First ★★ U

Comedy 1930 · US · BW · 69mins

Harold Lloyd raids his own gag store to refloat this feeble comedy after it runs aground during an over-long sea voyage. Stowing away on a Honolulu liner to press his romantic suit with Barbara Kent, Lloyd's timid go-getter gets himself trapped in a mail sack, which just happens to land on a builder's hoist outside a skyscraper. Although much of the high-rise slapstick that follows is borrowed from *Safety Last*, the business with the gyrating fire hose is both inspired and hilarious. However, it comes too late to save a picture hamstrung by Lloyd's evident discomfort with dialogue. [VIDEO]

Harold Lloyd *Harold Horne* • Robert McWade *John Tanner* • Lillianne Leighton *Mrs Tanner* • Barbara Kent *Mary* • Alec Francis [Alec B Francis] *Old timer* • Noah Young *Ship's officer* • Henry Hall (1) *Endicott* • Arthur Housman *Drunken clubman* ■ *Dir* Clyde Bruckman • *Scr* Felix Adler, Lex Neal, Paul Gerard Smith, from a story by John Grey, Alfred A Cohn, Clyde Bruckman

Felicia's Journey ★★★★ 12

Psychological thriller
1999 · UK/Can · Colour · 111mins

Pretty Irish innocent Felicia, made pregnant by a British soldier, travels to Birmingham to find her lover. There she is befriended by Hilditch, a factory catering manager and portly serial killer of young girls. All the tabloid elements of a lurid thriller are here, but Canadian director Atom Egoyan avoids the obvious in his adaptation of William Trevor's novel. The result is a small masterpiece of atmosphere and insight that reveals the extraordinary in the everyday, with performances by Elaine Cassidy (as shy but resilient Felicia) and Bob Hoskins (the creepy, mother-fixated Hilditch) that transform the story into a scary fairy tale. Egoyan has called his film "anti-Hitchcockian", and it certainly lacks the Master's thrills. However, it has a rewarding sense of alarm and disquiet that is all its own. [VIDEO] DVD

Bob Hoskins *Hilditch* • Elaine Cassidy *Felicia* • Claire Benedict *Miss Calligary* • Brid Brennan *Mrs Lysaght* • Peter McDonald *Johnny* • Gerard McSorley *Felicia's father* • Arsinée Khanjian *Gala* ■ *Dir* Atom Egoyan • *Scr* Atom Egoyan, from the novel by William Trevor

Felix the Cat: the Movie ★ U

Animated fantasy 1989 · US · Colour · 78mins

Felix the Cat made his debut as an animated short as far back as 1919, but this attempt to update the feline hero for a new generation is a monumental clanger and an insult to kids with even the merest of imaginations. Surrealism abounds as Felix goes on a quest to rescue a princess, encountering Mizards (mice with bodies of lizards) and a rhinoceros on a tightrope. The bland storyline is matched by uninspired animation which robs the character of all its period charm. This never looks like anything other than a TV cartoon padded out to feature length. [VIDEO]

Chris Phillips • Maureen O'Connell • Peter Neuman • Alice Playten • Susan Montanaro • Don Oriolo ■ *Dir* Tibor Hernadi • *Scr* Don Oriolo, Pete Brown, from a story and cartoon character created by Don Oriolo

Fellini's Roma ★★★

Experimental comedy documentary
1972 · It/Fr · Colour · 117mins

Posing as a documentary, this mix of memories, fantasies and idle musings confirms Federico Fellini's visual genius, while also exposing his reckless lack of intellectual rigour. Beginning with youthful impressions of the Eternal City gained from his home town of Rimini, Fellini recalls people and place as the fancy takes him (hence the film's much-criticised shapelessness). Whether reminiscing or chatting to the likes of Marcello Mastroianni, Anna Magnani and Gore Vidal, he makes a companionable, if occasionally overbearing guide. But it's the forties music-hall show, the unearthing of an ancient villa and the clerical fashion parade that reveal the maverick maestro close to his best. An Italian language film.

Federico Fellini • Peter Gonzales *Fellini, age 18* • Stefano Mayore *Fellini as a child* • Pia

De Doses *Princess* • Renato Giovanneli *Cardinal Ottaviani* • Fiona Florence *Young prostitute* • Anna Magnani • Gore Vidal • Marcello Mastroianni ■ *Dir* Federico Fellini • *Scr* Federico Fellini, Bernardino Zapponi

Fellow Traveller ★★★ 15
Political drama
1989 · UK/US · Colour · 97mins

The title refers to someone with Communist sympathies, and the film (partly financed by British television) deals with that terrible time in Hollywood when the blacklist was in force, a serious subject only rarely tackled by Hollywood itself – *The Front, Guilty by Suspicion*, and *The Way We Were*. The astute screenplay by Michael Eaton uses that favourite Hollywood device, that of two chums whose professional paths vary considerably. A genuinely political film, directed (by the under-rated Philip Saville) in anger, and played to perfection by a cast that includes Ron Silver, Hart Bochner and Daniel J Travanti. The look and feel of the fifties, and in particular the early birth pangs of commercial television in England are beautifully conjured up, and you'll never view Richard Greene's *The Adventures of Robin Hood* TV series in quite the same way again. Only the Imogen Stubbs character doesn't really work. ▣

Ron Silver *Asa Kaufman* • Imogen Stubbs *Sarah Aitchison* • Daniel J Travanti *Jerry Leavy* • Hart Bochner *Clifford Byrne* • Katherine Borowitz *Joan Kaufman* • Julian Fellowes *D'Arcy* • Richard Wilson *Sir Hugo Armstrong* ■ *Dir* Philip Saville • *Scr* Michael Eaton

Female ★★★
Romantic comedy drama
1933 · US · BW · 65mins

A splendid starring vehicle for the largely forgotten Ruth Chatterton, this comedy/drama presents her as an intelligent and liberated female who runs a car manufacturing company and seduces the better-looking male employees for amorous relief. Her astonishing mansion marks an early screen appearance for Frank Lloyd Wright's Ennis House in the Hollywood Hills. Skilfully directed by Michael Curtiz – with uncredited assistance from William A Wellman, the film rapidly loses conviction when dreary George Brent (Chatterton's real-life husband at the time) comes along and is supposed to bowl her over.

Ruth Chatterton *Alison Drake* • George Brent *Jim Thorne* • Lois Wilson *Harriet* • Johnny Mack Brown *George C Cooper* • Ruth Donnelly *Miss Frothingham* • Ferdinand Gottschalk *Pettigrew* • *Dir* Michael Curtiz • *Scr* Gene Markey, Kathryn Scola, from the novel by Donald Henderson Clarke

The Female Animal ★
Romantic drama
1958 · US · BW · 82mins

Saved from a serious injury by handsome George Nader, movie star Hedy Lamarr moves him into her beach house as both caretaker and lover. It's only a matter of time before her adopted daughter Jane Powell falls for him, too, as does former actress Jan Sterling. This inept and dreary movie is pulp melodrama of the worst kind, the sole attraction being a late-career look at Lamarr, famed for her extraordinary

beauty and brains, but – on this evidence – not her acting skills.

Hedy Lamarr *Vanessa Windsor* • Jane Powell *Penny Windsor* • Jan Sterling *Lily Frayne* • George Nader *Chris Farley* ■ *Dir* Harry Keller • *Scr* Robert Hill, from a story by Albert Zugsmith

The Female Bunch ★ 18
Drama
1969 · US · Colour · 80mins

Women's Lib meets Russ Meyer-style sexploitation in this insane movie shot at the Spahn ranch, a disused film set occupied by the Manson "family" around the time of the notorious murders. "Their law is the whip" ran the ad line about this group of man-hating women living on a secluded farm who run drugs across the Mexican border. You'd think a movie filled with bouts of lesbianism, drug-taking, nudity, sadism and *tom thumb* actor Russ Tamblyn having his face branded would be fun – wrong! And spare a thought for poor old Lon Chaney Jr in his last ever role as a hired hand. At least Al Adamson retains his record for making truly diabolical movies. Would you watch *Horror of the Blood Monsters* unless you really had to? As a grisly footnote Adamson was himself murdered at his Californian home in 1995. ▣

Russ Tamblyn *Bill* • Jennifer Bishop *Grace* • Lon Chaney Jr *Monty* • Nesa Renet *Sandy* • Geoffrey Land *Jim* • Regina Carrol *Waitress* ■ *Dir* Al Adamson, John Cardos • *Scr* Jale Lockwood, Brent Nimrod, from a story by Raphael Nussbaum

The Female Jungle ★
Crime drama
1955 · US · BW · 72mins

Lawrence Tierney stars as a police sergeant found drunk at the scene of an actress's murder in this below average "you won't care" whodunit, that's mainly of interest because it features the first significant film role of fifties sex bomb Jayne Mansfield. She was only paid $150 for her performance, but it typecast her as the dumb blonde/nymphomaniac for the rest of her tragically short life.

Lawrence Tierney *Sergeant Stevens* • John Carradine *Claude Almstead* • Jayne Mansfield *Candy Price* • Burt Kaiser *Alec Voe* • Kathleen Crowley *Peggy Voe* • James Kodl *Joe* ■ *Dir* Bruno VeSota • *Scr* Bruno VeSota, Burt Kaiser

Female on the Beach ★★
Crime drama
1955 · US · BW · 96mins

Joan Crawford plays a widow who moves in to a beach house and quickly falls in love with Jeff Chandler, who may have murdered the previous occupant. Like her previous hit, *Sudden Fear*, this successful melodrama kept Crawford's career moving, gave her some great opportunities to model some beachwear and to deliver some hilarious dialogue – "I wouldn't take you if you were covered in diamonds – upside down," she tells Chandler after a tiff. Things get pretty steamy towards the end, but the final product is silly rather than sexy.

Joan Crawford *Lynn Markham* • Jeff Chandler *Drummond Hall* • Jan Sterling *Amy Rawlinson* • Cecil Kellaway *Osbert Sorenson* • Judith Evelyn *Eloise Crandall* • Natalie Schafer

Queenie Sorenson ■ *Dir* Joseph Pevney • *Scr* Robert Hill, Richard Alan Simmons, from the play *The Besieged Heart* by Robert Hill

Female Perversions ★★ 18
Drama
1996 · US/Ger · Colour · 108mins

Susan Streitfeld makes her directorial debut with this raunchy by nature drama based on an analytical book by feminist Louise J Kaplan. Eve (Tilda Swinton) is a high-powered lawyer with judicial aspirations, who is outwardly a model of femininity but is plagued by neuroses. She has a stormy relationship with her sister Madelyn (Amy Madigan), a compulsive shoplifter. Secrets are unravelled and kit is taken off, but despite the promise of something interesting to come, it never actually arrives as Streitfeld gets bogged down in her own pretentiousness and symbolism. Disappointing. Contains swearing, sex scenes and some violence. ▣

Tilda Swinton *Evelyn "Eve" Stephens* • Amy Madigan *Madelyn Stephens* • Karen Sillas *Renee* • Frances Fisher *Annunciata* • Laila Robins *Emma* • Paulina Porizkova *Langley Flynn* ■ *Dir* Susan Streitfeld • *Scr* Susan Streitfeld, Julie Hebert, from the non-fiction book *Female Perversions: the Temptations of Emma Bovary* by Louise J Kaplan

Female Trouble ★★★★ 18
Underground satirical melodrama
1974 · US · Colour · 93mins

Along with *Pink Flamingos*, this is the film that gained cult director John Waters his trophy for spectacularly redefining melodrama. A twisted parallel of *Mildred Pierce*, it features the unreachably tawdry transvestite Divine on a perverse quest for self-realisation at whatever cost, following a disastrous Christmas morning in which her parents fail to deliver the requested cha-cha heels. The squeamish solo delivery of her baby is the first scene in what turns out to be a true mother-and-daughter-from-hell scenario, with Mink Stole in hyper tantrum mode as the insufferable brat Taffy. Waters's disregard for the genteel is in full force throughout, with the overflowing Edith Massey (a sight for sore eyes in her black satin catsuit) grossly endearing in a category of acting all her own. Those with a sensitive disposition be warned: this is an unhinged celebration of bad taste. ▣

Divine *Dawn Davenport/Earl Peterson* • David Lochary *Donald Dasher* • Mary Vivian Pearce *Donna Dasher* • Mink Stole *Taffy Davenport* • Edith Massey *Aunt Ida Nelson* • Cookie Mueller *Concetta* • Susan Walsh *Chiclet* • Michael Potter *Gater* ■ *Dir/Scr* John Waters

The Female Vampire ★
Erotic horror
1973 · Fr/Bel/Por · Colour · 90mins

More ponderous and artlessly shot sex and violence from the Ed Wood of Spain, Jesus Franco. In this ludicrous vampire tale, Franco favourite Lina Romay stars as a countess who seduces all and sundry with an unusual oral technique and shares a telepathic link with an Austrian novelist on holiday in Madeira. Franco dwells on badly executed bloodsucking, crass nudity and pointless zooms as if they

were going out of style. Which, of course, at the time they were. Yet this turned out to be one of his most popular poverty-row quickies. Contains violence, sex scenes and nudity.

Lina Romay *Countess Irina Karlstein* • Jack Taylor *Baron Von Rathony* • Jesus Franco *Roberts* • Jean-Pierre Bouyxou *Dr Orloff* ■ *Dir/Scr* Jesus Franco

The Feminine Touch ★★★
Comedy
1941 · US · BW · 97mins

This entertaining Rosalind Russell comedy vehicle has a knockout central idea: Russell is the wife of writer Don Ameche, who's just penned a book on jealousy, and she thinks he's fooling around with the lovely Kay Francis. Well, who wouldn't? There's lots of MGM gloss, and star-to-be Van Heflin in sterling support as the publisher who has his eye on Russell. Director Woody Van Dyke II piles on the pace, and the cast simply couldn't be more glamorous – watch how both Francis and Russell are exquisitely back-lit, and not just in their close-ups.

Rosalind Russell *Julie Hathaway* • Don Ameche *John Hathaway* • Kay Francis *Nellie Woods* • Van Heflin *Elliott Morgan* • Donald Meek *Captain Makepeace Liveright* • Gordon Jones *Rubber-legs Ryan* ■ *Dir* WS Van Dyke II [WS Van Dyke] • *Scr* George Oppenheimer, Edmund L Hartmann, Ogden Nash

The Feminine Touch ★★ U
Romantic drama
1956 · UK · Colour · 91mins

Also known in the USA as *The Gentle Touch*, this mediocre drama was among the last batch of films made at the famous Ealing Studios. Director Pat Jackson had made his name with realistic docudramas during the Second World War, but this tale of trainee nurses was a far cry from his earlier hospital picture *White Corridors*. Diana Wynyard stands out as Matron, but the few girls we follow are a pretty tepid bunch, struggling with rather too familiar personal and professional traumas. George Baker's romance with Belinda Lee also does little to enliven the proceedings.

George Baker *Dr Jim Alcott* • Belinda Lee *Susan Richards* • Delphi Lawrence *Pat Martin* • Adrienne Corri *Maureen O'Brien* • Henryetta Edwards *Ann Bowland* • Barbara Archer *Liz Jenkins* • Diana Wynyard *Matron* ■ *Dir* Pat Jackson • *Scr* Ian McCormick, from the book *A Lamp Is Heavy* by Sheila Mackay Russell

Une Femme Est une Femme ★★★ PG
Comedy drama
1961 · Fr · Colour · 79mins

French New Wave director Jean-Luc Godard's third feature is often described as a homage to the Hollywood musical. Shot in colour and CinemaScope, it is also a love letter to its radiant star Anna Karina, whom Godard married shortly after the film was completed. She plays a stripper who badly wants a child, and when her boyfriend Jean-Claude Brialy won't give her one, so to speak, she turns to his best friend, Jean-Paul Belmondo. The slight story is rather similar to Godard's compatriot François Truffaut's *Jules et Jim*, made the same year, and the star of that film, Jeanne Moreau, puts in a cameo appearance. In French with English subtitles. ▣

U = SUITABLE FOR ALL   **Uc** = SUITABLE FOR ALL, ESPECIALLY FOR YOUNG CHILDREN (VIDEO ONLY)   **PG** = PARENTAL GUIDANCE

Anna Karina *Angéla* • Jean-Claude Brialy *Emile Recamier* • Jean-Paul Belmondo *Alfred Lubitsch* • Nicole Paquin *Suzanne* • Marie Dubois *First prostitute* • Marion Sarraut *Second prostitute* • Jeanne Moreau *Woman in bar* ∎ *Dir* Jean-Luc Godard • *Scr* Jean-Luc Godard, from an idea by Geneviève Cluny

Femme Fatale ★★ 15

Thriller 1991 · US · Colour · 92mins

A rather unhappy flirtation with Hollywood for TV's *Pride and Prejudice* hero Colin Firth. There are some interesting ideas explored here, but the end result is a muddled mess. Firth plays an unbelievably naive Englishman abroad in Los Angeles who falls for the beautiful Lisa Zane, only for her to disappear suddenly. As Firth digs deeper into her vanishing act, he discovers she has a sinister past. Firth does his best with his material and there's good support from Lisa Blount and Billy Zane, but Ms Zane (Billy's sister in real life) lacks the lure of a true *femme fatale*. Contains swearing, violence and sex scenes. ▭

Colin Firth *Joe Prince* • Lisa Zane *Elizabeth/Cynthia/Maura* • Billy Zane *Elijah* • Scott Wilson *Dr Beaumont* • Lisa Blount *Jenny* • Suzanne Snyder *Andrea* • Pat Skipper *Ted* ∎ *Dir* Andre Guttfreund • *Scr* Michael Ferris, John D Brancato

Une Femme Française ★★ 18

Drama 1994 · Fr/UK/Ger · Colour · 94mins

Daniel Auteuil and Emmanuelle Béart's off-screen relationship terminated during the production of this uninvolving story, set either side of the Second World War. The merest hint of their private tensions might have sparked this ponderous melodrama into life, but Auteuil merely looks bemused, while Béart is asked to do little more than sulk. He plays a prisoner-of-war betrayed by his wife both during his incarceration and after their reconciliation; she plays the wife, who spends much of the time pouting seductively with her young German lover (Gabriel Barylli). The period trappings and the photography are lovely, but director Régis Wargnier sidesteps the fascinating topic of wartime collaboration altogether. Contains violence. ▭

Emmanuelle Béart *Jeanne* • Daniel Auteuil *Louis* • Gabriel Barylli *Mathias Behrens* • Jean-Claude Brialy *Arnoult* • Geneviève Casile *Solange* • Heinz Bennent *Andreas* • Michel Etcheverry *Charles* ∎ *Dir* Régis Wargnier • *Scr* Régis Wagnier, Alain Le Henry

La Femme Infidèle ★★★★

Thriller 1968 · Fr/It · Colour · 98mins

Director Claude Chabrol's masterly thriller stars the stunning Stéphane Audran as the unfaithful wife of the title, whose husband kills her lover, then dumps him in a lake. Owing much to Hitchcock (the disposal of the body recalls *Psycho*), this is an elegant, tense and wickedly funny satire on the middle classes, performed to perfection by Audran, Michel Bouquet as the jealous and decidedly creepy husband, and Maurice Ronet as the doomed lover. This was the first in a magnificent run of thrillers from Chabrol in which the main characters were always called Charles and

Hélène. In French with English subtitles.

Stéphane Audran *Hélène Desvallees* • Michel Bouquet *Charles Desvallees* • Maurice Ronet *Victor Pegala* • Serge Bento *Bignon* • Michel Duchaussoy *Police Officer Duval* • Guy Marly *Police Officer Gobet* ∎ *Dir/Scr* Claude Chabrol

La Femme Publique ★★★★

Crime drama 1984 · Fr · Colour · 105mins

Made shortly after he left his native Poland for France, Andrzej Zulawski's dazzling picture occasionally lacks focus, but there's no denying the ingenuity of its story, its Dostoevskian preoccupations and its delirious style. There's a *Pygmalion* feel to tyrannical director Francis Huster's relationship with ambitious actress Valérie Kaprisky. But the more bizarre incidents occur away from the set of *Les Possédés*, as Huster pursues the wife of Czech exile Lambert Wilson, who finds himself charged with the murder of a Lithuanian archbishop. Bouncing back from her disappointment in Jim McBride's *Breathless*, Kaprisky is a revelation. In French with English subtitles.

Francis Huster *Lucas Kesling* • Valérie Kaprisky *Ethel* • Lambert Wilson *Milan Mliska* • Diane Delor *Elena* • Roger Dumas *Photographer* ∎ *Dir* Andrzej Zulawski • *Scr* Andrzej Zulawski, Dominique Garnier

FernGully: the Last Rainforest ★★ U

Animated musical fantasy 1992 · Ausl · Colour · 72mins

Down in the forest something stirred – the sound of critics giving the bird to this eco-worthy cartoon, because many felt it force-fed its tale of planet-saving too strenuously. Unfairly, however, as the story of a fairy, a fruit bat and a tiny lumberjack battling a malevolent spirit bent on destruction is a well-meaning and thoroughly entertaining adventure for youngsters. Its target audience won't mind the preachiness of the tale and adults, even though they may be a little bored with it themselves, can be sure of the film's good intentions. ▭

Samantha Mathis *Crysta* • Jonathan Ward *Zak* • Robin Williams *Batty Koda* • Christian Slater *Pips* • Tim Curry *Hexxus* • Grace Zabriskie *Magi Lune* • Geoffrey Blake *Ralph* • Robert Pastorelli *Tony* ∎ *Dir* Bill Kroyer • *Scr* Jim Cox, from stories by Diana Young

Ferris Bueller's Day Off ★★★★ 15

Comedy 1986 · US · Colour · 98mins

Matthew Broderick worshipped by students, scourge of teachers decides to play truant and whisks reluctant chum Alan Ruck and girlfriend Mia Sara off to the big city for an adventure; uptight Dean of Students Jeffrey Jones is determined to catch him in the act. It's a simple story, but this remains the most fully rounded of writer/director John Hughes's teen comedies, although once again it's marred slightly by Hughes's familiar undercurrent of sentimentality. Broderick is remarkably likeable as the arrogant, spoilt brat, Ruck is excellent as his melancholy friend and Jones almost steals the show as he suffers the humiliations that would later be

heaped upon the burglars in the blockbuster Hughes-scripted *Home Alone*. The film also provides early outings for Jennifer Grey (*Dirty Dancing*) and Charlie Sheen as a deliquent. ▭

Matthew Broderick *Ferris Bueller* • Alan Ruck *Cameron Frye* • Mia Sara *Sloane Peterson* • Jeffrey Jones *Ed Rooney* • Jennifer Grey *Jeanie Bueller* • Cindy Pickett *Katie Bueller* • Lyman Ward *Tom Bueller* • Edie McClurg *School Secretary* • Charlie Sheen *Garth Volbeck* ∎ *Dir/Scr* John Hughes

Ferry to Hong Kong ★★ U

Drama 1958 · UK · Colour · 98mins

Directed on location by Lewis Gilbert, the script was extensively rewritten and then ad-libbed by Welles, who clashed loudly with co-star Jurgens. For Welles, this "holiday" – he boycotted the premiere and never saw the finished film – was his first visit to Macao where he hatched the idea of filming Isak Dinesen's *The Immortal Story*. Welles hit the markets for Chinese bric-a-brac and even hijacked Gilbert's camera equipment to shoot some background footage, which eventually found its way into his 1968 film. ▭

Curt Jurgens *Mark Conrad* • Orson Welles *Captain Hart* • Sylvia Syms *Liz Ferrers* • Jeremy Spenser *Miguel Henriques* • Noel Purcell *Joe Skinner* • Margaret Withers *Miss Carter* ∎ *Dir* Lewis Gilbert • *Scr* Vernon Harris, Lewis Gilbert

Festen ★★★ 15

Drama 1998 · Den · Colour · 105mins

Echoes of country house comedies like Jean Renoir's *La Règle du Jeu* and such savage social satires as Luis Buñuel's *The Discreet Charm of the Bourgeoisie* ring around the first feature made under film-making collective Dogma 95's "vow of chastity". A Danish patriarch celebrates his 60th birthday, but his son decides to reveal a few family secrets. But while the severity of the themes and the immediacy of the video imagery give the disastrous family reunion the same sort of visceral thrill induced by the first films of the *nouvelle vague*, this is more a shakycam soap opera than a mould-breaking masterpiece. However, any film that can tumble complacent chattering-class audiences out of their seats has to be applauded. In Danish with English subtitles.

Ulrich Thomsen *Christian* • Henning Mortizen *Helge* • Thomas Bo Larsen *Michael* • Paprika Steen *Helene* • Birthe Neuman *Elsa* • Trine Dyrholm *Pia* ∎ *Dir* Thomas Vinterberg • *Scr* Thomas Vinterberg, Mogens Rukov

Fetishes ★★★ 18

Documentary 1997 · UK · Colour · 77mins

Nick Broomfield's documentary about sadomasochism made its TV debut in defiance of the triumphant publicity tag "the film that Channel 4 dared not show". Having already made the controversial *Chicken Ranch*, which detailed the comings and goings at a real-life brothel, this wasn't the first time Broomfield had explored the sex sector. But the man who has also tackled Margaret Thatcher, Eugene Terreblanche and Courtney Love without batting an eyelid is clearly less

than comfortable with Mistress Raven and the other occupants of New York's Pandora's Box club. Or rather, he's fazed by the things that they do at the request of their clients. Disturbingly compelling, this is a judgement-free, if graphic, insight into a highly singular world. Contains coarse language and sex scenes. ▭

Dir Nick Broomfield

Le Feu Follet ★★★★ 15

Drama 1963 · Fr/It · BW · 103mins

Released as *The Fire within* in the States and sometimes called *Will o' the Wisp* in this country, Louis Malle's drama is widely regarded as one of his best. The story of an alcoholic who visits his friends in the hope of finding a reason to live could, in the wrong hands, have been an unbearably maudlin and melodramatic affair. But Malle shuns sentiment and turns this into a painfully truthful study of self-realisation. Maurice Ronet (the forgotten actor of the French New Wave) is outstanding as Alain Leroy, subtly earning our sympathy without ever really deserving it. In French with English subtitles.

Maurice Ronet *Alain Leroy* • Léna Skerla *Lydia* • Yvonne Clech *Madamoiselle Farnoux* • Hubert Deschamps *D'Averseau* • Jean-Paul Moulinot *Dr La Barbinais* • Mona Dol *Madame La Barbinais* • Jeanne Moreau *Jeanne* ∎ *Dir* Louis Malle • *Scr* Louis Malle, from the novel by Pierre Drieu la Rochelle

The Feud ★★★ 15

Comedy 1989 · US · Colour · 93mins

In small-town America, the Beeler and the Bullard families start a feud when Dolf Beeler brandishes a cigar in the Bud Bullard's non-smoking hardware store. The row escalates and the hardware store becomes a smoking one – it's burned down in an arson attack. Then a car is bombed, people get killed and, of course, in the tradition of *Romeo and Juliet*, there's a love affair across the divide. Set in a sunny Eisenhower era of happy families, optimism and cars that look like spaceships, this is a deftly-made black comedy. ▭

René Auberjonois *Reverton* • Joe Grifasi *Bud Bullard* • Ron McLarty *Dolf Beeler* • David Strathairn *The Stranger* • Gale Mayron *Bernice Beeler* • Scott Allegrucci *Tony Beeler* • Lynne Killmeyer *Eva Bullard* ∎ *Dir* Bill D'Elia • *Scr* Bill D'Elia, Robert Uricola, from the novel by Thomas Berger

Fever ★★★

Crime drama 1988 · Ausl · Colour · 86mins

Popular Australian actor Bill Hunter here plays a good detective who turns bad when he discovers a suitcase full of drug money. Gleefully returning home to share a new life with his wife, he unfortunately interrupts her in a bit of extra-marital lovemaking... with unforeseen consequences. An Australian *film noir* with a touch of the *Blood Simple* about it, there are excellent performances all around, with a twist some may see coming. Still, it's a fun caper.

Bill Hunter *Jack Welles* • Gary Sweet *Jeff* • Mary Regan *Leanne Welles* • Jim Holt *Morris* ∎ *Dir* Craig Lahiff • *Scr* John Emery

A Fever in the Blood ★★
Political comedy drama
1961 · US · BW · 118mins

A judge, a district attorney and a senator are all campaigning for State Governor. Unfortunately their involvement in a murder case may thwart their ambitions. Exactly how are the three gubernatorial candidates involved and is one of them the killer? With its corkscrew plot of murder, blackmail, sexual betrayal and other subterfuge, this is the sort of thing John Grisham turned into gold dust a few decades later. Directed by veteran Vincent Sherman, it's a workmanlike job with a decent cast headed by Efrem Zimbalist Jr, then the star of a hit TV series, 77 Sunset Strip – which was thought to enhance the film's box-office appeal.

Efrem Zimbalist Jr *Judge Leland Hoffman* • Angie Dickinson *Cathy Simon* • Jack Kelly *Dan Callahan* • Don Ameche *Senator AS Simon* • Ray Danton *Marker* • Herbert Marshall *Governor Thornwall* ■ *Dir* Vincent Sherman • *Scr* Roy Huggins, Harry Kleiner, from the novel by William Pearson

Fever Pitch ★★15
Gambling drama 1985 · US · Colour · 91mins

Poor old Ryan O'Neal. In the seventies he was the envy of Hollywood, starring in hits like *Love Story* and *Paper Moon*, but within a decade his career was seriously off the boil and only badly scripted roles like this as a sports writer who becomes addicted to gambling seem to have popped through his letterbox. To add to the misery, this film also marks a decline in fortunes for writer/director Richard Brooks, best known for classics like *Elmer Gantry*, *Cat on a Hot Tin Roof* and *The Blackboard Jungle*. Sadly, neither star nor director have done much since this disappointment proof, if it were needed, that the adage is true: you really are only as good, or as bad, as your last movie. Contains swearing.

Ryan O'Neal *Taggart* • Catherine Hicks *Flo* • Giancarlo Giannini *Charley* • Bridgette Andersen *Amy* • Chad Everett *Dutchman* • John Saxon *Sports editor* • Hank Greenspun *Sun Publisher* • Keith Hefner *Casino boss* ■ *Dir/Scr* Richard Brooks

Fever Pitch ★★★★15
Romantic comedy
1996 · UK · Colour · 98mins

No Arsenal fan will forget Michael Thomas's last gasp-goal at Anfield on 26 May 1989. That breakaway championship winner provides the rousing finale to this hugely entertaining reworking of Nick Hornby's runaway bestseller. But although the film is based on a football fanatic's memoir, don't despair – there's much more to this romantic comedy than football. It's a bit like a feature version of *Men Behaving Badly*, with Colin Firth and best buddy Mark Strong buzzing off to Highbury or being glued to the box, while girlfriend Ruth Gemmell and flatmate Holly Aird pass acerbic asides about how incapable the lads are of growing up. Football, fads, fashion aberrations and long-gone TV shows will ensure this story is instantly recognisable, not only to nearly every thirtysomething male in the country,

but also to their long-suffering female kin. While some felt that perhaps there wasn't enough football in the film, abandon all sense of betrayal, because Hornby wrote the screenplay himself and you can always return to your paperback once the credits start to roll. Contains swearing and sexual references. 🖵 DVD

Colin Firth *Paul Ashworth* • Ruth Gemmell *Sarah Hughes* • Neil Pearson *Paul's Dad* • Lorraine Ashbourne *Paul's Mum* • Mark Strong *Steve* • Holly Aird *Jo* • Ken Stott *Ted, the headmaster* • Stephen Rea *Ray, the governor* • Luke Aikman *Young Paul* ■ *Dir* David Evans • *Scr* Nick Hornby, from his book

A Few Good Men ★★★★15
Drama 1992 · US · Colour · 137mins

The ultimate rebel Jack Nicholson has a ball playing the ultimate establishment figure in this star-laden, rather old-fashioned courtroom drama. In fact, Nicholson's role of the obsessive, hard-nosed marine officer is little more than a scene-stealing cameo, and the two leads are Tom Cruise and Demi Moore, who play naval lawyers trying to discover the truth behind the death of a marine. It's crisply directed by Rob Reiner, who once again shows that he is comfortable with numerous styles of film-making and, if it becomes a little talky at times, the climactic fireworks between Nicholson and Cruise make for compulsive viewing. The fine supporting cast includes Kevin Bacon, Kevin Pollak and JT Walsh, and there's also a chilling cameo from Kiefer Sutherland. Contains swearing and violence. DVD

Tom Cruise *Lieutenant Daniel Kaffee* • Jack Nicholson *Colonel Nathan R Jessep* • Demi Moore *Lieutenant Commander Joanne Galloway* • Kevin Bacon *Captain Jack Ross* • Kiefer Sutherland *Lieutenant Jonathan Kendrick* • Kevin Pollak *Lieutenant Sam Weinberg* • James Marshall *Private First Class Louden Downey* • JT Walsh *Lieutenant Colonel Matthew Markinson* ■ *Dir* Rob Reiner • *Scr* Aaron Sorkin, from his play

Fiddler on the Roof ★★★★U
Musical comedy 1971 · US · Colour · 171mins

This film version of one of the greatest, most heartbreaking of all Broadway shows is perfectly acceptable, but given the subject matter and opportunities for movie magic it could have been magnificent. Director Norman Jewison tells the tragic saga of the expulsion of the Jews from the Ukraine rather flatly, and extremely long-windedly, but nevertheless as his own producer preserves intact most of the marvellous score, with *Sunrise, Sunset* being particularly well-mounted and moving. As Tevye, Sholom Aleichem's garrulous milkman, Topol is fine, but actually too young for the role. The generally unfamiliar supporting cast is exceptionally well-chosen, but the real gem is the soundtrack. One of two Oscars went to musical director John Williams for his adaptation of Jerry Bock and Sheldon Harnick's wonderful score, and the fiddler is Isaac Stern. The other Oscar went to British cameraman Oswald Morris's loving Panavision photography, shot through burnished (actually stockinged) lenses.

Not the perfect work it should have been, but well worth taping, for future generations to view, and learn from. 🖵 DVD

Topol *Tevye* • Norma Crane *Golde* • Leonard Frey *Motel* • Molly Picon *Yente* • Paul Mann *Lazar Wolf* • Rosalind Harris *Tzeitel* • Michele Marsh *Hodel* • Neva Small *Chava* • Paul Michael Glaser *Perchik* • Raymond Lovelock *Fyedka* ■ *Dir* Norman Jewison • *Scr* Joseph Stein, from his book, from stories by Sholom Aleichem

Fiddlers Three ★★
Comedy 1944 · UK · BW · 88mins

The follow-up to *Sailors Three* is a cheap and cheerful reworking of Eddie Cantor's *Roman Scandals*. A bolt of lightning transports stars Tommy Trinder, Sonny Hale and Wren Diana Decker back to ancient Rome, where she takes the eye of the emperor Nero, and Tommy has to resort to a Carmen Miranda disguise to save her. The gags are poor and the songs are even worse, but any escape from the war was welcome and, with Francis L Sullivan camping it up as Nero, there were a few cheerful digs at Mussolini and his allies along the way.

Tommy Trinder *Tommy* • Frances Day *Poppaea* • Sonnie Hale *Professor* • Francis L Sullivan *Nero* • Diana Decker *Lydia* • Elisabeth Welch *Thora* ■ *Dir* Harry Watt • *Scr* Harry Watt, Diana Morgan, Angus Macphail

The Field ★★★15
Drama 1990 · UK · Colour · 105mins

Critics and audiences alike were rather underwhelmed by Jim Sheridan's follow-up to the phenomenally successful *My Left Foot*. The writer/director's attempt to create a rural drama akin to those premiered in the heyday of Dublin's Abbey Theatre results in an overbrewed poteen that intoxicates only to leave you with a thick head and dulled senses. Richard Harris received an Oscar nomination for his imposing performance as the grouchy farmer fighting to save ''his'' land, but it is the understated playing of John Hurt and Brenda Fricker that provides the real backbone of this handsome, arresting production. Contains violence and swearing. 🖵

Richard Harris *''Bull'' McCabe* • Sean Bean *Tadgh McCabe* • Tom Berenger *Peter, the American* • Frances Tomelty *The widow* • Brenda Fricker *Maggie McCabe* • John Hurt *''Bird'' O'Donnell* • Ruth McCabe *First tinker woman* ■ *Dir* Jim Sheridan • *Scr* Jim Sheridan, from a play by John B Keane

Field of Dreams ★★★★PG
Fantasy drama 1989 · US · Colour · 101mins

A classic from the days when Kevin Costner made worthwhile movies rather than celluloid statements. Phil Alden Robinson's film is a delightful throwback to the fanciful ''feel good'' corn of Frank Capra, while Iowa farmer Costner is the epitome of dignified determination as he accedes to a ghostly voice and turns the field on which the family and livelihood depend into a baseball diamond. The underestimated Amy Madigan gives a good account of herself as his trusting wife, while Ray Liotta and Frank Whaley represent the spirit world with distinction. 🖵

Kevin Costner *Ray Kinsella* • Amy Madigan *Annie Kinsella* • Gaby Hoffman *Karin Kinsella* • Ray Liotta *''Shoeless'' Joe Jackson* • Timothy Busfield *Mark* • James Earl Jones *Terence Mann* • Burt Lancaster *Dr ''Moonlight'' Graham* • Frank Whaley *Archie Graham* ■ *Dir* Phil Alden Robinson • *Scr* Phil Alden Robinson, from the novel *Shoeless Joe* by WP Kinsella

Fiend without a Face ★★★
Science-fiction horror
1957 · UK · BW · 73mins

Canadian atomic experiments cause human thoughts to transform into brain-sucking creatures in a grisly little fifties number featuring unusually graphic special effects for the period. Arthur Crabtree's *Quatermass*-style shocker starts off pretty ordinarily but, once the flying spinal cords whip into throat-choking action, the screams you hear may well be your own! British to the core, despite the pseudo-American trappings and the presence of fading Hollywood actor Marshall Thompson taking centre stage.

Marshall Thompson *Major Jeff Cummings* • Terence Kilburn [Terry Kilburn] *Captain Chester* • Kynaston Reeves *Professor Walgate* • Stanley Maxted *Colonel Butler* • Michael Balfour *Sergeant Kasper* • Kim Parker *Barbara* ■ *Dir* Arthur Crabtree • *Scr* Herbert J Leder, from a story by Amelia Reynolds Long

The Fiendish Plot of Dr Fu Manchu ★PG
Comedy 1980 · US · Colour · 100mins

No matter which way you cut it, there's no escaping the fact that the last film Peter Sellers made was also his worst (mercifully he didn't live to see two later *Pink Panther* out-take abominations). It was a bad idea in the first place to have Sellers play both the Oriental master villain and his dogged pursuer, Nayland Smith, but he spends so much time in disguise that it's sometimes hard to remember who he's supposed to be. As the focus is so roundly on the star, the supporting cast (including Helen Mirren and Sid Caesar) has next to nothing to do. 🖵

Peter Sellers *Dr Fu Manchu/Nayland Smith* • Helen Mirren *Alice Rage* • David Tomlinson *Sir Roger Avery* • Sid Caesar *Joe Capone* • Stratford Johns *Ismail* • John Le Mesurier *Perkins* ■ *Dir* Piers Haggard • *Scr* Jim Moloney, Rudy Dochtermann, from characters created by Sax Rohmer

Fierce Creatures ★★12
Comedy 1997 · US/UK · Colour · 89mins

John Cleese reassembled the team from *A Fish Called Wanda* (including Kevin Kline, Jamie Lee Curtis and Michael Palin) for this soft-hearted caper. Cleese plays the new manager appointed by a Murdoch-style media mogul to jazz up a local menagerie by adopting a ''fierce creaures only'' policy. Fearing for the future of the zoo and reluctant to change, his keepers form a plan to promote their fluffy little favourites as maneaters. Once again Cleese is cast as a love machine (with Curtis as his object of desire), an inexplicable hurdle for all those who do not understand the attraction of the first movie. Sadly, the combination doesn't work as well here and, despite the valiant efforts of a host of

U = SUITABLE FOR ALL, UC = SUITABLE FOR ALL, ESPECIALLY FOR YOUNG CHILDREN (VIDEO ONLY), PG = PARENTAL GUIDANCE

familiar faces, that vital spark is largely missing. 📺

The Fiercest Heart ★★ U

Adventure 1961 · UK · Colour · 89mins

This decidedly anti-colonial tale, adapted from Stuart Cloete's novel by screenwriter Edmund H North, is really nothing more than a western transferred to the South African veld. Set in 1837, director George Sherman replaces wagon train adventure with a great Boer trek, while the usual fugitive outlaw figure becomes a political prisoner who escapes from a British internment camp and finds redemption in the arms of a pioneering woman. Stuart Whitman combines ruggedness and rigidity in about equal measure, and his beloved, Juliet Prowse, is just as inanimate. Thank heavens for Raymond Massey's performance as a community elder.

Stuart Whitman *Bates* • Juliet Prowse *Francina* • Ken Scott *Harry Carter* • Raymond Massey *Willem* • Geraldine Fitzgerald *Tante Maria* • Rafer Johnson *Nzobo* • Michael David *Barent* ■ *Dir* George Sherman • *Scr* Edmund H North, from the novel by Stuart Cloete

Fiesta ★★★

Musical 1947 · US · Colour · 102mins

This sumptuous MGM production filmed on location down Mexico way and in glorious Technicolor, is little more than a starring vehicle for ultra-glamorous Esther Williams. She looks ravishing in a torero's outfit in a sort of Shakespearean plot in which she has to disguise herself as her twin brother – dashing screen newcomer Ricardo Montalban. Fortunately Montalban falls for the equally ravishing Cyd Charisse, and the two of them get to indulge in a brace of fiery dance duets. He's actually a composer by trade, and Aaron Copland's *El Salon Mexico* suite appears as one of Ricardo's compositions. (Oh, and *La Bamba* also gets a look in.) Meanwhile, sister Esther finds romance with John Carroll. Tosh, of course, but done with style, and it's simply fabulous to look at. A reminder of the kind of movie that nobody knows how to make any more.

Esther Williams *Maria Morales* • Akim Tamiroff *Chato Vasquez* • Ricardo Montalban *Mario Morales* • John Carroll *Jose "Pepe" Ortega* • Mary Astor *Senora Morales* • Cyd Charisse *Conchita* ■ *Dir* Richard Thorpe • *Scr* George Bruce, Lester Cole

La Fièvre Monte à el Pao ★★★

Drama 1959 · Fr/Mex · BW · 100mins

Part potboiler, part acute political analysis, this cynical drama unfolds on an island off the coast of a Latin American republic with a large population of jailbirds and political prisoners from the mainland. When the governor is assassinated, Vásquez (Gérard Philipe), his former secretary and a man of ideals, takes care of

matters until a new governor (Jean Servais) is appointed. The two men do not see eye to eye, however, and Vásquez becomes governor, only to find that power forces him to betray his humane principles. The director's cynical message – that individuals are forced to bow to systems – comes through loud and clear, but Philipe, making his last film before his early death, seems unable to inject life into his somewhat ill-defined role. A French language film.

Gérard Philipe *Ramón Vásquez* • María Félix *Inés Rojas* • Jean Servais *Alejandro Gual* • Victor Junco *Indarte* • Roberto Cañedo *Coronel Olivares* • Andres Soler *Carlos Barreiro* • Domingo Soler *Juan Cárdenas* ■ *Dir* Luis Buñuel • *Scr* Luis Buñuel, Luis Alcoriza, Charles Dorat, Louis Sapin, Henry Castillou, from the novel by Henry Castillou

Fifth Avenue Girl ★★

Comedy 1939 · US · BW · 82mins

The girl is poor-but-honest Ginger Rogers (a tad too old for the role) who's "adopted" by millionaire Walter Connolly for a night to be his companion, in order to compensate himself for familial neglect. Some nice left-wing barbs in here, but overall there's a rather unsavoury and unfamiliar taste to director Gregory (*My Man Godfrey*) La Cava's misanthropic view of human behaviour, and at times Rogers's performance seems undirected. Her permanent expression of bewildered blankness is not totally ideal for this sudden rags-to-riches story. The ending also leaves a fair bit to be desired, but the dialogue and situations are surprisingly adult, and bear watching.

Ginger Rogers *Mary Grey* • Walter Connolly *Mr Borden* • Verree Teasdale *Mrs Borden* • James Ellison *Michael* • Tim Holt *Tim Borden* • Kathryn Adams *Katherine Borden* ■ *Dir* Gregory La Cava • *Scr* Allan Scott

The Fifth Element ★★★★ PG

Science-fiction action comedy 1997 · Fr · Colour · 121mins

Ancient evil returns to destroy the galaxy in director Luc Besson's ultra-hip, socially conscious and clever science-fiction action comedy. Laconic former government agent Bruce Willis is forced to save the universe when the secret key to stopping this happening literally falls into his cab in 23rd-century New York. A superb flight of imagination that soars into original terrain for an inventive roller-coaster ride, Besson's instant classic in the *Blade Runner* tradition is a stunning achievement delivering on all levels of slick satire, unusual visuals and futuristic thrills. If the Big Apple special effects don't amaze, the camp trip to the resort planet of Fhloston Paradise certainly will. Gary Oldman is great as haute-couture corruption personified. 📺 **DVD**

Bruce Willis *Korben Dallas* • Gary Oldman *Zorg* • Ian Holm *Cornelius* • Milla Jovovich *Leeloo* • Chris Tucker *Ruby Rhod* • Luke Perry *Billy* • Brion James *General Munro* • Lee Evans *Fog* ■ *Dir* Luc Besson • *Scr* Luc Besson, Robert Mark Kamen

The Fifth Floor ★

Psychological thriller 1980 · US · Colour · 87mins

Despite its title this is bargain-basement stuff about a woman mistakenly admitted to a mental hospital, after being poisoned at a disco. Populated by the usual crazies and a depraved orderly (Bo Hopkins), it's definitely not the place for a nice girl, particularly when she's sane. Even with a pre-cult appearance by Robert (Freddy Krueger) Englund, Howard Avedis's direction reaches no heights and is as predictable as a calendar.

Bo Hopkins *Carl* • Dianne Hull *Kelly McIntire* • Patti D'Arbanville [Patti D'Arbanville-Quinn] *Cathy Burke* • Sharon Farrell *Melanie* • Mel Ferrer *Dr Coleman* • Robert Englund *Benny* ■ *Dir* Howard Avedis • *Scr* Meyer Dolinsky, from a story by Howard Avedis, Marlene Schmidt

The Fifth Missile ★★ PG

Thriller 1986 · US · Colour · 139mins

An update of the nuclear drama *The Bedford Incident*, with David Soul weirdly cast as the unhinged captain of a nuclear submarine who wants to start a Third World War. Robert Conrad and Sam Waterston are among those who think this is a bad idea. Like most submarine dramas, it's claustrophobic and the scenery is boring. It's also small fry compared to later big-budget cinema versions on the same theme like *The Hunt for Red October* and *Crimson Tide*. 📺

Robert Conrad *Lt Commander Mark Van Meer* • Sam Waterston *Commander Allard Renslow* • Richard Roundtree *Commander Frederick Bryce* • Jonathan Banks *Ray Olsen* • Art La Fleur [Art LaFleur] *Meslinsky* • Dennis Holahan *Warden* • David Soul *Capt Kevin Harris* ■ *Dir* Larry Peerce • *Scr* Eric Bercovici, from the novel *The Gold Crew* by Thomas Scortia, Frank Robinson

The 5th Monkey ★★

Adventure 1990 · US · Colour · 95mins

Ben Kingsley's film career has taken some peculiar turns since his Oscar-winning portrayal of Gandhi in 1982. Here he finds himself deep in the Amazon rainforest attempting to sell some rare monkeys in order to make enough money to marry his true love. Written and directed by Eric Rochat (not to be confused with Eric Rochat of *A World without Pity* and *Autobus* fame), this meandering tale makes the most of the Brazilian landscape, but fails to sustain interest in Kingsley's ultimate goal, and its sermon on the need for conservation is overzealously preached. Contains violence.

Ben Kingsley *Cunda* • Mika Lins *Octavia* • Vera Fischer *Mrs Watts* • Silvia De Carvalho *Maria* • Carlos Kroeber *Mr Garcia* ■ *Dir* Eric Rochat • *Scr* Eric Rochat, from the novel *Le Cinquième Singe* by Jacques Zibi

The Fifth Musketeer ★★ 15

Historical adventure 1979 · Aus · Colour · 115mins

Yet another rehash of *The Man in the Iron Mask*, with Beau Bridges rather poorly cast in the dual role as Louis XIV and his incarcerated twin brother. Sylvia Kristel – famous as the heroine of the soft-porn *Emmanuelle* films – plus Ursula Andress join an impressive roster of slumming veterans, including

Rex Harrison, Olivia de Havilland and Jose Ferrer. Ken Annakin directs without fuss but the whole thing has the heaviness one expects from a Euro-pudding movie. 📺

Beau Bridges *King Louis/Philippe* • Sylvia Kristel *Marie-Thérèse* • Ursula Andress *Madame De La Vallière* • Cornel Wilde *D'Artagnan* • Ian McShane *Fourquet* • Lloyd Bridges *Aramis* • Alan Hale Jr *Porthos* • Olivia de Havilland *Queen Anne* • José Ferrer *Athos* • Rex Harrison *Colbert* ■ *Dir* Ken Annakin • *Scr* David Ambrose, from the novel *The Man in the Iron Mask* by Alexandre Dumas, from a screenplay by George Bruce

Fifty/Fifty ★★★ 15

Action adventure 1991 · US · Colour · 96mins

Directed by actor Charles Martin Smith (*American Graffiti*), this decent little action adventure concerns two wisecracking mercenaries taking a job from the CIA to overthrow a South East Asian dictator. Along the way they have to train a guerrilla army and spar romantically for the favour of the prettiest rebel soldier you'll ever care to see. The two tough guys are played by Peter Weller (in a rare straightforward hero role) and Robert Hays (best known from *Airplane!*), and they have a lot of chemistry together. The dialogue is surprisingly good, but in the end the setup is more fun than the payoff. 📺

Peter Weller *Jake Wyer* • Robert Hays *Sam French* • Charles Martin Smith *Martin Sprue* • Ramona Rahman *Suleta* • Lim Kay Tong *Akhantar* ■ *Dir* Charles Martin Smith • *Scr* Michael Butler, Dennis Shryack, Jeff Levine, LeeAnn Lanctos, Chris Wood

55 Days at Peking ★★★★ U

Historical drama 1963 · US · Colour · 147mins

An intelligent historical epic about the Boxer rebellion of 1900 when extremists besieged the compound of international diplomats. Producer Samuel Bronston had asked Charlton Heston to star in *The Fall of the Roman Empire* and had built the Roman forum in anticipation of Heston's agreement. But, when Heston declined, screenwriter Philip Yordan came up with the Chinese drama, Heston agreed to star in it, and Rome was promptly demolished to make way for Peking, one of the most spectacular sets ever created. Switching smoothly between the wider political sphere and the personal dilemmas of the key players Heston, David Niven, Ava Gardner the movie is a carefully balanced study of principle and courage in action, partly directed by Nicholas Ray who suffered a heart attack during production and whose work was completed by second unit director Andrew Marton and an uncredited Guy Green. 📺

Charlton Heston *Major Matt Lewis* • Ava Gardner *Baroness Natalie Ivanoff* • David Niven *Sir Arthur Robertson* • Flora Robson *Dowager Empress Tzu Hsi* • John Ireland *Sergeant Harry* • Harry Andrews *Father De Beam* ■ *Dir* Nicholas Ray, Andrew Marton, Guy Green • *Scr* Philip Yordan, Bernard Gordon, Robert Hamer

54 ★★★ 15

Drama 1998 · US · Colour · 89mins

Vividly capturing the atmosphere of Studio 54 and the "Anything Goes" ambience of the disco era, writer/director Mark Christopher's chronicle of the notorious seventies night club is too ambitious and let down by a formulaic plot. Ryan Phillippe is the hunky bartender from New Jersey who gains a surrogate family when he is sucked into the decadent, glitzy lifestyle of the spaced-out "In Crowd". Mike Myers is terrific as Steve Rubell, the club's permanently stoned, homosexual master-of-ceremonies. But it's the hedonistic circus atmosphere Christopher evokes that makes this survey so superficial. The result is a painless experience, held together in the style of *American Graffiti* by a brilliant array of classic disco songs. Contains swearing, drug abuse and sexual references. ▭

Ryan Phillippe *Shane O'Shea* • Salma Hayek *Anita* • Neve Campbell *Julie Black* • Mike Myers *Steve Rubell* • Sela Ward *Billie Auster* • Sherry Stringfield *Viv* • Cindy Crawford • Sheryl Crow • Donald Trump • Art Garfunkel • Peter Bogdanovich • Lorna Luft ■ *Dir/Scr* Mark Christopher

52 Pick-Up ★★★ 18

Crime thriller 1986 · US · Colour · 103mins

While the late nineties seemed to throw up an Elmore Leonard adaptation every other month (*Get Shorty, Jackie Brown, Out of Sight*), the eighties saw two versions of *52 Pick-Up*, both made by the same company. The first was *The Ambassador*, made in 1984; for the second, made two years later, they kept Leonard's original title and storyline and sensibly asked the novelist to write the script himself. Director John Frankenheimer is way below his best form (*The Manchurian Candidate, Ronin*) but still keeps the plot simmering, while Roy Scheider is excellent as the man whose mistress has been murdered because he won't pay the blackmailers. Fans of Leonard's sleazy world will not be disappointed. ▭

Roy Scheider *Harry Mitchell* • Ann-Margret *Barbara Mitchell* • Vanity *Doreen* • John Glover *Alan Raimy* • Robert Trebor *Leo Franks* • Lonny Chapman *Jim O'Boyle* • Kelly Preston *Cini* • Doug McClure *Mark Averson* ■ *Dir* John Frankenheimer • *Scr* John Steppling, Elmore Leonard, from the novel by Elmore Leonard

Fight Club ★★★★★ 18

Satirical drama 1999 · US · Colour · 134mins

Chuck Palahniuk's bestseller is boldly brought to the screen by *Se7en* director David Fincher and emerges as a shocking, provocative and highly amusing macho fantasy. Insomniac loser Edward Norton teams up with soap salesman Brad Pitt, who lives his life on the edge, to form a no-holds-barred fight club as an outlet for their directionless aggressions. The growing cult's Project Mayhem takes subversive vandalism into the outside world with a series of ludicrous acts of sabotage. Fincher's satirical fable brilliantly plays with cinematic conventions and climaxes with a shock twist (changed from the book). This charged slice of nihilistic angst is the nineties

male psyche, fuelled by elaborate production design, unconventional editing, startling images, and superlative acting from the three leads. You'll either love it or hate it. ▭

Brad Pitt *Tyler Durden* • Edward Norton *Narrator* • Helena Bonham Carter *Marla Singer* • Meat Loaf Aday [Meat Loaf] *Robert Paulsen* • Jared Leto *Angel Face* • Rachel Singer *Chloe* ■ *Dir* David Fincher • *Scr* Jim Uhls, from the novel by Chuck Palahniuk • *Cinematographer* Jeff Cronenweth • *Music* The Dust Brothers

A Fight for Jenny ★★ PG

Drama based on a true story 1986 · US · Colour · 94mins

Predictable, platitudinous, ponderous call them what you will, but TV movies are the true heirs of the "problem pictures" of the forties, when directors like Elia Kazan would have been drawn to this story of a mixed race couple seeking custody of the white wife's daughter from a previous marriage. Director Gilbert Moses isn't of Kazan's calibre and star Lesley Ann Warren outclasses co-star Philip Michael Thomas, but this is a tricky issue and the film's good intentions partly excuse its poor quality. ▭

Philip Michael Thomas *David Caldwell* • Lesley Ann Warren *Kelsey Wilkes* • Jaclyn-Rose Lester *Jennifer Wilkes* • William Atherton *Michael Rosen* ■ *Dir* Gilbert Moses • *Scr* Judy Merl, Paul Eric Myers, Duffy Bart

The Fighter ★

Drama 1952 · US · BW · 78mins

Jack London's short story *The Mexican* is turned into a nothing B-movie. Richard Conte becomes a prizefighter to raise money for the revolution against a local bigwig who is responsible for the slaughter of his village, including his sweetheart. He decides to take on a big name fighter. Conte is not leading man material, Vanessa Brown is the vague love interest and Lee J Cobb is busking between better assignments like *On the Waterfront*. Only James Wong Howe's camerawork has any class.

Richard Conte *Filipe Rivera* • Lee J Cobb *Durango* • Vanessa Brown *Kathy* • Frank Silvera *Paulino* • Roberta Haynes *Nevis* • Hugh Sanders *Roberts* ■ *Dir* Herbert Kline • *Scr* Herbert Kline, Aben Kandel, from the short story *The Mexican* by Jack London

Fighter Squadron ★★ U

Second World War drama 1948 · US · Colour · 94mins

This routine Warner Bros war flick is of moderate interest in that it stars the ever-watchable Edmond O'Brien and Robert Stack as the flyboys struggling against both clichés and Technicolor make-up. It's of more interest today as it features the extremely gauche premiere appearance of superstar-to-be Rock Hudson, cast on looks alone by legendary director Raoul Walsh, and whose single-line performance (requiring a phenomenal amount of takes to get right) is barely acceptable. Don't blink or you'll miss it. The rest of the movie just about passes muster, and British audiences will enjoy seeing Burbank, California, standing in for wartime England.

Edmond O'Brien *Maj Ed Hardin* • Robert Stack *Capt Stu Hamilton* • John Rodney *Col Bill*

Brickley • Tom D'Andrea *Sgt Dolan* • Henry Hull *Brig Gen Mike McCready* • Rock Hudson *Lieutenant* ■ *Dir* Raoul Walsh • *Scr* Seton I Miller, Martin Rackin

Fighting Back ★★★

Drama based on a true story 1980 · US · Colour · 95mins

Robert Urich (*Vegas*) stars in this interesting and often moving true-life drama about American football star Rocky Bleier, who returned to the sport after suffering serious injuries in the Vietnam war. Director Robert Lieberman keeps to the facts without wallowing in sentimentality, and he is ably assisted by a cast that includes Art Carney as Rocky's coach, *Police Academy* regular Bubba Smith and Bonnie Bedelia from *Die Hard*.

Robert Urich *Rocky Bleier* • Bonnie Bedelia *Aleta* • Art Carney *Art Rooney* • Richard Herd *Chuck Noll* • Howard Cosell • Steve Tannen *Terry Hanratty* • Bubba Smith *Jacobs* ■ *Dir* Robert Lieberman • *Scr* Jerry McNeely, from the book by Rocky Bleier, Terry O'Neil

Fighting Caravans ★★★ U

Western 1931 · US · BW · 88mins

This excellent, if dated, early Gary Cooper western features him as a young wagon train guide. Fresh from *Morocco* opposite Marlene Dietrich, he is here well paired with striking French actress Lili Damita. Ernest Torrence and Tully Marshall reprise the old-timers they played in *The Covered Wagon*, while Fred Kohler contributes some lively villainy that leads to a spectacular climactic attack by Indians as the travellers cross a river.

Gary Cooper *Clint Belmet* • Lili Damita *Felice* • Ernest Torrence *Bill Jackson* • Fred Kohler *Lee Murdock* • Tully Marshall *Jim Bridger* ■ *Dir* Otto Brower, David Burton • *Scr* Edward E Paramore Jr, Keene Thompson, Agnes Brand Leahy, from a novel by Zane Grey

A Fighting Choice ★★ PG

Drama 1986 · US · Colour · 90mins

Patrick Dempsey is the teenager who takes his parents (Beau Bridges and Karen Valentine) to court when they refuse to allow him to have a dangerous operation that may cure his epilepsy. Unfortunately, despite good performances from the leads, this has Disney written all over it, so all the interesting issues are buried in favour of sugary sentiment and weepy moments. ▭

Beau Bridges *Thad Taylor* • Karen Valentine *Meg Taylor* • Patrick Dempsey *Kellin Taylor* • Frances Lee McCain *Virginia Hagan* • Lawrence Pressman *Dr Tobin* ■ *Dir* Ferdinand Fairfax • *Scr* Craig Buck

Fighting Father Dunne ★

Drama 1948 · US · BW · 92mins

Simply awful drama, with Pat O'Brien in his customary role as a Catholic priest with a heart as big as Ireland. This time he fights on behalf of orphaned newsboys in St Louis and tries to find them a home. Based on a true story, it was made to prove that movie studios were not merely money machines but were at the service of humanity. However, this woeful effort is only for those in need of a 90-minute cringe.

Pat O'Brien *Father Peter Dunne* • Darryl Hickman *Matt Davis* • Charles Kemper *Emmett Mulvey* ■ *Dir* Ted Tetzlaff • *Scr* Martin Rackin, Frank Davis, from a story by William Rankin

Fighting for My Daughter ★★ 15

Drama based on a true story 1995 · US · Colour · 87mins

Lindsay Wagner as a hooker? Actually, her devoted fans can rest assured that she is only pretending, although how anybody could be taken in by her disguise is just one of the shaky premises of this made-for-TV fluff. Wagner is the devoted mother who begins to suspect that an ex-con is grooming her daughter (Renee Humphrey) for a career in the world's oldest profession. Piper Laurie delivers a typically grand performance as a judge, but director Peter Levin is overwhelmed by the corny and melodramatic script. Contains some swearing. ▭

Lindsay Wagner *Kate Kerner* • Piper Laurie *Judge Edna Burton* • Chad Lowe *Eric* • Kirk Baltz *Russell* • Deirdre O'Connell *Peggy* • Renee Humphrey *Jessie* ■ *Dir* Peter Levin • *Scr* Eric Blakeney

Fighting Justice ★★★ 15

Crime drama 1989 · US · Colour · 103mins

This under-rated courtroom thriller gives James Woods a rare good-guy role as a one-time radical lawyer who now scrapes a living defending drug dealers under dubious constitutional arguments. He rediscovers his idealism when he takes up the case of a young Korean, who claims he has been framed for a gangland murder. Woods turns in a edgy, passionate performance and is ably supported by Robert Downey Jr as his assistant. Although the script doesn't bear too much scrutiny, director Joseph Ruben screws every ounce of tension out of it. Contains violence, swearing and substance abuse. ▭

James Woods *Eddie Dodd* • Robert Downey Jr *Roger Baron* • Margaret Colin *Kitty Greer* • Yuji Okumoto *Shu Kai Kim* • Kurtwood Smith *Robert Reynard* • Tom Bower *Cecil Skell* ■ *Dir* Joseph Ruben • *Scr* Wesley Strick

The Fighting Kentuckian ★★★ U

Historical adventure 1949 · US · BW · 100mins

Lodged in the John Wayne canon between two of his finest performances in *She Wore a Yellow Ribbon* and *Sands of Iwo Jima* this is a genuine curio. Produced by the Duke himself, it details an interesting historical anomaly the settling in America of Napoleon's exiled officers and their relatives immediately after the defeat at Waterloo. The political aspect isn't really explored, though, merely serving as a background for a rollicking romance with lots of fighting. Cast intriguingly as Wayne's sidekick is Oliver Hardy, who acquits himself well without Stan Laurel; indeed, he's the best reason for viewing. ▭

John Wayne *John Breen* • Vera Ralston *Fleurette Demarchand* • Philip Dom *Colonel Georges Geraud* • Oliver Hardy *Willie Paine* •

Marie Windsor *Ann Logan* • John Howard (1) *Blake Randolph* • Hugo Haas *General Paul Demarchand* ■ *Dir/Scr* George Waggner

Fighting Mad ★★

Action drama   1976 · US · Colour · 87mins

A sleazy, low-budget effort from the Roger Corman factory, with Peter Fonda as an Arkansas rancher's son who declares war on big-business interests and does a Rambo when intimidation turns into murder. There are crooked senators, a corrupt cop and a mob of heavies who line up against Fonda's extended family of ordinary, decent folk. Paying a certain amount of lip service to environmental issues, this is really just an excuse to justify some vigilante violence and to allow novice writer/director Jonathan Demme a few opportunities to show off some fancy footwork. A far cry from Demme's *The Silence of the Lambs*. Contains violence, swearing and nudity.

Peter Fonda *Tom Hunter* • Lynn Lowry *Lorene Maddox* • John Doucette *Jeff Hunter* • Philip Carey *Pierce Crabtree* • Scott Glenn *Charlie Hunter* • Kathleen Miller *Carolee Hunter* ■ *Dir/Scr* Jonathan Demme

Fighting Man of the Plains ★★ U

Western   1949 · US · Colour · 93mins

Randolph Scott stars as a former Quantrill's Raider, cleaning up a town with the help of outlaw Jesse James, in this sturdy Fox western from skilled producer Nat Holt. As James, Holt cast newcomer Dale Robertson, who later achieved fame in such TV series as *Tales of Wells Fargo* and *The Iron Horse*. Look out for *Gone with the Wind*'s carpetbagger Victor Jory, who's third-billed here.

Randolph Scott *Jim Dancer* • Bill Williams *Johnny Tancred* • Victor Jory *Dave Oldham* • Jane Nigh *Florence Peel* • Douglas Kennedy *Ken Vedder* • Joan Taylor *Evelyn Slocum* • Dale Robertson *Jesse James* ■ *Dir* Edwin L Marin • *Scr* Frank Gruber

The Fighting Prince of Donegal ★★ U

Action adventure
1966 · UK · Colour · 105mins

The title tells all – buckles swashed and derring-do done in this adventure film. Peter McEnery is the rebel in Ireland during Elizabethan times, wooing Susan Hampshire and battling a villainous Gordon Jackson, leader of the British troops who kidnaps McEnery's true love and mother. Aimed directly at youngsters – who may well overlook the cut-out castle and the cast-offs dialogue – director Michael O'Herlihy's noisy movie is nothing like as sophisticated as children's TV had become by this time, but it's enjoyable enough for an afternoon matinée. 🖵

Peter McEnery *Red Hugh* • Susan Hampshire *Kathleen* • Tom Adams *Henry O'Neill* • Gordon Jackson *Capt Leeds* • Andrew Keir *MacSweeney* • Norman Wooland *Sir John Perrott* ■ *Dir* Michael O'Herlihy • *Scr* Robert Westerby, from the novel *Red Hugh, Prince of Donegal* by Robert T Reilly

The Fighting Seabees ★★★ U

War drama   1944 · US · BW · 99mins

Although denied military service during the Second World War, John Wayne did his fair share of fighting on screen in propaganda movies like this one, which is based on a true story. He stars as the boss of a construction company who orders his workers to take up arms against the invading Japanese. It's the one where Wayne's hot-headedness causes his buddy's death, leading him to demolish all the enemy in sight, blasting his way to glory. Well, Borden Chase's screenplay worked then, and it almost works now, and if you're a fan of the Duke, give it a try. By the way, Wayne's leading lady is the young Susan Hayward. 🖵

John Wayne *Wedge Donovan* • Susan Hayward *Constance Chesley* • Dennis O'Keefe *Lt Cmdr Robert Yarrow* • William Frawley *Eddie Powers* • Leonid Kinskey *Johnny Novasky* • Jim Kerrigan *Sawyer Collins* ■ *Dir* Edward Ludwig • *Scr* Borden Chase, Aeneas MacKenzie, from a story by Borden Chase

The Fighting 69th ★★ PG

First World War drama
1940 · US · BW · 86mins

James Cagney joins up for the First World War, but breaks down under fire in the trenches. His cowardice results in him sending up a star shell, giving away his regiment's position, causing many deaths, mostly those of the New York Irishmen in his unit. Fortunately there's a kindly, sympathetic priest at hand – good heavens, it's Pat O'Brien, what a surprise – who cures Cagney and gets him firing on all cylinders. A cynical piece of studio propaganda, efficiently directed by William Keighley, the man sacked from *The Adventures of Robin Hood* in 1938, a film which was originally to star Cagney. 🖵

James Cagney *Jerry Plunkett* • Pat O'Brien *Father Duffy* • George Brent *Wild Bill Donovan* • Jeffrey Lynn *Joyce Kilmer* • Alan Hale *Sgt Big Mike Wynn* • Frank McHugh *"Crepe Hanger" Burke* ■ *Dir* William Keighley • *Scr* Norman Reilly Raine, Fred Niblo Jr, Dean Franklin

Fighting Stock ★★

Comedy   1935 · UK · BW · 72mins

While at film company Gainsborough, producer Michael Balcon demonstrated a highly catholic taste in comedy. In addition to such music-hall stalwarts as George Formby and Will Hay, he also had a yen for the Aldwych farces of Ben Travers, whom Balcon hired to write this comedy. This is not one of the strongest Balcon/Travers collaborations, but aristocratic brigadier Tom Walls and bumbling nephew Ralph Lynn are on top of their game as they tackle a crotchety neighbour and deliver niece Marie Lohr from blackmailers during a stay in a country cottage. Tom Walls, as director, never fully grasped the difference between stage and screen direction, but he does a tidy job.

Tom Walls *Sir Donald Rowley* • Ralph Lynn *Sidney* • J Robertson Hare [Robertson Hare] *Duck* • Marie Lohr *Barbara Rivers* • Lesley Wareing *Eileen Rivers* • Veronica Rose *Diana Rivers* ■ *Dir* Tom Walls • *Scr* Ben Travers

The Fighting Sullivans ★★★★ U

Drama   1944 · US · BW · 111mins

Unbearably moving (because you know the outcome) true story of the five brothers of a single family who enlisted, fought, and died together in the Second World War (the American Navy consequently banned all family members from serving on the same ship). It makes you wonder if Steven Spielberg was aware of it when he made *Saving Private Ryan*. A superb cast does full justice to the tragedy of the brothers from Iowa, whose ship was sunk at Guadalcanal. Although the Sullivans are played by virtual unknowns, exceptionally fine acting is provided by top-billed Anne Baxter as the wife of Al Sullivan, the last to enlist, and in particular by Thomas Mitchell and Selena Royle as the boys' parents. *DVD*

Thomas Mitchell *Mr Sullivan* • Anne Baxter *Katherine Mary* • Selena Royle *Mrs Sullivan* • Edward Ryan *Al* • John Campbell *Frank* • James Cardwell *George* • John Alvin *Matt* • George Offerman Jr *Joe* • Trudy Marshall *Genevieve* • Ward Bond *Lieutenant* ■ *Dir* Lloyd Bacon • *Scr* Mary C McCall Jr, from a story by Edward Doherty, Jules Schermer

Figures in a Landscape ★★★

Thriller   1970 · UK · Colour · 108mins

A nightmare vision of a repressive future? A treatise on the survival of the fittest and the corruption of the innocent? A tale of celestial forces toying with humans? Take your pick from these possible meanings in Robert Shaw's reworking of Barry England's novel about two escaped prisoners (Shaw and Malcolm McDowell) who resort to violence to evade the dogged pursuit of a helicopter pilot. Director Joseph Losey cleverly uses the rugged landscape (superbly photographed by Henri Alekan) to show the hopelessness of their situation. By keeping the characters at a distance, however, he stops us sharing their plight.

Robert Shaw *MacConnachie* • Malcolm McDowell *Ansell* • Henry Woolf *Helicopter pilot* • Christopher Malcolm *Helicopter observer* • Pamela Brown *Widow* • Andrew Bradford *Soldier* ■ *Dir* Joseph Losey • *Scr* Robert Shaw, from the novel by Barry England • *Music* Richard Rodney Bennett

The File of the Golden Goose ★

Thriller   1969 · UK · Colour · 109mins

Sam Wanamaker was talented in many fields, but he was not a good film director as this (the first of his five feature outings behind the camera) testifies. Admittedly the ponderous tale of American agent Yul Brynner's pursuit of international counterfeiters is hardly riveting material, but it would be markedly less irksome to watch if it had not been so baldly padded out with uninspired tableaux of the London landscape. Only Charles Gray (cast once more as the svelte villain) enters into the Swinging Sixties spirit. The rest look as if they knew this goose was a turkey.

Yul Brynner *Peter Novak* • Charles Gray *Nick "the Owl" Harrison* • Edward Woodward *Peter*

Thompson* • John Barrie *Sloane* ■ *Dir* Sam Wanamaker • *Scr* John C Higgins, James B Gordon, from a story by John C Higgins

The File on Thelma Jordon ★★★

Film noir   1949 · US · BW · 100mins

Barbara Stanwyck is a murder suspect who works her spell on a hapless assistant DA, played to meek perfection by Wendell Corey. He has her acquitted, but discovers her true motives. It's as if Stanwyck had somehow survived *Double Indemnity* and this is what happened after she killed Fred MacMurray. In these thrillers Stanwyck has a terrific, deadly allure and the moody lighting and the music conspire with her, keeping the men fluttering around her like moths to a flame. A second-string *film noir* maybe, but director Robert Siodmak orchestrates it with tremendous flair.

Barbara Stanwyck *Thelma Jordon* • Wendell Corey *Cleve Marshall* • Paul Kelly *Miles Scott* • Joan Tetzel *Pamela Marshall* • Stanley Ridges *Kingsley Willis* • Richard Rober *Tony Laredo* ■ *Dir* Robert Siodmak • *Scr* Ketti Grings, from a story by Marty Holland

La Fille de l'Air ★★ 15

Action drama   1992 · Fr · Colour · 102mins

Béatrice Dalle is devastated when her ex-convict lover (Thierry Fortineau) is arrested and imprisoned for armed robbery. Having served time herself for complicity, she plots to free Fortineau with the help of his brother, a small-time crook. Maroun Bagdadi's film climaxes with a reconstruction of an actual jailbreak that took place in eighties France, and the action scenes are thrilling. Characterisation is thin on the ground, however, and the result is no more enjoyable than watching an episode of *Crimewatch UK*. In French with English subtitles. 🖵

Béatrice Dalle *Brigitte* • Hippolyte Girardot *Philippe* • Thierry Fortineau *Daniel* • Jean-Claude Dreyfus *Marcel* • Roland Bertin *Mr Lefort* ■ *Dir* Maroun Bagdadi • *Scr* Dan Franck, Florence Quentin, Maroun Bagdadi, from a book by Nadine Vaujour

Film ★★★

Experimental comedy drama
1965 · US · BW · 21mins

Written by playwright Samuel Beckett of *Waiting for Godot* fame, *Film* is notable not only for its ambiguity, but also for bringing Buster Keaton back from semi-retirement. Paring cinema down to its visual essentials, it's a parable of an old man fending off the futility of existence and his own obscurity. It hardly goes out of its way to explain itself but it's good to see Buster back again and wielding unusual silent power.

Buster Keaton *O* ■ *Dir* Alan Schneider • *Scr* Samuel Beckett • *Cinematographer* Boris Kaufman

The Filth and the Fury ★★★ 15

Music documentary
2000 · UK/US · Colour · 107mins

Director Julien Temple revisits *The Great Rock 'n' Roll Swindle* for a second look at the band with the gift of the gob: the Sex Pistols. Sidelining self-serving manager Malcolm McLaren, this punk retrospective combines comments from surviving band members with unseen archive footage and TV appearances, including the notorious encounter with Bill Grundy. The result is a more accurate and less sensationalised account of the era of safety-pinned, one-chord wonders. Fast and furious, this really is essential viewing for anyone who was there, anyone who wasn't there but wishes they were, and even for anyone who wasn't there and is glad they weren't.

Dir Julien Temple

Final Analysis ★★ 15
Psychological thriller
1992 · US · Colour · 119mins

With an alluring surface gloss that suggests more than is there, and a plot so clumsy that it regularly trips over itself, it is astonishing that the quality cast (Uma Thurman, Kim Basinger and, to a lesser extent, Richard Gere) is able to salvage anything from the wreckage of this film. Thurman is psychiatrist Gere's patient and Basinger is Thurman's married sister with whom she soon becomes involved. As the twists and turns in the story stretch credibility to breaking point, it's Basinger who brings character and determination to the heart of the film, at times making Gere look no more than a clothes horse. Contains violence, swearing and nudity. *DVD*

Richard Gere *Isaac Barr* • Kim Basinger *Heather Evans* • Uma Thurman *Diana Baylor* • Eric Roberts *Jimmy Evans* • Paul Guilfoyle *Mike O'Brien* • Keith David *Detective Huggins* ■ *Dir* Phil Joanou • *Scr* Wesley Strick, from a story by Robert Berger, Wesley Strick

Final Appeal ★★★ 15
Drama based on a true story
1993 · US · Colour · 92mins

Based on a true story, this has JoBeth Williams being tried for the murder of her husband, and choosing her reckless lawyer brother (the always watchable Brian Dennehy) to represent her. *The Big Chill* actress Williams cannot, unfortunately, carry a film by herself, and she is blown off the screen by Dennehy and co-star Lindsay Crouse each time they appear. An intermittently watchable drama that could have been excellent with a more convincing lead actress. Contains violence. 🖵

JoBeth Williams *Christine Biondi* • Brian Dennehy *Harry Sundquist* • Lindsay Crouse *Dana Cartier* • Tom Mason *Dr Ed Biondi* • Eddie Jones *Detective Ayers* ■ *Dir* Eric Till • *Scr* Philip Rosenberg

Final Approach ★ 15
Thriller   1991 · US · Colour · 96mins

This *Twilight Zone*-style science-fiction thriller tries for zest, but lacks any originality. Debut director Eric Steven Stahl emphasises technology over content in this tale, jarringly told (often in flashback) of a test pilot, played by the traditionally dour James B Sikking, who is interrogated after an accident involving a top secret plane. The always reliable Hector Elizondo plays the psychiatrist probing his past and

provides some comic relief to counterbalance the dull Sikking. Gimmicky and uninvolving, this is notable only for its pioneering use of digital sound.

James B Sikking *Colonel Jason J Halsey* • Hector Elizondo *Dr Dio Gottlieb* • Madolyn Smith Osborne [Madolyn Smith] *Casey Halsey* • Kevin McCarthy *General Geller* ■ *Dir* Eric Steven Stahl • *Scr* Eric Steven Stahl, Gerald Laurence

Final Chapter – Walking Tall ★ 18
Action crime drama
1977 · US · Colour · 108mins

As unpleasant a trilogy of films as you're ever likely to find are those based on the real-life exploits of Tennessee sheriff Buford Pusser, energetically wielding his baseball bat in the one-man fight against bad-doers. This was the second outing in the lead for Bo Svenson, who had taken over from Joe Don Baker, and he brings all of his non-star appeal to the role. Jack Starrett, director of *Cleopatra Jones* and TV series such as *Starsky and Hutch*, is buried by a clumsy script lurching between cornball schmaltz and hyper-violence. Alas, despite the untimely demise of the real Pusser, the world had to suffer a subsequent television movie and series. 🖵

Bo Svenson *Buford Pusser* • Margaret Blye [Maggie Blye] *Luan* • Forrest Tucker *Grandpa Pusser* • Lurene Tuttle *Grandma Pusser* • Morgan Woodward *The Boss* • Leif Garrett *Mike Pusser* ■ *Dir* Jack Starrett • *Scr* Howard B Kreitsek, Samuel A Peeples

Final Combination ★★ 18
Crime thriller   1993 · US · Colour · 89mins

A (failed) bid to turn British former WBC light middleweight boxing champ Gary Stretch into a Hollywood action star, this sometimes unsavoury serial killer outing also features hard working *Reservoir Dogs* cult actor Michael Madsen as the dogged cop on his trail. Stretch is actually quite menacing as a wandering parcel of psychotic knuckles who has left a trail of pulped faces across the USA. Detective Madsen teams up with journalist Lisa Bonet to set up an endgame full of twists. Directed by top music promo producer Nigel Dick, who also directed *Private Investigations*. Contains swearing, violence and sex scenes. 🖵

Michael Madsen *Det Matt Dickson* • Lisa Bonet *Catherine Briggs* • Gary Stretch *Richard Welton* • Tim Russ *Det Chuck Rowland* • Damian Chapa *Donato* • Carmen Argenziano *Lt Stein* • Eric DaRe *Bouncer* ■ *Dir* Nigel Dick • *Scr* Larry Golin, Jonathan Tydor

The Final Comedown ★★
Blaxploitation drama
1972 · US · Colour · 83mins

A fairly average slice of blaxploitation, although with a stronger political slant than usual. This stars Billy Dee Williams as a young black man who gets mixed up with a Black Panther style organisation who set out to make their mark in the cosy white middle-class suburbs. The political message is a little muddled and, as is often the case with these Blaxploitation thrillers, the seventies fashions provide the most entertainment.

Billy Dee Williams *Johnny Johnson* • D'Urville Martin *Billy Joe Ashley* • Celia Kaye *Rene Freeman* • Raymond St Jacques *Imir* ■ *Dir/Scr* Oscar Williams

The Final Conflict ★★ 18
Horror   1980 · US · Colour · 108mins

When *The Omen* was released in 1976 it was a real rival to *The Exorcist*, but it soon degenerated into a soppy formula. This second sequel finds Devil-child Damien as US Ambassador to the Court of St James, thus following in father's footsteps. Intending to do a Herod by killing every male child born on a certain day, Damien unleashes a load of special effects, obliging the priests to dust off the seven daggers of Megiddo yet again. The climax is mind-bogglingly silly, but not final enough because there was yet another sequel, *Omen 4: The Awakening*, in 1991. 🖵

Sam Neill *Damien Thorn* • Rossano Brazzi *Father DeCarlo* • Don Gordon *Harvey Dean* • Lisa Harrow *Kate Reynolds* • Barnaby Holm *Peter Reynolds* • Mason Adams *President* • Robert Arden *American Ambassador* ■ *Dir* Graham Baker • *Scr* Andrew Birkin, from characters created by Dave Seltzer

The Final Countdown
★★★ PG
Science-fiction adventure
1980 · US · Colour · 98mins

What would have happened if the Americans possessed modern aircraft carriers and nuclear weapons during the time of the attack on Pearl Harbor? That's the ingenious premise of this absorbing and never silly sci-fi thriller as Captain Kirk Douglas and Martin Sheen sail into a time-warp, and have the power to alter history at the touch of a button. Reminiscent of a *Twilight Zone* but on a big budget: the film was given unprecedented access to film aboard the USS *Nimitz*.

Kirk Douglas *Captain Matthew Yelland* • Martin Sheen *Warren Lasky* • Katharine Ross *Laurel Scott* • James Farentino *Commander Richard Owens* • Ron O'Neal *Commander Dan Thurman* • Charles Durning *Senator Samuel Chapman* • Victor Mohica *Black Cloud* ■ *Dir* Don Taylor • *Scr* David Ambrose, Gerry Davis, Thomas Hunter, Peter Powell

The Final Cut ★★ 18
Thriller   1988 · SAfr · Colour · 89mins

John Barrett, veteran stuntman and stand-in for action stars such as Chuck Norris, moves centre stage for this by-the-book but businesslike action thriller. Former cop Barrett gets involved in the murky world of snuff movies, whose ruthess operators will stop at nothing to protect their business. Despite the budget limitations and a largely unknown cast, Frans Nel ties up the package neatly and simply. 🖵

John Barrett • Matthew Stewardson • Michael Huff ■ *Dir* Frans Nel • *Scr* Emil Kolbe

The Final Cut ★★ 18
Action thriller   1995 · US · Colour · 95mins

The Keanu Reeves hit *Speed* sparked a brief craze for mad bomber movies, including this watchable straight-to-video thriller. A grizzled Sam Elliott plays a former bomb disposal expert

called in to find out who is blowing up members of his old squad, only to find himself becoming the prime suspect. The explosive set pieces are spectacular enough, though the plotting won't exactly tax the brain. 🖵

Sam Elliott *John Pierce* • Amanda Plummer *Rothstein* • John Hannah *Gilmore* • Matt Craven *Lloyd* • Charles Martin Smith *Captain Weldon Mamet* • Anne Ramsay *Sergeant Kathleen Hardy* ■ *Dir* Roger Christian • *Scr* Raul Inglis, from a story by Crash Leyland

Final Cut ★★★★ 18
Drama   1998 · UK · Colour · 93mins

A very edgy pseudo-documentary made on a minuscule budget and all the better for it. Jude Law plays Jude, an actor who has met a premature death; Sadie Frost is his wife, who screens his last piece of work at his wake. Jude's video systematically exposes his closest friends as not only flawed, but also back-stabbing and corrupt, and the fallout from their enforced viewing is compulsive to witness. The first of what the producers promise will be a series of hard-hitting low-budget Brit flicks, this is delightfully innovative and original both in its content and cinematography – with friends like these, who needs enemies? Contains swearing. 🖵 *DVD*

Ray Winstone *Ray* • Jude Law *Jude* • Sadie Frost *Sadie* • Holly Davidson *Holly* • John Beckett *John* • Mark Burdis *Mark* • Perry Benson *Tony* • Lisa Marsh *Lisa* ■ *Dir/Scr* Ray Burdis, Dominic Anciano

The Final Days ★★★★ U
Political drama 1989 · US · Colour · 144mins

Fans of Oliver Stone's *Nixon* can enjoy another portrayal of the flawed president in this drama originally shown on US television. This time it's veteran character actor Lane Smith playing Richard Nixon, from Watergate through to resignation disgrace, with Richard Kiley as Special White House Counsel and Theodore Bikel as Henry Kissinger. Directed by Richard Pearce with a real feel for gathering tension, this was based on Bob Woodward and Carl Bernstein's book, *All the President's Men*.

Lane Smith *Richard Nixon* • Richard Kiley *J Fred Buzhardt* • David Ogden Stiers *General Alexander Haig* • Ed Flanders *Leonard Garment* • Theodore Bikel *Henry Kissinger* ■ *Dir* Richard Pearce • *Scr* Hugh Whitemore, from a book by Bob Woodward, Carl Bernstein

Final Descent ★★★ PG
Disaster action adventure
1997 · US · Colour · 87mins

Former *Spenser: for Hire* star, Robert Urich, is piloting a new high-tech jumbo jet, when disaster strikes in the form of a small prop plane. With the damaged plane now forced to ascend, Urich must use his skill and instincts to correct the plane's flight path before the air pressure causes it to break up. Annette O'Toole, plays his second officer and love interest. Urich's thoroughly convincing performance transforms what could have been a run-of-the-mill plane crash movie into a taut adventure thriller that will have you on the edge of your seat. 🖵

Robert Urich *Glen "Lucky" Singer* • Annette O'Toole *Connie Phipps* • John de Lancie

Captain George W Bouchard • Ken Pogue *Ian Pryce* • Kevin McNulty *Henry Gibbons* ■ *Dir* Mike Robe • *Scr* Roger Young, from the book *The Glass Cockpit* by Robert P Davis

Final Destination ★★★ 15
Supernatural horror
2000 · US · Colour · 97mins

The X Files veteran James Wong makes his feature debut with this hugely entertaining post-modernist thriller, in which the principals are named after movie horror legends. It's as if the teen slasher and the disaster flick had met in the Twilight Zone. As Devon Sawa's premonition of a mid-air disaster comes explosively true and Death begins to stalk those who escaped by dint of being ejected from the plane along with our tormented hero. The premise is flawed and the exposition clumsy, but the methods of demise are as hilarious as they're ingenious, with Wong more intent on toying with our expectations than shocking outright.

Devon Sawa *Alex Browning* • Ali Larter *Clear Rivers* • Kerr Smith *Carter Horton* • Kristen Cloke *Valerie Lewton* • Seann William Scott *Billy Hitchcock* • Chad E Donella *Tod Waggner* ■ *Dir* James Wong • *Scr* Glen Morgan, James Wong, Jeffrey Reddick, Lara Fox, from a story by Jeffrey Reddick

The Final Heist ★★ 15
Thriller
1991 · US · Colour · 92mins

Jan-Michael Vincent once the star of the mini-series *The Winds of War* and the TV series *Airwolf* seems to have ended up in TV movie oblivion, generally playing the misunderstood action man role. Here, he's in trouble again. As a man who recovers stolen artefacts for an insurance company, he's forced to steal a priceless Van Gogh when his daughter is kidnapped. As usual, Vincent rises above the unoriginal material (the storyline is similar to a host of other movies) to make this quite a gripping "dad-to-the-rescue" thriller. 🎞

Jan-Michael Vincent *David King* • Gabrielle Lazure *Gabrielle Delon* • Michael Sinelnikoff *Mark Thomas* • Tom Rack *Cameron* • Amy Fulco *Gillian* ■ *Dir* George Mihalka • *Scr* Stephen Zoller, David Preston

Final Justice ★★ 15
Crime thriller
1998 · US · Colour · 87mins

When a jury frees her gay brother's killer, Annette O'Toole seeks revenge by abducting the morally deficient defence attorney. But the tables are turned after she is captured and goes on trial for kidnapping. What might have been an interesting piece of social commentary is instead reduced to stock situations, stereotypical characters and dismal dialogue. The only good thing to come out of this convoluted TV movie is that its stars, O'Toole and Michael McKean, found romance on the set and got married. Too bad their anniversary will always remind them of this clunky effort. Contains some swearing and sexual references. 🎞

Annette O'Toole *Gwen* • Michael McKean *Merle* • Brian Wimmer *Michael* • David Meyers • CCH Pounder *Danielle Kline* ■ *Dir* Tommy Lee Wallace • *Scr* Babs Greyhosky

Final Mission ★★ 15
Action thriller
1993 · US · Colour · 87mins

Not all the ideas work, but this straight-to-video thriller comes up with some nice spins on the *Top Gun* formula. The setting is a secret defence project where a group of crack flyers are undergoing a secret virtual reality programme. When some of his fellow pilots start to crack up, Billy Wirth suspects a conspiracy. There are good turns from Corbin Bernsen and Steve Railsback, but budgetary constraints mean that a lot of the ideas are never fully realised. 🎞

Billy Wirth *Tom Waters* • Corbin Bernsen *General Breslaw* • Elizabeth Gracen *Caitlin Cole* • Steve Railsback *Colonel Anderson* ■ *Dir* Lee Redmond • *Scr* Sam Montgomery, Lee Richmond, Ernst Sheldon Jr

The Final Programme ★★
Science-fiction fantasy
1973 · UK · Colour · 83mins

The sight of the misshapen messiah will certainly send shudders down the spine of those who have stuck with the stylised imagery and apocalyptic incidents that comprise this baffling adaptation of one of Michael Moorcock's "Jerry Cornelius" stories. But many more will have long since despaired of finding any tangible meaning in this fatally flawed fantasy that ends with a cruel joke at the expense of *2001: a Space Odyssey*. Patrick Magee, Graham Crowden and George Coulouris make fearsome adversaries, but Jon Finch's bid to save both his sister and the planet are confounded by director Robert Fuest's preoccupation with look over logic.

Jon Finch *Jerry Cornelius* • Jenny Runacre *Miss Brunner* • Hugh Griffith *Professor Hira* • Patrick Magee *Dr Baxter* • Sterling Hayden *Major Wrongway Lindbergh* • Graham Crowden *Dr Smiles* • George Coulouris *Dr Powys* ■ *Dir* Robert Fuest • *Scr* Robert Fuest, from the novel by Michael Moorcock

Final Round ★★ 18
Martial arts adventure
1993 · US · Colour · 78mins

Another teaming for martial arts video stars Lorenzo Lamas and Kathleen Kinmont, best known for the *Codename Assassin* movies. This is pretty tiresome stuff, with the seen-it-all-before story of Lamas and Kinmont being held against their will and forced to take part in a televised no-holds-barred cage fighting. Martial arts fans will probably enjoy the fight bouts but the bits in between are whole lot less interesting. 🎞

Lorenzo Lamas *Tyler Verdiccio* • Anthony de Longis *Delgado* • Kathleen Kinmont *Jordan* • Clark Johnson *Trevon* ■ *Dir* George Erschbamer • *Scr* Arne Olsen

The Final Test ★★★ U
Comedy
1953 · UK · BW · 87mins

Inspired by Don Bradman's famous second-ball dismissal in his final Test match, this charming film was adapted by Terence Rattigan from his own TV play. Jack Warner gives a no-nonsense performance as the old pro, only to be totally outplayed by Robert Morley as the poet who'd give anything to be a cricketer (much to the bewilderment of Warner's pretentious son, Ray

Jackson). Anthony Asquith directs with a straight bat, producing a picture that is as quintessentially English as *Test Match Special*. Cricketing legends including Len Hutton, Denis Compton and Alec Bedser have cameos.

Jack Warner *Sam Palmer* • Robert Morley *Alexander Whitehead* • Brenda Bruce *Cora* • Ray Jackson *Reggie Palmer* • Syd Thompson • Adrianne Allen *Aunt Ethel* • Len Hutton *Frank Jarvis* • Denis Compton • Alec Bedser ■ *Dir* Anthony Asquith • *Scr* Terence Rattigan, from his TV play

Final Verdict ★★★
Drama
1991 · US · Colour · 93mins

An interesting look at the law (and lawlessness) in California before the First World War, this drama is based on the memoirs of Adela "Nora" Rogers St Johns (played by Olivia Burnette), who as a girl often accompanied her criminal lawyer father when he was out working. The always reliable Treat Williams is immensely watchable as the father, and he is ably supported by the great Glenn Ford. Contains swearing.

Treat Williams *Earl Rogers* • Glenn Ford *Reverend Lowell Rogers* • Olivia Burnette *Nora Rogers* • Gretchen Corbett *Aunt Blanche* • Raphael Sbarge *Al Boyd* • Lance Kerwin *Harry Johnson* • Barton Heyman *Bill Jory* ■ *Dir* Jack Fisk • *Scr* Lawrence Roman, from the memoirs of Adela Rogers St Johns

Find the Lady ★ U
Crime thriller
1956 · UK · BW · 56mins

After a solid start assisting Lord Bernard Miles on *The Tawny Pipit*, former editor Charles Saunders never really established himself behind the camera and was saddled with too many bargain-basement B-movies like this one. Released a year after *The Ladykillers*, this is a straight variation on the theme of a gang of crooks holing up in an elderly woman's home. However, this time, Donald Houston and Mervyn Johns are forced to take Beverley Brooks's niece Kay Callard hostage to ensure their co-operation. Lacking in suspense and played without a hint of naturalism, this thriller does at least have the advantage of being mercifully brief.

Donald Houston *Bill* • Beverley Brooks *June* • Mervyn Johns *Mr Hust* • Kay Callard *Rita* • Maurice Kaufmann *Nicky* ■ *Dir* Charles Saunders • *Scr* Kenneth R Hayles, from a story by Paul Erickson, Dermot Palmer

Find the Lady ★ PG
Comedy
1976 · Can/UK · Colour · 85mins

Hardly a film to boost the reputation of British or Canadian movie-making, this politically incorrect comedy is packed with the kind of raucous humour that rocks pubs towards last orders. Reprising the roles they played in the truly awful *It Seemed Like a Good Idea at the Time*, John Candy and Lawrence Dane star as incompetent cops stomping their way through the upper classes in search of a missing socialite. It says much that the ever-likeable Candy outstays his welcome, and both he and Dane are given an object lesson in comic delivery by Peter Cook and Dick Emery. 🎞

Lawrence Dane *Detective Sergeant Roscoe Broom* • John Candy *Officer Kopek* • Mickey

Rooney *Trigger* • Dick Emery *Leo-Hugo* • Peter Cook *JK Lewenhak* • Alexandra Bastedo *Victoria* ■ *Dir* John Trent • *Scr* Kenneth R Hughes

Finders Keepers ★ U
Musical comedy
1966 · UK · Colour · 85mins

Five years after they made *The Young Ones*, Cliff Richard and Robert Morley were reunited for this dismal romp that, more significantly, marked the end of Cliff's screen collaboration with The Shadows. Written by Michael Pertwee, the story of a clean-cut combo who find an American atom bomb off the Spanish coast is too ridiculous to contemplate and, for once, Cliff doesn't have any decent songs to distract us from its shortcomings. The same year, United Artists released Elvis Presley's embarrassing *Frankie and Johnny*, proving once and for all that the teeny-bop pop musical was dead.

Cliff Richard *Cliff* • Robert Morley *Colonel Roberts* • Bruce Welch • Hank B Marvin • Brian Bennett • John Rostill • John Le Mesurier *Mr X* ■ *Dir* Sidney Hayers • *Scr* Michael Pertwee, from a story by George H Brown • *Music/Lyrics* The Shadows

Finders Keepers ★ 15
Comedy
1984 · US · Colour · 91mins

A deeply depressing blip on Richard Lester's directorial career, this misguided, laugh-free comedy caper is a poor man's *It's a Mad Mad Mad Mad World*. At least that had a starry cast; here we're stuck with lightweights Michael O'Keefe and Beverly D'Angelo, who find themselves caught in an increasingly hysterical chase for a fortune hidden in a coffin. Pamela Stephenson is among the large cast who bravely hide their embarrassment. Notable mainly for an early film appearance by Jim Carrey. 🎞

Michael O'Keefe *Michael Rangeloff* • Beverly D'Angelo *Standish Logan* • Pamela Stephenson *Georgiana Latimer* • Louis Gossett Jr *Century* • Ed Lauter *Josef Sirola* • Jim Carrey *Lane Biddlecoff* ■ *Dir* Richard Lester • *Scr* Ronny Graham, Terence Marsh, Charles Dennis, from the novel *The Next to Last Train Ride* by Charles Dennis

Finders Keepers, Lovers Weepers ★★
Drama
1968 · US · Colour · 69mins

An uncharacteristic crime drama from soft-core sex director Russ Meyer with too much moralising and a crueller edge than normal. Sleazy topless night club owner Paul Lockwood, his unfaithful wife and her bartender lover are held captive by two burglars employed by the tough brothel madam he's seeing on the sly. Sadly, Meyer's unpleasant psychodrama has little of his trademark titillation, sexual satire or broad humour. The sex-in-the-swimming-pool scene intercut with demolition derby footage reveals the level of cynical symbolism contained in this preachy minor work from the Priest of Soft Porn. A bust but not in the way one expects! Contains nudity.

Paul Lockwood *Paul* • Anne Chapman *Kelly* • Gordon Wescourt *Ray* • Duncan McLeod *Cal* • Robert Rudelson *Feeny* • Lavelle Roby *Claire* •

Jan Sinclair *Christiana* • Joey Duprez *Joy* • Nick Wolcuff *Nick* ■ *Dir* Russ Meyer • *Scr* Richard Zachary, from a story by Russ Meyer

Finding Graceland ★★

Road movie 1999 · US · Colour · 97mins

Depressed following the death of his wife, Johnathon Schaech takes to the road in his beaten-up car and picks up Harvey Keitel who insists he's the real Elvis. So do most of the awe-struck people they encounter on the road to Graceland in a whimsical saga about finding oneself and being true to your own feelings. Religious metaphor and *Blue Suede Shoes* nostalgia makes for an uneasy mix and it does teeter on the edge of open-mouthed stupidity for a lot of the time. But Elvis fans will love it for its messianic qualities and Bridget Fonda is wonderful as a Marilyn Monroe impersonator.

Harvey Keitel *Elvis* • Bridget Fonda *Ashley* • Johnathon Schaech *Byron Gruman* • Gretchen Mol *Beatrice Gruman* • David Stewart *Purvis* ■ *Dir* David Winkler • *Scr* Jason Horwitch, from a story by David Winkler, Jason Horwitch

Finding North ★★★ 15

Road movie 1997 · US · Colour · 94mins

Essentially a lower-octane, gender-bending version of *Forces of Nature*, Tanya Wexler's feature debut takes an off-the-beaten-track approach to the road movie. Mixing gentle character comedy with life-affirming revelation, it features John Benjamin Hickey as a man with a mission – a Texan quest set by his dead lover – who is joined by Wendy Makkena as a just-sacked, thirtysomething Brooklynite desperate to escape the clutches of her shrewish Jewish mother. Played to the pleasingly melancholic strains of a country soundtrack, the film tackles the Aids issue with sensitivity rather than insistence, and avoids unnecessary sentimentality. But the central relationship feels forced, with the sparky Makkena getting too little response from Hickey's self-pitying stuffed shirt. Contains swearing.

Wendy Makkena *Rhonda Portelli* • John Benjamin Hickey *Travis Furlong* • Anne Bobby *Debi* • Rebecca Creskoff *Gina* • Angela Pietropinto *Mama Portelli* ■ *Dir* Tanya Wexler • *Scr* Kim Powers

Finding the Way Home ★★

Drama 1991 · US · Colour

Sixty might seem a bit old for a mid-life crisis, but George C Scott is businessman Max Mittelmann, burdened with marital and financial problems. Salvation comes via an accident and temporary amnesia, which finds him working with a group of Latino farm labourers. Needless to say this causes him to reassess his life. This TV movie has more class than the banality of the idea might suggest, and Scott is always worth watching.

George C Scott *Max Mittelmann* • Hector Elizondo *Ruben* • Julie Carmen *Elena* • Beverly Garland *Arlene* • Julio Cedillo *Hector* • Jose Alcala *Luis* ■ *Dir* Rod Holcomb • *Scr* Scott Swanton, from the novel *Mittelmann's Hardware* by George Raphael Small

A Fine Madness ★★★

Black comedy 1966 · US · Colour · 105mins

This is probably the darkest screwball comedy ever made and it undoubtedly would have been bleaker still if studio boss Jack Warner hadn't demanded last-minute changes. Relishing the break from Bond, Sean Connery gives one of his most vigorous performances as a poet devoid of inspiration and driven to distraction by the women in his life. Often painfully funny, there's no escaping the fact that it's pretty misogynistic stuff, with Joanne Woodward and Jean Seberg doing well with a script that has no time for them. Director Irvin Kershner would reunite with Connery for his 007 comeback *Never Say Never Again*.

Sean Connery *Samson Shillitoe* • Joanne Woodward *Rhoda* • Jean Seberg *Lydia West* • Patrick O'Neal *Dr Oliver West* • Colleen Dewhurst *Dr Vera Kropotkin* • Clive Revill *Dr Menken* ■ *Dir* Irvin Kershner • *Scr* Elliot Baker, from his novel

A Fine Mess ★ PG

Comedy 1986 · US · Colour · 86mins

Had Blake Edwards swapped the word "hideous" for "fine", he would have been nearer the mark. Ted Danson hits an all-time career low (and if you've seen *Getting Even with Dad*, you know just how low that is!) as an actor who stumbles upon a plot to dope a horse before the big race, only to find himself hurtling around Los Angeles in some of the most shambolic chase sequences you've ever seen. Worse still are villains Richard Mulligan and Stuart Margolin, whose unrestrained mugging is embarrassing to watch.

Ted Danson *Spence Holden* • Howie Mandel *Dennis Powell* • Richard Mulligan *Wayne "Turnip" Farragalla* • Stuart Margolin *Maurice "Binky" Dzundza* • Maria Conchita Alonso *Claudia Pazzo* • Jennifer Edwards *Ellen Frankenthaler* • Paul Sorvino *Tony Pazzo* • Dennis Franz *Phil* ■ *Dir/Scr* Blake Edwards

A Fine Pair ★

Crime comedy 1969 · It · Colour · 89mins

This is hardly the sort of assignment that would suit a former assistant to Michelangelo Antonioni, so it's hardly surprising director Francesco Maselli never comes to terms with either the tone or the pacing of this crass crime caper. The basic premise is sound enough, with Claudia Cardinale suckering New York cop Rock Hudson into "returning" the priceless jewels that a thief·of her acquaintance has stolen from an Austrian villa. The break-in is typically intricate, but, with Hudson looking bored, the romantic by-play between the leads is tiresome. No wonder it's most often seen in a heavily cut 89-minute version. Italian dialogue dubbed into English.

Rock Hudson *Captain Mike Harmon* • Claudia Cardinale *Esmeralda Marini* • Tomas Milian *Roger* • Leon Askin *Chief Wellman* ■ *Dir* Francesco Maselli • *Scr* Francesco Maselli, Luisa Montagnana, Larry Gelbart, Virgil C Leone, from a story by Luisa Montagnana

Fine Things ★ PG

Melodrama 1990 · US · Colour · 137mins

Yet another soapy tale from the pen of the airport romance novelist. This time,

your hanky will get soggy at the traumas of a recently widowed man who has to fight for custody of his stepdaughter. Unfortunately, aside from Cloris Leachman, this is hampered by a C-movie cast and performances that make American daytime soaps look like *cinéma vérité*.

DW Moffett *Bernie Fine* • Tracy Pollan *Liz O'Reilly* • Judith Hoag *Molly Jones* • Cloris Leachman *Ruth Fine* • Noley Thornton *Jane* ■ *Dir* Tom Moore • *Scr* Peter Lefcourt, from the novel by Danielle Steele

The Finest Hour ★★ 15

Gulf war action thriller 1991 · US · Colour · 100mins

Before Rob Lowe discovered there was more fun to be had in sending up his smoothie image – *Wayne's World*, *Austin Powers: International Man of Mystery* – than in playing it straight, he found himself relegated to straight-to-video fare such as this tired thriller. He plays a cocky young SEAL recruit who falls out with his best buddy (Gale Hansen) over a girl, in between fighting the Iraqis. Melanie Griffith's less famous half-sister Tracy pops up in support. Director Shimon Dotan was aiming for another *Top Gun*, but this film lacks the flashy exhilaration of the Tony Scott original and the pretty locations fail to compensate for the hackneyed script. Contains swearing, violence and brief nudity.

Rob Lowe *Hammer* • Gale Hansen *Dean* • Tracy Griffith *Barbara* • Eb Lottimer *Bosco* • Baruch Dror *Greenspan* • Daniel Dieker *Albie* • Michael Fountain *Carter* ■ *Dir* Shimon Dotan • *Scr* Shimon Dotan, Stuart Schoffman

The Finger Points ★★

Crime drama 1931 · US · BW · 87mins

Richard Barthelmess stars as a low-paid newspaper reporter who compromises his integrity by allowing gang leaders to buy his silence. Like the curate's egg, this low-key crime drama is good in parts, a characteristic Depression-era offering from Warner Bros, the "social conscience" studio. Fay Wray, her encounter with King Kong yet to come, is the girl who attempts to get Barthelmess to mend his ways, Clark Gable appears as a gangster, and John Francis Dillon directs competently enough.

Richard Barthelmess *Breckenridge Lee* • Fay Wray *Marcia Collins* • Regis Toomey *Charlie "Breezy" Russell* • Clark Gable *Louis Blanco* • Robert Elliott *City editor* ■ *Dir* John Francis Dillon • *Scr* Robert Lord, from a story by John Monk Saunders, WR Burnett

Fingers ★★★★ 18

Psychological drama 1978 · US · Colour · 89mins

James Toback's directorial debut is a strangely erotic and ominously threatening drama about a concert pianist who also collects debts for the mob. The edgy direction and Harvey Keitel's compelling performance caught the attention of several major critics, including David Thomson and Pauline Kael, but the film did not find an audience. Toback is undeniably talented, but wayward, and his career never really got going, but as studio-

financed oddities go, this one is unmissable.

Harvey Keitel *Jimmy Angelelli* • Tisa Farrow *Carol* • Jim Brown *Deems* • Michael V Gazzo *Ben Angelelli* • Marian Seldes *Mother* • Carole Francis *Christa* • Georgette Muir *Anita* • Danny Aiello *Butch* ■ *Dir/Scr* James Toback

Fingers at the Window ★

Horror mystery 1942 · US · BW · 80mins

Mad, bad Basil Rathbone impersonates the head of an asylum and hypnotises the inmates to carry out a string of axe murders. Actor Lew Ayres and his girlfriend Laraine Day (stars of the popular *Dr Kildare* series at the time) follow the trail of the "Robot Murders" (as the posters hyped it) and bring Rathbone to justice. A very dated chiller, weakly directed by Charles Lederer, with a cast acting as if they were all indeed under hypnosis!

Lew Ayres *Oliver Duffy* • Laraine Day *Edwina Brown* • Basil Rathbone *Dr H Santelle* • Walter Kingsford *Dr Cromwell* • Miles Mander *Dr Kurt Immelman* ■ *Dir* Charles Lederer • *Scr* Rose Caylor, Lawrence P Bachmann, from a story by Rose Caylor

Finian's Rainbow ★★★ U

Musical 1968 · US · Colour · 139mins

Although it ran for 725 performances on Broadway, it's tempting to suggest that the reason this satirical musical took 21 years to make it to the screen was because studio executives recognised that its magic worked best on the stage. Even old hands would have struggled to balance the whimsical story of a leprechaun searching for his stolen gold with sharp insights into racism and greed. Directing his first film for a major studio, Francis Ford Coppola fumbles both fantasy and sermon. However, Fred Astaire, in one of his last starring roles, is as watchable as ever.

Fred Astaire *Finian McLonergan* • Petula Clark *Sharon McLonergan* • Tommy Steele *Og* • Don Francks *Woody* • Barbara Hancock *Susan the Silent* • Keenan Wynn *Judge Billboard Rawkins* ■ *Dir* Francis Ford Coppola • *Scr* EY Harburg, Fred Saidy, from their play

Finishing School ★★

Drama 1934 · US · BW · 70mins

Frances Dee has the leading role of the pupil at an exclusive girls' school who becomes pregnant, but most interest in this drama now resides in a perky performance by Ginger Rogers. She plays Dee's madcap roommate dispensing the wisecracks, and Billie Burke also has fun as Dee's selfish mother. RKO made the film a test of new directorial talent by teaming one of the film's writers, Wanda Tuchock, with an editor, George Nichols Jr. Only Nichols continued directing.

Frances Dee *Virginia Radcliff* • Billie Burke *Mrs Radcliff* • Ginger Rogers *Pony* • Bruce Cabot *MacFarland* • John Halliday *Mr Radcliff* • Beulah Bondi *Miss Van Alstyn* ■ *Dir* Wanda Tuchock, George Nichols Jr • *Scr* Wanda Tuchock, Laird Doyle, from a story by David Hempstead, from the play *These Days* by Katherine Clugston

U = SUITABLE FOR ALL   Uc = SUITABLE FOR ALL, ESPECIALLY FOR YOUNG CHILDREN (VIDEO ONLY)   PG = PARENTAL GUIDANCE

The Finishing Touch ★★ 18

Erotic crime thriller
1992 · US · Colour · 78mins

Shelley Hack took over from Kate Jackson on *Charlie's Angels*, but only lasted one season before being replaced by Tanya Roberts. Her career never really recovered, and it certainly wasn't helped by this generic thriller about an LA cop (Michael Nader) who teams up with his ex-wife (Hack) to hunt down a serial killer. Matters are complicated when Hack becomes friendly with one of the key suspects. Arnold Vosloo became a familiar Hollywood heavy with roles in *Hard Target* and *The Mummy*. ▣

Michael Nader *Sam Stone* • Shelley Hack *Hannah Stone* • Arnold Vosloo *Mikael Gant* • Art Evans *Lt Mormon* • Clark Johnson *Det Gilliam* • Ted Raimi *Det Arnold* ■ *Dir* Fred Gallo • *Scr* Anthony L Greene, from a story by Rodger S Grossman, Anthony L Greene

Fiorile ★★★★ 12

Drama 1993 · It/Fr/Ger · Colour · 113mins

Tracing an ancestral curse over 200 years, the three stories in this elegant outing possess all the passion and wonderment we've come to expect from the Taviani brothers. Related by a father to his children as they visit their grandfather, the accounts are neatly woven into the journey and punctuated by the kids' increasingly anxious questions. With the cast playing multiple roles, the action has a neorealist feel in spite of the period opulence, most evident in the Napoleonic episode. Magisterial film-making from one of cinema's most accomplished storytelling duos. In Italian with English subtitles. ▣

Claudio Bigagli *Corrado/Alessandro* • Galatea Ranzi *Elisabetta/Elisa* • Michael Vartan *Jean/Massimo* • Lino Capolicchio *Luigi* • Constanze Engelbrecht *Juliette* • Athina Cenci *Gina* ■ *Dir* Paolo Taviani, Vittorio Taviani • *Scr* Paolo Taviani, Vittorio Taviani, Sandro Petraglia, from a story by Paolo Taviani, Vittorio Taviani

Fire! ★★

Disaster movie 1977 · US · Colour · 97mins

Made-for-TV disaster movie about a forest fire, started by a convict, which threatens to engulf a mountain community. Expect lots of the usual mini-dramas and characters saying, "Don't I smell smoke?" before the inferno arrives. A better than average supporting cast – including tough-guy Ernest Borgnine, Vera Miles, Patty Duke Astin (the Oscar winner from *The Miracle Worker*) and even Ty Hardin, TV's Bronco Lane – is in the thick of it.

Ernest Borgnine *Sam Brisbane* • Vera Miles *Martha Wagner* • Patty Duke Astin [Patty Duke] *Dr Peggy Wilson* • Alex Cord *Dr Alex Wilson* • Donna Mills *Harriet Malone* • Lloyd Nolan *Doc Bennett* • Neville Brand *Larry Durant* • Ty Hardin *Walt Fleming* ■ *Dir* Earl Bellamy • *Scr* Norman Katkov, Arthur Weiss, from a story by Norman Katkov

Fire ★★★★ 15

Drama 1996 · Can/Ind · Colour · 107mins

Parodying the traditions of the traditional masala melodrama and opening Deepa Mehta's controversial "elements" trilogy, this was one of the first Indian films to depict adultery, pornography, masturbation and lesbianism. Deprived of love in a patriarchal society, Shabana Azmi succumbs to the advances of her equally neglected sister-in-law, Nandita Das, and embarks upon a romance that shatters their ultra-conservative family. With the exception of Ranjit Chowdhry's embittered servant, the males are rather crudely caricatured. But the female leads exhibit a courage that matches Mehta's bold discussion of such themes as arranged marriage, sexual emancipation, spiritual enslavement and disappointed ambition. Contains swearing and some sex scenes. ▣

Shabana Azmi *Radha* • Nandita Das *Sita* • Kulbhushan Kharbanda *Ashok* • Jaaved Jaaferi *Jatin* • Ranjit Chowdhry *Mundu* • Kushal Rekhi *Biji* ■ *Dir/Scr* Deepa Mehta

Fire and Ice ★★

Political thriller 1962 · Fr · BW · 100mins

An unremarkable story of jealousy and political zealotry, which offers passing insights into the concerns of the day, but now seems almost ridiculously earnest. Full of the kind of brooding, meaningful conversations seized upon by the detractors of arthouse cinema, it makes too little of the doomed romantic triangle that is formed when activist Jean-Louis Trintignant leaves his actress wife Romy Schneider in the care of liberal Henri Serre while he plots the assassination of a prominent politician. The players seem overwhelmed by director Alain Cavalier's gravitas; consequently, we are unconcerned by their tragedy. French dialogue dubbed into English..

Romy Schneider *Anne* • Jean-Louis Trintignant *Clément* • Henri Serre *Paul* • Diana Lepvrier *Cécile* • Pierre Asso *Serge* • Jacques Berlioz *Le Père* • Armand Meffre *André* • Clara Tambour *Marthe* ■ *Dir/Scr* Alain Cavalier

Fire and Ice ★★ PG

Animated fantasy 1983 · US · Colour · 78mins

After the failure of his *Lord of the Rings* adaptation, Ralph Bakshi might have felt justified in steering clear of sword-and-scorcery fare. Instead he teamed up with legendary fantasy artist Frank Frazetta and comic-book masters Roy Thomas and Gerry Conway for this showdown between good and evil set in mystical prehistoric times. With the figures being Rotoscoped (traced on to celluloid from live-action footage), the animation has a realistic feel, but it's the voice talents of the cast that truly bring alive the multitude of characters – hulky hero Larn (William Ostrander), imperilled Teegra (Maggie Roswell), malevolent sorceror Nekron (Stephen Mendel) and his scheming mother, Juliana (Susan Tyrrell). ▣

Susan Tyrrell *Juliana* • Maggie Roswell *Teegra* • William Ostrander *Taro/Larn* • Stephen Mendel *Nekron* • Clare Nono *Tutor* • Alan Koss *Envoy* • Hans Howes *Defender Captain* ■ *Dir* Ralph Bakshi • *Scr* Roy Thomas, Gerry Conway, from a story and characters created by Ralph Bakshi, Frank Frazetta

Fire and Rain ★ 15

Disaster drama based on a true story
1989 · US · Colour · 83mins

Even such accomplished actors as Angie Dickinson (*Police Woman*) and Charles Haid (*Hill Street Blues*'s Renko) can't save this dreadful disaster tale. Based on a book by Jerome Chandler, this story follows the 1985 Delta Airlines crash at Dallas/Ft Worth airport (only 15 people survived). A dull, overwrought melodrama with one depressing incident after another, the film shows rescue workers trying to save passengers, and the aftermath of their ordeal. ▣

Angie Dickinson *Beth Mancini* • Tom Bosley *Derryl Price* • David Hasselhoff *Dr Dan Meyer* • Susan Ruttan *Sandra Thompson* • Dean Jones *Jack Ayers* • Charles Haid ■ *Dir* Jerry Jameson • *Scr* Gary Sherman, from a book by Jerome Greer Chandler

Fire Down Below ★★

Romantic adventure
1957 · UK · Colour · 115mins

Corny, only vaguely watchable melodrama, with Jack Lemmon and Robert Mitchum as smuggling partners who fall out over Rita Hayworth – she presumably giving both men the sensation described in the title. Hayworth is on board Mitchum's ship, trying to get to the West Indies so she can get a passport, when the boat catches fire, creating much back-projected action. The film wastes its top-rank cast – Hayworth is still playing Gilda – and was shot in Britain on a tiny budget by producers Cubby Broccoli and Irving Allen.

Rita Hayworth *Irena* • Jack Lemmon *Tony* • Robert Mitchum *Felix* • Herbert Lom *Harbour master* • Bonar Colleano *Lt Sellers* • Anthony Newley *Miguel* ■ *Dir* Robert Parrish • *Scr* Irwin Shaw, from a novel by Max Catto

Fire Down Below ★★ 18

Action adventure
1997 · US · Colour · 100mins

He may be a recent convert to saving the earth, but Steven Seagal proves he is no tree-hugging peacenik in this straight-to-video eco-thriller. He is joined by Harry Dean Stanton and a grizzled Kris Kristofferson in a tale of environmental mayhem in rural Tennessee. He plays a federal agent on a twin mission to track down the killer of a colleague and destroy the industrialist who has been poisoning the local water supply. As usual Seagal's fists and boots do most of the talking, but fans will enjoy an unexpected treat as he warbles a folk song over the credits. Contains swearing and violence. ▣ **DVD**

Steven Seagal *Jack Taggart* • Marg Helgenberger *Sarah Kellogg* • Stephen Lang *Earl* • Brad Hunt *Orin Jr* • Kris Kristofferson *Orin Sr* • Harry Dean Stanton *Cotton* ■ *Dir* Felix Enriquez Alcala • *Scr* Jeb Stuart, Philip Morton, from a story by Jeb Stuart

A Fire Has Been Arranged ★★ U

Comedy 1935 · UK · BW · 70mins

Bud Flanagan and Chesney Allen are on leave from most of the Crazy Gang, playing former convicts who go back to retrieve their plunder only to find that it's now covered by a building. The film's title suggests their possible solution to this problem. As comedy it relies too much on Flanagan and Allen's very fragile star-quality, though it does contain a "turn" by the magnificent Robb Wilton. Fans of Michael Cimino's *Thunderbolt and Lightfoot*, starring Clint Eastwood and Jeff Bridges might notice some similarities in the plot.

Bud Flanagan [Dennis O'Keefe] *Bud* • Chesney Allen *Ches* • Mary Lawson *Betty* • Robb Wilton *Oswald* • Harold French *Toby* • Alastair Sim *Cutte* ■ *Dir* Leslie Hiscott • *Scr* H Fowler Mear, Michael Barringer, from a story by H Fowler Mear, James Carter

Fire, Ice and Dynamite ★★ PG

Action drama
1990 · W Ger · Colour · 101mins

Having turned in his Walther PPK after 1985's *A View to a Kill*, Roger Moore found himself back in Bond territory – but only in terms of the daft plot and emphasis on stunts. Moore plays a wealthy man who fakes his own death and sets up an elaborate series of Olympic-type sports contests pitting his step-children against his creditors. The winners will get their hands on his fortune. Director Willy Bogner was the cinematographer on the ski sequences in Bond films including *On Her Majesty's Secret Service* and *The Spy Who Loved Me* and this harmless time-waster is worth catching only for the stunning ski set pieces and for Moore's famous charm. ▣

Roger Moore *Sir George/McVay* • Connie de Groot *Lucy* • Geoffrey Moore *Dudley* • Simon Shepherd *Alexander* • Shari Belafonte-Harper [Shari Belafonte] *Serena* • Uwe Ochsenknecht *Victor* • Isaac Hayed ■ *Dir* Willy Bogner • *Scr* Tony Williamson, Willy Bogner

Fire in the Dark ★★★ PG

Drama 1991 · US · Colour · 93mins

Olympia Dukakis, who won a best supporting actress Oscar for *Moonstruck*, is on form again for her role here as an ageing widow coming to terms with life and the fact that her children don't seem to be prepared to look after her in her old age. Dukakis manages not to let the drama become saccharine, and instead gives a touching performance which conveys both humour and courage. ▣

Olympia Dukakis *Emily Miller* • Lindsay Wagner *Janet* • Jean Stapleton *Henny Dutton* • Ray Wise *Richard* • Edward Herrmann *Robert* ■ *Dir* David Jones • *Scr* David J Hill

A Fire in the Sky ★★ PG

Drama 1978 · US · Colour · 140mins

In true TV disaster movie fashion, the citizens of Phoenix, Arizona, react badly to the news that a comet is on a collision course with their city. The expected pandemonium breaks out and the cast either ignore the omens or start behaving badly. Shown on television prior to the cinema release of *Meteor*, this is pretty dull fare. Surprisingly, given that there is little destruction on show, this won an Emmy for best special effects. ▣

Richard Crenna *Jason Voight* • Elizabeth Ashley *Sharon Allan* • David Dukes *David Allan* • Joanna Miles *Jennifer Dreiser* • Lloyd Bochner *Paul Gilliam* ■ *Dir* Jerry Jameson • *Scr* Dennis Nemec, Michael Blankfort, from a story by Paul Gallico

Fire in the Sky ★★★ 🅂

Science-fiction drama
1993 · US · Colour · 104mins

It's a case from *The X Files* that Scully and Mulder missed: a small-town lumberjack vanishes in the woods and his colleagues claim he was kidnapped by aliens. Problem is, the investigating officer here is sceptical James Garner and he suspects foul play. Director Robert Lieberman wisely concentrates on the emotional impact of the event on a close-knit circle of friends and family, although the eventual revelation of the abduction is genuinely scary. DB Sweeney shines in the lead role and there's good support from *Terminator 2*'s Robert Patrick, *The Last Seduction*'s Peter Berg and Henry Thomas of *ET* and *Legends of the Fall* fame, although old pro Garner effortlessly steals every scene. Contains some swearing. ▣

DB Sweeney *Travis Walton* • Robert Patrick *Mike Rogers* • Craig Sheffer *Allan Dallis* • Peter Berg *David Whitlock* • Henry Thomas *Greg Hayes* • Bradley Gregg *Bobby Cogdill* • James Garner *Lieutenant Frank Watters* ■ *Dir* Robert Lieberman • *Scr* Tracy Tormé, from the book *The Walton Experience* by Travis Walton

Fire Maidens from Outer Space ★ 🅄

Science-fiction
1956 · UK · BW · 79mins

Just what the world needed – an even dafter British version of the infamous space exotica romp *Cat Women of the Moon*. Life is such a trial for the female lost civilization of Atlantis, stranded on the 13th moon of Jupiter. They wear bathing suits with little skirts, lie around in flames all day for extra energy, perform dances to Borodin's music and fight a lumpy-faced creature in ill-fitting tights. Instant has-been Anthony Dexter is the astronaut determined to rescue the alien damsels from this terrible existence. Despite the extensive use of classical music, beating Stanley Kubrick's similar *2001* ploy by more than a decade, this is bottom-of-the-barrel lunatic nonsense that has to be seen to be believed.

Anthony Dexter *Luther Blair* • Susan Shaw *Hestia* • Paul Carpenter *Larson* • Harry Fowler *Sydney Stanhope* • Jacqueline Curtiss *Duessa* • Sidney Tafler [Sydney Tafler] *Dr Higgins* ■ *Dir/Scr* Cy Roth

Fire over England ★★★★ 🅄

Historical epic
1937 · UK · BW · 91mins

This spectacular epic, set in the Elizabethan past, is memorable not just for early sword- and word-play by Laurence Olivier, but for its political context – it's a call to arms against the growing forces of Nazism in Europe. Olivier is the young nobleman seeking revenge for the death of his father at the hands of the Spanish Inquisition, and warning Queen Elizabeth (Flora Robson) about the imminent Armada invasion. Raymond Massey sneers a lot as Philip II of Spain, while director William K Howard's lavish production design works hard to divert attention from uneven dialogue matched to fervent jingoism. Great fun, though.

Laurence Olivier *Michael Ingolby* • Flora Robson *Queen Elizabeth* • Leslie Banks *Earl of Leicester* • Raymond Massey *Philip of Spain* • Vivien Leigh *Cynthia* • Morton Selten *Burleigh* • Lyn Harding *Sir Richard* • James Mason *Hillary Vane* ■ *Dir* William K Howard • *Scr* Clemence Dane, Sergei Nolbandov, from a novel by AEW Mason • *Photography* James Wong Howe • *Costume Design* Rene Hubert

Fire Sale ★★

Comedy
1977 · US · Colour · 88mins

Alan Arkin's second outing as a feature director is a wild farce that most contemporary critics denounced as distasteful. It's certainly on the dark side, with basketball coach Arkin adopting a troublesome black kid solely to secure him for his under-achieving team; meanwhile his brother Rob Reiner persuades crazed uncle Sid Caesar to torch the family department store by convincing him it's a Nazi stronghold. The plot is unfocused and the acting is often manically over the top. But it's the way Arkin labours over too many misfiring gags that really explains this clumsy comedy's refusal to catch light.

Alan Arkin *Ezra Fikus* • Rob Reiner *Russel Fikus* • Vincent Gardenia *Benny Fikus* • Anjanette Comer *Marion Fikus* • Barbara Dana *Virginia* • Sid Caesar *Sherman* ■ *Dir* Alan Arkin • *Scr* Robert Klane, from his novel

Fire! Trapped on the 37th Floor ★★

Disaster
1991 · US · Colour · 94mins

The Six Million Dollar Man himself, Lee Majors, is the chief firefighter trying to control a blaze in a Los Angeles office block in this drama based on a real-life disaster. *Knots Landing*'s Lisa Hartman is one of two people stranded by the flames. Although this is quite well handled, it isn't a patch on the ultimate edge-of-your-seat disaster movie, Irwin Allen's Oscar-winning blockbuster *The Towering Inferno*, made 17 years earlier.

Lee Majors *Captain Sterling* • Lisa Hartman *Susan* • Peter Scolari *Paul* • John Laughlin *Milner* • Kim Miyori *Willa* • Michael Beach *Perez* • David Dunard *Doyle* ■ *Dir* Robert Day • *Scr* Jeffrey Bloom

Fire with Fire ★★ 🅂

Romantic drama
1986 · US · Colour · 99mins

Dull tale of teenage angst which is not as salacious as it first sounds. Prim and proper Virginia Madsen's hormones go into overdrive when she catches sight of mean and moody junior convict Craig Sheffer (*A River Runs through It*), much to the disapproval of all those around her. Madsen and Sheffer do their best with the clichéd material and there's good support from Jon Polito (*Miller's Crossing*), but the story has been better told elsewhere. ▣

Virginia Madsen *Lisa Taylor* • Craig Sheffer *Joe Fisk* • Jon Polito *Boss* • Jeffrey Jay Cohen [JJ Cohen] *Mapmaker* • Kate Reid *Sister Victoria* • Jean Smart *Sister Marie* ■ *Dir* Duncan Gibbins • *Scr* Bill Phillips, Warren Skaaren, Paul Boorstin, Sharon Boorstin

The Fireball ★★ 🅄

Sports drama
1950 · US · BW · 83mins

Multi-talented diminutive dynamo Mickey Rooney is the star of this unappealing drama about an orphan with a complex about his height who sets out to become a roller-skating champion, exhibiting ruthless ambition along the way. Rooney fans will be familiar with Mickey's brash, cocky brilliance but, although his presence enlivens this lacklustre movie, the character he plays is an unattractive one. Tay Garnett (who had seen better days at MGM) directs for 20th Century-Fox, whose relatively unknown contract player Marilyn Monroe appears as a girl named Polly.

Mickey Rooney *Johnny Casar* • Pat O'Brien *Father O'Hara* • Beverly Tyler *Mary Reeves* • James Brown (2) *Allen* • Marilyn Monroe *Polly* • Ralph Dumke *Bruno Crystal* ■ *Dir* Tay Garnett • *Scr* Tay Garnett, Horace McCoy

Fireball 500 ★★★ 🅄

Action drama
1966 · US · Colour · 90mins

A beach party movie with those icons of sand, sea and swimwear – Frankie Avalon, Fabian and the adorable Annette Funicello. The two boys are rivals for the girl as they race souped-up cars for her pleasure and get into hot water with illicit booze. The whole thing exudes an innocence and charm, as well as some very twangy, singalong tunes. Perhaps not quite up to the standards of previous William Asher beach epics like the masterly *How to Fill a Wild Bikini*, this is still unmissable for sixties culture-vultures.

Frankie Avalon *Dave* • Annette Funicello *Jane* • Fabian *Leander* • Chill Wills *Big Jaw* • Harvey Lembeck *Charlie Bigg* • Julie Parrish *Martha* ■ *Dir* William Asher • *Scr* William Asher, Leo Townsend

Firebird 2015 AD ★

Science-fiction
1980 · US · Colour · 97mins

Petrol is in such short supply in the 21st century that the government orders all cars to be destroyed. When their owners start getting wiped out, too, it's up to illegal bands of motorcyclists to take the law into their own hands. Poorly written and directed, this *Mad Max* rip-off has minor futuristic fantasy touches but plenty of stunt action for those who like that sort of thing. Doug McClure probably wished he had stayed in *The Land That Time Forgot*.

Darren McGavin *Red* • Doug McClure *McVain* • George Touliatos *Indy* • Mary Beth Rubens *Jill* ■ *Dir* David M Robertson • *Scr* Barry Pearson, Biff McGuire, Maurice Hurley

The Firechasers ★★ 🅄

Crime thriller
1970 · UK · Colour · 101mins

Chad Everett (real name Raymond Cramton!) became a teen heart-throb in the US TV series *Medical Center*, which ran until the mid-seventies. His subsequent career included useful supporting roles in features and leading roles in half-baked programme-fillers such as this, a TV movie in America, and a supporting theatrical film over here. Director Sidney Hayers keeps up the pace as unlikely insurance investigator Everett hunts an arsonist throughout a London peopled with well-known British character actors. He's aided by lovely Anjanette Comer, and they make a glamorous, if improbable, twosome.

Chad Everett *Quentin Barnaby* • Anjanette Comer *Toby Collins* • Keith Barron *Jim Maxwell* • Joanne Dainton *Valerie Chrane* • Rupert Davies *Prentice* • Roy Kinnear *Roscoe* ■ *Dir* Sidney Hayers • *Scr* Philip Levene

Firecreek ★★★ 🄵🄶

Western
1968 · US · Colour · 99mins

James Stewart here succumbs to the notorious "yup-nope" syndrome, playing a monosyllabic part-time sheriff defending his fellow townsfolk from outlaw Henry Fonda and his gang of layabout thugs. Cast against type, Fonda obviously liked his role so much he became even more villainous for Sergio Leone's *Once upon a Time in the West*, released in Italy the same year. While this doesn't bear serious comparison with Leone's classic spaghetti western, it's entertaining enough. Contains some violence. ▣

James Stewart *Johnny Cobb* • Henry Fonda *Larkin* • Inger Stevens *Evelyn* • Gary Lockwood *Earl* • Dean Jagger *Whittier* • Ed Begley *Preacher Broyles* ■ *Dir* Vincent McEveety • *Scr* Calvin Clements

The Firefly ★★★ 🅄

Period musical
1937 · US · BW · 138mins

"There's a song in the air, but the gay senorita doesn't seem to care... " Yes, it's the *Donkey Serenade* movie, with Allan Jones singing his heart out to vivacious Jeanette MacDonald, winning her from stern Warren William during the Spanish Peninsular War, as she takes a break from her regular singing swain Nelson Eddy. MGM's production is so glossy and the film's length so nearly unendurable that its flimsy origins (an operetta by Rudolf Friml) are all but forgotten under Robert Z "Pops" Leonard's classy direction. Incidentally, the operetta of the same name has a completely different plot!

Jeanette MacDonald *Nina Maria Azara* • Allan Jones *Don Diego Manrique De Lara* • Warren William *Colonel De Rougemont* • Douglass Dumbrille *Marquis De Melito* ■ *Dir* Robert Z Leonard • *Scr* Frances Goodrich, Albert Hackett, Ogden Nash, from the operetta by Otto A Harbach • *Music* Rudolf Friml • *Music Director* Herbert Stothart

Firefox ★★ 🅂

Spy thriller
1982 · US · Colour · 119mins

Maybe it's some sort of contractual obligation, but Clint Eastwood (as director) every now and then delivers up a boring, emotionless film – *The Rookie* and *The Eiger Sanction* to name but two – and this violent Cold War affair is hard going for even the most dedicated of fans. Eastwood plays a disillusioned flier who is sent across the Iron Curtain to steal a new Russian jet and bring it home. The supporting Britpack (Warren Clarke, Freddie Jones, Ronald Lacey) hams it up for all it's worth, but, while there are some decent flying sequences, Eastwood's heart doesn't appear to be in it. Contains swearing. ▣

Clint Eastwood *Mitchell Gant* • Freddie Jones *Kenneth Aubrey* • David Huffman *Buckholz* • Warren Clarke *Pavel Upenskoy* • Ronald Lacey *Semelovsky* ■ *Dir* Clint Eastwood • *Scr* Alex Lasker, Wendell Wellman, from the novel by Craig Thomas

🅄 = SUITABLE FOR ALL 🅄🄴 = SUITABLE FOR ALL, ESPECIALLY FOR YOUNG CHILDREN (VIDEO ONLY) 🄿🄶 = PARENTAL GUIDANCE

Firehead ★★ 15

Science-fiction action adventure
1991 · US · Colour · 83mins

This dull thriller with mild fantasy overtones is notable for wasting a fine cast. Scientist Chris Lemmon (sounding and acting like his father Jack) and CIA agent Gretchen Becker team up to track down Soviet defector Brett Porter who can shoot laser beams from his eyes, move molecules and start fires. Christopher Plummer is the government bureaucrat-by-day/secret-society-leader-by-night who needs Porter to kill the president and start a Third World War. Martin Landau is a retired admiral and Lemmon's mentor. Peter Yuval's suspense adventure never knows quite what direction to move in and the result is a fuzzy muddle. Contains violence and swearing

Christopher Plummer *Colonel Garland Vaughn* • Chris Lemmon *Warren Hart* • Martin Landau *Admiral Pendleton* • Gretchen Becker *Melia Buchanan* • Brett Porter *Ivan Tibor* ■ *Dir* Peter Yuval • *Scr* Peter Yuval, Jeff Mandel

Firelight ★★★ 15

Romantic drama
1997 · US/UK · Colour · 99mins

Tissues at the ready for this sugary 19th-century tale of a mother's love. Swiss governess Sophie Marceau agrees to conceive a child for English aristocrat Stephen Dillane, who takes the child back to his wife. A few years later the pair cross paths again when he takes her on as nanny to their daughter which, unsurprisingly, opens can upon can of worms when the not-unattractive Marceau moves into the strange household of stiff-upper-lipped husband, bedridden wife and rebellious daughter. The two leads seem uncomfortable with their roles, but the story is interesting enough and is enlivened by a strong performance by Dominique Belcourt as their daughter, and a supporting cast which includes Joss Ackland. Contains some swearing and a sex scene.

Sophie Marceau *Elisabeth Laurier* • Stephen Dillane *Charles Godwin* • Kevin Anderson *John Taylor* • Lia Williams *Constance* • Dominique Belcourt *Louisa Godwin* • Joss Ackland *Lord Clare* • *Dir/Scr* William Nicholson

Fireman Save My Child ★★★

Sports comedy
1932 · US · BW · 67mins

Joe E Brown, who was to the mouth what Jimmy Durante was to the nose, is fairly amusing as a dopey, peanut-munching hick fireman who's also a crack baseball player. He manages to get to the big league, and is torn between the girl back home in Kansas and the sophisticated city girl. Naturally, simple values triumph at the end of this serio-comic movie. Brown, who was no mean ball player himself, had a clause written into his contract with Warner Bros which stated that they were to supply him with his own baseball team.

Joe E Brown *Smokey Joe Grant* • Evalyn Knapp *Sally Toby* • Lilian Bond [Lillian Bond] *June Farnum* • Guy Kibbee *Pop Devlin* • Richard Carle *Dan Toby* ■ *Dir* Lloyd Bacon •

Scr Ray Enright, Robert Lord, Arthur Caesar, from a story by Ray Enright, Robert Lord, Arthur Caesar, Lloyd Bacon

Fireman Save My Child ★★ U

Comedy
1954 · US · BW · 80mins

Abbott and Costello were the original stars of this slapdash comedy but their withdrawal made room for the less than stellar talents of Hugh O'Brian and Buddy Hackett. However, this silly tale set in an early 20th-century San Francisco fire department, is enlivened by the eccentric presence of Spike Jones and his City Slickers. The band attacks the *Poet and Peasant Overture, Dance of the Hours* and *In a Persian Market* in characteristically crazy style. The film bears no resemblance to the superior 1932 Joe E Brown comedy of the same name.

Spike Jones *Lieutenant McGinty* • His City Slickers *Firemen* • Buddy Hackett *Smokey* • Hugh O'Brian *Smitty* • Adele Jergens *Harry's wife* • Tom Brown *Captain Bill Peters* ■ *Dir* Leslie Goodwins • *Scr* Lee Loeb, John Grant

The Fireman's Ball ★★★★ U

Satirical comedy   1967 · Cz · Colour · 69mins

Director Milos Forman's last film in Czechoslovakia before his American exile begins as a gently mocking comedy of small-town manners, but ends as a blazing allegorical satire on the incompetence, insularity and ideological idiocy of the state. Amid the wealth of comic detail that surrounds the ball held to celebrate a veteran fire chief's retirement, it's easy to forget that the real theme of this socialist realist parody is the Stalinist purges of the fifties. But the chaotic beauty contest, the theft of the lottery prizes and the discomfort of the guest of honour can all be enjoyed without a deep knowledge of Czech politics. In Czech with English subtitles.

Vaclav Stockel *Fire Brigade Commander* • Josef Svet *Old Man* • Jan Vostrcil *Chairman of Committee* • Josef Kolb *Josef* • Frantisek Debelka *First committee member* • Josef Sebanek *Second committee member* ■ *Dir* Milos Forman • *Scr* Milos Forman, Ivan Passer, Jaroslav Papousek

Firepower ★★ 15

Action thriller   1979 · UK · Colour · 99mins

One of the easiest jobs in film criticism is to knock the work of Michael Winner. But he's not always deserved the pannings he's received and this fast-moving (if admittedly empty-headed) thriller is no worse than many other luxury location jaunts that have escaped without censure. From the opening scene in which Sophia Loren's husband is killed, to the highly predictable denouement, there are explosions and car chases aplenty. On the plus side, Loren and James Coburn do make an attractive couple. Winner also edited the film under the pseudonym Arnold Crust.

Sophia Loren *Adele Tasca* • James Coburn *Jerry Fanon/Eddie* • OJ Simpson *Catlett* • Eli Wallach *Sal Hyman* • Anthony Franciosa *Dr Felix* • Vincent Gardenia *Frank Hull* • Victor Mature *Harold Everett* ■ *Dir* Michael Winner • *Scr* Gerald Wilson, from a story by Bill Kerby, Michael Winner

Firepower ★★ 18

Science-fiction crime action
1993 · US · Colour · 90mins

Prolific straight-to-video director Richard Pepin splices together the sci-fi and fight contest genres for this predictably efficient thriller. Gary Daniels and Chad McQueen play a pair of futuristic cops who are forced into the fight ring when they go undercover in a no-go crime zone in 21st-century Los Angeles. Every post-apocalypse cliché is present and correct, but the fight sequences will satisfy undemanding fans of the genre.

Chad McQueen • Gary Daniels • George Murdock • Joseph Ruskin ■ *Dir* Richard Pepin • *Scr* Michael January

Fires on the Plain ★★★★★

Second World War drama
1959 · Jap · BW · 107mins

This is cinema's most terrifying study of the Second World War. Adapted by director Kon Ichikawa's wife, Natto Wada, from the novel by Shohei Ooka, Ichikawa's masterpiece has an other-worldly feel. Desperate, cannibalistic Japanese soldiers are left to fend for themselves on the Philippine island of Leyte, its desolate landscape littered with ominous fires. As the tubercular trooper who wanders the landscape in search of food and shelter, and whose infirmity delivers him from the hellish nightmare of survival, the almost wordless Eiji Funakoshi reacts to the atrocities he witnesses with such genuine horror that their impact becomes all the more immediate. In Japanese with English subtitles.

Eiji Funakoshi *Tamura* • Osamu Takizawa *Yasuda* • Mickey Curtis *Nagamatsu* • Mantaro Ushio *Sergeant* • Kyu Sazanka *Army surgeon* • Yoshihiro Hamaguchi *Officer* • Asao Sano *Soldier* • Masaya Tsukida *Soldier* • Hikaru Hoshi *Soldier* ■ *Dir* Kon Ichikawa • *Scr* Natto Wada, from the novel by Shohei Ooka

Fires Were Started ★★★★

Documentary drama 1943 · UK · BW · 63mins

Humphrey Jennings was the poet of the British Documentary Movement. Yet, he reined in his imaginative impulses to record the grim reality of the Blitz in what ranks among the finest Home Front films of the Second World War. As in all good propaganda, it's simplicity that makes the most impact. In depicting the men of the Auxiliary Fire Service as a dedicated team, whose camaraderie is evident both at work and play, Jennings is able to inspire audience confidence in their quiet heroism, while also extolling the essential humanity in their single-minded determination to conquer their enemy – fire.

Dir/Scr Humphrey Jennings

Fires Within ★★ 15

Romantic drama 1991 · US · Colour · 83mins

After leaving *LA Law*, Jimmy Smits made one so-what movie after another, and this well-meaning drama also did little for his prospects. What makes this doubly disappointing is that, firstly, it was made by the talented Australian director Gillian Armstrong and, secondly, its story of Cuban refugees in America throws up some fascinating

political points, which are evaded one after the other by the pedestrian script. Greta Scacchi as a Cuban housewife is a rotten bit of casting, but she, Smits and Vincent D'Onofrio (as her new lover) try to wring every ounce of significance out of the potentially interesting plot. Contains swearing.

Jimmy Smits *Nestor* • Greta Scacchi *Isabel* • Vincent D'Onofrio *Sam* • Luis Avalos *Victor Hernandez* • Bertila Damas *Estella Sanchez* • Bri Hathaway *Maribi* ■ *Dir* Gillian Armstrong • *Scr* Cynthia Cidre, Peter Barsocchini

Firestarter ★★★ 15

Supernatural drama
1984 · US · Colour · 109mins

Stephen King's work has suffered mixed fortune at the hands of film-makers and this early folly is not one of the better adaptations. A very young Drew Barrymore is the girl with very fiery thoughts which are seemingly connected to the sinister experiments dad and mum (David Keith and Heather Locklear) underwent. Despite a starry cast, there's little here in the way of frights or suspense.

David Keith *Andrew McGee* • Drew Barrymore *Charlie McGee* • Freddie Jones *Dr Joseph Wanless* • Heather Locklear *Vicky McGee* • Martin Sheen *Captain Hollister* • George C Scott *John Rainbird* • Art Carney *Irv Manders* • Louise Fletcher *Norma Manders* ■ *Dir* Mark L Lester • *Scr* Stanley Mann, from the novel by Stephen King • *Music* Tangerine Dream

Firestorm ★★ 15

Adventure   1998 · US · Colour · 85mins

Former American football star Howie Long is said to have been singled out for stardom by Rupert Murdoch himself, but on the evidence of this (it went straight to video here) there is still some way to go before he joins the front ranks of Hollywood's action stars. Pitched as a cross between *ConAir* and *Backdraft*, Long plays a daredevil bush fire fighter who finds himself caught up in a lethal forest blaze started by a group of escaped convicts hunting for their buried loot. William Forsythe effortlessly plays the show as psychotic robber but Scott Glenn and Suzy Amis are largely wasted in supporting roles, and director Dean Semler (cinematographer on *Waterworld* and *Dances with Wolves*) struggles away from the action sequences. Contains swearing and some violence.

Howie Long *Jesse* • Scott Glenn *Wynt* • William Forsythe *Shaye* • Suzy Amis *Jennifer* • Christianne Hirt *Monica* ■ *Dir* Dean Semler • *Scr* Chris Soth, Graham Yost

Firewalker ★★ 15

Western adventure
1986 · US · Colour · 100mins

It could be Chuck Norris's most embarrassing effort, because here he attempts to do something that he has absolutely no knack for – comedy. Neither does his co-star Louis Gossett Jr, though he at least keeps some dignity, even when he's forced to speak Pig Latin. The two stars play unlucky mercenary adventurers who are hired by Melody Anderson to find an ancient treasure south of the border, with danger, cardboard sets, and stereotypes at every twist and turn. Not even the most gifted comedian could generate laughs with the material here, and those tuning in expecting at least a moderate amount of karate action – or any kind of action – from Norris will be greatly disappointed. ▭

Chuck Norris *Max Donigan* • Louis Gossett Jr *Leo Porter* • Melody Anderson *Patricia Goodwyn* • Will Sampson *Tall Eagle* • Sonny Landham *El Coyote* • John Rhys-Davies *Corky Taylor* ■ *Dir* J Lee Thompson • *Scr* Robert Gosnell, from a story by Jeffrey M Rosenbaum, Norman Aladjem, Robert Gosnell

The Firm ★★★★ 15

Thriller 1993 · US · Colour · 148mins

After running rings around the US Navy in *A Few Good Men*, Tom Cruise returns to the courtroom for this big-screen adaptation of John Grisham's bestseller. The result is a lavish, star-studded legal thriller that is never less than engrossing. Cruise is a rising young lawyer who gets a dream job with a prestigious law firm only to discover that it offers more than just legal advice to one particularly sinister client. The ever excellent Gene Hackman is his jaded superior, but, as good as they are, the two stars are outshone by the seemingly never-ending parade of star supporting turns (Holly Hunter, Ed Harris, David Strathairn, Hal Holbrook and an unbilled *Goodfellas* reprise from Paul Sorvino). Director Sydney Pollack is as proficient as usual and just about manages to sustain the suspense throughout, even though the subject matter is fairly dry. Contains swearing, violence and a sex scene. ▭

Tom Cruise *Mitch McDeere* • Jeanne Tripplehorn *Abby McDeere* • Gene Hackman *Avery Tolar* • Hal Holbrook *Oliver Lambert* • Terry Kinney *Lamar Quinn* • Wilford Brimley *William Devasher* • Ed Harris *Wayne Tarrance* • Holly Hunter *Tammy Hemphill* • David Strathairn *Ray McDeere* ■ *Dir* Sydney Pollack • *Scr* David Rabe, Robert Towne, David Rayfiel, from the novel by John Grisham

First a Girl ★★★ U

Musical comedy 1935 · UK · BW · 88mins

A popular hit for British screen sweetheart Jessie Matthews, this tuneful comedy plunders a German film called *Viktor und Viktoria* and was itself later reworked by director Blake Edwards as a vehicle for his wife Julie Andrews as *Victor/Victoria*. Whichever way you look at it, this is a highly unconvincing tale of cross-dressing about a girl who impersonates a female impersonator – effectively a girl impersonating a man impersonating a girl. The ramifications don't bear thinking about, but Matthews brings it all off charmingly, singing and dancing her merry way in a relatively lavish Michael Balcon production, directed by Victor Saville without so much of a hint of unsavoury subtext – at least, not to its contemporary audiences. ▭

Jessie Matthews *Elizabeth* • Sonnie Hale *Victor* • Griffith Jones *Robert* • Anna Lee *Princess* • Alfred Drayton *McIntosh* • Constance Godridge *Darryl* • Martita Hunt *Seraphina* ■ *Dir* Victor Saville • *Scr* Marjorie Gaffney, from the play *Victor/Victoria* by Reinhold Schunzel

First Blood ★★ 15

Action drama 1982 · US · Colour · 125mins

Although he eventually metamorphosised into a hero of the free world, Rambo began as a mad, gun-obsessed loner. Of course, with all-American hero Sylvester Stallone in the title role there wasn't really any danger of the character being portrayed in a bad light and the result is a compromised thriller with a very dubious message. Rambo is a disaffected Vietnam veteran trying to get his life back together, who is driven over the edge by the constant harassment of bullying sheriff Brian Dennehy. Director Ted Kotcheff delivers the goods in the action stakes, but the apparently heroic status bestowed on Stallone's vigilante stance is still unpalatable. Contains swearing. *DVD*

Sylvester Stallone *John Rambo* • Richard Crenna *Colonel Trautman* • Brian Dennehy *Sheriff Will Teasle* • David Caruso *Mitch* • Jack Starrett *Galt* ■ *Dir* Ted Kotcheff • *Scr* Michael Kozoll, William Sackheim, Q Moonblood [Sylvester Stallone], from a book by David Morrell • *Music* Jerry Goldsmith

The First Deadly Sin ★★ 15

Mystery 1980 · US · Colour · 107mins

After a hiatus of ten years, Frank Sinatra returned to the screen as a cop on the verge of retirement whose last case is a series of grisly murders. Faye Dunaway plays his wife, who's in hospital connected to a dialysis machine. No prizes for guessing whodunit, and apart from some fairly gory details this is no different than a routine episode of *Kojak*. The very quick of eye might just be able to spot Bruce Willis wearing a big cap in a restaurant doorway. ▭

Frank Sinatra *Edward Delaney* • Faye Dunaway *Barbara Delaney* • David Dukes *Daniel Blank* • George Coe *Dr Bernardi* • Brenda Vaccaro *Monica Gilbert* • Martin Gabel *Christopher Langley* ■ *Dir* Brian G Hutton • *Scr* Mann Rubin, Lawrence Sanders

First Degree ★★ 18

Thriller 1995 · US · Colour · 87mins

Despite successfully re-inventing himself as a light comedian, Rob Lowe still occasionally plays it straight, as this moody thriller proves. He plays a detective investigating the murder of a top businessman who, rather unwisely, begins an affair with the man's sultry widow (Leslie Hope). It takes quite a while for the action to heat up, but the piece picks up speed towards the end, culminating in a dramatic and bloody finale. ▭

Rob Lowe *Detective Rick Mallory* • Leslie Hope *Hadley Pyne* • Joseph Griffin *Rico Perrini* • Tom McCamus *Amos* • Nadia Capone *Tina* ■ *Dir* Jeff Woolnough • *Scr* Ron Base

First Do No Harm ★★★ PG

Drama 1997 · US · Colour · 90mins

Only Meryl Streep could turn a standard disease-of-the-week TV movie into something special. Her mannered performance as a struggling mother trying to get the best treatment for her epileptic son while marital and financial problems rear their heads, is yet another of her wrenchingly emotional class acts. Based on a *Lorenzo's Oil*-type true story, Seth Adkins also shines as her afflicted son in a gruelling drama that informs about epilepsy, while making pertinent statements about society's attitude towards the condition. ▭

Meryl Streep *Lori Reimuller* • Fred Ward *Dave Reimuller* • Seth Adkins *Robbie Reimuller* • Margo Martindale *Marjean* • Allison Janney *Dr Abbasac* • Oni Faida Lampley *Marisha Warren* ■ *Dir* Jim Abrahams • *Scr* Ann Beckett

First Family ★★ 15

Comedy 1980 · US · Colour · 95mins

A disappointing debut for director Buck Henry, whose screenplays for *The Graduate* and *What's Up, Doc?* showed he was adept at both satire and screwball. Here he tackles political satire but without political sting. The absurd plot concerns the kidnapping of American president Bob Newhart's daughter, Gilda Radner, by an African tribe. Despite the comedy credentials of the strong cast, this witless witness to the wonders of the White House fails as entertainment. ▭

Gilda Radner *Gloria Link* • Bob Newhart *President Manfred Link* • Madeline Kahn *Constance Link* • Richard Benjamin *Press Secretary Bunthorne* • Bob Dishy *Vice President Shockley* • Buck Henry *Father Sandstone* ■ *Dir/Scr* Buck Henry

The First Great Train Robbery ★★★

Period crime thriller
1978 · UK · Colour · 107mins

Sumptuously shot on location in Ireland by Geoffrey Unsworth, this allegedly true heist movie is a kind of "Butch Connery and the Sutherland Kid". Written and directed by Michael Crichton from his own novel, it's a far cry from high-tech action adventures like *Jurassic Park*, as a pair of Victorian villains played by Sean Connery and Donald Sutherland set out to steal gold destined for the army in the Crimea, from a moving train. The stars seem to be enjoying themselves enormously, but Crichton fails to sustain the tension of the robbery and too often lets the comedy run unchecked. That said, it's a smashing piece of period escapism.

Sean Connery *Edward Pierce* • Donald Sutherland *Agar* • Lesley-Anne Down *Miriam* • Alan Webb *Edgar Trent* • Malcolm Terris *Henry Fowler* • Wayne Sleep *Clean Willy* • Michael Elphick *Burgess* ■ *Dir* Michael Crichton • *Scr* Michael Crichton, from his novel

First Kid ★★ PG

Comedy 1996 · US · Colour · 95mins

A sugary family comedy, presumably designed as a vehicle for American comedy favourite Sinbad. He plays a tough Secret Service agent who gets the thankless task of babysitting the President's spoilt son (Brock Pierce). However, it's not long before the big guy warms to his charge and starts teaching him some valuable life lessons. Predictable stuff, though the liberal splattering of slapstick will delight youngsters. ▭

Sinbad *Sam Simms* • Brock Pierce *Luke Davenport* • Blake Boyd *Dash* • Timothy Busfield *Woods* • Lisa Eichhorn *Linda Davenport* • James Naughton *President Davenport* • Sonny Bono ■ *Dir* David Mickey Evans • *Scr* Tim Kelleher

First Knight ★★★ PG

Adventure 1995 · US · Colour · 128mins

Following his success with *Ghost*, director Jerry Zucker focuses on another three-way romance in this retelling of the spiciest of Arthurian myths. If Kevin Costner can play Robin Hood with an American accent, then what's to stop Richard Gere giving Lancelot a Philadelphia twang? Gere is suitably dashing as the most independent knight of the Round Table, while Julia Ormond is ravishing as the constantly imperilled Guinevere. Stealing every scene, however, is Sean Connery, who, as a legend in his own lifetime, has no difficulty conveying the regal bearing of the once and future king. Very nineties, yet curiously and unashamedly old-fashioned. Contains some violence. ▭ *DVD*

Sean Connery *King Arthur* • Richard Gere *Lancelot* • Julia Ormond *Lady Guinevere* • Ben Cross *Malagant* • Liam Cunningham *Sir Agravaine* • Christopher Villiers *Sir Kay* ■ *Dir* Jerry Zucker • *Scr* William Nicholson

First Lady ★★★

Comedy 1937 · US · BW · 83mins

Classy, clever and sophisticated screen adaptation of the George S Kaufman/Katharine Dayton Broadway play, offering a strong role to the elegant Kay Francis as an ambitious politician's wife, schemingly shoving her secretary of state husband, Preston Foster, into a campaign against crooked judge Walter Connolly, as excellent as ever. There's little doubt that the message here is that Washington women are the real power behind the throne, but that's surely not news to Hillary Clinton or Nancy Reagan, or even Eleanor Roosevelt. A little wordy, and not overly cinematic, but well worth dipping into.

Kay Francis *Lucy Chase Wayne* • Anita Louise *Emmy Page* • Verree Teasdale *Irene Hibbard* • Preston Foster *Stephen Wayne* • Walter Connolly *Carter Hibbard* • Victor Jory *Senator Keane* ■ *Dir* Stanley Logan • *Scr* Rowland Leigh, from the play by George S Kaufman, Katharine Dayton

The First Legion ★★★ U

Drama 1951 · US · BW · 86mins

Charles Boyer gives a fine performance as the former criminal attorney turned priest who investigates an apparent miracle at a Jesuit seminary. Made entirely on location at a Spanish-style inn, this is one of director Douglas Sirk's lesser-known films from the fifties but it's skilfully directed, smoothly acted (though it takes time to accept comedian William Demarest as a Monsignor) and lighter in tone than might be expected. The ending is a mushy attempt to keep believers as well as sceptics happy.

Charles Boyer *Father Marc Arnoux* • William Demarest *Monsignor Michael Carey* • Lyle Bettger *Dr Peter Morrell* • Barbara Rush *Terry Gilmartin* • Leo G Carroll *Fr Paul Duquesne* ■ *Dir* Douglas Sirk • *Scr* Emmett Lavery

First Love ★★ U

Romance   1939 · US · BW · 84mins

Only significant now for Deanna Durbin receiving her first proper screen kiss, from Robert Stack in his movie debut no less – and that's about it. Hard to imagine the impact nowadays, but when singing superstar Durbin puckered up to receive her sensational smackeroo from handsome Stack, audiences were enthralled. As for the plot, it's a version of Cinderella with orphan Deanna hived off to an aunt and uncle. However, it's all rather charming, and Durbin does gets to belt out a few choice songs.

Deanna Durbin *Constance Harding* • Robert Stack *Ted Drake* • Eugene Pallette *James Clinton* • Helen Parrish *Barbara Clinton* • Lewis Howard *Walter Clinton* • Leatrice Joy *Grace Clinton* ■ *Dir* Henry Koster • *Scr* Bruce Manning, Lionel Houser

First Love ★★★★

Romance 1970 · W Ger/Swi · Colour · 92mins

A classy adaptation of the Turgenev story about an adolescent boy who becomes infatuated with the flirtatious girl next door. She plays with him, then rejects him. As he grows up, much the wiser, Europe maintains its terrible addiction to war. John Moulder-Brown is suitably callow-looking as the boy, while Dominique Sanda (fresh from her debut in Bresson's *A Gentle Creature* and about to star in *The Conformist*) is radiantly beautiful and alluring. Impeccably shot by Bergman's cameraman, Sven Nykvist, it marked the directing debut of Maximilian Schell; his style is a little academic at times, yet he assembles a fine supporting cast that includes playwright John Osborne.

John Moulder-Brown *Alexander* • Dominique Sanda *Sinaida* • Maximilian Schell *Father* • Valentina Cortese *Mother* • Marius Goring *Dr Lushin* • John Osborne *Maidanov* ■ *Dir* Maximilian Schell • *Scr* Maximilian Schell, John Gould, from a story by Ivan Turgenev

First Love ★★ 15

Romantic drama 1977 · US · Colour · 87mins

Based on a story Harold Brodkey wrote for *The New Yorker* magazine, this is a sentimental tale about a romance between college students William Katt and Susan Dey that turns sour when Katt discovers Dey is involved with a much older man. Because this was made in the seventies, there are lots of intense discussions about sex, and Dey looks uncomfortable leaving her *Partridge Family* goody two-shoes image behind to play a woman with at least two men on the go. Contains swearing. ▭

William Katt *Elgin Smith* • Susan Dey *Caroline* • John Heard *David* • Beverly D'Angelo *Shelley* • Robert Loggia *John March* • Tom Lacy *Professor Oxtan* • Swoosie Kurtz *Marsha* ■ *Dir* Joan Darling • *Scr* Jane Stanton Hitchcock, David Freeman, from the short story *Sentimental Education* by Harold Brodkey

First Man into Space ★★ PG

Science-fiction adventure
1958 · UK · BW · 73mins

Cosmic rays mutate Earth's first astronaut into a marauding monster with a taste for blood in this briskly efficient B-movie from the golden era of British science fiction. In a film bearing more than a passing resemblance to Hammer's *The Quatermass Experiment* with a dash of *Dracula* thrown in for good exploitative measure, director Robert Day goes for both pity and scares by engendering sympathy for the one-eyed malformation while delivering uneasy shocks. Lacklustre acting from Marshall Thompson doesn't help his cause, but Marla Landi screaming every time the slime-encrusted alien appears does add an unintentional streak of light entertainment. ▭

Marshall Thompson *Commander CE Prescott* • Marla Landi *Tia Francesca* • Bill Edwards *Lt Dan Prescott* • Robert Ayres *Captain Ben Richards* • Bill Nagy *Wilson* • Carl Jaffe *Dr Paul Von Essen* ■ *Dir* Robert Day • *Scr* John C Cooper, Lance Z Hargreaves, from a story by Wyott Ordung

First Men in the Moon ★★★ U

Science-fiction 1964 · UK · Colour · 98mins

Outstanding special effects from stop-motion magician Ray Harryhausen add further lustre to director Nathan Juran's colourfully engaging tale about a Victorian lunar expedition. Based on the HG Wells novel, Lionel Jeffries is splendid as the eccentric Professor Cavor using his anti-gravity paint invention to achieve lift-off into light-hearted adventure. Cavor, Edward Judd and Martha Hyer are then captured by insectoid creatures and menaced by a Moon caterpillar in this highly enjoyable flight of sheer fantasy. ▭

Edward Judd *Arnold Bedford* • Lionel Jeffries *Cavor* • Martha Hyer *Kate Callender* • Erik Chitty *Gibbs* • Betty McDowall *Maggie* ■ *Dir* Nathan Juran • *Scr* Nigel Kneale, Jan Read, from the novel by HG Wells

First Monday in October ★★★ 15

Comedy drama 1981 · US · Colour · 93mins

British veteran Ronald Neame's penultimate picture was produced by Paul Heller and Martha Scott and adapted by Jerome Lawrence and Robert E Lee from their own stage play. Consequently, there is far too much chat, even for a courtroom movie, but, if you plan your tea breaks for the segments in which the American political and legal systems are discussed, it's quite a likeable romantic comedy of sorts. Jill Clayburgh does a sterling job as the first female Supreme Court judge, whose strict principles alienate and then attract shabby liberal colleague Walter Matthau. The leads make better adversaries than possible partners and their jousting alone sustains the interest. Contains some swearing. ▭

Walter Matthau *Dan Snow* • Jill Clayburgh *Ruth Loomis* • Barnard Hughes *Chief Justice Crawford* • Jan Sterling *Christine Snow* • James Stephens *Mason Woods* ■ *Dir* Ronald Neame • *Scr* Jerome Lawrence, Robert E Lee, from their play

First Name: Carmen ★★ 18

Drama 1983 · Fr/Swi · Colour · 80mins

Forget Prosper Mérimée's novel or Bizet's opera. Ostensibly a film about a terrorist called Carmen X, this is actually a movie about the problems of making movies, interspersed with recitals of Beethoven string quartets and long sessions with director Jean-Luc Godard, sitting in a lunatic asylum and burbling on about himself, life and art. Maybe Godard thought this could be his *8½*, and that a few explicit sex scenes would somehow attract an audience. Some of it is actually rather charming, especially for those who have followed Godard's career since *A Bout de Souffle*. But for most viewers, *First Name: Carmen* will be a maddening and early switch-off. In French with English subtitles. ▭

Maruschka Detmers *Carmen X* • Jacques Bonnaffé *Joseph Bonnaffé* • Myriem Roussel *Claire* • Christophe Odent *Gang leader* • Jean-Luc Godard *Uncle Jean* • Hippolyte Girardot *Fred* ■ *Dir* Jean-Luc Godard • *Scr* Anne-Marie Miéville, adapted from the novel *Carmen* by Prosper Mérimée

The First of the Few ★★★ U

Second World War biographical drama
1942 · UK · BW · 113mins

Offered contracts and any number of enticing star roles after *Gone with the Wind*, Leslie Howard chose to leave Hollywood and return to England to fight a celluloid war against Germany. This was his epic, directing and starring as visionary aircraft designer RJ Mitchell, the father of the Spitfire. Rosamund John is his wife, David Niven the test pilot, and William Walton the composer whose music sums up an entire era of flying pictures. It was Howard's final screen performance: his plane was shot down in 1943 on a mission that immediately became shrouded in mystery – one that has never been explained. ▭

Leslie Howard *RJ Mitchell* • David Niven *Geoffrey Crisp* • Rosamund John *Diana Mitchell* • Roland Culver *Commander Bride* • Annie Firth [Anne Firth] *Miss Harper* • David Horne *Higgins* ■ *Dir* Leslie Howard • *Scr* Antone de Grunwald, Miles Malleson, from a story by Henry C James • *Source* • *Story* Kay Strueby

The First Power ★★ 18

Horror thriller 1990 · US · Colour · 94mins

In this over-familiar blend of hard-boiled cops on a mission, omens, killer nuns and psychics, detective Logan (Lou Diamond Phillips) catches the Pentagram Killer – so called because he carves that sign on his victims' chests – and sends him to the gas chamber. From there his demonic spirit transfers into a succession of weak bodies and continues the murderous spree. Phillips and clairvoyant Tracy Griffith (half-sister of Melanie) try to stop the carnage. Director Robert Resnikoff's derivative devilry has a few eerie moments and a couple of excellent stunts but they are mostly lost in a third-rate black mass of poor continuity, sloppy framing and a plot that makes less sense as it staggers its way towards a number of false endings. The realistic tone Resnikoff opts for kills every supernatural twist stone dead through lack of suitable moodiness. ▭

Lou Diamond Phillips *Russell Logan* • Tracy Griffith *Tess Seaton* • Jeff Kober *Patrick Channing* • Mykel T Williamson [Mykel T Williamson] *Detective Oliver Franklin* • Elizabeth Arlen *Sister Marguerite* ■ *Dir/Scr* Robert Resnikoff

The First Rebel ★★★ U

Western 1939 · US · BW · 70mins

Originally titled *Allegheny Uprising* and very sensibly retitled for the UK (who can pronounce Allegheny after all?), this super little pre-American War of Independence western benefited from its casting, reteaming the leads from *Stagecoach*, John Wayne and Claire Trevor. The former Ringo Kid smashes evil Brian Donlevy's illicit liquor trade as well as dealing with snarling British officer George Sanders, and finding the time to romance Trevor. Well, that's what made John Wayne John Wayne. The film is helped immensely by the somewhat expressionistic lighting from master cinematographer Nicholas Musuraca. ▭

John Wayne *Jim Smith* • Claire Trevor *Janie* • George Sanders *Captain Swanson* • Brian Donlevy *Callendar* • Wilfrid Lawson *MacDouglas* • Robert Barrat *Duncan* ■ *Dir* William A Seiter • *Scr* PJ Wolfson

The First Time ★★

Comedy 1969 · US · Colour · 89mins

A limp coming-of-age comedy about a teenager who cons his two friends into believing that Buffalo is a buzzing, switched-on place and that losing one's virginity there is as easy as falling off a log. It isn't, of course, and various comic complications ensue. In 1969 the three friends were played by unknowns which may have given the film some freshness. Sadly, the guys are still unknown which makes it of little interest to today's audiences. It's really just a pale imitation of *The Graduate* with the gorgeous Jacqueline Bisset as the rather intimidating seductress who isn't actually a prostitute, as the boys think.

Jacqueline Bisset *Anna* • Wes Stern *Kenny* • Rick Kelman *Mike* • Wink Roberts *Tommy* • Gérard Parkes *Charles* • Sharon Acker *Pamela* • Cosette Lee *Grandmother* • Vincent Marino *Frankie* ■ *Dir* James Neilson • *Scr* Jo Heims, Roger Smith, from a story by Bernard Bassey

First Time Felon ★★★ 15

Drama based on a true story
1997 · US · Colour · 105mins

The American concept of boot camps for young criminals has been championed by a number of British politicians. Perhaps they saw this TV movie. Omar Epps plays a young gang member who opts for the new justice programme after being convicted of drug-dealing. Initially rebellious, he and his fellow teens get the chance to prove themselves when they are called in to help a flood-threatened town. Actor turned director Charles S Dutton maintains a realistic, even tone throughout and elicits fine performances from his cast. Contains swearing and some violence. ▭

Omar Epps *Greg Yance* • Delroy Lindo *Calhoun* • Rachel Ticotin *McBride* • Justin Pierce *Eddie* • Lucinda Jenney *Sharon* • Jo D Jonz *Pookie* ■ *Dir* Charles S Dutton • *Scr* Daniel Therriault

First to Fight ★★ U

Second World War drama
1967 · US · Colour · 97mins

Chad Everett – a minor TV star and even less of a movie star – plays a marine who returns from Guadalcanal as a war hero, marries, becomes a drill instructor but craves to be back on the front line. Sent back to Pacific, Everett cracks up and turns into a dribbling wreck. Has marriage (to Marilyn Devin) and impending fatherhood made him lose his nerve? A young Gene Hackman is on hand to encourage Everett to further heroics. Never more than a B-movie, though a fairly costly one, this war drama pushes all the right patriotic buttons.

Chad Everett *Jack Connell* • Marilyn Devin *Peggy Sanford* • Dean Jagger *Lt Col Baseman* • Bobby Troup *Lt Overman* • Claude Akins *Capt Mason* • Gene Hackman *Sgt Tweed* ■ *Dir* Christian Nyby • *Scr* Gene L Coon

The First Travelling Saleslady ★★ U

Comedy 1956 · US · Colour · 92mins

You could charitably view this last gasp of what was once the great RKO empire as an early feminist tract, but actually it's a deadly dull, badly-paced "comedy" about a corset saleswoman out west reduced to hawking barbed wire. Played by the totally miscast Ginger Rogers and accompanied by the whimsical Carol Channing – proving here once and for all how totally unsuited she was to big screen leading roles – interest now would come from a very young and bronzed Clint Eastwood playing Channing's Cavalry boyfriend. Indeed he clearly outclasses nominal leading men Barry Nelson and David Brian. Director Arthur Lubin, who also produced this farrago allegedly once intended for Mae West, supervises matters as though he wishes he were somewhere else.

Ginger Rogers *Rose Gillray* • Barry Nelson *Charles Masters* • Carol Channing *Molly Wade* • David Brian *James Carter* • James Arness *Joel Kingdom* • Clint Eastwood *Jack Rice* ■ *Dir* Arthur Lubin • *Scr* Stephen Longstreet, Devery Freeman

The First Wives Club
★★★★ PG

Comedy 1996 · US · Colour · 98mins

Olivia Goldsmith's bestselling novel becomes a hilarious film by *Police Academy* director Hugh Wilson, featuring sparkling performances from Hollywood divas Goldie Hawn, Bette Midler and Diane Keaton. They play three wealthy New Yorkers all deserted by their husbands in favour of much younger women (including *Sex and the City*'s Sarah Jessica Parker and *Showgirls*' Elizabeth Berkley). Instead of sitting back and taking it, the trio unite to exact revenge and gain financial control, with Midler stealing the show from her two co-stars as the most deliciously vicious of them all. Terrific stuff. 📺

Goldie Hawn *Elise Elliot Atchison* • Bette Midler *Brenda Morelli Cushman* • Diane Keaton *Annie MacDuggan Paradise* • Maggie Smith *Gunilla Garson Goldberg* • Sarah Jessica Parker *Shelly* • Dan Hedaya *Morty Cushman* • Stockard Channing *Cynthia Swann Griffin* • Elizabeth Berkley *Phoebe LaVelle* ■ *Dir* Hugh Wilson • *Scr* Robert Harling, from the novel by Olivia Goldsmith

First Yank into Tokyo ★

Second World War action drama
1945 · US · BW · 82mins

Less than a month after the fall-out settled on the ruins of Hiroshima and Nagasaki, RKO rushed out this programme-filler about the atomic bomb. In fact, it was originally a drama about a new super-gun but a few twiddles to the dialogue and a few new scenes gave the film an unexpected immediacy. It's rubbish, of course, with Tom Neal playing a soldier who undergoes plastic surgery and sneaks back into Japan, where he was raised, to obtain weaponry information from a captive scientist.

Tom Neal *Major Ross* • Barbara Hale *Abby Drake* • Marc Cramer *Jardine* • Richard Loo *Colonel Okanura* • Keye Luke *Haan-Soo* • Leonard Strong *Major Nogira* ■ *Dir* Gordon Douglas • *Scr* J Robert Bren, from a story by J Robert Bren, Gladys Atwater

The First Year ★★★ U

Drama 1932 · US · BW · 81mins

Janet Gaynor and Charles Farrell were indisputably Hollywood's sweethearts in the immediate pre-sound era, and carried on as a strictly professional perfect screen couple for a while through the early talkie years. This is a well-scripted tale of a newlywed couple's attempt to settle down and, though both Gaynor and Farrell are a shade long in the tooth for the roles, they play together superbly, with great charm and élan, their relationship clearly honed on more famous movies such as *Seventh Heaven*. For today's audiences, though, the material may appear dated.

Janet Gaynor *Grace Livingston* • Charles Farrell *Tommy Tucker* • Minna Gombell *Mrs Barstow* • Leila Bennett *Hattie* • Dudley Digges *Dr Anderson* • Robert McWade *Fred Livingston* • George Meeker *Dick Loring* ■ *Dir* William K Howard • *Scr* Lynn Starling, from a play by Frank Craven

Firstborn ★★ 15

Drama 1984 · US · Colour · 96mins

In a prime example of a film that engages interest only to dramatically lose it with the denouement, Teri Garr is a divorcee with two sons who picks up a lover that her boys realise is totally unsavoury. However by playing on her self-doubt he manages to drive a wedge between the mother and her sons. Peter Weller (remember him as *Robocop*?) is excellent as the sinister suitor and Garr is convincing as the neurotic mother, but the plausible set-up is thrown away by actions more akin to *Death Wish* than this kind of domestic melodrama. 📺

Teri Garr *Wendy* • Peter Weller *Sam* • Christopher Collet *Jake* • Corey Haim *Brian* • Sarah Jessica Parker *Lisa* • Richard Brandon *Dad* ■ *Dir* Michael Apted • *Scr* Ron Koslow

A Fish Called Wanda ★★★★★ 15

Comedy 1988 · UK/US · Colour · 103mins

Audiences around the world were not alone in appreciating this sparkling British-set comedy, as stars John Cleese, Jamie Lee Curtis, Kevin Kline and Michael Palin so enjoyed the experience that they went on to make

a second feature together, the sadly disappointing *Fierce Creatures*. The comic credentials are impeccable, for not only were Cleese and Palin *Monty Python* colleagues, but director Charles Crichton was also responsible for those Ealing classics *Hue and Cry*, *The Lavender Hill Mob* and *The Titfield Thunderbolt*. The American pair more than play their part, however, with Kline wonderfully manic as the unhinged Otto, winning a best supporting actor Oscar in the process. Contains swearing, some violence, sex scenes and nudity. 📺 *DVD*

John Cleese *Archie Leach* • Jamie Lee Curtis *Wanda* • Kevin Kline *Otto* • Michael Palin *Ken* • Maria Aitken *Wendy* • Tom Georgeson *George* • Patricia Hayes *Mrs Coady* • Geoffrey Palmer *Judge* • Cynthia Caylor *Portia* ■ *Dir* Charles Crichton • *Scr* John Cleese, from a story by Charles Crichton, John Cleese

The Fish That Saved Pittsburgh ★★

Comedy 1979 · US · Colour · 104mins

A hopelessly muddled basketball comedy that attempts to cash in on the disco craze. The loosely plotted story focuses on a dire team that in desperation turns to the stars (the astrological ones, that is) in an attempt to get back on the winning track. Real-life basketball greats Kareem Abdul-Jabbar and Julius Erving are teamed with some talented comedy performers (Jonathan Winters, Stockard Channing) but no one really gets the chance to shine. Fans of seventies kitsch will dig the soundtrack.

Julius "Dr J" Erving *Moses Guthrie* • Jonathan Winters *HS/Harvey Tilson* • Meadowlark Lemon *Reverend Grady Jackson* • M Emmet Walsh *Wally Cantrell* • Stockard Channing *Mona Mondieu* • Kareem Abdul-Jabbar ■ *Dir* Gilbert Moses • *Scr* Jaison Starkes, Edmond Stevens, from a story by Gary Stromberg, David Dashev

The Fisher King ★★★★★ 15

Fantasy drama 1991 · US · Colour · 131mins

The Arthurian legend of a maimed warrior healed by the innocence of "a perfect fool" is given a magical update by director Terry Gilliam, tripping the light fantastic in his highly individual manner in this fantasy drama. Gilliam has an eerie knack of wringing visionary heart-tugging power from unsentimental if bizarre material, and Jeff Bridges's mythical search for redemption in the enchanted kingdom of New York fits the bill exactly. A magnificent perusal into what fires and feeds the soul, with super-tramp Robin Williams keeping his trademark zaniness in check until it really counts. But it's Oscar-winner Mercedes Ruehl's electrifying portrayal of moral betrayal that you'll remember long after the fade-out. Contains swearing, some violence and brief nudity. 📺

Robin Williams *Parry* • Jeff Bridges *Jack Lucas* • Amanda Plummer *Lydia* • Mercedes Ruehl *Anne Napolitano* • Michael Jeter *Homeless cabaret singer* • Adam Bryant *Radio engineer* • David Hyde Pierce *Lou Rosen* ■ *Dir* Terry Gilliam • *Scr* Richard LaGravenese

F.I.S.T. ★★★ PG

Drama 1978 · US · Colour · 130mins

Sylvester Stallone made a brave attempt to get away from his *Rocky* image in this unflattering portrayal of the American trade union movement. He plays Johnny Kovak, who rises to the leadership of the Federation of Interstate Truckers but finds that power corrupts. The result is not as one-dimensional as some of his recent roles have been and there are moments of real dramatic conviction. Director Norman Jewison supplies the visual punch to this drama based on articles by Joe *Basic Instinct* Eszterhas. Stallone is still outclassed by Rod Steiger and Peter Boyle, though. Contains swearing. 📺

Sylvester Stallone *Johnny Kovak* • Rod Steiger *Senator Andrew Madison* • Peter Boyle *Max Graham* • Melinda Dillon *Anna Zerinkas* • David Huffman *Abe Belkin* • Kevin Conway *Vince Doyle* • Tony LoBianco *Babe Milano* ■ *Dir* Norman Jewison • *Scr* Sylvester Stallone, Joe Eszterhas, from articles by Joe Eszterhas

Fist of Fury ★★★ 18

Martial arts drama
1972 · HK · Colour · 98mins

Despite a troubled shoot, this remains an essential Bruce Lee vehicle. Dating from his Hong Kong days, he plays a martial arts student who sets out to avenge the death of his beloved mentor. He uncovers a Japanese gangster-smuggling ring who killed his boxing master when he discovered their plots. The uninitiated will cringe at the dumb script and often amateurish direction, but the fight scenes, choreographed by Lee, are breathtaking and his athletic charisma will win over doubters. Cantonese dialogue dubbed into English. 📺

Bruce Lee *Chen Chen* • Nora Miao *Yuan Le-Erh* • James Tien *Fan Chun-Hsia* • Robert Baker *Russian boxer* • Maria Yi *Yen* ■ *Dir* Lo Wei • *Scr* Lo Wei

Fist of the North Star ★★ 18

Animated science-fiction adventure
1986 · Jap · Colour · 111mins

Based on a Japanese manga (comic book) of the same name, it was inevitable that this animated movie would gain instant cult status because of the extremely violent and gory deaths many of the grotesque characters suffer. One "hero" aims get his girlfriend back from the brute who beat him up and left him for dead, but there is not much else going on in this story about various martial arts factions and *Mad Max*-like gangs constantly at each other's throats in a post-apocalypse world. Still, it's better and more faithful to the original comic book than the live-action version made several years later (starring Gary Daniels). Japanese dialogue dubbed into English. 📺

John Vickery *Ken* • Melodee Spivack *Julia* • Wally Burr *Raoh* • Michael McConnohie *Shin* • Gregory Snegoff *Rei* • Tony Oliver *Bat* • Holly Sidell *Lynn* ■ *Dir* Toyoo Ashida • *Scr* Susumu Takahisa, from the graphic novels by Buronson Hara, Tetsuo Hara

U = SUITABLE FOR ALL   Uc = SUITABLE FOR ALL, ESPECIALLY FOR YOUNG CHILDREN (VIDEO ONLY)   PG = PARENTAL GUIDANCE

Fist of the North Star ★★ 18

Science-fiction martial arts adventure
1995 · US · Colour · 88mins

A very standard live-action version of the popular Japanese animated manga series written and directed by the team behind *Hellbound: Hellraiser II*. Martial arts star Gary Daniels is Kenshiro, the warrior on a mission to restore peace between the warring faction of the Northern and Southern Star, in his post-apocalyptic kingdom. Evil Southern Star chief Lord Shin (Costas Mandylor) has other ideas. Like a bad spaghetti western unceremoniously placed in a science-fiction setting, Tony Randel's direction fails to match the hyper-kinetic quality of the original cartoon despite plenty of goofy action spiced up with additional gore. ▭

Gary Daniels *Kenshiro* • Malcolm McDowell *Ryuken* • Costas Mandylor *Lord Shin* • Dante Basco *Bat* • Nalona Herron *Lynn* • Melvin Van Peebles *Asher* • Chris Penn [Christopher Penn] *Jackal* ■ *Dir* Tony Randel • *Scr* Peter Atkins, Tony Randel, from the graphic novels by Buronson Hara, Tetsuo Hara

A Fistful of Dollars

★★★★★ 15

Classic spaghetti western
1964 · It/W Ger/Sp · Colour · 95mins

Based on Akira Kurosawa's 1961 samurai classic *Yojimbo*, the first "spaghetti" western was directed by Sergio Leone. His daringly brilliant use of extreme close-up and compensational depth, and his unflinching depiction of violence, gave the western a new lease of life. Clint Eastwood, whose career to this point had been in American TV, most notably in the western series *Rawhide*, became an international superstar for his portrayal of the Man with No Name, insisting that much of his dialogue was cut to increase the drifter's air of mystery. Gian Maria Volonté (billed here as John Wells) lends excellent support as the snarling Ramon, and Ennio Morricone's minimalist score is a gem. ▭ **DVD**

Clint Eastwood *The Man with No Name* • Marianna Koch *Marisol* • John Wells [Gian Maria Volonté] *Ramon Rojo* • Pepe Calvo *Silvanito* • Wolfgang Lukschy *John Baxter* • Sieghardt Rupp *Esteban Rojo* • Antonio Prieto *Benito Rojo* • Margarita Lozano *Consuela Baxter* • Daniel Martin *Julian* • Carol Brown [Bruno Carotenuto] *Antonio Baxter* • Benito Stefanelli *Rubio* • Richard Stuyvesant [Mario Brega] *Chico* • Josef Egger *Piripero* ■ *Dir* Sergio Leone • *Scr* Sergio Leone, Duccio Tessari, Victor A Catena, G Schock, from the film *Yojimbo* by Akira Kurosawa, Ryuzo Kikushima, Hideo Oguni

A Fistful of Dynamite

★★★ 15

Spaghetti western
1971 · It · Colour · 132mins

A spaghetti western by master chef Sergio Leone, whose original title *Duck, You Sucker!* was perhaps more in tune with the film's jokey intentions, as peasant Rod Steiger becomes involved with fugitive IRA explosives expert James Coburn and the Mexican Revolution. There's nothing all that funny about Coburn as a walking arsenal, but Leone manages more laughs than you'd expect, thanks to the actors' unexpected gift for

deadpan comedy. Some dialogue dubbed into English. Contains violence and swearing. ▭

Rod Steiger *Juan Miranda* • James Coburn *Sean Mallory* • Romolo Valli *Dr Villega* • Maria Monti *Adolita* • Rik Battaglia *Santerna* • Franco Graziosi *Governor* ■ *Dir* Sergio Leone • *Scr* Sergio Leone, Luciano Vicenzoni, Sergio Donati, from a story by Sergio Leone

A Fistful of Fingers ★★ 15

Western spoof 1995 · UK · Colour · 77mins

Shot in Somerset on a miniscule budget, this spoof western from self-confessed Sam Raimi fan, director Edgar Wright makes up in *Monty Python* slapstick, *Airplane!*-style gags, Sergio Leone references and jokes about its cheapness what it lacks in hard cash. The Man With No Name, his face smeared in fake five o'clock shadow, pursues the outlaw Squint, wearing a false moustache, across the Mendips in Wright's game homage, using a mostly teenage cast, that plays like a surrealistic shoestring version of *Blazing Saddles*. Although most of the humour falls embarrassingly flat, it's hard not to enjoy the sheer gung ho ingenuity of this movie. ▭

Graham Low *No Name/Walter Marshall* • Martin Curtis *Running Sore* • Oliver Evans *The Squint* • Quentin Green *Jimmy James* • Jeremy Beadle • Nicola Stapleton *Pint-sized hussy* ■ *Dir/Scr* Edgar Wright

Fists in the Pocket

★★★★ 12

Drama 1965 · It · BW · 104mins

Shot on a shoestring, Marco Bellocchio's debut feature is an aggressive, semi-autobiographical assault on family life and bourgeois parochialism. Raging at the restrictions of small-town, middle-class life, the film uses epilepsy and blindness as symbols of social malaise to which teenager Lou Castel can only respond with increasingly frenzied acts of violence when he tries to escape the family by getting married. Typified by Castel's astonishing portrayal of pent-up fury, the bruising backstreet authenticity is amazing for its time. Thanks to Bellocchio's controlled direction and Alberto Marrama's no-nonsense imagery, this study of mental instability and murder is totally convincing. An Italian language film. Contains violence. ▭

Paola Pitagora *Giulia* • Lou Castel *Sandro* • Marino Mase *Augusto* • Liliana Gerace *The Mother* • Pier Luigi Troglio *Leone* • Jean MacNeil *Lucia* ■ *Dir/Scr* Marco Bellocchio

Fitzcarraldo ★★★★★ PG

Drama 1982 · W Ger · Colour · 150mins

A labour of love that, for German director Werner Herzog, became a love of labour. An obsessionalist like his hero, Herzog once said "I live my life or end my life with this project". It is the story of Fitzcarraldo, a man so determined to bring opera to the South American jungle that he hires local natives to haul his steamship over a mountain and build an opera house. Up a 40-degree incline, 320 tons were pushed and tugged by brute force – an actual endeavour which Herzog filmed. The result is a stunning achievement,

about which a documentary, *Burden of Dreams*, was made in 1982. What you see is what you get – a stupendous uplift of muscle and mind. In German with English subtitles. ▭

Klaus Kinski *Fitzcarraldo* • Claudia Cardinale *Molly* • Jose Lewgoy *Don Aquilino* • Paul Hittscher *Paul* • Miguel Angel Fuentes *Cholo* ■ *Dir/Scr* Werner Herzog

Fitzwilly ★★ U

Comedy 1967 · US · Colour · 102mins

What with Edith Evans compiling a dictionary for people who can't spell and butler Dick Van Dyke heading a crime syndicate to prevent her discovering that the family fortune has given out, *Fitzwilly* keeps threatening to turn into a gleeful screwball romp. That it fails to do so is mostly down to the killjoy direction of Delbert Mann, who doesn't seem to appreciate the comic potential of the situations and Isobel Lennart's gag-packed script. Van Dyke and Evans are good fun, and John McGiver provides practised support, but Barbara Feldon is a drip as Evans's secretary and a debuting Sam Waterston makes little impression.

Dick Van Dyke *Fitzwilliam* • Barbara Feldon *Juliet Nowell* • Edith Evans *Victoria Woodworth* • John McGiver *Albert* • Harry Townes *Mr Nowell* • Sam Waterston *Oliver* ■ *Dir* Delbert Mann • *Scr* Isobel Lennart, from the novel *A Garden of Cucumbers* by Poyntz Tyler

Five ★★★

Drama 1951 · US · BW · 90mins

Former radio producer turned exploitation merchant Arch Oboler has some interesting gimmick-laden films to his credit, most notably the first movie in 3-D, the notorious *Bwana Devil*. The gimmick here is both the title and the plot, which deals with the last five survivors after the Earth has been devastated by a (then topical) A-bomb blast. The trouble is, it's all rather static and cheap-looking, and it's awfully hard to care about these particular survivors, a group of unknowns who have remained as such. A story like this really needs star-power, as was the case in such post-apocalypse movies as *On the Beach* and *The World, the Flesh and the Devil*. However, the dialogue is clever and the situations, though contrived, are nonetheless intriguing. The bizarre whole is certainly a collector's item, though perhaps better suited to radio.

William Phipps *Michael* • Susan Douglas *Roseanne* • James Anderson *Eric* • Charles Lampkin *Charles* ■ *Dir/Scr* Arch Oboler

Five against the House ★★

Crime drama 1955 · US · BW · 83mins

A heist thriller, in which five students plan to rob an allegedly secure casino in Reno, cashing in on two winning movie formulas of the time: the "perfect robbery" and the "teenage-angst drama". Guy Madison makes a lacklustre hero, quite upstaged by Brian Keith as the psychotic member of the gang. There is a girl, of course Kim Novak, who was spotted by Columbia boss Harry Cohn when she flogged refrigerators under the name of "Miss Deepfreeze". Her allure, hardly chilling, plus Phil Karlson's zippy

direction, make for a decent B-movie with a ludicrously cod-Freudian ending.

Guy Madison *Al Mercer* • Kim Novak *Kay Greylek* • Brian Keith *Brick* • Alvy Moore *Roy* • William Conrad *Eric Berg* • Kerwin Mathews *Ronnie* ■ *Dir* Phil Karlson • *Scr* Stirling Silliphant, William Bowers, John Barnwell, from a story by Jack Finney

Five Branded Women ★★

Second World War drama
1960 · US/It/Yug · BW · 103mins

A stellar cast has far too little asked of it in this uncompromising exploration of Yugoslav resistance during the Second World War. The scene in which the women have their heads shaved for dallying with Nazi officer Steve Forrest is easily the most disturbing of the picture, as the later guerilla encounters differ little from the combat sequences seen in a dozen other war movies. Martin Ritt's direction doesn't shy away from the cruel realities of Partisan activity and draws committed performances from Silvana Mangano and Vera Miles particularly. However, its brutal intensity makes it rather heavy going.

Van Heflin *Velko* • Silvana Mangano *Jovanka* • Vera Miles *Daniza* • Barbara Bel Geddes *Marja* • Jeanne Moreau *Ljuba* • Richard Basehart *Captain Reinhardt* • Harry Guardino *Branco* • Carla Gravina *Mira* ■ *Dir* Martin Ritt • *Scr* Ivo Perilli, from the novel by Ugo Pirro

Five Came Back ★★★

Adventure drama 1939 · US · BW · 75mins

A gripping affair as pilot Chester Morris crashes his plane in the Andes and can only take off again with the titular five. Of the twelve on board, who will escape the dreaded headhunters of the Amazon? Lucille Ball? John Carradine? C Aubrey Smith? Wendy Barrie? A motley assortment of passengers, and, to be fair, *The Bridge of San Luis Rey* got there first and *The High and the Mighty* did it better, but this is still mesmerising, though showing its age now. Director John Farrow liked the plot so much he remade it in 1956 as *Back from Eternity*, making him one of a select group of Hollywood directors such as Hitchcock, DeMille and John Ford who remade their own movies.

Chester Morris *Bill* • Lucille Ball *Peggy* • Wendy Barrie *Alice Melhorne* • John Carradine *Crimp* • Allen Jenkins *Peter* • C Aubrey Smith *Prof Henry Spengler* ■ *Dir* John Farrow • *Scr* Jerry Cady, Dalton Trumbo, Nathanael West, from a story by Richard Carroll

5 Card Stud ★★★

Western 1968 · US · Colour · 102mins

When a cardsharp is lynched by the five men he cheated, the men themselves start dying mysteriously. This neat little mystery is really Agatha Christie's *Ten Little Indians* transposed to the Wild West, with Dean Martin as a cardplayer turned detective and Robert Mitchum as a preacher. Made during a brief fad for poker pictures (*The Cincinnati Kid*, *Kaleidoscope*, and *Big Deal at Dodge City* were others), it exists solely on the laconic charm of its two stars: Martin recalling his great days on *Rio Bravo* and Mitchum sending himself up as the menacing cleric from *The Night of the Hunter*.

Dean Martin *Van Morgan* • Robert Mitchum *Reverend Rudd* • Roddy McDowall *Nick Evers* • Inger Stevens *Lily Langford* • Katherine Justice *Nora Evers* • John Anderson *Marshal Dana* • Yaphet Kotto *Little George* ■ *Dir* Henry Hathaway • *Scr* Marguerite Roberts, from a novel by Roy Gaulden

Five Corners ★★★ 15

Thriller 1987 · US · Colour · 89mins

Produced by George Harrison's HandMade Films, it's the cast of this virtually unreleased movie that catches the eye: Jodie Foster, Tim Robbins and John Turturro. Directed by Tony Bill and written by John Patrick Shanley (who won an Oscar for his screenplay for *Moonstruck* the same year), it's set in the Bronx in 1964 where Foster has been nearly raped, Turturro emerges from jail for said crime, and Robbins is about to go south to join the civil rights movement. After much scene-setting, Turturro goes completely crazy. As a coming-of-age drama, it offers nothing new, and the film's shifts of mood from comedy to drama to horror are over-calculated, but the three young stars are always worth watching, especially Robbins, who is a dead ringer for the young Orson Welles. Contains violence and swearing.

Jodie Foster *Linda* • Tim Robbins *Harry Fitzgerald* • Todd Graff *James* • John Turturro *Heinz Sabantino* • Elizabeth Berridge *Melanie* • Rose Gregorio *Mrs Sabantino* ■ *Dir* Tony Bill • *Scr* John Patrick Shanley

Five Days from Home ★

Action drama 1978 · US · Colour · 108mins

With less than a week of his sentence to go, convicted killer TM Pryor escapes from jail in order to be with his critically ill son. George Peppard turned director for the first and last time with this drama in which he also takes the lead role as the ex-cop whose victim was his wife's lover. This makes him a more likeable character than a bank robber or a rapist, and certainly more sympathetic than snarling heavy Neville Brand who is hot on his trail. The sentimentality of the story will probably leave you feeling a bit nauseous.

George Peppard *TM Pryor* • Neville Brand *Inspector Markley* • Sherry Boucher *Wanda Dulac* • Victor Campos *Jose Stover* • Robert Donner *Baldwin* ■ *Dir* George Peppard • *Scr* William Moore

Five Days One Summer ★★ PG

Drama 1982 · US · Colour · 103mins

Fred Zinnemann's last film is a very personal tale, a Kay Boyle story with a theme similar to events in Zinnemann's own past, but not, alas, terribly obvious screen material. Of course, the director of *High Noon* and *From Here to Eternity* knows how to tell a tale, and the use of Alpine scenery is certainly striking, but the film never really builds up steam and isn't helped by the fragmentary story-telling and flashback structure. Despite the dignified stellar presence of Sean Connery, plus talented Lambert Wilson, the chemistry simply isn't there, and Betsy Brantley is wholly inadequate in a key role.

Sean Connery *Douglas* • Betsy Brantley *Kate* • Lambert Wilson *Johann* • Jennifer Hilary *Sarah* • Isabel Dean *Kate's mother* • Gérard Buhr *Brendel* • Anna Massey *Jennifer Pierce* ■ *Dir* Fred Zinnemann • *Scr* Michael Austin, from the short story *Maiden Maiden* by Kay Boyle

Five Easy Pieces ★★★★★ 15

Drama 1970 · US · Colour · 94mins

Movies like *Batman* and *Mars Attacks!* have done little for Jack Nicholson's career but his Oscar for *As Good As It Gets* restored some of the lustre to his reputation. Take a look at *Five Easy Pieces* and you'll see how good he used to be. He was lean and hungry then, fresh from *Easy Rider* and in cahoots with several of the best indie film-makers of the time: director Bob Rafelson, producer Bert Schneider and writers Carole Eastman and Robert Towne. In *Five Easy Pieces*, he's simply magnetic as Bobby Dupea, emotionally repressed and unable to adjust to the two worlds he inhabits among blue collar oil-riggers and the family home, a sort of Ibsen commune devoted to maths and Mozart. The film, superbly directed by Rafelson, shifts the late sixties hippy drop-out genre into the Ingmar Bergman class: it's cerebral, yes, but also moving and witty. It also has a classic scene when Nicholson orders a sandwich at a diner and asks the waitress to hold the chicken and just serve him the toast. DVD

Jack Nicholson *Robert Eroica Dupea* • Karen Black *Rayette Dipesto* • Susan Anspach *Catherine Van Ost* • Lois Smith *Partita Dupea* • Billy "Green" Bush [Billy Green Bush] *Elton* • Ralph Waite *Carl Fidelio Dupea* ■ *Dir* Bob Rafelson • *Scr* Adrien Joyce [Carole Eastman], from a story by Bob Rafelson, Joyce Rafelson

Five Finger Exercise ★

Melodrama 1962 · US · BW · 111mins

Peter Shaffer's stage play – a success at the time – turned into an embarrassing showcase for the rasping charm of Rosalind Russell, a culture vulture who's married to thick Jack Hawkins and fancies egghead German tutor Maximilian Schell, who tries to commit suicide because he feels alienated. The original, a sort of George Bernard Shaw-ish exercise in linguistics, was set in London but this is set on the Columbia backlot in Hollywood, and is hopelessly stagebound and constipated.

Rosalind Russell *Louise Harrington* • Jack Hawkins *Stanley Harrington* • Maximilian Schell *Walter* • Richard Beymer *Philip Harrington* ■ *Dir* Daniel Mann • *Scr* Frances Goodrich, Albert Hackett, from the play by Peter Shaffer

5 Fingers ★★★ U

Spy drama 1952 · US · BW · 107mins

Loosely based on fact, this spy thriller stars James Mason as the Albanian valet who, while serving the British Ambassador to Turkey, peddles secrets to the Germans. Michael Rennie is the detective trying to plug the leak, while Danielle Darrieux is a mysterious countess. Directed by Joseph L Mankiewicz in order to free himself from a contract with Fox (for whom he had made *All about Eve*), it's a sophisticated and often witty affair dominated by Mason's suave duplicity. Blacklisted screenwriter Michael Wilson found his structure retained but his dialogue extensively rewritten by Mankiewicz; the same thing happened again to Wilson on *Lawrence of Arabia* ten years later.

James Mason *Cicero* • Danielle Darrieux *Anna* • Michael Rennie *George Travers* • Walter Hampden *Sir Frederic* • Oscar Karlweis *Moyzisch* • Herbert Berghof *Col von Richter* • John Wengraf *Von Papen* ■ *Dir* Joseph L Mankiewicz • *Scr* Michael Wilson, from the book *Operation Cicero* by LC Moyzisch

Five Gates to Hell ★

War drama 1959 · US · BW · 88mins

Before he became known as the author of *King Rat* and *Tai-Pan*, James Clavell persuaded Fox to let him write, produce and direct this frenzied war melodrama. Seven Red Cross nurses are captured and abused by Indo-Chinese guerrillas, but live to wreak a violent revenge on their captors. The result is in such bad taste, it's surprising it didn't develop a cult following. Neville Brand does his best to create a rounded figure out of the warlord's lieutenant obsessed with Dolores Michaels's nurse.

Neville Brand *Chen Pamok* • Dolores Michaels *Athena* • Patricia Owens *Joy* • Ken Scott *Dr John Richter* • Nobu McCarthy *Chioko* ■ *Dir/Scr* James Clavell

Five Golden Dragons ★★ PG

Action crime drama 1967 · UK · Colour · 100mins

The most appealing thing about this unashamed slice of hokum are the villains – Christopher Lee, George Raft, Brian Donlevy and Dan Duryea as members of a secret sect in Hong Kong. The hero, Hollywood has-been Robert Cummings, washes up there and finds himself caught between the Dragons and local Mafioso. The cast includes Rupert Davies, then known to the film's entire audience as TV's Inspector Maigret. An outrageously hammy Klaus Kinski also pops up in this lively affair that fleeces everything from *The World of Suzie Wong* to the *Fu Manchu* films. Producer Harry Alan Towers also wrote the script under the pseudonym Peter Welbeck.

Robert Cummings *Bob Mitchell* • Rupert Davies *Comm Sanders* • Margaret Lee *Magda* • Klaus Kinski *Gert* • Brian Donlevy *Dragon* • Dan Duryea *Dragon* • Christopher Lee *Dragon* • George Raft *Dragon* ■ *Dir* Jeremy Summers • *Scr* Peter Welbeck [Harry Alan Towers] • *Cinematographer* John von Kotze

Five Graves to Cairo ★★★★

Second World War drama 1943 · US · BW · 96mins

Minor but hugely enjoyable Billy Wilder picture with Erich von Stroheim as Field Marshall Rommel, holed up in a fly-blown hotel during the North Africa campaign. Franchot Tone is a British spy posing as a club-footed waiter, Anne Baxter is a French maid, Peter Van Eyck a Nazi sadist and Fortunio Bonanova an Italian buffoon who bursts into opera – the whole movie is a sly transposition of *Aida*. Despite a few token shots of tanks in the desert, this is the Second World War played indoors as a game of charades, role-playing and racial stereotyping. Tense and hilarious, it's a smashing entertainment, and von Stroheim is utterly magnificent.

Franchot Tone *Cpl John Bramble* • Anne Baxter *Mouche* • Akim Tamiroff *Farid* • Erich von Stroheim *Field Marshal Rommel* • Peter Van Eyck *Lt Schwegler* • Fortunio Bonanova *General Sabastiano* • Miles Mander *British Colonel* ■ *Dir* Billy Wilder • *Scr* Charles Brackett, Billy Wilder, from the play *Hotel Imperial* by Lajos Biró

Five Guns West ★★ U

Western 1955 · US · Colour · 81mins

A piece of movie history was forged here with the directing debut of Roger Corman, who became the acknowledged master and exploiter of the B-movie and the sponsor of such talents as Bogdanovich, Coppola, Scorsese and Demme. It's a western, of course, a sort of Civil War spy story about a deserter, stolen gold, a list of Confederate agents – and five convicted murderers who are let out of jail to catch the deserter. Shot in colour and widescreen by Floyd Crosby – the cameraman on *High Noon* – and starring wooden John Lund and Dorothy Malone, it's unmissable for students of modern Hollywood.

John Lund *Govern Sturges* • Dorothy Malone *Shalee* • Mike Connors *Hale Clinton* • Bob Campbell *John Candy* • Jonathan Haze *Billy Candy* • Paul Birch *JC Haggard* • James Stone *Uncle Mime* • Jack Ingram *Jethro* • Larry Thor *Confederate captain* ■ *Dir* Roger Corman • *Scr* R Wright Campbell

The Five Heartbeats ★★★ 15

Musical drama 1991 · US · Colour · 121mins

Having made a sensational debut with the blistering satire *Hollywood Shuffle*, Robert Townsend slightly missed his step with this overlong, but still essentially enjoyable, tribute to African-American singing groups like the Dells (on whom this film is loosely based), who struggled in the shadow of Motown in the sixties. Although the music is very much of the period, the overall style is closer to the "I'm gonna play my own sound" bandleader biopics of the forties and fifties. The familiar round of minor gigs, auditions and disappointments is trotted out in textbook fashion, but it's lovingly done and slickly played. Contains violence and swearing.

Robert Townsend *Donald "Duck" Matthews* • Michael Wright *Eddie King Jr* • Leon *James Thomas "JT" Matthews* • Harry J Lennix *Terence "Dresser" Williams* • Tico Wells *Anthony "Choirboy" Stone* • Diahann Carroll *Eleanor Porter* ■ *Dir* Robert Townsend • *Scr* Robert Townsend, Keenen Ivory Wayans

Five Miles to Midnight ★★

Drama 1963 · US/Fr/It · BW · 108mins

In which Sophia Loren slowly goes stark, staring mad. Well, she is married to Anthony Perkins who unfortunately (for her) survives a plane crash and continues to torment her and everyone else who thinks he's dead. Meanwhile, he plans to take advantage of his timely demise by defrauding the insurance company – with the help of his unwilling spouse. In return, he promises to disappear from her life. Fans of melodrama will enjoy this juicy item that sometimes seems Hitchcockian in tone but most of the time exists in a world of its own.

Loren, as ever, looks like a marble statue and acts like one as well, while Perkins simply crosses his Norman Bates act from *Psycho* with Cary Grant's from *Suspicion*.

Sophia Loren *Lisa Macklin* • Anthony Perkins *Robert Macklin* • Gig Young *David Barnes* • Jean-Pierre Aumont *Alan Stewart* • Yolande Turner *Barbara Ford* ■ *Dir* Anatole Litvak • *Scr* Peter Viertel, Hugh Wheeler

The Five Pennies ★★★★ U

Musical biographical drama
1959 · US · Colour · 117mins

After the success of James Stewart in *The Glenn Miller Story*, glossy bandleader biopics enjoyed a brief vogue, and this dramatic but schmaltzy Paramount music-fest was one of the best. Danny Kaye is perfectly cast as cornettist "Red" Nichols, whose life seemed like a scriptwriter's invention. When his daughter Dorothy (played as a teenager by a wonderful Tuesday Weld) contracted polio, he threw away his instrument, only to enjoy a revival as her health improved. There's a super jam session with Louis Armstrong, plus some fine new songs, including a lovely *Lullaby in Ragtime* from the film's associate producer Sylvia Fine (Mrs Danny Kaye). All in all, an excellent example of a fifties studio crowd-pleaser.

Danny Kaye *Loring "Red" Nichols* • Barbara Bel Geddes *Bobbie Meredith* • Louis Armstrong • Bob Crosby *Wil Paradise* • Harry Guardino *Tony Valani* • Susan Gordon *Dorothy Nichols, aged six* • Tuesday Weld *Dorothy aged 12–14* • Bob Hope ■ *Dir* Melville Shavelson • *Scr* Melville Shavelson, Jack Rose, from a story by Robert Smith

The Five Senses ★★★★ 15

Drama
1999 · Can · Colour · 104 52s

The danger of making a film about genetic stereotyping is that contrivance will undermine inspiration. Yet Canadian director Jeremy Podeswa avoids any such pitfalls in this accomplished ensemble drama. Although it takes time to introduce us to the cake-maker with no taste, the cleaner with a nose for romance, the optician who's going deaf and the masseuse with an irresponsible teenage daughter, their stories soon interweave into a satisfying whole. With a splendid cast led by Mary-Louise Parker, this is a genuinely sensual experience which suggests people should trust their senses more and their emotions less. Contains swearing and sex scenes.

Mary-Louise Parker *Rona* • Pascale Bussières *Gail* • Richard Clarkin *Raymond* • Brendan Fletcher *Rupert* • Marco Leonardi *Roberto* • Nadia Litz *Rachel* • Molly Parker *Anna Miller* ■ *Dir/Scr* Jeremy Podeswa

Five Star Final ★★★

Crime drama
1931 · US · BW · 90mins

Ben Hecht and Charles MacArthur's Broadway play *The Front Page* was a huge hit and began a cycle of newspaper stories in which editors and reporters were either crusading heroes or as scummy as the people and crimes they exposed. *Five Star Final*, which was originally a Broadway hit by Louis Weitzenkorn, stars Edward G Robinson as a decent editor who is

ordered by his proprietor to sink the tone of the stories he prints into the gutter to raise his newspaper's circulation. Two suicides ensue when a scandal breaks on the front page. Wearing its social conscience on its rolled-up sleeve, the picture, directed by Mervyn LeRoy, remains gripping, and the excellent Robinson is well supported by HB Warner, Frances Starr and Boris Karloff as a shifty reporter named Isopod. What it lacks, though, is Hecht and MacArthur's bracing wit.

Edward G Robinson *Randall* • Marian Marsh *Jenny Townsend* • HB Warner *Michael Townsend* • Anthony Bushell *Philip Weeks* • George E Stone *Ziggie Feinstein* • Frances Starr *Nancy Voorhees Townsend* • Ona Munson *Kitty Carmody* • Boris Karloff *"Reverend" Vernon Isopod* ■ *Dir* Mervyn LeRoy • *Scr* Byron Morgan, Robert Lord, from the play *Late Night Final* by Louis Weitzenkorn

Five Steps to Danger ★★ U

Spy melodrama
1957 · US · BW · 80mins

This lame-brained B-thriller stars Ruth Roman as a "mystery woman" in possession of a secret code, who finds herself the target of communist agents. Werner Klemperer, the son of the famous conductor Otto, plays a shifty psychiatrist. The main reason for watching is Sterling Hayden, who is best remembered for *The Asphalt Jungle* and *The Killing*. Hayden was a major actor who never became a star; his career was handicapped by his "friendly" testimony before the anti-communist McCarthy hearings and by an obsession with the sea which took him on long and arduous voyages.

Ruth Roman *Ann Nicholson* • Sterling Hayden *John Emmett* • Werner Klemperer *Dr Simmons* • Richard Gaines *Dean Brant* • Charles Davis *Kirk* • Jeanne Cooper *Helen Bethke* ■ *Dir* Henry S Kesler • *Scr* Henry S Kesler, from a story by Donald Hamilton

The 5,000 Fingers of Dr T ★★★★★ U

Fantasy adventure
1953 · US · Colour · 88mins

Criminally neglected for far too long, producer Stanley Kramer's offbeat children's nightmare, co-written by Ted Geisel (better known as Dr Seuss), is one of the best surrealistic fantasies Hollywood has ever made. Tommy Rettig hates his piano lessons so much he dreams of being forced to play the world's largest keyboard by mad musician Dr Terwilliker (the nastily marvellous Hans Conried) along with 500 other captive boys. Look for the anti-communist propaganda (symbolised by the red smoke) as the children are slave-driven to ignite an atomic bomb by their manic playing. Hugely imaginative, fun, scary and visually dazzling – the sets and backdrops are simply stunning.

Peter Lind Hayes *Mr Zabladowski* • Tommy Rettig *Bart Collins* • Mary Healy *Mrs Collins* • Hans Conried *Dr Terwilliker* • John Heasley *Uncle Whitney* • Robert Heasley *Uncle Judson* • Noel Cravat *Sergeant Lunk* • Henry Kulky *Stroogo* ■ *Dir* Roy Rowland • *Scr* Ted "Dr Seuss" Geisel, Allan Scott, from a story by Ted "Dr Seuss" Geisel • *Cinematographer* Franz Planer • *Art Director* Rudolph Sternad

Five Weeks in a Balloon ★★ U

Comedy
1962 · US · Colour · 101mins

Pop go entertainment values in this Jules Verne adventure that is inflated beyond all probability by disaster movie maestro Irwin Allen, who here made the wrong sort of disaster. Cedric Hardwicke, singer Fabian and Red Buttons are members of a 19th-century British expedition floating over Africa, while Peter Lorre joins them for the dramatic ride. The inclusion of Fabian just shows how desperate the movie is to attract attention.

Red Buttons *Donald O'Shay* • Fabian *Jacques* • Barbara Eden *Susan Gale* • Cedric Hardwicke *Fergusson* • Peter Lorre *Ahmed* • Richard Haydn *Sir Henry Vining* ■ *Dir* Irwin Allen • *Scr* Charles Bennet, Irwin Allen, Albert Gail, from the novel by Jules Verne

Five Women around Utamaro ★★★★

Period melodrama
1946 · Jap · BW · 106mins

Returning to the theme of female emancipation that had preoccupied him in the mid-thirties, Kenji Mizoguchi was prevented from using this film to celebrate Japan's new-found democracy and the concept of liberation through eroticism by the production guidelines issued by the US occupying force. Consequently, he found himself the subtextual subject of this exploration of the complex relationships and social injustices that inspired the 18th-century Edo printmaker, Utamaro. In depicting the twilight world of the geishas and the artist's struggle for creative freedom, screenwriter Yoshikata Yoda provides a dramatic core that enables Mizoguchi to conduct formal experiments reflecting Utamaro's style. In Japanese with English subtitles.

Minosuke Bando *Utamaro* • Kotaro Bando *Seinosuke Koide* • Kinuyo Tanaka *Okita* • Kowasaki Hiroko *Oran* • Izuka Toshiko *Takasode* ■ *Dir* Kenji Mizoguchi • *Scr* Yoshikata Yoda, from the novel *Utamaro O Meguru Gonin no Onna* by Kanji Kunideda

Fixed Bayonets ★★★

War drama
1951 · US · BW · 91mins

War may be hell, but for writer/director Samuel Fuller it's also a character workout that can temper personalities for the worse or the better. In this familiar story of a lost platoon fighting a rearguard action in Korea, it is Richard Basehart who is fused by events into purposeful command. Although the film never reaches the poetic heights of Lewis Milestone's similar *A Walk in the Sun*, there's the same understanding that men in battle are really at war within themselves. It's a theme which makes up for a lot of phoney heroics in other flag-wavers.

Richard Basehart *Corporal Denno* • Gene Evans *Sergeant Rock* • Michael O'Shea *Sergeant Lonergan* • Richard Hylton *Wheeler* • Craig Hill *Lieutenant Gibbs* • Skip Homeier *Whitey* ■ *Dir* Samuel Fuller • *Scr* Samuel Fuller, from the novel by John Brophy

The Fixer ★★

Drama
1968 · US · Colour · 132mins

A lumbering epic starring Alan Bates as a Jewish opportunist in tsarist

Russia who claims to be a Gentile and insinuates his way into the management of a brick factory. There's a rape charge, imprisonment, humiliation and constant fear of exposure and a new wave of pogroms. Based on Bernard Malamud's novel, screenwriter Dalton Trumbo and director John Frankenheimer take on some mighty themes and turn them into a scaled-down *Doctor Zhivago*, complete with a tacky Maurice Jarre score. It's tedious and turgid, with great dollops of dialogue and some pretty picture postcard photography. The weird cast, which includes Dirk Bogarde, David Warner and Carol White, merely adds to the incongruity.

Alan Bates *Yakov Bok* • Dirk Bogarde *Bibikov* • Georgia Brown *Marfa Golov* • Hugh Griffith *Lebedev* • Elizabeth Hartman *Zinaida* • Ian Holm *Grubeshov* • David Warner *Count Odoevsky* • Carol White *Raisl* ■ *Dir* John Frankenheimer • *Scr* Dalton Trumbo, from the novel by Bernard Malamud • *Music* Maurice Jarre

The Fixer ★★★

Crime drama
1997 · US · Colour · 105mins

In addition to sharing an executive producer credit for this hard-hitting TV movie, Jon Voight also stars as a crooked lawyer who experiences a "road to Damascus" change of heart after he survives a potentially lethal accident. The only problem is, his corrupt clients refuse either to let him go straight or turn himself in. Voight, who impressed in *Heat* after several years in the Hollywood wilderness, has always been an imposing screen presence and his transformation from powerbroker to penitent is entirely convincing here. However, the over-neat ending is less credible and rather undermines the moral of the story. Contains swearing, violence, sex scenes and nudity.

Jon Voight *Jack Killoran* • Brenda Bakke *CJ* • JJ Johnston *Angelo* • Sara Botsford *Bonnie* ■ *Dir* Charles Carner [Charles Robert Carner] • *Scr* Charles Carner

Fixing the Shadow ★★★ 18

Crime drama
1994 · US · Colour · 96mins

This engrossing look at the machinations of undercover police work is uncomfortably shoe-horned into an imperfect update of the old American Indian legend of the title, about a young brave running from his shadow and then descending into the land of shadows to retrieve it. Charlie Sheen is the cop recruited by the FBI to infiltrate a biker gang who finds his life strangely mirroring the fable as he starts to lose his own identity during the investigation, and tries to maintain his cover by increasingly violent behaviour. Never quite achieving the depth, grit or emotional power it strives for, Sheen and Michael Madsen give the understated drama a strong through-line. ▭

Charlie Sheen *Dan* • Linda Fiorentino *Renee* • Michael Madsen *Blood* • Courtney B Vance *Conroy* • Rip Torn *Prescott* • Larry Ferguson *Kelly* ■ *Dir/Scr* Larry Ferguson

The Flame and the Arrow
★★★ **U**

Romantic swashbuckling adventure
1950 · US · Colour · 87mins

An exuberant swashbuckler and something of a dress rehearsal for *The Crimson Pirate* with Burt Lancaster as a Robin Hood-type character from northern Italy who sinks his teeth into a land-owning monster, played by Robert Douglas. Virginia Mayo is the love interest, but Lancaster's soul mate on the swinging chandeliers is Nick Cravat, his former circus partner, who was brought into the picture to ensure that the stunts went smoothly. The picture was heavily promoted by Warner Bros, who boasted that the stars did their own stunts and offered $1 million to anyone who could prove they didn't. When the gentlemen of the Cleveland press dared to doubt this, Lancaster and Cravat repeated their ''perch-pole'' stunt outside the newspaper building and did a radio interview at the same time.

Burt Lancaster *Dardo* • Virginia Mayo *Anne* • Robert Douglas *Alessandro* • Aline MacMahon *Nonna Bartoli* • Nick Cravat *Piccolo* ■ *Dir* Jacques Tourneur • *Scr* Waldo Salt, from his story *The Hawk and the Arrow*

Flame in the Streets ★★ **PG**

Drama   1961 · UK · Colour · 89mins

Released at a time when ''kitchen sink'' realism was all the rage, this adaptation by Ted Willis of his own play *Hot Summer Night* suffers from the uncomfortable worthiness that blighted the efforts of so many bourgeois British film-makers trying to tackle thorny social issues. John Mills rises above the old-fashioned liberalism to capture the confused bluster of the trade unionist who defends a black shop steward, but cannot tolerate the prospect of his daughter Sylvia Syms marrying Jamaican teacher Johnny Sekka. However, Brenda de Banzie's performance as his scornful, snobbish wife is badly misjudged. ▣

John Mills *Jacko Palmer* • Sylvia Syms *Kathie Palmer* • Brenda de Banzie *Nell Palmer* • Johnny Sekka *Peter Lincoln* • Earl Cameron *Gabriel Gomez* ■ *Dir* Roy Baker [Roy Ward Baker] • *Scr* Ted Willis, from his play *Hot Summer Night*

The Flame of New Orleans
★★

Comedy   1941 · US · BW · 79mins

A frothy comedy from French director René Clair, his first effort on his wartime sojourn in Hollywood. Phoney countess Marlene Dietrich leaves her rich but dull new husband Roland Young at the altar and sails away with rough-trade sea captain Bruce Cabot, disguising herself in the process. However, a shadowy figure from her European past appears and threatens her plans. This twist on the old gold-digger formula offers only middling entertainment, and shows just how ordinary Dietrich could be and how she needed rather more appealing leading men than Young and Cabot.

Marlene Dietrich *Claire Ledeux* • Bruce Cabot *Robert Latour* • Roland Young *Charles Giraud*

• Mischa Auer *Zolotov* • Andy Devine *First sailor* • Frank Jenks *Second sailor* ■ *Dir* René Clair • *Scr* Norman Krasna

Flame of the Barbary Coast
★★★ **U**

Western   1945 · US · BW · 91mins

This earthquake adventure isn't a patch on MGM's *San Francisco* but it was a big picture for Republic and it was trumpeted as the studio's ''tenth anniversary production''. John Wayne excels as cattleman Duke Fergus, competing with slimy Joseph Schildkraut for the attentions of Ann Dvorak. The low budget is evident in the ropey old stock shots and inadequate sets, though the production received Oscar nominations for its sound and score. ▣

John Wayne *Duke Fergus* • Ann Dvorak *Flaxen Tarry* • Joseph Schildkraut *Tito Morell* • William Frawley *Smooth Wylie* • Virginia Grey *Rita Dane* • Russell Hicks *Cyrus Danver* ■ *Dir* Joseph Kane • *Scr* Borden Chase

Flame Top ★★★

Biography   1980 · Fin · Colour · 150mins

One of the most expensive films ever made in Finland, this historical epic chronicles the life of the prolific and reclusive novelist, Maiju Lassila. Forced to flee St Petersburg after the murder of a Tsarist official, Lassila worked for the most part in abject poverty, enduring a tempestuous relationship with ex-actress Olga Esempio (passionately played by Rea Mauranen), before participating in the Bolshevik revolt in Helsinki. Faced with portraying such a complex character, Asko Sarkola is a touch too self-effacing. But the stately pacing lends suitable weight to unfamiliar events. In Finnish with English subtitles.

Asko Sarkola *Maiju Lassila* • Rea Mauranen *Olga Esempio* • Kari Franck *Publisher* • Esko Salminen *Stationmaster* • Ari Suonsuu *Errand boy* • Tuomo Railo *Olga's young son* ■ *Dir/ Scr* Pirjo Honkasalo, Pekka Lehto

Flaming Creatures ★★★

Underground satire   1962 · US · BW · 45mins

A seminal experimental gay movie that paved the way for the acceptance of underground culture (specifically Andy Warhol's work), a higher profile depiction of on-screen homosexuality and probably engineered the Manhattan midnight-movie-going cult. An elliptical mesh of tableaux featuring drag queens in various states of orgiastic behaviour, director Jack Smith's sexual apocalypse pilfers a kitsch range of Hollywood imagery from Marilyn Monroe and Josef von Sternberg to Maria Montez and Busby Berkeley movies (a sound montage of Montez dialogue accompanies the raw black-and-white footage) and shakes them up further with taboo-ridden acts of wanton lust. Groundbreaking in its day, a camp footnote now, but still interesting as a shock to the filmic system.

Francis Francine • Delores Flores • Joel Markman • Shirley ■ *Dir* Jack Smith

Flaming Star ★★★★ **PG**

Western   1960 · US · Colour · 88mins

Originally intended as a vehicle for Marlon Brando, this immensely dignified and astoundingly violent (for its time) western became the second movie after *King Creole* to prove Elvis Presley could act. Here he plays an unhappy misfit, who must take sides when his mother's people (he is half American Indian) decide to go on the warpath. The tension, under the brilliant direction of Don Siegel, is beautifully sustained, and the outdoor colour and CinemaScope photography is outstanding. This was to be the last shot Presley would get at a decent acting role with a major director – after this his film career took a major turn for the worse. The box-office receipts were reasonable but not startling, partly because the film totally lacked songs apart from the title number and a folksy dance tune, both in the opening minutes. ▣

Elvis Presley *Pacer Burton* • Steve Forrest *Clint Burton* • Barbara Eden *Roslyn Pierce* • Dolores Del Rio *Neddy Burton* • John McIntire *Sam Burton* • Rudolph Acosta *[Rodolfo Acosta] Buffalo Horn* ■ *Dir* Don Siegel • *Scr* Clair Huffaker, Nunnally Johnson, from the novel by Clair Huffaker

The Flamingo Kid ★★★ **15**

Comedy drama   1984 · US · Colour · 95mins

Garry Marshall didn't stray far from his *Happy Days* sitcom roots with this slight but affectionate teenage comedy drama set in the early sixties. Matt Dillon plays the working class kid, attempting to better himself by working at an exclusive private club, who finds himself in a paternal tug of war between rich smoothie Richard Crenna and his own blue-collar dad, played by Hector Elizondo. The period trappings are lovingly re-created, as are the sounds of the era, and the script is a cut above the norm. ▣

Matt Dillon *Jeffrey Willis* • Richard Crenna *Phil Brody* • Hector Elizondo *Arthur Willis* • Jessica Walter *Phyllis Brody* • Fisher Stevens *Hawk Ganz* • Brian McNamara *Steve Dawkins* ■ *Dir* Garry Marshall • *Scr* Garry Marshall, Neal Marshall, from a story by Neal Marshall

Flamingo Road ★★★

Melodrama   1949 · US · BW · 94mins

The second coming of Joan Crawford was a truly awesome sight. After leaving MGM under a cloud and winning her Oscar in 1945 for *Mildred Pierce* at Warner Bros, Crawford played a string of *femme fatale/grande dame* roles, making mincemeat of weak leading men, while women would come to sticky ends in a welter of retribution or redemption in melodramas that pleased audiences and dismayed critics. Here Crawford is reunited with her *Mildred Pierce* mentor, the brilliant director Michael Curtiz, portraying a carnival dancer stranded in deepest Florida, trapped between two men and swapping cheap philosophy with sinister sheriff Sydney Greenstreet. Immaculately produced and consummately well acted, this is a torrid treat.

Joan Crawford *Lane Bellamy* • Zachary Scott *Fielding Carlisle* • Sydney Greenstreet *Titus Semple* • David Brian *Dan Reynolds* • Gladys

George *Lute-Mae Sanders* • Virginia Huston *Annabelle Weldon* • Fred Clark *Doc Waterson* ■ *Dir* Michael Curtiz • *Scr* Robert Wilder, Edmund H North, from the play by Robert Wilder, Sally Wilder

Flap ★

Comedy drama   1970 · US · Colour · 105mins

You would need the world's most powerful microscope to spot any trace of the director of *The Third Man* in this utterly dismal effort. It stars Anthony Quinn as an Indian chief called Flapping Eagle who starts an uprising in order to draw attention to the economic plight of all native Americans. Dating from the same period as Dee Brown's book, *Bury My Heart at Wounded Knee*, Carol Reed's movie might have seemed timely and even controversial. But it's pitched as a slapstick comedy and Quinn's role as a drunken lecher is far more insulting than sympathetic.

Anthony Quinn *Flapping Eagle* • Claude Akins *Lobo Jackson* • Tony Bill *Eleven Snowflake* • Victor Jory *Wounded Bear Mr Smith* • Don Collier *Mike Lyons* • Shelley Winters *Dorothy Bluebell* ■ *Dir* Carol Reed • *Scr* Clair Huffaker

Flareup ★★ **15**

Drama   1969 · US · Colour · 93mins

A little-seen Raquel Welch vehicle which makes for diverting enough viewing. The star plays a Las Vegas dancer who attracts the unwelcome attentions of a psychopath, who rather unreasonably blames her for all his own personal problems. It's actually an early example of the *Fatal Attraction* genre that became so popular in the eighties and nineties, so it makes for an interesting curiosity. ▣

Raquel Welch *Michele* • James Stacy *Joe Brodnek* • Luke Askew *Alan Morris* • Don Chastain *Lieutenant Manion* • Ron Rifkin ''*Sailor*'' • Jean Byron *Jerri Benton* ■ *Dir* James Neilson • *Scr* Mark Rogers

The Flash ★★★ **PG**

Action fantasy   1990 · US · Colour · 89mins

A lesser-known DC Comics superhero gets the full works in the feature-length pilot episode of the short-lived US television series. John Wesley Shipp is the regular police chemist who is turned into a high-speed crime avenger thanks to a freak bolt of lightning and some chemicals. Soon he's running rings around a biker gang terrorising Central City, and being kept in check by caring Amanda Pays. The well-balanced blend of heroic thrills and sharp humour rarely flags, while the limited special effects never overwhelm the pretty simple narrative told in neat comic bubble style and established for a fast pace. ▣

John Wesley Shipp *Barry Allen/The Flash* • Amanda Pays *Christina McGee* • Michael Nader *Pike* • Tim Thomerson *Jay Allen* • Alex Desert *Julio* ■ *Dir* Robert Iscove • *Scr* Danny Bilson, Paul De Meo, from the comic strip character created by Gardner Fox, Harry Lampert • *Music* Danny Elfman

Flash ★★

Drama   1997 · US · Colour

Calling all animal lovers... this heartwarming family film will have you rooting for boy and beast. Lucas Black

U = SUITABLE FOR ALL   **Uc** = SUITABLE FOR ALL, ESPECIALLY FOR YOUNG CHILDREN (VIDEO ONLY)   **PG** = PARENTAL GUIDANCE

(*Sling Blade*) gives an affecting performance as a Georgia boy who becomes attached to a chestnut colt owned by a neighbouring farmer. But though his father buys the horse, the pair must endure a number of ordeals before everyone can live happily after. Predictable and schmaltzy, Monte Merrick's TV-movie script nevertheless touches the heart.

Lucas Black *Connor Strong* • Brian Kerwin *David Strong* • Ellen Burstyn *Laura Strong* ■ *Dir* Simon Wincer • *Scr* Monte Merrick

Flash Gordon ★★★ U

Science-fiction adventure
1936 · US · BW · 205mins

This is the feature-length condensation of the original 13-part *Flash Gordon* serial which inspired director George Lucas to create *Star Wars*. Breathless cliffhangers and vintage action meets cheesy special effects and hilarious overacting as charismatic hero Flash (former Olympic athlete Larry ''Buster'' Crabbe), along with Dale Arden (Jean Rogers) and Dr Zarkov (Frank Shannon), prevent Ming the Merciless (Charles Middleton) of the Planet Mongo conquering Earth. It's non-stop thrill-a-minute stuff (thanks to the ruthless editing) as Flash battles one adversary after another including Lion Men, Gocko the dragon-lizard monster and King Kala's underwater aliens. The best of the Crabbe trilogy of *Flash Gordon* films.

Larry ''Buster'' Crabbe *Flash Gordon* • Jean Rogers *Dale Arden* • Charles Middleton *Ming the Merciless* • Priscilla Lawson *Princess Aura* • John Lipson *King Vultan* • Richard Alexander *Prince Barin* • Frank Shannon *Dr Zarkov* ■ *Dir* Frederick Stephani • *Scr* Frederick Stephani, George Plympton, Basil Dickey, Ella O'Neill, from the comic strip by Alex Raymond

Flash Gordon ★★★ PG

Science-fiction comedy
1980 · US · Colour · 106mins

Aiming for the tongue-in-cheek frivolity of the fabulous Buster Crabbe adventures of the thirties, Mike Hodges's big-budget fantasy is great fun, providing you ignore the plot altogether and concentrate on the corny performances and cheesy special effects. Although Ornella Muti makes a wonderfully witty Princess Aura, it's Max von Sydow who runs away with the picture as the dastardly Emperor Ming. However, the sheer badness of Sam J Jones as Flash (whose dialogue had to be dubbed by another actor) and Melody Anderson as Dale Arden also adds to the charm of this expensive sci-fi pantomine. ▭ **DVD**

Sam J Jones [Sam Jones] *Flash Gordon* • Melody Anderson *Dale Arden* • Topol *Dr Hans Zarkov* • Max von Sydow *Emperor Ming* • Ornella Muti *Princess Aura* • Timothy Dalton *Prince Barin* • John Osborne *Arborian Priest* • Richard O'Brien *Fico* ■ *Dir* Mike Hodges • *Scr* Lorenzo Semple Jr, Michael Allin, from the characters created by Alex Raymond • *Music* Queen, Howard Blake

A Flash of Green ★★★★

Drama   1984 · US · Colour · 131mins

Ed Harris once again proves what a superb actor he is, in this drama with an ecological theme, based on the John D MacDonald novel. He plays a Florida reporter who betrays more than just his profession when he agrees to help a corrupt official win backing for a controversial housing development. Victor Nunez's (*Ulee's Gold*) film boasts both classy direction and a strong cast. Apart from the always bankable Harris, there is good support from Blair Brown, Richard Jordan, and John Glover. Gripping stuff.

Ed Harris *Jimmy Wing* • Blair Brown *Kate Hubble* • Richard Jordan *Elmo Bliss* • George Coe *Brian Hass* • Joan Goodfellow *Mitchie* • Jean De Baer *Jackie Halley* • John Glover *Ross Halley* ■ *Dir* Victor Nunez • *Scr* Victor Nunez, from the novel by John D MacDonald

Flashback ★★★ 15

Comedy action road movie
1990 · US · Colour · 103mins

An entertaining trip through flower power nostalgia, with Dennis Hopper having a ball sending up his old screen persona. He is a sixties' activist, on the run for two decades, who is finally nabbed by the FBI but then proceeds to run rings around his fresh-faced captor, Kiefer Sutherland. The stars spark off each other nicely and there are also some neat supporting turns from Richard Masur, Carol Kane and Michael McKean as frustrated middle-aged hippies. The script lacks any real satirical bite, but it is nice to see Hopper in one of his rare non-psycho roles and director Franco Amurri keeps the action zipping along. ▭

Kiefer Sutherland *John Buckner* • Dennis Hopper *Huey Walker* • Carol Kane *Maggie* • Cliff De Young *Sheriff Hightower* • Michael McKean *Hal* • Richard Masur *Barry* • Paul Dooley *Donald R Stark, FBI Director* ■ *Dir* Franco Amurri • *Scr* David Loughery

Flashdance ★★★ 15

Drama   1983 · US · Colour · 90mins

What a feeling... of déjà vu. The *Dirty Dancing* of its era stars Jennifer Beals as a welder by day and exotic dancer by night. But what she really, really wants is to join the Pittsburgh Ballet. Her dream ambition and fluffy romance with Michael Nouri looks welded together from other Hollywood fairy tales of fame and fortune, yet director Adrian Lyne caught the post-disco visual mood of the time to win over even the most cynical viewer. The title song (featuring Irene Cara) won an Oscar, while a major scandal developed when it was reported that Beals was doubled by Marine Jahan in the strenuous dance scenes. Contains swearing and nudity. ▭

Jennifer Beals *Alex Owens* • Michael Nouri *Nick Hurley* • Lilia Skala *Hanna Long* • Sunny Johnson *Jeanie Szabo* • Kyle T Heffner *Richie* ■ *Dir* Adrian Lyne • *Scr* Joe Eszterhas, Tom Hedley, from a story by Tom Hedley

Flashfire ★★ 18

Thriller   1993 · US · Colour · 84mins

This thriller starts well enough, with a ferocious blaze and the murder of much-decorated Billy Zane's partner. But invention is at a premium once Zane joins up with feisty hooker Kristin Minter, who witnessed the murder, and they have to rely on their wits to stay one step ahead of Zane's crooked colleagues and a gang of arsonists. Carelessly directed by Elliot Silverstein, this muddled tale of corruption and conspiracy comes to an abrupt and highly unsatisfactory conclusion. Contains swearing and violence. ▭

Billy Zane *Jack Flinder* • Louis Gossett Jr *Ben Durand* • Kristin Minter *Lisa Cates* • Louis Giambalvo *Al Sherwin* • Tom Mason *Art Cantrell* • Caroline Williams *Ann* ■ *Dir* Elliot Silverstein • *Scr* John Warren, Dan York

Flashpoint ★★ 15

Thriller   1984 · US · Colour · 89mins

Despite its title and the combustible chemistry of its two leads (Kris Kristofferson and Treat Williams as US border patrolmen), this is rather a damp squib with a final revelation route-mapped all too obviously. The guards, who fear replacement by computer techology, find a jeep buried in the desert complete with a skeleton and a lot of loot. They start making enquiries about where the cash came from, before keeping the money; soon both the baddies and the FBI (or are they one and the same?) are on their trail. There's a fascinatingly eerie sense of location, but the characters are as chaotic as the narrative, and the buddy-buddy theme means the girls hardly get a look-in. ▭

Kris Kristofferson *Bob Logan* • Treat Williams *Ernie Wiatt* • Kevin Conway *Brook* • Joaquin Martinez *Pedroza* • Rip Torn *Sheriff Wells* • Guy Boyd *Lambasino* ■ *Dir* William Tannen • *Scr* Michael Butler, Dennis Shryack, from the novel by George La Fountaine

Flatliners ★★★ 15

Supernatural thriller
1990 · US · Colour · 109mins

Is there life after death? Not with some of the acting on display here. Julia Roberts purses her bicycle-pedal lips and looks bemused in this gothic mix of old dark house and high-tech laboratory, as one of a group of medical students whose extracurricular experiments involve temporarily inducing their own deaths. Director Joel Schumacher puts more flash than flesh on the story, but still manages to deliver the expected chills with cool efficiency. Trouble is, the after-life stuff is rather too crudely clichéd. Contains swearing and sex scenes. ▭ **DVD**

Kiefer Sutherland *Nelson Wright* • Julia Roberts *Rachel Mannus* • Kevin Bacon *David Labraccio* • William Baldwin *Joe Hurley* • Oliver Platt *Randy Steckle* • Kimberly Scott *Winnie Hicks* • Joshua Rudoy *Billy Mahoney* ■ *Dir* Joel Schumacher • *Scr* Peter Filardi

The Flavour of Green Tea over Rice ★★★★

Drama   1952 · Jap · BW · 115mins

Yasujiro Ozu explores the nature of deceit and companionship in this wry yet ultimately touching study of arranged marriage. In showing how a discontented executive (Shin Saburi) and his free-spirited wife (Michiyo Kogure) work through the crisis in their relationship, he highlights the shifting social priorities of the postwar bourgeoisie while also evoking a fond nostalgia for the recent past. It remains a recognisably intimate Ozu offering, in spite of the diversity of locations, frequency of camera movements and rhythmic cutting. In Japanese with English subtitles.

Shin Saburi • Michiyo Kogure • Koji Tsuruta • Keiko Tsushima • Kuniko Miyake • Chikage Awashima • Chishu Ryu ■ *Dir* Yasujiro Ozu • *Scr* Yasujiro Ozu, Kogo Noda

The Flaw ★

Crime drama   1954 · UK · BW · 60mins

Director Terence Fisher, best known for his work at Hammer films, does all that can be expected with this ominously titled thriller that reunites him with John Bentley, who had starred in his previous outing, *Stolen Assignment*. Well-cast as a sinisterly suave racing driver, Bentley easily upstages Donald Houston, who is the lawyer trying to thwart Bentley's plans to bump off his wealthy wife, Rona Anderson. The feeble script betrays the fact this is pure B-fodder, re-made from a 1933 film, but adding nothing. ▭

John Bentley *Paul Oliveri* • Donald Houston *John Millway* • Rona Anderson *Monica Oliveri* • Doris Yorke *Mrs Bower* • Tonia Bern *Vera* ■ *Dir* Terence Fisher • *Scr* Brandon Fleming

Flawless ★★ 15

Comedy drama   1999 · US · Colour · 110mins

Utterly schematic, hopelessly old-fashioned and totally bogus, director Joel Schumacher's highly personal comedy drama nevertheless delivers some camp laughs along its uneven, shamelessly manipulative route. After suffering a stroke, homophobic security guard Robert De Niro is rehabilitated by street-smart drag queen Philip Seymour Hoffman. A meaningful relationship ensues as the macho patient learns the error of his bigoted ways. Deflating the simplistic morality fable is a vicious subplot involving stolen mob money that Hoffman may have hidden to pay for a sex-change operation. The two leads strive for emotional impact, but the superficial screenplay continually lets them down by substituting heartfelt truths with bitchy one-liners.

Robert De Niro *Walt Koontz* • Philip Seymour Hoffman *Rusty Zimmerman* • Barry Miller *Leonard Wilcox* • Wilson Jermaine Heredia *Cha-Cha* • Daphne Rubin-Vega *Tia* ■ *Dir/Scr* Joel Schumacher

A Flea in Her Ear ★★★

Farce   1968 · US/Fr · Colour · 94mins

Doppelgängers, mistaken identity, mad chases and misunderstandings abound in this movie adaptation (by *Rumpole* creator John Mortimer) of a Feydeau farce which had scored a considerable success in London at the National Theatre. Rex Harrison stars in the double role of barrister Victor Chandebisse and hotel porter Poche, and Rosemary Harris is Gabrielle, Victor's suspicious and jealous wife. The Anglo-French cast are all on form in this classic Gallic sex comedy which was considered quite risqué in its time (it was given an X certificate on release in the UK).

Rex Harrison *Victor Chandebisse/Poche* • Rosemary Harris *Gabrielle Chandebisse* • Louis Jourdan *Henri* • Rachel Roberts *Suzanne* • John Williams *Dr. Finache* • Grégoire Aslan *Max* • Edward Hardwick *Pierre* ■ *Dir* Jacques Charon • *Scr* John Mortimer, from the play by John Mortimer, from the play *La Puce à l'Oreille* by Georges Feydeau

Fled ★★ 18

Action thriller 1996 · US · Colour · 97mins

A far-fetched action thriller, starting from the same premise as 1958's *The Defiant Ones*, with one black and one white convict (Laurence Fishburne and Stephen Baldwin respectively) handcuffed together as they escape from a chain-gang. The exit has been organised with the knowledge of the law enforcement agencies, who have their sights set on a South American narcotics boss. Pathetic plotting has Fishburne falling for Salma Hayek and Baldwin (as a computer whizz, no less) having a stripper for a girlfriend. Director Kevin Hooks fills in the spaces with fist-fights and, of course, a visit to a strip joint. ▦

Laurence Fishburne *Charles Piper* • Stephen Baldwin *Mark Dodge* • Will Patton *Matthew Gibson* • Robert John Burke [Robert Burke] *Pat Schiller* • Robert Hooks *Lieutenant Clark* • Salma Hayek *Cora* ■ *Dir* Kevin Hooks • *Scr* Preston A Whitmore II

The Fleet's In ★★★ U

Musical comedy 1942 · US · BW · 93mins

A daft Paramount wartime crowd-pleaser in which shy sailor William Holden takes on a bet to kiss sultry night club chanteuse Dorothy Lamour. Funny newcomer Betty Hutton in support became a star virtually overnight, and Jimmy Dorsey and his Orchestra feature prominently. It's all very forties, but alas director Victor Schertzinger died before the movie opened. Nevertheless the plot would continue to be used in Paramount pictures right up to Elvis Presley's comeback film *GI Blues* in 1960.

Dorothy Lamour *The Countess* • William Holden (1) *Casey Kirby* • Eddie Bracken *Barney Waters* • Betty Hutton *Bessie* • Cass Daley *Cissie* • Gil Lamb *Spike* ■ *Dir* Victor Schertzinger • *Scr* Walter DeLeon, Ralph Spence, Sid Silvers, from the play *Sailor Beware!* by Kenyon Nicholson, Charles Robinson, from a story by Monte Brice, J Walter Ruben

Flesh ★★★★

Drama 1932 · US · BW · 95mins

A wonderfully melancholic study of tragic wrestler Wallace Beery and his obsessional passion for moll Karen Morley, who's emotionally involved with nasty Ricardo Cortez. This is full-blown melodrama via the Teutonic stylings of Emil Jannings, and is superbly directed by the great John Ford, someone never afraid to tackle meaty material. The insights into the world of professional wrestling are fascinating and revelatory, especially the differences in the "sport" between Germany (where the tale begins) and the USA, while the brilliant Beery produces another fine performance.

Wallace Beery *Polikai* • Karen Morley *Laura Nash* • Ricardo Cortez *Nicky* • Jean Hersholt *Mr Herman* • John Miljan *Joe Willard* • Vince Barnett *Waiter* ■ *Dir* John Ford • *Scr* Moss Hart, Leonard Praskins, Edgar Allan Woolf, from a story by Edmund Goulding

Flesh ★★★ 18

Cult erotic drama 1968 · US · Colour · 85mins

Set in the demimonde of male prostitutes and extroverted transvestites typical of producer Andy Warhol, director Paul Morrissey's gutter graphic sex farce was an early attempt by the pop art icon to cross over from underground cinema into the mainstream arena. With no story structure as such, Morrissey is content to focus on the fringe elements of society in a series of Manhattan vignettes, revolving around the nearly always naked Joe Dallesandro, who is either hustling gays to get money for his bad-tempered wife or having sex with assorted weirdos. Filmed cine-verité style with a host of non-actor Warhol superstars (Jackie Curtis, Candy Darling), it's a funny and frank walk on the wild side. ▦

Joe Dallesandro *Joe* • Geraldine Smith *Gerry* • John Christian *Young man* • Maurice Braddell *Artist* • Barry Brown *Boy on street* • Candy Darling *Blonde on sofa* • Jackie Curtis *Redhead on sofa* • Patti D'Arbanville [Patti D'Arbanville-Quinn] *Gerry's girl friend* ■ *Dir/Scr* Paul Morrissey

Flesh + Blood ★★★ 18

Historical epic 1985 · US/Neth · Colour · 121mins

Dutch director Paul Verhoeven's first Hollywood movie is a medieval epic which delivers the titular ingredients in proverbial buckets. It also boasts sumptuous music and splendid camerawork by Verhoeven regulars Basil Poledouris and Jan de Bont, who directed *Speed*. Much tougher and wittier than its rival *Highlander*, the film stars Rutger Hauer as a guerrilla warrior and Jennifer Jason Leigh as the virgin he kidnaps and rapes. (Naturally, she falls head over heels in love with him.) Shot in Spain (fans of *El Cid* will delight in revisiting Belmonte Castle), it's a spectacle that anticipates Verhoeven's later films (*RoboCop*, *Basic Instinct* and *Starship Troopers*) by pushing back the boundaries of sex and violence. ▦

Rutger Hauer *Martin* • Jennifer Jason Leigh *Agnes* • Tom Burlinson *Steven* • Jack Thompson *Hawkwood* • Fernando Hillbeck *Arnolfini* • Susan Tyrrell *Celine* ■ *Dir* Paul Verhoeven • *Scr* Paul Verhoeven, Gerald Soeteman, from a story by Gerald Soeteman • *Photography* Jan De Bont

Flesh and Bone ★★★★ 15

Drama 1993 · US · Colour · 121mins

Real-life husband and wife Dennis Quaid and Meg Ryan turn in two of their best ever performances in *The Fabulous Baker Boys* director Steve Kloves's unsettling modern *film noir*. James Caan is the psychotic cowhand who discovers his son Quaid is in love with the sole survivor of a family he murdered when she was a child. But will Ryan remember his face? Combining a fascinating fatalism with uncompromising black humour, this expert thriller evokes a haunting moodiness that never loses its grip as it turns up the subtle suspense to full throttle. An undeserved cinema failure. Contains swearing and sex scenes. ▦

Dennis Quaid *Arlis Sweeney* • Meg Ryan *Kay Davies* • James Caan *Roy Sweeney* • Christopher Rydell *Reese Davies* • Gwyneth Paltrow *Ginnie* • Scott Wilson *Elliot* ■ *Dir/Scr* Steve Kloves

Flesh and Fantasy ★★★

Supernatural portmanteau 1943 · US · BW · 92mins

New York wits Robert Benchley and David Hoffman link these three tales of the supernatural as they discuss dreams and elements of the supernatural. This leads into the three stories: the first is *Cinderella* with a twist, starring Betty Field and Robert Cummings; the second and best is an adaptation of Oscar Wilde's *Lord Arthur Saville's Crime* with Edward G Robinson shocked to learn from a spiritualist that he's about to become a murderer; and finally, Barbara Stanwyck's ghostly presence makes circus tightrope walker Charles Boyer lose his balance. Like all portmanteau films, a mixed blessing, but Julien Duvivier directs them all stylishly.

Edward G Robinson *Marshall Tyler* • Charles Boyer *Paul Gaspar* • Barbara Stanwyck *Joan Stanley* • Betty Field *Henrietta* • Robert Cummings *Michael* • Robert Benchley *Doakes* • David Hoffman *Davis* ■ *Dir* Julien Duvivier • *Scr* Ernest Pascal, Samuel Hoffenstein, Ellis St Joseph, from stories by Ellis St Joseph, Oscar Wilde (*Lord Arthur Saville's Crime,*), Laslo Vadnay

Flesh and the Devil ★★★★ U

Silent drama 1926 · US · BW · 112mins

Greta Garbo glows like a luminous icon of yearning with John Gilbert as one of her lovers in a film whose tremendous success was as much to do with the stars' off-screen affair as the story. Garbo – helped by William Daniels's lustrous camerawork – is a Countess-temptress who inspires a duel between her husband and a soldier, which – subtracted from its notorious sex scenes – was touched with the absurdity of the over-melodramatic. It was Garbo's third film for MGM, and director Clarence Brown poured her more than competently into the mould that the studio most wanted: that of a femme fatale. ▦

John Gilbert *Leo von Harden* • Greta Garbo *Felicitas von Eltz* • Lars Hanson *Ulrich von Kletzingk* • Barbara Kent *Hertha Prochvitz* • William Orlamond *Uncle Kutowski* • George Fawcett *Pastor Voss* ■ *Dir* Clarence Brown • *Scr* Benjamin F Glazer [Benjamin Glazer], from the novel *Es War; Roman in Zwei Banden* by Herman Sudermann

The Flesh and the Fiends ★★★

Horror 1959 · UK · BW · 93mins

An explicitly scary and darkly atmospheric retelling of the Burke and Hare story, with Peter Cushing exceptional as the coldly ambitious Dr Knox, who scandalises the medical profession when he strikes a fatal bargain with two grave robbers to supply him with fresh corpses for experiments. The grimy poverty of 19th-century Edinburgh provides a vivid background to this unflinching shocker, which uses stark black-and-white imagery to startling effect. An under-rated British chiller, greatly inspired by the "House of Hammer" look.

Peter Cushing *Dr Robert Knox* • Donald Pleasence *William Hare* • June Laverick *Martha* • George Rose *William Burke* • Dermot Walsh *Dr Geoffrey Mitchell* • Renee Houston

Helen Burke • Billie Whitelaw *Mary Patterson* ■ *Dir* John Gilling • *Scr* John Gilling, Leon Griffiths, from a story by John Gilling

Flesh Feast ★

Horror 1970 · US · Colour · 72mins

What do Hollywood glamour queens do when they retire? Play homicidal maniacs, of course. The trend started memorably with *What Ever Happened to Baby Jane?* but hit rock bottom with this tasteless and cheap mess of a movie. Lured back to the screen long after her glory days of the forties, Veronica Lake plays a scientist conducting anti-ageing experiments using live maggots that devour old skin tissue. An interesting approach to cosmetic surgery! This was Lake's last film and was filmed in Florida in what looks like director Brad F Grinter's sitting room.

Veronica Lake *Dr Elaine Frederick* • Phil Philbin *Ed Casey* • Heather Hughes *Kristine* • Martha Mischon • Yanka Mann • Dian Wilhite • Chris Martell ■ *Dir* Brad F Grinter • *Scr* Brad F Grinter, Thomas Casey

Flesh for Frankenstein ★★★ 18

Horror 1974 · US · Colour · 90mins

Explicit blood-letting and violence overwhelms director Paul Morrissey's shockingly funny exposé of the venal grime behind Victorian aristocracy. Udo Kier is wonderfully arrogant and bad-tempered as the Nietzschean Baron dismembering the local townspeople to build the perfect Aryan male and his female mate. Originally shown in excellent 3-D (the reason why sharp instruments are constantly being thrust into the camera) a strong stomach is still needed to witness the flattened down lurid gore and sickening splatter. Full of camp quotable dialogue and a particularly hilarious sex scene between Joe Dallesandro and Monique Van Vooren. ▦

Joe Dallesandro *Nicholas* • Udo Kier *Frankenstein* • Monique Van Vooren *Katrin* • Arno Juerging *Otto* • Srdjan Zelenovic *Man Monster* ■ *Dir* Paul Morrissey • *Scr* Paul Morrissey, Tonino Guerra

Flesh Gordon ★★ 18

Science-fiction sex comedy 1974 · US · Colour · 84mins

Only in Britain would this limp sex spoof of the Flash Gordon Saturday morning pictures adventure series have become a theatrical, and then later, video hit. Jason Williams in the title role, Suzanne Fields, John Hoyt and a cameo from real-life porn star Candy Samples supply the talent. The Earth is being bombarded with a sex ray from the Planet Porno, and Flesh Gordon is the man to save us from our naughty selves. Not hilarious, but harmless all the same. ▦

Jason Williams *Flesh Gordon* • Suzanne Fields *Dale Ardor* • Joseph Hudgins *Dr Flexi Jerkoff* • John Hoyt *Professor Gordon* • William Hunt [William Dennis Hunt] *Emperor Wang* • Craig T Brandy *(uncredited) Voice of the monster* • Candy Samples ■ *Dir* Howard Ziehm, Michael Benveniste • *Scr* Michael Benveniste

The Flesh Is Weak ★

Crime drama   1957 · UK · BW · 88mins

John Derek – the future husband of Ursula Andress, Linda Evans and Bo Derek – takes on the sordid role of a Soho racketeer. He has an affair with innocent country girl Milly Vitale, frames her and watches her go to jail. However, a journalist manages to get Vitale to talk about her corruptor. Pretending to be a socially responsible look at the world of prostitution and campaigning for its legalisation, this is actually a cheapo melodrama, scripted by Leigh Vance, the future writer of *The Avengers* TV series.

John Derek *Tony Giani* • Milly Vitale *Marissa Cooper* • William Franklyn *Lloyd Buxton* • Martin Benson *Angelo Giani* • Freda Jackson *Trixie* • Norman Wooland *Insp Kingcombe* ■ *Dir* Don Chaffey • *Scr* Leigh Vance

The Flesh of the Orchid ★★★

Drama   1974 · Fr/It/W Ger · Colour · 105mins

Adapted from the James Hadley Chase novel, this is less an exercise in hard-boiled fiction than in *Grand Guignol*. Exploiting expressionist visuals and allowing his cast to play at fever pitch, Patrice Chéreau clearly hopes to bring a sense of theatrical menace to his slow-burning tale of greed and revenge. Edwige Feuillère hits the right note of hysteria as the wicked aunt who has her niece consigned to an asylum in a bid to seize her inheritance, while Bruno Cremer is charismatically sinister as the stranger who helps confound her schemes. But Charlotte Rampling is less successful as the put-upon heiress who gets help from an unexpected source. French dialogue dubbed into English.

Charlotte Rampling *Claire* • Bruno Cremer *Louis* • Edwige Feuillère *Aunt* • Simone Signoret *Lady Vamos* • Hugues Quester *Son* • Alida Valli *Woman* ■ *Dir* Patrice Chéreau • *Scr* Jean-Claude Carrière, Patrice Chéreau, from the novel by James Hadley Chase

Fleshtone ★★ 🔞

Erotic thriller   1994 · US · Colour · 86mins

Before relaunching his acting career in *EastEnders*, Martin Kemp wiled away the years in straight-to-video land. In this thriller, one of his less distinguished efforts, he is somewhat unconvincingly cast as a painter who becomes a murder suspect when he gets hooked on a sex chat-line. It's the usual mix of soft lighting, mild eroticism and a plot twist you will see coming a mile off. ▭

Martin Kemp *Matthew Greco* • Lise Cutter • Tim Thomerson ■ *Dir/Scr* Harry Hurwitz

Fletch ★★★ 🅿🄶

Comedy adventure

1985 · US · Colour · 94mins

Chevy Chase, one of the original *Saturday Night Live* team and the embodiment of laid-back Los Angeles eighties humour, stars in the first of two outings as the investigative reporter with a sideline in disguises and witty repartee. Seized from Malibu beach (where he is disguised as a beach bum) by a millionaire who orders his own murder, Chase stumbles and bumbles through a corkscrew plot that

fits his comic frame like a bespoke suit. Sleek, glossy and often very funny indeed, the inventive script is by Andrew Bergman, who cut his teeth as a co-writer on *Blazing Saddles* and went on to direct *The Freshman* and *Honeymoon in Vegas*. ▭

Chevy Chase *IM Fletcher, "Fletch"* • Joe Don Baker *Chief Karlin* • Dana Wheeler-Nicholson *Gail Stanwyk* • Tim Matheson *Alan Stanwyk* • M Emmet Walsh *Dr Dolan* • George Wendt *Fat Sam* • Geena Davis *Larry* ■ *Dir* Michael Ritchie • *Scr* Andrew Bergman, from the novel by Gregory McDonald

Fletch Lives ★★ 🅿🄶

Comedy mystery   1989 · US · Colour · 90mins

Chevy Chase reprises his role as the daffy investigative reporter in this adult comedy, but this time he's not blessed with a sharp enough script. Fletch is one of those characters that you either find irresistibly funny and folksy, or merely the celluloid celebration of the nightmare passenger you find yourself sitting beside in a plane. If you tend firmly towards the latter, then this particular journey in the company of Mr Chase could be the equivalent of nonstop to Auckland in economy. The plot, such as it is, doesn't so much revolve around Chase in a variety of ill-fitting disguises, as spin mercilessly out of control. Contains swearing. ▭

Chevy Chase *Fletch* • Julianne Phillips *Becky Ann Culpepper* • Hal Holbrook *"Ham" Johnson* • R Lee Ermey *Jimmy Lee Farnsworth* • Richard Libertini *Frank Walker* • Randall "Tex" Cobb *Ben Dover* ■ *Dir* Michael Ritchie • *Scr* Leon Capetanos, from characters created by Gregory McDonald

Flight ★★

Action drama   1929 · US · BW · 116mins

Jack Holt and Ralph Graves had starred in Frank Capra's 1928 movie, *Submarine*, which was a silent picture released with music and sound effects. The team were reunited for this drama which was a genuine Capra talkie. Like *Submarine*, it's a military adventure, dealing with America's invasion of Nicaragua and because the US Navy cooperated fully with the production, loaning the unit its base and equipment in San Diego, the movie has some spectacular aerial sequences. Unfortunately the same cannot be said for the familiar love triangle storyline.

Jack Holt *Panama Williams* • Ralph Graves *Lefty Phelps* • Lila Lee *Elinor* • Alan Roscoe *Major* • Harold Goodwin *Steve Roberts* ■ *Dir* Frank Capra • *Scr* Howard J Green, Frank Capra, from a story by Ralph Graves

Flight Command ★★

Second World War drama

1940 · US · BW · 115mins

MGM prepared Americans for war by sending Robert Taylor aloft as a recently qualified Naval pilot who helps design a fog landing system, saving the squadron commander in the process and making widowed Ruth Hussey go all dewy-eyed. There's enough plot for a dozen movies, so emotions tend to suffer from serious air turbulence and even Red Skelton, in his second film, hasn't much time for his comedy schtick. And anyway, there's a serious job to be done in

trying to persuade American citizens to sign up for the war effort.

Robert Taylor (1) *Ensign Alan Drake* • Ruth Hussey *Lorna Gary* • Walter Pidgeon *Squadron Cdr Bill Gary* • Paul Kelly *Lt Cdr Dusty Rhodes* • Red Skelton *Lt "Mugger" Martin* ■ *Dir* Frank Borzage • *Scr* Wells Root, Cdr Harvey Haislip, from the story by Cdr Harvey Haislip, John Sutherland

Flight for Freedom ★★ 🅄

Romantic drama   1943 · US · BW · 101mins

Resembling Katharine Hepburn's 1933 *Christopher Strong*, this thinly disguised biopic is clearly based on noted aviatrix Amelia Earhart, and her last mysterious journey. Though the movie was sanctioned by Earhart's widower, publisher Charles Palmer Putnam, he wouldn't let RKO use her name, and you can't blame him after seeing this melodramatic nonsense. Rosalind Russell made her debut for the studio as the plucky, patriotic flier, cast opposite a happy-go-lucky Fred MacMurray, and a stern, long-suffering Herbert Marshall as the instructor who loves our heroine but gradually realises he's not really part of the picture. Preposterous stuff, leadenly directed and only worth watching for the look on Russell's face when she's told that her work will help the Allies in the coming war against Japan.

Rosalind Russell *Tonie Carter* • Fred MacMurray *Randy Britton* • Herbert Marshall *Paul Turner* • Edward Ciannelli *[Eduardo Ciannelli] Johnny Salvini* • Walter Kingsford *Admiral Graves* ■ *Dir* Lothar Mendes • *Scr* Oliver HP Garrett, SK Lauren, Jane Murfin, from a story by Horace McCoy

Flight from Ashiya ★★

Action drama

1964 · US/Jap · Colour · 102mins

A mega-macho trio – Yul Brynner, Richard Widmark, George Chakiris – are engulfed by sentimentality and self-doubt as members of a US rescue mission at sea. They're trying to save the survivors of a storm-battered cargo ship off the Japanese coast but all three have psychological problems to overcome before they can get to grips with the elements. Far from being a robust action adventure, the extensive flashback sequences turn this into a glorified high-seas soap.

Yul Brynner *Sgt Mike Takashima* • Richard Widmark *Col Glenn Stevenson* • George Chakiris *Lt John Gregg* • Suzy Parker *Lucille* • Shirley Knight *Caroline* • Danièle Gaubert *Leila* ■ *Dir* Michael Anderson • *Scr* Elliott Arnold, Waldo Salt, from the novel by Elliott Arnold

Flight from Glory ★★

Action drama   1937 · US · BW · 66mins

An RKO B-movie, inspired by the success of MGM's classier *Night Flight*, which boasted two Barrymores and Clark Gable flying air freight across the Andes. Here it's still the Andes, but the cast only gets as high up the stellar scale as Chester Morris and Van Heflin, who have both lost their licences in America and now fly supplies to a remote mountain mining camp. When they're not in the air, romance blossoms between head honcho Morris and Whitney Bourne, Heflin's new bride.

Chester Morris *Smith* • Whitney Bourne *Lee Wilson* • Onslow Stevens *Ellis* • Van Heflin *George Wilson* • Richard Lane *Hanson* • Paul Guilfoyle *Jones* ■ *Dir* Louis Friedlander [Lew Landers] • *Scr* David Silverstein, John Twist, from a story by Robert D Andrews

Flight from Justice ★★

Action drama   1993 · Can · Colour

One of the first English language excursions for French star Jean Reno a year before his breakthrough in *Leon*, this is a competent if unremarkable TV adventure tale. Reno plays an elite fighter pilot who goes to the aid of old comrade Bruce Boxleitner. Reno exudes his usual sleepy charm and there's good support from Carole Laure and Boxleitner, while director Don Kent makes fine use of the rugged Canadian landscape. Contains violence and swearing.

Jean Reno *Lieutenant Charlie Beck* • Bruce Boxleitner *Michael* • Carole Laure *Dr Ann Stephen* ■ *Dir* Don Kent • *Scr* Sylvain Saada, Robert Geoffrion

Flight 90: Disaster on the Potomac ★★ 🅿🄶

Drama based on a true story

1984 · US · Colour · 91mins

In January 1982, an Air Florida plane crashed into the Potomac river in Washington DC. This disaster movie sets out to describe the tragedy, and largely succeeds in its portrayal of the immediate aftermath, despite the use of a heated studio pool, complete with floating chunks of chilly polystyrene, substituting for the icy river. But writer John McGreevey struggles with the many subplots involving his sprawling cast, which includes Barry Corbin, Richard Masur and Ken Olin. ▭

Jeannetta Arnette [Jeanetta Arnette] *Nikki Felch* • Barry Corbin *Bert Hamilton* • Stephen Macht *Joe Stiley* • Dinah Manoff *Priscilla Tirado* • Richard Masur *Roger Olian* ■ *Dir* Robert Michael Lewis [Robert Lewis] • *Scr* John McGreevey

Flight of the Dove ★ 🔞

Romantic thriller   1995 · US · Colour · 88mins

Theresa Russell is a spy on the run. Scott Glenn is the explosives expert with a past she becomes romantically involved with. Can they outsmart the bad guys after her and live a happy life together? You won't really care in this bad movie raised to the level of mediocrity by the sheer force of the headliners' charisma. Former actor turned director Steve Railsback (*The Stunt Man*) loses the plot by focusing on clumsy erotica and banal action and the result is a wash-out. ▭

Scott Glenn *William* • Theresa Russell *Mary Ann/Alex Canis* • Lane Smith *Stephen* • Terence Knox *Jonathan* • Katherine Helmond *Dr Schilling* • Joe Pantoliano *Brezner* ■ *Dir* Steve Railsback • *Scr* Lewis A Greene

Flight of the Doves ★★★ 🅄

Adventure drama   1971 · UK · Colour · 97mins

Director Ralph Nelson followed the success of the controversial *Soldier Blue* with this charming piece of Irish whimsy, a strange choice of subject matter that may be too self-consciously cute for adult tastes. Beautifully shot on location by ace cinematographer

Harry Waxman, this blithe tale charts the trials and tribulations of a pair of Liverpudlian children who, quite unexpectedly, keep running into English character actors like Ron Moody, Stanley Holloway and Willie Rushton. There's a lovely performance from the marvellous Dorothy McGuire (*Claudia*, *The Spiral Staircase*), and Roy Budd's score is great. ▣

Ron Moody *Hawk Dove* • Jack Wild *Finn Dove* • Dorothy McGuire *Granny O'Flaherty* • Stanley Holloway *Judge Liffy* • Helen Raye *Derval Dove* • William Rushton *Tobias Cromwell* ■ Dir Ralph Nelson • Scr Frank Gabrielson, Ralph Nelson, from a novel by Walter Macken

Flight of the Innocent ★★ 🔞

Thriller   1993 · It/Fr · Colour · 100mins

After an arresting opening, in which a young boy witnesses the slaughter of both his family and a kidnapped child, Carlo Carlei's film lapses into a shameless sentimentality that fatally undermines the initial naturalism. Manuel Colao gives a remarkable performance as the Aspromontian hill urchin who seeks refuge in the city after fleeing Federico Pacifici's scarfaced outlaw because he is the only witness to a kidnapping. But he has one too many narrow escapes, and is accepted too readily by grieving parents Francesca Neri and Jacques Perrin, for this increasingly melodramatic tale to truly convince. Carlei's symbolism is heavy-handed and his cosy finale will satisfy no one. In Italian with English subtitles. ▣

Manuel Colao *Vito* • Francesca Neri *Marta Rienzi* • Jacques Perrin *Davide Rienzi* • Federico Pacifici *Scarface* • Sal Borgese [Salvatore Borgese] *Vito's Father* ■ Dir Carlo Carlei • Scr Carlo Carlei, Gualtiero Rosella, from a story by Carlo Carlei

Flight of the Intruder ★★ 🔞

War drama   1991 · US · Colour · 114mins

Gung-ho bombast is definitely macho director John Milius's forte. Unfortunately, it can't save this claustrophobic and endlessly talky drama, set during the winding-down stages of the Vietnam War. Milius co-wrote *Apocalypse Now*, but this moralistic study of the vainglorious US military effort isn't in the same class. The high-profile cast, including Danny Glover and Willem Dafoe, does what it can considering the ideological script, but it's fighting as much of a losing battle as the one depicted on screen.

Danny Glover *Commander Frank Camparelli* • Willem Dafoe *Lieutenant Commander Virgil Cole* • Brad Johnson *Lieutenant Jake* • Rosanna Arquette *Callie* ■ Dir John Milius • Scr Robert Dillon, David Shaber, from a novel by Stephen Coonts

Flight of the Navigator

        ★★★ 🔤

Science-fiction adventure
1986 · US · Colour · 85mins

An appealing children's adventure that has just enough quirky touches to keep adults involved as well. Joey Cramer is the youngster who goes missing at the age of 12, only to turn up eight years later completely unchanged. It soon becomes apparent that his disappearance is linked to alien space travel. The scenes where

Cramer attempts to get to grips with the fact that he has missed out on eight years of his life (his younger brother is now his elder) are neatly handled by director Randal Kleiser, who proves equally adept at the action sequences. A pre-stardom Pee-Wee Herman (aka Paul Reubens) provides the voice of Cramer's friendly robot. ▣

Joey Cramer *David Freeman* • Veronica Cartwright *Helen Freeman* • Cliff De Young *Bill Freeman* • Sarah Jessica Parker *Carolyn McAdams* • Howard Hesseman *Dr Faraday* ■ Dir Randal Kleiser • Scr Michael Burton, Matt MacManus, from a story by Mark H Baker

The Flight of the Phoenix

        ★★★★

Adventure   1966 · US · Colour · 141mins

James Stewart's plane crashes in the desert and when, after days in the sweltering heat, you think he might take a juicy bite out of Richard Attenborough, Peter Finch or Hardy Kruger to get some protein, a plan is hatched to build a smaller plane out of the wreckage. This survivalist epic has all the expected ingredients and more – Attenborough's nerves are shattered, Kruger is the embodiment of Germanic efficiency, Finch is stiff-upper-lipped, Jimmy Stewart is Charles Lindbergh with a wing down and all of them sweat and grow beards with customary skill. Director Robert Aldrich keeps things boiling for perhaps longer than is necessary but delivers a genuinely exciting climax.

James Stewart *Frank Towns* • Richard Attenborough *Lew Moran* • Peter Finch *Captain Harris* • Hardy Kruger *Heinrich Dorfmann* • Ernest Borgnine *Trucker Cobb* • Ian Bannen *Crow* • Ronald Fraser *Sergeant Watson* ■ Dir Robert Aldrich • Scr Lukas Heller, from the novel by Elleston Trevor

Flight to Fury   ★★

Crime adventure drama
1966 · US/Phil · BW · 80mins

Amazingly, Jack Nicholson wrote the script for this jungle potboiler on the ship that was taking him and the crew to the Philippines where the film was to be shot. By the time they landed in Manila, Nicholson had finished his first solo screenplay. Not surprisingly he wrote the best part for himself, that of a psychopathic gem smuggler, member of a gang whose plane crashes in the jungle where they fight bandits and each other over a cache of stolen diamonds. Directed on a shoestring budget with credible gusto by Monte Hellman, this was scarcely released into theatres and, like so many of Nicholson's pre-fame movies, is largely unmemorable.

Dewey Martin *Joe Gaines* • Fay Spain *Destiny Cooper* • Jack Nicholson *Jay Wickham* • Jacqueline Hellman [Jaclyn Hellman] *Gloria Walsh* ■ Dir Monte Hellman • Scr Jack Nicholson, from a story by Monte Hellman, Fred Roos

Flight to Mars   ★ 🔤

Science-fiction   1951 · US · Colour · 71mins

A ramshackle space opera in comic-strip style about mankind's first landing on Mars and the discovery of an advanced, dying underground civilisation plotting an Earth invasion

because they are running low on resources. Shot in 11 days by quickie merchants Monogram Studios, this uninspired pulp nonsense launched star Cameron Mitchell's B-movie career. Some chuckles are to be had from the Martian girls wearing silver miniskirts, but there's not much else. Mitchell's astronaut costume was a leftover from *Destination Moon*, a hit movie that this film tried to cash in on.

Marguerite Chapman *Alita* • Cameron Mitchell *Steve* • Arthur Franz *Jim* • Virginia Huston *Carol* • John Litel *Dr Lane* • Richard Gaines *Prof Jackson* ■ Dir Lesley Selander • Scr Arthur Strawn

Flight to Tangier   ★ 🔤

Action drama   1953 · US · Colour · 89mins

Joan Fontaine's career was on the slide when she agreed to star in this overly complicated chase melodrama, although Jack Palance must have welcomed the chance to play a romantic lead, abdicating the villainy to Robert Douglas. Set in contemporary Tangier, writer/director Charles Marquis Warren's picture is peopled by mysterious characters behaving strangely to the point where you couldn't care less what any of them are up to. It was originally made for screening in 3-D, which would have provided a welcome distraction.

Joan Fontaine *Susan* • Jack Palance *Gil Walker* • Corinne Calvet *Nicole* • Robert Douglas *Danzar* • Marcel Dalio *Gogo* ■ Dir/Scr Charles Marquis Warren

Flinch   ★★ 🔞

Thriller   1994 · Can · Colour · 88mins

A great title for a thriller which sadly fails to live up to expectation. Gina Gershon and Judd Nelson have the risible job of filling in for shop mannequins when their plastic friends are working elsewhere. In this capacity they witness a woman being strangled and soon have psycho killer Nick Mancuso on their tail. Deplorable dialogue and a stale performance from Nelson are perked up considerably by the feisty Gershon and fearsome Mancuso. Not one that'll have you holding your breath though. ▣

Judd Nelson *Harry Mirapolsky* • Gina Gershon *Daphne James* • Nick Mancuso *Miles* • Marilyn Norry *Vivian* • Frank Cassini *Fowler* ■ Dir George Erschbamer • Scr Tippi Dobrofsky, Neal H Dobrofsky

The Flintstones   ★★ 🔤

Comedy   1994 · US · Colour · 86mins

The casting is almost perfect, the re-creation of Bedrock is masterly and the special effects are clever without being overly intrusive. And yet this live-action version of the classic sixties TV cartoon series seems somewhat lacklustre – in fact, one critic's advice for those thinking of seeing the film was, "Yabba dabba don't!". Between them, the scriptwriting trio and director Brian Levant manage to lose the boisterous fun that made the Hanna-Barbera original so endearing, and not even John Goodman's exuberant Fred or Elizabeth Taylor's sly mother-in-law can atone. The comic slapstick will appeal to youngsters in the family, but,

a few Stone Age anachronisms apart, the film just isn't that funny. ▣ **DVD**

John Goodman *Fred Flintstone* • Elizabeth Perkins *Wilma Flintstone* • Rick Moranis *Barney Rubble* • Rosie O'Donnell *Betty Rubble* • Kyle MacLachlan *Cliff Vandercave* • Halle Berry *Miss Stone* • Elizabeth Taylor *Pearl Slaghoople* ■ Dir Brian Levant • Scr Tom S Parker, Jim Jennewein, Steven E de Sousa, from the animated TV series by William Hanna, Joseph Barbera

The Flintstones in Viva Rock Vegas   ★★★ 🔤

Comedy   2000 · US · Colour · mins

It's yabba-dabba-woo time as Fred and Barney first meet Wilma and Betty in a belated prequel to 1994's live-action original. First half is cuter and more kiddie friendly, with loads of those trademark retro gizmos; by contrast, the second half is duller, more plot-driven, and could tax pre-adolescent patience as Fred seeks to see off competition for well-off Wilma's hand by striking it rich in Vegas. Casting is variable. *The Full Monty*'s Mark Addy, as Fred, looks the part, but underplays it. Stephen Baldwin, as Barney, is too gormless and two feet too tall. Girls, though, are good, with *Ally McBeal*'s Jane Krakowski a nicely traditional Betty, and *Third Rock*'s Kristen Johnston an unexpectedly voluptuous Wilma. All told, though, this is a modern Stone Age family film that's smarter than your average prequel.

Mark Addy *Fred Flintstone* • Stephen Baldwin *Barney Rubble* • Kristen Johnston *Wilma Slaghoople* • Jane Krakowski *Betty O'Shale* • Joan Collins *Pearl Slaghoople* • Alan Cumming *The Great Gazoo/Mick Jagged* • Harvey Korman *Col Slaghoople* ■ Dir Brian Levant • Scr Harry Elfont, Deborah Kaplan, Jim Cash, Jack Epps Jr, from the animated TV series by William Hanna, Joseph Barbera

Flipper   ★★★ 🔤

Adventure   1963 · US · Colour · 86mins

There can hardly be a babyboomer in Britain who didn't follow the adventures of Flipper the dolphin on TV at one time or another during the sixties. Well, this is the film that inspired the series. Produced by Ivan Tors, who specialised in animal adventures, this is a delight from start to finish, with Luke Halpin excelling as the small boy who befriends and tames the mischievous, scene-stealing dolphin. It was remade in 1996, but if you're of a certain age, you'll probably prefer the original. ▣

Chuck Connors *Porter Ricks* • Luke Halpin *Sandy Ricks* • Kathleen Maguire *Martha Ricks* • Connie Scott *Kim Parker* • Jane Rose *Hettie White* • Joe Higgins *Mr LC Porett* ■ Dir James B Clark • Scr Arthur Weiss, from a story by Ricou Browning, Jack Cowden

Flipper   ★★ 🔤

Adventure   1996 · US · Colour · 91mins

Enjoyable formula stuff based on the sixties TV series about the friendship between a boy and his dolphin. Elijah Wood stars as Sandy, a typical teenager who would rather attend a Red Hot Chili Peppers concert in Philadelphia than spend the summer on an island near Florida with his fisherman uncle Porter (Paul Hogan). The island's fisherfolk turn nasty when

Sandy befriends a dolphin they suspect of eating all the local catch, but the tables are turned when the duo discovers a gang of hunters polluting the in-shore waters with toxic waste. Idyllic locations, an upbeat soundtrack and a talented dolphin (a combination of the real thing and animatronics) add up to a feel-good family film. ▭
Paul Hogan *Porter* • Elijah Wood *Sandy* • Jonathan Banks *Dirk Moran* • Luke Halpin *Bounty fisherman* • Bill Kelley *Tommy* • Chelsea Field *Cathy* • Isaac Hayes *Sheriff Buck Cowan* ■ *Dir* Alan Shapiro • *Scr* Alan Shapiro, from the film by Arthur Weiss, from a story by Ricou Browning, Jack Cowden

Flipper and the Pirates ★★★ PG
Drama adventure 1964 · US · Colour · 94mins

Despite Flipper's 1996 big-screen outing, in which Paul Hogan and Elijah Wood co-starred with an animatronic dolphin, nostalgia addicts and, now, their children still nurture affection for child actor Luke Halpin and his original versatile friend, who made their feature debut in 1963. This is the sequel (or should that be sea-quel?) to the original *Flipper*, elegantly photographed in Florida and the Bahamas that were almost certainly more fun to visit for the actors than the script was to read. The amiable cast, headed by Halpin, includes British visitors Pamela Franklin best known for her sinister role in *The Innocents* and Mrs Trevor Howard, Helen Cherry, both of whom look like they're having a thoroughly enjoyable time. Tom Helmore plays a blackmailed millionaire, and Flipper wins the day. Good, clean fun all round, but mainly for children. ▭
Luke Halpin *Sandy Ricks* • Pamela Franklin *Penny* • Tom Helmore *Sir Halsey Hopewell* • Helen Cherry *Julia* • Francesca Annis *Gwen* ■ *Dir* Leon Benson • *Scr* Art Arthur, from a story by Ivan Tors, from characters created by Ricou Browning, Jack Cowden

Flipping ★★★ 18
Crime drama 1996 · US · Colour · 98mins

Despite the off-putting title, this is an atmospheric crime thriller, set on the seedy streets of Hollywood. David Amos is Michael, one of group of tough-guy collectors working for local crime boss Leo (David Keith). The trouble starts when the boys decide they would be better off with Leo out of the way. An interesting twist is provided by Michael's unexpected relationship with cop Billy White. Sharply written and directed, *Flipping* is smarter than your average crime yarn. Contains swearing and violence. ▭
Keith David *Leo Richards* • David Proval *Billy White* • David Amos *Michael Moore* • Barry Primus *Joey* • Mike Starr *CJ* • Gene Mitchell *Shot* ■ *Dir/Scr* Gene Mitchell

Flirt ★★ 15
Comedy drama
1995 · US/Ger/Jap · Colour · 83mins

Independent director Hal Hartley has a vision as quirky as it is emotionally contained, and this is a whimsy in which the same idea is put through three transformations. New Yorker Bill Sage wonders if he should reject his lover, only to find a suicide attempt getting in the way; in Berlin, Dwight

Ewell wonders about his own future; in Tokyo Miho Nikaido (Hartley's wife) engages with a visiting film director (Hartley himself). Some emotional home truths are learned, but the structure is too self-conscious to appeal to those who aren't in on the joke. In English, German and Japanese with subtitles. ▭
Bill Sage *Bill (New York)* • Martin Donovan *Walter (New York)* • Parker Posey *Emily (New York)* • Dwight Ewell *Dwight (Berlin)* • Geno Lechner *Greta (Berlin)* • Miho Nikaido *Miho (Tokyo)* • Chikako Hara *Yuki (Tokyo)* • Hal Hartley *Hal (Tokyo)* ■ *Dir/Scr* Hal Hartley

Flirtation Walk ★★★ U
Musical comedy 1934 · US · BW · 98mins

Dedicated to the West Point Military Academy itself, this lively light-hearted musical (an early screenplay by future ace director Delmer Daves) goes a fair way to both glamourising and glorifying that legendary institution. It also provides an ideal arena for that likeable toothsome twosome of Dick Powell and Ruby Keeler (he's a cadet, she's the general's daughter) who get to croon and stroll along a very studio-bound vision of the eponymous "walk". Director Frank Borzage makes heavy weather of the simplistic plotting, but the film was popular enough to earn a surprising best picture Oscar nomination and is still a pleasant enough diversion, although the overt patriotism may rankle.
Dick Powell *Dick "Canary" Richard Palmer* • Grant Dorcy • Ruby Keeler *Kit Fitts* • Pat O'Brien *Scrapper Thornhill* • Ross Alexander *Oskie* • John Arledge *Spike* • John Eldredge *Lt Robert Biddle* • Henry O'Neill *Gen Jack Fitts* ■ *Dir* Frank Borzage • *Scr* Delmer Daves, from a story by Lou Edelman, Delmer Daves

Flirting ★★★★★ 15
Comedy drama 1989 · Ausl · Colour · 94mins

Director John Duigan began the coming-of-age story of Danny Embling in the wonderful *The Year My Voice Broke*, and continues it in this even more enjoyable and moving comedy drama. Noah Taylor reprises his role as the young boy who moves from his small Australian outback town to an all-boys boarding school. Across the lake is an all-girls school, and it is during one of the occasions where the two schools get together that he meets and falls in love with a beautiful young Ugandan pupil (Thandie Newton, making her film debut). A true gem, Duigan's film is also notable for a brief appearance by Nicole Kidman, back on her native soil. ▭
Noah Taylor *Danny Embling* • Thandie Newton *Thandiwe Adjewa* • Nicole Kidman *Nicola Radcliffe* • Bartholomew Rose *"Gilby" Fryer* • Felix Nobis *Jock Blair* • Josh Picker *"Baka" Bourke* • Marc Gray *Christopher Laidlaw* ■ *Dir/Scr* John Duigan

Flirting with Disaster ★★★ 15
Comedy road movie
1996 · US · Colour · 88mins

Less abrasive than *Spanking the Monkey*, David O Russell's second feature is a madcap, country-crossing comedy, which makes up in eccentric characterisation what it occasionally loses in control. As the orphan hoping

to trace his roots before naming his new baby, Ben Stiller is suitably neurotic as ditzy psychologist Téa Leoni leads him up endless blind alleys. But it's the cameos by adoptive parents Mary Tyler Moore and George Segal, and ageing hippies Alan Alda and Lily Tomlin that steal Stiller's thunder and further marginalise the under-used Patricia Arquette, who seeks solace with a bisexual FBI agent. Great screwball, shame about the slapstick. ▭
Ben Stiller *Mel Coplin* • Patricia Arquette *Nancy Coplin* • Téa Leoni *Tina Kalb* • Mary Tyler Moore *Mrs Coplin* • George Segal *Mr Coplin* • Alan Alda *Richard Schlicting* • Lily Tomlin *Mary Schlicting* • Josh Brolin *Tony* ■ *Dir/Scr* David O Russell

Floating Away ★★★
Drama 1998 · US · Colour · 105mins

In this surprisingly well done character piece, based on the novel *Sorrow Floats* by Tim Sandlin, an alcoholic woman (Roseanna Arquette) meets up with two recovering alcoholic men who are about to set off on a cross-country trip. She joins them, hoping to retrieve her child who has been placed with her estranged husband. Worthy performances are turned in by Arquette and her travelling companions Paul Hogan and Judge Reinhold (*Beverly Hills Cop*). A certain amount of self-help psychobabble prevails, but John Badham (*Saturday Night Fever*) handles this road movie competently.
Rosanna Arquette *Maurey* • Paul Hogan *Shane* • Judge Reinhold *Lloyd* ■ *Dir* John Badham • *Scr* Tim Sandlin, from his novel *Sorrow Floats*

Floating Weeds ★★
Drama 1959 · Jap · Colour · 119mins

Based on the same story that inspired his silent 1934 drama, *A Story of Floating Weeds*, this was among Yasujiro Ozu's weakest postwar pictures. For once his nostalgic yearnings seem to have got the better of him, as there are few contemporary resonances in this story of a travelling Kabuki player who hurts his mistress by interfering in the love life of his estranged son. In fact, the film is most notable for marking the director's only collaboration with Kenji Mizoguchi's regular cinematographer, Kazuo Miyagawa, who gives the seascapes a lustre that only occasionally illuminates the rest of the production. In Japanese with English subtitles.
Ganjiro Nakamura *Komajuro Arashi* • Haruko Sugimura *Oyoshi* • Hiroshi Kawaguchi *Kiyoshi* • Machiko Kyo *Sumiko* • Ayako Wakao *Kayo* • Chishu Ryu *Theatre owner* ■ *Dir* Yasujiro Ozu • *Scr* Yasujiro Ozu, Kogo Noda, from a story by Yasujiro Ozu, from the film *Ukigusa Monogatari* by Tadao Ikeda

The Flood ★★ U
Children's drama 1963 · UK · BW · 58mins

Based on a story by Frank Wells, this is another of those matinée specials so much beloved of the British film industry in the fifties and sixties. However, this one has more to offer (even to today's pre-teen sophisticates) than many of its ilk, as it follows six children learning how to fend for themselves after their isolated

farm is cut off by a freak flood. Dexterously handling his young cast and making effective use of his desolate location, Frederic Goode builds the tension steadily as the waters rise and the kids' spirits begin to sag.
Waveney Lee *Clarissa Weathersfield* • Christopher Ellis *Robin* • Frank Knight *Reg* • Jonathan Bergman *Bill Brasted* • Ian Ellis *Charles* ■ *Dir* Frederic Goode • *Scr* Jean Scott Rogers, from a story by Frank Wells

Flood! ★★ U
Disaster movie 1976 · US · Colour · 97mins

Making his first foray into TV movies, Irwin Allen here draws on the expertise he gained in producing disaster epics such as *The Poseidon Adventure* and *When Time Ran Out* to make the action in this wild-river tale as spectacular as the budget will allow. Robert Culp snarls to good effect as the reluctant hero, while Barbara Hershey looks suitably fraught as she attempts to lead the helpless victims to safety. Unfortunately, their efforts can't save this mediocre drama.
Robert Culp *Steve Banning* • Martin Milner *Paul Blake* • Barbara Hershey *Mary Cutler* • Richard Basehart *John Cutler* • Carol Lynley *Abbie Adams* • Roddy McDowall *Franklin* • Cameron Mitchell *Sam Adams* ■ *Dir* Earl Bellamy • *Scr* Don Ingalls, Arthur Weiss

The Flood ★★★
Drama 1993 · Rus/Fr · Colour · 97mins

This adaptation of Yevgyeni Zamyatin's novel is unusual in that it eschews revolutionary politics (although the shadow of the Bolshevik takeover casts its pall) to concentrate on the emotions experienced by a childless woman when her respectable husband falls for their adopted teenage daughter. Renowned for her ability to convey psychological depth, Isabelle Huppert gives an expert reading of the transformation of humiliation and acceptance into jealousy and recrimination, as she rebels against both her situation and a discriminatory society. Director Igor Minayev's visual sense is acute, although some may find his pacing too precise. A French language film.
Isabelle Huppert *Sofia* • Boris Nevzorov *Trofim* • Masha Lipkina *Ganka* • Svetlana Kryuchkova *Pelagia* ■ *Dir* Igor Minayev • *Scr* Jacques Baynac, Igor Minayev, from a novel by Yevgyeni Zamyatin

Flood: a River's Rampage ★★
Disaster movie 1997 · US · Colour

After he'd spent so much time up on Walton's Mountain, you might be forgiven for wondering how Richard Thomas would cope down in the valley with the mighty Mississippi getting ready to burst its banks. But, have no fear, our hero knows just what to do in this kind of emergency, especially when he has true love (and US Army engineer) Kate Vernon by his side. An unconvincing blend of the disaster movie and an old-fashioned family melodrama, this mediocre TV movie predictably suffers from not having the budget to create the special effects that make a blockbuster such as *Hard Rain* so watchable.

Richard Thomas *Herb Dellenbach* • Kate Vernon *Pat Malloy* ■ *Dir* Bruce Pittman • *Scr* Jonathan Rintels, Edward Hume

Floods of Fear ★★ 🔟

Drama   1958 · UK · BW · 80mins

Ealing Studios veteran (and *A Fish Called Wanda* director) Charles Crichton didn't do his reputation any favours with this sentimental melodrama. Basically an ensemble chamber piece revolving around four people trapped by floods in a gloomy house, the predictable plot barely keeps credibility afloat as an escaped convict eventually redeems himself through decisive action when tragedy looms. Well performed by an able cast – *Dallas* star Howard Keel, *Steptoe and Son's* Harry H Corbett, Cyril Cusack and, in particular, damsel in distress Anne Heywood – this is typical, and unremarkable, fifties British B-movie fare. Contains swearing and violence. 📼

Howard Keel *Donovan* • Anne Heywood *Elizabeth Matthews* • Cyril Cusack *Peebles* • Harry H Corbett *Sharkey* • John Crawford *Jack Murphy* • Eddie Byrne *Sheriff* • John Phillips *Dr Matthews* ■ *Dir* Charles Crichton • *Scr* Vivienne Knight, Charles Crichton, from the novel by John Hawkins, Ward Hawkins

The Floorwalker ★★★★★ 🔲

Silent comedy   1916 · US · BW · 24mins

Chaplin makes his brilliant most of a look-alike scenario, as he discovers he's a ringer for the floorwalker in a large department store. He indulges in some of his greatest pratfalls and seriously falls for Edna Purviance. Basically a series of revue turns, with him skidding and dancing around, it is more reliant on plot than many of his early films at this time. It's a frivolity, with escapades on the escalator, but nevertheless offers some acute insights into the almost Dickensian society of the day. 📼

Charles Chaplin *Tramp* • Edna Purviance *Secretary* ■ *Dir* Charles Chaplin • *Scr* Charles Chaplin, Vincent Bryan

Florian ★★ 🔲

Drama adventure   1940 · US · BW · 92mins

The title role is taken by a Lippizaner stallion, a member of Franz Josef's court and waited on hand and hoof by stable boy Robert Young. Like *Black Beauty*, all sorts of misadventures befall the horse. He goes from the circus, through the war and finally to America where he pulls a junk cart. But fear not, this is an MGM picture and Florian can't end up in the glue factory, can he? A real-life drama befell the production when second unit cameraman Richard Rosson went to Vienna and spent 34 days in jail as a guest of the Gestapo.

Robert Young *Anton* • Helen Gilbert *Diana* • Charles Coburn *Tramp* • Lee Bowman *Oliver* • Reginald Owen *Emperor Franz Josef* • Lucile Watson *Countess* • Irina Baronova *Trina* ■ *Dir* Edwin L Marin • *Scr* Noel Langley, James Kevin McGuinness, Geza Herczeg, from the novel by Felix Salten

Florida Straits ★★ 🔟

Action adventure
1986 · US/Can · Colour · 93mins

Raul Julia stars as a Cuban ex-prisoner in Florida who hires some men to help him return home and find his lost love. Except, of course, he's not really looking for a woman but for a pile of hidden loot. Despite the solid gold cast which includes Fred Ward and Antonio Fargas this drama from director Mike Hodges has a plot like a rusty old saucepan (full of holes) and a less-than-platinum script. Contains some violence and swearing. 📼

Raul Julia *Carlos Jayne* • Fred Ward *Lucky Boone* • Daniel Jenkins *Mac* • Jaime Sanchez *Innocente* • Victor Argo *Pablo* • Ilka Tanya Payan *Carmen* • Antonio Fargas *El Gato Negro* ■ *Dir* Mike Hodges • *Scr* Roderick Taylor

Floundering ★★

Drama   1994 · US · Colour · 97mins

The psychological aftermath of the LA riots is examined in an offbeat but muddled look at the unravelling life of one resident. James LeGros heads a eye-catching cast that includes John Cusack, Ethan Hawke, Billy Bob Thornton and Steve Buscemi, and Peter McCarthy's film certainly doesn't pull any punches in its portrayal of crumbling moral, social and political values. Unfortunately, the film's air of self-importance doesn't encourage identification with LeGros, nor do his pretentious ramblings about spirituality. Maybe the film will have more significance if you're actually from Los Angeles.

James LeGros *John Boyz* • John Cusack *JC* • Ethan Hawke *Jimmy* • Maritza Rivera *Elle* • Steve Buscemi *Ned* • Billy Bob Thornton *Gun clerk* ■ *Dir/Scr* Peter McCarthy

Flower Drum Song ★★ 🔲

Musical comedy 1961 · US · Colour · 132mins

Interminable and grotesquely over-produced (by the king of "camp" glamour Ross Hunter) this screen version of Rodgers and Hammerstein's Broadway success about life in San Francisco's Chinatown was woefully patronising and under-directed by Henry Koster. On Broadway, the tale had charm and style but this overblown and overlong movie just lies there and dies there. However, there's some bracing choreography from clever Hermes Pan and mercifully the endearing score has survived almost intact. Nominated in music and art direction categories at Oscar time, this lost out on everything – unsurprisingly – to *West Side Story*.

Nancy Kwan *Linda Low* • James Shigeta *Wang Ta* • Miyoshi Umeki *Mei Li* • Juanita Hall *Auntie* • Jack Soo *Sammy Fong* • Benson Fong *Wang Chi-Wang* • Reiko Sato *Helen Chao* ■ *Dir* Henry Koster • *Scr* Joseph Fields, from the novel by CY Lee and the book of the musical by Joseph Fields • *Cinematographer* Russell Metty • *Music/Lyrics* Richard Rodgers, Oscar Hammerstein II

The Flower of My Secret

★★★★ 🔟

Drama   1995 · Sp/Fr · Colour · 101mins

Truth versus fiction is the concern of this drama from Pedro Almodóvar, which constitutes a marked change of

pace for the cult Spanish director. Almodóvar tones down his usual camp satirical sensibilities to tell the engaging story of a romance novelist (Marisa Paredes) whose work is suffering because her marriage is falling apart. And that's not all: her best friend is betraying her, her half-blind mother and sister are driving her crazy, and her maid's son has plagiarised one of her manuscripts! Paredes gives an extraordinary performance as the writer in crisis, suffering gloriously in a lush tragi-comedy that boasts a scorching script, observant details, sharp visual contrasts and moments of truly biting humour. In Spanish with English subtitles. Contains swearing. 📼

Marisa Paredes *Leo* • Juan Echanove *Angel* • Imanol Arias *Paco* • Carmen Elias *Betty* • Rossy de Palma *Rosa* • Chus Lampreave *Mother* • Joaquin Cortes *Antonio* • Manuela Vargas *Blanca* ■ *Dir/Scr* Pedro Almodóvar

Flowers in the Attic ★★ 🔟

Horror   1987 · US · Colour · 87mins

VC Andrews's twisted Gothic bestseller gets a rather sanitised makeover in this big screen adaptation. Victoria Tennant is unconvincing in the villainous role of a loopy widow who keeps her own children (including Jeb Stuart Adams and Kristy Swanson, the original Buffy the Vampire Slayer) prisoners in a creepy old mansion while she plots to rid her parents (Louise Fletcher and Nathan Davis) of their fortune. Director Jeffrey Bloom raises the odd fright, but the finale is plain silly. 📼

Clare C Peck *Narrator* • Victoria Tennant *Corinne* • Kristy Swanson *Cathy* • Jeb Stuart Adams *Chris* • Louise Fletcher *Grandmother* • Ben Ganger *Cory* • Nathan Davis *Grandfather* ■ *Dir* Jeffrey Bloom • *Scr* Jeffrey Bloom, from the novel by VC Andrews

Flowers of Shanghai ★★★★

Period drama
1998 · Tai/Jap · Colour · 125mins

Adapted from Han Ziyun's 19th-century novel, this is a masterclass in studio stylisation from Taiwanese director Hou Hsiao-Hsien. His meticulous compositions and unobtrusive camera movements capture both the traditional atmosphere and the impending sense of change hanging over a Shanghai "flower house", which is more a place of education and intrigue than a brothel. This is a ruthless world of exploitation, enslavement and emotional blackmail, in which the women use everything at their disposal to retain the favour of their wealthy, but clearly discontented callers. Yet it is exquisitely depicted, with the studiously mannered performances reinforcing the achingly mournful tone. A Mandarin language film.

Tony Chiu-Wai Leung [Tony Leung (1)] *Wang Lingsheng* • Michiko Hada *Crimson* • Michelle Reis *Emerald* • Carina Lau *Pearl* • Jack Kao *Luo* • Vicky Wei [Wei Hsiao-Hui] *Jasmin* ■ *Dir* Hou Hsiao-Hsien • *Scr* Chu Tian-Wen, from the novel *Haishang hua liezhuang (Biographies of Flowers of Shanghai)* by Han Ziyun

Flubber ★★★ 🔲

Comedy   1997 · US · Colour · 90mins

Flubber continues Hollywood's recent obsession with souping-up the hit comedies of the sixties – in this case *The Absent Minded Professor* (1961) – with today's sophisticated special effects. Robin Williams is Philip Brainard, a scientist who becomes so immersed in creating a new energy source that he once again misses his own wedding. But this time he has an excuse, if only his long-suffering fiancée will listen, because he has invented Flubber – a substance like rubber which generates its own energy, wreaking havoc everywhere it goes. In fact it gives inanimate objects a life of their own, resulting in *Home Alone*-style attacks on baddies by everything from toy robots to bowling balls. Kids will lap it up. 📼 *DVD*

Robin Williams *Professor Philip Brainard* • Marcia Gay Harden *Sara Jean Reynolds* • Christopher McDonald *Wilson Croft* • Raymond J Barry *Chester Hoenicker* • Clancy Brown *Smith* ■ *Dir* Les Mayfield • *Scr* John Hughes, Bill Walsh, from the story *A Situation of Gravity* by Samuel W Taylor

Fluffy ★★ 🔲

Comedy   1965 · US · Colour · 91mins

The eponymous animal is a lion who has the misfortune to be engaged in research with Professor Tony Randall who – by way of that research – falls in love with Shirley Jones. We keep watching, hoping that Randall will rise above the script, and that Jones will burst into song; a waste of the two stars – and the lion.

Tony Randall *Daniel Potter* • Shirley Jones *Janice Claridge* • Edward Andrews *Griswald* • Ernest Truex *Claridge* • Jim Backus *Sergeant* • Frank Faylen *Catfish* • Howard Morris *Sweeney* ■ *Dir* Earl Bellamy • *Scr* Samuel Roeca

Fluke ★★★★ 🔣

Fantasy drama   1995 · US · Colour · 91mins

An excellent adaptation of James Herbert's fantasy adventure about a man protecting his family from villainous intent when reincarnated as a dog after a fatal car crash. Directed by co-writer Carlo Carlei in a breathtaking style complete with razzle-dazzle visuals, what basically sounds like a children's story becomes one accessible to adults thanks to a host of serious issues raised in a galvanising human context. Good voice-over work from Matthew Modine (as Fluke the mixed-breed puppy) and Samuel L Jackson (playing the wise, older dog, Rumbo) dovetails neatly with fine performances from human stars Nancy Travis and Eric Stoltz to craft a charming and touching tale sprinkled with special magic. 📼

Matthew Modine *Thomas Johnson/Fluke* • Nancy Travis *Carol Johnson* • Eric Stoltz *Jeff Newman* • Max Pomeranc *Brian Johnson* • Samuel L Jackson *Rumbo* ■ *Dir* Carlo Carlei • *Scr* Carlo Carlei, James Carrington, from the novel by James Herbert

The Fly ★★★ 🔟

Horror   1958 · US · Colour · 89mins

No match for the superior David Cronenberg remake, but still a slick slice of absurdist fifties' sci-fi in its own right. Based on a *Playboy* short story, with a script by *Shogun* writer James Clavell, the plot has matter-transmitter experiments giving Al Hedison (later David Hedison) the head and arm of a common house fly, while Vincent Price, as Hedison's brother, has histrionics about family curses. Enjoyably unsettling once past the inconsistencies of the premise, this plush flesh-crawler includes many marvellous moments – the fly's-eye prism view and the tiny half human/half fly trapped in a cobweb shrieking "Help me!". 🎞

Al Hedison [David Hedison] *Andre* • Patricia Owens *Helene* • Vincent Price *François* • Herbert Marshall *Inspector Charas* • Kathleen Freeman *Emma* • Betty Lou Gerson *Nurse Andersone* • Charles Herbert *Philippe* ■ *Dir* Kurt Neumann • *Scr* James Clavell, from a story by George Langelaan

The Fly ★★★★ 🔞

Horror   1986 · US · Colour · 91mins

It's easy to see why visceral visionary David Cronenberg wanted to remake the landmark 1958 chiller about scientific experiments in molecular teleportation. It plunges into the same primal territory he explored in *Shivers*, *Rabid* and *Videodrome* by regurgitating his deep-seated fears of ageing, disease, deformity and the beast within. Only Cronenberg can get away with working out his raw phobias on screen while being poignantly witty and repulsively entertaining at the same time. Jeff Goldblum's sensitive performance takes the edge off the grisly special effects, but many will find it hard to get past the gooey gore. Contains some swearing. 🎞

Jeff Goldblum *Seth Brundle* • Geena Davis *Veronica Quaife* • John Getz *Stathis Borans* • Joy Boushel *Tawny* • Les Carlson *Dr Cheevers* • George Chuvalo *Marky* • David Cronenberg *Gynaecologist* ■ *Dir* David Cronenberg • *Scr* Charles Edward Pogue, David Cronenberg, from a story by George Langelaan

The Fly II ★★ 🔞

Horror   1989 · US · Colour · 100mins

Exactly what you'd expect from special effects and make-up artist-turned-director Chris Walas – too much emphasis on gore galore and scant attention paid to plot. Not that there is one, really merely sketchy broad strokes showing Son of the Fly going berserk in a labyrinthine biochemical laboratory. Eric Stoltz does what he can encased in rubber as the misunderstood larva, but it goes without saying that this obvious sequel, inspired more by *Alien*, has none of the sly subtlety, horrific elegance or poignant humour David Cronenberg brought to his superior 1986 film. Still, the Muppet-style deformed dog is a laugh. Contains swearing and violence. 🎞

Eric Stoltz *Martin Brundle* • Daphne Zuniga *Beth Logan* • Lee Richardson *Anton Bartok* • John Getz *Stathis Borans* • Frank Turner *Dr Shepard* ■ *Dir* Chris Walas • *Scr* Mick Garris, Jim Wheat, Frank Darabont, Ken Wheat, from a story by Mick Garris

Fly Away Home ★★★★ 🅄

Drama based on a true story
1996 · US · Colour · 102mins

No one captures the inspirational beauty of nature better than director Carroll Ballard, who also made *Never Cry Wolf* and the excellent *Black Stallion*. Working from a true story, this exhilarating picture gets off to a painful start with a fatal road accident. But the mood changes from despair to determination as Anna Paquin channels her grief into the rearing of some orphan goslings, learning to fly a microlight plane to guide her feathered family to its winter breeding ground. With selfless support from Jeff Daniels as Paquin's inventor father and from the geese themselves (stealing every scene, whether waddling comically or flying majestically), this impeccably photographed film is an unbounded delight. 🎞 **DVD**

Jeff Daniels *Thomas Alden* • Anna Paquin *Amy Alden* • Dana Delany *Susan Barnes* • Terry Kinney *David Alden* • Holter Graham *Barry Strickland* ■ *Dir* Carroll Ballard • *Scr* Robert Rodat, Vince McKewin, from the autobiography by Bill Lishman

Fly by Night ★★

Crime   1942 · US · BW · 74mins

Unassuming little thriller with B-movie regular Richard Carlson and former child star Nancy Kelly as two innocents suddenly ensnared in the world of espionage and a mysterious weapon known only as G-32. Carlson is accused of killing an inventor, and escapes to try and prove his innocence. Making only his second US movie, director Robert Siodmak makes the most of his slender resources and produces an Americanised blend of Hitchcock's *The 39 Steps* and *The Man Who Knew Too Much*.

Nancy Kelly *Pat Lindsey* • Richard Carlson *Jeff Burton* • Albert Basserman *Dr Storm* • Martin Kosleck *George Taylor* • Nestor Paiva *Grube* • Walter Kingsford *Heydt* ■ *Dir* Robert Siodmak • *Scr* Jay Dratler, F Hugh Herbert, from a story by Ben Roberts, Sidney Sheldon

The Flying Deuces ★★ 🅄

Comedy   1939 · US · BW · 64mins

Notwithstanding a script co-written by silent star Harry Langdon and direction by comedy specialist A Edward Sutherland, this is one of the weaker Laurel and Hardy pictures. Mostly pilfered from the four-reeler *Beau Hunks* and the feature *Bonnie Scotland*, the comic material is simply spread too thinly, and time hangs heavily between the Paris opening, the pair's jaunty dance on arrival at the Foreign Legion fort and the careering plane finale. The boys make the best of what is available but the disappointment for fans is painful. 🎞 **DVD**

Stan Laurel *Stan* • Oliver Hardy *Ollie* • Jean Parker *Georgette* • Reginald Gardiner *François* • Charles Middleton *Commandant* ■ *Dir* A Edward Sutherland • *Scr* Ralph Spence, Alfred Schiller, Charles Rogers, Harry Langdon

Flying down to Rio ★★★ 🅄

Musical   1933 · US · BW · 85mins

When it was first shown, the stars of this film were glamorous Dolores Del

Rio and dashing Gene Raymond, backed by perfect Depression-era deco sets and design and imaginative choreography. But the real significance and most of the pleasure of this film today lies in the casting of two featured players (originally billed fourth and fifth) who, although they knew each other in their pre-Hollywood days in New York, had never danced together until this movie. And when they did, screen history was made. Their names were Fred Astaire and Ginger Rogers, and the highlight here is the 18-minute-long *Carioca*. They made nine more films together and gave more pleasure to audiences than, arguably, any other partnership in movie history. Sit back, watch, and marvel at their evident pleasure at working with each other. 🎞

Dolores Del Rio *Belinha* • Gene Raymond *Roger Bond* • Fred Astaire *Fred Ayres* • Ginger Rogers *Honey Hale* • Raul Roulien *Julio Ribeiro* ■ *Dir* Thornton Freeland • *Scr* Cyril Hume, HW Hanemann, Erwin Gelsey, from a play by Anne Caldwell, from a story by Lou Brock

The Flying Eye ★★★ 🅄

Adventure   1955 · UK · BW · 53mins

The special effects may look like something cobbled together on *Blue Peter*, but who could resist a film in which a character called Colonel Audacious and his trusty sidekick Bunstuffer use a model plane with an all-seeing TV eye to confound some enemy spies? Adapted from a novel by John Newton Chance, this ripping yarn was one of the Children's Film Foundation's most enjoyable offerings, with Geoffrey Sumner revelling in the role of the eccentric inventor and David Hannaford contributing some oafish derring-do. It's dated, of course, but will evoke pleasant memories for ex-Saturday matinée aficionados.

David Hannaford *Bunstuffer* • Julia Lockwood *Angela* • Harcourt Williams *Professor* • Ivan Craig *Mayer* • Geoffrey Sumner *Col Audacious* ■ *Dir* William C Hammond • *Scr* William C Hammond, Ken Hughes, Darrell Catling, from a novel by John Newton Chance

Flying 55 ★★ 🅄

Crime drama   1939 · UK · BW · 71mins

As with so many horse-racing melodramas, this Edgar Wallace story is pretty heavy going until we reach the course, when all the clichés and caricatures are forgotten in that frantic dash for the line. Wallace could never be accused of stinting on incident as family feuds, race fixing, blackmail and romance are all brought under starters' orders by no-nonsense director, Reginald Denham. Derrick de Marney and Nancy Burne are the stars, but it's Marius Goring who contributes the only worthwhile performance.

Derrick de Marney *Bill Urquhart* • Nancy Burne *Stella Barrington* • Marius Goring *Charles Barrington* • John Warwick *Jebson* • Peter Gawthorne *Jonas Urquhart* • DA Clarke-Smith *Jacques Gregory* ■ *Dir* Reginald Denham • *Scr* Victor M Greene, Vernon Clancey, Kenneth Horne, from the novel by Edgar Wallace

Flying Leathernecks ★★ 🄟🄶

Second World War action drama
1951 · US · Colour · 97mins

Another disappointing early work from Nicholas Ray, whose *Rebel without a Cause* remains a key movie of the fifties. This is a trite reworking of many themes (and characters) familiar from films like Howard Hawks's masterly *Air Force* (1943). John Wayne and, particularly, Robert Ryan seem ill-at-ease in their leading roles, flying studio mock-ups of planes against Technicolor back-projection and dutifully conveying a gung-ho spirit without any real enthusiasm. Acting honours are stolen by veteran Jay C Flippen, well cast as a wily sergeant, however this is just corny, obvious and not really good enough. 🎞

John Wayne *Major Dan Kirby* • Robert Ryan *Captain Carl Griffin* • Don Taylor *Lieutenant "Cowboy" Blithe* • William Harrigan *Curan* • Jay C Flippen *Master Sergeant Clancy* ■ *Dir* Nicholas Ray • *Scr* James Edward Grant, from a story by Kenneth Gamet

The Flying Scot ★ 🅄

Crime thriller   1957 · UK · BW · 70mins

The most noteworthy thing about this crime programme-filler is that it was scripted by Norman Hudis, who wrote six *Carry On* films. As with most British B-movies of the period, a clutch of transatlantic stars were imported to raise the profile, but neither Canadians Lee Patterson and Kay Callard, nor American Alan Gifford could do much to distract from the mediocrity of this train robbery thriller in which they set out to rob the train of the title, but face unexpected obstacles.

Lee Patterson *Ronnie* • Kay Callard *Jackie* • Alan Gifford *Phil* • Margaret Withers *Lady* • Mark Baker *Gibbs* • Jeremy Bodkin *Charlie* ■ *Dir* Compton Bennett • *Scr* Norman Hudis, from a story by Ralph Smart, Jan Read

Flying Tigers ★★ 🄟🄶

Second World War drama
1942 · US · BW · 97mins

A very average wartime John Wayne feature, singing the praises of the American Volunteer Group, the mercenaries who fought for China's freedom against superior Japanese odds in the days before Pearl Harbor. Director David Miller provides some well-staged action sequences, but Wayne and his co-star John Carroll struggle with the contrived plot. This kind of adventure would have benefited from a major studio and the combined star power of, say, Spencer Tracy and Clark Gable. 🎞

John Wayne *Jim Gordon* • John Carroll *Woody Jason* • Anna Lee *Brooke Elliott* • Paul Kelly *Hap Davis* • Mae Clarke *Verna Bales* • Edmund MacDonald *Blackie Bales* ■ *Dir* David Miller • *Scr* Kenneth Gamet, Barry Trivers, from a story by Kenneth Gamet

Flynn ★★★ 🔞

Biographical adventure drama
1995 · Ausl · Colour · 95mins

Even if only half of the stories are true, dashing screen legend Errol Flynn packed enough incident into his lifetime to provide material for at least three movies. This Australian biography concentrates on his pre-Hollywood, hell-raising days, with Guy Pearce (*LA*

Confidential) enjoying himself as the young Flynn, a rampant womaniser, gold prospector and possible killer. Steven Berkoff and John Savage also get into the spirit of things, while director Frank Howson whips it along at an entertaining pace. ▭

Guy Pearce *Errol Flynn* • Steven Berkoff *Klaus Reicher* • John Savage *Joe Stromberg* • Claudia Karvan *Penelope Watts* • Will Gluth *Professor Flynn* ■ *Dir* Frank Howson • *Scr* Frank Howson, Alister Webb

The Fog ★★★ **15**
Chiller 1980 · US · Colour · 85mins

Not director John Carpenter at the peak of his form, but a reasonable enough shocker involving spectral pirates cloaked by supernatural mists terrorising a coastal town. Losing dramatic focus by switching between two heroines who never meet – disc jockey Adrienne Barbeau (then married to Carpenter) and Jamie Lee Curtis (starring with real-life mum Janet Leigh for the first time) – Carpenter leans hard on cheap scare tactics (people jumping out of the dark) more than subtle suspense. However, some sequences do turn the tension dial up quite high. ▭

Adrienne Barbeau *Stevie Wayne* • Hal Holbrook *Father Malone* • Jamie Lee Curtis *Elizabeth Solley* • Janet Leigh *Kathy Williams* • Tom Atkins *Nick Castle* • John Houseman *Machen* ■ *Dir* John Carpenter • *Scr* John Carpenter, Debra Hill • *Cinematographer* Dean Cundey • *Music* John Carpenter

Fog Island ★
Mystery 1945 · US · BW · 69mins

Uninviting tale about the search for treasure on an isolated isle, with character actors George Zucco and Lionel Atwill wading through fog-shrouded dullness, not alleviated by the cumbersome direction. Zucco plays a once-rich man who invites those he thinks are responsible for his downfall to his island. Morse later directed the American scenes inserted into *Godzilla*.

George Zucco *Leo Grainger* • Lionel Atwill *Alec Ritchfield* • Jerome Cowan *Kavanaugh* • Sharon Douglas *Gail* • Veda Ann Borg *Sylvia* ■ *Dir* Terry Morse • *Scr* Pierre Gendron, from the story by Bernadine Angus

Fog over Frisco ★
Crime drama 1934 · US · BW · 69mins

No great star in the clutches of the studio system suffered so much poor material as did Bette Davis at Warner Bros (she eventually sued the studio, and lost), and this ludicrous crime melodrama is a prime example. Bravely directed by William Dieterle and Daniel Reed, the movie is notable for its pace, created by a succession of skilfully employed wipes and quick dissolves, which hasten 69 minutes of drivel to a speedy end. As a San Francisco heiress and archetypal bad girl, Davis flounces and emotes with breathtaking conviction, lighting a fiery path through the inane plot and cardboard characters that surround her. It's often unintentionally funny: watch it and relish Margaret Lindsay as Davis's loyal sister, bravely maintaining dignity as she utters dialogue that beggars belief. ▭

Bette Davis *Arlene Bradford* • Margaret Lindsay *Val Bradford* • Lyle Talbot *Spencer Carleton* • Arthur Byron *Everett Bradford* • Hugh Herbert *Izzy Wright* • Douglass Dumbrille *Joshua Maynard* ■ *Dir* William Dieterle, Daniel Reed • *Scr* Robert N Lee, Eugene Solow, from the story by George Dyer

Folies Bergère ★★★
Musical 1935 · US · BW · 104mins

This super 20th Century-Fox musical revolves around one of the studio's many stock plots. Here it's the one about mistaken identity, also used in *That Night in Rio* and *On the Riviera*, both of which are virtual remakes of this. Maurice Chevalier is in his prime here as both Folies star and pompous aristocrat, getting involved with Folies co-star Ann Sothern and beautiful baroness Merle Oberon, whose scenes in this film slow down the pace somewhat. Nevertheless, the musical numbers are elaborate, and there's a knockout (though tasteless) dance finale which won choreographer Dave Gould an Oscar.

Maurice Chevalier *Eugene Charlier/Baron Cassini* • Merle Oberon *Baroness Genevieve Cassini* • Ann Sothern *Mimi* • Walter Byron *Rene* • Lumsden Hare *Gustave* • Eric Blore *François* ■ *Dir* Roy Del Ruth • *Scr* Bess Meredyth, Hal Long, from the play *The Red Cat* by Hans Adler, Rudolph Lothar

Folks! ★ **15**
Comedy 1992 · US · Colour · 108mins

Director Ted Kotcheff and writer Robert Klane – the guys who brought us *Weekend at Bernie's* – smite viewers once again with this terrible ''comedy'', which drove a stake into the heart of Tom Selleck's career. He plays Jon, a successful broker whose world falls apart when he is investigated for insider trading and has his bank accounts frozen. It couldn't come at a worse time: his mother needs medical care, while senile old Dad (Don Ameche) makes them homeless when he accidentally burns the house down. Senility and attempted suicide are used to supposed comic effect as Selleck wanders around in various states of disarray, probably wondering what on earth he did to end up in this dreadful film. ▭

Tom Selleck *Jon Aldrich* • Don Ameche *Harry Aldrich* • Anne Jackson *Mildred Aldrich* • Christine Ebersole *Arlene Aldrich* • Wendy Crewson *Audrey Aldrich* • Robert Pastorelli *Fred* ■ *Dir* Ted Kotcheff • *Scr* Robert Klane

Follow a Star ★★ **U**
Comedy 1959 · UK · BW · 99mins

If you're reckless enough to follow the plot of this Norman Wisdom comedy, you'll find faint echoes of *Singin' in the Rain*. Very faint. Norman is the tailor's assistant whose voice fading celebrity Jerry Desmonde mimes to, without rewarding the little man's services. Norman's humour knows no restraint or timing, which makes him schmaltzily tedious, especially as he can only sing in the presence of his wheelchair-bound girlfriend June Laverick. But he has wonderful backing from British stalwarts such as Hattie Jacques, John Le Mesurier, Richard Wattis and Fenella Fielding. Perhaps he should have mimed to them. ▭

Norman Wisdom *Norman Truscott* • June Laverick *Judy* • Jerry Desmonde *Vernon Carew* • Hattie Jacques *Dymphna Dobson* • Richard Wattis *Dr Chatterway* • John Le Mesurier *Birkett* • Fenella Fielding *Lady Finchington* ■ *Dir* Robert Asher • *Scr* Jack Davies, Henry Blyth, Norman Wisdom

Follow Me ★★
Detective comedy 1971 · UK · Colour · 95mins

Adapted from Peter Shaffer's play *The Public Eye*, this one-hour comedy is inexcusably strung out to 95 minutes by the playwright and the director, Carol Reed. While some of this time is justifiably taken up with photographer Christopher G Challis's loving images of London, too much is occupied with Topol's ham-fisted buffoonery. He plays a detective hired by priggish accountant Michael Jayston to spy on his free-spirited wife. Mia Farrow's innocent perambulations have an undeniable charm as she plays the misunderstood wife.

Mia Farrow *Belinda* • Topol *Julian Cristoforou* • Michael Jayston *Charles* • Margaret Rawlings *Mrs Sidley* • Annette Crosbie *Miss Framer* ■ *Dir* Carol Reed • *Scr* Peter Shaffer, from his play *The Public Eye*

Follow Me, Boys! ★★★ **U**
Romantic comedy 1966 · US · Colour · 115mins

In a far cry from his *film noir* tough-guy stance in the forties, the hit TV series *My Three Sons* gave actor Fred MacMurray a completely new avuncular image, and he spent much of his later career portraying a worried, but basically imperturbable, good guy at Disney. Here he plays a scout leader in a small-town saga of rather limited charm. As ever in Disney films of this period, the supporting cast is full of seasoned veterans, none more impressive than silent movie great Lillian Gish. The Technicolor is nice but to be honest, it's a long slog through the corn, though Vera Miles couldn't be better as MacMurray's wife and watch out for young Kurt Russell. ▭

Fred MacMurray *Lemuel Siddons* • Vera Miles *Vida Downey* • Lillian Gish *Hetty Seibert* • Charlie Ruggles [Charles Ruggles] *John Everett Hughes* • Elliott Reid *Ralph Hastings* • Kurt Russell *Whitey* ■ *Dir* Norman Tokar • *Scr* Louis Pelletier, MacKinley Kantor

Follow That Bird ★★★ **U**
Comedy 1985 · US · Colour · 84mins

Fans of *Sesame Street* will be thrilled with this adventure, which features everyone's favourite resident, Big Bird. The yellow feathered one has been evicted from the street, so he goes off on a long adventure, making new friends along the way while his friends back home desperately search for him. It's strictly for the under-fives, but adults will nonetheless be entertained by celebrity cameos from such luminaries as Sandra Bernhard, Chevy Chase and John Candy. The non-human cast, meanwhile, includes all the old favourites, with Oscar the Grouch, Kermit the Frog, Bert, Ernie and the Cookie Monster all getting their 15 minutes of fame. ▭

Carroll Spinney *Big Bird/Oscar* • Jim Henson *Kermit the Frog/Ernie* • Frank Oz *Cookie Monster/Bert/Grover* • Paul Bartel *Grouch cook* • Sandra Bernhard *Grouch waitress* • John Candy *State trooper* • Chevy Chase *Newscaster* • Joe Flaherty *Sid Sleaze* ■ *Dir* Ken Kwapis • *Scr* Tony Geiss, Judy Freudberg

Follow That Dream ★★★ **U**
Musical drama 1962 · US · Colour · 105mins

An easy-going rustic drama, with Elvis Presley cast as wide-eyed country boy Toby Kwimper, in a film adapted by *His Girl Friday* screenwriter Charles Lederer from Richard Powell's novel *Pioneer, Go Home*. This was not actually intended as a vehicle for Elvis, the real stars are Arthur O'Connell and a troublesome homestead but it benefits from Presley's gentle, laid-back performance as an unsophisticated young hillbilly. Director Gordon Douglas seems at a loss over what to do during Elvis's (too) few songs, and directs him lying down and looking rather uncomfortable most of the time, especially during the obvious miming of the title number. Still, there's pleasure in watching Presley resist the charms of Joanna Moore, or flirt with cute Anne Helm.

Elvis Presley *Toby Kwimper* • Arthur O'Connell *Pop Kwimper* • Anne Helm *Holly Jones* • Joanna Moore *Alicia Claypoole* • Jack Kruschen *Carmine* ■ *Dir* Gordon Douglas • *Scr* Charles Lederer, from the novel *Pioneer, Go Home* by Richard Powell

Follow the Boys ★★★★ **U**
Musical comedy 1944 · US · BW · 119mins

A wonderful nostalgic treat that has now become a quintessential wartime artefact. This all-star review produced by ace packager Charles K Feldman was released by Universal as a tribute to the US forces (the ''boys'' of the title). It actually has a plot of sorts, with George Raft and Vera Zorina splitting up – somewhat improbably – so that Raft can organise USO shows, but, oh what shows! Here's Orson Welles famously sawing Marlene Dietrich in half, WC Fields demonstrating his great *Ziegfeld Follies* pool hall routine and Jeanette MacDonald reviving *Beyond the Blue Horizon*. Perhaps most potently, Dinah Shore sings one of the most popular – and most beautiful – of all wartime ballads, Jule Styne and Sammy Cahn's *I'll Walk Alone*. Other talent on display includes the likes of The Andrews Sisters, Artur Rubinstein, Maria Montez, Randolph Scott, and Sophie Tucker performing *Some of These Days*. Of course it's a little long, but what would you cut?

George Raft *Tony West* • Vera Zorina *Gloria Vance* • Grace McDonald *Kitty West* • Charles Grapewin [Charley Grapewin] *Nick West* • George Macready *Walter Bruce* • Jeanette MacDonald • Orson Welles • Marlene Dietrich • Donald O'Connor • WC Fields • Lon Chaney Jr • Randolph Scott • Dinah Shore • The Andrews Sisters • Artur Rubinstein • Maria Montez • Sophie Tucker ■ *Dir* Edward Sutherland [A Edward Sutherland] • *Scr* Lou Breslow, Gertrude Purcell

Follow the Boys ★★ **U**
Romantic comedy 1963 · US · Colour · 95mins

Sequel of sorts to MGM's popular 1960 teenage romp *Where the Boys Are* (itself ludicrously remade in 1984)

substituting the French Riviera for Florida's Fort Lauderdale and reuniting two of the female stars that made the first one so sassy – swingin' Connie Francis and kooky Paula Prentiss. It's a pleasure to look at in but frankly it smacks of desperation, with the cast too old for this would-be romp. Still, it's always good to see performers of the calibre of Russ Tamblyn and Janis Paige go through their paces, and the colourful locations make up a little for the sheer sappiness of the plot. Delectable French actress Dany Robin is left all at sea, though. Not to be confused with the all-star 1944 extravaganza of the same title.

Connie Francis *Bonnie Pulaski* • Paula Prentiss *Toni Denham* • Ron Randell *Cmdr Ben Bradville* • Janis Paige *Liz Bradville* • Russ Tamblyn *Lt "Smitty" Smith* • Dany Robin *Michele* ■ *Dir* Richard Thorpe • *Scr* David T Chantler, David Osborn, from a story by Lawrence P Bachmann

Follow the Fleet ★★★★ U

Musical 1936 · US · BW · 110mins

Shore-leave sailors Fred Astaire and Randolph Scott breeze into town and fall for sisters Ginger Rogers and Harriet Nelson (billed here as Harriet Hilliard). The plot revolving around the Scott/Hilliard characters had dominated the stage play *Shore Leave* and the Broadway show and film of *Hit the Deck*, on which sources this film was based. But here it plays second fiddle to the romance between the swaggering Astaire and the equally sassy Rogers. The settings might not be the Art Deco delights of the couple's other pictures and not all of Irving Berlin's songs would make his greatest hits compilation, but the song-and-dance duo are as captivating as ever and *Let's Face the Music and Dance* ranks as one of their finest routines. [video]

Fred Astaire *"Bake" Baker* • Ginger Rogers *Sherry Martin* • Randolph Scott *Bilge Smith* • Harriet Hilliard [Harriet Nelson] *Connie Martin* • Astrid Allwyn *Iris Manning* • Harry Beresford *Captain Ezra Hickey* • Russell Hicks *Jim Nolan* • Lucille Ball *Kitty Collins* • Betty Grable *Showgirl* ■ *Dir* Mark Sandrich • *Scr* Dwight Taylor, Allan Scott, from the play *Shore Leave* by Hubert Osborne, from the musical *Hit the Deck* by Herbert Fields

Follow the Leader ★★

Comedy adventure 1944 · US · BW · 64mins

The East Side Kids were headed for a wartime rut by the time they delivered this instalment, a reiteration of their usual shtick as Muggs and Glimpy (that's Leo Gorcey and Huntz Hall, not yet the Bowery Boys) try to flush out a bad 'un from among the kids. In Second World War Hollywood, that's a subtext which means watch out for informers or fifth columnists in your neighbourhood). There's nothing particularly notable here, except for an appearance by toughie Jack LaRue, before he crossed the big pond to star in *No Orchids for Miss Blandish*. The whole cycle was rejigged as *The Bowery Boys* in 1946, providing work for Gorcey, Hall and the boys for the next ten years.

Leo Gorcey *Muggs McGinnis* • Huntz Hall *Glimpy Freedhoff* • Dave Durand *Danny* • Bud Gorman *James Aloysius "Skinny" Bogerty* • Bobby Stone *Speed* • Jimmy Strand *Dave* • Gabriel Dell *WW "Fingers" Belmont* • Jack LaRue *Larry* • Joan Marsh *Millie McGinnis* ■ *Dir* William Beaudine • *Scr* William X Crowley, Beryl Sachs, from a story by Ande Lamb

Follow the River ★★★

Western drama 1995 · US · Colour

Surprisingly few movies have been set during America's colonial era, and while this TV movie may not be of the calibre of John Ford's *Drums along the Mohawk* or Michael Mann's *The Last of the Mohicans*, it still makes for absorbing viewing. As the pregnant mother captured by the Shawnees, Sheryl Lee gives an unexpectedly gutsy performance, teaming well with Ellen Burstyn. Director Martin Davidson efficiently explores the clashing cultures and the role of women in pioneering society, making the most of the stunning Blue Ridge scenery.

Sheryl Lee *Mary Ingles* • Ellen Burstyn *Gretel* • Tim Guinee *Will Ingles* • Eric Schweig *Wildcat* ■ *Dir* Martin Davidson • *Scr* Jennifer Miller, from the novel by James Alexander Thorn

Following ★★★ 15

Thriller 1998 · UK · BW · 70mins

Shot around Soho at weekends on 16mm monochrome, Christopher Nolan's feature debut is a tortuous flashback thriller that, regrettably, attempts one twist too many. The opening segment is filled with sinister promise, as people-watching wannabe novelist Jeremy Theobald is played at his own game by Alex Haw, a burglar who claims to be able to define his victims' personalities by their possessions. Alarm bells sound once Lucy Russell joins the fray, however, as intriguing character study is abandoned for structural and narrative contrivance. For all the deadpanning of a committed cast, this is ultimately a misfire, but a fascinating and unusual one nonetheless.

Jeremy Theobald *The young man* • Alex Haw *Cobb* • Lucy Russell *Blonde* • John Nolan *Policeman* • Dick Bradsell *Bald guy* • Gillian El-Kadi *Home owner* • Jennifer Angel *Waitress* • Nicolas Carlotti *Barman* ■ *Dir/Scr* Christopher Nolan

Following Her Heart ★★

Romantic drama 1994 · US · Colour

Ann-Margret and co-star George Segal add a little class to this slight but well-made TV drama. She plays an unhappily married woman who with the help of a pen pal dreams of a new life as a country and western songwriter in Nashville. Oscar-winner Lee Grant (*Shampoo*) has been directing since the early eighties, and she coaxes believable performances from a cast that also includes Brenda Vaccaro, while trying her best to keep sentimentality at bay.

Ann-Margret *Ingalill Lindquist* • George Segal *Harry* • Brenda Vaccaro *Cecile* ■ *Dir* Lee Grant • *Scr* Merry Helm

Folly to Be Wise ★★★

Comedy 1952 · UK · BW · 91mins

Based on the James Bridie play that gently mocked the popular BBC radio debate programme *The Brains Trust*, this Frank Launder and Sidney Gilliat comedy seems so satisfied with its central idea that it neglects to flesh it out with wit. The various members of the splendid cast seem all too aware that they are marking time between those marvellous moments when army chaplain Alastair Sim loses control of his squabbling panellists, but they are powerless to raise the tempo. Nevertheless, Roland Culver and Elizabeth Allan are good value as the sparring spouses, and Martita Hunt does well in another of her celebrated *grande dame* turns.

Alastair Sim *Captain Paris* • Roland Culver *George Prout* • Elizabeth Allan *Angela Prout* • Martita Hunt *Lady Dodds* • Miles Malleson *Dr Hector McAdam* • Colin Gordon *Professor James Mutch* • Edward Chapman *Joseph Byres* ■ *Dir* Frank Launder • *Scr* Frank Launder, John Dighton, from the play *It Depends What You Mean* by James Bridie

Food of Love ★★ 15

Romantic comedy
1997 · UK/Fr · Colour · 108mins

A poor relation to *In the Bleak Midwinter*, this romantic comedy set in the world of amateur dramatics subjects a willing cast to situations and dialogue worthier of a weekend playwright than someone of Stephen Poliakoff's reputation. Wearily touching on such themes as the town and country divide, middle-age regret and the continuing relevance of theatre, the action follows banker Richard E Grant's attempt to relive an idyllic summer by taking his long-disbanded thesping troupe back to a sleepy rural village for a production of *Twelfth Night*. What follows is as cringingly predictable as the bittersweet subplots involving Grant and Natalie Baye and former lovers Joe McGann and Juliet Aubrey.

Richard E Grant *Alex Salmon* • Nathalie Baye *Michèle* • Joe McGann *Sam* • Juliet Aubrey *Madeline* • Lorcan Cranitch *Luke* • Penny Downie *Mary* • Holly Davidson *Jessica* • Tameka Empson *Alice* • Sylvia Syms *Mrs Harvey-Brown* ■ *Dir/Scr* Stephen Poliakoff

The Food of the Gods ★★ 18

Science-fiction 1975 · US · Colour · 84mins

This "revenge of nature" thriller owes much to big bug movies of the fifties like *Them!* but lacks the charm that made those schlock classics so memorable. Still, it's tough to dislike a movie that incorporates giant chickens and rats in its tale of a remote island where a mystery substance has caused the creatures to grow to an abnormal size. Based loosely on the HG Wells novel, the special effects that are so crucial in making a picture like this work are variable at best, but director Bert I Gordon conjures up some gruesome set-piece deaths such as a man stung to death by a giant wasp. Ultimately this wears out its welcome – once you've seen one giant chicken you've seen them all. [video]

Marjoe Gortner *Morgan* • Pamela Franklin *Lorna Scott* • Ralph Meeker *Jack Bensington* • Ida Lupino *Mrs Skinner* • Jon Cypher *Brian* • Belinda Balaski *Rita* • Tom Stovall *Tom* • John McLiam *Mr Skinner* ■ *Dir* Bert I Gordon • *Scr* Bert I Gordon, from the novel by HG Wells

The Fool ★★★ U

Drama 1990 · UK · Colour · 140mins

Beautifully detailed account of Victorian life in London, with Derek Jacobi as Frederick, the humble clerk, who leads a double life by also posing as Sir John, a businessman who's accepted in high social circles – a gem of paste in a chandelier of diamonds. Director Christine Edzard who, in 1987, had reconstructed Charles Dickens' *Little Dorritt* to great acclaim, here needs a stronger narrative. A superb cast can't prevent the characters from resembling the Cruikshank-illustrated cartoons of Victorian social historian Henry Mayhew.

Derek Jacobi *Sir John/Mr Frederick* • Cyril Cusack *The Ballad Seller* • Ruth Mitchell *The Girl* • Maria Aitken *Lady Amelia* • Irina Brook *Georgiana Shillibeer* • Paul Brooke *Lord Paramount* • Richard Caldicot *Duke* • Rosalie Crutchley *Mrs Harris* • Patricia Hayes *The Dowager* ■ *Dir* Christine Edzard • *Scr* Christine Edzard, Olivier Stockman

Fool for Love ★★★ 15

Drama 1985 · US · Colour · 102mins

Kim Basinger acts her sexual socks off in Robert Altman's adaptation of a theatrical production that works well as a piece of cinema, while still retaining its stifling atmosphere. Sam Shepard takes the starring role in his own play, about a past, semi-incestuous love that overshadows the present, and lends a special power to his role as a cowboy hick, driven by furies that would not disgrace a Greek tragedy. Co-star Harry Dean Stanton, as an eccentric old man, also proves how satisfying good character acting can be. Contains some violence and swearing. [video]

Sam Shepard *Eddie* • Kim Basinger *May* • Harry Dean Stanton *Old man* • Randy Quaid *Martin* • Martha Crawford *May's mother* • Louise Egolf *Eddie's mother* • Sura Cox *Teenage May* • Jonathan Skinner *Teenage Eddie* ■ *Dir* Robert Altman • *Scr* Sam Shepard, from his play

The Fool Killer ★★★

Period thriller 1965 · US · BW · 101mins

The story of an orphan boy's adventures just after the end of the Civil War proves to be an unusual experience. Initially the boy – played by actor Eddie Albert's son, Edward – runs into a reclusive eccentric named Dirty Jim Jelliman (Henry Hull, relishing the role) who tells him yarn after yarn about the Fool Killer, a legendary slayer of idiots. The boy then encounters Anthony Perkins, a traumatised former soldier who may or may not be the eponymous axe-wielder. Surely not? A labour of love for all concerned, with Perkins doing what he does best.

Anthony Perkins *Milo Bogardus* • Edward Albert *George Mellish* • Dana Elcar *Mr Dodd* • Henry Hull *Dirty Jim Jelliman* • Salome Jens *Mrs Dodd* • Charlotte Jones *Mrs Ova Fanshawe* • Arnold Moss *Rev Spotts* ■ *Dir* Servando Gonzalez • *Scr* David Friedkin, Morton Fine, from a novel by Helen Eustis

Foolin' Around ★★ PG

Romantic comedy
1980 · US · Colour · 95mins

Another would-be zany comedy, with not-too-bad performances from the stars, but a silly script. Gary Busey, best known for his star turn in *The Buddy Holly Story*, plays an innocent farm boy turned student who woos gorgeous Annette O'Toole. Of course, she turns out to be very rich and already engaged to another man. Busey was in his mid-30s when he played this role, but he tries his best despite this miscasting, and the uneven direction. The supporting cast includes two US sitcom stars of the seventies – Cloris Leachman (*The Mary Tyler Moore Show*) and Tony Randall (*The Odd Couple*). 🖵

Gary Busey *Wes McDaniels* • Annette O'Toole *Susan Carlson* • John Calvin *Whitley* • Eddie Albert *Daggett* • Cloris Leachman *Samantha Carlson* • Tony Randall *Peddicord* • Michael Talbott *Clay* ■ *Dir* Richard T Heffron • *Scr* Mike Kane, David Swift

Foolish Heart ★★

Romantic drama
1998 · Arg/Bra/Fr · Colour · 132mins

Clearly autobiographical but clumsily constructed, this is a two-act melodrama that neither involves nor convinces. Originally devised by Hector Babenco as a big Hollywood production, the film begins with Argentine teenager Juan (Walter Quiroz) tasting first love with the mentally unstable Maria Luiza Mendonca during a project to photograph the human soul. Settling for fame as a movie director, the adult Juan (Miguel Angel Sola) returns home to visit his ailing father and embarks on another affair, this time with the impoverished Xuxa Lopes. Full of undeveloped plot strands and sketchily-drawn characters, this is a highly personal but somewhat impenetrable picture. A Spanish language film.

Miguel Angel Sola *Juan as an adult* • Walter Quiroz *Juan as an adolescent* • Maria Luiza Mendonca *Ana* • Xuxa Lopes *Lilith* ■ *Dir* Hector Babenco • *Scr* Hector Babenco, Ricardo Piglia, from a idea by Hector Babenco

Foolish Wives ★★★

Silent drama
1920 · US · BW · 107mins

A legendary silent movie which cost more and took longer to make than DW Griffith's epic *Intolerance*. Originally running for five hours, it's an incredibly lavish study of corruption and sexual obsession, set largely in the casinos, hotels, cafés and boudoirs of Monte Carlo and ends, appropriately enough for a satire, in the city's sewers. A fake count seduces rich ladies, but when he tries it with an ambassador's wife he runs out of luck. Today's viewers will have problems with the pacing, the wayward plotting and the acting styles, but director Erich von Stroheim's vision of decadence still seems impressive. Billed by the studio as the "First Million Dollar Movie" and helped by rumours of censorship, it was a big hit.

Rudolph Christians *Andrew J Hughes* • Miss Du Pont *Helen, his wife* • Maude George *Princess Olga Petschnikoff* • Mae Busch *Princess Vera Petschnikoff* • Erich von Stroheim *Count Sergius Karamzin, Captain of Third Hussars, Imperial Russian Army* ■ *Dir* Erich von Stroheim • *Scr* Erich von Stroheim, Marian Ainslee (titles)

Fools ★

Romantic drama 1970 · US · Colour · 93mins

This dumb (and aptly titled) drama, set in San Francisco, is about the romance between an ageing star of horror

movies and the neglected wife of a lawyer. Indifferently written, directed and acted, it's a shoddy vehicle for its two "name" stars – Jason Robards and Katharine Ross, who just three years earlier was the runaway bride escaping down the aisle with Dustin Hoffman in *The Graduate*.

Jason Robards [Jason Robards Jr] *Matthew South* • Katharine Ross *Anais* • Scott Hylands *David Appleton* • Marc Hannibal *Dog owner* ■ *Dir* Tom Gries • *Scr* Robert Rudelson

Fools for Scandal ★★

Comedy
1938 · US · BW · 80mins

Mervyn LeRoy directs Carole Lombard (sublime) and Fernand Gravet (engaging) in this mind-bendingly silly romantic comedy which starts out very well indeed in a cardboard, studio-built Paris. The action then moves to London, where penniless French aristocrat and master chef Gravet pursues famous movie star Lombard in an attempt to woo her away from her stuffy insurance man (Ralph Bellamy). The piece progressively disintegrates but there are some laughs along the way, and the stars, particularly Lombard, almost survive the chaos into which they are thrown.

Carole Lombard *Kay Winters* • Fernand Gravet *René* • Ralph Bellamy *Phillip Chester* • Allen Jenkins *Dewey Gibson* • Isabel Jeans *Lady Paula Malverton* • Marie Wilson *Myrtle* • Marcia Ralston *Jill* ■ *Dir* Mervyn LeRoy, Bobby Connolly • *Scr* Herbert Fields, Joseph Fields, Irving Brecher, from the play *Return Engagement* by Nancy Hamilton, James Shute, Rosemary Casey

Fool's Gold ★★ U

Western
1946 · US · BW · 63mins

Silent screen matinée idol William Boyd achieved a memorable second career in the sound era as the black-clad, silver-haired cowboy gentleman with the improbable name of Hopalong Cassidy, a character based on a series of frontier tales by writer Clarence E Mulford. The movies were little more than cheap programme fillers, but the character whose popularity was fuelled by comic books and personal appearances was immensely dignified and endearing, and movies like this one, in which "Hoppy" is memorably teamed with sidekick Andy Clyde, were fast-paced, fun, and mercifully short in duration. The series would find a whole new audience on television, making William Boyd a very rich cowboy actor.

William Boyd *Hopalong Cassidy* • Andy Clyde *California Carlson* • Rand Brooks *Lucky Jenkins* • Robert Emmett Keane *Professor Dixon* • Jane Randolph *Jessie Dixon* • Steve Barclay [Stephen Barclay] *Bruce Landy* ■ *Dir* George Archainbaud • *Scr* Doris Schroeder, from characters created by Clarence E Mulford

Fools of Fortune ★★★ 15

Drama
1990 · UK · Colour · 104mins

It's the twenties in Ireland, and the wealthy Quinton family are shocked when their rural splendour is shattered by the British army of the time, the Black and Tans, who burn the house and massacre some of the family. Survivors include Julie Christie and her son, Iain Glen, whose childhood sweetheart grows into Mary Elizabeth Mastrantonio. But politics continue to

play a major role in this absorbing but curiously reticent family saga from the director of *Cal*, another film based on the troubles in Ireland. Author William Trevor's book *Felicia's Journey* was made into a critically-acclaimed film nine years later. 🖵

Iain Glen *Willie Quinton* • Mary Elizabeth Mastrantonio *Marianne* • Julie Christie *Mrs Quinton* • Michael Kitchen *Mr Quinton* • Niamh Cusack *Josephine* • Tom Hickey *Father Kilgarriff* • John Kavanagh *Johnny Lacy* • Mick Lally *Mr Derenzy* • Niall Toibin *Lanigan* ■ *Dir* Pat O'Connor • *Scr* Michael Hirst, from the novel by William Trevor

Fools' Parade ★★★

Melodrama
1971 · US · Colour · 97mins

James Stewart plays a habitual criminal who is released after 40 years in jail and wants to claim $25,000 of prison pay that he has banked legitimately. But the bank manager has run off with it, forcing Stewart back to his old ways. The star chews up the scenery, while George Kennedy, Strother Martin and a young Kurt Russell offer expert support.

James Stewart *Mattie Appleyard* • George Kennedy *Doc Council* • Anne Baxter *Cleo* • Strother Martin *Lee Cottrill* • Kurt Russell *Johnny Jesus* ■ *Dir* Andrew V McLaglen • *Scr* James Lee Barrett, from the novel by Davis Grubb

Fools Rush In ★★★ 12

Romantic comedy
1997 · US · Colour · 104mins

Ignored on its cinema release, this romantic comedy is well worth seeking out. *Friends* star Matthew Perry is a New Yorker on business in Las Vegas who has a one night stand with sultry Mexican Salma Hayek, only for her to reappear three months later to tell him she's pregnant with his baby. The road to true happiness is littered with problems, which form the basis for the rest of the movie, with her traditional parents (and his snobby Wasp-ish ones) being the butt of many a joke along the way. The likeable Perry and sultry Hayek make an attractive couple and are ably supported by Jill Clayburgh, Jon Tenney and Matthew's real-life dad, John Bennett Perry (playing, of course, Matthew's dad). An unexpected treat. Contains sexual references. 🖵

Matthew Perry *Alex* • Salma Hayek *Isabel* • Jon Tenney *Jeff* • Carlos Gomez *Chuy* • Tomas Milian *Tomas* • Siobhan Fallon *Lanie* • John Bennett Perry *Richard* ■ *Dir* Andy Tennant • *Scr* Katherine Reback, from a story by Joan Taylor, Katherine Reback

Footlight Glamour ★★ U

Comedy
1943 · US · BW · 67mins

By 1943, the *Blondie* series of musical comedies, based on the comic strip by Chic Young, had begun to run out of steam. So, in a bid to lure unsuspecting audiences into theatres, Columbia dropped the heroine's title from the 13th and 14th entries, *It's a Great Life* and this cornball comedy. The tactic failed, however, and the story of Penny Singleton and Arthur Lake's encounter with Thurston Hall and his stagestruck daughter, Ann Savage, won few friends and the series was cancelled. However, a flood of letters prompted the studio to

relaunch Blondie Bumstead and her hapless husband Dagwood in *Leave It to Blondie* in 1945.

Penny Singleton *Blondie Bumstead* • Arthur Lake *Dagwood Bumstead* • Larry Simms *Alexander Bumstead* • Ann Savage *Vicki Wheeler* • Jonathan Hale *JC Dithers* • Thurston Hall *Randolph Wheeler* ■ *Dir* Frank R Strayer • *Scr* Karen DeWolfe, Connie Lee, from the comic strip *Blondie* by Chic Young

Footlight Parade ★★★★ U

Musical
1933 · US · BW · 99mins

James Cagney, hoofer extraordinaire, is better remembered for being the thirties' top gangster than as a rival to Fred Astaire. This typically fast-paced Warner Bros extravaganza is a showcase for Cagney at full pelt, playing an extrovert (what else?) producer staging those now-forgotten prologues to the main feature. In this movie, Cagney has the benefit of the genius choreography of Busby Berkeley at his peak. Highlights include Cagney as a sailor searching for his *Shanghai Lil*, *Honeymoon Hotel* and the spectacular *By a Waterfall*, all production numbers that could only have been created on a Warner Bros soundstage. Witty, well cast and as brash as they come, this is a real treat. 🖵

James Cagney *Chester Kent* • Joan Blondell *Nan Prescott* • Dick Powell *Scotty Blair* • Ruby Keeler *Bea Thorn* • Guy Kibbee *Silas Gould* ■ *Dir* Lloyd Bacon, Busby Berkeley • *Scr* Manuel Seff, James Seymour, from a story by Robert Lord, Peter Milne

Footlight Serenade ★★ U

Musical
1942 · US · BW · 80mins

Not to be confused with Warner Bros's wonderful *Footlight Parade*, this is an average wartime 20th Century-Fox Betty Grable vehicle, though with a little more humour than most of its ilk. The film contains some very pleasing performances, including a lightly self-mocking one from hulk Victor Mature as a Broadway-bound boxer. Phil Silvers and Jane Wyman are also impressive, but Grable is not at her best, and her leading man is the terminally bland John Payne. This cries out for colour and a decent score.

John Payne *Bill Smith* • Betty Grable *Pat Lambert* • Victor Mature *Tommy Lundy* • Jane Wyman *Flo Laverne* • James Gleason *Bruce McKay* • Phil Silvers *Flap* • Cobina Wright Jr *Estelle Evans* • June Lang *June* • Frank Orth *Doorman* • Mantan Moreland *Dresser* ■ *Dir* Gregory Ratoff • *Scr* Robert Ellis, Helen Logan, Lynn Starling, from the story *Dynamite* by Fidel LaBarba, Kenneth Earl

Footloose ★★ 15

Musical drama
1984 · US · Colour · 99mins

Essentially a souped up Elvis Presley musical with a daft plot to match, this movie features Kevin Bacon as a free-spirited teenager fighting small-minded minister John Lithgow in a small town where rock 'n' roll and dancing are illegal. Equally appealing are Lori Singer, Dianne Wiest, Christopher Penn and Sarah Jessica Parker, who really do perform wonders with a story that hits the drivel button and becomes overly sentimental far too frequently. While Kenny Loggins may not be your first choice to write songs for a rock musical, his tunes aren't half bad (the

U = SUITABLE FOR ALL   Uc = SUITABLE FOR ALL, ESPECIALLY FOR YOUNG CHILDREN (VIDEO ONLY)   PG = PARENTAL GUIDANCE

title track got to number six in the UK charts), and the energy raised during the finger-snapping dance numbers is surprisingly infectious. Contains swearing and brief nudity. 📼

Kevin Bacon *Ren MacCormack* • Lori Singer *Ariel Moore* • John Lithgow *Reverend Moore* • Dianne Wiest *Vi Moore* • Christopher Penn *Willard* • Sarah Jessica Parker *Rusty* • John Laughlin *Woody* • Elizabeth Gorcey *Wendy Jo* ■ *Dir* Herbert Ross • *Scr* Dean Pitchford

Footrot Flats: the Dog's Tale ★★★
Animation   1986 · NZ · Colour · 71mins

Down Under, Murray Ball's newspaper cartoon strip *Footrot Flats* is as big as *The Gambols*, and this feature film became one of New Zealand's biggest-ever releases. In the Northern Hemisphere, the antics of Wal and Dog are virtually unknown. Here, the nice-but-dim sheep farmer with a passion for rugby crosses swords with the fearsome Crocopigs and Murphy's hellhounds, aided and abetted by his loyal canine companion. John Clarke, memorable as Sam Neill's best friend in *Death in Brunswick*, supplies the voice of Wal, while Dog is voiced by Peter Rowley. An acquired taste, perhaps, but well worth a watch, especially with a tube or two.

John Clarke *Wal* • Peter Rowley *Dog* • Rawiri Paratene *Rangi* • Fiona Samuel *Cheeky Hobson/Pongo* • Peter Hayden *Cooch/Irish Murphy* • Dorothy McKegg *Aunt Dolly* ■ *Dir* Murray Ball • *Scr* Murray Ball, Tom Scott

Footsteps in the Dark ★★
Comedy mystery   1941 · US · BW · 96mins

Flat-footed comedy thriller with Errol Flynn looking distinctly uncomfortable in a suit and bow-tie as the investment banker who moonlights as a mystery writer called FX Pettijohn, which sounds like a nom de plume for WC Fields. Flynn's Holmesian character cruises the streets, discovers a murder and sets out to solve it. Warner Bros, buckling under Flynn's demands to be relieved of his swashbuckles, clearly had in mind a breezy *Thin Man*-style adventure and missed by yards, if not miles. The supporting cast includes Alan Hale, Ralph Bellamy, and Brenda Marshall as Flynn's wife.

Errol Flynn *Francis Warren* • Brenda Marshall *Rita Warren* • Ralph Bellamy *Dr Davis* • Alan Hale *Inspector Mason* • Lee Patrick *Blondie White* • Allen Jenkins *Wilfred* • Lucile Watson *Mrs Archer* • William Frawley *Hopkins* ■ *Dir* Lloyd Bacon • *Scr* Lester Cole, John Wexley, from the play *Blondie White* by Ladislaus Fodor, Bernard Merivale, Jeffrey Dell

Footsteps in the Fog ★★★
Thriller   1955 · UK/US · Colour · 89mins

Handsome Stewart Granger and his then wife, the lovely Jean Simmons, returned to Britain at the peak of their international stardom for this suspenseful and atmospheric Victorian melodrama. In a Columbia Studios tale of lust and blackmail, the under-rated Granger is particularly effective as the murderer, his unique combination of matinée idol looks and ability to appear at ease in period clothing being used to good effect. The Technicolor photography and the clever Shepperton studio interiors also complement him

perfectly. A fine British supporting cast does sterling work, and Rank starlet Belinda Lee is suitably glamorous. Well worth catching.

Stewart Granger *Stephen Lowry* • Jean Simmons *Lily Watkins* • Bill Travers *David MacDonald* • Ronald Squire *Alfred Travers* • Finlay Currie *Inspector Peters* • Belinda Lee *Elizabeth Travers* • William Hartnell *Herbert Moresby* • Frederick Leister *Doctor Simpson* ■ *Dir* Arthur Lubin • *Scr* Dorothy Reid, Leonore Coffee, Arthur Pierson, from the novel *The Interruption* by WW Jacobs

For a Few Dollars More ★★★★★ 15
Classic spaghetti western
1965 · It/W Ger/Sp · Colour · 125mins

The second instalment of Sergio Leone's *Dollars* trilogy is the best and most influential of the three. Honing the stylised visuals and dark humour of the original, Leone takes this opportunity to develop such future genre staples as the uneasy alliance against a common foe and the three-way shoot out. But, while the pursuit of bandit Gian Maria Volonté by bounty hunters Clint Eastwood (motivated by greed) and Lee Van Cleef (driven by revenge) forms the core of the action, it's the attention to everyday detail and the symbols of a passing era (religion and the railroad) that give this operatic classic its distinctive aura. Some dialogue dubbed into English. 📼
DVD

Clint Eastwood *Man with No Name* • Lee Van Cleef *Colonel Douglas Mortimer* • Gian Maria Volonté *Indio* • Jose Egger *Old man over railway* • Rosemary Dexter *Colonel's sister* • Mara Krup *Hotel manager's wife* • Klaus Kinski *Hunchback* ■ *Dir* Sergio Leone • *Scr* Sergio Leone, Luciano Vincenzoni, from a story by Sergio Leone, from a story by Fulvio Morsella • *Music* Ennio Morricone

For Better and for Worse ★★
Romantic comedy
1993 · Fr/US · Colour · 89mins

There's nothing worse than a low-concept comedy in which the central contrivance is matched only by the decrepitude of the dialogue. This, for example, was progressing along quite nicely as a wedding nerves romp, with some broad class divide satire thrown in for good measure. But, then, screenwriter Tony Gilroy has the groom's practical joking buddy send an invitation to the Pope, which, of course, is accepted in a bid to improve the Papacy's public image. Patrick Dempsey and Kelly Lynch strive to give the proceedings some momentum, but the result is as lightweight as a handful of confetti.

Patrick Dempsey *Robert Faldo* • Kelly Lynch *Catherine Vernet* • Gérard Rinaldi *Touchet* • Marion Peterson *Françoise* • Catherine Alcover *Carmina Faldo* • Nicolas Vogel *Joseph Faldo* • Marianne Borgo *Nathalie Vernet* ■ *Dir* Paolo Barzman • *Scr* Tony Gilroy

For Better, for Worse ★★★ U
Romantic comedy
1954 · UK · Colour · 84mins

Almost comforting in its snug predictability, this adaptation of Arthur Watkyn's stage play is now more

noteworthy for its unworldly, sit-comic depiction of young bourgeois marriage than its actual entertainment value. There's a definite rapport between impoverished Dirk Bogarde and his bride, Susan Stephen, but the reliance on disapproving in-laws, nosey neighbours and dodgy tradesmen for laughs could easily have worn thin were it not for the effortlessly accomplished support from the likes of Cecil Parker, Dennis Price and Eileen Herlie. Comedy wasn't really director J Lee Thompson's forte, but he keeps things pottering along nicely.

Dirk Bogarde *Tony Howard* • Susan Stephen *Anne Purves* • Cecil Parker *Anne's father* • Eileen Herlie *Anne's mother* • Dennis Price *Debenham* • Sidney James *Foreman* ■ *Dir* J Lee Thompson • *Scr* J Lee Thompson, from the play by Arthur Watkyn

For Better or Worse ★★★ 12
Romantic comedy
1995 · US · Colour · 85mins

Also known as *Stranger Things*, this comedy marked the directorial debut of *Seinfeld* co-star Jason Alexander. While there's no shortage of kooky characters and slick wisecracks, the storyline takes some swallowing as love-scarred loser Alexander finds himself on the lam with his new sister-in-law (Lolita Davidovich) after his crooked brother (James Woods) bungles a robbery. It's overly reliant on Alexander's manic melancholia, and the farce is too often encumbered by pathos. But Davidovich is pleasingly feisty, and there's a wonderful double act from Joe Mantegna and Jay Mohr as the world's dumbest gangsters. Look out, too, for cameos from Rob Reiner and Rip Torn. Contains violence and some swearing. 📼

Jason Alexander *Michael Makeshift* • James Woods *Reggie* • Lolita Davidovich *Valerie* • Joe Mantegna *Stone* • Jay Mohr *Dwayne* • Beatrice Arthur *Beverly* • Robert Constanzo *Landlord* • Rip Torn *Tex* • Rob Reiner ■ *Dir* Jason Alexander • *Scr* Jeff Nathanson

For Ever Mozart ★★
Experimental drama
1996 · Fr/Swi · Colour · 85mins

This wayward effort from Jean-Luc Godard consists of four short films glued together – "which do not necessarily form a whole" – but could also be called "30 people in search of a story". Most viewers might well be in search of the exit after 20 minutes or so which is, loosely, about the conflict in Bosnia and about the film-making process. Thus businessmen, philosophers, film producers and Serbian fighters spout on about the war and the importance of culture. It's the movie an idealistic 19-year-old student might have made, but Godard was 65 at the time. The Mozart music is gloriously uplifting, though; the world premiere was held in Sarajevo. In French with English subtitles.

Madeleine Assas *Camille, the director's daughter* • Frédéric Pierrot *Jerome, Camille's lover* • Ghalia Lacroix *Dzamila, Camille and Vicky's Arab maid* • Vicky Messica *Vicky Vitalis, the director* ■ *Dir/Scr* Jean-Luc Godard

For Heaven's Sake ★★★★
Silent comedy   1926 · US · BW · 58mins

After several years at Pathé, Harold Lloyd made his debut for Paramount with this sprightly slapstick classic, in which he took the "comedy of thrills" to new heights in a dazzling finale featuring a double-decker bus careering through the tightest city streets. Although playing a millionaire's son, Lloyd is still in characteristic go-getting mood as he sets out to woo Jobyna Ralston by supporting her father's mission. Although the scenes in the Bowery slums were intended to have some social impact, the emphasis is firmly on the comic, but none of the gags come close to the brilliance of the closing chase.

Harold Lloyd *J Harold Manners, the Uptown Boy* • Jobyna Ralston *Hope, the Downtown Girl* • Noah Young *Bull Brindle, the Roughneck* • James Mason *[Jim Mason] The Gangster* • Paul Weigel *Brother Paul, the optimist* ■ *Dir* Sam Taylor • *Scr* John Grey, Ted Wilde, Clyde Bruckman

For Heaven's Sake ★★★
Fantasy comedy   1950 · US · BW · 86mins

A bizarre but eminently watchable fantasy, saved from ignominy by the splendidly tongue-in-cheek acting of Clifton Webb and Edmund Gwenn as a pair of unlikely angels sent to watch over the unborn baby of Joan Bennett and Robert Cummings. What distinguishes this tale from other less successful "visitors from above" sagas is the spicy, gloriously witty script and the deft, easy direction of George Seaton. It was the heyday of this kind of fantasy movie and *For Heaven's Sake* is a typically slick example of the genre.

Clifton Webb *Charles* • Joan Bennett *Lydia Bolton* • Robert Cummings *Jeff Bolton* • Edmund Gwenn *Arthur* • Joan Blondell *Daphne* • Gigi Perreau *Item* • Jack LaRue *Tony* • Harry Von Zell *Tex* • Tommy Rettig *Joe* ■ *Dir* George Seaton • *Scr* George Seaton, from the play *May We Come In?* by Harry Segall

For Hire ★★ 15
Crime thriller   1997 · Can · Colour · 94mins

A nifty crime thriller with a superior plotline, with Rob Lowe as an aspiring actor who forms a friendship with shady author Joe Mantegna, only to find himself the prime suspect in a murder. Lowe is as bland as ever, but the reliable Mantegna more than compensates and director Jean Pellerin manages to keep you guessing right up to the end. Contains some swearing and violence. 📼

Rob Lowe *Mitch Lawrence* • Joe Mantegna *Lou Webber* • Charles Powell *Joe Watson* • Bronwen Booth *Faye Lawrence* • Steve Adams *Tom Kellman* ■ *Dir* Jean Pellerin • *Scr* Karen Erbach, Leah M Kerr, from a story by Karen Erbach, Leah M Kerr

For Keeps ★★ 15
Comedy drama   1987 · US · Colour · 94mins

Molly Ringwald finds life tough as a teenage wife and mother when she gets pregnant by boyfriend Stan (Randall Batinkoff). Career and college ambitions have to be sacrificed and their relationship comes under enormous strain. Written by the team who collaborated on *About Last*

Night... , this is lacking in depth or realism, with Ringwald portrayed as a special case rather than the archetypal girl-next-door. The intimate scenes between the two leads do have genuine heart though. ▭

Molly Ringwald *Darcy Elliot* • Randall Batinkoff *Stan Bobrucz* • Kenneth Mars *Mr Bobrucz* • Miriam Flynn *Mrs Elliot* • Conchata Ferrell *Mrs Bobrucz* • John Zarchen *Chris* • Sharon Brown *Lila* ■ *Dir* John G Avildsen • *Scr* Tim Kazurinsky, Denise DeClue

For Love of a Child ★★ 🅟🅖
Drama   1990 · US · Colour · 93mins

Michael Tucker, best known for his long-running role in *LA Law*, takes the lead in this competent, unambitious made-for-TV drama. He plays a contented suburbanite who enjoys a good business and personal friendship with neighbour Kevin Dobson (*Kojak*'s sidekick Crocker). All that changes when Tucker's daughter dies in a tragic accident in his friend's swimming pool. It's sensitively played by the cast, but the direction lacks flair. ▭

Michael Tucker *Peter Stillwell* • Kevin Dobson *Hank Bolen* • Belinda Montgomery [Belinda J Montgomery] *Terry Stillwell* • Karen Austin *Donna Bolen* • Olivia Burnette *Mickey Bolen* • Staci Keanan *Kathy Stillwell* ■ *Dir* Kevin James Dobson • *Scr* Allan Sloane, Phil Penningroth, from a story by Tom Ackerman, Norm Lenzer

For Love of Ivy ★★ 🅟🅖
Romantic comedy
1968 · US · Colour · 100mins

Having taken Hollywood by storm with *In the Heat of the Night* and *Guess Who's Coming to Dinner*, Sidney Poitier clearly wanted to take a break from hard-hitting civil rights dramas. Daniel Mann's film is a much lighter affair, though there is still an underlying message. Poitier co-stars with Abbey Lincoln as a couple who are brought together by a liberal white family desperate to keep their treasured home-help. Despite a couple of good scenes between Poitier and Beau Bridges, this worthy attempt at depicting everyday black life veers uncomfortably between the preachy and the patronising. ▭

Sidney Poitier *Jack Parks* • Abbey Lincoln *Ivy Moore* • Beau Bridges *Tim Austin* • Nan Martin *Doris Austin* • Lauri Peters *Gena Austin* • Carroll O'Connor *Frank Austin* • Leon Bibb *Billy Talbot* ■ *Dir* Daniel Mann • *Scr* Robert Alan Aurthur, from a story by Sidney Poitier

For Love of the Game ★★ 🄻🄴
Sports drama   1999 · US · Colour · 138mins

Kevin Costner is the legendary but ageing baseball pitcher desperate to prove there's life in the old dog yet in this glossy but overblown sports drama. A distracted Costner strives to focus long enough to pitch the perfect game, but is hampered by injuries and distracted by thoughts of partner Kelly Preston, who's made a sudden decision to dump him. Lacking the edge and humour of such earlier Costner sports outings as *Tin Cup* and *Bull Durham*, this is long-winded and over-sentimental, while British audiences may not be sufficiently familiar with the intricacies of baseball to appreciate its nuances. The attractive leads just about carry it off,

though director Sam Raimi's debut, *The Evil Dead*, now seems many World Series ago.

Kevin Costner *Billy Chapel* • Kelly Preston *Jane Aubrey* • John C Reilly *Gus Sinski* • Jena Malone *Heather* • Brian Cox *Gary Wheeler* • JK Simmons *Frank Perry* • Vin Scully • Steve Lyons ■ *Dir* Sam Raimi • *Scr* Dana Stevens, from a novel by Michael Shaara

For Love or Money ★★
Comedy   1963 · US · Colour · 107mins

Oh dear, one of those would-be Swinging Sixties comedies from Universal, all gloss and glitz, but with little charm or humour. Despite the presence of a glowing Mitzi Gaynor, clever Gig Young and watchable Thelma Ritter, this attempt at levity is sunk by a desperately unfunny performance from a totally miscast Kirk Douglas, as the attorney hired by Ritter to find husbands for her three daughters. There's also a nice end-of-career cameo from William Bendix, but the satire on contemporary American themes – modern art, bodybuilding, Madison Avenue – seems tired, and the execution of the plot isn't really wacky enough. Director Michael Gordon might have been hoping for another *Pillow Talk*, but Douglas's grimacing would sink a battleship.

Kirk Douglas *Deke Gentry* • Mitzi Gaynor *Kate Brasher* • Gig Young "Sonny" John Dayton Smith • Thelma Ritter *Chloe Brasher* • Julie Newmar *Bonnie Brasher* • William Bendix *Joe Fogel* ■ *Dir* Michael Gordon • *Scr* Michael Morris, Larry Markes

For Love or Money   ★★ 🅟🅖
Romantic comedy
1984 · US · Colour · 90mins

Not to be confused with either the 1963 Kirk Douglas/Mitzi Gaynor comedy or the 1993 Michael J Fox one released here as *The Concierge* this is a daft TV movie about a man and a woman who have to pretend to fall for each other after being chosen to appear on a TV game show. A likeable performance by Suzanne Pleshette, better known for playing the sensible wife in TV's long-running *Bob Newhart Show*, helps make this lightweight fare passable. ▭

Suzanne Pleshette *Joanna Piper* • Gil Gerard *Mike Coyne* • Jamie Farr *Larry Melody* • Ray Walston *Eddie Eppes* • Lawrence Pressman *Dr Herb Frobisher* • Barney Martin *George Piper* ■ *Dir* Terry W Hughes [Terry Hughes] • *Scr* James S Henerson

For Me and My Gal ★★★★ 🅄
Medical   1942 · US · BW · 103mins

A fabulous star vehicle for Judy Garland, who glows with talent and basks in the best songs and production values that MGM could bestow on her. The studio also gave her a new leading man, a dancer with a neon smile who had impressed Broadway critics as John O'Hara's heel in *Pal Joey*. His name? Gene Kelly, here making a stunning movie debut. Director Busby Berkeley, on top form and for once shorn of his kaleidoscopic box of tricks, uses his leads brilliantly: the sheer charm of the title number and *When You Wore a Tulip* should be what cinema is all about. Kelly's character is not the

most endearing ever, but the plot's engrossing, nonetheless.

Judy Garland *Jo Hayden* • George Murphy *Jimmy K Metcalf* • Gene Kelly *Harry Palmer* • Marta Eggerth *Eve Minard* • Ben Blue *Sid Simms* • Horace McNally [Stephen McNally] *Bert Waring* • Keenan Wynn *Eddie Milton* • Richard Quine *Danny Hayden* ■ *Dir* Busby Berkeley • *Scr* Richard Sherman, Fred F Finklehoffe, Sid Silvers, Jack McGowan, Irving Brecher, from the story *The Big Time* by Howard Emmett Rogers • *Cinematographer* William Daniels

For Pete's Sake   ★★ 🅟🅖
Comedy   1974 · US · Colour · 86mins

One of those specially constructed star vehicles (but this time the wheels fell off with Barbra Streisand on board) that arrived with much ballyhoo and crept away shamefacedly after a major critical mauling. Streisand can be very funny if given a tight script, but here she looks bewildered and lost as a debt-ridden wife forced to mix in unsavoury company. Director Peter Yates, who gave us such gems as *Bullitt* and *The Janitor*, seems to have left his film-making skills at home. The entire movie smacks of shoving a famous name into a hastily put together dollar earner. Except it wasn't. Contains swearing. ▭

Barbra Streisand *Henry* • Michael Sarrazin *Pete* • Estelle Parsons *Helen* • Molly Picon *Mrs Cherry* • William Redfield *Fred* • Louis Zorich *Nick* • Vivian Bonnell *Loretta* • Heywood Hall Broun *Judge Hiller* ■ *Dir* Peter Yates • *Scr* Stanley Shapiro, Maurice Richlin

For Queen and Country
★★★ 🄸🄵
Thriller   1988 · UK/US · Colour · 100mins

Scriptwriter Martin Stellman made his directorial debut with this odd drama set against the gloomy backdrop of the Thatcher years of mid-eighties Britain. In an unusual bit of casting (perhaps the producers needed a Hollywood name to get funding), Denzel Washington stars as the Caribbean-born Falklands war veteran who returns home to his grim South London council estate, only to be told he is no longer a British citizen. It's all rather depressing stuff, but Stellman's own script captures the mood of the time intelligently and it is backed up by a nice (if unevenly accented) performance by Washington, who once again holds your attention from the first frame to the last. ▭

Denzel Washington *Reuben* • Dorian Healy *Fish* • Amanda Redman *Stacey* • George Baker *Kilcoyne* • Bruce Payne *Colin* • Sean Chapman *Bob* • Geff Francis *Lynford* • Craig Fairbrass *Challoner* ■ *Dir* Martin Stellman • *Scr* Martin Stellman, Trix Worrell

For Richer or Poorer ★★ 🄻🄴
Comedy   1997 · US · Colour · 110mins

TV stars Kirstie Alley (*Cheers*, *Veronica's Closet*) and Tim Allen (*Home Improvement*) star in this sitcom-style comedy about a bickering married couple who hide out in an Amish community because the Inland Revenue Service is after them for unpaid taxes. *Witness* made valid comparisons between modern life and that of the rural Amish, but the accent here is on laughs. Allen and Alley don

the costumes, leave their materialistic life behind and, of course, rekindle the love they lost while he was making money and she was getting manicures. Unfortunately, the theme of leaving the rich world behind to find yourself has been done better in everything from the classic *Sullivan's Travels* to the Goldie Hawn comedy *Overboard*. They were much funnier, too. Contains some swearing. ▭

Tim Allen *Brad Sexton* • Kirstie Alley *Caroline Sexton* • Jay O Sanders *Samuel Yoder* • Michael Lerner *Phil Kleinman* • Wayne Knight *Bob Lachman* ■ *Dir* Bryan Spicer • *Scr* Jana Howington, Steve LuKanic

For the Boys   ★★ 🄸🄵
Drama   1991 · US · Colour · 138mins

Bette Midler scooped an Oscar nomination and gave one of the best performances of her career in this otherwise overblown showbiz drama that traces the love-hate relationship of a comedy duo who only ever seem to speak to each other when America is at war. You'd expect better material from *River's Edge* screenwriter Neal Jimenez and Woody Allen's longtime collaborator Marshall Brickman, but the action sags badly when Midler is off screen. Given little to do but sulk, smarm and shout, James Caan looks distinctly uncomfortable throughout, but never more so than during his routines with the Divine Miss M. Definitely not one for the boys. Contains swearing. ▭

Bette Midler *Dixie Leonard* • James Caan *Eddie Sparks* • George Segal *Art Silver* • Patrick O'Neal *Shephard* • Christopher Rydell *Danny* • Arye Gross *Jeff Brooks* • Norman Fell *Sam Schiff* • Rosemary Murphy *Luanna Trott* ■ *Dir* Mark Rydell • *Scr* Marshall Brickman, Neal Jimenez, Lindy Laub, from the story by Neal Jimenez, Lindy Laub

For the First Time   ★★ 🅄
Musical romance
1959 · US/It/W Ger · Colour · 97mins

Actually, for the last time, since this was chubby tenor Mario Lanza's final movie. He had decided not to fulfil a concert commitment for mobster Lucky Luciano, and tragically was discovered dead in a hospital bed soon afterwards. The incidents apparently were not connected. Still, Lanza's relatively slimline here, and this is the one where he falls for a deaf girl and belts out *Ave Maria* to her, to test whether she can actually hear. He also performs *Vesti La Giubba* among others, while the Technirama camera follows him to attractive effect throughout Europe's key musical cities.

Mario Lanza *Tonio "Tony" Costa* • Johanna Von Koczian *Christa Bruckner* • Zsa Zsa Gabor *Gloria de Vadnuz* • Kurt Kasznar *Ladislas Tabory* • Hans Sohnker *Professor Albert Bruckner* • Peter Capell *Leopold Huebner* • Renzo Cesana *Angelo* ■ *Dir* Rudolph Maté • *Scr* Andrew Solt

For the Future: the Irvine Fertility Scandal   ★★ 🄻🄴
Crime drama based on a true story
1996 · US · Colour · 86mins

In this troubling true-life story, doctors at the University of California's fertility unit were accused of stealing patients' eggs and implanting them in surrogate

mothers. Marilu Henner, as one of the victims involved, and Linda Lavin, as an employee of the unit who helped expose the scandal, bring the tale to life with their committed performances. With the whole surrogacy issue currently under review in this country, this is a timely reminder of how the system can be abused. Contains some strong language.

Marilu Henner *Debbie Challender* • Linda Lavin *Marilyn Killane* • Randle Mell *John Challender* • Castulo Guerra *Dr Ricardo Asch* ■ *Dir* David Jones • *Scr* Stephanie Liss

For the Love of Aaron ★★★

Drama based on a true story
1993 · US · Colour

Along with the likes of Lindsay Wagner, Meredith Baxter is one of the icons of TV's true-story land and this weepie will undoubtedly keep her fans satisfied. Baxter plays a mentally unstable woman, battling to regain her sanity and to keep custody of her young child (Keegan Macintosh). It's a serviceable enough concept and Baxter gives it her all, although director John Kent Harrison lets the drama slide into sentimentality.

Meredith Baxter *Margaret Gibson* • Keegan Macintosh *Aaron Gibson* • Joanna Gleason *Shirley* • Nick Mancuso *Stuart Singer* • John Kapelos *Dr Teplitsky* • Malcolm Stewart *Duncan Miller* ■ *Dir* John Kent Harrison • *Scr* Peter Silverman, Margaret Gibson, from a story by Glen MacPherson

For the Love of Ada ★★

Comedy 1972 · UK · Colour · 88mins

The seventysomething romance of Ada Cresswell and Walter Bingley never made for scintillating sitcom viewing, even though the 1970 TV series was popular in its day. This movie spin-off, set on the couple's first wedding anniversary, is leisurely in the extreme, as writers Vince Powell and Harry Driver struggle to find ways to fill the extra hour. Yet the by-play between widow Irene Handl and Wilfred Pickles (as the gravedigger who'd buried her husband) is engaging enough, and there's some practised comic support from daughter Barbara Mitchell and football crazy son-in-law Jack Smethurst. A nice memento for fans, but too gentle for modern tastes.

Irene Handl *Ada Bingley* • Wilfred Pickles *Walter Bingley* • Barbara Mitchell *Ruth Pollit* • Jack Smethurst *Leslie Pollit* • Arthur English *Arthur* • Andria Lawrence *Sandra* • Larry Martyn *Brian* ■ *Dir* Ronnie Baxter • *Scr* Harry Driver, Vince Powell

For the Love of Benji ★★ U

Adventure 1977 · US · Colour · 83mins

Three years after *Benji*, his surprise hit, director Joe Camp finally got round to making a second film about the cute little stray who's smarter than the average hound. Providing support for Higgins, the performing dog (a stand-in for the original, incidentally), Patsy Garrett and Cynthia Smith return for this perfectly acceptable adventure, set amid the splendours of Athens, in which our canine hero escapes from the clutches of a spy ring with a secret code written on his paw. The plot could have used a touch more imagination, but this sequel is much better than the later additions to the cycle.

Patsy Garrett *Mary* • Cynthia Smith *Cindy* • Allen Fiuzat *Paul* • Ed Nelson *Chandler Dietrich* • Art Vasil *Stelios* • Peter Bowles *Ronald* • Bridget Armstrong *Elizabeth* ■ *Dir* Joe Camp • *Scr* Joe Camp, from a story by Ben Vaughn, Joe Camp

For the Love of Mary ★★

Musical comedy 1948 · US · BW · 90mins

Deanna Durbin stars as a telephonist at the White House, striking up a relationship with the president (never seen) after she suffers an attack of hiccups. He helps her to sort out her romantic problems, involving Don Taylor, Edmond O'Brien and Jeffrey Lynn. Directed by Frederick De Cordova, this is characteristic Durbin flimflam, allowing the star to break into song from time to time and providing fairly painless entertainment. However, Durbin getting into a nonsensical, fairytale situation at 27 doesn't hold the same delightful appeal as Durbin at the centre of events in her teens, and this unremembered movie proved to be one of her two last.

Deanna Durbin *Mary Peppertree* • Edmond O'Brien *Lt Tom Farrington* • Don Taylor *David Paxton* • Jeffrey Lynn *Phillip Manning* • Ray Collins *Harvey Elwood* • Hugo Hass *Gustav Heindel* • Harry Davenport *Justice Peabody* ■ *Dir* Frederick De Cordova • *Scr* Oscar Brodney

For the Love of Mike ★★ U

Western 1960 · US · Colour · 88mins

Have several hankies handy when this little film unspools. Danny Bravo is a young native American boy who enters his horse in a race so he can win the prize money to build a new church. It's enough to bring tears to the eyes of local priest Richard Basehart, local doctor Stuart Erwin and, indeed, to Bravo's horse, but no one has told the local mountain lion (who does everything but wear a black hat) that little Danny is off limits as prey. But let us not be cynical: this is a story that celebrates the human spirit, directed with Bressonian intensity by George Sherman who used to churn out early John Wayne westerns.

Richard Basehart *Father Phelan* • Stuart Erwin *Dr Mills* • Arthur Shields *Father Walsh* • Armando Silvestre *Tony Eagle* • Elsa Cardenas *Mrs Eagle* • Michael Steckler *Ty Corbin* • Rex Allen *Rex Allen* • Danny Bravo *Michael* ■ *Dir* George Sherman • *Scr* DD Beauchamp

For Their Own Good ★★★ PG

Drama based on a true story
1993 · US · Colour · 91mins

The thorny issue of a woman's right to have a family versus the employer's interests, is given a new twist in this TV movie. Produced by Jon Avnet (director of *Fried Green Tomatoes at the Whistle Stop Cafe*) this stars Elizabeth Perkins as a young woman who challenges her employer's ultimatum that she agree to a sterilisation or lose her job. A strong cast includes Charles Haid (*Hill Street Blues*) and Laura San Giacomo, still best known for *sex, lies, and videotape*. Thought-provoking stuff.

Elizabeth Perkins *Sally Thompson* • Charles Haid *Frank Souter* • Gary Basaraba *Roy Wheeler* • Laura San Giacomo *Jo Mandell* • CCH Pounder *Naomi Brinker* • Kelli Williams *Erma* • David Purdham *Jim Davis* ■ *Dir* Ed Kaplan • *Scr* Ed Kaplan, from a story by Clifford Campion, William Wages

For Those in Peril ★★★ U

Second World War drama
1943 · UK · BW · 66mins

Documentarist Harry Watt and future Ealing comedy scribe TEB Clarke united for this flagwaver. Charles Crichton made his directorial debut with this bullish tale about the rivalry between David Farrar's air-sea rescue unit and a bigger patrol boat. The action sags a little as ace pilot Ralph Michael has to learn the importance of teamwork. However, the scenes in which he races against time to fish survivors out of the drink before a Nazi craft reaches them have an exciting, pseudo-newsreel feel to them, thanks to Douglas Slocombe's fine photography.

David Farrar *Murray* • Ralph Michael *Rawlings* • Robert Wyndham *Leverett* • John Slater *Wilkie* • John Batten *Wireless operator* • Robert Griffith *Griffiths* • Peter Arne *Junior officer* • James Robertson-Justice *Operations room officer* ■ *Dir* Charles Crichton • *Scr* Harry Watt, JOC Orton, TEB Clarke, from a story by Richard Hillary

For Valour ★★

Comedy 1937 · UK · BW · 94mins

Adapted for the screen from his own hit play, this Ben Travers comedy keeps promising to burst into life, but is eventually snuffed out by the endless round of deceptions and misunderstandings that were the trademark of his celebrated Aldwych productions. Expert farceurs Tom Walls and Ralph Lynn are as happy as sandboys in their dual roles but, while Walls plays father and son with the customary glint in his eye, Lynn fails to bring the same vim to the part of a Boer War veteran as he does to his shady, silly-ass grandson.

Tom Walls *Doubleday/Charlie Chisholm* • Ralph Lynn *Major Pyke/Willie Pyke* • Veronica Rose *Phyllis Chisholm* • Joan Marion *Clare Chester* • Hubert Harben *Mr Gallop* • Henry Longhurst *Inspector Harding* ■ *Dir* Tom Walls • *Scr* Ben Travers, from his play

For Whom the Bell Tolls ★★★ U

War drama 1943 · US · Colour · 124mins

Gary Cooper and Ingrid Bergman turn Ernest Hemingway's classic of the Spanish Civil War into a star vehicle made for two, while director Sam Wood scrubs this tale – about an American who joins a loyalist partisan group – clean of political taint (there's no mention of Franco, for example). The focus on Cooper's love for the much-abused Bergman works well enough because of the quality of the two actors. However, it was Katina Paxinou's performance as an ancient peasant woman that won the Oscar, perhaps for the sense of reality she brought to the overall sanitisation.

Ingrid Bergman *Maria* • Gary Cooper *Robert Jordan* • Akim Tamiroff *Pablo* • Katina Paxinou *Pilar* • Vladimir Sokoloff *Anselmo* • Arturo De Cordova *Agustin* • Mikhail Rasumny *Rafael* ■ *Dir* Sam Wood • *Scr* Dudley Nichols, from the novel by Ernest Hemingway

For Your Eyes Only ★★★ PG

Spy adventure 1981 · UK · Colour · 122mins

Number 12 in the 007 series provides no real surprises, with the exception perhaps of Roger Moore, who gets the chance to show a little bit more grit than usual. The plot revolves around the hunt for a device from a sunken nuclear submarine, with French star Carole Bouquet providing a little class as the girl who may hold the key to the puzzle. If Julian Glover is rather subdued as the number one villain, there is a colourful turn from *Fiddler on the Roof* star Topol as a rogue with shifting loyalties, and the eagle-eyed will spot Charles Dance as a killer. Bond veteran John Glen ensures that the set pieces are spectacular enough and thankfully plays down the silly gadgetry.

Roger Moore *James Bond* • Carole Bouquet *Melina* • Topol *Columbo* • Lynn-Holly Johnson *Bibi* • Julian Glover *Kristatos* • Cassandra Harris *Lisl* • Jill Bennett *Brink* • Michael Gothard *Locque* • Lois Maxwell *Moneypenny* • Desmond Llewelyn *"Q"* • Charles Dance *Claus* • Janet Brown *Prime Minister* ■ *Dir* John Glen • *Scr* Richard Maibaum, Michael G Wilson, from the short stories *For Your Eyes Only* and *Risico* by Ian Fleming

Forbidden ★★

Melodrama 1932 · US · BW · 87mins

Despite the torrid-sounding title this is not a TV movie but an undistinguished entry in the Frank Capra canon. Barbara Stanwyck is spinster Lulu Smith, who goes on a cruise and falls for married district attorney Adolphe Menjou. Regardless of the script, Capra could usually be relied upon to bring a unique lightness and brisk wit to any storyline. In this case he fails, the only redeeming features being the performance of Stanwyck and fine photography from Joseph Walker who worked on Capra classics such as *It Happened One Night* and *Mr Smith Goes to Washington*.

Barbara Stanwyck *Lulu Smith* • Adolphe Menjou *Bob Grover* • Ralph Bellamy *Al Holland* • Dorothy Peterson *Helen* • Thomas Jefferson *Winkinson* ■ *Dir* Frank Capra • *Scr* Jo Swerling, from a story by Frank Capra

Forbidden ★★

Crime drama 1953 · US · BW · 84mins

Tough-guy Tony Curtis is dispatched to Macao by a gang of criminals to bring back, by force if necessary, Joanne Dru, the widow of a racketeer who possesses incriminating evidence against them. Much cross and double-cross later, involving among other things Macao's chief criminal (Lyle Bettger), the plot complications are resolved and love triumphs. Directed by the once-great European cameraman-turned-director Rudolph Maté, this sub-*noir* gangster film-cum-romance is, as you would expect, good-looking and technically proficient, but otherwise downbeat and dreary.

Tony Curtis *Eddie Darrow* • Joanne Dru *Christine Lawrence* • Lyle Bettger *Justin Keit* • Marvin Miller *Cliff Chalmer* • Victor Sen Yung *Allan* • Alan Dexter *Barney* ■ *Dir* Rudolph Maté • *Scr* William Sackheim, Gil Doud, from a story by William Sackheim

Forbidden ★★ PG

Drama based on a true story
1985 · UK/US/W Ger · Colour · 109mins

Jürgen Prochnow plays a Jew who has a passionate affair with a German aristocrat during the Second World War. Playing the German countess who loves and hides Prochnow from the Gestapo is Jacqueline Bisset, a radiantly beautiful actress whose career has always lacked momentum. Prochnow is best known for his powerful performance as the U-Boat captain in *Das Boot*, and director Anthony Page was once one of London's foremost stage directors, but their efforts here produce a distinctly average effort. ▭

Jacqueline Bisset *Nina Von Halder* • Jürgen Prochnow *Fritz Friedlander* • Irene Worth *Ruth Friedlander* • Peter Vaughan *Major Stauffel* ■ *Dir* Anthony Page • *Scr* Leonard Gross, from his book *The Last Jews in Berlin*

Forbidden Cargo ★★ PG

Crime drama 1954 · UK · BW · 82mins

Joyce Grenfell plays a bird-watcher named Lady Flavin Queensway in this cosy but not exactly exciting thriller about drug smuggling. Customs agent Nigel Patrick tries to stop our dope smugglers from polluting our shores, supported by a cast of British stalwarts that includes Elizabeth Sellars, Jack Warner and Terence Morgan. Director Harold French is probably best known for his work with David Lean on *Major Barbara*, while editor Anne V Coates won an Oscar for another Lean movie *Lawrence of Arabia*. ▭

Nigel Patrick *Michael Kenyon* • Elizabeth Sellars *Rita Compton* • Terence Morgan *Roger Compton* • Jack Warner *Alec White* • Greta Gynt *Madame Simonetta* • Theodore Bikel *Max* • Joyce Grenfell *Lady Flavin Queensway* ■ *Dir* Harold French • *Scr* Sydney Box

Forbidden Island ★★

Adventure 1959 · US · Colour · 65mins

An adventure star of the thirties and forties, Jon Hall is a little bit long in the tooth for this slice of hokum about skin-divers and a sunken treasure ship. The divers fall out in their search for a priceless emerald but the problem, as ever, with these underwater malarkies is that it's hard to fathom who's who behind the masks. Critics at the time were hard pressed to decide whether the colour process was deliberately stylised or just messed up in the lab.

Jon Hall *Dave Courtney* • Nan Adams *Joanne* • John Farrow *Stuart Godfrey* • Jonathan Haze *Jack Mautner* • Greigh Phillips *Dean Pike* ■ *Dir/Scr* Charles B Griffith

Forbidden Nights ★★ PG

Romantic drama based on a true story
1990 · US · Colour · 88mins

A run-of-the-mill romantic drama in which Melissa Gilbert (of *Little House on the Prairie* fame) stars as an American teacher who falls for a radical student in late seventies' China. It's an interesting but under-used setting for a production that bears the trademark slickness of Waris Hussein, a director whose credits include the lavish *Henry VIII and His Six Wives*. ▭

Melissa Gilbert *Judith Shapiro* • Robin Shou *Liang Heng* • Victor K Wong [Victor K Wong] *Comrade Ho* • Ma Tzi *Li Dao* • Beulah Quo *Vice Dean Yin* • Khigh Dhiegh *Lu Ming* • Augustine Lam *Ma Soong* ■ *Dir* Waris Hussein • *Scr* Tristine Rainer, from a story by David Henry Hwang, from the article *The Rocky Course of Love in China* by Judith Shapiro

Forbidden Planet ★★★★★ U

Classic science-fiction adventure
1956 · US · Colour · 94mins

What unknown terror roams the planet Altair-4 killing everyone apart from tormented scientist Morbius (Walter Pidgeon) and his daughter Altaira (Anne Francis)? Starship commander Leslie Nielsen (long before he turned *Airplane!* comedian) finds out in one of the finest science-fiction films ever made. Loosely based on Shakespeare's *The Tempest*, which explains its overall intelligence, this is an enthralling eye-popper featuring super monster effects created by Disney animators and outstanding technology that includes the unforgettable Robby the Robot, the subterranean Krell city, Morbius's futuristic home and an impressive array of space vehicles. The *2001* of the fifties. ▭

Walter Pidgeon *Dr Morbius* • Anne Francis *Altaira* • Leslie Nielsen *Commander Adams* • Warren Stevens *Lieutenant "Doc" Ostrow* • Jack Kelly *Lieutenant Farman* • Richard Anderson *Chief Quinn* • Earl Holliman *Cook* • Marvin Miller *Robby the Robot* ■ *Dir* Fred McLeod Wilcox [Fred M Wilcox] • *Scr* Cyril Hume, from a story by Irving Block, Allen Adler

Forbidden Territory ★★

Adventure based on a true story
1997 · US · Colour · 96mins

There are some acts that are just impossible to follow and so definitive were the performances of Spencer Tracy and Cedric Hardwicke in 1939's *Stanley and Livingstone* that it took nearly 60 years for anyone else to attempt reprising the roles. Unfortunately, Aidan Quinn is miscast as the intrepid reporter who transformed his fortunes with his expedition to find the missing Scottish missionary, who is played with suitable piety by Nigel Hawthorne. Director Simon Langton adequately exploits the African scenery and draws a showy cameo out of Edward Fox, but this TV movie lacks the drive of Henry King's original. Contains swearing.

Aidan Quinn *Henry Morton Stanley* • Nigel Hawthorne *David Livingstone* • Edward Fox *Markham* • Fay Masterson *Alice* ■ *Dir* Simon Langton • *Scr* John Pielmeier

Forbidden Valley ★★ U

Western 1938 · US · BW · 67mins

One of those perfectly competent but utterly routine westerns made by Universal, starring the amiable Noah Beery Jr. Here he plays a boy living in a remote mountain hideaway because his father, Samuel S Hinds, has been wrongly accused of murder. Beery's isolated existence begins to change when he encounters wealth in the pert shape of Frances Robinson. Look out for Glenn Strange as the ominously named Corlox – six years later he would take the role of the monster in Universal's *House of Frankenstein*. This was re-made in colour as *Sierra* in 1950 with Audie Murphy.

Noah Beery Jr *Ring* • Frances Robinson *Wilda* • Fred Kohler Sr [Fred Kohler] *Regan* • Alonzo Price *Indian Joe* • Samuel S Hinds *Hazzard* • Stanley Andrews *Lanning* • Spencer Charters *Dr Scudd* ■ *Dir* Wyndham Gittens • *Scr* Wyndham Gittens, from the novel *Mountains Are My Kingdom* by Stuart Hardy

Force Majeure ★★★

Drama 1989 · Fr · Colour · 86mins

Pierre Jolivet began his career co-scripting Luc Besson's *The Last Battle* and *Subway* before turning to directing. This is a dark deliberation on the contention that the modern age is not a time of heroes. Patrick Bruel and François Cluzet are the holidaying friends who face a moral dilemma when a fellow backpacker is sentenced to death for drug-trafficking. In a film in which dialogue is at a premium, much depends on the physical performances of the cast, and Bruel and Cluzet manage to convey a range of contradictory emotions without ever resorting to histrionics. Difficult and often self-conscious, but give it a go. In French with English subtitles.

Patrick Bruel *Philippe* • François Cluzet *Daniel* • Kristin Scott Thomas *Katia* • Alan Bates *Malcolm* • Sabine Haudepin *Jeanne* • Thom Hoffman *Hans* • Lucienne Hamon *Philippe's mother* • Marc Jolivet *Journalist* ■ *Dir* Pierre Jolivet • *Scr* Pierre Jolivet, Oliver Schatzky

Force of Arms ★★

Second World War drama
1951 · US · BW · 98mins

William Holden and Nancy Olson – the almost-lovers from *Sunset Boulevard* – are reunited in this war movie, directed by the man who made *Casablanca*. In fact, it's a remake of Hemingway's *A Farewell to Arms*, first filmed in 1932 and updated to the Second World War. Holden's GI falls for Olson's nurse during the Italian campaign; he is then reported missing after a terrible battle. It's nothing special, despite Holden's romantic appeal. A further remake followed in 1957, reverting to Hemingway's original title.

William Holden (1) *Peterson* • Nancy Olson *Eleanor* • Frank Lovejoy *Maj Blackford* • Gene Evans *McFee* • Dick Wesson *Klein* • Paul Picerni *Sheridan* • Katherine Warren *Maj Waldron, WAC* • Ross Ford *Hooker* ■ *Dir* Michael Curtiz • *Scr* Orin Jannings, from the story *Italian Story* by Richard Tregaskis

Force of Evil ★★★★ PG

Film noir 1948 · US · BW · 74mins

A truly remarkable one-off, a quintessential *film noir* filmed on authentic New York locations by the great cinematographer George Barnes with dialogue in blank verse, co-written and directed by Abraham Polonsky. The plot revolves around corruption in the numbers racket, and holding it all together is a remarkably intense performance by John Garfield, doing some of his career best screen work here. But, be warned, this bleak and sordid philosophical allegory may not be to everyone's taste. Polonsky was blacklisted following the McCarthy witch-hunt and did not direct again until 1969. ▭

John Garfield *Joe Morse* • Beatrice Pearson *Doris Lowry* • Thomas Gomez *Leo Morse* • Howland Chamberlin *Freddy Bauer* • Roy Roberts *Ben Tucker* • Marie Windsor *Edna Tucker* • Paul McVey *Hobe Wheelock* • Tim Ryan *Johnson* ■ *Dir* Abraham Polonsky • *Scr* Abraham Polonsky, Ira Wolfert, from the novel *Tucker's People* by Ira Wolfert

A Force of One ★★ 15

Martial arts 1979 · US · Colour · 85mins

Between the death of Bruce Lee and the emergence of Jackie Chan, martial arts fans had to make do with the plank of wood that was Chuck Norris, the six-times world karate champion. Displaying all his customary charm, the hairy one is characteristically cast as a Vietnam vet fighting cop-killing drug dealers in a small Californian town. Paul Aaron's follow-up to *Good Guys Wear Black* is unpretentious action fare for the not-too-bothered brigade. Despite its screenplay by *Shaft* author Ernest Tidyman, this has about as much life as an opponent who's just been felled by Norris. ▭

Jennifer O'Neill *Detective Mandy Rust* • Chuck Norris *Matt Logan* • Clu Gulager *Dunne* • Ron O'Neal *Rollins* • Bill Wallace *Jerry Sparks* • Eric Laneuville *Charlie Logan* • James Whitmore Jr *Moskowitz* • Clint Ritchie *Melrose* ■ *Dir* Paul Aaron • *Scr* Ernest Tidyman, from a story by Pat Johnson

Force 10 from Navarone ★★ 15

Second World War drama
1978 · UK · Colour · 113mins

A totally unnecessary and remarkably belated follow-up to producer Carl Foreman's massive 1961 smash hit, *The Guns of Navarone*. The cast here is no match for Gregory Peck, David Niven and Anthony Quinn in the original; this time round, a tired Robert Shaw (in his penultimate picture), a pre-superstardom Harrison Ford and a mannered Edward Fox are faced not only with the enemy, but also with a cliché-ridden script. Director Guy Hamilton's uninspired movie begins with the climax of the earlier film, then spends an inordinate amount of time before reaching its own explosive finale. Fans of the James Bond series may recognise Barbara Bach and Richard Kiel in supporting roles. Contains swearing ▭

Robert Shaw *Mallory* • Harrison Ford *Barnsby* • Edward Fox *Miller* • Barbara Bach *Maritza* • Franco Nero *Lescovar* • Carl Weathers *Weaver* • Richard Kiel *Drazac* • Angus MacInnes *Reynolds* ■ *Dir* Guy Hamilton • *Scr* Robin Chapman, from a story by Carl Foreman, from the novel by Alistair MacLean

Forced March ★★★ 15

Drama 1989 · US/Hun · Colour · 99mins

Not the thick-ear action flick the title suggests, but an ambitious film within a film about a fading US actor who travels to Hungary to star in a biography of a Hungarian-Jewish poet who died during the Holocaust. Rick King's film mixes scenes of the actor making the film with scenes from the film he's making; it also explores the cast members' varying commitment to the project. Style sometimes gets in the way of content, but this remains a powerful drama, with Chris Sarandon impressive at the head of a predominantly European cast. 📺

Chris Sarandon *Kline/Miklos Radnoti* • Renée Soutendijk *Myra* • Josef Sommer *Father* • John Seitz *Hardy* ■ *Dir* Rick King • *Scr* Dick Atkins, Charles K Bardosh

Forced Vengeance ★★ 18

Martial arts thriller
1982 · US · Colour · 85mins

Chuck Norris may yet learn that slick karate chops and macho grunting are no substitute for acting. Looking for the most part here as if he's reading his lines off another actor's forehead, Norris only begins to add any character to the film when he stops talking and gets on with the action. At that point, the tightly choreographed martial arts sequences, the movie's sole blessing, come into their own. Contains swearing and nudity. 📺

Chuck Norris *Josh Randall* • Mary Louise Weller *Claire Bonner* • Camila Griggs *Joy Paschal* • Michael Cavanaugh *Stan Raimondi* • David Opatoshu *Sam Paschal* ■ *Dir* James Fargo • *Scr* Franklin Thompson

Forces of Nature ★★ 15

Comedy   1998 · US · Colour · 106mins

Unfortunately, the forces at work in this romantic comedy starring Sandra Bullock and Ben Affleck fail to muster much chemistry between the two attractive leads. He is fine as the strait-laced groom-to-be who has a *Planes, Trains and Automobiles*-style trip to his wedding. But Bullock is a little miscast as the quirky gal he hooks up with, who may tempt him away from his waiting bride (*ER's* Maura Tierney). All the cast members (including the fabulous Steve Zahn as Affleck's gormless pal) work hard, but director Bronwen Hughes never brings enough farcical humour, or any sense of impending catastrophe, to the adventure. Amusing, but not as good as it could have been.

Sandra Bullock *Sarah* • Ben Affleck *Ben* • Maura Tierney *Bridget* • Steve Zahn *Alan* • Blythe Danner *Virginia* • Ronny Cox *Hadley* • Michael Fairman *Richard* • *Dir* Bronwen Hughes • *Scr* Marc Lawrence

Forces' Sweetheart ★ U

Comedy   1953 · UK · BW · 73mins

Having starred with Peter Sellers and Spike Milligan in *Down among the Dead Men* the previous year, Harry Secombe and Michael Bentine re-team for this dismally unfunny uniform debacle. Hy Hazell is the object of everyone's attention, while veteran comic Freddie Frinton has the few good lines there are. Directed with his customary lack of brio by journeyman Maclean Rogers.

Hy Hazell *Judy James* • Harry Secombe *Private Llewellyn* • Michael Bentine *Flight Lt Robinson* • Freddie Frinton *Aloysius Dimwitty* • John Ainsworth *Lt Robinson* • Kenneth Henry *Tommy Tupp* ■ *Dir/Scr* MacLean Rogers

A Foreign Affair ★★★★

Romantic comedy drama
1948 · US · BW · 116mins

Iowa congresswoman Jean Arthur is sent to postwar Berlin to check on things, and runs into a thriving black market, corrupt GIs and a seductive

Marlene Dietrich who's having affairs with an American army captain and a former Nazi. Not for nothing is Arthur's character called Frost and the question is, will she melt? Brimming with great lines, the film's weakness is John Lund as the US soldier. but its strength is Arthur's brave performance and director Billy Wilder's take on the ruins of the city he once lived in. Only he could have toured the bomb sites and stuck *Isn't It Romantic?* on the soundtrack. Comedies come no blacker or harsher than this.

Jean Arthur *Phoebe Frost* • Marlene Dietrich *Erika von Schluetow* • John Lund *Capt John Pringle* • Millard Mitchell *Col Rufus J Plummer* • Bill Murphy *Joe* • Stanley Prager *Mike* • Peter Von Zerneck *Hans Otto Birgel* ■ *Dir* Billy Wilder • *Scr* Charles Brackett, Billy Wilder, Richard Breen, Robert Harari, from a story by David Shaw • *Costume Designer* Edith Head

Foreign Affaires ★★ U

Comedy   1935 · UK · BW · 69mins

Written by Ben Travers in the style of his Aldwych farces, this hit-and-miss affaire was produced by Michael Balcon, who would later sponsor the legendary Ealing comedies. The accomplished team of Tom Walls and Ralph Lynn trot out their familiar mannerisms as the artful gambler and silly-ass car dealer who find themselves being duped in a crooked Nice casino. However, as was so often the case, it's the estimable Robertson Hare who steals the show, with his shockable pomposity and his immaculate comic timing. Walls also directs, but his theatrical expertise renders the action stiff and stagey. 📺

Tom Walls *Capt Archibald Gore* • Ralph Lynn *Jefferson Darby* • Robertson Hare *Mr Hardy Hornett* • Norma Varden *Mrs Hardy Hornett* • Marie Lohr *Mrs Cope* • Diana Churchill *Sophie* ■ *Dir* Tom Walls • *Scr* Ben Travers

Foreign Affairs ★★★ 18

Romantic drama   1993 · US · Colour

Despite the Mills & Boon title and the presence of Stephanie Beacham in the cast, this adaptation of Alison Lurie's novel is actually high quality made-for-cable fare. Joanne Woodward is Vinnie, a middle-aged New England academic embarking on a research trip to the UK. On the plane she meets Chuck Mumpson (Brian Dennehy) a compatriot who doesn't appear to be her ideal companion – even on a transatlantic flight. But love blossoms in the most unlikely places. 📺

Joanne Woodward *Vinnie Miner* • Brian Dennehy *Chuck Mumpson* • Eric Stoltz *Fred Turner* • Ian Richardson *Edwin* • Stephanie Beacham *Rosemary Radley* • Robert Hands *David Hewson* ■ *Dir* Jim O'Brien • *Scr* Chris Bryant, from the novel by Alison Lurie

Foreign Body ★ 15

Comedy   1986 · UK · Colour · 106mins

A comedy which manages to be both unfunny and offensive. Victor Banerjee stars as Indian immigrant Ram Das, who gets a job as a bus conductor in England until he is convinced by his cousin (Warren Mitchell, complete with blacked-up face) to pose as a private doctor. Despite an impressive best-of-British cast this is fumbled at every turn. Blame can be attached to

scriptwriter Celine La Freniere, and to an out-of-his-depth Banerjee, but one wonders why director Ronald Neame (best known for *The Poseidon Adventure* and *The Prime of Miss Jean Brodie*) ever signed on for this one. 📺

Victor Banerjee *Ram Das* • Warren Mitchell *IQ Patel* • Amanda Donohoe *Susan Partridge* • Eve Ferret *Norah Plumb* • Geraldine McEwan *Lady Ammanford* • Trevor Howard *Dr Stirrup* • Denis Quilley *Prime Minister* • Anna Massey *Miss Furze* ■ *Dir* Ronald Neame • *Scr* Celine La Freniere, from a novel by Roderick Mann

Foreign Correspondent ★★★★ PG

Spy thriller   1940 · US · BW · 115mins

An immensely pleasurable spy story, set on the eve of the Second World War and ending with American reporter Joel McCrea warning of the danger to come. Director Alfred Hitchcock makes the most of some great set pieces, many of which are now acknowledged as key moments in the Hitchcock canon: an Amsterdam assassination (on a huge interior set) as umbrellas close ranks in the rain; tense moments inside a vast Dutch windmill; a plane crash where the air supply on board is slowly draining away; a remarkable sequence in Westminster Cathedral. The plot's twists and turns are cleverly and wittily maintained, and the supporting cast is impeccably chosen, notably Edmund Gwenn as a most untrustworthy bodyguard and Albert Basserman whose kidnap kick-starts the plot. It's the propagandist aspects which have dated the film, and it is also impaired by the lightweight casting of McCrea (Hitch wanted Gary Cooper) and Laraine Day in the leading roles. No matter, this is still marvellous Hitchcock, with the Master clearly at his most playful. 📺

Joel McCrea *Johnny Jones/Huntley Haverstock* • Laraine Day *Carol Fisher* • Herbert Marshall *Stephen Fisher* • George Sanders *Scott Ffolliott* • Albert Basserman *Van Meer* • Robert Benchley *Stebbins* • Edmund Gwenn *Rowley* • Eduardo Ciannelli *Krug* ■ *Dir* Alfred Hitchcock • *Scr* Charles Bennett, Joan Harrison, James Hilton, Robert Benchley • *Cinematographer* Rudolph Maté

Foreign Intrigue ★★

Spy drama   1956 · US · Colour · 99mins

Shot on location in Europe, this stars a trenchcoat-clad Robert Mitchum at his most laconic in a movie whose murky plot and even murkier colour photography leave much to be desired. This was allegedly based on the Cold War experiences of its writer/producer/director Sheldon Reynolds, whose adventures formed the basis for a TV series from which this plodding film is a spin-off. On its original release, this main feature was overshadowed by its supporting B-movie *The Killing* directed by the then-unknown movie genius Stanley Kubrick.

Robert Mitchum *Dave Bishop* • Genevieve Page *Dominique* • Ingrid Tulean [Ingrid Thulin] *Brita* • Frederick O'Brady *Spring* • Eugene Deckers *Sandoz* • Inga Tidblad *Mrs Lindquist* ■ *Dir* Sheldon Reynolds • *Scr* Sheldon Reynolds, Harry Jack Bloom, Gene Levitt

Foreign Student ★★ 15

Drama   1994 · US/Fr · Colour · 91mins

A variation on the formula of Hollywood reworking foreign movies, this American co-produced melodrama was adapted from the bestselling memoirs of French film-maker Philippe Labro. Debuting director Eva Sereny capably captures the atmosphere of mid-fifties Virginia, but Robin Givens is too modern to convince as the black teacher being romanced by visiting student Marco Hofschneider. The book's fond nostalgia has been turned into mildly sensationalist sentiment, and any sense of passion or social insight has been lost by Menno Meyjes's trite script. Contains swearing and nudity. 📺

Robin Givens *April* • Marco Hofschneider *Philippe Le Clerc* • Rick Johnson *Cal Cate* • Charlotte Ross *Sue Ann* • Edward Herrmann *Zach Gilmore* ■ *Dir* Eva Sereny • *Scr* Menno Meyjes, from the novel by Philippe Labro

The Foreman Went to France ★★★ U

Second World War comedy drama
1941 · UK · BW · 81mins

Having learned his craft under Alfred Hitchcock, Charles Frend edited some of the most impressive British pictures of the thirties, including *Goodbye, Mr Chips*. He later graduated to direction during the Second World War and shot three of the most interesting docudramas of the conflict. Made between *The Big Blockade* and *San Demetrio, London*, this engaging flag-waver was based on the true-life exploits of Melbourne Johns, who crossed the Channel to smuggle vital machine tools back to Blighty. Clifford Evans and Constance Cummings tackle the mission with suitable gravitas, while troopers Gordon Jackson and Tommy Trinder provide some welcome light relief.

Tommy Trinder *Tommy* • Constance Cummings *Anne* • Clifford Evans *Fred Carrick* • Robert Morley *French mayor* • Gordon Jackson *Jock* • Ernest Milton *Stationmaster* ■ *Dir* Charles Frend • *Scr* John Dighton, Angus MacPhail, Leslie Arliss, from a story by JB Priestley • *Music* William Walton

Forever ★

Fantasy mystery   1993 · US · Colour · 93mins

Movie fact meets movie fiction in this low-grade supernatural thriller which seeks to exploit the real-life unsolved murder of Irish-born director William Desmond Taylor in twenties Hollywood. When a rock video director moves into the former home of a murdered film-maker he cranks up an old moviola and the celluloid personalities inside come to life, including Mary Pickford and "Fatty" Arbuckle. It sounds great, but a messy script and cack-handed direction consign it to the bin, and stars Sean Young and Sally Kirkland look embarrassed to be in this mishmash of spooky chills, rock video, Hollywood history and soft-core porn.

Sally Kirkland *Angelica* • Sean Young *Mary Miles Minter* • Keith Coogan *Ted Dickson* • Diane Ladd *Mabel Normand* • Terence Knox *Wallace Reid* • Nicholas Guest *Billy Baldwin* • Ashley Hester *Mary Pickford* ■ *Dir* Thomas Palmer Jr • *Scr* Jackelyn Giroux, Thomas Palmer Jr

Forever Amber ★★★ U
Historical melodrama
1947 · US · Colour · 132mins

Otto Preminger's lavish costume drama was based on Kathleen Winsor's notorious novel about a sultry wench romping from bed to bed on her way up the social ladder in the time of Charles II. Amber is portrayed with competent efficiency by Linda Darnell, who was one of Hollywood's biggest stars of the forties, but, after Fox ended her studio contract, a virtual unknown by the late fifties. The film may be short on finesse but it is long on period colour and Hollywood production values, which certainly make it worth sitting down to.

Linda Darnell *Amber St Clair* • Cornel Wilde *Bruce Carlton* • Richard Greene *Lord Almsbury* • George Sanders *King Charles II* • Richard Haydn *Earl of Radcliffe* • Jessica Tandy *Nan Britton* • Anne Revere *Mother Red Cap* ■ *Dir* Otto Preminger • *Scr* Philip Dunne, Ring Lardner Jr, Jerome Cady, from the novel by Kathleen Winsor

Forever and a Day ★★★★
Historical drama 1943 · US · BW · 104mins

No less than 21 writers – ranging from Christopher Isherwood to RC Sheriff – are credited with writing this all-star curio, plus seven directors and a mere four cameramen. It charts the history of a London mansion from 1804 to the Blitz, when it was converted into a residential hotel; as many stars as possible enter its impressive portals. An uneven film, obviously, and a bit rushed, but some episodes are outstanding and the whole enterprise is to be commended: everyone worked for free and profits were given to various Anglo-American war charities.

Anna Neagle *Miriam (Susan)* • Ray Milland *Bill Trimble* • Claude Rains *Pomfret* • C Aubrey Smith *Adm Trimble* • Dame May Whitty *Mrs Trimble* • Gene Lockhart *Cobblewick* • Ray Bolger *Sentry* • Edmund Gwenn *Stubbs* • Lumsden Hare *Fitts* • Stuart Robertson *Lawyer* • Charles Coburn *Sir William* • Jessie Matthews *Mildred* • Charles Laughton *Bellamy* • Montagu Love *Sir John Bunn* • Reginald Owen *Mr Simpson* • Cedric Hardwicke *Dabb* • Buster Keaton *Dabb's assistant* • Ida Lupino *Jenny* • Merle Oberon *Marjorie* ■ *Dir* René Clair, Edmund Goulding, Cedric Hardwicke, Frank Lloyd, Victor Saville, Robert Stevenson, Herbert Wilcox • *Scr* Charles Bennett, CS Forester, Lawrence Hazard, Michael Hogan, WP Lipscomb, Alice Duer Miller, John Van Druten, Alan Campbell, Peter Godfrey, SM Herzig, Christopher Isherwood, Gene Lockhart, RC Sherriff, Claudine West, Norman Corwin, Jack Hartfield, James Hilton, Emmett Lavery, Frederick Lonsdale, Donald Ogden Stewart, Keith Winters

Forever, Darling ★★ U
Comedy 1956 · US · Colour · 90mins

Lucille Ball and Desi Arnaz's second attempt to become stars of the big screen together after the popular and stylish Vincente Minnelli-directed *The Long, Long Trailer* was this unfunny lark, in which guardian angel James Mason attempts to sort out the tribulations in their screen marriage. It doesn't sound particularly funny, and it wasn't, despite having Alexander Hall as director, who'd already had notable success with angels in *Here Comes Mr Jordan* and *Down to Earth*. Mason is a joy to watch, (even if he does look

embarrassed about the material), but it's an unworthy vehicle for American TV's greatest stars.

Lucille Ball *Susan Vega* • Desi Arnaz *Lorenzo Xavier Vega* • James Mason *Guardian angel* • Louis Calhern *Charles Y Bewell* • John Emery *Dr Edward R Winter* • John Hoyt *Bill Finlay* • Natalie Schafer *Millie Opdyke* ■ *Dir* Alexander Hall • *Scr* Helen Deutsch

Forever England ★★ PG
First World War drama
1935 · UK · BW · 67mins

This was the first fictional film made with the full co-operation of the Royal Navy, including ships and technical advisors, and, not surprisingly, the Senior Service emerges with all colours flying. After a slow start spent sketching our hero's background, director Walter Forde cranks up the pace as able seaman John Mills is rescued from the wreck of HMS *Rutland* by the German battleship *Zeithen*. His escape, and the way in which he delays the damaged ship's repair by picking off the crew from his hideout on the Galapagos island of Resolution, is crude but exciting. 📺

John Mills *Albert Brown* • Betty Balfour *Elizabeth Brown* • Barry MacKay *Lt Somerville* • Jimmy Hanley *Ginger* • Howard Marion-Crawford *Max* ■ *Dir* Walter Forde • *Scr* Michael Hogan, Gerard Fairlie, JOC Horton, from a novel by CS Forester

Forever Female ★★★
Comedy 1953 · US · BW · 93mins

Adapted and updated out of all recognition from an old JM Barrie play, this comedy about the Broadway theatre is haunted by the ghost of *All about Eve* (1950), but is nonetheless bitchy, witty and romantic in its own right. A chic Ginger Rogers plays an ageing Broadway actress, married to producer Paul Douglas. Desperate to regain her former star status, Rogers competes with ambitious youngster Patricia Crowley for the lead in a new play, and falls for its author, William Holden, en route to the movie's resolution. Polished entertainment, directed by old hand Irving Rapper of *Now Voyager* fame.

Ginger Rogers *Beatrice Page* • William Holden (1) *Stanley Krown* • Paul Douglas *E Harry Phillips* • Patricia Crowley *[Pat Crowley] Clara Mootz* • James Gleason *Eddie Woods* • Jesse White *Willie Wolfe* • Marjorie Rambeau ■ *Dir* Irving Rapper • *Scr* Julius J Epstein, Philip G Epstein, from the play *Rosalind* by JM Barrie

Forever Lulu ★ 18
Comedy adventure
1987 · US · Colour · 86mins

Yikes, is this bad! Fresh-faced debutant Alec Baldwin must have wondered what sort of business he was getting into as he watched Israeli director Amos Kollek cobble together this unmitigated disaster of a movie. It was much worse for German star Hanna Schygulla because she had placed an international reputation on the line (although heaven only knows why). Debbie Harry got it right, however – cameo, get paid and run. Released on video as *Crazy Streets*, this is a fish-out-of-water story that should have been thrown back. Contains swearing and nudity 📺

Hanna Schygulla *Elaine Hines* • Deborah Harry *Lulu* • Alec Baldwin *Buck* • Annie Golden *Diana* • Paul Gleason *Robert* • Dr Ruth Westheimer • Raymond Serra *Alphonse* • George Kyle *Pepe* ■ *Dir/Scr* Amos Kollek

Forever Young ★★ 15
Drama 1984 · UK · Colour and BW · 80mins

Originally made for the *First Love* TV series, this tangled tale of faded fame and unresolved differences is told via a series of bitterly nostalgic flashbacks. Although Nicholas Gecks is now a priest and James Aubrey a teacher, they were once part of a fifties rock band. Their rivalry resurfaces, as reunion bonhomie is replaced by competition for the attention of single mother Karen Archer, which has a traumatic effect on her altar boy son. As you'd expect, given that Ray Connolly wrote *That'll Be the Day* and *Stardust*, the monochrome memoirs make more impact than the modern-day melodrama. 📺

James Aubrey *James* • Nicholas Gecks *Father Michael* • Alec McCowen *Father Vincent* • Karen Archer *Mary* • Joseph Wright *John* • Liam Holt *Paul* • Jane Forster *Cathy* ■ *Dir* David Drury • *Scr* Ray Connolly

Forever Young ★★ PG
Romantic fantasy 1992 · US · Colour · 97mins

Mel Gibson obviously had to dig deep to find the enthusiasm to carry off this tired role of a cryogenic Rip Van Winkle who wakes 53 years after he has been frozen and forgotten. Hollywood used to churn out this kind of fluff with practised ease and it's a pity director Steve Miner couldn't have found the same winning formula in Mel's time capsule, but the reunions are touching, Jamie Lee Curtis provides charming support, and we're spared the usual smug time-lapse jokes. 📺 *DVD*

Mel Gibson *Daniel McCormick* • Jamie Lee Curtis *Claire* • Elijah Wood *Nat* • Isabel Glasser *Helen* • George Wendt *Harry* • Joe Morton *Cameron* • Nicholas Surovy [Nicolas Surovy] *John* ■ *Dir* Steve Miner • *Scr* Jeffrey Abrams

Forget-Me-Not ★★ U
Romantic drama 1936 · UK · BW · 68mins

In spite of the plea in the title, this badly dated melodrama is all too forgettable. Co-directed by Zoltan Korda and Stanley Irving, it begins on board a ship and spends the rest of its time inside hotel rooms and opera houses as Joan Gardner tries to choose between sailor Ivan Brandt and widowed singer Beniamino Gigli, whose appeal lies wholly in his magical voice. The direction is manipulative, the script sentimental and the performances painful, but if a little sugar-coated culture is your thing then you could do worse. 📺

Beniamino Gigli *Enzo Curti* • Joan Gardner *Helen* • Ivan Brandt *Hugh Anderson* • Hugh Wakefield *Curti's manager* • Jeanne Stuart *Irene* ■ *Dir* Zoltan Korda, Stanley Irving • *Scr* Hugh Gray, Arthur Wimperis

Forget Mozart ★★★
Historical detective thriller
1985 · Cz/W Ger · Colour · 93mins

As anyone who has seen *Amadeus* will know, slighted court composer Antonio Salieri considered himself responsible for Mozart's death. But masons, music-hall managers, monarchs – among others – all come under investigation in this complex costume thriller, as secret policeman Armin Mueller-Stahl seeks a darker explanation that will satisfy his conspiracy theories. While it lacks the scale of Milos Forman's Oscar-winner, this is still a stylish picture, with director Slavo Luther allowing the evidence to build into a case that is at least plausible, even though it may have as much to do with fact as the various theories on Jack the Ripper. In German with English subtitles.

Max Tidof *Mozart* • Armin Mueller-Stahl *Count Pergen* • Catarina Raacke *Konstanze* • Wolfgang Preiss *Swieten* • Uwe Ochsenknecht *Schikaneder* • Winfried Glatzeder *Salieri* ■ *Dir* Slavo Luther • *Scr* Zdenek Mahler

Forget Paris ★★★ 12
Romantic comedy
1995 · US · Colour · 97mins

This romantic comedy has a cosily familiar feel to it – perhaps that's because it has borrowed its anecdotal flashback structure from *Broadway Danny Rose*, its initial premise from *Avanti!* and much of what happens thereafter from *When Harry Met Sally...* There are some nice moments, but Debra Winger isn't really cut out for comedy and Billy Crystal is clearly treading water, while whatever wit and insight the film has is diminished by the nagging sense of déjà vu. The basketball sequences are admittedly funny, but co-writer/producer/director Crystal is so much in the thrall of Billy Wilder and Woody Allen that he rather loses touch with his own inimitable style. 📺

Billy Crystal *Mickey Gordon* • Debra Winger *Ellen Andrews* • Joe Mantegna *Andy* • Cynthia Stevenson *Liz* • Richard Masur *Craig* • Julie Kavner *Lucy* ■ *Dir* Billy Crystal • *Scr* Billy Crystal, Lowell Ganz, Babaloo Mandel

Forgotten Prisoners: the Amnesty Files ★★★ 15
Political drama 1990 · US · Colour · 88mins

A well intentioned TV movie about a lawyer (Ron Silver) who volunteers to travel to Istanbul with Amnesty International and fight the government bureaucracy detaining three political prisoners. Scenes of torture in a Turkish prison are harrowing, while the fine supporting cast lends credibility and texture. Shot in Budapest, director Robert Greenwald creates a polished look to this technically accomplished film and breathes life into the subject matter. 📺

Ron Silver *Jordan Ford* • Hector Elizondo *Hasan Demir* • Roger Daltrey *Howard Storm* • Leslee Udwin *Nuray Azim* ■ *Dir* Robert Greenwald • *Scr* Rex Weiner, Cindy Myers, from a story by Cindy Myers

Forgotten Sins ★★ 15

Drama based on a true story
1996 · US · Colour · 87mins

John Shea is the father who finds his life turning into a nightmare after his grown-up daughters accuse him of abuse, following therapy to release repressed memories. Unfortunately, this controversial subject – such cases are common in America – is treated in rather trivial fashion by this TV movie. That said, Shea and Willam Devane (playing the sociologist involved in the case) do give well-rounded performances. ▭

William Devane *Dr Richard Ofshe* • John Shea *Matthew Bradshaw* • Bess Armstrong *Roberta Bradshaw* • Dean Norris *Carl Messenger* • Brian Markinson *Lowell Hart* ■ *Dir* Dick Lowry • *Scr* TS Cook, from articles in *The New Yorker* by Lawrence Wright

The Formula ★★ 15

Thriller
1980 · US · Colour · 112mins

Although Steve Shagan and John G Avildsen had gelled on *Save the Tiger*, this thriller about a Nazi process for synthetic fuel prompted such an acrimonious bust-up that Avildsen campaigned to remove his name from the credits. At stake was the relative emphasis to be placed on the narrative and on the theory that the oil business was exploiting the world by suppressing this ingenious formula. The veracity of the background "facts" is dubious in the extreme, but the thesis is more logical than the plot, featuring George C Scott as a baffled detective and Marlon Brando as a mumbling tycoon. ▭

George C Scott *Lieutenant Barney Caine* • Marlon Brando *Adam Steiffel* • Marthe Keller *Lisa* • John Gielgud *Dr Abraham Esau* • GD Spradlin *Clements* ■ *Dir* John G Avildsen • *Scr* Steve Shagan, from his novel

Forrest Gump ★★★★ 12

Comedy drama 1994 · US · Colour · 136mins

Winner of six Oscars, including best picture, actor and director, *Forrest Gump* was a box-office blockbuster in America, though its simple-minded patriotism was greeted with a certain cynicism in Europe. Gump, played by Tom Hanks, is a chump: a semi-literate everyman who drifts through recent American history (Vietnam, the civil rights movement, assassinations, Watergate) and emerges triumphant. He's an athlete, war hero and hokey southern savant, a one-man palliative for a nation's political and moral bankruptcy. His personal credo is "Life is like a box of chocolates. You never know what you're going to get", and that's as profound as the movie gets. But Hanks's performance is truly remarkable and, this being a Robert Zemeckis film, the effects are stunning: Gump meeting people like JFK and Nixon is amazingly believable, and Gary Sinise as an amputee combines brilliant acting with state-of-the-art technology. Contains some violence, swearing, drug abuse and nudity. ▭

Tom Hanks *Forrest Gump* • Gary Sinise *Lieutenant Dan Taylor* • Robin Wright [Robin Wright Penn] *Jenny Curran* • Sally Field *Mrs Gump* • Mykel T Williamson *Benjamin Buford "Bubba" Blue* • Rebecca Williams *Nurse at*

park bench • Michael Conner Humphreys *Young Forrest* ■ *Dir* Robert Zemeckis • *Scr* Eric Roth, from the novel by Winston Groom

Forsaking All Others ★★★

Comedy 1934 · US · BW · 82mins

Clark Gable and Joan Crawford team up yet again for this smart MGM comedy. Gable wants to propose to childhood friend Crawford, but she's engaged to Robert Montgomery. Need you ask about the outcome? The under-rated WS "Woody" Van Dyke directs adroitly, while Crawford seems to undergo more costume changes than in her entire career (and that's saying something). The ineffable Charles Butterworth offers a beautifully timed supporting performance, while the feline Frances Drake plays Montgomery's other woman.

Joan Crawford *Mary Clay* • Clark Gable *Jeff Williams* • Robert Montgomery *Dill Todd* • Charles Butterworth *Shep* • Billie Burke *Paula* • Frances Drake *Connie* • Rosalind Russell *Eleanor* ■ *Dir* WS Van Dyke • *Scr* Joseph L Mankiewicz, from a play by Edward Barry Roberts, Frank Morgan Cavett

The Forsyte Saga ★★ U

Melodrama 1949 · US · Colour · 112mins

While Greer Garson looks splendid as "That Forsythe Woman" (the US title of the film), the courageously cast Errol Flynn is by far the best thing in this stilted picture, giving a performance of considerable restraint and depth. The leaden pace shown here proves that imported British director Compton Bennett's *The Seventh Veil* was just a lucky fluke, as the *Saga* is barely touched upon and, despite the high production values, this spiritually undernourished, empty feature is no match for the later BBC serial.

Errol Flynn *Soames Forsyte* • Greer Garson *Irene Forsyte* • Walter Pidgeon *Young Jolyon Forsyte* • Robert Young *Philip Bosinney* • Janet Leigh *June Forsyte* • Harry Davenport *Old Jolyon Forsyte* ■ *Dir* Compton Bennett • *Scr* Ivan Tors, James B Williams, Arthur Wimperis, from the novel *The Man of Property*, the first book in the trilogy *The Forsyte Saga* by John Galsworthy

Fort Algiers ★★ U

Adventure 1953 · US · BW · 79mins

A Foreign Legion adventure showcasing exotic Yvonne De Carlo (born Peggy Middleton in Vancouver) and dashing Argentinian Carlos Thompson. The stars quickly became a couple in real life, but here they pale beside big Raymond Burr, swarthy Anthony Caruso and angst-ridden Leif Erickson as the heavies. Of course, the Arabs are bad, the French are dashing, and Yvonne's a secret agent posing as a cabaret singer – get the picture? Time-wasting nonsense, though De Carlo's now-forgotten song *I'll Follow You* is nice.

Yvonne De Carlo *Yvette* • Carlos Thompson *Jeff* • Raymond Burr *Amir* • Leif Erickson *Kalmani* • Anthony Caruso *Chavez* • John Dehner *Major Colle* ■ *Dir* Lesley Selander • *Scr* Theodore St John, Frederick Stephani

Fort Apache ★★★★ U

Western 1948 · US · BW · 128mins

The first of three remarkable films director John Ford made about the US cavalry. It's a satisfying, finely crafted

work, not least because of Ford's ability to create a tangible sense of time and place in a displaced community against the majestic surroundings of his beloved Monument Valley. Ford regular Henry Fonda is particularly outstanding – cast against type as martinet officer Owen Thursday. Thursday is an embittered man set on a tragic course and clearly modelled on George Armstrong Custer. He breaks a peace deal with Apache leader Cochise, an agreement that was originally engineered by Kirby York, here played by John Wayne in one of his finest, most delicate portrayals. The life of the cavalry – its music, its women, its mythology – is all superbly realised by director Ford, who, in one simple shot of a soldier reading his Bible, confirms his greatness. ▭

John Wayne *Captain York* • Henry Fonda *Lieutenant Colonel Owen Thursday* • Shirley Temple *Philadelphia Thursday* • Pedro Armendariz *Sergeant Beaufort* • Ward Bond *Sergeant Major Michael O'Rourke* • George O'Brien *Captain Collingwood* • John Agar *Lieutenant Michael O'Rourke* • Victor McLaglen *Sergeant Festus Mulcahy* • Miguel Inclan *Chief Cochise* ■ *Dir* John Ford • *Scr* Frank S Nugent, from the story *Massacre* by James Warner Bellah • *Cinematographer* Archie Stout • *Music* Richard Hageman

Fort Apache, the Bronx ★★★★

Crime drama 1981 · US · Colour · 123mins

Hard-boiled, and hard-pressed, cop Paul Newman tries to control crime on New York's mean streets in a tremendously exciting thriller laced with taut suspense and grisly shocks making *NYPD Blue* look like *Dixon of Dock Gree*. Even cult *Hairspray* director John Waters singled out for high praise former sleaze-queen Pam Grier's electric performance as a psychotic hooker – just watch for that razor blade between her teeth. Highly controversial (the Bronx community complained about misrepresentation), but still highly recommended. Contains swearing, violence and brief nudity. ▭

Paul Newman *John Murphy* • Edward Asner [Ed Asner] *Captain Dennis Connolly* • Ken Wahl *Corelli* • Danny Aiello *Morgan* • Rachel Ticotin *Isabella* • Pam Grier *Charlotte* • Kathleen Beller *Theresa* • Tito Goya *Jumper/Detective* • Miguel Pinero *Hernando* • Jaime Tirelli *Jose* ■ *Dir* Daniel Petrie • *Scr* Heywood Gould

Fort Saganne ★★★★ 15

Historical adventure
1984 · Fr · Colour · 173mins

This long and lavish desert adventure pulls out all the stops for location shooting, almost rivalling *Lawrence of Arabia*, and casts four of France's biggest stars: Gérard Depardieu and Philippe Noiret, but also Catherine Deneuve and Sophie Marceau in token romantic diversions. The result is an exhausting but often impressive drama in which Depardieu's legionnaire expands the French Empire from the back of a camel just prior to the First World War. Acting honours go to Noiret's ambitious and choleric officer, but the star of the show is cameraman Bruno Nuytten, whose images of the sand seas of Mauritania will take your breath away. In French with English subtitles. ▭

Gérard Depardieu *Charles Saganne* • Philippe Noiret *Dubreuilh* • Catherine Deneuve *Louise Tissot* • Sophie Marceau *Madeleine De Saint Ilette* • Michel Duchaussoy *Baculard* ■ *Dir* Alain Corneau • *Scr* Alain Corneau, Henri DeTurenne, Louis Gardel, from the novel by Louis Gardel

Fort Worth ★★ U

Western 1951 · US · Colour · 80mins

The last film of veteran director Edwin L Marin (*Show Business*, *Johnny Angel*) is little more than a routine western, with a fairly innocuous plot that deals with the coming of newsprint to the west. Rugged Randolph Scott makes a most unlikely newspaper editor, and his predictable reversion to gunplay denudes the movie of any real suspense. But it's never less than watchable, despite a substandard supporting cast and colourless leading ladies in Phyllis Thaxter and Warner contractee Helena Carter.

Randolph Scott *Ned Britt* • David Brian *Blair Lunsford* • Phyllis Thaxter *Flora Talbot* • Helena Carter *Amy Brooks* • Dick Jones [Dickie Jones] *Luther Wick* ■ *Dir* Edwin L Marin • *Scr* John Twist, from his story *Across the Panhandle*

Fortress ★★★ 18

Science-fiction action thriller
1992 · Ausl/US · Colour · 91mins

An entertaining science-fiction thriller, with Christopher Lambert sent to a maximum security prison for conceiving a second child – a crime in director Stuart Gordon's imaginatively rendered totalitarian future. There he suffers high-tech torture and intense corruption while planning a daring break out. Violent, inventive (watch out for the Intestinator and the Mind Wipe Chamber!) and lots of intriguing fun, *Re-Animator* man Gordon makes this fantasy *Great Escape* meets *Prisoner Cell Block H* a suspenseful roller-coaster ride, despite its pulp limitations. You can't fail to be swept away by its excess verve as the action is cranked up to ever more fast and furious levels. Contains violence, sweaing, and some nudity. ▭ **DVD**

Christopher Lambert *John Brennick* • Kurtwood Smith *Prison Director Poe* • Loryn Locklin *Karen Brennick* • Lincoln Kilpatrick *Abraham* • Clifton Gonzalez *Nino* ■ *Dir* Stuart Gordon • *Scr* Steve Feinberg, Troy Neighbors

The Fortune ★★

Comedy 1975 · US · Colour · 87mins

Stockard Channing easily outshines Warren Beatty and Jack Nicholson, while David Shire's jazz arrangements are a major delight, in this occasionally tacky story set in the twenties. Nicholson and Beatty are two incompetent con-men trying to extract money from an heiress. Director Mike Nichols's impressive track-record includes *The Graduate* and *Primary Colors* but here his style seems tastelessly gauche. But there are moments of atmosphere to savour – plus Ms Channing.

Jack Nicholson *Oscar* • Warren Beatty *Nicky* • Stockard Channing *Freddie* • Florence Stanley *Mrs Gould* • Richard B Shull *Chief Detective* • Tom Newman *John the barber* ■ *Dir* Mike Nichols • *Scr* Adrien Joyce

Fortune and Men's Eyes★★

Prison drama
1971 · US/Can · Colour · 102mins

Homosexual activity and brutality in men's prisons were the themes of John Herbert's powerful Broadway play. However, although Herbert himself wrote the screenplay, the film version is far more exploitative, and seems to have lost the plea for prison reform on the way. Nevertheless, it still packs a certain punch, given its story of a young man having to submit to being sodomised regularly by his "protector". Surprisingly, for a movie that portrays such horrifying conditions, the film was given the assistance of the Canadian government. The original director Jules Schwerin was replaced by Harvey Hart, and many scenes had to be reshot.

Wendell Burton *Smitty* • Michael Greer *Queenie* • Zooey Hall *Rocky* • Danny Freedman *Mona* • Larry Perkins *Screwdriver* • James Barron *Holyface Peters* • Lazaro Perez *Catso* • Jon Granik *Sgt Gritt* ■ *Dir* Harvey Hart • *Scr* John Herbert, from his play

The Fortune Cookie

★★★★ U

Comedy
1966 · US · BW · 120mins

Billy Wilder's first teaming of Walter Matthau and Jack Lemmon crackles regularly throughout. Matthau is amoral lawyer "Whiplash Willie" who sees an opportunity to cash in when his brother-in-law, hapless cameraman Harry (Lemmon) is injured at a football game. Typically mining his drama from the collision between affectionate comedy and spiky cynicism, Wilder squeezes telling performances from his two stars. Matthau's lugubrious eccentricity, not to mention his delivery of comic gems won him an Oscar for best supporting actor, while Lemmon conveys the chaotic decency familiar from his role in *The Apartment*. ▭

Jack Lemmon *Harry Hinkle* • Walter Matthau *Willie Gingrich* • Ron Rich *Luther "Boom-Boom" Jackson* • Cliff Osmond *Mr Purkey* • Judi West *Sandy Hinkle* ■ *Dir* Billy Wilder • *Scr* Billy Wilder, I AL Diamond

Fortune Is a Woman

★★

Mystery
1956 · UK · BW · 94mins

Adapted from a novel by Winston Graham (of *Poldark* fame), this fair-to-middling thriller by the inseparable duo of Frank Launder and Sidney Gilliat is all plot and no point. Borrowing from a thousand and one *films noirs*, it follows the misfortunes of Jack Hawkins, an insurance assessor whose investigation of a series of fires draws him into murder, marriage and blackmail with a fatalistic inevitability. Hawkins lacks the vulnerability that Edward G Robinson brought to similar films like *The Woman in the Window*, while Arlene Dahl's *femme fatale* lacks the allure that would make such a dangerous liaison worth the risk.

Jack Hawkins *Oliver Branwell* • Arlene Dahl *Sarah Moreton* • Dennis Price *Tracey Moreton* • Violet Farebrother *Mrs Moreton* • Ian Hunter *Clive Fisher* • Christopher Lee *Charles Highbury* ■ *Dir* Sidney Gilliat • *Scr* Sidney Gilliat, Frank Launder, Val Valentine, from the novel by Winston Graham

40 Carats

★★ PG

Comedy
1973 · US · Colour · 108mins

Based like its 1969 predecessor *Cactus Flower* on a Broadway transfer of a French play, this would-be sprightly comedy suffers from severe central miscasting. Swedish import Liv Ullmann, in the role played on stage by Lauren Bacall, doesn't fit into the sophisticated New York whirl presented here, and no matter how hard she tries, her affair with younger Edward Albert remains unconvincing. But debonair Gene Kelly, as her ex-husband, is a joy to discover in this wisp of fluff, despite his awkward toupee. ▭

Liv Ullmann *Ann Stanley* • Edward Albert *Peter Latham* • Gene Kelly *Billy Boylan* • Binnie Barnes *Maud Ericson* • Deborah Raffin *Trina Stanley* ■ *Dir* Milton Katselas • *Scr* Leonard Gershe, from the play by Jay Presson Allen, Pierre Barillet, Jean-Pierre Gredy

48 HRS

★★★★ 15

Action thriller
1982 · US · Colour · 89mins

Trading Places apart, Eddie Murphy has never been better than in this, his exhilarating debut, still one of the best "buddy" cop thrillers to be made. Murphy is the con who is sprung from prison by racist cop Nick Nolte in an attempt to track down psychopathic duo James Remar and Sonny Landham, who have escaped from a chain gang and are now back in town. Nolte and Murphy are perfectly paired: the latter all smooth charm and wisecracks, the former the rough, gruff straight man. Murphy's taming of a redneck bar deserves its place in the cinematic history books, while director Walter Hill also delivers the goods in the action stakes with some beautifully orchestrated shoot-ups and chases. Followed by an uninspired retread *Another 48 Hours* in 1990. Contains swearing, violence and brief nudity. ▭

Nick Nolte *Detective Jack Cates* • Eddie Murphy *Reggie Hammond* • Annette O'Toole *Elaine* • Frank McRae *Captain Haden* • James Remar *Albert Ganz* ■ *Dir* Walter Hill • *Scr* Roger Spottiswoode, Walter Hill, Larry Gross, Steven E de Souza

Forty Guns

★★★

Western
1957 · US · BW · 78mins

Samuel Fuller was one of American cinema's true mavericks who eventually found a comfortable base at 20th Century-Fox, turning out a series of lurid melodramas that later achieved cult status, including this stylishly photographed CinemaScope western. Barbara Stanwyck (slightly too old) plays a ruthless Arizona rancher who is a law unto herself, until marshal Barry Sullivan (who hasn't killed a soul in ten years) turns up. It's all good fun, and, in its fairly short running time, not a second is wasted.

Barbara Stanwyck *Jessica Drummond* • Barry Sullivan *Griff Bonnell* • Dean Jagger *Ned Logan* • John Ericson *Brockie Drummond* ■ *Dir/Scr* Samuel Fuller

The 49th Man

★★★ U

Spy drama
1953 · US · BW · 72mins

Worried about a foreign power smuggling an atomic bomb into the US, the Navy plans an elaborate hoax to test the readiness of the security services. That's one twist in the plot; the next is such a humdinger that one becomes genuinely concerned for the survival of Nevada and for the devious mind of the screenwriter, Harry Essex, who also wrote two sci-fi schlock classics, *It Came from Outer Space* and *Creature from the Black Lagoon*. Designed to reassure Middle America about communist invasion and atomic terrorism, this B-movie has a sense of urgency and suitably awed acting from the likes of John Ireland, a heavy who, for once, washes up on the right side of the law.

John Ireland *John Williams* • Richard Denning *Paul Regan* • Suzanne Dalbert *Margo Wayne* • Robert Foulk *Commander Jackson* • Touch Connors [Mike Connors] *Lt Magrew* • Richard Avonde *Buzz Olin* ■ *Dir* Fred F Sears • *Scr* Harry Essex, from a story by Ivan Tors

49th Parallel

★★★★ U

Second World War drama
1941 · UK · BW · 116mins

Sponsored by the Ministry of Information and 18 months in the making, this is one of the best propaganda films produced in Britain during the Second World War. With a stellar cast and a rousing score by Ralph Vaughan Williams, Michael Powell and Emeric Pressburger's gripping action drama thoroughly merited its Oscar for best original story and its nominations for best picture and screenplay. Eric Portman gives the finest performance of his career as the officer of a bombed U-boat who has to lead his surviving crew across the Canadian wilderness to neutral America. Leslie Howard adds a dash of humour, while Laurence Olivier's French-Canadian accent has to be heard to be believed. ▭

Eric Portman *Lt Ernst Hirth* • Laurence Olivier *Johnnie Barras* • Leslie Howard *Philip Armstrong Scott* • Anton Walbrook *Peter* • Raymond Massey *Andy Brock* • Glynis Johns *Anna* • Niall MacGinnis *Vogel* ■ *Dir* Michael Powell • *Scr* Rodney Ackland, Emeric Pressburger, from a story by Emeric Pressburger • *Cinematographer* Freddie Young • *Editor* David Lean

Forty Pounds of Trouble

★★★ U

Comedy
1962 · US · Colour · 105mins

An immensely likeable reworking of the Damon Runyon tale, filmed in 1934 and 1980 as *Little Miss Marker* and in 1949 as *Sorrowful Jones*. This time it's amiable Tony Curtis as the gambling house manager who's left holding the baby, a situation that prompts nightclub chanteuse Suzanne Pleshette to lure him away from his ex-wife. The film has all the gloss you'd expect from a Universal feature of the period; it also boasts a typically voracious performance from the great Phil Silvers as Curtis's boss. What's surprising, given its lightness of content, is that it marked the feature debut of Canadian director Norman Jewison, later responsible for such worthy classics as *In the Heat of the Night* and *Fiddler on the Roof*.

Tony Curtis *Steve McLuskey* • Phil Silvers *Bernie Friedman* • Suzanne Pleshette *Chris Lockwood* • Claire Wilcox *Penny Piper* • Larry Storch *Floyd* • Howard Morris *Julius* ■ *Dir* Norman Jewison • *Scr* Marion Hargrove, from the short story *Little Miss Marker* by Damon Runyon

42nd Street

★★★★★ U

Musical
1933 · US · BW · 85mins

One of the most important and enjoyable musicals of all time, this sizzling Warner Bros movie is also one of the best loved of the early talking pictures. The film is recognised as a masterpiece, not merely for its racy dialogue and lavish costumes, or for its now-classic "newcomer goes on instead of indisposed star" plot, but also for affording kaleidoscope choreographer Busby Berkeley a chance to show off in such superb numbers as *Shuffle Off to Buffalo* and *You're Getting to Be a Habit with Me*. The production cost a mammoth $400,000 and it shows. This is as entertaining as it gets, with a knockout cast headed by Warner Baxter as the stressed Broadway director and Bebe Daniels as his star. Dick Powell and Ruby Keeler (then married to Warners legend Al Jolson) feature in roles that would turn them into household favourites, and a newcomer called Ginger Rogers plays Anytime Annie "The only time she said no", she didn't hear the question!". A real treat. ▭

Warner Baxter *Julian Marsh* • Bebe Daniels *Dorothy Brock* • Ruby Keeler *Peggy Sawyer* • Dick Powell *Billy Lawler* • George Brent *Pat Denning* • Una Merkel *Lorraine Fleming aka Lolly* • Ginger Rogers *Ann aka Anytime Annie Lowell* • Guy Kibbee *Abner Dillon* ■ *Dir* Lloyd Bacon • *Scr* James Seymour, Rian James, from a novel by Bradford Ropes • *Producer* Darryl F Zanuck • *Cinematographer* Sol Polito • *Music/Lyrics* Harry Warren, Al Dubin

Forty Thousand Horsemen

★★

First World War drama
1941 · Ausl · BW · 80mins

For 30 years, Charles Chauvel was Australia's first and possibly only major director. It was Chauvel who, in 1933, gave Errol Flynn his screen debut as Fletcher Christian in the docu-drama *In the Wake of the Bounty*. *Forty Thousand Horsemen* was Chauvel's big movie about the Australian Light Horse regiment's role in Palestine during the First World War. The action easily outclasses the quieter moments, involving a romance between an Aussie soldier and a beautiful French girl, which are rather poorly acted. It was remade in 1987 as *The Lighthorsemen*.

Grant Taylor *Red Gallagher* • Betty Bryant *Juliet Rouget* • Chips Rafferty *Jim* • Pat Twohill *Larry* • Harvey Adams *Von Hausen* • Eric Reiman *Von Schiller* • Joe Valli *Scotty* ■ *Dir* Charles Chauvel • *Scr* Elsa Chauvel

La Forza del Destino

★★ U

Opera
1949 · It · BW · 102mins

The least assured of the operas filmed by veteran director Carmine Gallone in the immediate postwar period, this tale of forbidden love, unsuspecting camaraderie and bitter revenge is also considered one of Verdi's lesser works. However, legendary baritone Tito Gobbi stars as the rebel who is forced to flee to Europe after killing his lover's disapproving father. The plot

marginalises Nelly Corradi (voiced by Caterina Mancini) by having her become a penitent hermit and the denouement, is wildly melodramatic. But the relationship between Gobbi and her soldier brother, Gino Sinimberghi (sung by Galliano Masini) is well developed. In Italian with English subtitles.

Caterina Mancini • Galliano Masini • Tito Gobbi • Nelly Corradi • Gino Sinimberghi ■ *Dir* Carmine Gallone

Foster and Laurie ★★★

Police drama based on a true story
1975 · US · Colour · 100mins

In 1972, a fanatical organisation murdered two New York patrolmen as part of its campaign to unnerve and undermine confidence within the city's police department. In this TV-movie version of the story, Perry King and Dorian Harewood give impressive performances as the two victims, Rocco Laurie and his partner Gregory Foster, revealing the men behind the badge as well the dedication to duty that cost them their lives. Talia Shire (of *The Godfather* and *Rocky* fame) and Jonelle Allen do well as their respective wives and there's an all-too-brief appearance from a young James Woods as a junkie. With a stirring score by Lalo Schifrin, this is an unusually effective mix of fact and melodrama. Contains violence

Perry King *Rocco Laurie* • Dorian Harewood *Gregory Foster* • Talia Shire *Adelaide Laurie* • Jonelle Allen *Jacqueline Foster* • Roger Aaron Brown *Sims* • Victor Campos *Dealer* • James Woods *Addict* ■ *Dir* John Llewellyn Moxey • *Scr* Albert Ruben, from a book by Al Silverman

Foul Play ★★★ PG

Comedy thriller 1978 · US · Colour · 110mins

An incredibly silly but very enjoyable comedy, with Goldie Hawn as the librarian who discovers a plot to kill the visiting Pope. Chevy Chase has one of his best roles as the detective who doesn't believe Hawn's life is in danger, and the cast also features Burgess Meredith and Dudley Moore having a whale of a time in between car chases and assassination attempts. Written and directed by Colin Higgins, who also made *Nine to Five*. Contains some swearing. ▭

Goldie Hawn *Gloria Mundy* • Chevy Chase *Tony Carlson* • Dudley Moore *Stanley Tibbets* • Burgess Meredith *Mr Hennesey* • Rachel Roberts *Gerda Casswell* • Brian Dennehy *Fergie* ■ *Dir/Scr* Colin Higgins

The Fountain ★★

First World War drama
1934 · US · BW · 80mins

Creaky and dated melodrama faithfully (but slowly) directed by John Cromwell about a married Dutch woman who falls for a handsome British officer billeted on her family during the First World War. This tedious tale is redeemed somewhat by the casting – particularly the superbly serene but under-rated Ann Harding – and the conflict engendered when her German husband, Paul Lukas, returns. The makings of a worthwhile drama are all in place, but the telling is unexciting in the extreme. Still, it does retain a certain period fascination.

Ann Harding *Julie Von Narwitz* • Brian Aherne *Lewis Allison* • Paul Lukas *Rupert Von Narwitz* • Jean Hersholt *Baron Van Leyden* • Ralph Forbes *Ballater* ■ *Dir* John Cromwell • *Scr* Jane Murfin, Samuel Hoffenstein, from the novel by Charles Morgan

The Fountain ★★★

Comedy 1988 · USSR · Colour · 100mins

Faintly recalling the French tenement pictures of the thirties, with its mock realist portrait of everyday life, Yuri Mamin's satire cheekily compares the Soviet state to a dilapidated apartment block, which begins to crumble further when Kazakh farmer Asankul Kuttubaev comes to stay with his daughter and her bureaucrat husband. The symbolism of this *perestroika* comedy is blatant. But there is an irresistible charm about the havoc wreaked by this innocent abroad, as he approaches modern appliances with a mixture of awe and disgust at what he sees as reckless waste. In Russian with English subtitles.

Zhanna Kerimtaeva *Maya* • Viktor Mikhailov *Mitrofanov* • Asankul Kuttubaev *Kerbabaev* • Sergei Dontsov *Lagutin* ■ *Dir* Yuri Mamin • *Scr* Vladimir Vardunas

The Fountainhead ★★ PG

Drama 1949 · US · BW · 112mins

An overblown but unflamboyant (owing to an overuse of studio interiors) Warner Bros adaptation of controversial writer Ayn Rand's peculiar retelling of the story of the great architect Frank Lloyd Wright. Gary Cooper plays the architect – here rechristened Howard Roark – looking as though he'd be more at home in a western. His scenes with co-star Patricia Neal do sizzle, though, and we now know that they were a secret couple in real life. Director King Vidor, not exactly known for understatement (*Duel in the Sun, War and Peace*) does what he can with the dubious text. The film was successfully revived theatrically in the late nineties, for an audience that had never seen the great "Coop" in anything else. The film's unsubtle symbolism is hysterical to watch, and the "message" of the individual versus society is completely muffed. Contains some violence.

Gary Cooper *Roark* • Patricia Neal *Dominique* • Raymond Massey *Gail Wynand* • Robert Douglas *Ellsworth Toohey* • Kent Smith *Peter Keating* • Henry Hull *Henry Cameron* • Ray Collins *Enright* ■ *Dir* King Vidor • *Scr* Ayn Rand, from her novel

Four Adventures of Reinette and Mirabelle ★★★★ U

Drama 1986 · Fr · Colour · 94mins

Concentrating on the contrasting attitudes of two talkative teens, this rare non-series picture from French auteur Eric Rohmer makes light of its miniscule budget and inexperienced cast to provide another richly layered and hugely satisfying drama. A sophisticated spin on the town and country mouse fable, this is a film of incidents rather than adventures, with the eccentric Joëlle Miquel landing herself in scrapes that alternately amuse and irritate her more sophisticated Parisian pal, Jessica

Forde. The most diverting of their inspired improvisations is the encounter with a pompous waiter, but the endless stream of chat is never less than absorbing. In French with English subtitles. ▭

Joëlle Miquel *Reinette* • Jessica Forde *Mirabelle* • Philippe Laudenbach *Waiter* • Yasmine Haury *Kleptomaniac* • Marie Rivière *Hustler* • Béatrice Romand *Inspector* • Géraud Courant *Inspector* ■ *Dir/Scr* Eric Rohmer

4 Clowns ★★★★ U

Comedy compilation 1970 · US · BW · 95mins

From innocence to insolence – they don't make them like this any more. Robert Youngson's compilation of comic cuts from the early days of film comedy reveals Laurel and Hardy, Buster Keaton and the undervalued Charley Chase (in his magnificent *Limousine Love*, among others) as creatures of infinite grace and wit. You can even forgive the film's sometimes patronising ho-ho commentary for showing us the dizzying standards from which so many of today's comedians have fallen. Here's a golden age which has lost none of its lustre.

Buster Keaton • Charley Chase • Stan Laurel • Oliver Hardy ■ *Dir* Robert Youngson

Four Daughters ★★★★ U

Romance 1938 · US · BW · 89mins

A big-box office winner in its day, and deservedly so. Claude Rains is simply wonderful as the musical father watching over the lives and loves of his four disparate daughters. This is a prime example of what can be achieved with an ostensibly soapy outline: small-town life with all its foibles, but with a top-notch cast that includes John Garfield in his first role. What could have been an exercise in hoary old clichés and character stereotyping emerges as a fascinating, subtle look at the complexities of parenthood and community life.

Claude Rains *Adam Lemp* • May Robson *Aunt Etta* • Priscilla Lane *Ann Lemp* • Lola Lane *Thea Lemp* • Rosemary Lane *Kay Lemp* • Gale Page *Emma Lemp* • Dick Foran *Ernest* ■ *Dir* Michael Curtiz • *Scr* Julius J Epstein, Lenore Coffee, from the novel *Sister Act* by Fannie Hurst

Four Days in September ★★★★

Historical drama
1997 · Bra · Colour · 105mins

Returning home after a decade in the States, Bruno Barreto landed an Oscar nomination for this involved political drama, that was based on the autobiography of revolutionary-turned-journalist Fernando Gabeira. Set in 1969, with Brazil under a military dictatorship, the film recalls the abduction of American ambassador Charles Burke Elbrick by the MR-8 movement in a bid to secure the release of 15 political prisoners and publicise their cause. Playing fair with all the participants (including tormented torturer Marco Ricca), this is a gripping reconstruction, with the friendship between Alan Arkin as the ambassador and Pedro Cardoso as the journalist humanising, but not romanticising, a tense situation. In Portuguese with English subtitles.

Alan Arkin *Charles Burke Elbrick* • Pedro Cardoso *Fernando Gabeira/Paulo* • Fernanda Torres *Maria* • Luiz Fernando Guimaraes *Marcao* • Claudia Abreu *Renee* • Nelson Dantas *Toledo* • Matheus Nachtergaele *Jonas* ■ *Dir* Bruno Barreto • *Scr* Leopoldo Serran, from the novel *O Que E Isso, Companheiro?* by Fernando Gabeira

The Four Days of Naples ★★★★

Second World War drama
1962 · It · BW · 119mins

The raw courage of a proud people rising against the Nazi yoke is brought home with eloquence and power in this Oscar-nominated drama from director Nanni Loy. Comparisons with Roberto Rossellini's *Rome, Open City* are somewhat flattering, but what this account of the events of September 1943 shares with that neorealist masterpiece is a sense of immediacy, as the Neopolitan population rebelled against a dictate that all males between the ages of five and 50 should be dispatched to labour camps. The ensemble playing is exceptional, with the standout being Domenico Formato as the barricade boy-hero, Gennaro Capuozzo. In Italian with English subtitles.

Lea Massari *Maria* • Jean Sorel *Livornese* • Franco Sportelli *Professor Rosati* • Charles Belmont *Sailor* • Gian Maria Volonté *Stimolo* • Frank Wolff *Salvatore* • Domenico Formato *Gennaro Capuozzo* ■ *Dir* Nanni Loy • *Scr* Pasquale Festa Campanile, Massimo Franciosa, Nanni Loy, Carlo Benari, from a story by Vasco Pratolini, Pasquale Festa Campanile, Massimo Franciosa

The Four Deuces ★★

Crime drama 1976 · US · Colour · 89mins

Jack Palance here takes on an almost benevolent aspect as a gangland boss during the Prohibition era – both his gang and and his gambling establishment bear the name of the film's title. What redeems him this time is the love he bears for Carol Lynley and it's this romance which gives the film's violent action and romance its raison d'être. Altogether an oddball spin on the genre with the Prohibition atmosphere well established and Palance, as usual, giving good value.

Jack Palance *Vic* • Carol Lynley *Wendy* • Warren Berlinger *Chico* • Adam Roarke *Ross* • EJ Peaker *Lory* ■ *Dir* William H Bushnell Jr • *Scr* C Lester Franklin, from a story by Don Martin

The Four Diamonds ★★★

Fantasy drama 1995 · US · Colour · 96mins

The story on which this rousing adventure is based was written by Christopher Millard as he battled the cancer that killed him at 14. If *The Wizard of Oz* was an unconscious influence on his tale, it certainly provided the impetus for this Disney TV movie, in which the young boy's family and the doctor treating him take on the principal roles in his tale of chivalry and black magic. Thomas Guiry acquits himself admirably as the knight searching for the four diamonds of courage, honesty, wisdom and strength. But it's Christine Lahti who steals the show with a wonderful display of pantomimic malevolence as the wicked sorceress.

Thomas Guiry *Christopher Millard/Squire Millard* • Christine Lahti *Dr Burke/Sorceress/Raptannehan* • Kevin Dunn *Charles Millard/Charles the Mysterious* • Jayne Brook *Irma Millard/Hermit of the Lagoon* ■ *Dir* Peter Werner • *Scr* Todd Robinson, from a short story by Christopher Millard

Four Eyes and Six-Guns ★★★

Comedy western 1992 · US · Colour · 92mins

A daft-as-a-brush TV movie that looks, on paper, like a recipe for goggle-eyed embarrassment but is, in fact, a bit of a giggle. Judge Reinhold – Eddie Murphy's sidekick in the *Beverly Hills Cop* movies – is wonderfully funny (lots of mad, timid eye-blinking) as the naive optician from "back east" who comes to the aid of Wyatt Earp (Fred Ward), whose sight is failing. This is hilarious stuff, largely owing to the careful playing of the leads, but also to a zippy, hectic pace, which never allows the jokes to let up for a second. In other words, if a certain gag doesn't take your fancy, don't worry there'll be another along in a minute. Infantile and hugely enjoyable.

Judge Reinhold *Ernest Albright* • Fred Ward *Wyatt Earp* • Patricia Clarkson *Lucy Laughton* • M Emmet Walsh *Mayor Thornbush* • John Schuck *Charlie Winniger* ■ *Dir* Piers Haggard • *Scr* Leon Prochnik

Four Feathers ★★★

Silent adventure 1929 · US · BW · 81mins

This spectacular version of AEW Mason's famous novel was the last major Hollywood film to be made without any spoken dialogue, carrying only music and sound effects. Richard Arlen is the young officer given white feathers for displaying cowardice by three fellow soldiers – William Powell, Clive Brook and Theodore von Eltz – and his fiancée, played by Fay Wray in an early association with the *King Kong* team of Ernest B Schoedsack and Merian C Cooper. They began their film careers making wild-life documentaries and spent a year in Africa filming dramatic sequences with hippos and baboons – scenes that are well integrated into the story of Arlen redeeming himself in action.

Richard Arlen *Harry Faversham* • Fay Wray *Ethne Eustace* • Clive Brook *Lt Durrance* • William Powell *Capt Trench* • Theodore von Eltz *Lt Castleton* • Noah Beery Sr [Noah Beery] *Slave trader* • Zack Williams *Idris* • Noble Johnson *Ahmed* ■ *Dir* Merian C Cooper, Ernest B Schoedsack, Lothar Mendes • *Scr* Howard Estabrook, Hope Loring, from the novel by AEW Mason • *Producer* David Selznick [David O Selznick]

The Four Feathers ★★★★★ U

Classic adventure
1939 · UK · Colour · 110mins

The fourth screen version of AEW Mason's rousing adventure is one of the finest films made by the Korda brothers – producer Alexander, director Zoltan and art director Vincent. Everything about it is spot on: the tightly constructed script by RC Sherriff, Lajos Biro and Arthur Wimperis; the rich colours and evocative location work of

cinematographers Georges Perinal, Osmond Borradaile and Jack Cardiff; the perfectly paced editing of William Hornbeck and Henry Cornelius; and the pounding score by Miklos Rozsa. And we've not even begun to extol the virtues of the performances of John Clements, Ralph Richardson and C Aubrey Smith. It's a gem! 📖

John Clements *Harry Faversham* • Ralph Richardson *Captain John Durrance* • C Aubrey Smith *General Burroughs* • June Duprez *Ethne Burroughs* • Allan Jeayes *General Faversham* • Jack Allen *Lieutenant Willoughby* • Donald Gray *Peter Burroughs* • Frederick Culley *Dr Sutton* ■ *Dir* Zoltan Korda • *Scr* RC Sherriff, Lajos Biró, Arthur Wimperis, from the novel by AEW Mason

The Four Feathers ★★ U

War adventure 1978 · US · Colour · 100mins

Given that the 1939 version is one of the all-time greats of British cinema, this TV remake was on a hiding to nothing. Beau Bridges looks out of place, but gives it his best shot as the disgraced officer who redeems himself when he goes undercover as a tribesman to help his three old military chums who have accused him of cowardice. The sterling efforts of a mainly British cast, including Robert Powell and Simon Ward, can't erase memories of earlier – and better – adaptations. 📖

Beau Bridges *Harry Faversham* • Jane Seymour *Ethne Eustace* • Robert Powell *Jack Durrance* • Simon Ward *William Trench* • Harry Andrews *General David Faversham* • Richard Johnson *Abou Fatma* ■ *Dir* Don Sharp • *Scr* Gerald DiPego, from the novel by AEW Mason

4 for Texas ★★

Comedy western
1963 · US · Colour · 114mins

One of the series of Rat Pack movies with numbers in their titles, this overlong, over-indulgent western romp is really quite amusing, despite tiresome Clan antics, as rivals Frank Sinatra and Dean Martin team up to defeat the baddies (banker Victor Buono and gunslinger Charles Bronson), who steal the only acting honours available to be stolen. No film that ropes in the talents of Martin and Bronson could be totally unwatchable and at least Sinatra had the good sense to hire a decent director. However, there's little *The Dirty Dozen's* Robert Aldrich could do with this farrago in western guise, except take the proffered fee.

Frank Sinatra *Zack Thomas* • Dean Martin *Joe Jarrett* • Anita Ekberg *Elya Carlson* • Ursula Andress *Maxine Richter* • Charles Bronson *Matson* • Victor Buono *Harvey Burden* • Edric Connor *Prince George* ■ *Dir* Robert Aldrich • *Scr* Teddi Sherman, Robert Aldrich

Four Frightened People ★★

Adventure 1934 · US · BW · 77mins

Silly but entertaining survivalist melodrama, shot partly in Hawaii, with Claudette Colbert, Herbert Marshall and others hacking through the Malayan jungle because an on-board epidemic forces them to jump from a Dutch coastal steamer. Even away from Ancient Rome, Cecil B DeMille still asks Colbert to strip off and take a bath – DeMille, you will recall, got Colbert bathing in ass's milk in *The*

Sign of the Cross, and she was semi-naked throughout *Cleopatra*.

Claudette Colbert *Judy Cavendish* • Herbert Marshall *Arnold Ainger* • Mary Boland *Mrs Mardick* • William Gargan *Stewart Corder* • Leo Carrillo *Montague* ■ *Dir* Cecil B DeMille • *Scr* Bartlett Cormack, Lenore Coffee, from the novel by E Arnot Robertson

Four Girls in White ★★

Drama 1939 · US · BW · 73mins

MGM clearly released this hospital melodrama hoping to repeat the success of its new *Doctor Kildare* series. However, the nursing quartet of the title spend as much time flirting with the doctors and orderlies as they do ministering to their patients. Sara Haden is suitably starchy as the martinet matron and Una Merkel and Buddy Ebsen provide some cornball comic relief. But the main focus falls on the rivalry between Florence Rice and single mother Mary Howard for the attention of Doctor Alan Marshal, which ends with a tragedy that will have you reaching for the tissues.

Florence Rice *Norma Page* • Una Merkel *Gertie Robbins* • Ann Rutherford *Patricia Page* • Mary Howard *Mary Forbes* • Alan Marshal *Dr Stephen Melford* ■ *Dir* S Sylvan Simon • *Scr* Dorothy Yost, from a story by Nathalie Bucknall, Endre Boehm

Four Guns to the Border ★★ U

Western 1954 · US · Colour · 82mins

Youthful Rory Calhoun and Colleen Miller convey some unusually uninhibited (for the time) moments of passion in this otherwise routine western, handsomely photographed by Russell Metty. The title refers to Calhoun and his three pals, who rob a bank and hightail it for Mexico, only to be sidetracked into rescuing Miller and her old rancher father from an Apache ambush. Most notable is the steamy love scene between the leads, but there's good supporting work from older players Walter Brennan (as the girl's crusty father), John McIntire and Nina Foch. Actor Richard Carlson does a capable job as director.

Rory Calhoun *Ray Cully* • Colleen Miller *Lolly Bhumer* • George Nader *Bronco* • Walter Brennan *Simon Bhumer* • Nina Foch *Maggie Flannery* • John McIntire *Dutch* ■ *Dir* Richard Carlson • *Scr* George Van Marter, Franklin Coen, from a story by Louis L'Amour

The Four Horsemen of the Apocalypse ★★★

Silent First World War drama
1921 · US · BW · 114mins

To interest modern audiences in this classic of the silent cinema, one has to say that Latin heart-throb Rudolph Valentino was the Leonardo DiCaprio of his day. Actually, Valentino was infinitely bigger than DiCaprio could ever be – but you get the picture. So much of this film is rubbish, and the stuff about two brothers fighting on opposing sides in the First World War is extremely tedious. However, in those scenes where Valentino dances the tango or simply glowers dangerously, one is suddenly confronted with one of the most powerful of screen legends. Director Rex Ingram handles the apocalyptic climax very well.

Rudolph Valentino *Julio Desnoyers* • Alice Terry *Marguerite Laurier* • Pomeroy Cannon *Madariaga, the Centaur* • Josef Swickard *Marcelo Desnoyers* • Brinsley Shaw *Celendonio* • Alan Hale *Karl von Hartrott* • Bridgetta Clark *Dona Luisa* • Mabel Van Buren *Elena* ■ *Dir* Rex Ingram • *Scr* June Mathis, from the novel *Los Cuatro Jinetes del Apocalipsis* by Vicente Blasco Ibáñez

The Four Horsemen of the Apocalypse ★★★

Second World War drama
1962 · US · Colour · 153mins

Based on an unreadable novel by Vicente Blasco Ibáñez, this study of an Argentinian family torn apart by war became indelibly famous as the silent movie in which Rudolph Valentino danced the tango and catapulted to stardom. However, despite the array of talent on display and some stunning CinemaScope photography, this would-be extravaganza stubbornly remains earthbound. It's not helped by the grievous miscasting of the usually dependable Glenn Ford in the Valentino role, while updating the story to the Second World War doesn't wash. But the vision of the Four Horsemen from the Book of Revelations, riding to the strains of André Previn's potent score, is genuinely impressive.

Glenn Ford *Julio Desnoyers* • Ingrid Thulin *Marguerite Laurier* • Charles Boyer *Marcelo Desnoyers* • Lee J Cobb *Julio Madariaga* • Paul Henreid *Etienne Laurier* ■ *Dir* Vincente Minnelli • *Scr* Robert Ardrey, John Gay, from the novel *Los Cuatro Jinetes del Apocalipsis* by Vicente Blasco Ibáñez • *Cinematographer* Milton Krasner

The 400 Blows ★★★★★ PG

Drama 1959 · Fr · BW · 95mins

Former critic François Truffaut made his feature debut with this largely autobiographical drama. Made for a mere $75,000, it has echoes of Jean Vigo's *Zéro de Conduite*, although the influence of Jean Renoir and Italian neorealism is also evident. Introducing the character of Antoine Doinel (who would feature in another four Truffaut outings), the story paints a grimly authentic portrait of troubled adolescence, with 13-year-old actor Jean-Pierre Léaud effortlessly conveying both mischief and vulnerability in the lead role. Packed with familiar New Wave faces, the film won Truffaut the best director's prize at Cannes and sent ripples around world cinema with its audacious freeze-frame finale. In French with English subtitles. 📖

Jean-Pierre Léaud *Antoine Doinel* • Claire Maurier *Mme Doinel* • Albert Rémy *M Doinel* • Guy Decomble *Teacher* • Patrick Auffay *René Bigey* • Georges Flamant *M Bigey* ■ *Dir* François Truffaut • *Scr* François Truffaut, Marcel Moussy, from a story by François Truffaut • *Cinematographer* Henri Decaë

Four in the Morning ★★★★

Drama 1965 · UK · BW · 93mins

The title's a clever pun, since the film deals with the time of a young girl's drowning, and with the (unrelated) trials and tribulations of two unnamed couples. Acclaimed in its day as a sharp slice of British neorealism, talented director/writer Anthony

U = SUITABLE FOR ALL   Uc = SUITABLE FOR ALL, ESPECIALLY FOR YOUNG CHILDREN (VIDEO ONLY)   PG = PARENTAL GUIDANCE

Simmons has done nothing quite as good, although his location work on *Black Joy* and *The Optimists of Nine Elms* is also impressive. Judi Dench won a Bafta award for her role, while Ann Lynn, Norman Rodway and Brian Phelan have seldom been better. The bleak score by John Barry is superb.

Ann Lynn *Girl* • Brian Phelan *Boy* • Judi Dench *Wife* • Norman Rodway *Husband* • Joe Melia *Friend* ■ *Dir/Scr* Anthony Simmons

The Four Just Men ★★★

Drama 1939 · UK · BW · 87mins

Gathering war clouds cast their shadows over this adaptation of novelist Edgar Wallace's ingenious imperial thriller. Produced by Michael Balcon at Ealing, it defiantly suggests that Britain could never fall under the sway of a dictator. But in all other respects it's a rollicking *Boys' Own* adventure, with some of the most fiendishly comic-book murders you will ever see. Hugh Sinclair, Frank Lawton, Griffith Jones and Francis L Sullivan unite gallantly to prevent treacherous Basil Sydney from helping enemy agents sabotage the Suez Canal. But the romance between Jones and Anna Lee needlessly sidetracks the otherwise hugely entertaining sub-Hitchcockian antics.

Hugh Sinclair *Humphrey Mansfield* • Griffith Jones *James Brodie* • Francis L Sullivan *Leon Poiccard* • Frank Lawton *Terry* • Anna Lee *Ann Lodge* • Alan Napier *Sir Hamar Ryman MP* ■ *Dir* Walter Forde • *Scr* Angus MacPhail, Sergei Nolbandov, Roland Pertwee, from a novel by Edgar Wallace

4 Little Girls ★★★★ 15

Documentary 1997 · US · BW and Colour · 112mins

Spike Lee's Oscar-nominated account of the murder of four young African-Americans by white supremacist bombers is as chilling as it is compelling. Using interviews, cuttings and archive footage to establish the segregational fervour that existed in Birmingham, Alabama in 1963, Lee not only describes how Carol Denise McNair, Cynthia Wesley, Addie Mae Collins and Carole Rosamund Robertson met their fate, but also suggests how much poorer the world has been for their loss. The arrogance of Klan killer Robert Chambliss is hard to bear, but nothing prepares you for the morgue photographs of the dead girls. A history lesson that cannot be ignored. ▱

Dir Spike Lee

Four Men and a Prayer ★★★

Mystery drama 1938 · US · BW · 85mins

In spite of a slow start and a humdrum romantic diversion, this is a serviceable adventure mystery from master director John Ford. The gung-ho quartet of the title are the sons of old soldier C Aubrey Smith, who come face to face with a gang of gun-runners while investigating their father's death. Although George Sanders and William Henry have some fun back in Blighty, Richard Greene and David Niven get rather bogged down feuding over Loretta Young in Buenos Aires. The Brits are solid, but it's the acting of

supports Alan Hale and John Carradine that catches the eye.

George Sanders *Wyatt Leigh* • David Niven *Christopher Leigh* • Richard Greene *Geoff Leigh* • William Henry *Rodney Leigh* • Loretta Young *Lynn Cherrington* • C Aubrey Smith *Colonel Loring Leigh* • Alan Hale *Furnoy* • John Carradine *General Adolfo Arturo Sebastian* ■ *Dir* John Ford • *Scr* Richard Sherman, Sonya Levien, Walter Ferris, from the novel by David Garth

The Four Musketeers
★★★ PG

Historical comedy adventure 1974 · Pan/Sp · Colour · 101mins

This sequel was shot at the same time as its more illustrious predecessor, but without the knowledge of its cast, who sued producer Alexander Salkind for back-pay. Subtitled *The Revenge of Milady*, the action brings Faye Dunaway to the fore, as she seeks to trap the dashing blades by imprisoning Michael York's beloved, Raquel Welch. The original cast is obviously still in the swing of things and there is a nice demonstration of screen villainy from Christopher Lee, but director Richard Lester can't resist tilting the swashbuckling into slapstick, with uneven results. The costumes were nominated for an Oscar. ▱

Oliver Reed *Athos* • Faye Dunaway *Milady de Winter* • Michael York *D'Artagnan* • Raquel Welch *Constance Bonancieux* • Richard Chamberlain *Aramis* • Frank Finlay *Porthos* • Simon Ward *Duke of Buckingham* • Christopher Lee *Rochefort* • Charlton Heston *Cardinal Richelieu* • Geraldine Chaplin *Anne of Austria* ■ *Dir* Richard Lester • *Scr* George MacDonald Fraser, from the novel *The Three Musketeers* by Alexandre Dumas

Four Nights of a Dreamer
★★★

Drama 1971 · Fr/It · Colour · 82mins

Having made his colour debut with *A Gentle Creature*, Robert Bresson returned to Dostoyevsky for this exploration of obsessive passion and the romantic treachery of nocturnal Paris. But whereas Luchino Visconti's version of *White Nights* used theatrical settings and soft-focus imagery to heighten the impossible innocence of the artist's love for the girl he dissuades from suicide, Bresson achieves an erotic realism that makes the promise of lasting love all the more tantalising and impossible. Sensitively played by Guillaume Des Forêts and Isabelle Weingarten, but with its occasionally precious visuals and stilted dialogue, this is one of Bresson's few disappointments. In French with English subtitles.

Isabelle Weingarten *Marthe* • Guillaume Des Forêts *Jacques* • Jean-Maurice Monnoyer *The lodger* • Giorgio Maulini • Lydia Biondi [Lidia Biondi] *Marthe's mother* ■ *Dir* Robert Bresson • *Scr* Robert Bresson, from the story *White Nights* by Fyodor Dostoyevsky

The Four Poster ★★

Comedy drama 1953 · US · BW · 102mins

Although they were married in real life, Rex Harrison and Lilli Palmer were not perhaps the ideal couple to star in this adaptation of Jan de Hartog's play. (Two other thespian couples, Hume Cronyn and Jessica Tandy, and Michael

Denison and Dulcie Gray had already filled the roles on stage.) Spanning 45 years of marriage, this boudoir drama requires a little more raw emotion than the sophisticated spouses were prepared to invest, especially in the scene of the death of their soldier son. Informative, as well as amusing, the seven animated intrascenes were created by the UPA studio duo of John Hubley and Paul Julian.

Rex Harrison *John* • Lilli Palmer *Abby* ■ *Dir* Irving Reis • *Scr* Allan Scott, from the play by Jan de Hartog • *Music* Dmitri Tiomkin

Four Rooms ★ 18

Portmanteau comedy drama 1995 · US · Colour · 93mins

Proof that wonderkid Quentin Tarantino is fallible. He's the driving force behind this horribly botched portmanteau movie and he also directs and stars in *The Man from Hollywood* segment. Set in the same hotel, the four stories are loosely linked by inept bellboy Tim Roth (apparently in Jerry Lewis mode). Allison Anders's story of a witches coven is slight and silly; Alexandre Rockwell fares little better in a farcical yarn of a lover's tiff; while Tarantino's effort barely passes muster as an anecdote. The best of the bunch is Robert Rodriguez's *The Misbehavers*, a cartoon-like tale of Roth playing babysitter to a gangster's psychopathic children. The cast includes Bruce Willis, Madonna, Amanda De Cadenet and Salma Hayek, but while they obviously had a ball, you won't. ▱

Tim Roth *Ted the Bellhop* • Lawrence Bender *Long Hair Yuppy Scum* • Marisa Tomei *Margaret* • Madonna *Elspeth* • Amanda De Cadenet *Diana* • Antonio Banderas *Man* • Salma Hayek *TV dancing girl* • Quentin Tarantino *Chester* • Bruce Willis *Leo* ■ *Dir/Scr* Allison Anders, Alexandre Rockwell, Robert Rodriguez, Quentin Tarantino

The Four Seasons ★★★★ 15

Comedy drama 1981 · US · Colour · 103mins

Alan Alda's directorial debut is as waspishly decent-hearted as you'd expect from the hero of TV's *M*A*S*H*, with its exploration of American middle-class habits. Three married couples regularly take their holidays together, but find this complacent routine faltering when one husband falls for a younger woman. A rather stodgy narrative is transcended by fine performances from Carol Burnett, Len Cariou, Sandy Dennis, Jack Weston and, especially, Alda himself. Contains some swearing and brief nudity ▱

Alan Alda *Jack Burroughs* • Carol Burnett *Kate Burroughs* • Len Cariou *Nick Callan* • Sandy Dennis *Anne Callan* • Rita Moreno *Claudia Zimmer* • Jack Weston *Danny Zimmer* • Bess Armstrong *Ginny Newley* • Elizabeth Alda *Beth* • Beatrice Alda *Lisa* ■ *Dir/Scr* Alan Alda

Four Sons ★★★★

Silent First World War drama 1928 · US · BW · 100mins

This heartbreaking opus from the great director John Ford, about a widow whose sons fight on opposite sides during the First World War, is a formidable piece of cinema. There are few more moving moments than those in which the postman (superbly delineated by Albert Gran) arrives

bearing news of the sons, while the long-suffering Bavarian mother is brilliantly portrayed by Margaret Mann. The climactic sequence of her finally arriving at New York's Ellis Island will leave no handkerchief dry, and was amazingly influential on film-makers as diverse as Elia Kazan (*America, America*) and Francis Ford Coppola (*The Godfather Part II*). Fox remade the story in 1940, but the addition of sound and the efforts of director Archie Mayo could not improve on Ford's film.

James Hall *Joseph Bernle* • Margaret Mann *Mother Bernle* • Earle Foxe *Von Stomm* • Charles Morton *Johann Bernle* • Francis X Bushman Jr [Ralph Bushman] *Franz Bernle* • George Meeker *Andres Bernle* • Albert Gran *Letter Carrier* ■ *Dir* John Ford • *Scr* Philip Klein, HH Caldwell (titles), Katherine Hilliker (titles), from the story *Grandmother Bernle Learns Her Letters* by Ida Alexa Ross Wylie

Four Sons ★★

Second World War drama 1940 · US · BW · 88mins

A remake of a 1928 silent picture, updated to cover Hitler's inexorable march into Czechoslovakia, an event which has a cataclysmic impact on a mother and her four sons. One flees to America, one becomes a Nazi, another joins the resistance and the youngest fights for the Third Reich in Poland. Guess which one survives? Co-written (with Milton Sperling) by John Howard Lawson (one of the original Hollywood Ten blacklisted during the McCarthy era) and directed by Archie Mayo, it probably served its propagandist purpose well enough in 1940, even though Hitler's march across Europe dated it before release, but it seems schematic nowadays.

Don Ameche *Chris* • Eugenie Leontovich *Frau Bernie* • Mary Beth Hughes *Anna* • Alan Curtis *Karl* • George Ernest *Fritz* • Robert Lowery *Joseph* • Lionel Royce *Max Sturm* ■ *Dir* Archie Mayo • *Scr* John Howard Lawson, Milton Sperling, from a story by IAR Wylie

Four Times That Night ★★

Erotic drama 1972 · It/W Ger · Colour · 90mins

This sex comedy was a distinct change of pace for Italian horror maestro Mario Bava. Scripted by Mario Moroni and Charles Ross, it clearly owes its genesis to Akira Kurosawa's landmark treatise on the nature of real and cinematic truth, *Rashomon*, as various witnesses try to account for the scratches that appear on Brett Halsey's forehead following a date with Daniela Giordano. This might have been a sordid little story had not Bava and his assistant Sandro Battelli taken such a playful approach, but even then, it's definitely only a minor work. Italian dialogue dubbed into English.

Daniela Giordano *Tina* • Brett Halsey *Gianni* • Michael Hinz *Sergio* • Dick Randall *Duccio* ■ *Dir* Mario Bava • *Scr* Mario Moroni, Charles Ross

Four Weddings and a Funeral ★★★★★ 15

Comedy 1994 · UK · Colour · 112mins

One of the most successful British productions of all time, in all honesty, it's little more than a glorified sitcom but there is no denying it is funny, charming, at one point disarmingly poignant, and never anything less than hugely enjoyable. Mike Newell directs with an understatement that allows the rich humour in Richard Curtis's script to shine through. Hugh Grant and Andie MacDowell will probably never better their performances, while the support playing, particularly of Bafta-winning Kristin Scott Thomas and Simon Callow, is of a very high order. This is the sort of divine comedy that Grant should have confined himself to! Contains swearing. 📺 **DVD**

Hugh Grant *Charles* • Andie MacDowell *Carrie* • Kristin Scott Thomas *Fiona* • James Fleet *Tom* • Simon Callow *Gareth* • John Hannah *Matthew* • David Bower *David* • Charlotte Coleman *Scarlett* • Corin Redgrave *Hamish* • Rowan Atkinson *Father Gerald* • Anna Chancellor *Henrietta* • Rosalie Crutchley *Mrs Beaumont* ■ *Dir* Mike Newell • *Scr* Richard Curtis

Four Wives ★★

Drama   1939 · US · BW · 110mins

John Garfield caused a sensation in *Four Daughters* playing a brash misfit and musical genius who kills himself. This sequel keeps his memory alive as his young widow (Priscilla Lane) discovers she will be having his baby. Garfield also returns as a ghostly vision; elsewhere Rosemary Lane romances Eddie Albert's young doctor, while Claude Rains's other two daughters (Lola Lane, Gale Page) have their own crosses to bear. The result is trite, overlong and indifferently acted, but director Michael Curtiz generates warmth between the characters and his fluid camera style keeps up the momentum.

Priscilla Lane *Ann Lemp Borden* • Rosemary Lane *Kay Lemp* • Lola Lane *Thea Lemp Crowley* • Gale Page *Emma Lemp* • Claude Rains *Adam Lemp* • John Garfield *Mickey Borden* ■ *Dir* Michael Curtiz • *Scr* Julius J Epstein, Philip G Epstein, Maurice Hanline, from the story *Sister Act* by Fannie Hurst

Four's a Crowd ★★🄤

Romantic comedy 1938 · US · BW · 91mins

Errol Flynn as a PR man, Rosalind Russell as an ace reporter, Patric Knowles as a playboy newspaper proprietor and Olivia de Havilland as an heiress. Blend thoroughly and hand to Michael Curtiz for careful cooking. Sadly, though, the result lacks the sparkle promised by the cast and director, and the script is merely a rehash of other, better, pictures notably *The Front Page* and *Nothing Sacred* which gives it a rather jaded air. It was also a box-office failure, mainly because audiences would not accept Flynn in anything except swashbucklers or war movies.

Errol Flynn *Robert "Bob" Kensington Lansford* • Olivia de Havilland *Lorri Dillingwell* • Rosalind Russell *Jean Christy* • Patric Knowles *Patterson Buckley* • Walter Connolly *John P Dillingwell* • Hugh Herbert *Silas Jenkins* ■ *Dir* Michael Curtiz • *Scr* Casey Robinson, Sid Herzig, from the novel *All Rights Reserved* by Wallace Sullivan

Fourteen Hours ★★★★

Drama based on a true story
1951 · US · BW · 91mins

An exciting suspense drama about Richard Basehart threatening to end it

all from a New York skyscraper, gutwrenchingly directed by Henry Hathaway and based on a real-life incident. The crowd of onlookers that gathers becomes a character in itself, with stars-to-be on view including Debra Paget and Jeffrey Hunter, plus the debut of young Grace Kelly, playing an estranged wife who is prompted by Basehart's plight to take another crack at marriage. Agnes Moorehead and Robert Keith are particularly effective as the would-be suicide's parents, but the movie's actual top-liner is tough cop Paul Douglas.

Paul Douglas *Dunnigan* • Richard Basehart *Robert Cosick* • Barbara Bel Geddes *Virginia* • Debra Paget *Ruth* • Agnes Moorehead *Mrs Cosick* • Robert Keith *Mr Cosick* ■ *Dir* Henry Hathaway • *Scr* John Paxton, from the story *The Man on the Ledge* by Joel Sayre

1492: Conquest of Paradise ★★★★🄖

Historical drama
1992 · US/Sp/Fr/UK · Colour · 149mins

Three big films were made to mark the 500th anniversary of the discovery of the New World – a catastrophic *Carry On*, the dire *Christopher Columbus: the Discovery* and Ridley Scott's *1492: Conquest of Paradise*. Despite a rather wobbly first hour, when it's hard to understand Gérard Depardieu's accent or make out Sigourney Weaver's scheming Spanish queen in the gloomy light, the picture gathers momentum with the voyage, captures in dazzling imagery the actual discovery, and then produces a horrific and masterly final segment as Columbus returns on a second voyage to preside over slaughter and the raising of a giant church bell. Those looking for an old-style adventure should look elsewhere, for this is a dark, bloody and brooding piece about colonial exploitation. Woefully under-rated by many critics, it was shot in Spain and Costa Rica, looks like the millions it cost to make (and lost) and boasts an eerily atmospheric score by Vangelis. Contains violence. 📺

Gérard Depardieu *Christopher Columbus* • Armand Assante *Sanchez* • Sigourney Weaver *Queen Isabel* • Loren Dean *Older Fernando* • Angela Molina *Beatrix* • Fernando Rey *Marchena* • Michael Wincott *Moxica* • Tcheky Karyo *Pinzon* • Kevin Dunn *Captain Mendez* ■ *Dir* Ridley Scott • *Scr* Roselyne Bosch

The Fourth Man ★★★★

Psychological black comedy thriller
1983 · Neth · Colour · 102mins

An early nightmarish, and typically allegorical, fantasy from Dutch director Paul Verhoeven (*Robocop*, *Basic Instinct*) and cinematographer-turned-director Jan De Bont (*Speed*, *Twister*). Homosexual writer Jeroen Krabbé suffers horrific premonitions after he meets attractive blonde Renée Soutendijk, whose last three husbands have all died in mysterious circumstances. Is he to be her fourth victim, lured into her black widow's web by her attractive bisexual lover Thom Hoffman? Obliquely eerie, explicitly erotic and perversely hilarious, this intricate symbolic shocker is a double-edged Dutch treat. In Dutch with English subtitles.

Jeroen Krabbé *Gerard Reve* • Renée Soutendijk *Christine Halsslag* • Thom Hoffman *Herman* • Dolf de Vries *Dr De Vries* • Geert De Jong *Ria* ■ *Dir* Paul Verhoeven • *Scr* Gerard Soeteman, from a novel by Gerard Reve • *Cinematographer* Jan De Bont

The Fourth Protocol ★★🄖

Spy thriller   1987 · UK · Colour · 113mins

Before getting his big break as 007, Pierce Brosnan tried his hand at life on the other side of the wall, playing a dastardly Russian spy out to blow up an American airbase in England. Michael Caine is the less-than-super agent out to stop him, and a familiar cavalcade of British actors (plus the odd visiting American) is on hand to help or hinder him. Based on the Frederick Forsyth bestseller, but what made for diverting reading while on the way to the sun now appears tired and not particularly relevant. Contains swearing, violence and nudity. 📺

Michael Caine *John Preston* • Pierce Brosnan *Major Valeri Petrofsky* • Joanna Cassidy *Irina Vassilieva* • Ned Beatty *General Borisov* • Ray McAnally *General Karpov* ■ *Dir* John Mackenzie • *Scr* Frederick Forsyth, Richard Burridge, from the novel by Frederick Forsyth

The Fourth War ★★🄖

Thriller   1990 · US · Colour · 86mins

It's November 1988 and Roy Scheider is a gung-ho Vietnam veteran who embarks on a private war with Soviet hothead Jürgen Prochnow (himself an embittered casualty of Afghanistan) after he witnesses the death of a defector during one of his reckless sorties beyond the checkpoint. It's quite some time since the films of John Frankenheimer have done anything but disappoint and the hand of the director of such Cold War classics as *The Manchurian Candidate* and *Seven Days in May* is nowhere to be seen in this dreary piece of macho posturing set on the Czech/West German border. Contains violence and swearing. 📺

Roy Scheider *Colonel Jack Knowles* • Jürgen Prochnow *Colonel NA Valachev* • Tim Reid *Lieutenant Colonel Timothy Clark* • Lara Harris *Elena Novotna* • Harry Dean Stanton *General Roger Hackworth* ■ *Dir* John Frankenheimer • *Scr* Stephen Peters, Kenneth Ross, from the novel by Stephen Peters

The Fourth Wish ★★★

Drama   1976 · Ausl · Colour · 107mins

This Australian film about childhood death and parental resolve never once comes close to easy sentiment but instead allows genuine feelings to emerge with sensitivity and force. Because his 12-year-old son is dying from leukaemia, a father tries to grant him his every wish. John Meillon impressively balances his interpretation of the father between anxiety and determination.

John Meillon *Casey* • Robert Bettles *Sean* • Robyn Nevin *Connie* • Julie Hamilton *Jenny* • Brian Anderson *Wally* • Anne Haddy *Dr Kirk* ■ *Dir* Don Chaffey • *Scr* Michael Craig

The Fox ★★★

Drama   1967 · US · Colour · 110mins

From glamour girl to drama diva, Anne Heywood formerly Violet Pretty made

the transition in fine style marrying producer Raymond Stross and starring in this sexually risky adaptation of the DH Lawrence novella. It details the long-term relationship of lesbians Ellen (Heywood) and Jill (Sandy Dennis) that's disrupted by the arrival of handyman Paul (Keir Dullea) not so much a fox as a cat among pigeons in the lonely farmhouse that is the women's love-nest. Dennis's twitchiness is almost laughable at times, but Heywood's portrayal of dominance threatened by aching insecurity is memorably poignant.

Sandy Dennis *Jill* • Keir Dullea *Paul* • Anne Heywood *Ellen March* • Glyn Morris *Realtor* ■ *Dir* Mark Rydell • *Scr* Lewis John Carlino, Howard Koch, from the novella by DH Lawrence

Fox and His Friends ★★★★

Drama   1975 · W Ger · Colour · 123mins

Director Rainer Werner Fassbinder also plays the title role of an unemployed carnival worker in this unusual and penetrating melodrama. Picked up by an antique dealer after winning the lottery and introduced into an effete bourgeois homosexual milieu, he is exploited, abused and driven to despair. The working class victim was based on Armin Meier, one of Fassbinder's former lovers, a young butcher to whom the film is dedicated. Eerily, the film anticipated Armin's suicide by four years. Although an honest portrayal of homosexual relationships, Fassbinder's absorbing film is ultimately more concerned with class exploitation. In German with English subtitles.

Rainer Werner Fassbinder *Fox* • Peter Chatel *Eugen* • Karl-Heinz Bohm [Karlheinz Böhm] *Max* • Harry Baer *Philip* • Adrian Hoven *Father* • Ulla Jacobsson *Mother* • Christiane Maybach *Hedwig* ■ *Dir* Rainer Werner Fassbinder • *Scr* Christian Hohoff, Rainer Werner Fassbinder

The Fox and the Hound ★★★🄤

Animated adventure
1981 · US · Colour · 80mins

Disney animation was still reckoned to be in the doldrums when this charming tale of animal friendship was produced, and it probably has a lower profile than it deserves. A young hound pup is befriended by a fox cub and they become firm chums. Once grown, the hound warns his foxy friend to keep away from the hunt and his cruel master, but the fox proves his courage when he saves the hound from a marauding bear. Hound returns the favour when his wild friend is pursued by the pack in a family parable about the power of friendship. 📺

Mickey Rooney *Tod* • Kurt Russell *Copper* • Pearl Bailey *Big Mama* • Jack Albertson *Amos Slade* • Sandy Duncan *Vixey* ■ *Dir* Art Stevens, Ted Berman, Richard Rich • *Scr* Larry Clemmons, Ted Berman, Peter Young, Steve Hulett, David Michener, Burny Mattinson, Earl Kress, Vance Gerry, from the novel by Daniel P Mannix

Fox Movietone Follies of 1929 ★★

Musical 1929 · US · BW and Colour · 80mins

This was Fox's riposte to MGM's *Broadway Melody* and *Hollywood Revue* of 1929 and to Warner Bros' *Show of Shows* and *On with the Show*, all of which were star-packed extravaganzas designed to show off the new wonder of the age. Fox really went to town with this one: not only did it use early Technicolor, but the film was also shot in the 70mm process called Grandeur, with a separate soundtrack offering fantastic sound quality. Pity they didn't take as much care over the laboured plot, substandard songs and corny dance routines. For collectors of historic movie curios only.

John Breeden *George Shelby* • Lola Lane *Lila Beaumont* • DeWitt Jennings *Jay Darrell* • Sharon Lynne *Ann Foster* • Arthur Stone *Al Leaton* • Stepin Fetchit *Swifty* • Warren Hymer *Martin* ■ *Dir* David Butler, Marcel Silver • *Scr* David Butler, William K Wells

Foxes ★★★ 15

Drama   1980 · US · Colour · 101mins

Ex-TV commercial director Adrian Lyne made his feature film debut with this slick 1979 movie about four teenage girls and their problems with life and men. A young Jodie Foster is Jeanie, the straight arrow sorting out her friends, which include podgy, unloved Madge (Marilyn Kagan), compulsive liar Deirdre (Kandice Stroh), and abused hooker Annie (ex-Runaways singer and member Cherie Currie). Foster's *Bugsy Malone* co-star Scott Baio provides the male interest, but it's really one to watch for the girls, who all overcome a clichéd script to give a good depiction of what it was like to be a teenager at the end of the seventies. ▭

Jodie Foster *Jeanie* • Scott Baio *Brad* • Sally Kellerman *Mary* • Randy Quaid *Jay* • Marilyn Kagan *Madge* • Kandice Stroh *Deirdre* • Lois Smith *Mrs Axman* • Adam Faith *Bryan* • Cherie Currie *Annie* ■ *Dir* Adrian Lyne • *Scr* Gerald Ayres • *Producer* David Puttnam, Gerald Ayres

The Foxes of Harrow ★★

Historical drama   1947 · US · BW · 117mins

This overlong adaptation of Frank Yerby's popular Southern novel would have benefited from more sensible casting, Technicolor photography and a more involved director than John M Stahl at the helm. Rex Harrison is miscast as the Irish rogue who gambles his way to the top, while Maureen O'Hara plays her role with a grimness which suggests how unhappy she must have been to be subjected to her co-star's infamous on-set arrogance. The production values are undoubtedly attractive, however, and the art direction was unsurprisingly nominated for an Oscar.

Rex Harrison *Stephen Fox* • Maureen O'Hara *Odalie D'Arceneaux* • Richard Haydn *Andre LeBlanc* • Victor McLaglen *Capt Mike Farrell* • Vanessa Brown *Aurore D'Arceneaux* • Patricia Medina *Desiree* • Gene Lockhart *The Vicomte* ■ *Dir* John M Stahl • *Scr* Wanda Tuchock, from the novel by Frank Yerby • *Art Director* Lyle Wheeler, Maurice Ransford

Foxfire ★★

Romantic drama   1955 · US · Colour · 91mins

A soppy concoction with Jeff Chandler as a half-breed Apache, a mining engineer digging for gold in Arizona and settling down to married bliss with… Jane Russell? Yes, it's love across the cultural divide, but despite the

improbability of the match, it carries on without batting an eyelid. The trade magazine *Variety* apparently described Chandler as "churlish", "surly" and generally a bit of a heel. On the other hand, he did sing the theme song, wich was co-written with Mr Pink Panther himself, Henry Mancini.

Jane Russell *Amanda* • Jeff Chandler *Jonathan Dartland* • Dan Duryea *Hugh Slater* • Mara Corday *Maria* • Robert Simon *Ernest Tyson* • Frieda Inescort *Mrs Lawrence* • Barton MacLane *Jim Mablett* ■ *Dir* Joseph Pevney • *Scr* Ketti Frings, from a novel by Anya Seton

Foxfire ★★★

Drama   1987 · US · Colour · 118mins

Not the 1955 Jane Russell movie, but a 1987 TV-movie adaptation of the Broadway play, featuring husband-and-wife team Hume Cronyn (who co-wrote the stage play with Susan Cooper) and Jessica Tandy. Tandy won a Tony for the role on stage, and an Emmy for her performance here as an independent-minded widow unwilling to abandon her home in the Blue Ridge Mountains, in memory of her dead husband. It's an often moving tale, beautifully performed by Tandy and Cronyn. Country music star John Denver, who died in 1997 in a plane crash, also features.

Jessica Tandy *Annie Nations* • Hume Cronyn *Hector Nations* • John Denver *Dillard Nations* • Gary Grubbs *Prince Carpenter* • Harriet Hall *Holly* • Collin Wilcox-Paxton *Madge Burton* • Joshua Bryson *Heckie* ■ *Dir* Jud Taylor • *Scr* Susan Cooper, Hume Cronyn, from the play by Susan Cooper, Hume Cronyn

Foxfire ★★★ 18

Drama   1996 · US · Colour · 97mins

Four teenage girls discover their common strengths when they tire of an abusive teacher and the negligent school system that ignores them. Hedy Burress is the film's focus, with the ever-smirking Angelina Jolie as "Legs", the independent wanderer who floats into the lives of the other girls just as they need that extra push into rebellion. The male characters are painted rather flatly as either abusive or obtuse, mostly to give the girls more incentive to revolt. This probably would have had more impact if, like the book that inspired it, the film had been set in its original fifties milieu. Contains swearing, violence and sexual situations. ▭

Hedy Burress *Maddy Wirtz* • Angelina Jolie *Legs Sadovsky* • Jenny Lewis *Rita Faldes* • Jenny Shimizu *Goldie Goldman* • Sarah Rosenberg *Violet Kahn* ■ *Dir* Annette Haywood-Carter • *Scr* Elizabeth White, from the novel by Joyce Carol Oates

Foxhole in Cairo ★★

Spy drama   1960 · UK · BW · 83mins

Unremarkable wartime espionage drama, with James Robertson-Justice and Adrian Hoven as British and German spies playing hide and seek with the plans for El Alamein. Fenella Fielding makes a sexy Jewish resistance fighter saved by Robertson-Justice, who prevents the Desert Fox from winning the Battle of Algiers. Albert Lieven is a convincing Rommel

and if you blink you'll miss Michael Caine as a German soldier.

James Robertson-Justice *Captain Robertson DSO* • Adrian Hoven *John Eppler* • Niall MacGinnis *Radek* • Peter Van Eyck *Count Almazy* • Fenella Fielding *Yvette* • Albert Lieven *Rommel* • Michael Caine *Weber* ■ *Dir* John Moxey [John Llewellyn Moxey] • *Scr* Leonard Mosley, Donald Taylor, from the novel *The Cat and the Mice* by Leonard Mosley

Foxy Brown ★★ 18

Blaxploitation thriller   1974 · US · Colour · 87mins

"Don't mess aroun' with Foxy Brown" read the shoutline for Pam Grier's fourth collaboration with director Jack Hill. However, far more revealing is the poster copy that sums up the slam-bam nature of one of blaxploitation's low points: "She's got drive and that ain't jive. She don't bother to bring 'em back alive!" Posing as a hooker to snare the drug dealers who killed her cop boyfriend, Grier is so preoccupied with kinky sex and violence she has to leave what little acting there is to Antonio Fargas, who plays her dopey brother. ▭

Pam Grier *Foxy Brown* • Antonio Fargas *Link Brown* • Peter Brown *Steve Elias* • Terry Carter *Michael Anderson* • Kathryn Loder *Katherine Wall* • Harry Holcombe *Judge Fenton* • Juanita Brown *Claudia* ■ *Dir/Scr* Jack Hill

Fragment of Fear ★★ 15

Thriller   1970 · UK · Colour · 91mins

The poster promised "A Phantasmagoria of Fright", but director Richard C Sarafian's disappointing adaptation of John Bingham's novel delivers very little of anything. The initial premise is promising. Writer David Hemmings is investigating the murder of his aunt (Flora Robson) in Pompeii. The problem is, he's a reformed drug addict, and clues to the mystery keep being complicated by weird hallucinations. Is he going insane? A Euro-pudding cast – Gayle Hunnicutt, Wilfrid Hyde White, Adolfo Celi – provide some answers before the whole flimsy farrago falls apart. ▭

David Hemmings *Tim Brett* • Gayle Hunnicutt *Juliet Bristow* • Flora Robson *Lucy Dawson* • Wilfrid Hyde White *Mr Copsey* • Daniel Massey *Major Ricketts* • Adolfo Celi *Bardoni* ■ *Dir* Richard C Sarafian • *Scr* Paul Dehn, from the novel by John Bingham

Framed ★★

Crime drama   1947 · US · BW · 82mins

Even after *Gilda*, Glenn Ford was still serving time on the treadmill of Columbia's programme-fillers, this one a crime thriller in which he's an unemployed mining engineer who becomes the fall-guy for a bank robbery. He is set up by robber Janis Carter, who uses him because he looks like her accomplice Barry Sullivan, but she ends up falling for Ford instead. The blonde Miss Carter was formerly an opera singer, who ended up hosting TV game shows in the fifties.

Glenn Ford *Mike Lambert* • Janis Carter *Paula Craig* • Barry Sullivan *Stephen Price* • Edgar Buchanan *Jeff Cunningham* • Karen Morley *Mrs Price* • Jim Bannon *Jack Woodworth* ■ *Dir* Richard Wallace • *Scr* Ben Maddow, from the story by Jack Patrick

Framed ★ 18

Action crime   1975 · US · Colour · 100mins

You've seen this one a billion times before but never one more grauitously violent. Nashville gambler Joe Don Baker is put in jail for accidentally killing a sheriff and, after being paroled, goes after the corrupt cops who set him up. This is a typical seventies revenge saga characterised by reprehensible *Death Wish* viciousness. Unsurprising, really, as director, writer and star had previously collaborated on *Walking Tall*. ▭

Joe Don Baker *Ron Lewis* • Conny Van Dyke *Susan Barrett* • Gabriel Dell *Vince Greeson* • John Marley *Sal Viccarrone* ■ *Dir* Phil Karlson • *Scr* Mort Briskin, from a novel by Art Powers, Mike Misenheimer

Framed ★★ 15

Comedy   1990 · US · Colour · 87mins

Jeff Goldblum has often been the sole reason for watching a mediocre movie, following such successes as David Cronenberg's *The Fly* with misfires like Mel Smith's romantic comedy *The Tall Guy*. Here once again he is the only sign of life in a caper which negotiates the AZ of predictability. In the guise of an art forger framed in more ways than one, Goldblum scatters the film with quirkiness and humour, but Kristin Scott Thomas has too little to work with as his double-crossing girlfriend. Contains swearing. ▭

Jeff Goldblum *Wiley* • Kristin Scott Thomas *Kate* • Todd Graff *Pete* • Abdul Salaam El Razzac *Agent Joak* • Michael Lerner *Elliot Shane* • James Hong *Mr Chang* ■ *Dir* Dean Parisot • *Scr* Gary Rosen

Frameup ★★★

Crime comedy drama   1993 · US · Colour and BW · 91mins

Doomed young killers have long fascinated American directors (*Badlands*, *Natural Born Killers*) but this little-seen gem is one of the bleakest examinations of the subject. Howard Swain is the small-time crook who hooks up with bored waitress Nancy Carlin to make a new life in California. Their aimless road trip takes in sex, sightseeing and – finally – murder. Unlike other movies with similar themes, writer/director Jon Jost shows absolutely no sympathy for his pathetic leads, and although that provokes some uncomfortable laughs, his jarring vision chills to the bone.

Howard Swain *Ricky Lee Gruber* • Nancy Carlin *Beth-Ann Bolet* ■ *Dir/Scr* Jon Jost

Frances ★★★★ 15

Biography   1982 · US · Colour · 133mins

Jessica Lange is mesmerising in this uneven biopic of the spirited, politically outspoken thirties actress Frances Farmer, who fell from grace in Hollywood and ended up institutionalised in an asylum where she later underwent a lobotomy. Although the film only touches on the problems in Hollywood which Frances faced, instead focusing on her hospitalisations, this is an often riveting drama which benefits from a superb central performance from Lange (who at times looks eerily like Farmer), and solid support from Sam Shepard

(as Farmer's love) and Kim Stanley as her fame-hungry mother.

Jessica Lange *Frances Farmer* • Sam Shepard *Harry York* • Kim Stanley *Lillian Farmer* • Bart Burns *Ernest Farmer* • Christopher Pennock *Dick Steele* • James Karen *Judge* • Gerald S O'Loughlin *Lobotomy doctor* ■ Dir Graeme Clifford • Scr Eric Bergren, Christopher DeVore, Nicholas Kazan

The Franchise Affair ★★

Mystery 1950 · UK · BW · 88mins

Adapted from the novel by Josephine Tey (which was itself based on actual events), this tale of superstition and recrimination should keep us guessing right up to the moment the mystery is sensationally cleared up. But the presence of postwar British cinema's golden couple, Michael Denison and Dulcie Gray, deprives the story of much of its suspense. As one of the women accused of kidnap and torture by the hysterical Ann Stephens, Gray fails to generate sufficient ambiguity, while lawyer Denison's clipped decency lacks the indignation that might have injected some much-needed impetus.

Michael Denison *Robert Blair* • Dulcie Gray *Marion Sharpe* • Anthony Nicholls *Kevin McDermott* • Marjorie Fielding *Mrs Sharpe* • Athene Seyler *Aunt Lin* • Ann Stephens *Betty Kane* ■ Dir Lawrence Huntington • Scr Robert Hall, Lawrence Huntington, from the novel by Josephine Tey

Francis ★★ U

Comedy 1949 · US · BW · 90mins

The adventures of Francis the talking mule (voiced by Chill Wills) proved so successful that they led to an unofficial comedy series, critically unloved but massively popular with the picture-going public. In this first entry, the pesky mule helps Donald O'Connor become a war hero. O'Connor felt that being Francis's stooge cost him true stardom, and he may not have been far wrong. The series was used to try out new studio contractees – look out for Anthony (later Tony) Curtis in this one – while director Arthur Lubin later worked with another talking horse on TV's *Mr Ed*.

Donald O'Connor *Lt Peter Stirling* • Patricia Medina *Maureen Gelder* • ZaSu Pitts *Valerie Humpert* • Ray Collins *Colonel Hooker* • John McIntire *General Stevens* • Anthony Curtis [Tony Curtis] *Captain Jones* • Chill Wills *Francis* ■ Dir Arthur Lubin • Scr David Stern, from his novel

Francis Gary Powers: the True Story of the U-2 ★★★ U

Cold war drama 1976 · US · Colour · 98mins

Based on Gary Powers's memoirs, this TV movie stars Lee Majors as the pilot who became the small change of history when he was shot down over Russia during a spy mission. Majors is surprisingly effective as a man caught up in the seemingly irresistible forces of the Cold War. His complex relationship with Soviet interrogator (Nehemiah Persoff) strips the glamour from a James Bond-like situation, revealing the victimisation Powers suffered both then and later back home in America.

Lee Majors *Francis Gary Powers* • Noah Beery [Noah Beery Jr] *Oliver Powers* • Nehemiah Persoff *Rudenko* • Brooke Bundy *Mrs Powers* • William Daniels *Bissell* ■ Dir Delbert Mann • Scr Robert E Thompson, from the book *Operation Overflight* by Francis Gary Powers

Francis, God's Jester ★★★★ U

Drama 1950 · It · BW · 96mins

Based on the writings of St Francis of Assisi and shot with such a firm grasp of period and place that it feels like a newsreel of 13th-century Italy, this truly inspiring picture is not a saintly homage, but a neorealist study in faith and human decency. Director Roberto Rossellini draws extraordinary performances from his mainly non-professional cast, notably from Nazario Gerardi, who was himself a Franciscan friar. Ironically, the only weak link is established star Aldo Fabrizi's eye-rolling villainy as a local warlord. Co-authored by Italian director Federico Fellini, the script focuses on the simple joys of life rather than theology and is guaranteed to raise the spirits. In Italian with English subtitles..

Aldo Fabrizi *Nicolaio* • Arabella Lemaitre *Saint Clair* • Brother Nazario Gerardi *Saint Francis* ■ Dir Roberto Rossellini • Scr Roberto Rossellini, Federico Fellini

Francis of Assisi ★ U

Biographical drama 1961 · US · Colour · 105mins

This stilted biopic of the patron saint of animals has a woefully miscast Bradford Dillman as Francis – only Pat Boone or Frankie Avalon could have been worse. Even more surprising is that Michael Curtiz should have agreed to direct it. Those expecting cuddly creatures will be disappointed, as this focuses on the life of Francis the warrior who, like El Cid before him, sorts out rival Christians and Arabs while fighting for Sicily's liberation before going into retreat.

Bradford Dillman *Giovanni Di Bernardone* • Dolores Hart *Clare Scefi* • Stuart Whitman *Paolo* • Pedro Armendariz *Sultan* ■ Dir Michael Curtiz • Scr Eugene Vale, James Forsyth, Jack Thomas, from the novel *The Joyful Beggar* by Louis De Wohl

Frank and Jesse ★★ 15

Western 1995 · US · Colour · 101mins

Writer/director Robert Boris assembled a willing young cast for what he clearly intended to be a revisionist western. But, the life and crimes of Frank and Jesse James have been re-examined so many times that there is little left to say. Boris predictably gives Rob Lowe's Jesse a conscience and suggests the James, Younger and Ford brothers were victims of a society that betrayed them after the South's defeat in the Civil War. But, more interestingly, he also explores the corruption and brutality of the forces of law and order, respresented by William Atherton's egotistical detective.

Rob Lowe *Jesse James* • Bill Paxton *Frank James* • Randy Travis *Cole Younger* • William Atherton *Allan Pinkerton* • Todd Field *Bob Younger* • Alexis Arquette *Charlie Ford* • Dana Wheeler-Nicholson *Annie* • Maria Pitillo *Zee James* ■ Dir/Scr Robert Boris

Frankenhooker ★★★ 18

Comedy horror 1990 · US · Colour · 80mins

A terrifying tale of sluts and bolts! Cult director Frank Henenlotter (of *Basket Case* notoriety) sewed together one of his best lampoons with this madcap gore parody revealing his usual bad taste and warped sense of humour. Mad inventor James Lorinz accidentally chops up his girlfriend in a power lawnmower accident, saves her head and finds body parts to remake her from prostitutes addicted to the supercrack drug he's developed. Although paying homage to the bizarre sexy shockers of Spanish director Jesus Franco, and pushing cartoon violence to the limit, Henenlotter's trump card is Lorinz, who turns in a charismatic performance laden with wit and pathos.

James Lorinz *Jeffrey Franken* • Patty Mullen *Elizabeth* • Louise Lasser *Jeffrey's Mom* • Charlotte Helmkamp *Honey* • Joseph Gonzalez *Zorro* • Shirley Stoler *Spike* • Lia Chang *Crystal* ■ Dir Frank Henenlotter • Scr Frank Henenlotter, Robert Martin

Frankenstein ★★★★★ PG

Classic horror 1931 · US · BW · 68mins

"It's Alive!" Shocking in its day, and still a genuinely creepy experience, director James Whale's primitive yet enthralling interpretation of Mary Shelley's classic tale of man playing God is the most influential genre movie ever made. Its success kick-started the golden age of horror for Universal Studios and provided inspiration for scores of imitators and successors. Boris Karloff breathes miraculous life into his definitive monster portrayal: the most touching moment is the creature reaching up to grasp a ray of sunlight. A superb cast, imaginative set design and Whale's innovative direction using bizarre camera angles create a remarkably tense and melancholy atmosphere.

Colin Clive *Dr Frankenstein* • Mae Clarke *Elizabeth* • Boris Karloff *The Monster* • John Boles *Victor* • Edward Van Sloan *Dr Waldman* • Dwight Frye *Fritz, The Dwarf* • Frederick Kerr *Baron* • Lionel Belmore *Burgomaster* • Michael Mark *Ludwig, peasant father* ■ Dir James Whale • Scr Garrett Fort, Francis Edwards Faragoh, John L Balderston, Robert Florey, from the novel by Mary Shelley, from the play by Peggy Webling • Cinematographer Arthur Edeson • Art Director Charles D Hall • Make-up Jack Pierce

Frankenstein ★★

Horror 1973 · US · Colour · 130mins

The same year as he directed *Dracula*, Dan Curtis produced and co-wrote this doggedly undistinguished version of the Mary Shelley classic as a two-part, three-hour mini-series. Much of the threadbare padding is thankfully missing in the cut-down video version starring miscast Robert Foxworth as the rebellious baron and gentle giant Bo Svenson as his sympathetic monster. Hammy performances can't disguise the cheapness of the enterprise or the pedestrian direction by Glenn Jordan.

Robert Foxworth *Dr Frankenstein* • Susan Strasberg *Elisabeth* • Bo Svenson *Creature* • Heidi Vaughan *Agatha* • Philip Bourneuf • Alphonse Frankenstein ■ Dir Glenn Jordan • Scr Sam Hall, Richard Landaur, from the novel by Mary Shelley

Frankenstein ★★★ 15

Horror 1992 · US/UK · Colour · 111mins

Made for cable television by David Wickes, the writer/producer/director of the TV mini-series *Jack the Ripper* and *Jekyll & Hyde*, this faithful adaptation of the classic tale is remarkably similar in tone and style to Kenneth Branagh's *Mary Shelley's Frankenstein* (1994). Patrick Bergin is good as the Baron who duplicates his own body into the unfinished Randy Quaid, and John Mills plays the blind hermit. Shot in England and Poland, this richly ornate version is told as one long flashback to a ship's captain.

Patrick Bergin *Victor Frankenstein* • Randy Quaid *The Monster* • John Mills *Delacey* • Lambert Wilson *Clerval* • Fiona Gillies *Elizabeth* ■ Dir David Wickes • Scr David Wickes, from the novel by Mary Shelley

Frankenstein and the Monster from Hell ★★ 15

Horror 1973 · UK · Colour · 90mins

The sixth Hammer *Frankenstein* is a stylish return to their fifties' gothic roots, and is a fitting end to the series. Peter Cushing returned as the obsessed Baron Frankenstein, this time creating a new monster (Dave Prowse) from the lunatic inmates of Carlsbad's asylum for the criminally insane. Hammer protégé Shane Briant engagingly plays his willing disciple, while Madeline Smith stars as a mute girl in this efficiently horrifying exercise, packed with gruesome close-ups and laboratory black humour.

Peter Cushing *Baron Frankenstein* • Shane Briant *Dr Simon Helder* • Dave Prowse *Creature* • Madeline Smith *Sarah, the Angel* • Bernard Lee *Tarmut* • Norman Mitchell *Policeman* • Patrick Troughton *Body snatcher* ■ Dir Terence Fisher • Scr John Elder [Anthony Hinds]

Frankenstein Created Woman ★★★ 15

Horror 1966 · UK · Colour · 87mins

Considered by Hammer aficionados to be the best Frankenstein made by the House of Horror, this offbeat entry finds the good doctor experimenting with soul transference. Re-animating the corpse of a young girl (Susan Denberg), the ever-dependable Peter Cushing gives it the soul of her boyfriend, who was wrongly guillotined for murder. The chilling result is a vengeful creature luring his/her enemies to remote places, promising romance and delivering death instead. Terence Fisher's neat balance of fairy-tale fear, psychological horror, murky sexuality and engaging lunacy makes this a fine addition to the genre.

Peter Cushing *Baron Frankenstein* • Susan Denberg *Christina* • Thorley Walters *Dr Hertz* • Robert Morris *Hans* • Peter Blythe *Anton* • Barry Warren *Karl* • Derek Fowlds *Johann* • Alan MacNaughtan *Kleve* ■ Dir Terence Fisher • Scr John Elder [Anthony Hinds]

U = SUITABLE FOR ALL Uc = SUITABLE FOR ALL, ESPECIALLY FOR YOUNG CHILDREN (VIDEO ONLY) PG = PARENTAL GUIDANCE

Frankenstein Meets the Wolf Man ★★★
Horror   1943 · US · BW · 73mins

The fifth feature in Universal's series was the first time two celebrity monsters shared the screen. Picking up where both *The Wolfman* (1941) and *The Ghost of Frankenstein* (1942) left off, this entertaining sequel has werewolf Lon Chaney Jr seeking out the dead Frankenstein's diary, containing the cure for his lycanthropy, and stumbling across the monster (Bela Lugosi in his only appearance as the creature) encased in ice. Not particularly horrific, director Roy William Neill's monster mish-mash is still charming fun because of the skilled acting, cheap thrills and trademark Universal back-lot atmosphere.

Lon Chaney Jr *The Wolf Man/Lawrence Talbot* • Ilona Massey *Baroness Elsa Frankenstein* • Patric Knowles *Dr Mannering* • Lionel Atwill *Mayor* • Bela Lugosi *Monster* • Maria Ouspenskaya *Maleva* ■ *Dir* Roy William Neill • *Scr* Curt Siodmak

Frankenstein Meets the Devil Fish ★★
Monster horror
1964 · Jap/US · Colour · 87mins

One of the more inventive re-workings of the *Frankenstein* myth collapses into a typical Toho monster battle in *Godzilla* director Inoshiro Honda's daffy spectacular. A young kid eats the Hiroshima-infected heart of the Frankenstein monster and grows into a 30-foot tall mutated caveman, who eventually saves Japan's rebuilding programme from the rampaging dinosaur Baragon. Nick Adams is the friendly American scientist in a ridiculous, yet enormously fun, addition to the Japanese monster hall of fame.

Nick Adams *Dr James Bowen* • Tadao Takashima *Scientist* • Kumi Mizuno *Woman doctor* ■ *Dir* Inoshiro Honda • *Scr* Kaoru Mabuchi, from a synopsis by Jerry Sohl, from a story by Reuben Bercovitch

Frankenstein Must Be Destroyed ★★★ 18
Horror   1969 · UK · Colour · 96mins

The fifth of Hammer's Frankenstein series is graced by an incisive performance from Peter Cushing, up to his old tricks as the Baron performing brain transplants. Freddie Jones is astonishing as the anguished victim of the transplant, whose wife fails to recognise him and rejects him, prompting a revenge plan. The gothic gore is once more directed with spirited skill and economy by Terence Fisher (his fourth in the series), although the most memorable Grand Guignol scare has a buried body bursting through the earth because of a broken water pipe. ▭

Peter Cushing *Baron Frankenstein* • Simon Ward *Dr Karl Holst* • Veronica Carlson *Anna Spengler* • Freddie Jones *Prof Richter* • Thorley Walters *Insp Frisch* ■ *Dir* Terence Fisher • *Scr* Bert Batt, from a story by Anthony Nelson Keys, Bert Batt

Frankenstein – 1970 ★
Horror   1958 · US · BW · 82mins

This hugely inept plummet into gothic fakery is significant only in the fact that for the first time in his career Boris Karloff played the Baron and not the creature. Karloff is the grandson of the deceased and disfigured (courtesy of Nazi torturers) Baron Frankenstein, who finds himself so strapped for cash to buy an atomic reactor with which to resuscitate his latest creation that he allows a television crew into the family castle for a touch of *Through the Keyhole* Transylvanian-style. A total waste of time. Howard W Koch directs as if in a coma, with Karloff hamming it up as if it were an Olympic event.

Boris Karloff *Baron Victor von Frankenstein* • Tom Duggan *Mike Shaw* • Jana Lund *Carolyn Hayes* • Don "Red" Barry [Donald Barry] *Douglas Row* ■ *Dir* Howard W Koch • *Scr* Richard Landau, George Worthing Yates, from a story by Aubrey Schenck, Charles A Moses

Frankenstein: the College Years ★★ PG
Comedy   1991 · US · Colour · 88mins

Lightweight but mildly amusing spin on Mary Shelley's venerable horror classic, which is firmly pitched at a family audience. William Ragsdale (*Fright Night*), and Christopher Daniel Barnes play a pair of medical students who inadvertently create their own monster, which they name Frank N Stein. It's a long way from the original, but it's attractively played by the two leads, and there is solid support from Larry Miller. ▭

William Ragsdale *Mark Chrisman* • Christopher Daniel Barnes *Jay Butterman* • Larry Miller *Albert Loman* • Vincent Hammond *Frank N Stein* • Andrea Elson *Andi Richmond* ■ *Dir* Tom Shadyac • *Scr* Bryant Christ, John Trevor Wolff

Frankenstein: the True Story ★★★★
Horror   1973 · US · Colour · 122mins

Kenneth Branagh's 1994 version of the classic horror tale made much of its fidelity to the source novel, but this earlier version (made for US television) remains among the most faithful of the *Frankenstein* adaptations. The production is notable for the sympathy with which the monster is portrayed by Michael Sarrazin, minus the once obligatory nuts and bolts, and his relationship with his creator (Leonard Whiting) has a tragic resonance. The film is intelligently scripted by Christopher Isherwood and boasts a distinguished cast of supporting players including John Gielgud, Ralph Richardson and a pre-*Doctor Who* Tom Baker.

James Mason *Dr Polidori* • Leonard Whiting *Dr Victor Frankenstein* • David McCallum *Henry Clerval* • Jane Seymour *Agatha/Prima* • Michael Sarrazin *The creature* • Nicola Pagett *Elizabeth Fanschawe* • Ralph Richardson *Mr Lacey* • John Gielgud *Chief Constable* • Tom Baker *Sea captain* ■ *Dir* Jack Smight • *Scr* Christopher Isherwood, Don Bachardy, from the novel by Mary Shelley

Frankenstein Unbound ★★★ 18
Science-fiction horror
1990 · US · Colour · 82mins

After nearly 20 years in retirement Roger Corman returned to directing with an engagingly loopy rewriting of the Frankenstein myth. Based on the novel by Brian W Aldiss, this camp confection jumbles time travel, Mary Shelley's circle of friends, her monstrous fictional creation, dream sequences and an apocalyptic future for a mind-boggling baroque soap opera. More fun, and far scarier, than any other recent *Frankenstein* you might care to mention, Corman's endearing reliance on his trademark terror skills means it feels like he's never been away. Contains violence and sex scenes. ▭

John Hurt *Dr Joseph Buchanan* • Raul Julia *Dr Victor Frankenstein* • Bridget Fonda *Mary Godwin Shelley* • Jason Patric *Lord Byron* • Michael Hutchence *Percy Shelley* • Nick Brimble *The Monster* ■ *Dir* Roger Corman • *Scr* Roger Corman, FX Feeney, from the novel by Brian W Aldiss

Frankie & Johnny ★★ U
Musical   1966 · US · Colour · 83mins

No, not Al Pacino and Michelle Pfeiffer in a diner, but the Elvis Presley film version of the old jazz/folk song standard. This is gaudy and bright, but, like most of Presley's films from this period, it has an air of having just been thrown together. The Mississippi riverboat setting is undeniably attractive, but it's simply inexcusable to use repeat footage of the title number in the finale reprise. Presley and Donna Douglas (Elly May in the *Beverly Hillbillies*) pair sweetly together, and the songs pass muster, with *Hard Luck* being the standout, but this is merely a pleasant time-filler. ▭

Elvis Presley *Johnny* • Donna Douglas *Frankie* • Harry Morgan *Cully* • Sue Ane Langdon *Mitzi* • Nancy Kovack *Nelly Bly* • Audrey Christie *Peg* ■ *Dir* Frederick De Cordova • *Scr* Alex Gottlieb, from a story by Nat Perrin

Frankie & Johnny ★★★★ 15
Romantic drama
1991 · US · Colour · 112mins

A moving and often very funny romantic drama, with Al Pacino and Michelle Pfeiffer as the short-order cook and the waitress who fall hesitantly in love. It does take a major suspension of the imagination to see this gorgeous duo as lonely hearts rejects, but they act their way out of the hole. Pfeiffer in particular shows what a fine actress she can be with a good script. What lifts this particular romantic tale above the dross is the realistic air of vulnerability and fear that characterises the halting affair. Contains swearing. ▭

Michelle Pfeiffer *Frankie* • Al Pacino *Johnny* • Hector Elizondo *Nick* • Nathan Lane *Tim* • Jane Morris *Nedda* • Greg Lewis *Tino* • Al Fann *Luther* • Kate Nelligan *Cora* ■ *Dir* Garry Marshall • *Scr* Terrence McNally, from his play *Frankie and Johnny in the Clair de Lune*

Frankie Starlight ★★★ 15
Romantic comedy
1995 · US/Ire · Colour · 96mins

Is this offbeat drama, based on the reminiscences of a dwarf novelist, a charmer that slipped through the net or trifling whimsy? Co-scripted by Chet Raymo from his novel, and clearly influenced by *My Left Foot*, the film has its moments, as wartime refugee Anne Parillaud falls for Irish customs officer Gabriel Byrne and then Texan drifter Matt Dillon. There are also two splendid performances from Alan Pentony and Corban Walker as the young and adult Frankie, the son whose love of stars and fascination with his mother's amours result in a bestseller. It's all amiable enough, but promises more than it delivers. Contains swearing and nudity ▭

Anne Parillaud *Bernadette De Bois* • Matt Dillon *Terry Klout* • Gabriel Byrne *Jack Kelly* • Rudi Davies *Emma Kelly* • Georgina Cates *Young Emma* • Corban Walker *Frank Bois* ■ *Dir* Michael Lindsay-Hogg • *Scr* Chet Raymo, Ronan O'Leary, from the novel *The Dork of Cork* by Chet Raymo

Frank's Greatest Adventure ★★
Satire   1967 · US · Colour · 78mins

Shot in 1965, shown at Cannes in 1967 and shelved until 1969, this satire is the first solo feature by the director of *The Right Stuff* and *The Unbearable Lightness of Being*, Philip Kaufman. It was also the first screen appearance by Jon Voight, who plays a Mafia victim who dreams of coming back from the dead to wipe everyone out in comic-strip fashion. It's very much a product of its time, influenced by the French New Wave and Godard in particular, and feels rather dated now.

Jon Voight *Frank/False Frank* • Monique Van Vooren *Plethora* • Joan Darling *Lois* • Severn Darden *Doctor/Claude* • Anthony Holland *Alfred* • Lou Gilbert *Boss* • Ben Carruthers *The Cat* ■ *Dir/Scr* Philip Kaufman

Frantic ★★★★ 15
Thriller   1988 · US · Colour · 114mins

A variation on the Dirk Bogarde 1950 film *So Long at the Fair*, Roman Polanski makes this account of doctor Harrison Ford looking for his missing wife in an antagonistic Paris deeply disturbing. When Ford's wife Betty Buckley disappears from their hotel suite, reality becomes nightmare and solid citizen Ford resorts to increasingly desperate measures to find her. Emmanuelle Seigner, as a punkish free spirit, is a major flaw, but as a whole the movie is a bad dream of surreal, often funny, conviction. It's a Hitchcockian idea, but Polanski embellishes it with his own baleful theme of the uneasy nature of human existence. Contains swearing, brief nudity and drug use. ▭ *DVD*

Harrison Ford *Dr Richard Walker* • Emmanuelle Seigner *Michelle* • Betty Buckley *Sondra Walker* • John Mahoney *Williams* • Jimmy Ray Weeks [Jimmie Ray Weeks] *Shaap* • Yorgo Voyagis *Kidnapper* • David Huddleston *Peter* • Gérard Klein *Gaillard* • Jacques Ciron *Hotel manager* ■ *Dir* Roman Polanski • *Scr* Gérard Brach, Roman Polanski

Frantz Fanon: Black Skin White Mask ★★★
Documentary   1996 · UK/Fr · Colour · 70mins

Isaac Julien's portrait of the author of the freedom's fighter's "bible", *The Wretched of the Earth*, is a skilful combination of archive footage, contemporary interviews and dramatic reconstructions. Equally compelling as his earlier *Looking for Langston*, if erring slightly towards the hagiographic, Julien's film traces Fanon's life from his youth on Martinique, through his experience of fighting for France in the Second World War, to his gradual politicisation as a psychiatrist in Algeria during its struggle for independence. The staged elements aren't particularly persuasive, however, and Colin Salmon's static performance isn't helped along by the pious dialogue.

Colin Salmon *Frantz Fanon* • Al Nedjari *Algerian patient* • John Wilson *French policeman* • Ana Ramalho *French woman* • Noirín Ní Dubhgaill *Fanon's companion* ■ *Dir* Isaac Julien • *Scr* Isaac Julien, Mark Nash

Frasier, the Sensuous Lion
★

Comedy   1973 · US · Colour · 97mins

Once upon a time there was a lion in a California safari park that became famous because he sired 37 cubs from a harem of seven lionesses. The real Frasier died in 1972 but such was his fame that the park's proprietors conceived this crackpot movie in which Frasier starts talking in the manner of Francis, the Talking Mule. Michael Callan plays the animal behaviourist who becomes Frasier's buddy and confidante, learning what makes him such a great sexual athlete.

Michael Callan *Marvin Feldman* • Katherine Justice *Allison Stewart* • Victor Jory *Frasier (voice only)* • Frank DeKova *The man* ■ *Dir* Pat Shields • *Scr* Jerry Kobrin, from a story by Sandy Dore

Fratelli e Sorelle
★★★

Comedy drama   1992 · It/US · Colour

The work of director Pupi Avati is virtually unknown outside his native Italy yet he's one of their best talents. Even those horror fans who championed Avati's gothic opus *House with the Windows that Laugh* are in for a welcome surprise with this wry and penetrating social drama. It's the tale of two Italian boys who are transplanted to the States when their mother leaves her cheating husband to stay with her sister in St Louis. Observing the different ways in which these strangers in a strange land cope with their new situation, Avati has produced a complex, well observed and richly detailed study of the family in all its extended forms. In Italian with English subtitles.

Franco Nero *Franco* • Paola Quattrini *Lea* • Anna Bonaiuto *Gloria* • Lino Capolicchio *Aldo* • Christopher Marsh *Steve* ■ *Dir* Pupi Avati • *Scr* Stefano Accorsi, Pupi Avati

Fraternity Row
★★★ 15

Drama   1977 · US · Colour · 94mins

A fascinating insight into upper-echelon America in the mid-fifties, this low-budget drama is a laudable blend of raw talent and professional nous. Director Thomas J Tobin and writer/producer Charles Gray Allison were able to draw on Hollywood guidance to complete this picture, performed and shot by undergraduates at the University of Southern California. Although veteran Cliff Robertson provided the narration, only Robert Emhardt had much acting experience; indeed, Wendy Phillips and Gregory Harrison were making their feature debuts in this troubling, true-life study of fraternity ritual. Scott Newman,

Paul's son, died in a drink/drugs accident the following year. 🖿

Peter Fox *Rodger Carter* • Gregory Harrison *Zac Sterling* • Scott Newman *Chunk Cherry* • Nancy Morgan *Jennifer Harris* • Wendy Phillips *Betty Ann Martin* • Robert Emhardt *Brother Bob Abernathy* • Cliff Robertson *Narrator* ■ *Dir* Thomas J Tobin • *Scr* Charles Gary Allison

Fraternity Vacation
★ 15

Comedy   1985 · US · Colour · 89mins

Yet another cheap teen comedy attempting to hijack the success of *Animal House* and *Porky's*. This one features a young Tim Robbins, who today possibly wishes he was holding the negative in one hand and a flaming torch in the other. Beer, sex, beer, wet T-shirts and beer all feature fairly prominently in this slender tale of college delinquents pursuing girls. There's a fleeting appearance from Britt Ekland, but surely the best reason to avoid this movie are the songs by Bananarama.

Stephen Geoffreys *Wendell Tvedt* • Sheree J Wilson *Ashley Taylor* • Cameron Dye *Joe Gillespie* • Leigh McCloskey *Charles "Chas" Lawlor III* • Tim Robbins *Larry "Mother" Tucker* • Britt Ekland *Evette* ■ *Dir* James Frawley • *Scr* Lindsay Harrison

Frauds
★★ 15

Black comedy   1992 · Ausl · Colour · 89mins

This cartoonish farce gave Phil Collins his wackiest, blackest film role to date, although in the end it has to go down as a missed opportunity. The pop star plays a mysterious insurance broker who begins to terrorise a suburban family (Hugo Weaving and Josephine Byrnes) when they resort to a financial scam to get themselves out of a business mess. Collins is occasionally very creepy, but director Stephan Elliott (*The Adventures of Priscilla, Queen of the Desert*) backs off when he could have gone for the jugular. Contains violence and swearing. 🖿

Phil Collins *Roland* • Hugo Weaving *Jonathan* • Josephine Byrnes *Beth* • Peter Mochrie *Michael Allen* • Helen O'Connor *Margaret* • Andrew McMahon *Young Matthew* • Rebel Russell *Mother* • Colleen Clifford *Mrs Waterson* ■ *Dir/Scr* Stephan Elliott

Fraulein Doktor
★★

Wartime spy drama   1968 · It/Yug · Colour · 100mins

Brimming with the excesses that rendered so many sixties co-productions pompous fakes, this is a hopelessly melodramatic account of the exploits of a real-life double (which had previously been filmed as *Mademoiselle Docteur* in 1936). Eschewing his trademark realism, Italian director Alberto Lattuada here depicts espionage as a sexily glamorous game rather than a perilous round of treachery and deceit. Suzy Kendall shines as she plots the death of Lord Kitchener and seeks the formula for a hideous poisonous gas, but the excitement is only sporadic, in spite of some vivid battle scenes.

Suzy Kendall *Fraulein Doktor* • Kenneth More *Colonel Foreman* • James Booth *Meyer* • Capucine *Dr Saforet* • Alexander Knox *General Peronne* ■ *Dir* Alberto Lattuada • *Scr* Duilio Coletti, Stanley Mann, H AL Craig, Vittoriano Petrilli, Alberto Lattuada, from a story by Vittoriano Petrilli

Freaked
★★★ 15

Comedy horror   1993 · US · Colour · 81mins

Bill & Ted star Alex Winter co-directs this idiotic "tour de farce" on warp-drive with Tom Stern, his partner on the MTV series *The Idiot Box*. Winter also plays the arrogant Hollywood celebrity and spokesperson for a toxic chemical being pawned off to the Third World as a fertiliser. On a South American promotional tour, his entourage meet crazy Freak Show owner Randy Quaid, who uses the product to turn Winter into a headlining half man/half scaly beast. Forget the insane story, just laugh out loud at the amiable absurdity, and unsubtle send-ups of everything from *The Twilight Zone* to *Hollywood Squares*. Brooke Shields, Mr T (the Bearded Lady) and Keanu Reeves (uncredited as the Dog Boy) make eye-opening appearances. 🖿

Alex Winter *Ricky Coogin* • Megan Ward *Julie* • Michael Stoyanov *Ernie* • Keanu Reeves *The Dog Boy (uncredited)* • Randy Quaid *Elijah C Skuggs* • William Sadler *Dick Brian* • Mr T *Bearded Lady* • Brooke Shields *Skye Daley* ■ *Dir/Scr* Alex Winter, Tom Stern

Freaks
★★★★ 15

Horror   1932 · US · BW · 62mins

Still banned in some countries, and suppressed in others for decades, this unique classic from Tod Browning, director of the original *Dracula*, remains one of the most nightmarish yet compassionate horror movies ever made. Browning cleverly draws the viewer into an enclosed carnival society (featuring real circus anatomical oddities essentially playing themselves) with its attendant bonds, codes and rituals, and then chillingly shows what happens when a "normal" human – conniving trapeze artist Olga Baclanova – breaks them with a swindling scam. A deserved cult masterpiece, this tale of the macabre with its blood-freezing shock ending is incredible, disturbing and, once seen, never forgotten. 🖿

Wallace Ford *Phroso* • Leila Hyams *Venus* • Olga Baclanova *Cleopatra* • Rosco Ates [Roscoe Ates] *Roscoe* • Henry Victor *Hercules* • Harry Earles *Hans* • Daisy Earles *Frieda* • Rose Dione *Madame Tetrallini* • Daisy Hilton *Siamese Twin* • Violet Hilton *Siamese Twin* ■ *Dir* Tod Browning • *Scr* Willis Goldbeck, Leon Gordon, Edgar Allan Woolf, Al Boasberg, from the book *Spurs* by Clarence Tod Robbins • *Cinematographer* Merritt B Gerstad • *Art Director* Cedric Gibbons

Freaky Friday
★★★ U

Comedy   1976 · US · Colour · 94mins

One of the very early body-swap movies, this was a precursor to *Vice Versa* and the blockbuster *Big*. This one undeservedly sank without trace, although it contains an effervescent performance from Jodie Foster, who switches places with her mother for a day. It's one of those movies that starts at a brisk trot, lapses into walking pace and winds up misfiring through sheer lack of gags. However, it's well worth catching for the performances of Foster and Barbara Harris as the mum. 🖿

Barbara Harris *Ellen Andrews* • Jodie Foster *Annabel Andrews* • John Astin *Bill Andrews* • Patsy Kelly *Mrs Schmauss* • Dick Van Patten

Harold Jennings • Vicki Schreck *Virginia* • Sorrell Booke *Mr Dilk* ■ *Dir* Gary Nelson • *Scr* Mary Rodgers, from her book

Freaky Friday
★★

Comedy   1995 · US · Colour

Shelley Long and Gaby Hoffmann have the thankless task of trying to top the double act of Barbara Harris and Jodie Foster – the stars of the 1976 version of Mary Rodgers's book. But co-writer/director Melanie Mayron (*thirtysomething*) has produced a lively reworking for TV of this familiar body-swap story, in which mystical necklaces cause a mother and daughter to change places. The supporting cast includes Carol Kane, Eileen Brennan and Sandra Bernhard, but Long, still desperately trying to prove there's life after *Cheers*, overcooks the comedy.

Shelley Long *Ellen Andrews* • Gaby Hoffmann *Annabelle Andrews* • Asher Metchik *Ben Andrews* • Alan Rosenberg *Bill* • Eileen Brennan *Principal Handel* • Sandra Bernhard *Frieda Debny* • Carol Kane *Miss Futterman* • Catlin Adams *Mrs Barab* ■ *Dir* Melanie Mayron • *Scr* Stu Krieger, Melanie Mayron, from the film and the book by Mary Rodgers

Freddie as FRO7
★★ U

Animated spoof adventure   1992 · UK · Colour · 90mins

Technically, this ill-advised foray into full-length feature animation can't be faulted: the visuals are sumptuous, and a distinguished cast of British actors provide the voices. The story, however, which revolves around a James Bond-style superagent who also happens to be a frog, is just plain daft, and there is little of the knowing humour which makes the new features from Walt Disney popular with adults as well as kids. 🖿

Ben Kingsley *Freddie the Frog* • Jenny Agutter *Daffers* • John Sessions *Scotty* • Brian Blessed *El Supremo* • Nigel Hawthorne *Brigadier G* • Michael Hordern *King* • Phyllis Logan *Nessie* • Jonathan Pryce *Trilby* • Billie Whitelaw *Messina* ■ *Dir* Jon Acevski • *Scr* Jon Acevski, David Ashton

Freddy's Dead: the Final Nightmare
★★ 18

Horror   1991 · US · Colour · 88mins

Before Wes Craven dragged his seminal *Nightmare on Elm Street* saga into another realm altogether with his re-energised *New Nightmare* (1994), the series had already ground to a tired halt. This gimmick-laden sixth instalment about the child-molesting dream-stalker's exploits in nightmare land is a virtual rehash of *A Nightmare on Elm Street 3: Dream Warriors*, with an astonishingly lame 3-D climax tacked on. Roseanne (Barr), Johnny Depp (who starred in the original) and Alice Cooper make cameo appearances to little effect. 🖿

Robert Englund *Freddy Krueger* • Lisa Zane *Maggie Burroughs* • Shon Greenblatt *John* • Lezlie Deane *Tracy* • Ricky Dean Logan *Carlos* • Breckin Meyer *Spencer* • Yaphet Kotto *Doc* ■ *Dir* Rachel Talalay • *Scr* Michael DeLuca, from a story by Rachel Talalay, from characters created by Wes Craven

Free and Easy ★★
Comedy   1930 · US · BW · 73mins

Buster Keaton's career wobbled with his first sound film and never recovered. His great days as a silent comedian in creative charge of his work were over. His grave voice suited his demeanour, but MGM put him in a musical comedy as the hick who escorts Anita Page's beauty contest winner to Hollywood. They see celebrities at a premiere and he runs through the studio, bursting in on films in production and giving glimpses of stars and directors at work. It has none of the clever construction of Keaton's earlier comedies and it's a young Robert Montgomery who ends up getting the girl.

Buster Keaton *Elmer Butts* • Anita Page *Elvira* • Trixie Friganza *Ma* • Robert Montgomery *Larry* • Fred Niblo *Director* • Edgar Dearing *Officer* • Gwen Lee • John Miljan • Lionel Barrymore • Cecil B DeMille ■ *Dir* Edward Sedgwick • *Scr* Richard Schayer, Al Boasberg, Paul Dickey

Free Money ★
Comedy   1998 · Can · Colour · 95mins

Moronic comedy with Marlon Brando reaching a career-low as a religious-nut prison warden and a wasted cast that includes Charlie Sheen, Mira Sorvino, Donald Sutherland and blink-and-you'll-miss-them cameos from David Arquette and Martin Sheen. This unfunny shambles starts with the double wedding of Brando's identical twin daughters, and it's downhill from there. Attempts at quirkiness fall totally flat, and the nonsensical plot developments include the dumbest prison break you've ever seen.

Marlon Brando *Sven the Swede* • Mira Sorvino *Agent Karen Polarski* • Charlie Sheen *Bud* • Donald Sutherland *Judge Rolf Rausenberg* • Thomas Haden Church *Larry* • David Arquette ■ *Dir* Yves Simoneau • *Scr* Anthony Peck, Joseph Brutsman

Free of Eden ★
Drama   1999 · US · Colour · 98mins

Sidney Poitier produced and stars in this contrived TV film, with his daughter Sydney, in one of her first acting roles, and Cosby's Phylicia Rashad. Poitier is a former schoolteacher, now a successful New York financier. An ex-pupil, now a high-school dropout, seeks him out and a unlikely teacher/student relationship begins. Preachy and sanctimonious, with stereotypical characters, this is like a very inferior To Sir with Love.

Sidney Poitier *Will Cleamons* • Sydney Poitier *Nicole* • Phylicia Rashad *Desiree* • Robert Hooks *Joe Sherman* • Khalil Kain *Taurus* • Saundra McClain *Ruthie Turner* • Anthony Sherwood *Frank* • Nefta Perry *Crystal* ■ *Dir* Leon Ichaso • *Scr* Yule Caise, Delle Chatman

A Free Soul ★★★
Drama   1931 · US · BW · 93mins

When San Francisco society girl (Norma Shearer), brought up to defy convention by her adored and adoring lawyer father (Lionel Barrymore), rejects a perfect suitor (Leslie Howard) for a liaison with a gangster (Clark Gable), the lives of father and daughter are almost destroyed. MGM wheeled

out the big guns and high style for this melodrama which, seen today, is both gripping and fascinating. Shearer – then married to MGM production boss Irving Thalberg – picked up one of her several Oscar nominations, as did director Clarence Brown. The best actor award went to Barrymore, who makes a climactic 14-minute courtroom speech.

Norma Shearer *Jan Ashe* • Leslie Howard *Dwight Winthrop* • Lionel Barrymore *Stephen Ashe* • Clark Gable *Ace Wilfong* • James Gleason *Eddie* • Lucy Beaumont *Grandma Ashe* • Claire Whitney *Aunt Helen* ■ *Dir* Clarence Brown • *Scr* John Meehan, from the novel by Adela Rogers St John, from the play by Willard Mack

Free Willy ★★★ U
Adventure   1993 · US · Colour · 107mins

This is a magnificent children's picture that knows exactly what strings to pull and when. Australian director Simon Wincer combines animatronic models with shots of Keiko, the real-life killer whale that plays Willy, with great skill. The action away from the aqua park is suffocated by political correctness, family-bonding scenes and hammed-up villainy, but it's pretty hard to resist once Keiko and Jason James Richter are on screen together. ■ *DVD*

Jason James Richter *Jesse* • Lori Petty *Rae Lindley* • Jayne Atkinson *Annie Greenwood* • August Schellenberg *Randolph Johnson* • Michael Madsen *Glen Greenwood* ■ *Dir* Simon Wincer • *Scr* Keith A Walker, Corey Blechman

Free Willy 2: the Adventure Home ★★ U
Adventure   1995 · US · Colour · 93mins

After all the fuss that followed the revelation that the real Willy was being kept in less than adequate conditions, the producers of this sequel decided to take no chances and used mostly model whales. Unfortunately, they opted for a plastic replica plot, too, with Jason James Richter once more standing between the friendly orca and some unscrupulous adults, this time with sassy half-brother Francis Capra in tow. This is so full of sentiment, it makes Lassie movies look positively heartless; the recovery of the lost harmonica is bad enough, but that first kiss yeucch! ■

Jason James Richter *Jesse* • Francis Capra *Elvis* • Mary Kate Schellhardt *Nadine* • August Schellenberg *Randolph* • Michael Madsen *Glen* • M Emmet Walsh *Wilcox* ■ *Dir* Dwight Little [Dwight H Little] • *Scr* Karen Janszen, Corey Blechman, John Mattson, from characters created by Keith A Walker, Corey Blechman

Free Willy 3: the Rescue ★★★ U
Adventure   1997 · US · Colour · 81mins

Although Jason James Richter returns for this third instalment, he's too old to be taught any new eco-lessons. Now it's ten-year-old Vincent Berry, who learns the value of life and liberty from Willy the killer whale. But rather than simply set illegally-fishing father against born-again son, director Sam Pillsbury taps into the American hunter male myth and makes Patrick Kilpatrick's re-evaluation a real wrench

from tradition rather than just a sentimental change of heart. The whales are clearly the big attraction, but this is also a subtly argued message movie. ■

Jason James Richter *Jesse* • August Schellenberg *Randolph* • Annie Corley *Drew* • Vincent Berry *Max* • Patrick Kilpatrick *Wesley* • Tasha Simms *Mary* ■ *Dir* Sam Pillsbury • *Scr* John Mattson, ffrom characters created by Keith A Walker, Corey Blechman

Freebie and the Bean ★★★ 18
Action comedy   1974 · US · Colour · 107mins

James Caan and Alan Arkin star in an early variation on the buddy cops routine that is dominated by a clutter of car crashes as our heroes pursue big-time mobster Jack Kruschen. Hugely tasteless (there are a flurry of racist jokes from Caan about Arkin's chicano origins), this is a film where most of the characters are treated with contempt, but director Richard Rush puts so much energetic inventiveness into the turbulence you're almost convinced he doesn't mean it. Contains violence and swearing. ■

Alan Arkin *Bean* • James Caan *Freebie* • Loretta Swit *Meyers's wife* • Jack Kruschen *Red Meyers* • Mike Kellin *Lt Rosen* • Linda Marsh *Freebie's girl* • Valerie Harper *Bean's wife* ■ *Dir* Richard Rush • *Scr* Robert Kaufman, from a story by Floyd Mutrux

Freedom Radio ★★ PG
Second World War drama
1941 · UK · BW · 89mins

Raymond Huntley, one of the finest comic stooges the British cinema possessed, is the sole reason for watching this outdated and often unintentionally funny flag-waver. Here he plays a truly sinister Nazi, but the rest of the cast are simply dreadful as they spout platitudes in clipped stage accents that are totally unsuited to their middle-European characters. Clive Brook and Derek Farr are embarrassingly earnest as the heads of a pirate radio station, but topping them is Diana Wynyard's ludicrously naive collaborator. ■

Clive Brook *Roder* • Diana Wynyard *Irena Roder* • Raymond Huntley *Rabenau* • Derek Farr *Hans Glaser* • Joyce Howard *Elly* • Howard Marion-Crawford *Kummer* • John Penrose *Otto* ■ *Dir* Anthony Asquith • *Scr* Anatole de Grunwald, Basil Woon, Jeffrey Dell, Louis Golding, Gordon Wellesley, Bridget Boland, Roland Pertwee, from the story by Wolfgang Wilhelm, George Campbell

Freedom Road ★★ PG
Historical drama
1979 · US · Colour · 186mins

Two years after starring in The Greatest, Muhammad Ali appeared in this sprawling saga, originally a mini-series, edited down for release outside the United States. Ali, who rejected his original name of Cassius Clay because it was a slave name, plays ex-slave Gideon Jackson, who becomes a delegate to a state convention charged with rewriting the constitution of South Carolina. This is evidently intended to be a Spartacus for the modern era (both are based on novels by Howard Fast) but with a happy ending instead of the crucifixion. It was directed by the Hungarian-born director Jan Kadar, who

died shortly after the film was completed. ■

Muhammad Ali *Gideon Jackson* • Kris Kristofferson *Abner Lait* • Ron O'Neal *Francis Cardozo* • Edward Herrmann *Stephen Holms* • Barbara-O Jones [Barbara O Jones] *Rachel Jackson* • Alfre Woodard *Katie* ■ *Dir* Jan Kadar • *Scr* David Zelag Goodman, from a novel by Howard Fast

Freedom Road: the Vernon Johns Story ★★★
Biographical drama
1994 · US · Colour · 100mins

This is a powerful and at times hard-hitting TV movie about the early days of the civil rights movement. Set in Alabama during the late forties and early fifties, it's held together by a towering performance from James Earl Jones. As the preacher urging his apathetic congregation to lobby for drastic social change, Jones proves himself capable of both determined dignity and electrifying oratory. Although opposed by church elders and the white authorities alike, the Rev Vernon Johns's crusade would inspire the young Martin Luther King. With its message as relevant as ever, this is both uplifting and provocative stuff.

James Earl Jones *Reverend Vernon Johns* • Mary Alice *Altona Johns* • Joe Seneca *Deacon Wilkes* • Cissy Houston *Rose* • Nicole Leach *Baby Dee* • Tommy Hollis *Coach Hill* ■ *Dir* Kenneth Fink • *Scr* Kevin Arkadie, from the story by Leslie Lee, Gary Steele

Freefall ★★ 18
Action adventure 1994 · US · Colour · 96mins

Eric Roberts and Jeff Fahey were two of the most reliable draws on video throughout the nineties and this thriller catches them in good form. Set in Africa, Roberts gets the good guy role, coming to the assistance of snapper Pamela Gidley who is caught up in a complex international conspiracy. Fahey exudes villainy with his usual style, while John Irvin's gritty direction makes good use of the stunning locations. ■

Eric Roberts *Grant Orion* • Jeff Fahey *Dex Dellum* • Pamela Gidley *Katy Mazur* • Ron Smerczak *John Horner* ■ *Dir* John Irvin • *Scr* David Zito, Les Weldon

Freefall: Flight 174 ★★ PG
Drama based on a true story
1995 · US · Colour · 93mins

Clearly cloned from the Airport series, this in-flight entertainment is one of TV moviedom's better efforts, helped by the fact that it's based on an incident which occurred in 1983. William Devane, Shelley Hack and Mariette Hartley are put through their panic-station paces as Flight 174 mysteriously runs out of fuel in mid-air and the tense search begins for a landing site. Those with a fear of flying should be warned off, but everybody else will find enough low-rent suspense and ham acting on offer to make this an enjoyable time-waster.

William Devane *Captain Bob Pearson* • Shelley Hack *Lynn Brown* • Scott Hylands *Maurice Quintal* • Mariette Hartley *Beth Pearson* • Nicholas Turturro *Al Williams* ■ *Dir* Jorge Montesi • *Scr* Lionel Chetwynd, from the book *Freefall* by William Hoffer, Marilyn Hoffer

Freejack ★★ 🔲

Science-fiction adventure
1992 · US · Colour · 105mins

Based on an imaginative and surprising novel, this opts instead for sci-fi cliché and obvious thrills as Emilio Estevez is plucked from near-death in a racing accident to house the brain of a future-age Anthony Hopkins. Mick Jagger in his first big screen dramatic role since 1970's *Performance* and *Ned Kelly* suitably interprets his devious mercenary as a cynical yobbo, but it's a sin not to give talent like Hopkins and Rene Russo meatier roles. Contains swearing and violence. ▣

Emilio Estevez *Alex Furlong* • Rene Russo *Julie Redlund* • Mick Jagger *Vacendak* • Anthony Hopkins *McCandless* • Jonathan Banks *Michelette* • David Johansen *Brad* • Amanda Plummer *Nun* • Grand L Bush *Boone* ■ *Dir* Geoff Murphy • *Scr* Steven Pressfield, Ronald Shusett, Dan Gilroy, from a story by Steven Pressfield, Ronald Shusett, from the novel *Immortality Inc* by Robert Sheckley

Freeway ★★ 🔲

Thriller   1988 · US · Colour · 86mins

Casual and lethal snipings on the Los Angeles freeway lead a nurse (Darlanne Fluegel) into vengeful pursuit of the Bible-citing killer of her other half. The only clue she has is that the gunman is constantly ringing up a radio psychiatrist prior to shooting his next victim. It all sounds rather garish and gaudy, but director Francis Delia just makes it slow and cumbersome – rather like the acting. ▣

Darlanne Fluegel *Sarah "Sunny" Harper* • James Russo *Frank Quinn* • Richard Belzer *Dr David Lazarus* • Michael Callan *Lieutenant Boyle* • Billy Drago *Edward Anthony Heller* • Joey Palese *Detective Gomez* ■ *Dir* Francis Delia • *Scr* Francis Delia, Darrell Fetty

Freeway ★★★★ 🔲

Thriller   1996 · US · Colour · 97mins

This deeply twisted version of *Little Red Riding Hood* brought the exceptionally talented Reese Witherspoon to the attention of a wider audience. She plays a feisty young teenager from a dysfunctional family who sets off to find her grandmother, falling foul of psycho Bob Wolverton (Kiefer Sutherland) en route. Witherspoon is a revelation as the foul-mouthed teenage rebel, Sutherland is great as her nemesis, and there are enjoyable cameos from Amanda Plummer, Dan Hedaya and Brooke Shields. It went straight to video in the UK, but don't let that put you off. ▣

Kiefer Sutherland *Bob Wolverton* • Reese Witherspoon *Vanessa* • Brooke Shields *Mimi Wolverton* • Wolfgang Bodison *Detective Breer* • Dan Hedaya *Detective Wallace* • Amanda Plummer *Ramona* ■ *Dir/Scr* Matthew Bright

The Freeway Killings ★★ 🔲

Crime drama   1987 · US · Colour · 138mins

This is a feature-length sequel to the *Police Story* series, which ran for some 80 episodes in the mid-seventies before being succeeded by the even longer running spin-off *Police Woman*. The common link between the two series was Angie Dickinson, who returns in this instantly forgettable TV movie that leaves the unmistakeable

taste of reheated leftovers. Not even actors of the quality of Ben Gazzara, Richard Crenna and Tony LoBianco can raise above the predictable. Contains violence. ▣

Richard Crenna *Deputy Chief Robert Devers* • Ben Gazzara *Captain Tom Wright* • Angie Dickinson *Officer Anne Cavanaugh* • Don Meredith *Sergeant Foley* • Tony LoBianco *Sergeant Diangelo* ■ *Dir* William A Graham • *Scr* Mark Rodgers, from the TV series by Joseph Wambaugh

Freeze Frame ★★

Adventure   1989 · US · Colour · 78mins

Shannen Doherty plays another precocious kid in this would-be perky adventure about a student who uncovers corruption in her town while working as a reporter for her high school TV station. It's as ludicrous as it sounds, and only *Hill Street Blues* veteran Charles Haid brings any realism to his role. After proving that she could outbitch the best with her turn in *Heathers*, it's a shame that Doherty had to resort to lightweight stuff like this. Contains some violence.

Shannen Doherty *Lindsay Scott* • Charles Haid *Dr Michael Scott* • Robyn Douglass *Victoria Case* ■ *Dir/Scr* William Bindley

French Cancan ★★★ 🔲

Musical drama   1955 · Fr · Colour · 99mins

Director Jean Renoir's return to France after 15 years and his reunion with fellow legend Jean Gabin – they worked together on the classic *La Grande Illusion* among others – was not the cinema event buffs would hope, but there is still much to treasure in this exuberant tribute to the Moulin Rouge. The story – Gabin sets out to turn laundress Françoise Arnoul into a star – would not have been out of place in a glitzy Hollywood musical, but Renoir lovingly brings the glamorous world of the celebrated cancan to glorious life. In French with English subtitles. ▣

Jean Gabin *Danglard* • Maria Felix *La Belle Abesse* • Françoise Arnoul *Nini* • Jean-Roger Caussimon *Baron Walter* • Gianni Esposito *Prince Alexandre* • Philippe Clay *Casimir* ■ *Dir* Jean Renoir • *Scr* Jean Renoir, from an idea by André-Paul Antoine

The French Connection 🔲★★★★★ 🔲

Crime drama   1971 · US · Colour · 99mins

Gene Hackman's bruising, vigilante portrayal of the New York cop "Popeye" Doyle won him an Oscar – and deservedly so. Director William Friedkin also took an Academy Award, as did the crackling script. It's a police procedural about two cops (Hackman and Roy Scheider) discovering the biggest haul of narcotics in police records, organised by a French mastermind (Fernando Rey) who's as cool and imperturbable as the police are overworked and fractious. Full of exciting set-pieces, including an elevated-railway car chase which is overwhelmingly tense as the duo desperately, and obsessively, try to get their man. Contains violence, swearing and nudity. ▣

Gene Hackman *Jimmy "Popeye" Doyle* • Fernando Rey *Alain Charnier* • Roy Scheider *Buddy Russo* • Tony LoBianco *Sal Boca* •

Marcel Bozzuffi *Pierre Nicoli* • Frederic De Pasquale *Devereaux* • Bill Hickman *Mulderig* ■ *Dir* William Friedkin • *Scr* Ernest Tidyman, from the novel by Robin Moore • *Cinematographer* Owen Roizman

French Connection II ★★★ 🔲

Thriller   1975 · US · Colour · 119mins

John Frankenheimer's sequel to *The French Connection* is less credible than its predecessor, but it's still a cracking thriller. New York cop "Popeye" Doyle (Gene Hackman brilliantly reprising his Oscar-winning role) blunders into the French operation (Bernard Fresson in charge) to uncover heroin-tsar Fernando Rey's drugs ring. There's a disturbing sequence as Hackman goes "cold turkey" following his enforced drug addiction, but after that it's revenge and violence all the way as he tries to recover and go after arch-enemy Rey. Contains violence, swearing and drug abuse. ▣

Gene Hackman *"Popeye" Doyle* • Fernando Rey *Alain Charnier* • Bernard Fresson *Barthélemy* • Jean-Pierre Castaldi *Raoul Diron* • Charles Millot *Miletto* • Pierre Collet *Old Pro* • Alexandre Fabre *Young Tail* ■ *Dir* John Frankenheimer • *Scr* Robert Dillon, Laurie Dillon, Alexander Jacobs, from a story by Laurie Dillon, Robert Dillon

French Dressing ★★★

Comedy   1964 · UK · BW · 100mins

Ken Russell passed up the chance to direct the Cliff Richard musical *Summer Holiday*, choosing to break into feature films with this charming story partly inspired by Jacques Tati's *Monsieur Hulot's Holiday*. A deck-chair attendant (James Booth) at the seaside resort of Gormleigh-on-Sea (Herne Bay in disguise) aims to brighten things up by organising a film festival with a Bardot-like film star (Marisa Mell). Despite a nice cast, it was panned by critics at the time – humour of this *Carry On* kind was beyond our ken but now it seems rather cherishable.

James Booth *Jim* • Roy Kinnear *Henry* • Marisa Mell *Françoise Fayol* • Alita Naughton *Judy* • Bryan Pringle *Mayor* • Robert Robinson • Norman Pitt *Westebourne Mayor* • Henry McCarthy *Bridgemouth Mayor* ■ *Dir* Ken Russell • *Scr* Peter Myers, Ronald Cass, Peter Brett, Johnny Speight (additional dialogue), from a story by Peter Myers, Ronald Cass

French Kiss ★★★ 🔲

Romantic comedy   1995 · US · Colour · 106mins

This is one of director Lawrence Kasdan's most insubstantial movies, but if you banish *The Big Chill* and *The Accidental Tourist* from your mind, you can still enjoy this amiably fluffy confection. Meg Ryan, in her trademark "ever-so-ditzy" mode, sets off for France to reclaim wandering fiancé Timothy Hutton only to find herself stuck with slobby French thief Kevin Kline. The latter's role was reported to have been created for Gérard Depardieu, but Kline acquits himself well as the Gallic rogue and the chemistry between him and Ryan is spot on. Contains swearing ▣

Meg Ryan *Kate* • Kevin Kline *Luc* • Timothy Hutton *Charlie* • Jean Reno *Jean-Paul* •

François Cluzet *Bob* • Susan Anbeh *Juliette* • Renee Humphrey *Lilly* ■ *Dir* Lawrence Kasdan • *Scr* Adam Brooks

The French Lieutenant's Woman ★★★★ 🔲

Romantic drama
1981 · UK · Colour · 118mins

Director Karel Reisz and screenwriter Harold Pinter here take on the near-impossible filming of John Fowles's complex novel. Two stories are told in parallel, one of an affair between a disgraced Victorian governess and an English gentleman, and the other the relationship between the two film actors portraying the Victorian couple. Jeremy Irons and Meryl Streep feature in the dual roles. The historic tale is often interrupted by the antics of the modern duo, which seem prosaic by comparison. However, Victorian morality seeps hauntingly into every frame of the main story, which is decked out in convincing period detail and hangs on two scorching performances from Irons and Streep. Contains swearing, sex scenes and brief nudity. ▣

Meryl Streep *Sarah Woodruff/Anna* • Jeremy Irons *Charles Smithson/Mike* • Hilton McRae *Sam* • Leo McKern *Dr Grogan* • Emily Morgan *Mary* • Charlotte Mitchell *Mrs Tranter* • Lynsey Baxter *Ernestina Freeman* • Jean Faulds *Cook* ■ *Dir* Karel Reisz • *Scr* Harold Pinter, from the novel by John Fowles • *Cinematographer* Freddie Francis • *Music* Carl Davis

The French Line ★★ 🔲

Musical comedy   1954 · US · Colour · 98mins

Notorious in its day for Jane Russell's censor-provoking costume – the one with the crafty gaps in it – this was originally shot in 3-D to enhance Russell's assets. It was eventually released flat, which is how this would-be comedy well and truly falls. The songs are lacklustre, the support cast is second rate and Russell, sadly, is past her prime. But today the film does contain a quaint period charm, and watch closely for Marilyn (soon to become Kim) Novak's siren debut as a fashion model.

Jane Russell *Mary Carson* • Gilbert Roland *Pierre DuQueene* • Arthur Hunnicutt *"Waco" Mosby* • Mary McCarty *Annie Farrell* • Joyce MacKenzie *Myrtle Brown* ■ *Dir* Lloyd Bacon • *Scr* Mary Loos, Richard Sale, from a story by Matty Kemp, Isabel Dawn

A French Mistress ★★ 🔲

Comedy   1960 · UK · BW · 93mins

Roy Boulting was past his comic prime by the time he made this underwhelming boys' school comedy, produced, as ever, by twin brother John, and co-scripted by longtime partner Jeffrey Dell. All those familiar faces should at least have given the action a certain cosy appeal, but veterans such as Cecil Parker, James Robertson-Justice and Raymond Huntley are left high and dry by a script that is little more than a bumper collection of sniggering bike-shed jokes about sex and French women. ▣

Cecil Parker *Headmaster* • James Robertson-Justice *Robert Martin* • Ian Bannen *Colin Crane* • Agnes Laurent *Madeleine Lafarge* • Raymond Huntley *Reverend Edwin Peake* • Irene Handl *Staff Sergeant Hodges* • Edith

Sharpe *Matron* • Kenneth Griffith *Mr Meade* • Dir Roy Boulting • Scr Roy Boulting, Jeffrey Dell, from the play by Robert Monro

French Silk ★★
Thriller 1993 · Can · Colour

A glossy but shallow TV thriller set against a supposedly glamorous backdrop of supermodels and the fashion industry. Susan Lucci is the lingerie queen who gets her knickers in a twist when she finds herself the prime suspect in a murder investigation. The cast includes other US television regulars such as Lee Horsley and Shari Belafonte, but, despite the racy subject matter, the end result is bland.

Susan Lucci *Claire* • Lee Horsley *Cassidy* • Shari Belafonte *Martine* • Sarah Marshall *Claire's mother* • Jim Metzler *Alister Petrie* • Joe Warfield *Andre Philippe* • Paul Rosenberg *Leon* • Taylor Simpson *Ariel Bird* ■ Dir Noel Nosseck • Scr Carol Monpere, from the novel by Sandra Brown

French Twist ★★★ 18
Comedy 1995 · Fr · Colour · 102mins

Josiane Balasko (who played Gérard Depardieu's homely lover in *Trop Belle pour Toi*) wrote, directed and stars in this well-meaning but uneven French sex comedy. She plays Marijo, whose car breaks down near the home of Loli (Victoria Abril) and her philandering husband Laurent (Alain Chabat). Loli invites Marijo in, and it's not long before the two women are expressing their mutual appreciation of each other, much to the anger of Laurent. All three leads play their roles with farcical verve, but they are let down by Balasko's script. Sexy and amusing this is, but hilarious and original it is not. In French with English subtitles. Contains swearing and nudity. ▭

Victoria Abril *Loli* • Josiane Balasko *Marijo* • Alain Chabat *Laurent* • Ticky Holgado *Antoine* • Miguel Bose *Diego* • Catherine Hiegel *Dany* • Catherine Samie *Prostitute* • Catherine Lachens *Sopha* • Michèle Bernier *Solange* ■ Dir/Scr Josiane Balasko

Frenchman's Creek ★★★
Period romantic adventure
1944 · US · Colour · 113mins

Following the Oscar-winning success of *Rebecca*, Hollywood snapped up Daphne du Maurier's tale of an aristocratic woman who leaves her husband, goes to Cornwall and falls for a French pirate. Mitchell Leisen's direction typically concentrates on the colour scheme, the sets and costumes – he was once an art director – while the story rolls along by itself. Joan Fontaine is ideally cast as the imperious woman in the throes of passion but she's handicapped by the dullest of leading men – Leisen had wanted Ray Milland, but got Ralph Forbes as the spineless husband and Arturo De Cordova as the pirate.

Joan Fontaine *Lady Dona St Columb* • Arturo De Cordova *French Pirate* • Basil Rathbone *Lord Rockingham* • Nigel Bruce *Lord Godolphin* • Cecil Kellaway *William* • Ralph Forbes *Harry St Columb* ■ Dir Mitchell Leisen • Scr Talbot Jennings, from the novel by Daphne du Maurier • Costume Designer Raoul Pène du Bois

Frenzy ★★★★ 18
Thriller 1972 · UK · Colour · 110mins

Alfred Hitchcock's penultimate film saw him return to his British roots with this thriller about a necktie murderer causing havoc in London. Jon Finch plays the chief suspect but, typically, Hitchcock is more interested in black humour than a simple whodunit; lots of typical Hitchcockian touches are on show – a roving, restless camera, dark shots of fleeing footsteps on the edge of our view, a shocking corpse when least expected... *Sleuth* author Anthony Shaffer wrote the screenplay and there's plenty of other local talent on display, including Alec McCowen and the excellent Billie Whitelaw. While some regard this as inferior fare, it remains an unsettling piece. ▭

Jon Finch *Richard Blaney* • Barry Foster *Robert Rusk* • Alec McCowen *Chief Inspector Oxford* • Barbara Leigh-Hunt *Brenda Blaney* • Anna Massey *Babs Milligan* • Vivien Merchant *Mrs Oxford* • Bernard Cribbins *Felix Forsythe* • Billie Whitelaw *Hetty Porter* • Jean Marsh *Monica Bailing* ■ Dir Alfred Hitchcock • Scr Anthony Shaffer, from the novel *Goodbye Piccadilly, Farewell Leicester Square* by Arthur LaBern • Cinematographer Gilbert Taylor

Frequency ★★★★ 15
Fantasy thriller 2000 · US · Colour · 118mins

Changing the past to alter the present is the intriguing premise of this diverting thriller. Via an ancient ham radio set, Jim Caviezel (*The Thin Red Line*) is able to speak to his beloved fireman dad (Dennis Quaid) across 30 years of time, on the day before the latter is due to die in a warehouse blaze. Forewarned by Caviezel, Quaid escapes his fate, but his survival changes history: suddenly, Caviezel's mum (Elizabeth Mitchell) no longer exists! Combining a relationship yarn with a race-against-time bid to hunt down a killer, *Frequency* plays like a big-budget episode of *The Twilight Zone*. Paradoxes appear as the film gets increasingly complex, but Quaid and Caviezel give fine performances and director Gregory Hoblit's (*Primal Fear*) only serious misjudgement is an unforgivably slushy finale.

Dennis Quaid *Frank Sullivan* • Jim Caviezel [James Caviezel] *John Sullivan* • André Braugher *Satch DeLeon* • Elizabeth Mitchell *Julia Sullivan* • Noah Emmerich *Gordo Hersch* • Shawn Doyle *Jack Shepard* ■ Dir Gregory Hoblit • Scr Toby Emmerich

Frequent Flyer ★★
Drama 1996 · US · Colour · 92mins

Dashing airline pilot Jack Wagner leads a successful triple life with three wives in three different towns. The material seems ripe for a sex farce, but instead this slightly po-faced drama examines the devastating emotional fall-out on the affected women – Shelley Hack, Joan Severance and Nicole Eggert – when his bigamous ways are revealed. The performances are credible enough and the direction from Alan Metzger is efficient. Contains some swearing.

Jack Wagner *Nick Rawlings* • Shelley Hack *Jobeth Rawlings* • Nicole Eggert *Miriam Wells* • Joan Severance *Alison Rawlings* • Elizabeth Ruscio *Pat Kelsey* ■ Dir Alan Metzger • Scr D Victor Hawkins, Tom Nelson

Fresh ★★★★ 18
Drama 1994 · US · Colour · 108mins

The stale, overdone subject of drug-pushing kids is wonderfully enlivened by Boaz Yakin's direction and Sean Nelson's quietly contained performance as the 12-year-old black kid trying to extricate himself from dope-dealing and help his junkie sister by using psychological moves learned from his chess-playing father. The absence of moralising and macro posturing gives authenticity and poignancy to the film. Yakin's movie may be set in the ghetto, but its message is universal. ▭

Sean Nelson *Fresh* • Giancarlo Esposito *Esteban* • Samuel L Jackson *Sam* • N'Bushe Wright *Nicole* • Ron Brice *Corky* • Jean LaMarre *Jake* • Jose Zuniga *Lt Perez* • Luis Lantigua *Chuckie* ■ Dir/Scr Boaz Yakin

Fresh Horses ★★ 15
Romantic drama 1988 · US · Colour · 98mins

Andrew McCarthy co-stars with *Pretty in Pink* flame Molly Ringwald in this doom-laden story of ill-matched lovers. McCarthy is university student Matt, who has a good marriage in prospect until he meets Jewel (Ringwald), at which point common sense deserts him. She turns out to be an underage bride from the wrong side of the tracks, whose husband (Viggo Mortensen) may be a murderer. These and a few other problems eventually cool even Matt's ardour, but not before he's broken off his engagement. Far too superficial to work, McCarthy is very bland and Ringwald too one-dimensional to pull this off.

Molly Ringwald *Jewel* • Andrew McCarthy *Matt Larkin* • Patti D'Arbanville [Patti D'Arbanville-Quinn] *Jean McBaine* • Ben Stiller *Tipton* • Doug Hutchinson *Sproles* ■ Dir David Anspaugh • Scr Larry Ketron, from his play

The Freshman ★★★★★ U
Silent comedy 1925 · US · BW · 69mins

The bespectacled comic innocence of Harold Lloyd here takes a tumble that does him no harm at all, as the nerdish new college student who, via a series of accidents, becomes an all-star football player and so wins the hand of Jobyna Ralston. A classic of Lloyd's "Cinderfella" kind of humour – the poor boy who makes good – and there are some sly digs at the way an American educational institute values brawn instead of brain to raise funds. The final game is a knockout in more ways than one. ▭

Harold Lloyd *Harold "Speedy" Lamb* • Jobyna Ralston *Peggy* • Brooks Benedict *College cad* • James Anderson *Chester A "Chet" Trask* • Hazel Keener *College belle* • Joseph Harrington *College tailor* • Pat Harmon *The coach* • Charles Stevenson *Assistant coach* ■ Dir Fred C Newmeyer, Sam Taylor • Scr John Grey, Ted Wilde, Tim Whelan, Sam Taylor, Clyde Bruckman, Lex Neal, Jean Havez

The Freshman ★★★★ PG
Comedy drama 1990 · US · Colour · 98mins

Here's a chance to see a mellow Marlon Brando in his greatest comedy performance. It's a case of self-parody as he plays a godfather figure making film student Matthew Broderick an offer he can't refuse: a job as a

delivery boy, carting around exotic animals including a giant lizard. Writer/director Andrew Bergman's glorious spoof of Mafia ways spends too long satirising film-study pretension, but spins its screwball antics along at such a pace you can forgive it almost anything. Contains swearing. ▭

Marlon Brando *Carmine Sabatini* • Matthew Broderick *Clark Kellogg* • Bruno Kirby *Victor Ray* • Penelope Ann Miller *Tina Sabatini* • Frank Whaley *Steve Bushak* • Jon Polito *Chuck Greenwald* • Paul Benedict *Arthur Fleeber* ■ Dir/Scr Andrew Bergman

Freud ★★
Biography 1962 · US · BW · 140mins

Montgomery Clift – even with whiskers – seems the wrong choice to play Sigmund Freud, the father of psychoanalysis, while John Huston's style as director is far too direct to depict Freud's intricate early years. The nervous collapse of a young woman (Susannah York) helped the young doctor formulate his theory that the sexual instinct was the basis of human personality, leading to the revelation that came to be known as the Oedipus Complex. Everyone works hard to convince, but Clift's own twitchiness suggests he's a suitable case for treatment, and the use of dream sequences seems a curious cop-out.

Montgomery Clift *Sigmund Freud* • Susannah York *Cecily Koertner* • Larry Parks *Dr Joseph Breuer* • Susan Kohner *Martha Freud* • Eric Portman *Dr Theodore Meynert* ■ Dir John Huston • Scr Charles Kaufman, Wolfgang Reinhardt, from a story by Charles Kaufman

Friday ★★★ 15
Comedy 1995 · US · Colour · 87mins

Less preachy and more laid-back view of the "boyz" from the 'hood, with rapper Ice Cube and Chris Tucker (in one of his first major roles) navigating an ordinary day in the ghetto through a haze of dope. Their love of the latter sees them fall foul of gun-toting gangsters, while the unemployed pair also have to endure lectures from their relatives, jealous partners and the neighbourhood bully. Director F Gary Gray (*The Negotiator*), sidesteps some of the usual clichés of the genre to deliver an affectionate, fresh portrait of inner city life.

Ice Cube *Craig* • Chris Tucker *Smokey* • Nia Long *Debbie* • Tiny "Zeus" Lister Jr [Tom "Tiny" Lister Jr] *Deebo* • John Witherspoon *Mr Jones* • Anna Maria Horsford *Mrs Jones* • Regina King *Dana* • Paula Jai Parker *Joi* ■ Dir F Gary Gray • Scr Ice Cube, DJ Pooh

Friday Foster ★★★ 18
Blaxploitation crime drama
1975 · US · Colour · 86mins

Pam Grier – star of *Jackie Brown* – is here seen in an early role as a black "superwoman". She plays a fearless magazine photographer (a character taken from a comic strip) who blunders into a St Valentine's Day-style massacre involving a black millionaire. Grier is joined by a terrific black cast: Yaphet Kotto (cop), Godfrey Cambridge (crook), Eartha Kitt (fashion designer), Scatman Crothers (minister). The villainous mastermind (Jim Backus) is white, though.

Pam Grier *Friday Foster* • Yaphet Kotto *Colt Hawkins* • Godfrey Cambridge *Ford Malotte* • Thalmus Rasulala *Blake Tarr* • Eartha Kitt *Madame Rena* • Jim Backus *Enos Griffith* • Scatman Crothers *Reverend Noble Franklin* ■ *Dir* Arthur Marks • *Scr* Orville H Hampton, Arthur Marks, from a story by Arthur Marks

Friday the Thirteenth

★★★★ U

Drama   1933 · UK · BW · 82mins

After a bus crashes, the preceding day in the lives of six passengers unfolds, before revealing which ones survive. The formula goes at least as far back as Thornton Wilder's 1927 novel *The Bridge of San Luis Rey*, but it's an intriguing one that is given an entertaining workout here. The episodes are neatly tied together with an adroit mixture of comedy and drama, while the top-notch cast includes Jessie Matthews and co-writer Emlyn Williams as a cunningly insinuating villain.

Jessie Matthews *Milly* • Emlyn Williams *Blake* • Sonnie Hale *Alf* • Cyril Smith *Fred* • Eliot Makeham *Jackson* • Ursula Jeans *Eileen Jackson* • Max Miller *Joe* • *Dir* Victor Saville • *Scr* GH Moresby-White, Sidney Gilliat, Emlyn Williams

Friday the 13th

★★★ 18

Horror   1980 · US · Colour · 90mins

Essentially a cheap rural rip-off of John Carpenter's hugely influential *Halloween*, this mix of bloody horror and teenage terror from low-budget sleaze merchant Sean Cunningham blazed the trail for the stalk-and-slash vogue of the eighties. A catalogue of gruesome slaughter follows the re-opening of Camp Crystal Lake, long closed after a brutal unsolved murder. There are plenty of gory scares, while the audience is allowed to sympathise with the counsellors under repeated attack from a mystery assailant. The *Carrie*-inspired jolt ending left the door open for numerous sequels.

Betsy Palmer *Mrs Voorhees* • Adrienne King *Alice* • Harry Crosby *Bill* • Laurie Bartram *Brenda* • Mark Nelson *Ned* • Jeannine Taylor *Marcie* • Robbi Morgan *Annie* • Kevin Bacon *Jack* • Ari Lehman *Jason Voorhees* ■ *Dir* Sean S Cunningham • *Scr* Victor Miller

Friday the 13th Part 2

★★ 18

Horror   1981 · US · Colour · 83mins

The first sequel to the surprise horror hit is a virtual retread of the original, except that it introduces maniac icon Jason Voorhees (here played by Warrington Gillette) into the mayhem mix, eager to butcher another camp full of sex-starved counsellors. No real surprises, just plenty of methodical murders with graphic impaling being the favourite. Steve Miner directs by the numbers because, in this mean-spirited slasher, it's the splatter that matters, not the dead-end cast.

Amy Steel *Ginny* • John Furey *Paul Holt* • Adrienne King *Alice* • Kirsten Baker *Terry* • Stuart Charno *Ted* • Warrington Gillette *Jason Voorhees* • Walt Gorney *"Crazy Ralph"* ■ *Dir* Steve Miner • *Scr* Ron Kurz, from characters created by Victor Miller

Friday the 13th Part III

★★ 18

Horror   1982 · US · Colour · 91mins

Jason donned his famous hockey mask for the first time in director Steve Miner's formula rehash of slasher gold. This time Jason carves his gory way through a crew of dim-witted teenagers renting a house on the shores of his beloved Camp Crystal Lake. Originally shot in 3-D to disguise the creative bankruptcy, Miner's body count machine still fails to tap into the dormant insecurities that made the original so potent.

Dana Kimmell *Chris* • Paul Kratka *Rick* • Tracie Savage *Debbie* • Jeffrey Rogers *Andy* • Catherine Parks *Vera* • Richard Brooker *Jason Voorhees* ■ *Dir* Steve Miner • *Scr* Martin Kitrosser, Carol Watson, from characters created by Victor Miller, Ron Kurz

Friday the 13th: the Final Chapter

★★ 18

Horror   1984 · US · Colour · 91mins

The plot is as negligible as ever, the sex-obsessed teenagers interchangeable and the grisly murders all twists on the old favourites in director Joseph (*Rosemary's Killer*) Zito's take on the Camp Crystal Lake blueprint. Special make-up genius Tom Savini gives the body count an extra dimension of charnel house nausea as machete-wielding Jason goes on the rampage again. Incredibly, Zito manages to create tension prior to each shock demise, and he also provides a truly nightmarish denouement. Crispin Glover of *Back to the Future* fame stars.

Crispin Glover *Jimmy* • Erich Anderson *Rob* • Judie Aronson *Samantha* • Peter Barton *Doug* • Kimberly Beck *Trish* • Corey Feldman *Tommy* ■ *Dir* Joseph Zito • *Scr* Barney Cohen, from a story by Bruce Hidemi Sakow, from characters created by Victor Miller, Ron Kurz, Martin Kitrosser, Carol Watson

Friday the 13th: a New Beginning

★★★ 18

Horror   1985 · US · Colour · 87mins

Has Jason returned from the dead? Or is there a copycat killer doing a good impersonation of the Camp Crystal Lake nemesis? The setting for the fifth instalment in the series is a rural rehab centre where Tommy Jarvis (John Shepherd) is still haunted by the memory of the hockey-masked murderer. Director Danny Steinmann tries hard to breathe fresh life into the hackneyed proceedings with a tongue-in-cheek script and more characterisation than the series is usually noted for. Beginning and ending with stylish nightmares, this features less blood than usual because at the time the slasher genre was coming under attack from worried liberals and the press.

Melanie Kinnaman *Pam* • John Shepherd *Tommy Jarvis* • Shavar Ross *Reggie* • Marco St John *Sheriff Cal Tucker* • Richard Young *Matt Peters* • Juliette Cummins *Robin* ■ *Dir* Danny Steinmann • *Scr* Martin Kitrosser, David Cohen, Danny Steinmann, from a story by Martin Kitrosser, David Cohen

Friday the 13th Part VI: Jason Lives

★★★ 18

Horror   1986 · US · Colour · 87mins

A witty parody of a James Bond credits sequence immediately sets the tone for director Tom McLoughlin's slick and exuberant Jason sequel. Cleverly mining the undercurrent of humour inherent in the gory series, McLoughlin makes sure Jason's roller-coaster tracks are well-oiled and run smoothly in this vigorous, vivid and creepy instalment. When Tommy Jarvis (Thom Mathews) digs up his grave to prove Jason's really dead, a bolt of lightning hits the corpse and turns it into a zombie. Cue inventive deaths galore and textbook scares that still elicit a shiver or two. Contains violence.

Thom Mathews *Tommy Jarvis* • Jennifer Cooke *Megan Garris* • David Kagen *Sheriff Garris* • Kerry Noonan *Paula* • Renee Jones *Sissy* • Tom Fridley *Cort* • CJ Graham *Jason Voorhees* ■ *Dir* Tom McLoughlin • *Scr* Tom McLoughlin, from characters created by Victor Miller

Friday the 13th Part VII: the New Blood

★ 18

Horror   1988 · US · Colour · 84mins

Victim hears noise. Stops. Turns. Turns back. Jason appears from nowhere holding a machete/axe/spike... The Jason formula hits rock bottom with this static, boring and threadbare episode, directed by B-movie make-up man John Carl Buechler. *New Blood* contains virtually no blood; the only new addition to the nihilism is a telekinetic girl who may be able to destroy Jason with her psychic powers. Buechler's direction might be faceless, but Jason goes about his gory business unmasked in this, the weakest *Friday the 13th* of all.

Lar Park-Lincoln *Tina* • Kevin Blair [Kevin Spirtas] *Nick* • Terry Kiser *Dr Crews* • Susan Jennifer Sullivan *Melissa* • Heidi Kozak *Sandra* • Kane Hodder *Jason* • William Butler *Michael* • Staci Greason *Jane* ■ *Dir* John Carl Buechler • *Scr* Daryl Haney, Manuel Fidello

Friday the 13th Part VIII: Jason Takes Manhattan

★★★ 18

Horror   1989 · US · Colour · 96mins

Director Rob Hedden's stylish attack on the Jason franchise lifts the fear formula a cut and a slash above the average. The title is a misnomer: it takes ages for Jason to carve up the Big Apple. Having been revived by an underwater electrical cable, he stows aboard a pleasure cruiser taking Crystal Lake graduates to New York. It's fun seeing the hockey-masked murderer stalking rat-infested mean streets instead of leafy glades, but this crisply photographed scare-fest surprisingly doesn't milk the new location for extra chills.

Jensen Daggett *Rennie Wickham* • Scott Reeves *Sean Robertson* • Peter Mark Richman *Charles McCulloch* • Barbara Bingham *Colleen Van Deusen* • Kane Hodder *Jason* ■ *Dir* Rob Hedden • *Scr* Rob Hedden, from characters created by Victor Miller

Fried Green Tomatoes at the Whistle Stop Cafe

★★★★ PG

Drama   1991 · US · Colour · 124mins

Jessica Tandy received an Oscar nomination for her portrayal of a feisty old-timer in the American South, telling tales about the bigotry she encountered during her youth in the thirties. Kathy Bates is almost as good as Tandy, playing a modern-day housewife and frump in the dumps, who visits Tandy in a nursing home and finds inspiration in her memories of the past. Essentially a story about friendship between two pairs of women, then and now, this could be classified as an intelligent woman's picture, but it should also be enjoyed by all. A truly uplifting and gratifying experience. Contains some violence and swearing. ⊞ DVD

Mary Stuart Masterson *Idgie Threadgoode* • Mary-Louise Parker *Ruth* • Kathy Bates *Evelyn Couch* • Jessica Tandy *Ninny Threadgoode* • Gailard Sartain *Ed Couch* • Stan Shaw *Big George* • Cicely Tyson *Sipsey* • Gary Basaraba *Grady* ■ *Dir* Jon Avnet • *Scr* Fannie Flagg, Carol Sobieski, from the novel by Fannie Flagg

Frieda

★★★ PG

Drama   1947 · UK · BW · 94mins

Although there were plenty of tales of brave wartime resistance, few film-makers ventured into the darker territory of commitment to Nazism. Basil Dearden's bold bid to understand collaboration and the need to forgive, lapses into stereotype and melodrama rather too quickly. Yet the story of RAF officer David Farrar who returns to Blighty with Mai Zetterling – the German girl who helped him when he was a prisoner of war– still touches a few raw nerves. Glynis Johns, as the sympathetic sister-in-law, and Albert Lieven and Flora Robson as the unyielding patriots provide solid support.

David Farrar *Robert Dawson* • Glynis Johns *Judy Dawson* • Mai Zetterling *Frieda Dawson* • Flora Robson *Nell Dawson* • Albert Lieven *Richard Mannsfeld* ■ *Dir* Basil Dearden • *Scr* Ronald Millar, Angus Macphail, from the play by Ronald Millar

Friendly Enemies

★★ U

Second World War drama
1942 · US · BW · 95mins

The title refers to two Germans who have been living in the USA for 40 years when the country enters the Second World War. Charles Winninger plays the one sympathetic to his fatherland's cause and Charles Ruggles his friend who supports the USA. The two old pros get a few laughs, but their tiresome verbal battles take up too much screen time until Winninger sees the light and joins his friend to trap a spy. It doubtless seemed timely in 1942 to resurrect this property, originally a play written in 1918, but director Allan Dwan can do little to compensate for the static nature of the piece.

Charles Winninger *Karl Pfeiffer* • Charlie Ruggles [Charles Ruggles] *Heinrich Block* • James Craig *William Pfeiffer* • Nancy Kelly *June Block* • Otto Kruger *Anton Miller* • Ilka

U = SUITABLE FOR ALL, Uc = SUITABLE FOR ALL, ESPECIALLY FOR YOUNG CHILDREN (VIDEO ONLY), PG = PARENTAL GUIDANCE

Gruning *Mrs Pfeiffer* ■ *Dir* Allan Dwan • *Scr* Adelaide Heilbron, from the play by Samuel Shipman, Aaron Hoffman

Friendly Fire ★★★★

Drama based on a true story
1979 · US · Colour · 147mins

The American media is obsessed with conspiracy theories. So it should come as no surprise to learn that this TV movie, chronicling the real-life efforts of Peg Mullen to compel Washington to reveal the circumstances of her son's death in Vietnam, won four Emmys, including best drama. Although both leads took acting awards, Carol Burnett's unswerving commitment is less subtly shaded than Ned Beatty's performance as her husband, torn between patriotism and the truth. With fine support from Sam Waterston and Timothy Hutton, this is a disturbing insight into both war and the state's ability to distort facts.

Carol Burnett *Peg Mullen* • Ned Beatty *Gene Mullen* • Sam Waterston *CDB Bryan* • Dennis Erdman *Sgt Michael Mullen* • Sherry Hursey *Mary Mullen* • Timothy Hutton *John Mullen* • Fanny Spiess *Pat Mullen* ■ *Dir* David Greene • *Scr* Fay Kanin, from the novel by CDB Bryan

Friendly Persuasion ★★★★ U

Drama 1956 · US · Colour · 137mins

A marvellously humane study of an Indiana Quaker family during the American Civil War, with pacifist Gary Cooper in one of his finest later performances. Under William Wyler's direction the story takes its time to unravel, but it's a film of great charm, with impressive performances from Dorothy McGuire as Cooper's wife and a young Anthony Perkins as the son with whom he clashes. The movie also boasts a superb score from Dmitri Tiomkin, plus ravishing location colour photography from Ellsworth Fredericks. It rightly received six Oscar nominations, including one for its blacklisted and uncredited screenwriter, Michael Wilson.

Gary Cooper *Jess Birdwell* • Dorothy McGuire *Eliza Birdwell* • Marjorie Main *Widow Hudspeth* • Anthony Perkins *Josh Birdwell* • Richard Eyer *Little Jess* • Robert Middleton *Sam Jordan* • Phyllis Love *Mattie Birdwell* ■ *Dir* William Wyler • *Scr* Michael Wilson (uncredited), from the novel by Jessamyn West • *Cinematographer* Ellsworth Fredericks • *Music* Dmitri Tiomkin

Friends ★ 15

Drama 1971 · UK · Colour · 96mins

This is one of those innocent teenage movies where sweet fumbling results in pregnancy puzzlement. Films like this usually take place on a South Seas island, but this time around it's a deserted beach in France. There's a lot of soft focus, numerous log-fires, connubial bliss by the cartload and an Elton John soundtrack. Both sets of parents eventually pitch up to administer smacks all round, but not before the audience has been left feeling rather ill. 🖭

Sean Bury *Paul Harrison* • Anicee Alvina *Michelle LaTour* • Ronald Lewis *Harrison* • Tony Robins *Mrs Gardner* ■ *Dir* Lewis Gilbert • *Scr* Jack Russell, Vernon Harris, from a story by Lewis Gilbert

Friends ★★ 15

Drama 1993 · UK/Fr · Colour · 104mins

The versatile Kerry Fox (*Shallow Grave, An Angel at My Table*) stars as Sophie, one of three friends who meet at university in South Africa. Fox is from a rich area of Johannesburg, while Michele Burgers is a poor Afrikaner and Dambisa Kente is a Zulu. This is one of those dramas in which important political and social issues are used as a background to the central theme of friendship. Here that friendship is severely tested when Fox's character plants a bomb as part of her anti-apartheid activities. Director Elaine Proctor's debut feature is strong on setting and politics but the characters unfortunately lack the depth of their surroundings. 🖭

Kerry Fox *Sophie* • Dambisa Kente *Thoko* • Michele Burgers *Aninka* • Marius Weyers *Johan* • Tertius Meintjes *Jeremy* • Dolly Rathebe *Innocentia* • Wilma Stockenstrom *Iris* ■ *Dir/Scr* Elaine Proctor

Friends and Lovers ★★

Romantic drama 1931 · US · BW · 66mins

Adolphe Menjou and Laurence Olivier are British officers in India, rivals for the affections of *femme fatale* Lili Damita, whose blackmailing husband, Erich von Stroheim, isn't averse to a spot of blackmail. This risible melodrama has only one thing going for it – its intriguing cast. Interesting to see the 24-year-old Olivier, in one of his first Hollywood films, Damita (who would wed Errol Flynn four years later) and the always-hypnotic, monocled von Stroheim. Director Victor Schertzinger was co-credited with Max Steiner for the score.

Adolphe Menjou *Captain Roberts* • Lili Damita *Alva Sangrito* • Laurence Olivier *Lieutenant Nichols* • Erich von Stroheim *Victor Sangrito* • Hugh Herbert *McNellis* • Frederick Kerr *General Armstrong* ■ *Dir* Victor Schertzinger • *Scr* Wallace Smith, Jane Murfin, from the novel *Le Sphinx a Parlé* by Maurice De Kobra

Friends at Last ★★★ PG

Drama 1995 · Can/US · Colour · 87mins

It's not often Kathleen Turner turns up in TV movie and her star presence lifts this weepie melodrama above the norm. Turner plays a wife whose marriage breaks down as her hardworking journalist husband (Colm Feore) begins to find success. However, following their divorce Turner and Feore are forced to re-evaluate their lives when Turner is diagnosed as having cancer. It's a long way from the vampy roles that made her name, but Turner makes the most of the emotional material, even if director John David Coles takes it a little too slowly for its own good. Contains strong language. 🖭

Kathleen Turner *Fanny Conlon* • Colm Feore *Phillip Conlon* • Krista Marie Bonura *Diana, age eight* • Megan Bouchard *Diana, age 11* • Sarah Paulson *Diana, age 21* • Faith Prince *Celia* • Julie Khaner *Blair* ■ *Dir* John David Coles • *Scr* Susan Sandler

The Friends of Eddie Coyle
★★★★

Crime drama 1973 · US · Colour · 102mins

Robert Mitchum plays an ageing small-time gangster and cynical police informer who is relentlessly pursued by the mobsters he's betrayed. In a quality cast, Peter Boyle stands out as the hit man and so-called "friend" who's given the job of eliminating Mitchum. Peter Yates, the British director who forged his Hollywood reputation with the incredible car chase in *Bullitt*, gives this crime drama a more subtle power, turning the story into a fable about urban violence. After this benchmark performance Mitchum had the ability to give his characters a loser's edge and a new depth of understanding. Contains violence and swearing. 🖭

Robert Mitchum *Eddie Coyle* • Peter Boyle *Dillon* • Richard Jordan *Dave Foley* • Steven Keats *Jackie* • Alex Rocco *Scalise* • Joe Santos *Artie Van* • Mitchell Ryan *Waters* ■ *Dir* Peter Yates • *Scr* Paul Monash, from the novel by George V Higgens

Fright ★★ 18

Thriller 1971 · UK · Colour · 83mins

Employing mental illness as fodder for horror movies, however unsettling, can produce masterpieces like *Psycho* and *Repulsion*. But the sense of exploitation is all too evident in this unpleasant tale of a young babysitter terrorised by an escaped lunatic. Ian Bannen jumps through hoops in an effort to make his role convincing but Peter Collinson's formulaic direction reduces him to just another anonymous nutter. As the terrified heroine, Susan George merely alternates between pouting and screaming. Brutal in depiction and implication, this is one for undemanding scare-hounds. 🖭

Susan George *Amanda* • Honor Blackman *Helen* • Ian Bannen *Brian* • John Gregson *Dr Cordell* • George Cole *Jim* • Dennis Waterman *Chris* • Tara Collinson *Tara* ■ *Dir* Peter Collinson • *Scr* Tudor Gates

Fright Night ★★★★ 18

Horror 1985 · US · Colour · 102mins

Hugely entertaining horror spoof in which teenage B-movie buff William Ragsdale becomes convinced that new neighbour Chris Sarandon is a vampire responsible for a spate of brutal killings. Only when best pal Stephen Geoffreys has become Sarandon's slave and girlfriend Amanda Bearse has also fallen under his spell, does Ragsdale succeed in enlisting the help of "fearless" TV vampire hunter Roddy McDowall to end his reign of terror. Neatly parodying Hitchcock and John Hughes movies, writer/director Tom Holland litters his rattling story with as many laughs as jolts. Contains violence and swearing. 🖭

Chris Sarandon *Jerry Dandridge* • William Ragsdale *Charley Brewster* • Amanda Bearse *Amy Peterson* • Roddy McDowall *Peter Vincent* • Stephen Geoffreys *Evil Ed* • Jonathan Stark *Billy Cole* • Dorothy Fielding *Judy Brewster* ■ *Dir/Scr* Tom Holland

Fright Night Part 2 ★★ 18

Comedy horror 1988 · US · Colour · 99mins

The original *Fright Night* breathed a bit of knowing humour into the vampire genre, but this is an uninspired retread from horror sequel specialist Tommy Lee Wallace, also responsible for the dire *Halloween 3*. William Ragsdale returns as student Charley Brewster, who uncovers another coven of vampires when he falls for sexy Julie Carmen. Roddy McDowall also reprises his role as fearful vampire slayer Peter Vincent, but he can't breathe life into the worn-out script or Wallace's shapeless direction. 🖭

Roddy McDowall *Peter Vincent* • William Ragsdale *Charley Brewster* • Julie Carmen *Regine* • Traci Lin *Alex* • Jonathan Gries *Louie* ■ *Dir* Tommy Lee Wallace • *Scr* Tommy Lee Wallace, Tim Metcalfe, Miguel Tejada-Flores, from the characters created by Tom Holland

The Frightened City ★★ PG

Crime drama 1961 · UK · BW · 93mins

Limping along years after Hollywood's postwar exterior-location thrillers such as *The Naked City*, this British attempt at the genre just about manages to hold the interest. The story is about London gangsters falling out over a protection racket, and features a young Sean Connery (when he had hair) and a pre-*Pink Panther* Herbert Lom at his most seedily sinister. 🖭

Herbert Lom *Waldo Zhernikov* • John Gregson *Detective Inspector Sayers* • Sean Connery *Paddy Damion* • Alfred Marks *Harry Foulcher* ■ *Dir* John Lemont • *Scr* Leigh Vance, from a story by Leigh Vance, John Lemont

The Frightened Man ★★

Crime drama 1952 · UK · BW · 70mins

This is a dreary little quota quickie which draws on all the stock situations one associates with British B-thrillers. Director John Gilling makes solid use of the down-at-heel locations, but he fails to inject any suspense into the story (which he wrote) of a botched jewel robbery. Given little support by the rest of the cast, Dermot Walsh tries hard as the junk dealer's son who's thrown out of university and drawn into a life of crime.

Dermot Walsh *Julius Roselli* • Barbara Murray *Amanda* • Charles Victor *Mr Roselli* • John Blythe *Maxie* • Michael Ward *Cornelius* • Thora Hird *Vera* ■ *Dir/Scr* John Gilling

The Frighteners ★★★★ 15

Supernatural comedy thriller
1996 · NZ/US · Colour · 105mins

Peter Jackson, the director of *Braindead* and *Heavenly Creatures* explores the shockingly unhealthy paranormal bond between two lovers with record-breaking murder in mind. Hitting exactly the right balance between black comedy and jet-black chills, this cross between *Casper* and *The Silence of the Lambs* is another ghoulish masterpiece from the Kiwi eccentric, showcasing a dazzling array of computer-generated ghosts and blood-freezing poltergeist activity. Michael J Fox is ingeniously cast against type as a pseudo psychic dealing with all the nasty hereafter horror in a merrily menacing spectre spectacular. 🖭 **DVD**

Michael J Fox *Frank Bannister* • Trini Alvarado *Lucy Lynskey* • Peter Dobson *Ray Lynskey* • John Astin *The Judge* • Jeffrey Combs *Milton Dammers* • Dee Wallace Stone *Patrica Bradley* ■ *Dir* Peter Jackson • *Scr* Fran Walsh, Peter Jackson

Frightmare ★★ 18

Horror   1981 · US · Colour · 82mins

Horror movie stalwart Ferdy Mayne never quite hit the Hammer heights of, say, Christopher Lee. He's well cast here as an old horror movie icon, based perhaps upon his best known role, that of the sinister count in Roman Polanski's *The Fearless Vampire Killers*, whose body is kidnapped by members of a horror film society. When his widow holds a séance the actor's reanimated corpse picks off the kids one by one in *Friday the 13th* style. An uneasy blend of homage, laughs and standard teens-in-jeopardy bloodletting that would have done better in the hands of someone like Wes Craven. ▭

Ferdinand Mayne [Ferdy Mayne] *Conrad* • Luca Bercovici *Saint* • Nita Talbot *Mrs Rohmer* • Leon Askin *Wolfgang* • Jennifer Starrett *Meg* • Barbara Pilavin *Etta* • Carlene Olson *Eve* ■ *Dir/Scr* Norman Thaddeus Vane

The Fringe Dwellers ★★★ PG

Drama   1985 · Ausl · Colour · 97mins

Director Bruce Beresford has succeeded only in drawing the sting from Nene Gare's controversial study of middle-class snobbery and Aboriginal exclusion. Good intentions abound in this story of a teenage girl who is determined to rouse her idle father into action so that they can move into a new housing development. But the characterisations are too broad, with nearly all the whites being loathsome and the Aborigines being cheerful in their poverty. However, Kristina Nehm gives a striking performance as the ambitious Trilby, with Ernie Dingo impressive as her shiftless lover.

Kristina Nehm *Trilby Comeaway* • Justine Saunders *Mollie Comeaway* • Bob Maza *Joe Comeaway* • Kylie Belling *Noonah Comeaway* • Denis Walker *Bartie Comeaway* ■ *Dir* Bruce Beresford • *Scr* Bruce Beresford, Rhoisin Beresford, from the novel by Nene Gare

Frisco Kid ★★

Adventure   1935 · US · BW · 77mins

James Cagney sports curly hair and wing collars in this 1890s tale of the notorious Barbary Coast in San Francisco. The story of a young sailor's rise to prominence in the world of saloons, gamblers and corrupt politicians is strictly routine, with the heroine the owner of a crusading newspaper fighting to clean up the city. Even with the fast cutting we expect from Warner Bros, and a brief running time, the tale still flags and it's the dynamic Cagney who keeps it afloat. The extras include several former silent screen actors, hired at the caring Cagney's insistence.

James Cagney *Bat Morgan* • Margaret Lindsay *Jean Barrat* • Ricardo Cortez *Paul Morra* • Lili Damita *Bella Morra* • Donald Woods *Charles Ford* • Barton MacLane *Spider Burke* • George E Stone *Solly* ■ *Dir* Lloyd Bacon • *Scr* Warren Duff, Seton I Miller

The Frisco Kid ★★ PG

Comedy western   1979 · US · Colour · 113mins

A comedy drama that isn't as comic as it thinks it is, nor as dramatic as it should be. Gene Wilder stars as a novice rabbi sent to San Francisco and befriended by cowboy Harrison Ford on the way. There are some laughs to be had in the gaffes, but director Robert Aldrich – who made one of the great nuclear parables with *Kiss Me Deadly* (1955) – inserts some violent action sequences into the episodic plot that jar with what should have been a much gentler affair. ▭

Gene Wilder *Avram* • Harrison Ford *Tommy* • Ramon Bieri *Mr Jones* • Val Bisoglio *Chief Gray Cloud* • George DiCenzo *Darryl Diggs* • Leo Fuchs *Chief Rabbi* • Penny Peyser *Rosalie* • William Smith *Matt Diggs* ■ *Dir* Robert Aldrich • *Scr* Michael Elias, Frank Shaw

Frisk ★★

Erotic thriller   1995 · US · Colour · 88mins

Adapted from Dennis Cooper's controversial novel, director Todd Verow's explicit shocker explores a gay man's increasingly baroque fantasies of sex and murder after he picks up a willing masochist. Intended as a serious look at the differing attitudes society has towards pain and pleasure, Verow's matter-of-fact approach renders the startling issues he tackles pointlessly dull instead of riveting. Lifting the lid on sexual practices rarely dealt with on film and opening up the "snuff" debate is one thing, but unless you are a master director (like David Cronenberg, for example), using such extreme imagery quickly becomes exploitation rather than argument. Contains swearing, sex and violence.

Michael Gunther *Dennis* • Raoul O'Connell *Kevin* • Jaie Laplante *Julian* • Mark Ewert *Young Dennis* • James Lyons *Gypsy Pete* • Dustin Schell *Snuff photographer* ■ *Dir* Todd Verow • *Scr* Todd Verow, George LaVoo, Jim Dwyer, from the novel by Dennis Cooper

Fritz the Cat ★★★ 18

Animated erotic comedy   1972 · US · Colour · 75mins

Radical and largely successful attempt on the part of director Ralph Bakshi to translate the underground comic character invented by Robert Crumb to the big screen. Fritz is an innocent at large in the times that are a "a-changin'" at the fag end of the hippy wave. He rapidly discovers the joys of sex and student politics, before bumping painfully into various downsides of the counterculture like hard drugs and biker gangs. Quite shocking at the time, this remains a fun period artefact. ▭

Skip Hinnant *Fritz the Cat* • Rosetta LeNoire • John McCurry • Judy Engles ■ *Dir* Ralph Bakshi • *Scr* Ralph Bakshi, from the character created by Robert Crumb

Frog Dreaming ★★★

Fantasy adventure   1985 · Ausl · Colour · 93mins

In spite of a troubled shoot, this is an intriguing blend of childhood imagination and local mythology. *ET*'s Henry Thomas gives a similarly wide-eyed performance as the gadget-obsessed American orphan who becomes fascinated with the legend of a fire-breathing spirit who supposedly inhabits an unmapped lake near his Australian guardian's bush home. Capturing both the bravado, ingenuity and timidity of youth, without any of the cloying sentimentality that blights so many Hollywood rites of passage pictures, this is a far-fetched fantasy, but nonetheless enjoyable.

Henry Thomas *Cody Walpole* • Tony Barry *Gaza* • Rachel Friend *Wendy* • Tamsin West *Jane* • John Ewart *Sergeant Ricketts* • Dennis Miller *Mr Cannon* ■ *Dir* Brian Trenchard-Smith • *Scr* Everett DeRoche

The Frog Prince ★★★ 15

Romantic comedy   1984 · UK · Colour · 86mins

This charming tale of cross-cultural courtship is set in the pre-Swinging Sixties. Cartoonist Posy Simmonds's semi-autobiographical screenplay may indulge in a little cheap caricature where both the plainspeaking and bohemian French folk are concerned, but it, nevertheless, captures the hesitancy and naive emotionalism of first love with genuine insight and affection. Making Paris seem romantic is hardly an onerous task, but director Brian Gilbert turns the city into a key character, rather than just the beautiful backdrop to mousey exchange student Jane Snowden's relationship with the dashing Alexandre Sterling. ▭

Jane Snowden *Jenny* • Alexandre Sterling *Jean-Philippe* • Jacqueline Doyen *Mme Peroche* • Raoul Delfosse *Monsieur Peroche* • Jeanne Herviale *Mme Duclos* ■ *Dir* Brian Gilbert • *Scr* Posy Simmonds, Brian Gilbert, from the story by Posy Simmonds

The Frogmen ★★★ U

Second World War action drama   1951 · US · BW · 96mins

Warners' veteran director Lloyd Bacon fetched up after the war at 20th Century-Fox as a sort of hack-of-all-trades. He has the benefit here of the studio's starry roster of male actors (everyone except Gregory Peck and Tyrone Power) in a realistic and tense suspense drama about Pacific underwater demolition teams during the Second World War. Richard Widmark is the tough commander whose men resent him – naturally though, led by Dana Andrews, they eventually come to understand his uncompromising methods. Interesting to watch Fox's next wave of leading men Jeffrey Hunter and Robert Wagner stealing scenes from the veterans.

Richard Widmark *Lieutenant Commander John Lawrence* • Dana Andrews *Flannigan* • Gary Merrill *Lieutenant Commander Pete Vincent* • Jeffrey Hunter *Creighton* • Warren Stevens *Hodges* • Robert Wagner *Lieutenant Franklin* ■ *Dir* Lloyd Bacon • *Scr* John Tucker Battle, from a story by Oscar Millard

Frogs ★★

Horror   1972 · US · Colour · 90mins

One of the many ecologically-correct horror films of the seventies and one of the silliest. Ray Milland is the wheelchair-bound Southern patriarch whose birthday celebrations are disrupted by a revolt of the swamp creatures who has tried to eliminate with DDT and insecticides. The intelligent frog population also enrol snakes, bugs and snapping turtles to leap around attacking the obvious upper-class types on their private island. Those who find such creatures scary will be suitably terrified.

Ray Milland *Jason Crockett* • Sam Elliott *Pickett Smith* • Joan Van Ark *Karen Crockett* • Adam Roarke *Clint Crockett* • Judy Pace *Bella Berenson* ■ *Dir* George McCowan • *Scr* Robert Hutchison, Robert Blees, from a story by Robert Hutchison

From Beyond ★★ 18

Science-fiction horror   1986 · US · Colour · 81mins

Following his gross-out hit *Re-Animator*, Stuart Gordon reunited leads Jeffrey Combs and Barbara Crampton in another HP Lovecraft-based splatter-fest. This sometimes crude clash of horror and sci-fi elements stars Combs as a typically unhinged scientist, whose experiments with the Resonator spark off the usual orgy of murder and mutilation, turning him into a mutated creature with increasingly rubbery effect. This demented tale is sloppily directed, but once it gets going you can't fault its energy and audacity. ▭

Jeffrey Combs *Crawford Tillinghast* • Barbara Crampton *Dr Katherine McMichaels* • Ken Foree *Bubba Brownlee* • Ted Sorel *Dr Edward Pretorius* ■ *Dir* Stuart Gordon • *Scr* Dennis Paoli, Stuart Gordon, Brian Yuzna, from the story by HP Lovecraft

From beyond the Grave ★★★ 15

Horror   1973 · UK · Colour · 94mins

Devilish antiques dealer Peter Cushing sells evil artefacts to unsuspecting shoppers in an above average anthology from British studio Amicus, linking four R Chetwynd-Hayes horror stories. Haunted mirrors, demonic oak doors, invisible elementals and black magic provide the shudder basics for director Kevin Connor, who complements each distinctive tale with atmospheric flourishes and eerie production values. Dotty psychic Margaret Leighton is a stand-out in the enthusiastic cast. ▭ *DVD*

Peter Cushing *Proprietor* • David Warner *Edward Charlton* • Wendy Allnutt *Pamela* • Donald Pleasence *Underwood* • Ian Bannen *Christopher Lowe* • Diana Dors *Mabel Lowe* • Angela Pleasence *Emily* • Margaret Leighton *Madame Orloff* • Ian Carmichael *Reggie Warren* • Ian Ogilvy *William Seaton* • Lesley-Anne Down *Rosemary Seaton* ■ *Dir* Kevin Connor • *Scr* Raymond Christodoulou, Robin Clarke, from the short story collection *The Unbidden* by R Chetwynd-Hayes

From Dusk till Dawn ★★★★ 18

Horror adventure   1995 · US · Colour · 103mins

Delivering everything you'd expect from a splatter-action horror bearing scriptwriter Quentin Tarantino's name, director Robert Rodriguez's in-your-face shocker juggles sharp dialogue, excessive violence, great special effects and bad taste with stylish verve. Tarantino and George Clooney are two crooks heading south of the border, who take preacher Harvey Keitel's family hostage and end up under attack from bloodthirsty vampires, undead strippers and Hell's

U = SUITABLE FOR ALL Uc = SUITABLE FOR ALL, ESPECIALLY FOR YOUNG CHILDREN (VIDEO ONLY) PG = PARENTAL GUIDANCE

Angels when they hide out at a sleazy Mexican bar. Energetic film-making and engaging performances keep this hilarious gore-fest firing on all its raucously tongue-in-cheek cylinders. Contains violence, swearing and nudity 🎞 **DVD**

Harvey Keitel *Jacob Fuller* • George Clooney *Seth Gecko* • Quentin Tarantino *Richard Gecko* • Juliette Lewis *Kate Fuller* • Richard "Cheech" Marin *Border guard/Chet Pussy/ Carlos* • Fred Williamson *Frost* • Salma Hayek *Santanico Pandemonium* • Marc Lawrence *Old timer* ■ *Dir* Robert Rodriguez • *Scr* Quentin Tarantino, from a story by Robert Kurtzman

From Hell It Came ★★

Horror   1957 · US · BW · 70mins

Not a problem which pops up too often in *Gardeners' Question Time* – what do you do with a man-eating, walking tree? This is the dilemma facing Tod Andrews and Tina Carver when an island paradise becomes haunted by a sapling seeking revenge. The unknowns in the cast do their best to keep a straight face, but this really is one for trash fans.

Tod Andrews *Dr William Arnold* • Tina Carver *Dr Terry Mason* • Linda Watkins *Mrs Kilgore* • John McNamara *Dr Howard Clark* • Gregg Palmer *Kimo* • Robert Swan *Witch doctor Tano* ■ *Dir* Dan Milner • *Scr* Richard Bernstein, from a story by Richard Bernstein, Jack Milner

From Hell to Texas ★★★ 🆄

Western   1958 · US · Colour · 99mins

Cowboy Don Murray accidentally kills a man and is relentlessly pursued by RG Armstrong as the victim's vengeful father, hence the movie's more familiar UK title *Manhunt*. Murray's open, innocent face is perfect for this allegorical western, vividly directed by Henry Hathaway. The main interest today lies in the casting of Dennis Hopper, whose final confrontation with Murray is as taut as it is unpredictable, and Hathaway brilliantly frames the antagonists against the landscape.

Don Murray *Tod Lohman* • Diane Varsi *Juanita Bradley* • Chill Wills *Amos Bradley* • Dennis Hopper *Tom Boyd* • RG Armstrong *Hunter Boyd* • Jay C Flippen *Jake Leffertfinger* ■ *Dir* Henry Hathaway • *Scr* Robert Buckner, Wendell Mayes, from the book *The Hell Bent Kid* by Charles O Locke

From Hell to Victory ★★

Second World War drama
1979 · Fr/It/Sp · Colour · 102mins

Even if you don't think much of his film, you have to applaud Umberto Lenzi for the shrewd selection of his pseudonym, Hank Milestone. Lewis Milestone was the director of *All Quiet on the Western Front* which is, some 70 years later, still one of the greatest war movies ever made. In Lenzi's film, a group of friends of various nationalities face separation on the eve of the Second World War. They plan an annual reunion of course, but how many of them will survive? The battle sequences are well mounted, but the highlight is George Hamilton's laughable French accent.

George Peppard *Brett Rosson* • George Hamilton *Maurice* • Horst Buchholz *Jurgen Dietrich* • Jean-Pierre Cassel *Dick Sanders* • Capucine *Nicole Levine* • Sam Wanamaker

Ray MacDonald ■ *Dir* Hank Milestone [Umberto Lenzi] • *Scr* Umberto Lenzi, Jose Luis Martinez Molls, Gianfranco Clerici

From Here to Eternity ★★★★★ 🄿🄶

Wartime drama   1953 · US · BW · 113mins

James Jones's bestseller was thought to be unfilmable – too sexy and too anti-militaristic for a start but, as written by Daniel Taradash and directed by Fred Zinnemann, it became a classic and a box-office smash, nominated for 13 Oscars and winning eight of them. Set in the run-up to and during the Japanese attack on Pearl Harbor, it deals with life in the US forces overseas – the sexually predatory sergeant (Burt Lancaster), the frustrated wife (Deborah Kerr), the peace-loving bugler (Montgomery Clift), the persecuted Italian GI (Frank Sinatra) and the sadistic stockade sergeant (Ernest Borgnine). Lancaster and Kerr's embrace in the pounding surf gained instant fame, while Sinatra put up a noisy campaign to win the role against the wishes of studio boss Harry Cohn. 🎞

Burt Lancaster *Sergeant Milton Warden* • Deborah Kerr *Karen Holmes* • Montgomery Clift *Robert E Lee Prewitt* • Frank Sinatra *Angelo Maggio* • Donna Reed *Alma/Lorene* • Ernest Borgnine *Sergeant "Fatso" Judson* • Philip Ober *Captain Dana Holmes* • Jack Warden *Corporal Buckley* ■ *Dir* Fred Zinnemann • *Scr* Daniel Taradash, from the novel by James Jones • *Cinematographer* Burnett Guffey • *Editor* William Lyon

From Hollywood to Deadwood ★★

Detective spoof   1989 · US · Colour · 90mins

Two gumshoes are hired to find an actress who's gone missing in mid-production in this spoof on the private-eye genre from writer/director Rex Pickett. Evidently there was no time for retakes or a more considered script, as Pickett struggles to make the most of the interplay between Scott Paulin and Jim Haynie. Consequently, the few genuinely wry jabs at Hollywood's expense become lost amid the road-movie clichés as Paulin and Haynie's search becomes a frantic cross-country chase. Contains swearing, violence and sex scenes.

Scott Paulin *Raymond Savage* • Jim Haynie *Jack Haines* • Barbara Schock *Lana Dark* • Jurgen Doeres *Steve Reese* • Chris Mulkey *Nick Detroit* • Mike Genovese *Ernie November* • Campbell Scott *Bobby* ■ *Dir/Scr* Rex Pickett

From Mao to Mozart: Isaac Stern in China ★★★★

Music documentary
1980 · US · Colour · 83mins

Winner of the Oscar for best documentary feature, Murray Lerner's reverential, yet revealing record of Isaac Stern's 1979 goodwill tour to China is remarkable on a number of levels. Apart from the violin virtuoso's eloquent playing, it is interesting to see the enthusiasm with which he was received and the passion for Western music that has been fostered under the communist system. There are sombre moments too, such as the old academic's memoir of the Cultural Revolution. But the scenes at the

Peking Opera and those featuring the phenomenal child prodigies, give the film a sociological fascination to complement its sublime music.

Dir Murray Lerner • *Cinematographer* Nic Knowland, Nick Doob, David Bridges • *Editor* Tom Haneke

From Noon till Three ★★ 🄸🄵

Comedy western   1976 · US · Colour · 95mins

An eccentric western, with Charles Bronson as an amateur gunfighter who returns from the dead after his former mistress (Jill Ireland) has embellished his clumsy exploits and turned him into a money-making legend. Combining elements of *The Man Who Shot Liberty Valance*, *The Life and Times of Judge Roy Bean* and *Cat Ballou*, writer/ director Frank D Gilroy turns in a movie with few laughs and even fewer action highlights. Bronson, cast against type, lacks the necessary lightness for the role or the drunkenness of Lee Marvin in *Cat Ballou*. Film music buffs should look out for a brief cameo by Elmer Bernstein. 🎞

Charles Bronson *Graham Dorsey* • Jill Ireland *Amanda Starbuck* • Douglas V Fowley [Douglas Fowley] *Buck Bowers* • Stan Haze *Ape* • Damon Douglas *Boy* • Hector Morales *Mexican* • Elmer Bernstein *Songwriter* ■ *Dir* Frank D Gilroy • *Scr* Frank D Gilroy, from his novel

From Russia with Love ★★★★ 🄿🄶

Spy adventure   1963 · UK · Colour · 110mins

Ian Fleming received a useful boost to his sales when President Kennedy listed *From Russia with Love* as one of his ten favourite books. It is also one of the most popular Bond movies and a terrific thriller in its own right, owing much to Hitchcock and Carol Reed's *The Third Man* in its marvellous atmosphere of foreign intrigue. Superbly shot on location in a pre-touristy Istanbul, and closely following Fleming's original story, the film has Sean Connery duped into smuggling a top secret communist decoding machine, plus blonde Russian Embassy clerk Daniela Bianchi, from Turkey to the west via the Orient Express. Lotte Lenya is unforgettable as lesbian villain Rosa Klebb, and hit man Robert Shaw commits a terrible *faux pas* in front of 007 by ordering red wine with fish. 🎞 **DVD**

Sean Connery *James Bond* • Daniela Bianchi *Tatiana Romanova* • Pedro Armendariz *Kerim Bey* • Lotte Lenya *Rosa Klebb* • Robert Shaw *Red Grant* • Bernard Lee "M" • Eunice Gayson *Sylvia* • Walter Gotell *Morzeny* • Lois Maxwell *Miss Moneypenny* • Francis De Wolff *Vavra* • Desmond Llewelyn *Major Boothroyd* ■ *Dir* Terence Young • *Scr* Richard Maibaum, Johanna Harwood, from the novel by Ian Fleming • *Music* John Barry

From the Earth to the Moon ★★ 🆄

Science-fiction adventure
1958 · US · Colour · 99mins

Producer Ben Bogeaus's deal with Howard Hughes included the Allan Dwan series and this clunky sci-fi drama. This scrappily-budgeted Jules Verne adaptation offers some pleasure to those who like watching a cast of seemingly-inebriated veterans lurch

through the material. Joseph Cotten plays the scientist who invents Power X (sounds like a detergent, but isn't), a power source that enables him to travel to the moon.

Joseph Cotten *Victor Barbicane* • George Sanders *Stuyvesant Nicholl* • Debra Paget *Virginia Nicholl* • Don Dubbins *Ben Sharpe* ■ *Dir* Byron Haskin • *Scr* Robert Blees, James Leicester, from the novel by Jules Verne

From the Edge of the City ★★★ 🄸🄸

Drama   1998 · Gr · Colour · 93mins

If this stark study of disenfranchised Russian émigrés operating on the outskirts of Athens proves anything, it's that, as far as cinema is concerned, the counterculture of the streets is the same no matter where you are. In following the misfortunes of a gang of pill-popping, petty thieving rent boys, director Constantinos Giannaris employs a technique that combines neorealistic episodes with talking head interviews and frantic time-lapse codas. While this adds immediacy to the authenticity, it distracts from the dramatic implications of Stathis Papadopoulos's dangerous liaison with frosty prostitute Theodora Tzimou and her ambitious pimp, Dimitris Papoulidis. In Greek with English subtitles.

Stathis Papadopoulos *Sasha* • Costas Cotsianidis *Cotsian* • Panagiotis Chartomatsidis *Panagiotis* • Dimitris Papoulidis *Giorgos* • Theodora Tzimou *Natasha* • Anestis Polychronidis *Anestis* ■ *Dir/Scr* Constantinos Giannaris

From the Files of Joseph Wambaugh: a Jury of One ★★★ 🄸🄵

Drama   1992 · US · Colour · 88mins

The films spawned by the novels of Joseph Wambaugh have provided a gritty antidote to the mindless action thrillers so beloved of Hollywood. This TV-movie version unsurprisingly smoothes off the rough edges, but it remains an absorbing drama about a detective (John Spencer) whose life disintegrates after he accidentally kills a fellow police officer during a robbery. However, an investigation into gang murders offers the chance of redemption. It's not in the same league as Wambaugh's *The Onion Field*, but it's sympathetically played and fans of *NYPD Blue* will love it. 🎞

John Spencer *Detective Mike Mulick* • Eddie Velez *Tommy Alomar* • Rachel Ticotin *Christine Avila* • Cheryl Paris *Rita* • Eugene Clark *Detective Dick Price* • Sal Lopez *Al Ramirez* ■ *Dir* Alan Metzger • *Scr* David J Kinghorn

From the Hip ★ 🄸🄵

Courtroom comedy drama
1987 · US · Colour · 106mins

Oh dear, what has happened to Judd Nelson's career? From Brat Pack success in films like *The Breakfast Club*, he has been reduced to making rubbish like this third-rate comedy. He's not the only one who would probably like to forget this tale of a lawyer who will do anything to clear his client of murder – it's safe to assume co-stars Elizabeth Perkins and John

Hurt will have deleted it from their CVs as well. 🖵

Judd Nelson *Robin Weathers* • Elizabeth Perkins *Jo Ann* • John Hurt *Douglas Benoit* • Darren McGavin *Craig Duncan* ■ *Dir* Bob Clark • *Scr* David E Kelley, Bob Clark, from a story by David E Kelley

From the Life of the Marionettes ★★★★

Drama
1980 · W Ger · BW and Colour · 104mins

Ingmar Bergman's second film made during his tax exile in Germany is superior to the misconceived *The Serpent's Egg* (1977). Opening with the murder of a prostitute in a blood-red room, most of the film is shot in stark monochrome with an intense whiteness in the dream sequences. Balanced between the distancing device of Brechtian titles and the use of large closeups, Bergman created a tightly controlled case history in the German idiom. Many of the thoughts of the characters are delivered via speeches, most notably a monologue by an ageing gay man, a rarity in Bergman's female-dominated *oeuvre*. In German with English subtitles. 🖵

Robert Atzorn *Peter Egermann* • Christine Buchegger *Katarina Egermann* • Martin Benrath *Mogens Jensen* • Rita Russek *Ka* • Lola Müthel *Cordelia Egermann* ■ *Dir/Scr* Ingmar Bergman • *Cinematographer* Sven Nykvist • *Art Director* Rolf Zehetbauer

From the Mixed-Up Files of Mrs Basil E Frankweiler ★★★

Adventure drama 1995 · US · Colour · 92mins

Adapted from the novel by EL Konigsberg, this is a TV-movie remake of the 1973 children's film, which was also known as *The Hideaways*. Taking over the title role from Ingrid Bergman, a rather imperious Lauren Bacall has her work cut out to prevent young Jean Marie Barnwell and Jesse Lee from stealing the picture, as they seek her advice in determining whether a statue in New York's Metropolitan Museum of Art is a genuine Michelangelo. It's rather highbrow for youngsters, but director Marcus Cole cleverly turns it into an accessible detective mystery.

Lauren Bacall *Mrs Basil E Frankweiler* • Jean Marie Barnwell *Claudia* • Jesse Lee *Jamie* • M Emmet Walsh *Morris* • Miriam Flynn *Mrs Kincaid* ■ *Dir* Marcus Cole • *Scr* Betty Goldberg, from the novel by EL Konigsberg

From the Pole to the Equator ★★★ PG

Experimental documentary compilation
1987 · It/W Ger · Tinted · 97mins

Born in 1874, Luca Comerio was the official photographer to the Italian Royal Family, before turning to film-making in 1905. Over the next 23 years, he covered the globe capturing news events like the 1911 invasion of Libya as well as making travelogues in areas as varied as the South Pole, India, Africa and Central Asia. This stylised compilation of his most representative imagery took over three years to assemble. Yervant Gianikian and Angela Ricci Lucchi sifted through miles of footage, which they then stretch-printed and tinted to produce a

mesmerising – and often disconcerting – memoir of a bygone age of sporting savagery and imperial exploitation. With English subtitles.. 🖵

Dir Yervant Gianikian, Angela Ricci Lucchi

From the Terrace ★★ PG

Drama
1960 · US · Colour · 143mins

The combination of pedestrian direction and predictable plotting undermines Mark Robson's adaptation of John O'Hara's sprawling novel. Paul Newman goes through the motions as a Wall Street whizkid who defies his well-heeled family to marry Joanne Woodward, only to risk losing her when he has a fling with Ina Balin. Newman is upstaged by his female co-stars, with Myrna Loy particularly effective playing against type as a boozing matriarch. Screenwriter Ernest Lehman gives the impression of tackling weighty themes, but this is little more than a glitzy soap opera. 🖵

Paul Newman *Alfred Eaton* • Joanne Woodward *Mary St John* • Myrna Loy *Martha Eaton* • Ina Balin *Natalie* • Leon Ames *Samuel Eaton* • Elizabeth Allen *Sage Rimmington* ■ *Dir* Mark Robson • *Scr* Ernest Lehman, from the novel by John O'Hara

From This Day Forward ★★★

Drama
1946 · US · BW · 95mins

Mark Stevens stars as an unemployed ex-serviceman looking back to the days during the Depression when he met and married Joan Fontaine in this classy piece of escapism from RKO. Stevens struggles with his role, but his rather feeble performance is offset by the charm of Fontaine, even if you have suspend disbelief to accept her as a working-class New Yorker. Once over that hurdle, relax and enjoy the sheer professionalism of the Hollywood dream factory.

Joan Fontaine *Susan* • Mark Stevens *Bill* • Rosemary De Camp *Martha* • Henry Morgan [Harry Morgan] *Hank* • Wally Brown *Jake* • Bobby Driscoll *Timmy* ■ *Dir* John Berry • *Scr* Hugo Butler, Garson Kanin, Edith R Sommer, Charles Schee, from the novel *All the Brides Are Beautiful* by Thomas Bell

The Front ★★★ 15

Comedy drama 1976 · US · Colour · 90mins

Woody Allen too bland? Surprisingly, that's how he comes across in this Martin Ritt-directed exposé of Hollywood during the witch-hunt days of the fifties, playing a cashier who agrees to lend his name as a cover for blacklisted scriptwriters. Allen simply puts his usual neurotic personality on hold until his character starts believing he's as good as the authors he's helping. Allen is dwarfed both physically and dramatically by Zero Mostel, whose anxiety is twice the size of his bulk. 🖵

Woody Allen *Howard Prince* • Zero Mostel *Hecky Brown* • Herschel Bernardi *Phil Sussman* • Michael Murphy *Alfred Miller* • Andrea Marcovicci *Florence Barrett* ■ *Dir* Martin Ritt • *Scr* Walter Bernstein

The Front Page ★★★

Comedy drama 1931 · US · BW · 102mins

Ben Hecht and Charles MacArthur's stage success of 1928 was a natural

for a movie adaptation: set mainly in the pressroom of a Chicago court-house, it's a gift for actors. Adolphe Menjou plays the powerful editor, Walter Burns, and Pat O'Brien is his ace reporter, Hildy Johnson. Then condemned prisoner George E Stone gives Hildy a scoop, diverting him from his fiancée. Spraying smart dialogue at the speed of Chicago's machine-guns, it carries its age with dignity. Remade – with a sex-change operation (Hildy becomes a woman) – as *His Girl Friday* in 1940, by Billy Wilder in 1974, and again in *Switching Channels* in 1988, by this time set in a TV newsroom.

Adolphe Menjou *Walter Burns* • Pat O'Brien *Hildy Johnson* • Mary Brian *Peggy* • Edward Everett Horton *Bensinger* • Walter Catlett *Murphy* ■ *Dir* Lewis Milestone • *Scr* Bartlett Cormack, Ben Hecht (uncredited), Charles Lederer (uncredited), from the play by Ben Hecht, Charles MacArthur

The Front Page ★★★

Comedy drama 1974 · US · Colour · 104mins

Director Billy Wilder had already made one classic newspaper movie *Ace in the Hole* before he tackled Ben Hecht and Charles MacArthur's play, previously filmed in 1931. Preserving nearly half the play's dialogue, Wilder and his co-writer, IAL Diamond, created a breathless, Faustian farce. Jack Lemmon stars as Hildy Johnson, the hotshot reporter who's intent on getting married despite the fact that he has clearly sold his soul to the Devil incarnate, satanic editor Walter Burns, played by Walter Matthau. Lemmon and Matthau are on top form, and their "cigarette me" scene is creepily effective, but 104 minutes of screaming and shouting, no matter how clever the dialogue, gets a bit wearing.

Jack Lemmon *Hildy Johnson* • Walter Matthau *Walter Burns* • Carol Burnett *Mollie Malloy* • Susan Sarandon *Peggy Grant* • Vincent Gardenia *Sheriff* • David Wayne *Bensinger* • Allen Garfield *Kruger* ■ *Dir* Billy Wilder • *Scr* Billy Wilder, IAL Diamond, from the play by Ben Hecht, Charles MacArthur

Front Page Story ★★★ PG

Drama
1953 · UK · BW · 94mins

Back in the days when Rupert was only a bear in Fleet Street and British newspapers engaged in rivalries that were almost gentlemanly compared with today, editor Jack Hawkins has to choose between his job and his marriage to Elizabeth Allan, who sits at home and wonders where it all went wrong. Cosily dated, but an interesting sign of its times. 🖵

Jack Hawkins *John Grant* • Elizabeth Allan *Susan Grant* • Eva Bartok *Mrs Thorpe* • Derek Farr *Teale* • Michael Goodliffe *Kennedy* ■ *Dir* Gordon Parry • *Scr* Jay Lewis, Jack Howells, William Fairchild, Guy Morgan, from the novel *Final Night* by Robert Gaines

Front Page Woman ★★★

Comedy drama 1935 · US · BW · 83mins

Julia Roberts and Nick Nolte starred in 1994's *I Love Trouble*, an inferior variation on this thirties picture starring Bette Davis and George Brent. It's a tale about two newspaper hounds, constantly trying to out-scoop and out-

quip each other, before deciding to settle their professional differences in the traditional way of romantic comedies. It wins no prizes for realism in its depiction of newspaper life, but at least it scores some points for correctness ahead of its time on the working woman issue, and there's a good deal of enjoyment to be had en route to the rather predictable finale.

Bette Davis *Ellen Garfield* • George Brent *Curt Devlin* • Roscoe Karns *Toots* • Winifred Shaw *Inez Cordova* • Joseph Crehan *Spike Kiley* ■ *Dir* Michael Curtiz • *Scr* Roy Chanslor, Lillie Hayward, Laird Doyle, from the novel *Women Are Bum Newspapermen* by Richard Macauley

La Frontera ★★★ 15

Political drama
1991 · Chil/Sp · Colour · 115mins

Deftly revealing character through locale, Ricardo Larrain's debut feature (which won a Silver Bear at the Berlin Film Festival) is a precisely paced study of the loneliness of principle. As the Chilean maths teacher exiled to a coastal town that was once swept away by a tidal wave, Patricio Contreras unassumingly combines commitment and resignation. There's much amusement to be had in the way he taunts his doltish police guards, but the core of the film lies in his tentative relationship with Gloria Laso, the daughter of a fugitive from Franco's Spain, and his uneasy friendship with a priest. In Spanish with English subtitles. 🖵

Patricio Contreras *Ramiro Orellana* • Gloria Laso *Maite* • Hector Noguera *Father Patricio* • Alonso Venegas *Delegate* • Aldo Bernales *Diver* ■ *Dir* Ricardo Larrain • *Scr* Ricardo Larrain, Jorge Goldenberg

Frontier Badmen ★★ U

Western
1943 · US · BW · 77mins

The bland Robert Paige is surrounded by a highly watchable cast, notably the tormented Diana Barrymore, alcoholic daughter of John, as the romantic lead. Lon Chaney Jr features as a mean hired gun with a streak of sheer sadism unusual in a family-themed movie of this type, and Paige's sidekick is a young Noah Beery Jr, best remembered today for *The Rockford Files* TV series.

Robert Paige *Steve* • Anne Gwynne *Chris* • Noah Beery Jr *Jim* • Diana Barrymore *Claire* • Leo Carrillo *Chinito* • Andy Devine *Slim* • Lon Chaney Jr *Chango* ■ *Dir* Ford Beebe • *Scr* Gerald Geraghty, Morgan B Cox

Frontier Gal ★★★

Comedy western 1945 · US · Colour · 84mins

This romantic western was one of the movies that made a star out of exotic lovely Yvonne De Carlo. Tight-lipped leading man Rod Cameron is De Carlo's rugged co-star, and the splendidly batty plot involves bandit Cameron marrying De Carlo and going on the run for six years, then returning to discover that he's now a father before ultimately throwing the villain over a cliff. Don't ask. The roles were originally intended for the equally exotic Maria Montez and bland Jon Hall, but De Carlo and Cameron are marginally more watchable, if less showy. De Carlo would gain icon status

U = SUITABLE FOR ALL   Uc = SUITABLE FOR ALL, ESPECIALLY FOR YOUNG CHILDREN (VIDEO ONLY)   PG = PARENTAL GUIDANCE

in *The Munsters* TV series, but Cameron was relegated to B-westerns.

Yvonne De Carlo *Lorena Dumont* • Rod Cameron *Johnny Hart* • Andy Devine *Big Ben* • Fuzzy Knight *Fuzzy* • Sheldon Leonard *Blackie* • Andrew Tombes *Judge Prescott* ■ *Dir* Charles Lamont • *Scr* Michael Fessier, Ernest Pagano

Frontier Horizon ★★ U
Western   1939 · US · BW · 54mins

After being loaned out for *Stagecoach*, this was John Wayne's last appearance in the *Three Mesquiteers* series before Republic finally promoted him to A-features. Filmed as *New Frontier*, it is retitled for TV showings to avoid confusion with *The New Frontier* (1935). The dreary-as-usual plot has Wayne, Ray Corrigan and Raymond Hatton saving settlers from taking worthless land. The only point of interest is the young Phyllis Isley, who would transform herself into a major star under the name of Jennifer Jones.

John Wayne *Stony Brooke* • Ray Corrigan *Tucson Smith* • Raymond Hatton *Rusty Joslin* • Phyllis Isley [Jennifer Jones] *Celia* ■ *Dir* George Sherman • *Scr* Betty Burbridge, Luci Ward, from characters created by William Colt McDonald

Frontier Marshal ★★★
Western   1939 · US · BW · 71mins

A marvellously authentic-looking version of the Wyatt Earp legend, the first sound western for director Allan Dwan. This take on the tale is based on Stuart Lake's novel and stars the stone-faced Randolph Scott as the man who cleaned up the West, with debonair Cesar Romero as the doom-laden Doc Holliday, renamed for some reason as Doc Halliday. Despite a cracking pace and some exciting moments, this is nowhere near as effective, or affecting, as John Ford's *My Darling Clementine* (which also features the same actor Charles Stevens as the same drunken Indian!), or even John Sturges's *Gunfight at the OK Corral*. It may not be historically correct, but it's undeniably entertaining, and mercifully brief in the telling.

Randolph Scott *Wyatt Earp* • Nancy Kelly *Sarah Allen* • Cesar Romero *Doc Halliday* • Binnie Barnes *Jerry* • John Carradine *Ben Carter* • Edward Norris *Dan Blackmore* • Lon Chaney Jr *Pringle* ■ *Dir* Allan Dwan • *Scr* Sam Hellman, from the novel *Wyatt Earp, Frontier Marshal* by Stuart N Lake

Frontier Outlaws ★★★ U
Western   1944 · US · BW · 58mins

Former Olympic gold medallist Buster Crabbe made 36 B-westerns for poverty row studio PRC from 1941 to 1946. This brisk 58-minute affair is one of the best, with enough action and humour to please all enthusiasts of old-fashioned, uncomplicated shoot-'em-ups. Crabbe's comic sidekick in all these films was played by Al "Fuzzy" St John, former Sennett comedian and nephew of "Fatty" Arbuckle, but there are more laughs than usual between the action episodes in this, due to a great courtroom turn by Emmett Lynn as an unconventional judge.

Buster Crabbe [Larry "Buster" Crabbe] *Billy Carson* • Al St John *Fuzzy Jones* • Frances Gladwin *Pat* • Marin Sais *Ma Clark* • Charles King *Barlow* ■ *Dir* Sam Newfield • *Scr* Joe O'Donnell

Frostfire ★★★
Adventure   1994 · Can · Colour

Among the most prolific makers of TV movies, British actor-turned-director David Greene puts the Arctic landscape to good use in this intriguing adventure. Mosha Cote makes an impressive debut as the young Inuit who suspects dirty work is afoot when the mysteriously ill woman he rescues from the icy wilds is inexplicably replaced by an impostor for TV coverage of the story. Combining conspiracy theory with suspense, outdoor action and Inuit folklore, this is well-crafted entertainment.

Robert Clothier *Rupert Kromick* • Mosha Cote *Nelson Nagarauk* • Wendy Crewson *Virginia* ■ *Dir* David Greene • *Scr* Marc Strange

Frozen Assets ★★ 15
Comedy   1992 · US · Colour · 97mins

If you were going to make a comedy about a sperm bank, you would think the only way to go is over the top. But director George Miller – no, not the *Mad Max* man, but the one responsible for *Andre* – was unable or unwilling to enter the realms of cheerful tastelessness, and the result is a tepid comedy. Corbin Bernsen is the city high-flier who finds himself in charge of a small-town bank in Oregon that doesn't deal in the usual commodities. Shelley Long spars with Bernsen, but an embarrassingly eccentric turn from Larry Miller hardly helps matters, and this misfire was deposited straight into the video market in the UK. Contains swearing.

Shelley Long *Dr Grace Murdock* • Corbin Bernsen *Zach Shepard* • Larry Miller *Newton Patterson* • Dody Goodman *Mrs Patterson* • Matt Clark *JF Hughes* ■ *Dir* George Miller (1) • *Scr* Don Klein, Thomas Kartozian

Fudge-a-Mania ★★★ U
Comedy   1995 · US · Colour · 88mins

This energetic made-for-TV family film, based on the well-loved children's books by Judy Blume, features Luke Tarsitano as the eponymous Fudge, a mischievous little boy who seems determined to make life a misery for his older brother while on a family holiday. Directed by Bob Clark, the film also stars Jake Richardson and Eve Plumb, here re-united with her screen mother (Florence Henderson) from the TV series *The Brady Bunch*.

Florence Henderson *Muriel* • Darren McGavin *Buzzy Tubman Sr* • Eve Plumb *Ann Hatcher* • Jake Richardson *Peter Hatcher* • Luke Tarsitano *Fudge* • Forrest Witt *Warren Hatcher* • Nassira Nicola *Sheila Tubman* ■ *Dir* Bob Clark • *Scr* Bob Clark, from the novel by Judy Blume

The Fugitive ★★★★ PG
Drama   1947 · US · BW · 99mins

Director John Ford's mesmerising version of *The Power and the Glory* – Graham Greene's novel about a "whisky priest"– was seriously compromised in content by the censorship of the time. But, despite the fact that the central relationship is no longer a sexual one and Henry Fonda's priest is not an alcoholic, it remains resolutely convincing. Pedro Armendariz is particularly fine as the mustachioed police lieutenant, and Dolores Del Rio smoulders as the woman, but the real star of this brooding opus is the magnificent outdoor photography from Gabriel Figueroa.

Henry Fonda *Fugitive* • Dolores Del Rio *Native woman* • Pedro Armendariz *Police lieutenant* • J Carrol Naish *Police informer* • Leo Carrillo *Chief of police* • Ward Bond *El Gringo* ■ *Dir* John Ford • *Scr* Dudley Nichols, from the novel *The Power and the Glory* by Graham Greene

The Fugitive ★★★★ 15
Thriller   1993 · US · Colour and BW · 124mins

The original TV series of *The Fugitive* starring David Janssen ran for 120 episodes between 1963–67, and attracted a cult following. This big screen adaptation bears little resemblance to the series, but for once this is a blessing. Director Andrew Davis (*Above the Law, Under Siege*), takes the bare bones of the series and comes up with an unstoppable juggernaut, in which the suspense never lets up and where the set pieces (notably the spectacular train crash and Ford's daredevil dive into the dam) are truly epic. Harrison Ford is fine as the innocent surgeon who is wrongfully convicted of the murder of his wife and sets off to find the real killer. But the movie is stolen from under his nose by an Oscar-winning turn from Tommy Lee Jones, as the marshal doggedly pursuing the wanted man. Contains violence and swearing. **DVD**

Harrison Ford *Dr Richard Kimble* • Tommy Lee Jones *Deputy Marshal Samuel Gerard* • Sela Ward *Helen Kimble* • Julianne Moore *Dr Anne Eastman* • Joe Pantoliano *Cosmo Renfro* ■ *Dir* Andrew Davis • *Scr* Jeb Stuart, David Twohy, from a story by David Twohy, from characters created by Roy Huggins

Fugitive from Justice ★★ 15
Drama   1996 · US · Colour · 90mins

If it isn't a deviant dad, it's a drug-addled mama in another TV movie about parents kidnapping their own children to save them from an abusive spouse. You know the beginning and you know where this awkwardly directed drama is going. Chris Noth (*Sex and the City*) does his best as a concerned father who fears that his boozy ex-wife (Loryn Locklin) and her low-life boyfriend are abusing and neglecting his infant daughter. Singer Natalie Cole plays the head of the underground group that helps Noth.

Chris Noth [Christopher Noth] *Larry Coster* • Peter MacNicol *Roy Dowd* • Stepfanie Kramer *Loretta Gaines* • Natalie Cole *Latisha Corbett* ■ *Dir* Chuck Bowman • *Scr* Joel Oliansky, Kurt Inderbitzen, Victoria Karess

The Fugitive Kind ★★ 15
Drama   1960 · US · BW · 116mins

Another emotional tale from Tennessee Williams, directed by Sidney Lumet, with Marlon Brando as a guitar-playing drifter who falls into the lap of Anna Magnani, a lonely woman trapped in a marriage to a dying man. There are subplots aplenty, and Joanne Woodward as well, but you get the feeling it's Williams throwing out his dirty washing and seeing how it fails. Magnani, known in Italy as "la Lupa" or "the She-Wolf", had won an Oscar for another film based on a Williams play, 1955's *The Rose Tattoo*. But, despite such prestige casting, audiences sensed a downer and stayed away in droves.

Marlon Brando *Val Xavier* • Anna Magnani *Lady Torrance* • Joanne Woodward *Carol Cutrere* • Maureen Stapleton *Vee Talbot* • Victor Jory *Jabe Torrance* ■ *Dir* Sidney Lumet • *Scr* Tennessee Williams, Meade Roberts, from the play *Orpheus Descending* by Tennessee Williams

Fugitive Nights: Danger in the Desert ★★★
Crime thriller   1993 · US · Colour · 95mins

The tentative pilot for a possible series, this above-average TV movie was written and produced by Joseph Wambaugh author of *The Onion Field*. His authorial presence lends gravitas to an otherwise fairly routine up-market/down-market mismatched cop scenario, as Palm Springs detective Teri Garr and hard-drinking Sam Elliott team up to track down a mysterious fugitive before the bad guys get there first. The leads both deliver their usual solid performances, but the whole is somewhat unadventurous.

Teri Garr *Brenda Burrows* • Sam Elliott *Lynn Cutter* • Thomas Haden Church *Nelson Hareem* • Warren Frost *Clive Devon* • Geno Silva *Fugitive* • Barbara Babcock *Rhonda Devon* • Raymond J Barry *Jack Graves* • TJ Castronovo *John Lugo* ■ *Dir* Gary Nelson • *Scr* Joseph Wambaugh, from his novel

Full Body Massage ★★★
Drama   1995 · US · Colour · 93mins

It seems a terrible waste for a director as distinctive and stylish as Nicolas Roeg to be mired in cable TV land. This is an eminently watchable piece, but there's a sense of treading water about such a low-key, stagey drama following the relationship between the rich Mimi Rogers and her masseur (Bryan Brown). It's essentially a two-hander and low on action, but the two leads make the most of the intelligent script from Dan Gurskis. Contains violence, swearing and nudity.

Mimi Rogers *Nina* • Bryan Brown *Fitch* • Christopher Burgard *Douglas* • Elizabeth Barondes *Alice* • Patrick Neil Quinn *Andy* ■ *Dir* Nicolas Roeg • *Scr* Dan Gurskis

Full Circle ★★
Horror   1977 · UK/Can · Colour · 97mins

Director Richard Loncraine's competent adaptation of Peter Straub's novel is a slow-moving, supernatural tale more concerned with atmosphere than action. Mia Farrow is an unstable mother who, feeling responsible for the choking death of her daughter, leaves her husband (Keir Dullea). Moving into an eerie house haunted by the spirit of a moody child, she becomes even more guilt-stricken and obsessed. Loncraine's subtle and lyrical chiller has its admirers, but most viewers will be three steps ahead of the catatonic Farrow and be wondering what all the fuss is about.

Mia Farrow *Julia Lofting* • Keir Dullea *Magnus Lofting* • Tom Conti *Mark* • Jill Bennett *Lily* • Robin Gammell *David Swift* • Cathleen Nesbitt *Mrs Rudge* • Anna Wing *Mrs Flood* ■ *Dir* Richard Loncraine • *Scr* Dave Humphries, from the novel *Julia* by Peter Straub

Full Confession ★★

Crime drama　　1939 · US · BW · 72mins

A B-movie combination of *I Confess* and *The Informer*, with Victor McLaglen starring in a part reminiscent of his Oscar-winning role in the latter. He plays a ruthless killer who tells a priest of his crime. Since an innocent man (Barry Fitzgerald) is under sentence of death, can the priest convince McLaglen to confess? The interesting theme is marred by the script's heavy-handed piety and sanctimonious soul-searching, which John Farrow's slow-paced direction fails to counteract. It is intriguing to see Joseph Calleia, best known as a screen villain, convincingly portraying the priest.

Victor McLaglen *McGinnis* • Sally Eilers *Molly* • Joseph Calleia *Father Loma* • Barry Fitzgerald *Michael O'Keefe* • Elisabeth Risdon *Norah O'Keefe* ■ *Dir* John Farrow • *Scr* Jerry Cady, from a story by Leo Birinski

Full Contact ★★★★ 18

Action thriller　　1992 · HK · Colour · 92mins

Chow Yun-Fat is Jeff, the Bangkok bouncer who takes violent revenge after an arms raid leads to a double-cross in this frantic "heroic bloodshed" thriller. Simon Yam, as gay arms dealer Judge dominates proceedings and Anthony Wong plays Jeff's duplicitous friend Sam. This is a film of flying metal, whether in the form of speeding cars, bikes or bullets. Ringo Lam's direction is electrifying, topping the armoured car robberies with a sensational nightclub shootout, in which the camera takes on the perspective of the bullets. In Cantonese with English subtitles. Contains violence and swearing

Chow Yun-Fat *Jeff* • Simon Yam *Judge* • Ann Bridgewater *Mona* • Anthony Wong *Sam* • Bonnie Fu *Virgin* • Frankie Chin *Deano* ■ *Dir* Ringo Lam • *Scr* Nam Yin

A Full Day's Work ★★

Black comedy　　1973 · Fr · Colour · 95mins

Jean-Louis Trintignant is probably best remembered as the racing driver in the classic French romance *A Man and a Woman*, but his directorial debut finds him at the opposite end of the spectrum. An undistinguished black comedy, it follows the murderous exploits of baker Jacques Dufilho, as he exacts his revenge on the jurors who sent his son to his death. As far as "chopping list" films go we're not exactly in Vincent Price territory. French dialogue dubbed into English.

Jacques Dufilho *Gaston Rousseau, baker* • André Falcon *Director* • Luce Marquand *Mother* • Vittorio Caprioli *Mangiacavalo* ■ *Dir/Scr* Jean-Louis Trintignant

Full Eclipse ★★★ 18

Action horror thriller
1993 · US · Colour · 93mins

This imaginative werewolf romp is given lashings of style by horror director Anthony Hickox, which compensates for the general lack of blood-spilling enforced by its TV movie status. Hard-bitten urban cop Mario Van Peebles is tricked by Patsy Kensit into joining Bruce Payne's elite corps of crime-busting lycanthropes. A simple injection turns him into a furry vigilante with an appetite for criminal-ripping frenzies, performed with Hong Kong-inspired élan in a film redolent with creepy atmosphere.

Mario Van Peebles *Max Dire* • Patsy Kensit *Casey Spencer* • Bruce Payne *Adam Garou* • Anthony John Denison *Jim Sheldon* • Victoria Rowell *Anna Dire* • John Verea *Ramon Perez* ■ *Dir* Anthony Hickox • *Scr* Richard Christian Matheson, Michael Reaves

Full Exposure: the Sex Tapes Scandal ★ 18

Thriller　　1989 · US · Colour · 91mins

An intriguing title for a dreadful thriller about a lawyer investigating the murder of a prostitute who leaves behind some incriminating evidence. *Knots Landing*'s Lisa Hartman, the doyenne of the TV movie, is capable enough, but even she can't hide the fact that this is a ridiculous and badly plotted movie with a script that should have been consigned to the "reject" pile. Contains nudity.

Lisa Hartman *Sarah Dutton* • Anthony Denison [Anthony John Denison] *Lieutenant James Thompson* • Vanessa L Williams *Valentine* • Jennifer O'Neil *Debralee* ■ *Dir* Noel Nosseck • *Scr* Stephen Zito

Full Fathom Five ★★

Action thriller　　1990 · US · Colour · 82mins

Roger Corman once again demonstrates his unerring ability (or luck) when it comes to spotting directorial talent. Carl Franklin is now acclaimed for his thrillers *One False Move* and *Devil in a Blue Dress*, but back in 1990 he was a jobbing TV actor, known mainly for a semi-regular role in *The A-Team*. This blatant cash-in on *The Hunt for Red October* features cult icon Michael Moriarty as a submarine skipper on the trail of stolen nuclear craft. It's pretty undistinguished fare, although it obviously taught Franklin something.

Michael Moriarty *McKenzie* • Maria Rangel *Justine* • Diego Bertie *Miguel* • German Gonzales *Sebastian* ■ *Dir* Carl Franklin • *Scr* Bart Davis, from his novel

Full Metal Jacket ★★★★★ 18

War drama　　1987 · UK · Colour · 111mins

Stanley Kubrick's penultimate film is a harrowing, foul-mouthed and violent Vietnam war drama. But, unlike the rainforest horrors of *Apocalypse Now* or *Platoon*, Kubrick's film begins with a long training camp sequence in America before moving to a bombed-out Vietnamese city. While its message is simple – innocent young Americans are taught to be machine-like killers – its technique is extraordinary. Because Kubrick refuses to travel any distance, it was shot

entirely in Britain, with palm trees uprooted from Spain and Matthew Modine and a cast of relative unknowns uprooted from Hollywood. Kubrick created a huge and spectacular outdoor set, though some sequences, it must be said, lack tropical realism. The performances are superb, especially Lee Ermey as the drill sergeant with a colourful vocabulary, Vincent D'Onofrio as the pathetic Private Pyle and Modine as the cynical recruit named Joker.

Matthew Modine *Private Joker* • Adam Baldwin *Animal Mother* • Vincent D'Onofrio *Leonard Lawrence, Private Gomer Pyle* • Lee Ermey [R Lee Ermey] *Gunnery Sergeant Hartman* • Dorian Harewood *Eightball* • Arliss Howard *Private Cowboy* ■ *Dir* Stanley Kubrick • *Scr* Stanley Kubrick, Michael Herr, Gustav Hasford, from the novel *The Short-Timers* by Gustav Hasford • *Art Director* Anton Furst

The Full Monty ★★★★★ 15

Comedy　　1997 · UK/US · Colour · 87mins

When the going gets tough, the tough get go-going, as Robert Carlyle – a divorced father trying to maintain joint custody of his son – forms a strip act along with a group of other unemployed Sheffield steelworkers in director Peter Cattaneo's highly engaging, genuinely poignant and hilarious full-frontal comedy drama. Well endowed with side-splitting laughter, mined by a superb ensemble cast, it's about men's emotional shortcomings as much as their *Dirty Dancing* techniques. The many many wonderful moments include the Chippendales of the North inadvertently gyrating to the radio in a dole queue – simply inspired. Contains swearing and some nudity.

Robert Carlyle *Gaz* • Tom Wilkinson *Gerald* • Mark Addy *Dave* • Lesley Sharp *Jean* • Emily Woof *Mandy* • Steve Huison *Lomper* • Paul Barber *Horse* • Hugo Speer *Guy* • Deirdre Costello *Linda* • Bruce Jones *Reg* ■ *Dir* Peter Cattaneo • *Scr* Simon Beaufoy

Full Moon High ★★★ 15

Comedy horror　　1982 · US · Colour · 90mins

Horror specialist Larry Cohen ventures into comedy with this parody of such fifties' B-movies as *I Was a Teenage Werewolf*. But it's also a sort of *Back to the Future* with fangs, as Adam Arkin returns from Transylvania after years in a lycanthropic wilderness to discover that his old high school buddies have changed almost as drastically as he has. Playing down the special effects in order to concentrate on the social spoofing, this is a surprisingly sharp and funny film, with Arkin (son of the excellent Alan, who also cameos) proving that anything Michael J Fox can do...

Adam Arkin *Tony Walker* • Elizabeth Hartman *Miss Montgomery* • Ed McMahon *Mr Walker* • Kenneth Mars • Roz Kelly • Joanne Nail • Pat Morita • Louis Nye ■ *Dir/Scr* Larry Cohen

Full Moon in Blue Water ★★ 15

Comedy drama　　1988 · US · Colour · 90mins

Only Gene Hackman saves this comedy drama from totally sinking. He plays Floyd, the owner of a run-down Texas bar, who is obsessed by his long-lost wife despite the efforts of Teri Garr to

grab him for herself. Full of the kind of eccentrics usually found in a Tennessee Williams play, the production veers too clumsily between engaging realism and overblown melodrama. Contains swearing.

Gene Hackman *Floyd* • Teri Garr *Louise* • Burgess Meredith *The General* • Elias Koteas *Jimmy* • Kevin Cooney *Charlie* • David Doty *Virgil* • Gil Glasgow *Baytch* ■ *Dir* Peter Masterson • *Scr* Bill Bozzone

Full Moon in Paris ★★★★ 15

Romantic comedy　　1984 · Fr · Colour · 97mins

The fourth film in Eric Rohmer's *Comedies and Proverbs* series is a sublime example of the trouble we land ourselves in every time we open our mouths. In this delightful tale – surely no other film-maker has depicted with such consistency and accuracy exactly what it means to be human – Pascale Ogier backfires when she's sucked into a new social world full of temptations and regrets. The daughter of popular star Bulle Ogier, Pascale won the best actress award at Venice, only to die shortly afterwards at the tragically young age of 24. In French with English subtitles.

Pascale Ogier *Louise* • Fabrice Luchini *Octave* • Tcheky Karyo *Rémi* • Christian Vadim *Bastien* • Virginie Thévenet *Camille* • Thérèse Liotard *Marianne* • Noël Coffman *Stanislas* ■ *Dir/Scr* Eric Rohmer

Full of Life ★★★

Comedy drama　　1956 · US · BW · 90mins

The delightful Judy Holliday was rarely upstaged, but this warm family comedy is stolen by pudgy Salvatore Baccaloni, the Metropolitan Opera bass making his screen debut with a superb performance as her father-in-law. The film covers the final few days in Holliday's pregnancy with her first child, and the problems that arise when her husband's well-meaning but interfering Italian Catholic father comes to fix a hole in their floor. Holliday's anxieties are human and believable and, although Richard Conte lacks the light touch as Holliday's writer husband, the film has a beguiling charm.

Judy Holliday *Emily Rocco* • Richard Conte *Nick Rocco* • Salvatore Baccaloni *Papa Rocco* • Esther Minciotti *Mama Rocco* • Joe De Santis *Father Gondolfo* ■ *Dir* Richard Quine • *Scr* John Fante, from his novel

The Full Treatment ★★

Mystery drama　　1961 · UK · BW · 120mins

Known in the US as *Stop Me before I Kill!*, this sees racing driver Ronald Lewis follow his marriage to Diane Cilento with a serious head injury. French psychiatrist Claude Dauphin is supposed to be helping Lewis with some serious psychological problems but he's actually more interested in pursuing Cilento. The adult theme and a few sexy scenes earned this film an X certificate back in the early sixties but it looks mild enough now and far too long.

Claude Dauphin *Dr David Prade* • Diane Cilento *Denise Colby* • Ronald Lewis *Alan*

U = SUITABLE FOR ALL　**Uc** = SUITABLE FOR ALL, ESPECIALLY FOR YOUNG CHILDREN (VIDEO ONLY)　**PG** = PARENTAL GUIDANCE

Colby • Françoise Rosay *Madame Prade* ■ *Dir* Val Guest • *Scr* Val Guest, Ronald Scott Thorn, from the novel by Ronald Scott Thorn

The Fuller Brush Man ★★
Comedy   1948 · US · BW · 91mins

Red Skelton's style of slapstick comedy isn't to all tastes but this is a better example than most. As a novice brush salesman, he has some fine moments going door-to-door but the picture is overburdened with a plot which makes him a murder suspect and involves a war surplus racket before the engaging climax in which the comic and his girlfriend (Janet Blair) are on the run from the heavies in a warehouse.

Red Skelton *Red Jones* • Janet Blair *Ann Elliot* • Don McGuire *Keenan Wallick* • Hillary Brooke *Mildred Trist* • Trudy Marshall *Sara* ■ *Dir* S Sylvan Simon • *Scr* Frank Tashlin, Devery Freeman, from a story by Roy Huggins

Fun ★★ 18
Drama
1994 · Can/US · Colour and BW · 99mins

Resembling Peter Jackson's infinitely superior *Heavenly Creatures*, which brought Kate Winslet to Hollywood's attention, director Rafal Zielinski's tale of two precocious teenagers committing murder to cement their friendship makes no effort to endear the gruesome girls to the viewer. That flaw, coupled with laughable psychology and a cop-out climax, severely undermines the *vérité* style that the director was aiming for; despite a tightly constructed plot in black and white for the present, glorious colour for the flashbacks and horribly compelling central performances from Alicia Witt and Renee Humphrey.

Renee Humphrey *Hilary* • Alicia Witt *Bonnie* • William R Moses *John* • Leslie Hope *Jane* • Ania Suli *Mrs Farmer* ■ *Dir* Rafal Zielinski • *Scr* James Bosley, from his play

Fun and Fancy Free ★★★ U
Animation   1947 · US · Colour · 69mins

Disney's wholehearted support for the war effort and the consequent diversion of the studio's resources, resulted in a series of packaged shorter cartoons during the late forties. This pairing of just two stories is one of the better pictures from that period. Jiminy Cricket's tale about Bongo the wandering bear is based on a Sinclair Lewis story, while Edgar Bergen's retelling of *Jack and the Beanstalk* with Mickey, Donald and Goofy playing penniless farmers, is notable for being the last time Disney supplied the voice of Mickey.

Dinah Shore *Narrator* • Edgar Bergen • Luana Patten • Anita Gordon *The Singing Harp* • Cliff Edwards *Jiminy Cricket* • Billy Gilbert *The Giant* • Clarence Nash *Donald Duck* ■ *Dir* Jack Kinney, Bill Roberts, Hamilton Luske, William Horgan • *Scr* Homer Brightman, Eldon Dedini, Lance Nolley, Tom Oreb, Harry Reeves, Ted Sears, from a story by Sinclair Lewis

Fun in Acapulco ★★ U
Musical   1963 · US · Colour · 92mins

Elvis performs a decidedly sub-standard score in a back-projected Mexico – though *Bossa Nova Baby* was

a minor hit. The women are pretty sensational: here's Ursula Andress, fresh from *Dr No*; and beautiful Elsa Cardenas as a sexy lady bullfighter, no less. Director Dick Thorpe once guided the King through the untamed *Jailhouse Rock* – the results are much tamer here. Paul Lukas (winner of the best actor Oscar for *Watch on the Rhine*) is also on hand, stealing the show as a batty chef.

Elvis Presley *Mike Windgren* • Ursula Andress *Margarita Dauphine* • Elsa Cardenas *Dolores Gomez* • Paul Lukas *Maximillian* • Larry Domasin *Raoul Almeido* ■ *Dir* Richard Thorpe • *Scr* Allan Weiss

Fun with Dick and Jane ★★★
Comedy   1977 · US · Colour · 99mins

The humour inherent in the title is somewhat lost on British audiences, since it's the name of a basic primary school book in the States. Dick (George Segal in top comic form) becomes unemployed, and with the help of his wife (Jane Fonda), decides to turn to crime. It's funny at first, but being out of work isn't much of a laugh really, and the gags become hard to sustain despite director Ted Kotcheff's pleasant handling of the situation. Contains swearing.

George Segal *Dick Harper* • Jane Fonda *Jane Harper* • Ed McMahon *Charlie Blanchard* • Dick Gautier *Dr Will* • Allan Miller *Loan company manager* ■ *Dir* Ted Kotcheff • *Scr* David Giler, Jerry Belson, Mordecai Richler, from the story by Gerald Gaiser

The Funeral ★★★ 18
Crime drama   1996 · US · Colour · 95mins

Probably the most conventional, formal film in Abel Ferrara's nineties canon, this crime drama, scripted by his longtime collaborator Nicholas St John, nevertheless touches upon familiar themes of guilt and redemption. Christopher Walken, for once relatively low-key, is the head of a gangster family trying to come to grips with the death of younger brother Johnny (Vincent Gallo). Walken's subtle turn is matched by fine performances from Chris Penn, Isabella Rossellini and Annabella Sciorra. A little talky at times, *The Funeral* remains a thoughtful slow-burner and an intriguing flipside to the director's more lurid melodramas. Contains swearing, sex scenes and violence.

Christopher Walken *Ray Tempio* • Chris Penn [Christopher Penn] *Chez Tempio* • Vincent Gallo *Johnny* • Benicio Del Toro *Gaspare* • Annabella Sciorra *Jeanette* • Isabella Rossellini *Clara* • Gretchen Mol *Helen* ■ *Dir* Abel Ferrara • *Scr* Nicholas St John

Funeral Ceremony ★★★
Drama   1969 · Cz · BW

Following the Soviet invasion of Czechoslovakia in 1968, four films were "banned forever" and several more were withdrawn without ever being screened. Twenty years after it was made, Zdenek Sirovy's powerful drama finally emerged as a result of the Velvet Revolution. Jaroslava Ticha gives a performance of determination and dignity as the widow demanding that her husband should be buried in the village from which he was driven

during the Communist takeover of 1948. Josef Somr shows why he was one of the most significant figures of Czech cinema at the time. In Czech with English subtitles.

Jaroslava Ticha • Josef Somr ■ *Dir* Zdenek Sirovy • *Scr* Zdenek Sirovy, from the novel by Eva Kanturkova

Funeral in Berlin ★★★ PG
Spy drama   1966 · UK · Colour · 97mins

Following the success of *The Ipcress File*, Michael Caine returned as Harry Palmer in this dense thriller that is so full of ingenious plotlines that you need to have your wits about you to follow what's going on. Caine goes behind the Iron Curtain to persuade communist spy boss Oscar Homolka to defect, only to run into Israeli agent Eva Renzi who is tracking down Nazi war criminals. The film blends action with sardonic humour and, if Guy Hamilton's directorial style is rather dour, he skilfully sustains the suspense.

Michael Caine *Harry Palmer* • Eva Renzi *Samantha Steel* • Paul Hubschmid *Johnny Vulkan* • Oscar Homolka *Colonel Stok* • Guy Doleman *Ross* • Rachel Gurney *Mrs Ross* ■ *Dir* Guy Hamilton • *Scr* Evan Jones, from the novel by Len Deighton

The Funhouse ★★★ 18
Horror   1981 · US · Colour · 88mins

Director Tobe Hooper has lots of fun pulling the rug out from under the viewer's feet in this under-rated "frightmare". Four bored teenagers are challenged to spend the night in a spooky ghost train at the local carnival. Trouble is, a mutant albino wearing a Frankenstein mask knows they saw him kill a gypsy fortune teller and wants to eradicate all witnesses to his crime. It's full of clever twists and turns, and Hooper elicits great tension from the simple cat-and-mouse concept – the climax in the funhouse machine room comes close to scaling the terror heights he attained in *The Texas Chain Saw Massacre*.

Elizabeth Berridge *Amy Harper* • Cooper Huckabee *Buzz* • Miles Chapin *Richie* • Largo Woodruff *Liz* • Shawn Carson *Joey Harper* ■ *Dir* Tobe Hooper • *Scr* Larry Block

Funny about Love ★★ 15
Comedy drama   1990 · US · Colour · 97mins

Despite the title, there is very little that is amusing in this lukewarm comedy. And that's quite surprising, considering the combined talents of a cast that includes Gene Wilder, Christine Lahti, Mary Stuart Masterson and Robert Prosky. Like John Travolta's *Perfect*, this project was based on a magazine article – probably not a good omen for director Leonard Nimoy or his stars. Contains swearing.

Gene Wilder *Duffy Bergman* • Christine Lahti *Meg Lloyd* • Mary Stuart Masterson *Daphne Delillo* • Robert Prosky *Emil T Bergman* • Stephen Tobolowsky *Dr Hugo Blatt* ■ *Dir* Leonard Nimoy • *Scr* Norman Steinberg, David Frankel, from the article *Convention of the Love Goddesses* by Bob Greene

Funny Bones ★★★★ 15
Comedy drama
1994 · US/UK · Colour · 127mins

A wry and caustic examination of the nature of comedy from *Hear My Song* writer/director Peter Chelsom. Oliver Platt plays Tommy Fawkes, the son of legendary comedian George Fawkes, who arrives in Blackpool, his father's old stamping ground, from Las Vegas, ostensibly to watch new talent. However he's really come to buy comedy material which he intends to pass off as his own back home in America. In Blackpool, not only does he find out that his own father stole a lot of his original act from Thomas and Bruno Parker, he also discovers he has a long lost brother in Bruno's son Jack (Lee Evans). And Jack has "funny bones" – he's effortlessly funny – whereas Tommy isn't. While it may be too quirky for some, this is worth sticking with for the moments where it all comes together as a glorious whole. Contains swearing.

Oliver Platt *Tommy Fawkes* • Jerry Lewis *George Fawkes* • Lee Evans *Jack Parker* • Leslie Caron *Katie Parker* • Richard Griffiths *Jim Minty* • Oliver Reed *Dolly Hopkins* • George Carl *Thomas Parker* • Freddie Davies *Bruno Parker* ■ *Dir* Peter Chelsom • *Scr* Peter Chelsom, Peter Flannery

Funny Face ★★★★ U
Musical comedy 1957 · US · Colour · 103mins

With glowing Technicolor (photography by Ray June) and great Gershwin tunes, director Stanley Donen has created a film that looks as elegant today as it did when it first appeared. A satire on fashion magazines, the fabulous Fred Astaire stars as photographer Dick Avery (Richard Avedon was the film's consultant), who finds the face of his dreams (Audrey Hepburn) in a Greenwich Village bookstore. Kay Thompson stands out as an imperious magazine editor – it takes real style to compete with the likes of Hepburn and Astaire. The only questionable scenes are the ones in which the three leads end up in Paris and ridicule Emile Flostre (played by Michel Auclair), a dead ringer for Jean-Paul Sartre – the anti-intellectualism is unworthy of Donen. Otherwise it's scintillating, magical and above all romantic.

Audrey Hepburn *Jo Stockton* • Fred Astaire *Dick Avery* • Kay Thompson *Maggie Prescott* • Michel Auclair *Prof Emile Flostre* • Robert Flemyng *Paul Duval* • Dovima *Marion* ■ *Dir* Stanley Donen • *Scr* Leonard Gershe, from his musical libretto *Wedding Day*

Funny Farm ★★ PG
Comedy   1988 · US · Colour · 97mins

Doffing his cap to *Mr Blandings Builds His Dream House*, Chevy Chase plays a sports hack who finds himself wrestling with life in the country. Quite why esteemed director George Roy Hill (*Butch Cassidy and the Sundance Kid*) would want to build a film around the cheesy charm of Chase is beyond understanding. However, his smart mouth, wraparound smirk and Tinseltown teeth do join forces to provide a degree of relaxed enjoyment, even when the gags stop being funny, which they too often do. By contrast, the final sequence is blessed with a comic vitality missing from much of the film. Contains some swearing. ▭

Chevy Chase *Andy Farmer* • Madolyn Smith *Elizabeth Farmer* • Joseph Maher *Michael Sinclair* • Jack Gilpin *Bud Culbertson* • Brad Sullivan *Brock* • MacIntyre Dixon *Mayor Barclay* ■ *Dir* George Roy Hill • *Scr* Jeffrey Boam, from the book by Jay Cronley

Funny Games ★★★🔞

Thriller 1997 · Aus · Colour · 104mins

Austrian director Michael Haneke's controversial cautionary tale is lauded in some circles for being an uncompromising study of on-screen violence and, in others, as the worst type of exploitation that panders to the same base instincts it purports to lay bare. Two young men inveigle their way into the holiday home of a middle-class family and subject them to degrading torture and sickening humiliation in Haneke's deconstruction of terror that's radical and thought-provoking, but also too clever by half. This is a powerful "shockumentary" that's hard to watch – deliberately. Definitely not for the faint-hearted. In German with English subtitles. Contains violence and swearing. ▭

Susanne Lothar *Anna* • Ulrich Mühe *Georg* • Frank Giering *Peter* • Arno Frisch *Paul* • Stefan Clapczynski *"Schorschi"* • Doris Kuntsmann *Gerda* • Christoph Bantzer *Fred* • Wolfgang Gluck *Robert* ■ *Dir/Scr* Michael Haneke

Funny Girl ★★★★🇺

Musical 1968 · US · Colour · 141mins

Charlton Heston recalls asking director William Wyler if he had any problems with Barbra Streisand on *Funny Girl*. "Nah, not really," said Wyler, "considering it's the first film she ever directed." This was a spectacular switch from stage to screen for Streisand, whose film debut portraying fame-seeking Fanny Brice earned her a joint Oscar for best actress (she shared the honour with Katharine Hepburn). The film is a marvellous musical comedy and Streisand is given fine support by the ultra-smooth Omar Sharif. Wyler's penultimate picture was actually his first attempt at a musical, and its success led to a sequel *Funny Lady* seven years later. ▭

Barbra Streisand *Fanny Brice* • Omar Sharif *Nick Arnstein* • Kay Medford *Rose Brice* • Anne Francis *Georgia James* • Walter Pidgeon *Florenz Ziegfeld* • Lee Allen *Eddie Ryan* • Mae Questel *Mrs Strakosh* ■ *Dir* William Wyler • *Scr* Isobel Lennart, from the musical by Jule Styne, Bob Merrill, Isobel Lennart

Funny Lady ★★★🅿🅶

Musical 1975 · US · Colour · 132mins

Barbra Streisand returned to the role for which she won her joint 1968 best actress Oscar, continuing the fictionalised story of Ziegfeld Follies star Fanny Brice and producer Ray Stark (the man behind *Funny Girl*). This sequel suffers a little in the hands of choreographer-turned-director Herbert Ross, who can't quite control the clichés of the plot or the rowdy performance of James Caan. Still, the musical numbers are fine, particularly Streisand's rendition of *I Found a Million Dollar Baby in a Five and Ten Cent Store*, which makes full use of the Panavision frame, and there's

some fancy footwork from Ben Vereen, plus a welcome guest appearance from *Funny Girl* co-star Omar Sharif. ▭

Barbra Streisand *Fanny Brice* • James Caan *Billy Rose* • Omar Sharif *Nick Arnstein* • Roddy McDowall *Bobby* • Ben Vereen *Bert Robbins* • Carole Wells *Norma Butler* ■ *Dir* Herbert Ross • *Scr* Arnold Schulman, Jay Presson Allen, from a story by Arnold Schulman

The Funny Man ★★🔞

Horror comedy 1994 · UK · Colour · 88mins

Monty Python meets Freddy Krueger in a predictable drip-feed of gore, gags and groans in this horror tale spoof. Benny Young wins a haunted house in a poker game with Christopher Lee, and then falls prey to its fourth dimensional evil spirit incarnated as a demented jester. The harlequin from hell (Tim James) then indulges in wickedly droll murders as Young's friends are systematically disembowelled and dismembered. Debut director Simon Sprackling's slapdash comic strip shows some brutal invention, but for the most part it's a childish, witless endeavour. Contains swearing and violence. ▭

Tim James *The Funny Man* • Christopher Lee *Callum Chance* • Ingrid Lacey *Tina Taylor* • Matthew Devitt *Johnny Taylor* • Chris Walker *Morgan "Hard Man"* • George Morton *Alan "Crap Puppeteer"* • Rhona Cameron *Thelma Fudd* ■ *Dir/Scr* Simon Sprackling

A Funny Thing Happened on the Way to the Forum ★★★🅿🅶

Musical comedy 1966 · US/UK · Colour · 93mins

This toga-clad musical farce about ancient Roman scandals was inspired by Frankie Howerd's popular TV series, *Up Pompeii*. Richard Lester's undisciplined direction takes its cue from the great comic line-up: Zero Mostel as the slave seeking freedom; Phil Silvers as a Bilko-like brothel keeper; Jack Gilford as Hysterium; and the great Buster Keaton, in one of his last feature films, as a man who's lost his children. Ramshackle it may be but it retains the verve and humour of its Broadway origins. ▭

Zero Mostel *Pseudolus* • Phil Silvers *Lycus* • Jack Gilford *Hysterium* • Buster Keaton *Erronius* • Michael Crawford *Hero* • Annette Andre *Philia* • Patricia Jessel *Domina* • Michael Hordern *Senex* ■ *Dir* Richard Lester • *Scr* Melvin Frank, Michael Pertwee, from the musical by Burt Shevelove, Larry Gelbart • *Cinematographer* Nicolas Roeg • *Music/Lyrics* Stephen Sondheim

The Furies ★★★★

Western 1950 · US · BW · 108mins

This intense, highly-charged account of power, passion, rivalry and revenge has much in common with Greek tragedy and is full of far-from-subtle Freudian elements. (Watch how Walter Huston and Barbara Stanwyck, as a father and daughter perpetually at odds, ease their faces closer until it seems they are about to kiss.) Expertly written by Charles Schnee and brilliantly directed by Anthony Mann, the film is powerfully performed by Stanwyck, Huston and Judith Anderson. Franz Waxman's rousing score and Victor Milner's Oscar-

nominated photography add to the pleasures of an overwrought but totally compelling piece.

Barbara Stanwyck *Vance Jeffords* • Walter Huston *TC Jeffords* • Wendell Corey *Rip Darrow* • Judith Anderson *Florence Burnett* • Gilbert Roland *Juan Herrera* • Thomas Gomez *El Tigre* • Beulah Bondi *Mrs Annaheim* ■ *Dir* Anthony Mann • *Scr* Charles Schnee, from the novel by Niven Busch

A Further Gesture ★★🔞

Political thriller 1996 · UK/Ger/Jap/Ire · Colour · 96mins

Director Robert Dornhelm's main claim to fame is that he made Grace Kelly's last film: a 25-minute, never-seen short. But he contributes little except melancholy to this barely coherent political thriller. A moody Stephen Rea plays an escaped IRA prisoner who flees to the US and gets further embroiled in violence when he is asked by a group of Guatemalan immigrants to assist in an assassination attempt. There's precious little insight and even less drama to be found in Ronan Bennett's screenplay. Contains swearing and violence. ▭

Stephen Rea *Dowd* • Alfred Molina *Tulio* • Rosana Pastor *Monica* • Brendan Gleeson *Richard* • Jorge Sanz *Paco* • Pruitt Taylor Vince *Scott* • Frankie McCafferty *Danny* ■ *Dir* Robert Dornhelm • *Scr* Ronan Bennett, from an idea by Stephen Rea

Further up the Creek ★★🇺

Comedy 1958 · UK · BW · 84mins

Made in something of a hurry by director Val Guest, as he sought to cash in on the success of *Up the Creek*, this sequel suffers from both indifferent plotting and the absence of Peter Sellers from the role of the scheming bosun. Exploiting the sale of his ship to the ruler of Algerocco by flogging tickets for a Mediterranean cruise, Frankie Howerd works every gag, as the floating con trick is suddenly called to action stations. But, he was not a natural before the movie camera and comes off second best alongside such practised performers as David Tomlinson and Lionel Jeffries.

David Tomlinson *Lt Fairweather* • Frankie Howerd *Bos'n* • Shirley Eaton *Jane* • Thora Hird *Mrs Galloway* • Lionel Jeffries *Steady Barker* ■ *Dir* Val Guest • *Scr* Val Guest, John Warren, Len Heath

Fury ★★★

Silent adventure 1923 · US · BW

Reuniting the star (Richard Barthelmess), director (Henry King) and writer (Edmund Goulding) of the massively successful *Tol'able David*, this is an all-stops-out melodrama set aboard a sailing ship and at the docks of London and Glasgow. Barthelmess plays the son of Tyrone Power (senior) whose wife, Dorothy Gish, has run off with another man – which proves to be upsetting for everyone. It was a big hit with twenties audiences, who loved its heaving emotions and its vividly filmed depiction of life at sea.

Richard Barthelmess *Boy Leyton* • Tyrone Power *Captain Leyton* • Pat Hartigan *Morgan* • Barry Macollum *Looney Luke* • Dorothy Gish *Minnie* • Jessie Arnold *Boy's mother* ■ *Dir* Henry King • *Scr* Edmund Goulding

Fury ★★★★

Crime drama 1936 · US · BW · 92mins

Austrian-born director Fritz Lang's first American movie is a searing indictment of lynch law based on a true case. The film is given tremendous intensity by the naturalistic performances of leads Spencer Tracy, as the man unjustly accused, and Sylvia Sidney as his fiancée. This is an uncomfortable film to watch, with Joseph Ruttenberg's lighting deliberately expressionistic, an unusual style for Hollywood's high-gloss studio MGM. The second half fails to carry the earnest conviction of the opening scenes, however, and a bizarre manic thrust takes over, perhaps intended to symbolise the unchannelled fury of the mob.

Spencer Tracy *Joe Wilson* • Sylvia Sidney *Katherine Grant* • Walter Abel *District Attorney* • Bruce Cabot *Kirby Dawson* • Edward Ellis *Sheriff* • Walter Brennan *"Bugs" Meyers* • George Walcott *Tom* ■ *Dir* Fritz Lang • *Scr* Bartlett Cormack, Fritz Lang, from the story *Mob Rule* by Norman Krasna

The Fury ★★★★🔞

Horror 1978 · US · Colour · 113mins

Brian De Palma found himself in familiar territory with this follow-up to *Carrie* – an adaptation of John Farris's telekinetic conspiracy thriller. Adopting a broader suspense canvas than he'd utilised before (the action and slow motion sequences remain the best he's ever crafted), De Palma's gorgeous horror adventure concerns two teens with psychic powers who become pawns between spy factions. Ingeniously plotted, extravagantly staged and beautifully balanced between apocalyptic goriness and full-blooded pyrotechnic imagery, this nail-biting shocker is De Palma's most under-rated movie. ▭

Kirk Douglas *Peter Sandza* • John Cassavetes *Childress* • Carrie Snodgress *Hester* • Charles Durning *Dr Jim McKeever* • Amy Irving *Gillian Bellaver* • Fiona Lewis *Dr Susan Charles* • Andrew Stevens *Robin Sandza* • Carol Rossen *Dr Ellen Lindstrom* ■ *Dir* Brian De Palma • *Scr* John Farris, from his novel

Fury at Furnace Creek ★★🇺

Western 1948 · US · BW · 87mins

When General Blackwell (Robert Warwick) is accused of instigating an Indian massacre, his sons Victor Mature and Glenn Langan are determined to clear his name. The solution lies in the boom town of Furnace Creek where the head of a mining syndicate, well played by Albert Dekker, is revealed as the arch villain. The story originally saw service as a tale of gunrunning in India, in John Ford's *Four Men and a Prayer* (1938). Glenn Langan was a late substitute for George Montgomery, but Coleen Gray makes a vivacious heroine.

Victor Mature *Cash* • Coleen Gray *Molly Baxter* • Glenn Langan *Rufe* • Reginald Gardiner *Capt Walsh* • Albert Dekker *Leverett* ■ *Dir* H Bruce Humberstone • *Scr* Charles G Booth, Winston Miller, from a story by David Garth

Fury at Showdown ★★★

Western 1957 · US · BW · 75mins

His pretty-boy days behind him, John Derek (just turned 30) gives an intense

🇺 = SUITABLE FOR ALL   🇺ᴄ = SUITABLE FOR ALL, ESPECIALLY FOR YOUNG CHILDREN (VIDEO ONLY)   🅿🅶 = PARENTAL GUIDANCE

performance as a complex cowboy in this atmospheric western. Derek tries to live down his reputation as a gunfighter by running a cattle ranch, while villains pressure him into selling his property with predictable results. Directed with punch by Gerd Oswald and photographed beautifully by Joseph LaShelle, the film is quite an achievement considering it was shot in only five days.

John Derek *Brock Mitchell* • John Smith *Miley Sutton* • Carolyn Craig *Ginny Clay* • Nick Adams *Tracy Mitchell* • Gage Clarke *Chad Deasey* ■ *Dir* Gerd Oswald • *Scr* Jason James, from the novel by Lucas Todd

Fury at Smugglers Bay ★★★ U

Period adventure   1961 · UK · BW · 98mins

Any tale of Cornish piracy is bound to invite comparisons with Alfred Hitchcock's *Jamaica Inn*. But this does a minor disservice to writer/director John Gilling's rumbustious yarn, in which squire Peter Cushing and his gung-ho son, John Fraser, take on Bernard Lee and his band of smuggling cut-throats. This 1790s adventure is tantamount to an English western, with a saloon brawl, sword-wielding showdowns and a last-minute rescue. However, the peripheral characters are more subtly shaded, with Miles Malleson's comic nobleman and George Coulouris's abused outsider being particularly well realised.

John Fraser *Chris Trevenyan* • Peter Cushing *Squire Trevenyan* • Bernard Lee *Black John* • June Thorburn *Jenny Trevenyan* • Michèle Mercier *Louise Lejeune* • George Coulouris *François Lejeune* • Miles Malleson *Duke of Avon* ■ *Dir/Scr* John Gilling

Future Cop ★★

Police comedy drama
1976 · US · Colour · 78mins

Veteran policeman Ernest Borgnine is assigned a new partner, who just happens to be an android, in this TV movie. The one-joke premise is that the new cop, Michael Shannon, has a few glitches in his programme and keeps screwing up at the most inopportune times. Borgnine rises to the reasonably funny occasion, Shannon doesn't, and Jud Taylor directs with little panache and feel for the subject matter. A short-lived TV series followed, as well as another forgettable TV movie, the wittily titled *Cops and Robin*.

Ernest Borgnine *Joe Cleaver* • Michael Shannon [Michael J Shannon] *John Haven* • John Amos *Sgt Bundy* • John Larch *Forman* • Herbert Nelson *Klausmeier* • Ronnie Claire Edwards *Avery* ■ *Dir* Jud Taylor • *Scr* Anthony Wilson

Future Schlock ★

Futuristic political satire
1984 · Ausl · Colour · 75mins

Conservative suburbanites imprison non-conformists in a walled-up ghetto after a 21st-century Australian civil war in this blunted political satire. The comedy revs up slightly when rebel prisoners escape to harass their straight-laced captors with vicious pranks. *Mad Max* and *National Lampoon's Animal House* are thrown into this quasi-fantasy blender, but

directors Barry Peak and Chris Kiely can't compete with either and the title says it all.

Mary-Anne Fahey *Sarah* • Michael Bishop *Bear* • Tracey Callander *Ronnie* • Tiriel Mora *Alvin* ■ *Dir/Scr* Barry Peak, Chris Kiely

Futuresport ★★ 15

Science-fiction action drama
1998 · US · Colour · 86mins

This glossily unimaginative TV movie borrows so liberally from the far superior *Rollerball* as to appear totally redundant. Set in the future, a violent game is created in a bid to ease gang tensions, a sort of amalgam of basketball and rugby played on levitating skateboards with an electrified ball. The trio of stars Dean (*Superman*) Cain, Vanessa L Williams and Wesley Snipes add much needed lustre to Ernest Dickerson's join-the-dots direction. Contains swearing and violence, with some sexual references. 📺 *DVD*

Wesley Snipes *Obike Fixx* • Dean Cain *Tremaine "Tre" Ramzey* • Vanessa L Williams *Alex Torres* • Bill Smitrovich *Coach Douglas Freeman* • Adrian Hughes ■ *Dir* Ernest R Dickerson • *Scr* Robert Hewitt Wolfe, from a story by Steve Dejarnatt, Robert Hewitt Wolfe

Futureworld ★★★ PG

Science-fiction thriller
1976 · US · Colour · 102mins

The follow-up to the excellent *Westworld*, this sci-fi thriller is one of the most inventive sequels of the Hollywood blockbuster era. With more than a nod in the direction of Don Siegel's classic *Invasion of the Body Snatchers*, the action concerns the replacement of the world's ruling elite by lookalike robots. This was one of the first pictures to perfect the use of 3-D computer animation, with the video-screen image of Peter Fonda produced by computer mapping. Less explosive than its predecessor, this is nevertheless an unnerving watch. 📺

Peter Fonda *Chuck Browning* • Blythe Danner *Tracy Ballard* • Arthur Hill *Duffy* • Yul Brynner *Gunslinger* • John Ryan [John P Ryan] *Dr Schneider* • Stuart Margolin *Harry* • Jim Antonio *Ron* • Allen Ludden *Game show host* ■ *Dir* Richard T Heffron • *Scr* Mayo Simon, George Schenck

Fuzz ★★

Detective comedy
1972 · US · Colour · 93mins

Evan Hunter adapted this cynical cop comedy from one of the *87th Precinct* stories he wrote under his pseudonym Ed McBain. A series of vignettes involving a quartet of Boston cops is linked by ingenious bombings carried out by Yul Brynner. The stand-out scenes involve Burt Reynolds and Jack Weston posing as nuns, and Tom Skerritt and Raquel Welch trying to concentrate on a stakeout while sharing a sleeping bag. The characterisation is rounded and the station-house atmosphere well established, but the Keystone-style mayhem is slightly ham-fisted. 📺

Burt Reynolds *Detective Carella* • Jack Weston *Detective Meyer* • Tom Skerritt *Detective Kling* • Yul Brynner *The Deaf Man* • Raquel Welch *Detective McHenry* • James McEachin

Detective Brown ■ *Dir* Richard A Colla • *Scr* Evan Hunter, from the novel by Ed McBain [Evan Hunter]

The Fuzzy Pink Nightgown ★★ U

Comedy   1957 · US · BW · 87mins

Inspired by a true-life incident when actress Marie McDonald was purportedly kidnapped, then discovered wandering in the desert, this mild comedy tells a similar tale of a movie star (Jane Russell) kidnapped just before the release of her new film, *The Kidnapped Heiress*. Predictably, no one will believe the incident is not a publicity stunt and, just as predictably, Russell falls for handsome kidnapper Ralph Meeker. Russell took the blame for the film's commercial failure, stating that she insisted on black and white rather than colour and told director Norman Taurog to play up the romance at the expense of comedy. Since the film was produced by her then-husband, her wishes were obeyed, though surprisingly she allowed herself to be photographed in an unbecoming blonde wig for the first half of the movie.

Jane Russell *Laurel Stevens* • Ralph Meeker *Mike Valla* • Keenan Wynn *Dandy* • Adolphe Menjou *Arthur Martin* ■ *Dir* Norman Taurog • *Scr* Richard Alan Simmons, from the novel by Sylvia Tate

GI Blues ★★★ U

Musical   1960 · US · Colour · 99mins

Elvis Presley had been away for two years, heroically doing his military service, including a spell in Germany, and this comeback film was intended to capitalise on that. This movie substantially shifted Elvis's image – from the teenage rebel of *King Creole* to the all-American soldier boy –. It's a family-orientated remake of an old Paramount chestnut *The Fleet's In*. Sultry Juliet Prowse is the dancer he loses his heart to after he woos her for a $300 bet, and the songs are classy. Apart from the title track, there's *Wooden Heart* and *Didya Ever?*; there's also a reminder of *Blue Suede Shoes*. 📺

Elvis Presley *Tulsa McCauley* • James Douglas *Rick* • Robert Ivers *Cookey* • Juliet Prowse *Lili* • Leticia Roman *Tina* • Sigrid Maier *Marla* • Arch Johnson *Sergeant McGraw* • The Jordanaires ■ *Dir* Norman Taurog • *Scr* Edmund Beloin, Henry Garson

GI Jane ★★★ 15

Action drama
1997 · US/UK · Colour · 119mins

Demi Moore built up her body but forgot to spend equal time on her acting skills for this high-octane, low-on-brains action film from *Blade Runner* director Ridley Scott. Moore is Lieutenant Jordan O'Neil, who becomes the first woman to train with the mucho macho Navy SEALS as part of a government experiment. Expect lots of lingering shots of a very buff Demi flexing muscles, shaving her head and kicking male butt in between impressively co-ordinated scenes of the guys-and-gal training. But don't expect much in the way of great moments in acting, apart from a suitably gruff performance from Viggo Mortensen as Moore's poetry-reciting superior. Contains swearing, violence and brief nudity. 📺

Demi Moore *Lt Jordan O'Neil* • Viggo Mortensen *Master Chief John Urgayle* • Anne Bancroft *Lillian DeHaven* • Jason Beghe *Royce* • Daniel Von Bargen *Theodore Hayes* • John Michael Higgins *Chief of Staff* • Kevin Gage *Instructor Pyro* • David Warshofsky *Instructor Johns* • David Vadim *Cortez* ■ *Dir* Ridley Scott • *Scr* David Twohy, Danielle Alexandra, from a story by Danielle Alexandra

"G" Men ★★★

Crime drama   1935 · US · BW · 84mins

A typically gritty Warner Bros gangster melodrama from the studio's greatest period, with James Cagney on the side of justice for once. Director William Keighley, who also co-directed *The Adventures of Robin Hood*, keeps the action cracking along, and there's terrific support from all those regular

Warners character players, plus Ann Dvorak from *Scarface* as Cagney's former girlfriend. But no one else really gets a look in, as this is Cagney's movie, a vehicle to show off the abilities of one of cinema's most talented stars in one of his best roles, fast talking, tough, and terrific.

James Cagney *James "Brick" Davis* • Ann Dvorak *Jean Morgan* • Margaret Lindsay *Kay McCord* • Robert Armstrong *Jeff McCord* • Barton MacLane *Brad Collins* • Lloyd Nolan *Hugh Farrell* • William Harrigan *McKay* • Edward Pawley *Danny Leggett* ■ *Dir* William Keighley • *Scr* Seton I Miller, from the novel *Public Enemy No 1* by Gregory Rogers

Gable and Lombard ★

Biographical romance
1976 · US · Colour · 131mins

A tragic romance is presented more like a screwball comedy in this disastrous biopic that shamefully insults its subjects. James Brolin is rigidly unconvincing as Clark Gable, while Jill Clayburgh brims over with anachronistic energy as Carole Lombard, the sparky actress who stole the King of Hollywood's heart and then broke it when she was killed in a plane crash on a wartime bond rally. Allen Garfield impresses as Louis B Mayer, the MGM mogul who disapproved of Gable's adulterous affair, but director Sidney J Furie fails to capture either the atmosphere of the period or the uniqueness of the relationship.

James Brolin *Clark Gable* • Jill Clayburgh *Carole Lombard* • Allen Goorwitz [Allen Garfield] *Louis B Mayer* • Red Buttons *Ivan Cooper* • Joanne Linville *Ria Gable* • Melanie Mayron *Dixie* • Carol McGinnis *Noreen* • Noah Keen *A Broderick* ■ *Dir* Sidney J Furie • *Scr* Barry Sandler

Gabriel over the White House ★★★

Political fantasy   1933 · US · BW · 94mins

A witty and highly distinctive political satire starring Walter Huston as Judson Hammond, who, as a rather corrupt president, survives an accident, is visited by the Archangel Gabriel and goes on to save America from the Depression and gangsters. The picture's simple-minded patriotism has to be seen to be believed, though the film went through some political cartwheels of its own during production in order to assuage MGM boss Louis B Mayer's political sympathies. Despite its many flaky elements, this picture has actually worn better than some of Frank Capra's political dramas.

Walter Huston *Judson Hammond* • Arthur Byron *Jasper Brooks* • Karen Morley *Pendota Molloy* • Franchot Tone *Hartley Beekman* • Dickie Moore *Jimmy Vetter* • C Henry Gordon *Nick Diamond* • Joanne Landau *John Bronson* • Samuel Hinds [Samuel S Hinds] *Dr Eastman* • William Pawley *Borell* • Jean Parker *Alice Bronson* • Claire Dubrey *Nurse* ■ *Dir* Gregory La Cava • *Scr* Carey Wilson, Bertram Bloch, from the novel *Rinehard* by TF Tweed

Gaby ★★

Wartime romantic drama
1956 · US · Colour · 97mins

The third screen version of the play *Waterloo Bridge*, though still hidebound by censorship, was updated to the Second World War. It stars a beguiling Leslie Caron (after *Lili* and before *Gigi*)

as the ballerina forced to become a prostitute through circumstance. John Kerr is gauche as her beau, but then who could ever erase memories of Robert Taylor and Vivien Leigh in the classic 1940 version? It was folly for MGM to try, though the film does have a quaint fifties sheen. Unfortunately, the pacing of *Beau Brummell* director Curtis Bernhardt is slow, and the overall effect is dull.

Leslie Caron *Gaby* • John Kerr *Gregory Y Wendell* • Cedric Hardwicke *Mr Carrington* • Taina Elg *Elsa* • Margalo Gillmore *Mrs Carrington* • Scott Marlowe *Jan* • Ian Wolfe *Registrar* • Joe Di Reda *Allen* • Ruta Lee *Denise* ■ *Dir* Curtis Bernhardt • *Scr* Albert Hackett, Frances Goodrich, Charles Lederer, from the film *Waterloo Bridge* by SN Behrman, Paul H Rameau, George Froeschel, from the play by Robert E Sherwood

Gadjo Dilo ★★★ 15

Drama   1997 · Fr · Colour · 101mins

Director Tony Gatlif completes the "Gypsy Triptych" he began with *Les Princes* (1982) and *Latcho Drom* (1993) with this striking, if sentimentalised drama. As the young Parisian seduced by culture shock, Romain Duris seems too eager to conform. But Izidor Serban is mischievously grizzled as his surrogate father, and Rona Hartner brings a fierce sense of self-worth to the role of the enticing Romanian firebrand. While it seeks to score social points, this is more a celebration of the Romany lifestyle than a plea for greater tolerance. Laced with raucous humour and plenty of toe-tapping music, it's a heartfelt tribute to the vibrancy and tenacity of a much-misunderstood people. In French with English subtitles. Contains swearing, sex scenes and sexual references.

Romain Duris *Stéphane* • Rona Hartner *Sabina* • Izidor Serban *Izidor* • Ovidiu Balan *Sami* • Angela Serban *Angela* • Aurica Ursan *Aurica* • Vasile Serban *Vasile* • Ioan Serban *Ioan* ■ *Dir/Scr* Tony Gatlif

Le Gai Savoir ★

Documentary drama
1968 · Fr · Colour · 95mins

This film marked Godard's irrevocable break with narrative cinema. It's supposed to be an adaptation of Swiss philosopher Jean Jacques Rousseau's novel about education, *Emile* – at least, that's what French TV commissioned. However, it consists mainly of Jean-Pierre Léaud and Juliet Berto sitting in a black void of a TV studio beneath a transparent umbrella to protect them from atomic radiation. Their chat consists of naive slogans, Maoist ideas and general ranting about the media and capitalism. Pretentious, incredibly boring and infuriating, it should never be the first Godard film anyone sees (if so, it will be the last), and should also be seen in the context of the Paris student revolt of 1968. In French with English subtitles.

Juliet Berto *Patricia Lumumba* • Jean-Pierre Léaud *Emile Rousseau* ■ *Dir* Jean-Luc Godard • *Scr* Jean-Luc Godard, from the book *Emile* by Jean Jacques Rousseau

Gaiety George ★★★

Period musical biography
1946 · UK · BW · 98mins

Richard Greene, best known to a generation as TV's Robin Hood, here portrays the father figure of Edwardian musical comedy, George Edwardes, famous for his Gaiety Girls. He's called George Howard here, renamed perhaps because Greene totally fails to evoke Edwardes's trademark flamboyance and Irish vitality. A pallid Ann Todd doesn't add much as the love interest, and the film cries out for colour. However, the period atmosphere is well re-created, ingénue Hazel Court is particularly mesmerising, and the whole is not unwatchable.

Richard Greene *George Howard* • Ann Todd *Kathryn Davis* • Peter Graves (2) *Carter* • Hazel Court *Elizabeth Brown* • Leni Lynn *Florence Stephens* • Ursula Jeans *Isobel Forbes* • Morland Graham *Morris* • Frank Pettingell *Grindley* ■ *Dir* George King, Freddie Carpenter, Leontine Sagan • *Scr* Katherine Strueby, Basil Woon, from a story by Richard Fisher, Peter Cresswell

Gaily, Gaily ★★

Period comedy   1969 · US · Colour · 106mins

Released as *Chicago, Chicago* in the UK, this account of screenwriter Ben Hecht's early career should have been a stingingly satirical portrait of the Windy City at its breeziest. Instead, it's a crass comedy with the laughs writ large and the playing wildly over the top. Beau Bridges grows in confidence as the cub reporter who discovers that Melina Mercouri's "hotel" is a brothel and that every bigwig in town frequents it. But only Brian Keith, as his world-weary Irish mentor, offers him any support as the story becomes increasingly improbable. Director Norman Jewison spends more time showing off his gaudy period sets.

Beau Bridges *Ben Harvey* • Melina Mercouri *Queen Lil* • Brian Keith *Francis X Sullivan* • George Kennedy *Axel P Johanson* • Hume Cronyn *"Honest" Tim Grogan* • Margot Kidder *Adeline* • Wilfrid Hyde White *Governor* ■ *Dir* Norman Jewison • *Scr* Abram S Ginnes, from the memoirs by Ben Hecht

Gal Young Un ★★

Drama   1979 · US · Colour · 105mins

An early indie production from Victor Nunez, the future director of *Ruby in Paradise* and *Ulee's Gold*. Set in the thirties in the backwoods of Florida, the story concerns a woman who has chosen to live a simple and solitary existence. A young bootlegger and con man, who comes out of nowhere, becomes romantically involved with her and fleeces her of her modest savings. Trouble is, the woman endures all this hardship and a lot of abuse rather than lose the man and be on her own again. She even tolerates him taking a lover, the "gal young un" of the title. Slow to unfold, earnest in tone and uneven in performance, it was produced, directed, written, photographed and edited by Nunez.

Dana Preu *Mattie Siles* • David Peck *Trax* • J Smith *Elly* • Gene Densmore *Storekeeper* • Jennie Stringfellow *Edna* • Tim McCormack *Blaine* • Casey Donovan *Jeb Lantry* • Mike Garlington *Eddy Lantry* • Marshall New *Edgar* •

Bruce Cornwell *Phil* ■ *Dir* Victor Nunez • *Scr* Victor Nunez, from a story by Marjorie Kinnan Rawlings • *Cinematographer* Victor Nunez

Galaxina ★★

Science-fiction spoof   1980 · US · Colour

This *Star Wars* spoof features lowbrow comedy, duff special effects, an awkward *Alien* parody and a central performance by Dorothy Stratten, murdered by her estranged husband on the very day it received its American premiere. The doomed starlet is the robot navigator on board a police spaceship, who gets sent on a mission to recover possession of the powerful Blue Star crystal. Few laughs and even fewer thrills are raised thanks to an unfocused script and haphazard direction by Z-movie maestro William Sachs. A sad epitaph for Stratten whose life story was turned into the acclaimed Bob Fosse movie *Star 80*.

Dorothy Stratten *Galaxina* • Stephen Macht *Thor* • Ronald Knight *Ordric* • Lionel Smith *Maurice* • Tad Horino *Sam Wo* • Nancy McCauley *Elexia* • Avery Schreiber *Captain Butt* ■ *Dir/Scr* William Sachs

Galaxy Quest ★★★★ PG

Science-fiction spoof
1999 · US · Colour · 102mins

In this enormously entertaining send-up of the *Star Trek* universe, a bunch of actors from a cult sci-fi TV show are mistaken for the real thing and recruited to defend a dying alien race. It's an inspired premise, fired into orbit by a fantastic script, sublime visual effects and an absolutely perfect cast, including Tim Allen, Sigourney Weaver and Alan Rickman, hysterical as a grumpy British actor who hates his half-reptilian character. The story is so cleverly executed and the characters so nicely fleshed-out that it not only succeeds as a *Trek* spoof, a satire on the acting profession and a parody of science-fiction fans, but also as an original space saga in its own right.

Tim Allen *Jason Nesmith/Commander Peter Quincy Taggart* • Sigourney Weaver *Gwen DeMarco/Lt Tawny Madison* • Alan Rickman *Alexander Dane/Dr Lazarus* • Tony Shalhoub *Fred Kwan/Tech Sgt Chen* • Sam Rockwell *Guy Fleegman* • Daryl Mitchell *Tommy Webber/Laredo* • Enrico Colantoni *Mathesar* • Robin Sachs *Sarris* • Patrick Breen *Quellek* ■ *Dir* Dean Parisot • *Scr* Robert Gordon, David Howard, from a story by David Howard

Galileo ★★★

Historical biography
1974 · UK/Can · Colour · 144mins

After fiddling on the roof for so long, Topol steps down to take on the role of the 17th-century Italian mathematician and astronomer whose heretical theories of the universe brought him into dangerous confrontation with the Roman Catholic church and the Inquisition. Adapted from the play by Bertolt Brecht and directed by Joseph Losey, this is a rather static production from the America Film Theatre. However, the actors, including Edward Fox, Michel Lonsdale and Tom Conti, enliven a debate animated by vivid argument.

Chaim Topol [Topol] *Galileo Galilei* • Edward Fox *Cardinal Inquisitor* • Colin Blakely *Priuli* • Georgia Brown *Ballad singer's wife* • Clive Revill *Ballad singer* • Margaret Leighton *Court lady* • John Gielgud *Old cardinal* • Michael Gough *Sagredo* • Michel Lonsdale *Cardinal Barberini (later Pope)* • Tom Conti *Andrea Sarti as a man* ■ *Dir* Joseph Losey • *Scr* Barbara Bray, Joseph Losey, Charles Laughton, from the play by Bertolt Brecht

The Gallant Hours ★★ U
Second World War biography
1960 · US · BW · 111mins

James Cagney gives a sober, po-faced performance as legendary American war hero Admiral William F Halsey, paying homage on bended knee to the man's formidable reputation. A strong cast, including Robert Montgomery Jr, Dennis Weaver and Ward Costello, admirably fleshes out the tale, but this all-American farrago centres firmly on Cagney, whose portrayal displays great grit but little light or shade. It's one of those movies that falls into the trap of believing you cannot criticise a man with a chest full of medals. 💬

James Cagney *Admiral William F Halsey Jr* • Dennis Weaver *Lt Commander Andy Lowe* • Ward Costello *Captain Harry Black* • Richard Jaeckel *Lt Commander Roy Webb* • Les Tremayne *Captain Frank Enright* • Robert Burton *Major General Roy Geiger* • Raymond Bailey *Major General Archie Vandegrift* ■ *Dir* Robert Montgomery • *Scr* Frank D Gilroy, Beirne Lay Jr

Gallant Lady ★★★
Melodrama 1934 · US · BW · 81mins

An unmarried mother (Ann Harding) is forced to give up her baby son for adoption. Travelling abroad five years later, she meets a widower (Otto Kruger) who is about to marry a woman whom her five-year-old son (Dickie Moore) intensely dislikes. No prizes for guessing who the boy really is, or who Kruger marries in the end. Melodramas about self-sacrificing mother love were popular in the thirties. Though this is not the best example of the genre, it's stylishly directed by Gregory La Cava and engages the heart thanks to Harding, one of Hollywood's most sympathetic and gifted actresses.

Ann Harding *Sally Wyndham* • Clive Brook *Dan Pritchard* • Otto Kruger *Philip Lawrence* • Tullio Carminati *Count Carnini* • Dickie Moore *Deedy* ■ *Dir* Gregory La Cava • *Scr* Sam Mintz, from a story by Gilbert Emery, Douglas Doty, Franc Rhodes

Gallipoli ★★★★ PG
First World War drama
1981 · Ausl · Colour · 106mins

Gallipoli is Australia's *Alamo* or *Dunkirk*, and serves as a national monument to the courage of the men who fought and died there during the First World War. It is stirring stuff, despite the fact that it takes an awfully long time to get to the battlefield. So, for over an hour, Mel Gibson stars in a Down Under version of *Chariots of Fire*, running a race across the scorching desert and then heading off to Egypt for some basic training, before the script ships everyone off to the Dardanelles as cannon fodder. There they're ordered to hold the line against impossible odds. This is director Peter Weir's least characteristic film, but its success led him to Hollywood and films such as *Witness* and *Dead Poets Society*. Contains some swearing. 💬

Mel Gibson *Frank Dunne* • Mark Lee *Archy Hamilton* • Bill Hunter *Major Barton* • Bill Kerr *Uncle Jack* • Robert Grubb *Billy Lewis* • Tim McKenzie *Barney Wilson* • David Argue "*Snowy*" • Ron Graham *Wallace Hamilton* ■ *Dir* Peter Weir • *Scr* David Williamson, from a story by Peter Weir, from the book *The Broken Years* by Bill Gammage and war histories by CEW Bean

Gallivant ★★★★ 15
Documentary 1996 · UK · Colour · 103mins

Cruelly overlooked on its original release, this offbeat documentary has more incident and intelligence than a barrow-load of blockbusters. Compiled from over 50 hours of interviews and travelogue footage, Andrew Kötting's odyssey around the British coastline is made all the more enchanting by the frank opinions of his grandmother, Gladys, and the courage of his daughter, Eden, who makes light of Joubert's Syndrome to communicate in sign language. With its experimental use of different camera angles and speeds, the style is occasionally fussy, but the eccentric encounters are priceless and highly revealing of our gloriously diverse national characteristics. Contains swearing.

Dir/Scr Andrew Kötting

Gambit ★★★ U
Crime comedy 1966 · US · Colour · 108mins

Falling into the trap of lighting up each surprise in neon well in advance, director Ronald Neame ensures that the unexpected here quickly becomes the expected and so contributes to the shallowness of the plot. However, events are regularly chirped up by Michael Caine and Shirley MacLaine, who feed their natural frivolity and nimble comic timing into the roles of a cockney crook and his Eurasian showgirl-turned-accomplice. Herbert Lom is also good fun as the hapless target of their wheeze.

Shirley MacLaine *Nicole* • Michael Caine *Harry Deane* • Herbert Lom *Shahbandar* • Roger C Carmel *Ram* • Arnold Moss *Abdul* • John Abbott *Emile* • Richard Angarola *Colonel Salim* • Maurice Marsac *Hotel clerk* ■ *Dir* Ronald Neame • *Scr* Alvin Sargent, Jack Davies, from the novel by Sidney Carroll

The Gamble ★★★ 15
Period drama 1988 · It · Colour · 100mins

An entertaining costume romp in the *Tom Jones* vein, with Matthew Modine as an impoverished nobleman who wagers his life in a bid to to win back the family fortune from sinister countess Faye Dunaway. Though no great shakes, this is made with a certain panache and sensibly acted with tongues firmly in cheeks by the cast, which also includes Jennifer Beals. It's the sort of film they don't make much any more – one or two moments make you wonder why. An English/Italian language film. 💬

Matthew Modine *Francesco* • Jennifer Beals *Olivia* • Faye Dunaway *Countess* • Corinne Cléry ■ *Dir* Carlo Vanzina • *Scr* Enrico Vanzina, Carlo Vanzina, Livia Giampalmo, from a novel by Alberto Ongaro

The Gambler ★★★★ 18
Drama 1974 · US · Colour · 106mins

Quoting Dostoyevsky's gambling compulsion as an excuse for his own obsession, James Caan gives a remarkable performance as the university lecturer in hock to loan sharks for his debts. This was director Karel Reisz's most effective movie of those made during his brief stay in Hollywood; he was obviously not as at home in California as he was "up north" (see *Saturday Night and Sunday Morning*). It's a film that takes its time, but supporting actors such as Lauren Hutton, Paul Sorvino and Burt Young give necessary substance to the movie's style. Contains swearing. 💬

James Caan *Axel Freed* • Lauren Hutton *Billie* • Paul Sorvino *Hips* • Morris Carnovsky *AR Lowenthal* • Jacqueline Brookes *Naomi* • Burt Young *Carmine* • Carmine Caridi *Jimmy* • Vic Tayback *One* • Steven Keats *Howie* ■ *Dir* Karel Reisz • *Scr* James Toback

The Gambler ★★★ 15
Drama 1997 · UK/Neth/Hun · Colour · 93mins

A starry cast and some beautiful locations enhance this adaptation of Fyodor Dostoyevsky's autobiographical novel. Hungarian director Karoly Makk employs the unusual device of the "novel within the film" to show how the writer came to pen his intense study of gambling fever. Stylistically, however, Makk has overloaded his dice and goes for broke on far too many occasions. Rising above the wordy script and the stiff staging, Michael Gambon and Jodhi May fascinate as the author and his young muse. However, the most remarkable performance comes from dual Oscar winner Luise Rainer, appearing in her first film in 54 years. Contains some swearing and a sex scene. 💬

Michael Gambon *Fyodor Dostoyevsky* • Jodhi May *Anna Snitkina* • Polly Walker *Polina* • Dominic West *Alexei* • John Wood *The General* • Johan Leysen *De Grieux* • Angeline Ball *Mlle Blanche* • Tom Jansen *Stellovsky* • Luise Rainer *Grandmother* • Gijs Scholten von Asschat *Maikov* ■ *Dir* Karoly Makk • *Scr* Katharine Ogden, Charles Cohen, Nick Dear, from the novel by Fyodor Dostoyevsky

The Gambler and the Lady ★★
Crime drama 1952 · UK · BW · 72mins

What went on behind the scenes of this Hammer production is far more interesting than the on-screen action. Although Pat Jenkins has his name on the picture, a variety of sources claim that Hollywood hack Sam Newfield co-directed; others assert that horror maestro Terence Fisher also had a hand in its making. The film itself is an unremarkable crime tale about a hard-bitten American gambler (Dane Clark) who discovers the English aristocracy is a much tougher nut to crack than the underworld.

Dane Clark *Jim Forster* • Kathleen Byron *Pat* • Naomi Chance *Lady Susan Willens* • Meredith Edwards *Dave* • Anthony Forwood *Peter Willens* • Eric Pohlmann *Arturo Colonna* • Julian Somers *Licasi* • Anthony Ireland *Farning* • Enzo Cottichia *Angelo Colonna* ■ *Dir* Pat Jenkins, Sam Newfield • *Scr* Sam Newfield

The Gamblers ★ U
Comedy drama 1969 · US · Colour · 91mins

A lacklustre caper movie starring Suzy Kendall, a pretty blonde who married Dudley Moore and probably got the roles previously offered to Julie Christie and Susannah York. Supposedly based on a Gogol play, it was filmed in the spectacular Croatian seaboard city of Dubrovnik where gamblers, con men and other dubious characters gather. As well as the usual Europudding cast, creating a gaggle of accents, it features a bulging swag-bag of movie plunder – a scene lifted from *Topkapi*, a joke from *The Pink Panther*, a Korean bodyguard from *Goldfinger* and so on. Kendall doesn't have a lot to do except model some fancy frocks.

Suzy Kendall *Candace* • Don Gordon *Rooney* • Pierre Olaf *Cozzier* • Kenneth Griffith *Broadfoot* • Stuart Margolin *Goldy* • Richard Woo *Koboyashi* • Massimo Serato *Del Isolla* • Faith Domergue *Signora Del Isolla* • Relja Basic *Yakov* ■ *Dir* Ron Winston • *Scr* Ron Winston, from a play by Nikolai Gogol

Gambling Lady ★★★
Drama 1934 · US · BW · 66mins

Here's tough and sexy Barbara Stanwyck, on her way to becoming one of Hollywood's great ladies, cast as a professional gambler born on the wrong side of the tracks who enters high society through marriage to posh Joel McCrea. This is one of those swiftly-paced, tightly-knit melodramas that leave you gasping at the end of a comparatively short running time. Pat O'Brien is actually the nominal co-star, but McCrea has the more important role, and looks good with Stanwyck – he would later appear opposite her in *Banjo on My Knee*, and, more notably, *Union Pacific*. Watch the Park Avenue gambling sequence closely – that's a young Tyrone Power at the table.

Barbara Stanwyck *Lady Lee* • Joel McCrea *Garry Madison* • Pat O'Brien *Charlie Lang* • C Aubrey Smith *Peter Madison* • Claire Dodd *Sheila Aiken* • Philip Reed *Steve* • Philip Faversham *Don* • Robert Barrat *Mike Lee* ■ *Dir* Archie Mayo • *Scr* Ralph Block, Doris Malloy, from a story by Doris Malloy

The Game ★★★ 15
Thriller 1997 · US · Colour · 122mins

When hard-nosed businessman Michael Douglas is given the ultimate birthday present by his brother (Sean Penn) – the chance to play an all-encompassing "reality game" that promises life-changing consequences – he gets swept into what he perceives as a paranoid conspiracy. Douglas is perfectly cast as the increasingly desperate pawn in *Se7en* director David Fincher's visually stylish thriller, which cranks up the suspense and continually questions what's real and what isn't. Soon, however, we come to expect the unexpected, and the initially fascinating concept becomes a glossy trivial pursuit. Contains swearing, sexual references and some violence. 💬

Michael Douglas *Nicholas Van Orton* • Sean Penn *Conrad Van Orton* • Deborah Kara Unger *Christine* • James Rebhorn *Jim Feingold* • Peter Donat *Samuel Sutherland* • Carroll Baker *Ilsa* • Anna Katarina *Elizabeth* • Armin Mueller-Stahl *Anson Baer* ■ *Dir* David Fincher • *Scr* John Brancato, Michael Ferris

A Game for Vultures ★★ 18

Political drama 1979 · UK · Colour · 108mins

Political strife in Rhodesia in the late seventies is the backdrop for this dull and dusty home-grown epic. Richard Roundtree (*Shaft*) plays black freedom fighter Gideon Marunga, increasingly angry at the British sanctions. Richard Harris finds it impossible to resist the charms of Joan Collins, while Ray Milland and Denholm Elliott round off a cast that's rather better than the movie merits. This film's heart may be in the right place, but such a worthy subject deserved rather worthier movie-making – and a less pretentious approach. 💬

Richard Harris *David Swansey* • Richard Roundtree *Gideon Marunga* • Joan Collins *Nicolle* • Ray Milland *Colonel Brettle* • Sven-Bertil Taube *Larry Prescott* • Denholm Elliott *Raglan Thistle* • Jana Cilliers *Ruth Swansey* ∎ *Dir* James Fargo • *Scr* Phillip Baird, from the novel by Michael Hartmann

The Game Is Over ★

Drama romance 1966 · Fr/It · Colour · 98mins

Jane Fonda's second film with director/husband Roger Vadim was this mildly scandalous, updated version of Zola's novel *La Curée*, in which Fonda falls passionately in love with her stepson, played by the long forgotten Peter McEnery. She asks her husband for a divorce, but while she is away he pressures the stepson into a marriage with the daughter of a banker. Panned at the time, it nevertheless gave Fonda her biggest role to date and allowed Vadim plenty of opportunities to photograph her semi-naked.

Jane Fonda *Renée Saccard* • Peter McEnery *Maxime Saccard* • Michel Piccoli *Alexandre Saccard* • Tina Marquand [Tina Aumont] *Anne Sernet* • Jacques Monod *M Sernet* • Simone Valerie *Mme Sernet* • Luong Ham-Chau *Mr Chou* ∎ *Dir* Roger Vadim • *Scr* Roger Vadim, Jean Cau, Bernard Frechtman, from the novel *La Curée* by Emile Zola

A Game of Death ★★

Thriller 1945 · US · BW · 72mins

Although modestly effective in its own low-budget way, director Robert Wise's version of writer Richard Connell's horror adventure yarn *The Most Dangerous Game* suffers in comparison to the classic 1932 interpretation by directors Irving Pichel and Ernest B Schoedsack. Edgar Barrier takes on the role of Kreiger, the Nazi lunatic hunting shipwreck survivors for sadistic sport on his isolated island. John Loder is the novelist washed up on his shores who turns the hunter into the hunted, with a certain degree of suspense.

John Loder *Rainsford* • Audrey Long *Ellen* • Edgar Barrier *Kreiger* • Russell Wade *Robert* • Russell Hicks *Whitney* • Jason Robards *Captain* • Gene Stutenroth [Gene Roth] *Pleshke* • Noble Johnson *Carib* • Robert Clarke *Helmsman* ∎ *Dir* Robert Wise • *Scr* Norman Houston, from the story *The Most Dangerous Game* by Richard Connell

Game of Death ★★ 18

Martial arts drama
1978 · HK · Colour · 92mins

When Bruce Lee died suddenly in 1973, the industry he helped bring to a wider audience lost no time in churning out a string of shabby, vaguely tasteless exploitation pieces. This is one of the best known of his posthumous releases and one of the worst. The Lee character – predominantly stand-in Kim Tai Jong – finds himself up against a ruthless gangster (Dean Jagger), who kidnaps his girlfriend (Colleen Camp). The makers originally claimed the film would be drawing on 100 minutes of never-before-seen footage, but precious little seems to have made it to the screen and, apart from a beautifully edited end sequence featuring Lee at his best, this is an embarrassing mess. Chuck Norris is in there, too. Contains swearing. 💬

Bruce Lee *Billy Lo* • Gig Young *Jim Marshall* • Dean Jagger *Dr Land* • Hugh O'Brian *Steiner* • Robert Wall *Carl Miller* • Colleen Camp *Ann Morris* • Kareem Abdul-Jabbar *Hakim* ∎ *Dir* Robert Clouse • *Scr* Jan Spears

Gamera ★★

Monster adventure 1965 · Jap · BW · 86mins

Created by the Daiei Studio to rival Toho's *Godzilla*, Gamera is a giant prehistoric fire-breathing turtle, which is awakened by an atomic blast and spins its way to Tokyo, destroying all in its path. As with the original *Godzilla*, American stars Albert Dekker and Brian Donlevy make their appearance, in footage specially shot for the international market, as government officials liaising with the Japanese authorities to trap the super-turtle in a rocket and blast it to Mars. Although competent in every standard Japanese monster-movie department, *Gamera* never really caught on outside its home turf despite numerous wacky sequels and a spectacular high-tech refit in the nineties. Japanese dialogue dubbed into English.

Albert Dekker *Secretary of Defense* • Brian Donlevy *General Terry Arnold* • Diane Findlay *Sergeant Susan Embers* • John Baragrey *Captain Lovell* • Dick O'Neill *General O'Neill* • Eiji Funakoshi *Dr Hidaka* • Harumi Kiritachi *Kyoke* • Yoshiro Uchida *Toshio* ∎ *Dir* Noriyaki Yuasa • *Scr* Fumi Takahashi, Richard Kraft, from an idea by Yonejiro Saito

Games ★★

Psychological drama
1967 · US · Colour · 100mins

Despite a multiplication of psychological double-crosses, Curtis Harrington's mystery drama never really involves us in the Manhattan machinations of fortune-hunting husband James Caan and his gullible wife Katharine Ross. Simone Signoret is the amateur medium who becomes embroiled in their fun and games, peering into a crystal ball as murky as the plot. Had Harrington been concerned more with pace and less with style, the film might have worked.

Simone Signoret *Lisa* • James Caan *Paul* • Katharine Ross *Jennifer* • Don Stroud *Norman* • Kent Smith *Harry* • Estelle Winwood *Miss Beattie* • Marjorie Bennett *Nora* • Ian Wolfe *Dr Edwards* ∎ *Dir* Curtis Harrington • *Scr* Gene Kearney, from a story by Curtis Harrington, George Edwards

The Games ★ PG

Sports drama 1970 · UK · Colour · 92mins

What real-life athletes such as technical adviser Gordon Pirie made of Michael Winner's sporting drama about the build-up to the marathon at the Rome Olympics is anybody's guess. It's hard to know where to look, really. At the so-obvious cardboard cut-out crowds? At the mind-boggling casting of Michael Crawford as an ace marathon runner? Or at Ryan O'Neal as an all-round American good guy, competing despite a heart condition? Only Stanley Baker and Jeremy Kemp as trainers emerge with any credit in this sprawling mess of a movie. 💬

Michael Crawford *Harry Hayes* • Stanley Baker *Bill Oliver* • Ryan O'Neal *Scott Reynolds* • Charles Aznavour *Pavel Vendek* • Jeremy Kemp *Jim Harcourt* • Elaine Taylor *Christine* • Athol Compton *Sunny Pintubi* • Fritz Wepper *Kovanda* ∎ *Dir* Michael Winner • *Scr* Erich Segal, from a novel by Hugh Atkinson

Gandhi ★★★★★ PG

Epic biographical drama
1982 · UK · Colour · 180mins

In 1963 Indian diplomat Motilal Kothari approached Richard Attenborough to make a film about Gandhi. Nearly 20 years later he realised his dream, using a script by John Briley and benefiting from a truly inspirational performance by Ben Kingsley. The picture has an epic sweep, beginning with Gandhi's assassination and flashing back to the seeds of Indian independence. A *Who's Who* of British acting is present and very correct (sardonic John Gielgud, chilling Edward Fox, sociable John Mills), but it's Kingsley you remember, alongside Roshan Seth, who makes a strong impression as the scheming Nehru. Eight Oscars, and a triumph for Attenborough. Contains violence. 💬

Ben Kingsley *Mahatma Gandhi* • Candice Bergen *Margaret Bourke-White* • Edward Fox *General Dyer* • John Gielgud *Lord Irwin* • Trevor Howard *Judge Broomfield* • John Mills *The Viceroy* • Martin Sheen *Walker* • Rohini Hattangady *Kasturba Gandhi* • Roshan Seth *Pandit Nehru* ∎ *Dir* Richard Attenborough • *Scr* John Briley • *Cinematographer* Billy Williams, Ronnie Taylor • *Editor* John Bloom • *Costume Designer* John Mollo, Bhanu Athaiya • *Production Designer* Stuart Craig

Gang Busters ★★

Crime drama 1955 · US · BW · 71mins

William H Clothier, best known for his work on John Ford's later westerns, served as both cinematographer and co-producer on this minor crime drama. He certainly makes the most of the Oregon locations to give the action a documentary feel, but director Bill Karn lacks the visual imagination to inject much life into a slow-moving story that was adapted from a popular radio drama. Given a rare leading role after dozens of western supports, Myron Healey acquits himself well as Public Enemy No 4, who seems to spend as much time breaking out of jails as he does committing crimes.

Myron Healey *John Omar Pinson* • Don C Harvey *Detective Walsh* • Sam Edwards *Long* • Frank Gerstle *Detective Fuller* • Frank Richards *Slug Bennett* • Kate MacKenna *Aunt Jenny* • Rusty Wescoatt *Mike* • William Justine *Louie* ∎ *Dir* Bill Karn • *Scr* Phillips H Lord

Gang in Blue ★★★

Police drama 1996 · US · Colour · 97mins

Following their writing/directing collaboration on 1995's *Panther*, father and son Melvin and Mario Van Peebles went a few steps further, jointly producing, directing and starring in this police thriller. Mario plays an idealistic policeman who discovers a secret brotherhood of racists at work within his department and sets out to bring them to justice. With a heavyweight supporting cast, which includes JT Walsh and Stephen Lang, this is an impassioned and intelligent film whose gloss doesn't compromise its integrity. Contains violence, swearing and sex scenes.

Mario Van Peebles *Michael Rhoades* • Melvin Van Peebles *Andre Speier* • Josh Brolin *Keith Debruler* • Cynda Williams *Anita Bayard* • Stephen Lang *Moose Tavola* • JT Walsh *Sergeant William Eyer* • Zach Grenier *Beckstrom* ∎ *Dir* Mario Van Peebles, Melvin Van Peebles • *Scr* Rick Natkin, David Fuller

Gang Related ★★★★ 15

Crime drama 1997 · US · Colour · 106mins

Tupac Shakur's final film offers a glimpse of what a fine, subtle actor he was becoming before his tragic early death. The acclaimed rap star plays a detective who, with partner James Belushi, has established a lucrative scam ripping off and killing drug dealers and pronouncing the deaths as "gang related". However, it all goes pear-shaped when their latest victim turns out to be an undercover drugs agent and the derelict they attempt to frame (Dennis Quaid) is discovered to have a surprising past. Belushi sweats sleaze as the murderously corrupt cop. Writer/director Jim Kouf delivers the goods thriller-wise, while mining an unexpected seam of gallows humour. Contains swearing, violence and some nudity. 💬 **DVD**

James Belushi *Detective Frank K Divinci* • Tupac Shakur *Detective Rodriguez* • Lela Rochon *Cynthia Webb* • Dennis Quaid *William Dane McCall/"Joe Doe"* • James Earl Jones *Arthur Baylor* • David Paymer *Elliot Goff* • Wendy Crewson *Helen Eden* • Gary Cole *Richard Simms* ∎ *Dir/Scr* Jim Kouf

The Game of Love ★★ 15

Comedy drama 1987 · US · Colour · 93mins

A sort of *Cheers* without the gags, this ensemble piece focuses on the trials and tribulations of the regulars who frequent the singles bar Henry's, run by the wise Ken Olin (*thirtysomething*). His troubled customers include Robert Rusler, a clerk torn between two women, an ageing pilot (Max Gail) and Olin's bed-hopping brother (*Hill Street Blues's* Ed Marinaro). Director Bobby Roth leaps smoothly between the interlocking story strands but he can't hide the soapy nature of the material. Nevertheless, it is sharply played by the cast, also includes Belinda Bauer and Janet Margolin. 💬

Ed Marinaro *Hayden Fox* • Ken Olin *Henry Fox* • Max Gail *Sam Davies* • Belinda Bauer *Pamela Ahlberg* • Tracy Nelson *Jamie Davies* • Robert Rusler *Kenny* • Janet Margolin *Chris* • Emily Longstreth *Kim* ∎ *Dir* Bobby Roth • *Scr* Steven Humphrey, Sue Grafton

U = SUITABLE FOR ALL   Uc = SUITABLE FOR ALL, ESPECIALLY FOR YOUNG CHILDREN (VIDEO ONLY)   PG = PARENTAL GUIDANCE

The Gang That Couldn't Shoot Straight ★★★ 15

Crime comedy 1971 · US · Colour · 92mins

This slapstick comedy about New York mobsters stars Jerry Orbach as the incompetent hood who makes a disastrous series of attempts to bump off a local Mafioso, played by gravel-voiced Lionel Stander. Directed at breakneck pace by James Goldstone and written by Waldo Salt, with an ear for the local South Brooklyn wisecrack, it's a bit hit and miss, but it's hard to dislike a mobster movie that features a cycle race and a lion on the loose. Stander is tremendous and Jo Van Fleet is ludicrously over the top, but most eyes will be on Robert De Niro, having a ball as one of the Italian cyclists who becomes an illegal immigrant and a bogus priest.

Jerry Orbach *Kid Sally* • Leigh Taylor-Young *Angela* • Jo Van Fleet *Big Momma* • Lionel Stander *Baccala* • Robert De Niro *Mario* • Irving Selbst *Big Jelly* • Herve Villechaize *Beppo* ■ *Dir* James Goldstone • *Scr* Waldo Salt, from the novel by Jimmy Breslin

Gang War ★★★

Crime drama 1958 · US · BW · 71mins

Sixteen years before the controversial *Death Wish*, Charles Bronson turned vigilante in this little-known crime thriller. Having witnessed a gangland murder, Bronson testifies in court and later finds his pregnant wife has been murdered in a revenge attack. When the police fail to arrest the killers, Bronson goes up against the mob himself, only to find... Well, this movie has a peculiarly ironic ending that makes Bronson's personal crusade a mere blip on the natural course of American capitalism. Despite some naff scenes and a few dodgy performances, this B-movie is well worth seeking out.

Charles Bronson *Alan Avery* • Kent Taylor *Bryce Barker* • Jennifer Holden *Marie* • John Doucette *Maxie Matthews* • Gloria Henry *Edie Avery* • Gloria Grey *Marsha Brown* • Barney Phillips *Sam Johnson* • Ralph Manza *Axe Duncan* ■ *Dir* Gene Fowler Jr • *Scr* Louis Vittes, from the novel *The Hoods Take Over* by Ovid Demaris

The Gang's All Here ★★★

Comedy melodrama 1939 · UK · BW · 78mins

This film's title is the reason why Busby Berkeley's 1943 Hollywood extravaganza of the same name was released as *The Girls He Left Behind* in the UK (while this film was released as *The Amazing Mr Forrest* in the US). This Jack Buchanan vehicle is a sequel to his earlier *Smash and Grab*, which attempted to turn Buchanan and Elsie Randolph into a British Nick and Nora Charles (*The Thin Man*). He plays John Forrest, an insurance investigator who routs an American gang in a London nightclub with Googie Withers. Jack and Googie make a very smart coupling, and this flick was a big hit, its style aided by the presence of American director Thornton Freeland (*Flying Down to Rio*) and the likes of Edward Everett Horton, Jack LaRue and Otto Kruger in the cast.

Edward Everett Horton *Treadwell* • Otto Kruger *Mike Chadwick* • Jack Buchanan *John Forrest* • Jack LaRue *Alberni* • Googie Withers *Alice Forrest* • Syd Walker *Younce* • David Burns *Beretti* • Walter Rilla *Prince Homouska* ■ *Dir* Thornton Freeland • *Scr* Ralph Spence

The Gang's All Here ★★ U

Musical 1943 · US · Colour · 103mins

Better known in the UK by the title *The Girls He Left Behind*, this is a mesmerisingly awful chunk of camp kitsch, designed and filmed in Technicolor so garish you'd be forgiven for thinking you'd fallen into a box of chocolates. The undoubted highlight is the preposterous Carmen Miranda performing *The Lady in the Tutti Frutti Hat* while chorus girls do the most extraordinary things with giant bananas. This farrago proves that director Busby Berkeley left his taste behind him at MGM and Warner Bros when he decamped to 20th Century-Fox. Painfully dated now, the film nominally stars Alice Faye, who sings *A Journey to a Star*. Band leader Benny Goodman also sings (and plays), but the wartime utility leading men Phil Baker and James Ellison are, frankly, pathetic. Charlotte Greenwood and Edward Everett Horton compensate, but not much.

Alice Faye *Eadie Allen* • Carmen Miranda *Dorita* • Phil Baker *Phil Baker* • Eugene Pallette *Mr Mason Sr* • Charlotte Greenwood *Mrs Peyton Potter* • Edward Everett Horton *Peyton Potter* ■ *Dir* Busby Berkeley • *Scr* Walter Bullock, from a story by Nancy Winter, George Root Jr, Tom Bridges

The Gangster ★

Film noir 1947 · US · BW · 83mins

A gloomy and largely unrevealing attempt to psychoanalyse a criminal mind. Barry Sullivan is the gangland leader who tries to be a nicer human being, but finds people still crossing the street to avoid him. Sullivan, never a front-rank actor, tries hard to give his character (incongruously named Shubunka) the sort of energy and strange appeal that Edward G Robinson, Paul Muni and James Cagney brought to similar roles in the thirties. Sadly, he comes across as merely tedious, leaving Akim Tamiroff and Belita (a former ice-skater and down-market Sonja Henie) to try to lighten things up. This dime-budget production is dudsville all the way.

Barry Sullivan *Shubunka* • Belita *Nancy Starr* • Joan Lorring *Dorothy* • Akim Tamiroff *Nick Jammey* • Henry Morgan [Harry Morgan] *Shorty* • John Ireland *Karty* • Fifi D'Orsay *Mrs Ostroleng* • Virginia Christine *Mrs Karty* • John Kellogg *Sterling* ■ *Dir* Gordon Wiles • *Scr* Daniel Fuchs, from his novel *Low Company*

Gangster No 1 ★★★ 18

Crime thriller 2000 · UK · Colour · mins

Following in the wake of *Lock, Stock and Two Smoking Barrels*, Paul McGuigan's thriller is another tale of London gangsters, though this time without the humour. As studies of pure evil go, however, it's very convincing. Malcolm McDowell plays a crime lord who, concerned that a mob boss he once double-crossed is about to be released from prison, looks back on the sixties antics of his gang. Flashbacks show him played by the impressive Paul Bettany, whose psychotic behaviour leads to much blood-letting. This central section is stylistically superb, but the film is fatally flawed by the fact that both boss David Thewlis and his moll (Saffron Burrows) are badly aged for the final section. The gratuitous violence and profanity also leave a nasty taste in the mouth.

Malcolm McDowell *Gangster 55* • David Thewlis *Freddie Mays* • Paul Bettany *Young Gangster* • Saffron Burrows *Karen* • Kenneth Cranham *Tommy* • Jamie Foreman *Lennie Taylor* • Andrew Lincoln *Maxie King* ■ *Dir* Paul McGuigan • *Scr* Johnny Ferguson, from the play by Louis Mellis, David Scinto

Gangster Story ★★★

Crime drama 1959 · US · BW · 70mins

Inside every great Hollywood actor there's a would-be director trying to get out. Clint Eastwood, Mel Gibson and Kevin Costner are but three recent examples. Fans of Walter Matthau may be surprised to find that the untidy half of *The Odd Couple* made his directing debut as far back as 1959. He also stars in this crime drama as gangster Jack Martin, who finds himself in conflict with local hood Bruce McFarlan when he tries to muscle in on his territory. Not Oscar-winning stuff, but competent and absorbing.

Walter Matthau *Jack Martin* • Carol Grace *Carol* • Bruce McFarlan *Earl Dawson* • Garrett Wallberg *Adolph* • Raiken Ben Ari *Hood* ■ *Dir* Walter Matthau • *Scr* Paul Purcell, from a story by Richard Grey, VJ Rhems

Gangway ★★★ U

Musical 1937 · UK · BW · 86mins

Try as they might, British producers of the thirties always managed to be just out of time in their attempts to emulate the Hollywood musical. Jessie Matthews, therefore, didn't have much to beat to be hailed as the queen of the British equivalent, but her energy and charm enabled her to elevate the most mundane material and win fans on both sides of the Atlantic. The second of three films directed by her then husband Sonnie Hale, this lively crime comedy of errors benefits not only from her willing lead, but also from the expert support of Nat Pendleton and Alastair Sim.

Jessie Matthews *Pat Wayne* • Barry MacKay *Inspector Bob Deering* • Olive Blakeney *Nedda Beaumont* • Liane Ordeyne *Greta Brand* • Patrick Ludlow *Carl Freemason* • Nat Pendleton *"Smiles" Hogan* • Noel Madison *Mike Otterman* • Alastair Sim *Taggett* ■ *Dir* Sonnie Hale • *Scr* Lesser Samuels, Sonnie Hale, from a story by Dwight Taylor

Ganja and Hess ★★★

Blaxploitation horror
1973 · US · Colour · 86mins

Lauded in some circles as one of the best movies to explore black culture seriously within a genre context and seen by others as just a dull vampire tale, director Bill Gunn's spiritual contemplation on African myth versus Christianity was severely cut and tampered with on its initial release and retitled *Blood Couple*. Duane Jones (of *Night of the Living Dead* fame) is an anthropologist studying the ancient religion of Myrthia. When he's stabbed by a sacrificial dagger, he becomes addicted to blood and resistant to death, and starts having visions of his native Africa. Thoughtful and thought-provoking, Gunn's offbeat tale is a haunting experience if one is prepared to forgive its slow patches.

Duane Jones *Dr Hess Green* • Marlene Clark *Ganja Meda* • Bill Gunn *George* • Sam Waymon *Reverend Luther Williams* • Leonard Jackson *Archie* • Candece Tarpley *Girl in bar* • Richard Harrow *Dinner guest* • John Hoffmeister *Jack Sargent* ■ *Dir/Scr* Bill Gunn

Gaolbreak ★ U

Drama crime 1962 · UK · BW · 62mins

The Cinematograph Act, passed by Parliament in 1927, was supposed to help the British film industry by ensuring that cinemas presented a quota of home-made features each year. The problem was, cash was too scarce to produce prestige pictures and what resulted were the much maligned "quota quickies", many of which had barely enough plot to make a TV episode, let alone keep a cinema audience happy. Studios such as Butcher's specialised in this kind of cheapie, in which a typically down-at-heel crime story is spiced up by a subplot about an unwanted pregnancy. Everyone was grateful for the work, but this output didn't help the reputation of the British film industry.

Peter Reynolds *Eddie Wallis* • Avice Landone *Mrs Wallis* • David Kernan *Len Rogerson* • Carol White *Carol Marshall* • David Gregory *Ron Wallis* • John Blythe *Slim* • Robert Desmond *Page* • Geoffrey Hibbert *Dr Cambus* ■ *Dir* Francis Searle • *Scr* AR Rawlinson

Garam Hawa ★★★★

Drama 1973 · Ind · Colour · 146mins

Also known as *Scorching Winds*, this is the highly impressive debut feature from the socially committed Indian film-maker MS Sathyu. Set in northern India shortly after partition in 1947, it explores the problems faced by those Muslims who chose to stay rather than emigrate to the new state of Pakistan. Balraj Sahni (who died shortly after filming) gives a towering performance as the shoemaker whose family suffers in the face of prejudicial new laws and his refusal to leave his heritage behind. An Urdu language film.

Balraj Sahni *Salim Mirza* • Shaukat Azmi *Jamila Mirza* • Gita *Amina* • Farouque Shaikh *Sikander* • Dinanath Zutshi *Halim Mirza* ■ *Dir* MS Sathyu • *Scr* Kaifi Azmi, Shama Zaidi, from a story by Ismat Chugtai

The Garbage Pail Kids Movie ★ PG

Comedy 1987 · US · Colour · 91mins

The movie spin-off from the Topps Company's bubble gum trading cards series is purposely offensive rubbish. The alien kids, who rejoice in names such as Greaser Greg and Nat Nerd, land on Earth in a dustbin and end up in Anthony Newley's shop. Unfortunately Newley's assistant takes the lid off the dustbin, subjecting us to a bad-taste mix of mean-spirited pranks, grotesque humour and knockabout violence. Director Rod Amateau's lousy movie is supposed to be mindless trash and sadly achieves that aim. In fact, garbage is putting it mildly.

Anthony Newley *Captain Manzini* • MacKenzie Astin *Dodger* • Katie Barberi *Tangerine* • Ron MacLachlan *Juice* • Kevin Thompson *Ali Gator*

• Phil Fondacaro *Greaser Greg* • Robert Bell [Robert N Bell] *Foul Phil* • Larry Green *Nat Nerd* • Arturo Gil *Windy Winston* ■ *Dir* Rod Amateau • *Scr* Rod Amateau, Melinda Palmer

Garbo Talks ★★★ 15

Comedy drama 1984 · US · Colour · 100mins

Director Sidney Lumet's fondness for social outsiders goes back to his first film, *12 Angry Men*, and the pattern continues with *Garbo Talks*, in which Anne Bancroft plays an affable but certifiable eccentric. The New York housewife is obsessed with the titular film star and addicted to supporting lost causes, as a result of which she is continually getting arrested. Ron Silver is suitably long-suffering as her exasperated but devoted son and Bancroft makes her character wholly credible. The result is a charming, if uneven film.

Anne Bancroft *Estelle Rolfe* • Ron Silver *Gilbert Rolfe* • Carrie Fisher *Lisa Rolfe* • Catherine Hicks *Jane Mortimer* • Steven Hill *Walter Rolfe* • Howard Da Silva *Angelo Dokakis* • Dorothy Loudon *Sonya Apollinar* ■ *Dir* Sidney Lumet • *Scr* Larry Grusin

La Garce ★★

Drama 1984 · Fr · Colour · 90mins

Actress Christine Pascal (*'Round Midnight*) also directed a handful of films, of which this was the second. This provocative drama dabbles in extreme situations, coldly enacted by a main trio of thoroughly resistible characters. Isabelle Huppert's attempt to adopt a new personality after she is raped by cop Richard Berry is confounded by her decision to abandon her gangster lover (Vittorio Mezzogiorno) on her assailant's release from jail. Pascal deserves credit for striving for such unpalatable truth, but, for once, Huppert fails to get to grips with the complexities of her character. French dialogue dubbed into English.

Isabelle Huppert *Aline/Edith* • Richard Berry *Lucien Sabatier* • Vittorio Mezzogiorno *Max* • Jean Benguigui *Rony* • Jean-Claude Leguay *Brunet* • Daniel Jegou *Dujarric* • Jenny Cleve *Mme Beffroit* • Jean-Pierre Bagot *Beffroit* ■ *Dir* Christine Pascal • *Scr* Andre Marc Delocque-Fourcaud, Laurent Heynemann, Pierre Fabre, Christine Pascal

Garde à Vue ★★★★

Crime drama 1981 · Fr · Colour · 88mins

John Wainwright's novel, *Brainwash*, is the inspiration for this tense murder investigation. By confiding the bulk of the action to a provincial police station, Claude Miller is able to control not only the steady flow of secrets and lies, but also the suspense levels, as detectives Lino Ventura and Guy Marchand seek to uncover prominent lawyer Michel Serrault's role in the rape and murder of a young girl. There are improbabilities in the plot, but such is the conviction of the exchanges that they serve only to deepen the mystery. In French with English subtitles.

Lino Ventura *Inspector Antoine Gallien* • Michel Serrault *Jérôme Martinaud* • Guy Marchand *Inspector Marcel Belmont* • Romy Schneider *Chantal Martinaud* • Didier Agostini *Young policeman* • Patrick Depeyrat *1st policeman* • Pierre Maguelon *Adami* • Serge Malik *Mechanic* ■ *Dir* Claude Miller • *Scr* Claude Miller, Jean Herman, from the novel *Brainwash* by John Wainwright

The Garden ★★ 15

Experimental drama
1990 · UK · BW and Colour · 88mins

Director Derek Jarman's uncompromising experimental work is alternately moving, annoying and boring. Christianity, the media, police brutality, advertising, Aids, old age and repression are just some of the topics that make up this angry, non-narrative view of homosexual discrimination. Using camp, weird and shocking imagery (two lovers tortured by a cop dressed as Santa Claus, a drag queen stoned by debutantes in slow motion, Jesus walking by a nuclear power station), Jarman's political treatise is a graphically dense look at gay counterculture. Michael Gough (Alfred in the *Batman* films) supplies the narration.

Tilda Swinton *Madonna* • Johnny Mills *Lover* • Kevin Collins *Lover* • Pete Lee-Wilson *Devil* • Spencer Leigh *Mary Magdalene/Adam* • Jody Graber *Young boy* • Roger Cook *Christ* • Jessica Martin *Singer* • Michael Gough *Narrator* ■ *Dir/Scr* Derek Jarman

The Garden of Allah ★★★

Silent romance 1927 · US · BW · 82mins

The second of the three screen versions of Robert Hitchens's novel was shot on location in North Africa and at the famous Victorine studio in Nice. Directing wife Alice Terry, Rex Ingram allows the camera to caress her face without capturing the barest flicker of emotion. As the monk who abandons his vocation to run away and marry her, Ivan Petrovich at least manages to express some of the torment experienced by the Trappist lured from the right path by worldly temptation. However, it's Marcel Vibert's sinister Arab who steals this stylish but ultimately limp melodrama.

Alice Terry *Domini Enfilden* • Ivan Petrovich *Father Adrien/Boris Androvsky* • Marcel Vibert *Count Anteoni* • HH Wright *Lord Rens* ■ *Dir* Rex Ingram • *Scr* Willis Goldbeck, from the novel by Robert Hichens

The Garden of Allah ★★

Romantic melodrama
1936 · US · Colour · 85mins

Many movies are damned by film critics, only to find widespread popularity with the cinema-going public. Few of these are actual junk; this film, by contrast, actually is total garbage. From a novel that was already dated on publication, directed by a Polish émigré (Richard Boleslawski) with little sense of style or pace, and phoney beyond endurance in narrative and execution, *The Garden of Allah* doesn't even appeal on the "so bad it's good" front. The two leads (Marlene Dietrich and Charles Boyer) look uncomfortable and awkward as they attempt to mouth unspeakable platitudes. These criticisms notwithstanding, the use of early Oscar-winning Technicolor photography is sumptuous.

Marlene Dietrich *Domini Enfilden* • Charles Boyer *Boris Androvsky* • Basil Rathbone *Count Anteoni* • C Aubrey Smith *Father Roubier* • Tilly Losch *Irena* • Joseph Schildkraut *Batouch* ■ *Dir* Richard Boleslawski • *Scr* WP Lipscomb, Lynn Riggs, from the novel by Robert Hichens • *Cinematographer* Harold Rosson

Garden of Evil ★★

Western 1954 · US · Colour · 98mins

This loose rehash of *The Treasure of the Sierra Madre* squanders its cast and devotes its energies to capturing the scenery with the new CinemaScope lens. The script has Susan Hayward convincing adventurers Gary Cooper and Richard Widmark that "there's gold in them thar hills" – as well as a husband buried in the mine they're seeking. Indian attacks impede their progress and their return, while Hayward makes the chaps break out in sweaty rivalry. A western that searches for biblical parallels, to no avail.

Gary Cooper *Hooker* • Susan Hayward *Leah Fuller* • Richard Widmark *Fiske* • Cameron Mitchell *Luke Daly* • Hugh Marlowe *John Fuller* • Rita Moreno *Singer* • Victor Manuel Mendoza *Vicente Madariaga* • Fernando Wagner *Captain* ■ *Dir* Henry Hathaway • *Scr* Frank Fenton, from a story by Fred Freiberger, William Tunberg

The Garden of the Finzi-Continis ★★★★★

Second World War drama
1971 · It/W Ger · Colour · 95mins

Based on Giorgio Bassani's semi-autobiographical novel and the winner of the 1971 best foreign film Oscar, this sobering drama is something of a companion piece to Roberto Benigni's *Life Is Beautiful*. Eschewing both the neorealist flourishes that forged his reputation and the melodramatic excesses that marred it, Vittorio De Sica brilliantly employs flashbacks to explain the confidence of a Jewish family in their belief that Fascism will never breach the walls of their Ferrara home. Rarely has inevitability been so suspensefully presented – or faith in a doomed way of life so well portrayed – as in this exquisitely played and genuinely moving masterpiece. In Italian with English subtitles.

Dominique Sanda *Micol* • Lino Capolicchio *Giorgio* • Helmut Berger *Alberto* • Fabio Testi *Malnate* • Romolo Valli *Giorgio's father* • Raffaele Curi *Ernesto* • Camillo Angelini-Rota *Micol's father* • Katina Viglietti *Micol's mother* • Inna Alexeieff *Micol's grandmother* ■ *Dir* Vittorio De Sica • *Scr* Cesare Zavattini, Vittorio Bonicelli, Ugo Pirro, Giorgio Bassani, from the novel by Giorgio Bassani

Garden of the Moon ★★ U

Musical 1938 · US · BW · 93mins

Busby Berkeley's dull direction of his last musical for Warner Bros is a far cry from the glorious inventiveness he brought to the musical numbers of *42nd Street* or *Gold Diggers of 1933*. Set in a nightclub called the Garden of the Moon run by a pushy and obnoxious Pat O'Brien, this spotlights John Payne as a bandleader and singer (after Dick Powell refused to play the role) with Margaret Lindsay's publicity agent as his love interest. The most memorable of the songs is *The Girl Friend of the Whirling Dervish*.

Pat O'Brien *John Quinn* • Margaret Lindsay *Toni Blake* • John Payne *Don Vincente* • Johnnie Davis *Slappy Harris* • Melville Cooper *Maurice* • Isabel Jeans *Mrs Lornay* • Mabel Todd *Mary Stanton* • Penny Singleton *Miss Calder* ■ *Dir* Busby Berkeley • *Scr* Jerry Wald, Richard Macaulay, from the story by H Bedford-Jones, John Barton Browne

The Gardener ★

Horror 1972 · US · Colour · 97mins

This mind-boggling trash was filmed in Puerto Rico and didn't see the light of day until the early eighties. One-time Andy Warhol superstar Joe Dallesandro is a gardener with a wonderful gift for rearing exotic plants, but his female employers aren't enjoying such good health. It's hard to stay awake but the ending, in which Dallesandro turns into a tree, has to be seen to be believed.

Katharine Houghton *Ellen Bennett* • Rita Gam *Helena Boardman* • Joe Dallesandro *Carl the gardener* • James Congdon *John Bennett* ■ *Dir/Scr* James H Kay III

Gardens of Stone ★★★ 15

War drama 1987 · US · Colour · 106mins

If "war is hell" was the message of Francis Coppola's 1979 Vietnam epic, *Apocalypse Now*, then "war is senseless" must be the message of the director's return to the subject of the Vietnam War in this quieter, more sombre film, set on the home front. James Caan gives a powerful performance as the combat veteran whose ambivalence towards the war and the military is combined with a romantic interest in an anti-war journalist, played by Anjelica Huston. The film was marred by the tragic death of Coppola's son, Giancarlo, in a boating accident during production.

James Caan *Sgt Clell Hazard* • James Earl Jones *Sgt Major "Goody" Nelson* • DB Sweeney *Private Jackie Willow* • Anjelica Huston *Samantha Davis* • Dean Stockwell *Capt Homer Thomas* • Mary Stuart Masterson *Rachel Field* • Dick Anthony Williams *Sgt Slasher Williams* • Lonette McKee *Betty Rae* ■ *Dir* Francis Coppola [Francis Ford Coppola] • *Scr* Ronald Bass, from the novel by Nicholas Proffitt

The Garment Jungle ★★★

Crime drama 1957 · US · BW · 87mins

A good hard-hitting example of fifties Hollywood realism, this tackles the subject of labour unions in the clothing business. It is almost a pro-union retort by Columbia to the studio's own anti-union *On the Waterfront*, three years earlier. As in the earlier movie, Lee J Cobb is the heavy – this time, however, not as a corrupt union official, but as a union-bashing boss involved with gangster Richard Boone. The original (uncredited) director Robert Aldrich was taken off the film towards the end of shooting and replaced by Vincent Sherman.

Lee J Cobb *Walter Mitchell* • Kerwin Mathews *Alan Mitchell* • Gia Scala *Theresa Renata* • Richard Boone *Artie Ravidge* • Valerie French *Lee Hackett* • Robert Loggia *Tulio Renata* • Joseph Wiseman *Kovan* • Harold J Stone *Tony* ■ *Dir* Vincent Sherman, Robert Aldrich • *Scr* Harry Kleiner, from the article *Gangsters in the Dress Business* by Lester Velie

Gas ★

Comedy 1981 · Can · Colour · 94mins

This Canadian comedy about the effects of a phoney petrol shortage on a small American town piles on the automobile pile-ups in the vain hope

544

U = SUITABLE FOR ALL Uc = SUITABLE FOR ALL, ESPECIALLY FOR YOUNG CHILDREN (VIDEO ONLY) PG = PARENTAL GUIDANCE

that such destruction will somehow be fun. Donald Sutherland is less than adequately served by his role as Nick the Noz, a disc jockey so laid-back he's practically flat. Les Rose directs, if that's what you call splicing together car wrecks. The deviants in David Cronenberg's film *Crash* are the only ones who'd find this enjoyable.

Donald Sutherland *Nick the Noz* • Susan Anspach *Jane Beardsley* • Howie Mandel *Matt Lloyd* • Sterling Hayden *Duke Stuyvesant* • Sandee Currie *Sarah Marshall* • Peter Aykroyd *Ed Marshall* • Keith Knight *Ira* • Helen Shaver *Rhonda* ■ *Dir* Les Rose • *Scr* Richard Wolf, from a story by Richard Wolf, Susan Scranton

Gas, Food, Lodging
★★★★ **15**

Drama   1992 · US · Colour · 101mins

Brooke Adams is the single mother trying to hold down a job at a diner while coping with teenage daughters who are growing up too fast in writer/ director Allison Anders's intelligent family drama. Anders works wonders with a low budget and sketches a gritty, sympathetic portrait of lost dreams and the daily struggle of small-town American life. The cast, with Ione Skye and Fairuza Balk as the daughters, is exemplary, and there's even a turn from the usually wooden James Brolin. Disappointingly, Anders has often struggled to live up to this early promise. Contains swearing and sex scenes. ▭

Brooke Adams *Nora Roberts* • Ione Skye *Trudi* • Fairuza Balk *Shade* • James Brolin *John Evans* • Robert Knepper *Dank* • David Landsbury *Hamlet Humphrey* • Chris Mulkey *Raymond* • Adam Biesk *Brett* ■ *Dir* Allison Anders • *Scr* Allison Anders, from the novel *Don't Look and It Won't Hurt* by Richard Peck

Gasbags
★★★ **U**

Second World War comedy
1940 · UK · BW · 77mins

Intended to boost wartime morale, this is the best film ever made by the Crazy Gang, the British comedy team led by Bud Flanagan and Chesney Allen. The plot includes a flying fish-and-chip shop, while the geriatric-looking Moore Marriott – a veteran of innumerable Will Hay films – plays a prisoner of war with plans for a secret weapon tattooed on his back. No wonder the Gang have designs on him. Director Marcel Varnel has just the right surreal touch to make it work and leave audiences laughing.

Bud Flanagan [Dennis O'Keefe] *Bud* • Chesney Allen *Ches* • Jimmy Nervo *Cecil* • Teddy Knox *Knoxy* • Charlie Naughton *Charlie* • Jimmy Gold *Goldy* • Moore Marriott *Jerry Jenkins* • Wally Patch *Sergeant Major* ■ *Dir* Marcel Varnel • *Scr* Val Guest, Marrott Edgar, from the story by Val Valentine, Ralph Smart

Gaslight
★★★ **PG**

Drama thriller   1940 · UK · BW · 80mins

Nowadays, most viewers will probably be more familiar with George Cukor's 1944 adaptation of Patrick Hamilton's stage success than with this British original. The Hollywood version is easily the better picture, with MGM's vision of Victorian London more atmospheric than the rough-and-ready one cobbled together here by British National. Diana Wynyard is streets

behind Ingrid Bergman (who won an Oscar) as the terrorised wife, but Anton Walbrook is splendidly sinister and it is a great story. MGM bought up the prints of this to ensure that its remake had the field to itself. ▭

Anton Walbrook *Paul Mallen* • Diana Wynyard *Bella Mallen* • Cathleen Cordell *Nancy* • Robert Newton *Ullswater* • Frank Pettingell *Rough* • Jimmy Hanley *Cobb* • Minnie Rayner *Elizabeth* • Mary Hinton *Lady Winterbourne* ■ *Dir* Thorold Dickinson • *Scr* Ar Rawlinson, Bridget Boland, from the play *Angel Street* by Patrick Hamilton

Gaslight
★★★★ **PG**

Melodrama   1944 · US · BW · 108mins

Ingrid Bergman won her first best actress Oscar as the socialite slowly being driven mad (or is she really mad?) by suave husband Charles Boyer. Based on a Patrick Hamilton stage success called *Angel Street*, this was released in Britain as *The Murder in Thornton Square*, to avoid confusion with the equally famous 1940 British version with Anton Walbrook and Diana Wynyard. MGM actually tried to suppress the first film when they remade it as this super glossy Bergman vehicle. It's a bit dated now, but still has much to offer, notably George Cukor's intelligent direction, which, combined with production designer Cedric Gibbons's terrific Victorian setting (the interior decoration won an Oscar), offers the radiant Bergman a shameless opportunity that she seizes with all the acting tricks at her disposal. ▭

Charles Boyer *Gregory Anton* • Ingrid Bergman *Paula Alquist* • Joseph Cotten *Brian Cameron* • Dame May Whitty *Miss Thwaites* • Angela Lansbury *Nancy Oliver* • Barbara Everest *Elizabeth Tompkins* • Eustace Wyatt *Budge* ■ *Dir* George Cukor • *Scr* John Van Druten, Walter Reisch, John L Balderston, from the play *Angel Street* by Patrick Hamilton

Gas-s-s-s, or It Became Necessary to Destroy the World in Order to Save It
★★

Comedy   1970 · US · Colour · 79mins

A nerve gas leak in Alaska kills everyone over 25 in this hopelessly surreal comedy from cult director Roger Corman. However, the expected Utopia doesn't materialise in a free-wheeling romp that features Hell's Angels, Che Guevara, Edgar Allan Poe and Martin Luther King. Talia Shire, Ben Vereen, Bud Cort and Cindy Williams all make appearances in this time-capsule oddity, but Corman takes aim at too many hip targets and doesn't hit any of them successfully. After the film was heavily cut by his usual distributors, AIP, Corman set up his own production company, New World.

Robert Corff *Coel* • Elaine Giftos *Cilla* • Pat Patterson *Demeter* • George Armitage *Billy the Kid* • Alex Wilson *Jason* • Alan Braunstein *Dr Drake* • Ben Vereen *Carlos* • Cindy Williams *Marissa* • Bud Cort *Hooper* • Talia Shire *Coralie* • Country Joe and the Fish *FM Radio* ■ *Dir* Roger Corman • *Scr* George Armitage

The Gate
★★★ **15**

Horror   1987 · US/Can · Colour · 82mins

Three kids (Stephen Dorff, Christa Denton and Louis Tripp) inadvertently

open the gateway to hell in their back yard and unleash a horde of demonic midgets who are making way for the arrival of the Devil himself. Although full of plot holes bigger than the one in the garden, director Tibor Takacs's low-budget trip though *Gremlins* and *Poltergeist* territory has enough verve and gall to drag it above the usual level of lightweight, popcorn horror fodder despite every twist being telegraphed well in advance. Even though it sports an episodic mix-and-match story, dazzling special effects make *The Gate* worth a look. ▭

Stephen Dorff *Glen* • Christa Denton *Al* • Louis Tripp *Terry* • Kelly Rowan *Lori Lee* • Jennifer Irwin *Linda Lee* • Deborah Grover *Mom* • Scot Denton *Dad* • Ingrid Veninger *Paula* • Sean Fagan *Eric* ■ *Dir* Tibor Takacs • *Scr* Michael Nankin

Gate of Hell
★★★★★

Historical drama 1953 · Jap · Colour · 91mins

Winner of an Oscar for best costume and an honorary statuette, as well as the Grand Prix (now Palme d'Or) at Cannes, this is one of the most sumptuously coloured films ever made. Shooting in Eastmancolor and employing the theories of "synaesthesia" learned from Sergei Eisenstein, director Teinosuke Kinugasa lovingly sculpts each image, whether it's from a battle or the doomed courtship of Machiko Kyo by the heroic samurai, Kazuo Hasegawa. Amid such physical beauty, it's too easy to forget the majesty of the performances, particularly Kyo's proud wife, who refuses to submit to either the lust of her suitor or the conventions of her time. In Japanese with English subtitles.

Machiko Kyo *Lady Kesa* • Kazuo Hasegawa *Moritoh* • Isao Yamagata *Wataru* • Koreya Senda *Kiyomori* • Yataro Kurokawa *Shigemori* • Kikue Mohri *Sawa* • Kotaro Bando *Rokuroh* • Jun Tazaki *Kogenta* ■ *Dir* Teinosuke Kinugasa • *Scr* Teinosuke Kinugasa, from the play *Jigokumon* by Kan Kikuchi

Gates of Paris
★★★ **U**

Drama   1957 · Fr/It · BW · 100mins

Based on René Fallet's novel, *La Grande Ceinture*, René Clair's last film before his New Wave denunciation is an unexpectedly serious and grossly under-rated near neighbour of Marcel Carné's *Le Jour Se Lève*. Yet his return to poetic realism is only partially successful. Léon Barsacq's claustrophobic interiors are derivative to the point of cliché, while the *ménage à trois* of dipsomaniac drifter Pierre Brasseur, his girlfriend Dany Carrel and fugitive killer Henri Vidal can only end in tragedy. However, there are flashes of the old inspiration, with troubadour Georges Brassens (in his only film) acting as a roving commentator on the action. In French with English subtitles.

Pierre Brasseur *Juju* • Georges Brassens *L'Artiste* • Henri Vidal *Pierre Barbier* • Dany Carrel *Maria* • Raymond Bussières *Alphonse* • Amédée Paolo *Juju* ■ *Dir* René Clair • *Scr* René Clair, Jean Aurel, from the novel *La Grande Ceinture* by René Fallet

A Gathering of Eagles
★★ **U**

Drama   1963 · US · Colour · 115mins

Colonel Rock Hudson arrives at a Strategic Air Command base, where he has control over nuclear warheads but not, it seems, over his indolent men or wife. This soggy drama wants to be a Cold War version of *From Here to Eternity*, but it's let down by Hudson's boring performance and a generally weak supporting cast. The film needs Elizabeth Taylor or Ava Gardner as the wife; instead it has Mary Peach, best known as Laurence Harvey's girlfriend in *Room at the Top*.

Rock Hudson *Col Jim Caldwell* • Rod Taylor *Hollis Farr* • Mary Peach *Victoria Caldwell* • Barry Sullivan *Col Fowler* • Kevin McCarthy *Gen Kirby* • Henry Silva *Col Garcia* • Leora Dana *Mrs Fowler* • Robert Lansing *Sgt Banning* ■ *Dir* Delbert Mann • *Scr* Robert Pirosh, from a story by Sy Bartlett

A Gathering of Old Men
★★★

Drama   1987 · US · Colour · 91mins

An above-average race relations thriller. Based on the novel by Ernest J Gaines, it details the anonymous shooting of a redneck Louisiana farmer. Plantation owner Holly Hunter rounds up all her hands, most of whom are black, only to find each in possession of the potential murder weapon and all of them admitting to the murder. Despite the plodding pace, the film exceeds expectation due to witty and dry scripting from Charles Fuller and the superb ensemble performances from Louis Gosset Jr, Joe Seneca, Julius Harris and Woody Strode.

Louis Gossett Jr *Mathu* • Richard Widmark *Mapes* • Holly Hunter *Candy Marshall* • Will Patton *Lou Dimes* • Joe Seneca *Clatoo* • Woody Strode *Yank* • Tiger Haynes *Booker* • Papa John Creach *Jacob* • Julius Harris *Coot* ■ *Dir* Volker Schlöndorff • *Scr* Charles Fuller, from the novel by Ernest J Gaines

Gator
★★ **15**

Action adventure
1976 · US · Colour · 111mins

Burt Reynolds resurrected Gator McKlusky, the demon driver character he created in *White Lightning*, for his directorial debut, a so-so action thriller. The moonshining ex-con is forced by federal agents to nail an old school friend who's now a corrupt politician. Surprisingly good-humoured, this features unconventional performances from Jack Weston and Jerry Reed. Reynolds employs more subtlety, both in front of and behind the camera, than one would expect from such a formula endeavour. ▭

Burt Reynolds *Gator McKlusky* • Jack Weston *Irving Greenfield* • Lauren Hutton *Aggie Maybank* • Jerry Reed *Bama McCall* • Alice Ghostley *Emmeline Cavanaugh* • Dub Taylor *Mayor Caffrey* • Mike Douglas *Governor* ■ *Dir* Burt Reynolds • *Scr* William Norton

Gattaca
★★★★ **15**

Science-fiction thriller
1997 · US · Colour · 102mins

Before screenplay writer Andrew Niccol stood the science-fiction genre on its end with *The Truman Show*, he had already shaken it up with this superlative futuristic thriller, which he also directed. It's built around the controversial subject of genetic engineering. Vincent Freeman (Ethan Hawke) is the imperfect human with ambitions of joining a space mission, who illegally exchanges identities with Jerome (Jude Law), a paraplegic with perfect DNA. How he does this armed with blood and urine samples is ingeniously shown by Niccol, who mints a new genre vocabulary with his utterly absorbing, intelligent and suspenseful story. Stunningly designed, this cautionary tale with a twist has Hawke, Law and Uma Thurman giving career-best performances. Contains swearing and some violence. ▭ **DVD**

Ethan Hawke *Jerome/Vincent* • Uma Thurman *Irene* • Jude Law *Eugene/Jerome* • Gore Vidal *Director Josef* • Xander Berkeley *Lamar* • Elias Koteas *Antonio* • Ernest Borgnine *Caesar* • Alan Arkin *Detective Hugo* • Loren Dean *Anton* ■ *Dir/Scr* Andrew Niccol

The Gaucho ★★★

Silent swashbuckling drama
1927 · US · BW and Colour · 96mins
The last but one of Douglas Fairbanks's silent swashbucklers, a virtual rehash of his two *Zorro* films, was based on a story by Fairbanks himself, using his customary pseudonym of Elton Thomas. Set in South America, it gives Fairbanks the chance to demonstrate his athletic skills while saving the peasants from exploitation. Fairbanks's wife, Mary Pickford, makes a brief appearance as Our Lady of the Shrine. Mexican actress Lupe Velez, who plays the heroine, was originally spotted in a Laurel and Hardy one-reeler; she was married to Johnny Weismuller, the screen Tarzan, for five years and committed suicide in 1944.

Douglas Fairbanks *The Gaucho* • Lupe Velez *The Mountain Girl* • Geraine Greear *Girl of the Shrine* • Eve Southern *Girl of the Shrine, as a child* • Gustav von Seyffertitz *Ruiz, the Usurper* • Mary Pickford *Our Lady of the Shrine* ■ *Dir* F Richard Jones • *Scr* Lotta Woods, from a story by Douglas Fairbanks [Elton Thomas]

The Gauntlet ★★★ 🔞

Action crime drama
1977 · US · Colour · 104mins
Clint Eastwood stars in this effective action adventure as a discredited and dim cop escorting prostitute Sondra Locke to a trial in Phoenix, Arizona, with mobsters and corrupt officials trying to stop them. The shoot-outs prove less engaging than the mismatched couple's smart-talking infighting and, as director, Eastwood selflessly highlights his then-girlfriend Locke's acting range with understanding and precision – interesting to see in the light of their subsequent acrimonious lawsuit. Clint blurs the line between law enforcement and the way the mob conducts its business to provide extra food for thought in a compelling and well-paced tale. Contains violence, swearing and nudity. ▭ **DVD**

Clint Eastwood *Ben Shockley* • Sondra Locke *Gus Mally* • Pat Hingle *Josephson* • William Prince *Blakelock* • Bill McKinney *Constable* • Michael Cavanaugh *Feyderspiel* • Carole Cook *Waitress* ■ *Dir* Clint Eastwood • *Scr* Michael Butler, Dennis Shryack

Gawain and the Green Knight ★★ 🆄

Fantasy 1973 · UK · Colour · 107mins
With his first feature, *I, Monster*, Stephen Weeks reworked the Jekyll and Hyde story and this second effort takes on Arthurian legend. Made on the slenderest of resources, it's almost a children's film that falls somewhere between *Excalibur* and *Monty Python and the Holy Grail* and doesn't quite get up again. Murray Head is an appealing hero as Gawain, while the Green Knight – headless from the start – is played by the imposing Nigel Green, who died shortly after the film was completed. Weeks complained long and loud that the film was re-edited by the distributor and, in 1983, he had a second crack at the story as *Sword of the Valiant*.

Murray Head *Gawain* • Nigel Green *Green Knight* • Ciaran Madden *Linet* • Robert Hardy *Sir Bertilak* • David Leland *Humphrey* • Anthony Sharp *King* • Ronald Lacey *Oswald* • Murray Melvin *Seneschal* ■ *Dir* Stephen Weeks • *Scr* Stephen Weeks, Philip Breen

The Gay Adventure ★★

Portmanteau drama 1949 · UK · BW · 74mins
This rather insipid portmanteau picture, made in 1949 but held up for four years, follows three men travelling from France to London. They are an "ooh-la-la" Frenchman (Jean-Pierre Aumont), an "oh I say" Englishman (Richard Murdoch) and a "gee whiz" American (Burgess Meredith). They each fantasise differently about the same blonde they see on the train. The object of their lust is played by Paula Valenska, a wooden actress who was clearly not destined to be the next Marlene Dietrich, despite the efforts of producer Anatole De Grunwald. The original British title was *Golden Arrow*, but that probably sounded a bit too much like a western to American ears.

Burgess Meredith *Dick* • Jean-Pierre Aumont *Andre Marchand* • Paula Valenska *Suzy/Sonia/Hedy* • Kathleen Harrison *Isobel* • Richard Murdoch *David Felton* • Julian D'Albie *Waterhouse* • Jose de Almeyda *Jones* ■ *Dir* Gordon Parry • *Scr* Paul Darcy, Sid Colin, Anatole De Grunwald

The Gay Bride ★★

Comedy crime drama
1934 · US · BW · 80mins
In her only appearance for MGM, the sublime Carole Lombard is wasted in this mishmash of crime melodrama and comedy, directed by Jack Conway. The future Mrs Clark Gable is the mercenary Mary, who marries gangster Nat Pendleton solely for his money and in anticipation of his early death. He duly gets himself killed and she moves on to another sucker. The supporting cast includes ZaSu Pitts, and the script, by successful playwrights Sam and Bella Spewack, promises much. But it runs out of steam and direction far too soon to hold our interest.

Carole Lombard *Mary* • Chester Morris *Office boy* • ZaSu Pitts *Mirabelle* • Leo Carrillo *Mickey* • Nat Pendleton *Shoots Magiz* • Sam Hardy *Dingle* • Walter Walker *MacPherson* • Joe Twerp *Lafcadio* ■ *Dir* Jack Conway • *Scr* Bella Spewack, Sam Spewack, from the story *Repeal* by Charles Francis Coe

The Gay Caballero ★★ 🆄

Western 1940 · US · BW · 57mins
This is Cesar Romero's third outing as the ever so slightly camp cowboy, the Cisco Kid, a role that suited the gay Romero perfectly. Running at less than an hour, it tells of Romero and his sidekick Chris-Pin Martin arriving in town and discovering that the Kid is presumed dead. While the plot about land rights seems hard-pressed to fill the time, this does offer B-movie spills and thrills and a good villainess in Janet Beecher.

Cesar Romero *Cisco Kid* • Sheila Ryan *Susan Wetherby* • Robert Sterling *Billy Brewster* • Chris-Pin Martin *Gordito* • Janet Beecher *Kate Brewster* • Edmund MacDonald *Joe Turner* • Jacqueline Dalya *Carmelita* • Montague Shaw *George Wetherby* ■ *Dir* Otto Brower • *Scr* Albert Duffy, John Larkin, from a story by Walter Bullock, Albert Duffy, from characters created by O Henry

The Gay Deception ★★★ 🆄

Romantic comedy 1935 · US · BW · 77mins
This romantic comedy gained an Academy Award nomination for best original story but it now seems a routine concoction. Francis Lederer is the prince working incognito as a bellboy in a New York hotel to study its methods, and Frances Dee is the lottery winner from out of town who checks in determined to inject some luxury into her life. William Wyler's smooth direction, some clever comic details and spirited supporting work, by Akim Tamiroff, Alan Mowbray and Luis Alberni among others, overcome the weak casting of the lead roles.

Francis Lederer *Sandro* • Frances Dee *Mirabel* • Benita Hume *Miss Channing* • Alan Mowbray *Lord Clewe* • Akim Tamiroff *Spellek* • Lennox Pawle *Consul General* • Adele St Maur *Lucille* • Luis Alberni *Ernest* ■ *Dir* William Wyler • *Scr* Stephen Morehouse Avery, Don Hartman

The Gay Desperado ★★

Musical comedy 1936 · US · BW · 88mins
Leo Carrillo is the small-time Mexican bandit who loves Hollywood gangster pictures and decides to remodel his gang on American lines. He also loves music and finds a way to get tenor Nino Martini to join his merry band. Ida Lupino is the heiress kidnapped along with her fiancé, James Blakeley. It's moderately engaging to see what a brilliant director (Rouben Mamoulian) makes of this broad comedy material and the images are often stunning, but the songs are second-rate and the humour becomes tiresome.

Ida Lupino *Jane* • Nino Martini *Chivo* • Leo Carrillo *Braganza* • Harold Huber *Campo* • James Blakeley *Bill* • Stanley Fields *Butch* ■ *Dir* Rouben Mamoulian • *Scr* Wallace Smith, from a story by Leo Birinski

The Gay Divorcee ★★★★

Musical comedy 1934 · US · BW · 103mins
Though Hollywood censorship refused to acknowledge that a divorce could possibly be gay – in the old-fashioned sense of the word – and changed the name from the musical, the title of this movie version reverted back to *The Gay Divorce* in Britain. The knock-out follow-up to *Flying down to Rio* pairs Astaire with perky Ginger Rogers in the leading roles for the first time – and

how they shine. The plot's froth, but who cares since the score includes the Cole Porter classic *Night and Day* and the sensational Oscar-winning *The Continental*. The sets (including a very deco Brighton) are ingenious, and the supporting cast is witty and well chosen. Watch out also for a pre-stardom Betty Grable, performing *Let's K-nock K-nees* with the redoubtable Edward Everett Horton. ▭

Fred Astaire *Guy Holden* • Ginger Rogers *Mimi* • Alice Brady *Aunt Hortense* • Edward Everett Horton *Egbert* • Erik Rhodes *Rodolfo Tonetti* • Eric Blore *Waiter* • Betty Grable *Hotel guest* ■ *Dir* Mark Sandrich • *Scr* George Marion Jr, Dorothy Yost, Edward Kaufman, from the musical by Dwight Taylor, Cole Porter

The Gay Falcon ★★★

Murder mystery 1941 · US · BW · 66mins
Leslie Charteris, the creator of *The Saint*, sued RKO for plagiarism after George Sanders (who had previously played Simon Templar) took on the role of Michael Arlen's debonair detective, Gay Lawrence (The Falcon). Despite the similarities, this fast-moving thriller delighted audiences and spawned 15 sequels over the next eight years. Cruising through the case, Sanders not only proves his chauffeur (Allen Jenkins) innocent of murder and diamond robbery, but also revels in having Wendy Barrie and Anne Hunter squabble over him. After four murders there aren't many suspects left, but the fun comes from watching Sanders rather than working out whodunit.

George Sanders *Gay Lawrence/The Falcon* • Wendy Barrie *Helen Reed* • Allen Jenkins *Goldy* • Anne Hunter *Elinor* • Gladys Cooper *Maxine* • Edward Brophy *Bates* • Arthur Shields *Waldeck* • Damian O'Flynn *Weber* ■ *Dir* Irving Reis • *Scr* Lynn Root, Frank Fenton, from the character created by Michael Arlen

Gay Purr-ee ★★★ 🆄

Animated musical adventure
1962 · US · Colour · 84mins
This sophisticated and witty cartoon reunited Judy Garland with the composers from *The Wizard of Oz*, Harold Arlen and EY "Yip" Harburg. Mewsette the cat (voiced by Garland) leaves her country home seeking excitement in the big city (Paris) and soon runs into trouble. The songs include *Little Drops of Rain*, and *Paris Is a Lonely Town*. Adults will enjoy spotting the Impressionist landscapes used in some scenes.The kids may prefer that later feline adventure, Disney's *The Aristocats*, which was probably influenced by this film's character and style.

Judy Garland *Mewsette* • Hermione Gingold *Mme Rubens-Chatte* • Robert Goulet *Jaune-Tom* • Red Buttons *Robespierre* • Paul Frees *Meowrice* ■ *Dir* Abe Levitow • *Scr* Chuck Jones, Dorothy Jones, Ralph Wright

The Gay Sisters ★★★

Drama 1942 · US · BW · 109mins
A Warner Bros melodrama from the days when gay meant, well, gay. The title is ironic as Barbara Stanwyck, Geraldine Fitzgerald and Nancy Coleman are the conniving titular trio, bent on deviously securing an inheritance through Stanwyck secretly marrying sturdy George Brent. A supporting actor called Byron Barr

played a character named Gig Young in this, and subsequently changed his professional name to that of his character. Warners was renowned for so-called "women's pictures" like this one and they were often directed by Irving Rapper, who is best known today for *Now, Voyager.*

Barbara Stanwyck *Fiona Gaylord* • George Brent *Charles Barclay* • Geraldine Fitzgerald *Evelyn Gaylord* • Donald Crisp *Ralph Pedloch* • Byron Barr [Gig Young] *Gig Young* • Nancy Coleman *Susanna Gaylord* • Gene Lockhart *Herschell Gibbon* • Larry Simms *Austin* ▪ *Dir* Irving Rapper • *Scr* Lenore Coffee, from the novel by Stephen Longstreet

The Gazebo ★★★
Black comedy   1959 · US · BW · 101mins

There's a small summerhouse in the grounds of a country estate under which there may – or may not be – a dead body. Likeable stars Glenn Ford and Debbie Reynolds are super together; they were to pair up again soon after for the same director, George Marshall, in the limp *It Started with a Kiss*, but here they're close to their box-office prime and both are enchanting. They're nearly acted off the screen, though, by character stars John McGiver and Doro Merande.

Glenn Ford *Elliott Nash* • Debbie Reynolds *Nell Nash* • Carl Reiner *Harlow Edison* • John McGiver *Sam Thorpe* • Mabel Albertson *Mrs Chandler* • Martin Landau *The Duke* • Doro Merande *Matilda* • Bert Freed *Lieut Joe Jenkins* • ZaSu Pitts *Mrs MacGruder* ▪ *Dir* George Marshall • *Scr* George Wells, from a play by Alec Coppel, from a story by Myra Coppel, Alec Coppel

The Geisha Boy ★★★U
Comedy   1958 · US · Colour · 101mins

Jerry Lewis's frantic, jerk-around comedy style here got its most suitable director, who saw him simply as a cartoon with no connection to real life. That's because Frank Tashlin used to be a cartoonist himself, so the sight gags are often hilarious. The comedy works less well when third-rate magician Lewis joins an army tour of Japan and gets lumbered with a kid. Yet even when the twee flies thick and fast, there's some fun to be had. Suzanne Pleshette and Marie McDonald are very easy on the eye.

Jerry Lewis *Gilbert Wooley* • Marie McDonald *Lola Livingston* • Robert Kazuyoshi Hirano *Mitsuo Watanabe* • Nobu Atsumi McCarthy [Nobu McCarthy] *Kimi Sikita* • Sessue Hayakawa *Mr Sikita* • Barton MacLane *Major Ridgley* • Suzanne Pleshette *Betty Pearson* • Ryuzo Demura *Ichiyama* ▪ *Dir* Frank Tashlin • *Scr* Frank Tashlin, from a story by Rudy Makoul

The Gendarme in New York ★U
Comedy   1965 · Fr/It · Colour · 101mins

The second in Jean Girault's series of coarse, chaotic comedies makes the mistake of taking Sergeant Cruchot and his brigade of buffoons away from home. The plot has the St Tropez squad representing France at an international police conference in New York. Clearly the decision to decamp to the Big Apple was dictated by hopes of attracting an American audience, but not only is the resulting farce less funny than its predecessor, the film

also proved a misfire at the French box office. Louis De Funès works hard, but it looks as if he couldn't get the gags through customs. French dialogue dubbed into English.

Louis De Funès *Sergeant Ludovic Cruchot* • Geneviève Grad *Nicole* • Michel Galabru *Gerber* • Jean Lefebvre *Fougasse* ▪ *Dir* Jean Girault • *Scr* Jacques Vilfrid, Richard Balducci, Jean Girault, from a story by Richard Balducci

The Gendarme of St Tropez ★★U
Comedy   1964 · Fr/It · Colour · 94mins

This was the first of six frantic farces starring Louis De Funès as the blusteringly incompetent Sergeant Ludovic Cruchot. French critics detested the series, though they initially proved hugely popular with the public. There's the vaguest hint of Clouseau in this first misadventure, as De Funès arrives to take up his new post and launches a crusade against the local nudists. However, much of the action is taken up with the apprehension of a gang of art thieves, thanks more to Cruchot's daughter (Geneviève Grad) than the efforts of his own Keystone-style cops. French dialogue dubbed into English.

Louis De Funès *Sergeant Ludovic Cruchot* • Geneviève Grad *Nicole Cruchot* • Michel Galabru *Gerber* • Jean Lefebvre *Fougasse* • Christian Marin *Merlot* • Daniel Cauchy *Richard* • Jean-Paul Bertrand *Eddie* • Frank Vilcour *Jean-Luc* ▪ *Dir* Jean Girault • *Scr* Richard Balducci, Jacques Vilfrid, Jean Girault, from the story by Richard Balducci

The Gendarme Wore Skirts ★
Comedy   1982 · Fr/It · Colour · 99mins

The *Gendarme of St Tropez* series never quite plumbed the depths of the *Police Academy* movies, but they came close with this final, undistinguished farce. Made four years after *The Spacemen of St Tropez* flopped, the film – in which Sergeant Cruchot's incompetent squad are sent into total disarray by the arrival of some female recruits – also proved to be Louis De Funès's last picture. As his loyal adjutant, Michel Galabru does his best to bolster the woeful script, but not even the assistance of Tony Aboyantz can disguise the fact that director Jean Girault has finally run out of ideas. French dialogue dubbed into English.

Louis De Funès *Sergeant Ludovic Cruchot* • Michel Galabru *Inspector Gerber* • Maurice Risch *Beaupied* • Jacques François *Colonel* ▪ *Dir* Jean Girault, Tony Aboyantz • *Scr* Jacques Vilfrid

The Gene Krupa Story ★★★
Musical biography   1959 · US · BW · 101mins

Ringo Starr, eat your heart out! The Beatles' trip-hammer drummer could take lessons from this biopic, alternatively called *Drum Crazy*. It tells the story of Krupa (Sal Mineo), the greatest jazz percussionist of his time, who was convicted on a drugs charge and then found that success drained away in the aftermath of the scandal. It's a whitewash job as far as it can be, but the jazz soundtrack is more than adequate.

Sal Mineo *Gene Krupa* • Susan Kohner *Ethel Maguire* • James Darren *Eddie Sirota* • Susan Oliver *Dorissa Dinell* • Yvonne Craig *Gloria Corregio* • Lawrence Dobkin *Speaker Willis* • Celia Lovsky *Mother* • Red Nichols ▪ *Dir* Don Weis • *Scr* Orin Jannings

The General ★★★★★U
Silent comedy   1927 · US · BW · 73mins

Buster Keaton's greatest movie is, some would argue, the finest silent screen comedy ever made. Stone-faced engineer Buster loves his vast steam locomotive, "The General", almost as much as his girlfriend (Marion Mack). When he is rejected by the Confederate Army, Mack brands him a coward and breaks off the engagement. Later, he risks all to pursue the train with her on board when it's stolen by Yankee spies. The humour ranges from the gentle to the exhilarating, while the drama of the railtrack-chase has a visual beauty that puts this comedy into the category of true classic. Buster Keaton's genius was not just in the nuts and bolts of invention, but in the creation of an endearing character. 📼 **DVD**

Buster Keaton *Johnnie Gray* • Glen Cavender *Capt Anderson* • Jim Farley *Gen Thatcher* • Frederick Vroom *Southern General* • Marion Mack *Annabelle Lee* • Charles Smith *Her father* ▪ *Dir* Buster Keaton, Clyde Bruckman • *Scr* Al Boasberg, Charles Smith, from a story by Buster Keaton, Clyde Bruckman, from the novel *The Great Locomotive Chase* by William Pittinger

The General ★★★★★15
Biographical drama   1998 · Ire/UK · BW · 118mins

"Dublin's favourite gangster" was the contemporary description of Martin Cahill, known as "The General". Here he's portrayed in a towering performance by Brendan Gleeson as a mythic hero for writer/producer/director John Boorman. Cahill was shot to death in 1994 and this biography tracks back to show how – with the Hollyfield estate as his personal fiefdom – he lived with his beloved wife (Maria Doyle Kennedy) and her equally beloved sister (Angeline Ball) while leading a gang that raided post offices and stole priceless paintings, bringing him into conflict with police inspector Ned Kenny (Jon Voight). Caught between the Brits and the Provos, Cahill is shown as a man of intermittent brutality while courting popular acclaim. Contains swearing, violence and sexual references. 📼

Brendan Gleeson *Martin Cahill* • Adrian Dunbar *Noel Curley* • Sean McGinley *Gary* • Maria Doyle Kennedy *Frances* • Angeline Ball *Tina* • Jon Voight *Inspector Ned Kenny* • Eanna MacLiam *Jimmy* • Tom Murphy *Willie Byrne* ▪ *Dir* John Boorman • *Scr* John Boorman, from the non-fiction book *The General: Godfather of Crime* by Paul Williams

General Della Rovere ★★★★
Second World War drama   1959 · It/Fr · BW · 131mins

The winner of the Golden Lion at Venice in 1959, this film relies totally on the astonishing performance of Vittorio De Sica. In attempting to recapture the neorealist glories of *Rome, Open City*, director Roberto

Rossellini overstages the authenticity and misses the naturalism that characterised the performances in his epoch-making film. So it falls to one-time matinee idol De Sica to bring some life and truth to this sentimental tale. He's a swindler who is forced by the Nazis to impersonate a murdered resistance leader and, inspired by the selflessness of his new comrades, becomes a hero instead of betraying them. The result is moving, darkly comic and inspirational. In Italian with English subtitles.

Vittorio De Sica *Bardone/Grimaldi* • Hannes Messemer *Colonel Mueller* • Sandra Milo *Olga* • Giovanna Ralli *Valeria* • Anne Vernon *Chiara Fassio* • Vittorio Caprioli *Banchelli* • Ivo Garrani *Fabrizio* ▪ *Dir* Roberto Rossellini • *Scr* Roberto Rossellini, Sergio Amidei, Diego Fabbri, Indro Montanelli, from a story by Indro Montanelli

The General Died at Dawn ★★
Adventure   1936 · US · BW · 97mins

The general is a Chinese warlord (a very cheesy, ah-so Akim Tamiroff) and Gary Cooper is a mercenary whose plans to assist the oppressed peasants are thwarted by Madeleine Carroll robbing him on a train. There's a lot of plot here but, rather than treat it as a thick slice of hokum, with performances to match, playwright Clifford Odets, working on his first film, and director Lewis Milestone try and say great things about the human condition. The dialogue is mock-poetic mudcake that sticks to everything. The film received three Oscar nominations: for photography; for its score; and for Tamiroff as best supporting actor, the first year such a category existed.

Gary Cooper *O'Hara* • Madeleine Carroll *Judy Perrie* • Akim Tamiroff *General Yang* • Dudley Digges *Mr Wu* • Porter Hall *Peter Perrie* • William Frawley *Brighton* • JM Kerrigan *Leach* • Philip Ahn *Oxford* ▪ *Dir* Lewis Milestone • *Scr* Clifford Odets, from a novel by Charles G Booth • *Cinematographer* Victor Milner • *Music* Werner Janssen

The General Line ★★★★
Silent political drama
1929 · USSR · BW · 90mins

Shot either side of his ill-received revolutionary masterpiece, *October*, this was a determined effort on the part of Sergei Eisenstein to return to official favour by enthusiastically promoting the Kremlin's policy of collectivisation. However, the experiments in tonal montage, which characterise Eisenstein's last silent feature, met with disapproval and he elected to go on a prolonged sabbatical odyssey. Certainly there is a constructivist fervour about the scene that involves a mechanical cream separator. But much else in the film recalls the rural poetry of Dovzhenko's *Earth*, while Marfa Lapkina's weatherworn face triumphantly proclaims the effectiveness of the casting principle of typage.

Marfa Lapkina *Marfa* • M Ivanin *Marfa's son* • Vasia Buzenkov *A komsomol, manager of dairy co* • Nejnikov *Mitrochkin, teacher* • Chukamariev *Kulak, peasant proprietor* • Kostia Vasiliev *Tractor driver* ▪ *Dir/Scr* Sergei Eisenstein, Grigori V Aleksandrov

The General's Daughter
★★★ 18

Mystery thriller
1999 · US/Ger · Colour · 112mins

This moderately absorbing military whodunit is let down by the lazy hamming of star John Travolta. He plays an armed forces cop called in to investigate the horrific rape and murder of a woman officer (Leslie Stefanson), who also happens to be the daughter of heavyweight military man James Cromwell. However, as Travolta and colleague Madeleine Stowe start digging, they find some nasty skeletons in Stefanson's closet. Travolta aside, the performances are strong, with James Woods effortlessly stealing the show as one of the prime murder suspects. *Con Air* director Simon West demonstrates that there is more to him than grand destruction, yet the wayward script's derivative twists and turns weaken what should have been a hard-hitting drama. Contains violence and swearing. ▭

John Travolta *Paul Brenner* • Madeleine Stowe *Sarah Sunhill* • James Cromwell *General Campbell* • Timothy Hutton *Colonel Kent* • Leslie Stefanson *Elisabeth Campbell* • Daniel Von Bargen *Chief Yardley* • Clarence Williams III *Colonel Fowler* • James Woods *Colonel Moore* ▪ *Dir* Simon West • *Scr* Christopher Bertolini, William Goldman, from the novel by Nelson DeMille

A Generation
★★★★ 12

Second World War drama
1954 · Pol · BW · 83mins

Director Andrzej Wajda made his debut with this solemn tale of love, patriotism and party unity that opened the war trilogy completed by *Kanal* and *Ashes and Diamonds*. As much influenced by personal zeal as the socialist realism that the Polish state expected of its film-makers, this is a naive picture. But such is Wajda's commitment and his pictorial sense that we are carried along with the story of Tadeusz Lomnicki, the young woodworker whose passion for Urszula Modrzynska leads to his involvement with the resistance, the Warsaw ghetto and the communist agenda. Bursting with potential, the film also launched the acting careers of Roman Polanski and Zbigniew Cybulski. In Polish with English subtitles. ▭

Tadeusz Lomnicki *Stach* • Urszula Modrzynska *Dorota* • Janusz Janczar *Sekula* • Ryszard Kotas *Jacek* • Roman Polanski *Mundek* • Zbigniew Cybulski *Kostek* ▪ *Dir* Andrzej Wajda • *Scr* Bohdan Czeszko

Generation
★★

Comedy
1969 · US · Colour · 90mins

Hollywood found it difficult to provide a suitable vehicle for David Janssen to match his success in the TV series *The Fugitive* and *Harry O*. This generation-gap comedy, which betrays its Broadway origins, is not one of the high points of his career. Janssen plays an advertising executive, about to become a grandfather, who is horrified when his determined daughter decides to ignore convention and opts for a home birth. Watch out for Pete Duel (Hannibal Heyes in *Alias Smith and Jones*) in a small part.

David Janssen *Jim Bolton* • Kim Darby *Doris Bolton Owen* • Carl Reiner *Stan Herman* • Peter Duel *Walter Owen* • Andrew Prine *Winn Garand* • James Coco *Mr Blatto* • Sam Waterston *Desmond* • David Lewis *Arlington* ▪ *Dir* George Schaefer • *Scr* William Goodhart, from his play

Generation X
★★★ 15

Science-fiction adventure
1996 · US/Can · Colour · 86mins

Filmed as a pilot for a TV series, this entertaining sci-fi romp was executive produced by Stan Lee, on whose *Marvel* comic characters the action is based. A band of mutant misfits is called in to save the planet after mad scientist Matt Frewer perfects the ability to infiltrate people's dreams. Everyone is clearly enjoying themselves enormously, notably *Staying Alive* star Finola Hughes as "White Queen" Emma Frost. Turning the low budget to his advantage, designer Douglas Higgins has fashioned some wonderfully kitsch sets, although the same constraints render the special effects much less effective. ▭

Matt Frewer *Russell Tresh* • Finola Hughes *Emma "White Queen" Frost* • Jeremy Ratchford *Sean "Banshee" Cassidy* • Agustin Rodriguez *Angelo "Skin" Espinosa* • Heather McComb *Jubilation "Jubilee" Lee* • Randall Slavin *Kurt "Refrax" Pastorious* • Amarilis Monet "M" *St Croix* • Suzanne Davis *Arlee "Buff" Hicks* ▪ *Dir* Jack Sholder • *Scr* Eric Blakeney, Scott Lobdell, from the comic book by Chris Bachalo

Genesis II
★★

Science-fiction adventure
1973 · US · Colour · 74mins

Star Trek creator Gene Roddenberry failed to strike similar gold with this contrived tale involving Alex Cord as the lone survivor of a post-millennium holocaust, watching as the Earth is re-created by two opposing factions. Not to be taken as seriously as it takes itself, this sci-fi adventure clearly owes more to *Flash Gordon* than *Star Trek*. British director John Llewellyn Moxey does what he can, in his own second incarnation as a director of formulaic American fare after a career in low-budget chillers in the UK. Nothing featuring Mariette Hartley is totally unwatchable, however.

Alex Cord *Dylan Hunt* • Mariette Hartley *Lyra-a* • Ted Cassidy *Isiah* • Percy Rodrigues *Dr Isaac Kimbridge* • Harvey Jason *Singh* • Titos Vandis *Yuloff* • Bill Striglos *Dr Kellum* • Lynne Marta *Harper-Smythe* ▪ *Dir* John Llewellyn Moxey • *Scr* Gene Roddenberry

Genevieve
★★★★★ U

Comedy
1953 · UK · Colour · 82mins

Mocking many of the character traits that supposedly made this nation great, *Genevieve* is one of the most quintessentially British of British films. The good-natured round of confrontations and calamities that befall John Gregson, Dinah Sheridan, Kenneth More and Kay Kendall are familiar to generations of movie-goers and, even though each disaster is more predictable than the last, there is unending pleasure to be had in observing the reactions of the childish, overzealous chauvinists and their teasing, long-suffering partners. The

performances are a joy, the soundtrack unforgettable. ▭ **DVD**

Kenneth More *Ambrose Claverhouse* • John Gregson *Alan McKim* • Dinah Sheridan *Wendy McKim* • Kay Kendall *Rosalind Peters* • Geoffrey Keen *First traffic policeman* • Harold Siddons *Second traffic policeman* • Reginald Beckwith *JC Callahan* • Joyce Grenfell *Hotel proprietress* ▪ *Dir* Henry Cornelius • *Scr* William Rose • *Music* Larry Adler

Genghis Khan
★ PG

Biographical adventure
1964 · US/UK/ W Ger/Yug · Colour · 119mins

This shoddy-looking movie is one of those "sub-epics" that shoot for the prestige and grandeur of *Ben-Hur* or *El Cid* yet fall dismally short. Omar Sharif is woefully miscast as the Mongol invader, riding across Yugoslavian locations and hacking extras to bloody bits in Henry Levin's slow-moving film; Jack Palance would have been a better choice. A superior supporting cast, however, offers a few blushes — James Mason and Robert Morley are especially silly as Chinamen. ▭

Omar Sharif *Temulin-Genghis Khan* • Stephen Boyd *Jamuga* • James Mason *Kam Ling* • Eli Wallach *Shah of Khwarezm* • Françoise Dorléac *Bortei* • Telly Savalas *Shan* • Robert Morley *Emperor of China* • Yvonne Mitchell *Katke* • Woody Strode *Sengal* ▪ *Dir* Henry Levin • *Scr* Clarke Reynolds, Beverly Cross, from a story by Berkely Mather

A Gentle Creature
★★★★

Psychological drama
1969 · Fr · Colour · 88mins

Based on a story by his constant inspiration, Fyodor Dostoyevsky, this is Robert Bresson's first film in colour. The purity of his vision remains intact, however, as he once more employs the blend of naturalistic acting and precise, symbolic composition that established him as one of cinema's most rigorous auteurs. Dominique Sanda makes a remarkable debut as the wife whose suicide prompts a sequence of flashbacks, as her pawnbroker husband Guy Frangin seeks clues to her despair. Open to any number of possible interpretations, this is more pessimistic than Bresson's earlier works, but the essential humanism is still evident. In French with English subtitles.

Dominique Sanda *The wife* • Guy Frangin *The husband* • Jane Lobre *Anna* ▪ *Dir* Robert Bresson • *Scr* Robert Bresson, from the short story *A Gentle Soul* by Fyodor Dostoyevsky

Gentle Giant
★ U

Adventure
1967 · US · Colour · 92mins

When seven-year-old Clint Howard befriends a cuddly black bear cub, his daddy (Dennis Weaver) and mummy (Vera Miles) are surprisingly unperturbed. Set in Florida, this is a Disney-style animal adventure aimed primarily at uncritical youngsters. Clint Howard (the younger brother of child actor-turned-director Ron Howard) is such a precocious child that you almost wish mummy bear would show up to get her baby back. The movie was deemed successful enough to spawn a TV series called *Gentle Ben*.

Dennis Weaver *Tom Wedloe* • Vera Miles *Ellen Wedloe* • Ralph Meeker *Fog Hanson* • Clint Howard *Mark Wedloe* • Huntz Hall *Dink* • Rance Howard *Tater* • Frank Schuller *Charlie* •

Ric O'Feldman *Mate* ▪ *Dir* James Neilson • *Scr* Edward J Lakso, Andy White, from the novel *Gentle Ben* by Walt Morey

The Gentle Gunman
★★★ U

Drama
1952 · UK · BW · 82mins

Dirk Bogarde wrote that this "wasn't a film I particularly wanted to make". Nonetheless, playing an IRA activist who wants to step up the war against the British in 1941, he still does a good job as a man tormented by doubts. There are no doubts, though, for his brother (John Mills) who sees the war against the Nazis as more important and is put on IRA trial for his pains. It's this too-balanced approach to the Irish dilemma that makes Basil Dearden and Michael Relph's otherwise thoughtful film too glib for its own good and our conviction.

John Mills *Terence Sullivan* • Dirk Bogarde *Matt Sullivan* • Robert Beatty *Shinto* • Elizabeth Sellars *Maureen Fagan* • Barbara Mullen *Molly Fagan* • Eddie Byrne *Flynn* • Joseph Tomelty *Dr Brannigan* • Gilbert Harding *Henry Truethorne* • James Kenney *Johnny Fagan* ▪ *Dir* Basil Dearden, Michael Relph • *Scr* Roger MacDougall, from his play

The Gentle Rain
★

Romantic drama
1966 · US/Bra · Colour · 110mins

In Rio de Janeiro, a neurotic American girl falls for a man who has lost his power of speech following a traumatic accident. It scores points for the unusual subject matter, but what should have been a tender tale about the problems of speaking and non-speaking people relating to each other becomes a routine and ultimately discreditable melodrama. Christopher George and Lynda Day do their best with less than credible material and the somewhat contrived ending.

Christopher George *Bill Patterson* • Lynda Day [Lynda Day George] *Judy Reynolds* • Fay Spain *Nancy Masters* • Maria Helena Dias *Gloria* • Lon Clark *Harry Masters* • Barbara Williams *Girl friend* • Robert Assumpaco *Hotel manager* ▪ *Dir* Burt Balaban • *Scr* Robert Cream

The Gentle Sex
★★★ U

Second World War drama
1943 · UK · BW · 88mins

Seen over half a century after the event, Leslie Howard's final film as a director (sharing the credit with the prolific Maurice Elvey) seems unbearably patronising in its depiction of the contribution made to the war effort by seven socially diverse women, who volunteer for the Auxiliary Territorial Service on the same day. Yet it served its purpose as both a morale booster and as a recruitment advertisement, thanks to some astute appeals to the patriotic spirit and some spunky asides. The topnotch cast includes Barbara Waring as a catty snob and Lilli Palmer as a timid German immigrant. Howard was killed when his plane was shot down later in 1943, while he was on a secret mission to Portugal. ▭

Joan Gates *Gwen* • Jean Gillie *Good Time Dot* • Joan Greenwood *Betty* • Joyce Howard *Ann Lawrence* • Rosamund John *Maggie Fraser* • Lilli Palmer *Erna* • Barbara Waring *Joan* • John Justin *David Sheridan* ▪ *Dir* Leslie Howard,

U = SUITABLE FOR ALL, **Uc** = SUITABLE FOR ALL, ESPECIALLY FOR YOUNG CHILDREN (VIDEO ONLY) **PG** = PARENTAL GUIDANCE

Maurice Elvey • *Scr* Moie Charles, Aimee Stuart, Roland Pertwee, Phyllis Rose, from a story by Moie Charles

The Gentle Trap ★

Thriller 1960 · UK · BW · 61mins

An utterly threadbare British B-movie about an apprentice locksmith who goes on the run from the police and local gangsters. It was made by the low-budget production company Butcher's, and everyone involved accordingly made a hash of it. Only devoted fans of its leading actor Spencer Teakle and actress Felicity Young, who plays a rather feeble *femme fatale*, will bother to watch.

Spencer Teakle *Johnny Ryan* • Felicity Young *Jean* • Dorinda Stevens *Mary* • Martin Benson *Ricky Barnes* • Dawn Brooks *Sylvia* • Arthur Hewlett *Sam* • Alan Edwards *Al Jenkins* • Hugh Latimer *Vic Carter* ■ *Dir* Charles Saunders • *Scr* Brock Williams, Alan Osborne, from the story by Guido Coen

A Gentleman after Dark ★

Crime drama 1942 · US · BW · 76mins

Miriam Hopkins's career on screen was on the wane when she teamed up with Brian Donlevy in this low-budget melodrama. She attacks her role with the usual relish, playing Flo Melton, a woman who isn't averse to a spot of blackmail. Husband Donlevy is prepared to break out of jail and sacrifice everything in order to deal with her and protect the honour of their daughter. This story, already filmed in 1928 and 1936 as *Forgotten Faces*, was long past its sell-by date.

Brian Donlevy *Harry Melton* • Miriam Hopkins *Flo Melton* • Preston Foster *Tom Gaynor* • Harold Huber *Stubby* • Philip Reed *Eddie* • Gloria Holden *Miss Clark* ■ *Dir* Edwin L Marin • *Scr* Patterson McNutt, George Bruce, from a story by Richard Washburn Child

A Gentleman at Heart ★★ U

Comedy 1942 · US · BW · 66mins

Cesar Romero is given a rare chance to play the lead – rather than a loser in love to one of Fox's musical stars. He clearly enjoys himself in this slight comedy about shady dealings in the art world. As the bookie who discovers sculptors aren't the only chisellers where fine art is concerned, Romero more than holds his own against such notorious scene-stealers as Milton Berle. J Carrol Naish is also in fine fettle as a forger dashing off old masters to order, but Carole Landis is slightly miscast as the gallery manager who Romero romances.

Cesar Romero *Tony Miller* • Carole Landis *Helen Mason* • Milton Berle *Lucky Cullen* • J Carrol Naish *Gigi* • Richard Derr *Stewart Haines* • Rose Hobart *Claire Barrington* • Jerome Cowan *Finchley* • Elisha Cook Jr *Genius* ■ *Dir* Ray McCarey • *Scr* Lee Loeb, Harold Buchman, from the story *Masterpiece* by Paul Hervey

Gentleman Jim ★★★ U

Biographical drama 1942 · US · BW · 100mins

Errol Flynn stars as James J Corbett, the real-life bank clerk who went on to become the first official heavyweight champion of the world. While Flynn regarded this performance as one of his best, there is disagreement as to whether the film's portrayal of a brash extrovert is a true reflection of its inspiration's personality. Despite claiming to be based on Corbett's autobiography, the movie is somewhat fictionalised. However, the actual fights are re-created with some care and it's pacily directed by action maestro Raoul Walsh. As well as taking on the likes of Ward Bond in the ring, Flynn also spars outside the arena with the haughty Alexis Smith. [video]

Errol Flynn *James J Corbett* • Alexis Smith *Victoria Ware* • Jack Carson *Walter Lowrie* • Alan Hale *Pat Corbett* • John Loder *Clinton DeWitt* • William Frawley *Billy Delaney* • Minor Watson *Buck Ware* • Ward Bond *John L Sullivan* ■ *Dir* Raoul Walsh • *Scr* Vincent Lawrence, Horace McCoy, from the autobiography *The Roar of the Crowd* by James J Corbett

Gentleman's Agreement ★★★★

Drama 1947 · US · BW · 118mins

An eye-opener in its day, this exposure of racial prejudice in high society still has the power to compel. The story of magazine writer Gregory Peck passing himself off as a Jew to reveal anti-Semitism is not violently confrontational, but it is successful in showing that the subtle malaise is not recognised as such by the people who sustain it. Writer Moss Hart pressed all the politically correct postwar buttons, adapting Laura Z Hobson's controversial bestseller for rising young director Elia Kazan. While it's one of Peck's finest performances, other members of the cast produce work of a similarly high standard – the confused liberal Dorothy McGuire, the soured poseur Celeste Holm and the cynically bitter ex-serviceman John Garfield. Twentieth Century-Fox gave this blast at bigotry all the hype it needed and the result was Academy awards and nominations all round.

Gregory Peck *Phil Green* • Dorothy McGuire *Kathy* • John Garfield *Dave* • Celeste Holm *Anne* • Anne Revere *Mrs Green* • June Havoc *Miss Wales* • Albert Dekker *John Minify* • Jane Wyatt *Jane* ■ *Dir* Elia Kazan • *Scr* Moss Hart, from the novel by Laura Z Hobson

Gentlemen Marry Brunettes ★★

Musical comedy 1955 · US · Colour · 106mins

Jeanne Crain and Jane Russell, showing a lot of leg and cleavage, play dual roles as brunette showgirl sisters in Paris and their blonde mother and aunt, who were the toast of Paris in the twenties. Despite the gorgeous costumes by Travilla and Christian Dior, the Technicolor and CinemaScope, the chic Parisian settings and some good songs, this is a feeble farrago. The uninspired screenplay was by Richard Sale and Mary Loos – not to be confused with Anita Loos, who wrote the story on which it is based.

Jane Russell *Bonnie Jones/Mimi Jones* • Jeanne Crain *Connie Jones/Mitzi Jones* • Alan Young *Charlie Biddle/Mr Biddle Sr* • Scott Brady *David Action* • Rudy Vallee • Guy Middleton *Earl of Wickenware* • Eric Pohlmann *Monsieur Ballard* • Ferdy Mayne *Monsieur Dufond* ■ *Dir* Richard Sale • *Scr* Mary Loos, Richard Sale, from the story *But Gentlemen Marry Brunettes* by Anita Loos

Gentlemen Prefer Blondes ★★★★ PG

Musical comedy 1953 · US · Colour · 87mins

Marilyn Monroe's star was well into the ascendant when she portrayed writer Anita Loos's gold-digging Lorelei Lee in this scintillating 20th Century-Fox musical, cannily directed by Howard Hawks who had a clever understanding of how to exploit Monroe's star power. Watch how even co-star Jane Russell is entranced by the blonde bombshell during their duets. Monroe particularly shines in the superbly photographed (Harry J Wild) and brilliantly choreographed (Jack Cole) production numbers, most notably *Diamonds Are a Girl's Best Friend*. The movie opens with a scene that uses the sparkling Technicolor to best effect, as Monroe and Russell announce that they're just *Two Little Girls from Little Rock*, and it simply takes off from there. The men are underused and the third act is a flat and contrived letdown, but make no mistake – this is the movie that consolidated Monroe's stardom. [video]

Marilyn Monroe *Lorelei Lee* • Jane Russell *Dorothy Shaw* • Charles Coburn *Sir Francis Beekman* • Elliott Reid *Malone* • Tommy Noonan *Gus Esmond* • George Winslow *Henry Spofford III* • Taylor Holmes *Gus Esmond Sr* ■ *Dir* Howard Hawks • *Scr* Charles Lederer, from the play by Anita Loos, Joseph Fields, from the novel by Anita Loos

Genuine Risk ★ 18

Crime thriller 1990 · US · Colour · 85mins

Three years before *The Last Seduction*, Peter Berg was already getting involved with the wrong kind of woman in this thriller with *noir* overtones. Berg plays Henry, an ex-con, gambler and all-round slacker who reluctantly takes a job with gangster Terence Stamp's outfit. Unfortunately, Berg's current lover Michelle Johnson is also bestowing her sexual favours on the villainous Stamp. The denouement is, as you might imagine, not for those of a delicate disposition. With MK Harris and Stamp on board, this should have been a lot better. But the plot details are utterly predictable, and Johnson remains little more than a cipher. [video]

Terence Stamp *Paul Hellwart* • Peter Berg *Henry* • Michelle Johnson *Girl* • MK Harris *Cowboy Jack* • Teddy Wilson *Billy* • Sid Haig *Curly* ■ *Dir* Kurt Voss • *Scr* Kurt Voss, from a story by Larry J Rattner

Geordie ★★★ U

Drama 1955 · UK · Colour · 95mins

Scripted by those bastions of postwar British cinema, Frank Launder and Sidney Gilliat, this is a pleasing picture, yet unlike its central character it never really develops into anything substantial. The story of a Scottish gamekeeper's son who body-builds his way to the Olympics was given relevance by the 1956 Melbourne games, but, shorn of its topicality, the film is too dependent on that old British standby, whimsy, to rank among the best British comedies. Bill Travers could do with a little more charm to add to his brawn, but Alastair Sim is on hand to pep up the humour. [video]

Alastair Sim *Laird* • Bill Travers *Geordie MacTaggart* • Norah Gorsen *Jean Donaldson* • Molly Urquhart *Geordie's mother* • Francis De Wolff *Henry Samson* • Jack Radcliffe *Rev McNab* ■ *Dir* Frank Launder • *Scr* Frank Launder, Sidney Gilliat, from the novel by David Walker

George and Mildred ★ 15

Comedy 1980 · UK · Colour · 89mins

Back in the mists of time, a curse was obviously placed on all attempts to bring British TV sitcoms to the big screen. No matter how hilarious a programme was on the telly, it scarcely raised a titter in cinemas. Brian Murphy and Yootha Joyce were consistently funny as the Ropers, first in *Man about the House* and then in their own series *George and Mildred*. But this desperate, smutty comedy of errors is no laughing matter. Made a year after the series ended, it was a sad finale for Yootha Joyce, who died before the film was released. [video]

Yootha Joyce *Mildred Roper* • Brian Murphy *George Roper* • Stratford Johns *Harry Pinto* • Norman Eshley *Jeffrey Fourmile* • Sheila Fearn *Ann Fourmile* • Kenneth Cope *Harvey* • David Barry *Elvis* ■ *Dir* Peter Frazer Jones • *Scr* Dick Sharples, from the characters created by Brian Cooke, Johnnie Mortimer

George Balanchine's The Nutcracker ★★ U

Ballet 1993 · US · Colour · 92mins

Director Emile Ardolino regularly collaborated with the great choreographer George Balanchine, but his version of Tchaikovsky's popular children's ballet remains stubbornly stagebound. Shooting from the stalls, Ardolino fails to capture the energy of the dancers, while the clumsily incorporated close-ups interfere with the action when they should be clarifying the emotions of the characters. Macaulay Culkin trained at the School of American Ballet and appeared in two stage versions of *The Nutcracker*, but he doesn't do much here as the prince who guides Jessica Lynn Cohen through his toyland kingdom. Kevin Kline's narration was a late addition, intended to make the story more accessible.

Kevin Kline *Narrator* • Macaulay Culkin *Nutcracker Prince* • Bart Robinson Cook *Herr Drosselmeier* • Jessica Lynn Cohen *Marie* • Darci Kistler *Sugarplum Fairy* • Damian Woetzel *Cavalier* • Kyra Nichols *Dewdrop* • Wendy Whelan *Coffee* • Margaret Tracey *Marzipan* ■ *Dir* Emile Ardolino • *Scr* Susan Cooper, from the story by ETA Hoffman

George in Civvy Street ★

Comedy 1946 · UK · BW · 88mins

From 1937-43 George Formby was Britain's biggest box-office draw and most of his hits had been directed by Marcel Varnel, who also made the best films of Will Hay, the Crazy Gang and Arthur Askey. This sad final collaboration, in which George returns from the army to run a dilapidated pub, is dispiritingly uninspired and out of date, and the songs are a poor echo of Formby's earlier hits. Even an *Alice in Wonderland* dream sequence, with costumes based on the original John Tenniel illustrations, lacks charm. Formby made no more films after this, and Varnel was killed the following year in a car crash.

George Formby *George Harper* • Rosalyn Boulter *Mary Colton* • Ronald Shiner *Fingers* • Ian Fleming *Uncle Shad* • Wally Patch *Sprout* • Philippa Hiatt *Lavender* • Enid Cruickshank *Miss Gummidge* • Mike Johnson *Toby* ■ *Dir* Marcel Varnel • *Scr* Peter Fraser, Ted Kavanagh, Max Kester, Gale Pedrick, from the story by Howard Irving Young

George of the Jungle ★★★ 🆄

Comedy adventure
1997 · US · Colour · 87mins

This engagingly stupid spin on *Tarzan* packs in enough dim-witted slapstick to raise a chuckle from even the most sophisticated grown-ups and took over $100 million in the US. Brendan Fraser (*The Mummy*) is George, who has been brought up by a group of brainy gorillas led by Ape (voiced by John Cleese). Unfortunately none of their intelligence seems to have rubbed off on George, who has an unfortunate habit of swinging into trees and has an elephant that thinks it's a dog. The fun slows down a little when he gets whisked back to the States by heiress Leslie Mann, but director Sam Weisman largely stays true to the film's comic strip origins. 🖭 *DVD*

Brendan Fraser *George* • Leslie Mann *Ursula Stanhope* • Thomas Haden Church *Lyle Van de Groot* • Richard Roundtree *Kwame* • Greg Cruttwell *Max* • Holland Taylor *Beatrice Stanhope* • Kelly Miller *Besty* • John Cleese *Ape* ■ *Dir* Sam Weisman • *Scr* Dana Olsen, Audrey Wells, from a story by Dana Olsen, from the characters created by Jay Ward

The George Raft Story ★★

Biographical drama 1961 · US · BW · 105mins

Ray Danton stars in this biopic of the Broadway dancer turned racketeer turned Hollywood actor, who made his name as the coin-spinning hood in *Scarface*. Raft could never really duck charges of illegal activities and his movie career faded in the fifties, as did his business career – Castro closed down his casino in Havana and Scotland Yard refused him permission to visit his business interests in London. Since this biopic was made when Raft was alive and kicking, it is necessarily uncontroversial and, therefore, somewhat dull.

Ray Danton *George Raft* • Jayne Mansfield *Lisa Lang* • Julie London *Sheila Patton* • Barrie Chase *June* • Barbara Nichols *Texas Guinan* • Frank Gorshin *Moxie Cusack* • Margo Moore *Ruth Harris* • Brad Dexter *Benny Siegel* • Neville Brand *Al Capone* ■ *Dir* Joseph M Newman • *Scr* Wilbur Crane

George Washington Slept Here ★★ 🆄

Comedy 1942 · US · BW · 91mins

Although this is one of Jack Benny's better comedies, he's still somewhat miscast as the Manhattanite whose wife purchases a surprise new home – a house in the country in which Washington reputedly stayed. Far from idyllic, their new home lacks everything from running water to walls, and Benny naturally hates it. Directed by William Keighley, this film version of George S Kaufman and Moss Hart's Broadway play is too calculated and predictable to be more than superficially amusing but it was just what wartime audiences wanted. Ann Sheridan is ebulliant as

the wife and Percy Kilbride reprises his stage role as the caretaker.

Jack Benny *Bill Fuller* • Ann Sheridan *Connie Fuller* • Charles Coburn *Uncle Stanley* • Percy Kilbride *Mr Kimber* • Hattie McDaniel *Hester* • William Tracy *Steve Eldridge* • Joyce Reynolds *Madge* • Lee Patrick *Rena Leslie* ■ *Dir* William Keighley • *Scr* Everett Freeman, from the play by George S Kaufman, Moss Hart

George White's 1935 Scandals ★★★ 🆄

Musical 1935 · US · BW · 84mins

Ziegfeld's biggest rival, Broadway impresario George White, directs himself in this sequel to the previous year's *George White's Scandals*. Not surprisingly, he plays a Broadway impresario discovering small-town talent Alice Faye and making her into a star. The stage acts are enjoyable enough – comedian Ned Sparks, singer Cliff Edwards and tap-dancing Eleanor Powell making her debut. The inevitable love triangle here involves Faye, Powell and James Dunn. Of course, the backstage story is predictable but it's all very agreeable.

Alice Faye *Honey Walters* • James Dunn *Eddie Taylor* • Ned Sparks *Elmer White* • Lyda Roberti *Manya* • Cliff Edwards *Dude Holloway* • Arline Judge *Midgie Malone* • Eleanor Powell *Marilyn Collins* • Emma Dunn *Aunt Jane* ■ *Dir* George White • *Scr* Jack Yellin, Patterson McNutt, from an idea by George White

George White's Scandals ★★★

Musical 1934 · US · BW · 83mins

George White's annual music revues had become a Broadway fixture by the early thirties, so it seemed a good idea to put on a film version, with the impresario taking on the roles of producer, co-director and even actor. The result is merely a hackneyed backstage musical, but it gave Alice Faye a starring role in her first picture (after Lilian Harvey backed out) and her alluring performance, especially singing the *Nasty Man* number, won her a contract with Fox. Rudy Vallee and Jimmy Durante are the other topliners. This was popular enough to be followed by two more screen *Scandals*, in 1935 and 1945.

Rudy Vallee *Jimmy Martin* • Jimmy Durante *Happy McGillicuddy* • Alice Faye *Kitty Donnelly* • Adrienne Ames *Barbara Loraine* • Gregory Ratoff *Nicholas Mitwoch* • Cliff Edwards *Stew Hart* • George White ■ *Dir* George White, Thornton Freeland, Harry Lachman • *Scr* Jack Yellen, from a story by George White

George White's Scandals ★★ 🆄

Musical 1945 · US · BW · 94mins

After two screen versions of Broadway impresario George White's musical revues in the mid-thirties, this belated follow-up was directed by Felix E Feist, with White producing. It's a patchy affair that provides a fine showcase for the nutty comedy of Joan Davis, including her take-off of *grande dames* of the theatre. Among the many guest performers are Gene Krupa and his band performing *Bolero in the Jungle*. George White doesn't appear this time, but he's impersonated by Glenn Tryon.

Joan Davis *Joan Mason* • Jack Haley *Jack Williams* • Phillip Terry *Tom McGrath* • Glenn Tryon *George White* • Martha Holliday *Jill Martin* • Margaret Hamilton *Clarabell* • Ethel Smith *Ethel Smith* ■ *Dir* Felix E Feist [Felix Feist] • *Scr* Hugh Wedlock, Howard Snyder, Parke Levy, Howard J Green, from a story by Hugh Wedlock, Howard Snyder

George's Island ★★

Adventure 1991 · Can · Colour · 89mins

This Canadian family film about a modern-day search for buried treasure is a muddled mix of pirate quest and foster-home drama. Ian Bannen is a class above everyone else, as the eccentric ex-sailor whose tales of Captain Kidd unlock his grandson's imagination. But the humour is flat and often nasty, and the story – which has more than a hint of the dark fantasies of Roald Dahl – is as entertaining as a long walk off a short plank.

Ian Bannen *Captain Waters* • Sheila McCarthy *Cloata Birdwood* • Maury Chaykin *Mr Droonfield* • Nathaniel Moreau *George Waters* • Vicki Ridler *Bonie* • Brian Downey *Mr Beane* • Irene Hogan *Mrs Beane* • Gary Reinike *Captain Kidd* ■ *Dir* Paul Donovan • *Scr* Paul Donovan, Maura O'Connell

Georgette Meunier ★★

Satire 1988 · W Ger · Colour · 82mins

One to file under "bizarre". Directors Tania Stöcklin and Cyrille Rey-Coquais were seemingly under the illusion that they were creating a profound feminist statement on celluloid. In fact, apart from the odd striking image, this is a *pfennig*-dreadful in which Georgette (Tiziana Jelmini) is transformed into an ordinary girl engaged in an incestuous relationship with her brother into a merciless murderess who kills with kisses. Some might attribute the film's theatrically stylised look to budgetary constraints, but by vacillating between polemic and *Grand Guignol*, the debut directors shroud the film in an archness that renders it utterly irresistible. In German with English subtitles.

Tiziana Jelmini *Georgette* • Thomas Schunke *Emile* • Dina Leipzig *Esmeralda* • Miklos Königer *Leopold Zsoldos* • Frank Kunkel *Insect specialist* • Kio Cornel *Singer* • Joe Rey-Coquais *Adonis* ■ *Dir* Tania Stöcklin, Cyrille Rey-Coquais • *Scr* Tania Stöcklin, Cyrille Rey-Coquais, Felix Schneider-Henninger

Georgia ★★★ 🆅

Mystery thriller 1988 · Ausl · Colour · 89mins

Australian director Ben Lewin attempts to merge Michelangelo Antonioni's *Blow Up* with Akira Kurosawa's *Rashomon* in this overambitious thriller. The opening is neat and intriguing, as a series of photographs puts tax fraud investigator Judy Davis on the track of a murderer. But, as the different witnesses give their versions of events through fragmentary flashbacks, it becomes clear that Lewin is cheating on us. Rather than tackling the themes of truth and perception explored in *Blow Up* and *Rashomon*, he uses the film director's sleight of hand to hide the fact that his mystery isn't that mysterious. Davis's typically solid performance just about holds things together. Contains some violence, swearing and nudity. 🖭

Judy Davis *Nina Bailey/Georgia White* • John Bach *William Karlin* • Julia Blake *Elizabeth* • Marshall Napier *Frank LeMat* • Alex Menglet *Laszlo* • Lewis Fiander *Scarlatti* • Roy Baldwin *Librarian* • Keryn Boyer *First policewoman* ■ *Dir* Ben Lewin • *Scr* Ben Lewin, Joanna Murray-Smith, Bob Weis

Georgia ★★★

Musical drama
1995 · US/Fr · Colour · 113mins

Jennifer Jason Leigh and Mare Winningham compete in acting their socks off in this interesting, performance-led film from director Ulu Grosbard (*Straight Time*). Winningham is Georgia, the successful folk singer with a husband and children, while Leigh is Sadie, her more destructive, erratic and unpredictable sister, who sings in clubs but remains undiscovered. Written by Leigh's mother, Barbara Turner, the film has some uncomfortable moments, notably a long and painful scene in which Leigh murders an old Van Morrison song. But it's worth persevering with for the impressive lead performances.

Jennifer Jason Leigh *Sadie* • Mare Winningham *Georgia* • Ted Levine *Jake* • Max Perlich *Axel* • John Doe *Bobby* • John C Reilly *Herman* • Jimmy Witherspoon *Trucker* • Jason Carter *Chasman* ■ *Dir* Ulu Grosbard • *Scr* Barbara Turner

Georgia, Georgia ★★

Drama 1972 · US/Swe · Colour · 84mins

A tale of pride and prejudice, written for the screen by author Maya Angelou, about a controversial mixed-race relationship between a black singer and a white photographer. The subject matter now looks somewhat dated, but the passion of the writing and performances still shines through. The most familiar cast name is Dirk Benedict, star of the TV series *Battlestar Galactica* and *The A-Team*.

Diana Sands *Georgia Martin* • Dirk Benedict *Michael Winters* • Minnie Gentry *Alberta Anderson* • Roger Furman *Herbert Thompson* • Terry Whitmore *Bobo* • Diana Kjaer *Brigit* ■ *Dir* Stig Bjorkman • *Scr* Maya Angelou

Georgy Girl ★★★★ 🆅

Comedy drama 1966 · UK · BW · 94mins

At the time a sexual show-stopper, this can now be seen as an unconscious parody of Swinging Sixties chic. It is saved from mere shock novelty by Lynn Redgrave's performance as the dowdy girl pursued by older employer James Mason, but finding her own identity looking after the illegitimate baby of flatmate Charlotte Rampling. Former TV director Silvio Narizzano piles on the tricks of cinematic trendiness, but it's the acting that stabilises the story into something memorable from a boringly self-conscious era. 🖭

Lynn Redgrave *Georgy* • James Mason *James Leamington* • Alan Bates *Jos* • Charlotte Rampling *Meredith* • Bill Owen *Ted* • Clare Kelly *Doris* • Denise Coffey *Peg* • Rachel Kempson *Ellen* ■ *Dir* Silvio Narizzano • *Scr* Margaret Forster, Peter Nichols, from the novel by Margaret Forster

🆄 = SUITABLE FOR ALL   🆅 = SUITABLE FOR ALL, ESPECIALLY FOR YOUNG CHILDREN (VIDEO ONLY)   🅿🅶 = PARENTAL GUIDANCE

The German Sisters ★★★
Political drama
1981 · W Ger · Colour · 106mins

Returning to themes already explored in *Sisters, or the Balance of Happiness*, Margarethe von Trotta based this provocative drama on the true-life experiences of Christiane and Gudrun Ensslin. While this is a highly politicised film, there is also a pronounced personal emphasis, with magazine editor Jutta Lampe being shaken from her bourgeois lethargy by the state's insistence that the Stammheim prison death of her hunger-striking terrorist sister (Barbara Sukowa) was suicide. Highlighting the need for continuity and courage in the protest against social injustice, von Trotta also examines what causes individuals from identical backgrounds to depart in such radically different directions. A German language film.

Jutta Lampe *Juliane* • Barbara Sukowa *Marianne* • Rüdiger Vogler *Wolfgang* • Doris Schade *Mother* • Vérénice Rudolph *Sabine* • Luc Bondy *Werner* • Franz Rudnick *Father* • Julia Biedermann *Marianne aged 16* • Ina Robinski *Juliane aged 17* ■ *Dir/Scr* Margarethe von Trotta

Germany in Autumn ★★★
Portmanteau documentary drama
1978 · W Ger · Colour and BW · 123mins

With its title bitterly evoking the idealism of *Heimat*, this portmanteau piece is an instant reaction to the events that rocked West Germany in the autumn of 1977: the storming of the hijacked plane at Mogadishu; the mysterious deaths of the Baader-Meinhof trio at Stammheim jail; and the murder of kidnapped industrialist Hans Martin Schleyer. Supervised by the father of New German cinema, Alexander Kluge, it's a mix of fictional and documentary vignettes from nine leading film-makers, with Rainer Werner Fassbinder's chilling conversation with his pro-authoritarian mother and Volker Schlöndorff's media spoof being the highlights. In German with English subtitles.

Hannelore Hoger • Katja Rupé • Hans Peter Cloos • Angela Winkler • Franzisca Walser • Vadim Glowna • Helmut Griem • Dieter Laser ■ *Dir* Alf Brustellin, Bernhard Sinkel, Hans Peter Cloos, Katja Rupé, Rainer Werner Fassbinder, Alexander Kluge, Beate Mainka-Jellinghaus, Maximiliane Mainka, Peter Schubert, Edgar Reitz, Volker Schlöndorff • *Scr* Heinrich Böll, Peter Steinbach, Alf Brustellin, Bernhard Sinkel, Hans Peter Cloos, Katja Rupé, Rainer Werner Fassbinder, Alexander Kluge, Beate Mainka-Jellinghaus, Maximiliane Mainka, Peter Schubert, Edgar Reitz, Volker Schlöndorff

Germany, Year Zero ★★★★
Drama 1947 · It/W Ger/Fr · BW · 74mins

The number of studio-shot scenes in the concluding part of director Roberto Rossellini's war trilogy, which also includes *Rome, Open City* and *Paisan*, shows that he was already moving away from the neorealist style. Yet the documentary footage of a decimated Berlin is still enormously powerful, especially when compared to the coverage of that other vanquished, but unscathed, capital in *Rome, Open City*. The shadow of Nazism hovers over this chilling depiction of desperation, as

12-year-old Edmund Moeschke scavanges among the ruins to feed his family. His murder of his ailing father is harrowing, but the tiny human details with which Rossellini invests the crime make it somehow forgivable, a testament to his film-making skill. In German with English subtitles.

Edmund Moeschke *Edmund* • Franz Kruger *Edmund's father* • Barbara Hintz *Eva* • Werner Pittschau *Karlheinz* ■ *Dir* Roberto Rossellini • *Scr* Roberto Rossellini, Carlo Lizzani, Max Kolpet, from a story by Roberto Rossellini

Germinal ★★★ 15
Historical drama
1993 · Fr/Bel/It · Colour · 151mins

Emile Zola's grimly realistic novel did much to highlight the miseries of French miners in the 1860s. In his pursuit of authenticity for this screen version of the tale, director Claude Berri broke the budget record for a French film. There's no doubt that the mining village is a masterpiece of period design and Yves Angelo's photography is often breathtaking, but the scale and sheen of the production in many ways count against this dour study of exploitative capitalism and stoic (rather than heroic) labour. Gérard Depardieu turns in another towering performance, but it's Miou-Miou and Judith Henry, as his wife and daughter, who impress most. In French with English subtitles. Contains violence, sex scenes and nudity. ▭

Renaud *Etienne Lantier* • Gérard Depardieu *Maheu* • Miou-Miou *Maheude* • Jean Carmet *Bonnemort* • Judith Henry *Catherine Maheu* • Jean-Roger Milo *Chaval* • Laurent Terzieff *Souvarine* • Jean-Pierre Bisson *Rasseneur* ■ *Dir* Claude Berri • *Scr* Claude Berri, Arlette Langmann, from the novel by Emile Zola

Geronimo ★★ U
Western 1939 · US · BW · 87mins

Although recycling action footage and basic plots was standard Hollywood practice, this lavish-looking Paramount western, with a B-feature cast headed by Preston Foster, is a real cheat. Its writer/director, the obscure Paul H Sloane, took his storyline from *The Lives of a Bengal Lancer*, integrated spectacular highlights from big-budget pictures such as *The Plainsman* and *Wells Fargo*, and gave the title character little screen time. At least he's portrayed by a real native American, Chief Thundercloud, and Gene Lockhart is on hand to give one of his patented studies of villainy.

Preston Foster *Captain Starrett* • Ellen Drew *Alice Hamilton* • Andy Devine *Sneezer* • William Henry *Lt Steele* • Ralph Morgan *Gen Steele* • Gene Lockhart *Gillespie* • Marjorie Gateson *Mrs Steele* • Chief Thundercloud *Geronimo* ■ *Dir/Scr* Paul H Sloane

Geronimo ★★★ PG
Western 1962 · US · Colour · 98mins

Today, Chuck Connors might not seem a politically correct choice to play the famous Apache leader, but back in the sixties this was the kind of role that consolidated the star power of the former professional baseball player. Connors looks good and acquits himself well and the landscapes – shot by Mexican cinematographer Alex Phillips – are stunning. Unfortunately,

the script strays from the facts of the shameful story and fails to improve upon history, with the defeat of the great warrior reduced to "cowboys and Indians" level. The eclectic casting is interesting, however, including Adam West (TV's Batman) and the ever-reliable Denver Pyle as a corrupt congressman. ▭

Chuck Connors *Geronimo* • Kamala Devi *Teela* • Ross Martin *Mangus* • Pat Conway *Maynard* • Adam West *Delahay* • Lawrence Dobkin *General Crook* • Denver Pyle *Senator Conrad* ■ *Dir* Arnold Laven • *Scr* Pat Fielder, from a story by Arnold Laven, Pat Fielder

Geronimo ★★★★ 12
Western 1993 · US · Colour · 110mins

Many critics questioned whether Walter Hill's version of the story of the legendary Chiricahua Apache was actually about him at all. However, screenwriter John Milius has always used a secondary voice as a device to gain a deeper insight into his central characters. The narration, provided here by Matt Damon's Lieutenant Britton Davis, presents us with the wider picture from which to draw our conclusions. The film also caused a fuss over its depiction of the native Americans. Milius and Hill present the massacres perpetrated by both sides as part and parcel of the struggle for nationhood and should be seen in the context of the times. While many will find this uncomfortable to watch, there's no denying the quality of Joe Alves's painstakingly authentic design or the lovingly re-created period feel of Lloyd Ahern's cinematography. The acting is also first rate, with Wes Studi magnificent in the title role. Contains violence and swearing. ▭

Jason Patric *Lieutenant Charles Gatewood* • Gene Hackman *Brigadier General George Crook* • Robert Duvall *Al Sieber* • Wes Studi *Geronimo* • Matt Damon *Lieutenant Britton Davis* • Rodney A Grant *Mangas* • Kevin Tighe *Brigadier General Nelson Miles* • Steve Reevis *Chato* ■ *Dir* Walter Hill • *Scr* John Milius, Larry Gross, from a story by John Milius

Geronimo ★★ 15
Western 1993 · US · Colour · 100mins

This TV movie premiered the same week that Walter Hill's *Geronimo* opened in cinemas. Drawing on historical records and American Indian traditions, director Roger Young's account somewhat distorts the facts in its effort to avoid the clichéd movie depiction of the great Chiricahua Apache warrior and his methods. The three leads perform admirably in depicting Goyathalay (to give him his real name) during key episodes in 1829-1909: his teenage encounter with the Mexican army; his infamous battles with the US cavalry; and his despairing old age, as he witnesses the life he had fought for slowly disappearing. ▭

Joseph Runningfox *Geronimo* • Nick Ramus *Mangas Coloradas* • Michelle St John *Ishton* • August Schellenberg *Cochise* • Michael Greyeyes *Juh* • Ryan Black *Young Geronimo* • Tailinh Forest Flower *Alope* • Kimberly Norris Chelchaye • Jimmy Herman *Old Geronimo* ■ *Dir* Roger Young • *Scr* JT Allen

Gert and Daisy's Weekend ★★ U
Second World War comedy
1941 · UK · BW · 79mins

Elsie and Doris Waters had been radio stars for some 15 years before they made this rare sortie in front of the movie camera. Starring as the cockney tittle-tattles Gert and Daisy, they escort some East End evacuees to a country house, where the kids end up as chief suspects in a jewel robbery. The sisters usually wrote their own material and took great pains to be original. Consequently, they look distinctly unhappy with the rehashed gags penned by director Maclean Rogers and his co-writer Kathleen Butler. It hasn't dated well, but those who lived through evacuation will perhaps find something to smile at.

Elsie Waters *Gert* • Doris Waters *Daisy* • Iris Vandeleur *Ma Butler* • John Slater *Jack Densham* • Elizabeth Hunt *Maisie Butler* • Wally Patch *Charlie Peters* • Annie Esmond *Lady Plumtree* • Aubrey Mallalieu *Barnes* • Gerald Rex *George the Terror* ■ *Dir* Maclean Rogers • *Scr* Maclean Rogers, Kathleen Butler

Gertrud ★★★★★ PG
Drama 1964 · Den · BW · 112mins

Carl Theodor Dreyer was a filmic genius who never shied away from controversial themes or unconventional techniques. This film is a troubling study of a married woman (played with great passion by Nina Pens Rode) who is prepared to sacrifice all in the impossible pursuit of love. In spite of the intimacy and intensity of the action, Dreyer opted to shoot in long takes with little camera movement, in order to emphasise the power of the words and performances. Much maligned on its release, this mesmerising picture was subsequently hailed as one of the most remarkable achievements of a brilliant career. In Danish with English subtitles. ▭

Nina Pens Rode *Gertrud Kanning* • Bendt Rothe *Gustav Kanning* • Ebbe Rode *Gabriel Lidman* • Baard Owe *Erland Jansson* • Axel Strobye *Axel Nygren* • Vera Gebuhr *Kanning's maid* • Anna Malberg *Kanning's mother* ■ *Dir* Carl Theodor Dreyer • *Scr* Carl Theodor Dreyer, from a play by Hjalmar Soderberg

Gervaise ★★★
Drama 1956 · Fr · BW · 115mins

René Clément's film is a solid version of Zola's *L'Assommoir*, which dealt with the ravages of alcoholism among the working classes of 19th-century Paris. Gervaise is an 18-year-old washerwoman who is abandoned by the father of her two children. She then marries a roofing contractor, who turns to drink after an accident leaves him incapacitated. When Gervaise's first lover (Armand Mestral) returns, further catastrophes and humiliations ensue. As Gervaise, Maria Schell (older sister of Maximilian Schell) gives a performance that won her a prize at the Venice Festival but was widely criticised as an exercise in technique, lacking in emotional conviction. In French with English subtitles.

Maria Schell *Gervaise* • François Périer *Henri Coupeau* • Suzy Delair *Virginie* • Mathilde Casadesus *Madame Boche* • Armand Mestral

Lantier • Jacques Harden *Goujet* ■ Dir René Clément • Scr Jean Aurenche, Pierre Bost, from the novel *L'Assommoir* by Emile Zola

Get Back ★★★ PG

Music documentary
1991 · UK · Colour and BW · 85mins

Having compiled the moving scrapbook that was shown on giant screens before each concert, Richard Lester was the natural choice for this rockumentary account of Paul McCartney's 1990 world tour. Valiantly attempting to update the busy visual style he pioneered on *A Hard Day's Night*, he slightly overdoes the trickery and spends a tad too long behind the scenes. However, his coverage of the gigs is exemplary, with Macca and his superb band rattling through Beatles anthems and solo favourites with genuine pleasure. ▭

Dir Richard Lester

Get Carter ★★★★ 18

Crime drama 1971 · UK · Colour · 106mins

This terrific, tough British thriller hides its story of raw revenge behind some fascinating Newcastle-upon-Tyne locations, courtesy of cinematographer Wolfgang Suschitzky. Its impact is undiminished since it was first seen in 1971. Michael Caine is at his most impassively impressive as the London gangster who goes north after his brother is murdered and finds his teenage niece involved in a blue film racket. Playwright John Osborne, appearing here as a North East crime boss, has a razor-slash presence, while director Mike Hodges keeps a firm hand on the surly proceedings. A welcome change from the American-set thrillers of today, this is sex and death with a British accent. ▭

Michael Caine *Jack Carter* • John Osborne *Cyril Kinnear* • Ian Hendry *Eric Paice* • Britt Ekland *Anna Fletcher* • Bryan Mosley *Cliff Brumby* • Geraldine Moffat *Glenda* • Dorothy White *Margaret* • Alun Armstrong *Keith* ■ Dir Mike Hodges • Scr Mike Hodges, from the novel *Jack's Return Home* by Ted Lewis

Get Cracking ★★ U

Second World War comedy
1943 · UK · BW · 97mins

In the late thirties and early forties, George Formby had been virtually the only home-grown talent who could match the popularity of the major Hollywood stars at the British box office. But by 1942 his star was showing signs of waning. *Get Cracking* is pleasant enough, but it's hardly vintage Formby. The comedy, a forerunner of TV's *Dad's Army*, finds George typically giving his all, in a somewhat substandard story of rival village Home Guard units trying to outdo each other on manoeuvres.

George Formby *George Singleton* • Edward Rigby *Sam Elliott* • Frank Pettingell *Alf Pemberton* • Ronald Shiner *Everett Manley* • Dinah Sheridan *Mary Pemberton* • Wally Patch *Sgt Joe Preston* • Mike Johnson *Josh* ■ Dir Marcel Varnel • Scr L du Garde Peach

Get Crazy ★★★ 18

Musical comedy 1983 · US · Colour · 88mins

A long-time employee of the legendary music venue Fillmore East in New

York, director Allan Arkush was the right man for this rock-flavoured satire. A spoof comedy, in which a New Year's Eve concert is threatened by a trio of villains (Ed Begley Jr, Bobby Sherman and Fabian), it has actors playing musicians and vice versa. Malcolm McDowell plays a Mick Jagger-like character named Reggie Wanker, while Lou Reed appears as Dylan clone Auden. The cast is also speckled with dozens of cult-movie mini-celebs, such as Mary Woronov and Dick Miller. *The Blues Brothers* it ain't, but it's still good cartoonish fun. ▭

Malcolm McDowell *Reggie Wanker* • Allen Goorwitz [Allen Garfield] *Max Wolfe* • Daniel Stern *Neil* • Gail Edwards *Willy Loman* • Miles Chapin *Sammy Fox* • Ed Begley Jr *Colin Beverly* • Lou Reed *Auden* • Bobby Sherman *Mark* • Fabian Forte [Fabian] *Marv* • Mary Woronov *Violetta* • Dick Miller *Susie's dad* ■ Dir Allan Arkush • Scr Danny Opatoshu, Henry Rosenbaum, David Taylor

Get off My Back ★★

Drama 1965 · US · BW · 106mins

Usually associated with glossy comedies such as *Sex and the Single Girl* or *Paris When It Sizzles*, Richard Quine made this curio about a drug rehab centre called Synanon, founded by Charles Dederich in California in the late fifties. Using real Synanon residents as well as actors, its very obvious message is driven by subplots and incidents that could come from any Hollywood melodrama. Dederich, played by Edmond O'Brien, was the film's chief adviser. Slinky Eartha Kitt puts in an interesting performance as a former heroin addict.

Chuck Connors *Ben* • Stella Stevens *Joaney* • Alex Cord *Zankie Albo* • Richard Conte *Reid* • Eartha Kitt *Betty Coleman* • Edmond O'Brien *Chuck Dederich* • Barbara Luna *Mary* • Alejandro Rey *Chris* ■ Dir Richard Quine • Scr Ian Bernard, S Lee Pogostin, from a story by Barry Oringer, S Lee Pogostin

Get on the Bus ★★★ 15

Road movie 1996 · US · Colour · 116mins

On 16 October 1995, African-American men from all over the United States converged on Washington DC to unite in a historic moment of goodwill, known as the "Million Man March". This event serves as the inspiration for another controversial look at racial politics from *adult terrible* Spike Lee. The focus is on 12 angry men from different backgrounds (cop, prisoner, student, gay couple, Denzel Washington wannabe) who travel from Los Angeles to the rally, embarking on personal voyages of discovery during the three-day bus trip. Though this reasonably absorbing road movie is less confrontational than Spike Lee's usual output, the message is still hammered home. ▭

Richard Belzer *Rick* • De'Aundre Bonds *Junior* • AndréBraugher *Flip* • Thomas Jefferson Byrd *Evan Thomas Sr* • Gabriel Casseus *Jamal* • Albert Hall *Craig* • Hill Harper *Xavier* • Harry Lennix [Harry J Lennix] *Randall* • Bernie Mac *Jay* ■ Dir Spike Lee • Scr Reggie Rock Bythewood

Get out Your Handkerchiefs ★★★

Comedy 1977 · Fr/Bel · Colour · 108mins

The winner of the Oscar for best foreign film, this outrageous comedy continues where Bertrand Blier's 1974 film *Les Valseuses* left off. Gérard Depardieu and Patrick Dewaere are reunited for a savage satire on the conventionality of middle-class life and the cosiness of commercial cinema. Depardieu reins in his natural ebullience as the husband who devotes himself to finding lovers for his discontented wife, Carol Laure, thus allowing 13-year-old Riton to steal the picture as the missing piece in their bizarre *ménage à trois*. Occasionally wildly wide of the mark, this provocative picture has something to offend everyone. In French with English subtitles.

Gérard Depardieu *Raoul* • Patrick Dewaere *Stephane* • Carole Laure *Solange* • Riton Christian Beloeil *Mrs Beloeil* • Jean Rougerie *Mr Beloeil* • Sylvie Joly *Passerby* ■ Dir/Scr Bertrand Blier

Get Real ★★ 15

Drama 1998 · UK/SA · Colour · 106mins

Beautiful Thing meets *Grange Hill*, but that isn't a recommendation. What's a 16-year-old school boy to do when he lives in Basingstoke, knows he's "dodgy" (in other words, gay) and fancies the head boy? Those are the problems facing Steven Carter (Ben Silverstone) as he grapples with hiding his sexuality being bullied at school and trying to study, while gazing adoringly at sports hero John Dixon (Brad Gorton). Director Simon Shore merely joins up the gay soap-opera dots he's inherited from screenwriter Patrick Wilde's fringe play *What's Wrong with Angry?* and, despite encouraging an engaging central performance from Silverstone, does little more than indulge in a certain clichéd angst. ▭

Ben Silverstone *Steven Carter* • Brad Gorton *John Dixon* • Charlotte Brittain *Linda* • Stacy A Hart *Jessica* • Kate McEnery *Wendy* • Patrick Nielsen *Mark* • Tim Harris *Kevin* • James D White *Dave* ■ Dir Simon Shore • Scr Patrick Wilde, from his play *What's Wrong with Angry?*

Get Shorty ★★★★ 15

Drama 1995 · US · Colour · 100mins

This adaptation of Elmore Leonard's novel explores the murky world of Hollywood's links to organised crime. John Travolta plays the Florida loan shark Chili Palmer, who arrives in Hollywood to collect a bad debt from Gene Hackman's sleazeball movie producer and decides to stay, importing his strong-arm methods into movie production. Made in the wake of *Pulp Fiction*, *Get Shorty* was the first attempt by a major studio to cash in on Quentin Tarantino's style. The performances by the impressive cast are exquisite: the jowly Travolta has tremendous charm but also considerable menace; Danny DeVito plays a movie star to perfection; and Hackman is a sheer delight as the purveyor of schlocky monster movies. Add Rene Russo and unbilled cameos by Bette Midler and Harvey Keitel and

you have a snazzy treat. Contains violence and swearing. ▭ **DVD**

John Travolta *Chili Palmer* • Gene Hackman *Harry Zimm* • Rene Russo *Karen Flores* • Danny DeVito *Martin Weir* • Dennis Farina *Ray "Bones" Barboni* • Delroy Lindo *Bo Catlett* • James Gandolfini *Bear* • Jon Gries [Jonathan Gries] *Ronnie Wingate* ■ Dir Barry Sonnenfeld • Scr Scott Frank, from the novel by Elmore Leonard

Get Smart, Again! ★★ PG

Spy spoof 1989 · US · Colour · 93mins

The amiable, jokey spy spoofs of the sixties, both on film and TV, were generally slap-happy events, full of amusingly improbable action, yet rarely barbed enough to be satirical or lean enough to be witty. The television series *Get Smart*, about an agent whose idiocy sparked the comedy, was one such example. In the second film version of this series, Maxwell Smart and sidekick Agent 99 embrace once more the giddy days of spying when they take on old adversaries KAOS. Expect the usual all-action clowning, crazed zeal and daft accomplices in this relaxed canter through all kinds of nonsense. ▭

Don Adams *Maxwell Smart* • Barbara Feldon *Agent 99* • Dick Gautier *Hymie* • John Delancie *Major Waterhouse* • Harold Gould *Nicholas Dimente* • Robert Karvelas *Larrabee* • Dave Ketchum *Agent 13* • Bernie Kopell *Siegfried* ■ Dir Gary Nelson • Scr Leonard B Stern, Mark Curtiss, Rod Ash, from the TV series *Get Smart* by Mel Brooks, Buck Henry

Get to Know Your Rabbit ★★

Satirical comedy 1972 · US · Colour · 91mins

Bored with corporate politics, Tom Smothers abandons his conformist job to become an itinerant tap-dancing magician, with a little help from Orson Welles. He soon finds that his change of lifestyle hasn't freed him from the exploitative, money-obsessed world he is trying to escape. Director Brian De Palma's first big-budget feature is an overlong, uninspired parable for the time, with stagey performances from Smothers, Katharine Ross and Orson Welles. A banal black comedy of social mores, this was edited against De Palma's wishes and only a few flashes of his visual talent remain.

Tom Smothers *Donald Beeman* • John Astin *Mr Turnbull* • Suzanne Zenor *Paula* • Samantha Jones *Susan* • Allen Goorwitz [Allen Garfield] *Vic* • Katharine Ross *Girl* • Orson Welles *Mr Delasandro* ■ Dir Brian De Palma • Scr Jordan Crittenden

Get Yourself a College Girl ★★

Musical comedy 1964 · US · Colour · 86mins

Student Mary Ann Mobley gets into trouble when she's exposed as the songwriter of some disreputable – but supposedly groovy – tunes. Fortunately, an ambitious senator (Willard Waterman) is around to help out – in exchange for some youth "cred" with the voters. This would-be fun teen picture is saved by the appearance of a strange melange of musicians, including early Britpoppers the Dave Clark Five and the Animals, lounge chanteuse Astrud Gilberto and cool

U = SUITABLE FOR ALL   Uc = SUITABLE FOR ALL, ESPECIALLY FOR YOUNG CHILDREN (VIDEO ONLY)   PG = PARENTAL GUIDANCE

jazz man Stan Getz. Beware: there are some scenes of the dreaded twist.

Mary Ann Mobley *Terry* • Joan O'Brien *Marge* • Chris Noel *Sue* • Nancy Sinatra *Lynne* • Chad Everett *Gary* • Fabrizio Mioni *Armand* • Willard Waterman *Senator Hubert Morrison* ■ *Dir* Sidney Miller • *Scr* Robert E Kent

The Getaway ★★★★ 18

Thriller 1972 · US · Colour · 117mins

A gripping, landmark thriller, directed by the master of screen violence, Sam Peckinpah, this is based on a novel by Jim Thompson and scripted by Walter Hill, who later directed *48 Hours*. Steve McQueen and Ali MacGraw bungle a bank robbery and head off to Mexico, pursued by a gang of gunmen, a wounded gangster and an army of cops. It's a modern western, a tough, disconcerting fable about the barren landscapes of the Texan desert and the human soul. The charismatic McQueen slaps MacGraw around and seems only to experience passion through violence and stolen loot. In real life, the stars fell in love and married. Contains swearing. ▭

Steve McQueen *"Doc" McCoy* • Ali MacGraw *Carol McCoy* • Ben Johnson *Jack Benyon* • Sally Struthers *Fran Clinton* • Al Lettieri *Rudy Butler* • Slim Pickens *Cowboy* • Richard Bright *Thief* • Jack Dodson *Harold Clinton* ■ *Dir* Sam Peckinpah • *Scr* Walter Hill, from the novel by Jim Thompson

The Getaway ★★★ 18

Thriller 1994 · US · Colour · 110mins

This remake of Sam Peckinpah's 1972 thriller reuses much of Walter Hill's original script. It's directed by Roger Donaldson and stars Alec Baldwin and Kim Basinger in the roles played originally by Steve McQueen and Ali MacGraw. Baldwin isn't in the same league as McQueen, but Donaldson's picture has flair and the female leads stand up to comparison. The story (from Jim Thompson's bleak novel) has a fair amount of tension, and the south western locations have an arid, end-of-the-line symbolism. James Woods's appearance is a welcome bonus. Contains swearing, violence, sex scenes and nudity. ▭

Alec Baldwin *Carter "Doc" McCoy* • Kim Basinger *Carol McCoy* • Michael Madsen *Rudy Travis* • James Woods *Jack Benyon* • David Morse *Jim Deer Jackson* • Jennifer Tilly *Fran Carvey* • James Stephens *Harold Carvey* • Richard Farnsworth *Slim* ■ *Dir* Roger Donaldson • *Scr* Walter Hill, Amy Jones, from the novel by Jim Thompson

Getting Away with Murder ★ 15

Comedy 1996 · US/Can · Colour · 87mins

It's a special sort of director who takes a talented comic cast – including Dan Aykroyd, Jack Lemmon and Lily Tomlin – and still manages to turn in a completely unfunny comedy. (Writer/director Harvey Miller also made the Steve Guttenberg flop *Bad Medicine*.) The problem here is that the material is weird rather than wacky, as professor Aykroyd discovers that his neighbour (Lemmon) is a Nazi war criminal and decides to murder him. Perhaps he should have taken pot shots at the writer instead, as things veer into bad-taste territory when

Aykroyd discovers his victim wasn't really a Nazi. Nasty, tasteless and decidedly unfunny. ▭

Dan Aykroyd *Jack Lambert* • Lily Tomlin *Inga Mueller* • Jack Lemmon *Max Mueller/Luger* • Bonnie Hunt *Gail Holland* • Brian Kerwin *Marty Lambert* • Jerry Adler *Judge* • Andy Romano *Psychiatrist* ■ *Dir/Scr* Harvey Miller

Getting Even ★★ 18

Action thriller 1986 · US · Colour · 86mins

This uninspired hostage drama has a plot that ultimately stretches audience credibility too far. Joe Don Baker, who has made a career out of playing bullish villains, is an insane industrialist threatening to unleash a deadly flesh-eating gas upon the population of Dallas unless he's paid $50 million. (There are shades here of the storyline to future blockbuster *The Rock*.) Edward Albert is the rival businessman hot on his heels. Dwight H Little displays numerous directorial inadequacies by allowing the pace to lag, but delivers a rip-snorting final reel featuring dazzling aerial stunts. ▭

Edward Albert *Taggar* • Audrey Landers *Paige Starsen* • Joe Don Baker *King Kenderson* • Rod Pilloud *Doc* • Billy Streater *Ryder* • Blue Deckert *Kurt* • Caroline Williams *Molly* ■ *Dir* Dwight H Little • *Scr* M Phil Senini, Eddie Desmond, J Michael Liddle

Getting Even with Dad ★★ PG

Comedy 1994 · US · Colour · 104mins

Home Alone's Macaulay Culkin again proves more than a match for a whole bunch of adults with criminal tendencies in this inoffensive, if grindingly obvious comedy. This time the victim of his machinations is his dad, crooked Ted Danson, who Culkin is trying to steer on to the straight and narrow. However, most of the humiliation is saved for Danson's inept sidekicks, Saul Rubinek and Gailard Sartain. Howard Deutch is a proficient enough second-division director, but he lets things get too gooey, and the awkwardly ageing Culkin (approaching adolescence) no longer possesses the charm of old. Contains swearing. ▭

Macaulay Culkin *Timmy* • Ted Danson *Ray* • Glenne Headly *Theresa* • Saul Rubinek *Bobby* • Gailard Sartain *Carl* • Sam McMurray *Alex* • Hector Elizondo *Lt Romayko* • Sydney Walker *Mr Wankmueller* ■ *Dir* Howard Deutch • *Scr* Tom S Parker, Jim Jennewein

Getting Gertie's Garter ★★

Comedy 1945 · US · BW · 73mins

The Broadway hit by Wilson Collison and Avery Hopwood was made into a silent feature in 1927. In this later version of the bedroom-and-hayloft farce Dennis O'Keefe plays Ken, the newly-married scientist desperately trying to retrieve an engraved diamond-studded garter he gave his old flame Gertie, played by Marie "The Body" McDonald. His wife, played by Sheila Ryan, and Gertie's fiancé, Barry Sullivan, naturally misunderstand the situation. Under the smooth direction of Allan Dwan, the players extract every possible ounce of fun.

Dennis O'Keefe *Ken* • Marie McDonald *Gertie* • Barry Sullivan *Ted* • Binnie Barnes *Barbara* • Sheila Ryan *Patty* • J Carrol Naish *Charles, the butler* • Jerome Cowan *Billy* • Vera Marshe

Anna, the maid ■ *Dir* Allan Dwan • *Scr* Allan Dwan, Karen DeWolf, from the play by Wilson Collison, Avery Hopwood

Getting Gotti ★★ 15

Crime drama based on a true story
1994 · US · Colour · 89mins

It was inevitable that Mafia boss John Gotti, a gangster obsessed with celebrity, would end up being filmed. This is the lesser of two biopics (the other was *Gotti*), released on video in the UK at much the same time, with Anthony John Denison as the infamous "Teflon Don". Events are seen from the perspective of the obsessed district attorney (Lorraine Bracco) who fought for years to nail the media-friendly mobster. It's an interesting tale and is reasonably well played, although the treatment is a little too low-key for such a larger-than-life character. ▭

Lorraine Bracco *Diane Giacalone* • Anthony John Denison *John Gotti* • Ellen Burstyn *Jo Giacalone* • Kathleen Laskey *Cassie* • August Schellenberg *Willie Boy Johnson* • Kenneth Welsh *Bennett* • Jeremy Ratchford *Harvey Sanders* • Ron Gabriel *Gravano* ■ *Dir* Roger Young • *Scr* James S Henerson

Getting In ★★★

Black comedy thriller
1994 · US · Colour · 94mins

This black comedy marked the directorial debut of Doug Liman (*Swingers*). Gabriel Higgs (Stephen Mailer) is bound by family tradition to go to Johns Hopkins College to study medicine. A lacklustre exam performance sees him resorting to blackmail to eliminate the five people ahead of him on the reserve list. Unfortunately they're dropping down dead instead and, before he knows it, Gabriel's a murder suspect. *Friends* star Matthew Perry and *Ally McBeal's* Calista Flockhart are among the strong supporting cast. Great gags make this enjoyable to watch.

Stephen Mailer *Gabriel Higgs* • Kristy Swanson *Kirby Watts* • Andrew McCarthy *Rupert Grimm* • Dave Chappelle *Rom* • Matthew Perry *Randall Burns* • Calista Flockhart *Amanda Morel* ■ *Dir* Doug Liman • *Scr* PJ Posner, Joel Posner, Jonathan Lewin

Getting It Right ★★ 15

Romantic comedy
1989 · US · Colour · 97mins

A decade before her mould-breaking role in *Fight Club*, Helena Bonham Carter unsuccessfully tried to shake her period drama image in this uneven comedy. Jesse Birdsall (slightly out of his depth) is Gavin Lamb, an inexperienced young man who finds himself pursued by three women, including Bonham Carter and Jane Horrocks. Based on Elizabeth Jane Howard's novel, this probably worked better on the page than it does on screen, but a classy cast (including Lynn Redgrave, Peter Cook and John Gielgud) makes it worth a look. ▭

Jesse Birdsall *Gavin Lamb* • Helena Bonham Carter *Lady Minerva Munday* • Peter Cook *Mr Adrian* • John Gielgud *Sir Gordon Munday* • Jane Horrocks *Jenny* • Lynn Redgrave *Joan* • Shirley Anne Field *Anne* • Pauline Quirke *Muriel Sutton* ■ *Dir* Randal Kleiser • *Scr* Elizabeth Jane Howard, from her novel

The Getting of Wisdom ★★★ PG

Period drama 1977 · Ausl · Colour · 97mins

Film-makers during the Australian New Wave of the seventies had a flair for giving costume movies a resounding contemporary relevance. Here Bruce Beresford provides a few choice insights into the miseries of school life and the pain of lonely adolescence. He re-creates the atmosphere of a repressive turn-of-the-century boarding school with some care, but misses the sense of danger found in the original autobiographical novel by Henry Handel Richardson that caused a scandal on its publication. Susannah Fowle does well as the new pupil whose "passion" for chaplain John Waters and intense friendship with senior girl Hilary Ryan reveal the tensions beneath the school's prim exterior. ▭

Susannah Fowle *Laura Tweedle Rambotham* • Barry Humphries *Reverend Strachey* • John Waters *Reverend Robert Shepherd* • Sheila Helpmann *Mrs Gurley* • Patricia Kennedy *Miss Chapman* • Kerry Armstrong *Kate Horner* • Celia De Burgh *MP* • Kim Deacon *Lilith Gordon* ■ *Dir* Bruce Beresford • *Scr* Eleanor Witcombe, from the novel by Henry Handel Richardson [Ethel Florence Richardson]

Getting Out ★★★ 15

Drama 1993 · US · Colour · 88mins

Rebecca De Mornay looked set for a major career after her role as the nanny from hell in *The Hand That Rocks the Cradle*, but she chose a complete change of pace for this TV drama the following year. She plays a hard-bitten ex-con who is trying to make a new life for herself and her child but can't seem to escape from her past. She's both credible and moving in the lead role and more than holds her own against canny scene-stealer Ellen Burstyn. Director John Korty keeps the film pleasingly free from the sugary excesses of other like-minded productions. Contains some violence. ▭

Rebecca De Mornay *Arlene Holsclaw* • Ellen Burstyn *Arlene's mother* • Robert Knepper *Carl* ■ *Dir* John Korty • *Scr* Eugene Corr, Ruth Shapiro, from the play by Marsha Norman

Getting Straight ★★★ 15

Comedy drama 1970 · US · Colour · 119mins

Made on the back of *Easy Rider* and the anti-Vietnam War campaign, this was one of several "campus movies" that enabled studio executives to look cool and save money on ties. Elliott Gould – who, after *MASH*, briefly became a counterculture hero – plays a Vietnam veteran. Resuming his university education, he becomes embroiled in campus politics and involved with fashion victim Candice Bergen. Harrison Ford makes an early appearance in a film that is very much of its time, though even by today's standards the sex scenes seem quite steamy. ▭

Elliott Gould *Harry Bailey* • Candice Bergen *Jan* • Robert F Lyons *Nick* • Jeff Corey *Dr Willhunt* • Max Julien *Ellis* • Cecil Kellaway *Dr Kasper* • Jon Lormer *Vandenburg* • Leonard Stone *Lysander* • Harrison Ford *Jake* ■ *Dir* Richard Rush • *Scr* Robert Kaufman, from the novel by Ken Kolb

Getting Up and Going Home ★★

Romantic drama 1992 · US · Colour · 92mins

Tom Skerritt finds his reserves of calm dignity severely tested in this midlife-crisis TV-movie adaptation of Robert Anderson's novel. He plays Jack Montgomery, a successful lawyer who realises his marriage to Blythe Danner isn't enough. This leads to romantic entanglements with two other women, but Skerritt manages to convince us that his character's behaviour is born more out of loneliness and confusion than wanderlust.

Tom Skerritt *Jack Montgomery* • Blythe Danner *Lily Montgomery* • Roma Downey *Kimberly Stevens* • Julianne Phillips *Janet Huntley* • Bruce Kirby *Oliver Benson* • Gary Frank *Scott Stevens* • Dorian Harewood *Ted Owens* ■ *Dir* Steven Schachter • *Scr* Peter Nelson, from the novel by Robert Anderson

Gettysburg ★★★ PG

Historical war drama
1993 · US · Colour · 259mins

Ted Turner's company produced this ambitious account of the bloody battle of July 1863, which cost some 7,000 lives and secured final victory for the Union. With a running time considerably longer than *Gone with the Wind* – Turner's favourite movie – *Gettysburg* has time to consider both points of view, but it has only been going for 45 minutes before the cannons start firing. Undeniably spectacular in parts and dull in others (much like the real battle, in fact), it makes the strategy of the battle clear but takes some liberties with the actual events. Turner makes an uncredited cameo appearance as a Confederate who gets shot when answering the call to advance. ▣

Tom Berenger *Lieutenant General James Longstreet (Confederate)* • Martin Sheen *General Robert E Lee (Confederate)* • Stephen Lang *Major General George E Pickett (Confederate)* • Richard Jordan *Brigadier General Lewis A Armistead (Confederate)* • George Lazenby *Brigadier General J Johnston Pettigrew (Confederate)* • Jeff Daniels *Colonel Joshua Lawrence Chamberlain (Federal)* • Sam Elliott *Brigadier General John Buford (Federal)* • C Thomas Howell *Lieutenant Thomas D Chamberlain (Federal)* • Maxwell Caulfield *Colonel Strong Vincent (Federal)* ■ *Dir* Ronald F Maxwell • *Scr* Ronald F Maxwell, from the novel *The Killer Angels* by Michael Shaara

Ghidrah, the Three-Headed Monster ★★★

Science-fiction horror
1965 · Jap · Colour · 73mins

Ghidrah (or Ghidorah as Japanese movie-goers correctly know him) is a three-headed, fire-breathing dragon which lands on Earth and causes the usual global destruction. Godzilla (in his first adventure as a good monster) defends the planet, with help from Mothra and Rodan (Toho Studios's other big earners), defeating Ghidrah in a spectacular battle on Mount Fuji. With higher production values and better visual effects than normal, this engaging behemoth bash established the use of various monsters in combat combinations, which would increase in goofiness over the years. Japanese dialogue dubbed into English.

Yosuke Natsuki *Shindo* • Yuriko Hoshi *Naoko* • Hiroshi Koizumi *Professor Murai* • Takashi Shimura *Dr Tsukamoto* ■ *Dir* Ishiro Honda [Inoshiro Honda] • *Scr* Shinichi Sekizawa

Ghost ★★★★ 15

Romantic drama
1990 · US · Colour · 121mins

This romantic and glossy mix of the sentimental and the supernatural reaps higher rewards than Patrick Swayze's acting ability deserves. He's the murdered banker trying to warn girlfriend Demi Moore she's in mortal danger via psychic Whoopi Goldberg, who provides the comic moments so necessary to lighten the potentially maudlin atmosphere. In fact, she did it so well, she won a best supporting actress Oscar. The special effects are a real treat, the love-beyond-the-grave theme is touching and Swayze's ascent into heaven is a wonderful piece of schmaltz. Contains swearing and violence. ▣

Patrick Swayze *Sam Wheat* • Demi Moore *Molly Jensen* • Whoopi Goldberg *Oda Mae Brown* • Tony Goldwyn *Carl Bruner* • Rick Aviles *Willie Lopez* • Gail Boggs *Louise* ■ *Dir* Jerry Zucker • *Scr* Bruce Joel Rubin

The Ghost and Mr Chicken ★★ U

Comedy mystery 1966 · US · Colour · 89mins

Don Knotts made one of his more successful ventures on to the silver screen with this comedy chiller. He plays Luther Heggs, a typesetter for a local newspaper who yearns to be a proper journalist. He finally gets his big break with a piece about a supposedly haunted house, where two mysterious deaths took place 20 years earlier. The bad news for Luther is that he has to spend a night in the house. While not on a par with *The Ghost Breakers* or *The Cat and the Canary*, the movie has its moments thanks to Knotts.

Don Knotts *Luther Heggs* • Joan Staley *Alma* • Liam Redmond *Kelsey* • Dick Sargent *Beckett* • Skip Homeier *Ollie* • Reta Shaw *Mrs Maxwell* • Lurene Tuttle *Mrs Miller* • Philip Ober *Simmons* ■ *Dir* Alan Rafkin • *Scr* James Fritzell, Everett Greenbaum

The Ghost and Mrs Muir ★★★★ U

Romantic fantasy 1947 · US · BW · 99mins

This wonderfully romantic ghost story has ethereally beautiful Gene Tierney beguiled by bewhiskered sea captain Rex Harrison, himself long dead. A marvellously lyrical Bernard Herrmann score helps underline the poignancy of this enchanting tale, and Philip Dunne's literate screenplay avoids all the pitfalls normally associated with such delicate material. The movie is also enhanced by a particularly well-chosen cast, including George Sanders as Tierney's would-be suitor, and Natalie Wood as Tierney's young daughter Anna (Vanessa Brown portrays her in later years). Today, the settings and pace may look studio-bound, but they suit the theatricality of the subject, and there's no question that this superb original is far better than its spin-off TV series. ▣

Gene Tierney *Lucy Muir* • Rex Harrison *Captain Daniel Gregg* • George Sanders *Miles Fairley* • Edna Best *Martha* • Vanessa Brown

Anna • Anna Lee *Mrs Fairley* • Robert Coote *Coombe* • Natalie Wood *Young Anna* ■ *Dir* Joseph L Mankiewicz • *Scr* Philip Dunne, from the novel by RA Dick

The Ghost and the Darkness ★★★ 15

Period action adventure
1996 · US · Colour · 109mins

What a way to run a railway! Big-game hunter Michael Douglas and Irish engineer Val Kilmer have quite a job on their hands trying to rid the under-construction East African track in Victorian times from two human-guzzling lions, which have terrified native labourers into absenteeism. Director Stephen Hopkins tells the story – based on Colonel Patterson's book *The Man-Eaters Of Tsavo* – in a manner that leaks tension. But the lions themselves are wonderful anti-colonial villains – you don't want to mess with these maulers! ▣

Michael Douglas *Remington* • Val Kilmer *John Patterson* • Bernard Hill *Dr Hawthorne* • John Kani *Samuel* • Tom Wilkinson *Beaumont* • Om Puri *Abdullah* • Emily Mortimer *Helena Patterson* ■ *Dir* Stephen Hopkins • *Scr* William Goldman, from the book *The Man-Eaters of Tsavo* by John Patterson

The Ghost Breakers ★★★★

Comedy mystery 1940 · US · BW · 83mins

Made to capitalise on the success the previous year of Bob Hope's comedy *The Cat and the Canary*, this lightning paced follow-up is even better than its money-spinning predecessor. Once again Hope and Paulette Goddard find themselves shacked up in a supposedly haunted house – this time it's her inherited mansion in an exotic Cuban locale. The same pleasing recipe of thrills, laughs and romance keep the potboiler simmering nicely with the added bonus of some truly spooky moments amid the fun.

Bob Hope *Larry Lawrence* • Paulette Goddard *Mary Carter* • Richard Carlson *Geoff Montgomery* • Paul Lukas *Parada* • Willie Best *Alex* • Pedro De Cordoba *Havez* • Anthony Quinn *Ramon/Francisco* ■ *Dir* George Marshall • *Scr* Walter De Leon, from the play by Paul Dickey, Charles W Goddard

The Ghost Camera ★★ U

Crime mystery 1933 · UK · BW · 64mins

Say what you like about the much-maligned "quota quickie" (and, to be honest, most of them were pretty dreadful), they proved an invaluable training ground for some of this country's most talented individuals. Director Bernard Vorhaus clearly doesn't fit into that category, but his stars Ida Lupino, then a mere 15 years old, and a scarcely more experienced John Mills, together with editor (and future director) David Lean, certainly do. Unfortunately, much of the action of this mystery is dominated by Henry Kendall as the chemist-turned-sleuth seeking to use photographic evidence to prove Mills innocent of murder. However, the reliable Felix Aylmer helps pep up the court scenes. ▣

Henry Kendall *John Grey* • Ida Lupino *Mary Elton* • John Mills *Ernest Elton* • S Victor Stanley *Albert Sims* • George Merritt *Inspector* • Felix Aylmer *Coroner* • Davina Craig *Amelia*

Wilkinson • Fred Groves *Barnaby Rudd* ■ *Dir* Bernard Vorhaus • *Scr* H Fowler Mear, from a story by J Jefferson Farjeon

Ghost Catchers ★★★

Musical comedy 1944 · US · BW · 68mins

While it never quite recaptures the manic mayhem of the hilarious *Hellzapoppin'*, this is another riot of mirth and melody from stars Ole Olsen and Chic Johnson. Adapted from the story *High Spirits*, co-written by director Edward F Cline, the plot is as transparent as a spectre and the action pauses rather too readily for a song. But Chic and Ole are on rattlingly good form as they help the family in the mansion adjoining their nightclub solve their spook problem. Expertly exploiting Universal's genius for eerie atmosphere, Cline also draws on some expert supporting players, notably Leo Carillo and Lon Chaney Jr.

Ole Olsen *Ole* • Chic Johnson *Chic* • Gloria Jean *Melinda* • Martha O'Driscoll *Susanna* • Leo Carrillo *Jerry* • Andy Devine *Bear* • Lon Chaney Jr *Horsehead* • Kirby Grant *Clay* ■ *Dir* Edward F Cline [Edward Cline] • *Scr* Edmund L Hartmann, from the story *High Spirits* by Milt Gross, Edward F Cline [Edward Cline]

Ghost Dad ★ PG

Comedy fantasy 1990 · US · Colour · 80mins

Bill Cosby has had a disastrous time trying to transfer his TV popularity to the big screen. After the ill-conceived spy spoof *Leonard, Part 6* came this equally daft supernatural comedy which, despite the efforts of director Sidney Poitier, also went straight to video over here. Cosby plays a harassed businessman who is killed in a car accident and discovers he's been missing out on the joys of family life. Cosby mugs away for all he's worth, but good gags are few and far between. Contains some swearing. ▣

Bill Cosby *Elliot Hopper* • Kimberly Russell *Diane Hopper* • Denise Nicholas *Joan* • Ian Bannen *Sir Edith Moser* • Christine Ebersole *Carol* • Barry Corbin *Mr Collins* • Salim Grant *Danny Hopper* • Brooke Fontaine *Amanda Hopper* ■ *Dir* Sidney Poitier • *Scr* Chris Reese, Brent Maddock, SS Wilson, from a story by SS Wilson, Brent Maddock

Ghost Dog: the Way of the Samurai ★★★ 15

Crime drama 1999 · US/Fr · Colour · 115mins

Inspired by Jean-Pierre Melville's *Le Samourai*, Jim Jarmusch's quirky crime drama creates a world of such deadpan solemnity that humour exists solely in the eye of the beholder. Forest Whitaker is perfectly at home here, as a bushido-obsessed hit man who communicates with his boss by pigeon and doesn't speak a word of his ice cream-selling best friend's language. The word laconic doesn't do justice to the film's tempo – though the outbursts of explosive violence as Whitaker jousts with mobsters John Tormey and Henry Silva tend to spoil the ambience. Contains violence.

Forest Whitaker *Ghost Dog* • John Tormey *Louie* • Cliff Gorman *Sonny Valerio* • Henry Silva *Vargo* • Isaach de Bankole *Raymond* • Tricia Vessey *Louise Vargo* • Gene Ruffini *Old consigliere* ■ *Dir/Scr* Jim Jarmusch

U = SUITABLE FOR ALL   Uc = SUITABLE FOR ALL, ESPECIALLY FOR YOUNG CHILDREN (VIDEO ONLY)   PG = PARENTAL GUIDANCE

The Ghost Goes West

★★★ U

Comedy   1935 · UK · BW · 78mins

One of the prestige pictures with which producer Alexander Korda hoped to capture a corner of the US market. Adapted from a story in *Punch*, it is a lightweight fantasy that gets by thanks to some expert playing and the assured touch of director René Clair, who was making his English language debut after a decade of making comedies in his native France. Although Clair's frothy style is somewhat stifled by Korda's delusions of grandeur, he coaxes an impish performance out of Robert Donat as the ghost haunting a Scottish castle transported to Florida by vulgar millionaire Eugene Pallette. ▭

Robert Donat *Murdoch/Donald Glourie* • Jean Parker *Peggy Martin* • Eugene Pallette *Joe Martin* • Elsa Lanchester *Lady Shepperton* • Ralph Bunker *Ed Bigelow* • Patricia Hilliard *Shepherdess* • Everley Gregg *Gladys Martin* ■ *Dir* René Clair • *Scr* Robert E Sherwood, René Clair, Geoffrey Kerr, from the story *Sir Tristram Goes West* by Eric Keown

A Ghost in Monte Carlo ★★

Period romantic drama 1990 · UK/US · Colour

Fans of Barbara Cartland's rich settings, English poise and tales of improbable innocents ensnared by lascivious men may well enjoy this sugary contrivance, which is adapted from one of her novels. Others may find it unintentionally funny, as a decent cast headed by Oliver Reed, Sarah Miles and Lysette Anthony is forced to recite slabs of dialogue to camera in what is, sadly, an unmoving romantic drama. Done well, this kind of romp can be entertaining, but director John Hough's made-for-TV effort falls well short of the mark.

Lysette Anthony *Mistral* • Sarah Miles *Emilie* • Oliver Reed *Rajah* • Marcus Gilbert *Lord Robert Stanford* • Christopher Plummer *Grand Duke Ivan* • Samantha Eggar *Jeanne* • Fiona Fullerton *Lady Violet* • Jolyon Baker *Prince Nicholas* • Joanna Lumley *Lady Drayton* • Lewis Collins *Lord Drayton* • Gareth Hunt *Dulton* ■ *Dir* John Hough • *Scr* Terence Feely, from the novel by Barbara Cartland

The Ghost in the Invisible Bikini

★★ PG

Comedy horror   1966 · US · Colour · 79mins

Exploitation movies don't come much brighter and bolder than this. Part *Beach Party* flick, part horror, this follow-up of sorts to *Dr Goldfoot and the Girl Bombs* was equally ambitious but shorter on imagination and signalled the end of the *Beach Party* cycle. Forget the plot, some aimless drivel about newly deceased Boris Karloff trying to gain entry into heaven by doing a good deed. The real fun comes from watching an eclectic cast go through their paces, including Karloff, Nancy Sinatra and Basil Rathbone who, despite his advanced years, allegedly handled his own stunts in a sword fight with teen idol Tommy Kirk. Director Don Weis graduated to television in the seventies. ▭

Tommy Kirk *Chuck Phillips* • Deborah Walley *Lili Morton* • Aron Kincaid *Bobby* • Quinn O'Hara *Sinatra* • Jesse White *J Sinister Hulk* • Harvey Lembeck *Eric Von Zipper* • Nancy

Sinatra *Vicki* • Basil Rathbone *Reginald Ripper* • Boris Karloff *Hiram Stokely, the corpse* ■ *Dir* Don Weis • *Scr* Louis M Heyward, Elwood Ullman, from a story by Louis M Heyward

Ghost in the Machine

★★★ 18

Science-fiction horror
1993 · US · Colour · 91mins

A byte-sized horror thriller from Rachel Talalay about a serial killer whose death during a freak electrical storm transforms him into a computer virus. His evil spirit then murderously stalks through Cleveland's communication networks using Karen Allen's lost address book. Engaging and fast-paced, it's a very contemporary tale, laced with inventive mayhem and cool wit, sparsely augmented by well-executed special effects. Contains swearing and violence. ▭

Karen Allen *Terry Munroe* • Chris Mulkey *Bram* • Ted Marcoux *Karl* • Wil Horneff *Josh Munroe* • Jessica Walter *Elaine* • Brandon Quintin Adams [Brandon Adams] *Frazer* • Rick Ducommun *Phil* • Nancy Fish *Karl's landlord* ■ *Dir* Rachel Talalay • *Scr* William Davis, William Osborne

Ghost in the Noonday Sun

★★ PG

Comedy adventure
1973 · UK · Colour · 88mins

The history behind the making of this film is far more interesting than the tired shambles that eventually ended up on screen. Peter Sellers's career was at a low ebb at the time and the star hoped this desperately unfunny pirate romp about hidden treasure would revive it. He was wrong – the whole sorry mess never found its way inside cinemas. Modest laughs are to be had, especially during Spike Milligan's brief appearance, but this poor man's *Treasure Island* is for Sellers completists only. ▭

Peter Sellers *Dick Scratcher* • Anthony Franciosa *Pierre* • Spike Milligan *Bombay* • Clive Revill *Bay of Algier* • Peter Boyle *Ras Mohammed* • Richard Willis *Jeremiah* • James Villiers *Parsley-Freck* ■ *Dir* Peter Medak • *Scr* Evan Jones, Spike Milligan

Ghost in the Shell ★★★★ 15

Animated science-fiction
1995 · Jap/UK · Colour · 82mins

This is a hypnotic, animated fusion of thrilling, highly cinematic action sequences and philosophical soul-searching. Dynamic use of traditional cel techniques and computer-aided artwork, a vivid *Blade Runner*-esque landscape and a curvy cyborg heroine make this even more of a visual feast than the previous *manga* benchmark *Akira*. The fluid elegance of the animation is matched by Kenji Kawai's haunting music and, although the script gets bogged down in its own artfulness, there's moody atmosphere here to match that in any Ridley Scott movie. An *anime* to convert the unconverted. Japanese dialogue dubbed into English. ▭ **DVD**

Richard George *Bateau* • Mimi Woods *Kusanagi* • William Frederick *Aramaki* • Abe Lasser *Puppet master* • Christopher Joyce *Togusa* • Mike Sorich *Ishikawa* ■ *Dir* Mamoru Oshii • *Scr* Kazunori Ito, from the graphic novel *Kokaku Kidotai* by Shirow Masamune

The Ghost of Frankenstein

★★

Horror   1942 · US · BW · 67mins

Technically and artistically second-rate, the fourth episode in Universal's *Frankenstein* series sees Bela Lugosi back for a second stint as the vengeful Ygor. His brain gets transplanted by mistake into Lon Chaney Jr's creature by Dr Frankensein's second son, Cedric Hardwicke. Sloppy sequel continuity means characters who died in the previous *Son of Frankenstein* suddenly appear without explanation. The scant running time is bolstered by scenes from the original 1931 classic. Creaky more than creepy.

Lon Chaney Jr *Monster* • Sir Cedric Hardwicke [Cedric Hardwicke] *Frankenstein* • Ralph Bellamy *Erik* • Lionel Atwill *Dr Bohmer* • Bela Lugosi *Ygor* • Evelyn Ankers *Elsa* • Janet Ann Gallow *Cloestine* • Barton Yarborough *Dr Kettering* ■ *Dir* Erle C Kenton • *Scr* Scott Darling, from the story by Eric Taylor

The Ghost of St Michael's

★★★★ U

Comedy thriller   1941 · UK · BW · 82mins

Will Hay is back before the blackboard and on the trail of Nazi spies in this spooky comedy. Hay and his class of likely lads are evacuated to a castle on the Isle of Skye, which is haunted by a ghost whose skirling bagpipes are a portent of death. While the mystery is moderately baffling, the highlights are the classroom showdowns in which Hay's academic shortcomings are gleefully exposed by brainbox Charles Hawtrey. Hay is on fine form, but the entire ensemble cast is splendid, particularly Raymond Huntley as a suspicious teacher and John Laurie as the school janitor.

Will Hay *William Lamb* • Claude Hulbert *Hilary Teasdale* • Charles Hawtrey *Percy Thorne* • Raymond Huntley *Mr Humphries* • Felix Aylmer *Dr Winter* • Elliot Mason *Mrs Wigmore* • John Laurie *Jamie* • Hay Petrie *Procurator Fiscal* • Roddy Hughes *Amberley* ■ *Dir* Marcel Varnel • *Scr* Angus Macphail, John Dighton

The Ghost Ship

★★★

Chiller   1943 · US · BW · 69mins

A successful plagiarism suit kept this film from acclaimed low-budget producer Val Lewton (*I Walked with a Zombie*) out of circulation for a long time. It proves to be a highly effective psychological thriller rather than just another horror picture. Under Mark Robson's direction, the normally heroic Richard Dix gives a powerful performance as the mentally deranged ship's captain whose crew members die in mysterious circumstances. Young third officer, Russell Wade, rumbles his secret but can't convince any of his crew mates. When Dix's behaviour goes over the edge, Wade even ends up fearing for his own life.

Richard Dix *Captain Stone* • Russell Wade *Tom Merriman* • Edith Barrett *Ellen Roberts* • Ben Bard *Bowns* • Edmund Glover *Jacob Winslow, "Sparks"* • Skelton Knaggs *Finn* • Tom Burton *Benson* • Steve Winston *Ausman* ■ *Dir* Mark Robson • *Scr* Donald Henderson Clarke, from a story by Leo Mittler

Ghost Ship

★ U

Chiller   1952 · UK · BW · 71mins

Buying a vessel that's haunted, even at a bargain price, is asking for trouble, as the young couple played by Dermot Walsh and Hazel Court find out in this waterlogged British B-feature. After they discover that the previous owner killed his spouse and her lover on board, they're on their way to laying the ship's ghost. Co-writer/director (as well as producer) Vernon Sewell, who was able to combine film-making with a love of the sea, probably had more fun than the audience. ▭

Dermot Walsh *Guy* • Hazel Court *Margaret* • Hugh Burden *Dr Fawcett* • John Robinson *Dr Martineau* • Joss Ambler *Yard manager* • Joan Carol *Mrs Martineau* • Hugh Latimer *Peter* • Mignon O'Doherty *Mrs Manley* ■ *Dir* Vernon Sewell • *Scr* Vernon Sewell, Philip Thornton

Ghost Story

★★

Horror   1974 · UK · Colour · 87mins

This is more an arty mood piece than a fully fledged horror outing by Stephen Weeks, one-time British genre hopeful and director of the equally idiosyncratic *I, Monster* and *Gawain and the Green Knight*. In England in the thirties, a trio of friends are invited to test whether an ancestral mansion is haunted or not. One of them comes under the influence of an enigmatic doll, which relays psychic images of past events, including the incarceration of an innocent woman in the local asylum. Unexceptional special effects make this an interesting failure.

Larry Dann *Talbot* • Murray Melvin *McFayden* • Vivian Mackerall *Duller* • Marianne Faithfull *Sophy* • Anthony Bate *Dr Borden* • Penelope Keith *Rennie* • Leigh Lawson *Robert* • Sally Grace *Girl* ■ *Dir* Stephen Weeks • *Scr* Rosemary Sutcliff, Stephen Weeks

Ghost Story

★★ 18

Chiller   1981 · US · Colour · 105mins

Peter Straub's bestselling novel about four old-timers haunted by supernatural reminders of a past dark secret makes for pretty slow going here. Badly adapted by *Carrie* scriptwriter Lawrence D Cohen from the convoluted book, it's more a gothic soap opera than a horror film; in fact, most of the special effects were edited out prior to release. Yet it's worth watching for the skilled performances of veterans Fred Astaire, Melvyn Douglas, John Houseman and Douglas Fairbanks Jr (even if they're all miscast) and for the gifted Alice Krige as the central spectre. Contains nudity. ▭

Fred Astaire *Ricky Hawthorne* • Melvyn Douglas *John Jaffrey* • Douglas Fairbanks Jr *Edward Wanderley* • John Houseman *Sears James* • Craig Wasson *Don/David* • Patricia Neal *Stella* • Alice Krige *Alma/Eva* ■ *Dir* John Irvin • *Scr* Lawrence D Cohen, from the novel by Peter Straub

Ghost Town

★★★ 18

Horror western   1988 · US · Colour · 81mins

"The good, the bad and the Satanic" ran the more than apt tagline for this inventive mix of western, ghost story and conventional splatter movie. Television actor Franc Luz stars as a sheriff who tracks down a missing girl to a zombie-populated town and finds himself drawn into a *High Noon*-style showdown with an evil gunslinger. Debut director Richard Governor achieves an eerie ghost town atmosphere and displays a deft talent for surreal touches, such as portraying death in the guise of a sightless card player dealing aces to doomed men, or having Luz sharpening his sheriff's badge into a Ninja death star. 🔲

Franc Luz *Langley* • Catherine Hickland *Kate* • Jimmie F Skaggs *Devilin* • Penelope Windust *Grace* • Bruce Glover *Dealer* • Zitto Kazann *Blacksmith* • Blake Conway *Harper* ■ *Dir* Richard Governor • *Scr* Duke Sandefur, from a story by David Schmoeller

The Ghost Train ★★★ U
Comedy mystery   1931 · UK · BW · 71mins

Walter Forde was clearly a big fan of this comedy chiller as, almost a decade after completing this version, he remade it as a wartime flag-waver with Arthur Askey. Based on the play by Arnold Ridley (Private Godfrey in *Dad's Army*), this story of a haunted country station may now seem short on suspense, but there are still laughs a-plenty as the husband-and-wife team of Jack Hulbert and Cicely Courtneidge take on a gang of smugglers bringing commie propaganda into England. The supporting cast is also first class.

Jack Hulbert *Teddy Deakin* • Cicely Courtneidge *Miss Bourne* • Ann Todd *Peggy Murdock* • Cyril Raymond *Richard Winthrop* • Allan Jeayes *Dr Sterling* • Donald Calthrop *Saul Hodgkin* • Angela Baddeley *Julia Price* • Henry Caine *Herbert Price* ■ *Dir* Walter Forde • *Scr* Angus Macphail, Lajos Biró, Sidney Gilliat, from the play by Arnold Ridley

The Ghost Train ★★★ U
Comedy mystery   1941 · UK · BW · 81mins

Arthur Askey and Richard Murdoch, the stars of the hit radio show *Band Waggon*, were reunited for this flag-waving remake of the classic play by Arnold Ridley (Private Godfrey in *Dad's Army*). Including the Will Hay version, *Oh, Mr Porter!*, this was the fourth reworking of the story about a haunted country station and, try as director Walter Forde might to inject some atmosphere, there's a predictability about both the proceedings and the comedy. Askey was never at his best on screen and his energetic overacting has dated badly, though Kathleen Harrison and Raymond Huntley are typically excellent. 🔲

Arthur Askey *Tommy Gander* • Richard Murdoch *Teddy Deakin* • Kathleen Harrison *Miss Bourne* • Morland Graham *Dr Sterling* • Linden Travers *Julia Price* • Peter Murray Hill *Richard Winthrop* • Carole Lynn *Jackie Winthrop* • Raymond Huntley *John Price* ■ *Dir* Walter Forde • *Scr* Marriott Edgar, Val Guest, JOC Orton, Sidney Gilliat, from the play by Arnold Ridley

Ghost Writer ★★ PG
Supernatural comedy   1989 · US · Colour · 89mins

Laughs, not chills are the order of the day in this inferior comedy mystery starring real-life sisters Audrey and July Landers. When a journalist rents a beach house for a dose of quiet relaxation, she discovers it's haunted by the ghost of a murdered starlet. Together the writer and spectral actress team up to hunt down her

killer. The plot is timid and the direction perfunctory, but it's fun seeing David Doyle, Bosley in *Charlie's Angels*, head the supporting cast. 🔲

Audrey Landers *Angela Reid* • Judy Landers *Billie Blaine* • Jeff Conaway *Tom Farrell* • Anthony Franciosa *Vincent Carbone* • David Doyle *Herb Baxter* • Joey Travolta *Bee-Jay* ■ *Dir/Scr* Kenneth J Hall

Ghostbusters ★★★★ PG
Supernatural comedy   1984 · US · Colour · 100mins

The often dazzling, special-effects-driven slapstick tends to overshadow the fact that there are some slyer, more sophisticated laughs on offer in this blockbusting family comedy. Bill Murray is terrifically deadpan and sleazy as the dubious leader of a troupe of ghostbusters (the film's writers Dan Aykroyd and Harold Ramis, plus Ernie Hudson) who are called into action when ancient spirits are let loose in New York. Sigourney Weaver shows an admirably light touch as a possessed cellist, and Rick Moranis also scores in his breakthrough movie. Director Ivan Reitman stages some spectacular set pieces, including an enjoyably daft finale with a giant marshmallow man. The concept was so successful that the film spawned a cartoon series and almost the entire team reunited for a sequel. Contains swearing. 🔲 **DVD**

Bill Murray *Dr Peter Venkman* • Dan Aykroyd *Dr Raymond Stantz* • Sigourney Weaver *Dana Barrett* • Rick Moranis *Louis Tully* • Annie Potts *Janine Melnitz* • Ernie Hudson *Winston Zeddemore* • William Atherton *Walter Peck* ■ *Dir* Ivan Reitman • *Scr* Dan Aykroyd, Harold Ramis

Ghostbusters II ★★★ PG
Supernatural comedy   1989 · US · Colour · 103mins

Having reassembled almost the entire team behind the first blockbuster, director Ivan Reitman was not prepared to mess with a successful formula. This time the self-styled ghostbusters – Bill Murray, Dan Aykroyd, Harold Ramis and Ernie Hudson – are called back into service when evil, emanating from a painting Sigourney Weaver's boss Peter MacNicol has been restoring, awakens spirits around New York. The effects are bigger and more spectacular than in the original, Murray once again shines as the shyster scientist and there is an expanded role for Rick Moranis. But Ramis and Aykroyd's script fails to sparkle and there is very little new to show for all the big-budget endeavour. Contains swearing. 🔲 **DVD**

Bill Murray *Dr Peter Venkman* • Dan Aykroyd *Dr Raymond Stantz* • Sigourney Weaver *Dana Barrett* • Harold Ramis *Dr Egon Spengler* • Rick Moranis *Louis Tully* • Ernie Hudson *Winston Zeddemore* • Annie Potts *Janine Melnitz* • Peter MacNicol *Janosz Poha* • Harris Yulin *Judge* ■ *Dir* Ivan Reitman • *Scr* Dan Aykroyd, Harold Ramis

Ghosts Can't Do It ★ 18
Erotic supernatural fantasy   1990 · US · Colour · 83mins

Execrable soft-core nonsense from director John Derek and his wife Bo. Billionaire Anthony Quinn commits suicide after a heart attack ruins his

sex life with wife Kate (Bo Derek). The ludicrous plot then sees him return in ghostly form with a plan to kill handsome Leo Damien and take over his body so they can resume their erotic odyssey. Former Catwoman Julie Newmar pops up and Donald Trump plays himself, but they can't save this indescribably bad fantasy fiasco, geared around Bo taking off her clothes, swimming naked, wearing wet T-shirts and talking inanely to thin air. The fourth film made by the Derek team, this is the worst of the lot. 🔲

Bo Derek *Kate* • Anthony Quinn *Scott* • Leo Damien *Fausto* • Don Murray *Winston* • Julie Newmar *Angel* ■ *Dir/Scr* John Derek

Ghosts from the Past ★★★ 15
Drama based on a true story   1996 · US · Colour · 125mins

Released as *Ghosts of Mississippi* in America, Rob Reiner's fact-based drama stars Alec Baldwin as Bobby DeLaughter, the lawyer attempting to bring to justice the murderer of Medgar Evers, a black civil rights leader killed on his driveway 30 years before. A white man named Byron De La Beckwith (an over-the-top James Woods) had been charged with the crime, but was released when two white juries could not unanimously find him guilty. It's a moving true story, and the cast – which also includes Whoopi Goldberg as Evers's widow and William H Macy – are all excellent. However, there is something uninvolving about Reiner's direction, which fails to make the story as compelling or passionate as it should be and instead gives it the feel of a superior TV movie. 🔲

Alec Baldwin *Bobby DeLaughter* • Whoopi Goldberg *Myrlie Evers* • James Woods *Byron De La Beckwith* • Craig T Nelson *Ed Peters* • Susanna Thompson *Peggy Lloyd* • Lucas Black *Burt DeLaughter* • Joseph Tello *Drew DeLaughter* • Alexa Vega *Claire DeLaughter* • William H Macy *Charlie Crisco* ■ *Dir* Rob Reiner • *Scr* Lewis Colick

Ghosts in the Night ★★ U
Comedy   1943 · US · BW · 64mins

Bela Lugosi's second outing with the East Side Kids was something of a comedown from his first – the more than mediocre *Spooks Run Wild*. Ignore the title, as there isn't a single ghoul occupying that old deserted house. But there are plenty of fifth columnists, operating under the fanatical eye of spymaster Lugosi. Mugging in their usual unsubtle way, Huntz Hall and Leo Gorcey are torn between nabbing the Nazis and getting Hall's sister (played by Ava Gardner, on loan to Monogram from MGM) to the church on time. Understandably, Lugosi looks thoroughly unimpressed with both the plot and his co-stars.

Leo Gorcey *Muggs McGinnis* • Huntz Hall *Glimpy Williams* • Bobby Jordan *Danny* • "Sunshine Sammy" Morrison *Scruno* • Billy Benedict *Skinny/Benny* • Stanley Clements *Stash* • Bobby Stone *Rocky/Dave* • Bill Bates *"Sleepy" Dave* • Bela Lugosi *Emil* • Ava Gardner *Betty Williams Gibson* ■ *Dir* William Beaudine • *Scr* Kenneth Higgins

Ghosts – Italian Style ★★★
Comedy   1967 · Fr/It · Colour · 92mins

Every genre went "Italian style" in the sixties and this supernatural comedy is one of the better offshoots of that craze. Sophia Loren and Vittorio Gassman are an impoverished married couple offered free accommodation in an old palace. Of course, it's haunted. Meanwhile, Loren's would-be-lover, Mario Adorf, has also moved into the palace and much amusement ensues when Gassman mistakes him for a ghost. With Sophia looking stunning and loads of ectoplasmic energy emanating from the spiritual spoofing of social mores and Italian customs, Renato Castellani's romp scores much laughter from the hereafter. An Italian language film.

Sophia Loren *Maria* • Vittorio Gassman *Pasquale* • Mario Adorf *Alfredo* • Aldo Giuffre *Raffaele* • Margaret Lee *Sayonara* • Francesco Tensi *Professor Santanna* • Marcello Mastroianni *Headless ghost* ■ *Dir* Renato Castellani • *Scr* Renato Castellani, Adriano Baracco, Leo Benvenuti, Piero De Bernardi, Ernest Pintoff, from the play *Questi Fantasmi!* by Eduardo De Filippo

The Ghosts of Berkeley Square ★★★
Comedy   1947 · UK · BW · 100mins

This amiable adaptation of SJ Simon and Caryl Brahms's novel *No Nightingales* will delight film buffs and casual viewers alike. Robert Morley and Felix Aylmer are wonderfully mischievous as the bungling 18th-century assassins who are cursed to haunt a luxurious town house until it is visited by a reigning monarch. Amusing interludes along the way include Ernest Thesiger's attempt to prove they're a hoax and the ghosts being mistaken for First World War spies. It's not only a fine excuse for a galaxy of guest stars, but also a spirited flight of fancy that takes several sly swipes at the British cinema of the period.

Robert Morley *General Burlap* • Felix Aylmer *Colonel Kelsoe* • Yvonne Arnaud *Millie* • Robert Beaumont *King's equerry* • Madge Brindley *Matron* • Strelsa Brown *Rajah's Amazon attendant* • Harry Fine *1914 Colonel* • Ronald Frankau *Tex* • Ernest Thesiger *Investigator* ■ *Dir* Vernon Sewell • *Scr* James Seymour, from the novel *No Nightingales* by Caryl Brahms, SJ Simon

Ghosts...of the Civil Dead ★★★★ 18
Prison drama   1988 · Ausl · Colour · 92mins

Prison pictures don't come much tougher than this. Directed with reckless visual energy by one-time pop promo producer John Hillcoat, this drama casts an unflinching eye over the brutalities perpetrated by the staff of a state-of-the-art, maximum security prison, packed to the rafters with violent offenders. Everything from drugs and starvation to rape and self-mutilation is charted as the film, through a series of flashbacks, reveals the motives for an explosive riot that rips through the high-tech defences. Shot with a ruthless power, made all the more chilling by the relentlessly raw realism, this is a remarkable debut that is not for the faint-hearted. Contains violence and swearing. 🔲

U = SUITABLE FOR ALL   Ue = SUITABLE FOR ALL, ESPECIALLY FOR YOUNG CHILDREN (VIDEO ONLY)   PG = PARENTAL GUIDANCE

Dave Field *Wenzil* • Mike Bishop *David Yale* • Chris De Rose *Jack Grezner* • Nick Cave *Maynard* • Freddo Dierck *Robbins* • Vincent Gil *Ruben* • Bogdan Koca *Waychek* • Kevin Mackey *Glover* • Dave Mason *Lilly* ■ *Dir* John Hillcoat • *Scr* Nick Cave, Gene Conkie, Evan English, John Hillcoat, Hugo Race, John Flaus

The Ghoul ★★★★ PG

Horror   1933 · UK · BW · 69mins

Following his enormous success in the US, Boris Karloff returned home to England for this highly successful clone of *The Mummy*. Under eerily effective make-up, he's a cataleptic Egyptologist rising from the dead to recover a stolen talisman. Hugely atmospheric, if slow by today's standards, it has a macabre mood that eventually gives way to sinister slapstick; yet Karloff's commanding presence elevates it to the level of seminal British *Grand Guignol*. It also marks Ralph Richardson's first screen appearance, as a fake priest.

Boris Karloff *Professor Morlant* • Cedric Hardwicke *Broughton* • Ernest Thesiger *Laing* • Dorothy Hyson *Betty Harlow* • Anthony Bushell *Ralph Morlant* • Kathleen Harrison *Kaney* • Harold Huth *Aga Ben Dragore* • DA Clarke-Smith *Mahmoud* • Ralph Richardson *Nigel Hartley* ■ *Dir* T Hayes Hunter • *Scr* Roland Pertwee, John Hastings Turner, Rupert Downing, L du Garde Peach, from the novel and play by Dr Frank King, Leonard J Hines

The Ghoul ★★ 18

Horror   1975 · UK · Colour · 89mins

Shot on sets left over from *The Great Gatsby*, Freddie Francis's flapper frightfest (produced by his son Kevin) eschews gore in favour of more traditional terror. The unsavoury tale has defrocked minister Peter Cushing trying to keep his cannibal son locked in the attic. Then Hammer scream queen Veronica Carlson's car breaks down on the foggy moors and... you don't need to be a horror buff to guess the rest. A nice feeling for the twenties period atmosphere and a crazed performance from John Hurt give this fractured flick a few extra kicks.

Peter Cushing *Dr Lawrence* • John Hurt *Tom Rawlings* • Alexandra Bastedo *Angela* • Gwen Watford *Ayah* • Veronica Carlson *Daphne* • Stewart Bevan *Billy* • Ian McCulloch *Geoffrey* • Don Henderson *The Ghoul* ■ *Dir* Freddie Francis • *Scr* John Elder [Anthony Hinds]

Ghoulies ★★ 15

Comedy horror   1985 · US · Colour · 77mins

A tacky imitation of *Gremlins* from executive producer Charles Band, the self-styled B-movie king of eighties schlock and cheap straight-to-video horror. Under the spell of his satanist father, Peter Liapis invokes a black magic ritual in the family mansion and conjures up midget demons from another dimension which go on a teen-killing spree. The self-mocking tone and grisly gore may be emblematic of the sleaze-and-slash eighties but the ghoulies themselves – when they finally appear – look like a throwback to the rubber puppet monsters of the fifties. Low-grade trash with a cult cast, this features singer Michael Des Barres and David Lynch regular Jack Nance (*Eraserhead*).

Peter Liapis *Jonathan Graves* • Lisa Pelikan *Rebecca* • Michael Des Barres *Malcolm*

Graves • Jack Nance *Wolfgang* • Peter Risch *Grizzel* • Tamara De Treaux *Greedigut* • Scott Thomson *Mike* ■ *Dir* Luca Bercovici • *Scr* Luca Bercovici, Jefery Levy

Ghoulies II ★ 15

Comedy horror   1987 · US · Colour · 86mins

More witless mayhem, as the salivating little devils from *Ghoulies* join a travelling carnival show and murder anyone stupid enough to pay to see them in a sideshow attraction. The hand-puppet special effects look even cheesier this time round and, although it's more innocuous than the original, director Albert Band's weak sequel is a dully paced, poorly plotted morality tale, and is peopled by a decidedly uncharismatic cast.

Damon Martin *Larry* • Royal Dano *Uncle Ned* • Phil Fondacaro *Sir Nigel* • J Downing *P Hardin* • Kerry Remsen *Nicole* • Dale Wyatt *Dixie* ■ *Dir* Albert Band • *Scr* Dennis Paoli, from a story by Charlie Dolan

Ghoulies III: Ghoulies Go to College ★ 15

Comedy horror   1990 · US · Colour · 90mins

The razor-toothed Gremlin clones go to Glazier College to indulge their playfully murderous habits in this *Animal House*-style second sequel. When Professor Ragnar (Kevin McCarthy) uses a comic-book spell to summon up three demons, the rubber imps emerge from the toilet to play low-brow fraternity pranks involving topless girls in *Pscho* shower routines, underwear raids, a dash of sadomasochism and plenty of lavatorial humour. Influenced more *Porky's* than anything else, this atrocious horror comedy sinks the already lame series to a new low.

Kevin McCarthy *Professor Ragnar* • Evan MacKenzie *Skip Carter* • Patrick Labyorteaux *Mookey* • Marcia Wallace *Miss Boggs* • Griffin O'Neal *Blane* ■ *Dir* John Carl Buechler • *Scr* Brent Olson, from the characters created by Luca Bercovici, Jefery Levy

Ghoulies IV ★ 15

Comedy horror   1994 · US · Colour · 80mins

Peter Liapis returns as Jonathan Graves, the would-be wizard who first conjured up the little demons in the original *Ghoulies* movie. This finds him in slightly more conventional mode as a Los Angeles detective, with ex-girlfriend Stacie Randall now a satanist who's busy sacrificing victims to her demon god. Only two ghoulies are thankfully on show in this nonsensical sequel and they are played by masked dwarf actors, not the usual plastic-looking puppets. Instead, the special effects quotient is replaced by soft-core erotica with loads of scantily clad girls. Some may consider this an overall improvement on the juvenile japes of the series thus far.

Peter Liapis *Jonathan Graves* • Barbara Alyn Woods *Kate* • Stacie Randall *Alexandra* ■ *Dir* Jim Wynorski • *Scr* Mark Sevi

Ghunghat ★★★

Musical drama   1996 · Pak · Colour

In this typically convoluted musical drama from Pakistan, former international cricketer Mohsin Khan stars as a married man desperately trying to shrug off the unwanted

attentions of an overzealous admirer. Andaleeb, in her film debut, gives a spirited performance – despite having both her singing and dialogue dubbed – as Khan's young wife, embittered by her battle to preserve her honour. However, it's the experienced Shan, as the psychopathic cousin stalking Andaleeb, and the striking Saima, as a tantalising temptress, who make the biggest impression. In Urdu with English subtitles.

Mohsin Khan • Andaleeb • Shan • Saima • Arbaaz Khan • Reshan ■ *Dir* Syed Noor

Gia ★★★

Biographical drama
1998 · US · Colour · 117mins

Oscar-winner Angelina Jolie (*Girl, Interrupted*) gives an early knockout performance in this dark and provocative TV movie. She stars as Gia Carangi, whose rise to fame as a supermodel in the seventies brought tragedy as she became addicted to pills, cocaine and heroin. With its almost soft-core porn style, this is more an arthouse film then standard TV-movie fare. Strong performances by Mercedes Ruehl as Gia's mother and Faye Dunaway as her agent give it a powerful punch. Whatever your reservations about the subject matter, *Gia* deserves a look, if only for the multifaceted performance of Jolie. Contains sex scenes and drug abuse.

Angelina Jolie *Gia Carangi* • Elizabeth Mitchell *Linda* • Mercedes Ruehl *Kathleen Carangi* • Faye Dunaway *Wilhemina Cooper* • Kylie Travis *Stephanie* ■ *Dir* Michael Cristofer • *Scr* Michael Cristofer, Jay McInerney

Giant ★★★★ PG

Epic drama   1956 · US · Colour · 192mins

James Dean's last film before his fatal car crash reveals him more as an icon for the time than an actor. He just doesn't convince as the middle-aged Jett Rink in the final half of this drama based on Edna Ferber's homage to Texas. But director George Stevens, who won an Oscar for the film, manages to compress some of the swashbuckling magic of oil barons and land exploitation into the three hours-plus running time. A lustrous Elizabeth Taylor plays the object of Dean's unrequited passion – unfortunately for him, she's married to manly Rock Hudson. Those elements and a tremendous scene in which Dean strikes oil make it an adventure of epic proportions.

Elizabeth Taylor *Leslie Benedict* • Rock Hudson *Bick Benedict* • James Dean *Jett Rink* • Mercedes McCambridge *Luz Benedict* • Carroll Baker *Luz Benedict II* • Dennis Hopper *Jordan Benedict III* • Sal Mineo *Angel Obregon III* • Jane Withers *Vashti Snythe* • Chill Wills *Uncle Rawley* ■ *Dir* George Stevens • *Scr* Fred Guiol, Ivan Moffat, from the novel by Edna Ferber

The Giant Behemoth ★★★

Science-fiction   1959 · UK · BW · 71mins

Director Eugène Lourié cannibalised his own *The Beast from 20,000 Fathoms* and added sterling special effects by *King Kong* creator Willis O'Brien for another classic fifties giant-monster-on-the-loose fantasy. This time a prehistoric dinosaur is revived by an

atomic explosion and travels to London to wreak radioactive havoc. Gene Evans saves the city by shooting the creature down with a radium-filled torpedo – but not before London Bridge is destroyed in the exciting climax. Lourié builds suspense and mood through evocative lighting and excellent use of O'Brien's stop-motion puppet. The director recycled the same story again for *Gorgo*.

Gene Evans *Steve Karnes* • André Morell *Professor James Bickford* • John Turner *Ian Duncan* • Leigh Madison *Jeanie MacDougall* • Jack MacGowran *Dr Sampson* • Maurice Kaufmann *Submarine officer* • Henry Vidon *Tom* • Leonard Sachs *Scientist* ■ *Dir* Eugène Lourié, Douglas Hickox • *Scr* Eugène Lourié, Daniel James (uncredited), from a story by Robert Abel, Allen Adler

The Giant Gila Monster ★★

Science-fiction horror
1959 · US · BW · 74mins

A badly rear-projected giant lizard stomps through model Texan towns and terrorises the local teens, who always seem to be having hot-rod races or rock 'n' roll dance hall parties. The creature is eventually beaten by one brave lad who drives a hot rod packed with explosives into the beast's belly. Unintentionally amusing rather than scary, this is directed by Ray Kellogg, who also made the hilarious *The Killer Shrews*.

Don Sullivan *Chace Winstead* • Lisa Simone *Lisa* • Shug Fisher *Mr Harris* • Jerry Cortwright *Bob* • Beverly Thurman *Gay* • Don Flournoy *Gordy* • Clarke Browne *Chuck* • Pat Simmons *Sherry* ■ *Dir* Ray Kellogg • *Scr* Jay Sims, Ray Kellogg, from a story by Ray Kellogg

The Giant of Marathon ★★ U

Historical adventure
1960 · It · Colour · 90mins

Former Mr Universe Steve Reeves was one of the pillars of the Italian sword-and-sandal cycle, at its height in the late fifties. Rippling like an incoming tide, he abandons the role of Hercules (for which he was most famous) to squeeze his bronzed torso into the role of the Athenian warrior Philippides, who warns his fellow Greeks of a Persian invasion. It's not the worst of its kind by a long chalk, but it's sad to see B-movie maestro Jacques Tourneur, who directed such cult classics as *Cat People* and *Night of the Demon*, reduced to muscle-bound mediocrity like this.

Steve Reeves *Philippides* • Mylene Demongeot *Andromeda* • Daniela Rocca *Karis* • Ivo Garrani *Creuso* • Philippe Hersent *Callimaco* • Sergio Fantoni *Teocrito* • Alberto Lupo *Milziade* • Daniele Varga *Dario, King of the Persians* ■ *Dir* Jacques Tourneur • *Scr* Ennio De Concini, Augusto Frassinetti, Bruno Vailati, from an idea by Raffaello Pacini, Alberto Barsanti

The Giant Spider Invasion ★

Science-fiction horror
1975 · US · Colour · 75mins

A rash of outsize spider sightings are traced to Wisconsin, but greedy farmer Robert Easton, thinking the radioactive spiders' eggs from another dimension are jewels, won't let the authorities investigate until it's too late. This shoddily-made trash from schlock maestro Bill Rebane has bottom-of-the-barrel special effects, including a Volkswagen in hairy drag masquerading as the largest spider of all. It is irredeemable dreck, with the star cast wasted in pointless roles.

Barbara Hale *Dr Jenny Langer* • Steve Brodie *Dr Vance* • Leslie Parrish *Ev Kester* • Alan Hale Jr *Sheriff* • Robert Easton *Kester* • Kevin Brodie *Dave Perkins* • Christiane Schmidtmer *Helga* ■ *Dir* Bill Rebane, Richard L Huff • *Scr* Richard L Huff, Robert Easton

Gideon's Day ★★★★
Crime drama   1959 · UK · Colour · 90mins

A real original. This crime drama was based on a novel by John Creasey (writing as JJ Marric) and shot in England by western maestro John Ford. Shown in America as *Gideon of Scotland Yard*, this cynical romp is extremely entertaining and contains a marvellous performance from Jack Hawkins as the Gideon of the title, who is followed by the camera on what must be the busiest day of his life. Hawkins was the only British actor to star for the three greatest American directors of their day: William Wyler in *Ben-Hur*, Howard Hawks in *Land of the Pharaohs* and Ford here. ▭

Jack Hawkins *Inspector George Gideon* • Dianne Foster *Joanna Delafield* • Anna Lee *Kate Gideon* • Anna Massey *Sally Gideon* • Andrew Ray *PC Simon Farnaby-Green* • Cyril Cusack *Herbert "Birdy" Sparrow* • James Hayter *Mason* • Ronald Howard *Paul Delafield* ■ *Dir* John Ford • *Scr* TEB Clarke, from the novel by JJ Marric [John Creasey]

Gideon's Trumpet ★★★★ U
Courtroom drama based on a true story
1980 · US · Colour · 103mins

Henry Fonda is marvellous in this TV movie based on a true-life court case that enshrined the principle of free representation in American legal history. Although not the obvious choice to play a semi-literate convict, Fonda manages to bring off the characterisation with a bravado that is both winning and warm. In short, this is great acting. Also remarkably effective is José Ferrer as Fonda's lawyer Abe Fortas. John Houseman, who also executive produced, heads up a distinguished supporting cast that includes Dean Jagger and Fay Wray. In a much-maligned genre, this is an example of the TV movie at its best, tackling a subject that cinema might regard as uncommercial. ▭

Henry Fonda *Clarence Earl Gideon* • José Ferrer *Abe Fortas* • John Houseman *Chief Justice* • Fay Wray *Edna Curtis* • Sam Jaffe *1st Justice* • Dean Jagger *6th Justice* • Nicholas Pryor *Jacob* • William Prince *5th Justice* ■ *Dir* Robert Collins • *Scr* David W Rintels, from a story by Anthony Lewis

Gidget ★★★★ U
Romantic comedy
1959 · US · Colour · 95mins

A perfect period artefact, this quintessential California surf movie is actually much, much better than it should be – or was ever given credit for – largely thanks to the stylish (and wise) direction by Paul Wendkos. Sandra Dee is the titular heroine who's half-girl, half-midget. She became identified with the role, even though she didn't reprise it in the two sequels

or in the two completely different TV series. Her beaus are James Darren and Cliff Robertson, and there is a very real sense of enjoyment abroad when all three are together. The beach looks fabulous in CinemaScope and Eastmancolor and, if you let your hair down, you'll enjoy the period slang and good-time atmosphere.

Sandra Dee *Francie* • James Darren *Moondoggie* • Cliff Robertson *Kahoona* • Arthur O'Connell *Russell Lawrence* • Mary LaRoche *Dorothy Lawrence* • Joby Baker *Stinky* • Tom Laughlin *Lover Boy* ■ *Dir* Paul Wendkos • *Scr* Gabrielle Upton, from the novel by Frederick Kohner

Gidget Goes Hawaiian ★★
Romantic comedy
1961 · US · Colour · 101mins

There's a different Gidget (Deborah Walley had taken over from Sandra Dee), but otherwise things are much the same in this sequel to the surprise hit surf movie. Gidget and Jeff (nicknamed Moondoggie) split up after a misunderstanding and Gidget flies off with her parents to Hawaii, where she finds herself pursued by a number of boys and becomes a victim of gossip. Moondoggie turns up, and the rest is a tangle of rivalry, teenage jealousy and endless shots of surfing.

James Darren *Jeff* • Michael Callan *Eddie Horner* • Deborah Walley *Gidget* • Carl Reiner *Russ Lawrence* • Peggy Cass *Mitzie Stewart* • Eddie Foy Jr *Monty Stewart* • Vicki Trickett *Abby Stewart* ■ *Dir* Paul Wendkos • *Scr* Ruth Brooks Flippen, from the characters created by Frederick Kohner

Gidget Goes to Rome ★★ U
Romantic comedy
1963 · US · Colour · 103mins

Third film, third Gidget. This time Cindy Carol stars as the "girl midget", although continuity is assured by the reappearance of James Darren as boyfriend Jeff. Here the couple travel to Rome where their relationship is tested by the attentions of two locals – Paolo (Cesare Danova) and Daniela (Danielle de Metz). The *Gidget* series spawned a mini-industry, with TV movies and two series keeping the diminutive heroine on the small screen until the end of the eighties.

Cindy Carol *Gidget* • James Darren *Jeff* • Jessie Royce Landis *Aunt Albertina* • Cesare Danova *Paolo Cellini* • Danielle de Metz *Daniela Serrini* • Joby Baker *Judge* • Trudi Ames *Libby* ■ *Dir* Paul Wendkos • *Scr* Ruth Brooks Flippen, Katherine Eunson, Dale Eunson, from the characters created by Frederick Kohner

A Gift for Heidi ★★★
Adventure   1958 · US · Colour

It may be impossible to film Johanna Spyri's much-loved novel without lashings of sentimentality, but never has the little Alpine orphan found herself so immersed in sticky sweetness as in this glutinous fable. The gift in question is a set of carved wooden figures depicting Faith, Hope and Charity, the true meaning of which she comes to learn in the course of three tacky tales. Sandy Descher is just about bearable in the lead, but the most interesting piece of casting is Douglas Fowley as her white-bearded uncle. He's barely recognisable as the

actor who played the hysterical director in *Singin' in the Rain*.

Sandy Descher *Heidi* • Douglas Fowley *Alm Uncle* • Van Dyke Parks *Peter* • Peter Capell *Doc* • Erik Jelde *Ernst* • Susan Sainio *Clara* • Oswald Ursteins *Carlo* • Clancy Cooper *Dr Roth* ■ *Dir* George Templeton • *Scr* Eugene Vale, David Dortort, from the characters created by Johanna Spyri

The Gift Horse ★★ U
Second World War drama
1952 · UK · BW · 101mins

Packed with stock situations, this unremarkable naval drama starts in 1940 on the broken-down tub presented to gung-ho captain Trevor Howard as part of a 50-destroyer loan made to Britain by neutral America. The inevitable hostility that flares between Howard and his men, the Admiralty inquiry into negligence and the ramming raid on a Nazi dockyard in France are all staged with efficiency by director Compton Bennett. But the action lacks urgency, Howard looks bored by the proceedings and crew members Richard Attenborough, Hugh Williams and Bernard Lee have nothing new to show us. ▭

Trevor Howard *Lieutenant Commander Hugh Fraser* • Richard Attenborough *Dripper Daniels* • Sonny Tufts *Yank Flanagan* • James Donald *Lieutenant Richard Jennings* • Joan Rice *June Mallory* • Bernard Lee *Stripey Wood* • Dora Bryan *Glad* • Hugh Williams *Captain* ■ *Dir* Compton Bennett • *Scr* William Fairchild, William Rose, Hugh Hastings, from a story by Ivan Goff, Ben Roberts

The Gift of Love ★ U
Drama   1958 · US · Colour · 105mins

In 1946, Fox had a big hit with the very mushy *Sentimental Journey*, which worked because of the sincerity of Maureen O'Hara and the adroit direction of Walter Lang. This time round it's Lauren Bacall playing the dying wife who adopts a little girl to provide consolation for her husband after she's gone. Garish colour, the miscasting of Bacall and the crude direction of Jean Negulesco result in insufferable schmaltz. Robert Stack and Evelyn Rudie co-star.

Lauren Bacall *Julie Beck* • Robert Stack *Bill Beck* • Evelyn Rudie *Hitty* • Lorne Greene *Grant Allan* • Anne Seymour *McMasters* • Edward Platt *Dr Miller* • Joseph Kearns *Mr Rynicker* ■ *Dir* Jean Negulesco • *Scr* Luther Davis, from a story by Nelia Gardner White

The Gift of Love ★★
Drama   1994 · US · Colour

There are many films that ask you to suspend your disbelief, but surely none has made a more outrageous demand on your intelligence than this unashamedly manipulative TV movie. At the centre of the mawkish melodrama is a grieving mother whose dead son's heart is used in the transplant that saves her father's life. As if that isn't contrived enough, there's also a young runaway who makes Pollyanna look like a quitter. Andy Griffith and Blair Brown call on all their know-how to give more effective performances than this slush deserves. Director Paul Bogart can do – and should know – better.

Andy Griffith *Phil Doucet* • Blair Brown *Helen* • Will Friedle *Luke* • Olivia Burnette *Louise* • Penny Fuller *Leora* • Joyce Van Patten *Erika Magnussen* • Richard Herd *Charlie Magnussen* • Daniel Von Bargen *Mr Brady* ■ *Dir* Paul Bogart • *Scr* Robert W Lenski, from the novel *Set for Life* by Judith Freeman

The Gig ★★★ 15
Comedy drama   1985 · US · Colour · 87mins

This wistfully funny jazz movie, never released in Britain, has one of TV's *MASH* stars, Wayne Rogers, as a New York car dealer. He's been playing jazz trombone with a bunch of friends for years and books them into a swanky resort in the Catskill Mountains, the sort of place that usually hosts Jewish stand-ups and tea dances. Personally financed by its director, Frank D Gilroy, the film has a pleasingly sardonic edge, a tremendous sense of place and winning performances from Rogers, Cleavon Little (the belligerent black bass player), Andrew Duncan (piano), Jerry Matz (clarinet) and Daniel Nalbach (he drums by night, drills teeth by day). ▭

Wayne Rogers *Marty Flynn* • Cleavon Little *Marshall Wilson* • Andrew Duncan *Jack Larmon* • Daniel Nalbach *Arthur Winslow* • Jerry Matz *Aaron Wohl* • Warren Vache *Gil Macrae* • Joe Silver *Abe Mitgang* • Jay Thomas *Rick Valentine* • Stan Lachow *George* ■ *Dir/Scr* Frank D Gilroy

Gigi ★★★★★ PG
Musical   1958 · US · Colour · 119mins

Rightful winner of nine Academy Awards (including best picture), this is the last great musical from genius producer Arthur Freed (*Singin' in the Rain*). He coerced composers Lerner and Loewe into creating a screen original from Colette's tale following their sensational stage success with *My Fair Lady*. It's superbly cast – with Leslie Caron in the title role, Maurice Chevalier, who won a special Oscar, and Louis Jourdan – and immaculately designed for CinemaScope in Art Nouveau by Cecil Beaton. Impeccably directed by Vincente Minnelli, this is a sophisticated and entertaining musical treat. The story, about the training of a young girl to become a courtesan, is hardly the usual basis for a screen song-fest, but it's brilliantly and intelligently handled, with arguably the best sequences (Gaston's soliloquy, *I Remember It Well*) directed by the uncredited Charles Walters, who had previously guided Caron in *Lili*. ▭

Leslie Caron *Gigi* • Maurice Chevalier *Honore Lachaille* • Louis Jourdan *Gaston Lachaille* • Hermione Gingold *Mme Alvarez* • Eva Gabor *Liane D'Exelmans* • Jacques Bergerac *Sandomir* • Isabel Jeans *Aunt Alicia* • John Abbott *Manuel* ■ *Dir* Vincente Minnelli • *Scr* Alan Jay Lerner, from the play by Anita Loos, from the novel by Colette • *Cinematographer* Joseph Ruttenberg • *Editor* Adrienne Fazan • *Art Director* William A Horning, Preston Ames • *Costume Designer* Cecil Beaton • *Music/Lyrics* Frederick Loewe • *Lyrics* Alan Jay Lerner • *Music Director* Andre Previn

Gigot ★★★ U
Comedy drama   1962 · US · Colour · 104mins

Much abused when it first appeared, this charming latter-day fairy tale is a lasting testament to that great American love affair with Paris. Director

U = SUITABLE FOR ALL   Uc = SUITABLE FOR ALL, ESPECIALLY FOR YOUNG CHILDREN (VIDEO ONLY)   PG = PARENTAL GUIDANCE

Gene Kelly embraces the inherent sentimentality in the touching tale of a Parisian mute and, aided by a magnificent performance in the title role by former TV star Jackie Gleason, achieves an almost Chaplinesque work of great poignancy. Understandably, and unfortunately, the film was re-edited by 20th Century-Fox when they realised what Kelly had delivered, and Kelly and Gleason always claimed that the original cut (no longer in existence) was far better than the one that survives. Not for all tastes, certainly, but interesting nonetheless.

Jackie Gleason *Gigot* • Katherine Kath *Colette* • Gabrielle Dorziat *Madame Brigitte* • Jean Lefebvre *Gaston* • Jacques Marin *Jean* • Albert Remy *Alphonse* • Yvonne Constant *Lucille Duval* • Germaine Delbat *Madame Greuze* ■ *Dir* Gene Kelly • *Scr* John Patrick, from a story by Jackie Gleason

Gilda ★★★★★ PG
Classic film noir   1946 · US · BW · 104mins

"There never was a woman like Gilda!" shrieked the original poster (designed by James Bond title wizard Maurice Binder). And there never was anyone to capture the imagination like Rita Hayworth, whose first appearance in this movie is a classic star introduction. Highlights include her striptease (well, she takes off a glove!) to *Put the Blame on Mame* and her voluptuous vamping of callow Glenn Ford, whose perverse relationship with his former boss and Gilda's husband George Macready seems to circumvent the censors by a mile. Columbia's low-lit studio-bound Buenos Aires setting is quintessential forties *film noir*, and the whole is a remarkable example of the Hollywood system turning dross into pure gold. ▭ DVD

Rita Hayworth *Gilda* • Glenn Ford *Johnny Farrell* • George Macready *Ballin Mundson* • Joseph Calleia *Obregon* • Steven Geray *Uncle Pio* • Joseph Sawyer *[Joe Sawyer] Casey* • Gerald Mohr *Captain Delgado* ■ *Dir* Charles Vidor • *Scr* Marion Parsonnet, Jo Eisinger, from a story by EA Ellington

The Gilded Cage ★★
Thriller   1954 · UK · BW · 78mins

After a string of supporting roles for Universal in the early fifties, Alex Nicol earned a dubious promotion to leading man in this British thriller. It was also something of a comedown for Clifford Evans who, before war service intervened, seemed destined for great things after his performances in films such as *Love on the Dole*. Director John Gilling tries to push this tale of art theft and murder along at a decent pace, but spotting who framed Nichol's brother is hardly taxing.

Alex Nicol *Steve Anderson* • Veronica Hurst *Marcia Farrell* • Clifford Evans *Ken Aimes* • Ursula Howells *Brenda Lucas* • Elwyn Brook-Jones *Bruno* • John Stuart *Harding* • Michael Alexander *Harry Anderson* • Trevor Reid *Inspector Brace* ■ *Dir* John Gilling • *Scr* Brock Williams, from a story by Paul Erickson

The Gilded Lily ★★★
Comedy   1935 · US · BW · 82mins

This frothy Paramount comedy rode in on the back of the phenomenal success of Columbia's *It Happened One Night*. Critics and public alike were quick to make the connection with this

new vehicle for Claudette Colbert. She's delightful as a New York secretary having to make up her mind between two suitors: a charming, wealthy but caddish English aristocrat (Ray Milland) and a standard-issue American newspaper reporter (Fred MacMurray). Deftly directed by one-time Keystone Cop Wesley Ruggles, the movie launched MacMurray to stardom, while raising the British Milland's Hollywood profile.

Claudette Colbert *Lillian David* • Fred MacMurray *Peter Dawes* • Ray Milland *Charles Gray/Granville* • C Aubrey Smith *Lloyd Granville* • Eddie Craven *Eddie* • Luis Alberni *Nate* • Donald Meek *Hankerson* ■ *Dir* Wesley Ruggles • *Scr* Claude Binyon, from a story by Melville Baker, Jack Kirkland

Gimme Shelter ★★★★ 15
Music documentary   1970 · US · Colour · 91mins

Rightly considered to be more of a sixties watershed than Woodstock, the free concert given by the Rolling Stones at the Altamount Speedway in northern California will always be remembered for revealing the flip side of the decade of love and peace. The murder of a black spectator by a Hell's Angels bouncer during *Under My Thumb* and the violence that followed pervades this documentary, most memorably in the scene in which Mick Jagger and Charlie Watts view the incident on an editing machine. But there is also some mesmerising footage of the Stones, Jefferson Airplane and the Flying Burrito Brothers, and a slyly mocking portrait of showbiz lawyer Melvin Belli. ▭

Dir David Maysles, Albert Maysles, Charlotte Zwerin

Ginger & Fred ★★★★★ PG
Satirical comedy   1986 · It/Fr/W Ger · Colour · 122mins

Ginger Rogers tried to sue the production company behind this masterpiece from the great Italian director Federico Fellini – a move that now seems astonishingly myopic. The film itself pays tribute to Ginger; it also meditates on urban decay (exemplified by television's down-market values) while affirming the warmth of past love. Marcello Mastroianni and Giulietta Massina (Fellini's wife) play two elderly dancers who, having discreetly modelled themselves on Astaire and Rogers, are brought out of retirement for a TV show. Fellini's attack on tacky telly is as comic as it is wounding, but Mastroianni and Massina show that human emotion can win the day. In Italian with English subtitles. ▭

Giulietta Masina *Amelia Bonetti, "Ginger"* • Marcello Mastroianni *Pippo Botticella, "Fred"* • Franco Fabrizi *Show host* • Frederick von Ledenburg *Admiral* • Augusto Poderosi *Transvestite* • Martin Maria Blau *Assistant producer* • Jacques Henri Lartigue *Flying priest* ■ *Dir* Federico Fellini • *Scr* Federico Fellini, Tonino Guerra, Tullio Pinelli

Ginger in the Morning ★★ PG
Road movie romance   1973 · US · Colour · 90mins

A young Sissy Spacek plays the titular Ginger – a gangly, free-spirited teenage hitchhiker who gets a ride from lonely

travelling salesman Joe (Monte Markham). This road movie slides effortlessly into a romance, as the unlikely mutual attraction between the conservative Joe and the wild child Ginger grows apace. However, although the landscape is lovely, the action is minimal. Soon after, Spacek made *Badlands*, which made her a star – something this film failed to do. ▭

Monte Markham *Joe* • Sissy Spacek *Ginger* • Slim Pickens *Sheriff* • Mark Miller *Charlie* • Susan Oliver *Sugar* ■ *Dir* Gordon Wiles

The Gingerbread Man ★★★ 15
Crime thriller   1997 · US · Colour · 109mins

Robert Altman forsakes the scatter-shot storytelling technique of *Nashville* and *The Player* for a more conventional form of movie-making with this adaptation of a John Grisham story set in Savannah, Georgia. Kenneth Branagh brings a touch of Shakespearean bravado to the role of successful lawyer Rick Magruder, who becomes involved with a waitress (Embeth Davidtz) when she accuses her religiously eccentric father (Robert Duvall) of pursuing her. Soon Branagh feels compelled to kidnap his own children to save them from danger, while the menacing atmosphere grows along with the threat of impending floods. Altman's dictum that "film-making is playing jazz" makes *The Gingerbread Man* one of the better Grisham adaptations. Contains some swearing. ▭ DVD

Kenneth Branagh *Rick Magruder* • Embeth Davidtz *Mallory Doss* • Robert Downey Jr *Clyde Pell* • Daryl Hannah *Lois Harlan* • Robert Duvall *Dixon Doss* • Tom Berenger *Pete Randle* • Famke Janssen *Leeanne* • Clyde Hayes *Carl Alden* ■ *Dir* Robert Altman • *Scr* Al Hayes, from a story by John Grisham

The Girl ★★★ 18
Erotic thriller   1986 · Swe/UK · Colour · 103mins

The seduction of a leading lawyer by a 14-year-old schoolgirl is the focus of this soft-core slice of Euro erotica. Seduction leads to lust, passion and murder, though not necessarily in that order. Starring Franco Nero and Bernice Stegers, with Christopher Lee in a small supporting role, the film starts strongly in a *Lolita* vein, but the slackening pace of the second half leads it to become more of a Loll-ita. Oodles of sex and nudity, though, for those who like that sort of thing. ▭

Clare Powney *Pat, the girl* • Franco Nero *John Berg* • Bernice Stegers *Eva Berg* • Frank Brennan *Lindberg, reporter* • Mark Robinson *Hans, cab driver* • Clifford Rose *General Carlsson* • Rosie Jauckens *Mrs Carlsson* • Christopher Lee *Peter Storm* ■ *Dir* Arne Mattsson • *Scr* Ernest Hotch

Girl ★★★ 15
Comedy drama   1998 · US · Colour · 99mins

After a very promising comic start, in which the camera tracks down a suburban American street showing every garage full of aspiring but terrible teen rock bands, this quickly disintegrates and enters predictable territory. Dominique Swain (who played Lolita opposite Jeremy Irons) stars as a high school girl on the verge of

adulthood, who's only capable of reaching it after she sees her teenage dream for what it is. This journey involves her swooning and sleeping with ultra-cool, egocentric rock god Sean Patrick Flanery and then working through her disillusionment when she realises he's a selfish pig. Very much a debut feature from director Jonathan Kahn, this offers nothing that's original. Contains swearing.

Dominique Swain *Andrea Marr* • Sean Patrick Flanery *Todd Sparrow* • Summer Phoenix *Rebecca Farnhurst* • Tara Reid *Cybil* • Selma Blair *Darcy* • Channon Roe *Kevin* • Portia Di Rossi *Carla* • Rosemary Forsyth *Mother* ■ *Dir* Jonathan Kahn • *Scr* David E Tolchinsky, from the novel by Blake Nelson

A Girl Called Rosemarie ★★
Drama based on a true story   1996 · Ger · Colour · 133mins

Based on a true story, this is an efficient remake of Rolf Thiele's 1958 melodrama. However, Nina Hoss lacks the ability of her predecessor, Nadja Tiller, to dominate the unsavoury proceedings as the teenage delinquent whose habit of sleeping her way out of trouble resulted in her (still unsolved) murder. There's a wealth of plot to pack in, yet director Bernd Eichinger manages to locate the drama in an authentically seedy Frankfurt underworld, where Hoss encounters both blackmailing pimp Til Schweiger and mysterious Frenchman Mathieu Carrière. Accomplished, but detached. In German with English subtitles.

Nina Hoss *Rosemarie Nitribitt* • Heiner Lauterbach *Hartog* • Mathieu Carrière *Fribert* • Horst Krause *Bruster* • Hannelore Elsner *Marga* • Katja Flint *Christine* • Til Schweiger *Nadler* ■ *Dir* Bernd Eichinger • *Scr* Bernd Eichinger, Uwe Wilhelm

The Girl Can't Help It ★★★★ U
Satirical musical comedy   1956 · US · Colour · 97mins

Witty, stylish, clever and (by today's standards) extraordinarily sexist, this hilarious satire on the juke-box industry is the rock 'n' roll movie *par excellence*. Pneumatic Jayne Mansfield is supported (if that's the word) by more than a dozen major music acts, including Little Richard, Eddie Cochran, Fats Domino and Gene Vincent, singing *Be Bop a Lula*. But director Frank Tashlin's viewpoint is pure acid, and only balladeer Julie London is filmed without cynicism. The use of Scope is exemplary, and the movie is a perfect fifties piece. But the question still remains – how did Mr Average himself, Tom Ewell, get to co-star with such bombshells as Marilyn Monroe, Sheree North and Jayne Mansfield? ▭

Tom Ewell *Tom Miller* • Jayne Mansfield *Jerri Jordan* • Edmond O'Brien *Murdock* • Henry Jones *Mousey* • John Emery *Wheeler* • Juanita Moore *Hilda* ■ *Dir* Frank Tashlin • *Scr* Frank Tashlin, Herbert Baker

Girl Crazy ★★★ U
Musical comedy   1943 · US · BW · 98mins

A magnificent George and Ira Gershwin score and the teaming of the fabulous Judy Garland with the irrepressible Mickey Rooney make this worth seeing. Admittedly, its attitudes have dated badly and, despite Garland looking lovelier than ever, the Rooney/Garland romance really doesn't gel. Still, their duet on *Could You Use Me?* is particularly skilful and sophisticated, and *But Not for Me* has seldom been performed more touchingly. The Busby Berkeley cowboy finale is grossly overextended, though, drawing every ounce of charm from *I Got Rhythm*.

Mickey Rooney *Danny Churchill Jr* • Judy Garland *Ginger Gray* • Gil Stratton *Bud Livermore* • Robert E Strickland *Henry Lathrop* • Rags Ragland *"Rags"* • June Allyson *Speciality* • Nancy Walker *Polly Williams* • Guy Kibbee *Dean Phineas Armour* ■ *Dir* Norman Taurog • *Scr* Fred F Finklehoffe, Sid Silvers, Dorothy Kingsley, William Ludwig, from the play by George Gershwin, Ira Gershwin, Guy Bolton, Jack McGowan

The Girl from Mexico ★

Comedy 1939 · US · BW · 71mins

Lupe Velez revived her Hollywood screen career with this limp slapstick comedy that exploited her tempestuous Latin image. She's hired by Donald Woods's advertising executive to sing on the radio in New York and sneaks out on the town with Leon Errol's Uncle Matt, shouting herself hoarse at a wrestling match and ruining her audition the next day. The film went down so well with American small-town audiences that it started the *Mexican Spitfire* series, which starred Lupe and Leon Errol.

Lupe Velez *Carmelita Fuentes* • Donald Woods *Dennis Lindsey* • Leon Errol *Uncle Matt* • Linda Hayes *Elizabeth Price* • Donald MacBride *Renner* • Edward Raquello *Tony Romano* • Elisabeth Risdon *Aunt Della* • Ward Bond *Mexican Pete* ■ *Dir* Leslie Goodwins • *Scr* Lionel Houser, Joseph A Fields, from a story by Lionel Houser

The Girl from Missouri ★★★

Romantic comedy 1934 · US · BW · 71mins

Anita Loos (*Gentlemen Prefer Blondes*) co-scripted this sharp, witty comedy, which stars blonde bombshell Jean Harlow, Franchot Tone and comedian Patsy Kelly. The women play a couple of chorus-line girls on the lookout for husbands, with Harlow determined to snare a millionaire while preserving her virginity until the right man comes along. Spirited entertainment, this has an excellent supporting cast that includes Alan Mowbray and distinguished MGM stalwarts Lionel Barrymore and Lewis Stone.

Jean Harlow *Eadie Chapman* • Lionel Barrymore *TR Paige* • Franchot Tone *T "Tom" R Paige Jr* • Lewis Stone *Frank Cousins* • Patsy Kelly *Kitty Lennihan* • Alan Mowbray *Lord Douglas* • Clara Blandick *Miss Newberry* ■ *Dir* Jack Conway • *Scr* Anita Loos, John Emerson

The Girl from Petrovka ★

Romantic comedy
1974 · US · Colour · 104mins

Goldie Hawn and Anthony Hopkins adopt thick Russian accents for this pathetic Cold War comedy. La Hawnska grows disenchanted with life in Russia and is romanced by American foreign correspondent Hal Holbrook. Hopkins is a black marketeer, a sort of Harry Lime figure. Subplots proliferate, but the story goes nowhere quickly and has nothing to say about East-West relations. Filmed in Vienna, it was one of several clinkers produced by Richard D Zanuck and David Brown, best known for their monster hits *The Sting* and *Jaws*.

Goldie Hawn *Oktyabrina* • Hal Holbrook *Joe* • Anthony Hopkins *Kostya* • Grégoire Aslan *Minister* • Anton Dolin *Ignatievitch, ballet master* • Bruno Wintzell *Alexander* • Zoran Andric *Leonid* • Hanna Hertelendy *Judge* ■ *Dir* Robert Ellis Miller • *Scr* Allan Scott, Chris Bryant, from the novel by George Feifer

The Girl from 10th Avenue ★★★

Drama 1935 · US · BW · 69mins

A smashing first starring vehicle for wide-eyed Bette Davis, who grabs this daft melodrama between her teeth and never lets go. She's an honest working girl straightening out an alcoholic society type, while coping with the nuisance of a female nemesis who wants her man back. Bette remains unfazed, of course, and this leads to a verbal baiting, which precipitates a newspaper story causing the marriage to topple. It's great tosh, terrifically directed at a smart pace by Alfred E Green, who would later steer La Davis to her first Oscar with *Dangerous*. As the men, Ian Hunter and Colin Clive maintain dignity, but fail to hold a candle when Davis is on.

Bette Davis *Miriam Brady* • Ian Hunter *Geoffrey Sherwood* • Colin Clive *John Marland* • Alison Skipworth *Mrs Martin* • John Eldredge *Hugh Brown* • Philip Reed *Tony Hewlett* ■ *Dir* Alfred E Green • *Scr* Charles Kenyon, from the play *Outcast* by Hubert Henry Davies

Girl Happy ★★ PG

Musical 1965 · US · Colour · 90mins

Despite the Florida settings and a plethora of bikinis, this is one of Elvis Presley's weaker vehicles and a sign that worse was to come. The King plays Rusty Wells, a rock 'n' roll musician doubling up as a chaperone for mobster's daughter Shelley Fabares. Presley displays his customary charm and gives those remarkable tonsils a real work-out on generally unworthy material, notably *Puppet on a String* and *Do Not Disturb*. Director Boris Sagal went on to make the far superior apocalyptic sci-fi drama *The Omega Man*.

Elvis Presley *Rusty Wells* • Shelley Fabares *Valerie Frank* • Harold J Stone *Big Frank* • Gary Crosby *Andy* • Joby Baker *Wilbur* • Nita Talbot *Sunny Daze* • Mary Ann Mobley *Deena* • Fabrizio Mioni *Romano* ■ *Dir* Boris Sagal • *Scr* Harvey Bullock, RS Allen

The Girl He Left Behind ★★ U

Comedy 1956 · US · BW · 103mins

Studio chief Jack L Warner must have had high hopes of Tab Hunter and Natalie Wood as new stars, teaming them in both the western *The Burning Hills* and this army comedy. Under the direction of veteran David Butler, Hunter is well cast as a spoiled, insufferable and unwilling draftee in the peace-time army, who itches to get back to the girl he left behind (Wood). Naturally, Hunter grows up. The comedy is familiar stuff, the film as a whole overlong. But Wood is vivacious and there's strong support from Jessie Royce Landis and Murray Hamilton, who plays an exasperated sergeant.

Tab Hunter *Andy Sheaffer* • Natalie Wood *Susan Daniels* • Jessie Royce Landis *Madeline Sheaffer* • Jim Backus *Sergeant Hanna* • Henry Jones *Hanson* • Murray Hamilton *Sergeant Clyde* • Alan King *Maguire* • James Garner *Preston* • David Janssen *Captain Genaro* ■ *Dir* David Butler • *Scr* Guy Trosper, from the novel by Marion Hargrove

The Girl Hunters ★★

Mystery thriller 1963 · UK · BW · 97mins

Author Mickey Spillane plays his own creation, hard-boiled private eye Mike Hammer, in this all-American B-movie that, for tax reasons, was based and financed in Britain. However, little is made of a promising plot about murder and corruption in American politics, while Spillane is shown to have more ego than acting talent. British starlet Shirley Eaton takes a break from her usual *Carry On* roles to step into shoes more commonly filled by Barbara Stanwyck, playing a blonde *femme fatale* who, fatally, doesn't know one end of a shotgun from the other.

Mickey Spillane *Mike Hammer* • Shirley Eaton *Laura Knapp* • Scott Peters *Pat Chambers* • Hy Gardner • Lloyd Nolan *Art Rickerby* • Guy Kingsley Poynter *Dr Larry Snyder* • James Dyrenforth *Bayliss Henry* ■ *Dir* Roy Rowland • *Scr* Roy Rowland, Robert Fellows, from the novel by Mickey Spillane

The Girl in a Swing ★

Thriller 1988 · UK/US · Colour · 117mins

An interminable and incomprehensible suspense thriller, long on atmosphere but short on sense, about an antiques dealer who, while on business abroad, becomes besotted with a German girl and quickly weds her. He ignores the fact that she's prone to delusions and other bizarre behaviour. Based on a novel by *Watership Down* author Richard Adams, this wilfully and irritatingly odd film stars Meg Tilly, then the better-known sister of Jennifer, but now rather eclipsed by her younger sibling. Appearances in tosh like this may have had something to do with it.

Meg Tilly *Karin Foster* • Rupert Frazer *Alan* • Nicholas Le Prevost *The Vicar* • Elspet Gray *Mrs Dresland* • Lorna Heilbron *Flick* • Claire Shepherd *Angela* • Jean Boht *Mrs Taswell* • Sophie Thursfield *Deirdre* ■ *Dir* Gordon Hessler • *Scr* Gordon Hessler, from the novel by Richard Adams

The Girl in Black Stockings ★★

Murder mystery 1957 · US · BW · 75mins

Murder in a ritzy Utah resort hotel – with voluptuous blonde Mamie Van Doren as one of the female victims – places crippled hotel owner Ron Randell, his loving sister Marie Windsor, lawyer Lex Barker and a young Anne Bancroft under suspicion. Sheriff John Dehner investigates. Howard W Koch directs this efficient whodunit, which has its roots in the Agatha Christie-style formula of having contrasting characters walled up in a confined location who all appear to have a motive to kill.

Lex Barker *David Hewson* • Anne Bancroft *Beth Dixon* • Mamie Van Doren *Harriet Ames* • Ron Randell *Edmund Parry* • Marie Windsor *Julia Parry* • John Dehner *Sheriff Holmes* • John Holland *Norman Grant* • Diana Vandervlis *Louise Miles* ■ *Dir* Howard W Koch • *Scr* Richard Landau, from the story *Wanton Murder* by Peter Godfrey

A Girl in Every Port ★★

Silent comedy 1928 · US · BW

Director Howard Hawks would go on to better things, such as *Bringing Up Baby* and *To Have and Have Not*. This late silent-era vehicle for beefy Victor McLaglen (who would also have better material, winning the Oscar for *The Informer* in 1935), is nobody's finest hour. The title tells the story: sailors McLaglen and Robert Armstrong chase women, date women and brawl over women during their travels around the four corners of the globe. Coarse-grained and only mildly amusing, the film's best episode features the always extraordinary Louise Brooks.

Victor McLaglen *Spike Madden* • Maria Casajuana *Chiquita* • Natalie Joyce *Girl in Panama* • Dorothy Mathews *Girl in Panama* • Elena Jurado *Girl in Panama* • Louise Brooks *Marie, girl in France* • Francis McDonald *Gang leader* • Phalba Morgan *Lena, girl in Holland* • Robert Armstrong *Salami* ■ *Dir* Howard Hawks • *Scr* Howard Hawks, Seton I Miller, from the story by James Kevin McGuinness

A Girl in Every Port ★ U

Comedy 1952 · US · BW · 82mins

A dire experience for Groucho Marx enthusiasts, as he appears with a real moustache and without his brothers, scouring the horizon for non-existent laughlines. The low-budget farce casts him as a fast-talking sailor, with William Bendix as his dim-witted pal. The pair try to put over a horse-race scam involving two identical nags, one fast and the other slow. Dumb blonde Marie Wilson is another capable performer left high and dry.

Groucho Marx *Benny Linn* • Marie Wilson *Jane Sweet* • William Bendix *Tim Dunnevan* • Don DeFore *Bert Sedgwick* • Gene Lockhart *Garvey* • Dee Hartford *Millicent* • Hanley Stafford *Navy Lieutenant* • Teddy Hart *"High Life"* ■ *Dir* Chester Erskine • *Scr* Chester Erskine, from the story *They Sell Sailors Elephants* by Frederick Hazlitt Brennan

Girl in the Headlines ★★★

Crime drama 1963 · UK · BW · 93mins

This sleazy whodunit could have been compiled from a random leaf through the Sunday scandal sheets. At times it seems as if every known vice has been woven into the labyrinthine plot, which centres on the efforts of cop Ian Hendry to prise clues to the identity of a model's killer out of her friends and family. They include Margaret Johnston and Jeremy Brett, later to find renown as TV's Sherlock Holmes. Hendry's commitment and the Watsonesque support of his sergeant (Ronald Fraser) keep you curious.

Ian Hendry *Inspector Birkett* • Ronald Fraser *Sergeant Saunders* • Margaret Johnston *Mrs Gray* • Natasha Parry *Perlita Barker* • Jeremy Brett *Jordan Barker* • Kieron Moore *Herter* • Peter Arne *Hammond Barker* • Jane Asher *Lindy Birkett* • Rosalie Crutchley *Maude Klein* ■ *Dir* Michael Truman • *Scr* Vivienne Knight, Patrick Campbell, Laurence Payne

560 U = SUITABLE FOR ALL Uc = SUITABLE FOR ALL, ESPECIALLY FOR YOUNG CHILDREN (VIDEO ONLY) PG = PARENTAL GUIDANCE

The Girl in the News ★★★
Murder mystery 1940 · UK · BW · 78mins

Around the time of *Night Train to Munich* and *Kipps*, Carol Reed also churned out this workmanlike if rather transparent murder mystery, adapted from Roy Vickers's novel. Reunited with Reed after *Night Train*, Margaret Lockwood heads a starry British cast as a nurse, whose patients have the unfortunate habit of dying after being poisoned. It's a pretty thankless role and she adequately performs the task of looking bewildered and persecuted as required. Barry K Barnes is charged with the task of defending her and Emlyn Williams is the butler who may have crucial information.

Margaret Lockwood *Anne Graham* • Barry K Barnes *Stephen Farringdon* • Emlyn Williams *Tracy* • Roger Livesey *Bill Mather* • Margaretta Scott *Judith Bentley* • Wyndham Goldie *Edward Bentley* • Irene Handl *Miss Blaker* ■ *Dir* Carol Reed • *Scr* Sidney Gilliat, from the novel by Roy Vickers

The Girl in the Picture ★★ U
Crime drama 1956 · UK · BW · 63mins

Probably best known for his work at Disney in the sixties (*Greyfriars Bobby*, *The Three Lives of Thomasina*), director Don Chaffey was still cutting his teeth on British B-movies when he completed this lacklustre thriller. The girl of the title is Junia Crawford, whom crime reporter Donald Houston is convinced holds the key to the murder story he's covering. As mysteries go, this is on the elementary side. Houston, however, has an engaging sense of urgency, and there's some sterling support from Patrick Holt and Maurice Kaufmann.

Donald Houston *John Deering* • Patrick Holt *Inspector Bliss* • Maurice Kaufmann *Rod Molloy* • Junia Crawford *Pat Dryden* • Paddy Joyce *Jack Bates* • John Miller *Duncan* ■ *Dir* Don Chaffey • *Scr* Paul Rogers

The Girl in the Picture
★★★ 15
Romantic comedy 1985 · UK · Colour · 84mins

You can just imagine the pitch if this was being touted now: "It's the next *Four Weddings and a Funeral*, with the twist that the hero is actually a wedding photographer!" Sadly, this gentle comedy was made in 1985 – long before the global success enjoyed by Hugh Grant et al. John Gordon-Sinclair is the awkward snapper who falls in and out of love with the beautiful Irina Brook. It never quite captures the quirky charm of Gordon-Sinclair's hit *Gregory's Girl*, but the playing is superb and it remains thoroughly enjoyable in a quietly unassuming way. 🎞

John Gordon-Sinclair *Alan* • Irina Brook *Mary* • David McKay *Ken* • Gregor Fisher *Bill* • Caroline Guthrie *Annie* • Paul Young *Smiley* • Rikki Fulton *Minister* ■ *Dir/Scr* Cary Parker

The Girl in the Red Velvet Swing ★★ PG
Historical crime drama 1955 · US · Colour · 104mins

Remembered as the Hollywood debut, amid a fanfare of publicity, of Joan Collins, whose "come hither" charms

are its chief focus, this is a suspect retelling of the notorious murder of the brilliant American architect Stanford White in 1906. He was shot in full view of the Manhattan crowds by Harry K Thaw, the unstable husband of White's mistress, showgirl Evelyn Nesbit. The film deals with events from Thaw's perspective, dwelling on the expensive legal defence by which he escaped the death penalty. This is a superficial exercise, with Richard Fleischer's direction and Charles Brackett and Walter Reisch's script treating the whole thing as a soap opera. The young Collins makes a flashy and inadequate Nesbit. 🎞

Ray Milland *Stanford White* • Joan Collins *Evelyn Nesbit Thaw* • Farley Granger *Harry K Thaw* • Luther Adler *Delphin Delmas* • Cornelia Otis Skinner *Mrs Thaw* • Glenda Farrell *Mrs Nesbit* • Frances Fuller *Mrs White* ■ *Dir* Richard Fleischer • *Scr* Walter Reisch, Charles Brackett

Girl, Interrupted ★★★ 15
Drama based on a true story 1999 · US · Colour · 127mins

Set in a New England psychiatric institution in 1967, director/co-writer James Mangold's commendable drama has a similar agenda to Milos Forman's Oscar-winning classic *One Flew over the Cuckoo's Nest*, but never quite reaches the same peaks of poignancy. Mangold makes clever use of jarring narrative cuts to convey Winona Ryder's confused state of mind, Oscar winner Angelina Jolie is mesmerising as a pushy, pouting troublemaker, and Whoopi Goldberg does her best work in ages as a no-nonsense nurse. Yet there's a definite feeling the producers were hoping to set off brighter emotional fireworks than this well-intentioned but lightweight movie actually provides.

Winona Ryder *Susanna Kaysen* • Angelina Jolie *Lisa* • Brittany Murphy *Daisy* • Clea DuVall *Georgina* • Whoopi Goldberg *Valerie* • Jeffrey Tambor *Dr Potts* • Jared Leto *Tobias Jacobs* • Vanessa Redgrave *Dr Wick* ■ *Dir* James Mangold • *Scr* Anna Hamilton Phelan, James Mangold, Susan Shilliday, Lisa Loomer, from the memoirs of Susanna Kaysen

Girl Loves Boy ★
Drama 1937 · US · BW · 77mins

Not a very original title – but the action (if that's the right word) is even less inspired. Co-written by director Duncan Mansfield, this halting melodrama stars Eric Linden, whose career never really took off after he showed promise playing James Cagney's brother in 1932's *The Crowd Roars*. Here Linden's character gets his just desserts after he spurns the love of perky Cecilia Parker and chooses a gold-digging girl instead. There's only one way this kind of story could end, but it seems to take an eternity to reach its conclusion.

Eric Linden *Robert Conrad* • Cecilia Parker *Dorothy McCarthy* • Roger Imhof *Charles Conrad* • Dorothy Peterson *Mrs McCarthy* • Pedro De Cordoba *Signor Montefiori* • Bernadene Hayes *Sally* • Rollo Lloyd *Dr Williams* ■ *Dir* Duncan Mansfield • *Scr* Duncan Mansfield, Carroll Graham

The Girl Most Likely ★★★ U
Musical comedy 1957 · US · Colour · 94mins

A winsome musical remake of the 1941 RKO Ginger Rogers hit *Tom, Dick and Harry*, this is a stylish, fun musical, albeit in a minor key. It's the last feature of veteran Mitchell Leisen, directed with wit and verve, and well served by some super choreography from the great Gower Champion – he of the Gower and Marge Champion dance team and Broadway's *42nd Street*. Jane Powell is perfect as the girl who can't choose a mate, and comedian Kaye Ballard is terrific in her first movie as Powell's best friend. The guys – Cliff Robertson, Keith Andes, Tommy Noonan – are lightweight but charming. Entertaining fluff. 🎞

Jane Powell *Dodie* • Cliff Robertson *Pete* • Keith Andes *Neil* • Kaye Ballard *Marge* • Tommy Noonan *Buzz* • Una Merkel *Mom* • Kelly Brown *Sam* ■ *Dir* Mitchell Leisen • *Scr* Paul Jarrico (uncredited), Devery Freeman, from a story by Paul Jarrico (uncredited)

A Girl Named Tamiko ★★
Romantic drama 1962 · US · Colour · 110mins

Tough-guy director John Sturges was never really comfortable with melodrama. However, who could blame him for wanting to work in exotic Tokyo locations with lovely France Nuyen under the auspices of veteran producer Hal B Wallis? The film stars Laurence Harvey as a Russo-Chinese photographer who stops at nothing to get a US visa. It's all well made; unfortunately, it's also turgid, intractable and empty. That said, Gary Merrill, Michael Wilding, Martha Hyer (Mrs Wallis) and Miyoshi Umeki (who won an Oscar for *Sayonara*) help make it almost watchable.

Laurence Harvey *Ivan Kalin* • France Nuyen *Tamiko* • Martha Hyer *Fay Wilson* • Gary Merrill *Max Wilson* • Michael Wilding *Nigel Costairs* • Miyoshi Umeki *Eiko* • Steve Brodie *James Hatten* • Lee Patrick *Mary Hatten* ■ *Dir* John Sturges • *Scr* Edward Anhalt, from a novel by Ronald Kirkbride

The Girl Next Door ★★★ U
Musical comedy 1953 · US · Colour · 91mins

Dan Dailey is always a pleasure to watch, his easy-going screen persona reflecting a versatile talent and likeable personality that was too often wasted in lightweight vehicles such as this. He stars as a cartoonist whose quiet life is disrupted when chanteuse June Haver moves in next door. As with other movie cartoonists – Dean Martin in *Artists and Models*, Jack Lemmon in *How To Murder Your Wife* – work takes priority, until... There's nice support from crooner Dennis Day, best remembered from Jack Benny's TV and radio shows, and from the under-rated Cara Williams.

Dan Dailey *Bill Carter* • June Haver *Jeannie* • Dennis Day *Reed Appleton* • Billy Gray *Joe Carter* • Cara Williams *Rosie* • Natalie Schafer *Evelyn* • Clinton Sundberg *Samuels* • Hayden Rorke *Fields* ■ *Dir* Richard Sale • *Scr* Isobel Lennart, from a story by L Bush-Fekete, Mary Helen Fay

The Girl Next Door ★★
Psychological drama 1998 · US · Colour · 85mins

An unexceptional made-for-TV thriller that does at least provide an all too infrequent outing for former *Cagney and Lacey* star Sharon Gless. She plays a police psychologist called in to unravel the actions of a young woman (Tracey Gold), who is involved in a dangerous affair with an unhappily married policeman (Tom Irwin). Told largely in flashback, it's an intriguing enough tale, but the script and direction are nondescript.

Tracey Gold *Annie Nolan* • Sharon Gless *Dr Gayle Bennett* • Tom Irwin *Craig Mitchell* • Michael Dorn *Lieutenant Steve Driscoll* ■ *Dir* David Greene • *Scr* Mel Frohman

The Girl of the Golden West ★★★ U
Musical 1938 · US · Sepia · 120mins

For its hit team of Jeanette MacDonald and Nelson Eddy, MGM bought the rights to a hoary old David Belasco stage melodrama (but ignored Puccini's subsequent opera version). More than satisfactory for the duo's followers but hardly innovative in any way, this features MacDonald as the saloon proprietor in love with Eddy's dashing bandit and the object of sheriff Walter Pidgeon's affections. Sigmund Romberg and Gus Kahn wrote the score for the film; Jeannette also sings Gounod's *Ave Maria* to ensure a touch of class.

Jeanette MacDonald *Mary Robbins* • Nelson Eddy *Ramerez/Lt Johnson* • Walter Pidgeon *Sheriff Jack Rance* • Leo Carrillo *Mosquito* • Buddy Ebsen *Alabama* • Leonard Penn *Pedro* • Priscilla Lawson *Nina Martinez* • Bob Murphy *Sonora Slim* ■ *Dir* Robert Z Leonard • *Scr* Isabel Dawn, Boyce DeGaw, from the play by David Belasco

Girl of the Night ★★
Drama 1960 · US · BW · 90mins

Pert and pretty blonde Anne Francis made the most of her role as a reluctant prostitute relating her seamy adventures to oh-so-earnest psychiatrist Lloyd Nolan. She hopes these sessions will help her change her life. Based on a book called *The Call Girl* and presented as a "medical case history", this was quite outspoken for its time, athough it seems fairly tame by today's standards. The girl's tale, told in flashback, makes for dull viewing.

Anne Francis *Bobbie* • Lloyd Nolan *Dr Mitchell* • Kay Medford *Rowena* • John Kerr *Larry* • Arthur Storch *Jason Franklin Jr* • James Broderick *Dan Bolton* • Lauren Gilbert *Mr Shelton* • Eileen Fulton *Lisa* ■ *Dir* Joseph Cates • *Scr* Ted Berkman, Raphael Blau, from the book *The Call Girl* by Dr Harold Greenwald

The Girl on a Motorcycle ★★★ 15
Romantic drama 1968 · UK/Fr · Colour · 86mins

Considered terribly daring in its day, this quintessential sixties' movie catches Marianne Faithfull on the cusp between beauty and seedy decline. She is required to do little more than sneer, pout and wrap her leather-encased limbs around said bike, but this image alone reduced a generation of pseudo-hippy males to pop-eyed slavering wrecks. The plot is as wafer thin as Faithfull's waist but, with its gallery of cinematic icons of the day – including Alain Delon, Catherine Jourdan and Marius Goring – the movie is still a delicious-looking curiosity that encapsulates the freewheeling hedonism of the times. Contains swearing, sex scenes and nudity. 🎬

Marianne Faithfull *Rebecca* • Alain Delon *Daniel* • Roger Mutton *Raymond* • Marius Goring *Rebecca's father* • Catherine Jourdan *Catherine* • Jean Leduc *Jean* ▪ *Dir* Jack Cardiff • *Scr* Ronald Duncan, Gillian Freeman, from the novel *La Motocyclette* by Andre Pieyre de Mandiargues

Girl on Approval ★★★
Drama   1962 · UK · BW · 79mins
This pithy little feature was made by Eyeline Films for the then-new British film company Bryanston. About the angst of foster parenting, this film provides excellent roles for the hitherto under-used Rachel Roberts and suave James Maxwell as the parents, and Annette Whitley as the lass up for fostering. Perhaps a little too self-consciously worthy, it is most interesting today for its view of the mores and fashions of what feels like a bygone age. It's directed by Charles Frend, who was previously an extremely talented editor and is best known for *Scott of the Antarctic*.

Rachel Roberts *Anne Howland* • James Maxwell *John Howland* • Annette Whitley *Sheila* • John Dare *Stephen Howland* • Ellen McIntosh *Mary Gardner* • Michael Clarke *William Howland* ▪ *Dir* Charles Frend • *Scr* Kathleen White, Kenneth Cavander, from a story by Kathleen White

The Girl on the Boat ★★🅄
Comedy   1962 · UK · BW · 89mins
Realising he was too deep into the rut of slapdash slapstick, Norman Wisdom tried to extricate himself with this misplaced attempt to do something different. A sea-going comedy romance taken from a story by Bertie Wooster creator PG Wodehouse, it doesn't work for Wisdom, though it does for the less mannered professionals in support, such as Richard Briers, Millicent Martin and Athene Seyler. It was a bomb at the box office: Wisdom must have thought he could do nothing right. 🎬

Norman Wisdom *Sam* • Millicent Martin *Billie Bennett* • Richard Briers *Eustace Hignett* • Sheila Hancock *Jane* • Bernard Cribbins *Peters* • Athene Seyler *Mrs Hignett* • Philip Locke *Bream Mortimer* • Noel William Webster ▪ *Dir* Henry Kaplan • *Scr* Reuben Ship, from the novel by PG Wodehouse

The Girl on the Bridge ★★★🅵
Romantic drama   1999 · Fr · BW · 92mins
Three years after *Ridicule*, director Patrice Leconte filmed this romantic fantasy in shimmering black and white. Middle-aged knife thrower Daniel Auteuil talks the elfin Vanessa Paradis out of jumping off a bridge into the Seine, turning her desperation to his advantage by hiring her as his assistant. Their relationship deepens, and darkens, as they tour the south of France, although romance is hampered

by the flings she has at every port of call – not to mention the daggers he flings at her every night. With Marianne Faithfull warbling on the soundtrack and sumptuous visuals from Jean-Marie Dreujou, this is an elegant, nostalgic treat that's short enough to leave you wanting more. In French with English subtitles.

Vanessa Paradis *Adèle* • Daniel Auteuil *Gabor* • Demetre Georgalas *Takis* • Isabelle Petit-Jacques *The bride* • Frederic Pfluger *The contortionist* ▪ *Dir* Patrice Leconte • *Scr* Serge Frydman

Girl on the Run ★★🅄
Crime thriller   1958 · US · BW · 77mins
A programme filler that utilises the roster of contract actors Warner Bros built up for its many TV series in the fifties and early sixties. Made for US television but released in cinemas outside the USA as a supporting feature, this serves as a showcase for suave charmer Efrem Zimbalist Jr (from the studio's phenomenally successful television show *77 Sunset Strip*). His co-star here is Erin O'Brien, whose career never really took off. A pleasant enough crime thriller that's inoffensive, short and nothing special.

Efrem Zimbalist Jr *Stuart Bailey* • Erin O'Brien *Kathy Allen/Karen Shay* • Shepperd Strudwick *McCullough* • Edward Byrnes [Edd Byrnes] *Smiley* • Barton MacLane *Brannigan* • Ray Teal *Lieutenant Harper* • Vince Barnett *Janitor* ▪ *Dir* Richard L Bare • *Scr* Marion Hargrove, from a story by Roy Huggins

Girl Rush ★★
Musical comedy   1944 · US · BW · 64mins
This B-movie is a real curio, so it's a shame it isn't very good. Alan Carney and Wally Brown are the two vaudevillians stranded during the gold rush days in San Francisco, in an excuse for a plot that only really worked for stars such as Bing Crosby and Bob Hope in the *Road* movies. Of course, these films are not without interest. A look down the cast list reveals a young Robert Mitchum in a minor role, showing little promise of the great screen career to come. The leading lady is sexy singer Frances Langford, and ditzy Vera Vague (sometimes credited as Barbara Jo Allen) has some moments, but overall it's as daft as a brush.

Wally Brown *Jerry Miles* • Alan Carney *Mike Strager* • Frances Langford *Flo Daniels* • Robert Mitchum *Jimmy Smith* • Vera Vague [Barbara Jo Allen] *Susie Banks* • Paul Hurst *Muley* • Patti Brill *Claire* • Sarah Padden *Emma* ▪ *Dir* Gordon Douglas • *Scr* Robert E Kent, from a story by Laszlo Vadnay, Aladar Laszlo

The Girl Rush ★★★🅄
Musical comedy   1955 · US · Colour · 84mins
Rosalind Russell goes to Las Vegas to claim her inheritance in a hotel but things aren't quite what they seem. Her hotel is on the skids thanks to the efforts of James Gleason and Russell is labouring under the impression that she owns half of another establishment – actually owned by Fernando Lamas. Based on a story by Phoebe and Henry Ephron, who concocted *There's No Business Like Show Business*, this might have been

better if it had starred a brassier personality than Rosalind Russell – Jane Russell, perhaps.

Rosalind Russell *Kim Halliday* • Fernando Lamas *Victor Monte* • Eddie Albert *Elliot Atterbury* • Gloria DeHaven *Taffy Tremaine* • Marion Lorne *Aunt Clara* • James Gleason *Ether Ferguson* ▪ *Dir* Robert Pirosh • *Scr* Robert Pirosh, Jerome Davis, from a story by Henry Ephron, Phoebe Ephron

Girl Shy ★★★★★🅄
Silent comedy   1924 · US · BW · 88mins
A classic Harold Lloyd silent comedy, with a breathtaking chase sequence providing a memorable climax. The action gets off to a stuttering start but it's totally in keeping with Lloyd's character – a nervous tailor who overcomes his romantic timidity to write a book on love. But, when he learns that his girl is about to marry a bigamist, the pace hots up as Lloyd hurtles across town using every means of transport he can commander. It is both hilarious and frenetic, but what makes it so special is the precision of the editing. 🎬

Harold Lloyd *Harold Meadows, the Poor Boy* • Jobyna Ralston *Mary Buckingham, the Rich Girl* • Richard Daniels *Jerry Meadows, the Poor Man* • Carlton Griffith *Ronald Devore, the Rich Man* ▪ *Dir* Fred C Newmeyer, Sam Taylor • *Scr* from a story by Ted Wilde, Tim Whelan, Tommy Gray, Sam Taylor

Girl 6 ★★★★🔞
Comedy drama   1996 · US · Colour · 103mins
This light-hearted tale is free from the preachy philosophising often associated with film-maker Spike Lee. Theresa Randle gives the performance of her life as a struggling actress who decides to join a phone-sex agency after being asked to strip for casting director Quentin Tarantino. In the event, she becomes addicted to the buzz she gets from her conversations, as she takes on a variety of characters in order to feed the fantasies of her callers. This film lays itself wide open to every politically incorrect charge you could level at it, yet Lee manages to comment on society's dual standards with regard to sexploitation without detracting from the humour of the piece. Through it all, the poignancy of Randle's performance shines through. Contains swearing and nudity. 🎬

Theresa Randle *Girl 6* • Isaiah Washington *Shoplifter* • Spike Lee *Jimmy* • Jenifer Lewis *Boss 1, Lil* • Debi Mazar *Girl 39* • Peter Berg *Caller 1, Bob* • Michael Imperioli *Scary caller 30* • Dina Pearlman *Girl 19* • Naomi Campbell *Girl 75* • Gretchen Mol *Girl 12* • Madonna *Boss 3* • John Turturro *Murray the agent* ▪ *Dir* Spike Lee • *Scr* Suzan-Lori Parks

The Girl Who Had Everything ★
Crime drama   1953 · US · BW · 69mins
Elizabeth Taylor was hot from *Ivanhoe* and *A Place in the Sun* when MGM squandered her talents in this tepid remake of its torrid 1931 hit *A Free Soul*. Liz lacks the abandon required for the role of the spoiled daughter of a prosperous criminal lawyer who falls for his gangster client, Fernando Lamas. As the lawyer William Powell remains as suave as ever in his last role for the studio, while Lamas

struggles with the part of the shady Romeo. Under Richard Thorpe's static direction the film didn't work and was pared down to B-feature length.

Elizabeth Taylor *Jean Latimer* • Fernando Lamas *Victor Y Ramondi* • William Powell *Steve Latimer* • Gig Young *Vance Court* • James Whitmore *Charles "Chico" Menlow* • Robert Burton *John Ashmond* • William Walker *Julian* • Harry Bartell *Joe* ▪ *Dir* Richard Thorpe • *Scr* Art Cohn, from the novel *A Free Soul* by Adela Rogers St John

The Girl Who Knew Too Much ★★
Spy drama   1969 · US · Colour · 96mins
There's no sign of a Joker or a Riddler as the former Caped Crusader takes on the Red Menace. *Batman's* Adam West stars in this spy film as an ex-CIA man who comes out of retirement to investigate communist infiltration of the mob. Nancy Kwan and Buddy Greco co-star. The Cold War theme seems very dated now and this is one of many non-classics on West's CV.

Adam West *Johnny Cain* • Nancy Kwan *Revel Drue* • Nehemiah Persoff *Lieutenant Crawford* • Buddy Greco *Lucky Jones* • Robert Alda *Kenneth Allardice* • Patricia Smith *Tricia Grinaldi* • David Brian *Had Dixon* ▪ *Dir* Francis D Lyon • *Scr* Charles Wallace

The Girl Who Spelled Freedom ★★★🅄
Drama based on a true story
1986 · US · Colour · 90mins
Free Willy director Simon Wincer is the man behind the camera for this entertaining true tale about a Cambodian refugee family starting a new life in America. The story of how one of the family, who could speak no English on her arrival, went on to win a national spelling competition is convincingly told, thanks to Wincer's subtle direction and good performances by Wayne Rogers, Mary Kay Place and Kieu Chinh. 🎬

Wayne Rogers *George Thrash* • Mary Kay Place *Prissy Thrash* • Kieu Chinh *Phoen Yann* • Kathleen Sisk *Laura Thrash* • Jade Chinn *Linn Yann* • Margot Pinvidic *Mandy* • Susan Walden *Suanna* ▪ *Dir* Simon Wincer • *Scr* Christopher Knopf, David A Simons

The Girl with Brains in Her Feet ★★★🅵
Comedy drama   1997 · UK · Colour · 98mins
This endearing coming-of-age tale, set in Leicester, centres on a fleet-footed 13-year-old schoolgirl whose career in athletics seems set to run and run. But only weeks before a major sports meet, she veers off track as a result of the twin distractions of adolescent angst and a dysfunctional home life. The film's feel of the real, plus sterling performances from its cast of relative unknowns, more than compensate for the enigmatic and off-putting title.

Amanda Mealing *Vivienne Jones* • Joanna Ward *Jacqueline "Jack" Jones* • Jamie McIntosh *"Poor Bastard"* • Jodie Smith *Maxine* • Richard Claxton *Steve Green* • John Thomson *Mr Loughborough* • Gareth Tudor-Price *Mr Roundhead* ▪ *Dir* Roberto Bangura • *Scr* Jo Hodges

🅄 = SUITABLE FOR ALL   🆄c = SUITABLE FOR ALL, ESPECIALLY FOR YOUNG CHILDREN (VIDEO ONLY)   🅿🅶 = PARENTAL GUIDANCE

Girl with Green Eyes ★★★★ PG

Romantic drama   1963 · UK · BW · 92mins

Adapted by Edna O'Brien from her novel, *The Lonely Girl*, this sensitive tale of opposites is blessed with a highly literate script and affecting performances. Sixties starlets Rita Tushingham and Lynn Redgrave play the shopgirls who share a room but little else, until they meet shy and retiring writer Peter Finch. The decline in their relationship, as it transpires he prefers the mousey Tushingham to the blowsy Redgrave, is conveyed with great skill. Debutant director Desmond Davis wisely allows the cast to go about their business and captures the atmosphere of Dublin with the eye of an experienced cinematographer. 🖭

Peter Finch *Eugene Gaillard* • Rita Tushingham *Kate Brady* • Lynn Redgrave *Baba Brenan* • Marie Kean *Josie Hannigan* • Arthur O'Sullivan *Mr Brady* • Julian Glover *Malachi Sullivan* • TP McKenna *Priest* • Lislott Goettinger *Joanna* ■ *Dir* Desmond Davis • *Scr* Edna O'Brien, from her novel *The Lonely Girl*

The Girl with Red Hair ★★★ PG

Second World War drama
1981 · Neth · Colour · 113mins

The redhead in question is Hannie Schaft, a vigilante member of the Dutch resistance whose unconventional methods often brought her into conflict with her own superiors, as well as the Nazis. Renée Soutendijk plays her as an ordinary woman whose fierce patriotism drives her to abandon her ambitions and conquer a distaste for violence in order to become a ruthless killing machine. Debutant Ben Verbong directs with dignity and justified anger. While he occasionally allows his generally intelligent depiction of life under the Occupation to lapse into cliché, his adroit use of light and colour admirably captures the look of the period. In Dutch with English subtitles.

Renée Soutendijk *Hannie Schaft* • Peter Tuinman *Hugo* • Ada Bouwman *Tinka* • Robert Delhez *Floor* • Johan Leysen *Frans* • Loos Luca *An* • Adrian Brine *German Officer* • Lineke Rijxman *Judith* ■ *Dir* Ben Verbong • *Scr* Ben Verbong, Pieter De Vos, from the novel by Theun De Vries

Girlfriends ★★★★

Comedy drama   1978 · US · Colour · 87mins

Her work on Shirley MacLaine's Oscar-nominated documentary, *The Other Half of the Sky*, enabled Claudia Weill to fund this significant landmark in both women's film-making and American independent cinema. Smashing cosy studio stereotypes, she creates the kind of single women who might really dwell in rented apartments rather than exist solely in the hazy imagination of a Hollywood screenwriter. As wannabe photographer Susan, Melanie Mayron is fresh, honest and vulnerable, whether she's trying to break into the New York art scene or discussing men with her soon-to-be-married flatmate, Anita Skinner. Lightly played, keenly observed and superbly understated.

Melanie Mayron *Susan Weinblatt* • Eli Wallach *Rabbi Gold* • Anita Skinner *Anne Munroe* •

Bob Balaban *Martin* • Christopher Guest *Eric* • Gina Rogak *Julie* • Amy Wright *Ceil* ■ *Dir* Claudia Weill • *Scr* Vicki Polon, from a story by Claudia Weill, Vicki Polon

Les Girls ★★★ U

Musical   1957 · US · Colour · 109mins

This late MGM musical was selected for its year's Royal Film Performance, and there was much discussion about how the Queen would relate to a sexy musical about the British upper classes in Paris. Others wondered how British audiences would get the point of a send-up of Marlon Brando's *The Wild One* when the original was still banned in Britain. Today it's fun to watch, risqué and disarming, but not really sophisticated enough – though it certainly tries. The flashback structure doesn't help, but the girls – Mitzi Gaynor, Kay Kendall and Taina Elg – are delightful, and Gene Kelly is as watchable as ever. Director George Cukor seems uncomfortable with the material, though, and the Cole Porter score is disappointing. 🖭

Gene Kelly *Barry Nichols* • Mitzi Gaynor *Joy Henderson* • Kay Kendall *Lady Wren* • Taina Elg *Angele Ducros* • Jacques Bergerac *Pierre Ducros* • Leslie Phillips *Sir Gerald Wren* • Henry Daniell *Judge* • Patrick Macnee *Sir Percy* ■ *Dir* George Cukor • *Scr* John Patrick, from a story by Vera Caspary

Girls about Town ★★

Comedy drama   1931 · US · BW · 80mins

This curiosity from George Cukor's early career hardly stacks up against the director's later work, but it shows clear signs of his legendary skill with actresses in the vivacious performances of Kay Francis and Lilyan Tashman. The duo play gold-diggers who enjoy a lavish lifestyle courtesy of the businessmen they "entertain". Joel McCrea is well cast as the rich sucker from out of town who wants to marry Francis. The film pre-dates the Hays Office clampdown on morality in Hollywood, which explains the relative latitude in plot and dialogue.

Kay Francis *Wanda Howard* • Joel McCrea *Jim Baker* • Lilyan Tashman *Marie Bailey* • Eugene Pallette *Benjamin Thomas* • Alan Dinehart *Jerry Chase* • Lucille Webster Gleason *Mrs Benjamin Thomas* • Anderson Lawler *Alex Howard* • George Barbier *Webster* ■ *Dir* George Cukor • *Scr* Raymond Griffith, Brian Marlow, from a story by Zoe Akins

Girls at Sea ★★ U

Comedy   1958 · UK · Colour · 80mins

The thirties' film version of the stage farce *The Middle Watch*, which starred Jack Buchanan, was pretty bad, but beside this tepid remake it looks like a comedy classic. The cast does its level best to pep up the tired material, but there's only so much you can do with a story in which a captain has to keep his admiral from discovering three girls stranded on board after a dockside party. Ronald Shiner is cheeky and Michael Hordern is absent-mindedly authoritarian, while all the girls get to do is rush around in a state of undress. Try another form of naval gazing instead.

Guy Rolfe *Captain* • Ronald Shiner *Marine Ogg* • Michael Hordern *Admiral Hewitt* • Alan White *Commander* • Anne Kimbell *Mary* • Nadine

Tallier *Antoinette* • Fabia Drake *Lady Hewitt* • Mary Steele *Jill* • Teddy Johnson *Singer* ■ *Dir* Gilbert Gunn • *Scr* Gilbert Gunn, TJ Morrison, Walter C Mycroft, from the play *The Middle Watch* by Stephen King-Hall, Ian Hay

Girls Can Play ★

Crime drama   1937 · US · BW · 59mins

Rita Hayworth was several years away from her defining role in *Gilda* when she appeared in this forgettable B-movie. The plot – somewhat bizarrely – revolves around a booze racketeer (John Gallaudet) and the female baseball team that represents one of his more legitimate business interests. When one of the girls is murdered, a dull-witted cop (Guinn Williams) is assigned to the case.

Jacqueline Wells [Julie Bishop] *Ann Casey* • Charles Quigley *Jimmy Jones* • Rita Hayworth *Sue Collins* • John Gallaudet *Foy Harris* • George McKay *Sluggy* • Patricia Farr *Peanuts* • Guinn "Big Boy" Williams [Guinn Williams] *Lt Flannigan* • Joseph Crehan *Brophy* ■ *Dir* Lambert Hillyer • *Scr* Lambert Hillyer, from a story by Albert DeMond

Girls! Girls! Girls! ★★★ U

Musical   1962 · US · Colour · 94mins

One of Presley's more enjoyable romps, this has colourful locations, a serviceable (though silly) plot and the usual attractive co-stars, including cult sex bomb Stella Stevens, who also gets to sing. Elvis plays a tuna boat fisherman in Hawaii who shows his underlying toughness in a brief but particularly revealing scene in which he tries to seduce rich girl Laurel Goodwin. The hit song was the superb *Return to Sender* and the rest of the score is quite bearable, with well-appointed set pieces such as *We're Coming in Loaded* and *Thanks to the Rolling Sea*. 🖭

Elvis Presley *Ross Carpenter* • Stella Stevens *Robin Gantner* • Jeremy Slate *Wesley Johnson* • Laurel Goodwin *Laurel Dodge* • Benson Fong *Kin Yung* • Robert Strauss *Sam* • Guy Lee *Chen Yung* • Frank Puglia *Alexander Stavros* ■ *Dir* Norman Taurog • *Scr* Edward Anhalt, Allan Weiss, from a story by Allan Weiss

Girls in Prison ★★★ 15

Drama   1994 · US · Colour · 78mins

This is a campy, sleazy take on that old B-movie staple: women behind bars. Missy Crider plays a young woman wrongly convicted of murder, who teams up with Ione Skye and Bahni Turpin in prison to see off the fellow inmates and a hired assassin sent to kill her. In the hands of John McNaughton (*Henry: Portrait of a Serial Killer*), it's a lot raunchier than its fifties' prototypes, and McNaughton has a lot of fun staging the requisite shower scenes and cat fights. The three leads are a touch bland, but there is a strong supporting cast that includes Anne Heche, Jon Polito and Nicolette Scorsese. Contains swearing, violence and nudity.

Missy Crider *Aggie* • Bahni Turpin *Melba* • Ione Skye *Carol* • Anne Heche *Jennifer* • Jon Polito *Boss Johnson* • Richmond Arquette *Detective Campion* • Nicolette Scorsese *Suzy* • Nestor Serrano *Borcelino* • Tom Towles *Norman Stoneface* ■ *Dir* John McNaughton • *Scr* Samuel Fuller, Christa Lang

Girls in Uniform ★★★★ 18

Drama   1931 · Ger · BW · 110mins

Adapted from Christa Winsloe's play *Gestern und Heute*, this landmark in gay cinema may no longer scandalise. But it remains a touching love story, as neurotic Hertha Thiele falls under the spell of teacher Dorothea Wieck, her only source of solace in a cold Prussian boarding school. Demonstrating a sympathetic understanding of the misery of teenage isolation, director Leontine Sagan also emphasises the importance of the individual in a society ruled by the code of militarist uniformity. This subtly subversive picture was banned by the Nazis and many of its key personnel were forced into exile. In German with English subtitles. 🖭

Emilia Unda *The Principal* • Dorothea Wieck *Fraulein von Bernburg* • Hedwig Schlichter *Fraulein von Kesten* • Hertha Thiele *Manuela von Meinhardie* • Ellen Schwannecke *Ilse von Westhagen* ■ *Dir* Leontine Sagan • *Scr* Christa Winsloe, FD Andam, from the play *Gestern und Heute* by Christa Winsloe

Girls Just Want to Have Fun ★★★ PG

Musical comedy   1985 · US · Colour · 83mins

American teen flicks are never short of clichés, and this musical comedy is no exception, packing in most of the genre conventions on the way to its wildly over-the-top, all-dancing finale. However, another confident performance by Sarah Jessica Parker (*Honeymoon in Vegas*, *Miami Rhapsody*) rescues this outing from obscurity. Here she convincingly plays a high-school student who incurs her father's wrath by entering a dance competition. 🖭

Sarah Jessica Parker *Janey Glenn* • Helen Hunt *Lynne Stone* • Lee Montgomery *Jeff Malene* • Shannen Doherty *Maggie Malene* • Biff Yeager *Mr Malene* • Morgan Woodward *JP Sands* • Jonathan Silverman *Drew* ■ *Dir* Alan Metter • *Scr* Amy Spies

Girls' Night ★★★★ 15

Comedy drama
1997 · UK/US · Colour · 98mins

Scripted by Kay Mellor, who wrote TV's *Band of Gold*, this comedy drama enables Brenda Blethyn to give another demonstration of everywoman bravura. She stars alongside Julie Walters, who matches Blethyn in every scene. The pair play two northern girls who work in an electrics factory and have been friends since school. When Jackie discovers Dawn has cancer, she decides to take her pal to Las Vegas. There they meet cowboy Cody (Kris Kristofferson) and embark on an adventure to remember. What could have been a run-of-the-mill, disease-of-the-week TV movie ends up being much more, thanks to two impressive and moving performances from Blethyn and Walters. Contains sex scenes and some swearing. 🖭

Brenda Blethyn *Dawn Wilkinson* • Julie Walters *Jackie Simpson* • Sue Cleaver *Rita* • Kris Kristofferson *Cody* • Meera Syal *Carmen* • Margo Stanley *Irene* • Maggie Tagney *Anne Marie* • George Costigan *Steve Wilkinson* ■ *Dir* Nick Hurran • *Scr* Kay Mellor

Girls' Town ★

Drama 1959 · US · BW · 92mins

After her questionable lifestyle involves her in the death of a young guy, bad girl Mamie Van Doren is sent to a correctional institution run by nuns. Under their influence, her hard shell begins to crack and she uncovers the person who was really responsible for the incident. Trading off Van Doren's brassy, suggestive voluptuousness, the movie brings to mind a whole lexicon of adjectives, such as sleazy, tawdry and trashy. Its only point of interest is the inclusion of such musical luminaries as Mel Tormé, Paul Anka and The Platters in the cast.

Mamie Van Doren *Silver Morgan* • Mel Tormé *Fred Alger* • Paul Anka *Jimmy Parlow* • Ray Anthony *Dick Culdane* • Maggie Hayes *Mother Veronica* • Cathy Crosby *Singer* • Gigi Perreau *Serafina Garcia* • Elinor Donahue *Mary Lee Morgan* • Harold Lloyd Jr *Chip Gardner* ■ *Dir* Charles Haas • *Scr* Robert Smith, from a story by Robert Hardy Andrews

Girls Town ★★★ 15

Drama 1996 · US · Colour · 89mins

Made on a shoestring and largely improvised by the impressive ensemble, Jim McKay's small-town drama begins with a chillingly subtle opening sequence, in which evidence of a rape is planted in the soundtrack. From then on, however, it is inexorably drawn into melodrama, as three high school seniors decide to avenge the suicide of their best friend. Single mum Lili Taylor holds things together, with her relationship with abusive boyfriend John Ventimiglia providing greater dramatic interest than her antics with Bruklin Harris and Anna Grace. The plotting is shaky, but the dialogue rings true and leaves you with plenty to think about. ▣

Aunjanue Ellis *Nikki* • Bruklin Harris *Angela* • Anna Grace *Emma* • Lili Taylor *Patti Lucci* • Ramya Pratt *Tomy Lucci* • Asia Minor *Marlys Giovanni* • John Ventimiglia *Eddie* ■ *Dir* Jim McKay • *Scr* Jim McKay, Anna Grace, Bruklin Harris, Lili Taylor, Denise Casano

Giro City ★★★

Thriller 1982 · UK · Colour · 102mins

Glenda Jackson lends her talents to this social thriller, but not to much effect. Writer/director Karl Francis's film follows two members of a British investigative documentary team as they consider the plight of a Welsh farmer facing eviction, before going on to look into the activities of the IRA. But they end up having to compromise, in a film that has its heart is in the right place but lacks the substance or artistry to do its subjects justice.

Glenda Jackson *Sophie* • Jon Finch *O'Mally* • Kenneth Colley *Martin* • James Donnelly *James* • Emrys James *Tommy Williams* • Karen Archer *Brigitte* • Simon Jones *Henderson* • Huw Ceredig *Elwyn Davies* ■ *Dir/Scr* Karl Francis

Give a Girl a Break ★★★ U

Musical 1953 · US · Colour · 82mins

Directed by Stanley Donen and co-choreographed by Gower Champion, this is an enjoyable diversion from MGM's stable of musical talent and offers several dazzling dance routines to compensate for the totally unmemorable score. Champion plays the director of a forthcoming Broadway show from which the temperamental leading lady departs in a huff. The search for a replacement results in three possible contenders: mature Marge Champion (Gower's old flame and first choice); balletic Helen Woods (supported by the show's composer, Kurt Kasznar); and ingenue Debbie Reynolds, whose cause is championed by Gower's junior assistant, Bob Fosse. The plot keeps one guessing which girl will get the big break.

Marge Champion *Madelyn Corlane* • Gower Champion *Ted Sturgis* • Debbie Reynolds *Suzy Doolittle* • Helen Wood *Joanna Moss* • Bob Fosse *Bob Dowdy* • Kurt Kasznar *Leo Belney* • Richard Anderson *Burton Bradshaw* • William Ching *Anson Pritchett* ■ *Dir* Stanley Donen • *Scr* Albert Hackett, Frances Goodrich, from a story by Vera Caspary • *Choreographer* Gower Champion, Stanley Donen

Give 'Em Hell, Harry! ★★★

Comedy drama 1975 · US · Colour · 102mins

Actor James Whitmore's successful one-man show as US President Harry S Truman toured extensively in the USA and was brought to the screen by director Steve Binder. The timing seemed to be propitious. Richard Nixon was in disgrace after Watergate and Whitman's portrayal of Truman harked back to an era of cleaner, nobler politics. The 33rd US President, Truman was in office from 1945-53, ordering the bombing of Hiroshima and steering America through postwar prosperity and the first years of the Cold War. As for Whitmore, his virtuoso performance earned him an Oscar nomination. The film was recorded and edited together from two live performances in Seattle.

James Whitmore *Harry S Truman* ■ *Dir* Steve Binder • *Scr* Samuel Gallu

Give My Regards to Broadway ★★★ U

Musical 1948 · US · Colour · 88mins

Broadway movies with backstage emotions boiling over and the show going on regardless are a sub-genre all of their own, and this is one of the most amiable, even if it lacks the usual abundance of big production numbers. Charles Winninger is the old-timer who refuses to accept that the vaudeville tradition has had its day, and devotes his energy towards putting his children on the stage. Dan Dailey, as Winninger's son, proves yet again what a versatile actor he was.

Dan Dailey *Bert* • Charles Winninger *Albert* • Nancy Guild *Helen* • Charlie Ruggles [Charles Ruggles] *Toby* • Fay Bainter *Fay* • Barbara Lawrence *June* • Jane Nigh *May* • Charles Russell *Arthur Waldron Jr* • Sig Rumann [Sig Ruman] *Dir* Lloyd Bacon • *Scr* Samuel Hoffenstein, Elizabeth Reinhardt, from a story by John Klempner

Give My Regards to Broad Street ★★ PG

Musical 1984 · UK · Colour · 103mins

Widely condemned as a worthless ego trip, Paul McCartney's musical fantasy is a great idea for a concept video that had the misfortune to be made into a feature film. The plot – about an ex-con and some missing tapes – is negligible, the references to Fellini's 8½ are laughable, and some of the musical sequences lack inspiration (most notably the orchestral elongation of *Eleanor Rigby*, during which Paul, his wife Linda, Ringo Starr and Barbara Bach go on a Victorian picnic). However, fans will enjoy the Beatles classics and newer songs, such as *Ballroom Dancing*. ▣

Paul McCartney *Paul* • Bryan Brown *Steve* • Ringo Starr *Ringo* • Barbara Bach *Journalist* • Linda McCartney *Linda* • Tracey Ullman *Sandra* • Ralph Richardson *Jim* • George Martin *Record producer* • *Dir* Peter Webb • *Scr* Paul McCartney • *Music* Paul McCartney

Give Us the Moon ★★★ U

Comedy 1944 · UK · BW · 95mins

Made during the Second World War but set in the postwar future, this unusual British comedy is based on a Caryl Brahms and SJ Simon novel about a Soho club founded by a group of idlers who refuse to work. The satire is slight, but co-screenwriter and director Val Guest keeps it moving along nicely, and there's terrific work from stars Margaret Lockwood, Vic Oliver and Peter Graves. There's also a wonderfully brash performance from 14-year-old Jean Simmons as Lockwood's sister, demonstrating her future star quality even at that tender age. Other familiar faces include Max Bacon and Irene Handl.

Margaret Lockwood *Nina* • Vic Oliver *Sascha* • Peter Graves (2) *Peter Pyke* • Roland Culver *Ferdinand* • Max Bacon *Jacobus* • Frank Cellier *Pyke* • Jean Simmons *Heidi* • Irene Handl *Miss Haddock* ■ *Dir* Val Guest • *Scr* Val Guest, Howard Irving Young, Caryl Brahms, SJ Simon, from the novel *The Elephant Is White* by Caryl Brahms, by SJ Simon

Give Us This Day ★★

Drama 1949 · UK · BW · 119mins

Sam Wanamaker plays an Italian bricklayer in Brooklyn, whose dreams of owning his own house are brought crashing down by his naivety and the Depression. This movie pleads for our sympathy and every point is driven home with sledgehammer obviousness – it freely advertises its left-wing credentials because it was shot and financed in Britain. The director and writer had both been blacklisted as a result of the McCarthy witch-hunts – Dmytryk having already served a year in prison – and were living in exile along with Wanamaker who, though never blacklisted himself, thought it prudent to leave America.

Sam Wanamaker *Geremio* • Lea Padovani *Annunziata* • Kathleen Ryan *Kathleen* • Charles Goldner *Luigi* • Bonar Colleano *Julio* • William Sylvester *Giovanni* • Nino Pastellides *The Lucy* ■ *Dir* Edward Dmytryk • *Scr* Ben Barzman, from the novel *Christ in Concrete* by Pietro Di Donato

Give Us Tomorrow ★

Thriller 1978 · UK · Colour · 94mins

Compare this hopeless Home Counties hokum with either version of *The Desperate Hours*, and you'll see why British commercial cinema has never emerged from the shadow of Hollywood. In trying to re-create the tension of a hostage situation following a bungled bank job, writer/director Donovan Winter shies away from portraying intimidation and human drama and instead plunges us into a risible debate on the iniquities of the class system. Derren Nesbitt's villain is far less scary than Sylvia Syms's affronted suburbanite, whose resentment at her family's plight has an ominously Thatcherite ring.

Sylvia Syms *Wendy Hammond* • Derren Nesbitt *Ron* • James Kerry *Martin Hammond* • Donna Evans *Nicola Hammond* • Matthew Haslett *Jamie Hammond* • Alan Guy *Boy* • Victor Brooks *Superintendent* • Derek Anders *Inspector* ■ *Dir/Scr* Donovan Winter

The Given Word ★★★★

Drama 1962 · Bra · BW · 98mins

Adapted from a play by Dias Gomes, this scathing attack on the Brazilian Catholic Church is often claimed as a key entry in the *cinema nôvo* movement. But, with its theatrical structuring and traditional visuals, it owes more to the *chanchada* tradition of comic melodrama. However, the story of the farmer who vows to carry a cross to the local chapel in thanks for the recovery of his donkey still has the power to move and provoke. Director Anselmo Duarte exposes the unholy alliance of social corruption, political indolence and media manipulation that conspires to repress the impoverished people of Bahia. In Portuguese with English subtitles.

Leonardo Vilar *Ze* • Gloria Menezes *Rosa* • Dionisio Azevedo *Father Olavo* • Norma Bengell *Marli* • Geraldo D'el Rey *Bonitao/"Handsome"* • Roberto Ferreira *Dede* • Othon Bastos *Reporter* • Gilberto Marques *Galego* ■ *Dir* Anselmo Duarte • *Scr* Anselmo Duarte, from the play *O Pagador de Promessas* by Alfredo Dias Gomes

Gladiator ★★★ 15

Action drama 1992 · US · Colour · 97mins

Director Rowdy Herrington delivers exactly the sort of films you would expect from someone so named. His works tend to be brutish, no-nonsense slices of macho action, and this is one of the best. Cuba Gooding Jr plays a streetwise teenager who, along with *Twin Peaks* alumnus James Marshall, is lured into the world of illegal boxing by a memorably sleazy Brian Dennehy. The plot is riddled with clichés, but this is much grittier territory than the airbrushed world of the *Rocky* films. The two leads are aided by a talented line-up of fine character actors, including John Heard, Robert Loggia and Ossie Davis. Contains some violence, swearing and nudity. ▣

James Marshall *Tommy Riley* • Cuba Gooding Jr *Lincoln* • Brian Dennehy *Jimmy Horn* • Robert Loggia *Pappy Jack* • Ossie Davis *Noah* • Jon Seda *Romano* • Lance Slaughter *Shortcut* • John Heard *John Riley* ■ *Dir* Rowdy Herrington • *Scr* Lyle Kessler, Robert Mark Kamen

Gladiator ★★★★ 15

Historical epic 2000 · US · Colour · 155mins

Ridley Scott and the boys from DreamWorks have produced the first genuine Roman epic in 35 years. This is a virtual remake of *The Fall of the Roman Empire*, dealing with the transition of power from the sage-like Marcus Aurelius to his monstrous son, Commodus. The fictional hero, General Maximus, is Caesar's adopted heir, whom Commodus turns into an exile after killing his family. Becoming a gladiator, Maximus fights to avenge his loved ones and save the soul of Rome. The film's strengths are a fine script, which doesn't stint on the politics, and excellent performances from Richard Harris and Oliver Reed, in his final film, as a gladiator trainer. Also superb is Joaquin Phoenix as the paranoid Commodus, while Russell Crowe is utterly convincing as the Conan/Spartacus-like hero. As always with Scott, the visuals are fabulous.

Russell Crowe *Maximus* • Joaquin Phoenix *Commodus* • Connie Nielsen *Lucilla* • Oliver Reed *Proximo* • Derek Jacobi *Gracchus* • Djimon Hounsou *Juba* • Richard Harris *Marcus Aurelius* • David Schofield *Falco* • John Shrapnel *Gaius* ■ *Dir* Ridley Scott • *Scr* David Franzoni, John Logan, William Nicholson, from a story by David Franzoni • *Cinematographer* John Mathieson

The Glass Bottom Boat
★★★🅄

Romantic comedy · 1966 · US · Colour · 110mins

Doris Day shows a surprising affinity for satire in this Cold War spoof, starring as a publicist in a space laboratory who's falling in love with engineer boss Rod Taylor while writing a biography of him. Various governments are interested in Taylor's work and, as Day has a dog called Vladimir, she quickly becomes a Soviet suspect. Director Frank Tashlin was a former cartoonist and packs the film with sight gags, but Day rises above the slapstick.

Doris Day *Jennifer Nelson* • Rod Taylor *Bruce Templeton* • Arthur Godfrey *Axel Nordstrom* • John McGiver *Ralph Goodwin* • Paul Lynde *Homer Cripps* • Edward Andrews *General Wallace Bleecker* • Eric Fleming *Edgar Hill* • Dom De Luise *Julius Pritter* ■ *Dir* Frank Tashlin • *Scr* Everett Freeman

The Glass Cage
★

Crime drama   1955 · UK · BW · 75mins

John Ireland, best known for playing heavies in Hollywood B-movies, was lured to Britain for this low-budget crime drama. It's a promising but ultimately bungled yarn about a circus performer called the "Starving Man" (Eric Pohlmann) who fasts for a living. When he is found dead in his glass cage, investigations reveal that he had witnessed the murder of a blackmailer and was subsequently silenced by the killer. Honor Blackman co-stars.

John Ireland *Pel* • Honor Blackman *Jenny* • Geoffrey Keen *Stanton* • Eric Pohlmann *Sapolio* • Sidney James *Tony Lewis* • Liam Redmond *Lindley* • Sydney Tafler *Rorke* • Valerie Vernon *Bella* ■ *Dir* Montgomery Tully • *Scr* Richard Landau, from the novel *The Outsiders* by AE Martin

The Glass Cage
★★ 18

Erotic thriller   1996 · US · Colour · 91mins

Another offering of sex and sleaze scantily dressed up as a thriller. Directed with evident self-satisfaction by Michael Schroeder, this sordid tale of diamond smuggling and dirty dancing lurches from shoot-out to soft-core porn, while paying only passing attention to such trifles as character, originality and logic. As the gangster's moll condemned to gyrate at a New

Orleans strip joint, Charlotte Lewis just manages to keep her dignity. The same cannot be said of Eric Roberts, whose performance as a corrupt cop is more evidence of a faltering career. Contains violence, swearing, sex scenes, drug abuse and nudity. 🖭

Charlotte Lewis *Jaqueline* • Richard Tyson *Paul Yaeger* • Eric Roberts *Detective Montrachet* • Stephen Nicholas *Renzi* • Joseph Campanella *Lebeque* • Richard Moll *Ian Dexter* • Horacio Anthony *Marko* • Anthony Curtis *Anton* ■ *Dir* Michael Schroeder • *Scr* Peter Yurksaitis, David Keith Miller

Glass Houses
★

Erotic drama   1972 · US · Colour · 90mins

We're in *Bob & Carol & Ted & Alice* territory – minus the big stars – with this story about the sexual revolution, set in California. The plot throws in adultery, environmental concerns and a soupçon of incest but hovers close to soft-core porn and characters spend a lot of time in the hot-tub. Director Alexander Singer also worked on TV's *Lost in Space* and was associate producer of Kubrick's *The Killing*.

Bernard Barrow *Victor* • Deirdre Lenihan *Kim* • Jennifer O'Neill *Jean* • Ann Summers *Wife* • Phillip Pine *Ted* • Clarke Gordon *Novelist* ■ *Dir* Alexander Singer • *Scr* Alexander Singer, Judith Singer

The Glass Key
★★

Crime drama   1935 · US · BW · 77mins

A dated but still absorbing adaptation of Dashiell Hammett's novel, with George Raft as the henchman of an allegedly corrupt politician (Edward Arnold) accused of murdering a senator's son. The dialogue is pure "movie talk", sometimes hovering close to screwball comedy. There is a decent sense of intrigue, but the visual atmospherics associated with *film noir* are conspicuously absent – this was years before the style took root with *The Maltese Falcon*. The interesting cast includes Ray Milland (as the murder victim) whom Paramount consistently undervalued until his starring role in *The Lost Weekend*.

George Raft *Ed Beaumont* • Claire Dodd *Janet Henry* • Edward Arnold *Paul Madvig* • Rosalind Keith *Opal Madvig* • Ray Milland *Taylor Henry* • Robert Gleckler *Shad O'Rory* • Guinn "Big Boy" Williams [Guinn Williams] *Jeff* • Tammany Young *Clarkie* ■ *Dir* Frank Tuttle • *Scr* Kathryn Scola, Kubec Glasmon, Harry Ruskin, from the novel by Dashiell Hammett

The Glass Key
★★★★

Film noir   1942 · US · BW · 85mins

The second, and far superior, version of Dashiell Hammett's novel, with Alan Ladd and Veronica Lake following up their first hit together, *This Gun for Hire*. Ladd plays the bodyguard to Brian Donlevy's politician, uncovering a murder plot, while Lake seesaws provocatively between them, finally settling on Ladd in one of those legendary screen clinches. The story's focus on the bodyguard gave Akira Kurosawa the idea for his masterly 1961 samurai drama *Yojimbo* and that, in turn, was acknowledged by Sergio Leone as the inspiration for *A Fistful of Dollars*.

Brian Donlevy *Paul Madvig* • Veronica Lake *Janet Henry* • Alan Ladd *Ed Beaumont* •

Bonita Granville *Opal Madvig* • Richard Denning *Taylor Henry* • Joseph Calleia *Nick Varna* • William Bendix *Jeff* ■ *Dir* Stuart Heisler • *Scr* Jonathan Latimer, from the novel by Dashiell Hammett

The Glass Menagerie
★★★🅄

Drama   1950 · US · BW · 107mins

This early film version of Tennessee Williams's play relies as much on star power as the mesmeric dialogue and the involving quality of the story. Gertrude Lawrence stars as the faded Southern belle mother, living in a run-down St Louis apartment with crippled, introverted daughter Jane Wyman and rebellious son Arthur Kennedy. Kirk Douglas is the gentleman caller, whose visit changes the family completely – Lawrence believes Douglas will sweep Wyman off her feet and into a wedding. Director Irving Rapper is demonstrably restrained.

Jane Wyman *Laura Wingfield* • Kirk Douglas *Jim O'Connor* • Gertrude Lawrence *Amanda Wingfield* • Arthur Kennedy *Tom Wingfield* • Ralph Sanford *Mendoza* • Ann Tyrrell *Clerk* • John Compton *Young man* • Gertrude Graner *Woman instructor* ■ *Dir* Irving Rapper • *Scr* Tennessee Williams, Peter Berneis, from the play by Tennessee Williams

The Glass Menagerie
★★★ PG

Drama   1987 · US · Colour · 138mins

Paul Newman's reverent film version of one of Tennessee Williams's slighter fables stars his wife Joanne Woodward as a faded Southern belle and dominating mother who lives with her son Tom (John Malkovich) and her crippled daughter Laura (Karen Allen) in a delapidated St Louis apartment. Tom works in a warehouse to keep the family, while Laura spends her days polishing her collection of glass animals and wistfully waiting for a "gentleman caller" to whisk her away. Woodward's iron woman is a triumph, and Malkovich is easily her match. 🖭

Joanne Woodward *Amanda Wingfield* • John Malkovich *Tom Wingfield* • Karen Allen *Laura Wingfield* • James Naughton *The Gentleman Caller/Jim O'Connor* ■ *Dir* Paul Newman • *Scr* from a play by Tennessee Williams

The Glass Mountain
★★

Romantic drama   1949 · UK · BW · 107mins

In the second of their five screen twinnings, husband-and-wife team Michael Denison and Dulcie Gray experience a few marital difficulties after he returns from RAF duty obsessed with both an idea for an opera and Valentina Cortese, the partisan who rescued him from the mountain snow. The subject of couples forced apart because of differing wartime experiences is worthy of attention, but director Henry Cass struggles to prevent it being buried in an avalanche of sentimentality. The polished finale features members of Milan's celebrated La Scala company, performing music co-written by Federico Fellini's regular composer, Nino Rota.

Michael Denison *Richard Wilder* • Dulcie Gray *Ann Wilder* • Valentina Cortese *Alida* • Tito Gobbi *Tito* • Sebastian Shaw *Bruce McLeod* • Antonio Centa *Gino* • Sidney King *Charles* •

Elena Rizzieri *Singer* ■ *Dir* Henry Cass • *Scr* Joseph Janni, John Hunter, Emery Bonnet, John Cousins, Henry Cass

The Glass Shield
★★ 15

Police drama based on a true story
1995 · US/Fr · Colour · 105mins

A worthy if overelaborate thriller, this is based on a true story about the first black cop to be assigned to a Californian sheriff's department. Michael Boatman is the eager young recruit who finds himself contending with not only the racist attitudes of his all-white colleagues, but also a web of corruption that leads to the highest level. There's solid support from Lori Petty, rapper Ice Cube and old hand Michael Ironside, but director Charles Burnett occasionally gets too bogged down in the intricate plot to allow a real sense of excitement. 🖭

Michael Boatman *JJ Johnson* • Lori Petty *Deputy Deborah Fields* • Ice Cube *Teddy Woods* • Elliott Gould *Greenspan* • Richard Anderson *Massey* • Don Harvey *Deputy Bono* • Michael Ironside *Baker* • Michael Gregory *Roy Bush* • Bernie Casey *Locket* ■ *Dir* Charles Burnett • *Scr* Charles Burnett, from the screenplay *One of Us* by Ned Walsh

The Glass Slipper
★★🅄

Romantic fantasy 1955 · US · Colour · 93mins

This musical version of the Cinderella story, directed by Charles Walters, is solemnly narrated by Walter Pidgeon. It stars Leslie Caron and an awkwardly-cast Michael Wilding, who finds himself unsuitably involved in the ballet production numbers, choreographed by Roland Petit. These are, however, the highlights of an extraordinarily dull movie, in which Caron's heroine is perversely irritating, the ugly sisters even more perversely glamorous and Estelle Winwood's fairy godmother a winsome old bag.

Leslie Caron *Ella* • Michael Wilding *Prince Charles* • Keenan Wynn *Kovin* • Estelle Winwood *Mrs Toquet* • Elsa Lanchester *Widow Sonder* • Barry Jones *Duke* • Amanda Blake *Birdena* • Lisa Daniels *Serafina* ■ *Dir* Charles Walters • *Scr* Helen Deutsch

The Glass Wall
★★★

Drama   1953 · US · BW · 79mins

One of a handful of films made by Vittorio Gassman for MGM during his marriage to Shelley Winters. The Italian heart-throb plays an illegal immigrant in the USA, who is given refuge by social outcast Gloria Grahame and jazzman Jerry Paris. The atmospherically lit, documentary-style movie has a lively jazz score, and there are brief appearances by the likes of Jack Teagarden. It was the best of Gassman's Hollywood films. His marriage to Winters proved short-lived and he returned to Italy to resume his prestigious stage and screen career.

Vittorio Gassman *Peter* • Gloria Grahame *Maggie* • Ann Robinson *Nancy* • Douglas Spencer *Inspector Bailey* • Robin Raymond *Tanya* • Jerry Paris *Tom* • Elizabeth Slifer *Mrs Hinckley* ■ *Dir* Maxwell Shane • *Scr* Maxwell Shane, Ivan Tors

The Glass Web
★★

Crime drama   1953 · US · BW · 81mins

A TV producer is blackmailed by his former mistress: when she is

murdered, the case is featured on the producer's show, *Crime of the Week*. Made when television was beginning to eat into cinema attendances, Jack Arnold's drama was originally filmed in 3-D, a gimmick intended to lure audiences away from their TV sets. However, the plot is tortuous and unfolds slowly, while Edward G Robinson, playing another of the film's blackmail victims, is given little opportunity to show his talents.

Edward G Robinson *Henry Hayes* • John Forsythe *Don Newell* • Kathleen Hughes *Paula Ranier* • Marcia Henderson *Louise Newell* • Richard Denning *Dave Markson* • Hugh Sanders *Lieutenant Stevens* • Clark Howat *Bob Warren* • Dick Stewart *Everett* ■ *Dir* Jack Arnold • *Scr* Robert Blees, Leonard Lee, from the novel by Max Simon Ehrlich

Glastonbury the Movie
★★★ 🔞

Music documentary
1995 · UK · Colour · 96mins

What a contradiction this is – a documentary celebrating Britain's thriving counterculture that proudly proclaims itself to be the first feature completed with National Lottery funding. Employing widely differing styles and film techniques, and shot over a number of years, this tribute is more concerned with the antics of the audience than with the acts on stage. The sideshows around this site of Arthurian legend are revealing and occasionally entertaining, but the refusal to present the sights and sounds in a cohesive way deprives the footage of any anthropological value. However, fans of the bands featured won't have too many complaints. 🖵

Dir Robin Mahoney, William Beaton, Matthew Salkeld, Lisa Lake, Mike Sarne [Michael Sarne]

Gleaming the Cube ★★★🔞

Action adventure 1988 · US · Colour · 99mins

Despite the sometimes uneasy mix of children's caper and more adult action, this is, for the most part, an exhilarating ride. Christian Slater is the ace skateboarder who teams up with his chums and a reluctant detective (Steven Bauer) to discover who murdered his adopted Vietnamese brother. The pre-stardom Slater oozes charisma, there's solid support from Ed Lauter and Richard Herd, and the stunning skateboarding sequences are expertly choreographed by director Graeme Clifford. Contains mild swearing. 🖵 *DVD*

Christian Slater *Brian Kelly* • Steven Bauer *Detective Al Lucero* • Ed Lauter *Mr Kelly* • Micole Mercurio *Mrs Kelly* • Art Chudabala *Vinh Kelly* • Richard Herd *Ed Lawndale* • Tuan Le *Colonel Trac* • Min Luong *Tina Trac* ■ *Dir* Graeme Clifford • *Scr* Michael Tolkin

Glen or Glenda ★🔞

Drama 1953 · US · BW · 70mins

The poster for Tim Burton's 1994 biopic *Ed Wood* featured a pink angora sweater – a homage to this fifties gem. Edward D Wood Jr directs himself (billed as Daniel Davis) as Glen, the troubled transvestite who longs to share a wardrobe with his fiancée Dolores Fuller. The cross-dressing Wood aimed for a documentary realism

in this plea for understanding. However, his juxtaposition of painfully earnest psychiatrist Timothy Farrell and a sneering Bela Lugosi rattling on about big green dragons quickly reduces the entire exercise to excruciating farce. So bad, it's unmissable. Contains sexual references. 🖵

Bela Lugosi *The Spirit* • Lyle Talbot *Police Inspector Warren* • Timothy Farrell *Dr Alton* • Daniel Davis [Edward D Wood Jr] *Glen/Glenda* • Dolores Fuller *Barbara* • "Tommy" Haines *Alan/Ann* ■ *Dir/Scr* Edward D Wood Jr

Glengarry Glen Ross
★★★★★🔞

Drama 1992 · US · Colour · 96mins

Director James Foley, working with a highly resonant screenplay by David Mamet, brings a palpable cinematic tension to what could have been a dry, theatrical piece. Rarely moving outside the real-estate office where four salesmen are under pressure to sell more or lose their jobs, the film speaks forcefully about decency being snuffed out by desire, good men taking wrong turnings despite their best efforts and the stench of the American Dream gone mad. Al Pacino, Jack Lemmon, Alan Arkin and Ed Harris all give note-perfect ensemble performances, Alec Baldwin appears in a telling cameo and there's a major early role for Kevin Spacey. You can only gawp at such ability. Contains swearing. 🖵 *DVD*

Al Pacino *Ricky Roma* • Jack Lemmon *Shelley "The Machine" Levene* • Alec Baldwin *Blake* • Ed Harris *Dave Moss* • Alan Arkin *George Aaronow* • Kevin Spacey *John Williamson* • Jonathan Pryce *James Lingk* ■ *Dir* James Foley • *Scr* David Mamet, from his play

The Glenn Miller Story
★★★★🔵

Musical biographical drama
1953 · US · Colour · 107mins

Director Anthony Mann and star James Stewart made a series of stunning psychological westerns in the fifties (*Winchester '73, The Naked Spur*), yet this biopic of the legendary trombonist and band leader will always be their most fondly remembered collaboration. Whether struggling to find the style of swing that would set him apart from his contemporaries, enjoying the brief benefits of fame or romancing June Allyson, Stewart is so perfect for the role that it is hardly surprising many people are more familiar with his impersonation than they were with the real Glenn Miller. The supporting cast is impeccable and the music, adapted by Henry Mancini, is as bewitching as ever. 🖵

James Stewart *Glenn Miller* • June Allyson *Helen Burger Miller* • Charles Drake *Don Haynes* • George Tobias *Si Schribman* • Henry Morgan [Harry Morgan] *Chummy MacGregor* • Marion Ross *Polly Haynes* • Irving Bacon *Mr Miller* ■ *Dir* Anthony Mann • *Scr* Valentine Davies, Oscar Brodney

The Glimmer Man ★★🔞

Action thriller 1996 · US · Colour · 87mins

Sandwiched between his eco-warrior outings *On Deadly Ground* and *Fire Down Below*, this has Steven Seagal going back to the no-brainer action

thrillers that made his name. It's a partial success and an improvement on those two, but ultimately it lacks the streamlined thrills of his early films. Here, New Age cop Seagal is set on the trail of a serial killer, only to discover his murky government past coming back to haunt him. Keenen Ivory Wayans provides a lively foil as his partner. Brian Cox, however, only succeeds in butchering an American accent again as Seagal's former boss. Contains swearing. 🖵 *DVD*

Steven Seagal *Jack Cole* • Keenen Ivory Wayans *Jim Campbell* • Bob Gunton *Frank Deverell* • Brian Cox *Mr Smith* • John M Jackson *Donald* • Michelle Johnson *Jessica* • Stephen Tobolowsky *Christopher Maynard* ■ *Dir* John Gray • *Scr* Kevin Brodbin

Glitz ★🔞

Crime drama 1988 · US · Colour · 94mins

Before film versions of *Get Shorty* and *Out of Sight* revived his faith in Hollywood, Elmore Leonard endured several uninspired efforts to adapt his bestselling crime novels, including this dud from director Sandor Stern. Jimmy Smits warms up for his subsequent role in TV's *NYPD Blue* by playing a Miami cop whose girlfriend dies in mysterious circumstances. Unfortunately, Leonard's detailed, distinctive characters and surge of electricity have been swapped in the screenplay for bland clichés, so that the entire enterprise is shaky from frame one. Contains swearing. 🖵

Jimmy Smits *Vincent Mora* • Markie Post *Linda Moon* • John Diehl *Teddy Magyk* • Madison Mason *Dixie Davies* • Robin Strasser *Nancy Donovan* • Richard Schaal *Tommy Donovan* • James Purcell *Jackie Garbo* • Ken Foree *Delon "Moose" Johnson* • Tasia Valenza *Iris Ruiz* ■ *Dir* Sandor Stern • *Scr* Steven Zito, from the novel by Elmore Leonard

A Global Affair ★★🔵

Comedy 1964 · US · BW · 83mins

Bob Hope is a United Nations official who discovers that an abandoned baby is a good way to make yourself very popular with a bevy of international beauties. But is it Hope or the baby they're after? This is not a highlight of Bob's post-*Road* career and director Jack Arnold would probably have preferred to be remembered for *The Incredible Shrinking Man* or *The Mouse That Roared*.

Bob Hope *Frank Larrimore* • Lilo Pulver [Liselotte Pulver] *Sonya* • Michèle Mercier *Lisette* • Elga Andersen *Yvette* • Yvonne De Carlo *Dolores* • Miiko Taka *Fumiko* • Robert Sterling *Randy* • Nehemiah Persoff *Sigura* ■ *Dir* Jack Arnold • *Scr* Arthur Marx, Bob Fisher, Charles Lederer, from a story by Eugene Vale

La Gloire de Mon Père
★★★🔵

Biographical drama
1990 · Fr · Colour · 106mins

Drawn from film-maker Marcel Pagnol's autobiography, this is a handsome and beautifully acted piece of French heritage cinema. The kitsch quotient may be high, and director Yves Robert has clearly gone out of his way to please the crowd, but the cast is fine, with Philippe Caubère neatly capturing the arrogance of the *petit bourgeois* and Nathalie Roussel dishing out fond

reproaches with true maternal gentility. Even more impressive is Julien Ciamaca as the young Marcel, struggling to deal with his father's victory at *boules* and his celebrity after he bags a brace of partridge. Try not to let Vladimir Cosma's intrusive score spoil your enjoyment. In French with English subtitles. 🖵

Philippe Caubère *Joseph Pagnol* • Nathalie Roussel *Augustine Pagnol* • Thérèse Liotard *Aunt Rose* • Didier Pain *Uncle Jules* • Julien Ciamaca *Marcel aged 11* • Victorien Delamere *Paul aged 5* • Joris Molinas *Lili Des Bellons* • Paul Crauchet *Mond Des Parpaillouns* ■ *Dir* Yves Robert • *Scr* Lucette Andrei, Jérôme Tonnerre, Louis Nucera, Yves Robert, from the autobiography by Marcel Pagnol

Gloria ★★★★🔞

Thriller 1980 · US · Colour · 116mins

Oscar-nominated Gena Rowlands gives a formidably engaging performance as Gloria, a not-so-dumb broad living in the Bronx, who takes charge of a half-Puerto Rican boy (John Adames) whose parents have been killed by the Mafia. Holding an account book of gangster dealings, she and the boy go on the run from the mob, until she turns and stands her ground as a pistol-packing "mama". Director John Cassavetes deftly matches his trademark freewheeling camerawork to his wife Rowlands's brassy, endearing portrayal. As dramatic entertainment, *Gloria* is quite glorious. 🖵

Gena Rowlands *Gloria Swenson* • Tony Knesich *1st gangster* • Gregory Cleghorne *Kid in elevator* • Buck Henry *Jack Dawn* • John Adames *Phil Dawn* • Julie Carmen *Jeri Dawn* • Jessica Castillo *Joan Dawn* • Tom Noonan *2nd gangster* • Ronald Maccone *3rd gangster* ■ *Dir/Scr* John Cassavetes

Gloria ★★🔞

Crime drama 1998 · US · Colour · 107mins

Sharon Stone's attempt to emulate Gena Rowlands's hard-as-nails moll (who made her money turning tricks with executive gangsters in John Cassavetes's 1980 social thriller) is constantly undercut by veteran Sidney Lumet's lacklustre direction, as this Gloria, together with a small, orphaned Hispanic boy (Jean-Luke Figueroa) and a computer disc of Mafia info, is pursued by the mob. It's a pity for Stone's sake – she's an enterprising actress who should be admired for taking dramatic chances. Cardboard characters and cut-out situations are all that are left here, without any acknowledgement of Cassavetes's original – which does at least help to leave his memory untarnished.

Sharon Stone *Gloria* • Jean-Luke Figueroa *Nicky* • Jeremy Northam *Kevin* • Cathy Moriarty *Diane* • George C Scott *Ruby* • Mike Starr *Sean* • Barry McEvoy *Terry* • Don Billett *Raymond* • Bonnie Bedelia *Brenda* ■ *Dir* Sidney Lumet • *Scr* Steven Antin, from the film by John Cassavetes

Glory ★★★★🔞

Historical war drama
1989 · US · Colour · 117mins

This tale of the American Civil War is a long overdue tribute to America's first black regiment to go into combat, the 54th Massachusetts Voluntary Infantry. The details are culled partly from the letters of the 54th's commander,

🔵 = SUITABLE FOR ALL, 🔵ₑ = SUITABLE FOR ALL, ESPECIALLY FOR YOUNG CHILDREN (VIDEO ONLY) 🔞 = PARENTAL GUIDANCE

Colonel Robert Gould Shaw (played by Matthew Broderick), a sensitive 25-year-old (but already a veteran) from an abolitionist family who's determined to lead his men into full battle. His racist superiors won't even allow the soldiers boots, and the troops resent the white young man's leadership, especially runaway slave Denzel Washington. While there is stereotyping, such as the embarrassing scene in which Morgan Freeman, Washington and the rest of the black cast burst into spiritual harmonies, the lasting impression is of Washington's performance and the plight of the men in general. Fabulously photographed by Freddie Francis, it features brilliantly staged (and shockingly violent) battle scenes. Contains swearing. ▢ **DVD**

Matthew Broderick *Colonel Robert Gould Shaw* • Denzel Washington *Trip* • Morgan Freeman *John Rawlins* • Cary Elwes *Cabot Forbes* • Jihmi Kennedy *Sharts* • AndréBraugher *Thomas Searles* • John Finn *Sergeant Mulcahy* • Donovan Leitch *Charles Morse* ■ *Dir* Edward Zwick • *Scr* Kevin Jarre, from the books *Lay This Laurel* by Lincoln Kirstein and *One Gallant Rush* by Peter Burchard, and the letters of Robert Gould Shaw

Glory Alley ★

Drama   1952 · US · BW · 79mins

MGM was trying to find roles for Leslie Caron after *An American in Paris* and wanted to see if Ralph Meeker had the makings of a star. This stilted, dreary drama was no help to either of them; nor did it enhance the reputation of its veteran director, Raoul Walsh (*White Heat*, *High Sierra*). Meeker is the boxer accused of cowardice who goes off to become a hero in Korea. At least Caron's occupation as a burlesque dancer allows her to show off those skills and there are also enjoyable performances from Louis ''Satchmo'' Armstrong and Jack Teagarden.

Ralph Meeker *Socks Barbarrosa* • Leslie Caron *Angela* • Kurt Kasznar *Judge* • Gilbert Roland *Peppi Donnato* • John McIntire *Gabe Jordan* • Louis Armstrong *Shadow Johnson* • Jack Teagarden • Larry Gates *Dr Robert Ardley* ■ *Dir* Raoul Walsh • *Scr* Art Cohn

Glory & Honor ★★★ **PG**

Biographical adventure drama
1998 · US · Colour · 90mins

Not many people know that, when Captain Robert Peary claimed the honour of being the first man to reach the North Pole, he was accompanied by his African-American assistant. That's the premise of this high-quality TV movie about nonstop adventure in the icy wastes. Peary (Henry Czerny), who was obsessed with reaching the top of the world, was accompanied on all his expeditions by faithful manservant Matthew Henson (Delroy Lindo). The master/servant relationship was gradually eroded as the stalwart Henson turned out to be invaluable, and his willingness to learn Inuit ways was an important factor in the success of the team. Contains some swearing and brief nudity. ▢

Delroy Lindo *Matthew Henson* • Henry Czerny *Robert Peary* • Bronwen Booth *Josephine Peary* • Kim Staunton *Lucy Ross* ■ *Dir* Kevin Hooks • *Scr* Jeffrey Lewis, Susan Rhinehart, from a story by Robert Caputo

Glory Boy ★

Drama   1971 · US · Colour · 102mins

Disillusioned soldier Michael Moriarty brings two fellow Vietnam servicemen home to his father's dilapidated farm. Mitchell Ryan is the psychopathic sergeant who taunts Moriarty's patriotic father, played by veteran character actor Arthur Kennedy, and then forces himself on a young hitchhiker, Topo Swope (the daughter of Dorothy McGuire). Director Edwin Sherin allows a seemingly bold attempt to convey the dehumanising effect of the Vietnam War to degenerate into a sordid tale of rape and murder.

Michael Moriarty *Trubee Pell* • Arthur Kennedy *Walter Pell* • William Devane *Jimmy Pilgrim* • Mitchell Ryan *Sergeant Martin Flood* • Topo Swope *Helen* • Lloyd Gough *Dr Paul* • Ford Rainey *Sheriff Coleman* • Peter Donat *Car salesman* ■ *Dir* Edwin Sherin • *Scr* Stanford Whitmore, from the novel *The Old Man's Place* by John Sanford

The Glory Brigade ★★★ **U**

War drama   1953 · US · BW · 81mins

Victor Mature stars in this tale of conflict between American and Greek soldiers, fighting alongside one another during the Korean War. The film's portrayal of smart Americans and peasant Greeks seems dubious by today's standards, but director Robert D Webb specialised in action scenes and acquits himself well enough, while Lee Marvin makes a strong impression in an early starring role. The real Korean War ended only a month after this film was released.

Victor Mature *Lieutenant Sam Prior* • Alexander Scourby *Lieutenant Niklas* • Lee Marvin *Corporal Bowman* • Richard Egan *Sergeant Johnson* • Nick Dennis *Corporal Marakis* • Roy Roberts *Sergeant Chuck Anderson* • Alvy Moore *Private Stone* • Russell Evans *Private Taylor* ■ *Dir* Robert D Webb • *Scr* Franklin Coen

Glory Daze ★★

Comedy drama   1995 · US · Colour · 104mins

This pointless movie about pointless people will be of interest mainly to admirers of Ben Affleck and Matt Damon. Affleck takes the lead role as one of a gang of rich college seniors, all living in the same boarding house and fearing graduation day and the cruel realities of life beyond. There are a few laughs, but on the whole nothing much happens and a stream of bad language and scenes of boozing are supposed to make up for it. At least writer/director Rich Wilkes doesn't overdo the sentimentality. Look out for Damon and Matthew McConaughey in cameo roles.

Ben Affleck *Jack* • Sam Rockwell *Rob* • French Stewart *Dennis* • Alyssa Milano *Chelsea* • Megan Ward *Joannie* • Vinnie DeRamus *Mickey* • Matthew McConaughey *Rental truck guy* • Matt Damon *Edgar Pudwhacker* • Hong Vien *Slosh* ■ *Dir/Scr* Rich Wilkes

The Glory Guys ★★★

Western   1965 · US · Colour · 119mins

A large-budget and largely competent western, written by Sam Peckinpah, this focuses on a US cavalry action against the Indians and conflict within the ranks. Tom Tryon is pretty nondescript in the leading role, playing

a cavalry officer loath to send his recruits into combat. Andrew Duggan does better as the general who's less fussed at the prospect of losing a few men, while a young James Caan catches the eye as a bull-headed soldier. The typically brutal plot takes its time to unfold, but builds to a rousing finale.

Tom Tryon *Demas Harrod* • Harve Presnell *Sol Rogers* • Senta Berger *Lou Woodard* • Andrew Duggan *General McCabe* • James Caan *Dugan* • Slim Pickens *Gregory* • Michael Anderson Jr *Martin Hale* • Peter Breck *Hodges* • Robert McQueeny *[Robert McQueeney] Marcus* ■ *Dir* Arnold Laven • *Scr* Sam Peckinpah, from the novel *The Dice of God* by Hoffman Birney

The Glory Stompers ★★

Action drama   1967 · US · Colour · 85mins

Violence erupts between warring bikers when Dennis Hopper's Black Souls beat up Stompers leader Jody McCrea and take his girlfriend to be sold in a Mexican white-slave market. Jock Mahoney rescues McCrea and joins his old friend on the manhunt south of the border. This is nothing more than a hippy western substituting cowboys with Hell's Angels, horses with roaring choppers and campfire talk with a laughable love-in. Risible dialogue and mindless action puts this near the bottom of the very large rebel riders heap. Hopper did much better as the director (and star) of *Easy Rider* two years later, on a similar theme.

Dennis Hopper *Chino* • Jody McCrea *Darryl* • Chris Noel *Chris* • Jock Mahoney *Smiley* • Saundra Gayle *Jo Ann* • Robert Tessier *Magoo* • Astrid Warner *Doreen* • Gary Wood *Pony* ■ *Dir* Anthony M Lanza • *Scr* James Gordon White, John Lawrence

The Glove ★★

Crime action   1978 · US · Colour · 90mins

Convict Roosevelt ''Rosey'' Grier is equipped with a custom-built steel glove that can smash through people and solid metal. When he's not causing damage with his lethal appendage, Grier shows his philanthropic side to underprivileged kids. Ex-cop turned bounty hunter John Saxon is offered $20,000 for his recapture. This is an odd, before-its-time combination of science-fiction, action and social issues that fails to make its mark in each area it tries to embrace. Written and produced by Julian Roffman, director of the weird 3-D exploiter *The Mask*, and directed by former B-movie actor Ross Hagen, this bizarre effort is entertaining by default.

John Saxon *Sam Kellough* • Roosevelt Grier *[Rosey Grier] Victor Hale* • Joanna Cassidy *Sheila Michaels* • Joan Blondell *Mrs Fitzgerald* • Jack Carter *Walter Stratton* • Keenan Wynn *Bill Schwartz* • Aldo Ray *Prison guard* • Michael Pataki *Harry Iverson* ■ *Dir* Ross Hagen • *Scr* Hubert Smith, Julian Roffman

G:MT Greenwich Mean Time ★ **18**

Drama   1998 · UK · Colour · 91mins

This is unconvincing, painfully clichéd garbage about a bunch of London-based friends who are torn apart by everything from jealousy to paralysis. For two unbearable hours, the film leaps clumsily between half a dozen plot strands, as poorly defined

characters spew out corny dialogue and experience a couple of traumas each. While the rehabilitation of Charlie (Alec Newman) in hospital after a road accident is the film's best stab at conviction, it's overshadowed by Bean's (Benjamin Waters) hilarious descent from nice trumpeter to crack dealer. The decent drum 'n' bass soundtrack helps a little, but this is still nothing short of an ordeal.

Alec Newman *Charlie* • Melanie Gutteridge *Lucy* • Georgia MacKenzie *Rachel* • Chiwetel Ejiofor *Rix* • Steve John Shepherd *Sam* • Alicya Eyo *Bobby* • Benjamin Waters *Bean* • Anjela Lauren Smith *Sherry* ■ *Dir* John Strickland • *Scr* Simon Mirren

The Gnome-Mobile ★★★ **U**

Fantasy   1967 · US · Colour · 81mins

A whimsical fantasy in the Disney tradition of whiter-than-white family fun, packed with enchanting special effects and merry if instantly forgettable tunes from Buddy Baker and the Sherman brothers. Those ever-so-slightly annoying kids from *Mary Poppins*, Matthew Garber and Karen Dotrice, turn up again, this time protecting gnomes living in redwood forests from mindless lumber barons. Owing much to the Disney classic *Darby O'Gill and the Little People*, also directed by Robert Stevenson, this little-known live feature deserves better attention; kids will love it. Veteran Walter Brennan is a stand-out in a dual role and there's a knockout car chase finale. ▢

Walter Brennan *DJ Mulrooney/Knobby* • Tom Lowell *Jasper* • Matthew Garber *Rodney Winthrop* • Ed Wynn *Rufus* • Karen Dotrice *Elizabeth Winthrop* • Richard Deacon *Ralph Yarby* • Sean McClory *Horatio Quaxton* • Jerome Cowan *Dr Conrad Ramsey* ■ *Dir* Robert Stevenson • *Scr* Ellis Kadison, from the novel *The Gnomobile: a Gnice Gnew Gnarrative With Gnonsense, But Gnothing Gnaughty* by Upton Sinclair

Go ★★★★ **18**

Comedy crime drama
1999 · US · Colour · 98mins

Doug Liman's directorial debut, *Swingers*, was impressive; his follow-up film is even more so, intertwining three separate storylines to present a picture of mixed-up Los Angeles youth. It's Christmas Eve, and two supermarket checkout girls are desperately trying to raise some rent money by rather dubious means. A colleague drives with his mates to Las Vegas, but their good-time gambling quickly turns sour. In the meantime, two male soap stars become embroiled in a police sting and end up getting their fingers burnt. Katie Holmes, Sarah Polley, Jay Mohr and Scott Wolf are all on great form in an ensemble vision of twentysomething angst that boasts a superb soundtrack. Contains sex scenes and swearing. ▢ **DVD**

Katie Holmes *Claire Montgomery* • Sarah Polley *Ronna Martin* • Desmond Askew *Simon Baines* • Scott Wolf *Adam* • Jay Mohr *Zack* • Timothy Olyphant *Todd Gaines* • Jimmy Shubert *Victor Jr* • Nathan Bexton *Mannie* ■ *Dir* Doug Liman • *Scr* John August

The Go-Between ★★★★ PG

Period drama 1971 · UK · Colour · 111mins

Director Joseph Losey and writer Harold Pinter's wonderfully resonant adaptation of LP Hartley's classic Edwardian romance is a beautiful, beguiling and brilliant exposé of a repressive and manipulative class system. Julie Christie and Alan Bates excel as the upper-class girl and her farmer lover carrying on a clandestine relationship, unwittingly aided by young "postman" Dominic Guard, who delivers their letters. Gorgeously shot by Gerry Fisher on Norfolk locations, this is thought-provoking costume drama of the highest order. ▭

Julie Christie *Marian Maudsley* • Alan Bates *Ted Burgess* • Dominic Guard *Leo Colston* • Margaret Leighton *Mrs Maudsley* • Michael Redgrave *Leo, as an old man* • Michael Gough *Mr Maudsley* • Edward Fox *Hugh Trimingham* • Richard Gibson *Marcus Maudsley* ■ *Dir* Joseph Losey • *Scr* Harold Pinter, from the novel by LP Hartley

Go Chase Yourself ★★★ U

Comedy 1938 · US · BW · 70mins

A gullible bank clerk (Joe Penner) wins a posh caravan in a lottery and is subsequently hijacked by a trio of crooks. The ensuing ride increasingly careers out of control to create a crazy comic farrago that manages to include numerous characters and situations. A vehicle for Penner, a then popular comic star of American radio, this is one for fans of zany farce. A lively cast of RKO stalwarts, directed by Edward F Cline, includes Lucille Ball on the way up (she would one day buy the studio) as Penner's tough-cookie wife, Jack Carson, and Fritz Feld as a penniless count courting heiress June Travis.

Joe Penner *Wilbur Meely* • Lucille Ball *Carol Meely* • June Travis *Judith Daniels* • Richard Lane *Nails* • Fritz Feld *Count Pierre de Louis-Louis* • Tom Kennedy *Ice-Box* • Jack Carson *Warren Miles* ■ *Dir* Edward F Cline [Edward Cline] • *Scr* Paul Yawitz, Bert Granet, from a story by Walter O'Keefe

Go Fish ★★★★ 18

Romantic drama 1994 · US · BW · 79mins

Unpretentious, inoffensive and very funny, this ultra low-budget festival hit, about finding true love in the lesbian community, effortlessly cruises between queer politics and hip funkiness. It's all about the very Woody Allen-esque things that happen when terminally single Max goes on a blind date with the neurotic Ely just to please her best mates. Arty yet wholly accessible, this monochrome marvel works on numerous levels, touching many universal issues in the process. A genuinely hilarious heart-warmer. Contains swearing and nudity. ▭

VS Brodie *Ely* • Guinevere Turner *Max* • T Wendy McMillan *Kia* • Migdalia Melendez *Evy* • Anastasia Sharp *Daria* • Mary Garvey *Student/Jury member* • Daniela Falcon *Student/Jury member* • Tracy Kimme *Student/Jury member* ■ *Dir* Rose Troche • *Scr* Rose Troche, Guinevere Turner

Go for a Take ★ U

Comedy 1972 · UK · Colour · 89mins

A British comedy with minimal laugh potential. Reg Varney and Norman Rossington are waiters on the run from debt collectors who take refuge in a film studio, a scenario which leads to some amazingly unfunny sequences. It's enough to make the *Carry On* films seem as witty as Oscar Wilde. Stale from his success in *On the Buses*, Varney is embarrassingly eager to please – it's a pity that inspiration doesn't match aspiration.

Reg Varney *Wilfrid Stone* • Norman Rossington *Jack Foster* • Sue Lloyd *Angel Montgomery* • Dennis Price *Dracula* • Julie Ege *April* • Patrick Newell *Generous Jim* • David Lodge *Graham* • Jack Haig *Security man* ■ *Dir* Harry Booth • *Scr* Alan Hackney, from a story by Alan Hackney, Harry Booth

Go for Broke! ★

Second World War drama 1951 · US · BW · 90mins

The title was the war cry of the 442nd Regimental Combat Team, a unit made up of Japanese-Americans who fought alongside their fellow Americans against the Nazis. Van Johnson plays the lieutenant in charge of them, who overcomes his initial wariness when he sees how they fight in Italy. For years Hollywood had been casting Japanese as the cruellest of enemies, the cynical motivation behind this MGM effort was that, in the postwar era, Japan was becoming a major market for Hollywood movies, so a story like this was good publicity. But it's not an especially good drama. The real President Harry Truman appears at the end, dishing out medals.

Van Johnson *Lt Michael Grayson* • Lane Nakano *Sam* • George Miki *Chick* • Akira Fukunaga *Frank* • Ken K Okamoto *Kaz* • Henry Oyasato *O'Hara* • Harry Hamada *Masami* ■ *Dir/Scr* Robert Pirosh

Go into Your Dance ★★

Musical comedy drama 1935 · US · BW · 92mins

This was the only movie in which Al Jolson and his wife Ruby Keeler appeared together, but there was more chemistry on screen between Keeler and Dick Powell in other Warner Bros musicals. Nevertheless, Jolson and Keeler pleasantly deliver some tuneful numbers by Harry Warren and Al Dubin (who appear briefly as themselves), including *About a Quarter to Nine* and *She's a Latin from Manhattan*. The choreographer Bobby Connolly was no Busby Berkeley, but he does a reasonable job. The feeble plot attempted to combine two of Warners' specialities – the backstage musical and the gangster movie.

Al Jolson *Al Howard* • Ruby Keeler *Dorothy Wayne* • Glenda Farrell *Sadie Howard* • Helen Morgan *Luana Bell* • Barton MacLane *The Duke* • Sharon Lynne *Blonde* • Patsy Kelly *Irma* • Benny Rubin ■ *Dir* Archie Mayo • *Scr* Earl Baldwin, from a story by Bradford Ropes

Go, Johnny, Go! ★★

Musical 1959 · US · BW · 75mins

Rock legend Chuck Berry and disc jockey Alan Freed (who also produced the film) beat up the soundtrack to this otherwise dull effort. The *Pygmalion*-like storyline involves the transformation of an orphan (Jimmy Clanton) into a rock 'n' roll hero. The highlights are the songs, such as *Little Queenie*, and Ritchie Valens hitting his strident form in his only film appearance. (Valens's life was well portrayed by Lou Diamond Phillips in the film *La Bamba* 27 years later.)

Alan Freed • Jimmy Clanton *Johnny* • Sandy Stewart *Julie Arnold* • Chuck Berry • Herb Vigran *Bill Barnett* • Frank Wilcox *Mr Arnold* • Barbara Woodell *Mrs Arnold* • Milton Frome *Mr Martin* • Richie Valens ■ *Dir* Paul Landres • *Scr* Gary Alexander

Go, Man, Go! ★★ U

Drama sports 1953 · US · BW · 83mins

One of two films directed by James Wong Howe, the Cantonese-born cinematographer whose credits include *The Prisoner of Zenda*, *Sweet Smell of Success* and *Hud* (for which he won his second Oscar). It's the story of Abe Saperstein (played by Dane Clark), the man who founded the world famous, all-black Harlem Globetrotters basketball team. Sidney Poitier appears, along with some bona fide Globetrotters, and the message about racism retains its power.

Dane Clark *Abe Saperstein* • Pat Breslin [Patricia Breslin] *Sylvia Saperstein* • Sidney Poitier *Inman Jackson* • Ruby Dee *Irma Jackson* • The Harlem Globetrotters • Edmon Ryan *Zack Leader* • Bram Nossen *James Willoughby* • Anatol Winogradoff *Papa Saperstein* ■ *Dir* James Wong Howe • *Scr* Arnold Becker (front for Alfred Palca)

Go Naked in the World ★★

Drama 1961 · US · Colour · 103mins

MGM embarked on a series of lavish melodramas in the sixties. This tosh, in which Gina Lollobrigida is taken home to meet dad Ernest Borgnine by infatuated son Anthony Franciosa, is not the best example. There's no thrill at all when we discover that Borgnine, and most of the townsfolk, already know about Lollobrigida's shady background. Writer/director Ranald MacDougall doesn't have the experience to turn this into gold – it needed a Douglas Sirk or a Vincente Minnelli. Given an X certificate on its original release, the film looks pretty tame today, though it's a reminder of MGM's late heyday gloss.

Gina Lollobrigida *Giulietta Cameron* • Anthony Franciosa *Nick Stratton* • Ernest Borgnine *Pete Stratton* • Luana Patten *Yvonne Stratton* • Will Kuluva *Argus Diavolos* • Philip Ober *Josh Kebner* • John Kellogg *Cobby* • Nancy R Pollock *Mary Stratton* ■ *Dir* Ranald MacDougall • *Scr* Ranald MacDougall, from the novel by Tom T Chamales

Go Now ★★ 15

Drama romance 1995 · UK · Colour · 82mins

Jude director Michael Winterbottom tackles another gloomy subject in this grim, contemporary drama. Robert Carlyle is Nick, in love with Karen (Juliet Aubrey), randy and raucous. His life turns sour when he discovers he has multiple sclerosis. The film chronicles his physical deterioration and how the inability to lead a normal life affects both Nick's morale and his relationship with Karen. Winterbottom's interpretation is unsentimental to say the least, though he remains sympathetic. The film hammers home what an excruciating situation having an incurable illness is, but there is little redemption or hope on offer. Contains sex scenes and some swearing. ▭

Robert Carlyle *Nick Cameron* • Juliet Aubrey *Karen Walker* • James Nesbitt *Tony* • Sophie Okonedo *Paula* • John Brobbey *Geoff* • Darren Tighe *Dell* • Berwick Kaler *Sammy* • Sean McKenzie *George* ■ *Dir* Michael Winterbottom • *Scr* Paul Henry Powell, Jimmy McGovern

Go Tell It on the Mountain ★★★

Drama 1984 · US · Colour · 96mins

Adapted from James Baldwin's semi-autobiographical novel, this is a stagey but engrossing rite-of-passage picture set initially during the mid-thirties. James Bond III gives a mature performance as a teenager trying to come to terms with both his sexuality and a hostile stepfather, before his conversion to the Temple of the Fire Baptised. Rosalind Cash and Alfre Woodard feature in a superb supporting cast, but it's Paul Winfield as the uncompromising Gabriel who holds the attention. Stan Lathan directs with a touch too much reverence for his material, but nevertheless provides a sobering insight into the black experience in pre-civil rights America.

Paul Winfield *Gabriel Grimes* • Rosalind Cash *Aunt Florence* • James Bond III *John Grimes* • Roderic Wimberly *Roy Grimes* • Olivia Cole *Elizabeth Grimes* • Ving Rhames *Young Gabriel* • Alfre Woodard *Esther* • CCH Pounder *Deborah* • Linda Hopkins *Sister McCandless* ■ *Dir* Stan Lathan • *Scr* Gus Edwards, Leslie Lee, from the novel by James Baldwin

Go Tell the Spartans ★★★ 15

War drama 1977 · US · Colour · 110mins

One of the few American movies to deal in depth with the morality of the Vietnam conflict, which officially started as "policing" action in 1964 – the year in which the film is set. It plays like a transplanted western, with veteran Burt Lancaster starring as a military adviser beset with doubts about his mission and its value. The screenplay by Wendell Meyes (*In Harm's Way*) is both clever and perceptive, and director Ted Post (*Hang 'Em High*) does what he can, but the scale is limited and the supporting cast lacks gravitas. Nevertheless, the film ultimately contrives to be surprisingly moving. Despite its stern and earnest approach to its subject matter, this is peppered with witty lines invariably spat out with relish by Lancaster. Contains swearing. ▭

Burt Lancaster *Major Asa Barker* • Craig Wasson *Corporal Stephen Courcey* • Jonathan Goldsmith *Sergeant Oleonowski* • Marc Singer *Captain Al Olivetti* • Joe Unger *Lt Raymond Hamilton* • Dennis Howard *Corporal Abraham Lincoln* • David Clennon *Lt Finley Wattsberg* • Evan Kim *Cowboy* ■ *Dir* Ted Post • *Scr* Wendell Mayes, from the novel *Incident at Muc Wa* by Daniel Ford

Go to Blazes ★★ U

Comedy 1961 · UK · Colour · 79mins

As a panellist on the ever-popular *Call My Bluff*, Patrick Campbell displayed wit and erudition. However, neither quality is evident in Campbell's screenplay (co-written with Vivienne Knight) for this substandard comedy caper, which is now mainly of interest for providing Maggie Smith with only

her second screen role. The story of some clottish crooks who train themselves up as firemen in order to use the engine they've bought as a getaway vehicle is both derivative and dull. Comedian Dave King and Daniel Massey generate few comic sparks, but there's a fun cameo from Robert Morley as an obliging arsonist.

Dave King *Bernard* • Robert Morley *"Arson" Eddie* • Daniel Massey *Harry* • Dennis Price *Withers* • Coral Browne *Colette* • Norman Rossington *Alfie* • Maggie Smith *Chantal* • Miles Malleson *Salesman* • Finlay Currie *Judge* ■ *Dir* Michael Truman • *Scr* Patrick Campbell, Vivienne Knight, from a story by Peter Myers, Ronald Cass

Go toward the Light ★★★ PG
Drama based on a true story
1988 · US · Colour · 89mins

Terminator star Linda Hamilton gets serious in this moving but depressing tale of a family who have to come to terms with the fact that their haemophiliac child has Aids. The cast including Richard Thomas, Ned Beatty and Piper Laurie all give meaningful performances but, despite the significance of the subject matter, one is left wishing there were a few lighter moments to brighten what is a worthy but often morose drama.

Linda Hamilton *Claire Madison* • Richard Thomas *Greg Madison* • Piper Laurie *Grandma* • Ned Beatty *Grandpa* • Joshua Harris *Ben* ■ *Dir* Mike Robe • *Scr* Beth Polson, Susan Nanus, from the non-fiction book by Beth Polson, Chris Oyler, Laurie Becklund

Go West ★★★★ U
Silent comedy 1925 · US · BW · 69mins

All the great comedians have headed in this direction at some time or another, and Buster Keaton may have been exceptional – but he was no exception. This is, perhaps, the only one of his silent movies which tries for a touch of Chaplin-esque sentiment: he's called Friendless and his touching way with a favourite cow – he places the milking pail beneath her hoping she will milk herself – achieves a gingerly-handled tenderness. There's a great stampede of cattle at the end which Buster tries to stop, though the cops don't believe his story. As usual.

Buster Keaton *Friendless* • Howard Truesdale *Ranch owner* • Kathleen Myers *His daughter* • Ray Thompson *The foreman* ■ *Dir* Buster Keaton • *Scr* Raymond Cannon, from a story by Buster Keaton

Go West, Young Man ★★★
Comedy 1936 · US · BW · 79mins

The lines may not be as outrageous as in her earlier films, but Mae West is as physically suggestive as ever in her own adaptation of a Lawrence Riley play. Poking fun at herself, she plays a modern-day film star on tour to promote her new picture. She perks up at the sight of handsome Randolph Scott and decides to stay on and see what develops. The capable supporting cast includes Warren William as her manager and Lyle Talbot, who went on to appear in Ed Wood classics such as *Glen or Glenda*.

Mae West *Mavis Arden* • Warren William *Morgan* • Randolph Scott *Bud Norton* • Alice Brady *Mrs Struthers* • Elizabeth Patterson

Aunt Kate • Lyle Talbot *Francis X Harrigan* • Isabel Jewell *Gladys* • Margaret Perry *Joyce* ■ *Dir* Henry Hathaway • *Scr* Mae West, from the play *Personal Appearance* by Lawrence Riley

The Goalkeeper's Fear of the Penalty Kick ★★★★
Drama 1971 · Aus/W Ger · Colour · 101mins

In adapting his own novel for the screen, Peter Handke retains its existential aura of Camus, Sartre and Kafka. Yet, with goalkeeper Arthur Brauss exhibiting a passion for all things American, this is recognisably a Wim Wenders movie (indeed, it was the first to bring him international recognition). With its imagery focusing on vehicles and modes of communication, and a resolute refusal to justify Brauss's motives for killing a cinema cashier, this could be described as an existential thriller. Wenders invests seemingly inconsequential objects with an almost sinister significance to reflect his anti-hero's mental deterioration following that fateful spot kick. In German with English subtitles.

Arthur Brauss *Joseph Bloch* • Kai Fischer *Hertha Gabler* • Erika Pluhar *Gloria* • Libgart Schwarz *Maid* • Marie Bardischewski *Maria* • Michael Toost *Salesman* • Bert Fortell *Customs official* • Edda Kochl *Girl in Vienna* ■ *Dir* Wim Wenders • *Scr* Wim Wenders, Peter Handke, from a novel by Peter Handke

GoBots: Battle of the Rocklords ★ U
Science-fiction animation
1986 · US · Colour · 70mins

Yet another kid's animation movie that is little more than an extended commercial for a new line of toys. Hanna-Barbera, home of *Yogi Bear* and *The Flintstones*, provides the less-than-inspired animation, while the Tonka corporation provides the product – a range of robots that can be transformed into vehicles and spaceships. The plot is yet another tired *Star Wars* rehash, set in a futuristic world in which the GoBots and the beleaguered Rock People (living mineral creatures that can change from human form into stone) join forces to defeat an evil overlord. A host of familiar guest voices, including Telly Savalas and Roddy McDowall, bring class to what amounts to little more than an arcade game.

Margot Kidder *Solitaire* • Roddy McDowall *Nugget* • Michael Nouri *Boulder* • Telly Savalas *Magmar* • Ike Eisenmann *Nick* • Bernard Erhard *Cy-Kill* • Marilyn Lightstone *Crasher* • Morgan Paull *Matt* ■ *Dir* Don Lusk, Alan Zaslove, Ray Patterson • *Scr* Jeff Segal

God Bless the Child ★★★ 15
Drama 1988 · US · Colour · 93mins

Mare Winningham was one of the original Brat Pack but, apart from her Oscar-nominated turn in *Georgia*, she hasn't really realised her potential. However, she gives a truly moving performance in this superior TV movie as a woman who is forced to raise her daughter in a shelter for the homeless after she is abandoned by her husband. Grace Johnston excels as her gutsy seven-year-old, while Dorian Harewood is compassion itself as the social worker who befriends them.

Director Larry Elikann is a past master at this sort of human-interest drama and never allows sentiment to confuse the central issue.

Mare Winningham *Theresa Johnson* • Dorian Harewood *Calvin Reed* • Grace Johnston *Hillary Johnson* • Charlaine Woodard [Charlayne Woodard] • Obba Babatunde • L Scott Caldwell ■ *Dir* Larry Elikann • *Scr* Dennis Nemec

God Is My Co-Pilot ★★ U
Second World War drama
1945 · US · BW · 87mins

A wartime flag-waver extolling the heroism of Major General Channault's Flying Tigers outfit, which flew against the Japanese from Pearl Harbor to China. Channault himself is played by Raymond Massey, but the lead role goes to Dennis Morgan who flies, prays to his co-pilot and survives to guide us through the flashbacks. These include him being shot down and having to survive in enemy territory. The same story had already been told in John Wayne's first foray into the Second World War, 1942's *Flying Tigers*.

Dennis Morgan *Col Robert L Scott* • Dane Clark *Johnny Petach* • Raymond Massey *Maj Gen Chennault* • Alan Hale *"Big Mike" Harrigan* • Andrea King *Catherine Scott* • John Ridgely *Tex Hill* • Stanley Ridges *Col Meriam Cooper* • Craig Stevens *Ed Rector* ■ *Dir* Robert Florey • *Scr* Peter Milne, Abem Finkel, from the book by Col Robert L Scott

God Said, "Ha!" ★★
Comedy drama 1998 · US · Colour · 87mins

Julia Sweeney directs and stars in this recording of her self-penned one-woman stage show. Far from being lightweight stand-up comedy, this monologue takes us through Julia's experience of temporarily losing her independence as she nursed her cancer-stricken brother. To add to the trauma of his slow death and an invasion by her parents, Sweeney then discovered that she had a rare form of cervical cancer. Utilising only the most basic of sets, it seems very theatrical and rough round the edges, but the emotional honesty is affecting.

Julia Sweeney ■ *Dir* Julia Sweeney • *Scr* Julia Sweeney, from her play

God Told Me to ★★
Horror thriller 1976 · US · Colour · 91mins

The title is a sniper's justification for climbing to the top of a water tower in New York, loading up a high velocity rifle and casually popping innocent people in the street. Initially telling a story similar to that of Peter Bogdanovich's *Targets*, Larry Cohen's thriller (also known as *Demon*) spirals off into a weird world of sexual fantasy, religious fanaticism and even alien invasion. Lovers of movie schlock might well find their lusts satisfied, though audiences who value more prosaic things, such as decent photography, a script that makes sense and convincing performances, might find it somewhat lacking.

Tony LoBianco *Peter Nicholas* • Deborah Raffin *Casey Forster* • Sandy Dennis *Martha Nicholas* • Sylvia Sidney *Elizabeth Mullin* • Sam Levene *Everett Lukas* • Robert Drivas *David Morten* ■ *Dir/Scr* Larry Cohen

The Goddess ★★★
Drama 1958 · US · BW · 105mins

An excellent rendition of the "poor, working-class girl makes it in the movies" scenario, written with great depth and understanding by Paddy Chayefsky. Allegedly based on the life of Marilyn Monroe, and full of oblique references to abused childhoods and scenes of reckless pill-popping, this is nevertheless a serious attempt to explore the nature of female fame and sexual charisma. Kim Stanley turns in a fine performance as the ambitious starlet, who's part manipulative minx, part vulnerable victim, and she is ably supported by a fine cast.

Kim Stanley *Emily Ann Faulkner* • Betty Lou Holland *Mother* • Joan Copeland *Aunt* • Gerald Hiken *Uncle* • Burt Brinckerhoff *Boy* • Steven Hill *John Tower* • Gerald Petrarca *Minister* • Linda Soma *Bridesmaid* • Curt Conway *Writer* ■ *Dir* John Cromwell • *Scr* Paddy Chayefsky

The Godfather ★★★★★ 18
Crime drama 1972 · US · Colour · 168mins

Over 25 years on, *The Godfather* and its 1974 sequel look incontestably like American cinema's finest achievement since... well, certainly since 1972 and maybe since the Second World War. The production problems are well documented – how Paramount wanted a quickie, how Francis Ford Coppola came cheap and how he turned the picture into an epic, the only $100 million grosser with a brain. His first masterstroke was casting Marlon Brando, Al Pacino, James Caan, Robert Duvall and Diane Keaton, four relative unknowns and one known risk. His next masterstroke was to keep cool under fire, like Michael Corleone himself, turning Mario Puzo's pulp novel into art and showing how capitalism and crime go hand in hand. It's thrilling, romantic, tense and scary, a five-course meal that leaves you hungry for more. Contains violence, swearing and sex scenes.

Marlon Brando *Don Vito Corleone* • Al Pacino *Michael Corleone* • James Caan *Sonny Corleone* • Richard Castellano *Clemenza* • Robert Duvall *Tom Hagen* • Sterling Hayden *McCluskey* • John Marley *Jack Woltz* • Richard Conte *Barzini* • Diane Keaton *Kay Adams* ■ *Dir* Francis Ford Coppola • *Scr* Francis Ford Coppola, Mario Puzo, from the novel by Mario Puzo • *Cinematographer* Gordon Willis • *Production Designer* Dean Tavoularis • *Music* Nino Rota, Carmine Coppola

The Godfather, Part II ★★★★★ 18
Crime drama 1974 · US · Colour · 192mins

In *The Godfather*, Don Corleone's war hero son Michael (Al Pacino) turns into a man who orders death like room service. In *Part II*, Michael is a symbol of an America born of immigrant idealism and dying of corruption. Breathtaking in scope, *Part II* shows the early life of the Don, brilliantly portrayed by Robert De Niro, as he flees Sicily and sails for New York. These sequences have the grandeur of a silent movie by DW Griffith or Erich von Stroheim; the later sequences, with Michael in Cuba, are sometimes confusing. But the climax is as chilling as the look on Michael's face when he realises that even family members can be rubbed out. Despite its obvious

structural flaws (somewhat ironed out in the extended TV version), *Part II* is rivalled only by *Heaven's Gate* and *JFK* as the last great American picture show. Contains violence and some swearing.

Al Pacino *Michael Corleone* • Robert Duvall *Tom Hagen* • Diane Keaton *Kay Corleone* • Robert De Niro *Vito Corleone* • Talia Shire *Connie* • John Cazale *Fredo Corleone* • Lee Strasberg *Hyman Roth* • Michael V Gazzo *Frank Pentangeli* ■ *Dir* Francis Ford Coppola • *Scr* Francis Ford Coppola, Mario Puzo, from characters created by Mario Puzo • *Cinematographer* Gordon Willis • *Production Designer* Dean Tavoularis • *Music* Nino Rota, Carmine Coppola

The Godfather Part III
★★★ 🔞

Crime drama   1990 · US · Colour · 163mins

The Godfather was a masterpiece and so, too, was its sequel. Yet this third picture is merely a distant relative and was made for purely mercenary reasons (director Francis Ford Coppola reportedly needed the money for a personal project). Thanks to the badly bungled corkscrew plot – it's difficult to understand what's going on, apart from some vague corruption in the Vatican – one is left with the basic theme of Michael Corleone (Al Pacino) unable to renounce crime and being slowly transformed into a martyr. Pacino has some fine moments and Andy Garcia is frequently electrifying as Sonny Corleone's bastard son Vincent Mancini, the new don on the block. However, Coppola's own daughter, Sofia, who took over at the last minute from Winona Ryder, is embarrassing as Michael's daughter Mary. Contains violence and swearing. 🖵

Al Pacino *Michael Corleone* • Diane Keaton *Kay Adams* • Andy Garcia *Vincent Mancini* • Talia Shire *Connie Corleone Rizzi* • Eli Wallach *Don Altobello* • Joe Mantegna *Joey Zasa* • George Hamilton *BJ Harrison* • Bridget Fonda *Grace Hamilton* • Sofia Coppola *Mary Corleone* ■ *Dir* Francis Ford Coppola • *Scr* Francis Ford Coppola, Mario Puzo • *Cinematographer* Gordon Willis

Godmoney
★★★★

Drama   1997 · US · Colour · 94mins

A powerful, striking American indie film, this probably deserved better than an unheralded video release. Using a cast of unknowns, first-time director Darren Doane transforms a predictable tale of drug dealing into an arresting and chilling portrait of moral apathy in American suburbia. Newcomer Rick Rodney (a dead ringer for John Malkovich) is the New York youngster who arrives in Los Angeles, determined to put his criminal past behind him. But when he loses his job and money runs short, a tempting offer from an ambitious local drug dealer proves difficult to pass up. 🖵 *DVD*

Rick Rodney *Nathan* • Bobby Field *Matthew* • Christi Allen *Dana* • Stewart Teggart *Jason* • Chad Nell *John* • Sean Atkins *Jeff* ■ *Dir* Darren Doane • *Scr* Sean Atkins, Darren Doane, Sean Christopher Nelson

Gods and Monsters
★★★★★ 15

Biographical drama
1998 · US/UK · Colour · 94mins

Ian McKellen gives a brilliant performance as director James Whale – the "Father of Frankenstein", according to Christopher Bram's source novel – in Bill Condon's inventive biographical fantasy. A gay *Sunset Boulevard*, it explores the roots of the horror genre with peerless wit and deft assurance. Set during Whale's twilight years, when he was ostracised by Hollywood for being a box-office failure and a homosexual to boot, this deeply touching tribute to the director's life and work focuses on his ambiguous relationship with his gardener (Brendan Fraser). Condon mingles half-forgotten images of Whale's shadowy past and his experience of making *Bride of Frankenstein* with drug-raddled sexual hallucinations and the Mary Shelley myth to explain the "mysterious circumstances" surrounding the Gothic visionary's death. A poignant and elegant masterpiece. Contains swearing and sex scenes. 🖵 *DVD*

Ian McKellen *James Whale* • Brendan Fraser *Clayton Boone* • Lynn Redgrave *Hanna* • Lolita Davidovich *Betty* • Kevin J O'Connor *Harry* • David Dukes *David Lewis* • Brandon Kleyla *Young James Whale* • Pamela Salem *Sarah Whale* ■ *Dir* Bill Condon • *Scr* Bill Condon, from the novel *Father of Frankenstein* by Christopher Bram

God's Country
★★★★

Documentary   1985 · US · Colour · 90mins

Making his final foray into the documentary field, Louis Malle brought his trademark humanism to this study of the ultra-traditional farming community of Glencoe, Minnesota. The bulk of the action was filmed in 1979, when the aftershocks of Vietnam and Watergate could still be felt – even in this most isolated region, where patriarchy was synonymous with prejudice and a disconcerting lack of curiosity. Yet it's the closing segment, shot at the height of the Reagan era, that provides the most telling insights, as the fond-held hopes and schemes prove illusory. Touching and amusing, yet never patronising or cruel.

Louis Malle *Narrator* ■ *Dir* Louis Malle

God's Country and the Woman
★★ 🇺

Drama   1937 · US · Colour · 85mins

It's hard to get excited when the woman of the title turns out to be minor Warner Bros actress Beverly Roberts, playing opposite George Brent instead of his regular co-star (and rumoured squeeze) Bette Davis. Brent plays a hunky lumberjack, but the real reason for watching is God's country itself, stunningly photographed in an early (and now forgotten) example of glorious Technicolor, and almost justifying the daft plot and dialogue.

George Brent *Steve Russett* • Beverly Roberts *Jo Barton* • Barton MacLane *Bullhead* • Robert Barrat *Jefferson Russett* • Alan Hale *Bjorn Skalka* • Joseph King *Red Munro* • Joseph Crehan *Jordan* ■ *Dir* William Keighley • *Scr* Norman Reilly Raine, Peter Milne,

Charles Belden, from the novel by James Oliver Curwood • *Cinematographer* Tony Gaudio

God's Gun
★★ 🔞

Western   1977 · Is/It · Colour · 92mins

Here's a little-seen novelty: an Italian-styled western produced in Israel by cousins Yoram Globus and Menachem Golan, and directed by that veteran of the spaghetti genre, Frank Kramer. It stars three actors old enough to know that sometimes you just take the money – Lee Van Cleef, Jack Palance and Richard Boone. Played with very little conviction, this is naff exploitation only made tolerable by its grizzled cast and by the fact that Palance's son Cody is in there alongside his father. Contains violence and sex scenes. 🖵

Lee Van Cleef *Father John/Lewis* • Jack Palance *Sam Clayton* • Richard Boone *The Sheriff* • Sybil Danning *Jenny* • Leif Garrett *Johnny* • Cody Palance ■ *Dir* Frank Kramer [Gianfranco Parolini] • *Scr* Gianfranco Parolini, John Fonsecan

God's Little Acre
★★★

Melodrama   1958 · US · BW · 111mins

This is director Anthony Mann's version of Erskine Caldwell's steamy melodrama about a farmer in Georgia who thinks he's struck gold, except for that one acre he sets aside for the Almighty. What we have here is a giant metaphor, a sort of *Treasure of the Sierra Madre*, in which everyone is possessed by gold lust and just plain ordinary lust. As the farmer, Robert Ryan delivers a trademark performance of dignity unravelling as his family disintegrates. The picture lacks a decent female lead and is almost as pompous a family saga as, say, *Giant*, although it's not as elongated and the earth really does move.

Robert Ryan *Ty Ty Walden* • Aldo Ray *Will Thompson* • Tina Louise *Griselda* • Buddy Hackett *Pluto* • Jack Lord *Buck Walden* • Fay Spain *Darlin' Jill* • Vic Morrow *Shaw Walden* • Helen Wescott *Rosamund* ■ *Dir* Anthony Mann • *Scr* Philip Yordan, from the novel by Erskine Caldwell

The Gods Must Be Crazy
★★★ 🅿🄶

Comedy
1980 · Botswana/SAfr · Colour · 108mins

Now here's a film guaranteed to divide. There will be those who see it as inexcusably racist exploitation that mocks the traditions and expectations of the Kalahari bush tribe, whose peaceful existence is disturbed by a Coke bottle that drops from the sky. But others will applaud the barbed colonial satire that arises when N !xau ventures into civilisation to drop the contentious bottle off the edge of the world. Certainly audiences worldwide warmed to director Jamie Uys's slapstick style, turning this latter-day Keystone comedy into a cult smash. There are some crude laughs, but the juvenility is hard to ignore. 🖵 *DVD*

Paddy O'Byrne *Narration* • N !xau *Xixo* • Marius Weyers *Andrew Steyn* • Sandra Prinsloo *Kate Thompson* • Nic De Jager *Jack Hind* • Louw Verwey *Sam Boga* • Michael Thys *Mpudi* • Fanyana Sidumo *First Card* • Joe Seakatsie *Second Card* ■ *Dir/Scr* Jamie Uys

The Gods Must Be Crazy II
★★★ 🅿🄶

Comedy
1989 · US/Botswana/SAfr · Colour · 97mins

Considering his meagre resources, director Jamie Uys can hardly be blamed for the tackiness of the aerial effects in this sequel to his surprise box-office hit. He must also be commended for the patience with which he constructs his gags, several of which seem to take an age to pay off. However, the unsubtlety of his slapstick and the dubiousness of some of his cultural observation make this every bit as divisive a film as its predecessor. N !xau returns as the bushman confronting civilisation, this time after his children are accidentally abducted by poachers. Frantic fun or unforgivably offensive? You decide.

N !xau *Xixo* • Lena Ferugia *Dr Ann Taylor* • Hans Strydom *Dr Stephen Marshall* • Eiros *Xiri* • Nadies *Xisa* • Erick Bowen *Mateo* • Treasure Tshabalala *Timi* ■ *Dir/Scr* Jamie Uys

Gods of the Plague
★★★

Crime drama   1969 · W Ger · BW · 91mins

Rainer Werner Fassbinder's third feature, about a man released from prison who works his way back into the underworld, is a forceful homage to Hollywood *film noir*. However, despite the trenchcoats, trilbies and cigarette smoke, it is mainly a sombre meditation on the alienated postwar German generation. Fassbinder's cast, including Hanna Schygulla and future director Margarethe von Trotta, are exemplary. Fassbinder's lover of the time, Günther Kaufmann, the illegitimate son of a black GI and a Bavarian woman, plays a crook who dies whispering, "Life is so precious, even right now." In German with English subtitles.

Harry Baer *Franz* • Hanna Schygulla *Joanna* • Margarethe von Trotta *Margarethe* • Günther Kaufmann *Günther* • Carla Aulaulu *Carla* • Ingrid Caven *Magdalena Fuller* • Jan George *Cop* • Marian Seidowski *Marian* • Rainer Werner Fassbinder *Porno buyer* ■ *Dir/Scr* Rainer Werner Fassbinder

God's Will
★★

Comedy   1989 · US · Colour · 100mins

With both mum and dad in the business, there was always a chance that Domenica Cameron-Scorsese was going to end up in movies. Here she bravely holds together her screenwriter mother Julia Cameron's directorial debut as the orphan who invokes the help of her dead, divorced parents to spare her the nightmare of living with their new spouses. Daniel Region and Laura Margolis also try hard as the squabbling showbiz luvvies who resort to a little spooking to help their daughter. But the film never recovered from the theft of the soundtrack, as the dubbed dialogue sounds just too otherworldly.

Marge Kotlisky *God* • Daniel Region *Peter Potter* • Laura Margolis *Gillian Norwood* • Domenica Cameron-Scorsese *Victoria Potter* • Holly Fulger *Hedy* ■ *Dir* Julia Cameron

🅄 = SUITABLE FOR ALL   🅄🄴 = SUITABLE FOR ALL, ESPECIALLY FOR YOUNG CHILDREN (VIDEO ONLY)   🅿🄶 = PARENTAL GUIDANCE

The Godsend ★ 15

Horror   1980 · UK · Colour · 82mins

A family discovers that their adopted daughter is really a demon out to murder them one by one in this tepid, ultra-slow and raggedly acted *Omen*-style fantasy borrowing most of its plot elements from that film but doing little of note with them. Although beautifully photographed, and accenting the psychologically scary side of the story more than the gruesome details, this low-key item is handled like a soporific soap opera. Appropriately enough, director Gabrielle Beaumont's numerous TV assignments in the eighties included directing episodes of *Dynasty*. ▣

Malcolm Stoddard *Alan Marlowe* • Cyd Hayman *Kate Marlowe* • Angela Pleasence *Stranger* • Patrick Barr *Dr Collins* • Wilhelmina Green *Bonnie* ■ *Dir* Gabrielle Beaumont • *Scr* Olaf Pooley, from the novel by Bernard Taylor • *Cinematographer* Norman Warwick

Godspell ★★★ U

Musical   1973 · US · Colour · 101mins

This New York-set reworking of the Gospel according to St Matthew following a famous off-Broadway theatrical workshop production is an uneasy enchantment that's halfway between holy foolishness and hippy indulgence. Director David Greene's musical nevertheless has moments of infectious glee, as Gospel parables are narrated by a Christ figure (Victor Garber) in a Superman sweatshirt and workman's overalls. Though it won't make you turn on or drop out, it's worth tuning in. This innocent remnant of the flower-power era is far less calculated and mercenary than the same year's *Jesus Christ Superstar*.

Victor Garber *Jesus* • David Haskell *John/Judas* • Jerry Sroka *Jerry* • Lynne Thigpen *Lynne* • Katie Hanley *Katie* • Robin Lamont *Robin* • Gilmer McCormick *Gilmer* • Joanne Jonas *Joanne* • Jeffrey Mylett *Jeffrey* ■ *Dir* David Greene • *Scr* David Greene, John-Michael Tebelak, from the musical by John-Michael Tebelak, Stephen Schwartz

Godzilla ★★★

Monster horror   1954 · Jap/US · BW · 80mins

A gigantic dinosaur with radioactive breath is awakened by atomic testing and goes on a rampage, destroying Tokyo. The first, and best, of the long-running monster franchise from Toho Studios is sombre science fiction (in contrast to the kiddie-friendly sequels) and incorporates award-winning special effects by Eiji Tsuburaya into its nuclear-age allegory. Additional footage, directed by Terry Morse, featuring reporter Raymond Burr commenting on the manic mayhem, was spliced into a cut-down, dubbed version of the Japanese original. Director Ishiro Honda's original 98-minute masterpiece makes a plea for peace and no more A-bomb testing. The 80-minute Americanised version doesn't. Japanese dialogue dubbed into English.

Raymond Burr *Steve Martin* • Takashi Shimura *Dr Yamane* • Momoko Kochi *Emiko* • Akira Takarada *Ogata* • Akihiko Hirata *Dr Serizawa* • Sachio Sakai *Hagiwara* • Fuyuki Murakami *Dr Tabata* • Ren Yamamoto ■ *Dir* Terry Morse,

Inoshiro Honda • *Scr* Takeo Murata, Inoshiro Honda, from the story *Godzilla, King of the Monsters* by Shigeru Kayama

Godzilla ★★ PG

Monster horror   1984 · Jap · Colour · 87mins

After a decade in hibernation, the King of the Monsters returned as the villain to cause an international Cold War incident after trashing a Soviet submarine. Russia and America want the outsized nuisance destroyed, and Tokyo is nearly razed to the ground for the umpteenth time. Raymond Burr pops up as an intrepid reporter, just as he did in the original 1954 movie, in footage added for western markets. Elsewhere, it's business as usual – thin plot, inane dialogue, daft dubbing and cheap special effects. In Japanese with English subtitles. ▣

Raymond Burr *Steve Martin* • Keiju Kobayashi *Prime Minister Mitamura* • Ken Tanaka *Goro Maki* • Yasuko Sawaguchi *Naoko Okumura* • Shin Takuma *Hiroshi Okumura* • Eitaro Ozawa *Finance Minister Kanzaki* • Taketoshi Naito *Chief Cabinet Secretary Takegami* • Nobuo Kaneko *Home Affairs Minister Isomura* ■ *Dir* Kohji Hashimoto, RJ Kizer • *Scr* Shuichi Nagahara, Lisa Tomei, from a story by Tomoyuki Tanaka

Godzilla ★★ PG

Monster adventure
1997 · US · Colour · 132mins

In this dreary American overhaul from *Independence Day* director Roland Emmerich, Japan's favourite giant lizard crawls out of radioactive waters in the South Pacific and heads for New York. Resembling an over-produced version of *The Beast from 20,000 Fathoms*, Emmerich's blockbuster behemoth replaces man-in-suit special effects with dodgy computer digitals and sub-*Jurassic Park* thrills. What it doesn't replicate is the endearing charm the celebrated fire-breather had when he stomped through cardboard skyscrapers. The old Toho Studios fantasy adventures may have had lower budgets, but even the cheapest show more flair than this dismal monster mishmash. ▣ *DVD*

Matthew Broderick *Dr Niko Tatopoulos* • Jean Reno *Philippe Roaché* • Maria Pitillo *Audrey Timmonds* • Hank Azaria *Victor "Animal" Palotti* • Kevin Dunn *Colonel Hicks* • Michael Lerner *Mayor Ebert* • Harry Shearer *Charles Caiman* • Arabella Field *Lucy Palotti* ■ *Dir* Roland Emmerich • *Scr* Dean Devlin, Dean Emmerich, from a story by Ted Elliott, Terry Rossio, Dean Devlin, Roland Emmerich, from the character created by Toho Co Ltd

Godzilla Raids Again ★

Monster horror   1955 · Jap/US · BW · 77mins

The first *Godzilla* sequel finds the giant lizard under an assumed name – Gigantis, because Warner Bros neglected to secure the rights to the name Godzilla – as he battles the spiky-backed Angurus before stomping towards Tokyo and trashing Osaka en route. The usual shaky backdrops and hysterical civilian panic footage make less impact this time. It was eight years before Godzilla met King Kong to triumph again. Japanese dialogue dubbed into English.

Hiroshi Koizumi *Shoichi Tsukioka* • Setsuko Wakayama *Hedemi Yamaji* • Minoru Chiaki *Koji Kobayashi* ■ *Dir* Motoyoshi Oda, Hugo Grimaldi • *Scr* Takeo Murata, Sigeaki Hidaka

Godzilla vs Gigan ★★★

Monster horror   1972 · Jap · Colour · 85mins

More totally bonkers fantasy mayhem from Japan's Toho Studios, as Godzilla makes another appearance to save the planet from intergalactic domination. This time alien cockroaches plan to occupy the earth and summon Ghidorah, the three-headed dragon, and Gigan, a crimson-eyed metal bird with a chainsaw chest, to fight the Monster Island duo of Godzilla and Anzilla at a children's amusement park. For the first time, the monsters talk to each other, and a note of contemporary relevance is struck as shots of Tokyo depict the aliens' dying world. One of the better Godzilla efforts. Japanese dialogue dubbed into English. ▣

Haruo Nakajima *Godzilla* • Yukietsu Omiya *Angurus* • Kanta Ina *Ghidorah* • Kengo Nakayama • Hiroshi Ichikawa • Yuriko Hishimi ■ *Dir* Jun Fukuda • *Scr* Takeshi Kimura, Shinichi Skizawa

Godzilla vs King Ghidorah ★★★ PG

Monster horror   1991 · Jap · Colour · 102mins

One of the best of the entire 22-strong Japanese *Godzilla* series, this also boasts one of the saga's most complex plots. It involves time travellers from the future intervening in the 1944 nuclear events, causing the monster lizard's birth and creating his three-headed flying nemesis Ghidorah to defeat Japan and stop it becoming a future world power. The time-warp elements do cause some confusion but are easy to forgive in such an imaginative story, which also neatly fills in details of Godzilla's humble beginnings. All the monster battles are epic and exciting. Japanese dialogue dubbed into English. ▣

Anna Nakagawa *Emmy Kano* • Kosuke Toyohara *Kenichiro Terasawa* • Megumi Odaka *Miki Saegusa* • Kiwako Harada *Chiaki Moriyuma* • Shoji Kobayashi *Yuzo Tsuchiashi* ■ *Dir/Scr* Kazuki Omori

Godzilla vs Megalon ★★★ PG

Monster horror   1973 · Jap · Colour · 78mins

Megalon, a giant insect monster with drills for arms plus a death-ray head, and Gigan are teamed by the Seatopians to conquer the world in revenge for inflicting nuclear damage under the oceans. That's the cue for Godzilla to fight the monster menace and save Japan once more. Here Godzilla joins the brightly coloured Jet Jaguar robot for the barren desert battles, so part of the fun in watching cardboard model cities topple is missing. But hilariously risible dubbed dialogue, along the lines of "those damned Seatopians", more than makes up for the lack of stupid spectacle and the plot is interspersed with a sobering anti-pollution message. Japanese dialogue dubbed into English. ▣

Katsuhiko Sasaki *Professor Goro Ibuki* • Hiroyuki Kawase *Rokuro Ibuki* ■ *Dir* Jun Fukuda • *Scr* Jun Fukuda, Shinichi Sekizawa, Takeshi Kimura

Godzilla vs Mothra ★★★ PG

Monster horror   1992 · Jap · Colour · 102mins

Thirty years after Toho introduced Mothra in *Godzilla vs the Thing*, the studio virtually remade the same story in their attempt to modernise their monster dinosaur series for a new generation. It worked and this was a huge hit in Japan. Two tiny women, known as the Cosmos, summon up the creature Mothra to fight the evil Battra, who has been sent to destroy Earth. However, Godzilla appears and a three-way battle occurs in a fiery finale set in Tokyo. Good, colourful fun. Japanese dialogue dubbed into English. ▣

Tetsuya Bessho *Takuya Fujita* • Akiji Kobayashi *Ryuzo Dobashi* • Satomi Kobayashi *Masako Tezuka* • Takehiro Murata *Kenji Ando* • Megumi Odaka *Miki Saegusa* ■ *Dir* Takao Okawara • *Scr* Kazuki Omori

Godzilla vs the Cosmic Monster ★★

Monster horror   1974 · Jap · Colour · 79mins

You can't keep a good monster down, and for his 20th anniversary (and 14th film), Japan's Toho Studios created a worthy adversary for its money-making prehistoric lizard – a cyborg version of Godzilla himself. In this average entry in the variable series, Mechagodzilla is the secret weapon of ape-like aliens that are seeking world domination. Plenty of sparks fly in the extended cardboard battle scenes, and there are a couple of daft new creatures to smirk at, but it's pretty much children's comic book stuff. In Japanese with English subtitles.

Masaaki Daimon *Keisuke Shimizu* • Kazuya Aoyama *Masahiko Shimizu* ■ *Dir* Jun Fukuda • *Scr* Hiroyasu Yamamura, Jun Fukuda

Godzilla's Revenge ★

Monster horror   1969 · Jap · Colour · 70mins

A bullied schoolboy realises his dream of going to Monster Island, where he meets Godzilla and his son, Minya, who teach him how to be brave. Stripped of the serious A-bomb underpinnings that made early entries in the Toho series so rich in irony, the tenth *Godzilla* movie is a very sad affair. Insult is added to injury by the inclusion of battle scenes from earlier adventures such as *Son of Godzilla* and *Ebirah, Terror of the Deep* to save money on special effects. Japanese dialogue dubbed into English.

Kenji Sahara *Kenkichi Miki* • Tomonori Yazaki *Ichiro Miki* • Machiko Naka *Mrs Miki* • Sachio Sakai *Senbayashi* • Chotaro Togin *Assistant detective* • Yoshibumi Tajima *Policeman* ■ *Dir* Ishiro Honda [Inoshiro Honda] • *Scr* Shinichi Sekizawa

Gog ★★★

Science-fiction   1954 · US · Colour · 82mins

Don't let the Z-grade title put you off – this is actually a decent little sci-fi techno shocker that predates *2001: a Space Odyssey* by more than a decade in its depiction of a computer programmed to kill. It's produced by Ivan Tors, famous for TV shows such

as *Daktari*. Richard Egan leads an undistinguished cast, with people being bumped off by two malevolent robots let loose in a subterranean laboratory in New Mexico. Originally released in 3-D, this combines great Saturday matinee thrills with Cold War tension and topical fears about all-powerful machines.

Richard Egan *David Sheppard* • Constance Dowling *Joanna Merritt* • Herbert Marshall *Dr Van Ness* • John Wengraf *Dr Zeltman* • Philip Van Zandt *Dr Elzevir* • Valerie Vernon *Madame Elzevir* • Stephen Roberts *Major Howard* • Byron Kane *Dr Carter* ■ *Dir* Herbert L Strock • *Scr* Tom Taggart, Richard G Taylor, from a story by Ivan Tors

Goin' Coconuts ★★
Comedy adventure
1978 · US · Colour · 93mins

The all-singing, all-dancing Osmond family were an international pop phenomenon in the seventies. Two of the tribe, Donny and Marie Osmond, then graduated to their own TV show and – inevitably – a big-screen outing followed. This juvenile adventure finds the toothsome twosome under threat from villains in picturesque Hawaii, but the plot is of secondary importance as they deliver a clutch of songs before the obligatory happy ending.

Donny Osmond *Donny* • Marie Osmond *Marie* • Herbert Edelman *Sid* • Kenneth Mars *Kruse* • Crystin Sinclaire *Tricia* • Ted Cassidy *Mickey* • Marc Lawrence *Webster* • Khigh Dhiegh *Wong* • Harold Sakata *Ito* ■ *Dir* Howard Morris • *Scr* Raymond Harvey

Goin' South ★★★ PG
Western
1978 · US · Colour · 103mins

After making a respectable directorial debut in 1971 with *Drive, He Said*, Jack Nicholson planned a mystical western called *Moon Trap*. But the project didn't please the studios and Nicholson eventually turned to *Goin' South*, an amiable and wayward western in which he escapes the gallows and rides away with Mary Steenburgen. Steenburgen got the part after Jane Fonda turned it down – she felt it was another *Cat Ballou* – and after newcomers Jessica Lange and Meryl Streep were tested. Owing much to the eccentric *The Missouri Breaks*, which Nicholson appeared in two years earlier, it's easy to enjoy, even if his trademark leers are no substitute for real acting. The picture was a critical and commercial failure. ▭

Jack Nicholson *Henry Lloyd Moon* • Mary Steenburgen *Julia Tate* • Christopher Lloyd *Frank Towfield* • John Belushi *Hector* • Danny DeVito *Clyde/"Hog"* • Veronica Cartwright *Hermine* • Richard Bradford *Sheriff Andrew Kyle* • Jeff Morris *Big Abe* ■ *Dir* Jack Nicholson • *Scr* John Herman Shaner, Al Ramrus, Charles Shyer, Alan Mandel, from a story by John Herman Shaner

Goin' to Town ★★★
Musical comedy
1935 · US · BW · 74mins

Mae West writes herself another juicy role as a cattle baroness who makes a fortune from the timely acquisition of an oil field. Getting her man – in this case Paul Cavanagh – doesn't prove quite so easy, so Mae sets out to improve her social standing. She has a fine time mocking the hypocrisy of high society and memorably performs a

song from the opera *Samson and Delilah* by Saint-Saëns. The weak line-up of male performers – including Cavanagh, Ivan Lebedeff and Monroe Owsley – leaves Mae in full command of the proceedings.

Mae West *Cleo Borden* • Paul Cavanagh *Edward Carrington* • Gilbert Emery *Winslow* • Marjorie Gateson *Mrs Grace Brittony* • Tito Coral *Taho* • Ivan Lebedeff *Ivan Valadov* • Fred Kohler *Buck Gonzales* • Monroe Owsley *Fletcher Colton* ■ *Dir* Alexander Hall • *Scr* Mae West, from a story by Marion Morgan, George B Dowell

Going All the Way ★ 15
Drama
1997 · US · Colour · 98mins

A badly scripted, disappointing fifties-set drama from director Mark Pellington, this stars Jeremy Davies as the shy, nerdy photographer who makes friends with local jock Ben Affleck after they both return to their home town following service in the Korean War. They try and help each other overcome their neuroses. Rose McGowan, Amy Locane and Rachel Weisz are the girls providing the glamour, but even this impressive young cast can't save the film from being clichéd, tediously plotted and ultimately irritating. Contains swearing and sex scenes. ▭

Jeremy Davies *Sonny Burns* • Ben Affleck *Gunner Casselman* • Amy Locane *Buddy Porter* • Rose McGowan *Gail Thayer* • Rachel Weisz *Marty Pilcher* • John Lordan *Elwood Burns* • Bob Swan [Robert Swan] *Luke* • Jill Clayburgh *Alma Burns* • Lesley Ann Warren *Nina Casselman* ■ *Dir* Mark Pellington • *Scr* Dan Wakefield, from his novel

Going Ape! ★ U
Comedy
1981 · US · Colour · 87mins

The hit TV comedy series *Taxi* was still running when stars Tony Danza and Danny DeVito took time out to appear in this big-screen outing about a guy (Danza) who stands to inherit a fortune if he can successfully look after his late father's orang-utans. Writer/director Jeremy Joe Kronsberg made a name for himself with his script for *Every Which Way but Loose*, which teamed Clint Eastwood with loveable orang-utan Clyde. Here Kronsberg reached the logical (but erroneous) conclusion that if one orang-utan was funny, a whole bunch must be hilarious.

Tony Danza *Foster* • Jessica Walter *Fiona* • Stacey Nelkin *Cynthia* • Danny DeVito *Lazlo* • Art Metrano *Joey* • Frank Sivero *Bad Habit* • Rick Hurst *Brandon* • Howard Mann *Jules Cohen* ■ *Dir/Scr* Jeremy Joe Kronsberg

Going Berserk ★★ 15
Comedy
1983 · US/Can · Colour · 80mins

John Candy is reunited with some old chums from his Canadian TV days (Eugene Levy and Joe Flaherty) for this wildly erratic comedy. Candy plays a nice but dim driver engaged to the daughter of a politician who finds himself caught up in his prospective father-in-law's battle against a cult. Directed by David Steinberg, this is let down by a script with more misses than hits, but Candy is as effortlessly appealing as ever. ▭

John Candy *John Bourgignon* • Joe Flaherty *Chick Leff* • Eugene Levy *Sal di Pasquale* •

Alley Mills *Nancy Reese* • Pat Hingle *Ed Reese* • Ann Bronston *Patti Reese* • Eve Brent Ashe *Mrs Reese* • Elizabeth Kerr *Grandmother Reese* ■ *Dir* David Steinberg • *Scr* Dana Olsen, David Steinberg

Going Hollywood ★★ U
Musical comedy
1933 · US · BW · 77mins

Marion Davies and Bing Crosby co-star in this modest musical from MGM, which spawned the durable hit *Temptation* and included the lilting *Beautiful Girl* among its songs. The corny tale of a crooner, followed to Hollywood by a fan who poses as a French maid and supplants his current girlfriend and leading lady (Fifi D'Orsay), it provided Davies with an excellent showcase for her charm and her somewhat limited talents. It also disguises Crosby's lack of acting experience by letting him do what he did best – croon. Lennie Hayton conducts his orchestra and plays the piano on screen. Raoul Walsh, who's known for tougher, more substantial material, directs with a light touch.

Bing Crosby *Bill Williams* • Marion Davies *Sylvia Bruce* • Fifi D'Orsay *Lili Yvonne* • Stuart Erwin *Ernest P Baker* • Patsy Kelly *Jill Barker* • Bobby Watson *Jack Thompson* • Three Radio Rogues *Film electricians* ■ *Dir* Raoul Walsh • *Scr* Donald Ogden Stewart, from a story by Frances Marion

Going Home ★★★
Drama
1971 · US · Colour · 97mins

Having murdered his wife some years previously, Robert Mitchum comes out of jail only to be tracked down by his vengeance-seeking son (Jan-Michael Vincent). Brenda Vaccaro plays the woman caught between them in Herbert B Leonard's sombre drama, which sank without trace at the American box office and was never released in Britain. However, it's worth watching for Mitchum's brooding performance as the violent hunk and Korean War veteran who feels the pain he inflicts on others.

Robert Mitchum *Harry K Graham* • Brenda Vaccaro *Jenny* • Jan-Michael Vincent *Jimmy Graham* • Jason Bernard *Jimmy at six* • Sally Kirkland *Ann Graham* • Josh Mostel *Bonelli* • George DiCenzo *Sergeant* ■ *Dir* Herbert B Leonard • *Scr* Lawrence B Marcus

Going in Style ★★★ PG
Comedy
1979 · US · Colour · 94mins

Never shown at cinemas in the UK, this touching and very funny movie was part of the great second career coming of George Burns, made while he was producing his interminable *Oh, God!* sequels. This teams him with fellow veterans Art Carney and Lee Strasberg, father of the American Method school of acting, as three old-timers who decide to relieve their boredom by robbing a bank. This was the second feature directed by the talented Martin Brest, a film-maker whose films (including *Beverly Hills Cop*, *Midnight Run* and *Scent of a Woman*) are inexplicably better known than he is. Contains some swearing. ▭

George Burns *Joe* • Art Carney *Al* • Lee Strasberg *Willie* • Charles Hallahan *Pete* • Pamela Payton-Wright *Kathy* • Siobhan Keegan *Colleen* • Brian Neville *Kevin* • Constantine Hartofolis *Boy in park* ■ *Dir* Martin Brest • *Scr* Martin Brest, from a story by Edward Cannon

Going My Way ★★★★ U
Musical drama
1944 · US · Colour · 124mins

Although writer/producer/director Leo McCarey bagged three Oscars for this effortless piece of Catholic whimsy, its enduring charm rests with the Oscar-winning performances of Bing Crosby and Barry Fitzgerald (the last performer to be nominated in both acting categories for the same role). The sequences in which the inner-city urchins are transformed into angelic choirboys beggar belief, but the brisk by-play between the streetwise Father Crosby and the peppery Father Fitzgerald more than compensates. Crosby was later rewarded for his positive portrayal with a private audience at the Vatican.

Bing Crosby *Father "Chuck" O'Malley* • Risë Stevens *Genevieve Linden* • Barry Fitzgerald *Father Fitzgibbon* • Frank McHugh *Father Timothy O'Dowd* • James Brown (2) *Ted Haines Jr* • Gene Lockhart *Ted Haines Sr* • Jean Heather *Carol James* • Porter Hall *Mr Belknap* ■ *Dir* Leo McCarey • *Scr* Frank Butler, Frank Cavett, from a story by Leo McCarey

Going Places ★★★
Musical comedy
1938 · US · BW · 84mins

This piece of horse nonsense has Dick Powell masquerading as a famous jockey in order to drum up more business for his employers. Trouble is, he finds himself riding a temperamental horse who can only be soothed by the trumpet playing of Louis Armstrong. His antics do, however, impress the lovely Anita Louise. Forget the plot – this is yet another screen version of the play *The Hottentot*. Instead enjoy the great "Satchmo" in one of his rare featured roles, the Harry Warren/Johnny Mercer song *Jeepers Creepers*, and a musical cameo from the teenage Dandridge sisters (Vivian and Dorothy).

Dick Powell *Peter Mason/Peter Randall* • Anita Louise *Ellen Parker* • Allen Jenkins *Droopy* • Ronald Reagan *Jack Withering* • Walter Catlett *Franklin Dexter* • Harold Huber *Maxie* • Larry Williams *Frank* • Louis Armstrong *Gabe* ■ *Dir* Ray Enright • *Scr* Sig Herzig, Jerry Wald, Maurice Leo, Earl Baldwin, from the play *The Hottentot* by Victor Mapes, William Collier Sr

Going Undercover ★★
Spoof thriller
1984 · US · Colour · 89mins

This uneven comedy was made in 1984, but for some odd reason (because it was a clunker, perhaps?) remained unseen for four years. *Back to the Future* star Lea Thompson is the spoilt brat on a trip to Europe who is kept under surveillance by Chris Lemmon, a private eye so unskilled that she gets kidnapped right under his nose. Incredibly silly stuff, it's notable only for the supporting performances of Jean Simmons and Viveca Lindfors, who manage to rise above the otherwise poor material.

Chris Lemmon *Henry Brilliant* • Jean Simmons *Maxine De La Hunt* • Lea Thompson *Marigold De La Hunt* • Viveca Lindfors *Mrs Bellinger* • Mills Watson *Billy O'Shea* • Nancy Cartwright *Stephanie* ■ *Dir/Scr* James Kenelm Clarke

Gold ★★★

Adventure   1974 · UK · Colour · 123mins

This adventure, co-scripted (with Stanley Price) by Wilbur Smith from his own blockbuster novel *Goldmine*, was Britain's contribution to the seventies rash of disaster movies. Shot in South Africa (to the fury of anti-apartheid groups and various trade unions), the film oversimplifies its themes of racism and exploitation, but as an action-packed thriller it delivers the goods for most of its exhausting running time. As he seeks to prevent the sabotage that will send the price of gold soaring, Roger Moore is as wooden as a pit prop, but Bradford Dillman is a splendid villain and Susannah York invites sympathy as his duped wife. Contains some violence.

Roger Moore *Rod Slater* • Susannah York *Terry Steyner* • Ray Milland *Hurry Hirschfeld* • Bradford Dillman *Manfred Steyner* • John Gielgud *Farrell* • Tony Beckley *Stephen Marais* • Simon Sabela *Big King* • Bernard Horsfall *Kowalski* • *Dir* Peter Hunt • *Scr* Wilbur Smith, Stanley Price, from the novel *Goldmine* by Wilbur Smith

The Gold and Glory ★ 15

Drama   1984 · Ausl · Colour · 97mins

This dismal Australian athletics drama irresistibly recalls the hilarious cross-country hop in Michael Palin and Terry Jones's Ripping Yarn *Tomkinson's Schooldays*. The naive premise at the centre of this intelligence-insulting story is that music is for sissies, while real men pound across unforgiving terrain and win both the admiration of their tough-as-nails fathers and the hearts of sensitive young girls. No prizes for guessing who comes out on top. Quite what talented actors like Colin Friels and Nick Tate are doing in this kind of macho nonsense is anybody's guess. Run a mile rather than watch it.

Joss McWilliam *Steve Lucas* • Nick Tate *Jpe Lucas* • Josephine Smulders *Kerri Dean* • Robyn Nevin *Robyn Lucas* • Colin Friels *Adam Lucas* • Grant Kenny • Melanie Day *Gilda* • Melissa Jaffer *Ballet teacher* • *Dir* Igor Auzins • *Scr* Peter Schreck

Gold Diggers ★★

Musical   1983 · UK · BW · 95mins

Made by an all-female crew with everyone, including star Julie Christie, receiving the same daily wage, Sally Potter's debut feature is a bold statement on behalf of the cinematic sisterhood. Her monochrome deconstruction of the Hollywood musical is less laudable, however. Although Potter neatly reproduces such genre standards as the production number and the dream sequence, the symbolism is often so dense and self-satisfied that the viewer's response is more likely to be polite admiration than wholehearted enthusiasm. Potter called the film "a musical describing a female quest", but amid the flowing action the meaning is lost.

Julie Christie *Ruby* • Colette Laffont *Celeste* • Hilary Westlake *Ruby's mother* • David Gale *Expert* • Tom Osborn *Expert's assistant* • Jacky Lansley *Tap dancer* • George Yiasoumi *Stage manager* • *Dir* Sally Potter • *Scr* Lindsay Cooper, Rose English, Sally Potter

Gold Diggers in Paris ★★

Musical   1938 · US · BW · 98mins

"Forget the ballet, whether Paris likes it or not we're going to do it our way." It's these words and sentiments that lead to the typically lavish Busby Berkeley number, which is the highlight of this musical comedy. This last, and rarest, in the *Gold Diggers* series has the accent on comedy and music, rather than story, but fans of the girls may need no further recommendation.

Rudy Vallee *Terry Moore* • Rosemary Lane *Kay Morrow* • Hugh Herbert *Maurice Giraud* • Allen Jenkins *Duke Dennis* • Gloria Dickson *Mona* • Melville Cooper *Pierre LeBrec* • Mabel Todd *Leticia* • Fritz Feld *Luis Leoni* • *Dir* Ray Enright • *Scr* Earl Baldwin, Warren Duff, from a story by Jerry Wald, Richard Macaulay, Maurice Leo, Jerry Horwin, James Seymour

Gold Diggers of 1933 ★★★★

Musical   1933 · US · BW · 97mins

Some of the most powerful musical routines ever filmed are featured in this cracking Warner Bros opus, the first of the Busby Berkeley-choreographed series that followed his superb *42nd Street*. Ignore the Ruby Keeler/Dick Powell Broadway plot (though cherish the snappy dialogue) and concentrate on a real rarity, with song-and-dance direction that reflects the climate of the times. This is a movie of the Depression, mirroring the emotions of an audience sick and tired of breadlines, Prohibition and worthless currency. Particularly striking are *My Forgotten Man*, a lament for returning First World War veterans, and Ginger Rogers leading a chorus dressed in sexy pre-censorship gold-coin costumes singing *We're in the Money*. This is a vital, venerable classic and Berkeley's ground-breaking kaleidoscopic choreography continues to be a revelation.

Warren William *J Lawrence Bradford* • Joan Blondell *Carol King* • Aline MacMahon *Trixie Lorraine* • Ruby Keeler *Polly Parker* • Dick Powell *Brad Roberts* • Guy Kibbee *Peabody* • Ned Sparks *Barney Hopkins* • Ginger Rogers *Fay Fortune* • *Dir* Mervyn LeRoy • *Scr* Erwin Gelsey, James Seymour, David Boehm, Ben Markson, from the play *Gold Diggers of Broadway* by Avery Hopwood

Gold Diggers of 1935 ★★★ U

Musical comedy   1935 · US · BW · 90mins

Dance whiz Busby Berkeley finally got to direct the whole movie and not just the dancing sections, and created the celebrated *Lullaby of Broadway* number. In that Oscar-winning climax, singer Winifred Shaw describes the ultimately fragile existence of a New York chorus girl: "Sleep tight, baybee, milkman's on his way..." The excuse for the songs is a charity show at Adolphe Menjou's resort hotel, where Dick Powell is a desk clerk and Gloria Stuart (*Titanic*) is the object of his affections. But the real star of this show is Berkeley's amazing choreography.

Dick Powell *Dick Curtis* • Gloria Stuart *Amy Prentiss* • Adolphe Menjou *Nicoleff* • Glenda Farrell *Betty Hawes* • Grant Mitchell *Louis Lamson* • Dorothy Dare *Arline Davis* • Alice Brady *Mrs Mathilda Prentiss* • Winifred Shaw

Winny • *Dir* Busby Berkeley • *Scr* Manuel Seff, Peter Milne, from a story by Peter Milne, Robert Lord

Gold Diggers of 1937 ★★★ U

Musical comedy   1936 · US · BW · 102mins

The advent of film censorship placed a terrible burden on Warner Bros's potent *Gold Diggers* series. Not only was the generic title now highly suspect, but choreographer Busby Berkeley's use of semi-naked cavorting chorus girls also had to be curtailed. Consequently the production numbers in this film suffer from a lack of excitement, as well as from an obvious lack of budget. Nevertheless, the cast is likeable, even if baby-faced Dick Powell is beginning to grow tiresome in these sappy roles, and the Broadway source (a play called *Sweet Mystery of Life*) provided intelligent dialogue and a semi-decent plot.

Dick Powell *Rosmer Peek* • Joan Blondell *Norma Parry* • Glenda Farrell *Genevieve Larkin* • Victor Moore *JJ Hobart* • Lee Dixon *Boop Oglethorpe* • Osgood Perkins *Mory Wethered* • Charles D Brown *John Huge* • *Dir* Lloyd Bacon • *Scr* Warren Duff, from the play *Sweet Mystery of Life* by Richard Maibaum, Michael Wallace, George Haight

Gold Diggers of Broadway ★★★

Musical   1929 · US · Colour · 105mins

This early talkie no longer exists in its entirety. Some years ago, however, the British Film Institute found the final reel, which makes for nine minutes of fascinating viewing. Filmed in early two-strip Technicolor, it starts with a brief plot-wrapping scene between Nancy Welford and Conway Tearle. After a dazzling overhead shot of backstage activity, it launches into a climactic revue section. Lavishly staged against an impressionistic Parisian backdrop and enthusiastically performed by an array of speciality dance and acrobatic acts, even what little remains clearly indicates why the film was such a huge success on its initial release.

Nancy Welford *Jerry* • Conway Tearle *Stephen Lee* • Winnie Lightner *Mable* • Ann Pennington *Ann Collins* • Lilyan Tashman *Eleanor* • William Bakewell *Wally* • *Dir* Roy Del Ruth • *Scr* Robert Lord, from the play by Avery Hopwood • *Choreography* Larry Ceballos

Gold Diggers: the Secret of Bear Mountain ★★ PG

Adventure   1995 · US · Colour · 89mins

Moving from LA with her mother, Beth (Christina Ricci) is lonely and lost until she befriends fellow outcast and tomboy Jody (Anna Chlumsky). The two friends determine to run away and track down legendary gold in the caves beneath Bear Mountain. This is an utterly formulaic, Disney-esque tale, with stereotypes aplenty; its only redeeming features are the touching friendship between the two girls and Christina's inimitable charm. It's interesting to contrast Ricci's successful career in the late nineties (*The Ice Storm*, *The Opposite of Sex*) with her co-star's current obscurity.

Christina Ricci *Beth Easton* • Anna Chlumsky *Jody Salerno* • Polly Draper *Kate Easton* • Brian Kerwin *Matt Hollinger* • Diana Scarwid

Lynette Salerno • David Keith *Ray Karnisak* • Gillian Barber *Grace Briggs* • *Dir* Kevin James Dobson • *Scr* Barry Glasser

The Gold Express ★

Comedy crime drama
1955 · UK · BW · 58mins

In the thirties, Gaumont British was one of the jewels of the domestic industry. Alas, beneath the Rank umbrella, it fell on such hard times that this dismal quickie was par for its course. A poor imitation of *The Lady Vanishes*, this train-bound comedy thriller is devoid of thrills and utterly lacking in eccentricity – despite the presence of May Hallat and Ivy St Helier as a couple of dotty whodunit writers. The screwball by-play between honeymooning reporters Vernon Gray and Ann Walford is equally bogus, as they seek to prevent Patrick Boxill from swiping a consignment of gold.

Vernon Gray *Bob Wright* • Ann Walford *Mary Wright* • May Hallatt *Agatha Merton* • Ivy St Helier *Emma Merton* • Patrick Boxill *Mr Rover* • Charles Rolfe *George Phillips* • John Serret *Luke Dubois* • Delphi Lawrence *Pearl* • *Dir* Guy Fergusson • *Scr* Jackson Budd

Gold for the Caesars ★★ U

Adventure   1964 · Fr/It · Colour · 85mins

Based on a long-forgotten novel by Florence A Seward, this stagey sword-and-sandal adventure was directed by Sabatino Ciuffini and Riccardo Freda under the supervision of Hollywood veteran, Andre De Toth. The ancient Roman settings reek of studio artifice and the plot is short on surprises. But Jeffrey Hunter is suitably statuesque as the slave-come-architect, who is sent on a perilous mission to find the titular gold by treacherous proconsul Massimo Girotti. With Mylène Demongeot providing the glamour, this is a tolerable time-passer. Italian dialogue dubbed into English.

Jeffrey Hunter *Lacer* • Mylène Demongeot *Penelope* • Ron Randell *Rufus* • Massimo Girotti *Maximus* • Giulio Bosetti *Scipio* • Ettore Manni *Luna* • Georges Lycan *Malendi* • *Dir* Andre De Toth, Sabatino Ciuffini, Riccardo Freda • *Scr* Arnold Perl, Sabatino Ciuffini, from the novel by Florence A Seward

Gold in the Streets ★ 15

Drama   1996 · UK/Ire · Colour · 93mins

The immensely talented Aidan Gillen (*Queer as Folk*) and Ian Hart (*The End of the Affair*) co-star with James Belushi in this substandard tale of Irish illegal immigrants in New York. Screenwriter Noel Pearson and debut director Elizabeth Gill have sadly failed here on all fronts. This is a clichéd, glossy nostalgia piece at the expense of the Irish community. Belushi as bar-owner Mario, the main employer of the immigrants, holds his own, as does Hart, but the remaining cast are all one-dimensional stereotypes who missed out on accent coaching. One to be missed. Contains swearing.

Karl Geary *Liam* • James Belushi *Mario* • Ian Hart *Des* • Jared Harris *Owen* • Aidan Gillen *Paddy* • Louise Lombard *Mary* • Tom Hickey *Mr Costello* • Andrea Irvine *Breda* • Lorraine Pilkington *Rose* • *Dir* Elizabeth Gill • *Scr* Janet Noble, Noel Pearson, from the play *Away Alone* by Janet Noble

Gold Is Where You Find It ★★★ U

Western 1938 · US · Colour · 95mins

Gold-miners and wheat farmers argue it out in the Sacramento valley in this Technicolored slice of hokum, knocked off in three weeks by director Michael Curtiz. Warners toplined George Brent, who's rather a forgotten star nowadays. His moustachioed gallantry graced many an action pic and in real life he married as often as Henry VIII. His romantic sparring partner is Olivia de Havilland who's married to that inveterate scene-stealer, Claude Rains. Brent is a mining engineer who falls for de Havilland, who is a farmer's daughter – and farmers hate miners.

George Brent *Jared Whitney* • Olivia de Havilland *Serena Ferris* • Claude Rains *Col Ferris* • Margaret Lindsay *Rosanne Ferris* • John Litel *Ralph Ferris* • Tim Holt *Lanceford Ferris* • Barton MacLane *Slag Minton* ■ *Dir* Michael Curtiz • *Scr* Warren Duff, Robert Buckner, from the story by Clements Ripley

Gold of Naples ★★★★

Comedy drama 1954 · It · BW · 112mins

Here are four stories for the price of one, as great Italian director (and co-writer) Vittorio De Sica illustrates scenes of working-class life in Naples. Sophia Loren makes an early appearance as a philandering wife in *Pizza on Credit*; Silvana Mangano plays a prostitute in *Theresa*; Totò has problems with an unwanted house guest in *The Racketeer*; and De Sica finds himself upstaged by a kid in a tale about a very unsuccessful gambler. The kind of wholesome sentimentality that's good for what ails you. In Italian with English subtitles.

Totò *The husband* • Lianella Carrell *His wife* • Sophia Loren *Sofia, the wife* • Giacomo Furia *Rosario, the husband* • Alberto Farnese *Alfredo, the lover* • Vittorio De Sica *The Count* • Mario Passante *His valet* • Silvana Mangano *Theresa* ■ *Dir* Vittorio De Sica • *Scr* Cesare Zavattini, Vittorio De Sica, Giuseppe Marotta, from the novel by Giuseppe Marotta

Gold of the Seven Saints ★★ U

Western 1961 · US · BW · 88mins

Clint Walker and Roger Moore, stars of the western TV series *Cheyenne* and *Maverick* respectively, are here relocated to scenic Utah. They play fur trappers who strike it rich when they find the eponymous gold in this moderately entertaining retread of *The Treasure of the Sierra Madre*. Walker and Moore's couch potato fans were used to seeing them in colour, but Warners saved money by having the film shot in black and white.

Clint Walker *Jim Rainbolt* • Roger Moore *Shaun Garrett* • Leticia Roman *Tita* • Robert Middleton *Gondora* • Chill Wills *Doc Gates* • Gene Evans *McCracken* • Roberto Contreras *Armanderez* • Jack C Williams *Ames* • Art Stewart *Ricca* ■ *Dir* Gordon Douglas • *Scr* Leigh Brackett, Leonard Freeman, from the novel *Desert Guns* by Steve Frazee

The Gold Rush ★★★★★ U

Silent comedy 1925 · US · BW · 71mins

Charlie Chaplin allowed the copyright for this, the most light-hearted of his great features, to lapse in 1953 so that it passed into the public domain – a gift for audiences. As a prospector in the ice-bound gold fields – an outsider even in a world of outcasts – he falls yearningly for a contemptuous Georgia Hale, but finally claims the girl and the gold. The comedy dazzles (in scenes such as the dance of the bread rolls) and darkens (his starving comrade hallucinates that Charlie is a very edible chicken), but the ending is wonderfully affirmative, a fact that he couldn't help mocking. For the final embrace, shipboard photographers shout: "You've spoiled the picture!" Marvellously, though, he hadn't. ▭

Charles Chaplin *Lone prospector* • Mack Swain *Big Jim McKay* • Tom Murray *Black Larson* • Georgia Hale *Georgia* • Betty Morrissey *Georgia's friend* ■ *Dir/Scr* Charles Chaplin • *Cinematographer* Rollie Totheroh

Gold Rush Maisie ★★★ U

Comedy drama 1940 · US · BW · 81mins

Ann Sothern's comic vitality and warmth gave an added dimension to the character of Maisie Ravier, the sassy, scatter-brained, accident-prone heroine of the popular series of the forties. Here she is trying to make it as a singer in Gold Rush territory, where she comes across poor and hungry farmers. Typically Maisie, who always starts off looking after number one, helps the farmers out of their difficulties. One of the best of the series of ten movies, it successfully manages a switch in tone between comedy and drama.

Ann Sothern *Maisie Ravier* • Lee Bowman *Bill Anders* • Virginia Weidler *Jubie Davis* • John F Hamilton *Bert Davis* ■ *Dir* Edwin L Marin • *Scr* Mary C McCall Jr, Betty Reinhardt, from a story by Wilson Collison

The Golden Age of Buster Keaton ★★★★ U

Compilation 1975 · US · BW · 96mins

The genius of the most cinematic of all the silent clowns is celebrated in this hugely entertaining compilation. Director Jay Ward deserves a pat on the back for including rarely-seen footage from the early Fatty Arbuckle shorts in which Keaton began his film career, even though they seem to be playing on fast forward. In addition to classic scenes from such shorts as *The Playhouse* and *The Electric House*, there are more sustained sequences from Keaton's features that demonstrate not only his balletic skill and mastery of props, but also his unrivalled ability to develop a gag and his immaculate comic timing.

Buster Keaton ■ *Dir* Jay Ward

The Golden Age of Comedy ★★★★

Compilation 1958 · US · BW · 70mins

Containing material from both the Mack Sennett and Hal Roach archives, this was the first of Robert Youngson's slapstick compilations and it did much to restore Laurel and Hardy's then flagging reputation. Although there are clips featuring such clowns as Harry Langdon, Ben Turpin and Charley Chase, it's the Stan and Ollie excerpts that command the most attention. Two-reelers such as *The Second Hundred Years*, *You're Darn Tootin'*, *Two Tars* and *Double Whoopee* had scarcely been seen since the silent era, but not even their hilarity could match the anarchic brilliance of the pie fight from *The Battle of the Century*.

Dwight Weist *Narrator* • Ward Wilson *Narrator* ■ • *Scr* Robert Youngson • *Producer* Robert Youngson • *Music* George Steiner

Golden Balls ★★★ 18

Comedy 1993 · Sp · Colour · 88mins

The middle section of director Bigas Luna's "Iberian passion" trilogy (completed by *Jamon Jamon* and *The Tit and the Moon*) continues his bawdy contemplation on greed, food and sex. In another brazen performance, Spanish heart-throb Javier Bardem is a horny young buck who wants to erect a skyscraper in honour of himself and sees everyone as potential rungs towards that goal. He's also obsessed with stealing bidets, Julio Iglesias, Rolex watches and Salvador Dali in this fascinating study of sun-drenched selfishness and stubbornness. Sexually explicit and packed with unforgettable images, Luna's work equals that of the better known Pedro Almódovar in the kitsch-and-think drama department. In Spanish with English subtitles.

Javier Bardem *Benito Gonzalez* • Maria de Medeiros *Marta* • Maribel Verdu *Claudia* • Elisa Touati *Rita* • Raquel Bianca *Ana the maneater* • Alessandro Gassman *Melilla's friend* • Benicio Del Toro *Bob the friend from Miami* • Francesco Ma Dominedo *Mosca* ■ *Dir* Bigas Luna • *Scr* Bigas Luna, Cuca Canals

The Golden Blade ★★ U

Adventure fantasy 1953 · US · Colour · 79mins

Universal went in for camp and colourful exotic adventures, with simple good vs evil plots. Rock Hudson is Harun, the handsome and noble hero, George Macready (hiss!) is the nasty Grand Vizier, and Piper Laurie the Princess of Baghdad, the damsel in distress. Hard to believe that the cute though unexotic Laurie was the same actress who played the lonely, lame girl in *The Hustler* eight years later. More formulaic than most, it's still pleasantly escapist. Watch out for an early glimpse of Anita Ekberg, as one of the Princess's handmaidens.

Rock Hudson *Harun* • Piper Laurie *Princess Khairuzan* • Gene Evans *Hadi* • Kathleen Hughes *Bakhamra* • George Macready *Jafar* • Steven Geray *Barcus* • Edgar Barrier *Caliph* ■ *Dir* Nathan Juran • *Scr* John Rich

Golden Boy ★★★

Drama 1939 · US · BW · 99mins

A very famous play in its time, this tale has been copied and parodied ever since. The story of a violinist who also boxes was once considered a daringly left wing and extremely courageous work, bringing international fame and acclaim to its author Clifford Odets. But, in this watered-down movie version, the play's sting is largely missing and the New York tenement setting is sanitised. Lee J Cobb's performance as William Holden's dad is one of the worst pieces of character overacting in movie history. The film is cliché-ridden and very dated, and the only real reasons for watching now are the leads, with Barbara Stanwyck showing the ropes to an amazingly innocent Holden in the role that made him a star. Contains some violence.

Barbara Stanwyck *Lorna Moon* • William Holden (1) *Joe Bonaparte* • Adolphe Menjou *Tom Moody* • Lee J Cobb *Mr Bonaparte* • Joseph Calleia *Eddie Fuseli* • Sam Levene *Siggie* • Edward S Brophy [Edward Brophy] *Roxy Lewis* ■ *Dir* Rouben Mamoulian • *Scr* Lewis Meltzer, Daniel Taradash, Sara Y Mason, Victor Heerman, from the play by Clifford Odets

Golden Braid ★★★★ 15

Drama 1991 · Ausl · Colour · 87mins

Dutch-born director Paul Cox is one of the unsung heroes of Australian cinema. His slow-moving but intense films always draw you into their core and bind you into the troubled lives of his characters. This subtly powerful drama is based on a story by Guy de Maupassant, although Cox has changed the ending to suggest that madness is not the only escape from the agony of isolation. As the clock repairer who becomes infatuated with a lock of hair, Chris Haywood manages to be both sinister and sympathetic, as his passion detaches him from reality. A truly compelling picture. ▭

Chris Haywood *Bernard Simon* • Gosia Dubrowolska *Terese* • Paul Chubb *Joseph* • Norman Kaye *Psychiatrist* • Marion Heathfield *Housekeeper* • Monica Maughan *Antique-shop owner* • Robert Menzies *Ernst* • Jo Kennedy *Ernst's wife* • Paul Cox *Priest* ■ *Dir* Paul Cox • *Scr* Paul Cox, Barry Dickins, from the story *La Chevelure* by Guy de Maupassant

The Golden Child ★★ PG

Action comedy 1986 · US · Colour · 89mins

At this stage in his career, Eddie Murphy was certainly the golden boy of Hollywood with hits such as *Beverly Hills Cop* and *48 HRS* under his belt. However, not even he could save this horribly misconceived comedy adventure, in which he is cast rather improbably as a social worker who is asked to track down a Tibetan youngster (the "Golden Child") who holds the key to the world's survival. Murphy's quick-fire quips fall flat and Michael Ritchie's direction is best described as indifferent, while Charles Dance mugs away terribly as the baddie of the piece. Contains some violence and swearing. ▭

Eddie Murphy *Chandler Jarrell* • Charles Dance *Sardo Numspa* • Charlotte Lewis *Kee Nang* • Victor Wong *Old Man* • JL Reate *Golden Child* • Randall "Tex" Cobb *Til* • James Hong *Dr Hong* • Shakti *Kala* ■ *Dir* Michael Ritchie • *Scr* Dennis Feldman

The Golden Coach ★★★★ U

Period drama 1953 · Fr/Ital · Colour · 105mins

Despite a contrived storyline, gleaned from a play by Prosper Mérimée, this vibrant costume drama succeeds mainly because of Claude Renoir's stunning Technicolor photography. Suggesting both the untouched beauty of 18th-century Peru and the fabulous dream world of the stage, the imagery mirrors the radiance of Anna Magnani. She's the star of a touring *commedia dell'arte* troupe torn between a love for her art and the dictates of her heart.

Director Jean Renoir continued to explore the contrasts between drama and life in the rest of his unofficial "theatre" trilogy, *French Cancan* and *Elena et les Hommes*.

Anna Magnani *Camilla* • Odoardo Spadaro *Don Antonio* • Nada Fiorelli *Isabella* • Dante Rino *Harlequin* • Duncan Lamont *Viceroy* • George Higgins *Martinez* • Ralph Truman *Duke* ■ *Dir* Jean Renoir • *Scr* Jean Renoir, Renzo Avanzo, Jack Kirkland, Giulio Macchi, from the play *Le Carosse du Saint-Sacrement* by Prosper Mérimée

The Golden Disc ★ U
Musical 1958 · UK · BW · 77mins

The coffee bar was the only place to be seen in the early rock 'n' roll years, but it is almost impossible to see how they became teen meccas from this risible British pop picture. In the very worst "it's trad, dad" manner, it shows how Lee Patterson and Mary Steele jazz up her aunt's coffee shop with a record booth and the singing talents of odd-job man Terry Dene. The subplot, about Dene's record deal being hijacked by unscrupulous grown-ups, is made even more improbable by the lamentable quality of his soggy ballads. Well worth missing.

Lee Patterson *Harry Blair* • Mary Steele *Joan Farmer* • Terry Dene *Terry Dene* • Linda Gray *Aunt Sarah* • Ronald Adam *Mr Dryden* • Peter Dyneley *Mr Washington* • David Jacobs • David Williams *Recording engineer* ■ *Dir* Don Sharp • *Scr* Don Sharp, Don Nicholl, from a story by Gee Nicholl

Golden Earrings ★★
Spy drama 1947 · US · BW · 94mins

A British intelligence agent (Ray Milland), on a mission to get his hands on a secret Nazi formula for poison gas, is helped by an exotic gypsy (Marlene Dietrich), in whose caravan he finds sanctuary and romance. Despite stylish direction from Mitchell Leisen and the heavyweight (if not exactly harmonious) pairing of Milland and Dietrich, the ridiculous plot manages to be both camp and humourless. This marked Dietrich's return to the screen after an absence spent entertaining the troops during the Second World War. Second-billed to Milland, this drivel proved her glory days with von Sternberg were well and truly over. Not the best of comebacks.

Ray Milland *Col Ralph Denistoun* • Marlene Dietrich *Lydia* • Murvyn Vye *Zoltan* • Bruce Lester *Byrd* • Dennis Hoey *Hoff* • Quentin Reynolds • Reinhold Schunzel *Prof Krosigk* ■ *Dir* Mitchell Leisen • *Scr* Abraham Polonsky, Frank Butler, Helen Deutsch, from the novel by Yolanda Foldes

Golden Eighties ★★★
Musical drama
1986 · Fr/Be/Swi · Colour · 96mins

In the seventies, the feminist Belgian director Chantal Akerman was known for her rather glum and static minimalist films. So it came as a surprise when Akerman turned her hand to a somewhat kitsch musical, in which the themes of love, sex and commerce are closely linked. Most of the small-scale, bittersweet film takes place in a shopping mall and revolves around a clothes boutique and a hair salon, where the characters play out their destinies to the accompaniment

of an eclectic score and witty, sometimes raunchy lyrics. At its centre is the exquisite Delphine Seyrig, who tragically died four years later aged 58. In French with English subtitles.

Delphine Seyrig *Jeanne Schwartz* • Myriam Boyer *Sylvie* • Fanny Cottençon *Lili* • Lio *Mado* • Pascale Salkin *Pascale* • Charles Denner *Monsieur Schwartz* • Jean-Françoise Balmer *Monsieur Jean* • John Berry *Eli* • Nicolas Tronc *Robert Schwartz* ■ *Dir* Chantal Akerman • *Scr* Chantal Akerman, Leora Barish, Henry Bean, Pascal Bonitzer, Jean Gruault

Golden Gate ★★ 15
Crime drama 1994 · US · Colour · 86mins

Anyone who thinks that Matt Dillon is a one-trick actor should take a look at this moody period piece. Unfortunately, his astute performance as an eager law graduate discovering that working for the FBI doesn't automatically put him on the side of the good guys is rather wasted on such a disjointed and ultimately disappointing film. The un-American paranoia of the early fifties is well captured, but once Dillon secures a conviction against some Chinese workers sending money home to Hong Kong, both the tension and the pace slacken, and the scenes set during the sixties are lazily melodramatic. Contains swearing. ▭

Matt Dillon *Kevin Walker* • Joan Chen *Marilyn Song* • Bruno Kirby *Ron Pirelli* • Teri Polo *Cynthia* • Ma Tzi *Chen Jung Song* • Stan Egi *Bradley Ichiyasu* • Jack Shearer *FBI Chief* • Peter Murnik *Byrd* • George Guidall *Meisner* ■ *Dir* John Madden • *Scr* David Henry Hwang

Golden Girl ★★★ U
Musical drama 1951 · US · Colour · 108mins

Talented, chirpy Mitzi Gaynor is largely remembered today for her appearance as Nellie Forbush in the movie version of *South Pacific*, but she adorned a run of minor Technicolored musicals at 20th Century-Fox, of which this is fairly typical. Gaynor is Lotta Crabtree, a legendary and glamorous performer in the days of the Civil War, most noted for her popular song *Oh, Dem Golden Slippers*, which she sang all over the Old West before becoming the toast of New York. Gaynor is charming in the role, and Dale Robertson makes a laconically attractive, if rather weak leading man.

Mitzi Gaynor *Lotta Crabtree* • Dale Robertson *Tom Richmond* • Dennis Day *Mart* • James Barton *Mr Crabtree* • Una Merkel *Mrs Crabtree* • Raymond Walburn *Cornelius* • Gene Sheldon *Sam Jordan* • Carmen D'Antonio *Lola Montez* ■ *Dir* Lloyd Bacon • *Scr* Walter Bullock, Charles O'Neal, Gladys Lehman, from a story by Arthur Lewis, Albert Lewis, Edward Thompson

The Golden Hour ★★ U
Musical comedy 1941 · US · BW · 86mins

James Stewart sings with Horace Heidt and his Orchestra on his uncle Charles Winninger's radio show, while falling for Mary Gordon's lovely daughter Paulette Goddard. That's all there is to the plot, really, and Stewart later publicly declared this the worst of his films. Viewed today, it has a quaint period charm, though songs such as *With a Knife, a Fork and a Spoon* don't exactly light any fires. The US title, *Pot o' Gold*, was the name of a popular long-running radio show featuring

bandleader Heidt, and this film was made to capitalise on his appeal. ▭

James Stewart *Jimmy Haskell* • Paulette Goddard *Molly McCorkle* • Charles Winninger *CJ Haskell* • Mary Gordon *Ma McCorkle* • Frank Melton *Jasper* • Jed Prouty *Mr Louderman* • Dick Hogan *Willie McCorkle* ■ *Dir* George Marshall • *Scr* Walter De Leon, from a story by Monte Brice, Andrew Bennison, Harry Tugend, from an idea by Haydn Roth Evans, Robert Brilmayer

Golden Needles ★★
Martial arts action
1974 · US · Colour · 92mins

Soon after his ground-breaking collaboration with Bruce Lee, director Robert Clouse returned to Hong Kong for this so-so action adventure. The "golden needles" of the title make up a priceless artefact that is being hunted by a disparate group of people. Joe Don Baker, Burgess Meredith and Elizabeth Ashley top the cast but, although Clouse still stuffs the film with plenty of martial-arts mayhem, the mix of laughs and action never gels.

Joe Don Baker *Dan* • Elizabeth Ashley *Felicity* • Jim Kelly *Jeff* • Burgess Meredith *Winters* • Ann Sothern *Finzie* • Roy Chiao *Lin Toa* • Frances Fong *Su Lin* • Tony Lee *Kwan* ■ *Dir* Robert Clouse • *Scr* S Lee Pogostin, Sylvia Schnebel

Golden Rendezvous ★ 15
Action thriller 1977 · US · Colour · 97mins

John Vernon leads a terrorist assault on a floating casino, hoping his threat to nuke the vessel and its passengers will make the president of the United States hand over a ship full of gold bullion. Richard Harris plays the officer who puts his life on the line (as the actor puts his talent on hold) to foil the plot. This amateurish caper, based on the novel by Alistair MacLean, is *Goldfinger* at sea – without 007, Pussy Galore or a decent villain.

Richard Harris *John Carter* • Ann Turkel *Susan Beresford* • David Janssen *Charles Conway* • Burgess Meredith *Van Heurden* • John Vernon *Luis Carreras* • Gordon Jackson *Dr Marston* • Dorothy Malone *Elizabeth Taubman* • John Carradine *Fairweather* ■ *Dir* Ashley Lazarus • *Scr* Stanley Price, from the novel by Alistair MacLean

Golden Salamander ★★ U
Adventure 1949 · UK · BW · 90mins

The one thing you could usually never say about Trevor Howard was that he was a dull performer. However, he certainly was the wrong side of interesting in this utterly predictable thriller about gunrunning in the North African desert. Usually a dab hand at this sort of thing, director Ronald Neame is content to cruise in low gear, thus wasting the villainous potential of Herbert Lom, Jacques Sernas and Walter Rilla. The only compensations are wily Wilfrid Hyde White and 17-year-old Anouk Aimée, whose assured performance belies the fact that she was making only her third film.

Trevor Howard *David Redfern* • Anouk Aimée *Anna* • Herbert Lom *Rankl* • Miles Malleson *Douvet* • Walter Rilla *Serafis* • Jacques Sernas *Max* • Wilfrid Hyde White *Agno* • Peter Copley *Aribi* ■ *Dir* Ronald Neame • *Scr* Ronald Neame, Victor Canning, Lesley Storm, from a novel by Victor Canning

The Golden Voyage of Sinbad ★★★ U
Fantasy adventure
1973 · UK · Colour · 100mins

John Phillip Law – best known as the blind angel Pygar in *Barbarella* – takes over the role of the legendary seafarer from Kerwin Mathews, who'd impressed in *The 7th Voyage of Sinbad*. However, the actors and the plot once again end up playing second fiddle to the magnificent Dynamation sequences meticulously created by the godfather of special effects, Ray Harryhausen. Particularly memorable are the talking figurehead, the hideous centaur and the multi-armed statue that tests Sinbad's swordfighting skills to the maximum. ▭

John Phillip Law *Sinbad* • Caroline Munro *Margiana* • Tom Baker *Koura* • Douglas Wilmer *Vizier* • Martin Shaw *Rachid* • Grégoire Aslan *Hakim* • Kurt Christian *Haroun* • Takis Emmanuel *Achmed* ■ *Dir* Gordon Hessler • *Scr* Brian Clemens, from a story by Brian Clemens, Ray Harryhausen

GoldenEye ★★★★ 12
Spy adventure
1995 · UK/US · Colour · 124mins

When "M" says to James Bond, "I think you're a sexist, misogynist dinosaur, a relic of the Cold War," who can disagree? To ram home the point, "M" is played by a woman (Judi Dench) and a key scene is set in a Russian park that is now a dumping ground for statues of redundant communist heroes. However, Pierce Brosnan, on his first mission as 007, quickly establishes himself as the best Bond since Sean Connery and makes a fetish out of the old-fashioned values of loyalty and patriotism. There isn't a proper villain, but director Martin Campbell does provide a stunning chase between car and tank through the streets of St Petersburg. There are also splendid Bond girls, including Izabella Scorupco and feisty Famke Janssen, who kills by crushing her victims between her thighs. Contains violence. ▭ DVD

Pierce Brosnan *James Bond* • Sean Bean *Alec Trevelyan* • Izabella Scorupco *Natalya Simonova* • Famke Janssen *Xenia Onatopp* • Joe Don Baker *Jack Wade* • Judi Dench *"M"* • Robbie Coltrane *Valentin Zukovsky* • Tcheky Karyo *Dimitri Mishkin* • Desmond Llewelyn *"Q"* • Samantha Bond *Moneypenny* ■ *Dir* Martin Campbell • *Scr* Jeffrey Caine, Bruce Feirstein, from a story by Michael France

Goldengirl ★ 15
Drama sports 1979 · US · Colour · 100mins

Susan Anton is an athlete who is actually brainwashed and physically tortured into becoming a gold medal winner at the 1980 Moscow Olympics. The surprise is, she isn't a Soviet athlete, but an American. Electric shock treatment and mental torture are among the methods employed by her father, Curt Jurgens, and her shrink, Leslie Caron, while her agent, James Coburn, seems more interested in getting her into bed. Intended to reveal the corruption and commercialism in sport, the film looked especially stupid in 1980 after the USA boycotted the Moscow Olympics. Poor direction and a ridiculous script don't help. ▭

Susan Anton *Goldine Serafin* • James Coburn *Jack Dryden* • Curt Jurgens *Dr Serafin* • Leslie Caron *Dr Sammy Lee* • Robert Culp *Steve Esselton* • James A Watson Jr *Winters* • Harry Guardino *Valenti* • Ward Costello *Cobb* ■ *Dir* Joseph Sargent • *Scr* John Kohn, from the novel by Peter Lear

Goldfinger ★★★★★ PG

Spy adventure 1964 · UK · Colour · 105mins

The third in the series featuring Ian Fleming's indestructibly suave superspy is one of the slickest of all the Bond movies. Endlessly entertaining and effortlessly performed, it's packed with classic moments. These include: Shirley Eaton's legendary gold-plated death; the best name for any Bond girl in Pussy Galore (played to the hilt by ex-Avenger Honor Blackman); a brilliantly bizarre villain in Gert Frobe, who plans to irradiate Fort Knox to boost the value of his own gold supplies; Ken Adam's hilariously OTT weapon and gadget designs; and that legendary Shirley Bassey song. Oh yes: Sean Connery's not bad as 007 either. ▭ *DVD*

Sean Connery *James Bond* • Honor Blackman *Pussy Galore* • Gert Frobe *Auric Goldfinger* • Shirley Eaton *Jill Masterson* • Tania Mallett *Tilly Masterson* • Harold Sakata *Oddjob* • Bernard Lee *"M"* • Martin Benson *Solo* • Cec Linder *Felix Leiter* • Desmond Llewelyn *"Q"* • Lois Maxwell *Miss Moneypenny* ■ *Dir* Guy Hamilton • *Scr* Richard Maibaum, Paul Dehn, from the novel by Ian Fleming • *Music* John Barry • *Production Designer* Ken Adam

Goldstein ★★

Black comedy 1964 · US · BW · 82mins

This "far out" movie marked the directing debut of Philip Kaufman, who later wrote *The Outlaw Josey Wales* and *Raiders of the Lost Ark* and directed *The Right Stuff*. It's a very sixties satire with biblical overtones – it's actually based on the story of the prophet Elijah. Lou Gilbert plays the tramp who rises from Lake Michigan, shuffles around Chicago, clashes with abortionists, sculptors and other wacky people, and then sinks again. The sort of film that's bound to polarise opinions, it features a cameo appearance by Nelson Algren, author of *The Man with the Golden Arm*.

Lou Gilbert *Old man* • Ellen Madison *Sally* • Thomas Erhart *Sculptor* • Benito Carruthers [Ben Carruthers] *Jay* • Charles Fischer *Mr Nice* • Severn Darden *Doctor* • Nelson Algren ■ *Dir/Scr* Philip Kaufman, Benjamin Manaster

The Goldwyn Follies ★★★ U

Musical 1938 · US · Colour · 110mins

This might have been an unwatchable prize clunker, were it not for a few touches that lifted it from the mediocre to the special. Not least of these is the fact that it contains the last song ever written by the great George Gershwin, the hypnotically beautiful *Love Walked In*. However, it's performed unmercifully by the graceless tenor Kenny Baker, whose warbling is a matter of taste. Taste does not apply to the antics of the Ritz Brothers, Edgar Bergen and his dummy Charlie McCarthy, nor to a series of ballets by George Balanchine, involving his then wife Vera Zorina. All are astoundingly awful and prove that, though producer Samuel Goldwyn

thought himself the Hollywood Ziegfeld, there really was only one Florenz – the rest were just follies. ▭

Adolphe Menjou *Oliver Merlin* • The Ritz Brothers • Vera Zorina *Olga Samara* • Kenny Baker (2) *Danny Beecher* • Andrea Leeds *Hazel Dawes* • Helen Jepson *Leona Jerome* • Phil Baker *Michael Day* • Ella Logan *Glory Wood* • Edgar Bergen • Alan Ladd *Auditioning singer* ■ *Dir* George Marshall • *Scr* Ben Hecht, Sam Perrin, Arthur Phillips

The Golem ★★★★

Silent horror classic 1920 · Ger · BW · 85mins

This is the most eye-catching of the several versions of the ancient Jewish legend, mainly because of the Expressionist sets by Hans Poelzig, and the use of chiaroscuro to create a Gothic effect. Paul Wegener, who co-directed with Carl Boese, plays the clay monster created by a rabbi to help his people fight against the Emperor's expulsion of the Jews from the ghetto in 16th-century Prague. Wegener's lumbering gait was imitated by Boris Karloff in James Whale's *Frankenstein* (1931). Wegener, who had already played the Golem in the 1914 film version of the story, continued to act in films of the Nazi period.

Paul Wegener *The Golem* • Albert Steinrück *Rabbi Loew* • Lyda Salmonova *Miriam* • Ernst Deutsch *Famulus* • Otto Gebühr *Emperor* • Lothar Müthel *Florian* • Loni Nest *Child* ■ *Dir* Paul Wegener, Carl Boese • *Scr* Paul Wegener, Henrik Galeen, from the novel *Der Golem* by Gustav Meyrinck • *Cinematographer* Karl Freund

The Golem ★★★

Horror 1936 · Cz/Fr · BW · 83mins

Julien Duvivier's sound version of this classic horror story was shot in Prague, where the Jewish folk legend was said to have originated. Harry Baur is Emperor Rudolf II, whose persecution of the Jews causes the clay monster (the Golem) to reanimate and punish the oppressors. Ironically, Baur's own Jewish wife was arrested by the Nazis during the Second World War. Despite a good French cast, this lacks the atmosphere and narrative drive of Paul Wegener's 1920 film. However, those unfamiliar with the story will still find this scary and may also see parallels with Boris Karloff's more celebrated Monster. In French with English subtitles.

Harry Baur *Emperor Rudolf II* • Roger Karl *Chancellor Lang* • Germaine Aussey *Countess Strada* • Jany Holt *Rachel* • Charles Dorat *Rabbi Jacob* • Roger Duchesne *de Trignac* • Aimos [Raymond Aimos] *Toussaint* • Ferdinand Hart *The Golem* ■ *Dir* Julien Duvivier • *Scr* Julien Duvivier, André-Paul Antoine, JD Antoine, from the novel *Der Golem* by Gustav Meyrinck

Golem, the Spirit of Exile ★★

Drama 1992 · Ger/Fr · Colour · 105mins

With Hanna Schygulla assuming a variety of ethereal disguises, and cinematographer Henri Alekan producing his customarily sublime images, this treatise on the plight of the displaced has more in common with *Wings of Desire* than the silent, Expressionist versions of the old Jewish Golem myth. Unfortunately, writer/director Amos Gitai surrounds

the travails of Ophrah Shemesh's family with so many obscure references that it's almost impossible to identify with her problems. For all its sincerity, and notwithstanding cameos from directors Samuel Fuller and Bernardo Bertolucci, this is heavy going. In French with English subtitles.

Hanna Schygulla *Naomi* • Vittorio Mezzogiorno • Ophrah Shemesh ■ *Dir/Scr* Amos Gitai

Goliath and the Barbarians ★★15

Period adventure 1959 · It · Colour · 81mins

It's AD 568 and dastardly barbarians are on the rampage, raping and pillaging in downtown Verona. But Steve Reeves stands in their way, all rippling muscles and flashing teeth, keen to play tug of war with cart horses. Mr Reeves was a minor Arnold Schwarzenegger of his day, a former Mr Universe who enjoyed brief stardom when the Italians ripped off their own mythology in a series of deliriously awful epics that cost twice as much to publicise as they did to produce. The English dubbing, the cardboard sets and the lack of any technical proficiency make this peculiarly endearing. Italian dialogue dubbed into English. ▭

Steve Reeves *Emiliano* • Chelo Alonso *Londo* • Bruce Cabot *Alboyna* • Giulia Rubini *Sabina* • Livio Lorenzon *Igor* • Luciano Marin *Svevo* • Arturo Dominici *Delfo* • Furio Meniconi *Marco* ■ *Dir* Carlo Campogalliani • *Scr* Carlo Campogalliani, Gino Mangini, Nino Stresa, Giuseppe Taffarel, from a story by Emimmo Salvi, Gino Mangini

Gone Are the Days ★★★

Comedy drama 1963 · US · BW · 97mins

Actor Ossie Davis turned his heartfelt play *Purlie Victorious* into a screen vehicle for himself and his wife Ruby Dee. Davis plays a self-styled preacher who returns to his little Southern home town in order to start his own church. Despite opposition from a segregationist plantation owner, through various schemes and tricks he finally achieves his aim. Great performances from the committed cast make the most of the somewhat dated humour, pertinently used to underscore the racist thrust of the plot. Alan Alda made his film debut as one of the more liberal-thinking white characters.

Ossie Davis *Purlie Victorious* • Ruby Dee *Lutiebelle* • Sorrell Booke *Capt Cotchipee* • Godfrey Cambridge *Gitlow* • Hilda Haynes *Missy* • Alan Alda *Charlie Cotchipee* • Beah Richards *Idella* • Charles Welch *Sheriff* ■ *Dir* Nicholas Webster • *Scr* Ossie Davis, from his play *Purlie Victorious*

Gone Fishin' ★ PG

Comedy 1997 · US · Colour · 90mins

A misguided and truly abysmal comedy vehicle for *Lethal Weapon* co-stars Joe Pesci and Danny Glover, who play a couple of disaster-prone chums who set off on a fishing trip. Along the way the bumbling duo end up with a map to a missing fortune. As a result, they are pursued by a lethal con man (Nick Brimble) and the two women on his trail (Rosanna Arquette and Lynn Whitfield). The two talented stars can do nothing with the gag-free script. Two hours of unsuccessful fly fishing would

provide more entertainment than this disaster. ▭

Joe Pesci *Joe Waters* • Danny Glover *Gus Green* • Rosanna Arquette *Rita* • Lynn Whitfield *Angie* • Willie Nelson *Billy "Catch" Pooler* • Nick Brimble *Dekker Massey* • Gary Grubbs *Phil Beasly* • Carol Kane *Donna Waters* ■ *Dir* Christopher Cain • *Scr* Jill Mazursky *Cody* [Jill Mazursky], Jeffrey Abrams

Gone in 60 Seconds ★★

Crime action 1974 · US · Colour · 107mins

The versatile HB Halicki not only wrote, directed and starred in this grandaddy of the car-chase movie; he also supplied the vehicles, 93 of which ended up demolished – if you believe the pre-release hype. Influencing a range of films from *The Cannonball Run* to *Deathrace 2000*, Halicki's story of a ring of professional car thieves, culminates in the now classic 40-minute chase sequence. It was enough of a cult hit to warrant a sequel in 1989, during the filming of which Halicki was killed doing a stunt. By the way, the title refers to how long it takes to steal a car.

HB Halicki *Maindrian Pace* • Marion Busia *Pumpkin Chase* • Eugene *Eugene Chase* • James McIntyre *Stanley Chase* • George Cole *Atlee Jackson* • Ronald Halicki *Corlis Pace* ■ *Dir/Scr* HB Halicki

Gone in 60 Seconds ★★15

Action crime drama 2000 · US · Colour · 117mins

The car's the star in this boys-and-their-toys action drama which unfortunately lacks enough action to cover for the absence of plot. Nicolas Cage is a reformed car thief who agrees to pull off an impossible job – steal 50 top-of-the-range cars in four nights – for bad guy Christopher Eccleston, in return for brother Giovanni Ribisi's life. Cage ropes in his old crew – including ex-flame Angelina Jolie and silent-but-deadly Vinnie Jones – but it's over an hour before we get any stealing or crashing of any description. There's a nice chase at the end, though.

Nicolas Cage *Randall "Memphis" Raines* • Angelina Jolie *Sara "Sway" Wayland* • Giovanni Ribisi *Kip Raines* • Delroy Lindo *Det Roland Castlebeck* • Will Patton *Atley Jackson* • Christopher Eccleston *Raymond Calitri* • Chi McBride *Donny Astricky* • Robert Duvall *Otto Halliwell* ■ *Dir* Dominic Sena • *Scr* Scott Rosenberg, from the 1974 film

Gone to Earth ★★★★ PG

Period romantic drama 1950 · UK · Colour · 110mins

Michael Powell and Emeric Pressburger's weirdly compelling version of Mary Webb's novel about a Shropshire lass called Hazel Woodus, who communes with nature (notably a fox who lives in the mossy, mystical forest) and is at odds with the local community. Produced by Alexander Korda and David O Selznick, who saw it as a showcase for his wife, Jennifer Jones, it's a full-blooded melodrama, a piece of Celtic chemistry dominated by the unearthly beauty of Miss Jones. When Selznick saw the finished film he cut 30 minutes, retitled it *The Wild Heart* and ordered new scenes by director Rouben Mamoulian. Naturally

it flopped everywhere, but has lately been restored and revalued. 📼

Jennifer Jones *Hazel Woodus* • David Farrar *Jack Reddin* • Cyril Cusack *Edward Marston* • Esmond Knight *Abel Woodus* • Sybil Thorndike *Mrs Marston* • Hugh Griffith *Andrew Vessons* • Edward Chapman *Mr James* • Beatrice Varley *Aunt Prowde* • George Cole *Albert* ■ *Dir* Michael Powell, Emeric Pressburger • *Scr* Michael Powell, Emeric Pressburger, from the novel by Mary Webb

Gone with the Wind
★★★★★ 🅿🄶

Historical romantic drama
1939 · US · Colour · 220mins

Is this the greatest romance ever filmed? Or is it, as a recent critique suggested, a very long soap so bad that it would never get made today? Majority opinion still leans towards the former view of what remains probably the most popular Hollywood movie of all time. The epic adaptation of Margaret Mitchell's bestselling American Civil War novel spares no expense. Vivien Leigh, in turn, spares no emotion as the feisty southern belle, Scarlett O'Hara, while, as they say in the publicity campaigns, Clark Gable *is* Rhett Butler. Yes, to modern audiences it may seem sexist, racist, melodramatic, dated and overlong. But what's that against eight major Oscars and Hollywood immortality? 📼

Vivien Leigh *Scarlett O'Hara* • Clark Gable *Rhett Butler* • Leslie Howard *Ashley Wilkes* • Olivia de Havilland *Melanie Hamilton* • Hattie McDaniel *Mammy* • Thomas Mitchell *Gerald O'Hara* • Barbara O'Neil *Ellen O'Hara* • Laura Hope Crews *Aunt "Pittypat" Hamilton* ■ *Dir* Victor Fleming • *Scr* Sidney Howard, Ben Hecht (uncredited), Jo Swerling (uncredited), Oliver HP Garrett (uncredited), from the novel by Margaret Mitchell • *Producer* David O Selznick • *Cinematographer* Ernest Haller, Lee Garmes, Ray Rennahan • *Editor* Hal C Kern, James E Newcom • *Music* Max Steiner • *Production Designer* William Cameron Menzies

Good Burger
★ 🅿🄶

Comedy   1997 · US · Colour · 91mins

Young fans of TV channel Nickelodeon stars Kenan and Kel are about the only ones who will be remotely amused by this misjudged comedy. The duo work in a burger bar called, you guessed it, Good Burger. Obviously instructed by director Brian Robbins (who made the rap movie *The Show*) to overact themselves silly, the pair mug at every available opportunity while trying to save their little burger bar from being taken over by corporate bad guys. This appears to have been aimed at small kids who don't know better, but parents be warned: it does include some adult themes and occasionally cruel humour, to which fragile little minds should not be exposed. 📼

Kenan Thompson *Dexter Reed* • Kel Mitchell *Ed* • Abe Vigoda *Otis* • Sinbad *Mr Wheat* • Shar Jackson *Monique* • Dan Schneider *Mr Bailey* • Jan Schwieterman *Kurt Bozwell* • Ron Lester *Spatch* ■ *Dir* Brian Robbins • *Scr* Dan Schneider, Kevin Kopelow, Heath Seifert, from their characters

The Good Companions
★★★★ 🅄

Musical comedy   1933 · UK · BW · 112mins

Bet you didn't know this was the first talkie seen by a reigning British monarch. Adapted from the celebrated novel and play by JB Priestley, this charming musical comedy is full of surprises, not least of which is John Gielgud's facility for song and dance. Victor Saville directs with a light touch and strings together the many episodes with deceptive ease, conveying both the atmosphere of the Depression and the relief the Dinky Doos touring troupe brings to everyone. While Jessie Matthews is superb in the role that established her as an international star, Edmund Gwenn steals every scene he's in.

Jessie Matthews *Susie Dean* • Edmund Gwenn *Jess Oakroyd* • John Gielgud *Inigo Jolifant* • Mary Glynne *Miss Trant* • Percy Parsons *Morton Mitcham* • AW Baskcomb *Jimmy Nunn* • Dennis Hoey *Joe Brundit* ■ *Dir* Victor Saville • *Scr* WP Lipscomb, Angus Macphail, Ian Dalrymple, from the novel and play by JB Priestley

The Good Companions
★★★ 🅄

Musical comedy 1956 · UK · Colour · 107mins

JB Priestley's 1929 novel was first filmed in 1933 with John Gielgud and Jessie Matthews. This remake has a glittering array of female talent, including Celia Johnson, Joyce Grenfell, Rachel Roberts, Thora Hird and Janette Scott. The men (Eric Portman, John Fraser, Hugh Griffith, Alec McCowen and Anthony Newley) are less showy, but still prove how British movies of the time could cast in depth without having to offer roles to the acting knights of the realm. The story, about a concert party, has dated, and it's all a bit too polite, but the cast makes it well worth watching.

Eric Portman *Jess Oakroyd* • Celia Johnson *Miss Trant* • Janette Scott *Susie Dean* • John Fraser *Inigo Jolifant* • Hugh Griffith *Morton Mitcham* • Rachel Roberts *Elsie Longstaff/ Effie Longstaff* • Thora Hird *Mrs Oakroyd* • Alec McCowen *Albert* • Joyce Grenfell *Lady Parlitt* • Anthony Newley *Mulbrau* ■ *Dir* J Lee Thompson • *Scr* TJ Morrison, JL Hodgson, John Whiting, from the novel by JB Priestley

Good Day for a Hanging
★★ 🅄

Western   1958 · US · Colour · 85mins

The debonair but lightweight Fred MacMurray made a surprisingly believable western star at a low point in his career, before *The Shaggy Dog* and other Disney comedies revived it. Here he's the town marshal who thinks he's captured the sheriff's killer, played by a charismatic Robert Vaughn. Intending to carry out the execution he meets almost universal opposition – no one wants to believe that such a charmer could be guilty of murder. The lurid colour makes one yearn for old-fashioned black and white.

Fred MacMurray *Ben Cutler* • Maggie Hayes *Ruth Granger* • Robert Vaughn *The Kid* • Joan Blackman *Laurie Cutler* • James Drury *Paul Ridgely* • Wendell Holmes *Tallant Joslin* •

Edmon Ryan *William Selby* ■ *Dir* Nathan Juran • *Scr* Daniel B Ullman, Maurice Zimm, from a story by John Reese

The Good Die Young
★★★

Crime drama   1954 · UK · BW · 99mins

This well-crafted British heist thriller, atmospherically directed by Lewis Gilbert, stars Laurence Harvey as the leader of a quartet of ne'er-do-wells who team up to pull off a robbery that goes wrong. The talented cast also includes Gloria Grahame, Joan Collins, Stanley Baker, Robert Morley and Margaret Leighton, whose second husband was Harvey. Both Harvey and Leighton died young – Harvey of cancer at the age of 45, and Leighton as a result of multiple sclerosis, aged 54.

Laurence Harvey *Miles "Rave" Ravenscourt* • Gloria Grahame *Denise* • Richard Basehart *Joe* • Joan Collins *Mary* • John Ireland *Eddie* • René Ray *Angela* • Stanley Baker *Mike* • Margaret Leighton *Eve Ravenscourt* • Robert Morley *Sir Francis Ravenscourt* ■ *Dir* Lewis Gilbert • *Scr* Lewis Gilbert, Vernon Harris, from a novel by Richard Macauley

The Good Earth
★★★

Drama   1937 · US · BW · 137mins

Described by one critic as "the Lychees of Wrath", this saga about Chinese peasants won the second of two Oscars on the trot for MGM's Austrian import, Luise Rainer. Based on a doorstop novel by Pearl S Buck, it's a saga of rural hardship and greed, as a farmer battles against famine and the elements. It's a bit long and worthy, but it's redeemed by Rainer's moving portrayal and by a cleverly filmed plague of locusts. The few location shots of China were made in 1934 for another project by director George Hill, who then committed suicide. The film is unique in bearing the name of Irving Thalberg, MGM's wunderkind executive who died just prior to the film's release.

Paul Muni *Wang Lung* • Luise Rainer *O-Lan* • Walter Connolly *Uncle* • Tilly Losch *Lotus* • Charley Grapewin *Old father* • Jessie Ralph *Cuckoo* • Soo Yong *Aunt* • Keye Luke *Elder son* ■ *Dir* Sidney Franklin • *Scr* Talbot Jennings, Tess Schlesinger, Claudine West, Francis Marion, from the novel by Pearl S Buck • *Cinematographer* Karl Freund

The Good Fairy
★★★★

Comedy   1935 · US · BW · 100mins

This delightful comedy stars Margaret Sullavan at her least cloying as Luisa Ginglebusher, the "good fairy" who's released from an asylum and bursts into the life of Herbert Marshall's prickly, unsuccessful Budapest lawyer, liberating him from his dreary existence. The inventive script by Preston Sturges (adapted from the Ferenc Molnar play) abounds in slapstick, misunderstandings and verbal tomfoolery, while William Wyler's direction doesn't miss a trick. The good supporting cast includes that splendid character actor Eric Blore, who went on to appear in several Preston Sturges films.

Margaret Sullavan *Luisa "Lu" Ginglebusher* • Herbert Marshall *Dr Max Sporum* • Frank Morgan *Konrad* • Reginald Owen *Detlaff* • Alan Hale *Maurice Schlapkohl* • Beulah Bondi *Dr*

Schultz • Cesar Romero *Joe* • Eric Blore *Doctor Metz* ■ *Dir* William Wyler • *Scr* Preston Sturges, from the play by Ferenc Molnar

The Good Family
★★

Black comedy   1990 · US · Colour · 96mins

This TV movie might have been an attempt by Tony Curtis to give his later career a shade more gravitas, by joining forces with the queen of the psychobabble movie, Mary Tyler Moore. It's a lame tale about the deeply eccentric Schloss family and their wild and unpredictable ways. There's a classy TV cast, but the script wanders all over the place. After much beating of breasts and stupidity on a heroic scale, the audience is still none the wiser about what really makes this family tick. Plodding, if worthy.

Mary Tyler Moore *Paula Schloss* • Tony Curtis *Max Schloss* • Jonathon Brandmeier *Randy Schloss* • Kelly Curtis *Barbara* • Joseph Bologna *Ned Monk* • Andrew Hirsch *Michael Schloss* • Gabe Bologna *Young Ned* • Cal Gibson *Richard* ■ *Dir* Gino Tanasescu • *Scr* Steve Zacharias, Jeff Buhai

The Good Father
★★★★ 🄸🄵

Drama   1986 · UK · Colour · 86mins

Oscar-winner Anthony Hopkins gives another moving and impressive performance – this time as a bitter man dealing with his separation from his wife. Director Mike Newell (*Four Weddings and a Funeral*) and writer Christopher Hampton (*Dangerous Liaisons*) touch on a sensitive subject and handle it admirably. Hopkins's character feels he is a man with no rights – he sees his son only once a week. So he embarks on a crusade to help another wronged man (Jim Broadbent), whose ex-wife has decided to emigrate to Australia with their child. Hopkins handles the rage and the calm of his character with precision, and it remains hard to believe that it took until 1991's *The Silence of the Lambs* for him to be recognised as one of the world's finest screen actors. 📼

Anthony Hopkins *Bill Hooper* • Jim Broadbent *Roger Miles* • Harriet Walter *Emmy Hooper* • Frances Viner *Cheryl Langford* • Simon Callow *Mark Varda* • Joanne Whalley *Mary Hall* • Miriam Margolyes *Jane Powell* • Stephen Fry *Creighton* ■ *Dir* Mike Newell • *Scr* Christopher Hampton, from the novel by Peter Prince

The Good Guys and the Bad Guys
★★

Comedy western 1969 · US · Colour · 91mins

Despite the stirring presence of Robert Mitchum and a useful support cast, director Burt Kennedy completely fails to carry off this *Ride the High Country* clone for several reasons. Co-star George Kennedy (no relation) is a talented character actor – he won a best supporting actor Oscar for *Cool Hand Luke* – but he lacks the starpower to be a convincing adversary for Mitchum. There is also an uncomfortable sense of period, as cars and horses jostle in a ludicrous finale, and the comedic tone is very uncertain. No wonder it was reduced to co-feature status with *The Valley of Gwangi* on its British release.

Robert Mitchum *Marshal Flagg* • George Kennedy *Big John McKay* • Martin Balsam

Mayor Wilker • David Carradine *Waco* • Lois Nettleton *Mary* • Tina Louise *Carmel* • John Davis Chandler *Deuce* • John Carradine *Ticker* ▪ *Dir* Burt Kennedy • *Scr* Ronald M Cohen, Dennis Shryack

Good Guys Wear Black ★★🔞

Action thriller   1977 · US · Colour · 91mins

Another slick, monotonously violent starring vehicle for the perpetually wooden Chuck Norris, who was a video star before the term was even invented. Inevitably, he's a Vietnam veteran, this time facing an enemy closer to home when he discovers that his old unit are being bumped off one by one and he's next on the hit list. Ted Post directed Clint Eastwood to good effect in *Hang 'Em High* and *Magnum Force*, but his efforts here are no more than workmanlike and the acting is all over the place. ▭

Chuck Norris *John T Booker* • Anne Archer *Margaret* • Lloyd Haynes *Murray* • James Franciscus *Conrad Morgan* • Dana Andrews *Government man* • Jim Backus *Doorman* ▪ *Dir* Ted Post • *Scr* Bruce Cohn, Mark Medoff, from a story by Joseph Fraley

Good King Wenceslas ★★

Christmas drama   1994 · US · Colour

A competent, if rather uninspired, festive drama, based on an episode of Dark Ages history immortalised by the Christmas carol. It follows the trials and tribulations of Prince Wenceslas, who finds himself caught between his royal duties and his love of a beautiful woman. The cast includes Northern Irish actor John Hallam and *Rumpole of the Bailey* star Leo McKern, as well as familiar US TV-movie faces such as Stefanie Powers, Jonathan Brandis and Perry King. Michael Tuchner's direction may be a little perfunctory, but this is still entertaining enough fare.

Jonathan Brandis *Prince Wenceslas* • Stefanie Powers *The Queen* • Perry King *Tunna* • Joan Fontaine *Queen Ludmilla* • Leo McKern *Duke Phillip* • Oliver Milburn *Boleslav* • Charlotte Chatton *Johanna* • John Hallam *Gomom* ▪ *Dir* Michael Tuchner • *Scr* James Andrew Hall

Good Luck ★★★

Comedy drama   1996 · US · Colour · 98mins

A paraplegic (Gregory Hines) teams up with a bitter ex-pro football star (Vincent D'Onofrio), who lost his sight in an accident, to compete in a life-affirming white-water rafting race. With elements of both the buddy pic and the road movie, this comedy is all about people achieving their dreams and realising that disability needn't be tragic or a handicap to life. Some might find it a little too heavy on the schmaltz, but Richard LaBrie directs with a sure hand and he's helped by the strong rapport between the two leads. There's some sharp dialogue and amusing doses of black comedy – D'Onofrio picks up a girl in a bar but must rely on Hines's judgement as to her attractiveness and sincerity.

Gregory Hines *Bernard ''Bern'' Lemley* • Vincent D'Onofrio *Tony ''Ole'' Olezniak* • James Earl Jones *James Bing* • Max Gail *Farmer John* • Joe Theismann • Roy Firestone • Robert O'Reilly *Bartender* • Jack Rader *Drag queen* ▪ *Dir* Richard LaBrie • *Scr* Bob Comfort

Good Luck, Miss Wyckoff ★★🔞

Drama   1979 · US · Colour · 86mins

Anne Heywood, a repressed single schoolteacher, is raped by a young black janitor in Kansas in 1956. Despite her initially shocked reaction, she eventually gives in to the relationship, complicating her struggle to come to grips with her own sexuality. This grim and controversial portrayal of human sexuality was based on the novel by William Inge (*Splendor in the Grass*). Despite a strong cast, many viewers may find director Marvin Chomsky's handling of racial issues offensive rather than insightful. ▭

Anne Heywood *Evelyn Wyckoff* • Donald Pleasence *Dr Steiner* • Robert Vaughn *Dr Neal* • Carolyn Jones *Beth* • Dorothy Malone *Mildred* • Ronee Blakley *Betsy* • Dana Elcar *Mr Havermeyer* • Doris Roberts *Rene* ▪ *Dir* Marvin J Chomsky • *Scr* Polly Platt, from the novel by William Inge

A Good Man in Africa ★★🔞

Comedy drama   1993 · US · Colour · 90mins

Barely playing above the level of a second-rate *Carry On* movie, this tale of consular shenanigans in a small African republic is a sad misfire from Bruce Beresford (*Driving Miss Daisy*). William Boyd's screenplay, from his own novel, has Casanova diplomat Colin Friels blackmailed into ''persuading'' doctor Sean Connery to support president elect Lou Gossett Jr's building project. In a film that's ponderous and completely devoid of humour, with supremely bizarre casting, good man Connery is the only saving grace. Presumably Beresford thought that the crass, stereotypical shambles of a script passes for satire and insight. Contains swearing, sex scenes and nudity. ▭

Colin Friels *Morgan* • Sean Connery *Dr Murray* • Joanne Whalley-Kilmer [Joanne Whalley] *Celia* • Louis Gossett Jr *Adekunle* • John Lithgow *Fanshawe* • Diana Rigg *Chloe* • Sarah-Jane Fenton *Priscilla* • Jeremy Crutchley *Dalmire* ▪ *Dir* Bruce Beresford • *Scr* William Boyd, from his novel

Good Morning ★★★★

Comedy drama   1959 · Jap · BW · 94mins

Updating his own 1932 film *I Was Born, But...*, director Yasujiro Ozu has turned a feud between two small boys and their parents into a gently vibrant study of everyday life and a wittily wise treatise on the importance of communication. Shooting in his typically unobtrusive style, Ozu demonstrates again how fully he understands the human condition, as two businessmen face up to their shortcomings, a women is driven from her home by gossip and a couple hide their true feelings in platitudes. In the midst of this misunderstanding and misery, the boys refuse to speak until their folks accept the westernising influence of television. Masterly. A Japanese language film.

Koji Shidara *Minoru, the elder brother* • Masahiko Shimazu *Isamu, the younger brother* • Chishu Ryu *Father* • Kuniko Miyake *Mother* • Yoshiko Kuga *Aunt* • Keiji Sada *Teacher* •

Haruo Tanaka *Tatsuko* • Haruko Sugimura *Kikue, Tatsuko's wife* ▪ *Dir* Yasujiro Ozu • *Scr* Yasujiro Ozu, Kogo Noda

Good Morning... and Goodbye ★★

Exploitation drama   1967 · US · Colour · 78mins

This is one of exploitation maverick Russ Meyer's best sex morality fables, although devotees may be disappointed by the minimal nudity. In a return to the basics of his early work, Meyer lifts the seamy lid on rustic sexual desires, wants and shortcomings, as sexually frustrated Alaina Capri cheats on her rich farmer husband Stuart Lancaster with construction worker Patrick Wright. A forest trip to meet sorceress Haji gets the lead back in Lancaster's pencil and sorts out the muddled affairs. The film is wild, melodramatic and portentous in Meyer's trademark ''kitsch-and-think'' way.

Alaina Capri *Angel* • Stuart Lancaster *Burt* • Patrick Wright *Stone* • Haji *Sorceress* • Karen Ciral *Lana* • Don Johnson *Ray* • Tom Howland *Herb* • Megan Timothy *Lottie* ▪ *Dir* Russ Meyer • *Scr* John E Moran, from a story by Russ Meyer

Good Morning, Babylon ★★★★🔞

Period drama   1987 · It/Fr/US · Colour · 112mins

A deeply affecting and beautifully shot, if rather coolly observed tale of two Italian stonemason brothers who find they can no longer make a living restoring cathedrals in their native Tuscany. Arrriving in America around the time of the First World War, they end up working for DW Griffith on his epic *Intolerance*. In their first English language story, directors Paolo and Vittorio Taviani have created a deeply symbolic story, shot through with autobiographical resonance, which throws up complex issues of fraternal intimacy, emerging democracy, the role of the extended family and the disintegration of local communities. If this sounds a touch heavy – it is. At the same time, the film is imbued with such a lyrical love of film-making and sterling performances that you find yourself drawn into its web. In English and Italian with subtitles. ▭

Vincent Spano *Nicola Bonnano* • Joaquim de Almeida *Andrea Bonnano* • Greta Scacchi *Edna* • Désirée Becker *Mabel* • Omero Antonutti *Bonnano* • Charles Dance *DW Griffith* • Bérangère Bonvoisin *Mrs Griffith* ▪ *Dir* Paolo Taviani, Vittorio Taviani • *Scr* Tonino Guerra, Vittorio Taviani, Paolo Taviani, from an idea by Lloyd Fonvielle

Good Morning, Boys ★★★★🇺

Comedy   1937 · UK · BW · 74mins

Will Hay returns to his celebrated music-hall persona of the cynically incompetent schoolmaster in the first of several films he made with French director Marcel Varnel. Having to bluff furiously to remain one step ahead of a class that contains the ever-mischievous Graham Moffat, Hay is close to his peak as he lectures to a conference of educationalists, flirts with chanteuse Lilli Palmer and helps

prevent the theft of the *Mona Lisa*. However, nothing beats his turning a discussion on betting into a lesson on Agincourt to fool an aggressive governor (Martita Hunt). ▭

Will Hay *Dr Benjamin Twist* • Martita Hunt *Lady Bagshott* • Peter Gawthorne *Col Willoughby-Gore* • Graham Moffatt *Albert* • Fewlass Llewellyn *Dean* • Mark Daly *Arty Jones* • Peter Godfrey *Cliquot* • C Denier Warren *Henri Duval* • Lilli Palmer *Yvette* ▪ *Dir* Marcel Varnel • *Scr* Val Guest, Leslie Arliss, Marriott Edgard, Anthony Kimmins, from a story by Anthony Kimmins

Good Morning, Miss Dove ★★🇺

Drama   1955 · US · Colour · 107mins

Director Henry Koster had the biggest hit of his career with the first movie released in CinemaScope, *The Robe*, but prior to that he was better known as a purveyor of schmaltzy films starring Deanna Durbin, or whimsy like *The Bishop's Wife* and *Harvey*. This is an ideal subject for Koster, a warm-hearted tale (told in flashback) of how a small town feels about its spinster schoolmarm and how she affects the lives of everybody who crosses her path. Koster brings it off most effectively, even though star Jennifer Jones seems ill-cast as the prissy Miss Dove, a role that perhaps would have been better played by Greer Garson or Dorothy McGuire.

Jennifer Jones *Miss Dove* • Robert Stack *Tom Baker* • Kipp Hamilton *Jincey Baker* • Robert Douglas *Mr Porter* • Peggy Knudsen *Billie Jean* • Marshall Thompson *Mr Pendleton* • Chuck Connors *Bill Holloway* • Biff Elliott *Alex Burnham* • Jerry Paris *Maurice* ▪ *Dir* Henry Koster • *Scr* Eleanore Griffin, from the novel by Frances Gray Patton

Good Morning, Vietnam ★★★🔞

Biographical comedy drama   1987 · US · Colour · 116mins

Robin Williams got an Oscar nomination for giving what is essentially a stand-up comedy performance. He plays a motor-mouth disc jockey sent to Vietnam to entertain the GIs who, in the event, adds rather more salt, pepper and hot sauce to the place than the military brass would have liked. Based on the case of a real US armed forces DJ, the film is distinctive for being Hollywood's first Vietnam comedy and among the first movies to treat the Vietnamese themselves as real people. The action loses its way, however, whenever the film tries to get serious, but when Williams is behind the studio mike, it offers a decent showcase for his virtuoso talents. Contains violence and swearing. ▭ **DVD**

Robin Williams *Airman Adrian Cronauer* • Forest Whitaker *Private Edward Garlick* • Tran Tung Thanh *Tuan* • Chintara Sukapatana *Trinh* • Bruno Kirby *Lieutenant Steven Hauk* • Robert Wuhl *Marty Lee Dreiwitz* • JT Walsh *Sergeant-Major Dickerson* ▪ *Dir* Barry Levinson • *Scr* Mitch Markowitz

The Good Mother ★★★🔞

Drama   1988 · US · Colour · 104mins

Also known as *The Price of Passion*, this is a rather depressing tale about a divorced mother (Diane Keaton) who finds love and sexual fulfilment in the arms of Liam Neeson, only to have her ex-husband sue her for custody of her daughter because he is convinced Neeson is sexually abusing her. It's quite a serious subject for director Leonard Nimoy, who made the much more lightweight *Three Men and a Baby* to far better effect. There are good performances and it's an interesting subject, but the overall result is rather dreary drama. Contains swearing and nudity.

Diane Keaton *Anna Dunlap* • Liam Neeson *Leo Cutter* • Jason Robards Jr *Muth* • Ralph Bellamy *Grandfather* • Teresa Wright *Grandmother* • James Naughton *Brian Dunlap* • Asia Vieira *Molly* • Joe Morton *Frank Williams* ■ *Dir* Leonard Nimoy • *Scr* Michael Bortman, from the novel by Sue Miller

Good Neighbor Sam ★★★

Comedy 1964 · US · Colour · 130mins

A very funny, though overlong, Jack Lemmon farce, this has a familiar plot that involves him pretending to be married to sexy Romy Schneider in order to help her come into a small fortune. Slight enough, but spun out with a lot of sixties' fripperies, including a high degree of risqué – for then – gags and fashionable jokes about advertising and consumerism. Period TV faces Dorothy Provine, from *The Roaring Twenties*, and *Mannix*'s Michael Connors play Jack and Romy's other halves, and wily old Edward G Robinson is welcome as a business magnate (though he's not given enough screen time). Under-rated director David Swift keeps the whole glossy farrago afloat with aplomb.

Jack Lemmon *Sam Bissel* • Edward G Robinson *Simon Nurdlinger* • Romy Schneider *Janet Lagerlof* • Dorothy Provine *Minerva Bissel* • Michael Connors [Mike Connors] *Howard Ebbets* • Anne Seymour *Irene Krump* • Charles Lane [] *Jack Bailey* ■ *Dir* David Swift • *Scr* James Fritzell, Everett Greenbaum, David Swift, from the novel by Jack Finney

Good News ★★★★ U

Musical comedy 1947 · US · Colour · 89mins

One of the most delightful of the MGM musicals from a golden period, this is a Technicolor remake of the studio's 1930 black-and-white original. The college romp marked the directorial debut of *Meet Me in St Louis* choreographer Charles Walters, who would follow this movie with such greats as *Easter Parade* and *High Society*. Here, despite the presence of rather over-age students June Allyson and Peter Lawford, Walters injects real verve and genuine *joie de vivre* into such numbers as *Billion Dollar Baby* and *My Blue Heaven*. A real treat for fans of musicals.

June Allyson *Connie Lane* • Peter Lawford *Tommy Marlowe* • Patricia Marshall *Pat McClellan* • Joan McCracken *Babe Doolittle* • Ray McDonald *Bobby Turner* • Mel Tormé *Danny* • Robert Strickland [Robert E Strickland] *Peter Van Dyne III* • Donald MacBride *Coach Johnson* ■ *Dir* Charles Walters • *Scr* Betty Comden, Adolph Green, from the musical by Lawrence Schwab, Frank Mandel, BG De Sylva, Lew Brown, Ray Henderson

The Good Old Boys ★★★ PG

Western drama 1995 · US · Colour · 112mins

Tommy Lee Jones made his writing and directing debut with this period TV movie. He plays an itinerant cowboy who returns home in 1906 to his brother's struggling Texas farm, but finds it hard to settle down or be responsible. Will the call of the open range prove to be stronger than his love for Sissy Spacek? Jones proves he is not just a gifted actor but also a sensitive director, eliciting strong performances from a stellar cast that includes Frances McDormand, Sam Shepard and a soon-to-be discovered Matt Damon. There's no ropin' and ridin' or shootin' and dyin', but this atypical western will truly satisfy.

Tommy Lee Jones *Hewey Calloway* • Terry Kinney *Walter Calloway* • Frances McDormand *Eve Calloway* • Sissy Spacek *Spring Renfro* • Sam Shepard *Yarnell* • Wilford Brimley *CC Tarpley* • Matt Damon ■ *Dir* Tommy Lee Jones • *Scr* Tommy Lee Jones, JT Allen, from the novel by Elmer Kelton

The Good Policeman ★★★

Drama 1994 · US · Colour

Possessing a title that doesn't exactly tax the imagination or set the pulse racing, this is a typical "rule book out the window" story that has more than a little in common with the 1973 thriller *Serpico*. Ron Silver adds executive producing duties to his starring role in this solid TV movie about an unconventional New York cop (is there any other kind?) who finds his dealings with the mayor and his superiors every bit as perilous as his brushes with the Mafia and the city's petty criminals. Bristling with indignation, Silver brings his usual energy to an overfamiliar role, while Tony LoBianco, Blair Brown and Roy Dotrice provide accomplished support.

Ron Silver *Issac Sidel* • Tony LoBianco *Jerry Diangelis* • Joe Morton *Sweets Montgomery* • Blair Brown *Rebecca Karp* • Victor Slezak *Burt Bortlesman* • Lenny Venito *Joe Barbarossa* • Roy Dotrice *Cardinal O'Bannon* ■ *Dir* Peter Werner • *Scr* Jerome Charyn

Good Sam ★★ U

Comedy drama 1948 · US · BW · 114mins

Store manager Gary Cooper is such a universally soft touch that his marriage to Ann Sheridan suffers. After all his good deeds, the day finally arrives when Sam needs to be bailed out of his financial troubles. But will anyone come to his rescue? This comedy drama follows the pattern of the classic *It's a Wonderful Life*, but it suffers from being contrived and drawn out. Coop's good Samaritan is so exasperatingly stupid at times that it's hard to feel much sympathy for him. Similarly, Ann Sheridan seems too strong an actress to let him get away with it. Sadly, producer/director Leo McCarey, responsible for such classics as *Duck Soup* and *The Awful Truth*, had lost his light touch with comedy.

Gary Cooper *Sam Clayton* • Ann Sheridan *Lu Clayton* • Ray Collins *Rev Daniels* • Edmund Lowe *HC Borden* • Joan Lorring *Shirley Mae* • Clinton Sundberg *Nelson* • Minerva Urecal *Mrs Nelson* • Louise Beavers *Chloe* ■ *Dir* Leo McCarey • *Scr* Ken Englund, from a story by Leo McCarey, John Klorer

The Good Son ★★ 18

Drama 1993 · US · Colour · 82mins

Macaulay Culkin's comic treatment of the *Home Alone* burglars ably demonstrated his sadistic streak but here his cruelty is played very straight, with genuinely creepy results. He plays an outwardly friendly youngster who takes a murderous dislike to his cousin (Elijah Wood), who comes to stay when his mother dies and his father is away on business. Sadly, despite its controversial subject matter – the UK video release was delayed because of the tragic Jamie Bulger murder case – there's little attempt to explain Culkin's psychopathic behaviour. However, Wood is superb as the tortured Mark, and director Joseph Ruben lays on some slickly scary moments.

Macaulay Culkin *Henry Evans* • Elijah Wood *Mark Evans* • Wendy Crewson *Susan Evans* • David Morse *Jack Evans* • Daniel Hugh-Kelly *Wallace* • Jacqueline Brookes *Alice Davenport* • Quinn Culkin *Connie Evans* • Ashley Crow *Janice* ■ *Dir* Joseph Ruben • *Scr* Ian McEwan

The Good, the Bad and the Ugly ★★★★★ 18

Classic spaghetti western
1967 · It/Sp · Colour · 155mins

The concluding part of the "Dollars" trilogy is not only the most graphic, but it also ups the compassion and dark humour of the first two Sergio Leone films. The stylised violence of the genre is thrown into shocking relief by the bloody futility of the Civil War that intrudes on the lives of drifters Clint Eastwood, Lee Van Cleef and Eli Wallach. There is nothing new about the buried treasure plotline, but through the deceptively simple story, Leone dexterously weaves different strands of small- and large-scale human drama, drawing superb performances from the leads and providing a compelling feast for the viewer. ▦ **DVD**

Clint Eastwood *"Joe"/"Blondie"* • Eli Wallach *Tuco* • Lee Van Cleef *Setenza* ■ *Dir* Sergio Leone • *Scr* Sergio Leone, Luciano Vincenzoni, from a story by Agenore Incrocci, Furio Scarpelli, Luciano Vincenzoni, Sergio Leone • *Music* Ennio Morricone • *Cinematographer* Tonino Delli Colli

Good Time Girl ★★

Crime drama 1948 · UK · BW · 92mins

As the reform school rebel who hooks up with a gang of American crooks, Jean Kent created a screen image that she was never totally able to shake in this moody melodrama. It's adapted from the Arthur la Bern novel *Night Darkens the Streets*, which was itself inspired by a true-life incident. Kent's sneering, sultry performance must have seemed very daring in those dank postwar days, but nowadays her petulance seems more like posturing. Director David MacDonald allows the plot to meander in order to make the most obvious social observations.

Jean Kent *Gwen Rawlings* • Dennis Price *Red* • Herbert Lom *Max* • Bonar Colleano *American* • Peter Glenville *Jimmy the waiter* • Flora Robson *Chairman of juvenile court* • Diana Dors *Lyla Lawrence* • George Carney *Mr Rawlings* ■ *Dir* David MacDonald • *Scr* Muriel Box, Sydney Box, Ted Willis, from the novel *Night Darkens the Streets* by Arthur la Bern

Good Times ★★ PG

Musical 1967 · US · Colour · 91mins

William Friedkin, director of *The French Connection* and *The Exorcist*, made his feature debut with this silly but amusing piece of wish-fulfilment, which stars the then-married pop duo, Sonny and Cher. Although it has dated badly, this potted history of Hollywood movie styles is, in its own small way, quite a clever satire, at the expense of both Tinseltown and the audiences who'll watch any old rubbish. Naturally, Sonny and Cher get to sing *I Got You Babe*, even though it has absolutely nothing to do with the plot. George Sanders puts in a rather shamefaced guest appearance. ▦

Sonny Bono • Cher • George Sanders *Mordicus* • Norman Alden *Warren* ■ *Dir* William Friedkin • *Scr* Tony Barrett

Good to Go ★★ 15

Musical drama 1986 · US · Colour · 86mins

Singer Art Garfunkel's acting career seems to have hit a slump since 1980's *Bad Timing*. In this controversial drama, he plays a journalist investigating the go-go music scene in Washington, in the wake of a gang rape and murder. The police turn out to be pursuing their own agenda and Art ends up on the side of the music-loving gang. Sadly, Garfunkel is less than convincing and the music peppering the plot is annoying rather than enjoyable. But let's look on the positive side – at least Art doesn't warble *Bright Eyes* in this one. ▦

Art Garfunkel *SD Blass* • Robert DoQui *Max* • Harris Yulin *Harrigan* • Reginald Daughtry *Little Beats* • Richard Brooks *Chemist* • Paula Davis *Evette* • Richard Bauer *Editor* • Michael White *Gil Colton* ■ *Dir/Scr* Blaine Novak

The Good Wife ★★★ 15

Drama 1986 · Ausl · Colour · 93mins

In this moral tale of small-town lust, set in thirties Australia, Rachel Ward yearns to break free from her dreary home life with an indifferent husband (Bryan Brown). After a brief tumble with her brother-in-law, the good wife goes bad and hits town looking for romance and sex. Enter Sam Neill. The ensuing erotic fandango may not exactly be *Madame Bovary*, but Ward and Neill act up a storm, while Brown is a convincing reminder of why a nice girl might consider adultery. Contains swearing. ▦

Rachel Ward *Marge Hills* • Bryan Brown *Sonny Hills* • Sam Neill *Neville Gifford* • Steven Vidler *Sugar Hills* • Jennifer Claire *Daisy* • Bruce Barry *Archie* • Clarissa Kaye-Mason [Clarissa Kaye] *Mrs Jackson* • Carole Skinner *Mrs Gibson* ■ *Dir* Ken Cameron • *Scr* Peter Kenna

Good Will Hunting ★★★★★ 15

Drama 1997 · US · Colour · 121mins

Matt Damon and Ben Affleck wrote and starred in this unmissable, moving drama directed by Gus Van Sant (*My Own Private Idaho*, *To Die For*). Damon is Will, a wrong-side-of-the-tracks janitor at top college MIT who has an exceptional mind, and whose mathematical genius is discovered by one of the professors (Stellan Skarsgård) at the school. However, Will is an emotionally troubled young man, so a psychologist (Robin Williams) with problems of his own is brought in to help him. Skilfully directed and stunningly performed by Damon, Williams, Skarsgård, Affleck (as Will's best friend) and Minnie Driver (as Will's intellectual girlfriend), this is mesmerising from start to finish, and deservedly won Oscars for Damon and Affleck's screenplay as well as Williams's subtle performance. Contains swearing. ▭ **DVD**

Matt Damon *Will Hunting* • Robin Williams *Sean McGuire* • Ben Affleck *Chuckie* • Minnie Driver *Skylar* • Stellan Skarsgård *Lambeau* • John Mighton *Tom* • Rachel Majowski *Krystyn* • Colleen McCauley *Cathy* ■ *Dir* Gus Van Sant • *Scr* Matt Damon, Ben Affleck

The Good Woman of Bangkok ★★★
Documentary 1991 · Ausl · Colour · 82mins

While director Gough Lewis refused to reveal on screen that he slept with his subject during the making of *Sex: the Annabel Chong Story*, Dennis O'Rourke makes an open secret of his physical liaison with Thai prostitute Yaowalak Chonchanakun in this relentlessly uncomfortable pseudo-documentary. Shot over nine months on Super 8, the action alternates between interviews with the often exhausted (or possibly drug-addled) girl and discreetly filmed footage of the Bangkok sex industry in action. Any insights O'Rourke gains about the nature of love are buried beneath his sense of guilt at exploiting Yaowalak and acquiescing in the system that enslaves her.

Dir/Scr Dennis O'Rourke

Goodbye Again ★★★
Romantic drama 1961 · US · BW · 119mins

This is the film version of the book by once-fashionable, controversial novelist Françoise Sagan, *Aimez-Vous Brahms* (the movie's French title). It's sensitively but rather boringly brought to the screen by director Anatole Litvak, who did rather better by his star Ingrid Bergman in another collaboration of theirs, *Anastasia*, for which she won an Oscar. Bergman is loved by toy boy Anthony Perkins while really harbouring a deep passion for playboy Yves Montand. Perkins picked up an acting award at Cannes for his performance and, indeed, he's rather good, and the Paris locations are attractive. But the two-hour running time stretches a very slight tale a long way.

Ingrid Bergman *Paula Tessier* • Yves Montand *Roger Demarest* • Anthony Perkins *Philip Van Der Besh* • Jessie Royce Landis *Mrs Van Der Besh* • Jackie Lane *Maisie I* • Jean Clarke *Maisie II* • Michèle Mercier *Maisie III* • Pierre Dux *Maître Fleury* ■ *Dir* Anatole Litvak • *Scr* Samuel Taylor, from the novel *Aimez-Vous Brahms* by Françoise Sagan

Goodbye Charlie ★
Fantasy comedy 1964 · US · Colour · 116mins

Despite stylish direction from Vincente Minnelli, the presence of Debbie Reynolds and Tony Curtis, and stalwart support from Pat Boone and Walter Matthau (as a wealthy mother's boy and volatile Hungarian movie producer respectively), this film still comes a cropper. Based on a failed Broadway play by the usually reliable George

Axelrod, this witless heaven-and-earth tale has Reynolds struggling manfully to portray Charlie, a writer who, having been murdered by a jealous husband (Matthau), returns to earth as a beautiful girl. Charlie consorts with his/her best friend (Curtis) and is courted by Boone, to the discomfort of everyone – including the audience.

Tony Curtis *George Tracy* • Debbie Reynolds *Charlie Sorel/The Woman* • Pat Boone *Bruce Minton* • Joanna Barnes *Janie* • Ellen McRae [Ellen Burstyn] *Franny* • Laura Devon *Rusty* • Martin Gabel *Morton Craft* • Roger C Carmel *Inspector* • Walter Matthau *Sir Leopold Sartori* ■ *Dir* Vincente Minnelli • *Scr* Harry Kurnitz, from a play by George Axelrod

Goodbye, Columbus ★★★
Comedy 1969 · US · Colour · 101mins

Released in the wake of *The Graduate*, this adaptation of Philip Roth's novella stars Richard Benjamin as a librarian who woos pretty rich girl Ali MacGraw. Set in the affluent Jewish community of New York and the swanky Florida resort of Boca Raton, it's a comedy that spins on MacGraw's parents (Jack Klugman and Nan Martin) who dislike Benjamin because he's penniless. So far so conventionally entertaining, but the rest of the plot revolves around MacGraw's birth control method, or lack of it. Pretty daring for 1969, it seems pretty pointless now. Even so, it's nicely acted, cleverly observed and there's a knockout scene in a country club swimming pool. Contains some swearing, brief nudity and sex scenes.

Richard Benjamin *Neil Klugman* • Ali MacGraw *Brenda Patimkin* • Jack Klugman *Mr Patimkin* • Nan Martin *Mrs Patimkin* • Michael Meyers *Ron* • Lori Shelle *Julie Patimkin* • Royce Wallace *Carlotta* • Sylvie Strauss *Aunt Gladys* ■ *Dir* Larry Peerce • *Scr* Arnold Schulman, from the novella by Philip Roth

Goodbye Emmanuelle ★★ 18
Erotic drama 1977 · Fr · Colour · 94mins

Sylvia Kristel packs her suitcase for another suitably exotic location (the Seychelles) in this aimless retread through another thin story idea, which as usual is just a pretext for lots of soft-focus disrobing. Given that she has to do little but take her clothes off, it's probably best to just gloss over the glaring limitations of Kristel's acting, although the film still possesses a touch more class than the formulaic erotic thrillers on offer nowadays. French dialogue dubbed into English. Contains sex scenes and nudity. ▭

Sylvia Kristel *Emmanuelle* • Umberto Orsini *Jean* • Jean-Pierre Bouvier *Grégory* • Charlotte Alexandra *Chloë* • Jacques Doniol-Valcroze *Michel Cordier* • Olga Georges-Picot *Florence Cordier* ■ *Dir* François Leterrier • *Scr* François Leterrier, Monique Lange, from the characters created by Emmanuelle Arsan

The Goodbye Girl ★★★★ PG
Romantic comedy 1977 · US · Colour · 105mins

A Neil Simon script, Mike Nichols wielding the megaphone and Robert De Niro to star. It seemed nothing could stop *Bogart Slept Here* from becoming the movie of the year. But two weeks into production, the director and his star were at odds over everything from Method acting to comic timing. De Niro

was sacked and went off to make *Taxi Driver*, leaving Nichols to shut down the picture. Two years later, Richard Dreyfuss took the lead in what was now *The Goodbye Girl*, and Neil Simon's winter of discontent was made glorious summer by this unprepossessing son of New York. Dreyfuss is inspired, his gay Richard III the highlight of a wisecracking romantic comedy that barely pauses for breath. He's ably matched by Marsha Mason as the ex-chorus girl and single mother. Dreyfuss won an Oscar, a success De Niro still regards as the one that got away. ▭

Richard Dreyfuss *Elliott Garfield* • Marsha Mason *Paula McFadden* • Quinn Cummings *Lucy McFadden* • Paul Benedict *Mark Morgenweiss* • Barbara Rhoades *Donna Douglas* • Theresa Merritt *Mrs Crosby* ■ *Dir* Herbert Ross • *Scr* Neil Simon

Goodbye Lover ★★ 18
Comedy crime thriller 1997 · US · Colour · 97mins

Killing Fields director Roland Joffé tries to make this revenge tale amusing but fails. In the end, it's only worth catching for better-than-the-movie-deserves performances from TV alumni Don Johnson (*Miami Vice*) and Ellen DeGeneres (*Ellen*). The former stars as the rich businessman who is pushed over a balcony by his useless brother (Dermot Mulroney) and the sister-in-law (Patricia Arquette) with whom he was having an affair. As always with stories of cross and double-cross, there's a nosy cop (DeGeneres). DeGeneres gets the (only) good lines and delivers them with aplomb, but neither she nor the still-suave Johnson can save this from the "reject" pile. ▭ **DVD**

Patricia Arquette *Sandra Dunmore* • Dermot Mulroney *Jake Dunmore* • Ellen DeGeneres *Sgt Rita Pompano* • Mary-Louise Parker *Peggy Blaine* • Don Johnson *Ben Dunmore* • Ray McKinnon *Rollins* • Alex Rocco *Detective Crowley* ■ *Dir* Roland Joffé • *Scr* Ron Peer, Joel Cohen, Alec Sokolow

Goodbye, Mr Chips
★★★★★ U
Drama 1939 · UK/US · BW · 109mins

British star Robert Donat pipped Clark Gable's Rhett Butler to the best actor Oscar the year *Gone with the Wind* swept the awards with a marvellous portrayal of author James Hilton's crusty pedagogue. This is a warm-hearted, humanitarian work, beautifully filmed in England by MGM and a fine example of that great studio at its peak. Immaculately directed by the desperately under-rated Sam Wood (*A Night at the Opera*, *Kings Row*), the film introduced world audiences to Greer Garson, who replaced Norma Shearer overnight to become first lady of the MGM lot. Watch out, too, for *Casablanca*'s Paul Henreid and for young John Mills as one of Mr Chipping's boys. ▭

Robert Donat *Charles Chipping* • Greer Garson *Katherine Ellis* • Terry Kilburn *John Colley/Peter Colley* • John Mills *Peter Colley as a young man* • Paul Henreid *Max Staefel* • Judith Furse *Flora* • Lyn Harding *Dr Wetherby* • Milton Rosmer *Charteris* ■ *Dir* Sam Wood • *Scr* RC Sherriff, Claudine West, Eric Maschwitz, Sidney Franklin, from the novella by James Hilton • *Cinematographer* FA Young [Freddie Young] • *Art Director* Alfred Junge

Goodbye, Mr Chips ★ PG
Musical 1969 · UK · Colour · 152mins

Herbert Ross became one of Hollywood's most assured directors of light entertainment (*The Sunshine Boys*, *My Blue Heaven*), but he was very lucky indeed to get another chance after this nightmare of a debut. Rex Harrison and Richard Burton both had the sense to send Terence Rattigan's script back from whence it came, and not even an Oscar nomination can hide the fact that this is one of Peter O'Toole's least distinguished performances. The fact that John Williams and Leslie Bricusse were also nominated for best score is preposterous, as the songs in this musical adaptation of James Hilton's delightful novel are shocking. ▭

Peter O'Toole *Arthur Chipping* • Petula Clark *Katherine Bridges* • Michael Redgrave *Headmaster* • George Baker *Lord Sutterwick* • Sian Phillips *Ursula Mossbank* • Michael Bryant *Max Staefel* • Jack Hedley *William Baxter* ■ *Dir* Herbert Ross • *Scr* Terence Rattigan, from the novella by James Hilton

Goodbye, My Fancy ★★★ U
Romance drama 1951 · US · BW · 107mins

This is hardly the film for which Joan Crawford will be remembered. It is, however, a fascinating example of how miscasting can ruin an otherwise engaging story. Crawford is Agatha Reed, a congresswoman caught up in a romantic triangle while revisiting her old school to receive an honorary degree. Even her stellar power failed to make the picture play at the box office and her presence overbalances what was a pretty flimsy comedy in the first place. Robert Young and Frank Lovejoy are the love rivals but they can do nothing to repair the damage.

Joan Crawford *Agatha Reed* • Robert Young *Dr James Merrill* • Frank Lovejoy *Matt Cole* • Eve Arden *Woody* • Janice Rule *Virginia Merrill* • Lurene Tuttle *Ellen Griswold* • Howard St John *Claude Griswold* • Viola Roache *Miss Shackleford* ■ *Dir* Vincent Sherman • *Scr* Ivan Goff, Ben Roberts, from the play by Fay Kanin

Good-bye, My Lady ★★ U
Adventure drama 1956 · US · BW · 95mins

Brandon de Wilde, the wide-eyed youngster from *Shane*, stars in this cute but engaging story about an orphan boy who lives in the Mississippi swamps and befriends a dog with unusual gifts as a hunter. Turns out that the dog is a rare breed and its owner wants it back. Veteran director William A Wellman makes a tidy job of things, and it's far less syrupy than the Disney equivalent *Old Yeller*.

Walter Brennan *Uncle Jesse* • Phil Harris *Cash* • Brandon de Wilde *Skeeter* • Sidney Poitier *Gates* • William Hopper *Grover* • Louise Beavers *Bonnie* • Vivian Vance *Wife* ■ *Dir* William A Wellman • *Scr* Sid Fleischman, from a novel by James Street

Goodbye New York ★★ 15
Comedy 1984 · US · Colour · 90mins

A year before she starred in the hysterically funny *Lost in America* with Albert Brooks, Julie Hagerty made this pale precursor (which could have been subtitled *Lost in Israel*). After oversleeping on a Paris flight, Hagerty finds herself stranded in Israel. Instead

U = SUITABLE FOR ALL, Uc = SUITABLE FOR ALL, ESPECIALLY FOR YOUNG CHILDREN (VIDEO ONLY) PG = PARENTAL GUIDANCE

of getting the first plane back like any normal person, she ends up living on a kibbutz and falling in love with soldier Amos Kollek (who also directs). Hagerty, whose brand of kooky comedy could brighten up the dullest movie, is funny to watch, but you can't help wishing she had the material to match her talents. 📹

Julie Hagerty *Nancy Callaghan* • Amos Kollek *David* • Shmuel Shiloh *Moishe* • Aviva Ger *Ilana* • David Topaz *Albert* • Jennifer Babtist *Lisa* • Christopher Goutman *Jack* • Hanan Goldblat *Avi* ■ *Dir/Scr* Amos Kollek

Goodbye, Norma Jean ★★ 18
Biographical drama
1976 · US/Ausl · Colour · 93mins

A sleazy, sensationalist biopic of Norma Jean Baker, the young brunette who reinvented herself as that ultimate blonde screen icon, Marilyn Monroe. Misty Rowe plays Marilyn, and does an OK job. But she has never come close to matching Monroe's screen success and, after spending the eighties appearing in such broad teen comedies as *National Lampoon's Class Reunion* and *Meatballs 2*, she returned to the role of Monroe in a 1989 sequel *Goodnight, Sweet Marilyn*. 📹

Misty Rowe *Norman Jean Baker* • Terrence Locke *Ralph Johnson* • Patch Mackenzie *Ruth Latimer* • Preston Hanson *Hal James* • Marty Zagon *Irving Olbach* • Andre Philippe *Sam Dunn* ■ *Dir* Larry Buchanan • *Scr* Larry Buchanan, Lynn Shubert

The Goodbye People ★★
Comedy 1984 · US · Colour · 104mins

It's hard to understand how Herb Gardner came to make his directorial debut with this adaptation of his own stage play, nearly 20 years after it flopped on Broadway. Sentimentality drips off this indigestible mush like the ketchup oozing out of the hot dogs sold by Martin Balsam's retired Coney Island vendor. Both he and disgruntled toy maker Judd Hirsch try to cut down on the corn, but Gardner piles it on with relish. This "odd couple" comedy might have been more appetising had it possessed the same light touch that Fred Coe brought to *A Thousand Clowns* (1965), another Gardner play Balsam helped bring to the screen.

Judd Hirsch *Arthur Korman* • Martin Balsam *Max Silverman* • Pamela Reed *Nancie "Shirley" Scot* • Ron Silver *Eddie Bergson* • Michael Tucker *Michael Silverman* • Gene Saks *Marcus Soloway* ■ *Dir* Herb Gardner • *Scr* Herb Gardner, from his play

Goodbye Pork Pie ★★ 18
Road movie 1981 · NZ · Colour · 102mins

The first New Zealand feature to recoup its costs at the domestic box office is a road movie in the good old counterculture tradition. Indeed, there's a real coming-of-age feel as unlikely buddies Tony Barry and Kelly Johnson learn about life, love and responsibility on a cross-country trek that's littered with eccentric characters and angry lawmen. It's dated in places, the sexism is unforgiveable and the episodic structure stops it building up a real head of steam. Considering he was a first-time writer/director/producer, Geoff Murphy does

however pack the picture with plenty of action and offbeat humour. Contains swearing. 📹

Tony Barry *John* • Kelly Johnson *Gerry Austin* • Claire Oberman *Shirl* • Shirley Gruar *Sue* • Jackie Lowitt *Leslie Morris* • Don Selwyn *Kaitaia policeman* • Shirley Dunn *Car rental girl* • Paki Cherrington *Taxi driver* ■ *Dir* Geoff Murphy • *Scr* Geoff Murphy, Ian Mune

GoodFellas ★★★★★ 18
Crime drama 1990 · US · Colour · 139mins

Martin Scorsese's unflinching depiction of the attraction and the brutal reality of the Mafia lifestyle is a masterwork on every artistic level. Direction, script – based on Nicholas Pileggi's non-fiction book *Wiseguy* – photography, ensemble acting (Joe Pesci won a deserved Oscar, but he's matched by Robert De Niro and Ray Liotta) and driving pop and rock soundtrack seamlessly combine to dazzling effect in this instant classic. Crackling with raw energy, Scorsese's fascinating new take on themes explored in his earlier *Mean Streets* enthrals from the first violent frames to the stunning final image. Be prepared to be completely bowled over by a director in full control of topnotch material at the peak of his talents. Contains swearing, violence and drug abuse. 📹 **DVD**

Robert De Niro *James Conway* • Ray Liotta *Henry Hill* • Joe Pesci *Tommy DeVito* • Lorraine Bracco *Karen Hill* • Paul Sorvino *Paul Cicero* • Frank Sivero *Frankie Carbone* • Tony Darrow *Sonny Bunz* • Mike Starr *Frenchy* ■ *Dir* Martin Scorsese • *Scr* Nicholas Pileggi, Martin Scorsese, from the book *Wiseguy* by Nicholas Pileggi • *Cinematographer* Michael Ballhaus • *Editor* Thelma Schoonmaker

A Goofy Movie ★★ U
Animated musical
1995 · US · Colour · 74mins

Mickey Mouse's pal Goofy gets his own movie, but fans of the original short cartoons in which he was a co-star may be shocked to discover that Goofy is now a dad, and not a cool one either, preferring to drag his son off fishing rather than let him chat up girls. Unfortunately, the story is rather ordinary and the bland computer animation looks less interesting than anything kids can catch nowadays on TV. Sadly, sophisticated youngsters brought up on *The Simpsons* and *Rugrats* will probably give this a wide berth. 📹 **DVD**

Bill Farmer *Goofy* • Jason Marsden *Max* • Jim Cummings *Pete* • Kellie Martin *Roxanne* • Rob Paulsen *PJ* • Wallace Shawn *Principal Mazur* • Frank Welker *Bigfoot* • Kevin Lima *Lester* • Florence Stanley *Waitress* ■ *Dir* Kevin Lima • *Scr* Jymn Magon, Chris Matheson, Brian Pimental, from a story by Jymn Magon

The Goonies ★★★ PG
Adventure 1985 · US · Colour · 108mins

Before making it big directing Macaulay Culkin in *Home Alone*, Chris Columbus wrote the screenplay from a story by a certain Steven Spielberg for this good-natured children's romp, which features a gang of kids tackling pirates while searching for missing treasure. The tale rattles along like a juvenile *Raiders of the Lost Ark* and the young leads – including Martha Plimpton, Sean Astin and Corey Feldman – are likeable enough. There's also some

nice hamming from villains Anne Ramsey, Joe Pantoliano and Robert Davi. Contains some swearing and violence. 📹

Sean Astin *Mikey* • Josh Brolin *Brand* • Jeff Cohen *Chunk* • Corey Feldman *Mouth* • Kerri Green *Andy* • Martha Plimpton *Stef* • Ke Huy Quan *Data* • John Matuszak *Sloth* • Robert Davi *Jake* • Joe Pantoliano *Francis* • Anne Ramsey *Mama Fratelli* ■ *Dir* Richard Donner • *Scr* Chris Columbus, from a story by Steven Spielberg

The Goose Steps Out ★★★★ U
Second World War comedy
1942 · UK · BW · 84mins

A wonderful comedy in which Will Hay is sent to a Nazi academy to get hold of Frank Pettingell's plans for a gas bomb. As usual, Hay's academic shortcomings are soon exposed, this time by a class of Hitler Youth that includes Peter Ustinov, Charles Hawtrey and Barry Morse, but he still manages to insult Hitler at every turn, steal a sample bomb casing and pass on some bogus invasion plans before heading back to Blighty. The script by Angus Macphail and John Dighton is packed with morale-boosting jokes that still seem pretty fresh, and Hay is in prime form.

Will Hay *William Potts/Muller* • Frank Pettingell *Professor Hoffman* • Julien Mitchell *General Von Glotz* • Charles Hawtrey *Max* • Peter Croft *Hans* • Anne Firth *Lena* • Leslie Harcourt *Vagel* ■ *Dir* Will Hay, Basil Dearden • *Scr* Angus Macphail, John Dighton, from a story by Bernard Miles, Reginald Groves

Gor ★ 15
Action fantasy 1987 · US · Colour · 90mins

The sword-and-sorcery genre had well and truly run its course by the time Fritz Kiersch's lame-brained effort saw the light of day. Urbano Barberini is Cabot, a nerdy professor transported to a distant planet where he sets about freeing its people from the tyrannical slavery of their overlord, played by the under-used Oliver Reed. All the staple ingredients are present – sword duels, scenes of torture, pastiche erotica and the obligatory escape through catacombs – but any attempt at humour fails miserably. Jack Palance turns up at the end to introduce himself as the villain of the sequel, *Outlaw of Gor*. 📹

Urbano Barberini *Cabot* • Rebecca Ferratti *Talena* • Paul L Smith [Paul Smith] *Surbus* • Oliver Reed *Sarm* • Jack Palance *Xenos* ■ *Dir* Fritz Kiersch • *Scr* Rick Marx, Peter Welbeck [Harry Alan Towers], from the novel *Tarnsman of Gor* by John Norman

The Gorbals Story ★★
Drama 1949 · UK · BW · 74mins

During its golden age Hollywood made films with titles such as *The Philadelphia Story* and *The Palm Beach Story*. *The Gorbals Story* hardly arouses the same level of expectation. This is a grim affair in which Glaswegian artist Howard Connell recalls the tough tenement existence that not only shaped his talent, but almost drove him to murder. Adapted by director David MacKane from Robert McLeish's play, the film strives valiantly for authenticity, but the social

message is badly fumbled and the performances highly theatrical.

Howard Connell *Willie Mutrie* • Betty Henderson *Peggie Anderson* • Russell Hunter *Johnnie Martin* • Majorie Thomson *Jean Mutrie* • Roddy McMillan *Hector* • Isobel Campbell *Nora Reilly* • Jack Stewart *Peter Reilly* • Archie Duncan *Bull* ■ *Dir* David MacKane • *Scr* David MacKane, from the play by Robert McLeish

Gordon the Black Pirate ★★ U
Swashbuckling adventure
1961 · It · Colour · 82mins

Like many Italian swashbucklers of the period, the action here is brisk but predictable, while the tawdry surface opulence can't disguise the cheapness of the production. (Ricardo Montalban's pirate ship was actually a fishing boat.) However, Vincent Price – who apparently only agreed to star in the picture because it afforded him the opportunity to go art hunting – has a hissably good time as the governor's secretary with a nasty sideline in slavery. The actor made *Nefertite, Queen of the Nile* with producer Ottavio Poggi the same year. 📹

Ricardo Montalban *Gordon* • Vincent Price *Romero* • Giulia Rubini *Manuela* • Liana Orfei *Luana* • Mario Feliciani *Tortuga* ■ *Dir* Mario Costa • *Scr* John Byrne, Ottavio Poggi

Gordon's War ★★
Blaxploitation crime drama
1973 · US · Colour · 89mins

Vietnam veteran Paul Winfield returns home to Harlem and has to cope with his wife's death from a drug overdose. Declaring war on the ghetto underworld, he organises a strike force to rid the neighbourhood of pushers. This is a slickly packaged blaxploitation vigilante drama, shot on gritty locations and with more credible action and less comic-strip violence than most of its ilk. Director Ossie Davis is better known these days as an actor, appearing in Spike Lee's *School Daze* and *Do the Right Thing*.

Paul Winfield *Gordon* • Carl Lee *Bee* • David Downing *Otis* • Tony King *Roy* • Gilbert Lewis *Spanish Harry* • Carl Gordon *Luther the Pimp* • Nathan C Heard *Big Pink* • Grace Jones *Mary* • Adam Wade *Hustler* ■ *Dir* Ossie Davis • *Scr* Howard Friedlander, Ed Spielman

Gordy ★ U
Comedy adventure
1994 · US · Colour · 86mins

This excruciating children's drama about a talking pig was released a year before *Babe* made eating bacon a capital crime. Cute to the point of nausea, *Gordy* includes every barnyard cliché in the book as he escapes the slaughterhouse, tries to find his folks and saves the young heir to a corporation from drowning. Strangely enough its saving grace, for those who like that sort of thing, is a country and western soundtrack with stars such as Boxcar Willie and Roy Clark. It would be telling porkies to say Mark Lewis's film would charm anyone but the least demanding child. 📹

Michael Roescher *Hanky Royce* • Doug Stone *Luke MacAllister* • Kristy Young *Jinnie Sue MacAllister* • Deborah Hobart *Jessica Royce* • Tom Lester *Cousin Jake* • Tom Key *Brinks*

Ted Manson *Henry Royce* • Justin Garms *Gordy* ■ *Dir* Mark Lewis • *Scr* Leslie Stevens, from a story by Jay Sommers, Dick Chevillat

Gore Vidal's Billy the Kid ★★★ 15

Western 1989 · US · Colour · 93mins

In this cumbersomely monikered cable movie, Gore Vidal took another bash at the more-than-familiar story of Billy the Kid. He had already scripted the TV movie *The Death of Billy the Kid* in the fifties, which inspired the Paul Newman vehicle *The Left-Handed Gun*. Here, again, Vidal presents Billy as a crazy, mixed-up kid who was caught up in a Wild West maelstrom from which he could only emerge feet first. Val Kilmer gives William Bonney a certain baby-faced charm, but he never hints at the complexities revealed by Newman. Though nothing special, it's all well above usual TV-movie standards.

Val Kilmer *William H Bonney* • Duncan Regehr *Pat Garrett* • Julie Carmen *Celsa* • Ned Vaughn *Charlie* • Patrick Massett *Tom* • Wilford Brimley *Governor Lew Wallace* • René Auberjonois *Drunk* • Nate Esformes *Valdez* • Gore Vidal *Minister* ■ *Dir* William A Graham • *Scr* Gore Vidal

The Gorgeous Hussy ★★

Period drama 1936 · US · BW · 103mins

Joan Crawford scandalises Washington society as the innkeeper's daughter who becomes President Andrew Jackson's bit-on-the-side in Clarence Brown's period drama. Crawford wanted the part because she rather resented Norma Shearer getting all the juicy historical roles MGM had to offer. Audiences were apathetic, though, and Franchot Tone (Joan's husband on screen and in real life) came off badly as well. On one occasion, Tone, who disliked his part, arrived on set 90 minutes late and was treated to a tongue-lashing from his wife. The marriage ended soon afterwards.

Joan Crawford *Peggy O'Neal Eaton* • Robert Taylor (1) *Bow Timberlake* • Lionel Barrymore *Andrew Jackson* • Melvyn Douglas *John Randolph* • James Stewart *"Rowdy" Roderick Dow* • Franchot Tone *John Eaton* • Louis Calhern *Sunderland* • Alison Skipworth *Mrs Beall* • Beulah Bondi *Rachel Jackson* ■ *Dir* Clarence Brown • *Scr* Ainsworth Morgan, Stephen Morehouse Avery, from the book by Samuel Hopkins Adams

Gorgo ★★★ PG

Monster adventure
1960 · UK · Colour · 73mins

Seven years after making *The Beast from 20,000 Fathoms*, Eugene Lourie came to Britain for what turned out to be his swansong. This highly derivative film has borrowed from so many other monster movies that it is almost as much fun spotting the swipes (mostly from *King Kong* and the *Godzilla* series) as it is watching the picture itself. Special effects boffin Tom Howard's creatures are the sweetest rampaging dinosaurs you will ever see, and the model London landmarks trampled by Mrs Gorgo are risible. Bill Travers and William Sylvester manage to keep admirably straight faces as this eminently enjoyable tosh unfolds around them.

Bill Travers *Joe* • William Sylvester *Sam* • Vincent Winter *Sean* • Christopher Rhodes *McCartin* • Joseph O'Conor *Professor Hendricks* • Bruce Seton *Professor Flaherty* • Martin Benson *Dorkin* • Maurice Kauffman *Radio Reporter* ■ *Dir* Eugène Lourié • *Scr* John Loring [Robert L Richards], Daniel Hyatt [Daniel James], from their story

The Gorgon ★★★ 15

Horror 1964 · US · Colour · 79mins

Barbara Shelley, Hammer's best ever *femme fatale*, is possessed by the snake-tressed, stone-gazing spirit of the Greek mythological creature in director Terence Fisher's most poetic and under-rated fearful fairy tale. One of the House of Horror's outings that is totally unclassifiable, it relies less on its absurd story and more on provocative imagery. But, while it may fall short of the monstrous mark, the period atmosphere is powerfully evoked and it's made headier by the peerless Peter Cushing and Christopher Lee at the height of their dramatic authority.

Peter Cushing *Namaroff* • Christopher Lee *Meister* • Richard Pasco *Paul* • Barbara Shelley *Carla* • Michael Goodliffe *Heitz* • Patrick Troughton *Kanof* • Jack Watson *Eatoff* • Jeremy Longhurst *Bruno* ■ *Dir* Terence Fisher • *Scr* John Gilling, from a story by J Llewellyn Devine

Gorilla at Large ★★★

Thriller 1954 · US · Colour · 81mins

An above-average chiller, though probably not a film that star Anne Bancroft would regard as one of her career highlights. She still cuts a fine figure in her trapeze artist catsuit, in this tale of bizarre killings seemingly linked to fellow amusement park employee Cameron Mitchell (resplendent in a crummy gorilla costume). Director Harmon Jones uses as his backdrop the technicoloured splendour associated with fairgrounds and swells the story with a superb supporting cast, including Lee J Cobb, future *Ironside* actor Raymond Burr and, in an early career break, Lee Marvin. This was originally released in 3-D, so if things hurtle at you for no apparent reason, you'll know why.

Cameron Mitchell *Joey Matthews* • Anne Bancroft *Laverne Miller* • Lee J Cobb *Detective Sergeant Garrison* • Raymond Burr *Cyrus Miller* • Charlotte Austin *Audrey Baxter* • Peter Whitney *Kovacs* • Lee Marvin *Shaughnessy* • Warren Stevens *Mack* ■ *Dir* Harmon Jones • *Scr* Leonard Praskins, Barney Slater

Gorillas in the Mist ★★★★ 12

Biographical drama
1988 · US · Colour · 123mins

A fascinating account of Dian Fossey's ground-breaking research into the closed world of the gorilla, this has a tour de force performance from Sigourney Weaver in the lead role. She admirably presents a warts-and-all portrait of the woman who slowly gained access to a tribe of remote primates facing extinction. In this biopic, Fossey's passion for her gorillas is contrasted with her coldness as a human being and a commitment to her work that borders on obsessional. Michael Apted's direction is sympathetic and he makes the most of the jungle location. Bryan Brown is good as Weaver's lover, but the real acting accolades must go to the apes themselves. Contains some swearing.

Sigourney Weaver *Dian Fossey* • Bryan Brown *Bob Campbell* • Julie Harris *Roz Carr* • John Omirah Miluwi *Sembagare* • Iain Cuthbertson *Dr Louis Leakey* • Constantin Alexandrov *Van Vecten* • Waigwa Wachira *Mukara* • Iain Glen *Brendan* • David Lansbury *Larry* ■ *Dir* Michael Apted • *Scr* Anna Hamilton Phelan, from a story by Anna Hamilton Phelan, Tab Murphy, from the book by Dian Fossey and an article by Harold TP Hayes

Gorky Park ★★★ 15

Spy thriller 1983 · US · Colour · 123mins

This is based on an intriguing idea from the bestseller by Martin Cruz Smith. Moscow cop William Hurt – looking pained and acting sincere – investigates the case of three faceless corpses. Are the deaths due to Lee Marvin's business operation or are they a result of spy games? Dennis Potter's screenplay is a bit ponderous, but Michael Apted's direction makes the most of the plot convolutions and locations (with Helsinki standing in for Moscow).

William Hurt *Arkady Renko* • Lee Marvin *Jack Osborne* • Brian Dennehy *William Kirwill* • Ian Bannen *Iamskoy* • Joanna Pacula *Irina Asanova* • Michael Elphick *Pasha Pavlovich* • Richard Griffiths *Anton* • Rikki Fulton *Major Pribluda* • Alexei Sayle *Golodkin* ■ *Dir* Michael Apted • *Scr* Dennis Potter, from the novel by Martin Cruz Smith

G.O.R.P. ★

Comedy 1980 · US · Colour · 90mins

Before director Joseph Ruben made his name in the fantasy genre (*Dreamscape*, *The Stepfather*), he was an adept practitioner of good-natured exploitation fluff, often set in a high school milieu (*The Pom Pom Girls*). But this crudely unfunny summer camp comedy about Jewish jocks trying to get laid is the worst and most lightweight of the lot. Michael Lembeck and Dennis Quaid drown under an interminable onslaught of sexist gags, macho posturing and drug-related humour, which submerges the poor excuse for a plot at every limp turn.

Michael Lembeck *Kavell* • Dennis Quaid *Mad Grossman* • Philip Casnoff *Bergman* • Fran Drescher *Evie* • David Huddleston *Walrus Wallman* • Robert Trebor *Rabbi Blowitz* • Lou Wagner *Federman* ■ *Dir* Joseph Ruben • *Scr* Jeffrey Konvitz, from a story by Martin Zweiback, Jeffrey Konvitz

The Gospel According to St Matthew ★★★★★ U

Biblical epic 1964 · It/Fr · BW · 129mins

Eschewing the false grandeur of the traditional historical epic, Pier Paolo Pasolini employed a neorealist approach to reaffirm the immediate social significance of Christ's teaching. This unique collaboration between a Marxist director and the Catholic Church (which contributed to the budget) is remarkable not only for the powerful truth of its message, but also for the gentle conviction of Enrique Irazoqui's Jesus, as he rails against injustice and works miracles with a compassion that is absent from the more reverential Hollywood testaments. With the sublime classical score contrasting with the rugged beauty of Calabria, this is unquestionably the most relevant religious film ever made. Italian dialogue dubbed into English.

Enrique Irazoqui *Jesus Christ* • Margherita Caruso *Mary, as a girl* • Susanna Pasolini *Mary, as a woman* • Marcello Morante *Joseph* • Mario Socrate *John the Baptist* • Settimo Di Porto *Peter* • Otello Sestili *Judas* • Ferruccio Nuzzo *Matthew* ■ *Dir/Scr* Pier Paolo Pasolini • *Cinematographer* Tonino Delli Colli

Gossip ★★ 15

Thriller 1999 · US · Colour · 90mins

Three college roommates start a rumour about a prudish classmate having sex at a party. It quickly gets out of hand, leading to an accusation of rape and an innocent man's arrest. The gossip-mongers are then caught in the middle as they fight about whether or not to come clean. Dark secrets from the past also surface to complicate matters. The film benefits from striking visuals, but never fully capitalises on the dramatic potential of its premise. Similarly, the young cast is attractive but their performances are shallow, with James Marsden the only standout as the cynical Derrick.

James Marsden *Derrick* • Lena Headey *Cathy Jones* • Norman Reedus *Travis* • Kate Hudson *Naomi* • Joshua Jackson *Beau* • Marisa Coughlan *Sheila* • Edward James Olmos *Det Curtis* • Sharon Lawrence *Det Kelly* • Eric Bogosian *Professor Goodwin* ■ *Dir* David Guggenheim • *Scr* Theresa Rebeck, Gregory Poirier, from a story by Gregory Poirier

Gotcha! ★★★ 15

Comedy spy drama
1985 · US · Colour · 96mins

An uninspired, if watchable hybrid of the teen wish-fulfilment comedy and substandard John le Carré. A youthful Anthony Edwards impresses as a shy college kid who embarks upon a European vacation and gets involved with a spy ring, while Linda Fiorentino's turn as a sultry spy leaves one pondering why it took so long for her to blossom into a star. We've all seen it before – innocent abroad has an affair with a sophisticated older woman. However director Jeff Kanew offers plenty of frantic scurrying about and sharp one-liners to paper over the elements of *déjà vu*, if little in the way of actual danger and suspense. Put simply, it's "diet Hitchcock".

Anthony Edwards *Jonathan Moore* • Linda Fiorentino *Sasha Banicek/Cheryl Brewster* • Nick Corri *Manolo* • Alex Rocco *Al* • Marla Adams *Maria* • Klaus Loewitsch [Klaus Löwitsch] *Vlad* • Christopher Rydell *Bob Jensen* • Christie Claridge *Girl student* ■ *Dir* Jeff Kanew • *Scr* Dan Gordon, from a story by Paul G Hensler, Dan Gordon

Gothic ★★★ 18

Horror 1986 · UK · Colour · 83mins

Ken Russell's talent to abuse past icons goes wondrously berserk here, as he resurrects the notorious 19th-century literary booze-up of Byron, Shelley, Mary Godwin and Polidori at the Villa Diodati on the shores of Lake Geneva. It's this incestuous, laudanum-quaffing occasion that led to the writing of *Frankenstein* and, while Gabriel Byrne, Julian Sands and

Natasha Richardson take it seriously enough, Russell keeps undermining them with overwrought visual decadence. You feel you've been invited to the exorcism of some very private demons in this example of cinema as psychiatrist's couch. Contains swearing, violence and sex scenes. ▣

Julian Sands *Percy Bysshe Shelley* • Natasha Richardson *Mary Godwin* • Gabriel Byrne *Lord Byron* • Myriam Cyr *Claire* • Timothy Spall *Dr John Polidori* • Dexter Fletcher *Rushton* • Andreas Wisniewski *Fletcher* • Alec Mango *Murray* ■ *Dir* Ken Russell • *Scr* Stephen Volk

Goto, l'Ile d'Amour ★★★★
Fantasy drama
1968 · Fr · Colour and BW · 93mins

The surreal poetry that characterised Walerian Borowczyk's animation is clearly evident in his first live-action feature. Shot through with moments of extravagant colour, which lend a certain sinister enchantment to the cruel fairytale world of Goto, the heavily stylised visuals make the characters seem as insignificant as the array of symbolic objects (such as music boxes and phonographs) littered around the residence of Pierre Brasseur's cuckolded dictator. With its flycatchers, duels and acts of self-sacrifice, there's an operatic feel to the storyline, which is reinforced by the sublime Handel organ concerto and the theatricality of the performances. In French with English subtitles.

Pierre Brasseur *Goto III* • Ligia Branice *Glossia* • Ginette Leclerc *Gonasta* • René Dary *Gomor* • Jean-Pierre Andréani *Gono* • Michel Charrel *Grymp* ■ *Dir/Scr* Walerian Borowczyk • *Cinematographer* Paul Coteret

Gotti ★★ 18
Biographical crime drama
1996 · US · Colour · 117mins

Armand Assante gives a compelling and charismatic performance in this biopic of New York mobster, John Gotti, but he's let down by a poor script. The film traces the career of the "Teflon Don" from up-and-coming hit man to Mafia boss of the powerful Gambino crime family, battling wits with Federal agents. With its standard "mob-speak" dialogue and uninspired direction this doesn't offer too many insights into what made Gotti tick. Look out for Dominic Chianese and Vincent Pastore – both familiar from TV's *The Sopranos*. ▣

Armand Assante *John Gotti* • Anthony Quinn *Neil Dellacroce* • William Forsythe *Sammy Gravano* • Marc Lawrence *Carlo Gambino* • Richard Sarafian [Richard C Sarafian] *Paul Castellano* • Vincent Pastore *Angelo Ruggiero* • Dominic Chianese *Joe Armone* • Frank Vincent *Robert DiBernardo* ■ *Dir* Robert Harmon • *Scr* Steve Shagan, from a book by Jerry Capeci, Gene Mustain

The Governess ★★ 15
Period drama 1997 · UK/Fr · Colour · 109mins

Someone laced the corsets far too tight for this rigid drama set in the mid-1840s, in which Jewish girl Minnie Driver pretends to be a gentile so she can earn money for her family working as a governess. Her plan works and she takes a job with the Cavendish family on a remote Scottish island. It's not long, of course, before her undergarments are being tossed on the floor as she embarks on an affair with her stiff-upper-lipped, married employer (*The Full Monty*'s Tom Wilkinson), while also helping him with his scientific research in photography. Writer/director Sandra Goldbacher, while cleverly mixing the early images of photography with the growing relationship between the governess and her reluctant boss, never manages to convey any feeling of sensuality between the mismatched pair. ▣

Minnie Driver *Rosina DaSilva/Mary Blackchurch* • Tom Wilkinson *Mr Charles Cavendish* • Florence Hoath *Clementina Cavendish* • Jonathan Rhys-Meyers *Henry Cavendish* • Harriet Walter *Mrs Cavendish* • Arlene Cockburn *Lily Milk* • Emma Bird *Rebecca* ■ *Dir/Scr* Sandra Goldbacher

Government Girl ★★★ U
Second World War comedy
1943 · US · BW · 93mins

This simple but affecting tale of love among the armaments stars Sonny Tufts and Olivia de Havilland and follows the understated forties tradition of slipping a spot of satire in among standard wartime propaganda. The two main stars give us a lively, knockabout relationship (Tufts is a production expert and de Havilland a Washington secretary), but beneath the gloss and wisecracks is a heavier message about the stifling nature of government bureaucracy. Though not a classic, this is an above-average example of what was on plentiful offer at the time.

Olivia de Havilland *Smokey* • Sonny Tufts *Ed Browne* • Agnes Moorehead *Mrs Wright* • Anne Shirley *May* • Jess Barker *Dana* • James Dunn *Sergeant Joe* • Paul Stewart *Branch* • Harry Davenport *Senator MacVickers* ■ *Scr* Dudley Nichols, Budd Schulberg, from a story by Adela Rogers St John

Goya in Bordeaux ★★★★
Biographical drama
1999 · Sp/It · Colour · 102mins

Realising a long-cherished project, Carlos Saura has impeccably captured the increasingly tormented vision of the Spanish painter, who spent his declining years in French exile. The re-creation of the sombre canvases, which reflected the impact of both Goya's Napoleonic trauma and his insulating deafness, is achieved with imaginative authenticity by Vittorio Storaro, with the tableaux sequence depicting the "Disasters of War" engravings making the most impact. As the ageing Goya, impereately recalling court intrigue and his affair with duchess Maribel Verdu, Francisco Rabal excels. However, with a mastery of sound and dance complementing the beauty, the glory belongs to Saura. In Spanish with English subtitles.

Francisco Rabal *Goya* • Maribel Verdu *Duchess of Alba* • Jose Coronado *Goya as a young man* • Dafne Fernandez *Rosario* • Eulalia Ramón *Leocadia* • Joaquin Climent *Moratin* • Cristina Espinosa *Pepita Tudo* • Jose Maria Pou *Godoy* ■ *Dir/Scr* Carlos Saura

Grace & Glorie ★★★
Drama 1998 · US · Colour · 98mins

There's a whiff of *Fried Green Tomatoes* permeating this adaptation of Tom Ziegler's stage play, with Gena Rowlands assuming the role of the testy nursing-home inmate who decides to use her experience to help someone in greater pain than herself. Diane Lane plays the woman trying to rebuild her own life who decides to take care of the terminally ill Rowlands. This is an unashamedly sentimental TV movie, but Rowlands adds an unmistakeable touch of class.

Gena Rowlands *Grace Stiles* • Diane Lane *Glorie* • Neal McDonough *David* • Chris Beetem *Roy* • Carrie Preston *Charlene* • Emmy Rossum *Luanne* ■ *Dir* Arthur Allan Seidelman • *Scr* Grace McKeaney, from a play by Tom Ziegler

Grace of My Heart ★★★★★ 15
Romantic drama
1996 · US · Colour · 111mins

Smart, hip and glorious, director Allison Anders's affectionate hymn to those sixties songwriters who made New York's Brill Building the place to be doesn't miss a beat. Illeana Douglas touchingly plays a thinly disguised Carole King, anxious for fame as a singer rather than composer of girl group classics, whose string of failed relationships includes one with "surf pop" genius Matt Dillon. John Turturro's turn as a shadowy Phil Spector-like figure is absolutely brilliant, there's strong support from the likes of Patsy Kensit and Bridget Fonda, and the songs written expressly for the movie by Burt Bacharach, Lesley Gore and Elvis Costello are just perfect. Unmissable. ▣

Illeana Douglas *Denise Waverly/Edna Buxton* • Matt Dillon *Jay Phillips* • Eric Stoltz *Howard Caszatt* • Bruce Davison *John Murray* • Patsy Kensit *Cheryl Steed* • Jennifer Leigh Warren *Doris Shelly* • John Turturro *Joel Millner* • Chris Isaak *Matthew Lewis* • Bridget Fonda *Kelly Porter* ■ *Dir/Scr* Allison Anders

Grace Quigley ★★★ 15
Black comedy 1984 · US · Colour · 87mins

After seeing him murder her landlord, elderly widow Katharine Hepburn hires hit man Nick Nolte to kill aged friends and neighbours who would benefit from the euthanasia. Anthony Harvey's comedy is certainly ebony-hued, but the two stars carry it off in sprightly fashion. In the end, though, it all gets rather sentimental – a result, it appears, of being mauled by distributors prior to release. The film's original title was *The Ultimate Solution of Grace Quigley* – solutions don't get much more ultimate than this one. ▣

Katharine Hepburn *Grace Quigley* • Nick Nolte *Seymour Flint* • Kit Le Fever *Muriel* • Chip Zien *Dr Herman* • William Duell *Mr Jenkins* • Elizabeth Wilson *Emily Watkins* ■ *Dir* Anthony Harvey • *Scr* A Martin Zweiback

The Graduate ★★★★★ 15
Comedy 1967 · US · Colour · 101mins

This hilarious satire on America's bourgeoisie thrust the unknown Dustin Hoffman into the limelight and won a best direction Oscar for Mike Nichols. In his film debut, Hoffman is sensational as the innocent college graduate seduced by older married woman Anne Bancroft and then falling for her daughter Katharine Ross. The humour in Calder Willingham and Buck Henry's screenplay has the bite of a dry martini, Robert Surtees's stunning, innovative camerawork contributes telling visual ironies and the Simon and Garfunkel soundtrack perfectly captures the mood of disaffected youth seething beneath the laid-back exterior of sixties California. Nichols's Oscar was well deserved, launching him into the top rank of Hollywood directors, though the film missed out in six other categories – best picture, actor (Hoffman), actress (Bancroft), supporting actress (Ross), screenplay and cinematography. ▣ **DVD**

Dustin Hoffman *Benjamin Braddock* • Anne Bancroft *Mrs Robinson* • Katharine Ross *Elaine Robinson* • William Daniels *Mr Braddock* • Elizabeth Wilson *Mrs Braddock* • Murray Hamilton *Mr Robinson* • Brian Avery *Carl Smith* • Walter Brooke *Mr Maguire* ■ *Dir* Mike Nichols • *Scr* Calder Willingham, Buck Henry, from the novel by Charles Webb • *Cinematographer* Robert Surtees • *Editor* Sam O'Steen • *Production Designer* Richard Sylbert • *Music* Dave Grusin, Paul Simon

Graffiti Bridge ★★ 15
Musical 1990 · US · Colour · 86mins

After *Purple Rain*, this is the best film from the artist who was still then known as Prince. Not surprising, really, because it's a sequel of sorts, which finds him once again basically playing Prince, aka the Kid. His old nemesis from *Purple Rain*, Morris Day, and his band the Times return – this time they are warring nightclub owners – and once again steal the show. But despite an impressive array of musical talent (Mavis Staples, George Clinton), the tunes aren't quite as memorable this time around and, as a film director, Prince remains a brilliant musician. ▣

Prince *The Kid* • Ingrid Chavez *Aura* • Morris Day • Jerome Benton *Jerome* • Michael Bland • Damon Dickson • Mavis Staples *Melody Cool* • George Clinton ■ *Dir* Prince • *Scr* Prince

Grand Canyon ★★★★ 15
Drama 1991 · US · Colour · 128mins

After the critical mauling he received for his ill-judged black comedy *I Love You to Death*, writer/director Lawrence Kasdan returned to the ensemble territory of *The Big Chill*. However, the warm nostalgia of the latter is largely absent this time as Kasdan attempts to come to grips with the fear and violence afflicting modern-day Los Angeles. It's an ambitious task, and at times the script strays toward sentimental melodrama, but Kasdan's direction is as assured as ever. He is rewarded with excellent performances from Danny Glover, regular collaborator Kevin Kline, *Dances with Wolves*'s Mary McDonnell and Alfre Woodard. There's also a scene-stealing role for Steve Martin, who plays an arrogant film producer reportedly modelled on action master Joel Silver of *Lethal Weapon* fame. ▣

Danny Glover *Simon* • Steve Martin *Davis* • Kevin Kline *Mack* • Mary McDonnell *Claire* • Mary-Louise Parker *Dee* • Alfre Woodard *Jane* • Jeremy Sisto *Roberto* • Tina Lifford *Deborah* ■ *Dir* Lawrence Kasdan • *Scr* Lawrence Kasdan, Meg Kasdan

Grand Central Murder ★★

Mystery drama   1942 · US · BW · 73mins

An acceptable low-budget B-thriller, this looks like an RKO programme filler but was, in fact, made at the glossiest studio of all, MGM, which later had some success with better examples of the style, such as *Act of Violence*. The reliable, if slightly dog-eared Van Heflin stars as a private detective and Patricia Dane is a Broadway star whose downfall is charted in flashbacks. The settings are the railway sidings and the underground passages of New York's Grand Central Station, a dramatic location that has always attracted film-makers.

Van Heflin *"Rocky" Custer* • Patricia Dane *Mida King* • Cecilia Parker *Constance Furness* • Virginia Grey *Sue Custer* • Sam Levene *Inspector Gunther* • Samuel S Hinds *Roger Furness* ■ *Dir* S Sylvan Simon • *Scr* Peter Rurie, from a novel by Sue MacVeigh

Le Grand Chemin ★★★★15

Drama   1987 · Fr · Colour · 106mins

A sugary confection with a hard centre may not be to everyone's taste, but the crunches in this charming rite-of-passage picture make the melting moments all the more sweet. Anémone and Richard Bohringer both won Césars (the French equivalent of an Oscar) for their performances as a grief-stricken couple whose care of a nine-year-old Parisian boy results in a bitter tug of war for his affections. Young Antoine Hubert is endearingly wide-eyed throughout his introduction to the ways of grown-ups and Vanessa Guedj is quite wonderful as the knowing tomboy who acts as his guide. In French with English subtitles.

Anémone *Marcelle* • Richard Bohringer *Pelo* • Antoine Hubert *Louis* • Vanessa Guedj *Martine* • Christine Pascal *Claire* • Raoul Billerey *Priest* • Pascale Roberts *Yvonne* • Marie Matheron *Solange* ■ *Dir/Scr* Jean-Loup Hubert

Grand Hotel ★★★★★U

Drama   1932 · US · BW · 115mins

Based on the German play by Vicki Baum and its American version, the star-filled melodrama that is *Grand Hotel* became a blueprint for almost every glossy Hollywood soap opera that followed it. Greta Garbo, John and Lionel Barrymore, Joan Crawford and Wallace Beery vie for screen time as the various residents of the Berlin hotel, but it is art director Cedric Gibbons who deserves the plaudits for the luscious look of the film. One of the biggest projects in Hollywood at the time, the all-star cast caused MGM numerous problems as far as billing was concerned. In the end, the word "Garbo" appeared at the top of the bill to honour a clause stating she would have top billing, while the other actors were billed in alphabetical order below. ▱

Greta Garbo *Grusinskaya* • John Barrymore *The Baron Felix Benvenuto Frihern Von Gaigern* • Joan Crawford *Flaemmchen* • Wallace Beery *General Director Preysing* • Lionel Barrymore *Otto Kringelein* • Jean Hersholt *Senf* ■ • *Scr* William A Drake, from his play, from the play *Menschen im Hotel* by Vicki Baum • *Cinematographer* William Daniels • *Costume Designer* Adrian

Le Grand Jeu ★★★

Erotic romantic drama   1933 · Fr · BW · 115mins

Pierre-Richard Willm flees to Morocco to forget the Parisian society woman who has spurned him. His plan backfires when he meets a cabaret singer who is her double. The discovery eventually spells disaster for him. Marie Bell (in a dual role) co-stars in this French excursion into romantic melodrama which is somewhat fantastical, but is directed in fine style with loads of exotic and erotic atmosphere by Jacques Feyder and Marcel Carné. Françoise Rosay, Feyder's wife, also appears in the first of three successful films they made together. A French language film.

Marie Bell *Florence/Irma* • Pierre-Richard Willm *Pierre Martel* • Charles Vanel *Clément* • George Pitoeff *Nicolas* • Françoise Rosay *Blanche* ■ *Dir* Jacques Feyder, Marcel Carné • *Scr* Jacques Feyder, Charles Spaak

Grand Jury ★★

Crime drama   1976 · US · Colour · 100mins

Leslie Nielsen's career renaissance came in the early eighties with his portrayal of the staggeringly incompetent Frank Drebin in the TV series *Police Squad* – a role he won after his hilarious performance in *Airplane!*. Unfortunately, this feeble mid-seventies drama finds Mr Nielson in decidedly unfunny mode. Bruce Davison and Meredith MacRae are the naive young couple whose involvement in an insurance scam has disastrous consequences. Director Christopher Cain went on to make *Young Guns*.

Leslie Nielsen *John Williams* • Bruce Davison *Bobby Allen* • Meredith MacRae *Nancy Williams* • Larry Barton *Parking lot owner* • Myron Griffin *Inspector Hanes* • Alice Reinheart *Jury foreman* • Michael Rougas *Jimmy* ■ *Dir/Scr* Christopher Cain

Grand Prix ★★★PG

Drama   1966 · US · Colour · 162mins

One of the best motor-racing films ever made. Filmed in Cinerama-SuperPanavision – the Bugatti of screen ratios – it suffers badly from the confines of TV, especially during the frequent bursts into split-screen. But racing fans will adore the glimpses of Graham Hill, the banking at Monza and the sixties speed machines, which seem so flimsy and thin-tyred compared to the cars that race today. There are spectacular stunts, of course, but the human pile-ups between the races scrape the bottom of the drama cliché barrel. ▱

James Garner *Pete Aron* • Eva Marie Saint *Louise Frederickson* • Yves Montand *Jean-Pierre Sarti* • Toshiro Mifune *Izo Yamura* • Brian Bedford *Scott Stoddard* • Jessica Walter *Pat* • Antonio Sabato *Nino Barlini* • Françoise Hardy *Lisa* ■ *Dir* John Frankenheimer • *Scr* Robert Alan Aurthur, Bill Hanley • *Editor* Fredric Steinkamp, Henry Berman, Stewart Linder, Frank Santillo

Grand Slam ★★15

Comedy thriller   1990 · US · Colour · 59mins

A crude and rarely-seen pilot for a forgotten TV series that looks as if it tried to cash in on the success of the Robert De Niro comedy hit *Midnight Run*. Former *Dukes of Hazzard* star

John Schneider and Paul Rodriguez are the deeply unloveable bounty hunters who reluctantly team up to track down an escaped murderer on the trail of his missing loot. The bickering duo generate few laughs and director Bill L Norton shows no sign of escaping from the straitjacket of American TV. Contains some swearing. ▱

John Schneider *"Hardball" Bakelenekoff* • Paul Rodriguez *Pedro N Gomez* • Susan Walters *Ann* • Juan Fernandez *Aguilar* ■ *Dir* Bill L Norton • *Scr* Bob Clark

Grand Theft Auto ★★PG

Action comedy   1977 · US · Colour · 80mins

Ron Howard's full-length feature directing debut is very much a family affair. Made under the aegis of that canny judge of film talent Roger Corman, this was co-written by Howard's father Rance (who also appears) and offers a role for brother Clint. And while not strictly family, Ron's screen mum from *Happy Days* Marion Ross is also in there as well. Sadly, the film itself is less memorable and little more than an extended *Dukes of Hazzard* adventure. Another Corman protegé soon set for bigger things, Joe Dante, edited the film. ▱

Ron Howard *Sam Freeman* • Nancy Morgan *Paula Powers* • Marion Ross *Vivian Hedgeworth* • Peter Isacksen *Sparky* • Barry Cahill *Digby Powers* • Hoke Howell *Preacher* • Lew Brown *Jack Clepper* • Elizabeth Rogers *Priscilla Powers* ■ *Dir* Ron Howard • *Scr* Ron Howard, Rance Howard

La Grande Bouffe ★★★18

Satirical comedy   1973 · Fr · Colour · 124mins

Marco Ferreri's satire is like Buñuel's *The Discreet Charm of the Bourgeoisie* in reverse: where Buñuel's characters never quite get to their waiting feast, Ferreri's gather in a villa and gorge themselves on food, wine and women. This is not a picture for bulimics or the obese; nor is it as subversively funny as it might have been. Nevertheless, there are some great scenes – notably the moment when the ample buttocks of Andrea Ferreol are used to mould a vast slab of *mousse de foie gras*. In French with English subtitles. ▱

Marcello Mastroianni *Pilot* • Ugo Tognazzi *Chef* • Michel Piccoli *TV producer* • Philippe Noiret *Judge* • Andrea Ferreol *Teacher* • Monique Chaumette *Madeleine* • Florence Giorgetti *Anne* • Rita Scherrer *Anulka* ■ *Dir* Marco Ferreri • *Scr* Marco Ferreri, Rafael Arcona

La Grande Illusion ★★★★★U

Classic First World War drama   1937 · Fr · BW · 108mins

Critics vie to heap superlatives on Renoir's masterpiece and landmark of world cinema, but one of the film's highest accolades of all came from Nazi propaganda boss Josef Goebbels, who classified it as "Cinematographic Enemy No 1". Made on the eve of the Second World War but set in a German PoW camp during the First World War, it has also been called the ultimate anti-war film – no small claim since it does not contain a single battle scene, making its point with dialogue rather than action. Though not an easy film, in any sense, it's worth the effort. In French with English subtitles. ▱

Jean Gabin *Maréchal* • Erich von Stroheim *Von Rauffenstein* • Pierre Fresnay *Capt De Boeldieu* • Dalio *Rosenthal* • Dita Parlo *Peasant woman* • Julien Carette *Actor* • Gaston Modot *Engineer* • Jean Dasté *Schoolteacher* • Georges Peclet *French soldier* ■ *Dir* Jean Renoir • *Scr* Charles Spaak, Jean Renoir • *Cinematographer* Christian Matras • *Art Director* Lourié [Eugène Lourié]

Les Grandes Manoeuvres ★★★★U

Romantic comedy   1955 · Fr/It · Colour · 102mins

One of the most inspirational pioneers of French silent and early sound cinema, René Clair's critical fortunes had dipped dramatically by the time he made his first colour feature. Yet this is one of the glories of a career studded with delights. Combining wit and grace with comic impudence, Clair concocts a frothy comedy that turns into a poignant drama, as dragoon Gérard Phillipe realises that his reputation as a gadabout has thwarted his one chance of true love with Michèle Morgan, the divorcee who he wagered his comrades he could seduce. In French with English subtitles. ▱

Michèle Morgan *Marie Louise Riviere* • Gérard Philipe *Lt Armand de la Verne* • Brigitte Bardot *Lucie* • Yves Robert *Felix* • Jean Desailly *Victor Duverger* • Pierre Dux *Colonel* • Jacques François *Rudolph* • Lise Delamare *Jeanne* • Jacqueline Maillan *Juliette* ■ *Dir* René Clair • *Scr* René Clair, Jerome Geronimi, Jean Marsan, from a story by Courteline

Grandeur et Décadence d'un Petit Commerce de Cinéma ★★★

Drama   1986 · Fr · Colour · 90mins

Originally made for the French TV show, *Série Noire*, this contemptuous anti-thriller took former New Wave icon Jean-Luc Godard's determined bid to demythologise the movie-making process to a higher plain. Ostensibly seeking to greenlight an adaptation of a James Hadley Chase novel, failed auteur Jean-Pierre Léaud and producer Jean-Pierre Mocky end up ogling the auditioning starlets, while spouting theories and dropping the touchstone names of those ensconced in the cinematic pantheon. With Godard himself interrupting these rambling discourses to denounce everything from pretentiousness to Polanski, this is a scathing exposé of the commercial considerations underpinning even the most chaste arthouse project. A French language film.

Jean-Pierre Léaud *Gaspar Bazin* • Jean-Pierre Mocky *Jean Almereyda* • Marie Valéra *Eurydice* ■ *Dir* Jean-Luc Godard • *Scr* Jean-Luc Godard, from a novel by James Hadley Chase

Grandview, USA ★★15

Drama   1984 · US · Colour · 97mins

The cast may be a who's who of future stars, but the plot of this teen angst drama is right out of yesteryear. Set in the Midwest of the mid-eighties, the film follows Jamie Lee Curtis's bid to keep her father's demolition derby in business, while sidestepping the adoring advances of star driver Patrick Swayze. C Thomas Howell is also involved, but the smartest acting

comes from veterans Troy Donahue and M Emmet Walsh. Swayze's choreography is hardly ''dirty dancing'', however, and director Randal Kleiser fared better with *Grease*.

Jamie Lee Curtis *Michelle "Mike" Cody* • C Thomas Howell *Tim Pearson* • Patrick Swayze *Ernie "Slam" Webster* • Troy Donahue *Donny Vinton* • Jennifer Jason Leigh *Candy Webster* • William Windom *Bob Cody* • Carole Cook *Betty Welles* • M Emmet Walsh *Mr Clark* ■ *Dir* Randal Kleiser • *Scr* Ken Hixon

The Grapes of Wrath
★★★★★ PG

Drama   1940 · US · BW · 129mins

The classic adaptation of John Steinbeck's Depression-era novel, with Henry Fonda and the Joad family moving from the dust bowl of Oklahoma to the promised land of California. The scene when their home is bulldozed is heartrending and their fate as migrant workers has lasting power. Stupendously photographed by Gregg Toland, the film also has some weaknesses, notably a corny religious symbolism in place of Steinbeck's raw politics. When studio boss Darryl F Zanuck was persuading Steinbeck to endorse a happy ending, Zanuck was called away to deal with an even more urgent matter. ''*The Grapes of Wrath*,'' said Steinbeck, ''is unimportant compared to Shirley Temple's tooth.'' Oscars went to director John Ford and to Jane Darwell, unforgettable as Ma Joad.

Henry Fonda *Tom Joad* • Jane Darwell *Ma Joad* • John Carradine *Casey* • Charley Grapewin *Grandpa Joad* • Dorris Bowdon *Rosaham* • Russell Simpson *Pa Joad* • OZ Whitehead *Al* • John Qualen *Muley* • Eddie Quillan *Connie* • Zeffie Tilbury *Grandma Joad* ■ *Dir* John Ford • *Scr* Nunnally Johnson, from the novel by John Steinbeck • *Music* Alfred Newman • *Art Director* Richard Day, Mark-Lee Kirk

Grass: a Nation's Battle for Life
★★★★

Silent documentary   1925 · US · BW · 70mins

Although they are best remembered for *King Kong*, Merian C Cooper and Ernest B Schoedsack were renowned travel chroniclers during the silent era. The film is full of spectacular set pieces, such as the perilous crossing of the torrential Karun river and the final barefoot ascent. But there's a troublingly civilised arrogance about the possibility that, like their mentor, Robert Flaherty, the pair manipulated the action by urging 50,000 Bakhtiari nomads to take the most treacherous (and, thus, most cinematic) route across the Zardeh Kuh mountains in search of grazing land. Their Siamese picture, *Chang* (1927), is equally impressive, but much less exploitative.

Dir Merian Cooper [Merian C Cooper], Ernest B Schoedsack, Marguerite Harrison • *Cinematographer* Merian C Cooper, Ernest B Schoedsack

The Grass Harp
★★★ PG

Drama   1995 · US · Colour · 102mins

Charles Matthau's film based on Truman Capote's autobiographical novel may be old-fashioned, but it also has the polish that used to make studio pictures so irresistible. This may

be down to the fact that the script is co-written by Hollywood veteran Stirling Silliphant, but it's the exceptional ensemble that gives this memoir of a Deep South childhood in the late thirties its charm. As the chalk-and-cheese sisters who raise orphan Edward Furlong, Piper Laurie and Sissy Spacek bind together the episodic narrative. They also give it a credibility that makes Jack Lemmon and Walter Matthau's more outrageous turns delightful rather than damaging. Contains some swearing. 🖭

Piper Laurie *Dolly Talbo* • Sissy Spacek *Verena Talbo* • Walter Matthau *Judge Charlie Cool* • Edward Furlong *Collin Fenwick* • Nell Carter *Catherine Creek* • Jack Lemmon *Dr Morris Ritz* • Mary Steenburgen *Sister Ida* • Sean Patrick Flanery *Riley Henderson* ■ *Dir* Charles Matthau • *Scr* Stirling Silliphant, Kirk Ellis, from the novel by Truman Capote

The Grass Is Greener
★ PG

Romantic comedy
1960 · UK · Colour · 100mins

Too much talk, too little action and a miscast Robert Mitchum contribute to this disappointing screen adaptation of Hugh and Margaret Williams's West End hit. The plot rests on the romantic complications that ensue when American multi-millionaire Mitchum takes a tour of English earl Cary Grant's stately home and falls for his wife, played by Deborah Kerr. Meanwhile, Jean Simmons makes a play for Grant. Director Stanley Donen, usually at home with soufflé-light comedy romance, fails to rescue this one from its all-too-evident stage origins, a leaden script and uncharacteristically flat performances from both Grant and Kerr.

Cary Grant *Victor Rhyall* • Deborah Kerr *Hilary Rhyall* • Robert Mitchum *Charles Delacro* • Jean Simmons *Hattie* • Moray Watson *Sellers* ■ *Dir* Stanley Donen • *Scr* Hugh Williams, Margaret Williams, from their play

The Grasshopper
★

Drama   1970 · US · Colour · 95mins

Bored with her small-town life in British Columbia, Jacqueline Bisset becomes a Las Vegas showgirl and pop star's girlfriend. Then she moves to Los Angeles, gets beaten up and learns the meaning of life. Produced and scripted by Garry Marshall and Jerry Belson, the team behind the sitcoms *Happy Days* and *Mork and Mindy*, this is a flashily directed ''message movie'' dressed up with lots of sex and violence. The only consistent factors are Bisset's beauty and her jittery acting style. Contains swearing and scenes of violence.

Jacqueline Bisset *Christine* • Jim Brown *Tommy Marcott* • Joseph Cotten *Richard Morgan* • Corbett Monica *Danny* • Ramon Bieri *Roosevelt Dekker* • Christopher Stone *Jay Rigney* • Roger Garrett *Buck* • Stanley Adams *Buddy Miller* ■ *Dir* Jerry Paris • *Scr* Jerry Belson, Garry Marshall, from the novel *The Passing of Evil* by Mark McShane

Grave Secrets: the Legacy of Hilltop Drive
★★ 15

Horror   1992 · US · Colour · 93mins

This is allegedly based on a true story, although the more sceptical among you might say the participants have seen

Poltergeist too many times. David Soul and Patty Duke are the nice suburban couple who move into their dream home, only to discover that not only is it haunted but the development has been built on top of an ancient burial site. Being a TV movie, director John Patterson doesn't really get the chance to spring any real shocks and, although the true story angle makes it a bit of a curiosity, it's nowhere near as much fun as Tobe Hooper's 1982 exhilarating ride. 🖭

Jonelle Allen *Madeline Garrick* • David Selby *Shag Williams* • Patty Duke *Jean Williams* • David Soul *Sam Haney* ■ *Dir* John Patterson • *Scr* Gregory Goodell

Gravesend
★★★ 18

Drama   1995 · US · Colour · 81mins

Nineteen-year-old Salvatore Stabile's feature debut – made for just $5,000 – may feel like an early Martin Scorsese venture, but the legend above the title reads ''Oliver Stone presents''. The reason for his involvement? A breathless ''stash the stiff'' opus that frantically blends voice-overs, flashbacks, character profiles and graveyard humour. However, it never loses sight of the fact that this isn't just a madcap adventure for its quartet of Brooklyn buddies, but part of a dead-end nightmare. Steven Spielberg was so impressed with Stabile's work he offered him a contract at DreamWorks. Contains swearing and violence. 🖭

Thomas Brandise *Mikey* • Tom Malloy *Chicken* • Michael Parducci *Ray* • Tony Tucci *Zane* • Sean Quinn *Mark* • Carmel Altomare *Zane's mother* • Teresa Spinelli *Zane's grandmother* ■ *Dir/Scr* Salvatore Stabile

Graveyard Shift
★★★ 18

Supernatural horror
1986 · US/Can · Colour · 82mins

An intriguing modern-dress vampire movie that plays rather like *Taxi Driver* with a screenplay by Bram Stoker. Its bloodsucker hero, credibly brought to life (after death) by Silvio Oliviero, works nights as a New York cabbie – a great way to meet potential supper guests. Director Gerard Ciccoritti shows great flair for fetishist images (blood crawling down a stiletto heel) though his rock video-style technique ultimately grates. But the urban night-time setting is neatly evoked, despite the fact the film was actually shot in Toronto, which implausibly doubles for Manhattan. It was followed by an underwhelming sequel, *The Understudy: Graveyard Shift II*. 🖭

Silvio Oliviero *Stephen Tsepes* • Helen Papas *Michelle* • Cliff Stoker *Eric Hayden* • Dorin Ferber *Gilda* ■ *Dir* Gerard Ciccoritti [Gérard Ciccoritti] • *Scr* Gerard Ciccoritti

The Gravy Train
★★

Action comedy   1974 · US · Colour · 95mins

Stacy Keach and Frederic Forrest are brothers, both no-hopers and low-lifes, who join up with Barry Primus and rob an armoured car. When Primus runs away with all the money and Margot Kidder, he provides an ample excuse for an hour or so of vengeful bloodletting, as well as some social comments about the nightmare of the American Dream – the level of violence

is almost in the Sam Peckinpah class. The result is an efficient piece of work, pacily directed by Jack Starrett and co-written by one David Whitney – a pseudonym adopted by Terrence Malick, who had just made his directing debut with *Badlands*.

Stacy Keach *Calvin Dion* • Frederic Forrest *Russell Dion* • Margot Kidder *Margie* • Barry Primus *Tony* • Richard Romanus *Carlo* • Denny Miller *Rex* • Jack Starrett *Rancher* ■ *Dir* Jack Starrett • *Scr* Bill Kerby, David Whitney [Terrence Malick]

Gray Lady Down
★★★ PG

Disaster drama   1978 · US · Colour · 105mins

A flurry of clichés almost engulfs this aquatic thriller about a Charlton Heston-commanded nuclear submarine stuck on the edge of an ocean canyon and awaiting a Stacy Keach-commanded rescue mission. Everything that can happen does happen, from ramming by a Norwegian freighter to earth slides, but David Greene's direction transcends banalities with pace and panache, while Heston's authority is the sort that could walk on water. 🖭

Charlton Heston *Captain Paul Blanchard* • David Carradine *Captain Gates* • Stacy Keach *Captain Bennett* • Ned Beatty *Mickey* • Stephen McHattie *Murphy* • Ronny Cox *Commander Samuelson* • Dorian Harewood *Fowler* • Rosemary Forsyth *Vickie* ■ *Dir* David Greene • *Scr* Howard Sackler, James Whittaker, Frank P Rosenberg, from the novel *Event 1000* by David Lavallee

Grayeagle
★★ PG

Western   1977 · US · Colour · 99mins

Charles B Pierce is a truly independent film-maker, who frequently writes, produces and directs his movies, and has even been known to act as his own cinematographer. Here, he attempts a low-rent version of John Ford's classic *The Searchers*, this time telling the story from the Indians' point of view, with Ben Johnson (Ford's own discovery) in the lead and Natalie Wood's sister Lana as the girl kidnapped by the Cheyenne. Pierce himself appears in a small role, but unfortunately lacks both acting ability and charisma. With a cast that also includes Jack Elam, this isn't unwatchable, but its aspirations to worthiness soon become tiresome. 🖭

Ben Johnson *John Colter* • Iron Eyes Cody *Standing Bear* • Lana Wood *Beth Colter* • Jack Elam *Trapper Willis* • Paul Fix *Running Wolf* • Alex Cord *Grayeagle* • Jacob Daniels *Scar* • Jimmy Clem *Abe Stoud* • Charles B Pierce *Bugler* ■ *Dir/Scr* Charles B Pierce

Gray's Anatomy
★★★

Comedy   1996 · US/UK · Colour · 80mins

The writer and actor Spalding Gray is probably best known for his filmed monologue *Swimming to Cambodia*, inspired by his experiences as a minor cast member of *The Killing Fields*, and directed by Jonathan Demme. *Gray's Anatomy* is another such monologue, this time starting from Gray's discovery of a sight defect that required some drastic surgery. Steven Soderbergh (*sex, lies, and videotape*) films Gray at a desk, circling him and presenting a strange assortment of backdrops for the diverting and wildly discursive talk. Be warned: the film begins with some shocking images of eye injuries. Contains swearing.

Spalding Gray ■ *Dir* Steven Soderbergh • *Scr* Spalding Gray, Renée Shafransky, from their performance piece

Grease ★★★★ 🅟🅖

Musical 1978 · US · Colour · 105mins

Fresh from *Saturday Night Fever*, John Travolta was the biggest movie star in the world when he teamed with Olivia Newton-John to help turn one of Broadway's biggest ever hits into one of Hollywood's most successful musicals. The film aims to evoke nostalgia for a time before most of its audience would have been born – fifties' America with Rydell High as the setting for a rather slender tale of teenage love, pre-Vietnam innocence and DA hairdos. It succeeds in the task, thanks to some toe-tapping numbers, spritely hoofing and slick performances, not least by Stockard Channing as the most unruly teenager in town. 🖵

John Travolta *Danny Zucco* • Olivia Newton-John *Sandy Olsson* • Stockard Channing *Betty Rizzo* • Jeff Conaway *Kenickie* • Barry Pearl *Doody* • Michael Tucci *Sonny* • Kelly Ward *Putzie* ■ *Dir* Randal Kleiser • *Scr* Bronte Woodard, Allan Carr, from the musical by Warren Casey, Jim Jacobs

Grease 2 ★★ 🅟🅖

Musical 1982 · US · Colour · 109mins

An unprepossessing sequel to the massive John Travolta/Olivia Newton-John hit, this is notable for a great title song by the Four Tops and a then-unknown Michelle Pfeiffer in a clinging short skirt. This is the story of Rydell High some years on from those halcyon days of drainpipe trousers and stiff petticoats. The problem is that director and choreographer Patricia Birch tries to bring those high steppin', arm-waving innocent production values to an altogether grittier era of emerging sixties liberalism. It doesn't work. Look out for relatives of the stars – Liza Minnelli's step-sister Lorna Luft is the most "distinguished". 🖵

Michelle Pfeiffer *Stephanie* • Maxwell Caulfield *Michael* • Didi Conn *Frenchy* • Eve Arden *Ms McGee* • Sid Caesar *Coach Calhoun* • Adrian Zmed *Johnny Nogerilli* • Christopher McDonald *Goose* • Peter Frechette *Lou Dimucci* • Lorna Luft *Paulette Rebchuck* ■ *Dir* Patricia Birch • *Scr* Ken Finkleman

Greased Lightning ★★ 🅟🅖

Biographical comedy
1977 · US · Colour · 92mins

Richard Pryor never really looks comfortable in this story of the America's first black stock-car racing driver, Wendell Scott, who battled prejudice to reach the top of his chosen profession. It's a fascinating story, but the main problem is that it never makes up its mind whether it is a straightforward biopic or a comedy. However, the supporting cast, which includes Beau Bridges and black film icon Pam Grier (*Jackie Brown*), can't be faulted, and there's some strong racing footage. 🖵

Richard Pryor *Wendell Scott* • Beau Bridges *Hutch* • Pam Grier *Mary Jones* • Cleavon Little *Peewee* • Vincent Gardenia *Sheriff Cotton* • Richie Havens *Woodrow* • Julian Bond *Russell*

• Earl Hindman *Beau Welles* ■ *Dir* Michael Schultz • *Scr* Kenneth Voze, Lawrence DuKore, Melvin Van Peebles, Leon Capetanos

Greaser's Palace ★★

Satirical western drama
1972 · US · Colour · 91mins

Ostensibly a western parody, this plotless comedy extravaganza from film-maker Robert Downey chronicles the exploits of a Christ-like figure called Zoot Suit (Allan Arbus) who descends upon an unsuspecting town en route to becoming a singer. Its audacious, nutball approach is finally its undoing, becoming a technically proficient slice of allegorical pretentiousness. Downey didn't direct another film until 1980's dreadful *Up the Academy*.

Allan Arbus *Zoot Suit* • Albert Henderson *Seaweedhead Greaser* • Michael Sullivan *Lamy Greaser* • Luana Anders *Cholera Greaser* • James Antonio [Jim Antonio] *Vernon* • George Morgan *Coo Coo* • Ron Nealy *Ghost/Card Man* • Larry Moyer *Captain Good* ■ *Dir/Scr* Robert Downey

The Great Adventure ★★★ 🅤

Adventure 1953 · Swe · BW · 73mins

This internationally acclaimed drama from film-maker Arne Sucksdorff won a prize at the Cannes film festival in 1954. Set in Sweden, it tells the simple story of two boys who secretly befriend an otter over one winter's season but then find that the animal wants to return to the wild. Visually striking, this showed nature without any hint of Disney-esque sentiment. Veteran documentary film-maker Sucksdorff not only directed the film but also wrote, produced, edited, photographed and acted in it. In Swedish with English subtitles.

Anders Norborg *Anders* • Kjell Sucksdorff *Kjell* • Arne Sucksdorff *Father* • Norman Shelley *Narrator* • Gunnar Sjoberg *Narrator* ■ *Dir/Scr* Arne Sucksdorff

The Great American Broadcast ★★★ 🅤

Musical drama 1941 · US · BW · 91mins

A cheerfully fictionalised account of the early days of American radio, culminating in the first coast-to-coast hook-up of stations. This breezy Fox musical casts Jack Oakie and John Payne as ambitious entrepreneurs and Alice Faye as their singing star, with the trio going through the usual break-ups and reconciliations. With some catchy songs (by Mack Gordon and Harry Warren) and cameos by such wireless celebrities as Jack Benny and Rudy Vallee, it's a generous measure of relaxing entertainment.

Alice Faye *Vicki Adams* • Jack Oakie *Chuck Hadley* • John Payne *Rix Martin* • Cesar Romero *Bruce Chadwick* • James Newill *Singer* • The Four Ink Spots • The Nicholas Brothers • The Wiere Brothers ■ *Dir* Archie Mayo • *Scr* Don Ettlinger, Edwin Blum, Robert Ellis, Helen Logan

The Great American Cowboy ★★★

Documentary 1973 · US · Colour · 90mins

This Oscar-winning documentary takes an inside look at rodeo as a

professional sport. Spending months on the road with the riders travelling from one prize contest to the next, director Kieth Merrill and writer Douglas Kent Hall focus on a veteran star (Larry Mahan) and his younger rival (Phil Lyne). Subjective camerawork involves the audience in the thrills and spills of the arena, while slow-motion dissects the high-speed action. Overlong for all but rodeo devotees, it has the bonus of warm narration by retired cowboy star Joel McCrea.

Joel McCrea *Narrator* ■ *Dir* Kieth Merrill • *Scr* Douglas Kent Hall

The Great American Sex Scandal ★★

Comedy drama based on a true story
1990 · US · Colour · 94mins

It is difficult to sympathise with a put-upon accountant who is wrongly accused of cooking the books. Dramatic, it isn't. The "sex" comes much later as the jury attempts to find out who is ultimately responsible for the hapless accountant's fate. This is one of those made-for-TV movies that takes as its theme a real-life scenario, but embellishes it beyond all believability. Lynn Redgrave turns in a neat performance and the rest of the cast does its best with a decent slice of old hokum that never scratches deeper than the first layer of skin.

Barbara Bosson *Evelyn* • Ilene Graff *Marilyn* • Bill Kirchenbauer *Nick Grady* • Heather Locklear *Rita* • Lynn Redgrave *Abby* • William G Schilling *Harold* • Tracy Scoggins *Hope Hathaway* • Alan Thicke *Phil* ■ *Dir* Michael A Schultz [Michael Schultz] • *Scr* Rob Gilmer

The Great Balloon Adventure ★★

Adventure 1978 · US · Colour · 83mins

Katharine Hepburn waited two years for director Richard A Colla to finance this amiable family adventure, and then refused to take a penny in payment. The Hollywood veteran even insisted on doing her own stunts, after complaining that the stand-in dangling above the ground by a rope looked nothing like her. When asked why she took on the role of a junk dealer who helps a couple of boys rebuild their grandfather's balloon and re-create his famous circus act, she confessed that the film fulfilled a long-standing ambition to fly in a hot-air balloon.

Katharine Hepburn *Miss Pudd* • Kevin McKenzie *Alby* • Dennis Dimster *Chris* • Obie Joshua ■ *Dir* Richard A Colla • *Scr* Eugene Poinc, from a story by Maria L de Ossio, Eugene Poinc, Richard A Colla

Great Balls of Fire! ★★★ 🅕🅔

Musical biography
1989 · US · Colour · 107mins

There's a whole lotta shakin' goin' on in *The Big Easy* director Jim McBride's bright rock 'n' roll biography of Jerry Lee Lewis, played with style and flash by the always watchable Dennis Quaid. It's an entertaining romp, following Jerry Lee's life in the fifties up to his fall from grace in London after he married his 13-year-old cousin Myra (sweetly played by Winona Ryder). It's Quaid's on-the-edge performance and the music that makes this so much fun, plus the able support from Ryder,

Alec Baldwin (as the evangelist Jimmy Swaggart) and Trey Wilson. 🖵

Dennis Quaid *Jerry Lee Lewis* • Winona Ryder *Myra Gale Lewis* • John Doe *JW Brown* • Stephen Tobolowsky *John Phillips* • Trey Wilson *Sam Phillips* • Alec Baldwin *Jimmy Swaggart* • Joe Bob Briggs *Dewey "Daddy-O" Phillips* ■ *Dir* Jim McBride • *Scr* Jim McBride, Jack Baran, from the non-fiction book by Myra Lewis, Murray Silver

The Great Bank Robbery ★★ 🅤

Comedy western 1969 · US · Colour · 97mins

The idea of robbing a bank so safe that it's where the likes of Jesse James keep their loot is an amusing one, but a leaden screenplay from *The Exorcist's* William Peter Blatty and the desperately uneven direction of Hy Averback defeat the best efforts of the eclectic cast to bring the premise to life. Zero Mostel is disastrously miscast as a phoney evangelist, while "wooden" is too kind an adjective to describe the performances of Clint Walker and Kim Novak. Veterans Akim Tamiroff, Claude Akins and, especially, John Anderson almost save the day, but the relentless uncertainty of tone sinks even their best endeavours.

Zero Mostel *Reverend Pious Blue* • Kim Novak *Lyda Kabanov* • Clint Walker *Ben Quick* • Claude Akins *Slade* • Akim Tamiroff *Papa Pedro* • Larry Storch *Juan* • John Anderson *Kincaid* • Sam Jaffe *Brother Lilac* • Elisha Cook Jr *Jeb* ■ *Dir* Hy Averback • *Scr* William Peter Blatty, from the novel by Frank O'Rourke

The Great British Train Robbery ★★★

Crime drama 1966 · W Ger · BW · 104mins

Based on Peta Fordham's book *The Robbers' Tale: the Real Story of the Great Train Robbery*, this German movie is a surprisingly effective reconstruction of the audacious raid on a Royal Mail train that resulted in the theft of £2.6 million. Capturing the atmosphere of sixties London with sharp black-and-white photography, directors John Olden and Claus Peter Witt adopt a brisk, workmanlike style befitting the pseudo-documentary approach to the planning and execution of the robbery. Horst Tappert and the rest of the gang turn in unfussy performances and there is an end-of-career part for Isa Miranda. German dialogue dubbed into English.

Horst Tappert *Michael Donegan* • Hans Cossy *Patrick Kinsey* • Karl Heinz Hess *Geoffrey Black* • Günter Neutze *Archibald Arrow* • Hans Reiser *Thomas Webster* • Rolf Nagel *Gerald Williams* • Harry Engel *George Slowfoot* • Isa Miranda *Mona* ■ *Dir* John Olden, Claus Peter Witt • *Scr* Henry Kolarz, Robert Muller, from the book *The Robbers' Tale: the Real Story of the Great Train Robbery* by Peta Fordham

The Great Caruso ★★★★ 🅤

Musical biography
1951 · US · Colour · 104mins

A popular and sentimentalised biopic of the legendary tenor, a role MGM's own lyric tenor Mario Lanza was born to play. The ramshackle screenplay doesn't really matter as Lanza performs such full-blooded arias as *La Donna e Mobile*, *Celeste Aida* and *Vesti la Giubba* in that remarkable golden voice, although the actual hit

song from the movie was *The Loveliest Night of the Year*, sung by Lanza's co-star, Ann Blyth. This was Lanza's biggest success in an all-too-short career that ended with his early death at the age of 38. ▭

Mario Lanza *Enrico Caruso* • Ann Blyth *Dorothy Benjamin* • Dorothy Kirsten *Louise Heggar* • Jarmila Novotna *Maria Selka* • Richard Hageman *Carlo Santi* • Carl Benton Reid *Park Benjamin* ■ *Dir* Richard Thorpe • *Scr* Sonia Levien, William Ludwig, from a story by Dorothy Caruso

Great Catherine ★ U

Historical comedy
1968 · UK · Colour · 98mins
Based on a play by George Bernard Shaw, this farrago about the romantic life of the Empress of Russia is more like a *Carry On* movie transferred to St Petersburg. Peter O'Toole breezes through it all as an English Light Dragoons captain who finds himself in the Empress's bedchamber, while arthouse heroine Jeanne Moreau is hopelessly miscast as Catherine. The jokes are constantly telegraphed, and the flashy, tricksy direction roots the film in the Swinging Sixties.

Peter O'Toole *Captain Edstaston* • Zero Mostel *Patiomkin* • Jeanne Moreau *Catherine* • Jack Hawkins *Sir George Gorse* • Akim Tamiroff *Sergeant* • Marie Lohr *Dowager Lady Gorse* • Kenneth Griffith *Naryshkin* ■ *Dir* Gordon Flemyng • *Scr* Hugh Leonard, from the play *Great Catherine Whom Glory Still Adores* by George Bernard Shaw

Great Day ★ U

Drama
1944 · UK · BW · 79mins
As the village of Denley prepares to welcome First Lady Eleanor Roosevelt, alcoholic First World War veteran Eric Portman disgraces himself by stealing from a lady's purse. His daughter, Sheila Sim, dithers over whether she should marry her boss, while his wife, Flora Robson, dedicates herself to the Womens' Guild. This American-financed aberration, based on the play by Lesley Storm, feels like an episode of *Mrs Dale's Diary* and would have been better suited to the radio.

Eric Portman *Captain Ellis* • Flora Robson *Mrs Ellis* • Sheila Sim *Margaret Ellis* • Isabel Jeans *Lady Mott* • Walter Fitzgerald *John Tyndale* • Philip Friend *Geoffrey Winthrop* • Marjorie Rhodes *Mrs Mumford* ■ *Dir* Lance Comfort • *Scr* Wolfgang Wilhelm, John Davenport, from a play by Lesley Storm

A Great Day in Harlem ★★★★★ U

Music documentary
1994 · US · BW and Colour · 59mins
A famous photograph of 57 jazz musicians and a club owner outside a Harlem brownstone is the starting point for this stunningly inventive documentary. The shot covers every jazz generation up to 1958 and includes Dizzy Gillespie and Sonny Rollins. Director Jean Bach splices together voice-overs, snappy interviews, promotional films and home movies to unearth not just the spontaneity and uncertainty of jazz life, but also to home in on its passion, sensitivity and morality. Incidentally, it was *Kramer vs Kramer* director Robert Benton, then art director at *Esquire*, who commissioned the photograph.

Quincy Jones *Narrator* ■ *Dir* Jean Bach • *Scr* Jean Bach, Susan Peehl, Matthew Seig

Great Day in the Morning ★★★

Western   1956 · US · Colour · 91mins
Strikingly shot by William Snyder against the jaw-dropping landscape of the Colorado Territory, this eve-of-Civil-War western boasts a highly literate script and a redoubtable performance from Robert Stack as a southern maverick forced to choose between patriotism and his pocket. The dialogue is sharp-tongued, the action is serviceably staged and there is impressive support from Raymond Burr and Alex Nicol. But Jacques Tourneur, one of Hollywood's finest B-movie directors, was at a loss for the inspiration that would have transformed the film from the adequate into the admirable.

Robert Stack *Owen Pentecost* • Virginia Mayo *Ann Merry Alaine* • Ruth Roman *Boston Grant* • Alex Nicol *Stephen Kirby* • Raymond Burr *Jumbo Means* • Leo Gordon *Zeff Masterson* ■ *Dir* Jacques Tourneur • *Scr* Lesser Samuels, from the novel by Robert Hardy Andrews

The Great Diamond Robbery ★★ PG

Comedy crime   1953 · US · BW · 87mins
Red Skelton was one of the great American clowns. A vaudevillian, he became a radio favourite in the forties. But it was in film and television that his particular brand of gurning and slapstick really made its mark. He was already well established by the time he played a gullible diamond cutter conned by crooks, in what proved to be a disappointing end to his MGM career. Fortunately the comedian continued to enjoy huge success on the small screen where his own TV show ran for more than 20 years. ▭

Red Skelton *Ambrose C Park* • Cara Williams *Maggie Drumman* • James Whitmore *Remlick* • Kurt Kasznar *Tony* • Dorothy Stickney *Emily Drumman* • George Mathews *Duke Fargoh* ■ *Dir* Robert Z Leonard • *Scr* Laslo Vadnay, Martin Rackin, from a story by Laslo Vadnay

The Great Dictator ★★★★ U

Satirical comedy   1940 · US · BW · 124mins
Hitler didn't see the joke but he got the point. Charlie Chaplin's first dialogue feature was a satire on the anti-Semitic Nazi regime, with Chaplin in the dual role of a Jewish barber and dictator Adenoid Hynkel. The final speech, pleading for universal tolerance when the barber takes over from Hynkel, is mawkish outrage. Before that, however, we have had the glories of the barber shaving a customer in time to a Hungarian dance by Brahms contrasting with Hynkel's solo ballet with a globe of the world. Bliss, even though Chaplin said that, if he had known the real horror of the Nazis, he would never have made such a burlesque. ▭

Charlie Chaplin [Charles Chaplin] *Jewish barber/Hynkel, dictator of Tomania* • Paulette Goddard *Hannah* • Jack Oakie *Napaloni, dictator of Bacteria* • Reginald Gardiner *Schultz* • Henry Daniell *Garbitsch* • Billy Gilbert *Herring* • Grace Hayle *Madame Napaloni* •

Carter De Haven *Bacterian ambassador* ■ *Dir* Charlie Chaplin [Charles Chaplin] • *Scr* Charles Chaplin

The Great Elephant Escape ★★

Adventure   1995 · US · Colour · 93mins
Joseph Gordon-Levitt (*10 Things I Hate about You*) goes to Africa with his mum (Stephanie Zimbalist) where he befriends an orphaned elephant and she gets cosy with the infinitely less appealing Julian Sands. Shot on location in Kenya, this TV movie isn't exactly subtle but will appeal to animal lovers and those who believe that if you mistreat an elephant you should get your comeuppance.

Stephanie Zimbalist *Beverly Cunningham* • Joseph Gordon-Levitt *Matt Cunningham* • Leo Burmester *Harlo Ethridge* • Julian Sands *Clive Potter* ■ *Dir* George Miller (1) • *Scr* John Sweet, Christopher Canaan

The Great Escape ★★★★★ PG

Second World War action adventure
1963 · US · Colour · 172mins
Neither the passing of time nor the familiarity of its content have diminished the excitement of director John Sturges's terrific war film, an epic on the scale of his *Magnificent Seven* that was shot on authentic European locations. The climactic scenes are now rightly regarded as classic, and the characters have passed into folklore. Three of the "magnificent seven" are reunited (Steve McQueen, Charles Bronson and James Coburn) in a brilliant Anglo-American cast that couldn't be bettered, and Elmer Bernstein provides a march theme that is devastatingly moving in its aptly heroic simplicity. ▭ **DVD**

Steve McQueen *Hilts, "The Cooler King"* • James Garner *Hendley, "The Scrounger"* • Richard Attenborough *Bartlett, "Big X"* • Charles Bronson *Danny Velinski, "Tunnel King"* • Donald Pleasence *Blythe, "The Forger"* • James Donald *Ramsey, "The SBO"* • James Coburn *Sedgwick, "Manufacturer"* • Gordon Jackson *MacDonald, "Intelligence"* • David McCallum *Ashley-Pitt, "Dispersal"* ■ *Dir* John Sturges • *Scr* James Clavell, WR Burnett, from a book by Paul Brickhill

The Great Escape II: the Untold Story ★ PG

Second World War action adventure
1988 · US · Colour · 178mins
John Sturges's 1963 film, a box-office smash, can legitimately claim to be the greatest PoW movie of all time. Paul Wendkos's 1988 effort most certainly isn't. It's a remake of sorts which tacks on an extra hour or so in order to trace the surviving prisoners of war, as well as their German guards. Christopher Reeve plays a British officer, while the only cast member from the original film, Donald Pleasence, has inexplicably changed sides to become a Nazi soldier. ▭

Christopher Reeve *Major John Dodge* • Judd Hirsch *Captain Matthews* • Anthony Denison [Anthony John Denison] *Lt Mike Corey* • Charles Haid *Sgt MacKenzie* • Ian McShane *Roger Bushell* • Donald Pleasence *Dr Absalon* ■ *Dir* Paul Wendkos • *Scr* Walter Halsey Davis

Great Expectations ★★★★★ PG

Classic period drama
1946 · UK · BW · 113mins
This may be the best ever film adaptation of a Charles Dickens novel, not to mention the best film ever made by the best director Britain has ever produced – no small claim given that David Lean went on to make *The Bridge on the River Kwai, Doctor Zhivago* and *Lawrence of Arabia*. The film won Oscars for black-and-white cinematography and art direction, and was unlucky not to get nominations for best film, director and screenplay. In short, no mean movie, with John Mills, Bernard Miles, Jean Simmons and Alec Guinness (in his movie debut with the exception of a small part in *Evensong*, 12 years before) all first-rate. A must-see. ▭

John Mills *Pip as an adult* • Valerie Hobson *Estella as an adult* • Bernard Miles *Joe Gargery* • Francis L Sullivan *Jaggers* • Martita Hunt *Miss Havisham* • Finlay Currie *Abel Magwitch* • Alec Guinness *Herbert Pocket* • Ivor Barnard *Wemmick* • Anthony Wager *Pip as a child* • Jean Simmons *Estella as a child* ■ *Dir* David Lean • *Scr* David Lean, Ronald Neame, Anthony Havelock-Allan, Cecil McGivern, Kay Walsh, from the novel by Charles Dickens • *Cinematographer* Guy Green • *Art Director* John Bryan • *Editor* Jack Harris • *Art Director* Wilfred Shingleton

Great Expectations ★★ U

Period drama
1974 · US/UK · Colour · 118mins
Following the success of Carol Reed's version of *Oliver Twist*, it was only a matter of time before someone suggested another musical Dickens. Mercifully the songs were out – could you imagine *It's a Kind of Magwitch*? What's left is a retelling of Pip's progress in which the majority of scenes seem to be staged solely for the benefit of the big production number that never arrives and tell this superbly crafted story in the most simplistic way. Only Margaret Leighton's Miss Havisham rings true, with Michael York, Sarah Miles and James Mason miserably miscast. ▭

Michael York *Pip* • Sarah Miles *Estella* • Margaret Leighton *Miss Havisham* • James Mason *Magwitch* • Anthony Quayle *Jaggers* • Robert Morley *Pumblechook* • Joss Ackland *Joe Gargery* ■ *Dir* Joseph Hardy • *Scr* Sherman Yellen, from the novel by Charles Dickens

Great Expectations ★★★ U

Animated drama
1985 · Ausl · Colour · 69mins
One of a series of animated Dickens adaptations, this is a useful introduction for younger viewers to one of the author's most popular novels. Even taking into account the sensibilities of its audience, the film still wastes such key scenes as Pip's meeting with Magwitch in the marshes and the visits to Miss Havisham's creepy house. However, director Jean Tych does succeed in making London seem a far less inviting place than Joe Gargery's forge. ▭

Bill Kerr • Phillip Hinton • Simon Hinton • Barbara Hawley ■ *Dir* Jean Tych • *Scr* from the novel by Charles Dickens

Great Expectations ★★★ 🅸🅵

Romantic drama
1997 · US · Colour · 106mins

After the minor miracle he worked with *A Little Princess*, Alfonso Cuarón rather lost the plot with this Dickens update. Clearly keen to avoid comparison with David Lean's 1946 masterpiece, he opted for a loose retelling centred on the eerie Everglades and the New York art scene. But while he lashes on the style, he fumbles the book's underlying themes. He's also ill-served by his leads, with Ethan Hawke consumed by sensitivity and Gwyneth Paltrow too shallow to be a worthy object of obsession. So it's left to a gleefully deranged Anne Bancroft and a caringly criminal Robert De Niro to provide any actorly substance. Contains swearing and some violence. ▭

Ethan Hawke *Finnegan Bell* • Gwyneth Paltrow *Estella* • Hank Azaria *Walter Plane* • Chris Cooper *Joe* • Anne Bancroft *Nora Diggers Dinsmoor* • Robert De Niro *Lustig* • Josh Mostel *Jerry Ragno* • Kim Dickens *Maggie* ■ Dir Alfonso Cuarón • Scr Mitch Glazer, from the novel by Charles Dickens

The Great Flamarion ★★★

Film noir
1945 · US · BW · 78mins

In this imaginative low-budget *film noir*, the great Erich von Stroheim (then past his peak) teamed up with talented young director, Anthony Mann, who went on to direct a series of classic fifties westerns like *Winchester 73*. Von Stroheim has the title role of the vaudeville sharpshooter who, despite an unhappy history with women, makes the mistake of falling for his alluring young assistant, played by Mary Beth Hughes. Of course this is very bad news for Hughes's husband, played by Dan Duryea. The film was made on such a shoestring that a park scene had to be faked on a soundstage with just a bench, a lamp and thick fog.

Erich von Stroheim *Flamarion* • Mary Beth Hughes *Connie Wallace* • Dan Duryea *Al Wallace* • Steve Barclay [Stephen Barclay] *Eddie* • Lester Allen *Tony* ■ Dir Anthony Mann • Scr Anne Wighton, Heinz Herald, Richard Weil, from the story *Big Shot* by Vicki Baum

The Great Gabbo ★★★

Musical drama
1929 · US · BW · 92mins

Considering he arrived on the set of this hokey melodrama fully aware that the disaster of his extravagant melodrama *Queen Kelly* had all but signalled the end of his illustrious directing career, Erich von Stroheim gives an outstanding performance as the egomaniacal ventriloquist who allows his dummy to speak the words of his heart. Based on a story by Ben Hecht and directed with no little style by James Cruze, the film slows slightly in the second half to accommodate a number of vaudeville acts (which were originally shown in somewhat blurred colour). But it's impossible to take your eyes off von Stroheim

Erich von Stroheim *Gabbo* • Betty Compson *Mary* • Don Douglas *Frank* • Margie "Babe" Kane *Babe* ■ Dir James Cruze • Scr Hugh Herbert, from the story *The Rival Dummy* by Ben Hecht

The Great Garrick ★★★ 🆄

Comedy
1937 · UK · BW · 90mins

Brian Aherne is the famous 18th-century actor David Garrick, who tells his London audience that he's been invited to perform at the Comédie Française and intends to give the French a lesson in acting. Hearing this, French actors hatch a plot to discredit Garrick as he spends a night in Calais. This is a bright and breezy affair, although it amounts to little more than a charade. It's lavishly made by Warner Bros, with Aherne's future sister-in-law, Olivia de Havilland, adding to the fun, plus, in her second featured role, Lana Turner. The stylish direction is by James Whale.

Brian Aherne *David Garrick* • Olivia de Havilland *Germaine De Le Corbe* • Edward Everett Horton *Tubby* • Melville Cooper *M Picard* • Luis Alberni *Basset* • Lionel Atwill *Beaumarchais* • Marie Wilson *Nicolle* • Lana Turner *Auber* ■ Dir James Whale • Scr Ernest Vadja, from his play *Ladies and Gentleman*

The Great Gatsby ★★★ 🆄

Drama
1949 · US · BW · 91mins

Previously filmed in 1926, F Scott Fitzgerald's novel provides plenty of plot for a screenwriter to work with, but his silky style simply refuses to translate to the screen. Alan Ladd's limited acting technique almost accidentally conveys some of the mystery of the millionaire who becomes the toast of Long Island society. But while he valiantly attempts to look enigmatic, Betty Field blows the whole illusion with a gauche interpretation of Daisy Buchanan, the socialite whose murder of her husband's mistress leads to further tragedy. Elliott Nugent directs with some noirish touches, but can't counter screenwriter Richard Maibaum's verbosity.

Alan Ladd *Jay Gatsby* • Betty Field *Daisy Buchanan* • Macdonald Carey *Nick Carraway* • Ruth Hussey *Jordan Baker* • Barry Sullivan *Tom Buchanan* • Howard Da Silva *Wilson* • Shelley Winters *Myrtle Wilson* • Henry Hull *Dan Cody* • Carole Mathews *Ella Cody* ■ Dir Elliott Nugent • Scr Cyril Hume, Richard Maibaum, from the play by Owen Davis, from the novel by F Scott Fitzgerald

The Great Gatsby ★★★ 🅿🅶

Romantic drama
1974 · US · Colour · 135mins

Over an hour longer than the 1949 version, this was Paramount's third stab at bringing F Scott Fitzgerald's jazz-age classic to the screen. Robert Redford is unquestionably more handsome than Alan Ladd, but he's no more demonstrative or credible as the millionaire with a dark past. Mia Farrow, meanwhile, is better cast than Betty Field, though her Daisy Buchanan is more skittishly irresponsible than irresistibly infatuating. While Jack Clayton's direction is suitably languid, the lush imagery only reinforces the superficiality of Francis Ford Coppola's reverential script. ▭

Robert Redford *Jay Gatsby* • Mia Farrow *Daisy Buchanan* • Bruce Dern *Tom Buchanan* • Karen Black *Myrtle Wilson* • Scott Wilson *George Wilson* • Sam Waterston *Nick Carraway* • Lois Chiles *Jordan Baker* ■ Dir Jack Clayton • Scr Francis Ford Coppola, from the novel by F Scott Fitzgerald

The Great Georgia Bank Hoax ★★★

Comedy
1977 · US · Colour · 93mins

The Watergate scandal was still haunting the US when this satire about corruption in a Georgia bank was released. The lightweight plot was given added resonance by the (intentional) Watergate references, as one case of embezzlement leads to an even bigger scam by the bank's boss, Burgess Meredith. Richard Basehart and the always reliable Ned Beatty add a touch of class to proceedings.

Burgess Meredith *Jack* • Richard Basehart *Emanuel* • Ned Beatty *Julius* • Charlene Dallas *Cathy* • Paul Sand *Richard* • Michael Murphy *Manigma* • Constance Forslund *Patricia* ■ Dir/Scr Joseph Jacoby

Great Guns ★★ 🅿🅶

Comedy
1941 · US · BW · 70mins

Laurel and Hardy's first feature for 20th Century-Fox is a plodding army comedy with echoes of their own *Pack Up Your Troubles* and the Abbott and Costello hit *Buck Privates*, which had been released earlier the same year. Directed by Monty Banks, the veteran of comedies with George Formby and Banks's own wife Gracie Fields, the film has sadly too little Stan and Ollie and far too much of a romance between Sheila Ryan and Dick Nelson. It's vaguely vintage, so savour the laughs when they come. ▭

Stan Laurel *Stan* • Oliver Hardy *Ollie* • Sheila Ryan *Ginger Hammond* • Dick Nelson *Dan Forrester* • Edmund MacDonald *Hippo* • Charles Trowbridge *Colonel Ridley* • Ludwig Stossel *Dr Schickel* • Kane Richmond *Captain Baker* ■ Dir Monty Banks • Scr Lou Breslow

Great Guy ★★

Crime drama
1936 · US · BW · 73mins

James Cagney was in dispute with his regular employer, Warner Bros, when he appeared in this movie for minor studio, Grand National. This weak crime drama lacked the Warners gloss, but Cagney makes a point of abandoning his tough-guy image, playing an incorruptible weights-and-measures inspector who exposes a food scam to cheat customers. There is less than the usual violence, and he even allows himself to be bossed around by Mae Clarke, the actress who received his celebrated grapefruit massage in *The Public Enemy*.

James Cagney *Johnny Cave* • Mae Clarke *Janet Henry* • James Burke *Pat Haley* • Edward Brophy *Pete Reilly* • Henry Kolker *Conning* • Bernadene Hayes *Hazel Scott* ■ Dir John G Blystone • Scr Henry McCarty, Horace McCoy, Henry Johnson, Henry Ruskin, from the stories by James Edward Grant

The Great Impostor ★★ 🆄

Biographical comedy adventure
1960 · US · BW · 112mins

By the time he made this biopic of Ferdinand Waldo Demara Jr, a notorious real-life imposter, Tony Curtis had proved that he wasn't just a pretty face. But even his considerable comic gifts were not enough to sustain this episodic, mildly amusing comedy, in which he masquerades as a professor, a Trappist monk, a navy surgeon and (most impressively) a prison

administrator who manages to forestall a riot. It's a pity that in this potentially interesting case history, the character's motivations are never sufficiently explained.

Tony Curtis *Ferdinand Waldo Demara Jr* • Edmond O'Brien *Captain Glover* • Arthur O'Connell *Warden Chandler* • Gary Merrill *Pa Demara* • Robert Middleton *Brown* • Doodles Weaver *Farmer* ■ Dir Robert Mulligan • Scr Liam O'Brien, from the book by Robert Crichton

The Great Jewel Robber ★★

Crime drama based on a true story
1950 · US · BW · 91mins

David Brian, probably best known today for his starring role in the popular TV series *Mr District Attorney*, parades his burly talents on the other side of the law as the titular criminal of this efficient programme filler, based on a true story. The director is the under-rated British expatriate Peter Godfrey, who was beginning his decline from Warner Bros features through credits like this to work on TV series. This is pleasing enough, but nothing special.

David Brian *Gerard Dennis* • Marjorie Reynolds *Martha* • Jacqueline de Wit *Mrs Vinson* • Alice Talton [Alix Talton] *Brenda* • John Archer *Sampter* • Perdita Chandler *Peggy* • Robert B Williams *Captain Ryan* ■ Dir Peter Godfrey • Scr Borden Chase, from the story *The Life of Gerard Graham Dennis* by Borden Chase, GG Dennis

The Great John L ★

Biographical sports drama
1945 · US · BW · 96mins

Bing Crosby turned producer with this lumbering biopic of a heavyweight boxer who marries a vaudeville star, turns to drink and sinks ever lower from there. Crosby snapped hunky Greg McClure from a small theatre in Los Angeles to play the title role and tied him to a multi-picture contract. It's a demanding role, the sort that Tracy, Errol Flynn or Victor McLaglen could have eaten for breakfast, and McClure clearly isn't up to it. But worst of all, the story, telling of the boxer's loss of self respect and sudden rehabilitation, has that Crosby overlay of schmaltz.

Greg McClure *John L Sullivan* • Linda Darnell *Anne Livinstone* • Barbara Britton *Kathy Harkness* • Lee Sullivan *Mickey* • Otto Kruger *Richard Martin* • Wallace Ford *McManus* • George Mathews *John Flood* • Robert Barrat *Billy Muldoon* ■ Dir Frank Tuttle • Scr James Edward Grant

Great Land of the Small ★★★ 🆄

Fantasy
1987 · Can · Colour · 87mins

A children's fantasy that genuinely conveys the imagination and innocence of childhood by creating a credible child's world. It nonetheless pulls no emotional punches as it tells the fetching tale of two kids from the city who learn all about invisible creatures and rainbows from their grandmother in the country. They then encounter a hobbit-like creature and help him in his quest for his missing gold dust. ▭

Karen Elkin *Jenny* • Michael Blouin *David* • Michael J Anderson *Fritz* • Ken Roberts *Flannigan* • Lorraine Desmarais *Mother* ■ Dir Vojtech Jasny • Scr David Sigmund

🆄 = SUITABLE FOR ALL   🆄🅲 = SUITABLE FOR ALL, ESPECIALLY FOR YOUNG CHILDREN (VIDEO ONLY)   🅿🅶 = PARENTAL GUIDANCE

The Great Lie ★★★★
Romantic melodrama 1941 · US · BW · 107mins

One of the greatest of Bette Davis's films at Warner Bros, which were once termed "women's pictures" and are now recognised as being among the finest products of the studio system. Here Davis is given more than a run for her money by co-star Mary Astor, who collected the best supporting actress Oscar as Davis's rival in love for handsome George Brent, allegedly Davis's lover in real life. The titular lie involves the "ownership" of Brent's child, and both female stars pull out all the stops. Director Edmund Goulding knows better than to hold them back, and ladles on the Tchaikovsky to boot, since Astor's character is a concert pianist.

Bette Davis *Maggie* • Mary Astor *Sandra* • George Brent *Pete Van Allen* • Lucile Watson *Aunt Ada* • Hattie McDaniel *Violet* • Grant Mitchell *Joshua Mason* • Jerome Cowan *Jock Thompson* • Charles Trowbridge *Senator Greenfield* ■ *Dir* Edmund Goulding • *Scr* Lenore Coffee, from the novel *January Heights* by Polan Blanks

The Great Lover ★★★
Comedy 1949 · US · BW · 80mins

One of Bob Hope's better vehicles casts him as a scoutmaster trying to cope with a group of dedicated "child foresters" on a transatlantic liner. The diversions include the beautiful daughter (Rhonda Fleming) of a penniless duke, and a cardsharp who is murdering passengers. The risible script makes room for a brief but splendid cameo by Jack Benny, and Richard Lyon plays one of the youths, urging the unwilling Hope to give up cigarettes and women. "A boy forester never makes a mistake," he tells Hope, who replies: "Too bad your parents weren't foresters."

Bob Hope *Freddie Hunter* • Rhonda Fleming *Duchess Alexandria* • Roland Young *CJ Dabney* • Roland Culver *Grand Duke Maximillian* • Richard Lyon *Stanley* • Jim Backus *Higgins* ■ *Dir* Alexander Hall • *Scr* Edmund Beloin, Melville Shavelson, Jack Rose

The Great McGinty ★★★★
Comedy 1940 · US · BW · 83mins

Don't be put off just because this is a comedy about American politics with no star names. Writer Preston Sturges persuaded Paramount to let him make his directing debut for a ten-dollar fee, and the result is this delicious study in comic irony. It's the story of a penniless Irishman who rises through a corrupt party machine to become governor of a state, then is ruined in a crazy minute of honesty. Proving as brilliant a director as he was a writer, Sturges won the Oscar for best original screenplay and opened the doors for other writers like Billy Wilder to direct their work. Brian Donlevy attacks his role with gusto, while supporting players shine in every scene.

Brian Donlevy *Dan McGinty* • Muriel Angelus *Catherine McGinty* • Akim Tamiroff *Boss* • Allyn Joslyn *George* • William Demarest *Politician* • Louis Jean Heydt *Thompson* • Harry Rosenthal *Louis the bodyguard* • Arthur Hoyt *Mayor Tillinghast* ■ *Dir/Scr* Preston Sturges

The Great McGonagall ★ 15
Comedy 1974 · UK · Colour · 84mins

Whatever the shortcomings of the Victorian versifier – the unemployed Scot who was determined to be the Queen's laureate – he didn't deserve this snide, incoherent jeering. Comedians Spike Milligan and Peter Sellers lead with the machetes, carving fun out of a simple-minded man whose verses didn't scan and whose thoughts were banal, but it's the mutual admiration society of the principals that scores its own goal. ▭

Spike Milligan *William McGonagall* • Peter Sellers *Queen Victoria* • Julia Foster *Mrs McGonagall* ■ *Dir* Joseph McGrath • *Scr* Spike Milligan, Joseph McGrath

The Great Madcap ★★★
Comedy 1949 · Mex · BW · 90mins

The second film of Luis Buñuel's Mexican comeback began as a jobbing assignment, but ended up dictating the way the master surrealist would work for the remainder of his career, by teaching him the value of meticulous pre-planning. Some have sought anti-bourgeois satire in drunken patriarch Fernando Soler's revenge on the worthless family that tried to trick him into believing he had squandered his fortune. But the storyline of this gentle comedy is pure Hollywood, as hard work brings out the best in those previously content to exploit. In Spanish with English subtitles.

Fernando Soler *Ramiro* • Rosario Granados *Virginia* • Andres Soler *Ladislao* ■ *Dir* Luis Buñuel, Fernando Soler • *Scr* Luis Alcoriza, Janet Alcoriza, from a play by Adolfo Torrado

The Great Man ★★★
Drama 1956 · US · BW · 92mins

Echoes of *Citizen Kane* ring around this hollow, cynical drama, in which a media personality's shining reputation is tarnished during the preparation of a tribute. Impressing more as co-writer and director than as star, José Ferrer can do little about the predictable manner in which skeletons tumble out of various closets, but he draws wonderfully embittered performances from his expert cast. Ed Wynn is outstanding as the radio boss who discovered the "Studio King", though Julie London's abused singer, Dean Jagger's network boss and Keenan Wynn's self-seeking executive are also strong. Slick and satirical, but lacking the depth to be truly satisfying.

José Ferrer *Joe Harris* • Dean Jagger *Philip Carleton* • Keenan Wynn *Sid Moore* • Julie London *Carol Larson* • Joanne Gilbert *Ginny* • Ed Wynn *Paul Beaseley* • Jim Backus *Nick Cellantano* • Russ Morgan *Eddie Brand* ■ *Dir* José Ferrer • *Scr* Al Morgan, José Ferrer, from the novel by Al Morgan

The Great Man Votes ★★ U
Drama 1939 · US · BW · 71mins

Sharpish political satire about floating voter John Barrymore whose personal problems – widower, drunkard, two kids to raise – make him the target of spin doctors. Clearly influenced by the success of Capra's films, such as *Mr Smith Goes to Washington*, this is a showcase for Barrymore's bloated talent, though by this time he was several years and several bottles past his prime.

John Barrymore *Gregory Vance* • Peter Holden *Donald Vance* • Virginia Weidler *Joan Vance* • Katherine Alexander *Miss Billow* • Donald MacBride *Iron Hat McCarthy* • Bennie Bartlett *Dave McCarthy* • Brandon Tynan *Chester Ainslee* • Elisabeth Risdon *Phoebe Ainslee* ■ *Dir* Garson Kanin • *Scr* John Twist, from a story by Gordon Malherbe Hillman

The Great Man's Lady ★★★
Western 1942 · US · BW · 90mins

A melodramatic western epic, irritatingly told in flashback and featuring Barbara Stanwyck made-up as a 100-year-old woman (nearly 30 years before *Little Big Man* and Dustin Hoffman). It tells the saga of how Stanwyck backed husband Joel McCrea in forging a town out of the wilderness, only to disagree about the eventual coming of the railroad. Director William A Wellman is at home with this kind of material, and much of the staging is impressive despite the slow pace.

Barbara Stanwyck *Hannah Sempler* • Joel McCrea *Ethan Hoyt* • Brian Donlevy *Steely Edwards* • Katharine Stevens [KT Stevens] *Girl biographer* • Thurston Hall *Mr Sempler* • Lloyd Corrigan *Mr Cadwallader* • Etta McDaniel *Delilah* • Frank M Thomas *Senator Knobs* • Lillian Yarbo *Mandy* ■ *Dir* William A Wellman • *Scr* WL River, Adela Rogers St John, Seena Owen, from the story *The Human Side* by Vina Delmar

The Great Moment ★★★★
Biography 1944 · US · BW · 80mins

How do you make an entertaining tribute to the forgotten dentist who first discovered the anaesthetic? The great comedy writer/director Preston Sturges had the answer, but audiences didn't want to know, giving him his one flop among a string of hits that included *The Lady Eve* and *The Palm Beach Story*. Without sacrificing scientific detail, Sturges embellishes the situations with valid slapstick humour, conveying the horror of an amputation before anaesthesia through the fainting of an unprepared onlooker (William Demarest). According to Sturges, the great moment in the life of the dentist, sensitively portrayed by Joel McCrea, is not his discovery, but a gesture of great humanity which ends the film on an upbeat note.

Joel McCrea *WTG Morton* • Betty Field *Elizabeth Morton* • Harry Carey *Prof Warren* • William Demarest *Eben Frost* • Louis Jean Heydt *Dr Horace Wells* • Julius Tannen *Dr Jackson* • Edwin Maxwell *VP medical society* • Porter Hall *President Pierce* ■ *Dir* Preston Sturges • *Scr* Preston Sturges, from a biography by Rene Fulop-Miller

The Great Muppet Caper ★★★ U
Musical comedy 1981 · US · Colour · 97mins

Although crammed full of big names, this second Muppet movie is something of a disappointment. The parodies of the Busby Berkeley-esque production numbers are artfully staged and the byplay between Charles Grodin and Miss Piggy is charged with comic eroticism. But there are too many scenes that seem to be merely passing the time until the plot is ready to resume rolling. Kermit, Fozzie and Gonzo are particularly ill-served as the reporters investigating the theft of Diana Rigg's diamond. The song *The First Time It Happens* landed an Oscar nomination. ▭

Jim Henson *Kermit the Frog/Rowlf/Dr Teeth/Waldorf* • Frank Oz *Miss Piggy/Fozzie Bear/Animal* • Dave Goelz *Gonzo/Chester Rat/Bill the Frog/Zoot* • Charles Grodin *Nicky Holiday* • John Cleese *Neville* • Robert Morley *British gentleman* • Peter Ustinov *Truck driver* • Jack Warden *Editor* • Peter Falk *Tramp* ■ *Dir* Jim Henson • *Scr* Tom Patchett, Jay Tarses, Jerry Juhl, Jack Rose

The Great Northfield Minnesota Raid ★★★
Western 1972 · US · Colour · 91mins

Yet another foray into American folk-hero territory, in this case the bank heist by the Jesse James gang. It lacks pace but looks so purposefully authentic that you expect the brown-hued edges to curl like ancient photographs. Directed by Philip Kaufman, the film boasts Robert Duvall and Cliff Robertson in the leading roles of Jesse James and his cousin, Cole Younger. Robertson's moody anti-heroism is at one with the rain-soaked Northfield town in this, one of the first of the revisionist westerns. Contains violence, swearing and nudity.

Cliff Robertson *Cole Younger* • Robert Duvall *Jesse James* • Luke Askew *Jim Younger* • RG Armstrong *Clell Miller* • Dana Elcar *Allen* • Donald Moffat *Manning* • John Pearce *Frank James* ■ *Dir/Scr* Philip Kaufman

The Great O'Malley ★
Drama 1937 · US · BW · 71mins

Humphrey Bogart received his first star billing for this terrible Warners programmer, a grotesquely sentimentalised crime melodrama in which slum-dweller Bogart is forced into criminality because his daughter is crippled. Pat O'Brien, always ready with a little lecture on morality, is the Irish cop, on Bogart's case. There's something of a shock ending, though, while Bogart's daughter is played by a scene-stealing Sybill Jason, who also becomes a victim of O'Brien's intractability.

Pat O'Brien *James Aloysius O'Malley* • Humphrey Bogart *John Phillips* • Frieda Inescort *Mrs Phillips* • Henry O'Neill *Attorney for defence* • Hobart Cavanaugh *Pinky Holden* • Mary Gordon *Mrs O'Malley* • Sybil Jason *Barbara Phillips* ■ *Dir* William Dieterle • *Scr* Milton Krims, Tom Reed, from the story *The Making of O'Malley* by Gerald Beaumont

The Great Outdoors ★★ PG
Comedy 1988 · US · Colour · 86mins

John Hughes's attempt to re-create the success of the previous year's adult comedy *Planes, Trains and Automobiles* backfires with this routine outing. John Candy, the obnoxious one in the aforementioned *Planes*, gets to be the nice guy this time around, finding himself stuck on vacation with his appalling brother-in-law, Dan Aykroyd. The two stars do their best, but Hughes's script is a mechanical retread of past glories and director Howard Deutch fails to bring much inspiration to the lumbering slapstick. Look out for a pre-stardom Annette Bening in a supporting role. ▭

Dan Aykroyd *Roman Craig* • John Candy *Chet Ripley* • Stephanie Faracy *Connie Ripley* • Annette Bening *Kate Craig* • Chris Young *Buck Ripley* • Ian Giatti *Ben Ripley* • Hilary Gordon *Cara Craig* • Rebecca Gordon *Mara Craig* ■ *Dir* Howard Deutch • *Scr* John Hughes

The Great Pretender ★★ 🄿🄶

Thriller   1991 · US · Colour · 93mins

Bruce Greenwood stars as a journalist investigating a death, who uncovers local corruption in this pilot for a TV series that was never made. Scripted by executive producer Stephen J Cannell, this is a more serious adventure than Cannell's previous successes such as *The Rockford Files* and *The A-Team*, and Greenwood is certainly no James Garner or George Peppard (or, for that matter, Mr T). Nevertheless, it has its moments, and supporting actors Jessica Steen and Gregg Henry gamely hold the whole thing together. 🖵

Bruce Greenwood *Earl Brattigan* • Gregg Henry *Wilson Leer* • Jessica Steen *Kate Hightower* • Donald Moffat *Owen Milner* • Anaron Ipale *Panos Bratso* • Paul Guilfoyle *Martin Brinkman* ■ *Dir* Gus Trikonis • *Scr* Stephen J Cannell

The Great Race ★★★★ 🅄

Comedy   1965 · US · Colour · 153mins

Jack Lemmon sports one of the most dastardly moustaches this side of a Victorian melodrama to compete against clean-cut good guy Tony Curtis in a 1908 automobile race from New York to Paris. Director Blake Edwards pays homage to the cartoon characterisation and slapstick wackiness of silent comedies in this stylised and overlong, but lavish and entertaining comedy extravaganza. Lemmon overplays to particular comic effect as the hiss-worthy villain, and the score is by Henry Mancini. 🖵

Tony Curtis *The Great Leslie* • Jack Lemmon *Professor Fate* • Natalie Wood *Maggie Dubois* • Peter Falk *Max* • Keenan Wynn *Hezekiah* • Arthur O'Connell *Henry Goodbody* • Vivian Vance *Hester Goodbody* • Dorothy Provine *Lily Olay* ■ *Dir* Blake Edwards • *Scr* Arthur Ross, from a story by Arthur Ross, Blake Edwards

The Great Rock 'n' Roll Swindle ★★★★ 🄸🄸

Drama documentary
1979 · UK · Colour · 100mins

The rise and fall of the Sex Pistols is charted in director Julien Temple's docu-fiction account of the punk era in all its anarchic glory. Using backstage interviews, concert clips, newsreels, staged sequences and animation footage from their aborted vehicle *Who Killed Bambi?* (which "King Leer" Russ Meyer was set to direct), a fascinating and remarkably honest slice of rock history emerges from the swirling mass of material. All the relevant bases are touched on including *God Save the Queen*, the jaunt to Rio to visit Great Train Robber Ronnie Biggs, Nancy Spungen's manslaughter and Sid Vicious's death, with manager guru Malcolm McLaren shown as the ultimate manipulator of the masses and, on the evidence here, fully earning the title "King Con". 🖵

Malcolm McLaren *The Embezzler* • Sid Vicious *The Gimmick* • Johnny Rotten [John Lydon]

The Collaborator • Steve Jones *The Crook* • Paul Cook *The Tea-maker* • Ronald Biggs *The Exile* ■ *Dir/Scr* Julien Temple

The Great St Louis Bank Robbery ★★

Crime   1959 · US · BW · 89mins

Only the name of its leading actor rescues this minor hold-up picture from obscurity. The rest of the cast and crew on this production, based on the story of a real heist, never made it to the big time. The young Steve McQueen, pre-Hollywood stardom, shows his mettle as the youngster driving the getaway car for three professional criminals. The build-up to the robbery is rather protracted, but the climax is effectively handled.

Steve McQueen *George Fowler* • David Clarke *Gino* • Crahan Denton *John Egan* • Molly McCarthy *Ann* ■ *Dir* Charles Guggenheim, John Stix • *Scr* Richard T Heffron

The Great St Trinian's Train Robbery ★★ 🅄

Comedy   1966 · UK · Colour · 90mins

Although Frank Launder couldn't resist the temptation of returning to his old stamping ground in 1980's *The Wildcats of St Trinian's*, this should have been the last in the film series based on Ronald Searle's ghoulish schoolgirls, as it had clearly run out of steam. Frankie Howerd's limitations as a film actor are all too apparent in this feeble mix of vulgar comedy and Swinging Sixties satire. Richard Wattis does sterling work as the man from the ministry, but, try as they might, Dora Bryan, Reg Varney and Stratford Johns (providing the booming voice-over) can't hold a candle to the much-missed Alastair Sim and Joyce Grenfell. George Cole makes an all-too-brief appearance as Flash Harry. 🖵

Frankie Howerd *Alphonse Askett* • Reg Varney *Gilbert* • Desmond Walter-Ellis *Leonard Edwards* • Cyril Chamberlain *Maxie* • Stratford Johns *The Voice* • Richard Wattis *Bassett* • Dora Bryan *Amber Spottiswood* • George Cole *Flash Harry* ■ *Dir* Frank Launder, Sidney Gilliat • *Scr* Frank Launder, Ivor Herbert, from the drawings by Ronald Searle

The Great Santini ★★★ 🄿🄶

Drama   1979 · US · Colour · 110mins

This adaptation of Pat Conroy's novel has a title that suggests a story about an escapologist or a racing driver is in the offing. In fact, it tells of a retired fighter pilot called Bull Meechum (nicknamed "Santini"), whose drunkenness makes life a misery for his wife (Blythe Danner) and children. Like *The Prince of Tides*, also based on a Conroy original, it's a thick slice of Deep South angst and sour mash philosophy in which drink turns dialogue into poetry. But Robert Duvall is magnificent in the lead role and earned an Oscar nomination for his pains, as did Michael O'Keefe.

Robert Duvall *Bull Meechum* • Blythe Danner *Lillian Meechum* • Michael O'Keefe *Ben Meechum* • Stan Shaw *Toomer Smalls* • Lisa Jane Persky *Mary Anne Meechum* • Julie Anne Haddock *Karen Meechum* • Brian Andrews *Matthew Meechum* • Theresa Merritt *Arrabelle Smalls* ■ *Dir* Lewis John Carlino • *Scr* Lewis John Carlino, from the novel by Pat Conroy

The Great Scout & Cathouse Thursday ★★

Comedy western
1976 · US · Colour · 105mins

Set in Colorado in 1908, this is a coarse, crass and calamitous misjudgement. Yet it's worth watching to witness the battle of wills between Lee Marvin and Oliver Reed, in which the former strains every sinew to stop himself lapsing into caricatured mugging, while the latter tempts him to stray with an exhibition of unabashed showboating. Caught in the middle of this titanic struggle are Robert Culp, as the politician who once gypped the feuding duo, and Kay Lenz, as the homely hooker who takes a fancy to Marvin. Don Taylor clearly thinks he's serving up an offbeat treat, but he ain't. Contains violence and swearing.

Lee Marvin *Sam Longwood* • Oliver Reed *Joe Knox* • Robert Culp *Jack Colby* • Elizabeth Ashley *Nancy Sue* • Strother Martin *Billy* • Sylvia Miles *Mike* • Kay Lenz *Thursday* ■ *Dir* Don Taylor • *Scr* Richard Shapiro

The Great Sinner ★★

Romantic drama   1949 · US · BW · 109mins

Fyodor Dostoyevsky's *The Gambler* has defeated many a film-maker this side of the Russian border. In MGM's lushly upholstered version of the tale, two of the world's best-looking stars, Gregory Peck and Ava Gardner, are seemingly without a clue as to what they're supposed to be thinking or doing under the heavy hand of director Robert Siodmak. Peck looks none too comfortable in the period clothes, though Gardner's aristocrat is ravishing, sumptuously gowned and photographed. The result is hardly watchable, despite a magnificent supporting cast.

Gregory Peck *Fyodor Dostoyevsky* • Ava Gardner *Pauline Ostrovski* • Melvyn Douglas *Armand Le Glasse* • Walter Huston *General Ostrovski* • Ethel Barrymore *Granny* • Frank Morgan *Aristide Pitard* • Agnes Moorehead *Emma Getzel* • Ludwig Stossel *Hotel manager* ■ *Dir* Robert Siodmak • *Scr* Ladislas Fodor, Christopher Isherwood, from a story by Ladislas Fodor, Rene Fulop-Miller, from the story *The Gambler* by Fyodor Dostoyevsky

The Great Sioux Massacre ★★ 🅄

Historical western
1965 · US · Colour · 92mins

Sidney Salkow directs this virtual remake of his own *Sitting Bull*, made in 1954. One of the cinema's periodic examinations of Custer's Last Stand, this B-western re-creates the famous battle of the Little Big Horn. Philip Carey plays Custer as an idealist who is initially outspoken in his defence of north American Indian rights. Later he is forced to compromise these ideals in order to further his political ambitions in Washington. Michael Pate plays Sitting Bull, while Crazy Horse is played by Iron Eyes Cody, who had previously played the same role in the earlier Salkow effort.

Joseph Cotten *Major Reno* • Darren McGavin *Captain Benton* • Philip Carey *Col George Armstrong Custer* • Julie Sommars *Caroline Reno* • Nancy Kovack *Libbie Custer* • John Matthews *Dakota* • Michael Pate *Sitting Bull* •

Iron Eyes Cody *Crazy Horse* • ■ *Dir* Sidney Salkow • *Scr* Fred C Dobbs, from a story by Sidney Salkow, Marvin Gluck

The Great Sioux Uprising ★★ 🅄

Western   1953 · US · Colour · 80mins

This Civil War-era western brings a fresh perspective to some familiar situations – including horse rustling. Jeff Chandler is Jonathan Westgate, the new veterinarian in town, who discovers that prominent horse trader Lyle Bettger is up to no good. He's stealing animals from the Sioux Indians and selling them to the army. Chandler's efforts to help find him caught between the Indians and the local ranchers. Faith Domergue plays livery stable owner Joan Britton.

Jeff Chandler *Jonathan Westgate* • Faith Domergue *Joan Britton* • Lyle Bettger *Stephen Cook* • John War Eagle *Red Cloud* • Stephen Chase *Major McKay* • Stacy Harris *Uriah* ■ *Dir* Lloyd Bacon • *Scr* Melvin Levy, J Robert Bren, Gladys Atwater, from a story by J Robert Bren, Gladys Atwater

The Great Smokey Roadblock ★★ 🄸🄵

Action adventure 1977 · US · Colour · 85mins

Hard on the wheels of *Smokey and the Bandit* came this clapped-out vehicle for Henry Fonda, in which he's an ageing trucker making one last bid at a journey before being overtaken by his finance company. The oddballs rolling along with him hold some interest (a load of evicted prostitutes and Robert Englund out of *A Nightmare on Elm Street* make-up), but the decrepit pace eventually makes this a vehicle only a scrapyard could love. 🖵

Henry Fonda *Elegant John* • Eileen Brennan *Penelope* • Robert Englund *Beebo* • John Byner *Disc Jockey* • Austin Pendleton *Guido* • Susan Sarandon *Ginny* • Melanie Mayron *Lulu* • Marya Small *Alice* ■ *Dir/Scr* John Leone

The Great Texas Dynamite Chase ★★★

Crime drama   1976 · US · Colour · 88mins

Director Michael Pressman made his feature debut with this typically raucous offering (originally entitled *Dynamite Women*) from Roger Corman's New World company. Former *Playboy* model Claudia Jennings's feisty fugitive and Jocelyn Jones's bored bankteller are the prototype Thelma and Louise, but audiences will be divided about the validity of the "can't beat 'em, join 'em" morality, especially when the comic capers unexpectedly take on a darker tone.

Claudia Jennings *Candy Morgan* • Jocelyn Jones *Ellie Jo Turner* • Johnny Crawford *Slim* • Chris Pennock [Christopher Pennock] *Jake* • Tara Strohmeier *Pam Morgan* ■ *Dir* Michael Pressman • *Scr* David Kirkpatrick, Mark Rosin

The Great Waldo Pepper ★★★ 🄿🄶

Drama   1975 · US · Colour · 102mins

Reuniting Robert Redford with George Roy Hill, who directed both *Butch Cassidy* and *The Sting*, this is a clear case of a missed opportunity. Scripted by *Cassidy*'s William Goldman, the story of the former First World War

🅄 = SUITABLE FOR ALL   🅄🄲 = SUITABLE FOR ALL, ESPECIALLY FOR YOUNG CHILDREN (VIDEO ONLY)   🄿🄶 = PARENTAL GUIDANCE

pilot who lives on false deeds and reckless stunts should have provided biting insights into the nature of heroism and Hollywood's shameless predilection for myth-making. Instead, we get a self-pitying tale of a dreamer who has out-lived both his times and his usefulness. Redford effortlessly portrays Pepper's superficial charm, but lacks the depth to convey his torment. Disappointing, though the aerial sequences are stunning. [video]

Robert Redford *Waldo Pepper* • Bo Svenson *Axel Olsson* • Bo Brundin *Ernst Kessler* • Susan Sarandon *Mary Beth* • Geoffrey Lewis *Newton Potts* • Edward Herrmann *Ezra Stiles* ■ *Dir* George Roy Hill • *Scr* William Goldman, from a story by George Roy Hill

A Great Wall ★★★ PG

Drama 1985 · US · Colour · 95mins

Peter Wang caught the eye in Wayne Wang's *Chan Is Missing*. It's hardly surprising, therefore, that his debut as actor/director should share so many of the themes of his namesake's delightful drama *Dim Sum*, albeit as seen from the other side of the wall (as it were). Instead of exploring how Chinese emigrants cope with life in America, this film focuses on the culture shock experienced by a family of first generation American Chinese during a visit to the old country. Avoiding controversial issues, this is essentially a guided tour of Beijing with some gentle drama thrown in for good measure. In English and Mandarin with subtitles. [video]

Xiao Wang *Liu Yida* • Qinqin Li *Lili Chao* • Jian Xiu *Yu* • Sharon Iwai *Grace Fang* • Peter Wang *Leo Fang* ■ *Dir* Peter Wang • *Scr* Peter Wang, Shirley Sun

The Great Waltz ★★★★ U

Biographical drama 1938 · US · BW · 103mins

A splendid MGM retelling of the life of Johann Strauss, and not to be confused with the vastly inferior biopics of later years with similar titles. Romantic charmer Fernand Gravet stars as Strauss, with the composer here neglecting his wife (portrayed by the regrettably forgotten double Oscar-winner Luise Rainer) for an opera singer played by Miliza Korjus. Style is everything here, and cameraman Joseph Ruttenberg won the Oscar for best cinematography. But who directed this opulent extravaganza? The movie is credited to Frenchman Julien Duvivier, but he left about halfway through, and others, including WS Van Dyke II and Victor Fleming, replaced him. The great Josef von Sternberg took charge for the sumptuous finale.

Luise Rainer *Poldi Vogelhuber* • Fernand Gravet *Johann Strauss* • Miliza Korjus *Carla Donner* • Hugh Herbert *Hofbauer* • Lionel Atwill *Count Hohenfried* • Curt Bois *Kienzl* • Leonid Kinskey *Dudelman* ■ *Dir* Julien Duvivier • *Scr* Samuel Hoffenstein, Walter Reisch, from a story by Gottfried Reinhardt

The Great Waltz ★★ U

Musical 1972 · US · Colour · 133mins

Andrew L Stone followed up his Grieg biopic *Song of Norway* with a retread of the familiar saga of Johann Strauss. This version benefits from colour, Panavision and – predictably – some of the most beautiful waltzes this side of heaven. Horst Buchholz makes a valiant effort as young Johann, and there's a welcome on-screen appearance by Mary Costa, the singing voice of Princess Aurora in Walt Disney's animated *Sleeping Beauty*.

Horst Buchholz *Johann Strauss Jr* • Mary Costa *Jetty Treffz* • Rossano Brazzi *Baron Tedesco* • Nigel Patrick *Johann Strauss Sr* • Yvonne Mitchell *Anna Strauss* • James Faulkner *Josef Strauss* • Vicki Woolf *Lili Weyl* ■ *Dir/Scr* Andrew L Stone

The Great War ★★★★

First World War comedy drama
1959 · Fr/It · BW · 118mins

Alberto Sordi appeared in a number of films in 1959, but none as entertaining as this tragicomic Italian variation on that old Hollywood favourite, *What Price Glory?* Winning both the Golden Lion at Venice and the best director award for Mario Monicelli, this irreverent romp follows Sordi and fellow conscript Vittorio Gassman as they seek to distance themselves from the living hell of the trenches during the First World War. But whether squabbling over prostitute Silvana Mangano or enduring bungling officers, they make an irresistible team, especially when finally forced to abandon their essential cowardice in the face of the merciless Austrians. An Italian language film.

Vittorio Gassman *Giovanni Busacca* • Alberto Sordi *Oreste Jacovacci* • Silvana Mangano *Constantina* • Folco Lulli *Bordin* • Bernard Blier *Capitano Castelli* • Romolo Valli *Tenente Gallina* • Vittorio Sanipoli *Maggiore Venturi* • Nicola Arigliano *Giardino* • Mario Valdemarin *Aspirante Loquenzi* ■ *Dir* Mario Monicelli • *Scr* Mario Monicelli, Luciano Vincenzoni, Agenore Incrocci, Furio Scarpelli, from a story by Luciano Vincenzoni

The Great White Hope ★★★ 15

Biographical drama
1970 · US · Colour · 98mins

This heavyweight boxing fable, based on the real-life decline and fall of turn-of-the-century black champion Jack Johnson, has a knockout performance by James Earl Jones, but it only just gets by on points as drama and is undermined by an early form of political correctness. Director Martin Ritt wears his conscience too obviously on his sleeve in showing the bigotry that destroys Jones when he falls for a white woman (Jane Alexander), but all is forgiven with Jones's endearing mix of rage and gullibility. [video]

James Earl Jones *Jack Jefferson* • Jane Alexander *Eleanor* • Lou Gilbert *Goldie* • Joel Fluellen *Tick* • Chester Morris *Pop Weaver* • Robert Webber *Dixon* • Marlene Warfield *Clara* • RG Armstrong *Cap'n Dan* • Hal Holbrook *Cameron* ■ *Dir* Martin Ritt • *Scr* Howard Sackler, from his play

The Great White Hype ★★★ 15

Comedy drama 1996 · US · Colour · 86mins

This boxing comedy – a brave attempt at satirising the unsatirisable – boasts a heavy-hitting cast that includes boisterous Damon Wayans, sinister Samuel L Jackson and a typically oddball Jeff Goldblum. Wayans is James "the Grim Reaper" Roper, the black heavyweight champion of the world, who has beaten all there is to beat and is seeking new opponents. Step forward fair-skinned rocker Terry Conklin, who once beat Roper as an amateur, but has since given up the fight game. Jackson persuades him to go back into training again. There are some sharp observations among the many slapstick moments. [video]

Samuel L Jackson *Reverend Fred Sultan* • Jeff Goldblum *Mitchell Kane* • Peter Berg *Terry Conklin* • Jon Lovitz *Sol* • Damon Wayans *James "the Grim Reaper" Roper* • Corbin Bernsen *Peter Prince* • Richard "Cheech" Marin *Julio Escobar* ■ *Dir* Reginald Hudlin • *Scr* Tony Hendra, Ron Shelton

The Great Ziegfeld ★★★★ U

Musical 1936 · US · BW · 176mins

This sumptuously mounted MGM musical biography of Broadway's most flamboyant showman is perhaps slightly too long for today's tastes, but it thrilled cinema-goers at the time and won the best film Oscar. Luise Rainer also won the first of two successive Academy Awards as best actress for her performance here as Ziegfeld's wife, Anna Held (she won the following year for *The Good Earth*), and her famous telephone scene is a lesson in screen acting. Suave William Powell is the Great Flo, a role he reprised eight years later in *Ziegfeld Follies*.

William Powell *Florenz Ziegfeld* • Luise Rainer *Anna Held* • Myrna Loy *Billie Burke* • Frank Morgan *Billings* • Reginald Owen *Sampston* • Nat Pendleton *Sandow* • Virginia Bruce *Audrey Lane* • Ernest Cossart *Sidney* ■ *Dir* Robert Z Leonard • *Scr* William Anthony McGuire

The Greatest ★★★ PG

Biography 1977 · US/UK · Colour · 97mins

Who else but Muhammad Ali could have starred in this biopic? The charismatic boxer takes to the screen with ease, dancing through his early life as Cassius Clay before reliving the 1975 "Rumble in the Jungle" when he regained his world heavyweight title by defeating George Forman. Ali's induction into the Nation of Islam, his controversial evasion of the Vietnam draft and his subsequent ban from the ring is also given lengthy, if not particularly objective treatment. There is strong support from Ernest Borgnine, Robert Duvall and James Earl Jones as Malcolm X – not that Ali needs it – and rather than restaging the fights, the film sensibly uses archive footage. [video]

Muhammad Ali • Ernest Borgnine *Angelo Dundee* • John Marley *Dr Pacheco* • Lloyd Haynes *Herbert Muhammad* • Robert Duvall *Bill McDonald* • Ben Johnson *Hollis* • James Earl Jones *Malcolm X* ■ *Dir* Tom Gries • *Scr* Ring Lardner Jr, from the book *The Greatest: My Own Story* by Muhammad Ali, Herbert Muhammad, Richard Durham

The Greatest Gift ★★★ U

Drama 1974 · US · Colour · 100mins

Glenn Ford made one of his occasional TV-movie appearances in this pilot for what turned out to be a rather short-lived series. This is something of a Deep South reworking of the Don Camillo stories, with Ford as the kindly preacher resisting the fire and brimstone inclinations of his superiors while battling no-nonsense sheriff Harris Yulin for the hearts and minds of his impoverished flock. Set in the early forties, the film's folksy, *Waltons*-style feel is only marred by a moment of unexpected violence.

Glenn Ford *Reverend Holvak* • Julie Harris *Elizabeth Holvak* • Lance Kerwin *Ramey Holvak* • Harris Yulin *Hog Yancy* • Charles Tyner *Amos Goodloe* • Dabbs Greer *Deacon Hurd* • Cari Anne Warder *Julie Mae Holvak* • Albert Smith *Eli Wiggins* ■ *Dir* Boris Sagal • *Scr* Abby Mann [Ben Goodman], from the novel *Ramey* by Jack Farris

The Greatest Show on Earth ★★★★ U

Epic drama 1952 · US · Colour · 146mins

Well, perhaps not as great as all that, though it did win Cecil B DeMille an Oscar. The film is a jumbo-sized package of all the clichés that money can buy, as circus owner Charlton Heston strives to control the untamed emotions of Betty Hutton, Cornel Wilde and Gloria Grahame. James Stewart is the most original turn as a clown who, for reasons too complex to unfold, never takes off his make-up. As usual, DeMille megaphones his direction to let us know where we've been, where we are and where we're going. Nevertheless, this is a marvellous piece of entertainment. [video]

Charlton Heston *Brad* • James Stewart *Buttons, a clown* • Betty Hutton *Holly* • Dorothy Lamour *Phyllis* • Cornel Wilde *Sebastian* • Gloria Grahame *Angel* • Lyle Bettger *Klaus* • Lawrence Tierney *Henderson* • Henry Wilcoxon *Detective* • John Kellogg *Harry* • Rosemary Dvorak *Rosemary* • Bob Hope • Bing Crosby ■ *Dir* Cecil B DeMille • *Scr* Fredric M Frank, Barré Lyndon, Theodore St John, from a story by Theodore St John, Fredric M Frank, Frank Cavett

The Greatest Story Ever Told ★★★ U

Biblical drama 1965 · US · Colour · 190mins

George Stevens's epic re-telling of the life of Christ is a monumental achievement, given tremendous power by Max von Sydow's masterful portrayal of Jesus. Unfortunately, the film is fatally compromised by its cumbersome length and the casting of key players in every role. While the likes of Carroll Baker and Sidney Poitier work well, the inclusion of Pat Boone and, especially, John Wayne actually damages the fabric. It's a remarkable movie nonetheless, considering the fact that Stevens fell ill and the great David Lean took over the direction, reuniting with his *Lawrence of Arabia* actors José Ferrer and Claude Rains. [video]

Max von Sydow *Jesus* • Carroll Baker *Veronica* • Pat Boone *Young man at the tomb* • Charlton Heston *John the Baptist* • Martin Landau *Caiaphas* • Angela Lansbury *Claudia* • David McCallum *Judas Iscariot* • Roddy McDowall *Matthew* • Sal Mineo *Uriah* • Telly Savalas *Pontius Pilate* • John Wayne *Centurion* • Shelley Winters *Woman of no name* • Dorothy McGuire *Mary* • Robert Loggia *Joseph* • Claude Rains *Herod the Great* • José Ferrer *Herod Antipas* • Donald Pleasence *Dark hermit* ■ *Dir* George Stevens • *Scr* George Stevens, James Lee Barrett, from the book by Fulton Oursler and radio scripts by Henry Denker

Greed ★★★★★ PG
Classic silent drama 1925 · US · BW · 134mins

This is the epic that ensured that director Erich von Stroheim was, ever after, seen as a genius who could not be trusted. Made over two years, this adaptation of Frank Norris's novel *McTeague* was planned to last ten hours, but MGM executives took it away from its creator and cut it down to a more commercial size. As an exercise in vicious irony, it tells of McTeague (Gibson Gowland), an unqualified dentist about to marry ZaSu Pitts, who becomes a lottery winner but then refuses to spend any of the money. For von Stroheim, human beings were just predatory animals and the moral squalor is never more evident than in the wedding scenes. His obsession with realistic detail reached its zenith during the final scenes in Death Valley, where the actors suffered hugely for the director's art. 📼

Gibson Gowland *McTeague* • ZaSu Pitts *Trina* • Jean Hersholt *Marcus Schouler* • Chester Conklin *Mr Sieppe* • Sylvia Ashton *Mrs Sieppe* • Oscar Gottell *Sieppe Twin* • Otto Gottell *Sieppe Twin* • Frank Hayes *Old Grannis* ■ Dir Erich von Stroheim • Scr Erich von Stroheim, June Mathis, from the novel *McTeague* by Frank Norris • Cinematographer William Daniels, Ben F Reynolds

The Greed of William Hart ★★
Crime melodrama 1948 · UK · BW · 74mins

Tod Slaughter gives another of his outrageously over-the-top performances in this low-budget British horror picture, based on the real-life exploits of the infamous 19th-century grave-robbers, Burke and Hare. Henry Oscar is equally larger-than-life as his partner in crime. The melodramatic style of the piece verges on the comical nowadays, but, taken on its own terms, the sum of the parts verges on the adequate.

Tod Slaughter *William Hart* • Henry Oscar *Mr Moore* • Jenny Lynn *Helen Moore* • Winifred Melville *Meg Hart* • Patrick Addison *Hugh Alston* • Arnold Bell *Doctor Cox* ■ Dir Oswald Mitchell • Scr John Gilling

Greedy ★★★ 12
Comedy 1994 · US · Colour · 107mins

In this slightly black comedy, the money-grabbing relatives of ailing millionaire Kirk Douglas become apprehensive when the old boy hires a sexy nurse. Michael J Fox and Nancy Travis are among the vultures awaiting their inheritance, but British director Jonathan Lynn's comical jibes are neither heartless nor hectic enough to gain a full complement of laughs. Movie buffs will note that the family name is McTeague after Erich von Stroheim's 1925 silent classic *Greed*. Contains swearing. 📼

Michael J Fox *Daniel McTeague* • Kirk Douglas *Uncle Joe McTeague* • Nancy Travis *Robin Hunter* • Olivia D'Abo *Molly Richardson* • Phil Hartman *Frank* • Ed Begley Jr *Carl* • Jere Burns *Glen* ■ Dir Jonathan Lynn • Scr Lowell Ganz, Babaloo Mandel

The Greek Tycoon ★★ 15
Drama 1978 · US · Colour · 111mins

Glossy tosh of a kind that the TV mini-series has made infamous, this is about the romance between a Greek shipping magnate and an American president's wife – Aristotle Onassis and Jackie Kennedy by any other name. Anthony Quinn and Jacqueline Bisset fill in the characters as best they can, but it's the lush staging that wins the day. British helmer J Lee Thompson directs this sumptuous rubbish. Contains swearing. 📼

Anthony Quinn *Theo Tomasis* • Jacqueline Bisset *Liz Cassidy* • Raf Vallone *Spyros Tomasis* • Edward Albert *Nico Tomasis* • James Franciscus *James Cassidy* • Charles Durning *Michael Russell* ■ Dir J Lee Thompson • Scr Mort Fine, from a story by Mort Fine, Nico Mastorakis, Win Wells

The Green Berets ★★ PG
War drama 1968 · US · Colour · 136mins

Most of the films made about the American involvement in Vietnam are highly critical and were produced long after the American withdrawal from that shameful conflict. John Wayne, however, saw Vietnam as a new Alamo, staunch Republican that he was, and both starred in and co-directed this flag-waving action adventure, a unique example of auteurism going nowhere. There's no denying the epic sweep of the action scenes, but even for Duke fans this is heavy-going, thick-eared nonsense. Contains violence. 📼 DVD

John Wayne *Colonel Mike Kirby* • David Janssen *George Beckworth* • Jim Hutton *Sergeant Petersen* • Aldo Ray *Sergeant Muldoon* • Raymond St Jacques *Doc McGee* • Bruce Cabot *Colonel Morgan* • Jack Soo *Colonel Cai* • George Takei *Captain Nim* ■ Dir John Wayne, Ray Kellogg • Scr James Lee Barrett, from the novel by Robin Moore

Green Card ★★★ 15
Romantic comedy 1990 · Ausl/Fr · Colour · 102mins

Gérard Depardieu's much-anticipated English language debut was, to some extent, lost in the fuss created by the revelations about his felonious youth that appeared around the time of its release. This is not original, it's full of narrative improbabilities and it's not as funny as it should be. Yet Peter Weir's comedy is easy-going, has undeniable charm and features two thoroughly engaging performances, with Andie MacDowell winning you over to her initially cold, calculating Manhattanite. Weir is a little heavy-handed with the comic set pieces, but he develops the romance with some care and turns the immigration inquiry into a nail-biting tear-jerker. Contains swearing. 📼

Gérard Depardieu *George Faure* • Andie MacDowell *Brontë Parrish* • Bebe Neuwirth *Lauren Adler* • Gregg Edelman *Phil* • Robert Prosky *Brontë's lawyer* • Jessie Keosian *Mrs Bird* • Ethan Phillips *Gorsky* • Mary Louise Wilson *Mrs Sheehan* ■ Dir/Scr Peter Weir

The Green Cockatoo ★
Crime drama 1937 · UK · BW · 63mins

Sometimes even the greatest of talents don't add up to a successful movie. In this case the original story was by Graham Greene, the director

was the great production designer William Cameron Menzies and the film was produced by noted director William K Howard. John Mills is miscast as a singer who sets out to avenge the murder of his brother (Robert Newton). René Ray, who witnessed the killing, eventually leads Mills to the villains. A contrived and episodic imitation of a Hollywood gangster melodrama, set during one dark night in Soho.

John Mills *Jim Connor* • René Ray *Eileen* • Robert Newton *Dave Connor* • Charles Oliver *Terrell* • Bruce Seton *Madison* • Julian Vedey *Steve* • Allan Jeayes *Inspector* • Frank Atkinson *Butler* ■ Dir William Cameron Menzies • Scr Edward O Berkman, Arthur Wimperis, from a story by Graham Greene

Green Dolphin Street ★★
Adventure drama 1947 · US · BW · 141mins

This romantic drama should have been the studio's *San Francisco* of the forties with its epic earthquake (the special effects won an Oscar), but it lacked that film's dynamic stars, strong storyline and concise direction. Instead, it turned out to be a dreary and overlong tale of the dark-haired Lana Turner travelling from the Channel Islands to New Zealand to marry businessman Richard Hart, who really desires her sister, played by Donna Reed. Van Heflin is Hart's partner who secretly covets Turner. Despite a huge budget, it was filmed in black and white.

Lana Turner *Marianne Patourel* • Van Heflin *Timothy Haslam* • Donna Reed *Marguerite Patourel* • Richard Hart *William Ozanne* • Frank Morgan *Dr Edmund* • Edmund Gwenn *Octavius Patourel* • Dame May Whitty *Mother Superior* • Reginald Owen *Captain O'Hara* ■ Dir Victor Saville • Scr Samson Raphaelson, from a novel by Elizabeth Goudge

Green Eyes ★★★
Drama 1976 · US · Colour · 68mins

After his Oscar-nominated performance in Martin Ritt's under-rated rural drama *Sounder* (1972), Paul Winfield was regarded by some as the heir to Sidney Poitier. Viewers will be all the more puzzled by his failure to develop into a top-flight star after watching this superior TV movie. As a Vietnam veteran returning to find the child he left behind, Winfield once again proves himself to be an actor of great depth and sincerity. There's solid support from Rita Tushingham and Jonathan Lippe, while director John Erman ensures the moving material does not descend into pathos.

Paul Winfield *Lloyd Dubeck* • Rita Tushingham *Margaret Sheen* • Jonathan Lippe *Noel Cousins* • Victoria Racimo *Em Thuy* • Lemi Trung • Royce Wallace *Mrs Dubeck* • Robert DoQui *Hal* • Fred Sadoff *VA oficer* ■ Dir John Erman • Scr David Seltzer, from a story by Eugene Logan, David Seltzer

Green Fire ★★★ U
Romantic drama
1954 · US · Colour · 100mins

A glossy MGM adventure co-starring tanned Stewart Granger and sleek Grace Kelly, arguably the best-looking couple in movies since Vivien Leigh and Robert Taylor in *Waterloo Bridge*. In its day, this romp was accused of wasting Kelly's talents, but she's actually well cast as the plantation

owner who falls for tough emerald miner Granger, and their love scenes together sizzle, especially that kiss in the waterfall. The plot's a load of old hokum about slimy Murvyn Vye trying to steal Granger's emeralds (the "green fire" of the title), but there are some fine set pieces, including a memorable avalanche.

Stewart Granger *Rian Mitchell* • Grace Kelly *Catherine Knowland* • Paul Douglas *Vic Leonard* • John Ericson *Donald Knowland* • Murvyn Vye *El Moro* • Jose Torvay *Manuel* • Robert Tafur *Father Ripero* ■ Dir Andrew Marton • Scr Ivan Goff, Ben Roberts

Green for Danger ★★★★
Comedy thriller 1946 · UK · BW · 90mins

This is the kind of brisk, bright and thoroughly engaging entertainment that the British film industry has, sadly, forgotten how to make. But, then again, there are no more Alastair Sims to transform a passage of jovial banter into a moment of nail-biting suspense simply by slowing that melancholy Scottish accent and lowering those expressive oyster eyes. Gone, too, are such expert character actors as Leo Genn, whose ability to portray heroes and villains alike deepened the mystery in whodunits like this one, in which a patient is murdered on the operating table. Sidney Gilliat directs with a deliciously dark wit. 📼

Alastair Sim *Inspector Cockrill* • Sally Gray *Nurse Linley* • Trevor Howard *Dr Barney Barnes* • Rosamund John *Nurse Esther Sanson* • Leo Genn *Mr Eden* • Judy Campbell *Sister Marion Bates* • Megs Jenkins *Nurse Woods* • Moore Marriott *Joe Higgins* ■ Dir Sidney Gilliat • Scr Sidney Gilliat, Claude Guerney, from a novel by Christianna Brand

The Green Goddess ★
Adventure 1930 · US · BW · 80mins

With his fine voice and stage experience, George Arliss was considered ideally suited to make the transition to talkies, and this was a sound remake of his 1923 silent melodrama. He portrays a wily Rajah with a grudge against the British, who holds three Brits captive after they are fortunate enough to survive a plane crash. In its time, this was well received and hugely successful – Arliss gained a best actor Academy Award nomination (and won that same year for his performance in *Disraeli*). Be warned, though: the restrictions of early sound film-making, the stilted acting and the hoary melodramatic plot make this virtually unwatchable.

George Arliss *The Rajah* • HB Warner *Maj Crespin* • Alice Joyce *Lucilla Crespin* • Ralph Forbes *Doctor Traherne* • David Tearle *High temple priest* • Reginald Sheffield *Lt Cardew* ■ Dir Alfred E Green • Scr Julien Josephson, from the play by William Archer

Green Grass of Wyoming ★★ U
Drama 1948 · US · Colour · 84mins

Winding up the Flicka trilogy, this is yet another "how to do it" horsey picture, this time offering an insider's view of the highly competitive sport of trotting. Even though cinematographer Charles Clarke was nominated for an Oscar, it is comfortably the weakest of the series, eschewing wide-eyed innocence for a *Romeo and Juliet*-style romance between Peggy Cummins and Robert Arthur, respectively niece and son of implacable trotting rivals Charles Coburn and Lloyd Nolan. The veterans act the youngsters off the screen, but, as director Louis King seems to prefer young love to wrinkly badinage, we don't see enough of them.

Peggy Cummins *Carey Greenway* • Charles Coburn *Beaver* • Robert Arthur *Ken* • Lloyd Nolan *Rob McLaughlin* • Burl Ives *Gus* • Robert Adler *Joe* • Will Wright *Jake* ■ *Dir* Louis King • *Scr* Martin Berkeley, from the novel by Mary O'Hara

Green Grow the Rushes
★★ U

Comedy   1951 · UK · BW · 88mins

In his last home-grown picture before joining 20th Century-Fox, Richard Burton plays the leader of a gang of brandy smugglers in a nondescript and shameless reworking of Ealing's *Whisky Galore!* It was hardly a memorable parting gift: Burton was never an accomplished comedian and he struggles to make anything of his thin ration of jokes. But then Roger Livesey fares little better as the skipper of the boat whose activities have attracted the attention of three less-than-wise men from the ministry.

Richard Burton *Hammond* • Roger Livesey *Captain Biddle* • Honor Blackman *Meg* • Frederick Leister *Colonel Gill* • John Salew *Finch* • Colin Gordon *Fisherwick* • Geoffrey Keen *Prudhoe* • Cyril Smith *Hewitt* • Eliot Makeham *Urquhart* • Vida Hope *Polly* ■ *Dir* Derek Twist • *Scr* Howard Clewes, Derek Twist, from a novel by Howard Clewes

The Green Horizon
★★

Drama   1981 · Jap · Colour · 120mins

Noted for introducing *cinéma vérité* realism into his fictional features, director Susumu Hani spent much of the seventies making wildlife documentaries for Japanese television. So it wasn't too much of a stretch for him to combine both preoccupations in this mediocre melodrama, which looks superb (thanks to cinematographer/co-director Simon Trevor) but makes few emotional or intellectual demands. In what proved to be his final big-screen appearance, James Stewart was wasted as the owner of an African animal sanctuary whose peaceful idyll is disrupted when pilot Philip Sayer crash-lands in the jungle and promptly falls in love with Stewart's granddaughter.

James Stewart *Old Man* • Philip Sayer *Man* • Kathy *Girl* ■ *Dir* Susumu Hani, Simon Trevor • *Scr* Shintaro Tsuji, from a story by Shuji Terayama

Green Ice
★★ 15

Thriller   1981 · UK · Colour · 104mins

One of those films that doesn't realise the offence it is causing by making comedy thrills out of a national tragedy. Ryan O'Neal and Anne Archer are fine as the couple involved in a risky heist of gems to fill rebel coffers in Colombia, and Omar Sharif is an entertaining enough villain, but the general light-heartedness of tone sits awkwardly on a story involving torture and armed struggle. Perhaps that's taking it too seriously, but caper

movies shouldn't be made of such stern stuff. ▭

Ryan O'Neal *Joseph Wiley* • Anne Archer *Holbrook* • Omar Sharif *Meno Argenti* • Domingo Ambriz *Miguel* • John Larroquette *Claude* • Philip Stone *Kellerman* • Michael Sheard *Jaap* • Enrique Lucero *Lucho* ■ *Dir* Ernest Day • *Scr* Edward Anhalt, Ray Hassett, Anthony Simmons, Robert De Laurentis, from the book by Gerald Browne

A Green Journey
★★★

Drama   1990 · US · Colour · 100mins

Angela Lansbury and Denholm Elliott rescue this potentially schmaltzy *84 Charing Cross Road* clone, producing subtle performances when over-sentimentality threatens the drama. The elegant Lansbury is Agatha, a dedicated teacher from the American Midwest, and Elliott brings his trademark eccentricity and crusty outlook to the role of James, her Irish pen friend. In what is sometimes a laboured story, the two leads complement each other perfectly.

Angela Lansbury *Agatha McGee* • Denholm Elliott *James* • Robert Prosky *Bishop* ■ *Dir* Joseph Sargent • *Scr* Ron Cowen, Daniel Lipman, from a novel by John Hassler

Green Light
★★

Drama   1937 · US · BW · 84mins

A torrid tear-jerker with Errol Flynn as a surgeon who takes the blame when a patient dies on the operating table. Flynn then finds religion, uses his own body to experiment with a new vaccine and (there is more) falls in love with the dead patient's daughter. Based on a novel by Lloyd C Douglas, who also wrote the religious epic *The Robe*, it's sanctimony all the way, and pretty daft it is too. Made by Warner Bros to placate its restless star who was feeling trapped as an action hero, it co-stars Anita Louise and was directed by the master of cringe, Frank Borzage.

Errol Flynn *Dr Newell Paige* • Anita Louise *Phyllis Dexter* • Margaret Lindsay *Frances Ogilvie* • Cedric Hardwicke *Dean Harcourt* • Walter Abel *Dr John Stafford* • Henry O'Neill *Dr Endicott* • Spring Byington *Mrs Dexter* • Erin O'Brien-Moore *Pat Arlen* ■ *Dir* Frank Borzage • *Scr* Milton Krims, Lloyd C Douglas

The Green Man
★★★★ PG

Comedy   1956 · UK · BW · 76mins

If you ever doubted that Alastair Sim was the finest British screen comedian of the sound era, then here's the proof of his immense talent. As the assassin with the mournful smile, he gives a performance of rare genius that more than makes amends for the longueurs in Frank Launder and Sidney Gilliat's script. The sequence in which he persuades three old dears to cease their recital so that his radio bomb can finish off politician Raymond Huntley is a masterclass in the lost art of farce. Huntley also excels as the pompous target, but George Cole is overly bumbling as the vacuum-cleaner salesman who uncovers the plot. ▭

Alastair Sim *Hawkins* • George Cole *William Blake* • Jill Adams *Ann Vincent* • Avril Angers *Marigold* • Terry-Thomas *Boughtflower* • John Chandos *McKecknie* • Raymond Huntley *Sir Gregory Upshoot* ■ *Dir* Robert Day • *Scr* Sidney Gilliat, Frank Launder, from their play *Meet a Body*

Green Mansions
★★ U

Romantic adventure
1959 · US · Colour · 104mins

A rare opportunity to see Audrey Hepburn as Rima, the mystical "Bird Girl", communing with nature and winning the heart of Anthony Perkins in the Venezuelan jungle. Alas, the film (directed by the star's then husband, actor Mel Ferrer) is misconceived. A poor screenplay fails to capture the elusive magic of the fantasy novel from which it was adapted, and the whole thing is photographed in unattractive shades of green. However, the fragile doe-like beauty of the sublime Hepburn, followed around by a lookalike young deer, and an equally fragile, youthful Perkins, afford some fleeting pleasure.

Audrey Hepburn *Rima* • Anthony Perkins *Abel* • Lee J Cobb *Nuflo* • Sessue Hayakawa *Runi* • Henry Silva *Kua-Ko* • Nehemiah Persoff *Don Panta* • Michael Pate *Priest* ■ *Dir* Mel Ferrer • *Scr* Dorothy Kingsley, from the novel by William Henry Hudson

The Green Mile
★★★★ 18

Fantasy prison drama
1999 · US · Colour · 188mins

Set in a Louisiana prison in 1935, this overblown, sentimental fantasy is clearly aimed at the *Forrest Gump* audience. Tom Hanks plays a warden who forms a life-affirming relationship with a black prisoner, on death row for the murder of two little girls. Suspension of disbelief is essential if you're to enjoy Frank Darabont's reverential adaptation of Stephen King's 1996 novel. All the wardens are angels, bar one, while giant-sized newcomer Michael Clarke Duncan is too gentle to convince as a convicted child-killer. Yet Darabont, directing his first film since *The Shawshank Redemption*, manipulates our emotions masterfully, and only the very hard-hearted will remain dry-eyed throughout or unshocked by the harrowing execution scenes. Contains violence.

Tom Hanks *Paul Edgecomb* • David Morse *Brutus "Brutal" Howell* • Bonnie Hunt *Jan Edgecomb* • Michael Clarke Duncan *John Coffey* • James Cromwell *Warden Hal Moores* • Michael Jeter *Eduard Delacroix* • Graham Greene *Arlen Bitterbuck* • Doug Hutchison *Percy Wetmore* • Sam Rockwell *"Wild Bill" Wharton* • Harry Dean Stanton *Toot-Toot* ■ *Dir* Frank Darabont • *Scr* Frank Darabont, from the novel by Stephen King

The Green Pastures
★★★ U

Drama   1936 · US · BW · 91mins

Warner Bros's faithful screen version of playwright Marc Connelly's Pulitzer Prize-winning smash hit re-tells the Old Testament in terms of a Saturday night fishfry. Today this interpretation may irritate some, but in fact this all-black production works as effectively now as it did in its time, making the Bible accessible and giving work to many black artists. Rex Ingram plays De Lawd, and Eddie "Rochester" Anderson is a memorable Noah. This may not be to everyone's taste, but it would be difficult to find an audience unmoved by the stark simplicity of its telling, or the marvellous Hall Johnson Choir sounding forth with an array of well-loved, and nowadays generally neglected, negro spirituals.

Rex Ingram *De Lawd/Adam/Hezdrel* • Oscar Polk *Gabriel* • Eddie "Rochester" Anderson *Noah* • Frank Wilson *Moses* • George Reed *Mr Deshee* • Abraham Gleaves *Archangel* • Myrtle Anderson *Eve* • Al Stokes *Cain* • Edna M Harris *Zeba* ■ *Dir* Marc Connelly, William Keighley • *Scr* Marc Connelly, Sheridan Gibney, from the play by Marc Connelly, from the collection of stories *Ol' Man Adam an' His Chillun* by Roark Bradford

The Green Ray
★★★★ PG

Drama   1986 · Fr · Colour · 94mins

Unlike Eric Rohmer's previous films, the dialogue of this comedy of manners was almost entirely improvised by the actors. How one reacts to the film may depend to how one reacts to the character of the overly fastidious Delphine, played superbly by Marie Rivière. Not knowing what to do on her holidays, she goes to Cherbourg, then the mountains and then Biarritz, but is bored and depressed everywhere until she meets the man of her dreams. The title, taken from the Jules Verne novel, refers to the last ray of sunset, the green of which is supposed to make observers more aware of the feelings and perceptions of others. Rohmer's films have much the same effect. In French with English subtitles. ▭

Marie Rivière *Delphine* • Vincent Gauthier *Jacques* • Béatrice Romand *Béatrice* • Sylvie Richez *Sylvie* ■ *Dir* Eric Rohmer • *Scr* Eric Rohmer, Marie Rivière

The Green Room
★★★

Drama   1978 · Fr · Colour · 94mins

Alfred Hitchcock's *Vertigo* haunts this film, inspired by the works of Henry James. Director/co-writer François Truffaut also stars as the obituarist whose life is devoted to the memory of his beloved wife and the victims of the First World War. Such is the totality of his grief that even when he befriends Nathalie Baye, the best he can offer her is a chance to become a fellow mourner at his vigil. Peering through cinematographer Nestor Almendros's gloomy interiors, it's easy to see just how personal a project this was, but it's harder to share in Truffaut's obsessions. A French language film.

François Truffaut *Julien Davenne* • Nathalie Baye *Cecilia Mandel* • Jean Dasté *Bernard Humbert* • Jean-Pierre Moulin *Gérard Mazet* • Antoine Vitez *Bishop's secretary* • Jane Lobre *Madame Rambaud* • Monique Dury *Editorial secretary* ■ *Dir* François Truffaut • *Scr* François Truffaut, Jean Gruault, from the works of Henry James

The Green Scarf
★★

Mystery   1954 · UK · BW · 88mins

Based on a French novel called *The Brute* by popular thriller writer Guy des Cars, this murky murder mystery is set in Paris with an oh-so-British cast as French characters. Michael Redgrave is a lawyer defending a blind, deaf and dumb murder suspect (Kieron Moore) who, thinking his wife (Ann Todd) had killed her lover, confesses to the crime. Courtroom dramas seldom fail to hold the attention and this is no exception, despite the mechanical performances (including Redgrave's), lame script and uninspiring direction.

Michael Redgrave *Deliot* • Ann Todd *Solange* • Leo Genn *Rodelec* • Kieron Moore *Jacques* •

Richard O'Sullivan *Jacques as a child* • Jane Lamb *Solange as a child* • Ella Milne *Louise* • Jane Griffiths *Danielle* ■ *Dir* George More O'Ferrall • *Scr* Gordon Wellesley, from the novel *The Brute* by Guy des Cars

The Green Years ★★★

Drama   1946 · US · BW · 126mins

MGM didn't need top stars to have a huge box-office success with its film adaptation of AJ Cronin's popular novel. Set in Scotland, it's capably directed by Britain's Victor Saville. In his first major role, nine-year-old Dean Stockwell shines as the boy growing up in a hostile family environment and forging a close relationship with his extraordinary great-grandfather. A bearded Charles Coburn plays the alcoholic old codger so engagingly that he received his third Oscar nomination for best supporting actor.

Charles Coburn *Alexander Gow* • Tom Drake *Robert Shannon* • Beverly Tyler *Alison Keith* • Hume Cronyn *Papa Leckie* • Gladys Cooper *Grandma Leckie* • Dean Stockwell *Robert Shannon as a child* • Selena Royle *Mama Leckie* • Jessica Tandy *Kate Leckie* ■ *Dir* Victor Saville • *Scr* Robert Ardrey, Sonya Levien, from the novel by AJ Cronin

The Greengage Summer ★★★ PG

Romantic drama   1961 · UK · Colour · 95mins

Charmingly capturing the brilliance of youth and the beauty of champagne country, director Lewis Gilbert's adaptation of Rumer Godden's novel suffers only from a disappointingly trite ending. As the 16-year-old forced to take charge of her siblings when their mother falls ill, Susannah York radiates the innocent's new-found lust for life and, whether getting tipsy for the first time or suffering from the initial pangs of love, she is truly captivating. As the mystery man who steals her heart, Kenneth More allows her the space to mature, while also revealing a more cynical side in his dealings with his landlady lover, Danielle Darrieux.

Kenneth More *Eliot* • Danielle Darrieux *Madame Zizi* • Susannah York *Joss Grey* • Claude Nollier *Madame Corbet* • Jane Asher *Hester Grey* • Elizabeth Dear *Vicky Grey* • Richard Williams *Willmouse Grey* • David Saire *Paul* ■ *Dir* Lewis Gilbert • *Scr* Howard Koch, from the novel by Rumer Godden

Greenwich Village ★★★ U

Musical   1944 · US · Colour · 78mins

Jolly enjoyable Technicolor 20th Century-Fox musical, ostensibly set in the titular artists' quarter of New York City in the Roaring Twenties. But, since the speakeasy run by proprietor William Bendix features the fabulous Carmen Miranda and vivacious Vivian Blaine, we're clearly in the mid-forties, which means superb musical arrangements and the skimpiest of plots on which to hang them. Don Ameche is the hick composer hired by Bendix to write a show, but keep your eyes sharply peeled for a glimpse of the legendary Judy Holliday and *Singin' in the Rain* authors Betty Comden and Adolph Green.

Carmen Miranda *Princess Querida* • Don Ameche *Kenneth Harvey* • William Bendix *Danny O'Mara* • Vivian Blaine *Bonnie Watson*

• Felix Bressart *Moger* • Tony De Marco • Sally De Marco • BS Pully *Brophy* ■ *Dir* Walter Lang • *Scr* Earl Baldwin, Walter Bullock, Michael Fessier (adaptation), Ernest B Pagano (adaptation), from a story by Fred Hazlitt Brennan [Frederick Hazlitt Brennan]

Greetings ★★★ 18

Comedy drama   1968 · US · Colour · 87mins

The second feature from director Brian De Palma successfully explores the anti-establishment mood of the alienated sixties generation with serio-comic intensity. De Palma also manages to experiment with the very nature of cinema and indulge in what would soon become his technically brilliant hallmarks. The slight story – Robert De Niro and Gerrit Graham's efforts to get their best friend Jonathan Warden rejected by the Army draft – is a mere springboard to attack such political targets as Lyndon Johnson, the Vietnam War and the Warren Commission report on the assassination of John F Kennedy, using *cinéma vérité*, sexual obsession and voyeurism.

Jonathan Warden *Paul Shaw* • Robert De Niro *Jon Rubin* • Gerrit Graham *Lloyd Clay* • Richard Hamilton *Pop Artist* • Megan McCormick *Marina* ■ *Dir* Brian De Palma • *Scr* Charles Hirsch, Brian De Palma

Gregory's Girl ★★★★ 12

Romantic comedy   1980 · UK · Colour · 87mins

Near faultless film-making from Bill Forsyth, who latterly hasn't fulfilled this early promise under the auspices of Hollywood. As director, he keeps a wry eye on the triangle linking school goalkeeper John Gordon-Sinclair (then Gordon John), centre forward Dee Hepburn and her pal Clare Grogan. But it is as scriptwriter that he excels, capturing the anxieties and insecurities of teen love and the language of the playground with consummate skill. He also creates a glorious array of secondary characters, including Robert Buchanan and William Greenlees as Sinclair's lovelorn mates and Chic Murray as the laconic headmaster. Contains swearing. *DVD*

Gordon John Sinclair [John Gordon-Sinclair] *Gregory* • Dee Hepburn *Dorothy* • Jake D'Arcy *Phil Menzies* • Clare Grogan *Susan* • Robert Buchanan *Andy* • William Greenlees *Steve* • Chic Murray *Headmaster* • Alex Norton *Alec* ■ *Dir/Scr* Bill Forsyth

Gregory's Two Girls ★★ 15

Comedy   1999 · UK/Ger · Colour · 111mins

Bill Forsyth has clearly not forgiven Hollywood for his career eclipse, judging by the strong anti-American flavour that laces this sequel to his best-known film. There's still plenty of his quirky observational humour, though, which provides the perfect platform for John Gordon-Sinclair to give a genial performance of political awareness, social ineptitude and sexual timidity. Now a teacher at his old school, Gregory wavers between a crush on fifth-former Carly McKinnon and the advances of hot-blooded colleague, Maria Doyle Kennedy. Alas, the plot to expose local industrialist Dougray Scott's part in Third World repression is barely credible and takes an age to resolve. *DVD*

John Gordon-Sinclair *Gregory Underwood* • Dougray Scott *Fraser Rowan* • Maria Doyle Kennedy *Bel* • Carly McKinnon *Frances* • Hugh McCue *Douglas* • Kevin Anderson *Jon* • Fiona Bell *Maddy Underwood* • Martin Schwab *Dimitri* ■ *Dir/Scr* Bill Forsyth

Gremlins ★★★★ 15

Black comedy horror   1984 · US · Colour · 101mins

Although Steven Spielberg as executive producer ensures that things don't get too nasty, this remains a wonderfully anarchic affair that is probably one of Hollywood's blackest mainstream hits. Zach Galligan is the teenager who is given a cuddly exotic pet mogwai called Gizmo, but through carelessness unwittingly unleashes a viciously murderous swarm of little gremlins. There's no doubt whose side director Joe Dante is on and he gleefully trashes the view of small-town America portrayed by feel-good movies like *It's a Wonderful Life* (which is being screened on TV throughout the tale). Film buffs will delight in all the in-jokes and the long list of cameos, ranging from Roger Corman veteran Dick Miller to Spielberg himself. Contains violence and swearing. *DVD*

Zach Galligan *Billy Peltzer* • Phoebe Cates *Kate* • Hoyt Axton *Rand Peltzer* • Frances Lee McCain *Lynn Peltzer* • Polly Holliday *Mrs Deagle* • Keye Luke *Grandfather* • John Louie *Chinese Boy* • Dick Miller *Mr Futterman* ■ *Dir* Joe Dante • *Scr* Chris Columbus

Gremlins 2: the New Batch ★★★ 15

Comedy horror   1990 · US · Colour · 102mins

With Steven Spielberg's influence seemingly absent this time around, Joe Dante's anarchic view of life is given full rein in this chaotic but cracking sequel. The action is transplanted to a skyscraper in New York where mad scientist Christopher Lee inadvertently lets the evil gremlins loose to take over the entire building. As with the original, Dante bombards the screen with a never-ending stream of movie spoofs, slapstick violence and sly little treats for film buffs. Stars Phoebe Cates and Zach Galligan are back again, but most of the laughs come from the supporting players: Lee, John Glover, Robert Prosky and Roger Corman veteran Dick Miller. Contains swearing.

Zach Galligan *Billy Peltzer* • Phoebe Cates *Kate Beringer* • John Glover *Daniel Clamp* • Robert Prosky *Grandpa Fred* • Howie Mandel *Gizmo* • Tony Randall *"Brain" Gremlin* • Robert Picardo *Forster* • Christopher Lee *Dr Catheter* • Dick Miller *Murray Futterman* ■ *Dir* Joe Dante • *Scr* Charlie Haas, from characters created by Chris Columbus

Gremloids ★★★ PG

Science-fiction comedy   1990 · US · Colour · 86mins

In this reasonably successful low-budget *Star Wars* spoof, a navigation mistake lands cosmic bad guy Buckethead on Earth instead of in a galaxy far, far away. He's in hot pursuit of a princess who's run off with some secret radio transmissions. Buckethead (and indeed he does have a bucket on his head!) is the Darth Vader of director Todd Durham's

refreshing piece, which doesn't set its satirical sights too high and hits more targets dead on as a result.

Paula Poundstone *Karen* • Chris Elliott *Hopper* • Alan Marx *Max* ■ *Dir/Scr* Todd Durham

Grendel, Grendel, Grendel ★★★

Animated adventure   1981 · Ausl · Colour · 88mins

Briefly popular with the chattering classes, John Gardner's reworking of the legend of Beowulf was an ambitious choice for an animated feature. The graphics are bold and colourful, the songs (apart from the trite theme tune) slyly apposite and the voices packed with character – particularly impressive is Peter Ustinov's reading of the monster, transforming him from the scourge of Hrothgar's kingdom into the hapless victim of its superstition and intolerance. But, lacking either the intellectual weight of its source or the levity to make it child friendly, the film failed to find an audience.

Peter Ustinov *Grendel* • Keith Michell *Shaper* • Arthur Dignam *Beowulf* • Ed Rosser *King* ■ *Dir* Alexander Stitt • *Scr* Alexander Stitt, from the novel *Grendel* by John Gardner

The Grey Fox ★★★★ PG

Western   1982 · Can · Colour · 87mins

Richard Farnsworth, who once did stunts for Roy Rogers and won Oscar nominations for *Comes a Horseman* and *The Straight Story*, gives a marvellous performance in this low-budget Canadian picture. Emerging in 1901 after 33 years in jail, Bill Miner (Farnsworth) tries to pick up where he left off as one of the Old West's most notorious outlaws – but those days are long gone. Shot in pseudo-documentary style, which gives the film the flavour of old photographs and the oldest movie (*The Great Train Robbery*), this is a real charmer in the tradition of *The Wild Bunch* and *Butch Cassidy*.

Richard Farnsworth *Bill Miner/George Edwards* • Jackie Burroughs *Kate Flynn* • Wayne Robson *William "Shorty" Dunn* • Timothy Webber *Sergeant Fernie* • Ken Pogue *Jack Budd* • Gary Reineke *Detective Seavey* ■ *Dir* Phillip Borsos • *Scr* John Hunter

Grey Gardens ★★★

Documentary   1975 · US · Colour · 95mins

Edith Bouvier Beale (79) and daughter Edie (56) – aunt and cousin of Jacqueline Onassis – were filmed by David and Albert Maysles over a few weeks in their squalid, decaying 28-room Long Island mansion, which was officially declared a health hazard. An intriguing, rather voyeuristic "non-fiction feature" on the lives of two eccentric women, who may or may not be giving performances for the ever present camera, it raises questions about the unvarnished "truth" which the Maysles brothers' "Direct Cinema" claimed to represent. The result is curious, but a bit unnerving.

Dir Ellen Hovde, Muffie Meyer • *Cinematographer* David Maysles, Albert Maysles

U = SUITABLE FOR ALL   **Uc** = SUITABLE FOR ALL, ESPECIALLY FOR YOUNG CHILDREN (VIDEO ONLY)   **PG** = PARENTAL GUIDANCE

Greyfriars Bobby ★★★★ U

Drama based on a true story
1960 · US/UK · Colour · 91mins

Forget the accents and the shabby sets, this is Disney at its delightful best. The true story of the Skye terrier who refused to desert its master after his burial in an Edinburgh kirkyard is irresistible, and is here never allowed to become maudlin or tacky for a second. Laurence Naismith, Donald Crisp and Kay Walsh judge their performances to perfection and director Don Chaffey does well to restrain the enthusiasm of the youngsters. But no one's eyes will be anywhere other than on the little dog. Don't be ashamed to cheer when he's granted the freedom of the city.

Donald Crisp *John Brown* • Laurence Naismith *Mr Traill* • Alex Mackenzie *Old Jock* • Kay Walsh *Mrs Brown* • Andrew Cruickshank *Lord Provost* • Gordon Jackson *Farmer* ■ *Dir* Don Chaffey • *Scr* Robert Westerby, from the story by Eleanor Atkinson

Greyhounds ★★

Action drama 1994 · US · Colour · 92mins

Made as a pilot for a TV series that never materialised, this humdrum crime thriller is all the more disappointing bearing in mind the quality of its cast. Dennis Weaver, James Coburn, Pat Morita and Robert Guillaume play the four men (three retired lawyers and a ex-con) who are hired by ambitious DA Roxann Biggs to help solve a murder mystery. This is hardly a brain-teasing mystery, but it's the lack of spark between the leads that scuppers the project.

Dennis Weaver *Chance Wayne* • Robert Guillaume *Robert "Maximum Bob" Smith* • James Coburn *John Dolan* • Pat Morita *Akira "Moch" Mochizuki* • Roxann Biggs *Jojo Golina* • Joan Pringle *Ann Smith* • Richard Steinmetz *Cam Cavanaugh* ■ *Dir* Kim Manners • *Scr* Stephen J Cannell, from a story by Peter Lance, Jerome Beck, Fred Murphy

Greystoke: the Legend of Tarzan, Lord of the Apes ★★★ PG

Adventure 1984 · UK/US · Colour · 131mins

This claims to be the definitive screen version of Edgar Rice Burroughs's tale, but, despite a highly professional cast that includes Ralph Richardson, Ian Holm and James Fox, it is far too long and collapses badly in the middle. However, director Hugh Hudson creates a memorable Edwardian atmosphere, and the early scenes in the ape colony are moving and deftly handled. Christopher Lambert certainly looks the part, but is not a skilful enough actor to carry off the complexities of Tarzan's plight in this decidedly adult version of the tale. Contains brief nudity.

Christopher Lambert *John Clayton, Tarzan* • Ralph Richardson *Earl of Greystoke* • Ian Holm *Captain Phillipe D'Arnot* • James Fox *Lork Esker* • Andie MacDowell *Jane Porter* • Cheryl Campbell *Lady Alice Clayton* • John Wells *Sir Evelyn Blount* • Nigel Davenport *Major Jack Downing* • Ian Charleson *Jefferson Brown* • Richard Griffiths *Captain Billings* ■ *Dir* Hugh Hudson • *Scr* PH Vazak [Robert Towne], Michael Austin, from the novel *Tarzan of the Apes* by Edgar Rice Burroughs • *Cinematographer* John Alcott • *Make-up* Rick Baker • *Production Designer* Stuart Craig

Gribouille ★★★

Drama 1937 · Fr · BW · 86mins

French character actor Raimu, renowned for his association with Marcel Pagnol, here finds his generous nature gets him into trouble. As jury member Camille, he takes pity on accused killer Michèle Morgan and takes her into his home. Directed by Marc Allégret, this was the third film appearance of Morgan, then 17, who would mature into one of France's most beautiful and accomplished actresses. An American version of the story, *The Lady in Question*, was made in 1940 with Brian Aherne and Rita Hayworth. In French with English subtitles.

Raimu *Camille* • Jeanne Provost *Louise* • Michèle Morgan *Natalie* • Gilbert Gil *Claude* • Jean Worms *Presiding judge* • Carette [Julien Carette] *Lurette* ■ *Dir* Marc Allégret • *Scr* Marcel Achard, HG Lustig, from a story by Marcel Achard

Grid Runners ★★ 18

Science-fiction action
1996 · US · Colour · 86mins

This future shocker mixes martial arts action with virtual reality. The premise may have worked better as a graphic novel; on screen it is leadenly executed. Don "the Dragon" Wilson is the requisitely muscled hero getting to grips with an evil cyberspace kickboxer Dante (Michael Bernardo), who goes on the rampage after escaping from inside a computer game. The plodding script is worsened by the inclusion of a cast of no-hopers, save for the presence of sixties siren Stella Stevens, whose son Andrew handles the directorial chores.

Don "the Dragon" Wilson *David Quarry* • Michael Bernardo *Dante* • Stella Stevens *Mary* ■ *Dir/Scr* Andrew Stevens

Gridlock ★★ 15

Action thriller 1995 · US · Colour · 87mins

Baywatch meets *Die Hard*, and, yes, it turns out to be as ghastly a concoction as it sounds. David Hasselhoff is the lone maverick who sets out to foil a gang of super-criminals who are threatening to bring New York to a halt in order to ransack $100 billion from a bank. TV-movie specialist Sandor Stern does his best with a limited budget and manages to stage a few decent set pieces. However, Hasselhoff is as wooden as ever and there isn't even an Alan Rickman-style villain to distract the attention.

David Hasselhoff *Jack Gorski* • Miguel Fernandes • Kathy Ireland ■ *Dir* Sandor Stern • *Scr* Joe Ferullo, Scott Sturdeon, Sandor Stern

Gridlock'd ★★★ 18

Comedy 1996 · US/UK · Colour · 87mins

In writer/director Vondie Curtis-Hall's engaging look at inner city life, Tim Roth and Tupac Shakur play jazz musicians trying to kick heroin. The comedy mainly springs from the way they are shunted between civic centres and red-tape nightmares as they go on the rehab/welfare merry-go-round while on the run from gangsters. Despite the depressing subject matter, the angry sadness that underscores the outwardly comic playing gives this adsurdist buddy movie some neat twists. These are further elevated by nifty flashbacks and agreeable character observation.

Tim Roth *Stretch* • Tupac Shakur *Spoon* • Thandie Newton *Cookie* • Charles Fleischer *Mr Woodson* • Howard Hesseman *Blind man* • John Sayles *First cop* • Eric Payne *Second cop* ■ *Dir/Scr* Vondie Curtis-Hall

Il Grido ★★

Drama 1957 · US/It · BW · 116mins

Also known as *The Outcry*, this is a typically neorealist effort from Italian writer/director Michelangelo Antonioni. A factory worker and his child are abandoned by the mother and wander the industrialised Po Valley. Antonioni's use of a rugged-looking but bad American actor (Steve Cochran) in the lead was a mistake, though it was typical of Italian movies at the time. (They never recorded live sound or bothered about accents.) A minor work from a major director who hit his stride with his next film, *L'Avventura*.

Steve Cochran *Aldo* • Alida Valli *Irma* • Betsy Blair *Elvia* • Dorian Gray *Virginia* • Lyn Shaw *Andreina* ■ *Dir* Michelangelo Antonioni • *Scr* Michelangelo Antonioni, Elio Bartolini, Ennio De Concini, from a story by Michelangelo Antonioni

Grief ★★ 18

Comedy drama 1993 · US · Colour · 82mins

Five crazy days in the life of a TV company producing *The Love Judge* soap opera come under the spotlight in director Richard Glatzer's cheap but cheerful tale. Gay story editor Craig Chester is at the centre of the action, still mourning the Aids-related death of his lover while fancying seemingly heterosexual writer Alexis Arquette. Throw in the fact that his boss is played by Jackie Beat (in post-Divine mode) and it becomes clear this mildly amusing spoof of American pop culture – tacky soap scenes alternate with vapid reality – is working on a reasonably diverting level of its own. Contains swearing, sex scenes and nudity.

Craig Chester *Mark* • Jackie Beat *Jo* • Illeana Douglas *Leslie* • Lucy Gutteridge *Paula* • Alexis Arquette *Bill* • Carlton Wilborn *Jeremy* • Robin Swid *Kelly* ■ *Dir/Scr* Richard Glatzer

Grievous Bodily Harm ★★★ 18

Thriller 1987 · Ausl · Colour · 96mins

This rattling Australian thriller from director Mark Joffe certainly takes no prisoners. The bruising action never lets up, from the moment when crusading crime reporter Colin Friels discovers that a teacher's dead wife was a secret blue movie actress. Add a touch of corruption and a conspiracy theory to the brew and you have a highly potent picture, helped along by the gutsy performances of Friels, John Waters as the morbidly obsessed widower and Bruno Lawrence as a bent cop with a malicious glint in his eye. Not all the loose ends tie up, but don't let that worry you. Contains swearing and brief nudity.

Colin Friels *Tom Stewart* • Bruno Lawrence *Det Sgt Ray Birch* • John Waters *Morris Martin*
• Joy Bell *Claudine* • Chris Stalker *Allen* • Kim Gyngell *Mick* • Shane Briant *Stephen Enderby* ■ *Dir* Mark Joffe • *Scr* Warwick Hind

The Grifters ★★★★ 18

Crime thriller 1990 · US · Colour · 105mins

It's not quite a contradiction in terms to describe this adaptation of Jim Thompson's novel as a highly colourful *film noir*. Director Stephen Frears neatly alternates between the audacious scams executed by a trio of con artists, sudden moments of calculated violence and the intense rivalry that develops between expert bet chiseller Anjelica Huston, her ambitious son John Cusack and his scheming girlfriend Annette Bening. Cusack rather lets the side down with a lightweight performance, but the powerhouse playing of his Oscar-nominated co-stars keeps the attention riveted through every twist and turn. Contains swearing and nudity.

Anjelica Huston *Lilly Dillon* • John Cusack *Roy Dillon* • Annette Bening *Myra Langtry* • Pat Hingle *Bobo Justus* • Henry Jones *Simms* • JT Walsh *Cole* • Martin Scorsese *Narrator* ■ *Dir* Stephen Frears • *Scr* Donald E Westlake, from the novel by Jim Thompson

Grim Prairie Tales ★★★

Horror western 1990 · US · Colour · 86mins

A collection of stories grouped together by one theme, told by a city traveller and a mountain man (Brad Dourif and James Earl Jones) who meet on the desolate plains one night. The stories – a mixture of horror, western and comedy – are entertainingly performed by Marc McClure, William Atherton and Scott Paulin, but the real plaudits once again belong to Jones, the booming-voiced actor who supplied the vocals for Simba's father in *The Lion King*.

Brad Dourif *Farley* • James Earl Jones *Morrison* • Will Hare *Lee* • Marc McClure *Tom* • William Atherton *Arthur* • Lisa Eichhorn *Maureen* • Michelle Joyner *Jenny* • Wendy Cooke *Eva* • Scott Paulin *Martin* • Bruce M Fischer *Colochez* ■ *Dir/Scr* Wayne Coe

Grip of the Strangler ★★★

Mystery horror 1958 · US · BW · 81mins

Studying the 20-year-old murders of the "Haymarket Strangler", writer Boris Karloff becomes gruesomely possessed by the maniac responsible. Why? Because he *was* the maniac responsible! Karloff merely shuts one eye and bites his lower lip to become the madman in this pale Jekyll and Hyde clone. But while he shows his gift for changing personalities with the simplest shift of expression, whipping up minor scares in the process, the obvious low budget and simplistic script fail to give him much support.

Boris Karloff *James Rankin* • Jean Kent *Cora Seth* • Elizabeth Allan *Barbara Rankin* • Anthony Dawson *Detective Superintendent Burk* • Vera Day *Pearl* • Tim Turner *Kenneth McColl* • Diane Aubrey *Lily* ■ *Dir* Robert Day • *Scr* Jan Read, John C Cooper, from a story by Jan Read

The Grissom Gang ★★★

Thriller 1971 · US · Colour · 128mins

A thoroughly brutish and violent reworking of a notorious original, James Hadley Chase's novel *No*

Orchids for Miss Blandish, directed by Robert Aldrich, a major talent with a dark imagination. Disturbingly overlong to boot, this sombre epic remains relentlessly watchable thanks to a superb central performance from Kim Darby (*True Grit*) as the kidnapped heiress at the centre of the drama. The thugs are comic-book creations, buffoonish and degenerate, and producer/director Aldrich can't decide whether the movie is a comedy, a thriller or something in between.

Kim Darby *Barbara Blandish* • Tony Musante *Eddie Hagan* • Scott Wilson *Slim Grissom* • Irene Dailey *Ma Grissom* • Robert Lansing *Dave Fenner* ■ *Dir* Robert Aldrich • *Scr* Leon Griffiths, from the novel *No Orchids for Miss Blandish* by James Hadley Chase

Grizzly ★ 15

Adventure   1976 · US · Colour · 87mins

One of many *Jaws* rip-offs, this replaces the shark with a very angry, hungry and overgrown grizzly bear who gets his kicks snacking off the visitors to a nature reserve. The bear seems particularly partial to human offal – raw, without even a drop of a nice chianti. As the body count rises, park ranger Christopher George is joined in his heroic pursuit by helicopter pilot Andrew Prine and naturalist Richard Jaeckel. You'll root for the bear. ▭

Christopher George *Ranger* • Andrew Prine *Helicopter pilot* • Richard Jaeckel *Naturalist* • Joan McCall *Photographer* ■ *Dir* William Girdler • *Scr* Harvey Flaxman, David Sheldon

Grizzly Adams: the Treasure of the Bear ★★

Adventure   1995 · US · Colour · 98mins

This latest adventure of the bearded backwoodsman dabbles in native American folklore and cultural piracy, as well as the usual outdoor heroics, and is rather dark and involved for a family film. Aided by a grizzly named Samson, Tom Tayback (as Adams) takes on both the perils of Dark Mountain and the villainous Joseph Campanella to secure the liberty of a kidnapped professor and ensure the safe birth of the new chief of the Bear People. Director John Huneck makes effective use of the landscape, but all the stuff about spirits, superstitions and shamen will probably go over the heads of younger viewers.

Tom Tayback *Grizzly Adams* • Joseph Campanella *Hunnicutt* • Lindsay Bloom ■ *Dir* John Huneck, David Sheldon • *Scr* Larry Bischoff, William Brian Lowery

Grizzly Mountain ★★

Adventure   1997 · US · Colour · 96mins

Although the title and the presence of Grizzly Adams himself, Dan Haggerty, imply it, this lame backwoods tale is no relation to the movie and TV series that brought former animal trainer Haggerty his fame. Here, the time-travelling story finds jaded city kids Dylan Haggerty (Dan's son) and Nicole Lund being whisked back in time to the Wild West of the 1870s for some adventures with the now visibly ageing Haggerty Sr. The scenery is nice, but the plotting and performances leave a lot to be desired.

Dan Haggerty *Jeremiah* • Kim Morgan Greene *Betty* • Nicole Lund *Nicole Marks* • Martin Kove *Marshall Jackson* • Perry Stephens *Burt "Boss Man" Mann* • Dylan Haggerty *Dylan Marks* • Megan Haggerty *Megan Marks* ■ *Dir* Jeremy Haft • *Scr* Jeremy Haft, Peter White, from a story by Eric Parkinson

The Groove Tube ★★★ 18

Comedy satire   1974 · US · Colour · 72mins

This saucy upstart of a movie pokes fun at all aspects of US TV. A spin-off from the similarly-themed theatrical production, it consists of a series of sketches satirising such small-screen fare as children's programmes, sports broadcasts and adverts. As with most comedy ventures it is inconsistent, but its scatalogical approach means it does occasionally hit some worthwhile targets. With its X-rated, bad-taste style this can be seen as the forerunner to later shock comedies like *Kentucky Fried Movie* and *Dumb and Dumber.* ▭

Buzzy Linhart *The Hitchhiker* • Richmond Baier *The Girl* • Christine Nazareth *Theatre Girl* • Chevy Chase *The Fingers/Geritan/"Four Leaf Clover"* • Jennifer Welles *Geritan* • Ken Shapiro *Koko the Clown/Kramp TV Kitchen/The Dealer/Newscaster/"Just You, Just Me"* • Richard Belzer *President* ■ *Dir* Ken Shapiro • *Scr* Ken Shapiro, Lane Sarasohn

Grosse Pointe Blank ★★★ 15

Comedy drama   1997 · US · Colour · 102mins

A hitman (John Cusack) returns to his home town for a high-school reunion and another assassination, only to find conventional free-marketeers just as ruthless as he is. He also bumps into an old flame (Minnie Driver) he jilted on prom night ten years before. Named in tribute to John Boorman's cult thriller *Point Blank*, this uneasy black comedy from director George Armitage only really picks up speed halfway into the story. But the actors, including Dan Aykroyd and Cusack's older sister Joan, are really superior. ▭ **DVD**

John Cusack *Martin Q Blank* • Minnie Driver *Debi Newberry* • Alan Arkin *Dr Oatman* • Dan Aykroyd *Grocer* • Joan Cusack *Marcella* • Hank Azaria *Lardner* • K Todd Freeman *McCullers* • Mitchell Ryan *Mr Newberry* ■ *Dir* George Armitage • *Scr* Tom Jankiewicz, DV DeVincentis, Steve Pink, John Cusack, from a story by Tom Jankiewicz

The Grotesque ★ 18

Black comedy   1995 · UK · Colour · 93mins

Want to know how to turn a witty and original novel into a hackneyed bore in one easy lesson? Just watch director John-Paul Davidson's lamentable black comedy based on author Patrick McGrath's wildly acerbic tale about the class struggle in forties England. Basically the story of what happens when new butler Sting arrives at the house of eccentric explorer Alan Bates, this murderous social satire is stunningly conventional when it should have been a penetrating look at the macabre collapse of a certain kind of lifestyle. The cast do their best with the arch dialogue, but it's nowhere near good enough to elevate this self-conscious yawn above the status of made-for-TV mediocrity. ▭

Alan Bates *Sir Hugo Coal* • Sting *Fledge* • Theresa Russell *Lady Harriet Coal* • Lena Headey *Cleo Coal* • Steven Mackintosh *Sidney Giblet* • Anna Massey *Mrs Giblet* • Timothy Kightley *Harbottle* • Jim Carter *George Lecky* ■ *Dir* John-Paul Davidson • *Scr* Patrick McGrath, from his novel

Ground Zero ★★★ 15

Thriller   1987 · Ausl · Colour · 96mins

Although we're used to the way governments keep us in the dark, this political thriller from Australia still manages to shock with its story, based on fact, about a man seeking reasons for his father's death during British A-bomb testing in the outback in the fifties. Directors Michael Pattinson and Bruce Myles induce a feeling of paranoia using the niftiest of devices, while actors Colin Friels and Jack Thompson put genuine feeling into their roles as they lift the lid on past moral meltdown. It's Donald Pleasence, however, playing the hermit-like survivor of those nuclear trials, who manages to steal every scene he's in. Contains violence and swearing. ▭

Colin Friels *Harvey Denton* • Jack Thompson *Trebilcock* • Donald Pleasence *Prosper Gaffney* • Natalie Bate *Pat Denton* • Simon Chilvers *Commission president* • Neil Fitzpatrick *Hooking* • Bob Maza *Wallemare* • Peter Cummins *Ballantyne* • Stuart Faichney *ASIO agent* ■ *Dir* Michael Pattinson, Bruce Myles • *Scr* Jan Sardi, Mac Gudgeon

Groundhog Day ★★★★★ PG

Comedy fantasy   1993 · US · Colour · 96mins

Hollywood once produced three or four classic comedies each year. Nowadays we're lucky to get one a decade and this is a contender for the nineties. Bill Murray gives the best performance of his career as Phil Connors, the weatherman with attitude, trapped in a day he will remember for the rest of his life because, unless he can find some answers, it will *be* the rest of his life. Director Harold Ramis uses every cinematic trick in the book to keep what is essentially a one-gag movie brimming with life and fresh ideas. Stephen Tobolowsky is superb as a nerdy insurance salesman and, as Phil's producer, Andie MacDowell has never been better. Contains some strong language. ▭ **DVD**

Bill Murray *Phil Connors* • Andie MacDowell *Rita Hanson* • Chris Elliott *Larry* • Stephen Tobolowsky *Ned* • Brian Doyle-Murray *Buster* • Marita Geraghty *Nancy* • Angela Paton *Mrs Lancaster* • Rick Ducommun *Gus* ■ *Dir* Harold Ramis • *Scr* Danny Rubin, Harold Ramis, from a story by Danny Rubin

The Groundstar Conspiracy ★★

Drama   1972 · Can · Colour · 95mins

This effective thriller about spies in the space programme is really one of those high-gloss flicks Universal made to show off and use up its contract players, in this case George Peppard and Michael Sarrazin. Director Lamont Johnson handles the suspense with a firm touch and, though the script could have been tighter and the leading lady (Christine Belford) more distinguished, the Vancouver locations look splendid.

George Peppard *Tuxan* • Michael Sarrazin *Welles* • Christine Belford *Nicole* • Cliff Potts *Mosely* • James Olson *Stanton* • Tim O'Connor *Gossage* • James McEachin *Bender* • Alan Oppenheimer *Hackett* ■ *Dir* Lamont Johnson • *Scr* Matthew Howard, from the novel *The Alien* by LP Davies

The Group ★★★★

Drama   1966 · US · Colour · 146mins

Notable as one of the first films to show the emotional development of women as individuals and not just as lost souls awaiting salvation by men, this glitzy, glossy and extremely good drama is based on the iconoclastic blockbuster by Mary McCarthy. It is beautifully played by the likes of Candice Bergen, Jessica Walter and, particularly, Joan Hackett, whose ultimate fate is skilfully drawn. A soap opera-style movie that rather aptly features a pre-*Dallas* Larry Hagman.

Candice Bergen *Lakey* • Joan Hackett *Dottie* • Elizabeth Hartman *Priss* • Shirley Knight *Polly* • Joanna Pettet *Kay* • Mary-Robin Redd *Pokey* • Jessica Walter *Libby* • Larry Hagman *Harald* • Hal Holbrook *Gus Leroy* ■ *Dir* Sidney Lumet • *Scr* Sidney Buchman, from the novel by Mary McCarthy

Grumpier Old Men ★★ 12

Comedy   1996 · US · Colour · 96mins

Old stagers Walter Matthau and Jack Lemmon cruise through this unaccountably popular sequel to an equally moribund original, presumably on their way to another fat pay-cheque. Ann-Margret also returns from the first film, while Sophia Loren turns up as a much-married interloper who stirs up the boys' bile by buying their beloved bait shop and turning it into a restaurant. The grumpy pair forget their incessant feuding to wage war on the restaurant, but resourceful Loren outwits them before kindling a little love in Matthau's heart. It's good to see such troupers working again, but they deserve better material. ▭

Jack Lemmon *John Gustafson* • Walter Matthau *Max Goldman* • Ann-Margret *Ariel Gustafson* • Sophia Loren *Maria Ragetti* • Burgess Meredith *Grandpa Gustafson* • Daryl Hannah *Melanie Gustafson* • Kevin Pollak *Jacob Goldman* ■ *Dir* Howard Deutch • *Scr* Mark Steven Johnson, from his characters

Grumpy Old Men ★★★ 12

Comedy drama   1993 · US · Colour · 99mins

Jack Lemmon and Walter Matthau are one of the all-time great partnerships and this engaging comedy marked their seventh screen collaboration. In this high-concept tale, they are a gentler variation on Harry Enfield's Old Gits – warring senior citizens whose feuding escalates as they battle for the hand of Ann-Margret. Although the script isn't quite as strong as it could be, the chemistry between the two stars is irresistible and they are matched by an equally strong supporting cast including Burgess Meredith, Kevin Pollak and Ossie Davis. Contains some swearing. ▭

Jack Lemmon *John Gustafson* • Walter Matthau *Max Goldman* • Ann-Margret *Ariel Truax* • Burgess Meredith *Grandpa Gustafson* • Daryl Hannah *Melanie Gustafson* • Kevin Pollak *Jacob Goldman* • Ossie Davis *Chuck* • Buck Henry *Elliott Snyder* ■ *Dir* Donald Petrie • *Scr* Mark Steven Johnson

Guadalcanal Diary ★★★★
Second World War action drama
1943 · US · BW · 93mins

Richard Tregaskis's novel, an "I was there" account of the struggle to recapture the South Pacific island of Guadalcanal from the Japanese during the Second World War, was difficult to film without resorting to cliché. Nevertheless, 20th Century-Fox pulls out all the stops in the authenticity stakes, with superbly staged (and expensive) action sequences that war movie fans will lap up. Richard Jaeckel is exceptionally fine, and there's solid back-up from stars such as William Bendix, Anthony Quinn and Lloyd Nolan. Preston Foster offers some unusually unsentimental homilies as the padre and, overall, the movie contains a rare honesty as it eschews the usual Hollywood heroics.
Preston Foster *Father Donnelly* • Lloyd Nolan *Hook Malone* • William Bendix *Taxi Potts* • Richard Conte *Captain Davis* • Anthony Quinn *Jesus "Soose" Alvarez* • Richard Jaeckel *Private Johnny Anderson* • Roy Roberts *Captain Cross* • Lionel Stander *Butch* ■ *Dir* Lewis Seiler • *Scr* Lamar Trotti, Jerry Cady, from the diary by Richard Tregaskis

Guantanamera ★★ 15
Drama 1995 · Sp /Cu/Ger · Colour · 101mins

This road movie – the last project completed by Tomas Gutierrez Alea, Cuba's best-known director – has too many echoes of Alea's own *Death of a Bureaucrat* for comfort. The passing of a famous singer's funeral cortege across the island should have inspired some seething satire, but the swipes at petty officialdom, government propaganda and macho misanthropy are merely passing blows at easy targets. There's simply not enough tension in the developing romance between onetime lecturer Mirtha Ibarra and her gone-to-bad student Jorge Perugorria to hold our attention. Carlos Cruz is hissably callous as Ibarra's soulless husband, but this is a disappointing swansong.
Carlos Cruz *Adolfo* • Mirtha Ibarra [Mirta Ibarra] *Georgina* • Raul Eguren *Candido* • Jorge Perugorria *Mariano* • Pedro Fernandez *Ramon* • Luis Alberto Garcia *Tony* • Conchita Brando *Yoyita* ■ *Dir* Tomás Gutiérrez Alea, Juan Carlos Tabio • *Scr* Eliseo Alberto Diego, Tomás Gutiérrez Alea, Juan Carlos Tabio

The Guardian ★★ 18
Thriller 1984 · US · Colour · 93mins

Not the William Friedkin chiller about the psycho-nanny, but a drama from *The Count of Monte Cristo* director David Greene, set in a New York apartment building. After a murder takes place in their block, the residents decide to hire a former soldier as a "guardian" but get more than they bargained for. An impressive cast including Martin Sheen and Louis Gossett Jr helps save this film from daftness. Contains swearing.
Martin Sheen *Charlie Hyatt* • Louis Gossett Jr *John Mack* • Arthur Hill *Phil Julian* • Tandy Cronyn *Lynn Hyatt* • Simon Reynolds *Robbie Hyatt* • Kate Lynch *Fran* ■ *Dir* David Greene • *Scr* Richard Levinson, William Link

The Guardian ★★★ 18
Supernatural horror
1990 · US · Colour · 88mins

A po-faced horror offering from William Friedkin, the director who once frightened the life out of world audiences with *The Exorcist*. There's much pleasure to be had here, mainly from watching leading lady Jenny Seagrove in her first American starring role: the part is virtually unplayable, but, as the demonic nanny, Seagrove really makes us believe she's on nodding terms with hell. It could have been a lot more scary, but that's a minor quibble in a generally satisfying tale of the supernatural. Contains swearing and violence.
Jenny Seagrove *Camilla* • Dwier Brown *Phil* • Carey Lowell *Kate* • Brad Hall *Ned Runcie* • Miguel Ferrer *Ralph Hess* • Natalia Nogulich [Natalija Nogulich] *Molly Sheridan* • Pamela Brull *Gail Krasno* ■ *Dir* William Friedkin • *Scr* Stephen Volk, William Friedkin, Dan Greenburg, from the novel *The Nanny* by Dan Greenburg

Guardian Angels ★★
Comedy 1995 · Fr · Colour · 110mins

Director Jean-Marie Poiré followed up his blockbusting time-travel fantasy, *Les Visiteurs*, with this patchy comedy, which he co-scripted with that film's star, Christian Clavier. A mix of character comedy and perilous slapstick, the action centres on the shady-dealing Gérard Depardieu, who encounters his guardian angel while trying to protect a friend's son from the Triads and recover $14 million in stolen loot. Depardieu is in typically rollicking form, but it's Clavier, whose naive priest has a thoroughly resistible guardian angel of his own, who shamelessly steals the show. Subtle it's not, but there are laughs amidst the mugging. A French language film.
Gérard Depardieu *Antoine Carco* • Christian Clavier *Père Tarain* • Eva Grimaldi *Regina Podium* ■ *Dir* Jean-Marie Poiré • *Scr* Jean-Marie Poiré, Christian Clavier

Guarding Tess ★★★ 12
Comedy drama 1994 · US · Colour · 91mins

As the former First Lady from hell, Shirley MacLaine does almost too good a job of playing cantankerous president's widow Tess Carlisle, who confounds her secret service minder Doug Chesnic (Nicolas Cage) by asking for another spell of duty from him after he has already suffered three years of provocation. MacLaine is so believable in the leading role she's almost unendurable to watch, while Cage displays a sure comic touch. The film is attractively staged and entertaining until it finally lurches into melodrama. Contains violence and swearing.
Shirley MacLaine *Tess Carlisle* • Nicolas Cage *Doug Chesnic* • Austin Pendleton *Earl* • Edward Albert *Barry Carlisle* • James Rebhorn *Howard Shaeffer* • Richard Griffiths *Frederick* • John Roselius *Tom Bahlor* ■ *Dir* Hugh Wilson • *Scr* Hugh Wilson, Peter Torokvei

The Guardsman ★★★★
Comedy 1931 · US · BW · 81mins

The celebrated husband-and-wife acting team of Lynn Fontanne and Alfred Lunt repeated their stage roles in this screen version of Ferenc Molnar's romantic comedy. Tormented by jealousy, the husband tests his wife by disguising himself as a Russian officer and attempting to seduce her. Although very theatrical, the film survives as a cherishable testament to the couple's exceptional skills. It's clear to see why they were perhaps the most famous stage actors of their generation. The story was later remade as the musical *The Chocolate Soldier* in 1941.
Alfred Lunt *The Actor* • Lynn Fontanne *The Actress* • Roland Young *The Critic* • ZaSu Pitts *Liesl* • Maude Eburne *Mama* • Herman Bing *A Creditor* ■ *Dir* Sidney Franklin • *Scr* Ernst Vajda [Ernest Vajda], Claudine West, from the play by Ferenc Molnar

Guelwaar ★★★★
Political satire
1992 · Sen/Fr · Colour · 115mins

One of the best-known of black African film-makers, Ousmane Sembene forged his reputation with the searing satire of Senegalese life, *Xala*. He is no less scathing in this supremely controlled study of the conflicts of politics, language, religion and custom that divide a state proud of its independence and yet still reliant on overseas aid. The disappearance of a political dissident's corpse exposes all manner of contradictions as Catholic priests and Muslim imams feud over the burial, while the mayor and his chief of police fight to keep the truth about his death a secret. Third World cinema close to its best. In French with English subtitles.
Omar Seck *Gora* • Ndiawar Diop *Barthelemy* • Mame Ndoumbe Diop *Nogoy Marie Thioune* • Isseu Niang *Veronique* • Myriam Niang *Helene* ■ *Dir/Scr* Ousmane Sembene

La Guerre Est Finie
★★★★ 15
Drama 1966 · Fr/Swe · BW · 116mins

Typically overlapping the present, memory and imagination, Alain Resnais here offers a troubling study of the gulf between passive commitment and direct action. Written by the exiled Spanish author Jorge Semprun, the film focuses on the three days in which middle-aged revolutionary Yves Montand comes to recognise that his unswerving allegiance to the cause of overthrowing Franco is faltering. Montand gives a performance of great solemnity, and he is well supported by Ingrid Thulin as his loyal mistress and Geneviève Bujold as the student radical with whom he has a brief affair. In French with English subtitles.
Yves Montand *Diego* • Ingrid Thulin *Marianne* • Geneviève Bujold *Nadine* • Paul Crauchet *Roberto* • Jean Bouise *Ramon* • Jean Dasté *Chief* • Dominique Rozan *Jude* • Michel Piccoli *Customs inspector* • Françoise Bertin *Carmen* ■ *Dir* Alain Resnais • *Scr* Jorge Semprun

Guess What Happened to Count Dracula ★
Horror 1970 · US · Colour · 80mins

Not a lot actually. The Transylvanian vampire apparently changed his name to Count Adrian (Des Roberts) and took to hanging around a mod Sunset Strip disco called Dracula's Castle. Well, that's according to this atrocious exploitation quickie directed and written by Laurence Merrick and designed to steal *Count Yorga, Vampire*'s thunder at the box office. It didn't stand a chance and has been little seen since. But that's mainly because it's no good.
Des Roberts *Count Dracula* • Claudia Barron *Angelica* • John Landon *Guy* • Robert Branche *Dr Harris* • Frank Donato *Imp* • Sharon Beverly *Vamp* ■ *Dir/Scr* Laurence Merrick

Guess Who's Coming to Dinner ★★★★ PG
Comedy drama 1967 · US · Colour · 103mins

One biography suggests that Spencer Tracy treated Katharine Hepburn more harshly than schmaltzy legend might suggest. But you would not guess it from this, their last movie together, in which the alliance works to dovetailing perfection. They're a rich couple whose liberal principles are tested by the proposed marriage of their daughter to a black doctor. As he is Sidney Poitier, all intellectual politesse, there's never any doubt about the outcome. The film may have a foregone conclusion, but it's worth watching as the acting is so good. Tracy and an Oscar-winning Hepburn were a deceptively rare cinema double-act, who seemed genuinely fond of each other both on and off screen. Contains swearing.
Spencer Tracy *Matthew Drayton* • Sidney Poitier *John Prentice* • Katharine Hepburn *Christina Drayton* • Katharine Houghton *Joey Drayton* • Cecil Kellaway *Monsignor Ryan* • Beah Richards *Mrs Prentice* • Roy E Glenn Sr *Mr Prentice* • Isabell Sanford [Isabel Sanford] *Tillie* ■ *Dir* Stanley Kramer • *Scr* William Rose

Guest House Paradiso ★ 15
Comedy 1999 · UK · Colour · 86mins

Probably the best thing that can be said here is that *Bottom* fans won't be disappointed: essentially, this is a slightly expanded, big-screen version of the TV series, with slightly better sets and plenty of cartoon violence. For the uninitiated, however, this has to be the worse TV spin-off since *On the Buses* back in 1971. Stars Rik Mayall and Adrian Edmondson have no one to blame but themselves for this puerile farce: Edmondson directs, from a script he co-wrote with Mayall. The story, for what it's worth, finds sociopaths Richie and Eddie running a revolting hotel in the shadow of a nuclear power plant.
Rik Mayall *Richie Twat* • Adrian Edmondson *Eddie Elizabeth Ndingobaba* • Vincent Cassel *Gino Bolognese* • Hélène Mahieu *Gina Carbonara* • Bill Nighy *Mr Johnson* • Simon Pegg *Mr Nice* • Fenella Fielding *Mrs Foxfur* ■ *Dir* Adrian Edmondson • *Scr* Adrian Edmondson, Rik Mayall

Guest in the House ★
Drama 1944 · US · BW · 120mins

Anne Baxter stars as a mentally disturbed but beautiful young woman who falls for her doctor's brother (Ralph Bellamy). Baxter doesn't allow Bellamy's marriage or her own relationship with the doctor (Scott McKay) to stand in her way, as she wreaks appalling emotional havoc in the happy home. Directed by John Brahm with lots of atmosphere and an excellent cast, this poisonous, overlong and ludicrous drivel is all the more depressing because it compels one to keep watching.

Anne Baxter *Evelyn Heath* • Ralph Bellamy *Douglas Proctor* • Aline MacMahon *Aunt Martha* • Ruth Warrick *Ann Proctor* • Scott McKay *Dan Proctor* • Jerome Cowan *Mr Hackett* • Marie McDonald *Miriam* ■ *Dir* John Brahm • *Scr* Ketti Frings, from the play *Dear Evelyn* by Hagar Wilde, Dale Eunson

Guest Wife ★★ U

Comedy 1945 · US · BW · 84mins

A comedy variation on the eternal triangle theme – bachelor foreign correspondent must play married to keep his job, borrows banker friend's wife, inevitable complications ensue – is unfortunately short on intended laughs. An increasingly chaotic and unconvincing farce, directed with too heavy a hand by Sam Wood, in which only Claudette Colbert, at her sparkling best as the "borrowed" wife, rises above the material. Don Ameche's newspaperman looks uncomfortable and one-time screen cowboy Richard Foran's accommodating husband is just plain silly.

Claudette Colbert *Mary Price* • Don Ameche *Joe Parker* • Richard Foran *Christopher Price* • Charles Dingle *AT Worth* • Grant Mitchell *Detective* • Wilma Francis *Susy* ■ *Dir* Sam Wood • *Scr* Bruce Manning, John Klorer

A Guide for the Married Man ★★★ PG

Comedy 1967 · US · Colour · 87mins

Walter Matthau, married for years, suddenly breaks one of the Ten Commandments, he covets his neighbour's wife. Fortunately, his best friend, Robert Morse, is a philanderer himself, and more than willing to teach Matthau the art of having an affair and getting away with it. This is, clearly, a variation on *The Seven Year Itch*, for which Matthau, by the way, was first choice. There's plenty to enjoy in this comedy of sexual mores, which is most notable for its glorious gallery of guest spots including Lucille Ball, Jack Benny, Jayne Mansfield, Phil Silvers and Terry-Thomas. Gene Kelly directed, not that you'd notice.

Walter Matthau *Paul Manning* • Robert Morse *Ed Stander* • Inger Stevens *Ruth Manning* • Sue Anne Langdon [Sue Ane Langdon] *Irma Johnson* • Jackie Russell *Miss Harris* • Claire Kelly *Harriet Stander* • Linda Harrison *Miss Stardust* • Elaine Devry *Jocelyn Montgomery* ■ *Dir* Gene Kelly • *Scr* Frank Tarloff, from his book

The Guilt of Janet Ames ★★★

Psychological drama 1947 · US · BW · 81mins

Psychiatry was very much in fashion in stage and screen drama when this offbeat drama was made. Its fascinating premise also tapped into postwar guilt and paranoia, with Rosalind Russell as a woman whose husband was killed in the war when he threw himself on a grenade to save five comrades. She sets out to trace the men whose lives were spared to see if they were worthy of her husband's sacrifice. One of the men (Melvyn Douglas) cures her hysterical paralysis with hypnosis, though it turns out he's more in need of therapy than she is.

Rosalind Russell *Janet Ames* • Melvyn Douglas *Smithfield Cobb* • Sid Caesar *Sammy Weaver* • Betsy Blair *Katie* • Nina Foch *Susie Pierson* • Charles Cane *Walker* • Harry Von Zell *Carter* ■ *Dir* Henry Levin • *Scr* Louella MacFarlane, Allen Rivkin, Devery Freeman, from a story by Lenore Coffee

Guilty? ★★

Crime mystery 1956 · UK · BW · 94mins

Based on Michael Gilbert's novel *Death Has Deep Roots*, this might have been an enthralling thriller had director Edmond T Gréville had a more original plot to work with. There's certainly enough incident, as sleuthing attorney John Justin heads to Avignon to unearth the evidence that will clear Resistance heroine Andrée Debar of the murder of the lover whose wartime betrayal resulted in her incarceration in a concentration camp. But, instead of delving into the guilty secrets of France under the Nazi occupation, the story develops a more straightforward strand, involving an undercover agent played by Barbara Laage.

John Justin *Nap Rumbold* • Barbara Laage *Jacqueline Delbois* • Donald Wolfit *Judge* • Stephen Murray *Summers* • Norman Wooland *Pelton* • Frank Villard *Pierre Lemaire* • Andrée Debar *Vicki Martin* • Betty Stockfeld *Mrs Roper* ■ *Dir* Edmond T Gréville • *Scr* Maurice J Wilson, Ernest Dudley, from the novel *Death Has Deep Roots* by Michael Gilbert

Guilty as Charged ★★★ 18

Black comedy 1991 · US · Colour · 91mins

Rod Steiger revisits his homicidal persona from *No Way to Treat a Lady* in this black comedy. He's at his scenery-chewing best as mad religious tycoon Ben Kallin, dispatching criminals in his home-made electric chair. *South Park*'s Chef, Isaac Hayes, is one of Steiger's little helpers. It's all a shocker of some voltage, with Lauren Hutton looking aghast and director Sam Irvin making it stylish, if not plausible.

Rod Steiger *Ben Kallin* • Lauren Hutton *Liz Stanford* • Heather Graham *Kimberly* • Lyman Ward *Mark Stanford* • Isaac Hayes *Aloysius* • Zelda Rubenstein *Edna* • Erwin Keyes *Deek* ■ *Dir* Sam Irvin • *Scr* Charles Gale

Guilty as Sin ★★★ 15

Thriller 1993 · US · Colour · 102mins

Ever since his masterpiece *12 Angry Men*, director Sidney Lumet has had a taste for legal thrillers. And before it topples from high mystery to low melodrama, this film cops a plea for craftsmanship at least, with Rebecca De Mornay as the slick lawyer defending wife-killer Don Johnson, whose lethal duplicity involves the death of more than one woman. Larry Cohen's script is far more serrated than the *Jagged Edge* it resembles and so, prior to its succumbing to victim-in-peril clichés, is Lumet's handling of some suspenseful legal scenes. Contains violence and some swearing. **DVD**

Rebecca De Mornay *Jennifer Haines* • Don Johnson *David Greenhill* • Stephen Lang *Phil Garson* • Jack Warden *Moe Plimpton* • Dana Ivey *Judge Tompkins* • Ron White *Diangelo* ■ *Dir* Sidney Lumet • *Scr* Larry Cohen

Guilty by Suspicion ★★★ 15

Drama 1990 · US · Colour · 100mins

The investigation of the House Un-American Activities Committee into communism in Hollywood is one of the most shameful episodes in movie history. But the film folk whose careers were destroyed by the infamous blacklist deserve a better memorial than Irwin Winkler's well-intentioned but underachieving picture. Set at the height of the 1951 witch-hunt, the action centres on film-maker Robert De Niro's dilemma – lose everything he's worked for or betray the "fellow travellers" among his friends. Although rooted in fact, the film fails to generate the requisite atmosphere of fear and suspicion, and seems more of a liberal reproach than a searing indictment. Contains swearing.

Robert De Niro *David Merrill* • Annette Bening *Ruth Merrill* • George Wendt *Bunny Baxter* • Patricia Wettig *Dorothy Nolan* • Sam Wanamaker *Felix Graff* • Luke Edwards *Paulie Merrill* • Chris Cooper *Larry Nolan* • Ben Piazza *Darryl F Zanuck* • Martin Scorsese *Joe Lesser* ■ *Dir/Scr* Irwin Winkler

Guilty Bystander ★★

Film noir 1950 · US · BW · 91mins

Zachary Scott finds himself in familiar thriller territory as an ex-cop with a drink problem, a crummy job and a failed marriage. His problems escalate when his son is kidnapped and the convoluted storyline throws in smuggling for good measure. The supporting cast, including Broadway stalwarts Sam Levene and Kay Medford (the latter Oscar-nominated for her role in *Funny Girl*) lend strength to the flimsy plot, while there are telling contributions from Faye Emerson and Mary Boland.

Zachary Scott *Max Thursday* • Faye Emerson *Georgia* • Mary Boland *Smitty* • Sam Levene *Capt Tonetti* • J Edward Bromberg *Varkas* • Kay Medford *Angel* • Jed Prouty *Dr Elder* • Harry Landers *Bert* ■ *Dir* Joseph Lerner • *Scr* Don Ettlinger, from a novel by Wade Miller

Guilty Conscience ★★★★

Thriller 1985 · US · Colour · 104mins

The writing partnership of Richard Levinson and William Link was responsible for some of the most popular shows in recent TV history. They also penned dozens of TV movies, but few surpassed this taut drama in which Anthony Hopkins gives a bravura performance as a lawyer who cross-examines his alter ego to concoct the perfect plan to murder his wife. But while he is scheming and dreaming of a future with his mistress, other plots are being hatched behind his back. Blythe Danner and Swoosie Kurtz match Hopkins every step of the way in a chatty but clever thriller.

Anthony Hopkins *Arthur Jamison* • Blythe Danner *Louise Jamison* • Swoosie Kurtz *Jackie Willis* • Wiley Harker *Older man* • Ruth Manning *Older woman* ■ *Dir* David Greene • *Scr* Richard Levinson, William Link

Guilty Hands ★★★

Crime drama 1931 · US · BW · 60mins

Deliciously inventive, this crime drama stars Lionel Barrymore as the former district attorney attempting to commit

the perfect murder to prevent his daughter from marrying a playboy bounder. More usually a comic snob, Alan Mowbray must have been flattered to play the scoundrel, with no less a figure than Kay Francis as his mistress. Bayard Veiller's original screenplay comes up with an unforgettable way for Mowbray to settle the score, while WS Van Dyke's direction is visually accomplished.

Lionel Barrymore *Richard Grant* • Kay Francis *Marjorie West* • Madge Evans *Barbara Grant* • William Bakewell *Tommy Osgood* • C Aubrey Smith *Rev Hastings* • Polly Moran *Aunt Maggie* • Alan Mowbray *Gordon Rich* • Forrester Harvey *Spencer Wilson* ■ *Dir* WS Van Dyke • *Scr* Bayard Veiller, from his story

The Guinea Pig ★★ U

Drama 1948 · UK · BW · 93mins

Richard Attenborough makes light of his 20-odd years to play a boy half his age in this class-barrier melodrama that is as predictable and reassuring as a school dinner menu. Accepted by a top public school as part of an educational experiment, working-class Attenborough endures the raillery of classmates and family with practised angst as he passes from victim to insider with the help of teacher Robert Flemyng. Wallowing in the clichés of establishment privilege rather than questioning them, director Roy Boulting makes few demands of a cast that almost sleepwalks through familiar characterisations.

Richard Attenborough *Jack Read* • Sheila Sim *Lynne Hartley* • Bernard Miles *Mr Read* • Cecil Trouncer *Mr Hartley, housemaster* • Robert Flemyng *Nigel Lorraine* • Edith Sharpe *Mrs Hartley* • Joan Hickson *Mrs Read* • Peter Reynolds *Grimmett* ■ *Dir* Roy Boulting • *Scr* Warren Chetham Strode, Bernard Miles, from the play by Warren Chetham Strode

Guinevere ★★★

Romantic drama 1999 · US · Colour · 104mins

A knock-out performance from Canadian actress Sarah Polley (*Go, The Sweet Hereafter*) is the main reason for seeing this insightful, if sentimental coming-of-age saga. Polley plays affection-starved 21-year-old Harper Sloane, who meets middle-aged photographer Stephen Rea at her sister's wedding. Attracted by his bohemian charisma, she becomes his apprentice and lover. But does she really think she's something special? Or is she just another conquest? This familiar May-December romance contains as many deft broad strokes as it does missteps. However, the sheer force of Polley's multi-faceted accomplishment makes such mistakes easier to bear.

Stephen Rea *Connie Fitzpatrick* • Sarah Polley *Harper Sloane* • Jean Smart *Deborah Sloane* • Gina Gershon *Billie* • Jasmine Guy *Linda* • Francis Guinan *Alan Sloane* • Paul Dooley *Walter* ■ *Dir/Scr* Audrey Wells

Gulliver's Travels ★★ U

Animated fantasy 1939 · US · Colour · 76mins

An age in production, this animated version of Jonathan Swift's timeless satire owes more to the imagination of the Fleischer brothers than it does to the venerable Dublin dean's. The most serious failing is the time it takes for

U = SUITABLE FOR ALL, Uc = SUITABLE FOR ALL, ESPECIALLY FOR YOUNG CHILDREN (VIDEO ONLY), PG = PARENTAL GUIDANCE

Gulliver to embark on his Lilliputian adventures, with far too long being devoted to the pointless feud between kings Little of Lilliput and Bombo of Blefescu. The romance between David and Glory is also unnecessary and further complicates the artwork's stylistic inconsistencies, with their appearance contrasting sharply with the naturalistic Gulliver and the other more cartoony creations.

Dir Dave Fleischer • *Scr* Dan Gordon, Ted Pierce, Izzy Sparber, Edmond Seward, from a story by Edmond Seward, from the novel by Jonathan Swift

Gulliver's Travels ★ U
Animated satirical fantasy
1977 · UK/Bel · Colour · 76mins

Slicing out swathes of Jonathan Swift's priceless prose with much the same disrespectful glee as the Fleischer brothers' 1939 version, this dismal adaptation of the classic satirical odyssey is a distressing combination of dire songs, unutterable dialogue and one of the worst mergers of animated and live-action footage ever committed to celluloid. Richard Harris looks like a man enduring a nightmare as he tries desperately to interact with his clumsily drawn co-stars. The problem lies in trying to turn a sophisticated social tract into a kiddie entertainment. But even this dumbed-down, the story should have had a modicum of visual charm. Sadly, it doesn't. ▣

Richard Harris *Gulliver* • Catherine Schell *Girl* • Norman Shelley *Father* • Meredith Edwards *Uncle* ■ *Dir* Peter Hunt • *Scr* Don Black, from the novel by Jonathan Swift

The Gumball Rally ★★★ PG
Comedy adventure
1976 · US · Colour · 102mins

A precursor to such frantic cross-country races as *The Cannonball Run* and *Smokey and the Bandit*, this comedy adventure is a reasonable example of the genre, unhindered by a serious plot and full of tyre-squealing action. It's directed and produced by stuntman Chuck Bail and, though the actors are constantly upstaged by the customised autos, Michael Sarrazin and rival Tim McIntire do raise a few smiles as bungling cop Normann Burton desperately tries to stop their contest. Watch out for Raul Julia in a small role. ▣

Michael Sarrazin *Michael Bannon* • Normann Burton [Norman Burton] *Roscoe* • Gary Busey *Gibson* • John Durren *Preston* • Susan Flannery *Alice* • Harvey Jason *Lapchick* • Tim McIntire *Steve Smith* • Raul Julia *Franco* ■ *Dir* Chuck Bail • *Scr* Leon Capetanos, from a story by Leon Capetanos, Chuck Bail

Gumby: the Movie ★★
Animated fantasy adventure
1995 · US · Colour · 90mins

Having first demonstrated his genius for claymation with the abstract jazz fantasy, *Gumbasia*, Art Clokey became something of an institution on American television in the fifties with the adventures of a pliable green blob. The star of the show, Gumby, joins with his old pals – Pokey, Goo and co – to confound the attempt of their great rivals, the Blockheads, to replace his invaluable dog, Lowbelly, with an android hound. However, not even

heavy-handed references to *Star Wars* and *Terminator 2* can enliven this trip down memory lane, which culminates in a concert to raise the funds to save Gumby's neighbours from eviction.

Art Clokey *Pokey/Prickle/Gumbo* • Gloria Clokey *Goo* • Manny LaCarruba *Thinbuckle* • Alice Young *Ginger* • Janet MacDuff *Gumba* ■ *Dir* Art Clokey • *Scr* Art Clokey, Gloria Clokey, from characters created by Art Clokey

Gummo ★★★★ 18
Drama
1997 · US · Colour · 85mins

Abandoning any pretence of linear narrative, director Harmony Korine – writer of the highly controversial *Kids* – presents an impressionistic collection of grim insights into a neighbourhood recovering from a destructive tornado. Using a variety of techniques, including hand-held camerawork, *Gummo* follows two geeky adolescents, Jacob Reynolds and Nick Sutton, as they sniff glue, torture cats and gross out the locals. This extraordinary investigation into the tarnished American Dream and the desolate confusion caused by fast-food culture is repulsive, shocking and definitely not for the faint-hearted. Eventually, however, Korine penetrates the heart. Contains swearing. ▣

Jacob Sewell *Bunny Boy* • Nick Sutton *Tummler* • Lara Tosh *Girl in car* • Jacob Reynolds *Solomon* • Darby Dougherty *Darby* • Chloë Sevigny *Dot* • Carisa Glucksman *Helen* • Jason Guzak *Skinhead* • Casey Guzak *Skinhead* ■ *Dir/Scr* Harmony Korine

Gumshoe ★★★★ 15
Crime comedy
1971 · UK · Colour · 82mins

Director Stephen Frears made his feature debut with this wonderfully understated homage to *film noir*. Albert Finney excels as Eddie Ginley, the bingo caller who has dreams of writing like Dashiell Hammett and acting like Humphrey Bogart. Following the example of Woody Allen in *Play It Again, Sam*, screenwriter Neville Smith blends fond parody with an original story that has an undeniable charm of its own. But *Gumshoe* also has an unexpectedly hard edge, thanks to its tough themes of drugs and gunrunning and Frears's astute snapshots of Liverpool. Contains swearing and violence. ▣

Albert Finney *Eddie Ginley* • Billie Whitelaw *Ellen* • Frank Finlay *William* • Janice Rule *Mrs Blankerscoon* • Carolyn Seymour *Alison Wyatt* • Fulton Mackay *John Straker* • George Innes *Bookshop proprietor* • Wendy Richard *Anne Scott* • Maureen Lipman *Naomi* ■ *Dir* Stephen Frears • *Scr* Neville Smith

The Gumshoe Kid ★★
Comedy
1990 · US · Colour · 98mins

This goofy leftover from the eighties somehow got released in 1990 as a last gasp of "madcap" comedy before the plethora of movies made from *Saturday Night Live* sketches hit their mark. Cash-strapped amateur sleuth Jay Underwood is foisted on to his private detective uncle (Vince Edwards) by his family, but he is unwilling to trust the teenager with anything too taxing. However, through a series of stupid coincidences, Underwood ends up on the run from murderers with a woman (Tracy Scoggins) he was

assigned to watch. Don't waste your time snooping around this film.

Jay Underwood *Jeff Sherman* • Tracy Scoggins *Rita Benson* • Vince Edwards *Ben Sherman* • Arlene Golonka *Gracie Sherman* ■ *Dir* Joseph Manduke • *Scr* Victor Bardack

Gun Crazy ★★★★
Film noir
1949 · US · BW · 87mins

Now here's an unsung minor masterpiece. Highly influential on everybody from Jean-Luc Godard to Oliver Stone, this is a stylish *film noir* from director Joseph H Lewis, about a smouldering *femme fatale* (Peggy Cummins in the role of her life) who leads the psychotic, gun-fixated John Dall astray. Originally based on a *Saturday Evening Post* short story by MacKinlay Kantor, the taut screenplay is the work of Kantor, Millard Kaufman and the uncredited, and blacklisted, Dalton Trumbo. The plot was reworked less effectively in 1992's *Guncrazy*, which bizarrely removed the strong sexual undercurrent from the original.

John Dall *Bart Tare* • Peggy Cummins *Annie Laurie Starr* • Berry Kroeger *Packett* • Annabel Shaw [Anabel Shaw] *Ruby Tare* • Harry Lewis *Clyde Boston* • Morris Carnovsky *Judge Willoughby* • Stanley Prager *Bluey-Bluey* • Nedrick Young *Dave Allister* ■ *Dir* Joseph H Lewis • *Scr* MacKinlay Kantor, Millard Kaufman [Dalton Trumbo], from the story by MacKinlay Kantor in *The Saturday Evening Post*

Gun Duel in Durango ★★ U
Western
1957 · US · BW · 73mins

Rugged George Montgomery spent most of the fifties appearing as the hero of short and snappy minor westerns. This time he's the leader of a band of outlaws who decides it's time to change for the better. Before he can marry sweetheart Ann Robinson he has to prove himself, but his old gang have ways of persuading him to join them in another raid. Comfortably predictable – naturally, there is a final showdown – it is directed competently enough to please most western fans.

George Montgomery *Dan* • Ann Robinson *Judy* • Steve Brodie *Dunston* • Bobby Clark *Robbie* • Frank Ferguson *Sheriff Howard* • Donald Barry *Larry* • Denver Pyle *Ranger captain* ■ *Dir* Sidney Salkow • *Scr* Louis Stevens

Gun for a Coward ★★ U
Western
1957 · US · Colour · 88mins

An interesting western from that period in the fifties when juvenile delinquency was the byword and all Hollywood youths were crazy mixed-up kids. Jeffrey Hunter and Dean Stockwell are both excellent as the troubled teens coping with the death of their father, watched over by their older sibling, the reliable Fred MacMurray. This promises more than it delivers, despite a classy cast that includes Josephine Hutchinson.

Fred MacMurray *Will Keough* • Jeffrey Hunter *Bless Keough* • Janice Rule *Aud Niven* • Chill Wills *Loving* • Dean Stockwell *Hade Keough* • Josephine Hutchinson *Mrs Keough* • Betty Lynn *Claire* • Iron Eyes Cody *Chief* ■ *Dir* Abner Biberman • *Scr* R Wright Campbell

Gun Fury ★★★ U
Western
1953 · US · Colour · 78mins

Universal's new star Rock Hudson, loaned out here to Columbia, acquits himself adequately as a rancher whose fiancée (Donna Reed) is suddenly abducted. The film boasts a moody plot set out west, pitting the gauche, honest and upright Hudson against psychotic baddie Phil Carey (outstanding) and his cohorts Lee Marvin and Neville Brand. Originally filmed in the novelty of 3-D, this exciting psychological western was released without the 3-D gimmick in the UK, and one wonders if director Raoul Walsh had encouraged inexperienced star Hudson to overact to compensate for this. ▣

Rock Hudson *Ben Warren* • Donna Reed *Jennifer Ballard* • Phil Carey [Philip Carey] *Frank Slayton* • Roberta Haynes *Estella Morales* • Lee Marvin *Blinky* • Leo Gordon *"Jess Burgess"* • Neville Brand *Brazos* • Ray Thomas *Doc* ■ *Dir* Raoul Walsh • *Scr* Irving Wallace, Roy Huggins, from the novel *Ten against Caesar* by Kathleen B George, Robert A Granger

Gun Glory ★★ U
Western
1957 · US · Colour · 88mins

This last film British-born actor Stewart Granger made under his seven-year contract with MGM was a farewell without much glory. Granger, who was best as a swashbuckling hero, seems ill-at-ease as a gunfighter returning home to his ranch after some years away, to find that his wife has died and his teenage son is bitter towards him. Director Roy Rowland commits the cardinal casting sin of putting his plainly inadequate son Steve in the role of Granger's son. But the plot and the lovely Rhonda Fleming make this CinemaScope western quite watchable.

Stewart Granger *Tom Early* • Rhonda Fleming *Jo* • Chill Wills *Preacher* • Steve Rowland *Young Tom Early* • James Gregory *Grimsell* • Jacques Aubuchon *Sam Winscott* • Arch Johnson *Gunn* • William Fawcett *Martin* ■ *Dir* Roy Rowland • *Scr* William Ludwig, from the novel *Man of the West* by Philip Yordan

The Gun in Betty Lou's Handbag ★★★ 15
Comedy
1992 · US · Colour · 84mins

The decision to offer this comic slice of small-town life to director Allan Moyle might seem curious considering he is best known for those celebrations of teenage angst, *Pump Up the Volume* and *Empire Records*. However, he keeps this preposterous story ticking along nicely and coaxes an engaging performance out of Penelope Ann Miller as the timid librarian who finds a murder weapon and confesses to the crime to spice up her life. Contains swearing. ▣

Penelope Ann Miller *Betty Lou Perkins* • Eric Thal *Alex Perkins* • Alfre Woodard *Ann* • Julianne Moore *Elinor* • Andy Romano *Herrick* • Ray McKinnon *Frank* • William Forsythe *Beaudeen* • Cathy Moriarty *Reba* ■ *Dir* Allan Moyle • *Scr* Grace Cary Bickley

The Gun Runners ★★★
Crime adventure
1958 · US · Colour · 82mins

It's not often that the same story is well-filmed three times around, but this cheaply-made version of Ernest Hemingway's *To Have and Have Not* is creditably close to Howard Hawks's adaptation in 1944 and Michael Curtiz's *The Breaking Point* in 1950. The key again is a skilled director, Don Siegel, who draws a surprisingly persuasive performance from Audie Murphy as the hard-up fishing boat captain. Patricia Owens is good as his caring wife, Everett Sloane excellent as his drunken assistant, and Eddie Albert outstanding as the treacherous gunrunner who hires his boat.

Audie Murphy *Sam Martin* • Eddie Albert *Hanagan* • Patricia Owens *Lucy Martin* • Everett Sloane *Harvey* • Richard Jaeckel *Buzurki* • Jack Elam *Arnold* ■ Dir Don Siegel • Scr Daniel Mainwaring, Paul Monash, from the novel *To Have and Have Not* by Ernest Hemingway

Gun Smoke ★★★
Western   1931 · US · BW · 63mins

A truly unusual western that features rugged *Wings* star Richard Arlen in the leading role, but is better remembered for the performance of William "Stage" Boyd, stealing Arlen's thunder as a villainous deranged mobster out west. This Boyd was a star of the Broadway theatre (hence "Stage" to differentiate him from former Cecil B DeMille star William "Hopalong Cassidy" Boyd), whose career was given a boost by his performance in this film. In fact, this movie also began a short trend where machine guns vied with six-guns on the range.

Richard Arlen *Brad Farley* • William "Stage" Boyd *Kedge Darvis* • Mary Brian *Sue Vancey* • Eugene Pallette *Stub Wallack* • Charles Winninger *Tack Gillup* • Louise Fazenda *Hampsey Dell* • Brooks Benedict *Spot Skee* ■ Dir Edward Sloman • Scr Grover Jones, William McNutt

Gunbus ★ PG
Adventure   1986 · UK · Colour · 88mins

Scott McGinnis and Jeff Osterhage try valiantly to drum up some knockabout bonhomie here as Wild West outlaws enrolled in a British fighter squadron during the First World War, but everything from the stereotypical characters to the risible banter is against them. Bearing in mind the technical expertise of director Zoran Perisic, this adventure should at least have looked good. However, the aerial action is so inept that it only emphasises the shortcomings of this disappointing buddy movie. Contains some violent scenes. ▣

Scott McGinnis *Barney* • Jeff Osterhage *Luke* • Ronald Lacey *Fritz* • Miles Anderson *Bannock* • Valerie Steffen *Yvette* • Ingrid Held *Mitsou* • Keith Buckley *Commander von Schlussel* • Terence Harvey *Colonel Canning* ■ Dir Zoran Perisic • Scr Thom Keyes

Guncrazy ★★★ 15
Crime drama   1992 · US · Colour · 92mins

Tamra Davis, who had ridicule heaped upon her as the director of one of the worst films of 1996, *Billy Madison*, here does a better job with this tale of a teenage girl (Drew Barrymore) who falls for an ex-con. This occasionally tries to be a nineties version of the much more subtle *Badlands*, as the pair go on the run, firing guns aplenty,

but luckily Barrymore and co-stars James LeGros and Billy Drago keep their performances realistic. Contains violence and swearing. ▣

Drew Barrymore *Anita* • James LeGros *Howard* • Michael Ironside *Kincaid* • Ione Skye *Joy* • Billy Drago *Hank* • Joe Dallesandro *Rooney* ■ Dir Tamra Davis • Scr Matthew Bright

A Gunfight ★★★
Western   1971 · US · Colour · 89mins

In this offbeat western Kirk Douglas and Johnny Cash give excellent performances as two ageing gunfighters who have fallen on hard times. In response to speculation in the town, Douglas proposes that they should stage a gun duel and charge admission so that the survivor can make a fresh start. Tension mounts under Lamont Johnson's sharp direction of Harold Jack Bloom's screenplay, as we don't want either man to die. But the handling of the outcome is not entirely satisfactory.

Kirk Douglas *Will Tenneray* • Johnny Cash *Abe Cross* • Jane Alexander *Nora Tenneray* • Raf Vallone *Francisco Alvarez* • Karen Black *Jenny Simms* • Eric Douglas *Bud Tenneray* ■ Dir Lamont Johnson • Scr Harold Jack Bloom

Gunfight at Comanche Creek ★★ U
Western   1964 · US · Colour · 90mins

Audie Murphy follows in the footsteps of George Montgomery in a remake of the 1957 western *Last of the Badmen*. In this hybrid of a forties-style detective movie and the traditional western, detective Bob Gifford (Murphy) poses as an outlaw to infiltrate a particularly ruthless gang of robbers. Their cunning plan involves using escaped convicts to commit further crimes, and then killing them so they can collect the bounty. Murphy's lightweight style undermines the potential for suspense.

Audie Murphy *Bob Gifford* • Ben Cooper *Carter* • Colleen Miller *Abbie Stevens* • DeForest Kelley *Troop* • Jan Merlin *Nielson* • John Hubbard *Marshal Shearer* • Damian O'Flynn *Winton* • Susan Seaforth *Janie* ■ Dir Frank McDonald • Scr Edward Bernds

Gunfight at the OK Corral ★★★★ PG
Western   1957 · US · Colour · 117mins

Wyatt Earp and Doc Holliday were never better portrayed on screen than here, played by movie giants Burt Lancaster and Kirk Douglas respectively. The Leon Uris screenplay may veer towards the turgid in setting up the action, but once the gunplay starts the screen positively ignites: director John Sturges's shoot-out finale is a mesmerisingly fine piece of cinema, brilliantly photographed and edited. There's also a soaring, nostalgic title ballad by Frankie Laine, and a marvellously etched supporting performance from Jo Van Fleet as Holliday's woman. ▣

Burt Lancaster *Wyatt Earp* • Kirk Douglas *John H "Doc" Holliday* • Rhonda Fleming *Laura Denbow* • Jo Van Fleet *Kate Fisher* • John Ireland *Johnny Ringo* • Frank Faylen *Cotton Wilson* • Earl Holliman *Charles Bassett* • Dennis Hopper *Billy Clanton* • DeForest Kelley *Morgan Earp* • Lee Van Cleef *Ed Bailey* ■ Dir

John Sturges • Scr Leon Uris, from the article *The Killer* by George Scullin • Music Dmitri Tiomkin

Gunfight in Abilene ★★
Western   1967 · US · Colour · 85mins

Teen idol Bobby Darin heads a cast that includes Michael Sarrazin and a pre-*Airplane!* Leslie Nielsen in this very routine Universal western, from the period when the studio was making low-budget supporting features utilising its back lot and existing sets. Darin gives a capable performance as the disillusioned American Civil War veteran who's reluctantly recruited as the sheriff of Abilene by cattle baron Nielsen, but co-star Emily Banks is an unconvincing heroine and William Hale's direction is leaden.

Bobby Darin *Cal Wayne* • Emily Banks *Amy Martin* • Leslie Nielsen *Grant Evers* • Donnelly Rhodes *Joe Slade* • Don Galloway *Ward Kent* • Michael Sarrazin *Cord Decker* • Barbara Werle *Leann* ■ Dir William Hale • Scr Berne Giler, John DF Black, from the novel *Gun Shy* by Clarence Upson Young

The Gunfighter ★★★★ U
Western   1950 · US · BW · 81mins

Gregory Peck gives a performance of characteristic dignity and grit in this simmering western about the stark realities of frontier life. Having been forced to go for his gun by a barroom braggart, gunslinger Peck rides off to a neighbouring town to visit his estranged wife and son, only to find his presence resented by the locals and his life threatened by the brothers of his latest victim. Veteran director Henry King expertly strips away the glamour of the gunfighter to reveal a man who regrets his past, but knows killing is his only future. ▣

Gregory Peck *Jimmy Ringo* • Helen Westcott *Peggy Walsh* • Millard Mitchell *Sheriff Mark Strett* • Jean Parker *Molly* • Karl Malden *Mac* • Skip Homeier *Hunt Bromley* • Anthony Ross *Charlie* • Verna Felton *Mrs Pennyfeather* ■ Dir Henry King • Scr William Bowers, William Sellers, Nunnally Johnson, from a story by William Bowers, Andre De Toth

Gung Ho! ★ PG
Second World War drama
1943 · US · BW · 82mins

This military drama was a huge wartime hit for Universal with its rousing fictionalised re-creation of a highly successful August 1942 attack in which a battalion of specially picked marine raiders took a Pacific island back from the Japanese. The force's motto is "gung ho", a Chinese expression for working in harmony. Randolph Scott is suitably heroic as the tough commander Thorwald, and a young Robert Mitchum also appears. ▣

Randolph Scott *Col Thorwald* • Grace McDonald *Kathleen Corrigan* • Alan Curtis *John Harbison* • Noah Beery Jr *Kurt Richter* • J Carrol Naish *Lt Cristoforos* • David Bruce *Larry O'Ryan* • Bob Mitchum [Robert Mitchum] *"Pig-Iron" Matthews* ■ Dir Ray Enright • Scr Lucien Hubbard, from a story by Capt WS LeFrançois

Gung Ho ★★★ 15
Comedy   1986 · US · Colour · 107mins

Before he made the likes of *Apollo 13* and *Parenthood*, Ron Howard directed this small but often enjoyable comedy. Michael Keaton is the car factory foreman trying to create peace between the workers and the new Japanese owners of the plant, who, of course, want their employees to be punctual, correct and up at six in the morning doing exercises in the parking lot. Keaton is a deft hand at comedy, and he is capably supported by George Wendt (*Cheers*) and Coen Brothers regular John Turturro. ▣

Michael Keaton *Hunt Stevenson* • Mimi Rogers *Audrey* • George Wendt *Buster* • Gedde Watanabe *Kazihiro* • John Turturro *Willie* • Soh Yamamura [So Yamamura] *Mr Sakamoto* ■ Dir Ron Howard • Scr Lowell Ganz, Babaloo Mandel, from a story by Edwin Blum, Lowell Ganz, Babaloo Mandel

Gunga Din ★★★★★ U
Adventure   1939 · US · BW · 112mins

Absolutely spiffing action adventure, loosely based on the imperialist poem by Rudyard Kipling, but actually nicking its plot premise from the Broadway classic *The Front Page*, unconsciderately by the same authors as this original story, Ben Hecht and Charles MacArthur. Casting couldn't be bettered, as boyos Cary Grant, Douglas Fairbanks Jr and Victor McLaglen swashbuckle their way across the 19th-century Indian frontier, only to be ultimately rescued by the titular water boy Sam Jaffe. First choice director Howard Hawks was unavoidably detained, but replacement George Stevens (*Shane, Giant*) makes a superb job of handling the rumbunctious squaddies in his biggest budget movie to date. Dateless and timeless, this immensely enjoyable epic has stubbornly resisted any attempt at a remake, although Frank Sinatra's clan proffered a crude westernisation with *Sergeants Three*. ▣

Cary Grant *Cutter* • Victor McLaglen *MacChesney* • Douglas Fairbanks Jr *Ballantine* • Sam Jaffe *Gunga Din* • Joan Fontaine *Emmy* • Eduardo Ciannelli *Guru* • Montagu Love *Colonel Weed* ■ Dir George Stevens • Scr Joel Sayre, Fred Guiol, from a story by Ben Hecht, Charles MacArthur, from the poem by Rudyard Kipling

Gunhed ★★★ 12
Science-fiction action
1989 · Jap · Colour · 100mins

In 2025, the super computer Kyron-5 began hostilities with mankind. By 2083, fearless techno-bounty hunters assault the computer's Pacific Island HQ initiating the great Robot War. The only hope for man's future lies in the fabled fighting machine Unit 507, the last of the Gunheds. Can this adaptable bio-droid penetrate the island's dizzying battle levels for victory over the machine? A smash hit in Japan, director Masato Harada's dark vision of a hardware driven future may play like *Aliens* remodelled as a computer game, but it's an exciting helter-skelter action adventure, with few pauses for breath. A Japanese and English language film.

Landy Leyes *Gunhed* • Masahiro Takashima *Brooklyn* • Brenda Bakke *Sergeant Nim* • Yujin Harada *Steven* • Kaori Mizushima *Eleven* • Aya Enyoji *Bebe* • Mickey Curtis *Bancho* • James B Thompson *Balba* ■ *Dir* Masato Harada • *Scr* Masato Harada, James Bannon

Gunmen ★★★ 18

Action adventure 1994 · US · Colour · 90mins

Christopher Lambert, comedian Denis Leary and Patrick Stewart (*Star Trek: the Next Generation*) make for strange movie bedfellows, but it's this eclectic casting that lifts what is basically a trashy and gory B-movie thriller out of the ordinary. Lambert and Mario Van Peebles play a mismatched duo forced to team up to locate a boat that holds millions of dollars stolen off drugs lord Stewart; Leary and an army of swarthy bandits are also hot on their trail. The two stars spark off each other nicely and director Deran Sarafian stages some enjoyably ludicrous action set pieces. Contains swearing, violence, sex scenes and nudity. 📼

Christopher Lambert *Dani Servigo* • Mario Van Peebles *Cole Parker* • Denis Leary *Armor O'Malley* • Patrick Stewart *Loomis* • Kadeem Hardison *Izzy* • Sally Kirkland *Bennett* ■ *Dir* Deran Sarafian • *Scr* Stephen Sommers

Gunn ★★

Detective drama 1967 · US · Colour · 94mins

Blake Edwards's successful TV series of the early sixties, *Peter Gunn*, comes to the big screen with Craig Stevens reprising his role as the private investigator. The story involves Mafia treachery, offshore bordellos and exploding yachts, with Stevens waltzing through it with a girl on each arm. At times Edwards creates a lovely pastiche of forties Hollywood but for the most part this is a slick package that Edwards may have designed in the hope it might rival his successful *Pink Panther* franchise.

Craig Stevens *Peter Gunn* • Laura Devon *Edie* • Edward Asner [Ed Asner] *Jacoby* • Sherry Jackson *Samantha* • Helen Traubel *Mother* • Albert Paulsen *Fusco* • MT Marshall [Marion Marshall] *Daisy Jane* • J Pat O'Malley *Tinker* • Regis Toomey *"The Bishop"* ■ *Dir* Blake Edwards • *Scr* Blake Edwards, William Peter Blatty, from a story and characters created by Blake Edwards

Gunnar Hede's Saga ★★★★

Silent drama 1922 · Swe · BW · 70mins

One of the Swedish masterworks of director Mauritz Stiller, based on a novel by Selma Lagerlöf, this is the tale of an introspective young man who is cast off the family estate for befriending a young female violinist. He seeks to emulate his grandfather by bringing a vast herd of reindeer down from the snowy north but suffers a serious accident during the journey. This drive, with its stampede, puts the film in the epic class, but it is also concerned with dreams, hallucinations and the power of memory.

Einar Hanson *Gunnar Hede* • Pauline Brunius *Gunnar's mother* • Mary Johnson *Ingrid* • Adolf Olchansky *Mr Blomgren* • Stina Berg *Mrs Blomgren* • Hugo Björne *Gunnar's father* • Theckla Ahlander *Miss Stava* ■ *Dir* Mauritz Stiller • *Scr* Mauritz Stiller, from the novel *En Herrgårdssägen* by Selma Lagerlöf

Gunpoint ★★ PG

Western 1966 · US · Colour · 82mins

A late Audie Murphy vehicle, with the ageing baby-faced war hero playing a sheriff trying to capture a gang of train robbers who have taken a saloon girl hostage. Murphy is always watchable and there's expert support from grizzled western veterans Denver Pyle and Edgar Buchanan, but this unoriginal movie is little better than TV fodder. Director Earl Bellamy makes good use of its locations, but the low budget is very evident. 📼

Audie Murphy *Chad Lucas* • Joan Stanley *Uvalde* • Warren Stevens *Nate Harlan* • Edgar Buchanan *Bull* • Denver Pyle *Cap Hold* • Royal Dano *Ode* • Nick Dennis *Nicos* • William Bramley *Hoag* ■ *Dir* Earl Bellamy • *Scr* Willard Willingham, Mary Willingham

Gunpowder ★★ PG

Comedy thriller 1985 · UK · Colour · 81mins

Hopelessly dated spy thriller, complete with evil master criminals, suave agents and girls with suggestive names. There are plenty of familiar British faces in the cast, including David Gilliam and Gordon Jackson of *The Professionals* fame, but the movie raises more unintentional laughs than thrills. 📼

David Gilliam *Mike Gunn* • Martin Potter *Charles Powder* • Gordon Jackson *Sir Anthony Phelps* • Debra Burton *Coffee Carradine* • David Miller *Dr Vache* • Susan Rutherford *Penny Keynes* • Anthony Schaeffer *Lovell* • Rachel Laurence *Miss Belt* ■ *Dir* Norman J Warren • *Scr* Rory H MacLean

Guns at Batasi ★★★★

Drama 1964 · UK · BW · 104mins

Overlooked in 1964 as an routine piece of stiff-upper-lip-manship, this film is a fascinating epitaph for the British Empire and a whole slew of movies about Imperial derring-do. Set in an Africa well brushed by what Harold Macmillan called "the wind of change", it's the story of insurrection in a newly independent state and what the resident British army does about it. Staunchly traditional, it's also subversive and satirical, with a stand-out performance by Richard Attenborough as the apoplectic RSM.

Richard Attenborough *RSM Lauderdale* • Mia Farrow *Karen Ericksson* • Jack Hawkins *Lt Col Deal* • Flora Robson *Miss Barker-Wise* • John Leyton *Pte Wilkes* • Errol John *Lt Boniface* • Earl Cameron *Capt Abraham* ■ *Dir* John Guillermin • *Scr* Robert Holles, from his novel *The Siege of Battersea*

Guns for San Sebastian ★★ PG

Adventure drama 1968 · US/Fr/Mex/It · Colour · 106mins

Already pretty heavy going, this uncomfortable blend of social theology, coarse comedy and bruising action is made all the more intolerable by the sloppy dubbing. Not that the dialogue would have benefited much from a slicker job, as this adaptation of William Barby Faherty's novel *A Wall for San Sebastian* is full of bombastic pronouncements and glib posturings. Anthony Quinn is at full throttle as a mid-18th-century Mexican drifter posing as a priest. But Henri Verneuil handles the fighting with aplomb, and there's a brooding dignity about Charles Bronson's misguided loyalty. Ennio Morricone's score helps too. French dialogue dubbed into English. 📼

Anthony Quinn *León Alastray* • Anjanette Comer *Kinita* • Charles Bronson *Teclo* • Sam Jaffe *Father Joseph* • Silvia Pinal *Felicia* • Jorge Martinez DeHoyos *Cayetano* • Jaime Fernandez *Golden Lance* • Rosa Furman *Agueda* ■ *Dir* Henri Verneuil • *Scr* James R Webb, from the novel *A Wall For San Sebastian* by William Barby Faherty • *Music* Ennio Morricone

Guns in the Heather ★★ U

Spy adventure 1969 · US · Colour · 85mins

Disney decamped to Ireland for this so-so adventure, also known – less picturesquely – as *The Secret of Boyne Castle* and *Spy Busters*. Kurt Russell stars as student Rich Evans, who helps his brother, a CIA agent, prevent a defecting scientist from falling into the clutches of communist agents. Already a TV and movie veteran by the late sixties, the 18-year-old Russell gives the impression that the material is beneath him and, certainly, the routine round of sanitised set pieces and narrow squeaks hardly makes for gripping viewing. 📼

Glenn Corbett *Tom Evans* • Alfred Burke *Kersner* • Kurt Russell *Rich Evans* • Patrick Dawson *Sean O'Connor* • Patrick Barr *Lord Boyne* • Hugh McDermott *Carleton* • Patrick Westwood *Levick* ■ *Dir* Robert Butler • *Scr* Herman Groves, Charles Frend, from a novel by Lockhart Amerman

The Guns of August ★★★

First World War documentary 1964 · US · BW · 100mins

Governments on either side were slow to recognise the value of propaganda at the outbreak of the First World War. To his credit, producer/director Nathan Kroll was able to uncover a wealth of archive material, much of it previously unseen, for his adaptation of Barbara Tuchman's acclaimed, Pulitzer Prize-winning study of Europe on the precipice. Chronicling events from the funeral of Edward VII in 1910 to the armistice in 1918, the film presents an indelible image of what was meant to be the war to end all wars.

Fritz Weaver *Narrator* ■ *Dir* Nathan Kroll • *Scr* from the non-fiction work by Barbara W Tuchman

Guns of Darkness ★★★

Drama 1962 · UK · BW · 102mins

A minor film from director Anthony Asquith, but extremely interesting nonetheless, despite the all-too-obvious overuse of Elstree interiors, doubling for a swampy South America where pacifist planter David Niven and pregnant wife Leslie Caron find themselves aiding revolutionaries. As with Asquith's similar "moral dilemma" movies *Carrington VC* and *Orders to Kill*, this promises more intellectually as it delivers cinematically. Niven's motivation seems unclear, and his character's boorishness makes him hard to like, let alone understand, while Caron's part is seriously underwritten. There's excellent support, though, from David Opatoshu and James Robertson-Justice.

David Niven *Tom Jordan* • Leslie Caron *Claire Jordan* • James Robertson-Justice *Hugo Bryant* • David Opatoshu *President Rivera* • Derek Godfrey *Hernandez* • Richard Pearson *Bastian* • Eleanor Summerfield *Mrs Bastian* • Ian Hunter *Dr Swann* ■ *Dir* Anthony Asquith • *Scr* John Mortimer, from the novel *Act of Mercy* by Francis Clifford

Guns of Hate ★★

Western 1948 · US · BW · 61mins

Tim Holt had an extraordinary career, appearing in two of the greatest westerns ever, John Ford's *Stagecoach* and *My Darling Clementine*, and having key roles in two other classics, John Huston's *The Treasure of the Sierra Madre* and Orson Welles's *The Magnificent Ambersons*. He chose to reject conventional Hollywood stardom to ride the movie range in a series of programme fillers and to work with the horses he loved. In this very ordinary RKO B-western he sets out to find the killers of Jason Robards. It's distinguished only by terrific performances from Tony Barrett and Steve Brodie as the villains.

Tim Holt *Bob* • Nan Leslie *Judy* • Richard Martin *Chito* • Steve Brodie *Morgan* • Myrna Dell *Dixie* • Tony Barrett *Wyatt* • Jason Robards *Ben Jason* ■ *Dir* Lesley Selander • *Scr* Norman Houston, Ed Earl Repp

The Guns of Navarone ★★★★ PG

Second World War adventure 1961 · UK/US · Colour · 150mins

Classic wartime adventure about a commando raid to spike two whopping German guns which threaten HM Navy. Writer/producer Carl Foreman slightly overcooks the classical, Homeric parallels – this is a new Odyssey – and gets distinctly preachy when a traitor is unmasked. But mostly this is an exciting adventure of the old school that tackles back-projected storms at sea, cliff faces at Shepperton studios and cat-and-mouse games with the Nazis on location in Rhodes. Gregory Peck is grim-faced and stoical, and Anthony Quinn preps his Zorba routine, but the acting honours go to David Niven as the cynical, cowardly explosives expert. 📼

Gregory Peck *Capt Mallory* • David Niven *Cpl Miller* • Anthony Quinn *Andrea Stavros* • Stanley Baker *CPO Brown* • Anthony Quayle *Maj Franklin* • James Darren *Pappadimos* • Irene Papas *Maria* • Gia Scala *Anna* ■ *Dir* J Lee Thompson • *Scr* Carl Foreman, Alistair Maclean

Guns of the Magnificent Seven ★★

Western 1969 · US · Colour · 105mins

A second sequel to a great original, wisely retaining the majestic Elmer Bernstein score. This time out, Yul Brynner relinquishes his role of mercenary gunman Chris to George Kennedy, and the Mexican-set locations were actually filmed in Spain. Thankfully, this movie neither looks nor feels like a European western, despite the fact that it was made at the height of the spaghetti western's popularity. A touch of class is provided by Fernando Rey, veteran of many a Luis Buñuel film, as the revolutionary leader in need of rescue by Kennedy's gang. Contains violence.

George Kennedy *Chris* • James Whitmore *Levi Morgan* • Monte Markham *Keno* • Bernie Casey *Cassie* • Joe Don Baker *Slater* • Scott Thomas *PJ* • Fernando Rey *Quintero* ■ *Dir* Paul Wendkos • *Scr* Herman Hoffman

Guns of the Timberland ★ Ⓤ

Western　　　　1960 · US · Colour · 91mins

Alan Ladd is as wooden as the scenery in this feeble logging drama produced by Aaron Spelling (*Dynasty*). It does raise worthwhile environmental considerations, as Ladd and his team of lumberjacks want to remove forest cover to protect the inhabitants of a valley from huge mudslides. Unfortunately the cliché-ridden script resorts to a violent dispute between Ladd and his partner (Gilbert Roland) and a romance across the divide between Ladd and rancher Jeanne Crain. Frankie Avalon supplies the pop music interludes and the supporting cast includes Ladd's daughter, Alana.

Alan Ladd *Jim Hadley* • Jeanne Crain *Laura Riley* • Gilbert Roland *Monty Walker* • Frankie Avalon *Bert Harvey* • Lyle Bettger *Clay Bell* • Noah Beery Jr *Blackie* • Verna Felton *Aunt Sarah* • Alana Ladd *Jane Peterson* ■ *Dir* Robert D Webb • *Scr* Aaron Spelling, Joseph Petracca, from the novel by Louis L'Amour

Gunsight Ridge ★★ Ⓤ

Western　　　　1957 · US · BW · 85mins

A western starring Joel McCrea and containing a secret piano-playing villain called Velvet Clark can't be all bad, although it comes pretty close. The middle-aged McCrea is an undercover agent who rides a well-worn trail to track down the aforementioned Velvet (Mark Stevens), currently operating under the guise of a mine owner. McCrea ends up as the town's new sheriff after the previous incumbent meets with an accident, and he gets the girl (Joan Weldon). Director Francis D Lyon had won an Oscar for his editing work on *Body and Soul*, but he fails to breathe new life into this plot.

Joel McCrea *Mike* • Mark Stevens *Velvet Clark* • Joan Weldon *Molly* • Darlene Fields *Rosa* • Addison Richards *Sheriff Jones* • Carolyn Craig *Girl* • Robert Griffin *Babcock* • Slim Pickens *Hank Moss* ■ *Dir* Francis D Lyon • *Scr* Talbot Jennings, Elizabeth Jennings

The Gunslinger ★★ ᴾᴳ

Western　　　　1956 · US · Colour · 74mins

This early Roger Corman venture is a fitfully entertaining camp western featuring two female adversaries – shades of *Johnny Guitar* – and giving more emphasis to sex and violence than was customary at the time. Curvaceous Beverly Garland is the town marshal's widow who straps on his guns and badge after he's gunned down. Equally curvaceous Allison Hayes is the wicked saloon-keeper who hires John Ireland's gunslinger to kill Garland – but, wouldn't you know, he falls for her instead. The film's microbudget shows up in a saloon chorus line made up of only three girls. ▦

John Ireland *Cane Miro* • Beverly Garland *Rose Hood* • Allison Hayes *Erica Page* • Martin Kingsley *Gideon Polk* • Jonathan Haze *Jack Hays* • Chris Alcaide *Joshua Tate* •

Richard Miller [Dick Miller] *Jimmy Tonto* • Bruno VeSota *Zebelon Tabb* ■ *Dir* Roger Corman • *Scr* Charles B Griffith, Mark Hanna

Gunsmoke ★★ Ⓤ

Western　　　　1953 · US · Colour · 79mins

This routine western stars Audie Murphy as a gunslinger who has a change of heart when he's hired by a landowner to kill a rancher. The result is nothing special, but it does offer a chance to see Susan Cabot (*Sorority Girl*, *The Wasp Woman*) before she became a Roger Corman cult heroine. The use of the Marlene Dietrich song *See What the Boys in the Back Room Will Have* prompted Universal to remake *Destry Rides Again* the following year with Murphy in the James Stewart role. The film has absolutely nothing to do with the famous TV series of the same name.

Audie Murphy *Reb Kittredge* • Susan Cabot *Rita Saxon* • Paul Kelly *Dan Saxon* • Charles Drake *Johnny Lake* • Mary Castle *Cora DuFrayne* • Jack Kelly *Curly Mather* • Jesse White *Professor* • William Reynolds *Brazos* ■ *Dir* Nathan Juran • *Scr* DD Beauchamp, from the novel *Roughshod* by Norman A Fox

Gunsmoke: the Last Apache ★ ᴾᴳ

Western　　　　1990 · US · Colour · 90mins

The history of big-screen adaptations of TV shows is the story of taking sharp, focused ideas and turning them into blandness, or porridge. Joining this unhappy throng is *Gunsmoke: the Last Apache*, which takes its cue from a once well-loved TV series that ran for 20 years with the help of imposing James Arness. Here, once again playing US marshal Matt Dillon, he jumps into the saddle to save a daughter he never knew existed from the Apaches, only to find himself riding towards cheap sentiment, lumpy plotting and poorly defined characters. ▦

James Arness *Matt Dillon* • Richard Kiley *Chalk* • Michael Learned *Mike* • Hugh O'Brian *General Miles* • Amy Stock-Poynton *Beth Yardner* • Geoffrey Lewis *Bodine* ■ *Dir* Charles Correll • *Scr* Earl W Wallace

Gunsmoke: To the Last Man ★★ ⑮

Western　　　　1992 · US · Colour · 89mins

Of all the TV western series that have hit our screens since the fifties, *Gunsmoke* is usually regarded as the grandaddy of them all. Starring James Arness as Marshal Matt Dillon, it is closer to such psychological westerns as *High Noon* than the horse operas beloved of matinée audiences everywhere. This third TV movie spin-off is a pretty predictable affair, with cattle rustlers, feuding farmers and unforgiving vigilantes. Fittingly, the proceedings are shrouded in plenty of gun smoke, with Arness making light of his 68 years to cut an imposing figure as Dodge City's most famous lawman. ▦

James Arness *Matt Dillon* • Pat Hingle *Colonel Tucker* • Amy Stock-Poynton *Beth* • Matt Mulhern *Will McCall* • Jason Lively *Rusty Dover* • Joseph Bottoms *Tommy Graham* • Morgan Woodward *Abel Rose* • Mills Watson

Horse Trader • James Booth *Preacher* • Amanda Wyss *Lizzie Tewksbury* ■ *Dir* Jerry Jameson • *Scr* Earl W Wallace

The Guru ★★ Ⓤ

Satirical drama
1969 · US/Ind · Colour · 111mins

Made shortly after the Beatles sat at the feet of the Maharishi at Rishikesh, this heavy-handed satire on colliding cultures suffers from the fact that James Ivory appears to have little sympathy for any of the characters. Michael York's pop star is portrayed as shallow, while Rita Tushingham's hippy is an opportunistic groupie. Only sitar master and spiritual mentor Utpal Dutt is permitted any depth, but the subtle blend of humility and egotism owes more to his own canny delivery than the mocking bombast of the script.

Utpal Dutt *Ustad Zafar Khan* • Michael York *Tom Pickle* • Rita Tushingham *Jenny* • Aparna Sen *Ghazala* • Madhur Jaffrey *Begum Sahiba* • Barry Foster *Chris* ■ *Dir* James Ivory • *Scr* Ruth Prawer Jhabvala, James Ivory

Guru in Seven ★★ ⑱

Comedy　　　　1997 · UK · Colour · 102mins

Made for a mere £33,000, this is essentially an Asian *Alfie*. Rebelling against the social and racial prejudices of his parents, artist Nitin Chandra Ganatra bets his friends that he can bed a week's worth of women following his split from the love of his life, Ernestina Quarcoo. Director Shani Grewal takes this as an excuse to savage everything from Bollywood musicals to Punjabi economic expectation. But while he demonstrates that Asian males are just as laddish as their other racial counterparts, he fails in his bid to show older subcontinentals to be every bit as suburban as the rest of Britain's bourgeoisie. Contains swearing. ▦

Saeed Jaffrey *Mr Walia* • Jacqueline Pearce *Joan* • Nitin Chandra Ganatra *Sanjay* • Lea Rochelle *Nora* • Lynne Michelle *Candy* • Elle Lewis *Holly* • Amanda Pointer *Gaynor* • Ernestina Quarcoo *Jill* ■ *Dir* Shani Grewal [Shani S Grewal] • *Scr* Shani Grewal

Gus ★★ Ⓤ

Comedy　　　　1976 · US · Colour · 92mins

Disney family films of this cosily low-budget kind were an endangered species even when this was made. Younger viewers may still enjoy the gentle humour of this story about a football team taking on a mule which can kick a ball one hundred yards. Ed Asner and Don Knotts are the two-legged heroes. ▦

Ed Asner *Hank Cooper* • Don Knotts *Coach Venner* • Gary Grimes *Andy Petrovic* • Tim Conway *Crankcase* • Liberty Williams *Debbie Kovac* • Dick Van Patten *Cal Wilson* • Ronnie Schell *Joe Barnsdale* • Bob Crane *Pepper* ■ *Dir* Vincent McEveety • *Scr* Arthur Alsberg, Don Nelson, from a story by Ted Key

Guy ★★★ ⑱

Drama　　　1996 · UK /Ger · Colour · 90mins

Covering the same sort of territory as *The Truman Show* and *EDtv*, Michael Lindsay-Hogg's psychological thriller steers the subject matter into much darker territory. Hope Davis is the aspiring film-maker who decides to

make an ordinary stranger (Vincent D'Onofrio) the star of her new movie, provoking a complex battle of wills in which the lines between the subject and the film-maker become increasingly blurred. A small-scale but intriguing study of voyeurism. ▦

Vincent D'Onofrio *Guy* • Hope Davis "*The Camera*" • Kimber Riddle *Veronica* • Diane Salinger *Gail* • Richard Portnow *Al* • Valente Rodriguez *Low Rider* • Michael Massee *Mark* • John O'Donohue *Detective* • Lucy Liu [Lucy Liu] *Woman at newstand* ■ *Dir* Michael Lindsay-Hogg • *Scr* Kirby Dick

A Guy Named Joe ★★★

Wartime romantic drama
1944 · US · BW · 119mins

A supernatural morale-booster for wartime, this is an MGM glossy with all that great studio's polish. Spencer Tracy stars as an air force pilot who is killed on a mission. He returns in spirit to help the living – in particular his former girlfriend Irene Dunne and her admirer, new pilot Van Johnson. Victor Fleming directed the unification of the two with splendid aplomb, and fans of the film included Steven Spielberg, who re-made it as *Always* (1989).

Spencer Tracy *Pete Sandidge* • Irene Dunne *Dorinda Durston* • Van Johnson *Ted Randall* • Ward Bond *Al Yackey* • James Gleason *Col "Nails" Kilpatrick* • Lionel Barrymore *The General* • Barry Nelson *Dick Rumney* • Esther Williams *Ellen Bright* • Irving Bacon *Corporal* ■ *Dir* Victor Fleming • *Scr* Dalton Trumbo, from a story by Chandler Sprague, David Boehm, Frederick H Brennan

Guys and Dolls ★★★★ Ⓤ

Musical comedy 1955 · US · Colour · 143mins

When producer Sam Goldwyn set about filming one of the greatest of all Broadway musicals, he went after the best dancer he could find, his ideal Sky Masterson, Gene Kelly. Louis B Mayer wouldn't release Kelly to his rival, however, so Goldwyn went for the best actor in the movies. That's how Marlon Brando became the definitive Masterson, singing the Frank Loesser songs himself, cleverly choreographed by Michael Kidd, whose depiction of Broadway is one of the film's highlights. With Jean Simmons waking up to love with *If I Were a Bell*, and Frank Sinatra and Vivian Blaine as Nathan Detroit and Miss Adelaide, what more could you want? ▦

Marlon Brando *Sky Masterson* • Jean Simmons *Sarah Brown* • Frank Sinatra *Nathan Detroit* • Vivian Blaine *Miss Adelaide* • Robert Keith *Lieutenant Brannigan* • Stubby Kaye *Nicely-Nicely Johnson* • BS Pully *Big Jule* • Sheldon Leonard *Harry the Horse* • Regis Toomey *Arvide Abernathy* • Johnny Silver *Benny Southstreet* ■ *Dir* Joseph L Mankiewicz • *Scr* Joseph L Mankiewicz, from a musical by Abe Burrows, Jo Swerling, from short stories by Damon Runyon

The Guyver ★★

Science-fiction action
1992 · US · Colour · 92mins

One day you're saving the universe as Luke Skywalker in *Star Wars*, the next you're playing a CIA agent who turns into a cockroach. Such is the fate of Mark Hamill in this unintentionally hilarious movie based on a popular Japanese comic book. Co-directors Steve Wang and Joji Tani handle the action well in this tale of a college student who becomes an armour-plated superhero, courtesy of the titular device, and takes on monster-changing bad guys. Unfortunately, characterisation and dialogue play second-fiddle to a series of hilariously rubbery monsters.

Mark Hamill *Max* • Vivian Wu *Mizky* • Jack Armstrong *Sean* • David Gale *Balcus* • Michael Berryman *Lisker* • Jimmie Walker *Striker* • Spice Williams *Weber* • Peter Spellos *Ramsey* ■ *Dir* Steve Wang, Screaming Mad George [Joji Tani] • *Scr* Jon Purdy, from characters created by Yoshiki Takaya

Guyver 2: Dark Hero ★★★ 15
Science-fiction action
1994 · US · Colour · 95mins
The same mix of science fiction, genetic tampering, martial arts and weird creatures as the Japanese comic book-inspired original, director Steve Wang's rousing sequel is even more lunatic and action-packed. David Hayter takes over from Jack Armstrong as the armour-plated hero. This time he's after the Zoanoid aliens responsible for double-crossing archaeologist Kathy Christopherson as she unearths a cave-bound spaceship. Lots of acrobatic monster-bashing ensues with just enough eye-opening plot between each bout to keep the mind similarly amused. ▭

David Hayter *Sean Barker* • Kathy Christopherson *Cori* • Christopher Michael Atkins • Bruno Giannotta *Crane* • Stuart Weiss *Marcus* ■ *Dir* Steve Wang • *Scr* Nathan Long, from a story by Steve Wang, from characters created by Yoshiki Takaya

Gymkata ★ 18
Action adventure 1985 · US · Colour · 85mins
Former Olympic gymnast Kurt Thomas has the misfortune to find himself in the lead of this shambolic martial arts action adventure that attempts to retell the Robin Hood legend in the style of *The Arabian Nights*. Sent by a secret government agency to prevent the overthrow of the ruler of an almost medieval kingdom, he's soon up to his eyeballs in spies and crooked officials and, of course, head over heels in love with a kung-fu fighting princess. Contains swearing and violence. ▭

Kurt Thomas *Jonathan Cabot* • Tetchie Agbayani *Princess Rubali* • Richard Norton *Zamir* • Edward Bell *Paley* • John Barrett *Gomez* • Conan Lee *Hao* • Bob Schott *Thorg* • Buck Kartalian *The Khan* ■ *Dir* Robert Clouse • *Scr* Charles Robert Carnes, from the novel *The Terrible Game* by Dan Tyler Moore

Gypsy ★★★★ PG
Musical biography
1962 · US · Colour · 137mins
Rosalind Russell stars as Stephen Sondheim and Jule Styne's fabulous Rose Hovick, the mother (and-a-half) of real-life stripper Gypsy Rose Lee, in this marvellous presentation of one of the greatest of all Broadway shows. Purists may argue that Russell isn't Ethel Merman (star of the stage show), that some songs are missing, or that Mervyn LeRoy's direction is too "theatrical". Nevertheless, this is a bright, dazzling and above all entertaining movie. It contains a fabulous array of colourful showbiz characters and a performance by

Russell that will knock your socks off. There are other great moments, too: Natalie Wood's tender, touching *Little Lamb* and her final triumphant striptease, plus Paul Wallace's *All I Need Is the Girl*. ▭

Rosalind Russell *Rose* • Natalie Wood *Louise "Gypsy"* • Karl Malden *Herbie Sommers* • Paul Wallace *Tulsa* • Betty Bruce *Tessie Tura* • Parley Baer *Mr Kringelein* • Harry Shannon *Grandpa* ■ *Dir* Mervyn LeRoy • *Scr* Leonard Spigelgass, from the musical by Arthur Laurents, from the memoirs by Gypsy Rose Lee [Rose Louise Hovick]

Gypsy ★★★ PG
Musical drama 1993 · US · Colour · 136mins
Composers Jule Styne and Stephen Sondheim's musical interpretation of the life of stripper queen Gypsy Rose Lee was filmed in 1962 with the splendid Rosalind Russell in the role of the most monstrous showbusiness mother of them all, Mama Rose Hovick. In this re-creation made for US television, the score survives splendidly, and the great Jerome Robbins's choreography is faithfully duplicated by Bonnie Walker. Most things work, especially a touching, vulnerable performance from Cynthia Gibb as young Louise, but the whole founders on the central casting of Bette Midler as Mama Rose. She looks fine, but all the technique in the world can't conceal that she's not a skilled actress. ▭

Bette Midler *Rose Hovick* • Peter Riegert *Herbie* • Cynthia Gibb *Louise Hovick* • Jennifer Beck *June Hovick* • Ed Asner *Rose's father* ■ *Dir* Emile Ardolino • *Scr* Arthur Laurents, from his musical, from the memoirs by Gypsy Rose Lee [Rose Louise Hovick]

The Gypsy and the Gentleman ★★
Drama 1958 · UK · Colour · 107mins
This is hardly the sort of potboiler you would expect from a film-maker of Joseph Losey's calibre. By attempting to re-ceate the look of contemporary art, however, he brings some undeserved sophistication to this otherwise garish adaptation of Nina Warner Hooke's penny-dreadful, *Darkness I Love You*. Melina Mercouri roars through this Regency bodice-ripper with a demented glee that totally swamps Keith Michell's brooding aristocrat. With June Laverick and Lyndon Brook merely required to contribute some ineffectual simpering, the only worthwhile performances come from the mercenary Patrick McGoohan and the scheming Flora Robson.

Melina Mercouri *Belle* • Keith Michell *Deverill* • Patrick McGoohan *Jess* • June Laverick *Sarah* • Flora Robson *Mrs Haggard* • Lyndon Brook *John* • Clare Austin *Vanessa* • Helen Haye *Lady Ayrton* • Newton Blick *Ruddock* ■ *Dir* Joseph Losey • *Scr* Janet Green, from the novel *Darkness I Love You* by Nina Warner Hooke

Gypsy Colt ★★★ U
Drama 1954 · US · Colour · 71mins
Is there a 13-year-old horse-mad daughter in the house? If so, get those tissues at the ready for this endearing if rather treacly tale, which reworks *Lassie Come Home* for the equine fan.

A young horse owner is reduced to despair by her parents' decision to sell her much-loved pet to a racing stables, but love will out, even when it's on four sturdy legs. A highly professional film that presses all the right buttons.

Donna Corcoran *Meg MacWade* • Ward Bond *Frank MacWade* • Frances Dee *Em MacWade* • Lee Van Cleef *Hank* • Larry Keating *Wade Y Gerald* • Bobby Hyatt *Phil Gerald* • Nacho Galindo *Pancho* • Rodolfo Hoyos Jr [Rodolfo Hoyos] *Rodolfo* ■ *Dir* Andrew Marton • *Scr* Martin Berkeley, from a story by Eric Knight

The Gypsy Moths ★★★ 15
Action adventure
1969 · US · Colour · 102mins
Steve McQueen was to have starred in this gripping, if resolutely sombre romance, but then director John Frankenheimer cast Burt Lancaster and Deborah Kerr, reuniting the stars of *From Here to Eternity*. Lancaster is one of three skydivers who arrive in Kansas to perform their death-defying stunts. Thrilling in the air and depressing on the ground, it's a study of nobodies going nowhere, with Lancaster silently morose for most of the time while Kerr simmers. Gene Hackman, Sheree North and Bonnie Bedelia, in her screen debut, add to the general mood of listlessness. ▭

Burt Lancaster *Mike Rettig* • Deborah Kerr *Elizabeth Brandon* • Gene Hackman *Joe Browdy* • Scott Wilson *Malcolm Webson* • William Windom *V John Brandon* • Bonnie Bedelia *Annie Burke* • Sheree North *Waitress* ■ *Dir* John Frankenheimer • *Scr* William Hanley, from the novel by James Drought

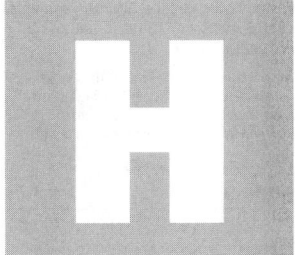

HM Pulham Esq ★★★★ U
Drama 1941 · US · BW · 119mins
It doesn't sound very exciting, but director King Vidor makes a memorable and moving film about a stuffy Bostonian who played safe and in old age regrets not marrying the love of his life. Robert Young showed new depths as the wistful Harry Pulham, while Hedy Lamarr demonstrated that she could be more than just a glamour figure as the advertising copywriter in New York who tries to liberate him from his stifling background of wealth and privilege. Vidor also wrote the script with his wife, Elizabeth Hill, and there's an uncredited walk-on part from Ava Gardner.

Hedy Lamarr *Marvin Myles* • Robert Young *HM Pulham Esq* • Ruth Hussey *Kay Motford* • Charles Coburn *Pulham Sr* • Fay Holden *Mrs Pulham* • Van Heflin *Bill King* • Leif Erickson *Rodney "Bo-Jo" Brown* ■ *Dir* King Vidor • *Scr* King Vidor, Elizabeth Hill, from the novel by John P Marquand • *Art Director* Cedric Gibbons

The H-Man ★★★
Science-fiction 1954 · Jap · Colour · 78mins
Taking time out from his *Godzilla/Rodan* industry, director Inoshiro Honda came up with one of his best movies. His Japanese answer to *The Blob* has men turning into oozing green slime after being exposed to a nuclear test zone. Rain washes some of the gelatinous residue into the Tokyo sewers where it proliferates to attack the population. Flame throwers set the city sewage system alight in a spectacular climax to an engaging fantasy chock-full of hallucinatory images and impressive visual effects. Honda's semi-sequel *The Human Vapor* (1964) failed to match the same extraordinary weirdness. Japanese dialogue dubbed into English.

Yumi Shirakawa *Girl* • Kenji Sahara *Detective* • Akihiko Hirata *Scientist* • Eitaro Ozawa *Inspector Tominaga* • Koreya Senda *Dr Maki* • Mitsuru Sato *Uchida* ■ *Dir* Inoshiro Honda • *Scr* Takeshi Kimura, Hideo Kaijo

Habit ★★★
Horror 1995 · US · Colour · 112mins
A New York alcoholic, played by writer/director Larry Fessenden with his front tooth missing, meets mysterious Meredith Snaider at a Halloween party and immediately starts having terrifying dreams, with the odd bite appearing on his body. Incredibly, Fessenden accomplishes something new with very familiar vampire material, combining creepy camerawork, scary atmospherics and mesmerising performances. Cleverly using a low budget to enhance the mood of his little-seen independent film,

Fessenden's unusual *Taxi Driver* meets *Lost Boys* affair is a rare treat and a cult movie in waiting.

Larry Fessenden *Sam* • Meredith Snaider *Anna* • Aaron Beall *Nick* • Patricia Coleman *Rae* • Heather Woodbury *Liza* • Jesse Hartman *Lenny* ■ *Dir/Scr* Larry Fessenden

Hackers ★★★ U

Thriller 1995 · US · Colour · 105mins

Teenage hackers uncover a massive computer fraud in director Iain Softley's romantic action adventure set against the intriguing backdrop of New York's cyber-culture. A standard industrial espionage chase thriller is given a stylish patina by its digital-age atmosphere, complete with often bewildering technical data and imaginative journeys down the information superhighway. New mouse on the mat Jonny Lee Miller and tough net surfer Angelina Jolie interface well as the console-crossed lovers trying to prove laptop supremacy. ▭ *DVD*

Jonny Lee Miller *Dade* • Angelina Jolie *Kate* • Jesse Bradford *Joey* • Matthew Lillard *Cereal Killer* • Laurence Mason *Nikon* • Renoly Santiago *Phantom Phreak* • Fisher Stevens *The Plague* • Wendell Pierce *Agent Dick Gill* ■ *Dir* Iain Softley • *Scr* Rafael Moreu

Hadley's Rebellion ★

Drama 1984 · US · Colour · 96mins

A young boy moves from Georgia to California, only to find his prep-school classmates are less than friendly. That is, until he takes up wrestling. Shallow, predictable and very much in the *Rocky* mould, the only redeeming feature seems to be the chemistry between Griffin O'Neal as Hadley and William Devane as his coach.

Griffin O'Neal *Hadley Hickman* • William Devane *Coach Ball* • Adam Baldwin *Bobo McKenzie* • Lisa Lucas *Linda Johnson* • Eric Boles *Mr Stevens* • Israel Juarbe *Manuel Hernandez* • Chad McQueen *Rick Stanton* ■ *Dir/Scr* Fred Walton

Hail Caesar ★

Comedy 1994 · US · Colour · 93mins

The most appalling thing about *Hail Caesar* is that it marks a low point in the career of Samuel L Jackson: he plays the postman who repeatedly suffers at the hands of the main character's dog. This crime is heinous enough; that it comes in the middle of so unrepentantly awful a film as this is a cruel twist of the knife. Anthony Michael Hall directs himself as Caesar, a too-cool rock 'n' roll wannabe who must prove himself to his girlfriend's father by working in dad's eraser factory. But then Caesar discovers that the factory is really manufacturing illegal plastic explosives. "Wackiness" ensues.

Anthony Michael Hall *Julius Caesar MacGruder* • Robert Downey Jr *Jerry* • Judd Nelson *Prisoner One* • Samuel L Jackson *Mailman* • Frank Gorshin *Mr DeWitt* • Nicholas Pryor *Mr Bidwell* • Leslie Danon *Annie* ■ *Dir* Anthony Michael Hall • *Scr* Robert Mittenthal, from a story by Mark Twain

Hail! Hail! Rock 'n' Roll! ★★★★ U

Music documentary 1987 · US · Colour · 115mins

Normally pop documentaries veer from on-stage electricity and dressing-room silliness to the rambling of band members posing as philosophers. *This Is Spinal Tap* did a superb spoof on all this. Now, avoiding all the pitfalls and pratfalls of the genre, comes one of the screen's most accomplished pop biographies ever, easily on a par with *The Last Waltz*. Making no attempt to gloss over Chuck Berry's brittle personality, his arrogance and petulance, it also brings out the racism Chuck experienced in his youth and examines the nature of his unique guitar sound. Telling comments by the likes of Little Richard and Bo Diddley are joined seamlessly to a big-blast concert at the Fox Theatre, St Louis, to celebrate Chuck's 60th birthday. ▭

Dir Taylor Hackford

Hail, Hero! ★★★

Drama 1969 · US · Colour · 87mins

Michael Douglas's screen debut benefits from the direction of David Miller, who was in the chair for *Lonely Are the Brave*, one of his father Kirk's best films. Something of a radical in his youth, Douglas Jr brings an authenticity to this tale about a boy who drops out of college to enlist for Vietnam, not because he believes in the war – he doesn't – but because of his hawkish parents, played by Arthur Kennedy and Teresa Wright. The pacifist message is often awkward and cringe-inducing, but one admires the film's ambition and honesty.

Michael Douglas *Carl Dixon* • Arthur Kennedy *Albert Dixon* • Teresa Wright *Santha Dixon* • John Larch *Mr Conklin* • Charles Drake *Senator Murchiston* • Mercer Harris *Jimmy* • Peter Strauss *Frank Dixon* ■ *Dir* David Miller • *Scr* David Manber, from the novel by John Weston • *Music/Lyrics* Gordon Lightfoot

Hail the Conquering Hero ★★★★★ U

Comedy 1944 · US · BW · 100mins

This extraordinarily daring wartime comedy stars Eddie Bracken as the dejected son of a dead First World War hero, prevented by hay fever from serving in the current conflict. When some battle veterans persuade him to return home and masquerade as a valiant marine to please his dear old mother, he receives a hero's welcome from the entire town. Writer/director Preston Sturges handles the mounting complications with dazzling dexterity and draws delightful performances from his favourite character actors, most notably William Demarest as the hard-boiled sergeant and Raymond Walburn as the pompous windbag of a mayor. Ella Raines also sparkles under Sturges's encouragement.

Eddie Bracken *Woodrow Truesmith* • Ella Raines *Libby* • Bill Edwards *Forrest Noble* • Raymond Walburn *Mayor Noble* • William Demarest *Sergeant* ■ *Dir/Scr* Preston Sturges

La Haine ★★★★ 15

Drama 1995 · Fr · BW · 97mins

Responsible for causing a scandal on its domestic release, this bruising portrait of disaffected youth confirmed its writer/director Mathieu Kassovitz as the *wunderkind* of French cinema. Presenting the housing schemes on the outskirts of Paris as hotbeds of racial hatred and social unrest, the film follows three lads from different ethnic backgrounds and explores how they spend their endless spare time and examines their response to a case of police brutality. Vincent Cassel is outstanding as the Jewish skinhead, but it's Kassovitz's restless camerawork and a script as funny as it is hard-hitting that make this such an impressive and important work. In French with English subtitles. Contains violence, swearing and drug abuse.

Vincent Cassel *Vinz* • Hubert Kounde *Hubert* • Saïd Taghmaoui *Saïd* • Karim Belkhadra *Samir* • Edouard Montoute *Darty* • François Levantal *Astérix* • Solo Dicko *Santo* • Marc Duret *Inspector "Notre Dame"* • Héloïse Rauth *Sarah* ■ *Dir/Scr* Mathieu Kassovitz

Hair ★★ 15

Musical 1979 · US · Colour · 116mins

If ever a musical is caught firmly in its time, then it's *Hair*. In this film version made in the late seventies, director Milos Forman fails to capture the enormous energy of the original stage show, which was a celebrated load of old nonsense even back in the mid-sixties. Anyone who had any pretensions to hippydom at the time will find their toes curling involuntarily at the memory, and those born since will be quite bemused at all the fuss. Made at least ten years too late or 30 years too early, the film has a general air of fustiness and anachronism, and, apart from Treat Williams's table-top dance, the leads have little to be proud of. Contains nudity. ▭

John Savage *Claude* • Treat Williams *Berger* • Beverly D'Angelo *Sheila* • Annie Golden *Jeannie* • Dorsey Wright *Hud* • Don Dacus *Woof* • Cheryl Barnes *Hud's fiancée* • Nicholas Ray *General* ■ *Dir* Milos Forman • *Scr* Michael Weller, from the musical by Gerome Ragni, James Rado, Galt MacDermot

The Hairdresser's Husband ★★★★ 15

Drama 1990 · Fr · Colour · 78mins

French director Patrice Leconte has never been a great respecter of political correctness, and this eccentric comedy sees him at his most dubious. If you can overcome his attitude to both women and Arabic culture then there are some utterly charming moments, as the wonderful Jean Rochefort delights in the delicate hands of hairdresser Anna Galiena. The scenes of a seaside childhood and the sudden tragic twist remain longest in the mind, along with Rochefort's marvellously impish performance. But Leconte's camera lingers on Galiena with a lecherous lens that is far removed from the sympathetic gaze of the title character in his previous film, *Monsieur Hire*. In French with English subtitles. Contains sex scenes. ▭

Jean Rochefort *Antoine* • Anna Galiena *Mathilde* • Roland Bertin *Antoine's father* •

Maurice Chevit *Agopian* • Philippe Clevenot *Morvoisieux* • Jacques Mathou *Monsieur Chardon* • Claude Aufaure *Customer* • Albert Delpy *Donecker* ■ *Dir* Patrice Leconte • *Scr* Claude Klotz, Patrice Leconte

Hairspray ★★★★ PG

Satire 1988 · US · Colour · 87mins

These days Ricki Lake has to deal with more than her fair share of eccentrics on her chat show, but she probably still hasn't come across anyone weirder than John Waters, who launched her into stardom with this kitsch classic. Waters tones down his usual excesses, but his mischievous black sense of humour is still very much to the fore in this affectionate salute to those Z-grade teen movies. Lake is the fun-loving Tracy Turnblad, who becomes the new teen dancing queen much to the horror of wealthy snobs Debbie Harry and Sonny Bono, who want their daughter to shine. The soundtrack is a constant delight, as is the eclectic cast, which ranges from Waters' regular Divine (his last movie) through to Pia Zadora. ▭

Ricki Lake *Tracy Turnblad* • Divine *Edna Turnblad/Arvin Hodgepile* • Sonny Bono *Franklin Von Tussle* • Ruth Brown *Motormouth Maybell* • Colleen Fitzpatrick *Amber Von Tussle* • Debbie Harry [Deborah Harry] *Velma Von Tussle* • Michael St Gerard *Link Larkin* • Jerry Stiller *Wilbur Turnblad* • Pia Zadora *Beatnik girl* ■ *Dir/Scr* John Waters

The Hairy Ape ★★

Drama 1944 · US · BW · 91mins

Many liberties are taken with Eugene O'Neill's twenties' play about dockyard politics, mainly to dilute its fairly blatant communism. The plot is further twisted into wartime flagwaver, with William Bendix as the "hairy ape", a resentful stoker on a ship that runs refugees from Lisbon to America. On-board lovers are snotty heiress Susan Hayward and ship's engineer John Loder, who clash when Hayward insists on being shown the boiler room and is horrified by the sight of Bendix. World war meets class war – match abandoned after an hour or so.

William Bendix *Hank Smith* • Susan Hayward *Mildred Douglas* • John Loder *2nd Engineer Tony Lazar* • Dorothy Comingore *Helen Parker* • Roman Bohnen *Paddy* ■ *Dir* Alfred Santell • *Scr* Robert D Andrews, Decla Dunning, from the play by Eugene O'Neill

Half a Sixpence ★★★★ U

Musical 1967 · UK · Colour · 139mins

Based on HG Wells's minor classic *Kipps*, this is one of the very few British musicals that doesn't have you squirming in your seat with embarrassment, for which we have to thank veteran Hollywood director George Sidney. Admittedly, the story drags once Tommy Steele and Julia Foster's relationship hits the rocks, but so much of what has gone on before is slickly staged and joyously played that you should forgive it this pause for breath. Rattling through David Heneker's catchy songs and hurling himself into Gillian Lynne's energetic dance routines, Steele has never been better on screen. ▭

Tommy Steele *Arthur Kipps* • Julia Foster *Ann* • Cyril Ritchard *Harry Chitterlow* • Penelope Horner *Helen Walsingham* • Elaine Taylor *Kate*

U = SUITABLE FOR ALL   Uc = SUITABLE FOR ALL, ESPECIALLY FOR YOUNG CHILDREN (VIDEO ONLY)   PG = PARENTAL GUIDANCE

• Grover Dale *Pearce* • Hilton Edwards *Shalford* ■ *Dir* George Sidney • *Scr* Beverley Cross, from the novel *Kipps* by HG Wells

Half Angel ★★ 🄴

Comedy 1951 · US · Colour · 75mins

Robert Riskin penned some of Frank Capra's most popular films, but he was sadly off form with this slight romantic frippery. Loretta Young lacks the frivolity to carry off the part of a starchy nurse whose true character only emerges during her frequent bouts of sleepwalking. There's little for Joseph Cotten and John Ridgely (as the suitors in love with the different aspects of her personality) to do but look on adoringly. Better known as a scriptwriter, director Richard Sale was out of his depth.

Loretta Young *Nora* • Joseph Cotten *John Raymond* • Cecil Kellaway *Mr Gilpin* • Basil Ruysdael *Dr Jackson* • Jim Backus *Michael Hogan* • Irene Ryan *Kay* • John Ridgely *Tim* • Therese Lyon *Mrs McCarey* ■ *Dir* Richard Sale • *Scr* Robert Riskin, from a story by George Carleton Brown

The Half-Breed ★★ 🄴

Western 1952 · US · Colour · 81mins

A very minor contribution to the cycle of films beginning with *Broken Arrow* in 1950, which challenged the usual western stereotypes favoured by Hollywood. Here the white villain wants the Apache reservation cleared of its inhabitants as there's gold for the taking. Robert Young, giving his usual polished performance as a gambler, helps Jack Buetel's eponymous hero defuse the situation, conveniently saving RKO the expense of staging a big battle scene, but disappointing fans eager for some rousing action.

Robert Young *Dan Craig* • Janis Carter *Helen* • Jack Buetel *Charlie Wolf* • Barton MacLane *Marshal* • Reed Hadley *Captain Jackson* • Damian O'Flynn *Captain Gilchrist* • Porter Hall *Ma Higgins* ■ *Dir* Stuart Gilmore • *Scr* Harold Shumate and Richard Wormser, from a story by Robert Hardy Andrews

Half Moon Street ★★★ 🄸

Political thriller 1986 · UK · Colour · 85mins

This eagerly awaited next movie from director Bob Swaim (*La Balance*) failed miserably at the theatrical box office, but it's hard to see why. Based on Paul Theroux's novel *Doctor Slaughter*, here's the ultra-sexy Sigourney Weaver as a prim Middle East scholar in the daytime and a call girl by night, while Michael Caine is Lord Bulbeck, the British diplomat who favours her favours. Adult and certainly different, there's a grim topicality about Arab wheelings and dealings in the Mayfair byway of the title, and the film's subsequent reputation will lead you to believe that it's a dog. It isn't. 🎞

Sigourney Weaver *Dr Lauren Slaughter* • Michael Caine *Lord Bulbeck* • Patrick Kavanagh *General Sir George Newhouse* • Faith Kent *Lady Newhouse* • Ram John Holder *Lindsay Walker* • Keith Buckley *Hugo Van Arkady* • Annie Hanson *Mrs Van Arkady* • Patrick Newman *Julian Shuttle* • Niall O'Brien *Captain Twilley* • Nadim Sawalha *Karim Hatami* ■ *Dir* Bob Swaim • *Scr* Edward Behr, Bob Swaim, from the novel *Doctor Slaughter* by Paul Theroux

The Half Naked Truth ★★★★

Comedy 1932 · US · BW · 77mins

The now almost forgotten Lee Tracy, a wonderfully fast-talking, sour-looking, wisecracking star of the thirties, is here at the top of his form as an unscrupulous publicity man. This delectable comedy, classily directed by Gregory La Cava, has Tracy scheming to make fiery Lupe Velez into an instant celebrity by blackmailing neurotic producer Frank Morgan. The cast also included frog-voiced Eugene Pallette and prissy Franklin Pangborn. Velez, known as the "Mexican Spitfire", soon to marry Johnny "Tarzan" Weissmuller, was to commit suicide, aged 36, in 1944.

Lee Tracy *Bates* • Lupe Velez *Teresita* • Eugene Pallette *Achilles* • Frank Morgan *Farrell* • Robert McKenzie *Col Munday* • Franklin Pangborn *Hotel manager* ■ *Dir* Gregory La Cava • *Scr* Gregory La Cava, Corey Ford, from a story by Ben Markson, HN Swanson, the novel *Phantom Fame* by David Freedman, Bartlett Cormack

Half Shot at Sunrise ★★ 🄴

Comedy 1930 · US · BW · 78

The first to admit that their films were never on a par with their stage shows, Bert Wheeler and Robert Woolsey deserve better than the anonymity in which they now languish. Their wisecracking interchanges were littered with risqué puns and their slapstick had plenty of zip. They were top-billed for the first time in this lively comedy about a couple of First World War soldiers who keep out of the clutches of the military police to sample the delights of Paris. Some of the gags miss the mark and the musical moments are an unnecessary intrusion, but it's mostly sparky stuff.

Bert Wheeler *Tommy* • Robert Woolsey *Gilbert* • John Rutherford *MP Sergeant* • George MacFarlane *Col Marshall* • Roberta Robinson *Eileen* ■ *Dir* Paul Sloane [Paul H Sloane] • *Scr* James Ashman Creelman, Anne Caldwell, Ralph Spence, from a story by James Ashman Creelman

Half-Baked ★ 🄸

Comedy 1998 · US · Colour · 78mins

An unwise and utterly unfunny attempt to resurrect a genre we'd hoped had disappeared into a cultural black hole along with flared trousers – the seventies drug comedy as typified by Cheech and Chong. Comedian Dave Chappelle stars as one of a gang of pothead pals dreaming up crazy schemes to spring a friend from prison. There are occasional lapses into amusement, but all too often it hits the obvious button. An abundance of cameos from the likes of Snoop Doggy Dogg and Willie Nelson don't help. Contains violence, drug abuse, nudity and swearing. 🎞

Dave Chappelle *Thurgood/Sir Smoka Lot* • Jim Breuer *Brian* • Guillermo Diaz *Scarface* • Harland Williams *Kenny* • Rachel True *Mary Jane* • Snoop Doggy Dogg *Scavenger Smoker* • Clarence Williams III *Samson Simpson* • Tommy Chong *Squirrel Master* • Willie Nelson *Historian Smoker* ■ *Dir* Tamra Davis • *Scr* Dave Chappelle, Neal Brennan

The Halfway House ★★★

Portmanteau drama 1943 · UK · BW · 95mins

Produced by Michael Balcon and directed by Basil Dearden, this is a halfway decent stab at the difficult art of the portmanteau picture – a selection of short stories linked by a common theme. In an admirable all-star cast, Mervyn and Glynis Johns are splendid as the ghostly hosts at a Welsh inn, where the guests are given the chance to re-evaluate their contribution to the war effort. Cowardice, black marketeering, family unity and the thorny issue of Irish neutrality are all explored in an intelligent piece of propaganda that still makes for optimistic entertainment.

Françoise Rosay *Alice Meadows* • Tom Walls *Captain Harry Meadows* • Mervyn Johns *Rhys* • Glynis Johns *Gwyneth* • Alfred Drayton *Oakley* • Esmond Knight *David Davies* • Richard Bird *Sub-lieutenant Richard French* • Philippa Hiatt *Margaret* • Sally Ann Howes *Joanna French* ■ *Dir* Basil Dearden • *Scr* Angus MacPhail, Diana Morgan, from the play *The Peaceful Inn* by Denis Ogden

Hallelujah ★★ 🄴

Black drama 1929 · US · BW · 105mins

Although plainly hampered by the primitive sound techniques, King Vidor received an Oscar nomination for this ground-breaking talkie. However, today it's impossible to escape the period racism in the tale of cotton-picker Daniel L Haynes, who twice finds redemption following a crime – once after killing his brother in a brawl and then, as a lapsed preacher, after murdering his mistress and her lover. Although MGM made much of the all-black cast, this was more to mollify white audiences than to make a social statement. Indeed, the colour prejudice is clearly evident, with the lighter-skinned Nina Mae McKinney being made to appear far more alluring than her co-stars.

Daniel L Haynes *Zeke* • Nina Mae McKinney *Chick* • William E Fountaine *Hot Shot* • Harry Gray *Parson* • Fannie Belle DeKnight *Mammy* • Everett McGarrity *Spunk* • Victoria Spivey *Missy Rose* ■ *Dir* King Vidor • *Scr* Wanda Tuchock, Ransom Rideout, from a story by King Vidor • *Music/Lyrics* Irving Berlin

Hallelujah, I'm a Bum ★★★ 🄴

Musical comedy 1933 · US · BW · 84mins

With its rhyming dialogue and witty songs by Rodgers and Hart, this Depression-set musical endeavoured to repeat the success of Rouben Mamoulian's *Love Me Tonight*, made the previous year. It didn't quite come off (director Lewis Milestone was really happier with tougher material), but is a brave attempt with some fine moments. Al Jolson is a hobo living in Central Park (with his sidekick Egghead, played by famed silent comic Harry Langdon) who falls in love with the girlfriend of the mayor (Frank Morgan) and tries to change his ways. SN Behrman's script, based on a story by Ben Hecht, is amusing and incisive, but the title song had to be filmed twice, the word "bum" being replaced by "tramp" for British audiences.

Al Jolson *Bumper* • Madge Evans *June Marcher* • Frank Morgan *Mayor Hastings* • Harry Langdon *Egghead* • Chester Conklin *Sunday* • Tyler Brooke *Mayor's secretary* ■ *Dir* Lewis Milestone • *Scr* SN Behrman, from a story by Ben Hecht • *Music/Lyrics* Richard Rogers, Lorenz Hart • *Music* Alfred Newman

The Hallelujah Trail ★★★ 🄴

Comedy western 1965 · US · Colour · 139mins

Beleaguered cavalry commander Burt Lancaster is under attack from as bizarre a collection of pressure groups as ever enlivened a spoof western. Lee Remick leads a brigade of temperance women trying to stop an overland shipment of whiskey from reaching Denver, while local Indians are equally eager to divert the barrels. Director John Sturges is free with the wagon-trail clichés, not always to great effect, but the film's worth a look, if only for Martin Landau's performance. 🎞

Burt Lancaster *Colonel Thadeus Gearhart* • Lee Remick *Cora Templeton Massingale* • Jim Hutton *Captain Paul Slater* • Pamela Tiffin *Louise Gearhart* • Brian Keith *Frank Wallingham* • Martin Landau *Chief Walks-Stooped-Over* • John Anderson *Sergeant Buell* ■ *Dir* John Sturges • *Scr* John Gay, from the novel by Bill Gulick

The Halliday Brand ★★

Western 1957 · US · BW · 77mins

A rather dreary psychological western from cult director Joseph H Lewis that bears all the hallmarks of a quick, cheap shoot and a poorly thought-through sub-Freudian screenplay. Having said that, Lewis fans may still find much to enjoy in this picture. In a short running time, sterling work is done by the classy lead quartet of Joseph Cotten, Ward Bond, Viveca Lindfors and Betsy Blair, but it's all very intense and brooding, and not terribly enlightening or enjoyable.

Joseph Cotten *Daniel* • Viveca Lindfors *Aleta* • Betsy Blair *Martha* • Ward Bond *Big Dan* • Bill Williams *Clay* • Jay C Flippen *Chad Burris* • Christopher Dark *Jivaro* • Jeanette Nolan *Nante* ■ *Dir* Joseph H Lewis • *Scr* George W George, George S Slavin

Halloween ★★★★ 🄸

Horror 1978 · US · Colour · 87mins

John Carpenter's terror trailblazer established the slasher trend for "calendar date" horror. But few of the clones it inspired had the same directorial flair, dazzling skill or irreverent wit as this "baby-sitter in jeopardy" jolter. Jamie Lee Curtis earned her "scream queen" coronet in Carpenter's deceptively clever trick-or-treat chiller, and Donald Pleasence carved a whole new career for himself through several variable sequels as the fearful psychiatrist chasing the indestructible and shuddersome killer Michael Myers. 🎞

Donald Pleasence *Dr Sam Loomis* • Jamie Lee Curtis *Laurie Strode* • Nancy Loomis *Annie* • PJ Soles *Lynda* • Charles Cyphers *Brackett* • Kyle Richards *Lindsey* • Brian Andrews *Tommy* • John Michael Graham *Bob* • Nancy Stephens *Marion* • Arthur Malet *Graveyard keeper* • Mickey Yablans *Richie* • Brent Le Page *Lonnie* • Tony Moran *Michael aged 21* ■ *Dir* John Carpenter • *Scr* Debra Hill, John Carpenter

Halloween II ★★ 🔞

Horror   1981 · US · Colour · 87mins

With the exception of *H20*, the sequels to John Carpenter's 1978 horror masterpiece have been universally awful. However, like the aforementioned 1998 version, this was the only one to feature the original star Jamie Lee Curtis, and is a better film for it. *Halloween II* takes up where the original finished, with Curtis being taken to hospital still in shock, but before long her indestructible nemesis is stalking her around the wards. Carpenter had a hand in the script, but this is a by-the-numbers retread and the direction of Rick Rosenthal lacks flair. 📺 **DVD**

Jamie Lee Curtis *Laurie* • Donald Pleasence *Sam Loomis* • Charles Cyphers *Leigh* • Jeffrey Kramer *Graham* • Lance Guest *Jimmy* • Pamela Susan Shoop [Pamela Shoop] *Karen* • Hunter Von Leer *Gary* ■ *Dir* Rick Rosenthal • *Scr* John Carpenter, Debra Hill

Halloween III: Season of the Witch ★ 🔟5

Horror   1982 · US · Colour · 91mins

This deserves a star for being the most original of all the *Halloween* sequels – the problem is that it's also one of the worst. Dumping the Michael Myers storyline, the film has mad toy mogul Dan O'Herlihy supplying children with lethal Halloween masks. Tom Atkins is the father who stumbles across O'Herlihy's evil plan. There are a few good gory bits, but the story is plain daft and the direction from Tommy Lee Wallace – John Carpenter's editor on the original *Halloween* and *The Fog* – is disappointing. Contains swearing and violence. 📺

Tom Atkins *Dr Dan Challis* • Stacey Nelkia *Ellie* • Dan O'Herlihy *Conal* • Ralph Strait *Buddy* • Michael Currie *Rafferty* • Jadeen Barbor *Betty* • Bradley Schachter *Little Buddy* ■ *Dir/Scr* Tommy Lee Wallace

Halloween 4: the Return of Michael Myers ★★ 🔞

Horror thriller   1988 · US · Colour · 88mins

After the misguided, Michael Myers-less *Halloween III*, it's back-to-basics time and the result is a competent but yawningly empty slasher thriller. Danielle Harris steps into the Jamie Lee Curtis role, playing one of the last surviving relatives of the caged psycho, who once again escapes and heads back to his home turf for some more blood-letting. By now, any genuine menace was seeping away fast. **DVD**

Donald Pleasence *Dr Loomis* • Ellie Cornell *Rachel Carruthers* • Danielle Harris *Jamie Lloyd* • George P Wilbur *Michael Myers* • Michael Pataki *Dr Hoffman* ■ • *Scr* Alan B McElroy, from a story by Dhani Lipsius, Larry Rattner, Benjamin Ruffner, Alan B McElroy

Halloween 5 ★★ 🔞

Horror   1989 · US · Colour · 96mins

More slashing by numbers, as Danielle Harris once again dodges nasty Uncle Michael Myers, who, surprise surprise, managed to survive this film's predecessor. Shot back to back with Part 4, the only link with John Carpenter's original is Donald Pleasence as the barking psychiatrist Dr Sam Loomis, named after a

character in *Psycho*. Otherwise, it's business as usual. 📺 **DVD**

Ellie Cornell *Rachel* • Beau Starr *Meeker* • Donald Pleasence *Dr Loomis* • Danielle Harris *Jamie* • Wendy Kaplan *Tina* • Donald L Shanks [Don Shanks] *Michael Myers* ■ *Dir* Dominique Othenin-Girard • *Scr* Michael Jacobs, Dominique Otherin-Girard, Shem Bitterman

Halloween 6: the Curse of Michael Myers ★ 🔞

Horror   1995 · US · Colour · 84mins

The worst of the series so far. Director Joe Chappelle tries to give menace by proxy to the laughable awfulness, reviving Carpenter's original *Halloween* score as a backdrop. It doesn't work, and neither do the revelations intended to explain Michael Myers's years of murder and mayhem. Donald Pleasence gives his usual reliable performance, but sadly the line of dialogue, "Not dead. Just very much retired", proved to be his epitaph: the infirm actor died shortly after shooting. Contains swearing, violence and sex scenes. 📺

Donald Pleasence *Dr Loomis* • Mitch Ryan [Mitchell Ryan] *Dr Wynn* • Marianne Hagan *Kara Strode* • Paul Rudd *Tommy Doyle* • Mariah O'Brien *Beth* • Kim Darby *Debra Strode* • George P Wilbur *Mike Myers* ■ *Dir* Joe Chappelle • *Scr* Daniel Farrands

Halloween H20: 20 Years Later ★★★ 🔞

Horror   1998 · US · Colour · 97mins

John Carpenter's classic 1978 chiller gets a nineties makeover, although in the hands of director Steve Miner, a veteran of horror franchises like *Friday the 13th* and *House*, the emphasis is still firmly on frights rather than in-jokes. Jamie Lee Curtis, back in the role that made her name, is now a recovering alcoholic and headteacher at an exclusive school. The problem is that the murderous and seemingly indestructible Michael is keen to celebrate the 20th anniversary of his first massacre. The older and wiser Curtis steals the show from the teenage TV pin-ups, but Miner's direction is merely efficient, rather than scary. Contains violence and swearing, with some sexual references. 📺

Jamie Lee Curtis *Laurie Strode/Keri Tate* • Michelle Williams *Molly* • Joseph Gordon-Levitt *Jimmy* • Josh Hartnett *John* • Adam Arkin *Will Brennan* • LL Cool J *Ronny* • Jodi Lyn O'Keefe *Sarah* • Adam Hann-Byrd *Charlie* • Janet Leigh *Norma* ■ *Dir* Steve Miner • *Scr* Robert Zappia, Matt Greenberg, from a story by Debra Hill, John Carpenter

The Halloween Tree ★★★★ 🇺

Animated fantasy 1993 · US · Colour · 69mins

Ray Bradbury's children's novel is superbly brought to the screen in this top-notch animation feature made for television by the Hanna-Barbera studio. Four children, who desperately want to help a sick friend, embark on a journey through the multicultural and religious history of All Hallows' Eve. Guided by Mr Moundshroud (voiced by Leonard Nimoy) they learn a 4,000-year history and moral lesson en route to a gallant sacrifice. Brilliantly adapted by

Bradbury, the combination of traditional Halloween imagery with the less globally well-known ones is as inventive as *Tim Burton's The Nightmare before Christmas*. 📺

Leonard Nimoy *Mr Moundshroud* ■ *Dir* Mario Piluso • *Scr* Ray Bradbury, from his novel

Halls of Anger ★★

Drama   1970 · US · Colour · 98mins

Formula film about a school riven with racial violence. The production boasts a certain class, but there's no lesson to be learned here that hasn't been taught in a dozen other movies with similar plots and settings. Some interest resides, though, in the cast – not leads Calvin Lockhart or Janet MacLachlan, but look further and you'll spot the likes of Rob Reiner, Ed Asner and a very young Jeff Bridges.

Calvin Lockhart *Quincy Davis* • Janet MacLachlan *Lorraine Nash* • James A Watson Jr *JT Watson* • Jeff Bridges *Douglas* • Rob Reiner *Leaky Couloris* • DeWayne Jesse *Lerone Johnson* • Patricia Stich *Sherry Vaughn* • Edward Asner [Ed Asner] *McKay* ■ *Dir* Paul Bogart • *Scr* John Shaner, Al Ramrus

Halls of Montezuma ★★★ 🇺

Second World War action drama
1950 · US · Colour · 108mins

This big-budget, ferociously patriotic 20th Century-Fox Second World War movie was directed by one of the all-time greats of the genre, Lewis Milestone, who was responsible for the original *All Quiet on the Western Front*, *A Walk in the Sun* and *Pork Chop Hill*. The action here isn't up to the standard of those classics, but it's extremely enjoyable, largely thanks to an excellent cast headed by Richard Widmark, and backed up by Jack Palance (still billed as Walter), a pre-*Dragnet* Jack Webb and Robert Wagner as the youngster of the outfit. The Technicolor photography is quite outstanding, and there's no unnecessary Hollywood romance in this one. 📺

Richard Widmark *Lieutenant Anderson* • Walter [Jack] Palance [Jack Palance] *Pigeon Lane* • Reginald Gardiner *Sergeant Johnson* • Robert Wagner *Coffman* • Karl Malden *Doc* • Richard Hylton *Corporal Conroy* • Richard Boone *Lieutenant Colonel Gilfilan* • Skip Homeier *Pretty Boy* • Don Hicks *Lieutenant Butterfield* • Jack Webb *Correspondent Dickerman* • Bert Freed *Slattery* ■ *Dir* Lewis Milestone • *Scr* Michael Blankfort • *Cinematographer* Winton C Hoch, Harry Jackson

Hambone and Hillie ★★★ 🔤

Comedy drama   1984 · US · Colour · 86mins

Heroic canines have always been popular with moviegoers, but few tales of four-pawed adventure have been as brutal as this cross-country epic, which includes an escaped convict's horrific assault on a pregnant woman and a dog's gruesome death. Thankfully there are more wholesome episodes, such as Hambone's friendships with a sentimental truck driver and a lonely paraplegic. As the grandmother hoping her lost hound will find his way home, the venerable Lillian Gish is adorable. That said, all eyes will be on the latter-day Lassie. 📺

Lillian Gish *Hillie Radcliffe* • Timothy Bottoms *Michael Radcliffe* • Candy Clark *Nancy Rollins* • OJ Simpson *Tucker* • Robert Walker [Robert Walker Jr] *Wanderer* • Jack Carter *Lester Burns* • Alan Hale [Alan Hale Jr] *McVickers* • Anne Lockhart *Roberta Radcliffe* ■ *Dir* Roy Watts • *Scr* Sandra K Bailey, Michael Murphey, Joel Soisson, from a story by Ken Barnett

Hamburger Hill ★★★★ 🔞

War drama   1987 · US · Colour · 104mins

Unjustly overshadowed by Oliver Stone's *Platoon* and Stanley Kubrick's *Full Metal Jacket*, John Irvin's *Hamburger Hill* is almost their equal. The story has the classic simplicity of a past era of war movies: troops of the 101st Airborne Division attack Hill 937 in the Ashau Valley, Vietnam, and after ten days and 11 assaults, when everyone has been put through the meat grinder, the hill is renamed after America's favourite fast food. Reducing the Vietnam war to the level of symbol is an efficient means of conveying the pointless sacrifice, and Irvin does the messy job superbly. Not for the lily-livered. Contains violence, swearing and brief nudity. 📺

Anthony Barrile *Languilli* • Michael Patrick Boatman [Michael Boatman] *Motown* • Don Cheadle *Washburn* • Michael Dolan *Murphy* • Don James *McDaniel* • Dylan McDermott *Sergeant Frantz* ■ *Dir* John Irvin • *Scr* James Carabatsos

Hamilton ★★★

Spy thriller   1998 · Swe · Colour · 127mins

Jan Guillou's Carl Hamilton is apparently the Scandinavian answer to Tom Clancy's Jack Ryan, and his bestsellers have been filmed a number of times and this is one of the most successful adaptions. *Fargo* star Peter Stormare enjoys the opportunity to be the eponymous hero who, along with sidekick Mats Langbacka, is on the trail of a Russian gang trying to unload a nuclear missile. There are also good supporting roles for Lena Olin and Mark Hamill, and award-winning commercials director Harald Zwart keeps the action racing along. In Swedish with English subtitles.

Mark Hamill *Mike Hawkins* • Lena Olin *Tessie* • Peter Stormare *Carl Hamilton* • Mats Langbacka *Ake Stalhandske* • Madeleine Elfstrand *Anna* • Thomas Hedengran *Gustavsson* • Mikael Ahlberg *Andersson* ■ *Dir* Harald Zwart • *Scr* Jonas Cornell, William Aldridge, from novels by Jan Guillou

Hamlet ★★★★★ 🇺

Classic tragedy   1948 · UK · BW · 147mins

Laurence Olivier directed himself in this astonishing Shakespeare adaptation, which won five Academy Awards. Desmond Dickinson's camerawork adds mood to the moment as Larry's blond-headed Prince Hamlet wanders around Elsinore Castle, ambiguously pursuing Ophelia (Jean Simmons), berating his mother Eileen Herlie and stalking his new stepfather Basil Sydney. (Olivier also played the ghost of Hamlet's father, to eerie effect.) For the sake of pace – and the film certainly has that! – adapter Alan Dent removes the supporting characters Rosencrantz and Guildenstern, while William Walton's music adds atmospheric lustre.

Despite all the cuts, this is a very great Dane. [video] DVD

Laurence Olivier *Hamlet* • Eileen Herlie *Gertrude* • Basil Sydney *Claudius* • Norman Wooland *Horatio* • Felix Aylmer *Polonius* • Terence Morgan *Laertes* • Jean Simmons *Ophelia* • Peter Cushing *Osric* • Stanley Holloway *Gravedigger* • Anthony Quayle *Marcellus* ■ *Dir* Laurence Olivier • *Scr* Alan Dent, from the play by William Shakespeare • *Costume Designer* Roger K Furse • *Art Director* Roger K Furse, Carmen Dillon

Hamlet ★★★★

Tragedy 1964 · USSR · BW · 150mins

The Russian version of Shakespeare's most famous tragedy was filmed by veteran director Grigori Kozintsev to commemorate the 400th anniversary of the playwright's birth. His treatment is a study of medieval state machinations, and is set in an Elsinore whose inhabitants are contained by an impressive fortress of stone and iron. It may lack the depth of other film versions, but the images, enriched by the dramatic Shostokovich music, are bold and powerful – as is the great Russian actor Innokenti Smoktunovsky's Prince of Denmark, a man of action and not a brooding dreamer. A Russian language film.

Innokenti Smoktunovsky *Hamlet* • Mikhail Nazvanov *King* • Elsa Radzin *Queen* • Yuri Tolubeyev *Polonius* • Anastasia Vertinskaya *Ophelia* • Vladimir Erenberg *Horatio* • C Olesenko *Laertes* • Vadim Medvedev *Guildenstern* • Igor Dmitriev *Rosencrantz* ■ *Dir* Grigori Kozintsev • *Scr* Grigori Kozintsev, Boris Pasternak, from the play by William Shakespeare

Hamlet ★★★ U

Tragedy 1969 · UK · Colour · 112mins

Until Kenneth Branagh appeared on the scene, Nicol Williamson had the distinction of being the cinema's only bearded Hamlet. But there all similarities between the two interpretations end, for, whereas Branagh has shot the play on lavish, expansive sets, Williamson and director Tony Richardson opted for extreme close-ups (although whether this is to intensify the drama or disguise the paucity of the Round House theatre backdrops isn't quite clear). While it might have made those in the back row feel part of the proceedings, Williamson's booming performance sits uncomfortably on the small screen. Compensations come from Roger Livesey's dual role as Lucianus and the Player King and Anthony Hopkins's Claudius. [video]

Nicol Williamson *Hamlet* • Gordon Jackson *Horatio* • Anthony Hopkins *Claudius* • Judy Parfitt *Gertrude* • Mark Dignam *Polonius* • Michael Pennington *Laertes* • Marianne Faithfull *Ophelia* • Ben Aris *Rosencrantz* • Clive Graham *Guildenstern* • Peter Gale *Osric* • Roger Livesey *Lucianus/Player King* • Michael Elphick *Captain* • Anjelica Huston *Court lady* ■ *Dir* Tony Richardson • *Scr* from the play by William Shakespeare

Hamlet ★★★★ PG

Tragedy 1990 · US · Colour · 128mins

After mixed reviews for his 1968 *Romeo and Juliet*, Franco Zeffirelli waited over 20 years – not counting his 1986 version of Verdi's opera *Otello* – before tackling the Bard again. Closer in spirit to Baz Luhrmann's *William Shakespeare's Romeo and Juliet* than Kenneth Branagh's meticulously faithful *Hamlet*, this is a surprisingly vigorous rendition of a play essentially about indecision and hesitancy. Mel Gibson is the screen's most muscular Prince of Denmark, but he gives a good account of himself, as does Helena Bonham Carter as the abused Ophelia – yet it's Alan Bates who most impresses as the villainous Claudius. Not one for the purists, but a laudable attempt to introduce Shakespeare to the blockbuster generation. Contains nudity. [video]

Mel Gibson *Hamlet* • Glenn Close *Queen Gertrude* • Alan Bates *Claudius* • Paul Scofield *Ghost* • Ian Holm *Polonius* • Helena Bonham Carter *Ophelia* • Stephen Dillane *Horatio* • Nathaniel Parker *Laertes* • Sean Murray *Guildenstern* • Michael Maloney *Rosencrantz* • Trevor Peacock *Gravedigger* • John McEnery *Osric* ■ *Dir* Franco Zeffirelli • *Scr* Franco Zeffirelli, Christopher De Vore, from the play by William Shakespeare

Hamlet ★★★ PG

Tragedy 1996 · US · Colour · 232mins

This monumental full-length, unabridged version of the play has Kenneth Branagh directing himself as the Prince. Admirable, and challenging, this is a very showbizzy staging – in addition to the leading players (such as Kate Winslet as Ophelia, Julie Christie's Gertrude, Derek Jacobi as Polonius), there is a veritable galaxy of star appearances to tweak the interest. While some critics might say this is not so much a movie as a chorus-line of talents, Branagh has to be admired for the ambition of this ravishingly beautiful staging, although his occasionally patronising direction can be irritating. [video]

Kenneth Branagh *Hamlet* • Derek Jacobi *Claudius* • Julie Christie *Gertrude* • Richard Briers *Polonius* • Kate Winslet *Ophelia* • Nicholas Farrell *Horatio* • Michael Maloney *Laertes* • Brian Blessed *Ghost* • Gérard Depardieu *Reynaldo* • Jack Lemmon *Marcellus* • Charlton Heston *Player King* • Rufus Sewell *Fortinbras* • Richard Attenborough *English Ambassador* • Timothy Spall *Rosencrantz* • Reece Dinsdale *Guildenstern* • John Gielgud *Priam* • Judi Dench *Hecuba* ■ *Dir* Kenneth Branagh • *Scr* Kenneth Branagh, from the play by William Shakespeare • *Production Designer* Tim Harvey • *Art Director* Desmond Crowe

Hamlet Goes Business ★★★★ PG

Comedy 1987 · Fin · BW · 85mins

Only Aki Kaurismäki could turn Shakespeare's most complex play into an offbeat drama about the rubber duck business. Transferring the action from Elsinore to a modern Finnish boardroom, the writer/director also shifts the thematic emphasis away from insanity and the inability to act and places it on cruelty and a wilful defiance of progress. Seeking revenge for the murder of his father, Pirkka-Pekka Petelius is like a character from a *film noir*, an impression reinforced by Timo Salminen's shadowy monochrome photography. All the *dramatis personae* are wickedly reinvented, as are the Bard's famous quotations. Add a stunning score, and the result is a palpable hit. In Finnish with English subtitles. [video]

Pirkka-Pekka Petelius *Hamlet* • Esko Salminen *Klaus* • Kati Outinen *Ophelia* • Elina Salo *Gertrud* • Esko Nikkari *Polonius* • Kari Väänänen *Lauri Polonius* • Hannu Valtonen *Simo* • Mari Rantasila *Helena* • Turo Pajala *Rosencrantz* • Aake Kalliala *Guildenstern* • Pentii Auer *Father/Ghost* ■ *Dir* Aki Kaurismäki • *Scr* Aki Kaurismäki, from the play by William Shakespeare

Hammersmith Is Out ★★

Drama 1972 · US · Colour · 114mins

Peter Ustinov's reputation may now rest on his skill as a raconteur, but he was once considered, with films such as *Private Angelo*, to be the British film industry's great white hope as a director. This makes it hard to see why. It's a bizarre story about madman Richard Burton escaping a mental hospital – run by a language-mangling Ustinov – to become a tycoon, with Elizabeth Taylor in tow. It may have been intended as a spoof, but it comes across as an ego indulgence.

Elizabeth Taylor *Jimmie Jean Jackson* • Richard Burton *Hammersmith* • Peter Ustinov *Doctor* • Beau Bridges *Billy Breedlove* • Leon Ames *General Sam Pembroke* • George Raft *Guido Scartucci* • Jose Espinoza *Duke* ■ *Dir* Peter Ustinov • *Scr* Stanford Whitmore

Hammett ★★★

Crime drama 1982 · US · Colour · 97mins

A flawed but fascinating crime drama from Wim Wenders – his first Hollywood movie, based on one of the key figures in the genre itself, Dashiell Hammett. In this fictionalised tale, Frederic Forrest plays the legendary novelist, down on his luck and entangled in corruption and blackmail involving a Chinese prostitute. The under-rated Forrest is quite superb and there are strong supporting turns from the likes of Peter Boyle and Marilu Henner. This was made under the auspices of Francis Ford Coppola's troubled Zoetrope studio, and its problems probably contributed to the movie's uneven tone, although Wenders still succeeds in summoning up an authentic *film noir* atmosphere.

Frederic Forrest *Hammett* • Peter Boyle *Jimmy Ryan* • Marilu Henner *Kit Conger/Sue Alabama* • Roy Kinnear *English Eddie Hagedorn* • Elisha Cook Jr *Eli the taxi driver* • Lydia Lei *Crystal Ling* • RG Armstrong *Lieutenant O'Mara* • Richard Bradford *Detective Bradford* ■ *Dir* Wim Wenders • *Scr* Ross Thomas, Dennis O'Flaherty, Thomas Pope, from the novel by Joe Gores

Hamsun ★★★

Biography
1996 · Den/Swe/Nor/Ger · Colour · 158mins

Cutting a Lear-like figure as a man who has outlived his times, Max von Sydow dominates this controversial study of the Nobel laureate whose admiration for Hitler led to him being branded a traitor after the liberation of Norway. However, as Jan Troell is keen to point out, Knut Hamsun was more concerned with denouncing British imperialism and advancing the cause of Norwegian independence than bolstering the hated regime of Vidkun Quisling. This is a fascinating study and Hamsun's meeting with Hitler is riveting. A Swedish language film.

Max von Sydow *Knut Hamsun* • Ghita Norby *Marie Hamsun* • Sverre Anker Ousdal *Vidkun Quisling* • Eindride Eidsvold *Tore Hamsun* • Gard B Eidsvold *Arild Hamsun* • Anette Hoff *Ellinor Hamsun* • Asa Soderling *Cecilia Hamsun* • Svein Erik Brodal *Holmboe* • Ernst Jacobi *Adolf Hitler* ■ *Dir* Jan Troell • *Scr* Per Olov Enquist, from the non-fiction book *Prosessen mot Hamsun* by Thorkild Hansen

Hana-Bi ★★★★ 18

Crime drama 1997 · Jap · Colour · 98mins

With its fragmentary structure intended to resemble the "fireworks" (the literal translation of Hana-Bi) of the title, this is definitely a detective film with a difference. Winner of the Golden Lion at Venice, it's a lyrical, compassionate tale as ex-cop Takeshi "Beat" Kitano (who also directs) seeks to care for both his dying wife and his partner, disabled while chasing a criminal. To counteract the grim reality of Kitano's problems back in the city, there are lengthy passages of contemplative silence and pastoral vistas, as well as symbolic paintings commenting on the action. Although there are still explosive sequences of gun-play, this is a far cry from earlier Kitano films such as *Sonatine*. In Japanese with English subtitles. Contains violence and some swearing. [video]

Takeshi Kitano *Yoshitika Nishi* • Kayoko Kishimoto *Miyuki (Nishi's wife)* • Ren Osugi *Horibe* • Susumu Terajima *Detective Nakamura* • Tetsu Watanabe *Tesuka (junkyard owner)* ■ *Dir/Scr* Takeshi Kitano

The Hand ★★★ 18

Horror 1981 · US · BW and Colour · 99mins

Hollywood bad boy Oliver Stone's second directorial effort was this fine psychological horror tale about cartoonist Michael Caine losing his hand in a freak car accident and the severed limb seeking violent revenge on all his enemies. Or is Caine committing the murders and simply hallucinating? What makes this dark fantasy more than just an angry, depressing and gory remake of the classic *The Beast with Five Fingers* is Stone's multi-dimensional and thoughtful script that explores the many facets of madness. This is the thinking man's horror film, with Caine's possible insanity shown through stylish cleverness, distorted angles and monochrome flashbacks. A misunderstood and under-rated film from Stone. Contains violence, swearing and nudity. [video]

Michael Caine *Jon Lansdale* • Andrea Marcovicci *Anne Lansdale* • Annie McEnroe *Stella Roche* • Bruce McGill *Brian Ferguson* • Viveca Lindfors *Doctor* • Rosemary Murphy *Karen Wagner* • Mara Hobel *Lizzie Lansdale* ■ *Dir* Oliver Stone • *Scr* Oliver Stone, from the novel *The Lizard's Tale* by Marc Brandel • *Cinematographer* King Baggott

Hand Gun ★★ 18

Crime thriller 1994 · US · Colour · 85mins

Treat Williams here rehearses his comeback role from *Things to Do in Denver When You're Dead*, although this movie's not quite in the same class. Williams plays a small-time crook who, with brother Paul Shulze, gets in over his head when his equally crooked father (Seymour Cassel) does a runner with the takings of a bank robbery. The cast features colourful character actors such as Michael

Rapaport and Joe Pesci's regular punch-bag, Frank Vincent, but the writing lacks focus and Whitney Ransick's direction is a tad overheated. Contains swearing, violence, sex scenes and nudity.

Treat Williams *George McCallister* • Seymour Cassel *Jack McCallister* • Paul Schulze *Michael McCallister* • Frank Vincent *Earl* • Anna Thomson [Anna Levine] *Laura* • Michael Imperioli *Benny* • Michael Rapaport *Lenny* • Star Jasper *Sally* ■ *Dir/Scr* Whitney Ransick

The Hand of Night ★

Horror 1966 · UK · Colour · 89mins

Hapless William Sylvester visits Morocco and is enticed into a den of vampires by beautiful Moorish princess Alizia Gur. Awkwardly combining the Dracula myth with middle-eastern mummy motifs, but bringing nothing of its own to the terror table except exotic locations, this tedious sub-Hammer horror filler is further eroded in the shock department by bland performances.

William Sylvester *Paul Carver* • Diane Clare *Chantal* • Alizia Gur *Marisa* • Edward Underdown *Gunther* • Terence de Marney *Omar* • William Dexter *Leclerc* ■ *Dir* Frederic Goode • *Scr* Bruce Stewart

The Hand That Rocks the Cradle ★★★★ 15

Thriller 1992 · US · Colour · 105mins

A psychological thriller with cool, Teutonic-looking Rebecca De Mornay as the "nanny from hell", wreaking havoc on the sunny designer family life of Annabella Sciorra and Matt McCoy. Director Curtis Hanson successfully plugs into every deep-seated fear of middle-class parents, with De Mornay doing a neat turn in icy malevolence wrapped up in the guise of responsible carer. This is pure hokum, of course, but extremely effective until the last 30 minutes, when the plot rapidly self-destructs. Contains violence, swearing and nudity. DVD

Annabella Sciorra *Claire Bartel* • Rebecca De Mornay *Mrs Mott/"Peyton Flanders"* • Matt McCoy *Michael Bartel* • Ernie Hudson *Solomon* • Julianne Moore *Marlene* • Madeline Zima *Emma Bartel* • John de Lancie *Doctor Mott* • Mitchell Laurance *Lawyer* ■ *Dir* Curtis Hanson • *Scr* Amanda Silver

A Handful of Dust ★★★★ PG

Period drama 1987 · UK · Colour · 114mins

In this glossily depressing adaptation of Evelyn Waugh's satire on the between-wars aristocracy, James Wilby stars as the dull, duty-bound estate owner cuckolded by his adulterous wife Kristin Scott Thomas and man-about-town Rupert Graves. Directed by Charles Sturridge with the same impeccable detail he brought to his TV adaptation of *Brideshead Revisited*, the impressive performances can't lighten a cynicism which tries to persuade us that the wages of goodness are death. DVD

James Wilby *Tony Last* • Kristin Scott Thomas *Brenda Last* • Rupert Graves *John Beaver* • Anjelica Huston *Mrs Rattery* • Judi Dench *Mrs Beaver* • Alec Guinness *Mr Todd* • Richard Beale *Ben* • Jackson Kyle *John Andrew* ■ *Dir* Charles Sturridge • *Scr* Charles Sturridge, Tim Sullivan, Derek Granger, from the novel by Evelyn Waugh

Handgun ★★★★ 18

Thriller 1983 · UK/US · Colour · 95mins

An intriguing if only partially successful attempt by British director Tony Garnett to redress the balance in favour of the female victim of male violence. Karen Young is excellent as the passive young woman whose experiences at the hands of Texan brute Clayton Day (another finely etched performance) turn her into a marauding vigilante. On the plus side, there are a great sense of menace and tension, good supporting performances and an intelligent, sensitive handling of tricky issues. The minus is Garnett's overall thesis that the way to handle violence is to strike back. However, this is still a minor classic. Contains violence, swearing and nudity.

Karen Young *Kathleen Sullivan* • Clayton Day *Larry Keeler* • Suzie Humphreys *Nancy* • Helena Humann *Miss Davis* • Ben Jones *Chuck* ■ *Dir/Scr* Tony Garnett

Handle with Care ★★ U

Drama 1958 · US · BW · 82mins

Dean Jones, that stalwart of Disney features during the sixties and seventies (*That Darn Cat*, *The Love Bug*) makes an earlier career stab at teen-idoldom in this undistinguished drama. As law student Zachary Davis, Jones investigates small-town crime in a legal process that allows such pupils to take on mock grand-jury work. Sincere, but boring.

Dean Jones *Zachary Davis* • Joan O'Brien *Mary Judson* • Thomas Mitchell *Mayor Dick Williston* • John Smith *Bill Reeves* • Walter Abel *Professor Bowdin* • Burt Douglas *Ray Crowder* ■ *Dir* David Friedkin • *Scr* David Friedkin, Morton Fine, from the teleplay *Mock Trial* by Samuel Grafton, Edith Grafton

The Handmaid's Tale ★★★ 18

Futuristic drama 1990 · US · Colour · 103mins

As a portrait of a depraved new world, this lacks the conviction to put the frighteners on us. Adapted from a Margaret Atwood bestseller, its heroine Kate (Natasha Richardson) lives in a born-again America run on puritanical lines in a polluted future. As one of the few fertile women around, she's ordered to bear Commander Robert Duvall a child for wife Faye Dunaway. The republic's religious rites and oppression of women echo some of today's theocratic fanaticisms, but it's a story that never gets its act or acting together, although Duvall is a formidable presence in this feminist protest. Contains violence, swearing and sex scenes.

Natasha Richardson *Kate* • Faye Dunaway *Serena Joy* • Aidan Quinn *Nick* • Elizabeth McGovern *Moira* • Victoria Tennant *Aunt Lydia* • Robert Duvall *Commander* • Blanche Baker *Ofglen* • Traci Lind *Ofwarren/Janine* • Zoey Wilson *Aunt Helena* ■ *Dir* Volker Schlöndorff • *Scr* Harold Pinter, from the novel by Margaret Atwood

Hands across the Table ★★★★

Romantic comedy 1935 · US · BW · 79mins

A manicurist and a penniless playboy, each determined to marry money and betrothed to dull but appropriately wealthy partners, meet, fall in love, and break off their engagements. The simple plot services a superior romantic comedy: sparkling, witty and marvellously played by Carole Lombard and Fred MacMurray, both of whose progress into top stardom was hastened by the film's box-office success. Ralph Bellamy and Astrid Allwyn are the future spouses who are thrown over, and Mitchell Leisen directs with the lightness of touch you would expect from a Paramount production of the period.

Carole Lombard *Regi Allen* • Fred MacMurray *Theodore Drew III* • Ralph Bellamy *Allen Macklyn* • Astrid Allwyn *Vivian Snowden* • Ruth Donnelly *Laura* • Marie Prevost *Nona* • William Demarest *Natty* ■ *Dir* Mitchell Leisen • *Scr* Herbert Fields, Norman Krasna, Vincent Lawrence, from the story *Bracelets* by Viña Delmar

Hands of Orlac ★★★

Silent crime horror 1924 · Aus · BW · 90mins

Made five years after his seminal horror outing, *The Cabinet of Dr Caligari*, Robert Wiene's adaptation of Maurice Renard's sensationalist novel suffers from an uncertainty of tone. For the most part, the action is staged in a realistic manner, thus making the moments of expressionist stylisation all the more incongruous. However, Conrad Veidt is mesmerising as the concert pianist living on his nerves after his shattered hands are replaced with those of a murderer. Equally compelling is Fritz Kortner's blackmailer, but not even he's prepared for the final twist.

Conrad Veidt *Orlac* • Fritz Kortner *Nera* • Carmen Cartellieri *Regine* • Paul Adkonas *Diener* ■ *Dir* Robert Wiene • *Scr* Louis Nerz, from the novel by Maurice Renard

The Hands of Orlac ★★★★

Horror 1960 · UK/Fr · BW · 101mins

Filmed twice before (most notably as *Mad Love* in 1935), this elegant version of Maurice Renard's psychological case study of murderous obsession still exerts a morbid fascination. Mel Ferrer is a little lightweight as the pianist given a convicted strangler's hands after a plane crash, but Christopher Lee is a remorseless revelation as the sadistic magician tormenting him, ensuring the chilling tension is maintained right up until the final surprise twist.

Mel Ferrer *Steven Orlac* • Christopher Lee *Nero* • Dany Carrel *Li-Lang* • Felix Aylmer *Dr Cochrane* • Basil Sydney *Siedelman* • Lucile Saint-Simon *Louise Cochrane* • Donald Wolfit *Prof Volcheff* • Donald Pleasence *Coates* ■ *Dir* Edmond T Gréville • *Scr* John Baines, Donald Taylor, Edmond T Gréville, from the novel by Maurice Renard

Hands of the Ripper ★★★ 15

Horror 1971 · UK · Colour · 81mins

Hammer films, like *Carry Ons*, divide audiences: though most film lovers regard them as poorly made tosh aimed at a very specific market, over the years a Hammer cult has emerged, giving a certain respectability to these cheap schlock flicks. This is one of the more entertaining of the later Hammers, piece of nonsense about Jack the Ripper's daughter who, having watched her dad dismember mama, goes slightly barmy whenever she gets kissed in a flickering light. Cue distinguished therapist Eric Porter, who tries to cure her but then starts covering up her murders. Porter is too serious for these proceedings; Vincent Price or Peter Cushing would have helped. Angharad Rees is a swell Ms Ripper, and the end result is helped by Ken Talbot's colour photography and by Peter Sasdy's restrained direction.

Eric Porter *Dr John Pritchard* • Angharad Rees *Anna* • Jane Merrow *Laura* • Keith Bell *Michael Pritchard* • Derek Godfrey *Dysart* • Dora Bryan *Mrs Golding* • Marjorie Rhodes *Mrs Bryant* • Lynda Baron *Long Liz* • Marjorie Lawrence *Dolly* • Norman Bird *Police inspector* • Margaret Rawlings *Madame Bullard* ■ *Dir* Peter Sasdy • *Scr* LW Davidson, from a story by Edward Spencer Shew

Hands over the City ★★★ U

Political drama 1963 · It · Colour · 99mins

Italian director Francesco Rosi imported American actor Rod Steiger to give weighty menace to the role of a property tycoon who manipulates civic politicians to let him develop his land, despite the effect on the people living there. Steiger gives a suitably overbearing performance as the ruthless millionaire in whom fascism has not died, but the film is too angry to articulate its arguments properly. It's still great dramatic entertainment, though. An Italian language film.

Salvo Randone *De Angeli* • Rod Steiger *Nottola* • Guido Alberti *Maglione* ■ *Dir* Francesco Rosi • *Scr* Francesco Rosi, Raffaele La Capria, Enzo Provenzale, Enzo Forcella

Hands Up! ★★★

Silent comedy 1926 · US · BW

Raymond Griffith, the debonair silent comedian who specialised in take-offs of traditional Hollywood fare, comes close to matching the best of Harold Lloyd and Buster Keaton in this delightfully brisk parody of the American Civil War. As a Confederate spy sent out west, Griffith displays considerable ingenuity in surviving firing squads and hostile tribes as he tracks down a stagecoach carrying gold to the Union side. He even finds a way of living happily ever after with both of his lady loves, played by Marion Nixon and Virginia Lee Corbin, who save him from a necktie party.

Raymond Griffith *Confederate spy* • Marion Nixon [Marian Nixon] *The girl he loves* • Virginia Lee Corbin *The other girl he loves* • Mack Swain *Mine owner* • Montague Love [Montagu Love] *Union general* • George Billings *Abraham Lincoln* • Noble Johnson *Sitting Bull* ■ *Dir* Clarence Badger • *Scr* Monty Brice, Lloyd Corrigan, from a story by Reginald Morris

Hang 'em High ★★★ 18

Western 1968 · US · Colour · 114mins

Clint Eastwood is once again a man of few words but many bullets in the first western he made back in America after Sergio Leone had virtually invented him – as a film star and a distinctive screen character – in the spaghetti westerns they made together. Eastwood does the strong, silent stuff with characteristic efficiency in a tale

of revenge and justice for all, which is perhaps more memorable as a staging post in Eastwood's career than as a landmark in the history of the western. Contains violence. [video] DVD

Clint Eastwood *Jed Cooper* • Inger Stevens *Rachel* • Ed Begley *Cap'n Wilson* • Pat Hingle *Judge Adam Fenton* • Arlene Golonka *Jennifer* • James MacArthur *Preacher* • Ruth White *Madam Peaches Sophie* • Bruce Dern *Miller* • Alan Hale Jr *Stone* • James Westerfield *Prisoner* • Dennis Hopper *Prophet* • Ben Johnson *Sheriff Dave Bliss* ■ *Dir* Ted Post • *Scr* Leonard Freeman, Mel Goldberg

Hangar 18 ★ PG

Science-fiction drama
1980 · US · Colour · 96mins

Two space shuttle astronauts witness a collision with a UFO that crash-lands in Texas. When the White House hides the wreck in a remote air base hangar, astronaut Gary Collins tries to uncover the conspiracy over the accident for which he is being blamed. Any resemblance to *Close Encounters* and the "Roswell incident" are purely intentional in another sluggish and slapdash slice of speculative science-fiction from the notorious Sunn Classics outfit, who exclusively made drive-in exploitation fare. [video]

Darren McGavin *Harry Forbes* • Robert Vaughn *Gordon Cain* • Gary Collins *Steve Bancroft* • Joseph Campanella *Frank Lafferty* • Pamela Bellwood *Sarah Michaels* ■ *Dir* James L Conway • *Scr* Steven Thornley, James L Conway, Tom Chapman, from a novel by Robert Weverka, Charles E Sellier

Hangfire ★★ 18

Action drama 1991 · US · Colour · 85mins

Efficient but unremarkable action film about a hostage crisis that starts when a group of escaped prisoners take over a small community in New Mexico. Chief escapee is Lee DeBroux, who's plausibly dangerous, while Jan-Michael Vincent represents the National Guard which arrives in force. Not to be outwitted, though, is the local sheriff, played by Brad Davis, who died shortly after the film was completed and was best known for his performance in *Midnight Express*. [video]

Brad Davis *Sheriff Ike Slayton* • Kim Delaney *Maria* • Ken Foree *Billy* • Lee DeBroux *Kuttner* • Jan-Michael Vincent *Johnson* • James Tolkan *Patch* • George Kennedy *Warden* • Yaphet Kotto *Lieutenant* • Lou Ferrigno *Smitty* ■ *Dir* Peter Maris • *Scr* Brian D Jeffries

Hangin' with the Homeboys ★★★ 15

Comedy drama 1991 · US · Colour · 85mins

Among the last films to be released in the 'hood sequence of urban black American movies that took US cinema by storm in the early nineties, this is the only one to focus on the interaction between black and Hispanic youths. Writer/director Joseph B Vasquez's third feature explores some overly familiar situations, but there is a real sense of life as it is lived in his depiction of a night in the lives of four friends from the Bronx. Much of this freshness is due to the fact that the young cast was encouraged to improvise. Stand-up comics Doug E Doug and Mario Joyner clearly relish the opportunity, but it's John Leguizamo and Nestor Serrano who give the more rounded performances. Contains violence, swearing and nudity. [video]

Doug E Doug *Willie* • Mario Joyner *Tom* • John Leguizamo *Johnny* • Nestor Serrano *Vinny* • Kimberly Russell *Vanessa* • Mary B Ward *Luna* • Reggie Montgomery *Rasta* • Christine Claravall *Daria* • Rosemarie Jackson [Rose Jackson] *Lila* ■ *Dir/Scr* Joseph B Vasquez

The Hanging Garden ★★★ 15

Drama 1997 · Can/UK · Colour · 91mins

A heavy-duty Canadian drama about a once fat and troubled teen who returns to the family home after ten years away. He's now fit, well adjusted and happily gay, but his homecoming prompts hauntings of his past and memories of his miserable adolescence. The leading role is taken by the unknown Chris Leavins, but watch out for Kerry Fox and *The Sweet Hereafter's* Sarah Polley among the supports. This is a tough watch, but an emotional drama worth persevering with nevertheless.

Chris Leavins *Sweet William* • Troy Veinotte *Sweet William, teenager* • Kerry Fox *Rosemary* • Sarah Polley *Rosemary, teenager* • Seana McKenna *Iris* • Peter MacNeill *Whiskey Mac* ■ *Dir/Scr*

The Hanging Tree ★★★★ PG

Western 1959 · US · Colour · 102mins

This is a superb western, set in and around a wild mining community, that climaxes in a moving demonstration of the power of love. Gary Cooper gives a magnificent performance as the spiritually wounded doctor who cares for Maria Schell's temporarily blind and abandoned Swiss immigrant. The lascivious attentions of Karl Malden add spice to the scenario and George C Scott, in his screen debut, also makes an impact as a fanatical healer. Director Delmer Daves does a wonderful job of evoking the frontier atmosphere with the able assistance of cameraman Ted McCord. [video]

Gary Cooper *Doc Joe Frail* • Maria Schell *Elizabeth Mahler* • Karl Malden *Frenchy Plante* • Ben Piazza *Rune* • George C Scott *Dr George Grubb* • Karl Swenson *Mr Flaunce* • Virginia Gregg *Mrs Flaunce* • John Dierkes *Society Red* ■ *Dir* Delmer Daves • *Scr* Wendell Mayes, Halsted Welles, from the novella by Dorothy M Johnson

Hanging Up ★★ 15

Comedy melodrama
1999 · US · Colour · 94mins

Delia Ephron's novel about three sisters dealing with their senile father (Walter Matthau) is translated to the screen by director Diane Keaton, who also stars as the eldest sibling. However, Keaton and her co-star Lisa Kudrow get very little screen time compared to Meg Ryan, the daughter who is usually responsible for dear old dad. The trio spend little time together, so the film ends up a lifeless and clichéd tale about Ryan's relationship with Matthau. The latter gets some good lines, but you'll yearn for more scenes like the deliciously bitchy one in which the girls turn on each other and blame one another for everything that's gone wrong in their lives.

Meg Ryan *Eve* • Diane Keaton *Georgia* • Lisa Kudrow *Maddy* • Walter Matthau *Lou* • Adam Arkin *Joe* • Duke Moosekian *Omar Kunundar* • Ann Bortolotti *Ogmed Kunundar* ■ *Dir* Diane Keaton • *Scr* Delia Ephron, Nora Ephron, from the novel by Delia Ephron

The Hangman ★★ U

Western 1959 · US · BW · 86mins

The writer of *Stagecoach* and one of Hollywood's most reliable directors team up for a psychological western in which Robert Taylor plays a marshal with a reputation for stringing people up. Jack Lord is Taylor's current quarry, though he's apparently gone straight and has a family. Then Taylor gets a lesson in humanity from local sheriff Fess Parker (TV's Davy Crockett). Those looking for bursts of action and spectacular scenery should search elsewhere, but others might appreciate this low-key study of a psychotic peace officer.

Robert Taylor (1) *Mackenzie Bovard* • Fess Parker *Sheriff Buck Weston* • Tina Louise *Selah Jennison* • Jack Lord *Johnny Bishop* • Shirley Harmer *Kitty Bishop* • Gene Evans *Big Murph* ■ *Dir* Michael Curtiz • *Scr* Dudley Nichols, from a story by Luke Short

Hangman's House ★★

Silent melodrama 1928 · US · BW · 72mins

One of John Ford's earlier essays on his beloved Ireland, this late silent production features one of the master director's favourite actors, Victor McLaglen, as the Irish patriot who kills a drunken wastrel in a duel, freeing his widow for the man she had always loved. However, the stars – June Collyer, Larry Kent, Earle Foxe – mean little and the story drags. The film's highlight these days is the glimpse of a very young John Wayne as an excited horse race spectator.

June Collyer *Connaught O'Brien* • Larry Kent *Dermott McDermott* • Earle Foxe *John Darcy* • Victor McLaglen *Citizen Hogan* • Hobart Bosworth *Lord Chief Justice O'Brien* • John Wayne ■ *Dir* John Ford • *Scr* Marion Orth, Philip Klein, from the novel by Brian Oswald Donn-Byrne

Hangmen Also Die ★★★

Second World War drama
1943 · US · BW · 138mins

A powerful piece of wartime propaganda begins in occupied Czechoslovakia with the assassination of notorious Nazi butcher Reinhard Heydrich. This is a consummate piece of committed film-making – devised by Bertolt Brecht and the film's director, Fritz Lang – in which the Nazis are portrayed as brutal but intelligent enemies who systematically murder Czech citizens until the perpetrator is delivered to them by the underground. It may take a while to accept Hollywood actors like Brian Donlevy, Walter Brennan and Dennis O'Keefe as Czechs, but the effort is worth it.

Brian Donlevy *Dr Franz Svoboda* • Walter Brennan *Prof Novotny* • Anna Lee *Mascha Novotny* • Gene Lockhart *Emil Czaka* • Dennis O'Keefe *Jan Horek* • Alexander Granach *Alois Gruber* • Margaret Wycherly *Aunt Ludmilla Novotny* ■ *Dir* Fritz Lang • *Scr* John Wexley, from a story by Fritz Lang, Bertolt Brecht

Hangover Square ★★★

Horror 1945 · US · BW · 77mins

Following his successful collaboration with director John Brahm and screenwriter Barré Lyndon on *The Lodger*, Laird Cregar again takes the role of a psychopathic killer haunting the fog-bound streets of London. Here the burly star plays a promising young composer who turns nasty whenever he hears harsh sounds. Linda Darnell and George Sanders (as singer and police psychologist respectively) co-star in this melodrama, but it is the score by the great Bernard Herrmann which stands out. Cregar died of a heart attack, aged 28, shortly after finishing this picture.

Laird Cregar *George Harvey Bone* • Linda Darnell *Netta Longdon* • George Sanders *Dr Allan Middleton* • Glenn Langan *Carstairs* ■ *Dir* John Brahm • *Scr* Barré Lyndon, from the novel by Patrick Hamilton

Hangup ★★

Crime drama 1973 · US · Colour · 92mins

Also known as *Super Dude*, this was veteran director Henry Hathaway's last film – and, possibly, his worst. Black policeman William Elliott saves a young heroin addict (Marki Bey) from herself and her dependency, but then leaves her when he finds out she was a hooker. However the consequences of his actions lead him to the drug ring that exploited her. A very unsympathetic hero, and a curious sense of moral outrage, make this a surly sort of thriller and Hathaway's usual action can't divert us from this unpleasantness.

William Elliott *Ken* • Marki Bey *Julie* • Cliff Potts *Lou* • Michael Lerner *Richards* • Wally Taylor *Sergeant Becker* ■ *Dir* Henry Hathaway • *Scr* Albert Maltz, Lee Lazich, from the novel *The Face of Night* by Bernard Brunner

Hanky Panky ★★ 15

Comedy thriller 1982 · US · Colour · 102mins

After the success of *Stir Crazy*, you could understand Gene Wilder and director Sidney Poitier wanting to reunite with Richard Pryor. When he pulled out, however, it might have been more advisable to cast an actor in the same comic mould rather than rewrite the role in a romantic vein for Gilda Radner. Clearly there were plenty of sparks off the screen between Wilder and Radner, who married shortly afterwards, but the script gives them nothing to feed off and the endless round of coincidences and bad Hitchcock parodies soon become wearisome. Richard Widmark provides some compensation as a snarling villain. [video]

Gene Wilder *Michael Jordon* • Gilda Radner *Kate Hellman* • Kathleen Quinlan *Janet Dunn* • Richard Widmark *Ransom* • Robert Prosky *Hiram Calder* • Josef Sommer *Adrian Pruitt* ■ *Dir* Sidney Poitier • *Scr* Henry Rosenbaum, David Taylor

Hannah and Her Sisters ★★★★★ 15

Comedy drama 1986 · US · Colour · 102mins

True creativity means that an artist can mine the same seam time and time again and still come up with something fresh. Targeting once again the arty, self-obsessed residents of neurotic New York with his familiar, exhilarating combination of melancholy sentiment and witty cynicism, Woody Allen relishes their foibles and celebrates their triumphs, backing up his tale with some touching period tunes. Michael Caine and Dianne Wiest (both Oscar-winners), not to mention Woody himself, playing a hypochondriac, can do no wrong. This is Allen in complete control of his enormous talent. Contains swearing. 🖾

Woody Allen *Mickey Sachs* • Michael Caine *Elliot* • Mia Farrow *Hannah* • Carrie Fisher *April* • Barbara Hershey *Lee* • Max von Sydow *Frederick* • Dianne Wiest *Holly* • Lloyd Nolan *Evan* • Maureen O'Sullivan *Norma* • Daniel Stern *Dusty* • Sam Waterston *David* • Tony Roberts *Mickey's ex-partner* • Julie Kavner *Gail* ■ *Dir/Scr* Woody Allen

Hanna's War ★★ 15

Biographical war drama
1988 · US · Colour · 143mins

Intended to prove that in the Second World War the Jews of central Europe were resistance fighters as well as helpless victims, Menahem Golan's biopic of the Hungarian poet Hanna Senesh is undermined by a crusty script and unsubtle characterisation. Recruited by squadron leader Anthony Andrews for a vital Balkan mission, Maruschka Detmers settles for a kind of designer heroism as she battles behind the lines before suffering at the hands of Donald Pleasence's sadistic torturer. His villainy is the best thing in this muddled melodrama, although Ellen Burstyn provides an admirable cameo as Hanna's betrayed mother. A noble idea, badly botched. 🖾

Ellen Burstyn *Katalin Senesh* • Maruschka Detmers *Hanna Senesh* • Anthony Andrews *Squadron Leader McCormack* • Donald Pleasence *Rosza Gabor* • David Warner *Captain Julian Simon* ■ *Dir* Menahem Golan • *Scr* Menahem Golan, Stanley Mann, from *The Diaries of Hanna Senesh* by Hanna Senesh, from the non-fiction book *A Great Wind Cometh* by Yoel Palgi

Hannibal ★ U

Historical adventure
1959 · It · Colour · 104mins

In this grotty historical epic, Victor Mature crosses the Alps to smash the Roman Empire, pausing along the way for a romantic dalliance with Rita Gam. Director Edgar G Ulmer is perhaps best known for B-movies such as *Detour* (1945), which won him a cult following in the seventies, but his work here won't win him any extra fans. The pace is sluggish, the acting is wooden, the scenery looks painted on and the battles are staged with about six extras and a few circus elephants, who look as bored as you probably will be. Italian dialogue dubbed into English.

Victor Mature *Hannibal* • Rita Gam *Sylvia* • Milly Vitale *Danila* • Rik Battaglia *Hasdrubal* • Franco Silva *Maharbal* • Mario Girotti [Terence Hill] *Quintilius* • Mirko Ellis *Mago* ■ *Dir* Edgar G Ulmer, Ludovico Bragaglia [Carlo Bragaglia] • *Scr* Mortimer Braus, from an idea by Allesandro Continenza, from a story by Ottavio Poggi

Hannibal Brooks ★★ U

Second World War comedy drama
1968 · UK · Colour · 101mins

If you were trying to escape from the Germans in the Second World War, surely the last thing you'd want is an elephant tagging along to slow things down. Yet that's what happens here, as PoW Oliver Reed tries to cross the Alps via pachyderm in Michael Winner's tepid stab at war comedy. Michael J Pollard and John Alderton join the antics, but the tale's extremely hard to swallow.

Oliver Reed *Hannibal Brooks* • Michael J Pollard *Packy* • Wolfgang Preiss *Colonel Von Haller* • Helmut Lohner *Willi* • Karin Baal *Vronia* • Peter Karsten *Kurt* • John Alderton *Bernard* ■ *Dir* Michael Winner • *Scr* Dick Clement, Ian La Frenais, from a story by Michael Winner, Tom Wright

Hannie Caulder ★★ 15

Western
1971 · UK · Colour · 81mins

It should have been a major feminist work, a mystic western about a raped and widowed frontierswoman taught to shoot by a lone bounty hunter. Trouble is, this is that rare anomaly, the British western, shot in Spain with all the associated problems of realism, not the least of which is the casting of Raquel Welch in the title role. Welch looks fine but she simply can't carry the picture, and she's not helped particularly by Burt Kennedy's casting. The photography is handsome, but the pace is slack, and the violence unpleasant. Connoisseurs of the ridiculous might enjoy Christopher Lee as a friendly gunsmith. Oh, and Diana Dors is in there somewhere – didn't she learn anything from her previous mistakes? 🖾

Raquel Welch *Hannie Caulder* • Robert Culp *Thomas Luther Price* • Ernest Borgnine *Emmett Clemens* • Strother Martin *Rufus Clemens* • Jack Elam *Frank Clemens* • Diana Dors *Madame* ■ *Dir* Burt Kennedy • *Scr* ZX Jones [David Haft Kennedy], from a story by Peter Cooper, from characters created by Ian Quicke, Bob Richards • *Cinematographer* Edward Scaife

Hanoi Hilton ★★ 15

War drama
1987 · US · Colour · 120mins

The Hanoi Hilton was the name given by the American inmates of Hoa Lo Prison in Hanoi, North Vietnam, during the war. Set far from the paddy fields and rivers of the usual Vietnam war movie, this drama covers ten years and many mini-dramas as PoWs arrive and discuss their experiences. Written directly for the screen, it has the setting and the talkiness of a play, but this is no literal piece. This is the politics of *Rambo* and is, doubtless, a real reflection of what many American prisoners felt. Stunted, uninvolving drama 🖾

Michael Moriarty *Williamson* • John Edwin Shaw *Mason* • Ken Wright *Kennedy* • Paul LeMat *Hubman* • David Soul *Oldham* • Stephen Davies *Miles* • Lawrence Pressman *Cathcart* ■ *Dir/Scr* Lionel Chetwynd

Hanover Street ★★ PG

Romantic Second World War drama
1979 · UK/US · Colour · 104mins

It's odd to find Peter Hyams directing this glossy Second World War weepie,

as he is more usually associated with sci-fi action adventures such as *2010* and *Timecop*. He's certainly more at home with battle sequences than romantic clinches, as is his star, Harrison Ford, who often looks distinctly uncomfortable as an American pilot whose air-raid encounter with nurse Lesley-Anne Down leads to trouble with her husband, Christopher Plummer. Apart from some lovely photography, it was all done much better in the 1940 Vivien Leigh/Robert Taylor vehicle, *Waterloo Bridge*. Contains swearing and nudity. 🖾

Harrison Ford *David Halloran* • Lesley-Anne Down *Margaret Sellinger* • Christopher Plummer *Paul Sellinger* • Alec McCowen *Major Trumbo* • Richard Masur *Lieutenant Jerry Cimino* • Michael Sacks *Lieutenant Martin Hyer* • Patsy Kensit *Sarah Sellinger* • Max Wall *Harry Pike* • Shane Rimmer *Colonel Ronald Bart* • Keith Buckley *Lieutenant Wells* • Sherrie Hewson *Phyllis* • John Ratzenberger *Sergeant John Lucas* ■ *Dir/Scr* Peter Hyams • *Cinematographer* David Watkin

Hans Christian Andersen ★★★★ U

Musical drama 1952 · US · Colour · 107mins

Children should enjoy this sentimental Hollywood fabrication of the life of the great storyteller, and sophisticated adults will appreciate the superb Frank Loesser songs, notably the charming *Inch-worm*, the unforgettable *Ugly Duckling* and the rollicking *Wonderful Wonderful Copenhagen*. They're all performed by star Danny Kaye, unusually subdued in possibly his best screen performance, a role that became identified with him. A big hit in its day, it's worthwhile recalling the stream of Scandinavian anti-Semitism that erupted back in the fifties over a Jew (Kaye) playing Denmark's treasured raconteur. 🖾

Danny Kaye *Hans Christian Andersen* • Farley Granger *Niels* • Jeanmaire [Zizi Jeanmaire] *Doro* • Joey Walsh [Joseph Walsh] *Peter* • Philip Tonge *Otto* • Erik Bruhn *The Hussar* • Roland Petit *The Prince* • John Brown *Schoolmaster* • John Qualen *Burgomaster* ■ *Dir* Charles Vidor • *Scr* Moss Hart, from a story by Myles Connolly

Hanussen ★★★★ 15

Drama 1988 · Hun/W Ger · Colour · 111mins

A searing indictment of misguided ambition, political corruption and the malleability of the masses, this film is the last and marginally least effective of the "stranger in his homeland" trilogy directed by István Szabó and starring Klaus Maria Brandauer. Here, the character vaunted and then victimised by a frightened regime is a war-wounded clairvoyant, whose fame is tarnished when he predicts the formation of the Third Reich. The period detail is flawless, the ensemble playing impeccable and Brandauer's performance mesmerising, but it lacks the subtle imagery and insight of its predecessors. In German with English subtitles. Contains violence, swearing and nudity. 🖾

Klaus Maria Brandauer *Klaus Schneider/"Erik-Jan Hanussen"* • Erland Josephson *Dr Bettelheim* • Ildiko Bansagi *Sister Betty* • Walter Schmidinger *Propaganda minister* • Karoly Eperjes *Captain Tibor Nowotny* •

Grazyna Szapolowska *Valery de la Meer* • Colette Pilz-Warren *Dagma* ■ *Dir* István Szabó • *Scr* István Szabó, Peter Dobai

The Happening ★★

Comedy 1967 · US · Colour · 91mins

Very much of its hippy period, it is indicative of the quality of this film that the title song by the Supremes has survived longer in popular culture than the movie it originates from. Anthony Quinn is his usual gruff self as a kidnapped gangster, and the period cast of George Maharis, Michael Parks and Robert Walker Jr is pleasantly supported by a young Faye Dunaway in her screen debut. It's forgettable stuff, really, except for a startling and unpleasant change of tone at the end. This is a comedy? Contains violence, swearing and nudity.

Anthony Quinn *Roc Delmonico* • George Maharis *Taurus* • Michael Parks *Sureshot* • Robert Walker Jr *Herby* • Martha Hyer *Monica Delmonico* • Faye Dunaway *Sandy* • Milton Berle *Fred* • Oscar Homolka *Sam* ■ *Dir* Elliot Silverstein • *Scr* Frank R Pierson, James D Buchanan, Ronald Austin, from a story by James D Buchanan, Ronald Austin

The Happiest Days of Your Life ★★★★ U

Comedy 1950 · UK · BW · 78mins

You can almost smell the school dinners in this wonderful comedy, adapted by John Dighton and Frank Launder from Dighton's play and directed by Launder (for once without longtime partner Sidney Gilliat). The bones of contention that arise when Margaret Rutherford's academy for young ladies is accidentally evacuated to a building already occupied by Alastair Sim's boys' school are beautifully observed, but the comic highlight is the precision with which the pupils scurry around the school to avoid groups of visiting VIPs. 🖾

Alastair Sim *Wetherby Pond* • Margaret Rutherford *Miss Whitchurch* • Joyce Grenfell *Miss Gossage* • Richard Wattis *Arnold Billings* • John Bentley *Richard Tassell* • Bernadette O'Farrell *Miss Harper* • Guy Middleton *Victor Hyde-Brown* • Edward Rigby *Rainbow* ■ *Dir* Frank Launder • *Scr* Frank Launder, John Dighton, from the play by John Dighton

The Happiest Millionaire ★★★ U

Musical 1967 · US · Colour · 158mins

This film has its place in history as the last one personally produced by Walt Disney. Yet why he felt this polished but hardly glittering picture should last over two and a half hours is anyone's guess, as it's far too long for most youngsters to take at a single sitting. The songs by the Sherman brothers aren't a patch on the ones that won them Oscars in *Mary Poppins*, while the Romeo and Juliet story never catches light, in spite of the presence of Fred MacMurray, Greer Garson, Geraldine Page and Tommy Steele, making his Hollywood debut as a Buttons-like matchmaker.

Fred MacMurray *Anthony J Drexel Biddle* • Tommy Steele *John Lawless* • Greer Garson *Mrs Cordelia Biddle* • Geraldine Page *Mrs Duke* • Gladys Cooper *Aunt Mary Drexel* • Hermione Baddeley *Mrs Worth* • Lesley Ann Warren *Cordy Biddle* • John Davidson *Angie*

U = SUITABLE FOR ALL   **Uc** = SUITABLE FOR ALL, ESPECIALLY FOR YOUNG CHILDREN (VIDEO ONLY)   **PG** = PARENTAL GUIDANCE

Duke • Paul Peterson *Tony Biddle* • Eddie Hodges *Livingston Biddle* ■ *Dir* Norman Tokar • *Scr* AJ Carothers, from the play by Kyle Crichton, from the book *My Philadelphia Father* by Kyle Crichton, Cordelia Drexel Biddle

Happily Ever After ★★ U

Animation 1990 · US · Colour · 71mins

You have to admire Filmation's cheek. At the same time they made this unofficial sequel to *Snow White and the Seven Dwarfs*, they were producing another Disney follow-up, *Pinocchio and the Emperor of the Night*. While the animation is competent, what lets down this stubbornly unmagical fairy tale is the laboured plot, in which Snow White is aided by the seven dwarfs' cousins after her prince is snatched away by the wicked queen's vengeful brother Lord Maliss. The one bright spot, however, are the voice-overs, with Malcolm McDowell sneerily villainous as Maliss, Irene Cara tunefully vulnerable as Snow White and Tracey Ullman delightfully winsome as Moonbeam. [video]

Dom DeLuise *Looking Glass* • Phyllis Diller *Mother Nature* • Zsa Zsa Gabor *Blossom* • Edward Asner [Ed Asner] *Scowl* • Sally Kellerman *Sunburn* • Irene Cara *Snow White* • Carol Channing *Muddy* • Tracey Ullman *Moonbeam/Thunderella* • Michael Horton *Prince* • Malcolm McDowell *Lord Maliss* ■ *Dir* John Howley • *Scr* Martha Moran, Robby London

Happiness ★★★★★ 18

Black comedy drama
1998 · US · Colour · 139mins

Todd Solondz's stunningly acted and scripted film contains an extraordinary tapestry of unusual men and women, who share two things in common: they feel lonely, isolated and crave love, and secondly they engage in shocking behaviour, including obscene phone calls, murder and paedophilia. What's so amazing about this tragi-comedy is the lack of a moral judgement, the pungent humour that emerges under the sickest of circumstances and the way we get drawn into and feel pity for these people's lives. The film's most controversial scene (the frankest of discussions between an unlikely child molester and his inquisitive son) will play on your mind for days. An uncomfortable movie experience. Contains sex scenes, strong sexual references and swearing.

Jane Adams *Joy Jordan* • Jon Lovitz *Andy Kornbluth* • Philip Seymour Hoffman *Allen* • Dylan Baker *Bill Maplewood* • Lara Flynn Boyle *Helen Jordan* • Louise Lasser *Mona Jordan* • Ben Gazzara *Lenny Jordan* • Jared Harris *Vlad* • Marla Maples *Ann Chambeau* • Elizabeth Ashley *Diane Freed* ■ *Dir/Scr* Todd Solondz

The Happiness Cage ★★

Drama 1972 · US · Colour · 92mins

In this slow-moving drama, army scientists use controversial shock therapy on overly aggressive soldiers who find it difficult to conform to army life. Ronny Cox and a pre-stardom Christopher Walken play two victims who respond to the pleasure-centre brain treatment in differing ways. Despite powerful moments, the movie never fully conquers its stage play origins, although it does manage to put across the trauma inherent in the experimental euphoria.

Christopher Walken *Private James Reese* • Joss Ackland *Dr Frederick* • Ralph Meeker *Major* • Ronny Cox *Miles* • Marco St John *Orderly* ■ *Dir* Bernard Girard • *Scr* Ron Whyte, from the play by Dennis Reardon

Happy ★★ U

Comedy musical 1933 · US · BW · 83mins

Rarely seen comic musical about boffin and hard-up musician Stanley Lupino and his attempts to find a market for his new invention. The star – whose daughter Ida would go on to Hollywood fame in later years – had a hand in the script as well so it's pretty much his show, and he delivers the goods with some lively playing from co-stars Laddie Cliff and Will Fyffe.

Stanley Lupino *Frank Brown* • Laddie Cliff *George* • Will Fyffe *Simmy* • Dorothy Hyson *Lillian* • Harry Tate *Dupont* • Renee Gadd *Pauline* • Gus McNaughton *Waller* ■ *Dir* Fred Zelnik • *Scr* Austin Melford, Arthur Woods, Frank Launder, Stanley Lupino, from the play *Es War Einmal ein Musikus* by Karl Notl, Jacques Bachrach, Alfred Hahm

Happy Anniversary ★★

Comedy 1959 · US · BW · 82mins

This David Niven comedy is, despite the title, little cause for celebration. Made in the days when television was a burgeoning rival to the cinema's ability to pull in mass audiences, this tale has Niven and Mitzi Gaynor as a happily married couple whose daughter (Patty Duke) reveals her father's past life on a children's TV show. Topical jokes for the time, but not now in these days of multi-media revolution.

David Niven *Chris Walters* • Mitzi Gaynor *Alice Walters* • Carl Reiner *Bud* • Loring Smith *Mr Gans* • Monique Van Vooren *Jeanette* • Phyllis Povah *Mrs Gans* • Patty Duke *Debbie Walters* ■ *Dir* David Miller • *Scr* Joseph Fields, Jerome Chodorov, from the play *Anniversary Waltz* by Jerome Chodorov

Happy Birthday, Gemini ★★

Comedy drama 1980 · US · Colour · 107mins

Director Richard Benner scored a notable hit in 1977 with the Canadian gay/drag movie *Outrageous*, which spawned an equally successful sequel *Too Outrageous* ten years later. In between Benner delivered this adaptation of Albert Innaurato's hit Broadway comedy about a man coming to terms with his sexuality. The stage play had drawn accusations of homophobia for some of its more extreme moments but the film avoided all such problems. The late Madeline Kahn does some of her best work here but she is somewhat swamped by the overall dullness of the piece.

Madeline Kahn *Bunny Weinberger* • Rita Moreno *Lucille Pompi* • Robert Viharo *Nick Geminiani* • Alan Rosenberg *Francis Geminiani* • Sarah Holcomb *Judith Hastings* • David Marshall Grant *Randy Hastings* ■ *Dir* Richard Benner • *Scr* Richard Benner, from the play *Gemini* by Albert Innaurato

Happy Birthday, Wanda June ★★★

Comedy 1971 · US · Colour · 105mins

When big-game hunter Rod Steiger returns from eight years in the Amazonian wilds, he finds his bimbo wife Susannah York educated, liberated and about to marry again – to either a pacifist doctor (George Grizzard) or a vacuum cleaner salesman (Don Murray). Kurt Vonnegut Jr's screenplay, based on his off-Broadway play about the modern world's need for heroes, is stuck in a theatrical mire, and there's nothing director Mark Robson can do to get it out. The result is a clash of symbols, in which style and content collide.

Rod Steiger *Harold Ryan* • Susannah York *Penelope Ryan* • George Grizzard *Dr Norbert Woodley* • Don Murray *Herb Shuttle* • William Hickey *Looseleaf Harper* • Steven Paul *Paul Ryan* • Pamelyn Ferdin *Wanda June* • Pamela Saunders *Mildred Ryan* ■ *Dir* Mark Robson • *Scr* Kurt Vonnegut Jr, from his play

The Happy Ending ★★

Melodrama 1969 · US · Colour · 111mins

An old-style women's melodrama – one of the last of the breed – made by tough-guy director Richard Brooks and starring his real-life wife, Jean Simmons, whose fine performance earned her Oscar and Golden Globe nominations. Bored with her husband of 16 years, Simmons drinks, watches movies on TV, then suddenly ups for the Bahamas and has a fling with a gigolo. This is a film that strains for significance rather than wallows in its contrivance: "they're more alive then we are," Simmons tells husband John Forsythe after watching Bogart and Bergman in a re-run of *Casablanca*.

Jean Simmons *Mary Wilson* • John Forsythe *Fred Wilson* • Shirley Jones *Flo* • Lloyd Bridges *Sam* • Teresa Wright *Mrs Spencer* • Dick Shawn *Harry Bricker* • Nanette Fabray *Agnes* • Robert Darin *Franco* • Tina Louise *Helen Bricker* ■ *Dir/Scr* Richard Brooks

Happy Ever After ★★ U

Comedy 1954 · UK · Colour · 84mins

David Niven got so little practice at playing cads that you can almost forgive him for being so bad here, as the gruff English landlord whose new regime drives his tenants to the point of murder. It's whimsy all the way in this amiable but underachieving film, which cries out for black comedy as the locals draw lots to see who will do the dirty deed. Unfortunately, none of the methods chosen to get rid of the squire demonstrate any imagination, and would-be assassins George Cole, Joseph Tomelty and Michael Shepley are forced to mug like crazy to raise a laugh. [video]

David Niven *Jasper O'Leary* • Yvonne De Carlo *Serena McGlusky* • Barry Fitzgerald *Thady O'Heggarty* • George Cole *Terence* • AE Matthews *General O'Leary* • Noelle Middleton *Kathy McGlusky* • Robert Urquhart *Dr Michael Flynn* • Michael Shepley *Major McGlusky* • Joseph Tomelty *Dooley* • Eddie Byrne *Lannigan* ■ *Dir* Mario Zampi • *Scr* Jack Davies, Michael Pertwee, LAG Strong

The Happy Family ★★★ U

Comedy 1952 · UK · BW · 88mins

One of those "they don't make 'em like this anymore" comic capers in which Stanley Holloway and Kathleen Harrison star as a shop-keeping couple refusing to move from their humble dwelling to accommodate the 1951 Festival of Britain. This is an innocent, gentle lark, harking back to an infinitely preferable if somewhat mythically rosy era when officialdom was bumptious but owlishly benign, and the "great unwashed" behaved like a troupe of good-hearted medieval tumblers. Watch out for a youthful George Cole.

Stanley Holloway *Henry Lord* • Kathleen Harrison *Lillian Lord* • Naunton Wayne *Mr Filch* • Dandy Nichols *Ada* • John Stratton *David* • Eileen Moore *Joan* • Shirley Mitchell *Marina* • Margaret Barton *Anne* • George Cole *Cyril* ■ *Dir* Muriel Box • *Scr* Muriel Box, Sydney Box, from the play by Michael Clayton Hutton

Happy Gilmore ★★ 12

Sports comedy 1996 · US · Colour · 88mins

Adam Sandler – now famed for such hits as *The Wedding Singer* and *The Waterboy* – has come on a bit since he made this knockabout sports comedy. The former *Saturday Night Live* regular was clearly hoping to follow in the footsteps of Mike Myers and Dan Aykroyd by taking the title role in this slapstick vehicle, about a second-rate ice hockey player whose thuggish tactics are the only thing keeping him on the team. When his slapshot is noticed by Carl Weathers and turned into a golfer's drive, Gilmore sees a way of earning enough cash on the fairway to save his old granny's home from the depredations of the IRS. It's no-brainer fare, but it does raise the odd chortle. Contains some mild swearing. [video] DVD

Adam Sandler *Happy Gilmore* • Christopher McDonald *Shooter* • Julie Bowen *Virginia* • Frances Bay *Grandma* • Carl Weathers *Chubbs* • Alan Covert [Allen Covert] *Otto* • Robert Smigel *IRS agent* • Bob Barker • Richard Kiel *Mr Larson* • Dennis Dugan *Doug Thompson* • Lee Trevino ■ *Dir* Dennis Dugan • *Scr* Tim Herlihy, Adam Sandler

Happy Go Lovely ★★ U

Musical 1950 · UK · Colour · 93mins

This lacklustre musical was shot in Britain with Hollywood journeyman Bruce Humberstone directing. Cesar Romero and Vera-Ellen were also imported to sugar the pill for American audiences, and they give polished performances as the down-at-heel producer and his protégée, although David Niven is less at home as the moody millionaire conned into financing their Edinburgh Festival show. TV stalwarts Gordon Jackson and John Laurie also appear. [video]

David Niven *BG Bruno* • Vera-Ellen *Janet Jones* • Cesar Romero *John Frost* • Bobby Howes *Charlie* • Diane Hart *Mae* • Gordon Jackson *Paul Tracey* • John Laurie *Jonskill* ■ *Dir* Bruce Humberstone [H Bruce Humberstone] • *Scr* Val Guest, Arthur Macrae, from a story by F Dammann, H Rosenfeld

Happy Go Lucky ★★ U

Musical romantic comedy
1943 · US · Colour · 81mins

New Yorker Mary Martin uses her savings for a trip to the Caribbean in search of a rich husband. She finds a suitable candidate in an eccentric millionaire (former crooner Rudy Vallee), but loses her heart to beachcomber Dick Powell. Martin and Powell are the nominal stars of this slimline escapist musical, but it's "incendiary blonde" Betty Hutton, also chasing a man (Eddie Bracken) in what passes for plot, who walks away with it. Her raucous rendition of *Murder He Says* will delight Hutton's followers; others might be less entranced. Curtis Bernhardt, taking time out from melodrama, directs.

Mary Martin *Marjory Stuart* • Dick Powell *Pete Hamilton* • Betty Hutton *Bubbles Hennessy* • Eddie Bracken *Wally Case* • Rudy Vallee *Alfred Monroe* • Mabel Paige *Mrs Smith* ■ *Dir* Curtis Bernhardt • *Scr* Walter DeLeon, Norman Panama, Melvin Frank, from a story by John Jacoby, Michael Uris • *Music/Lyrics* Frank Loesser, Jimmy McHugh, Henry J Sayers

The Happy Hooker ★★ 18

Comedy 1975 · US · Colour · 93mins

Liberally sprinkled with sex, satire and no little savvy, Xaviera Hollander's memoirs made her the toast of New York. However, this screen adaptation has reduced her bestselling insights to a series of cheap conquests in a battle of the sexes that is so one-sided the victors can hardly have cause for celebration. Playing the Big Apple's most famous madam as a sensible woman who is both protective of her girls and sympathetic towards her clients, Lynn Redgrave does a splendid job. But, Jean-Pierre Aumont aside, she gets little help from the rest of the cast. Contains swearing and nudity. ▣

Lynn Redgrave *Xaviera Hollander* • Jean-Pierre Aumont *Yves St Jacques* • Lovelady Powell *Madeleine* • Nicholas Pryor *Carl Gordon* • Elizabeth Wilson *Mrs Gordon* • Tom Poston *J Arthur Conrad* • Conrad Janis *Fred* • Richard Lynch *Cop* ■ *Dir* Nicholas Sgarro • *Scr* William Richert, from the book by Xaviera Hollander, Robin Moore, Yvonne Dunleavy

The Happy Hooker Goes to Washington ★★ 18

Comedy 1977 · US · Colour · 84mins

The original *Happy Hooker* was a pretty tame affair, and this too suffers from a surprising prudishness. Joey Heatherton steps into Lynn Redgrave's high heels and sexy outfits as the now-famous madam, who gets involved in national politics when she is called to Capitol Hill. There's a solid supporting cast, but laughs are few and far between. ▣

Joey Heatherton *Xaviera Hollander* • George Hamilton *Ward Thompson* • Ray Walston *Senator Sturges* • Jack Carter *Senator Caruso* ■ *Dir* William A Levey • *Scr* Robert Kaufman

The Happy Hooker Goes to Hollywood ★

Comedy 1980 · US · Colour · 85mins

Probably the raciest in the series (although that's not saying much) – but definitely the most hopeless – this boasts a new Xaviera Hollander in Martine Beswick, who this time decides to put her talents to use helping a film company facing extinction. The likes of Adam West and Phil Silvers should have known better, and it's neither steamy nor funny.

Martine Beswick *Xaviera Hollander* • Adam West • Phil Silvers • Richard Deacon • Edie Adams ■ *Dir* Alan Roberts • *Scr* Devi Goldenberg

Happy Hour ★ PG

Comedy 1987 · US · Colour · 83mins

ver wonder what happened to Jamie Farr after *M*A*S*H*? He ended up in this execrable comedy about a secret ingredient that makes beer drinkers up their consumption. The result is chaos as beer sales jump and beer is foisted on the young ("Mom, can I have some more in my cereal?") Scientists finally decide that the formula must be destroyed, which would have been good advice for this movie as well. ▣

Richard Gilliland *Blake Teegarden* • Jamie Farr *Crummy Fred* • Tawny Kitaen *Misty Roberts* • Ty Henderson *Bill* • Rich Little *Mr X* ■ *Dir* John De Bello • *Scr* John De Bello, Constantine Dillon, J Stephen Peace

Happy Is the Bride ★★★ U

Comedy 1958 · UK · BW · 84mins

Adapted from Esther McCracken's play, *Quiet Wedding* is one of the most fondly remembered British comedies of the Second World War. Directed by co-scriptwriter Roy Boulting, this remake hasn't the polish of Anthony Asquith's version, but what it lacks in style it almost makes up for in verve, as such practised *farceurs* as Cecil Parker, Terry-Thomas and Joyce Grenfell do their level best to complicate the arrangements for Ian Carmichael and Janette Scott's nuptials. Yet the plaudits must go to Athene Seyler, who steals the show in the same role she played in the original.

Ian Carmichael *David Chaytor* • Janette Scott *Janet Royd* • Cecil Parker *Arthur Royd* • Terry-Thomas *Policeman* • Joyce Grenfell *Aunt Florence* • Eric Barker *Vicar* • Edith Sharpe *Mildred Royd* • Elvi Hale *Petula* • John Le Mesurier *Chaytor* • Nicholas Parsons *John Royd* • Athene Seyler *Aunt Harriet* ■ *Dir* Roy Boulting • *Scr* Roy Boulting, Jeffrey Dell, from the play *Quiet Wedding* by Esther McCracken

Happy Land ★★ U

Drama 1943 · US · BW · 75mins

Don Ameche stars as an Iowa shopkeeper who loses his son in the Second World War and is consoled by the ghost of his own father, a veteran of the First World War. Intended to convince the bereaved that their loved ones have not died in vain, it's a fairly creepy and decidedly sudsy experience as Ameche is shown what a good life both he and his son have had. The film was shot in Santa Rosa, California, and used many residents as extras. These included the five-year-old Natalie Wood, who was immediately offered a contract by the director, Irving Pichel.

Don Ameche *Lew Marsh* • Frances Dee *Agnes* • Harry Carey *Gramp* • Ann Rutherford *Lenore Prentiss* • Cara Williams *Gretchen Barry* • Richard Crane *Rusty* • Henry Morgan [Harry Morgan] *Tony Cavrek* ■ *Dir* Irving Pichel • *Scr* Kathryn Scola, Julien Josephson, from the novel by MacKinlay Kantor

Happy Landing ★★★ U

Comedy musical 1938 · US · BW · 101mins

Norwegian Olympic Champion ice skater Sonja Henie was a petite blonde who rapidly became one of Hollywood's highest-ranking movie stars after her first two films struck gold for 20th Century-Fox. Here, the winsome Henie enjoys the company of two men and a nothing plot about a

bandleader's plane landing near Henie's house in a very Hollywood Norway, hence the title. But plots don't matter when Sonja skates, Ethel Merman sings and the two guys are amiable Don Ameche and handsome Cesar Romero. The film's easy to watch, undemanding entertainment, but Sonja connoisseurs avow that the score's not so hot as in other Henie vehicles. ▣

Sonja Henie *Trudy Erickson* • Don Ameche *Jimmy Hall* • Jean Hersholt *Herr Erickson* • Ethel Merman *Flo Kelly* • Cesar Romero *Duke Sargent* • Billy Gilbert *Counter man* • Wally Vernon *Al Mahoney* ■ *Dir* Roy Del Ruth • *Scr* Milton Sperling, Boris Ingster

Happy Mother's Day... Love, George ★★★

Mystery thriller 1973 · US · Colour · 90mins

Actor Darren McGavin's directorial debut was the last movie lounge singer Bobby Darin made before his untimely death. Darin is part of a solid cast in a very strange horror soap opera about Ron Howard returning to his boyhood Nova Scotia home to discover the identity of his father. His investigations uncover a twisted family tree and some gruesome murders as he traces his roots in the tranquil community. Striking visuals combine with the offbeat story to unusual effect and create an unusual genre item.

Patricia Neal *Cara* • Cloris Leachman *Ronda* • Bobby Darin *Eddie* • Tessa Dahl *Celia* • Ron Howard *Johnny* • Kathie Browne *Crystal* • Joseph Mascolo *Piccolo* • Simon Oakland *Ron Howard* ■ *Dir* Darren McGavin • *Scr* Robert Clouse • *Cinematographer* Walter Lassally

Happy New Year ★★

Crime caper 1974 · Fr/It · Colour · 114mins

Claude Lelouch would be a much better film-maker were he not such a fan of his own work. This tired treatise on the attraction of opposites is so self-satisfied that it even begins with a clip from *Une Homme et une Femme*, the identically themed opus that forged the director's international reputation. This glossy but empty picture focuses on the unlikely romance between rugged jewel thief Lino Ventura and Riviera sophisticate Françoise Fabian. The opening heist has its moments, but the rest is bogus bohemianism in the glutinous strains of Francis Lai's score. In French with English subtitles.

Lino Ventura *Simon* • Françoise Fabian *Françoise* • Charles Gérard *Charles* • Silvano Tranquilli *Italian lover* ■ *Dir* Claude Lelouch • *Scr* Claude Lelouch, Pierre Uytterhoeven

Happy New Year ★★★ 15

Comedy 1987 · US · Colour · 84mins

This engaging cross between a comedy, love story, heist picture and buddy movie is an undeservedly neglected American remake of Claude Lelouch's 1974 film. It boasts winning performances by Charles Durning and Peter Falk as two old partners in crime, planning the robbery of a Palm Beach jewellery store. Lelouch himself makes a brief early appearance, but the movie ultimately belongs to Falk, who dons a series of brilliant disguises, including one as an old woman – based on his own mum – that sees him turn in one of

Hollywood's finest drag acts since Dustin Hoffman's in *Tootsie*. ▣

Peter Falk *Nick* • Charles Durning *Charlie* • Wendy Hughes *Carolyn Benedict* • Tom Courtenay *Edward Sanders* • Tracy Brooks Swope *Nina* • Joan Copeland *Sunny* • Daniel Gerroll *Curator* • Bruce Malmuth *Police lieutenant* ■ *Dir* John G Avildsen • *Scr* Warren Lane [Nancy Dowd], from the 1974 film

The Happy Road ★★ U

Comedy drama 1956 · US · BW · 99mins

Gene Kelly's second movie of the seven he directed solo was filmed on location in France. In it, he stars as an American widower who is drawn to a French divorcée when their kids run away from their Swiss school and head for Paris. The children – particularly Brigitte Fossey in her second film after *Forbidden Games* – are not without charm, but the situations are predictable, and the view of the French is a bit too patronising.

Gene Kelly *Mike Andrews* • Barbara Laage *Suzanne Duval* • Michael Redgrave *General Medworth* • Bobby Clark *Danny Andrews* • Brigitte Fossey *Janine Duval* • Roger Treville *Dr Solaise* ■ *Dir* Gene Kelly • *Scr* Arthur Julian, Joseph Morhaim, Harry Kurnitz, from a story by Arthur Julian, Harry Kurnitz

Happy, Texas ★★★★ 12

Comedy 1999 · US · Colour · 91mins

Besides letting us know that Jeremy Northam (*An Ideal Husband*, *The Winslow Boy*) can unfreeze that stiff upper lip of his, this comedy of errors is a quiet and unexpected revelation. Escaped American convicts Harry Sawyer (Northam) and Wayne Wayne Wayne Jr (Steve Zahn) flee an overturned prison van and wind up in the Texan town of Happy, where they are mistaken for two gay carnival organisers who've been hired to help with a beauty contest for five-year-olds. The local (male) sheriff takes a shine to Sawyer, while Wayne falls for schoolteacher Illeana Douglas ("that whole gay thing is more of a hobby, really"). Director/co-writer Mark Illsley has made a small comic gem. ▣

Jeremy Northam *Harry Sawyer* • Steve Zahn *Wayne Wayne Wayne Jr* • Ally Walker *Josephine "Joe" McLintock* • Illeana Douglas *Ms Schaefer* • William H Macy *Sheriff Chappy Dent* • MC Gainey *Bob Maslow* • Ron Perlman *Nalhober* ■ *Dir* Mark Illsley • *Scr* Ed Stone, Mark Illsley, Phil Reeves

The Happy Thieves ★

Comedy crime drama 1962 · US · BW · 89mins

Richard Condon's first novel *The Oldest Confession* was an entertaining yarn which provided the basis for this unentertaining yawn. The cause lay in the fatigued direction by George Marshall and the full-of-holes script. Nor are matters helped by the uneasy pairing of Rex Harrison and Rita Hayworth as two art thieves attempting to steal a Goya from the Prado in Madrid. Needless to say, the robbery, like the film, fails to come off.

Rex Harrison *Jim Bourne* • Rita Hayworth *Eve Lewis* • Joseph Wiseman *Jean Marie Calbert* • Grégoire Aslan *Dr Munoz* • Alida Valli *Duchess Blanca* • Brita Ekman [Britt Ekland] *Mrs Pickett* ■ *Dir* George Marshall • *Scr* John Gay, from the novel *The Oldest Confession* by Richard Condon

U = SUITABLE FOR ALL Uc = SUITABLE FOR ALL, ESPECIALLY FOR YOUNG CHILDREN (VIDEO ONLY) PG = PARENTAL GUIDANCE

Happy Together ★★★ 15
Romantic comedy   1989 · US · Colour · 98mins

A sweet but slight comedy about a shy young writer (Patrick Dempsey) and a brash, aspiring actress (Helen Slater) who, owing to a mix-up, end up as roommates in an all-male college dormitory. Both leads are fine, but they don't have much to work with in what is effectively an entertaining if made-by-numbers comedy romance. Look for Brad Pitt in an early role. Contains swearing, sexual references and brief nudity. ▭

Patrick Dempsey *Christopher Wooden* • Helen Slater *Alexandra "Alex" Page* • Dan Schneider *Gooseflesh* • Kevin Hardesty *Slash* • Marius Weyers *Denny Dollenbacher* • Barbara Babcock *Ruth Carpenter* • Gloria Hayes *Luisa Dellacova* • Brad Pitt *Brian* • Aaron Harnick *Wally* • Ron Sterling *Trevor* ■ *Dir* Mel Damski • *Scr* Craig J Nevius

Happy Together ★★★ 15
Romantic drama   1997 · HK · Colour and BW · 92mins

Director Wong Kar-Wai's reputation rests on his genius for combining audacious imagery with human stories, but this adaptation of Manuel Puig's novel *The Buenos Aires Affair* is his least coherent or convincing film. The relationship between Leslie Cheung and Tony Leung, Hong Kong lovers on holiday in Argentina, is so destructive it's hard to empathise with either character when their conversations are so accusatory and their actions so self-interested. Christopher Doyle's photography is sumptuous, but Wong's direction is over-indulgent. The switches from monochrome to colour are neatly judged but too much is sacrificed to his stylistic preoccupations. In Spanish, Cantonese and Mandarin with English subtitles. Contains swearing, sex scenes and some violence. ▭

Leslie Kwok-Wing Cheung [Leslie Cheung] *Ho Po-Wing* • Tony Chiu-Wai Leung [Tony Leung (1)] *Lai Yiu-Fai* • Chang Chen *Chang* ■ *Dir* Wong Kar-Wai • *Scr* Wong Kar-Wai, from the novel *The Buenos Aires Affair* by Manuel Puig

Happy We ★★★
Drama   1983 · Swe · Colour · 111mins

Before he came to international attention in 1985, Swedish director Lasse Hallström was best known for his rockumentary *ABBA the Movie*. This comedy drama about the reunion of three university pals closely preceded his breakthrough hit *My Life as a Dog*. As they recall old times, re-enact the sketches they had performed in college revues and catch up on the disappointments and broken dreams of adulthood, you will inevitably be reminded of *The Big Chill* and *Peter's Friends*. Coaxing pleasing performances from his cast, Hallstrom treads the fine line between pertinence and sentiment with some skill. In Swedish with English subtitles.

Brasse Brannstrom *Thomas Bengtsson* • Ivan Oljelund *Erik Bengtsson* • Magnus Harenstam *Klasse Wallin* • Pia Green *Anna Wallin* • Lars Amble *Fredrik Wahlgren* ■ *Dir* Lasse Hallström • *Scr* Brasse Brannstrom, Lasse Hallström, Magnus Harenstam

Hara-Kiri ★★★
Silent drama   1928 · Fr · BW · 87mins

Although the history books tend to concentrate on the experiments of the impressionist and surrealist avant-garde, French commercial cinema in the late silent era was also capable of producing pictures of stunning visual beauty. This Oriental melodrama from director/star Marie-Louise Iribe is a case in point. However, the story of the wife who leaves her academic husband for a shogun's son was also rather daring, especially as she elects to die by her own hand to rejoin him in the afterlife, after he is killed trying to rescue a maiden from a ravine.

Marie-Louise Iribe *Nicole Daomi* • Constant Rémy *Professor Daomi Samura* • AndréBerley *Police inspector* • Liao Szi-Jen *Prince Fujiwara* • Labusquière *Ambassador* • Michaud *Guide* • Wuriu *Fujiwara's brother* • Toshi Komori *Marquis Awaji* ■ *Dir* Marie-Louise Iribe • *Scr* Pierre Lestringuez

Harakiri ★★★★
Drama   1962 · Jap · BW · 134mins

Masaki Kobayashi's extraordinary samurai drama is far darker than anything Akira Kurosawa made, which explains why it is not as immediately accessible. Shot in black-and-white widescreen, this epic explores and challenges the militaristic cult of the samurai who, by 1630, have been reduced to beggars and are disembowelling themselves. Since the film's premiere at Cannes in 1963, a legend grew about its violence on account of a scene where a young samurai commits ritual suicide using a bamboo sword. An unblinking and majestic piece of film-making. A Japanese language film.

Tatsuya Nakadai *Hanshiro Tsugumo* • Shima Iwashita *Miho Tsugumo* • Akira Ishihama *Motome Chijiiwa* • Yoshio Inaba *Jinai Chijiiwa* • Rentaro Mikuni *Kageyu Saito* ■ *Dir* Masaki Kobayashi • *Scr* Shinobu Hashimoto, from the novel by Yasuhiko Takiguchi • *Cinematographer* Yoshio Miyajima

Harbour Beat ★★ 15
Police drama   1990 · Ausl/UK · Colour · 87mins

Long before *Four Weddings* and *Sliding Doors*, John Hannah went Down Under for this variation on the buddy movie that failed to secure a cinematic release and received its premiere on Australian television. As a Glasgow cop with an over-developed sense of adventure, Hannah reveals a rarely seen mean streak as he teams with naive country boy Steven Vidler for a perilous case, in which treachery and deception go hand in hand with danger. Predictable, but directed with brash humour by David Elfick. Contains violence and swearing. ▭

John Hannah *Neal McBride* • Steven Vidler *Lance Cooper* • Gary Day *Gavin Walker* • Emily Simpson *Constable Simpson* • Bill Young *Sergeant Cimino* • Tony Poli *Andrew De Santos* • Angie Milliken *Simone* ■ *Dir* David Elfick • *Scr* Morris Gleitzman

Hard-Boiled ★★★★ 18
Crime action drama   1992 · HK · Colour · 122mins

Although *A Better Tomorrow* and *The Killer* caught the eye of the film buffs, this was the first film that really launched Hong Kong maestro John Woo in the UK. The plot is unashamedly formulaic – mismatched cops Chow Yun-Fat and Tony Leung join forces to track down a ruthless gunrunner. However, the sensuous flair Woo brings to the many stunning action sequences remains vibrantly fresh today, despite the clunking attempts of Hollywood directors to ape them, while the melodramatic playing and plotting brings an odd but touching humanity to the piece. Superb. In Cantonese with English subtitles. ▭

Chow Yun-Fat *Inspector Yuen ("Tequila")* • Tony Chiu-Wai Leung [Tony Leung (1)] *Tony* • Teresa Mo *Teresa* • Philip Chan *Superintendent Pang* • Anthony Wong *Johnny Wong* • Bowie Lam *Yuen's partner* • Kwan Hoi-Shan *Mr Hoi* ■ *Dir* John Woo • *Scr* Barry Wong, from a story by John Woo

Hard Choices ★★★ 18
Crime drama   1984 · US · Colour · 86mins

This strange amalgam of teenage crime and taboo romance is one of those surprising animals – a film that becomes less predictable as it unfolds. Beginning as a straightforward action thriller, it follows the troubles of 15-year-old Bobby (Gary McCleery) after he is caught driving a getaway car for his two brothers in a robbery that ends with the murder of a policeman. Margaret Klenck plays a worker with juvenile offenders who tries to help the boy, while actor–director John Sayles co-stars as a drug-pushing pal who comes to her aid. ▭

Margaret Klenck *Laura Stephens* • Gary McCleery *Bobby Lipscomb* • John Seitz *Sheriff Mavis Johnson* • John Sayles *Don* • John Snyder *Ben* • Martin Donovan *Josh* • JT Walsh *Deputy Anderson* • Spalding Gray *Terry Norfolk* ■ *Dir* Rick King • *Scr* Rick King, from a story by Robert Mickelson, Rick King

Hard Contract ★★
Crime drama   1969 · US · Colour · 105mins

A philosophically soft-centred morality play, with stone-faced James Coburn playing a professional killer at large in Europe, on the trail of three people he has agreed to kill for mysterious client Burgess Meredith. Coburn also has sexual hang-ups about the women (Lilli Palmer, Lee Remick) he encounters. Writer/director S Lee Pogostin takes what could have been a James Bond-style thriller and throttles it with too much chat, despite the fine cast.

James Coburn *John Cunningham* • Lee Remick *Sheila Metcalfe* • Lilli Palmer *Adrianne* • Burgess Meredith *Ramsey Williams* • Patrick Magee *Alexi* • Sterling Hayden *Michael Carlson* • Claude Dauphin *Maurice* • Helen Cherry *Evelyn Carlson* • Karen Black *Ellen* ■ *Dir/Scr* S Lee Pogostin

Hard Country ★★
Romantic drama   1981 · US · Colour · 104mins

The title of this drama could refer to the difficulties in making it in country music or it could refer to the tough life of small-town Texas. In the end, the plot revolves around *Urban Cowboy* type Kyle Richardson (Jan-Michael Vincent), who labours away at a factory by day and shakes his thing down at the saloon by night. His girlfriend Jodie, played by Kim Basinger (in her

movie debut), has to choose between settling down with Kyle or following her friend and role model Caroline (real-life country star Tanya Tucker) to the bright lights of California and a recording career. Predictable, but still watchable.

Jan-Michael Vincent *Kyle Richardson* • Kim Basinger *Jodie Lynn Palmer* • Michael Parks *Royce Richardson* • Gailard Sartain *Johnny Bob* • Tanya Tucker *Caroline Peters* • Daryl Hannah *Loretta Palmer* ■ *Dir* David Greene • *Scr* Michael Kane, from a story by Michael Kane, Michael Martin Murphey

A Hard Day's Night ★★★★★ U
Musical comedy   1964 · UK · BW · 89mins

At a time when Elvis and Cliff were still making old-style musicals, this progenitor of the modern music video smashed the mould. Satirising the endless round of banal inquisition, petty regulation and screaming adoration to which the Fab Four were subjected, this musical odyssey enabled them to mock authority and shirk duty without allowing such anti-establishment rebelliousness to detract from the working-class respectability of their "mop top" image. However, Richard Lester's film is not just a homage to Buster Keaton-style slapstick and Busby Berkeley spectacle; it's also a handbook of new wave film techniques, from Fellini and the *nouvelle vague* to Free Cinema and the Czech Film Miracle. ▭

John Lennon • Paul McCartney • George Harrison • Ringo Starr • Wilfrid Brambell *Grandfather* • Norman Rossington *Norm* • Victor Spinetti *TV director* • John Junkin *Shake* • Deryck Guyler *Police inspector* • Anna Quayle *Millie* • Kenneth Haigh *Simon* • Richard Vernon *Man on train* • Eddie Malin *Hotel waiter* • Robin Ray *TV floor manager* • Lionel Blair *TV choreographer* ■ *Dir* Richard Lester • *Scr* Alun Owen • *Cinematographer* Gilbert Taylor

Hard Drive ★★ 18
Erotic thriller   1994 · US · Colour · 88mins

Despite some nods towards current concerns with the internet, this is essentially another sleazy, soulless erotic thriller. Leo Damian plays a grown-up child star who now hides away from the public eye and spends his time surfing the net. He manages to find the perfect woman, but their fantasies soon get out of control and he finds himself up to his neck in murder and blackmail. Old troupers Edward Albert Jr and Stella Stevens are on hand to bring a little class to the affair, and a little bit more thought than normal has gone into the script. Ultimately, though, this is a formulaic erotic thriller. ▭

Leo Damian *Will Donovan* • Christina Fulton *Delilah/Dana* • Edward Albert *Chief of Examiners* • Matt McCoy *Jack* • Belinda Waymouth *Laura* • Stella Stevens *Susan* ■ *Dir* James Merendino • *Scr* James Merendino, from a story by Leo Damian

Hard Eight ★★★ 18
Drama   1996 · US · Colour · 97mins

The feature debut from Paul Thomas Anderson, director of *Boogie Nights*, is a minimally plotted mood piece featuring a magnetic central performance from Philip Baker Hall. He

plays the sweetly bumbling elderly professional gambler who takes dim-witted John C Reilly under his wing to teach him some of the tricks of the Las Vegas casino trade. All's well until Reilly falls for hooker Gwyneth Paltrow and she takes a client hostage. Despite the somewhat lethargic pace, this is a cool, sharply observed thriller that knows its own strengths and makes the most of them. ▭

Philip Baker Hall *Sydney* • John C Reilly *John* • Gwyneth Paltrow *Clementine* • Samuel L Jackson *Jimmy* • F William Parker *Hostage* • Philip Seymour Hoffman *Young craps player* ■ *Dir/Scr* Paul Thomas Anderson

Hard Evidence ★★

Action thriller 1994 · US · Colour · 100mins

An average thriller, with a reasonably gripping storyline woven around the usual shedding of clothes. Gregory Harrison (anyone still remember the TV series *Trapper John, MD*?) is the architect who falls under the spell of *femme fatale* Cali Timmins; the latter then gets her hooks into Harrison's wife (Joan Severance). There are no real stars in the cast, but the performances are solid enough and Michael Kennedy directs this TV movie with a modicum of confidence and style. Contains swearing, violence and sex scenes.

Gregory Harrison *Trent Turner* • Joan Severance *Madelyn Turner* • Cali Timmins *Dina Davis* • Andrew Airlie *Adam Russell* ■ *Dir* Michael Kennedy • *Scr* William Martell

Hard Evidence ★★★ 15

Thriller based on a true story
1994 · US · Colour · 90mins

Since the glossy inanities of *Charlie's Angels*, Kate Jackson has carved herself a nice little niche by appearing in worthy true-life TV dramas, and this is a typically competent example. In a story with similarities to Sissy Spacek's *Marie*, Jackson plays a single mother who lands a job with the Georgia Labor Department, only to discover that the bureaucracy is riddled with corruption. Dean Stockwell scores as Jackson's villainous boss. Jan Egleson's direction is a touch pedestrian, but the committed performances carry the day. Contains violence. ▭

Kate Jackson *Sandra Clayton* • John Shea *Tommy Marchant* • Dean Stockwell *Sam Caldwell* • Terry O'Quinn *Harris Wiley* • Beth Broderick *Melissa Brewer* • Rand Courtney *Shane* • Megan Gallagher *Shannon* ■ *Dir* Jan Egleson • *Scr* Richard Rashke

Hard, Fast and Beautiful ★★ U

Drama 1951 · US · BW · 78mins

Nice to find that most accomplished of character actresses, Claire Trevor, carrying a picture as the star. This was an early Ida Lupino venture as a director for her own independent production company, and Trevor gives a spot-on portrayal of a frustrated woman who pins all her hopes of worldly success on the tennis-playing skills of her daughter. Sally Forrest is competent enough as the youngster propelled into becoming a champion, but the film is a little too relentless and unvaried in its dramatic agenda.

Claire Trevor *Milly Farley* • Sally Forrest *Florence Farley* • Carleton Young *Fletcher Locke* • Robert Clarke *Gordon McKay* ■ *Dir* Ida Lupino • *Scr* Martha Wilkerson, from a novel by John R Tunis

Hard Feelings ★★★ 15

Drama 1981 · Can · Colour · 100mins

A quietly rewarding coming-of-age drama set in early sixties' America and featuring believable performances from a largely unknown cast. Carl Marotte is the confused adolescent who is getting to grips with his impending adulthood and social (and racial divides). Directed with low-key affection by Daryl Duke and co-written by John Herzfeld, who went on to make the terrific black comedy *Two Days in the Valley*. ▭

Charlaine Woodard [Charlayne Woodard] *Winona Lockhart* • Vincent Bufano *Russell Linwood* • Grand Bush [Grand L Bush] *Lathom Lockhart* • Lisa Langlois *Barbara Holland* • Allan Katz *Lee Bridgeman* ■ *Dir* Daryl Duke • *Scr* WD Richter, John Herzfeld, from the novel by Don Bredes

Hard Justice ★★ 18

Action thriller 1995 · US · Colour · 87mins

Hugely derivative but enjoyable thriller, which cheerfully appropriates most of John Woo and Co's best Hong Kong moves. David Bradley, who made his name in the *Cyborg Cop* franchise, is the undercover cop who infiltrates corrupt warder Charles Napier's prison, which is being used by gangsters as a clearing house for firearms. Bradley's position is jeopardised when gangster Yuji Okumoto, whom Bradley has recently had put behind bars, is transferred to the same cell block. Director Greg Yaitanes obviously did his Hong Kong homework and stages the many fight sequences with some flair. ▭

David Bradley (2) *Nick Adams* • Charles Napier *Warden Pike* • Yuji Okumoto *Jimmy Wong* ■ *Dir* Greg Yaitanes • *Scr* Nicholas Amendolare, Chris Bold

Hard Knocks ★★★

Drama 1980 · Ausl · Colour · 85mins

Tracy Mann won an Australian Oscar as best actress for her superb performance in this affecting drama, which focuses on her attempts to leave her criminal past behind and start over again. Her subtle performance is well backed up by familiar Australian character actors Bill Hunter, Max Cullen and Tony Barry, while the believable script from director Don McLennan and Hilton Bonner (who has a supporting role) was also nominated for an Australian Film Institute award.

Tracy Mann *Sam* • Bill Hunter *Brady* • Max Cullen *Newman* • Tony Barry *Barry* ■ *Dir* Don McLennan • *Scr* Don McLennan, Hilton Bonner

Hard Men ★★★ 18

Crime drama
1996 · UK/Fr · Colour and Tinted · 83mins

Three violent gangsters run a London numbers racket for Kray-inspired mobster Pops (played by real-life ex-con "Mad" Frankie Fraser). But one (Vincent Regan) wants out of the crooked game – family life beckons – so Pops orders his two remaining stooges to cut off the traitor's hand

and have it on his desk by the next morning. Clearly patterned after *Reservoir Dogs*, this oddly compelling and amusing journey through the greasy-spoon cafés and sleazy brothels of Soho is trashy pulp fiction, boldly executed by first-time writer/director JK Amalou. Lee Ross is great as the drug freak Speed. ▭

Vincent Regan *Tone* • Ross Boatman *Bear* • Lee Ross *Speed* • "Mad" Frankie Fraser *Pops* • Den • Ken Campbell *Mr Ross* • Mirella D'Angelo *Chantal* • Irene Ng *Suki* • Robyn Lewis *Lleila* ■ *Dir/Scr* JK Amalou

Hard Promises ★★ PG

Romantic comedy
1991 · US · Colour · 91mins

A forgettable comedy made slightly less so by an experienced cast, which includes Sissy Spacek, William Petersen, Peter MacNicol and Mare Winningham. Petersen is Sissy's ex-husband, who is invited to her upcoming wedding and is determined to disrupt the ceremony. Repeating his unlikeable schtick from *Cousins*, Petersen overpowers the rest of the cast with his relentless sliminess, which leaves you to wonder why Spacek's character married him in the first place. Populated with clichés instead of supporting characters. ▭

Sissy Spacek *Chris Coalter* • William Petersen *Joey Coalter* • Brian Kerwin *Walter Humphrey* • Mare Winningham *Dawn* • Jeff Perry *Pinky* • Olivia Burnette *Beth Coalter* • Peter MacNicol *Stuart Coalter* • Rip Torn ■ *Dir* Martin Davidson • *Scr* Jule Selbo

Hard Rain ★★ 15

Action thriller
1997 · US/UK/Jap/Ger/Den · Colour · 92mins

Christian Slater and Minnie Driver battle the elements in this slim, waterlogged but fast-paced adventure that throws bad guys together with the forces of nature after a flood envelops a small town on the same night a daring robbery takes place. Utterly preposterous in places, this nonetheless zips along merrily and offers the bonus of some impressively tongue-in-cheek performances from Morgan Freeman and Randy Quaid. Contains violence and swearing. ▭ *DVD*

Morgan Freeman *Jim* • Christian Slater *Tom* • Randy Quaid *Sheriff* • Minnie Driver *Karen* • Edward Asner [Ed Asner] *Charlie* • Richard Dysart *Henry* • Betty White *Doreen* • Michael Goorjian *Kenny* ■ *Dir* Mikael Salomon • *Scr* Graham Yost

The Hard Ride ★

Action drama 1971 · US · Colour · 92mins

A dismal *Easy Rider* rip-off with Robert Fuller (star of TV western *Wagon Train*) as the Vietnam veteran bringing his buddy's dead body home and finding that he has inherited a motorcycle. Fuller doesn't really know one end of a bike from another but, hey man, he's soon riding the highway and getting to know native Americans and gang lore while the soundtrack offers endless songs about peace and love. Burt Topper specialised in anti-war, anti-establishment youth movies, but never really got out of the drive-in arena.

Robert Fuller *Phil* • Sherry Bain *Sheryl* • Tony Russell *Big Red* • William Bonner *Grady* • Marshall Reed *Father Tom* • Mikel Angel *Ralls* ■ *Dir/Scr* Burt Topper

Hard Target ★★★ 18

Action thriller 1993 · US · Colour · 91mins

Cult Hong Kong director John Woo's Hollywood debut was regarded as a major disappointment by his die-hard fans, but it still remains leaps ahead of most American action fodder. It is also easily Jean-Claude Van Damme's best movie, even if Woo doesn't quite achieve the impossible and coax a performance out of him. Armed with the dodgiest haircut since Hoddle and Waddle in their Spurs' heyday (ask the football fan next to you), Van Damme plays an unemployed sailor who spoils the human hunting games of some wealthy millionaires when he fights back. The plotting is minimal, but Lance Henriksen and Arnold Vosloo make for terrific baddies and Woo orchestrates some stunning action set pieces – including a spectacular finale – with panache. Contains swearing and violence. ▭ *DVD*

Jean-Claude Van Damme *Chance Boudreaux* • Lance Henriksen *Emil Fouchon* • Yancy Butler *Natasha "Nat" Binder* • Wilford Brimley *Uncle Douvee* • Kasi Lemmons *Carmine Mitchell* • Arnold Vosloo *Pik Van Cleaf* • Bob Apisa *Mr Lopacki* • Chuck Pfarrer *Douglas Binder* ■ *Dir* John Woo • *Scr* Chuck Pfarrer

Hard Time ★★

Crime drama 1998 · US · Colour · 120mins

The acclaimed *Boogie Nights* gave Burt Reynolds's flagging career a much needed boost, but this average thriller, which he also directs, is closer in feel to the slew of forgettable material he starred in during the eighties. He plays a vaguely unstable cop who is framed for murder when a police drugs bust goes wrong. The strong supporting cast includes old sparring partner Charles Durning, Billy Dee Williams and Mia Sara, but while the handling of Reynolds the director is assured, his action-man lead performance is less convincing. Nonetheless, the film has gone on to spawn a number of sequels Stateside, a tribute of sorts to the durability of Reynolds's appeal.

Burt Reynolds *Logan McQueen* • Charles Durning *Duffy* • Robert Loggia *Martin* • Billy Dee Williams *Barker* • Mia Sara *Susan Myler* • Michael Buie *Higgs* ■ *Dir* Burt Reynolds • *Scr* David S Cass Sr, Steve Wesley

Hard to Get ★★★ U

Comedy 1938 · US · BW · 78mins

Yes, this is the *You Must Have Been a Beautiful Baby* movie, with crooner Dick Powell serenading the young and lovely Olivia de Havilland in a wacky screwball comedy from Warner Bros. She's rich, he's poor, as if you cared, and they're supported by a great cast of hand-picked eccentrics: Penny "Blondie" Singleton is charming as a kooky maid, and Charles Winninger, as Olivia's rich dad, is hysterically funny. Also along for the ride are such clever comic players as Allen Jenkins and Grady Sutton, both Warner veterans. Skilled and under-rated director Ray Enright keeps up the necessary pace.

Dick Powell *Bill Davis* • Olivia de Havilland *Margaret Richards* • Charles Winninger *Big Ben Richards* • Allen Jenkins *Roscoe* • Bonita Granville *Connie Richards* • Penny Singleton *Hattie* • Grady Sutton *Stanley Potter* ■ Dir Ray Enright • Scr Jerry Wald, Maurice Lee, Richard Macauley, from a screen story by Wally Klein, Joseph Schrank, from the story *Classified* by Stephen Morehouse Avery

Hard to Handle ★★★

Comedy 1933 · US · BW · 82mins

The original title *A Bad Boy* was dropped by Warner Bros, who feared audiences would expect a gangster movie. But, in this pacey Depression-era drama, James Cagney still fires on all cylinders as an entrepreneur and wittily refers back to his 1931 role in *The Public Enemy* by promoting grapefruit rather than squashing one into the face of his girlfriend, played here by bubbly blonde Mary Brian. Ruth Donnelly also makes an impression as Brian's mother, and director Mervyn LeRoy orchestrates some fine period trappings, including the sort of dance marathon later featured in *They Shoot Horses, Don't They?*.

James Cagney *Lefty Merrill* • Mary Brian *Ruth Waters* • Ruth Donnelly *Lil Waters* • Allen Jenkins *Radio announcer* • Claire Dodd *Marlene Reeves* • Gavin Gordon *John Hayden* ■ Dir Mervyn LeRoy • Scr Wilson Mizner, Robert Lord, from a story by Houston Branch

Hard to Hold ★ 15

Musical drama 1984 · US · Colour · 88mins

Pop sensation Rick Springfield made an ill-advised career move when he decided to appear in this humdrum vehicle tailored to his limited talents. He plays a spoilt teen idol who falls in love with feisty Janet Eilber, mainly because she hasn't got a clue that he's a big star. Poorly written, directed and acted, this cynical cash-in is neither a comedy nor a drama and is totally unbelievable because of the lack of any chemistry between the two supposed lovers. ▭

Rick Springfield *James Roberts* • Janet Eilber *Diana Lawson* • Patti Hansen *Nicky Nides* • Albert Salmi *Johnny Lawson* ■ Dir Larry Peerce • Scr Thomas Hedley, from a story by Richard Rothstein, Thomas Hedley

Hard to Kill ★★★ 18

Action thriller 1989 · US · Colour · 91mins

This was the movie that set action superstar Steven Seagal on his monosyllabic road to riches. He plays Mason Storm, a cop who is grievously wounded when a gang invades his marital bedroom and sprays it with gunfire. Storm survives, though his wife isn't so lucky. It takes seven years to recover from the ordeal, but he emerges stronger than ever and, after the usual period of fearsome solo martial-arts training, wreaks a terrible revenge on his attackers. Seagal stars alongside Kelly LeBrock, his real-life consort. ▭ **DVD**

Steven Seagal *Mason Storm* • Kelly LeBrock *Andy Stewart* • Bill Sadler [William Sadler] *Vernon Trent* • Frederick Coffin *Kevin O'Malley* • Bonnie Burroughs *Felicia Storm* • Andrew Bloch *Captain Dan Hulland* • Zachary Rosencrantz *Sonny Storm* • Dean Norris *Detective Sergeant Goodhart* ■ Dir Bruce Malmuth • Scr Steven McKay, Steven Pressfield, Ronald Shusett

Hard Traveling ★★ PG

Drama 1985 · US · Colour · 93mins

A very slow and laborious tale which relies on far too many flashbacks. Centred around the court case of JE Freeman in Depression America, the film explains how an ordinary, gentle man finds the love of his life but is driven to robbery and murder in order to survive and provide for her. Based on the background of director Dan Bessie and the novel *Bread and a Stone* written by his father, this well-meaning project has substance but little style. As far as courtroom dramas go this is mediocre fare. ▭

JE Freeman *Ed Sloan* • Ellen Geer *Norah Sloan* • Barry Corbin *Frank Burton* ■ Dir Dan Bessie • Scr Dan Bessie, from the novel *Bread and a Stone* by Alvah Bessie

The Hard Truth ★★★ 18

Crime drama 1994 · US · Colour · 96mins

Michael Rooker plays a cop suspended from duty for being trigger-happy with a psycho in this intriguing crime drama. His girlfriend (British actress Lysette Anthony) suggests they go into crime together and they set their sights on $3 million-worth of Mafia money that her corrupt boss has received. The daring pair recruit computer expert Eric Roberts to help them and an inevitable love triangle ensues. The plan then starts to go awry. Plenty of action, chases and a modicum of sex keep this on the simmer, if not the boil. Contains swearing and violence. ▭

Eric Roberts *Dr Chandler Etheridge* • Michael Rooker *Jonah Mantz* • Lysette Anthony *Lisa Kantrell* • Ray Baker *Hamilton Nichols* • Don Yesso *Luis Gisors* ■ Dir Kristine Peterson • Scr Jonathan Tydor

The Hard Way ★★★

Melodrama 1942 · US · BW · 109mins

Move over, Bette Davis! This was Ida Lupino's chance to carry a Warner Bros melodrama, and she does the job splendidly as the tough dame from the industrial slums who ruthlessly propels talented younger sister Joan Leslie to showbiz stardom. Incisively written by Daniel Fuchs and Peter Viertel, it is visually powerful thanks to ace cameraman James Wong Howe's strong influence on director Vincent Sherman. Joan Leslie seems a little too docile to be a top star – but then again if she had more drive, she wouldn't have needed big sister's assistance in the first place.

Ida Lupino *Helen Chernen* • Joan Leslie *Katherine Chernen* • Dennis Morgan *Paul Collins* • Jack Carson *Albert Runkel* • Gladys George *Lily Emery* • Faye Emerson *Waitress* • Paul Cavanagh *John Shagrue* ■ Dir Vincent Sherman • Scr Daniel Fuchs, Peter Viertel, from a story by Jerry Wald

The Hard Way ★

Thriller 1980 · Ire · Colour · 89mins

Having made one of the definitive studies of the professional killer in *Point Blank*, John Boorman, for some reason, felt the need to act as executive producer on this dispiriting Irish TV movie directed by Michael Dryhurst. Patrick McGoohan is an assassin for hire who plans to retire in Ireland after deciding he has lost the

pitiless detachment required for the job. However, he is lured back for a final hit by Lee Van Cleef, but relations between the two soon deteriorate. The scenery is breathtaking, but that scarcely compensates for the dour story and the lacklustre performances.

Patrick McGoohan *John Connor* • Lee Van Cleef *McNeal* • Edna O'Brien *Kathleen* ■ Dir Michael Dryhurst • Scr Richard F Tombleson, Kevin Grogan

The Hard Way ★★★★ 15

Action comedy 1991 · US · Colour · 106mins

Michael J Fox and James Woods have a wonderful time sending up their established screen personae in this cheerful, breezy comedy thriller. Fox is the pampered film star who wants to ditch his lightweight image with a grittier new role as a hard-nosed detective – and who better to teach him the ropes than real-life hard-nosed detective Woods? The two reluctant partners then get caught up in the hunt for a serial killer (an over-the-top Stephen Lang). Action specialist John Badham piles on the mayhem with the requisite car chases and explosive set pieces, but the real joy comes from the two stars, as Woods is nearly driven mad by Fox's determination to live his life. Annabella Sciorra is wasted as the love interest, but keep an eye out for rapper LL Cool J and Christina Ricci. Contains swearing. ▭

Michael J Fox *Nick Lang* • James Woods *John Moss* • Stephen Lang ''Party Crasher'' • Annabella Sciorra *Susan* • Delroy Lindo *Captain Brix* • Luis Guzman *Pooley* • Mary Mara *China* • LL Cool J *Billy* • John Capodice *Grainy* • Christina Ricci *Bonnie* • Penny Marshall *Angie* ■ Dir John Badham • Scr Daniel Pyne, Lem Dobbs, from a story by Lem Dobbs, Michael Kozoll

Hardcore ★★★ 18

Drama 1979 · US · Colour · 103mins

George C Scott stars as a Michigan Calvinist searching for his errant daughter who has become a porn actress in Los Angeles. Scott's search leads him through a warren of massage parlours, nude encounters and snuff movies, but he maintains a chilly aloofness, nursing his bigotry and heading towards that inevitable explosion of violence. Written and directed by Michigan Calvinist Paul Schrader, this flawed but generally impressive transposition of *The Searchers* inhabits the same sleazy yet redemptive world as Schrader's script for *Taxi Driver*.

George C Scott *Jake Van Dorn* • Peter Boyle *Andy Mast* • Season Hubley *Niki* • Dick Sargent *Wes DeJong* • Leonard Gaines *Ramada* ■ Dir/Scr Paul Schrader

The Harder They Come ★★ 15

Drama 1972 · Jam · Colour · 103mins

Jamaica's first indigenous feature become something of a cult hit and made a huge star of Jimmy Cliff, whose own experiences, to a degree, inform the plot. After a hard-hitting opening, however – in which keenly observed documentary detail captures both the exotic and ugly sides of Kingston – this reggae reworking of the old rags-to-riches story disappointingly

descends into banal blaxploitation. The struggle to make it in the music business is convincingly depicted, but director Perry Henzell loses his way when Cliff resorts to cop killing to boost his record sales. Whatever the film's shortcomings, though, the music is superb. With subtitles. ▭

Jimmy Cliff *Ivan* • Carl Bradshaw *Jose* • Basil Keane *Preacher* • Janet Bartley *Elsa* • Winston Stona *Police detective* • Bobby Charlton *Record company manager* • Ras Daniel Hartman *Pedro* ■ Dir Perry Henzell • Scr Perry Henzell, Trevor D Rhone

The Harder They Fall ★★★ 15

Sports drama 1956 · US · BW · 104mins

A riveting study of the hidden world of professional prize fighting, author Budd Schulberg's yarn is given added poignancy by the fact that his star is Humphrey Bogart in his last role, aged and mellowed and dying. Bogie is terrific as the washed-up sports columnist forced to work for boxing promoter Rod Steiger, and what a joy it is to revel in their contrasting acting styles: Bogey so casual and effortless, Steiger so Method and explosive. Mark Robson's direction and Philip Yordan's screenplay attempt rugged realism, but this is full-blooded Hollywood melodrama, and should be enjoyed as such. Watch out for some key fight figures, including Max Baer and Jersey Joe Walcott. ▭

Humphrey Bogart *Eddie Willis* • Rod Steiger *Nick Benko* • Jan Sterling *Beth Willis* • Mike Lane *Toro Moreno* • Max Baer *Buddy Brannen* • Jersey Joe Walcott *George* • Edward Andrews *Jim Weyerhause* • Harold J Stone *Art Leavitt* • Carlos Montalban *Luis Agrandi* ■ Dir Mark Robson • Scr Philip Yordan, from the novel by Budd Schulberg

Hardly Working ★★

Comedy 1981 · US · Colour · 91mins

Nine years after the disastrous *The Day the Clown Cried* (it was never given general release), Jerry Lewis produced this ''comeback'' comedy which should be marked ''return to sender''. Directed by Lewis to recoup his fortunes after his spell out of the limelight, it's about an unemployed circus clown who bumbles around looking for work and sympathy. Some good moments, but generally this is too self-pitying for comfort.

Jerry Lewis *Bo Hooper* • Susan Oliver *Claire Trent* • Roger C Carmel *Robert Trent* • Deanna Lund *Millie* • Harold J Stone *Frank Loucazi* ■ Dir Jerry Lewis • Scr Michael Janover, Jerry Lewis, from a story by Michael Janover

Hardware ★★★★ 18

Science-fiction horror 1990 · UK · Colour · 89mins

Sex, drugs and rock 'n' roll are the components greasing the splatter-punk engine of director Richard Stanley's impressive debut. His *Terminator*-style shocker with attitude is an amusing, gore-drenched thrill ride. Twenty-first century soldier of fortune Dylan McDermott gives his estranged sculptress girlfriend Stacey Travis a junked robot so she can weld the spare parts into surreal artwork. Neither know that the cyborg is really a scrapped prototype developed for future military warfare to kill without mercy – until it reconstructs itself and goes on the bloody rampage. A purposely trashy shock to the system, Stanley's nuts-and-bolts science-fiction slasher is meant to disturb, and does so without apology. ▣

Dylan McDermott *Mo* • Stacey Travis *Jill* • John Lynch *Shades* • William Hootkins *Lincoln* • Iggy Pop *Angry Bob* • Mark Northover *Alvy* ■ *Dir* Richard Stanley • *Scr* Richard Stanley, Mike Fallon, from the story *Shok!* from the comic book *Fleetway Comics 2000 AD* by Steve McManus, Kevin O'Neill

The Hardys Ride High ★★ 🆄

Comedy   1939 · US · BW · 80mins

The sixth in the long saga of the Hardy family. This time Mickey Rooney, Lewis Stone and company come into a $2 million inheritance and move to Detroit. The moral is that money and luxuries are no substitute for the small-town values and everyday joys of the Hardys' hometown of Carvel. Rooney, now 16, starts smoking and falls for a gold-digging chorus girl. Problem is, Rooney was actually 19 at the time, but looked about nine.

Mickey Rooney *Andy Hardy* • Lewis Stone *Judge James K Hardy* • Cecilia Parker *Marian Hardy* • Fay Holden *Mrs Emily Hardy* • Ann Rutherford *Polly Benedict* ■ *Dir* George B Seitz • *Scr* Kay Van Riper, Agnes C Johnson, William Ludwig, from characters created by Aurania Rouverol

Harem   ★★ 🅻

Romantic drama   1985 · Fr · Colour · 93mins

Obsession usually makes for good drama, but not this time. The kidnapping of Wall Street stockbroker Nastassja Kinski by enthralled Arab prince Ben Kingsley is an upmarket white-slave story that looks ravishing, though nobody really gets ravished. The trouble is, the prince is too sensitive for his own good or for his victim's bad. Rudolph Valentino in *The Sheik* wouldn't have stood for such nonsense. It all fizzles out in a welter of silly talk and a supposedly ironic ending – an ending that can't come soon enough. ▣

Nastassja Kinski *Diane* • Ben Kingsley *Selim* • Dennis Goldson *Massoud* • Zohra Segal *Affaf* • Michel Robin *Monsieur Raoul* • Julette Simpson *Zelide* • Karen Bowen *Mrs Green* ■ *Dir* Arthur Joffé • *Scr* Arthur Joffé, Tom Rayfiel, from a story by Arthur Joffé, Richard Prieur, Antonio B Hernandez

Harem Holiday   ★★ 🆄

Musical comedy   1965 · US · Colour · 81mins

Another sub-standard entry in the screen career of Elvis Presley. Here he plays a movie star who travels to the Middle East to attend the premiere of his latest film and gets caught up in a plot to assassinate a local ruler. The exotic locations add a frisson of interest to the usual formula, but this is negated by the lacklustre plot and forgettable songs. Cult TV fans may recognise co-star Mary Ann Mobley as the first actress to play *The Girl from UNCLE* on the small screen, before Stefanie Powers took the role. ▣

Elvis Presley *Johnny Tyronne* • Mary Ann Mobley *Princess Shalimar* • Fran Jeffries *Aishah* • Michael Ansara *Prince Dragna* • Jay

Novello *Zacha* • Philip Reed *King Toranshah* • Theo Marcuse *Sinan* • Billy Barty *Baba* ■ *Dir* Gene Nelson • *Scr* Gerald Drayson Adams

Harem Suare   ★★★

Historical drama
1999 · It/Fr/Tur · Colour · 106mins

Revisiting many of the themes from *The Turkish Bath* – forbidden love, ritual cleansing and the passage of long-established tradition – Ferzan Ozpetek here explores the political manoeuvrings occurring within the Sultan's palace against the backdrop of the Ottoman eclipse during the 1900s. Marie Gillain gives a spirited performance as the favoured courtesan Alex Descas comes to mirror her master's growing political impotence. With Valeria Golino in cameo support, this is a sensual account of a society in transition that also begs questions about the role of women in Turkey today. In French, Turkish and Italian with English subtitles.

Marie Gillain *Safiye* • Alex Descas *Nadir* • Lucia Bosé *Old Safiye* • Valeria Golino *Anita* • Malick Bowens *Midhat* • Christophe Aquilon *Sumbul* • Serra Yilmaz *Gulfidan* • Haluk Bilginer *Abdulhamit* ■ *Dir* Ferzan Ozpetek • *Scr* Gianni Romilo, Ferzan Ozpetek

Harlan County, USA   ★★★

Documentary   1976 · US · Colour · 103mins

Barbara Kopple's Oscar-winning documentary, which was years in the making, is a powerful and compelling record of the strike called at the Brookside colliery in Kentucky after management refused to recognise the workers' union status. It's a shrewdly compiled piece, but in spite of the expert manipulation, what emerges is a portrait of a community bursting with initiative, intelligence, camaraderie and a real sense of justice and self-worth. Exploring every aspect of Harlan life, Kopple gives particular attention to the miners' wives as they stand by their husbands on the picket line.

Dir/Scr Barbara Kopple

Harlem Nights   ★★ 🔞

Crime comedy   1989 · US · Colour · 110mins

Oh, dear. Eddie Murphy's directing debut and star vehicle hits engine trouble early on and conks out completely long before the home straight. The plan was to make a latter-day version of a thirties' gangster movie; the result has some nifty costumes, luscious sets and neat music, but, on almost every other count, it's a mess. As if Murphy's involvement were not already substantial enough, he also wrote the script and was executive producer. The result offers a simple message for the star: stick to acting. Contains swearing and violence. ▣

Eddie Murphy *Quick* • Richard Pryor *Sugar Ray* • Danny Aiello *Sergeant Phil Cantone* • Michael Lerner *Bugsy Calhoune* • Della Reese *Vera* • Redd Foxx *Bennie Wilson* • Berlinda Tolbert *Annie* • Stan Shaw *Jack Jenkins* • Jasmine Guy *Dominique La Rue* • Arsenio Hall *Crying man* ■ *Dir/Scr* Eddie Murphy • *Cinematographer* Woody Omens • *Production Designer* Lawrence G Paull • *Costume Designer* Joe I Tompkins

Harlequin   ★★

Drama   1980 · Ausl · Colour · 92mins

Director Simon Wincer's second feature is a downright odd attempt to update the story of Rasputin to eighties' Australia. Trading on the piercing eyes that made him so effective in *Jesus of Nazareth*, Robert Powell plays a charismatic healer who convinces senator David Hemmings and his wife that he can cure their son's leukaemia. This is typical of the kind of curio that Hemmings opted for as his once-glittering career went into a steep decline, and Wincer piles on the mystery without really developing the story. Hollywood veteran Broderick Crawford ,who won a best actor Oscar in 1949 for *All the King's Men*, pops up as Hemmings's spin doctor.

Robert Powell *Gregory Wolfe* • David Hemmings *Senator Nick Rast* • Carmen Duncan *Sandra Rast* • Broderick Crawford *Doc Wheelan* • Gus Mercurio *Mr Bergier* • Alan Cassell *Mr Porter* • Mark Spain *Alex Rast* ■ *Dir* Simon Wincer • *Scr* Everett De Roche

Harley Davidson and the Marlboro Man   ★ 🔞

Action adventure 1991 · US · Colour · 94mins

A blatant, dispiriting plug for leather and lung cancer with Mickey Rourke and Don Johnson as bikers who in 1996 (for some reason this is a futuristic thing) are mistaken for drug runners instead of the slimeballs they really are. Lacking the energy and exploitation thrills of the sixties' biker movies it tries to emulate, this is more like a retread of those dreadful *Cannonball Run* movies. ▣

Mickey Rourke *Harley Davidson* • Don Johnson *Marlboro* • Chelsea Field *Virginia Slim* • Daniel Baldwin *Alexander* • Giancarlo Esposito *Jimmy Jiles* • Vanessa Williams [Vanessa L Williams] *Lulu Daniels* • Robert Ginty *Thom* • Tia Carrere *Kimiko* ■ *Dir* Simon Wincer • *Scr* Don Michael Paul

Harlow   ★★

Biographical drama
1965 · US · Colour · 124mins

Not altogether believable biopic of the platinum blonde bombshell, with Jean Harlow viewed as an unhappy innocent trying to become a star in thirties' Hollywood while dodging the ever-present casting couch. However, the film did well at the box office, and Carroll Baker, Red Buttons (as Harlow's agent Arthur Landau) and Angela Lansbury (as Harlow's mother) rise above the limitations of the script. Not to be confused with the Carol Lynley film of the same name and year, which used "Electronovision", a process that involved shooting on video stock and gave poor results.

Carroll Baker *Jean Harlow* • Martin Balsam *Everett Redman* • Red Buttons *Arthur Landau* • Mike Connors *Jack Harrison* • Angela Lansbury *Mama Jean Bello* • Peter Lawford *Paul Bern* • Leslie Nielsen *Richard Manley* ■ *Dir* Gordon Douglas • *Scr* John Michael Hayes, from the non-fiction book *An Intimate Biography* by Irving Shulman, Arthur Landau

Harlow   ★

Biographical drama
1965 · US · Colour · 107mins

Made the same year as the marginally better biopic starring Carroll Baker as

Harlow, this exploitative film cashes in sad, sorry life of the Hollywood starlet. Lynley isn't up to the role and Ginger Rogers (who play's Jean's mother) really should have known better. The producers rushed to get this out before the Paramount film, and the sloppiness shows.

Carol Lynley *Jean Harlow* • Efrem Zimbalist Jr *William Mansfield* • Ginger Rogers *Mama Jean* • Barry Sullivan *Marino Bello* • Hurd Hatfield *Paul Bern* • Lloyd Bochner *Marc Peters* • Hermione Baddeley *Marie Dressler* ■ *Dir* Alex Segal • *Scr* Karl Tunberg

Harmful Intent   ★★★ 🅸

Thriller   1993 · US · Colour · 89mins

The film version of Robin Cook's *Coma* was an under-rated medical chiller, and while this made-for-TV version of another of his thrillers isn't quite in the same league, it's still a nerve-tingling affair. Tim Matheson is the doctor forced to go on the run when he is falsely accused of giving a pregnant woman a fatal dose of anaesthetic. With the help of Emma Samms he uncovers a frightening conspiracy. Matheson is fine as the wronged man, there are solid supporting turns from the likes of Robert Pastorelli and Alex Rocco, and director John Patterson manages to inject a good number of shocks and twists. ▣

Tim Matheson *Dr Jeffrey Rhodes* • Emma Samms *Kelly Everson* • Robert Pastorelli *Devlin O'Shea* • Alex Rocco *Mosconi* • Kurt Fuller *Bingham* • John Walcutt *Trent Harding* ■ *Dir* John Patterson • *Scr* Martha Weingartner, from the novel by Robin Cook

The Harness   ★★★

Romantic drama
1971 · US · Colour · 120mins

An excellent version of a heart-warming John Steinbeck story, offering a leading role to under-rated Lorne Greene, the Canadian actor best known as Ben Cartwright in *Bonanza*. Here he plays a farmer whose life is dominated by his sick wife until the arrival of two newcomers at his ranch. There are excellent supporting roles for Louise Latham as the wife and, especially, from Murray Hamilton. The rich photography is from one of the all-time Hollywood camera maestros, Russell Metty, whose career stretches from *Bringing Up Baby* to *Spartacus*, embracing *Touch of Evil* on the way. A TV movie of distinction from Universal, who pioneered films specifically made for the small screen.

Lorne Greene *Peter Randall* • Julie Sommars *Jennifer Shagaras* • Murray Hamilton *Roy Kern* • Lee H Montgomery [Lee Montgomery] *Tor Shagaras* • Louise Latham *Emma Randall* • Henry Beckman *Doc Marn* • Joan Tompkins *Millie Chappel* ■ *Dir* Boris Sagal • *Scr* Leon Tokatyan, Edward Hume, from a short story by John Steinbeck

Harold and Maude   ★★★★ 🅸

Drama   1972 · US · Colour · 87mins

Call it bad taste, but rarely has such a strange love affair been presented so charmingly as the one here between morbid young Harold (Bud Cort) and 79-year-old concentration camp survivor Maude (Ruth Gordon). Depressed by life, and rejected by his wealthy mother Vivian Pickles, the death-fascinated Harold drives a

🆄 = SUITABLE FOR ALL   🅻 = SUITABLE FOR ALL, ESPECIALLY FOR YOUNG CHILDREN (VIDEO ONLY)   🅿🅶 = PARENTAL GUIDANCE

hearse to funerals, meets the skittish Maude and falls in love. A cult classic, the film started life as a graduate thesis by Colin Higgins, whose landlady helped him to set it up for direction by Hal Ashby. The performances are a delightful bonus in a movie that, for all its eccentricities, likes people.

Ruth Gordon *Maude* • Bud Cort *Harold* • Vivian Pickles *Mrs Chasen* • Cyril Cusack *Glaucus* • Charles Tyner *Uncle Victor* • Ellen Geer *Sunshine Dore* • Eric Christmas *Priest* • G Wood *Psychiatrist* ■ *Dir* Hal Ashby • *Scr* Colin Higgins • *Music* Cat Stevens

Harper Valley P.T.A. ★★★

Comedy 1978 · US · Colour · 101mins

Ode to Billy Joe demonstrated the potential for pop ballads to inspire movies and the spicy comedy *Harper Valley P.T.A.*, based on Jeannie C Riley's song about small-town hypocrisy, continued the trend. Barbara Eden takes the lead as a sexy widow whose lifestyle offends the uptight members of the local Parent-Teachers Association, but turns the tables on them by exposing their own considerable foibles. A moderate hit theatrically, the film scored impressive ratings when it aired on US television and was promptly turned into a TV series with Eden re-creating her sassy movie role.

Barbara Eden *Stella Johnson* • Ronny Cox *Willis Newton* • Nanette Fabray *Alice Finely* • Susan Swift *Dee Johnson* • Louis Nye *Kirby Baker* • Pat Paulsen *Otis Harper Jr* ■ *Dir* Richard Bennett • *Scr* George Edwards, Barry Schneider, from the song by Tom T Hall

The Harrad Experiment ★

Drama 1973 · US · Colour · 97mins

James Whitmore and Tippi Hedren are a learned married couple who run Harrad College, a bastion of libertarian values where young people are obliged to live with each other and work out their sexual hang-ups. Doubtless Hollywood felt it was being terribly grown-up to tackle such a story, but it's relentlessly tedious and hardly likely to raise anything more than a smile, despite some rather coy nudity and dirty dialogue. Look closely as one of the students is played by a pre-*Miami Vice* Don Johnson, who later married Hedren's daughter Melanie Griffith (who also appears here in an uncredited bit part).

James Whitmore *Philip Tenhausen* • Tippi Hedren *Margaret Tenhausen* • Don Johnson *Stanley* • B Kirby Jr [Bruno Kirby] *Harry* • Laurie Walters *Sheila* • Melanie Griffith ■ *Dir* Ted Post • *Scr* Michael Werner, Ted Cassedy, from the novel by Robert H Rimmer

The Harrad Summer ★ 15

Drama 1974 · US · Colour · 100mins

Too much experience is less than a good thing, as this indifferent sequel to *The Harrad Experiment* about students at a sex-education college demonstrates. When the students return to their communities, they take their extra-curricular "homework" with them. Aimed, as the other film, to cash in on the *Kinsey Report*, leads Robert Reiser and Laurie Walters don't take any acting honours with this, while TV movie regular director Steven Hilliard Stern's name is more distinguished than his talents.

Robert Reiser *Stanley Kolasukas* • Laurie Walters *Sheila Grove* • Richard Doran *Harry Schacht* • Victoria Thompson *Beth Hillyer* • Emmaline Henry *Margaret Tonhausen* • Bill Dana *Jack Schacht* ■ *Dir* Steven Hilliard Stern • *Scr* Morth Thaw, Steve Zacharias

Harriet Craig ★★★

Psychological drama 1950 · US · BW · 94m

This is a rip-roaring vehicle for Joan Crawford, who ably demonstrates on screen all those "qualities" so vividly documented in *Mommie Dearest*. Crawford, as ever, tends to chew the scenery to achieve effect, in contrast to the superb Rosalind Russell in the earlier talkie version of the play on which this was based. Nevertheless, the star breathes life into this hoary old chestnut about a woman more taken by her possessions than by her family, and makes the whole dated premise a mesmerising experience.

Joan Crawford *Harriet Craig* • Wendell Corey *Walter Craig* • Lucile Watson *Celia Fenwick* • Allyn Joslyn *Billy Birkmire* • William Bishop *Wes Miller* • KT Stevens *Clare Raymond* • Raymond Greenleaf *Henry Fenwick* • Ellen Corby *Lottie* ■ *Dir* Vincent Sherman • *Scr* Anne Froelick, James Gunn, from the play *Craig's Wife* by George Kelly

Harriet the Spy ★★★ PG

Comedy 1996 · US · Colour · 97mins

Although a rather slow rendition of the popular children's novel by Louise Fitzhugh, the movie nevertheless has a lot of enthusiasm and nice performances going for it, which should enchant fans of the book. Harriet is the schoolgirl who spies on her friends and family, making copious observations about them in her secret notebook. Its hardly a surprise that, when the book falls into the wrong hands and Harriets scribblings are read out, her subjects are none too pleased. While not as colourful or zippily paced as the novel, this is a quirky film from director Bronwen Hughes, which benefits from a great group of kids and a warm adult performance from Rosie ODonnell as Harriet's nanny.

Michelle Trachtenberg *Harriet* • Rosie O'Donnell *Ole Golly* • Vanessa Lee Chester *Janie Gibbs* • Gregory Smith *Sport* • J Smith-Cameron *Mrs Welsch* • Robert Joy *Mr Welsch* • Eartha Kitt *Agatha K Plummer* ■ *Dir* Bronwen Hughes • *Scr* Douglas Petrie, Theresa Rebeck, from the novel by Louise Fitzhugh, adapted by Greg Taylor, Julie Talen

Harrison Bergeron ★★★

Science-fiction drama
1995 · Can · Colour · 99mins

Based on a short story by Kurt Vonnegut, this Canadian TV movie is set in 2053, some time after the second American Revolution when intelligence is controlled by electronic headbands that make everyone equally mediocre. But, no sooner has director Bruce Pittman established this arresting situation, than we dash headlong into the familiar territory already covered by such films as *Logan's Run* and *THX 1138*. Sean Astin just about holds the action together as the eponymous rebel as he passes from romantic interlude into political intrigue, and there's typically strong support from Christopher Plummer. You know how it will end, but it's worth a look, anyway. Contains violence and swearing.

Sean Astin *Harrison Bergeron* • Miranda de Pencier *Phillipa* • Christopher Plummer *Klaxon* • Buck Henry *Havlicek* • Eugene Levy *President McKloskey* • Howie Mandel *Charlie* • Andrea Martin *Heather Hoffman* ■ *Dir* Bruce Pittman • *Scr* Arthur Crimm, from the short story by Kurt Vonnegut

Harry and Son ★★ 15

Drama 1984 · US · Colour · 111mins

Paul Newman here stars, directs, co-writes and co-produces in a one-man band attempt to create a meaningful family melodrama. What we get is an awful lot of breast-beating, home truths and hysterical outbursts, but not much true understanding of why a father (Newman) and son (Robby Benson) find each other such fraught company in the first place. The members of a stellar cast (Joanne Woodward, Morgan Freeman, Ellen Barkin) stand around a lot, wringing their hands on the edge of the bear pit. Someone badly needed to divest Newman of one of his hats, but presumably nobody dared. Contains swearing and nudity.

Paul Newman *Harry Keach* • Robby Benson *Howard Keach* • Ellen Barkin *Katie* • Wilford Brimley *Tom* • Judith Ivey *Sally* • Ossie Davis *Raymond* • Morgan Freeman *Siemanowski* • Maury Chaykin *Lawrence* • Joanne Woodward *Lilly* ■ *Dir* Paul Newman • *Scr* Paul Newman, Ronald L Buck, from the novel *A Lost King* by Raymond DeCapite

Harry and Tonto ★★★★

Comedy 1974 · US · Colour · 115mins

Art Carney strikes a blow for the older generation – and won an Oscar in the process – with this story of a widower in his seventies who, after being evicted from his New York apartment, sets off on an odyssey across America with his cat Tonto. Intending to call on his grown-up children along the way, he ends up discarding a few prejudices. Paul Mazursky directs with a keen eye for characters, including Ellen Burstyn as a daughter who finds Harry's charm a bit too much, and Larry Hagman as a son forced to confront his own failure. Hitchhiker Melanie Mayron puts in a teenage flourish, but it's Carney's last hurrah which compels attention.

Art Carney *Harry* • Ellen Burstyn *Shirley* • Chief Dan George *Sam Two Feathers* • Geraldine Fitzgerald *Jessie* • Larry Hagman *Eddie* • Arthur Hunnicutt *Wade* • Melanie Mayron *Ginger* ■ *Dir* Paul Mazursky • *Scr* Paul Mazursky, Josh Greenfeld

Harry and Walter Go to New York ★★ U

Crime caper 1976 · US · Colour · 106mins

Vaguely influenced by the success of *The Sting*, this box-office dud admittedly has an attractive cast: James Caan and Elliott Gould as song-and-dance men turned safecrackers, Michael Caine as a sort of Mabuse-like mastermind and Diane Keaton as their ditzy confederate in an elaborate bank heist. Although money has been lavished on the re-creation of the New York of 1890, the script isn't nearly clever or funny enough.

James Caan *Harry Dighby* • Elliott Gould *Walter Hill* • Michael Caine *Adam Worth* • Diane Keaton *Lissa Chestnut* • Charles Durning *Rufus T Crisp* • Lesley Ann Warren *Gloria Fontaine* ■ *Dir* Mark Rydell • *Scr* John Byrum, Robert Kaufman

Harry in Your Pocket ★★★

Crime drama 1973 · US · Colour · 102mins

This is a film that boasts sleight-of-hand performing artist Tony Giorgio as its technical adviser (he also appears on-screen as a detective) and a plot concerning young Michael Sarrazin and Trish Van Devere learning how to pick a pocket or two. The stars find themselves under the tutelage of veteran pickpockets (or "cannons" as they are called here) – James Coburn, perfectly cast as a smoothie, and Walter Pidgeon, as a sleazy sophisticate, in one of the latter's better later roles. This heartfelt one-off is the only major credit of producer/director Bruce Geller, unless you count his 1976 TV movie *The Savage Bees*. Contains some strong language.

James Coburn *Harry* • Michael Sarrazin *Ray Houlihan* • Trish Van Devere *Sandy Coletto* • Walter Pidgeon *Casey* • Michael C Gwynne *Fence* • Tony Giorgio *First detective* ■ *Dir* Bruce Geller • *Scr* Ron Austin, James David Buchanan

Harry's War ★★★

Comedy 1981 · US · Colour · 98mins

It's a touch flattering to compare this throwback to thirties folksy comedies to the "everyman" classics of Frank Capra, even though it's positively packed to the rafters with Capra corn. So often the prissy nemesis of harmless heroes, Edward Herrmann here plays nicely against type as the postman who takes a stand against the Internal Revenue Service after it erroneously demands huge back taxes from his aunt, Geraldine Page. Writer/director Kieth Merrill is unquestioningly over-earnest in his celebration of small-town values, and a few more laughs wouldn't have gone amiss, but this is pleasantly uplifting entertainment.

Edward Herrmann *Harry Johnson* • Geraldine Page *Beverly Payne* • Karen Grassle *Kathy Johnson* • David Ogden Stiers *Ernie Scelera* • Salome Jens *Wilda Crawley* • Elisha Cook Jr *Sergeant Billy* ■ *Dir/Scr* Kieth Merrill

The Harvest ★★ 18

Thriller 1993 · US · Colour · 93mins

The illegal trade in body parts stands as a metaphor for the exploitative nature of Hollywood film-making in this flashy conspiracy thriller from debut director David Marconi. Playing fast and loose with traditional narrative structures, Marconi throws in flashbacks, dream sequences and episodes that could equally be real or simply part of wannabe writer Miguel Ferrer's latest screenplay. However, for all the intricacy of the plotting and the beauty of Emmanuel Lubezki's photography, too little attention is paid to either theme or characterisation. Contains violence, sex scenes, nudity and swearing.

Miguel Ferrer *Charlie Pope* • Leilani Sarelle Ferrer *Natalie Caldwell* • Henry Silva *Detective Topo* • Tim Thomerson *Steve Mobley* • Harvey Fierstein *Bob Lakin* • Anthony John Denison *Noel Guzmann* ■ *Dir/Scr* David Marconi

Harvest of Fire ★★★
Mystery drama   1996 · US · Colour

Any film about the Amish community is bound to draw some sort of comparison with Peter Weir's thriller *Witness*. Here FBI agent Lolita Davidovich goes to Iowa to investigate a series of barn burnings, but the solution of the crimes is of less importance to the success of Arthur Allan Seidelman's TV movie than the friendship that develops between the outsider and Amish widow Patty Duke. The drama is anything but original, but the performances of Davidovich and Duke are out of the top drawer. Contains some violence.

Lolita Davidovich *Sally* • Patty Duke *Annie* • JA Preston • Jean Louisa Kelly • Eric Mabius ■ *Dir* Arthur Allan Seidelman • *Scr* Richard Alfieri, Susan Nanus

Harvey ★★★★★ U
Comedy   1950 · US · BW · 107mins

James Stewart gives a knockout performance in a classic comic fantasy about tipsy Elwood P Dowd and his unusual friendship with Harvey, an invisible 6ft tall white rabbit. This is superb whimsy about the fine line between sanity and insanity, and Henry Koster directs this loving tribute to eccentricity and bar-room philosophy with a deft touch. Alongside the satiric misunderstandings, character mix-ups and revitalised clichés come poignant comments about humanity's lack of communication, which touch both the funny bone and the heart. Guaranteed to leave you with a smile on your face for ages afterwards. ▨

James Stewart *Elwood P Dowd* • Josephine Hull *Veta Louise Simmons* • Peggy Dow *Miss Kelly* • Charles Drake *Dr Sanderson* • Cecil Kellaway *Dr Chumley* • Victoria Horne *Myrtle Mae* • Jesse White *Wilson* • William Lynn *Judge Gaffney* • Wallace Ford *Lofgren* ■ *Dir* Henry Koster • *Scr* Mary Chase, Oscar Brodney, from the play by Mary Chase • *Cinematographer* William Daniels

Harvey ★★
Comedy   1996 · US · Colour

Have they no shame? The original *Harvey* is one of the all-time classic comedies, providing James Stewart with one of his more memorable roles, and it's hard to think how it could be improved. In this bland TV-movie version, Harry Anderson does his best as the cheerful drunk Elwood P Dowd, who insists that he has a giant white rabbit as a chum, and there is useful support from the likes of Swoozie Kurtz and Leslie Nielsen. But it's not a patch on the Stewart film and just makes you pine for the marvellous original.

Harry Anderson *Elwood P Dowd* • Swoosie Kurtz *Veta* • Leslie Nielsen *Dr Chumley* ■ *Dir* George Schaefer • *Scr* Joseph Dougherty, from the play by Mary Chase

The Harvey Girls ★★★ U
Musical comedy   1946 · US · Colour · 96mins

Once intended as a vehicle for Lana Turner, this Technicolored musical comedy became one of Judy Garland's greatest personal triumphs. The first half is undeniably spectacular and great fun, climaxing with a wonderful Oscar-winning set piece as Garland

and the company perform Harry Warren and Johnny Mercer's *On the Atchison, Topeka and the Santa Fe*, magnificently choreographed in railroad rhythm and directed with hardly a visible edit. When the story gets going, however, the plot is as cardboard as the scenery, and John Hodiak is a totally inadequate and lacklustre leading man. But the film belongs to Garland, and she is simply wonderful. ▨

Judy Garland *Susan Bradley* • John Hodiak *Ned Trent* • Ray Bolger *Chris Maule* • Preston Foster *Judge Sam Purvis* • Virginia O'Brien *Alma* • Angela Lansbury *Em* • Marjorie Main *Sonora Cassidy* • Chill Wills *HH Hartsey* • Kenny Baker (2) *Terry O'Halloran* • Cyd Charisse *Deborah* ■ *Dir* George Sidney • *Scr* Edmund Beloin, Nathaniel Curtis, Harry Crane, James O'Hanlon, Samson Raphaelson, from a story by Eleanore Griffin, William Rankin, from a novel by Samuel Hopkins Adams • *Music Director* Lennie Hayton • *Choreographer* Robert Alton

Harvey Middleman, Fireman ★★★
Comedy drama   1965 · US · Colour · 75mins

Ernest Pintoff made some very droll short cartoons, including *The Critic*, which won an Oscar. *Harvey Middleman, Fireman* was the first of his few features, starring the then (as now) unknown Gene Troobnick as a New York fireman. Troobnick is a happily married father of two, with a happy-go-lucky view of life. Until, that is, he rescues an attractive young woman from a fire, kisses her and then falls madly in love. Suddenly in turmoil, he even goes to a shrink, played by the monstrously hammy Hermione Gingold. It's a small, slight, charmingly cranky movie about moral conventions that came from nowhere and sadly stayed there.

Gene Troobnick *Harvey Middleman* • Hermione Gingold *Mrs Koogleman* • Patricia Harty *Lois* • Arlene Golonka *Harriet* • Will Mackenzie *Dinny* • Ruth Jaroslow *The mother* • Charles Durning *Dooley* ■ *Dir/Scr* Ernest Pintoff

Has Anybody Seen My Gal? ★★★
Musical comedy   1952 · US · Colour · 88mins

Millionaire Charles Coburn decides to check whether the family of the woman he loved many years ago, but who turned down his marriage proposal, is worthy of inheriting his fortune. Masquerading as an eccentric artist and taking a job as a soda jerk, he rents a room in the family house, arranges an anonymous gift of money for them, and gleefully watches the results. Breezily directed by Douglas Sirk, with a cast that includes Rock Hudson and Piper Laurie (and with James Dean in a bit part), this beguiling comedy owes much of its appeal to Coburn's performance.

Charles Coburn *Samuel Fulton* • Rock Hudson *Dan Stebbins* • Piper Laurie *Millicent Blaisdell* • Gigi Perreau *Roberta Blaisdell* • Lynn Bari *Harriet Blaisdell* • Larry Gates *Charles Blaisdell* • William Reynolds *Howard Blaisdell* • Skip Homeier *Carl Pennock* • James Dean *Youth* ■ *Dir* Douglas Sirk • *Scr* Joseph Hoffman, from a story by Eleanor H Porter

The Hasty Heart ★★★ U
Second World War drama
1949 · UK · BW · 106mins

In transferring John Patrick's hit play to the screen, Vincent Sherman remained faithful to the text, but neglected his duty as a film director by failing to challenge the eye as well as the ear. In an overblown but Oscar-nominated performance, Richard Todd dominates the action as a self-pitying Scot who makes life unbearable for his fellow patients in a Burmese field hospital. Patricia Neal also overdoes her angel of mercy act (although to a much lesser degree), but there is the compensation of seeing Ronald Reagan give one of his best performances as level-headed Yank.

Ronald Reagan *Yank* • Patricia Neal *Sister Margaret* • Richard Todd *Corporal Lachlan McLachlan* • Anthony Nicholls *Lieutenant Colonel Dunn* • Howard Marion-Crawford *Tommy* • Ralph Michael *Kiwi* • Alfie Bass *Orderly* ■ *Dir* Vincent Sherman • *Scr* Ranald MacDougall, from the play by John Patrick

Hatari! ★★★★ U
Adventure   1962 · US · Colour · 158mins

Howard Hawks's amiable safari romp – which he shot in East Africa – is ecologically sound, almost plotless, and so long that you can wander in and out of it with no sense of missing anything. But if you did, you would lose out on a wonderful and unique roller-coaster ride of fun and adventure, plus the sort of camaraderie between the likes of star John Wayne, director Hawks and writer Leigh Brackett that only long-term collaboration can produce. The movie also contains the best setting-a-dislocated-shoulder-by-hand scene ever. *Hatari!* has its detractors, but fie on them.

John Wayne *Sean Mercer* • Elsa Martinelli *Dallas* • Hardy Kruger *Kurt* • Red Buttons *Pockets* • Gérard Blain *Chip Maurey* • Michèle Girardon *Brandy* • Bruce Cabot *Indian* ■ *Dir* Howard Hawks • *Scr* Leigh Brackett, from a story by Harry Kurnitz

The Hatchet Man ★★
Crime melodrama   1932 · US · BW · 74mins

A year after Edward G Robinson played the title role in *Little Caesar*, he starred as Wong Low Get, an Oriental gangster, a terror of the Tongs. Loretta Young is in Chinese make-up, too, as Wong's ward and eventual bride, an event that causes the hatchets to come out. Sundry subplots and a trip to China, where J Carroll Naish is naturally a big cheese, fill in the screen time. Set in San Francisco, this melodrama aimed at being different from all those Chicago-set mob movies, and different it is. The flabby romance and unusually slow direction by William A Wellman produces a disappointing result.

Edward G Robinson *Wong Low Get* • Loretta Young *Toya San* • Dudley Digges *Nag Hong Fah* • Leslie Fenton *Harry En Hai* • Edmund Breese *Yu Chang* • Tully Marshall *Long Sen Yat* • J Carrol Naish *Sun Yat Sen* ■ *Dir* William Wellman [William A Wellman] • *Scr* JG Alexander, from the play *The Honourable Mr Wong* by Achmed Abdullah, David Belasco

Hatchet Man ★★★ 18
Thriller   1994 · US · Colour · 86mins

Two of video's biggest draws, Lance Henriksen and Eric Roberts, team up for this novel spin on *The Hitcher*. Essentially a two-hander, Henriksen plays a salesman travelling cross-country in a state being stalked by the serial killer of the title. When he reluctantly hooks up with sinister hitchhiker Roberts, it soon becomes apparent that both men have dark secrets to hide. Director Victor Salva edgily plays out the cat-and-mouse games between two dangerous men and is rewarded with relatively restrained performances from his leads. Contains violence, sex scenes, swearing and drug abuse. ▨

Lance Henriksen *Jack Powell* • Eric Roberts *Adrian (Dusty)* • Brion James *Sheriff Gordon* • Sasha Jenson *Gerald* • Ana Gabriel *Dahlia* ■ *Dir/Scr* Victor Salva

A Hatful of Rain ★★★
Drama   1957 · US · BW · 108mins

Don Murray stars as a Korean war veteran who keeps his heroin addiction a secret from his pregnant wife Eva Marie Saint. Described by director Fred Zinnemann as "the grimmest of all the films I ever made," this pioneering study of drug addiction remains a powerful experience, gaining enormously from the moody black-and-white CinemaScope photography of New York, its documentary detail and from Bernard Herrmann's music. The blacklisted Carl Foreman – who wrote Zinnemann's *High Noon* – wrote much of the script without screen credit.

Eva Marie Saint *Celia Pope* • Don Murray *Johnny Pope* • Anthony Franciosa *Polo* • Lloyd Nolan *John Pope Sr* • Henry Silva *Mother* • Gerald O'Loughlin [Gerald S O'Loughlin] *Chuck* • William Hickey *Apples* ■ *Dir* Fred Zinnemann • *Scr* Michael Vincent Gazzo, Alfred Hayes, Carl Foreman (uncredited), from the play by Michael Vincent Gazzo • *Cinematographer* Joe MacDonald

Hatter's Castle ★★★
Historical drama   1941 · UK · BW · 103mins

Although certain liberties were taken with AJ Cronin's novel, this is nevertheless an enthralling melodrama that combines an oppressive Gothic atmosphere with some untethered Victorian bombast. Overshadowing such stars in the making as Deborah Kerr and James Mason, Robert Newton gnaws at the exquisitely designed scenery as the Glasgow hatter who drives his family to the verge of madness in order to line his pockets and juggle his love life. Lance Comfort's direction is occasionally sensationalist, but he's wise to allow Newton his head, especially as such expert supports as Beatrice Varley (as his long-suffering wife) can more than cope with his scene-stealing.

Robert Newton *James Brodie* • Deborah Kerr *Mary Brodie* • Beatrice Varley *Mrs Brodie* • James Mason *Dr Renwick* • Emlyn Williams *Dennis* • Henry Oscar *Grierson* • Enid Stamp-Taylor *Nancy* ■ *Dir* Lance Comfort, James Carter • *Scr* Rodney Ackland, from the novel by AJ Cronin

Haunted ★

Horror   1976 · US · Colour

The spirit of a native American woman accused of witchcraft in the Civil War returns to an Arizona ghost town to persecute the descendants responsible for her plight. It's when Jim Negele falls in love with her reincarnation (Ann Michelle) that the curse swings properly into action. Incredibly literary dialogue, tasteful scares and pretentious direction are the only real curses worth mentioning with regards to this depressing flop.

Virginia Mayo *Michelle* • Aldo Ray • Jim Negele • Ann Michelle ■ *Dir/Scr* Michael DeGaetano

The Haunted ★★ 15

Thriller based on a true story
1991 · US · Colour · 87mins

A TV movie in the *Amityville Horror* vein, with a thin base and few extra toppings. It's the true story of the Smurl family, who claimed to suffer ten long years of demonic possession and poltergeist activity in their Pennsylvania home. The focus is on Janet Smurl, played by Sally Kirkland, who clung on to her faith while the church refused to believe her ghostly visions and exorcism pleas. Perfunctory direction at the outset does build towards a few chills, but not enough to warrant more than passing interest. 📼

Sally Kirkland *Janet Smurl* • Jeffrey DeMunn *Jack Smurl* • Louise Latham *Mary Smurl* • George D Wallace *John Smurl* • Joyce Van Patten *Cora Miller* • Diane Baker *Lorraine Warren* • Stephen Markle *Ed Warren* • William O'Connell *Father Kearney* • Allison Barron *Katie* ■ *Dir* Robert Mandel • *Scr* Darrah Cloud, from a non-fiction book by Robert Curran, Jack Smurl, Janet Smurl, Ed Warren, Lorraine Warren

Haunted ★★★ 15

Supernatural thriller
1995 · UK/US · Colour · 103mins

Right from the Edwardian prologue, a palpable air of malevolence hangs over this tale of murder, madness and memory. As the sceptic whose tragic past catches up with him as he investigates the supernatural at a Sussex stately home, Aidan Quinn gives a performance of substance and subtlety that perfectly complements the quirkier cameos of his co-stars. Kate Beckinsale makes a suitably creepy coquette and Anthony Andrews revels in his eccentricity, but topping the lot is Anna Massey's deliciously Danvers-esque nanny. Contains a sex scene and nudity. 📼

Aidan Quinn *David Ash* • Kate Beckinsale *Christina Mariell* • Anthony Andrews *Robert Mariell* • John Gielgud *Dr Doyle* • Anna Massey *Nanny Tess Webb* • Alex Lowe *Simon Mariell* • Geraldine Somerville *Kate* • Liz Smith *Old gypsy woman* ■ *Dir* Lewis Gilbert • *Scr* Tim Prager, Lewis Gilbert, Bob Kellet, from the novel by James Herbert

Haunted Honeymoon ★★ PG

Comedy horror   1986 · US · Colour · 79mins

Gene Wilder, who can often be relied upon to be funny as an actor, is here weighed down by his own directorial incompetence and by the fact that he borrows too heavily from other similar – but better – films in his attempt to emulate the earlier haunted-house scare movies. Those in mind of the classic Bob Hope vehicle *The Cat and the Canary* will be appalled at the lack of imagination and at the victory of noise over wit in this second-rate entry in the genre. Even Dom DeLuise can't save the day.

Gene Wilder *Larry Abbot* • Gilda Radner *Vickie Pearle* • Dom DeLuise *Aunt Kate* • Jonathan Pryce *Charles Abbot* • Paul L Smith *[Paul Smith] Dr Paul Abbot* • Peter Vaughan *Francis Sr* • Bryan Pringle *Pfister* • Roger Ashton-Griffiths *Francis Jr* • Jim Carter *Montego* ■ *Dir* Gene Wilder • *Scr* Gene Wilder, Terence Marsh

The Haunted House of Horror ★★

Horror   1969 · UK · Colour · 91mins

A psycho killer murders a Swinging Sixties' fashion victim at a happening in a suburban London mansion. Which of the thirtysomething actors playing teen revellers (including Frankie Avalon on a *Beach Party* vacation) is the crazed culprit? An effective shocker in its day – partly owing to some subtle gay overtones in the whodunit aspects of the plot, but the only screams of terror this elicits now come from the trendy outfits. Sexploitation horror maestro Michael Armstrong went on to direct the controversial witchfinder gore-fest *Mark of the Devil*.

Frankie Avalon *Chris* • Jill Haworth *Sheila* • Richard O'Sullivan *Peter* • Veronica Doran *Madge* • Julian Barnes *Richard* • Robin Stewart *Henry* • Mark Wynter *Gary* • Gina Warwick *Sylvia* • Clifford Earl *Police sergeant* ■ *Dir* Michael Armstrong • *Scr* Michael Armstrong, Peter Marcus

The Haunted Palace ★★★ 18

Horror   1963 · US · Colour · 83mins

Enjoy a double dose of horror from the guru of ghoul, Vincent Price, who plays two characters in Roger Corman's creepy tale of curses; although the title is borrowed from an Edgar Allan Poe poem, the tale is based on an HP Lovecraft story, *The Case of Charles Dexter Ward*. Price is at his deliciously evil best, wreaking terrible revenge on a local community. Horror veteran Lon Chaney Jr is also on hand to give his customary chilling support, playing Price's faithful servant. 📼

Vincent Price *Charles Dexter Ward/Joseph Curwen* • Debra Paget *Ann Ward* • Lon Chaney Jr *Simon Orne* • Frank Maxwell *Dr Marinus Willet* • Leo Gordon *Edgar Weeden* • Elisha Cook [Elisha Cook Jr] *Peter Smith* ■ *Dir* Roger Corman • *Scr* Charles Beaumont, from the story *The Case of Charles Dexter Ward* by HP Lovecraft

Haunted Summer ★★ 18

Historical romantic drama
1988 · US · Colour · 102mins

Yet another treatment of the meeting between poets Byron and Shelley, writer Mary Godwin and Dr Polidori in Italy in 1816. Despite the acting efforts of Philip Anglim, Laura Dern, Alice Krige and Eric Stoltz, this tale makes unconvincing history. Director Ivan Passer – who made cult favourite *Cutter's Way* –seems determined to lower the drama just as Ken Russell, with the similarly themed *Gothic*, upped it. 📼

Eric Stoltz *Percy Shelley* • Philip Anglim *Lord Byron* • Alice Krige *Mary Godwin* • Laura Dern *Claire Clairmont* • Alex Winter *John Polidori* • Peter Berling *Maurice* • Don Hodson *Rushton* ■ *Dir* Ivan Passer • *Scr* Lewis John Carlino, from the novel by Anne Edwards

The Haunting ★★★★★ 12

Horror   1963 · US · BW · 107mins

One of the best supernatural chillers ever made. Richard Johnson is the psychic researcher who brings along two mediums to help him investigate a monstrously haunted mansion steeped in spectral phenomena. All the more effective for keeping its horrors unseen, director Robert Wise's masterful adaptation of Shirley Jackson's *The Haunting of Hill House* is a subtle exercise in frighteningly invisible terror: all you see are pulsating walls and all you hear are loud pounding noises. Julie Harris shines as the spinster worst affected by the poltergeist events, whose psychological state is cleverly kept in question. 📼

Julie Harris *Eleanor Vance* • Claire Bloom *Theodora* • Richard Johnson *Dr John Markway* • Russ Tamblyn *Luke Sanderson* • Fay Compton *Mrs Sanderson* • Rosalie Crutchley *Mrs Dudley* • Lois Maxwell *Grace Markway* • Valentine Dyall *Mr Dudley* • Diane Clare *Carrie Fredericks* ■ *Dir* Robert Wise • *Scr* Nelson Gidding, from the novel *The Haunting of Hill House* by Shirley Jackson

The Haunting ★★ 12

Supernatural horror
1999 · US · Colour · 113mins

Nothing to scream over, and certainly nothing to shout about, director Jan De Bont's remake of Robert Wise's 1963 classic is a frightless wonder, which isn't the least bit scary despite using computer-generated animation to show all the poltergeist activity (effectively unseen in the original, but yawningly overblown here). Hokey in the extreme, with a daft script and numerous unintentional laughs, only the imposing and beautifully designed baroque sets (evoking *Citizen Kane* at every turn) impress in this shallow and artificial spookfest. 📼

Liam Neeson *Dr David Marrow* • Catherine Zeta-Jones *Theo* • Owen Wilson *Luke Sanderson* • Lili Taylor *Eleanor "Nell" Vance* • Bruce Dern *Mr Dudley* • Marian Seldes *Mrs Dudley* • Virginia Madsen *Jane* ■ *Dir* Jan De Bont • *Scr* David Self, from the novel *The Haunting of Hill House* by Shirley Jackson • *Production Designer* Eugenio Zanetti

Haunting Fear ★ 18

Horror drama   1990 · Colour · 84mins

A Poe-faced horror romp, loosely based on Edgar Allan's *The Premature Burial*, about a husband and mistress conniving to drive his wife (video "scream queen" Brinke Stevens) round the twist. Jan-Michael Vincent and Karen Black star in this schlocky horror picture show from B-movie master Fred Olen Ray, and you may recognise the faces of fright stalwarts Robert Quarry (*Count Yorga, Vampire*) and Michael Berryman (*Hills Have Eyes*) lurking about in the background. Two stars for fans of kitsch 'n' stinkers. One star for anyone else. 📼

Jan-Michael Vincent *Lt James Trent* • Karen Black *Dr Julia Harcourt* • Jay Richardson *Terry Monroe* • Michael Berryman *Mortician* • Brinke Stevens *Victoria Monroe* • Robert Quarry *Visconti* ■ *Dir* Fred Olen Ray • *Scr* Sherman Scott [Sam Newfield], from the short story *The Premature Burial* by Edgar Allan Poe

The Haunting of Helen Walker ★★★ 15

Supernatural period drama
1995 · US · Colour · 87mins

Valerie Bertinelli, the star of the eighties' sitcom *One Day at a Time*, looks somewhat out of place in this adaptation of Henry James's classic tale *The Turn of the Screw*. As you would expect of the prolific British TV dramatist Hugh Whitemore, this version includes a polished screenplay, but it lacks the palpable menace of Jack Clayton's 1961 version *The Innocents*. Diana Rigg, Michael Gough and Paul Rhys add a touch of class beyond the wildest dreams of most TV movies. Contains some swearing and sexual references. 📼

Valerie Bertinelli *Helen Walker* • Diana Rigg *Mrs Grose* • Florence Hoath *Flora Goffe* • Michael Gough *Barnaby* • Aled Roberts *Miles Goffe* • Paul Rhys *Edward Goffe* • Christopher Guard *Peter Quint* • Elizabeth Morton *Miss Jessel* • Tricia Thorns *Peggy* • Aisling Flitton *Connie* ■ *Dir* Tom McLoughlin • *Scr* Hugh Whitemore, from the novel *The Turn of the Screw* by Henry James

The Haunting of Lisa ★★★

Supernatural thriller
1996 · US · Colour · 99mins

TV-movie icon Cheryl Ladd takes the lead role in this watchable, if sanitised, slice of supernatural hokum. She plays a mother who is disturbed to discover that her nine-year-old daughter (Aemilia Robinson) is having visions of a mysterious woman who seems to hold the key to some brutal murders plaguing the city. Ladd is plucky in the lead role and there are adequate performances from an unfamiliar supporting cast. Director Don McBrearty develops a nice line in eerie suspense. Contains some swearing.

Cheryl Ladd *Ellen Downey* • Duncan Regehr *Mitchell Graham* • Wayne Northrop *Bob Marsden* • Don Allison *Father Aiken* • Aemilia Robinson *Lisa Downey* • Kate Lynch *Anne* ■ *Dir* Don McBrearty • *Scr* Don Henry

The Haunting of Morella ★★★

Horror   1990 · US · Colour · 87mins

Roger Corman recaptures the energy and essence of his own Poe series from the sixties in this production for his New Horizons company directed by schlock regular James Wynorski. David McCallum lends great authority to his role as a blind New England recluse whose witch wife was burned at the stake. Unfortunately, her spirit returns in the body of her grown-up daughter and a new reign of terror begins. Tarted up with modish gore, lesbianism and grisly violence, this hugely entertaining neo-Gothic romp is packed with cheap thrills and sacrificial blood-letting. Contains violence, sex scenes and nudity.

David McCallum *Gideon* • Nicole Eggert *Morella/Lenora* • Christopher Halsted *Guy* • Lana Clarkson *Coel Deveroux* • Maria Ford

Diane • Jonathan Farwell *Doctor Gault* ■ *Dir* Jim Wynorski • *Scr* RJ Robertson, from the story by Edgar Allan Poe

The Haunting of Seacliff Inn ★★ 15

Supernatural thriller
1994 · US · Colour · 89mins

Although this sounds like it should be a thirties Tod Slaughter barnstormer, it is in fact a recent TV movie about a couple who open a guesthouse in the hope of saving their failing marriage. There's nothing original about stories featuring old dark houses that are given a psychic pick-me-up by the arrival of new occupants, and try as director Walter Klenhard might, he simply doesn't have the script or the budget to pull off this corny chiller. Contains some swearing, violence and brief nudity. ▣

Ally Sheedy *Susan Enright* • William R Moses *Mark Enright* • Louise Fletcher *Dorothy O'Hara* • Lucinda Weist *Sara Warner* • Tom McCleister *John* ■ *Dir* Walter Klenhard • *Scr* Walter Klenhard, Tom Walla

The Haunting Passion ★ 15

Romantic drama 1983 · US · Colour · 91mins

Jane Seymour's presence in a film brings with it certain expectations of sappy romance, daft plotting and those luxuriant tresses. Seen here in her pre-Dr Quinn days, this has Seymour falling under the spell of a hunky ghost whose charms seem to outweigh – temporarily at least – those of her husband Gerald McRaney. This lifeless TV movie is not so much beyond the grave as beyond the pale; it doesn't haunt but it will bore. ▣

Jane Seymour *Julie Evans* • Gerald McRaney *Dan Evans* • Millie Perkins *Lois* • Ruth Nelson *Mrs Granville* • Paul Rossilli *Jonathan* • Ivan Bonar *Thorne Abbot* • Lisa Britt *Karen* ■ *Dir* John Korty • *Scr* Michael Berk, Douglas Schwartz

Hav Plenty ★★ 15

Romantic comedy
1998 · US · Colour · 83mins

"Newcomer Christopher Scott Cherot writes, directs and stars in this gauche romantic comedy. Such an egocentric creation can sometimes pay off but, as often as not, the film trips up on its own Freudian slip. Lee Plenty (Cherot) is an aspiring writer who is suffering from writer's block and living in his car until his rich friend Havilland Savage (Chenoa Maxwell) invites him to Washington DC for New Year's Eve. There the hapless Plenty is besieged in numerous ways by every woman in sight. That Hav and Plenty will make a lovely couple is a truth that seems to evade everyone except Hav's gran and, of course, the audience. Contains swearing and some violence. ▣

Christopher Scott Cherot *Lee Plenty* • Chenoa Maxwell *Havilland Savage* • Hill Harper *Michael Simmons* • Tammi Katherine Jones *Caroline Gooden* • Robinne Lee *Leigh Darling* ■ *Dir/Scr* Christopher Scott Cherot

Havana ★★★ 15

Romantic thriller
1990 · US · Colour · 138mins

Robert Redford's seventh collaboration with director Sydney Pollack was one of the box-office bombs of the nineties. But this *Casablanca* clone sits rather nicely on the small screen and makes for polished, if occasionally pedestrian, entertainment. As there's surprisingly little passion between Redford and his co-star Lena Olin, the main interest here lies in the excellence of the supporting cast, with Alan Arkin typically assured as a shady casino boss, Raul Julia convincing as Olin's pro-Communist husband and Tomas Milian truly unnerving as the brutal police chief. With a little judicious pruning, this could have been so much better. Contains swearing, violence and sex scenes. ▣ *DVD*

Robert Redford *Jack Weil* • Lena Olin *Roberta "Bobby" Duran* • Alan Arkin *Joe Volpi* • Tomas Milian *Menocal* • Daniel Davis *Marion Chigwell* • Tony Plana *Julio Ramos* • Betsy Brantley *Diane* • Lise Cutter *Patty* • Raul Julia *Arturo Duran* • Mark Rydell *Meyer Lansky* ■ *Dir* Sydney Pollack • *Scr* Judith Rascoe, David Rayfiel, from a story by Judith Rascoe

Havana Widows ★★

Comedy 1933 · US · BW · 63mins

In most respects this is a *Gold Diggers* movie with Joan Blondell, but one misses the songs and those suggestive Busby Berkeley dance routines. Blondell and Glenda Farrell play unemployed chorus girls on the loose in Cuba and looking for sugardaddies – after they lose their jobs and borrow some cash from their gangster friends. Mobsters and the usual showbiz intrigue make the tropicana setting somewhat superfluous, but for fans of this sort of movie it's probably still funny and charmingly raffish.

Joan Blondell *Mae Knight* • Glenda Farrell *Sadie Appleby* • Guy Kibbee *Deacon Jones* • Lyle Talbot *Bob Jones* • Allen Jenkins *Herman Brody* ■ *Dir* Ray Enright • *Scr* Earl Baldwin

Have Rocket, Will Travel ★★ U

Science-fiction comedy
1959 · US · BW · 76mins

As their movie contract with Columbia came to an end, the Three Stooges thought their careers were over, but this juvenile romp in outer space put them back on top as firm family favourites. The trio (with new Stooge Joe De Rita) play cleaners at a rocket base who accidentally send themselves to Venus, where they encounter a talking unicorn, a brain machine, a flame-throwing giant spider and doppelgangers of themselves. Silly, aimless fun substituting painful sight gags and weird sound effects for any shred of wit or invention.

Moe Howard *Moe* • Larry Fine *Larry* • Joe De Rita *Curley Joe* • Jerome Cowan *JP Morse* • Anna-Lisa *Dr Ingrid Naarveg* • Bob Colbert [Robert Colbert] *Dr Ted Benson* ■ *Dir* David Lowell Rich • *Scr* Raphael Hayes

Having Our Say: the Delany Sisters' First 100 Years ★★★

Biographical drama 1999 · US · Colour

The chronicle of African-American sisters Sadie and Bessie Delany, who lived into their hundreds, spawned this made-for-TV movie, a bestseller and a Broadway play. Derived from the interviews of *New York Times* journalist Amy Hill Hearth, the story relates their upbringing on a university campus, their acute experiences of racism and prejudice and their individual achievements in pioneering their careers as a teacher and dentist in New York City. A compelling tale, well performed and executed.

Diahann Carroll *Sarah L "Sadie" Delany* • Ruby Dee *Annie Elizabeth "Bessie" Delany* • Amy Madigan *Amy Hill Hearth* • Lisa Arrindell Anderson *Sadie in her 20s* • Mykel T Williamson *Papa Delany* • Lonette McKee *Mama Delany* ■ *Dir* Lynne Littman • *Scr* Emily Mann, from the book *Having Our Say* by Sarah L Delany, A Elizabeth Delany, Amy Hill Hearth

Having Wonderful Time ★★★

Romance 1938 · US · BW · 69mins

Arthur Kober's satirical play about Jewish New Yorkers on holiday in the Catskills lost much of its nuance in this movie version – despite being adapted by Kober himself – but it certainly benefited from a sparkling RKO cast, headed by the marvellous Ginger Rogers and Lucille Ball. The film is a veritable treasure trove for fans of the period: that's Dean Jagger as Ginger's brother, plus Eve Arden and Ann Miller among the holidaymakers. Red Skelton, billed as Richard, makes an impressive feature debut, and most of the folks at Camp Kare-Free, for that matter, will seem like old buddies.

Ginger Rogers *Teddy Shaw* • Douglas Fairbanks Jr *Chick Kirkland* • Peggy Conklin *Fay Coleman* • Lucille Ball *Miriam* • Lee Bowman *Buzzy Armbuster* • Eve Arden *Henrietta* • Dorothea Kent *Maxine* • Richard Skelton [Red Skelton] *Itchy Faulkner* • Dean Jagger *Charlie* ■ *Dir* Alfred Santell • *Scr* Arthur Kober, from his play

Hawaii ★★★ PG

Historical drama
1966 · US · Colour · 181mins

The fact that this adaptation of James Michener's novel was nominated for seven Oscars and won none is a clue that here is a big empty movie which middlebrow Hollywood felt had something significant to say. Packed with tempestuous love affairs, natural disasters, culture clashes and slick action sequences, the film does little more than transfer the familiar western pioneering theme to the Pacific island. This meander through 20 years of the 19th century would be intolerably dull without the towering performance of Max von Sydow, who almost makes his unyielding missionary sympathetic in spite of his monstrous views. ▣

Max von Sydow *Abner Hale* • Julie Andrews *Jerusha Bromley* • Richard Harris *Rafer Hoxworth* • Carroll O'Connor *Charles Bromley* • Elizabeth Cole *Abigail Bromley* • Diane Sherry *Charity Bromley* • Heather Menzies *Mercy Bromley* • Torin Thatcher *Reverend Thorn* • Gene Hackman *John Whipple* ■ *Dir* George Roy Hill • *Scr* Dalton Trumbo, Daniel Taradash, from the novel by James Michener

The Hawk ★★★ 15

Thriller 1992 · UK · Colour · 83mins

An intriguing home-grown movie which, rumour has it, was inspired by the Yorkshire Ripper investigation. Women in the North East are being killed and a housewife has noticed that each murder coincides with her husband scuttling away on business with his DIY hammer on walkabout from the shed. A talented clutch of thespians, including Helen Mirren, Owen Teale and Rosemary Leach, lend a somewhat over-bleak and murky thriller some much-needed depth and spark. Not quite of the calibre of Mirren's *Prime Suspect*, but worth a peek nonetheless. Contains swearing. ▣

Helen Mirren *Annie Marsh* • George Costigan *Stephen Marsh* • Rosemary Leach *Mrs Marsh* • Melanie Hill *Norma* • Owen Teale *Ken Marsh* • Clive Russell *Chief Inspector Daybury* • Christopher Madin *Matthew Marsh* • Marie Hamer *Jackie Marsh* • David Harewood *Sergeant Streete* • Pooky Quesnel *WPC Clarke* • Caroline Paterson *Jan* • John Duttine *John* • Nadim Sawalha *Bahnu* ■ *Dir* David Hayman • *Scr* Peter Ransley, from his novel

Hawk the Slayer ★ PG

Fantasy adventure
1980 · UK · Colour · 89mins

Not so much swords-and-sorcery as rubber rapiers and woeful witchcraft as good brother John Terry battles with bad brother Jack Palance for possession of a mystic blade. Gimmicky direction by Terry Marcel can't hide the low budget of this production, though Palance – once described by the late Dilys Powell as having the face of King Cobra – hisses and vows vengeance as though he were in a movie worthy of his venomous talents. It's a British Arthurian concept, debased by trite ideas and a banal approach. ▣

Jack Palance *Voltan* • John Terry *Hawk* • Bernard Bresslaw *Gort* • Ray Charleson *Crow* • Peter O'Farrell *Baldin* • Morgan Sheppard *Ranulf* • Cheryl Campbell *Sister Monica* • Annette Crosbie *Abbess* • Roy Kinnear *Innkeeper* • Warren Clarke *Scar* ■ *Dir* Terry Marcel • *Scr* Harry Robertson, Terry Marcel

Hawken's Breed ★★

Western 1989 · US · Colour · 93mins

Low-budget western that looks like it was shot in someone's back garden. The main interest resides in its always watchable star, Peter Fonda, sadly reduced to making B-movies like this during his "wilderness" years. Veteran cowboy actor Jack Elam also appears. Director Charles B Pierce specialises in genre no-budgeters – his other films include *The Legend of Boggy Creek* and the risible *The Norseman*.

Peter Fonda *Hawken* • Jack Elam *Tackett* • Bill Thurman *Jeb Kine* • Serene Hedin *Spirit* • Chuck Pierce Jr *Noel Hickman* • Sue Anne Langdon [Sue Ane Langdon] *Holly Clawson* • Dennis Fimple *Crawley* ■ *Dir/Scr* Charles B Pierce

Hawks ★★★ 15

Black comedy drama
1988 · UK · Colour · 105mins

Taking a break from his 007 capers, Timothy Dalton opted for this modest little black comedy set in London and the Netherlands. Dalton is the charismatic lawyer stricken with cancer, who lifts fellow sufferer Anthony Edwards (Dr Greene in the TV series *ER*) out of his gloom and whisks him away to Amsterdam for one final fling. Sentimentality is never far from the surface, but the enthusiastic playing of the two stars overcomes the

U = SUITABLE FOR ALL   Uc = SUITABLE FOR ALL, ESPECIALLY FOR YOUNG CHILDREN (VIDEO ONLY)   PG = PARENTAL GUIDANCE

more mawkish moments, and there are refreshing turns from Camille Coduri and Janet McTeer as the two English girls they meet on the continent. Contains swearing. 🖵

Timothy Dalton *Bancroft* • Anthony Edwards *Deckermensky, "Decker"* • Janet McTeer *Hazel* • Camille Coduri *Maureen* • Julie T Wallace *Ward sister* • Connie Booth *Nurse Jarvis* • Robert Lang *Walter Bancroft* • Jill Bennett *Vivian Bancroft* • Sheila Hancock *Regina* • Caroline Langrishe *Carol* ■ *Dir* Robert Ellis Miller • *Scr* Roy Clarke, from an idea by Barry Gibb, David English

Hawks and Sparrows ★★★★ PG

Fantasy   1966 · It · BW · 84mins

Working for the last time in monochrome, Pier Paolo Pasolini conceived this allegorical fantasy as a showcase for the legendary comic actor, Toto, and newcomer Ninetto Davoli. In addition to playing a couple of modern-day vagabonds, they also appear in a parable related by a talking crow, in which a pair of 12th-century monks are detailed by St Francis of Assisi to convert the birds to Christianity. Their lack of success in the parable is reflected back in the present day as Pasolini parodies Fellini, Rossellini and himself, and in so doing rejects Marxism, Catholicism and neorealism as the answer to Italy's problems. With excellent music from Ennio Morricone, this is one of the controversial director's more humorous offerings. Italian dialogue dubbed into English. 🖵

Totò *Innocenti Totò/brother Ciccillo* • Ninetto Davoli *Innocenti Ninetto/brother Ninetto* • Femi Benussi *Luna* • Rossana Di Rocco *Ninetto's friend* • Lena Lin Solaro *Urganda la Sconosciuta* ■ *Dir/Scr* Pier Paolo Pasolini

Hawk's Vengeance ★★ 18

Action adventure
1996 · Can · Colour · 92mins

Another proficient straight-to-video thriller with Gary Daniels, who plays an ex-special forces officer trying to find the killers of his stepbrother. The trail leads to a white supremacist gang, who also happen to dabble in the human-organs trade. Jayne Heitmeyer provides the female interest, while Daniels is almost overshadowed by chief villain Cass Magda, a genuine martial-arts expert who provides a masterclass in sword and stick fighting.

Gary Daniels *Solo* • Jayne Heitmeyer *Lizzie* • Cass Magda • Vlasta Vrana • Charles Biddle Jr ■ *Dir* Marc F Voizard • *Scr* Michael Ellis, John Maxwell

Hawmps ★★ PG

Comedy western
1976 · US · Colour · 113mins

Sounds funny: a cavalry troop switching to camels for transport. Despite being based on a true incident, the camel corps idea is not enough to sustain a film, and it shows. Slim Pickens, who rode the bomb to destruction in *Dr Strangelove*, joins the slapstick. How long can you watch before getting the hump? 🖵

James Hampton *Howard Clemmons* • Christopher Connelly *Uriah Tibbs* • Slim Pickens *Naman Tucker* • Denver Pyle *Colonel*

Seymour Hawkins • Gene Conforti *Hi Jolly* • Mimi Maynard *Jennifer Hawkins* • Jack Elam *Bad Jack Cutter* ■ *Dir* Joe Camp • *Scr* William Bickley, Michael Warren, from a story by Joe Camp, William Bickley, Michael Warren

Häxan ★★★★ 15

Silent horror documentary
1921 · Swe · BW · 87mins

Danish director Benjamin Christensen's documentary-style investigation into *Witchcraft through the Ages* (the English title) employs an array of cinematic devices, with etchings, manuscripts and re-enacted episodes (in which Christensen himself plays the Devil). Three years in the making, the film sees the witch as a harmless victim of a superstitious and repressive Church. This illuminating, frightening and amusing film was banned in some countries at the time, ostensibly because of its violence and nudity, but its anticlericalism might have weighed more heavily with the censors. It was Christensen's most famous film; he subsequently directed a few minor horror films in Hollywood in the late twenties. 🖵

Benjamin Christensen *The Devil/The fashionable doctor* • Ella La Cour *Karna, the witch* • Emmy Schönfeld *Karna's collaborator* • Kate Fabian *Lovesick maiden* ■ *Dir/Scr* Benjamin Christensen

A Hazard of Hearts ★★ PG

Romantic drama   1987 · UK · Colour · 89mins

Totally over the top and thoroughly enjoyable, this Barbara Cartland romantic thriller stars Helena Bonham Carter and Edward Fox. Helena plays tenacious Serena Staverly, who's sent to live with distant relative and harpy Diana Rigg. There she falls in love with emotionally frigid rake Marcus Gilbert and uncovers a dastardly smuggling plot. The end is inevitable – triumphant love and no tongues. Trashy, terrible but completely watchable, it's so bad you won't be able to turn it off, and there's a splendid cameo from Stewart Granger. 🖵

Diana Rigg *Lady Harriet Vulcan* • Edward Fox *Lord Harry Wrotham* • Helena Bonham Carter *Serena Staverly* • Fiona Fullerton *Lady Isabel Gillingham* • Neil Dickson *Nicholas* • Marcus Gilbert *Lord Vulcan* • Christopher Plummer *Sir Giles Staverly* • Stewart Granger *Old Vulcan* ■ *Dir* John Hough • *Scr* Terence Feely, from the novel by Barbara Cartland

The Hazing ★ 15

Drama   1977 · US · Colour · 84mins

Imagine *National Lampoon's Animal House* without the jokes or a decent director. That's this dud, which sounds like a horror film but isn't, although it does use the stalk-and-slash plot staple of a college fraternity initiation prank that goes wrong, killing a student. Director Douglas Curtis, in his debut outing, accents the campus students hushing up the death and how they crack under the pressure for his main narrative thrust. Despite the presence of Charlie Martin Smith (*The Untouchables*), there's little to recommend in this hazily executed melodrama. 🖵

Charlie Martin Smith [Charles Martin Smith] *Barney* • Jeff East *Craig* • Brad David *Rod* •

Kelly Moran *Wendy* • David Hayward *Carl* ■ *Dir* Douglas Curtis • *Scr* Bruce Shelley, David Ketchum

He Got Game ★★★★ 15

Sports drama   1998 · US · Colour · 130mins

This superb sports drama from writer/director Spike Lee sets out to prove that basketball is not just a game, but rather an essential part of the American way of life. From the opening shots of young men at obsessive play, set to music by Aaron Copland, Lee sets the tone of a world in which Jake Shuttlesworth (a powerful portrayal by Denzel Washington) is allowed out of prison – where he's serving a term for his wife's manslaughter – to talk his son Jesus (real-life pro Ray Allen), into becoming part of the prison warden's old college basketball team, and get himself paroled into the bargain. The confrontations feel real, the games have tension and the underlying message is universally scathing – sport is no longer for kudos, but purely for the money. Contains swearing, sex scenes and some violence. 🖵

Denzel Washington *Jake Shuttlesworth* • Ray Allen *Jesus Shuttlesworth* • Milla Jovovich *Dakota Burns* • Rosario Dawson *Lala Bonilla* • Hill Harper *Coleman "Booger" Sykes* • Ned Beatty *Warden Wyatt* • Jim Brown *Spivey* • Bill Nunn *Uncle Bubba* • John Turturro *Coach Billy Sunday* • Lonette McKee *Martha Shuttlesworth* ■ *Dir/Scr* Spike Lee

He Is My Brother ★

Adventure   1974 · US · Colour

Guess the ending from the title of this well-intentioned message picture that's badly miscast, languidly directed and hopelessly anodyne? One-time teen idol Bobby Sherman and his best friend Robbie Rist are shipwrecked on a South Sea Island leper colony and become the focal point of a religious power struggle, as love and courage conquer fear and superstition. Nice scenery, shame about the movie.

Bobby Sherman *Jeff* • Keenan Wynn *Dalton* • Robbie Rist *Randy* • Joaquin Martinez *Kahuna* • Benson Fong *Kiko* • Kathy Paulo *Luana* ■ *Dir* Edward Dmytryk • *Scr* David Pritchard

He Knows You're Alone ★★ 18

Thriller   1981 · US · Colour · 89mins

Recycling an idea from the Bela Lugosi shocker *The Corpse Vanishes* in 1942, this predictably heavy-handed slasher movie has a killer stalking brides-to-be, terrorising them with increasingly ugly games of cat-and-mouse. No real surprises here, unless you count the fact that the director Armand Mastroianni is the late Marcello's cousin, and a young Tom Hanks makes his film acting debut. Hanks paid sly homage to this career step in his feature-directing debut *That Thing You Do!* by insisting on filming at the exact same Staten Island locations used here. Contains violence. 🖵

Don Scardino *Marvin* • Caitlin O'Heaney *Amy Jensen* • Elizabeth Kemp *Nancy* • Tom Rolfing *Killer* • Lewis Arlt *Len Gamble* • Patsy Pease *Joyce* • James Rebhorn *Carl* • Tom Hanks *Elliot* • Paul Gleason *Daley* ■ *Dir* Armand Mastroianni • *Scr* Scott Parker

He Laughed Last ★★

Comedy   1956 · US · Colour · 76mins

Blake Edwards's second outing as a writer/director, co-scripted with Richard Quine, is a satire on the gangster movie. Lead actor is Frankie Laine, a recording star who's perhaps best known for singing the title number to TV's *Rawhide*, later used to fun effect in *The Blues Brothers*. Laine plays a nightclub owner whose employee Lucy Marlow is a dancer and hostess who inherits a mobster's fortune, much to the dismay of her policeman boyfriend. There are musical numbers, fun with gangster conventions and Marlow is a dish, but it doesn't disguise the fact that this is a dime-budget offering.

Frankie Laine *Gino Lupo* • Lucy Marlow *Rosemary Lebeau* • Anthony Dexter *Dominic* • Dick Long [Richard Long] *Jimmy Murphy* • Alan Reed *Big Dan Hennessy* ■ *Dir* Blake Edwards • *Scr* Blake Edwards, from a story by Blake Edwards, Richard Quine

He Ran All the Way ★★★

Crime drama   1951 · US · BW · 77mins

John Garfield's final role saw him give a typically intense performance as a thug on the run after a payroll robbery. Life seems to be improving when he (briefly) finds sanctuary with Shelley Winters. Then Garfield's tendency to panic leaves Winters to choose between her father and her lover. A happy ending seems unlikely, however, as was the case with the actor, whose career suffered during the Communist witch-hunts in fifties' Hollywood.

John Garfield *Nick* • Shelley Winters *Peg* • Wallace Ford *Mr Dobbs* • Selena Royle *Mrs Dobbs* • Gladys George *Mrs Robey* • Norman Lloyd *Al Molin* • Bobby Hyatt *Tommy Dobbs* ■ *Dir* John Berry • *Scr* Guy Endore, Hugo Butler, from the novel by Sam Ross

He Rides Tall ★★

Western   1964 · US · BW · 83mins

Tony Young was an American TV star in a violent (for its time) western series called *Gunslinger*, and Universal released two vehicles for him theatrically: this one, a stark, grim story that was X-rated in the UK, and a companion piece called *Taggart*. Both were directed by western veteran RG Springsteen, best remembered for *Come Next Spring*, and both went out as support features to little acclaim. This is the (marginally) better of the two, benefiting as it does from a fine late performance from the superb Dan Duryea, but Young simply didn't have what it takes to be a movie star.

Tony Young *Marshal Morg Rocklin* • Dan Duryea *Bart Thorne* • Jo Morrow *Kate McCloud* • Madlyn Rhue *Ellie Daniels* • RG Armstrong *Josh McCloud* ■ *Dir* RG Springsteen • *Scr* Charles W Irwin, Robert Creighton Williams, from a story by Charles W Irwin

He Said, She Said ★★★ 15

Comedy   1991 · US · Colour · 110mins

Watch out for a pre-*Basic Instinct* Sharon Stone as a sexy siren in this comedy about two warring TV talk show hosts (Kevin Bacon and Elizabeth Perkins) who carry on their relationship both in front of and behind the cameras. The film is split into two halves (one directed by Ken Kwapis, the other by his wife Marisa Silver) so you see the romance from each point of view. Both Bacon and Perkins are attractively amiable, but neither manages to sustain the comedy to the end and, after part one, it does get a bit tedious seeing the same events from a slightly different perspective. Contains some swearing. ▣

Kevin Bacon *Dan Hanson* • Elizabeth Perkins *Lorie Bryer* • Sharon Stone *Linda* • Nathan Lane *Wally Thurman* • Anthony LaPaglia *Mark* • Stanley Anderson *Mr Weller* • Brad Pitt ■ *Dir* Ken Kwapis, Marisa Silver • *Scr* Brian Hohlfeld, from his story

He Walked by Night ★★★ 🅿🄶
Thriller   1948 · US · BW · 78mins

One of those economic miracles – a B-thriller made for peanuts which manages to create some vivid images and a high degree of tension. Its success is mainly owing to ace cameraman John Alton, a master of black-and-white moodiness, while Anthony Mann is thought to have given credited director Alfred Werker a hand on some scenes. Richard Basehart stars as a thief who kills a cop and is tracked down by the Los Angeles police. Much emphasis is placed on detection methods and on Basehart's personality: a loner with a pet dog, obsessed by technical precision. It's a compelling character study that also delivers in terms of action, notably a shoot-out in the storm drains of LA. ▣

Richard Basehart *Davis Morgan* • Scott Brady *Sergeant Marty Brennan* • Roy Roberts *Captain Breen* • James Cardwell *Chuck Jones* • Whit Bissell *Reeves* ■ *Dir* Alfred Werker • *Scr* John C Higgins, Crane Wilbur, Harry Essex, from a story by Crane Wilbur • *Cinematographer* John Alton

He Was Her Man ★★★
Crime drama   1934 · US · BW · 70mins

Snappy, exuberant, Roaring Twenties-like thriller, with James Cagney as the safecracker who gives up a life of crime to scare off rivals who've been trying to put him inside. Joan Blondell is the wisecracker who stands by him and pulls him through, while Lloyd Bacon directs in the tradition of machine-gun macho.

James Cagney *Flicker Hayes* • Joan Blondell *Rose Lawrence* • Victor Jory *Nick Gardella* • Frank Craven *Pop Sims* • Harold Huber *JC Ward* • Russell Hopton *Monk* • Ralf Harolde *Red Deering* • Sarah Padden *Mrs Gardella* ■ *Dir* Lloyd Bacon • *Scr* Tom Buckingham, Niven Busch, from a story by Robert Lord

He Who Gets Slapped
★★★★
Silent drama   1924 · US · BW · 72mins

Lon Chaney Sr gives one of his best performances in the film version of Leonid Andreyev's Broadway success. *The Man of a 1,000 Faces* plays a disillusioned scientist whose professional disappointments force him to alter his appearance and join the circus as a clown. But instead of finding happiness and freedom in a world of total make-believe, he soon discovers a different grief lies hidden beneath the greasepaint and tinsel. Beautifully told, and flawlessly directed by Victor Sjöström (making his second

film in the US), this unsentimental and probing look at the Big Top is a poetic silent masterpiece.

Lon Chaney *Paul Beaumont/"He Who Gets Slapped"* • Norma Shearer *Consuelo* • John Gilbert *Bezano* • Tully Marshall *Count Mancini* • Marc MacDermott *Baron Regnard* • Ford Sterling *Tricaud* ■ *Dir* Victor Seastrom [Victor Sjöström] • *Scr* Carey Wilson, Victor Seastrom [Victor Sjöström], from the play *He, the One Who Gets Slapped* by Leonid Andreyev, translated by Gregory Zilboorg

He Who Rides a Tiger ★★
Crime drama   1965 · UK · BW · 102mins

This crime melodrama is a "kitchen sink" tale – overflowing with soap – that's as schizophrenic as its cat burglar protagonist, played by Tom Bell. One moment he's soft on orphans and the eager Judi Dench; the next he's stealing jewels from stately homes and erupting into demented violence. Bell admirably combines both personality traits in his performance, but the shifts from realism to romanticism in Trevor Peacock's script are less credible. And, while director Charles Crichton makes the most of his rundown urban locations, he can't decide whether to place the emphasis on suspense, sentiment or social comment.

Tom Bell *Peter Rayston* • Judi Dench *Joanne* • Paul Rogers *Superintendent Taylor* • Kay Walsh *Mrs Woodley* • Ray McAnally *Orphanage superintendent* • Jeremy Spenser *The Panda* • Peter Madden *Peepers Woodley* ■ *Dir* Charles Crichton • *Scr* Trevor Peacock

Head ★★★★ 🅿🄶
Musical comedy   1968 · US · Colour · 85mins

Bob Rafelson had been the brains behind the Monkees, the American pop group formed in the image of the Beatles specifically for an NBC TV series. With the band's popularity on the wane, he and co-writer Jack Nicholson fashioned this psychedelic romp that beefed up the usual bubblegum slapstick with Vietnam footage and old movie clips. It went over the heads of most fans in 1968, but it's essential viewing for anyone who knows all the words to the Monkees' theme tune. ▣

Annette Funicello *Minnie* • Timothy Carey *Lord High'n'Low* • Logan Ramsey *Officer Faye Lapid* • Abraham Sofaer *Swami* • Sonny Liston • Carol Doda *Sally Silicone* • Frank Zappa *Critic* • June Fairchild *Jumper* • Victor Mature *Big Victor* • Teri Garr *Testy True* • Peter Tork • David Jones • Micky Dolenz • Michael Nesmith ■ *Dir* Bob Rafelson • *Scr* Jack Nicholson, Bob Rafelson

Head above Water ★ 🄵🄵
Comedy mystery thriller
1996 · US/UK · Colour · 88mins

Jim Wilson, producer of Kevin Costner hits such as *The Bodyguard* and *Dances with Wolves*, came a cropper with this modest but thoroughly unfunny black comedy, a remake of the little known Norwegian film *Hodet over vannet* (1993). Harvey Keitel and Cameron Diaz are the mismatched newlyweds – she with a substance-abuse problem – who fast fall out when the latter's ex (Billy Zane) turns up. He falls asleep in her bed, but in trying to avoid embarrassment when Keitel returns from fishing, Diaz makes

a fatal mistake. Director Wilson never gets a handle on the underwritten script, and the talented performers are reduced to unfunny mugging. ▣

Harvey Keitel *George* • Cameron Diaz *Nathalie* • Craig Sheffer *Lance* • Billy Zane *Kent* • Shay Duffin *Policeman* • Mo Mo, the bird ■ *Dir* Jim Wilson • *Scr* Theresa Marie, from a film by Geir Eriksen, Eirik Ildahl

Head of the Family ★★ 🄵🄶
Horror   1996 · US · Colour · 78mins

Blake Bailey and his trailer-trash girlfriend Jacqueline Lovell want to get rid of her husband, so they turn to a large-brained evil genius in a wheelchair for help. The giant-headed mutant, and his family of moronic misfits, use mind control to send out zombies to do their nefarious bidding, but when Bailey gets greedy, they decide to teach the duo a lesson. A cheesy semi-porn horror outing that piles on the nudity along with the gore, it's sometimes funny, but most of the time just plain stupid, existing mainly to showcase the nubile talents of Lovell and fellow video "scream queen" Dianne Colazzo.

Blake Bailey *Lance* • Jacqueline Lovell *Loretta* • James Jones *Wheeler* • Bob Schott *Otis* • Dianne Colazzo *Ernestine* • Gordon Jennison Howard ■ *Dir* Robert Talbot • *Scr* Benjamin Carr, from a story by Robert Talbot

Head Office ★ 🄵🄵
Comedy   1986 · US · Colour · 87mins

In this trite comedy Judge Reinhold plays an inept bod, inveigled into a job in a top multinational company where he is used and abused, but still falls for his company director's daughter Lori-Nan Engler. Sadly Reinhold fails to be funny enough to carry the movie and the only sparky moments are down to support characters Don Novello and Richard Masur. For some strange reason both Rick Moranis and Danny DeVito are killed off in the first twenty minutes which is one of the movie's many mistakes. ▣

Eddie Albert *Helmes* • Danny DeVito *Stedman* • Lori-Nan Engler *Rachael* • Don King • Don Novello *Sal* • Judge Reinhold *Jack Issel* • Jane Seymour *Jane* • Wallace Shawn *Hoover* • Rick Moranis *Gross* ■ *Dir/Scr* Ken Finkleman

Head On ★★★
Comedy drama   1980 · Can · Colour · 86mins

Sally Kellerman and Stephen Lack star in this bizarre but sometimes intriguing drama about two drivers who are involved in a head-on crash and then become lovers. Both like playing dangerous games, both sexual and otherwise, and soon the stakes begin to rise as the film flits between tension and comedy. Originally known as *Fatal Attraction*, this is an interestingly quirky movie lent weight by the lead performances and the supporting cast, which includes John Huston.

Sally Kellerman *Michelle Keys* • Stephen Lack *Peter Hill* • John Huston *Clarke Hill* • Lawrence Dane *Frank Keys* • John Peter Linton *Gad Bernstein* • Hadley Kay *Stanley* • Robert Silverman *Michelle's analyst* • Maxwell Moffett *Henry* ■ *Dir* Michael Grant • *Scr* James Sanderson, Paul Illidge

Head On ★★■ 🄵🄶
Drama   1997 · Ausl · Colour · 104mins

Apart from calling it *Down Your Throat*, it's hard to see how writer/director Ana Kokkinos could have made her raw study of being young, gay and Greek in modern Melbourne any more abrasive. Both she and lead actor Alex Dimitriades deserve credit for making the central character so anti-heroic, as he spurns cultural identity and social stability for a nihilistic diet of drugs and rough trade. However, the wilful self-indulgence and repetitiveness of his lost night on the town so numbs the sensibilities, there's no outrage left by the time he's subjected to racially motivated police brutality along with his transvestite friend (Paul Capsis). In English and Greek with subtitles. Contains drug abuse, sex scenes and swearing.

Alex Dimitriades *Ari* • Paul Capsis *Johnny, "Toula"* • Julian Garner *Sean* • Elena Mandalis *Betty* • Tony Nikolakopoulos *Dimitri* • Damien Fotiou *Joe* • Eugenia Fragos *Sofia* • Dora Kaskanis *Dina* ■ *Dir* Ana Kokkinos • *Scr* Andrew Bovell, Ana Kokkinos, Mira Robertson, from the novel *Loaded* by Christos Tsiolkas

Head over Heels in Love
★★★ 🅄
Musical   1937 · UK · BW · 78mins

Having made her movie name under the direction of Victor Saville, Jessie Matthews went to work for her four-time co-star and then husband Sonnie Hale, whose first outing behind the camera this was. Adapted from a minor French play, the story centres on Jessie's inability to make up her mind between suitors Robert Flemyng and Louis Borell. Unfortunately, neither comes across as anyone to lose sleep over, and Hale's inexperience shows away from the musical numbers. But it's engaging enough, and Alfred Junge's sets give the film a sophistication too often missing from British musicals of the period. ▣

Jessie Matthews *Jeanne* • Robert Flemyng *Pierre* • Louis Borell *Marcel* • Romney Brent *Matty* • Helen Whitney Bourne *Norma* • Paul Leyssac *Max* • Eliot Makeham *Martin* ■ *Dir* Sonnie Hale • *Scr* Fred Thompson, Dwight Taylor, Marjorie Gaffney, from the play *Pierre ou Jac* by François de Crosset

Heads ★★★
Comedy thriller   1994 · Can · Colour · 99mins

At one time, Jon Cryer seemed destined for big things, but he has never really reached the same heights as *Pretty in Pink*. Nevertheless, he is as engaging as ever in this blackly comic mystery about an employee of a small-town paper who gets his big break as a journalist following a series of killings in the area. Cryer is well served by an exemplary supporting cast that includes Edward Asner, Jennifer Tilly and Roddy McDowall. However, director Paul Shapiro fails to make the most of the gruesome material. Contains swearing, violence and a sex scene.

Jon Cryer *Guy Franklin* • Nancy Drake *Emily* • Ed Asner *Ab Abbott* • Jennifer Tilly *Tina Abbot* • Roddy McDowall *Fibris Drake* ■ *Dir* Paul Shapiro • *Scr* Jay Stapleton, Adam Brooks

H.E.A.L.T.H. ★★★

Satirical comedy
1980 · US · Colour · 102mins

One of director Robert Altman's social comedies, which exemplifies the maxim that they shall have muesli wherever they go. It's set at a health food convention as its members try to elect a new president, though political corruption is Altman's target for satire. Among the wild and wacky women of whom Altman seems very fond are Glenda Jackson, Lauren Bacall – playing an 83-year-old virgin – and Carol Burnett. James Garner is engagingly macho in contrast. The pile-up of off-the-wall jokes does get a bit tiresome by the end, however.

Glenda Jackson *Isabella Garnell* • Carol Burnett *Gloria Burbank* • James Garner *Harry Wolff* • Lauren Bacall *Esther Brill* • Dick Cavett • Paul Dooley *Dr Gil Gainey* • Henry Gibson *Bobby Hammer* • Alfre Woodard *Hotel manager* ■ *Dir* Robert Altman • *Scr* Frank Barhydt, Paul Dooley, Robert Altman

Hear My Song ★★★★ 15

Comedy drama 1991 · UK · Colour · 109mins

Just when you think they don't make 'em like that any more, debutant director Peter Chelsom comes along and proves that they most certainly do. This is a delicious confection, with just the right amounts of ''Oirish'' whimsy, Scouse noise, bittersweet romance and broad comedy. Adrian Dunbar is the personification of impudent charm as the club owner seeking the tax-exiled tenor Josef Locke (played with gruff amiability by Ned Beatty). The Irish sequences get the nod over those set in Liverpool, but how could a run-in with a mystery singer hope to compete with a runaway cow? A treat – savour it. Contains some violence, swearing and nudity. 🎞

Ned Beatty *Josef Locke* • Adrian Dunbar *Micky O'Neill* • Shirley Anne Field *Cathleen Doyle* • Tara FitzGerald *Nancy Doyle* • William Hootkins *Mr X* • Harold Berens *Benny Rose* • David McCallum *Jim Abbott* • John Dair *Derek* • Norman Vaughan *Norman Vaughan* • James Nesbitt *Fintan O'Donnell* ■ *Dir* Peter Chelsom • *Scr* Peter Chelsom, Adrian Dunbar, from a story by Peter Chelsom

Hear No Evil ★ 15

Thriller 1993 · US · Colour · 92mins

A dismal stalker thriller – reminiscent of the Audrey Hepburn film *Wait until Dark* – has deaf personal trainer Jillian (Marlee Matlin, Oscar winner for *Children of a Lesser God*) being pursued by a cop (Martin Sheen) and a creepy man in black. Both of them want to get their hands on a rare coin she doesn't even know she has. It's tedious and annoying fare, packed with every cliché imaginable but little else of interest, even though the cast (which includes DB Sweeney) try to make the best of a bad situation. Contains violence and swearing.

Marlee Matlin *Jillian Shanahan* • DB Sweeney *Ben Kendall* • Martin Sheen *Lieutenant Philip Brock* • John C McGinley *Mickey O'Malley* ■ *Dir* Robert Greenwald • *Scr* RM Badat [Randall Badat], Kathleen Rowell, from a story by Danny Rubin, RM Badat [Randall Badat]

The Hearse ★★ 15

Horror 1980 · US · Colour · 95mins

Former mental case Trish Van Devere inherits a house from an aunt. When the house turns out to be haunted by a witch who looks exactly like her, she goes bonkers again. The plot is thickened by a hearse that drives itself and Joseph Cotten in his last real estate agent. Compared with *Rosemary's Baby*, *The Exorcist*, *The Omen* and *The Amityville Horror*, this wouldn't make a grasshopper jump, However, it's nicely made and features the veteran Cotten in his last major role. 🎞

Trish Van Devere *Jane Hardy* • Joseph Cotten *Walter Pritchard* • David Gautreaux *Tom Sullivan* • Donald Hotton *Rev Winston* • Med Flory *Sheriff* ■ *Dir* George Bowers • *Scr* Bill Bleich, from an idea by Mark Tenser

Heart ★ 15

Sports drama 1987 · US · Colour · 90mins

As a weary retread of one of the best boxing movies ever – Robert Wise's 1949 film *The Set-Up* – this has lost all grip. A pallid imitation of a vivid original, Brad Davis is the retired pugilist tricked into a comeback by slimy manager Steve Buscemi (*Reservoir Dogs*, *Fargo*), while girlfriend Frances Fisher looks on aghast. As well she might: despite Buscemi's performance, this low-budget film never even begins to be a contender. 🎞

Brad Davis *Eddie Brennan* • Frances Fisher *Jeannie* • Steve Buscemi *Nicky* • Robinson Frank Aub *Buddy* • Jesse Doran *Diddy* • Sam Grey *Leo* ■ *Dir* James Lemmo • *Scr* James Lemmo, Randy Jurgensen

Heart ★★★ 18

Psychological thriller
1997 · UK · Colour · 82mins

The song *Anyone Who Had a Heart* takes on grim meaning indeed in a gripping and highly unusual psychological thriller from the pen of ace TV scriptwriter Jimmy McGovern. In the *Cracker* creator's first work written expressly for the big screen, a devastated Saskia Reeves allows the heart of her beloved son, killed in an accident, to be given to Christopher Eccleston. It's when Reeves strikes up an uneasy relationship with Eccleston to ensure he is a worthy recipient that the really startling aspect of the story begins to take shape. For those not put off by some truly shocking twists or the graphic blood-letting and surgical detail, director Charles McDougall's dark passion play crackles with McGovern's distinctive style, black humour and emotional energy, complemented by moving turns from the two leads. Contains swearing, violence and sex scenes. 🎞

Christopher Eccleston *Gary Ellis* • Saskia Reeves *Marie Ann McCardle* • Kate Hardie *Tess Ellis* • Rhys Ifans *Alex Madden* • Anna Chancellor *Nicola Farmer* • Bill Paterson *Mr Kreitman* • Matthew Rhys *Sean McCardle* • Jack Deam *Policeman* ■ *Dir* Charles McDougall • *Scr* Jimmy McGovern

Heart and Souls ★★★ PG

Fantasy drama 1993 · US · Colour · 99mins

Four ghosts get the chance to tie up loose ends in their lives by taking over the body of uptight yuppie Robert Downey Jr, in *City Slickers* director Ron Underwood's touching flight of comedy fantasy. Once over the far-too-elaborate set-up, this becomes a cosy whimsical fable with fewer signposted twists than initially anticipated. Endearing and sentimental, the highlight is Downey Jr's fabulously funny and versatile performance, with Tom Sizemore, Alfre Woodard and Elisabeth Shue adding sparkling support. Contains some strong language. 🎞

Robert Downey Jr *Thomas Reilly* • Charles Grodin *Harrison Winslow* • Alfre Woodard *Penny Washington* • Kyra Sedgwick *Julia* • Tom Sizemore *Milo Peck* • David Paymer *Hal, the bus driver* • Elisabeth Shue *Anne* • Bill Calvert *Frank Reilly* • Lisa Lucas *Eva Reilly* ■ *Dir* Ron Underwood • *Scr* Brent Maddock, SS Wilson, from a story by Brent Maddock, SS Wilson, from a screenplay (unproduced) by Eric Hansen, Gregory Hansen

Heart Beat ★★

Biographical drama
1979 · US · Colour · 108mins

Ambitious but ultimately doomed attempt to shed light on the stars of the Beat Generation, despite some extraordinary performances from the talented cast. This loosely biographical tale focuses on the strange relationship between Jack Kerouac (John Heard) and the Cassadys (Nick Nolte and Sissy Spacek), but although all three have rarely been better, director John Byrum seems at a loss to know where to develop the story. A noble failure.

Nick Nolte *Neal Cassady* • Sissy Spacek *Carolyn Cassady* • John Heard *Jack Kerouac* • Ray Sharkey *Ira* • Ann Dusenberry *Stevie* • Margaret Fairchild *Mrs Kerouac* • Tony Bill *Dick* ■ *Dir* John Byrum • *Scr* John Byrum, from memoirs by Carolyn Cassady

Heart, Beating in the Dark ★★★

Drama 1982 · Jap · Colour

In director Shunichi Nagasaki's alarming drama, desperate lovers cling to each other and relive their lives in role-reversed flashbacks before their plight is explained in a startling conclusion. Shooting in Super-8, Nagasaki takes us so deeply into the emotions of his main characters that the sense of intruding quite overwhelms any shock we may feel from witnessing their aggressive acts of what can just about be called love. In Japanese with English subtitles. Contains violence and sex scenes.

Naito Takeshi *Ringo* • Muroi Shigeru *Iniko* ■ *Dir* Shunichi Nagasaki

Heart Condition ★★ 15

Action comedy 1990 · US · Colour · 95mins

Randall and Hopkirk (Deceased) is given a racial spin in this passable fantasy comedy, starring Bob Hoskins and Denzel Washington as the mismatched pair. Hoskins, with the transplanted heart of Washington inside him, investigates the latter's death. Writer/director James D Parriott doesn't quite pull off the invisibility gags, nor does he allow his talented stars enough space to fill their characters. Despite its flaws, its sentimental heart is in the right place, if slightly out of condition. Chalk this paranormal buddy movie up as a pleasant enough time-waster. Contains swearing and violence. 🎞

Bob Hoskins *Jack Moony* • Denzel Washington *Napoleon Stone* • Chloe Webb *Crystal Gerrity* • Roger E Mosley *Captain Wendt* • Ja'net DuBois *Mrs Stone* • Alan Rachins *Dr Posner* • Ray Baker *Harry Zara* • Jeffrey Meek *John Graham* ■ *Dir/Scr* James D Parriott

Heart Full of Rain ★★ 12

Drama 1997 · US · Colour · 87mins

Rick Schroder, Richard Crenna and Carroll Baker star in this tale of a young man's return to his parents' farm after leaving abruptly several years earlier. His mother and younger brother welcome him lovingly, but his father can't forgive him for deserting the family. However, when a massive storm threatens their home, father and son must cast aside their differences. A turgid melodrama that generates little tension, but good acting by a seasoned cast keeps it watchable. Contains some mild swearing, violence and a sex scene. 🎞

Richard Crenna *Arliss Dockett* • Rick Schroder *Isaiah Dockett* • Carroll Baker *Edith Pearl Dockett* • Gabriel Mick *Jacob Dockett* ■ *Dir* Roger Young • *Scr* Quinton Peeples

The Heart Is a Lonely Hunter ★★★★ PG

Drama 1968 · US · Colour · 118mins

Set in a small Southern town, this is a compelling version of novelist Carson McCullers's acute study of the anxieties and aspirations of a disparate group of troubled characters. Alan Arkin gives an Oscar-nominated performance as John Singer, the deaf-mute who tries to bring peace and consolation to a fellow mute, an impotent café owner, an adolescent tomboy (Sondra Locke), an alcoholic Marxist and a black doctor battling against injustice. Director Robert Ellis Miller makes the novel's points without the heavy-handedness typical of many movie adaptations, and debutants Stacy Keach and Locke (who was also nominated for an Academy Award) hold their own in a splendid supporting cast. 🎞

Alan Arkin *John Singer* • Laurinda Barrett *Mrs Kelly* • Stacy Keach *Blount* • Chuck McCann *Antonapoulos* • Biff McGuire *Mr Kelly* • Sondra Locke *Mick Kelly* • Percy Rodriguez *Dr Copeland* • Cicely Tyson *Portia* • Jackie Marlowe *Bubber Kelly* • Johnny Popwell *Willie* • Wayne Smith *Harry* ■ *Dir* Robert Ellis Miller • *Scr* Thomas C Ryan, from the novel by Carson McCullers

Heart like a Wheel ★★★ PG

Biography 1983 · US · Colour · 108mins

Shirley Muldowney is often described as the world's first woman racing driver, though because she drives hot-rods and dragsters she isn't recognised as such in Europe. This greasy, gutsy biopic covers a span of 25 years and gives Bonnie Bedelia (Bruce Willis's wife in the *Die Hard* movies) an acting challenge she passes with flying colours. Marriage, divorce and romance with her manager Beau Bridges are just some of the pitstops on the way to winning the world championship three times. The

---

real Muldowney served as the film's creative consultant. 🖳

Bonnie Bedelia *Shirley Muldowney* • Beau Bridges *Connie Kalitta* • Leo Rossi *Jack Muldowney* • Hoyt Axton *Tex Roque* • Bill McKinney *Don "Big Daddy" Garlits* • Anthony Edwards *John Muldowney (age 15–23)* • Dean Paul Martin *Sonny Rigotti* ■ *Dir* Jonathan Kaplan • *Scr* Ken Friedman

Heart of a Champion: the Ray Mancini Story ★★🅿🄶
Sports biography 1985 · US · Colour · 90mins

Embracing the rags-to-riches clichés of the American Dream, and almost deafening itself with the thunder of the obvious, this story of boxer Mancini's rise to fame never rises above the superficial. That's a shame, because the psyche of the real-life slugger was intriguing, spurred on as he was by his boxer father's failure to achieve glory. Still, in a film where executive producer Sylvester Stallone has choreographed the fight scenes, Robert Blake and his fellow actors go 15 rounds with some style, but without delivering the necessary blow. 🖳

Robert Blake *Lenny Mancini* • Doug McKeon *Ray "Boom Boom" Mancini* • Mariclare Costello *Ellen Mancini* • Tony Burton *Grif* • Ray Buktenica *Dave Wolf* • James Callahan *Father O'Neill* ■ *Dir* Richard Michaels • *Scr* Dennis Nemec

Heart of a Child ★★★🄵
Drama based on a true story 1994 · US · Colour · 88mins

It's a simple rule of thumb that, if a TV movie is about a heart-breaking medical crisis, it's based on a true story. The subject of this weepie kept the Canadian tabloids occupied for a couple of months as two mothers-to-be on opposite sides of the country learn that the only way one of their unborn babies can survive is by receiving the heart of the other. As the women facing the agonising decision, Michele Green and TV movie stalwart Ann Jillian give solid performances, while the versatile Rip Torn does well as the doctor advising them. 🖳

Ann Jillian *Alice Holc* • Michele Green *Karen Schouten* • Terry O'Quinn *Gordon Holc* • Bruce Greenwood *Fred Schouten* • Rip Torn *Dr Leonard Bailey* • Andrew Wheeler *Dr Cramer* • Cindy Girling *Dr Cynthia Adler* • Ric Reid *Terry Waterhouse* • William B Davis *Vern* ■ *Dir* Sandor Stern • *Scr* Susan Nanus

Heart of Darkness ★★★🄵
Drama 1993 · US · Colour · 101mins

Making a faithful screen adaptation of Joseph Conrad's brooding novella about madness and greed, which formed the basis for *Apocalypse Now*, was always going to be a bold step given that parallels would inevitably be drawn with Coppola's masterpiece. The story is certainly one familiar to film-goers – a man (Tim Roth) is sent up the Congo in a leaky steamboat to find the renegade Kurtz (John Malkovich in malevolent form), an ivory trader now mad prophet and self-acclaimed king. The eccentric visual flair associated with the once-mighty Nicolas Roeg made him the perfect choice for this straight-to-cable production, and he encourages exemplary performances from his two main leads. Overall,

though, this never manages to rise much above the ordinary. 🖳

Tim Roth *Marlow* • John Malkovich *Kurtz* • Isaach de Bankole *Mfumu* • James Fox *Gosse* • Morten Faldaas *Harlequin* • Patrick Ryecart *De Griffe* • Michael Fitzgerald *Harou* • Geoffrey Hutchings *Delcommune* • Peter Vaughan *Director* • Iman *Black Beauty* ■ *Dir* Nicolas Roeg • *Scr* Benedict Fitzgerald, from the novella by Joseph Conrad

Heart of Dixie ★🄸🄵
Drama 1989 · US · Colour · 91mins

Starring Ally Sheedy, Virginia Madsen and Phoebe Cates, this is fifties-style melodrama of the worst order. The girls are at college in the Deep South and are at odds with the racism and sexism of where they live. Romances ensue, consciousness is raised and the film improves briefly towards the end with the arrival of the first black student on campus. However, by this point you're sick of the oversimplification of the political issues. One to avoid, really. 🖳

Ally Sheedy *Maggie* • Virginia Madsen *Delia* • Phoebe Cates *Aiken* • Treat Williams *Hoyt* • Don Michael Paul *Boots* • Kyle Secor *Tuck* • Francesca Roberts *Keefi* ■ *Dir* Martin Davidson • *Scr* Tom McCown, from the novel *Heartbreak Hotel* by Ann Rivers Siddons

The Heart of Justice ★★★★🄸🄶
Mystery thriller 1992 · US · Colour · 87mins

Director Bruno Barreto coaxed a superbly subtle performance out of Dennis Hopper in the quietly moving romantic drama *Acts of Love*. This is an earlier collaboration, but it is an equally classy affair, with Eric Stoltz as a journalist who sets out to unravel the mysterious murder of well known novelist Hopper. Barreto also secures a clutch of superb portrayals from the likes of William H Macy, Bradford Dillman, Jennifer Connelly and Joanna Miles, and look out, too, for a delightful cameo from Vincent Price. Contains some swearing, violence and sexual references. 🖳

Jennifer Connelly *Emma Burgess* • Bradford Dillman *Mr Burgess* • Dermot Mulroney *Elliot Burgess* • Dennis Hopper *Austin Blair* • Vincent Price *Shaw* • Eric Stoltz *David Leader* • William H Macy *Booth* • Joanna Miles *Mrs Burgess* • Harris Yulin *Keneally* • Keith Reddin *Simon* ■ *Dir* Bruno Barreto • *Scr* Keith Reddin

Heart of Midnight ★🄸🄶
Horror thriller 1988 · US · Colour and BW · 106mins

A sick fantasy that's neither sick nor fantastic enough, director Matthew Chapman's degrading attempt to be meaningful in a horror thriller context is a pretentiously arty bore. Jennifer Jason Leigh is the woman on the verge of a nervous breakdown who inherits a tacky LA nightclub-cum-brothel from a debauched uncle. Before you can say Roman Polanski's *Repulsion*, she's raped by three workmen, giant eye-balls crash into her bedroom and she hears noises behind the walls. Is she hallucinating? Who cares? Only a cameo from the fabulous Brenda Vaccaro save this daft psychodrama from being a complete write-off. 🖳

Jennifer Jason Leigh *Carol Rivers* • Peter Coyote *Sharpe/Larry* • Gale Mayron *Sonny* •

Sam Schact *Uncle Fletcher* • Denise Dummont *Mariana* • Frank Stallone *Ledray* • Steve Buscemi *Eddy* • Brenda Vaccaro *Betty Rivers* ■ *Dir* Matthew Chapman • *Scr* Matthew Chapman, Everett DeRoche

The Heart of the Matter ★★★
Drama 1953 · UK · BW · 105mins

Graham Greene's tale of wartime infidelity and tortured conscience in Sierra Leone has, like its protagonist, not been faithful to its source. The religious and moral dilemma facing the adulterous police commissioner Scobie has been downplayed to concentrate on the human tragedy of a doomed love triangle. With the innocent intensity of her emotions clearly displayed, Maria Schell gives the best performance of the three leads, contrasting with the over-indulgent tantrums of Elizabeth Allan and the muted angst of Trevor Howard.

Trevor Howard *Harry Scobie* • Elizabeth Allan *Louise Scobie* • Maria Schell *Helen* • Denholm Elliott *Wilson* • Peter Finch *Father Rank* • Gérard Oury *Yusef* • George Coulouris *Portuguese captain* ■ *Dir* George More O'Ferrall • *Scr* Ian Dalrymple, Lesley Storm, from the novel by Graham Greene

Heartaches ★★🄸🄵
Comedy 1981 · Can · Colour · 88mins

A decade before *Thelma and Louise* hit the road, this Canadian movie covered similar ground. Pregnant Annie Potts decides to walk out on her husband Robert Carradine rather than face up to the reality of the baby's paternity. She teams up with kooky Margot Kidder (best known for her role as Lois Lane in *Superman*) for a series of misadventures, in a well-played if slightly predictable comic tale of gals doing it for themselves. 🖳

Margot Kidder *Rita Harris* • Annie Potts *Bonnie Howard* • Robert Carradine *Stanley Howard* • Winston Rekert *Marcello Di Stassi* • Guy Sanvido *Aldo* • Arnie Achtman *Alvin* ■ *Dir* Donald Shebib • *Scr* Terence Heffernan

Heartbeat ★★
Romantic comedy 1946 · US · BW · 101mins

In 1942 Ginger Rogers, aged 30, played a 12-year-old girl for laughs in *The Major and the Minor*. Four years later, it was no laughing matter when she attempted to convince as a teenage French escapee from a reform school who becomes a pickpocket. At least Danielle Darrieux, in the same role in the superior 1939 version *Battements de Coeur*, was in her early twenties at the time. In a film that strains vainly for charm, only Basil Rathbone – as Ginger's mentor in the art of picking pockets – provides any.

Ginger Rogers *Arlette* • Jean-Pierre Aumont *Pierre* • Adolphe Menjou *Ambassador* • Basil Rathbone *Prof Aristide* • Melville Cooper *Roland Medeville* • Mikhail Rasumny *Yves Cadubert* ■ *Dir* Sam Wood • *Scr* Morrie Ryskind, Roland Leigh, from the film *Battement de Coeur* by Hans Wilhelm, Max Kolpé, Michel Duran

Heartbeat ★★🅿🄶
Romantic drama 1992 · US · Colour · 88mins

What do heavily moistened lips, tans as burnished as copper pans and

several heaving cleavages signify? Yet another Danielle Steel blockbuster, busting its extremely unsubtle way on to our screens. Two lovelorn TV producers get their edits in a twist, as they do, and both are already carrying enough emotional baggage to kit out the safari department at Harrods. Remove your brain and enjoy. 🖳

John Ritter *Bill Grant* • Polly Draper *Adrian Townsend* • Nancy Morgan *Zelda* • Kevin Kilner *Steven Townsend* ■ *Dir* Michael Miller • *Scr* Jan Worthington, from the novel by Danielle Steel

Heartbeeps ★★★🅄
Science-fiction comedy 1981 · US · Colour · 74mins

Love means never having to say you're soldered in an under-rated sci-fi comedy featuring a rare screen performance from cult *Taxi* star Andy Kaufman (immortalised recently by Jim Carrey in *Man in the Moon*) and a welcome movie outing for Broadway diva Bernadette Peters. Set in 1995, they play servant robots who meet in a factory, fall in love, run away and hide out in a junkyard where they have a robot baby. Full of charming details – an entertainment robot programmed to tell jokes – and honest sentiment, Stan Winston's mechanical makeovers were deservedly Oscar-nominated. 🖳

Andy Kaufman *Val* • Bernadette Peters *Aqua* • Randy Quaid *Charlie* • Kenneth McMillan *Max* • Melanie Mayron *Susan* • Christopher Guest *Calvin* • Dick Miller *Watchman* ■ *Dir* Allan Arkush • *Scr* John Hill • *Music* John Williams

Heartbreak Hotel ★★🄸🄵
Fantasy drama 1988 · US · Colour · 96mins

A fistful of movies have sought to evoke the spirit of Elvis Presley, including films such as Jim Jarmusch's *Mystery Train* and even Tony Scott's Quentin Tarantino-scripted *True Romance*. Here, the whimsical plotline has youngster Charlie Schlatter dragging Elvis home to cheer up mom Tuesday Weld. Unfortunately, David Keith, as Elvis, neither looks nor moves remotely like the man, and the whole flimsy premise is quick to collapse. Writer/director Chris Columbus has real problems with both style and tone, but his failure here didn't stop him going on to great success with *Home Alone* and *Mrs Doubtfire*. Contains violence and swearing. 🖳

David Keith *Elvis Presley* • Tuesday Weld *Marie Wolfe* • Charlie Schlatter *Johnny Wolfe* • Angela Goethals *Pam Wolfe* • Jacque Lynn Colton *Rosie Pantangellio* • Chris Mulkey *Steve Ayres* ■ *Dir/Scr* Chris Columbus

The Heartbreak Kid ★★★🅿🄶
Comedy 1972 · US · Colour · 101mins

A marvellously witty, and genuinely disturbing black comedy, scripted by Neil Simon from a Bruce Jay Friedman short story, is given extra potency by the casting of director Elaine May's own daughter Jeannie Berlin as the Jewish wife jettisoned for a blonde "shikse" on her honeymoon. As the husband, Charles Grodin is brilliant, equalling his *Midnight Run* best, and Cybill Shepherd is well cast as the other woman, while veteran Eddie Albert is the very antagonistic father.

🅄 = SUITABLE FOR ALL   🅄c = SUITABLE FOR ALL, ESPECIALLY FOR YOUNG CHILDREN (VIDEO ONLY)   🅿🄶 = PARENTAL GUIDANCE

The acid cruelty of the first part of the film is not, alas, sustained throughout, and, frankly, neither is the plotline, which fails to reach any kind of climax. But there's more than enough left to satisfy sophisticated audiences. ▢

Charles Grodin *Lenny Cantrow* • Cybill Shepherd *Kelly Corcoran* • Jeannie Berlin *Lila Kolodny* • Eddie Albert *Mr Corcoran* • Audra Lindley *Mrs Corcoran* • William Prince *Colorado Man* • Augusta Dabney *Colorado Woman* • Mitchell Jason *Cousin Ralph* ■ Dir Elaine May • Scr Neil Simon, from the story *A Change of Plan* by Bruce Jay Friedman

The Heartbreak Kid ★★★
Romantic drama   1993 · Ausl · Colour

Not the Charles Grodin comedy, but an Australian rites-of-passage drama that explores the prejudices against age-gap romances. Claudia Karvan and Alex Dimitriades give convincing performances as the middle-class teacher and the teenage student for whom she breaks her close family ties. Director Michael Jenkins makes clever use of a handheld camera to disguise the material's stage origins and makes several telling points about Melbourne's Greek community and their place in Australian society.

Claudia Karvan *Christina* • Alex Dimitriades *Nick* • Nico Lathouris *George* • Steve Bastoni *Dimitri* • Doris Younane *Evdokia* • George Vidalis *Vasili* • Louis Mandylor *Eleni* • William McInnes *Southgate* ■ Dir Michael Jenkins • Scr Michael Jenkins, Richard Barrett

Heartbreak Ridge ★★★ 15
War drama   1986 · US · Colour · 124mins

A grizzled gunnery sergeant trains a batch of rookie soldiers in readiness for the US assault on Grenada in this typically hard-nosed vehicle for Clint Eastwood to strut his stern stuff. He's the reason to watch this by-the-numbers contemporary war epic, which recycles many vintage clichés of the genre, from the misfit recruit gaining dignity to the virgin platoon's first bitter taste of battle on the beaches. The old, die-hard veteran versus the modern major gets an airing, too, in a movie the US Department of Defense openly condemned – "drill sergeants are not permitted by regulations to swear at recruits". Contains violence and swearing. ▢

Clint Eastwood *Sergeant Thomas Highway* • Marsha Mason *Aggie* • Everett McGill *Major Powers* • Moses Gunn *Sergeant Webster* • Eileen Heckart *Little Mary* • Bo Svenson *Roy Jennings* • Boyd Gaines *Lieutenant Ring* • Mario Van Peebles *"Stitch" Jones* • Arlen Dean Snyder *Master Sergeant Choozoo* ■ Dir Clint Eastwood • Scr James Carabatsos

Heartbreakers ★★★ 18
Romantic comedy
1984 · US · Colour · 94mins

Although it provides in passing a snapshot of Reagan's America, this perceptive drama ends up concentrating more on wounded individuals than prevailing social trends. Ostensibly, it's about the corners that artist Peter Coyote and businessman Nick Mancuso have painted themselves into. However, good as they are as the self-obsessed thirtysomethings who can't commit to anything that might impinge upon their precious personal freedom, it's gallery

clerk Carole Laure and model Carol Wayne who hold the piece together. An impressive debut from writer/director Bobby Roth. Contains swearing and sex scenes.

Peter Coyote *Blue* • Nick Mancuso *Eli* • Carole Laure *Liliane* • Max Gail *King* • Kathryn Harrold *Cyd* • Carol Wayne *Candy* • James Laurenson *Terry Ray* • Jamie Rose *Libby* ■ Dir/Scr Bobby Roth

Heartburn ★★★ 15
Comedy drama   1986 · US · Colour · 104mins

Based on the best-selling novel by *When Harry Met Sally...* scriptwriter Nora Ephron about her tempestuous marriage to Watergate journalist Carl Bernstein, this comedy drama has Meryl Streep as the cookery writer who marries columnist Jack Nicholson, only to discover that life isn't always happy ever after when he has an affair while she's pregnant. Nicholson gets all the best lines and does well with what is essentially a rather shallow part with few redeeming features, but Streep is somewhat at sea with her role and ends up a rather unsympathetic character. Slickly directed by Mike Nichols, with music from Carly Simon. ▢

Meryl Streep *Rachel Samstat* • Jack Nicholson *Mark Forman* • Jeff Daniels *Richard* • Maureen Stapleton *Vera* • Stockard Channing *Julie* • Richard Masur *Arthur* • Catherine O'Hara *Betty* • Steven Hill *Harry* • Milos Forman *Dmitri* • Natalie Stern *Annie* • Karen Akers *Thelma Rice* ■ Dir Mike Nichols • Scr Nora Ephron, from her autobiographical novel

Heartland ★★★★
Historical western
1979 · US · Colour · 95mins

Based on the memoirs of Elinore Randall Stewart, this portrait of pioneer life on the Wyoming frontier circa 1910 is perhaps the cinema's truest reflection of the female experience of the west. Bringing the wealth of historical detail to vibrant life is Conchata Ferrell as a widow who progresses from housekeeper to wife as she comes to understand the terse determination of rancher Rip Torn. Never flinching from the grim realities of the daily grind, former documentarist Richard Pearce manages to find moments of raw joy amid the hardships caused by the cruel climate and unyielding land. Exhausting and memorable. ▢

Rip Torn *Clyde Stewart* • Conchata Ferrell *Elinore Randall* • Barry Primus *Jack* • Lilia Skala *Grandma Landauer* • Megan Folsom *Jerrine* • Amy Wright *Clara Jane* • Jerry Hardin *Cattle buyer* • Mary Boylan *Ma Gillis* ■ Dir Richard Pearce • Scr Beth Ferris, from the books and papers by Elinore Randall Stewart

Hearts and Minds ★★★★
Documentary   1974 · US · Colour · 111mins

America's failure of arms in Vietnam is still a running sore in the hearts and minds of the US military and the American people. Director Peter Davis's Oscar-winning documentary twists the knife again, trying to unravel why the Americans became involved with the whole bloody business, and its honesty and full-frontal recording of experiences made it a hot potato for distributors at the time. That it can

now be seen shows just how far times and politics can change.

Dir Peter Davis

Heart's Desire ★★
Musical   1935 · UK · BW · 79mins

Producers made repeated efforts during the thirties to balance their usual musical froth with some serious culture. Grace Moore, Lily Pons and Richard Tauber were just three operatic luminaries who were in demand with film-makers. Here Tauber plays a Viennese beer-garden singer who is persuaded to leave home and love to perform on the London stage, but then finds himself attracted to a glamorous socialite. Obviously, acting did not come naturally, but there is no denying the quality of the tenor's voice even though the songs and arias are presented without a flicker of flair.

Richard Tauber *Joseph Steidler* • Leonora Corbett *Frances Wilson* • Kathleen Kelly *Anna* • Paul Graetz *Florian* • Carl Harbord *Oliver Desmond* • George Graves *Granville Wilson* • Diana Napier *Diana Sheraton* • Frank Vosper *Van Straaten* • Viola Tree *Lady Bennington* ■ Dir Paul Stein [Paul L Stein] • Scr Bruno Frank, L Du Garde Peach, Roger Burford, Jack Davies Jr, Clifford Grey, from a story by Lioni Pickard

Hearts of Darkness: a Film-Maker's Apocalypse ★★★★ 15
Documentary   1991 · US · Colour · 91mins

An enthralling documentary about the making of Francis Ford Coppola's Vietnam drama *Apocalypse Now*. Using new interviews and footage shot on location by Coppola's wife, Eleanor, this is a catalogue of madness and inspiration in the jungles of the Philippines that ranges from an overweight and unprepared Marlon Brando, the firing of Harvey Keitel, Martin Sheen's heart attack, previously unseen footage (a superb sequence in a French plantation house which Coppola foolishly cut) to crises such as typhoons and President Marcos withdrawing his helicopters to fight a real war. With contributions from Coppola, screenwriter John Milius, and a characteristically incoherent Dennis Hopper, this is an unmissable treat for fans of the movie and, indeed, for anyone interested in the cinema. Contains swearing. ▢

Dir/Scr Fax Bahr, George Hickenlooper

Hearts of Fire ★ 15
Drama   1987 · US · Colour · 91mins

Hilariously bad rock movie and an unfortunate swan song for the talented director Richard Marquand (*Jagged Edge*). Fiona Flanagan, who didn't quite enjoy the same success as the character she plays here, is the aspiring young musician torn between a woefully miscast Rupert Everett and a monosyllabic Bob Dylan. It would make a worthy companion piece to *This Is Spinal Tap*, but, sadly, it is intended to be serious and there's no respite in the bland soundtrack. Contains swearing. ▢

Rupert Everett *James Colt* • Bob Dylan *Billy Parker* • Fiona Flanagan *Molly McGuire* • Ian Dury *Bones* • Richie Havens *Pepper Ward* •

Julian Glover *Alfred* • Suzanne Bertish *Anne Ashton* ■ Dir Richard Marquand • Scr Scott Richardson, Joe Eszterhas

Hearts of the West ★★★★ PG
Western   1975 · US · Colour · 102mins

Inspired by the experiences of writer Zane Grey and shot in the style of a thirties western series, this is a wonderfully inventive and richly nostalgic picture. Jeff Bridges stars as an unpublished writer of western stories who discovers he's being conned by gangsters. By chance he falls in with a film crew, becoming a stuntman and, briefly, a star. Bridges is excellent in the lead, but he's almost upstaged by Andy Griffith's performance as a fellow stuntman. The likeable result is sure to appeal to fans of B-westerns and Hollywood lore in general. ▢

Jeff Bridges *Lewis Tater* • Andy Griffith *Howard Pike* • Donald Pleasence *AJ Nietz* • Blythe Danner *Miss Trout* • Alan Arkin *Kessler* • Richard B Shull *Stout crook* • Herbert Edelman *Polo* • Alex Rocco *Earl* ■ Dir Howard Zieff • Scr Rob Thompson

Hearts of the World ★★★
Silent First World War drama
1918 · US · BW · 152mins

After making his epic *Intolerance*, DW Griffith wrote, produced and directed this picture as a contribution to the war effort in 1918, incorporating documentary footage and scenes shot at the Front. It stars Lillian Gish and Robert Harron as two lovers and shows the devastating effect of the war on one small French village. Griffith's feeling for his characters overcomes the contrivances of the plot and moments of sentimentality. Technical adviser Erich von Stroheim is also seen as a Prussian officer, while making his first screen appearance as the teenager with a wheelbarrow is a young Noël Coward.

Adolphe Lestina *Grandfather* • Josephine Crowell *Mother* • Lillian Gish *Girl* • Robert Harron *Boy* • Dorothy Gish *Little Disturber* • Erich von Stroheim *German soldier* • Noël Coward *Boy with wheelbarrow* ■ Dir DW Griffith • Scr M Gaston de Tolignac [DW Griffith], Capt Victor Marier [DW Griffith]

Hearts on Fire ★★
Drama   1992 · US · Colour · 95mins

A fraught TV movie, originally titled *In Sickness and in Health*, about a husband who falls in love with the nurse he employs to care for his ailing wife. Tom Skerritt, a decent jobbing actor best known for his Captain Dallas in *Alien*, plays the husband; Lesley Ann Warren plays the unfortunate wife and Marg Helgenberger plays the seductive carer.

Lesley Ann Warren *Anita Mattison* • Tom Skerritt *Jarrett Mattison* • Marg Helgenberger *Mickey* • Robyn Lively *Holly Mattison* • Ray Baker *Sam* • Lisa Blount *Carmen* ■ Dir Jeff Bleckner • Scr Alan Hines, Joyce Eliason, from a story by Joyce Eliason

Heat ★★ 🔞
Cult drama 1972 · US · Colour · 96mins

Underground icon Joe Dallesandro plays a former child actor-turned-hustler, and Sylvia Miles a fading minor movie star, in director Paul Morrissey's *Sunset Boulevard* revisited which is given the usual tacky Andy Warhol spin. Andrea Feldman adds further bizarre twists and trashy turns to the ''Hollyweird'' parody as Miles's daughter. Sometimes hilariously camp, sometimes just very ordinary, this was the most commercially successful of Warhol's bad taste trilogy, which also featured including *Flesh* and *Trash*. 🖵
Sylvia Miles *Sally* • Joe Dallesandro *Joe* • Pat Ast *Motel Owner* • Andrea Feldman *Jessica* • Ray Vestal *Movie Producer* • PJ Lester *Sally's former husband* ■ *Dir* Paul Morrissey • *Scr* Paul Morrissey, John Hollowell

Heat ★ 🔞
Crime drama 1987 · US · Colour · 96mins

Once the world's biggest box office draw, poor Burt Reynolds was reduced to the status of ''Burt who?'' until *Boogie Nights* revived his name. His fall from grace isn't difficult to comprehend on the evidence of this drab, squalid action movie. Reynolds, relying on his trademark toughie-with-a-heart-of-gold persona, plays a freelance bodyguard who's up against Las Vegas slimeballs, but dreams of one day retiring. A muddled, violent and humourless experience with director Dick Richards pushing all the predictable buttons. 🖵
Burt Reynolds *Mex* • Karen Young *Holly* • Peter MacNicol *Cyrus Kinnick* • Howard Hesseman *Pinchus Zion* • Neill Barry *Danny DeMarco* • Diana Scarwid *Cassie* • Joseph Mascolo *Baby* ■ *Dir* Dick Richards • *Scr* William Goldman, from his novel

Heat ★★★★★ 15
Crime thriller 1995 · US · Colour · 163mins

Directed by Michael Mann, this crime thriller about a cop (Al Pacino) and a robber (Robert De Niro) is epic in scale and in length at just under three hours. Though punctuated by bursts of virtuoso action including a running battle in downtown LA that ranks as one of the best action scenes ever filmed, it is the unusual emphasis on the characters which impresses, especially De Niro as the calm, methodical loner whose personal credo is to arrange his life so that he can abandon everything in 30 seconds when the heat is on, including his sidekick, Val Kilmer. Pacino, by contrast, is more of a cliché: angst-ridden and onto his third marriage. We've seen it before and you catch Pacino acting all the time, especially in his set-piece meeting with De Niro. It's also a pity that after so much brilliance, Mann should succumb to a derivative ending and a tidy if bloody resolution in which the wrong man gets killed. 🖵 **DVD**
Al Pacino *Vincent Hanna* • Robert De Niro *Neil McCauley* • Val Kilmer *Chris Shiherlis* • Jon Voight *Nate* • Tom Sizemore *Michael Cheritto* • Diane Venora *Justine* • Amy Brenneman *Eady* • Ashley Judd *Charlene* • Mykel T Williamson *Drucker* • Wes Studi *Casals* • Natalie Portman *Lauren* ■ *Dir/Scr* Michael Mann • *Cinematographer* Dante Spinotti

Heat and Dust ★★★ 15
Drama 1982 · UK · Colour · 124mins

Ex-BBC researcher Julie Christie travels to India to investigate her late great-aunt Olivia (Greta Scacchi) who caused a scandal in the twenties – and it doesn't take long for us to guess that she became rather too familiar with an Indian. Adapting her own novel, Ruth Prawer Jhabvala produces a new twist on EM Forster's *A Passage to India*, using two characters and separate time zones to express similar ideas about cultural collision. It's arty and undeniably exotic, with Christie and Scacchi refusing to be upstage by the ravishing Rajastani scenery that director James Ivory throws at us. 🖵
DVD
Julie Christie *Anne* • Christopher Cazenove *Douglas* • Greta Scacchi *Olivia Rivers* • Julian Glover *Mr Crawford* • Susan Fleetwood *Mrs Crawford* • Shashi Kapoor *The Nawab* • Madhur Jaffrey *The Begum* • Nickolas Grace *Harry* • Zakir Hussain *Inder Lal* • Barry Foster *Major Minnies* • Amanda Walker *Lady Mackleworth* • Patrick Godfrey *Dr Saunders* ■ *Dir* James Ivory • *Scr* Ruth Prawer Jhabvala, from her novel

Heat and Sunlight ★★
Drama 1988 · US · BW · 98mins

In his feature *Signal 7*, Rob Nilsson not only employed a purely improvisational technique, but also pioneered the method of shooting on video before transferring the results to celluloid. He repeats the trick in this disappointing follow-up, which is atmospherically scored by David Byrne and Brian Eno. However, the lack of a coherent screenplay means the action is too often allowed to ramble, although, when scenes do ignite, there is palpable tension, as Nilsson's pathologically jealous photographer is consumed by violent rages that are invariably directed at Consuelo Faust, the dancer with whom he's been having an affair.
Rob Nilsson *Mel Hurley* • Consuelo Faust *Carmen* • Don Bajema *Mitch* • Ernie Fosselius *Bobby* ■ *Dir/Scr* Rob Nilsson • *Music/Lyrics* David Byrne, Brian Eno, Mark Adler, David Schickele, Michael Small

Heat Wave ★★★
Drama based on a true story
1990 · US · Colour · 92mins

This Emmy award-winning TV movie is based on actual events that occurred during the civil rights riots that turned the Watts district of Los Angeles into a battleground in the summer of 1965. As an ambitious journalist who is branded a race traitor for his coverage of the story for a paper with a predominantly white readership, Blair Underwood gives a performance of dignity and integrity that invites comparisons with Sidney Poitier. Cicely Tyson and James Earl Jones are typically impressive, while director Kevin Hooks assuredly blends discussion of the social issues with explosive action.
Cicely Tyson *Ruthana Richardson/Motherdear* • Blair Underwood *Robert Richardson* • James Earl Jones *Junius Johnson* • Sally Kirkland *Mrs Canfield* • Margaret Avery *Roxie Turpin* • Vondie Curtis-Hall *Clifford Turpin* ■ *Dir* Kevin Hooks • *Scr* Michael Lazarou

Heathers ★★★★ 🔞
Black comedy 1989 · US · Colour · 98mins

Don't allow the fact that Michael Lehmann directed *Hudson Hawk* to put you off his stunning debut with this movie about an all-girl high-school clique terrorising fellow students. Their actions prompt Winona Ryder and Christian Slater to engineer a rash of deaths to break the clique's hold on their schoolmates. Beneath the hip, lip-glossed surface of this devastatingly witty black comedy lurks a serious satire on peer-group pretensions and other teen movies. But the message never gets in the way of the snappy dialogue or on-target jabs at the in-crowd lunacy of high-school life. See it and you'll never drink mineral water again! Contains violence, swearing and sex scenes. 🖵
Winona Ryder *Veronica Sawyer* • Christian Slater *Jason ''JD'' Dean* • Shannen Doherty *Heather Duke* • Lisanne Falk *Heather McNamara* • Kim Walker *Heather Chandler* • Penelope Milford *Pauline Fleming* • Glenn Shadix *Father Ripper* • Lance Fenton *Kurt Kelly* • Patrick Labyorteaux *Ram Sweeney* ■ *Dir* Michael Lehmann • *Scr* Daniel Waters

The Heat's On ★★ U
Musical comedy 1943 · US · BW · 78mins

After her lively sparring match with WC Fields in *My Little Chickadee*, Mae West was off-screen for nearly four years until producer/director Gregory Ratoff persuaded her to return in this musical comedy, supported by Victor Moore and Almira Sessions. West herself was in fine shape but the script wasn't, especially after she had rewritten her part to make it more sympathetic. In fact, her role as a Broadway sex siren seems dated and her time on screen is quite limited.
Mae West *Fay Lawrence* • Victor Moore *Hubert Bainbridge* • William Gaxton *Tony Ferris* • Lester Allen *Mouse Beller* • Mary Roche *Janey Bainbridge* • Almira Sessions *Hannah Bainbridge* • Hazel Scott • Alan Dinehart *Forrest Stanton* • Lloyd Bridges *Andy Walker* ■ *Dir* Gregory Ratoff • *Scr* Fitzroy Davis, George S George, Fred Schiller, from a story by Boris Ingster, Lou Breslow

Heatseeker ★ 🔞
Science-fiction action
1995 · US · Colour · 87mins

Straight-to-video veteran Albert Pyun strikes again! Human boxer Keith Cooke is forced to fight an android adversary in the low-tech world of 2019 in this cyber-killer drivel. A vague William Gibson-style cyber-punk ethos is attempted, but that route soon peters out along with any viewer interest. Quite why Pyun is so prolific in the science-fiction movie industry is a complete mystery.
Norbert Weisser *Tung* • Keith Cooke *Chance O'Brien* • Gary E Daniels [Gary Daniels] *Xao* ■ *Dir* Albert Pyun • *Scr* Albert Pyun, Christopher Borkgren, from a story by Albert Pyun

Heatwave ★★★ 15
Drama based on a true story
1983 · Ausl · Colour · 90mins

Militant liberal Judy Davis protests the crime-related gentrification of downtown Sydney, only to get caught up in political intrigue and romance with an ambitious architect (Richard

Moir). Davis gives a typically fine performance, while director Phillip Noyce (*Dead Calm*, *Patriot Games*) expertly tightens the suspense screws to produce a memorably disturbing finish. Set against a sultry Christmas backdrop, this jet-black thriller is based on a true property scandal.
Judy Davis *Kate* • Richard Moir *Steven* • Chris Haywood *Peter* • Bill Hunter *Robert* • John Gregg *Phillip* • Anna Jemison *Victoria* • John Meillon *Freddy* • Dennis Miller *Mick* ■ *Dir* Phillip Noyce • *Scr* Phillip Noyce, Phillip Noyce, Marc Rosenberg, Mark Stiles, Tim Gooding

Heaven ★★ 🔞
Documentary 1987 · US · Colour · 59mins

Actress Diane Keaton's first film as director is a sweet idea gone sour. A variety of ordinary people – boxing promoter Don King being an exception – are interviewed and asked to explain their views on death and a possible afterlife. However, despite some intriguing old film clips, Keaton's patronising narration and ludicrously affected camera angles deflate the airy bubble of an idea that needed a more affectionate, light-handed touch. 🖵
Dir Diane Keaton • *Cinematographer* Joe Kelly, Frederick Elmes

Heaven and Earth ★★★★ 🔞
War drama 1993 · US · Colour · 103mins

After *Platoon* and *Born on the Fourth of July*, Oliver Stone turns his attention to the Vietnamese themselves, in particular a village girl named Le Ly Hayslip (Hiep Thi Le) who endures the horrors of the war only to marry a psychotic American soldier (Tommy Lee Jones) who takes her to California. Unjustly slated by the critics, the picture shows all of Stone's brilliance in creating scenes of unusual vividness – it's horrifying, beautiful, ugly and moving all at the same time. It is also, at times, an unsettling black comedy about cultural and religious rituals that switches from Buddhist shrines in rice paddies to consumerist shrines in supermarkets. There hasn't been such a great politicised melodrama since the heyday of Otto Preminger. Contains violence and swearing.
Tommy Lee Jones *Sergeant Steve Butler* • Joan Chen *Mama* • Haing S Ngor *Papa* • Hiep Thi Le *Le Ly* • Debbie Reynolds *Eugenia* ■ *Dir* Oliver Stone • *Scr* Oliver Stone, from the non-fiction books *When Heaven and Earth Changed Places* by Le Ly Hayslip, Jay Wurts and *Child of War, Woman of Peace* by Le Ly Hayslip, James Hayslip

Heaven Can Wait ★★★★★★
Fantasy comedy 1943 · US · Colour · 112mins

A witty satire masquerading as a Fox family saga, this movie gets its title from the prologue where the Devil (Laird Cregar) sits in judgement on Don Ameche's Henry Van Cleve. This is as good as Ameche gets; not only is he perfectly cast, but also brilliantly directed by the comic genius Ernst Lubitsch, working in colour for the first time. The film has great warmth, charm and honesty, and grows on you until, at the end, you're sorry to leave. Gene Tierney has never looked lovelier –and that's *really* saying something– nor *The Merry Widow* used more emotively.

U = SUITABLE FOR ALL   Uc = SUITABLE FOR ALL, ESPECIALLY FOR YOUNG CHILDREN (VIDEO ONLY)   PG = PARENTAL GUIDANCE

Each viewing confirms this film's growing status as a classic.

Gene Tierney *Martha* • Don Ameche *Henry Van Cleve* • Charles Coburn *Hugo Van Cleve* • Marjorie Main *Mrs Strabel* • Laird Cregar *His Excellency, the Devil* • Spring Byington *Bertha Van Cleve* • Allyn Joslyn *Albert Van Cleve* ■ *Dir* Ernst Lubitsch • *Scr* Samson Raphaelson, from the play *Birthdays* by Lazlo Bus-Fekete • *Cinematographer* Edward Cronjager

Heaven Can Wait ★★★★ PG

Fantasy comedy 1978 · US · Colour · 96mins

An updated version of the 1941 film *Here Comes Mr Jordan*, this is one of the few remakes that is almost as good as the original. Warren Beatty co-directs and stars as the football supremo accidentally selected to die after a car accident. Realising he has been called before his time, Beatty bargains with celestial James Mason and gets the chance to live again but in someone else's body, that of a wealthy businessman whose wife is plotting to kill him. Well played, well written (by Beatty and Elaine May) and well directed, this is one of the highlights of Beatty's career. [image]

Warren Beatty *Joe Pendleton* • Julie Christie *Betty Logan* • James Mason *Mr Jordan* • Jack Warden *Max Corkle* • Charles Grodin *Tony Abbott* • Dyan Cannon *Julia Farnsworth* • Buck Henry *Escort* • Vincent Gardenia *Krim* ■ *Dir* Warren Beatty, Buck Henry • *Scr* Elaine May, Warren Beatty, from the play by Harry Segall

Heaven Is a Playground ★★ 15

Sports drama 1991 · US · Colour · 102mins

No sporting cliché is left unturned for this well-cast but disappointing basketball drama. DB Sweeney is the idealistic lawyer who helps the equally idealistic coach (*Hill Street Blues*'s Michael Warren) with a talented but troublesome cadre of players from the ghetto and protect them from sleazy sports shark Richard Jordan. There's no faulting the committed paying, but the script and direction of Randall Fried lack focus. [image]

DB Sweeney *Zack* • Michael Warren *Byron* • Richard Jordan *Racine* • Victor Love *Truth* • Bo Kimble *Matthew* • Janet Julian *Dalton* ■ *Dir* Randall Fried • *Scr* Randall Fried, from the non-fiction book by Rick Telander

Heaven Knows, Mr Allison ★★★★ U

Second World War drama
1957 · US · Colour · 106mins

This is a rare gem: a marvellously touching two-hander, beautifully acted by the sublime duo of Robert Mitchum and Deborah Kerr in their prime. The tale is simplicity itself: she's a nun and he's a marine, and they're stranded on a Japanese-occupied Pacific island during the Second World War. Echoes reverberate of the much-loved *African Queen*, also directed by John Huston, who here wisely lets the stars bring their magic touch to the clever screenplay. This is an early 20th Century-Fox CinemaScope feature, and the compositions and locations are superbly handled by the great English cameraman Ossie Morris, while Russell Lloyd's editing is dynamic, especially in the exciting bravado raids by Mitchum into enemy territory.

Deborah Kerr *Sister Angela* • Robert Mitchum *Mr Allison* ■ *Dir* John Huston • *Scr* John Huston, John Lee Mahin

Heaven Only Knows ★★

Western fantasy 1947 · US · BW · 98mins

An angel descends from heaven to the Wild West to attend to the soul of a psychotic saloon keeper and get him married to a demure schoolteacher. The bar owner, also a ruthless killer, arrived on earth without a soul and the angel tries to put this right. Robert Cummings makes a relatively human angel in this western spin on *It's A Wonderful Life*, whose more mawkish elements are tempered by a vague sense of humour.

Robert Cummings *Mike* • Brian Donlevy *Duke* • Marjorie Reynolds *Ginger* • Jorja Cartwright *Drusilla* • Bill Goodwin *Plumber* • Stuart Erwin *Sheriff* • John Litel *Reverend* • Peter Miles *Speck O'Donnell* ■ *Dir* Albert S Rogell • *Scr* Art Arthur, Ernest Haycox, Rowland Leigh, from the story by Aubrey Wisberg

Heaven Tonight ★★ 15

Musical drama 1990 · Ausl · Colour · 93mins

The feature film debut from *Neighbours* and *LA Confidential* star Guy Pearce, this follows the familiar tale of a young man falling out with his family when he embarks on a musical career. The twist this time is that the biggest obstacle is his father John Waters, a sixties rock legend who is less than enamoured by the fact that his boy is now getting all the attention. The two leads are fine, but the machinations of the music business lack realism and the songs are awful. It's hard to believe either would have become pop stars, whatever the decade. [image]

John Waters *Johnny Dysart* • Rebecca Gilling *Annie Dysart* • Guy Pearce *Paul Dysart* • Kim Gyngell *Baz Schultz* ■ *Dir* Pino Amenta • *Scr* Frank Howson, Alister Webb

Heavenly Bodies ★★ 15

Musical drama 1985 · Can · Colour · 85mins

A daft and rather bizarre attempt to cash in on the aerobics explosion of the early eighties. The story is set around a dance studio, where the young owner finds herself in all sorts of difficulty when she rebuffs the charms of an egocentric rival. It's pretty risible stuff, leadenly directed by Lawrence Dane, and a clutch of distinctly forgettable tunes hardly helps matters. For aerobics fans, John Travolta's *Perfect* is probably the definitive movie about the sport. Contains swearing and nudity. [image]

Cynthia Dale *Samantha* • Richard Rebiere *Steve* • Walter George Alton *Jack* • Laura Henry *Debbie* • Stuart Stone *Joel* • Patricia Idlette *KC* • Pam Henry *Patty* • Linda Sorenson *TV Producer* ■ *Dir* Lawrence Dane • *Scr* Lawrence Dane, Ron Base

The Heavenly Body ★★

Romantic comedy 1943 · US · BW · 94mins

The title not only refers to Hedy Lamarr, making her first attempt at light comedy, but also the heavens above in this contrived wartime comedy. William Powell exercises his perfectly honed comedy skills to little avail as the eccentric astronomer whose nocturnal gazing causes him to neglect Lamarr as his wife. After she takes up astrology, the predicted arrival of a tall, dark stranger duly occurs when James Craig's air raid warden comes knocking at the door.

William Powell *William B Whitley* • Hedy Lamarr *Vicky Whitley* • James Craig *Lloyd X Hunter* • Fay Bainter *Margaret Sibyll* • Henry O'Neill *Professor Stone* • Spring Byington *Nancy Potter* ■ *Dir* Alexander Hall • *Scr* Michael Arlen, Walter Reisch, Harry Kurnitz, from a story by Jacques Thery

Heavenly Creatures ★★★★ 18

Psychological drama based on a true story
1994 · NZ · Colour · 97mins

This is the film that launched the career of Kate Winslet, who within three years of starring in this New Zealand fact-based drama was starring in *Titanic*, the highest-grossing film ever. It also transformed the fortunes of director Peter Jackson, who went from making ingenious schlock-horrors such as *Bad Taste* and *Braindead* to directing such high-tech Hollywood-backed chillers as *The Frighteners*. The real star of this masterly mix of nostalgia, innocence and menace, however, is Melanie Lynskey, who is mesmerising as the matricidal half of the teenage duo who scandalised a nation in the early fifties. Although Winslet and Lynskey dominate the film, they are splendidly supported by Diana Kent and Clive Merrison as Juliet's parents, and by Sarah Peirse as Pauline's ill-fated mother. Contains violence and swearing. [image]

Melanie Lynskey *Pauline Parker* • Kate Winslet *Juliet Hulme* • Sarah Peirse *Honora Parker* • Diana Kent *Hilda Hulme* • Clive Merrison *Henry Hulme* • Simon O'Connor *Herbert Reiper* ■ *Dir* Peter Jackson • *Scr* Peter Jackson, Frances Walsh

The Heavenly Kid ★★ 15

Comedy fantasy 1985 · US · Colour · 87mins

A dim teenage spin on *Heaven Can Wait*, which finds fifties rock 'n' roll rebel Lewis Smith earning his chance to book a place in Heaven if he helps out confused eighties teenager Jason Gedrick. Richard Mulligan fares the best in a lightweight cast, but all concerned are let down by the lazy script. [image]

Lewis Smith *Bobby* • Jason Gedrick *Lenny* • Jane Kaczmarek *Emily* • Richard Mulligan *Rafferty* • Mark Metcalf *Joe* • Beau Dremann *Bill* ■ *Dir* Cary Medoway • *Scr* Cary Medoway, Martin Copeland

Heavenly Pursuits ★★★ 15

Satirical comedy 1986 · UK · Colour · 86mins

A delightful British film about miracles and religion, sharply written and directed by Charles Gormley. Tom Conti is the teacher at a Glasgow Catholic school who gets caught up in possible miraculous goings-on and then finds himself at the mercy of his colleagues and the media in this well-realised satire. Odd and often hilarious, this treat of a movie features terrific performances from a cast which includes David Hayman, Helen Mirren and *Trainspotting*'s Ewen Bremner. [image]

Tom Conti *Vic Mathews* • Helen Mirren *Ruth Chancellor* • David Hayman *Jeff Jeffries* • Brian Pettifer *Father Cobb* • Jennifer Black *Sister* • Dave Anderson *Headmaster* • Tom Busby *Monseigneur Brusse* • Ewen Bremner *Stevie Deans* ■ *Dir/Scr* Charles Gormley

Heavens Above! ★★ PG

Comedy 1963 · UK · BW · 113mins

Based on an idea by, of all people, Malcolm Muggeridge, this is only a minor entry on the CVs of both Peter Sellers and the Boulting brothers. The satire at the expense of the Church of England is too gentle, the resolution is beyond contrivance and the church-goers are clumsy stereotypes. The petty snobberies and prejudices of the devout were first pointed out in the New Testament, and the script here has nothing new to add to the debate. As a prison chaplain ministering to the well heeled, Sellers wallows in whimsy, leaving centre stage to Irene Handl and Eric Sykes's gypsy family. [image]

Peter Sellers *Reverend John Smallwood* • Cecil Parker *Archdeacon Aspinall* • Isabel Jeans *Lady Despard* • Eric Sykes *Harry Smith* • Bernard Miles *Simpson* • Brock Peters *Matthew* • Ian Carmichael *The other Smallwood* • Irene Handl *Rene Smith* ■ *Dir* John Boulting • *Scr* John Boulting, Frank Harvey, from an idea by Malcolm Muggeridge

Heaven's Burning ★★★★ 18

Road movie 1997 · Ausl/Jap · Colour · 95mins

After cracking Hollywood with his charismatic turn in *LA Confidential*, Russell Crowe headed Down Under for this stunning but criminally overlooked Australian thriller. He plays a getaway driver with a conscience who forms an odd relationship with Youki Kudoh, an unhappy Japanese woman trying to dump her possessive husband. The pair are forced to go on the run pursued by the cops, Crowe's psychopathic ex-colleagues and Kudoh's even crazier spouse. Director Craig Lahiff makes stunning use of spare Australian locations and fashions a moving, melancholic romance that is peppered with shocking bursts of violence. Contains violence, swearing and nudity. [image]

Russell Crowe *Colin O'Brien* • Youki Kudoh *Midori Takada* • Kenji Isomura *Yukio Takada* • Ray Barrett *Cam O'Brien* • Robert Mammone *Mahood* • Petru Gheorghiu *Boorjan* ■ *Dir* Craig Lahiff • *Scr* Louis Nowra

Heaven's Gate ★★★

Western 1980 · US · Colour · 148mins

Michael Cimino's legendary western soared over budget and was so thoroughly trashed by the New York critics that the bankrupted studio, United Artists, withdrew the film and cut it by an hour. Sadly, this is the version usually seen today. While some of the director's ambition still shines through – notably the wondrous photography, the set-piece battle and the roller-skating dance – the story, about a Wyoming range war between cattlemen and persecuted immigrants, makes little sense. The full version, however, is a superb, five-star achievement. [image]

Kris Kristofferson *James Averill* • Christopher Walken *Nathan D Champion* • John Hurt *Billy Irvine* • Sam Waterston *Frank Canton* • Brad Dourif *Mr Eggleston* • Isabelle Huppert *Ella Watson* • Joseph Cotten *Reverend Doctor* • Jeff Bridges *John H Bridges* • Richard Masur

Cully • Terry O'Quinn *Captain Minardi* • Mickey Rourke *Nick Ray* ■ *Dir/Scr* Michael Cimino • *Cinematographer* Vilmos Zsigmond

Heaven's Prisoners ★★★ 15
Thriller   1996 · US · Colour · 126mins

Alec Baldwin stars as ex-New Orleans cop Dave Robicheaux, hero of several crime thrillers by James Lee Burke: a man at odds with himself over his alcoholism, loss of faith and love of violence. This is adapted from the second in the series, in which Robicheaux rescues a small girl from a lagoon air-crash and thinks he's spiritually saved, only to find he's up to his neck in drug smuggling and murder. Baldwin is a little too engaging in the lead, and the plot becomes a rather routine tale of vengeance, but along the way director Phil Joanou keeps a good deal of the novel's sinister atmosphere, and Eric Roberts makes a suitably charming villain. Contains violence, swearing, sex scenes and nudity. ▭

Alec Baldwin *Dave Robicheaux* • Kelly Lynch *Annie Robicheaux* • Mary Stuart Masterson *Robin Gaddis* • Eric Roberts *Bubba Rocque* • Teri Hatcher *Claudette Rocque* • Vondie Curtis-Hall *Minos P Dautrieve* • Badja Djola *Batist* • Samantha Lagpacan *Alafair* • Joe Viterelli *Didi Giancano* ■ *Dir* Phil Joanou • *Scr* Harley Peyton, Scott Frank, from the novel by James Lee Burke

Heavy ★★★★ 15
Drama   1995 · US · Colour · 100mins

The coming-of-age of an overweight, thirtysomething pizza chef may not seem like a very promising viewing experience. But writer/director James Mangold's marvellous feature debut has a ring of truth few real-life dramas manage. Pruitt Taylor Vince is exceptional as the withdrawn gentle giant who must cross emotional thresholds he never dared acknowledge. The drama is set in motion when Vince's imperious mother (Shelley Winters) decides to match him with new waitress Liv Tyler. Often unbearably poignant, the attention to small details pays heartfelt dividends in this sensitive and defiantly low-key triumph. Contains swearing. ▭

Pruitt Taylor Vince *Victor* • Liv Tyler *Callie* • Shelley Winters *Dolly* • Deborah Harry *Delores* • Joe Grifasi *Leo* • Evan Dando *Jeff* • David Patrick Kelly *Grey man in hospital* • Marian Quinn *Darlene* ■ *Dir/Scr* James Mangold

Heavy Metal ★★ 15
Animated science-fiction fantasy
1981 · US · Colour · 86mins

This cult favourite from the eighties, based on an American comic book, now looks a tad dated. A mix of mythical imagery and X-rated animation, this compendium of stories was eagerly lapped up by American teens, but it pales in comparison to the amoral savagery of nineties Japanese *anime*, while the AOR rock soundtrack is quaint rather than subversive. Nevertheless, the animation is still striking and a talented cast of American comics provide voices. ▭ **DVD**

Richard Romanus *Harry Canyon* • Susan Roman *Girl/Satellite* • John Candy *Desk sergeant* • Marilyn Lightstone *Queen/Whore* • Jackie Burroughs *Katherine* • George Touliatos

Pilot • Harold Ramis *Zeke* ■ • *Scr* Dan Goldberg, Len Blum, from a comic strip by Richard Corben, Angus McKie, Dan O'Bannon, Thomas Warkentin, Berni Wrightson • *Music* Elmer Bernstein

Heavy Petting ★★ 15
Documentary   1988 · US · Colour · 71mins

As hard as it would seem to make a boring documentary about sex, director Obie Benz and his conceptual collaborator, Pierce Rafferty, have done just that. This supposedly humorous look at American sexual mores uses newsreel footage, school education shorts, film and television clips as well as personal reminiscences about dating and masturbation, from such personalities as Spalding Gray, Allen Ginsberg, William Burroughs and Sandra Bernhard, to extremely dull effect. Scenes from feature films mingle with fifties sitcom clips and pop songs with little rhyme, reason or amusement. Remarkably facile, kitsch and uninformative, this is far too safe for a sex documentary. ▭

Dir Obie Benz • *Scr* Suzanne Fenn, Lianne Halfron, from an idea by Pierce Rafferty

Heavyweights ★ PG
Comedy   1995 · US · Colour · 93mins

Sickly teen movie from the Disney studio about a health farm, Camp Hope, where overweight kids go to diet. The camp is taken over by a maniacal fitness guru who forces the kids to endure humiliation, starvation and abuse. Buried deep beneath the cringe-inducing sequences is a satire about commercialism, since it transpires that the kids are to become part of a wider merchandising scheme. If this comes your way, avoid. ▭

Tom McGowan *Pat* • Aaron Schwartz *Gerry* • Shaun Weiss *Josh* • Tom Hodges *Lars* • Leah Lail *Julie* • Paul Feig *Tim* • Kenan Thompson *Roy* • David Bowe *Chris Donelly* ■ *Dir* Steven Brill • *Scr* Judd Apatow, Steven Brill

Heck's Way Home ★★★
Adventure   1995 · Can · Colour · 91mins

This cross between a Lassie movie and Disney's *The Incredible Journey* is splendid entertainment for all ages. Everyone will be rooting for plucky pooch Heck as he escapes from the clutches of snivelling dogcatcher Alan Arkin and treks across country to find his 11-year-old master, Chad Krowchuk, before his parents emigrate from Canada to Australia. It's classic race-against-time stuff, set against stupendous scenery. Michael Scott directs with tremendous energy and Arkin is a suitably hissable villain.

Chad Krowchuk • Michael Riley • Shannon Lawson • Don Francks • Gabe Khouth • Alan Arkin ■ *Dir* Michael Scott

Hedd Wyn ★★★ 12
Biographical drama
1992 · UK · Colour · 114mins

Despite being the first film in Welsh to receive an Oscar nomination, Paul Turner's biopic has a typically British period polish. Yet it also has a commitment to language and a pride in national culture that is both unfashionable and refreshing. Huw Garmon gives a respectful performance

as Ellis Evans, the teenage poet who wrote under the name of "Hedd Wyn" before dying in the First World War. It's the war scenes, though, that give the film a power and poignancy to rival that of the trench poem *Yr Arwr (The Hero)* which posthumously won Evans the Chair at the National Eisteddfod, a prize he'd always coveted. In Welsh with English subtitles. Contains some strong language.

Huw Garmon *Ellis Evans/Hedd Wyn* • Sue Roderick *Lizzie Roberts* • Judith Humphreys *Jini Owen* • Nia Dryhurst *Mary Catherine Hughes* • Grey Evans *Evan Evans* ■ *Dir* Paul Turner • *Scr* Alan Llwyd

Hedda ★★★★ PG
Drama   1975 · UK · Colour · 102mins

Glenda Jackson earned her fourth and final Oscar nomination in this filmed record of her RSC triumph as Ibsen's heroine, the bored and pregnant wife of an egghead several rungs down from her on the social ladder. Jackson gives a powerful interpretation of the role, making it very much a part of the then-emerging women's movement, as does Trevor Nunn's own adaptation. Directing his first film for the cinema (he directed *Anthony and Cleopatra* for TV in 1974), Nunn commendably resists the chance to "open up" the play by keeping the action mostly within the gloomy brown walls of the Tesman drawing room. ▭

Glenda Jackson *Hedda* • Peter Eyre *George Tesman* • Timothy West *Judge Brack* • Jennie Linden *Thea Elvsted* • Patrick Stewart *Ejlert Lovborg* • Constance Chapman *Julie* • Pam St Clement *Bertha* ■ • *Scr* Trevor Nunn, from the play *Hedda Gabler* by Henrik Ibsen

Heidi ★★★ U
Drama   1937 · US · BW · 84mins

One of Shirley Temple's most popular films, expertly directed by tough veteran Allan Dwan, on a relatively big budget that allows for expansive Christmas settings and a sleigh chase in the snow. Temple is excellent as the orphan nobody wants and, despite her awkward interpretation as a Dutch girl in one particular musical number, her Swiss miss is convincing. Of course, some may find themselves feeling rather nauseous as Heidi helps a distressed sick girl to walk, causes butler Arthur Treacher to lose his dignity and clowns with an organ-grinder's monkey. ▭

Shirley Temple *Heidi* • Jean Hersholt *Adolph Kramer* • Arthur Treacher *Andrews* • Helen Westley *Blind Anna* • Pauline Moore *Elsa* • Thomas Beck *Pastor Schultz* • Mary Nash *Fraulein Rottenmeier* • Sig Rumann [Sig Ruman] *Police captain* ■ *Dir* Allan Dwan • *Scr* Walter Ferris, Julien Josephson, from the novel by Johanna Spyri

Heidi ★★★
Drama   1965 · Aus/W Ger · Colour · 94mins

One of the most-filmed children's classics is given a colourful makeover by Werner Jacobs in this lively German-language version. Defiantly resisting the example of such twee predecessors as Shirley Temple, Eva Maria Singhammer radiates homely vivacity as the little Alpine girl who is kidnapped from her beloved grandfather (Gustav Knuth) so she can

rally the flagging spirits of disabled Gertraud Mittermayr in Frankfurt. Starting off rather like a junior rustic idyll, the central city segment of Johanna Spyri's tale is given some much-needed melodramatic steel by Margot Trooger's frosty governess. German dialogue dubbed into English.

Eva Maria Singhammer *Heidi* • Gertraud Mittermayr *Klara* • Gustav Knuth *Alp-Oehi* • Lotte Ledl *Dete* • Ernst Schroder *Sesemann* • Margot Trooger *Miss Rottenmeier* • Rolf Moebius *Dr Klassen* • Rudolf Vogel *Sebastian* ■ *Dir* Werner Jacobs • *Scr* Richard Schweizer, Michael Hallen (adaptation), from the novel by Johanna Spyri

The Heidi Chronicles ★★★ 12
Comedy drama   1995 · US · Colour · 92mins

Nothing to do with Johanna Spyri's Alpine heroine, but a TV-movie version of Wendy Wasserstein's hit play that not only won a Tony award, but also the Pulitzer Prize. Although Wasserstein's adaptation doesn't always break free from its stage shackles, the dialogue crackles with bons mots and provocative feminist statements. Spanning 30 years, from college days to discontented middle age, the story focuses on the friendship between Jamie Lee Curtis, gay paediatrician Tom Hulce and fashion-conscious Kim Cattrall. The stars acquit themselves admirably under Paul Bogart's sensible direction, but Peter Friedman catches the eye as Curtis's shifty journalist beau. ▭

Jamie Lee Curtis *Heidi Holland* • Tom Hulce *Peter* • Kim Cattrall *Susan* • Peter Friedman *Scoop* ■ *Dir* Paul Bogart • *Scr* Wendy Wasserstein, from her play

Heidi's Song ★★ U
Animated musical
1982 · US · Colour · 90mins

After numerous live-action versions, Johanna Spyri's much-loved classic gets the cartoon treatment in this sugary, critter-strewn offering. This was a rare feature outing for the Hanna-Barbera studio, which had concentrated on TV shows such as *The Flintstones* and *Top Cat* after its production of countless Tom and Jerry shorts. But little of the old magic is evident in this lacklustre adaptation, which is not helped by the abundance of substandard songs from the usually reliable Sammy Cahn and Burton Lane. Margery Gray does what she can as Heidi, while Sammy Davis Jr adds a little pizzazz as Head Ratte. ▭

Lorne Greene *Grandfather* • Margery Gray *Heidi* • Sammy Davis Jr *Head Ratte* • Peter Cullen *Gruffle* • Roger DeWitt *Peter* • Richard Erdman *Herr Sessmann* • Fritz Feld *Sebastian* ■ *Dir* Robert Taylor • *Scr* Joseph Barbera, Robert Taylor, Jameson Brewer, from the novel by Johanna Spyri

Heimat ★★★★★ 15
Drama
1984 · W Ger · BW and Colour · 923mins

It took over five years to shoot the 923 minutes that make up this monumental mosaic of 20th-century German history, and it was worth every second. Set in a village in the Hunsrück uplands, Edgar Reitz's masterpiece chronicles the life of the

U = SUITABLE FOR ALL   Uc = SUITABLE FOR ALL, ESPECIALLY FOR YOUNG CHILDREN (VIDEO ONLY)   PG = PARENTAL GUIDANCE

farming family into which Marita Breuer marries in 1919, paying as much attention to local detail as to the great events that shaped the nation's destiny. Wrongly dismissed in some quarters as high-class soap opera, the story not only eschews cheap melodramatics, but also meticulously develops its characters, who are played with uniform excellence by the huge cast. Also shown in 11 parts on TV, this stunningly photographed epic (with monochrome being tantalisingly embossed with patches of colour) was followed by the disappointingly inferior *Second Heimat*. In German with English subtitles.

Michael Lesch *Paul Simon* • Marita Breuer *Maria Wiegand* • Gertrud Bredel *Katharina Simon* • Willi Burger *Mathias Simon* • Rüdiger Weigang *Eduard Simon* • Karin Kienzler *Pauline Simon* • Arno Lang *Robert Krober* ■ *Dir* Edgar Reitz • *Scr* Edgar Reitz, Peter Steinbach • *Cinematographer* Gernat Roll

Heimkehr ★★★★

Silent romantic drama
1928 · Ger · BW · 110mins

Joe May pioneered the German movie serial and directed numerous feature films, as well as launching the career of Fritz Lang, before creating what many regard as his masterpiece. This tragic melodrama, which bears the hallmark of both UFA (the German national production body) stylisation and Hollywood gloss, has more in common with FW Murnau's *Sunrise* than May's own follow-up, the grittily realistic street drama, *Asphalt*. A tale of doomed wartime romance sees Dita Parlo caught between Gustav Fröhlich and Lars Hanson. Produced by Erich Pommer, it's expertly photographed by Gunther Rittau, who would go on to shoot *The Blue Angel* two years later.

Lars Hanson *Richard* • Dita Parlo *Anna* • Gustav Fröhlich *Karl* ■ *Dir* Joe May • *Scr* Fred Majo, Dr Fritz Wendhauser, from the novel *Karl und Anna* by Leonhard Franck

The Heiress ★★★★★ U

Drama 1949 · US · Colour · 114mins

An immaculately cast and brilliantly directed movie adaptation of Henry James's novel *Washington Square*. Olivia de Havilland quite rightly won her second Academy Award as the plain spinster seeking affection from fortune hunter Montgomery Clift. Clift also gives a finely controlled performance of great subtlety and, though both he and de Havilland are too good-looking for their roles, it is this quintessential Hollywood factor that keeps you riveted to the screen. As de Havilland's autocratic father, Ralph Richardson delivers arguably his finest screen work, and these flawless casting choices contribute to what is surely the most satisfying screen adaptation of James's original story.

Olivia de Havilland *Catherine Sloper* • Montgomery Clift *Morris Townsend* • Ralph Richardson *Dr Austin Sloper* • Miriam Hopkins *Lavinia Penniman* • Vanessa Brown *Maria* • Mona Freeman *Marian Almond* • Selena Royle *Elizabeth Almond* • Ray Collins *Jefferson Almond* • Betty Linley *Mrs Montgomery* ■ *Dir* William Wyler • *Scr* Ruth Goetz, Augustus Goetz, from their play, from the novel *Washington Square* by Henry James • *Music* Aaron Copland • *Costume Designer* Edith Head, Gile Steele • *Art Director* John Meehan

The Heist ★★★

Crime comedy 1971 · US · Colour · 120mins

Known as *$ (Dollars)* in the USA, Richard Brooks's crime comedy has much in common with *Rififi* and *The Italian Job*. Never anything less than hugely enjoyable, this often frantic caper stars Warren Beatty as a bank security expert dedicated to crime and Goldie Hawn as his happy hooker accomplice. Although there is little chemistry between the leads and Brooks's direction is occasionally over-elaborate, the thefts from the deposit boxes of three criminal heavies are conducted with training-manual precision, while the finale has all the intricacy of a Buster Keaton chase.

Warren Beatty *Joe Collins* • Goldie Hawn *Dawn Divine* • Gert Fröbe [Gert Fröbe] *Mr Kessel* • Robert Webber *Attorney* • Scott Brady *Sarge* • Arthur Brauss *Candy Man* • Robert Stiles *Major* ■ *Dir/Scr* Richard Brooks

The Heist ★★★ 15

Crime drama 1989 · US · Colour · 93mins

One from Pierce Brosnan's post-*Remington Steele*, pre-Bond career hiatus, this is a sharply plotted, engaging crime caper. Brosnan plays a topnotch thief out to carry out an ingenious robbery at a racetrack, now guarded by his old partner in crime (Tom Skerrit) who betrayed him years earlier. The fine supporting cast includes Wendy Hughes, Noble Willingham and Robert Prosky, and director Stuart Orme smoothly navigates the labyrinthine plotting. [VIDEO]

Pierce Brosnan *Neil Skinner* • Tom Skerritt *Ebet Berens* • Wendy Hughes *Sheila* • Noble Willingham *Stuckey* • Robert Prosky *Dancer* • Tom Atkins *Detective Leland* ■ *Dir* Stuart Orme • *Scr* David Fuller, Rick Natkin

Hélas pour Moi ★★

Drama 1993 · Fr/Swi · Colour · 85mins

The English title is *Oh, Woe Is Me* and it's a reworking of the ancient Greek myth of Alcmene and Amphitryon. Gérard Depardieu drifts around a rainy Swiss lakeside village soliciting opinions on everything from love to the war in Bosnia. His body is then borrowed by God. It looks slapped together in a day or so, with Depardieu appearing as if in homage to Godard's earlier achievements, such as *A Bout de Souffle*. Wonderful music by Beethoven, Bach and Shostakovich gives the illusion of beauty. A French language film.

Gérard Depardieu *Simon Donnadieu* • Laurence Masliah *Rachel Donnadieu* • Bernard Verley *Abraham Klimt* • Jean-Louis Loca *Max Mercure* • François Germond *Pastor* • Jean-Pierre Miquel *Other Pastor* ■ *Dir* Jean-Luc Godard • *Scr* Jean-Luc Godard, from the play *Amphitryon 38* by Jean Giraudoux

The Helen Morgan Story ★★★

Musical biography 1957 · US · BW · 118mins

Although Ann Blyth bears no resemblance to Helen Morgan and doesn't sing (Gogi Grant does the dubbing), she gives a sincere and effective performance as the great torch singer. This biopic plays fast and loose with the facts of Morgan's tumultuous life, but has considerable Prohibition-era atmosphere through the moody black-and-white photography of Ted McCord allied to the fast-paced direction of Michael Curtiz. Paul Newman scores as the opportunist who weaves in and out of her life.

Ann Blyth *Helen Morgan* • Paul Newman *Larry* • Richard Carlson *Wade* • Gene Evans *Whitey Krause* • Alan King *Ben* • Cara Williams *Dolly* ■ *Dir* Michael Curtiz • *Scr* Oscar Saul, Dean Reisner, Stephen Longstreet, Nelson Gidding

Helen of Troy ★★★ U

Drama 1955 · US/It · Colour · 113mins

One of Tinseltown's rare excursions into Greek myth – Hollywood has always preferred Christians, Romans and hungry lions. Based partly on Homer, it was filmed in Italy by Robert Wise, the future director of *West Side Story* and *The Sound of Music*, and boasts a weird cast: Jacques Sernas as Paris and Rossana Podesta as Helen are a lacklustre romantic couple, while Stanley Baker's Achilles is a real heel. Janette Scott and even Brigitte Bardot add support, and future 007 designer Ken Adam provides the decor.

Rossana Podesta *Helen* • Jacques Sernas *Paris* • Cedric Hardwicke *Priam* • Stanley Baker *Achilles* • Niall MacGinnis *Menelaus* • Nora Swinburne *Hecuba* • Harry Andrews *Hector* • Brigitte Bardot *Andraste* ■ *Dir* Robert Wise • *Scr* John Twist, Hugh Gray

The Helicopter Spies ★★ U

Spy adventure 1968 · US · Colour · 94mins

The hilarious staccato-speak and all-action breeziness of *The Man from UNCLE* are handled with flair by David McCallum and Robert Vaughn in a feature that has been skilfully plucked from an episode of the comic-book TV series. Even the ham-fisted clichés (dotty scientist, for example) are part of the fun. Still, no amount of leaping around the world can disguise the creakiness of the presentation.

Robert Vaughn *Napoleon Solo* • David McCallum *Illya Kuryakin* • Carol Lynley *Annie* • Bradford Dillman *Luther Sebastian* • Lola Albright *Azalea* • John Dehner *Dr Kharmusi* • Leo G Carroll *Mr Waverly* ■ *Dir* Boris Sagal • *Scr* Dean Hargrove

Hell and High Water ★★★ U

Action spy drama
1954 · US · Colour · 102mins

A splendid submarine movie starring Richard Widmark that makes the best of the confined surroundings to pump up the atmosphere. Twentieth Century-Fox boss Darryl F Zanuck didn't want to spend too much time on this one, so he entrusted it to jobbing director Samuel Fuller. The film became yet another heady Fuller brew, full of action, espionage, romance and cardboard characterisation. The result is, of course, immensely enjoyable and a feast for Fuller fans. The supporting cast helps hide the fact that the female lead (Bella Darvi, Zanuck's mistress at the time) can't act.

Richard Widmark *Adam Jones* • Bella Darvi *Denise* • Victor Francen *Professor Montel* • Cameron Mitchell *"Ski" Brodski* • Gene Evans *Chief Holter* • David Wayne *Dugboat Walker* • Stephen Bekassy *Neuman* ■ *Dir* Samuel Fuller • *Scr* Jesse L Lasky Jr, Samuel Fuller, from a story by David Hempstead

Hell below Zero ★★★ U

Adventure 1954 · UK · Colour · 86mins

Alan Ladd took advantage of the tax break that helped US stars if they spent 18 months in Europe by making a series of British movies aimed at the international market, including this action adventure based on the Hammond Innes novel *White South*. It's smoothly directed by another American, the excellent and under-rated Mark Robson, and the oh-so-cool Ladd is terrific pitted against assorted grim-faced whalers in the Antarctic wastes. The exciting action sequences became the signature of co-producer Albert R Broccoli and co-writer Richard Maibaum, whose collaboration, principally on the James Bond series of movies, continued until Maibaum's death in 1991. [VIDEO]

Alan Ladd *Duncan Craig* • Joan Tetzel *Judie Nordahl* • Basil Sydney *Bland* • Stanley Baker *Erik Bland* • Joseph Tomelty *Captain McPhee* • Niall MacGinnis *Dr Howe* • Jill Bennett *Gerda Peterson* • Peter Dyneley *Miller* ■ *Dir* Mark Robson • *Scr* Alec Coppel, Max Trell, Richard Maibaum, from the novel *The White South* by Hammond Innes

Hell Bent for Glory ★★

First World War drama
1957 · US · BW · 91mins

Also known as *Lafayette Escadrille*, this First World War saga was a deeply personal project for director William Wellman, who had himself been an ace fighter pilot with the Lafayette Flying Corps. Wellman's high hopes were dashed, however, when Paul Newman dropped out. He was replaced by the blond and tanned Malibu lifeguard Tab Hunter, who really doesn't cut it as a war hero. Clint Eastwood gets an early featured role as one of Wellman's flying chums, and Wellman himself is played by his son.

Tab Hunter *Thad Walker* • Etchika Choureau *Renee* • Marcel Dalio *Drillmaster* • David Janssen *Duke Sinclaire* • Paul Fix *US General* • Veola Vonn *The Madam* • Will Hutchins *Dave Putnam* • Clint Eastwood *George Moseley* • Bill Wellman Jr *Bill Wellman* ■ *Dir* William A Wellman • *Scr* AS Fleischman, from the story *C'est la Guerre* by William A Wellman

Hell Bent for Leather ★★ U

Western 1960 · US · Colour · 81mins

An uninspired Audie Murphy western given a novel moral twist by the fact that evil marshal Stephen McNally just keeps on pursuing our baby-faced hero even though he knows he's innocent. Felicia Farr (Mrs Jack Lemmon in real life) is the girl Murphy enlists to help him, and there are some mean hombres in tow including sleek Robert Middleton and steel-eyed Jan Merlin. It also gains from being filmed in CinemaScope, and from the presence of old-time western hero Bob Steele.

Audie Murphy *Clay* • Felicia Farr *Janet* • Stephen McNally *Deckett* • Robert Middleton *Ambrose* • Rad Fulton *Moon* • Jan Merlin *Travers* • Bob Steele *Jared* ■ *Dir* George Sherman • *Scr* Christopher Knopf, from a novel by Ray Hogan

Hell Boats ★

Wartime drama
1970 · UK/US · Colour · 95mins

A feeble Second World War drama, made for peanuts and with a poor cast. James Franciscus is top-billed as an American lieutenant commander in the Royal Navy, who arrives in the Mediterranean to find an undisciplined rabble and a lonely wife, played by Elizabeth Shepherd. Things blow up (German supply dumps) and things break down (actors' accents and relationships) as the script tries to re-stage sequences from *The Dirty Dozen* via wobbly back projection.

James Franciscus *Lt Commander Tom Jeffords* • Elizabeth Shepherd *Alison Ashurst* • Ronald Allen *Commander Roger Ashurst* • Reuven Bar Yotam *CPO Yacov* • Mark Hawkins *Lt Barlow* ■ *Dir* Paul Wendkos • *Scr* Anthony Spinner, Donald Ford, Derek Ford, from a story by SS Schweitzer

Hell Camp ★★ 18

Thriller 1987 · US · Colour · 95mins

A disappointing slice of straight-to-video fodder – released in the States as *Opposing Force* – that fails to deliver on an intriguing premise. Tom Skerritt and Lisa Eichhorn are among the military guinea pigs undergoing tests in the field to see how they stand up to being prisoners of war. The problem is that bonkers camp boss Anthony Zerbe starts taking the experiments a little too seriously. Despite a better-than-average cast, this is a by-the-numbers thriller, directed with little flair by Eric Karson. Contains violence, swearing and nudity. ▦

Tom Skerritt *Major Logan* • Lisa Eichhorn *Lieutenant Casey* • Anthony Zerbe *Becker* • Richard Roundtree *Sergeant Stafford* • Robert Wightman *General McGowan* • John Considine *General MacDonald* • George Kee Cheung [George Cheung] *Tuan* ■ *Dir* Eric Karson • *Scr* Gil Cowan

Hell Comes to Frogtown ★ 15

Science-fiction action adventure
1988 · US · Colour · 82mins

This is almost the ultimate in dumb movie plotlines. Professional wrestler "Rowdy" Roddy Piper stars as Sam Hell, the last potent man alive, who is chosen to rescue and impregnate various buxom maidens held captive by mutant frog folk. The directors never allow anything as trivial as common sense to get in the way of the fun, with most of the *Carry On*-style jokes focusing on Piper's "below the belt" equipment. Bad enough to be beyond criticism: how can you hate a movie which includes such immortal lines as "Eat lead, froggies!" ▦

Roddy Piper *Sam Hell* • Sandahl Bergman *Spangle* • Cec Verrell *Centinella* • William Smith *Captain Devlin/Count Sodom* • Rory Calhoun *Looney Tunes* • Nicholas Worth *Bull* • Kristi Somers *Arabella* ■ *Dir* RJ Kizer, Donald G Jackson • *Scr* Randall Frakes, from a story by Donald G Jackson, Randall Frakes

Hell Divers ★★ U

Action drama 1932 · US · BW · 108mins

This overlong action drama casts Clark Gable and Wallace Beery as a pair of tough officers in the US Navy. Dorothy Jordan is the woman who comes between them, though their rivalry is resolved when Beery sacrifices all to save Gable's life. The narrative mostly consists of endless flying missions that get less impressive the further the film progresses. Director George Hill, best known for his silent drama *The Big House*, later shot himself while making *The Good Earth*.

Clark Gable *Steve* • Wallace Beery *Windy* • Conrad Nagel *Duke* • Dorothy Jordan *Ann* • Marjorie Rambeau *Mame Kelsey* • Marie Prevost *Lulu* • Cliff Edwards *Baldy* ■ *Dir* George Hill • *Scr* Harvey Gates, Malcolm Stuart Boylan, JK McGuinness, Ralph Graves, from a story from Lt Cdr Frank Wead

Hell Drivers ★★★★

Thriller 1957 · UK · BW · 107mins

A gripping British thriller with a cutting edge of social reality from former Hollywood director Cy Endfield (billed here as C Raker Endfield). Stanley Baker stars as the ex-con given the job of driving lorries at perilous speeds to meet the deadlines of a haulage company, who uncovers a racket run by his unprincipled manager. There's a splendid performance from Patrick McGoohan as a lethal rival driver and a marvellous co-starring role for Herbert Lom. Watch out, too, for a young, pre-Bond Sean Connery.

Stanley Baker *Tom Yately* • Herbert Lom *Gino* • Peggy Cummins *Lucy* • Patrick McGoohan *Red* • William Hartnell *Cartley* • Wilfrid Lawson *Ed* • Sidney James *Dusty* • Jill Ireland *Jill* • Alfie Bass *Tinker* • Gordon Jackson *Scottie* • David McCallum *Jimmy Yately* • Sean Connery *Johnny* ■ *Dir* C Raker Endfield [Cy Endfield] • *Scr* John Kruse, C Raker Endfield [Cy Endfield]

Hell Hath No Fury ★★ 18

Thriller 1991 · US · Colour · 85mins

Based on the bestselling novel *Smithereens*, this predictable thriller gains points from the stand-out performances of its two female leads, *I Dream of Jeannie* star Barbara Eden and Loretta Swit, who also has *M*A*S*H* as "Hot Lips" in the TV series *M*A*S*H*. Eden is the wife whose life falls apart when her husband is murdered, while Swit's manic performance as the psychotic out to frame her makes Glenn Close's *Fatal Attraction* turn look like an audition for *Blue Peter*. ▦

Barbara Eden *Terri Ferguson* • Loretta Swit *Connie Stewart* • David Ackroyd *Stanley Ferguson* • Kim Zimmer *Marlene* • Amanda Peterson *Michelle* • Richard Kline *Milton* • Jim Haynie *Cantrell* • Stephen Lee *Bruce Gossiter* ■ *Dir* Thomas J Wright • *Scr* Beau Bensink, from the novel *Smithereens* by BW Battin

Hell in the Pacific ★★★★ PG

Second World War drama
1968 · US · Colour · 101mins

Director John Boorman touches the primitive nerve of mankind at odds with itself and nature (anticipating his masterpiece, *Deliverance*, four years later) in this story of an American pilot and a Japanese sailor marooned on an island in wartime. The catchpenny title masks the solidly psychological nature of the action, as Lee Marvin displays a dramatic complexity rarely seen in his other works, while Toshiro Mifune exhibits honour as a sword that cuts both ways. The dynamics of the pair forcibly having to share their lives makes for compelling viewing. ▦

Lee Marvin *US marine pilot* • Toshiro Mifune *Japanese naval officer* ■ *Dir* John Boorman • *Scr* Alexander Jacobs, Eric Bercovici, from a story by Reuben Bercovitch

Hell Is a City ★★★ PG

Thriller 1959 · UK · BW · 91mins

Made when Hammer wasn't just a house of horror, this brisk crime thriller was filmed on location in Manchester. Studio executives were so worried that the locals would resent this portrait of their city that Mancunian screenings were prefaced by a speech from a neighbourhood bobby assuring all that the film-makers didn't really equate their home with the inferno. Stanley Baker bristles with northern grit as the inspector out to nab the escaped convict whose crimes include murder and robbing bookie Donald Pleasence. Director Val Guest demonstrates a flair for docudramatic realism and no-nonsense pacing that is at odds with his earlier screenplay writing collaborations on Will Hay films. ▦

Stanley Baker *Inspector Martineau* • John Crawford *Don Starling* • Donald Pleasence *Gus Hawkins* • Maxine Audley *Julia Martineau* • Billie Whitelaw *Chloe Hawkins* • Joseph Tomelty *Furnisher Steele* • George A Cooper *Doug Savage* ■ *Dir* Val Guest • *Scr* Val Guest, from a novel by Maurice Proctor

Hell Is for Heroes ★★★

Second World War adventure
1962 · US · BW · 89mins

Having already won a screenwriting Oscar for *Battleground* (1949), Robert Pirosh here came up with an even more uncompromising insight into the terrifying uncertainty and sudden brutality of frontline life. Never one to shy away from violence, director Don Siegel builds steadily towards the pitiless battle sequences by allowing us to get to know the members of the small unit ordered to overpower a German pillbox, whose only hope of survival is to mislead the Germans into believing they are a much more substantial force. Steve McQueen is overly intense and Bob Newhart's comic monologue a mite ill-judged, but James Coburn is superb.

Steve McQueen *Reese* • Bobby Darin *Private Corby* • Fess Parker *Sergeant Pike* • Harry Guardino *Sergeant Larkin* • James Coburn *Corporal Henshaw* • Mike Kellin *Private Kolinsky* • Joseph Hoover *Captain Loomis* • Bill Mullikin *Private Cumberly* • LQ Jones *Sergeant Frazer* • Bob Newhart *Private Driscoll* ■ *Dir* Don Siegel • *Scr* Robert Pirosh, Richard Carr, from a story by Robert Pirosh

Hell on Frisco Bay ★★

Crime thriller 1955 · US · Colour · 98mins

Alan Ladd stars as the former cop framed and jailed on a manslaughter charge, who is seeking revenge on the violent racketeer responsible, played by Edward G Robinson. Ladd is aided by a first-rate cast, including Joanne Dru as his wife, Fay Wray as a faded film star and Paul Stewart as her lover and Robinson's right-hand man. Jayne Mansfield has a bit in a nightclub and Rod Taylor makes an early appearance. Frank Tuttle directs.

Alan Ladd *Steve Rollins* • Edward G Robinson *Victor Amato* • Joanne Dru *Marcia Rollins* • William Demarest *Dan Bianco* • Nestor Paiva *Lou Fiaschetti* • Perry Lopez *Mario Amato* • Paul Stewart *Joe Lye* • Fay Wray *Kay Stanley* • Jayne Mansfield *Blonde* • Stanley Adams *Hammy* • Rodney Taylor [Rod Taylor] *Brodie Evans* ■ *Dir* Frank Tuttle • *Scr* Sydney Boehm, Martin Rackin, from the magazine serial *The Darkest Hour* by William P McGivern

Hell Ship Mutiny ★ U

Adventure drama 1957 · US · BW · 66mins

In the 1940s, the well-built and handsome Jon Hall was a kind of male Dorothy Lamour, only instead of a sarong, he was mostly seen in a loincloth. Though still handsome in his forties, Hall remained fully clothed, despite the South Seas setting, in this rather dire low-budget Republic adventure. He's a ship's captain helping a princess rid her island of thieves. There is some minor consolation in that the heavies include John Carradine and Peter Lorre.

Jon Hall *Captain Knight* • John Carradine *Malone* • Peter Lorre *Lamouet* • Roberta Haynes *Mareva* • Mike Mazurki *Ross* • Charles Mauu *Tula* ■ *Dir* Lee Sholem, Elmo Williams • *Scr* DeVallon Scott, Wells Root

Hell to Eternity ★★★

Second World War drama
1960 · US · BW · 133mins

Based on a true story of Second World War hero Guy Gabaldon, the film presents a slightly different angle on the war – how the Californian Japanese community was affected by the bombing of Pearl Harbour. Most of the movie, however, is the usual slam-bang battle stuff, until Jeffrey Hunter – with divided loyalties due to his upbringing by Japanese foster parents – uses his knowledge of his adopted tongue to get an enemy battalion to surrender. Two of his buddies are David Janssen (*The Fugitive*) and Vic Damone, best known as a crooner.

Jeffrey Hunter *Guy Gabaldon* • David Janssen *Bill* • Vic Damone *Pete* • Patricia Owens *Sheila* • Miiko Taka *Ester* • Sessue Hayakawa *General Matsui* • George Takei *George* ■ *Dir* Phil Karlson • *Scr* Ted Sherdeman, Walter Roeber Schmidt, from a story by Gil Doud

Hell Up in Harlem ★ 18

Crime drama 1973 · US · Colour · 90mins

The weak sequel to *Black Caesar* finds Fred Williamson fighting both his father and the mob for control of Harlem. When the Mafia kidnap his children, he leads a posse of frogmen against mob headquarters in the Florida Keys. Plenty of double-crossing mayhem and hand-held camera action fail to enliven the usually reliable director Larry Cohen's blaxploitation caper. ▦

Fred Williamson *Tommy Gibbs* • Julius Harris *Papa Gibbs* • Gloria Hendry *Helen Bradley* • Margaret Avery *Sister Jennifer* • D'Urville Martin *Reverend Rufus* • Tony King *Zach* ■ *Dir/Scr* Larry Cohen

The Hell with Heroes ★

Crime drama 1968 · US · Colour · 101mins

Most definitely not to be confused with the Steve McQueen war movie *Hell Is for Heroes*, this is an eminently missable adventure, as Rod Taylor and Peter Duel try to make a dishonest buck after the Second World War by smuggling contraband. Harry Guardino plays Mr Big and Claudia Cardinale his

mistress, a thankless role with which she looks suitably bored. TV director Joseph Sargent made his big-screen debut here and seems determined to cram in as much redundant casbah footage as possible, perhaps in homage to *Pépé le Moko*.

Rod Taylor *Brynie MacKay* • Claudia Cardinale *Elena* • Harry Guardino *Lee Harris* • Kevin McCarthy *Colonel Wilson* • Peter Duel *Mike Brewer* • William Marshall *Al Poland* • Don Knight *Pepper* ■ *Dir* Joseph Sargent • *Scr* Halsted Welles, Harold Livingston, from a story by Harold Livingston

Hellborn ★★ 🔞
Crime drama 1961 · US · Colour · 75mins

An undercover cop in drag, a judge warning the audience of the dangers of pornography and a beauty queen cornered by a sadistic psycho killer – what else could this be but another poverty row, sexploitation quickie from Ed Wood Jr, famously acknowledged as the world's worst director? The last film directed by the cult auteur of *Plan 9 for Outer Space* has Michael "Dino" Fantini going berserk watching a stag movie and turning into a sex maniac. Although an interesting artefact from the early "adults only" days, this ludicrous grindhouse affair is a typical Wood mix of tease, tastelessness and tacky acting. 📺

Kenne Duncan *Lieutenant Matt Carson* • James "Duke" Moore *Sergeant Randy Stone* • Jean Fontaine *Gloria Henderson* • Carl Anthony *Johnny Ryde* • Dino Fantini *Dirk Williams* • Jeanne Willardson *Mary Smith* ■ *Dir/Scr* Edward D Wood Jr

Hellbound ★ 🔞
Action adventure 1993 · US · Colour · 90mins

Two Chicago police officers investigating a (literally) heart-wrenching murder end up in Israel where the concerned authorities are convinced a supernatural being is the root cause. The worst film made by martial arts star Chuck Norris, this cheaply made, slapdash mess has virtually no action or sense to warrant its existence, while the unpleasant streak of Arab racism leaves a nasty taste in the mouth. Contains violence, nudity and swearing. 📺

Chuck Norris *Shatter* • Calvin Levels *Jackson* • Christopher Neame *Lockley* • Sheree J Wilson *Leslie* • Jack Adalist *Krieger* • Ori Levy *Rabbi Shindler* • Erez Atar *Bezi* ■ *Dir* Aaron Norris • *Scr* Donald Thompson, Brent Friedman, from a story by Ian Rabin, Anthony Ridio, Brent Friedman

Hellbound: Hellraiser II ★★ 🔞
Horror 1988 · UK · Colour · 89mins

Allegory is replaced by the just plain gory in the first sequel to Clive Barker's groundbreaking macabre masochistic myth about the dark angels of hell and their Faustian bargains. Kenneth Cranham is the demented doctor anxious to meet the Cenobite messengers, while asylum inmate Ashley Laurence (still recovering from *Hellraiser* events) is forced to fight the invoked demons for her father's soul. Routinely directed by Tony Randel, some disturbing eeriness is conjured up between the blood-soaked illogicalities and outlandish inconsistencies. Contains violence and swearing. 📺 **DVD**

Ashley Laurence *Kirsty Cotton* • Clare Higgins *Julia* • Kenneth Cranham *Dr Channard* • Imogen Boorman *Tiffany* • William Hope *Kyle Macrae* • Oliver Smith *Browning* • Sean Chapman *Uncle Frank* • Doug Bradley *Pinhead* ■ *Dir* Tony Randel • *Scr* Peter Atkins, from a story by Clive Barker

Hellcats of the Navy ★★ 🅄
Second World War drama 1957 · US · BW · 77mins

A barely average war movie, filled with phoney back-projected battles and an equally phoney performance from Ronald Reagan, as a submarine commander who offers moral homilies to his crew on a mission to look for Japanese mines. After a skirmish, Reagan is forced to leave one of his men behind, while a crass romance with comely nurse Nancy Davis (his real-life wife and the future First Lady) complicates matters further. Apart from their future appearances on the world stage, this would be the only time they acted together. 📺

Ronald Reagan *Commander Casey Abbott* • Nancy Davis *Helen Blair* • Arthur Franz *Lieutenant Commander Don Landon* • Robert Arthur *Freddy Warren* • William Leslie *Lieutenant Paul Prentice* • William Phillips [William "Bill" Phillips] *Carroll* • Harry Lauter *Wes Barton* ■ *Dir* Nathan Juran • *Scr* David Lang, Raymond T Marcus [Bernard Gordon], from a story by David Lang, from the book *Hellcats of the Sea* by Charles A Lockwood, Hans Christian

Heller in Pink Tights ★★★
Western 1960 · US · Colour · 100mins

George Cukor, renowned as a woman's director in Hollywood, might seem an unlikely choice to direct a western, but this is an unlikely example of the genre, dealing as it does with a group of travelling theatricals, led by stunning Sophia Loren. Anthony Quinn and Steve Forrest flex their emotions as rivals for La Loren, but the real star is Cukor's skill as a film-maker. The production design is superb, and Loren and her troupe, whether on-stage or off-stage, look great in Technicolor.

Sophia Loren *Angela Rossini* • Anthony Quinn *Tom Healy* • Margaret O'Brien *Della Southby* • Steve Forrest *Clint Mabry* • Eileen Heckart *Lorna Hathaway* • Edmund Lowe *Manfred "Doc" Montague* • Ramon Novarro *De Leon* ■ *Dir* George Cukor • *Scr* Dudley Nichols, Walter Bernstein, from the novel *Heller with a Gun* by Louis L'Amour • *Art Director* Hal Pereira

Hellfighters ★★ 🅿🅖
Adventure 1969 · US · Colour · 115mins

John Wayne douses oilfield fires while trying to dampen the passion his daughter (Katharine Ross) feels for his young partner (Jim Hutton). Based on the exploits of fire-fighter Red Adair, the film's technical adviser, this old-style action movie would have suited Howard Hawks, but Andrew V McLaglen's effort hardly sets the world alight with its perfunctory action and tacked-on romance. Vera Miles, who was secretly in love with Wayne in *The Searchers*, here plays his ex-wife, while buffs will spot the similarities between this and the 1998 asteroid epic, *Armageddon*. 📺

John Wayne *Chance Buckman* • Katharine Ross *Tish Buckman* • Jim Hutton *Greg Parker* • Vera Miles *Madelyn Buckman* • Jay C Flippen *Jack Lomax* • Bruce Cabot *Joe Horn* • Edward Faulkner *George Harris* ■ *Dir* Andrew V McLaglen • *Scr* Clair Huffaker

The Hellfire Club ★★ 🅄
Historical adventure 1961 · UK · Colour · 93mins

Depravity, debauchery and devil worship? There's nothing of the sort in this would-be horror flick, in which such sins are sadly bleached of any lurid content. Keith Michell stars as the dispossessed son who returns to claim his degenerate father's estate, only to be challenged by his cousin Peter Arne, who's up to all kinds of dirty tricks by virtue of his Hellfire Club membership. The club was, in fact, a group of 18th-century aristocrats bent on the violation of local maidens while praying to Satan and all his works, but any relationship between the real story and this hokum is coincidental.

Keith Michell *Jason* • Adrienne Corri *Isobel* • Peter Cushing *Merryweather* • Kai Fischer *Yvonne* • Peter Arne *Thomas* • David Lodge *Timothy* • Bill Owen *Martin* • Miles Malleson *Judge* ■ *Dir* Robert S Baker, Monty Berman • *Scr* Leon Griffiths, Jimmy Sangster, from a story by Jimmy Sangster

Hellgate ★★ 🅄
Western 1952 · US · Colour · 87mins

Hellgate is a remote prison in New Mexico where the brutal regime in the 1860s is made worse by the desert heat. Sterling Hayden plays the wrongly imprisoned veterinary surgeon, persecuted by the harsh and embittered commandant portrayed by Ward Bond, in this unremittingly grim production. Written and directed by Charles Marquis Warren, this low-budget western becomes too reminiscent of John Ford's much superior *The Prisoner of Shark Island*, and the true story behind it, when the vet's medical skills come in handy during a deadly epidemic.

Sterling Hayden *Gil Hanley* • Joan Leslie *Ellen Hanley* • Ward Bond *Lt Tod Vorhees* • Jim Arness [James Arness] *George Redfield* • Marshall Bradford *Doctor Pelham* • Peter Coe *Jumper Hall* • Richard Paxton *George Nye* • John Pickard *Gundy Boyd* ■ *Dir* Charles Marquis Warren • *Scr* Charles Marquis Warren, from a story by Charles Marquis Warren, John C Champion

Hello Again ★★★ 🅿🅖
Black comedy 1987 · US · Colour · 92mins

Making it to the big screen from TV's *Cheers*, Shelley Long – Sam Malone's high-minded barmaid – is rather small-time in one of those supernatural plots that were popular after *Ghostbusters*. She's a plastic surgeon's plastic wife, who chokes to death and returns to a much-altered life thanks to her medium sister. Long's brittle vivacity crumples under an overload of whimsy, though Judith Ivey, as the spaced-out, hippy sister, tunes us in to the cosmos to some comical effect. Contains some swearing. 📺

Shelley Long *Lucy Chadman* • Gabriel Byrne *Kevin Scanlon* • Judith Ivey *Zelda* • Corbin Bernsen *Jason Chadman* • Sela Ward *Kim Lacey* • Austin Pendleton *Junior Lacey* ■ *Dir* Frank Perry • *Scr* Susan Isaacs

Hello, Dolly! ★★★★ 🅄
Musical 1969 · US · Colour · 139mins

Despite Barbra Streisand's underaged Dolly Levi, this lavish 20th Century-Fox movie version of the long-running Broadway hit is a wondrous treat under Gene Kelly's expert direction, and now looks like the virtual last gasp of the great era of costly Hollywood musicals. Among the twinkling, shining stars are Britain's own Michael Crawford and the man who had taken the title song to number one in the US charts five years earlier, Louis "Satchmo" Armstrong himself. The design, use of colour and, particularly, the marvellous score are quite breathtaking, and the film won three Oscars. 📺

Barbra Streisand *Dolly Levi* • Walter Matthau *Horace Vandergelder* • Michael Crawford *Cornelius Hackl* • Louis Armstrong *Orchestra leader* • Marianne McAndrew *Irene Molloy* • EJ Peaker *Minnie Fay* • Danny Lockin *Barnaby Tucker* • Joyce Ames *Ermengarde* ■ *Dir* Gene Kelly • *Scr* Ernest Lehman, from the musical *Hello, Dolly!* by Jerry Herman, Michael Stewart, from the play *The Matchmaker* by Thornton Wilder • *Cinematographer* Harry Stradling • *Music* Lenny Hayton, Lionel Newman • *Production Designer* John De Cuir

Hello Down There ★★ 🅄
Comedy 1969 · US · Colour · 97mins

This would-be comedy comes across as a sort of underwater *Swiss Family Robinson*, with Tony Randall as the designer of a submersible house who agrees to test it out on his wife and children. The plethora of generation gap jokes soon grates on the nerves, as do the bratty adolescent cast members, including a young Richard Dreyfuss, but there's no denying an ingenious premise that should dazzle the youngsters. Director Jack Arnold was reunited with his *Creature from the Black Lagoon* colleague Ricou Browning, who helped co-ordinate the diving sequences.

Tony Randall *Fred Miller* • Janet Leigh *Vivian Miller* • Jim Backus *TR Hollister* • Roddy McDowall *Nate Ashbury* • Merv Griffin • Ken Berry *Mel Cheever* • Kay Cole *Lorrie Miller* • Richard Dreyfuss *Harold Webster* • Harvey Lembeck *Sonarman* ■ *Dir* Jack Arnold • *Scr* Frank Telford, John McGreevey, from a story by Ivan Tors, Art Arthur

Hello, Frisco, Hello ★★ 🅄
Period musical 1943 · US · Colour · 98mins

After time off for motherhood, Alice Faye returned in another Fox period musical with her regular co-stars of the time, John Payne and Jack Oakie. But this is not in the same league as *Tin Pan Alley* or *The Great American Broadcast*. The script is routine stuff about Payne's impresario making a singing star out of Faye on the turn-of-the-century Barbary Coast and how she repays the debt when he's down on his luck. To supplement the period numbers, Mack Gordon and Harry Warren wrote *You'll Never Know*, an Oscar-winning song about separated lovers with a wartime relevance that helped the film to box-office success.

Alice Faye *Trudy Evans* • John Payne *Johnny Cornell* • Jack Oakie *Dan Daley* • Lynn Bari *Bernice Croft* • Laird Cregar *Sam Weaver* • June Havoc *Beulah Clancy* • Ward Bond *Sharkey* ■ *Dir* H Bruce Humberstone • *Scr* Robert Ellis, Helen Logan, Richard Macauley

Hello – Goodbye ★

Comedy 1970 · US/UK · Colour · 100mins

In this pre-Frank Spencer comic role, Michael Crawford plays Harry England, a man obsessed with luxury cars, an interest which embroils him in a love affair while on a trip to France. Only later does he discover the object of his affection is actually the wife of the wealthy baron who employs him. A meandering romantic comedy which is more like a Skoda than a Bentley. They should have taken a train.

Michael Crawford *Harry England* • Geneviève Gilles *Dany* • Curt Jurgens *Baron De Choisis* • Ira Fürstenberg *Evelyne* • Lon Satton *Cole* • Peter Myers *Bentley* • Mike Marshall *Paul* ■ *Dir* Jean Negulesco • *Scr* Roger Marshall

Hello, Hemingway ★★★

Drama 1990 · Cub · Colour · 88mins

Set in the pre-Castro Cuba that played host to the exiled Ernest Hemingway (whose elusive presence lingers just off screen), this rites-of-passage drama draws its inspiration from the author's Pulitzer prize-winning masterpiece, *The Old Man and the Sea*. However, director Fernando Perez doesn't overdo the parallels between the obsessive fisherman's battles with the elements and Elvis-besotted teenager Laura de la Uz's bid to land the scholarship in the States that will enable her to break away from her impoverished family and increasingly politicised boyfriend. In Spanish with English subtitles.

Laura de la Uz *Larita* • Raul Paz *Victor* • Herminia Sanchez *Josefa* • Caridad Hernandez *Rosenda* • Enrique Molina *Manolo* • Maria Isabel Diaz *Flora* • Micheline Calvert *Miss Amalia* • Marta Del Rio *Doctor Martinez* ■ *Dir* Fernando Perez • *Scr* Maydo Royero

Hello Sister! ★★★

Drama 1933 · US · BW · 55mins

It is a sad fact that most of the nine movies directed by Erich von Stroheim were subject to a great deal of interference. Previously he had been profligate with studio money, but he completed *Walking Down Broadway*, his first and last sound film, on time and within budget. Yet 20th Century-Fox, with some reshoots and re-editing, released it under the crass title of *Hello Sister!* Pity, because there are enough bizarre touches in this uncharacteristically simple tale of boy meets girl on Broadway, to display von Stroheim's touch. But he removed his name from the credits, and was to spend the rest of his life as an actor, never to direct again.

ZaSu Pitts *Millie* • Boots Mallory *Peggy* • James Dunn *Jimmy* • Terrance Ray *Mac* • Minna Gombell *Mona* • Hattie McDaniel *Black woman in apartment house* ■ *Dir* Erich von Stroheim • *Scr* Erich von Stroheim, Leonard Spigelgass, Geraldine Nomis, Harry Ruskin, Maurine Watkins, from the play *Walking Down Broadway* by Dawn Powell • *Cinematographer* James Wong Howe

Hellraiser ★★★ 18

Horror 1987 · UK · Colour · 89mins

Popular horror writer Clive Barker transferred his trademark perverse chills visually intact to the screen in his directorial debut. A surreal, claustrophobic and graphic shocker about the consequences of opening a Chinese puzzle box, the film allows Barker to introduce a dark new mythology to the genre as well as the Cenobites, leather-clad, disfigured angels from hell with intriguing concepts of dimensional pleasure and pain. Despite his uneven direction and the odd Cricklewood locations, this absorbing sadomasochistic chiller really delivers the gruesome goods. Contains violence and swearing. 🔲 **DVD**

Andrew Robinson *Larry Cotton* • Clare Higgins *Julia Cotton* • Ashley Laurence *Kirsty Swanson* • Sean Chapman *Frank Cotton* • Oliver Smith *Frank the Monster* • Doug Bradley *Lead Cenobite* ■ *Dir* Clive Barker • *Scr* Clive Barker, from his novella *The Hellbound Heart*

Hellraiser III: Hell on Earth ★★★ 18

Horror 1992 · US · Colour · 89mins

Pinhead, the Cenobite superstar of author Clive Barker's bloody brainchild, tempts new disciples down the path of perverse pleasure in this distinct improvement on *Hellbound: Hellraiser II*. Here, director Anthony Hickox's high-energy horror comic strip is hot-wired by a keen visual sense and big dipper drive. More a supernatural sadomasochistic action thriller than the murky Gothic nightmares of the previous two episodes, this kamikaze kaleidoscope of carnage is funny, original and unpredictable. Contains violence, swearing, sex scenes, drug abuse and nudity. 🔲 **DVD**

Terry Farrell *Joey Summerskill* • Doug Bradley *Pinhead/Elliott Spencer* • Paula Marshall *Terri* • Kevin Bernhardt *JP Monroe* • Ken Carpenter *Doc/Camerahead* • Peter Boynton *Joey's father* • Aimee Leigh *Sandy* ■ *Dir* Anthony Hickox • *Scr* Peter Atkins, from a story by Peter Atkins, Tony Randel, from characters created by Clive Barker

Hellraiser: Bloodline ★★★ 18

Horror 1996 · US · Colour · 81mins

Showing clear signs of the studio tinkering that made director Kevin Yagher take his name off the credits, the ragged third sequel to author Clive Barker's Cenobite saga still does the blood-drenched business. Blending past, present and future together by exploring the evil origins of the lament configuration box (the key to unlocking the pleasures of Hell), genre icon Pinhead (Doug Bradley) takes sadomasochism into space in this audacious episode. Wacky, way-out and creepy, this is nowhere near the disaster it's made out to be. Contains swearing and violence. 🔲

Bruce Ramsay *Phillipe Lemarchand/John Merchant/Paul Merchant* • Valentina Vargas *Angelique* • Doug Bradley *Pinhead* ■ *Dir* Alan Smithee [Kevin Yagher] • *Scr* Peter Atkins

Hell's Angels ★★★ U

First World War drama 1930 · US · BW and Colour · 91mins

Howard Hughes's legendary air epic was almost completed as a silent movie, then virtually remade as a talkie. After sacking several directors, Hughes finally directed it himself and, despite good reviews and huge queues, the film cost too much to show a profit. The First World War aerial combat scenes remain spectacular and are the reason why Hughes made the film in the first place. Jean Harlow is still sexy down the decades, but Ben Lyon and James Hall are terribly stilted as the brothers who fight the war, and for Harlow.

Ben Lyon *Monte Rutledge* • James Hall *Roy Rutledge* • Jean Harlow *Helen* • John Darrow *Karl Amstedt* • Lucien Prival *Baron von Kranz* • Frank Clarke *Lt von Bruen* • Roy Wilson *Baldy* • Douglas Gilmore *Capt Redfield* ■ *Dir* Howard Hughes, Marshall Neilan, Luther Reed • *Scr* Joseph Moncure March, Harry Behn (adaptation), Howard Estabrook (adaptation), from a story by Marshall Neilan, Joseph Moncure March

Hell's Angels on Wheels ★★★ 18

Action drama 1967 · US · Colour · 79mins

A cult biker movie, originally banned by the British censors and full of carnage and copulation. Jack Nicholson plays a character called Poet (as characters were called in those days) who falls in with Adam Roarke's gang. As with his later film *The Stunt Man*, director Richard Rush uses a barrage of camera tricks, frenzied cutting and other "look at me" gimmicks which here help to enhance the boy-meets-biker girl story. 🔲

Jack Nicholson *Poet* • Adam Roarke *Buddy* • Sabrina Scharf *Shill* • Jana Taylor *Abigale* • John Garwood *Jock* • Richard Anders *Bull* • Mimi Machu *Pearl* • James Oliver *Gypsy* ■ *Dir* Richard Rush • *Scr* R Wright Campbell

Hell's Half Acre ★★

Crime drama 1954 · US · BW · 90mins

In this complicated crime drama, Wendell Corey is the reformed racketeer in Honolulu, involved in murder and blackmail, who hides out in the tough slum district of the city that gives the film its title. Evelyn Keyes is a further complication as the long abandoned wife who comes looking for him. Some skilful location shooting and the efforts of a good cast keep it moderately interesting.

Wendell Corey *Chet Chester* • Evelyn Keyes *Dona Williams* • Elsa Lanchester *Lida O'Reilly* • Marie Windsor *Rose* • Nancy Gates *Sally Lee* • Leonard Strong *Ippy* • Jesse White *Tubby Otis* • Keye Luke *Chief Dan* • Philip Ahn *Roger Kong* ■ *Dir* John H Auer • *Scr* Steve Fisher • *Cinematographer* John L Russell

Hell's Highway ★★★

Drama 1932 · US · BW · 60mins

A hard-hitting exposé of life in an American prison camp in the South, this is one of three notable films that writer Rowland Brown managed to direct in a career blighted by a reputation for truculence. This little-known rival to *I Was a Fugitive from a Chain Gang* has a hackneyed storyline, but the powerful performances from Richard Dix (convict) and C Henry Gordon (sadistic chief guard), its stark atmosphere and some of the incidents (such as the death of a deaf-mute who does not hear the posse demanding his surrender) stick in the mind.

Richard Dix *Frank "Duke" Ellis* • Tom Brown *Johnny Ellis* • Louise Carter *Mrs Ellis* • Rochelle Hudson *Mary Ellen* • C Henry Gordon *Blacksnake Skinner* • Warner Richmond *Pop-*

Eye Jackson • Sandy Roth *Blind Maxie* ■ *Dir* Rowland Brown • *Scr* Samuel Ornitz, Robert Tasker, Rowland Brown

Hell's House ★★

Crime 1932 · US · BW · 74mins

Strictly lower-order B-picture fare, made with no apparent flair by an obscure director named Howard Higgin. The movie concerns a youth (Junior Durkin) whose association with a racketeer (Pat O'Brien) lands him, though innocent of a crime, in a reform school run by abusive overseers. Junior's girlfriend is played by Bette Davis in one of the many inferior roles visited on her during her Warner Bros contract. At little over an hour, the movie is an undemanding time-filler.

Junior Durkin *Jimmy Mason* • Pat O'Brien *Kelly* • Bette Davis *Peggy Gardner* • Junior Coghlan *Shorty* • Charley Grapewin *Uncle Henry* • Emma Dunn *Aunt Emma* • Morgan Wallace *Frank Gebhardt* ■ *Dir* Howard Higgin • *Scr* Paul Gangelin, B Harrison Orkow, from the story by Howard Higgin

Hell's Island ★★

Crime 1955 · US · Colour · 84mins

With its rather shabby hero (a DA sacked because of a drink problem who becomes a bouncer), an overweight mastermind, a shady lady and a missing, priceless jewel, you realise rather quickly that this is a rehash of *The Maltese Falcon*. Set on a Caribbean island, where these B-list adventurers search for a big chunk of ruby which might have been lost in a place crash, it crams in a lot of sidebar plots and VistaVision scenery, all efficiently, if anonymously directed by Phil Karlson, who was later offered the first James Bond film, *Dr No*.

John Payne *Mike Cormack* • Mary Murphy *Janet Martin* • Francis L Sullivan *Barzland* • Eduardo Noriega *Inspector Pena* • Arnold Moss *Paul Armand* • Walter Reed *Lawrence* ■ *Dir* Phil Karlson • *Scr* Maxwell Shane, from a story by Jack Leonard, Martin M Goldsmith

The Hellstrom Chronicle ★★★

Drama documentary 1971 · US · Colour · 89mins

The microscopic action and doom-laden predictions contained in this stylised documentary reveal a sinister side to the insect antics of *Microcosmos*. Yes, the deadly purpose behind Walon Green's film is to warn us that bugs will eventually rule the planet, as they have an evolutionary durability that we can only dream of. However, it would be easier to take this unpalatable message more seriously were it not delivered by such a flagrantly bogus expert. Lawrence Pressman's performance as Nils Hellstrom is just irritatingly smug and distracts from the excellence of the photography, which clearly won this undeserving curio its Oscar.

Lawrence Pressman *Professor Hellstrom* ■ *Dir* Walon Green • *Scr* David Seltzer • *Music* Lalo Schifrin • *Cinematographer* Helmuth Barth, Walon Green, Vilis Lapenieks, Ken Middleham, Heinz Sielmann

U = SUITABLE FOR ALL   Uc = SUITABLE FOR ALL, ESPECIALLY FOR YOUNG CHILDREN (VIDEO ONLY)   PG = PARENTAL GUIDANCE

Hellzapoppin' ★★★★ U

Comedy   1941 · US · BW · 80mins

This surreal, almost plotless film version of vaudevillians Ole Olsen and Chic Johnson's famous long-running Broadway hit is a genuine one-off. Of course, it's virtually impossible to re-create characters on screen who wreak havoc in the theatre, so a number of cinematic devices have been incorporated to hilarious effect – the actual projectionist showing the movie is turned into an on-screen character (almost). Some of these gags work on TV, but many don't, and the place to revel in this forerunner of *The Goon Show* and Monty Python is really in the cinema, where it approaches comic masterpiece status. ▭

Ole Olsen *Ole* • Chic Johnson *Chic* • Martha Raye *Betty* • Hugh Herbert *Quimby* • Jane Frazee *Kitty* • Robert Paige *Jeff* • Mischa Auer *Pepi* • Richard Lane *The director* • Elisha Cook Jr *Selby* ■ *Dir* HC Potter • *Scr* Warren Wilson, Nat Perrin, Alex Gottlieb, from a story by Nat Perrin, from the play by Ole Olsen, Chic Johnson • *Music/Lyrics* Sammy Fain, Charles Tobias

Help! ★★★★ U

Musical comedy   1965 · UK · Colour · 91mins

A disappointment after the exhilarating *A Hard Day's Night*, the second Beatles feature is still hugely enjoyable. Sweeping John, George, Paul and Ringo from Swiss ski-slopes to the beaches of the Bahamas, this extremely silly story follows the attempts of an Eastern cult (led by Leo McKern and Eleanor Bron) to recover a ceremonial ring that has ended up on Ringo's finger. Pop classics (*Ticket to Ride* and the title song) abound and there are plenty of sharp one-liners. Nevertheless, the grander scale and the needs of the story prevent director Richard Lester from repeating the wisecracking familiarity of the first Fab Four film. ▭

John Lennon *John* • Paul McCartney *Paul* • Ringo Starr *Ringo* • George Harrison *George* • Leo McKern *Clang* • Eleanor Bron *Ahme* • Victor Spinetti *Foot* • Roy Kinnear *Algernon* ■ *Dir* Richard Lester • *Scr* Marc Behm, Charles Wood, from a story by Marc Behm

Hemingway's Adventures of a Young Man ★★

Adventure drama
1962 · US · Colour · 142mins

Loosely assembled from ten of the autobiographical Nick Adams stories and the Italian segment of *A Farewell to Arms*, this is an ill-judged, miscast odyssey that seeks to combine the artistry of Ernest Hemingway's fiction with the macho posturing of his private life. As the titular seeker-after-experience, Richard Beymer's struggle to impose his personality on the proceedings is hampered by a script containing too many opportunities for scene-stealing cameos. Paul Newman's grotesque boxer, Fred Clark's exploitative entrepreneur and Eli Wallach's kindly orderly impress, though the standouts are Arthur Kennedy and Jessica Tandy as the hero's parents.

Richard Beymer *Nick Adams* • Diane Baker *Carolyn* • Corinne Calvet *Contessa* • Fred Clark *Mr Turner* • Dan Dailey *Billy Campbell* •

James Dunn *Telegrapher* • Juano Hernandez *Bugs* • Arthur Kennedy *Dr Adams* • Ricardo Montalban *Major Padula* • Paul Newman *Ad Francis* • Susan Strasberg *Rosanna* • Jessica Tandy *Mrs Adams* • Eli Wallach *John* ■ *Dir* Martin Ritt • *Scr* AE Hotchner, from stories by Ernest Hemingway

Hemoglobin ★★★ 18

Horror   1997 · US/Can · Colour · 88mins

Troubled John Strauss (Roy Dupuis) and his wife visit a remote North American island in an attempt to find descendants of his twin ancestors who had lived there hundreds of years before. There they meet a clan of strange mutants with rather unsavoury eating habits. This is a slick and sick story of hereditary horror from Dan O'Bannon and Ron Shusett, the scriptwriters of *Alien*. Romance, vampirism and incest are all touched on in this bizarre stomach-churner with Rutger Hauer's performance keeping a tight rein on the scare tactics. Contains graphic violence and sex scenes. ▭

Rutger Hauer *Dr Marlowe* • Roy Dupuis *John Strauss* • Kristin Lehman *Kathleen Strauss* • Jackie Burroughs *Lexie Krongold* • Joanna Noyes *Byrde* • Felicia Shulman *Yolanda* ■ *Dir* Peter Svatek • *Scr* Charles Adair, Dan O'Bannon, Ronald Shusett

Hen in the Wind ★★★

Melodrama   1948 · Jap · BW · 90mins

The tale of a wife who is forced into prostitution to pay her son's hospital bills while her husband fights at the front sounds more suitable for Kenji Mizoguchi than Yasujiro Ozu. However, while this allegorical study of postwar Japan may not be thematically typical of Ozu's work, it certainly bears his stylistic imprint. Spurning reliance on symbolic close-ups, the imagery is notable for its compositional precision and the use of cutting to establish spatial relationships. With its nostalgic yearnings for the past and a pragmatic approach to the future, this is also an astute discourse on the loss of national innocence. In Japanese with English subtitles.

Kinuyo Tanaka *Tokiko* • Shuji Sano *Shuichi Amamiya* • Chishu Ryu *Kazuichiro Satake* • Takeshi Sakamoto *Hikozo Sakai* • Kuniko Miyake • Chieko Murata *Akiko Ida* • Eijiro Tono • Koji Mitsuo ■ *Dir* Yasujiro Ozu • *Scr* Yasujiro Ozu, Ryosuke Saito

Henna ★★★ PG

Drama   1990 · Ind/Pak · Colour · 180mins

An epic Indian tale of love that crosses the borders between India and Pakistan. Just before his marriage, Chander (Rishi Kapoor) is swept away at sea and wakes up in the care of a young girl, Henna (Zeba). He finds that he has no memory of his past life. A storm on their wedding night returns Chander's memory and he realises he must go back to India, though he's now wanted by the police as a spy. The traditional virtues of the Indian cinema are readily apparent (songs, costumes and sparkle) and the film is put together with considerable charm, making it accessible to audiences unfamiliar with the genre. In Hindi and Urdu with English subtitles.

Zeba *Henna* • Rishi Kapoor *Chander* • Ashuini Bhave *Chandni* • Saeed Jaffrey ■ *Dir* Randhir Kapoor • *Scr* Jainendra Jain, from a story by Khodzhi Ahmad Abbas, J Sathe

Hennessy ★★★★ 15

Political thriller   1975 · UK · Colour · 99mins

Controversial in its time – because it showed the Royal Family under threat – this seventies drama still has a full charge of suspense, with Rod Steiger as the embittered Belfast man intent on blowing up the state opening of Parliament to avenge the accidental slaughter of his family. Actor Richard Johnson (on whose story the film is based) is working with Trevor Howard to bring down this lone terrorist on behalf of MI5, while the IRA's Eric Porter is in pursuit as well. After a lifetime of hackery, director Don Sharp turns in his best movie, while Steiger gives a consummate portrayal of a righteously vengeful man. ▭

Rod Steiger *Hennessy* • Lee Remick *Kate Brooke* • Richard Johnson *Tobin, IRA Leader* • Peter Egan *Williams* • Ian Hogg *Gerry* ■ *Dir* Don Sharp • *Scr* John Gay, from a story by Richard Johnson

Henry & June ★★★ 18

Biographical erotic drama
1990 · US · Colour · 130mins

Director Philip Kaufman followed up *The Unbearable Lightness of Being* with this intellectually erotic depiction of the bizarre relationship between author Henry Miller (Fred Ward), his wife June (Uma Thurman) and the writer Anaïs Nin (Maria de Medeiros). Based on Nin's diaries, it's a rather slow and stilted film whose main interest now lies in its cast, which, as well as a young Thurman, includes Richard E Grant as Nin's bland husband and Kevin Spacey as Henry's friend. Nowhere near as sexy as the original publicity led viewers to believe, it became notorious more for its subject matter than for what actually appears on screen. ▭ **DVD**

Fred Ward *Henry Miller* • Uma Thurman *June Miller* • Maria de Medeiros *Anaïs Nin* • Richard E Grant *Hugo* • Kevin Spacey *Osborn* • Jean-Philippe Ecoffey *Eduardo* • Bruce Myers *Jack* • Jean-Louis Buñuel *Publisher/Editor* ■ *Dir* Philip Kaufman • *Scr* Philip Kaufman, Rose Kaufman, from the diaries of Anaïs Nin

Henry Fool ★★★ 18

Comedy drama   1997 · US · Colour · 131mins

Writer/director Hal Hartley is one of the quirkiest and most original of independent film-makers, and in this effort, the winner of the best screenplay at Cannes, he is on fine form. It's about a shy garbage collector and his promiscuous sister whose humdrum lives are changed for ever by the arrival of the charismatic rogue, Henry Fool, who moves into the basement of their house with the apparent intention of putting the finishing touches to his memoirs. The end product is a strangely compelling and, at times, hysterically funny fable, with a cast that does justice to the director's talent for discovering high drama in even the humblest of characters. Contains swearing, sexual references and some violence. ▭

Thomas Jay Ryan *Henry Fool* • James Urbaniak *Simon Grim* • Parker Posey *Fay* • Maria Porter *Mary* • James Saito *Mr Deng* • Kevin Corrigan *Warren* • Liam Aiken *Ned* • Camille Paglia ■ *Dir/Scr* Hal Hartley

Henry: Portrait of a Serial Killer ★★★★★ 18

Psychological horror
1986 · US · Colour · 77mins

Instead of a cultured, super-intelligent serial killer like Hannibal Lecter, John McNaughton's disturbing debut offers us a piece of poor white trash (Michael Rooker) who drifts anonymously from city to city, murdering at random. With no discernible motive or modus operandi, no one knows he is a mass murderer until he lets flatmate and fellow ex-con Tom Towles in on his gruesome hobby. McNaughton's rough, non-judgemental direction gives the film a chilling documentary feel, while the killer's use of a camcorder asks some uncomfortable questions about voyeurism and the nature of screen violence. A modern classic. ▭

Michael Rooker *Henry* • Tom Towles *Otis* • Tracy Arnold *Becky* • Mary Demas *Dead Woman/Dead Prostitute/Hooker* • Anne Bartoletti *Waitress* ■ *Dir* John McNaughton • *Scr* Richard Fire, John McNaughton

Henry: Portrait of a Serial Killer, Part II ★★

Psychological horror
1996 · US · Colour · 85mins

With director John McNaughton gone, this sequel immediately has two strikes against it, though it does end up being somewhat better than one might think. Neil Giuntoli takes over as Henry, continuing his travels around the country until he finds menial work in one location. When he finds out his boss is a professional arsonist, they start exchanging trade secrets and help each other out. Director Charles Parello tries hard to duplicate the original movie's mood (right down to duplicating the style of the opening credits) and his script focuses more on the mentally unbalanced characters than gore; the problem is this had already been done in the first movie.

Neil Giuntoli *Henry* • Rich Komenich *Kai* • Kate Walsh *Cricket* • Carri Levinson *Louisa* • Daniel Allar *Rooter* • Penelope Milford *Woman in woods* ■ *Dir/Scr* Charles Parello

Henry VIII and His Six Wives ★★★ PG

Historical drama
1972 · UK · Colour · 120mins

As one has the right to expect, the costumes and locations for this film version of the acclaimed BBC TV series *The Six Wives of Henry VIII* are superb. However, the story suffers from being compressed into just over two hours (the series ran for six 90-minute episodes), and, while it is understandable to focus on Anne Boleyn and the break with Rome, it overbalances the action to the detriment of the later wives. Keith Michell gives a textbook portrayal of Henry, but he is outshone by Bernard Hepton as Cranmer and Donald Pleasence as Cromwell. ▭

Keith Michell *King Henry VIII* • Frances Cuka *Catherine of Aragon* • Charlotte Rampling *Anne Boleyn* • Jane Asher *Jane Seymour* • Jenny Bos *Anne of Cleves* • Lynne Frederick *Catherine Howard* • Barbara Leigh-Hunt *Catherine Parr* • Donald Pleasence *Thomas Cromwell* • Michael Gough *Norfolk* • Brian Blessed *Suffolk* • Bernard Hepton *Archbishop Cranmer* • Michael Goodliffe *Thomas More* ■ *Dir* Waris Hussein • *Scr* Ian Thorne

Henry V ★★★★★ U
Classic historical drama
1944 · UK · Colour · 131mins

Having failed to secure the services of William Wyler or Carol Reed, Laurence Olivier embarked on his directorial debut with some misgivings. David O Selznick had already refused to allow Olivier's wife Vivien Leigh to play Katharine as he didn't want his star in a bit part, and the war had necessitated the shooting of the Agincourt scenes in Ireland to find enough extras. Dislocating his ankle while filming the ambush scene, Olivier still handled the battle sequences with a skill that belied his inexperience. Released to great acclaim with victory over Hitler in sight, the film chimed in with the nation's ebullience and it remains a colourful and rousing spectacle. *DVD*

Laurence Olivier *King Henry V* • Robert Newton *Ancient Pistol* • Leslie Banks *Chorus* • Renée Asherson *Princess Katharine* • Esmond Knight *Fluellen* • Leo Genn *Constable of France* • Ralph Truman *Montjoy, a French Herald* • Harcourt Williams *King Charles VI of France* ■ *Dir* Laurence Olivier • *Scr* Laurence Olivier, Alan Dent, from the play by William Shakespeare • *Cinematographer* Robert Krasker • *Art Director* Paul Sheriff • *Costume Designer* Roger Furse

Henry V ★★★★ PG
Historical drama
1989 · UK · Colour · 131mins

It's hard to recall the furore that greeted this film on its original release. Almost everyone compared first-time director Kenneth Branagh with Laurence Olivier, who made his own debut behind the camera with the same play 45 years earlier. The knives were clearly out for the pretender to Olivier's throne, yet he produced a version that was as much of its time as Olivier's had been. Instead of the booming patriotism befitting the wartime flag-waver that was served up by Olivier, Branagh decided to focus on the savagery and futility of war. He thoroughly merited his best actor Oscar nomination, though his inclusion in the direction category was more than a little flattering, his showy use of camera and slow motion too often betraying the naivety of the debutant.

Kenneth Branagh *Henry V* • Derek Jacobi *Chorus* • Brian Blessed *Exeter* • Ian Holm *Captain Fluellen* • Paul Scofield *French King* • Michael Maloney *Dauphin* • Alec McCowen *Ely* • Emma Thompson *Katherine* • Richard Briers *Bardolph* • Robert Stephens *Pistol* • Robbie Coltrane *Sir John Falstaff* • Judi Dench *Mistress Quickly* ■ *Dir* Kenneth Branagh • *Scr* Kenneth Branagh, from the play by William Shakespeare

Her Alibi ★★ PG
Comedy thriller 1989 · US · Colour · 90mins

Director Bruce Beresford, whose career has featured high points like *Breaker Morant* and *Driving Miss Daisy* and low points like *A Good Man in Africa*, here hits another trough with this uneven comedy thriller. Designed to continue Tom Selleck's rise in the movies after his success in *Three Men and a Baby*, it's a rather ludicrous tale that needs more than just a well-known actor and an actress model (Paulina Porizkova) in the lead roles. A talented cast, a decent script and something more than the "I think my girlfriend's going to kill me" plot would also have made a big difference. Contains swearing.

Tom Selleck *Phil Blackwood* • Paulina Porizkova *Nina Ionescu* • William Daniels *Sam* • James Farentino *Frank Polito* • Hurd Hatfield *Troppa* • Patrick Wayne *Gary Blackwood* • Tess Harper *Sally Blackwood* ■ *Dir* Bruce Beresford • *Scr* Charlie Peters

Her Cardboard Lover ★ U
Romantic drama 1942 · US · Colour · 92mins

Robert Taylor and Norma Shearer, under George Cukor's direction, co-star as a penniless songwriter in love with a millionairess who hires him as a secretary-cum-bodyguard to inflame the jealousy of her on-again/off-again lover, George Sanders. Despite its illustrious stars and director, this is a candidate for one of the worst films ever made. Taylor smiles a lot, Shearer – in her final film – sobs and twitters and Sanders looks uncomfortable, as well he might. To call the script witless is an understatement, and how MGM could pour such lavish resources into such rubbish must forever remain a mystery.

Norma Shearer *Consuelo Croyden* • Robert Taylor (1) *Terry Trindale* • George Sanders *Tony Barling* • Frank McHugh *Chappie Champagne* • Elizabeth Patterson *Eva* • Chill Wills *Judge* ■ *Dir* George Cukor • *Scr* John Collier, Anthony Veiller, William H Wright, Jacques Deval, from the play *Her Cardboard Lover* by Valerie Wyngate, PG Wodehouse, from the play *Dans Sa Cadeur Naïve* by Jacques Deval

Her Costly Affair ★★
Thriller 1996 · US · Colour

Bonnie Bedelia adds a bit of class to this otherwise depressingly formulaic made-for-TV thriller. She plays a college professor who enjoys a brief affair with a toy-boy pupil of hers, only to discover he is bottom of the class when it comes to rejection. The stalwart Bedelia is believable in an unsympathetic role, and there is an equally credible turn from former *Beverly Hills 90210* star Brian Austin Green. However, the direction and writing are strictly by the numbers.

Bonnie Bedelia *Dr Diane Weston* • Brian Austin Green *Jeff* • Joe Spano *Carl Weston* • Roma Maffia *Sally Canter* • Gina Philips *Tess Weston* • Steven Gilborn *Dr Sorenson* ■ *Dir* John Patterson • *Scr* Carmen Culver

Her Deadly Rival ★★★ 15
Crime drama 1995 · US · Colour · 87mins

In this stranger-than-fiction story, poor Harry Hamlin finds his 12-year marriage falling apart when he begins receiving provocative phone calls and expensive gifts from a mysterious woman. Although he protests his innocence, his spouse– an emotional performance by Annie Potts – and colleagues start to doubt him and when his wife turns up dead, he becomes the prime murder suspect. A well-directed thriller that will keep you guessing until the end.

Harry Hamlin *Jim Landsford* • Annie Potts *Kris Landsford* • Roma Maffia *Officer Caldwell* • Lisa Zane *Lynne* • DL Anderson *Connie* ■ *Dir* James Hayman • *Scr* Dan Vining

Her Hidden Truth ★★ PG
Drama 1995 · US · Colour · 85mins

This is one of those "procession of death" pictures, in which everyone involved in a murder case is slowly bumped off until you are left with just a couple of characters, one of whom is the hero. Kellie Martin stars as a teenager who escapes after eight years in a detention centre in order to prove that someone else lit the fire that killed members of her family. Director Daniel Lerner tries to shroud the action in mystery, but this isn't the most taxing of whodunits. Contains violence and swearing.

Kellie Martin *Billie Calhoun* • Antonio Sabato Jr *Matt* • Ken Howard *Jack Devereaux* • Reed Diamond *Clay Devereaux* • Bruce Weitz *Lieutenant Levine* • Cindy Pickett *Laney Devereaux* • Gordon Clapp *Father Paul* ■ *Dir* Daniel Lerner • *Scr* Pamela K Long

Her Husband's Affairs ★★★
Comedy 1947 · US · BW · 83mins

The witty team of Ben Hecht and Charles Lederer provided better and worse screenplays than this screwball comedy with the misleading title. The "affairs" indicated are actually business ventures involving advertising man Franchot Tone, in which his wife, Lucille Ball, predating her *I Love Lucy* character, interferes. The comedy comes from an unlikely source – the quest to create the perfect embalming fluid – but it's Edward Everett Horton who provides most of the fun in yet another film that pokes fun at the world of advertising.

Lucille Ball *Margaret Weldon* • Franchot Tone *William Weldon* • Edward Everett Horton *JB Cruikshank* • Mikhail Rasumny *Prof Glinka* • Gene Lockhart *Peter Winterbottom* • Nana Bryant *Mrs Winterbottom* • Jonathan Hale *Governor Fox* ■ *Dir* S Sylvan Simon • *Scr* Ben Hecht, Charles Lederer

Her Last Chance ★★ 15
Drama 1996 · US · Colour · 86mins

Kellie Martin and Patti LuPone star in this timely and poignant story of a boozy teenage drug addict who is thrown into rehab by her exasperated mother after a bad LSD trip. With the help of a no-nonsense counsellor (*Dharma and Greg*'s Jenna Elfman) she struggles to confront her problems and achieve sobriety. This TV movie would have done better to stay with the serious nature of addiction, recovery and peer pressure. Instead it turns into a rather inconsequential murder mystery. Contains drug abuse and some swearing.

Kellie Martin *Alex Saxen* • Patti LuPone *Joanna Saxen* • Jonathan Brandis *Preston* • Tony Lucca *Cody* • Jenna Elfman *Leslie* ■ *Dir* Richard A Colla • *Scr* Kathleen Rowell

Her Life as a Man ★★ PG
Comedy drama 1984 · US · Colour · 92mins

A *Tootsie* in reverse TV movie, with Robyn Douglass donning male drag to work as a sportswriter. Although based on a true story published in the *Village Voice*, this gender-bender anecdote has far too many unintentionally comic moments to be taken seriously despite the well-meaning efforts of a valiant cast, who at least try and give the story some dignity. The inclusion of Joan Collins in the cast adds even more unnecessary camp mirth.

Robyn Douglass *Carly Perkins/Carl Parsons* • Marc Singer *Mark Rogers* • Laraine Newman *Barbara* • Miriam Flynn *Sheila* • Robert Culp *Dave Fleming* • Joan Collins *Pam Dugan* ■ *Dir* Robert Ellis Miller • *Scr* Joanna Crawford, Diane English, from the article in *The Village Voice* by Carol Lynn Mithers

Her Majesty Love ★★★
Musical comedy 1931 · US · BW · 75mins

The presence of the inimitable WC Fields (for once minus the bibulous cynicism) enlivens this lightweight musical comedy, which marked the official Hollywood debut of William Dieterle, who'd spent the previous year making German-language versions of US box-office hits. Demonstrating the juggling genius that sustained his vaudeville career, Fields upstages Broadway star Marilyn Miller, whose marriage prospects are dashed when he reveals that he is a barber and she's a barmaid at a Berlin cabaret. It's an amiable frippery, blessed with expert support from Leon Errol and those silent slapstick stalwarts Ford Sterling and Chester Conklin.

Marilyn Miller *Lia Toerrek* • Ben Lyon *Fred von Wellingen* • WC Fields *Lia's father* • Ford Sterling *Otmar* • Leon Errol *Baron von Schwarzdorf* • Chester Conklin *Emil* • Harry Stubbs *Hanneman* • Maude Eburne *Aunt Harriette* ■ *Dir* William Dieterle • *Scr* Robert Lord, Arthur Caesar, Henry Blanke, Joseph Jackson, from a play by R Bernauer, R Oesterreicher

Her Man ★★
Drama 1930 · US · BW · 85mins

An unconvincing blend of *Anna Christie* and *Min and Bill*, this wearying waterfront melodrama has little to recommend it. Helen Twelvetrees plays a café hostess whose brief encounter with sailor Ricardo Cortez reaches its inevitable happy ending after his bout of fisticuffs with her brutal boss. James Gleason and his barroom cronies provide a few lighter moments and the lovers' day out has a certain charm. But director Tay Garnett can do little to rescue this stilted affair that has the look of a silent and the creaky dialogue of an early talkie.

Helen Twelvetrees *Frankie* • Marjorie Rambeau *Annie* • Ricardo Cortez *Johnnie* • Phillips Holmes *Dan* • James Gleason *Steve* • Franklin Pangborn *Sport* • Harry Sweet *Eddie* ■ *Dir* Tay Garnett • *Scr* Tom Buckingham, from a story by Howard Higgin, Tay Garnett

U = SUITABLE FOR ALL, ESPECIALLY FOR YOUNG CHILDREN (VIDEO ONLY) PG = PARENTAL GUIDANCE

Her Twelve Men ★★

Comedy   1954 · US · BW · 90mins

With the golden age of Hollywood disappearing, MGM had begun the process of cutting back on their contract stars and this light-hearted fluff marked the turn of Mrs Miniver, alias Greer Garson. After several years of mediocre vehicles and with age creeping up on her, her swansong came with this glutinously sentimental but otherwise inoffensive film about a schoolteacher whose patience and sweet nature has the desired effect on a bunch of difficult young schoolboys. Robert Ryan and Barry Sullivan co-star with the gracious Garson under the experienced control of Robert Z Leonard, once one of the studio's premier directors of women.

Greer Garson *Jan Stewart* • Robert Ryan *Joe Hargrave* • Barry Sullivan *Richard Y Oliver Sr* • Richard Haydn *Dr Avord Barrett* • Barbara Lawrence *Barbara Dunning* • James Arness *Ralph Munsey* • Rex Thompson *Homer Curtis* • Tim Considine *Richard Y Oliver Jr* ■ *Dir* Robert Z Leonard • *Scr* William Roberts, from the story *Miss Baker's Dozen* by Louise Baker

Her Wedding Night ★★

Comedy   1930 · US · BW · 78mins

Frank Tuttle remade his own 1925 silent *Miss Bluebeard* here, with Clara Bow replacing Bebe Daniels in the lead. Working from the Avery Hopwood play *Little Miss Bluebeard*, Tuttle concocts a frenzied farce, in which Bow, the original It Girl, plays a movie star whose stay in an Italian riviera town results in a ride on a romantic merry-go-round with a composer of sentimental ditties. The pair end up mistakenly getting married while checking into what they think is a hotel. Although Bow is clearly uncomfortable with dialogue, this still has its fun moments.

Clara Bow *Norma Martin* • Ralph Forbes *Larry Charters* • Charlie Ruggles [Charles Ruggles] *Bertie Bird* • Skeets Gallagher *Bob Talmadge* • Geneva Mitchell *Marshall* • Rosita Moreno *Lulu* • Natalie Kingston *Eva* ■ *Dir* Frank Tuttle • *Scr* Henry Myers, from the play *Little Miss Bluebeard* by Avery Hopwood

Herbie Goes Bananas ★★ U

Comedy   1980 · US · Colour · 88mins

After three breezy episodes in ten years, this fourth film about Herbie the Love Bug was the one that finally put the skids under the series. The novelty of having a Volkswagen Beetle with a mind of its own was already showing signs of wearing off in *Herbie Goes to Monte Carlo*, when an "exotic" location was used to cover the holes in the plot. However, the sights of South America are not enough to distract us from the flimsiness of this story, as Herbie rubs bumpers with a gang of smugglers on his way to Brazil. ▭

Cloris Leachman *Aunt Louise* • Charles Martin Smith *Davie Johns* • John Vernon *Prindle* • Stephan W Burns *Pete Stanchek* • Elyssa Davalos *Melissa* • Garay III *Joaquin Paco* • Harvey Korman *Captain Blythe* • Richard Jaeckel *Shepard* ■ *Dir* Vincent McEveety • *Scr* Don Tait, from characters created by Gordon Buford

Herbie Goes to Monte Carlo ★★★ U

Comedy   1977 · US · Colour · 100mins

The third in Disney's series about the VW Beetle with a mind of its own is rather predictable, though still entertaining. This time out, Herbie is reunited with driver Dean Jones and falls for a powder-blue Lancia (driven by Julie Sommars) during the Paris to Monte Carlo rally. Putting a headstrong intelligence under the bonnet of a car has been a winning formula, but there are only a few touches here that rise above the mechanical. ▭

Dean Jones *Jim Douglas* • Don Knotts *Wheely Applegate* • Julie Sommars *Diane Darcy* • Jacques Marin *Inspector Bouchet* • Roy Kinnear *Quincey* ■ *Dir* Vincent McEveety • *Scr* Arthur Alsberg, Don Nelson, from characters created by Gordon Buford

Herbie Rides Again ★★★ U

Comedy   1974 · US · Colour · 84mins

The sequel to Disney's smash hit *The Love Bug*, this is the second of four films featuring the Volkswagen Beetle with a mind of its own. Director Robert Stevenson and scriptwriter/producer Bill Walsh return to ensure the action remains fast, furious and very funny. The original cast may have departed, but in its place are such seasoned veterans as Keenan Wynn and Helen Hayes, who are tremendous value as the tycoon determined to build an enormous skyscraper and the dotty dear who won't leave the old homestead. The effects may have dated somewhat, but the film is still in perfect working order. ▭

Helen Hayes *Mrs Steinmetz* • Stefanie Powers *Nicole Harris* • Ken Berry *Willoughby Whitfield* • John McIntire *Mr Judson* • Keenan Wynn *Alonzo Hawk* • Huntz Hall *Judge* ■ *Dir* Robert Stevenson • *Scr* Bill Walsh, from a story by Gordon Buford

Hercules ★★★ U

Fantasy adventure   1957 · It · Colour · 98mins

This film launched the immensely popular Italian film genre known as "peplum", although it is better known worldwide as the "sword and sandal" cycle. Ex-Mr Universe Steve Reeves cuts an imposing figure in the title role, though there was more to him than just bulging biceps. In lesser hands, the scenes in which he longs to become mortal might have induced giggling, and there is a definite spark between him and Sylva Koscina as his beloved, Iole. Italian dialogue dubbed into English. ▭

Steve Reeves *Hercules* • Sylva Koscina *Iole* • Gianna Maria Canale *Antea* • Fabrizio Mioni *Jason* • Ivo Garrani *Pelias* • Arturo Dominici *Eurysteus* ■ *Dir* Pietro Francisci • *Scr* Pietro Francisci, Ennio de Concini, Gaio Frattini, from a story by Pietro Francisci

Hercules ★ PG

Adventure fantasy   1983 · US · Colour · 99mins

A bizarre, misguided throwback to those dubbed monstrosities of the fifties and sixties, this would-be epic attempts to cash in on the brief craze for sword-and-sorcery nonsense in the early eighties. Lou Ferrigno (*The Incredible Hulk*) gets to wear slightly more clothing than in his old TV show. Unfortunately he has more dialogue as well, while the effects are pretty ropey.

Lou Ferrigno *Hercules* • Mirella D'Angelo *Circe* • Sybil Danning *Arianna* • Ingrid Anderson *Cassiopea* • William Berger *King Minos* • Brad Harris *King Augeas* ■ *Dir* Lewis Coates [Luigi Cozzi] • *Scr* Lewis Coates [Luigi Cozzi]

Hercules ★★★ U

Animated musical
1997 · US · Colour · 91mins

As a dumbed-down version of the Greek myth this Disney animation has its moments, but few that will appeal to students of legend. Here Hercules, son of almighty Zeus, is brought up as a mortal, thanks to the machinations of Underworld ruler Hades, and has to pass tests to prove both his manhood and his godhood. Some of the draughtsmanship of the animation is wonderful, as are the voice-overs of James Woods and Danny DeVito, but the powerful original idea is sapped by the need to make it a teenage comic strip cartoon. ▭

Charlton Heston *Narrator* • Tate Donovan *Hercules* • Danny DeVito *Phil* • James Woods *Hades* • Susan Egan *Meg* • Rip Torn *Zeus* • Samantha Eggar *Hera* ■ *Dir* John Musker, Ron Clements • *Scr* Ron Clements, John Musker, Donald McEnery, Bob Shaw, Irene Mecchi, from an idea by Joe Haidar • *Production Designer* Gerald Scarfe

Hercules II ★ 15

Action adventure fantasy
1983 · US · Colour · 88mins

The second misbegotten attempt by Italian hack director Luigi Cozzi to marry *Star Wars*-style fantasy with sword-and-sandal epic is no better than the first. Made at the same time as the original *Hercules* but released two years later, this time the task of strongman Lou Ferrigno is to find some lost thunderbolts hidden among a welter of lousy special effects. Although initially colourful and unintentionally funny, both sources of entertainment value soon wear off.

Lou Ferrigno *Hercules* • Milly Carlucci *Urania* • Sonia Viviani *Glaucia* • William Berger *King Minos* • Carlotta Green *Athena* • Claudio Cassinelli *Zeus* ■ *Dir* Lewis Coates [Luigi Cozzi] • *Scr* Lewis Coates [Luigi Cozzi]

Hercules in New York ★★ PG

Adventure comedy
1969 · US · Colour · 87mins

Expelled from Mount Olympus by jealous dad Zeus, Hercules ends up in New York during the psychedelic sixties riding a chariot up Broadway and wrestling bears in Central Park zoo. This one-joke spectacle was conceived as a pastiche of cheap sword-and-sandal epics, and would have been quickly forgotten had it not starred one Arnold Strong (real name Schwarzenegger) in his first film role. Then at peak form as Mr Universe, Arnie is stripped of his voice (through bad dubbing), his clothes and all dignity as he amiably parades through a poor man's *Crocodile Dundee*. ▭

Arnold Strong [Arnold Schwarzenegger] *Hercules* • Arnold Stang *Pretzie* • Deborah Loomis *Helen* • James Karen *The Professor* • Ernest Graves *Zeus* • Tanny McDonald *Juno* •

Taina Elg *Nemesis* • Michael Lipton *Pluto* ■ *Dir* Arthur A Seidelman [Arthur Allan Seidelman] • *Scr* Aubrey Wisberg

Hercules Returns ★★★ 15

Comedy   1993 · Ausl · Colour · 76mins

A one-joke film – but a joke that's so good it just about sustains the whole running time of the film. David Argue, Bruce Spence and Mary Coustas are battling to reopen a classic cinema, much to opposition of slimy businessman Michael Carman, who plots to destroy their opening night by providing them with an Italian version of an old Hercules epic. It falls to the intrepid trio to provide all the voices themselves. The plotting is tenuous, but the redubbed beefcake epic is a constant delight. ▭

David Argue *Brad McBain* • Michael Carman *Sir Michael Kent* • Mary Coustas *Lisa* • Bruce Spence *Sprocket* • Brendon Suhr *King* ■ *Dir* David Parker • *Scr* Des Mangan, from his live show *Double Take Meet Hercules*

Hercules Unchained ★★ U

Fantasy adventure
1959 · It/Fr · Colour · 92mins

Photographed by future horror director Mario Bava, this was the first of many sequels to the sword-and-sandal epic that made one-time Mr Universe, Steve Reeves, a movie star. Here he is reunited with Sylva Koscina only to be parted from her again when she is abducted by a Theban giant (played by former boxing champion Primo Carnera). Reeves also has to escape the clutches of Lydian queen Sylva Lopez, so it's action all the way, campily staged with disastrously dubbed dialogue. Italian dialogue dubbed into English. ▭

Steve Reeves *Hercules* • Sylva Koscina *Iole* • Sylva Lopez *Omphale, Queen of Lydia* • Primo Carnera *Antaeus* • Patrizia Della Rovere *Penelope* ■ *Dir* Pietro Francisci • *Scr* Pietro Francisci, Ennio De Concini

The Herd ★★★★

Political drama   1978 · Tur · Colour · 118mins

Contrasting the traditional methods of simple, superstitious shepherds and the entrenched rivalry between their nomadic tribes with the corruption, injustice and inhumanity of contemporary consumer society, this calamitous odyssey from the plains of Anatolia to the backstreets of Ankara is an unflinchingly scathing portrait of modern Turkey. Written in prison (where he was serving 19 years for killing a magistrate in a café brawl), this was the picture that brought the nation's most important film-maker, Yilmaz Güney, to international attention. Like its successor, *The Enemy*, it was directed by Zeki Ökten in exact accordance with its author's exhaustively detailed notes. In Turkish with English subtitles.

Tarik Akan *Sirvan* • Melike Demirag *Berivan* • Tuncel Kurtiz *Hamo* ■ *Dir* Zeki Ökten • *Scr* Yilmaz Güney • *Cinematographer* Izzet Akay

Here Come the Co-Eds ★★★ U

Musical comedy   1945 · US · BW · 90mins

Lively musical comedy featuring Bud Abbott and Lou Costello as two

incident-prone nincompoops who get jobs as caretakers at a staid girls school. The pair create their normal slapstick mayhem and the snobbish atmosphere of the school crumbles before them. Well established by this time, they breeze through this well constructed vehicle, which is zany even by their own wacky standards. Lon Chaney Jr, famous for his horror roles, can also be spotted down the cast in a slightly less ghoulish role than normal.

Bud Abbott *Slats McCarthy* • Lou Costello *Oliver Quackenbush* • Peggy Ryan *Patty* • Martha O'Driscoll *Molly McCarthy* • June Vincent *Diane Kirkland* • Lon Chaney Jr *"Strangler" Johnson* • Donald Cook *Larry Benson* ■ *Dir* Jean Yarbrough • *Scr* Arthur T Horman, John Grant, from a story by Edmund L Hartmann

Here Come the Girls ★★★

Musical comedy 1953 · US · Colour · 77mins

A terrific black musical comedy as Bob Hope, "the oldest chorus boy in the business", gets his big break standing in for star crooner Tony Martin, whom one "Jack the Slasher" is threatening to kill. The central premise is not fully realised by director Claude Binyon, but the turn-of-the-century setting is attractive, the Technicolor is luscious, and there's a funny turn from veteran Fred Clark as an irascible impresario.

Bob Hope *Stanley Snodgrass* • Tony Martin *Allen Trent* • Arlene Dahl *Irene Bailey* • Rosemary Clooney *Daisy Crockett* • Millard Mitchell *Albert Snodgrass* • William Demarest *Dennis Logan* • Fred Clark *Harry Fraser* • Robert Strauss *Jack the Slasher* ■ *Dir* Claude Binyon • *Scr* Edmund Hartmann, Hal Kanter, from a story by Edmund Hartmann • *Cinematographer* Lionel Lindon

Here Come the Huggetts ★★★

Comedy 1948 · UK · BW · 92mins

Following the success of Carol Reed's *Bank Holiday*, Jack Warner and Kathleen Harrison's Huggett clan were given a picture of their own by the Rank front office. Directed by Ken Annakin with such a keen eye for the everyday that the film almost has sociological value, this prototype soap is enlivened by the antics of Diana Dors, the blonde bombshell niece who disrupts the placid suburban household. Peter Rogers (who produced the *Carry On* series) is one of the scriptwriting quintet, so the drama is liberally sprinkled with laughs. *Vote for Huggett* and *The Huggetts Abroad* quickly followed.

Jack Warner *Joe Huggett* • Kathleen Harrison *Ethel Huggett* • Jane Hylton *Jane Huggett* • Susan Shaw *Susan Huggett* • Petula Clark *Pat Huggett* • Diana Dors *Diana Hopkins* • Jimmy Hanley *Jimmy* • David Tomlinson *Harold Hinchley* ■ *Dir* Ken Annakin • *Scr* Mabel Constanduros, Denis Constanduros, Peter Rogers, Muriel Box, Sydney Box, from characters created by Godfrey Winn

Here Come the Munsters ★★PG

Comedy 1995 · US · Colour · 85mins

A lame and laboured TV movie attempt to emulate the charming sixties sitcom *The Munsters*. Here the frightful family get involved with Norman Hyde (Max Grodenchik) and his alter ego Brent

Jekyll (Jeff Trachta). Uneasily caught between *Brady Bunch* campness and *Addams Family* mordant satire, the jokes in this handsome-looking monster mishmash come thick and slow. The new cast aren't a patch on their originals who – except for the late Fred Gwynne – make brief and touching cameo appearances. ⊞

Edward Herrmann *Herman Munster* • Veronica Hamel *Lily Munster* • Robert Morse *Grandpa* • Christine Taylor *Marilyn* • Mathew Botuchis *Eddie Munster* • Mary Woronov *Mrs Dimwitty* • Max Grodenchik *Norman Hyde* • Amanda Bearse *Mrs Pearl* ■ *Dir* Robert Ginty • *Scr* Bill Prady, Jim Fisher, Jim Staahl

Here Come the Waves ★★U

Second World War musical comedy 1944 · US · BW · 99mins

One among too many disposable musicals springing from the war effort, this one offers two Betty Huttons for the price of one. Bing Crosby is a crooner who joins the navy with heroic aims, but only sees action in the entertainment unit where he must handle shows put on by the navy's distaff side, including twin sisters both played by Hutton. After a predictable flood of broad comedy situations involving mistaken identity, Crosby ends up with one of the twins. The movie's main claim to fame is the Oscar-nominated song, *Accentuate the Positive*.

Bing Crosby *Johnny Cabot* • Betty Hutton *Susan Allison/Rosemary Allison* • Sonny Tufts *Windy* • Ann Doran *Ruth* • Gwen Crawford *Tex* • Noel Neill *Dorothy* • Catherine Craig *Lieutenant Townsend* ■ *Dir* Mark Sandrich • *Scr* Allan Scott, Ken Englund, Zion Myers • *Music* Harold Arlen • *Lyrics* Johnny Mercer

Here Comes Mr Jordan ★★★★U

Fantasy comedy 1941 · US · BW · 89mins

A clever, charming and ingenious fantasy that was a popular hit in its day, starring a slightly miscast but nevertheless excellent Robert Montgomery as "Flying Pug" Joe Pendleton, who following an air crash is accidentally rushed to heaven before his allotted due date, and who has to be found a new body until his official time is up. The preposterous plot is brilliantly constructed and charmingly performed, with character actor James Gleason in a career-best role as the fighter's manager. Claude Rains (as the eponymous Mr Jordan) and Edward Everett Horton keep the whimsical whole effortlessly down-to-earth. ⊞

Robert Montgomery *Joe Pendleton* • Evelyn Keyes *Bette Logan* • Claude Rains *Mr Jordan* • Rita Johnson *Julia Farnsworth* • Edward Everett Horton *Messenger No 7013* • James Gleason *Max Corkle* ■ *Dir* Alexander Hall • *Scr* Sidney Buchman, Seton I Miller, from the play *Heaven Can Wait* by Harry Segall

Here Comes the Groom ★★U

Comedy 1951 · US · BW · 113mins

Despite a fine cast headed by Bing Crosby, Jane Wyman, Franchot Tone and an excellent Alexis Smith, this Frank Capra comedy about a newsman who imports two war orphans in order to win back a former fiancée, is a

disappointment. It came from a bad period in the director's career and his leaden approach betrays his lack of confidence in the material. But the film does include the year's Oscar-winning song, Hoagy Carmichael and Johnny Mercer's *In The Cool, Cool, Cool of the Evening*.

Bing Crosby *Pete* • Jane Wyman *Emmadel Jones* • Alexis Smith *Winifred Stanley* • Franchot Tone *Wilbur Stanley* • James Barton *Pa Jones* • Louis Armstrong • Dorothy Lamour ■ *Dir* Frank Capra • *Scr* Virginia Van Upp, Liam O'Brien, Myles Connolly, from a story by Robert Riskin, Liam O'Brien

Here Comes the Navy ★★U

Adventure comedy 1934 · US · BW · 88mins

In effect, this is little more than a recruitment poster for the US Navy, with James Cagney pressed into heroic peacetime service by a studio worried about his image as a racketeer or sociopath. Cagney is also paired for the first time with Pat O'Brien, who steals Cagney's girl; Cagney joins the navy and woos O'Brien's sister, played by Gloria Stuart. There are a few songs to boot, and the whole forgettable thing is smoothly packaged by Lloyd Bacon, director of *42nd Street* and *Footlight Parade*.

James Cagney *Chesty O'Connor* • Pat O'Brien *Biff Martin* • Gloria Stuart *Dorothy Martin* • Frank McHugh *Droopy* • Dorothy Tree *Gladys* ■ *Dir* Lloyd Bacon • *Scr* Ben Markson, Earl Baldwin, from a story by Ben Markson

Here Comes the Sun ★★U

Musical comedy 1945 · UK · BW · 83mins

Director John Baxter made his name with such gritty working-class dramas as *Love on the Dole*. Yet he supplies exactly the required lightness of touch for this amiable musical comedy. What makes the film particularly interesting is that it marked the last screen teaming for more than a decade of those Crazy Gang stalwarts, Bud Flanagan and Chesney Allen, who dropped from the limelight the following year because of Allen's arthritis. The plot is confusing, revolving around a newspaper owner's forged will, but the stars' charming routines ably compensate. ⊞

Bud Flanagan [Dennis O'Keefe] *Corona Flanagan* • Chesney Allen *Ches Allen* • Elsa Tee *Helen Blare* • Joss Ambler *Bradshaw* • Dick Francis *Governor* • John Dodsworth *Roy Lucas* ■ *Dir* John Baxter • *Scr* Geoffrey Orme, from a story by Bud Flanagan [Dennis O'Keefe], Reginald Purdell

Here on Earth ★★

Drama 1993 · Por · Colour · 105mins

Something of a misfire at the 1993 Venice film festival, *Here on Earth* is not an easy watch. Its central theme is that misery is not the preserve of any one particular group of people, but there's too little to draw you in to either the story of a rich man whose world falls apart after the death of his father or that of a couple of hard-up lovers who are driven to murder. Portuguese director Joao Botelho is a unique talent, but this isn't perhaps the best introduction for those coming fresh to his work. In Portuguese with English subtitles. Contains swearing.

Luis Miguel Cintra *Miguel Chagas* • Jessica Weiss *Isabel* • Pedro Hestnes *Antonio* • Rita Dias *Cecilia* • Isabel De Castro *Miguel's mother* • Ines Medeiros *Prostitute* • Henrique Viana *Inspector* ■ *Dir/Scr* Joao Botelho

Here on Earth ★★

Romantic drama 2000 · US · Colour · 98mins

Saccharine high-school romance with LeeLee Sobieski as a small town girl torn between rich kid Chris Klein and farm boy Josh Hartnett. Sobieski and Klein approach their roles with dewy-eyed earnestness, while Hartnett gives the film its only solid performance. Director Mark Piznarski too often uses pop music to intensify the drama rather than trust his actors with the task. The result is a movie that's more like a music video.

LeeLee Sobieski *Samantha* • Chris Klein *Kelley* • Josh Hartnett *Jasper* • Michael Rooker *Malcolm Arnold* • Annie Corley *Betsy Arnold* • Bruce Greenwood *Earl Cavanaugh* • Annette O'Toole *Jo Cavanaugh* ■ *Dir* Mark Piznarski • *Scr* Michael Seitzman

Here We Go Again ★★U

Comedy 1942 · US · BW · 76mins

Unlikely though the concept sounds, ventriloquism was really big on the wireless in the forties. In the US, Edgar Bergen and his cheeky rascal Charlie McCarthy graduated from their own radio show to appear in a clutch of movies in the thirties and forties. This one features fellow radio favourites Fibber and Molly McGee (Jim and Marian Jordan) who are celebrating their 20th anniversary with a second honeymoon.

Edgar Bergen • Jim Jordan *Fibber McGee* • Marian Jordan *Molly McGee* • Harold Peary *Gildersleeve* • Ginny Simms *Jean* • Bill Thompson *Wimple* • Gale Gordon *Caldwalder* ■ *Dir* Allan Dwan • *Scr* Paul Gerard Smith, Joe Bigelow, from a story by Paul Gerard Smith, from the radio series *Fibber McGee and Molly* by Don Quinn

Here We Go round the Mulberry Bush ★★

Comedy 1967 · UK · Colour · 96mins

One of those Swinging Sixties curios that abound with white boots, sooty eyes, pelmet skirts and *Thunderbirds*-style dancing. Originally a rather slight but charming novel by Hunter Davies about a young bloke who longs to acquire his very own dolly bird, it has been turned into an English Tourist Board commercial, extolling the delights of fab young Britain. The book's teeth have been firmly extracted and replaced instead by the soft gums of nonstop swingdom.

Barry Evans *Jamie McGregor* • Judy Geeson *Mary Gloucester* • Angela Scoular *Caroline Beauchamp* • Sheila White *Paula* • Adrienne Posta *Linda* • Vanessa Howard *Audrey* • Diane Keen *Claire* • Denholm Elliott *Mr Beauchamp* • Christopher Timothy *Spike* ■ *Dir* Clive Donner • *Scr* Hunter Davies, from his novel

Hero ★★★U

Documentary 1987 · UK/Mex · Colour · 82mins

In 1986, Mexico became the first nation to host the World Cup twice. Although it's best remembered here for the "Hand of God" incident that took

Argentina into the semi-finals, this was Diego Maradona's tournament for all the right reasons, too, most notably the mesmeric solo efforts against England and Belgium. But while these are included in Tony Maylam's official record, too many other key moments are omitted because he elected to follow ten key players rather than cover each match. Nevertheless, it remains a passable memoir for fans. ▣

Michael Caine *Narrator* ■ *Dir* Tony Maylam • *Music* Rick Wakeman

A Hero Ain't Nothin' but a Sandwich ★★★

Drama 1978 · US · Colour · 107mins

Ralph Nelson, a director with a penchant for "human" themes (*Charly, Lilies of the Field*), made this honest, well-mounted film about the travails of a black teenage boy (Larry B Scott) drawn into drug addiction, and the effect on his caring parents (Cicely Tyson, Paul Winfield) and concerned white schoolteacher (David Groh). He produced an admirable attempt to address the social and educational problems of black urban society, which was happily devoid of sensationalism. However, the film is also talky, earnest and, on the whole, disappointingly dull.

Cicely Tyson *Sweets* • Paul Winfield *Butler* • Larry B Scott *Benjie* • Helen Martin *Mrs Bell* • Glynn Turman *Nigeria* • David Groh *Cohen* • Kevin Hooks *Tiger* ■ *Dir* Ralph Nelson • *Scr* Alice Childress, from her novel

Hero and the Terror ★ 15

Action thriller 1988 · US · Colour · 92mins

Possibly due to the declining returns on his movies in the late eighties, Chuck Norris chose to play a softer hero here – a troubled cop still traumatised from his experience capturing a vicious serial killer (Jack O'Halloran) in his past, while dealing with the upcoming birth of his girlfriend's child. The stress increases when "the Terror", as he's known, escapes and resumes his savage spree. While Norris is to be applauded for trying something different – by playing a more likeable and believable hero – it comes at the expense of a boring and mostly uneventful story that has hardly any karate action. ▣

Chuck Norris *O'Brien* • Brynn Thayer *Kay* • Steve James *Robinson* • Jack O'Halloran *Simon Moon* • Jeffrey Kramer *Dwight* • Ron O'Neal *Mayor* ■ *Dir* William Tannen • *Scr* Dennis Shryack, Michael Blodgett, from the novel by Michael Blodgett

Hero at Large ★★★ PG

Comedy 1980 · US · Colour · 93mins

A daft but occasionally funny comedy, with amiable John Ritter becoming a real-life hero after foiling a crime while dressed up as superhero Captain Avenger. What is more interesting than the quickfire action on screen is the cast, which includes a pre-stardom Anne Archer and the excellent Kevin Bacon, who found fame four years later with *Footloose*. The director is Martin Davidson, best known for *Eddie and the Cruisers*.

John Ritter *Steve Nichols* • Anne Archer *J Marsh* • Bert Convy *Walter Reeves* • Kevin McCarthy *Calvin Donnelly* • Harry Bellaver

Eddie • Anita Dangler *Mrs Havacheck* • Jane Hallaren *Gloria* • Kevin Bacon ■ *Dir* Martin Davidson • *Scr* AJ Carothers

Hero of Babylon ★★

Historical adventure 1963 · It · Colour · 98mins

The *Goliath* series was just one of the many sword-and-sandal cycles that kept the world's musclemen and the Italian film industry busy in the early sixties. Also known as *Goliath, King of Slaves*, this all-action adventure stars Gordon Scott as the rippling renegade fighting injustice and tyranny in the ancient city of Babylon. Having already played such superheroes as Tarzan, Maciste and Hercules, Scott made a suitable successor to ex-Mr Universe Steve Reeves, going on to play the character again in *Goliath and the Vampires* and *Goliath and the Black Hercules*. Laughably bad in places, but then that's part of the fun. In Italian with English subtitles.

Gordon Scott • Michael Lane [Mike Lane] • Geneviève Grad • Moira Orfei • Piero Lulli ■ *Dir* Siro Marcellini • *Scr* Gianpaolo Callegari, Siro Marcellini, Albert Valentin

The Heroes ★★★

Adventure 1968 · US/Iran · Colour · 96mins

The alternative title of this US-Iranian co-production, *The Invincible Six*, gives the clue to its origins. It's a rehash of *The Magnificent Seven*, with Stuart Whitman leading a band of renegade mercenaries who take pity on a village at the mercy of bandits. Veteran director Jean Negulesco puts urgency into the action and, although it's in no way the equal of the illustrious western classic, it's tense enough of its kind.

Stuart Whitman *Tex* • Elke Sommer *Zari* • Curt Jurgens *The Baron* • Ian Ogilvy *Ronald* • Behrooz Vosugi *Jahan* • Lon Satton *Mike* • Isarco Ravaioli *Giorgio* • James Mitchum *Nazar* ■ *Dir* Jean Negulesco • *Scr* Guy Elmes, Chester Erskine, from the novel *The Heroes of Yucca* by Michael Barrett

The Heroes ★★

Adventure 1972 · It/Fr/Sp · Colour · 110mins

Rod Steiger leads a band of post-Second World War misfits in pursuit of some loot stolen by former hooker Rosanna Schiaffino in this lacklustre Italian movie. The cast is interesting – Rod Taylor, Claude Brasseur, Terry-Thomas – but director Duccio Tessari doesn't know what to do with them except have them spout clichés in North African locations. Italian dialogue dubbed into English.

Rod Steiger *Günther von Lutz* • Rosanna Schiaffino *Katrin* • Rod Taylor *Bob Robson* • Claude Brasseur *Raphael Tibaudet* • Terry-Thomas *John Cooper* • Gianni Garko *Schreiber* • Aldo Giuffrè *Spartaco* ■ *Dir* Duccio Tessari • *Scr* Luciano Vincenzoni, Sergio Donati, from a novel by Albert Kantof

Heroes ★★ 15

Comedy drama 1977 · US · Colour · 107mins

Henry Winkler was the star of the TV show *Happy Days* when he was given the role of a traumatised Vietnam veteran who escapes from hospital with dreams of running a worm farm in California. On the road he meets and falls in love with Sally Field, herself a

TV star on the rise. Written by Vietnam veteran James Carabatsos, it's a late straggler in the long run of counter-culture movies that never delivers either as a comedy or a drama. The main interest now is the supporting role by Harrison Ford, who made this immediately after *Star Wars*. ▣

Henry Winkler *Jack Dunne* • Sally Field *Carol Bell* • Harrison Ford *Kenny Boyd* • Val Avery *Bus Driver* • Olivia Cole *Jane Adcox* • Hector Elias *Dr Elias* • Dennis Burkley *Gus* • Tony Burton *Chef* ■ *Dir* Jeremy Paul Kagan • *Scr* James Carabatsos

The Heroes of Telemark ★★★ U

Second World War thriller 1965 · UK · Colour · 123mins

Reluctant scientist Kirk Douglas and fiery resistance fighter Richard Harris have to overcome their hatred of each other, as well as the Germans, to sabotage an atomic bomb project in this brawny war story set in Norway in 1942. Director Anthony Mann avoids getting bogged down with technical information and sustains a nail-biting tension throughout the daredevil mission. While some in the supporting cast seem disaffected, Anton Diffring convinces as a steely-eyed Nazi officer. The night sequences are particularly striking, although Robert Krasker's photography throughout will have you positively pining for the fjords. ▣

Kirk Douglas *Dr Rolf Pedersen* • Richard Harris *Knut Straud* • Ulla Jacobsson *Anna* • Michael Redgrave *Uncle* • David Weston *Arne* • Anton Diffring *Major Frick* • Eric Porter *Terboven* • Mervyn Johns *Colonel Wilkinson* ■ *Dir* Anthony Mann • *Scr* Ivan Moffat, Ben Barzman

Heroes Stand Alone ★ 18

War drama 1989 · US · Colour · 79mins

This little-seen war drama from the Roger Corman stable has Chad Everett leading a team of mercenaries to pick up survivors from an American plane which has crashed during an illegal flight over a wartorn Central American country. Mark Griffiths's film is critical of American involvement in the region and portrays interfering Cubans and Russians in a favourable light. The Peruvian locations are attractive, as is Elsa Olivero. ▣

Chad Everett *Zack Duncan* • Bradford Dillman *Walt Simmons* • Rick Dean *Willie* • Michael Chieffo *Killer* • Elsa Olivero *Rosa* ■ *Dir* Mark Griffiths • *Scr* Thomas McKelvey Cleaver

Heroines of Evil ★★★

Drama 1979 · Fr · Colour · 88mins

This is another trio of immoral tales from Walerian Borowczyk, although he seems more preoccupied this time with the luxuriant look of the film than the moral implications of his taboo-riven anecdotes. Set in Renaissance Rome, *Margherita* focuses on the murder of a prominent banker and the painter Raphael by the latter's model lover. But this tale of lust and greed has nothing on the bestial insinuation of both *Marceline* (in which a girl exacts the ultimate revenge on the parents who killed her pet rabbit) and *Marie* (in which a kidnap victim is rescued by her trusty hound). In French with English subtitles.

Marina Pierro *Margherita Luti* • François Guétary *Raphael Sanzio* • Jean-Claude Dreyfus *Bini* • Jean Martinelli *Pope* • Pierre Benedetti *Mad painter* • Philippe Desboeuf *Doctor* • Gaëelle Legrand *Marceline Cain* • Pascale Christophe *Marie* ■ *Dir* Walerian Borowczyk • *Scr* Walerian Borowczyk, from the short story *Le Sang et l'Agneau* by Andre Pieyre de Mandiargues and the non-fiction book *Promenades dans Rome* by Stendhal

Hero's Island ★★★

Action drama 1962 · US · Colour · 94mins

A rather weird historical movie, part children's film and part symbolic drama, set on an island off the coast of the Carolinas in the early 1700s. Two former slaves and their children go to live on the island, but the father is murdered by marauding fishermen. Castaway James Mason offers his help but because the woman is deeply religious he agrees to non-violence until there's no other alternative. Big themes bump into each other – religion, pacifism, slavery – but none are fully developed in a typically flawed effort from writer/director Leslie Stevens, a marginal but fascinating talent who also conceived the TV series *McCloud* and *The Outer Limits*.

James Mason *Jacob Webber* • Kate Manx *Devon Mainwaring* • Neville Brand *Kingstree* • Rip Torn *Nicholas* • Warren Oates *Wayte* • Robert Sampson *Enoch* • Harry Dean Stanton *Dixey* ■ *Dir/Scr* Leslie Stevens

Hers to Hold ★★★

Romance 1943 · US · BW · 93mins

Having reached her twenties, Deanna Durbin was successfully relaunched as a young adult, playing a society figure in this romantic comedy which boosted the war effort with its scenes in a real aircraft factory. She sings the very popular *Say a Prayer for the Boys Over There* as well as Cole Porter's *Begin the Beguine* and a song from Bizet's *Carmen*. Joseph Cotten is her rather mature romantic interest, while Charles Winninger and Nella Walker play her parents for the third time.

Deanna Durbin *Penelope Craig* • Joseph Cotten *Bill Morley* • Charles Winninger *Judson Craig* • Evelyn Ankers *Flo Simpson* • Gus Schilling *Rosey Blake* • Nella Walker *Dorothy Craig* • Ludwig Stossel *Binns* • Samuel S Hinds *Dr Crane* ■ *Dir* Frank Ryan • *Scr* Lewis R Foster, from a story by John D Klorer

He's My Girl ★★ 15

Romantic comedy 1987 · US · Colour · 99mins

This cross-dressing farce should be called "Some Like It Tepid". TK Carter is Reggie who, pretending to be his best mate David Hallyday, wins a trip to Hollywood. The problem is the winners need to be a couple. Cue Reggie becoming Regina and the two friends getting into a *Twelfth Night* set of love wrangles and misunderstandings on holiday. The only aspect of interest is Jennifer Tilly as a rather lovely waitress – the rest is just plain silly, with Carter's attempts at botched femininity being neither farcical nor funny. ▣

TK Carter *Reggie/Regina* • David Hallyday *Bryan* • David Clennon *Mason Morgan* • Misha McK *Tasha* • Jennifer Tilly *Lisa* •

Warwick Sims *Simon Sledge* ■ *Dir* Gabrielle Beaumont • *Scr* Charles Bohl, Taylor Ames, from a story by Taylor Ames

Hester Street ★★★★ PG
Period drama 1975 · US · BW · 89mins

This marvellously evocative study of Jewish immigrant life in turn-of-the-century New York, mainly told in delightfully subtitled Yiddish, features an outstanding lead performance from the Oscar-nominated Carol Kane. She plays Gitl, the wife of Steven Keats, summoned from the old country after he has been in America for a dangerous few years. Unsurprisingly she finds him a changed man, so she sets out to make her own way in the New World. Electing to film in black-and-white, director Joan Micklin Silver creates a world previously only seen in old photos and such Hollywood forays as *Funny Girl* and *Rhapsody in Blue*. Her film feels so real you can smell the herrings. In English and Yiddish with subtitles. ▭

Steven Keats *Jake* • Carol Kane *Gitl* • Mel Howard *Bernstein* • Dorrie Kavanaugh *Mamie* • Doris Roberts *Kavarsky* • Stephen Strimpell *Peltner* • Lauren Frost *Fanny* • Paul Freedman *Joey* ■ *Dir* Joan Micklin Silver • *Scr* Joan Micklin Silver, from the story *Yekl* by Abraham Cahan • *Cinematographer* Kenneth Van Sickle

Hexed ★★ 15
Comedy thriller 1993 · US · Colour · 88mins

One of the first attempts to send up the *Fatal Attraction*/*Basic Instinct* genre, this is a patchy affair enlivened by the enthusiastic playing of the cast. Arye Gross is a compulsive liar working at a hotel whose fantasy world is interrupted when he gets mixed up with murderous *femme fatale* Claudia Christian. Director Alan Spencer produced the TV spoof *Sledge Hammer!*, but he struggles to bring the brainless charm of that series to this big-screen outing. However, Gross is an accomplished comedy player, and there's nice support from Hal Hartley favourite Adrienne Shelly. ▭

Arye Gross *Matthew Welsh* • Claudia Christian *Hexina* • Adrienne Shelly *Gloria O'Connor* • Ray Baker *Victor Thummell* • R Lee Ermey *Detective Ferguson* • Michael E Knight *Simon Littlefield* ■ *Dir/Scr* Alan Spencer

Hey Babu Riba ★★★
Romantic drama
1986 · Yug · Colour · 109mins

Flashing back from the funeral of the girl who epitomised the innocence of fifties Yugoslavia, this is a film of laboured symbolism and clumsy nostalgia. Yet, while the violation of the teenage Gala Videnovic by a swaggering Party activist might lack subtlety, the exuberant fun she has with the four Belgrade lads who made up her rowing team is slyly staged by director Jovan Acin. He cleverly contrasts the fact that the promises of freedom made in the music and movies flooding in from America were just as empty as those peddled by the communists. In Serbo-Croat with English subtitles.

Gala Videnovic *Miriana Zivkovic/"Esther"* • Relja Bacic *Glen* • Nebojsa Bakocevic *Young*

Glen • Marko Todorovic *Sacha* • Dragan Bjelogrlic *Young Sacha* • Srdjan Todorovic *Young Kicha* ■ *Dir/Scr* Jovan Acin

Hey Boy! Hey Girl! ★ U
Musical 1959 · US · BW · 80mins

Hey Rubbish! This is one of those inane zero-budget musicals with singer Keely Smith emotionally blackmailing Louis Prima and his band, the Witnesses. She's only going to sing with them if they'll play at the church fête with which she's associated. The result is pretty lacklustre and, considering Prima and Smith were married and working together at the time, you'd expect better.

Louis Prima • Keely Smith *Dorothy Spencer* • James Gregory *Father Burton* • Henry Slate *Marty Moran* • Kim Charney *Buzz* • Barbara Heller *Grace Dawson* ■ *Dir* David Lowell Rich • *Scr* Raphael Hayes, James West

Hey! Hey! USA ★★ U
Comedy 1938 · UK · BW · 88mins

Made without the assistance of his regular stooges, Moore Marriott and Graham Moffatt, this is one of Will Hay's least memorable outings. Removed from his familiar milieu, he seems uncomfortable with the material and strives too hard for laughs. The film casts him as a stowaway on board a transatlantic liner who poses as a famous history professor to stop gangsters Edgar Kennedy and David Burns kidnapping a millionaire's son. Only Hay's trademark bluffing during a radio lecture comes close to matching his earlier work; the remainder is given over to some formulaic slapstick and Kennedy's shameless mugging. ▭

Will Hay *Benjamin Twist* • Edgar Kennedy *Bugs Leary* • David Burns *Tony Ricardo* • Eddie Ryan *Ace Marco* • Fred Duprez *Cyrus Schultz* • Paddy Reynolds *Mrs Schultz* • Tommy Bupp *Bertie Schultz* • Arthur Goullet *Gloves Johnson* ■ *Dir* Marcel Varnel • *Scr* Marriott Edgar, Val Guest, JOC Orton

Hey, Let's Twist! ★★★ U
Musical 1961 · US · BW · 78mins

Who remembers Joey Dee? When this film was made he was one of the hottest names in pop music, having introduced, with his group the Starliters, the Twist at the Peppermint Lounge in New York. An energetic, pint-sized performer, Dee made two films (the other was *Two Tickets to Paris*) which are fascinating sociological time capsules capturing the start of the Swinging Sixties.

Joey Dee • Teddy Randazzo *Rickey Dee* • Kay Armen *Angie* • Zohra Lampert *Sharon* • Dino Di Luca *Papa* ■ *Dir* Greg Garrison • *Scr* Hal Hackady

Hi, Gang! ★★ U
Second World War comedy
1941 · UK · BW · 96mins

Married Hollywood film stars Bebe Daniels and Ben Lyon were hugely popular in Britain, particularly during the Second World War, when they stayed in England to entertain the public and the troops, rather than escape to the relative safety of the US. This film was a spin-off from their famous radio series, a spirited romp from Gainsborough Pictures, featuring

Bebe and Ben as radio personalities for rival broadcasting companies. The film also featured the wonderful pair Graham Moffatt and Moore Marriott, stalwart supporters of many comedy stars including the great Will Hay. ▭

Bebe Daniels *The Victory Girl* • Ben Lyon *Her Other Half* • Vic Oliver *Nuisance with the ideas* • Moore Marriott *Uncle Jerry* • Graham Moffatt *Albert* • Felix Aylmer *Lord Amersham* ■ *Dir* Marcel Varnel • *Scr* Val Guest, Marriott Edgar, JOC Orton, Howard Irving Young, from the radio series by Bebe Daniels, Ben Lyon

Hi Honey, I'm Dead ★★ U
Comedy drama 1991 · US · Colour · 88mins

Having been announced as a director to watch following his first feature, the offbeat Jane Fonda/Donald Sutherland comedy *Steelyard Blues* in 1973, Alan Myerson's career never really got off the ground, hitting its lowest point in the late eighties with the truly awful fourth sequel in the *Police Academy* series. Looking to revive his fortunes in the realm of the TV movie, here Myerson turns his hand to a reincarnation romp. Curtis Armstrong plays the arrogant yuppie who dies in an accident caused by his own cost-cutting, only to find that he has returned as a tramp. Armstrong is an amiable lead, but he can't lift this comedy above the average. ▭

Curtis Armstrong *Arnold Pishkin* • Catherine Hicks *Carol Stadler* • Kevin Conroy *Brad Stadler* • Paul Rodriguez *Ralph* • Joseph Gordon-Levitt *Josh* ■ *Dir* Alan Myerson • *Scr* Carl Kleinschmitt

The Hi-Jackers ★★
Crime drama 1963 · UK · BW · 69mins

This low-budget crime thriller from the Butcher's studio is set in the rough-and-ready world of trucking. However, British lorry drivers don't have the cinematic glamour of their American counterparts, so identifying the familiar British faces – Anthony Booth (Tony Blair's father-in-law), Patrick Cargill, Glynn Edwards – is the main point of interest in this very dated movie.

Anthony Booth *Terry McKinley* • Jacqueline Ellis *Shirley* • Derek Francis *Jack Carter* • Patrick Cargill *Inspector Grayson* • Glynn Edwards *Bluey* • David Gregory *Pete* • Harold Goodwin *Scouse* • Anthony Wager *Smithy* • Arthur English *Bert* ■ *Dir/Scr* Jim O'Connolly

Hi-Life ★★★
Comedy drama 1998 · US · Colour · 82mins

Sadly, despite a good cast of young American actors, this ordinary comedy-drama plays more like a soap than a serious big-screen picture. Actor Eric Stoltz owes $900 to vicious bookie Charles Durning after the dosh. He borrows the money from girlfriend Moira Kelly, telling her it's to pay for sister Daryl Hannah's abortion. Kelly's brother, bartender Campbell Scott, is drawn into the whole confusing affair as the net begins to close around Stoltz's elaborate deceit. This is one that Stoltz, Campbell and Hannah will be happy to forget.

Campbell Scott *Ray* • Eric Stoltz *Jimmy* • Daryl Hannah *Maggie* • Moira Kelly *Susan* • Katrin Cartlidge *April* • Charles Durning *Fatty* • Peter Riegert *Miner* ■ *Dir/Scr* Roger Hedden

The Hi-Lo Country ★★★ 15
Western drama 1998 · US · Colour · 114mins

Woody Harrelson and the impressive Billy Crudup are bosom-buddy cowboys who run a ranch together in the American west after the Second World War. Their friendship becomes sorely tested when Harrelson begins an affair with the object of Crudup's desire, Patricia Arquette. This is a sumptuous, sprawling western from director Stephen Frears and producer Martin Scorsese, who last collaborated on *The Grifters*. But, while beautifully shot, there is little new here in a familiar tale of best friends clashing over love. Both female leads – Arquette and Penelope Cruz – are two-dimensional; often a flaw in the traditional western, but inexcusable in a nineties take on the genre. Contains violence and sex scenes.

Woody Harrelson *Big Boy Matson* • Billy Crudup *Pete Calder* • Patricia Arquette *Mona Birk* • Cole Hauser *Little Boy Matson* • Penelope Cruz *Josepha O'Neil* • Enrique Castillo *Levi Gomez* • Darren Burrows *Billy Harte* • Sam Elliott *Jim Ed Love* ■ *Dir* Stephen Frears • *Scr* Walon Green, from the novel by Max Evans • *Cinematographer* Oliver Stapleton

Hi, Mom! ★★★★
Comedy 1970 · US · BW and Colour · 86mins

In director Brian De Palma's sex-fixated, counterculture satire, Robert De Niro's character from *Greetings* returns to make a semi-pornographic film about his neighbours and bomb a laudromat in the name of revolutionary politics. Meanwhile his best friend (Gerrit Graham) gets involved with a radical theatre troupe. The final reel is given over to a brilliantly extended sequence of said troupe's confrontational play, *Be Black, Baby*, where fact, fiction, theatre and film merge with stunning docudrama realism. In what is clearly an early incarnation of his Travis Bickle character from *Taxi Driver*, De Niro reveals the charismatic form that would mark his later career.

Robert De Niro *Jon Rubin* • Jennifer Salt *Judy Bishop* • Lara Parker *Jeannie Mitchell* • Gerrit Graham *Gerrit Wood* • Nelson Peltz *Playboy* • Charles Durnham [Charles Durning] *Superintendent* • Allen Garfield *Joe Banner* ■ *Dir* Brian De Palma • *Scr* Brian De Palma, from a story by Charles Hirsch, Brian De Palma

Hi, Nellie! ★★★
Crime comedy 1934 · US · BW · 75mins

Here's a novelty: the often bewhiskered Paul Muni in a contemporary role as a tough newspaper editor demoted to the lonely-hearts column. It's a far cry from the roles of Louis Pasteur and Emile Zola that Muni was to play later, but a terrific example of the tough, fast-paced, beautifully-made newspaper movie that Warner Bros did so well. And who could resist a cast that boasts wisecracking Glenda Farrell (as Muni's ex) and cynical comedian Ned Sparks? Skilled Mervyn LeRoy directs with the style and verve that enabled him to knock off several movies a year. If the tale somehow seems familiar, there are three remakes (at least) of this very same slim plot.

U = SUITABLE FOR ALL   Uc = SUITABLE FOR ALL, ESPECIALLY FOR YOUNG CHILDREN (VIDEO ONLY)   PG = PARENTAL GUIDANCE

Paul Muni *Bradshaw* • Glenda Farrell *Gerry* • Douglass Dumbrille *Harvey Dawes* • Robert Barrat *Brownell* • Ned Sparks *Shammy* • Hobart Cavanaugh *Fullerton* • Pat Wing *Sue* ■ *Dir* Mervyn LeRoy • *Scr* Sidney Sutherland, Abem Finkel, from a story by Roy Chanslor

Hickey and Boggs ★★★
Thriller 1972 · US · Colour · 111mins

Re-enacting their cynical, laconic roles as rundown private eyes from the *I Spy* TV series, Bill Cosby and Robert Culp extend the concept without losing pace or interest as they stumble upon a lethal *femme fatale* while searching for the proceeds of a Pittsburgh bank robbery. Walter Hill's first venture into feature scriptwriting, allied with Culp's own direction, keep this as crisp as a cracker, though some plot points are annoyingly mysterious. Look out for James Woods in an early role. Contains violence and swearing.

Bill Cosby *Al Hickey* • Robert Culp *Frank Boggs* • Rosalind Cash *Nyona* • Sheila Sullivan *Edith Boggs* • Isabel Sanford *Nyona's mother* • Ta-Ronce Allen *Nyona's daughter* • Lou Frizzell *Lawyer* • James Woods *Lt Wyatt* ■ *Dir* Robert Culp • *Scr* Walter Hill

The Hidden ★★★★ 18
Science-fiction horror
1987 · US · Colour · 92mins

A rip-roaring buddy movie with an extra-terrestrial twist. LAPD cop Michael Nouri and his alien partner Kyle MacLachlan investigate a series of weird crimes, and find the culprit responsible is a renegade slug-like creature from MacLachlan's home planet which invades earthly bodies and makes them commit nasty mayhem. Beginning in frantic top gear, director Jack Sholder keeps the high-energy proceedings rattling along, yet still manages to find time for sharp and meaningful character interplay between the fun-packed, gross-out special effects. A minor gem. ▭

Michael Nouri *Tom Beck* • Kyle MacLachlan *Lloyd Gallagher* • Ed O'Ross *Cliff Willis* • William Boyett *Jonathan Miller* • Clu Gulager *Lieutenant Ed Flynn* • Claudia Christian *Brenda Lee Van Buren* • Clarence Felder *Lieutenant John Masterson* • Richard Brooks *Sanchez* ■ *Dir* Jack Sholder • *Scr* Bob Hunt

The Hidden II ★★ 18
Science-fiction horror
1994 · US · Colour · 89mins

This hopelessly second-rate sequel to the brilliant 1987 original, set 15 years later, finds Raphael Sbarge taking on the Kyle MacLachlan benevolent alien role. This time he searches out the daughter (Kate Hodge) of the Michael Nouri character to help him defeat the shape-shifting slug-like alien menace organising a mass spawning at a warehouse rave. Very talky, ineptly comic and shamelessly using the best footage from the first film, this soon falls into formula chase theatrics. ▭

Raphael Sbarge *MacLachlan* • Kate Hodge *Juliet* • Michael Nouri *Detective Beck* ■ *Dir/Scr* Seth Pinsker

Hidden Agenda ★★★ 15
Political thriller 1990 · UK · Colour · 97mins

Ken Loach's movies tend to be rather preachy, but the better ones, including this investigation into a murdered American civil rights activist in Northern Ireland, engage both the mind and the heart. American activist Frances McDormand teams up with British cop Brian Cox to get at the truth and uncover a huge conspiracy. This is a tense and tough depiction of the Troubles during the eighties: Loach brings a keen sense of time and place to the important issues he raises, while McDormand and Cox strike just the right acting notes. Contains violence, swearing and nudity. ▭

Frances McDormand *Ingrid Jessner* • Brian Cox *Peter Kerrigan* • Brad Dourif *Paul Sullivan* • Mai Zetterling *Moa* • Bernard Bloch *Henri* • John Benfield *Maxwell* • Jim Norton *Brodie* ■ *Dir* Ken Loach • *Scr* Jim Allen

Hidden City ★★ 15
Thriller 1987 · UK · Colour and BW · 107mins

Produced by Channel 4, Stephen Poliakoff's first feature as director is weighed down by confusion. It follows the search by sociologist Charles Dance and obsessive Cassie Stuart for a piece of government film which may contain a sinister secret. The consequent investigation leads our intrepid duo to further discarded bureaucratic items hidden in a maze of tunnels beneath the city of London. Formidably filled with menace, there are just too many plotlines, which prevent this debut achieving high status. However, Poliakoff's script goes some way to removing the audience's objections to these implausibilities, creating a menacing and seedy vision of London.

Charles Dance *James Richards* • Cassie Stuart *Sharon Newton* • Bill Paterson *Anthony* • Richard E Grant *Brewster* • Alex Norton *Hillcombe* • Tusse Silberg *Barbara* • Richard Ireson *Schoolmaster* • Saul Jephcott *Curtis* ■ *Dir/Scr* Stephen Poliakoff

The Hidden Eye ★★
Crime mystery 1945 · US · BW · 69mins

Edward Arnold stars as the blind detective, Captain Duncan Maclain, whose guide dog, a German shepherd named Friday, helps solve a trio of slayings and prevents a fourth. The clue common to all the murders is a perfume which the dog recognises. Arnold's character, plus dog, first appeared in director Fred Zinnemann's second feature *Eyes in the Night*, but this sequel, directed by Richard Whorf, fails to realise its potential.

Edward Arnold *Captain Duncan Maclain* • Frances Rafferty *Jean Hampton* • William "Bill" Phillips *Marty Corbell* • Ray Collins *Philip Treadway* • Paul Langton *Harry Gifford* ■ *Dir* Richard Whorf • *Scr* George Harmon Coxe, Harry Ruskin, from characters created by Baynard Kendrick

Hidden Fear ★★
Crime 1957 · US · BW · 83mins

Directed by the now-fashionable Andre De Toth, this B-picture is about the hunt for a killer in Copenhagen. Benefitting from on-location filming, it's interesting only because it features so many stars – John Payne, Alexander Knox, Conrad Nagel – who had lost their glimmer by this time. Fox musical regular Payne only made three more features before his death in 1989.

John Payne *Mike Brent* • Alexander Knox *Hartman* • Conrad Nagel *Arthur Miller* • Natalie Norwick *Susan Brent* • Anne Neyland *Virginia Kelly* ■ *Dir* Andre De Toth • *Scr* Andre De Toth, John Ward Hawkins

Hidden Fears ★★
Psychological thriller
1993 · US · Colour · 90mins

Years after the public, brutal and unsolved murder of her husband by two ruffians, Maureen (Meg Foster) learns the identity of the murderers – just as the eyewitnesses begin to die. Foster tries to warn the remaining bystanders, but her TV appeal to flush out the two redneck brothers only serves to put them on her trail. Though the hillbillies are too cartoon-like, solid acting performances and a nice twist ending make this thriller worth a look.

Meg Foster *Maureen Dietz* • Frederic Forrest *Mike* • Bever-Leigh Banfield *Helen* • Marc Macaulay *Marty Van Beeber* • Patrick Cherry *Calvin Van Beeber* ■ *Dir* Jean Bodon • *Scr* Stuart Kaminsky, from the novel *Exercise in Terror* by Stuart Kaminsky

The Hidden Fortress
★★★★★ PG
Adventure 1958 · Jap · BW · 138mins

Akira Kurosawa was the master of the *chambara*, a swordplay film invariably set during Japan's civil wars, in which a wandering samurai unswervingly adheres to the Bushido code. His regular collaborator Toshiro Mifune takes on the role in this expert blend of comedy and adventure that marked the director's first use of widescreen technology. Kurosawa always regarded this film (about a warrior who helps a dismissive princess and a pair of prattling peasants smuggle gold through enemy territory) as his favourite project. It also clearly made an impact on George Lucas, who cited it as a source of inspiration for *Star Wars*. In Japanese with English subtitles. Contains violence. ▭

Toshiro Mifune *Rokurota* • Misa Uehara *Lady Yukihime* • Minoru Chiaki *Tahei* • Kamatari Fujiwara *Matashichi* • Susumu Fujita *Hyoe Tadokoro* • Takashi Shimura *Izumi* ■ *Dir* Akira Kurosawa • *Scr* Ryuzo Kikushima, Hideo Oguni, Shinobu Hashimoto, Akira Kurosawa

Hidden Homicide ★ U
Murder mystery 1958 · UK · BW · 81mins

Like a lot of British B-movies, this bargain-basement thriller would have worked as a TV episode. Spun out to feature length, however, the gaping holes in the narrative logic and the inadequacy of the direction become glaringly apparent. Director Tony Young badly fumbles this story of a writer who is so convinced by the circumstantial evidence surrounding his uncle's death, he begins to consider himself a suspect. Griffith Jones lacks the vulnerability to convince in the lead.

Griffith Jones *Michael Cornforth* • Patricia Laffan *Jean* • James Kenney *Oswald Castellan* • Bruce Seton *Bill Dodd* • Maya Koumani *Marian* • Robert Raglan *Ashbury* • Richard Shaw *Wright* • Charles Farrell *Mungo Peddey*

■ *Dir* Tony Young • *Scr* Tony Young, Bill Luckwell, from the novel *Murder at Shinglestrand* by Paul Capon

Hidden in America ★★★
Drama 1996 · US · Colour · 96mins

This gritty made-for-TV drama was executive-produced by Jeff Bridges, who made the film in co-operation with the End Hunger Network. Brother Beau stars as a redundant factory worker and widower unable to support his family but just too proud to accept help from his sick daughter's doctor (Bruce Davison). A well-made and meaningful piece, despite the occasional sermonising, which softens into a hopeful conclusion.

Beau Bridges *Bill Januson* • Bruce Davison *Dr Michael Millerton* • Shelton Dane *Robbie Januson* • Jena Malone *Willa Januson* • Alice Krige *Dee* • Josef Sommer *Edward Millerton* • Frances McDormand *Gus* • Jeff Bridges *Vincent* ■ *Dir* Martin Bell • *Scr* Peter Silverman, Michael de Guzman

Hide and Seek ★★ U
Comedy thriller 1963 · UK · Colour · 92mins

After a decade top-lining some of the wittiest social satires ever made in the UK, Ian Carmichael's fortunes were already on the wane by the time he starred in this leaden comedy thriller. Had full-blooded suspense been the order of the day, director Cy Endfield might have been more at home. But Carmichael wasn't really his kind of actor and he mishandles the jokier aspects of the plot, in which a scientist working on a top secret project is presumed to have defected when, in actuality, he's been kidnapped.

Ian Carmichael *David Garrett* • Janet Munro *Maggie* • Curt Jurgens *Hubert Marek* • George Pravda *Frank Melnicker* • Kieron Moore *Paul* • Hugh Griffith *Wilkins* • Derek Tansley *Chambers* • Judy Parfitt *Chauffeur* ■ *Dir* Cy Endfield • *Scr* David Stone, Robert Foshko, from a story by Harold Greene

Hide in Plain Sight
★★★★ PG
Crime drama 1980 · US · Colour · 87mins

Actor James Caan made an impressive directorial debut with this gutsy, unfussily acted account of the father who goes in search of his children after his wife (who is now involved with a renegade gangster) becomes part of the witness protection programme. Based on actual events, the action is shrewdly paced to reflect the painfully slow progress made by Caan's untutored factory worker in attempting to glean information from an uncaring, jobsworthing system. Yet, in striving to convey his character's frustration, Caan places more emphasis on his socio-political message than on the human interest angle. ▭

James Caan *Thomas Hacklin Jr* • Jill Eikenberry *Alisa Hacklin* • Robert Viharo *Jack Scolese* • Joe Grifasi *Matty Stanek* • Barbra Rae *Ruthie Hacklin Scolese* • Kenneth McMillan *Sam Marzetta* • Josef Sommer *Jason R Reid* • Danny Aiello *Sal Carvello* ■ *Dir* James Caan • *Scr* Spencer Eastman, from a book by Leslie Waller

Hideaway ★★ 18

Horror thriller   1995 · US · Colour · 102mins

After a near-death experience in a car crash, antiques dealer Jeff Goldblum develops a psychic link to a satanist serial killer in this confusing psychological horror thriller, co-scripted by *Se7en*'s screenwriter Andrew Kevin Walker from the Dean R Koontz novel. It's devoid of any real terror or suspense, though good computer-generated visual effects go a long way in maintaining the interest. However, the dispassionate Goldblum prevents any empathy with his quandary and the low-key approach of director Brett Leonard flattens any rich potential the premise might have had. Contains violence, swearing and nudity. 🖭 *DVD*

Jeff Goldblum *Hatch Harrison* • Christine Lahti *Lindsey Harrison* • Alicia Silverstone *Regina Harrison* • Jeremy Sisto *Vassago* • Alfred Molina *Dr Jonas Nyebern* • Rae Dawn Chong *Rose Orwetto* ■ *Dir* Brett Leonard • *Scr* Andrew Kevin Walker, Neal Jimenez, from the novel *Hideaway* by Dean R Koontz

The Hideaways ★★ U

Drama   1973 · US · Colour · 105mins

Originally shown under the cumbersome title *From the Mixed-Up Files of Mrs Basil E Frankweiler*, this was heavily touted as the comeback, after three years, of Ingrid Bergman. It's a flimsy tale about two perfectly dressed, perfectly dentured, perfectly behaved children (you know the sort) who have the run of New York's Metropolitan Museum and wonder if a Michelangelo sculpture is a fake or not. Bergman plays a white-haired eccentric who may have a clue to the sculpture's origin.

Ingrid Bergman *Mrs Frankweiler* • Sally Prager *Claudia* • Johnny Doran *Jamie* • George Rose *Saxonburg* • Richard Mulligan *Mr Kincaid* • Georgann Johnson *Mrs Kincaid* • Madeline Kahn *Schoolteacher* ■ *Dir* Fielder Cook • *Scr* Blanche Hanalis, from the novel *From The Mixed-Up Files of Mrs Basil E Frankweiler* by EL Konigsburg

Hideous Kinky ★★★ 15

Drama   1998 · UK/Fr · Colour · 94mins

Kate Winslet followed her headline-grabbing role in the blockbuster *Titanic* with the lead in this lower-profile film, based on the book by Esther Freud. She plays young mother Julia, who decides to uproot her two young daughters and seek adventure and possibly romance in the Morocco of 1972. While Julia's journey is quite interesting and full of colour, the tale of expatriate life in Marrakesh is often repetitive, with one too many scenes having Julia's older daughter Bea bleating about the fact that she hates all this free-living. Both Julia and Bea come off as two selfish children determined to get their own way, leaving the heart of the film to Julia's youngest, Lucy, played with skill by little Carrie Mullan. 🖭 *DVD*

Kate Winslet *Julia* • Said Taghmaoui *Bilal* • Bella Riza *Bea* • Carrie Mullan *Lucy* • Pierre Clémenti *Santoni* • Abigail Cruttenden *Charlotte* ■ *Dir* Gillies MacKinnon • *Scr* Billy MacKinnon, from the novel by Esther Freud

Hideous Sun Demon ★ PG

Science-fiction horror
1955 · US · BW · 71mins

Scientist Robert Clarke is exposed to nuclear radiation and turns into a scaly lizard-like monster when exposed to the sun's rays. Wordy dialogue, hopeless acting, wonky photography and a soundtrack that later turned up in *Night of the Living Dead* have made this farcical science-fiction fantasy a cult hit in the *Plan 9 from Outer Space* so-bad-it's-funny tradition. 🖭

Robert Clarke *Dr Gilbert McKenna Pitnik* • Patricia Manning *Ann Russell Polly* • Nan Peterson *Trudy Osborne Bunny* • Patrick Whyte *Dr Frederick Buckell Major* • Bill Hampton *Police Lieutenant* ■ *Dir* Robert Clarke, Thomas Boutross, Craig Mitchell • *Scr* ES Seeley Jr, Doane Hoag, Craig Mitchell, Robert Clarke, Phil Hiner

Hider in the House ★★ 18

Thriller   1989 · US · Colour · 103mins

Until it breaks down the believability barrier, director Matthew Patrick's unusual psycho thriller is tightly constructed and grippingly written. Former mental institution inmate Gary Busey hides in the home of well-to-do Mimi Rogers and Michael McKean, obsessively spies on them and eventually intervenes in their personal affairs. It's when he's found out that the all-too-familiar maelstrom of mayhem begins and the early sharpness, focusing touchingly on family values and loss, is dulled by clichés of the genre. Yet Busey and Rogers raise enormous empathy before the plot degenerates into a stock shocker. Contains violence, swearing, sex scenes and nudity. 🖭

Gary Busey *Tom Sykes* • Mimi Rogers *Julie Dryer* • Michael McKean *Phil Dryer* • Kurt Christopher Kinder *Neil Dryer* • Candy Hutson [Candace Hutson] *Holly Dryer* • Bruce Glover *Gary Hufford* ■ *Dir* Matthew Patrick • *Scr* Lem Dobbs

Hiding Out ★★ 15

Comedy thriller   1987 · US · Colour · 98mins

Jon Cryer has rarely found the right vehicle for his comedic talents and, although this provides him with a rare starring role, it founders on a lame, unconvincing script. He plays a stockbroker who, finding himself on the run from the mob, decides to hide out as a college student. Given that he looks far too young as a bearded adult, this charade works wonders, but complications ensue when a fellow student (Annabeth Gish) falls for him. Director Bob Giraldi seems unsure whether this is a teen comedy or a light-hearted thriller. Contains some violence and swearing. 🖭

Jon Cryer *Andrew Morenski* • Keith Coogan *Patrick Morenski* • Annabeth Gish *Ryan Campbell* • Gretchen Cryer *Aunt Lucy* • Oliver Cotton *Killer* • Claude Brooks *Clinton* • Lou Walker *Ezzard* ■ *Dir* Bob Giraldi • *Scr* Joe Menosky, Jeff Rothberg

The Hiding Place ★★

Second World War drama
1975 · US · Colour · 146mins

Produced by Billy Graham's Evangelistic Association, this rather flat story of Dutch Christians giving shelter to persecuted Jews during the Second World War, wears its heart, but not its art, on its sleeve. Julie Harris and Arthur O'Connell – in his final film role – are just too well-scrubbed to pass for wartime citizens, despite the quality of their performances. This is certainly a moving experience, but it never really gets anywhere.

Julie Harris *Betsie ten Boom* • Eileen Heckart *Katje* • Arthur O'Connell *Casper ten Boom* • Jeannette Clift *Corrie ten Boom* • Robert Rietty *Willem ten Boom* • Pamela Sholto *Tine* • Paul Henley *Peter ten Boom* ■ *Dir* James F Collier • *Scr* Allan Sloane, Lawrence Holben, from the non-fiction book by Corrie Ten Boom, John Sherrill, Elizabeth Sherrill

High and Low ★★★★ 12

Crime drama
1963 · Jap · BW and Colour · 143mins

Akira Kurosawa's genius for literary adaptation also included hard-boiled pulp, as he proves with this reworking of Ed McBain's *King's Ransom*. It begins on a single set, as Toshiro Mifune's corrupt tycoon debates whether to pay the ransom demanded for the chauffeur's son, who was mistakenly kidnapped instead of his own offspring. But then the action opens out to follow the police on their desperate hunt around the seedier parts of town. Displaying a masterly control of mood and visual style, Kurosawa is more concerned with the morality of the case than its safe solution. However, this is still a riveting and tense thriller. In Japanese with English subtitles. 🖭

Toshiro Mifune *Kingo Gondo* • Kyoko Kagawa *Reiko, Gondo's wife* • Tatsuya Mihashi *Kawanishi* • Yutaka Sada *Aoki, the chauffeur* • Tatsuya Nakadai *Inspector Tokuro* • Takashi Shimura *Director* ■ *Dir* Akira Kurosawa • *Scr* Akira Kurosawa, Ryuzo Kikushima, Hideo Oguni, Eijiro Hisaita, from the novel *King's Ransom* by Ed McBain [Evan Hunter]

The High and the Mighty ★★ U

Drama   1954 · US · Colour · 146mins

As a crippled airplane flies through the sky, having passed the point of no return, it is up to washed-up pilot John Wayne (in a role originally intended for Spencer Tracy) to save the day. Director William A Wellman seems restrained by the CinemaScope format, and Ernest K Gann, adapting his novel to the screen, writes mundane flashbacks which dissipate the tension. Shallow characterisation doesn't help, either. A big hit in its day, this forerunner of the *Airport* series gained Oscar nominations for Wellman and supporting actresses Claire Trevor and Jan Sterling, while Dimitri Tiomkin won for his dramatic score.

John Wayne *Dan Roman* • Claire Trevor *May Holst* • Laraine Day *Lydia Rice* • Robert Stack *Sullivan* • Jan Sterling *Sally McKee* • Phil Harris *Ed Joseph* • Robert Newton *Gustave Pardee* • David Brian *Ken Childs* • Paul Kelly *Flaherty* ■ *Dir* William A Wellman • *Scr* Ernest K Gann, from his novel

High Anxiety ★★★ 15

Parody   1977 · US · Colour · 93mins

This parody of Alfred Hitchcock's greatest hits rather sums up the strengths and weaknesses of Mel Brooks's films. By opting for the best known scenes in *Spellbound*, *Vertigo*, *North by Northwest* and *Psycho*, he settles for easy laughs and thus misses the chance to kid around with the real aficionados. Moreover, not enough thought has gone into the non-spoof scenes, many of which run out of steam, like the Freudian lecture delivered in euphemisms owing to the presence of a young child. There are many funny moments, but perhaps Hitch was just too self-mocking to be spoofable. Contains swearing. 🖭

Mel Brooks *Richard H Thorndyke* • Madeline Kahn *Victoria Brisbane* • Cloris Leachman *Nurse Diesel* • Harvey Korman *Doctor Charles Montague* • Ron Carey *Brophy* • Howard Morris *Professor Lilloman* • Dick Van Patten *Doctor Wentworth* • Jack Riley *Desk clerk* ■ *Dir* Mel Brooks • *Scr* Mel Brooks, Ron Clark, Rudy DeLuca, Barry Levinson

High Art ★★★★ 18

Drama   1998 · US · Colour · 97mins

An intimate, skilfully observed study of the complex relationship between two neighbours, one a previously famous photographer (Ally Sheedy), the other an assistant editor of a photography magazine (Radha Mitchell). Despite its themes of drug abuse and lesbianism, this is far from being a sensationalist drama, while the gradual deepening of the ambitious, strong-willed Mitchell's attraction to and fascination with the drained, almost lifeless Sheedy is given credibility by the thoughtful script and stripped-bare performances. The gaunt Sheedy, barely recognisable from her teenage *Breakfast Club* days, expresses emotions that her erstwhile co-stars Emilio Estevez, Judd Nelson and Molly Ringwald can only dream of. Contains swearing, sex scenes and drug abuse. 🖭

Ally Sheedy *Lucy Berliner* • Radha Mitchell *Syd* • Patricia Clarkson *Greta* • Gabriel Mann *James, Syd's boyfriend* • Bill Sage *Arnie* • Ahr Duong *Dominique, "Frame" editor* • Tammy Grimes *Vera, Lucy's mother* • David Thornton *Harry, Syd's boss* ■ *Dir/Scr* Lisa Cholodenko

High-ballin' ★★ 15

Action   1978 · US/Can · Colour · 98mins

Produced by exploitation studio AIP, this low-budget trucking epic followed in the wake of Burt Reynolds's *Smokey and the Bandit* and went head-to-head with Sam Peckinpah's *Convoy*. Jerry Reed, who appeared in three *Smokey* films, is joined this time by biker Peter Fonda and female trucker Helen Shaver. The real star, though, is the massive rig that bowls down the freeway causing mayhem while our three heroes resist various hijackers, bootleggers and the corrupt trucking boss played by Chris Wiggins. 🖭

Peter Fonda *Rane* • Jerry Reed *Duke* • Helen Shaver *Pickup* • Chris Wiggins *King Carroll* • Michael Ironside *Butch* ■ *Dir* Peter Carter • *Scr* Paul Edwards, from a story by Richard Robinson, Stephen Schneck

High Barbaree ★★

Second World War drama
1947 · US · BW · 90mins

In this Second World War yarn, Van Johnson steers his downed navy seaplane towards High Barbaree, a fabled Pacific island his uncle once told him about. Co-pilot Cameron Mitchell keeps him company while he tells his story, which leads to

flashbacks re-creating Johnson's life back home with sweetheart June Allyson. Based on a novel by Charles Nordhoff and James Norman Hall, authors of *Mutiny on the Bounty* and other South Seas yarns, this is less a war movie than a soupy romance.

Van Johnson *Alec Brooke* • June Allyson *Nancy Fraser* • Thomas Mitchell *Capt Thad Vail* • Marilyn Maxwell *Diana Case* • Henry Hull *Dr Brooke* • Claude Jarman Jr *Alec, age 14* • Cameron Mitchell *Lt Moore* ■ *Dir* Jack Conway • *Scr* Anne Morrison Chaplin, Whitfield Cook, Cyril Hume, from the novel by Charles Nordhoff, James Norman Hall

High Boot Benny ★★★★ 15
Thriller 1993 · Ire · Colour · 78mins
In keeping with the principles of the non-sectarian school at the centre of his controversial drama, writer/director Joe Comerford tries to be even-handed, and he avoids many of the situations inherent in films about the Troubles. Frances Tomelty does well as the idealistic matron, as does Marc O'Shea as the confused teenager from Northern Ireland who seeks refuge south of the border. The tarring and feathering scene and the brutal army reprisal finale will chill to the marrow. ▭

Marc O'Shea *Benny* • Frances Tomelty *Matron* • Alan Devlin *Manley* • Annie Farr *Dorothy* • Seamus Ball *Father Bergin* • Fiona Nicholas *Orphan* ■ *Dir/Scr* Joe Comerford

The High Bright Sun ★★ PG
Wartime drama 1965 · UK · Colour · 109mins
This attempt to make emotional drama (army officer Dirk Bogarde's love for archaeology student Susan Strasberg) out of a national crisis (the Cypriot struggle against British occupation) results in one of the most stilted and wooden movies that Bogarde ever made for Rank. Director Ralph Thomas hammers away at the obvious and rapidly loses credibility, while Ian Stuart Black's dialogue is awesomely improbable. Bogarde, though, pulls the film up by its bootstraps. Contains some swearing and violence. ▭

Dirk Bogarde *Major McGuire* • George Chakiris *Haghios* • Susan Strasberg *Juno Kozani* • Denholm Elliott *Baker* • Grégoire Aslan *Skyros* • Colin Campbell *Emile* • Joseph Furst *Dr Andros* • Katherine Kath *Mrs Andros* ■ *Dir* Ralph Thomas • *Scr* Ian Stuart Black, Bryan Forbes, from the novel by Ian Stuart Black

The High Cost of Loving ★★ U
Comedy 1958 · US · BW · 87mins
That splendid actress Gena Rowlands, who found fame in husband John Cassavetes's powerful films, made an inauspicious screen debut in this tame domestic comedy directed by and co-starring José Ferrer. A celebrated stage and screen actor, Ferrer also directed seven so-so films. His fifth effort tells of a husband who thinks he is losing his office job, and whose wife fails to tell him she's expecting a baby.

José Ferrer *Jim Fry* • Gena Rowlands *Virginia Fry* • Joanne Gilbert *Syd Heyward* • Jim Backus *Paul Mason* • Bobby Troup *Steve Heyward* • Philip Ober *Herb Zorn* • Edward Platt *Eli Cave* • Charles Watts *Boylin* ■ *Dir* José Ferrer • *Scr* Rip Van Ronkel, from a story by Milo Frank Jr, Rip Van Ronkel

The High Country ★
Romantic adventure
1981 · Can · Colour · 101mins
Poor old Timothy Bottoms. After winning rave reviews for his role as the teenager coming of age in *The Last Picture Show*, he was reduced to making tedious, unoriginal dramas like this. He plays an escaped prisoner dragging Linda Purl through the mountains in what is essentially an excuse for director Harvey Hart to film lots of impressive Canadian scenery in between the mediocre chase scenes.

Timothy Bottoms *Jim* • Linda Purl *Kathy* • George Sims *Larry* • Jim Lawrence *Casey* • Bill Berry *Carter* • Walter Mills *Clem* • Paul Jolicoeur *Red* • Dick Butler *Herbie* ■ *Dir* Harvey Hart • *Scr* Bud Townsend

The High Crusade ★★ 15
Science-fiction comedy
1994 · US/Ger · Colour · 86mins
Before making American blockbusters such as *Independence Day*, director Roland Emmerich produced this lame combination of *Star Wars* and *Monty Python and the Holy Grail*. During the Crusades, a spaceship lands outside the castle of knight Rick Overton. When his trusty army defeats the laser gun-wielding aliens, he decides to use the craft to get to the Holy Land quickly and save the day. Unfortunately events take an even more bizarre turn as the slapstick and anachronistic humour stubbornly refuse to gel with the cheap science-fiction elements. The hyperkinetic insanity becomes tiresome.

Rick Overton *Sir Roger* • John Rhys-Davies *Brother Parvus* • Patrick Brymer *Red John* • Debbie Lee Carrington *Branithar* • Michael Des Barres *Monsieur du Lac* ■ *Dir* Holger Neuhäuser, Klaus Knoesel • *Scr* Robert G Brown, from a novel by Poul Anderson, Jürgen Egger

High Desert Kill ★★★ 15
Science-fiction thriller
1989 · US · Colour · 88mins
An intriguing sci-fi chiller in which a group of hunters falls prey to a sinister alien force in the New Mexican desert. Craggy Chuck Connors (in one of his last roles) and Marc Singer are among the threatened marksmen and director Harry Falk makes great use of the desolate landscape. The superior screenplay is from TS Cook, who co-wrote the Oscar-nominated script for *The China Syndrome* (1979). Contains some violence. ▭

Anthony Geary *Dr Jim Cole* • Marc Singer *Brad Mueller* • Chuck Connors *Stan Brown* • Micah Grant *Ray Bettencamp* • Vaughn Armstrong *Paul Bettencamp* • Lori Birdsong *Terry* ■ *Dir* Harry Falk • *Scr* TS Cook

High Fidelity ★★★★ 15
Comedy drama
2000 · US/UK · Colour · 113mins
Don't fret about the fact that Stephen Frears has transposed Nick Hornby's novel from north London to downtown Chicago. This slickly scripted, knowingly played and cameo-stewn comedy stands, on its merits, as an *Alfie* for the millennial generation. As the owner of a failing vinyl emporium, John Cusack combines reluctant self-awareness with genuine delusion as

he attempts to reconcile the loss of girlfriend Iben Hjejle to lusty neighbour Tim Robbins by dating singer Lisa Bonet. However, it's when directly addressing the viewer or compulsively compiling Top Five lists with co-workers Jack Black and Todd Louiso that Cusack, and the film, come alive.

John Cusack *Rob Gordon* • Iben Hjejle *Laura* • Todd Louiso *Dick* • Jack Black *Barry* • Lisa Bonet *Marie De Salle* • Catherine Zeta-Jones *Charlie* • Joan Cusack *Liz* • Tim Robbins *Ian* • Lili Taylor *Sarah* • Natasha Gregson Wagner *Caroline* ■ *Dir* Stephen Frears • *Scr* DV DeVincentis, Steve Pink, John Cusack, Scott Rosenberg, from the novel by Nick Hornby

High Flight ★★ U
Action drama 1957 · UK · Colour · 105mins
The training of jet pilots in peacetime makes for a dull subject, despite some capably-staged midair crises. For dramatic take-off, therefore, this British-made film relies on the tense relationship between Ray Milland's commanding officer and Kenneth Haigh's rebellious young cadet. Haigh must have seemed ideal casting, having just made his name on stage as Jimmy Porter in *Look Back in Anger*. But he curiously lacks screen presence, and the part would have been much better played by Anthony Newley, seen here as a fellow cadet.

Ray Milland *Wing Commander David Rudge* • Bernard Lee *Flight Sergeant Harris* • Kenneth Haigh *Tony Winchester* • Anthony Newley *Rodger Endicott* • Kenneth Fortescue *John Fletcher* • Sean Kelly *Cadet Day* • Helen Cherry *Louise* • Leslie Phillips *Squadron Leader Blake* • John Le Mesurier *Commandant* ■ *Dir* John Gilling • *Scr* Joseph Landon, Ken Hughes, from a story by Jack Davies

High Heels ★★★ 18
Black comedy 1991 · Sp · Colour · 108mins
After a string of cult hits, it was inevitable that Pedro Almodóvar would eventually take a false step, and it came in *High Heels*. Abandoning his trademark Euro-trash style, he attempted to tackle more serious themes in this disconcerting melodrama that owes more to the films of Douglas Sirk and Rainer Werner Fassbinder than to the blend of sex, kitsch, and comedy typical of his more outrageous pictures. Unfortunately, he is so hell-bent on presenting a weighty treatise on families, the media and the price of fame that he allows too many scenes to become morose. The performances of Marisa Paredes and Victoria Abril just about save the day. In Spanish with English subtitles. ▭

Victoria Abril *Rebecca* • Marisa Paredes *Becky del Paramo* • Miguel Bose *Judge Dominguez/ Femme Letal/Hugo* • Pedro Diez del Corral *Alberto* • Feodor Atkine *Manuel* • Ana Lizaran [Anna Lizaran] *Margarita* • Rocio Munoz *Little Rebecca* • Mairata O'Wisiedo *Judge's mother* ■ *Dir/Scr* Pedro Almodóvar

High Hell ★★
Action adventure 1957 · US · BW · 85mins
One of those cheaply-made thrillers that always sound more enticingly full of menace than they really are. This one is all about a mine-owner's wife who takes a fancy to her husband's partner. The problems start when all

three find themselves trapped in a snowbound hut high up in the Canadian Rockies. John Derek stars alongside familiar British faces Patrick Allen and Jerold Wells.

John Derek *Craig Rhodes* • Elaine Stewart *Lenore Davidson* • Patrick Allen *Luke Fulgham* • Jerold Wells *Charlie Spence* • Al Mulock *Frank Davidson* • Rodney Burke *Danny Rhodes* • Colin Croft *Dell Malverne* ■ *Dir* Burt Balaban • *Scr* Irve Tunick, from the novel *High Cage* by Steve Frazee

High Hopes ★★★★ 15
Comedy drama 1988 · UK · Colour · 107mins
Mike Leigh's long-awaited big-screen follow-up to *Bleak Moments*, which appeared 17 years earlier, presents an amusing and affecting, if sometimes grim slice in the life of three couples in Thatcher's Britain: a working-class couple with counter-cultural pretensions, an obnoxious up-market twosome, and a pair of consumerist vulgarians. Caricatures they may be, and the plot tends towards the slender. Yet Leigh's unique blend of improvisation, invention and satire – what might be called misanthropy with a comic twist – combine to distinctive and telling effect. Contains swearing and sex scenes. ▭

Philip Davis *Cyril Bender* • Ruth Sheen *Shirley* • Edna Doré *Mrs Bender* • Philip Jackson *Martin Burke* • Heather Tobias *Valerie Burke* • Lesley Manville *Laetitia Boothe-Braine* • David Bamber *Rupert Boothe-Braine* • Jason Watkins *Wayne* ■ *Dir/Scr* Mike Leigh

High Lonesome ★★ U
Western 1950 · US · Colour · 81mins
Sociologically interesting cross between a western and a juvenile problem picture, with the snarling, brooding John Barrymore Jr, son of "the Great Profile", as a teenager with a conscience. It's directed by writer Alan LeMay, better known today for penning the book on which *The Searchers* is based. Alas, LeMay is no cinematic craftsman, and this film really needed an understanding director like Nicholas Ray or Elia Kazan, both of whom did similar work with other, more famous examples of broody male youth.

John Barrymore Jr [John Drew Barrymore] *Cooncat* • Chill Wills *Boatwhistle* • John Archer *Pat Farrell* • Lois Butler *Meagan Davis* • Kristine Miller *Abbey Davis* • Basil Ruysdael *Horse Davis* • Jack Elam *Smiling Man* • Dave Kashner *Roper* ■ *Dir/Scr* Alan LeMay

High Lonesome ★★★
Music documentary
1993 · US · Colour and BW · 95mins
Fans of Kentucky's special brand of music will enjoy this documentary. The main focus is on 82-year-old Bill Monroe, "the father of bluegrass", who fused local hillbilly music with Scots-Irish traditions brought by immigrants to the Kentucky coal fields. The music then developed and led to its acceptance at Nashville's Grand Ole Opry. The post-war period concentrates on the legendary Flatt and Scruggs, and the use of TV in spreading their music.

Dir Rachel Liebling • *Scr* Rachel Liebling

High Mountain Rangers ★★ PG

Action adventure 1987 · US · Colour · 89mins

The usual good guy/bad guy clichés make their presence felt in this rather ordinary action adventure. The only point of interest in this otherwise mundane mountain romp is that Robert Conrad not only stars, directs and contributes to the script, but has his two sons up on the screen, with his daughter executive-producing the entire show. In a film that never really rises above the prosaic, spotting family similarities becomes fascinating. 🖭

Robert Conrad *Jesse Hawkes* • Christian Conrad *Matt Hawkes* • Shane Conrad *Cody Hawkes* • Russell Todd *Cutler* • Todd Allen *Shepard* • Eugene Williams *Hart* • Tom Towles *TJ Cousins* ■ *Dir* Robert Conrad • *Scr* David J Kinghorn, from a story by David J Kinghorn, Robert Conrad

High Noon ★★★★★ U

Classic western 1952 · US · BW · 84mins

This is the film that put director Fred Zinnemann on the Hollywood A-list, revived the career of Gary Cooper and made Grace Kelly a star. If that's not enough, this multiple Oscar-winner was also one of the first psychological westerns, breaking the mould of the gun-toting tales that had dominated the genre since the early silent era. It was also a highly controversial film, being seen as an attack on those who deserted their colleagues during the communist witch-hunts that turned Hollywood into a place of fear between 1947 and 1951. 🖭

Gary Cooper *Will Kane* • Grace Kelly *Amy Kane* • Thomas Mitchell *Jonas Henderson* • Lloyd Bridges *Harvey Pell* • Katy Jurado *Helen Ramirez* • Otto Kruger *Percy Mettrick* • Lon Chaney Jr *Martin Howe* • Henry Morgan [Harry Morgan] *William Fuller* • Lee Van Cleef *Jack Colby* ■ *Dir* Fred Zinnemann • *Scr* Carl Foreman, from the story *The Tin Star* by John W Cunningham • *Cinematographer* Floyd Crosby • *Music* Dmitri Tiomkin • *Editor* Elmo Williams, Harry Gerstad

High Plains Drifter ★★★★ 18

Western 1973 · US · Colour · 100mins

Sex, sadism and the supernatural are loosely bundled in Clint Eastwood's stylishly self-conscious western: man-with-no-name satire or fable of mystic revenge, take your pick. Eastwood looms out of the desert, a mirage of retribution who stood by while an town's inhabitants who stood by while their honest sheriff was whipped to death. Eastwood seems, not altogether successfully, to be paying off debts to his former mentor, Sergio Leone – gratitude he can only express obliquely via the occult references on this distinctive variation on the spaghetti western genre. Contains violence and swearing. 🖭

Clint Eastwood *The Stranger* • Verna Bloom *Sarah Belding* • Mariana Hill [Marianna Hill] *Callie Travers* • Mitchell Ryan *Dave Drake* • Jack Ging *Morgan Allen* • Stefan Gierasch *Mayor Jason Hobart* ■ *Dir* Clint Eastwood • *Scr* Ernest Tidyman • *Cinematographer* Bruce Surtees

High Pressure ★★

Comedy 1932 · US · BW · 72mins

William Powell stars as a racketeer who falls for an inventor's scheme to convert sewage into artificial rubber. He sets up a corporation and sells stocks to raise some cash, romancing Evelyn Brent along the way. Powell breezes through this nonsense, which is not quite a gangster picture and not quite good enough for director Mervyn Le Roy (*Little Caesar, Five Star Final*).

William Powell *Gar Evans* • Evelyn Brent *Francine* • George Sidney *Colonel Ginsburg* • Frank McHugh *Mike Donoghey* • Guy Kibbee *Clifford Gray* • Evalyn Knapp *Helen* • Ben Alexander *Geoffrey* • Harry Beresford *Dr Rudolph* ■ *Dir* Mervyn LeRoy • *Scr* Joseph Jackson, from the story *Hot Money* by SJ Peters and the play by Aben Kandell

The High Price of Passion ★

Drama based on a true story
1986 · US · Colour · 100mins

A sordid little TV movie with Richard Crenna, who deserves better material, as a university professor who becomes dangerously obsessed with gold-digging hooker Karen Young. Sort of *The Blue Angel* meets *Of Human Bondage* really, but offering no similar insights into the human condition. In addition, TV censorship effectively prevents this from being a genuinely disturbing drama, even in the hands of experienced TV director Larry Elikann.

Richard Crenna *William Douglas* • Karen Young *Robin Benedict* • Sean McCann *John Benedict* • Terry Tweed *Shirley Benedict* • Wayne Best *Keefe* ■ *Dir* Larry Elikann • *Scr* Mel Frohman, from the novel *The Ruling Passion* by Russell M Glitman

High Risk ★★

Action adventure 1981 · US · Colour · 91mins

Laughable action adventure about four chums who decide that the solution to their money woes is a quick trip to Colombia to lift a fortune from a drugs kingpin. Naturally, things don't go quite according to plan. It boasts a pretty good cast – James Coburn, James Brolin, Anthony Quinn, Lindsay Wagner – but the sheer implausibility of the tale make it hard to feel involved.

James Brolin *Stone* • Cleavon Little *Rockney* • Bruce Davison *Dan* • Chick Vennera *Tony* • Anthony Quinn *Mariano* • Lindsay Wagner *Olivia* • James Coburn *Serrano* • Ernest Borgnine *Clint* ■ *Dir/Scr* Stewart Raffill

High Road to China ★★★ PG

Action adventure
1983 · US · Colour · 100mins

Tom Selleck was offered the lead in *Raiders of the Lost Ark*, but had to refuse because he was contracted to the TV show *Magnum PI*. Instead he starred in this *Raiders* wannabe, playing a First World War flying ace who helps spoiled rich girl Bess Armstrong track down her missing father. While low on special effects, thanks to zippy direction from Brian G Hutton (*Where Eagles Dare, Kelly's Heroes*) this romps along merrily in the style of forties Saturday matinées, while Selleck cuts quite a dash as the suave, wise-cracking hero. 🖭

Tom Selleck *O'Malley* • Bess Armstrong *Eve Tozer* • Jack Weston *Struts* • Wilford Brimley *Bradley Tozer* • Robert Morley *Bentik* • Brian Blessed *Suleiman Khan* • Cassandra Gava *Alessa* ■ *Dir* Brian G Hutton • *Scr* Sandra Weintraub Roland, S Lee Pogostin, from the novel by Jon Cleary

High School ★★★

Documentary 1968 · US · BW · 75mins

For over three decades, Fred Wiseman, a leading exponent of Direct Cinema or *cinéma vérité*, has entered various institutions with his hand-held camera, shot a vast amount of footage, and edited it down dispassionately, being careful not to make a subjective point. However, in his second documentary (the first, *Titicut Follies*, was set in an insane asylum), he eavesdrops on a middle-class school in Philadelphia and seems to be exposing the deadly conformity of the place. Concentrating mostly on student-teacher relationships, it has too narrow a focus, but is a fascinating study nevertheless.

Dir/Scr Frederick Wiseman • *Cinematographer* Richard Leiterman • *Editor* Frederick Wiseman

High School Confidential ★★★

Cult drama 1958 · US · BW · 85mins

The patriotic and paternalistic Louis B Mayer would have turned in his grave had he seen this deeply subversive, hugely exploitative MGM offering about school kids getting high on marijuana. It also packs in gang warfare, hot-rod racing, alcoholism, plenty of sex and a note of seriousness when lead delinquent, Russ Tamblyn, turns out to be a narcotics agent. Jan Sterling plays an English teacher and that fifties icon, Mamie Van Doren, turns up as Tamblyn's lascivious aunt. Rock star Jerry Lee Lewis has a cameo appearance as himself.

Russ Tamblyn *Tony Baker* • Jan Sterling *Arlene Williams* • John Drew Barrymore *JI Coleridge* • Mamie Van Doren *Gwen Dulaine* • Diane Jergens *Joan Staples* • Jerry Lee Lewis ■ *Dir* Jack Arnold • *Scr* Lewis Meltzer, Robert Blees, from a story by Robert Blees

High School High ★★ 15

Comedy 1996 · US · Colour · 81mins

This hit-and-miss spoof is chiefly aimed at the Michelle Pfeiffer hit *Dangerous Minds*, but also takes drive-by shots at all and sundry. Jon Lovitz is the idealistic teacher determined to make a difference at a school so crime-ridden the headmistress has to appeal at assembly for the return of kidnapped tutors. It's good to see perennial sidekick Lovitz in a lead role, but both the script and the supporting performances are patchy. According to the credits the film is produced by "the artist formerly known as David Zucker", the man responsible for ground-breaking comedy classics such as *Airplane!* and *The Naked Gun*. 🖭

Jon Lovitz *Clark* • Tia Carrere *Victoria* • Louise Fletcher *Mrs Doyle* • Mekhi Phifer *Griff* • Malinda Williams *Natalie* • Guillermo Diaz *Paco* • Lexie Bigham *Two Bags* • Gil Espinoza *Alonzo* ■ *Dir* Hart Bochner • *Scr* David Zucker, Robert LoCash, Pat Proft

High School USA ★ PG

Comedy 1983 · US · Colour · 91mins

Two years away from *Back to the Future* and film stardom, Michael J Fox was finding success in the *Family Ties* series while still grinding away in TV movies like this one. It's an unfunny comedy set in a school where young

Fox – 22 at the time – is the goody-two-shoes. A host of would-be bratpackers (including Crispin Glover and *ER*'s Anthony Edwards) play fellow students, to little comic effect. 🖭

Michael J Fox *Jay-Jay Manners* • Nancy McKeon *Beth Franklin* • Anthony Edwards *Beau Middleton* • Todd Bridges *Otto Lipton* • Angela Cartwright *Miss D'Angelo* • Bob Denver *Milton Feld* • Dwayne Hickman *Mr Plaza* • Lauri Hendler *Nadine* ■ *Dir* Rod Amateau • *Scr* Alan Eisenstock, Larry B Mintz

High Season ★★ 15

Satirical drama 1987 · UK · Colour · 90mins

Oddly old-fashioned, romantic fluff, with Jacqueline Bisset as a photographer on the Greek island of Rhodes. Clare Peploe's film chronicles her encounters with all manner of people who need shooting – though not necessarily with a camera – including obnoxious tourists, spies and an egocentric ex-hubby. The main interest lies in the picture-postcard views of both the island and Miss Bisset, and in a classy supporting cast which includes James Fox, Robert Stephens and Kenneth Branagh. 🖭

Jacqueline Bisset *Katherine* • James Fox *Patrick* • Irene Papas *Penelope* • Sebastian Shaw *Basil Sharp* • Kenneth Branagh *Rick Lamb* • Lesley Manville *Carol Lamb* • Robert Stephens *Konstantinis* ■ *Dir* Clare Peploe • *Scr* Clare Peploe, Mark Peploe

High Sierra ★★★ PG

Film noir 1941 · US · BW · 100mins

The film that unquestionably turned character actor Humphrey Bogart into a fully-fledged star. Bogie, in a role turned down by George Raft, plays melancholic gangster "Mad Dog" Roy Earle, making his last stand from a log cabin in the landscape of the title. The plot's actually a bit daft, and there's some risible nonsense with a disabled girl (the excellent Joan Leslie) and a dog. But screenwriters John Huston and WR Burnett (*Little Caesar*) have, on the whole, fashioned a pacy melodrama for director Raoul Walsh to get his teeth into. 🖭

Humphrey Bogart *"Mad Dog" Roy Earle* • Ida Lupino *Marie Garson* • Alan Curtis *Babe Kozak* • Arthur Kennedy *Red Hattery* • Joan Leslie *Velma* • Henry Hull *"Doc" Banton* • Barton MacLane *Jake Kranmer* • Henry Travers *Pa* ■ *Dir* Raoul Walsh • *Scr* John Huston, WR Burnett, from the novel by WR Burnett

High Society ★★★★ U

Musical comedy 1956 · US · Colour · 102mins

A musical remake of the 1940 film *The Philadelphia Story* that was a gigantic smash hit, particularly in Britain. This glowing, late MGM musical offers many joys, notably the only teaming of crooners Bing Crosby and Frank Sinatra, and the delightful Grace Kelly in a role she was born to play, namely that of a spoiled rich brat. Sinatra and Celeste Holm make a snappy pair of journalists, but Crosby seems ill-at-ease, and jazz great Louis Armstrong is reduced to the role of chorus and stooge. There are nine Cole Porter songs, including the classics *Who Wants to be a Millionaire?* and *Well, Did You Evah?* 🖭

Bing Crosby *CK Dexter-Haven* • Grace Kelly *Tracy Lord* • Frank Sinatra *Mike Connor* •

Celeste Holm *Liz Imbrie* • John Lund *George Kittredge* • Louis Calhern *Uncle Willie* • Sidney Blackmer *Seth Lord* • Louis Armstrong ■ *Dir* Charles Walters • *Scr* John Patrick, from the play *The Philadelphia Story* by Philip Barry • *Music* Johnny Green, Saul Chaplin

High Spirits ★★★ 15
Supernatural comedy
1988 · US · Colour · 93mins

A ghost-busting cross between *Fawlty Towers* and *Blithe Spirit*, Neil Jordan's boil-in-the-bag *Beetle Juice* goes for Ealing whimsy and easy laughs and, incredibly, manages both in spite of such a slender plot. Peter O'Toole hits the right note of craziness as a "haunted" castle owner whose staff of fake spectres battle real poltergeists during the American tourist season, with suitably madcap results. However, too many desperate characters veer off into so many disparate subplots that complete *Carry On Screaming*-style satisfaction is never achieved. ▣

Peter O'Toole *Peter Plunkett* • Daryl Hannah *Mary Plunkett* • Steve Guttenberg *Jack* • Beverly D'Angelo *Sharon* • Liam Neeson *Martin Brogan* • Ray McAnally *Plunkett Senior* • Liz Smith *Mrs Plunkett* • Jennifer Tilly *Miranda* • Peter Gallagher *Brother Tony* • Connie Booth *Marge* ■ *Dir/Scr* Neil Jordan

High Stakes ★★ 18
Romantic thriller 1989 · US · Colour · 82mins

Sally Kirkland, as a New York prostitute, gives a superbly sensitive performance and almost redeems this story of her attempt to rescue her daughter from the mob, while falling in love with a Wall Street operator. Not particularly thrilling material, though Kirkland puts in a portrayal beyond the call of duty. Any other interest is provided by an early appearance from Sarah Michelle Gellar (from TV's *Buffy the Vampire Slayer*), plus a pre-*Misery* role for Kathy Bates.

Sally Kirkland *Melanie "Bambi" Rose* • Robert LuPone *John Stratton* • Richard Lynch *Slim* • Sarah Gellar [Sarah Michelle Gellar] *Karen* • Kathy Bates *Jill* • WT Martin *Bob* • Eddie Earl Hatch *Earl* ■ *Dir/Scr* Amos Kollek

High Tide ★★★ 15
Drama 1987 · Ausl · Colour · 101mins

One of those Australian movies of the late eighties, before the days of *Muriel's Wedding* and *The Adventures of Priscilla, Queen of the Desert*, that almost drowned in its own dour political correctness. But this bleak tale of a woman who unexpectedly discovers her long-abandoned daughter is saved by the stirring, emotionally loaded central performance of Judy Davis, one of the most fascinating and adventurous actors working today, whose well-documented eccentricity has prevented her achieving major star status. This often thoughtful, intelligent film shows us once again what a charismatic celluloid presence she can be. Contains swearing. ▣

Judy Davis *Lilli* • Jan Adele *Bet* • Claudia Karvan *Ally* • Colin Friels *Mick* • John Clayton *Col* • Frankie J Holden *Lester* • Monica Trapaga *Tracey* • Mark Hembrow *Mechanic* ■ *Dir* Gillian Armstrong • *Scr* Laura Jones

High Tide at Noon ★★
Drama 1957 · UK · BW · 110mins

Since his graduation to features in the early fifties, one-time documentarist Philip Leacock had mostly impressed, yet he came unstuck with this *Romeo and Juliet* story set alongside the Nova Scotia fishing banks. Leacock surveys the local scenery with a keen eye, but his handling of the melodramatic ructions caused by Betta St John's rejection of Patrick McGoohan and Michael Craig in favour of outsider William Sylvester is less sure. With the accents all over the place, it's St John's sad, largely silent return to the deserted village that provides the film's most poignant moment.

Betta St John *Joanna MacKenzie* • William Sylvester *Alec Douglas* • Michael Craig *Nils* • Patrick McGoohan *Simon Breck* • Flora Robson *Donna* • Alexander Knox *Stephen* ■ *Dir* Philip Leacock • *Scr* Neil Paterson, from the novel by Elizabeth Ogilvie • *Scr* Eric Cross

High Time ★★ U
Musical comedy 1960 · US · Colour · 102mins

Sammy Cahn and Jimmy Van Heusen picked up an Oscar nomination for their song *The Second Time Around*, but that's the only bright spot in Blake Edwards's twee comedy. Bing Crosby ladles on the charm as the millionaire widower who heads back to college for some long overdue education, but can only raise a giggle by suffering indignities like dressing up as Scarlett O'Hara. Cosby gets to romance pouting professor Nicole Maurey, but he's clearly aware the script is ludicrously lightweight. Fabian and Tuesday Weld play his unhip fellow students.

Bing Crosby *Harvey Howard* • Fabian *Gil Sparrow* • Tuesday Weld *Joy Elder* • Nicole Maurey *Helene Gauthier* • Richard Beymer *Bob Bannerman* • Yvonne Craig *Randy Pruitt* • Patrick Adiarte *TJ Padmanagham* ■ *Dir* Blake Edwards • *Scr* Tom Waldman, Frank Waldman, from a story by Garson Kanin

High Velocity ★
Action drama 1977 · US · Colour · 105mins

This is exploitation movie-making at its crassest. Both Ben Gazzara and Paul Winfield are utterly wasted as hard-boiled Vietnam vets hired to rescue a corporate tycoon (Keenan Wynn) kidnapped by a guerilla force. Amid the substandard action scenes director Remi Kramer tries to make a point about foreign businesses in Third World countries corrupting officials, but offers no genuine insight. At least he manages a decent car chase in his one and only directorial assignment.

Ben Gazzara *Clifford Baumgartner* • Britt Ekland *Mrs Andersen* • Paul Winfield *Watson* • Keenan Wynn *Mr Andersen* • Alejandro Rey *Alejandro Martel* ■ *Dir* Remi Kramer • *Scr* Remi Kramer, Michael J Parsons

High Wall ★★★
Crime drama 1947 · US · BW · 98mins

Stylish, angst-ridden *film noir* with Robert Taylor as the traumatised war veteran and possible wife killer who falls in love with his psychiatrist, Audrey Totter. She recommends brain surgery and truth-drugs; Taylor realises that if he has the surgery he will be

judged sane and tried for murder. As the flashbacks roll past, we realise everyone has a sexual hang-up that the war just made worse. Taylor looks convincingly ravaged throughout, and Herbert Marshall makes a splendidly shady character who commits murder with a delicate twist of his umbrella.

Robert Taylor (1) *Steven Kenet* • Audrey Totter *Dr Ann Lorrison* • Herbert Marshall *Willard I Whitcombe* • Dorothy Patrick *Helen Kenet* • HB Warner *Mr Slocum* • Warner Anderson *Dr George Poward* • Moroni Olsen *Dr Phillip Dunlap* ■ *Dir* Curtis Bernhardt • *Scr* Sydney Boehm, Lester Cole, from the novel and play by Alan R Clark, Bradbury Foote

High, Wide and Handsome ★★★★ U
Western musical 1937 · US · BW · 110mins

Decidedly offbeat but entertaining, this epic period musical dramatises the efforts of prospectors, led by Randolph Scott, to exploit oil under their land. The astonishing climax, in which a pipeline is constructed over a hill in Pennsylvania, involves an entire circus and its elephants thwarting a band of saboteurs. A screen original by Oscar Hammerstein II, who wrote lyrics to some wonderful songs with music by Jerome Kern, it has continually inventive direction by Rouben Mamoulian. Memorable performances are drawn from Irene Dunne as the medicine show singer who marries Scott's farmer-turned-oilman and Akim Tamiroff as the wily saloon keeper. ▣

Irene Dunne *Sally Watterson* • Randolph Scott *Peter Cortlandt* • Dorothy Lamour *Molly Fuller* • Elizabeth Patterson *Grandma Cortlandt* • Raymond Walburn *Doc Watterson* • Charles Bickford *Red Scanlon* • Akim Tamiroff *Joe Varese* ■ *Dir* Rouben Mamoulian • *Scr* Oscar Hammerstein II, George O'Neil

A High Wind in Jamaica ★★★
Adventure 1965 · UK · Colour · 105mins

Alexander Mackendrick's penultimate picture is a solidly crafted adaptation of Richard Hughes's bestseller about a gnarled pirate who finds himself playing nursemaid to a group of young stowaways. Although occasionally becalmed during its more melodramatic passages, it is still marvellous entertainment. Anthony Quinn is fine in the action sequences but doesn't always convince, but James Coburn is on top form as his first mate and cinematographer Douglas Slocombe's seascapes are often very beautiful.

Anthony Quinn *Juan Chavez* • James Coburn *Zac* • Benito Carruthers [Ben Carruthers] *Alberto* • Lila Kedrova *Rosa* • Deborah Baxter *Emily Thornton* • Viviane Ventura *Margaret Fernandez* • Martin Amis *John Thornton* • Roberta Tovey *Rachel Thornton* • Gert Frobe *Dutch captain* ■ *Dir* Alexander Mackendrick • *Scr* Stanley Mann, Ronald Harwood, Denis Cannan, from the novel by Richard Hughes

Higher and Higher ★★★ U
Musical 1943 · US · BW · 86mins

Frank Sinatra's first starring vehicle after becoming America's most popular teenage crooner, in which the thin one (as he then was) performs *I Couldn't Sleep a Wink Last Night* and *A Lovely Way to Spend an Evening*, among

others. French import Michèle Morgan was originally top-billed in this bright and breezy adaptation of the Broadway hit, and Jack Haley (the Tin Man in *The Wizard of Oz*) re-creates his New York starring role. Among the cheerful supporting cast, watch out for two of today's veteran performers, Mel Tormé and Victor Borge, neither of whom really cut it as movie players.

Michèle Morgan *Millie* • Frank Sinatra *Frank* • Jack Haley *Mike* • Leon Errol *Drake* • Marcy McGuire *Mickey* • Victor Borge *Sir Victor Fitzroy Victor* • Mary Wickes *Sandy* • Elisabeth Risdon *Mrs Keating* • Barbara Hale *Katherine* • Mel Tormé *Marty* ■ *Dir* Tim Whelan • *Scr* Jay Dratler, Ralph Spence, William Bowers, Howard Harris, from the play by Gladys Hurlbut, Joshua Logan

Higher Learning ★★★ 15
Drama 1995 · US · Colour · 123mins

Director John Singleton's third feature depicts a university campus as social microcosm. In a place where race and peer pressure matter more than intelligence and individuality, only professor Laurence Fishburne seems capable of thinking for himself. However, his idealistic belief seems curiously naive alongside the terrified eagerness with which freshmen Michael Rapaport, Omar Epps and Kristy Swanson seek to fit into their new environment. Cole Hauser is chillingly effective as the white supremacist skinhead who reveals Rapaport's potential for violence, while Jennifer Connelly gives the most adult performance. Contains swearing, violence and drug abuse. ▣

Omar Epps *Malik Williams* • Kristy Swanson *Kristen Connor* • Michael Rapaport *Remy* • Jennifer Connelly *Taryn* • Ice Cube *Fudge* • Tyra Banks *Deja* • Cole Hauser *Scott Moss* • Laurence Fishburne *Professor Maurice Phipps* ■ *Dir/Scr* John Singleton

Highlander ★★★ 15
Action fantasy 1986 · US · Colour · 111mins

So confused as to be hilariously watchable, director Russell Mulcahy's cult fantasy wavers between sci-fi, horror flick and music video as 16th-century Scottish clansman Christopher Lambert is schooled into being an immortal swordsman by Sean Connery for eternal battles with the evil Kurgan (Clancy Brown). There are some great sword-lunging duels (the best, in fact, is in a Madison Square Garden garage at the beginning, but the plot itself is never as pointedly directed. Contains violence, swearing and nudity. ▣

Christopher Lambert *Connor MacLeod* • Roxanne Hart *Brenda Wyatt* • Clancy Brown *Kurgan* • Sean Connery *Ramirez* • Beatie Edney *Heather* • Alan North *Lieutenant Frank Moran* • Sheila Gish *Rachel Ellenstein* ■ *Dir* Russell Mulcahy • *Scr* Gregory Widen, Peter Bellwood, Larry Ferguson, from a story by Gregory Widen

Highlander II: the Quickening ★★ 15
Action fantasy 1990 · US · Colour · 85mins

Despite some absurdly silly casting (Christopher Lambert as a Scotsman?), the first *Highlander* went on to become a worldwide smash and was hoots of fun into the bargain. Director Russell Mulcahy was on board again for this second instalment, but this time around it just doesn't click, even though both Lambert and Sean Connery return from the original. The two leads once again exude charisma, if not credible accents, and Ironside is splendid as the baddie, but there's not enough flash this time to cover the lack of substance. Contains swearing and violence. ▣

Christopher Lambert *Connor MacLeod* • Sean Connery *Juan Villa-Lobos Ramirez* • Virginia Madsen *Louise Marcus* • Michael Ironside *General Katana* • Allan Rich *Alan Neyman* • John C McGinley *Blake* ■ *Dir* Russell Mulcahy • *Scr* Peter Bellwood, from a story by Brian Clemens, William N Panzer, from characters created by Gregory Widen

Highlander III: the Sorcerer
★ ▣

Action fantasy
1995 · Can/Fr/UK · Colour · 93mins
Just when you thought the *Highlander* saga couldn't sink any further into diluted caricature and empty rock video flash, along comes the terminally dreary second sequel to Russell Mulcahy's inventive original. This time immortal Christopher Lambert must battle ancient evil magician Mario Van Peebles over the fate of his adopted son in a flaccid fantasy that makes a lot of noise but not a lot of sense. Contains swearing, violence and sex scenes. ▣

Christopher Lambert *Connor MacLeod/Russel Nash* • Mario Van Peebles *Kane* • Deborah Unger [Deborah Kara Unger] *Alex Johnson/Sarah* • Mako *Nakano* • Raoul Trujillo *1st warrior* • Jean-Pierre Pérusse *2nd warrior* • Martin Neufeld *Stenn* ■ *Dir* Andy Morahan [Andrew Morahan] • *Scr* Paul Ohl, from a story by William N Panzer, Brad Mirman, from characters created by Gregory Widen

Highly Dangerous ★★★ ▢

Comedy thriller 1950 · UK · BW · 88mins
Eric Ambler's playful script is the main reason for watching this lively espionage adventure, although there's also some wonderful character acting from Wilfrid Hyde White and Michael Hordern. Margaret Lockwood is particularly sprightly as an entomologist caught up in intrigue behind the Iron Curtain by reporter Dane Clark. Director Roy Ward Baker imparts the same jaunty mix of thrills and comedy that he brought to such hit TV shows as *The Avengers*, but he doesn't always succeed in persuading American actor Clark (making his British screen debut) to drop the Hollywood pizzazz.

Margaret Lockwood *Frances Gray* • Dane Clark *Bill Casey* • Marius Goring *Anton Razinski* • Naunton Wayne *Hedgerley* • Wilfrid Hyde White *Luke* • Eugene Deckers *Alf* • Olaf Pooley *Assistant* • Michael Hordern *Rawlings* ■ *Dir* Roy Ward Baker • *Scr* Eric Ambler

Highpoint ★★ ▣

Thriller 1979 · Can · Colour · 86mins
Richard Harris takes a job with Christopher Plummer, who has stolen $10 million and is now being pursued by both the Mafia and the CIA. A muddled thriller with the high point being a climactic tussle on top of a Toronto skyscraper. It's exciting enough but hardly worth enduring the rest of this routine film for. Kate Reid

and Beverly D'Angelo complete a cast that's rather classier than the movie merits. ▣

Richard Harris *Louis Kinney* • Christopher Plummer *James Hatcher* • Beverly D'Angelo *Lise Hatcher* • Kate Reid *Rachel Hatcher* • Peter Donat *Don Maranzella* • Robin Gammell *Banner* • Saul Rubinek *Centino* ■ *Dir* Peter Carter • *Scr* Richard Guttman, Ian Sutherland

Highway Patrolman ★★★ ▣

Crime thriller 1991 · Mex · Colour · 100mins
English director Alex Cox does his cult reputation no harm at all with this evocative Spanish language thriller, filmed in Mexico where he now resides. Well-known Latin American actor Roberto Sosa plays an idealistic cop who learns that his new job is not quite the noble career he had in mind. How disillusionment leads to corruption and worse is the prime concern of Cox's morality tale, filmed extensively with a hand-held camera using single long takes. The technique communicates the characters' mounting emotions all the more vividly, as well as bringing out the best in the barren locations. In Spanish with English subtitles. Contains violence, swearing and sex scenes. ▣

Roberto Sosa *Pedro Rojas* • Bruno Bichir *Anibal* • Zaide Silvia Gutierrez *Griselda* • Vanessa Bauche *Maribel* • Pedro Armendariz Jr *Sgt Barreras* • Malena Doria *Abuela* ■ *Dir* Alex Cox • *Scr* Lorenzo O'Brien

Highway 61 ★★★

Road movie 1992 · Can · Colour · 110mins
This offbeat comedy hasn't the same raw edge as the director and leads' thriller *Roadkill*, but it's dark enough, as rock 'n' roll roadie Valerie Buhagiar persuades good-natured barber Don McKellar to drive her brother's coffin across the Canadian border and down to New Orleans. Everyone along the road has "eccentric" written into their job description, but none of them is quite as weird as Earl Pastko who, as "Satan", does tricks with polaroids of those he's persuaded to sell their souls. Sparky, quirky and fun. Contains violence, swearing, sex scenes, drug abuse and nudity.

Valerie Buhagiar *Jackie Bangs* • Don McKellar *Pokey Jones* • Earl Pastko *Mr Skin/"Satan"* • Peter Breck *Mr Watson* • Art Bergmann *Otto* • Johnny Askwith *Claude* ■ *Dir* Bruce McDonald • *Scr* Don McKellar, from a story by Don McKellar, Bruce McDonald, Allan Magee

Highway to Hell ★★★ ▣

Horror comedy 1992 · US · Colour · 90mins
An oddball horror comedy that pits the hordes of hell against a young eloping couple. An uneven contest you might think, but not when it's Chad Lowe whose fiancée is kidnapped by a cop from hell and who has just 24 hours to spring her from the underworld. Sounds daft, but director Ate De Jong manages to deliver enough inventive visuals, including a three-headed dog and literal "hand" cuffs, to keep you decently entertained. Ben Stiller turns up dressed, bizarrely, as Attila the Hun. It's that kind of movie. ▣

Patrick Bergin *Beezle* • Chad Lowe *Charlie Sykes* • Kristy Swanson *Rachel Clark* • Adam Storke *Royce* • Pamela Gidley *Clara* • Richard

Farnsworth *Sam* • Jarrett Lennon *Adam* • Ben Stiller *Cook/Attila the Hun* ■ *Dir* Ate De Jong • *Scr* Brian Helgeland

Hijacked: Flight 285 ★★★

Action thriller 1996 · US · Colour
The midair hostage thriller has experienced something of a revival in recent years. Yet, while *Executive Decision*, *Con Air*, *Turbulence* and *Air Force One* received the publicity, this TV movie pretty much steals a march on all of them. The introductions keep the action on the ground and at a slow pace. But once convicted killer Anthony Michael Hall seizes control and demands a $20 million ransom the pace begins to pick up. Contains some violence.

Ally Sheedy *Deni Patton* • Anthony Michael Hall *Peter Cronin* • James Brolin *Ron Showman* • Perry King *Frank Layton* • Hudson Leick *Shayna Loring* • James Lancaster *Andrew Leary* • Barbara Stock *Veronica Mitchell* • Michael Gross *Ben* ■ *Dir* Charles Correll • *Scr* David E Peckinpah

Hijacking Hollywood ★★★

Comedy 1997 · US · Colour · 93mins
This cute satire about movie-making has Henry Thomas as Kevin, a starstruck newcomer who turns up in Hollywood to try and get work from distant relative Mark Metcalf, a major producer. However, fed up with an endless number of menial chores, mostly associated with the new blockbuster *Moby Dick 2: Ahab's Revenge*, Thomas decides to hold the production to ransom by stealing essential master footage. Constantly amusing, this is an independent comedy that deserves greater exposure.

Henry Thomas *Kevin Conroy* • Scott Thompson *Russell* • Mark Metcalf *Michael Lawrence* • Neil Mandt *Tad* • Nicole Gian *Sarah Lawrence* • Helen Duffy *Mother* ■ *Dir* Neil Mandt • *Scr* Neil Mandt, Jim Rossow

Hilary and Jackie ★★★★ ▣

Biographical drama 1998 · UK · Colour · 117mins
Emily Watson excels at portraying the often difficult, selfish and driven cellist Jaqueline du Pré in this controversial biopic of the unusual relationship between her and sister Hilary (Rachel Griffiths). Loosely based on Hilary's (and their brother Piers's) biography, the film is a fascinating, no-holds-barred account of Jackie's musical career and private life. While many column inches have been devoted to the incident when Jackie asks Hilary whether she can sleep with her husband, and then does so, the film – thanks to Watson's mesmerising performance – should be lauded for its fascinating realisation of Jackie's talent and almost destructive personality. Contains occasional swearing and some sex scenes. ▣
DVD

Emily Watson *Jacqueline "Jackie" du Pré* • Rachel Griffiths *Hilary du Pré* • David Morrissey *Kiffer Finzi* • James Frain *Daniel Barenboim* • Charles Dance *Derek du Pré* • Celia Imrie *Iris du Pré* • Rupert Penry-Jones *Piers du Pré* ■ *Dir* Anand Tucker • *Scr* Frank Cottrell Boyce, from the non-fiction book *A Genius in the Family* by Hilary du Pré, Piers du Pré

Hilda Crane ★

Melodrama 1956 · US · Colour · 87mins
Free-thinking Hilda (Jean Simmons), who escaped the suffocating clutches of her unloving, rigidly conventional family, returns from New York for her small home town two marriages and several men later. Broke, disillusioned and unhappy, she makes a third "respectable" marriage, plunging herself into further disaster... A really dismal "woman's picture", paralysed by a combination of cliché and cop-out. Simmons struggles with, some success, in her showy role.

Jean Simmons *Hilda Crane* • Guy Madison *Russell Burns* • Jean-Pierre Aumont *Jacques de Lisle* • Judith Evelyn *Mrs Crane* • Evelyn Varden *Mrs Burns* • Peggy Knudsen *Nell Bromley* • Gregg Palmer *Dink* • Richard Garrick *Dr Francis* ■ *Dir* Philip Dunne • *Scr* Philip Dunne, from a play by Samuel Raphaelson

The Hill ★★★★ ▣

Prison drama 1965 · UK · BW · 118mins
After *Goldfinger*, Sean Connery was determined to extend his range beyond James Bond. Hitchcock's *Marnie* gave him the opportunity; *Woman of Straw* followed and was less successful. Then director Sidney Lumet cast him in *The Hill* and Connery cast his fake hair to the wind for the first time. It's a terse, tough picture about an army prison in North Africa where the inmates are forced to march up and down a phoney hill. It's the Greek myth of Sisyphus with a vengeance, an impudent symbol for British colonial impotence in the sixties, though it's set during the Second World War. Contains some strong language and violence. ▣

Sean Connery *Joe Roberts* • Harry Andrews *Sergeant Major Wilson* • Ian Bannen *Harris* • Roy Kinnear *Monty Bartlett* • Ian Hendry *Staff Sergeant Williams* • Michael Redgrave *Medical Officer* • Alfred Lynch *George Stevens* • Ossie Davis *Jacko King* • Jack Watson *Jock McGrath* ■ *Dir* Sidney Lumet • *Scr* Ray Rigby, RS Allen, from their play

A Hill in Korea ★★★ ▣

War drama 1956 · UK · BW · 68mins
A British patrol is caught behind enemy lines during the Korean War – a conflict given hardly a moment's thought by the British cinema. Badly made on Portuguese locations and containing reams of sermonising dialogue, it's nevertheless made watchable by the presence of future stars Robert Shaw and Michael Caine, who actually spent their national service in Korea and was the film's largely ignored military adviser. ▣

George Baker *Lieutenant Butler* • Harry Andrews *Sergeant Payne* • Stanley Baker *Corporal Ryker* • Michael Medwin *Private Docker* • Ronald Lewis *Private Wyatt* • Robert Shaw *Lance-Corporal Hodge* • Michael Caine *Private Lockyer* ■ *Dir* Julian Amyes • *Scr* Ian Dalrymple, Anthony Squire

Hill's Angels ★ ▢

Comedy 1979 · US · Colour · 95mins
This slow-moving tale, released in the US as *The North Avenue Irregulars*, is typical of the poor product that Disney came up with during the seventies. The story, in which naive young priest Edward Herrmann organises his

women parishioners to combat organised crime after one of them loses the church funds at the racetrack, is a poorly realised excuse for a string of madcap chase scenes. At least the cast is sensible enough not to take it seriously. ▭

Edward Herrmann *Michael Hill* • Barbara Harris *Vickie* • Susan Clark *Anne* • Karen Valentine *Jane* • Michael Constantine *Marv* • Cloris Leachman *Claire* • Patsy Kelly *Rose* ■ *Dir* Bruce Bilson • *Scr* Don Tait, from a book by the Reverend Albert Fay Hill

The Hills Have Eyes ★★★★ 18

Horror   1978 · US · Colour · 89mins

Drawing inspiration from the myth of Sawney Bean and his Scottish cannibal clan, director Wes Craven crafted the best of his early low-budget horror epics. Desert mutants lay murderous siege to stranded innocent campers in the *Scream* maestro's exploration of depravity and the survival instinct. Using mirror images of two families at the opposing extremes of humanity, Craven's sharp sense of suspense and his willingness to take shock images to their limits carries a potent charge. The introduction of the extraordinary-looking Michael Berryman to the roster of unpleasant characters only adds extra punch to the terror. ▭

John Steadman *Fred* • Janus Blythe *Ruby* • Arthur King *Mercury* • Russ Grieve *Big Bob Carter* • Virginia Vincent *Ethel Carter* • Susan Lanier *Brenda Carter* • Dee Wallace [Dee Wallace Stone] *Lynne Wood* • Michael Berryman *Pluto* ■ *Dir/Scr* Wes Craven

The Hills Have Eyes Part II ★ 18

Horror   1985 · US · Colour · 86mins

Lightning doesn't strike twice for director Wes Craven, who ill-advisedly goes back to the desert cannibals versus middle-class Americans theme for his hack sequel. This time a busload of youths (including two survivors from the first nightmare) break down in the Yucca Valley en route to a motorcycle rally and are forced to battle the homicidal barbarians from the first film. Consign this one to the sequel scrapheap. ▭

Michael Berryman *Pluto* • Tamara Stafford *Cass* • Kevin Spirtas *Kevin Blair* • Janus Blythe *Ruby* ■ *Dir/Scr* Wes Craven

Hills of Home ★★★ U

Adventure   1948 · US · Colour · 96mins

Marvellous Lassie vehicle, in which the world's most famous collie stars in a reworking of the canine classic *Greyfriars Bobby*, itself a source for the following year's *Challenge to Lassie*. Edmund Gwenn is the kindly Scottish doctor who tries to cure our heroine of her aversion to water, veteran Donald Crisp plays his friend, and Janet Leigh is simply lovely to look at. Director Fred M Wilcox, best known for *Forbidden Planet*, proves that, with this movie and *The Secret Garden*, he could direct dogs and children as well as robots.

Edmund Gwenn *Dr William MacLure* • Donald Crisp *Drumsheugh* • Tom Drake *Tammas Milton* • Janet Leigh *Margit Mitchell* • Rhys Williams *Mr Milton* • Reginald Owen *Hopps* ■

Dir Fred Wilcox [Fred M Wilcox] • *Scr* William Ludwig, from the sketches *Doctor of the Old School* by Ian MacLaren

Hills of Kentucky ★★★

Silent adventure   1927 · US · BW

One-time prop boy, director Howard Bretherton was credited with over 100 features during his career, including several B-westerns with William "Hopalong" Boyd and Buck Jones. This Rin-Tin-Tin adventure was only his second outing and his inexperience occasionally shows through. Yet the action sequences are thrilling, particularly the legendary plunge into the waterfall by the dog star to rescue Dorothy Dwan from certain death.

Jason Robards *Steve Harley* • Dorothy Dwan *Janet* • Tom Santschi *Ben Harley* • Nanette *Nanette* ■ *Dir* Howard Bretherton • *Scr* Edward Clark, from the story *The Untamed Heart* by Dorothy Yost

The Hillside Stranglers ★★★ 18

Crime drama based on a true story   1989 · US · Colour · 95mins

Better-than-average, tough TV movie detailing the real-life hunt for serial killers who terrorised Los Angeles in the late seventies. Richard Crenna heads the cast as the world-weary investigator, and he is ably supported by Dennis Farina (*Get Shorty*) and a young Billy Zane (*Dead Calm*). Despite being hampered by the usual restrictions of the format, director Steven Gethers scores points for his attention to detail and his refusal to sensationalise the subject matter. ▭

Richard Crenna *Detective Sgt Bob Grogan* • Billy Zane *Kenny Bianchi* • Dennis Farina *Angelo Buono* • Tony Plana *Detective Mike Hernandez* • James Tolkan *Lt Ed Henderson* ■ *Dir/Scr* Steven Gethers

Himalaya ★★★ PG

Adventure drama   1999 · Nep/Swi/Fr/UK · Colour · mins

Travel writer Eric Valli made his feature debut with this Oscar-nominated ethnographical odyssey, which was also released as *Caravan*. Drawing on his own experiences, the wizened Thilen Lhondup gives a supremely naturalistic performance as the Nepalese salt trader who relies on traditional wisdom to get his yak herd to market across some of the world's most inhospitable terrain. Yet, for all Thilen's simple courage and the visual splendour of the mountainscapes, this poetic tribute to the hardy spirit of a remarkable people is disappointingly short on dramatic incident. In Tibetan with English subtitles.

Thilen Lhondup *Tinlé* • Lhakpa Tsamchoe *Péma* • Gurgon Kyap *Karma* • Karma Tensing Nyima Lama *Norbou* • Karma Wangiel *Passang* ■ *Dir* Eric Valli • *Scr* Nathalie Azoulai, Olivier Dazat, Louis Gardel, Jean-Claude Guillebaud, Jacques Perrin • *Cinematographer* Eric Guichard, Jean-Paul Meurisse

The Hindenburg ★★ PG

Disaster drama   1975 · US · Colour and BW · 109mins

The seventies cycle of disaster movies came crashing down amid the debris

of this box-office bomb that has all the pace and substance of the famous German airship itself. The destruction of the *Hindenburg* as it reached New Jersey at the end of a transatlantic flight in 1937 sent shock waves around the world. However, in trying to combine their sabotage theory with the kind of soap-opera characterisation established in *Airport*, scriptwriters Nelson Gidding, Richard A Levinson and William Link have succeeded only in producing a colossal bore. ▭

George C Scott *Colonel Ritter* • Anne Bancroft *The Countess* • William Atherton *Boerth* • Roy Thinnes *Martin Vogel* • Gig Young *Edward Douglas* • Burgess Meredith *Emilio Pajetta* ■ *Dir* Robert Wise • *Scr* Nelson Gidding, Richard A Levinson, William Link, from the book by Michael M Mooney

Hindle Wakes ★★ PG

Romantic melodrama   1952 · UK · BW · 70mins

A weak adaptation of Stanley Houghton's theatrical warhorse about cross-class love in the early years of the century. The story of a Lancashire mill lass who refuses to marry the boss's son after spending her summer factory holiday with him at Blackpool is hardly likely to raise the eyebrows of the prudish or the pulse rate of the thrill-seeker. ▭

Lisa Daniely *Jenny Hawthorne* • Leslie Dwyer *Chris Hawthorne* • Brian Worth *Alan Jeffcote* • Sandra Dorne *Mary Hollins* • Ronald Adam *Nat Jeffcote* • Joan Hickson *Mrs Hawthorne* ■ *Dir* Arthur Crabtree • *Scr* John Baines, from the play by Stanley Houghton

Hindustan Ki Kasam ★★ PG

Drama   1999 · Ind · Colour · 146mins

Despite being a box-office smash, the critics found little to applaud in this overwrought melodrama set during the 1971 Indo-Pakistani war. Even stars of the calibre of Amitabh Bachchan and Prem Chopra are out of sorts. Considering writer/director Veeru Devgan was supposedly intent on fostering better relations between the feuding neighbours, he takes a pronouncedly anti-Pakistani stance in relating the tale of the novelist who is mistaken for his twin brother, who happens to be a nationalist assassin. Although strewn with special effects, the action is often clumsily staged. A Hindi language film. Contains some mild violence and swearing.

Amitabh Bachchan • Ajay Devgan • Manisha Koirala • Prem Chopra ■ *Dir* Veeru Devgan • *Scr* Hriday-Janak, Tanveer Khan

The Hired Gun ★★ U

Western   1957 · US · BW · 63mins

It makes a bit of a change to find a western in which a female plays the key role, and Anne Francis makes the most of her opportunity as the woman, wrongly convicted of murder, who cheats the hangman by escaping across the border into Mexico. Co-star Rory Calhoun is the gunman hired to bring her back, who comes to believe in her innocence and sets about proving it. Calhoun formed his own production company to make this picture but seemingly forgot to tell veteran director Ray Nazarro that he wasn't shooting another B-western.

Rory Calhoun *Gil McCord* • Anne Francis *Ellen Beldon* • Vince Edwards *Kell Beldon* • John Litel *Mace Beldon* • Chuck Connors *Judd Farrow* • Robert Burton *Nathan Conroy* ■ *Dir* Ray Nazarro • *Scr* David Lang, Buckley Angell

The Hired Hand ★★★ 15

Western   1971 · US · Colour · 86mins

Peter Fonda (son of Henry) had some clout in Hollywood when this post-hippy western was made, having produced and starred as "Captain America" in the cult hit *Easy Rider* two years earlier. In addition to starring here, Fonda also makes a fine job of directing this cold, almost existential western about a wife (the superb Verna Bloom) torn between two drifters, her husband Fonda and the older Warren Oates. This has all the clever bleakness and cyclical sense of destiny now associated with its writer, Alan Sharp, and is richly rewarding in its portrayal of the tough reality of frontier life. Some audiences might prefer more action, though. ▭

Peter Fonda *Harry Collings* • Warren Oates *Arch Harris* • Verna Bloom *Hannah Collings* • Robert Pratt *Dan Griffin* • Severn Darden *McVey* • Ted Markland *Luke* • Owen Orr *Mace* ■ *Dir* Peter Fonda • *Scr* Alan Sharp

The Hired Heart ★★

Romantic drama   1997 · US · Colour · 90mins

Penelope Ann Miller (*Kindergarden Cop*, *Awakenings*) and TV movie regular Brett Cullen star in this homespun romantic drama. Two years after her husband's death, a small-town doctor continues to grieve, throwing herself into her work. When her well-intentioned father-in-law begins sending every eligible bachelor to her office with a marriage proposal, she decides to hire an escort to pose as her boyfriend in order to thwart his meddling. It's lightweight but engaging, and the leads work well together.

Penelope Ann Miller *Garnet Hadley* • Brett Cullen *Bryan* • Barry Corbin *Mike Hadley* • Allison Hossack *Virginia* ■ *Dir* Jeremy Kagan [Jeremy Paul Kagan] • *Scr* Jeff Elison

Hired to Kill ★ 18

Action adventure   1990 · US · Colour · 92mins

The preposterous plot of this action thriller is so outrageous even Austin Powers would balk at its lack of credibility. Brian Thompson is cast as a soldier of fortune whose mission to overthrow a tinpot island dictator involves disguising himself as a gay fashion designer with a hit squad of female mercenaries all dressed as fashion models. Happens everyday, right? Stalwarts Oliver Reed – relishing his role as a sadistic secret police chief – and George Kennedy were somehow persuaded to appear. ▭

Brian Thompson *Frank Ryan* • Oliver Reed *Michael Bartos* • José Ferrer *Rallis* • George Kennedy *Thomas* • Michelle Moffett *Ana* ■ *Dir* Nico Mastorakis, Peter Rader • *Scr* Nico Mastorakis, Kirk Ellis, Fred C Perry, from a story by Nico Mastorakis

Hired Wife ★★★

Comedy drama   1940 · US · BW · 95mins

Indispensable, caring, efficient secretary Rosalind Russell proposes a marriage of convenience to her boss,

Brian Aherne, so that his tax situation can benefit by putting his property in his wife's name. He's preoccupied with advertising model Virginia Bruce, but when she disappears into the arms of John Carroll, Aherne accepts Russell's offer. What follows is comfortingly predictable in this slimly plotted romantic comedy, elevated into delightful froth by Aherne's charm and Russell's splendid performance.

Rosalind Russell *Kendal Browning* • Brian Aherne *Stephen Dexter* • Virginia Bruce *Phyllis Walden* • Robert Benchley *Roger Van Horn* • John Carroll *Jose* ■ *Dir* William A Seiter • *Scr* Richard Connell, Gladys Lehman, from a story by George Beck

The Hireling ★★★★🅿🅶

Drama   1973 · UK · Colour · 103mins

Set in the socially divided Britain of 1923, this adaptation of an LP Hartley novel makes up in elegance and ideas for what it lacks in drama. Neurotic, upper-class Sarah Miles hires the services of chauffeur Robert Shaw, and their working relationship helps to restore some balance in her fraught existence. However, his adoration for his mistress soon adds a touch of agitation to the mix. Director Alan Bridges's period piece has a topical relevance about who is really in the driving seat, but the drama is too crass to be affecting. ▭

Robert Shaw *Leadbetter* • Sarah Miles *Lady Franklin* • Peter Egan *Captain Hugh Cantrip* • Elizabeth Sellars *Lady Franklin's mother* • Caroline Mortimer *Connie* • Patricia Lawrence *Mrs Hansen* ■ *Dir* Alan Bridges • *Scr* Wolf Mankowitz, from the novel by LP Hartley

Hiroshima, Mon Amour

★★★★🅿🅶

Drama   1959 · Fr · BW · 100mins

Alain Resnais's first feature stunned audiences in 1959, and together with Jean-Luc Godard's *A Bout de Souffle* and François Truffaut's *The 400 Blows* it heralded the French New Wave. The story tells of a French actress who has an affair in Hiroshima with a Japanese architect while recalling an earlier, wartime affair with a German soldier. Marguerite Duras's script is about collaboration as well as reconciliation, while Resnais weaves time zones, silence and sound, and juxtaposes lush images of seduction with shocking documentary footage of survivors of the atomic bomb. In French with English subtitles. ▭

Emmanuelle Riva *Elle* • Eiji Okada *Lui* • Bernard Fresson *L'Allemand* • Stella Dassas *La Mère* • Pierre Barbaud *Le Père* ■ *Dir* Alain Resnais • *Scr* Marguerite Duras

Hiroshima: Out of the Ashes ★★★🅸🅵

Historical drama 1990 · US · Colour · 94mins

A respectful, quietly moving drama about the first use of the atomic bomb, which views its appalling aftermath through the eyes of survivors. The stellar cast includes Catholic priest Max von Sydow, American PoW Judd Nelson, Pat Morita and Kim Miyori. John McGreevey's script, partly based on *Hiroshima Diary* by Michihiko Hachiya, is a tad heavy-handed, but the direction of Peter Werner is suitably sober. ▭

Max von Sydow *Father Siemes* • Judd Nelson *Lieutenant Pete Dunham* • Pat Morita *Yoodo Toda* • Mako *Moritaki* • Ben Wright *Lieutenant Tom Reese* • Tamlyn Tomita *Sally* ■ *Dir* Peter Werner • *Scr* John McGreevey, from *Hiroshima Diary* by Michihiko Hachiya

His Bodyguard ★🅸🅵

Thriller   1998 · US · Colour · 84mins

Whitney Houston isn't anywhere to be found in this film, which must unfortunately rely on the thespian charms of Anthony Natale, Mitzi Kapture (*Baywatch*) and Robert Guillaume (*Benson*). A tycoon hires a female bodyguard to protect his adult deaf-mute son who witnessed the theft of an experimental and potentially lucrative drug from his bio-engineering firm. She moves in with her client and love blossoms. However the thugs are still out there... The script (co-written by *Dynasty*'s Emma Samms) is so pat and shallow it's actually aggravating. Contains violence and swearing. ▭

Mitzi Kapture *Jenny Farrell* • Anthony Natale *Sam* • Michael Copeman *Feld* • Robert Guillaume *Garrett* ■ *Dir* Artie Mandelberg • *Scr* Emma Samms, Bennett Cohen, from a story by Emma Samms

His Brother's Wife ★★★

Melodrama   1936 · US · BW · 91mins

When Robert Taylor's medical scientist goes off to the jungle to find a cure for spotted fever, Barbara Stanwyck, with whom he has had a whirlwind romance, is so enraged that she takes revenge by marrying his brother. Eventually, of course, she repents and turns up in the tropics to assist her true love, whereupon the melodrama escalates into situations so absurd and dialogue so risible as to become treasurable. The stars, whose real-life romance was news (they would marry in 1939), play this hokum for all its worth.

Barbara Stanwyck *Rita Wilson Claybourne* • Robert Taylor (1) *Chris Claybourne* • Jean Hersholt *Professor "Pop" Fahrenheim* • Joseph Calleia *"Fish-Eye"* • John Eldredge *Tom Claybourne* • Samuel S Hinds *Dr Claybourne* ■ *Dir* WS Van Dyke • *Scr* Leon Gordon, John Meehan, from a story by George Auerbach

His Butler's Sister ★★🅤

Musical comedy   1943 · US · BW · 93mins

No longer the winsome teenager who saved Universal Studios' bacon, but a winsome 22-year-old with her fine singing voice intact, Deanna Durbin stars as a small-town girl with ambitions to be a great singer. She goes to New York to seek the help of composer Franchot Tone, only to be put to work as a maid by his butler, Pat O'Brien. Complications ensue before the inevitable resolution. The star gets to sing several numbers (including *Nessun Dorma*) in this delightful nonsense, which Frank Borzage directs in the right spirit.

Deanna Durbin *Ann Carter* • Franchot Tone *Charles Gerard* • Pat O'Brien *Martin* • Akim Tamiroff *Popoff* • Walter Catlett *Kalb* • Elsa Janssen *Severina* ■ *Dir* Frank Borzage • *Scr* Samuel Hoffenstein, Betty Reinhardt

His Double Life ★★

Comedy   1933 · US · BW · 63mins

Largely forgotten, this slight and amiable screen version of Arnold Bennett's novel *Buried Alive* is intriguingly cast. Delightfully fussy character actor Roland Young is the reclusive painter who adopts the identity of his dead valet, and former silent star Lillian Gish makes an isolated comeback as the woman who weds the already-married Young under his assumed identity. However, the best version of this oft-filmed story is unquestionably *Holy Matrimony* with Monty Woolley and Gracie Fields.

Lillian Gish *Alice* • Roland Young *Priam Farrel* • Lumsden Hare *Oxford* • Lucy Beaumont *Mrs Leek* • Charles Richman *Witt* ■ *Dir* Arthur Hopkins • *Scr* Arthur Hopkins, Clara Beranger, from the story *Buried Alive* by Arnold Bennett

His Girl Friday ★★★★★🅤

Classic comedy   1939 · US · BW · 91mins

The fastest-talking comedy in the history of Hollywood, this brilliant reworking of the classic newspaper play *The Front Page* by director Howard Hawks is the perfect vehicle for Cary Grant (never better) and Rosalind Russell (never tougher) and is still achingly funny today. Limited for most of the time to two sets (the newspaper office and the pressroom at the jail), the film's great strength is the interplay between the two leads, as former spouses who are having a tough time remaining apart. It also boasts one of the blackest comedy situations ever, as a small-time loser finds himself up against city corruption and imminent execution. Clever, witty and extremely satisfying. ▭

Cary Grant *Walter Burns* • Rosalind Russell *Hildy Johnson* • Ralph Bellamy *Bruce Baldwin* • Gene Lockhart *Sheriff Hartwell* • Helen Mack *Mollie Malloy* • Porter Hall *Murphy* • Ernest Truex *Roy Bensinger* • Cliff Edwards *Endicott* ■ *Dir* Howard Hawks • *Scr* Charles Lederer, from the play *The Front Page* by Ben Hecht, Charles MacArthur

His Kind of Woman ★★★🅸🅸

Film noir   1951 · US · BW · 114mins

An interesting and enjoyably overheated melodrama from the Howard Hughes regime at RKO, this overlong, unwieldy movie shows signs of the great one's tinkerings: scenes don't make sense, obvious exteriors were filmed indoors, cast members come and go and Robert Mitchum looks bored. However, the whole is still entertaining, with a fine sense of parody that has won the movie quite a cult following. Mitchum's relationship with Jane Russell is genuinely provocative, but the movie is hijacked by Vincent Price at his posturing best. Contains some violence. ▭

Robert Mitchum *Dan Milner* • Jane Russell *Lenore Brent* • Vincent Price *Mark Cardigan* • Tim Holt *Bill Lusk* • Charles McGraw *Thompson* • Raymond Burr *Nick Ferraro* ■ *Dir* John Farrow • *Scr* Frank Fenton, Jack Leonard, from the story *Star Sapphire* by Gerald Drayson Adams

His Lordship ★★★🅤

Crime drama   1936 · UK · BW · 68mins

Character star George Arliss's great days were behind him when he

returned to his native England to take on a dual role in this political potboiler which is only held together by the sheer strength of Arliss's presence. The film's stage derivation seeps through the whole enterprise, and the combination of *Boys' Own* heroics and the politics of war is as hard to take today as it probably was then. But Arliss was undeniably a star, and those who only know his historical roles may enjoy seeing him in a contemporary part. In the USA, this was renamed *Man of Affairs*. ▭

George Arliss *Richard/Lord Dunchester* • Romilly Lunge *Bill Howard* • René Ray *Vera* • Jessie Winter *Lady Dunchester* • John Ford *Ibrahim* ■ *Dir* Herbert Mason • *Scr* Maude T Howell, L du Garde Peach, Edwin Greenwood, from the play *The Nelson Touch* by Neil Grant

His Majesty O'Keefe ★★★🅤

Swashbuckling adventure   1953 · US · Colour · 89mins

Burt Lancaster is in fine, devil-may-care form as a sea captain teaching islanders how to be enterprising and beat off pirates, while himself picking up a Polynesian girl (Joan Rice) as queen to his king. Its colonial message – naive natives ruled by intrepid white man – is dubiously patronising, but its good-natured breeziness defies serious criticism. Byron Haskin directs.

Burt Lancaster *Captain David O'Keefe* • Joan Rice *Dalabo* • André Morell *Alfred Tetins* • Abraham Sofaer *Fatumak* • Archie Savage *Boogulroo* • Benson Fong *Mr Chou* • Teresa Prendergast *Kakofel* ■ *Dir* Byron Haskin • *Scr* Borden Chase, James Hill, from a novel by Lawrence Klingman, Gerald Green

His New Job ★★★

Silent comedy   1915 · US · BW

In this uncharacteristic Chaplin short, his first for the Essanay studio, he disregarded the company's highly organised working methods and improvised a comedy about film-making based on what he saw around him. It shows Charlie seeking a job at a studio, quashing competition from cross-eyed Ben Turpin, and creating mayhem on the set of a costume film where Gloria Swanson (uncredited) is among the extras. This was Chaplin's first collaboration with cameraman Rollie Totheroh, with whom he worked regularly for the next 30 years.

Charles Chaplin *Film Extra* • Ben Turpin *Film Extra* • Charlotte Mineau *Actress* • Leo White • Gloria Swanson ■ *Dir/Scr* Charles Chaplin

His Woman ★★

Drama   1931 · US · BW · 76mins

Gary Cooper, the unlikely captain of a tramp steamer, rescues a baby from a drifting vessel at sea and decides to keep it. Advertising for female help on the return journey to New York, he gets Claudette Colbert, a girl with a shady past. Filmed only two years previously as the silent *Sal of Singapore*, the story (based on Dale Collins's novel, *The Sentimentalists*) was not improved by this version with its mediocre script and direction. Cooper is at his most expressionless, though Colbert, as usual, gives it everything.

Gary Cooper *Captain Sam Whalan* • Claudette Colbert *Sally Clark* • Averell Harris *Mate Gatson* • Richard Spiro *Sammy the baby* •

🅤 = SUITABLE FOR ALL   🅤c = SUITABLE FOR ALL, ESPECIALLY FOR YOUNG CHILDREN (VIDEO ONLY)   🅿🅶 = PARENTAL GUIDANCE

Hamtree Harrington *Aloysius* • Sidney Easton *Mark* • Douglass Dubrille *Alisandroe* • Raquel Davido *Maria Estella* ■ *Dir* Edward Sloman • *Scr* Adelaide Heilbron, Melville Baker, from the novel *The Sentimentalists* by Dale Collins

L'Histoire d'Adèle H ★★★

Biographical drama
1975 · Fr · Colour · 97mins

In what was only her fourth feature, the 19-year-old Isabelle Adjani comes remarkably close to conveying the desolation of a passionate older woman broken by her own determination. She plays Victor Hugo's daughter Adèle, who followed a young English soldier (Bruce Robinson) from Nova Scotia to Barbados, despite the fact that her love was unreciprocated. Working from Adèle's coded notebooks, director François Truffaut relies heavily on Adjani's crestfallen beauty and the oppressive majesty of Nestor Almendros's photography to suggest the heroine's agonising hope and incipient madness. In French with English subtitles.

Isabelle Adjani *Adèle Hugo* • Bruce Robinson *Lt Albert Pinson* • Sylvia Marriott *Mrs Saunders* • Joseph Blatchley *Mr Whistler* • Reuben Dorey *Mr Saunders* • M White *Colonel White* • Cal Hathwell *Lt Pinson's Batman* • Ivry Gitlis *Hypnotist* ■ *Dir* François Truffaut • *Scr* François Truffaut, Jean Gruault, Suzanne Schiffman, from *Le Journal d'Adèle Hugo* by Adèle Hugo, Frances V Guille

Une Histoire Inventée ★★★

Comedy 1990 · Can · Colour · 100mins

Also known as *An Imaginary Tale*, this is an occasionally amusing, but mostly jumbled ensemble piece from French Canadian director André Forcier. Recalling the precisely interwoven narratives of directors like Henry Jaglom or Alan Rudolph, the film focuses on a handful of disparate Montrealites, whose everyday lives are packed with more eccentric occurrences than most people could pack into a lifetime. The best moments are provided by the precious production of *Othello*, played before pensioners bussed in by a mobster, and the beauty who keeps countless ex-lovers at her beck and call. In French with English subtitles.

Jean Lapointe *Gaston* • Louise Marleau *Florence* • Charlotte Laurier *Soledad* • Marc Messier *Lentaignes* • Jean-François Pichette *Tibo* • France Castel *Alys* ■ *Dir* André Forcier • *Scr* André Forcier, Jacques Marcotte

Une Histoire Simple ★★★

Drama 1978 · Fr · Colour · 107mins

Although this study of bourgeois foibles received an Oscar nomination for best foreign film, director Claude Sautet is rather guilty of revisiting old haunts without having anything particularly new to show us. However, no one depicts the suffocating ennui of a seemingly successful life with such surety, and here he's excellently served by Romy Schneider, who won a César for her portrayal of a liberated woman who aborts lover Claude Brasseur's baby only to become pregnant by ex-husband, Bruno Cremer. The trappings of contentment are mercilessly mocked, but the main fascination lies in observing Schneider

and her loyal quartet of friends. In French with English subtitles.

Romy Schneider *Marie* • Bruno Cremer *Georges* • Claude Brasseur *Serge* • Arlette Bonnard *Gabrielle* • Sophie Daumier *Esther* • Eva Darlan *Anna* • Francine Bergé *Francine* • Roger Pigaut *Jerome* • Madeleine Robinson *Marie's mother* ■ *Dir* Claude Sautet • *Scr* Claude Sautet, Jean-Loup Dabadie

Histoires Extraordinaires ★★★★

Portmanteau horror
1967 · Fr/It · Colour · 121mins

Out of the three episodes based on the macabre tales by Edgar Allan Poe, the third – the only modern-day one, directed by Federico Fellini – is far and away the best, though it's pretty familiar Fellini territory. It stars Terence Stamp as a British actor in Rome who bets his head he can escape having an accident. Louis Malle's telling of *William Wilson*, about a man (Alain Delon) who kills his doppelgänger, is handsome and straightforward; while Roger Vadim saw to it that his wife Jane Fonda wore revealing clothes and caused an incestuous *frisson* by casting her brother Peter as her lover.

Jane Fonda *Countess Frederica Metzengerstein* • Peter Fonda *Baron Wilhelm* • Alain Delon *William Wilson/His double* • Brigitte Bardot *Giuseppina* • Terence Stamp *Toby Dammit* • Vincent Price *Narrator* ■ *Dir* Roger Vadim, Louis Malle, Federico Fellini • *Scr* Roger Vadim, Pascal Cousin, from the story *Metzengerstein* by Edgar Allan Poe; Louis Malle, Daniel Boulanger, from the story *William Wilson* by Edgar Allan Poe; Federico Fellini, Bernardino Zapponi, from the story *Never Bet the Devil Your Head* by Edgar Allan Poe

History Is Made at Night ★★★

Drama 1937 · US · BW · 97mins

This bizarre piece of fluff from melodrama maestro Frank Borzage finds Charles Boyer in good form as a waiter, jewel thief and restaurateur who saves Jean Arthur from her abusive marriage to shipping magnate Colin Clive. The story moves from Paris to New York, involves kidnapping and seduction, and ends rather darkly, on a sinking ship, with a confession of murder followed by a suicide. It's a lot to fit in one movie, which might explain the various loose ends – though this hardly seems to matter.

Charles Boyer *Paul Dumond* • Jean Arthur *Irene Vail* • Leo Carrillo *Cesare* • Colin Clive *Bruce Vail* • Ivan Lebedeff *Michael* • George Meeker *Norton* ■ *Dir* Frank Borzage • *Scr* Gene Towne, Graham Baker, from their story

History Is Made at Night ★

Spy comedy
1999 · UK /Fr/Ger/Fin · Colour · 94mins

It's hard to believe that the director of *Darkness in Tallinn* could have made this dismal spy caper. Even the weakest of the countless sixties Bond spoofs were more amusing than Ilkka Jarvilaturi's ill-conceived comedy, which manages the seemingly impossible feat of making Irène Jacob look incompetent. Besides disrobing at regular intervals, she overplays every situation, although she's not helped by her partner in ignominy, the usually reliable Bill Pullman. He resorts to

mugging in an effort to salvage a plot in which his CIA agent conspires with Jacob's Russian to humiliate her bosses and his rookie sidekick.

Bill Pullman *Harry* • Irène Jacob *Natasha* • Bruno Kirby *Max* • Glenn Plummer *Dave* • Udo Kier *Ivan* ■ *Dir* Ilkka Jarvilaturi • *Scr* Patrick Amos, from a story by Jean-Pierre Gorin, Patrick Amos

The History of Mr Polly ★★★★ U

Drama 1948 · UK · BW · 91mins

This is a splendid adaptation of HG Wells's charming comic novel by writer/director Anthony Pelissier that is pleasingly faithful to its source and enormously entertaining. John Mills gives one of the finest performances of his career as the draper whose search for contentment involves him in an unhappy marriage and a feud at a country inn. The supporting cast is impeccable, with Betty Ann Davies neatly switching from giggling cousin to grousing wife, and Moore Marriott inch-perfect as wizened Uncle Pentstemon. The scenes with Christabel on the wall don't quite come off, but the encounters with Polly's ghastly family and the duel with Finlay Currie are well staged. ▣

John Mills *Alfred Polly* • Sally Ann Howes *Christabel* • Megs Jenkins *Plump woman* • Finlay Currie *Uncle Jim* • Diana Churchill *Annie* • Betty Ann Davies *Miriam* • Edward Chapman *Mr Johnson* • Shelagh Fraser *Minnie* • Moore Marriott *Uncle Pentstemon* ■ *Dir* Anthony Pelissier • *Scr* Anthony Pelissier, from the novel by HG Wells

History of the World Part 1 ★★ 15

Comedy 1981 · US · Colour · 88mins

Mel Brooks's full-frontal assault on how we got where we are today has something to offend everyone: Moses drops five of the original 15 commandments and Brooks, as a waiter at the Last Supper, asks: "Are you all together or is it separate cheques?" From a hilarious Spanish Inquisition number to a "Jews in space" routine, it's vaudeville at its most vulgar with broader strokes than Monty Python, but without the smugness. So what happened to *History of the World Part 2*? Don't ask. Contains some swearing. ▣

Mel Brooks *Moses/Comicus/Torquemada/ Jacques/King Louis XVI* • Dom DeLuise *Emperor Nero* • Madeline Kahn *Empress Nympho* • Harvey Korman *Count de Monet* • Cloris Leachman *Madame de Farge* • Ron Carey *Swiftus* • Gregory Hines *Josephus* • Pamela Stephenson *Mademoiselle Rimbaud* • Sid Caesar *Chief caveman* • Orson Welles *Narrator* ■ *Dir/Scr* Mel Brooks

Hit! ★★★

Crime 1973 · US · Colour · 134mins

One of the better blaxploitation thrillers directed by the frustratingly erratic Sidney J Furie. There are shades of *French Connection II* in the plotting, which finds lawman Billy Dee Williams taking on the Gallic gangsters he blames for his daughter's death. However, this more than stands up in its own right, with Williams's compelling turn well supported by

Richard Pryor. It's a touch overlong, but riveting nevertheless.

Billy Dee Williams *Nick Allen* • Richard Pryor *Mike Willmer* • Paul Hampton *Barry Strong* • Gwen Welles *Sherry Nielson* • Warren Kemmerling *Dutch Schiller* • Janet Brandt *Ida* ■ *Dir* Sidney J Furie • *Scr* Alan R Trustman, David M Wolf

The Hit ★★★★ 18

Thriller 1984 · UK · Colour · 93mins

Twelve years after his directing debut, *Gumshoe*, Stephen Frears's second big-screen outing is a surreal comedy-thriller – a blend of cockney characters with a dash of Buñuel and spaghetti western. Terence Stamp is a supergrass exiled in Spain, where hit men John Hurt and Tim Roth track him down and take him to Paris to be killed. The twist is that Stamp is cool about the whole thing and seems to think it's his destiny, while the hoods are as jumpy as fleas. Charismatic acting, the endless road across the Spanish plain and the expected twist make for stylish entertainment. ▣

John Hurt *Braddock* • Tim Roth *Myron* • Terence Stamp *Willie Parker* • Fernando Rey *Policeman* • Laura Del Sol *Maggie* • Bill Hunter *Harry* • Lennie Peters *Mr Corrigan* ■ *Dir* Stephen Frears • *Scr* Peter Prince

Hit and Run ★★★ PG

Drama 1999 · US · Colour · 88mins

Margaret Colin finds her life shattered when she accidentally hits a child with her car. After leaving the scene to call for help, she returns only to hear the outraged reaction from onlookers who believe it's a hit-and-run and decides to keep quiet. As her life falls apart she must wrestle with her conscience as well as the detective who suspects her. Director Dan Lerner, writer Karen Stillman's thoughtful script and Colin's intense but restrained performance keep this TV movie tale of an innocent woman trapped by circumstance effective throughout.

Margaret Colin *Joanna Kendall* • Drew Pillsbury *Doug Kendall* • Lisa Vidal *Meredith Reed* ■ *Dir* Dan Lerner • *Scr* Karen Stillman

Hit List ★★★

Thriller 1984 · Fr · Colour · 90mins

Annie Girardot and François Marthouret are best known in France as comedy players, which makes their performances all the more commendable in this bruising vigilante picture all the more commendable. The plot has Marthouret's kindly cop keeping his distance while grieving mother Girardot picks off the gangsters responsible for her daughter's death. Alain Bonnot's second feature rather revels in the violent nature of the revenge, but – thanks to Girardot's chillingly calculated portrayal – the film's power comes more from the ferocity of her hatred than the bloodiness of her retribution. French dialogue dubbed into English.

Annie Girardot *Jeanne* • François Marthouret *Kalinsky* • Bernard Brieux *David* • Sandrine Dumas *Nathalie* • Pascal Tedes *Jacky* • Paul Crauchet *Pierre* ■ *Dir* Alain Bonnot • *Scr* Alain Bonnot, André G Brunelin, Marie-Thérèse Cuny, from the novel *Nathalie, ou la Punition* by Gérard Moreau

Hit List ★★ 🔞

Action thriller 1988 · US · Colour · 83mins

This is the epitome of the straight-to-video movie, a ragbag of formula thrills and recycled material from better films. William Lustig peppers his tale of a professional kidnapping gone wrong with bursts of unpleasant violence and, after a tight opening, allows the script to merely become an excuse for a succession of shootouts and chases. Lance Henriksen scores as the psychopathic hit man, but the revenge-seeking Jan-Michael Vincent gives a marvellous impersonation of an oak desk. ▭

Jan-Michael Vincent *Jack Collins* • Leo Rossi *Frank DeSalvo* • Lance Henriksen *Chris Caleek* • Charles Napier *Tom Mitchum* • Rip Torn *Vic Luca* • Jere Burns *Jared Riley* ■ *Dir* William Lustig • *Scr* John Goff, Peter Brosnan, from a story by Aubrey K Rattan

The Hit List ★★ 15

Thriller 1993 · US · Colour · 93mins

Not the Jan-Michael Vincent action tale, but yet another straight-to-video outing for Jeff Fahey. This time he's a top assassin (is there any other kind?) in the pay of lawyer James Coburn, spearhead of an anti-drugs campaign. However, Fahey's devotion to duty goes to the wall when he falls for his latest client Yancy Butler, who wants him to rub out the man who killed her husband. This is one of those thrillers where no one is what they seem and plot contrivance is obligatory. The action fizzes along, but the script and direction lack conviction. Contains violence, swearing, sex scenes and nudity. ▭

Jeff Fahey *Charlie Pike* • Yancy Butler *Jordan Henning* • James Coburn *Peter Mayhew* • Michael Beach *Detective Akin* • Randy Oglesby *Detective Wilcher* • Charles Lanyer *Captain Debont* • Sherman Howard *Bishop* ■ *Dir* William Webb • *Scr* Reed Steiner

Hit the Deck ★★★★ U

Musical 1955 · US · Colour · 112mins

The sailors-on-shore-leave theme may be familiar, but this version of the 1927 stage hit (with a totally new story) is immensely entertaining. Though no *On the Town*, and made when MGM's musical department was winding down, it still has all the studio know-how and a delightful cast. Jane Powell, Vic Damone and Tony Martin do well by the melodies – including *More than You Know* and *Hallelujah!* – Debbie Reynolds and Russ Tamblyn romp through an inventive routine in a fun-house, and best of all there's the irrepressible Ann Miller getting every ounce of humour from the lively script.

Jane Powell *Susan Smith* • Tony Martin *Chief Boatswain's Mate William F Clark* • Debbie Reynolds *Carol Pace* • Walter Pidgeon *Rear Admiral Daniel Xavier Smith* • Vic Damone *Rico Ferrari* • Gene Raymond *Wendell Craig* • Ann Miller *Ginger* • Russ Tamblyn *Danny Xavier Smith* ■ *Dir* Roy Rowland • *Scr* Sonya Levien, William Ludwig, from the musical by Herbert Fields, from the play *Shore Leave* by Hubert Osborne

Hit the Dutchman ★

Crime drama
1992 · US/USSR · Colour · 116mins

Flat-footed gangster movie with Bruce Nozick as the Jewish bootlegger straight out of the pen and into the rackets again with Legs Diamond (Will Kempe). The cast is in the straight-to-video league, though director Menahem Golan first announced the project in 1974 to star George Segal. A major drawback is the location – this movie claims to be set in New York, but it was shot rouble-cheap in Moscow, which supposedly resembles Brooklyn in the twenties.

Bruce Nozick *Dutch Shultz* • Christopher Bradley *Vincent "Mad Dog" Coll* • Eddie Bowz *Joey Noey* • Will Kempe *Legs Diamond* • Sally Kirkland *Emma, Dutch's mother* • Jeff Griggs *Peter Coll* ■ *Dir* Menahem Golan • *Scr* Joseph Goldman, from a story by Alex Simon

Hit the Ice ★★★ U

Musical comedy 1943 · US · BW · 82mins

This was made when the comedy team of Abbott and Costello were the top money-makers for Universal Studios, which in turn gave them good production values, amusing tailor-made scripts and sterling musical support. Bud and Lou are press photographers who get involved with gangsters at a ski resort (cue some inventive slapstick on the ice rink). The crooks include two of Hollywood's finest villains, Sheldon Leonard (who went on to become a TV producer) and Marc Lawrence.

Bud Abbott *Flash Fulton* • Lou Costello *"Tubby" McCoy* • Ginny Simms *Marcia Manning* • Patric Knowles *Dr Bill Elliot* • Elyse Knox *Peggy Osborne* • Joe Sawyer *Buster* • Marc Lawrence *Phil* • Sheldon Leonard *"Silky Fellowsby"* ■ *Dir* Charles Lamont • *Scr* Robert Lees, Frederic I Rinaldo, John Grant, from a story by True Boardman

Hit the Saddle ★

Western 1937 · US · BW · 61mins

This B-western from the initial batch of Republic's Three Mesquiteers series has leads Ray Corrigan and Robert Livingston fighting wild horse thieves and falling out over a disreputable saloon entertainer. Max Terhune is the third Mesquiteer, supplying comic relief with his ventriloquist act. Aficionados of the series do not rate this one highly, but it has acquired added interest because the beer hall floozie is Rita Hayworth, back in the days when she was Rita Cansino.

Robert Livingston *Stony Brooke* • Ray Corrigan *Tucson Smith* • Max Terhune *Lullaby Joslin* • Rita Cansino [Rita Hayworth] *Rita* • JP McGowan *Rance McGowan* • Edward Cassidy *Sheriff Miller* ■ *Dir* Mack V Wright • *Scr* Oliver Drake, from characters created by William Colt MacDonald

Hitched ★★★

Western comedy 1973 · US · Colour · 73mins

This TV movie, a sequel to 1971's *Lock, Stock and Barrel*, is a western comedy directed by Boris Sagal, the former cameraman who, two years earlier, made one of the best sci-fi films of the time, *The Omega Man*. A very young Sally Field and Tim Matheson are the newlyweds searching for each other across terrain as

treacherous as the outlaws who accuse Matheson of being a horse thief. The wonderfully villainous Neville Brand makes this less cutesy than it might have been.

Sally Field *Roselle Bridgeman* • Tim Matheson *Clare Bridgeman* • Neville Brand *Banjo Reilly* • Slim Pickens *Sam Dawson/Bart Dawson* • John Anderson *Williams* • John Fiedler *Henry* • Denver Pyle *Ben Barnstable* ■ *Dir* Boris Sagal • *Scr* Richard Alan Simmons

The Hitcher ★★★★ 🔞

Thriller 1986 · US · Colour · 97mins

No sooner does C Thomas Howell pick up hitchhiker Rutger Hauer against his better judgement than director Robert Harmon's feature debut revs into high homicidal gear. As it turns out, his icy passenger is a serial killer who quickly embroils his ride in a harrowing desert intrigue by implicating him in his sick crimes. Jennifer Jason Leigh, as the waitress who believes Howell's story, adds humanity along the way. Despite the film's huge lapses in logic and moments of wild self-parody, the paranoiac plot twists and grim body count generate some genuinely gruesome suspense. Something of a cult film, thanks to its surreal style and Hauer's inimitable presence.

Rutger Hauer *John Ryder* • C Thomas Howell *Jim Halsey* • Jennifer Jason Leigh *Nash* • Jeffrey DeMunn *Captain Esteridge* ■ *Dir* Robert Harmon • *Scr* Eric Red

The Hitch-Hiker ★★★★

Film noir 1953 · US · BW · 71mins

Ida Lupino made history as the only woman to direct a *film noir* with this wilderness thriller, which was developed from a news story by Daniel Mainwaring (who was denied a credit by RKO president Howard Hughes because of his political radicalism). Making the desert seem every bit as threatening as the urban jungle, Lupino draws a performance of crackling malevolence from William Talman, as the serial killer physically and mentally scarred by his abusive childhood. Equally authentic is the impotent terror of weekend fishermen Edmond O'Brien and Frank Lovejoy, the hostages ordered to make for Mexico.

Edmond O'Brien *Roy Collins* • Frank Lovejoy *Gilbert Bowen* • William Talman *Emmett Myers* • Jose Torvay *Captain Alvarado* • Sam Hayes *Sam* • Wendell Niles *Wendell* ■ *Dir* Ida Lupino • *Scr* Collier Young, Ida Lupino, Robert Joseph, from a story by Daniel Mainwaring (uncredited)

Hitler ★★

Biographical drama 1962 · US · BW · 102mins

According to this heavy-handed, often risible Freudian biopic of the Nazi dictator, the cause of the Second World War was Hitler's mother fixation. He is attracted to his niece and Eva Braun because of their resemblance to his mother. Richard Basehart brings a fair amount of intensity and hysteria to the title role, but most of the film is just sensationalist and phoney.

Richard Basehart *Adolf Hitler* • Cordula Trantow *Geli Raubal* • Maria Emo *Eva Braun* • Martin Kosleck *Joseph Goebbels* • John Banner *Gregor Strasser* • Martin Brandt

General Guderian • John Wengraf *Dr Morell* • John Mitchum *Hermann Goering* ■ *Dir* Stuart Heisler • *Scr* Sam Neuman, E Charles Straus

Hitler: the Last Ten Days ★★ PG

Second World War drama
1973 · UK · Colour · 100mins

Alec Guinness is Hitler trapped in his bunker while Berlin burns above him. It's a brave, incredibly detailed performance, but the film's Italian writer/director Ennio De Concini conspires against him, going for the obvious (cuts to black-and-white documentary footage). He also unwisely adds hindsight in Simon Ward's Hauptmann Hoffman, who not only invades the bunker armed with battalions of postwar guilt, but also plants political doubts in the mind of Eva Braun, played by German actress Doris Kunstmann.

Alec Guinness *Adolf Hitler* • Simon Ward *Hauptmann Hoffmann* • Adolfo Celi *General Krebs* • Diane Cilento *Hanna Reitsch* • Gabriele Ferzetti *Field Marshal Keitel* • Eric Porter *General Von Greim* • Doris Kunstmann *Eva Braun* • Joss Ackland *General Burgdorf* ■ *Dir* Ennio De Concini • *Scr* Ennio De Concini, Maria Pia Lenco, Wolfgang Reinhardt, Ivan Moffat, from the non-fiction book *The Last Days of the Chancellery* by Gerhard Boldt

Hitler's Children ★★★

Second World War drama
1943 · US · BW · 81mins

Edward Dmytryk's drama purports to show how the Nazi regime punished women for refusing to bear babies for the Third Reich. Sterilisation and public lashing are two of the penalties dished out in what is either outright exploitation or earnest education, depending on your point of view. Bonita Granville is one of the persecuted women, while Tim Holt plays her Nazi officer boyfriend who puts a stop to the floggings. This box-office goldmine is surely one of the weirdest propaganda movies ever made; a year later the same team produced a Japanese equivalent entitled *Behind the Rising Sun*.

Tim Holt *Karl* • Bonita Granville *Anna* • Kent Smith *Prof Nichols* • Otto Kruger *Colonel Henkel* • HB Warner *Bishop* • Lloyd Corrigan *Franz Erhart* ■ *Dir* Edward Dmytryk • *Scr* Emmett Lavery, from the non-fiction book *Education for Death* by Gregor Ziemer

Hitler's Madman ★★★

Second World War drama
1943 · US · BW · 83mins

The first Hollywood picture of melodrama king Douglas Sirk is a B-movie about the assassination of the Nazi, Reinhard Heydrich, and the savage reprisals which left the Czech village of Lidice razed to the ground. Made a short time after the actual events it depicted, the film has an urgency about it, if little of the director's later finesse. Sirk reputedly met Heydrich in Berlin in the twenties and remembered his expressive face and Shakespearean style of declaiming – which may explain John Carradine's performance as the Nazi monster. Ava Gardner pops up briefly as one of Lidice's martyred population.

John Carradine *Heydrich* • Patricia Morison *Jarmila* • Alan Curtis *Karel* • Ralph Morgan

U = SUITABLE FOR ALL   **Uc** = SUITABLE FOR ALL, ESPECIALLY FOR YOUNG CHILDREN (VIDEO ONLY)   **PG** = PARENTAL GUIDANCE

Hanka • Howard Freeman *Himmler* • Ludwig Stossel *Mayor Bauer* • Edgar Kennedy *Nepomuk* • Ava Gardner *Katy Chotnik* ∎ *Dir* Douglas Sirk • *Scr* Peretz Hirshbein, Melvin Levy, Doris Malloy, from a story by Emil Ludwig, Albrecht Joseph, from the story *Hangmen's Village* by Bart Lytton

The Hitman ★★ 18
Crime action thriller
1991 · US · Colour · 89mins

This vehicle for the ageing Chuck Norris at least benefits from significantly better direction than his other movies of the period, as brother Aaron Norris gives the proceedings a sharp, atmospheric look and a harder edge to the sporadic violence. Chuck Norris, however, does not give his character – a cop who goes undercover into the Mafia after nearly being killed in the line of duty – the hard, bitter edge that's needed, being his usual bland self. Extra time devoted to the manipulative subplot concerning Norris befriending a lonely African-American boy doesn't help.

Chuck Norris *Cliff Garret/Danny Grogan* • Michael Parks *Ronny "Del" Delaney* • Al Waxman *Marco Luganni* • Alberta Watson *Christine De Vera* • Salim Grant *Tim Murphy* • Ken Pogue *Chambers* • Marcel Sabourin *Andre Lacombe* ∎ *Dir* Aaron Norris • *Scr* Don Carmody, Robert Geoffrion

Ho! ★★
Crime drama   1968 · Fr · Colour · 110mins

In yet another flashy, trashy crime thriller from his sixties period, Jean-Paul Belmondo is a former race car star turned getaway driver who gets involved in a gang power struggle. His decision to go it alone incurs the wrath of girlfriend Joanna Shimkus, as well as fellow gang members. Over-plotted doesn't start to describe the ridiculous round of arrests, escapes, press exposés, robberies and shoot-outs that follows. By failing to keep either events or the gregarious Belmondo in check, director Robert Enrico allows the film to descend into chaos. French dialogue dubbed into English..

Jean-Paul Belmondo *Ho* • Joanna Shimkus *Benedite* • Sydney Chaplin *Canter* • Alain Mottet *Paul* • Paul Crauchet *Briand* ∎ *Dir* Robert Enrico • *Scr* Pierre Pelegri, Lucienne Hamon, Robert Enrico, from the novel by José Giovanni

Hoa-Binh ★★★
War drama   1970 · Fr · Colour · 90mins

Famed as the New Wave's most inventive cinematographer, Raoul Coutard was also a veteran war cameraman, and he brought that experience to bear on his even-handed, Oscar-nominated directorial debut. Couched in melodramatic terms, this is nevertheless an uncompromisingly authentic account of the everyday ramifications of the American invasion. Forced to accept menial work to support his sister, young Phi San gives a dignified and determined performance, which is counterpointed by the senseless savagery of the war footage.

Phi San *Hung* • Xvar Ha Moi *Mother* • Le Qynh *Father* • Danièle Delorme *Nurse* ∎ *Dir* Raoul Coutard • *Scr* Raoul Coutard, from the novel *La Colonne de Cendres* by Françoise Lorrain

A Hobo's Christmas ★★★ U
Seasonal drama   1987 · US · Colour · 93mins

Adorable old crusty Barnard Hughes, best known to younger viewers as Grandpa in *The Lost Boys*, plays a tramp who returns to the family he deserted 20 years before in this warm and cuddly seasonal tale. Hughes is always watchable, and he is supported by a capable cast that includes Gerald McRaney and Wendy Crewson. A Christmas movie that's more of a cracker than most. ▭

Barnard Hughes *Chance* • William Hickey *Cincinnati Harold* • Gerald McRaney *Charlie* • Wendy Crewson *Laurie* • Jamie Mills *Cathy* ∎ *Dir* Will Mackenzie • *Scr* Jeb Rosebrook

Hobson's Choice ★★★★ U
Classic comedy   1953 · UK · BW · 102mins

Winner of the British Academy Award for best British film in 1954, this is a splendid adaptation of the celebrated Harold Brighouse play. The role of the Salford cobbler at war with his wilful daughter is tailor-made for Charles Laughton (who had previously enjoyed much stage success in the role of Henry Horatio Hobson), and he gives one of his very best performances. The slick by-play between the leads belies the fact that Laughton detested Brenda de Banzie as Maggie and resented John Mills for landing the son-in-law part he wanted to go to Robert Donat. Director David Lean handles cast and material with equal care, judging the moments of comedy and poignancy perfectly. ▭

Charles Laughton *Henry Horatio Hobson* • John Mills *Willie Mossop* • Brenda de Banzie *Maggie Hobson* • Daphne Anderson *Alice Hobson* • Prunella Scales *Vicky Hobson* • Richard Wattis *Albert Prosser* • Derek Blomfield *Freddy Beenstock* • Helen Haye *Mrs Hepworth* • Joseph Tomelty *Jim Heeler* ∎ *Dir* David Lean • *Scr* David Lean, Norman Spencer, Wynyard Browne, from the play by Harold Brighouse

Hockey Night ★★
Drama   1984 · Can · Colour · 74mins

Likeable comedy, less exploitative than it could have been, about a pretty girl who becomes the goalie of a boys' hockey team in a small Canadian town. The film is pitched at early teens, so don't expect too many jokes about scoring own goalies! Megan Follows stars, but the best-known name in the cast is Rick Moranis.

Megan Follows *Cathy Yarrow* • Rick Moranis *Coach Willy Leipert* • Sean McCann *Mr Kozak* • Gail Youngs *Alice Yarrow* • Yannick Bisson *Spear Kozak* • Henry Ramer *Bill Moss* ∎ *Dir* Paul Shapiro • *Scr* Paul Shapiro, Jack Blum

Hocus Pocus ★★★ PG
Black comedy   1993 · US · Colour · 92mins

An unusually black comedy from Disney, this nevertheless makes for patchy entertainment. Three witches – Bette Midler, *Sister Act's* Kathy Najimy and Sarah Jessica Parker – are resurrected by a group of youngsters on Halloween and proceed to cause mayhem as they plot their revenge against the community that condemned them to death three centuries earlier. The three stars are the best thing about the movie and

they get to do one stunning musical number, a version of *I Put a Spell on You*. The youngsters, led by Thora Birch, acquit themselves admirably, but director Kenny Ortega seems unsure of the tone of the piece. ▭ **DVD**

Bette Midler *Winifred Sanderson* • Sarah Jessica Parker *Sarah Sanderson* • Kathy Najimy *Mary Sanderson* • Omri Katz *Max* • Thora Birch *Dani* • Vinessa Shaw *Allison* • Amanda Shepherd *Emily* ∎ *Dir* Kenny Ortega • *Scr* Neil Cuthbert, Mick Garris, from a story by Mick Garris, David Kirschner

Hoffa ★★★ 15
Biographical drama
1992 · US · Colour · 134mins

Although this purports to be a biopic of Jimmy Hoffa, one of the most controversial figures in American trade union history, it is dangerous to take it too seriously. Danny DeVito's character seems to be a figment of screenwriter David Mamet's imagination, and too little light is shed on Hoffa's alleged involvement with the Mob. However, as a study of a man devoted to his cause, it is a powerful piece of drama, and DeVito directs with an impressive epic sweep. Jack Nicholson dominates the screen as the belligerent Teamsters' boss, and Kevin Anderson is magnificently incisive as Robert Kennedy. Flawed but forceful. Contains swearing, violence and nudity. ▭

Jack Nicholson *James R Hoffa* • Danny DeVito *Bobby Ciaro* • Armand Assante *Carol D'Allesandro* • JT Walsh *Frank Fitzsimmons* • John C Reilly *Pete Connelly* • Frank Whaley *Young kid* • Kevin Anderson *Robert Kennedy* ∎ *Dir* Danny DeVito • *Scr* David Mamet

Hoffman ★ 15
Sex comedy   1970 · UK · Colour · 106mins

Not even Peter Sellers, in obsequious mode, can make this tale of middle-aged Hoffman, blackmailing Sinead Cusack to stay for a week in his apartment, anything other than tediously peculiar, if not downright perverse. Adapted by Ernest Gebler from his novel, it's a sex comedy that's not very sexy or comic. Not so much permissive as dismissive. ▭

Peter Sellers *Benjamin Hoffman* • Sinead Cusack *Janet Smith* • Jeremy Bulloch *Tom Mitchell* • Ruth Dunning *Mrs Mitchell* • David Lodge *Foreman* ∎ *Dir* Alvin Rakoff • *Scr* Ernest Gebler, from his novel

The Holcroft Covenant ★★ 15
Spy thriller   1985 · UK · Colour · 107mins

Oh, dear. It's Michael Caine chasing his father's Nazi legacy either to atone for or rebuild Hitler's empire. It's easy to blame once-talented director John Frankenheimer (*The Manchurian Candidate*) for making this farrago unwatchable, but the more likely obstacle is that the source material – Robert Ludlum's airport lounge thriller – is cinematically intractable. The locations look good, Lilli Palmer is tragically graceful, and Anthony Andrews manfully struggles with an impossible role in Caine's brother. ▭

Michael Caine *Noel Holcroft* • Anthony Andrews *Johann Tennyson von Tiebolt* • Victoria Tennant *Helden Tennyson von Tiebolt* • Lilli Palmer *Althene Holcroft* • Mario Adorf *Jurgen Maas/Erich Kessler* • Michael

Lonsdale [Michel Lonsdale] *Manfredi* ∎ *Dir* John Frankenheimer • *Scr* George Axelrod, Edward Anhalt, John Hopkins, from the novel by Robert Ludlum

Hold Back the Dawn ★★★★
Romantic comedy drama
1941 · US · BW · 116mins

A smashing comedy drama with Charles Boyer as a wartime refugee who marries schoolmarm Olivia de Havilland as a means of gaining entry into the US. Paulette Goddard is his partner in the deception and his chosen companion on his wedding night. Set largely on the US-Mexican border, in one of those fly-blown hotels filled with ''characters'', this is a very witty but also rather dark charade, written by Charles Brackett and Billy Wilder just before Wilder became a director himself.

Charles Boyer *Georges Iscovescu* • Olivia de Havilland *Emmy Brown* • Paulette Goddard *Anita Dixon* • Victor Francen *Van Den Luecken* • Walter Abel *Inspector Hammock* • Curt Bois *Bonbois* • Rosemary De Camp *Berta Kurz* ∎ *Dir* Mitchell Leisen • *Scr* Charles Brackett, Billy Wilder, from a story by Ketti Frings

Hold Back the Night
★★★★ 15
Drama   1999 · UK/It · Colour · 99mins

A powerful little drama about a strong-willed teenager (Christine Tremarco) who, while fleeing an abusive father, hooks up with two similarly restless souls: a grungy environmental protester (Stuart Sinclair Blyth) and a terminally ill woman (Sheila Hancock) whose dying wish is to see the sunrise at Orkney's Ring of Brodgar. Strong performances, believable characters and a script that doesn't offer easy answers combine to create an affecting journey. Tremarco's defensive, aloof behaviour often makes her difficult to care for, but then this isn't a story which shies away from risks, and it's a brave film that favours psychological plausibility above easy audience engagement. Contains swearing and drug abuse. ▭ **DVD**

Christine Tremarco *Charleen* • Stuart Sinclair Blyth *Declan* • Sheila Hancock *Vera* • Richard Platt *Michael* • Julie Ann Watson *Jackie* • Kenneth Colley *Bob* • Tommy Tiernan *John* ∎ *Dir* Phil Davis • *Scr* Steve Chambers

Hold Me, Thrill Me, Kiss Me ★★★ 18
Comedy   1992 · US · Colour · 92mins

Legend has it independent writer/director Joel Hershman set out to make a movie as tasteless, tacky and vulgar as anything Hollywood could make, only for much less money. He succeeded. Adrienne Shelley, Max Parrish, Sean Young and Diane Ladd star in a quirky, sleazy comedy about a drifter who hooks up with a nymphomaniac stripper and her nice-as-spice sister, only to find depravity and violence coming at him from not such an unexpected quarter. Eccentrically watchable. Contains swearing and sex scenes. ▭

Max Parrish *Eli/Bud/Fritz* • Adrienne Shelley *Dannie* • Sean Young *Twinkle* • Diane Ladd *Lucille* • Andrea Naschak [April Rayne] *Sabra* • Ania Suli *Olga* ∎ *Dir/Scr* Joel Hershman

Hold My Hand ★★

Comedy   1938 · UK · BW · 76mins

Stanley Lupino takes the lead in the film version of his stage play. Lupino plays Eddie Marston, whose generous offer to risk money financing his ward's newspaper backfires on him when he's accused of embezzlement. There are the usual romantic entanglements in a short, sharp romp that's absolutely typical of its time. The great comedian Fred Emney, whose long career extended into the seventies, appears as Lord Milchester.

Stanley Lupino *Eddie Marston* • Fred Emney *Lord Milchester* • Barbara Blair *Jane Howard* • Sally Gray *Helen* • Polly Ward *Paula Pond* • Bertha Belmore *Lady Milchester* • Jack Melford *Pop Currie* • John Wood *Bob Crane* ■ *Dir* Thornton Freeland • *Scr* Clifford Grey, Bert Lee, William Freshman, from the play by Stanley Lupino

Hold That Blonde ★★

Crime comedy   1945 · US · BW · 76mins

This patchy screwball comedy is short on originality and cruelly exposes the limitations of Eddie Bracken, here playing a kleptomaniac intent on preventing Veronica Lake from pinching a priceless Romanov bracelet. Bracken throws himself into every double take and slapstick set piece. Yet, for all his enthusiasm, he's totally upstaged by the sinister duo of Albert Dekker and George Zucco. Director George Marshall makes the most of the breakneck chases and throws in some sly class satire, but not even Lake can make this a gem.

Veronica Lake *Sally Martin* • Eddie Bracken *Ogden Spencer Trulow III* • Albert Dekker *Inspector Callahan* • Frank Fenton *Mr Phillips* • George Zucco *Pavel Sorasky* • Donald MacBride *Mr Kratz* ■ *Dir* George Marshall • *Scr* Walter DeLeon, Earl Baldwin, E Edwin Moran, from the play by Paul Armstrong

Hold That Co-Ed ★★★

Musical comedy   1938 · US · BW · 80mins

The "Great Profile", John Barrymore, made some six movies in 1938. Four years later he was dead, a burnt-out alcoholic once regarded as the greatest stage performer of his time. Unfortunately, talkies arrived too late for him as his finest screen portrayals were in the days of silent cinema. However, his own need for cash and the public's morbid curiosity never stopped the flamboyant Barrymore from working, and here he walks away with the movie as a bluff governor who sponsors a college football team to win votes. It's not *Hamlet*, but it's all jolly good fun, and the old ham is a complete delight to watch under George Marshall's fast-paced direction.

John Barrymore *Governor* • George Murphy *Rusty* • Marjorie Weaver *Marjorie* • Joan Davis *Lizzie* • Jack Haley *Wilbur* • George Barbier *Breckenridge* • Ruth Terry *Edie* • Donald Meek *Dean Thatcher* ■ *Dir* George Marshall • *Scr* Karl Tunberg, Don Ettinger, Jack Yellen, from a story by Karl Tunberg, Don Ettinger

Hold That Ghost ★★★

Comedy   1941 · US · BW · 86mins

A superior Abbott and Costello comedy that finds the zany duo inheriting a supposedly haunted mansion, thanks to a gangster's will. The heroes intend to turn the place into a restaurant, but once on the premises they encounter all sorts of spooky phenomena. Musical relief is provided by the boys' regular collaborators, the Andrews Sisters. Over the years this type of comedy chiller would provide the double act with some of their finest celluloid moments as the boys encountered Universal Pictures' full gallery of classic monsters.

Bud Abbott *Chuck Murray* • Lou Costello *Ferdinand Jones* • Richard Carlson *Dr Jackson* • Evelyn Ankers *Norma Lind* • Joan Davis *Camille Brewster* • Marc Lawrence *Charlie Smith* ■ *Dir* Arthur Lubin • *Scr* Robert Lees, Frederic I Rinaldo, John Grant

Hold-Up ★★

Crime drama   1985 · Fr/Can · Colour · 114mins

Even a tightly focused performance by Jean-Paul Belmondo can't hide the grinding predictability of a film in which a trio of bank robbers have more trouble with themselves than the law. Belmondo's natural ease and early appearance in a clown suit (in order to rob the bank) might help you stay the distance. Female lead Kim Cattrall is better than her track record (*Police Academy*, *Porky's*) suggests. The film was later remade by Bill Murray under the title *Quick Change*. French dialogue dubbed into English.

Jean-Paul Belmondo *Grimm* • Guy Marchand *Georges* • Kim Cattrall *Lise* • Jean-Pierre Marielle *Labrosse* • Tex Konig *Lasky* • Jacques Villeret *Cab driver* ■ *Dir* Alexandre Arcady • *Scr* Alexandre Arcady, Francis Veber, Daniel Saint-Harmont, from the novel *Quick Change* by Jay Cronley

Hold Your Man ★★★

Melodrama   1933 · US · BW · 88mins

Clark Gable and blonde bombshell Jean Harlow co-star as a charming, womanising petty gangster and a seemingly tough young woman who, after much fencing and wisecracking, fall in love. But things go wrong when he accidentally kills a man. Sam Wood directs this bizarre and unsettling mix of comedy, romance and melodrama, which strains credibility to the limit but still makes for satisfying entertainment.

Jean Harlow *Ruby Adams* • Clark Gable *Eddie Hall* • Stuart Erwin *Al Simpson* • Dorothy Burgess *Gypsy* • Muriel Kirkland *Bertha Dillon* • Garry Owen *Slim* • Barbara Barondess *Sadie Kline* • Paul Hurst *Aubrey Mitchell* ■ *Dir* Sam Wood • *Scr* Anita Loos, Howard Emmett Rogers, from a story by Anita Loos

The Hole ★★★

Drama   1998 · Tai/Fr · Colour · 90mins

Whereas in *The River*, director Tsai Ming-Liang presented water as a cause of corruption and pain, here it ebbs back towards its traditional symbolism as a source of life and a force for good. Stranded in a Taipei gripped by a mystery millennial virus, Lee Kang-Sheng becomes obsessed with his downstairs neighbour, Yang Kuei-Mei, after a clumsy plumber leaves a hole in his floor. Interspersed with musical reveries, performed by Yang in ironic tribute to the fifties singer Grace Chang, this is a delightfully quirky film, in which the minimalism of ennui gives way to the gentle magic of romance. A Mandarin language film.

Yang Kuei-Mai *Woman downstairs* • Li Kangsheng *Man upstairs* • Miao Tien *Salesman* • Tong Hsiang-Chu *Plumber* • Lin Hui-Chin *Neighbour* ■ *Dir* Tsai Ming-Liang • *Scr* Tsai Ming-Liang, Yang Ping-Ying

A Hole in the Head ★★ U

Comedy   1959 · US · Colour · 120mins

Set in Miami Beach, Frank Capra's penultimate film stars Frank Sinatra as a widower whose hotel, the Garden of Eden, is threatened with closure. Edward G Robinson is Sinatra's brother, while Eleanor Parker plays a wealthy widow who may be the answer to his prayers. Based on Arnold Schulman's play, it's crudely sentimental and desperately dated, as demonstrated by Carolyn Jones's irritating role as Sinatra's beatnik girlfriend. The undoubted high spot is Ol' Blue Eyes singing *High Hopes*, a song which he used to croon at JFK's campaign fundraisers.

Frank Sinatra *Tony Manetta* • Edward G Robinson *Mario Manetta* • Eddie Hodges *Ally Manetta* • Eleanor Parker *Mrs Rogers* • Carolyn Jones *Shirl* ■ *Dir* Frank Capra • *Scr* Arnold Shulman, from his play

A Hole Lot of Trouble ★★

Comedy   1969 · UK · Colour · 27mins

Veteran producer/director Francis Searle ended his career with a number of comedy shorts (all about 30 minutes long) designed to accompany features in the dying days of the double bill. Such shorts took a simple idea and exploited the potential to the maximum – Eric Sykes's *The Plank* is arguably the perfect example. Here, Arthur Lowe and friends explore the comic potential surrounding a group of workman digging a hole.

Arthur Lowe *Whitehouse* • Bill Maynard *Bill* • Tim Barrett *Longbottom* • Victor Maddern *Percy* • Brian Weske *Digby* • Leslie Dwyer *Evangelist* • Ken Parry *Charles* • Hani Borelle *Fenella* ■ *Dir* Francis Searle • *Scr* Ian Flintoff

Holiday ★★★

Romantic comedy   1930 · US · BW · 83mins

This is a capable filming of Philip Barry's hit Broadway comedy, with Robert Ames as the young nonconformist who rescues Ann Harding from an oppressive life in high society. Mary Astor is her sister, while Monroe Owsley is her weak brother drowning in drink. Under Edward H Griffith's direction, Ann Harding gained an Oscar nomination, though this adaptation has been thoroughly eclipsed by George Cukor's definitive 1938 version with Katharine Hepburn.

Ann Harding *Linda Seton* • Mary Astor *Julia Seton* • Edward Everett Horton *Nick Potter* • Robert Ames *Johnny Case* • Hedda Hopper *Susan Potter* • Monroe Owsley *Ned Seton* • William Holden (2) *Edward Seton* ■ *Dir* Edward H Griffith • *Scr* Horace Jackson, from the play by Philip Barry

Holiday ★★★★★ U

Romantic comedy   1938 · US · BW · 91mins

This absolutely magical entertainment – an expert brew of comedy, pathos, romance and social comment – comes courtesy of the team which, two years later, would reunite to make *The Philadelphia Story*: screenwriter Donald Ogden Stewart, working from a play by Philip Barry; director George Cukor; and Cary Grant and Katharine Hepburn, he at his most thoughtful and charming, she never more beautiful or touching. Previously filmed in 1930, it's the tale of a man (Grant) who falls in love with a girl (Doris Nolan). When she turns out to be from the top drawer of mega-wealthy New York society, he finds himself enmeshed in more than he bargained for – especially after her sister (Hepburn) takes a shine to him. The stars sparkle in the midst of a superb supporting cast. 🔲

Cary Grant *Johnny Case* • Katharine Hepburn *Linda Seton* • Doris Nolan *Julia Seton* • Lew Ayres *Ned Seton* • Edward Everett Horton *Nick Potter* • Henry Kolker *Edward Seton* • Binnie Barnes *Laura Cram* ■ *Dir* George Cukor • *Scr* Donald Ogden Stewart, Sidney Buchman, from the play by Philip Barry

Holiday Affair ★★★ U

Seasonal drama   1949 · US · BW · 86mins

An absolutely charming yet little-known RKO Christmas movie, with widowed single mum Janet Leigh torn between Robert Mitchum and Wendell Corey (that's a contest?) and, not surprisingly, drawn to the one her son prefers. There's a sweet opening sequence and a nice sense of New York at Christmas time that's a touch reminiscent of *Miracle on 34th Street*. Mitchum reveals what a subtle actor he could be, and Leigh proves herself yet again to be one of the most delectable of cinematic charmers. Cynics should steer well clear but, if you're in the right mood, this is delightful seasonal entertainment.

Robert Mitchum *Steve* • Janet Leigh *Connie* • Wendell Corey *Carl* • Gordon Gebert *Timmy* • Griff Barnett *Mr Ennis* • Esther Dale *Mrs Ennis* • Henry O'Neill *Mr Crowley* • Henry Morgan [Harry Morgan] *Police lieutenant* ■ *Dir* Don Hartman • *Scr* Isobel Lennart, from the story *Christmas Gift* by John D Weaver

Holiday Affair ★★★ U

Seasonal romance   1996 · US · Colour · 85mins

Get out the mistletoe, ignite the Yule log and wallow in Cynthia Gibb's romantic dilemma. In this remake of the 1949 Janet Leigh-Robert Mitchum film, Gibb is the widowed mother who finds herself torn between marriage to her financially secure lawyer boyfriend and a relationship with a handsome department store salesman. To add to her problems, one of her suitors is leaving town on New Year's Eve – for good. This sugary Christmas romantic triangle in the *Miracle on 34th Street* vein lacks Kris Kringle but still adds up to a cheerful holiday diversion. 🔲

Cynthia Gibb *Jodie* • David James Elliott *Steve Mason* • Curtis Blanck *Timmy* • Tom Irwin *Paul Davis* • Al Waxman *Mr Crowley* ■ *Dir* Alan Myerson • *Scr* Ara Watson, Sam Blackwell, from the 1949 film, from the story *Christmas Gift* by John D Weaver

Holiday Camp ★★★ U

Comedy drama   1947 · UK · BW · 93mins

Directed by Ken Annakin, this compendium of interlinked stories was more notable for its scripting credits than for the quality of the writing. Ted

Willis, Sydney and Muriel Box and Peter Rogers were among the contributors but, although many of the episodes are reasonably diverting, none of them gives the stars enough to chew on. What is fascinating, however, is the picture of camp life, which should keep *Hi-De-Hi!* fans entertained. Jack Warner and Kathleen Harrison steal the show as the Huggetts, who went on to feature in three more movies as well as their own radio show. ▢

Flora Robson *Esther Harmon* • Dennis Price *Squadron Leader Hardwicke* • Jack Warner *Joe Huggett* • Kathleen Harrison *Ethel Huggett* • Hazel Court *Joan Martin* • Peter Hammond *Harry Huggett* • Yvonne Owen *Angela Kirby* • Jimmy Hanley *Jimmy Gardner* • Esma Cannon *Elsie Dawson* ■ *Dir* Ken Annakin • *Scr* Sidney Box, Peter Rogers, Denis Constanduros, Mabel Constanduros, Ted Willis, from a story by Godfrey Winn

Holiday for Lovers ★★ U

Romantic comedy   1959 · US · Colour · 102mins

At a time when B-movies were overrun with delinquent juveniles, this old-fashioned family comedy had nothing more to offer than a couple of hormonally zestful bobby-soxers. Screenwriter Luther Davis and director Henry Levin do nothing to drag Ronald Alexander's play into the rock 'n' roll era, preferring instead to dabble in coy innuendo as Jill St John and Carol Lynley chase the chaps during stuffy Clifton Webb and sensible Jane Wyman's South American vacation. There are moving picture postcards from Brazil and Peru, a bullfight and a drunken scene for Webb to show his humanity. Alas, there are no laughs.

Clifton Webb *Robert Dean* • Jane Wyman *Mary Dean* • Jill St John *Meg Dean* • Carol Lynley *Betsy Dean* • Paul Henreid *Eduardo Barroso* • Gary Crosby *Paul Gattling* • Wally Brown *Joe* ■ *Dir* Henry Levin • *Scr* Luther Davis, from the play by Ronald Alexander

Holiday in Mexico ★★★ U

Musical   1946 · US · Colour · 127mins

Made to help cement America's Good Neighbour policy, this epic MGM musical actually never left the Culver City soundstages; the clever Hanna-Barbera animated title sequence establishes the only "authentic" Mexican flavour. Nevertheless, there's much to enjoy, despite the overlength that director George Sidney was prone to in the forties. It's effectively a vehicle for delightful ingénue Jane Powell, who (unbelievably!) develops a crush on much older pianist José Iturbi. But there's also some knockout piano choreography, created by youngster Stanley Donen.

Walter Pidgeon *Jeffrey Evans* • José Iturbi *Jose Iturbi* • Roddy McDowall *Stanley Owen* • Ilona Massey *Toni Karpathy* • Xavier Cugat *Xavier Cugat* • Jane Powell *Christine Evans* • Hugo Haas *Angus* ■ *Dir* George Sidney • *Scr* Isobel Lennart, from a story by William Kozlenko

Holiday Inn ★★★★ U

Musical comedy   1942 · US · BW · 100mins

Classic, well-loved musical that paired Crosby and Astaire for the first time, playing a song-and-dance team. The ingenious but wafer-thin plot sees

Crosby split from the act to run an inn which only opens on public holidays, but this is basically a vehicle for some wonderful Irving Berlin songs and some magical Astaire dance routines. Most of the songs celebrate the aforementioned public holidays, but one in particular – Crosby's rendition of *White Christmas* – really caught the public imagination, making his version of the song one of the most successful recordings of all time. ▢

Bing Crosby *Jim Hardy* • Fred Astaire *Ted Hanover* • Marjorie Reynolds *Linda Mason* • Virginia Dale *Lila Dixon* • Walter Abel *Danny Reid* • Louise Beavers *Mamie* • John Gallaudet *Parker* • James Bell *Dunbar* ■ *Dir* Mark Sandrich • *Scr* Claude Binyon, Elmer Rice, from an idea by Irving Berlin • *Choreographer* Danny Dare

Holiday on the Buses ★ PG

Comedy   1973 · UK · Colour · 82mins

The third movie culled from the hit TV series is one of the worst films you'll see this or any other year. Having been sacked from the bus depot, Stan and Jack fetch up at a Welsh holiday camp, where (surprise, surprise) their boss turns out to be old Blakey himself. The film's only achievement is to pack into 85 minutes more smutty sniggering than the entire oeuvre of Beavis and Butt-head, yet without an ounce of the dumb duo's wit. All the regulars are on board, but only guest players Arthur Mullard and Queenie Watts make any impression. ▢

Reg Varney *Stan Butler* • Stephen Lewis *Inspector Blake* • Bob Grant *Jack* • Doris Hare *Mrs Butler* • Michael Robbins *Arthur* • Anna Karen *Olive* • Wilfrid Brambell *Bert* • Arthur Mullard *Wally Briggs* ■ *Dir* Bryan Izzard • *Scr* Ronald Wolfe, Ronald Chesney, from their TV series *On the Buses*

Holidays on the River Yarra ★★★

Drama   1991 · Ausl · Colour · 88mins

This was part of the Melbourne urban cinema boom of the early nineties, along with Geoffrey Wright's controversial *Romper Stomper*. Leo Berkeley's edgy drama does not depict the extremity of right-wing sentiment found in Wright's film, but still portrays a city of unemployment, racial tension and disillusionment. Not content with voicing their views about various ethnic minorities at home, the lads here get involved in a far-fetched scheme to overthrow the reformist government of a small African island. While its realism is decidedly diminished by the doltishness of several minor characters, this is still a disturbing study of disaffection.

Craig Adams *Eddie* • Luke Elliot *Mick* • Alex Menglet *Big Mac* • Sheryl Munks *Valerie* • Kim Gyngell *Stewie* • Ian Scott *Frank* • Chris Askey *Eric* ■ *Dir/Scr* Leo Berkeley

Hollow Point ★★ 15

Thriller   1987 · US · Colour · 90mins

The name Peckinpah in the credits sets the pulse racing, until you realise it's not the great Sam, but David Peckinpah who wrote the story and co-wrote the screenplay for this run-of-the-mill thriller. Billy Drago is suitably malicious as the killer out for revenge after he is fingered by special needs

teacher Linda Purl. But when she takes up arms to defend herself, the story loses all touch with reality. The subplot involving Purl and an autistic child is tacky, while Yaphet Kotto is underused as the cop on the case. ▢

Linda Purl *Susan Andrews* • Yaphet Kotto *Lieutenant Tyrell* • Terry Lester *Dan Edwards* • Billy Drago *Eddie Reeves* • Gail Edwards *Alice* • Rick Lenz *Chris Fowler* ■ *Dir* Bruce Seth Green • *Scr* Robert Crais, David Peckinpah, from a story by David Peckinpah

Hollow Point ★★ 18

Crime comedy   1996 · US/Can · Colour · 98mins

Thomas Ian Griffith, star of action fare such as *Excessive Force*, plays this "both guns blazing" adventure for laughs with the help of *Wayne's World* babe Tia Carrere. Sidney J Furie directs, but his camera trickery and Griffith's gun-toting prowess are overshadowed by the two more accomplished members of the cast, *Third Rock from the Sun's* John Lithgow and, with his tongue very firmly in his cheek, Donald Sutherland. Contains violence, swearing and brief nudity. ▢ **DVD**

Tia Carrere *Diane Norwood* • Thomas Ian Griffith *Max Perish* • Donald Sutherland *Garrett Lawton* • John Lithgow *Thomas Livingston* • David Hemblen *Oleg Krezinsky* • Carl Alacchi *Alberto Capucci* ■ *Dir* Sidney J Furie • *Scr* James H Stewart, Robert Geoffrion

Hollow Reed ★★★ 15

Drama   1995 · UK/Ger · Colour · 101mins

With a subject that's usually the preserve of the TV movie, this drama gains little from being made for the cinema, but the performances make it memorable. As directed by Angela Pope, the film is tensely moving when it concentrates on estranged gay doctor Martin Donovan, who is trying to save his son, Sam Bould, from what he believes are the attacks of ex-wife Joely Richardson's live-in lover, Jason Flemyng. However, the subsequent courtroom scenes become a gay rights manifesto during which genuine grievances over-ripen into dishonest special pleading. Contains violence, swearing and nudity. ▢

Martin Donovan *Martyn Wyatt* • Ian Hart *Tom Dixon* • Joely Richardson *Hannah Wyatt* • Sam Bould *Oliver Wyatt* • Jason Flemyng *Frank Donally* • Shaheen Khan *Dr Razmu* • Kelly Hunter *Jamie's mum* ■ *Dir* Angela Pope • *Scr* Paula Milne, from a story by Neville Bolt

Hollow Triumph ★★★ PG

Film noir   1948 · US · BW · 79mins

Producer/star Paul Henreid plays a gangster on the run from gamblers he's robbed. He murders a lookalike psychiatrist and assumes his identity, even inflicting a scar on his face to complete the resemblance. The story takes some swallowing but offers ingenious twists and, in true fatalistic *film noir* fashion, shows that no matter how hard you try, you can't escape your fate. The dramatic photography is the work of John Alton, one of the masters of *film noir*, who is given full rein by director Steve Sekely.

Joan Bennett *Evelyn Hahn* • Paul Henreid *John Muller* • Eduard Franz *Frederick Muller* • Leslie

Brooks *Virginia Taylor* • John Qualen *Swangron* ■ *Dir* Steve Sekely • *Scr* Daniel Fuchs, from the novel by Murray Forbes

The Holly and the Ivy ★★★ U

Seasonal drama   1952 · UK · BW · 83mins

A family drama whose stage origins are all too obvious. Vicar Ralph Richardson gathers his children around him at Christmas in his Norfolk rectory, only for the festive spirit to be dampened by a startling revelation. Almost inevitably, Celia Johnson is on hand like a thick cardigan to provide comfort, yet, despite the clunky direction by George More O'Ferrall, the outcome is bleaker than you expect.

Ralph Richardson *Reverend Martin Gregory* • Celia Johnson *Jenny Gregory* • Margaret Leighton *Margaret Gregory* • Denholm Elliott *Michael "Mick" Gregory* • John Gregson *David Patterson* • Hugh Williams *Richard Wyndham* ■ *Dir* George More O'Ferrall • *Scr* Anatole de Grunwald, from the play by Wynard Browne

Hollywood ★★ U

Silent comedy drama   1923 · US · BW · 30mins

One of the biggest productions of the silent period to exploit the insatiable appetite of picturegoers for glimpses of the film capital, this Paramount comedy put little-known players in the lead roles to contrast with the celebrities who appeared as themselves, including Cecil B DeMille, Mary Pickford, Gloria Swanson and Will Rogers. As the young would-be star from the Midwest who has no success in Hollywood while her entire family is offered work, Hope Drown was aptly named: she was never seen again.

Hope Drown *Angela Whitaker* • Luke Cosgrave *Joel Whitaker* • George K Arthur *Lem Lefferts* • Ruby Lafayette *Grandmother Whitaker* • Roscoe Arbuckle *[Roscoe "Fatty" Arbuckle] Fat man in casting director's office* • Gertrude Astor • Mary Astor • Agnes Ayres • Charles Chaplin • Betty Compson • Cecil B DeMille • Douglas Fairbanks • Mary Pickford • ZaSu Pitts • Will Rogers • Gloria Swanson ■ *Dir* James Cruze • *Scr* from a story by Frank Condon, Tom Geraghyt [Thomas J Geraghty]

Hollywood Boulevard ★★★ 18

Comedy   1976 · US · Colour · 78mins

Roger Corman agreed to finance this parody of his own cash-strapped movie-making style, provided Allan Arkush and Joe Dante could complete it for less than $90,000. Ten days later (and $10,000 under budget), they submitted this patchy but often hilarious pastiche, in which New World (Corman's production company) becomes Miracle Pictures and Corman classics like *Death Race 2000* are given a whole new lease of life. Candice Rialson proves a good sport , while veterans like Paul Bartel sieze the opportunity to send up the Corman canon. An inferior sequel followed in 1989. ▢

Candice Rialson *Candy Wednesday* • Mary Woronov *Mary McQueen* • Rita George *Bobbi Quackenbush* • Jeffery Kramer *Patrick Hobby* • Dick Miller *Walter Paisley* • Richard Doran *Producer* • Paul Bartel *Erich Von Leppe* ■ *Dir* Joe Dante, Allan Arkush • *Scr* Patrick Hobby

Hollywood Canteen ★★★ U

Musical comedy   1944 · US · BW · 125mins

This Warner Bros contribution to the war effort was the studio's top-grossing hit of 1944, thanks to the cornucopia of stars who strut their stuff or play themselves. The line-up, to mention a mere few, includes the Andrews Sisters, Jack Benny, Joan Crawford, Bette Davis, Peter Lorre, Roy Rogers and Trigger, Barbara Stanwyck and Jimmy Dorsey and his Band. The plot? Soldiers Robert Hutton and Dane Clark spend their unforgettable leave at the Hollywood Canteen. Written and directed by Delmer Daves, it's a feeble excuse for a fascinating entertainment

Robert Hutton *Slim* • Dane Clark *Sergeant* • Janis Paige *Angela* • Jonathan Hale *Mr Brodel* • Barbara Brown *Mrs Brodel* • Bette Davis • John Garfield • Joan Leslie • Jack Benny • Joan Crawford • Sydney Greenstreet • Peter Lorre • Barbara Stanwyck • Jane Wyman • Roy Rogers ■ *Dir/Scr* Delmer Daves

Hollywood Cavalcade ★★★ U

Drama   1939 · US · Colour · 88mins

Amiable and colourful slice of early Hollywood life, loosely based on the Mack and Mabel story (Mack Sennett, pioneer director, and Mabel Normand, early comedy superstar), pairing 20th Century-Fox's blonde Alice Faye and cheery Don Ameche, both coiffed and frocked totally, and shamefully, out of period. Still, the re-creations of silent movie days are fun, and the great Buster Keaton appears, as indeed does the real Mack Sennett (who also supervised the direction of the silent sequences). Al Jolson himself reprises his ground-breaking role from *The Jazz Singer*, so there's a fair amount of pleasure to be had.

Alice Faye *Molly Adair* • Don Ameche *Michael Linnett Connors* • J Edward Bromberg *Dave Spingold* • Alan Curtis *Nicky Hayden* • Stuart Erwin *Pete Tinney* • Jed Prouty *Chief of Police* ■ *Dir* Irving Cummings • *Scr* Irving Pascal, from a story by Hilary Lynn, Brown Holmes, from an idea by Lou Breslow

Hollywood Confidential ★★ 15

Crime drama   1997 · US · Colour · 88mins

A moderately enjoyable, tongue-in-cheek suspense yarn in which Edward James Olmos leads an ad hoc group of ex-FBI, CIA and other acronymical folk who bring the corrupt, the crooked and the lewd to book. In this case they go to Hollywood and assist a spoilt hotshot movie director with girl trouble. There are elements of *The A-Team* grafted onto *The Saint*, with amusing performances from the boys, plus the glamorous Charlize Theron. Contains some violence, swearing and sexual references. ▭

Edward James Olmos *Stan Navarro* • Rick Aiello *Joey di Rosa* • Anthony Yerkovich *Jack Hansen* • Richard T Jones *Dexter* • Brendan Kelly *Mike Mooney* • Charlize Theron *Sally* • Angela Alvarado *Teresa* ■ *Dir* Reynaldo Villalobos • *Scr* Anthony Yerkovich

The Hollywood Detective
★★ PG

Crime drama   1989 · US · Colour · 83mins

Telly Savalas will always be associated with the role of Theo Kojak, yet here he bites the hand that fed him lollipops in a so-so spoof of the kind of TV series that gave him cult status. Savalas plays an unemployed TV detective who finds himself in trouble when he investigates a real crime. The script fires too many blanks, but Savalas gives it his best shot. ▭

Telly Savalas *Harry Bell* • Helene Udy *Lois Wednesday* • Greg Mullavey *Mike Maglin* • Joe Dallesandro *Jerry Brazil* • Tom Reese *Lieutenant Vic Grabowski* • James Green *Eddie Northcott* • George Coe *Syd Kurl* • Herman Poppe *Marvin Morris* ■ *Dir* Kevin Connor • *Scr* Christopher Crowe

Hollywood Harry ★★

Crime   1985 · US · Colour · 96mins

The first (and so far) only film from cult favourite Robert Forster, whose career was revitalised by *Pulp Fiction*. A warm salute to the classic gumshoe movies of the past, Forster also stars as the private eye of the title, hired to find a rich man's daughter who has disappeared into the seamier side of Hollywood. Forster's real-life daughter Kate pops up in a supporting role.

Robert Forster *Harry* • Kate Forster *Danielle* • Joe Spinell *Max* • Shannon Wilcox *Candy* • Pete Shrum *Clapper* • Redmond Gleeson *Skeeter* • Read Morgan *Farmer* ■ *Dir* Robert Forster • *Scr* Curt Allen

Hollywood High ★

Comedy   1976 · US · Colour · 81mins

A forerunner to the teenage sex comedies of the eighties, this still somehow manages to be even worse than what was to follow. Forget about the plot: the movie is basically a collection of vignettes concerning four loose-living teenage girls going from place to place and having (or trying) to have sex with their boyfriends. The only attempt at creating a character comes with a parody of Fonzie (called the Fenz) from *Happy Days*, though he does nothing but blurt out lines like "Fenzi needs another beer!"

Marcy Albrecht *Bebe* • Sherry Hardin *Candy* • Rae Sperling *Monica* • Kevin Mead *The Fenz* • John Young *Mike* ■ *Dir* Patrick Wright

Hollywood Hot Tubs ★★ 15

Sex comedy   1984 · US · Colour · 98mins

Not the worst of the teen sex comedies so popular in the eighties, but don't take that as a recommendation. A sort of California version of *Adventures of a Plumber's Mate*, this tracks the adventures of a young teenager who gets an adolescent's dream job: fixing jacuzzis at the homes of rich Hollywood women. It's directed by prolific sex comedy maker Chuck Vincent. A sequel followed six years later. ▭

Donna McDaniel *Leslie Maynard* • Michael Andrew *Jeff* • Paul Gunning *Eddie* • Katt Shea [Katt Shea Ruben] *Dee Dee* • Edy Williams *Desire* • Jewel Shepard *Crystal* ■ *Dir* Chuck Vincent • *Scr* Mark Borde, Craig McDonnell

Hollywood Hotel ★★

Musical   1937 · US · BW · 100mins

Warner Bros musicals by 1937 had lost the big budgets and the vitality of such hits as *42nd Street* and *Dames*, even though Busby Berkeley was still directing and Dick Powell was still performing in them. This feeble story has Powell as a musician seeking success in Hollywood. Fortunately, it is rescued from complete mediocrity by the appearances of Benny Goodman and his orchestra and by the fine Johnny Mercer–Richard Whiting songs *Hooray for Hollywood* and *Silhouetted in the Moonlight*.

Dick Powell *Ronnie Bowers* • Rosemary Lane *Virginia* • Lola Lane *Mona Marshall* • Hugh Herbert *Chester Marshall* • Ted Healy *Fuzzy* • Glenda Farrell *Jonesy* • Johnnie Davis *Georgia* • Benny Goodman • Susan Hayward *Starlet at table* • Ronald Reagan *Radio announcer* • Carole Landis *Hat check girl* ■ *Dir* Busby Berkeley • *Scr* Jerry Wald, Maurice Leo, Richard Macauley

Hollywood Madam ★★ 18

Erotic thriller   1994 · US · Colour · 80mins

If Shannon Tweed is the queen of the erotic thriller, Shannon Whirry is her heir apparent. Here, Whirry plays a *femme fatale* who lures detective Michael Nouri into a web of sexual intrigue and murder involving high-class call girls and his own ex-wife. Director Fred Gallo gives it a glossy surface sheen but the plotting and execution is strictly routine. Contains violence, swearing, sex scenes and nudity ▭

Michael Nouri *Jimmy Scavetti* • Robert Costanzo *Charley* • Shannon Whirry *Lori* • Crystal Chappell *Elizabeth Henly* • Karen Kopins *Fiona* • Charles Grant *Scott Henly* ■ *Dir* Fred Gallo • *Scr* Dennis Manuel

Hollywood or Bust ★★★★ U

Comedy   1956 · US · Colour · 94mins

The 17th and last film teaming Dean Martin and Jerry Lewis shows no visible signs of the rapidly approaching on-set cracks in the relationship. Brilliant comic director Frank Tashlin indulges the duo and himself in a frantically stylised, often surreal, trek across the USA, ending in the movie capital of the title. This is a remarkably lavish and well-designed comedy, but the real highlight comes before the titles, as Lewis pays heartfelt tribute to movie fans around the world. Hard to believe, but this jape started life as a road movie for Humphrey Bogart and Shirley Booth called *Route 66*.

Dean Martin *Steve Wiley* • Jerry Lewis *Malcolm Smith* • Anita Ekberg • Pat Crowley *Terry Roberts* • Maxie Rosenbloom *"Bookie" Benny* ■ *Dir* Frank Tashlin • *Scr* Erna Lazarus, from her story *Beginner's Luck*

Hollywood Party ★★★ U

Musical comedy
1934 · US · BW and Colour · 65mins

Among the most gloriously miscalculated follies of the early sound era, this MGM extravaganza was originally intended to showcase the cream of the studio's star roster. Instead, it ended up being a manic montage of cockeyed comic cuts spinning off from fading movie icon Jimmy Durante's attempt to persuade Jack Pearl to sell him some lions for

his next picture. Introduced by special guest Mickey Mouse, a Technicolor musical segment, *The Hot Chocolate Soldiers*, impressed contemporary audiences, but the hilarious tit-for-tat egg smashing sequence, featuring Lupe Velez and Laurel and Hardy, is the biggest highlight today. ▭

Stan Laurel *Stan* • Oliver Hardy *Ollie* • Jimmy Durante *Schnarzan the Shouting Conqueror* • Mrs Jean Durante • Lupe Velez *Lupe Velez/ Jaguar Woman* • Ted Healy • Moe Howard *Moe* • Curly Howard *Curly* • Larry Fine *Larry* ■ *Dir* Richard Boleslawski, Allan Dwan, Roy Rowland • *Scr* Howard Dietz, Arthur Kober

Hollywood Revue ★★★★

Musical   1929 · US · BW · 114mins

Despite some now dated and rather tedious sequences, this Oscar-nominated movie is a historical document and a "must see" for anyone with a taste for early Hollywood, musicals, MGM stars and variety programmes. It was one of the first plotless revues to showcase a studio's stars, and Paramount, Fox and Warners soon followed suit. Lavishly staged under Charles Reisner's direction, the line-up of luminaries includes Lionel Barrymore, Joan Crawford, Buster Keaton, Laurel and Hardy, Bessie Love and Jack Benny. The range of acts embraces everything from Shakespeare (John Gilbert and Norma Shearer in a scene from *Romeo and Juliet*) to a variety of musical numbers of which the highlight is a spectacular treatment of "Singin' in the Rain", unveiled here 23 years before Gene Kelly performed it.

John Gilbert • Norma Shearer • Joan Crawford • Bessie Love • Marion Davies • Lionel Barrymore • Ann Dvorak *Chorus girl* • Gus Edwards • Oliver Hardy • Jack Benny *Emcee* • Conrad Nagel *Emcee* ■ *Dir* Charles Reisner • *Scr* Al Boasberg, Robert E Hopkins

Hollywood Shuffle ★★★★ 15

Satire   1987 · US · Colour · 77mins

Shot for just $100,000, this spot-on satire slams Uncle Tom, Rochester and Superfly types alike as it swipes at the way in which Hollywood has (and continues to) miscast and misuse its African-American talent. Forgive it for falling flat occasionally, because hilarious scenes like the "act black" training school, the "boyz from the 'hood" review show and the great roles "done black" dream sequence all more than compensate with their razor-sharp wit and insight. The man to thank for this gem is co-writer/director Robert Townsend, who also shines as a struggling actor forced to choose between a part and his principles. Contains swearing. ▭

Robert Townsend *Bobby Taylor* • Anne-Marie Johnson *Lydia* • Starletta DuPois *Bobby's mother* • Helen Martin *Bobby's grandmother* • Craigus R Johnson *Stevie Taylor* • Ludie Washington *Tiny* • Keenen Ivory Wayans *Donald* ■ *Dir* Robert Townsend • *Scr* Keenen Ivory Wayans, Robert Townsend

Hollywood Vice Squad ★★ 18

Action comedy   1986 · US · Colour · 96mins

When Robin Wright runs away from home and into Hollywood's porn industry and prostitution racket, her mother (Trish Van Devere) solicits the help of police captain Ronny Cox. This plot may be recognised as Paul Schrader's *Hardcore* which starred George C Scott who happened – in that thing called real life – to be Van Devere's husband. Pitched as a spoof, Penelope Spheeris's film has several additional casting in-jokes, notably Cox who basically repeats his role from the *Beverly Hills Cop* films. Carrie Fisher has fun with her role as a sort of "Dirty Harry in a dress" while John Travolta's brother Joey also makes a brief appearance. ▣

Ronny Cox *Captain Jensen* • Frank Gorshin *Walsh* • Leon Isaac Kennedy *Hawkins* • Trish Van Devere *Pauline Stanton* • Carrie Fisher *Betty Melton* • Ben Frank *Daley* • Evan Kim *Chang* • Robin Wright [Robin Wright Penn] *Lori Stanton* • Joey Travolta *Stevens* ■ Dir Penelope Spheeris • Scr James J Docherty

Holocaust 2000 ★★★

Science-fiction horror
1977 · It/UK · Colour · 101mins

The coming of the Antichrist is the theme of Alberto De Martino's spaghetti horror film, in which Kirk Douglas flexes his sense of morality and does battle with the Devil. Meanwhile his cherub-faced son Simon Ward is committing obnoxious acts that are anything but angelic. Derivative of such supernatural successes as *The Omen*, its special effects only spark distaste, but its acts of Revelation bring on the goosebumps.

Kirk Douglas *Robert Caine* • Agostina Belli *Sara Golan* • Simon Ward *Angel Caine* • Anthony Quayle *Professor Griffith* • Virginia McKenna *Eva Caine* • Alexander Knox *Meyer* ■ Dir Alberto De Martino • Scr Sergio Donati, Alberto De Martino, Michael Robson, from a story by Sergio Donati, Alberto De Martino

Holy Man ★★ PG

Comedy drama 1998 · US · Colour · 109mins

A satire on consumerism that comes across as sell-out rather than thought-provoking, with Eddie Murphy as a cross-legged guru who's discovered by a desperate TV shopping channel. His innocent philosophical musings are not only a bonus for ailing ratings but also teach materialistic Jeff Goldblum and Kelly Preston the value of love. However, after nearly two hours, Murphy's cheeky chappie persona starts to get wearisome. Contains some swearing ▣ *DVD*

Eddie Murphy *"G"* • Jeff Goldblum *Ricky Hayman* • Kelly Preston *Kate Newell* • Robert Loggia *John McBainbridge* • Jon Cryer *Barry* • Eric McCormack *Scott Hawkes* • Morgan Fairchild • James Brown (1) *James Brown* ■ Dir Stephen Herek • Scr Tom Schulman

Holy Matrimony ★★★★ U

Comedy 1943 · US · BW · 85mins

In this superior adaptation of the Arnold Bennett novel, Monty Woolley excels as the gruff English painter who passes himself off as his dead butler to escape the unwanted attentions of the art world. He is ably supported by Gracie Fields, in her full Hollywood debut, as the no-nonsense wife who stands by him when the truth emerges. Weepie specialist John M Stahl simply has to point the camera, as much as

his work has been done for him in Nunnally Johnson's literate and smoothly developed script.

Monty Woolley *Priam Farll* • Gracie Fields *Alice Challice* • Laird Cregar *Clive Oxford* • Una O'Connor *Mrs Leek* • Alan Mowbray *Mr Pennington* • Melville Cooper *Dr Caswell* ■ Dir John M Stahl • Scr Nunnally Johnson, from the novel *Buried Alive* by Arnold Bennett

Holy Matrimony ★ PG

Comedy 1994 · US · Colour · 89mins

A dire comedy from former *Star Trek* star Leonard Nimoy, which suffers from a clutch of one-note performances and unlikeable characters. After Havana (Patricia Arquette) and Peter (Tate Donovan) rob a county fair, they hide out in the Hutterite (like the Amish, only more conservative!) community where Peter grew up. However, when Peter dies, Hutterite tradition means that Havana has to marry his younger brother – even though he (*Third Rock from the Sun*'s Joseph Gordon-Levitt) is just 12 years old. A whole host of talents are out of their depth, with only Gordon-Levitt escaping the project relatively unscathed. ▣

Patricia Arquette *Havana* • Joseph Gordon-Levitt *Zeke* • Armin Mueller-Stahl *Uncle Wilhelm* • Tate Donovan *Peter* • John Schuck *Markowski* • Lois Smith *Orna* • Courtney B Vance *Cooper* ■ Dir Leonard Nimoy • Scr David Weisberg, Douglas S Cook

Holy Smoke ★★★ 18

Drama 1999 · US · Colour · 114mins

After the class-crossing passion of *Titanic* and her emergence as a star, Kate Winslet lets her hair down (and a lot more besides) in this lampoon on Australian bigotry from Jane Campion (*The Piano*). Winslet plays Ruth, the daughter of a white trash family from Sydney who becomes a disciple of an Indian guru. Fearful of his influence over her, Ruth's family hires an American "exit counsellor" and cult buster (Harvey Keitel), who takes her to the outback and tries to break her spirit. Both funny and dramatic, this *Smoke* really does get in your eyes.

Kate Winslet *Ruth Barron* • Harvey Keitel *PJ Waters* • Julie Hamilton *Miriam* • Tim Robertson *Gilbert* • Sophie Lee *Yvonne* • Dan Wyllie *Robbie* • Pam Grier *Carol* ■ Dir Jane Campion • Scr Jane Campion, from the autobiographical work *My Guru and His Disciple* by Christopher Isherwood

Homage ★★★

Psychological thriller
1995 · US · Colour · 97mins

There's nothing like a slice of deep-fried Deep South melodrama, and, while it never really succeeds in throwing off its stage origins, this still makes for entertainingly overheated viewing. Blythe Danner is the faded southern belle locked in a strange relationship with handyman Frank Whaley, until her actress daughter Sheryl Lee arrives to turn up the sexual tension another few degrees. The three stars are superb, and Mark Medoff, best known for *Children of a Lesser God*, does his best to open up his own play. Contains violence, sex scenes and swearing.

Blythe Danner *Katherine Samuel* • Frank Whaley *Archie Landrum* • Sheryl Lee *Lucy*

Samuel • Bruce Davison *Joseph Smith* • Danny Nucci *Gilbert Tellez* ■ Dir Ross Kagan Marks • Scr Mark Medoff, from his play *The Homage That Follows*

Hombre ★★★★ PG

Western 1967 · US · Colour · 106mins

Paul Newman has said that his best movies all start with an "H", and this fine, grim western bears him out. This is a *Stagecoach* variation, assembling differing characters for a trek through Arizona, played by a very distinguished cast including veteran Fredric March and a gnarled Richard Boone. Only import Diane Cilento (Sean Connery's ex-wife) seems ill-at-ease in a pivotal role. The movie is beautifully shot by veteran photographer James Wong Howe, and Newman's piercing blue eyes have seldom been more prominently featured. The plot has many valid points to make about incipient racism, and the film is deeply rewarding. Contains swearing. ▣

Paul Newman *John Russell* • Fredric March *Favor* • Richard Boone *Grimes* • Diane Cilento *Jessie* • Cameron Mitchell *Braden* • Barbara Rush *Adra Favor* • Martin Balsam *Mendez* ■ Dir Martin Ritt • Scr Irving Ravetch, Harriet Frank Jr, from the novel by Elmore Leonard

Hombre Mirando al Sudeste ★★★

Drama 1986 · Arg · Colour · 105mins

With the notable exception of Leopoldo Torre-Nilsson in the sixties and, more recently, Luis Puenzo, Argentinian cinema has produced surprisingly few directors of world renown. With this, his third film, Eliseo Subiela enjoyed box-office success in the Americas, although it was little seen in Europe. Also known as *Man Looking Southeast*, it's a mystical political parable in which opposition to the state is equated with insanity, but it shifts from satire to sinister comment with some ease. There are fine performances from Hugo Soto as a Christ-like patient who claims to come from outer space and Lorenzo Quinteros as the doctor seeking to certify him. In Spanish with English subtitles. Contains nudity.

Lorenzo Quinteros *Dr Dennis* • Hugo Soto *Rantes* • Ines Vernengo *Beatriz* • Cristina Scaramuzza *Nurse* • Rubens W Correa *Dr Prieto* ■ Dir/Scr Eliseo Subiela

Home Alone ★★★★ PG

Comedy 1990 · US · Colour · 98mins

A modest Christmas comedy that became one of the highest grossing pictures of all time. Writer/producer John Hughes and director Chris Columbus tuned in to two key elements: the fantasy of Steven Spielberg's *ET*, its children triumphing over adult adversity, and the perennial chase of Tom and Jerry cartoons. Thus Macaulay Culkin, then ten years old and already in his fifth picture, is the youngster left stranded by his parents who fly to Paris for the holiday. He pigs out on junk food, watches videos and then copes heroically with two burglars (Joe Pesci and Daniel Stern), crying "Yes!" when he zaps them. Surprisingly violent in a cartoon-like way, it's a celebration of

enterprise that captured the heart of every child on the planet. ▣

Macaulay Culkin *Kevin McAllister* • Joe Pesci *Harry* • Daniel Stern *Marv* • John Heard *Peter* • Roberts Blossom *Marley* • Catherine O'Hara *Kate* • John Candy *Gus Polinski* ■ Dir Chris Columbus • Scr John Hughes

Home Alone 2: Lost in New York ★★★ PG

Comedy 1992 · US · Colour · 115mins

Yep, Kevin McCallister (Macaulay Culkin) has managed to ditch his family again, this time getting on the wrong plane and ending up alone in New York while they are heading for Florida. And, armed with Dad's wallet, he enjoys all of life's luxuries at the Plaza hotel until he runs into those two inept burglars Harry and Marvin (Joe Pesci and Daniel Stern) once again. Unfortunately, what worked in the first film is not quite as entertaining here. Still, as slapstick escapism goes, this is well engineered stuff. ▣

Macaulay Culkin *Kevin McCallister* • Joe Pesci *Harry Lyme* • Daniel Stern *Marvin Murchins* • Catherine O'Hara *Kate McCallister* • John Heard *Peter McCallister* • Devin Ratray *Buzz* • Hillary Wolf *Megan* • Maureen Elisabeth Shay *Linnie* ■ Dir Chris Columbus • Scr John Hughes, from his characters

Home Alone 3 ★★★ PG

Comedy 1997 · US · Colour · 98mins

This time it's cute little Alex D Linz whose befuddled parents have mistakenly left him on his own in the house, when an international espionage team come calling to steal back a top secret computer chip hidden in his new toy. Pity the hapless baddies as the plucky boy devises ingenious booby traps and performs engaging heroics to foil them. Writer John Hughes's third neatly-plotted variation on the same theme is good knockabout fun, with Linz a winning replacement for Macaulay Culkin, some genuine laughs, and not too much saccharine or Tom-and-Jerry brutality. Contains slapstick violence and some mild swearing.

Alex D Linz *Alex Pruitt* • Olek Krupa *Beaupre* • Rya Kihlstedt *Alice* • Lenny Von Dohlen *Jernigan* • David Thornton *Unger* • Haviland Morris *Karen Pruitt* • Kevin Kilner *Jack Pruitt* ■ Dir Raja Gosnell • Scr John Hughes

Home and Away ★ U

Comedy 1956 · UK · BW · 92mins

No, not a feature-length version of the Australian soap, but a non-Huggett reunion for Jack Warner and Kathleen Harrison. Written and directed by Vernon Sewell, this contrived tale of a widow trying to cheat a fortune out of the pools is meant to be whimsical and slightly wicked. However, it ends up merely frantic and unfunny, with the Warner-Harrison partnership having one of its few off days. The supporting cast is surprisingly strong, but the film still founders – a shame, as it proved to be Leslie Henson's final picture. ▣

Jack Warner *George Knowles* • Kathleen Harrison *Elsie Harrison* • Lana Morris *Mary Knowles* • Charles Victor *Ted Groves* • Thora Hird *Margie Groves* • Leslie Henson *Uncle Tom* ■ Dir Vernon Sewell • Scr Vernon Sewell, RF Delderfield, from the play *Treble Trouble* by Heather McIntyre

The Home and the World
★★★★ U

Historical drama
1984 · Ind · Colour · 139mins

Throughout his career, Indian director Satyajit Ray turned to the works of his mentor, Rabindranath Tagore, for inspiration. Victor Banerjee loses his wife (Swatilekha Chatterjee) after he breaks with the tradition of seclusion and introduces her to a dashing patriot (Soumitra Chatterjee) in this compelling conversation piece, based on Tagore's novel, exploring the dangers inherent in both repression and liberation. One of the few true auteurs of world cinema, Ray also wrote the script and composed the score. However, while the leads give immaculate performances and the director never used colour better, the film is not quite a masterwork. In Bengali with English subtitles.

Soumitra Chatterjee *Sandip Mukherjee* • Victor Banerjee *Nikhilesh Choudhury* • Swatilekha Chatterjee *Bimala Choudhury* • Gopa Aich *Sister-in-law* • Jennifer Kapoor *Miss Gilby* ■ Dir Satyajit Ray • Scr Satyajit Ray, from a novel by Rabindranath Tagore

Home at Seven
★★★ U

Mystery
1952 · UK · BW · 81mins

Adapted from RC Sherriff's West End hit, this was Ralph Richardson's sole venture as a film director, and a pretty fair job he makes of it, too. He also re-creates his stage role as the timid bank clerk whose dose of amnesia coincides with a murder and a robbery. The strength of the picture is that you're never quite sure whether he's bluffing or baffled, and the secret is tightly kept right to the end. It's more than a mite stagey, though, with wife Margaret Leighton and doctor Jack Hawkins particularly guilty of overseasoning the ham. ▭

Ralph Richardson *David Preston* • Margaret Leighton *Janet Preston* • Jack Hawkins *Dr Sparling* • Frederick Piper *Mr Petherbridge* • Diana Beaumont *Ellen* • Meriel Forbes *Peggy Dobson* • Michael Shepley *Major Watson* • Margaret Withers *Mrs Watson* ■ Dir Ralph Richardson • Scr Anatole de Grunwald, from the play by RC Sherriff

Home before Dark
★★

Drama
1958 · US · BW · 136mins

Only Jean Simmons's most ardent fans will obtain any great pleasure from this long-winded and bleak psychological drama. As the wife recovering from a mental breakdown, she returns to her unloving college professor husband (Dan O'Herlihy), a stepsister (Rhonda Fleming) in whom her husband is more interested and a domineering stepmother (Mabel Albertson). However, a handsome, sympathetic colleague (Efrem Zimbalist Jr) of her husband helps in her readjustment. Reminiscent of those thrillers in which leading ladies were nearly driven insane for their wealth, this Mervyn LeRoy production tries to be more subtle but ends up merely dull.

Jean Simmons *Charlotte Bronn* • Dan O'Herlihy *Arnold Bronn* • Rhonda Fleming *Joan Carlisle* • Efrem Zimbalist Jr *Jake Diamond* • Mabel Albertson *Inez Winthrop* • Steve Dunne *Hamilton Gregory* • Joan Weldon *Frances*

Barrett ■ Dir Mervyn LeRoy • Scr Robert Bassing, Eileen Bassing, from the novel *Home before Dark* by Eileen Bassing

Home Fires Burning
★★★

Drama
1989 · US · Colour · 93mins

Robert Inman, casting an affectionate glance back towards the golden age of Frank Capra, has no trouble translating the spirit of his novel into a screenplay for director Glenn Jordan. Expertly capturing the detail of American small-town manners and mores, Inman allows the spirit of a country rattled by the Second World War to seep through the personal drama. Barnard Hughes (*The Lost Boys*) is well cast as the Georgia editor who spits opinions with great relish, only to find his confidence eroded by imminent change.

Barnard Hughes *Jake Tibbetts* • Sada Thompson *Pastine Tibbetts* • Robert J Prosky [Robert Prosky] *Rosh Benefield* • Bill Pullman *Henry Tibbetts* • Elizabeth Berridge *Francine Tibbetts* • Neil Patrick Harris *Lonnie Tibbetts* ■ Dir Glenn Jordan • Scr Robert Inman, from his novel

Home for Christmas
★★ U

Comedy drama
1990 · US · Colour · 96mins

As far as Hollywood is concerned, this is the season to be tacky and few films have packed in as many overripe ingredients as this gooey confection. That game old trouper Mickey Rooney stars as the petty crook whose bungled car theft leads to the most magical Christmas of his life. This blend of whimsy and wish fulfilment was old hat when Rooney was a child star, but at least then there were directors capable of turning this kind of mawkish melodrama into wholesome family entertainment. Sadly, Peter McCubbin is not that good, but the end result is still quite quaint. ▭

Mickey Rooney *Elmer* • Chantellese Kent *Amanda* • Simon Richards *Reg* ■ Dir Peter McCubbin • Scr Peter Ferri, Peter McCubbin

Home for the Holidays
★★★ 15

Comedy drama
1995 · US · Colour · 98mins

Jodie Foster follows up her quirky directorial debut (*Little Man Tate*) with this uneven comedy drama about a group of grown-up kids returning to the family home for a Thanksgiving that, of course, is filled with romance, rows, misunderstandings and strange behaviour. Despite the occasional awkward switches between comedy and sentiment, this works most of the time thanks to the impressive cast (which includes Holly Hunter, Robert Downey Jr, Anne Bancroft, Charles Durning and Claire Danes as Hunter's daughter). One of those films which makes you thankful that your own family is relatively normal. Contains some swearing. ▭

Holly Hunter *Claudia Larson* • Robert Downey Jr *Tommy Larson* • Anne Bancroft *Adele Larson* • Charles Durning *Henry Larson* • Dylan McDermott *Leo Fish* • Geraldine Chaplin *Aunt Glady* • Steve Guttenberg *Walter Wedman* • Claire Danes *Kitt* ■ Dir Jodie Foster • Scr WD Richter, from a short story by Chris Radant

Home Free All
★★

Comedy drama
1983 · US · Colour · 92mins

Stewart Bird's one and only feature is a depressing and incoherent mess about two childhood friends in New York City who meet again as adults and try to make sense out of their unproductive and neurotic lives. Predictably, they just end up making things worse as an ill-fated affair only creates more confusion. The action is punctuated with ethnic jokes that, were they really required in the film, should at least have been wittier.

Allan Nicholls *Barry Simon* • Roland Caccavo *Al* • Maura Ellyn *Cathy* • Shelley Wyant *Rita* • Lucille Rivin *Lynn* • Lorry Goldman *Marvin* • Janet Burnham *Chastity* • JoséRamon Rosario *Custodian* • Chazz Palminteri *Hijacker* ■ Dir/Scr Stewart Bird

Home Fries
★ 12

Drama
1998 · US · Colour · 89mins

Drew Barrymore in a romantic comedy should be a sure bet, but this mix of romance, ill-conceived black humour and very little comedy must be the only blot on her post-child star CV. While her burgeoning romance with Luke Wilson (she's a pregnant waitress, he's her Lamaze partner) works quite nicely, it's mixed in with an odd subplot (he and his brother scared their stepdad to death – literally) that doesn't work at all. Barrymore does her best, but there's little humour or romance to work with, and even fans of the former *ET* star will be left with a bad taste in their mouths. Contains some mild swearing, sexual references and violence. ▭

Drew Barrymore *Sally* • Jake Busey *Angus* • Catherine O'Hara *Mrs Lever* • Shelley Duvall *Mrs Jackson* • Luke Wilson *Dorian* • Kim Robillard *Billy* ■ Dir Dean Parisot • Scr Vince Gilligan

Home from the Hill
★★★

Drama
1960 · US · Colour · 149mins

A splendid MGM melodrama, lengthy but nevertheless totally engrossing. Robert Mitchum delivers one of his finest performances as the Texas patriarch whose sons turn his domestic life inside out. In its day this movie was notable for the star-making performances of two Georges (Peppard and Hamilton) as Mitch's offspring, one legitimate, the other not. This is from the same period in flamboyant director Vincente Minnelli's career as *Some Came Running*, and shares with it a loving use of CinemaScope and an intense use of colour. Sit back with a box of chocolates and enjoy.

Robert Mitchum *Captain Wade Hunnicutt* • Eleanor Parker *Hannah Hunnicutt* • George Peppard *Rafe Copley* • George Hamilton *Theron Hunnicutt* • Everett Sloane *Albert Halstead* • Luana Patten *Libby Halstead* ■ Dir Vincente Minnelli • Scr Irving Ravetch, Harriet Frank Jr, from the novel by William Humphrey

Home Front
★ PG

Comedy
1987 · US · Colour · 88mins

Released in the United States as *Morgan Stewart's Coming Home*, this is yet another entry on the CV of Alan Smithee, the "person" who carries the can when the disgruntled director actually made the film removes his or

her name from the credits. And you have to admit that removing their names was a wise move here on the part of co-directors Terry Winsor and Paul Aaron, for this teenage comedy is excruciatingly awful. A second star could be awarded for the gallantry of Lynn Redgrave and Jon Cryer, who try to haul the crude story out of the gutter. Contains swearing. ▭

Jon Cryer *Morgan Stewart* • Lynn Redgrave *Nancy Stewart* • Nicholas Pryor *Senator Tom Stewart* • Viveka Davis *Emily* • Paul Gleason *Jay Springsteen* • Andrew Duncan *General Fenton* ■ Dir Alan Smithee [Terry Winsor], Alan Smithee [Paul Aaron] • Scr Ken Hixon, David Titcher

Home in Indiana
★★★ U

Drama
1944 · US · Colour · 103mins

A beguiling 20th Century-Fox horse-racing melodrama, beautifully shot by Edward Cronjager in glorious Technicolor. An unusually top-billed Walter Brennan, who had won an Oscar for a similar movie, Fox's *Kentucky*, seems to enjoy himself watching over two relative newcomers, Jeanne Crain and June Haver. Lon McCallister, who plays Brennan's young orphaned nephew, swiftly established himself as a star in this movie, but his film career only lasted another nine years. Director Henry Hathaway handles the climactic trotting race superbly, and, if it all seems familiar, Fox remade it in 1957 as the Pat Boone vehicle *April Love*.

Walter Brennan *JP "Thunder" Bolt* • Lon McCallister *Sparke Thorton* • Jeanne Crain *Char* • June Haver *Cri-Cri* • Charlotte Greenwood *Penny* • Ward Bond *Jed Bruce* • Charles Dingle *Godaw Boole* • Robert Condon *Gordon Bradley* ■ Dir Henry Hathaway • Scr Winston Miller, from the novel *The Phantom Filly* by George Agnew Chamberlain

Home Is Where the Hart Is
★

Comedy
1987 · US/Can · Colour · 94mins

Following his success in the *Airplane!* movies, Leslie Nielsen turned from playing straight roles to almost exclusively appearing in comedies. Unfortunately some of his choices reflected rather dubious judgement, and this is one such project. The story concerns a centenarian, Slim Hart, and his conniving nurse, who has her eye on his inheritance. Slim's twin sons, who aren't exactly spring chickens themselves, try to thwart her plans. Funny man Martin Mull also appears but can't rescue this damp squib.

Valri Bromfield *Belle Haimes* • Stephen E Miller *Rex Haines* • Martin Mull *Carson Boundy* • Eric Christmas *Martin Hart* • Ted Stidder *Art Hart* • Deanne Henry *Selma Dodge* • Leslie Nielsen *Sheriff Nashville Schwartz* • Joe Austin *Slim "Pappy" Hart* ■ Dir/Scr Rex Bromfield • Music/Lyrics Long John Baldry

Home Movies
★★★ U

Comedy
1979 · US · Colour · 90mins

Brian DePalma was teaching at New York's Sarah Lawrence College when he conceived the idea for this bold but misfiring comedy about a film-making guru who encourages his students to live as the stars of their own movies. Relishing the role of "the Maestro", Kirk Douglas turns in a devilish

performance, made all the more effective by DePalma's neat tactic of shooting many of his scenes in the style of a self-aggrandising film diary. But the picture belongs to Keith Gordon as a nerd goaded into seizing editorial control of his sad existence by poaching his brother's fiancée.

Kirk Douglas *Dr Tuttle, "the Maestro"* • Nancy Allen *Kristina* • Keith Gordon *Denis* • Gerrit Graham *James* • Vincent Gardenia *Dr Byrd* ■ *Dir* Brian De Palma • *Scr* Robert Harders, Gloria Norris, Kim Ambler, Dana Edelman, Stephan LeMay, Charles Loventhal, from a story by Brian DePalma

A Home of Our Own ★★★ PG

Drama   1993 · US · Colour · 100mins

Oscar-winner Kathy Bates (*Misery*) gives another sterling performance, this time as a downtrodden mother determined to keep a roof over the heads of her children in this sixties-set drama. Discovering that her eldest son Edward Furlong has turned to petty crime, she decides to uproot her brood from LA and ends up in Idaho, determined to find a home for her family without taking charity. It's an often depressing tale, bolstered by warm performances from Bates and Furlong and understated direction from Tony Bill, but it ultimately gets bogged down in its own relentlessness. ▨

Kathy Bates *Frances Lacey* • Edward Furlong *Shayne Lacey* • Soon-Teck Oh *Mr Munimura* • Tony Campisi *Norman* • Amy Sakasitz *Annie Lacey* • Miles Feulner *Murray Lacey* • Clarissa Lassig *Lynn Lacey* • TJ Lowther *Craig Lacey* ■ *Dir* Tony Bill • *Scr* Patrick Duncan

Home of the Brave ★★★

Drama   1949 · US · BW · 86mins

Is one form of racial discrimination as bad as another? Since anti-Semitism had received a wide airing in recent movies, producer Stanley Kramer, director Mark Robson and writer Carl Foreman changed the theme of Arthur Laurents's Second World War play to attack prejudice against black people instead. In this low-budget drama, set on a South Pacific island held by the Japanese, James Edwards is excellent as the black soldier whose biggest enemy is a bigoted corporal (Steve Brodie). When his best friend is killed, Edwards's legs become paralysed, and it is up to Jeff Corey's army psychiatrist to find a solution.

Douglas Dick *Maj Robinson* • Steve Brodie *TJ* • Jeff Corey *Doctor* • Lloyd Bridges *Finch* • Frank Lovejoy *Mingo* • James Edwards *Moss* ■ *Dir* Mark Robson • *Scr* Carl Foreman, from the play by Arthur Laurents

Home of the Brave ★★ U

Experimental concert movie
1986 · US · Colour · 91mins

If you liked performance artist Laurie Andersen's 1981 Top Ten hit *O Superman*, you may find this multi-media concert film fascinating. If not, her unconventional warbling and post-hippy presentation will seem a pretentious bore. That said, Andersen's unorthodox music is mixed with a nice line in eccentric humour and accompanied by a well-staged array of colourful visuals, while cult

author William S Burroughs adds to the rarefied feel.

Dir/Scr Laurie Anderson

Home Page ★★★

Documentary   1998 · US · Colour · 99mins

Having impressed with *The Heck with Hollywood*, documentary maker Doug Block turned his attention to the internet with this portrait of young "web guru" Justin Hall, whose homepage diary not only evangelises the Net creed, but also reveals his most intimate thoughts and actions. Just about everyone Hall encounters in awe of his site status. But, having become hooked himself in the course of production, Block wisely avoids depicting these online obsessives as nerds in desperate need of a life, and presents their enthusiasm and eccentricities with the baffled respect their expertise merits.

Dir Doug Block • *Scr* Doug Block, Deborah Rosenberg

Home Remedy ★★

Comedy   1987 · US · Colour · 91mins

Richie Rosenbaum (Seth Barrish) is trying to embrace the joy of solitude, only to find his peace shattered by annoying neighbour, Nancy (Maxine Albert). What starts off as a prolonged argument soon grows into something far more dangerous. This was Maggie Greenwald's first feature film, made after her apprenticeship as assistant sound editor on such projects as John Hughes's *Weird Science*. New Yorker Greenwald was living in LA when she started writing the story, using this as her setting before realising that it was essentially an east coast tale. An oddball debut from an intriguing talent.

Seth Barrish *Richie Rosenbaum* • Maxine Albert *Nancy Smith* • Richard Kidney *PJ Smith* • David Feinman *Moshe* • John Tsakonas *Donnie* • Alexa *Mary* • Cynde Kahn *Bambi* ■ *Dir/Scr* Maggie Greenwald

Home, Sweet Home ★★★

Silent drama   1914 · US · BW · 62mins

Now here's a genuine rarity: a major but little-known feature film made by the great director DW Griffith between his better-known movies *Judith of Bethulia* and *The Birth of a Nation*. This was the film that consolidated Griffith's reputation and established the cinema as a mature art form and supreme entertainment experience. Slight by the standards of what was to come, this heavily sentimentalised biopic of composer John Howard Payne (writer of the song that gives the film its title) features a marvellous line-up of most of Griffith's favourite stars. Henry B Walthall is Payne and the luminous Lillian Gish his long-suffering sweetheart. It looks quaint today, but parts were risible even then, especially the hell-to-heaven "flying" finale. However, it still makes fascinating cinema, shot through with innovation and moments of superb playing.

Henry B Walthall *John Howard Payne* • Josephine Crowell *Mother* • Lillian Gish *Sweetheart* • Dorothy Gish *Sister* ■ *Dir* DW Griffith • *Scr* HE Aitken, DW Griffith, from the song by John Howard Payne

Home Sweet Home ★★

Musical comedy   1945 · UK · BW · 93mins

Both Nicolette Roeg and Tony Pendrell were making only their second big-screen appearances in this slight musical comedy, and their inexperience shows. Not that music-hall favourite Frank Randle was any more familiar with the camera, as this was his first venture away from the four *Somewhere in* comedies. However, his slack-jawed clowning provides the only real interest in this backstage Cinderella story, in which orphaned Roeg is forced to tread the boards after Pendrell's stuffy parents block their marriage.

Nicolette Roeg *Jacqueline Chantry* • Frank Randle *Frank* • Tony Pendrell *Eric Wright* • HF Maltby *Colonel Wright* • Hilda Bayley *Mrs Wright* • Cecil Fredericks *Webster* • Stan Little *Young Herbert* • Bunty Meadows *Bunty* ■ *Dir* John E Blakeley • *Scr* Roney Parsons, Anthony Toner, Frank Randle

Home to Danger ★★

Mystery   1951 · UK · BW · 67mins

A young woman (Rona Anderson) inherits an estate when her father commits suicide and is immediately attacked by a mysterious assailant. As the corpses mount up, so do the suspects in this standard whodunit, produced by B-movie specialist Lance Comfort and directed by Terence Fisher, who later hit his stride with his pioneering Hammer horrors. The cast is of some interest, too: Guy Rolfe, an imposing stage actor who looked best in chain mail or a toga; Alan Wheatley, who played the Sheriff of Nottingham in ITV's *Robin Hood* series; and Stanley Baker in an early role.

Guy Rolfe *Robert* • Rona Anderson *Barbara* • Francis Lister *Wainwright* • Alan Wheatley *Hughes* • Bruce Belfrage *Solicitor* • Stanley Baker *Willie Dougan* ■ *Dir* Terence Fisher • *Scr* John Temple-Smith, Francis Edge

Homeboy ★★ 15

Drama   1988 · US · Colour · 110mins

Touted as the new Brando, Mickey Rourke ended up making talent-wasting movies like this pet project about a boxer. Despite the presence of a scene-stealing Christopher Walken, it's Rourke's narcissism that dominates as he slouches into battle with an expressionless face and an intimidating faith in his ability to enthral. It was a mistaken faith, however, which is why we no longer hear from him these days, except when people ask "Whatever happened to Mickey Rourke?" ▨

Mickey Rourke *Johnny Walker* • Christopher Walken *Wesley Pendergrass* • Debra Feuer *Ruby* • Thomas Quinn *Lou* • Kevin Conway *Grazziano* • Antony Alda *Ray* • Jon Polito *Moe Fingers* ■ *Dir* Michael Seresin • *Scr* Eddie Cook, from a story by Mickey Rourke

Homeboys at the Beach ★★

Comedy drama   1998 · Fr · Colour · 90mins

Djamel Bensalah's feature debut bursts with energy and flirts with realism, but has little sense of restraint or quality control. Arriving in Biarritz having won a video competition, a mixed race quartet of Parisian suburbanites discover there's

more to life than gawping at babes. The trouble is, their abrasive attitude and a mix of snobbery and racism (both perceived and actual) prevents them from finding out what it is. The film offers little beneath its surface nihilism, although Jamel Debbouze impresses as the only lad to learn from his experiences. In French with English subtitles.

Jamel Debbouze *Youssef* • Julien Courbey *Mike* • Lorant Deutsch *Christophe* • Stéphane Soo Mongo *Stéphane* • Olivia Bonamy *Lydie* • Mariù Roversi *Christelle* • Julia Vaidis Bogard *Lea* ■ *Dir/Scr* Djamel Bensalah

Homeboyz ★★ 18

Action drama   1992 · US · Colour · 96mins

This trip through the crime-ridden barrios of Los Angeles is rough but carries more punch than other bigger-budgeted productions. The story gets few marks for originality – a policeman is riven by old loyalties to his family and friends – but it is enthusiastically acted by the unknown cast and assembled with some attention to detail by Lindsay Norgard. ▨

David Garrison *Murphy* • Todd Bridges *Johnny Davis* • Ron Odriozola *Emilio* • Keo Michaels *Hector* • Sigrid Salazar *Vanessa* ■ *Dir* Lindsay Norgard • *Scr* Peter Foldy

Homecoming ★★

Medical romance   1948 · US · BW · 112mins

MGM knew it would be enough to put Clark Gable together with Lana Turner for the crowds to flock in and didn't try very hard to make a worthwhile picture. Gable is the smug society doctor, married to Anne Baxter, who joins the medical corps, falls in love with Lana Turner's nurse while serving overseas and comes to dedicate himself to helping others. Anne Baxter gives the sharpest performance on view with John Hodiak (then her husband in real life) heading the rest of the cast. The glossy, long-winded direction by Mervyn LeRoy unfortunately has none of the liveliness of his work in the thirties.

Clark Gable *Ulysses Delby Johnson* • Lana Turner *Lt Jane "Snapshot" McCall* • Anne Baxter *Penny Johnson* • John Hodiak *Dr Robert Sunday* • Ray Collins *Lt Col Avery Silver* • Gladys Cooper *Mrs Kirby* • Cameron Mitchell *Monkevickz* • Art Baker *Williams* ■ *Dir* Mervyn LeRoy • *Scr* Paul Osborn, Jan Lustig, from the story *The Homecoming of Ulysses* by Sidney Kingsley

The Homecoming ★★★★

Drama   1973 · US/UK · Colour · 114mins

One of theatrical director Peter Hall's rare forays into film, this adaptation of Harold Pinter's play is more an account of a performance than a breakout from the restraint of the stage. But it's still white hot with bitterness, resentment and rancid randiness as north London butcher Paul Rogers makes mincemeat of his family (Cyril Cusack, Ian Holm, Michael Jayston, Terence Rigby) while Vivien Merchant flaunts her high-tease power to stunning effect. Pinter's dialogue has never been so enigmatic, menacing or comic.

Cyril Cusack *Sam* • Ian Holm *Lenny* • Michael Jayston *Teddy* • Vivien Merchant *Ruth* • Terence Rigby *Joey* • Paul Rogers *Max* ■ *Dir* Peter Hall • *Scr* Harold Pinter, from his play

Homecoming ★★★
Drama   1996 · US · Colour · 105mins

Distinguished actress Anne Bancroft won praise for her portrayal of a crotchety grandmother in this sentimental TV movie. When their mother abandons them in a strange city, teenager Kimberlee Peterson and her three younger siblings are forced to begin a long and difficult journey in search of a home. They embark on a 500-mile trek that ultimately leads them to the cantankerous grandmother they never knew. Up-and-coming star Peterson more than holds her own opposite the imposing Bancroft.

Anne Bancroft *Abigail "Ab" Tillerman* • Kimberlee Peterson *Dicey Tillerman* • Trevor O'Brien *James Tillerman* • Hanna Hall *Maybeth Tillerman* • William Greenblatt *Sammy Tillerman* • Bonnie Bedelia *Eunice* • Anna Louise Richardson *Liza Tillerman* ■ *Dir* Mark Jean • *Scr* Christopher Carlson, Mark Jean, from the novel by Cynthia Voigt

The Homecoming: a Christmas Story ★★★
Seasonal drama   1971 · US · Colour

Earl Hamner Jr's influential novel, which had already been the basis for *Spencer's Mountain* (a soapy effort with Henry Fonda and Maureen O'Hara), went on to provide the heart of *The Homecoming*, which itself went on to become *The Waltons*. Now that your brain's in a knot, just enjoy the simple pleasures of this TV film which, unlike *Spencer's Mountain* and *The Waltons*, generally sidesteps sentimentality for real emotional truth. Patricia Neal brings power and class to the role of mother Olivia.

Patricia Neal *Olivia Walton* • Richard Thomas *John-Boy Walton* • Edgar Bergen *Grandpa Walton* • Ellen Corby *Grandma Walton* • Cleavon Little *Hawthorne Dooley* • Dorothy Stickney *Emily Baldwin* • William Windom *Charlie Snead* • Andrew Duggan *John Walton* ■ *Dir* Fielder Cook • *Scr* Earl Hamner Jr, from his novel

Homegrown ★★★ 18
Comedy drama   1998 · US · Colour · 97mins

A Cheech and Chong movie for the Tarantino generation? Not exactly, but this tale of reefer madness does have the same sharp turns from hilarity to horror, plus a starry, eclectic supporting cast (Ted Danson, Jamie Lee Curtis, John Lithgow and Judge Reinhold) who pop up with atypical characterisations. After the brutal murder of their drug dealer boss, drug harvesters Billy Bob Thornton, Hank Azaria and Ryan Phillippe decide to carry on as normal and keep the profits for themselves. The "Class A" cast and the ensuing twists and turns bring a lively buzz to proceedings. Contains swearing and drug abuse. ▣

Billy Bob Thornton *Jack* • Hank Azaria *Carter* • Kelly Lynch *Lucy* • Ryan Phillippe *Harlan* • John Lithgow *Malcolm/Robert* • Jon Bon Jovi *Danny* • Jamie Lee Curtis *Sierra Kahan* • Judge Reinhold *Policeman* • Ted Danson *Gianni* ■ *Dir* Stephen Gyllenhaal • *Scr* Stephen Gyllenhaal, Nicholas Kazan, from a story by Stephen Gyllenhaal, Jonah Raskin

Homer ★★
Drama   1970 · US · Colour · 90mins

Liberal helpings of sex, drugs and rock 'n' roll – everything stereotypical of late sixties America – is thrown into this jumble. All the themes had already been thoroughly explored by the time John Trent's film about the young generation was released, though there is a decent soundtrack which includes Led Zeppelin, Cream and the Byrds.

Don Scardino *Homer Edwards* • Alex Nicol *Mr Edwards* • Tisa Farrow *Laurie Grainger* • Lenka Peterson *Mrs Edwards* • Ralph Endersby *Hector* • Trudy Young *Sally* • Arch McDonnell *Mr Grainger* • Jan Campbell *Mrs Grainger* ■ *Dir* John Trent • *Scr* Claude Harz, from a story by Claude Harz, Matt Clark

Homer and Eddie ★★ 15
Road movie   1989 · US · Colour · 95mins

After *About Last Night* and *Red Heat*, it looked as if James Belushi could be on track for a promising comic career. But with this mediocre 1989 road movie, it looked like that career had already taken a wrong turn. His co-star, Whoopi Goldberg, fares no better in this tale of a con artist (Goldberg) who takes a mentally handicapped man (Belushi) across country so he can visit his dying father. In the right hands, this could have been so much better, but director Konchalovsky blunders at every turn. ▣

James Belushi *Homer Lanza* • Whoopi Goldberg *Eddie Cervi* • Anne Ramsey *Edna* • Karen Black *Belle* • Beah Richards *Linda Cervi* ■ *Dir* Andrei Konchalovsky • *Scr* Patrick Cirillo

Hometown Boy Makes Good ★★★ 15
Comedy   1990 · US · Colour · 84mins

Fans of *ER* will undoubtedly relish the sight of Anthony Edwards pretending to the folks back home that he is a fully qualified doctor. Those with longer memories, though, will recognise that the real inspiration for this lightweight comedy is the Preston Sturges classic, *Hail the Conquering Hero*. However, where Eddie Bracken had Sturges's razor-sharp dialogue to deliver, Edwards has to make do with Allen Rucker's amiable blend of duplicity and doltishness as he finds himself continuing his pretence to the citizens of his small Minnesota town. ▣

Anthony Edwards *Boyd Geary* • Grace Zabriskie *Helen Geary* • Chris Mulkey *Al Swearingen* • Cynthia Bain *Merle Lee Swearingen* ■ *Dir* David Burton Morris • *Scr* Allen Rucker

Hometown USA ★★ 15
Comedy   1979 · US · Colour · 92mins

The son of a world heavyweight champion and known to millions as Jethro in *The Beverly Hillbillies*, Max Baer Jr made his third outing as a director with this predictable paean to the days when rebels didn't have causes and cars were used exclusively for parking and "chickie" runs. The period trappings may be overly familiar, and the direction occasionally slipshod and the humour decidedly on the coarse side, but there are amusing moments along the way as David Wilson and Brian Kerwin try to help Gary Springer

improve his luck with girls, only to end up dating them themselves. ▣

Gary Springer *Rodney C Duckworth* • David Wilson *Recil Calhoun* • Brian Kerwin *TJ Swackhammer* • Pat Delaney *Marilyn* ■ *Dir* Max Baer Jr • *Scr* Jesse Vint

Homeward Bound: the Incredible Journey ★★★ U
Adventure   1993 · US · Colour · 84mins

It seemed invidious to remake the 1963 Disney true-life adventure classic *The Incredible Journey*, especially with talking animals. But while the original remains the superior picture, this is still a treat for children, thanks to the astonishing performances of its animal cast. The vocal talents of Michael J Fox, Sally Field and Don Ameche certainly help pep up the pets' personalities, although you expect more of a screenwriter like Caroline Thompson than a series of playground-level wisecracks. Nevertheless, good family fare. ▣ *DVD*

Michael J Fox *Chance* • Sally Field *Sassy* • Don Ameche *Shadow* • Kim Greist *Laura* • Robert Hays *Bob* • Benj Thall *Peter* • Veronica Lauren *Hope* • Kevin Chevalia *Jamie* ■ *Dir* Duwayne Dunham • *Scr* Caroline Thompson, Linda Wolverton, from the film *The Incredible Journey* by James Algar, from the novel by Sheila Burnford

Homeward Bound II: Lost in San Francisco ★★ U
Adventure   1996 · US · Colour · 85mins

The title isn't the only thing this sequel almost shares with *Home Alone 2: Lost in New York*. The opening conceit is also similar, with an airport mix-up resulting in an accidental abandonment. However, with Shadow and Sassy to help him, Chance isn't alone for long. Indeed, romance is soon in the air as our heroic trio are befriended by a pack of street dogs. Ralph Waite admirably replaces the late Don Ameche as the sagacious Shadow, but not all the casting is as felicitous: the decision to have strays voiced by African-American actors has unfortunate racist overtones. ▣ *DVD*

Michael J Fox *Chance* • Sally Field *Sassy* • Ralph Waite *Shadow* • Robert Hays *Bob* • Kim Griest *Laura* • Veronica Lauren *Hope* ■ *Dir* David R Ellis • *Scr* Chris Hauty, from a story by Chris Hauty, Julie Hickson, from characters created by Sheila Burnford

Homicidal ★★★ 12
Horror   1961 · US · BW · 87mins

William Castle's grisly gender-switch thriller was the first and most obvious *Psycho* clone (some contemporary critics even preferred it to the Hitchcock classic), taking transvestite terror to its illogical conclusion. A weird tale of decapitations, delirious dementia and dysfunctional drag, time has watered down Castle's sneaky surprises and tongue-in-cheek denouement. But, while you won't need his fun "Fright Break" – 45 seconds to leave the cinema if too nervous to cope with the climax – Castle's prowess at powerhouse panic still rustles up some scares. ▣

Glenn Corbett *Karl* • Patricia Breslin *Miriam Webster* • Jean Arless [Joan Marshall] *Emily/*

Warren • Eugenie Leontovich *Helga* • Alan Bunce *Dr Jonas* • Richard Rust *Jim Nesbitt* ■ *Dir* William Castle • *Scr* Robb White

Homicide ★★★★ 15
Crime thriller   1991 · US · Colour · 96mins

David Mamet's third outing as writer/ director is a tough look at racial prejudice inside and outside the police force. Much of the look and feel of the picture derives from the style of Sidney Lumet, who directed Mamet's script of *The Verdict* in 1982. Mamet's roots as a playwright are evident in some scenes, but there's no denying the power of the whole piece as Joe Mantegna's Jewish cop investigates murder and a drug cartel, and finds organised anti-Semitism and an underground Jewish resistance movement. Its conclusions are bleak, yet reaching them makes for absorbing viewing. Contains violence and swearing.

Joe Mantegna *Bob Gold* • William H Macy *Tim Sullivan* • Natalija Nogulich *Chava* • Ving Rhames *Randolph* • Vincent Guastaferro *Lieutenant Senna* • Rebecca Pidgeon *Ms Klein* ■ *Dir/Scr* David Mamet

L'Homme de Ma Vie ★★★ 15
Drama   1992 · Fr/Can · Colour · 98mins

Many viewers will only have come across the Portuguese actress Maria de Medeiros in Philip Kaufman's *Henry and June* or Quentin Tarantino's *Pulp Fiction*. However, this amusing adult comedy from Jean-Charles Tacchella affords her the chance to demonstrate the talent that had long since established her as a top European star. As the flighty twentysomething searching for the rich man of her dreams, she is both kittenish and capricious, greeting each heartbreak with a shrug and a new dress. The action sags briefly in the middle, but Tacchella mostly keeps things light and breezy, and Thierry Fortineau and Jean-Pierre Bacri make admirable foils. In French with English subtitles.. ▣

Maria de Medeiros *Aimée* • Thierry Fortineau *Maurice* • Jean-Pierre Bacri *Malcolm* • Anne Letourneau *Catherine* • Ginette Garcin *Arlette* ■ *Dir/Scr* Jean-Charles Tacchella

Hondo ★★★ PG
Western   1953 · US · Colour · 79mins

A fine colourful western, originally made in 3-D, which explains the odd look of certain segments, notably the marvellous title sequence where John Wayne just keeps on walking off the screen and, supposedly, into the audience. Wayne, in his prime, plays a grim, buckskin-clad cavalry scout who comes across Oscar-nominated Geraldine Page and her son Lee Aaker and eventually helps them fend off some Indians. There is a strange tendency for some scenes to fade into black as though not fully completed by director John Farrow, yet this is still a mature, good-looking western with an excellent script by James Edward Grant. ▣

John Wayne *Hondo Lane* • Geraldine Page *Angie* • Ward Bond *Buffalo* • Michael Pate *Vittoro* • James Arness *Lennie* • Rodolfo Acosta *Silva* • Leo Gordon *Ed Lowe* • Lee

Aaker *Johnny* ■ *Dir* John Farrow • *Scr* James Edward Grant, from the story *The Gift of Cochise* by Louis L'Amour

Honest ★★ 18

Crime caper 2000 · UK · Colour · 110mins

Directed by one half of the Eurythmics and starring three of the four members of All Saints, this crime caper is part vanity project, part nostalgic throwback to the kitsch excesses of the Swinging Sixties. Melanie Blatt and real-life siblings Natalie and Nicole Appleton play three East End sisters who support their stay-at-home dad (James Cosmo) by dressing up as fellas and robbing London's great and good. Things go pear-shaped when they fall foul of mob boss Corin Redgrave and Nicole falls for American student Peter Facinelli. Though atrociously acted, ineptly plotted and directed with little sense of pace, period or plausibility, Dave Stewart's calamitous movie has a perverse fascination that renders it strangely, compulsively watchable.

Nicole Appleton *Gerry Chase* • Natalie Appleton *Mandy Chase* • Melanie Blatt *Jo Chase* • Peter Facinelli *Daniel Wheaton* • James Cosmo *Tommy Chase* • Jonathan Cake *Andrew Pryce-Stevens* • Corin Redgrave *Duggie Ord* ■ *Dir* David A Stewart • *Scr* David A Stewart, Dick Clement, Ian La Frenais

The Honest Courtesan ★★★ 15

Period romance 1998 · US · Colour · 108mins

Catherine McCormack co-stars with the glamorous city of Venice in this picturesque feminist fable, based on Margaret Rosenthal's biography of real-life 16th-century courtesan and poet Veronica Franco. McCormack lusts after impoverished aristocrat Rufus Sewell and an education, but is denied both by the prejudices of the time. Mother Jacqueline Bisset advises her to become a high-class prostitute as the only way to gain access to the tuition she craves and the man she desires. Director Marshall Herskovitz splashes out on atmosphere (a canal five foot deep with 22 million gallons of water was built) and McCormack delivers her witty lines with aplomb, but the climax is too melodramatic to be credible. Contains swearing and sex scenes. ▭

Catherine McCormack *Veronica Franco* • Rufus Sewell *Marco Venier* • Oliver Platt *Maffio Venier* • Moira Kelly *Beatrice Venier* • Fred Ward *Domenico Venier* • Jacqueline Bisset *Paola Franco* ■ *Dir* Marshall Herskovitz • *Scr* Jeannine Dominy, from the biography by Margaret Rosenthal

Honey I Blew Up the Kid ★★★ U

Comedy fantasy 1992 · US · Colour · 85mins

After nerdy scientist Rick Moranis accidentally pumps up his son into a 50ft giant, this film is reduced to a one-note romp that almost creaks to a halt. However, until then, there is a well-sustained spirit of infectious enthusiasm, bug-eyed innocence and wild lunacy that harks back to the "creature features" of the fifties. The central idea of a normally harmless child running amok in the adult world is strong, and Moranis is reliably goofy. ▭

Rick Moranis *Wayne Szalinski* • Marcia Strassman *Diane Szalinski* • Robert Oliveri *Nick Szalinski* • Daniel Shalikar *Adam Szalinski* • Joshua Shalikar *Adam Szalinski* • Lloyd Bridges *Clifford Sterling* • John Shea *Hendrickson* • Keri Russell *Mandy* ■ *Dir* Randal Kleiser • *Scr* Thom Eberhardt, Peter Elbling, Garry Goodrow, from a story by Garry Goodrow, from characters created by Stuart Gordon, Brian Yuzna, Ed Naha

Honey, I Shrunk the Kids ★★★★ U

Comedy fantasy 1989 · US · Colour · 89mins

The Absent-Minded Professor meets *The Incredible Shrinking Man* in a joyous, innocuous and thrilling Walt Disney adventure that will appeal to both young and old. Rick Moranis makes you laugh long and loud as the wacky inventor whose molecular reducer shrinks his two kids, and the children next door, to the size of Tom Thumb's thumb. How they cope with giant insects and water sprinklers in their hazardous garden-turned-jungle makes for epic chills and spills, doubling as a neat eco-learning quest in the best Disney tradition. ▭ **DVD**

Rick Moranis *Wayne Szalinski* • Matt Frewer *Big Russ Thompson* • Marcia Strassman *Diane Szalinski* • Kristine Sutherland *Mae Thompson* • Thomas Brown [Thomas Wilson Brown] *Little Russ Thompson* • Jared Rushton *Ron Thompson* ■ *Dir* Joe Johnston • *Scr* Ed Naha, Tom Schulman, from a story by Stuart Gordon, Brian Yuzna, Ed Naha

The Honey Pot ★★★

Comedy 1967 · UK/US/It · Colour · 150mins

Amusing if laboured, Joseph L Mankiewicz's reworking of Ben Jonson's *Volpone* came via Thomas Sterling's novel *The Evil of the Day* and Frederick Knott's play *Mr Fox of Venice*. The idea of having millionaire Rex Harrison test the loyalty of former lovers Edie Adams, Capucine and Susan Hayward by pretending to be dying is just as Jonson intended. But the intricate comedy could do without the contrived murder mystery that is unconvincingly tacked on here. Mankiewicz's dialogue has none of the original musicality and wit, yet Harrison valiantly tries to sparkle and Maggie Smith is fun as Hayward's nurse.

Rex Harrison *Cecil Fox* • Susan Hayward *Mrs Lone-Star Crockett Sheridan* • Cliff Robertson *William McFly* • Capucine *Princess Dominique* • Edie Adams *Merle McGill* • Maggie Smith *Sarah Watkins* • Adolfo Celi *Inspector Rizzi* ■ *Dir* Joseph L Mankiewicz • *Scr* Joseph L Mankiewicz, from the novel *The Evil of the Day* by Thomas Sterling, from the play *Mr Fox of Venice* by Frederick Knott

Honey, We Shrunk Ourselves ★★ PG

Science-fiction comedy 1997 · US · Colour · 71mins

Despite the presence of original star Rick Moranis, the concept was clearly running out of steam by the time Disney made this straight-to-video second sequel to *Honey, I Shrunk the Kids*. This time it's the adults who get downsized as Moranis, together with his wife, brother and sister-in-law, are miniaturised by his shrinking machine. The effects are fine, and director Dean Cundey (cinematographer on *Jurassic*

Park), keeps the action bustling along, but it still feels old hat. ▭ **DVD**

Rick Moranis *Wayne Szalinski* • Eve Gordon *Diane Szalinski* • Robin Bartlett *Patty Szalinski* • Allison Mack *Jenny Szalinski* • Jake Richardson *Gordon Szalinski* • Bug Hall *Adam Szalinski* ■ *Dir* Dean Cundey • *Scr* Karey Kirkpatrick, Nell Scovell, Joel Hodgson, from characters created by Stuart Gordon, Brian Yuzna, Ed Naha

Honeymoon ★★

Romantic dance drama 1959 · Sp/UK · Colour · 90mins

A dancer (Ludmila Tcherina) who has sacrificed her career for marriage to a possessive husband (Anthony Steel), is drawn to return to the stage while honeymooning in Spain where the great Antonio dances. The innovative film-maker Michael Powell, unable to resist Antonio's invitation to make a film with him, came unstuck with this loosely scripted Anglo-Spanish co-production, which ends up as part travelogue, part dance film. Regarded as a rare disaster from the director of *The Red Shoes*, it nonetheless ravishes the eye and provides an opportunity to see Antonio perform his signature *zapateado*.

Anthony Steel *Kit* • Ludmila Tcherina *Anna* • Antonio • Leonide Massine ■ *Dir* Michael Powell • *Scr* Michael Powell, Luis Escobar, Gregorio Martinez Sierra

Honeymoon Academy ★★ 15

Spy spoof 1990 · US · Colour · 89mins

This spy spoof starring *Sex and the City*'s Kim Cattrall is like a distaff version of *True Lies*, with Cattrall as the undercover agent who has kept her business a secret from her fiancé (he thinks she's a travel agent). When the pair marry, Cattrall gives up her job and intends to settle down into a normal life, but her boss has one last dangerous assignment for her to carry out. It's a rather obvious comedy, but the two leads are good value. ▭

Kim Cattrall *Chris Nelson* • Robert Hays *Sean McDonald* • Leigh Taylor-Young *Doris Kent* • Jonathan Banks *Pitt* • Christopher Lee *Lazos* ■ *Dir* Gene Quintano • *Scr* Gene Quintano, Jerry Lazarus, from a story by Gene Quintano

Honeymoon Hotel ★★

Comedy 1964 · US · Colour · 88mins

A bachelor (Robert Morse) is stood up at the altar and decides to go on the Caribbean honeymoon anyway. In place of the bride, he takes his pal Robert Goulet (making his movie debut as a playboy salesman) and the usual romantic complications ensue. It could have been a sophisticated sex comedy in the hands of a Billy Wilder, but this farce never manages to grow up. Even Elsa Lanchester as a confused chambermaid can't do much to save it.

Robert Goulet *Ross Kingsley* • Nancy Kwan *Lynn Hope* • Robert Morse *Jay Menlow* • Jill St John *Sherry* • Keenan Wynn *Mr Sampson* • Elsa Lanchester *Chambermaid* ■ *Dir* Henry Levin • *Scr* RS Allen, Harvey Bullock

Honeymoon in Vegas ★★★★ 15

Romantic comedy 1992 · US · Colour · 91mins

Nicolas Cage is in loveably dopey form here, as he finally proposes to his long-suffering girlfriend Sarah Jessica Parker (also excellent) only to see crooked gambler James Caan win her in a poker game. Director Andrew Bergman remains a much under-rated talent, and he expertly blends the classic elements of farce with a healthy dash of eccentricity to produce a delightful comedy. As Cage embarks on an epic journey to Hawaii and back to Las Vegas to reclaim his fiancée, who is gradually falling for the wealthy Caan, Bergman largely steers clear of the gloopy sentimentality that mars so many other romantic comedies and stages a stunning finale with parachuting Elvis impersonators. Contains some swearing. ▭

Nicolas Cage *Jack Singer* • James Caan *Tommy Korman* • Sarah Jessica Parker *Betsy Nolan/Donna* • Pat Morita *Mahi* • Johnny Williams *Johnny Sandwich* • John Capodice *Sally Molars* • Anne Bancroft *Bea Singer* ■ *Dir/Scr* Andrew Bergman

The Honeymoon Killers ★★★★ 18

Crime drama based on a true story 1969 · US · BW · 102mins

A fat and lonely spinster from Alabama latches on to a Spanish-born gigolo. Posing as brother and sister, they murder elderly women for their money. Based on the real-life case of Martha Beck and Ray Fernandez, who were both executed in 1951, this cult, low-budget thriller immerses us not only in the psychology of the murderous pair, but also in the dreadful lives and trash culture of their victims. It's a chilling, utterly compelling picture and a one-off classic by its otherwise unknown director, Leonard Kastle. François Truffaut consistently named it as one of his favourite films. ▭

Shirley Stoler *Martha Beck* • Tony LoBianco *Ray Fernandez* • Mary Jane Higby *Janet Fay* • Doris Roberts *Bunny* • Delphine Downing *Kip McArdle* ■ *Dir/Scr* Leonard Kastle

The Honeymoon Machine ★★ U

Comedy 1961 · US · Colour · 86mins

Naval lieutenant Steve McQueen misappropriates his ship's computer by using it to cheat at roulette in the Venice casino. However, there are three spanners in the works: admiral's daughter Brigid Bazlen, McQueen's former girlfriend (Paula Prentiss) and the Russians who think the Third World War is being launched. This is what passed in 1961 as a saucy Cold War comedy, but *Dr Strangelove* it isn't. McQueen was never at his best in this sort of thing and it needed Cary Grant or Tony Curtis to make it work.

Steve McQueen *Lt Fergie Howard* • Brigid Bazlen *Julie Fitch* • Jim Hutton *Jason Eldridge* • Paula Prentiss *Pam Dunstan* • Dean Jagger *Admiral Fitch* • Jack Weston *Signalman Burford Taylor* ■ *Dir* Richard Thorpe • *Scr* George Wells, from the play *The Golden Fleecing* by Lorenzo Semple Jr

---

Honeysuckle Rose ★★ 🔞

Drama   1980 · US · Colour · 114mins

Willie Nelson, the man who wrote *Crazy* for Patsy Cline in the sixties, became better known in later years for his battles with the IRS over back taxes. By that time he had also embarked on a film career, and this low-key entry was an early effort. In a bold piece of casting, Nelson plays a country and western star whose love for his wife (Dyan Cannon) and son is jeopardised by his career and alcoholic excesses. A crisis looms when Amy Irving, the daughter of his friend and ex-band member takes up with the grizzly old bear. 🖵

Willie Nelson *Buck* • Dyan Cannon *Viv* • Amy Irving *Lily* • Slim Pickens *Garland* • Joey Floyd *Jamie* • Charles Levin *Sid* • Priscilla Pointer *Rosella* ■ *Dir* Jerry Schatzberg • *Scr* Carol Sobieski, William D Wittliff, John Binder, from the story *Intermezzo* by Gösta Steven, Gustaf Molander

Hong Kong '97 ★★ 🔞

Action adventure 1994 · US · Colour · 86mins

Hong Kong in the days leading up to China's takeover of the colony makes for an intriguing setting, but that aside this is a straightforward shoot-em-up thriller with men in smart suits wasting hordes of bad guys in trendy slow-motion. Robert Patrick plays an assassin for a major corporation who has just completed his last job, the murder of a Chinese general. As this has happened the day before the Chinese finally take over the colony, there is much uproar, but he quickly realises his enemies are far closer to home. Video stalwarts Brion James (with a dodgy Brit accent) and Tim Thomerson co-star. 🖵

Robert Patrick *Reginald Cameron* • Brion James *Simon Alexander* • Wen Ming-Na *Katie Chun* • Tim Thomerson *Jack McGraw* ■ *Dir* Albert Pyun • *Scr* Randall Fontana

The Honkers ★★★

Drama   1971 · US · Colour · 102mins

James Coburn plays an ageing rodeo rider who returns to his home town after a lengthy absence to discover his long-suffering wife has taken up with another man and wants a divorce. At first, Coburn approaches the theme as cautiously as if it were a bucking bronco, but eventually he comes to terms with the role and puts in a competent performance. Actor-turned-director Steve Ihnat, who died shortly after completing the film, obviously intended it to be a thoughtful western, but to achieve this the project needed a more adventurous approach. Contains swearing and drug abuse.

James Coburn *Lew Lathrop* • Lois Nettleton *Linda Lathrop* • Slim Pickens *Clete* • Anne Archer *Deborah Moon* • Richard Anderson *Royce* • Ted Eccles *Bobby Lathrop* • Ramon Bieri *Jack Ferguson* ■ *Dir* Steve Ihnat • *Scr* Steve Ihnat, Stephen Lodge

Honky Tonk ★★★

Romantic adventure
1941 · US · BW · 104mins

There is tangible on-screen chemistry between "king of the movies" Clark Gable and up-and-coming sexpot Lana Turner, and their scenes together here sizzle. The framework is an amiable adventure with Gable as a con man and Turner the judge's daughter he falls for. There's lively support from Claire Trevor and Marjorie Main, and Chill Wills is endearing as Gable's sidekick, but it all gets far too talky around the middle, and doesn't really recover. However, as a souvenir of two great Hollywood stars in their prime and as a reminder of what MGM was capable of, this will do nicely.

Clark Gable *Candy Johnson* • Lana Turner *Elizabeth Cotton* • Frank Morgan *Judge Cotton* • Claire Trevor *"Gold Dust" Nelson* • Marjorie Main *Mrs Varner* • Albert Dekker *Brazos Hearn* • Chill Wills *Sniper* ■ *Dir* Jack Conway • *Scr* Pandro S Berman, John Sanford

Honky Tonk Freeway ★ 🔞

Comedy   1981 · US · Colour · 102mins

This shambolic, unfunny farce by British director John Schlesinger concerns a small Florida town, desperately in need of trade, that goes to any lengths to ensure it's not to be bypassed by a new motorway. William Devane is the mayor orchestrating the tourist-catching antics, while Beau Bridges, Teri Garr and Jessica Tandy act like crazy as the trippers invade. Grotesque. 🖵

Beau Bridges *Duane Hansen* • William Devane *Mayor Calo* • Hume Cronyn *Sherm* • Beverly D'Angelo *Carmen Shelby* • Teri Garr *Ericka* • Howard Hesseman *Snapper* • Geraldine Page *Sister Mary Clarise* • Jessica Tandy *Carol* ■ *Dir* John Schlesinger • *Scr* Edward Clinton

Honkytonk Man ★★ 🔞

Drama   1982 · US · Colour · 117mins

Clint Eastwood made this a family affair by featuring his son, Kyle, as the teenage nephew under the spell of an alcoholic country singer returned to rural roots. But that nepotism was as much of a mistake (Kyle's acting is never really up to the demands of the role), however well intentioned, as the idea that Eastwood himself could pass for a vocalist. He can do many things, such as produce and direct himself in this drama, but a singer he's not. This fatal flaw destabilises the whole movie and leaves us with little belief in his character or intentions. Contains swearing and a sex scene. 🖵

Clint Eastwood *Red Stovall* • Kyle Eastwood *Whit* • John McIntire *Grandpa* • Alexa Kenin *Marlene* • Verna Bloom *Emmy* • Matt Clark *Virgil* • Barry Corbin *Derwood Arnspriger* • Jerry Hardin *Snuffy* ■ *Dir* Clint Eastwood • *Scr* Clancy Carlile, from his novel

Honolulu ★★

Musical   1939 · US · BW · 82mins

A movie star (Robert Young) changes places with a plantation owner in Honolulu (also played by Young) and romances a dancer (Eleanor Powell) whom he meets on board an ocean liner. Some great dancing from the leggy and accomplished Powell, a couple of lively numbers and the appearance of George Burns and Gracie Allen partially enliven this otherwise dead musical, with its forgettable score and pedestrian direction from Edward Buzzell.

Eleanor Powell *Dorothy March* • Robert Young *Brooks Mason/George Smith* • George Burns *Joe Duffy* • Gracie Allen *Millie de Grasse* •
Clarence Kolb *Horace Grayson* • Jo Ann Sayers *Nurse* ■ *Dir* Edward Buzzell • *Scr* Herbert Fields, Frank Partos

Honor among Lovers ★★

Drama   1931 · US · BW · 75mins

A trifling romantic comedy, worth seeing for its always appealing stars: Claudette Colbert as the secretary wooed by playboy exec Fredric March but marrying Monroe Owsley instead. March fires her and predicts her marriage will quickly dissolve, but changes his mind and offers them both a job. Made by Hollywood's foremost – indeed only – woman director at the time, Dorothy Arzner, it has the timbre of a Broadway play though, as *Variety* said, "It is not on such a high plane that it will sail over the heads of the peasantry."

Claudette Colbert *Julia Traynor* • Fredric March *Jerry Stafford* • Monroe Owsley *Philip Craig* • Charles Ruggles *Monty Dunn* • Ginger Rogers *Doris Blake* • Avonne Taylor *Maybelle* • Pat O'Brien *Conroy* ■ *Dir* Dorothy Arzner • *Scr* Austin Parker, Gertrude Purcell, from the story by Austin Parker

Honor Thy Father and Mother: the Menendez Killings ★★★ 🔞

Drama based on a true story
1994 · US · Colour · 93mins

Before OJ Simpson, there were the Menendez brothers, whose lengthy trial displaced the soap operas from prime-time TV. America was obsessed by the case because the people involved were comfortably middle-class and lived in Beverly Hills. Oliver Stone planned a feature film about it, but eventually two TV movies were made. This one is a reasonable blend of docudrama and standard urban horror with Billy Warlock and David Beron portraying the brothers accused of killing their parents, played by James Farentino and Jill Clayburgh. Contains swearing and violence. 🖵

James Farentino *Jose Menendez* • Jill Clayburgh *Kitty Menendez* • Bill Warlock *[Billy Warlock] Lyle Menendez* • David Beron *Erik Menendez* • Susan Blakely *Leslie Abramson* • Erin Gray *Pamela Bozanich* ■ *Dir* Paul Schneider • *Scr* Michael J Murray, from the book *Blood Brothers; The Inside Story of the Menendez Murders* by Ron Soble, John Johnson

Honor Thy Mother ★★★ 🔞

Crime drama based on a true story
1992 · US · Colour · 89mins

An enjoyable, sensationalist true-story drama, focusing on one of those diabolical family murder plots. William McNamara is the fresh-faced student who sets out to dispose of his wealthy mother (played by Sharon Gless) and stepfather in order to lay his hands on their money. His mother somehow manages to survive, and it is left to detective Brian Wimmer to find the culprit. It's competently directed by TV movie specialist David Greene. 🖵

Sharon Gless *Bonnie Von Stein* • William McNamara *Chris Pritchard* • Matthew Faison *Leith Von Stein* • Brian Wimmer *Detective Pete Murphy* • Suzanne Ventulett *Angela Pritchard* • Dion Anderson *Agent Reed* ■ *Dir* David Greene • *Scr* Richard DeLong Adams, Robert L Freedman, from the non-fiction book *Blood Games* by Jerry Bledsoe

The Honorary Consul ★★★ 🔞

Drama   1983 · UK · Colour · 99mins

Michael Caine gives what was hailed at the time as the performance of his life in this Graham Greene story about an alcoholic British consul in a corrupt South American backwater, who's mistakenly kidnapped only to find that nobody wants to raise the ransom for his return. Bob Hoskins makes the most of his role as a police chief, but Richard Gere, as a doctor looking for his missing father, battles with an English accent and loses. It could have been much better without John Mackenzie's stolid direction. Contains swearing and sex scenes. 🖵

Michael Caine *Charley Fortnum* • Richard Gere *Dr Plarr* • Bob Hoskins *Colonel Perez* • Elpidia Carrillo *Clara* • Joaquim de Almeida *Leon* • A Martinez *Aquino* • Stephanie Cotsirilos *Marta* ■ *Dir* John Mackenzie • *Scr* Christopher Hampton, from the novel by Graham Greene

Honour among Thieves ★★★★

Crime drama   1954 · Fr/It · BW · 87mins

Based on a novel by Albert Simonin, this brooding study of dishonour among thieves established the vogue for gangster films in 1950s France. Jean Gabin won the best actor prize at Venice for his performance as Max the Liar – a world-weary hood on his last blag – who is forced to make impossible choices when his longtime partner, René Dary, is held for ransom by ruthless rival, Lino Ventura. Director Jacques Becker stages the Orly raid and the final confrontation efficiently enough, but his main interest lies in the dynamic that drives these luxury-loving mobsters to acts of clinical violence and guilt-free treachery. In French with English subtitles.

Jean Gabin *Max* • René Dary *Riton* • Jeanne Moreau *Josy* • Dora Doll *Lola* • Lino Ventura *Angelo* • Paul Frankeur *Pierrot* ■ *Dir* Jacques Becker • *Scr* Jacques Becker, Albert Simonin, Maurice Griffe, from a novel by Albert Simonin

Hoodlum ★★ 🔞

Period crime drama
1997 · US · Colour · 124mins

Laurence Fishburne had a supporting role in 1984's *The Cotton Club*, as a black gangster fighting Dutch Schultz's attempts to take over the Harlem numbers racket. Here the same bloody story takes centre stage, with Fishburne again refusing to bow down to Schultz, played by Tim Roth in foul-mouthed, psychopathic form. Andy Garcia is crime boss Lucky Luciano, pondering which side of the fence to sit on. Fishburne is as charismatic as ever, but the script takes some swallowing, while director Bill Duke takes an age to get the action pumping. Contains violence and some swearing. 🖵

Laurence Fishburne *Ellsworth "Bumpy" Johnson* • Tim Roth *Dutch Schultz* • Vanessa L Williams *Francine Hughes* • Andy Garcia *Lucky Luciano* • Cicely Tyson *Stephanie "Queen" St Clair* • Clarence Williams III *Bub Hewlett* ■ *Dir* Bill Duke • *Scr* Chris Brancato

U = SUITABLE FOR ALL   **Uc** = SUITABLE FOR ALL, ESPECIALLY FOR YOUNG CHILDREN (VIDEO ONLY)   **PG** = PARENTAL GUIDANCE

Hoodlum Empire ★★
Crime drama   1952 · US · BW · 97mins

This nickel-and-dime gangster picture was knocked out quickly by Republic Studios following the 1950 report by the Senate Crime Investigating Committee. Chaired by Senator Este Kefauver, the report not only exposed organised crime, but also severely criticised Hollywood violence and its glamorisation of criminals. Accordingly, the film takes pains to establish its serious credentials and moral strength as Brian Donlevy, playing a Kefauver clone, digs deep into the syndicate's dark secrets.

Brian Donlevy *Senator Bill Stephens* • Forrest Tucker *Charley Pignatalli* • Claire Trevor *Connie Williams* • Vera Ralston *Marthe Dufour* • Luther Adler *Nick Mancani* • John Russell *Joe Gray* • Gene Lockhart *Senator Tower* • Grant Withers *Rev Andrews* ■ *Dir* Joseph Kane • *Scr* Bruce Manning, Bob Considine

The Hoodlum Priest ★★★
Drama   1961 · US · BW · 102mins

Don Murray produced and pseudonymously co-wrote this social problem picture and stars as the Jesuit priest who helps juvenile delinquents and ex-cons by establishing halfway houses for them. One of these rehabilitating hoodlums, Keir Dullea, does well until he gets trapped into robbery and murder. Working like a religious *Rebel without a Cause*, the blend of piety and profanity is often hard to take, though Dullea is excellent in his screen debut and Murray's commitment is obvious.

Don Murray *Rev Charles Dismas Clark* • Cindi Wood *Ellen Henley* • Larry Gates *Louis Rosen* • Keir Dullea *Billy Lee Jackson* • Logan Ramsey *George Hale* • Don Joslyn *Pio Gentile* • Sam Capuano *Mario Mazziotti* ■ *Dir* Irvin Kershner • *Scr* Don Deer [Don Murray], Joseph Landon

The Hoodlum Saint ★
Drama   1946 · US · BW · 91mins

This disjointed comedy drama with a religious angle is one of the few real duds of William Powell's long stay at MGM. He appears as a disillusioned First World War veteran who carves out a fortune for himself but disappoints the girl he loves, played by Esther Williams (who should never have left the water). Powell tells old friends in need of help to appeal to St Dismas, the "hoodlum saint", but then his own luck runs out. Angela Lansbury is the perkiest performer on view.

William Powell *Terry Ellerton O'Neill* • Esther Williams *May Lorrison* • Angela Lansbury *Dusty Millard* • James Gleason *Sharp* • Lewis Stone *Father Nolan* ■ *Dir* Norman Taurog • *Scr* Frank Wead, James Hill

Hoods ★★
Comedy   1998 · US · Colour · 90mins

A talented cast is left high and dry in this misfiring Mafia movie, which oscillates between comedy and drama. Joe Mantegna is the mob killer with a conscience who begins to question his lifestyle when he is given a contract he can't bring himself to fulfil. He is as good as always, and he's ably supported by the likes of Kevin Pollack, Joe Pantoliano and Jennifer

Tilly, but Mark Malone's film wears its quirkiness too obviously on its sleeve.

Joe Mantegna *Angelo* • Seymour Cassel *Chief* • Jennifer Tilly *Mary* • Vincent Berry *Carmine Bellarosa* • Joseph Maher *Dr Alstrich* ■ *Dir* Mark Malone • *Scr* Mark Malone, Dennis Klein

The Hook ★★
War drama   1963 · US · Colour · 97mins

At the end of the Korean War, three GIs rescue a North Korean from the sea and are ordered to execute him. A thought-provoking situation – the ethics involved in the difference between soldiers killing on the battlefield and face-to-face execution – is weighed down by endless debate and contrived circumstances. But the performances from Kirk Douglas, Nick Adams and Robert Walker Jr (here making his screen debut) are suitably powerful.

Kirk Douglas *Sergeant PJ Briscoe* • Robert Walker Jr *Private OA Dennison* • Nick Adams *Private VR Hackett* • Enrique Magalona *The prisoner* • Nehemiah Persoff *Captain Van Ryn* ■ *Dir* George Seaton • *Scr* Henry Denker, from the novel *L'Hameçon* by Vahé Katcha

Hook ★★★ Ⓤ
Fantasy adventure
1991 · US · Colour · 135mins

Purists will shudder at what Steven Spielberg has done to JM Barrie's classic tale, but their protests are likely to be ignored by those children who prefer old-fashioned derring-do to be brightened up with some trimmings. In this take on *Peter Pan*, Robin Williams is the grown-up Pan, a ruthless business pirate who has no time for his family and no memory of his magical past. That all changes, however, when his children are kidnapped and he gets a visit from Tinkerbell (Julia Roberts). As good as Williams is, the film is stolen by an almost unrecognisable Dustin Hoffman, whose Hook is suitably pantomimic yet oddly sympathetic. The scenes between him and Bob Hoskins as Smee are a delight and, although the sentimentality gets a little sticky at times, this remains rousing entertainment. ▭ DVD

Dustin Hoffman *Captain James Hook* • Julia Roberts *Tinkerbell* • Bob Hoskins *Smee* • Maggie Smith *Granny Wendy* • Caroline Goodall *Moira Banning* • Charlie Korsmo *Jack* • Phil Collins *Inspector Good* ■ *Dir* Steven Spielberg • *Scr* Jim V Hart, Malia Scotch Marmo, from a story by Jim V Hart, Nick Castle, from characters created by JM Barrie • *Music* John Williams • *Art Director* Norman Garwood • *Set Designer* Garrett Lewis • *Costume Designer* Anthony Powell

Hook, Line and Sinker ★★ Ⓤ
Comedy   1969 · US · Colour · 87mins

Things turned sour for Jerry Lewis following the hit comedy *The Disorderly Orderly* (1964), as his later films were a motley bunch of misfires. *Hook, Line and Sinker* falls into this category. Lewis plays a man who finds out he is dying and goes on a globe-trotting spending spree, only to discover later that the diagnosis was wrong. Hugely in debt, he then decides to fake his own death. An unusually mean-spirited film that highlights the difficulty directors had in catching the Lewis genius. Always at his best when directing himself, it took Martin

Scorsese to use him brilliantly years later in Lewis's comeback triumph, *The King of Comedy*. ▭

Jerry Lewis *Peter Ingersoll* • Peter Lawford *Dr Scott Carter* • Anne Francis *Nancy Ingersoll* • Pedro Gonzales-Gonzales *Perfecto* • Jimmy Miller *Jimmy* • Jennifer Edwards *Jennifer* ■ *Dir* George Marshall • *Scr* Rod Amateau, from a story by David Davis, Rod Amateau

Hoop Dreams ★★★★ ⑫
Sports documentary
1994 · US · Colour · 170mins

American basketball films may not be the most riveting entertainment for the average British viewer. However, this three-hour documentary – cut down from 250 hours of footage – that follows the fortunes of two inner city Chicago kids whose only way out is through basketball, packs an enormous emotional punch. Film-maker Steve James not only displays an impassioned commitment to these central characters and their desires but also lays them bare so that our empathy is fully engaged. An often simple subject which is full of riches. Contains some swearing.

Dir Steve James • *Scr* Steve James, Fred Marx, Peter Gilbert • *Cinematographer* Peter Gilbert

Hooper ★★★★ ⓅⒼ
Action comedy   1978 · US · Colour · 95mins

One of the best movies to exploit Burt Reynolds's brand of wise-guy charm, in which he's an over-the-hill stuntman determined to become a legend by completing a final outrageous feat – a record-breaking leap across a collapsed bridge in a jet-fuelled car. All this to convince young rival Jan-Michael Vincent, doubtful girlfriend Sally Field and obnoxious film-maker Robert Klein of his greatness. The director, Hal Needham, was himself a former stuntman, which may explain why there are so many chariot rides, helicopter jumps and barroom brawls. Contains some swearing. ▭

Burt Reynolds *Sonny Hooper* • Jan-Michael Vincent *Ski* • Sally Field *Gwen* • Brian Keith *Jocko* • John Marley *Max Berns* • Robert Klein *Roger Deal* • James Best *Cully* • Adam West *Adam* ■ *Dir* Hal Needham • *Scr* Thomas Rickman, Bill Kerby, from a story by Walt Green, Walter S Herndon

Hooray for Love ★★
Musical   1935 · US · BW · 75mins

This minor backstage musical only really comes to life when Bill Robinson tapdances his way onto the screen supported by Fats Waller and others. Gene Raymond stars as the rich college kid who sinks all his wealth into a stage show starring the girl he loves, a singer played by Ann Sothern. Lionel Stander is amusing as a Russian orchestra conductor while Thurston Hall (as Sothern's con-man father) is seen starting an incredibly active period as a Hollywood character actor after being off screen since the early twenties.

Ann Sothern *Pat* • Gene Raymond *Doug* • Bill Robinson *Bill* • Thurston Hall *Commodore* • Pert Kelton *Trixie* • Georgia Caine *Duchess* • Lionel Stander *Chowsky* ■ *Dir* Walter Lang • *Scr* Lawrence Hazard, Ray Harris, from a story by Marc Lachmann

Hopalong Cassidy ★★
Western   1935 · US · BW · 60mins

The first of a series of westerns that ran for nearly 20 years on film and television in which former silent star William Boyd established a new career as Hopalong Cassidy, the silver-haired knight of the range. Bill Cassidy is shot in the leg during this bland story of feuding ranchers and rustlers and a nickname is born. Jimmy (later James) Ellison appears as his young screen partner for the first of eight times.

William Boyd *Bill "Hopalong" Cassidy* • Jimmy Ellison [James Ellison] *Johnny Nelson* • Paula Stone *Mary Meeker* • Robert Warwick *Jim Meeker* • Charles Middleton *Buck Peters* • Frank McGlynn Jr *Red Connors* ■ *Dir* Howard Bretherton • *Scr* Doris Schroeder, Harrison Jacobs, from the novel by Clarence E Mulford

Hope ★★ ⓅⒼ
Drama   1997 · US · Colour · 91mins

Goldie Hawn's directorial debut was made for cable television and is a predictable affair. A Deep South tale of segregation, set against the backdrop of the 1962 Cuban missile crisis, it features Jena Malone as a small-town teenager coming to terms with both the racism of the times and her own family's behaviour. Malone's performance is the major saving grace as script and direction are perfunctory, to say the least. ▭

Christine Lahti *Emma Percy* • Jena Malone *Lilly Kate Burns* • Catherine O'Hara *Muriel MacSwain* • Jeffrey D Sams *Jediah Walker* • JT Walsh *Ray Percy* • Mary Ellen Trainor *Mazie Burns* ■ *Dir* Goldie Hawn • *Scr* Kerry Kennedy

Hope and Glory ★★★★★ ⑮
Second World War drama
1987 · UK · Colour · 107mins

War may be hell if you're a grown-up, but it's a wheeze if you're nine years old and living in suburban London during the Blitz. Anyway, that's how it looks to the young hero of director John Boorman's whimsical, funny, nostalgic, semi-autobiographical memoir of family life in the Second World War. Sebastian Rice-Edwards gives an extraordinarily confident performance in the lead role, and he's matched by Geraldine Muir, playing his five-year-old sister. Sammi Davis as their rebellious elder sibling, meanwhile, gives a poignant portrayal of the teenager caught between sexual awakening and the savage truths of the day. The film is on the episodic side, and Sarah Miles and Ian Bannen might both have toned down their eccentric portrayals a notch, but these are minor quibbles in a delightful movie. Contains swearing. ▭

Sebastian Rice-Edwards *Bill Rohan* • Geraldine Muir *Sue Rohan* • Sarah Miles *Grace Rohan* • David Hayman *Clive Rohan* • Sammi Davis *Dawn Rohan* • Susan Wooldridge *Molly* • Jean-Marc Barr *Bruce* • Ian Bannen *Grandfather George* ■ *Dir/Scr* John Boorman • *Cinematographer* Philippe Rousselot

Hope Floats ★★ ⓅⒼ
Romance   1998 · US · Colour · 109mins

Sandra Bullock (who also executive-produced) stars as Birdee, who finds out on a Ricki Lake-style talk show that her husband has been unfaithful. So she decides to return to the small hometown where she was once a beauty queen to get over the pain with her mother (Gena Rowlands) and young daughter at her side. There's far too much moping and sobbing before she realises the boy next door (Harry Connick Jr) is now rather hunky, and director Forest Whitaker seems to think over an hour of wallowing is more interesting than the few amusing scenes of budding romance and bickering between mother and daughter. Contains some swearing and sexual references. ▭

Sandra Bullock *Birdee Pruitt* • Harry Connick Jr *Justin Matisse* • Gena Rowlands *Ramona Calvert* • Mae Whitman *Bernice Pruitt* • Michael Paré *Bill Pruitt* • Cameron Finley *Travis* • Kathy Najimy *Toni Post* • Bill Cobbs *Nurse* • Rosanna Arquette *Connie* ■ *Dir* Forest Whitaker • *Scr* Steven Rogers

Hoppity Goes to Town ★★ 🆄🄲

Animation   1941 · US · Colour · 74mins

Partially inspired by Frank Capra's *Mr Deeds Goes to Town*, this was one of the first animated features not to be based on a classic children's fable. However, the weakness in the storyline was to prove the film's undoing. Neither Hoppity the grasshopper's battle with the villainous C Bagley Beetle for the attentions of the drippy Honey Bee nor the insect colony's need to find new lodgings are enchanting enough to fire the imagination or hold the attention. The artwork is pleasing, but the voice-overs are as feeble as the songs, from the usually dependable Frank Loesser and Hoagy Carmichael. ▭

Dir David Fleischer [Dave Fleischer] • *Scr* David Fleischer, Dan Gordon, Isidore Sparber, William Turner, Mike Meyer, Graham Place, Bob Wickersham, Cal Howard

Hopscotch ★★★ 🄸🄵

Spy comedy   1980 · US · Colour · 100mins

CIA operative Miles Kendig (Walter Matthau) takes revenge for being demoted to a desk job by leaking his memoirs, chapter by chapter, to other intelligence agencies. Of course, he has to be stopped, but not before leading ex-boss Ned Beatty on a merry chase around the world. There are some splendid performances – Glenda Jackson, Herbert Lom, Sam Waterston – but it's Matthau who carries it all with his unique brand of serene cynicism. ▭

Walter Matthau *Miles Kendig* • Glenda Jackson *Isobel von Schmidt* • Sam Waterston *Cutter* • Ned Beatty *Myerson* • Herbert Lom *Mikhail Yaskov* • David Matthau *Ross* ■ *Dir* Ronald Neame • *Scr* Brian Garfield, Bryan Forbes, from the novel by Brian Garfield

Horizons West ★★

Western   1952 · US · Colour · 80mins

Cult director Budd Boetticher needed a much bigger budget, a far better script and another hour to do justice to this story of three brothers who become rivals after the Civil War. While Rock Hudson and James Arness are content to plough their parcels of land, Robert Ryan becomes a ruthless empire builder. Julia Adams, meanwhile, is the widow caught up in their sibling rivalry. Ryan gives a decent performance, but the film lacks the scorched visuals of

Boetticher's best work (*Comanche Station*, *Ride Lonesome*).

Robert Ryan *Dan Hammond* • Julia Adams [Julie Adams] *Lorna Hardin* • Rock Hudson *Neal Hammond* • John McIntire *Ira Hammond* • Judith Braun *Sally* • Raymond Burr *Cord Hardin* • James Arness *Tiny* • Dennis Weaver *Dandy Taylor* ■ *Dir* Budd Boetticher • *Scr* Louis Stevens

The Horn Blows at Midnight ★★★

Comedy   1945 · US · BW · 77mins

On his subsequent radio and television shows, comedian Jack Benny got a good deal of comic mileage from mentioning this movie to its detriment. This film is by no means as bad as Benny would have you believe: it's certainly preposterous, and grossly whimsical, but its tale of a dopey trumpeter who dreams that he's an angel dispatched to Earth and able to destroy it with one blast of his horn, is not so absurd after all. Benny himself is excellent and there's fine support, particularly a cameo from camp hotel detective Franklin Pangborn.

Jack Benny *Athanael* • Alexis Smith *Elizabeth* • Dolores Moran *Fran* • Allyn Joslyn *Osidro* • Reginald Gardiner *Archie Dexter* • Guy Kibbee *The Chief* • John Alexander *Doremus* • Franklin Pangborn *Sloan* • Margaret Dumont *Miss Rodholder* • Bobby Blake *Junior* ■ *Dir* Raoul Walsh • *Scr* Sam Hellman, James V Kern, from an idea by Aubrey Wisberg

The Hornet's Nest ★★ 🅄

Crime comedy   1955 · UK · BW · 64mins

This is a slight comedy from the days of double-bills when a second feature could be brief. June Thorburn and Marla Landi play Pat and Terry, two models who get more than they bargained for when they set up home on a barge. Unbeknown to them, a jewel thief has hidden his ill-gotten gains on board and is determined to get the goods back at all cost.

Paul Carpenter *Bob Bartlett* • June Thorburn *Pat* • Marla Landi *Terry Savarese* • Charles Farrell *Posh Peterson* • Larry Burns *Alfie* ■ *Dir* Charles Saunders • *Scr* Allan Mackinnon, from a story by John Roddick

Hornet's Nest ★★

Second World War drama   1970 · US · Colour · 109mins

Routine war outing with Rock Hudson as an American paratrooper who leads a group of Italian children against a dam controlled by the Nazis. No bouncing bombs here, just layers of cuteness and a superfluous love interest in the shape of Italian sex siren Sylva Koscina who plays a German nurse. The idea that kids can become killers with a moral purpose hardly figures in the script by SS Schweitzer, while Phil Karlson's direction barely conceals the improbabilities. Nice scenery, though.

Rock Hudson *Captain Turner* • Sylva Koscina *Bianca* • Mark Colleano *Aldo* • Sergio Fantoni *Von Hecht* • Jacques Sernas *Major Taussig* • Giacomo Rossi Stuart *Schwalberg* ■ *Dir* Phil Karlson • *Scr* SS Schweitzer, from a story by SS Schweitzer, Stanley Colbert

The Horrible Dr Hichcock ★★

Horror   1962 · It · Colour · 76mins

One of two Italian horror films (the other is *The Spectre*) featuring the eponymous British surgeon. This one was originally released in the UK, heavily cut, as *The Terror of Dr Hichcock*. Reputedly in homage to Hammer, storms rage, mists swirl and doors creak as Dr H's new bride is haunted by the ghost of his first wife. The casual viewer will find it all preposterous, but cultists revere this as one of the most stylish works of director Riccardo Freda. The Hichcocks are played by Robert Flemyng and scream queen Barbara Steele. Italian dialogue dubbed into English. ▭

Robert Flemyng *Dr Bernard Hichcock* • Barbara Steele *Cynthia* • Teresa Fitzgerald [Maria Teresa Vianello] *Margaret* • Harriet White *Martha* • Montgomery Glenn *Dr Kurt Lowe* ■ *Dir* Robert Hampton [Riccardo Freda] • *Scr* Julyan Perry [Ernesto Gastaldi]

Horror Express ★★★ 🄸🄵

Horror   1972 · UK/Sp · Colour · 83mins

A rattlingly good chiller set on the Trans-Siberian railway at the turn of the century, where what is believed to be a frozen Missing Link starts to revive in the presence of classic horror movie stars Peter Cushing and Christopher Lee, here playing rival anthropologists. The suspense is kept to a maximum by the clever and beautifully timed editing of Robert Dearberg, who deserves better movies: just study the opening sequence and guess how little material he had to work with. As in the previous year's *Pancho Villa*, director Eugenio (Gene) Martin is unable to control Telly Savalas, who this time chews the scenery as the leader of a group of Cossacks. Shame. ▭

Christopher Lee *Prof Alexander Saxton* • Peter Cushing *Dr Wells* • Telly Savalas *Kazan* • Silvia Tortosa *Irina* • Alberto de Mendoza *Inspector* ■ *Dir* Eugenio Martin • *Scr* Armand D'Usseau, Julian Halevey [Julian Zimet], from a story by Eugenio Martin

Horror Hospital ★★ 🆒🄸🄱

Comedy horror   1973 · US · Colour · 88mins

Combining audience preoccupations with medicine and terror, director Antony Balch attempts to spoof the usual horror contents by taking them so far over the edge that they self-destruct. There's a Rolls-Royce with scythes, belligerent bikers and, of course, a burns-scarred mad scientist, plus Robin Askwith (*Confessions of a Window Cleaner*) as an aspiring rock musician seeking a rest cure. The result is an almost unwatchable mess, but try to stay the course: the psychological subtext is fascinating. Contains some swearing. ▭

Michael Gough *Dr Storm* • Robin Askwith *Jason Jones* • Vanessa Shaw *Judy Peters* • Ellen Pollock *Aunt Harris* • Skip Martin *Frederick* • Dennis Price *Mr Pollack* ■ *Dir* Antony Balch • *Scr* Antony Balch, Alan Watson

The Horror of Frankenstein ★★ 🄸🄵

Horror comedy   1970 · UK · Colour · 91mins

Ralph Bates was no substitute for Peter Cushing in Hammer's feeble

attempt to remake their classic *Curse of Frankenstein*. He overplays the good/bad doctor as ridiculously evil in this throwaway comic variation on the well-worn theme. Nor was David Prowse any replacement for sympathetic Christopher Lee as the Monster. Writer/director Jimmy Sangster displays little subtlety, accenting instead the black humour in a very lowbrow entry, even considering the poor quality of Hammer's dated seventies output. ▭

Ralph Bates *Victor Frankenstein* • Kate O'Mara *Alys* • Graham James *Wilhelm* • Veronica Carlson *Elizabeth* • Bernard Archard *Elizabeth's father* • Dennis Price *Grave robber* • Joan Rice *Grave robber's wife* • David Prowse [Dave Prowse] *Monster* ■ *Dir* Jimmy Sangster • *Scr* Jimmy Sangster, Jeremy Burnham, from characters created by Mary Shelley

Hors la Vie ★★★★ 🄸🄵

Biographical drama   1991 · Fr/It/Bel · Colour · 93mins

Based on the real-life experiences of Roger Auque, this compelling drama provides a graphic insight into the plight of the political hostage, with Hippolyte Girardot magnificent in the role of the abducted French photographer. Lebanese director Maroun Bagdadi expertly conveys the claustrophobia, uncertainty and sheer terror of being at the mercy of people willing to kill for their cause. Yet he wisely avoids presenting the captors as inhuman fanatics, while also resisting the temptation to justify their actions with long tracts of rhetorical propaganda. In French and Arabic with English subtitles. ▭

Hippolyte Girardot *Patrick Perrault* • Rafic Ali Ahmad *Walid, "Chief"* • Hussein Sbeity *Omar* • Habib Hammoud *Ali, "Philippe"* • Magdi Machmouchi *Moustaph* ■ *Dir* Maroun Bagdadi • *Scr* Maroun Bagdadi, from the non-fiction book by Roger Auque, Patrick Forestier

Horse Feathers ★★★★★★

Comedy   1932 · US · BW · 70mins

In their penultimate movie for Paramount Pictures Groucho, Chico, Harpo and, this time around, Zeppo, display a wonderful disarray of puns, slapstick and misunderstandings as Groucho becomes head of a college that needs to win a crucial football game. Chico operates out of a speakeasy in which speech is not at all easy, while dogcatcher Harpo strums a melancholy melody. A classic which is still timeless and unmissable.

Groucho Marx *Professor Wagstaff* • Harpo Marx • Chico Marx • Zeppo Marx • Thelma Todd *Connie Bailey* • David Landau *Jennings* • James Pierce *Mullens* • Nat Pendleton *McCarthy* ■ *Dir* Norman Z McLeod • *Scr* Bert Kalmar, Harry Ruby, SJ Perelman

The Horse in the Gray Flannel Suit ★★ 🅄

Comedy drama   1968 · US · Colour · 112mins

The poster line "All's fair in love and woah" gives you some idea of the quality of this strained Disney offering. The ever-willing Dean Jones is back in harness for this silly story about an advertising executive who uses his daughter's pet nag to help sell a brand of stomach pill. Director Norman Tokar

was one of the studio's most reliable live-action directors, but even he fails to get the pace above a canter. Look out for a young Kurt Russell. ▣

Dean Jones *Fred Bolton* • Diane Baker *Suzie Clemens* • Lloyd Bochner *Archer Madison* • Fred Clark *Tom Dugan* • Ellen Janov *Helen Bolton* • Morey Amsterdam *Charlie Blake* • Kurt Russell *Ronnie Gardner* ■ *Dir* Norman Tokar • *Scr* Louis Pelletier, from the novel *The Year of the Horse* by Eric Hatch

The Horse Soldiers ★★★ PG

War drama 1959 · US · Colour · 114mins

This stirring Civil War epic was not liked on its release by fans of the great western director John Ford: it's not really a western and it seemed dramatically unconvincing. Today, however, Ford's marvellous set pieces are genuinely thrilling, and there's nostalgic value in seeing two great movie stars (John Wayne and William Holden) teamed so cleverly. The film is based on a true incident (the 1863 Grierson raid deep into the South to cut supply lines to Vicksburg), and Ford tells the tale straight, but the sequence that stays in the memory is that of the Southern military cadets being ordered to lay down their young lives for the cause to the sound of fife and drum. ▣

John Wayne *Colonel John Marlowe* • William Holden (1) *Major Henry Kendall* • Constance Towers *Hannah Hunter* • Althea Gibson *Lukey* • Hoot Gibson *Brown* • Anna Lee *Mrs Buford* ■ *Dir* John Ford • *Scr* John Lee Mahin, Rackin Martin, from the novel by Harold Sinclair

Horse Thief ★★★★ PG

Drama 1986 · Chi · Colour · 86mins

Fifth-generation director Tian Zhuangzhuang combined a preoccupation with cinematic technique and his reverence for the forbidding majesty of the Tibetan plains in this stunningly photographed study of life in one of China's most marginalised communities. Yet against the harsh conditions that force Rigzin Tseshang to steal horses in order to feed his family, the film tenders the consolation provided by Buddhism and its exquisitely mystical ceremonies. Employing a range of transitional and optical devices, Tian not only reveals the relevance of religion to these hardy people, but also the importance of the cultural continuity that Beijing is so determined to suppress. In Mandarin with English subtitles.

Rigzin Tseshang *Norbu* • Dan Jiji *Dolma* • Jamco Jayang *Tashi* • Gaoba *Nowre* ■ *Dir* Tian Zhuangzhuang • *Scr* Rui Zhang

The Horse Whisperer ★★★ PG

Drama 1998 · US · Colour · 162mins

Robert Redford won the protracted Hollywood bidding war over the movie rights to British author Nicholas Evans's bestseller about a Montana cowboy who cures traumatised horses. Directing himself for the first time, Redford fits the role as snugly as those faded denims, watched glowingly by Kristin Scott Thomas, a natural choice after her role in *The English Patient*. She's a New Yorker with a daughter and a horse, both disabled in a horrendous road accident. So,

leaving husband Sam Neill behind, they trot off to Montana to see horse shrink Redford. The story's blend of Disney wildlife film and adult romance is bizarre and, at nearly three hours, far too long. But the Montana scenery is stunning and, against your better judgement, you often feel a lump in the throat. ▣ **DVD**

Robert Redford *Tom Booker* • Kristin Scott Thomas *Annie MacLean* • Sam Neill *Robert MacLean* • Dianne Wiest *Diane Booker* • Scarlett Johansson *Grace MacLean* • Chris Cooper *Frank Booker* ■ *Dir* Robert Redford • *Scr* Eric Roth, Richard LaGravenese, from the novel by Nicholas Evans

The Horseman on the Roof ★★★ 15

Period drama 1995 · Fr · Colour · 130mins

At the time the most expensive film ever made in France, Jean-Paul Rappeneau's follow-up to *Cyrano de Bergerac* was too burly for the costume crowd and too deep for the slam-bang brigade. Adapted from the novel by Jean Giono, this tale of 19th-century politics and plague is full of arresting set pieces. Yet there is little narrative cohesion beside the predictable course of the romance between dashing revolutionary Olivier Martinez and Juliette Binoche, the loyal wife searching a decimated Provence for her ageing husband. Evocatively shot by Thierry Arbogast, the action is further hindered by showy guest turns from the usually excellent Gérard Depardieu and Jean Yanne. In French with English subtitles. ▣

Juliette Binoche *Pauline De Théus* • Olivier Martinez *Angelo* • Laura Marioni *Carla* • Paul Chevillard *Giacomo* • Richard Sammel *Franz* • Claudio Amendola *Maggionari* • Gérard Depardieu *Police Commissioner* • Jean Yanne *Door to door salesman* ■ *Dir* Jean-Paul Rappeneau • *Scr* Jean-Paul Rappeneau, Nina Companeez, Jean-Claude Carrière, from the novel by Jean Giono

The Horsemen ★★

Drama 1971 · US · Colour · 100mins

You don't see much buzkashi on *Grandstand*, do you? This is the Afghan sport in which a headless calf's carcass is kicked about by men on horses until either someone wins (according to rules seemingly made up on the spot) or no other player is left alive. It's a natural subject for John Frankenheimer, who had previously made *Grand Prix*, but the lack of a story proves to be a problem. Omar Sharif and Jack Palance are the buzkashi rivals, losing leg and face respectively, while the horses and calves look sheepish.

Omar Sharif *Uraz* • Leigh Taylor-Young *Zereh* • Jack Palance *Tursen* • David De Mukhi • Peter Jeffrey *Hayatal* • Mohammed Shamsi *Osaman Bey* • Saeed Jaffrey *District Chief* ■ *Dir* John Frankenheimer • *Scr* Dalton Trumbo, from a novel by Joseph Kessel

The Horse's Mouth ★★★ U

Comedy 1958 · UK · BW · 94mins

Alec Guinness earned an Oscar nomination for his droll adaptation of Joyce Cary's celebrated novel. He also turns in a solid performance as Gulley Jimson, the irascible, self-obsessed artist whose decision to paint a mural

arouses the curiosity of friends and foes alike. John Bratby's paintings cleverly reflect the character's temperament and they have been beautifully shot by Arthur Ibbetson, whose use of colour is painterly indeed. The problem is that the focus is so firmly on Guinness that the other characters are left on the sideline.

Alec Guinness *Gulley Jimson* • Kay Walsh *Coker* • Renee Houston *Sarah* • Mike Morgan *Nosey* • Robert Coote *Sir William Beeder* ■ *Dir* Ronald Neame • *Scr* Alec Guinness, from the novel by Joyce Cary

Horton Foote's Alone ★★★

Drama 1997 · US · Colour · 107mins

Foote's unique voice of the American heartland dominates in his story of lonely farmer Hume Cronyn's deliberation on whether to sell his land and retire after the death of his wife. His shiftless nephews, who own half the property, and their wives are all for the sale, especially when a Texas oil man wants to buy the mineral rights. A dilemma occurs when an old pal and ex-tenant farmer, unhappily retired in Houston, asks to come back to live on the farm. Under the solid direction of British director Michael Lindsay-Hogg, the star-studded cast (James Earl Jones, Frederic Forrest, Shelley Duvall) bring this dysfunctional family to life in vivid, believable strokes.

Hume Cronyn *John Webb* • James Earl Jones *Grey* • Ed Begley Jr *Gerald* • Chris Cooper *Gus Jr* • Shelley Duvall *Estelle* • Hallie Foote *Agnes* • Frederic Forrest *Carl* • Roxanne Hart *Grace Ann* • Piper Laurie *Lillie* ■ *Dir* Michael Lindsay-Hogg • *Scr* Horton Foote

The Hospital ★★ 15

Black comedy 1971 · US · Colour · 98mins

Paddy Chayefsky won an Oscar for his script for this manic black comedy, but it's hard to see why the Academy would be taken in by its heavy-handed satire, crude characterisation and undisciplined structure. Frankly, it's a mess and a more talented director than Arthur Hiller would have been pressed to make anything of it. However, towering above all of this is a sensational performance from George C Scott as the surgeon who conquers his mid-life crisis while murder, magic and madness rage around him. Having rejected his Oscar for *Patton*, Scott received another nomination as an act of revenge by the Academy. ▣

George C Scott *Dr Herbert Bock* • Diana Rigg *Barbara Drummond* • Barnard Hughes *Drummond* • Andrew Duncan *William Mead* • Nancy Marchand *Head Nurse Christie* • Stephen Elliott *Sundstrom* ■ *Dir* Arthur Hiller • *Scr* Paddy Chayefsky

The Hostage ★★★

Thriller 1966 · US · Colour · 80mins

The big surprise about *The Hostage* is that Roger Corman's name isn't on it. One of scores of independent features made in the sixties, it has all of Corman's credentials: a dime budget, bleak locations, bags of energy, and John Carradine and Harry Dean Stanton in key roles. It's a crime story with a twist, about a six-year-old boy trapped in a removal van which contains a corpse. Shot in Iowa, it's tensely directed by Russell S Doughton

and co-edited by Gary Kurtz, later the producer of *Star Wars*.

Don O'Kelly *Bull* • Harry Dean Stanton *Eddie* • John Carradine *Otis Lovelace* • Danny Martins *Davey Cleaves* • Ron Hagerthy *Steve Cleaves* ■ *Dir* Russell S Doughton • *Scr* Robert Laning, from the novel by Henry Farrell

Hostage ★★ 15

Drama 1988 · US · Colour · 89mins

Comedian Carol Burnett gets serious in this drama about a woman who is kidnapped by a 19-year-old girl who has escaped from prison following a false conviction. The girl is played by Burnett's real-life daughter Carrie Hamilton, but this is worth catching simply to see a young, pre-Warren Beatty Annette Bening proving she wasn't always as good as she was in *American Beauty*. ▣

Carol Burnett *Martha* • Carrie Hamilton *Bonnie Lee* • Annette Bening *Jill* ■ *Dir* Peter Levin • *Scr* Stephen H Foreman

Hostage ★★★ 18

Action spy drama 1992 · UK · Colour · 96mins

This British-made spy thriller about Machiavellian double dealing in Whitehall too often resembles John le Carré on speed. Sam Neill, who himself would have made an interesting James Bond, stars as a disgruntled agent sent to Argentina to rescue a British subject held captive by guerillas, only to fall in love with former 007 girl Talisa Soto. A mildly diverting and topical international morality play from acclaimed television director Robert Young is enlivened by a solid supporting cast, while James Fox camps it up gloriously as a hypocritical Whitehall mandarin. ▣

Sam Neill *John Rennie* • Talisa Soto *Joanna* • James Fox *Hugo Paynter* • Art Malik *Kalim Said* • Cristina Higueras *Gabriella* • Michael Kitchen *Fredericks* ■ *Dir* Robert Young • *Scr* Arthur Hopcraft, from the novel *No Place to Hide* by Ted Allbeury

Hostage for a Day ★★ PG

Comedy 1994 · US · Colour · 88mins

Notable mainly as John Candy's one stab at directing, this unadventurous comedy went straight to video and makes for very mild entertainment indeed. Former *Cheers* star George Wendt is the financially-strapped suburbanite who stages his own kidnapping to make some money, only to watch helplessly as events spiral out of control. It's well played, but the cast can do little with a distinctly average script. ▣

George Wendt *Warren Kooey* • Robin Duke *Elizabeth Kooey* • Christopher Templeton *Diane St Clair* • John Candy *Yuri Petrovich* • Peter Torokvei *Ron Fyfe* • John Vernon *VD Regan* ■ *Dir* John Candy • *Scr* Robert Crane, Kari Hildebrand, Peter Torokvei

Hostage: the Christine Maresch Story ★★ 18

Drama based on a true story 1982 · Ausl · Colour · 88mins

Couched in terms more suited to a sensationalist TV movie, this Australian production unashamedly employs melodramatic symbolism to emphasise the unbelievable truth of its true-life subject. Director Frank Shields secures a full-throttle performance from Ralph Schicha, as the brutal husband who not only subjects wife Kerry Mack to endless domestic violence, but also forces her to participate in the bank raids that sustain his neo-Nazi activities. Although there are references to the Baader-Meinhof group, ultimately the film is clearly less interested in politics than in the tempestuous marriage. ▢

Kerry Mack *Christine Maresch* • Ralph Schicha *Walter Maresch* • Gabriella Barraket *Mandy* • Judy Nunn *Mrs Lewis* ■ *Dir* Frank Shields • *Scr* Frank Shields, John Lind

Hostages ★★★
Second World War drama
1943 · US · BW · 87mins

Not a particularly good war movie, but a rare chance to see Luise Rainer, winner of consecutive best actress Oscars for *The Great Ziegfeld* and *The Good Earth*. She is superb, though the real revelation is bulky William Bendix as leader of the Czech Resistance. The rest of the imported cast (Paul Lukas, Oscar Homolka, Katina Paxinou) seem to be having as much trouble with their accents as with the plot. Director Frank Tuttle later fell foul of the McCarthyite witch-hunt. He wasn't blacklisted, but his career was never the same.

Arturo De Cordova *Paul Breda* • Luise Rainer *Milada Pressinger* • William Bendix *Janoshik* • Roland Varno *Jan Pavel* • Oscar Homolka *Lev Pressinger* • Katina Paxinou *Maria* • Paul Lukas *Rheinhardt* • Fred Giermann *Captain Patzer* • Felix Basch *Doctor Wallerstein* ■ *Dir* Frank Tuttle • *Scr* Lester Cole, Frank Butler, from the novel by Stefan Heym

Hostages ★★★★
Documentary drama
1993 · US/UK · Colour · 105mins

Scripted by novelist Bernard MacLaverty, this is a gruelling and uncompromising account of the five-year incarceration endured by western hostages Terry Anderson, Tom Sutherland, Frank Reed, John McCarthy, Terry Waite and Brian Keenan after they were abducted in the Lebanon by a group of Hezbollah fundamentalists. Although director David Wheatley also includes actuality footage and reconstructions of the families' frustrated efforts to secure the sextet's release, it's the scenes set in the Beirut hideout that make the biggest dramatic impact. Played with conviction by a superior cast, this is a worthy tribute to the courage and determination of all involved.

Harry Dean Stanton *Frank Reed* • Colin Firth *John McCarthy* • Josef Sommer *Tom Sutherland* • Ciaran Hinds *Brian Keenan* • Jay O Sanders *Terry Anderson* • Conrad Asquith *Terry Waite* • Kathy Bates *Peggy Say* • Natasha Richardson *Jill Morrell* ■ *Dir* David Wheatley • *Scr* Bernard MacLaverty

Hostile Force ★★
Action adventure
1996 · Ger/US · Colour · 91mins

A fast-moving but rather dim German/US co-production, in which Cynthia Geary co-stars as a former cop turned security guard who gets caught up in a tense hostage situation. Geary is OK in one of the lead roles, but the only familiar face is that of former Brat Packer Andrew McCarthy, while the

direction from Michael Kennedy is efficient but uninspired.

Andrew McCarthy *Mike, "Rabbit"* • Cynthia Geary *Lucy James* • Wolf Larson *Tony Reineke* • Hannes Jaenicke *Jeff* • Cali Timmins *Janice Simmons* • Brent Stait *Wendel Pone* ■ *Dir* Michael Kennedy • *Scr* Michael January

Hostile Guns ★★ Ⓤ
Western   1967 · US · Colour · 91mins

This is a slightly superior outing in producer AC Lyles's western series based on the nostalgic appeal of veteran players. A strong and simple storyline helps, as does the presence of George Montgomery and Yvonne De Carlo, who both show plenty of life – he as the marshal, she as an old flame who's one of four prisoners he's transporting across the desert in a wagon. Close behind are the kinfolk (headed by John Russell) of one of the convicts, waiting for the right moment to rescue him. Tab Hunter, in his mid-thirties, represents youth.

George Montgomery *Gid McCool* • Yvonne De Carlo *Laura Mannon* • Tab Hunter *Mike Reno* • Brian Donlevy *Marshal Willett* • John Russell *Aaron* • Leo Gordon *Hank Pleasant* • Robert Emhardt *RC Crawford* • Pedro Gonzalez-Gonzales *Angel* ■ *Dir* RG Springsteen • *Scr* Steve Fisher, Sloan Nibley, from a story by James Edward Grant, Sloan Nibley

Hostile Hostages ★★★ 15
Black comedy   1994 · US · Colour · 92mins

Those unfamiliar with stand-up comedian Denis Leary may have problems tuning into his hard-smoking, aggressively acerbic persona. Yet here his considerable comic talents are brilliantly shoehorned into a highly amusing attack on contemporary "relationship management" which takes effective side-swipes at the American class system. Leary plays a small-time thief holding a dysfunctional family hostage at Christmas who ends up getting caught in the middle of their multiple feuds and neuroses. Judy Davis and Kevin Spacey give Leary solid support as the "couple from Hell" in director Ted Demme's bitingly dark comedy.

Denis Leary *Gus* • Judy Davis *Caroline* • Kevin Spacey *Lloyd* • Robert J Steinmiller Jr *Jesse* • Glynis Johns *Rose* • Raymond J Barry *Huff* • Christine Baranski *Connie* ■ *Dir* Ted Demme • *Scr* Richard LaGravenese, Marie Weiss, from a story by Marie Weiss

Hostile Intent ★★ 18
Action thriller   1997 · US · Colour · 86mins

An innocent day of war games goes very wrong in this mix of *Deliverance*-style action and conspiracy paranoia. Rob Lowe stars as the computer boffin who has come up with the hack-proof computer guard. Taking time off for a weekend of war games, his team is picked off by a sinister foe using real bullets. The presence of Lowe and John Savage gives it a veneer of respectability and the direction of Jonathan Heap lifts it slightly above most straight-to-video thrillers. Contains swearing and violence. ▢

Rob Lowe *Cleary* • Sofia Shinas *Gina* • James Kidnie *Agent Adams* • John Savage *Bear* • Saul Rubinek *Kendall* • Louis Del Grande *Soames* • Ronn Sarosiak *Gordon* ■ *Dir* Jonathan Heap • *Scr* Manny Coto

Hostile Intentions ★★ 18
Thriller   1995 · US · Colour · 85mins

Occasionally dubious in tone, this is nevertheless a lively slice of girl power. Tia Carrere, Tricia Leigh Fisher and Lisa Dean Ryan head down Mexico way for a wild weekend only to fall foul of the corrupt local cops. When one of them attempts to rape Fisher, the girls blast their way out of jail, sparking a violent cross-country race for the border. The *Thelma & Louise* comparisons – in fact much of the script – don't bear close scrutiny, but it belts along at a helter-skelter pace. Contains violence, nudity, swearing and drug abuse. ▢

Tia Carrere *Nora* • Tricia Leigh Fisher *Maureen* • Lisa Dean Ryan *Caroline* • Carlos Gomez *Juan* ■ *Dir/Scr* Catherine Cyran

Hostile Waters ★★ PG
Thriller based on a true story
1996 · US/UK · Colour · 91mins

A heavyweight cast gives this real-life submarine disaster story a sheen of class. The setting is the Reagan era, when a Russian sub collided with an American one in the Caribbean. This film traces the heroic attempts of the Soviet crew to repair their badly damaged craft, while the US worries about a potential nuclear catastrophe. Rutger Hauer, Martin Sheen and Max von Sydow head the topnotch cast in this TV movie, and director David Drury keeps the tension factor high. ▢

Rutger Hauer *Captain Britanov* • Martin Sheen *Aurora Skipper* • Max von Sydow *Admiral Chernavin* • Rob Campbell *Sergei Preminin* • Harris Yulin *Admiral Quinn* • Regina Taylor *Lieutenant Curtis* ■ *Dir* David Drury • *Scr* Troy Kennedy Martin, from research by Tom Mangold, Peter Huchthausen, William Cran

Hostile Witness ★★ Ⓤ
Courtroom drama
1968 · UK · Colour · 100mins

Ray Milland directs and stars in this interesting, if disappointing tale of a barrister vowing revenge against the hit-and-run driver who killed his daughter. But he ends up questioning his own sanity when he finds himself in the dock for the murder of his neighbour. This was written for the screen by Jack Roffey from his own play, and it shows: the script reads as though it is meant for the stage and the actors emote as if they are playing to a live audience.

Ray Milland *Simon Crawford QC* • Sylvia Syms *Sheila Larkin* • Felix Aylmer *Mr Justice Osborne* • Raymond Huntley *John Naylor* • Geoffrey Lumsden *Major Hugh Maitland* • Norman Barrs *Charles Milburn* ■ *Dir* Ray Milland • *Scr* Jack Roffey, from his play

Hostile Witness ★★★
Courtroom drama
1987 · US · Colour · 134mins

Sam Waterston stars in an interesting, if rather tedious political drama, in which a Middle Eastern terrorist is kidnapped and brought back to the United States to stand trial for murder. It's essentially an excuse for director Jeff Bleckner to get preachy about terrorism and, although he is as dependable as ever in the lead role, Waterston hasn't the scope to give a performance anywhere near the

standard of his Oscar-nominated contribution to *The Killing Fields*.

Sam Waterston *James Delmore* • Ron Leibman *Sion Resnik* • Robert Davi *Salim Ajami* • Joe Morton *Kevin Tandy* • Jo Henderson *Judge Bonner* • Stephen Lee *Bradford Ellis* ■ *Dir* Jeff Bleckner • *Scr* Richard Levinson, William Link

Hot Blood ★★★
Musical romance 1956 · US · Colour · 85mins

"Be there when Jane Russell shakes her tambourines!" the posters implored, and she certainly did, flaunting the gypsy stereotype in this overly heated Romany romance. Russell and Cornel Wilde are LA gypsies forced by their families into an arranged marriage. Naturally, they fight like crazy at first, until the predictable reconciliation. However, the risible aspects are compensated for by director Nicholas Ray's dramatic use of colour and expert use of the CinemaScope screen. Ray also managed to get animated performances from the usually wooden leads, who perform their musical numbers with gusto.

Jane Russell *Annie Caldash* • Cornel Wilde *Stephan Torino* • Luther Adler *Marco Torino* • Joseph Calleia *Papa Theodore* • Mikhail Rasumny *Old Johnny* • Nina Koshetz *Nita Johnny* • Helen Westcott *Velma* • Jamie Russell *Xano* ■ *Dir* Nicholas Ray • *Scr* Jesse Lasky Jr, from a story by Jean Evans

Hot Dog – The Movie ★ 18
Comedy   1984 · US · Colour · 94mins

Not a sausage or a bun in sight, yet this remains cinema's equivalent of fast food: indigestible and utterly unmemorable. This typically crude example of the eighties party movie, distinguished by some eye-catching ski footage, stars David Naughton as one of many horny adolescents contesting the world freestyle championship ("hot-dogging" is a form of choreographed skiing). Blatantly sexist – 1982's *Playboy* playmate Shannon Tweed and other similarly unclad ladies are there like so much tinsel on a Christmas tree – and aimed squarely at the youth market, this plays like some tired old Hollywood executive's idea of what teens want to see. ▢

David Naughton *Dan* • Patrick Houser *Harkin* • Tracy N Smith *Sunny* • John Patrick Reger *Rudi Garmischt* • Frank Koppola *Squirrel* • James Saito *Kendo* • Shannon Tweed *Sylvia Fonda* ■ *Dir* Peter Markle • *Scr* Mike Marvin

Hot Enough for June ★★★
Spy satire   1963 · UK · Colour · 98mins

James Bond is dead! Long live Nicolas Whistler – or at least that's what this spy spoof would have us believe. Everything here is just on the unfunny side of clever; for instance, the American title *Agent 8* is a reference both to Federico Fellini's $8\frac{1}{2}$, released earlier the same year, and the fact that this was the eighth collaboration between director Ralph Thomas and Dirk Bogarde. Cheerfully sending up his own Rank image as much as that of Bond, Bogarde merely passes muster, for the real star of the show is Robert Morley as the spymaster who equates espionage with the Eton wall game.

Dirk Bogarde *Nicolas Whistler* • Sylva Koscina *Vlasta Simenova* • Robert Morley *Cunliffe* • Leo McKern *Simenova* • Roger Delgado *Josef* • John Le Mesurier *Allsop* • Richard Vernon *Roddinghead* ■ *Dir* Ralph Thomas, Ralph Thomas • *Scr* Lukas Heller, from the novel *Night of Wenceslas* by Lionel Davidson

Hot Lead and Cold Feet ★★ U

Comedy western 1978 · US · Colour · 85mins

Jim Dale had laboured for years in the *Carry On* films and also collared an Oscar nomination for writing the lyrics to the theme song for *Georgy Girl*. Perhaps sensing another Michael Crawford, who made it big (briefly) in Hollywood, Dale was snapped up by Disney for this kiddie western. He plays three parts: grumpy patriarch Jasper Bloodshy and his two sons, one nerdy and feeble, the other a gunslinger. Prepare, though, to wade through several tons of Disney treacle as Dale earns every cent of his fee. American TV comic Don Knotts was cast to assist box-office revenue. ▭

Jim Dale *Eli/Wild Billy/Jasper Bloodshy* • Karen Valentine *Jenny* • Don Knotts *Denver Kid* • Jack Elam *Rattlesnake* • John Williams *Mansfield* • Darren McGavin *Mayor Ragsdale* • Warren Vanders *Boss Snead* • Debbie Lytton *Roxanne* ■ *Dir* Robert Butler • *Scr* Joseph L McEveety, Arthur Alsberg, Don Nelson, from a story by Rod Piffath

Hot Millions ★★★ U

Comedy caper 1968 · UK · Colour · 106mins

A large, disparate cast of famous faces, from Maggie Smith to Bob Newhart, pulls out some moderately funny stops in this bubbly, engaging tale of manipulative Peter Ustinov parting a large multinational from a sizeable portion of its shekels. Ustinov is thankfully given a large, containing script to curb his worst excesses, the jokes come thick and relatively fast, and there is a charming jauntiness. The enterprise tends to run dangerously low on steam towards the end, but it grabs the attention with a considerable degree of style.

Peter Ustinov *Marcus Pendleton/Caesar Smith* • Maggie Smith *Patty Terwilliger* • Karl Malden *Carlton J Klemper* • Bob Newhart *Willard C Gnatpole* • Robert Morley *Caesar Smith* • Cesar Romero *Customs Officer* ■ *Dir* Eric Till • *Scr* Ira Wallach, Peter Ustinov

Hot Money ★★

Adventure 1979 · Can · Colour · 78mins

There are only a handful of performers in cinema history whose mere presence can raise the quality of a film by at least a couple of notches. Orson Welles is one of the few, and he alone makes this tepid Canadian heist comedy worth bothering with. Sadly, we see too little of him as the sheriff to crooked deputy Michael Murphy. It's contrived, unfunny and clear to see why the film was withheld for five years – but at least there's Orson.

Orson Welles *Sheriff* • Michael Murphy *Burt* ■ *Dir* Selig Usher • *Scr* Carl DeSantis, Phyllis Camesano, Joel Cohen, Neil Cohen

Hot Pursuit ★★ 15

Comedy 1987 · US · Colour · 88mins

This movie serves as a reminder of John Cusack's career before he enjoyed success with such hits as Woody Allen's *Bullets over Broadway* and the Al Pacino political drama *City Hall*. Here, Cusack plays a college boy in pursuit of his girlfriend who has gone on holiday with her parents; as one might expect, his journey is beset with silly disasters. It's essentially an attempt to reprise the actor's first hit – Rob Reiner's *The Sure Thing* – but, although Cusack is always engaging to watch, this film has none of the charm or wit of that delightful comedy. ▭

John Cusack *Dan Bartlett* • Wendy Gazelle *Lori Cronenberg* • Monte Markham *Bill Cronenberg* • Shelley Fabares *Buffy Cronenberg* • Jerry Stiller *Victor Honeywell* • Ben Stiller *Chris Honeywell* • Robert Loggia *Mac MacLaren* ■ *Dir* Steven Lisberger • *Scr* Steven Lisberger, Steven Carabatsos, from a story by Steven Lisberger

Hot Resort ★ 18

Comedy 1985 · US · Colour · 87mins

There's not much in the way of humour in this teen comedy concerning four American youths who get up to various sexual shenanigans while working at a Caribbean resort hotel. Poor old Frank Gorshin wanders in and out of the virtually plotless story, while Bronson Pinchot shows none of the comic talent that would later make him famous. Cannon Pictures basically used the same plot for the execrable *Hot Chili* in the very same year. ▭

Tom Parsekian *Marty* • Debra Kelly *Liza* • Bronson Pinchot *Brad* • Michael Berz *Kesey* • Dan Schneider *Chuck* • Samm-Art Williams *Bill Martin* • Marcy Walker *Franny* • Frank Gorshin *Mr Green* ■ *Dir* John Robins • *Scr* John Robins, Boaz Davidson, Norman Hudis, from a story by Paul Max Rubenstein

The Hot Rock ★★★★ U

Crime caper 1972 · US · Colour · 100mins

This caper movie, based on a novel by Donald E Westlake, is not without its flaws, but it boasts a sense of finesse and fun that other films in the genre sadly lack. Robert Redford and George Segal head a quartet of criminals bent on stealing a fabulous diamond from the Brooklyn Museum. Inevitably, their ineptitude at robbery is a reflection of their incompetence at living. Peter Yates, working from a William Goldman script that shouldn't have split the tale into four distinct parts, directs without momentum but achieves interest through his actors' considerable expertise. Hot stuff.

Robert Redford *John Dortmunder* • George Segal *Andrew Kelp* • Zero Mostel *Abe Greenberg* • Ron Leibman *Murch* • Paul Sand *Alan Greenberg* • Moses Gunn *Dr Amusa* ■ *Dir* Peter Yates • *Scr* William Goldman, from a novel by Donald E Westlake

Hot Shot ★★

Drama 1986 · US · Colour · 89mins

Fever Pitch aside, football has been poorly treated by movie-makers and, while being by no means the worse, this run-of-the-mill American take provides more unintentional laughs than genuine drama. Pele, who obviously got the film bug during

Escape to Victory, plays a football legend who is called to help a youngster embrace the greatest game. Look for early appearances by a pre-stardom Mario Van Peebles, Jimmy Smits and Billy Warlock.

Jim Youngs *Jimmy Kristidis* • Pele *Santos* • David Groh *Jerry Norton* • Mario Van Peebles *Hoffman* • Bill Warlock [Billy Warlock] *Vinnie Fortino* • Jimmy Smits *Stars team member* ■ *Dir* Rick King • *Scr* Rick King, Joe Sauter

Hot Shots! ★★★ PG

Spoof action 1991 · US · Colour · 81mins

If ever a movie was ripe for sending up, then *Top Gun* was it, and, although this lacks the charm of classic spoofs *Airplane!* and *The Naked Gun*, there are enough good gags on show to win over those who wished Tom Cruise had gone down in flames. This time director Jim Abrahams goes solo without the Zucker brothers, but he still displays the same cheerful lack of taste and subtlety, and finds time to poke fun at movies ranging from *The Fabulous Baker Boys* through to *Dances with Wolves*. Charlie Sheen enjoys himself as the ludicrously macho fighter pilot hero, although Lloyd Bridges bags the most laughs as the altogether untogether commanding officer. Contains swearing. ▭

Charlie Sheen *Sean "Topper" Harley/Rhett Butler/Superman* • Cary Elwes *Kent Gregory* • Valeria Golino *Ramada Thompson/Scarlett O'Hara/Lois Lane* • Lloyd Bridges *Admiral Benson* • Kevin Dunn *Lieutenant Commander Block* • William O'Leary *Pete "Dead Meat" Thompson* • Kristy Swanson *Kowalski* • Efrem Zimbalist Jr *Wilson* • Jon Cryer *Jim "Wash Out" Pfaffenbach* ■ *Dir* Jim Abrahams • *Scr* Pat Proft, Jim Abrahams

Hot Shots! Part Deux ★★ PG

Spoof action 1993 · US · Colour · 82mins

The law of diminishing laughs applies to Jim Abrahams and Pat Proft's self-conscious parody of the *Rambo* series, with Charlie Sheen reprising his role of the superhero with zero tolerance for the enemy. The late Lloyd Bridges also returns, this time as the US president, but this sequel is too reminiscent of its predecessor to be either original or terribly amusing. Still, there are some laughs to be had and British comedy favourite Rowan Atkinson makes a brief appearance. More inventiveness would have helped, though. Contains swearing. ▭

Charlie Sheen *Topper Harley* • Lloyd Bridges *Tug Benson* • Valeria Golino *Ramada Rodham Hayman* • Richard Crenna *Colonel Denton Walters* • Brenda Bakke *Michelle Rodham Huddleston* • Miguel Ferrer *Harbinger* • Rowan Atkinson *Dexter Hayman* ■ *Dir* Jim Abrahams • *Scr* Jim Abrahams, Pat Proft

Hot Spell ★★★

Drama 1958 · US · BW · 88mins

This rather stagey family melodrama, set in New Orleans, was the last of the five films that Shirley Booth made before returning to the stage and TV. As in her first film, *Come Back, Little Sheba* in 1952, for which she won the best actress Oscar, Booth plays a distressed housewife dreaming of better days. Her sensitive performance is contrasted with Anthony Quinn's bombastic one as her philandering husband. Shirley MacLaine, on the

verge of real stardom, is touching as the couple's daughter, and Eileen Heckart provides some humour as a neighbour. Sub-Tennessee Williams it may be, but it offers a certain amount of minor pleasure.

Shirley Booth *Alma Duval* • Anthony Quinn *Jack Duval* • Shirley MacLaine *Virginia Duval* • Earl Holliman *Buddy Duval* • Eileen Heckart *Fan* • Clint Kimbrough *Billy Duval* • Warren Stevens *Wyatt* • Jody Lawrance *Dora May* ■ *Dir* Daniel Mann • *Scr* James Poe, from the play *Next of Kin* by Lonnie Coleman

The Hot Spot ★★★ 18

Black comedy thriller 1990 · US · Colour · 124mins

Don Johnson is the drifter, holed up in a small Texas town, who falls for bad girl Virginia Madsen and good girl Jennifer Connelly. Director Dennis Hopper turns in a faithful tribute to the *film noir* thrillers of old, but, this being the nineties, he ups the sexual content a number of degrees. There are lots of fans, dust and people sweating, and Madsen smoulders away furiously to good effect. While not quite so convincing, Johnson is still suitably mean and brooding as the fall guy, and there's neat support from Charles Martin Smith and William Sadler. Contains violence, swearing, sex scenes and nudity. ▭

Don Johnson *Harry Madox* • Virginia Madsen *Dolly Harshaw* • Jennifer Connelly *Gloria Harper* • Charles Martin Smith *Lon Gulik* • William Sadler *Frank Sutton* • Jerry Hardin *George Harshaw* • Barry Corbin *Sheriff* ■ *Dir* Dennis Hopper • *Scr* Nona Tyson, Charles Williams, from the novel *Hell Hath No Fury* by Charles Williams

Hot Stuff ★★ 15

Comedy 1979 · US · Colour · 87mins

In the seventies US police established numerous undercover fencing set-ups which resulted in the recovery of over a billion dollars worth of stolen goods and led to thousands of arrests. Co-scripted by ace crime writer Donald E Westlake, this cop comedy takes that sting as its starting point and weaves around it a tale of double dealing involving the Mafia. Dom DeLuise directs and stars as Ernie Fortunato, a cop badly in need of some success. The sharp script and pacy style ensures interest is maintained, but it seems to be less than the sum of its parts and should have been better. ▭

Dom DeLuise *Ernie Fortunato* • Jerry Reed *Doug Van Horne* • Suzanne Pleshette *Louise Webster* • Luis Avalos *Ramon* • Ossie Davis *Captain Geibarger* • Marc Lawrence *Carmine* • Richard Davalos *Charles* ■ *Dir* Dom DeLuise • *Scr* Michael Kane, Donald E Westlake

Hot Summer Night ★★

Crime drama 1957 · US · BW · 85mins

Experienced television director David Friedkin shot this tightly scripted drama in just nine days. Although it lacks the grit of other contemporary crime B-movies, there's an atypically anti-media slant to this tale of the ambitious reporter who risks the life of his wife in his efforts to further his career by interviewing the leader of a notorious bank gang. However, we're so used to seeing Leslie Nielsen parodying situations like these that some of the riper dialogue has an unintentionally comic ring.

Leslie Nielsen *William Joel Partain* • Colleen Miller *Irene Partain* • Edward Andrews *Lou Follett* • Jay C Flippen *Oren Kobble* • James Best *Kermit* • Paul Richards (1) *Elly Horn* • Robert Wilke [Robert J Wilke] *Tom Ellis* ■ *Dir* David Friedkin • *Scr* Morton Fine, David Friedkin, from a story by Edwin P Hicks

Hot Target ★★ 18
Crime thriller   1985 · NZ · Colour · 91mins

A rather predictable and ham-fisted attempt at a gripping thriller, this New Zealand film tries to cover its clichéd tracks with twists and turns aimed at confusing the viewer. Simone Griffeth is the wife planning to get rid of husband Bryan Marshall with the help of a lover, unaware that her accomplice is actually a thief setting her up. Are you still with us? A *film noir* that's more bland than black. Contains swearing and nudity. ▢

Simone Griffeth *Christine Webber* • Steve Marachuk *Greg Sandford* • Bryan Marshall *Clive Webber* • Peter McCauley *Detective Inspector Nolan* ■ *Dir* Denis Lewiston • *Scr* Denis Lewiston, from a story by Gerry O'Hara

Hot to Trot ★ PG
Comedy   1988 · US · Colour · 79mins

It's typical of this confused and confusing comedy that the director's name, Michael Dinner, could so easily be mistaken for Michael Winner, the British film-maker. But however bad his movies, Winner has too much expertise to be responsible for this outdated tat, in which Bobcat Goldthwait gets tips from a talking horse (voiced by John Candy) and thinks he's on to a whinnying streak. Unsurprisingly, he's not. ▢

Bobcat Goldthwait *Fred Chaney* • Dabney Coleman *Walter Sawyer* • Jim Metzler *Boyd Osborne* • Cindy Pickett *Victoria Peyton* • Virginia Madsen *Allison Rowe* • John Candy *Don* ■ *Dir* Michael Dinner • *Scr* Stephen Neigher, Hugo Gilbert, Charlie Peters, from a story by Stephen Neigher, Hugo Gilbert

The Hot Touch ★
Romantic thriller
1982 · Can/Fr · Colour · 92mins

Roger Vadim was once the *enfant terrible* of French cinema. Yet, by the early eighties, he was reduced to accepting third-rate assignments across the Atlantic. Surely even a cursory glance at this script would have saved him a trip, as this art-scam thriller is as bogus as the paintings churned out by Wayne Rogers for crooked dealer, Patrick Macnee. Only the sinister commission from the psychopathic Lloyd Bochner – to replace a series of pictures lost in the war – has anything going for it.

Wayne Rogers *Danny Fairchild* • Marie-France Pisier *Dr Emillienne Simpson* • Lloyd Bochner *Severo* • Samantha Eggar *Samantha O'Brien* • Patrick Macnee *Vincent Reblack* • Melvyn Douglas *Max Reich* • Gloria Carlin *Kelly* • Allan Kolman *Lincoln Simpson* ■ *Dir* Roger Vadim • *Scr* Peter Dion, from a story by Peter Dion

Hot Water ★★★ U
Silent comedy   1924 · US · BW · 53mins

Harold Lloyd's previous comedy, *Girl Shy*, was eight reels long and had

theatre owners complaining about the gaps between the pratfalls. Lloyd got the message and took the scissors to *Hot Water*, cutting out the intricate plotting and concentrating on his trademark stunts. The story is simple: Lloyd is a newly married man coping with shopping, traffic and, naturally, his mother-in-law. This isn't one of Lloyd's best films, though his bespectacled character always has charm and there's a brilliant scene in a traffic jam when he's encumbered by a turkey that he's won in a raffle.

Harold Lloyd *Hubby* • Jobyna Ralston *Wifey* • Josephine Crowell *Mother-in-law* • Charles Stevenson *Brother-in-law* • Pat Harmon *Straphanger* • Andy DeVilla *Cop* • Mickey McBan *Brother-in-law* ■ *Dir* Sam Taylor, Fred C Newmeyer • *Scr* Thomas J Gray, Tim Whelan, John Grey, Sam Taylor

Hotel ★★
Drama   1967 · US · Colour · 108mins

Rivals fight for the ownership of a deluxe hotel, the St Gregory in New Orleans, as sundry guests, each with a personalised mini-drama in their luggage, check in and out. These include Merle Oberon as an English duchess whose husband is being blackmailed for murder, Karl Malden as a frustrated thief who keeps stealing credit cards instead of cash, and a black couple who are acting as agents provocateur for the Civil Rights movement. Arthur Hailey based his novel on New Orleans's Fairmont Hotel but this adaptation lacks the glamour and the big stars to carry it off.

Rod Taylor *Peter McDermott* • Catherine Spaak *Jeanne* • Karl Malden *Keycase* • Melvyn Douglas *Trent* • Kevin McCarthy *O'Keefe* • Merle Oberon *Duchess* • Richard Conte *Dupere* • Michael Rennie *Duke of Lanbourne* • Carmen McRae *Christine, the singer* ■ *Dir* Richard Quine • *Scr* Wendell Mayes, from the novel by Arthur Hailey

Hotel ★★★
Drama   1983 · US · Colour

With its five-star settling and transient guests, Arthur Hailey's novel is a natural for a TV series, and this pilot is rather better than the 1967 film version. Where the book was based in New Orleans, the location here is California; this time around the eponymous hostelry is owned by Bette Davis and managed by James Brolin. The result is glossy, vacuous and very entertaining, mainly due to Davis's scene-stealing performance. Sadly, a stroke stopped Davis from appearing in the subsequent series; her role was ironically taken by Anne Baxter, who famously usurped her in *All About Eve* three decades earlier.

Bette Davis *Laura Trent* • James Brolin *Peter McDermott* • Connie Sellecca *Christine Francis* • Shari Belafonte-Harper [Shari Belafonte] *Julie Gillette* • Morgan Fairchild *Guest* • Mel Tormé *Guest* ■ *Dir* Jerry London • *Scr* John Furia, Barry Oringer, from the novel by Arthur Hailey

Hotel Berlin ★
Second World War drama
1945 · US · BW · 98mins

An updated, retitled adaptation of Vicki Baum's 1943 novel *Berlin Hotel*, which, like her more famous *Grand Hotel*, observes the comings and the goings of the guests in said hotel as

the Allies close in. In this case, it's mainly a Nazi packing up at war's end and preparing to leave for South America with a plan to start another world war, and a Noble prize-winning scientist whose life has been destroyed by the Nazis. Warner Bros hoped they had another *Casablanca* on their hands; they didn't.

Helmut Dantine *Martin Richter* • Andrea King *Lisa Dorn* • Raymond Massey *Arnim Von Dahnwitz* • Faye Emerson *Tillie Weiler* • Peter Lorre *Johannes Koenig* • Alan Hale *Hermann Plottke* • George Coulouris *Joachim Helm* ■ *Dir* Peter Godfrey, Jack Gage • *Scr* Jo Pagano, Alvah Beassie, from the novel *Berlin Hotel* by Vicki Baum

Hotel Colonial ★★ 15
Adventure thriller
1987 · US/It · Colour · 101mins

A beautifully shot but ultimately insubstantial melodrama set in Latin America. John Savage plays an American out of his depth when he travels to Colombia to discover the truth behind his brother's reported death and comes up against the sinister Robert Duvall. Rachel Ward plays the love interest and all three produce capable performances, but the meandering script lacks gravitas. ▢

John Savage *Marco Venieri* • Robert Duvall *Carrasco* • Rachel Ward *Irene Costa* • Massimo Troisi *Werner* ■ *Dir* Cinzia Torrini • *Scr* Enzo Monteleone, Cinzia Torrini, Ira R Barmak, Robert Katz, from a story by Enzo Monteleone • *Cinematographer* Giuseppe Rotunno

Hotel de Love ★★★ 15
Romantic comedy
1996 · Ausl/US · Colour · 92mins

This unusually well-constructed Australian romantic comedy has much of the style of *Muriel's Wedding* and features British beauty Saffron Burrows, Pippa Grandison and old stager Ray Barrett. Twin brothers Rick and Stephen fall for high school goddess Melissa (Burrows), who leads them a merry dance before heading off to college. Matters come to a head a decade later when Melissa and her timid fiancé check into the honeymoon hotel where Rick is working as a bellhop. It's a lightweight affair, but it exudes a certain charm. ▢

Aden Young *Rick Dunne* • Saffron Burrows *Melissa Morrison* • Simon Bossell *Stephen Dunne* • Pippa Grandison *Alison Leigh* • Ray Barrett *Jack Dunne* • Julia Blake *Edith Dunne* • Peter O'Brien *Norman* • Belinda McLory *Janet* ■ *Dir/Scr* Craig Rosenberg

Hôtel du Nord ★★★
Drama   1938 · Fr · BW · 84mins

A brooding study of France on the verge of a precipice, this may not be Marcel Carné's most accomplished work, but it's still undeniably affecting. Though without the services of regular screenwriter, Jacques Prévert, Carné could still rely on designer Alexandre Trauner to reproduce the atmospheric settings that were essential to his poetic realist style. Indeed, the tatty interiors and quaintly rundown canal landmarks are the real stars of a film that only comes fitfully to life. Doomed lovers Annabella and Jean-Pierre Aumont are just a touch too tragic, while Arletty and Louis Jouvet are a

little too unbridled in their villainy. In French with English subtitles.

Annabella *Renée* • Arletty *Raymonde* • Louis Jouvet *M Edmond* • Jean-Pierre Aumont *Pierre* • Jeanne Marken *Louise Lecouvreur* • André Brunot *Emile Lecouvreur* • Bernard Blier *Prosper* ■ *Dir* Marcel Carné • *Scr* Marcel Carné, Henri Jeanson, Jean Aurenche (adaptation), from the novel by Eugène Dabit

Hôtel du Paradis ★★★ 15
Drama   1986 · UK/Fr · Colour · 113mins

Jana Bokova may have been working with an experienced cast, but her thoughtful study of isolation and thwarted ambition still displays a maturity rare in debutante directors. In an impudent yet fondly poignant reference to his own career, Fernando Rey plays an actor taking one last stab at legitimacy after wasting his talent in escapist entertainments. His fellow residents – among them Fabrice Luchini's frustrated film-maker and Hugues Quester's penurious thespian – are no less acquainted with disappointment, however. The tone is melancholic, but it's the restraint and attention to detail that makes this film so unexpectedly affecting. French dialogue dubbed into English.

Fernando Rey *Joseph* • Bérangère Bonvoisin • Hugues Quester *Maurice* • Marika Rivera *Marika* • Carola Regnier *Sarah* • Raul Gimenez *Emilio* • Michael Medwin *English producer* • Fabrice Luchini *Arthur* ■ *Dir/Scr* Jana Bokova

Hotel Imperial ★★★
Silent First World War drama
1927 · US · BW · 84mins

The noted Swedish director Mauritz Stiller arrived in Hollywood in 1925 with his protégée, Greta Garbo. He could not fit in with the studio system and only completed two pictures for Paramount in two-and-a-half years, the first being this powerful drama of wartime espionage and romance. Visually striking with its vast hotel setting and beautifully paced, it stars Pola Negri in an unusually restrained performance as the hotel chambermaid who helps an Austrian officer trapped behind Russian lines. Billy Wilder updated the story to the Second World War for *Five Graves to Cairo*.

Pola Negri *Anna Sedlak* • James Hall *Lieutenant Paul Almasy* • George Siegmann *General Juschkiewitsch* • Max Davidson *Elias Butterman* • Michael Vavitch *Tabakowitsch* ■ *Dir* Mauritz Stiller • *Scr* Jules Furthman, from the story *Szinmu Negy Felvonasban* by Lajos Biro • *Cinematographer* Bert Glennon

The Hotel New Hampshire ★★★ 18
Comedy drama   1984 · US · Colour · 103mins

On its original release, there was anything but a critical consensus on this adaptation of John Irving's expansive novel. Many blamed the book for the film's episodic structure and the sensationalist nature of the fates that befall the central characters. Others praised writer/director Tony Richardson for the fidelity of his approach. Led by Rob Lowe, Jodie Foster and Beau Bridges, the cast does its best, although the characters are a pretty hard bunch to sympathise with, particularly Nastassja Kinski's Susie, who regularly retreats into a

bear suit to calm her nerves. David Watkin's photography is a bonus, however. Contains swearing, sex scenes and violence. ▪

Rob Lowe *John Berry* • Jodie Foster *Franny Berry* • Paul McCrane *Frank Berry* • Beau Bridges *Win Berry* • Lisa Banes *Mary Berry* • Jennie Dundas *Lilly Berry* • Seth Green *Egg Berry* • Nastassja Kinski *Susie the Bear* • Wallace Shawn *Freud* • Wilford Brimley *"Iowa Bob" Berry* • Joely Richardson *Waitress* • Matthew Modine • Amanda Plummer ▪ *Dir* Tony Richardson • *Scr* Tony Richardson, from the novel by John Irving

Hotel Paradiso ★★

Comedy 1966 · US/UK · Colour · 100mins

Adapted by producer/director Peter Glenville and Jean-Claude Carrière from Georges Feydeau and Maurice Desvallières's famous stage farce *L'Hôtel du Libre Echange*, this is a classic example of how what might be hilarious in the theatre can end up being a dead duck on the screen. The action is so flatly directed that not even that great editor Anne Coates can inject any pace into the endless round of bedroom toing and froing that should have been as funny as it is frantic. Robert Morley blusters to reasonable effect, but neither Alec Guinness nor Gina Lollobrigida looks comfortable pursuing their affair.

Alec Guinness *Benedict Boniface* • Gina Lollobrigida *Marcelle Cot* • Robert Morley *Henri Cot* • Peggy Mount *Angelique Boniface* • Akim Tamiroff *Anniello* • Marie Bell *La Grande Antoinette* • Derek Fowldes [Derek Fowlds] *Maxime* ▪ *Dir* Peter Glenville • *Scr* Jean-Claude Carrière, Peter Glenville, from the play *L'Hôtel du Libre Echange* by Georges Feydeau, Maurice Desvallières

Hotel Reserve ★★★ U

Thriller 1944 · UK · BW · 88mins

British B-picture master Lance Comfort was always strong on atmosphere, if weak on plot. So it's the ambience that wins out in this subdued thriller which he directed, with Victor Hanbury and Max Greene, from an Eric Ambler novel. As a refugee hunts for a Nazi spy among guests at a French hotel, a directory of the time's character actors – from James Mason via Lucie Mannheim to Raymond Lovell – opens up, together with a flock of clichés. It's the atmosphere that intrigues, though.

James Mason *Peter Vadassy* • Lucie Mannheim *Madame Suzanne Koche* • Raymond Lovell *Monsieur Robert Duclos* • Julien Mitchell *Monsieur Beghin* • Clare Hamilton *Miss Mary Skelton* • Martin Miller *Herr Walter Vogel* • Herbert Lom *Monsieur André Roux* • Frederick Valk *Herr Emil Schimler* ▪ *Dir* Victor Hanbury, Lance Comfort, Max Greene • *Scr* John Davenport, from a novel by Eric Ambler

Hotel Sahara ★★★ U

Second World War comedy
1951 · UK · BW · 87mins

A marvellous comedy idea: during the desert campaign in the Second World War, Peter Ustinov's hotel is utilised at various times by British, German, Italian and French forces. Naturally, proprietor Ustinov manages to accommodate them all, plus a few visiting Arabs as well. Very funny, and played at a fast and furious pace by a wonderful cast, notably Yvonne De

Carlo as Ustinov's fiancée, the redoubtable David Tomlinson and splendid character actors Bill Owen, Sidney Tafler, Roland Culver and Eugene Deckers.

Yvonne De Carlo *Yasmin Pallas* • Peter Ustinov *Emad* • David Tomlinson *Captain "Puffin" Cheynie* • Roland Culver *Major Bill Randall* • Albert Lieven *Lt Gunther Von Heilicke* • Bill Owen *Private Binns* • Sidney Tafler [Sydney Tafler] *Corporal Pullar* • Eugene Deckers *French Spahi Officer* ▪ *Dir* Ken Annakin • *Scr* Patrick Kirwan, George H Brown

Hotel Sorrento ★★ 15

Drama 1994 · Ausl · Colour · 107mins

Family drama from Down Under about the ties that threaten to unbind when one of three sisters writes a tell-all book about life in their home town, the Aussie seaside resort of Sorrento. The book purports to be fiction, but the other two siblings reckon there's more than a few grains of uncomfortable truth in it. It's nicely acted by Joan Plowright, Caroline Goodall and *Strictly Ballroom*'s Tara Morice, but the material is dull and the pace is plodding.

Caroline Goodall *Meg Moynihan* • Caroline Gillmer *Hilary Moynihan* • Tara Morice *Pippa Moynihan* • Joan Plowright *Marge Morrisey* • John Hargreaves *Dick Bennett* • Ray Barrett *Wal Moynihan* • Ben Thomas *Troy Moynihan* • Nicholas Bell *Edwin* ▪ *Dir* Richard Franklin • *Scr* Richard Franklin, Peter Fitzpatrick, from the play by Hannie Rayson

Hotel Terminus: the Life and Times of Klaus Barbie ★★★★★

Documentary
1987 · US/Fr · BW and Colour · 267mins

Having been denied an Oscar for *The Sorrow and the Pity*, Marcel Ophüls finally received his due reward for this damning study of the unholy alliance of political expediency and anti-Semitic corruption that allowed former Gestapo chief Klaus Barbie (the so-called "Butcher of Lyons") to spend over 30 contented years in Bolivia, in spite of the enormity of his crimes against humanity. In the course of interviews with victims, enemies, collaborators and others, it becomes clear that Barbie had many willing accomplices – and only some wore Nazi uniforms. An epic historical documentary, perhaps, but also a moral indictment of timeless resonance. In English, French, German and Spanish with subtitles.

Jeanne Moreau *Narrator* ▪ *Dir* Marcel Ophüls

Houdini ★★★ U

Biography 1953 · US · Colour · 105mins

This is the first of five films real-life married couple Tony Curtis and Janet Leigh – the so-called "elite of the milkshake set" – made together. As the famous escapologist Harry Houdini, Curtis is half-naked for most of the early scenes, a treat for his teenage fans at the time. When he finds Mrs Houdini, he pays the rent by dreaming up ever more ambitious stunts, leading to his fatal accident in 1926 when he drowned upside down in a locked water tank. The movie covers some 40 years, though Curtis and Leigh age no more than 40 minutes. However, that

won't stop you enjoying this entertaining hagiography.

Tony Curtis *Houdini* • Janet Leigh *Bess* • Torin Thatcher *Otto* • Angela Clarke *Mrs Weiss* • Stefan Schnabel *Prosecuting attorney* • Ian Wolfe *Fante* • Sig Ruman *Schultz* • Michael Pate *Dooley* • Connie Gilchrist *Mrs Schultz* ▪ *Dir* George Marshall • *Scr* Philip Yordan, from a biography by Harold Kellock

Houdini ★★ PG

Biography 1998 · Colour · 90mins

A well-mounted, but wholly inaccurate, TV biopic about world famous illusionist Harry Houdini which charts his immigration to America, rapid rise in show business as an ace escapologist and then seance debunker, his relationship with his tetchy wife Bess, and finally his tragic death. A bland central performance by Johnathon Schaech does nothing to uncover the real man behind the magician, and the fuzzy soap opera dramatics of his domestic life divert attention from his contribution to the vaudeville industry. The atmosphere of the turn-of-the-century show-business world is neatly executed, but once Houdini's career takes off the movie loses its way and becomes just another mundane showbiz fable. ▭

Johnathon Schaech *Harry Houdini* • Stacy Edwards *Bess Houdini* • George Segal *Beck* • Paul Sorvino *Blackburn* • Rhea Perlman *Esther* • David Warner *Sir Arthur Conan Doyle* • Mark Ruffalo *Theo* ▪ *Dir/Scr* Pen Densham

Hound Dog Man ★★★ U

Musical 1959 · US · Colour · 86mins

Before such singer/actors as Sting or Madonna, there was Fabian, a good-looking teen idol who charmingly acknowledged that, despite carefully constructed hit records, he couldn't sing. This movie marked his screen debut, straight into a leading role in an amiable, rustic near-western from 20th Century-Fox. The title is deliberately redolent of Elvis Presley, but actually means what it says: Fabian hangs around the farm with some dogs. Under talented director Don Siegel's watchful eye (Siegel would handle Elvis himself in *Flaming Star* a year later), this is a beautifully filmed drama, and Fabian acquits himself remarkably well.

Fabian *Clint* • Carol Lynley *Dony* • Stuart Whitman *Blackie Scantling* • Arthur O'Connell *Aaron Mckinney* • Dodie Stevens *Nita Stringer* ▪ *Dir* Don Siegel • *Scr* Fred Gipson, Winston Miller, from the novel by Fred Gipson

The Hound of the Baskervilles ★★★★★ PG

Classic mystery 1939 · US · BW · 79mins

Follow the paw-prints of this enormous beast and be enthralled by the classiest Sherlock Holmes movie in the B-picture canon. Basil Rathbone is on terrific form as Holmes, leaving Nigel Bruce as Watson spluttering behind. When the game's afoot, the moors are scarfed in fog and the last of the Baskerville line is in dire danger. Surprisingly for 1939, Holmes's final words are "Quick Watson – the needle!", a reference to his drug addiction. But audiences of the time scarcely knew that; they must have thought he'd taken up sewing. ▭

Basil Rathbone *Sherlock Holmes* • Nigel Bruce *Dr Watson* • Richard Greene *Sir Henry Baskerville* • Wendy Barrie *Beryl Stapleton* • Lionel Atwill *James Mortimer MD* • John Carradine *Barryman* • Barlowe Borland *Frankland* • Beryl Mercer *Mrs Jenifer Mortimer* ▪ *Dir* Sidney Lanfield • *Scr* Ernest Pascal, from the novel by Sir Arthur Conan Doyle

The Hound of the Baskervilles ★★★★ PG

Classic mystery 1959 · UK · Colour · 83mins

Thrilling Hammer horror and the fabulous logic of Sir Arthur Conan Doyle are the perfect match in what was the first Sherlock Holmes adventure after the Universal series ended in 1946, and also the first in colour. It weaves a darkly romantic Gothic spell around the dread Hound from Hell, stalking the foggy moors on the lookout for cursed Baskerville family members. Peter Cushing gives one of his finest performances as the Baker Street sleuth and Christopher Lee is on top haunted form as Sir Henry in an atmospheric tour de force which Holmes scholars consider the definitive version of the tale. ▭

Peter Cushing *Sherlock Holmes* • André Morell *Dr Watson* • Christopher Lee *Sir Henry* • Marla Landi *Cecile* • Ewen Solon *Stapleton* • Francis De Wolff *Dr Mortimer* • Miles Malleson *Bishop Frankland* • John Le Mesurier *Barrymore* • David Oxley *Sir Hugo Baskerville* ▪ *Dir* Terence Fisher • *Scr* PeterBryan, from the novel by Sir Arthur Conan Doyle

The Hound of the Baskervilles ★★

Detective mystery
1972 · US · Colour · 90mins

This poorly scripted TV pilot for a proposed Sherlock Holmes television series is appallingly directed, with no sense of atmosphere whatsoever. Yet it remains watchable thanks to the casting of the two leads: the ageing Stewart Granger shares Holmes's arrogance and humour, though physically is nothing like the gaunt detective, and Bernard Fox does well as Dr Watson. William Shatner looks hopelessly out of period, however.

Stewart Granger *Sherlock Holmes* • Bernard Fox *Dr Watson* • William Shatner *George Stapleton* • Anthony Zerbe *Dr John Mortimer* • Sally Ann Howes *Laura Frankland* • John Williams *Arthur Frankland* ▪ *Dir* Barry Crane • *Scr* Robert E Thompson, from the novel by Sir Arthur Conan Doyle

The Hound of the Baskervilles ★ PG

Parody 1977 · UK · Colour · 81mins

Andy Warhol's one-time collaborator Paul Morrissey directed this woeful lampoon of Sir Arthur Conan Doyle's most celebrated story. In addition to scripting duties, Peter Cook also takes on the role of Baker Street's finest, while Dudley Moore doubles up as the doggedly dim Watson and Holmes's mother. Never did the duo look so bereft of inspiration as they watch gag after gag refuse to respond to the ministrations of such comic geniuses as Spike Milligan, Kenneth Williams and Terry-Thomas. Contains some swearing. ▭

Peter Cook *Sherlock Holmes* • Dudley Moore *Dr Watson/Mrs Holmes/Mrs Spiggott* •

Denholm Elliott *Stapleton* • Joan Greenwood *Beryl Stapleton* • Terry-Thomas *Dr Mortimer* • Max Wall *Mr Barrymore* • Irene Handl *Mrs Barrymore* • Kenneth Williams *Sir Henry Baskerville* • Roy Kinnear *Seldon* • Prunella Scales *Glynis* • Penelope Keith *Massage parlour receptionist* • Spike Milligan *Baskerville police force* ■ *Dir* Paul Morrissey • *Scr* Peter Cook, Dudley Moore, Paul Morrissey, from the novel by Sir Arthur Conan Doyle

The Hound of the Baskervilles ★★★ 🔞

Detective mystery
1983 · US · Colour · 95mins

There had already been one exceptional version of this classic Sherlock Holmes mystery with Basil Rathbone as Baker Street's finest. Indeed, there had even been an admirable one with Peter Cushing, a negligible one featuring Stewart Granger and a quite execrable one starring Peter Cook. Yet director Douglas Hickox still deemed it necessary to trek across Dartmoor for a further encounter with the accursed Baskervilles and their pesky pooch. Head and shoulders above a cast of familiar British faces, Ian Richardson goes for the sardonic approach as Holmes, but there's nothing really new here. Who's next? 🎬

Ian Richardson *Sherlock Holmes* • Donald Churchill *Dr Watson* • Denholm Elliott *Dr Mortimer* • Nicholas Clay *Jack Stapleton* • Martin Shaw *Sir Henry Baskerville* • Glynis Barber *Beryl Stapleton* • Edward Judd *Mr Barrymore* • Eleanor Bron *Mrs Barrymore* ■ *Dir* Douglas Hickox • *Scr* Charles Pogue, from the novel by Sir Arthur Conan Doyle

The Hounds of Zaroff ★★★★

Classic horror
1932 · US · BW · 63mins

Also known to moviegoers as *The Most Dangerous Game*, this teaming of star Fay Wray and co-director Ernest Schoedsack predates their classic *King Kong*, and traverses similar action territory, with the genius of composer Max Steiner vividly illuminating both movies. Richard Connell's story was a natural for filming, but none of the subsequent versions live up to the sheer exuberance of this 63-minute cracker. Leslie Banks's mad Count Zaroff remains hard to replicate and the theme of hunting human game was never quite so chilling as here. No question, this is the best movie version of the tale.

Joel McCrea *Bob Rainsford* • Fay Wray *Eve Trowbridge* • Leslie Banks *Count Zaroff* • Robert Armstrong *Martin Trowbridge* • Steve Clemento *Tartar servant* • Noble Johnson *Tartar servant* ■ *Dir* Ernest B Schoedsack, Irving Pichel • *Scr* James A Creelman, from a story by Richard Connell

The Hour before the Dawn ★★

Second World War spy drama
1944 · US · BW · 74mins

Franchot Tone is a pacifist English lord who weds his Austrian servant, sultry Veronica Lake, not realising she is a German spy helping the Nazis plan an invasion of England. It sounds like fun, but this propaganda piece, made at the height of the Second World War, is unremittingly earnest and none too convincing. Adapted from one of

Somerset Maugham's lesser works, it puts too much strain on Lake's histrionic reserves, while Tone seems bemused by the whole business.

Franchot Tone *Jim Hetherton* • Veronica Lake *Dora Bruckmann* • John Sutton *Roger Hetherton* • Binnie Barnes *May Hetherton* • Henry Stephenson *Gen Hetherton* • Philip Merivale *Sir Leslie Buchannan* ■ *Dir* Frank Tuttle • *Scr* Michael Hogan, Lesser Samuels, from the novel by W Somerset Maugham

The Hour of Decision ★★

Mystery drama
1957 · UK · BW · 80mins

This tidy little whodunit may not break the mould, but it packs in more than its fair share of surprises. Here the obligatory Hollywood star-on-the-skids is Jeff Morrow, who plays a journalist discovering his wife is implicated in a murder because of an adulterous affair. Fresh from her high-profile performance in Hammer's *The Curse of Frankenstein*, Hazel Court seems a little distracted, though Morrow gets better support from Lionel Jeffries and Anthony Dawson. Norman Hudis penned the script; a year later he achieved a kind of screen immortality by co-writing the first *Carry On* film.

Jeff Morrow *Joe Sanders* • Hazel Court *Peggy Sanders* • Lionel Jeffries *Elvin Main* • Anthony Dawson *Garry Bax* • Mary Laura Wood *Olive Bax* • Carl Bernard *Inspector Gower* • Vanda Godsell *Eileen Chadwick* ■ *Dir* C Pennington Richards • *Scr* Norman Hudis

Hour of the Assassin ★★★ 🔞

Political thriller
1987 · US · Colour · 88mins

This political thriller is directed by Luis Llosa, with Peru standing in for a mythical South American country. Erik Estrada is sent there to kill a newly-elected democratic president, while Robert Vaughn is the CIA agent whose orders are to stop the assassin at any cost. No subtleties here, but the film has an exciting Costa-Gavras flavour and has quite a few surprises in its cartridge belt. 🎬

Erik Estrada *Martin Fierro* • Robert Vaughn *Sam Merrick* • Alfredo Alvarez Calderón *Ortiz* • Orlando Sacha *Folco* • Reynaldo Arenas *Paladoro* • Lourdes Berninzon *Adriana* ■ *Dir* Luis Llosa • *Scr* Matt Leipzig

Hour of the Gun ★★★★

Western
1967 · US · Colour · 100mins

A superb follow-up to his own *Gunfight at the OK Corral* from director John Sturges, this film starts where the previous movie climaxed, and charts the moral decline of lawman Wyatt Earp from upright marshal to relentless avenger. He's portrayed brilliantly by a grim James Garner, in a far cry from his customary jolly screen image. Doc Holliday is also perfectly played by Jason Robards, providing a marvellous contrast to Garner's Earp. This movie, with its fine use of Panavision and its memorable Jerry Goldsmith score, prefigures the darker, anti-romantic westerns that were to come, notably those of director Sam Peckinpah.

James Garner *Wyatt Earp* • Jason Robards [Jason Robards Jr] *Doc Holliday* • Robert Ryan *Ike Clanton* • Albert Salmi *Octavius Roy* • Charles Aidman *Horace Sullivan* • Steve Ihnat

Warshaw • Jon Voight *Curly Bill Brocius* ■ *Dir* John Sturges • *Scr* Edward Anhalt • *Cinematographer* Lucien Ballard

The Hour of the Pig ★★★ 🔞

Comedy drama
1993 · UK/Fr · Colour · 107mins

British director Leslie Megahey here dares to be different to such a degree that the odd outbreak of perfunctory or off-target acting matters not one jot. He has successfully created a distinctive other world, specifically a medieval France which is defined by upper-class corruption, peasant superstition and ecclesiastical apathy. This ludicrous mixture of dark comedy and original thrills is revealed through the story of a smart Paris lawyer (Colin Firth) who has to defend a pig on a charge of murder. Though sometimes creaking under the burden of its own ideas, the film is nonetheless intelligent and wonderfully dotty. 🎬

Colin Firth *Richard Courtois* • Ian Holm *Albertus* • Donald Pleasence *Pincheon* • Amina Annabi *Samira* • Nicol Williamson *Seigneur Jehan d'Auferre* • Michael Gough *Magistrate Boniface* • Harriet Walter *Jeannine* ■ *Dir/Scr* Leslie Megahey

Hour of the Star ★★★★ 🔞

Drama
1985 · Bra · Colour · 95mins

Directed by a 52-year-old mother of nine, this debut stands as Third Cinema's most remarkable example of magical neorealism. Working from a novella by Clarice Lispector, Suzana Amaral graphically depicts Sao Paolo's grinding poverty, while still managing to invest her film with brave humour and touching humanity. Marcelia Cartaxo deservedly won the best actress prize at Berlin for her performance as the virginal, cola-drinking typist, whose dreams of celebrity and romance are confounded as much by society's expectations as her own lack of self-esteem and the swaggering ignorance of her boorish boyfriend. In Portuguese with English subtitles.

Marcelia Cartaxo *Macabea* • José Dumont *Olimpico* • Tamara Taxman *Gloria* • Fernanda Montenegro *Mme Carlotta* ■ *Dir* Suzana Amaral • *Scr* Suzana Amaral, Alfredo Oroz, from a novella by Clarice Lispector

The Hour of the Wolf ★★★

Psychological drama
1967 · Swe · BW · 89mins

This relentlessly ominous study of the price of artistic creativity comprises a series of gothic flashbacks inspired by Liv Ullmann's discovery of the diary belonging to her missing and much-tormented husband, Max von Sydow. With Sven Nykvist's camera surreally conjuring up expressionist horror, von Sydow is mocked by the ghoulish members of Erland Josephson's household and subjected to visions of demons and phantoms from his past. Even a puppet presentation of *The Magic Flute* has sinister overtones. Nevertheless, we expect more of Bergman than eerie set pieces. A Swedish language film.

Max von Sydow *Johan Borg* • Liv Ullmann *Alma Borg* • Erland Josephson *Baron von Merkens* • Ingrid Thulin *Veronica Vogler* ■ *Dir/Scr* Ingmar Bergman

Hourglass ★★ 🔞

Thriller
1996 · US · Colour · 87mins

Since his Brat Pack glory days, C Thomas Howell has remained largely mired in straight-to-video land, although for this one he has to take most of the blame – he wrote and directed it as well taking the lead role. A would-be erotic thriller, the auteur plays a successful fashion designer who gets into all sorts of difficulties when he falls under the spell of *femme fatale* Sofia Shinas. Old chums Kiefer Sutherland and Lou Diamond Phillips pop up in uncredited cameos, giving it a little bit more class than it deserves. Contains violence, swearing, sex scenes and drug abuse. 🎬

C Thomas Howell *Michael Jardine* • Ed Begley Jr *Detective Dish* • Timothy Bottoms *Jurgen Brauner* • Sofia Shinas *Dara Jensen* • Terry Kiser *Henry Jardine* • Kiefer Sutherland • Lou Diamond Phillips ■ *Dir* C Thomas Howell • *Scr* C Thomas Howell, Darren Dalton

The Hours and Times ★★★★ 🔞

Drama
1992 · US · BW · 54mins

Shortly after the birth of his son Julian, and at the end of the 1963 UK tour that saw the start of Beatlemania around the country, John Lennon accompanied the band's manager, Brian Epstein, on a short holiday to Spain. This highly plausible, carefully written and superbly played film takes its starting point from rumours of what might (or might not) have occurred during the trip. Ian Hart is magnificent as the cynical Lennon, who is torn between his affection for a man to whom he owed so much and his insatiable urge to mock. David Angus also impresses as the timid, homosexual Epstein, but the real credit goes to writer/director Christopher Münch. Contains swearing and nudity. 🎬

David Angus *Brian Epstein* • Ian Hart *John Lennon* • Stephanie Pack *Marianne* • Robin McDonald *Quinones* • Sergio Moreno *Miguel* ■ *Dir/Scr* Christopher Münch

House ★★ 🔞

Horror comedy
1986 · US · Colour · 88mins

The Amityville Horror meets *First Blood* in this straightforward haunted house chiller furnished with effective fun-fuelled scares. Blocked author William Katt (clearly playing a Stephen King clone) moves into a Gothic mansion previously owned by his nutty late aunt to work on his Vietnam memoirs. Soon strange phenomena and rubbery creatures from a sinister netherworld are roaming the floors. Director Steve Miner ably steers between broad humour and beastly visitations for tame shock value. 🎬 **DVD**

William Katt *Roger Cobb* • George Wendt *Harold Gorton* • Richard Moll *Big Ben* • Kay Lenz *Sandy* • Mary Stavin *Tanya* • Michael Ensign *Chet Parker* ■ *Dir* Steve Miner • *Scr* Ethan Wiley, from a story by Fred Dekker

House! ★★ 🔞

Comedy
2000 · UK · Colour · 89mins

A rundown seafront bingo hall faces closure due to the twin threats of a leaking roof and competition from a new superhall. The establishment's

U = SUITABLE FOR ALL   **Uc** = SUITABLE FOR ALL, ESPECIALLY FOR YOUNG CHILDREN (VIDEO ONLY)   **PG** = PARENTAL GUIDANCE

only hope lies in a lucrative national lotto game and an usherette's psychic ability to influence the way balls fall. Youngsters Kelly Macdonald and Jason Hughes give spirited performances, as do veterans Freddie Jones and Miriam Margolyes. But they're hogtied by a weak script and ham-fisted handling which fails to generate tension, even during the climactic big-game finale.

Kelly Macdonald *Linda* • Jason Hughes *Gavin* • Freddie Jones *Mr Anzani* • Miriam Margolyes *Beth* • Mossie Smith *Kay* • Bruce Forsyth • Keith Chegwin ■ *Dir* Julian Kemp • *Scr* Jason Sutton, from an idea by Eric Styles

House II: the Second Story
★ 15

Horror   1987 · US · Colour · 84mins

Built on even shakier foundations than its predecessor, director Ethan Wiley's dumb fright farce starts out as a bad John Hughes teen comedy and ends up like a demented episode of *Bonanza*. The convoluted plot has Arye Gross and Lar Park Lincoln moving into their great-great-grandfather's property and digging up the legendary old West outlaw for a crystal skull with magical properties. Zombie Gramps then leads the duo on a wild chase through endless alternate universes – stops include a ghost town and a prehistoric jungle – to battle an uninspired array of rubber creatures. ▭ *DVD*

Arye Gross *Jesse McLaughlin* • Jonathan Stark *Charlie* • Royal Dano *Gramps* • Bill Maher *John* • John Ratzenberger *Bill Towner* • Lar Park Lincoln *Kate* • Amy Yasbeck *Lana* • Gregory Walcott *Sheriff* • Dwier Brown *Clarence* ■ *Dir/Scr* Ethan Wiley

House III: The Horror Show
★ 18

Horror   1989 · US · Colour · 91mins

This grisly tale of a mass murderer sent to the electric chair who returns after death to terrorise the cop who brought him to justice bears more than a cursory resemblance to the equally turgid Wes Craven vehicle *Shocker*, released the same year. Coincidence? Genre favourite Brion James plays the killer with tongue so firmly in cheek one wonders if director James Isaac wanted to create another Freddy Krueger. Instead he's delivered a jumbled movie that between the bouts of predictable action is a solid bore. Yet another sequel, *House IV: Home Deadly Home*, followed in 1992. ▭

Lance Henriksen *Lucas McCarthy* • Brion James *Max Jenke* • Rita Taggart *Donna McCarthy* • Dedee Pfeiffer *Bonnie McCarthy* • Aron Eisenberg *Scott McCarthy* • Thom Bray *Peter Campbell* ■ *Dir* James Isaac • *Scr* Allyn Warner, Leslie Bohem, Alan Smithee

House Arrest
★★★ PG

Comedy   1996 · US · Colour · 104mins

This odd but surprisingly watchable comedy takes a fresh look at the impact of marital discord. Worried that their parents are about to get a divorce, Kyle Howard and Amy Sakasitz decide drastic action is needed. So they lock them in the basement, together with their chum's bickering mum and dad. Pretty soon other pupils are queueing up for their unique marriage guidance programme. The performances of both adults and

youngsters are uniformly strong and, although sentimentality isn't kept entirely at bay, it still makes for thoughtful entertainment. ▭

Jamie Lee Curtis *Janet Beindorf* • Kevin Pollak *Ned Beindorf* • Kyle Howard *Grover Beindorf* • Russel Harper *TJ Krupp* • Amy Sakasitz *Stacy Beindorf* • Wallace Shawn *Vic Finley* • Jennifer Love Hewitt *Brooke Figler* • Jennifer Tilly *Cindy Figler* ■ *Dir* Harry Winer • *Scr* Michael Hitchcock

House by the River
★★★

Film noir   1950 · US · BW · 87mins

Based on AP Herbert's novel, this has been described as Fritz Lang's most Teutonic American picture. However, the surfeit of atmosphere can't atone for the lack of suspense in this tired treatise on the old adage, "murder will out". The byplay between evil novelist Louis Hayward and his envious, lame brother Lee Bowman is effective, but the romance between Bowman and his prissy sister-in-law (Jane Wyatt) is less convincing. Making moody use of light and shade, Lang ingeniously involves us more deeply than the plot merits.

Louis Hayward *Stephen Byrne* • Lee Bowman *John Byrne* • Jane Wyatt *Marjorie Byrne* • Dorothy Patrick *Emily Gaunt* • Ann Shoemaker *Mrs Ambrose* • Jody Gilbert *Flora Bantam* • Sarah Padden *Mrs Beach* ■ *Dir* Fritz Lang • *Scr* Mel Dinelli, from the novel by AP Herbert

House Calls
★★ PG

Comedy   1978 · US · Colour · 93mins

Co-written by Julius J Epstein, who was one of the trio responsible for *Casablanca*, this hospital romance can't decide whether it wants to be a scorching screwball or a cosy sitcom. Making her Hollywood debut, Glenda Jackson is way below her *Touch of Class* form as a divorcee seeking commitment from Walter Matthau's newly footloose widower. But then, under Howard Zieff's lacklustre direction, no one emerges from this muddled comedy with much credit. Doctors Richard Benjamin and Art Carney fare worse than most, with the latter's endless round of surgical mishaps being particularly unfunny. ▭

Walter Matthau *Dr Charley Nicholas* • Glenda Jackson *Ann Atkinson* • Art Carney *Dr Amos Willoughby* • Richard Benjamin *Dr Norman Soloman* • Candice Azzara [Candy Azzara] *Ellen Grady* • Dick O'Neill *Irwin Owett* ■ *Dir* Howard Zieff • *Scr* Julius J Epstein, Alan Mandel, Charles Shyer, Max Shulman, from a story by Max Shulman, Julius J Epstein

The House in Nightmare Park
★★ PG

Comedy thriller   1973 · UK · Colour · 91mins

Oooer missus! One of the few low points in comedian Frankie Howerd's career is this failed fright farce, which invites poor comparisons with Bob Hope's horror comedy classic *The Cat and the Canary*. Howerd, who aptly plays a ham actor, is invited to perform at Ray Milland's creepy stately home and discovers he's heir to the family fortune. As the corpses pile up, so do the lame gags. Hammer director Peter Sykes fails to blend chills with chortles, but it's really not his fault. Howerd's stagey brand of vaudeville requires live audience spontaneity; remove that and he becomes a mere

buffoon drowning in a sea of desperate camera mugging. ▭

Frankie Howerd *Foster Twelvetrees* • Ray Milland *Stewart Henderson* • Hugh Burden *Major Reginald Henderson* • Kenneth Griffith *Ernest Henderson* • John Bennett *Patel* • Rosalie Crutchley *Jessica Henderson* • Ruth Dunning *Agnes Henderson* • Elizabeth MacLennan *Verity* ■ *Dir* Peter Sykes • *Scr* Clive Exton, Terry Nation

A House in the Hills
★ 18

Thriller   1993 · US · Colour · 86mins

Helen Slater should have stuck with being Supergirl instead of providing potential fodder for Internet voyeurs. Here she stars as an actress house-sitting for millionaire rose collector James Laurenson. Mistakenly taken for the millionaire's wife, she is accosted and held hostage by Michael Madsen who has an agenda of his own, having been conned by Laurenson. Mix into the mishmash a subplot concerning a murdered next-door neighbour and you've seen it all before (apart from a naked Slater of course). Contains violence, nudity and swearing. ▭

Michael Madsen *Mickey* • Helen Slater *Alex Weaver* • James Laurenson *Ronald Rankin* • Elyssa Davalos *Sondra Rankin* • Jeffrey Tambor *Willie* ■ *Dir* Ken Wiederhorn • *Scr* Ken Wiederhorn, Miguel Tejada-Flores

House in the Woods
★★★

Thriller   1957 · UK · BW · 62mins

Expanding on its story source, this is an unexpectedly tense British B-movie from a little-known director. Playing a painter who many suspect of slaughtering his spouse, Ronald Howard reveals an undetected flair for villainy as he lurks around the country hideaway he's leased to writer Michael Gough and wife Patricia Roc. Logic is not Munden's strong suit, but he more than compensates with his eerie exploitation of both the cottage's shadowy interiors and its isolated setting.

Ronald Howard *Spencer Rowland* • Patricia Roc *Carol Carter* • Michael Gough *Geoffrey Carter* • Andrea Troubridge *Mrs Shellaby* • Bill Shine *Col Shellaby* • Norah Hammond *Mrs Bletchley* ■ *Dir* Maxwell Munden • *Scr* Maxwell Munden, from the short story *Prelude to Murder* by Walter C Brown

House of America
★★★ 15

Drama   1996 · UK/Neth · Colour and BW · 93mins

By combining stylised colour with sun-tinted monochrome, first-time director Marc Evans cleverly contrasts the post-industrial Welsh wilderness with the wide-open spaces of the American neverland described by Jack Kerouac. But the film – about three kids who grow up in a rundown mining village believing their father has found the good life across the Atlantic – quickly descends into tabloid caricature. Insanity and incest take priority over the potentially more interesting story of the shunned younger brother, trying to fit into a society that has seen the very bedrock on which its machismo was founded cut out from underneath it. Contains swearing, sex scenes and some violence. ▭

Sian Phillips *Mam* • Steven Mackintosh *Sid Lewis* • Lisa Palfrey *Gwenny Lewis* • Matthew

Rhys *Boyo Lewis* • Richard Harrington *Cat* ■ *Dir* Marc Evans • *Scr* Edward Thomas, from his play

House of Angels
★★★★ 15

Comedy drama   1992 · Swe · Colour · 114mins

Scandinavian culture is littered with tales of respectable rural folk resisting devious city slickers. But Colin Nutley slyly inverts that scenario in this gentle satire, in which the entrenched prejudices of the countrysiders are held up to ridicule. Caricature is almost inevitable in the depiction of the locals, appalled by the fact that cabaret star Helena Bergström and her leather-clad biker buddy, Rikard Wolff, have decided to live on the farm inherited from her rich grandfather. But it is in this struggle between progress and self-seeking traditionalism that the film's whimsical charm lies. In Swedish with English subtitles. Contains sex scenes and swearing.

Helena Bergström *Fanny Zander* • Rikard Wolff *Zac* • Per Oscarsson *Erik Zander* • Sven Wollter *Axel Flogfält* • Viveka Seldhahl *Rut Flogfält* • Reine Brynolfsson *Fleming Collmert* • Jakob Eklund *Mårten Flogfält* • Ernst Günther *Gottfried Pettersson* ■ *Dir/Scr* Colin Nutley

House of Angels II: The Second Summer
★★

Comedy   1994 · Swe · Colour · 137mins

They say you should never go home, but that's exactly where director Colin Nutley should have allowed Helena Bergström and Rikard Wolff to go. Instead he sweeps them off to New York in this contrived sequel. Admittedly, their options were limited, their farmhouse having burned down while they were away on tour. But their adventures in the Big Apple with Tord Pettersson and his emigrant brother are less than riveting, especially as they are frequently interrupted when the action switches back to Sweden and the locals' search for the identity of Bergström's father. In Swedish with English subtitles.

Helena Bergström *Fanny* • Rikard Wolff *Zac* • Sven Wollter *Axel* • Ernst Günther *Gottfried* • Tord Pettersson *Ivar* • Reine Brynolfsson *Vicar* ■ *Dir/Scr* Colin Nutley

House of Bamboo
★★★

Crime drama   1955 · US · Colour · 102mins

Director Samuel Fuller was often described as a Hollywood maverick. In fact, he functioned more than adequately as a house director of action movies at 20th Century-Fox, and proved adept at making tightly budgeted films look costly, using widescreen photography and exotic locations and themes. This thick-ear crime drama is one of his better efforts, boasting good performances from three well-cast Hollywood leading men (Robert Ryan, Robert Stack, Cameron Mitchell) and some striking Tokyo photography from cameraman Joe MacDonald. Japanese leading lady Shirley Yamaguchi is also particularly appealing, providing a warmth usually missing in Fuller's violent world.

Robert Ryan *Sandy Dawson* • Robert Stack *Eddie Kenner/Spanier* • Shirley Yamaguchi *Mariko* • Cameron Mitchell *Griff* • Brad Dexter

Captain Hanson • Sessue Hayakawa *Inspector Kita* • *Dir* Samuel Fuller • *Scr* Harry Kleiner, Samuel Fuller

The House of Bernarda Alba ★★★ 🅸🅵

Drama 1987 · Sp · Colour · 103mins

While still laying the blame for Franco's tyranny on the prejudices of the bourgeoisie, Marcel Camus's adaptation of Federico Garcia Lorca's play places more emphasis on the melodramatic tensions that build up after a handsome suitor intrudes upon the solitary mourning which a widow imposes on her five daughters following their father's death. Meticulously opening out the action without diluting its intensity, Camus conjures up some evocative visuals and draws thoughtful performances from Irene Gutierrez Caba and her frustrated brood. While this cauldron of repressed emotions simmers nicely, however, it never quite boils over in the way the playwright intended. A Spanish language film.

Irene Gutierrez Caba *Bernarda Alba* • Ana Belén *Adela* • Florinda Chico *Poncia* • Enriqueta Carballeira *Angustias* • Vicky Peña *Martirio* • Aurora Pastor *Magdalena* • Mercedes Lezcano *Amelia* • Rosario Garcia-Ortega *Maria Josefa* ■ *Dir* Mario Camus • *Scr* Mario Camus, Antonio Larreta, from the play by Federico Garcia Lorca

House of Blackmail ★★ 🅄

Crime drama 1953 · UK · BW · 71mins

Maurice Elvey was the most prolific director in British cinema history, making over 300 features after his debut in 1913. Unfortunately, this low-budget B-movie, in which a hitchhiker finds himself in trouble after taking a lift from a woman who's being blackmailed, is not one of his best efforts. We could do with more surprises, but the pace is unrelenting and there are typically solid performances from Mary Germaine, William Sylvester and John Arnatt.

William Sylvester *Jimmy* • Mary Germaine *Carol Blane* • Alexander Gauge *John Markham* • John Arnatt *Peter Carter* • Dennis Shaw [Denis Shaw] *Bassett* • Ingeborg Wells *Emma* ■ *Dir* Maurice Elvey • *Scr* Allan MacKinnon

House of Cards ★★

Political thriller 1968 · US · Colour · 104mins

Lacklustre political thriller set in France, where a rich right-wing group who feel betrayed over Algerian independence are plotting to take over the country and execute De Gaulle. George Peppard is the innocent American in Paris who tumbles the plot, and Orson Welles is briefly imposing as a zillionaire French publisher who is financing it. Sadly, the promising idea (with its premonitions of *The Day of the Jackal*) is rather undermined by some hammy acting and a tendency to stage scenes in front of some tourist location or other.

George Peppard *Reno Davis* • Inger Stevens *Anne de Villemont* • Orson Welles *Claude Leschenhaut* • Keith Michell *Hubert Morillon* • Ralph Michael *Claude de Gonde* • Maxine Audley *Matilde Vosiers* • William Job *Bernard Bourdon* • Peter Bayliss *Edmond Vosier* ■ *Dir* John Guillermin • *Scr* Irving Ravetch, Harriet Frank Jr, from a novel by Stanley Ellin

House of Cards ★ 🅸🅵

Drama 1993 · US · Colour · 108mins

When Kathleen Turner's archaeologist husband falls to his death from a Mayan pyramid in Mexico, she packs up and returns to the States where her six-year-old daughter begins to behave very strangely. Child psychologist Tommy Lee Jones is brought in to help. At first, you think the little girl is going to take us into Stephen King territory; instead, it leads only to the usual clichéd drama. It is sad to see Jones and Turner wasting their time in this movie. 📼

Kathleen Turner *Ruth Matthews* • Tommy Lee Jones *Dr Jake Beerlander* • Asha Menina *Sally Matthews* • Shiloh Strong *Michael Matthews* • Esther Rolle *Adelle* ■ *Dir* Michael Lessac • *Scr* Michael Lessac, from a story by Michael Lessac, Robert Jay Litz

House of Dark Shadows ★★★★ 🅸🅴

Gothic horror 1970 · US · Colour · 92mins

The first of two movie offshoots from the popular US daytime horror soap *Dark Shadows*, featuring a number of series regulars, is one of the best horror movies of the seventies. Eighteenth-century vampire Barnabas Collins (Jonathan Frid) rises from his Maine grave to convert all the residents of the family mansion to his evil bloodsucking ways. Lavish production values, stunning photography, great special effects and moments of pure bone-chilling shock make this a resonant delight, exquisitely directed by series producer Dan Curtis.

Jonathan Frid *Barnabas Collins* • Joan Bennett *Elizabeth Collins Stoddard* • Grayson Hall *Dr Julia Hoffman* • Kathryn Leigh Scott *Maggie Evans* • Roger Davis *Jeff Clark* • Nancy Barrett *Carolyn Stoddard* • John Karlen *Willie Loomis* • Louis Edmonds *Roger Collins* ■ *Dir* Dan Curtis • *Scr* Sam Hall, Gordon Russell • *Cinematographer* Arthur J Ornitz

House of Dracula ★★

Horror 1945 · US · BW · 67mins

Not to be confused with *House of Frankenstein*, this sequel stars Glenn Strange as Frankenstein's monster, Lon Chaney Jr as the Wolf Man and, most impressively, the elegant John Carradine as Count Dracula. Needless to add, they are all splendid to watch under the famously copyrighted Universal make-up. It's the plot that's tiresome, as Onslow Stevens tries to "cure" the monsters of their evil qualities by resorting to science. Erle C Kenton's direction keeps things suitably murky, however, and that Universal house style always adds pleasure to the experience.

Lon Chaney Jr *Lawrence Talbot* • John Carradine *Count Dracula* • Martha O'Driscoll *Miliza Morell* • Lionel Atwill *Inspector Holtz* • Jane Adams *Nina* • Onslow Stevens *Dr Edelman* • Ludwig Stossel *Ziegfried* • Glenn Strange *The Monster* ■ *Dir* Erle C Kenton • *Scr* Edward T Lowe

House of Evil ★ 🅸🅵

Horror 1968 · Mex/US · Colour · 72mins

Boris Karloff wanders around a castle equipped with a torture dungeon in one of the four little-seen Mexican cheapies the master of the macabre made just prior to his death in 1969. The plot is very much in the vein of *The Old Dark House* with many of the cast coming to sticky ends. All the south of the border scenes were shot by director Juan Ibanez, while Jack Hill directed the Los Angeles-based interiors with Karloff. 📼

Boris Karloff *Mathias Morthevald* • Julissa *Lucy Durand* • Andres Garcia *Carlos Bisler* • Beatriz Baz *Cordelia Rush* • Quintin Bulnes *Dr Emerich Horvath* ■ *Dir* Juan Ibanez, Jack Hill • *Scr* Jack Hill, Luis Enrique Vergara, from the story *The Fall of the House of Usher* by Edgar Allan Poe

House of Evil ★★★ 🅸🅱

Horror 1983 · US · Colour · 87mins

Although basically another *Friday the 13th* retread, the feature debut of Mark Rosman avoids most of the obvious pitfalls that plague the slasher genre to emerge as a skilfully-made shocker. An end-of-term slumber party turns into a bloody nightmare when a sorority group unlock the dark secret of their out-to-lunch housemother. Numerous innovative touches – Kathryn McNeil fighting off her unknown assailant while under drug-induced hallucinations – elevate this perceptive, low-gore entry above its contemporaries.

Kathryn McNeil *Katherine* • Eileen Davidson *Vicki* • Janis Zido *Liz* • Robin Meloy *Jeanie* • Harley Kozak *Diane* • Jodie Draigie *Morgan* • Ellen Dorsher *Stevie* • Lois Kelso Hunt *Mrs Slater* • Christopher Lawrence *Dr Beck* ■ *Dir* Mark Rosman • *Scr* Mark Rosman, Bobby Fine

The House of Fear ★★

Murder mystery 1944 · US · BW · 69mins

Not one of the best of the Basil Rathbone-Nigel Bruce forays into Sherlock Holmes territory, but it nevertheless contains an ending worthy of a good Agatha Christie mystery. "The Good Comrades", a men's club based in a Scottish mansion, are being killed off one by one and Watson himself is kidnapped. Holmes even seems to regret his disappearance; however, as Bruce had declined into oafish bumbling by this time, we sadly do not.

Basil Rathbone *Sherlock Holmes* • Nigel Bruce *Dr Watson* • Aubrey Mather *Alastair* • Dennis Hoey *Lestrade* • Paul Cavanagh *Simon Merrivale* • Holmes Herbert *Alan Cosgrave* ■ *Dir* Roy William Neill • *Scr* Roy Chanslor, from the story *The Adventures of the Five Orange Pips* by Sir Arthur Conan Doyle

House of Frankenstein ★★★

Horror 1944 · US · BW · 70mins

The sequel to *Frankenstein Meets the Wolf Man* adds John Carradine as Dracula into the engaging Universal monster mix. Mad doctor Boris Karloff escapes from prison when the wall is struck by lightning and, with hunchback J Carrol Naish, seeks revenge on those who put him there. For this he enlists the help of the trio of vintage horror characters: Dracula, Frankenstein's monster and the Wolf Man. Glenn Strange plays the monster and Lon Chaney Jr the Wolf Man in a bundle of laughs and nostalgic suspense.

Boris Karloff *Dr Gustav Niemann* • Lon Chaney Jr *Lawrence Stewart Talbot* • J Carrol Naish *Daniel* • John Carradine *Count Dracula* • Anne Gwynne *Rita Hussman* • Peter Coe *Carl Hussman* • Lionel Atwill *Inspector Arnz* • Glenn Strange *The Monster* ■ *Dir* Erle C Kenton • *Scr* Edward T Lowe, from the story *The Devil's Brood* by Curt Siodmak

House of Games ★★★★ 🅸🅵

Psychological thriller 1987 · US · Colour · 97mins

After several notable plays and the screenplays for *The Postman Always Rings Twice*, *The Verdict* and *The Untouchables*, David Mamet became a director with this delectably clever parlour-game picture, which should delight connoisseurs of thrillers and cryptic crosswords. It's rather low on directorial flair, but high on literacy and performance values. Mamet's then-wife, Lindsay Crouse, plays a psychiatrist confronting the gambler (Joe Mantegna) who drove one of her patients to near-suicide. A card game results, with psychiatrist and gambler realising how similar their respective trades are. The joker in the pack is Mamet himself: this deck is well and truly stacked with bluff, double-bluff and a thrilling ace-in-the-hole finale. Contains violence and swearing. 📼

Lindsay Crouse *Margaret Ford* • Joe Mantegna *Mike* • Mike Nussbaum *Joey* • Lilia Skala *Dr Littauer* • JT Walsh *Businessman* ■ *Dir* David Mamet • *Scr* David Mamet, from a story by David Mamet, Jonathan Katz

The House of Mirth ★★ 🅿🅶

Romance 2000 · UK · Colour · 140mins

Edith Wharton's wonderful novel about a woman striving for financial and intellectual independence in a conservative, upper-crust society is faithfully brought to the screen by Terence Davies. Too faithfully, in fact: Davies directs at such a slow pace that much of the plot and characters seem rather lifeless. Gillian Anderson, from TV's *The X Files*, has a good shot at playing the heroine, though in the end she lacks the power required. Despite the budget limitations (Glasgow standing for turn-of-the-century New York, for example), the film's look is impressive.

Gillian Anderson *Lily Bart* • Eric Stoltz *Lawrence Selden* • Anthony LaPaglia *Sim Rosedale* • Laura Linney *Bertha Dorset* • Terry Kinney *George Dorset* • Dan Aykroyd *Gus Trenor* • Elizabeth McGovern *Carry Fisher* • Eleanor Bron *Mrs Peniston* • Jodhi May *Grace Stepney* ■ *Dir* Terence Davies • *Scr* Terence Davies, from the novel by Edith Wharton

House of Mortal Sin ★★★

Horror 1975 · UK · Colour · 104mins

A hugely under-rated shocker from cult director Pete Walker. Anthony Sharp gives an extraordinary performance as a Catholic priest who sublimates his desires by violating the sanctity of the confessional and torturing his distressed victims with guilt. Anyone trying to stop his course of "divine justice" is murdered by such diverse means as incense burners and poisoned holy wafers. Walker stalwart Sheila Keith is on hand to give this warped morality tale its clever twist.

Anthony Sharp *Father Xavier Meldrum* • Susan Penhaligon *Jenny Welch* • Stephanie Beacham

Vanessa Welch • Norman Eshley *Father Bernard Cutler* • Sheila Keith *Miss Brabazon* • Hilda Barry *Mrs Meldrum* • Stuart Bevan *Terry* ■ *Dir* Peter Walker • *Scr* David McGillivray

House of Mystery ★★★

Supernatural fantasy
1961 · UK · BW · 55mins

This is a neat little spine-tingler from writer/director Vernon Sewell, who was a dab hand at summoning up demons from beyond. Some aficionados insist that if it ain't Hammer it ain't horror, but there are plenty of uneasy moments in this haunting story, in which a couple of newlyweds learn the grim secret of their dream house from the resident spook himself.

Jane Hylton *Stella Lemming* • Peter Dyneley *Mark Lemming* • Nanette Newman *Joan Trevor* • Maurice Kaufmann *Henry Trevor* • Colin Gordon *Burdon* • Molly Urquhart *Mrs Bucknall* ■ *Dir* Vernon Sewell • *Scr* Vernon Sewell, from a play by Pierre Mills, C Vylars

House of Numbers ★★

Crime drama   1957 · US · BW · 91mins

Some of this implausible but quite ingenious thriller was shot in San Quentin prison, the eponymous house of the title. Behind bars is a bad guy, who is helped in his escape by his good twin brother. As both are played by Jack Palance, fans of the ever-watchable lean and mean star get a double helping particularly as he effectively differentiates the two characters. Based on a novel by Jack Finney, it needed more pace than director Russell Rouse provided.

Jack Palance *Bill Judlow/Arnie Judlow* • Barbara Lang *Ruth Judlow* • Harold J Stone *Henry Nova* • Edward Platt *Warden* ■ *Dir* Russell Rouse • *Scr* Russell Rouse, Don Mankiewicz, from a novel by Jack Finney

The House of Rothschild ★★★

Biographical drama   1934 · US · BW · 94mins

How the Rothschild dynasty rose from German ghetto obscurity to become the foremost banking house in Europe is a fascinating study of international monetary intrigue, early 19th century-style. Set against a lavishly mounted backdrop of the Napoleonic Wars, commanding George Arliss plays two key roles – family patriarch Mayer and his son, Nathan – while Boris Karloff eschews monster make-up in this rather entertaining history lesson.

George Arliss *Mayer Rothschild/Nathan Rothschild* • Boris Karloff *Count Ledrantz* • Loretta Young *Julie Rothschild* • Robert Young *Captain Fitzroy* • C Aubrey Smith *Duke of Wellington* • Arthur Byron *Baring* • Helen Westley *Gudula Rothschild* • Reginald Owen *Herries* ■ *Dir* Alfred Werker • *Scr* Nunnally Johnson, from a play by George Humbert Westley

House of Secrets ★★

Thriller   1956 · UK · Colour · 97mins

A box-office sleeper in its day, this patchy thriller will probably seem threadbare to modern audiences. But director Guy Green uses Paris locations well and keeps the story ticking along. Groomed by Rank as the successor to Dirk Bogarde, Michael Craig never quite lived up to the

reputation generated by the studio press office. However, as a naval officer impersonating his counterfeiting lookalike, he manages to hold his own in the company of such excellent character players as Anton Diffring and Gerard Oury.

Michael Craig *Larry Ellis* • Julia Arnall *Diane* • Brenda de Banzie *Madame Ballu* • Barbara Bates *Judy* • David Kossoff *Van de Heide* • Gérard Oury *Pindar* • Geoffrey Keen *Burleigh* • Anton Diffring *Lauderbache* ■ *Dir* Guy Green • *Scr* Robert Buckner, Bryan Forbes, from the novel *Storm over Paris* by Sterling Noel

House of Secrets ★★ 15

Thriller   1993 · US · Colour · 88mins

A terribly misconceived attempt to put a new spin on the classic French thriller *Les Diaboliques*. This time Cicely Tyson and Melissa Gilbert are the scheming wife and mistress who think they've murdered their partner (Bruce Boxleitner), but his body disappears. Being made for TV, there's very little in the way of suspense and shocks, and *Little House on the Prairie*'s Gilbert, who later married Boxleitner, is badly miscast. ▭

Melissa Gilbert *Marion Ravinel* • Bruce Boxleitner *Dr Frank Ravinel* • Kate Vernon *Laura Morrell* • Michael Boatman *Sergeant Joe DuBois* • Cicely Tyson *Evangeline* ■ *Dir* Mimi Leder • *Scr* Andrew Laskos, from the novel *Celle Qui N'était Plus* by Pierre Boileau, Thomas Narcejac

A House of Secrets and Lies ★★ 15

Drama   1992 · US · Colour · 90mins

Connie Selleca stars as a TV presenter who is persuaded by one of her guests that she should no longer tolerate husband Kevin Dobson's extra-marital dalliances and become her own woman. Even this briefest of outlines should leave you in little doubt that this is not one of the most original TV movies ever presented for your delectation. It's like watching a segment of *Ricki Lake* or *The Oprah Winfrey Show* but, while there is some fascination in seeing actual people lay bare their souls, there is less interest in watching a B-league cast wring their hands and furrow their brows. ▭

Connie Selleca *Susan Cooper* • Kevin Dobson *Jack Evans* • Grace Zabriskie *Ruby Bryant* • Peter Jurasik *Steve* • Georgann Johnson *Anita Cooper* • Geoffrey Nauffts *Brian* • Ken Jenkins *Ed Norwood* • Charles Siebert *Dr Hirsch* ■ *Dir* Paul Schneider • *Scr* Diana Gould, Linda Schreyer, from a story by Linda Schreyer, Connie Selleca

The House of Seven Corpses ★★★

Horror   1973 · US · Colour · 90mins

An effective low-budget horror movie about making a low-budget horror movie. John Carradine is the creepy caretaker of a haunted house where a film crew (made up of such veteran B-movie actors as Faith Domergue) is stalked by a real-life zombie while shooting an occult thriller. It's always enjoyable watching actors play actors, especially bad ones, and director Paul Harrison throws in some genuine scares and surprises to add to the cheap fun. He also sustains the tense

atmosphere, until a truly horrific climax.

John Ireland *Eric Hartman* • Faith Domergue *Gayle* • John Carradine *Mr Price* • Carole Wells *Anne* • Jerry Strickler *David* • Ron Foreman *Ron* ■ *Dir/Scr* Paul Harrison

House of Strangers ★★★

Crime drama   1949 · US · BW · 100mins

Famous for a prolonged wrangle over a screenwriting credit and a protest from the Bank of America, which funded most of Hollywood's studios, this crime drama features Edward G Robinson as a man who achieves the American Dream by becoming a successful banker but is then arrested for malpractice. Three of his sons take over and prevent him from resuming his responsibilities. Richard Conte's affair with Susan Hayward is a dramatic dead end and you feel the picture would have been better as a gangster thriller about the Mafia. Despite these flaws, Robinson's performance and the subversive theme make it well worth watching.

Edward G Robinson *Gino Monetti* • Susan Hayward *Irene Bennett* • Richard Conte *Max Monetti* • Luther Adler *Joe Monetti* • Paul Valentine *Pietro Monetti* • Efrem Zimbalist Jr *Tony* ■ *Dir* Joseph L Mankiewicz • *Scr* Philip Yordan, from the novel *I'll Never Go There Any More* by Jerome Weidman

House of the Long Shadows ★★ 15

Horror   1983 · UK · Colour · 97mins

Vincent Price, Christopher Lee, Peter Cushing and John Carradine team up for the first and last time in this miscalculated update of the creaky horror classic *Seven Days to Baldpate* from director Peter Walker. Desi Arnaz Jr is the author who bets publisher Richard Todd he can write a novel in 24 hours while holed up in an eerie Welsh mansion populated by the celebrated foursome. Tongue-in-cheek thrills and soft horror make little impact in a camp romp that wastes the talents of all involved. ▭

Vincent Price *Lionel* • Peter Cushing *Sebastian* • Christopher Lee *Corrigan* • Desi Arnaz Jr *Kenneth Magee* • Richard Todd *Sam Allison* • John Carradine *Lord Grisbane* • Julie Peasgood *Mary Norton* ■ *Dir* Peter Walker • *Scr* Michael Armstrong, from the novel *Seven Keys to Baldpate* by Earl Derr Biggers

The House of the Seven Hawks ★ U

Crime thriller   1959 · UK · BW · 91mins

Workhorse director Richard Thorpe had just completed some uncredited second unit work on MGM's epic *Ben-Hur* when he was sent by the studio to Britain and Holland to direct this bland B-movie. Based on a Victor Canning caper, this story of a horde of Nazi diamonds lost since the war stars Robert Taylor, also slumming as the heroic ship's skipper who rumbles the plot. Everyone apart from Taylor speaks in thick European accents, while the cast includes that legendary actor/manager, Donald Wolfit.

Robert Taylor (1) *John Nordley* • Nicole Maurey *Constanta Sluiter* • Linda Christian *Elsa* • Donald Wolfit *Van Der Stoor* • David Kossoff

Wilhelm Dekker ■ *Dir* Richard Thorpe • *Scr* Jo Eisinger, from the novel *The House of the Seven Flies* by Victor Canning

The House of the Spirits ★★ 15

Drama
1993 · Por/Den/Ger/US · Colour · 132mins

Some novels are so popular that they prove irresistible to film-makers. Yet Isabel Allende's classic tale of dynastic rivalry and magic realism is one of those books that, for all the temptations, should have been left well alone. Although he had already made his name for imaginative imagery with the Oscar-winning *Pelle the Conqueror*, Danish director Bille August chose an impossibly difficult text for his first English-language film. His own script (which takes monumental liberties with the original) is desperately pedestrian, but it's the casting that condemns this prestige project, with even the chameleon-like Meryl Streep struggling to create a truly rounded character. Contains violence, swearing and nudity. ▭

Jeremy Irons *Esteban Trueba* • Meryl Streep *Clara Del Valle* • Glenn Close *Ferula* • Winona Ryder *Blanca* • Antonio Banderas *Pedro* • Vincent Gallo *Esteban Garcia* • Vanessa Redgrave *Nivea* • Maria Conchita Alonso *Transito* • Armin Mueller-Stahl *Severo* ■ *Dir* Bille August • *Scr* Bille August, from the novel by Isabel Allende

The House of Usher ★ 18

Horror   1988 · US · Colour · 87mins

None of the refined terror of Roger Corman's superb version of the Poe tale is in evidence in this stupefying and sleazy modern-day redefinition of the doomed Usher family's desperate desire to continue their bloodline. Instead, Oliver Reed hams it up a storm as the super-sensitive Roderick Usher, who has his marriage sights set on his nephew's intended (Romy Windsor), while Donald Pleasence, one-handed but with a rotary tool replacement, doesn't leave any of the cheap scenery unchewed. This is a depressing mixture of rape, murder, torture and severed body parts, from producer Harry Alan Towers, who specialised in offensive trash. ▭

Oliver Reed *Roderick Usher* • Romy Windsor *Molly McNulty* • Rufus Swart *Ryan Usher* • Norman Coombes *Mr Derrick* • Anne Stradi *Mrs Derrick* • Carole Farquhar *Gwen* • Philip Godewa *Dr Bailey* ■ *Dir* Alan Birkinshaw • *Scr* Michael J Murray, from the story *The Fall of the House of Usher* by Edgar Allan Poe

House of Wax ★★★★ PG

Horror   1953 · US · Colour · 84mins

Director Andre De Toth's close remake of *The Mystery of the Wax Museum* (1933) is an exciting and diverting shocker that established Vincent Price as a major horror star. Price brilliantly portrays a mad masked sculptor – his mind and body deformed in a museum blaze staged by his insurance-hungry partner – who returns to dip human corpses in boiling wax for display in his turn-of-the century chamber of horrors. Charles Bronson plays Price's mute assistant in this atmospheric *Grand Guignol* masterpiece, one of the most effective (and profitable) movies ever to use the 3-D gimmick. ▭

Vincent Price *Professor Henry Jarrod* • Frank Lovejoy *Lieutenant Tom Brennan* • Phyllis Kirk *Sue Allen* • Carolyn Jones *Cathy Gray* • Paul Picerni *Scott Andrews* • Roy Roberts *Matthew Burke* • Charles Buchinsky [Charles Bronson] *Igor* ■ *Dir* Andre De Toth • *Scr* Crane Wilbur, from a play by Charles Belden

House of Whipcord ★★
Exploitation horror
1974 · UK · Colour · 101mins

Dismayed by the permissive society, a dithery old judge and his stern mistress turn their home into a house of correction where girls of loose morals (and looser costumes) are imprisoned, chastised, flogged and finally hanged. Most newspaper critics who bothered to see this exploitation movie soundly rubbished it. However, a minority saw it as an allegory about censorship and the Mary Whitehouse brigade, and a satire on Britain's right wing who wished to see the return of capital punishment.

Barbara Markham *Mrs Wakehurst* • Patrick Barr *Justice Bailey* • Ray Brooks *Tony* • Ann Michelle *Julia* • Penny Irving *Ann-Marie Di Vernay* • Sheila Keith *Walker* • Dorothy Gordon *Bates* • Robert Tayman *Mark Desade* • David McGillivray *Caven* ■ *Dir* Peter Walker • *Scr* David McGillivray, from a story by Pete Walker

House of Women ★
Prison drama
1962 · US · BW · 85mins

A major studio like Warner Bros is much too strait-laced to produce an out-and-out exploitation movie, though that was the pitch for this story of women convicts that went out on a double-bill with *Samar*, a tale of male political prisoners in the Philippines in the 19th century. But back to the women, chief among whom is Shirley Knight, sentenced to five years for robbery even though she's pregnant and just about as saintly as Mother Teresa or Mary Pickford. Compared to Jonathan Demme's *Caged Heat*, this is a Women's Institute tea party.

Shirley Knight *Erica* • Andrew Duggan *Warden Cole* • Constance Ford *Sophie Brice* • Barbara Nichols *Candy Kane* • Margaret Hayes *Zoe* ■ *Dir* Walter Doniger • *Scr* Crane Wilbur

The House of Yes ★★★
Comedy drama 1997 · US · Colour · 87mins

Another offbeat offering featuring indie film favourite Parker Posey. It's a black comedy set in Washington DC, in which Josh Hamilton stars as Posey's all-American twin brother, returning to his dysfunctional family home for Thanksgiving with his fiancée Tori Spelling. Posey – who is convinced that she is Jackie Onassis and loves her brother in more than just a filial way – is not pleased and decides to re-enact the JFK assassination, with real bullets. This witty walk on the wild side contains strong performances and an edgy sense of humour.

Parker Posey *Jackie-O* • Josh Hamilton *Marty* • Tori Spelling *Lesly* • Freddie Prinze Jr *Anthony* • Geneviève Bujold *Mrs Pascal* • Rachael Leigh Cook *Young Jackie-O* • David Love *Young Marty* ■ *Dir* Mark Waters • *Scr* Mark Waters, from the play by Wendy MacLeod

House on Bare Mountain ★★
Horror   1962 · US · Colour · 61mins

Nudies meet the nasties in the first topless monster flick from exploitation maestro Lee Frost (credited as RL Frost). Co-producer Bob Cresse (another sleaze icon) plays Granny Good, narrating the tale of the day her School for Good Girls was invaded by the Wolf Man, Frankenstein and Dracula. The undressed cast is clearly drunk as tepid scares punctuate the daily routine of nude art classes, bare sunbathing and naked jogging. A tacky and tawdry classic.

Bob Cresse *Granny Good* • Hugh Cannon *Krakow* • Laura Eden *Prudence Bumgartner* • Warren Ames *The monster* • Jeffrey Smithers *Dracula* ■ *Dir* RL Frost [Lee Frost] • *Scr* Denver Scott

The House on Carroll Street ★★★ PG
Thriller   1987 · US · Colour · 96mins

A convincingly robust Kelly McGillis is the political activist in an slender plot about senator Mandy Patinkin smuggling Nazis into America. Hounded out of her job by the McCarthyite tendency, she takes work reading to Jessica Tandy and begins to notice strange goings-on across the way. Jeff Daniels ably plays the FBI agent she enlists to solve the mystery. Sub-Hitchcock it may be, but this is still an enjoyable offering. 💬

Kelly McGillis *Emily Crane* • Jeff Daniels *Cochran* • Mandy Patinkin *Ray Salwen* • Jessica Tandy *Miss Venable* • Jonathan Hogan *Alan* • Remak Ramsay *Senator Byington* ■ *Dir* Peter Yates • *Scr* Walter Bernstein

House on Haunted Hill ★★★
Horror   1958 · US · BW · 74mins

In terms of sheer silly spookiness, this William Castle production has never been equalled, as Vincent Price tries to scare overnight guests to death at a creepy mansion. Originally featuring "Emergo" – a plastic skeleton flown over people's heads in the audience – the script matches that gimmick in terms of subtlety. But there's no denying that Castle's directorial crassness does actually supply some genuinely frightening moments. Decapitated heads, witches and acid vats add even more fun to a slick shocker, performed with zest by Price.

Vincent Price *Frederick Loren* • Carol Ohmart *Annabelle Loren* • Richard Long *Lance Schroeder* • Alan Marshal *Dr David Trent* • Elisha Cook [Elisha Cook Jr] *Watson Pritchard* ■ *Dir* William Castle • *Scr* Robb White

House on Haunted Hill ★★★ 18
Horror   1999 · US · Colour · 92mins

Held together by stylish direction from William Malone, some genuinely nasty jolts and a keen sense of genre history, this big-budget remake of the 1958 classic compares favourably with the original. The simple plot has theme park developer Geoffrey Rush (here doing a creditable Vincent Price impression) offering a group of strangers $1 million to spend the night in a supposedly spook-infested, Art

Deco asylum. Malone captures the essence of the fifties frightener while updating the shocks with computer effects and grisly gore.

Geoffrey Rush *Stephen Price* • Famke Janssen *Evelyn Price* • Taye Diggs *Eddie* • Peter Gallagher *Blackburn* • Chris Kattan *Pritchett* • Ali Larter *Sara* • Bridgette Wilson *Melissa Marr* ■ *Dir* William Malone • *Scr* Dick Beebe, from a story by Robb White

The House on 92nd Street ★★★★ U
Spy drama   1945 · US · BW · 87mins

Produced by Louis de Rochemont – co-founder/producer of the influential American newsreel *The March of Time* – this semi-documentary espionage thriller started a trend in postwar Hollywood for true-life crime dramas notable for their realism, "voice of doom" narration and understated use of authentic locations. Readily taking to the documentary style, director Henry Hathaway sets a cracking pace as double agent William Eythe keeps federal agent Lloyd Nolan informed about the activities of a Nazi spy ring operated from New York by Signe Hasso and Gene Lockhart.

William Eythe *Bill Dietrich* • Lloyd Nolan *Inspector George A Briggs* • Signe Hasso *Elsa Gebhardt* • Gene Lockhart *Charles Ogden Roper* • Leo G Carroll *Colonel Hammersohn* ■ *Dir* Henry Hathaway • *Scr* Barre Lyndon, Charles G Booth, John Monks Jr, from a story by Charles G Booth

The House on Telegraph Hill ★★★★
Thriller   1951 · US · BW · 92mins

A richly layered *film noir*, starring Richard Basehart as the manipulative guardian of a young heir, and outwardly vulnerable but inwardly steely Valentina Cortese as the war refugee who enters the US on the purloined papers of the boy's dead mother. Basehart and Cortese interact splendidly, with little being said but much atmospherically hinted at, and the movie throbs with a dark subtext on human fallibility.

Richard Basehart *Alan Spender* • Valentina Cortese *Victoria Kowelska* • William Lundigan *Major Marc Anders* • Fay Baker *Margaret* • Gordon Gebert *Chris* ■ *Dir* Robert Wise • *Scr* Elick Moll, Frank Partos, from the novel *The Frightened Child* by Dana Lyon

The House on the Waterfront ★★
Crime adventure 1955 · Fr · Colour · 96mins

Although he was 50 when he made this sub-aquatic thriller, Jean Gabin was still very much an icon of the French screen. Alas, not even his distinctive brand of melancholic machismo could buoy this downbeat tale of the diver who discovers a woman's body while searching for contraband and sets out to prevent the perpetrator from repeating his crime. The underwater sequences (directed by Louis Malle) are handled capably enough, but Edmond T Gréville is much more comfortable with the affair between Gabin's partner, Henri Vidal, and Andrée Debar, whom deranged Jean-Roger Caussimon has nominated as his next target. A French language film.

Jean Gabin *Le Captain Le Quévic* • Andrée Debar *Martine* • Henri Vidal *Michel* • Jean-Roger Caussimon *M Black* • Gaby Basset *The bistrot proprietor* • Robert Berri *L'Hercule* ■ *Dir* Edmond T Gréville • *Scr* Jacques Viot

The House on Trubnaya Square ★★★★★
Silent satirical comedy
1928 · USSR · BW · 81mins

Although this was the film that launched the great Vera Maretskaya's career, co-star Vladimir Fogel died only a year later. His knowing performance as a hairdresser with ideas above his station is one of the many pleasures of this glorious silent comedy. Whether craning down the side of the titular tenement or roving Moscow's streets, Yevgeni Alexeyev's camera picks up every delicious detail of the rustic Maretskaya's rebellion against her employer's refusal to let her join a housemaid's union. Visually vibrant, satirically astute and packed with wonderfully observed characters, this is Boris Barnet's finest hour.

Vera Maretskaya *Parasha Pitounova* • Vladimir Fogel *Golikov* • Yelena Tyapkina *Mrs Golikova* • Vladimir Batalov *Semyen Byvalov* ■ *Dir* Barnet • *Scr* Boris Zorich, Anatoly Marienhof, Vadim Shershenevich, Victor Shklovsky, Nikolai Erdman

House Party ★★★★ 15
Comedy   1990 · US · Colour · 99mins

Acting as a lighter alternative to those hard, unsettling visions of modern black America from the likes of Spike Lee and John Singleton, this fresh comedy makes no attempt to pander to a more mainstream audience but remains a hugely enjoyable affair, even if you don't know your hip from your hop. Rap duo Kid 'n' Play (Christopher Reid and Christopher Martin) take the lead roles, the former playing a grounded high school student who will stop at nothing to get to a party at his best friend's house. Directed at a frenetic pace by Reginald Hudlin, this boasts a terrific soundtrack, cameos from a host of rap stars and a scene-stealing performance from Robin Harris as Kid's grumpy dad. Contains swearing. 💬

Christopher Reid *Kid* • Christopher Martin *Play* • Robin Harris *Pop* • Martin Lawrence *Bilal* • Tisha Campbell *Sidney* • Adrienne-Joi Johnson [AJ Johnson] *Sharane* • Paul Anthony *Stab* • Bowlegged Lou *Pee-Wee* ■ *Dir/Scr* Reginald Hudlin

House Party 2 ★★ 15
Comedy   1991 · US · Colour · 90mins

The original *House Party* was a surprise hit around the world, but this shallow sequel failed to recapture the same magic. Kid 'n' Play (Christopher Reid and Christopher Martin) return once again, but this time in the slightly more grown-up surroundings of college. To ease some financial worries, they decide to hold another massive party which is the cue for further hip-hop cameos. Reid and Martin are likeable leads and the support cast includes Iman and Martin Lawrence, but the magnificently surly presence of the late Robin Harris (who played Kid's father in the first *House Party*) is sorely missed. Contains swearing. 💬

Christopher Reid *Kid* • Christopher Martin *Play* • Queen Latifah *Zora* • Iman *Sheila* • Eugene Allen *Groove* • George Anthony Bell *Reverend Simms* • Martin Lawrence *Bilal* ■ *Dir* George Jackson, Doug McHenry • *Scr* Rusty Cundlieff, Daryl G Nickens, from characters created by Reginald Hudlin

House Party 3 ★★ 15

Comedy   1994 · US · Colour · 89mins

Kid 'n' Play rap on through to another, third *House Party*, but by now the comedy beats are flagging. This time Kid (Christopher Reid) is ready to put his partying days behind him and marry his girlfriend (Tisha Campbell), much to the concern of long-time partner Play (Christopher Martin). Meanwhile, the duo are intent on signing up a hot new female act, played by real-life R 'n' B band TLC. Fans of the first two instalments won't be disappointed by the mix of rap and raunch, but the plotting and direction are haphazard and the tack factor high. 🎬

Christopher Reid *Kid* • Christopher Martin *Play* • David Edwards *Stinky* • Angela Means *Veda* • Tisha Campbell *Sydney* • Ketty Lester *Aunt Lacy* • Chris Tucker *Johnny Booze* ■ *Dir* Eric Meza • *Scr* Takashi Bufford, from a story by David Toney, Takashi Bufford, from characters created by Reginald Hudlin

The House That Dripped Blood ★★★

Horror   1971 · UK · Colour · 101mins

One of the best compendium films from Amicus (Hammer's main horror rival at the time), directed with imaginative flair by Peter Duffell and featuring Christopher Lee and Peter Cushing in tailor-made roles as two of the four tenants of the menacing title abode. Robert Bloch's satisfying tales of terror involve possession, mysterious waxworks, voodoo and vampirism for an effective mix of spine-tingling sincerity, creepy atmospherics and witty send-ups of the genre.

Denholm Elliott *Charles* • Joanna Dunham *Alice* • Peter Cushing *Philip* • Joss Ackland *Rogers* • Christopher Lee *Reid* • Nyree Dawn Porter *Ann* • Jon Pertwee *Paul* • Ingrid Pitt *Carla* • John Bennett *Holloway* • John Bryans *Stoker* ■ *Dir* Peter Duffell • *Scr* Robert Bloch

The House That Would Not Die ★★

Horror   1970 · US · Colour · 75mins

This so-so spine-tingler has a fine pedigree, coming from the producer of *Dynasty* and *Melrose Place* (Aaron Spelling), the director of above-average TV fare such as *City of the Dead* (John Llewellyn Moxey), and the author of *What Ever Happened to Baby Jane?* (Henry Farrell). Despite the talented line-up, however, it's a routine TV movie which piles on the supernatural elements in distinctly old-fashioned ways. Barbara Stanwyck stars as a woman who inherits an Amish house with hot and cold running ghosts.

Barbara Stanwyck *Ruth Bennett* • Richard Egan *Pat McDougal* • Michael Anderson Jr *Stan Whitman* • Katherine Winn [Kitty Winn] *Sara Dunning* • Doreen Lang *Sylvia Wall* • Mabel Albertson *Delia McDougal* ■ *Dir* John Llewellyn Moxey • *Scr* Henry Farrell, from the novel *Ammie, Come Home* by Barbara Michaels

The House Where Evil Dwells ★ 18

Horror   1982 · US · Colour · 83mins

The 19th-century ghosts of a cuckolded Japanese samurai, his unfaithful wife and her lover terrorise a young couple when they move into their Kyoto haunted house. After US diplomat and old family friend Doug McClure arrives on the scene, the three are doomed to re-enact the spiritual love triangle. Another predictable horror outing from Kevin Connor, the director of the equally lacklustre *Warlords of Atlantis*, its soft-core sex, low-key gore and an attack by large crabs (!) do nothing to keep the boredom at bay. 🎬

Edward Albert *Ted* • Susan George *Laura* • Doug McClure *Alex* • Amy Barrett *Amy* • Mako Hattori *Otami* • Toshiyuki Sasaki *Shugoro* • Toshiya Maruyama *Masanori* • Okajima Tsuyako *Witch* • Henry Mitowa *Zen Monk* ■ *Dir* Kevin Connor • *Scr* Robert Suhosky, from the novel by James Hardiman

Houseboat ★★★★ U

Romantic comedy drama
1958 · US · Colour · 105mins

A delightfully played, relatively unsophisticated comedy based on a slim but oh-so-romantic premise, as lovely Sophia Loren takes charge of lawyer Cary Grant's three children and, eventually of course, Grant himself. Beautifully photographed by Ray June, who made a similarly fabulous job of *Funny Face*, this is a real easy-on-the-eye glamfest that also contains a fabulous supporting performance from Harry Guardino as a handyman in wolf's clothing. Needless to say, Grant sails through the movie with accomplished ease.

Sophia Loren *Cinzia Zaccardi* • Cary Grant *Tom Winston* • Martha Hyer *Carolyn Gibson* • Harry Guardino *Angelo Donatello* • Eduardo Ciannelli *Arturo Zaccardi* • Murray Hamilton *Alan Wilson* ■ *Dir* Melville Shavelson • *Scr* Melville Shavelson, Jack Rose

Houseguest ★★ PG

Comedy   1995 · US · Colour · 104mins

This so-so vehicle for Sinbad – the American comedy star, not the *Brookside* regular – went straight to video this side of the pond. In this variation on a familiar theme, the nautically named comedian plays a petty con artist on the run from the mob who, passing himself off as the long-lost chum of uptight lawyer Phil Hartman, moves in with his family. Sinbad's free-wheeling style raises the odd giggle, and he works well with Hartman. However, Randall Miller's direction is uninspired, and the result is a pretty predictable affair. 🎬

Sinbad *Kevin Franklin* • Phil Hartman *Gary Young* • Kim Greist *Emily Young* • Chauncey Leopardi *Jason Young* • Talia Seider *Sarah Young* ■ *Dir* Randall Miller • *Scr* Lawrence Gay, Michael DiGaetano

Household Saints ★★★

Comedy drama   1993 · US · Colour · 124mins

Executive produced by Jonathan Demme, this is a quirky tale of Italian-American Catholics in New York. Vincent D'Onofrio wins Tracey Ullman in a pinochle game and they marry.

Though bullied by his mother (Judith Malina), she gives birth to a daughter (Lili Taylor). As Taylor grows, so do her love for Jesus and her obsession with her saintly namesake, St Teresa. Director Nancy Savoca portrays three generations of comic and tragic family life with tenderness and empathy.

Tracey Ullman *Catherine Falconetti* • Vincent D'Onofrio *Joseph Santangelo* • Lili Taylor *Teresa* • Judith Malina *Carmela Santangelo* • Michael Rispoli *Nicky Falconetti* • Victor Argo *Lino Falconetti* • Michael Imperioli *Leonard Villanova* • Rachael Bella *Young Teresa* ■ *Dir* Nancy Savoca • *Scr* Nancy Savoca, Richard Guay, from the novel by Francine Prose

The Householder ★★★ U

Comedy   1963 · US/Ind · BW · 101mins

Adapted from her own novel by Ruth Prawer Jhabvala and produced by Ismail Merchant, James Ivory's debut feature launched one of the most successful teams in cinema history. Bearing in mind that the production nearly collapsed through lack of funds, this account of mummy's boy Shashi Kapoor's troubled early marriage to Leela Naidu is admirably authentic. Yet it took some editing assistance from Satyajit Ray (who would also score *Shakespeare Wallah*) to give the narrative its sense of drama and pace. Rough edges remain, but the camerawork of Ray regular Subrata Mitra is deeply sensitive and the performances are touchingly honest.

Shashi Kapoor *Prem Sagar* • Leela Naidu *Indu* • Harindranath Chattopadhyaya *Mr Chadda* • Durga Khote *The Mother* • Pro Sen *Sohanlal* ■ *Dir* James Ivory • *Scr* Ruth Prawer Jhabvala, from her novel

The Housekeeper's Daughter ★★

Crime comedy   1939 · US · BW · 79mins

The only fireworks in this lowbrow murder farce come at the end when they're let off by drunken crime reporter Adolphe Menjou and press photographer William Gargan. It's one of many slapstick moments in this feature-length product from the Hal Roach fun factory, directed by Roach himself. Joan Bennett is the housekeeper's daughter with a shady past, and John Hubbard is the novice reporter up against Marc Lawrence's gang boss. Newcomer Hubbard failed as a leading man, however – unlike the debuting Victor Mature.

Joan Bennett *Hilda* • Adolphe Menjou *Deakon Maxwell* • John Hubbard *Robert Randall* • William Gargan *Ed O'Malley* • George E Stone *Benny* • Peggy Wood *Olga* • Donald Meek *Editor Wilson* • Marc Lawrence *Floyd* • Lilian Bond [Lillian Bond] *Gladys* • Victor Mature *Lefty* ■ *Dir* Hal Roach • *Scr* Rian James, Gordon Douglas, from a story by Donald Henderson Clarke

Housekeeping ★★★★ PG

Comedy drama   1987 · US · Colour · 111mins

Director Bill Forsyth has been sadly underused by the American film industry, particularly after his Robin Williams vehicle *Being Human* floundered because of creative differences. Yet it all started so well with this charming and superbly controlled study of the way in which children manage to survive even the

most outrageous whims of the adults entrusted with their care. Sara Walker and Andrea Burchill are splendid as the young sisters who seem to have immunised themselves against the upheavals that periodically shatter their world, while Christine Lahti has never been better as the dippy aunt who appears to be their saviour. Contains swearing.

Christine Lahti *Aunt Sylvie* • Sara Walker *Ruth* • Andrea Burchill *Lucille* • Anne Pitoniak *Lily* • Barbara Reese *Nona* • Bill Smillie *Sheriff* • Wayne Robson *Mr French* • Margot Pinvidic *Helen* ■ *Dir* Bill Forsyth • *Scr* Bill Forsyth, from the novel by Marilynne Robinson

Housemaster ★★★

Comedy drama   1938 · UK · BW · 95mins

This adaptation of the Ian Hay play brought actor Otto Kruger over from America for the role of his life, as the housemaster victimised by the school's head after disciplinary measures result in a revolt of the pupils. Irish-born director Herbert Brenon was responsible for silent screen hits such as *Beau Geste*, but it was the Oscar-nominated *Sorrell and Son* that demonstrated his empathy with the nuances of the English class system, evident in *Housemaster*. Watch for Cecil Parker in an early role, and also Jimmy Hanley who was on the brink of his screen career.

Otto Kruger *Charles Donkin* • Diana Churchill *Rosemary Faringdon* • Phillips Holmes *Philip de Courville* • Joyce Barbour *Barbara Fane* • René Ray *Chris Faringdon* • Cecil Parker *Sir Berkeley Nightingale* • Jimmy Hanley *Travers* ■ *Dir* Herbert Brenon • *Scr* Dudley Leslie, Elizabeth Meehan, from the play *Bachelor Born* by Ian Hay

HouseSitter ★★★ PG

Romantic comedy
1992 · US · Colour · 97mins

A likeable, if somewhat silly romantic comedy, with Goldie Hawn at her dippiest and Steve Martin as a staid architect whose life she overturns. Martin is recovering from rejection by the love of his life (Dana Delany) when he meets Hawn, who decides to help his convalescence by moving into the dream house he has built but left empty after getting the elbow from his dream woman. When Hawn tells the neighbourhood that she's his new wife, the comic complications pile on, to generally amusing effect. 🎬

Steve Martin *Newton Davis* • Goldie Hawn *Gwen* • Dana Delany *Becky* • Julie Harris *Edna Davis* • Donald Moffat *George Davis* • Peter MacNicol *Marty* • Richard B Shull *Ralph* ■ *Dir* Frank Oz • *Scr* Mark Stein, from a story by Mark Stein, Brian Grazer

Housewife ★

Drama   1972 · US · Colour · 91mins

Made in 1972 and called *Bone*, then *Beverly Hills Nightmare*, and released in Britain in 1979 as *Dial Rat for Terror*, this piece of schlock now appears as the altogether more chilling *Housewife*. It's a horror film from Larry Cohen – director of *It's Alive!* – and stars Yaphet Kotto, a lot of cockroaches, a dead rat in a swimming pool and a Beverly Hills couple going bananas. The film's pretensions have to be seen to be believed, for there's an allegory about wealth and white

privilege lurking among the wooden performances and silly shock effects. Contains violence, swearing, sex scenes and nudity.

Yaphet Kotto *Bone* • Andrew Duggan *Bill* • Joyce Van Patten *Bernadette* • Jeannie Berlin *Girl* ■ *Dir/Scr* Larry Cohen

How Awful about Allan ★★

Psychological thriller
1970 · US · Colour · 90mins

Adapted by Henry Farrell from his own novel, this chiller could easily have turned into hysterical nonsense in the hands of a lesser director. Yet not even the underestimated Curtis Harrington can conceal the shortcomings in this story of a blind man (Anthony Perkins) who feels responsible for the fire that killed his father. When he moves in with his sympathetic sister (Julie Harris), he is tormented by eerie voices and an unseen menace. Perkins, playing the victim for once, conjures up a real sense of bemused terror, but the sinister atmosphere is not sustained.

Anthony Perkins *Allan Colleigh* • Julie Harris *Katherine Colleigh* • Joan Hackett *Olive* • Kent Smith *Raymond Colleigh* • Kenneth Lawrence *Allan as a child* • Jeanette Howe *Katherine as a child* • Robert H Harris *Dr Ellins* • Bill Erwin *Dr Ames* ■ *Dir* Curtis Harrington • *Scr* Henry Farrell, from his novel

How Do I Love Thee? ★★ PG

Comedy drama 1970 · US · Colour · 108mins

For reasons best known to themselves, the producers of this laborious comedy chose the line immediately preceding that in the Elizabeth Browning poem for the title of this film version of Peter DeVries's novel *Let Me Count the Ways*. Jackie Gleason was perhaps not the most fortuitous choice to play an unrepentant atheist in keen debate with his philosophy professor son, as anyone who has seen the deadly dull *Nothing in Common* will know. Maureen O'Hara and Shelley Winters do little more than referee this talkathon, which is rarely worth listening to. 🔲

Jackie Gleason *Stanley Waltz* • Maureen O'Hara *Elsie Waltz* • Shelley Winters *Lena Mervin* • Rosemary Forsyth *Marion Waltz* ■ *Dir* Michael Gordon • *Scr* Everett Freeman, Karl Tunberg, from the novel *Let Me Count the Ways* by Peter DeVries

How Green Was My Valley ★★★★★ U

Drama 1941 · US · BW · 117mins

This magnificent Oscar-winning family saga may seem a trifle dated, with its superb, but phoney, studio re-creations of the valleys of South Wales. But there's no denying its power to move as well as entertain audiences, as director John Ford lovingly details life in the pits and valleys of Richard Llewellyn's famous autobiographical novel. Ford rightly won the best director Oscar and the movie won best picture, but often overlooked is the sincerity of the film's hand-picked cast, notably sturdy Walter Pidgeon and fiery Ford regular Maureen O'Hara. The best supporting actor Oscar went to Donald Crisp's patriarch. This is precisely the kind of movie that gave Hollywood film-making supremacy in its heyday. 🔲

Walter Pidgeon *Mr Gruffydd* • Maureen O'Hara *Angharad* • Donald Crisp *Mr Morgan* • Roddy McDowall *Huw* • Anna Lee *Bronwyn* • John Loder *Ianto* • Sara Allgood *Mrs Morgan* • Barry Fitzgerald *Cyfartha* ■ *Dir* John Ford • *Scr* Philip Dunne, from the novel by Richard Llewellyn • *Cinematographer* Arthur C Miller

How I Got Into College ★★★ 15

Comedy 1989 · US · Colour · 83mins

This romantic teen comedy stars Corey Parker as a lovestruck, non-academic sort who plans to enrol in the same college as the girl he worships (Lara Flynn Boyle). The trouble is, he's not the college type. Luckily the college in question is about to launch a new initiative allowing some "ordinary" guys to enter their hallowed halls. Witty, and likeable juvenile fare, above average for the genre. 🔲

Anthony Edwards *Kip* • Corey Parker *Marlon* • Lara Flynn Boyle *Jessica* • Finn Carter *Nina* • Charles Rocket *Leo* • Christopher Rydell *Oliver* • Philip Baker Hall *Dean Patterson* ■ *Dir* Savage Steve Holland • *Scr* Terrel Seltzer

How I Spent My Summer Vacation ★★ U

Thriller 1967 · US · Colour · 89mins

Made as a TV movie of the week by Universal, who pioneered such things, this confused would-be thriller was renamed *Deadly Roulette* and released in cinemas here largely because of its extremely attractive cast. A boyish Robert Wagner stars as a former soldier who seeks revenge on sophisticated, wealthy Peter Lawford following an incident when Lawford humiliated him; others aboard for the ride include Lola Albright, Jill St John and a dapper Walter Pidgeon.

Robert Wagner *Jack Washington* • Peter Lawford *Ned Pine* • Lola Albright *Mrs Pine* • Walter Pidgeon *Lewis Gannet* • Jill St John *Nikki Pine* • Michael Ansara *Pucci* ■ *Dir* William Hale • *Scr* Gene Kearney

How I Won the War ★★★★ 12

Black comedy 1967 · UK · Colour · 105mins

John Lennon's decision to take a break from the Beatles and accept the part of Private Gripweed was the major talking point when this film was initially released. Based on Patrick Ryan's biting attack on the follies of war and brass-hat incompetence, Richard Lester's feature broadens the satire and throws in a little surrealism and slapstick to make the subtleties of the book suitably cinematic. Getting by with a little help from his friends, Michael Crawford is admirably gung ho as the head of the special cricket pitch unit. Contains violence. 🔲

Michael Crawford *Lt Ernest Goodbody* • John Lennon *Gripweed* • Roy Kinnear *Clapper* • Lee Montague *Sgt Transom* • Jack MacGowran *Juniper* • Michael Hordern *Grapple* • Jack Hedley *Melancholy musketeer* • Karl Michael Vogler *Odlebog* ■ *Dir* Richard Lester • *Scr* Charles Wood, from the novel by Patrick Ryan

How Stella Got Her Groove Back ★★★ 15

Romantic comedy drama
1998 · US · Colour · 119mins

Based on the novel by Terry McMillan, this is a companion piece to the earlier *Waiting to Exhale*, which also starred Angela Bassett. Here she plays single mother Stella, who is encouraged by her best friend (Whoopi Goldberg) to escape her downbeat existence for a holiday in Jamaica. It's there that she meets half-her-age hunk Taye Diggs, and the audience is treated to picture-postcard shots of both their romance and the island itself. You'll want to book a holiday to the Caribbean before the film is over, but you won't be as enchanted with the characters only briefly sketched. Contains some swearing and sex scenes. 🔲

Angela Bassett *Stella* • Whoopi Goldberg *Delilah* • Regina King *Vanessa* • Taye Diggs *Winston Shakespeare* • Suzzanne Douglas *Angela* • Michael J Pagan *Quincy* • Sicily *Chantel* • Richard Lawson *Jack* ■ *Dir* Kevin Rodney Sullivan [Kevin Sullivan] • *Scr* Ronald Bass, Terry McMillan, from the novel by Terry McMillan

How Sweet It Is! ★

Comedy 1968 · US · Colour · 97mins

An unspeakably tasteless and witless comedy about two married Americans discovering sex in Europe, hoping to bring excitement to their marriage and maturity to their teenage offspring. Debbie Reynolds canoodles with Maurice Ronet at James Garner's expense, while Paul Lynde and Terry-Thomas share the few laughs on offer. Jerry Paris directs with a total lack of sophistication, allowing the usually reliable Garner to mug shamelessly.

James Garner *Grif Henderson* • Debbie Reynolds *Jenny Henderson* • Maurice Ronet *Philippe Maspere* • Terry-Thomas *Gilbert Tilly* • Paul Lynde *The Purser* • Marcel Dalio *Louis* ■ *Dir* Jerry Paris • *Scr* Garry Marshall, Jerry Belson, from the novel *The Girl in the Turquoise Bikini* by Muriel Resnik

How the West Was Won ★★★★ PG

Epic western 1962 · US · Colour · 157mins

One of only two narrative films made in three-camera Cinerama; if you look very carefully you can see the joins in its widescreen version, which are especially noticeable down the tree trunks. Of the three credited directors, Henry Hathaway shot the all-star Rivers, Plains and Outlaws sections, while George Marshall filmed that dangerous stunt-work on the railroad, and the great John Ford directed the splendid American Civil War sequence. The majestic score is by Alfred Newman, and was used again to witty comic effect in *Romancing the Stone*, but the total impact will inevitably be dwarfed on television. 🔲

James Stewart *Linus Rawlings* • John Wayne *General William T Sherman* • Gregory Peck *Cleve Van Valen* • Henry Fonda *Jethro Stuart* • Carroll Baker *Eve Prescott* • Lee J Cobb *Marshal Lou Ramsey* • Carolyn Jones *Julie Rawlings* • Karl Malden *Zebulon Prescott* • George Peppard *Zeb Rawlings* • Robert Preston *Roger Morgan* • Debbie Reynolds *Lilith Prescott* • Eli Wallach *Charlie Gant* • Richard Widmark *Mike King* • Walter Brennan *Colonel Hawkins* • Raymond Massey *Abraham*

Lincoln • Agnes Moorehead *Rebecca Prescott* • Thelma Ritter *Agatha Clegg* • Spencer Tracy *Narrator* ■ *Dir* John Ford, Henry Hathaway, Richard Thorpe • *Scr* James R Webb, from articles in *Life Magazine* • *Cinematographer* William Daniels, Milton Krasner, Charles Lang Jr [Charles Lang], Joseph LaShelle

How to Be a Woman and Not Die in the Attempt ★★★ 15

Comedy drama 1991 · Sp · Colour · 85mins

Wry and amusing comedy, in which the pain in Spain falls mainly on the wife. Carmen Maura plays a working wife and mum who finally takes umbrage at her workaholic hubby's chauvinistic belief that she should not only bring home a wage, but also be solely responsible for bringing up their three kids. Waspishly written and beautifully acted, especially by the ever-excellent Maura, this is proof that quality films from Spain don't have to have the name "Almodóvar" attached to them. In Spanish with English subtitles. 🔲

Carmen Maura *Carmen* • Antonio Resines *Antonio* ■ *Dir* Ana Belén • *Scr* Carmen Rico-Godoy, from her novel

How to Be Very, Very Popular ★★★ U

Musical comedy 1955 · US · Colour · 89mins

This mediocre musical saw Betty Grable bring down the curtain on a career in which she had been everything the title said. But the 38-year-old star is soundly upstaged in her swan song by Sheree North, a blond bombshell 16 years her junior making only her fourth feature. Bearing a passing resemblance to both the earlier *She Loves Me Not* and the later *Some Like It Hot*, the film gave writer/producer/director Nunnally Johnson the excuse to keep his stars in the skimpiest of costumes. Not even that old scene stealer Charles Coburn could beat that sort of competition.

Betty Grable *Stormy* • Sheree North *Curly* • Robert Cummings *Wedgewood* • Charles Coburn *Tweed* • Tommy Noonan *Eddie* • Orson Bean *Toby* • Fred Clark *Mr Marshall* • Charlotte Austin *Midge* ■ *Dir* Nunnally Johnson • *Scr* Nunnally Johnson, from a play by Howard Lindsay, from a novel by Edward Hope and a play by Lyford Moore, Harlan Thompson

How to Beat the High Cost of Living ★★★

Comedy 1980 · US · Colour · 96mins

Long before they got together on the small screen in the sitcom *Kate and Allie*, Susan Saint James and Jane Curtin teamed up on this caper comedy. Along with Jessica Lange, they play old schoolfriends who find themselves seriously in need of money, thanks mainly to the incompetence of their menfolk. The three hatch a plot to steal thousands of dollars from a giant plastic moneyball set up as a publicity stunt in their hometown shopping mall. More comedy than drama, but the three leads play appealing characters. 🔲

Susan Saint James *Jane* • Jane Curtin *Elaine* • Jessica Lange *Louise* • Richard Benjamin *Albert* • Eddie Albert *Max* • Cathryn Damon

U = SUITABLE FOR ALL,   **Uc** = SUITABLE FOR ALL, ESPECIALLY FOR YOUNG CHILDREN (VIDEO ONLY)   **PG** = PARENTAL GUIDANCE

Natalie • Dabney Coleman *Jack Heintzel* ■ *Dir* Robert Scheerer • *Scr* Robert Kaufman, from a story by Leonora Thuna

How to Break Up a Happy Divorce ★★

Drama   1976 · US · Colour · 74mins

The old, old story of a girl plotting her man's return by making him jealous is given a sprightly, farcical twist by Barbara Eden leaving Larry Hagman to fend for himself in *I Dream of Jeannie*. She is the divorcee showing her husband what he's missing by dating a slick man-about-town. Peter Bonerz and Hal Linden, as the men in her life, make you wonder why she bothers, but Eden is a treat to watch, whatever the quality of her material and co-stars.

Barbara Eden *Ellen Dowling* • Hal Linden *Tony Bartlett* • Peter Bonerz *Carter Dowling* • Marcia Rodd *Eve* • Harold Gould *Mr Henshaw* • Betty Bressler *Mrs Henshaw* • Liberty Williams *Jennifer Hartman* ■ *Dir* Jerry Paris • *Scr* Gerald Gardner, Dee K Caruso

How to Commit Marriage ★

Comedy   1969 · US · Colour · 95mins

In this self-conscious, dire comedy, Bob Hope and Jane Wyman play about-to-be-divorced parents. When their daughter Joanna Cameron brings home her fiancé, they try to pretend all is well. But the boy's father (Jackie Gleason) becomes suspicious, their charade is revealed and the wedding is called off. The kids then turn to an eastern mystic in an embarrassing attempt to cross the comedy of Hope and Gleason with the "anything goes" style of the Swinging Sixties.

Bob Hope *Frank Benson* • Jackie Gleason *Oliver Poe* • Jane Wyman *Elaine Benson* • Leslie Nielsen *Phil Fletcher* • Maureen Arthur *Lois Gray* • Joanna Cameron *Nancy Benson* • Tim Matheson *David Poe* ■ *Dir* Norman Panama • *Scr* Ben Starr, Michael Kanin

How to Fill a Wild Bikini ★ U

Musical comedy 1965 · US · Colour · 92mins

The fifth in AIP's beach party series is the biggest washout of the lot. With Frankie Avalon away on naval reserve duty, he's limited to a cameo role as the suspicious coastguard who calls on witch doctor Buster Keaton to ensure that Annette Funicello doesn't fall into the clutches of beefcake Dwayne Hickman. Boasting some of the worst song-and-dance routines ever committed to celluloid (take a bow, Brian Donlevy and Harvey Lembeck). Notable only for the guest appearances of Mickey Rooney, Beach Boy Brian Wilson and, in a corny in-joke finale, *Bewitched* star Elizabeth Montgomery.

Annette Funicello *Dee Dee* • Dwayne Hickman *Ricky* • Brian Donlevy *BD* • Harvey Lembeck *Eric Von Zipper* • Beverly Adams *Cassandra* • Buster Keaton *Bwana* • Mickey Rooney *Peachy Keane* • Frankie Avalon *Frankie* • Brian Wilson *Beach boy* • Elizabeth Montgomery *Witches' witch* ■ *Dir* William Asher • *Scr* William Asher, Leo Townsend

How to Frame a Figg ★

Comedy   1971 · US · Colour · 103mins

This clumsy, unsubtle vehicle for American comedian Don Knotts has

him typecast as a simple-minded fellow – the eponymous Mr Figg – who's batted back and forth between rival, crooked politicians. This won't mean much to British audiences; it didn't mean much to American audiences, either. However, cult TV fans may recognise TV's Batgirl, Yvonne Craig.

Don Knotts *Hollis Figg* • Joe Flynn *Kermit Sanderson* • Edward Andrews *Mayor Chisolm* • Elaine Joyce *Ema Lethakusic* • Yvonne Craig *Glorianna* • Frank Welker *Prentiss Gates* ■ *Dir* Alan Rafkin • *Scr* George Tibbles, from a story by Don Knotts, Edward J Montagne

How to Get Ahead in Advertising ★★★ 15

Satirical comedy 1989 · UK · Colour · 90mins

After the truly wonderful *Withnail & I*, this comic follow-up, which reunited Richard E Grant with writer/director Bruce Robinson, proved something of a disappointment. Grant is the troubled advertising executive who develops an evil alter ego: a boil which can not only talk but is intent on taking over his whole body. There are some neat, surreal touches from Robinson, another manic performance from Grant and a solid supporting cast, which includes Rachel Ward, Richard Wilson and Susan Wooldridge. However, the evil side of advertising is too broad and too obvious a target for Robinson to get his teeth into. Contains swearing and some nudity. ⊡

Richard E Grant *Dennis Bagley* • Rachel Ward *Julia Bagley* • Richard Wilson *Bristol* • Jacqueline Tong *Penny Wheelstock* • John Shrapnel *Psychiatrist* • Susan Wooldridge *Monica* ■ *Dir/Scr* Bruce Robinson

How to Make a Monster ★★ PG

Horror   1958 · US · BW and Colour · 73mins

When a Hollywood make-up effects man is told horror is passé, he applies special drugged cosmetics to the actors playing Frankenstein's creature and the Werewolf in his last movie so they'll think they really are monsters and murder the meddlesome moguls. Cue the re-use of old fright masks, props and veteran stars from AIP successes such as *I Was a Teenage Werewolf*, affectionately mocking the genre in which the film's real-life co-writer Herman Cohen originally found fame as a producer. A must for fifties schlock fans. ⊡

Robert H Harris *Pete Dummond* • Paul Brinegar *Rivero* • Gary Conway *Tony Mantell* • Gary Clarke *Larry Drake* • Malcolm Atterbury *Richards* ■ *Dir* Herbert L Strock • *Scr* Kenneth Langtry, Herman Cohen

How to Make an American Quilt ★★★ 12

Drama   1995 · US · Colour · 111mins

A low-key but enjoyable film for the girls, based on the book by Whitney Otto, directed by Jocelyn Moorhouse (*A Thousand Acres*), and featuring moving performances from the female-dominated cast. Winona Ryder is the marriage-shy young woman who listens while her older relatives recount tales of love and disappointment as they add squares to a growing and symbolic quilt. Some of the episodic tales work better than others, but all are

interesting and there are moving performances from both young (Samantha Mathis, Claire Danes) and more senior (Anne Bancroft, Ellen Burstyn, Jean Simmons, poet Maya Angelou) cast members. ⊡

Winona Ryder *Finn* • Ellen Burstyn *Hy* • Anne Bancroft *Glady Joe* • Kate Capshaw *Sally* • Dermot Mulroney *Sam* • Maya Angelou *Anna* • Alfre Woodard *Marianna* • Jean Simmons *Em* • Kate Nelligan *Constance* • Rip Torn *Arthur* • Samantha Mathis *Young Sophia* • Adam Baldwin *Finn's father* • Claire Danes *Young Glady Joe* ■ *Dir* Jocelyn Moorhouse • *Scr* Jane Anderson, from the novel by Whitney Otto • *Music* Thomas Newman

How to Marry a Millionaire ★★★★ PG

Comedy   1953 · US · Colour · 91mins

A fabulously cast and wickedly witty reworking of that much-filmed 20th Century-Fox standby, the one about the three gals seeking rich husbands, dusted off, smartened up and photographed in Fox's stunning new screen process, CinemaScope, the better to fill the frame with glorious shapes – and when those shapes belong to the new queen of the Fox lot, Marilyn Monroe, departing royalty Betty Grable, and worldly-wise Lauren Bacall, who could ask for more? Well, there is more. This film was the first shot in Scope, and it's preceded by an introductory orchestral sequence specially designed to show off the wonders of the then-new magnetic stereophonic sound. ⊡

Betty Grable *Loco* • Marilyn Monroe *Pola* • Lauren Bacall *Schatze Page* • David Wayne *Freddie Denmark* • Rory Calhoun *Eben* • Cameron Mitchell *Tom Brookman* • Alex D'Arcy *J Stewart Merrill* • Fred Clark *Waldo Brewster* • William Powell *JD Hanley* ■ *Dir* Jean Negulesco • *Scr* Nunnally Johnson, from the plays *The Greeks Had a Word for It* by Zoe Akins and *Loco* by Dale Eunson, Katherine Albert • *Music* Alfred Newman

How to Murder a Millionaire ★

Comedy   1990 · US · Colour · 97mins

Joan Rivers is the millionaire's wife who suspects her husband is trying to kill her in this woeful comedy adventure. A cast that includes Alex Rocco, Morgan Fairchild and David Ogden Stiers cannot save the movie from being a one-joke wonder, and Rivers, never the most subtle comedian, plays every weak laugh as if it was the best joke she'd ever heard.

Joan Rivers *Irma Summers* • Alex Rocco *Walter Summers* • Morgan Fairchild *Loretta* • David Ogden Stiers *Gilbert* • Telma Hopkins *Teresa* • Meshach Taylor *Danny* ■ *Dir* Paul Schneider • *Scr* Mark Edward Edens

How to Murder a Rich Uncle ★★★ U

Black comedy   1957 · UK · BW · 79mins

Glorious memories of *Kind Hearts and Coronets* are occasionally stirred by this black comedy about the English aristocracy. Nigel Patrick – who also directed with an uncredited Max Varnel – stars as Sir Henry Clitterburn, down on his uppers, who plots to murder visiting Canadian uncle Charles Coburn in order to inherit a bundle. His plans go awry, of course. There's lots to

enjoy here, including a lovely gallery of English eccentrics – notably a harumphing Wendy Hiller and little old Katie Johnson from *The Ladykillers* – and making his second credited screen appearance is a certain Michael Caine.

Nigel Patrick *Henry* • Charles Coburn *Uncle George* • Wendy Hiller *Edith* • Katie Johnson *Alice* • Anthony Newley *Edward* • Athene Seyler *Grannie* • Noel Hood *Aunt Marjorie* • Michael Caine *Gilrony* ■ *Dir* Nigel Patrick • *Scr* John Paxton, from the play *Il Faut Tuer Julie* by Didier Daix

How to Murder Your Wife ★★★★ PG

Comedy   1965 · US · Colour · 113mins

Confirmed bachelor Jack Lemmon wakes up after a night on the town married to luscious Virna Lisi, much to the dismay of his faithful butler Terry-Thomas, in director Richard Quine's brilliant politically incorrect comedy. Thereafter, strip-cartoonist Lemmon's action-man character Bash Brannigan becomes cosily domesticated. To placate his fans, who want Brannigan restored to bachelorhood, Lemmon kills off his cartoon hero's wife; but then Lisi disappears and Lemmon finds himself accused of murder. Scenes to cherish involve the "galopita-galopita" machine and the courtroom pressing of an imaginary button, while the long-married double act of Eddie Mayehoff and Claire Trevor shows just how far the battle of the sexes can go. ⊡

Jack Lemmon *Stanley Ford* • Virna Lisi *Mrs Ford* • Terry-Thomas *Charles* • Claire Trevor *Edna* • Eddie Mayehoff *Harold Lampson* • Sidney Blackmer *Judge Blackstone* • Max Showalter *Tobey Rawlins* • Jack Albertson *Dr Bentley* • Alan Hewitt *District attorney* ■ *Dir* Richard Quine • *Scr* George Axelrod

How to Save a Marriage and Ruin Your Life ★★

Comedy   1968 · US · Colour · 102mins

Dean Martin hits on a brilliant plan to save his friend's marriage in this convoluted comedy. Eli Wallach is cheating on his wife Katharine Bard, and Martin's rescue strategy involves seducing Wallach's mistress himself. Unfortunately he's got the wrong girl. From this one simple mix-up a muddle of gigantic proportions develops and the plot – hardly on an even keel from the beginning – lists hopelessly out of control. Stella Stevens as the wrongly-identified "mistress" tries her hardest.

Dean Martin *David Sloane* • Stella Stevens *Carol Corman* • Eli Wallach *Harry Hunter* • Anne Jackson *Muriel Laszlo* • Betty Field *Thelma* • Jack Albertson *Mr. Slotkin* • Katharine Bard *Mary Hunter* ■ *Dir* Fielder Cook • *Scr* Stanley Shapiro, Nate Monaster

How to Steal a Million ★★★ U

Crime comedy 1966 · US · Colour · 118mins

The third film that *Roman Holiday* director William Wyler made with Audrey Hepburn is a heist caper set in the Paris art world, with Hepburn hiring Peter O'Toole to steal her father's fake Cellini Venus. Overlong and overwritten, the picture shows its age in the Swinging Sixties decor and the generally rather frantic mood. But there are compensations in the supporting cast, with Charles Boyer and Marcel Dalio evoking the sophistication of those thirties comedies of Ernst Lubitsch. American vulgarity, meanwhile, is supplied by greedy art collector Eli Wallach, the replacement for George C Scott, whom Wyler fired after only one day of shooting. ▫

Audrey Hepburn *Nicole Bonnet* • Peter O'Toole *Simon Dermott* • Eli Wallach *David Leland* • Hugh Griffith *Charles Bonnet* • Charles Boyer *De Solnay* • Fernand Gravey [Fernand Gravet] *Grammont* • Marcel Dalio *Senor Paravideo* • Jacques Marin *Chief guard* ■ *Dir* William Wyler • *Scr* Harry Kurnitz, from the story *Venus Rising* by George Bradshaw

How to Steal the World ★★
Spy spoof 1968 · US · Colour · 89mins

Stretched to feature length from a couple of TV episodes by Norman Hudis (the pioneering *Carry On* scriptwriter), this was the last *Man from UNCLE* picture produced by MGM, with Robert Vaughn and David McCallum looking very bored after four years of tongue-in-cheek espionage. Barry Sullivan runs through all the tricks of arch-villainy as a rogue agent, abducting five mind-control experts whose knowledge is central to his plans for world domination. Despite guests of the calibre of Eleanor Parker and Leslie Nielsen, the series ended on a distinctly flat note.

Robert Vaughn *Napoleon Solo* • David McCallum *Illya Kuryakin* • Barry Sullivan *Robert Kingsley* • Leslie Nielsen *Gen Harmon* • Eleanor Parker *Margitta* ■ *Dir* Sutton Roley • *Scr* Norman Hudis

How to Succeed in Business without Really Trying ★★★★ Ⓤ
Musical comedy 1967 · US · Colour · 116mins

A superb film re-creation of Frank Loesser and Abe Burrows's wonderfully acerbic stage musical, with all of Bob Fosse's original choreography preserved on film by Dale Moreda. Robert Morse repeats his Broadway role in a marvellously wicked, devastatingly funny part as a ruthless window cleaner who claws his way to the top of World Wide Wickets, the company run by, of all people, crooner Rudy Vallee. A surprising success considering the source book by Shepherd Mead, which seemed an unlikely base for a musical, let alone one this terrific. This also has to be the only musical where the hero sings the love song to himself. ▫

Robert Morse *J Pierpont Finch* • Michele Lee *Rosemary Pilkington* • Rudy Vallee *JB Biggley* • Anthony Teague *Bud Frump* • Maureen Arthur *Hedy LaRue* • Murray Matheson *Benjamin Ovington* ■ *Dir* David Swift • *Scr* David Swift, from the musical by Abe Burrows, Willie Gilbert, Jack Weinstock, from the novel by Shepherd Mead • *Music/Lyrics* Frank Loesser

How U Like Me Now ★★
Romantic comedy
1992 · US · Colour · 109mins

Darryl Roberts wrote, produced and directed this low-budget feature set in Chicago's African-American community. Darnell Williams is a smart guy bored with his nine-to-five job and at cross-purposes with his live-in lover Salli

Richardson, who is more interested in social climbing. As the couple's relationship disintegrates their friends offer "battle of the sexes"-style counselling. In the end, though, this is all rather two-dimensional.

Darnell Williams *Thomas* • Salli Richardson *Valerie* • Daniel Gardner *Spoony* • Raymond Whitefield *Alex* • Debra Crable *Michelle* • Darryl Roberts *BJ* • Byron Stewart *Pierre* ■ *Dir/Scr* Darryl Roberts

Howard, a New Breed of Hero ★★ PG
Comedy fantasy 1986 · US · Colour · 105mins

Marvel Comics meets George Lucas's Industrial Light and Magic, and an uneasy, bland alliance it is, too, with Howard T Duck transported to mid-eighties punkland. Howard takes to the dreadful music of the time and feisty chanteuse Lea Thompson, but fails to ignite any form of discernible plot line or audience response. The movie remains a tedious mess until the final few reels, when Mr Lucas's boys throw some highly dynamic special effects into the burbling pot. Alas, it's too late to save a pretty execrable movie. Contains mild swearing. ▫

Lea Thompson *Beverly Switzler* • Tim Robbins *Phil Blumburtt* • Jeffrey Jones *Dr Jenning* • Paul Guilfoyle *Lieutenant Welker* • Liz Sagal *Ronette* • Dominique Davalos *Cal* • Holly Robinson *KC* • Tommy Swerdlow *Ginger Moss* ■ *Dir* Willard Huyck • *Scr* Willard Huyck, Gloria Katz, from a character created by Steve Gerber

Howards End ★★★★★ PG
Period drama 1992 · UK · Colour · 140mins

This adaptation of EM Forster's novel is the best film made by the long-time team of director James Ivory, producer Ismail Merchant and writer Ruth Prawer Jhabvala, with an elegance that never hides grim insights into the upper middle-classes. Matriarchal Ruth Wilcox (Vanessa Redgrave) dies after writing a letter bequeathing her country home, Howards End, to new friend Margaret Schlegel (Emma Thompson). But the note is destroyed by the Wilcox family snobs-in-residence, whose head (Anthony Hopkins) then falls in love with Margaret. Meanwhile, the low expectations of the clerking classes are dismally exemplified by Leonard Bast (Samuel West), whose affair with Margaret's sister Helen (Helena Bonham Carter) leads to tragedy. From Bast's dank lodgings to Howards End's cosy rurality, the perfect period detail is not an end in itself, but allows Hopkins and Thompson to create extraordinarily convincing portraits. One of the finest conversions of a novel to cinema. ▫ **DVD**

Anthony Hopkins *Henry Wilcox* • Emma Thompson *Margaret Schlegel* • Helena Bonham Carter *Helen Schlegel* • Vanessa Redgrave *Ruth Wilcox* • James Wilby *Charles Wilcox* • Samuel West *Leonard Bast* • Prunella Scales *Aunt Juley* • Jemma Redgrave *Evie Wilcox* • Nicola Duffett *Jacky Bast* ■ *Dir* James Ivory • *Scr* Ruth Prawer Jhabvala, from the novel by EM Forster

The Howards of Virginia ★★★ Ⓤ
Historical epic 1940 · US · BW · 110mins

The clash between the forces of conservatism and the emergence of the American democratic spirit form the stuff of this historical epic. Set before and during the American Revolution, it also encompasses a love story between a progressive Virginian (Cary Grant) and the daughter (Martha Scott) of a wealthy reactionary (Cedric Hardwicke). Directed with confident sweep by Frank Lloyd, Oscar winner for *Cavalcade* (1933), this handsomely mounted film is itself a cavalcade of events that includes the Boston Tea Party. Yet, for all its incident, political ideas and careful attention to period, it's less than compelling, and the debonair Grant is patently miscast. ▫

Cary Grant *Matt Howard* • Martha Scott *Jane Peyton Howard* • Sir Cedric Hardwicke [Cedric Hardwicke] *Fleetwood Peyton* • Alan Marshal *Roger Peyton* • Richard Carlson *Thomas Jefferson* • Paul Kelly *Captain Jabez Allen* • Irving Bacon *Tom Norton* • Elisabeth Risdon *Aunt Clarissa* • Alan Ladd *Neighbour* ■ *Dir* Frank Lloyd • *Scr* Sidney Buchman, from the novel *The Tree of Liberty* by Elizabeth Page

The Howling ★★★★ 18
Horror 1981 · US · Colour · 86mins

Co-writer John Sayles and director Joe Dante have huge fun turning werewolf clichés on their head in this rare beast – a horror film that gore fans and film buffs can enjoy. For the former, there is Rob Bottins's amazing make-up and a witty plot in which a sceptical TV journalist (Dee Wallace) uncovers a werewolf colony. For the latter, Dante touches his cap to monster greats of the past by naming key characters after cult horror directors such as Terry (Terence) Fisher and Fred (Freddie) Francis. Contains violence, swearing and nudity. ▫

Dee Wallace [Dee Wallace Stone] *Karen White* • Patrick Macnee *Dr George Waggner* • Dennis Dugan *Chris* • Christopher Stone *R William "Bill" Neill* • Belinda Balaski *Terry Fisher* • Kevin McCarthy *Fred Francis* • John Carradine *Erle Kenton* • Slim Pickens *Sam Newfield* • Elisabeth Brooks *Marsha* • Robert Picardo *Eddie* • Dick Miller *Walter Paisley* ■ *Dir* Joe Dante • *Scr* John Sayles, Terence H Winkless, from the novel by Gary Brandner

Howling II: Your Sister Is a Werewolf ★★ 18
Horror 1984 · US · Colour · 86mins

After the sly wit of Joe Dante's 1981 original, director Philippe Mora opts for a very camp spin for the first of an innumerable number of sequels. The setting is Transylvania, with Reb Brown setting out to track down the werewolf queen (Sybil Danning). Even the presence of Christopher Lee fails to impress, though the mix of loopy gore and clumsy parody exerts a bizarre charm. ▫

Christopher Lee *Stefan Crosscoe* • Annie McEnroe *Jenny Templeton* • Reb Brown *Ben White* • Sybil Danning *Stirba* • Marsha A Hunt *Mariana* • Judd Omen *Vlad* ■ *Dir* Philippe Mora • *Scr* Robert Sarno, Gary Brandner, from the novel *The Howling* by Gary Brandner

The Howling III ★★ 18
Horror comedy 1987 · Ausl · Colour · 94mins

It was pretty much downhill for *The Howling* franchise as soon as the first sequel came out, with subsequent films appropriating the transformation effects but little of the wit and humour of Joe Dante's original. This entry is notable for being perhaps the daftest of all the sequels, and for that reason is almost watchable in a perverse sort of way. It's a sort of "Tie Me Werewolf Down Sport", with researcher Barry Otto investigating a marsupial branch of the lycanthropic family Down Under, complete with pouches for the little 'uns. Director Philippe Mora, who also directed the first sequel, even finds room for an appearance by Dame Edna Everage and manages the occasional sly dig at the horror genre. For the most part, though, it's an erratic mess. (Three more sequels followed.) Contains violence and swearing. ▫

Barry Otto *Professor Harry Beckmeyer* • Imogen Annesley *Jerboa* • Dasha Blahova *Olga Gorki* • Max Fairchild *Thylo* • Ralph Cotterill *Professor Sharp* • Leigh Biolos *Donny Martin* • Frank Thring *Jack Citron* • Barry Humphries *Dame Edna Everage* ■ *Dir* Philippe Mora • *Scr* Philippe Mora, from the novel by Gary Brandner

Huck and the King of Hearts ★★★
Adventure 1993 · US · Colour · 103mins

A very loose, modern adaptation of the classic Mark Twain story. In this appealing family tale, a cardsharp and his young pal Huck travel across America searching for Huck's grandfather. Director Michael Keusch's film gains much from its likeable cast, which includes *Dances with Wolves's* Graham Greene, Dee Wallace Stone and Chauncey Leopardi as Huck.

Chauncey Leopardi *Billy "Huck" Thomas* • Graham Greene *Jim* • Dee Wallace Stone *Aunt Darlene* • Joe Piscopo *Max* • Gretchen Becker *Lisa* • Ed Trotta *Ed* • John Astin *Zach* ■ *Dir* Michael Keusch • *Scr* Christopher Sturgeon, from the novel *The Adventures of Huckleberry Finn* by Mark Twain

Huckleberry Finn ★★
Adventure drama 1931 · US · BW · 79mins

Jackie Coogan became a hugely popular child star after appearing with Chaplin in *The Kid* and Paramount had initial success in re-launching him, before the onset of puberty, in the early sound period in the title role of *Tom Sawyer* in 1930. Here he plays Tom again with Junior Durkin as Huck; together the duo save two young girls from falling into the hands of a pair of rascals. The film has some antiquated charm but Coogan can't match the pugnacity of Mickey Rooney in the 1939 version.

Jackie Coogan *Tom Sawyer* • Mitzi Green *Becky Thatcher* • Junior Durkin *Huckleberry Finn* • Jackie Searl [Jackie Searle] *Sid Sawyer* • Clarence Muse *Jim* • Clara Blandick *Aunt Polly* ■ *Dir* Norman Taurog • *Scr* Grover Jones, William Slavens McNutt, from the novel *The Adventures of Huckleberry Finn* by Mark Twain

Huckleberry Finn ★★★ U

Musical   1974 · US · Colour · 109mins

Reader's Digest, of all publications, flirted with film production in the seventies, and to its credit produced two very watchable Mark Twain movies. Both movies were shot on location and handsomely filmed in Panavision, and both had totally forgettable scores by the Sherman brothers, then coming off a roll with *Mary Poppins* and *The Jungle Book*. There's some clever casting in this one, particularly David Wayne and Harvey Korman as the river con men, but political correctness dilutes Paul Winfield's all-too-noble Jim. Veteran J Lee Thompson directs adequately, but the whole is without sparkle. Contains swearing. ▱

Jeff East *Huckleberry Finn* • Paul Winfield *Jim* • Harvey Korman *King* • David Wayne *Duke* • Arthur O'Connell *Colonel Grangerford* • Gary Merrill *Pap* • Natalie Trundy *Mrs Loftus* • Lucille Benson *Widder Douglas* ■ *Dir* J Lee Thompson • *Scr* Robert B Sherman, Richard M Sherman, from the novel *The Adventures of Huckleberry Finn* by Mark Twain

The Hucksters ★★★ U

Drama   1947 · US · BW · 110mins

To launch Deborah Kerr's Hollywood career, MGM surrounded her with a mighty cast of stars: Clark Gable, Sydney Greenstreet, Adolphe Menjou and Ava Gardner. The story, about the sharp practices of Madison Avenue advertising types, has dated badly; MGM wasn't in the business of criticising big business, even something as symbolically trivial as Greenstreet's bathroom soap empire. Gable joins the firm and gets the job of persuading 25 society women to endorse the soap. As a star package it has still has bags of glamour and some sparkling wit. ▱

Clark Gable *Victor Albee Norman* • Deborah Kerr *Kay Dorrance* • Sydney Greenstreet *Evan Llewellyn Evans* • Adolphe Menjou *Mr Kimberly* • Ava Gardner *Jean Ogilvie* • Keenan Wynn *Buddy Hare* • Edward Arnold *Dave Lash* • Aubrey Mather *Valet* ■ *Dir* Jack Conway • *Scr* Luther Davis, Edward Chodorov, George Wells, from the novel by Frederic Wakeman

Hud ★★★★★ 12

Drama   1963 · US · BW · 107mins

A powerhouse drama about family strife with Paul Newman as the heedless, sexually aggressive rancher's son, whose nephew Brandon de Wilde (echoing his role in *Shane*) looks on with horror and envy as Hud trashes towns and relationships. He is the only person with any real charisma, yet Martin Ritt's direction maintains a discreet critical distance from him. This is a masterly film, featuring Newman's finest ever screen performance and Oscar-winning roles for Patricia Neal and Melvyn Douglas as Newman's idealistic father. ▱

Paul Newman *Hud Bannon* • Patricia Neal *Alma Brown* • Melvyn Douglas *Homer Bannon* • Brandon de Wilde *Lon Bannon* • John Ashley *Hermy* • Whit Bissell *Burris* • Crahan Denton *Jesse* • Val Avery *Jose* ■ *Dir* Martin Ritt • *Scr* Irving Ravetch, Harriet Frank Jr, from the novel *Horseman, Pass By* by Larry McMurtry • *Cinematographer* James Wong Howe

Hudson Hawk ★★ 15

Action comedy   1991 · US · Colour · 95mins

Bruce Willis helped write the story and the title song of this so-called action comedy, in which he stars as a retired cat burglar who is persuaded to return to his criminal activities. There are some good action scenes, especially during the heist of a Leonardo da Vinci artefact, but Willis is not a strong enough screen presence to rise above the poor material. Richard E Grant and Sandra Bernhard are awful as the villains. Contains swearing and violence. ▱ *DVD*

Bruce Willis *Hudson Hawk* • Danny Aiello *Tommy Five-Tone* • Andie MacDowell *Anna Baragli* • James Coburn *George Kaplan* • Richard E Grant *Darwin Mayflower* • Sandra Bernhard *Minerva Mayflower* • David Caruso *Kit Kat* ■ *Dir* Michael Lehmann • *Scr* Steven E de Souza, Daniel Waters, from a story by Bruce Willis, Robert Kraft

Hudson's Bay ★★★

Historical adventure 1940 · US · BW · 95mins

This rather spurious historical romance ended up as one of 20th Century-Fox's no-expense-spared backlot historical pageants. It features Fox's lovely contract star Gene Tierney and, on loan from Warner Bros, the distinguished and fashionable Paul Muni; they are surrounded by Fox's forties repertory company including Laird Cregar and Vincent Price. The trouble is that the director is Irving Pichel. Though competent enough, this saga of the founder of the Hudson's Bay Trading Company really needed a John Ford or a Henry King to bring some sense of scale to the drama.

Paul Muni *Pierre Radisson* • Gene Tierney *Barbara Hall* • Laird Cregar *Gooseberry* • John Sutton *Lord Edward Crew* • Virginia Field *Nell Gwynn* • Vincent Price *King Charles II* ■ *Dir* Irving Pichel • *Scr* Lamar Trotti

The Hudsucker Proxy ★★★★ PG

Comedy drama 1994 · US · Colour · 106mins

This is a throwback to the good old days of the screwball comedy. When Joel and Ethan Coen pay tribute to a period or a style of film-making, however, they never slavishly re-create. In *The Hudsucker Proxy* they marry the go-get-'em attitudes of the thirties to fashion a parable that might just have something to say about America in the nineties. This is a classic "little man against the system" scenario, with Tim Robbins wonderfully ingenuous as the mail room nobody who hits gold when he invents the Hula-Hoop. In attempting to portray the kind of heartless villains associated with Edward Arnold and Eugene Pallette, Paul Newman mistakes excessive for comic, unlike Jennifer Jason Leigh, whose impression of Rosalind Russell doing a Katharine Hepburn is a hoot. ▱

Tim Robbins *Norville Barnes* • Jennifer Jason Leigh *Amy Archer* • Paul Newman *Sidney J Mussburger* • Charles Durning *Waring Hudsucker* • John Mahoney *Chief* • Jim True *Buzz* • William Cobbs *[Bill Cobbs] Moses* • Bruce Campbell *Smitty* ■ *Dir* Joel Coen • *Scr* Joel Coen, Ethan Coen, Sam Raimi

Hue and Cry ★★★★ U

Comedy   1947 · UK · BW · 78mins

After this early effort, director Charles Crichton went on to greater acclaim for making *The Lavender Hill Mob* and, more recently, *A Fish Called Wanda*. However there's much to enjoy in this slight but entertaining Ealing comedy caper – the first of the genre from the famous studio – as Alastair Sim and a gang of East End urchins set out to thwart some fiendish crooks. A fun frolic from a more innocent age, with some evocative location footage of postwar London .

Alastair Sim *Felix H Wilkinson* • Harry Fowler *Joe Kirby* • Valerie White *Rhona* • Jack Warner *Jim Nightingale* • Frederick Piper *Mr Kirby* • Heather Delaine *Mrs Kirby* • Douglas Barr *Alec* ■ *Dir* Charles Crichton • *Scr* TEB Clarke

Huey Long ★★★

Documentary 1985 · US · Colour and BW

A documentary portrait of Huey P Long, governor and senator of Louisiana from 1928 to 1935, when he was assassinated. Long's short career has few equals in modern America. He called himself "Kingfish" (he promised to make every man a king) and ran Louisiana as his private fiefdom. Directed by Ken Burns, this is a thorough and compelling portrait of a demagogue who inspired the 1949 feature film *All the King's Men*. Paul Newman played Long's brother, also a Louisiana governor, in the 1989 film *Blaze*.

David McCullough *Narrator* ■ *Dir* Ken Burns • *Scr* Geoffrey C Ward

The Huggetts Abroad ★ U

Comedy   1949 · UK · BW · 83mins

Having first encountered the Huggetts in *Holiday Camp*, it's somewhat apt that we should bid them farewell at the end of another sojourn. However, it's with relief not regret that we part company with Jack Warner, Kathleen Harrison et al, as this brief series had clearly run out of steam. It's one contrivance after another once Warner chucks his job and hauls the family off to South Africa, and the result is desperately unfunny and dull. ▱

Jack Warner *Joe Huggett* • Kathleen Harrison *Ethel Huggett* • Susan Shaw *Susan Huggett* • Petula Clark *Pet Huggett* • Dinah Sheridan *Jane Huggett* • Hugh McDermott *Bob McCoy* • Jimmy Hanley *Jimmy* ■ *Dir* Ken Annakin • *Scr* Mabel Constanduros, Denis Constanduros, Ted Willis, Gerard Bryant

Hugo Pool ★★

Romantic comedy drama 1997 · US · Colour · 93mins

The trials and tribulations of an LA pool-cleaner form the basis of this comedy drama, directed by Robert Downey and featuring his infamous son. Alyssa Milano is Hugo, whose thriving business forces her to draft in mum Cathy Moriarty and dad Malcolm McDowell, plagued (respectively) with alcohol and gambling problems. This inadequate pair accompany Hugo on her rounds as she meets the usual assortment of weird customers, including Downey Jr's movie director and Sean Penn's drifter. More wacky than humorous, this is a disappointing

story of talented actors in search of a script.

Alyssa Milano *Hugo* • Malcolm McDowell *Henry* • Sean Penn *Strange Hitchhiker* • Robert Downey Jr *Franz* • Cathy Moriarty *Minerva* • Patrick Dempsey *Floyd Gaylen* • Richard Lewis *Chick Chicalini* ■ *Dir* Robert Downey • *Scr* Robert Downey, Laura Downey

Hullabaloo over Georgie and Bonnie's Pictures ★★★

Comedy   1979 · UK/Ind · Colour · 83mins

Originally commissioned for television, this Merchant-Ivory team production was shot without a completed script and occasionally loses its way. Centred around princes, palaces, *objets d'art* and those who would exploit them, this minor entry in an illustrious canon is as delicate as the miniatures that dealers Larry Pine and Peggy Ashcroft try to prize away from maharajah Victor Bannerjee and his sister, Aparna Sen. Playful it may be, but it's still a worthwhile discussion of the function and value of art.

Peggy Ashcroft *Lady Gwyneth* • Victor Banerjee *Georgie* • Aparna Sen *Bonnie* • Saeed Jaffrey *Sri Narain* • Jane Booker *Lynn* ■ *Dir* James Ivory • *Scr* Ruth Prawer Jhabvala

Human Cargo ★★

Crime   1936 · US · BW · 87mins

Feeble romantic drama with Brian Donlevy and Claire Trevor as rival newshounds trying to unmask a gang smuggling aliens (the human variety) into the USA. Made by Fox, it lacks the tabloid, crusading spirit of the Warner Bros equivalents – *Five Star Final*, for instance – while the class difference between the two stars seems derived from *It Happened One Night*. The rough-hewn Donlevy is hardly in Gable's league as the romantic hero, however. Rita Hayworth, billed as Rita Cansino, makes an early appearance.

Claire Trevor *Bonnie Brewster* • Brian Donlevy *Packy Campbell* • Alan Dinehart *Lionel Crocker* • Ralph Morgan *District Attorney Cary* • Helen Troy *Susie* • Rita Cansino *[Rita Hayworth] Carmen Zoro* ■ *Dir* Allan Dwan • *Scr* Jefferson Parker, Doris Malloy, from the novel *I Will Be Faithful* by Kathleen Shepard

The Human Comedy ★★★★ U

Second World War drama
1943 · US · BW · 116mins

This beautifully realised adaptation of William Saroyan's novel looks at life in an American small town during the Second World War. Mickey Rooney gives a moving performance as the high school student turned telegraph boy around whom the everyday events revolve. Director Clarence Brown shamelessly pulls the heartstrings by leaning heavily on nostalgia, religion, family responsibility and patriotism, as he fills the screen with instantly recognisable characters everyone has met at one time or another. An emotionally engaging masterpiece of admirable simplicity.

Mickey Rooney *Homer Macauley* • Frank Morgan *Willie Grogan* • James Craig *Tom Spangler* • Marsha Hunt *Diana Steed* • Fay Bainter *Mrs Macauley* • Ray Collins *Mr Macauley* • Van Johnson *Marcus Macauley* •

Donna Reed *Bess Macauley* ■ *Dir* Clarence Brown • *Scr* Howard Estabrook, from the novel by William Saroyan

The Human Condition
★★★★★★

Epic war drama   1958 · Jap · BW · 579mins

Adapted from Gomikawa's six-part novel, Masaki Kobayashi's epic masterpiece reflects his own experiences as a pacifist in Japan during the Second World War. Four years in the making and running for a mammoth 579 minutes, Masaki Kobayashi's heart-rending anti-war trilogy was a controversial project; the Shochiku studio was reluctant to bankroll it, but was rewarded with a work of unparalleled power and poignancy. Sent to supervise a Manchurian copper mine, Tatsuya Nakadai attempts to curb brutal overseer Eitaro Ozawa's maltreatment of the enslaved Chinese workforce, only to find himself dispatched to the front without a chance to take leave of his wife, Michiyo Aratama. This harrowing exploration of the savage horror of combat is ambitious, shocking and unforgettable. In Japanese with English subtitles.

Tatsuya Nakadai *Kaji* • Michiyo Aratama *Michiko* • Ineko Arima *Yang Chun Lan* • So Yamamura *Okishima* • Akira Ishihama *Chen* • Shinji Nambara *Kao* • Eitaro Ozawa *Okazaki* ■ *Dir* Masaki Kobayashi • *Scr* Zenzo Matsuyama, Masaki Kobayashi, from the novel *Ningen No Joken* by Jumpei Gomikawa

Human Desire
★★★

Film noir   1954 · US · BW · 90mins

Emile Zola's bleak novel about the murderous triangle that engulfs a train driver, a stationmaster and his wife seems tailor-made for the screen. But just as the powerful themes and images had confounded Jean Renoir in *La Bête Humaine* in 1938, so they eluded Fritz Lang in this *film noir* that was prevented from exploring the book's seamier side by the strictures of the Hollywood Production Code. Lang's preoccupation with the sights, sounds and symbolism of the railway yards too often leaves the emotions and motives of the characters stranded in the sidings.

Glenn Ford *Jeff Warren* • Gloria Grahame *Vicki Buckley* • Broderick Crawford *Carl Buckley* • Edgar Buchanan *Alec Simmons* • Kathleen Case *Ellen Simmons* • Peggy Maley *Jean* ■ *Dir* Fritz Lang • *Scr* Alfred Hayes, from the novel *La Bête Humaine* by Emile Zola • *Cinematographer* Burnett Guffey

The Human Factor
★★☆

Action thriller   1975 · UK · Colour · 92mins

This action film aspires to the status of political conspiracy thriller, but it's really little more than *Death Wish* with a CIA subplot. George Kennedy is the NATO bigwig based in Naples whose family is wiped out by terrorists. Kennedy plays war games for a living, so he decides to put his theories into practice and hit the vengeance trail – with rather messy consequences. The multi-national supporting cast includes John Mills and Rita Tushingham. 🖵

George Kennedy *John Kinsdale* • John Mills Mike McAllister • Raf Vallone *Dr Lupo* • Arthur Franz *General Fuller* • Rita Tushingham *Janice*

Meredith • Barry Sullivan *Edmonds* • Haydée Politoff *Pidgeon* ■ *Dir* Edward Dmytryk • *Scr* Tom Hunter, Peter Powell

The Human Factor
★★★ 15

Spy drama   1979 · UK/US · Colour · 110mins

Faithfully adapted by Tom Stoppard, this espionage thriller has all the complexities of characterisation and plot one expects from a Graham Greene "entertainment". But Otto Preminger (who completed the picture with his own cash after the backers withdrew) never really comes to terms with the notions of honour, isolation and Englishness that underpin the novel. The cast sustain the suspense, with Nicol Williamson admirable as the double agent whose favour for an old friend has dire consequences for both family and colleagues. The most memorable performance, however, comes from Robert Morley as a killer who delights in his work. 🖵

Nicol Williamson *Maurice Castle* • Richard Attenborough *Colonel John Daintry* • Joop Doderer *Cornelius Muller* • John Gielgud *Brigadier Tomlinson* • Derek Jacobi *Arthur Davis* • Robert Morley *Doctor Percival* • Ann Todd *Castle's mother* • Iman *Sarah* ■ *Dir* Otto Preminger • *Scr* Tom Stoppard, from the novel by Graham Greene

Human Feelings
★★

Comedy   1978 · US · Colour · 96mins

This very early outing for Billy Crystal, made when he was just a rising star in the TV comedy *Soap*, was intended as a pilot for a series. Crystal plays an angel who is sent to Earth to find good in sin city Las Vegas; if he fails, God (or, as here, Mrs G) will reduce it to rubble. Nancy Walker enjoys herself as the Almighty, but the film's TV origins are very apparent and it would have worked better as a brief comedy sketch. Look out for Armand Assante, also in a very early role.

Nancy Walker *God/Mrs G* • Billy Crystal *Miles Gordon* • Pamela Sue Martin *Verna Gold* • Squire Fridell *Phil Sawyer* • Donna Pescow *Gloria Prentice* • Armand Assante *Johnny Turner* • Richard Dimitri *Garcia* ■ *Dir* Ernest Pintoff • *Scr* Henry H Bloomstein

Human Highway
★ 12

Fantasy musical comedy   1982 · US · Colour · 83mins

Here's a painful lesson for studios – never allow pop stars the money to make their own films. What was hippy icon Neil Young thinking about when he dreamt up this abysmal anti-nuke comedy about a pair of gas station attendants (Young and Russ Tamblyn) working in the shadow of a nuclear power plant. Apparently four years in the making, this embarrassment includes a dream sequence featuring New Wave pop group Devo and a climactic musical number where the cast sing as they ascend toward heaven. Even Dennis Hopper as a truck stop restaurant cook can't save this one. 🖵

Neil Young *Lionel Switch* • Russ Tamblyn *Fred Kelly* • Dean Stockwell *Otto Quartz* • Dennis Hopper *Cracker* • Charlotte Stewart *Charlotte Goodnight* • Sally Kirkland *Katherine* • Geraldine Baron *Irene* ■ *Dir* Bernard Shakey [Neil Young], Dean Stockwell • *Scr* Bernard Shakey [Neil Young], Jeanne Fields, Dean Stockwell, Russ Tamblyn, James Beshears

The Human Jungle
★★ PG

Police drama   1954 · US · BW · 78mins

This unremarkable police drama, filmed in the pseudo-documentary style of *The Naked City*, stars Gary Merrill, whose main claims to fame are as Bette Davis's husband and as an unsuccessful Senatorial candidate. Here he plays a police captain in charge of a tough neighbourhood called "The Heights" in an otherwise unidentified metropolis. Much of the running time is given over to police procedure, though Chuck Connors makes his mark as a killer. 🖵

Gary Merrill *Danforth* • Jan Sterling *Mary* • Paula Raymond *Pat Danforth* • Emile Meyer *Rowan* • Regis Toomey *Geddes* • Lamont Johnson *Lannigan* • Chuck Connors *Swados* ■ *Dir* Joseph M Newman • *Scr* William Sackheim, Daniel Fuchs, from a story by William Sackheim

Human Traffic
★★★ 18

Comedy drama   1999 · UK/Ire · Colour · 95mins

Director Justin Kerrigan's debut movie is a valiant attempt to put across the atmosphere of Britain's club scene, with its story of five friends who go out on a lost, drug- and drink-filled weekend in the dance halls of Cardiff. Jip (John Simm) can't get it together with girls and confides in friend Lulu (Lorraine Pilkington) as their night out turns into two days of frenzied rave-up. *Trainspotting* it isn't, but the spirited acting from the talented youngsters and the inspired visuals come out of the screen like a chemical rush. Contains swearing, sexual references and drug abuse. 🖵 **DVD**

John Simm *Jip* • Lorraine Pilkington *Lulu* • Shaun Parkes *Koop* • Danny Dyer *Moff* • Nicola Reynolds *Nina* • Dean Davies *Lee* • Jan Anderson *Karen Benson* • Jo Brand *Mrs Reality* • Howard Marks ■ *Dir/Scr* Justin Kerrigan • *Cinematographer* Dave Bennett

L'Humanité
★★★ 18

Drama   1999 · Fr · Colour · mins

Due to its frustrating lack of incident and pedestrian pacing, Bruno Dumont's film found little favour at Cannes, even though non-professionals Emmanuel Schotte and Severine Caneele took the main acting awards. Yet, like the equally unpopular *Rosetta*, this long-drawn-out investigation into the rape and murder of an 11-year-old girl exerts a macabre fascination, not least because of Schotte's eccentric turn as the thin-skinned cop whose methods are definitely unconventional. Dumont makes effective use of the Pas de Calais's soul-destroying landscape and draws a vigorously earthy performance from Caneele. In French with English subtitles.

Emmanuel Schotte *Pharaon de Winter* • Severine Caneele *Domino* • Philippe Tullier *Joseph* • Ghislain Ghesquiere *Police chief* ■ *Dir/Scr* Bruno Dumont

Humoresque
★★★★ U

Melodrama   1946 · US · BW · 119mins

Wonderful Warner Bros tosh containing a fine performance from Joan Crawford as a rich, autocratic patron to intense violinist John Garfield. Based on a

Fannie Hurst story, it contains some of the most riotously preposterous dialogue ever: check out Crawford's reply when asked if she likes classical music. Shades of *Golden Boy* abound, not surprisingly since the screenplay is co-written by Clifford Odets, on whose play that film was based; but this is better, and not just because Garfield's violin playing is dubbed by the great Isaac Stern. Lovers of melodrama will enjoy this immensely. 🖵

Joan Crawford *Helen Wright* • John Garfield *Paul Boray* • Oscar Levant *Sid Jeffers* • J Carrol Naish *Rudy Boray* • Joan Chandler *Gina* • Tom D'Andrea *Phil Boray* • Peggy Knudsen *Florence* • Ruth Nelson *Esther Boray* ■ *Dir* Jean Negulesco • *Scr* Clifford Odets, Zachary Gold, from a story by Fannie Hurst

The Hunchback
★★ 12

Gothic drama   1997 · US · Colour · 96mins

Despite lacklustre make-up, Mandy Patinkin's exceptionally sympathetic portrayal of Quasimodo is the only point of interest in this television version of Victor Hugo's tale. Although director Peter Medak is clearly more interested in bringing the man-behind-the-monster angle to the fore, he sadly understates the main thrust of the story and supplies little of the Parisian spectacle one expects to be part of any redefinition of the oft-told tale. Richard Harris is suitably menacing as Dom Frollo and Salma Hayek acquits herself nicely as the gypsy Esmeralda, but it's a flawed account of the Notre Dame fable. 🖵

Mandy Patinkin *Quasimodo* • Salma Hayek *Esmeralda* • Richard Harris *Dom Frollo* • Edward Atterton *Gringoire* • Benedick Blythe *Phoebus* • Nigel Terry *King Louis* • Jim Dale *Clopin* • Trevor Baxter *Chief lawyer* ■ *Dir* Peter Medak • *Scr* John Fasano, from the novel *Notre Dame de Paris* by Victor Hugo

The Hunchback of Notre Dame
★★★★ PG

Classic silent drama   1923 · US · BW · 86mins

The first film version of Victor Hugo's classic tale is a masterpiece of the silent era. It showcases magnificent sets and Lon Chaney's definitive take on deformed bell-ringer Quasimodo, with a secret infatuation for gypsy girl Esmeralda. From under a 72-pound rubber hump, and with his face covered by lumps of putty, the grotesque Chaney gives an eloquent performance, full of pathos and yearning, which dominates the screen despite all the other epic trappings. It's for his inimitable genius alone that this sprawling saga is now most fondly remembered. 🖵

Lon Chaney *Quasimodo* • Ernest Torrence *Clopin* • Patsy Ruth Miller *Esmeralda* • Norman Kerry *Phoebus* • Kate Lester *Mme De Gondelaurier* • Brandon Hurst *Jehan* • Raymond Hatton *Gringoire* • Tully Marshall *Louis XI* • Nigel De Brulier *Dom Claude* ■ *Dir* Wallace Worsley • *Scr* Edward T Lowe Jr, Perley Poore Sheehan, from the novel *Notre Dame de Paris* by Victor Hugo

The Hunchback of Notre Dame
★★★★★ PG

Classic gothic drama   1939 · US · BW · 116mins

For many, Disney and Lon Chaney notwithstanding, Charles Laughton is the cinema's definitive Quasimodo, and his poignant performance reveals more subtleties with every re-viewing. Laughton captures the tragic soul of Notre Dame's famous bell-ringer, and both his make-up and speech patterns are truly convincing. This is a splendidly RKO enterprise, with spectacular crowd scenes and superb supporting performances, notably from a sensual Maureen O'Hara as Esmeralda the gypsy, and a callow Edmond O'Brien as the youthful romantic lead. Two major future directors had a big hand in this epic – Jacques Tourneur handled the crowds and Robert Wise was the film's editor. 📼

Charles Laughton *Quasimodo* • Maureen O'Hara *Esmeralda* • Cedric Hardwicke *Frollo* • Thomas Mitchell *Clopin* • Edmond O'Brien *Gringoire* • Alan Marshal *Phoebus* • Walter Hampden *Claude* ■ *Dir* William S Dieterle [William Dieterle] • *Scr* Sonya Levien, Bruno Frank, from the novel *Notre Dame de Paris* by Victor Hugo • *Cinematographer* Joseph August [Joseph H August] • *Art Director* Van Nest Polglase

The Hunchback of Notre Dame ★★

Gothic drama 1956 · Fr/It · Colour · 103mins

This sadly misbegotten version of the Victor Hugo classic features Anthony Quinn as Quasimodo under a ton of make-up and Gina Lollobrigida, as Esmeralda, struggling beneath the weight of her own inadequacy. At least the Technicolor and widescreen presentation makes the film an interesting visual experience. The unfortunate director was veteran Jean Delannoy, whose track record is more prestigious than this clumsy adaptation would have us believe.

Gina Lollobrigida *Esmeralda* • Anthony Quinn *Quasimodo* • Jean Danet *Capt Phoebus* • Alain Cuny *Claude Frollo* • Philippe Clay *Clopin Trouillefou* • Danielle Dumont *Fleur de Lys* • Robert Hirsch *Gringoire* • Jean Tissier *Louis XI* ■ *Dir* Jean Delannoy • *Scr* Jacques Prévert, Jean Aurenche, from the novel *Notre Dame de Paris* by Victor Hugo • *Cinematographer* Michel Kelber

The Hunchback of Notre Dame ★★★★ PG

Gothic drama 1982 · US · Colour · 97mins

One of the best adaptations of Victor Hugo's classic tale of the misshapen Parisian bell-ringer and his ill-fated love for the gypsy girl Esmeralda. A brilliant and authentically literate script by John Gay is seized on with relish by Anthony Hopkins and Derek Jacobi (playing Quasimodo and Dom Claude Frollo respectively) who both give their difficult characters a warmth and sympathy beyond their tragic and villainous dimensions. Wonderful period production values are the icing on the cake. 📼

Anthony Hopkins *Quasimodo* • Derek Jacobi *Dom Claude Frollo* • Lesley-Anne Down *Esmerelda* • John Gielgud *Charmolue* • Robert Powell *Phoebus* • David Suchet *Trouillefou* • Tim Pigott-Smith *Philippe* • Nigel Hawthorne *Esmerelda trial magistrate* ■ *Dir* Michael Tuchner • *Scr* John Gay, from the novel *Notre Dame de Paris* by Victor Hugo

The Hunchback of Notre Dame ★★★★ U

Animated musical drama
1996 · US · Colour · 96mins

This animated version of the Victor Hugo classic is one of the better of the nineties Disney movies. As with previous versions, it's the tale of Quasimodo, the deformed keeper of the Notre Dame bells and his unrequited love for Esmeralda, a gypsy whose actions lead to her persecution. Darker and more adult than previous Disney animations, there's still room for three mischievous and mobile gargoyles – Victor, Hugo and Laverne – while Tom Hulce, Demi Moore and Kevin Kline provide voice-overs to match the poignancy of the drama. 📼

Tom Hulce *Quasimodo* • Demi Moore *Esmeralda* • Kevin Kline *Phoebus* • Jason Alexander *Hugo* • Mary Kay Bergman *Quasimodo's mother* • Corey Burton *Brutish guard* ■ *Dir* Gary Trousdale, Kirk Wise • *Scr* Irene Mecchi, Bob Tzudiker, Noni White, Jonathan Roberts, Will Finn, Tab Murphy, from a story by Tab Murphy, from the novel *Notre Dame de Paris* by Victor Hugo

A Hungarian Fairy Tale ★★★ PG

Surreal drama 1986 · Hun · BW · 97mins

This is an imaginative allegory based on the myth that a giant bird will descend on Hungary to rescue it in times of trouble. The nation appears here in the person of a small boy who is searching for the father he has never known. Beautifully shot in glowing monochrome, the film balances its precise socio-political commentary with moments of charming fantasy and black humour. Director Gyula Gazdag is not always in control of the material, but it is nevertheless a compelling watch. In Hungarian with English subtitles.

David Vermes *Andris* • Maria Varga *Maria* • Husak Frantisek *Antal Orban* • Pal Hetenyi *Hungarian voice* • Eszter Csakanyi *Young woman* • Peter Trokan *Teacher* • Szilvia Toth *Tunde* • Judit Pogany *Tunde's mother* • Geza Balkay *Tunde's stepfather* • Gabor Reviczky *Tunde's father* ■ *Dir* Gyula Gazdag • *Scr* Gyula Gazdag, Miklos Gyorffy, Kata Tolmer

Hunger ★★★★

Drama 1966 · Den/Nor/Swe · BW · 110mins

In adapting Knut Hamsun's first novel, Danish director Henning Carlsen has produced a compelling character study that delves into the mind of an artist on the verge of both physical and mental collapse. Per Oscarsson won the best actor prize at Cannes for his agonisingly truthful performance as a writer in turn-of-the-century Norway, whose poverty and creative anxiety are compounded by the callous indifference of an affluent flirt (a vibrantly coquettish Gunnel Lindblom) who humiliates him just as he has reason to hope for better times. A Norwegian/Swedish language film.

Per Oscarsson *The Writer* • Gunnel Lindblom *Ylajali* • Sigrid Horne-Rasmussen *Landlady* • Osvald Helmuth *Pawnbroker* • Henki Kolstad *Editor* ■ *Dir* Henning Carlsen • *Scr* Henning Carlsen, Peter Seeberg, from the novel *Sult* by Knut Hamsun

The Hunger ★★★ 18

Horror 1983 · US · Colour · 92mins

Scientist Susan Sarandon replaces ageing David Bowie in vampire Catherine Deneuve's affections in director Tony Scott's visually sumptuous adaptation of Whitley Strieber's enigmatic bestseller. Set against a generally effective backdrop of immortal decadence, embodying several centuries of glossy fashion and culture, this MTV-influenced undead tale emphasises style over content, despite an understated mix of sly humour, sexual mystery and clever make-up illusion. Contains violence, swearing and nudity. 📼

Catherine Deneuve *Miriam* • David Bowie *John Blaylock* • Susan Sarandon *Sarah Roberts* • Cliff De Young *Tom Haver* • Beth Ehlers *Alice Cavender* • Dan Hedaya *Lieutenant Allegrezza* ■ *Dir* Tony Scott • *Scr* Ivan Davis, Michael Thomas, from the novel by Whitley Strieber

Hungry Hill ★★ PG

Drama 1947 · UK · BW · 97mins

Daphne du Maurier and future James Bond director Terence Young share a writing credit for this adaptation of du Maurier's novel, but the plot-packed, melodramatic excesses of the book seem slightly ludicrous on the screen. Moreover, the flowery language often sounds ridiculous when uttered in the blarney brogue adopted by many of the cast. Margaret Lockwood admirably plays against type as the local firebrand tamed by the cruelty of the copper-mining family into which she marries. However, Brian Desmond Hurst's direction is typically florid and flabby, while the painted backdrops are just atrocious. 📼

Margaret Lockwood *Fanny Ross* • Dennis Price *Greyhound John* • Cecil Parker *Copper John* • Michael Denison *Henry Brodrick* • Dermot Walsh *Wild Johnnie* • FJ McCormick *Old Tim* • Eileen Crowe *Bridget* • Jean Simmons *Jane Brodrick* ■ *Dir* Brian Desmond Hurst • *Scr* Daphne du Maurier, Terence Young, Francis Crowdy, from the novel by Daphne du Maurier • *Cinematographer* Desmond Dickinson

Hunk ★★★ PG

Comedy 1987 · US · Colour · 98mins

Computer nerd Steve Levitt makes a pact with Devil's emissary Deborah Shelton (*Dallas*) so he can become a beach bum with pecs appeal in this intermittently charming comedy fantasy that effectively expands on the maxim "beauty's only skin deep". A pleasant enough time-waster, with gorgeous bodies of both sexes to ogle at, and James Coco puts in a fine turn as the time-travelling Satan with a neat line in amusing historical references. 📼

John Allen Nelson *Hunk Golden* • Steve Levitt *Bradley Brinkman* • Deborah Shelton *O'Brien* • Rebeccah Bush *Sunny* • James Coco *Dr D* • Robert Morse *Garrison Gaylord* ■ *Dir/Scr* Lawrence Bassoff

The Hunt ★★★★★

Drama 1966 · Sp · BW · 88mins

Director Carlos Saura has fashioned a pitiless and scathing assault on a society and the attitudes that shaped it. His contempt scorches into the celluloid like the heat in which a trio of Civil War veterans go rabbit shooting on the arid site of a former battlefield.

Equal scorn is poured on aristocratic and nouveau riche sensibilities, as a combination of vanity, snobbery, fiscal envy and politico-sexual repression drive the unrepentant Falangists to acts of savagery that leave their young companion rigid with indolent incomprehension. Deservedly, Saura's impeccable control of performance, pace and atmosphere earned him the best director prize at Berlin. In Spanish with English subtitles.

Ismael Merlo *José* • Alfredo Mayo *Paco* • Jose Maria Prada *Luis* • Emilio Gutiérrez Caba *Enrique* • Fernando Sanchez Polack *Juan* • Violeta Garcia *Nina* ■ *Dir* Carlos Saura • *Scr* Angelino Fons, Carlos Saura

The Hunt for Red October ★★★★ PG

Thriller 1990 · US · Colour · 129mins

This submarine drama marks the first screen appearance of Jack Ryan, the US agent subsequently played by Harrison Ford in *Patriot Games* and *Clear and Present Danger*. Here, Alec Baldwin as Ryan plays a distinct second fiddle to Sean Connery, charismatic as ever as the Russian commander who sparks an international crisis when he starts heading his sub straight for the USA. As the superpowers engage in the usual round of accusations and denials, it's left to Baldwin to figure out whether Connery is defecting or preparing to attack. John McTiernan's no-frills direction ensures that the tension rarely slips below pressure-cooker level. Contains violence. 📼

Sean Connery *Captain Marko Ramius* • Alec Baldwin *Jack Ryan* • Scott Glenn *Captain Bart Mancuso* • Sam Neill *Captain Vasily Borodin* • James Earl Jones *Admiral James Greer* • Joss Ackland *Andrei Lysenko* • Richard Jordan *Jeffrey Pelt* • Peter Firth *Ivan Putin* • Tim Curry *Dr Petrov* • Courtney B Vance *Seaman Jones* • Stellan Skarsgård *Captain Tupolev* ■ *Dir* John McTiernan • *Scr* Larry Ferguson, Donald Stewart, from the novel by Tom Clancy

Hunted ★★ PG

Drama 1952 · UK · BW · 81mins

This cross-country adventure stop-starts too often to engross, but it benefits from the effortless rapport between Dirk Bogarde and Jon Whiteley as a pair of runaways whose friendship is forged in adversity. Fleeing after the murder of his wife's lover, Bogarde makes a credible fugitive, particularly when threatening his young companion, who thinks he's burned down his foster parents' home. Director Charles Crichton makes the most of the various locales, but there's a predictability about the round of encounters and escapes. 📼

Dirk Bogarde *Chris Lloyd* • Jon Whiteley *Robbie* • Elizabeth Sellars *Magda Lloyd* • Kay Walsh *Mrs Sykes* • Frederick Piper *Mr Sykes* • Julian Somers *Jack Lloyd* • Jane Aird *Mrs Campbell* • Jack Stewart *Mr Campbell* • Geoffrey Keen *Detective Inspector Deakin* • Joe Linnane *Pawnbroker* ■ *Dir* Charles Crichton • *Scr* Jack Whittingham, from the story by Michael McCarthy

The Hunted ★★ 18

Action thriller 1995 · US · Colour · 105mins

In this proficient action thriller, video favourite Christopher Lambert plays a businessman based in the Far East who becomes the target of a crazed ninja gang after accidentally witnessing a murder. Help comes in the form of a modern-day samurai warrior (Yoshio Harada), who's looking to settle a centuries-old feud. Director JF Lawton ensures there's plenty of swordsmanship and violent action scenes, while the performances are a cut above the norm for this sort of genre flick. Contains violence, nudity and a sex scene. 🎬

Christopher Lambert *Paul Racine* • John Lone *Kinjo* • Joan Chen *Kirina* • Yoshio Harada *Takeda* • Yoko Shimada *Mieko* • Mari Natsuki *Junko* ■ *Dir/Scr* JF Lawton

The Hunted ★★ 15

Thriller 1998 · US/Can · Colour · 91mins

This instantly forgettable adventure is constructed around a similar premise to the infinitely superior *A Simple Plan*. Mädchen Amick stars as an insurance investigator searching for a crashed plane carrying a stolen $12 million. Stranded in mountainous terrain after wrecking her jeep, her only ally appears to be recluse Harry Hamlin – but can he be trusted? It's adequately performed and directed, but low on surprises. Contains violence and some mild swearing. 🎬

Harry Hamlin *Doc Kovac* • Mädchen Amick *Samantha "Sam" Clark* • Hannes Jaenicke *Jan Kroeger* • Enuka Okuma *Tracy* • Robert Moloney *Dorse* • Peter Lacroix *Ranger McNulty* • Fulvio Cecere *Detective Cuneo* • Peter Bryant *Uniformed officer* ■ *Dir* Stuart Cooper • *Scr* Bennett Cohen, David Ives

The Hunter ★★ 15

Action thriller based on a true story
1980 · US · Colour · 98mins

Steve McQueen's final film is a badly muffed attempt to update the classic western bounty-hunter story. Known for his doggedness and unconventional methods, Ralph "Papa" Thorson brought thousands of fugitives to justice during his career, and McQueen was obviously attracted to his all-action style and his offbeat personality. However, as directed by Buzz Kulik, the movie is not much more than a series of crash-bang pursuits with the eccentric Thorson being the only rounded character. 🎬

Steve McQueen *Ralph "Papa" Thorson* • Eli Wallach *Ritchie Blumenthal* • Kathryn Harrold *Dotty* • Ben Johnson *Sheriff Strong* • Tracey Walter *Rocco Mason* • Levar Burton *Tommy Price* • Richard Venture *Spota* ■ *Dir* Buzz Kulik • *Scr* Ted Leighton, Peter Hyams, from the non-fiction book by Christopher Keane

The Hunters ★★★

War drama 1958 · US · Colour · 107mins

Back in the Korean War after his role in *One Minute to Zero*, Robert Mitchum plays a fighter pilot who falls for the wife of his colleague. The final film to be produced and directed by the actor Dick Powell, this could be dismissed as a naive piece of anti-communist propaganda, were it not for Mitchum's characteristically mesmeric presence and for some splendidly orchestrated aerial action sequences. Robert Wagner and Richard Egan swell the US military ranks, while the two-timing wife is played by May Britt, a Swedish-born

beauty of dubious talent who retired in 1960 after marrying Sammy Davis Jr.

Robert Mitchum *Major Cleve Saville* • Robert Wagner *Lieutenant Ed Pell* • Richard Egan *Colonel "Dutch" Imil* • May Britt *Kristina* • Lee Philips *Lieutenant Carl Abbott* • John Gabriel *Lieutenant Corona* • Stacy Harris *Colonel "Monkey" Moncavage* ■ *Dir* Dick Powell • *Scr* Wendell Mayes, from the novel by James Salter

Hunting ★★★

Drama 1992 · Ausl · Colour · 97mins

Atmospherically shot around Melbourne, this thriller keeps threatening to turn into something exceptional only to lapse back into mediocrity at all the wrong moments. John Savage seems to be in a different film from everyone else for the first third of the action as he arrives from the States to rescue his struggling business, but there's definitely a spark in the love scenes he shares with secretary Kerry Armstrong. However, the stand-out sequence involves ex-*Neighbours* star Guy Pearce. Contains violence, nudity and sex scenes.

John Savage *Michael Bergman* • Guy Pearce *Sharp* • Kerry Armstrong *Michelle Harris* • Rebecca Rigg *Debbie McCormack* • Jeffrey Thomas *Larry Harris* • Rhys McConnochie *Bill Stockton* ■ *Dir/Scr* Frank Howson

The Hunting Party ★ 18

Western 1971 · UK · Colour · 104mins

Not just tripe, but a production that is also lewd and crude. It is sad to see the great Gene Hackman slumming in this British-made, Spanish-shot western, as a vicious Texan tycoon hunting down Oliver Reed and his gang, who have kidnapped his wife, Candice Bergen. Hackman has a high-powered rifle on his side; all Reed has is a leering expression. In their different ways, the stars survived this crass calamity, but who has heard of director Don Medford since? Contains violence and nudity. 🎬

Oliver Reed *Frank Calder* • Candice Bergen *Melissa Ruger* • Gene Hackman *Brandt Ruger* • Simon Oakland *Matthew Gunn* • Mitchell Ryan *Doc Harrison* • LQ Jones *Hog Warren* • GD Spradlin *Sam Bayard* • William Watson *Loring* • Ronald Howard *Watt Nelson* ■ *Dir* Don Medford • *Scr* William Norton, Gilbert Alexander, Lou Morheim, from a story by Gilbert Alexander, Lou Morheim

Hurlyburly ★★ 18

Drama 1998 · US · Colour · 122mins

Fourteen years after it was critically acclaimed on Broadway, David Rabe's hard-hitting play about moral bankruptcy in Hollywood ends up on screen a dated bore. An outstanding cast makes the most of Rabe's razor-sharp dialogue, which covers all offensive bases from dark misogyny to cynical drug-taking. Alas, Anthony Drazan's static direction fails to lift the stagey material, and all attempts to open out this fear and self-loathing talkfest fail miserably. Kevin Spacey, giving his most subtle performance, and Anna Paquin, in her first adult role, bolster Sean Penn's star turn. Overall, though, this is a draining and mind-numbing experience.

Sean Penn *Eddie* • Kevin Spacey *Mickey* • Robin Wright Penn *Darlene* • Meg Ryan *Bonnie* • Chazz Palminteri *Phil* • Garry Shandling *Artie* • Anna Paquin *Donna* ■ *Dir* Anthony Drazan • *Scr* David Rabe, from his play

The Hurricane ★★★ PG

Disaster adventure 1937 · US · BW · 99mins

John Ford grudgingly took on this screen adaptation of Charles Nordhoff and James Norman Hall's South Seas yarn about a vendetta between a native sailor and the governor of Tahiti, whose problems are solved by the timely intervention of some spectacularly inclement weather. Raymond Massey, Mary Astor and Dorothy Lamour (most fetching in her trademark sarong) star, and the resulting melodrama offers fair entertainment, some cornball symbolism and a special effects storm shot on the Goldwyn back lot. 🎬

Dorothy Lamour *Marama* • Jon Hall *Terangi* • Mary Astor *Madame Germaine De Laage* • C Aubrey Smith *Father Paul* • Thomas Mitchell *Dr Kersaint* • Raymond Massey *Governor Eugene De Laage* • John Carradine *Jailer* ■ *Dir* John Ford • *Scr* Dudley Nichols, Oliver HP Garrett, from the novel *The Hurricane* by Charles Nordhoff, James Norman Hall

Hurricane ★

Drama 1979 · US · Colour · 91mins

A dismal rehash of John Ford's 1937 movie, itself no great shakes, with missionaries thumping their bibles while their daughters fornicate with native boys. To make this would-be epic, producer Dino De Laurentiis built the entire town of Pago Pago on the Polynesian island of Bora Bora, as well as a luxury hotel to house the cast and crew. He also hired Roman Polanski to direct, but his sexual misadventure in Los Angeles forced his retirement from the project and Jan Troell took over. Costing around $20 million, it's one of Hollywood's mega-flops, and the hurricane itself amounts to little more than a breeze. 🎬

Jason Robards [Jason Robards Jr] *Captain Charles Bruckner* • Mia Farrow *Charlotte Bruckner* • Max von Sydow *Dr Bascomb* • Trevor Howard *Father Malone* • Timothy Bottoms *Jack Sanford* • James Keach *Sergeant Strang* ■ *Dir* Jan Troell • *Scr* Lorenzo Semple Jr, from the novel by Charles Nordhoff, James Norman Hall

The Hurricane ★★★★ 15

Biographical drama
1999 · US · Colour · 145mins

Thirty-three years after *In the Heat of the Night*, veteran director Norman Jewison tackles bigotry and prejudice again in this true story of racial injustice. Denzel Washington stars as Rubin "Hurricane" Carter, the boxer who was framed for three murders and sentenced to three life terms. Bob Dylan wrote a song about the case, and countless petitions were organised on his behalf. But it took a teenage boy named Lesra Martin (Vicellous Reon Shannon) to liberate Carter after 19 years of wrongful imprisonment. Washington initially makes Carter a prickly character, but his gradual progression from hate-filled loner to dignified role model is powerful.

Denzel Washington *Rubin "Hurricane" Carter* • Vicellous Reon Shannon *Lesra Martin* • Deborah Kara Unger *Lisa* • Liev Schreiber *Sam* • John Hannah *Terry* • Dan Hedaya *Vincent Della Pesca* • Debbi Morgan *Mae Thelma Carter* • Clancy Brown *Lt Jimmy Williams* • Rod Steiger *Judge Sarokin* ■ *Dir* Norman Jewison • *Scr* Armyan Bernstein, Dan Gordon, Christopher Cleveland, from the autobiography *The Sixteenth Round* by Rubin "Hurricane" Carter and the biography *Lazarus and the Hurricane* by Sam Chaiton, Terry Swinton • *Cinematographer* Roger Deakins

The Hurricane Express ★★ U

Action drama 1932 · US · BW · 76mins

As one chase and pile-up follows another, this may look like an old serial – which is exactly what it was originally. The storyline suffers in the condensation to feature length and, as the mysterious train-smashing Wrecker has the uncanny trick of wearing face masks that fool people into mistaking him for somebody else, the plot becomes more confusing than a railway timetable. There seems to have only been one take of every scene and a very young John Wayne is often woeful as the avenging hero.

John Wayne *Larry Baker* • Shirley Grey *Gloria Martin/Gloria Stratton* • Conway Tearle *Stevens* • Tully Marshall *Mr Edwards* ■ *Dir* Armand Schaefer, JP McGowan • *Scr* George Morgan, JP McGowan, from a story by Colbert Clark, Barney A Sarecky, Wyndham Gittens

Hurricane Streets ★★★ 15

Drama 1997 · US · Colour · 84mins

A triple winner at the Sundance Film Festival (for best dramatic picture, director and cinematography), this is a gripping, gritty little drama. The impressively mature Brendan Sexton III stars as a 15-year-old petty thief with aspirations of a better life that are beyond the New York gang he belongs to. He carries the weight of the film as the tough teen hampered by a poor upbringing, severe asthma and his girlfriend's overprotective father. Writer/director Morgan J Freeman (not that Morgan Freeman) has a better grasp of urban dialogue and expressive camerawork than he does focused storytelling, but it's still a very creditable debut. Contains swearing, violence and drug abuse. 🎬

Brendan Sexton III *Marcus* • Shawn Elliott *Paco* • Jose Zuniga *Kramer* • David Roland Frank *Chip* • Carlo Alban *Benny* • Antoine McLean *Harold* • Mtume Gant *Louis* • Lynn Cohen *Lucy* • Edie Falco *Joanna* ■ *Dir/Scr* Morgan J Freeman • *Cinematographer* Enrique Chediak

The Hurried Man ★★

Melodrama 1977 · Fr · Colour

Very loosely based on a novel by Paul Morand, this jet-setting melodrama will certainly intrigue fans of *Lovejoy*, though not everyone will warm to its glossy visuals and overwrought action. Besotted with beauty and recklessly devil-may-care, antique dealer Alain Delon is prepared to pay the ultimate price for a rare Etruscan vase. The byplay between Delon and partner Michel Duchaussoy is lively, but Edouard Molinaro's intense direction suggests he was trying too hard to

U = SUITABLE FOR ALL   **Uc** = SUITABLE FOR ALL, ESPECIALLY FOR YOUNG CHILDREN (VIDEO ONLY)   **PG** = PARENTAL GUIDANCE

shake his reputation for comedy. French dialogue dubbed into English.

Alain Delon *Pierre* • Mireille Darc *Edwige* • Michel Duchaussoy *Justin* • Monica Guerritore *Sister* ■ *Dir* Edouard Molinaro • *Scr* M Rheims, from a novel by Paul Morand

Hurry Sundown ★

Drama   1967 · US · Colour · 145mins

Whoever would have thought that Otto Preminger could have turned out such a stinker as this? There's little pleasure in watching this overlong adaptation of a doorstop novel, which totally miscasts Michael Caine as a ruthless southerner, replete with menacing accent and surly scowl as he tries to buy up most of Georgia. A feisty Jane Fonda's along for the ride, John Phillip Law is vacant and wan, Faye Dunaway is blowsy and tiresome, Robert Hooks is noble and dull – and they've got the more interesting roles!

Michael Caine *Henry Warren* • Jane Fonda *Julie Ann Warren* • John Phillip Law *Rad McDowell* • Faye Dunaway *Lou McDowell* • Robert Hooks *Reeve Scott* • Beah Richards *Rose Scott* • George Kennedy *Sheriff Coombs* • Burgess Meredith *Judge Purcell* ■ *Dir* Otto Preminger • *Scr* Thomas C Ryan, Horton Foote, from the novel by KB Gliden

Hurry Up, or I'll Be 30 ★★ 15

Comedy   1973 · US · Colour · 83mins

In this extremely low-budget would-be comedy, John Lefkowitz tries to sort out his life in time for that ageist deadline, totally unaided by Brooklyn-born director Joseph Jacoby. This film's real (if any) interest today lies in the fact that hidden away in the cast list is pint-sized wonder Danny DeVito. Even in his tiny role here, DeVito's more interesting than leading man Lefkowitz could ever be. Contains some swearing. 📺

John Lefkowitz *George Trapani* • Linda De Coff *Jackie Tice* • Ronald Anton *Vince Trapani* • Maureen Byrnes *Flo* • Danny DeVito *Petey* • David Kirk *Mr Trapani* • Frank Quinn *Mark Lossier* • Selma Rogoff *Mrs Trapani* ■ *Dir* Joseph Jacoby • *Scr* David Wiltse, Joseph Jacoby, from a story by Joseph Jacoby

Hurt Penguins ★★

Romantic comedy
1992 · Can · Colour · 98mins

Not even a cameo from Mamas and Papas star Denny Doherty can do much to improve the credibility of this bizarrely-titled romantic comedy, set against the backdrop of the Canadian music industry. Michele Muzzi and Daniel Kash star as a couple of aspiring singers whose determination to make it to the top leads Muzzi into a gold-digging marriage with the deadly dull George King. Pleasantly done, but don't be surprised if you find your attention wandering. Contains strong language.

Michele Muzzi *Harriet Swan* • Daniel Kash *Nick Piccione* • George King *Jeremy Finch* • Myra Fried *Robin Sommerfeld* • Denny Doherty *Bilbo Roberts* ■ *Dir* Robert Bergman, Myra Fried • *Scr* Myra Fried

Husbands ★

Drama   1970 · US · Colour · 141mins

There are few things more tedious in cinema than flailing improvisation.

Considering the talent involved here and the fact that this study of middle-aged melancholy followed on directly from the triumphant *Faces*, this self-indulgent wallow from John Cassavetes is doubly disappointing. Coping with the death of their buddy through booze, nostalgia and sex (in a totally bogus panic trip to London), New Yorkers Cassavetes, Peter Falk and Ben Gazzara cut depressing figures of suburban manhood. But we could accept them more readily if they weren't so obviously three arrogant actors imposing their angst and art upon us. A fraudulent folly.

Ben Gazzara *Harry* • Peter Falk *Archie* • John Cassavetes *Gus* • Jenny Runacre *Mary Tynan* • Jenny Lee Wright *Pearl Billingham* • Noelle Kao *Julie* • Leola Harlow *Leola* • Meta Shaw *Annie* ■ *Dir/Scr* John Cassavetes

Husbands and Wives
★★★★ 15

Comedy drama   1992 · US · Colour · 103mins

Throughout this excellent enterprise, Woody Allen employs a hand-held camera to convey the intensity and instability of the key relationship on screen, that between himself and Mia Farrow as a successful but troubled media couple. Sadly, the technique has the effect of nailing you to your seat and leaving you gasping for air. Otherwise this dissection of two relationships (the other is between Sydney Pollack and Judy Davis) is piled high with wit and vigour as it comments on the foibles of the artsy self-obsessed of midtown Manhattan. In a film released at the time of Woody and Mia's own troubles, rich ideas and strong performances abound. Contains swearing. 📺

Woody Allen *Gabe Roth* • Mia Farrow *Judy Roth* • Judy Davis *Sally* • Sydney Pollack *Jack* • Juliette Lewis *Rain* • Lysette Anthony *Sam* • Liam Neeson *Michael* • Blythe Danner *Rain's mother* ■ *Dir/Scr* Woody Allen

Hush ★ 12

Thriller   1998 · US · Colour · 91mins

Don't let the classy cast (Jessica Lange, Gwyneth Paltrow) fool you: this is a truly awful film which has probably been scrubbed from both actresses' CVs. Paltrow is the young woman who marries mummy's boy Johnathon Schaech (*That Thing You Do!*), only to find when they visit the family home that Mother (Lange) will do just about anything to keep her boy close at hand. This should have been played much more for laughs or scares, whereas instead it's just done ludicrously seriously. Paltrow and Lange desperately try to inject a bit of class, while Schaech gives a loyal imitation of a plank. 📺 **DVD**

Jessica Lange *Martha Baring* • Gwyneth Paltrow *Helen* • Johnathon Schaech *Jackson Baring* • Nina Foch *Alice Baring* • Debi Mazar *Lisa* • Kaiulani Lee *Sister O'Shaughnessy* • David Thornton *Gavin* • Hal Holbrook *Dr Hill* ■ *Dir* Jonathan Darby • *Scr* Jonathan Darby, Jane Rusconi, from a story by Jonathan Darby

Hush... Hush, Sweet Charlotte ★★★ 15

Gothic drama   1964 · US · BW · 132mins

Having revived the careers of Bette Davis and Joan Crawford in the

Hollywood melodrama *What Ever Happened to Baby Jane?* director Robert Aldrich was anxious to recall them for *Hush... Hush, Sweet Charlotte*. While Davis readily agreed, sensing another triumph, Crawford cried off, so Aldrich cast Olivia de Havilland. The result is a delirious slice of American Gothic about two warring cousins and an inheritance. All the Deep South conventions are present – shadowy mansion, thrumming insects, secrets in the closet – in a heady brew for fans of Hollywood's golden age. 📺

Bette Davis *Charlotte* • Olivia de Havilland *Miriam* • Joseph Cotten *Drew* • Agnes Moorehead *Velma* • Cecil Kellaway *Harry* • Victor Buono *Big Sam* • Mary Astor *Jewel Mayhew* • Wesley Addy *Sheriff* • George Kennedy *Foreman* ■ *Dir* Robert Aldrich • *Scr* Henry Farrell, Lukas Heller

Hush Little Baby ★★ 15

Thriller   1993 · US · Colour · 109mins

Diane Ladd's crazed performance in David Lynch's *Wild at Heart* helped resurrect her career and here she virtually reprises the role, playing an overprotective mother who meets up with her long-lost daughter and will stop at nothing to prevent anyone coming between them again. Ladd's spirited portrayal is let down by a faceless support cast and uninspired direction. Contains violence. 📺

Diane Ladd *Edie* • Wendel Meldrum *Susan Nolan* • Geraint Wyn Davies *Martin Nolan* • Illya Woloshyn *Dylan* • Ingrid Veninger *Meg* • Norma Edwards *Verna* • Dave Nichols *Officer* • Paul Soles *Dewey* ■ *Dir* Jorge Montesi • *Scr* Julie Moskowitz, Gary Stephens

Hussy ★★ 18

Drama   1979 · UK · Colour · 90mins

Muddled melodrama, with Helen Mirren as a nightclub hostess and part-time prostitute who gets involved with drugs and gangsters, but who manages finally to forge a new life for herself and her kids. Mirren does her best to transcend mediocre material, but can't work miracles. The best thing one can say about the film is that it re-creates well the seedy, druggy atmosphere of British nightclubs of the period. Contains swearing, violence and sex scenes. 📺

Helen Mirren *Beaty Simons* • John Shea *Emory* • Daniel Chasin *Billy Simons* • Murray Salem *Max* • Paul Angelis *Alex* • Jenny Runacre *Vere* • Patti Boulaye *Tama* • Marika Rivera *Nadine* ■ *Dir/Scr* Matthew Chapman

Hustle ★★★★ 15

Thriller   1975 · US · Colour · 114mins

The term *film noir* has been much misused in recent times, with any brooding thriller seemingly eligible for the tag, but this is the real thing. Director Robert Aldrich gives this seedy story the same sense of corruption, depravity and urban alienation that made his 1955 masterpiece *Kiss Me Deadly* so memorable. Aldrich is reunited with his *Mean Machine* star Burt Reynolds, whose world-weary detective can barely rouse himself to mumble the sour asides contained in Steve Shagan's uncompromising script. Catherine Deneuve is less sure-footed, but Ben Johnson, Eddie Albert

and Ernest Borgnine provide sinister support. Contains swearing. 📺

Burt Reynolds *Lt Phil Gaines* • Catherine Deneuve *Nicole Britton* • Eddie Albert *Leo Sellers* • Ben Johnson *Marty Hollinger* • Eileen Brennan *Paula Hollinger* • Ernest Borgnine *Santoro* • Paul Winfield *Sgt Louis Belgrave* ■ *Dir* Robert Aldrich • *Scr* Steve Shagan

The Hustler ★★★★★ 15

Drama   1961 · US · BW · 129mins

The Hustler is showing its age nowadays: all that mock-poetic, soul-searching dialogue and the alcoholic heroine are firmly rooted in fifties' social realism. However, as a showcase for Paul Newman's best screen performance to date, this is still a masterpiece, with Newman, Jackie Gleason and George C Scott striking sparks in the perfectly captured pool-hall atmosphere. The picture is streets ahead of Martin Scorsese's flashy sequel, *The Color of Money*, for which Newman finally won his deserved Oscar. 📺

Paul Newman "*Fast*" *Eddie Felson* • Jackie Gleason *Minnesota Fats* • Piper Laurie *Sarah Packard* • George C Scott *Bert Gordon* • Myron McCormick *Charlie Burns* • Murray Hamilton *Findlay* • Michael Constantine *Big John* ■ *Dir* Robert Rossen • *Scr* Sidney Carroll, Robert Rossen, from the novel by Walter Tevis • *Cinematographer* Eugen Schüfftan

Hustling ★★★

Drama   1975 · US · Colour · 118mins

Based on a book by magazine journalist Gail Sheehy, this drama has lost much of its power to shock since it first aired in 1975. However, there is still much to recommend this crusading TV movie. Lee Remick is totally credible as the reporter who hits the streets to expose the iniquities of a Manhattan prostitution ring, and there's particularly impressive support from hooker Jill Clayburgh (who picked up an Emmy nomination) and the menacing Fran Rocco.

Lee Remick *Fran Morrison* • Jill Clayburgh *Wanda* • Melanie Mayron *Dee Dee* • Alex Rocco *Swifty* • Burt Young *Gustavino* ■ *Dir* Joseph Sargent • *Scr* Fay Kanin, from a non-fiction book by Gail Sheehy

Hyènes ★★★

Drama   1992 · Sen · Colour · 113mins

A strain of indigenous magic realism has run through much sub-Saharan and west African cinema in the nineties. The Senegalese director Djibril Diop Mambety employs it in this symbolic drama that focuses on the clash between progress and tradition and the blurred line between proud nationhood and post-colonial dependence. The story revolves around a returning wealthy woman who offers untold riches to her fellow villagers if they help her wreak vengeance on the former lover who once drove her into exile. Ultimately, it fails to deliver what it promises, but this is still challenging stuff. In French with English subtitles.

Mansour Diouf *Dramaan* • Ami Diakhate *Linguere* • Mahouredia Gueye *The Mayor* • Issa Ramagelissa Samb *The Professor* ■ *Dir* Djibril Diop Mambety • *Scr* Djibril Diop Mambety, from the play *The Visit* by Friedrich Durrenmatt

The Hypnotist ★★
Crime drama   1957 · UK · BW · 89mins

Responsible for dozens of crime quickies in the *Scotland Yard* featurette series, the Irish-born director Montgomery Tully was one of the key figures in the British B-movie industry during the fifties and sixties. This is one of his better efforts, as psychiatrist Roland Culver attempts to frame disturbed test pilot Paul Carpenter for the murder of his wife. Culver does a nice line in evil manipulation and Patricia Roc is typically spirited as the girlfriend standing by her man, but poor old Carpenter probably needed to be hypnotised to give a decent performance.

Roland Culver *Dr Francis Pelham* • Patricia Roc *Mary Foster* • Paul Carpenter *Val Neal* • William Hartnell *Inspector Rose* • Kay Callard *Susie* • Ellen Pollock *Barbara Barton* • Gordon Needham *Sergeant Davies* • Martin Wyldeck *Dr Bradford* • Oliver Johnston *Dr Kenyon* ■ *Dir* Montgomery Tully • *Scr* Montgomery Tully, from a play by Falkland Cary

I Accuse! ★★★ U
Drama historical   1958 · UK · BW · 99mins

José Ferrer directs and stars in this rarely-shown drama about the famous treason trial in France which saw Alfred Dreyfus framed and sentenced to life imprisonment on Devil's Island. As Dreyfus, Ferrer makes a compelling hero and he is supported by a fine cast of stalwarts. Gore Vidal's screenplay was intended, perhaps, as an allegory about the McCarthy era. The black-and-white photography is by Freddie Young, who went on to win three Oscars for his work with David Lean, the first for *Lawrence of Arabia*.

José Ferrer *Alfred Dreyfus* • Anton Walbrook *Major Esterhazy* • Viveca Lindfors *Lucie Dreyfus* • Leo Genn *Major Picquart* • Emlyn Williams *Emile Zola* • David Farrar *Mathieu Dreyfus* • Donald Wolfit *General Mercier* • Herbert Lom *Major Dupaty De Clam* ■ *Dir* José Ferrer • *Scr* Gore Vidal, from the non-fiction book *Captain Dreyfus – a Story of Mass Hysteria* by Nicholas Halasz

I Aim at the Stars ★★ U
Biographical drama 1960 · US · BW · 106mins

Was it right for the Americans to employ a German scientist who had worked for Hitler on the US space programme? Was it possible for a man who invented the devastating V-2 rocket for the Nazis to have been apolitical? These are the compelling questions raised and then fudged in this tame biopic of rocket expert Wernher von Braun. According to the film, von Braun's only ambition was to explore outer space. Unfortunately, despite Curt Jurgens's earnest performance, we never learn much about the man's inner space.

Curt Jurgens *Wernher von Braun* • Victoria Shaw *Maria* • Herbert Lom *Anton Reger* • Gia Scala *Elizabeth Beyer* • James Daly *Major William Taggert* • Adrian Hoven *Mischke* ■ *Dir* J Lee Thompson • *Scr* Jay Dratler, from a story by George Froeschel, U Wolter, HW John

I Am a Camera ★★
Comedy drama   1955 · UK · BW · 100mins

A hugely disappointing film adaptation of John Van Druten's stage version of Christopher Isherwood's celebrated Berlin tales. John Collier must shoulder most of the blame for his drab script that completely misses the decadence and sordid charm of the underside of pre-war German society. Laurence Harvey's lack of technique is cruelly exposed playing Isherwood, but Julie Harris makes a spirited Sally Bowles. Stick to *Cabaret*.

Julie Harris *Sally Bowles* • Laurence Harvey *Christopher Isherwood* • Shelley Winters *Natalia Landauer* • Ron Randell *Clive* • Lea Seidl *Fraulein Schneider* • Anton Diffring *Fritz* ■ *Dir* Henry Cornelius • *Scr* John Collier, from

the play *I Am a Camera* by John Van Druten, from the short story collection *The Berlin Stories* by Christopher Isherwood

I Am a Dancer ★★ U
Documentary 1972 · Fr/UK · Colour · 88mins

While ballet fans will rejoice at the prospect of seeing Rudolph Nureyev and Margot Fonteyn give a full performance as Armand and Marguerite, those hoping to learn more about the Russian maestro and his art will be sorely disappointed. Given the amount of access permitted director Pierre Jourdain, one might have expected more than a few rehearsal sequences. But, then, how could Jourdain have possibly provided an in-depth analysis when he clearly had difficulty keeping the leaping star in full shot? ▥

Dir/Scr Pierre Jourdain

I Am a Fugitive from a Chain Gang ★★★★
Classic drama   1932 · US · BW · 93mins

The title tells all in terms of plot, but it gives no indication of the power generated by the Oscar-nominated performance of Paul Muni, as the war veteran framed for a hold-up and sentenced to work in a Georgia chain gang at the mercy of sadistic guards. One of the most forceful of Warner Bros's conscience-shaking cycle of movies in the thirties, it exposed a pitiless regime. Director Mervyn LeRoy pushed audiences of the day to the limits of endurance, just as the autobiographical novel, on which his film was based, had done for its readers.

Paul Muni *James Allen* • Glenda Farrell *Marie Woods* • Helen Vinson *Helen* • Noel Francis *Linda* • Preston Foster *Pete* • Allen Jenkins *Barney Sykes* • Berton Churchill *Judge* • Edward Ellis *Bomber Wells* • David Landau *Warden* ■ *Dir* Mervyn LeRoy • *Scr* Howard J Green, Brown Holmes, Sheridan Gibney, from the autobiography *I Am a Fugitive from a Georgia Chain Gang* by Robert E Burns

I Am Curious – Yellow ★★★ 18
Erotic drama comedy
1967 · Swe · BW · 116mins

Although it played a key role in undermining US censorship rules, Vilgot Sjoman's mix of soft-core sex and political satire is merely a curio now that its power to shock has diminished. The vox pops that sociologist Lena Nyman conducts on the streets of Stockholm are quite revealing of mid-sixties Swedish attitudes to class, civil rights and Vietnam. But the stylised couplings with boyfriend Sjoman and car salesman Börje Ahlstedt, while contextual, seem designed purely to titillate. The follow-up *I Am Curious – Blue* (the colours are those of the Swedish flag), made less impact. In Swedish with English subtitles. Contains sex scenes and nudity. ▥

Lena Nyman *Lena* • Peter Lindgren *Rune, Lena's father* • Börje Ahlstedt *Borje* • Vilgot Sjoman *Director* • Chris Wahlstrom *Rune's friend* ■ *Dir/Scr* Vilgot Sjoman

I Am Frigid... Why? ★★
Erotic drama   1972 · Fr · Colour · 88mins

Director Max Pécas was one of the pioneers of Euro-eroticism before he turned to that curiously popular French genre, the military comedy, in the mid-eighties. Also known as *She Should Have Stayed in Bed*, this soft-core trash centres around a gardener's daughter who experiments with boarding school lesbianism and high society prostitution in an effort to regain the sexual fervour lost after she was raped. The solution to her woes is dubious at best, while the rest is all stylised fumble and tumble. French dialogue dubbed into English. Contains sex scenes and nudity.

Sandra Jullien [Sandra Julien] *Doris* • Marie-George Pascal *Carla Chambon* • Jean-Luc Terrade *Eric Chambon* • Anne Kerylen *Eva* • Thierry Murzeau *Luc* • Virginie Vignon *Patricia* ■ *Dir/Scr* Max Pécas

I Am the Cheese ★★
Psychological thriller
1983 · US · Colour · 95mins

Robert Jiras made his name as a make-up artist on a string of hits, many of them with Warren Beatty. Here he went behind the cameras for the first (and last) time for a respectful adaption of the novel by Robert Coumier (who also has a cameo). The story focuses on the attempt of a psychiatrist (Robert Wagner) to unlock the long buried memories of a traumatised adolescent (Robert MacNaughton). The same source material would inspire the 1992 film *Lapse of Memory*.

Robert MacNaughton *Adam* • Hope Lange *Betty Farmer* • Don Murray *David Farmer* • Robert Wagner *Dr Brint* • Cynthia Nixon *Amy* ■ *Dir* Robert Jiras • *Scr* David Lange, Robert Jiras, from the novel by Robert Cormier

I Am the Law ★★★
Crime drama   1938 · US · BW · 83mins

Edward G Robinson stars as a law professor appointed as a special prosecutor to flush out urban racketeers, in one of those films where everyone who has information to deliver is bumped off before they can divulge it. The climax is truly weird as Robinson shows home movies and shots of the electric chair to his gathered suspects in a circus tent. Interestingly, New York's *Herald Tribune* found Robinson's moral rhetoric unconvincing at the time.

Edward G Robinson *John Lindsay* • Barbara O'Neil *Jerry Lindsay* • John Beal *Paul Ferguson* • Wendy Barrie *Frankie Ballou* • Otto Kruger *Eugene Ferguson* • Arthur Loft *Tom Ross* ■ *Dir* Alexander Hall • *Scr* Jo Swerling, from a story by Fred Allhoff

I Believe in You ★★★ U
Drama   1952 · UK · BW · 94mins

Michael Relph and Basil Dearden ladle on the good intentions in this unusual drama about the probation service, only to spoil everything by emphasising the patronising conceit that the proletariat will always be ignorant ne'er-do-wells without the guiding influence of the kindly middle classes. Cecil Parker turns from a bumbling do-gooder into a hard-nosed champion of

the underprivileged as he helps Harry Fowler and Joan Collins to stumble back on to the straight and narrow. Incapable of giving a bad performance, Celia Johnson is disappointingly sidelined once Parker finds his feet.

Celia Johnson *Matty* • Cecil Parker *Henry Phipps* • Godfrey Tearle *Mr Pyke* • Harry Fowler *Hooker* • George Relph *Mr Dove* • Joan Collins *Norma* • Laurence Harvey *Jordie* • Sidney James *Sergeant Brodie* ■ *Dir* Michael Relph, Basil Dearden • *Scr* Jack Whittingham, Nicholas Phipps, Michael Relph, Basil Dearden, from the novel *Court Circular* by Sewell Stokes

I Bought a Vampire Motorcycle ★★★ 18

Horror comedy 1989 · UK · Colour · 100mins

What TV director Dirk Campbell's homegrown horror spoof lacks in budget, finesse, genuine scares and acting, it more than makes up for in a wealth of clever ideas that gives a neat spin on formula undead mythology. After buying a possessed antique motorbike, which uses blood for petrol and won't kick-start during daylight hours, sleazy rider Neil Morrissey enlists the help of priest Anthony Daniels (better known as C3PO from *Star Wars*) to exorcise the splatter machine cutting a swathe through Birmingham's highways and hospitals. Cheesy gore, a garlic-breathed detective (Michael Elphick) and tasteless visual gags add to the lunatic fun in this unusually adventurous camp chiller. ▭

Neil Morrissey *Nick Oddie, "Noddy"* • Amanda Noar *Kim* • Michael Elphick *Inspector Cleaver* • Anthony Daniels *Priest* • Andrew Powell *Roach* • George Rossi *Chopper* • Midge Taylor *First Road Toad* • Daniel Peacock *Buzzer* • Burt Kwouk *Fu King owner* ■ *Dir* Dirk Campbell • *Scr* Mycal Miller, John Wolskel

I Can Get It for You Wholesale ★★★ U

Drama 1951 · US · BW · 88mins

A fairly tough adaptation of Jerome Weidman's colourful bestseller about the rag trade, toned down for the screen but providing a superb leading role for dynamic Susan Hayward. She's the gal who goes from seamstress to model to head of a fashion house, and still can't make up her mind whether she wants amiable Dan Dailey or suave George Sanders, who virtually repeats his *All about Eve* performance. This is the same tale that, in its musical incarnation on Broadway, featured a young unknown who brought the house down nightly with the song *Miss Marmelstein* – Barbra Streisand.

Susan Hayward *Harriet Boyd* • Dan Dailey *Teddy Sherman* • George Sanders *Noble* • Sam Jaffe *Cooper* • Randy Stuart *Marge* • Marvin Kaplan *Four Eyes* • Harry Von Zell *Savage* ■ *Dir* Michael Gordon • *Scr* Abraham Polonsky, Vera Caspary, from the novel by Jerome Weidman

I Confess ★★★★ PG

Drama 1953 · US · BW · 90mins

Dismissed by the critics and shunned by the public, this is perhaps Alfred Hitchcock's most under-rated film. In many ways, it shares the transference-of-guilt theme he had explored in his previous movie, *Strangers on a Train*.

But what alienated many audiences was an unfamiliarity with the codes of Catholicism that prevent a priest from betraying the secrets of the confessional. Seen today, this is a classic Hitchcock "wrong man" story, which makes marvellous use of its Quebec settings. Montgomery Clift's haunted look is ideal, but some of his Method mannerisms jar. Talky, serious and difficult, but long overdue for reappraisal. ▭

Montgomery Clift *Father Michael William Logan* • Anne Baxter *Ruth Grandfort* • Karl Malden *Inspector Larrue* • Brian Aherne *Willy Robertson* • OE Hasse *Otto Keller* • Dolly Haas *Alma Keller* • Roger Dann *Pierre Grandfort* • Charles Andre *Father Millais* ■ *Dir* Alfred Hitchcock • *Scr* George Tabori, William Archibald, from the play *Nos Deux Consciences* by Paul Anthelme

I Could Go On Singing ★★★ U

Musical 1963 · UK · Colour · 95mins

Judy Garland's last film, originally called *The Lonely Stage*, is a London-based melodrama attractively shot on location and co-starring the sympathetic Dirk Bogarde. Most of the movie is very average, pieced together when the star's illnesses made it necessary to finish the project in a hurry – the padding, when she was unavailable for filming, is all too obvious, hence interminable travelogue shots of London. However, what this picture does contain is arguably the finest example of improvisational screen acting ever: a single take set in a hospital where Garland and her character merge in a shattering moment of rare movie honesty. No wonder director Ronald Neame dared not try a second take. ▭

Judy Garland *Jenny Bowman* • Dirk Bogarde *David Donne* • Jack Klugman *George Kogan* • Aline MacMahon *Ida* • Gregory Phillips *Matt* • Pauline Jameson *Miss Plimpton* ■ *Dir* Ronald Neame • *Scr* Mayo Simon, from a story by Robert Dozier

I Could Read the Sky ★★★

Drama 2000 · UK/Ire · Colour · 84mins

Nichola Bruce's debut feature is a lyrical evocation of an Irish exile's life as he looks back from his spartan London bedsit on his youth and his itinerant struggle to find work over the water. Although Stephen Rea and Maria Doyle Kennedy contribute telling cameos, it's the performance of writer Dermot Healy, as the regret-scarred narrator, that dominates proceedings. As Healy guides us through the lost moments that shaped him, Bruce re-creates the fragmentary imperfection of memory by superimposing events into an elliptical, almost abstract diary of a mind.

Stephen Rea • Dermot Healy • Maria Doyle Kennedy • Brendan Coyle • Geraldine Fitzgerald ■ *Dir* Nichola Bruce • *Scr* Timothy O'Grady, Nichola Bruce, from the novel by Steve Pyke, Timothy O'Grady

I Cover the Waterfront ★★

Drama 1933 · US · BW · 75 mins

Journalist Ben Lyon romances Claudette Colbert as a means to expose her father (Ernest Torrence, who died before the film's release), a

suspected smuggler of Chinese immigrants. Smart-aleck dialogue between Lyon and Colbert vies with various seaborne chases, and there's a surprise appearance from a shark that carries off someone's leg. James Cruze's film invites comparison with Howard Hawks's similarly themed *Tiger Shark*, which came out the year before.

Claudette Colbert *Julie Kirk* • Ben Lyon *Joseph Miller* • Ernest Torrence *Eli Kirk* • Hobart Cavanaugh *McCoy* • Maurice Black *Ortegus* • Harry Beresford *Old Chris* • Purnell Pratt *John Phelps* ■ *Dir* James Cruze • *Scr* Wells Root, Jack Jevne, from a novel by Max Miller

i.d. ★★★★ 18

Drama 1994 · UK/Ger · Colour · 103mins

This is a remarkable debut by director Philip Davis, also known as an actor in films such as *Quadrophenia* and *High Hopes*. Although some of the asides about racism in football ring a little hollow and not all of his extras resemble hardened thugs, Davis presents a highly credible picture of what anthropologist Desmond Morris has described as the soccer tribe defending its patch. Reece Dinsdale gives an eye-opening performance as the dedicated policeman who turns into a rabid hooligan, and the support from pub personnel Warren Clarke (now star of *Dalziel and Pascoe*) and Saskia Reeves and peaches-and-cream girlfriend Claire Skinner is also impressive. Riveting and disturbingly possible. Contains violence, swearing and sex scenes. ▭

Reece Dinsdale *John* • Richard Graham *Trevor* • Claire Skinner *Marie* • Sean Pertwee *Martin* • Saskia Reeves *Lynda* • Warren Clarke *Bob* • Philip Glenister *Charlie* • Perry Fenwick *Eddie* ■ *Dir* Philip Davis [Phil Davis] • *Scr* Vincent O'Connell, from a story by James Bannon

I Didn't Do It ★★

Comedy thriller 1945 · UK · BW · 99mins

Made in Britain for Columbia, this was George Formby's penultimate picture. The toothy grin, gormless tenacism and the cheeky songs that had seen him through 18 features were now wearing more than a little thin and this eminently forgettable comedy whodunit did little to reverse his box-office decline. Even with five screenwriters on the job, this story in which he turns detective to prove his innocence after he is accused of the murder of an Australian acrobat is too short on gags or clues to hold the attention. Even the usually dependable comedy director Marcel Varnel was confounded by this mediocre mystery.

George Formby *George Trotter* • Billy Caryll *Pa Tubbs* • Hilda Mundy *Ma Tubbs* • Gaston Palmer *Le Grand Gaston* • Jack Daly *Terry O'Rourke* • Carl Jaffe *Hilary Vance* • Ian Fleming *Inspector Twyning* ■ *Dir* Marcel Varnel • *Scr* Norman Lee, Howard Irving Young, Stephen Black, Peter Fraser, Michael Vaughan

I Died a Thousand Times ★★

Crime drama 1955 · US · Colour · 109mins

In this cheesy remake of *High Sierra*, Jack Palance steps into Humphrey Bogart's shoes as "Mad Dog" Earl, the hard-boiled gangster who wants to finish a lifetime of crime with a spectacular heist. It was a by-the-

numbers story when Raoul Walsh tackled it back in 1941 and it proves even more tired in director Stuart Heisler's barely competent caper. Palance is certainly no Bogie, but the topnotch supporting cast is a movie buff's delight and well worth catching.

Jack Palance *Roy Earle* • Shelley Winters *Marie Gibson* • Lori Nelson *Velma* • Lee Marvin *Babe* • Earl Holliman *Red* • Perry Lopez *Louis Mendoza* • Pedro Gonzalez [Pedro Gonzalez-Gonzales] *Chico* • Lon Chaney Jr *Big Mac* • Dennis Hopper *Joe* ■ *Dir* Stuart Heisler • *Scr* WR Burnett, from his novel *High Sierra*

I Don't Buy Kisses Anymore ★★

Romantic comedy 1992 · US · Colour · 112mins

Long-suffering *Seinfeld* star Jason Alexander gets a rare leading role in this slender but warmly performed romantic comedy. He plays a shy bachelor who strikes up a friendship with smart student Nia Peeples, who unbeknown to him, sees him as perfect case study for her course. However, things get complicated when Alexander begins falling in love with her. There are nice supporting turns from Eileen Brennan, Lou Jacobi and Lainie Kazan and, while no laugh fest, it will leave you smiling.

Jason Alexander *Bernie Fishbine* • Nia Peeples *Theresa Garabaldi* • Lainie Kazan *Sarah Fishbine* • Lou Jacobi *Irving Fein aka Gramps* • Eileen Brennan *Frieda* ■ *Dir* Robert Marcarelli • *Scr* Jonnie Lindsell

The I Don't Care Girl ★★★ U

Biographical musical drama
1952 · US · Colour · 77mins

An under-written but entertaining biopic of Broadway club sensation Eva Tanguay, portrayed zappily by talented 20th Century-Fox contract star Mitzi Gaynor. Best remembered today as Nellie Forbush in the movie of *South Pacific*, and still happily performing live across the USA, Mitzi's not bad at all, and she's certainly helped by some rich Technicolor and smart co-stars David Wayne and Oscar Levant. Director Lloyd Bacon made the seminal *42nd Street* two decades earlier, but you'd never guess it from this.

Mitzi Gaynor *Eva Tanguay* • David Wayne *Ed McCoy* • Oscar Levant *Bennett* • Bob Graham *Larry* • Craig Hill *Keene* ■ *Dir* Lloyd Bacon • *Scr* Walter Bullock

I Don't Want to Be Born ★★

Horror 1975 · UK · Colour · 92mins

Joan Collins is cursed by a dwarf and gives birth to a killer baby in Britain's hilariously cheap answer to *Rosemary's Baby*, which also goes under the intriguing titles *It's Growing inside Her* and *The Devil within Her*. Donald Pleasence delivers the tiny terror who begins childhood by drowning his nanny and then moves on to dunking dead mice in teacups. Naturally poor Joanie can't understand why her toddler is a little demon. Veteran horror director Peter Sasdy's bargain-basement Hammer is irresistible trash from sinister start to foolish finish. An absolute hoot.

Joan Collins *Lucy Carlesi* • Eileen Atkins *Sister Albana* • Donald Pleasence *Dr Finch* • Ralph Bates *Gino Carlesi* • Caroline Munro *Mandy* •

Hilary Mason *Mrs Hyde* ■ *Dir* Peter Sasdy • *Scr* Stanley Price, from a story by Nato De Angeles

I Dood It ★★★ U
Musical comedy   1943 · US · BW · 102mins

Astonishing to find that Vincente Minnelli (*Meet Me in St Louis, An American in Paris*) directed this awkwardly contrived semi-musical from MGM, with Red Skelton as the tailor's assistant wooing actress Eleanor Powell from afar, by wearing his clients' clothes and looking a desirable fashion-plate. The title comes from Skelton's radio catch-phrase and there are some bright spots among the grey; such as some well-staged numbers and the song *Taking a Chance on Love*. Basically, it's a retread of Buster Keaton's *Spite Marriage*.

Red Skelton *Joseph Rivington Renolds* • Eleanor Powell *Constance Shaw* • Richard Ainley *Larry West* • Patricia Dane *Surelia Brenton* • Sam Levene *Ed Jackson* • Thurston Hall *Kenneth Lawlor* ■ *Dir* Vincente Minnelli • *Scr* Sig Herzig, Fred Saidy

I Dream of Jeanie ★★ U
Biographical musical drama
1952 · US · Colour · 90mins

Republic picked on the work of the popular 19th-century songwriter Stephen Foster for this low-budget musical biopic, because it was in the public domain and wouldn't cost anything. However, Foster's life was far too depressing, so writer Alan LeMay concocted a lighter version in which the impractical dreamer is rescued from his financial problems by a wiser brother. Filmed in the studio's erratic Trucolor process, it is packed with Foster's works, belted out by Ray Middleton as minstrel star Edwin P Christy, Bill Shirley as Foster, and others. Eileen Christy is pleasant as Foster's true love, his Jeanie with the light brown hair.

Ray Middleton *Edwin P Christy* • Bill Shirley *Stephen Foster* • Muriel Lawrence *Inez McDowell* • Eileen Christy *Jeanie McDowell* • Lynn Bari *Mrs McDowell* • Richard Simmons [Richard Simmons] *Dunning Foster* ■ *Dir* Allan Dwan • *Scr* Alan LeMay

I Dream of Jeannie... 15 Years Later ★★
Fantasy comedy   1985 · US · Colour

An unwise attempt to resurrect one of the most popular US sitcoms of the sixties, a series which put Larry Hagman on the way to TV stardom. Presumably his *Dallas* duties meant he was unable to return for this project and his place this time around was taken by Wayne Rogers (who played Trapper John in the TV series *M*A*S*H* from 1972–5). Bill Daily returns as his air force colleague, while the mischievous but loyal genie Barbara Eden creates more havoc. However, the concept looks stretched as a feature TV film.

Barbara Eden *Jeannie/Jeannie II* • Wayne Rogers *Tony Nelson* • Bill Daily *Captain Roger Healey* • Hayden Rorke *Dr Alfred Bellows* • John Bennett Perry *Wes Morrison* • MacKenzie Astin *TJ* • Dody Goodman *Scheherazade* ■ *Dir* William Asher • *Scr* Irma Kalish, from a story by Dinah Kirgo, Julie Kirgo, Irma Kalish, from characters created by Sidney Sheldon

I Dream Too Much ★★
Musical comedy   1935 · US · BW · 97 mins

This RKO musical comedy was only Henry Fonda's third film, and he's badly miscast. Fred Astaire's costume doesn't look very good on him, and he simply doesn't convince us he's the composer of Jerome Kern songs such as *I'm the Echo, The Jockey on the Carousel* and the title number. Hank's co-star is the French opera star Lily Pons, who made only two more films yet had a town in Maryland named after her. Lucille Ball also makes a fleeting appearance – and she ended up owning the studio!

Lily Pons *Jonathan Street* • Lily Pons *Annette Street* • Eric Blore *Roger Briggs* • Osgood Perkins *Paul Darcy* • Lucien Littlefield *Mr Dilley* • Lucille Ball *Gwendolyn Dilley* ■ *Dir* John Cromwell • *Scr* James Gow, Edmund North, from a story by Elsie Finn, David G Wittels

I Escaped from Devil's Island ★★
Prison drama   1973 · US · Colour · 86mins

Following hard on the heels of *Papillon* came this less self-important yarn in which Jim Brown leads a bunch of decidedly over-nourished men across the ocean and into the jungle. They leave behind the creature comforts of the French penal colony, journey on a raft made from animal skins, and encounter lepers, bare-breasted native girls and their own animal instincts. Made by Roger Corman's studio, it smacks its lips over the violence that exists in prison and outside.

Jim Brown *Le Bras* • Christopher George *Davert* • Rick Ely *Jo-Jo* • Richard Rust *Zamorra* ■ *Dir* William Witney • *Scr* Richard L Adams

I Even Met Happy Gypsies ★★★★
Drama   1967 · Yug · Colour · 90mins

Along with Bostjan Hladnik, Aleksandar Petrovic was the driving force behind the Novi Film movement which, in the early sixties, sought to steer Yugoslav cinema away from socialist realism. Following his revisionist, Oscar-nominated war picture, *Three*, he received another best foreign film nomination for this docu-dramatic insight into the lifestyle of the gypsies of the Vojvodnia region, which also won the Special Jury Prize at Cannes. With a cast including non-professional performers speaking their own language (Serbo-Croat, Slovak and Romany), Petrovic illuminates the story of the feather trader who saves a girl from her abusive stepfather with a wealth of authentic detail. In Serbian with English subtitles.

Bekim Fehmiu *Bora* • Olivera Vuco *Lence* • Bata Zivojinovic *Mirta* • Gordana Jovanovic *Tisa* • Mija Aleksic *Father Pavle* • Rahela Ferari *Nun* • Severin Bijelic *Religious peasant* • Etelka Filipovski *Bora's wife* • Milorad Jovanovic *Toni* ■ *Dir/Scr* Aleksandar Petrovic

I Found Stella Parish ★★
Weepie   1935 · US · BW · 84 mins

An unashamed assault on the tear ducts, this hoary melodrama rather went against the Warner Bros grain, substituting the customary hard-edged realism for a little soft-soap and

glamour. Bedecked in gowns by the legendary costume designer Orry-Kelly and playing against cavernous sets, Kay Francis emotes for all she's worth as the stage diva prepared to sacrifice almost everything to prevent her daughter from learning of her misdeeds on the way to the top. Directed with the excessive earnestness that regrettably blighted his later career, Mervyn LeRoy flatters Francis in every shot. However, Ian Hunter and Paul Lukas still manage to make an impression.

Kay Francis *Stella Parish* • Ian Hunter *Keith Lockridge* • Paul Lukas *Stephen Norman* • Sybil Jason *Gloria Parish* • Jessie Ralph *Nana* • Joseph Sawyer [Joe Sawyer] *Chuck* ■ *Dir* Mervyn LeRoy • *Scr* Casey Robinson, from the story by John Monk Saunders

I Heard the Owl Call My Name ★★★ U
Drama   1973 · US · Colour · 74mins

Adapted without condescension or overt sentimentality by director Daryl Duke, from the novel by Margaret Craven, this superior TV movie makes powerful use of the British Columbian coastscape to emphasise the grinding poverty of the native Indians who dwell there and the enormity of the task facing Tom Courtenay, as the inexperienced Anglican priest sent to minister to them. With humble support from Dean Jagger, as the bishop who sustains the novice's faith, as ignorance and isolation sap his morale, Courtenay achieves a sincerity and compassion that stands in stark contrast to his more cynical kitchen-sink persona. ▭

Tom Courtenay *Father Tark Brian* • Dean Jagger *Bishop* • Paul Stanley *Jim Wallace* • Marianne Jones *Keetah* • George Clutesi *George P Hudson* • Keith Pepper *Alan Spencer* ■ *Dir* Daryl Duke • *Scr* Gerald Di Pego, from the novel by Margaret Craven

I Hired a Contract Killer ★★★ 15
Comedy thriller
1990 · Fin/Swe · Colour · 74mins

Aki Kaurismäki made his English language debut with this doggedly downbeat slice of black comedy. Importing his inimitable sense of perspective and timing to London, the man many see as Finland's finest director transforms the city into a hostile urban wilderness. It's here that discarded civil servant Jean-Pierre Léaud seeks refuge from the hit man he no longer requires, having fallen for flowerseller Margi Clarke. Kaurismäki keeps the performances edgy with short scenes and minimalist dialogue, opting for a melancholic rather than suspenseful air. A minor work, but moody and amusing all the same. ▭

Margi Clarke *Margaret* • Jean-Pierre Léaud *Henri Boulanger* • Kenneth Colley *Killer* • Trevor Bowen *Department head* • Imogen Claire *Secretary* • Nicky Tesco *Pete* • Charles Cork *Al* ■ *Dir/Scr* Aki Kaurismäki

I Know What You Did Last Summer ★★★ 15
Horror thriller   1997 · US · Colour · 96mins

Aimed squarely at the teenage TV audience, director Jim Gillespie's stalk-and-slash saga gives *Scream* writer

Kevin Williamson the chance to revive his favourite psycho-killer clichés. Four bright college graduates cover up a hit-and-run accident, only to have the dark tragedy rear its head a year later when a hook-wielding masked fisherman starts decimating their number. Beautifully photographed, Gillespie's chiller nevertheless trades on out-dated thrills all the way through to its creak-and-shriek showdown. The biggest shock is how completely ordinary it all is. ▭ *DVD*

Jennifer Love Hewitt *Julie James* • Sarah Michelle Gellar *Helen Shivers* • Ryan Phillippe *Barry Cox* • Freddie Prinze Jr *Ray Bronson* • Muse Watson *Benjamin Willis/Fisherman* • Bridgette Wilson *Elsa Shivers* • Anne Heche *Melissa Egan* ■ *Dir* Jim Gillespie • *Scr* Kevin Williamson, from the novel by Lois Duncan

I Know Where I'm Going ★★★★★ U
Romantic comedy   1945 · UK · BW · 87mins

Of all the classics produced by Michael Powell and Emeric Pressburger, this may be the most unsung but it's undoubtedly the most entrancing. As the headstrong young woman and the laird who distracts her from her stuffy fiancé, Wendy Hiller and Roger Livesey are both superb, and there's canny support from Pamela Brown, John Laurie and Finlay Currie. Alfred Junge's sets cleverly blend Hebridean and Art Deco, while the photography of Erwin Hillier is as beautiful as it is atmospheric. But it's the expert mix of romance and comedy, arresting use of the landscape and respectful fascination with the local culture that make this so compelling. ▭

Wendy Hiller *Joan Webster* • Roger Livesey *Torquil* • Pamela Brown *Catriona Potts* • Nancy Price *Mrs Crozier* • John Laurie *John Campbell* • George Carney *Mr Webster* • Walter Hudd *Hunter* • Captain Duncan Mackechnie *Captain "Lochinvar"* ■ *Dir/Scr* Michael Powell, Emeric Pressburger

I Like It like That ★★★ 15
Romantic comedy
1994 · US · Colour · 102mins

Written and directed by Spike Lee alumnus Darnell Martin, this is a rare look at the lives of the Latino population jostling for space in the Bronx. At the centre of this engaging film is Lauren Velez, who gets the chance to prove she's more than just a homebird when her husband is jailed and she lands a job with a record label. The racial mix is just a tad too cosy and the message that men are all the same no matter what their colour is stated too blandly. But Martin knows her patch and coaxes a lovely performance from the sassy Velez. Contains violence, swearing, sex scenes, drug abuse and nudity. ▭

Lauren Velez *Lisette Linares* • Jon Seda *Chino Linares* • Tomas Melly *Li'l Chino Linares* • Desiree Casado *Minnie Linares* • Isaiah Garcia *Pee Wee Linares* • Jesse Borrego *Alexis* • Griffin Dunne *Stephen Price* ■ *Dir/Scr* Darnell Martin

I Live in Fear ★★★ PG
Drama   1955 · Jap · BW · 98mins

Shot at the height of the Cold War and a mere decade after the atomic assault on Japan, Akira Kurosawa's

U = SUITABLE FOR ALL   Uc = SUITABLE FOR ALL, ESPECIALLY FOR YOUNG CHILDREN (VIDEO ONLY)   PG = PARENTAL GUIDANCE

drama about life under the shadow of the bomb was originally conceived as a satire and an uncertainty of tone fatally undermines its purpose. By having ageing industrialist Toshiro Mifune descend into dementia, his desire to escape the holocaust by relocating his sneering family to a Brazilian hideaway can too easily be dismissed as senile paranoia instead of prescient warning. However, muddled humanism aside, Kurosawa's command of alternating montage sequences and fluid long takes is exemplary. A Japanese language film. ▭

Toshiro Mifune *Kiichi Nakajima* • Eiko Miyoshi *Toyo Nakajima* • Haruko Togo *Yoshi* • Takashi Shimura *Harada* ■ *Dir* Akira Kurosawa • *Scr* Akira Kurosawa, Shinobu Hashimoto, Hideo Oguni

I Live in Grosvenor Square ★ U

Romance 1945 · UK · BW · 114mins

An expensive, ridiculous and tediously overstretched romantic drama in which Anna Neagle, a duke's granddaughter, switches her affections from Rex Harrison's army major to Dean Jagger's American-air-force sergeant. It's unbelievable that the dull Jagger could oust the charismatic Rex, or that Rex would be such a generous loser – but it's typical of the way the entire production panders to the American market, where it played as *A Yank in London*.

Anna Neagle *Lady Patricia Fairfax* • Rex Harrison *Maj David Bruce* • Dean Jagger *Sgt John Patterson* • Robert Morley *Duke of Exmoor* • Jane Darwell *Mrs Patterson* • Nancy Price *Mrs Wilson* ■ *Dir* Herbert Wilcox • *Scr* Nicholas Phipps, William D Bayles, from a story by Maurice Cowan

I Live My Life ★★

Romantic comedy 1935 · US · BW · 85m

Animosity turns to amorousness (as you knew it would) when a rich, bored society girl and a humble archaeologist who disdains her friends and her lifestyle fall in love. Joan Crawford and Brian Aherne star in this desperately routine film, directed with a surprising lack of brio by WS Van Dyke. Designer clothes and sophisticated cocktail parties lend a fleeting and superficial gloss to the tepid screenplay, written by Joseph L Mankiewicz, who would go on to far, far better things – *All about Eve*, for example.

Joan Crawford *Kay* • Brian Aherne *Terry* • Frank Morgan *Bentley* • Aline MacMahon *Betty* • Eric Blore *Grove* ■ *Dir* WS Van Dyke • *Scr* Joseph L Mankiewicz, Gottfried Reinhardt, Ethel Borden, from the short story *Claustrophobia* by Abbie Carter Goodloe • *Music* Dimitri Tiomkin [Dmitri Tiomkin]

I Love a Man in Uniform ★★★ 18

Psychological thriller
1993 · Can · Colour · 94mins

Canadian director David Wellington's first feature divided audiences on its initial release, who couldn't decide whether it was merely provocative or just plain disturbing. Whatever your opinion, there is no denying that star Tom McCamus is mesmerising as the struggling actor who lands the role of a tough-talking cop on a TV show, only to

find that reality and make-believe blur when he starts patrolling the streets in his uniform, passing himself off as a real policeman. Fascinating, although the ending is somewhat disappointing. Contains violence and swearing. ▭

Tom McCamus *Henry Adler* • Brigitte Bako *Charlie Warner* • Kevin Tighe *Frank* • David Hemblen *Father* • Alex Karzis *Bruce* • Graham McPherson *Mr Pearson* • Daniel Maclvor *Director* • Wendy Hopkins *Casting director* ■ *Dir/Scr* David Wellington

I Love a Soldier ★★

Second World War romantic drama
1944 · US · BW · 106mins

Director Mark Sandrich must have longed for the good old days while handling this mediocre weepie for, while Paulette Goddard and Sonny Tufts may have looked good together, they were definitely no Fred and Ginger (whom he directed five times at RKO). Reteaming after their unexpected success in *So Proudly We Hail!*, the leads occasionally spark into life, as Tufts's dashing GI melts the hardened heart of Goddard's war-effort welder. But she fails to convince as the going gets tougher and she has to give Sonny the brush off, so he can keep his mind on killing the enemies of democracy.

Paulette Goddard *Eva Morgan* • Sonny Tufts *Dan Gilgore* • Mary Treen *Cissy Grant* • Walter Sande *Stiff Banks* • Ann Doran *Jenny* • Beulah Bondi *Etta Lane* ■ *Dir* Mark Sandrich • *Scr* Allan Scott

I Love Melvin ★★★★ U

Musical 1953 · US · Colour · 77mins

An undervalued little musical, with Donald O'Connor and Debbie Reynolds reunited after the success of the previous year's *Singin' in the Rain* and at the top of their form again here. O'Connor plays a photographer's assistant who cons Reynolds by telling her she's in line to be a cover girl. There are some charming duos – O'Connor's skating slides are a sight to behold – and plenty of zip to spare.

Donald O'Connor *Melvin Hoover* • Debbie Reynolds *Judy Leroy* • Una Merkel *Mom Schneider* • Richard Anderson *Harry Flack* • Allyn Joslyn *Pop Schneider* • Les Tremayne *Mr Hennenman* • Noreen Corcoran *Clarabelle* ■ *Dir* Don Weis • *Scr* George Wells, Ruth Brooks Flippen, from a story by Laslo Vadnay

I Love My... Wife ★★

Comedy 1970 · US · Colour · 95mins

A credit sequence charting Elliott Gould's progress from sexual novice to hopeful bridegroom gets this adult comedy off to a lively start. However, no sooner has disillusion set in than the inspiration dries up, and what might have been an amusing insight into the sexual insecurities of the post-sixties male becomes an assault on women in general and Brenda Vaccaro in particular. Gould's distinctive brand of world-weary cynicism should have been ideal for a dissection of modern marriage, but writer Robert Kaufman's one-liners are as smugly predictable as his coarsely satirical observations.

Elliott Gould *Dr Richard Burrows* • Brenda Vaccaro *Jody Borrows* • Angel Tompkins

Helene Donnelly • Dabney Coleman *Frank Donnelly* • Joan Tompkins *Grandma Dennison* ■ *Dir* Mel Stuart • *Scr* Robert Kaufman

I Love Trouble ★★★ PG

Comedy thriller 1994 · US · Colour · 117mins

If you can get your head round the idea of Julia Roberts as a ruthlessly ambitious newspaper reporter, then there's plenty to enjoy in this frivolous thriller. However, it's much too long and far too deliberate to fulfil its ambition of re-creating the screwball style that made the thirties battle-of-the-sexes comedies such a delight. Nick Nolte is closer to the mark as the cynical hack tinkering with old columns to lighten the load, but neither the rivalry nor the romance between the stars seems particularly convincing. ▭

Nick Nolte *Peter Brackett* • Julia Roberts *Sabrina Peterson* • Saul Rubinek *Sam Smotherman* • James Rebhorn *The Thin Man* • Robert Loggia *Matt Greenfield* • Kelly Rutherford *Kim* • Olympia Dukakis *Jeannie* • Marsha Mason *Senator Gayle Robbins* ■ *Dir* Charles Shyer • *Scr* Nancy Meyers, Charles Shyer

I Love You Again ★★★★

Romantic comedy 1940 · US · BW · 98mins

An absolutely hysterical MGM screwball comedy with super-sophisticates William Powell and Myrna Loy taking a break from their *Thin Man* series in an ingeniously written farce, in which amnesiac Powell spends the whole movie trying to persuade his wife, Loy, not to divorce him in order to marry her forties version of a toyboy. It's Powell's film, as he essays pratfalls and double takes with great *élan* in this superb comedic tour de force. Director Woody "one-take" Van Dyke II just lets Powell get on with it, and here the accomplished *farceur* is at his very best. Don't miss.

William Powell *Larry Wilson/George Carey* • Myrna Loy *Kay Wilson* • Frank McHugh *Doc Ryan* • Edmund Lowe *Duke Sheldon* • Donald Douglas *[Don Douglas] Herbert* • Nella Walker *Kay's mother* ■ *Dir* WS Van Dyke II [WS Van Dyke] • *Scr* Charles Lederer, George Oppenheimer, Harry Kurnitz, from a story by Leon Gordon, Maurine Watkins, from a novel by Octavus Roy Cohen

I Love You, Alice B Toklas ★★

Satirical comedy 1968 · US · Colour · 93mins

Even when Peter Sellers was at the height of his popularity, and could seemingly do no wrong, director Hy Averback's satirical comedy was a dubious proposition. Despite promising early scenes in which asthmatic lawyer Sellers is at odds with his pushy girlfriend (the brilliant Joyce Van Patten), it all falls apart when Sellers eats marijuana-spiked cookies and becomes a hippy dropout. Very much of its time, this provided a Hollywood breakthrough for screenwriters Paul Mazursky and Larry Tucker after years of contributing to TV series such as *The Monkees*. Contains brief nudity.

Peter Sellers *Harold* • Jo Van Fleet *Mother* • Leigh Taylor-Young *Nancy* • Joyce Van Patten *Joyce* • David Arkin *Herbie* • Herbert Edelman *Murray* • Louis Gottlieb *Guru* ■ *Dir* Hy Averback • *Scr* Paul Mazursky, Larry Tucker

I Love You, I Love You Not ★★

Drama 1997 · US/UK · Colour · 89mins

Claire Danes stars as a withdrawn teenager, Daisy, falling for the school jock (Jude Law) at her New York school. It all goes horribly wrong when her classmates discover her grandmother, Jean Moreau, is a Holocaust survivor and their anti-Semitism kicks in. Grandmother and granddaughter share their respective suffering – Danes playing Moreau in the flashback sequences in Germany. While the message – that persecution and anti-Semitism persist – is an important one, it's far better explored in films such as *Schindler's List* and *Sophie's Choice*.

Jeanne Moreau *Nana* • Claire Danes *Daisy* • Jude Law *Ethan* • Carrie Slaza *Jane* • Jerry Tanklow *Mr Gilman* • James Van Der Beek *Tony* ■ *Dir* Billy Hopkins • *Scr* Wendy Kesselman, from a play by Wendy Kesselman

I Love You to Death ★★ 15

Black comedy based on a true story
1990 · US · Colour · 93mins

One of those unfortunate efforts which looks a wow on paper – great plot, great director, grade-A comic cast – but which sinks like a celluloid *Titanic* under the weight of more ham than a butcher's shop. Based on a gift of a true story (woman tries desperately to kill unfaithful hubby, but he seems clottishly indestructible), yet everyone appears inexplicably hellbent on pressing the destruct button. A dreadful waste of all concerned. Contains violence ▭

Kevin Kline *Joey Boca* • Tracey Ullman *Rosalie Boca* • Joan Plowright *Nadja* • River Phoenix *Devo* • William Hurt *Harlan James* • Keanu Reeves *Marlon James* • Miriam Margolyes *Joey's mother* ■ *Dir* Lawrence Kasdan • *Scr* John Kostmayer

I Married a Dead Man ★★★

Drama 1983 · Fr · Colour · 110 mins

This drama of mistaken identity was previously filmed as *No Man of Her Own* in 1950 and, more recently, as *Mrs Winterbourne* in 1996. Nathalie Baye plays a pregnant woman who, after surviving a train crash, finds herself mistaken for one of its many victims. It is in the interests of her and the unborn child not to reveal the truth, but she soon finds herself in over her head. Baye is superb and the scenes with her and her newborn child bring tears to the eyes. French dialogue dubbed into English.

Nathalie Baye *Helene/Patricia* • Francis Huster *Pierre* • Richard Bohringer *Frank* • Madeleine Robinson *Lena* • Guy Tréjan *Monsieur Meyrand* ■ *Dir* Robin Davis • *Scr* Patrick Laurent, from a novel by William Irish [Cornell Woolrich]

I Married a Monster from Outer Space ★★★

Science-fiction horror
1958 · US · BW · 77mins

Soon-to-be-wed Tom Tryon has his body taken over by a rhubarb-faced alien in Gene Fowler Jr's smartly directed paranoia classic: substitute Gloria Talbott's UFO-duplicated husband for a red in her bed and the true anti-

Communist undercurrent becomes apparent. Fowler worked as an editor for Fritz Lang, and the German expressionist influence is evident in the use of shadows and weird angles to heighten the atmospheric tension. Despite its outrageously exploitative title, this is intelligent, well packaged science fiction.

Tom Tryon *Bill Farrell* • Gloria Talbott *Marge Farrell* • Peter Baldwin *Swanson* • Robert Ivers *Harry* • Chuck Wassil *Ted* • Valerie Allen *B Girl* • Ty Hungerford *Mac* • Ken Lynch *Dr Wayne* ■ *Dir* Gene Fowler Jr • *Scr* Louis Vittes

I Married a Strange Person ★★★

Comedy animation
1997 · US · Colour · 76mins

Acclaimed for the crayon-drawn *Your Face* and *One of Those Days*, Bill Plympton is revered by his fellow animators. It's easy to see why from this feature, which can be summed up in a single word – strange! Newlyweds Grant and Kerry Boyer seem blissfully happy until a pair of ducks fly into their satellite dish, transforming the TV into a malevolent machine that gives Grant the power to turn his fantasies into reality. Combining moments of mock horror (such as when a neighbour is attacked by his lawn) and surreal humour, this makes for perfect late-night escapism.

Chris Michaelson • Tom Larson • Richard Spore • Chris Cooke ■ *Dir* Bill Plympton • *Scr* Bill Plympton, PC Vey

I Married a Witch ★★★★

Fantasy comedy 1942 · US · BW · 76mins

This was one of the films French director René Clair made in Hollywood during his wartime exile. It's a comedy about a witch who is reincarnated in order to persecute the ancestor of the judge who condemned her to be burned at the stake 300 years earlier. The fact that the descendant, played by Fredric March, is running for political office is curiously prescient of the McCarthy witchhunts that occurred some five years later. Veronica Lake was usually typecast as a sultry *femme fatale*, but as the witch she shows a real flair for whimsy.

Fredric March *Wallace Wooley* • Veronica Lake *Jennifer* • Robert Benchley *Dr Dudley White* • Susan Hayward *Estelle Masterson* • Cecil Kellaway *Daniel* • Elizabeth Patterson *Margaret* • Robert Warwick *JB Masterson* ■ *Dir* René Clair • *Scr* Robert Pirosh, Marc Connelly, Dalton Trumbo, from the novel *The Passionate Witch* by Thorne Smith, Norman Matson

I Married a Woman ★★ U

Comedy 1958 · US · BW and Colour · 83mins

After a decade as the blonde bombshell of British cinema, Diana Dors graces this Hollywood comedy with her considerable assets – with mixed results. She does well enough as a pouting lovely who tries to put the pep back into her marriage, but co-star Gobel, a top American TV comedian, is an eminently resistible personality whose bungling wimp routine adds considerably to the burden of watching this desperately unfunny charade. The only thing of interest is a Technicolor cameo from an ill-at-ease John Wayne.

Diana Dors *Janice* • George Gobel *Marshall Briggs* • Adolphe Menjou *Sutton* • Jessie Royce Landis *Mother* • Nita Talbot *Miss Anderson* • William Redfield *Eddie* • Steve Dunne *Bob* • John McGiver *Girard* • John Wayne • Angie Dickinson *Screen wife* ■ *Dir* Hal Kanter • *Scr* Goodman Ace

I Married an Angel ★ U

Fantasy musical romance
1942 · US · BW · 83mins

This disastrous end to the Jeanette MacDonald/Nelson Eddy partnership is for die-hard devotees only. Mangling a hit Broadway musical by Richard Rodgers and Lorenz Hart, MGM miscast Eddy as a Budapest playboy while MacDonald fares little better, being restrained for most of the picture as an angel dreamed up by Eddy. A lighter, more satirical thrust might have improved matters, but director WS Van Dyke (at the end of his career) doesn't seem to have found much humour in Anita Loos's script.

Jeanette MacDonald *Anna Zador/Brigitta* • Nelson Eddy *Count Willie Palaffi* • Binnie Barnes *Peggy* • Edward Everett Horton *Peter* • Reginald Owen *Herman "Whiskers" Rothbart* ■ *Dir* WS Van Dyke • *Scr* Anita Loos, from the musical by Richard Rodgers, Lorenz Hart, from the play by Vaszary Janos

I Met Him in Paris ★★★

Romantic comedy 1937 · US · BW · 86 mins

A formula vehicle for Claudette Colbert, but the formula her fans wanted and expected, this comedy finds her taking a well-earned vacation from a boring fiancée in a familiar Paramount-designed Paris. There she's courted by two more men, and ends up on the Swiss ski slopes with both. Will she choose morose and cynical playwright Melvyn Douglas or charming smoothie playboy Robert Young? En route to the answer, Claude Binyon's screenplay crackles with barbed wit, delivered in best high-comedy style by the sparring trio. The film is bathed in the sheen of sophistication that was Paramount's hallmark in the thirties.

Claudette Colbert *Kay Denham* • Melvyn Douglas *George Potter* • Robert Young *Gene Anders* • Lee Bowman *Berk Sutter* • Mona Barrie *Helen Anders* • George Davis *Cutter driver* ■ *Dir* Wesley Ruggles • *Scr* Claude Binyon, from the story by Helen Meinardi

I Met My Love Again ★★★

Romantic drama 1938 · US · BW · 77mins

The romance of a youthful small-town couple is shattered when she is swept off her feet and elopes with a writer. Widowed ten years later, she returns home with her daughter and, to the disapproval of the over-protective townsfolk, tries to take up with her former love, now a college professor. This is basically soap opera elevated by a first-rate cast, with Henry Fonda and Joan Bennett as the lovers trying to resurrect their relationship. It is co-directed by Joshua Logan, making his first film.

Joan Bennett *Julie Wier Shaw* • Henry Fonda *Ives Towner* • Louise Platt *Brenda Lane* • Alan Marshal *Michael Shaw* • Dame May Whitty *Aunt William* • Alan Baxter *Tony* ■ *Dir* Arthur Ripley, Joshua Logan • *Scr* David Hertz, from the novel *Summer Lightning* by Allene Corliss • *Cinematographer* Hal Mohr

I, Monster ★★ 12

Horror 1971 · UK · Colour · 77mins

Dr Jekyll and Mr Hyde become Dr Marlowe and Mr Blake in a vapid attempt to give a Freudian psychological interpretation to Robert Louis Stevenson's oft-told tale. Christopher Lee is convincing as the doctor meddling with a schizophrenic formula, and the Victorian London atmosphere is well captured, but director Stephen Weeks's inexperience means that any complex themes are quickly abandoned, and the end result is flatter than you might expect. ▭

Christopher Lee *Dr Marlowe/Mr Blake* • Peter Cushing *Utterson* • Mike Raven *Enfield* • Richard Hurndall *Lanyan* • George Merritt *Poole* • Kenneth J Warren *Dean* • Susan Jameson *Diane* ■ *Dir* Stephen Weeks • *Scr* Milton Subotsky

I Never Promised You a Rose Garden ★★★★ 18

Drama 1977 · US · Colour · 88mins

Anthony Page's adaptation of Joanne Greenberg's semi-autobiographical bestseller never explores mental illness in any real depth, but is still a highly sympathetic study of someone facing up to its consequences. This Roger Corman production is steered away from any melodramatic pitfalls by Kathleen Quinlan's exemplary performance, as a teenage schizophrenic plagued by sexually charged fantasies and recurrent thoughts of suicide. Bibi Andersson is equally impressive as her intuitive psychiatrist, and the contributions of the supporting cast are universally excellent – even though some of Quinlan's fellow inmates are played for dubious light relief. ▭

Bibi Andersson *Dr Fried* • Kathleen Quinlan *Deborah Blake* • Ben Piazza *Mr Blake* • Lorraine Gary *Mrs Blake* • Darlene Craviotto *Carla* • Reni Santoni *Hobbs* • Susan Tyrrell *Lee* ■ *Dir* Anthony Page • *Scr* Lewis John Carlino, Gavin Lambert, from a novel by Hannah Green [Joanne Greenberg]

I Never Sang for My Father ★★★★

Drama 1969 · US · Colour · 92mins

An immensely moving screen version of Robert Anderson's sensitive play, scripted by the playwright himself, giving a superb career-best role to Melvyn Douglas as an ageing, domineering father. The truly remarkable aspect of this film is that it came out of a Hollywood not exactly noted for making movies about real-life responsibilities, such as caring for ageing parents. Gene Hackman, as the suffering adult son, and Estelle Parsons, as the daughter made an outcast because she married a Jew, are also outstanding. Gilbert Cates's direction manages to make this both depressing and uplifting at the same time, and, though resolutely theatrical, it remains compulsively watchable.

Melvyn Douglas *Tom Garrison* • Gene Hackman *Gene Garrison* • Dorothy Stickney *Margaret Garrison* • Estelle Parsons *Alice* • Elizabeth Hubbard *Peggy* • Lovelady Powell *Norma* ■ *Dir* Gilbert Cates • *Scr* Robert W Anderson, from his play

I Only Want You to Love Me ★★★

Drama based on a true story
1976 · W Ger · Colour · 104mins

Made for television during a creative crisis on *Satan's Brew*, this is one of Rainer Werner Fassbinder's most accessible, yet deceptively simple films. Based on actual events, this intellectually rigorous and expertly staged melodrama not only explores the modern tendency towards the breakdown of familial communication, but also the way in which material gestures have come to replace demonstrations of affection. Workaholic builder Vitus Zeplichal cuts a genuinely tragic figure as his emotional inarticulacy reduces him from doting son to crazed killer. In German with English subtitles.

Vitus Zeplichal *Peter* • Elke Aberle *Erika* • Alexander Allerson *Father* • Erni Mangold *Mother* • Johanna Hofer *Erika's grandmother* • Wolfgang Hess *Building superintendent* ■ *Dir/Scr* Rainer Werner Fassbinder

I Ought to Be in Pictures ★★★★ 15

Comedy 1982 · US · Colour · 102mins

Neil Simon has adapted this all-laughing, all-crying drama from his own stage play. It comes complete with a performance by Dinah Manoff which avoids direct sentimentality – but which still involves us emotionally – as the Hollywood-struck girl. She travels to Tinseltown to track down her father (Walter Matthau) who's now living with a forgiving girlfriend (Ann-Margret). He used to be a screenwriter but these days seems interested mainly in drinking and gambling. Herbert Ross directs with level-headed cool, letting Simon's script do all the work. ▭

Walter Matthau *Herbert Tucker* • Ann-Margret *Stephanie* • Dinah Manoff *Libby* • Lance Guest *Gordon* • Lewis Smith *Soldier* • Martin Ferrero *Monte Del Rey* ■ *Dir* Herbert Ross • *Scr* Neil Simon, from his play

IP5 ★ 15

Drama 1992 · Fr · Colour · 114mins

The French cinema movement called *cinema du look* came to a shuddering halt with this atrocious, self-referential road movie from Jean-Jacques Beineix. Sadly it was the swansong of Yves Montand, who died just days after "dying" in this film and whose gaunt expression is far more haunting than any of the director's stylised, yet undeniably handsome, imagery. Half-baked social and ecological theories abound, as Montand joins graffiti artist Olivier Martinez and rapper Sekkou Sall in a search of the Island of Pachyderms (hence the film's title, this being Beineix's fifth film), where he spent his idyllic, if incestuous, childhood. Alternately painful and embarrassing to watch. In French with English subtitles. ▭

Yves Montand *Léon Marcel* • Olivier Martinez *Tony* • Sekkou Sall *Jockey* • Geraldine Pailhas *Gloria* • Colette Renard *Clarisse/Monique* ■ *Dir* Jean-Jacques Beineix • *Scr* Jean-Jacques Beineix, Jacques Forgeas, from a film by Jacques Forgeas

IQ ★★★★ U
Romantic comedy
1995 · US · Colour · 91mins

When Meg Ryan pulls into Tim Robbins's garage, it's love at first sight for the mechanic. But this romantic tale has an added twist, for Ryan happens to be the niece of one Albert Einstein (as portrayed by Walter Matthau). Since Ryan is engaged to the pompous Stephen Fry (an unlikely bit of casting), Matthau decides to use his grey cells in the match-making department – a different theory of relativity – and help Robbins win the affections of Ryan. It is immaculately set in the fifties and the stars are well supported by the likes of Gene Saks (who directed Matthau in *The Odd Couple*) and Lou Jacobi, making it another treat from the director of *Roxanne*, Fred Schepisi.

Meg Ryan *Catherine Boyd* • Tim Robbins *Ed Walters* • Walter Matthau *Albert Einstein* • Lou Jacobi *Kurt Godel* • Gene Saks *Boris Podolsky* • Joseph Maher *Nathan Liebknecht* • Stephen Fry *James Moreland* • Tony Shalhoub *Bob Walters* ■ *Dir* Fred Schepisi • *Scr* Andy Breckman, Michael Leeson, from a story by Andy Breckman

I Remember Mama ★★★★ U
Drama
1948 · US · BW · 128mins

San Francisco in the 1900s is the setting for this reassuringly cosy story of a family of Norwegian immigrants and their struggles for survival. Irene Dunne brings her usual class and charm to the role of the matriarch who holds it all together and Barbara Bel Geddes is the daughter who records it all in her diary. Directed by George Stevens with a warm heart and a diverting way with a cliché, it also has a knockout performance by Cedric Hardwicke as a rundown old actor who reads from his own (unpublished) works but never seems to be able to pay the rent.

Irene Dunne *Mama* • Barbara Bel Geddes *Katrin* • Oscar Homolka *Uncle Chris* • Philip Dorn *Papa* • Sir Cedric Hardwicke [Cedric Hardwicke] *Mr Hyde* • Edgar Bergen *Mr Thorkelson* ■ *Dir* George Stevens • *Scr* DeWitt Bodeen, from a play by John Van Druten, from the novel *Mama's Bank Account* by Kathryn Forbes

I Saw What You Did ★★
Thriller
1965 · US · BW · 81mins

Two teenage girls (Andi Garrett, Sarah Lane), alone one night in a large and fairly isolated house, play a prank on a number of strangers by phoning random numbers and announcing, "I saw what you did, I know who you are." When one of the calls is taken by a man who has just murdered his wife, the joke turns sour. Made by schlock-horror merchant William Castle, this routine suspense programmer does have its moments, as the wife-killer (John Ireland) sets out to find the perpetrator of the threatening phone call. Joan Crawford is also on hand to emote as Ireland's demanding lover.

Joan Crawford *Amy Nelson* • John Ireland *Steve Marak* • Leif Erickson *Dave Mannering* • Patricia Breslin *Ellie Mannering* • Andi Garrett *Libby* • Sharyl Locke *Tess* • Sarah Lane *Kit* ■ *Dir* William Castle • *Scr* William P McGivern, from the novel *Out of the Dark* by Ursula Curtiss

I See a Dark Stranger ★★★ U
Second World War drama
1946 · UK · BW · 107mins

Having penned *The Lady Vanishes* for Alfred Hitchcock and *Night Train to Munich* for Carol Reed, Frank Launder and Sidney Gilliat struck out on their own for this tale of wartime treachery. But uncertain handling mars an otherwise diverting romp, in which Deborah Kerr's Irish republican sympathies lead her, unwittingly, to spy for the Nazis. Her feisty devotion to the cause carries the film through its more implausible moments, but she struggles to get much response from an unusually taciturn Trevor Howard. A touch too clever for its own good, but rattling entertainment all the same.

Deborah Kerr *Bridie Quilty* • Trevor Howard *Lieutenant David Bayne* • Raymond Huntley *Miller* • Liam Redmond *Timothy* ■ *Dir* Frank Launder • *Scr* Wolfgang Wilhelm, Sidney Gilliat, Frank Launder

I See Ice ★★ U
Comedy
1938 · UK · BW · 78mins

This typical George Formby vehicle sees the Lancashire comedian cast as a property man in an ice ballet production who, in his spare time, is an obsessive amateur photographer. Sporting a bow tie that conceals a mini-camera, George sets forth to snap candid photos and gets in all sorts of comical messes. Fast-paced, British comedy with all the usual ingredients of the time: romance, gangsters, misunderstandings and buckets of slapstick. An undemanding, unexceptional presentation but not without a certain period charm. ▭

George Formby *George Bright* • Kay Walsh *Judy Gaye* • Betty Stockfeld *Mrs Hunter* • Cyril Ritchard *Paul Martine* • Garry Marsh *Galloway* ■ *Dir* Anthony Kimmins • *Scr* Anthony Kimmins, Austin Melford

I Shot Andy Warhol ★★★★ 18
Biographical drama
1995 · US/UK · Colour · 99mins

Valerie Solanas was famous for 15 minutes when she tried to assassinate Pop Art king Andy Warhol in 1968. Director Mary Harron's endlessly fascinating case history delves into the complex personality of the lesbian feminist author and finally makes sense of what tipped her over the edge into paranoid fantasy. Rarely do films capture a cultural era as precisely as this evocative saga, which does it masterfully with a sure, sophisticated style and with wit and drama to spare. Lili Taylor is flawless as the angrily disruptive urban guerrilla and Jared Harris is just perfect as the white-wigged Warhol. It's Stephen Dorff's electrifying take on transvestite superstar Candy Darling, however, that is certain to swivel most heads. Contains swearing, sex scenes and drug abuse. ▭

Lili Taylor *Valerie Solanas* • Jared Harris *Andy Warhol* • Stephen Dorff *Candy Darling* • Martha Plimpton *Stevie* • Danny Morgenstern *Jeremiah Newton* • Lothaire Bluteau *Maurice Girodias* • Tahnee Welch *Viva* ■ *Dir* Mary Harron • *Scr* Mary Harron, Daniel Minahan • *Music* John Cale

I Shot Jesse James ★★★ U
Western
1949 · US · BW · 72mins

Samuel Fuller gained his first directing opportunity with this low-budget western told in the emphatic, headline style for which he would become noted. His script takes a characteristically offbeat approach to a familiar situation – the assassination of Jesse James – by telling it from the point of view of Bob Ford, played by John Ireland. He was the "dirty little coward" of ballad fame who took advantage of Jesse's friendship and hospitality to shoot him in the back of the head. Fuller attempts to make it the tragedy of someone who has killed a man he loved, but such a flawed character evokes little concern.

Preston Foster *John Kelley* • Barbara Britton *Cynthy Waters* • John Ireland *Bob Ford* • Reed Hadley *Jesse James* • J Edward Bromberg *Kane* • Victor Kilian *Soapy* ■ *Dir* Samuel Fuller • *Scr* Samuel Fuller, from articles by Homer Croy

I Spy Returns ★★ PG
Spy adventure
1994 · US · Colour · 92mins

This TV movie reunites Bill Cosby and Robert Culp, the stars of the sixties *I Spy* series that was notable for its pairing of a black and a white actor. Over a quarter of a century after the last show, Cosby and Culp return to secret service duty, as they babysit their offspring on their first assignment in Vienna. Director Jerry London, whose finest hour was the epic mini-series *Shogun*, makes the most of the city's stunning sights, while generating enough tension to offset the quips. Culp and Cosby reel back the years, but the joke does wear a little thin by the end. ▭

Bill Cosby *Alexander "Scotty" Scott* • Robert Culp *Kelly Robinson* • George Newbern *Bennett Robinson* • Salli Richardson *Nicole Scott* • Jonathan Hyde *Baroodi* ■ *Dir* Jerry London • *Scr* Michael Norell from characters created by Morton Fine and David Friedkin

I Start Counting ★★
Crime drama
1970 · UK · Colour · 107mins

Director David Greene forged a reputation for thrills with *The Shuttered Room* and *The Strange Affair*, but he taxed the patience with this manipulative whodunit. There are so many dead ends in this adaptation of Audrey Erskine Lindop's sinuous novel that it soon becomes a matter of indifference whether Bryan Marshall is responsible for the series of sex attacks near his home. Much more intriguing, however, is the effect the slayings have on his foster sister, Jenny Agutter, whose hero worship is both disturbing and potentially deadly. Agutter was even more impressive in her next two pictures, *The Railway Children* and *Walkabout*.

Jenny Agutter *Wynne* • Bryan Marshall *George* • Clare Sutcliffe *Corrine* • Simon Ward *Conductor* • Gregory Phillips *Len* • Lana Morris *Leonie* ■ *Dir* David Greene • *Scr* Harris Richard, from a novel by Audrey Erskine Lindop

I Still Dream of Jeannie ★★
Comedy
1991 · US · Colour · 96mins

Barbara Eden reprises her original TV role as Jeannie, the glamorous genie with an astronaut husband who was never allowed to show her navel. Despite playing the role for five years in the sixties, and again in a 1985 TV pilot for a proposed comeback series, she clearly can't resist another stab. Reluctantly convinced that her husband will not be returning from his last mission, Eden has to find a new master or be forced to return to Mesopotamia. Hardly the most politically correct of scenarios, but what's a girl to do? Follow her original co-star Larry Hagman and find a popular soap opera would be good advice on this unfunny evidence.

Barbara Eden *Jeannie Nelson/Jeannie II* • Bill Daily *Roger Healey* • Ken Kercheval *Mr Simpson* • Christopher Bolton *Tony Jr* • Al Waxman *General Wescott* ■ *Dir* Joseph Scanlan [Joseph L Scanlan] • *Scr* April Kelly, from characters created by Sidney Sheldon

I Still Know What You Did Last Summer ★ 18
Horror
1998 · US/Ger · Colour · 96mins

Noisy, flashy and deadly dull, *Judge Dredd* director Danny Cannon's sequel to *I Know What You Did Last Summer* features the return of college beauty in peril Jennifer Love Hewitt, this time fighting off the masked fisherman during hurricane season in the Bahamas. Without the horror-nerd energy of co-writer Kevin Williamson's original script, this plotless slab of wet T-shirt terror drearily alternates between the sou'westered spectre freaking out his victims with fake scares and viciously hooking them by the throat. Dismal. ▭ **DVD**

Jennifer Love Hewitt *Julie James* • Freddie Prinze Jr *Ray Bronson* • Brandy Norwood [Brandy] *Karla Wilson* • Mekhi Phifer *Tyrell* • Muse Watson *Ben Willis* • Bill Cobbs *Estes* ■ *Dir* Danny Cannon • *Scr* Trey Callaway, Kevin Williamson, Lois Duncan

I Take This Woman ★
Drama
1940 · US · BW · 97mins

Intended as a vehicle for MGM's latest acquisition, Hedy Lamarr, this quickly became one of those films notorious for its troubled and protracted production history. Lamarr is the suicidal girl who marries Spencer Tracy to forget her failed romance with Kent Taylor. Tracy, a physician committed to his work with the poor, now finds himself transformed into a fashionable doctor in order to provide his wife with the luxuries to which she is accustomed. The two stars are excellent but the material is unbearably trite.

Spencer Tracy *Karl Decker* • Hedy Lamarr *Georgi Gragore* • Verree Teasdale *Mme Maresca* • Kent Taylor *Phil Mayberry* • Mona Barrie *Sandra Mayberry* • Paul Cavanagh *Bill Rodgers* ■ *Dir* WS Van Dyke • *Scr* James Kevin McGuiness, from a story by Charles MacArthur

I Thank a Fool ★★
Drama
1962 · UK · Colour · 99mins

Relishably hoary old melodrama based on a novel in the *Jane Eyre* mould by

Audrey Erskine Lindop. Woman with a past (Susan Hayward) becomes entangled with her old nemesis, barrister (Peter Finch), and his mentally ill wife (Diane Cilento). But who is doing what to whom? Euthanasia always provides a controversial plot point; the rest is murder/mystery from another age, with ripe dialogue by *Ben-Hur* writer Karl Tunberg. The stellar cast do their best in one of MGM's prestige British productions, but audiences were unimpressed.

Susan Hayward *Christine Allison* • Peter Finch *Stephen Dane* • Diane Cilento *Liane Dane* • Cyril Cusack *Captain Ferris* • Kieron Moore *Roscoe* • Athene Seyler *Aunt Heather* • Richard Wattis *Ebblington* • Peter Sallis *Sleazy doctor* • Joan Hickson *Landlady* ■ *Dir* Robert Stevens • *Scr* Karl Tunberg, from a novel by Audrey Erskine Lindop

I Thank You ★★ U
Musical comedy   1941 · UK · BW · 77mins

If there's one genre in which the British cinema has a tendency to fail, it's the musical comedy. Here, Marcel Varnel has an expert cast at his disposal, but not even Arthur Askey and Richard Murdoch, plus Will Hay old boys Moore Marriott and Graham Moffatt, can warm up this tepid "upstairs-downstairs" charade.

Arthur Askey *Arthur* • Richard Murdoch *Stinker* • Lily Morris *Lady Randall* • Moore Marriott *Pop Bennett* • Graham Moffatt *Albert* • Peter Gawthorne *Dr Pope* • Kathleen Harrison *Cook* • Felix Aylmer *Henry Potter* ■ *Dir* Marcel Varnel • *Scr* Val Guest, Marriott Edgar, from a story by Howard Irving Young

I, the Jury ★
Crime thriller   1953 · US · BW · 87mins

Mickey Spillane was a former trampoline artist and narcotics agent who turned to thriller writing in 1947 with *I, the Jury*. At the time, the novel's violence was shocking, as was the blinkered morality of its thuggish private eye Mike Hammer as he avenges his friend's murder. UA signed Spillane to a four-film deal. They may have lavished 3-D on the movie but the cast is barely adequate and the novel is watered down. It flopped but Hammer's next cinematic exploit, *Kiss Me Deadly*, was a masterpiece.

Biff Elliot *Mike Hammer* • Preston Foster *Captain Pat Chambers* • Peggie Castle *Charlotte Manning* • Margaret Sheridan *Velda* • Alan Reed *George Kalecki* • Frances Osborne *Myrna* ■ *Dir* Harry Essex • *Scr* Harry Essex, from a novel by Mickey Spillane

I, the Jury ★★ 18
Crime thriller   1982 · US · Colour · 102mins

A remake of the first Mike Hammer movie, updating Mickey Spillane's yarn so that Hammer's murdered friend is now a Vietnam veteran. The sex and violence is closer to Spillane's original and the movie fittingly has the ambience of a penny dreadful and a trashy B-movie. As Hammer, Armand Assante also looks the part – menacing and thick – and the body count is high. The women in the cast seem simply required to get their clothes off as often as possible.

Armand Assante *Mike Hammer* • Barbara Carrera *Dr Charlotte Bennett* • Laurene Landon *Velda* • Alan King *Charles Kalecki* •

Geoffrey Lewis *Joe Butler* • Paul Sorvino *Detective Pat Chambers* ■ *Dir* Richard T Heffron • *Scr* Larry Cohen, from the novel by Mickey Spillane

I, the Worst of All ★★★★
Historical drama
1990 · Arg · Colour · 105mins

Argentinian director Maria Luisa Bemberg is probably best known in this country for *Miss Mary*, a stylish period tale starring Julie Christie. This historical drama has none of the gloss of that film yet, with its stark and striking lighting designs, its symbolically lavish costumes and delicately nuanced performances, *I, the Worst of All* is a deeply affecting study of Sister Juana Ines de la Cruz, one of the most important religious poets of the 17th century and the author of the anonymously ascribed *Defence of Women*. Recalling some of the themes of Alain Cavalier's *Thérèse*, this is a brave and beautiful film. In Spanish with English subtitles.

Assumpta Serna *Sister Juana Ines de la Cruz* • Dominique Sanda *Vice-Reine Maria Luisa* • Hector Alterio *Viceroy* • Lautaro Murua *Archbishop of Mexico* • Alberto Segado *Father Miranda* ■ *Dir* Maria Luisa Bemberg • *Scr* Maria Luisa Bemberg, Antonio Larreta, from the essay *The Traps of Faith* by Octavio Paz, from the book *Sor Juana: Her Life and Her World* by Octavio Paz

I Wake Up Screaming ★★★★ PG
Film noir   1941 · US · BW · 78mins

A great title (though it was changed to *Hotspot* in the UK) for what in hindsight turned out to be one of 20th Century-Fox's key *films noirs*. It contains a quintessential plot about a beautiful murdered actress and a grab-bag of seedy, unusual suspects. A crackingly good film, superbly cast with forties icons such as Victor Mature, Elisha Cook Jr and Laird Cregar, and a sympathetic non-singing Betty Grable is also excellent as the victim's sister. Added resonance comes from the fact that the dead girl is Carole Landis, who herself died in tragic circumstances. In all, a clever and fast-moving atmospheric thriller with a sordid undertone that leaves you wanting more.

Betty Grable *Jill Lynn* • Victor Mature *Frankie Christopher* • Carole Landis *Vicky Lynn* • Laird Cregar *Ed Cornell* • William Gargan *Jerry McDonald* • Alan Mowbray *Robin Ray* • Elisha Cook Jr *Harry Williams* ■ *Dir* H Bruce Humberstone • *Scr* Dwight Taylor, from the novel by Steve Fisher

I Walk Alone ★★★
Crime melodrama   1947 · US · BW · 97mins

Burt Lancaster and Kirk Douglas (both still relative novices here) give solid performances in this bruising *film noir* about ex-bootleggers who fall out over their spoils. Wendell Corey also impresses as the spineless accountant, who is murdered after helping Douglas build his empire while Lancaster is doing time. Based on Theodore Reeves's play *Beggars Are Coming to Town*, the action is kept nicely on the boil by Byron Haskin, who handles the violent set pieces and the romantic interludes and the musical numbers with equal assurance.

Burt Lancaster *Frankie Madison* • Kirk Douglas *Noll Turner* • Lizabeth Scott *Kay Lawrence* • Wendell Corey *Dave* • Kristine Miller *Mrs Richardson* • George Rigaud *Maurice* ■ *Dir* Byron Haskin • *Scr* Charles Schnee, Robert Smith, John Bright, from the play *Beggars Are Coming to Town* by Theodore Reeves

I Walk the Line ★★ 15
Crime thriller   1970 · US · Colour · 92mins

When upright Tennessee sheriff Gregory Peck falls for a white trash, in-bred moonshiner's daughter (Tuesday Weld), his career goes quickly on the skids. There's more than a touch of Tennessee Williams's *Baby Doll* to this torrid tale, and maybe a dash of *In the Heat of the Night* as well, but Peck seems badly miscast and that cripples the story from the beginning. On the plus side, there are some hokey country tunes from Johnny Cash, and director John Frankenheimer creates a convincing Deep South ambience despite the fact that much of the film was shot in northern California.

Gregory Peck *Sheriff Henry Tawes* • Tuesday Weld *Alma McCain* • Estelle Parsons *Ellen Haney* • Ralph Meeker *Carl McCain* • Lonny Chapman *Bascomb* • Charles Durning *Hunnicutt* • Jeff Dalton *Clay McCain* ■ *Dir* John Frankenheimer • *Scr* Alvin Sargent, from the novel *An Exile* by Madison Jones

I Walked with a Zombie ★★★★ PG
Horror   1943 · US · BW · 65mins

Is the invalid wife of a Haitian plantation owner (Tom Conway) really the victim of a voodoo curse? In her quest to find out, nurse Frances Dee uncovers dark family secrets in cult producer Val Lewton's ingenious reworking of *Jane Eyre*. Jacques Tourneur's direction creates palpable fear and tension in a typically low-key nightmare from the Lewton fright factory. The lighting, shadows, exotic setting and music all contribute to the immensely disturbing atmosphere, making this stunning piece of poetic horror a classic of the genre.

Tom Conway *Paul Holland* • Frances Dee *Betsy* • James Ellison *Wesley Rand* • Edith Barrett *Mrs Rand* • Christine Gordon *Jessica Holland* • James Bell *Dr Maxwell* • Richard Abrams *Clement* ■ *Dir* Jacques Tourneur • *Scr* Curt Siodmak, Ardel Wray, from a story by Inez Wallace • *Editor* Mark Robson

I Wanna Hold Your Hand ★★★
Comedy   1978 · US · Colour · 98mins

This gentle comedy, set in 1964, focuses on four New Jersey teenagers who are obsessed with meeting the Beatles, just as the Fab Four are about to make their debut on TV's *Ed Sullivan Show*. You don't get the Beatles of course, but there are lots of shots of winkle-pickered shoes and the movie has bags of ingenuity and charm. Of course, if Zemeckis remade it today he could have the real Beatles pasted into the story, in the manner of the special effects he developed in *Forrest Gump*. Steven Spielberg acted as executive producer.

Nancy Allen *Pam Mitchell* • Bobby DiCicco *Tony Smerko* • Marc McClure *Larry Dubois* • Susan Kendall Newman *Janis Goldman* •

Theresa Saldana *Grace Corrigan* • Wendie Jo Sperber *Rosie Petrofsky* ■ *Dir* Robert Zemeckis • *Scr* Robert Zemeckis, Bob Gale • *Executive Producer* Steven Spielberg • *Music* The Beatles

I Want Him Back ★★ 15
Romantic comedy
1990 · US · Colour · 88mins

Elliott Gould and Brenda Vaccaro are teamed for the third time after *I Love My Wife* and *Capricorn One* in this frequently embarrassing TV movie, which also rejoices in the title of *Stolen: One Husband*. As the spurned wife who embarks, with her friend Vaccaro in tow, on a tug-of-war to win back her menopausal husband, Valerie Harper plays every scene at full throttle, thus frittering away any sympathy we may have for the plight of her character. After an intriguing directorial debut with *Sticky Fingers*, this is a disappointing effort from former actress Catlin Adams.

Valerie Harper *Katherine Slade* • Elliott Gould *Martin Slade* • Brenda Vaccaro *Lisa Jarrett* • Bruce Davison *Dr Peter Foley* • Brenda Bakke *Samantha Laurel* • Julie Warner *Jennie Slade* ■ *Dir* Catlin Adams • *Scr* Anna Sandor, William Gough

I Want to Go Home ★
Satirical comedy   1989 · Fr · Colour · 110mins

This could be called "An American Cartoonist in Paris". Written by American humourist Jules Feiffer, it stars Adolph Green, co-writer of *On the Town*, *Singin' in the Rain* and *The Band Wagon*. Despite this obvious talent it really doesn't work at all, not even when Gérard Depardieu crops up as a university don. The involvement of Alain Resnais – one of the most deeply intellectual of French directors – is explained by his lifelong love of comics: he toiled for years to make a film of the cartoon-strip *Harry Dickson* with Dirk Bogarde.

Adolph Green *Joey Wellman* • Gérard Depardieu *Christian Gauthier* • Linda Lavin *Lena Apthrop* • Micheline Presle *Isabelle Gauthier* • John Ashton *Harry Dempsey* ■ *Dir* Alain Resnais • *Scr* Jules Feiffer

I Want to Live! ★★★★ 15
Biographical crime melodrama
1958 · US · BW · 116mins

Four-time loser Susan Hayward finally won an Oscar for her riveting portrayal of Barbara Graham, whose wretched life saw her descend into prostitution, fraud, perjury and drug addiction before she was finally convicted of murder. She was framed, according to the stance taken here on the notorious 1955 case, reinforcing the anti-capital punishment argument of director Robert Wise's campaigning opus. It's the depiction of Graham's brave march to her gas chamber execution that won over Academy Award voters to Hayward's side. In those classic moments, she expertly communicates the cruelty and criminality of the death penalty.

Susan Hayward *Barbara Graham* • Simon Oakland *Ed Montgomery* • Virginia Vincent *Peg* • Theodore Bikel *Carl Palmberg* • Wesley Lau *Henry Graham* ■ *Dir* Robert Wise • *Scr* Nelson Gidding, Don Mankiewicz, from articles by Ed Montgomery, from letters by Barbara Graham

I Want What I Want ★

Drama   1971 · UK · Colour · 105mins

Is it strange for a film producer to cast his own wife as a man who has a sex change operation? You can judge for yourself after watching this movie, in which producer Raymond Stross finds such a role for his spouse Anne Heywood – a former beauty queen whose real name was Violet Pretty. Heywood starts out as a Roy and ends up as a Wendy but nothing – not even some hideous make-up, silly clothes and a deep voice – can disguise the fact that she's a woman from start to finish. Not a very helpful contribution to a little-understood subject.

Anne Heywood *Roy/Wendy* • Harry Andrews *Father* • Jill Bennett *Margaret Stevenson* • Paul Rogers *Mr Waites* • Michael Coles *Frank* ■ *Dir* John Dexter • *Scr* Gillian Freeman, from a novel by Geoff Brown

I Want You ★★★ U

Drama   1951 · US · BW · 97mins

Producer Samuel Goldwyn's attempt to follow up the critical and popular success of his seven Oscar-winning 1946 masterpiece *The Best Years of Our Lives* resulted in this similarly themed movie, this time portraying the effects of the Korean War on American small-town families. The screenplay by novelist Irwin Shaw (*The Young Lions*, *Two Weeks in Another Town*) is excellent, and the performances ring touching and true. This is very much a period artefact, fascinating to watch today and, incidentally, inspired by the induction of Goldwyn's own son. The title is the US Army's recruiting slogan.

Dana Andrews *Martin Greer* • Dorothy McGuire *Nancy Greer* • Farley Granger *Jack Greer* • Peggy Dow *Carrie Turner* • Robert Keith *Thomas Greer* • Mildred Dunnock *Sarah Greer* ■ *Dir* Mark Robson • *Scr* Irwin Shaw, from stories by Edward Newhouse

I Want You ★★ 18

Thriller   1998 · UK · Colour · 83mins

Michael Winterbottom's turgid sexual melodrama is meant to be a deep psychological study into erotic compulsion, manipulation, bitterness and betrayal, but the director misses every target by miles. After serving nine years for murder, Alessandro Nivola heads back to his home town to pursue ex-girlfriend Rachel Weisz. Something unspeakable connects them – but what? The answer is easy to guess, and it's not worth wading through all the empty emotions and dire dialogue to find out. Contains swearing and sex scenes. ▭

Labina Mitevska *Smokey* • Rachel Weisz *Helen* • Alessandro Nivola *Martin* • Luka Petrusic *Honda* • Carmen Ejogo *Amber* • Ben Daniels *DJ Bob* ■ *Dir* Michael Winterbottom • *Scr* Eoin McNamee

I Wanted to See Angels ★★★

Drama   1992 · Rus · Colour · 83mins

Nothing could prepare you for the stark portrait of Moscow on the edge painted here by Sergei Bodrov. Essentially, this is a grim love story in which a disillusioned biker and a street kid cling together for survival in a place held hostage by the latest fad and by the forces of crime. But what is most striking about the film is Bodrov's gritty style and his determination to show the seediness and the hopelessness of Boris Yeltsin's Russia. In Russian with English subtitles.

Alexei Baranov • Natasha Ginko • Lea Akeojakova • Alex Jarkov ■ *Dir* Sergei Bodrov • *Scr* Sergei Bodrov, Carolyn Cavallero

I Wanted Wings ★★

Action drama   1941 · US · BW · 133mins

Ray Milland, William Holden and Wayne Morris join the army air corps and head for Texas for their training as fighter pilots. The script – co-written by future Bond writer Richard Maibaum – is top-heavy with plot as the three men work out their romantic entanglements, learn to fly, bond in buddy-buddy fashion and still keep us guessing as to who survives. Veronica Lake (billing herself as that for the first time) is the local beauty, though director Mitchell Leisen apparently thought she had no talent and bullied her, so that the scene when she goes hysterical in a plane was hardly acting at all.

Ray Milland *Jeff Young* • William Holden (1) *Al Ludlow* • Wayne Morris *Tom Cassidy* • Brian Donlevy *Capt Mercer* • Constance Moore *Carolyn Bartlett* • Veronica Lake *Sally Vaughn* ■ *Dir* Mitchell Leisen • *Scr* Richard Maibaum, Beirne Lay Jr, Sig Herzig, from a story by Eleanore Griffin, Frank Wead, from the non-fiction book by Lt Beirne Lay Jr • *Special Effects* Gordon Jennings, Faricot Edouart, Louis Mesenkop

I Was a Communist for the FBI ★★ U

Thriller   1951 · US · BW · 81mins

Although based on a *Saturday Evening Post* article given by undercover agent Matt Cvetic to journalist Pete Martin, this Red-baiting propaganda was clearly couched in fictional terms, thus making its Oscar nomination in the documentary feature category all the more puzzling. Shot as a *film noir*, it's too soused with political bile to be an effective thriller, no matter how much director Gordon Douglas cranks up the suspense. Frank Lovejoy is a steelworker recruited by the FBI to infiltrate his communist union but his tepid romance with communist teacher Dorothy Hart is an unnecessary distraction. As an insight into the hysteria that gripped America in the early days of the Cold War, however, it's an invaluable document.

Frank Lovejoy *Matt Cvetic* • Dorothy Hart *Eve Merrick* • Philip Carey *Mason* • Dick Webb *Crowley* • James Millican *Jim Blandon* • Ron Hagerty *Dick Cvetic* ■ *Dir* Gordon Douglas • *Scr* Crane Wilbur, from the article *I Posed as a Communist for the FBI* by Matt Cvetic, Pete Martin

I Was a Male War Bride ★★★★★ U

Romantic comedy   1949 · US · BW · 101mins

A hilarious comedy of errors, with French army officer Cary Grant marrying American WAC Ann Sheridan and attempting to get to the States using the postwar "war bride" bill. Director Howard Hawks wrings every ounce of humour from this bizarre situation, making splendid use of European locations (with interiors filmed at Shepperton Studios), and his cast could scarcely be improved upon. This is one of Grant's cleverest, most subtle performances, but the breezy Sheridan is more than a match for him: just watch that timing in the "sleeplessness in the guest house" sequence, and the increasing sense of frustration as an uncredited Lionel Murton tells Grant again and again, "you can't sleep here" (the film's British release title).

Cary Grant *Captain Henri Rochard* • Ann Sheridan *Lieutenant Catherine Gates* • William Neff *Captain Jack Rumsey* • Marion Marshall *WAC* • Randy Stuart *WAC* • Eugene Gericke *Tony Jowitt* ■ *Dir* Howard Hawks • *Scr* Charles Lederer, Leonard Spigelgass, Hagar Wilde, from the article *Male War Bride Trial to Army* in the *Baltimore Sun* by Henri Rochard

I Was a Shoplifter ★★

Crime drama   1950 · US · BW · 74mins

A gang blackmails kleptomaniacs into becoming professional thieves in this moderately engaging drama. Scott Brady stars as an undercover cop, while Mona Freeman plays the judge's daughter who is recruited by the ring. The film was denounced as "a course in shoplifting" by a censor in Atlanta, who promptly banned it. Interest is added by the appearances of two future stars: Tony (here Anthony) Curtis as a lecherous killer, and Rock Hudson as a store detective.

Scott Brady *Jeff Andrews* • Mona Freeman *Faye Burton* • Andrea King *Ina Perdue* • Anthony Curtis [Tony Curtis] *Pepe* • Charles Drake *Herb Klaxon* • Gregg Martell *The champ* • Rock Hudson *Si Swanson* ■ *Dir* Charles Lamont • *Scr* Irwin Gielgud, from his story

I Was a Spy ★★ U

Spy drama   1934 · UK · BW · 86mins

Fans of vintage British cinema will enjoy this sprightly espionage yarn, set during the First World War and bearing a close resemblance to the Mata Hari legend. The lovely Madeleine Carroll plays Martha Cnockhaert, a Belgian nurse who goes undercover with fellow spy Herbert Marshall and gets caught trying to sabotage a German munitions dump. Conrad Veidt, exiled from his homeland following the victory of the Nazis, plays a villainous German officer. Carroll went on to work with Hitchcock on *The 39 Steps* and *The Secret Agent*. ▭

Madeleine Carroll *Martha Cnockhaert McKenna* • Conrad Veidt *Commandant Oberaertz* • Herbert Marshall *Stephan* • Gerald Du Maurier *Doctor* • Edmund Gwenn *Burgomaster* • Nigel Bruce *Scotty* ■ *Dir* Victor Saville • *Scr* WP Lipscomb

I Was a Teenage Frankenstein ★★★ 15

Horror   1957 · US · BW and Colour · 73mins

If *I Was a Teenage Werewolf* has one of the most famous exploitation titles of all time, this quickie sequel contains some of the best-remembered dialogue: "Answer me, you have a civil tongue in your head. I know, I sewed it in there." As the resident evil scientist, horror dependable Whit Bissell swaps lucrative lycanthropy for ugly monster-making using car-crash cadavers. Immensely idiotic, naturally, but sometimes incredibly effective (especially the lively, colour climax), this lurid hokum has an unexpectedly neat line in self-parody. ▭

Whit Bissell *Professor Frankenstein* • Phyllis Coates *Margaret* • Robert Burton *Dr Karlton* • Gary Conway *Teenage Monster* • George Lynn *Sergeant Burns* • John Cliff *Sergeant McAffee* • Marshall Bradford *Dr Randolph* ■ *Dir* Herbert L Strock • *Scr* Kenneth Langtry

I Was a Teenage Werewolf ★★ 15

Horror   1957 · US · BW · 75mins

Rebel without a Cause meets *The Wolf Man* in a trend-setting cult classic, complete with rock 'n' roll, rumbles and teen traumas. Michael Landon (yes, Little Joe Cartwright from *Bonanza* himself) is the troubled student who tears his classmates to shreds after therapy administered by mad scientist Whit Bissell regresses him to his primal past. The suspense is minimal, the production values low, and the time-lapse special effects are hokey, but, even if this seminal shocker now only scrapes by on quaint nostalgia, its title will always be a part of horror history. ▭

Michael Landon *Tony* • Yvonne Lime *Arlene* • Whit Bissell *Dr Alfred Brandon* • Tony Marshall *Jimmy* • Dawn Richard *Theresa* • Barney Phillips *Detective Donovan* • Ken Miller *Vic* ■ *Dir* Gene Fowler Jr • *Scr* Ralph Thornton

I Was an Adventuress ★★★

Comedy drama   1940 · US · BW · 80mins

What fun this should have been, with scene-stealers Peter Lorre and Erich von Stroheim playing confidence tricksters who are abandoned by their partner-in-crime, seductive Vera Zorina, when she finds true love. The settings are lavish, and the pair's efforts to get the team back together generate enough twists to keep one watching. Alas, Gregory Ratoff's direction fails to add the necessary sparkle. Zorina's balletic skills are showcased in the final reel with an excerpt from *Swan Lake* choreographed by her husband, George Balanchine.

Zorina [Vera Zorina] *Countess Tanya Vronsky* • Richard Greene *Paul Vernay* • Erich von Stroheim *Andre Desormeaux* • Peter Lorre *Polo* • Sig Rumann [Sig Ruman] *Herr Protz* • Fritz Feld *Henri Gautier* • Cora Witherspoon *Aunt Cecile* ■ *Dir* Gregory Ratoff • *Scr* Karl Tunberg, Don Ettlinger, John O'Hara, from the film *J'Etais une Aventurière* by Jacques Companeez, Herbert Juttke, Hans Jacoby, Michael Duran • *Cinematographer* Leon Shamroy, Edward Cronjager

I Was Born, but... ★★★★★

Silent comedy drama   1932 · Jap · BW · 100m

Yasujiro Ozu established himself among Japan's greatest film-makers with this exemplary *shomin-geki* or lower-middle-class domestic movie. Coaxing wondrously natural performances from Hideo Sugawara and Tokkankozo, Ozu fashions a minutely observed silent comedy, in which the brothers' disgust at their father's subservience to his boss prompts them to go on hunger strike. The opening segment is played almost entirely in dumb show, although the captions used to explain the harsh realities of the adult world are never intrusive and reinforce the film's ironic take on childhood innocence and life's little injustices.

Hideo Sugawara *Older son, Ryoichi* • Tokkankozo *Younger son, Keiji* • Tatsu Saito *Father, Yoshi* • Mitsuko Yoshikawa *Mother* • Takeshi Sakamoto *Boss* • Seiji Nishimura *Schoolmaster* ■ *Dir* Yasujiro Ozu • *Scr* Akira Fushimi, James Maki [Yasujiro Ozu], Geibei Ibushiya • *Cinematographer* Hideo Shigehara

I Was Happy Here ★★★

Drama 1966 · UK · BW · 90mins

A bittersweet story of Irish disenchantment, this reminds us just how good Sarah Miles could be, even if she hasn't made many films of late. Here she is Cass, the girl who leaves her home and boyfriend in Ireland for the bright lights of London only to find an unhappy marriage with Julian Glover. When she next returns to own country, Cass has to confront her mixed feelings about her former home. Directed by Desmond Davis from a story by Edna O'Brien, the character's winsomeness can be a bit cloying, but Miles is impressive as the wide-eyed innocent who makes us sympathise with her contrary nature.

Sarah Miles *Cass* • Cyril Cusack *Hogan* • Julian Glover *Dr Matthew* • Sean Caffrey *Colin Foley* • Marie Kean *Barkeeper* • Eve Belton *Kate* • Cardew Robinson *Gravedigger* ■ *Dir* Desmond Davis • *Scr* Desmond Davis, Edna O'Brien, from the story *A Woman by the Seaside* by Edna O'Brien

I Was Monty's Double ★★★★U

Second World War drama 1958 · UK · BW · 96mins

The Second World War as fought on the pages of popular fiction is littered with doubles planted as decoys to divert the enemy away from a vital theatre of operation. But, as so often, it is the truth that provides the best stories. John Guillermin's film gains credibility not only because the title role is played by General Montgomery's double himself, ME Clifton James, but also because his autobiography has been so skilfully adapted by Bryan Forbes. Astute, unassuming and extremely slick.

John Mills *Major Harvey* • Cecil Parker *Colonel Logan* • Patrick Allen *Colonel Matthers* • Patrick Holt *Colonel Dawson* • Leslie Phillips *Major Tennant* • Michael Hordern *Governor of Malta* • Marius Goring *Neilson* • Barbara Hicks *Hester* • Sidney James *YMCA porter* ■ *Dir* John Guillermin • *Scr* Bryan Forbes, from a non-fiction book by ME Clifton James

I Went Down ★★★15

Crime comedy 1997 · Ire/UK/Sp · Colour · 102mins

Although the absurd is never far beneath its surface, this dark Irish crime comedy also has plenty to say about loyalty, greed and the pitfalls of macho posturing. Writer Conor McPherson asks a great deal of director Paddy Breathnach by packing so much incident into his script and the cycle of revenge, kidnaps, escapes and double-crosses prevents the action from gaining much momentum. But the exchanges between doltish hit man Brendan Gleeson and his reluctant accomplice Peter McDonald are often splutteringly funny, and there's a nice

turn from Peter Caffrey as their quarry. A misfire, perhaps, but a hugely entertaining one. Contains violence, swearing and a sex scene.

Peter McDonald *Git Hynes* • Antoine Byrne *Sabrina Bradley* • David Wilmot *Anto* • Michael McElhatton *Johnner Doyle* • Brendan Gleeson *Bunny Kelly* • Joe Gallagher *Steo Gannon* • Peter Caffrey *Frank Grogan* • Conor McPherson *Loser in nightclub* ■ *Dir* Paddy Breathnach • *Scr* Conor McPherson

I Will... I Will... for Now ★★15

Romantic comedy 1976 · US · Colour · 103mins

...well, no, perhaps not. The expected chemistry between Diane Keaton and Elliott Gould fails to spark in this cack-handed marital farce which climaxes in a sex-clinic for little reason other than the fact that, like Everest, it's there – and just as enormous a stereotype to scale. The supporting cast includes Victoria Principal, still a couple of years away from her big career break in *Dallas*.

Elliott Gould *Les Bingham* • Diane Keaton *Katie Bingham* • Paul Sorvino *Lou Springer* • Victoria Principal *Jackie Martin* • Robert Alda *Dr Magnus* ■ *Dir* Norman Panama • *Scr* Norman Panama, Albert E Lewin

I Woke Up Early the Day I Died ★★

Crime comedy 1998 · US · Colour · 89mins

Tim Burton's mesmerising biopic of Edward D Wood prompted renewed interest in the man many regard as the worst director of all time, so it probably made commercial sense to Aris Iliopulos to dust off one of his supposedly lost screenplays and film it for a new generation. Alas, this semi-homage to the bargain basement style of film-making that was Wood's trademark fails to gel. Its slim tale of an escaped lunatic (Billy Zane, who also produced) perpetrating a robbery only to lose all the cash is done in a Chaplin-esque silent movie way, heavy on the slapstick, but sadly low on attention grabbing. The one point of interest is a veritable flood of cameos.

Billy Zane *The Thief* • Ron Perlman *Cemetary caretaker* • Tippi Hedren *Maylinda* • Andrew McCarthy *Cop* • Will Patton *Preacher* • Carel Struycken *Undertaker* ■ *Dir* Aris Iliopulos • *Scr* Edward D Wood Jr

I Wonder Who's Killing Her Now? ★★★

Comedy 1975 · US · Colour · 87mins

An amusing, little-seen independent production written by a former associate of Woody Allen, though its approach is closer to the zaniness of Mel Brooks's films. Estranged hubby Bob Dishy hires someone to murder his wife, in order to collect the insurance to pay off his debts. When the policy is cancelled, he tries to cancel the hit, but finds out the man hired someone to do the job... who hired someone else... who hired someone else... and so on. Dishy gives a hilarious performance, expertly handling his character's fast-talking, half-truths and outright lies. The supporting cast of oddball characters help keep things buoyant when the

screenplay's output of laughs sputters in the second half.

Bob Dishy • Bill Dana • Joanna Barnes • Vito Scotti • Richard Libertini ■ *Dir* Steven Hilliard Stern • *Scr* Mickey Rose

I Wonder Who's Kissing Her Now ★★★U

Biographical musical 1947 · US · Colour · 104mins

Agreeable, if not exactly memorable, film biography of Joe Howard, a vaudeville singer and tunesmith in the 1890s. Mark Stevens plays Howard, while Lenore Aubert is the European star who entices him with her charms. The beauty of making a movie about a hit songwriter is that you don't have to send out for any new tunes, and Howard's own, including the title song, make easy listening.

Mark Stevens *Joe Howard* • June Haver *Katie* • Martha Stewart *Lulu Madison* • Reginald Gardiner *Will Hough* • Lenore Aubert *Fritzi Barrington* • William Frawley *Jim Mason* • Gene Nelson *Tommy Yale* ■ *Dir* Lloyd Bacon • *Scr* Lewis R Foster, Marion Turk

Ice ★★18

Action crime thriller 1994 · US · Colour · 87mins

Former porn star Traci Lords had by this stage improved on her previously poor acting skills. Though not great, she is better than one might expect as a professional thief who teams up with her husband to relieve a Mafia hood of some diamonds. When her husband gets "iced" in the process, Lords's life gets very complicated as she tries to fend off the advances of an amorous cop and find her brother who's run off with the gems. As with other PM Entertainment efforts, there are shootouts and broken glass enough for several movies; a lot of it is fun, but a lot also lacks the necessary juice. It would take a few more efforts before PM hit its stride.

Traci Lords *Ellen Reed* • Zach Galligan *Rick* • Michael Bailey Smith *Courier* • Floyd Levine *Det Prine* • Jamie Alba *Det Little* • Jean Pflieger *Jeweller* • Phillip Troy *Charley* ■ *Dir* Brooke Yeaton • *Scr* Sean Dash

Ice Castles ★★★PG

Romantic sports drama 1978 · US · Colour · 104mins

What would have been a perfect vehicle for thirties ice star Sonja Henie feels quaintly old-fashioned in a late seventies setting. With Lynn-Holly Johnson emoting almost as well as she skates, however, Donald Wrye's sentimental melodrama exercises a curious fascination. This owes much to Colleen Dewhurst's sharp performance as the Iowa skating coach who grooms her protégée for Olympic stardom. Tom Skerritt also impresses as Johnson's farmer father, though Robby Benson is something of an irritant as the boyfriend who has to deal with her fame before helping her through a shattering injury.

Robby Benson *Nick Peterson* • Lynn-Holly Johnson *Alexis Winston* • Colleen Dewhurst *Beulah Smith* • Tom Skerritt *Marcus Winston* • Jennifer Warren *Deborah Macland* • David Huffman *Brian Dockett* ■ *Dir* Donald Wrye • *Scr* Donald Wrye, Gary L Baim, from a story by Gary L Baim

Ice Cold in Alex ★★★★PG

Second World War drama 1958 · US · BW · 124mins

The film in which John Mills swigs the most famous glass of beer in movie history – probably! And how well he's earned it, having steered clear of the bottle, Axis troops and a desert full of mines to bring an ambulance to safety after the fall of Tobruk in 1942. No less deserving are crew members Sylvia Syms, Diane Clare, Harry Andrews and Anthony Quayle, who tolerate both his temper and his temperance. Based on a true-life incident, this is a one-premise picture, but director J Lee Thompson keeps the action tense and every jolt felt in the vehicle's cabin will throw you to the edge of your armchair.

John Mills *Captain Anson* • Sylvia Syms *Sister Diane Murdoch* • Anthony Quayle *Captain Van der Poel* • Harry Andrews *MSM Pugh* • Diane Clare *Sister Denise Norton* • Richard Leech *Captain Crosbie* ■ *Dir* J Lee Thompson • *Scr* Christopher Landon, TJ Morrison, from the novel by Christopher Landon

The Ice Follies of 1939 ★★★

Musical 1939 · US · BW and Colour · 83mins

The three-star rating is strictly for the ice-skating, some of it spectacularly executed by the dazzling International Ice Follies company, for which the rest of this movie is a thin excuse. The almost nonexistent plot has James Stewart as an ice-skater and Joan Crawford as his actress wife, suffering marital strife when she is offered a Hollywood contract. Neither the stars, nor the stalwart support of MGM character actors such as Lewis Stone can rescue the pathetic script, which is not improved by Reinhold Schunzel's dreary direction.

Joan Crawford *Mary McKay* • James Stewart *Larry Hall* • Lew Ayres *Eddie Burgess* • Lewis Stone *Douglas Tolliver* • Lionel Stander *Mort Hodges* ■ *Dir* Reinhold Schunzel • *Scr* Leonard Praskins, Florence Ryerson, Edgar Allan Woolf, from a story by Leonard Praskins • *Music* Roger Edens

Ice Palace ★★

Drama 1960 · US · Colour · 143mins

Edna Ferber has had many of her novels turned into films, *Giant* (1956) being perhaps the most memorable. This is a markedly less successful saga about the social development of Alaska. Filtered through the friendship-become-enmity of pioneers Richard Burton and Robert Ryan, it's a lengthy plod through the early years of the 20th century – a less than enthralling journey.

Richard Burton *Zeb Kennedy* • Robert Ryan *Thor Storm* • Carolyn Jones *Bridie Ballantyne* • Martha Hyer *Dorothy Kennedy* • Jim Backus *Dave Husack* • Ray Danton *Bay Husack* • Diane McBain *Christine Storm* • Karl Swenson *Scotty Ballantyne* • George Takei *Wang* ■ *Dir* Vincent Sherman • *Scr* Harry Kleiner, from a novel by Edna Ferber

The Ice Pirates ★★★15

Science-fiction adventure 1984 · US · Colour · 89mins

Although little more than an Errol Flynn-type intergalactic swashbuckler, this slight space opera is good inventive fun even if it does err on the crudely silly side. Space pirate Robert Urich searches the universe for the prized commodity of water, gets captured, falls in love with princess Mary Crosby and escapes with her to search for her father on a mysterious planet covered in water. Great art direction and neat special effects – the clever time-warp birth sequence, the castration device and the robot pimp – augment the constant stream of smart-aleck remarks and sexual innuendo. Off-the-wall and amusing even if it is more *Carry On* than *Star Wars*. ▣

Robert Urich *Jason* • Mary Crosby *Princess Karina* • Anjelica Huston *Maida* • Michael D Roberts *Roscoe* • John Matuszak *Killjoy* • Ron Perlman *Zeno* • John Carradine *Supreme Commander* ■ *Dir* Stewart Raffill • *Scr* Stewart Raffill, Stanford Sherman

The Ice Runner   ★★15

Prison thriller
1993 · US/UK/USSR · Colour · 122mins

US agent Jeffrey (Edward Albert) is double-crossed by his own side and sentenced to a long stretch in a harsh Russian prison – a virtual death sentence. Fortunately the train crashes en route, giving Jeffrey a chance to take over the identity of another prisoner and end up in another jail. If this all sounds like a re-run of lots of other prision movies, the action takes a left turn with the introduction of the dead prisoner's wife, Olga Kabo, who falls in love with Jeff. This Cold War drama is out of the ordinary, but lacks any real focus. ▣

Edward Albert *Jeffrey West* • Victor Wong *Fyodor* • Eugene Lazarev *Kolya* • Sergei Ruban *Gorsky* • Olga Kabo *Lena* • Alexander Kuznitzov *Petrov* • Basil Hoffman *JC Kruck* ■ *Dir* Barry Samson • *Scr* Joyce Warren, Clifford Coleman, Joshua Stallings

Ice Station Zebra   ★★★U

Adventure   1968 · US · Colour · 139mins

For a time, the action in this Cold War thriller, based on the Alistair MacLean novel, is as stiff as the title, as a far-off Polar outpost becomes a magnet for Russian and American forces out to recover some satellite photographs. Then it thaws into activity, mainly because Patrick McGoohan, as a British agent, arrives on the scene to stir Rock Hudson out of his cryogenic slumber. McGoohan is very welcome, Ernest Borgnine overacts unrestrainedly, and director John Sturges – who also filmed another MacLean title, *The Satan Bug*, to slightly better effect – ensures a steady treatment. ▣

Rock Hudson *Commander James Ferraday* • Ernest Borgnine *Boris Vaslov* • Patrick McGoohan *David Jones* • Jim Brown *Captain Leslie Anders* • Tony Bill *Lt Russell Walker* • Lloyd Nolan *Admiral Garvey* • Alf Kjellin *Colonel Ostrovsky* ■ *Dir* John Sturges • *Scr* Douglas Heyes, from the story by Harry Julian Fink, from the novel by Alistair MacLean

The Ice Storm   ★★★★★15

Drama   1997 · US · Colour · 107mins

Director Ang Lee's accomplished adaptation of Rick Moody's novel about two disfunctional New England families, surprisingly failed to make an impact on the Oscar voters. Set in 1973, Lee painstakingly focuses on

period details as the backdrop to the increasingly complicated relationships between neighbouring families the Carvers and the Hoods. Ben Hood (Kevin Kline) is cheating on his wife (Joan Allen) with bored neighbour Janey Carver (Sigourney Weaver), while their teenage children are experimenting with their own sexual desires. The drama climaxes with the beautifully realised (by cinematographer Frederick Elmes) ice storm. Outstanding performances from the adults are matched by those of the younger cast members. Unmissable. ▣ **DVD**

Kevin Kline *Ben Hood* • Sigourney Weaver *Janey Carver* • Joan Allen *Elena Hood* • Christina Ricci *Wendy Hood* • Elijah Wood *Mikey Carver* • Henry Czerny *George Clair* • Adam Hann-Byrd *Sandy Carver* • Katie Holmes *Libbets Casey* • Tobey Maguire *Paul Hood* ■ *Dir* Ang Lee • *Scr* James Schamus, from the novel by Rick Moody

Iceman   ★★★★PG

Science-fiction drama
1984 · US · Colour · 96mins

Two of Universal's most successful pictures are recalled in this fascinating sci-fi outing. With an opening that echoes *Frankenstein* and a plotline reminiscent of *ET*, Fred Schepisi's film couldn't have much better role models. While its subject matter is hardly new, the approach is refreshingly intelligent. John Lone gives a remarkable performance as the primitive man rescued from a 40,000-year incarceration in ice, registering fear, bewilderment, trust and curiosity with shifts of expression so subtle they cannot fail to convince. As the scientists monitoring his progress, Timothy Hutton and Lindsay Crouse also underplay to good effect. ▣

Timothy Hutton *Dr Stanley Shephard* • Lindsay Crouse *Dr Diane Brady* • John Lone *Charlie* • Josef Sommer *Whitman* • David Strathairn *Dr Singe* • Philip Akin *Dr Vermeil* • Danny Glover *Loomis* • Amelia Hall *Mabel* ■ *Dir* Fred Schepisi • *Scr* Chip Proser, John Drimmer, from a story by John Drimmer

The Iceman Cometh   ★★18

Drama   1973 · US · Colour · 239mins

Eugene O'Neill's massive play, first performed in 1946, is a gift for actors and a challenge for audiences: set in Harry Hope's bar – meeting and drinking place for drop-outs and other transients – it's a talk-fest that seems to last forever. If one swallows the major implausibility of drunken hobos being articulate and poetic in everything they say, you will adore every one of its four hours and admire the performances of the powerhouse cast. But most people will prefer the Lee Marvin of *Point Blank* or the Robert Ryan of *The Wild Bunch*. ▣

Lee Marvin *Theodore "Hickey" Hickman* • Fredric March *Harry Hope* • Robert Ryan *Larry Slade* • Jeff Bridges *Don Parritt* • Bradford Dillman *Willie Oban* • Sorrell Booke *Hugo Kalmar* ■ *Dir* John Frankenheimer • *Scr* Thomas Quinn Curtiss, from the play by Eugene O'Neill

The Icicle Thief   ★★★PG

Satirical comedy
1989 · It · Colour and BW · 81mins

A bravura blend of colour, monochrome, animation, neorealism

and commercial gloss, this astute satire on the ruin of cinema by television ends up being just a tad too clever for its own good. Co-writer/director Maurizio Nichetti gives an increasingly manic performance as the director who sees his homage to the postwar classic *Bicycle Thieves* being mixed up with some commercials during a special TV screening. While the interaction of the characters from these diametrically opposed fictional worlds amuses in a *Purple Rose of Cairo* kind of way, it's the response of the typical Italian family that gives the film its cutting edge. In Italian with English subtitles. ▣

Maurizio Nichetti *Antonio Piermattei/Maurizio Nichetti* • Caterina Sylos Labini *Maria Piermattei* • Federico Rizzo *Bruno Piermattei* • Matteo Augardi *Paolo Piermattei* • Renato Scarpa *Don Italo* ■ *Dir* Maurizio Nichetti • *Scr* Maurizio Nichetti, Mauro Monti

I'd Climb the Highest Mountain   ★★★U

Drama   1951 · US · Colour · 86mins

A clumsy and off-putting title for a charming slice of 20th Century-Fox period Americana. The slim plot in these movies seldom matters, and here a vivacious Susan Hayward narrates a series of vignettes about her marriage to a young minister (an undercast William Lundigan), all filmed in the Blue Ridge Mountains of Georgia where the original Corra Harris novel was set. The supporting cast is well chosen, with character actors like Gene Lockhart, Ruth Donnelly and Alexander Knox most welcome, lending the film a spurious authenticity.

Susan Hayward *Mary Thompson/Narrator* • William Lundigan *William Thompson* • Rory Calhoun *Jack Stark* • Barbara Bates *Jenny Brock* • Gene Lockhart *Mr Brock* • Lynn Bari *Mrs Billywith* • Ruth Donnelly *Glory White* • Kathleen Lockhart *Mrs Brock* • Alexander Knox *Salter* ■ *Dir* Henry King • *Scr* Lamar Trotti, from the novel by Corra Harris

I'd Rather Be Rich   ★★★U

Romantic comedy
1964 · US · Colour · 95mins

To cheer up her ailing grandfather (Maurice Chevalier), Sandra Dee agrees to introduce him to her fiancé (Andy Williams). But when he's delayed, she asks Robert Goulet to impersonate him. Thoroughly likeable remake of the Charles Laughton/Deanna Durbin comedy, *It Started with Eve*. Surprisingly, given how engaging he is, this is Andy Williams's only screen performance to date, though he sang and wrote songs for other movies. Controversy surrounds the legend that it was his voice doubling for Lauren Bacall's singing in *To Have and Have Not* – Howard Hawks later claimed it really was Bacall. Here Williams gets to sing *Almost There*, which subsequently became a hit on both sides of the Atlantic.

Sandra Dee *Cynthia Dulaine* • Robert Goulet *Paul Benton* • Andy Williams *Warren Palmer* • Maurice Chevalier *Philip Dulaine* • Gene Raymond *Martin Wood* • Charles Ruggles *Dr Charles Crandall* • Hermione Gingold *Miss Grimshaw* ■ *Dir* Jack Smight • *Scr* Oscar Brodney, Norman Krasna, Leo Townsend

Idaho Transfer   ★

Science-fiction   1973 · US · Colour · 87mins

Director Peter Fonda was still in hippy *Easy Rider* message mode with this well-intentioned but ridiculous science-fiction parable. Some present day kids take part in an experiment with a time machine that "teleports" them to Idaho in 2044, where they plan to start a new civilisation. None of them are emotionally equipped for the job, and anarchy soon rears its head as they become savages without leadership. Bleak, boring and unfocused, Fonda clearly can't direct the bland cast or give any dramatic edge to the rambling plot. ▣

Kelley Bohanan *Karen* • Kevin Hearst *Ronald* • Caroline Hildebrand *Isa* • Keith Carradine *Arthur* • Dale Hopkins *Leslie* ■ *Dir* Peter Fonda • *Scr* Thomas Matthiesen

An Ideal Husband   ★★★U

Comedy   1947 · UK · Colour · 92mins

Oscar Wilde's clever writing is subtly interpreted here by Alexander Korda in this class production of one of his more famous drawing-room comedies. A stellar list of the day's witty players (Paulette Goddard, C Aubrey Smith, Michael Wilding) lends a dash of celluloid pizzazz to the stylish melting pot. The downside is the rather plodding pace that seems to handcuff the players and their words. ▣

Paulette Goddard *Mrs Cheveley* • Michael Wilding *Viscount Goring* • Hugh Williams *Sir Robert Chiltern* • Diana Wynyard *Lady Chiltern* • C Aubrey Smith *Earl of Caversham* • Glynis Johns *Mabel Chiltern* • Constance Collier *Lady Markby* • Christine Norden *Mrs Marchmont* • Harriette Johns *Lady Basildon* • Fred Groves *Phipps* ■ *Dir* Alexander Korda • *Scr* Lajos Biró, from the play by Oscar Wilde

An Ideal Husband   ★★★★PG

Comedy   1999 · UK/US · Colour · 93mins

While it shares the wit and wisdom of Alexander Korda's 1947 version, writer/director Oliver Parker's adaptation of Oscar Wilde's 1895 play has the dual advantage of impeccable casting and, in the end-of-the-nineties climate of parliamentary sleaze, topicality. This British period piece is visually spot-on, but Parker's energetic opening out of the action occasionally seems a little excessive. What matters most, however, are the performances, with Rupert Everett standing out among an exemplary cast. This amusing tale of political intrigue is no longer scandalous, yet retains its power to disconcert. **DVD**

Cate Blanchett *Lady Gertrude Chiltern* • Minnie Driver *Mabel Chiltern* • Rupert Everett *Arthur Goring* • Julianne Moore *Mrs Laura Cheveley* • Jeremy Northam *Sir Robert Chiltern* • John Wood *Lord Caversham* • Lindsay Duncan *Lady Markby* • Peter Vaughan *Phipps* • Jeroen Krabbé *Baron Arnheim* ■ *Dir* Oliver Parker • *Scr* Oliver Parker, from the play by Oscar Wilde

Identification of a Woman
   ★★★18

Drama   1982 · It · Colour · 122mins

Throughout his career Michelangelo Antonioni has been preoccupied with transient love and urban alienation, and this was clearly a retreat into familiar territory following the lukewarm reception that his video experiment, *The Oberwald Mystery*, received. Alluding to Fellini's creative dilemma in $8\frac{1}{2}$ and mocking Hollywood's obsession with all things extraterrestrial, Antonioni treats the artistic and romantic problems of director Tomas Milian with a knowing irony. However, as the sequences in the fog and backwaters of Venice suggest, this is also a genuine lament for the decline in meaningful communication both between people and between the film-maker and his audience. In Italian with English subtitles. ▭

Tomas Milian *Niccolò* • Christine Boisson *Ida* • Daniela Silverio *Mavi* • Marcel Bozzuffi *Mario* • Lara Wendel *Girl at pool* • Veronica Lazar *Carla Farra* ■ *Dir* Michelangelo Antonioni • *Scr* Michelangelo Antonioni, Gérard Brach, Tonino Guerra, from a story by Michelangelo Antonioni • *Editor* Michelangelo Antonioni • *Cinematographer* Carlo Di Palma

The Idiot ★★
Drama 1951 · Jap · BW · 165 mins

Famous for his versions of Shakespeare's *Macbeth* (*Throne of Blood*, 1957) and *King Lear* (*Ran*, 1985), Kurosawa's attempt to adapt Dostoyevsky is far less successful. The story is updated and transposed to snowbound Okinawa where a prince and his emotionally unstable friend share a woman. Dostoyevsky's original novel was always difficult, but the Japanese version makes even stronger demands on its audience in terms of its weird performances and cultural context. Massive studio cuts don't help either, though it still runs for nearly three hours. In Japanese with English subtitles.

Masayuki Mori *Kinji Kameda, the Idiot* • Toshiro Mifune *Denkichi Akama* • Setsuko Hara *Taeko Nasu* • Takashi Shimura *Ono, the father* • Yoshiko Kuga *Ayako Ono* ■ *Dir* Akira Kurosawa • *Scr* Eijiro Hisaita, Akira Kurosawa, from the novel by Feodor Mikhailovich Dostoyevsky

Idiot Box ★★★ 18
Comedy 1996 · Ausl · Colour · 81mins

Debunking the much-posited contention that the media scars impressionable minds, writer/director David Caesar's throbbing comedy adopts the abrasive approach of *Trainspotting*. But, rather than merely ridiculing the slacker lifestyle, it also launches a swingeing assault on the macho cult of superiority to which the Australian male still clings in spite of unemployment, female emancipation and his own drunkenindolence. Ben Mendelsohn and Jeremy Sims are outstanding as the Aussie answer to Beavis and Butt-head, whose indiscriminate viewing prompts them to attempt a doomed bank robbery. Often anarchically funny, the use of TV theme tunes to underscore the action is a masterstroke. Contains swearing and scenes of violence. ▭

Ben Mendelsohn *Kev* • Jeremy Sims *Mick* • John Polson *Jonah* • Robyn Loau *Lani* • Graeme Blundell *Detective Eric* • Deborah Kennedy *Detective Loanne* • Stephen Rae *Colin* ■ *Dir/Scr* David Caesar

The Idiots ★★★★ 18
Comedy drama 1998 · Den · Colour · 114mins

The third film to emerge from the Dogma 95 collective (following director Lars von Trier's own *Breaking the Waves* and 1998's *Festen*), *The Idiots* utilises the group's complete rejection of film-making artifice to maximum effect and creates a uniquely unsettling experience. Von Trier thrusts his hand-held camera in the midst of a bunch of Danish drop-outs, who test the waters of cultural acceptance by pretending to be mentally disabled in all manner of public places. Although uncomfortably comic in its portrayal of people feigning disability, the disturbing (and for a few seconds pornographic) content is balanced by mesmerising naturalistic performances, emotionally engaging situations and an ultimately liberating message. In Danish with English subtitles.

Bodil Jorgensen *Karen* • Jens Albinus *Stoffer* • Anne Louise Hassing *Susanne* • Troels Lyby *Henrik* • Nikolaj Lie Kaas *Jeppe* • Louise Mieritz *Josephine* • Henrik Prip *Ped* • Luis Mesonero *Miguel* ■ *Dir/Scr* Lars von Trier • *Cinematographer* Lars von Trier

Idiot's Delight ★★★
Comedy 1939 · US · BW · 105m

Robert E Sherwood adapted (and softened) his own Broadway play as a vehicle for Clark Gable and Norma Shearer. This now somewhat dated mix of romance, comedy, and anti-war flag waving, offers the treasurable sight of Gable dancing on screen for the first and last time. He plays a hoofer who, with his all-girl dancing troupe, finds himself stranded in a European hotel as war threatens to break out. There, his old flame (Shearer) turns up in the guise of a Russian countess, complete with foreign accent. Impeccably directed by Garbo's favourite, Clarence Brown, with a value-for-money supporting cast.

Norma Shearer *Irene Fellara* • Clark Gable *Harry Van* • Edward Arnold *Achille Weber* • Charles Coburn *Dr Waldersee* • Joseph Schildkraut *Capt Kirvline* • Burgess Meredith *Quillery* ■ *Dir* Clarence Brown • *Scr* Robert E Sherwood, from his play

The Idle Class ★★★★ U
Silent comedy drama 1921 · US · BW · 26mins

Charlie Chaplin has an early dig at the aristocracy and he's in fine comic form playing a dual role alongside Edna Purviance. The story revolves around various opportunities for Chaplin to play extremes of character – an arrogant, drunken, wealthy husband and an endearing, sensitive but, obviously, impoverished tramp – but he still manages to deliver some strong observations on social inequalities with both piquance and intelligence. ▭

Charles Chaplin *Tramp/Husband* • Edna Purviance *Wife* • Mack Swain *Father* • Henry Bergman *Tramp/Cop* • John Rand *Tramp/Guest* • Rex Storey *Robber/Guest* ■ *Dir/Scr* Charles Chaplin

Idle Hands ★★★★ 18
Comedy horror 1999 · US · Colour · 88mins

The Beast with Five Fingers is given an energetic *Scream!* update in a

delightful slasher flick casting a winking eye on genre clichés and cannily redefining them into first class popcorn entertainment. Lazy college kid Devon Sawa can't control his supernaturally possessed hand and ends up killing his best friends without knowing it – a case of the left hand not knowing what the right hand is up to. Director Rodman Flender, who accurately pushes the jump-scare button on numerous remarkable occasions and always hits the funny bone dead on. A welcome surprise. Contains violent scenes. ▭ **DVD**

Devon Sawa *Anton* • Seth Green *Mick* • Elden Henson *Pnub* • Jessica Alba *Molly* • Christopher Hart *The Hand* • Vivica A Fox *Debi* • Jack Noseworthy *Randy* • Katie Wright *Tanya* ■ *Dir* Rodman Flender • *Scr* Terri Hughes, Ron Milbauer

The Idol ★★
Drama 1966 · UK · BW · 109mins

One of the many ludicrous London-set melodramas to appear in the sixties, this would-be profound psychological study centres on a good-looking young American student (Michael Parks) who is drawn to the girlfriend of his pal John Leyton. Unfortunately, Leyton's mother (Jennifer Jones) also finds herself drawn to the young lothario. At this point, the likelihood of a happy ending seems remote and, indeed, is. Enjoyable if you're in the right mood and John Dankworth's music is always worth listening to.

Jennifer Jones *Carol* • Michael Parks *Marco* • John Leyton *Timothy* • Jennifer Hilary *Sarah* • Guy Doleman *Martin Livesey* • Natasha Pyne *Rosalind* ■ *Dir* Daniel Petrie • *Scr* Millard Lampell, from a story by Ugo Liberatore

The Idolmaker ★★★★ 15
Drama 1980 · US · Colour · 113mins

This exposé of the American pop music industry of the late fifties tears the dream to pieces mercilessly. Starring in a tale clearly inspired by the way singer Frankie Avalon was built up, only to be succeeded by Fabian (another in the same mould), both Peter Gallagher and Paul Land are eagerly naive. They play youngsters at the mercy of Ray Sharkey, who is quite brilliant as an unscrupulous entrepreneur (based on Avalon and Fabian's real-life manager Bob Marcucci, here credited as technical adviser). First-time feature director Taylor Hackford has glossed it with a sceptical shine and makes sure the facts never obscure the bitter-pill entertainment. Contains some swearing ▭

Ray Sharkey *Vincent Vacarri* • Tovah Feldshuh *Brenda Roberts* • Peter Gallagher *Guido, "Caesare"* • Paul Land *Tommy Dee* • Joe Pantoliano *Gino Pilato* • Maureen McCormick *Ellen Fields* • John Aprea *Paul Vacarri* ■ *Dir* Taylor Hackford • *Scr* Edward Di Lorenzo

if... ★★★★ 15
Drama 1968 · UK · BW and Colour · 111mins

Clearly indebted to Jean Vigo's *Zero for Conduct*, this striking story of schoolboy revolt was originally offered to Nicholas Ray in the hope that he would produce a British equivalent to his classic *Rebel without a Cause*. With its surrealistic elements, it was

something of a departure for *This Sporting Life* director Lindsay Anderson, but he succeeds in both capturing the atmosphere and absurdities of public school life and investing the satire with plenty of venom. Malcolm McDowell gives a blistering performance in what is undoubtedly a key film in British cinema history, but it's now just starting to show its age. Contains violence and nudity. ▭

Malcolm McDowell *Mick Travers* • David Wood *Johnny* • Richard Warwick *Wallace* • Christine Noonan *The Girl* • Rupert Webster *Bobby Philips* • Robert Swann *Rowntree* • Hugh Thomas *Denson* • Peter Jeffrey *Headmaster* • Mona Washbourne *Matron* • Arthur Lowe *Mr Kemp, housemaster* • Charles Sturridge *Markland* ■ *Dir* Lindsay Anderson • *Scr* David Sherwin, from the (unproduced) *Scr Crusaders* by David Sherwin, John Howlett • *Cinematographer* Miroslav Ondricek

If a Man Answers ★★
Romantic comedy 1962 · US · Colour · 95mins

After *Gidget*, Sandra Dee went on to further stardom in the *Tammy* films for producer Ross Hunter. Here Hunter teamed her with real-life husband, teen heart-throb Bobby Darin. Dee is Chantal Stacey, a Franco/American who marries Eugene Wright (Darin) and soon feels neglected. Her mother's helpful advice for saving the marriage includes treating hubby like a pet dog, and then inventing an imaginary lover to make him jealous. Fortunately Darin doesn't hold it against her. Too cute for its own good perhaps, but on the whole harmless fun.

Sandra Dee *Chantal Stacey* • Bobby Darin *Eugene Wright* • Micheline Presle *Maman Stacey* • John Lund *John Stacey* • Cesar Romero *Robert Swan/Adam Wright* • Stefanie Powers *Tina* ■ *Dir* Henry Levin • *Scr* Richard Morris, from a novel by Winifred Wolfe

If I Had a Million ★★★
Comedy drama 1932 · US · BW · 88m

Paramount put its top directors, writers and stars into this episodic film built around various people's reaction to being handed a cheque for one million dollars. Charles Laughton has the most memorable response as the humble office clerk resigning his position in style, while Charlie Ruggles and WC Fields are also handed memorable comic sequences. On the more sentimental side, Wynne Gibson scores as the prostitute who knows how to indulge herself. Gary Cooper and George Raft are among the other stars, and a sensibly short running time means the idea doesn't overstay its welcome.

Richard Bennett *John Glidden* • Charlie Ruggles [Charles Ruggles] *Henry Peabody* • Wynne Gibson *Violet Smith* • George Raft *Edward Jackson* • WC Fields *Rollo* • Alison Skipworth *Emily La Rue* • Gene Raymond *John Wallace* • Frances Dee *Mary Wallace* • Charles Laughton *Phineas V Lambert* • Gary Cooper *Steven Gallagher* • Jack Oakie *Mulligan* • May Robson *Mary Walker* • Blanche Frederici *Mrs Garvey* ■ *Dir* Stephen Roberts, James Cruze, Norman Z McLeod, Norman Taurog, H Bruce Humberstone, Ernst Lubitsch, William A Seiter, Lothar Mendes • *Scr* Claude Binyon, Malcolm Stuart Boylan, Harvey Gates, Joseph L Mankiewicz, Oliver HP Garrett, Grover Jones, William Slavens McNutt, Whitney Bolton, Robert Sparks, Joseph L

U = SUITABLE FOR ALL   **Uc** = SUITABLE FOR ALL, ESPECIALLY FOR YOUNG CHILDREN (VIDEO ONLY)   **PG** = PARENTAL GUIDANCE

Mankiewicz, Lawton Mackall, Robert Sparks, Joseph L Mankiewicz, from the novel *Windfall* by Robert D Andrews, Grover Jones, William Slavens McNutt

If I Were Free ★★
Romance 1933 · US · BW · 65

A London antique shop owner (Irene Dunne), who has suffered an appalling marriage (to Nils Asther), falls in love with a lawyer (Clive Brook), taking refuge in alcohol from his unhappy marriage to a wife who refuses to divorce him. Adapted from John Van Druten's play *Behold, We Live!*, this glum and plodding drama is directed by Elliott Nugent, more at home with comedy but with no room to raise a smile here. The journey to the happy ending, though slow, is mercifully short, and the stars (and supporting players) give impeccable performances, almost as though they believe what they are saying.

Irene Dunne *Sarah Casanove* • Clive Brook *Gordon Evers* • Nils Asther *Tono Casanove* • Henry Stephenson *Hector Stribling* • Vivian Tobin *Jewel Stribling* ■ *Dir* Elliott Nugent • *Scr* Dwight Taylor, from the play *Behold, We Live!* by John Van Druten. • *Cinematographer* Edward Cronjager • *Music* Max Steiner

If I Were King ★★★★ U
Adventure 1938 · US · BW · 100mins

A sparklingly witty and polished historical romp, this gives plum roles to Ronald Colman as the romantic poet and audacious rogue François Villon and to Basil Rathbone as the wily, cackling French monarch, Louis XI, who allows Villon to save him from losing his throne. Preston Sturges's screenplay provides dialogue that is a constant delight, and no one has declaimed poetry better on screen than Colman. Frank Lloyd's direction is admirably brisk and Ellen Drew shines as the ordinary girl who loves Villon without reservation. A rare delight.

Ronald Colman *François Villon* • Basil Rathbone *Louis XI* • Frances Dee *Katherine de Vaucelles* • Ellen Drew *Huguette* • CV France *Father Villon* • Henry Wilcoxon *Captain of the Watch* • Heather Thatcher *Queen* ■ *Dir* Frank Lloyd • *Scr* Preston Sturges, from the play by Justin Huntly McCarthy

If It's Tuesday, This Must Be Belgium ★★
Comedy 1969 · US · Colour · 98mins

A party of "oh, wow" Americans fly in to Heathrow for a whirlwind tour of Europe, taking in all the familiar sights. Their courier is chirpy cockney Ian McShane, whose eyes are on the female tourists rather than the cultural highspots, and the clichés are as thick as the accents. As a send-up of the package tour, it's mild-mannered and moderately amusing, with the best moments provided by a dizzying array of cameos from the likes of Joan Collins and the pop singer Donovan, who also composed the score.

Suzanne Pleshette *Samantha Perkins* • Ian McShane *Charlie* • Mildred Natwick *Jenny Grant* • Murray Hamilton *Fred Ferguson* • Sandy Baron *John Marino* • Michael Constantine *Jack Harmon* • Norman Fell *Harve Blakely* • Patricia Routledge *Mrs Featherstone* • Donovan • Anita Ekberg • Ben Gazzara • John Cassavetes • Robert Vaughn • Joan

Collins ■ *Dir* Mel Stuart • *Scr* David Shaw, inspired by a cartoon from *The New Yorker,magazine* • *Music/Lyrics* Donovan

If Lucy Fell ★★ 15
Romantic comedy 1996 · US · Colour · 88mins

Writer/director/star Eric Schaeffer overstretches himself somewhat with this uneven romantic comedy. It's about two friends, Joe and Lucy (played by Schaeffer and *Sex and the City*'s Sarah Jessica Parker), who have made a pact to jump off the Brooklyn Bridge together if neither finds love before Lucy's 30th birthday, which is now only a month away. Their attempts at finding the ideal partner include Ben Stiller and Elle Macpherson, but you can work out who their true soul mate will be well before the end of the movie. Sugary sweet and inexcusably predictable. Contains some swearing and sexual references. [VIDEO]

Sarah Jessica Parker *Lucy Ackerman* • Eric Schaeffer *Joe MacGonaughgill* • Ben Stiller *Bwick Elias* • Elle Macpherson *Jane Lindquist* • James Rebhorn *Simon Ackerman* • Robert John Burke [Robert Burke] *Handsome man* ■ *Dir* Eric Schaeffer • *Scr* Eric Schaeffer, from a story by Tony Spiridakis, Eric Schaeffer

If Only ★★★ 15
Fantasy comedy romance 1998 · Sp/Fr/Can/UK/Lux · Colour · 90mins

In this twentysomething romantic comedy Douglas Henshall stars as the "resting" actor who loses the love of his life, Lena Headey, after a stupid infidelity. Unwittingly encountering a means to turn back time, he returns to the past to try to rectify his mistake. But in spite of strong and convincing performances from Headey and Henshall and the lovely Penelope Cruz, the time travel device is a source of weakness and acts as an irritation to an otherwise entertaining movie. Look out for a nice cameo from Elizabeth McGovern. Contains swearing. [VIDEO]

Lena Headey *Sylvia Weld* • Douglas Henshall *Victor Bukowski* • Penelope Cruz *Louise* • Gustavo Salmeron *Rafael* • Mark Strong *Dave Summers* • Charlotte Coleman *Alison Hayes* • Elizabeth McGovern *Diane* ■ *Dir* Maria Ripoll • *Scr* Rafa Russo

If These Walls Could Talk ★★★ 15
Drama 1996 · US · Colour · 97mins

Two of Hollywood's biggest stars, Cher and Demi Moore, weigh in to the abortion debate with this surprisingly gritty compendium about the subject. The three tales in this film, deal with unwanted pregnancies from the fifties to the present. In the first story, Moore plays a woman taking desperate measures at a time when abortion was illegal; in the second, Sissy Spacek is the seventies' mother and wife who divides her family when she contemplates abortion; while Cher takes centre stage and makes her directorial debut in the concluding story about a woman doctor facing the wrath of anti-abortionists. Although made for TV, this takes a measured, intelligent look at a controversial issue and does not fall into the trap of preaching. [VIDEO]

Demi Moore *Claire Donnelly* • Shirley Knight *Mary Donnelly* • Catherine Keener *Becky* •

Jason London *Kevin Donnelly* • Sissy Spacek *Barbara Ryan Barrows* • Xander Berkeley *John Barrows* • Hedy Burress *Linda Barrows* • Janna Michaels *Sally Barrows* • Cher *Dr Beth Thompson* • Anne Heche *Christine Cullen* • Eileen Brennan *Tessie* • Jada Pinkett [Jada Pinkett Smith] *Patti* • Lindsay Crouse *Frances White* ■ *Dir* Nancy Savoca, Cher • *Scr 1952* : *Scr* Nancy Savoca, from a story by Susan Nanus, Earl Wallace, from material by Stuart Kaplan, *1974* : *Scr* Nancy Savoca, I Marlene King, *1996* : *Scr*,Nancy Savoca, Pamela Wallace, from a story by Pamela Wallace

If These Walls Could Talk 2 ★★
Drama 2000 · US · Colour · 96mins

These three intimate portraits of the lesbian experience in America cross over three different decades from the sixties to the millennium, and are as uneven as they are groundbreaking. *1961* is the standout and features a daring performance by Vanessa Redgrave as the surviving member of a 50-year lesbian relationship who must face the loss of her life partner. Almost too good of an act for the next two tales to follow. *1972* stars Chloë Sevigny in a provocative, semi-amusing piece about a group of gay college coeds who come to view their own prejudices as they become politicised in the early years of the feminist movement. Last and least is, *2000*. Produced and directed by Hollywood's leading lesbian couple Anne Heche and Ellen DeGeneres (who also stars), this wannabe comedy about two lesbians going to any and all lengths to have a baby, still doesn't "deliver" even with the presence of Sharon Stone.

Vanessa Redgrave *Edith* • Chloë Sevigny *Amy* • Sharon Stone *Fran* • Ellen DeGeneres *Kal* ■ *Dir* Jane Anderson, Martha Coolidge • *Scr* Jane Anderson, Sylvia Sichel, from a story by Sylvia Sichel

If Winter Comes ★★
Drama 1947 · US · BW · 96mins

Previously made back in 1923 with Percy Marmont in the lead, this is an unashamedly sentimental adaptation of ASM Hutchinson's potboiler about an outwardly respectable publisher suspected by his neighbours of driving a pregnant girl to suicide. As the only friend of waif Janet Leigh, Walter Pidgeon's husband is caught between his demanding wife (Angela Lansbury) and his passionate mistress (Deborah Kerr). For all the suffering and stiff upper lips on show, however, this is a thoroughly resistible melodrama, and Victor Saville's unshaded direction makes few demands on either our minds or our heartstrings.

Deborah Kerr *Nona Tybar* • Walter Pidgeon *Mark Sabre* • Angela Lansbury *Mabel Sabre* • Janet Leigh *Effie Bright* • Binnie Barnes *Natalie Bagshaw* • Dame May Whitty *Mrs Perch* ■ *Dir* Victor Saville • *Scr* Marguerite Roberts, Arthur Wimperis, from the novel by ASM Hutchinson

If You Could Only Cook ★★★★
Comedy 1935 · US · BW · 70 mins

Here's a real find. Somewhere between directing Astaire and Rogers in *Roberta* and a slew of Shirley Temple and Deanna Durbin vehicles,

William A Seiter fashioned this screwball gem, with Herbert Marshall and delectable, bell-voiced Jean Arthur posing as butler and cook in a mobster's house. The movie opened in London bearing the fraudulent legend "A Frank Capra Production" on the advertising. Bill Seiter's reaction to this ploy is unrecorded, but Capra was furious, and persuaded studio boss Harry Cohn to buy him the Broadway hit *You Can't Take It with You* in lieu of settlement.

Herbert Marshall *Jim Buchanan* • Jean Arthur *Joan Hawthorne* • Leo Carrillo *Mike Rossini* • Lionel Stander *Flash* • Alan Edwards *Bob Reynolds* • Frieda Inescort *Evelyn Fletcher* • Gene Morgan *Al* ■ *Dir* William A Seiter • *Scr* Howard J Green, Gertrude Purcell, from the story by F Hugh Herbert

If You Knew Susie ★★ U
Musical comedy 1948 · US · BW · 90mins

Eddie Cantor's last film proper (following this he only made cameo appearances) reunites him with Joan Davies, with whom he enjoyed a considerable hit in *Show Business*. Unfortunately he fails to repeat that success here, but the film does have its moments. Cantor and Davis are the retired song-and-dance act who discover, by chance, that the Government owes the family a fortune in back interest payments.

Eddie Cantor *Sam Parker* • Joan Davis *Susie Parker* • Allyn Joslyn *Mike Garrett* • Charles Dingle *Mr Whitley* • Phil Brown *Joe Collins* ■ *Dir* Gordon M Douglas [Gordon Douglas] • *Scr* Warren Wilson, Oscar Brodney, Bud Pearson, Lester A White

Ikinai ★★★★
Road movie 1998 · Jap · Colour · 100mins

It soon becomes clear from watching Hiroshi Shimizu's directorial debut that he has learned a great deal from his mentor, Takeshi Kitano. Leavening the quirky comedy with poignant drama, this perfectly paced road movie concerns a group of world-weary men on a New Year bus tour that will culminate in the "accident" they hope will guarantee their dependents a healthy insurance payout. But the unscheduled arrival of a life-loving young woman prompts some to rethink their decision. Poking gentle fun at Japanese attitudes to tourism, duty and death, this is a constant delight and a masterclass in ensemble acting. In Japanese with English subtitles.

Dankan *Aragaki* • Nanako Ōkouchi *Nakano* • Toshinori Omi *Kimura* • Ippei Soda *Ozawa* • Yoichi Nukumizu *Yashiro* • Great Gidayu *Nose* • Hiroyuki Kishi *Mochizuki* • Takashi Mitsuhashi *Komatsu* ■ *Dir* Hiroshi Shimizu • *Scr* Dankan, from the novel *Futeiki Basu no Kyaku* by Fumio Nakahara.

Ikiru ★★★★★ PG
Drama 1952 · Jap · BW · 141mins

Director Akira Kurosawa is celebrated for his samurai dramas, notably *Rashomon* and *Seven Samurai*, but many critics regard this contemporary drama as his greatest achievement. The story would appear to have many pitfalls: a meek civil servant is told he has terminal cancer, so he gets drunk, confronts the emptiness of his life and finally makes amends by turning a

derelict city area into a children's playground. This is almost the preserve of the American TV movie – crassly manipulative – but such is the delicacy of Kurosawa's direction, and the discreet power of Takashi Shimura's performance, that you will be moved to tears. In Japanese with English subtitles. ▭

Takashi Shimura *Kanji Watanabe* • Nobuo Kaneko *Mitsuo Watanabe, Kanji's son* • Kyoko Seki *Kazue Watanabe, Mitsuo's wife* • Makoto Kobori *Kiichi Watanabe, Kanji's brother* • Kumeko Urabe *Tatsu Watanabe* ■ *Dir* Akira Kurosawa • *Scr* Akira Kurosawa, Shinobu Hashimoto, Hideo Oguni

I'll Be Home for Christmas
★★★ PG

Comedy   1998 · US · Colour · 82mins

Think *Planes, Trains and Automobiles* set at Christmas instead of Thanksgiving and without the comic talents of Steve Martin or John Candy. A vehicle for *Home Improvement* teen actor Jonathan Taylor Thomas, this is watchable enough if you're in the festive mood, as he's clearly having fun as the smart aleck college kid who finds himself stranded in the desert, wearing a Santa suit (don't ask), and facing a bizarre journey back to his family home for the holidays. While the nightmare trip home has been done better there are some laughs to be had. ▭

Jonathan Taylor Thomas *Jake* • Jessica Biel *Allie* • Adam LaVorgna *Eddie* • Gary Cole *Jake's father* • Eve Gordon *Carolyn* • Lauren Maltby *Tracey* ■ *Dir* Arlene Sanford • *Scr* Harris Goldberg, Tom Nursall, from a story by Michael Allin

I'll Be Seeing You
★★ PG

Romantic drama   1944 · US · BW · 85mins

Over-egged schmaltz from the David O Selznick stable, and not a patch on his *Since You Went Away* the same year. Nevertheless, it's professionally made, as you'd expect from a major movie of its period. Ginger Rogers is impossibly cast as the girl let out of jail for Christmas, who falls for disturbed, shell-shocked soldier Joseph Cotten. The tale is basically junk, despite the valiant efforts of the two leads. The title song is a lovely and evocative wartime ballad, and deserved better than being attached to this tosh. ▭

Ginger Rogers *Mary Marshall* • Joseph Cotten *Zachary Morgan* • Shirley Temple *Barbara Marshall* • Spring Byington *Mrs Marshall* • Tom Tully *Mr Marshall* ■ *Dir* William Dieterle • *Scr* Marion Parsonnet, from the play *Double Furlough* by Charles Martin

I'll Be Your Sweetheart
★★★

Musical   1945 · UK · BW · 104mins

Having cornered the market in costume dramas, Gainsborough had a tilt at period musicals with this passable imitation of glossy Fox fripperies. Unfortunately, Michael Rennie is too stolid to convince as a tunesmith stomping the streets of *fin de siècle* London to find a publisher for his ditties. More at home, however, are Garry Marsh, as an unscrupulous sheet music pirate, and Margaret Lockwood, as the blowsy music hall star who helps Rennie smash a

system that made profits for everyone but the songwriters themselves. Val Guest directs with brio, but the songs he's saddled with are second-rate.

Margaret Lockwood *Edie Storey* • Michael Rennie *Bob Fielding* • Vic Oliver *Sam Kahn* • Peter Graves (2) *Jim Knight* • Moore Marriott *George le Brunn* • Frederick Burtwell *Pacey* • Maudie Edwards *Mrs Jones* ■ *Dir* Val Guest • *Scr* Val Guest, Val Valentine

I'll Be Yours
★★ U

Comedy   1947 · US · BW · 93mins

Deanna Durbin at 26 was still playing do-gooders with a penchant for breaking into song. Here she sings four of them in the course of persuading meat-packer Adolphe Menjou to employ struggling lawyer Tom Drake by pretending the young man is her jealous husband. The film is a remake of *The Good Fairy* (1935), which had been adapted by Preston Sturges from Ferenc Molnár's play, and starred Margaret Sullavan. This time around, with the element of fantasy abandoned and Durbin no Sullavan, the result is a lacklustre semi-musical, signalling the approaching end of Durbin's moneymaking film career.

Deanna Durbin *Louise Ginglebusher* • Tom Drake *George Prescott* • William Bendix Wechsberg • Adolphe Menjou *J Conrad Nelson* • Walter Catlett *Mr Buckingham* • Franklin Pangborn *Barber* ■ *Dir* William A Seiter • *Scr* Felix Jackson, from the film *The Good Fairy* by Preston Sturges, from the play *The Good Fairy* by Ferenc Molnár, from the adaptation and translation *The Good Fairy* by Jane Hinton

I'll Cry Tomorrow
★★★★

Biographical musical drama
1955 · US · BW · 118mins   U

A fine MGM biopic starring the tempestuous redhead Susan Hayward in one of the two biographical roles most identified with her, the other being her Oscar-winning performance as condemned murderess Barbara Graham in *I Want to Live!* in 1958. Here, Hayward is tormented actress and self-confessed dipsomaniac Lillian Roth – she starred with the Marx Brothers in *Animal Crackers*. Some may think that Hayward over-acts the drunk scenes, but most will find her performance to be vulnerable and honest: as an actress, she was certainly a great movie star. Helen Rose's superb costume design won an Oscar. There's a strong supporting cast, too, with Jo Van Fleet outstanding, and the whole is a superior example of the Hollywood star biopic.

Susan Hayward *Lillian Roth* • Richard Conte *Tony Bardeman* • Eddie Albert *Burt McGuire* • Jo Van Fleet *Katie Roth* • Don Taylor *Wallie* • Ray Danton *David Tredman* • Margo *Selma* ■ *Dir* Daniel Mann • *Scr* Helen Deutsch and Jay Richard Kennedy, from the book by Lillian Roth, Mike Connolly, Gerold Frank

I'll Do Anything
★★★ 12

Comedy drama   1994 · US · Colour · 111mins

Terms of Endearment, Broadcast News and *As Good As It Gets* all garnered director James L Brooks wonderful reviews, Oscar nods and box-office kudos. This swept-under-the-carpet folly achieved exactly the opposite, even though it's a reasonably well observed and often funny comedy about

Hollywood, with Nick Nolte playing a struggling actor trying to juggle his career with single-parent duties. Brooks filmed the movie as a musical, but all the songs were cut out after preview audiences gave it the thumbs down. The end result holds up surprisingly well despite the obvious holes where the songs have been dropped. A real oddity that's well worth watching. Contains swearing and nudity. ▭

Nick Nolte *Matt Hobbs* • Whittni Wright *Jeannie Hobbs* • Albert Brooks *Burke Adler* • Julie Kavner *Nan Mulhanney* • Joely Richardson *Cathy Breslow* • Tracey Ullman *Beth Hobbs* • Ian McKellen *John Earl McAlpine* ■ *Dir/Scr* James L Brooks

I'll Get You for This
★★

Crime drama   1950 · UK · BW · 89mins

George Raft in his mid-fifties was no longer in demand for starring roles in Hollywood, so he worked for less money in Europe, beginning with this corny adaptation of a James Hadley Chase thriller set in Italy. Raft is convincing enough as an American gambler and dances as smoothly as ever with Coleen Gray's American tourist, but looks puffed out fleeing from a murder frame-up.

George Raft *Nick Cain* • Coleen Gray *Kay Wonderly* • Enzo Staiola *Toni* • Charles Goldner *Massine* • Walter Rilla *Mueller* • Martin Benson *Sperazza* • Peter Illing *Ceralde* ■ *Dir* Joseph M Newman • *Scr* George Callahan, William Rose, from the novel *I'll Get You for This* by James Hadley Chase

Ill Met by Moonlight
★★★★ U

Second World War drama
1956 · UK · BW · 104mins

Although Michael Powell and Emeric Pressburger's inimitable movies often had wartime settings, not many could be called simply war films. This, however, is a rare exception and a very satisfying example of the genre to boot. Loosely based on a real operation in the Second World War, the action finds Dirk Bogarde on stirring form as a British officer given the task of working with the partisans in occupied Crete to kidnap the local German commander (Marius Goring). Fine acting, rugged scenery and a trenchant score all add to the film's attractions. The Americans gave it the more prosaic title of *Night Ambush*.

Dirk Bogarde *Major Paddy Leigh Fermor* • Marius Goring *General Karl Kreipe* • David Oxley *Captain Billy Stanley Moss* • Cyril Cusack *Sandy* • Laurence Payne *Manoli* • Wolfe Morris *George* • Michael Gough *Andoni Zoidakis* ■ *Dir* Michael Powell, Emeric Pressburger • *Scr* Michael Powell, Emeric Pressburger, from the book by W Stanley Moss • *Music* Mikis Theodorakis

I'll Never Forget What's 'Is Name
★★★

Comedy drama   1967 · UK · Colour · 98mins

After a string of Swinging Sixties satires, Michael Winner rather ran out of steam with this scathing look at the world of advertising. Substituting style for substance, the director allows the plot to ramble in places, although he redeems himself with a finale of triumphant vulgarity. Oliver Reed is

moodily unconvincing as the commercials director with literary pretensions, but Orson Welles is corpulently corrupt as the man who leads him back down the path of transient achievement and empty glamour. Carol White, meanwhile, is brassily vulnerable as Reed's secretary. This is so nearly spot-on; instead it ends up being frustratingly inconsequential.

Orson Welles *Jonathan Lute* • Oliver Reed *Andrew Quint* • Carol White *Georgina* • Harry Andrews *Gerald Slater* • Michael Hordern *Headmaster* • Wendy Craig *Louise Quint* • Marianne Faithfull *Josie* • Frank Finlay *Chaplain* • Edward Fox *Walter* ■ *Dir* Michael Winner • *Scr* Peter Draper

I'll See You in My Dreams
★★★ U

Musical biography 1951 · US · BW · 105mins

One of Doris Day's best vehicles, a rags-to-riches biopic based on the life of Gus Kahn, one of Tin Pan Alley's most popular songwriters. Kahn's played here by the likeable Danny Thomas, in one of his several attempts at movie stardom – he eventually found fame on American television. Day plays his wife, vying with Patrice Wymore for Thomas's charms. Michael Curtiz, always seriously undervalued as a director of musicals, despite credits such as *White Christmas*, *Yankee Doodle Dandy* and *King Creole*, gives this film a warmly human style that's thankfully unpretentious. Doris Day on top-form is a delight, and the songs, which include *Makin' Whoopee!* and *It Had to Be You*, really suit her. ▭

Doris Day *Grace LeBoy Kahn* • Danny Thomas *Gus Kahn* • Frank Lovejoy *Walter Donaldson* • Patrice Wymore *Gloria Knight* • James Gleason *Fred* • Mary Wickes *Anna* • Jim Backus *Sam Harris* ■ *Dir* Michael Curtiz • *Scr* Melville Shavelson, Jack Rose, from a story by Grace Kahn, Louis F Edelman

I'll Take Romance
★★★

Musical   1937 · US · BW · 85mins

Billed on its original advertisements as "Her Greatest Romance!", this was the last American film and penultimate movie of the Metropolitan Opera's lyric soprano, Nashville-born Grace Moore. This is a pleasant enough trifle viewed today, one of those silly plots about a kidnapped opera star, but the story doesn't really matter, existing only as an excuse for Miss Moore to sing some arias and the particularly attractive title song.

Grace Moore *Elsa Terry* • Melvyn Douglas *James Guthrie* • Helen Westley *Madame Della* • Stuart Erwin *"Pancho" Brown* • Margaret Hamilton *Margot* • Walter Kingsford *William Kane* • Richard Carle *Rudi* ■ *Dir* Edward H Griffith • *Scr* George Oppenheimer, Jane Murfin, from a story by Stephen Morehouse Avery

I'll Take Sweden
★★

Romantic comedy
1965 · US · Colour · 96mins

Set in the sixties, when Sweden meant "S-E-X" to a generation of film-goers, this limp comedy has an effervescing Bob Hope sadly deflated by a weak script and inept direction (*Bedtime for Bonzo*'s Frederick De Cordova). Hope is Tuesday Weld's father, desperate to

break up her relationship with Frankie Avalon, so he decamps to Sweden with daughter in tow. New love blossoms, to limited comic effect, but you can listen to Frankie Avalon sing a few songs.

Bob Hope *Bob Holcomb* • Tuesday Weld *JoJo Holcomb* • Frankie Avalon *Kenny Klinger* • Dina Merrill *Karin Grandstedt* • Jeremy Slate *Erik Carlson* ■ *Dir* Frederick De Cordova • *Scr* Nat Perrin, Bob Fisher, Arthur Marx, from a story by Nat Perrin

Illegal ★★★

Crime melodrama   1955 · US · BW · 87mins

A gripping thriller with Edward G Robinson as the DA who, after sending an innocent man to the chair, changes sides and becomes a lawyer, defending a racketeer. Scripted by WR Burnett (who wrote the classic gangster novel *Little Caesar* which Robinson also starred in), the story has some startling twists. With its strong performances and tightly controlled bursts of violence, this is another low-budget miracle from Lewis Allen, who also directed that marvellous assassination thriller, *Suddenly*, in 1954.

Edward G Robinson *Victor Scott* • Nina Foch *Ellen Miles* • Hugh Marlowe *Ray Borden* • Jayne Mansfield *Angel O'Hara* • Albert Dekker *Frank Garland* • Howard St John *EA Smith* • Ellen Corby *Miss Hinkel* • DeForest Kelley *Clary* ■ *Dir* Lewis Allen • *Scr* WR Burnett, James R Webb, from the play *The Mouthpiece* by Frank J Collins

Illegal Entry: Formula for Fear ★★ 18

Thriller   1993 · US · Colour · 83mins

Sabryn Genet, from the long-running American soap *The Young and the Restless*, gets top billing (with her surname spelled as Gene'T for some unknown reason) in this faintly steamy thriller. Genet becomes the unwitting holder of a major scientific discovery by her father and finds herself on the run from a number of sinister parties all eager to lay their hands on the recipe. It zips along nicely, despite the attempts to spice up the action with some unnecessary sex scenes. 🎞

Sabryn Genet [Gene'T *Sabryn*] *Tracie* • Gregory Vignolle *Adam Wright* • Barbara Lee Alexander *Pamela Raby* • Carol Hoyt *Catherine Reese* • Arthur Roberts *CA Wright* ■ *Dir* Henri Charr • *Scr* John B Pfeifer

Illegal in Blue ★★ 18

Erotic thriller   1995 · US · Colour · 93mins

Cop Dan Gauthier tries to do the right thing by reporting the disappearance of some confiscated money and finds himself on suspension. While moonlighting as a taxi driver, he meets disturbed nightclub singer Stacey Dash. They begin a passionate affair but things get complicated when her husband is murdered and Dash is the prime suspect. A failed attempt at *film noir* in the manner of *The Last Seduction*, this atmospheric thriller makes up for in sexiness what it lacks in coherence. Contains swearing, violence and sex scenes. 🎞

Stacey Dash *Kari* • Dan Gauthier *Chris* • Louis Giambalvo *Lieutenant Cavanaugh* • Trevor

Goddard *Mickey Fuller* • Michael Durrell *Michael Snyder* • David Groh *DA Frank Jacobi* ■ *Dir* Stu Segall • *Scr* Noel Hynd

Illegally Yours ★ PG

Romantic comedy   1988 · US · Colour · 102mins

Rob Lowe revived his flagging career in the nineties with tongue-in-cheek performances in *Wayne's World* and *Austin Powers: the Spy Who Shagged Me*, but he was still in a trough when he made this dreadful romantic comedy. Lowe is Richard Dice, who finds himself serving on a jury that is trying his ex-girlfriend. Dire in the extreme, this is a film that both Lowe and director Peter Bogdanovich would doubtless prefer to forget. And you will want to as well. 🎞

Rob Lowe *Richard Dice* • Colleen Camp *Molly Gilbert* • Kenneth Mars *Hal B Keeler* • Harry Carey Jr *Wally Finnegan* ■ *Dir* Peter Bogdanovich • *Scr* MA Stewart, Max Dickens

Illicit ★★

Romantic drama   1931 · US · BW · 76m

A glum and unmemorable weepie, dredged up by Warners as a vehicle for newly emerging name Barbara Stanwyck, the movie recounts the love affair and subsequent marriage of Stanwyck and James Rennie. Married life, however, spells the death of romance and the onset of boredom and infidelity. The future great star of melodrama does what she can with the material, which was given a controversial makeover two years later to become *Ex-Lady*, for another up-and-coming melodrama queen, Bette Davis.

Barbara Stanwyck *Anne Vincent* • James Rennie *Dick Ives* • Ricardo Cortez *Price Baines* • Natalie Moorhead *Margie True* • Charles Butterworth *Georgie Evans* • Joan Blondell *Helen "Duckie" Childers* ■ *Dir* Archie Mayo • *Scr* Harvey Thew, from the play by Edith Fitzgerald, Robert Riskin

Illicit Dreams ★★ 18

Erotic thriller   1994 · US · Colour · 90mins

Fans of Shannon Tweed's much seen body will be pleased to note that it makes several prominent appearances in this otherwise silly erotic thriller, which mixes a bit of new-age nonsense into the standard soft-core mix. Tweed plays a woman locked in a loveless marriage to cold millionaire Joe Cortese; she establishes a psychic link with Mr Right (Andrew Stevens, who also directed), with dangerous consequences. Contains swearing, violence and sex scenes. 🎞

Andrew Stevens *Nick* • Shannon Tweed *Moira* • Joe Cortese *Daniel* • Stella Stevens *Cicily* ■ *Dir* Andrew Stevens • *Scr* Karen Kelly

illtown ★★★

Crime drama   1996 · US · Colour · 94mins

A disturbing, harrowing look at the reality of drug dealing, this excellent adaption of the novel *The Cocaine Kids* also works as a compellingly offbeat thriller. Michael Rappaport and Lili Taylor are superb as the nice couple from the suburbs who also co-ordinate a team of teenagers who supply drugs to clubbers. However, their cosily amoral lifestyle is threatened by the arrival of former partner Adam Trese.

Michael Rapaport *Dante* • Lili Taylor *Micky* • Adam Trese *Gabriel* • Tony Danza *D'Avalon* • Isaac Hayes *George* • Saul Stein *Gunther* ■ *Dir* Nick Gomez • *Scr* Nick Gomez, from the book *The Cocaine Kids* by Terry Williams

Illumination ★★★★

Drama   1972 · Pol · Colour · 91mins

Krzysztof Zanussi's fourth feature chronicles the academic and sentimental education of a doctorate student, whose friends seem to live unquestioningly while he spends his time searching for answers in the physical laws of the universe. He passes such milestones as his first affair, the death of a friend, marriage, fatherhood, military service and the discovery that he has a fatal heart disease. The insertion of documentary passages and self-conscious stylisation affects the accessibility of Zanussi's contentions, but this is a bold attempt to say something serious about the human condition in a provocative and cinematic manner. In Polish with English subtitles.

Stanislaw Latallo *Franciszek Retman* • Monika Denisiewicz-Olbrzychska *Agnieszka* • Malgorzata Pritulak *Malgosia* • Edward Zebrowski *Doctor* • Jan Skotnicki *Patient* ■ *Dir/Scr* Krzysztof Zanussi

Illusions ★★ 15

Thriller   1992 · US · Colour · 98mins

Dynasty glamour pusses Heather Locklear and Emma Samms are reunited for this glossy, faintly ridiculous made-for-TV thriller. Locklear plays a woman just out of psychiatric care who suspects sister-in-law Samms is trying to drive her around the bend again. There's a good supporting cast (Ned Beatty, Susannah York, Robert Carradine) but the predictable plot seeps with clichés. 🎞

Robert Carradine *Greg* • Heather Locklear *Jan* • Emma Samms *Laura* • Ned Beatty *George* • Susannah York *Dr Sanders* ■ *Dir* Victor Kulle • *Scr* Peter Colley, from the play *I'll Be Back before Midnight* by Peter Colley

The Illustrated Man ★★★★ 15

Science-fiction fantasy   1969 · US · Colour · 98mins

Despite Rod Steiger inventing dialogue as he goes along, and the original author, Ray Bradbury, being angered by the producers' refusal to let him in on filming, this fantasy fable from director Jack Smight works surprisingly well. Steiger is in moody mode as an Everyman whose futuristic adventures are depicted in tattoos over a large part of his body. Claire Bloom, then Steiger's real-life wife, shares the drama if not the star billing, which Steiger deserved if only for the daily make-up routine of four hours of painful application. Contains violence and nudity. 🎞

Rod Steiger *Carl* • Claire Bloom *Felicia* • Robert Drivas *Willie* • Don Dubbins *Pickard* • Jason Evers *Simmons* • Tim Weldon *John* ■ *Dir* Jack Smight • *Scr* Howard B Kreitsek, from the book by Ray Bradbury

Illustrious Corpses ★★★★★

Political thriller   1976 · It · Colour · 120mins

A dazzling conspiracy thriller which begins with the assassination of a public prosecutor. There's a funeral, another assassination, then another before cop Lina Ventura – Italy's Robert Mitchum – gets on to the case, discovering that everything is rotten in the corridors of power. Inviting comparison with Hollywood movies such as *Executive Action* and *The Parallax View*, director Francesco Rosi's cynicism about Italian politics makes for a shocking and dispiriting denouement, while his preference for staging scenes amid architectural and sculptural echoes of the Roman Empire implies that history teaches us nothing. In Italian with English subtitles.

Lino Ventura *Inspector Rogas* • Alain Cuny *Judge Rasto* • Paolo Bonacelli *Dr Maxia* • Marcel Bozzuffi *Indolent Man* • Tina Aumont *Prostitute* • Max von Sydow *Chief Magistrate Riches* • Fernando Rey *Minister of Justice* ■ *Dir* Francesco Rosi • *Scr* Francesco Rosi, Tonino Guerra, Lino Jannuzzi, from the novel *Il Contesto* by Leonardo Sciascia

I'm All Right Jack ★★★★★ U

Satirical comedy   1959 · UK · BW · 100mins

The Boulting Brothers' sparkling comedy of industrial manners reunites many of the cast of their 1956 national-service classic *Private's Progress*. The scene this time is a factory where Dennis Price and Richard Attenborough are once more knee-deep in shady dealings and in need of naive Ian Carmichael to unwittingly carry them through. Terry-Thomas also returns from the earlier film, this time playing the personnel manager driven to distraction by Carmichael's incompetence. But stealing the entire show is Peter Sellers as the union official chained to the rule book, whose faith in communism is inspired by thoughts of "all them cornfields and ballet in the evenings". 🎞

Ian Carmichael *Stanley Windrush* • Peter Sellers *Fred Kite* • Terry-Thomas *Major Hitchcock* • Richard Attenborough *Sidney de Vere Cox* • Dennis Price *Bertram Tracepurcel* • Margaret Rutherford *Aunt Dolly* • Irene Handl *Mrs Kite* • Liz Fraser *Cynthia Kite* • John Le Mesurier *Waters* ■ *Dir* John Boulting • *Scr* Frank Harvey, Alan Hackney, John Boulting, from the novel *Private Life* by Alan Hackney

I'm Dancing as Fast as I Can ★★★ 15

Drama   1982 · US · Colour · 101mins

Powerful drama, with Jill Clayburgh terrific as a pill-popping documentary film-maker who decides to go cold turkey and kick her habit. The film graphically portrays the physical and mental consequences of her gutsy decision. Unfortunately, the production is weaker than the performances – but what performances! And what a cast! In addition to Clayburgh, look out for powerhouse turns from Nicol Williamson, Daniel Stern, Dianne Wiest, Joe Pesci, John Lithgow and Geraldine Page. 🎞

Jill Clayburgh *Barbara Gordon* • Nicol Williamson *Derek Bauer* • Dianne Wiest *Julie Addison* • Joe Pesci *Roger* • Geraldine Page *Jean Martin* • Daniel Stern *Jim* • John Lithgow

Brunner ■ *Dir* Jack Hofsiss • *Scr* David Rabe, from the novel by Barbara Gordon • *Cinematographer* Jan De Bont

I'm Dangerous Tonight
★★ 18

Horror 1990 · US · Colour · 88mins

You could be forgiven for thinking you've already come across this story in another filmic guise. Made four years before the Jim Carrey vehicle *The Mask*, this humble TV movie about a red cloak that transforms the personality of its owner comes from no less a director than Tobe Hooper of *The Texas Chain Saw Massacre* fame. Mädchen Amick, who has struggled to make an impact since playing Shelly in *Twin Peaks*, stars as the girl-next-door blissfully unaware she is wearing a cursed Aztec cloak. Sadly, she lacks presence as a leading player, while Anthony Perkins and Dee Wallace Stone are wasted in support.

Mädchen Amick *Amy O'Neill* ■ Anthony Perkins *Professor Buchanan* • R Lee Ermey *Captain Aickman* • Natalie Schafer *Gram* • Daisy Hall *Gloria* • Mary Frann *Martha* • Dee Wallace Stone *Wanda Thatcher* ■ *Dir* Tobe Hooper • *Scr* Bruce Lansbury, Philip John Taylor, from a short story by Cornell Woolrich

I'm Gonna Git You Sucka
★★★ 15

Blaxploitation spoof
1988 · US · Colour · 84mins

Sending up the blaxploitation movies of the seventies is a hard thing to carry off since the originals now look pretty funny anyway. Keenen Ivory Wayans makes a fair attempt, as he writes, directs and stars in this daft tale about a man returning from the army to find his brother has overdosed on gold medallions. Of course, he must take revenge against Mr Big (John Vernon) who sold the chains to his sibling. The film features some of the best known blaxploitation stars, including Bernie Casey, Antonio Fargas and *Shaft* composer Isaac Hayes. Sometimes the humour is so obvious you feel you're being hit over the head with a sledgehammer, but anyone who thought *Dumb and Dumber* was too subtle will be doubled up with mirth. Contains swearing, violence, sex scenes and nudity.

Keenen Ivory Wayans *Jack Spade* • Bernie Casey *John Slade* • Antonio Fargas *Flyguy* • Steve James *Kung Fu Joe* • Isaac Hayes *Hammer* • Clu Gulager *Lieutenant Baker* ■ *Dir/Scr* Keenen Ivory Wayans

I'm Losing You
★★★

Drama 1998 · US · Colour · 102mins

Writer/director Bruce Wagner has adapted his own novel about the wealthy but misery-plagued Krohn family of Los Angeles. Patriarch Frank Langella discovers he has terminal cancer but decides not to tell his family. Meanwhile son Andrew McCarthy, a "resting" actor, feuds with ex-wife Gina Gershon over their daughter. Langella's adopted daughter/niece Rosanna Arquette has just made a disturbing discovery about how her parents really died. Sharp scripting and a strong cast give this soapy film more depth than its *Dynasty*-type plot might suggest.

Frank Langella *Perry Needham Krohn* • Amanda Donohoe *Mona Deware* • Rosanna Arquette *Rachel Krohn* • Buck Henry *Philip Dragom* • Elizabeth Perkins *Aubrey* • Andrew McCarthy *Bertie Krohn* • Gina Gershon *Lidia* • Ed Begley Jr *Zev* ■ *Dir/Scr* Bruce Wagner, Bruce Wagner

I'm No Angel
★★★★

Comedy 1933 · US · BW · 87 mins

The third, best, and most profitable of Mae West's films (said to have hauled Paramount out of financial difficulties), in which the buxom, blonde vulgarian plays Tira, a carnival entertainer determined to climb the social ladder "wrong by wrong". In the course of the action, Mae gets acquitted of murder, sings several songs, does a lion-taming act, and sues Cary Grant, the object of her affections, for breach of promise. Wesley Ruggles directs the lively proceedings, which, thanks to the Legion of Decency having not yet been formed, are generously loaded with the star's *double entendres*.

Mae West *Tira* • Cary Grant *Jack Clayton* • Gregory Ratoff *Benny Pinkowitz* • Edward Arnold *Big Bill Barton* • Ralf Haralode *Slick Wiley* • Kent Taylor *Kirk Lawrence* • Gertrude Michael *Alicia Hatton* ■ *Dir* Wesley Ruggles • *Scr* Mae West, Harlan Thompson, from the (unproduced) • *Scr The Lady and the Lions* by Lowell Brentano

I'm Not Rappaport
★★★ 12

Comedy drama 1996 · US · Colour · 129mins

A park bench provides the setting for some stimulating verbal exchanges between Walter Matthau and Ossie Davis in this pleasing demonstration of "grey power". They play octogenarian pensioners who join forces to battle against the way relatives and institutions try to pigeon-hole them because of their age. Written and directed by Herb Gardner, from his Broadway play, this is a fine example of stars lifting a drama out of the realm of cliché through a mix of pratfalls and poignancy. Gerry Mulligan provides the jazz score.

Walter Matthau *Nat* • Ossie Davis *Midge* • Amy Irving *Clara* • Craig T Nelson *The Cowboy* • Boyd Gaines *Danforth* • Martha Plimpton *Laurie* • Guillermo Diaz *J C* • Elina Lowensohn *Clara Lemlich* ■ *Dir* Herb Gardner • *Scr* Herb Gardner, from his play

The Image
★★★★ 15

Drama 1990 · US · Colour · 89mins

An interesting and provocative look at TV journalism, with Albert Finney in fine form as the megalomaniac broadcaster who will do anything for good ratings. More hard-hitting than *Broadcast News*, and almost as impressive as *Network*, *The Image* also boasts a fine cast including Kathy Baker, John Mahoney (best known for his work in the *Frasier* TV series), Marsha Mason and Spalding Gray. Also watch out for a young Brad Pitt in one of his earlier (and smaller) roles. Contains swearing and nudity.

Albert Finney *Jason Cromwell* • Marsha Mason *Jean Cromwell* • John Mahoney *Irv Mickelson* • Swoosie Kurtz *Joanne Winslow-Darvish* • Kathy Baker *Marcie Guilford* • Spalding Gray *Frank Goodrich* • Brad Pitt *Steve Black* ■ *Dir* Peter Werner • *Scr* Brian Rehak

The Imagemaker
★★ 15

Political comedy drama
1986 · US · Colour · 89mins

An American president's former spin doctor takes a turn for the worse following the death of his wife. Roger Blackwell (Michael Nouri) finds himself in possession of an audio tape which could damage his former boss. Ostensibly about government corruption and media manipulation, this is a disappointing addition to the genre. Director Hal Weiner misses out on an opportunity to portray the intricacies of White House life, more interestingly explored in the context of satirical movies like *Wag the Dog*.

Michael Nouri *Roger Blackwell* • Anne Twomey *Molly Grainger* • Jerry Orbach *Byron Caine* • Jessica Harper *Cynthia* • Farley Granger *Ambassador* ■ *Dir* Hal Weiner • *Scr* Dick Goldberg, Hal Weiner

Images
★★★★

Psychological drama
1972 · Ire · Colour · 103mins

Director Robert Altman is probably best known for weaving multiple plotlines round his ensemble casts in films such as *Nashville*, *Short Cuts* and *Pret-a-Porter*. This disturbing portrait of the collision between fantasy and reality in the mind of schizophrenic Susannah York isn't his most accessible work but it's worth making the effort. York and husband René Auberjonois find their country weekend is disrupted by her violent hallucinations. York won the best actress award at the 1972 Cannes film festival for her stunning performance, which is complemented by Altman's innovative direction and Vilmos Zsigmond's photography.

Susannah York *Cathryn* • René Auberjonois *Hugh* • Marcel Bozzuffi *Rene* • Hugh Millais *Marcel* • Cathryn Harrison *Susannah* ■ *Dir* Robert Altman • *Scr* Robert Altman, from the story *In Search of Unicorns* by Susannah York

Imaginary Crimes
★★★ PG

Drama 1994 · US · Colour · 100mins

Harvey Keitel gives one of his most nuanced performances here as a single parent trying to support his family and raise two daughters in sixties Oregon. Always on the verge of "something big" that will make his fortune, Keitel is slowly revealed to be a self-centred con man. Fairuza Balk is also a stand-out as his elder daughter, an aspiring writer, who relates the tale in flashback. These are great characters; shame about the soap-opera, softly, softly approach.

Harvey Keitel *Ray Weiler* • Fairuza Balk *Sonya* • Kelly Lynch *Valery* • Vincent D'Onofrio *Mr Webster* • Diane Baker *Abigail Tate* • Chris Penn [Christopher Penn] *Jarvis* • Amber Benson *Margaret* ■ *Dir* Anthony Drazan • *Scr* Kristine Johnson, Davia Nelson, from the novel by Sheila Ballantyne

Imagine: John Lennon
★★★ 15

Documentary
1988 · US · Colour and BW · 99mins

Employing a format similar to the one used in the *Anthology* series, this solidly crafted documentary traces the career of John Lennon before and after the Beatles. In addition to TV and archive footage, the film includes home-movie material from the seventies, which is far more arresting than the familiar scenes of the Fab Four running through their hits before crowds of Beatlemaniacs. Soundbites from interviews given by Lennon from the early sixties onwards being deftly shaped into an informative narrative. Few new facts emerge, but it is still a must for fans.

John Lennon *Narrator* ■ *Dir* Andrew Solt • *Scr* Sam Egan, Andrew Solt

Imitation General
★★ U

War comedy 1958 · US · BW · 88mins

Sergeant Glenn Ford faces a dilemma when his commanding officer is killed in action. He decides to impersonate him, fearing that morale would decline if news of the general's death got around. Using his new authority, Ford issues various orders and advances the war effort by several months. It's pitched as a wartime comedy but lacks a sharp enough satirical bite to make the point that it's the uniform that counts, not the jerk inside it.

Glenn Ford *Master Sergeant Murphy Savage* • Red Buttons *Corporal Chan Derby* • Taina Elg *Simone* • Dean Jones *Corporal Terry Sellers* • Kent Smith *Brigadier General Charles Lane* ■ *Dir* George Marshall • *Scr* William Bowers, from a story by William Chamberlain

Imitation of Life
★★★★★

Melodrama 1934 · US · BW · 111 mins

In the vein of melodrama known as "a woman's picture", *Imitation of Life*, masterfully directed by John M Stahl, was an exemplary and irresistible contribution to the genre, and earned an Oscar nomination for best picture. The versatile and accomplished Claudette Colbert stars as the struggling widow and mother of a small daughter who joins forces with her black maid (Louise Beavers), also the mother of a small daughter, to revitalise their lives and fortunes by opening a successful pancake business. Trouble strikes on all fronts when Beavers's light-skinned daughter grows up and sets out to pass for white with devastating consequences, and Colbert's teenage daughter falls in love with her mother's beau (Warren William). A superb weepie with a moral lesson about racism.

Claudette Colbert *Beatrice "Bes" Pullman* • Warren William *Stephen Archer* • Ned Sparks *Elmer* • Louise Beavers *Delilah Johnson* ■ *Dir* John M Stahl • *Scr* William Hurlbut, from a novel by Fannie Hurst

Imitation of Life
★★★★ U

Melodrama 1959 · US · Colour · 123mins

This wonderfully mawkish weepie from Douglas Sirk is transformed into a vehicle for a self-parodying Lana Turner. The film was a huge hit in its day, Turner having just weathered both *Peyton Place* and a major murder scandal. The daft plot doesn't bear serious thought (Turner and her daughter both in love with the same man?), but the racial elements are delicately handled, if stereotypical, and surprisingly unchanged from the previous 1934 Claudette Colbert version. The colour and gowns are sumptuous and the cast a joy to

ⓤ = SUITABLE FOR ALL   ＵⒸ = SUITABLE FOR ALL, ESPECIALLY FOR YOUNG CHILDREN (VIDEO ONLY)   PG = PARENTAL GUIDANCE

behold. But the mood swings of Turner's character are hard to accept on any level other than the wildly melodramatic, and that's how this picture works best.

Lana Turner *Lora Meredith* • John Gavin *Steve Archer* • Sandra Dee *Susie, age 16* • Dan O'Herlihy *David Edwards* • Susan Kohner *Sarah Jane, age 18* • Robert Alda *Allen Loomis* • Juanita Moore *Annie Johnson* ■ *Dir* Douglas Sirk • *Scr* Eleanore Griffin, Allan Scott, from a novel by Fannie Hurst • *Cinematographer* Russell Metty • *Costume Designer* Bill Thomas, Jean Louis

Immaculate Conception
★★★ **15**

Drama   1991 · UK · Colour · 117mins

Exotic drama, with Melissa Leo as a wife desperate to get pregnant but who only succeeds after visit to a mystic Indian fertility sect. She rates it as a miracle and embraces both baby and religion to the exclusion of all else. Hubby James Wilby feels cold-shouldered as a result and jumps to the understandable conclusion that the conception may have been rather less immaculate than his wife let on. This is offbeat subject matter but it is handsomely mounted, with good performances from the two attractive leads and strong backing from Indian support cast. In English and Urdu with subtitles. ▭

James Wilby *Alister* • Melissa Leo *Hannah* • Ronny Jhutti *Kamal* • Shabana Azmi *Samira* ■ *Dir/Scr* Jamil Dehlavi

Immediate Family   ★★★ **15**

Drama   1989 · US · Colour · 95mins

An absorbing if schematic family drama, distinguished by an impressive cast. Glenn Close and James Woods play a wealthy childless couple who decide to adopt Mary Stuart Masterson's baby. But Masterson suddenly changes her mind, preferring to bring up the baby in near poverty with her boyfriend, Kevin Dillon. The script by Barbara Benedek pushes all the expected buttons; Jonathan Kaplan, who made *The Accused* and *Love Field*, directs; and there's a small role for Jane Greer, *femme fatale* of films noirs long ago. ▭

Glenn Close *Linda Spector* • James Woods *Michael Spector* • Mary Stuart Masterson *Lucy Moore* • Kevin Dillon *Sam* • Jane Greer *Michael's mother* ■ *Dir* Jonathan Kaplan • *Scr* Barbara Benedek

The Immigrant   ★★★★★ **U**

Silent comedy drama
1917 · US · BW · 20mins

One of the funniest, and bleakest, of Charlie Chaplin's early silents, with the steel of his social comment supporting the humour as he enters America, penniless and only just recovering from seasickness. Images of exclusion abound – a shot of the Statue of Liberty is followed by the immigrants being herded like cattle. Chaplin's social concerns put him closer to the writings of Charles Dickens than to the work of his fellow comedians. There's underlying bitterness here, sweetened only by his love for Edna Purviance. It's rare to find a comedy so profoundly affecting. ▭

Charles Chaplin *An immigrant* • Edna Purviance *An immigrant* • Albert Austin *Russian immigrant/a diner* • Stanley Sanford *Gambler-thief* • Eric Campbell *Head waiter* ■ *Dir/Scr* Charles Chaplin

Immoral Mr Teas   ★★ **18**

Erotic comedy   1959 · US · Colour · 62mins

The very first nudie-cutie movie from *Playboy* photographer-turned-cult director Russ Meyer is a landmark sexploitation classic. Before this coy tale of a delivery man (Meyer's army buddy Bill Teas) with the ability to see fully-clothed women naked appeared, the soft-core sex industry consisted of either pseudo-documentaries warning of the dangers of sexual activity or nudist colony romps. Meyer's silent farce, with a leering voice-over narration, changed all that and influenced an entire generation of smut peddlers. A badly dated but vital history lesson in the evolution of the sex film. ▭

Bill Teas *Mr Teas* • Ann Peters • Marily Wesley • Mischele Roberts • Dawn Danielle • Edward J Lakso *Narrator* • Peter A DeCenzie ■ *Dir/Scr* Russ Meyer

Immortal Bachelor   ★★

Comedy   1980 · It · Colour · 112mins

Often hilarious and frequently racy, this Neapolitan farce finds cleaning woman Monica Vitti on trial for murdering her philandering husband, Giancarlo Giannini. Meanwhile, jury member Claudia Cardinale fantasises about Vitti's predicament in relation to her own marriage to boring Vittorio Gassman. The quartet of fine Italian comedy stars help to move director Marcello Fondato's slight skit up a few entertainment notches. But only just… In Italian with English subtitles.

Claudia Cardinale *Gabriella Sansoni* • Vittorio Gassman *Andrea Sansoni* • Giancarlo Giannini *Gino Benacio* • Monica Vitti *Tina Candela* ■ *Dir* Marcello Fondato • *Scr* Marcello Fondato, Francesco Scardamaglia

Immortal Beloved   ★★★★ **15**

Historical biography
1994 · UK/US · Colour · 115mins

The director of gruesome horror flick *Candyman* might seem an unlikely biographer of Beethoven, but, in seeking to identify the "immortal beloved" addressed in the composer's will, Bernard Rose has produced a respectful and imaginative study. It's an audacious mixture of *Citizen Kane* and *Amadeus*, with some *Fantasia*-like musical sequences added. Cinema has rarely given classical music such a chance to weave its spell. Gary Oldman gives a bravura performance, although some scenes might have been played with a touch more moderato. Contains nudity. ▭

Gary Oldman *Ludwig van Beethoven* • Jeroen Krabbé *Anton Schindler* • Isabella Rossellini *Countess Anna Maria Erdödy* • Johanna Ter Steege *Johanna van Beethoven* • Valeria Golino *Julia Guicciardi* • Miriam Margolyes *Frau Streicher* ■ *Dir/Scr* Bernard Rose

The Immortal Sergeant   ★★★

Second World War drama
1943 · US · BW · 90mins

Decent Second World War flagwaver, with soldier Henry Fonda and other platoon members lost in the desert wastes of Libya. It's a story of survival in which sergeant Thomas Mitchell has the homing instincts of a pigeon, if not the stamina of a camel, enabling Fonda to become a hero by leading his people to safety. Meanwhile, assorted airborne Germans are on hand to provide bursts of action, and Maureen O'Hara appears in flashback so as not to make this an all-boy affair. Well shot by cinematographer Arthur Miller, a master of black and white.

Henry Fonda *Colin* • Maureen O'Hara *Valentine* • Thomas Mitchell *Sergeant Kelly* • Allyn Joslyn *Cassity* • Reginald Gardiner *Benedict* • Melville Cooper *Pilcher* • Bramwell Fletcher *Symes* ■ *Dir* John M Stahl • *Scr* Lamar Trotti, from the novel by John Brophy

The Immortal Story   ★★★ **15**

Black drama   1968 · Fr · Colour · 54mins

A weird little Orson Welles movie, lasting under an hour and made for French TV. The parable-like story is by Isak Dinesen (author of *Out of Africa*) and concerns a Macao trader who hires a young sailor to sleep with his "wife" – who isn't his wife at all, but a whore. Welles revels in the role of the trader. Jeanne Moreau is as good as one expects but Norman Eshley as the sailor has an impossible task – to be pretty and plausible at the same time. It's easy to be cynical about it, but it's undeniably atmospheric. A French language film. ▭

Orson Welles *Mr Clay* • Jeanne Moreau *Virginie Ducrot* • Roger Coggio *Elishama Levinsky–the Clerk* • Norman Eshley *Paul–the Sailor* • Fernando Rey *Merchant in Street* ■ *Dir* Orson Welles • *Scr* Orson Welles, Louise de Vilmorin, from the story by Isak Dinesen

The Immortals   ★★★ **18**

Action crime thriller
1995 · US · Colour · 93mins

Although essentially another dose of the post-Tarantino "thieves meet up after illegal activities for a large helping of double-cross and death", this has an interesting cast for a film of its rather limited stature, plus an unexpected and enjoyably ludicrous twist that ties all the central characters together. Hamming it up as the assorted criminal stereotypes are the likes of Eric Roberts, Tony Curtis (the mob boss, naturally), Tia Carrere, Joe Pantoliano and William Forsythe. Fun, if you catch it in the right mood. Contains swearing, violence and brief nudity. ▭

Eric Roberts *Jack* • Tia Carrere *Gina* • Tony Curtis *Dominic* • Joe Pantoliano *Pete* • Kevin Bernhardt *Billy* • Brian Finney *George* • Kieran Mulroney *Kerry* • William Forsythe *Tim* ■ *Dir* Brian Grant • *Scr* Kevin Bernhardt, from a story by Elie Samaha.

Impact   ★★★

Crime melodrama   1949 · US · BW · 111mins

Tough stuff, as Brian Donlevy's wife and lover plan on getting rid of him, but it's not quite as easy as it seems.

There's a terrific supporting cast here, including Charles Coburn, Anna May Wong and Mae Marsh, but you'll find yourself rooting for Donlevy, so often cast as the heavy earlier in his career. It's a clever movie, that doesn't quite make it as an A-feature, but with a good deal more class and style than most B-movies.

Brian Donlevy *Walter Williams* • Ella Raines *Marsha Peters* • Charles Coburn *Lieutenant Quincy* • Helen Walker *Irene Williams* • Anna May Wong *Su Lin* • Mae Marsh *Mrs Peters* ■ *Dir* Arthur Lubin • *Scr* Dorothy Reid, Jay Dratler

Impact   ★★ **U**

Crime drama   1963 · UK · BW · 64mins

Co-written by star Conrad Phillips and director Peter Maxwell, this filler, produced in a matter of days on a shoestring budget, contains no surprises in the plot as ace reporter Phillips is set up as a train robber by vengeful club boss George Pastell. Maxwell just about keeps what action there is ticking over, but he is fighting a losing battle with a cast that is substandard, even for a B movie.

Conrad Phillips *Jack Moir* • George Pastell *The Duke* • Ballard Berkeley *Bill Mackenzie* • Linda Marlowe *Diana* ■ *Dir* Peter Maxwell • *Scr* Peter Maxwell, Conrad Phillips

Impasse   ★★

Adventure   1969 · US · Colour · 99mins

"I was then offered a film called *Impasse* – a good word for where my career was," wrote Burt Reynolds in his autobiography. Filmed in the Philippines, Richard Benedict's film is a stale, derivative action tale about a crock of gold buried by four GIs during the Second World War. Reynolds plays a shady trader based in Manila who persuades the soldiers to regroup and reclaim it. The result is a sort of *Treasure of the Sierra Madre*, minus the style and the great acting.

Burt Reynolds *Pat Morrison* • Anne Francis *Bobby Jones* • Lyle Bettger *Hansen* • Rodolfo Acosta *Draco* • Jeff Corey *Wombat* • Clarke Gordon *Trev Jones* • Miko Mayama *Mariko* ■ *Dir* Richard Benedict • *Scr* John C Higgins

Imperative   ★★★

Drama
1982 · W Ger/Fr · BW and Colour · 96mins

Coming between his key Solidarity era, *The Contract* (1980), and the Golden Lion-winning *A Year of the Quiet Sun* (1984), this is one of Krzysztof Zanussi's least-known films. It follows the trials of disillusioned academic Robert Powell, whose search for elusive truths in religion makes for absorbing if rather bleak viewing.

Robert Powell *Augustin* • Brigitte Fossey *Yvonne* • Sigfrit Steiner *Professor* • Matthias Habich *Theologist* • Leslie Caron *Mother* ■ *Dir/Scr* Krzysztof Zanussi

The Imperfect Lady   ★

Period drama   1947 · US · BW · 97mins

This lavishly mounted damp squib of a drama miscasts the essentially demure Teresa Wright as a music hall dancer of Victorian London. Ray Milland's aristocratic politician eventually persuades her to marry him but this coincides with a nasty scandal when Wright is the only alibi for accused murderer Anthony Quinn. Can their relationship survive if she does the right thing by Quinn? Apparently Paulette Goddard was considered for the lead role – which might have made the picture worth watching.

Ray Milland *Clive Loring* • Teresa Wright *Millicent Hopkins* • Cedric Hardwicke *Lord Belmont* • Virginia Field *Rose Bridges* • Anthony Quinn *Jose Martinez* • Reginald Owen *Mr Hopkins* ■ *Dir* Lewis Allen • *Scr* Karl Tunberg, from a story by Ladislas Fodor

Imperial Venus ★★★
Historical drama 1963 · It/Fr · Colour · 140m

A far cry from those immortal classics *L'Eternel Retour* (1943) and *La Symphonie Pastorale* (1946), this sweeping costume drama was clearly a jobbing assignment for Jean Delannoy, whose prospects had suffered greatly from comparisons with the young Turks of the New Wave. There's undeniable splendour in this account of the life and loves of Napoleon's sister, Paolina, but the absence of passion renders it a stilted and stuffy affair. Like many sixties movies from the Continent, it was made in English alongside the foreign-language version.

Gina Lollobrigida *Paolina* • Stephen Boyd *Jules de Canouville* • Gabriele Ferzetti *Freron* • Raymond Pellegrin *Napoleon* • Micheline Presle *Josephine* • Massimo Girotti *Leclerc* ■ *Dir* Jean Delannoy • *Scr* Jean Delannoy, Jean Aurenche, Rodolphe M Arlaud, Leonardo Benvenuti, Piero De Bernardi, John Michael Hayes

The Impersonator ★★
Crime mystery 1962 · UK · BW · 63mins

Signing an American star for a British movie has always been considered a surefire way of attracting international attention. Whereas today's imports are of the calibre of Julia Roberts, back in the sixties our cash-strapped companies had to make do with the likes of minor character actor John Crawford. To give him his due, he's the best thing in this unsettling study of insularity, playing an airman stationed near a sleepy country community who becomes the prime suspect when a number of women die in suspicious circumstances. It's shoestring stuff, but still better than most of its kind.

John Crawford *Jimmy Bradford* • Jane Griffiths *Ann Loring* • Patricia Burke *Mrs Lloyd* • John Salew *Harry Walker* • John Dare *Tommy Lloyd* ■ *Dir* Alfred Shaughnessy • *Scr* Alfred Shaughnessy, Kenneth Cavender

Implicated ★★
Erotic thriller 1994 · US · Colour · 85mins

An erotic thriller of the kind that has made director Jim Wynorski a well-known name in the straight-to-video business. Here, Wynorski hooks up with *Beastmaster 2* stars Marc Singer and Wings Hauser for a seedy story about a fraud investigator who becomes "emotionally" involved with the widow of the embezzler he's been tracking. But detective Johnny Williams is convinced that Singer and Shannon Tweed are up to something much more sinister than making whoopee. With not a single unexpected twist in sight, this is neither titillating nor thrilling. Contains violence, swearing, sex scenes and nudity.

Marc Singer *Pete Starky* • Shannon Tweed *Carla Duvall* • Wings Hauser *Leeland Duvall* • Johnny Williams *Marv Riker* ■ *Dir* Jim Wynorski • *Scr* William C Martell

The Importance of Being Earnest ★★★★ [U]
Comedy drama 1952 · UK · Colour · 91mins

As old as cinema itself, *The Importance of Being Earnest* celebrated its centenary in 1995. Shot in sumptuous Technicolor, Anthony Asquith's respectful adaptation of Oscar Wilde's sparkling comedy of errors thankfully rarely breaks free of its theatrical origins, the steady direction keeping Wilde's polished barbs and *bons mots* firmly to the fore and providing an invaluable record of an expert cast at work. Michael Redgrave and Michael Denison are clipped and composed as the gentlemen of leisure, whose innocent deceptions imperil their romantic aspirations towards the coquettish Joan Greenwood and Dorothy Tutin. But upstaging them all is Dame Edith Evans as Lady Bracknell, whose quavering "A handbag" is one of cinema's great moments. [📺] **DVD**

Michael Redgrave *Jack Worthing* • Michael Denison *Algernon Moncrieff* • Edith Evans *Lady Bracknell* • Dorothy Tutin *Cecily Cardew* • Joan Greenwood *Gwendolen Fairfax* • Margaret Rutherford *Miss Prism* ■ *Dir* Anthony Asquith • *Scr* Anthony Asquith, from the play by Oscar Wilde • *Costume Designer* Beatrice Dawson

The Importance of Being Earnest ★★
Comedy drama 1992 · US · Colour · 123mins

A modern take on one of Oscar Wilde's most celebrated plays. Although set in London, the period is contemporary and the African-American cast make no attempt to get their tongues round British accents. The film suffers from the usual problems of trying to "open up" a stage play, and the low-budget tape-to-film look doesn't help. The cast includes Brock Peters (*To Kill a Mockingbird*, *Carmen Jones*) and former *ER* actress CCH Pounder, but this is an experiment that doesn't really work. Fans of Wilde's play are probably better off seeking out the 1952 version.

Brock Peters *Doctor Chausible* • CCH Pounder *Miss Prism* • Obba Babatunde *Lane* • Wren T Brown *Algernon* • Chris Calloway *Gwendolyn* • Lanei Chapman *Cecily* ■ *Dir* Kurt Baker • *Scr* Peter Andrews, Kurt Baker, from the play by Oscar Wilde

The Important Man ★★★★
Drama 1961 · Mex · BW · 100mins

Best known for his collaborations with working-class icon Pedro Infante, Mexican director Ismael Rodriguez teamed with Japanese superstar Toshiro Mifune for this adaptation of the novel by Rogelio Barriga Rivas. Mifune excels as the coarse peasant, who, in spite of abusing his family and consorting with other women, has set his heart on being elected "chief for a day" in a forthcoming religious festival. Strikingly photographed by camera ace Gabriel Figueroa, this Oscar-nominated neorealist drama refuses either to sentimentalise the harsh rural conditions or excuse the boorish

behaviour of its anti-heroic protagonist. A Spanish language film.

Toshiro Mifune *Animas* • Flor Silvestre *Catania* • Antonio Aguilar *Tadeo* ■ *Dir* Ismael Rodriguez • *Scr* Ismael Rodriguez, Vincente Orona Jr, from the novel *La Mayordomia* by Rogelio Barriga Rivas

The Impostor ★★★ [U]
Second World War drama 1944 · US · BW · 57mins

The Nazi invasion of France inadvertently saves condemned murderer Jean Gabin when an air raid hits. Literally keeping his head, he impersonates a French soldier and transforms himself into a resistance hero in North Africa, bravely launching an attack on an Italian desert base. Made by French wartime exiles in Hollywood, this is a relatively rare French flagwaver, with part of its plot seemingly drawn from *Casablanca*, and a charismatic performance by Gabin, who was France's answer to Humphrey Bogart.

Jean Gabin *Clement* • Richard Whorf *Lt Varenne* • Allyn Joslyn *Bouteau* • Ellen Drew *Yvonne* • Peter Van Eyck *Hafner* • Ralph Morgan *Col De Bolvan* ■ *Dir* Julien Duvivier • *Scr* Julien Duvivier, Marc Connelly, Lynn Starling, Stephen Longstreet • *Music* Dimitri Tiomkin [Dmitri Tiomkin]

The Impostors ★★★ [15]
Period comedy 1998 · US · Colour · 97mins

Actor Stanley Tucci followed his critically acclaimed directorial debut, *Big Night*, with this farcical comedy (originally titled *Ship of Fools*), in which he and the under-rated Oliver Platt star as two out-of-work actors in the Depression who stow away on a luxury liner populated with eccentric passengers. A spoof on classics like *Grand Hotel*, the film features some rather old-fashioned slapstick, which often works well thanks to the timing skills of the eclectic cast. Tucci has gathered an array of familiar faces and, in the most hilarious turns of all, Billy Connolly (as a frisky tennis player), Steve Buscemi (as a suicidal performer named Happy) and Tucci's *Big Night* co-director Campbell Scott (as the Nazi-esque Meistrich). Enjoyable but uneven. Contains some swearing. [📺]

Oliver Platt *Maurice* • Stanley Tucci *Arthur* • Walker Jones *Maitre d'* • Jessica Walling *Attractive woman* • David Lipman *Baker* • E Katherine Kerr *Gertrude* • George Guidall *Claudius* • William Hill *Bernardo* • Alfred Molina *Jeremy Burtom* • Lili Taylor *Lily* • Steve Buscemi *Happy Franks* • Isabella Rossellini *Queen (veiled woman)* • Billy Connolly *Sparks* • Hope Davis *Emily* • Campbell Scott *Meistrich* • Woody Allen ■ *Dir/Scr* Stanley Tucci

Impromptu ★★★ [15]
Biographical romantic comedy 1991 · UK · Colour · 102mins

Either you'll relish the opportunity to see Hugh Grant as Chopin and Julian Sands as Liszt, or else you'll reach for the channel changer the moment James Lapine's period romance begins. If you choose the latter option, however, you'll miss Judy Davis's superb performance as notorious female novelist George Sand, who flits from love affair to duel with a wondrous disregard for the conventions

of 19th-century society. There's some splendid casting here, not least Ralph Brown of *Withnail & I* fame as Eugene Delacroix and Emma Thompson as the Duchess d'Antan. It's not exactly history, but it's still hugely enjoyable. [📺]

Judy Davis *George Sand* • Hugh Grant *Frederic Chopin* • Mandy Patinkin *Alfred DeMusset* • Bernadette Peters *Marie d'Agoult* • Julian Sands *Franz Liszt* • Ralph Brown *Eugene Delacroix* • Georges Corraface *Felicien Mallefille* • Anton Rodgers *Duke d'Antan* • Emma Thompson *Duchess d'Antan* • Anna Massey *George Sand's mother* ■ *Dir* James Lapine • *Scr* Sarah Kernochan

Improper Channels ★★
Comedy 1981 · Can · Colour · 91mins

A comedy about child abuse? Rest assured, this Canadian screwball isn't as sinister as it sounds: five-year-old Sarah Stevens's injuries are merely the result of a scrape in her father's camper. Officious social worker Monica Parker thinks otherwise, however, and dad Alan Arkin has to reunite with his estranged wife, Mariette Hartley, to retrieve the tot from care. Director Eric Till accentuates the ridiculousness of the situation. Unfortunately, the screenplay's attempts to put a message across not only feel preachy, but also slow down the farce.

Alan Arkin *Jeffrey Martley* • Mariette Hartley *Diana Martley* • Monica Parker *Gloria Washburn* • Sarah Stevens *Nancy Martley* • Danny Higham *Jack* • Richard Farrell *Fraser* ■ *Dir* Eric Till • *Scr* Ian Sutherland, Adam Arkin, Morrie Ruvinsky, from a story by Morrie Ruvinsky

Improper Conduct ★★ [18]
Erotic thriller 1994 · US · Colour · 91mins

Back in 1983 Steven Bauer looked to be on the brink of stardom with his role as Al Pacino's best chum in *Scarface*. Sadly, things didn't seem to quite click and since then he's largely found himself stuck in straight-to-video dross such as this erotic thriller, which, unconvincingly, also tries to provide a serious indictment of sexual harassment. Lee Ann Beaman plays a woman who sets out to avenge the hounding of her sister (Tahnee Welch, who appeared in *Cocoon* and is Raquel Welch's daughter) who was driven out of her job after turning down the advances of the boss's son-in-law; Bauer is the lawyer friend who reluctantly helps her. Contains violence, swearing and sex scenes [📺]

Steven Bauer *Sam* • Tahnee Welch *Ashley* • John Laughlin *Michael* • Nia Peeples *Bernadette* • Lee Anne Beaman *Kay* • Stuart Whitman *Mr Frost* ■ *Dir* Jag Mundhra • *Scr* Carl Austin, from a story by Jag Mundhra

An Impudent Girl ★★★★ [15]
Drama 1985 · Fr · Colour · 92mins

This is a typically insightful study of burgeoning youth from director Claude Miller. In only her third feature, Charlotte Gainsbourg is both rebellious and vulnerable as the teenager seeking an escape from her monotonous home life by hooking up with her idol, teenage pianist Clothilde Baudon. Their misadventures are more painful and revelatory than those featured in most rites-of-passage pictures, largely because the doubts

[U] = SUITABLE FOR ALL [Uc] = SUITABLE FOR ALL, ESPECIALLY FOR YOUNG CHILDREN (VIDEO ONLY) [PG] = PARENTAL GUIDANCE

and dreams the girls harbour are so normal. However, the film derives much of its honesty from the exceptional performance of Gainsbourg, whose expressions and emotions always ring true. In French with English subtitles. ▭

Charlotte Gainsbourg *Charlotte Castang* • Bernadette Lafont *Leone* • Jean-Claude Brialy *Sam* • Raoul Billerey *Antoine* • Clothilde Baudon *Clara Bauman* ■ *Dir* Claude Miller • *Scr* Claude Miller, Luc Béraud, Bernard Stora, Annie Miller

Impulse ★★
Crime thriller 1955 · UK · BW · 80mins

Routine British second-feature, although Arthur Kennedy (five times nominated for an Oscar) is a cut above the average imported American lead. Kennedy has a fling with nightclub singer Constance Smith, who involves him in a crime. Producers Robert S Baker and Monty Berman began with B-films like this, moved into Hammer-style horror, and ended up developing several major TV series. Screenwriter "Jonathan Roach" is actually director Cy Endfield, taking refuge in the UK from the McCarthy witch-hunts.

Arthur Kennedy *Alan Curtis* • Constance Smith *Lila* • Joy Shelton *Elizabeth Curtis* • Jack Allen *Freddie* • James Carney *Jack Forrester* • Cyril Chamberlain *Gray* ■ *Dir* Charles de Lautour • *Scr* Lawrence Huntington, Jonathan Roach [Cy Endfield], John Gilling, from a story by Carl Nystrom, from a story by Robert S Baker

Impulse ★
Crime thriller 1975 · US · Colour · 89mins

Film historians seeking the quintessential ham performance by William Shatner would be advised to choose this mid-seventies effort, made during Shatner's lowest career point after *Star Trek*. Ruth Roman's little girl can't convince her that her new boyfriend (guess who) is really a psychotic murderer. Shatner, sporting a different hairstyle in almost every shot, jumps up and down as if he has to go to indescribable expressions, and uses his famous stop/start enunciation to ludicrous extremes. His performance alone makes this a must for bad movie fans, but if you need further incentive, there's an appearance by Harold "Oddjob" Sakata as Karate Pete.

William Shatner *Matt Stone* • Ruth Roman *Julia Marstow* • Jennifer Bishop *Ann Moy* • Kim Nicholas *Tina Moy* • Harold Sakata *Karate Pete* • James Dobson *Clarence* ■ *Dir* William Grefe • *Scr* Tony Crechales

Impulse ★★★ 18
Thriller 1984 · US · Colour · 86mins

This sharp, under-rated slice of horror manages to put a sly spin on a familiar scenario. In a typical small town, the residents are starting to behave a little oddly; there's nothing particularly outlandish in their actions, it is just that they seem to be giving in to their baser instincts. Tim Matheson is the outsider who begins to think that something is up, and he is well supported by relative newcomers Meg Tilly and Bill Paxton, plus scene-stealing veteran Hume Cronyn. ▭

Tim Matheson *Stuart* • Meg Tilly *Jennifer* • Hume Cronyn *Dr Carr* • John Karlen *Bob Russell* • Bill Paxton *Eddie* • Amy Stryker *Margo* • Claude Earl Jones *Sheriff* • Robert Wightman *Howard* ■ *Dir* Graham Baker • *Scr* Bart Davis, Don Carlos Dunaway

Impulse ★★★ 18
Psychological thriller 1990 · US · Colour · 104mins

Actor-turned-director Sondra Locke is probably still best known for her acrimonious split from then-partner Clint Eastwood in the late eighties. The attendant publicity has somewhat overshadowed her subsequent career, which is perhaps unfair, as she brings a deft hand to this rather gloomy look at LA cops and hookers. Theresa Russell gives one of her best film performances as a hard-boiled undercover cop. There is a lot that is very ordinary about this movie and it has no great insights to impart, but Russell's dramatic presence ensures that it succeeds, nonetheless. Contains swearing, violence, sex scenes and nudity. ▭

Theresa Russell *Lottie Mason* • Jeff Fahey *Stan Harris* • George Dzundza *Joe Morgan* • Alan Rosenberg *Charley Katz* • Nicholas Mele *Rossi* • Eli Danker *Dimarjian* ■ *Dir* Sondra Locke • *Scr* John De Marco, Leigh Chapman, from a story by John De Marco

In a Lonely Place ★★★★★ PG
Classic film noir 1950 · US · BW · 89mins

In one of the very best dramas ever made about the movie industry, Humphrey Bogart stars as a jaded, heavy-drinking Hollywood screenwriter who becomes the prime suspect in the murder of hat-check girl Martha Stewart. This dark, gripping *film noir* gives Bogart a tremendous role that allows him to be sympathetic and sinister at the same time, a complex character teetering on the brink of destruction. His co-star and soulmate here is Gloria Grahame, then director Nicholas Ray's wife, though the part was specifically written for Bogart's wife, Lauren Bacall, whom Warner Bros refused to loan out. ▭

Humphrey Bogart *Dixon Steele* • Gloria Grahame *Laurel Gray* • Frank Lovejoy *Brub Nicolai* • Carl Benton Reid *Captain Lochner* • Art Smith *Mel Lippman* • Jeff Donnell *Sylvia Nicolai* ■ *Dir* Nicholas Ray • *Scr* Andrew Solt, from a story by Edmund H North, from the novel by Dorothy B Hughes • *Cinematographer* Burnett Guffey

In a Shallow Grave ★★ 15
Romantic drama 1988 · US · Colour · 87mins

A worthy, if sometimes overly melodramatic tale from the respected American Playhouse team. Based on the novel by James Purdy, Michael Biehn – cast very much against type – plays a bitter war hero who becomes fascinated with a young man (Patrick Dempsey) working for him. A study in class and sexual tension, it's beautifully acted, if directed at a slack pace. ▭

Michael Biehn *Garnet Montrose* • Maureen Mueller *Georgina Rance* • Michael Beach *Quintas Pearch* • Patrick Dempsey *Potter Daventry* • Thomas Boyd Mason *Edgar Doust* ■ *Dir* Kenneth Bowser • *Scr* Kenneth Bowser, from the novel by James Purdy

In a Stranger's Hand ★★★ 15
Thriller 1991 · US · Colour · 89mins

A chilling mystery of kidnapping and murder, directed by David Greene, the Manchester-born film-maker better known for such seventies' movies as *Godspell* and *The Count of Monte Cristo*, and, in an earlier life as an actor, for appearing in the classic 1950 PoW film *The Wooden Horse*. Robert Urich, a seasoned TV-movie veteran, gives another trusty performance as a man who decides not to get involved after witnessing a girl's kidnap. But fate has other ideas. Contains violence and drug abuse. ▭

Robert Urich *Jack Bauer* • Megan Gallagher *Laura McKillin* • Brett Cullen *Peter Harmon* • Vondie Curtis-Hall *Detective Gary Hopkins* ■ *Dir* David Greene • *Scr* Matthew Bombeck, from the story *The Last Stop* by Matt Benjamin

In a Year of 13 Moons ★★★★ 18
Drama 1978 · W Ger · Colour · 119mins

Inspired by the suicide of his lover, Armin Meier, this was one of Rainer Werner Fassbinder's most personal statements: as well as writer/director, he acted as cinematographer, designer and editor. The film also ranks among his most uncompromising condemnations of conformity, with transsexual Volker Spengler's desire to find emotional and social acceptance a root cause of his/her misery. Fassbinder refuses to let us identify with the characters and employs harshly lit and cluttered visuals to distract from the dialogue. Jarring, pessimistic and played with terrifying candour, this is a unique and disconcerting experience. In German with English subtitles. ▭

Volker Spengler *Elvira Weishaupt* • Ingrid Caven *Red Zora* • Gottfried John *Anton Saitz* • Elisabeth Trissenaar *Irene* • Eva Mattes *Marie-Ann* ■ *Dir/Scr* Rainer Werner Fassbinder

In All Innocence ★★ 15
Drama 1998 · Fr · Colour · 101mins

It's hard to believe this adaptation of Georges Simenon's novel was made by the same Pierre Jolivet who directed that intense morality tale, *Force Majeure*. Gone is the depth of characterisation and the probing intellect; in their place comes a designer *noir* style that makes comparisons with the original 1958 Claude Autant-Lara film, *En Cas de Malheur*, all the more unflattering. In the absence of psychological truth, actorly earnestness scarcely atones. Yet Carole Bouquet is credibly crushed as her lawyer husband Gérard Lanvin defends wild child Virginie Ledoyen on a robbery charge, only to fall for her charms in the process. In French with English subtitles. ▭

Gérard Lanvin *Michel* • Virginie Ledoyen *Cécile* • Carole Bouquet *Viviane* • Guillaume Canet *Vincent* • Aurelie Verillon *Samira* • Denis Podalydes *Martorel* ■ *Dir* Pierre Jolivet • *Scr* Roselyne Bosch, from the novel *En Cas de Malheur* by Georges Simenon

In & Out ★★★★ 12
Comedy 1997 · US · Colour · 86mins

Kevin Kline stars as the soon-to-be-married small town teacher who is outed by an ex-pupil-turned-Hollywood-star (Matt Dillon) during his televised Oscar acceptance speech. Inspired by Tom Hanks' *Philadelphia* acceptance speech (in which he thanked his gay professor), this has some very funny moments as Kline, his wedding-obsessed mother (Debbie Reynolds) and surprised fiancée (Joan Cusack) struggle with the fact he may be gay, and there's a nice supporting turn from Tom Selleck as the openly gay reporter who comes to town to cover the story. Thanks to Kline's sharp but moving performance, what could have been a stereotypical or even camp role is actually a fleshed out and sensitive one. Contains swearing ▭

Kevin Kline *Howard Brackett* • Joan Cusack *Emily Montgomery* • Tom Selleck *Peter Malloy* • Matt Dillon *Cameron Drake* • Debbie Reynolds *Berniece Brackett* • Glenn Close • Whoopi Goldberg • Jay Leno ■ *Dir* Frank Oz • *Scr* Paul Rudnick

In Bed with Madonna ★★★ 15
Music documentary 1991 · US · BW and Colour · 113mins

Shot during the 1990 "Blond Ambition" tour and released as *Truth or Dare* in the States, this is hardly an intimate portrait of Madonna as she's so aware of the presence of the camera that it's performance all the way. The on-stage concert sequences, for all their colour and polish, are positively dull beside the monochrome backstage scenes, in which no one is spared the Ciccone wrath (even God gets His ear bent before every show). The shredding of Kevin Costner is a treat, but on the downside there's the rudeness to her childhood friend. Perhaps most revealing are the scenes with then boyfriend Warren Beatty. Contains swearing. ▭

Dir Alek Keshishian

In Broad Daylight ★★★ 15
Drama based on a true story 1991 · US · Colour · 90mins

Brian Dennehy once again acts everyone else off the screen in this over-the-top drama as the local bad guy who decides to shoot just about everyone in his small town after his daughter is arrested for shoplifting. He is ably supported by Marcia Gay Harden and Cloris Leachman, but even two such experienced actresses can't compete with Dennehy's growling, vengeful performance. Contains violence. ▭

Brian Dennehy *Len Rowan* • Cloris Leachman *Ruth Westerman* • Marcia Gay Harden *Adina Rowan* • Chris Cooper *Jack Wilson* ■ *Dir* James Steven Sadwith • *Scr* William Hanley, from a book by Harry MacLean

In Caliente ★★
Romantic musical 1935 · US · BW · 84mins

"The lady in red, the fellas adore the lady in red..." and that's about all there is to adore in this lacklustre Warner Bros romantic vehicle for star Dolores Del Rio. Despite routines from ace choreographer Busby Berkeley, this musical never really gets off Warner's backlot, and leading man Pat O'Brien lacks the requisite lightness for this type of fluff. Nevertheless, for collectors of Warner musicals from this period, this one's a rarity, and it does at least feature the redoubtable Edward Everett Horton. Don't expect too much, that's all.

Dolores Del Rio *Rita Gomez* • Pat O'Brien *Larry MacArthur* • Leo Carrillo *Jose Gomez* • Edward Everett Horton *Harold Brandon* • Glenda Farrell *Clara* • Phil Regan *Pat Casey* ■ *Dir* Lloyd Bacon • *Scr* Jerry Wald, Julius J Epstein, from the story *Caliente* by Ralph Block, Warren Duff • *Choreographer* Busby Berkeley

In Celebration ★★★
Drama   1974 · UK · Colour · 131mins

Director Lindsay Anderson reunites the cast of London's Royal Court production for this screen version of David Storey's play. Three sons (Alan Bates, James Bolam, Brian Cox) return to their Northern roots for the 40th wedding anniversary celebrations of parents Bill Owen and Constance Chapman. While all three have exceeded the career achievements of their miner father, their homecoming brings the usual saga of angst, buried resentments and skeletons in the closet. While its stage origins do hinder the pace of the action, this is wryly observant, and well acted, particularly by Alan Bates.

Alan Bates *Andrew Shaw* • James Bolam *Colin Shaw* • Brian Cox *Steven Shaw* • Constance Chapman *Mrs Shaw* • Gabrielle Daye *Mrs Burnett* • Bill Owen *Mr Shaw* ■ *Dir* Lindsay Anderson • *Scr* David Storey, from his play

In Cold Blood ★★★★
Crime drama based on a true story
1967 · US · BW · 134mins

Truman Capote's book about two young real-life murderers was a shocking bestseller in its day, and thought impossible to bring to the screen. Yet writer/director Richard Brooks did deliver this harrowing movie adaptation, remarkably faithful to its source and featuring two relatively unknown actors as the youngsters who wiped out a Kansas family during a robbery. The mood is properly dour and relentless, and the use of actual locations superb. The supporting cast is full of well-known Hollywood players, with the likes of John Forsythe, Will Geer and Paul Stewart ensuring that the grim subject matter remains resolutely unsensationalised. Contains violence and swearing.

Robert Blake *Perry Smith* • Scott Wilson *Dick Hickock* • John Forsythe *Alvin Dewey* • Paul Stewart *Reporter* • Gerald S O'Loughlin *Harold Nye* • Jeff Corey *Hickock's father* • John Gallaudet *Roy Church* • James Flavin *Clarence Duntz* ■ *Dir* Richard Brooks • *Scr* Richard Brooks, from the non-fiction book by Truman Capote • *Cinematographer* Conrad Hall

In Country ★★★ 15
Drama   1989 · US · Colour · 110mins

This was Bruce Willis's first real stab at proving himself a serious actor, and he delivers a credibly moody performance as a disturbed Vietnam veteran trying to piece his life together after the conflict. Emily Lloyd also

emerges with honours in one of her first American roles. However, both are let down by a meandering script that never quite gets to grips with the subject matter and uneven direction from the usually reliable Norman Jewison (director of *Moonstruck* among other hits). Contains violence. 🖵

Bruce Willis *Emmett Smith* • Emily Lloyd *Samantha Hughes* • Joan Allen *Irene* • Kevin Anderson *Lonnie Malone* • Richard Hamilton *Grampaw* • Judith Ivey *Anita Stevens* ■ *Dir* Norman Jewison • *Scr* Frank Pierson, Cynthia Cidre, from the novel by Bobbie Ann Mason

The In Crowd ★★ PG
Romantic dance drama
1988 · US · Colour · 95mins

Donovan Leitch (son of Donovan and brother of Ione Skye) stars in this sixties-set rock 'n' roll drama as the wannabe singer/dancer who becomes an overnight star. Good attention to period detail and a great R 'n' B soundtrack make this both instantly feel good and instantly forgettable. Both *Hairspray* and *Dirty Dancing* achieve the same objective but have had more subsequent durability.

Donovan Leitch *Del Green* • Joe Pantoliano *Perry Parker* • Jennifer Runyon *Vicky* • Wendy Gazelle *Gail* • Sean Gregory Sullivan *Popeye* • Bruno Kirby *Norris* ■ *Dir* Mark Rosenthal • *Scr* Lawrence Konner, Mark Rosenthal

In Custody ★★ U
Drama   1993 · UK · Colour · 120mins

If only Ismail Merchant had kept this adaptation of Anita Desai's novel for his second outing as a director, we might have been talking four stars here instead of two. After 30 years as producer to James Ivory, he finally seized the directorial reins on a project that was obviously close to his heart, but simply lacked the experience to bring it fully to life. The story, about an academic seeking to record the work of a dissolute Urdu poet, is thought-provoking, touching and often very amusing, but the picture lacks pace and focus. In Urdu with English subtitles. 🖵

Shashi Kapoor *Nur* • Sameer Mitha *Manu* • Neena Gupta *Sarla* • Rupinder Kaur *Mrs Bhalla* • Om Puri *Deven* • Shahid Masood *Dhanu* • Tiblu Khan *Student* ■ *Dir* Ismail Merchant • *Scr* Anita Desai, Shahrukh Husain, from the novel by Anita Desai

In Dark Places ★★ 18
Erotic thriller   1997 · US · Colour · 92mins

Joan Severance plays the long-lost half sister of Bryan Kestner, a man without a care in the world until his naughty sibling returns to his life. Before long he has lost his job, his fiancée and even a couple of friends, who also fall under her spell. It's classier than the usual Shannon Tweed fodder, but that's not saying much, and suspense consistently takes a back seat to the sexual exploits. Contains swearing, sex scenes and nudity. 🖵

Joan Severance *Chapelle Donaldi* • Bryan Kestner *Chaz Donaldi* • John Vargas *Karl* ■ *Dir* James Burke • *Scr* HJ Crane

In Dreams ★★ 18
Psychological chiller
1998 · US · Colour · 96mins

Neil Jordan proves again what an inconsistent director he can be with this wildly contrived chiller. The visuals are impressively stylised, as Jordan summons up the nightmare world in which New England resident Annette Bening becomes trapped as she finds her mind invaded by the thoughts of a serial killer. Yet his handling of the various flashbacks and reveries is haphazard in the extreme, creating tension by sleight of hand (and an obsession with apples) rather than plot progression or sustained atmosphere. Hugely disappointing. Contains violent scenes and swearing. 🖵

Annette Bening *Claire Cooper* • Katie Sagona *Rebecca Cooper* • Aidan Quinn *Paul Cooper* • Robert Downey Jr *Vivian Thompson* • Stephen Rea *Doctor Silverman* ■ *Dir* Neil Jordan • *Scr* Bruce Robinson, Neil Jordan, from the novel *Doll's Eyes* by Bari Wood

In Enemy Country ★★
Second World War drama
1968 · US · Colour · 106mins

This uninspired Second World War hokum from Universal utilised the studio's backlot when its TV series weren't in production. Still, star Tony Franciosa copes manfully, going undercover to dispose of a Nazi torpedo factory, while British interest centres on import Tom Bell and the very artificial European setting. Producer/director Harry Keller does a serviceable job, however, and scores some points for effort.

Tony Franciosa [Anthony Franciosa] *Colonel Charles Waslow-Carton* • Anjanette Comer *Denise Marchois* • Guy Stockwell *Lieutenant Colonel Philip Braden* • Paul Hubschmid *Baron Frederich von Wittenberg* • Tom Bell *Captain Ian Peyton-Reid* ■ *Dir* Harry Keller • *Scr* Edward Anhalt, from a story by Sy Bartlett

In God We Trust ★ 15
Comedy   1980 · US · Colour · 92mins

Marty Feldman gets it horribly wrong as writer, director and star of this dismally unfunny comedy about a naive monk who receives a crash course in worldliness when he goes to Hollywood on a fundraising mission for his monastery. Blatant in its satire and inept in its characterisation, the film misses every one of its social and religious targets. Louise Lasser emerges with a modicum of credit for imbuing her blowsy hooker with some humanity, but Richard Pryor does himself no favours as God in a film that's beyond salvation. 🖵

Marty Feldman *Brother Ambrose* • Peter Boyle *Dr Melmoth* • Louise Lasser *Mary* • Richard Pryor *God* • Andy Kaufman *Armageddon T Thunderbird* • Wilfrid Hyde White *Abbot Thelonius* • Severn Darden *Priest* ■ *Dir* Marty Feldman • *Scr* Marty Feldman, Chris Allen

In God's Hands ★ 12
Sports adventure drama
1998 · US · Colour · 93mins

Soft-core director Zalman King takes a change of pace with this saga concerning three beach bum surfers (played by three real-life champion surfers) traveling halfway around the world looking for great waves. That

sentence essentially covers the entire plot of the movie, which never has a clear direction or purpose except to show reels of surfing action. The footage is expertly photographed, but with little else going on, the movie literally becomes a lesser version of *The Endless Summer*, with no attempt to explore the personality of the typical nomad surfer. *DVD*

Patrick Shane Dorian *Shane* • Matt George *Mickey* • Mathew Stephen "Matty"Liu *Keoni* • Shaun Thompson *Wyatt* ■ *Dir* Zalman King • *Scr* Zalman King, Matt George

In Harm's Way ★★★★ PG
Second World War action drama
1965 · US · BW · 160mins

Producer/director Otto Preminger had a rough critical ride in the sixties, not least for this marvellous Second World War epic, which begins with the Japanese attack on Pearl Harbour. The fine hand-picked cast includes John Wayne and Kirk Douglas as naval officers suffering mixed fortunes during and after the attack. Both are tremendous, and they are well supported by Patricia Neal, Brandon de Wilde and Dana Andrews. The main flaw is that the special effects in the later sea battles look unconvincing (they were shot using models). Nevertheless, the film has great scale (and a great score by Jerry Goldsmith), and, unusually, the characters aren't dwarfed by the canvas. It's a long haul, but it's well worth your perseverance. 🖵

John Wayne *Captain Rockwell Torrey* • Kirk Douglas *Commander Paul Eddington* • Patricia Neal *Lieutenant Maggie Haynes* • Tom Tryon *Lieutenant William McConnel* • Paula Prentiss *Bev McConnel* • Slim Pickens *Chief Petty Officer Culpepper* • George Kennedy *Colonel Gregory* • Henry Fonda *Cincpac Admiral* ■ *Dir* Otto Preminger • *Scr* Wendell Mayes, from the novel by James Bassett

The In-Laws ★★★ PG
Comedy   1979 · US · Colour · 98mins

Arthur Hiller's frantic screwball variation on the buddy theme is never quite as funny as it thinks it is, but the laughs keep coming thanks to the inspired pairing of Alan Arkin and Peter Falk. Determined to stand by his daughter's prospective father-in-law, Arkin's New York dentist heads off to South America to help Falk's eccentric CIA agent recover some stolen Treasury plates. Screenwriter Andrew Bergman's digs at dictator Richard Libertini and his tinpot republic are hardly in the "good neighbour" tradition, but the fun lies in the way the Falk lures Arkin into ever more ludicrous situations. 🖵

Peter Falk *Vince Ricardo* • Alan Arkin *Sheldon Kornpett* • Richard Libertini *General Garcia* • Nancy Dussault *Carol Kornpett* • Penny Peyser *Barbara Kornpett* • Arlene Golonka *Jean Ricardo* • Ed Begley Jr *Barry Lutz* ■ *Dir* Arthur Hiller • *Scr* Andrew Bergman

In like Flint ★★
Spy spoof   1967 · US · Colour · 114mins

This sub-James Bond adventure, a sequel to *Our Man Flint*, sees James Coburn return as the stone-faced spy. The plot concerns a group of women on the Virgin Islands planning to rule the world, hence the presence of a bevy of beauties, and plenty of insipid innuendo. It's often laughable, though Lee J Cobb does bring a touch of class to the crass proceedings.

James Coburn *Derek Flint* • Lee J Cobb *Cramden* • Jean Hale *Lisa* • Andrew Duggan *President Trent* • Anna Lee *Elisabeth* • Hanna Landy *Helena* • Totty Ames *Claire* ■ *Dir* Gordon Douglas • *Scr* Hal Fimberg

In Love and War ★★★
Second World War drama
1958 · US · Colour · 104mins

A 20th Century-Fox film designed to show off the studio's talented roster of contract players in a formulaic amalgam of *The Young Lions* and *Three Coins in the Fountain*. It's a pleasingly clichéd wartime melodrama, offering showy roles to Robert Wagner and Jeffrey Hunter, both looking far more fifties than forties, though Bradford Dillman scores highest as the thoughtful member of a trio of marines experiencing both romance and conflict. The women, as played by the splendid Dana Wynter, Hope Lange and Sheree North, emerge with credit, and there's a nice acting cameo from period satirist Mort Sahl.

Robert Wagner *Frankie O'Neill* • Dana Wynter *Sue Trumbell* • Jeffrey Hunter *Nico Kantaylis* • Hope Lange *Andrea Lenaine* • Bradford Dillman *Alan Newcombe* • Sheree North *Lorraine* • France Nuyen *Kalai Ducanne* ■ *Dir* Philip Dunne • *Scr* Edward Anhalt, from the novel *The Big War* by Anton Myrer

In Love and War ★★★[15]
Drama based on a true story
1987 · US · Colour · 92mins

James Woods, a master at repressed emotion, is generally careful to keep his intensity in check and his performances within the bounds of believability. Here, as a US Navy pilot who is being held and tortured by the Vietnamese, he adds to his list of electric roles, yet is ill-served by Paul Aaron, whose direction is alternately long-winded and flat. [VIDEO]

James Woods *Jim Stockdale* • Jane Alexander *Sybil Stockdale* • Dr Haing S Ngor [Haing S Ngor] *Major Bui*, *"Cat"* • Concetta Tomei *Doyen Salsig* • Steven Vincent Leigh *Big Ugh* ■ *Dir* Paul Aaron • *Scr* Carol Schreder, from a book by Jim Stockdale, Sybil Stockdale

In Love and War ★★[15]
Romantic First World War drama
1996 · US · Colour · 108mins

A typically humane but sadly uninvolving biographical drama from director Richard Attenborough. Set during the First World War, it centres on the romance between a young Ernest Hemingway, injured in combat, and the nurse who cares for him. One of the film's problems is the total lack of chemistry between its stars, Chris O'Donnell and Sandra Bullock, both hopelessly miscast and bringing a touch of LA mall culture to the trenches. Despite some attractive location photography in Italy, the whole project seems curiously stillborn; eclipsed by the thematically similar *The English Patient*, it was a critical and box-office bomb. [VIDEO]

Chris O'Donnell *Ernest Hemingway* • Sandra Bullock *Agnes von Kurowsky* • Ingrid Lacey *Elsie "Mac" MacDonald* • MacKenzie Astin *Henry Villard* • Emilio Bonucci *Domenico*

Caracciolo • Ian Kelly *Jimmy McBride* • Alan Bennett *Porter* ■ *Dir* Richard Attenborough • *Scr* Anna Hamilton Phelan, Clancy Sigal, Allan Scott, from a story by Allan Scott, Dimitri Villard, from the biography *Hemingway in Love and War* by Henry S Villard, James Nagel

In My Daughter's Name
★★★[15]
Courtroom drama 1992 · US · Colour · 92mins

Also known as *Overruled*, this harrowing tale of legal loopholes and vigilante justice is a cut above the average TV movie. Donna Mills gives a heartfelt performance as a mother driven to extremes after seeing her teenage daughter's killer walk free. It's plain throughout that it is American law that is on trial and it's hard not to side with Mills as she becomes a victim of the system that failed her. Director Jud Taylor keeps the courtroom scenes simmering, particularly when Mills is confronted with John Rubinstein, the family attorney who is now her prosecutor. [VIDEO]

Donna Mills *Laura Elias* • John Getz *Michael Elias* • John Rubinstein *Ben Worrall* • Lee Grant *Maureen Leeds* • Ron Frazier *Lipton's attorney* ■ *Dir* Jud Taylor • *Scr* Mimi Rothman Schapiro, Bill Wells, from a story by Sharon Michaels

In My Sister's Shadow
★★[PG]
Drama thriller 1999 · US · Colour · 89mins

Joan (Nancy McKeon) is cursed by having a younger and more attractive sister, Laurie (Alexandra Wilson). Things look up when Joan begins secretly dating her sibling's ex, Thomas McCarthy, but it's not long before her emotionally disturbed and dangerous boyfriend shows his true colours as he stalks Laurie and her new beau. This supposedly "fact-based" thriller is populated by unattractive characters who never rise from the role of victims, and so fails to deliver or a believable portrait of stalker/prey psychologies. As the girls' mother, Janet Leigh brings some much-needed Hollywood class to the film, but it's not enough to redeem it from dreary pointlessness. [VIDEO]

Nancy McKeon *Joan Conner* • Thomas McCarthy *Michael* • Alexandra Wilson *Laurie Conner* • Mark Dobies *Mark* • Janet Leigh *Kay Conner* ■ *Dir* Sandor Stern • *Scr* Dan Vining, Ronni Kern, from a story by Rob Fresco

In Name Only ★★★[U]
Drama 1939 · US · BW · 90mins

A great cast in a superior soapy drama, as unhappily married Cary Grant falls for widow Carole Lombard and tries to free himself from the clutches of his social-climbing wife, Kay Francis. There's a fine moment when Grant's parents – Nella Walker and Charles Coburn – are allowed an insight into Francis's true character, leaving little doubt as to the outcome of the plot. Of the extraordinary crop of films made in Hollywood in 1939, this conventional melodrama is often overlooked, but, despite rather slow-moving direction from John Cromwell, it's well worth a viewing. [VIDEO]

Carole Lombard *Julie Eden* • Cary Grant *Alec Walker* • Kay Francis *Maida Walker* • Charles Coburn *Mr Walker* • Helen Vinson *Suzanne* •

Katherine Alexander *Laura* • Jonathan Hale *Dr Gateson* • Maurice Moscovich *Dr Muller* • Nella Walker *Mrs Walker* ■ *Dir* John Cromwell • *Scr* Richard Sherman, from the novel *Memory of Love* by Bessie Brewer

In Old Arizona ★★★
Western 1929 · US · BW · 94m

This big-budget first western talkie is the best screen representation of the Cisco Kid, the colourful creation of master storyteller O Henry. In an Oscar-winning performance, Warner Baxter plays the caballero with an infectious zest, all flashing teeth and flashing spurs, stealing hearts and stagecoach strongboxes with equal abandon, while Edmund Lowe plods behind as the lawman who can never quite get his man. In the best role of her career, Dorothy Burgess makes a spirited Mexican senorita, while the ending has a sharp O Henry-ish twist. Director Raoul Walsh lost an eye during the filming which was completed by Irving Cummings.

Edmund Lowe *Sgt Mickey Dunne* • Dorothy Burgess *Tonia Maria* • Warner Baxter *The Cisco Kid* • J Farrell MacDonald *Tad* ■ *Dir* Raoul Walsh, Irving Cummings • *Scr* Tom Barry, from a story by O Henry

In Old California ★★[PG]
Western 1942 · US · BW · 87mins

A very routine Republic western with the rather odd casting of John Wayne as a pharmacist who finds himself entangled in the evil schemes of a local gunman. To hold your interest, there's Binnie Barnes as a spirited saloon hostess and died-in-the-wool villain Albert Dekker. The film lacks a film director's hand, so practised comic actors Patsy Kelly and Edgar Kennedy have plenty of opportunities to scene-steal. [VIDEO]

John Wayne *Tom Craig* • Binnie Barnes *Lacey Miller* • Albert Dekker *Britt Dawson* • Helen Parrish *Ellen Sanford* • Patsy Kelly *Helga* ■ *Dir* William McGann • *Scr* Gertrude Purcell, Frances Hyland, from a story by J Robert Bren, Gladys Atwater

In Old Chicago ★★★[U]
Historical disaster drama
1937 · US · BW · 91mins

Twentieth Century-Fox's answer to MGM's *San Francisco*, released a year earlier, but Tyrone Power is no Clark Gable and the Chicago fire of 1871 is a storm in a teacup compared with MGM's stupendously filmed earthquake. There is a lot of scene-setting and subplotting family virtues set beside political corruption before a cow kicks over a kerosene lamp and the special effects team makes the Windy City go up in smoke. Alice Faye, warbling a few songs, will keep her fans happy, while Alice Brady, as Power's mother, won an Oscar as best supporting actress. [VIDEO]

Tyrone Power *Dion O'Leary* • Alice Faye *Belle Fawcett* • Don Ameche *Jack O'Leary* • Alice Brady *Molly O'Leary* • Andy Devine *Pickle Bixby* ■ *Dir* Henry King • *Scr* Lamar Trotti, Sonya Levien, from the story *We the O'Learys* by Niven Busch

In Old Kentucky ★★★
Comedy 1935 · US · BW · 85mins

The homespun personality of Will Rogers made him one of the most popular stars of early talkies, and his amiable performance holds together this occasionally simple-minded tale of country folk and racehorse rivalries. Whether learning to tap-dance or trying to make a purchase at a fashion house, Rogers is always engaging. Sadly this was to be his last film: he was killed in a plane crash shortly after its completion.

Will Rogers *Steve Tapley* • Dorothy Wilson *Nancy Martingale* • Russell Hardie *Dr Lee Andrews* • Charles Sellon *Ezra Martingale* • Bill Robinson *Wash Jackson* ■ *Dir* George Marshall • *Scr* Sam Hellman, Gladys Lehman, from the play by Charles T Dazey

In Old Montana ★★
Western 1939 · US · BW · 61mins

Spectrum was a "poverty row" outfit churning out westerns as supporting fillers. This is a typical example, featuring singing cowboy Fred Scott. There's some action in this one, but unfortunately far too much plot. The sets and costumes, not to mention stories, were continuously reused in this material, and director Raymond K Johnson churned out 18 of these B westerns between 1931 and 1941 to little distinction. For fans only.

Fred Scott *Fred Dawson* • Jean Carmen *June Allison* • John Merton *Ed Brandt* • Harry Harvey *Doc Flanders* • Walter McGrail *Joe Allison* ■ *Dir* Raymond K Johnson • *Scr* Jackson Parks, Homer King Gordon, Raymond K Johnson, Barney Hutchinson

In Person ★★
Musical romantic comedy
1935 · US · BW · 87mins

In between *Top Hat* and *Follow the Fleet*, Ginger Rogers took a break from Fred Astaire by co-starring with the non-dancing, non-singing and, some would say, non-acting George Brent. In this rather feeble musical comedy, Rogers plays a temperamental film star escaping her fans by adopting a disguise and fleeing to a mountain resort in the company of Brent. No prizes for guessing what happens. Ginger has a couple of pleasant dance routines, choreographed by Hermes Pan, the dance director on the Astaire/Rogers movies, which only served to remind audiences of Fred's absence.

Ginger Rogers *Carol Corliss aka Miss Colfax* • George Brent *Emory Parks* • Alan Mowbray *Jay Holmes* • Grant Mitchell *Judge Thaddeus Parks* ■ *Dir* William A Seiter • *Scr* Allan Scott, from a novel by Samuel Hopkins Adams • *Choreographer* Hermes Pan

In Pursuit of Honor ★★★[12]
Drama based on a true story
1995 · US · Colour · 105mins

Shot on location in the Antipodes, this superior TV movie tells the story of one of the most shameful incidents in US military history. In 1935, General Douglas MacArthur (who went on to become a Second World War legend) ordered the destruction of 500 horses as part of a modernisation programme. However, a group of soldiers defied his orders and tried to herd the animals to Canada. Ken Olin directs with

considerable assurance, while Don Johnson and Craig Sheffer lead a solid cast. A pity Rod Steiger feels the need to show off. ▣

Don Johnson *Sergeant Major Libbey* • Craig Sheffer *Lieutenant Marshall Buxton* • Rod Steiger *Colonel Stuart* • Gabrielle Anwar *Jessica Stuart* • Bob Gunton *Hardesty* • James B Sikking *General Douglas MacArthur* ■ *Dir* Ken Olin • *Scr* Dennis Lynton Clark

In Search of Famine ★★★★

Drama   1980 · Ind · Colour · 124mins

A Calcutta film crew arrives in a remote village to document the devastating 1943 famine, but is greeted with unexpected suspicion and hostility by the poverty-stricken villagers. Unable to bridge this gap of understanding, the visitors return home empty-handed. One of Indian cinema's most insightful recorders of the country's social fabric, Mrinal Sen has created a lively film, no less profound for revealing the underlying comedy springing from the cultural divide between the protagonists. An excellent piece, this won the special jury prize at Berlin. A Bengali language film.

Dhritiman Chatterjee *Director* • Smita Patil *Actress* • Sreela Majumdar *Woman* • Gita Sen *Widow* • Dipankar Dey *Villager* ■ *Dir* Mrinal Sen • *Scr* Mrinal Sen

In Search of Gregory ★★

Psychological drama
1970 · UK/It · Colour · 89mins

Having co-written such seminal pictures as *L'Avventura* and *Blow Up*, it's not surprising echoes of Michelangelo Antonioni abound in this cryptic tale from Tonino Guerra. Unfortunately, director Peter Wood doesn't have the master's genius for expressing emotion through landscape, so Julie Christie's Genevan odyssey is more maddening than enigmatic. Enchanted by her father Adolfo Celi's description of a handsome house guest, Christie imagines him to be the same man whose picture she sees at the airport (Michael Sarrazin). It's an intriguing idea – a romance in which the lovers never meet – but it needs firmer handling than this.

Julie Christie *Catherine* • Michael Sarrazin *Gregory* • John Hurt *Daniel* • Adolfo Celi *Max* • Roland Culver *Wardle* • Tony Selby *Taxi driver* • Jimmy Lynn *Air steward* ■ *Dir* Peter Wood • *Scr* Tonino Guerra, Lucile Laks

In Search of the Castaways ★★★ Ⓤ

Fantasy adventure
1961 · US/UK · Colour · 94mins

Based on the novel *Captain Grant's Children*, this was Disney's second dip into the works of Jules Verne, but it can't be compared with the splendid *20,000 Leagues under the Sea*. Hayley Mills stars as a tigerish teen who ropes Maurice Chevalier and Wilfrid Hyde White into helping search for her father. But, as the action moves from South America to Australia, the cast becomes increasingly irrelevant to director Robert Stevenson subjects it to all manner of natural disasters. Unfortunately, the effects have dated badly and the meandering story rarely thrills. ▣

Maurice Chevalier *Professor Jacques Paganel* • Hayley Mills *Mary Grant* • George Sanders *Thomas Ayrton* • Wilfrid Hyde White *Lord Glenarvan* • Michael Anderson Jr *John Glenarvan* ■ *Dir* Robert Stevenson • *Scr* Lowell S Hawley, from the novel *Captain Grant's Children* by Jules Verne

In the Arms of a Killer

★★ 15

Crime thriller   1992 · US · Colour · 90mins

Ex-*Charlie's Angels* star and TV movie queen Jaclyn Smith is the detective who falls in love with a murder suspect in this predictable but well-played thriller. John Spencer and *Flashdance*'s Michael Nouri provide the macho elements, but it is really Smith (who must be taking a magic potion as she doesn't look a day over 30) who steals the show. ▣

Jaclyn Smith *Maria Quinn* • John Spencer *Vincent Cusack* • Michael Nouri *Dr Brian Venible* • Sandahl Bergman *Nurse Henninger* ■ *Dir/Scr* Robert Collins

In the Army Now ★ PG

Comedy   1994 · US · Colour · 88mins

Pauly Shore is something of an acquired taste, but one thing that counts in his favour is his willingness to strain every sinew in the hope of raising a laugh. Alas, he's got no chance in this marvel of military mayhem, thanks to the eight writers who toiled on the lamentable script. Comedy seems to have been the last thing on their minds when they penned this barmy story about a doltish shop assistant who finds himself in the middle of a US mission against Libya. No satire, no farce, no wit – just whimsical slapstick. ▣

Pauly Shore *Bones Conway* • Andy Dick *Jack Kaufman* • Lori Petty *Christine Jones* • David Alan Grier *Fred Ostroff* • Esai Morales *Sergeant Stern* ■ *Dir* Daniel Petrie Jr • *Scr* Daniel Petrie Jr, Fax Bahr, Adam Small, Ken Kaufman, Stu Krieger, from a story by Steve Zacharias, Jeff Buhai, Robbie Fox

In the Belly of the Whale

★★★

Drama   1984 · W Ger · Colour · 97mins

Made a year before she scored an international hit with the sex comedy *Men*, Doris Dörrie's second directorial outing is an assured melodrama in which cop Peter Sattmann is forced to join forces with his estranged wife when their daughter disappears. Dörrie challenges traditional assumptions about male-female relationships, but here she also manages to juggle satire and suspense as the bickering couple reluctantly agree to a truce in order to save the young girl's life. It takes a while to settle, but give it time. German dialogue dubbed into English.

Janna Marangosoff *Carla* • Eisi Gulp *Rick* • Silvia Reize *Marta* • Peter Sattmann *Frank* ■ *Dir* Doris Dörrie • *Scr* Michael Juncker, Doris Dörrie

In the Best Interest of the Child ★★★★ 15

Drama   1990 · US · Colour · 90mins

An affecting TV movie about the tricky subject of child sexual abuse that manages to provide reasonable entertainment without being tasteless.

This is undoubtedly owing to the talent of the three leads – Meg Tilly, Ed Begley Jr and Michele Greene – who bring their characters to achingly convincing life. There is nothing obvious or trite here, and a gripping screenplay treats the subject matter with delicacy, but not undue deference. Don't miss. ▣

Meg Tilly *Jennifer Colton* • Ed Begley Jr *Howard Feldon* • Michele Greene *Nora Harold* • Marta Woodward *Mandy Colton* ■ *Dir* David Greene • *Scr* Hal Sitowitz

In the Best Interest of the Children ★★★ 15

Drama based on a true story
1992 · US · Colour · 90mins

A heart-wrenching and thought-provoking American TV drama, based on the true story of the two-year battle by a manic depressive single mother to retain custody of her five children. Sarah Jessica Parker turns in a fine lead performance, while powerful direction and a superior screenplay make this far more than a routine tear-jerker, and force not just the characters, but also the viewer, into making almost impossible choices about what is, indeed, in the best interest of the children. ▣

Sarah Jessica Parker *Callie Cain* • Sally Struthers *Patty Payne* • Elizabeth Ashley *Carla Scott* ■ *Dir* Michael Ray Rhodes • *Scr* Peter Nelson, Jud Kinberg

In the Bleak Midwinter

★★★ 15

Comedy drama   1995 · UK · BW · 94mins

After the grand-standing and faintly embarrassing excesses of *Mary Shelley's Frankenstein*, Kenneth Branagh returns to his roots for this gentle and modestly amusing dig at theatrical pretensions. With Branagh opting to remain behind the camera, the leading role goes to Michael Maloney, who plays a struggling actor attempting to stage a Christmas production of *Hamlet* with a bitchy, egocentric group of luvvies. Branagh regular Richard Briers has a ball with the material. There's even a distinctly toned-down cameo from Joan Collins. However, the stunning black-and-white cinematography cannot disguise the slightness of the material. ▣

Michael Maloney *Joe Harper* • Richard Briers *Henry Wakefield* • Hetta Charnley *Molly* • Joan Collins *Margaretta D'Arcy* • Nicholas Farrell *Tom Newman* • Celia Imrie *Fadge* • Jennifer Saunders *Nancy Crawford* • Julia Sawalha *Nina* • John Sessions *Terry Du Bois* ■ *Dir/Scr* Kenneth Branagh

In the Blink of an Eye

★★★ 12

Drama based on a true story
1996 · US · Colour · 85mins

A fine made-for-TV drama, which manages successfully to blur the lines between real life and art. Director Micki Dickoff's movie is based on her own experiences, with Veronica Hamel playing the campaigning film-maker who takes up the case of a former childhood friend (Mimi Rogers) languishing in prison for a murder she did not commit. The two female leads give commanding performances and Dickoff manages to distance herself

sufficiently from the action to produce a tense and fiery examination of the iniquities of the American legal system. Contains swearing and violence. ▣

Veronica Hamel *Micki Dickoff* • Mimi Rogers *Sunny Jacobs* • Piper Laurie *Kay Trafero* • Polly Bergen *Murial* • Carlos Gomez *Jose Quinon* ■ *Dir* Micki Dickoff • *Scr* Rama Laurie Stagner, Dan Witt

In the Company of Darkness ★★★ 15

Psychological thriller based on a true story
1992 · US · Colour · 90mins

Yet another examination of the sinister world of the serial killer, this time given a tough edge by the performance of Helen Hunt as a rookie policewoman who befriends the killer. Hunt manages to make a difficult role almost believable by giving her character an appealing mixture of courage and vulnerability. She is ably assisted by Jeff Fahey, although both are forced to work against an occasionally plodding script. For those who stick with it, however, there is a rather good denouement. ▣

Helen Hunt *Gina Pulasky* • Jeff Fahey *Will McCaid* • Steven Weber *Kyle Timler* • Juan Ramirez *Machado* ■ *Dir* David Anspaugh • *Scr* John Leekley

In the Company of Men

★★★★ 18

Drama   1997 · US · Colour · 93mins

Brave, hard-hitting and controversial, director Neil LaBute's pitch-black comedy detailing the complexities of office politics and male rivalry is a deliberately uncomfortable viewing experience. Aaron Eckhart and Matt Malloy are exceptional as the two white-collar workers betting on who can seduce the most vulnerable girl in their office – deaf Stacy Edwards – and then dump her as an exercise in revenge against the fair sex. LaBute indulges in blatant misogyny and painful honesty to put his acerbic points across in a provocative and compelling shocker. Contains swearing. ▣

Aaron Eckhart *Chad* • Stacy Edwards *Christine* • Matt Malloy *Howard* • Emily Cline *Suzanne* • Jason Dixie *Keith, intern* ■ *Dir/Scr* Neil LaBute

In the Cool of the Day ★★

Drama   1963 · US · Colour · 91mins

Terminally ill New Yorker Jane Fonda runs off to Greece with her husband's business partner, Peter Finch, who in turn is fleeing from the wife he scarred in a car crash. This romantic tragedy aspires to the level of Greek myth but amounts to little more than Greek piffle. Worth watching, however, for the locations, such as the glorious ancient site of Delphi, all beautifully shot by cameraman Peter Newbrook, fresh from second unit work on *Lawrence of Arabia*.

Jane Fonda *Christine Bonner* • Peter Finch *Murray Logan* • Angela Lansbury *Sibyl Logan* • Arthur Hill *Sam Bonner* • Constance Cummings *Mrs Gellert* • Alexander Knox *Frederick Bonner* • Nigel Davenport *Leonard* • John Le Mesurier *Dr Arraman* ■ *Dir* Robert Stevens • *Scr* Meade Roberts, from the novel by Susan Ertz

In the Custody of Strangers ★★ 15

Drama 1982 · US · Colour · 90mins

An off-the-peg situation – boy is jailed for drunkenness, finds himself sharing a cell with hardcore psychos, parents fight to get him out – redeemed by an impressive cast. Martin Sheen plays dad and his real-life son, Emilio Estevez, plays his fictional son, while Jane Alexander, a fine actress who never quite makes it to the lead role, plays Mrs Sheen. The script, however, often scrapes the bottom of the cliché barrel.

Martin Sheen *Frank Caldwell* • Jane Alexander *Sandy Caldwell* • Emilio Estevez *Danny Caldwell* • Kenneth McMillan *Al Caruso* • Ed Lauter *Judge Halloran* ■ *Dir* Robert Greenwald • *Scr* Jennifer Miller

In the Deep Woods ★★ 18

Thriller 1992 · US · Colour · 91mins

As Patricia Arquette's career took off in films such as *True Romance* and *Beyond Rangoon*, her older sister Rosanna's seemed to be in decline – one minute she was in the hit *Desperately Seeking Susan*, the next she was making tepid thrillers like this one. She stars as an author of children's books who finds herself caught up in the investigation into a friend's murder. As you'd expect, Anthony Perkins plays someone who just might be a bit on the sinister side in this occasionally scary thriller.

Rosanna Arquette *Joanna Warren* • Anthony Perkins *Paul Miller* • Will Patton *Agent Eric Gaines* • DW Moffett *Frank* • Chris Rydell [Christopher Rydell] *Tommy Warren* ■ *Dir* Charles Correll • *Scr* Robert Nathan, Robert Rosenblum, from the novel *In the Deep of the Woods* by Nicholas Conde

In the Doghouse ★★ U

Comedy 1961 · UK · BW · 93mins

Long before James Herriot, Alex Duncan appeared on the bestseller lists with *It's a Vet's Life*. Adapted by Michael Pertwee, it makes a fine vehicle for Leslie Phillips, who has to resort to his trademark charm to atone for his misadventures in a new country practice. However, he also gets to reveal an unexpected action-man side as he thwarts a horse-smuggling ring run by his deadly rival (James Booth). Despite booming support from Hattie Jacques, this patchy film is perhaps most significant for bringing down the curtain on the career of Peggy Cummins, who made her first film back in 1940 at the age of 15.

Leslie Phillips *Jimmy Fox-Upton* • Peggy Cummins *Sally* • Hattie Jacques *Primrose Gudgeon* • James Booth *Bob Skeffington* • Dick Bentley *Mr Peddle* • Colin Gordon *Dean* • Joan Heal *Mrs Peddle* • Fenella Fielding *Miss Fordyce* ■ *Dir* Darcy Conyers • *Scr* Michael Pertwee, from the novel *It's a Vet's Life* by Alex Duncan

In the Doghouse ★★ U

Comedy 1998 · US · Colour · 86mins

This delightful family film stars Matt Frewer as the hapless head of a family whose adorable dog causes his master to get fired from his job. Fortunately the mischievous mutt becomes an unlikely new breadwinner when he is "discovered" by talent agent Rhea Pearlman, who casts him in a film. But disaster strikes again when, before shooting begins, a rival trainer snatches the new dog star.

Rhea Perlman *Phyllis Markowitz* • Matt Frewer *Scott Wagner* • Allison Hossack *Jenna Wagner* • Trevor Morgan *Dylan Wagner* ■ *Dir* George Miller (1) • *Scr* Paul Bernbaum

In the French Style ★★★

Romance 1963 · US/Fr · BW · 105mins

Seeing what an impact Jean Seberg made in *A Bout de Souffle*, Hollywood sent her back to Paris for this trend-chasing, slightly risqué movie based on two short stories by Irwin Shaw, who also produced here. As an American art student in Paris, Seberg has affairs with young student Philippe Forquet and journalist Stanley Baker before finally settling on someone else. Seberg is beautiful and convincing as the new independent woman, quite a contrast to a Hollywood still churning out Doris Day comedies.

Jean Seberg *Christina James* • Stanley Baker *Walter Beddoes* • Addison Powell *Mr James* • Jack Hedley *Bill* • Maurice Teynac *Baron* • James Leo Herlihy *Dr John Haislip* ■ *Dir* Robert Parrish • *Scr* Irwin Shaw, from his short stories *In the French Style* and *A Year to Learn the Language*

In the Gloaming ★★★★

Drama 1997 · US · Colour · 61mins

Although Christopher Reeve's recent on-screen appearance in a TV remake of *Rear Window*, this TV movie, while much less publicised, was equally courageous. The disabled star made his directorial debut with this short, but superbly realised, drama. Boasting a five-star cast, it centres on Aids patient Robert Sean Leonard's homecoming and the very different welcomes he receives from mother Glenn Close, father David Strathairn and sister Bridget Fonda. With a poignant cameo from Whoopi Goldberg as a live-in nurse, this is a painfully truthful study of a family facing tragedy and the need to express emotions before it's too late.

Glenn Close *Janet* • Robert Sean Leonard *Danny* • Bridget Fonda *Anne* • Whoopi Goldberg *Myrna* • David Strathairn *Martin* ■ *Dir* Christopher Reeve • *Scr* Will Scheffer, from the short story by Alice Elliott Dark

In the Good Old Summertime ★★★ U

Musical comedy 1949 · US · Colour · 102mins

A charming MGM remake, this time with music, of their romantic classic *The Shop around the Corner*. The film provides a vocal and comedy showcase for the great Judy Garland (she replaced a pregnant June Allyson) ,who teams up with Van Johnson in a warm-hearted Technicolor extravaganza. Garland is remarkably touching as the enamoured pen pal who doesn't realise that colleague Johnson is her secret letter lover, and there are some terrific moments where the plot actually takes a hiatus to let Garland perform in front of an on-screen audience. The child with Garland and Johnson in the closing sequence is Garland's real-life daughter, Liza Minnelli.

Judy Garland *Veronica Fisher* • Van Johnson *Andrew Larkin* • SZ "Cuddles" Sakall [SZ Sakall] *Otto Oberkugen* • Spring Byington *Nellie Burke* • Clinton Sundberg *Rudy Hansen* • Buster Keaton *Hickey* • Liza Minnelli ■ *Dir* Robert Z Leonard • *Scr* Samson Raphaelson, Frances Goodrich, Ivan Tors, Albert Hackett, from the play *The Shop around the Corner* by Miklos Laszlo

In the Heat of the Night ★★★★★ 15

Crime drama 1967 · US · Colour · 105mins

Winner of five Oscars, including best picture, this powerhouse drama of racial tension in the Deep South was released at the height of the civil rights movement and a year before the assassination of Martin Luther King. Sidney Poitier is the immaculately dressed Philadelphia cop who is wrongly arrested for murder while changing trains in a small town in Mississippi, ruled by Rod Steiger's rancid, racist police chief. The plot is a set-up, a stacked deck, yet the atmosphere is palpably unpleasant, and Poitier and Steiger have a field day. A major movie for its time, it spawned two further films featuring Poitier's character and a television series.

Sidney Poitier *Virgil Tibbs* • Rod Steiger *Bill Gillespie* • Warren Oates *Sam Wood* • Quentin Dean *Dolores Purdy* • James Patterson *Purdy* • William Schallert *Webb Schubert* • Jack Teter *Philip Colbert* • Lee Grant *Mrs Leslie Colbert* ■ *Dir* Norman Jewison • *Scr* Stirling Silliphant, from the novel by John Ball • *Cinematographer* Haskell Wexler • *Editor* Hal Ashby • *Music* Quincy Jones

In the Kingdom of the Blind ★ 18

Crime thriller 1994 · US · Colour · 93mins

Dumb, derivative crime drama, consisting of tiresome speeches and endless shouting, swearing and beatings. Star/writer/director Nick Vallelonga (a chubby Joe Mantegna without the talent) seems to have a penchant for violent confrontations, but not an eye for realism, nor an ear for dialogue. Crime boss William Petersen only gets two scenes, although that's one more than Michael Biehn, who's bizarre opening monologue has nothing to do with the rest of the movie. Straight-to-video fare of the lowest order. Contains some swearing and violence.

Nick Vallelonga *Al* • William L Petersen [William Petersen] *Tony C* • Michael Biehn *Jackie Ryan* • Leo Rossi *Moran* • Paul Winfield *Papa Joe* ■ *Dir/Scr* Nick Vallelonga

In the Lake of the Woods ★★★ 15

Drama 1996 · US · Colour · 87mins

Starting out as a political melodrama and ending up as a nightmare journey through some long-suppressed memories, this study of American self-doubt from director Carl Schenkel is a cut above most TV movies. Slaughtered on the hustings after news leaks of his involvement in a Vietnam War massacre, Peter Strauss's life goes into free fall when his wife Kathleen Quinlan vanishes and he becomes the prime suspect. Strauss's descent from arrogance to bewilderment is highly convincing. Contains violence.

Peter Strauss *John Waylan* • Kathleen Quinlan *Kathy Waylan* • Peter Boyle *Tony Carbo* ■ *Dir* Carl Schenkel • *Scr* Philip Rosenberg, from the novel by Tim O'Brien

In the Line of Duty: the FBI Murders ★★★ 18

Crime drama based on a true story 1988 · US · Colour · 92mins

David Soul and Michael Gross, both cast against their usual nice-guy persona, are chilling as the disturbed gun nuts who have convinced their wives that they are actually working for the CIA but are in fact terrorising Miami with their brutal armed robberies. The FBI, led by Ronny Cox (the baddie in the original *RoboCop* film), is on their case but the psychopathic duo are not giving up without a fight. The direction from Dick Lowry is sober and unsensational, although the sudden jolts of violence are surprisingly graphic for a made-for-TV movie.

David Soul *Mike Platt* • Michael Gross *Bill Matix* • Ronny Cox *Ben Grogan* • Doug Sheehan *FBI Commander Gordon McNeill* ■ *Dir* Dick Lowry • *Scr* Tracy Keenan Wynn

In the Line of Duty: Mob Justice ★★

Crime drama based on a true story 1991 · US · Colour · 93mins

Since his star billing in *Pulp Fiction*, Samuel L Jackson is unlikely to be cast in a film, only, as here, to be found rubbed out in a back-street long before it ends. Jackson brings his sense of brooding determination to the role of the DEA agent who has gone undercover to buy drugs, specifically from mob operative Gus Farace. As Farace, Tony Danza, clearly aspiring towards a more sinister image, never quite offloads the eager innocence which brought him fame in *Taxi*.

Ted Levine *Charles Rose* • Tony Danza *Gus Farace* • Samuel Jackson [Samuel L Jackson] *Everett Hatcher* • Dan Lauria • Nicholas Turturro ■ *Dir* Peter Markle • *Scr* Dick Beebe

In the Line of Duty: the Twilight Murders ★★ 18

Crime drama based on a true story 1991 · US · Colour · 90mins

A suitably mean and tough role for Rod Steiger as the leader of an extremist cop-killing gang on the run from the FBI. Based on a true story, the film is hyped up with the usual elements of action and suspense. The political twist helps prevent it from being just another "good guys chase bad guys" thriller.

Rod Steiger *Gordon Kahl* • Michael Gross *Richard Mayberly* • Christopher Rich *Scott Faul* • Gary Basaraba *Deputy Leland Wolf* ■ *Dir* Dick Lowry • *Scr* Michael Petryni

In the Line of Duty: Siege at Marion ★★★

Crime drama based on a true story 1992 · US · Colour · 96mins

The tale of one of the longest sieges in FBI history, this is certainly one of the better based-on-a-true-story TV movies, and it is mostly down to the calibre of the cast and the tension-building skill of director Charles Haid, still best known as one of the stars of *Hill Street Blues*. *St Elsewhere's* Ed Begley Jr and *NYPD Blue's* Dennis Franz are among the officers who surround a farm where two fanatics with an arsenal of guns and explosives are refusing to give themselves up. Contains swearing.

Ed Begley Jr *Lieutenant Fred House* • Tess Harper *Vicky Singer* • Dennis Franz *Bob Bryant* • Paul LeMat *Douglas Bodrero* • Kyle Secor *Adam Swapp* • William H Macy *Ray Daniels* ■ *Dir* Charles Haid • *Scr* Rick Husky

In the Line of Duty: Ambush in Waco ★★★▣

Crime drama based on a true story
1993 · US · Colour · 88mins

When a major tragedy is breaking in the States, it seems that TV executives often beat the emergency services to the scene to sign up those all-important film rights. The competition must have been tough for this true story: this movie was started even before the notorious siege of the Christian fundamentalist stronghold in Waco, Texas, had reached its tragic conclusion. Timothy Daly stars as David Koresh, the psychotic leader of the cult who takes on the might of law and order. Gripping, although faintly distasteful, stuff, efficiently directed by Dick Lowry. Contains violence and some swearing. ▢

Timothy Daly *David Koresh* • Dan Lauria *Bob Blanchard* • Neal McDonough *Jason* • Marlee Shelton [Marley Shelton] *Laura* • Kent Broadhurst *Cole* • Anne Gee Byrd *Sue Llamas* • William O'Leary *Adrian* ■ *Dir* Dick Lowry • *Scr* Phil Penningroth

In the Line of Duty: the Price of Vengeance ★★▣

Crime drama based on a true story
1994 · US · Colour · 88mins

This exceptionally plodding thriller is of primary interest for featuring Dean Stockwell in one of his more grim-faced incarnations. This time round, a policeman seeks revenge following the death of his partner a family man and loyal friend and proceeds to administer justice without bothering about a trial. It's all rather predictable, but if you enjoy police thrillers this one will probably be acceptable entertainment. Contains some violence. ▢

Dean Stockwell *Jack Lowe* • Michael Gross *Tom Williams* • Mary Kay Place *Norma Williams* • Brent Jennings *Johnny Moore* ■ *Dir* Dick Lowry • *Scr* Keith Ross Leckie

In the Line of Duty: Hunt for Justice ★★★▣

Crime drama based on a true story
1995 · US · Colour · 87mins

Nicholas Turturro, best known for his role in *NYPD Blue*, plays another enthusiastic young cop who is reluctantly teamed with an FBI man (*Chicago Hope's* Adam Arkin) to track down a gang of domestic terrorists. The two leads bicker away in predictable but entertaining fashion, and veteran TV movie director Dick Lowry generates a persuasive amount of tension without falling back on

spectacular set pieces. Look out, too, for another familiar TV face, Dan Lauria, the dad from *The Wonder Years*. Contains some swearing and violence. ▢

Adam Arkin *Damian ''Val''Valentino* • Nicholas Turturro *Detective Mike Garrett* • Dan Lauria *Philip Lamonaco* • Melissa Leo *Carol Manning* ■ *Dir* Dick Lowry • *Scr* John Miglis, from a draft by Joe Cacaci

In the Line of Duty: Kidnapped ★★★▣

Crime drama based on a true story
1995 · US · Colour · 87mins

Dabney Coleman is one of the unsung heroes of Hollywood, equally at home in comedy or dramatic roles. Here he gets a role he can really get his teeth into with this gripping police thriller, playing a serial abductor who begins a deadly cat-and-mouse game with frustrated FBI man Timothy Busfield. The two leads are backed up by strong supporting performances and no-nonsense direction from Bobby Roth. Contains some violence. ▢

Dabney Coleman *Arthur Milo* • Timothy Busfield *Agent Pete Honeycutt* • Lauren Tom *Lily Yee* • Tracey Walter *Oliver Tracy* • Barbara Williams *Beth Honeycutt* ■ *Dir* Bobby Roth • *Scr* Thomas Baum

In the Line of Duty: Smoke Jumpers ★★▣

Crime drama based on a true story
1996 · US · Colour · 87mins

Despite its fascinating subject matter – the true story of daredevil parachuting firefighters – this is formulaic fare. Adam Baldwin plays the airborne fireman who is forced to re-evaluate his gung-ho career after falling for ex-firefighter and single mother Lindsay Frost. The action scenes are gripping enough, but veteran TV-movie director Dick Lowry spends too much time exploring the domestic trials and tribulations of his two stars. ▢

Adam Baldwin *Don Mackey* • Lindsay Frost *Rene* • Timothy Carhart *Tom Classen* • Rob Youngblood *Timmerman* ■ *Dir* Dick Lowry • *Scr* Gy Waldron, Stephen Harrigan

In the Line of Fire ★★★★▣

Thriller 1993 · US · Colour · 123mins

A sight you thought you'd never see: Clint Eastwood in tears. Not many, but they're there. And that's just one of the novelties in this hugely enjoyable thriller in which Eastwood is a secret service agent who is not only visibly ageing – a fact that he admits to his younger lover, Rene Russo – but is also shamed by his past inability to save President Kennedy from assassination. That's why he's so obsessed with John Malkovich, would-be killer of the current First Executive. Eastwood reveals the same vulnerability that made his performance in *Unforgiven* so compelling and convincing. The Oscar-nominated Malkovich makes an admirable adversary, taunting Clint in much the same manner that Scorpio did in *Dirty Harry*. Contains swearing, violence and sex scenes. ▢ **DVD**

Clint Eastwood *Frank Horrigan* • John Malkovich *Mitch Leary* • Rene Russo *Lilly Raines* • Dylan McDermott *Al D'Andrea* • Gary Cole *Bill Watts* • Fred Dalton Thompson *Harry*

Sargent* • John Mahoney *Sam Campagna* ■ *Dir* Wolfgang Petersen • *Scr* Jeff Maguire • *Music* Ennio Morricone

In the Meantime, Darling ★★

Wartime comedy 1944 · US · BW · 71mins

The newly-wed young wife (Jeanne Crain) of an army officer (Frank Latimore), forced by army rules to live with other wives in a hotel near the military camp, kicks against the rules of the establishment, clashes with her fellow residents and falls into misunderstandings with her husband before he is shipped overseas and she comes to terms with reality. A potentially interesting idea is dissipated by an uninspired, indecisive script. Viennese-born Otto Preminger, with only a couple of American B-pictures behind him, would make his mark with *Laura* immediately after this very indifferent offering.

Jeanne Crain *Maggie* • Frank Latimore *Lt Daniel Ferguson* • Eugene Pallette *HB Preston* • Mary Nash *Mrs Preston* • Stanley Prager *Lt Red Pianatowski* ■ *Dir* Otto Preminger • *Scr* Arthur Kober, Michael Uris

In the Mouth of Madness ★★★▣

Horror 1994 · US · Colour · 91mins

Part homage to HP Lovecraft, part lampoon of Stephen King, John Carpenter's treatise on the psychological power of horror begins well, only to descend rapidly into genre cliché. The idea that a novel can turn its readers into demons might have been further developed, but screenwriter Michael De Luca is more interested in subjecting insurance fraud investigator Sam Neill to the bizarre goings-on in missing author Jürgen Prochnow's home town of Hobbs End. The coffee shop axe attack and the scene in the movie theatre are confidently handled, but bookend sequences in an asylum aren't enough to put this in the *Caligari* class. Contains swearing and violence. ▢

Sam Neill *John Trent* • Jürgen Prochnow *Sutter Cane* • Julie Carmen *Linda Styles* • Charlton Heston *Jackson Harglow* • David Warner *Dr Wrenn* • John Glover *Saperstein* ■ *Dir* John Carpenter • *Scr* Michael De Luca

In the Name of the Father ★★★★▣

Biographical drama
1993 · Ire/UK/US · Colour · 127mins

A stirring and exceptionally well acted, though controversial, rendering of Gerry Conlon's book about the grave miscarriage of justice suffered by the Guildford Four. Daniel Day-Lewis is highly impressive as Conlon, a naive young Irishman who couldn't blow his own hat off, fingered by corrupt police for the terrorist bombings along with three equally unlikely friends. The rest, as they say, is history and, as portrayed by director Jim Sheridan, it comes rattling out packing an enormous dramatic punch. Pete Postlethwaite is brilliant as Conlon's bemused and hapless father ,and the only false note is struck by Emma Thompson, hopelessly miscast (albeit Oscar-nominated) as the Four's

solicitor. Don't miss. Contains violence, swearing and drug abuse. ▢

Daniel Day-Lewis *Gerry Conlon* ■ Emma Thompson *Gareth Peirce* • Pete Postlethwaite *Guiseppe Conlon* • John Lynch *Paul Hill* • Mark Sheppard *Paddy Armstrong* • Beatie Edney *Carole Richardson* • Marie Jones *Sarah Conlon* • Britta Smith *Annie Maguire* • Corin Redgrave *Robert Dixon* ■ *Dir* Jim Sheridan • *Scr* Terry George, Jim Sheridan

In the Name of the Pope King ★★★★

Historical drama 1977 · It · Colour · 107mins

Set during the mid-19th century, this lavish historical drama focuses on the resistance of the Papal States to the cause of Italian unification. As the magistrate seeking to use his dwindling influence to save his son – an imprisoned member of Garibaldi's rebel army – Nino Manfredi gives a performance of abject despair, as he comes to recognise his personal and political impotence. Recalling Luchino Visconti in his magisterial use of colour and attention to historical detail, Luigi Magni not only evokes the grandeur of the Vatican, but also makes accessible the intricate political and theological issues at stake. In Italian with English subtitles.

Nino Manfredi *Don Colombo* • Danilo Mattei *Cesare Costa* • Carmen Scarpitta *Contessa Flaminia* • Giovanella Grifeo *Teresa* ■ *Dir/Scr* Luigi Magni

In the Navy ★★

Musical comedy 1941 · US · BW · 85mins

Abbott and Costello made such an impact as bumbling army recruits in *Buck Privates* that Universal immediately repeated the formula with another service comedy. Dick Powell plays a popular crooner who, fed up with the good life, enlists in the navy (under a false name) where he encounters misfit sailors Abbott and Costello. They help and hinder him as he tries to shake off a smart female reporter who sees through his guise. The Andrews Sisters (a big hit in *Buck Privates*) are on hand again, enlivening the proceedings with a few songs.

Bud Abbott *Smokey Adams* • Lou Costello *Pomeroy Watson* • Dick Powell *Tommy Halstead* • Claire Dodd *Dorothy Roberts* • The Andrews Sisters *The Andrews Sisters* ■ *Dir* Arthur Lubin • *Scr* Arthur T Horman, John Grant, from the story *They're in the Navy Now* by Arthur T Horman

In the Presence of Mine Enemies ★★

Drama 1996 · US · Colour · 100mins

Armin Mueller-Stahl stars here as a rabbi in the Warsaw ghetto, trying to keep himself and his Jewish community alive during the Nazi occupation. Charles Dance bravely takes on the role of the SS officer. The movie was directed by Joan Micklin Silver, best known for her two previous studies of New York's Jewish community – *Hester Street* and *Crossing Delancey*.

Armin Mueller-Stahl *Adam Heller* • Charles Dance *Captain Richter* • Elina Lowensohn *Rachel Heller* ■ *Dir* Joan Micklin Silver

U = SUITABLE FOR ALL **Uc** = SUITABLE FOR ALL, ESPECIALLY FOR YOUNG CHILDREN (VIDEO ONLY) **PG** = PARENTAL GUIDANCE

In the Realm of the Senses ★★★★ 18

Erotic drama based on a true story
1976 · Fr/Jap · Colour · 105mins

Based on a notorious murder case that scandalised Japan in the thirties, Nagisa Oshima's tale of puissant passion is also a complex study of gender status and oppression. However, as in *Last Tango in Paris*, the eroticism is so hardcore it has invariably prevented a considered assessment of the writer/director's achievement. Laced with cultural and historical allusions and imagery as beautiful as it is powerful, the film follows geisha Eiko Matsuda and her over Tatsuya Fuji as they willingly risk death in a bid to find individual fulfilment in a militarist society. In Japanese with English subtitles.

Tatsuya Fuji *Kichi-zo* • Eiko Matsuda *Sada* • Aoi Nakajima *Toku* • Meika Seri *Maid Matsuko* • Taiji Tonoyama *Old beggar* ■ *Dir/Scr* Nagisa Oshima

In the Shadow of a Killer ★★ PG

Crime thriller   1992 · US · Colour · 90mins

Poor old Scott Bakula. Although he found fame in the TV series *Quantum Leap*, he doesn't seem to have much success elsewhere, appearing in such turkeys as the Bruce Willis movie *Color of Night* and, regrettably, this crime thriller. It's a fact-based tale, with Bakula as a detective opposed to the death penalty who finds himself pressured from all sides after he arrests a Mafia cop killer. Unfortunately, there's not enough tension to sustain interest, and even Bakula fans will be put off by the one-note character he portrays.

Scott Bakula *David Mitchell* • Lindsay Frost *Tracy Mitchell* • Miguel Ferrer *Walzer* • JT Walsh *Leo Kemeny* ■ *Dir* Alan Metzger • *Scr* Phil Rosenberg

In the Shadow of Evil ★★ 15

Thriller   1995 · US · Colour · 89mins

The cast is splendid, the idea intriguing, but this TV movie fails to capitalise on either and ends up being yet another tepid thriller. The under-rated Treat Williams is a cop whose amnesia, after a road accident, threatens to allow a serial killer to go free. Margaret Colin also impresses as the psychiatrist who helps Williams reconstruct his memory. William H Macy, *ER*'s ex-chief of surgery, turns in typically assured support, but director Daniel Sackheim might have upped the suspense a couple of notches. Contains some violence.

Treat Williams *Jack Brenner* • Margaret Colin *Dr Molly Nostrand* • Timothy Busfield *Detective Walt Keller* • Joe Morton *Lieutenant Danny Royce* • William H Macy *Dr Frank Teague* • Brad Greenquist *Willy Sommers* ■ *Dir* Daniel Sackheim • *Scr* Robert Nathan, Raymond Hartung, from a story by Raymond Hartung

In the Soup ★★

Comedy   1936 · UK · BW · 72mins

Director Henry Edwards does little to disguise the theatrical origins of this comic warhorse, which shows just how reliant Ralph Lynn was on his fellow Aldwych farceurs. Without Tom Walls's wiles and Robertson Hare's pomposity, Lynn's silly-ass antics have a third-rate Bertie Wooster feel as he and Judy Gunn pose as servants in order to prevent his old colonial uncle discovering their marriage and disinheriting them. That said, Ralph Lumley's play throws up a couple of amusing set pieces.

Ralph Lynn *Horace* • Judy Gunn *Kitty* • Morton Selten *Abernathy Ruppershaw* • Nelson Keys *Emile Moppert* • Bertha Belmore *Madame Moppert* ■ *Dir* Henry Edwards • *Scr* H Fowler Mear, from a play by Ralph Lumley

In the Soup ★★★ 15

Comedy   1992 · US · Colour · 95mins

An unusual angle on the struggle to bring script to screen marks Alexandre Rockwell's larger-than-life comedy out from the many other indie films about indie films. The twist is that writer Steve Buscemi's pretentious 500-page epic is to be financed by hoodlum Seymour Cassel, who embarks on various criminal activities to raise the $250,000 budget. Good casting and some bright ideas, but the movie-making theme seems to fall by the wayside as Cassel pulls Buscemi into his unwholesome activities. As a result, the film loses its satirical edge. However, Cassel's energetic performance is a treat.

Steve Buscemi *Aldolpho Rollo* • Seymour Cassel *Joe* • Jennifer Beals *Angelica* • Pat Moya *Dang* • Will Patton *Skippy* • Jim Jarmusch *Monty* • Carol Kane *Barbara* ■ *Dir* Alexandre Rockwell • *Scr* Alexandre Rockwell, Tim Kissell

In the Spirit ★★★ 18

Comedy   1990 · US · Colour · 90mins

Screwball black comedy, with Peter Falk and Elaine May as houseguests of nutty new-age mystic Marlo Thomas. The couple need brass balls rather than crystal ones when unforeseen circumstances make them targets of a killer who's already polished off the prostitute next door. Great cast (Olympia Dukakis also appears), but irritating material, and characters you're as likely to loathe as to love. Watch out for a single-scene cameo from Melanie Griffith as the not-so-happy hooker.

Jeannie Berlin *Crystal* • Marlo Thomas *Reva Prosky* • Elaine May *Marianne Flan* • Olympia Dukakis *Sue* • Peter Falk *Roger Flan* • Melanie Griffith *Lureen* ■ *Dir* Sandra Seacat • *Scr* Jeannie Berlin, Laurie Jones

In the White City ★★★★ 15

Drama   1983 · Swi/Por · Colour · 108mins

Duality lies at the heart of Alain Tanner's intriguing existential drama. Sailor Bruno Ganz loves two women in contrasting locations – his Swiss wife, Julia Vonderlinn, and Teresa Madruga, the chambermaid he meets in Lisbon. Even the footage is two-tone, as it juxtaposes traditional 35mm with the Super-8 home movies that Ganz shoots as he survives various misadventures while wandering the schizophrenic city, which blithely casts off its warming daylight welcome for the forbidding shadows of night. Superbly controlled and atmospherically scored, this is an endlessly questioning study of emotional disquiet. In French with English subtitles.

Bruno Ganz *Paul* • Teresa Madruga *Rosa* • Julia Vonderlinn *Elisa* • Jose Carvalho *Bar proprietor* • Victor Costa *Bartender* ■ *Dir/Scr* Alain Tanner

In This Our Life ★★★

Melodrama   1942 · US · BW · 96mins

A rip-roaring Warner Bros melodrama directed by then newcomer John Huston, with an excellent cast including (watch closely) a cameo from his father Walter as a bartender, and tiny appearances from the likes of Humphrey Bogart and Peter Lorre. The scenery is chewed to bits by Bette Davis, who manages to destroy the life of her sister Olivia de Havilland and then destroys herself. There's some amazing plotting, as the wonderfully nasty Davis is involved in a hit-and-run and tries to lay the blame on the son of her black cook, not to mention driving Dennis Morgan to suicide (he was de Havilland's husband; she stole him), and trying to get back her jilted beau George Brent. Super stuff, not to be taken at all seriously.

Bette Davis *Stanley Timberlake* • Olivia de Havilland *Roy Timberlake* • George Brent *Craig Fleming* • Dennis Morgan *Peter Kingsmill* • Charles Coburn *William Fitzroy* • Hattie McDaniel *Minerva Clay* • Walter Houston *Bartender* ■ *Dir* John Huston • *Scr* Howard Koch, John Huston, from the novel by Ellen Glasgow • *Cinematographer* Ernie Haller [Ernest Haller] • *Music* Max Steiner

In Too Deep ★★ 18

Erotic crime thriller
1990 · Ausl · Colour · 101mins

A flawed thriller set against the backdrop of the Melbourne music scene. The story focuses on Hugo Race (occasional Nick Cave collaborator), a small time crook dreaming of a music career who has lucked into some evidence of government corruption. He attempts to stay one step ahead of the cops while resolving his relationship with jazz singer Samantha Press. Melbourne probably has never looked quite so exotic. Cave fans should keep an eye out for his old Birthday Party guitarist Rowland S Howard in a small role.

Hugo Race *Mack Donnelly* • Santha Press *Wendy Lyall* • Rebekah Elmaloglou *JoJo Lyall* • John Flaus *Miles* • Dominic Sweeney *Dinny* ■ *Dir* John Tatoulis, Colin South • *Scr* Deborah Parsons

In Too Deep ★★ 18

Action thriller   1999 · US · Colour · 93mins

This run-of-the-mill cops and robbers flick is distinguished by strong performances from Omar Epps and rapper/thespian LL Cool J. Epps is a young undercover cop who gets in over his head while investigating LL's charismatic drug lord. He is soon torn between duty and their budding friendship. LL Cool J plays a likeable villain, an interesting combination of kindness and malice. Beyond the acting, however, this movie offers no surprises, and an unnecessary romance between Epps and Nia Long severely impedes the pace.

Omar Epps *Jeff Cole/J Reid* • LL Cool J *Dwayne "God" Gittens* • Nia Long *Myra* • Pam Grier *Detective Angela Wilson* • Stanley Tucci *Preston Boyd* ■ *Dir* Michael Rymer • *Scr* Michael Henry Brown, Paul Aaron

In Which We Serve ★★★★★ U

Second World War drama
1942 · UK · BW · 109mins

Co-directed by the debuting David Lean, Noël Coward's naval epic is a wartime propaganda film about the thinly disguised maritime exploits of Lord Louis Mountbatten that has matured to become a paean to a lost world. Told in flashback, as a group of stranded sailors awaits rescue after the sinking of their ship, the film is immensely moving, and contains definitive performances from Coward himself and Celia Johnson, all chintz, beauty and stoicism in her film debut. Watch out, too, for screen bows from Richard Attenborough, Daniel Massey and an 11-week-old Juliet Mills. A box-office hit in its day, the film was awarded a special Oscar, given to Coward for his "outstanding production achievement". DVD

Noël Coward *Captain "D"* • John Mills *O/S "Shorty" Blake* • Bernard Miles *CPO Walter Hardy* • Celia Johnson *Alix Kinross* • Joyce Carey *Mrs Hardy* • Kay Walsh *Freda Lewis* • Derek Elphinstone *Number One* • Frederick Piper *Edgecombe* • Geoffrey Hibbert *Joey Mackridge* • George Carney *Mr Blake* • Michael Wilding *"Flags"* • Richard Attenborough *Young stoker* ■ *Dir* Noël Coward, David Lean • *Scr* Noël Coward, from the experiences of Lord Louis Mountbatten

Inadmissible Evidence ★★★

Drama   1968 · UK · BW · 95mins

Just because you're paranoid doesn't mean to say you don't have enemies. Nicol Williamson re-creates his role from John Osborne's stage play as the solicitor who fears he's being persecuted by everyone. The fact that he treats his wife (Eleanor Fazan), mistress (Jill Bennett) and colleagues with equal contempt seems to have escaped him. Williamson's tour de force of invective loses some of its impact on screen as director Anthony Page presents the speeches in fragmented form. But the solicitor's long and angry journey still makes its sombre point.

Nicol Williamson *Bill Maitland* • Eleanor Fazan *Anna Maitland* • Jill Bennett *Liz* • Peter Sallis *Hudson* • David Valla *Jones* • Eileen Atkins *Shirley* • Lindsay Anderson *Barrister* ■ *Dir* Anthony Page • *Scr* John Osborne, from his play

Inauguration of the Pleasure Dome ★★★

Underground experimental
1954 · US · Colour · 36mins

Another of Kenneth Anger's medium-length ciné-poems expressing his vision of the occult. The film has gone through several incarnations – the first had a soundtrack by Harry Parch, the second uses Janacek's *Glagolithic Mass* to better effect. In 1966, Anger then added an opening reading of Coleridge's *Kubla Khan* accompanied by stills of Satanist guru Aleister Crowley and talismanic symbols, which became known as the *Sacred*

Mushroom Edition. One does not have to share Anger's esoteric philosophy to relish his imagery, often outrageously camp and pretentious as it is. ▭
Anaïs Nin *Astarte* • Curtis Harrington *Cesare the Somnambulist* ■ *Dir/Scr* Kenneth Anger • Music Leos Janacek

Incendiary Blonde ★★★
Biographical musical
1945 · US · Colour · 113mins

An explosive Technicolor musical biopic giving a somewhat selective account of the colourful life of Texas Guinan, infamous nightclub queen of the Prohibition era, whose famous catchphrase was "Hello suckers!". Lavishly mounted by Paramount, the movie is lively and entertaining, jam-packed with songs, including *It Had to Be You*, and lots of incident involving bootlegging gangsters, one of whom (Arturo De Cordova) is Texas's lover. Betty Hutton's most significant role to date saw the star hurling herself at the material – both dramatic and musical – with the force of a neutron bomb, leaving viewers either deafened and exhausted, or thoroughly exhilarated.
Betty Hutton *Texas Guinan* • Arturo De Cordova *Bill Romero Kilgannon* • Charlie Ruggles [Charles Ruggles] *Cherokee Jim* • Albert Dekker *Joe Cadden* ■ *Dir* George Marshall • *Scr* Claude Binyon, Frank Butler, from the biography *Life of Texas Guinan* by Thomas Guinan, WD Guinan

Incense for the Damned ★★
Horror   1970 · UK · Colour · 86mins

Based on Simon Raven's novel *Doctors Wear Scarlet*, this little-seen oddity clearly fails to surmount its production problems. The low budget ran out in Cyprus, planned re-shoots never happened, so it was hastily patched together and subsequently disowned by horror maestro Robert Hartford-Davis, who signed it "Michael Burrowes". Yet flashes of imagination shine through as Patrick Macnee helps doomed starlet Imogen Hassall save her fiancé Patrick Mower from Greek satanists. Vampirism as an extension of sexual perversion is just one of the potent issues raised in this rare collector's item. Contains sex scenes, drug abuse and nudity.
Patrick Macnee *Major Longbow* • Peter Cushing *Dr Goodrich* • Alex Davion *Tony Seymour* • Johnny Sekka *Bob Kirby* • Madeline Hinde *Penelope* • Patrick Mower *Richard Fountain* • Edward Woodward *Holmstrom* • David Lodge *Colonel* ■ *Dir* Michael Burrowes [Robert Hartford-Davis] • *Scr* Julian More, from the novel *Doctors Wear Scarlet* by Simon Raven

Inchon ★
War drama   1981 · S Kor · Colour · 140mins

Dollar for dollar and with adjustments for inflation, this is the biggest flop in the history of the cinema. Financed to the tune of $46 million by the Church of the Reverend Sung Myung Moon, it's a vast re-creation of a major battle in the Korean war. Laurence Olivier as Douglas MacArthur leads a peculiar cast, while ex-Bond director Terence Young juggles the explosions and romantic interludes. It opened briefly, received a critical mauling and has barely been seen again.

Laurence Olivier *General Douglas MacArthur* • Jacqueline Bisset *Barbara Hallsworth* • Ben Gazzara *Major Frank Hallsworth* • David Janssen *David Feld* ■ *Dir* Terence Young • *Scr* Robin Moore, Laird Koenig, from a story by Paul Savage, Robin Moore

The Incident ★★★
Drama   1967 · US · BW · 107mins

This neatly compressed drama began as a live TV play called *Ride with Terror* but the planned Hollywood version, to be produced by Joseph E Levine, never came off. Tony Musante and Martin Sheen (in his screen debut) play two New York delinquents who make life a misery for the passengers on a subway train, including GI Beau Bridges, pensioner Thelma Ritter and bullied wife Jan Sterling. This structure – the 16 passengers representing a cross section of life in the big smoke – is filmed with considerable attack as the thugs taunt and expose the flaws in everyone's characters.
Tony Musante *Joe Ferrone* • Martin Sheen *Artie Connors* • Beau Bridges *Private First Class Felix Teflinger* • Jack Gilford *Sam Beckerman* • Thelma Ritter *Bertha Beckerman* • Brock Peters *Arnold Robinson* • Ruby Dee *Joan Robinson* • Donna Mills *Alice Keenan* ■ *Dir* Larry Peerce • *Scr* Nicholas E Baehr, from his play *Ride with Terror*

The Incident ★★★ PG
Courtroom drama   1990 · US · Colour · 94mins

Walter Matthau's twilight debut venture into TV movies, and a highly honourable one which ably illustrates his oft-forgotten straight acting skills. We are so used to the rubber-faced grumpy buffoon that Matthau's stirring portrayal of a small-time war lawyer defending a German PoW is almost shocking in its disciplined precision. The finely tuned script by Michael and James Norell is a big help, as is a fine supporting cast that includes Robert Carradine. ▭
Walter Matthau *Harman Cobb* • Susan Blakely *Billie* • Robert Carradine *Prosecutor Domsczek* • Peter Firth *Wilhelm Geiger* • Barnard Hughes *"Doc" Hansen* • Harry Morgan *Judge Bell* ■ *Dir* Joseph Sargent • *Scr* Michael Norell, James Norell

Incident at Phantom Hill ★★ U
Western   1966 · US · Colour · 87mins

From a period when Universal was making co-features to support its "A" product, invariably starring or trying out contract artists or television names, this stars *Laramie's* Robert Fuller opposite veteran baddie Dan Duryea. The tale of stolen bullion, hostile Apaches and the like is decked out in Technicolor to very little avail. The director is former floor assistant Earl Bellamy, whose technique is strictly TV, but old-timers Duryea and *Rio Bravo's* Claude Akins keep it just about watchable.
Robert Fuller *Matt Martin* • Jocelyn Lane *Memphis* • Dan Duryea *Joe Barlow* • Tom Simcox *Adam Long* • Linden Chiles *Dr Hanneford* • Claude Akins *Krausman* ■ *Dir* Earl Bellamy • *Scr* Frank Nugent, Ken Pettus, from a story by Harry Tateleman

Incident in a Small Town ★★★
Drama   1993 · US · Colour · 85mins

Walter Matthau returns in the third of his Harmon J Cobb small screen outings – the previous two were *The Incident* and *Against Her Will* – as the wily, lawyer working courtroom miracles in postwar America. The relaxed playing of the veteran leads is the best thing about this, although director Delbert Mann also manages to inject a few surprises into the murder mystery.
Walter Matthau *Harmon J Cobb* • Harry Morgan *Judge Stoddard Bell* • Stephanie Zimbalist *Lily* • Nick Stahl *John* • Bernard Behrens *Judge Greeves* • Lori Hallier *Madeleine* • David Nerman *Frank* ■ *Dir* Delbert Mann • *Scr* Cindy Myers

Incognito ★ 15
Thriller   1997 · US · Colour · 103mins

Director John Badham (*Saturday Night Fever, Stakeout*) takes a good cast and a reasonably interesting concept and comes up with this deeply disappointing thriller. You can hardly blame stars like Rod Steiger, who literally phones in his brief role as the artist father of art forger Jason Patric. The plot involves Patric's decision to accept a fortune to fake a Rembrandt and the mayhem that ensues. Irène Jacob provides the love interest but lovers of art and good movies should give this one a wide berth. Contains some swearing. ▭
Jason Patric *Harry Donovan* • Irène Jacob *Marieke Van Den Broeck* • Thomas Lockyer *Alistair Davies* • Ian Richardson *Turley – Prosecutor* • Rod Steiger *Milton A Donovan* • Miriam Karlin *Saleswomam in paint shop* ■ *Dir* John Badham • *Scr* Jordan Katz

The Incredible Hulk Returns ★★ PG
Fantasy adventure
1988 · US · Colour · 93mins

Bursting from the pages of Marvel Comics on to our TV screens in 1978, the Incredible Hulk was, briefly, essential viewing for children everywhere. But, by the time this TV movie appeared a decade later, audiences had grown out of his superheroic exploits, in much the same way that Bill Bixby grew out of his clothes (and turned into snarling Lou Ferrigno) every time he had a temper tantrum. Convinced that mere mortals were no longer a match for the far-from-jolly green giant, the producers brought in another Marvel regular, the mighty Thor, to provide the villainy. The plot is as tatty as Bixby's ripped shirt, but it's undemanding fun. ▭
Bill Bixby *David Banner* • Lou Ferrigno *The Incredible Hulk* • Lee Purcell *Maggie Shaw* • Tim Thomerson *Le Beau* • Eric Kramer [Eric Allan Kramer] *Thor* ■ *Dir/Scr* Nicholas Corea

The Incredible Journey ★★★★ U
Adventure   1963 · US · Colour · 76mins

Not only is this easily the best of Disney's true-life adventures, but it's also far superior to the studio's dumbed down 1993 remake, *Homeward Bound: the Incredible Journey*. Syn (as Tao the cat), Muffey (Bodger the bull terrier) and Rink

(Luath the labrador) are outstanding as the abandoned pets who make their way across the treacherous Canadian wilderness to reunite with their owners. On the way they encounter danger in the form of bears, mountain lions and a disgruntled porcupine. Subtly narrated by Rex Allen, this is only slightly spoiled by the wooden performances of the humans in the cast. Compelling family viewing. ▭
Rex Allen *Narrator* • Emile Genest *John Longridge* • John Drainie *Professor Jim Hunter* • Tommy Tweed *Hermit* • Sandra Scott *Mrs Hunter* • Syme Jago *Nervi Hurmi* • Marion Finlayson *Elizabeth Hunter* ■ *Dir* Fletcher Markle • *Scr* James Algar, from the novel by Sheila Burnford

The Incredible Melting Man ★★ 18
Horror   1977 · US · Colour · 85mins

Astronaut Alex Rebar returns from Saturn a changed man. His flesh is decomposing and he finds he's developed a taste for human flesh. A deliberate throwback to such cheap fifties' frights as *The First Man into Space*, hack writer/director William Sachs's films provides little of interest outside the tried and tested old-school format, apart from showcasing Oscar winner (*An American Werewolf in London*) Rick Baker's oozing, slimy and putrefying make-up to stunning effect. ▭
Alex Rebar *Melting Man* • Burr DeBenning *Dr Ted Nelson* • Myron Healey *General Perry* • Michael Alldredge *Sheriff Blake* • Ann Sweeny *Judy Nelson* • Lisle Wilson *Dr Loring* • Jonathan Demme *Matt* ■ *Dir/Scr* William Sachs • *Make-up* Rick Baker

The Incredible Mr Limpet ★★
Fantasy comedy animation
1964 · US · Colour · 102mins

Don Knotts stars as meek clerk Henry Limpet, who's obsessed with fish, in this part live action, part animated wartime fantasy. When he is turned down for the navy because of his short-sightedness Henry is despondent. Later, at Coney Island, he falls off the dock into the ocean and is miraculously transformed into an animated fish. In his new guise, he finds fulfilment by guiding US vessels pursuing German U-boats. This sentimental sub-Disney tale will be of interest only to undemanding children and fans of comic actor Don Knotts.
Don Knotts *Henry Limpet* • Carole Cook *Bessie Limpet* • Jack Weston *Lt George Stickle* • Andrew Duggan *Adm Harlock* ■ *Dir* Arthur Lubin • *Scr* Jameson Brewer, John C Rose, Joe DiMona, from the novel *Mr Limpet* by Theodore Pratt

The Incredible Sarah ★★
Biographical drama
1976 · UK · Colour · 105mins

Oscar-winning British actress Glenda Jackson hams it up as famous French actress Sarah Bernhardt, in a performance that hardly hints at a great future in politics. Despite many obvious errors of judgement, director Richard Fleischer was clearly at the end of his creative tether with this humdrum *Reader's Digest*-backed look at Bernhardt's life, so all he can do is

to provide some entertainment value. He only just succeeds.

Glenda Jackson *Sarah Bernhardt* • Daniel Massey *Sardou* • Yvonne Mitchell *Mam'selle* • Douglas Wilmer *Montigny* • David Langton *Duc De Morny* • Simon Williams *Henri De Ligne* ■ *Dir* Richard Fleischer • *Scr* Ruth Wolff

The Incredible Shrinking Man ★★★★★

Science-fiction   1957 · US · BW · 91mins

A must-see classic, directed by the master of fifties' science fiction, Jack Arnold, and derived from the thought-provoking novel by genre luminary Richard Matheson. Grant Williams slowly shrinks after passing through a radioactive cloud and, on the way down, sees his marriage disintegrate and is terrorised by the pet cat and a basement spider. A cogent comment on the plight of the "little man", Arnold's superlative thriller still retains its irony, shock and power. Williams gives a sensitive portrayal of a man hounded by the media and consigned to a freak's world, whose descent into nothingness provides a memorable climax.

Grant Williams *Scott Carey* • Randy Stuart *Louise Carey* • April Kent *Clarice* • Paul Langton *Charlie Carey* • Raymond Bailey *Dr Thomas Silver* • William Schallert *Dr Arthur Bramson* ■ *Dir* Jack Arnold • *Scr* Richard Matheson, from his novel *The Shrinking Man*

The Incredible Shrinking Woman ★★★

Comedy   1981 · US · Colour · 88mins

A very odd spoof on the wonderful *The Incredible Shrinking Man*, brought bang up to date with some neat special effects but lacking the shock value of the original. Lily Tomlin is very funny as the housewife accidentally sprayed with a new perfume and ending up the size of the germs she tries so hard to eradicate in her home. This is a pleasing little jaunt through highly familiar territory, directed with flair and a light touch by Joel Schumacher. But nothing comes close to the astounding originality of the 1957 classic. Contains swearing. ▭

Lily Tomlin *Pat Kramer/Judith Beasley* • Charles Grodin *Vance Kramer* • Ned Beatty *Dan Beame* • Henry Gibson *Dr Eugene Nortz* ■ *Dir* Joel Schumacher • *Scr* Jane Wagner, from the novel *The Shrinking Man* by Richard Matheson

The Incredible Two-Headed Transplant ★

Science-fiction horror
1971 · US · Colour · 87mins

This low-budget nonsense is so laughably bad as to have garnered a minor cult reputation among trash horror movie fans. Bruce Dern is perfectly cast as a deranged scientist who grafts the head of a murderer on to the body of a retarded giant who – predictably – goes on a Frankenstein-style rampage. Anthony M Lanza, unsurprisingly, never directed another film again, although acclaimed make-up effects artist Rick Baker (*An American Werewolf in London*) was responsible for the gorilla suit.

Bruce Dern *Roger* • Pat Priest *Linda* • Casey Kasem *Ken* • Albert Cole *Cass* • John Bloom *Danny* ■ *Dir* Anthony M Lanza • *Scr* James Gordon White, John Lawrence

The Incredibly Strange Creatures Who Stopped Living and Became Mixed-up Zombies ★★

Horror comedy   1963 · US · Colour · 82mins

This legendary turkey was billed as the "First Monster Musical" and features such awful production numbers as *The Mixed-up Zombie Stomp*, complete with tacky striptease routines. Cash Flagg (director Ray Dennis Steckler's alter ego) falls under the sinister spell of a sideshow fortune-teller who throws acid in her patron's faces and then confines them to cages where they become rabid zombies ready to break loose when the rock songs begin. A heady mix of carnival freaks, beatniks, voodoo and knife-murders, this unbelievably messy romp has something for every follower of trash. Originally shown in "Hallucinogenic Hypnovision" – whatever that means.

Cash Flagg [Ray Dennis Steckler] *Jerry* • Carolyn Brandt *Marge Neilson* • Brett O'Hara *Madame Estrella* • Atlas King *Harold* ■ *Dir* Ray Dennis Steckler • *Scr* Gene Pollock, Robert Silliphant, from a story by EM Kevke

The Incredibly True Adventures of Two Girls in Love ★★★ 15

Romantic comedy drama
1995 · US · Colour · 91mins

Likeable same-sex love story, about the romance between two girls from widely differing social and financial backgrounds. One is a working-class lesbian who lives with other lesbians, including her mum. The other is from a wealthy background, hugely popular, and complete with boyfriend. Burgeoning romance arouses wrath from both sets of friends and relatives. Engaging performances and sensitive plot-handling ensure you'll be rooting for the triumph of true love. And, of course, triumph it does. ▭

Laurel Holloman *Randy Dean* • Nicole Parker [Nicole Ari Parker] *Evie Roy* • Maggie Moore *Wendy* • Kate Stafford *Rebecca Dean* • Sabrina Artel *Vicky* • Toby Poser *Lena* ■ *Dir/Scr* Maria Maggenti

Incubus ★★★ 18

Horror   1965 · US · BW · 88mins

William Shatner speaking Esperanto and sharing screen time with someone calling himself Incubus. No, it's not a "lost" episode of *Star Trek* but a rare experimental art movie that was unavailable for years until a print belatedly became available. Best described as a kind of Swedish art movie filmed in California, this finds Shatner in the land of Nomen Tuum, where he's under threat from Allyson Ames's witch and the devil's little helper, Incubus. Shatner actually handles his part and the Esperanto dialogue well, and the black-and-white photography by Conrad Hall (Oscar winner for *Butch Cassidy*) is alternately stunning and haunting. Eventually, it gets silly towards the end, but it's definitely not the laugh fest you might

expect. In Esperanto with English subtitles. ▭

William Shatner *Marc* • Milos Milos *Incubus* • Allyson Ames *Kia* • Eloise Hardt *Amael* • Robert Fortier *Olin* ■ *Dir/Scr* Leslie Stevens

Indecent Behavior ★★ 18

Erotic thriller   1993 · US · Colour · 94mins

Shannon Tweed is the undisputed queen of the erotic thriller and this proved to be one of her most popular films. The story is completely daft: Tweed plays an extremely unlikely sex therapist, under suspicion when one of her patients dies, who becomes involved with the detective investigating the case. The plot is largely an excuse for Tweed and a string of her female patients to get up to some ludicrously stylised sex sessions set to a sub-MTV soundtrack. It's actually pretty funny, but for all the wrong reasons. Contains violence, swearing, sex scenes and nudity. ▭

Shannon Tweed *Rebecca Mathis* • Gary Hudson *Nick Sharkey* • Michelle Moffett *Carol Lefter* • Lawrence Hilton-Jacobs *Lou Parsons* • Jan-Michael Vincent *Tom Mathis* ■ *Dir* Lawrence Lanoff • *Scr* Rosalind Robinson

Indecent Behavior 2 ★★ 18

Erotic thriller   1994 · US · Colour · 90mins

Given her criminal exploits in the first film, it possibly wasn't the wisest idea to give saucy shrink Shannon Tweed community service in a psychiatrist's office. However, this is the starting point for another largely pointless exercise in soft-focus erotica, as Tweed gets mixed up with another oddball collection of sexually frustrated clients. Tweed disrobes with her usual enthusiasm but Chad McQueen (son of Steve) makes the fatal mistake of taking it all a little too seriously. Daft. Contains sex scenes, violence, swearing and nudity. ▭

Shannon Tweed *Dr Rebecca Mathis* • James Brolin *Dr Liam* • Chad McQueen *Darrell Martine* • Elizabeth Sandifer *Shoshana Reed* ■ *Dir* Carlo Gustaff • *Scr* Mike Snyder, Phoebe Caulfield, Joyce James

Indecent Proposal ★★★★ 15

Drama   1993 · US · Colour · 112mins

Would you pay $1 million to sleep with Demi Moore? Robert Redford thinks she's worth it, as he puts the proposal to Moore's husband Woody Harrelson after learning they need the money. The interesting "would *you* do it?" premise of Adrian Lyne's film goes slightly awry as the moral issues are dumped in favour of all three main characters simply showing how selfish they are. This is probably best seen as a good example of the excesses and emptiness of the early nineties. But, with a cast like this, who are we to quibble? Contains swearing, sex scenes and nudity. ▭

Robert Redford *John Gage* • Demi Moore *Diana Murphy* • Woody Harrelson *David Murphy* • Seymour Cassel *Mr Shackelford* • Oliver Platt *Jeremy* • Billy Connolly *Auction Emcee* • Joel Brooks *Realtor* • Pierre Epstein *Van Buren* • Sheena Easton • Herbie Hancock ■ *Dir* Adrian Lyne • *Scr* Amy Holden Jones, from the novel by Jack Engelhard

Indecent Seduction ★★★ 15

Drama based on a true story
1996 · US · Colour · 87mins

Alan Metzger has a decent track record in TV movies and here succeeds in keeping the lid on what might easily have been a censorious melodrama. Not that this study of the seedier aspects of high-school life is perfect. But it plays shrewdly on the screen image of Gary Cole (the dad in the *Brady Bunch* films) by making him appear all too human as the popular basketball coach who is accused of having an affair with 14-year-old student Nicholle Tom. With solid support from Mary Kay Place, this is provocative and credible. Contains sex scenes and swearing. ▭

Gary Cole *Coach Pete Nash* • Mary Kay Place *Betty Ann Dustin* • Nicholle Tom *Amy Dustin* • Alyson Hannigan *Kelly* • Sara Rue *Kimberly* ■ *Dir* Alan Metzger • *Scr* Diana Gould, from the article *The Seduction of Jane Doe* by Skip Hollandsworth

Independence Day ★★★ 15

Drama   1983 · US · Colour · 109mins

A perfectly realised slice of small-town life from director Robert Mandel, who would later gain some cult credibility by directing the pilot for *The X Files*. Adapted by Alice Hoffman from her own novel, the story features Kathleen Quinlan as a bored young woman torn between making a new life for herself and her developing relationship with David Keith. Their co-stars, who include Frances Sternhagen, Diane Wiest and Richard Farnsworth, offer subtle support ,and Mandel's direction is unobtrusive and sympathetic.

Kathleen Quinlan *Mary Ann Taylor* • David Keith *Jack Parker* • Frances Sternhagen *Carla Taylor* • Cliff De Young *Les Morgan* • Dianne Wiest *Nancy Morgan* • Richard Farnsworth *Evan* ■ *Dir* Robert Mandel • *Scr* Alice Hoffman

Independence Day ★★★★ 12

Science-fiction adventure
1996 · US · Colour · 138mins

Alien invasion has long fascinated movie audiences but no film has presented the destruction of the Earth on such an epic scale before this preposterously successful smash, directed by Roland Emmerich, came along, and blitzed everything before it at the box office. Of course, when we say the Earth, we really mean the United States. The story is simple: gigantic alien spacecraft hover above major cities and set about destroying everything below, but most of the effort goes on the mind-boggling set pieces of mass destruction. So what of the actors? Well, Will Smith, playing the wisecracking fighter pilot, was the big winner, with his charismatic performance making him one of the biggest box-office draws in the western world. Jeff Goldblum, Hollywood's most unlikely action star, delivers a variation of his boffin role in *Jurassic Park*. Of the females, Vivica A Fox fares the best. But this is, after all, a special effects, not an acting, showcase, and a darn entertaining one at that. ▭

Will Smith *Captain Steve Hiller* • Bill Pullman *President Thomas J Whitmore* • Jeff Goldblum *David Levinson* • Mary McDonnell *Marilyn Whitmore* • Judd Hirsch *Julius Levinson* •

Robert Loggia *General William Grey* • Randy Quaid *Russell Casse* • Margaret Colin *Constance Spano* • Harvey Fierstein *Marty Gilbert* • Adam Baldwin *Major Mitchell* • Vivica A Fox *Jasmine Dubrow* ■ *Dir* Roland Emmerich • *Scr* Dean Devlin, Roland Emmerich

The Indian Fighter ★★★ PG
Western   1955 · US · Colour · 88mins

Kirk Douglas stars in this under-rated and beautifully made western, which was the first film to be produced by Douglas's own company, Bryna. Its classy eroticism is exemplified by the casting of Italian star Elsa Martinelli as Douglas's maid, though Diana Douglas (Kirk's ex-wife and Michael's mum) also appears as a settler with more than a passing interest in the leading man. He is in his buckskinned prime, full of virile derring-do and flashing teeth, as he leads an Oregon-bound wagon train through "Injun" territory, helping a fort survive an attack in one particularly well-staged sequence. Writers Ben Hecht and Frank Davis show an honest respect for native American culture. ▭

Kirk Douglas *Johnny Hawks* • Elsa Martinelli *Onahti* • Walter Abel *Captain Trask* • Walter Matthau *Wes Todd* • Diana Douglas *Susan Rogers* • Lon Chaney Jr *Chivington* ■ *Dir* Andre De Toth • *Scr* Frank Davis, Ben Hecht, from a story by Ben Kadish [Robert L Richards]

The Indian in the Cupboard ★★★★★ PG
Fantasy adventure
1995 · US · Colour · 92mins

Wrapping culture-clash comedy up with *Honey, I Shrunk the Kids*-style special effects, director Frank Oz's assured version of the Lynne Reid Banks novel is low-key fantasy with a high grade impact. A young boy discovers that an old cupboard given to him on his birthday can animate his playthings in this enchanting family fable. Ultimately he must learn responsibility when he brings his toy Indian (well played by rap artist Litefoot) to life and starts treating him like a human Action Man. Muppet maestro Oz and his screenwriter Melissa Mathison never get too heavy, condescending or cloying with their sweet-natured message, and the results are funny, inspiring and moving. ▭

Hal Scardino *Omri* • Litefoot *Little Bear* • Lindsay Crouse *Jane* • Richard Jenkins *Victor* • Rishi Bhat *Patrick* • Steve Coogan *Tommy* ■ *Dir* Frank Oz • *Scr* Melissa Mathison, from the novel by Lynne Reid Banks

The Indian Runner ★★★ 15
Drama   1991 · US · Colour · 121mins

Sean Penn took everyone by surprise with this, his writing and directorial debut. It's a remarkably assured, mature drama, inspired by the Bruce Springsteen song *Highway Patrolman*, and follows the troubled relationship between David Morse and his disturbed younger brother (an electrifying Viggo Mortensen). The story is slight but Penn's commitment to his tragic characters shines through and his direction is pleasingly unflashy, aside from sudden jolts of violence. Contains swearing. ▭

David Morse *Joe Roberts* • Viggo Mortensen *Frank Roberts* • Valeria Golino *Maria Roberts* • Patricia Arquette *Dorothy* • Charles Bronson *Father* • Sandy Dennis *Mother* • Dennis Hopper *Caesar* • Jordan Rhodes *Randall* ■ *Dir* Sean Penn • *Scr* Sean Penn, from the song *Highway Patrolman* by Bruce Springsteen

Indian Summer ★★★★ 15
Comedy drama   1993 · US · Colour · 93mins

Several things stand out about this *Big Chill* in an adventure holiday camp. There is a wonderful sense of place and a bittersweet atmosphere of remembrance and regret generated by director Mike Binder, who also wrote the semi-autobiographical script. There is also the quality of the ensemble acting, in which no one tries to steal a march on any other member of the cast. However, Alan Arkin is particularly impressive as the camp director who invites his favourite guests to spend a final summer in the woods before he's closed down. Contains swearing, sex scenes and drug abuse. ▭

Alan Arkin *Uncle Lou* • Matt Craven *Jamie Ross* • Diane Lane *Beth Warden/Claire Everett* • Bill Paxton *Jack Belston* • Elizabeth Perkins *Jennifer Morton* • Kevin Pollak *Brad Berman* • Sam Raimi *Stick Coder* ■ *Dir/Scr* Mike Binder

The Indian Tomb ★★★
Adventure drama
1959 · W Ger/Fr/It · Colour · 95mins

The second half of Fritz Lang's two-part film (the first being *The Tiger of Eschnapur*) tells an exotic tale, evoking the world of silent serials. German architect Harald Berger and beautiful Indian dancer Seeta (unconvincingly played by Hollywood actress Debra Paget) face further perils as their romance is threatened by love rival Chandra (Walter Reyer). Lang's straight-faced approach provides some unintentional laughs, but it has its magical moments. In German with English subtitles.

Debra Paget *Seeta* • Walter Reyer *Chandra* • Paul Hubschmid *Harald Berger* • Claus Holm *Dr Walter Rhode* • Sabine Bethmann *Irene Rhode* • Valery Inkijinoff *Yama* ■ *Dir* Fritz Lang • *Scr* Fritz Lang, Werner Jörg Lüddecke, Thea von Harbou, from an idea by Thea von Harbou, from a novel by Richard Eichberg

Indian Uprising ★ U
Western   1951 · US · Colour · 75mins

In a feeble roundup of the situations being explored in bigger and better westerns of the period, George Montgomery plays the cavalry captain who's temporarily stripped of his command while trying to keep the peace between settlers and Indians. Villains are after the gold on the Indian reservation and that stirs up Geronimo, as played by Mexican actor Miguel Inclan. Inclan will be familiar to some as Cochise in John Ford's *Fort Apache* – the kind of film you'd like to be watching instead.

Eddy Waller *Sagebrush* • George Montgomery *Captain Case McCloud* • Audrey Long *Norma Clemson* • Carl Benton Reid *John Clemson* • Miguel Inclan *Geronimo* ■ *Dir* Ray Nazaro • *Scr* Kenneth Gamet, Richard Schayer, from a story by Richard Schayer

Indiana Jones and the Temple of Doom ★★★★ PG
Action adventure
1984 · US · Colour · 112mins

In retrospect, the least interesting episode of the rousing *Raiders* trilogy so far (an Atlantic-set fourth is on the way). Steven Spielberg's tribute to the classic cliffhanger serials of his youth is a trifle overblown and unsubtle, but it still has great sets, fun performances and terrific action – the stand-out, a wild ride through an Indian mine. Harrison Ford, consistently engaging as Indy, goes a long way in making up for the inferior story and often gruesome gags. ▭

Harrison Ford *Indiana Jones* • Kate Capshaw *Willie Scott* • Ke Huy Quan *Short Round* • Amrish Puri *Mola Ram* • Roshan Seth *Chatter Lal* • Philip Stone *Captain Blumburtt* • Roy Chiao *Lao Che* • David Yip *Wu Han* ■ *Dir* Steven Spielberg • *Scr* Willard Huyck, Gloria Katz, from a story by George Lucas, from characters created by George Lucas, Philip Kaufman • *Music* John Williams

Indiana Jones and the Last Crusade ★★★★★ PG
Action adventure
1989 · US · Colour · 121mins

The Temple of Doom saw the Indiana Jones series lurch off the rails a little, but all was restored with the third movie. The masterstroke here was the introduction of Sean Connery as Indy's crotchety dad, and the snappy by-play between him and Harrison Ford adds a wonderful new twist to the adventure. The quest this time is for the Holy Grail, no less, and finds Jones reunited with old chums, such as Denholm Elliott, and old enemies, namely the Nazis (Julian Glover this time…). As usual the action is on an epic scale and delivered with breathless enthusiasm and much panache by director Steven Spielberg. There is also a neat framing sequence in the beginning, with River Phoenix as the young Indy, that explains such things as our hero's fear of snakes. Contains swearing and violence. ▭

Harrison Ford *Indiana Jones* • Sean Connery *Dr Henry Jones* • Denholm Elliott *Marcus Brody* • Alison Doody *Dr Elsa Schneider* • John Rhys-Davies *Sallah* • Julian Glover *Walter Donovan* • River Phoenix *Young Indy* • Alexei Sayle *Sultan* ■ *Dir* Steven Spielberg • *Scr* Jeffrey Boam, from a story by George Lucas, Menno Meyjes, from characters created by George Lucas, Philip Kaufman • *Music* John Williams • *Cinematographer* Douglas Slocombe

Indianapolis Speedway ★★
Action drama   1939 · US · BW · 85m

Despite being a remake of the Jimmy Cagney/Howard Hawks hit *The Crowd Roars*, this car-racing drama fails on the first lap. As the champion driver who tries too hard to look after his kid brother, Pat O'Brien lacks Cagney's bravado and energy while director Lloyd Bacon displays none of Hawks's feeling for the material. Potential star John Payne is no more than adequate as the younger brother with racing fever but Ann Sheridan shows why Warner Bros were promoting her as "the Oomph Girl".

Pat O'Brien *Joe Greer* • Ann Sheridan *Frankie Merrick* • John Payne *Eddie Greer* • Gale Page

Lee Mason • Frank McHugh *Spud Connors* ■ *Dir* Lloyd Bacon • *Scr* Sig Herzig, Wally Klein, from the story *The Roar of the Crowd* by Howard Hawks, William Hawks • *Cinematographer* Sid Hickox

Indictment: the McMartin Trial ★★★★ 18
Courtroom drama based on a true story
1995 · US · Colour · 125mins

The basic storyline is a staple of the true story genre, but this starry production, executive produced by Oliver Stone, puts it in a different league altogether. The film is based on a case in the US, in which a family that ran a private day care centre were accused of child abuse. James Woods is the lawyer assigned to defend one of the accused (Henry Thomas), while Mercedes Ruehl is the ruthless prosecutor. The A-list cast are uniformly superb but what distinguishes this drama is the way director Mick Jackson keeps the viewer guessing as to what actually happened to the children. ▭

James Woods *Danny Davis* • Mercedes Ruehl *Lael Rubin* • Henry Thomas *Ray Buckey* • Shirley Knight *Peggy Buckey* • Sada Thompson *Virginia McMartin* • Lolita Davidovich *Kee McFarlane* • Mark Blum *Wayne Satz* • Alison Elliott *Peggy Ann Buckey* • Chelsea Field *Christine Johnson* ■ *Dir* Mick Jackson • *Scr* Abby Mann, Myra Mann

Indien ★★
Comedy drama   1993 · Aus · Colour · 90mins

One of the few Austrian pictures of recent times to gain any sort of international recognition, this sentimental comedy/drama was widely tipped for a best foreign film Oscar. Directed by Paul Harather and co-scripted with his two stars, Josef Hader and Alfred Dorfer, the story chronicles the changing relationship between two government hotel inspectors as they sample the facilities in various establishments. In true *Odd Couple* fashion there's plenty of sparring from the ill-matched couple. In German with English subtitles.

Josef Hader *Heinzi Bösel* • Alfred Dorfer *Kurt Fellner* ■ *Dir* Paul Harather • *Scr* Paul Harather, Josef Hader, Alfred Dorfer, from a play by Josef Hader, Alfred Dorfer

Indiscreet ★★★
Romantic comedy   1931 · US · BW · 92mins

One of Gloria Swanson's more successful attempts to extend her career into talkies, this comedy drama features her as the woman with a past who attempts to protect her younger sister (Barbara Kent) from the attentions of rakish Monroe Owsley. He's actually an ex-lover of Swanson's, and Kent is none too pleased when she finds out. Meanwhile Swanson has a budding romance with Ben Lyon's impulsive author. Largely scripted by the songwriting team of DeSylva, Brown and Henderson (who throw in a couple of lightweight numbers for Swanson to perform), this is a bright rehash of familiar situations, directed imaginatively by Leo McCarey.

Gloria Swanson *Geraldine Trent* • Ben Lyon *Tony Blake* • Monroe Owsley *Jim Woodward* • Barbara Kent *Joan Trent* • Arthur Lake *Buster*

U = SUITABLE FOR ALL   Uc = SUITABLE FOR ALL, ESPECIALLY FOR YOUNG CHILDREN (VIDEO ONLY)   PG = PARENTAL GUIDANCE

Collins • Maude Eburne *Aunt Kate* ■ *Dir* Leo McCarey • *Scr* BG DeSylva, Lew Brown, Ray Henderson, from their story *Obey That Impulse*

Indiscreet ★★★ PG
Romantic comedy
1958 · UK/US · Colour · 99mins

Two of the screen's most elegant stars provide much of the pleasure in this glossy romantic comedy. The plot twists and turns of Norman Krasna's original New York-located witty play *Kind Sir* have been transplanted to foggy London by talented Anglophile director Stanley Donen. Ingrid Bergman is an actress looking for love, and bachelor Cary Grant's pretending he's married, and together the two of them evoke delightfully sensuous memories of that kiss in *Notorious* over a decade earlier. Highlights include Grant dancing a superb Highland reel, and a witty supporting performance from David Kossoff as a chauffeur in disguise. Utterly charming. ▭

Cary Grant *Philip Adams* • Ingrid Bergman *Anna Kalman* • Cecil Parker *Alfred Munson* • Phyllis Calvert *Margaret Munson* • David Kossoff *Carl Banks* ■ *Dir* Stanley Donen • *Scr* Norman Krasna, from his play *Kind Sir*

Indiscreet ★★ PG
Romantic comedy
1988 · US/UK · Colour · 101mins

What did Robert Wagner and Lesley-Anne Down hope to gain from this remake of Stanley Donen's patchy, but nonetheless hugely enjoyable, 1958 adaptation of Norman Krasna's hit play? It was surely obvious that they would be compared to the original stars, Cary Grant and Ingrid Bergman, and would be found wanting. Watch if only to remember just how good Grant and Bergman really were. ▭

Robert Wagner *Philip Adams* • Lesley-Anne Down *Anne Kingston* ■ *Dir* Richard Michaels • *Scr* Walter Lockwood, Sally Robison, from the 1958 film *Indiscreet* by Norman Krasna, from his play *Kind Sir*

Indiscreet ★★ 15
Crime mystery 1998 · US · Colour · 96mins

This second-string thriller has nothing to do with the Cary Grant/Ingrid Bergman film of 1958. Instead it stars Luke Perry as a detective who finds himself a murder suspect when the millionaire husband of the woman he's been hired to follow winds up dead. Routine video fodder, flattered by a cast that includes Adam Baldwin and Peter Coyote. Contains swearing and some sex scenes. ▭

Luke Perry *Michael Nash* • Gloria Reuben *Eve Dodd* • Lisa Edelstein *Beth Sussman* • Peter Coyote *Detective Roos* • Laura Rogers *Katie Johnson* • Adam Baldwin *Jeremy* ■ *Dir* Marc Bienstock • *Scr* Vladimir Nemirovsky

Indiscretion of an American Wife ★★★ U
Drama 1954 · US/It · BW · 63mins

Director Vittorio De Sica's claustrophobic study of the end of a brief encounter was originally released in a double bill with Luis Buñuel's *The Adventures of Robinson Crusoe.* Brilliantly filmed in stark black and white in Rome's famous Stazione Terminale, the story brings together

Jennifer Jones and Montgomery Clift as lovers who can't bear to make the final break. The stars are filmed in magnificent close-ups, their anxiety almost palpable. Jones's husband, David O Selznick, recut this movie considerably, but it has a raw truth about it that is still deeply moving. ▭

Jennifer Jones *Mary Forbes* • Montgomery Clift *Giovanni Doria* • Gino Cervi *Commissioner* • Richard Beymer *Paul, Mary's nephew* ■ *Dir* Vittorio De Sica • *Scr* Cesare Zavattini, Luigi Chiarini, Giorgio Prosperi, Truman Capote, from a story by Cesare Zavattini

Indiscretion of an American Wife ★★ U
Romantic drama 1998 · US · Colour · 63mins

This TV movie remake of the Jennifer Jones/Montgomery Clift vehicle is nice to look at but devoid of emotion or passion. Anne Archer is the neglected wife of a diplomat (Michael Murphy) posted to Rome, who falls in love with a wealthy Italian wine maker, played by Italian actor Andrea Occhipinti. This leads to the usual adulterer's dilemma, as Archer feels she must choose between passion for her new lover and commitment to her marriage vows. Archer's stiff performance suggests she could have used a few more glasses of vino. Do yourself a favour and rent the original. ▭

Anne Archer *Julia Burton* • Michael Murphy *Russell Burton* • Andrea Occhipinti *Matteo Corbinelli* • Belinda Sinclair *Libby* ■ *Dir* George Kaczender • *Scr* Emily Tracy

Indochine ★★★★ 15
Period romance 1991 · Fr · Colour · 151mins

Winner of the Oscar for best foreign language film, this epic drama set in French Indochina in the thirties also won five Césars, including best actress for the imperious Catherine Deneuve and best supporting actress for Dominique Blanc. Having hooked us on a melodramatic love triangle involving Deneuve, her teenage daughter and a handsome naval officer, the picture plunges us into a breathless adventure as the daughter encounters the brutal realities of French rule when she follows the officer to his far-flung base. In French with English subtitles. Contains violence, swearing, sex scenes and drug abuse. ▭

Catherine Deneuve *Eliane* • Vincent Perez *Jean-Baptiste* • Dan Pham Linh *Camille* • Jean Yanne *Guy* • Dominique Blanc *Yvette* • Henri Marteau *Emile* • Carlo Brandt *Castellani* ■ *Dir* Régis Wargnier • *Scr* Erik Orssenna, Louis Gardel, Catherine Cohen, Régis Wargnier

Inevitable Grace ★
Psychological thriller
1994 · US · Colour · 103mins

In this weak psychological thriller, a psychiatrist finds herself drawn to the attractive husband of one of her patients. This isn't a good career move, especially when the husband is played by Maxwell Caulfield, giving his usual block-of-wood performance. The only point of interest comes from the opportunity of seeing whether Jack Nicholson's daughter Jennifer has inherited any of his talent. The answer to that question is no, but in fairness this formula vehicle would sink anyone's enthusiasm.

Maxwell Caulfield *Adam Cestare* • Stephanie Knights *Lisa Kelner* • Jennifer Nicholson *Veronica* • Tippi Hedren *Dr Marcia Stevens* • Sylvia B Suarez *Simone* • Samantha Eggar *Britt* ■ *Dir/Scr* Alex Canawati

Inferno ★★★
Drama 1953 · US · Colour · 83mins

Sharply directed by Britain's Roy Ward Baker, this ingenious thriller rests securely on the performance of Robert Ryan as the millionaire playboy left to die in the desert with a broken leg by his wife and her lover. Most of the film covers Ryan's heroic efforts to survive the extremes of temperature, hunger and natural hazards. This was one of the most effective pictures ever made for showing in 3-D, which emphasised the vastness of the desert, but the avoidance of gimmicky effects means that it works almost as well shown flat.

Robert Ryan *Carson* • Rhonda Fleming *Geraldine Carson* • William Lundigan *Joseph Duncan* • Larry Keating *Emory* • Henry Hull *Sam Elby* • Carl Betz *Lieutenant Mark Platt* ■ *Dir* Roy Ward Baker • *Scr* Francis Cockrell • *Cinematographer* Lucien Ballard

Inferno ★★★★ 18
Horror 1980 · It · Colour · 101mins

Italian director Dario Argento follows up *Suspiria* with this slightly demented but compulsive shocker. Student Leigh McCloskey returns to New York from Rome following the untimely demise of his girlfriend. His sister has discovered that her apartment building has some malevolent occupants whose supernatural powers result in a number of violent deaths. Argento creates enough striking moments to offset inconsistencies in the plot. Italian dialogue dubbed into English. ▭

Leigh McCloskey *Mark Elliot* • Irene Miracle *Rose Elliot* • Eleonora Giorgi *Sara* • Daria Nicolodi *Countess Elise* ■ *Dir* Dario Argento • *Scr* Dario Argento, from a story by Dario Argento • *Music* Keith Emerson

The Infiltrator ★★★ 18
Political thriller 1995 · US · Colour · 88mins

This intense thriller is based on the true story of Yaron Svoray an Israeli-born reporter. Svoray (Oliver Platt) travels to Germany to investigate neo-Nazism and infiltrates a skinhead gang. As Platt gets closer to uncovering the leaders of these right-wing fanatics, the full horror of their violent, hate-mongering movement becomes clear. Platt's convincing performance is particularly effective in this powerful drama. Contains swearing and violence, including a sexual assault. ▭

Oliver Platt *Yaron Svoray* • Arliss Howard *Eaton* • Peter Riegert *Rabbi Cooper* • Alan King *Rabbi Hier* • Tony Haygarth *Gunther* • Michael Byrne *Creutz* • Julian Glover *Bielert* • Alex Kingston *Anna* ■ *Dir* John Mackenzie • *Scr* Guy Andrews, from a story by Robert J Avrech, Guy Andrews, from the non-fiction book *In Hitler's Shadow: an Israeli's Amazing Journey inside Germany's Neo-Nazi Movement* by Yaron Svoray, Nick Taylor

Infinity ★★★
Biographical romantic drama
1996 · US · Colour · 119mins

Matthew Broderick both stars in and directs this feature about Nobel Prize-

winning physicist Richard Feynman, who worked on the development of the atomic bomb. The opening half, where Broderick meets and romances Patricia Arquette in pre- Second World War New York, is both touching and powerful. Unfortunately Arquette contracts TB at a time when Broderick is committed to the Manhattan Project, placing him in difficult position. He marries her anyway. It's an above average debut (scripted by Broderick's mother, Patricia) but viewers of a non-technical disposition might have preferred more emphasis on the romance and less on the science.

Matthew Broderick *Richard Feynman* • Patricia Arquette *Arline Greenbaum* • Peter Riegert *Mel Feynman* • Dori Brenner *Tutti Feynman* • Peter Michael Goetz *Dr Hellman* ■ *Dir* Matthew Broderick • *Scr* Patricia Broderick, from the memoirs *Surely You're Joking, Mr Feynman!* and *What Do You Care What Other People Think?* by Richard Feynman

Inflammable ★★ 18
Crime thriller 1994 · US · Colour · 85mins

Since making his mark as the cyborg in *Terminator 2: Judgment Day*, Robert Patrick has struggled to avoid stereotyping. Too often he finds himself in adrenalin-pumping but empty thrillers such as this, where he stars as an FBI agent who takes the law into his own hands when his family is butchered by a drugs gang. As director Joseph Merhi lets the corpses build up at an alarming rate, Patrick gives his all, but to little avail. Contains violence, swearing and drug abuse. ▭

Robert Patrick *Jeff Douglas* • Titus Welliver *Manta* • Mick Fleetwood *Vitch* • Miles O'Keeffe *Kowalski* • Kristen Meadows *Megan* ■ *Dir* Joseph Merhi • *Scr* Jacobsen Hart

Inflammable ★★★
Thriller 1995 · US · Colour

Marg Helgenberger follows in the footsteps of Demi Moore in *A Few Good Men* in this tense TV movie, as a rookie naval lawyer falling foul of her male superiors. Sent to the supply vessel USS *Laramie* to investigate an attempted rape, she provokes their quarry into brutally covering their tracks. No prizes for guessing that captain Kris Kristofferson, who is initially uncooperative, eventually becomes her heart's desire. However, this teasing tale of shipboard treachery isn't always so transparent, as director Peter Werner archly combines protocol and passion with the mystery and misogyny inherent in the plot.

Marg Helgenberger *Lieutenant Kathleen Dolan* • Kris Kristofferson *Captain Gutherie* ■ *Dir* Peter Werner • *Scr* Leo Garen, Harrison Starr

Information Received ★★
Thriller 1962 · UK · BW · 77mins

Routine British crime movie in which Scotland Yard show rather more enterprise than usual, foiling an underworld gang by substituting an informer as the safe-cracker imported from America for a big job. The bogus one is played by William Sylvester, who later found fleeting fame as Dr Heywood Floyd, the dull scientist in *2001: a Space Odyssey*. Top billing, though, goes to Sabina Sesselmann, a starlet with an alluring name but not

enough talent to carry her much further.

Sabina Sesselmann *Sabina Farlow* • William Sylvester *Rick Hogan* • Hermione Baddeley *Maudie* • Edward Underdown *Drake* • Robert Raglan *Supt Jeffcote* • Frank Hawkins *Sgt Jarvie* ■ *Dir* Robert Lynn • *Scr* Paul Ryder, from a story by Berkely Mather • *Cinematographer* Nicolas Roeg

The Informer ★★★ PG

Drama   1935 · US · BW · 91mins

This screen version of Liam O'Flaherty's novel is an art film with a vengeance. Given a low budget, director John Ford had a free hand to film this grim story set in Dublin in 1922 during the Irish Civil War. Gypo Nolan (Victor McLaglen), driven by poverty to inform against the IRA, is then racked by guilt as he faces inevitable retribution. Ford adopted a heavily stylised approach with overt symbolism and won an Academy Award along with leading actor McLaglen, screenwriter Dudley Nichols and composer Max Steiner. While Ford's less pretentious works are much to be preferred, this is still a powerful picture of great historic interest. ▣

Victor McLaglen *Gypo Nolan* • Heather Angel *Mary McPhillip* • Preston Foster *Dan Gallagher* • Margot Grahame *Katie Madden* • Wallace Ford *Frankie McPhillip* ■ *Dir* John Ford • *Scr* Dudley Nichols, from the novel by Liam O'Flaherty • *Music* Max Steiner

The Informers ★★ 12

Crime drama   1963 · UK · BW · 100mins

Nowadays British crime films of the fifties and sixties look rather quaint, with the dogged attempts of performers to either act tough and growl in East End argot as they plan their blags, or portray the clipped decency of the Scotland Yard flatfoot. Not for us the ruthless lowlifes and cynical cops of the Hollywood B-movie. While eminently watchable (it's certainly got an impressive cast), this police procedural crime drama from director Ken Annakin is a case in point. Nigel Patrick is the archetypal inspector in a mac, while Frank Finlay is as brutal as a pantomime villain. Allan Cuthbertson also merits a mention as Patrick's snivellingly ambitious second-in-command. ▣

Nigel Patrick *Chief Insp Johnnoe* • Margaret Whiting *Maisie* • Colin Blakely *Charlie Ruskin* • Derren Nesbitt *Bertie Hoyle* • Frank Finlay *Leon Sale* • Catherine Woodville *Mary Johnnoe* • Harry Andrews *Supt Bestwick* • Allan Cuthbertson *Smythe* ■ *Dir* Ken Annakin • *Scr* Alun Falconer, Paul Durst, from the novel *Death of a Snout* by Douglas Warner

Inherit the Wind ★★★★ U

Courtroom drama   1960 · US · BW · 123mins

A stirring title for a fairly gripping courtroom drama, inspired by the real-life trial in 1925 of a young Tennessee teacher charged with giving lessons on the Darwinian theory of evolution in a state school. Very much a drama of words and ideas, the film was a critical hit but a commercial flop in its day. Yes, the plot meanders and even drags at points, but ultimately it engrosses thanks to major-league performances from Spencer Tracy and Fredric March as the opposing lawyers

in what became known as the "Scopes Monkey Trial''. ▣

Fredric March *Matthew Harrison Brady* • Spencer Tracy *Henry Drummond* • Gene Kelly *EK Hornbeck* • Florence Eldridge *Mrs Brady* • Dick York *Bertram T Cates* • Donna Anderson *Rachel Brown* • Harry Morgan *Judge* • Elliott Reid *Davenport* ■ *Dir* Stanley Kramer • *Scr* Nathan E Douglas [Nedrick Young], Harold Jacob Smith, from the play by Jerome Lawrence, Robert E Lee • *Cinematographer* Ernest Laszlo • *Music* Ernest Gold

Inherit the Wind ★★ PG

Courtroom drama   1988 · US · Colour · 91mins

Kirk Douglas and Jason Robards are no match for Fredric March and Spencer Tracy in this only moderate TV-movie remake of the superior 1960 courtroom drama of the same name, based on the real-life trial in 1925 of a teacher accused of promoting Darwin's theory of evolution. We can all feel smug at the preposterousness of it all, but the truth is that there is probably no shortage of American Christian fundamentalists who would enjoy bringing a similar prosecution today. ▣

Kirk Douglas *Matthew Harrison Brady* • Jason Robards Jr *Henry Drummond* • Kyle Secor *Bertram Cates* • Darren McGavin *EK Hornbeck* • Jean Simmons *Lucy Brady* • Megan Follows *Rachel Brown* • Don Hood *Mayor* • Michael Ensign *Reverend Jeremiah Brown* • John Harkins *Judge* ■ *Dir* David Greene • *Scr* John Gay, from the play by Jerome Lawrence, Robert E Lee

Inherit the Wind ★★★★

Courtroom drama
1999 · US · Colour · 127mins

An all-star line-up, including Jack Lemmon, George C Scott, Piper Laurie and Beau Bridges, make this drama about the famous 1925 "Scopes Monkey Trial" compelling viewing. A schoolteacher – derided for expounding Darwinian theory – is arrested and tried in a case that soon generates national interest. A stocky courtroom drama ensues and forms the bulk of what was originally a stage play of the same name. Attention to twenties period detail and heavyweight performances make this a way-above-average, made-for-television drama.

Jack Lemmon *Henry Drummond* • George C Scott *Matthew Harrison Brady* • Beau Bridges *EK Hornbeck* • Piper Laurie *Sarah Brady* • Lane Smith *Reverend Jeremiah Brown* ■ *Dir* Daniel Petrie Sr [Daniel Petrie] • *Scr* Nedrick Young, Harold Jacob Smith, from the play by Jerome Lawrence, Robert E Lee

The Inheritance ★★★ 18

Drama   1976 · It · Colour · 98mins

Dominique Sanda, the pale-skinned, doe-eyed, slinky beauty from *The Conformist* and *The Garden of the Finzi-Continis*, has a juicy role here as a social climber with her eyes on a fortune owned by one of Italy's grandest and richest families. First she marries one of the sons; then she seduces his father, the lusty patriarch played by Anthony Quinn. Sadly, Quinn's life force soon runs dry as Sanda wears him out in bed. He does, though, bequeath her the entire estate, which doesn't make for harmonious family relations. Veteran director Mauro Bolognini directs this

moral tale with his usual elegance and with more than a touch of the Viscontis. Italian dialogue dubbed into English. ▣

Anthony Quinn *Gregorio Ferramonti* • Fabio Testi *Mario Ferramonti* • Dominique Sanda *Irene* • Luigi Proietti *Pippo Ferramonti* • Adriana Asti *Teta Ferramonti* ■ *Dir* Mauro Bolognini • *Scr* Ugo Pirro, Sergio Bazzini

The Inheritor ★★

Thriller   1973 · Fr · Colour · 112mins

Jean-Paul Belmondo enjoys appeal with both arthouse and commercial audiences, but his choice of assignments often puts a strain on their loyalty. In this jet-setting political thriller, Belmondo plays the heir to a business empire who suspects that his father's death in a plane crash was no accident. When he investigates further, with the help of a magazine journalist, he finds evidence of fascist activity close to home and his own life in danger. This being a French movie there are the usual romantic sideshows complicating an already over-fussy plot, but this is as glitzy and empty as a TV mini-series. French dialogue dubbed into English.

Jean-Paul Belmondo *Cordell* • Carla Gravina *Liza* • Jean Rochefort *Berthier* • Charles Denner *David* • Maureen Kerwin *Lauren* • Michel Beaune *Lambert* ■ *Dir* Philippe Labro • *Scr* Philippe Labro, Jacques Lanzmann

The Inheritors ★★★ 15

Drama   1997 · Aus · Colour · 94mins

By combining the style of the Hollywood range war movie with that of the German *Heimat* (or homeland) film, Austrian director Stefan Ruzowitzky has come up with what he terms "an Alpine western". Set just after the First World War, the story centres on a group of peasants who defy their foreman by refusing to sell the land they've inherited to a rich farmer. Sprinkled with coarse country humour and shot to capture the changing colours of the seasons, the action errs towards the melodramatic, while the acting is too determinedly rustic. Yet the stylised realism is ideal for such a stark study of liberty and progress. In German with English subtitles.

Simon Schwarz *Lukas* • Sophie Rois *Emmy* • Lars Rudolph *Severin* • Julia Gschnitzer *Old Nane* • Ulrich Wildgruber *Danninger* ■ *Dir/Scr* Stefan Ruzowitzky

L'Inhumaine ★★★★

Silent melodrama
1923 · Fr · BW and Tinted · 130mins

While not perhaps the most ambitious or accomplished experiment of the French Impressionist era, this is certainly the most artful. With a score by Darius Milhaud, exteriors designed by Robert Mallet-Stephens, a Cubist laboratory by Fernand Léger, and Georgette Leblanc's apartment given an Art Deco look by Alberto Cavalcanti, Marcel L'Herbier's silent (and in some prints tinted) melodrama has avant-garde written all over it. However, the tale of the singer who is saved from the clutches of maharajah Philippe Hériat by noble scientist Jaque Catelain is also notable for its audacious visual abstraction and the precision of its rapid cross-cutting.

Georgette Leblanc *Claire Lescot* • Jaque Catelain *Einar Norsen* • Marcelle Pradot *L'Innocente* • Philippe Hériat *Djorah de Manilha* • Léonid Walter de Malte *Kranine* ■ *Dir* Marcel L'Herbier • *Scr* Marcel L'Herbier, from a story by Pierre Mac Orlan [Pierre Dumarchais], mme Georgette Leblanc-Maeterlink • *Art Director* Alberto Cavalcanti, Fernand Léger, Claude Autant-Lara, Robert Mallet-Stevens • *Costume Designer* Paul Poiret • *Music* Darius Milhaud

The Initiation ★★ 18

Horror   1984 · US · Colour · 92mins

Melrose Place star Daphne Zuniga is the amnesiac sorority sister up to her pretty neck in bad-taste college pranks in this tacky *Nightmare on Elm Street* clone. The "Repressed Desires" costume party has to be seen to be believed, but nothing else is worth the same effort in this lame stalk-and-slash item, where most of the horror takes place off screen. *Psycho* star Vera Miles adds a touch of class to the murderous mayhem. ▣

Vera Miles *Frances Fairchild* • Clu Gulager *Dwight Fairchild* • Daphne Zuniga *Kelly Terry* • James Read *Peter* • Marilyn Kagan *Marcia* • Patti Heider *Nurse* • Robert Dowdell *Jason Randall* • Frances Peterson *Megan* ■ *Dir* Larry Stewart • *Scr* Charles Pratt Jr

Initiation ★★★ 15

Adventure   1987 · Ausl · Colour · 87mins

This Australian culture-clash drama is considerably better than much of the dross that reaches the shelves of our local video stores. Director Michael Pearce is asking a lot when he expects us to swallow some aspects of this story, in which a teenager from Brooklyn is reunited with his long-lost Vietnam vet dad, who is now flying consignments of dope to make ends meet. However, Bruno Lawrence can put across most things with conviction and young Rodney Harvey gives a fine account of himself. The scenery, by the way, is breathtaking. Contains violence and swearing. ▣

Bruno Lawrence • Rodney Harvey • Arna Maria Winchester • Miranda Otto • Bobby Smith ■ *Dir* Michael Pearce • *Scr* Jim Barton

Inn for Trouble ★★ U

Comedy   1960 · UK · BW · 98mins

This movie spin-off from *The Larkins*, the popular sitcom of the late fifties, moved the family away from 66 Sycamore Street and into a country pub, and that's where the problems begin. One of the series' great strengths was its portrait of a typical urban neighbourhood, populated with familiar characters. A whole new world had to be created here, however, with only Pa and Ma (David Kossoff and Peggy Mount) and Eddie (Shaun O'Riordan) providing continuity. Even the presence of Leslie Phillips and Charles Hawtrey can't make up for the general lifelessness.

Peggy Mount *Ada Larkins* • David Kossoff *Alf Larkins* • Leslie Phillips *John Belcher* • Glyn Owen *Lord Bill Osborne* • Yvonne Monlaur *Yvette* • Charles Hawtrey *Silas* • AE Matthews *Sir Hector Gore-Blandish* • Shaun O'Riordan *Eddie Larkins* • Ronan O'Casey *Jeff Rogers* ■ *Dir* CM Pennington-Richards • *Scr* Fred Robinson, from his TV series *The Larkins*

U = SUITABLE FOR ALL   Uc = SUITABLE FOR ALL, ESPECIALLY FOR YOUNG CHILDREN (VIDEO ONLY)   PG = PARENTAL GUIDANCE

The Inn of the Sixth Happiness ★★★★ PG

Biographical romantic drama
1958 · UK · Colour · 151mins

Ingrid Bergman's screen appeal was usually based on the vulnerability of her characters, so for her to present the tenacity and courage of Gladys Aylward, the domestic servant who set out to bring Christianity to the peasants of China, was a considerable challenge. It's a glamorised portrayal (and one with which Aylward was not completely satisfied), but it's also a gritty and completely sympathetic performance, backed by some exceptional support playing, notably from Athene Seyler. ▭

Ingrid Bergman *Gladys Aylward* • Curt Jurgens *Captain Lin Nan* • Robert Donat *Mandarin* • Ronald Squire *Sir Francis Jamison* • Noel Hood *Miss Thompson* • Athene Seyler *Mrs Lawson* • Burt Kwouk Li ■ *Dir* Mark Robson • *Scr* Isobel Lennart, from the novel *The Small Woman* by Alan Burgess

The Inner Circle ★★★ 15

Drama 1991 · It/US · Colour · 131mins

While Nikita Mikhalkov remained in Russia and went on to win an Oscar for the sublime *Burnt by the Sun*, his brother Andrei Konchalovsky rather slipped into a cinematic backwater during his US exile. He returned home to shoot this muddled but nevertheless intriguing story about a nobody who allows delusions of grandeur to destroy his life after he is appointed as Stalin's projectionist. Tom Hulce gives an intelligent performance as Ivan, while Lolita Davidovich is truly touching as his wife, prepared to risk everything for the sake of a Jewish orphan. ▭

Tom Hulce *Ivan Sanshin* • Lolita Davidovich *Anastasia Sanshin* • Bob Hoskins *Beria* • Aleksandr Zbruev *Stalin* • Feodor Chaliapin Jr *Professor Bartnev* ■ *Dir* Andrei Konchalovsky • *Scr* Andrei Konchalovsky, Anatoli Usov

Innerspace ★★★ PG

Science-fiction comedy
1987 · US · Colour · 114mins

This botched attempt to update *Fantastic Voyage* is probably director Joe Dante's worst movie, but it's still a notch above the usual Hollywood fodder. Dennis Quaid is the hot-shot military man who is miniaturised and mistakenly pumped into the body of lowly supermarket clerk Martin Short. The effects are excellent and Dante's sly humour shines through occasionally, but it lacks the anarchy of his best work and Short's hysterics eventually begin to grate. Contains some swearing. ▭

Dennis Quaid *Lt Tuck Pendelton* • Martin Short *Jack Putter* • Meg Ryan *Lydia Maxwell* • Kevin McCarthy *Victor Scrimshaw* • Fiona Lewis *Dr Margaret Canker* • Vernon Wells *Mr Igoe* ■ *Dir* Joe Dante • *Scr* Jeffrey Boam, Chip Proser, from a story by Chip Proser

Innocence Unprotected ★★★★ U

Drama 1968 · Yug · BW and Colour · 76mins

Consisting of fond flashbacks, gentle satire and an uplifting tribute to human indomitability, this unique film is an endless delight. Combining newsreel footage of the Nazi occupation, clips from Yugoslavia's second talkie, *Innocence Unprotected* (1942), and interviews with surviving members of the cast and crew, director Dusan Makavejev enables us to appreciate both the historical importance of this hoary melodramatic film, and the pride of its makers in confounding the Gestapo to produce a heartfelt statement of national defiance. In Serbian with English subtitles. ▭

Dragoljub Aleksic *Acrobat Aleksic* • Ana Milosavljevic *Nada the orphan* • Vera Jovanovic *Wicked Stepmother* • Bratoljub Gligorijevic *Mr Petrovic* • Ivan Zivkovic *Aleksic's brother* • Pera Milosavljevic *Servant* ■ *Dir/Scr* Dusan Makavejev

The Innocent ★★★ 15

Drama 1984 · UK · Colour · 95mins

Set in the Yorkshire Dales, this coming-of-age saga takes place in the early thirties against the backdrop of the Depression. The central character, Tim (Andrew Hawley), suffers from epilepsy, and his problems are compounded by his constantly arguing parents and an ongoing affair between a family friend and a married woman. It sometimes seems as if *Kes* has bumped into *The Go-Between*, and it's certainly a change of pace for John MacKenzie, director of *The Long Good Friday*. His film also features early appearances from Liam Neeson and Miranda Richardson.

Andrew Hawley *Tim Dobson* • Kika Markham *Mrs Dobson* • Kate Foster *Win* • Liam Neeson *John Carns* • Patrick Daley *Eddie King* • Paul Askew *Stanley* • Tom Bell *Frank Dobson* • Miranda Richardson *Mary Turner* ■ *Dir* John MacKenzie • *Scr* Ray Jenkins, from the novel *The Aura and the Kingfisher* by Tom Hart

The Innocent ★★ 15

Thriller 1993 · UK/Ger · Colour · 113mins

Despite its impressive cast, this brooding, rather old-fashioned Cold War thriller never really grips. In an odd bit of casting, the always impressive American actor Campbell Scott plays an English technician in fifties Berlin who gets caught up in a tortuous espionage plot instigated by CIA man Anthony Hopkins, here saddled with an unconvincing US accent. Isabella Rossellini supplies the glamour as the woman Scott falls for, but, while director John Schlesinger expertly captures the grey chill of the time and place, he gets a little lost in the detail. All in all, an honourable failure. ▭

Anthony Hopkins *Bob Glass* • Isabella Rossellini *Maria* • Campbell Scott *Leonard Markham* • Ronald Nitschke *Otto* • Hart Bochner *Russell* • James Grant *MacNamee* • Jeremy Sinden *Captain Lofting* • Richard Durden *Black* ■ *Dir* John Schlesinger • *Scr* Ian McEwan, from his novel

The Innocent ★★★

Crime thriller 1993 · US · Colour · 107mins

Executive producer Kelsey Grammer, famous as TV's Frasier Crane, here casts himself as an LA detective trying to wheedle out clues from an autistic child, sole witness to a violent crime. This sounds like the 1998 Bruce Willis film *Mercury Rising*, and indeed there are major similarities in plot and content. The scale here is more intimate, though, and Grammer is quite excellent, once you detach the comedy baggage he brings to the table.

Kelsey Grammer *Frank Barlow* • Keegan McIntosh *Gregory White* • Polly Draper *Pamela Sutton* • Dean Stockwell *Jason Flaboe* • Jeff Kober *Tinsley* • Gary Werntz *Bates* ■ *Dir* Mimi Leder • *Scr* David Venable

Innocent Blood ★★★ 15

Comedy horror 1992 · US · Colour · 110mins

Blood flies everywhere as the horror movie and the gangster film collide head on in this atmospheric offering from John Landis. From the moment Anne Parillaud sinks her teeth into hoodlum Robert Loggia, it's clear that this isn't going to be your average vampire chiller. The whole production drips with style as Loggia chomps his way towards fulfilling his ambition of controlling the underworld by means of the undead. Parillaud slinks through the picture, falling for Anthony LaPaglia in the process, but it's the excesses of Loggia and crooked lawyer Don Rickles that command the attention. Contains violence, swearing, sex scenes and nudity. ▭

Anne Parillaud *Marie* • Anthony LaPaglia *Joe Gennaro* • Robert Loggia *Sal "The Shark" Macelli* • David Proval *Lenny* • Rocco Sisto *Gilly* • Don Rickles *Emmanuel Bergman* • Chazz Palminteri *Tony* • Tony Sirico *Jacko* ■ *Dir* John Landis • *Scr* Michael Wolk

Innocent Bystanders ★★ 18

Spy thriller 1972 · UK · Colour · 106mins

We're in 007 territory again with this spy thriller from *The Italian Job* director Peter Collinson. This time our rather more fallible superhero is played by Stanley Baker, with boss Donald Pleasence sending him on a mission to locate a missing Russian scientist. A strong cast also includes Geraldine Chaplin and Dana Andrews, but those of a delicate disposition may find this defector drama leans too heavily on sadism and violence. ▭

Stanley Baker *John Craig* • Geraldine Chaplin *Miriam Loman* • Donald Pleasence *Loomis* • Dana Andrews *Blake* • Sue Lloyd *Joanna Benson* • Derren Nesbitt *Andrew Royce* • Vladek Sheybal *Aaron Kaplan* • Warren Mitchell *Omar* ■ *Dir* Peter Collinson • *Scr* James Mitchell, from the novel by James Munro [James Mitchell]

Innocent Lies ★★ 18

Crime mystery 1995 · UK/Fr · Colour · 84mins

It's odd that this supposedly steamy mix of incest and fascism should claim to have been inspired by the country house whodunits of Agatha Christie. Patrick Dewolf's period curio is much darker and far less well-constructed than anything concocted by the grand old lady of crime. Indeed, this is played at such a hysterical pitch that you could be forgiven for thinking it was a parody. As the cop investigating the death of his colleague, Adrian Dunbar behaves most peculiarly, especially in the presence of the deranged Gabrielle Anwar. Only Joanna Lumley emerges with any credit as her viciously snobby mother. Contains sex scenes and violence. ▭

Adrian Dunbar *Alan Cross* • Florence Hoath *Angela Cross* • Sophie Aubry *Solange Montfort* • Joanna Lumley *Lady Helena Graves* • Gabrielle Anwar *Celia Graves* • Alexis Denisof

Christopher Wood • Stephen Dorff *Jeremy Graves* ■ *Dir* Patrick Dewolf • *Scr* Kerry Crabbe, Patrick Dewolf

An Innocent Man ★★★ 18

Crime thriller 1989 · US · Colour · 108mins

Tom Selleck attempted to toughen up his image with this hard-edged thriller, but it was only a partial success. He plays an airline mechanic who is framed by two bent cops and finds himself in prison, where he nurses a desire for revenge. Director Peter Yates is an old hand when it comes to this sort of thing, and he stages the action scenes with some panache. Selleck, however, isn't entirely convincing as the innocent man who is transformed from a nice middle-class chap to a hard-bitten inmate. Contains violence and swearing. ▭

Tom Selleck *Jimmie Rainwood* • F Murray Abraham *Virgil Cane* • Laila Robins *Kate Rainwood* • David Rasche *Mike Parnell* • Richard Young *Danny Scalise* • Badja Djola *John Fitzgerald* • Todd Graff *Robby* ■ *Dir* Peter Yates • *Scr* Larry Brothers

Innocent Moves ★★★★ PG

Biographical drama
1993 · US · Colour · 105mins

Released in the US as *Searching for Bobby Fischer*, this chess drama marked the directorial debut of Steven Zaillian, who had just completed scriptwriting duties on *Schindler's List*. This true story was adapted from the autobiographical novel by Fred Waitzkin and not only reveals the unexpectedly ruthless side of competitive chess, but also explores the dangers of parents using children to fulfil their own ambitions. James Horner's score is way off-key, but Conrad Hall's Oscar-nominated photography is as impressive as the acting, with young Max Pomeranc, himself a top-ranking player, upstaging the likes of Joe Mantegna and Ben Kingsley.

Max Pomeranc *Josh Waitzkin* • Joe Mantegna *Fred Waitzkin* • Joan Allen *Bonnie Waitzkin* • Ben Kingsley *Bruce Pandolfini* • Laurence Fishburne *Vinnie* • Robert Stephens *Poe's teacher* • David Paymer *Kalev* ■ *Dir* Steven Zaillian • *Scr* Steven Zaillian, from the novel by Fred Waitzkin

The Innocent Sleep ★★★ 15

Mystery thriller 1995 · UK · Colour · 95mins

Rupert Graves strays from EM Forster territory to play a homeless man in this downbeat British thriller, set in London's Cardboard City. Graves is enjoying the five-star facilities of a warehouse underneath Tower Bridge when he realises that an assassination is in progress. He manages to get away but, when he goes to the police, he discovers that the detective heading the investigation was actually involved in the killing. Scott Michell's direction catches the downtrodden atmosphere of London's underworld, and he's helped by a good cast that includes Annabella Sciorra, Michael Gambon, John Hannah and Franco Nero. ▭

Annabella Sciorra *Billie Hayman* • Rupert Graves *Alan Terry* • Michael Gambon *Matheson* • Franco Nero *Cavani* • John Hannah *James* • Oliver Cotton *Lusano* • Tony Bluto *Thorn* • Paul Brightwell *Pelham* ■ *Dir* Scott Michell • *Scr* Ray Villis

L'Innocente ★★★★ 🔲15

Period drama 1976 · It · Colour · 123mins

Luchino Visconti's last film is one of his best and was clearly the inspiration behind Martin Scorsese's The Age of Innocence. Based on Gabriele D'Annunzio's acclaimed novel, the film saw the baroque director returning to his favourite theme: the decline of turn-of-the-20th-century Italian aristocracy and its implications for today's society. Giancarlo Giannini plays the adulterous Sicilian gentleman who is mortified by his wife's own sexual misconduct, in this stately, visually stunning meditation on mores and manners, while Laura Antonelli is magnificent as the unfaithful spouse. An Italian language film. 🔲

Giancarlo Giannini Tullio Hermil • Laura Antonelli Giuliana Hermil • Jennifer O'Neill Teresa Raffo • Rina Morelli Tullio's mother • Massimo Girotti Count Stefano Egano • Didier Haudepin Federico Hermil • Marie Dubois Princess ■ Dir Luchino Visconti • Scr Suso Cecchi D'Amico, Enrico Medioli, Luchino Visconti, from a novel by Gabriele D'Annunzio

The Innocents ★★★★

Horror 1961 · UK · BW · 99mins

As this terrifying and undeservedly neglected picture proves, there was much more to British cinema in the early sixties than angry young men prowling round the grim north. Truman Capote and John Mortimer both had a hand in the script for this adaptation of Henry James's The Turn of the Screw, and the film bristles with menace as it draws you inexorably towards its chilling conclusion. Never has horror looked so beautiful, with Freddie Francis reinforcing the eerie atmosphere with his unforgettable photography. Deborah Kerr is excellent as the haunted governess, Pamela Franklin and Martin Stephens send shivers down the spine as her sinister charges and Peter Wyngarde as Quint is evil personified.

Deborah Kerr Miss Giddens • Michael Redgrave Uncle • Peter Wyngarde Peter Quint • Megs Jenkins Mrs Grose • Martin Stephens Miles • Pamela Franklin Flora • Clytie Jessop Miss Jessel • Isla Cameron Anna ■ Dir Jack Clayton • Scr William Archibald, Truman Capote, John Mortimer, from the novella The Turn of the Screw by Henry James

Innocents in Paris ★★★

Comedy 1953 · UK · BW · 102mins

Considering the quality of the cast, this episodic British comedy could have been a great deal funnier than it is. Following a party of tourists on their weekend in Paris, Anatole de Grunwald's script has a pseudo-Ealing cosiness that prevents it from throwing caution to the wind and becoming downright comic. There are neat touches from Alastair Sim seeking to inebriate a Soviet politician and from Margaret Rutherford as an amateur artist at the Louvre, but Claire Bloom's romance, Ronald Shiner's parade, Jimmy Edwards's indoor cricket match and James Copeland's bekilted misadventures lack a vital spark.

Alastair Sim Sir Norman Barker • Margaret Rutherford Gladys Inglott • Ronald Shiner Dicky Bird • Claire Bloom Susan Robbins • Claude Dauphin Max de Lorne • Laurence Harvey François • Jimmy Edwards Captain

George Stilton • James Copeland Andy MacGregor • Gaby Bruyere Josette ■ Dir Gordon Parry • Scr Anatole de Grunwald

Inserts ★★★ 🔲18

Drama 1975 · UK/US · Colour · 111mins

An intriguing but ultimately disappointing drama about thirties Hollywood, where has-been director Richard Dreyfuss is making a porno movie with a gay actor and a former silent movie queen. The decision to limit the picture to a small cast and a single interior set at a British studio may be in homage to Harold Pinter or Samuel Beckett, or it may just betray a lack of finance. Even so, one sorely misses the soft light and the waving palms of Hollywood, and Bob Hoskins with an American accent doesn't help matters. Dreyfuss, though, is excellent, creating a richly complex character. 🔲

Richard Dreyfuss Boy Wonder • Jessica Harper Cathy • Stephen Davies Rex • Veronica Cartwright Harlene • Bob Hoskins Big Mac ■ Dir/Scr John Byrum

Inside ★★★ 🔲18

Political drama 1996 · US · Colour · 90mins

Eric Stoltz stars as a South African liberal who is mentally and physically tortured by army officer Nigel Hawthorne. Ten years later, after the fall of apartheid, Hawthorne is himself interrogated by human rights investigator Louis Gossett Jr. Shot in South Africa by Arthur Penn, this is a powerful, impressively acted and claustrophobic drama. It was produced by the Hallmark greetings card company for American TV. 🔲

Eric Stoltz Marty Strydom • Nigel Hawthorne Colonel Kruger • Louis Gossett Jr Questioner • Ian Roberts Guard Moolman • Ross Preller Guard Potgieter • Jerry Mofokeng Mzwaki ■ Dir Arthur Penn • Scr Bima Stagg

Inside Daisy Clover ★★ 🔲15

Drama 1965 · US · Colour · 123mins

Gavin Lambert's novel about the turbulent career of a precocious Hollywood musical star of the thirties had potential to be a lot of fun. Unfortunately in the hands of director Robert Mulligan it treads an uncomfortable line between satire and drama, with disappointing results. Natalie Wood, by then a movie veteran of more than 20 years, is Daisy and Robert Redford plays her handsome husband, whose sexual orientation makes him less than an ideal spouse. The two stars reteamed soon after for This Property Is Condemned. 🔲

Natalie Wood Daisy Clover • Christopher Plummer Raymond Swan • Robert Redford Wade Lewis • Roddy McDowall Walter Baines • Ruth Gordon The Dealer • Katharine Bard Melora Swan ■ Dir Robert Mulligan • Scr Gavin Lambert, from his novel

Inside Edge ★★ 🔲18

Action crime thriller 1992 · US · Colour · 84mins

Michael Madsen isn't exactly cast against type in this clichéd crime flick. He plays renegade cop Montana, whose methods – while effective – bring him into conflict with his department. Sexy siren Rosie Vela, working for local hood Gio (Richard

Lynch) seduces Montana into working with her boss to advance his own career while eliminating the boss's competition. It follows all the usual conventions, from the crusty chief of police to the partner who is doomed from the moment he walks on screen. There are a few surprises en route, but overall it's pretty predictable. 🔲

Michael Madsen Richard Montana • Richard Lynch Mario Gio • Rosie Vela Lisa Zamora • George Jenesky Hip-Hop • Tony Peck Dan Nealy ■ Dir Warren Clark • Scr Vincent Gutierrez, William Tannen, from a screenplay by Vincent Gutierrez

The Inside Man ★★ 🔲15

Political thriller 1984 · Swe/UK · Colour · 89mins

Two years before his career-reviving performance in David Lynch's Blue Velvet, Dennis Hopper turned up in this Anglo-Swedish co-production as a CIA agent assigned to track down a top-secret laser device stolen from a grounded Russian submarine. Actor-turned-director Tom Clegg cut his teeth on such homegrown crime yarns as McVicar and Sweeney 2; more recently, he directed Sean Bean in the Gulf War drama Bravo Two Zero. 🔲

Dennis Hopper Miller • Hardy Kruger Mandell • Gösta Ekman (2) Larsson • Kare Molder Kallin • David Wilson Baxter • Celia Gregory Theresa ■ Dir Tom Clegg • Scr Alan Plater, from a story by Tom Clegg, William Aldridge, from the novel The Fighter by Harry Kullman

Inside Monkey Zetterland ★★

Comedy drama 1992 · US · Colour · 93mins

Director Jefery Levy piles on the frantic screwball farce in his semi-autobiography, with little lasting effect. Steve Antin is the struggling screenwriter/playwright constantly being bewildered and confused by his eccentric extended family. There's his lesbian sister, the gay terrorist tenants and the celebrity-chasing neighbours played by the camp-friendly Patricia Arquette, Sandra Bernhard, Ricki Lake and Rupert Everett. A promising debut from Levy, but overdone to a distracting degree.

Steve Antin Monkey Zetterland • Patricia Arquette Grace Zetterland • Sandra Bernhard Imogene • Sofia Coppola Cindy • Tate Donovan Brent Zetterland • Rupert Everett Sasha • Katherine Helmond Honor Zetterland • Bo Hopkins Mike Zetterland • Ricki Lake Bella • Debi Mazar Daphne • Martha Plimpton Sophie ■ Dir Jefery Levy • Scr Steve Antin

Inside Moves: the Guys from Max's Bar ★★★

Drama 1980 · US · Colour · 112mins

This study of disability suffers from the same surfeit of sentiment that blights so many Hollywood attempts to be liberal and profound. Husband-and-wife team Valerie Curtin and Barry Levinson have scripted several eye-opening scenes, however, while director Richard Donner brings a touch of realism to proceedings by de-glamorising his already-seedy Los Angeles locations. Diana Scarwid was nominated for a best supporting actress Oscar, but it's the relationship between failed suicide John Savage

and would-be basketball star David Morse that provides the dramatic core.

John Savage Roary • David Morse Jerry Maxwell • Diana Scarwid Louise • Amy Wright Ann • Tony Burton Lucius Porter • Bill Henderson Blue Lewis • Steve Kahan Burt • Jack O'Leary Max Willatowski ■ Dir Richard Donner • Scr Valerie Curtin, Barry Levinson, from a novel by Todd Walton

Inside Out ★★ 🔲PG

Adventure 1975 · UK · Colour · 93mins

Telly Savalas's popularity at the time as TV cop Kojak ensured this routine caper movie a modest audience in cinemas. It's a blatant rip-off of another Savalas picture, The Dirty Dozen, with several dubious types going after a stash of Nazi gold in the Cold War era. Most of the story, though, is concerned with the springing from jail of a former Nazi who has vital information. James Mason and Robert Culp bring some extra class to the proceedings. Contains some violence and swearing. 🔲

Telly Savalas Harry Morgan • James Mason Ernst Furben • Robert Culp Sly Wells • Aldo Ray Sergeant Prior • Gunter Meisner Schmidt • Adrian Hoven Dr Maar • Wolfgang Lukschy Reinhard Holtz ■ Dir Peter Duffell • Scr Judd Bernard, Stephen Schneck

The Insider ★★★★★ 🔲15

Drama based on a true story 1999 · US · Colour · 157mins

Big Tobacco comes under the spotlight in Michael Mann's virtuoso ethical drama, based on the true case of a whistle-blower whose life was ruined when he decided to tell all to 60 Minutes. Russell Crowe plays Jeffrey Wigand, the sacked executive who went public with his firm's dark secrets, only to find his interview canned by network heads terrified of a potentially catastrophic law suit. Al Pacino sears the screen as Lowell Bergman, the producer who broke the story, while Christopher Plummer is superb as anchorman Mike Wallace. Mann has little interest in his female characters – Diane Venora is criminally underused as Wigand's wife Liane – but if you're searching for signs of intelligent life in Hollywood, look no further than this dazzling exposé of money, morals and the media.

Al Pacino Lowell Bergman • Russell Crowe Jeffrey Wigand • Christopher Plummer Mike Wallace • Diane Venora Liane Wigand • Philip Baker Hall Don Hewitt • Lindsay Crouse Sharon Tiller • Debi Mazar Debbie De Luca • Stephen Tobolowsky Eric Kluster • Gina Gershon Helen Caperelli • Michael Gambon Thomas Sandefur • Rip Torn John Scanlon • Michael Moore (2) ■ Dir Michael Mann • Scr Eric Roth, Michael Mann, from the article The Man Who New Too Much by Marie Brenner

Insignificance ★★★★ 🔲15

Comedy drama 1985 · UK · Colour · 104mins

Director Nicolas Roeg's wild, wacky and wonderful chamber piece is an exploration of love, life and the whole damn thing. Set in a hotel room in 1954, Roeg assembles four characters who bear a striking resemblance to celebrities of that era. Theresa Russell is "Marilyn Monroe", whose interest in Michael Emil's "Einstein" extends beyond his theory of relativity. Tony Curtis is the Joe McCarthy clone, while

Gary Busey is the Joe DiMaggio figure still pining for Marilyn. 🖭

Gary Busey *Ballplayer* • Tony Curtis *Senator* • Michael Emil *Professor* • Theresa Russell *Actress* • Will Sampson *Elevator attendant* • Patrick Kilpatrick *Driver* ■ *Dir* Nicolas Roeg • *Scr* Terry Johnson, from his play

Insomnia ★★★ 15

Psychological crime thriller
1997 · Nor · Colour · 95mins

Debutant director Erik Skjoldbjaerg pulls off something of a generic coup here, by staging a *film noir* in the relentless glare of the midnight sun. Set in an isolated town on the polar extremities, the action begins with a hunt for the killer of a teenage girl. But, once city cop Stellan Skarsgård accidentally shoots his colleague during a bungled ambush, the emphasis shifts to his struggle to remain focused on the case while battling his suppressed sense of guilt. Dazzlingly photographed by Erling Thurmann-Andersen, this taut thriller stints on narrative complexity, but it packs quite a psychological punch. In Norwegian with English subtitles. Contains some sex scenes.

Stellan Skarsgård *Jonas Engström* • Sverre Anker Ousdal *Erik Vik* • Bjørn Floberg *Jon Holt* • Gisken Armand *Hilde Hagen* • Maria Bonnevie *Ane* • Maria Mathiesen *Tanja Lorentzen* ■ *Dir* Erik Skjoldbjaerg • *Scr* Nikolaj Frobenius, Erik Skjoldbjaerg • *Cinematographer* Erling Thurmann-Andersen

Inspecteur Lavardin ★★★ 15

Crime   1986 · Fr/Swi · Colour · 100mins

Chabrol's sequel to *Cop au Vin*, with Jean Poiret repeating his role as the unorthodox policeman. This time he investigates the murder of a famous Catholic writer whose naked body – with the word "pig" on a buttock – is found on a beach. Then Lavardin discovers that the victim's wife, Bernadette Lafont, is an ex-girlfriend of his and the chief suspect. What follows is often quite grisly, decked out with eccentric characters and a cast that includes Jean-Claude Brialy. In French with English subtitles.

Jean Poiret *Inspector Jean Lavardin* • Bernadette Lafont *Hélène Mons* • Jean-Claude Brialy *Claude Alvarez* • Jacques Dacqmine *Raoul Mons* • Hermine Claire *Véronique Manguin* ■ *Dir* Claude Chabrol • *Scr* Claude Chabrol, Dominique Roulet

The Inspector ★★★

Drama   1962 · UK · Colour · 111mins

Having lost his Jewish fiancée to the Nazis, Dutch police inspector Stephen Boyd saves another Jewish girl (Dolores Hart) immediately after the war and attempts to smuggle her to Palestine. Bizarrely, they board a canal boat and end up in Morocco... The Americans pick them up in Tangier and ask the girl, who suffered torture in the death camps, to testify at the Nuremberg trials. A melodrama that doesn't quite obscure its more serious intentions, this is worth watching because of its unusually impressive supporting cast.

Stephen Boyd *Peter Jongman* • Dolores Hart *Lisa Held* • Leo McKern *Brandt* • Hugh Griffith *Van der Pink* • Donald Pleasence *Sgt Wolters* • Harry Andrews *Ayoob* • Robert Stephens

Dickens • Marius Goring *Thorens* • Finlay Currie *De Kooi* ■ *Dir* Philip Dunne • *Scr* Nelson Gidding, Jan de Hartog

An Inspector Calls ★★★★ PG

Drama   1954 · UK · BW · 76mins

While it's a gripping night out at the theatre, JB Priestley's celebrated play loses some of its impact on screen. The revelations made by the unwelcome visitor seem so much less shocking away from the intimate confines of the stage, especially as the use of flashback to reveal the family's guilty secrets deprives us of their reactions as the truth emerges. Yet this is a highly polished production, made all the more irresistible by another superb performance from Alastair Sim. 🖭

Alastair Sim *Inspector Poole* • Arthur Young *Arthur Birling* • Olga Lindo *Sybil Birling* • Eileen Moore *Sheila Birling* • Bryan Forbes *Eric Birling* • Brian Worth *Gerald Croft* • Jane Wenham *Eva Smith* ■ *Dir* Guy Hamilton • *Scr* Desmond Davis, from the play by JB Priestley

Inspector Clouseau ★★★ U

Comedy   1968 · UK · Colour · 91mins

Although Peter Sellers seemed to have the character copyright on the gauche, Gallic policeman, this oddity had Alan Arkin accent-ing the more positive aspects of the role as Clouseau arrives in a tediously swinging London to investigate the aftermath of the Great Train Robbery. Arkin is certainly a better straight actor than Sellers was, and he has a fine backing of such British stalwarts as Frank Finlay and Beryl Reid. But he doesn't have Sellers's sense of self-importance which is so very necessary for laughs. Nevertheless, this is worth looking at for variety's sake. 🖭

Alan Arkin *Inspector Jacques Clouseau* • Frank Finlay *Superintendent Weaver* • Beryl Reid *Mrs Weaver* • Delia Boccardo *Lisa Morrel* • Patrick Cargill *Sir Charles Braithwaite* • Barry Foster *Addison Steele* ■ *Dir* Bud Yorkin • *Scr* Tom Waldman, Frank Waldman, from a character created by Blake Edwards, Maurice Richlin

Inspector Gadget ★★ U

Comedy action adventure
1999 · US · Colour · 75mins

As mindless a Hollywood movie as you're ever likely to find, this screen version of the "cuddly cyborg" cartoon series abandons all plot after the first reel and devotes its energies to beating us senseless with a succession of slapstick effects sequences. Matthew Broderick's performance as the computerised cop is so bland he barely exists, while the script is witless, ineptly structured and solely reliant on Gadget's extendable bits and bobs. For undemanding kids only. 🖭

Matthew Broderick *Inspector Gadget/ RoboGadget/John Brown* • Rupert Everett *Sanford Scolex* • Joely Fisher *Brenda/ RoboBrenda* • Michelle Trachtenberg *Penny* ■ *Dir* David Kellogg • *Scr* Kerry Ehrin, Zak Penn, from a story by Dana Olsen, Kerry Ehrin, from characters created by Andy Heyward, Jean Chalopin, Bruno Bianchi

The Inspector General ★★★ U

Musical comedy 1949 · US · Colour · 101mins

Splendid Danny Kaye vehicle, ostensibly based on the Gogol play about a wandering buffoon mistaken for the visiting dignitary of the title. Warner Bros prepared this as a musical, importing Deanna Durbin's director Henry Koster, and giving Kaye free rein by commissioning songs from Mrs Kaye – the clever Sylvia Fine – and the brilliant Johnny Mercer. The numbers aren't particularly outstanding, but their tongue-twisting lyrics and use of romantic pathos served the star well, and he continued to use one particular musical sequence in his cabaret act for many years afterwards.

Danny Kaye *Georgi* • Walter Slezak *Yakov* • Barbara Bates *Leza* • Elsa Lanchester *Maria* • Gene Lockhart *The mayor* • Alan Hale *Kovatch* ■ *Dir* Henry Koster • *Scr* Philip Rapp, Harry Kurnitz, from the play by Nikolai Gogol

The Inspectors ★★★

Action thriller 1998 · US · Colour · 105mins

The thrill-a-minute lives of a couple of US postal inspectors form the subject of this TV movie, which can genuinely be said to deliver the goods. Not that things start out all that brightly, as veteran mail cop Louis Gossett Jr is saddled with Jonathan Silverman, a Harvard rookie full of ideas but short on experience. However, once they begin investigating a Baltimore letter bomb, the story begins to bite, with the clues repeatedly leading to dead ends. First-class it's not, but with steady direction from Brad Turner and good by-play between the leads it's still something of a surprise package.

Louis Gossett Jr *Inspector Hank Barnes* • Jonathan Silverman *Inspector Alex Urbina* • Tobias Mehler *Drew Carrigan* • Greg Thirloway *Inspector Frank Hughes* • JR Bourne *Dwayne* ■ *Dir* Brad Turner • *Scr* Bruce Zimmerman

Inspiration ★★ U

Drama   1931 · US · BW · 73mins

Parisian artist's model Yvonne (Greta Garbo) and trainee diplomat Andre (Robert Montgomery) fall in love, but the relationship runs into trouble when he learns of her past lovers. The only inspired element in this turgid drivel is Garbo herself, whose luminous presence and exquisite suffering almost rise above the material. Garbo and Montgomery were never teamed again after this picture.

Greta Garbo *Yvonne* • Robert Montgomery *Andre Martel* • Lewis Stone *Delval* • Marjorie Rambeau *Lulu* • Judith Vosselli *Odette* • Beryl Mercer *Marthe* • John Miljan *Coutant* • Edwin Maxwell *Julian Montell* • Oscar Apfel *Vignaud* ■ *Dir* Clarence Brown • *Scr* Gene Markey, from a treatment by James Forbes, from the novel *Sappho* by Alphonse Daudet

Instinct ★★ 15

Psychological drama
1999 · US · Colour · 118mins

What caused anthropologist Ethan Powell (Anthony Hopkins) to go on a murderous rampage while studying gorillas in Rwanda? That's what idealistic psychiatrist Theo Caulder (Cuba Gooding Jr) tries to find out

when Hopkins is finally arrested and placed in a mental institution in *Phenomenon* director Jon Turteltaub's plodding treatise on animal-versus-human instincts. Loosely based on Daniel Quinn's novel *Ishmael*, the film naturally features a fine performance from Hopkins as the intellectually frozen man resorting to the law of the jungle for justice. Yet Turteltaub's odd mixture of *Gorillas in the Mist* and *One Flew over the Cuckoo's Nest* is hardly riveting because it's mainly constructed as a series of prison interviews. Contains violence and swearing. 🖭

Anthony Hopkins *Ethan Powell* • Cuba Gooding Jr *Theo Caulder* • Donald Sutherland *Ben Hillard* • Maura Tierney *Lyn Powell* • George Dzundza *Dr John Murray* • John Ashton *Guard Dacks* ■ *Dir* Jon Turteltaub • *Scr* Gerald DiPego, from his story, from the novel *Ishmael* by Daniel Quinn

Institute Benjamenta, or This Dream People Call Human Life ★★ PG

Drama   1995 · UK · BW · 100mins

The first live-action film from the talented Brothers Quay animation team both confounds and intrigues. Mark Rylance is an aspiring butler who attends a mysterious school to learn the rituals of service, but soon finds his training consists of an endless repetition of one single lesson. Alternately fascinating and banal, this hotchpotch of ideas and images is a sub-Cocteau treatise on the meaning and futility of life. It boasts good performances, atmospheric direction and evocative Hampton Court locations, and is strangely hypnotic in a tedious way. 🖭

Mark Rylance *Jakob von Gunten* • Alice Krige *Lisa Benjamenta* • Gottfried John *Johannes Benjamenta* • Daniel Smith *Kraus* • Joseph Alessi *Pepino* • Jonathan Stone *Hebling* ■ *Dir* Timothy Quay, Stephen Quay • *Scr* Alan Passes, Brothers Quay, from the novella *Jakob von Gunten, and other texts* by Robert Walser

The Intelligence Men ★★★ U

Comedy   1965 · UK · Colour · 98mins

Morecambe and Wise found the transition from TV celebrities to film stars a difficult one to make. They were not helped by the fact that, for their big-screen debut, Sid Green and Dick Hills (scriptwriters of their ITV series at the time) failed to marry the familiar Eric and Ernie characteristics that kept audiences in stitches week after week with the demands of what is, in all honesty, a pretty duff spy spoof. When they do manage to rise above the material, they are very funny indeed, and nearly two hours in their company could never be considered time wasted. 🖭

Eric Morecambe *Eric* • Ernie Wise *Ernie Sage* • William Franklyn *Colonel Grant* • April Olrich *Madame Petrovna* • Richard Vernon *Sir Edward Seabrook* • Gloria Paul *Gina Carlotti* • Warren Mitchell *Prozoroff* ■ *Dir* Robert Asher • *Scr* SC Green, RM Hills, from a story by Peter Blackmore

Intent to Kill ★★

Thriller   1958 · UK · BW · 88mins

The man who photographed *Black Narcissus*, *A Matter of Life and Death*, *The Red Shoes* and *The African Queen* – Jack Cardiff – turned director with this B-thriller, set in Montreal. Critics at the time wondered why he bothered. Richard Todd plays a brain surgeon whose marital problems pale into insignificance when he's asked to operate on a South American leader (Herbert Lom) who is the target for assassins. Forget about Lom's record on human rights – not the film's concern – and concentrate instead on the mechanics of thriller-making.

Richard Todd *Dr Bob McLaurin* • Betsy Drake *Nancy Ferguson* • Herbert Lom *Juan Menda* • Warren Stevens *Finch* • Carlo Justini *Francisco Flores* • Paul Carpenter *O'Brien* • Alexander Knox *Dr McNeil* • Lisa Gastoni *Carla Menda* • Peter Arne *Kral* ■ *Dir* Jack Cardiff • *Scr* Jimmy Sangster, from a novel by Michael Bryan

Intent to Kill ★ 18

Crime action thriller
1992 · US · Colour · 94mins

If you can believe in ex-porn star Traci Lords as a nonconformist policewoman going after a drug dealer who's trying to retrieve a lost dope shipment, you'll believe the rest of this predictable action thriller. Yaphet Kotto plays Traci's captain and wins all the acting honours, but Traci gets to wear the more alluring outfits when she poses as a hooker. Otherwise this formula B-movie is notable for its high quota of graphic violence. Contains violence, nudity and drug abuse. 🖭 *DVD*

Traci Lords *Vicki Stewart* • Yaphet Kotto *Captain Jackson* • Scott Patterson *Al* • Angelo Tiffe *Salvador* ■ *Dir/Scr* Charles T Kanganis

Interceptor ★ 15

Action thriller   1992 · US · Colour · 89mins

Stealth bomber pilot Andrew Divoff springs into action when high-tech terrorist Jürgen Prochnow aims to steal the prized prototype jets. The end result is a predictable action adventure, which looks like a bargain basement cross between *Die Hard* and *Broken Arrow*. The characters here are two-dimensional, the thrills are very cheap and the on-screen gaffes are numerous. In his first film, director Michael Cohn shows little of the idiosyncratic flair he would later bring to his Sigourney Weaver showcase, *Snow White: a Tale of Terror*. 🖭

Andrew Divoff *Captain Christopher Winfield* • Jürgen Prochnow *Phillips* • Elizabeth Morehead *Major Janet Morgan* • J Kenneth Campbell *Engineer* • Jon Cedar *Elliot* ■ *Dir* Michael Cohn • *Scr* Michael Ferris, John Brancato

Interiors ★★★ 15

Psychological melodrama
1978 · US · Colour · 87mins

Coming between Woody Allen's great comic masterpieces *Annie Hall* and *Manhattan*, this intense drama baffled fans and divided critics on its original release. The influence of Ingmar Bergman is unmistakeable, but there are also echoes of Chekhov and Eugene O'Neill in this story of a family thrown into turmoil. Allen's stylish compositions and his astute handling of the cast are impressive, but the script lacks weight and some of the more searching scenes topple over into melodrama. Oscar-nominated Geraldine Page dominates the proceedings as the domineering, mentally disturbed mother, though EG Marshall and Maureen Stapleton also register in unassuming support. ■

Kristin Griffith *Flyn* • Mary Beth Hurt *Joey* • Richard Jordan *Frederick* • Diane Keaton *Renata* • EG Marshall *Arthur* • Geraldine Page *Eve* • Maureen Stapleton *Pearl* • Sam Waterston *Michael* ■ *Dir/Scr* Woody Allen • *Cinematographer* Gordon Willis

Interlude ★

Romantic drama   1957 · US · Colour · 88mins

A virtually unwatchable romantic drama, based on a James M Cain story, featuring a miscast June Allyson as a woman who falls for married conductor Rossano Brazzi in Munich. Instead of having a wonderful sensual adventure, she wastes time trying to decide between Brazzi and unappealing doctor Keith Andes. Cult figure Douglas Sirk provides heavy-handed and humourless direction, and the substandard plot compounds these failings. Munich looks nice in CinemaScope, though.

June Allyson *Helen Banning* • Rossano Brazzi *Tonio Fischer* • Marianne Cook *Reni* • Françoise Rosay *Countess Reinhart* • Keith Andes *Dr Morley Dwyer* ■ *Dir* Douglas Sirk • *Scr* Daniel Fuchs, Franklin Coen, Inez Cocke, from the film *When Tomorrow Comes* by Dwight Taylor, from the novel *Serenade* by James M Cain

Interlude ★★★ PG

Romantic drama
1968 · US · Colour · 108mins

A charming remake of that hoary old romance about a wide-eyed innocent abroad who falls for a sophisticated married musician, previously filmed (as *When Tomorrow Comes*) with Irene Dunne and Charles Boyer, and lugubriously with June Allyson and Rossano Brazzi. Here the casting is nearly perfect, with dashing intellectual Oskar Werner, one of the stars of *Jules et Jim*, as the baton-wielder, and Barbara Ferris as the young reporter who becomes entranced by him. The film benefits from a fine supporting cast, especially Virginia Maskell as the conductor's wife.

Oskar Werner *Stefan Zelter* • Barbara Ferris *Sally* • Virginia Maskell *Antonia* • Donald Sutherland *Lawrence* • Nora Swinburne *Mary* • Alan Webb *Andrew* • Bernard Kay *George Selworth* ■ *Dir* Kevin Billington • *Scr* Lee Langley, Hugh Leonard

Intermezzo ★★★★

Romance   1936 · Swe · BW · 88 mins

A famous violinist employs a young pianist to give his daughter lessons, but falls in love with her, leaves his wife, and embarks on a concert tour with the girl as his accompanist. Directed by one of Sweden's foremost filmmakers of the period, Gustaf Molander, and starring that country's most distinguished leading man, Gösta Ekman, this classy bittersweet romantic drama is notable for instigating the international career of Ingrid Bergman. David Selznick saw the film and, two years later, invited the relative unknown to Hollywood to star in an English-language remake. The rest, as they say, is history. In Swedish with English subtitles.

Gösta Ekman (1) *Holger Brandt* • Inga Tidblad *Margit Brandt* • Ingrid Bergman *Anita Hoffman* • Hasse Ekman *Åke Brandt* • Britt Hagman *Ann-Marie Brandt* ■ *Dir* Gustav Molander [Gustaf Molander] • *Scr* Gustav Molander, Gosta Stevens

Intermezzo ★★★★ PG

Romance   1939 · US · BW · 69mins

Also known as *Escape to Happiness*, this was producer David O Selznick's remake of the Swedish movie which also starred Ingrid Bergman. Originally only intending to purchase the story, Selznick was persuaded to also import Miss Bergman, who here makes her American debut, and her natural beauty was the movie's initial sales gimmick. The tale of obsessive love is old hat, but is remarkably and touchingly well played by Bergman and Leslie Howard. The film was to have been directed by William Wyler, who Selznick allegedly fired in order to hire the Russian émigré Gregory Ratoff, who owed Selznick and could therefore forfeit his director's salary to pay off his gambling debt. 🖭

Ingrid Bergman *Anita Hoffman* • Leslie Howard *Holger Brandt* • Edna Best *Margit Brandt* • John Halliday *Thomas Stenborg* • Cecil Kellaway *Charles Moler* • Enid Bennett *Greta Stenborg* • Ann E Todd *Ann Marie* • Douglas Scott *Eric Brandt* ■ *Dir* Gregory Ratoff • *Scr* George O'Neil, from the film by Gustav Molander, Gosta Stevens

Internal Affairs ★★★ 18

Crime thriller   1990 · US · Colour · 109mins

The Untouchables co-star Andy Garcia is the cop transferred to Internal Affairs, determined to prove that fellow police officer Richard Gere is corrupt in this often gripping thriller from *Leaving Las Vegas* director Mike Figgis. Gere is especially good as the dishonest and often violent cop, but, in the end, this film focuses more on Gere's general nastiness than the interesting vendetta between the pair. Contains violence, swearing and sex scenes. 🖭

Richard Gere *Dennis Peck* • Andy Garcia *Sergeant Raymond Avilla* • Nancy Travis *Kathleen Avilla* • Laurie Metcalf *Sergeant Amy Wallace* • Richard Bradford *Lieutenant Sergeant Grieb* • William Baldwin *Van Stretch* ■ *Dir* Mike Figgis • *Scr* Henry Bean

International House ★★★

Comedy   1933 · US · BW · 70mins

In this great, if paper-thin, antique comedy, WC Fields arrives by autogyro at a hotel in China where a giant television is about to be unveiled. Many popular radio performers of the day turn up to take part in the celebrations, including Rudy Vallee, George Burns and Gracie Allen, while Cab Calloway sings *Reefer Man*. Bela Lugosi appears as a Russian general in a rollicking good show that will appeal to nostalgia lovers.

WC Fields *Professor Quail* • Bela Lugosi *General Petronovich* • Stuart Erwin *Tommy Nash* • Sari Maritza *Carol Fortescue* • George Burns *Dr Burns* • Gracie Allen *Nurse Allen* • Rudy Vallee • Cab Calloway ■ *Dir* Edward Sutherland [A Edward Sutherland] • *Scr* Frances Martin, Walter DeLeon, from a story by Lou Heifetz, Neil Brant

International Lady ★ U

Second World War spy drama
1941 · US · BW · 102mins

Hungarian-born Ilona Massey, who enjoyed a brief career as an opera singer, is the "international lady" in this overlong piece of lighthearted wartime hokum. She's the spy who passes coded messages to the Nazis through the songs she broadcasts. George Brent's government agent and Basil Rathbone's Scotland Yard detective are both hot on her trail.

George Brent *Tim Hanley* • Ilona Massey *Carla Nillson* • Basil Rathbone *Reggie Oliver* • Gene Lockhart *Sidney Grenner* ■ *Dir* Tim Whelan • *Scr* Howard Estabrook, from a story by E Lloyd Sheldon, Jack DeWitt

International Settlement ★★ U

Thriller   1938 · US · BW · 70mins

With his long-standing enthusiasm for films torn from the day's headlines, Fox studio chief Darryl F Zanuck ordered one to exploit the Japanese invasion of China. For speedy production ahead of rivals, he handed it to his B-feature unit as a "special" to star Dolores Del Rio and George Sanders, previously teamed in *Lancer Spy*. Sanders is the adventurer in Shanghai's International Settlement district where he is first shot at, then saved by Del Rio's French nightclub singer. Newsreel footage of the bombing of Shanghai is incorporated into the climax.

George Sanders *Del Forbes* • Dolores Del Rio *Lenore Dixon* • June Lang *Joyce Parker* • Dick Baldwin *Wally Burton* • John Carradine *Murdock* • Keye Luke *Dr Wong* ■ *Dir* Eugene Forde • *Scr* Lou Breslow, John Patrick, from a story by Lynn Root, Frank Fenton

International Velvet ★★ PG

Drama   1978 · US/UK · Colour · 110mins

More than 30 years on from the MGM classic *National Velvet*, Elizabeth Taylor has grown into Nanette Newman, lives with Christopher Plummer and has ambitions for her niece, Tatum O'Neal, to win an Olympic equestrian title. Writer/director/producer Bryan Forbes considered the title "puerile" and lost his fight to change it, but this movie, a concoction devised by a near-destitute MGM, was probably a lost cause anyway. Despite some good moments, such as the crisis on a transatlantic flight when a horse goes berserk, everything is far too sugary and aimed at Americans intent on a touring holiday of Ye Olde England. 🖭

Tatum O'Neal *Sarah Brown* • Christopher Plummer *John Seaton* • Anthony Hopkins *Captain Johnny Johnson* • Nanette Newman *Velvet Brown* • Peter Barkworth *Pilot* • Dinsdale Landen *Mr Curtis* • Sarah Bullen *Beth* ■ *Dir* Bryan Forbes • *Scr* Bryan Forbes, suggested by the novel *National Velvet* by Enid Bagnold

The Internecine Project ★★

Thriller   1974 · UK · Colour · 88mins

A selection of gravel-voiced actors including James Coburn and Keenan

Wynn accompany actress Lee Grant in this lukewarm espionage thriller. Despite some awful dialogue, Coburn still manages to play the hard-edged plot with his tongue in his cheek, and he got his own back 17 years later when he parodied roles like this as a murder-happy spy in *Hudson Hawk*. Contains violence and swearing.

James Coburn *Robert Elliot* • Lee Grant *Jean Robertson* • Harry Andrews *Albert Parsons* • Ian Hendry *Alex Hellman* • Michael Jayston *David Baker* • Keenan Wynn *EJ Farnsworth* ■ Dir Ken Hughes • Scr Barry Levinson, Jonathan Lynn, from the novel *Internecine* by Mort W Elkind • Cinematographer Geoffrey Unsworth

Internes Can't Take Money ★★★

Medical drama   1937 · US · BW · 77mins

A young hospital doctor helps a gangster's widow find her missing child in a modest programme filler that stars Joel McCrea as the sympathetic medic and the wonderful Barbara Stanwyck as the mother. The film was an unexpected box-office hit for Paramount, but the studio badly missed the boat: it was MGM that picked up Max Brand's Dr Kildare character, cast Lew Ayres in the role and made a series of highly successful features over a nine-year period.

Barbara Stanwyck *Janet Haley* • Joel McCrea *James Kildare* • Lloyd Nolan *Hanlon* • Stanley Ridges *Innes* • Gaylord Pendleton [Steve Pendleton] *Interne Jones* • Lee Bowman *Interne Weeks* • Irving Bacon *Jeff* ■ Dir Alfred Santell • Scr Rian James, Theodore Reeves, from a story by Max Brand

The Interns ★★

Romantic drama   1962 · US · BW · 119mins

All sorts of sexual shenanigans go on behind the screens at a big American hospital when four newly-qualified doctors arrive for work. Clearly intended as the flipside of Doctor Kildare's squeaky-clean adventures, this movie was advertised at the time as being really adult and racy. It wasn't then and it isn't now, and the only reason to watch is the cast.

Michael Callan *Dr Considine* • Cliff Robertson *Dr John Paul Otis* • James MacArthur *Dr Lew Worship* • Nick Adams *Dr Sid Lackland* • Suzy Parker *Lisa Cardigan* • Haya Harareet *Mado* • Anne Helm *Mildred* • Stefanie Powers *Gloria* • Buddy Ebsen *Dr Sidney Wohl* • Telly Savalas *Dr Riccio* • Katherine Bard *Nurse Flynn* ■ Dir David Swift • Scr Walter Newman, David Swift, from a novel by Richard Frede

Interpol ★

Crime thriller   1957 · UK · BW · 91mins

Known as *Pickup Alley* in the US, this feeble thriller about tracking down a dope-peddling syndicate by the international police force boasted that it was filmed in London, Paris, Athens, Naples, Rome, Lisbon and New York. It looks as though they sometimes forgot to take the script with them. Trevor Howard obviously relishes acting the master villain for a change, though co-stars Victor Mature and Anita Ekberg don't try to act at all.

Victor Mature *Charles Sturgis* • Anita Ekberg *Gina Broger* • Trevor Howard *Frank McNally* •

Bonar Colleano *Amalio* • Alec Mango *Salko* ■ Dir John Gilling • Scr John Paxton, from the novel by AJ Forrest

Interrogation ★★★★

Political drama   1982 · Pol · Colour · 118mins

Although set in the last days of Stalinism, the parallels with the Solidarity era meant that Ryszard Bugaski's harrowing drama was immediately banned on its release in Poland. When it was eventually reissued, Krystyna Janda won the best actress prize at Cannes in 1990 for her performance as the falsely accused cabaret artist, who is pitilessly tortured on account of her sexual liaison with a major implicated in anti-government activity. In Polish with English subtitles.

Krystyna Janda *Antonia Dziwisz* • Adam Ferency *Morawsky* • Janusz Gajos *Zawada* • Agnieszka Holland *Witowska* • Olgierd Lukaszewicz ■ Dir Ryszard Bugajski • Scr Ryszard Bugajski, Janusz Dymek

The Interrupted Journey ★

Crime drama   1949 · UK · BW · 85mins

There's nothing more frustrating than a thriller that pulls the rug out from under you after you've invested so much emotion in it. Written by Michael Pertwee, this tale of the unexpected plays so many tricks on the viewer that it soon becomes impossible to identify with the plight of novelist Richard Todd, whose inability to choose between wife Valerie Hobson and mistress Christine Norden spells disaster for his fellow passengers on a speeding express. Director Daniel Birt's efforts to invest the action with some disconcerting visuals are undermined by the cheapness of the production and the gimmicky script.

Richard Todd *John North* • Valerie Hobson *Carol North* • Christine Norden *Susan Wilding* • Tom Walls *Mr Clayton* • Dora Bryan *Waitress* • Arnold Ridley *Saunders* ■ Dir Daniel Birt • Scr Michael Pertwee

Interrupted Melody ★★★★ U

Biographical drama   1955 · US · Colour · 105mins

A lush and expensive MGM biographical drama about the Australian singer Marjorie Lawrence, who contracted polio at the peak of her career. It's marvellously played by under-rated redhead Eleanor Parker – star of *Scaramouche*, *Detective Story* and *Caged* among others, but mainly remembered these days as the baroness in *The Sound of Music*. Eileen Farrell supplies Parker's singing voice, and the writers, William Ludwig and Sonya Levien, won an Oscar for best adapted screenplay. Glenn Ford is superb as the doctor who inspires the singer in her fight against the disease, and the supporting cast is led by a young Roger Moore.

Glenn Ford *Dr Thomas King* • Eleanor Parker *Marjorie Lawrence* • Roger Moore *Cyril Lawrence* • Cecil Kellaway *Bill Lawrence* • Eileen Farrell ■ Dir Curtis Bernhardt • Scr William Ludwig, Sonya Levien, from the book by Marjorie Lawrence

Intersection ★★★ 15

Drama   1994 · US · Colour · 94mins

Few will remember the glossy French movie *Les Choses de la Vie*, of which this is an even glossier remake. Richard Gere is a well-groomed architect, married to Sharon Stone and having an affair with journalist Lolita Davidovich. The usual *ménage à trois*, then, with designer labels, capped teeth, smart furniture and doting daughter, all droolingly shot and written like a TV soap. The trick is to give Gere's dilemma (Sharon or Lolita?) some resonance, so a stunningly staged car smash takes centre stage and takes the decision out of his hands. Impossible to film in Britain as we have roundabouts. Contains swearing, sex scenes and brief nudity. 📺

Richard Gere *Vincent Eastman* • Sharon Stone *Sally Eastman* • Lolita Davidovich *Olivia Marshak* • Martin Landau *Neal* • Jenny Morrison *Meaghan Eastman* ■ Dir Mark Rydell • Scr David Rayfiel, Marshall Brickman, from the novel *Les Choses de la Vie* by Paul Guimard, from the film *Les Choses de la Vie* by Paul Guimard, Jean-Loup Dabadie, Claude Sautet

Interval ★★★

Romantic drama   1973 · US/Mex · Colour · 85mins

Returning to the screen after six years, a well-preserved 62-year-old Merle Oberon starred in, produced and co-edited this soapy tale of a wealthy globetrotting woman on holiday in Mexico who meets and falls in love with a painter 20 years her junior. Her final film, directed stolidly in a colourful location by Daniel Mann, was a case of life imitating bad art, because Oberon, then living in Mexico, fell for her young, Dutch-born co-star, Robert Wolders, who soon became her fourth husband.

Merle Oberon *Serena Moore* • Robert Wolders *Chris* • Claudio Brook *Armando Vertiz* • Russ Conway *Fraser* • Charles Bateman *Husband* ■ Dir Daniel Mann • Scr Gavin Lambert

Interview with the Vampire: the Vampire Chronicles ★★★ 18

Horror   1994 · US · Colour · 117mins

When the highly anticipated movie version of Anne Rice's cult novel finally came to the screen, it was a decidedly anaemic affair. All sumptuously dressed up with nowhere really interesting to go, director Neil Jordan's lavish adaptation is a stylised horror tale lacking the emotional depth and jet-black darkness of the doom-laden tome that was such a chic and fashionable read in the seventies. Still, Tom Cruise is fine as the vampire Lestat, whose close relationship with handsome Brad Pitt forms an erotic twist on the Dracula legend. It's Antonio Banderas who gives the most full-blooded performance as the bisexual Armand in a beautifully mounted production, low on divine decadence but high on evocative elegance. Contains violence, swearing and nudity. 📺 **DVD**

Tom Cruise *Lestat de Lioncourt* • Brad Pitt *Louis Pointe du Lac* • Antonio Banderas *Armand* • Stephen Rea *Santiago* • Christian

Slater *Daniel Malloy* • Kirsten Dunst *Claudia* • Domiziana Giordano *Madeleine* ■ Dir Neil Jordan • Scr Anne Rice, from her novel *Interview with the Vampire*

Intervista ★★★★ 15

Biographical documentary drama 1987 · It · Colour · 106mins

A breathless, brilliant insight into the vanities and inanities of the motion picture business from the inimitable Federico Fellini. A curio rather than a classic, it sweeps the viewer from the eighties to the Cinecittà film studio of over 60 years ago, when a wide-eyed youth from Rimini came to Rome to make his name. Packed with clips from screen gems and constantly blurring the line between past and present, studio reality and cinematic illusion, the action is climaxed by a wickedly staged reunion between Marcello Mastroianni and Anita Ekberg, the stars of Fellini's classic *La Dolce Vita*. In Italian with English subtitles. 📺

Federico Fellini • Marcello Mastroianni • Anita Ekberg • Sergio Rubini *Reporter* • Maurizio Mein ■ Dir Federico Fellini • Scr Federico Fellini, Gianfranco Angelucci

Intimate Relations ★★★ 15

Comedy drama based on a true story 1995 · UK/Can · Colour · 95mins

This fifties-set drama lifts the lid on the lusty bedroom antics of the supposedly staid Brits. Rupert Graves is sailor Harold Guppy, who takes a room as a boarder in the home of the seemingly normal Beasley family. It's not long, before Mrs Marjorie Beasley (a great, almost sinister turn from Julie Walters) and her teenage daughter are vying for his horizontal affections, and hapless Harold finds himself out of his depth. Writer/director Philip Goodhew's debut feature is quirky and engrossing fare with a very dark edge. Contains swearing and a violent scene.

Julie Walters *Marjorie Beasley* • Rupert Graves *Harold Guppy* • Matthew Walker *Stanley Beasley* • Laura Sadler *Joyce Beasley* • Holly Aird *Deirdre* • Les Dennis *Maurice Guppy* ■ Dir/Scr Philip Goodhew

The Intimate Stranger ★★

Mystery drama   1956 · UK · BW · 95mins

This was the second film made in England by the blacklisted Hollywood director Joseph Losey, working under the pseudonym of Walton, which was his middle name. Blacklisted writer Howard Koch had written the script about an American film producer in London who is married to the daughter of the studio chief and is being blackmailed by a woman whose letters suggest she might be his mistress. In fact, he doesn't know who she is. It's a feeble effort with poor performances and cardboard sets, but the theme of the story – illusion, paranoia, guilt — are fascinating when set beside Losey's own predicament.

Richard Basehart *Reggie Wilson* • Mary Murphy *Evelyn Stewart* • Constance Cummings *Kay Wallace* • Roger Livesey *Ben Case* • Faith Brook *Lesley Wilson* • Mervyn Johns *Ernest Chapple* • Vernon Greeves *George Merns* • Andre Mikhelson *Steve Vadney* ■ Dir Joseph Walton [Joseph Losey] • Scr Peter Howard [Howard Koch], from the novel *Pay the Piper* by Paul Howard

Into the Arms of Danger ★

Drama 1997 · US · Colour · 90mins

Why do makers of TV movies always have to take otherwise credible stories to such ludicrous extremes? Had this drama stuck with either the tale of Morgan Fairchild's relationship with creepy boyfriend Michael Woods or daughter Chandra West's dealings with exploitative photographer Ricky Paull Goldin, then it might have made for provocative viewing. However, by combining the two strands and then having Fairchild turn into the maternal avenger, any serious issues get forgotten as excess is piled on excess. Contains swearing.

Morgan Fairchild *Diana* • Chandra West *Carly* • Michael Woods *Bob Lenic* • Ricky Paull Goldin *Brad Winters* ■ *Dir* Chuck Bowman • *Scr* John Robert Bensink

Into the Badlands ★★ 15

Supernatural portmanteau western 1991 · US · Colour · 84mins

More might have been expected from this portmanteau made-for-cable movie, which gathers together three supernatural cowboy tales from writers including the fine western novelist Will Henry. But, frankly, it's a mess, unredeemed by an interesting cast that features Helen Hunt, Dylan McDermott and Mariel Hemingway. Bruce Dern as a bounty hunter holds the trio of stories together – in fact, it's Dern's narration that provides most of the pleasure. Watch by all means, but don't expect too much.

Bruce Dern *TL Barston* • Mariel Hemingway *Alma Heusser* • Dylan McDermott *McComas* • Helen Hunt *Blossom* ■ *Dir* Sam Pillsbury • *Scr* Dick Beebe, Marjorie David, Gordon Dawson, from short stories by Will Henry, Marcia Muller, Bryce Walton

Into the Homeland ★★ 15

Drama 1987 · US · Colour · 110mins

This attempt to twin an attack on racism with a tale of personal redemption regularly promises to burst out of its familiar straitjacket but finally never shows the courage of its ambition. Powers Boothe, an actor sadly absent from key roles since his triumphs in *Southern Comfort* and *The Emerald Forest*, is an ex-cop who is galvanised from drunkeness when his daughter disappears.

Powers Boothe *Jackson Swallow* • C Thomas Howell *Tripp Winston* • Paul LeMat *Derrick Winston* • Arye Gross *Joel Baskin* ■ *Dir* Lesli Linka Glatter • *Scr* Anna Hamilton Phelan

Into the Night ★★ 15

Comedy thriller 1985 · US · Colour · 114mins

John Landis came a bit of a cropper with this lacklustre comedy caper, although it has aged better than some of his efforts. The then relatively unknown Jeff Goldblum and Michelle Pfeiffer take the lead roles: Goldblum the innocent bystander who inadvertently gets caught up with smuggler Pfeiffer and Arab terrorists. The action bustles along amusingly enough and Landis stuffs the pictures with cameos from everyone from David Bowie to Roger Vadim. ▣

Jeff Goldblum *Ed Okin* • Michelle Pfeiffer *Diana* • Stacey Pickren *Ellen Okin* • Bruce

McGill *Charlie* • Kathryn Harrold *Christie* • Carl Perkins *Mr Williams* • David Bowie *Colin Morris* • Richard Farnsworth *Jack Caper* • John Landis *Savak 4* • Dan Aykroyd • Roger Vadim *Monsieur Melville* ■ *Dir* John Landis • *Scr* Ron Koslow

Into the Sun ★★ 15

Action adventure 1992 · US · Colour · 96mins

Anthony Michael Hall's career started slipping the minute he started losing his geeky teenage looks, and this was one of his failed bids to relaunch himself as an action star. It's still worth a look, though, if only for a smarter-than-usual premise. Hall is the pampered Hollywood star researching a new film role who is reluctantly taken under the wing of maverick air force ace Michael Paré. Soon the pair find themselves caught up in a real-life war. There are shades of the similarly themed comedy *The Hard Way* in the beginning, although the film degenerates into *Rambo*-style clichés once the stars are caught behind enemy lines. ▣

Anthony Michael Hall *Tom Slade* • Michael Paré *Captain Paul Watkins* • Deborah Maria Moore [Deborah Moore] *Major Goode* • Terry Kiser *Mitchell Burton* • Brian Haley *Lieutenant DeCarlo* ■ *Dir* Fritz Kiersch • *Scr* John Brancato, Michael Ferris, from their story

Into the West ★★★ PG

Fantasy 1992 · Ire/UK · Colour · 102mins

A charming, unusually cast fable about two children who run away to the wild Irish hills on a white stallion, pursued by Gabriel Byrne and Ellen Barkin, playing gypsies. Set against some majestic scenery, this is partly a children's film that harks back to the genteel era of Ealing comedy, and partly an excursion into Gaelic myth, ably written by Jim Sheridan (of *My Left Foot* fame) and sensitively handled by Mike Newell, later the director of *Four Weddings and a Funeral*. It's poetic and sometimes weirdly comic. ▣

Gabriel Byrne *Papa Riley* • Ellen Barkin *Kathleen* • Ciaran Fitzgerald *Ossie Riley* • Ruaidhri Conroy *Tito Riley* • David Kelly *Grandpa Ward* • Johnny Murphy *Tracker* ■ *Dir* Mike Newell • *Scr* Jim Sheridan, from a story by Michael Pearce

Into Thin Air ★★★ 15

Drama based on a true story 1985 · US · Colour · 92mins

Lassiter director Roger Young is the man behind the camera of this intriguing fact-based drama about a teenage boy who goes missing, and the authorities' lack of interest in finding him. A strong cast, including Ellen Burstyn and Robert Prosky, makes what could have been a daft weepie into a strong, often gripping movie. Inspired by the Canadian documentary *Just Another Missing Kid*, this was initially known as *Brian Walker, Please Call Home*. ▣

Ellen Burstyn *Joan Walker* • Robert Prosky *Jim Conway* • Sam Robards *Stephen Walker* • Nicholas Pryor *Larry Walker* • Patricia Smith *Olga Conway* • Tate Donovan *Brian Walker* ■ *Dir* Roger Young • *Scr* George Rubino

Into Thin Air: Death on Everest ★★ PG

Drama based on a true story 1997 · US · Colour · 86mins

The events of a fatal Everest expedition of 1996 are documented in this TV movie, based on Jon Krakauer's book. Rival mountaineering guides (Peter Horton and Nathaniel Parker) team up to lead a group of international climbers up Mount Everest. Approaching the summit, and far from the safety of their tents, they are hit by a powerful blizzard. Make sure you remember what colour parkas the actors are wearing, otherwise you'll have no idea who's who in the overly swaddled cast. Solid technical credits all round help make this a tense experience, giving a reasonably authentic sense of the dangers faced by the participants of this ill-fated expedition.

Peter Horton *Scott Fischer* • Nathaniel Parker *Rob Hall* • Christopher McDonald *Jon Krakauer* • Richard Jenkins *Beck Weathers* • Tim Dutton *Andy Harris* • Ned Vaughn • Richard Rees ■ *Dir* Robert Markowitz • *Scr* Robert J Avrech, from the non-fiction book *Into Thin Air* by Jon Krakauer

Intolerance ★★★★★ U

Classic silent drama 1916 · US · BW · 120mins

A magnificent and deeply significant achievement of early cinema, this sprawling multi-layered epic helped define storytelling in the movies, with its early use of such devices as parallel action and the dramatic close-up. Made as a riposte by genius director DW Griffith to those who accused him of racism after his ground-breaking *The Birth of a Nation*, this analyses the effects of intolerance in four tales set throughout the ages, which are interspersed with the eternal image of a mother (Lillian Gish) and baby. The Babylonian sequences are as notorious as they are astounding, with gigantic sets almost dwarfing the rampant violence and nudity, but the contemporary tale is exciting and touching, too. Seen restored in a beautifully tinted and toned copy, with a fine score, this is one of the most satisfying films ever made; timeless and still stunning in its revolutionary and assured use of the medium.

Lillian Gish *The woman who rocks the cradle* • Mae Marsh *The Dear One* • Fred Turner *Father* • Robert Harron *Boy* • Howard Gaye *Christ* • Lillian Langdon *Mary* • Olga Grey *Mary Magdalene* • Margery Wilson *Brown Eyes* • Frank Bennett (1) *Charles IX* • Josephine Crowell *Catherine de Midici* • Constance Talmadge *Mountain girl* • Alfred Paget *Belshazzar* • Seena Owen *Attarea* ■ *Dir/Scr* DW Griffith

Intrigue ★ PG

Adventure 1947 · US · BW · 69mins

Wandering aimlessly around Shanghai after the Second World War, former tough-guy pilot George Raft finds himself working for a black-marketeering outfit. When, however, Raft discovers that the gang's food-price fixing is causing suffering to orphans, he sets out to remedy the situation. Edwin L Marin's direction has no discernible influence over the cliché-ridden and totally unbelievable

plot, or the now ageing Raft's impassive performance. ▣

George Raft *Brad Dunham* • June Havoc *Tamara Baranoff* • Helena Carter *Linda Arnold* • Tom Tully *Marc Andrews* • Marvin Miller *Ramon* • Dan Seymour *Karidian* ■ *Dir* Edwin L Marin • *Scr* Barry Trivers, George Slavin, from a story by George Slavin

The Intruder ★★★★ U

Drama 1953 · UK · BW · 81mins

An intriguing idea – why would a wartime hero become a peacetime thief? – played out rather mechanically by director Guy Hamilton, but performed with some force by officer Jack Hawkins, who finds a former member of his regiment (Michael Medwin) burgling his home. Hamilton was still honing his craft here after assisting on *The Third Man*, but he went on to be a fine action director with credits that include *Battle of Britain* and four of the James Bond series. ▣

Jack Hawkins *Wolf Merton* • Hugh Williams *Tim Ross* • Michael Medwin *Ginger Edwards* • George Cole *John Summers* • Dennis Price *Leonard Perry* • George Baker *Adjutant* • Richard Wattis *Schoolmaster* • Dora Bryan *Dora Bee* ■ *Dir* Guy Hamilton • *Scr* Robin Maugham, John Hunter, Anthony Squire, from the novel *Line on Ginger* by Robin Maugham

The Intruder ★★★ 15

Drama 1961 · US · Colour · 79mins

A remarkable one-off from horror producer/director Roger Corman, turning his hand to this stark tale of bigotry in the Deep South based on a controversial novel by screenwriter Charles Beaumont. William Shatner, in a role that's light years away from Captain Kirk, is the *agent provocateur* who incites racist riots in opposition to the then new US school integration. As Shatner's character's true motives are revealed, the film becomes particularly effective and genuinely unsettling. Not a success in its day, it has achieved a certain cult notoriety and is well worth seeking out. ▣

William Shatner *Adam Cramer* • Frank Maxwell *Tom McDaniel* • Beverly Lunsford *Ella McDaniel* • Robert Emhardt *Verne Shipman* • Jeanne Cooper *Vi* ■ *Dir* Roger Corman • *Scr* Charles Beaumont, from his novel

Intruder in the Dust ★★★

Drama 1949 · US · BW · 86mins

A solid adaptation of William Faulkner's novel about a black man (Juano Hernandez) who faces a lynch mob after he's accused of shooting a white man. He isn't guilty, of course, but his pride and obvious contempt for the justice system harm his case. Director Clarence Brown, best known for his work with Garbo, refuses to let hysteria invade the picture and he gets marvellous atmosphere from his location shooting in Oxford, Mississippi, Faulkner's home town.

David Brian *John Gavin Stevens* • Claude Jarman Jr *Chick Mallison* • Juano Hernandez *Lucas Beauchamp* • Porter Hall *Nub Gowrie* • Will Geer *Sheriff Hampton* ■ *Dir* Clarence Brown • *Scr* Ben Maddow, from the novel by William Faulkner

U = SUITABLE FOR ALL   Uc = SUITABLE FOR ALL, ESPECIALLY FOR YOUNG CHILDREN (VIDEO ONLY)   PG = PARENTAL GUIDANCE

Invader ★★ 15

Science-fiction action adventure
1991 · US · Colour · 91mins

A bargain-basement but quietly ambitious sci-fi thriller that should keep conspiracy theorists happy with its tale of an alien artificial intelligence system taking over a US air-force base and plotting Armageddon. Scandal sheet reporter Hans Bachmann (never heard of before or since) discovers what's going on and, with the Pentagon understandably sceptical, teams up with defence department agent A Thomas Smith to kick some UFO butt. Explosions for the sake of them and bouts of weak humour dampen the best efforts of director Philip J Cook. ▭

Hans Bachmann *Frank McCall* • A Thomas Smith *Captain Harry Anders* • Rick Foucheux *Colonel Faraday* • John Cooke *General Anheiser* ■ *Dir/Scr* Philip J Cook

The Invader ★★ 15

Science-fiction thriller
1997 · US · Colour · 92mins

Pregnant school teacher Sean Young is carrying the "Eve" infant of a threatened alien race. As good alien Ben Cross tries to protect her, bad alien Nick Mancuso cons cop Daniel Baldwin (also Young's boyfriend) into helping him find Cross. Mancuso's intentions are strictly murderous. Although rather pointless and silly, with director Mark Rosman playing down the action side of things and focusing on the unconvincing alien love triangle aspect, this fast-moving science-fiction thriller plays down the *Terminator* references in favour of fish-out-of-water comedy. Acting beyond the call of duty ensures the one-dimensional characters register effectively. Contains some violence. ▭

Sean Young *Annie* • Ben Cross *Renn* • Daniel Baldwin *Jack* • Nick Mancuso *Willard* • Lynda Boyd *Gail* • Tim Henry *Older cop* • Robert Andre *McNeil* ■ *Dir/Scr* Mark Rosman

Invaders from Mars ★★★★ PG

Science-fiction drama
1953 · US · Colour · 77mins

William Cameron Menzies helped to design *Gone with the Wind* and directed *Things to Come*, and his Martian fairy tale has achieved cult status because of its distorted sets and abstract surrealism. Yes, you can see the zips on the aliens' suits, and, yes, the paranoia scares are strictly kids' stuff. But that's precisely why this pulp science-fiction nightmare has built up a following. For it perfectly depicts, from a child's point of view, the ultimate horror of having no one to trust and nowhere to turn – a fear that will strike a chord of recognition in anyone who's ever trembled behind the living-room sofa. ▭

Helena Carter *Dr Pat Blake* • Arthur Franz *Dr Stuart Kelston* • Jimmy Hunt *David MacLean* • Leif Erickson *George MacLean* • Hillary Brooke *Mary MacLean* ■ *Dir* William Cameron Menzies • *Scr* William Cameron Menzies, Richard Blake, John Tucker Battle, from a story by John Tucker Battle

Invaders from Mars ★★★ PG

Science-fiction   1986 · US · Colour · 94mins

Director Tobe Hooper, best known for *The Texas Chain Saw Massacre*, skirts a fine line between kitsch and spoof in his big-budget remake of the 1953 B-movie. Clinging closely to the original primal paranoia story of a young boy's neighbourhood suddenly being overrun by aliens, Hooper's deadpan sci-fi comedy provides good scares, great visual design and Stan Winston's wonderfully wild Martian monster special effects. High points are the expedition into the blob-like Martians' subterranean lair, Oscar-winner Louise Fletcher snacking on live frogs, and Hunter Carson and his real-life mother Karen Black working well together as a team. ▭

Karen Black *Linda* • Hunter Carson *David Gardner* • Timothy Bottoms *George Gardner* • Laraine Newman *Ellen Gardner* • James Karen *General Wilson* • Louise Fletcher *Mrs McKeltch* ■ *Dir* Tobe Hooper • *Scr* Dan O'Bannon, Don Jakoby, Richard Blake

Invasion ★★ PG

Science-fiction thriller
1965 · UK · BW · 77mins

Aliens put an invisible force field around a secluded country hospital in this endearingly daffy British oddity, which must feature the cheapest alien takeover in history. Edward Judd is the scientist battling the extraterrestrial Oriental women in spacesuits, in an efficiently made and, yes, mildly exciting slice of cut-price science fiction. Director Alan Bridges imbues the Home Counties atmosphere with a peculiar ambience that's astonishingly heady at times, too. ▭

Edward Judd *Dr Vernon* • Yoko Tani *Lystrian leader* • Valerie Gearon *Dr Claire Harlan* • Lyndon Brook *Brian Carter* • Tsai Chin *Nurse Lim* ■ *Dir* Alan Bridges • *Scr* Roger Marshall, from a story by Robert Holmes

Invasion of Privacy ★★★ 18

Psychological thriller
1996 · US · Colour · 90mins

A mentally unbalanced man (Johnathan Schaech) kidnaps the woman (Mili Avital) carrying his child to prevent her from having an abortion in director Anthony Hickox's gripping and stylish genre-hopping thriller. How he becomes an unlikely pro-life icon in the ensuing courtroom battle is smartly written by horror scripter supremo Larry Cohen, best-known for *It's Alive*. Hickox makes marvellous use of split-screen, heightening tension in the latter exciting stages. And yes, that is supermodel Naomi Campbell making an appearance. ▭

Johnathon Schaech *Josh Taylor* • Mili Avital *Theresa Barnes* • Naomi Campbell *Cindy Carmichael* • David Keith *Sergeant Rutherford* • Tom Wright *Devereux* • Charlotte Rampling *Deidre Stiles* • RG Armstrong *Mr Logan* ■ *Dir* Anthony Hickox • *Scr* Larry Cohen

Invasion of the Astro-Monster ★★ U

Science-fiction adventure
1965 · Jap · Colour · 90mins

More commonly known as *Monster Zero*, this marked Godzilla's fifth film appearance and his change of status from Japan's evil enemy to much-loved national institution. The incomprehensible plot is something about Godzilla and Rodan being shipped off in space bubbles to Planet X so they can defeat three-headed Ghidrah. But don't bother trying to work out the alien double-cross, just enjoy the usual cheesy special effects, atrocious dubbing and Nick Adams (re-creating his astronaut role from *Frankenstein Conquers the World*) trying to look as if his scenes weren't shot separately in the States. ▭

Nick Adams *Glenn* • Akira Takarada *Fuji* • Kumi Mizuno *Namikawa* ■ *Dir* Inoshiro Honda • *Scr* Shinichi Sekizawa

Invasion of the Body Snatchers ★★★★★ PG

Classic science-fiction thriller
1956 · US · BW · 80mins

Pods from outer space land in a small Californian town and start replicating the inhabitants, turning them into brainwashed slaves, in director Don Siegel's chilling science-fiction tale. This classic of the genre (co-scripted by an uncredited Sam Peckinpah) reflects the blacklisting hysteria of the McCarthy era, as Siegel tersely piles on the nightmare with pulse-pounding briskness. Although expertly remade since, the original is still the most striking, with a justly famous scalp-freezing ending. ▭ **DVD**

Kevin McCarthy *Miles Bennell* • Dana Wynter *Becky Driscoll* • Larry Gates *Danny* • King Donovan *Jack* • Carolyn Jones *Theodora* • Jean Willes *Sally* • Ralph Dumke *Nick* • Virginia Christine *Wilma* ■ *Dir* Don Siegel • *Scr* Daniel Mainwaring, Sam Peckinpah, from the novel *The Body Snatchers* by Jack Finney

Invasion of the Body Snatchers ★★★ 15

Science-fiction thriller
1978 · US · Colour · 110mins

It was always going to be hard to better Don Siegel's fifties' classic, but director Philip Kaufman does succeed in summoning up a different but equally chilling air of paranoia in this remake, set in a coldly impersonal San Francisco. Donald Sutherland is the health inspector who begins to worry that people are acting weirdly normal, and there is solid support from Brooke Adams and a young Jeff Goldblum, plus a creepy turn from Leonard Nimoy. Kaufman also throws in some neat in-jokes in the shape of cameos from Siegel and the star of the original, Kevin McCarthy. Contains some swearing. ▭

Donald Sutherland *Matthew Bennell* • Brooke Adams *Elizabeth Driscoll* • Leonard Nimoy *Dr David Kibner* • Veronica Cartwright *Nancy Bellicec* • Jeff Goldblum *Jack Bellicec* • Kevin McCarthy *Running man* • Robert Duvall *Priest on swing* ■ *Dir* Philip Kaufman • *Scr* WD Richter, from the novel *The Body Snatchers* by Jack Finney

Invasion of the Saucer Men ★

Science-fiction comedy
1957 · US · BW · 69mins

A "so-bad-it's-almost-good" sci-fi quickie where aliens inject Hicksville teens with alcohol so they'll be arrested for drink driving. Well, it's one way to take over the world, but won't it take rather a long time? Fifties monster enthusiasts will salivate over the giant-headed "hell creatures" with bug-eyes and bulging exposed brains, while fans of the sixties TV series *Batman* will recognise Frank Gorshin (the Riddler) as the con man planning to keep a dead alien in his ice box. They really don't come any worse, wretched, or as unintentionally funny as this Martian mash, incredibly remade as *The Eye Creatures* in 1965.

Steven Terrell *Johnny* • Gloria Castillo *Joan* • Frank Gorshin *Joe* • Raymond Hatton *Larkin* ■ *Dir* Edward L Cahn • *Scr* Robert J Gurney Jr, Al Martin, from a story by Paul Fairman

Invasion Quartet ★ U

Second World War comedy
1961 · UK · BW · 91mins

MGM's British department showed just how far its reputation had plummeted since the glory days of the late thirties with this woeful wartime farrago. One might have had higher hopes for a script by Jack Trevor Story and John Briley, but what they serve up here is a preposterous tale about a ragtag outfit sent into Nazi-occupied France to knock out a gun aimed directly at Dover. Expedition leader Bill Travers makes light of being one-legged, but, while cohorts John Le Mesurier and Grégoire Aslan provide serviceable support, Spike Milligan simply doesn't register as a barmy boffin.

Bill Travers *Major Freddie Oppenheimer* • Spike Milligan *Lt Godfrey Pringle* • John Le Mesurier *Colonel* • Grégoire Aslan *Major Pierre Debrie* • Maurice Denham *Dr Barker* • Millicent Martin *Sister Kay Manning* ■ *Dir* Jay Lewis • *Scr* Jack Trevor Story, John Briley, from a story by Norman Collins

Invasion USA ★★

Drama   1952 · US · BW · 73 mins

Patrons in a New York bar are hypnotised by a weird stranger (Dan O'Herlihy) into believing America has been attacked by communist nuclear weapons. The customers react accordingly, some taking their own lives. The reason for this theme? To prove the nation must always be prepared for such an event. A laughable slice of Cold War hysteria, ineptly handled by director Alfred E Green, with cheap special effects and a reliance on newsreel footage, which makes it appear even shoddier.

Gerald Mohr *Vince* • Peggie Castle *Carla* • Dan O'Herlihy *Mr Ohman* • Robert Bice *George Sylvester* • Tom Kennedy *Bartender* ■ *Dir* Alfred E Green • *Scr* Robert Smith, from the story by Robert Smith, Franz Spencer

Invasion USA ★ 18

Action adventure
1985 · US · Colour · 107mins

Cold War paranoia brings out the jingoistic worst in American hardman Chuck Norris, resulting in a prime slice of hammy action. Norris plays Matt Hunter, a retired CIA man who discovers a band of marauding Russian terrorists have invaded the United States and are killing innocent people and spreading panic all across Florida. Acting completely alone, Hunter massacres entire divisions of Ruskies who have no answer to his

overwhelming, warrior-like skills. Even for its Reaganite times, this is complete trash.

Chuck Norris *Matt Hunter* • Richard Lynch *Rostov* • Melissa Prophet *McGuire* • Alexander Zale *Nikko* • Alex Colon *Tomas* ■ *Dir* Joseph Zito • *Scr* Chuck Norris, James Bruner, from a story by Aaron Norris, James Bruner

Inventing the Abbotts
★★★ 15

Drama   1997 · US · Colour · 102mins

Pat O'Connor's follow-up to *Circle of Friends* isn't quite as enjoyable, but is a pleasant enough distraction. Joaquin Phoenix and Billy Crudup star as two working-class brothers in fifties Illinois who share a fascination for the neighbouring (and wealthy) Abbott family, and two of the daughters – Jennifer Connelly and Liv Tyler in particular. While there is a tentative romance between Phoenix and Tyler, it's overshadowed by deception and resentment between the families, which ultimately gives the film a depressing tone. Nice performances, though, from the young cast, and Will Patton and Kathy Baker in supporting roles. Contains swearing. ▭

Joaquin Phoenix *Doug Holt* • Billy Crudup *Jacey Holt* • Liv Tyler *Pamela Abbott* • Will Patton *Lloyd Abbott* • Kathy Baker *Helen Holt* • Jennifer Connelly *Eleanor Abbott* • Michael Sutton *Steve* • Joanna Going *Alice Abbott* ■ *Dir* Pat O'Connor • *Scr* Ken Hixon, from the story by Sue Miller

Invention of Destruction
★★★★

Fantasy   1958 · Cz · BW · 95mins

Adapted from a Jules Verne novel, this ingenious fantasy (with its pirates, volcanoes, submarines, underwater cycles, hidden laboratories and rocket cannon) also borrows liberally from *20,000 Leagues under the Sea* and *The Mysterious Island*. There's also a hint of Méliès in Karel Zeman's audacious blend of animation, puppetry, models, glass shots and live-action, which evokes the glorious 19th-century illustrations of the novel. The story of villainous aristocrat Miroslav Holub's attempt to steal the explosive developed by professor Arnost Navratil and his intrepid assistant, Lubor Tokos, is action-packed. But it's also a thoughtful treatise on the misappropriation of science. In Czech with English subtitles.

Arnost Navratil *Prof Roche* • Lubor Tokos *Simon Hart* • Miroslav Holub *Argitas* • Frantisek Slegr *Pirate captain* • Vaclav Kyzlink *Serke* ■ *Dir* Karel Zeman • *Scr* Karel Zeman, from the novel *Face au Drapeau* by Jules Verne

Investigation of a Citizen above Suspicion
★★★ 18

Crime drama   1970 · It · Colour · 109mins

This Kafkaesque drama, which won the 1970 Oscar for best foreign film, caused a storm of protest when it was released in its native Italy. Exploring the nation's fascist legacy, director Elio Petri pulls no punches in his depiction of a police chief who murders his mistress and then taunts his underlings with a string of clues. While Gian Maria Volonté is chilling as the

contemptuous cop, Petri seems as pleased with the scam as his protagonist. He overloads the symbolism and drives home his political points when a craftiness commensurate with Ennio Morricone's score would have sufficed. In Italian with English subtitles. ▭

Gian Maria Volonté *Police Inspector* • Florinda Bolkan *Augusta Terzi* • Salvo Randone *Plumber* • Gianni Santuccio *Police commissioner* • Arturo Dominici *Mangani* ■ *Dir* Elio Petri • *Scr* Elio Petri, Ugo Pirro

Invisible Child
★★ PG

Drama   1999 · US · Colour · 87mins

Taking the *Harvey* concept of an invisible friend one step further, this TV movie gives us a mother with an imaginary middle child. Rita Wilson's family conspires in her shared fantasy, even hiring a nanny to help with their "three" children. Things start to unravel when the nanny becomes concerned for the wellbeing of the eldest daughter and decides to alert the authorities. This uncomfortable blend of fantasy and family drama treats mental illness far too lightly, with director Joan Micklin Silver (*Crossing Delancey*) seemingly uncertain of the right tone, veering clumsily between sweetness and melodrama. ▭

Rita Wilson *Annie Beeman* • Victor Garber *Tim Beeman* • Mae Whitman *Rebecca "Doc"Beeman* • David Dorfman *Sam Beeman* ■ *Dir* Joan Micklin Silver • *Scr* David Field, from a story by Ron Bass, David Field

Invisible Ghost
★ PG

Horror   1941 · US · BW · 60mins

With his old studio, Universal, pulling out of horror, Bela Lugosi signed with Poverty Row outfit Monogram. The first of several pictures he made for them, this is technically the best (director Joseph H Lewis went on to make several highly regarded *film noir* classics, notably *Gun Crazy*). But the plot, outlandish even by 1941 standards, now exhibits a naivety worthy of Ed Wood, Lugosi's last employer. Doctor Lugosi thinks he's under the spell of dead wife Betty Compson and a series of murders ensues. At least it's short.

Bela Lugosi *Dr Charles Kessler* • Polly Ann Young *Virginia* • John McGuire *Ralph/Paul* • Clarence Muse *Evans* ■ *Dir* Joseph H Lewis • *Scr* Helen Martin, Al Martin

The Invisible Kid
★ 15

Science-fiction comedy   1988 · US · Colour · 92mins

Weird Science meets *Porky's* as nerd student Grover (Jay Underwood) stumbles onto an invisibility formula and uses it to wander into the girls' locker rooms and cause havoc. A juvenile fantasy laden with dumb jock gags and inane sexist humour. Karen Black, queen of the B-movie cameo, wastes her talents once more playing Grover's air-head mother, who's obsessed with cable television trash. Stuff similar to this, in fact. ▭

Jay Underwood *Grover Dunn* • Karen Black *Mom* • Wally Ward [Wallace Langham] *Milton McClane* • Chynna Phillips *Cindy Moore* ■ *Dir/Scr* Avery Crounse

The Invisible Man
★★★★★ PG

Classic science-fiction horror   1933 · US · BW · 68mins

Claude Rains is one of the most undervalued stars of Hollywood's Golden Age. It's ironic that a familiar face that few could put a name to, should have made that name in a film in which he spent most of the action swathed in bandages or invisible. In truth, the success of this superb adaptation of HG Wells's novel is down to John P Fulton and John Mescall's pioneering special effects and the eerie atmosphere conjured up by horror master James Whale, as playful pranks give way to megalomania and murder. A minor classic. ▭

Claude Rains *Jack Griffin, the Invisible Man* • Gloria Stuart *Flora Cranley* • William Harrigan *Dr Kemp* • Henry Travers *Dr Cranley* • Una O'Connor *Mrs Hall* ■ *Dir* James Whale • *Scr* RC Sherriff, Philip Wylie (uncredited), from the novel by HG Wells • *Cinematographer* Arthur Edeson • *Art Director* Charles D Hall

The Invisible Man
★★

Science-fiction fantasy   1975 · US · Colour · 74mins

This pilot film for a short-lived TV series stars David McCallum as a scientist involved in laser research who stumbles upon the secret of invisibility. Deciding to keep it from the military, he flees with interested parties in hot pursuit. A by-the-numbers TV movie, only notable now for writer/producer Steve Bochco's involvement. He went on to become the creative force behind such landmark TV shows as *Hill Street Blues, NYPD Blue* and *Murder One*.

David McCallum *Dr Daniel Weston* • Melinda Fee *Kate Weston* • Jackie Cooper *Walter Carison* • Henry Darrow *Dr Nick Maggio* • Alex Henteloff *Rick Steiner* ■ *Dir* Robert Michael Lewis [Robert Lewis] • *Scr* Steven Bochco, from a story by Steven Bochco, Harve Bennett, from the novel by HG Wells

The Invisible Man Returns
★★★

Science-fiction thriller   1940 · US · BW · 81mins

The first sequel to the Claude Rains classic, while more modestly scaled than its predecessor, still receives a first-class treatment from director Joe May and, in many instances, surpasses the visual magic of the original. Vincent Price replaces Rains and gets his first starring role as a man condemned to hang for a murder he didn't commit. He persuades the brother of the man who created the invisible serum to give him a dose so he can find the real killer. Price's rich theatrical voice assures his invisible man a credible presence in a diverting tale filled with comedy, drama and eerie moments.

Sir Cedric Hardwicke [Cedric Hardwicke] *Richard Cobb* • Vincent Price *Geoffrey Radcliffe* • Nan Grey *Helen Manson* • John Sutton *Dr Frank Griffin* ■ *Dir* Joe May • *Scr* Curt Siodmak, Lester Cole, Cecil Belfrage, from a story by Curt Siodmak, Joe May

The Invisible Ray
★★★

Science-fiction horror   1936 · US · BW · 82mins

The film that introduced Boris Karloff to a role he would visit throughout his

career – that of a sympathetic scientist whose remarkable discovery makes him a threat to society. Here, as Dr Janos Rukh, he becomes contaminated by a radioactive meteor found in Africa and learns his touch means death. When he suspects Dr Benet (Bela Lugosi) of trying to take the credit for his discovery, the "Radium X" substance within the meteor causes him to go insane and seek vengeance. Innovative special effects for its era and the ever-dependable "gruesome twosome" supplying the thrills.

Boris Karloff *Dr Janos Rukh* • Bela Lugosi *Dr Felix Benet* • Frances Drake *Diane Rukh* • Frank Lawton *Ronald Drake* • Walter Kingsford *Sir Francis Stevens* • Beulah Bondi *Lady Arabella Stevens* ■ *Dir* Lambert Hillyer • *Scr* John Colton, from a story by Howard Higgin, Douglas Hodges • *Special Effects* John P Fulton

Invisible Strangler
★

Horror   1976 · US · Colour · 85mins

Shot in 1976 as *The Astral Factor*, it's not hard to see why this confusing would-be chiller was kept on the shelf until 1984. A boy strangles his mother when she tells him she wishes she had have had an abortion. Imprisoned in a mental asylum, he learns an ancient Buddhist technique for becoming invisible and escapes death row to murder all the people responsible for his sentence. Robert Foxworth is the cop assigned to track him down. A terrible script and amateur-hour direction condemn the viewer to hard labour as well.

Robert Foxworth *Lieutenant Charles Barrett* • Stefanie Powers *Candy Barrett* • Elke Sommer *Chris* • Sue Lyon *Miss De Long* • Leslie Parrish *Coleen Hudson* ■ *Dir* John Florea • *Scr* Arthur C Pierce, from the story by Arthur C Pierce, Earle Lyon

Invisible Stripes
★★

Crime drama   1940 · US · BW · 81mins

A routine and deeply moralistic gangster story, in which George Raft is determined to go straight when he comes out of prison... well, maybe for ten minutes at least. The great William Holden, in his second significant screen role, plays Raft's volatile younger brother, and their mother is played by, of all people, Flora Robson – who was aged 37 at the time and wears rubber wrinkles. And, this being a Warner Bros picture, Humphrey Bogart is in it as well, as a trigger-happy killer. Director Lloyd Bacon keeps things moving.

George Raft *Cliff Taylor* • Humphrey Bogart *Chuck Martin* • William Holden (1) *Tim Taylor* • Jane Bryan *Peggy* • Flora Robson *Mrs Taylor* • Paul Kelly *Ed Kruger* • Lee Patrick *Molly Daniels* ■ *Dir* Lloyd Bacon • *Scr* Warren Duff, Jonathan Finn, from the book by Warden Lewis E Lawes

The Invitation
★★★★

Comedy drama   1973 · Swi · Colour · 99mins

Demonstrating a narrative fluidity and a fondness for its characters, regardless of their foibles, director Claude Goretta evokes the great Jean Renoir with this gentle take on petty bourgeois values. As the penpusher who invites his workmates to a garden party at his newly acquired country house, Michel Robin is a study in gracious timidity.

Ultimately, though, all his guests prove to be archetypes as the sun and wine lower their office defences. Flitting from benevolent boss to flighty secretary to boorish joker, Goretta deftly reveals the person behind the persona with the help of a fine ensemble cast. Slight but delectable. In French with English subtitles.

Jean-Luc Bideau *Maurice* • Jean Champion *Alfred* • Pierre Collet *Pierre* • Jacques Rispal *Rene* • Cecile Vassort *Aline* • Rosine Rochette *Helene* • Corinne Coderey *Simone* ■ *Dir* Claude Goretta • *Scr* Claude Goretta, Michel Viala

Invitation to a Gunfighter ★★★★ U

Western   1964 · US · Colour · 88mins

George Segal is a Confederate soldier who returns from the war to find the Union townspeople have seized his farm and hired a gunfighter to kill him. Written and directed by Richard Wilson, an associate of Orson Welles back in the Mercury theatre and *Citizen Kane* days, it's an allegory about political exile and conformity that spends too much time in debate at the expense of action. Nevertheless, it's lifted by a knockout performance from Yul Brynner as the elegant, Creole gunfighter Jules Gaspard D'Estaing – a role he turned into an android for the sci-fi film *Westworld*. 📺

Yul Brynner *Jules Gaspard D'Estaing* • Janice Rule *Ruth Adams* • Brad Dexter *Kenarsie* • Alfred Ryder *Doc Barker* • Mike Kellin *Tom* • George Segal *Matt Weaver* ■ *Dir* Richard Wilson • *Scr* Richard Wilson, Elizabeth Wilson, Alvin Sapinsley, from a story by Hal Goodman, Larry Klein

Invitation to the Dance ★★★ U

Dance musical   1956 · US · Colour · 62mins

Gene Kelly's personal and most ambitious undertaking is a pure dance film, which he conceived, choreographed and directed. It comprises three different ballets starring Kelly and an impressive assembly of American and European dancers. Of these, *Ring around the Rosy* (music by André Previn) is the most successful and entertaining segment, concerning a bracelet which passes through many hands before coming back to its original owner. The finale, *Sinbad the Sailor*, danced to Rimsky-Korsakov's *Scheherazade*, in which Kelly dances with animated cartoon characters (and Carol Haney's Scheherazade), is the most innovative and experimental.

Igor Youskevitch *The lover* • Claire Sombert *The loved* • Gene Kelly *The clown* • David Paltenghi *The husband* • Daphne Dale *The wife* • Igor Youskevitch *The artist* • Gene Kelly *The marine* • Carol Haney *Scheherazade* • Gene Kelly *Sinbad* • Tamara Toumanova *Streetwalker* • Tommy Rall *Boyfriend* ■ *Dir/ Scr* Gene Kelly • *Choreographer* Gene Kelly

Invitation to the Wedding ★ PG

Romantic comedy
1983 · UK · Colour · 88mins

Incredibly inept and unfunny romantic comedy, one of several in the eighties that exploited American obsession with British aristocracy. A senile bishop

(Ralph Richardson, indulging his real-life passion for motorbikes) mistakenly weds the daughter of an impoverished earl to a visiting American. The dull confusion is compounded by the arrival of a Texan evangelist played, astoundingly, by John Gielgud, whose self-confessed inability with accents is well demonstrated. The celebration, without a trace of irony, of class prejudice and blood sports, passé in 1983, is now positively shocking.

Ralph Richardson *Bishop Willy* • John Gielgud *Clyde Ormiston* • Paul Nicholas *David Anderson* • Susan Brooks *Lady Anne* ■ *Dir/ Scr* Joseph Brooks

Invocation of My Demon Brother ★★★ 15

Experimental horror
1969 · US · Colour · 11mins

Underground filmmaker Kenneth Anger described his 11-minute short as "the shadowing forth of Our Lord Lucifer as the Powers of Darkness gather at a midnight mass". A homage to Satanist guru Aleister Crowley, it uses dynamic montage to Mick Jagger's Moog synthesiser soundtrack, rejecting narrative. Anger himself plays the Magus, while Bobby Beausoleil is Lucifer, who appears at the climax. In between are shots of a Satanic ritual, a Rolling Stones concert and GIs leaping from helicopters in Vietnam. Only for those who are in tune with Anger's homoerotic sensibility and perverse but striking visual style. 📺

Speed Hacker *Wand-bearer* • Lenore Kendel *Deaconess* • William Beutel *Deacon* • Kenneth Anger *Magus* • Anton Szandor La Vey *Satan* • Bobby Beausoleil *Lucifer* ■ *Dir/Scr* Kenneth Anger • *Music* Mick Jagger

The Ipcress File ★★★★ PG

Spy thriller   1965 · UK · Colour · 102mins

Len Deighton's first spy novel had everything except a name for its off-the-peg hero. Producer Harry Saltzman decided on Harry Palmer and cast the virtually unknown Michael Caine. Designed as a counterpart to the Bond movies, which Saltzman also co-produced, the story uncovers KGB operatives in the British secret service and enables Caine to talk Bermondsey, wear glasses and cook his own meals, things that Sean Connery would never do. Instead of the *Orient Express*, it's the Central Line. It's cunning, calculated and still works, thanks to some droll humour, John Barry's marvellously twangy score, Sidney J Furie's energetic direction and spot-on performances by Guy Doleman and Nigel Green as bowler-hatted spooks. Contains some swearing. 📺 **DVD**

Michael Caine *Harry Palmer* • Nigel Green *Dalby* • Guy Doleman *Major Ross* • Sue Lloyd *Jean Courtney* • Gordon Jackson *Jock Carswell* • Aubrey Richards *Radcliffe* • Frank Gatliff *Bluejay* ■ *Dir* Sidney J Furie • *Scr* Bill Canaway, James Doran, from the novel by Len Deighton • *Cinematographer* Otto Heller ■ *Art Director* Ken Adam

Iphigenia ★★★

Drama   1976 · Gr · Colour · 128mins

Having already made *Elektra* and *The Trojan Women*, Michael Cacoyannis completed his Euripidean trilogy with

this Oscar-nominated adaptation of *Iphigenia in Aulis*. In spite of the fragmentary nature of the source, the story of the ill-fated Athenian expedition to rescue Helen of Troy still makes for compelling viewing. However, Cacoyannis's overindulgence in directorial flourishes somewhat undermines the efforts of a sterling cast, with Costa Kazakos impressive as Agamemnon, the king who decides to sacrifice his daughter to appease the gods. But it's Irene Papas as his wife who dominates the proceedings. In Greek with English subtitles.

Irene Papas *Clytemnestra* • Costa Kazakos *Agamemnon* • Costa Carras *Menelaus* • Tatiana Papamoskou *Iphigenia* • Christos Tsangas *Ulysses* • Panos Michalopoulos *Achilles* • Angelos Yannoulis *Servant* ■ *Dir* Michael Cacoyannis • *Scr* Michael Cacoyannis, from the play *Iphigenia in Aulis* by Euripides • *Editor* Michael Cacoyannis

Irene ★★★ U

Musical comedy
1940 · US · BW and Colour · 81mins

Desperate for a musical success to show that there was life after Fred Astaire and Ginger Rogers, RKO threw money at this slight confection that was bought as a vehicle for the duo before they parted company in 1939. The studio was rewarded with its third biggest hit of the year, but there was nothing remarkable about this Cinderella story. Indeed, the songs are a pretty sorry batch. Director Herbert Wilcox coaxes a reasonably frothy performance from his wife, Anna Neagle, but Ray Milland looks distinctly uncomfortable. 📺

Anna Neagle *Irene O'Dare* • Ray Milland *Don Marshall* • Billie Burke *Mrs Vincent* • Alan Marshal *Bob Vincent* • Arthur Treacher *Betherton* • Roland Young *Mr Smith* ■ *Dir* Herbert Wilcox • *Scr* Alice Duer Miller, from the musical comedy by James H Montgomery

Irish Eyes Are Smiling ★★ U

Biographical musical comedy
1944 · US · Colour · 89mins

A musical comedy based very loosely on the life of turn-of-the-century songwriter Ernest R Ball, who's played rather one-dimensionally by Dick Haymes. After its opening scenes in Cleveland, the story moves to New York as Ball searches for fame and fortune and falls in love with a burlesque entertainer (June Haver). Standard fare, though Monty Woolley livens things up with his boisterous portrayal of a Broadway producer.

Monty Woolley *Edgar Brawley* • June Haver *Mary "Irish" O'Brien* • Dick Haymes *Ernest R Ball* • Anthony Quinn *Al Jackson* ■ *Dir* Gregory Ratoff • *Scr* Earl Baldwin, John Tucker Battle, from a story by EA Ellington

The Irishman ★★★★

Drama   1978 · Ausl · Colour · 108mins

British actor Michael Craig, so long under contract to Rank, had to emigrate to Australia to get a role as big and beefy as this. He's Paddy Doolan, a teamster so resistant to change that he prefers his team of horses to anything mechanical. Stubborn and doomed he may be, but we're willing him to succeed through battles against progress and the sad skirmishes of a family at war with

itself. Donald Crombie directs with a sharp eye for period detail (the twenties) and Michael Craig does him proud. The 20 giant Clydesdale horses are the ultimate scene-stealers, though.

Michael Craig *Paddy Doolan* • Robyn Nevin *Jenny Doolan* • Simon Burke *Michael Doolan* • Lou Brown *Will Doolan* • Bryan Brown *Eric Haywood* ■ *Dir* Donald Crombie • *Scr* Donald Crombie, from a novel by Elizabeth O'Conner

Irma la Douce ★★★★ 15

Comedy   1963 · US · Colour · 137mins

Billy Wilder took a hit Broadway musical, cut out all the songs and still came up trumps with this near-classic comedy. Jack Lemmon plays a priggish *gendarme* who dons a variety of improbable but hilarious disguises to save the soul (if not the virtue) of Shirley MacLaine's Parisian hooker. Set in and around the Les Halles food market, brilliantly re-created on a Hollywood sound stage by art director Alexander Trauner, it's a puzzle of a picture about morality and redemption, energetically performed by its two leads. The film was originally to have starred Elizabeth Taylor, but Wilder chose to reunite the stars of his 1960 Oscar-winner, *The Apartment*; Charles Laughton was also signed to play the café owner, but he died just as shooting started. Blink and you'll miss James Caan making his screen debut as one of MacLaine's clients. 📺

Jack Lemmon *Nestor* • Shirley MacLaine *Irma La Douce* • Lou Jacobi *Moustache* • Bruce Yarnell *Hippolyte* • Herschel Bernardi *Inspector LeFevre* • Hope Holliday *Lolita* • Bill Bixby *Tattooed sailor* ■ *Dir* Billy Wilder • *Scr* Billy Wilder, IAL Diamond, from the play by Alexander Breffort, from the musical by Marguerite Monnot • *Music* André Previn • *Cinematographer* Joseph LaShelle

Iron and Silk ★★★

Biographical drama
1990 · US · Colour · 94mins

What an unexpected little gem this is. American college graduate Mark Salzman travelled to China in 1982 to teach English and learn the martial arts from the celebrated kung-fu master Pan Qingfu. Both men play themselves in this pleasing adaptation of Salzman's bestselling book, which not only recounts his travels, but also his romantic encounter with a local girl (beautifully played by Vivian Wu). Blending gentle comedy with serious cultural observations, the film is directed with considerable care by Shirley Sun, and special mention should also be made of cinematographer James Hayman for his stunning images of Hangzhou. In English and Mandarin with subtitles.

Mark Salzman *Teacher Mark* • Pan Qingfu *Teacher Pan* • Jeanette Lin Tsui *Teacher Hei* • Vivian Wu *Ming* • Sun Xudong *Sinbad* • Zheng Guo *Mr Song* • To Funglin *Old Sheep* ■ *Dir* Shirley Sun • *Scr* Shirley Sun, Mark Salzman, from Salzman's book

The Iron Curtain ★★

Historical spy drama 1948 · US · BW · 86mins

Taking its title from Winston Churchill's famous Fulton, Missouri, speech of March 1946, this early Cold War drama is a pseudo-documentary, its grave tone alerting us to imminent communist takeover if not for the efforts of Dana Andrews and Gene Tierney. It seems the Soviets are up to no good in Canada, where spies and atomic secrets lie thick on the ground. Andrews is a Soviet dissident who wants to defect with his wife Tierney. Planning to stop them are June Havoc and Berry Kroeger as hard-line Stalinist spies. The story is based on fact, hence the low-key and, unfortunately, rather dull approach from director William A Wellman.

Dana Andrews *Igor Gouzenko* • Gene Tierney *Anna Gouzenko* • June Havoc *Karanova* • Berry Kroeger *Grubb* • Edna Best *Mrs Foster* • Stefan Schnabel *Dr Norman* ■ *Dir* William A Wellman • *Scr* Milton Krims, from the memoirs of Igor Gouzenko

Iron Eagle ★★ 15

Action adventure
1985 · US · Colour · 111mins

One of the better *Top Gun* cash-ins, although it hardly deserved the long-running video franchise it grew into. Jason Gedrick is the teenage flyer who goes on his own secret mission to rescue his dear old dad who is being held by David Suchet, the head of a nasty unnamed Arabian country. Louis Gossett Jr, reprising his gruff but tender Oscar-winning turn from *An Officer and a Gentleman*, is the sympathetic serviceman who breaks the rules to help him by teaching him to fly and stealing a couple of F-16s. Utter tosh, of course, but the flying sequences are quite good. Contains violence and swearing. ▭

Louis Gossett Jr *"Chappy" Sinclair* • Jason Gedrick *Doug Masterson* • David Suchet *Minister of Defence* • Tim Thomerson *Ted Masterson* ■ *Dir* Sidney J Furie • *Scr* Sidney J Furie, Kevin Elders

Iron Eagle II ★★ PG

Action adventure 1988 · US · Colour · 95mins

For the second instalment of the long-running franchise, the focus is firmly on the grown-ups with Louis Gossett Jr back taking centre stage as flying expert Chappy Sinclair. This time he is given the task of bringing together a squabbling squad of American and Russian flyers to train them to destroy a nuclear missile base in another unnamed Arab country. Naturally, there is tension between the two sets of pilots. As with the first, the flying sequences look good, and there's a fair bit of ground warfare too, but the clichéd chest-beating of the politics is harder to stomach. Contains violence and swearing. ▭

Louis Gossett Jr *Brigadier General Charles "Chappy" Sinclair* • Mark Humphrey *Captain Matt Cooper* • Stuart Margolin *General Stillmore* • Alan Scarfe *Colonel Vladimir Vardovsky* ■ *Dir* Sidney J Furie • *Scr* Sidney J Furie, Kevin Elders

Iron Eagle IV ★ 12

Action adventure
1995 · Can · Colour · 91mins

The *Iron Eagle* franchise struggled to number four on the back of Louis Gossett Jr's enduring popularity in the role of air-force general Chappy Sinclair (retired). He is now running an air school for young offenders and, while out on a routine flight, they discover the local air base is being used by

criminals involved with toxic chemicals. The authorities don't believe them, so it's time to take matters into their own hands. File under innocuous, as only Gossett Jr's performance is worth watching. ▭

Louis Gossett Jr *Chappy Sinclair* • Al Waxman *General Kettle* • Jason Cadieux *Doug Masters* • Joanne Vannicola *Wheeler* ■ *Dir* Sidney J Furie • *Scr* Michael Stokes

The Iron Giant ★★★★ U

Animated science-fiction adventure
1999 · US · Colour · 83mins

It might not have the Disney stamp, but this wonderful version of Ted Hughes's children's fable is still the best animated film of 1999. A first-class achievement in cartoon virtuosity, it liberally borrows images from fifties comic book art and conventions from the era's science-fiction movies to stunning effect. To a soundtrack of *American Graffiti*-style hits, this heavy metal *ET* tells the riveting tale of nine-year-old Hogarth, the giant alien robot he saves from electrical overload, and the fiercely protective relationship that develops between them. But it's when a Communist-hating FBI agent arrives, convinced the walking Meccano set poses a Cold War threat, that the real thrills begin. With political allegory for the adults, and dazzling visuals and excitement galore for the kids, this poignant fairy tale is outstanding on every artistic level. ▭ **DVD**

Jennifer Aniston *Annie Hughes* • Harry Connick Jr *Dean McCoppin* • Vin Diesel *The Iron Giant* • James Gammon *Marv Loach/Floyd Turbeaux* • Cloris Leachman *Mrs Tensedge* • Christopher McDonald *Kent Mansley* • John Mahoney *General Rogard* • Eli Marienthal *Hogarth Hughes* • M Emmet Walsh *Earl Stutz* ■ *Dir* Brad Bird • *Scr* Tim McCanlies, Andy Brent Forrester [Brent Forrester], from a story by Brad Bird, from the novel by Ted Hughes

The Iron Glove ★★ U

Period adventure 1954 · US · Colour · 76mins

Unless you're a Robert Stack fan, there's little to recommend this period tomfoolery about a young pretender to the throne of King George I. To be fair, Bob swashes a mean buckle; he also gets to romance the lovely Ursula Theiss, who later became Robert Taylor's second wife. The Technicolor's nice, the running time is mercifully short and Alan Hale Jr is on hand to remind audiences of his father, who he so uncannily resembled.

Robert Stack *Charles Wogan* • Ursula Thiess *Ann Brett* • Richard Stapley *James Stuart* • Charles Irwin *James O'Toole* • Alan Hale Jr *Patrick Gaydon* • Leslie Bradley *Duke of Somerfield* ■ *Dir* William Castle • *Scr* Jesse L Lasky Jr, DeVallon Scott, Douglas Heyes, from a story by Robert E Kent, Samuel J Jacoby

The Iron Horse ★★★★★

Silent epic western 1924 · US · BW · 131mins

Already a veteran of more than 40 films by the tender age of 29, John Ford established himself as a major talent with this colossal tale of railroads, romance and revenge. The pioneering work on the first transcontinental railroad brings with it greed, villainy and murder as Davy Brandon's surveyor father is murdered, supposedly by Indians. The adult Davy

(George O'Brien) later returns to discover the real culprit. Although brimming over with incident, it's the re-creation of the pioneering West that earns the film its place in cinema history. Twentieth Century-Fox spared no expense to give a ring of authenticity to the gaudy saloons, the dusty cattle drives and the murderous raids, but it's Ford's affinity for the period and its people that brings the scene to life.

George O'Brien *Davy Brandon* • Madge Bellamy *Miriam Marsh* • Cyril Chadwick *Peter Jesson* • Fred Kohler *Bauman* • Gladys Hulette *Ruby* • James Marcus *Judge Haller* ■ *Dir* John Ford • *Scr* Charles Kenyon, from a story by John Russell, Charles Kenyon

The Iron Maiden ★★ U

Comedy 1962 · UK · Colour · 97mins

The *Carry On* boys are behind this terrible British comedy, which attempts to marry *The Maggie* and *The Titfield Thunderbolt*, and succeeds only in creating a thundering bore. Yet again we have grown men going weak at the knees over a piece of clapped-out machinery, but here it's a traction engine instead of a boat or a train and, frankly, it has none of the same romance. Off to a slow start, the picture falls away towards the middle and finishes with a traction race of earth-juddering dullness.

Michael Craig *Jack Hopkins* • Anne Helm *Kathy Fisher* • Jeff Donnell *Mrs Fisher* • Alan Hale Jr *Paul Fisher* • Noel Purcell *Admiral Sir Digby Trevelyan* ■ *Dir* Gerald Thomas • *Scr* Vivian A Cox, Leslie Bricusse, from a story by Harold Brooks, Kay Bannerman

The Iron Major ★★ U

Drama 1943 · US · BW · 85mins

Pat O'Brien had played the famous football coach Knute Rockne in a highly successful 1940 biopic at Warner Bros. Three years later RKO Radio's executives had the brainwave of pitching him into this wartime propaganda piece about another real-life football coach, Frank Cavanaugh, who became a First World War hero. Nicknamed the Iron Major after he survived severe injuries received at the front, he returned to football until becoming blind. But O'Brien is too bland for leading roles – he was much better in small doses supporting the likes of James Cagney.

Pat O'Brien *Frank Cavanaugh* • Ruth Warrick *Florence Ayres* • Robert Ryan *Father Donovan* • Leon Ames *Robert Stewart* • Russell Wade *Manning* • Bruce Edwards *Lt Jones* ■ *Dir* Ray Enright • *Scr* Aben Kandel, Warren Duff, from a book by Florence Cavanaugh

The Iron Man ★★

Sports drama 1931 · US · BW · 81mins

Between his classic *Dracula* and his masterpiece *Freaks*, Tod Browning made this conventional boxing drama about a lightweight on his way to the title. Playing the boxer is Lew Ayres, then famous for his role in *All Quiet on the Western Front*, who must somehow cope with the demands of his manager as well as the duplicity of his wife, played by Jean Harlow. Critics weren't entirely enthusiastic about Harlow's performance, but her move to MGM a

year later saw her brief but spectacular career really take off.

Lew Ayres *Young Mason* • Robert Armstrong *George Regan* • Jean Harlow *Rose Mason* • John Miljan *Paul H Lewis* • Eddie Dillon [Edward Dillon] *Jeff* • Mike Donlin *McNeil* ■ *Dir* Tod Browning • *Scr* Francis Edward Faragoh, from a novel by WR Burnett

The Iron Mask ★★

Swashbuckling adventure
1929 · US · BW · 95mins

A fair swashbuckler, with Douglas Fairbanks repeating his 1921 role as the noble swordsmith D'Artagnan in *The Three Musketeers*, and still done very much in the style of a silent picture. In fact, *The Iron Mask* was heavily touted as Fairbanks's first talkie, though the actor, who never really enjoyed an intimate relationship with a microphone, only spoke a brief prologue and an epilogue to appease the studio. In later years, film historians argued that Fairbanks himself had never used his own voice, citing as evidence the fact that his son, Douglas Fairbanks Jr, had revoiced the film for a 1940 re-issue.

Douglas Fairbanks *D'Artagnan* • Belle Bennett *The Queen Mother* • Marguerite De La Motte *Constance* • Dorothy Revier *Milady De Winter* • Vera Lewis *Mme Peronee* • Rolfe Sedan *Louis XIII* ■ *Dir* Allan Dwan • *Scr* Elton Thomas, from the novel *The Three Musketeers* by Alexandre Dumas, from the novel *The Viscount of Bragelonne* by Alexandre Dumas

Iron Maze ★★★ 15

Mystery thriller
1991 · US/Jap · Colour · 97mins

Jeff Fahey is a more talented actor than his largely straight-to-video career would indicate, and he gives one of his best performances in this moody, downbeat thriller. Fahey plays a blue-collar worker implicated in the attempted murder of a Japanese businessman bent on closing down a steelworks. The excellent JT Walsh is the sceptical cop investigating the crime, while Bridget Fonda is the interloper's American bride who may have been having an affair with Fahey. It's a little self-important for its own good, but director Hiroaki Yoshida accurately captures the bleakness of a small town dying. ▭

Jeff Fahey *Barry* • Bridget Fonda *Chris* • Hiroaki Murakami *Junichi Sugita* • JT Walsh *Jack Ruhle* • Gabriel Damon *Mikey* • John Randolph *Mayor Peluso* • Peter Allas *Eddie* ■ *Dir* Hiroaki Yoshida • *Scr* Tim Metcalfe, from the short story *In The Grove* by Ryunosuke Akutagawa, from a story by Hiroaki Yoshida

The Iron Mistress ★★★

Biographical drama
1952 · US · Colour · 108mins

Steely-eyed Alan Ladd stars as Jim Bowie, famed inventor of the knife (the "iron mistress" that bears his name), in this would-be rip-roaring Warner Bros adventure. Trouble is, the screenplay isn't as sharp as the knife itself, and there's a fair bit of romantic padding holding up the action, as Ladd gets rejected by Virginia Mayo only to fall for Phyllis Kirk en route to his destiny at the Alamo. There's a distinct run-of-the-mill feeling to the tale, but of course that won't matter to Ladd fans.

Alan Ladd *Jim Bowie* • Virginia Mayo *Judalon de Bornay* • Joseph Calleia *Juan Moreno* • Phyllis Kirk *Ursula de Veramendi* ■ *Dir* Gordon Douglas • *Scr* James R Webb, from a story by Paul I Wellman

The Iron Petticoat ★★★★ U
Romantic comedy
1956 · UK · Colour · 90mins
...it's what's under the Iron Curtain! There's a fabulous and unexpected chemistry between Katharine Hepburn as a Russian aviatrix and Bob Hope as an American serviceman that's a sheer joy to observe in this latter-day version of *Ninotchka*, filmed in England from a clever screenplay by Hollywood veteran Ben Hecht. A wonderful supporting cast excels under the direction of under-rated British great Ralph Thomas, and, with the Cold War long over, the attitudes expressed in this movie now seem hilarious for being so outdated. ▣
Katharine Hepburn *Vinka Kovelenko* • Bob Hope *Chuck Lockwood* • James Robertson-Justice *Colonel Sklarnoff* • Robert Helpmann *Ivan Kropotkin* • David Kossoff *Dr Dubratz* • Sidney James *Paul* ■ *Dir* Ralph Thomas • *Scr* Ben Hecht, from a story by Harry Saltzman

The Iron Sheriff ★★★ U
Western   1957 · US · BW · 73mins
Another in a number of minor but competent westerns that were raised by the presence of Sterling Hayden's rugged, blond looks in the mid- to late fifties. As a sheriff, Hayden sets out to prove that his son (Darryl Hickman) is innocent of robbery and murder, even though he has substantial evidence against him. What the film lacks in suspense, it makes up for in the playing and the intriguing moral dimension. Hickman made a brief movie comeback in *Network*.
Sterling Hayden *Sheriff Galt* • Constance Ford *Claire* • John Dehner *Pollock* • Kent Taylor *Quincy* • Darryl Hickman *Benjie* ■ *Dir* Sidney Salkow • *Scr* Seeleg Lester

The Iron Triangle ★★★ 18
War action adventure
1988 · US · Colour · 86mins
One of a handful of American films which attempt to present all sides of the Vietnam war as fully developed characters. Political arguments are also largely ignored since this is a war between people who kill each other, take each other prisoner, and sometimes find it hard to continue the killing. Narrator Beau Bridges plays an American captain who loathes the cruelty of his allies, the South Vietnamese, and is then taken prisoner; the Oscar-winner from *The Killing Fields*, Haing S Ngor, plays a North Vietnamese officer. ▣
Beau Bridges *Captain Keene* • Haing S Ngor *Captain Tuong* • Johnny Hallyday *Jacques* • James Ishida *Khoi* ■ *Dir* Eric Weston • *Scr* Eric Weston, John Bushelman, Larry Hilbrand

Iron Will ★★★ U
Adventure   1994 · US · Colour · 104mins
Disney drew on a true story for this cracking piece of family entertainment. Set in 1917, it stars MacKenzie Astin as the South Dakota teenager who enters the world's toughest dog-sled

marathon both to prevent the loss of the family farm following the death of his dad and to pay for his education. Naturally, all manner of dangers and disasters face him on the 522-mile trek from Canada to Minnesota, especially when just about every other competitor is a dyed-in-the-wool rogue. With action aplenty and a neat supporting turn from Kevin Spacey as a mythologising journalist, this should keep young and old amused. ▣
MacKenzie Astin *Will Stoneman* • Kevin Spacey *Harry Kingsley* • David Ogden Stiers *JP Harper* • August Schellenberg *Ned Dodd* • Brian Cox *Angus McTeague* ■ *Dir* Charles Haid • *Scr* John Michael Hayes, Djordje Milicevic, Jeff Arch

Ironweed ★★★ 15
Drama   1987 · US · Colour · 136mins
Like a famished carnivore, Jack Nicholson sinks his teeth into this meaty role as Depression-era alcoholic drifter Francis Phelan. He is haunted by memories of the events that led to his current state of degradation – most tragically the accidental death of his baby son. Bag-lady Meryl Streep sees hope in his survival, but Hector Babenco's film is a grim odyssey with only the strong performances of Oscar-nominees Nicholson and Streep to sustain it. ▣
Jack Nicholson *Francis Phelan* • Meryl Streep *Helen Archer* • Carroll Baker *Annie Phelan* • Michael O'Keefe *Billy Phelan* • Diane Venora *Peg Phelan* • Fred Gwynne *Oscar Reo* • Tom Waits *Rudy* ■ *Dir* Hector Babenco • *Scr* Wiliam Kennedy, from his novel

Irreconcilable Differences ★★★★ 15
Comedy drama   1984 · US · Colour · 108mins
A highly engaging comedy about the way success changes everything, written by the *Baby Boom* team of Charles Shyer (also making his directorial debut) and Nancy Meyers. Ryan O'Neal and Shelley Long star as the bright young couple who lose sight of what's important as they prosper in Tinseltown – so much so, their nine-year-old daughter sues them for divorce. Way ahead of its time and full of sharp Hollywood satire, the entire bittersweet story is told in flashback as witness-stand testimony. Movie buffs will especially love it, and watch for an early appearance by Sharon Stone as the gold-digger after O'Neal. Contains swearing and nudity. ▣
Ryan O'Neal *Albert Brodsky* • Shelley Long *Lucy Van Patten Brodsky* • Drew Barrymore *Casey Brodsky* • Sam Wanamaker *David Kessler* • Allen Garfield *Phil Hanner* • Sharon Stone *Blake Chandler* ■ *Dir* Charles Shyer • *Scr* Nancy Meyers, Charles Shyer

Irresistible Force ★★ 15
Police drama   1993 · US · Colour · 74mins
Cynthia Rothrock is the highest profile female martial arts star, but she has never looked like following colleagues such as Jean-Claude Van Damme into the mainstream. In this thriller about a gang of terrorists who take control of a shopping mall full of VIPs, she at least gets a better-than-average supporting cast, and the fight scenes will undoubtedly keep her fans happy. However, the plotting is strictly routine

and Rothrock herself sadly remains a charisma-free zone. ▣
Stacy Keach *Harris Stone* • Cynthia Rothrock *Charlotte "Charlie" Heller* • Paul Winfield *Commander Tooley* ■ *Dir* Kevin Hooks • *Scr* Carleton Eastlake

Is Paris Burning? ★★★
Second World War drama
1966 · US/Fr · BW · 165mins
"Is Paris burning?" asks Adolf Hitler as the French Resistance rattles the Nazi occupiers and prepares the city for liberation. Conceived on the same lines as *The Longest Day*, this multi-lingual war epic boasts an all-star cast and contains some spectacular scenes of fighting along the boulevards of the eponymous capital. Maurice Jarre's jangly music maintains the momentum, while Gore Vidal and Francis Ford Coppola were just two of the writers who laboured on the episodic script. A French/German/English language film.
Jean-Paul Belmondo *Morandat* • Yves Montand *Bizien* • Orson Welles *Nordling* • Charles Boyer *Monod* • Leslie Caron *Françoise Labe* • Jean-Pierre Cassel *Henri Karcher* • Alain Delon *Jacques Chaban-Delmas* • Kirk Douglas *Patton* • Glenn Ford *Bradley* • Robert Stack *Sibert* • Anthony Perkins *Warren* • Simone Signoret *Caféproprietress* ■ *Dir* René Clément • *Scr* Francis Ford Coppola, Gore Vidal, Jean Aurenche, Pierre Bost, Claude Brule, Marcel Moussy, Beate von Molo, from the book by Larry Collins, Dominique LaPierre • *Music* Maurice Jarre

Is There Sex after Death? ★★★
Comedy   1971 · US · Colour · 97mins
Mining a similar vein to the following year's Woody Allen film *Everything You Always Wanted to Know about Sex (but Were Afraid to Ask)* this was a series of skits, jokes and sketches, taking sex as their theme. Bawdier than the Allen movie, *Is There Sex after Death?* definitely deserved its R (Restricted) rating and would have been unmemorable if it wasn't for the wonderful performance by Buck Henry as Dr Manos, one of our guides to the weird and wonderful world of sex. This is an oddity worth seeking out for fans of vulgar and decidedly non-PC humour.
Buck Henry *Dr Manos* • Alan Abel *Dr Rogers* • Marshall Efron *Vince Domino* • Holly Woodlawn • Robert Downey Sr *Robert Downey* • Jim Moran *Dr Elevenike* • Rubin Carson ■ *Dir/Scr* Jeanne Abel, Alan Abel • *Editor* Jeanne Abel

Isaac Littlefeathers ★★
Drama   1984 · Can · Colour · 94mins
A strange one this: a half-Canadian Indian boy, deserted by his hockey-player father, is raised by a Jewish shopkeeper, and later discovers that his mixed heritage does not sit well with the neighbouring families. It's a "film with a message", the point being that we should love each other no matter what the differences are. Unfortunately that message is obscured by the melodramatic plot, which sees the feuding neighbours resorting to ludicrous acts like kidnapping and arson.

Lou Jacobi *Abe Kapp* • William Korbut *Isaac Littlefeathers* • Scott Hylands *Jesse Armstrong* • Lorraine Behnan *Golda Hersh* ■ *Dir* Les Rose • *Scr* Les Rose, Barry Pearson

Isadora ★★★★
Biographical drama
1968 · UK · Colour · 138mins
Vanessa Redgrave superbly and insolently scandalises as Isadora Duncan, the improvisational and influential dancer whose life and career helped jazz up an earlier Jazz Age. She moves from James Fox to Jason Robards to Ivan Tchenko before her bizarre death – a broken neck caused by her scarf becoming entangled in the wheel of a sports car. Director Karel Reisz uses Isadora's life to celebrate a free-and-speakeasy era. Redgrave was Oscar-nominated for best actress but lost out to Barbra Streisand.
Vanessa Redgrave *Isadora Duncan* • James Fox *Gordon Craig* • Jason Robards [Jason Robards Jr] *Paris Singer* • Ivan Tchenko *Sergei Essenin* • John Fraser *Roger* • Bessie Love *Mrs Duncan* ■ *Dir* Karel Reisz • *Scr* Melvyn Bragg, Clive Exton, from the autobiography *My Life* by Isadora Duncan, from the non-fiction book *Isadora Duncan: an Intimate Portrait* by Sewell Stokes

Ishtar ★ PG
Comedy   1987 · US · Colour · 102mins
Intended as a tribute to the Hope/Crosby *Road* movies, this has gone down in movie history as one of the grossest miscalculations of the blockbuster era. Even if you find it in yourself to accept the oddball casting of Warren Beatty and Dustin Hoffman as a couple of tone deaf songwriters, it's impossible to forgive the triteness and racial insensitivity of writer/director Elaine May's crass script. ▣
Warren Beatty *Lyle Rogers* • Dustin Hoffman *Chuck Clarke* • Isabelle Adjani *Shirra Assel* • Charles Grodin *Jim Harrison* • Jack Weston *Marty Freed* • Tess Harper *Willa* • Carol Kane *Carol* ■ *Dir/Scr* Elaine May

The Island ★★★★
Drama   1961 · Jap · BW · 96mins
Already an established figure within Japanese cinema, Kenji Mizoguchi's protégé, Kaneto Shindo, garnered international acclaim for this austere study of the struggle for survival of a family farming a wild, isolated island. Always willing to experiment with theme and form, Shindo eliminated speech from this intense drama, as if to suggest both the couple's intuitive unity of purpose and the unjustifiable expenditure of effort when all their energies were needed to work the intractable land and fetch fresh water from the mainland.
Nobuko Otowa *Toyo* • Taiji Tonoyama *Senta* • Shinji Tanaka *Taro* • Masanori Horimoto *Jiro* ■ *Dir/Scr* Kaneto Shindo • *Cinematographer* Kiyoshi Kuroda

The Island ★★ 18
Adventure   1980 · US · Colour · 108mins
This isn't so much a comedown as a plunge to the depths for Peter Benchley, the author of *Jaws*, who adapted this quite ridiculous picture from his own novel. It beggars belief that legendary composer Ennio Morricone, the usually dependable

Michael Caine and more than capable director Michael Ritchie frittered away their talents on this tale of 17th-century pirates caught in the Bermuda Triangle. It's not quite bad enough to be a bona fide turkey, but it's pretty awful all the same. 🎬

Michael Caine *Blair Maynard* • David Warner *Jean-David Nau* • Angela Punch McGregor *Beth* • Frank Middlemass *Dr Windsor* • Don Henderson *Rollo* • Dudley Sutton *Dr Brazil* • Colin Jeavons *Hizzoner* ■ *Dir* Michael Ritchie • *Scr* Peter Benchley, from his novel

Island ★★

Psychological drama
1989 · Ausl · Colour · 93mins
Dutch-born film-maker Paul Cox has emerged as a challenging Australian director, bringing a European slant to bear on a film industry primarily influenced by Hollywood. It's all the more disappointing, therefore, that this complex allegory, shot in Greece with an international cast, should fall so flat so often. Following the fortunes of three women on an island refuge, the film suffers from a pompous and paper-thin script, and a mishmash of acting styles that often makes it appear as if the characters are playing in completely different pictures. Contains swearing.

Eva Sitta *Eva* • Irene Papas *Marquise* • Anoja Weerasinghe *Sahana* • Chris Haywood *Janis* • Norman Kaye *Henry* ■ *Dir/Scr* Paul Cox

The Island at the Top of the World ★★★ U

Adventure   1974 · US · Colour · 89mins
You'd be forgiven for thinking this Disney adventure's source was Jules Verne (it is, in fact, based on a novel called *The Lost Ones* by Ian Cameron), but there's no question that this offering falls below the studio's usual high standards. However, the film is certainly not the unmitigated disaster that many critics considered it to be. Donald Sinden holds things together as an Edwardian explorer who sets out to rescue his son's Arctic expedition. Sinden's clash with a long lost Viking tribe stretches credibility to breaking point, but the effects are pretty fair for their day, with the voyage by airship nicely done. 🎬

Donald Sinden *Sir Anthony Ross* • David Hartman *Professor Ivarsson* • Jacques Marin *Captain Brieux* • Mako *Oomiak* • David Gwillim *Donald Ross* ■ *Dir* Robert Stevenson • *Scr* John Whedon, from the novel *The Lost Ones* by Ian Cameron

Island in the Sky ★★ U

Action adventure   1953 · US · BW · 109mins
One of the chilliest films ever made. John Wayne is the pilot of a transport plane that makes an emergency landing on a frozen lake. He keeps the crew in shape while they endure six days of waiting to be rescued. The realism of the photography is dissipated by the clichéd characters, but Wayne is suitably heroic. Director William A Wellman, writer Ernest K Gann, John Wayne and most of the technical crew went on to make another drama of a plane in trouble, *The High and the Mighty*, which was at least in warm colour.

John Wayne *Captain Dooley* • Lloyd Nolan *Stutz* • Walter Abel *Colonel Fuller* • James Arness *McMullen* ■ *Dir* William A Wellman • *Scr* Ernest K Gann, from his novel

Island in the Sun ★★

Drama   1957 · US/UK · Colour · 119mins
Daring and critically abused in its day, this exotic concoction was former Fox head Darryl F Zanuck's first film as an independent producer, and he spared no expense: classy cast, fabulous locations, top director in Robert Rossen, major source novel but, alas, not enough time or thought went into the script. It's daft-as-a-brush matinée tosh, really, but author Alec Waugh's tale of interracial sensuality deserved a more sensitive cinematic adaptation. Still, Harry Belafonte glowers at Joan Fontaine over a shared cocktail, James Mason goes suitably nuts as the crazed Maxwell Fleury, and Dorothy Dandridge and Joan Collins smoulder in the Caribbean heat.

James Mason *Maxwell Fleury* • Joan Fontaine *Mavis* • Joan Collins *Jocelyn* • Harry Belafonte *David Boyeur* • Dorothy Dandridge *Margot Seaton* ■ *Dir* Robert Rossen • *Scr* Alfred Hayes, from the novel by Alec Waugh

The Island of Dr Moreau ★★★ 15

Science-fiction horror
1977 · US · Colour · 94mins
HG Wells's story about a mad scientist living on a remote island was filmed in 1932 with Charles Laughton as *Island of Lost Souls* and in 1996 with Marlon Brando. This first remake stars Burt Lancaster as the lunatic who thinks he's sane, conducting genetic experiments for the sake of mankind. Michael York shows up, unwisely, as does Barbara Carrera and Lancaster's acrobatic sidekick from the fifties, Nick Cravat. While never trying to be a classic, it's still a ripping yarn with a moral gloss and Lancaster's taciturn evil is often frightening. Contains brief nudity. 🎬

Burt Lancaster *Dr Moreau* • Michael York *Andrew Braddock* • Nigel Davenport *Montgomery* • Barbara Carrera *Maria* • Richard Basehart *Sayer of the law* • Nick Cravat *M'ling* • John Gillespie *Tigerman* ■ *Dir* Don Taylor • *Scr* John Herman Shaner, Al Ramrus, from the novel by HG Wells

The Island of Dr Moreau ★ 12

Science-fiction horror
1996 · US · Colour · 91mins
The third, and worst, version of the HG Wells classic fantasy about mad Doctor Moreau (Marlon Brando) genetically reshaping the animal kingdom to form a new species of man in a remote tropical paradise. Badly miscast – David Thewlis, Val Kilmer and Brando all give lousy performances – and hopelessly directed by John Frankenheimer (who stepped in four days after writer Richard Stanley was fired), this jungle jumble is a horrible miscalculation from start to finish. Brando's Popemobile-style entrance and Stan Winston's hokey creature effects are just two of the laughter-inducing embarrassments contained in this pretentious terror turkey. 🎬

Marlon Brando *Dr Moreau* • Val Kilmer *Montgomery* • David Thewlis *Edward Douglas* • Fairuza Balk *Aissa Moreau* • Daniel Rigney *Hyena-Swine* • Temuera Morrison *Azazello* ■ *Dir* John Frankenheimer • *Scr* Richard Stanley, Ron Hutchinson, from the novel by HG Wells

Island of Lost Souls ★★★★★ 12

Science-fiction horror
1932 · US · BW · 67mins
Banned in Britain for 21 years, the first, and best, version of HG Wells's provocative fantasy *The Island of Dr Moreau* is one of the best chillers ever made. Few horror films have as many terrifying facets or the harsh maturity of director Erle C Kenton. It's the uncompromising tale of doctor Charles Laughton grafting animals on to men in his tropical House of Pain to change evolution. Shot on beautiful sets, adding enormous atmospheric gloominess to the quite shocking and repellent imagery, Laughton turns in a memorably sadistic performance as the scarily mad scientist. Equally unforgettable is Bela Lugosi as the Sayer of the Law: "What is the law – are we not men!!''.

Robert Kortman *Hogan* • Alan Ladd *Ape man* • Randolph Scott *Ape man* • Larry "Buster" Crabbe *Ape man* • Joe Bonomo *Ape man* • Charles Laughton *Dr Moreau* • Richard Arlen *Edward Parker* • Leila Hyams *Ruth Walker* • Bela Lugosi *Sayer of the Law* • Kathleen Burke *Lota, the panther woman* ■ *Dir* Erle C Kenton • *Scr* Philip Wylie, Waldemar Young, from the novel *The Island of Dr Moreau* by HG Wells • *Cinematographer* Karl Struss

Island of Love ★★ U

Comedy   1963 · US · Colour · 100mins
This smutty and unfunny comedy was a non-starter from the word go, squandering the talents of Tony Randall and Walter Matthau, and leaving Warner Bros with egg on its face. It was a limp conclusion to a three-picture deal with the studio for stage director Morton DaCosta, who had brilliantly transferred *Auntie Mame* and *The Music Man* from stage to screen. Robert Preston gave a great performance as a confidence trickster in *The Music Man*, and he's a con artist here, too, but this time he's without good material.

Robert Preston *Steve Blair* • Tony Randall *Paul Ferris* • Georgia Moll [Giorgia Moll] *Elena Harakas* • Walter Matthau *Tony Dallas* • Betty Bruce *Cha Cha Miller* ■ *Dir* Morton Da Costa • *Scr* David R Schwartz, from a story by Leo Katcher

Island of Terror ★★ PG

Science-fiction horror
1966 · UK · Colour · 83mins
Bone marrow-sucking monsters are the by-product of cancer-cure research in this long-on-logic but high-on-hysteria chiller cheapie, directed by the ever-efficient Terence Fisher on a busman's holiday from Hammer Studios. Making the most of the isolated Irish setting and infusing the colourful carnage with a neat line in macabre humour (scientist Peter Cushing mutilating his own body to save himself, for instance), it's a reasonably tense offering, with the tentacled silicate creatures more fun than most of their B-feature sci-fi ilk. 🎬

Peter Cushing *Dr Stanley* • Edward Judd *Dr David West* • Carole Gray *Toni Merrill* • Eddie Byrne *Dr Landers* • Sam Kydd *Constable Harris* ■ *Dir* Terence Fisher • *Scr* Edward Andrew Mann, Alan Ramsen

Island of the Blue Dolphins ★★★ U

Drama   1964 · US · Colour · 99mins
A Disney-style children's film about a native American girl forced to leave her home on an island off the California coast, after her father is murdered by white trappers. She goes back to save her brother but, when he falls prey to wild animals, she is left alone there with just a wild dog for company. Despite some weaknesses, this is well above average for its type and has hints of *Nanook of the North* and *Tabu*.

Celia Kaye *Karana* • Larry Domasin *Ramo* • Ann Daniel *Tutok* • George Kennedy *Aleut captain* ■ *Dir* James B Clark • *Scr* Ted Sherdeman, Jane Klove, Robert B Radnitz, from the novel by Scott O'Dell

Islands in the Stream ★★★

Drama   1977 · US · Colour · 115mins
With his grey beard, gravelly voice and perpetual squint, George C Scott is ideally cast and riveting to watch as the grizzled fisherman and sculptor who prefers to sit out the Second World War in the Bahamas. Based on Ernest Hemingway's posthumously published novel, this story of a curmudgeonly father who has a troubled relationship with his wife (Claire Bloom) and three sons is rather self-important. But the scenery is pretty to look at, and Jerry Goldsmith's score is one of his very best.

George C Scott *Thomas Hudson* • David Hemmings *Eddy* • Gilbert Roland *Captain Ralph* • Susan Tyrrell *Lil* • Richard Evans *Willy* • Claire Bloom *Audrey* ■ *Dir* Franklin J Schaffner • *Scr* Denne Bart Petitclerc, from the novel by Ernest Hemingway

Isle of Fury ★★

Adventure drama   1936 · US · BW · 60mins
As an established star, Humphrey Bogart tended to gloss over his appearance in films. Admittedly this adaptation of W Somerset Maugham's novel *The Narrow Corner* isn't one of his image-making roles but it's not that bad either. Bogart is the fugitive who marries Margaret Lindsay and tries to start a new life on a South Seas island. Trouble arrives in the shape of detective Donald Woods who's come to track down Bogart and takes an unhealthy interest in his wife.

Humphrey Bogart *Val Stevens* • Margaret Lindsay *Lucille Gordon* • Donald Woods *Eric Blake* • EE Clive *Dr Hardy* • Paul Graetz *Capt Deever* ■ *Dir* Frank McDonald • *Scr* Robert Andrews, William Jacobs, from the novel *The Narrow Corner* by W Somerset Maugham

Isle of the Dead ★★★ 15

Horror   1945 · US · BW · 68mins
Quarantined on a Greek island during the 1912 Balkan war, General Nikolas Pherides (Boris Karloff) is convinced the group he's looking after will succumb to the "vrykolaka", an ancient vitality-draining vampire. Director Mark Robson's film is creepy and claustrophobic, while intelligently

U = SUITABLE FOR ALL   Ua = SUITABLE FOR ALL, ESPECIALLY FOR YOUNG CHILDREN (VIDEO ONLY)   PG = PARENTAL GUIDANCE

raising issues about modern ideals versus pagan superstition. Karloff and a tough-talking Katherine Emery are both outstanding in this intense and imaginative miniature – another minor gem from cult producer Val Lewton's fright factory. 🎞️

Boris Karloff *General Ferides* • Ellen Drew *Thea* • Marc Cramer *Oliver* • Katherine Emery *Mrs St Aubyn* • Jason Robards *Albrecht* ■ Dir Mark Robson • Scr Ardel Wray, Josef Mischel (uncredited), inspired by the painting *The Isle of the Dead* by Arnold Boecklin

Isn't It Romantic ★★ U

Period comedy drama
1948 · US · BW · 72mins

Hearts are set a-flutter in the household of ex-Civil War officer Roland Culver, the father of three daughters (Veronica Lake, Mona Freeman, Mary Hatcher) when handsome smoothie Patric Knowles turns up on the doorstep, causing Veronica to jilt fiancé Billy De Wolfe. The most memorable thing about this innocuous semi-musical is the durable Rodgers and Hart title song. Lake, her famous "peek-a-boo" hairstyle necessarily abandoned for the period, was making her last appearance under her seven-year Paramount contract.

Veronica Lake *Candy* • Mona Freeman *Susie* • Mary Hatcher *Rose* • Billy De Wolfe *Horace Frazier* • Roland Culver *Major Euclid Cameron* • Patric Knowles *Richard "Rick" Brannon* ■ Dir Norman Z McLeod • Scr Josef Mischel, Richard L Breen, from the novel *Gather Ye Rosebuds* by Jeannette Covert Nolan

Isn't It Shocking? ★★★★

Black comedy thriller
1973 · US · Colour · 73mins

Made just a year after he started playing Hawkeye in *M*A*S*H*, this unconventional thriller was something of a change of pace for Alan Alda. That's not to say there isn't a vein of dark humour running throughout Lane Slate's teleplay, but there's little time for wisecracks as Alda's New England sheriff investigates the suspicious deaths of several elderly residents. With wonderfully eccentric support from Louise Lasser and Ruth Gordon, this is as much a study in small-town manners as it is a whodunit.

Alan Alda *Sheriff Dan Barnes* • Louise Lasser *Blanche* • Edmond O'Brien *Justin Oates* • Ruth Gordon *Marge Savage* • Will Geer *Dr Lemuel Lovell* • Dorothy Tristan *Doc Lovell* ■ Dir John Badham • Scr Lane Slate

Isn't Life Wonderful ★★★

Silent romantic drama
1924 · US · BW · 90mins

Even with a phoney happy ending, the world wasn't interested in seeing a downbeat film that portrayed the wretched hunger and poverty of ordinary people in Germany after the First World War. Master film-maker DW Griffith lost his independence as a result of its failure, but it is a striking picture, shot on location in Germany with many local inhabitants as extras. Carol Dempster stars as a Polish refugee and Neil Hamilton is her lover, a soldier who returns ill from the front.

Carol Dempster *Inga* • Neil Hamilton *Paul* • Helen Lowell *Grandmother* • Erville Alderson

Professor • Frank Puglia *Theodor* ■ Dir DW Griffith • Scr DW Griffith, from the short story *Isn't Life Wonderful!* by Maj Geoffrey Moss

Isn't Life Wonderful! ★★ U

Comedy
1952 · UK · Colour · 83mins

If your image of Donald Wolfit is all bluster and eyebrows, you won't recognise him in this whimsical comedy based on the once popular novel *Uncle Willie and the Bicycle Shop*. There's something of the Clarence Day memoir *Life with Father* about this unremarkable period piece, as Cecil Parker presides over the antics of his underachieving kin. However, his grouchy snobbery quickly wears thin and there's precious little about his whimpering son Peter Asher, hopeless nephew Robert Urquhart or tipsy brother-in-law Wolfit to make us take their side.

Cecil Parker *Father* • Donald Wolfit *Uncle Willie* • Eileen Herlie *Mother* • Peter Asher *Charles* • Eleanor Summerfield *Aunt Kate* • Dianne Foster *Virginia* ■ Dir Harold French • Scr Brock Williams, from his novel *Uncle Willie and the Bicycle Shop*

Isn't She Great ★★ 15

Biographical comedy
1999 · US · Colour · 95mins

No she isn't! The incredible life of Jacqueline Susann, late author of the landmark bestseller *Valley of the Dolls*, gets short shrift in a trashy biography that reduces her achievements and personal tragedies to mere rags-to-riches anecdotes. Played by Bette Midler with one eye on theatrical mugging and the other on her hardcore gay audience, Susann goes from lousy actress to celebrity writer thanks to the undying devotion of her press agent husband, Irving Mansfield (a miscast Nathan Lane). Aside from the neat period detail, outrageous outfits and camp support from Stockard Channing, director Andrew Bergman's strangely affected showbiz saga veers from vapid farce to stale banality.

Bette Midler *Jacqueline Susann* • Nathan Lane *Irving Mansfield* • Stockard Channing *Florence Maybelle* • David Hyde Pierce *Michael Hastings* • John Cleese *Henry Marcus* • Sarah Jessica Parker *Tira Gropman* ■ Dir Andrew Bergman • Scr Paul Rudnick, from the article *Wasn't She Great* by Michael Korda • Music Burt Bacharach

Istanbul ★★ U

Adventure drama 1957 · US · Colour · 84mins

Not even Errol Flynn's presence can redeem this adventure drama, a remake of the Fred MacMurray/Ava Gardner movie *Singapore* (1947). Flynn plays a rover who returns to the eponymous city to recover some loot, only to find that his wife has lost both her memory and the sought-after gems. Flynn described this later as "just one of those things", though at least we get Nat King Cole singing *When I Fall in Love*.

Errol Flynn *Jim Brennan* • Cornell Borchers *Stephanie Bauer/Karen Fielding* • John Bentley *Inspector Nural* • Torin Thatcher *Douglas Fielding* • Leif Erickson *Charlie Boyle* • Peggy Knudsen *Marge Boyle* • Nat King Cole *Danny Rice* ■ Dir Joseph Pevney • Scr Seton I Miller, Barbara Gray, Richard Alan Simmons, from a story by Seton I Miller

Istanbul Express ★ U

Spy adventure 1968 · US · Colour · 93mins

Gene Barry, then famous as the star of the TV series *Burke's Law*, plays a secret agent who goes to Paris, boards the *Orient Express* to Venice and Istanbul and... well, hasn't he seen *From Russia with Love*? The plot and the performances are just as phoney as the dismal travelogue footage back-projected on to every scene.

Gene Barry *David London* • John Saxon *Cheval* • Senta Berger *Mila Darvos* • Tom Simcox *Leland McCord* • Mary Ann Mobley *Peggy Coopersmith* ■ Dir Richard Irving • Scr Richard Levinson, William Link

It ★★★ U

Silent comedy drama
1927 · US · BW · 76mins

Clara Bow became a major star as the "It Girl" in this delightful romantic comedy of the flapper age, directed by Clarence Badger (although Josef von Sternberg filled in while Badger was ill). "It" was a quality devised by the novelist Elinor Glyn that had most to do with sex appeal, which Bow had in abundance as part of her strikingly uninhibited acting style. The story is mild: Clara's the store clerk who makes a play for her boss, Antonio Moreno, because he has "it", but there is a striking subplot when she's suspected of being an unmarried mother. Handsome newcomer Gary Cooper can be seen in a bit role as a newspaper reporter. 🎞️

Clara Bow *Betty Lou* • Antonio Moreno *Cyrus Waltham* • William Austin *Monty* • Gary Cooper *Newspaper reporter* • Elinor Glyn ■ Dir Clarence Badger • Scr Hope Loring, Louis D Lighton, Elinor Glyn, from the story by Elinor Glyn

It Ain't Hay ★★ U

Comedy 1943 · US · BW · 80mins

Damon Runyon's short story *Princess O'Hara* provided the basis for this Abbott and Costello comedy. Runyon, the great comic chronicler of show people, gossip columnists and gangsters, used a unique twisted vernacular in his writing, and such idiosyncrasies have always proved difficult to translate to the screen. This time Bud and Lou must find a replacement race horse after a candy snack has fatal consequences. Originally made in 1935 (as *Princess O'Hara*) as a vehicle for veteran comedian Leon Errol.

Bud Abbott *Grover Mockridge* • Lou Costello *Wilbur Hoolihan* • Grace McDonald *Kitty McGloin* • Cecil Kellaway *King O'Hara* • Eugene Pallette *Gregory Warner* • Patsy O'Connor *Peggy, Princess O'Hara* ■ Dir Erle C Kenton • Scr Allen Boretz, John Grant, from the short story *Princess O'Hara* by Damon Runyon

It All Came True ★★★

Musical comedy 1940 · US · BW · 96mins

Why gangster Humphrey Bogart is hiding out in a boarding house whose tenants consist totally of hand-picked eccentric character actors is neither here nor there: the following year he would hit his stardom stride with *High Sierra* and *The Maltese Falcon*, and there would be no looking back. Top-billed over Bogie, and rightly so, is the

simply magnificent Ann Sheridan. She just picks up this movie, rolls it up under her arms, while chanting such ditties as *The Gaucho Serenade* and *Angel in Disguise*.

Ann Sheridan *Sarah Jane Ryan* • Jeffrey Lynn *Tommy Taylor* • Humphrey Bogart *Grasselli (Chips Maguire)* • ZaSu Pitts *Miss Flint* • Una O'Connor *Maggie Ryan* • Jessie Busley *Mrs Nora Taylor* • John Litel *Mr Roberts* ■ Dir Lewis Seiler • Scr Michael Fessier, Lawrence Kimble, from the *Hearst's International-Cosmopolitan* short story *Better than Life* by Louis Bromfield

It All Starts Today ★★★★ 12

Drama 1999 · Fr · Colour · 118mins

The winner of the international critics prize at Berlin, this film recalls the fluid starkness of Bertrand Tavernier's police thriller *L.627*, as the camera restlessly prowls headmaster Philippe Torreton's school to witness how his staff make light of financial constraints to fascinate and protect their pupils. Whether challenging an abusive "uncle", encouraging youngsters or lambasting the mayor, Torreton is outstanding in his energy and insight. Apart from the disappointingly cosy and optimistic conclusion, this is social drama at its best. In French with English subtitles.

Philippe Torreton *Daniel Lefebvre* • Maria Pitarresi *Valéria* • Nadia Kaci *Samia Damouni* • Véronique Ataly *Madame Liénard* ■ Dir Bertrand Tavernier • Scr Dominique Sampiero, Tiffany Tavernier, Bertrand Tavernier

It Always Rains on Sunday ★★★

Crime drama 1947 · US · BW · 91mins

One of Ealing Studio's more successful non-comedies, this fine adaptation of Arthur La Bern's novel offers the attraction of a series of well-known character actors in a saga of interconnecting lives. Set against a drab city locale, brilliantly re-created in the studio. Top-billed Googie Withers is particularly outstanding as the ex-lover of convict John McCallum (they got married a year later in real life!), and the depiction of East End life is well delineated by faces like Sydney Tafler and John Slater. Generally recognised today as a breakthrough movie in the portrayal of the English working class on screen, much of the credit should go to clever director and co-writer Robert Hamer, better known for directing Ealing's one undisputed masterpiece, *Kind Hearts and Coronets*.

Googie Withers *Rose Sandigate* • Edward Chapman *George Sandigate* • Susan Shaw *Vi Sandigate* • John McCallum *Tommy Swann* • Patricia Plunkett *Doris Sandigate* • Sydney Tafler *Morry Hyams* • John Slater *Lou Hyams* ■ Dir Robert Hamer • Scr Angus MacPhail, Robert Hamer, Henry Cornelius, from the novel by Arthur La Bern

It Came from beneath the Sea ★★★ U

Science-fiction adventure
1955 · US · BW · 75mins

Careless atomic testing spawns a giant octopus in this classic monster flick, which includes stop-motion special effects from the great Ray

Harryhausen. But radiation wasn't the cause of the suction-cup horror having a shortage of titanic tentacles – the ridiculously low budget saw to that! As the killer calamari rampages through San Francisco to destroy the Golden Gate bridge, B-movie star Kenneth Tobey still finds time to battle biologist Donald Curtis for vampy Faith Domergue's charms. Predictable tosh, but good fifties fun. ▣

Kenneth Tobey *Pete Mathews* • Faith Domergue *Lesley Joyce* • Ian Keith *Admiral Burns* • Donald Curtis *John Carter* • Dean Maddox Jr *Adam Norman* ■ *Dir* Robert Gordon • *Scr* George Worthing Yates, Hal Smith, from a story by George Worthing Yates

It Came from Outer Space
★★★★ PG

Science-fiction drama
1953 · US · BW · 76mins
Based on Ray Bradbury's short story *The Meteor*, this early 3-D classic was the first of many brilliant sci-fi films from director Jack Arnold, who went on to make *Tarantula* and *The Incredible Shrinking Man*. An alien spaceship lands in the Arizona desert, and its giant-eyed occupants adopt human identities while they repair their vessel. Astronomer Richard Carlson sees it happen, but no one believes him. Top heavy on eerie atmosphere and incorporating a neat plea for interracial tolerance, Arnold's tale uses stylish flourishes – including a fish-eye lens to simulate the aliens' point-of-view – resulting in a film that's as good as fifties science fiction gets. ▣

Richard Carlson *John Putnam* • Barbara Rush *Ellen Fields* • Charles Drake *Sheriff Matt Warren* • Russell Johnson *George* ■ *Dir* Jack Arnold • *Scr* Harry Essex, from the short story *The Meteor* by Ray Bradbury

It Came from Outer Space II
★ PG

Science-fiction drama
1996 · US · Colour · 84mins
This lacklustre update of Jack Arnold's 1953 classic has Brian Kerwin witnessing the arrival of the aliens while on a desert photo assignment. It is not too long before the blue rocks scattered from the spacecraft are causing havoc in the local community, where the townsfolk are being replicated by aliens. Just to add to the fun, the temperatures are soaring and the water supply is disappearing. Proof positive that 40 years of technical advances can't compensate for poor production values, boring characters and a complete lack of thrills. File this under "don't bother". ▣

Brian Kerwin *Jack Putnam* • Elizabeth Pena *Ellen Fields* • Jonathan Carrasco *Stevie Fields* • Bill McKinney *Roy Minter* • Adrian Sparks *Alan Paxson* • Howard Morris *Ben Cully* • Mickey Jones *Chance Madison* • Lauren Tewes *Carolee Minter* ■ *Dir* Roger Duchowny • *Scr* Jim Wheat, Ken Wheat, from the film *It Came from Outer Space* by Harry Essex, from the short story *The Meteor* by Ray Bradbury

It Conquered the World ★ PG

Science-fiction drama
1956 · US · BW · 68mins
Monster flicks never come dafter than this. Get ready to scream with laughter as a gravitationally challenged, fanged

carrot from Venus crawls around the Los Angeles countryside like a snail on valium. It clearly couldn't conquer the world even if It tried! Hence It prepares to turn us dumb earthlings into zombie slaves with the aid of what are supposed to be electronic bat-mites but which more closely resemble drunken boomerangs. One of quickie director Roger Corman's all-time worst films, yet cult fans will enjoy it for exactly that reason. ▣

Peter Graves (1) *Paul Nelson* • Beverly Garland *Claire Anderson* • Lee Van Cleef *Tom Anderson* • Sally Fraser *Joan Nelson* ■ *Dir* Roger Corman • *Scr* Lou Rusoff

It Could Happen to You
★★★ PG

Romantic comedy based on a true story
1994 · US · Colour · 97mins
With a title and a scenario worthy of Frank Capra, this cosy little romantic comedy is, incredibly, based on a true story. Nicolas Cage (reuniting with his *Honeymoon in Vegas* director, Andrew Bergman) plays a good-hearted cop. Rosie Perez also gives one of her usual performances, shrieking the place down as she discovers hubby Cage has divided his lottery winnings with waitress Bridget Fonda. But this is a case of familiarity breeding content, as both Cage and Perez are on top form, as is the fetchingly shy Fonda. Charming and disarming. Contains some swearing. ▣ DVD

Nicolas Cage *Charlie Lang* • Bridget Fonda *Yvonne Biasi* • Rosie Perez *Muriel Lang* • Wendell Pierce *Bo Williams* • Isaac Hayes *Angel* • Red Buttons *Zakuto* ■ *Dir* Andrew Bergman • *Scr* Jane Anderson

It Grows on Trees ★★ U

Fantasy comedy   1952 · US · BW · 84mins
Ditzy suburban housewife Irene Dunne, married to Dean Jagger, finds that two trees she had planted in her garden are sprouting dollar bills. The Treasury Department pronounces the money legal tender, and she embarks on a massive spending spree, only to discover that the bank notes, like leaves, fade and die. A whimsical and repetitive little fable, that falls somewhere between a feel-good movie and a simplistic moral tale. It was an unworthy final film for Dunne, one of the screen's most gracious, well-loved and versatile of leading ladies during the thirties and forties, who went into retirement after this.

Irene Dunne *Polly Baxter* • Dean Jagger *Phil Baxter* • Joan Evans *Diane Baxter* • Richard Crenna *Ralph Bowen* • Edith Meiser *Mrs Pryor* • Sandy Descher *Midge Baxter* ■ *Dir* Arthur Lubin • *Scr* Leonard Praskins, Barney Slater

It Happened at the World's Fair
★★★ PG

Musical   1962 · US · Colour · 100mins
A lightweight but enjoyable Elvis film, made in the wake of *Blue Hawaii's* box-office tidal wave. Here Elvis gets involved with a Chinese child, romances nurse Joan O'Brien and gets kicked in the shins by little Kurt Russell, who would grow up to portray Elvis himself on screen in the biopic *Elvis the Movie*. And all this against the colourful background of the Seattle World's Fair. Elvis's big song from this

film, *One Broken Heart for Sale*, was one of the few Presley singles not to reach the top ten, indicating that, although the talent was still strong, the fans weren't buying. ▣

Elvis Presley *Mike Edwards* • Joan O'Brien *Diane Warren* • Gary Lockwood *Danny Burke* • Vicky Tiu *Sue-lin* • Kurt Russell ■ *Dir* Norman Taurog • *Scr* Si Rose, Seaman Jacobs

It Happened Here ★★★★ PG

Drama   1963 · UK · BW · 96mins
A fascinating speculation on what might have happened if Hitler had successfully invaded Britain. It is also one of the most heroic films ever made, begun by teenagers Kevin Brownlow and Andrew Mollo in 1956 as a hobby. There are major flaws, naturally, mainly in the performances and the often naive writing, but forgive them. Instead, marvel at the provocative sight of the Third Reich goose-stepping down Whitehall and chill to the fascist overthrow of Little England. ▣

Pauline Murray *Pauline* • Sebastian Shaw *Dr Richard Fletcher* • Fiona Leland *Helen Fletcher* • Honor Fehrson *Honor Hutton* • Percy Binns *Immediate Action Commandant* ■ *Dir* Kevin Brownlow, Andrew Mollo • *Scr* Kevin Brownlow, Andrew Mollo, from an idea by Kevin Brownlow

It Happened in Brooklyn
★★★ U

Musical   1947 · US · BW · 102mins
It happened to Frank Sinatra and Kathryn Grayson, reunited after *Anchors Aweigh* in as lightweight a piece of fluff as you're ever likely to see. The great Jimmy Durante virtually stops the show in a fabulous duet with Sinatra called *The Song's Gotta Come from the Heart*. The piano work is that of a very young André Previn, and Gloria Grahame's in there, too. All that was really needed was a decent director and Technicolor, but MGM was on one of its economy drives. As it is, it's just a jolly little musical movie.

Frank Sinatra *Danny Webson Miller* • Kathryn Grayson *Anne Fielding* • Jimmy Durante *Nick Lombardi* • Peter Lawford *Jamie Shellgrove* • Gloria Grahame *Nurse* ■ *Dir* Richard Whorf • *Scr* Isobel Lennart, from a story by John McGowan

It Happened in Rome ★★ U

Comedy   1956 · It · Colour · 95mins
Well, actually, some of it happened in Venice and Florence as well. The trouble is, none of it is particularly interesting or original, as June Laverick, Isabelle Corey and Ingeborg Schoener city-hop in the hope of romance and adventure. The only truly significant feature of this tepid tourist advert is that it was co-written by the famous partnership of Age and Scarpelli, who penned some of the best films made by art-house directors Mario Monicelli and Ettore Scola.

June Laverick *Margaret* • Isabelle Corey *Josette* • Ingeborg Schoener *Hilde* • Vittorio De Sica *The Count* • Isabel Jeans *Cynthia* • Massimo Girotti *Ugo Parenti* ■ *Dir* Antonio Pietrangeli • *Scr* Dario Fo, Antonio Pietrangeli

It Happened on Fifth Avenue
★★

Musical comedy   1947 · US · BW · 114mins
Not a lot happens, in actual fact, in this interminably long and rather juvenile comedy that requires the same staying power as watching paint dry. Take one glib talking tramp, a bevy of his friends and an empty New York mansion in which they all decide to play toffs until they are rumbled, with a galaxy of performances ranging from the merely banal to the downright execrable. This is death by whimsy.

Don DeFore *Jim Bullock* • Gale Storm *Trudy O'Connor* • Charlie Ruggles [Charles Ruggles] *Michael O'Connor* • Victor Moore *McKeever* ■ *Dir* Roy Del Ruth • *Scr* Everett Freeman, Vick Knight, from a story by Herbert Clyde Lewis, Frederick Stephani

It Happened One Night
★★★★★ U

Romantic comedy   1934 · US · BW · 100mins
It started out as a minor film called *Night Bus* and MGM decided to punish its errant star Clark Gable by sending him over to Columbia to play the reporter. And what happened? As classy and charming a romantic comedy as you're ever likely to see, winning Oscars in all key departments – best film, director, stars, screenplay – thanks to whizkid director Frank Capra and a marvellous foil to Gable in leading lady Claudette Colbert. Incidentally, Gable changed American fashion overnight in the scene where he strips off his shirt and reveals that he's not wearing a vest! The scene where runaway heiress Colbert hitches a lift and the infamous "Walls of Jericho" bedroom sequence have great charm, and confirm this stand-out movie's claims to classic status. ▣

Claudette Colbert *Ellie Andrews* • Clark Gable *Peter Warne* • Roscoe Karns *Oscar Shapeley* • Henry Wadsworth *Drunk boy* • Claire McDowell *Mother* • Walter Connolly *Alexander Andrews* • Alan Hale *Danker* ■ *Dir* Frank Capra • *Scr* Robert Riskin, from the story *Night Bus* by Samuel Hopkins Adams

It Happened to Jane ★★★ U

Comedy   1959 · US · Colour · 97mins
This bright and breezy comedy from the quirky, witty and under-rated director Richard Quine stars Doris Day as the "Jane from Maine" who becomes a national heroine when she sues Ernie Kovacs's grasping railroad boss for putting her lobster farm at risk. Jack Lemmon is on hand as Day's feckless lawyer, but the movie is stolen by Kovacs, whose performance, with hindsight, is clearly a caricature of legendary Columbia Studios head, Harry Cohn. (Did he get the joke?)

Doris Day *Jane Osgood* • Jack Lemmon *George Denham* • Ernie Kovacs *Harry Foster Malone* • Steve Forrest *Larry Hall* • Teddy Rooney *Billy Osgood* • Russ Brown *Uncle Otis* ■ *Dir* Richard Quine • *Scr* Norman Katkov, from a story by Max Wilk, Norman Katkov

It Happened Tomorrow
★★★★

Fantasy drama   1944 · US · BW · 85mins
A clever and very enjoyable fantasy, with a difficult theme handled expertly

by French émigré director René Clair, who had demonstrated his understanding of American whimsy two years earlier with *I Married a Witch*. Reporter Dick Powell finds his career taking off when he's given the scoop on tomorrow's news – before it actually happens. Set in the 1890s, the strong cast includes veteran Jack Oakie as a mind-reader and Linda Darnell as Powell's girlfriend. The movie was Oscar-nominated for its score.

Dick Powell *Larry Stevens* • Linda Darnell *Sylvia* • Jack Oakie *Cigolini* • Edgar Kennedy *Inspector Mulrooney* • John Philliber *Pop Benson* • Edward Brophy *Jake Schomberg* ■ *Dir* René Clair, Music Director Robert Stolz

It Happens Every Spring ★★★ U

Sports comedy   1949 · US · BW · 81mins

An original (if blinkered) little comedy about chemistry professor Ray Milland inventing a substance that causes baseballs to veer away from the bats. Obviously, he then gives up the distinguished groves of academe to become a star pitcher. This daffy nonsense is endearingly played by Milland and co-stars Jean Peters and Paul Douglas. The inventive screenplay is by Valentine Davies, who had just won an Oscar for his original story *Miracle on 34th Street*.

Ray Milland *Vernon Simpson* • Jean Peters *Deborah Greenleaf* • Paul Douglas *Monk Lanigan* • Ed Begley *Stone* • Ted De Corsia *Dolan* ■ *Dir* Lloyd Bacon • *Scr* Valentine Davies, from a story by Valentine Davies, from the short story *The Sprightly Adventures of Instructor Simpson* by Shirley W Smith

It Lives Again ★★★ 15

Horror   1978 · US · Colour · 86mins

Director Larry Cohen's sequel to his own cult classic *It's Alive* doesn't quite hit the same subversive targets as a forceful indictment of society's misuse of atomic power and drugs, but as a gory action thriller it certainly delivers. Frederic Forrest and Kathleen Lloyd are the expectant parents who get a shock when their offspring turns out to be a fanged and clawed mutant terror tot. The mayhem takes an even weirder turn when the infant joins up with two other pint-sized baby-faced killers to wreak murderous havoc after their hide-out is discovered. Hardly subtle, but played with a winning conviction well above the call of duty. [video]

Frederic Forrest *Eugene Scott* • Kathleen Lloyd *Jody Scott* • John P Ryan *Frank Davis* • John Marley *Mallory* • Andrew Duggan *Dr Perry* • Eddie Constantine *Dr Forrest* • James Dixon *Detective Perkins* ■ *Dir/Scr* Larry Cohen

It Rains on Our Love ★★★

Romantic crime drama
1946 · Swe · BW · 95mins

Following the poor reception of *Crisis*, Ingmar Bergman turned independent for this adaptation of a play by Norwegian Oskar Braaten. Shades of Vigo and the French poetic realists colour this simple story, in which ex-jailbird Birger Malmsten and actress-turned-prostitute Barbro Kollberg

receive a little help from umbrella-wielding fairy godfather Gosta Cederlund in their battle against the caprices of a hypocritical, bureaucratic society. The action is never allowed to lapse into cheap melodrama and Bergman even manages to end on a note of unforced optimism. In Swedish with English subtitles.

Barbro Kollberg *Maggi* • Birger Malmsten *David* • Gosta Cederlund *Gentleman with umbrella* • Julia Caesar *Mrs Ledin* • Gunnar Björnstrand ■ *Dir* Ingmar Bergman • *Scr* Herbert Grevenius, Ingmar Bergman

It Should Happen to You ★★★★ U

Comedy   1954 · US · BW · 83mins

Two inimitable personalities and talents, *Born Yesterday's* Judy Holliday and, making his film debut, Jack Lemmon, are paired to delightful effect in this original, satirical romantic comedy, faultlessly directed by George Cukor. Holliday is small-town girl Gladys Glover who arrives in the crowded anonymity of the Big Apple. Longing to be a "somebody", she hires a prominent billboard on which she has her name displayed. Soon the whole town's talking, among them businessman Peter Lawford who covets Gladys's prime advertising site. The leads are superb, the movie just short of a perfect classic. [video]

Judy Holliday *Gladys Glover* • Peter Lawford *Evan Adams III* • Jack Lemmon *Pete Sheppard* • Michael O'Shea *Brod Clinton* • Vaughn Taylor *Entrikin* • Connie Gilchrist *Mrs Riker* ■ *Dir* George Cukor • *Scr* Garson Kanin

It Shouldn't Happen to a Dog ★★ U

Crime comedy   1946 · US · BW · 69mins

Doberman pinscher owners everywhere will be jealous of the skills displayed by this film's hero, an 85lb four-year-old called Rodney – but then he did share the same owners as Lassie. It's a pity that Rodney couldn't put more bite into this mild comedy in which he's mistakenly blamed for taking part in a hold-up, then helps his owner, an undercover policewoman (Carole Landis), and a reporter (Allyn Joslyn) round up a band of gangsters.

Carole Landis *Julia Andrews* • Allyn Joslyn *Henry Barton* • Margo Woode *Olive Stone* • Henry Morgan *[Harry Morgan] Gus Rivers* • Reed Hadley *Mike Valentine* ■ *Dir* Herbert I Leeds • *Scr* Eugene Ling, Frank Gabrielson, from the short story by Edwin Lanham

It Shouldn't Happen to a Vet ★★ U

Drama   1979 · UK · Colour · 88mins

Neither *All Creatures Great and Small* nor this amiable sequel were as successful as James Herriott's original memoirs or the long-running BBC television series. Yet this Yorkshire comedy is, nevertheless, a pleasingly unpretentious entertainment that can be enjoyed by the whole family. The formula of pre-war country cosiness, bawdy humour, folksy characterisation and animal emergency is meticulously repeated as John Alderton capably steps into the wellies vacated by Simon Ward, while Colin Blakely hammily takes over from Anthony

Hopkins, leaving Lisa Harrow alone to return from the first venture. [video]

John Alderton *James Herriot* • Colin Blakely *Siegfried Farnon* • Lisa Harrow *Helen Herriot* • Bill Maynard *Hinchliffe* • Paul Shelley *Richard Carmody* • Richard Pearson *Granville Bennett* ■ *Dir* Eric Till • *Scr* Alan Plater

It Started in Naples ★★

Romantic comedy
1960 · US · Colour · 99mins

Lawyer Clark Gable travels to Italy to settle his late brother's estate and runs into vengeful and hysterical Italians, Sophia Loren and lots of travelogue shots of Capri and the Amalfi coast. This is probably one of those movies where the cast and crew had more fun than the audience who watch their antics, and it's not a patch on Billy Wilder's similarly-themed *Avanti!*. Loren, however, is a vivacious delight in a role that was originally written for Capri's most famous resident, Gracie Fields.

Clark Gable *Mike Hamilton* • Sophia Loren *Lucia* • Marietto *Nando* • Vittorio De Sica *Mario Vitale* • Paolo Carlini *Renzo* ■ *Dir* Melville Shavelson • *Scr* Melville Shavelson, Jack Rose, Suso Cecchi d'Amico, from a story by Michael Pertwee, Jack Davies

It Started with a Kiss ★★★

Comedy   1959 · US · Colour · 103mins

When army sergeant Glenn Ford meets nightclub singer Debbie Reynolds, instant combustion leads to a hasty marriage. To test his affections she withholds sexual favours, though the couple come to a loving accommodation in time for the final fade. Filmed on eye-catching Spanish locations, George Marshall's comedy relies on innuendo and double entendre for its laughs, with extra amusement provided by Eva Gabor as a marquesa lusting after Ford. Reynolds, pursued by a wealthy bullfighter, relishes the opportunity to escape her wholesome image in this slice of good, clean, dirty fun.

Glenn Ford *Sergeant Joe Fitzpatrick* • Debbie Reynolds *Maggie Putnam* • Eva Gabor *Marquesa de la Rey* • Gustavo Rojo *Antonio Soriano* • Fred Clark *General O'Connell* ■ *Dir* George Marshall • *Scr* Charles Lederer, from a story by Valentine Davies

It Started with Eve ★★★ U

Musical comedy   1941 · US · BW · 90mins

Deanna Durbin, everybody's ideal teenager, was blossoming into young womanhood when she starred opposite Charles Laughton in this delightful romantic comedy. Laughton plays a crusty millionaire whose deathbed wish is to meet his son's fiancée. Therefore, the son, Robert Cummings, picks up hat-check girl Durbin to impersonate his bride-to-be for a day. Naturally, Laughton takes a shine to her and recovers. While the plot thickens, Deanna's bell-like tones are heard in three songs.

Deanna Durbin *Anne Terry* • Charles Laughton *Jonathon Reynolds* • Robert Cummings *J "Johnny" Reynolds Jr* • Guy Kibbee *Bishop* • Margaret Tallichet *Gloria Pennington* ■ *Dir* Henry Koster • *Scr* Norman Krasna, Leo Townsend, from the story *Almost an Angel* by Hans Kräly

It Takes Two ★★ U

Romantic comedy
1995 · US · Colour · 96mins

A bland twist on *The Parent Trap*, this story has two identical-in-appearance girls from opposite sides of the tracks (US TV stars Mary-Kate and Ashley Olsen) teaming up to bring their single parents (Kirstie Alley and Steve Guttenberg) together. So cute it will make your teeth ache. Very missable unless you're a little girl aged six. [video]

Kirstie Alley *Diane Barrows* • Steve Guttenberg *Roger Callaway* • Mary-Kate Olsen *Amanda Lemmon* • Ashley Olsen *Alyssa Callaway* • Philip Bosco *Vincenzo* ■ *Dir* Andy Tennant • *Scr* Deborah Dean Davis

It! The Terror from beyond Space ★★★

Science-fiction thriller
1958 · US · BW · 69mins

A rocket-ship crew returning from an interplanetary mission is menaced by a blood-drinking reptilian stowaway in this low-budget classic from science fiction's golden age. If the plot sounds familiar, it's because Edward L Cahn's briskly directed shocker is frequently cited as the blueprint for Ridley Scott's *Alien*. Ray "Crash" Corrigan wears the scaly rubber suit as the Martian monster, ably menacing Marshall Thompson and his fellow astronauts in a fifties' relic that still delivers some decent scares.

Marshall Thompson *Colonel Carruthers* • Shawn Smith *Ann Anderson* • Kim Spalding *Colonel Van Heusen* • Ann Doran *Mary Royce* • Dabbs Greer *Eric Royce* • Ray Corrigan *"It"* ■ *Dir* Edward L Cahn • *Scr* Jerome Bixby

It Was a Wonderful Life ★★

Documentary   1992 · US · Colour · 82mins

Nominated for awards at a number of festivals, this documentary about homeless women, while moving, is ultimately a shallow treatment of an agonisingly complicated issue. The women who are the focus of the film struggle against their destitution, but as they all have come from relatively "normal" backgrounds, their plight does not reflect the true nature or breadth of homelessness in the United States. Directed by Michèle Ohayon and narrated by Jodie Foster, this film is ultimately too one-sided to explore the issue with any great insight.

Jodie Foster *Narration* ■ *Dir* Michèle Ohayon

It Was Him or Us ★★

Drama   1995 · US · Colour

A well-meaning yet predictable made-for-TV movie about domestic violence. Ann Jillian plays a former victim-turned-counsellor who becomes convinced that her estranged daughter (Monique Lanier) is drifting into a dangerous relationship with Richard Grieco. Director Robert Iscove does his best with a cliché-ridden script and produces a suitably tense finale. Grieco delivers a believably sleazy turn and there is a reliable performance from Richard Masur, but it's hard to work up much sympathy for Jillian. Contains violence.

Ann Jillian *Peggy Pomeroy* • Richard Grieco *Gene* • Monique Lanier *Carrie* • Richard Masur ■ *Dir* Robert Iscove • *Scr* Richard Lawton

It! ★★
Horror 1966 · UK · Colour · 95mins

Director Herbert J Leder made this dismal attempt to resurrect the legend of the Golem monster – most famously filmed in 1920 by Paul Wegener – for Swinging Sixties audiences. Roddy McDowall is an assistant museum curator, living with the mummified corpse of his mother (*Psycho* has a lot to answer for), who revives the original Golem to do his psychopathic bidding. A confused mix of black humour and horror, this is distinctly lacking in style, invention or (crucially) budget, as evidenced in the monster's less than awesome destruction of a London bridge. At least the Golem itself is well realised and lives to fight another day surviving, of all things, an atomic blast!

Roddy McDowall *Arthur Pimm* • Jill Haworth *Ellen Grove* • Paul Maxwell *Jim Perkins* • Aubrey Richards *Professor Weal* • Ernest Clark *Harold Grove* • Oliver Johnston *Trimingham* ■ *Dir/Scr* Herbert J Leder

The Italian Connection ★
Crime action thriller
1973 · US/It/W Ger · Colour · 87mins

This typically derivative Italian thriller is a curiously bloodless affair, despite the requisite high body count. Director Fernando Di Leo, who worked on *A Fistful of Dollars*, directs this tale about Mafia inter-gang feuding with a breathless predictability. Luckily Mario Adorf is aggressively believable as a small-time thug framed for a six-million-dollar heroin heist and pursued by avenging hit men. Stylistically flat, this is clumsily dubbed to boot. Italian dialogue dubbed into English.

Mario Adorf *Luca Canali* • Henry Silva *Dave* • Woody Strode *Frank* • Adolfo Celi *Don Vito* • Luciana Paluzzi *Eva* • Sylva Koscina *Lucia* • Cyril Cusack *Corso* ■ *Dir* Fernando Di Leo • *Scr* Fernando Di Leo, Augusto Finocchi, Ingo Hermann, from a story by Fernando Di Leo

The Italian Job ★★★ PG
Crime comedy thriller
1969 · UK/US · Colour · 95mins

Smashing vehicle stunt work distinguishes this Swinging Sixties romp from Paramount, with interiors filmed at our very own Twickenham Studios. Unfortunately, despite a fine cast headed by criminals Michael Caine, Noël Coward and Benny Hill, the script doesn't quite come off. If the characters had been a little better developed and the director a little less determinedly flashy, this could have been a minor classic. That said, this is a mightily popular movie, helped by the soundtrack from Quincy Jones, the editing by John Trumper, and the marvellous Coward, who masterminds the whole wheeze from his prison cell. Contains some swearing, violence and sexual references. ▣

Michael Caine *Charlie Croker* • Noël Coward *Mr Bridger* • Benny Hill *Professor Simon Peach* • Raf Vallone *Altabani* • Tony Beckley *Freddie* • Rossano Brazzi *Beckerman* • Maggie Blye *Lorna* • Irene Handl *Miss Peach* • John Le Mesurier *Governor* ■ *Dir* Peter Collinson • *Scr* Troy Kennedy Martin • *Cinematographer* Douglas Slocombe

Italian Movie ★★★
Romantic comedy 1994 · US · Colour

Fans of *Moonstruck* and *Big Night* could do worse than check out this lively romantic comedy from director Roberto Monticello. With more shrugs and hand gestures than the entire *Godfather* trilogy, the film follows Caprice Benedetti's frantic attempts to discover why husband Michael Dellafemina's sexual prowess is on the wane. Add some financial problems, in the form of creditor James Gandolfini, and you have a spicy dish that should appeal to most tastes.

Michael Dellafemina *Leonardo* • Caprice Benedetti *Anna* • Janet Sarno *Nina* • James Gandolfini *Angelo* ■ *Dir* Roberto Monticello • *Scr* Angela Sciddurlo Rago, Eugenia Bone

An Italian Straw Hat ★★★★★
Silent comedy 1927 · Fr · BW · 60mins

The leading proponent of comic theory, Henri Bergson, considered this the near perfect film, and while others complained that its satirical assault on bourgeois sensibilities was lightweight, it's impossible not to be intoxicated by this balletic silent masterpiece. Taken at a pace to rival Mack Sennett, yet full of Chaplinesque subtlety, René Clair's adaptation of Eugène Labiche and Marc Marcel's stage success bursts out on to the streets of Paris, as Albert Préjean meets with an unexpected problem en route to his wedding. His horse has eaten a lady's hat and he is now desperately seeking a replacement. The characters may well be mere pantomimic puppets, but the precision of their movement is a joy to behold.

Albert Préjean *Fadinard* • Olga Tchekowa *Anaïs de Beauperthuis* • Marise Maïa *The bride* • Alice Tissot *A cousin* • Jim Gérald *Beauperthuis* ■ *Dir* René Clair • *Scr* René Clair, from the play *Un Chapeau de Paille d'Italie* by Eugène Labiche, Marc Michel

It's a Big Country ★ U
Drama 1951 · US · BW · 88mins

MGM's flag-waving series of eight episodes intended to illustrate the richness and diversity of American life scores straight zeroes, except for Gary Cooper's monologue about Texas, directed by Clarence Brown, which is momentarily amusing. Yawn at the mawkish or pointless material in which stars like Fredric March and Gene Kelly appear. An obvious embarrassment before release, the picture was cut down to a standard running time.

Ethel Barrymore *Mrs Brian Patrick Riordan* • Keefe Brasselle *Sgt Maxie Klein* • Nancy Davis *Miss Coleman* • Van Johnson *Adam Burch* • Gene Kelly *Icarus Xenophon* • Janet Leigh *Rosa Szabo* • Fredric March *Papa Esposito* ■ *Dir* Richard Thorpe, John Sturges, Charles Vidor, Don Weis, Clarence Brown, William A Wellman, Don Hartman • *Scr* William Ludwig, Helen Deutsch, Isobel Lennart, Allen Rivkin, George Wells, Dore Schary, Dorothy Kingsley

It's a Boy ★★ U
Comedy 1933 · UK · BW · 77mins

America's most dapper farceur, Edward Everett Horton, was imported by producer Michael Balcon for this rather pedestrian adaptation of a long-running West End smash. Mugging and double-

taking for all he's worth, Horton strikes the perfect note of manic fluster when his wedding to Wendy Barrie is disrupted by the arrival of a blackmailer posing as his illegitimate son. With fibs, misunderstandings and the lively Leslie Henson adding to the fun, this should have been a highly amusing romp. However, Tim Whelan's direction pays too much deference to the stage settings, and his comic timing is all to pot. ▣

Leslie Henson *James Skippett* • Edward Everett Horton *Dudley Leake* • Heather Thatcher *Anita Gunn* • Alfred Drayton *Eustace Bogle* ■ *Dir* Tim Whelan • *Scr* Austin Melford, Leslie Howard Gordon, John Paddy Carstairs, from the play by Austin Melford, Franz Arnold, Ernst Bach

It's a Date ★★★ U
Musical comedy 1940 · US · BW · 103mins

A famous actress (Kay Francis) has to face competition when a part she was hoping to get is offered instead to her ambitious daughter (Deanna Durbin). Love intervenes in the person of millionaire Walter Pidgeon, but will he choose Durbin or her mother? Now aged 19 and making her seventh feature film, Durbin reveals a more experienced grip on the art of acting, and some maturity in her singing of the usual rag-bag of songs (*Loch Lomond, Musetta's Waltz* from *La Bohème, Ave Maria* for the umpteenth time!) that embellishes her films. Note the presence of SZ "Cuddles" Sakall, soon to become a Hollywood fixture with his fractured English and huggy-bear personality, here making his American debut.

Deanna Durbin *Pamela Drake* • Kay Francis *Georgia Drake* • Walter Pidgeon *John Arlen* • Samuel S Hinds *Sidney Simpson* • SZ Sakall *Carl Ober* ■ *Dir* William A Seiter • *Scr* Norman Krasna, from a story by Jane Hall, Frederick Kohner, Ralph Block

It's a Gift ★★★★★
Classic comedy 1934 · US · BW · 71mins

Shades of Bacchus! It's the inimitable WC Fields in his most perfectly formed movie. Brilliantly conceived (by Fields himself, alias Charles Bogle), and beautifully structured (by director Norman Z McLeod), this is a milestone in screen comedy, and an emphatic must-see if you've decided you don't care for Fields or have never seen him before. The lengthy two-reel sequence on the porch is one of the funniest sustained sketches in sound cinema, and the store scene with Charles Sellon as blind Mr Muckle has to be seen to be believed. Kumquats will never be the same again.

WC Fields *Harold Bissonette* • Jean Rouveroi *Mildred Bissonette* • Julian Madison *John Durston* • Kathleen Howard *Amelia Bissonette* • Baby LeRoy *Baby Dunk* • Josephine Whittell *Mrs Dunk* ■ *Dir* Norman Z McLeod • *Scr* Jack Cunningham, from a story by Charles Bogle [WC Fields], from the play *The Comic Supplement (of American Life)* by JP McEvoy

It's a Grand Life ★★ U
Comedy 1953 · UK · BW · 106mins

Vulgar Lancashire music-hall star Frank Randle – a household name throughout Britain at the time thanks to his weekly strip in the well-loved *Film Fun* comic – had an appeal north

of Watford that seldom stretched southwards, let alone abroad, and his brand of parochial humour was looking dated by the time he made this quaint and cheap army caper. If you've never seen him, give this a chance. But if you have an aversion to music-hall stars on celluloid, give up, for Randle has neither the wit of George Formby nor the warmth of Gracie Fields, and by the time this movie was made he was looking tired and rather grubby. Still, the object of his fancy here is a young Diana Dors, and keen fifties' watchers might enjoy catching a rare glimpse of pianist Winifred Atwell.

Frank Randle *Private Randle* • Diana Dors *Corporal Paula Clements* • Dan Young *Private Young* • Michael Brennan *Sergeant Major O'Reilly* • Jennifer Jayne *Private Desmond* ■ *Dir* John E Blakeley • *Scr* HF Maltby, Frank Randle, from a story by HF Maltby

It's a Great Day ★★ U
Comedy 1955 · UK · BW · 70mins

The Grove Family was one of BBC television's great popular successes, a series that today would be termed soap opera, but then was a compulsive, if low-key, studio-bound rendering of the busy but uninvolving goings-on of a very average suburban family. The excellent Ruth Dunning and Edward Evans were Gladys and Bob Grove, and the acting honours, and the popularity stakes, were hijacked by formidable Nancy Roberts as Gran. This is a cheaply made feature version of the show, produced quickly and efficiently by Butcher's Films with the original cast, and now looks like a perfect period artefact.

Ruth Dunning *Gladys Grove* • Edward Evans *Bob Grove* • Sidney James *Harry Mason* • Vera Day *Blondie* • Sheila Sweet *Pat Grove* • Peter Bryant *Jack Grove* • Nancy Roberts *Gran* ■ *Dir* John Warrington • *Scr* Roland Pertwee, Michael Pertwee, from their TV series *The Grove Family*

It's a Great Feeling ★★★ U
Musical comedy 1949 · US · Colour · 84mins

Just about everyone who happened to have been passing through the Warners lot seems to have been roped into this ever-so-gentle Tinseltown spoof. With Jack Carson and Dennis Morgan playing themselves as a couple of likely lads, there's much fun to be had with the whole idea of on-screen persona. However, it's Doris Day who shines as the waitress they trawl round the studio as the latest singing sensation. For all the star-spotting and backslapping aside, not a lot happens to hold the attention. It's worth sticking with, though, if only to see Errol Flynn play Doris's Wisconsin sweetheart, Jeffrey Bushfinkle.

Doris Day *Judy Adams* • Dennis Morgan • Jack Carson • Bill Goodwin *Arthur Trent* • Gary Cooper • Joan Crawford • Errol Flynn *Jeffrey Bushfinkle* • Sydney Greenstreet • Danny Kaye • Patricia Neal • Eleanor Parker • Ronald Reagan • Edward G Robinson • Jane Wyman • Raoul Walsh • Michael Curtiz • King Vidor ■ *Dir* David Butler • *Scr* Jack Rose, Melville Shavelson, from a story by IAL Diamond

U = SUITABLE FOR ALL   Uc = SUITABLE FOR ALL, ESPECIALLY FOR YOUNG CHILDREN (VIDEO ONLY)   PG = PARENTAL GUIDANCE

It's a Mad Mad Mad Mad World ★★★ U

Comedy 1963 · US · Colour · 148mins

Director/producer Stanley Kramer assembled the cream of Hollywood's comic talent for this monumental and mostly entertaining chase caper. Yet it's the ever-versatile Spencer Tracy – in his penultimate film and clearly unwell – who catches the eye as the henpecked detective at the front of the race to find a stash of stolen cash. It's also rather ironic that the film was nominated for an editing Oscar, for, while the plethora of breakneck stunts undeniably have pace and precision, the action badly needed cutting by at least 80 minutes. Eventually, the passing parade of cameos begins to offer fewer pleasant surprises and the slapstick descends from the comedic into the chaotic.

Spencer Tracy *Captain CG Culpeper* • Milton Berle *J Russell Finch* • Sid Caesar *Melville Crump* • Buddy Hackett *Benjy* • Ethel Merman *Mrs Marcus* • Mickey Rooney *Ding Bell* • Dick Shawn *Sylvester Marcus* • Phil Silvers *Otto Meyer* • Terry-Thomas *J Algernon Hawthorne* • Jonathan Winters *Lennie Pike* ■ *Dir* Stanley Kramer • *Scr* William Rose • *Cinematographer* Ernest Laszlo • *Music* Ernest Gold

It's a Wonderful Life ★★★★★ U

Classic fantasy drama
1946 · US · BW · 130mins

Easily the finest Christmas movie ever made, Frank Capra's masterpiece still has much to say about community spirit and is a film with much more to it than feel-good sentimentality. George Bailey is Mr Deeds, John Doe and Mr Smith rolled into one, and only James Stewart could have given him the suicidal self-doubt that gnaws away at his essential decency. As with all good morality tales, the villain has to be exceptional too and Lionel Barrymore is at the peak of his powers as Potter. The term Capraesque is too often misapplied. So forget the imitations and revel in the genuine article.

DVD

James Stewart *George Bailey* • Donna Reed *Mary Hatch* • Lionel Barrymore *Mr Potter* • Thomas Mitchell *Uncle Billy* • Henry Travers *Clarence* • Beulah Bondi *Mrs Bailey* • Frank Faylen *Ernie* • Ward Bond *Bert* ■ *Dir* Frank Capra • *Scr* Frances Goodrich, Albert Hackett, Frank Capra, Jo Swerling, from the story *The Greatest Gift* by Philip Van Doren Stern • *Music* Dmitri Tiomkin

It's a Wonderful World ★★★★

Comedy 1939 · US · BW · 85mins

This is a brilliantly funny but overlooked screwball comedy, nearly the last of its kind, in which James Stewart and wacky Claudette Colbert spend their time despising each other (until the final reel, that is). He's a private eye on the run, and she's a poet and they're looking for a killer, and... well, that's screwball enough. This is a screen original, written by the great Ben Hecht from his and Herman J Mankiewicz's story, and directed with skill and considerable pace by WS "Woody One-Take" Van Dyke II.

Claudette Colbert *Edwina Corday* • James Stewart *Guy Johnson* • Guy Kibbee *Captain*

Streeter • Nat Pendleton *Sergeant Koretz* • Frances Drake *Vivian Tarbel* ■ *Dir* WS Van Dyke II [WS Van Dyke] • *Scr* Ben Hecht, from a story by Ben Hecht, Herman J Mankiewicz

It's a Wonderful World ★ U

Musical comedy 1956 · UK · Colour · 89mins

An anxious-to-please British musical comedy from director Val Guest. Set in the era before the advent of rock 'n' roll, the film follows the fortunes of composers Terence Morgan and George Cole, who, tired of being rejected in favour of more trendy music, pin their hopes of success on re-jigging a popular song. The music is not to everyone's taste, with Mylene Nicole's performance with Ted Heath's band striking the lowest note of all.

Terence Morgan *Ray Thompson* • George Cole *Ken Miller* • Kathleen Harrison *Miss Gilly* • Mylene Nicole [Mylene Demongeot] *Georgie Dubois* • James Hayter *Bert Fielding* • Harold Lang *Mervyn Wade* ■ *Dir/Scr* Val Guest

It's Alive ★★★ 18

Horror 1974 · US · Colour · 87mins

This breakthrough "mutant baby" movie marked the first time director Larry Cohen employed shock horror tactics to deal with serious social issues. Unsafe fertility drugs are blamed when Sharon Farrell's hideous newborn offspring, complete with claws and fangs, slaughters all the medics in the delivery room and embarks on a murder spree, leaving its still protective parents to face the publicity, and the shame. Cohen's absorbing, grisly and cleverly written brainchild provides food for thought while still delivering the chilling and often repugnant goods. Oscar-winning make-up man Rick Baker designs the baby, and the movie features one of Bernard Herrmann's last scores.

John Ryan [John P Ryan] *Frank Davies* • Sharon Farrell *Lenore Davies* • Andrew Duggan *Professor* • Guy Stockwell *Clayton* • James Dixon *Lieutenant Perkins* ■ *Dir/Scr* Larry Cohen

It's Alive III: Island of the Alive ★★★ 18

Horror 1987 · US · Colour · 91mins

Topical issues, socially conscious humour and a great performance by Michael Moriarty (one of director Larry Cohen's rep company regulars) make this a worthy successor to the previous two killer mutant baby shockers. Moriarty plays a third-rate actor who deals with his mixed-up feelings about fathering one of the vicious tots by going to court to stop them being destroyed and getting them quarantined to a Florida island. But when cynical media exploitation still dogs their existence, he joins an expedition to the island to help them, only to find they've grown collectively more eager to take revenge on an uncaring society. A lively, absorbing and scary indictment crafted with Cohen's usual care and attention.

Michael Moriarty *Steve Jarvis* • Karen Black *Ellen Jarvis* • Laurene Landon *Sally* • Gerritt Graham *Ralston* • James Dixon *Dr Perkins* • Neal Israel *Dr Brewster* ■ *Dir/Scr* Larry Cohen • *Music* Laurie Johnson, Bernard Herrmann

It's All Happening ★★ U

Musical 1963 · UK · Colour · 96mins

Well, if it is, it's nothing to get excited about. This sentimental hokum feels like it was something Norman Wisdom rejected before being turned into a vehicle for Tommy Steele. With a cheeky grin never far from his face, Steele masterminds a talent show to raise funds for the local orphanage. The songs sound as though they were knocked out on a slow afternoon on Denmark Street, London's very own Tin Pan Alley.

Tommy Steele *Billy Bowles* • Angela Douglas *Julie Singleton* • Michael Medwin *Max Catlin* • Jean Harvey *Delia* • Bernard Bresslaw *Parsons* ■ *Dir* Don Sharp • *Scr* Leigh Vance

It's All True ★★★★

Political documentary drama
1993 · Fr/Bra · BW · 85mins

In 1942, the day after he shot the last scene of *The Magnificent Ambersons*, Orson Welles flew to Brazil to make a semi-documentary, *It's All True*, which was to be anti-Nazi propaganda financed by the State Department. The film was never finished; meanwhile, RKO cut *Ambersons* behind Welles's back, sacking him on his return and destroying his Hollywood career. This film mixes interviews, Welles's exhilarating footage of the Rio carnival and a reconstruction of one story in the intended documentary. It's a riveting piece of cinema archaeology, an unmissable treat for buffs and historians alike that also sheds new light on the *Ambersons* fiasco.

Dean Beville *Narration* • Miguel Ferrer *Narration* • Orson Welles • Joseph Biroc • Elizabeth Wilson • Richard Wilson ■ *Dir* Richard Wilson, Myron Meisel, Bill Krohn • *Scr* Bill Krohn, Richard Wilson, Myron Meisel, from a story by Robert J Flaherty

It's Always Fair Weather ★★★★ U

Musical comedy 1955 · US · Colour · 101mins

Originally intended as a follow-up to *On the Town*, this wonderfully sardonic musical failed to find much critical approval or public acclaim on its original release. Now, in these more cynical times, we can appreciate this masterwork for what it is: a genuinely clever satire on all things American. Television is the main target here, but Madison Avenue advertising and the sports world take their fair share of knocks, as wartime buddies Gene Kelly, Dan Dailey and Michael Kidd plan a reunion, only to find they've nothing in common, until TV hostess Dolores Gray unites them against her.

Gene Kelly *Ted Riley* • Dan Dailey *Doug Halterton* • Cyd Charisse *Jackie Leighton* • Dolores Gray *Madeline Bradville* • Michael Kidd *Angie Valentine* • David Burns *Tim* ■ *Dir* Gene Kelly, Stanley Donen • *Scr* Betty Comden, Adolph Green

It's Great to Be Young ★★★★ U

Musical comedy 1956 · UK · Colour · 93mins

A light-hearted comedy with a remarkable level of energy and a superb sense of pace. John Mills stars as trumpet-playing, jazz-loving Mr Dingle, whose enforced resignation

from Angel Hill school leads to a (very minor) revolution. The kids, led by Jeremy Spenser and Dorothy Bromiley, are charming, and, thanks to an excellent Ted Willis screenplay, the adults are utterly believable, as is the studio construction of the fictional school. The only sour note, if you stop and think about it, is that this film was clearly written and filmed before the coming of rock 'n' roll. Rebellious kids forming a school jazz band in England in 1956? Please!

John Mills *Dingle* • Cecil Parker *Frome* • John Salew *Routledge* • Elizabeth Kentish *Mrs Castle* • Mona Washbourne *Miss Morrow* • Mary Merrall *Miss Wyvern* • Jeremy Spenser *Nicky* • Dorothy Bromiley *Paulette* ■ *Dir* Cyril Frankel • *Scr* Ted Willis

It's Hard to Be Good ★★ U

Comedy 1948 · UK · BW · 100mins

A product of the Rank system, Jimmy Hanley had been in movies since the mid-thirties when he took the lead in this British comedy. The premise is interesting – making Hanley a war hero-turned-idealist whose every attempt to preach peace and goodwill backfires disastrously – but it needed a sharper touch from writer/director Jeffrey Dell. He merely repeats the basic idea instead of developing it, so that the situations become predictable, descending from satire to slapstick.

Jimmy Hanley *Capt James Gladstone Wedge* • Anne Crawford *Mary* • Raymond Huntley *Williams* • Geoffrey Keen *Sgt Todd* • Elwyn Brook-Jones *Budibent* • David Horne *Edward Beckett* ■ *Dir/Scr* Jeffrey Dell

It's in the Air ★★ U

Comedy 1938 · UK · BW · 83mins

George Formby's toothy grin, innuendo-laden songs and jaunty ukelele-strumming delighted UK audiences of the thirties and forties. In a string of films following similar lines, underdog Formby would triumph against long odds and usually walk off with the girl. Some of his most popular vehicles found him dashing about on motorbikes or in uniform, and here these elements are combined, with George Brown (Formby) a motorcycle enthusiast who finds himself mistaken for an RAF pilot.

George Formby *George Brown* • Polly Ward *Peggy* • Garry Marsh *Commanding officer* • Julien Mitchell *Sergeant-Major* • Jack Hobbs *Corporal Craig* • C Denier Warren *Sir Philip Bargrave* ■ *Dir/Scr* Anthony Kimmins

It's in the Bag ★★

Comedy 1945 · US · BW · 87mins

There's nothing quite like this idiosyncratic comedy, co-scripted by Alfred Hitchcock's wife, Alma Reville. It starts off with a clever Fred Allen voice-over mocking the credits and continues with various vaudeville-style sketches that are patchy fun, tending to overstay their welcome. The familiar link is a search for money hidden in one of five chairs. Two of the episodes focus on Jack Benny and his meanness and William Bendix mocking his tough guy image as a sissy gangster.

Fred Allen *Fred Floogle* • Jack Benny • William Bendix • Binnie Barnes *Eve Floogle* • Robert

Benchley *Parker* ■ *Dir* Richard Wallace • *Scr* Lewis R Foster, Fred Allen, Jay Dratler, Alma Reville

It's Love Again ★★★ U

Musical comedy   1936 · UK · BW · 80mins

The ever-delightful Jessie Matthews is in fine fettle in this frothy concoction that perfectly showcases both her musical talent and her vivacious comic personality. As a showgirl posing as a big-game-hunting socialite, she runs rings round columnist Robert Young. Lacking the glamour of a Hollywood musical (in spite of some impossibly chic Art Deco sets), this is still a pleasurable romp, with Sonnie Hale (Matthews's real-life husband at the time) amusing as the rival reporter responsible for the scam and Robb Wilton hilarious as Young's valet. ▭

Jessie Matthews *Elaine Bradford* • Robert Young *Peter Carlton* • Sonnie Hale *Freddie Rathbone* • Ernest Milton *Archibald Raymond* • Robb Wilton *Boy* • Sara Allgood *Mrs Hopkins* ■ *Dir* Victor Saville • *Scr* Marion Dix, Lesser Samuels, Austin Melford

It's Love I'm After ★★★

Romantic comedy   1937 · US · BW · 90mins

A very funny Bette Davis/Leslie Howard vehicle that crackles with sophisticated one-liners, plus much histrionic raising of eyebrows and waving of hands courtesy of a plot that revolves around a warring pair of famous Shakespearean actors. Davis shows us what a consummate all-rounder she is, demonstrating a flair for deft comic timing, and even the normally lugubrious Howard joins in with verve and gusto. The theatre-land setting provides ample opportunity for lively humour, and Olivia de Havilland is the perfect foil as Howard's besotted fan.

Leslie Howard *Basil Underwood* • Bette Davis *Joyce Arden* • Olivia de Havilland *Marcia West* • Eric Blore *Digges* • Patric Knowles *Henry Grant* ■ *Dir* Archie Mayo • *Scr* Casey Robinson, from the story *Gentleman after Midnight* by Maurice Hanline

It's Magic ★★★

Romantic musical
1948 · US · Colour · 98mins

The sudden withdrawal of Betty Hutton (who had herself replaced Judy Garland) is the most significant thing about this breezy Warners musical, as it gave big band singer Doris Day the chance to take her first featured role. The stars of this Caribbean cruise confection were supposed to be Jack Carson and Janis Paige, but time hangs heavy between Day's all-too-brief appearances. Versatile though he was, director Michael Curtiz was never totally comfortable with the musical genre, which explains why Busby Berkeley was brought back to the studio to handle the dance routines.

Doris Day *Georgia Garrett* • Jack Carson *Peter Virgil* • Janis Paige *Elvira Kent* • Don DeFore *Michael Kent* • Oscar Levant *Oscar Farrar* • Fortunio Bonanova *Plinio* • Eric Blore *Ship's doctor* ■ *Dir* Michael Curtiz • *Scr* Julius J Epstein, Philip G Epstein, Ial Diamond, from the story *Romance in High C* by S Pondal Rios, Carlos A Olivari

It's My Life ★★★★★

Drama   1962 · Fr · BW · 83mins

Jean-Luc Godard's New Wave masterpiece concerns a prostitute who maintains a sort of spiritual integrity before falling victim to gangsters. Abandoning conventional narrative, Godard offers the story as twelve chapters and names his heroine Nana, after Zola's heroine; he also has her go to the cinema to see Carl Theodor Dreyer's legendary silent classic about another martyr, Joan of Arc. The then frank depiction of sex earned the film a certain notoriety, not to mention the application of the British censor's scissors. Now, though, what's most noticeable is Godard's technique and the luminous photography of Anna Karina, who had just become the director's wife and here gives a marvellous performance. In French with English subtitles.

Anna Karina *Nana Kleinfrankenheim* • Sady Rebbot *Raoul* • AndréS Labarthe *Paul* • Guylaine Schlumberger *Yvette* • Jean-Luc Godard *Voice* ■ *Dir* Jean-Luc Godard • *Scr* Jean-Luc Godard, with additional dialogue by Judge Marcel Sacotte, from the short story *The Oval Portrait* by Edgar Allen Poe

It's My Party ★★ 15

Comedy drama   1996 · US · Colour · 105mins

Architect Eric Roberts learns he is about to lose his long battle against Aids and decides to throw a two-day pre-suicide farewell party surrounded by family and friends. But his guests are uncomfortable in the highly-charged atmosphere where opinions collide, secrets spill and old wounds heal. Everyone struggles to accept Robertss fate, and their own. Unsympathetic characters clash with heavy sentiment in director Randal Kleiser's well-meaning comedy drama, which quickly wears out its celebratory welcome. ▭

Eric Roberts *Nick Stark* • George Segal *Paul Stark* • Marlee Matlin *Daphne Stark* • Roddy McDowall *Damian Knowles* • Olivia Newton-John *Lina Bingham* • Lee Grant *Amalia Stark* ■ *Dir/Scr* Randal Kleiser

It's My Turn ★★ 15

Romantic comedy
1980 · US · Colour · 86mins

Diana Ross sings *It's My Turn* and she might be talking about the disappointing career trajectory of leading lady Jill Clayburgh, who started the eighties with this predictable romantic drama and is now guesting in TV's *Ally McBeal*. Clayburgh's in a relationship with Charles Grodin but then goes to a wedding and meets retired baseball player Michael Douglas. Difficult decisions lie ahead. While nicely performed, this never really gets going and ultimately offers no more depth than a TV soap. ▭

Jill Clayburgh *Kate Gunzinger* • Michael Douglas *Ben Lewin* • Charles Grodin *Homer* • Beverly Garland *Emma* • Steven Hill *Jacob* • Daniel Stern *Cooperman* • Dianne Wiest *Gail* ■ *Dir* Claudia Weill • *Scr* Eleanor Bergstein

It's Never Too Late ★★★ U

Comedy   1956 · UK · Colour · 95mins

An amiable comedy, with genteel Phyllis Calvert as a materfamilias whose scriptwriting talents are discovered by a Hollywood producer, but who finds she can only write when she's surrounded by her chaotic family. This is very much of its time, with its West End origins masked by skilful art direction, but the period cast is a British film fan's delight. Director Michael McCarthy whips up a fair old storm in this particular teacup, and, although nothing really happens, there's a great deal of pleasure to be had from watching Calvert attempt to rule over her unruly household.

Phyllis Calvert *Laura Hammond* • Patrick Barr *Charles Hammond* • Susan Stephen *Tessa Hammond* • Guy Rolfe *Stephen Hodgson* • Jean Taylor-Smith *Grannie* • Sarah Lawson *Anne* • Irene Handl • Shirley Anne Field ■ *Dir* Michael McCarthy • *Scr* Edward Dryhurst, from the play by Felicity Douglas

It's Never Too Late to Mend ★★

Melodrama   1937 · UK · BW · 95mins

Another over-ripe slice of melodrama for Tod Slaughter to sink his teeth into and, once again, he has a ball hamming things up. In this tale, based on a play by Charles Reade and Arthur Shirley, he is a nasty aristocrat trying to get his evil way with a sweet young thing. To stand any chance he has to get rid of her lover, which he does by having him framed for a crime he did not commit and incarcerated in a brutal prison. Don't expect any surprises and you won't be disappointed.

Tod Slaughter *Squire Meadows* • Marjorie Taylor *Susan Merton* • Jack Livesey *Tom Robinson* • Ian Colin *George Fielding* • Lawrence Hanray *Lawyer Crawley* • DJ Williams *Farmer Merton* • Roy Russell *Reverend Eden* • Johnny Singer *Joseph* ■ *Dir* David MacDonald • *Scr* HF Maltby, from a play by Charles Reade, Arthur Shirley

It's Not Cricket ★★★ U

Comedy   1948 · UK · BW · 71mins

Basil Radford and Naunton Wayne first displayed their passion for cricket as Charters and Caldicott in Alfred Hitchcock's sparkling spy thriller *The Lady Vanishes* in 1938. Here (in one of the last of their 11 features together) they play Bright and Early, who become private detectives after they are cashiered from the army for allowing Nazi Maurice Denham to slip through their fingers. The misadventures of the bungling double act are pleasing enough, but the humour has about as much depth as the England batting order. ▭

Basil Radford *Major Bright* • Naunton Wayne *Captain Early* • Susan Shaw *Primrose Brown* • Maurice Denham *Otto Fisch* • Alan Wheatley *Felix* • Diana Dors *Blonde* ■ *Dir* Alfred Roome, Roy Rich • *Scr* Bernard McNab, Gerard Bryant and Lyn Lockwood

It'$ Only Money ★★★ U

Comedy   1962 · US · BW · 83mins

It always proved difficult to capture the essential Jerry Lewis on film and, outside of France where he is regarded as a genius, the concensus is that he was a brilliant comic who never fully translated his skills to screen. Director Frank Tashlin worked a number of times with Lewis, with mixed results, and this is one of their better collaborations. Lewis plays Lester March, a TV repair man who yearns to be a detective and persuades a real detective to let him join an investigation into a missing heir. Less slapstick than usual but still with one or two stand-out comedy routines.

Jerry Lewis *Lester March* • Zachary Scott *Gregory DeWitt* • Joan O'Brien *Wanda Paxton* • Mae Questel *Cecilia Albright* • Jesse White *Pete Flint* • Jack Weston *Leopold* ■ *Dir* Frank Tashlin • *Scr* John Fenton Murray

It's That Man Again ★★ U

Comedy   1942 · UK · BW · 80mins

By the time Tommy Handley starred in this disappointing backstage vehicle, his radio show, *ITMA*, was attracting 40 million listeners each week, all desperate to laugh away their wartime blues. However, the Liverpool-born comic's fast-talking style felt forced when shackled to the demands of a storyline, and his weaknesses as a physical comedian restricted the type of business he was able to carry off. Thus, while casting him as the devious mayor of Foaming-at-the-Mouth seemed sound enough, the events that follow his acquisition of a bombed-out London theatre feel like so much padding. ▭

Tommy Handley *Mayor Handley* • Greta Gynt *Stella Ferris* • Jack Train *Lefty/Funf* • Sidney Keith *Sam Scram* ■ *Dir* Walter Forde • *Scr* Howard Irving Young, Ted Kavanagh, from the radio series *ITMA* by Ted Kavanagh

It's the Old Army Game ★★★

Silent farce   1926 · US · BW · 70mins

Some of the best sequences from this WC Fields silent comedy were refined and re-used in his great 1934 talkie *It's a Gift*, where his raspy voice and the sound effects added considerably to the impact. Still, there's much merriment to be had here as a younger-looking, dark-haired Fields (as small-town pharmacist Elmer Prettywillie) attempts to obtain a decent night's sleep, and a family excursion to a Florida estate leads to general devastation. Plus there's the considerable bonus of the luminous Louise Brooks as his assistant.

WC Fields *Elmer Prettywillie* • Louise Brooks *Mildred Marshall* • Blanche Ring *Tessie Overholt* • William Gaxton *George Parker* ■ *Dir* Edward Sutherland [A Edward Sutherland] • *Scr* Tom J Geraghty, J Clarkson Miller, from the play *It's the Old Army Game* by Joseph Patrick McEvoy, from theatrical sketches by Joseph Patrick McEvoy, WC Fields

It's Trad, Dad ★★★ U

Musical comedy   1961 · UK · BW · 73mins

Richard Lester had already worked with the anarchic Goons on television and on film, and thus was no stranger to madcap mayhem. This flair was on show in this film (also known as *Ring-a-Ding Rhythm*). It's a light-hearted musical romp with the simple message that rock 'n' roll is good for you. Soulful voiced Helen Shapiro and clean-cut Craig Douglas star as a couple of kids trying to mount a music show, despite protests from the pompous mayor. Among the acts featured are rock 'n' roller Chubby Checker and teen idol Del Shannon.

Helen Shapiro *Helen* • Craig Douglas *Craig* • Felix Felton *Mayor* • Arthur Mullard *Police chief* • Timothy Bateson *Coffeeshop owner* • Derek Nimmo *Head waiter* ■ *Dir* Richard Lester • *Scr* Milton Subotsky

It's Turned Out Nice Again
★★★ U

Comedy   1941 · UK · BW · 79mins

George Formby's famous catchphrase was pressed into service for the title of this mischievous comedy, which proved to be his last assignment for Ealing Studios. Formby enjoys himself as a go-ahead ideas man at an underwear factory whose ambitious plans get his fellow knicker workers in a twist, but the action too often gets bogged down in a predictable subplot in which his smothering ma tries to break up his romance with Peggy Bryan. Director Marcel Varnel keeps it skipping along.

George Formby *George Pearson* • Peggy Bryan *Lydia Pearson* • Edward Chapman *Uncle Arnold* • Elliot Mason *Mrs Pearson* • Wilfrid Hyde White *Removal man* ■ *Dir* Marcel Varnel • *Scr* Austin Melford, John Dighton, Basil Dearden, from the play *As You Were* by Hugh Mills, Wells Root

Ivan the Terrible, Part I
★★★ PG

Historical drama   1944 · USSR · BW · 94mins

This is the first part of an intended trilogy about Ivan the Fourth, the warrior-tsar who virtually created the Russian empire in the 16th century. Like influential director Sergei Eisenstein's earlier *Battleship Potemkin* and *Alexander Nevsky*, this is textbook stuff if only for the reason that Eisenstein wrote the textbooks himself – influential tomes called *Film Sense* and *Film Form* – which laid down theories of composition and editing. But time has not been kind to Eisenstein's work and the plain fact is that one must endure masses of padding as well as histrionic acting between the impressive set pieces, when battleground action and Prokofiev's music, which was written specifically for the film, are artfully fused. In Russian with English subtitles. ▭

Nikolai Cherkassov *Tsar Ivan IV* • Serafima Birman *The Boyarina Efrosinia Staritskaya, Tsar's Aunt* • Pavel Kadochnikov *Vladimir Andreyevich Staritsky* • Mikhail Zharov *Malyuta Skuratov* ■ *Dir/Scr* Sergei Eisenstein • *Cinematographer* Andrei Moskvin, Edouard Tissé • *Art Director* Isaac Shpinel

Ivan the Terrible, Part II
★★★ PG

Historical drama   1946 · USSR · BW and Colour · 81mins

This second part of director Sergei Eisenstein's intended trilogy was completed in early 1946, by which time Eisenstein was recuperating from a heart attack. Emphasising the personal over the public aspect of the Tsar's life, the film was shown to Eisenstein's ultimate boss, Stalin, who banned it because Ivan's bodyguard and the secret service were portrayed like the "Ku Klux Klan and Ivan himself was… weak and indecisive, somewhat like Hamlet." The film remained unshown until 1958, by which time Eisenstein had been dead

for ten years. Sadly, it's even stodgier than its predecessor and contains some weird colour sequences towards the end, in which Ivan denounces all enemies of Russia. In Russian with English subtitles. ▭

Nikolai Cherkassov *Tsar Ivan IV* • Serafima Birman *The Boyarina Efrosinia Staritskaya, Tsar's Aunt* • Pavel Kadochnikov *Vladimir Andreyevich Staritsky* • Mikhail Zharov *Malyuta Skuratov* ■ *Dir/Scr* Sergei Eisenstein • *Music* Sergei Prokofiev

Ivana Trump's For Love Alone
★

Drama   1996 · US · Colour

Michael Lindsay-Hogg once directed the Beatles in the documentary *Let It Be*, a phrase he might have done well to recall when he was offered this TV-movie adaptation of Ivana Trump's loosely autobiographical novel. Sanna Vraa flounces through the piece as the Czech skier who strikes it lucky with millionaire Stephen Collins and becomes the toast of American society. Madeline Kahn and Trevor Eve are among those in the support cast who look ill-at-ease with their roles.

Stephen Collins *Adam Graham* • Sanna Vraa *Katrinka Kovar* • Trevor Eve *Mark* ■ *Dir* Michael Lindsay-Hogg • *Scr* Claire Labine, from the novel by Ivana Trump

Ivanhoe
★★★★ U

Epic swashbuckling adventure
1952 · UK · Colour · 102mins

A justifiable box-office smash in what was, with hindsight, one of MGM's greatest years, this rollicking Technicolor swashbuckler remains the definitive screen version of Sir Walter Scott's memorable medieval classic. The cast and the action sequences are almost perfect; though suitably handsome, American Robert Taylor is a little dull as Sir Wilfred of Ivanhoe, but Elizabeth Taylor as Rebecca is at her loveliest, Emlyn Williams is wonderfully theatrical as Wamba, and villains George Sanders, Robert Douglas and, especially, lean and mean Guy Rolfe as Prince John are superb. Interestingly, Scott's sub-theme about anti-Semitism in 1190 England is not glossed over, making this one of the few fifties movies to deal openly with such a tricky subject. ▭

Robert Taylor (1) *Ivanhoe* • Elizabeth Taylor *Rebecca* • Joan Fontaine *Rowena* • George Sanders *De Bois-Guilbert* • Emlyn Williams *Wamba* • Robert Douglas *Sir Hugh De Bracy* ■ *Dir* Richard Thorpe • *Scr* Marguerite Roberts (uncredited), Noel Langley, from the novel by Sir Walter Scott, adapted by Aeneas MacKenzie

Ivan's Childhood
★★★★★ PG

Second World War drama
1962 · USSR · BW · 90mins

Winner of the Golden Lion at Venice, Andrei Tarkovsky's debut feature – about a 12-year-old boy (Kolya Burlyaev) who becomes a spy to revenge himself on the Nazis who killed his family – may surprise those familiar only with his later philosophical treatises. The film would be indistinguishable from many other examples of Soviet socialist realism, were it not for the chilling clarity since Vadim Yusov's photography and the

visual flourishes that decorate the action. Even without these elements, however, this is still a shrewd insight into the reckless courage of youth and the grotesque poetry of combat. In Russian with English subtitles. ▭

Kolya Burlyaev *Ivan* • Valentin Zubkov *Capt Kholin* • E Zharikov *Lt Galtsev* • S Krylov *Cpl Katasonych* ■ *Dir* Andrei Tarkovsky • *Scr* Vladimir Bogomolov, Mikhail Papava

I've Always Loved You
★★ U

Drama   1946 · US · Colour · 117mins

Hollywood's great early romanticist and first ever Oscar-winning director, Frank Borzage, came unstuck with this offering towards the end of his long career. It stars Philip Dorn as a brilliant concert conductor torn between love and jealousy of his latest protégée, Catherine McLeod – and that's about the size of the almost invisible plot, attached to a tedious and overlong script. The film does, however, offer a feast of musical interludes, encompassing Rachmaninov, Chopin, Beethoven, Bach and others, and the off-screen piano playing of the great Artur Rubinstein.

Philip Dorn *Leopold Goronoff* • Catherine McLeod *Myra Hassman* • William Carter *George Sampter* • Maria Ouspenskaya *Mme Goronoff* • Felix Bressart *Frederick Hassman* ■ *Dir* Frank Borzage • *Scr* Borden Chase, from the short story *Concerto* by Borden Chase • *Cinematographer* Tony Gaudio

I've Gotta Horse
★★ U

Musical comedy   1965 · UK · Colour · 92mins

Billy Fury, one of Britain's answers to Elvis back in the sixties, deserved better than this dumb confection, which failed to do for him what similar threadbare flicks did for Cliff Richard. *Coronation Street* fans might enjoy watching Amanda Barrie in her movie heyday. However, nothing can take your mind off the terrible plot, as singer Fury misses rehearsals to watch his racehorse run in the Derby.

Billy Fury *Billy* • Amanda Barrie *Jo* • Michael Medwin *Hymie Campbell* • Marjorie Rhodes *Mrs Bartholemew* • Bill Fraser *Mr Bartholemew* • Peter Gilmore *Jock* • Jon Pertwee *Costumer's assistant* • Michael Cashman *Peter* ■ *Dir* Kenneth Hume • *Scr* Ronald Wolfe, Ronald Chesney, from a story by Kenneth Hume, Larry Parnes

I've Heard the Mermaids Singing
★★★ 15

Comedy drama   1987 · Can · Colour · 79mins

A modest movie which competently tackles the hoary theme of a young woman's self-discovery. This is a very able first-time effort from writer/ director Patricia Rozema and is notable for introducing Sheila McCarthy as the scatty lead who works in a deeply chic art gallery. McCarthy drew high critical acclaim for her strong, winning performance, but this initial praise failed to translate itself into further meaty roles. The movie has an unfortunate tendency to take itself too seriously at points but, overall, this is a laudable, enjoyable and often highly original movie. ▭

Sheila McCarthy *Polly Vandersma* • Paule Baillargeon *Gabrielle St Peres* • Ann-Marie

MacDonald *Mary Joseph* • John Evans *Warren* • Brenda Kamino *Japanese waitress* • Richard Monette *Clive* ■ *Dir/Scr* Patricia Rozema

Ivory Hunters
★★ PG

Adventure drama   1990 · US · Colour · 94mins

This ecologically sound but dramatically suspect drama sends John Lithgow and Isabella Rossellini into the African bush to expose the illegal trade in ivory. Unfortunately, this worthy cause is hampered by some redundant sub-plots and mini-dramas along the way. Lithgow seems to be playing Ernest Hemingway or John Huston, which is not so much ivory as irony. Produced for American cable TV by the wildlife organisation, the Audabon Society. ▭

John Lithgow *Robert Carter* • Isabella Rossellini *Maria DiConti* • James Earl Jones *Inspector Nkuru* • Tony Todd *Jomo* • Olek Krupa *Marcel Dettienne* ■ *Dir* Joseph Sargent • *Scr* Bill Bozzone, Richard Guttman, from a story by Bradley T Winter

Ivy
★★

Drama   1947 · US · BW · 98mins

You couldn't ask for a better mounted, more visually accomplished example of period melodrama set in Edwardian England than this account of Joan Fontaine as the determined Ivy. She poisons her husband (Richard Ney) and pins the blame on her lover (Patric Knowles) to clear the way for her conquest of Herbert Marshall's bachelor millionaire, but she reckons without Sir Cedric Hardwicke's Scotland Yard inspector. Unfortunately, writer Charles Bennett and director Sam Wood fail to create any suspense and Ivy's ultimate fate is an irritating contrivance.

Joan Fontaine *Ivy Lexton* • Patric Knowles *Dr Roger Gretorex* • Herbert Marshall *Miles Rushworth* • Richard Ney *Jervis Lexton* • Sir Cedric Hardwicke [Cedric Hardwicke] *Inspector Orpington* ■ *Dir* Sam Wood • *Scr* Charles Bennett, from the novel *The Story of Ivy* by Marie Belloc Lowndes

Izzy and Moe
★★★ U

Comedy   1985 · US · Colour · 92mins

The irresistible comedy team of Jackie Gleason and Art Carney (*The Honeymooners*) reunite in this delightful TV movie. They play a pair of ex-vaudevillians who become Federal Prohibition officers and put their theatrical experience to good use pursuing bootleggers. While the plot is slight, the movie is a showcase for the remarkable comedic talents of Gleason and Carney. Capably directed by former child star Jackie Cooper (*The Champ*), this is amusing escapism. ▭

Jackie Gleason *Isadore ''Izzy''Einstein* • Art Carney *Morris ''Moe''Smith* • Cynthia Harris *Dallas Carter* • Zohra Lampert *Esther* • Dick Latessa *Lieutenant Murphy* • Thelma Lee *Mrs Pearlman* • Drew Snyder *Sergeant John McCoy* ■ *Dir* Jackie Cooper • *Scr* Robert Boris • *Music* Jackie Gleason

JD's Revenge ★★ 18
Blaxploitation horror
1976 · US · Colour · 91mins

Cheap and cheerful horror chiller that is neither good nor bad enough to become a true cult classic but has its supporters nevertheless. Glynn Turman is the college boy whose body becomes inhabited by a dead gangster from the Prohibition days who soon turns the unwilling lad into a ruthless killer. Lou Gossett pops up as a priest and delivers the film's best performance, although it's put together with confidence by Arthur Marks. ▭

Glynn Turman *Ike* • Joan Pringle *Christella* • Louis Gossett Jr *Reverend Bliss* • Carl Crudup *Tony* • James Louis Watkins *Carl* • Alice Jubert *Roberta/Betty Jo* ■ *Dir* Arthur Marks • *Scr* Jaison Starkes

J Edgar Hoover ★★★
Biography 1987 · US · Colour · 110mins

His eyes glinting with malevolence and megalomania, Treat Williams revels in the opportunity to play the FBI chief, who was not only feared by America's criminals, but by anyone who challenged his status quo. Considering how many lives Hoover ruined, this could easily have turned into a merciless character assassination. However, Robert Collins's movie is more interested in exploring how a democracy could have allowed such a vitriolic figure to acquire so much power. Based on William G Sullivan and William S Brown's lid-blowing book *My 30 Years in Hoover's FBI*, this is flawed but fascinating.

Treat Williams *J Edgar Hoover* • Rip Torn *Lyndon Johnson* • David Ogden Stiers *Franklin D Roosevelt* • Robert Harper *Clyde Tolson* • Louise Fletcher *Annie M Hoover* • Art Hindle *John F Kennedy* • James F Kelly *Robert F Kennedy* • Charles Hallahan *Joseph McCarthy* ■ *Dir* Robert Collins • *Scr* Robert Collins, from the non-fiction book *My 30 Years in Hoover's FBI* by William S Brown, William G Sullivan

JFK ★★★★ 15
Thriller 1991 · US · Colour · 180mins

It's pretty clear that what we have here is an overblown and factually shaky version of the events surrounding the assassination of John F Kennedy. It's also more than obvious that director Oliver Stone takes his self-appointed position as the chronicler of recent US history far too seriously to be objective or concise. Yet, before you dismiss this review as just another conspiracy against Stone and his star Kevin Costner, let's remember that the cover-up theory has lost none of its fascination more than 35 years after the event. What's so remarkable about the film is how deftly Stone conveys such a wealth of information and how

he manages to ensure every character makes an impact. The Oscar-winning photography and editing are superb, and the ensemble is a triumph of casting. A clear case of unmissable cinema. Contains swearing, violence and drug abuse. ▭ **DVD**

Kevin Costner *Jim Garrison* • Sissy Spacek *Liz Garrison* • Joe Pesci *David Ferrie* • Tommy Lee Jones *Clay Shaw* • Gary Oldman *Lee Harvey Oswald* • Jay O Sanders *Lou Ivon* • Michael Rooker *Bill Broussard* • Laurie Metcalf *Susie Cox* • Gary Grubbs *Al Oser* • John Candy *Dean Andrews* • Jack Lemmon *Jack Martin* • Walter Matthau *Senator Russell Long* • Ed Asner *Guy Bannister* • Donald Sutherland *Colonel X* • Kevin Bacon *Willie O'Keefe* • Brian Doyle-Murray *Jack Ruby* ■ *Dir* Oliver Stone • *Scr* Oliver Stone, Zachary Sklar, from the non-fiction book *On the Trail of the Assassins* by Jim Garrison, from the non-fiction book *Crossfire: the Plot That Killed Kennedy* by Jim Marrs • *Cinematographer* Robert Richardson • *Music* John Williams

JLG/JLG – Self Portrait in December ★★★
Experimental documentary
1994 · Fr/Swi · Colour · 65mins

Shot in winter around his Swiss home on Lake Léman, this short Jean-Luc Godard documentary is a self-portrait of the *enfant terrible* who once rocked cinema on its heels, only to be marginalised (albeit partly through his own connivance) by the art form he helped transform. Discussing his diverse sources of inspiration, Godard appears secure in his reputation as a film-maker who has experimented with the moving image while making heartfelt and often controversial political and artistic statements. Constantly referencing his own output and works that continue to influence him, this is an eloquent dissertation from one of cinema's few philosopher-poets. In French with English subtitles.

Dir/Scr Jean-Luc Godard

JW Coop ★★★
Drama 1971 · US · Colour · 112mins

After winning the best actor Oscar for *Charly*, Cliff Robertson used his clout to produce, direct, write and star in this story of a rodeo rider who, after spending ten years in jail, finds himself adrift in a more commercialised and cynical world. Robertson is excellent as the eponymous cowboy, but the film shows its age by confronting him with tiresome hippies who advocate free love and soya beans instead of beef. Coop went to jail for passing a forged cheque; in 1977, Robertson blew the whistle on Columbia executive David Begelman who was himself passing forged cheques, creating the biggest Hollywood scandal in years.

Cliff Robertson *JW Coop* • Geraldine Page *Mama* • Cristina Ferrare *Bean* • RG Armstrong *Jim Sawyer* • RL Armstrong *Tooter Watson* ■ *Dir* Cliff Robertson • *Scr* Cliff Robertson, Gary Cartwright, Bud Shrake

Jabberwocky ★★ PG
Comedy fantasy 1977 · UK · Colour · 100mins

Inspired by the Lewis Carroll poem, Terry Gilliam's debut feature is an uneven mix of medieval tomfoolery and crude Monty Python humour. Fellow Python Michael Palin plays the hero who, to prove his worth and win the

hand of a fair maiden, sets out to kill the fearsome "manxome foe". The production design is stunning, and the look of the Jabberwock is based on the illustrations that Sir John Tenniel created for Carroll's original book. For all that, Gilliam's grim fantasy barely raises itself above the tiresome. ▭

Michael Palin *Dennis Cooper* • Max Wall *King Bruno* • Deborah Fallender *Princess* • John Le Mesurier *Chamberlain* • Annette Badland *Griselda Fishfinger* • Warren Mitchell *Mr Fishfinger* • Brenda Cowling *Mrs Fishfinger* • Harry H Corbett *Squire* • Rodney Bewes *Other Squire* • Bernard Bresslaw *Landlord* ■ *Dir* Terry Gilliam • *Scr* Terry Gilliam, Charles Alverson, from the poem *Jabberwocky* by Lewis Carroll

J'Accuse ★★★
Drama 1938 · Fr · BW · 95mins

As war loomed, Abel Gance reworked his 1919 classic to warn again of the follies of conflict. The poet is (over)played by Victor Francen, who vows to promote pacifism after surviving the slaughter of his trench patrol. However, his invention of unbreakable glass is misappropriated by the government and he is forced to summon the First World War dead from their graves to march across the country to persuade world leaders to outlaw fighting forever. Again the finale is the most moving and spectacular aspect of the picture, which is too often sidetracked by Francen's rivalry with Jean Max for Renée Devillers. In French with English subtitles.

Victor Francen *Jean Diaz* • Jean Max *Henri Chimay* • Delaître *François Laurin* • Renée Devillers *Helene* • Line Noro *Edith* ■ *Dir* Abel Gance • *Scr* Abel Gance, Steve Passeur

Jack ★★★ PG
Comedy drama 1996 · US · Colour · 108mins

In *Big*, Tom Hanks played a boy in the body of a man. *Jack* repeats the trick by casting Robin Williams as a 10-year-old who looks like a 40-year-old, the result of an ageing disorder that has made his body mature at an incredible rate. Diane Lane and Brian Kerwin give subtle performances as Jack's confused parents, and there's a sweet contribution from actress/singer Jennifer Lopez as his teacher. Unfortunately, Williams goes over the top again and his exuberance is unchecked by director Francis Ford Coppola, who proved with *Peggy Sue Got Married* that he wasn't the deftest hand at quirky fare. At least the film's heart is in the right place. ▭ **DVD**

Robin Williams *Jack Powell* • Diane Lane *Karen Powell* • Brian Kerwin *Brian Powell* • Jennifer Lopez *Miss Marquez* • Bill Cosby *Lawrence Woodruff* • Fran Drescher *Dolores Durante* • Michael McKean *Paulie* ■ *Dir* Francis Ford Coppola • *Scr* James DeMonaco, Gary Nadeau

Jack Ahoy! ★★★
Comedy 1934 · UK · BW · 70mins

This was a huge success in its day for jovial, lantern-jawed Jack Hulbert, and is one of a series of hits that still amuse today. Here, Hulbert sings *The Hat's on the Side of My Head* and gets kidnapped by Chinese revolutionaries! There's a nice pace and an easy-going air of geniality brought to this maritime

caper by skilled director Walter Forde, and its sheer breeziness is infectious.

Jack Hulbert *Jack Ponsonby* • Nancy O'Neil *Patricia Fraser* • Alfred Drayton *Admiral Fraser* • Tamara Desni *Conchita* • Henry Peterson *Larios* • Sam Wilkinson *Dodger* ■ *Dir* Walter Forde • *Scr* Jack Hulbert, Leslie Leslie Arliss, Gerard Fairlie, Austin Melford, from a story by Sidney Sidney Gilliat

Jack & Sarah ★★★ 15
Romantic comedy drama
1995 · UK · Colour · 105mins

A refreshing British spin on an ever-popular formula: men coping with babies. Richard E Grant is the high-flying lawyer who becomes a bumbling single father when his wife dies in childbirth; Samantha Mathis is the visiting American who is roped into being the child's nanny and falls for her employer. Grant and Mathis are appealing leads, but it is the classy hamming of Ian McKellen and Judi Dench that steals the show, with director Tim Sullivan just about keeping sentimentality at bay. Contains swearing. ▭

Richard E Grant *Jack* • Samantha Mathis *Amy* • Judi Dench *Margaret* • Ian McKellen *William* • Cherie Lunghi *Anna* • Eileen Atkins *Phil* • Imogen Stubbs *Sarah* • David Swift *Michael* • Laurent Grevill *Alain* • Kate Hardie *Pamela* ■ *Dir/Scr* Tim Sullivan

Jack Be Nimble ★★★ 18
Horror thriller 1992 · NZ · Colour · 91mins

Maybe it's all the sheep and empty spaces, but New Zealand has a good track record on horror (think *Death Warmed Up*, *Bad Taste*, *The Ugly*) and this creepily gothic offering is a satisfyingly twisted affair. Alexis Arquette is Jack, a young man who embarks on a monstrous plan of revenge with the help of a hypnosis machine, after suffering years of abuse at the hands of brutal foster parents. Sarah Smuts-Kennedy plays his equally long-suffering – and now long lost – sister, while "Mr NZ Cinema" Bruno Lawrence makes one of his last appearances. It's an uneven ride but writer/director Garth Maxwell conjures up some disturbing imagery. ▭

Alexis Arquette *Jack* • Sarah Smuts-Kennedy *Dora* • Bruno Lawrence *Teddy* • Tony Barry *Clarrie* • Elizabeth Hawthorne *Clarrie's wife* • Brenda Simmons *Mrs Birch* • Gilbert Goldie *Mr Birch* • Tricia Phillips *Anne* • Paul Minifie *Kevin* ■ *Dir/Scr* Garth Maxwell

The Jack Bull ★★★★
Western 1999 · US · Colour · 116mins

John Badham's unheralded but outstanding western was written by Dick Cusack and stars his son, John, as the horse dealer whose animals are mistreated by a neighbouring rancher. When the neighbour is backed up by the courts, Cusack launches an armed insurrection on the eve of Wyoming's bid for statehood. The story is based on Heinrich Von Kleist's *Michael Kohlhaas* and it gains rather than loses by its transposition to the American West. Cusack's Myrl Redding has the tragic overtones of a Thomas Hardy hero, a man to whom dreadful things happen, even in the best of times. This is a beautifully staged, unrelentingly sombre movie with a satisfying political complexity.

U = SUITABLE FOR ALL   **Uc** = SUITABLE FOR ALL, ESPECIALLY FOR YOUNG CHILDREN (VIDEO ONLY)   **PG** = PARENTAL GUIDANCE

John Cusack *Myrl Redding* • John Goodman *Judge Tolliver* • LQ Jones *Henry Ballard* • Miranda Otto *Cora* • John C McGinley *Woody* • John Savage *Slater* • Rodney A Grant *Billy* ■ *Dir* John Badham • *Scr* Dick Cusack, from the book *Michael Kohlhaas* by Heinrich Von Kleist

Jack Frost ★★ PG

Fantasy comedy drama
1998 • US • Colour • 97mins

Charmless fantasy fable about a rock musician dad resurrected as a snowman to watch over his son. Michael Keaton as a sinister-looking snowboarding Frost-dad requires a leap of imagination. Everything else is pretty unbelievable too, from the fake looking snow-creation (substandard work from Jim Henson's Creature Shop) to the inanity of Keaton's fatherly assistance. If it had been played as broad farce it might have worked. Unfortunately, the four scriptwriters decided to aim for the emotional resonance of *Ghost*, coating the whole movie in sickly icing. Contains some strong language. ▭
DVD

Michael Keaton *Jack Frost* • Kelly Preston *Gabby Frost* • Joseph Cross *Charlie Frost* • Mark Addy *Mac* • Henry Rollins *Sid Gronic* • Dweezil Zappa *John Kaplan* ■ *Dir* Troy Miller • *Scr* Steve Bloom, Jonathan Roberts, Mark Steven Johnson, Jeff Cesario, from a story by Mark Steven Johnson

Jack London ★★

Biographical adventure
1944 • US • BW • 93mins

A biopic of the novelist whose adventure stories have made many a movie. As the writer, Broadway actor Michael O'Shea is not ideal casting – you need someone like Clark Gable to pull off this globe-trotting, hard-drinking womaniser – while the film's emphasis on the Japanese-American conflict of 1904 is milked for its then contemporary relevance. Susan Hayward barely registers as London's wife and on whose memoir the film is loosely based.

Michael O'Shea *Jack London* • Susan Hayward *Charmain Kittredge* • Osa Massen *Freda Maloof* • Harry Davenport *Prof Hilliard* • Frank Craven *Old Tom* • Virginia Mayo *Mamie* • Ralph Morgan *George Brett* ■ *Dir* Alfred Santell • *Scr* Ernest Pascal, from the biography *The Book of Jack London* by Charmain London

Jack London's The Call of the Wild ★★★

Adventure 1996 • Can • Colour • 91mins

Yet another version of this story about the dog with the heart of an ox. Richard Dreyfuss is the narrator upon whom director Peter Svatek relies to bring London's richly evocative words to the screen and get into the mind of its canine legend, Buck. The actors, headed by Rutger Hauer as John Thornton, are not so well-served, though the famous sled-race scene is as heartstopping as ever.

Rutger Hauer *John Thornton* • Luc Morissette *Perrault* • Richard Dreyfuss *Narrator/Burarator* • Charles Powell *Hal* • Robert Pierre Cote *François* • Burke Lawrence *Charles* ■ *Dir* Peter Svatek • *Scr* Graham Ludlow, from the novel by Jack London

Jack of Diamonds ★★★ U

Crime drama
1967 • US/W Ger • Colour • 107mins

A heist movie that – appropriately enough – steals its best ideas from earlier movies, specifically *Topkapi*, while George Hamilton's role as an elegant, sophisticated cat burglar harks back to Cary Grant in Hitchcock's *To Catch a Thief*. Pinch some more bits from *The Pink Panther* and *How to Steal a Million* and you get a campy, quite amusing yarn about some dazzling diamonds and a robbery that doesn't go quite according to plan. Hamilton appears to be enjoying himself, Joseph Cotten plays his mentor and there are three glamour queens playing themselves, draped in baubles: Carroll Baker, Zsa Zsa Gabor and Lilli Palmer.

George Hamilton *Jeff Hill* • Joseph Cotten *Ace of Diamonds* • Marie Laforêt *Olga* • Maurice Evans *Nicolai* • Alexander Hegarth *Brugger* • Carroll Baker • Zsa Zsa Gabor • Lilli Palmer ■ *Dir* Don Taylor • *Scr* Jack DeWitt, Sandy Howard, Robert J Loseph

Jack Reed: a Search for Justice ★★★ 12

Police drama 1994 • US • Colour • 91mins

Hard-working Brian Dennehy is involved in just every about every part of this addition to the popular Jack Reed series serving as director, as well as co-producer and co-writer. In this one, he finds that the nightclub owner he suspects of murdering a young employee has powerful friends in the local establishment. Dennehy is as bruisingly charismatic as ever, there's able support from regulars Charles S Dutton and Susan Ruttan, and a nice supporting turn from Miguel Ferrer. ▭

Brian Dennehy *Jack Reed* • Susan Ruttan *Arlene Reed* • Charles S Dutton *Charles Silvera* • Miguel Ferrer *Win Carter* • Charles Hallahan *Roy Galvin* ■ *Dir/Scr* Brian Dennehy

Jack Reed: Badge of Honor ★★★ 15

Police drama 1993 • US • Colour • 89mins

Following the success of the mini-series featuring Chicago cop Jack Reed, Brian Dennehy returns as the uncompromising lawman in this above average TV movie. Called in on what looks like an open-and-shut case of murder, Dennehy is blocked at every turn by the FBI because his chief suspect is its star witness in a vital arms smuggling trial. It's not all crime fighting, however, as Dennehy and his screen wife, Susan Ruttan recognisable from *LA Law* also care for the murder victim's son. William Sadler does well as the x-ray technician with a decidedly dodgy past, but it's Dennehy who dominates the proceedings. ▭

Brian Dennehy *Jack Reed* • Susan Ruttan *Arlene Reed* • William Sadler *David Anatole* • Alice Krige *Joan Anatole* • RD Call *Lieutenant Lloyd Butler* ■ *Dir* Kevin Connor • *Scr* Andrew Andrew Laskos

Jack Reed: Death and Vengeance ★★ 15

Police drama 1996 • US • Colour • 86mins

Another eminently watchable entry in Brian Dennehy's successful made-for-

TV cop franchise. This one finds Dennehy's bluff detective uncovering local Government corruption while tracking the killers of his partner, only to find himself being framed for murder. Susan Ruttan returns as Reed's long-suffering wife as does other series regular Charles S Dutton, while Dennehy handles all his chores – script, direction, performance – with his usual no-nonsense reliability. ▭

Brian Dennehy *Jack Reed* • Charles S Dutton *Charles Silvera* • Susan Ruttan *Arlene Reed* • Anthony Zerbe *Sanford Miller* ■ *Dir* Brian Dennehy • *Scr* Bill Phillips, Brian Dennehy

Jack the Bear ★★ 15

Drama 1993 • US • Colour • 94mins

This heavy-handed modern fairy tale was directed by Marshall Herskovitz, who cut his teeth on TV's *thirtysomething*. The idea that real and imaginary terrors are often indistinguishable in the mind of a child is hardly an original one and this contrived tosh draws no startling conclusions, which is all the more disappointing as it's supposed to be a chiller. Danny DeVito hurls himself into the role of the widowed father, whose job as a horror show host does little to ease the fears of his son, who is impressively played by the film's major plus factor, Robert J Steinmiller Jr. ▭

Danny DeVito *John Leary* • Robert J Steinmiller Jr *Jack Leary* • Miko Hughes *Dylan Leary* • Gary Sinise *Norman Strick* • Art LaFleur *Mr Festinger* • Stefan Gierasch *Grandpa Glickes* • Erica Yohn *Grandma Glickes* ■ *Dir* Marshall Herskovitz • *Scr* Steven Zaillian, from the novel *Jack the Bear* by Dan McCall

Jack the Giant Killer ★★★

Fantasy 1962 • US • Colour • 94mins

Having already made *Attack of the 50ft Woman*, former Oscar-winning art director Nathan "Jerry" Juran tried for the same heights, metaphorically speaking, with this charming and enjoyable children's fairy tale. Juran is reunited with Kerwin Matthews, his star in *The Seventh Voyage of Sinbad*, and succeeds in creating a genuinely original romp for kids of all ages. Incidentally, on reissue the title lost its "Jack" and songs were bizarrely added to the soundtrack.

Kerwin Mathews *Jack* • Judi Meredith *Princess Elaine* • Torin Thatcher *Pendragon* • Walter Burke *Garna* • Roger Mobley *Peter* • Don Beddoe *Imp in bottle* ■ *Dir* Nathan Juran • *Scr* Orville H Hampton, Nathan Juran, from a story by Orville H Hampton

Jack the Ripper ★★★

Crime drama 1958 • UK • BW • 82mins

Made cheaply, this likeable little shocker received "A" treatment on release, thus promoting "stars" Lee Patterson and Eddie Byrne to feature players, albeit very briefly. Canadian actor Patterson had quite a following in Britain during the late fifties, thanks to a string of now forgotten programme fillers, and here his presence lends weight to the infamous tale. The film's stark title and its inevitable X certificate brought the producing/directing team of Bob Baker and Monty Berman a box-office hit. The spooky

atmosphere is well maintained, and the cheapness doesn't show.

Lee Patterson *Sam Lowry* • Eddie Byrne *Inspector O'Neill* • Betty McDowall *Anne Ford* • Ewen Solon *Sir David Rogers* • John Le Mesurier *Dr Tranter* • George Rose *Clarke* ■ *Dir* Robert S Baker, Monty Berman • *Scr* Jimmy Sangster, from a story by Peter Hammond

Jack the Ripper ★★★ 15

Crime drama 1988 • UK • Colour • 183mins

This intriguing, if somewhat protracted, speculation on Jack the Ripper's identity stars Michael Caine as Inspector Abberline, the real-life Scotland Yard detective who investigated the gruesome murders of East End prostitutes in the late 1880s. The fine supporting cast includes Jane Seymour, Armand Assante, Harry Andrews and Lewis Collins, while director and co-writer David Wickes revels in the foggy, gaslit ambience of Victorian London. ▭

Michael Caine *Inspector Abberline* • Armand Assante *Richard Mansfield* • Jane Seymour *Emma Prentice* • Lewis Collins *Sergeant George Godley* • Susan George *Cathy Eddowes* • Harry Andrews *Coroner* • Lysette Anthony *Mary Jane Kelly* ■ *Dir* David Wickes • *Scr* Derek Marlowe, David Wickes

The Jackal ★★★ 18

Action thriller 1997 • US • Colour • 119mins

Fred Zinnemann's *The Day of the Jackal* gets the Bruce Willis treatment courtesy of director Michael Caton-Jones. The classic thriller about an assassin at large has been relocated to America and now comes equipped with all kinds of techno-props which add nothing at all to the original's ruthless efficiency. Willis supplants Edward Fox, as the killer – and, surprisingly, doesn't make too bad a job of it. Willis, Richard Gere (as an IRA terrorist) and Russian intelligence officer Diane Venora compete for the Meryl Streep Most Authentic Foreign Accent award. Contains swearing and violence. ▭

Bruce Willis *The Jackal* • Richard Gere *Declan Mulqueen* • Sidney Poitier *FBI Deputy Director Carter Preston* • Diane Venora *Major Valentina Koslova* • Mathilda May *Isabella* • JK Simmons *Witherspoon* ■ *Dir* Michael Caton-Jones • *Scr* Chuck Pfarrer, from the film *The Day of the Jackal* by Kenneth Ross

Jackie Brown ★★★★ 15

Crime thriller 1997 • US • Colour • 147mins

Imaginatively dragging Elmore Leonard's bestseller *Rum Punch* into his own post-modern universe peppered with quirky dialogue and cinematic references, director Quentin Tarantino makes his re-energised crime thriller a homage to, and an updating of, seventies pulp blaxploitation fiction. Black icon Pam Grier is great as the air hostess pressured into an entrapment scam after being arrested for illegal cash smuggling, who decides to use her feminine wiles to outsmart everyone wanting to exploit or kill her. Tarantino draws maximum suspense from a superb cast and an array of visual techniques such as staging a key scene three times from three different points of view. A breathlessly exciting crime drama cut to a fabulous array of funk classics. Contains swearing, some violence, drug abuse and a sex scene. 🎬 *DVD*

Pam Grier *Jackie Brown* • Samuel L Jackson *Ordell Robbie* • Robert Forster *Max Cherry* • Bridget Fonda *Melanie* • Michael Keaton *Ray Nicolette* • Robert De Niro *Louis Gara* • Michael Bowen *Mark Dargus* • Lisa Gay Hamilton *Sheronda* • Tommy "Tiny" Lister Jr [Tom "Tiny" Lister Jr] *Winston* • Hattie Winston *Simone* • Denise Crosby *Public defender* ◼ *Dir* Quentin Tarantino • *Scr* Quentin Tarantino, from the novel *Rum Punch* by Elmore Leonard

Jackie Chan's First Strike ★★ 🔞12

Action adventure 1996 · HK · Colour · 80mins

Placing less emphasis on kung fu action (although it does feature an amazing fight involving a step-ladder) and more on spectacular stunts, this Jackie Chan comedy thriller is a Bond-esque romp shot on location all over the globe. A pretty idiotic plot sees Chan playing a Hong Kong cop who is hired by both the CIA and Russian intelligence to recover a stolen nuclear warhead. As ever, the storyline is a thin excuse to string together a series of breathtaking action sequences. Cantonese dialogue dubbed into English. 🎬 *DVD*

Jackie Chan *Jackie* • Jackson Lou Tsui • Chen Chun Wu *Annie* • Bill Tung *Uncle Bill* • Jouri Petrov *Colonel Gregor Yegorov* ◼ *Dir* Stanley Tong • *Scr* Stanley Tong, Nick Tramontane, Greg Mellot, Elliot Tong

Jackie Stewart: Weekend of a Champion ★★★★

Documentary 1971 · UK · Colour · 80mins

Formula One fans musn't miss this excellent and sometimes quirky profile of Jackie Stewart as he prepares for the Monaco Grand Prix in 1971, the year he won his second World Championship. The film was produced by Roman Polanski – like Stewart, one of the smart set and a racing fanatic who wanders around the pits and the track, getting the inside story. Way above the standard of the usual sports documentary, it probes the mind and the frayed nervous system of a racing driver, and vividly captures the mad F1 circus at its most glamorous venue.

Dir/Scr Frank Simon

Jackie's Back! ★★

Comedy 1999 · US · Colour · 120mins

A well-intentioned but uneven spoof which stars singer Jenifer Lewis (*The Preacher's Wife*) as a former child star-turned-one-hit wonder who decides to make her singing comeback. Tim Curry overacts a bit, but has fun as a pompous English documentarian assigned to chronicle the difficult diva on the eve of her career-reviving concert in Hollywood.

Jenifer Lewis *Jackie Washington* • Tim Curry *Edward Whatsett St John* • Tom Arnold *Marv* • Loretta Devine *Snookie* • Whoopi Goldberg *Ethyl* • Julie Hagerty *Pammy* ◼ *Dir* Robert Townsend • *Scr* Mark Alton Brown, Dee LaDuke

Jacknife ★★★ 15

Drama 1988 · US · Colour · 98mins

Robert De Niro returns to the traumas of Vietnam in this talky, yet engrossing, drama. He plays an ex-serviceman who has finally come to terms with the conflict, setting out to help his old friend Ed Harris, who is still deeply disturbed by his experiences of the war. Apart from a few, not entirely convincing, wartime flashbacks, director David Jones concentrates on the interplay between De Niro and Harris, and they both make the most of Stephen Metcalfe's perceptive script. Not in the same league as *The Deer Hunter*, but a modest, rewarding experience, nevertheless. Contains swearing. 🎬

Robert De Niro *Joseph "Megs" Megessey* • Ed Harris *Dave* • Kathy Baker *Martha* • Charles S Dutton *Jake* • Elizabeth Franz *Pru Buckman* • Tom Isbell *Bobby Buckman* • Loudon Wainwright III *Ferretti* • Sloane Shelton *Shirley* ◼ *Dir* David Jones • *Scr* Stephen Metcalfe, from his play *Strange Snow*

The Jackpot ★★★ U

Comedy 1950 · US · BW · 86mins

James Stewart wins a cash bonanza on a radio quiz show and finds that his life changes in many unexpected ways. To his dismay, he discovers he has to sell the prizes to pay the taxes on them. Lightweight comedy fluff, still timely in the National Lottery era, with Stewart turning on his effortless charm to lift the innocent fun up a few likeable notches.

James Stewart *Bill Lawrence* • Barbara Hale *Amy Lawrence* • James Gleason *Harry Summers* • Fred Clark *Mr Woodruff* • Alan Mowbray *Leslie* • Patricia Medina *Hilda Jones* • Natalie Wood *Phyllis Lawrence* • Tommy Rettig *Tommy Lawrence* ◼ *Dir* Walter Lang • *Scr* Phoebe Ephron, Henry Ephron, from an article by John McNulty

Jack's Back ★★ 18

Mystery thriller 1988 · US · Colour · 92mins

James Spader enjoys himself in dual roles in this modern, nasty spin on the Jack the Ripper story. The setting is eighties Los Angeles, where the Victorian serial killer's crimes are being visited upon a new generation. When suspicion falls on Spader, his twin brother (Spader again) sets out to prove the authorities wrong. The improbable plotting might raise some eyebrows, but director Rowdy Herrington summons up a fair amount of suspense. 🎬

James Spader *John/Rick Wesford* • Cynthia Gibb *Christine Moscari* • Rod Loomis *Dr Sidney Tannerson* • Rex Ryon *Jack Pendler* • Robert Picardo *Dr Carlos Battera* • Jim Haynie *Sergeant Gabriel* • Wendell Wright *Captain Walter Prentis* ◼ *Dir/Scr* Rowdy Herrington

Jackson County Jail ★★★★

Chase drama 1976 · US · Colour · 83mins

A stunning example of exploitation, artfully using the genre's stark conventions to make cogent comments on society. In one of her strongest roles, Yvette Mimieux is an LA executive who drives across country to New York only to have a disastrous encounter with southern "justice" after she is beaten up by the hitchhikers she has picked up. Michael Miller

directs his gripping feminist B-movie with raw-edged grit and a clear eye for action, while co-star Tommy Lee Jones backs up Mimieux to the hilt. Upsetting, but highly recommended. Contains violence and swearing.

Yvette Mimieux *Dinah Hunter* • Tommy Lee Jones *Coley Blake* • Robert Carradine *Bobby Ray* • Frederic Cook *Hobie* • Severn Darden *Sheriff Dempsey* • Nan Martin *Allison* • Mary Woronov *Pearl* • Howard Hesseman *David* ◼ *Dir* Michael Miller • *Scr* Donald Stewart

Jacob ★★★

Biblical drama 1994 · US/It/Ger · Colour

Old Testament movies are invariably overwritten affairs in which reverence for the source stilts the drama. Here, screenwriter Lionel Chetwynd can't resist the grandiose language, but he makes a decent job of packing what is a sprawling and, at times, improbable tale into this TV movie. Filmed in Morocco, the story of Jacob's feud with his brother Esau, his complicated love life in exile and his eventual return and renaming, is directed with gravitas by Peter Hall. Matthew Modine brings a certain charm to the title role, but the more interesting performances come from veterans Joss Ackland, Irene Papas and Giancarlo Giannini.

Matthew Modine *Jacob* • Lara Flynn Boyle *Rachel* • Sean Bean *Esau* • Joss Ackland *Isaac* • Juliet Aubrey *Leah* • Irene Papas *Rebekah* • Giancarlo Giannini *Laban* ◼ *Dir* Peter Hall • *Scr* Lionel Chetwynd

Jacob's Ladder ★★ 18

Thriller 1990 · US · Colour · 108mins

What's causing Vietnam veteran Tim Robbins's nightmare hallucinations as he wanders New York trying to figure out their mystical meaning? You'll be halfway up Adrian Lyne's shaky ladder before the *Fatal Attraction* director even thinks you're ready to climb the first rung! Although this rough assembly of horror clichés is tautly scripted by *Ghost* writer Bruce Joel Rubin, Lyne orchestrates his satanic flashdance into an overly pretentious mess of distorted *Platoon* images and Biblical red herrings. And any fantasy resorting to Al Jolson's song *Sonny Boy* to tug at the emotions is clearly in dire trouble. Contains violence, swearing and nudity. 🎬

Tim Robbins *Jacob Singer* • Elizabeth Pena *Jezzie* • Danny Aiello *Louis* • Matt Craven *Michael* • Pruitt Taylor Vince *Paul* • Jason Alexander *Donald Geary* • Macaulay Culkin *Gabe* • Eriq La Salle *Frank* ◼ *Dir* Adrian Lyne • *Scr* Bruce Joel Rubin

Jacqueline ★★ U

Drama 1956 · UK · BW · 89mins

John Gregson was among the most sympathetic of postwar British actors, but even he tries the patience in this Belfast-based reworking of *Pollyanna*. With good intentions endlessly lapsing into self-pity, Gregson overdoes the pathos as the shipyard worker who is plunged into the depths of despair when he loses his job as a result of vertigo. There's a similar lack of restraint about Jacqueline Ryan (whose mother, Kathleen, co-stars) as the daughter who tries to land him a longed-for farm job. Although it was based on the novel *A Grand Man*, this

mawkish melodrama owes more to the films of Shirley Temple than the imagination of Catherine Cookson, even though Cookson had a hand in the script. 🎬

John Gregson *Mike McNeil* • Kathleen Ryan *Elizabeth McNeil* • Jacqueline Ryan *Jacqueline McNeil* • Noel Purcell *Mr Owen* • Cyril Cusack *Mr Flannagan* • Maureen Swanson *Maggie* • Tony Wright *Jack McBride* • Liam Redmond *Mr Lord* • Maureen Delaney *Mrs McBride* ◼ *Dir* Roy Baker [Roy Ward Baker] • *Scr* Patrick Kirwan, Liam O'Flaherty, Patrick Campbell, Catherine Cookson, from the novel *A Grand Man* by Catherine Cookson

Jacquot de Nantes ★★★★★ PG

Biography 1991 · Fr · Colour and BW · 114mins

Agnès Varda's tribute to her late husband, Jacques Demy, was considered too cosy and sentimental in some quarters. But this is a genuinely fond and often moving portrait of the film-maker as a young man. The sequences depicting how Demy painstakingly created his earliest animated efforts are compelling and superbly convey the nascent passion for cinema that would result in such classics as *The Umbrellas of Cherbourg*. It's to Varda's credit that the film works both as biography and drama, but perhaps her finest achievement is in coaxing such a charming performance out of the inexperienced Philippe Maron. In French with English subtitles. 🎬

Philippe Maron *Jacquot 1* • Edouard Joubeaud *Jacquot 2* • Laurent Monnier *Jacquot 3* • Brigitte De Villepoix *Marilou, Mother* • Daniel Dublet *Raymond, Father* • Clement Delaroche *Yvon 1* ◼ *Dir* Agnès Varda • *Scr* Agnès Varda, from a story by Jacques Demy

Jade ★ 18

Erotic thriller 1995 · US · Colour · 91mins

William Friedkin's slick direction can't hide the trashy heart of this Joe Eszterhas scripted one-dimensional psycho thriller, which *NYPD Blue* TV actor David Caruso banked on to make him a star. No such luck. He's the assistant district attorney taking on the case of old flame Linda Fiorentino, a clinical psychologist who might be leading a double life as a murderous prostitute. Chazz Palminteri is the third part of a murky triangle. No one emerges with credit from this absurd farrago that's drenched in off-putting cinematic excess. Contains violence, sex scenes and swearing. 🎬

David Caruso *David Corelli* • Linda Fiorentino *Trina Gavin* • Chazz Palminteri *Matt Gavin* • Richard Crenna *Governor Edwards* • Michael Biehn *Bob Hargrove* • Donna Murphy *Karen Heller* ◼ *Dir* William Friedkin • *Scr* Joe Eszterhas

Jagged Edge ★★★★ 18

Thriller 1985 · US · Colour · 104mins

Because writer Joe Eszterhas has continually reworked the same basic formula (hero/heroine falls for murder suspect), it's easy to forget how startling the scenario was when it was first employed in this compelling thriller. Glenn Close is the defence attorney haunted by a case from her past when the wrong man went to jail, who falls in love with her client (Jeff Bridges), a charming publisher accused of brutally murdering his wealthy wife. Director Richard Marquand never misses a beat, gleefully tossing in red herrings and keeping the viewer constantly wondering whether Bridges is innocent or guilty. There are expert support turns from a foul-mouthed Robert Loggia and Peter Coyote, and it remains an enthralling, if a tad incredible, ride. Contains violence, swearing and brief nudity. ▦

Jeff Bridges *Jack Forrester* • Glenn Close *Teddy Barnes* • Peter Coyote *Thomas Krasny* • Robert Loggia *Sam Ransom* • John Dehner *Judge Carrigan* • Lance Henriksen *Frank Martin* • Leigh Taylor-Young *Virginia Howell* • Marshall Colt *Bobby Slade* ■ *Dir* Richard Marquand • *Scr* Joe Eszterhas

Jaguar Lives! ★ 🔟
Martial arts action
1979 · US · Colour · 82mins

The kung fu craze had long since expired by the time this lacklustre 007 spoof hit cinemas. Falling into the "never-heard-of-him" category is Joe Lewis as Jaguar, an agent skilled in hand-to-hand combat who sets out to smash an international drug ring, while three former Bond villains – Donald Pleasence, Christopher Lee and Joseph Wiseman – ham it up pointlessly. Director Ernest Pintoff was originally a cartoonist: it should be back to the drawing board for him. ▦

Joe Lewis *Jonathan Cross/Jaguar* • Christopher Lee *Adam Caine* • Donald Pleasence *General Villanova* • Barbara Bach *Anna* • Capucine *Zina Vanacore* • Joseph Wiseman *Ben Ashir* • Woody Strode *Sensei* ■ *Dir* Ernest Pintoff • *Scr* Yabo Yablonsky

Jail Bait ★★ 🅿🄶
Crime   1954 · US · BW · 68mins

Despite the sexploitation title, schlockmeister Ed Wood Jr's follow-up to his legendary *Glen or Glenda* is an unusual crime melodrama with a surprise ending. Gangster Timothy Farrell coerces the plastic surgeon father of the accomplice he's killed to alter his face so he can avoid detection. Like every Wood film, the facts behind it are more entertaining than actually watching it: Bela Lugosi was too ill to play the surgeon so silent star Herbert Rawlinson took over only to die the day after filming, while future *Hercules* star Steve Reeves makes his feature debut. ▦

Lyle Talbot *Inspector Johns* • Dolores Fuller *Marilyn Gregor* • Steve Reeves *Lieutenant Bob Lawrence* • Herbert Rawlinson *Dr Boris Gregor* • Theodora Thurman *Loretta* • Timothy Farrell *Vic Brady* ■ *Dir* Edward D Wood Jr • *Scr* Alex Gordon, Edward D Wood Jr

Jail Bait ★★★
Drama   1972 · W Ger · Colour · 100mins

Franz-Xaver Kroetz so despised this adaptation of his play that he gained an injunction forcing director Rainer Werner Fassbinder to remove two scenes he felt particularly betrayed his characters. Ultimately, Fassbinder made a show of disowning it himself, but this flawed film (which was originally made for German television) is far from a failure.Teenage lust and the chasm between the generations are the central themes, but this is also

a homage to Hollywood's rebellious youth pictures of the fifties. A boy is sent to prison for a sexual relationship with an underage girl, but continues it on his release. The violence and treachery are shocking, but perhaps the most disturbing aspect is the ease with which fascist values were still being disseminated among the lower middle-classes of Germany at the time. In German with English subtitles.

Eva Mattes *Hanni Schneider* • Harry Baer *Franz Bermeier* • Jorg von Liebenfels *Erwin Schneider, Hanni's father* • Ruth Drexel *Hilda Schneider, Hanni's mother* ■ *Dir* Rainer Werner Fassbinder • *Scr* Rainer Werner Fassbinder, from the play by Franz-Xaver Kroetz

Jail Busters ★★ 🅄
Prison comedy   1955 · US · BW · 61mins

The Bowery Boys were getting a bit long in the tooth and their routines had grown beards, but that didn't stop them churning out four low-budget comedies a year with undiminished energy in the mid-fifties. Here, three of the team put themselves behind bars to help a reporter expose corruption. An attempt by the prison psychiatrist to interview Huntz Hall is predictably amusing. The joke at the end of the escape tunnel was much funnier when Laurel and Hardy and Will Hay emerged with it in the thirties, however.

Huntz Hall *Horace Debussy "Sach"Jones* • Leo Gorcey *Terrence Aloysius "Slip"Mahoney* • Bernard Gorcey *Louie Dumbrowski* • Barton MacLane *Guard Jenkins* • Anthony Caruso *Ed Lannigan* • Percy Helton *Warden BW Oswald* ■ *Dir* William Beaudine • *Scr* Edward Bernds, Elwood Ullman

Jailbirds ★★ 🔟
Comedy adventure
1991 · US · Colour · 94mins

Dyan Cannon (still best known for her role in *Bob and Carol and Ted and Alice*, and her short marriage to Cary Grant), and Phylicia Rashad (Bill Cosby's wife in *The Cosby Show*), star as a couple of women on the run after escaping from prison. Both the leads are amiable enough, but the idea was better served by the hysterical *Midnight Run* with Charles Grodin and Robert De Niro, and the buddy-buddy aspect of the film is nothing new either. ▦

Dyan Cannon *Rosie Lacroix* • Phylicia Rashad *Janice Grant* • Dakin Matthews *Sheriff Dobbs* • David Knell *Deputy Baxter* • Ahmad Rashad *Larry* • Bethany Wright *Loretta* ■ *Dir* Burt Brinckerhoff • *Scr* Craig Heller, Guy Shulman, Marcia Midkiff, from a story by Marcia Midkiff

Jailbreak ★★
Thriller   1997 · US · Colour · 89mins

This may not go down as the greatest film with which Roger Corman was associated (he serves as executive producer), but it certainly lives up to his reputation for no-nonsense, fast-moving, low-budget entertainment. It also bears the Corman hallmark by virtue of the fact that it vaguely resembles his earlier *Jackson County Jail* (1976), in which the wrongfully arrested Yvette Mimieux went on the run with suspected killer Tommy Lee Jones. Ally Sheedy and David Carradine step into the roles for director Victoria Muspratt, who keeps the action brisk and bruising. Also

known as *Crossroads of Destiny* and *Macon County Jail*. Contains violence, swearing and a sex scene.

Ally Sheedy *Susan Reed* • David Carradine *Coley* • Charles Napier *Sheriff Dempsey* • Todd Kimsey *Hobie* ■ *Dir* Victoria Muspratt • *Scr* Victoria Muspratt, Donald E Stewart

The Jailbreakers ★
Crime drama   1960 · US · BW · 63mins

This utterly predictable bargain-basement melodrama is something of a one-man effort, with Alex Grasshoff producing as well as directing from his own script, which pits Robert Hutton and Mary Castle against a gang of escaped convicts who have fetched up in a ghost town to search for their $400,000 stash. Grasshoff was later known as the producer of the documentary, *Young Americans* (1967), which was stripped of its Oscar after it was declared ineligible for being released outside the designated year.

Robert Hutton *Tom* • Mary Castle *June* • Michael O'Connell *Lake* • Gabe Delutri *Joe* • Anton Van Stralen *Steam* • Toby Hill *Karen* ■ *Dir/Scr* Alex Grasshoff

Jailbreakers ★★ 🔞
Drama   1994 · US · Colour · 72mins

This TV movie reveals just how far William Friedkin's fortunes have fallen since he created his masterpiece *The Exorcist*. As part of a US series that revisits the drive-in flicks of the fifties and sixties, this teen drama bears only a passing resemblance to the 1960 Robert Hutton vehicle. As the cheerleader whose eye for jewellery lands her biker boyfriend in jail, Shannen Doherty plays a very different college kid from her *Beverly Hills 90210* persona. But once Antonio Sabato Jr has escaped and the lovebirds hit the road, the action quickly loses its direction. Hugely disappointing. Contains swearing, sex scenes and some violence. ▦

Shannen Doherty *Angel Norton* • Antonio Sabato Jr *Tony* • Vince Edwards *Mr Norton* • Adrienne Barbeau *Mrs Norton* • Talbert Morton *Whale* ■ *Dir* William Friedkin • *Scr* Debra Hill, Gogi Vorgan

Jailhouse Rock ★★★★ 🅄
Musical drama   1957 · US · BW · 97mins

Elvis Presley's glorious third movie, after *Love Me Tender* and *Loving You*, when that snarl and that talent were for once harnessed to a suitable plot under the experienced reins of veteran MGM director Richard Thorpe. Presley plays an ex-con whose subsequent Hollywood success proves him to be too big for his britches, causing old cellmate Mickey Shaughnessy to lay him flat with a blow to his money-spinning larynx. Elvis creates a most unlikeable character in Vince Everett, at the same time revealing an acting talent on a par with that of James Dean, only previously hinted at in his first two movies. Leading lady Judy Tyler was tragically killed in a car crash soon after shooting was completed (this was only her second film after starring on Broadway), and Presley couldn't bear to watch this film for that reason. ▦

Elvis Presley *Vince Everett* • Judy Tyler *Peggy Van Alden* • Mickey Shaughnessy *Hunk Houghton* • Vaughn Taylor *Mr Shores* • Jennifer Holden *Sherry Wilson* • Dean Jones *Teddy Talbot* • Anne Neyland *Laury Jackson* • Mike Stoller *Pianist* ■ *Dir* Richard Thorpe • *Scr* Guy Trosper, from a story by Ned Young

Jake Lassiter: Justice on the Bayou ★★
Crime drama   1995 · US/It/Ger · Colour

Following the exploits of an American footballer-turned-lawyer, this TV movie was adapted from Paul Levine's thriller. It's not in the same league as John Grisham, but it's not bad, with Gerald McRaney clearly relishing the title role, coming to the aid of a surgeon friend implicated in the death of a wealthy patient. Robert Loggia puts in a scene-stealing performance, and all the usual genre ingredients – sex, drugs and larceny are in place. Contains violence and sex scenes.

Gerald McRaney *Jake Lassiter* • Robert Loggia *Dr Charlie Riggs* • James B Sikking *Dr Roger Salisbury* • Tracy Scoggins *Melanie Corrigan* • Daphne Ashbrook *Susan Corrigan* ■ *Dir* Peter Markle • *Scr* David Israel, from the novel *To Speak for the Dead* by Paul Levine

Jake Spanner, Private Eye ★★
Detective drama 1989 · US · Colour · 97mins

This light detective drama starring Robert Mitchum gets off to a promising start, but quickly descends into predictable clichés. Mitchum, in a role he has done better before, is a has-been detective, hired by an old gangster enemy to help with a ransom drop. But the kidnapping is a fake, and the gumshoe discovers that what's really going on is drug dealing. This was a family affair for Mitchum: supporting roles are played by his brother and his son, but multiple Mitchums cannot lift this drab mystery out of mediocrity.

Robert Mitchum *Jake Spanner* • Stella Stevens *Sandra Summers* • Dick Van Patten *The Commodore* • John Mitchum *JP Spanner* • James Mitchum *Kevin Spanner* ■ *Dir* Lee H Katzin • *Scr* Andrew J Fenady, from the novel *The Old Dick* by LA Morse

Jake Speed ★★ 🔟
Comedy adventure
1986 · US · Colour · 100mins

A barely acceptable rip-off of *Romancing the Stone* and *Raiders of the Lost Ark* about a girl who vanishes in Paris and the fictional, paperback detective who sets out to find her. While Karen Kopins as the girl's sister and Wayne Crawford are hardly a match for Kathleen Turner and Michael Douglas, the white-slave-trader villain gives John Hurt ample opportunity to go way over the top in malarial malevolence. The story flits around the globe from Paris to Africa and picks up a touch of the *Casablanca*s towards the end. No new clichés here, as Sam Goldwyn might have said, but a certain self-conscious style. ▦

Wayne Crawford *Jake Speed* • Dennis Christopher *Desmond Floyd* • Karen Kopins *Margaret Winston* • John Hurt *Sid* • Leon Ames *Pop* ■ *Dir* Andrew Lane • *Scr* Wayne Crawford, Andrew Lane

Jakob the Liar ★★ 🔢

Second World War comedy drama
1999 · US · Colour · 116mins

For Robin Williams, more is less. The greater he lays on the schmaltz, the fewer tears we shed in response. As Jakob, a fantasist living in a Jewish ghetto in war-torn Poland, he pulls out all the emotional stops – unlike Roberto Benigni in the similar *Life Is Beautiful* – but the result falls far short of tragic resonance. Latching on to an overheard suggestion that all is going badly on the German front, Jakob finds he has to keep feeding his eager compatriots morsels of hope. Such fine actors as Armin Mueller-Stahl and Alan Arkin are enmeshed in a web of optimistic deceit that soon becomes as unconvincing as Williams himself. Contains some violence and wartime horror. ▢ *DVD*

Robin Williams *Jakob Heym* • Alan Arkin *Frankfurter* • Bob Balaban *Kowalsky* • Hannah Taylor Gordon *Lina* • Michael Jeter *Avron* • Armin Mueller-Stahl *Professor Kirschbaum* • Liev Schreiber *Mischa* • Nina Siemaszko *Rosa Frankfurter* ■ *Dir* Peter Kassovitz • *Scr* Peter Kassovitz, Didier Decoin, from the book *Jakob der Lügner* by Jurek Becker

Jalopy ★★ 🅄

Comedy
1953 · US · BW · 61mins

Another in the long line of Bowery Boys shoestring pictures, which offered cheap laughs and a few thrills. This time the streetwise "boys", now well into their thirties, led as usual by Leo Gorcey – a tough, pug-nosed, little punk – and the tall and gormless Huntz Hall, enter an auto race after discovering a type of super fuel. The usual slapstick antics ensue. The Bowery Boys, who averaged four features a year, continued with this sort of harmless nonsense throughout the fifties.

Leo Gorcey *Terrence Aloysius "Slip" Mahoney* • Huntz Hall *Horace Debussy "Sach" Jones* • Bernard Gorcey *Louie Dumbrowski* • Robert Lowery *Skid Wilson* • Leon Belasco *Professor Bosgood Elrod* • Richard Benedict *Tony Lango* ■ *Dir* William Beaudine • *Scr* Tim Ryan, Jack Crutcher, Edmond Seward Jr, Bert Lawrence, from a story by Tim Ryan, Jack Crutcher

Jamaica Inn ★★ 🅿🅶

Historical drama
1939 · UK · BW · 94mins

Alfred Hitchcock's last picture before his departure for Hollywood is the least of his three Daphne Du Maurier adaptations (*Rebecca* and *The Birds* being the others). Charles Laughton's self-indulgent performance as the piratical squire goes some way to explaining the film's failure, but Hitch's evident lack of interest in the character's dual nature is mostly to blame. It isn't a completely lost cause, however: Maureen O'Hara is spirited yet vulnerable in her first major role, while art director Tom N Moraham's reconstruction of Regency Cornwall brings a touch of authenticity to an otherwise lacklustre production. ▢

Charles Laughton *Sir Humphrey Pengallan* • Maureen O'Hara *Mary Yelland* • Leslie Banks *Joss Merlyn* • Emlyn Williams *Harry the Peddler* • Robert Newton *Jem Trehearne* • Wylie Watson *Salvation Watkins* ■ *Dir* Alfred Hitchcock • *Scr* Sidney Gilliat, Joan Harrison, JB Priestley, Alma Reville, from the novel *Jamaica Inn* by Daphne du Maurier

Jamaica Run ★★ 🅄

Adventure
1953 · US · Colour · 92mins

Ray Milland – who never quite cut it as an action-romantic hero – skippers a schooner in the Caribbean, courting Arlene Dahl whose family live in a great mansion on Jamaica. But it seems that the provenance of the estate is in doubt and may lie at the bottom of the sea, locked in a shipwreck. Pitched as a straightforward action film, it has some good points: location shooting, a competently handled underwater fight and a splendidly Gothic episode when the house erupts in flames.

Ray Milland *Patrick Fairlie* • Arlene Dahl *Ena Dacey* • Wendell Corey *Todd Dacey* • Patric Knowles *William Montague* • Laura Elliot *Janice Clayton* ■ *Dir* Lewis R Foster • *Scr* Lewis R Foster, from the novel *The Neat Little Corpse* by Max Murray

James and the Giant Peach ★★★★ 🅄

Animated fantasy adventure
1996 · US · Colour · 85mins

For a writer of children's stories, Roald Dahl undoubtedly had a dark imagination. Here, though, there will only be squeals of delight as James and his insect allies escape from a killer shark, skeleton pirates and a couple of awful aunts as they ride a giant peach to the city where dreams come true. It took three years to combine the live-action sequences with state-of-the-art model animation, and the latter is greatly assisted by the personality-packed voices of Susan Sarandon, Richard Dreyfuss, Simon Callow and David Thewlis. However, it's Joanna Lumley and Miriam Margolyes as the ghastly Spiker and Sponge who steal this wonderfully pantomimic show. ▢ *DVD*

Paul Terry *James* • Joanna Lumley *Aunt Spiker* • Miriam Margolyes *Aunt Sponge* • Pete Postlethwaite *Old Man* • Simon Callow *Grasshopper* • Richard Dreyfuss *Centipede* • Jane Leeves *Ladybug* • Susan Sarandon *Spider* • David Thewlis *Earthworm* ■ *Dir* Henry Selick • *Scr* Steven Bloom, Jonathan Roberts, from the novel by Roald Dahl

James Baldwin: the Price of the Ticket ★★★ 🅿🅶

Documentary
1989 · US · Colour · 86mins

James Baldwin was born black, poor and homosexual, yet he became one of the most celebrated American writers and civil rights activists of his up-tight era. Combining his expressive and controversial public speeches with rare archive footage, home movies and family (including interviews with his brother David, and writers Maya Angelou and William Styron), director Karen Thorsen provides a powerful and moving document into his life, works and beliefs, which skilfully puts across his insightful mind and keen, irrepressible spirit.

Dir Karen Thorsen

The James Dean Story ★★ 🅿🅶

Documentary
1957 · US · BW · 81mins

An early film from Robert Altman (co-directing with George W George) it relates the now familiar story of the fifties star, who died too young after starring in only three movies. It makes use of archive material in a way that tries to inject drama into the documentary process – there's a stylised depiction of the fatal car crash – but because there's very little revelation, the overall effect is one of a boring whitewash. ▢ *DVD*

Martin Gabel *Narrator* ■ *Dir* George W George, Robert Altman • *Scr* Stewart Stern

James Dean – the First American Teenager ★★★ 🔢

Documentary
1975 · UK · Colour · 77mins

Writer/director Ray Connolly, who sprayed *Stardust* with sharp pop insights, here unravels the James Dean legend with an attractive mixture of objectivity and affection. Without resorting to cheap sentimentality, this documentary successfully deals with Dean's huge social impact and endurance as an icon, while also pinning down the facts of his life, and death. Interviews with colleagues and co-stars like Natalie Wood, Dennis Hopper and Sammy Davis Jr, as well as rare screen-test footage, provide added spice. ▢

Stacy Keach *Narrator* ■ *Dir/Scr* Ray Connolly

The James Gang ★★ 🔢

Comedy drama
1997 · UK/Can · Colour · 94mins

A knowing soundtrack from Bernard Butler and a gutsy performance from Helen McCrory are the only plus points in this willing, but otherwise sadly under-realised debut from director Mike Barker and screenwriter Stuart Hepburn. As the single mum who responds to a house fire by embarking on a hand-to-mouth crime spree, McCrory very nearly binds together the ramshackle sequence of stylised set pieces. But too many misfires as McCrory's shiftless, karaoke-singing partner can keep this lumbering road movie off the hard shoulder. Contains swearing, nudity and sex scenes. ▢

John Hannah *Spendlove James* • Helen McCrory *Bernadette James* • Jason Flemyng *Frank James* • Toni Collette *Julia Armstrong* • Darren Brownlie *Spendlove Jr* • David Brownlie *Spendlove Jr* • Lauren McMurray *Geraldine James* • Lauren McCracken *Jessica James* ■ *Dir* Mike Barker • *Scr* Stuart Hepburn, from an idea by Andrew Eaton, Paul Lee

Jamon Jamon ★★★★ 🔢

Erotic comedy drama
1992 · Sp · Colour · 90mins

Forget the over-hyped Pedro Almodóvar, director Bigas Luna represents the cutting edge of Spanish cinema with his warm, witty and wise exploration of flamenco love and desire. The first of a trilogy – completed by *Golden Balls* and *The Tit and the Moon* – Luna's fast and frantic passion play rides a carnal carousel, with macho star discovery Javier Bardem posing in underwear, eating ham (*jamon*) and bullfighting in the nude. Call it paella porn or Andalucian art, it's uniquely entertaining and very hot stuff indeed. In Spanish with English subtitles. Contains violence, swearing and drug abuse ▢

Penelope Cruz *Silvia* • Anna Galiena *Carmen* • Javier Bardem *Raul* • Stefania Sandrelli *Conchita* • Juan Diego *Manuel* • Jordi Mollà *Jose Luis* ■ *Dir* Bigas Luna • *Scr* Cuca Canals, Bigas Luna

Jane and the Lost City ★ 🅿🅶

Action adventure 1987 · UK · Colour · 88mins

The *Daily Mirror's* famous comic-strip heroine searches for lost diamonds, a lost city and a lost script somewhere in darkest Africa, in a painfully cheap comedy dredging the bottom of the *Carry On* barrel for its seaside postcard puns. Watching the accident-prone Jane lose her clothes in awkwardly telegraphed set-ups may keep some viewers attentive, but even Jasper Carrott, in no less than three unfunny roles, can't save this wretched effort from being anything other than a witless fiasco. ▢

Sam Jones *"Jungle Jack" Buck* • Maud Adams *Lola Pagola* • Jasper Carrott *Heinrich* • Kirsten Hughes *Jane* • Graham Stark *Tombs* • Robin Bailey *Colonel* • Ian Roberts *Carl Donner* ■ *Dir* Terry Marcel • *Scr* Mervyn Haisman, from a story by Mervyn Haisman, Terry Marcel, Harry Robertson, from characters in the *Jane* cartoon created by Norman Pettin the *Daily Mirror*

Jane Austen in Manhattan ★★★

Comedy 1980 · US/UK · Colour · 111mins

When an unknown playlet by Jane Austen is auctioned in New York, it's bought by a rich foundation and two directors fight for the right to produce it on stage – as an operetta or as a trendy piece of avant-garde. Never more than an arty contrivance, this James Ivory piece celebrates acting, performance and sheer eccentricity in a series of vignettes designed to indulge his cast. In this regard it's good to see Anne Baxter get probably her best role since *All about Eve*, in what was her final feature film. Meanwhile Sean Young makes her film debut as Ariadne Charlton.

Anne Baxter *Liliana Zorska* • Robert Powell *Pierre* • Michael Wager *George Midash* • Tim Choate *Jamie* • John Guerrasio *Gregory* • Katrina Hodiak *Katya* • Kurt Johnson *Victor Charlton* • Sean Young *Ariadne Charlton* ■ *Dir* James Ivory • *Scr* Ruth Prawer Jhabvala, from the libretto *Sir Charles Grandison* by Jane Austen, Samuel Richardson • *Producer* Ismail Merchant

Jane Austen's Mafia ★★ 🔢

Spoof 1998 · US · Colour · 83mins

Jim Abrahams's Mafia spoof is in the same vein as his earlier hits *Airplane* and *The Naked Gun*, with sadly similar jokes. That it works at all is only due to convincing performances from Olympia Dukakis, Jay Mohr, Christina Applegate and the sorely missed Lloyd Bridges, who plays a Don Corleone figure training his son (Mohr) to take over the family business. However, there comes a time when he's disposable, so fellow hoods send a

temptress to woo Mohr away from his family and girlfriend (Applegate). You might say it's high time someone sent up *The Godfather*; you won't after seeing this. ▭

Jay Mohr *Anthony Cortino* • Billy Burke *Joey Cortino* • Christina Applegate *Diane* • Pamela Gidley *Pepper Gianini* • Olympia Dukakis *Sophia* • Lloyd Bridges *Vincenzo Cortino* ■ *Dir* Jim Abrahams • *Scr* Jim Abrahams, Greg Norberg, Michael McManus

Jane Eyre ★★★★ PG

Classic drama 1943 · US · BW · 96mins

From *Tudor Rose* through *Back Street* to *Mary Poppins*, British director Robert Stevenson has shown an unusual talent in his warmly sympathetic treatment of films about women. This typical 20th Century-Fox period melodrama is a fine example of his work, though many will persist in attributing the film's virtues to Orson Welles, who might have made a fine job of directing it, given the chance. Welles's Edward Rochester is suitably awesome, dominating his scenes (naturally), but, unfortunately, slowing the pace whenever he appears. Joan Fontaine, still recovering from a severe double dose of Alfred Hitchcock – *Rebecca* and *Suspicion* – is fine, though wan, in the title role. Watch for a young Elizabeth Taylor in a small but telling part early in the film. ▭

Orson Welles *Edward Rochester* • Joan Fontaine *Jane Eyre* • Margaret O'Brien *Adele* • Peggy Ann Garner *Jane, as a child* • John Sutton *St Rivers* • Sara Allgood *Bessie* • Henry Daniell *Brockelhurst* • Agnes Moorehead *Mrs Reed* • Elizabeth Taylor *Helen Burns* ■ *Dir* Robert Stevenson • *Scr* Aldous Huxley, Robert Stevenson, John Houseman, from the novel by Charlotte Brontë

Jane Eyre ★★★

Period romantic drama 1970 · UK · Colour · 110mins

Charlotte Brontë's wish-fulfilling novel about the Yorkshire governess and her forbidden love for the haunted and out-of-her-class Mr Rochester, is tastefully done by director Delbert Mann. Though made for television, it boasts the heavyweight presence of George C Scott who is suitably dark and moody, while Susannah York is a plain Jane with attitude. Diverting, but it would be better to read the book.

George C Scott *Edward Rochester* • Susannah York *Jane Eyre* • Ian Bannen *St John Rivers* • Jack Hawkins *Mr Brocklehurst* • Nyree Dawn Porter *Blanche Ingram* ■ *Dir* Delbert Mann • *Scr* Jack Pulman, from the novel by Charlotte Brontë

Jane Eyre ★★★ PG

Period romantic drama 1996 · Fr/It/UK/US · Colour · 116mins

William Hurt's thoughtful, subdued interpretation of Mr Rochester makes its own gently neurotic contribution to the Brontë movie canon – to add to the more boisterous variations already provided by Orson Welles and George C Scott – in Franco Zeffirelli's stylish and atmospheric take on the famous novel. Zeffirelli lays on sufficient simmering passion to make it interesting, yet at the same time brings the romantic longings of the two lead characters down to a more mundane, human level. Charlotte

Gainsbourg was seen by some, however, as too feisty for the role of Jane. The scenes in the orphanage are well done, and there's an eclectic supporting cast including and Maria Schneider in a rare recent role. Disappointing for aficionados of the novel, this is probably best viewed as a youngster's primer to the text. ▭

William Hurt *Rochester* • Charlotte Gainsbourg *Jane Eyre* • Joan Plowright *Mrs Fairfax* • Anna Paquin *Young Jane* • Geraldine Chaplin *Miss Scatherd* • Billie Whitelaw *Grace Poole* • Maria Schneider *Mrs Rochester* • Fiona Shaw *Mrs Reed* • Elle MacPherson *Blanche Ingram* ■ *Dir* Franco Zeffirelli • *Scr* Hugh Whitemore, Franco Zeffirelli, from the novel by Charlotte Brontë

Janek: a Silent Betrayal ★★

Crime drama 1994 · US · Colour

Richard Crenna stars as the world-weary New York cop Frank Janek, investigating a series of murders and discovering that the trail leads to Broadway in this TV movie. There's the novelty value of seeing theatre actors like Cliff Gorman and Philip Bosco in their element, and William Shatner is also along for the ride, playing an arrogant stage producer. The original story about a possessed brownstone is by William Bayer, author of *The Great Movies*, one of the better books about the film industry. Contains violence and swearing.

Richard Crenna *Lieutenant Frank Janek* • William Shatner *Alex Bodosh* • Helen Shaver *Monique Dessler* • Cliff Gorman *Sergeant Aaron Greenberg* • Philip Bosco *Chief Wycoff* • Gordon Currie *Rick Wheeler* ■ *Dir* Robert Iscove • *Scr* Edward De Blasio, from a story by William Bayer

Jane's House ★★★

Romantic drama 1994 · US · Colour · 90mins

James Woods is usually called on by Hollywood to play psychopaths, but here he can be found in relatively restrained form in this slight but absorbing drama, produced by the king of glossy TV series, Aaron Spelling. Woods plays a widower trying to raise a son and daughter, whose tentative romance with Anne Archer sparks off family ructions. Glenn Jordan, who was responsible for one of the finest made-for-TV movies of recent years, *Barbarians at the Gate*, directs the proceedings sympathetically and elicits credible performances from the leads.

James Woods *Paul Moore* • Anne Archer *Mary Cole* • Graham Beckel *Charlie* • Missy Crider *Hilary* • Diane D'Aquila *Marion* ■ *Dir* Glenn Jordan • *Scr* Eric Roth, from the novel by Robert Kimmel Smith

Janice Beard 45 WPM ★★★★ 15

Romantic comedy 1999 · UK · Colour · 81mins

Clare Kilner's highly impressive debut feature is quirky, original and extremely touching. Scottish newcomer Eileen Walsh stars as Janice, a plain Jane whose life revolves around her attempts to get her severely agoraphobic mother out the front door. In desperation, Janice heads for London and a temp job under the not-so-kind eye of a bitchy Patsy Kensit. There she develops a relationship with

postboy Rhys Ifans and becomes unwittingly embroiled in a plot to steal vital documents from her company. The retro look, innovative cinematography and spot-on script combine to make a film brimming with humour and heart.

Rhys Ifans *Sean* • Patsy Kensit *Julia* • David O'Hara *O'Brien* • Eileen Walsh *Janice Beard* • Sandra Voe *Mimi* • Frances Gray *Violet* • Zita Sattar *Jane* • Amelia Curtis *June* ■ *Dir* Clare Kilner • *Scr* Clare Kilner, Ben Hopkins

The January Man ★★ 15

Crime thriller 1989 · US · Colour · 97mins

One of those gritty thrillers that start out beckoning the finger of promise but end up in a right old mess. Kevin Kline is eminently watchable as the ex-New York cop with relationship angst who is hunting a serial killer. Susan Sarandon as the estranged wife of the police commissioner is quietly superb as always. The script is by the talented John Patrick Shanley, and it bears all the hallmarks of an accomplished scribe with no firm producer's hand on the tiller. In other words, gallons of chutzpah with no place to go. Disappointing. ▭

Kevin Kline *Nick Starkey* • Susan Sarandon *Christine Starkey* • Mary Elizabeth Mastrantonio *Bernadette Flynn* • Harvey Keitel *Frank Starkey* • Danny Aiello *Captain Vincent Alcoa* • Rod Steiger *Mayor Eamon Flynn* • Alan Rickman *Ed* • Faye Grant *Allison Hawkins* ■ *Dir* Pat O'Connor • *Scr* John Patrick Shanley

Japanese War Bride ★★

Drama 1952 · US · BW · 90mins

Shirley Yamaguchi plays the Japanese nurse who falls in love with Don Taylor, the American soldier she nurses back to health in Korea. Unfortunately, life at home in their Californian farming community isn't so harmonious, as Yamaguchi is almost destroyed by the hostility she faces as his wife. Although Marie Windsor is on her best vindictive form as the husband's jealous sister-in-law, this is a low pressure effort from director King Vidor.

Shirley Yamaguchi *Tae Shimizu* • Don Taylor *Jim Sterling* • Cameron Mitchell *Art Sterling* • Marie Windsor *Fran Sterling* • James Bell *Ed Sterling* • Louise Lorimer *Harriet Sterling* ■ *Dir* King Vidor • *Scr* Catherine Turney, from a story by Anson Bond

Jarrapellejos ★★★

Drama 1987 · Sp · Colour · 107mins

For once including the all-too-human village priest among the oppressed, this is an involved and involving melodrama. Faithfully re-creating the atmosphere of rural Spain around 1910, Antonio Giménez-Rico weaves this story of aristocratic covetousness and corruption with a steady hand. Antonio Ferrandis gives a strutting performance as the lustful landowner willing to abuse the law and destroy reputations to satiate his lust and keep his reckless nephew out of trouble. Juan Diego is equally impressive as the artist/teacher, whose love for Aitana Sanchez-Gijon leads to her tragic and brutally depicted death. In Spanish with English subtitles.

Antonio Ferrandis • Juan Diego • Lydia Bosch • Aitana Sanchez-Gijon ■ *Dir* Antonio Gimenéz-Rico • *Scr* Antonio Gimenéz-Rico, Manuel Gutierrez Aragon

Jason and the Argonauts ★★★ U

Fantasy adventure 1963 · UK · Colour · 99mins

A lively adventure, based on the Greek myth, in which our hero (a wooden Todd Armstrong) sails in search of the Golden Fleece and encounters gods, demons and Honor Blackman playing chess with the destiny of men. Made at the time when Hollywood was plundering Roman history at vast expense, this British picture went further back in time and created a niche of its own – the special effects epic masterminded by Ray Harryhausen, whose sword-wielding skeletons, Neptune in a studio jacuzzi and giant man of bronze thrilled adults and children alike. The tepid colour is a drawback, the stirring music by Bernard Herrmann a plus. ▭ **DVD**

Todd Armstrong *Jason* • Nancy Kovack *Medea* • Gary Raymond *Acastus* • Laurence Naismith *Argus* • Niall MacGinnis *Zeus* • Michael Gwynn *Hermes* • Jack Gwillim *King Aeetes* • Honor Blackman *Hera* ■ *Dir* Don Chaffey • *Scr* Jan Reed, Beverly Cross

Jason Goes to Hell: the Final Friday ★★★ 18

Horror 1993 · US · Colour · 84mins

The spirit of Jason Voorhees is whisked back to Crystal Lake via a series of deadly soul transferences in director Adam Marcus's affectionate milking of *Friday the 13th* imagery, hewn from the past eight chapters and cleverly turned inside out for a new, improved joy ride. Affectionately witty, inventively shocking and shot through with a gleaming high-tone style, Marcus delivers the slasher goods and supplies edge-of-the-seat thrills on a par with the original film. The supernatural jumping-off points, only hinted at prior to this episode, bring a fresh dimension to the Jason myth, shrewdly lubricated by the grisly gore and superior slime. ▭

John D LeMay *Steven Freeman* • Kari Keegan *Jessica Kimble* • Kane Hodder *Jason Voorhees* • Steven Williams *Creighton Duke* • Steven Culp *Robert Campbell* • Erin Gray *Diana Kimble* • Rusty Schwimmer *Joey B* ■ *Dir* Adam Marcus • *Scr* Dean Lorey, Jay Huguely, from a story by Adam Marcus, Jay Huguely

Jason's Lyric ★★★ 18

Drama 1994 · US · Colour · 115mins

Directed by Doug McHenry, who co-produced *New Jack City*, this curiously old-fashioned film attempts to put a new slant on the African-American experience. Although it revisits the familiar "going bad in the ghetto" theme, this feels more like a Hollywood problem picture of the late forties than an explosion of justifiable anger. This is mostly down to the fact that McHenry places as much emphasis on Allen Payne's sweet romance with Jada Pinkett as he does on his relationship with tearaway brother Bokeem Woodbine, who seems to have inherited the troubled mind of their dead father, played in flashback by Forest Whitaker. Uncertain but uplifting. Contains violence, swearing, sex scenes and nudity. 📼

Allen Payne *Jason Alexander* • Jada Pinkett [Jada Pinkett Smith] *Lyric Greer* • Forest Whitaker *Maddog* • Bokeem Woodbine *Joshua Alexander* • Suzzanne Douglas *Gloria Alexander* • Anthony "Treach"Criss *Alonzo* ■ *Dir* Doug McHenry • *Scr* Bobby Smith Jr

Jassy ★★★ PG
Drama 1947 · UK · Colour · 97mins

Two years after she took the nation by storm in *The Wicked Lady*, Margaret Lockwood was still being presented as Britain's celluloid "bad girl". Here she plays a gypsy dancing girl, all bandanas and golden earrings. This is by no means as silly as it sounds, even though the Gainsborough gang's all here, including Dennis Price hamming it up to the limit. Our Margaret's a bad girl all right, and murder is on the menu, but this time we are given hints at the heart beneath the tarty exterior. Great fun. 📼

Margaret Lockwood *Jassy Woodroffe* • Patricia Roc *Dilys Helmar* • Dennis Price *Christopher Hatton* • Dermot Walsh *Barney Hatton* • Basil Sydney *Nick Helmar* • Nora Swinburne *Mrs Hatton* • John Laurie *Woodroffe* ■ *Dir* Bernard Knowles • *Scr* Dorothy Christie, Campbell Christie, Geoffrey Kerr, from the novel *Jassy* by Norah Lofts

Java Head ★★★
Romantic drama 1935 · UK · BW · 70m

While one of two brothers (Ralph Richardson) settles down to marriage and is given the management of the fleet by his ship-owning father (Edmund Gwenn), the other (John Loder) seeks adventure in faraway climes. He returns with a Chinese bride (Anna May Wong), but the realisation that he still loves his childhood sweetheart (Elizabeth Allan), brings tragedy. This British-made combination of adventure, romance and melodrama, set in Bristol and at sea in the mid-19th century, boasts a fine cast who play it for all its worth. The film had the distinction of being edited by Thorold Dickinson and David Lean.

Anna May Wong *Taou Yen* • Elizabeth Allan *Nettie Vollar* • John Loder *Gerrit Ammidon* • Edmund Gwenn *Jeremy Ammidon* • Ralph Richardson *William Ammidon* • Herbert Lomas *Barzil Dunsack* • George Curzon *Edward Dunsack* ■ *Dir* J Walter Ruben • *Scr* Martin Brown, Gordon Wellesley, from the novel by Joseph Hergesheimer

Jawbreaker ★★ 15
Black comedy 1999 · US · Colour · 84mins

Heathers-style black comedy about a trio of high school "It" girls, whose birthday prank on their best friend goes horribly wrong. Writer/director Darren Stein has a flair for striking cartoon visuals, but the plot soon runs out and the film's tone is excessively cold and cruel. Its strongest asset is the bright young cast, headed by Rose McGowan's malicious super-bitch and Judy Evans Greer's convincing transformation from mousy nerd to sexy blonde bombshell. Contains swearing and sex scenes 📼 DVD

Rose McGowan *Courtney Shayne* • Rebecca Gayheart *Julie Freeman* • Julie Benz *Marcie Fox* • Judy Evans Greer *Fern Mayo* • Chad Christ *Zach Tartak* • Charlotte Roldan *Liz Purr* • Pam Grier *Detective Vera Cruz* • Carol Kane *Miss Sherwood* ■ *Dir/Scr* Darren Stein

Jaws ★★★★★ PG
Action adventure 1975 · US · Colour · 118mins

Peter Benchley's pulp bestseller turns into the scariest sea saga ever filmed, thanks to director Steven Spielberg creating maximum suspense in the first dark moments and then maintaining the momentum with brilliant sleight-of-hand direction. The tale of a Great White shark invading a New England resort and the modern-day Captain Ahab (Robert Shaw) employed by the stricken community to kill it is now a classic of the horror adventure genre. John Williams's Oscar-winning music and excellent performances from Roy Scheider and Richard Dreyfuss add to the ingeniously mounted tension, cleverly playing on all our deepest primeval fears. Contains violence, mild swearing and brief nudity. 📼 DVD

Roy Scheider *Brody* • Robert Shaw *Quint* • Richard Dreyfuss *Hooper* • Lorraine Gary *Ellen Brody* • Murray Hamilton *Vaughn* • Carl Gottlieb *Meadows* • Jeffrey C Kramer [Jeffrey Kramer] *Hendricks* • Susan Backlinie *Chrissie* • Jonathan Filley *Cassidy* ■ *Dir* Steven Spielberg • *Scr* Peter Benchley, Carl Gottlieb, Howard Sackler, from the novel by Peter Benchley • *Music* John Williams • *Editor* Verna Fields • *Cinematographer* Bill Butler • *Production Designer* Joe Alves

Jaws 2 ★★★ PG
Action adventure 1978 · US · Colour · 110mins

Three years after those infamous shark attacks, another Great White swims into police chief Roy Scheider's resort town to cause more havoc in this shameless sequel. Director Jeannot Szwarc tries to ape Steven Spielberg's imaginative style and visceral terror, but any suspense he attempts to build comes unglued because it floats in all-too-familiar waters. You just know how everyone is going to react from the stars to the director and even the mechanical shark! Still, despite mayor Murray Hamilton not learning any lessons from previous events, stalwart Scheider is in full control of this blasé follow-up that lacks the bite of the original classic. 📼

Roy Scheider *Police Chief Martin Brody* • Lorraine Gary *Ellen Brody* • Murray Hamilton *Mayor Larry Vaughan* • Joseph Mascolo *Len Peterson* • Jeffrey Kramer *Deputy Jeff Hendricks* • Collin Wilcox *Dr Lureen Elkins* • Ann Dusenberry *Tina Wilcox, Miss Amity* • Mark Gruner *Mike Brody* • Barry Coe *Andrews* ■ *Dir* Jeannot Szwarc • *Scr* Carl Gottlieb, Dorothy Tristan (uncredited), from characters created by Peter Benchley

Jaws III ★★ 15
Action adventure 1983 · US · Colour · 94mins

Called *Jaws III* for television and denuded of the one gimmick (3-D) that made it – arguably – acceptable in theatres, this hapless opus stands as a testament to the law of diminishing returns. (Unfortunately there was a truly awful follow-up in *Jaws the Revenge*.) Director credit goes to Joe

Alves, the production designer of Spielberg's great original, and therefore the man responsible for creating the mechanical shark, but it's quite clear from this effort that he's no director, as a group of moderate talents act all at sea – feel sorry for the likes of jobbing Dennis Quaid and Louis Gossett Jr, both ill-cast and extremely under-directed. 📼

Dennis Quaid *Mike Brody* • Louis Gossett Jr *Calvin Bouchard* • Bess Armstrong *Kathryn Morgan* • Simon MacCorkindale *Philip FitzRoyce* • John Putch *Sean Brody* • Lea Thompson *Kelly Ann Bukowski* • PH Moriarty *Jack Tate* ■ *Dir* Joe Alves • *Scr* Richard Matheson, Carl Gottlieb, from a story by Guerdon Trueblood, from characters created by Peter Benchley

Jaws of Satan ★
Horror 1979 · US · Colour · 92mins

A demon king cobra is sent from Hell to terrorise priest Fritz Weaver because of sins committed by his ancestors against Druids. The satanic serpent also commands others of its species to run amok while the local community idly stand by because they want their new dog track to open on schedule. A shoddy killer snake movie that might have elicited some scares had the obvious glass panes protecting the actors not been visible in every stunt shot. Amateurish, with an early appearance by Christina Applegate.

Fritz Weaver *Father Farrow* • Gretchen Corbett *Dr Maggie Sheridan* • Jon Korkes *Paul Hendricks* • Norman Lloyd *Monsignor* ■ *Dir* Bob Claver • *Scr* Gerry Holland, from a story by James Callaway

Jaws the Revenge ★ 15
Action adventure 1987 · US · Colour · 86mins

The one where the big rubber shark gets to attack an aircraft... and that's far from being the only silly thing about this fourth and most preposterous entry in the series. Michael Caine probably could have sold his grandmother for the money but, hey, the Bahamas (the setting for most of the film) is lovely in summer so he delivers a cheerfully irrelevant cameo instead. Lorraine Gary, the only link apart from the shark with the fine original, is annoyingly neurotic, while the plot – this time the shark gets personal – is laughably inept. Contains some swearing and violence. 📼

Lorraine Gary *Ellen Brody* • Lance Guest *Michael Brody* • Mario Van Peebles *Jake* • Karen Young *Carla Brody* • Michael Caine *Hoagie* • Judith Barsi *Thea Brody* ■ *Dir* Joseph Sargent • *Scr* Michael de Guzman, from characters created by Peter Benchley

The Jayhawkers ★★
Western 1959 · US · Colour · 103mins

This western pitches Jeff Chandler, as the leader of a private army of raiders called the Jayhawkers, against Fess Parker as the former jailbird who, for reasons of personal revenge, agrees to put a stop to Chandler's empire-building ambitions. With his Napoleon complex, a dislike for all women except his mother, and a strong affection for his adversary, Jeff Chandler is far more colourful than homespun Fess Parker, who shouldn't have stopped playing Davy Crockett.

Although handsomely shot by Loyal Griggs and vigorously scored by Jerome Moross, this is a long-winded, dramatically muddled bore.

Jeff Chandler *Luke Darcy* • Fess Parker *Cam Bleeker* • Nicole Maurey *Jeanne Dubois* • Herbert Rudley *Governor William Clayton* • Jimmy Carter *Paul* • Leo Gordon *Jake* ■ *Dir* Melvin Frank • *Scr* Melvin Frank, Joseph Petracca, Frank Fenton, Al Bezzerides

The Jayne Mansfield Story ★ PG
Biography 1980 · US · Colour · 91mins

Loni Anderson, Burt Reynolds's ex-missus, plays the rather tragic figure of the fifties sex symbol whose ample proportions helped to market her as a poor man's Marilyn Monroe. In this questionably accurate made-for-TV biopic, Mansfield is portrayed as a hard nut who will do anything for stardom. Starring opposite Anderson is Arnold Schwarzenegger as her body-builder husband Mickey Hargitay. Everybody has to start somewhere. 📼

Loni Anderson *Jayne Mansfield* • Arnold Schwarzenegger *Mickey Hargitay* • Ray Buktenica *Bob Garrett* • Kathleen Lloyd *Carol Sue Peters* • GD Spradlin *Gerald Conway* ■ *Dir* Dick Lowry • *Scr* Charles Dennis, Nancy Gayle, from the book *Jayne Mansfield and the American Fifties* by Martha Saxton

Jazz on a Summer's Day ★★★ U
Musical documentary 1959 · US · Colour · 87mins

Considering this is a record of the 1958 Newport Jazz Festival, it's telling that two of the most arresting sets come from rocker Chuck Berry and gospel singer Mahalia Jackson. However, you'll be equally enthralled by the performances of Anita O'Day and such jazz legends as Louis Armstrong, Thelonious Monk and Dinah Washington. Photographer Bert Stern's direction may be a touch self-serving, and Aram Avakian's editing takes in too many shots of the crowd and the nearby America's Cup trials. But they still manage to capture the relaxed atmosphere of the gig and the evident enjoyment of the artists.

Dir Bert Stern

The Jazz Singer ★★★ U
Musical drama 1927 · US · BW · 84mins

In the autumn of 1927, a historic premiere took place in New York when Al Jolson spoke the prophetic words, "You ain't heard nothing yet!" in the first feature with spoken dialogue. Warner Bros had gambled everything on this "talker" that would transform cinema forever. Actually, there is very little dialogue in this crude and schmaltzy film about a cantor's son torn between a life in the theatre and the synagogue. It is Jolson's dynamic singing of *Toot, Toot, Tootsie* and *My Mammy*, recorded by the Vitaphone process on disc and synchronised to the action, that breathes life into a film whose pioneering aspect is its main interest. There were unnecessary remakes in 1952 (with Danny Thomas) and 1980 (with Neil Diamond). 📼

Al Jolson *Jakie Rabinowitz/Jack Robin* • May McAvoy *Mary Dale* • Warner Oland *Cantor*

U = SUITABLE FOR ALL   Uc = SUITABLE FOR ALL, ESPECIALLY FOR YOUNG CHILDREN (VIDEO ONLY)   PG = PARENTAL GUIDANCE

Rabinowitz • Eugenie Besserer *Sara Rabinowitz* • Bobby Gordon *Jakie at thirteen* • Otto Lederer *Moishe Yudelson* • Cantor Josef Rosenblatt • Richard Tucker *Harry Lee* • Myrna Loy *Chorus girl* • William Demarest *Buster Billings* ■ *Dir* Alan Crosland • *Scr* Alfred A Cohn, Jack Jarmuth, from the play *Day of Atonement* by Samson Raphaelson

The Jazz Singer   ★★★ 🅤

Musical drama   1952 · US · Colour · 106mins

The oft-filmed story of the cantor's son who can't choose between showbiz and Yom Kippur. This is an unnecessary, though likeable, updated remake – the main problem being the star chosen, Danny Thomas, lacked the warmth the tale needs. Another Danny, Kaye, would have been perfect, as would director Michael Curtiz's discovery Doris Day instead of the anodyne Peggy Lee, in one of her two feature leads (the other was in *Pete Kelly's Blues*, for which she was Oscar-nominated). Not as bad, though, as the later version with Neil Diamond.

Danny Thomas *Jerry Golding* • Peggy Lee *Judy Lane* • Mildred Dunnock *Mrs Golding* • Eduard Franz *Cantor Golding* • Tom Tully *McGurney* • Alex Gerry *Uncle Louie* • Allyn Joslyn *George Miller* • Harold Gordon *Rabbi Roth* ■ *Dir* Michael Curtiz • *Scr* Frank Davis, Leonard Stern, Lewis Meltzer, from the play *Day of Atonement* by Samson Raphaelson

The Jazz Singer   ★★ 🅟🅖

Musical drama   1980 · US · Colour · 110mins

A "rocked-up" remake of the world's first talkie. *Cracklin' Rosie* man Neil Diamond updates the old Al Jolson role, playing a cantor's son who wants to make it big in the rock business. Laurence Olivier takes the money and runs as his understandably dubious dad. Given the "rocky" nature of the film, the title now seems pretty meaningless. But, then, that description could be applied to the whole film which, though adequate, remains more a monument to the egomania of musicians than a significant contribution to world cinema. 📼

Neil Diamond *Jess Robin/Yussel Rabinovitch* • Laurence Olivier *Cantor Rabinovitch* • Lucie Arnaz *Molly Bell* • Catlin Adams *Rivka Rabinovitch* • Franklyn Ajaye *Bubba* • Paul Nicholas *Keith Lennox* • Sully Boyar *Eddie Gibbs* ■ *Dir* Richard Fleischer • *Scr* Herbert Baker, Stephen H Foreman, from the play *Day of Atonement* by Samson Raphaelson

Je T'Aime, Je T'Aime   ★★★

Science-fiction fantasy drama
1968 · Fr · Colour · 94mins

Returning to the subjects of lapsing time and unreliable memory that had informed all his earlier features, Alain Resnais harnessed that old sci-fi standby, the time machine, to bring an extra dimension to this intriguing study of lost happiness, despair and death. Unfortunately, as the suicide survivor dispatched to retrace his past, Claude Rich struggles to make an impact amid the fragmentary recollections of his affair with Olga Georges-Picot, for whose demise he may be responsible. There may be a fantastical poetry about the enterprise, but it's also a searching investigation into the insignificance of human existence. In French with English subtitles.

Claude Rich *Claude Ridder* • Olga Georges-Picot *Catrine* • Anouk Ferjac *Wiana Lust* • Marie-Blanche Vergnes *Young woman* ■ *Dir* Alain Resnais • *Scr* Jacques Sternberg, Alain Resnais

Je, Tu, Il, Elle   ★★★★

Drama   1974 · Bel · BW · 90mins

Compulsive eating and a craving for sex go hand in hand in this psychological drama from Chantal Akerman. The debuting director's decision to play the lead is not only courageous, but also reinforces her status as a symbol for universal womanhood, as she struggles to make the transition from adolescence into adulthood. The opening letter-writing sequence, in which she constantly munches sugar, is every bit as erotic as the encounters with trucker Niels Arestrup and her female lover, Claire Wauthion. Recalling the work of Left Bank auteurs like Marguerite Duras, this is a powerful, non-narrative study of anguish and identity. In French with English subtitles.

Chantal Akerman *Julie* • Niels Arestrup *Truck-driver* • Claire Wauthion *Woman's lover* ■ *Dir/Scr* Chantal Akerman

Je Vous Aime   ★★

Comedy   1980 · Fr · Colour · 105mins

Although this involved melodrama sets up Catherine Deneuve as an icon of independent womanhood, the men in her life are so weak that ditching them seems more like common sense than an act of female empowerment. Employing a complex network of flashbacks and excruciating exchanges, director Claude Berri shows how Deneuve assembled her entourage, demonstrating admirable control of his material, but makes Deneuve seem cold and strident rather than assuredly self-contained. The result is polished but resistible. In French with English subtitles.

Catherine Deneuve *Alice* • Jean-Louis Trintignant *Julien* • Gérard Depardieu *Patrick* • Serge Gainsbourg *Simon* • Alain Souchon *Claude* • Christian Marquand *Victor* • Isabelle Lacamp *Dorothée* ■ *Dir* Claude Berri • *Scr* Claude Berri, Michel Grisolia

Je Vous Salue, Marie   ★★★

Drama   1984 · Fr/Swi/UK · Colour · 86mins

In this impudent updating of the immaculate conception, Mary, the daughter of a garage owner, discovers she is pregnant even though she has never slept with her boyfriend, cab driver Joseph. Jean-Luc Godard's film was predictably condemned by the Pope, while various religious groups threatened cinemas and TV stations with blasphemy suits. But the picture itself is a charming, delicate and poetic piece about the mystery of Creation and the mystique of womankind, all set to heavenly music by Bach and Dvorak. In French with English subtitles.

Myriem Roussel *Marie* • Thierry Rode *Joseph* • Philippe Lacoste *Angel Gabriel* • Manon Anderson *Girl* • Juliette Binoche *Juliette* • Malachi Jara Kohan *Jesus* • Dick Arthur • Johan Leysen *Professor* • Anne Gautier *Eva* ■ *Dir/Scr* Jean-Luc Godard

Jealousy, Italian Style   ★★★★

Comedy drama   1970 · It · Colour · 106mins

Marcello Mastroianni won the Best Actor prize at Cannes for his work in this scattershot satire, which takes aim at just about every aspect of Italian life. The plot is a hybrid of high opera and low Fellini; Mastoianni's doltish Communist bricklayer is a close cousin of that great clown, Toto; and Monica Vitti's flower-seller is a knowing parody of a neo-realist waif. Caught between them is Giancarlo Giannini's pizza cook, who displays the same glib charm Mastroianni had in the famous Cinecittà sex comedies of the early sixties. Italian dialogue dubbed into English.

Marcello Mastroianni *Oreste* • Monica Vitti *Adelaide* • Giancarlo Giannini *Nello* • Manolo Zarzo *Uto* • Marisa Merlini *Silvana* • Hercules Cortez *Ambleto di Meo* • Josefina Serratosa *Antonia* ■ *Dir* Ettore Scola • *Scr* Furio Scarpelli, Age [Agenore Incrocci], Ettore Scola

Jean de Florette   ★★★★★ 🅟🅖

Drama   1986 · Fr/It · Colour · 115mins

The first part of Claude Berri's adaptation of Marcel Pagnol's novel *L'Eau des Collines* is, quite simply, a tour de force. The screenplay (by Berri and Gérard Brach) is wholly cinematic, Bruno Nuytten's shimmering cinematography avoids mere pictorialism, while Berri's direction captures both the pace of the changing seasons and the unique atmosphere of Provence. The acting is also of the highest order. Gérard Depardieu is perhaps a little too insistent in asserting the worthiness of the hunchback, but Yves Montand and Daniel Auteuil are outstanding as the scheming Soubeyrans. In French with English subtitles.. Contains swearing and sexual references. 📼

Yves Montand *César Soubeyran, Le Papet* • Gérard Depardieu *Jean De Florette [Cadoret]* • Daniel Auteuil *Ugolin Soubeyran, "Galinette"* • Elisabeth Depardieu *Aimée Cadoret* • Ernestine Mazurowna *Manon Cadoret* • Marcel Champel *Pique-bouffigue* ■ *Dir* Claude Berri • *Scr* Gérard Brach, Claude Berri, from the novel *L'Eau des Collines* by Marcel Pagnol

Jeanne Dielman, 23 Quai du Commerce, 1080 Bruxelles   ★★★★

Drama   1975 · Bel/Fr · Colour · 225mins

Chantal Akerman made her name with this audacious exploration of bourgeois feminism. Delphine Seyrig gives a studied display of dispassionate normalness as the widowed housewife who makes ends meet by working afternoons as a prostitute. By shooting in long takes to capture each task in minute, real-time detail, Akerman renders the act of sleeping with a client just one more chore in Seyrig's daily routine. Yet, these rhythmic repetitions make the disrupted schedule of the third day, with its climactic act of violence, all the more compellingly disturbing. In French with English subtitles.

Delphine Seyrig *Jeanne Dielman* • Jan Decorte *Sylvain Dielman* • Henri Storck *First caller* • Jacques Doniol-Valcroze *Second caller* • Yves Bical *Third caller* • Chantal Akerman *Voice of neighbour* ■ *Dir/Scr* Chantal Akerman

Jeanne Eagels   ★★

Biographical drama 1957 · US · BW · 108mins

Kim Novak does a good job of bringing out the anxieties of the twenties stage (and screen) star Jeanne Eagels in this biopic. Three top screenwriters laboured on the dreary and contrived script but director George Sidney brings considerable visual flair to dramatic highlights – like the suicide of rival actress Elsie Desmond, played by Virginia Grey. Jeff Chandler supports as the carnival operator who pops in and out of Eagels's life.

Kim Novak *Jeanne Eagels* • Jeff Chandler *Sal Satori* • Agnes Moorehead *Madame Neilson* • Charles Drake *John Donahue* • Larry Gates *Al Brooks* • Virginia Grey *Elsie Desmond* • Gene Lockhart *Equity board president* • Joe De Santis *Frank Satori* ■ *Dir* George Sidney • *Scr* Daniel Fuchs, Sonya Levien, John Fante, from a story by Daniel Fuchs

Jeanne la Pucelle   ★★★★★★

Historical biographical drama
1994 · Fr · Colour · 237mins

Divided into two installments – *Les Batailles* and *Les Prisons* – Jacques Rivette's sprawling account of Joan of Arc's rise and fall demonstrates once more his mastery of the epic form. Refusing to indulge in mere period pageantry or religious speculation, he has produced a cinematic portrait to rank alongside those of Carl Theodor Dreyer (*The Passion of Joan of Arc*, 1928) and Robert Bresson (*Le Procès de Jeanne d'Arc*, 1962). As the Maid of Orleans, Sandrine Bonnaire glows with the strength of her conviction, whether rallying the troops of Dauphin André Marcon or testifying to the heavenly source of the voices that inspired her. Gaining in power throughout, this awesome achievement is both historically authentic and dramatically affecting. In French with English subtitles.

Sandrine Bonnaire *Jeanne* • André Marcon *Charles, Dauphin of France* • Jean-Louis Richard *Le Tremoille* • Marcel Bozonnet *Regnault de Chartres* • Didier Sauvegrain *Raoul de Gaucourt* • Jean-Pierre Lorit *Jean d'Alencon* ■ *Dir* Jacques Rivette • *Scr* Pascal Bonitzer, Christine Laurent

Jeannie   ★★★ 🅤

Romantic comedy   1941 · UK · BW · 100mins

Known to millions as Janet in *Dr Finlay's Casebook*, Barbara Mullen made a hugely promising (but ultimately false) start to her film career in this charming comedy. As the bonny Scottish girl at the centre of a romantic tug-of-war between sales rep Michael Redgrave and wastrel Albert Lieven, she strikes a perfect balance between worldly innocence and innate sense. Redgrave revels in the chance to display his sadly underused gift for comedy, while Lieven oozes smarmy charm. It's somewhat strange that no-one objected to this film on its release, as it celebrates the glories of Vienna, then an enemy city.

Barbara Mullen *Jeannie McLean* • Michael Redgrave *Stanley Smith* • Wilfrid Lawson *James McLean* • Albert Lieven *Count Erich Von Wittgenstein* • Gus McNaughton *Angus Whitelaw* • Googie Withers *Laundry girl* ■ *Dir* Harold French • *Scr* Anatole de Grunwald, Roland Pertwee, Aimee Stuart, from a play by Aimee Stuart

Jefferson in Paris ★★★ 🔞

Period drama 1995 · US · Colour · 133mins

Nick Nolte bursts through the usual polite tapestry woven by director James Ivory and producer Ismail Merchant, in a study of the hypocrisy inherent in the lifestyle of US president-to-be Thomas Jefferson. Jefferson was a man of upright conviction, yet was a mass of contradictions. He drafted the Declaration of Independence asserting that all men are created equal and, while appointed American ambassador to France in the late 18th century, had an affair with a married artist (Greta Scacchi) and children by his household slave (Thandie Newton). That Nolte makes the man at all tolerable is an indication of his acting skills although, despite his efforts, he can't hide the fact that he is too modern a performer for this period role. Contains brief nudity. 🎬

Nick Nolte *Thomas Jefferson* • Greta Scacchi *Maria Cosway* • Jean-Pierre Aumont *D'Hancarville* • Simon Callow *Richard Cosway* • Seth Gilliam *James Hemings* • Thandie Newton *Sally Hemings* • James Earl Jones *Madison Hemings* • Michael Lonsdale [Michel Lonsdale] *Louis XVI* • Gwyneth Paltrow *Patsy Jefferson* • Estelle Eonnett *Polly Jefferson* ■ *Dir* James Ivory • *Scr* Ruth Prawer Jhabvala

Jeffrey ★★★★ 🔞

Romantic comedy
1995 · US · Colour · 89mins

Paranoid gay man Steven Weber turns celibate due to the Aids threat, and then meets the hunk of his dreams, Michael T Weiss, who is HIV-positive. Adapted from Paul (*The Addams Family*) Rudnick's Obie-winning off-Broadway play, director Christopher Ashley's poignant adaptation is not only daring and sympathetic but extremely funny: a pitch-perfect look at New York gay society facing a common enemy with suitably mordant humour and bitchy cross-bearing. Patrick Stewart is a knockout as the flamboyant queen who advises Weber to take a chance rather than opt out of life altogether. 🎬 **DVD**

Steven Weber *Jeffrey* • Michael T Weiss *Steve* • Irma St Paule *Mother Teresa* • Patrick Stewart *Robert Klein Skip Winkley* • Christine Baranski *Ann Marwood Bartle* • Bryan Batt *Darius* • Sigourney Weaver *Debra Moorhouse* • Nathan Lane *Father Dan* • Olympia Dukakis *Mrs Marcangelo* ■ *Dir* Christopher Ashley • *Scr* Paul Rudnick, from the play by Paul Rudnick

Jekyll and Hyde ★★ 🔞

Horror 1989 · UK/US · Colour · 94mins

The much-filmed horror classic gets an unconvincing American TV movie makeover, and finds Michael Caine going through the motions as split personality Victorian gentleman Dr Henry Jekyll and his evil counterpart Mr Edward Hyde. Cheryl Ladd is out of her depth as his concerned girlfriend, Sara Crawford. Despite a sterling cast of Brits (Joss Ackland, Ronald Pickup, Lionel Jeffries), David Wickes's direction is uninspired and the surfeit of all-enveloping fog and chirpy cockneys soon becomes wearying. 🎬

Michael Caine *Dr Henry Jekyll/Mr Edward Hyde* • Cheryl Ladd *Sara Crawford* • Joss Ackland *Dr Lanyon* • Ronald Pickup *Jeffrey Utterson* • Kim Thomson *Lucy* • Lionel Jeffries

Mr Jekyll • Diane Keen *Annabel* ■ *Dir* David Wickes • *Scr* David Wickes, from the novel *The Strange Case of Dr Jekyll and Mr Hyde* by Robert Louis Stevenson

Jekyll and Hyde... Together Again ★★ 🔞

Horror spoof 1982 · US · Colour · 83mins

Satirical comedy show *Saturday Night Live* was famous for spawning a number of careers and a host of film spin-offs. It also gave rise to a number of imitators, arguably the best of which was *Fridays*, a similarly trendy late-night mix of jokes and sketches. That show in turn gave rise to the spin-off *Jekyll and Hyde... Together Again*, a movie designed to cash in on the popularity of Mark Blankfield's creation, a drug-crazed pharmacist. Here he plays a surgeon who changes personalities whenever he sniffs a strange powder. The transformation from small screen to big, however, wasn't so successful. 🎬

Mark Blankfield *Jekyll/Hyde* • Bess Armstrong *Mary* • Krista Errickson *Ivy* • Tim Thomerson *Dr Lanyon* • Michael McGuire *Dr Carew* ■ *Dir* Jerry Belson • *Scr* Monica Johnson, Harvey Miller, Jerry Belson, Michael Leeson, from the novel *The Strange Case of Dr Jekyll and Mr Hyde* by Robert Louis Stevenson

J'Embrasse Pas ★★★ 🔞

Drama 1991 · Fr · Colour · 110mins

Although they're always technically impeccable, the films of André Téchiné are invariably rather cold and detached. Consequently, it's hard to identify here with Manuel Blanc, the country mouse who comes to Paris hoping to make it in the movies and ends up on the streets as a rent boy. Clearly Blanc is faced with an impossible task in trying to salvage scenes from the excellent Philippe Noiret, but his own acting deficiencies don't help. Emmanuelle Béart provides some soul amid the degradation and desperation, yet this is very much a film that promises fulfilment without delivering. In French with English subtitles. Contains swearing. 🎬

Philippe Noiret *Romain* • Emmanuelle Béart *Ingrid* • Manuel Blanc *Pierre* • Hélène Vincent *Evelyne* • Yvan Desny [Ivan Desny] *Dimitri* • Christophe Bernard *Le Mac* ■ *Dir* André Téchiné • *Scr* André Téchiné, Jacques Nolot, Michel Grisolia, from a story by Jacques Nolot

Jennie Gerhardt ★★★

Melodrama 1933 · US · BW · 85mins

From the silent *Way Down East* to *The Valley of Decision*, and countless times between, romantic melodrama weepies involving a humble maid with a past and the son of the household seldom disappoint. This one, from a novel by Theodore Dreiser, stars Sylvia Sidney, who suffered so painfully in Dreiser's *An American Tragedy* and who once famously said of her career that she was "paid by the tear". She plays a victim of poverty, who falls pregnant but loses the father to an accident before they can marry. Finding work as a maidservant, she and Donald Cook fall in love, but her past presents an obstacle. Adequate direction, excellent supporting cast.

Sylvia Sidney *Jennie Gerhardt* • Donald Cook *Lester Kane* • Mary Astor *Letty Pace* • Edward

Arnold *Senator Brander* • HB Warner *William Gerhardt* • Louise Carter *Mrs Gerhardt* ■ *Dir* Marion Gering • *Scr* SK Lauren, Frank Partos, from the novel by Theodore Dreiser

Jennifer ★★

Crime drama 1953 · US · BW · 73mins

The careers of married couple Ida Lupino and Howard Duff were at a low ebb when they made this slow-moving mystery in which Lupino, as a woman who has taken on the job of caretaker at a gloomy mansion, spends endless periods wandering the house in a quest to find out what happened to her predecessor, who mysteriously disappeared. The under-nourished sets, starkly lit for James Wong Howe's camera, betray the modest budget and the mystery's solution proves anti-climactic. The film's only distinction is that it served to introduce the classic torch song *Angel Eyes*, sung by its composer Matt Dennis.

Ida Lupino *Agnes* • Howard Duff *Jim* • Robert Nichols *Orin* • Mary Shipp *Lorna* • Ned Glass *Grocery clerk* • Kitty McHugh *Landlady* • Russ Conway *Gardener* • Lorna Thayer *Grocery clerk* • Matt Dennis ■ *Dir* Joel Newton • *Scr* Virginia Myers

Jennifer ★ 🔞

Horror 1978 · US · Colour · 86mins

A terrible *Carrie* imitation with snakes substituted for telekinesis. Abused by her religious fanatic father Jeff Corey, withdrawn Lisa Pelikan also puts up with continual harassment from her high school classmates. It isn't long before she's using her supernatural power to call on the serpent gods to attack her tormentors. *Psycho*'s John Gavin, American game show host Bert Convey and Hollywood glamour queen Nina Foch are on hand to elicit scares, but fail miserably. 🎬

Lisa Pelikan *Jennifer Baylor* • Bert Convy *Jeff Reed* • Nina Foch *Mrs Calley* • Amy Johnston *Sandra Tremayne* ■ *Dir* Brice Mack • *Scr* Kay Cousins Johnson, from a story by Steve Krantz

Jennifer Eight ★★★ 🔞

Thriller 1992 · US · Colour · 119mins

A thriller that disappeared without trace, despite the fact that the leads are Andy Garcia and star Uma Thurman. Thurman is effective as a blind woman who hears a murder and may be in danger herself, while Garcia gives his usual charismatic turn as the cop convinced the case is linked to one he fouled up years before. The blind murder-witness scenario was done better in Michael Apted's 1994 thriller *Blink*, partly because it had fewer far-fetched twists than this one, but there's still plenty to keep followers of thrillers and fans of the two stars happy. Contains swearing, violence and sex scenes. 🎬

Andy Garcia *John Berlin* • Uma Thurman *Helena Robertson* • Lance Henriksen *Freddy Ross* • Kathy Baker *Margie Ross* • Graham Beckel *John Taylor* • Kevin Conway *Citrine* • John Malkovich *St Anne* • Perry Lang *Travis* ■ *Dir/Scr* Bruce Robinson

Jennifer on My Mind ★★

Black comedy 1971 · US · Colour · 85mins

Ghastly drugs film, one of many made as the Summer of Love crashed and

burned, with Michael Brandon and Tippy Walker as rootless drifter and rich girl who become pot-smoking partners when they meet up in Venice, then graduate to harder stuff when they get back home. The dire script is by Erich Segal, of *Love Story* fame, and earns a second star solely because of an early small role for Robert De Niro, who prophetically plays a taxi driver five years before he'd play a far more famous one for Martin Scorsese.

Michael Brandon *Marcus* • Tippy Walker *Jenny* • Lou Gilbert *Max* • Steve Vinovich *Ornstein* • Robert De Niro *Gypsy cab driver* ■ *Dir* Noel Black • *Scr* Erich Segal, from the novel *Heir* by Roger L Simon

Jenny ★★ 🔞

Drama 1969 · US · Colour · 88mins

A young film-maker (Alan Alda) comes up with a novel way to dodge the draft, by proposing marriage to an unmarried pregnant woman (Marlo Thomas). Unsurprisingly, to all but the cast, their relationship of convenience begins to deepen. Thomas, as the eponymous Jenny, and Alda are pleasant leads as usual, but this is not quite the deep Vietnam-era drama it aspires to be. Harry Nilsson contributes a song. 🎬

Marlo Thomas *Jenny* • Alan Alda *Delano* • Marian Hailey *Kay* • Elizabeth Wilson *Mrs Marsh* • Vincent Gardenia *Mr Marsh* • Stephen Strimpell *Peter* • Fay Bernardi *Woman* • Charlotte Rae *Bella Star* ■ *Dir* George Bloomfield • *Scr* George Bloomfield, from a story by Diana Gould

Jenny Kissed Me ★★★ 🔞

Drama 1984 · Ausl · Colour · 99mins

Best known for the spooky children's film *Frog Dreaming* and a spate of brutal Hollywood action films, director Brian Trenchard-Smith here offers a sordid slice of Melbourne life. Ten-year-old Jenny, played by Tamsin West, has a close relationship with mother Deborra-Lee Furness's boyfriend, Ivar Kants. Although events overstep the bounds of credibility, the drama is just about held together by the director's uncompromising portrait of inner-city squalor and by Furness's compelling performance as she is driven into prostitution and drugs by despair.

Deborra-Lee Furness *Carol Grey* • Ivar Kants *Lindsay Fenton* • Tamsin West *Jenny Grey* • Paula Duncan *Gaynor Roberts* • Steven Grives *Mal Evans* ■ *Dir* Brian Trenchard-Smith • *Scr* Judith Colquhoun, Warwick Hind, Alan Lake

Jeopardy ★★★

Melodrama 1953 · US · BW · 68mins

This suspense melodrama, written by Mel Dinelli from a radio play by Maurice Zimm, was one of the last films John Sturges directed before he established his reputation with *Escape from Fort Bravo*. During a camping vacation on a remote Mexican beach, husband and father Barry Sullivan is pinioned in the water by fallen timber. With just four hours before the tide comes in, wife Barbara Stanwyck drives off to find assistance. Unfortunately, she runs into fleeing killer Ralph Meeker. Despite its slender running time, credibility flies out the window about halfway through. Until then, however, this is a taut and exciting little movie, with Stanwyck gutsy and subtle.

Barbara Stanwyck *Helen Stilwin* • Barry Sullivan *Doug Stilwin* • Ralph Meeker *Lawson* • Lee Aaker *Bobby Stilwin* • Bud Wolfe *Lieutenant's driver* • Saul Gorss *Captain's driver* • Bob Castro *Machine gunner* • Paul Fierro *Mexican lieutenant* ■ *Dir* John Sturges • *Scr* Mel Dinelli, from the radio play *A Question of Time* by Maurice Zimm

Jeremiah Johnson ★★★ PG

Western adventure
1972 · US · Colour · 111mins

"Liver-eatin' Johnson" was what this real-life trapper was called, named after a particularly Hannibal Lecter-ish habit that is totally absent from this homogenised, ecologically sound and politically correct near-western. It's a pretty but ultimately boring epic, in which a miscast (too young, too intelligent) Robert Redford struggles through a semi-allegorical screenplay, poorly fashioned by John Milius and Edward Anhalt from two excellent accounts. Despite sterling support from Will Geer and *Calamity Jane's* Allyn Ann McLerie, the movie simply doesn't jell, and Warner Bros delayed its release in favour of Redford's *The Candidate*. ▭ **DVD**

Robert Redford *Jeremiah Johnson* • Will Geer *Bear Claw* • Stefan Gierasch *Del Gue* • Allyn Ann McLerie *Crazy woman* • Charles Tyner *Robidoux* • Josh Albee *Caleb* • Joaquin Martinez *Paints His Shirt Red* • Paul Benedict *Reverend* ■ *Dir* Sydney Pollack • *Scr* John Milius, Edward Anhalt, from the novel *Mountain Man* by Vardis Fisher, from the story *Crow Killer* by Raymond W Thorp

Jeremy ★

Romance   1973 · US · Colour · 90mins

Dripping with sentimentality, this is *Love Story* without the style, and how it won writer/director Arthur Barron a prize at Cannes for Best First Feature is anybody's guess. Robby Benson and Glynnis O'Connor play a budding cellist and ballet student respectively whose burgeoning romance is threatened by parental intervention. What makes this so hard to watch with a straight face are the trite protestations and the achingly tasteful approach to sex. (The chess game seduction is a minor kitsch classic.) What's more, with imagery straight out of a glossy magazine, the film seems to contradict its own anti-bourgeois sentiments.

Robby Benson *Jeremy* • Glynnis O'Connor *Susan* • Len Bari *Ralph* • Leonardo Cimino *Cello teacher* • Ned Wilson *Susan's father* • Chris Bohn *Jeremy's father* • Pat Wheel *Jeremy's mother* ■ *Dir/Scr* Arthur Barron

Jericho ★★★★

Drama   1991 · Ven · Colour · 90mins

Released to coincide with the celebrations marking the 500th anniversary of Columbus's voyage to the Americas, this revisionist Venezuelan drama could almost be considered an exercise in historical ethnography, such is the authenticity of its portrait of life among the native Indians. Particularly fascinating is the extended, untranslated sequence in which Dominican friar Cosme Cortazar is compelled to decipher the language and customs of the tribe that rescues him after he is separated from a

murderous band of conquistadores. Strikingly photographed by Andrés Agustí, writer/director Luis Alberto Lamata's debut contrasts accepted notions of civilisation and savagery with unforced veracity. In Spanish with English subtitles..

Cosme Cortazar *Santiago* ■ *Dir/Scr* Luis Alberto Lavata

Jericho Fever ★★ PG

Thriller   1993 · US · Colour · 85mins

Telegenic stars Stephanie Zimbalist and Perry King head the cast of this by-the-numbers TV thriller, which finds a mixed bag of spies, cops and medics on the trail of a gang of terrorists carrying a deadly disease. The two leads are likeable enough and director Sandor Stern, best known for scripting the first *Amityville Horror* hit, keeps the action cracking along at a moderately enjoyable pace. ▭

Stephanie Zimbalist *Bonnie Whitney* • Perry King *Michael Whitney* • Branscombe Richmond *Elgin Sweetroot* • Alan Scarfe *Klaus Bausen* • Elyssa Davalos *Bettina Fuentes* ■ *Dir* Sandor Stern • *Scr* IC Rapoport, from a story by IC Rapoport, Sandor Stern

The Jerk ★★★★ 15

Comedy   1979 · US · Colour · 89mins

Has Steve Martin made a funnier film? Fans of this insist he hasn't, as Martin takes on the role of simple-minded and naive Navin Johnson, who suddenly discovers that his black parents aren't his natural kith and kin. He takes his dog and leaves the plantation to make his way in a world which is as loopy as him. There are some heavenly jokes (especially the one where he makes a fortune inventing an absurd nose support for spectacles), and Martin is in best "manic" mode. ▭

Steve Martin *Navin Johnson* • Bernadette Peters *Marie Kimball* • Catlin Adams *Patty Bernstein* • Mabel King *Mother* • Richard Ward *Father* • Dick Anthony Williams *Taj* • Bill Macy *Stan Fox* • M Emmet Walsh *Madman* • Dick O'Neill *Frosty* • Carl Reiner ■ *Dir* Carl Reiner • *Scr* Steve Martin, Carl Gottlieb, Michael Elias

The Jerky Boys ★

Comedy   1995 · US · Colour · 82mins

From the same bad-taste school as *Wayne's World*'s comes this TV sitcom, cartoon, comic book and platinum market-posting duo. Johnny Brennan and Kamal Ahmed play the moronic pair of phone pranksters, who use crank calls to be sociable and bluff their way into Mafia high society, incurring the wrath of New York crime boss Alan Arkin. This featherlight nonsense shows a distinct lack of comic inspiration. Cameos by Tom Jones, Ozzy Osbourne and William Hickey don't help.

Johnny Brennan [John G Brennan] *Johnny Brennan* • Kamal Ahmed • Alan Arkin *Lazarro* • William Hickey *Uncle Freddy* • Alan North *Mickey* • Brad Sullivan *Worzic* • James Lorinz *Brett Weir* • Suzanne Shepherd *Mrs B* ■ *Dir* James Melkonian • *Scr* James Melkonian, Rich Wilkes, John G Brennan [Johnny Brennan], Kamal Ahmed

Jerry and Tom ★★★

Black comedy   1998 · Can · Colour · 105mins

Character actor Saul Rubinek takes a stroll into Tarantino territory – well he did have a killer cameo in *True Romance* – for this pleasingly black and quite stylish slice of North American indie cinema. The film opens with two hit men Jerry (Sam Rockwell) and Tom (Joe Mantegna) waiting to complete their latest assignment with the desperately wisecracking Peter Riegert. We then flash back in time to see how the two became partners. Rubinek (who also has a brief Hitchcock cameo) seamlessly blends the flashbacks together and still finds time to put some flesh on the bones of the duo's victims.

Joe Mantegna *Tom* • Sam Rockwell *Jerry* • Charles Durning *Vic* • Maury Chaykin *Billy* • Peter Riegert *Stanley* • William H Macy *Karl* • Ted Danson *Guy who loved Vicki* ■ *Dir* Saul Rubinek • *Scr* Rick Cleveland

Jerry Maguire ★★★★★ 15

Sports comedy romance
1996 · US · Colour · 133mins

Writer/director Cameron Crowe – who made the wonderfully moving teenage romance *Say Anything* – here balances the best performance of Tom Cruise's career with a clutch of superb supporting turns. Add a witty and tear-jerking script and the result is an unusual romantic-comedy-drama. Cruise is Jerry Maguire, a sports agent who, guilt-ridden one night about how he and his colleagues treat sport stars as commodities, writes a mission statement which effectively costs him his job. It's his relationships with his sole remaining client (a superb, Oscar-winning turn from Cuba Gooding Jr), the woman who stands by him (Renee Zellweger) and her adorable son (Jonathan Lipnicki) that bring an infectious warmth to a film that introduced the world to the oft-quoted: "Show me the money!" ▭ **DVD**

Tom Cruise *Jerry Maguire* • Cuba Gooding Jr *Rod Tidwell* • Renee Zellweger *Dorothy Boyd* • Kelly Preston *Avery Bishop* • Jerry O'Connell *Frank Cushman* • Jay Mohr *Bob Sugar* • Bonnie Hunt *Laurel Boyd* • Regina King *Marcee Tidwell* • Jonathan Lipnicki *Ray Boyd* • Todd Louiso *Chad the nanny* • Eric Stoltz *Ethan Valhere* ■ *Dir/Scr* Cameron Crowe

Jersey Girl ★★ 15

Romantic comedy
1992 · US · Colour · 91mins

In this bland reworking of better romantic comedies such as *Pretty Woman* and *Working Girl*, Jami Gertz (*Twister*) stars as a girl from New Jersey who's looking for a way out of her mundane existence. The opportunity arrives when she bumps into businessman Dylan McDermott (*The Practice*) at a Manhattan Mercedes showroom. Director David Burton Morris's movie falls down through lack of star power. Gertz comes across as a whining opportunist, and her scenes with McDermott lack the requisite chemistry. It does have a certain charm, but not enough to make it compelling viewing. ▭

Jami Gertz *Toby Mastallone* • Dylan McDermott *Sal* • Sheryl Lee *Tara* • Joseph Bologna *Bennie Mastallone* • Joseph Mazzello

Jason • Aida Turturro *Angie* • Molly Price *Cookie* ■ *Dir* David Burton Morris • *Scr* Gina Wendkos

Jerusalem ★★★

Period drama   1996 · Swe · Colour · 166mins

Bille August adapted this epic of rural discontent and religious fervour from the novel by Nobel Prize-winning author, Selma Lagerlöf, who had based her story on the actual 19th-century trek made by a group of Swedes to Jerusalem after they encountered the famed revivalist, Hellgum. Although Sven-Bertil Taube impresses as the impassioned preacher, it's the director's then wife, Pernilla August, who carries the drama as she feuds with Ulf Friberg for control of the family farm. This handsome period piece is occasionally sluggish, in spite of a surfeit of subplots. Made with funding from all the Scandinavian countries and Iceland. In Swedish with English subtitles.

Ulf Friberg *Ingmar* • Maria Bonnevie *Gertrud* • Pernilla August *Karin* • Max von Sydow *Vicar* • Olympia Dukakis *Mrs Gordon* • Reine Brynolfsson *Tim* • Lena Endre *Barbro* • Jan Mybrand *Gabriel* • Sven-Bertil Taube *Hellgum* ■ *Dir* Bille August • *Scr* Bille August, from the novel by Selma Lagerlöf

The Jerusalem File ★ PG

Political thriller
1972 · US/Is · Colour · 92mins

Made four years after his 1968 debut, *The Sergeant*, John Flynn's second feature is a cynical slice of anti-Arab propaganda. Although it purports to steer a middle course, the script's sympathies clearly lie with the Israeli characters encountered by archaeology student Bruce Davison as he picks his way through the intricacies of the Middle Eastern situation in the aftermath of the Six Day War. Raoul Coutard's photography has an immediacy that perfectly complements the seriousness of the subject, but the sporadic outbursts of *Boys' Own* adventure sit uncomfortably with the political proselytising. ▭

Bruce Davison *David* • Nicol Williamson *Lang* • Daria Halprin *Nurit* • Donald Pleasence *Samuels* • Ian Hendry *Mayers* • Koya Yair Rubin *Barak* ■ *Dir* John Flynn • *Scr* Troy Kennedy Martin • *Cinematographer* Raoul Coutard

Jesse ★★ PG

Drama based on a true story
1988 · US · Colour · 93mins

One of Lee Remick's final screen performances was in this worthy drama, playing a local nurse, loved by her community, who is suddenly found to have been practising without a licence. A court case looms with Remick, her husband and the whole town going on trial. The wordy script is by James Lee Barrett, who wrote *The Greatest Story Ever Told* and *The Green Berets*. Shot in the desert wastes of Arizona, though claiming to be set in California's Death Valley, one just wishes it could have been a better picture near the end of Remick's fine career. ▭

Lee Remick *Jesse Maloney* • Scott Wilson *Sam Maloney* • Albert Salmi *Sheriff Sommers*

• Priscilla Lopez *Martha* • Richard Erdman *Dr Adams* • Richard Marcus *Ray Butler* ■ *Dir* Glenn Jordan • *Scr* James Lee Barrett

Jesse James ★★★★ U

Classic western 1939 · US · Colour · 105mins

A western that virtually canonises notorious outlaw Jesse James, here sympathetically portrayed by Tyrone Power as a glamorous Robin Hood-style figure of the Old West, riding out to right wrongs alongside his brother Frank, played by Henry Fonda. The rich 20th Century-Fox Technicolor is superb, and whether the real Jesse was as dashing or handsome as Power is irrelevant: this is stirring stuff, brilliantly directed by Henry King, one of the great masters of on-screen Americana. Nunnally Johnson's screenplay ignores most of the facts, but who cares? ▣

Tyrone Power *Jesse James* • Henry Fonda *Frank James* • Nancy Kelly *Zee* • Randolph Scott *Will Wright* • Henry Hull *Major Rufus Cobb* • Brian Donlevy *Barshee* • John Carradine *Bob Ford* ■ *Dir* Henry King • *Scr* Nunnally Johnson, from historical data asembled by Rosalind Schaeffer, Jo Frances James

Jessica ★ 18

Comedy 1962 · US/It/Fr · Colour · 104mins

After her striking performance opposite John Wayne in *Rio Bravo*, Angie Dickinson deserved a major big-screen career but the right parts were never written for her. Instead, she ended up in films like this limp farce, playing the American midwife in a Sicilian village who prompts the jealous women into a *Lysistrata*-like love strike to get rid of her: no babies, no work. This was considered naughty enough in its day to be X-certificated for adults only. ▣

Angie Dickinson *Jessica* • Maurice Chevalier *Father Antonio* • Noël-Noël *Old Crupi* • Gabriele Ferzetti *Edmondo Raumo* • Sylva Koscina *Nunzia Tuffi* • Agnes Moorehead *Maria Lombardo* ■ *Dir* Jean Negulesco • *Scr* Edith Sommer, from the novel *The Midwife of Pont Clery* by Flora Sandstrom

Jesus ★★

Biblical drama 1979 · US · Colour · 121mins

Brian Deacon joins the pantheon of screen Christs, but this time it certainly isn't the greatest story ever told. Despite the compulsion of the title, this straightforward account of the life of Jesus Christ, narrated by Alexander Scourby, has little going for it apart from its enduring appeal to those of the Christian faith. Location filming does little to enhance the work of the undistinguished cast, while the producers were the biblically-named Genesis Project.

Alexander Scourby *Narrator* • Brian Deacon *Jesus* • Rivka Noiman *Mary* • Joseph Shiloah [Joseph Shiloach] *Joseph* ■ *Dir* Peter Sykes, John Kirsh • *Scr* Barnet Fishbein, from the Gospel of St Luke

Jesus Christ Superstar ★★ PG

Musical 1973 · US · Colour · 102mins

Andrew Lloyd Webber and Tim Rice's groundbreaking musical chronicling the last seven days of Jesus Christ works better on stage than screen, judging from director Norman Jewison's worthy adaptation. The score is brilliant, and Ted Neeley, Carl Anderson and Yvonne Elliman give great performances. However, they're undermined by Jewison's attempts to give the Passion Play a mod credibility: a busload of students arriving in the desert to put on a show, for example, or Judas ducking jet fighters halfway through a song. The result is a disappointment that would look less infantile and shallow without such a wrong-headed, anachronistic approach. ▣

Ted Neeley *Jesus Christ* • Carl Anderson *Judas Iscariot* • Yvonne Elliman *Mary Magdalene* • Barry Dennen *Pontius Pilate* • Bob Bingham *Caiaphas* ■ *Dir* Norman Jewison • *Scr* Melvyn Bragg, Norman Jewison, from the musical *Jesus Christ Superstar* by Tim Rice, from the musical *Jesus Christ Superstar* by Andrew Lloyd Webber • *Cinematographer* Douglas Slocombe

Jesus of Montreal ★★★★ 18

Satirical drama 1989 · Can · Colour · 114mins

Having charted *The Decline of the American Empire* in his previous picture, Québecois director Denys Arcand turned his attention to the Kingdom of God in this scathing satire. Mammon and the mores of the modern world also come in for some serious denunciation as actor Lothaire Bluteau revives the spirit of Christ the Social Radical while revamping a long-running passion play. Touching on everything from religious hypocrisy and artistic integrity, to petty bureaucracy and the public's insatiable appetite for sensation, this compelling parable forces you to re-evaluate as you laugh, although the contrived ending dissipates some of the impact. In French with English subtitles. ▣

Lothaire Bluteau *Daniel* • Catherine Wilkening *Mireille* • Johanne-Marie Tremblay *Constance* • Rémy Girard *Martin* • Robert Lepage *Rene* • Gilles Pelletier *Father Leclerc* • Yves Jacques *Richard Cardinal* • Denys Arcand *The Judge* ■ *Dir/Scr* Denys Arcand

Jesus' Son ★★★ 18

Road movie 1999 · US/Can · Colour · 107mins

The hero of Alison Maclean's rambling road movie, based on stories by cult author Denis Johnson, is known merely as "FH". Suffice to say that this is not exactly a term of endearment – more an indication of Billy Crudup's cluelessness as he embarks on a drug-fuelled odyssey through seventies America. Less a coherent drama than a collection of bizarre vignettes, the bitty narrative introduces a rogue's gallery of misfits whose unpredictable behaviour embroils FH in all manner of criminal activity. Not as hip as Gus Van Sant's *Drugstore Cowboy*, this is still an accomplished follow-up to the director's eye-catching debut, *Crush*.

Billy Crudup *FH* • Samantha Morton *Michelle* • Greg Germann *Dr Shanis* • Denis Leary *Wayne* • Jack Black *Georgie* • Will Patton *John Smith* • Holly Hunter *Mira* • Dennis Hopper *Bill* ■ *Dir* Alison Maclean • *Scr* Elizabeth Cuthrell, David Urrutia, Oren Moverman, from a book of short stories by Denis Johnson

Jet Attack ★ U

War drama 1958 · US · BW · 68mins

One of the six B-programme-fillers director Edward L Cahn delivered in 1958, this is interesting chiefly for its use of faded names John Agar (the former Mr Shirley Temple) and Audrey Totter rather than its plot about a jet scientist whose plane is shot down over Korea. A Edward L Cahn season would reveal most of his films to be low-grade junk. This is no exception.

John Agar *Tom Arnett* • Audrey Totter *Tanya* • Gregory Walcott *Bill* • James Dobson *Sandy* • Leonard Strong *Major Wan* ■ *Dir* Edward L Cahn • *Scr* Orville H Hampton, from a story by Mark Hanna

Jet over the Atlantic ★★

Adventure thriller 1960 · US · BW · 92mins

A gas bomb on board a flight from Spain to New York threatens to asphyxiate all the passengers. As the back projected clouds float past, the cast get on with the business of holding their breath and praying for a miracle. Their unlikely saviour turns out to be convicted murderer, Guy Madison, a former pilot, who is in the custody of FBI agent George Raft. Also on board is reptilian George Macready as an English nobleman. Not as much fun as *Airplane!* or even *Airport* but Madison does his heroic best.

Guy Madison *Brett Matoon* • Virginia Mayo *Jean Gurney* • George Raft *Stafford* • Ilona Massey *Madame Galli-Cazetti* • George Macready *Lord Robert Leverett* • Anna Lee *Ursula Leverett* ■ *Dir* Byron Haskin • *Scr* Irving H Cooper

Jet Pilot ★★ U

Romantic drama 1957 · US · Colour · 108mins

Intended as a rehash of *Ninotchka*, this rubbishy airborne yarn has John Wayne as a US airman and Janet Leigh as a Russian pilot who wants to defect. The resulting mess of crass anti-communist propaganda and cringe-inducing romance was the work of producer Howard Hughes, who owned RKO and had a fetish about planes and breasts. The film took 17 months to shoot and was completed around 1950; Hughes then delayed its release by a further six years. Worth seeing as a curiosity.

John Wayne *Colonel Shannon* • Janet Leigh *Anna* • Jay C Flippen *Major General Black* • Paul Fix *Major Rexford* • Richard Rober *George Rivers* • Roland Winters *Colonel Sokolov* ■ *Dir* Josef von Sternberg • *Scr* Jules Furthman

Jet Storm ★★

Drama 1959 · UK · BW · 97mins

On a plane to New York, Richard Attenborough accuses a fellow passenger of killing his daughter in a hit-and-run accident. When Captain Stanley Baker investigates, it emerges that Attenborough has planted a bomb onboard. Cue general hysteria. Despite the other flyers' inevitable mini-dramas – David Kossoff's Holocaust survivor, for instance – this is a star turn for Attenborough, who brings a convincing complexity to the role of bomber and bereft father. The film's constant moralising and eventual pay-off are hard to swallow, however.

Richard Attenborough *Ernest Tilley* • Stanley Baker *Captain Bardow* • Hermione Baddeley *Mrs Satterly* • Bernard Braden *Otis Randolf* • Diane Cilento *Angelica Como* • Barbara Kelly *Edwina Randolf* • David Kossoff *Dr Bergstein* • Virginia Maskell *Pam Leyton* • Harry Secombe *Binky Meadows* ■ *Dir* Cy Endfield • *Scr* Cy Endfield, Sigmund Miller, from a story by Sigmund Miller

La Jetée ★★★★★ PG

Classic science-fiction 1962 · Fr · BW · 26mins

Composed almost exclusively of still photographs, Chris Marker's classic of post-apocalyptic sci-fi makes for unforgettable viewing. Beginning with the childhood memory of a woman's face, the film traces Davos Hanich's efforts to uncover the meaning of this haunting image. Exploring many of the themes found in the *ciné-romans* of Alain Resnais, Marker uses photomontage to dazzling and disturbing effect, but even more devastating is the one simple but indelible live-action sequence. This unique exploration of time, memory and vision provided the inspiration for Terry Gilliam's *Twelve Monkeys*. In French with English subtitles. ▣

Hélène Chatelain *The woman* • Davos Hanich *The man* • Jacques Ledoux *The experimenter* • Jean Négroni *Narrator* ■ *Dir/Scr* Chris Marker • *Editor* Jean Ravel • *Music* Trevor Duncan

Jetsons: the Movie ★★★ U

Science-fiction animation 1990 · US · Colour · 78mins

Hanna-Barbera's less successful flipside of *The Flintstones* were the Space Age equivalent. Atom-powered ovens, robot vacuum cleaners, jet-propelled cars and flying saucer-shaped houses, the Jetson family has it all. What the film doesn't have is a strong story, just a thinly disguised environmental tract about furry space creatures losing their homes due to an asteroid mining operation. The songs are instantly forgettable, the ecology issue is no substitute for the original sixties'-themed whimsy but, fortunately, the animation is colourful and inventive enough to amuse the kids. ▣

George O'Hanlon *George Jetson* • Mel Blanc *Mr Spacely* • Penny Singleton *Jane Jetson* • Tiffany *Judy Jetson* • Patric Zimmerman *Elroy Jetson* • Don Messick *Astro* • Jean Vanderpyl *Rosie the Robot* ■ *Dir* William Hanna, Joseph Barbera • *Scr* Dennis Marks, additional dialogue Carl Sautter

Le Jeune Werther ★★★ 15

Drama 1992 · Fr · Colour · 90mins

As those familiar with *Ponette* will know, Jacques Doillon has a rare gift for directing youngsters. Indeed, there isn't an adult in sight in this canny updating of Goethe's novel, *The Sorrows of Young Werther*. Determined to know why their classmate committed suicide, Ismaël Jolé-Ménébhi and Thomas Brémond soon find themselves experiencing the same pangs of unrequited love for the elusive Miren Capello. True to the Romantic spirit of the original, yet echoing the argot and attitudes of nineties French youth, this rite-of-passage picture captures the

U = SUITABLE FOR ALL   Uc = SUITABLE FOR ALL, ESPECIALLY FOR YOUNG CHILDREN (VIDEO ONLY)   PG = PARENTAL GUIDANCE

innocence of first love while remaining refreshingly free from corny sentiment. In French with English subtitles.

Ismaël Jolé-Ménébhi *Ismael* • Marabelle Rousseau *Mirabelle* • Thomas Brémond *Theo* • Miren Capello *Miren* • Faye Anastasia *Faye* • Pierre Mezerette *Pierre* • Simon Clavière *Simon* ■ *Dir* Jacques Doillon • *Scr* Jacques Doillon, from the novel *The Sorrows of Young Werther* by JW von Goethe

Les Jeux Interdits ★★★★★

Drama 1953 · Fr · BW · 83mins

Named Best Foreign Language Film at the 1952 Oscars and awarded the Golden Lion at Venice, this is the most moving study of childhood innocence ever made. Delicately treading the line between insight and sentimentality, René Clément coaxes wondrous performances out of five-year-old Brigitte Fossey and eleven-year-old Georges Poujouly (found in a camp for underprivileged kids) as the orphan and farmer's boy who cope with the traumas of the Nazi occupation by building a cemetery for animals, which they sanctify with totems taken from the neighbouring graveyard. Simple, poetic and painfully honest, this is one of the gems of French cinema. In French with English subtitles.

Georges Poujouly *Michel Dolle* • Brigitte Fossey *Paulette* • Amédée *Francis Gouard* • Laurence Badie *Berthe Dolle* • Suzanne Courtal *Madame Dolle* • Lucien Hubert *Dolle, the father* • Jacques Marin *Georges Dolle* • Andre Wasley *Gouard, the father* ■ *Dir* René Clément • *Scr* René Clément, Jean Aurenche, Pierre Bost, Francois Boyer, from the novel *Les Jeux Inconnus* by Francois Boyer

Jew Süss ★★★

Period drama 1934 · UK · BW · 105mins

Lion Feuchtwanger's pro-Jewish 1925 novel was adapted for this comparatively lavish British production with an obvious regard to the rise of Fascism in Germany. Set in 18th-century Württemberg, Joseph "Jew Suss" Oppenheimer has risen to a position of power and influence in the Jewish community, but how will he react to the accusation that he is not really a Jew? The great German actor Conrad Veidt, exiled in England with his Jewish wife, is splendid in the title role, and the rest of the cast, including Cedric Hardwicke and Gerald du Maurier, though very British, are good.

Conrad Veidt *Joseph "Jew Suss" Oppenheimer* • Benita Hume *Marie Auguste* • Frank Vosper *Duke Karl Alexander* • Cedric Hardwicke *Rabbi Gabriel* • Gerald Du Maurier *Wessensee* • Pamela Ostrer *Naomi Oppenheimer* • Paul Graetz *Landauer* ■ *Dir* Lothar Mendes • *Scr* Dorothy Farnum, AR Rawlinson, from the novel *Jud Süss* by Lion Feuchtwanger

The Jewel of the Nile ★★★★ PG

Action adventure
1985 · US · Colour · 101mins

The sequel to *Romancing the Stone* re-teams stars Michael Douglas, Kathleen Turner and Danny DeVito, and does so without falling into too many of the usual sequel pitfalls (making the same movie over again, for instance). It starts a few months after Douglas whisked Turner off on his dream boat at the end of the first film, but she has already become bored with all the lovey-dovey stuff and jumps at the chance of hitting the exploration trail once again, at odds with Douglas but determined to get even as he chases after a gem called the Jewel of the Nile, with DeVito in hot pursuit. The three leads clearly have fun, and the action and snappy one-liners come thick and fast, making this one of those rare sequels that's not too far short of the quality of the original. Contains some swearing.

Michael Douglas *Jack* • Kathleen Turner *Joan* • Danny DeVito *Ralph* • Spiros Focas *Omar* • Howard Jay Patterson *Barak* • Randall Edwin Nelson *Karak* • Samuel Ross Williams *Arak* • Timothy Daniel Furst *Sarak* • Hamid Fillali *Rachid* ■ *Dir* Lewis Teague • *Scr* Mark Rosenthal, Lawrence Konner, from characters created by Diane Thomas

Jewel Robbery ★★★

Romantic comedy 1932 · US · BW · 63mins

There's hardly time to catch your breath in this tight little Warner Bros movie from a period when the studio was at its height and pace was everything. Debonair Raffles-like gentleman burglar William Powell robs a jewellery store, locks up the proprietor and a smart customer, and starts making up to the latter's wife, the impossibly elegant Kay Francis who – wouldn't you guess? – longs for a little excitement in her bored life. It's not quite Lubitsch, but sophisticated and immensely enjoyable.

William Powell *Robber* • Kay Francis *Baroness Teri Von Horhenfels* • Hardie Albright *Paul* • Andre Luguet *Count André* • Henry Kolker *Baron Franz Von Horhenfels* • Spencer Charters *Johann Christian Lenz* ■ *Dir* William Dieterle • *Scr* Erwin Gelsey, from the play by Ladislaus Fodor

Jezebel ★★★★ U

Romantic melodrama
1938 · US · BW · 100mins

An absolute cracker and arguably Bette Davis's best role – one which she fervently hoped would win her Scarlett in the following year's *Gone with the Wind*. She had to settle for the consolation of a best actress Oscar for her role here as a beautiful but spoilt southern belle who goes completely over the top in her efforts to make her fiancé Henry Fonda jealous. This is a classic in a golden era of such overblown period blockbusters, directed by William Wyler, with whom Davis was said to be infatuated, and co-starring other luminaries of the genre, such as Henry O'Neill and Donald Crisp. Do not miss.

Bette Davis *Julie Morrison* • Henry Fonda *Preston Dillard* • George Brent *Buck Cantrell* • Margaret Lindsay *Amy Bradford Dillard* • Fay Bainter *Aunt Belle Massey* • Richard Cromwell *Ted Dillard* • Donald Crisp *Dr Livingstone* • Henry O'Neill *General Theopholus Bogardus* ■ *Dir* William Wyler • *Scr* Clements Ripley, Abem Finkel, John Huston, Robert Bruckner, from the play by Owen Davis Sr • *Cinematographer* Ernest Haller • *Music* Max Steiner • *Costume Designer* Orry-Kelly

Jigsaw ★★

Crime drama 1949 · US · BW · 72mins

Franchot Tone is a crusading DA, fighting racketeers who have bumped off a journalist and who will rack up several further corpses before the end. The group, however, is prepared for Tone and sends a female operative to seduce him. This heavy-handed blend of violence and moralising is worth watching for some unbilled cameos from Henry Fonda, John Garfield and Marlene Dietrich, who did the film as a favour to her friend Mercedes McCambridge, the wife of the film's director, Fletcher Markle. As his own tribute to Dietrich, Markle then had a scene set in a New York nightclub called the Blue Angel.

Franchot Tone *Howard Malloy* • Jean Wallace *Barbara Whitfield* • Myron McCormick *Charles Riggs* • Marc Lawrence *Angelo Agostini* • Winifrid Lenihan *Mrs Hartley* • Marlene Dietrich *Nightclub patron* • Henry Fonda *Nightclub waiter* • John Garfield *Street loiterer* ■ *Dir* Fletcher Markle • *Scr* Fletcher Markle, Vincent McConnor, from the story by John Roeburt

Jigsaw ★★★

Mystery drama 1962 · UK · BW · 108mins

This satisfying murder mystery benefits from the reassuring presence of Jack Warner as the detective on the case. Set in Brighton, director Val Guest adopts an unsensational, pseudo-documentary approach that concentrates on the often laborious details of police procedure as the identity of dead woman is ascertained and her killer is slowly unmasked. Among the cast of familiar British faces, American actress Yolande Donlan – Mrs Val Guest – is excellent as a spinster who narrowly misses being a murder victim.

Jack Warner *Det Insp Fellows* • Ronald Lewis *Det Sgt Wilks* • Yolande Donlan *Jean Sherman* • Michael Goodliffe *Clyde Burchard* • John Le Mesurier *Mr Simpson* • Moira Redmond *Joan Simpson* ■ *Dir* Val Guest • *Scr* Val Guest, from the novel *Sleep Long, My Love* by Hillary Waugh

Jigsaw ★

Mystery drama 1968 · US · Colour · 96mins

Spartacus author Howard Fast once wrote a novel called *Fallen Angel*. It was filmed in 1965 as *Mirage* from a screenplay by Peter Stone, who wrote the brilliant *Charade*. It was an amnesia-based thriller that was hard to follow and easy to forget. *Jigsaw* is a remake, reworked by Ranald MacDougall under the pseudonym Quentin Werty which is the QWERTY on a typewriter keyboard. There is one major change to the story: instead of amnesia, the hero's problem is an overdose of LSD which makes him unable to remember who was murdered, and why.

Harry Guardino *Arthur Belding* • Bradford Dillman *Jonathan Fields* • Hope Lange *Helen Atterbury* • Pat Hingle *Lew Haley* • Diana Hyland *Sarah* • Victor Jory *Dr Edward Arkroyd* • Paul Stewart *Dr Simon Joshua* • Susan Saint James *Ida* ■ *Dir* James Goldstone • *Scr* Quentin Werty [Ranald MacDougall], from the film *Mirage* by Peter Stone, from the novel *Fallen Angel* by Howard Fast

Jigsaw ★★

Crime thriller 1972 · US · Colour · 100mins

Although this pilot succeeded in securing a TV series, only eight of the proposed 50 episodes were ever made. From the evidence on display here, it's fairly easy to see why. As a lieutenant with the Missing Persons Bureau, James Wainwright lacks both the dynamism and the quirkiness to win us over, despite finding himself in a pretty sticky situation when he is framed for the murder of a top-ranking state official. Vera Miles, a favourite of Alfred Hitchcock, deserved better than playing second fiddle in underplotted thrillers like this.

James Wainwright *Lt Frank Dain* • Vera Miles *Lilah Beth Cummings* • Andrew Duggan *Harrison Delando* • Edmond O'Brien *Det Ed Burtelson* • Marsha Hunt *Dr Gehlen* ■ *Dir* William A Graham • *Scr* Robert E Thompson

The Jigsaw Man ★★★ 15

Spy drama 1984 · UK · Colour · 90mins

This was another outing for Laurence Olivier and Michael Caine, but this Cold War thriller is not a fraction as effective as their *Sleuth* 12 years before. The story, about a British traitor whose face is surgically altered by the Russians so that he can be sent back on a mission, doesn't convince and, like the most irritating of jigsaws, a lot of plot-pieces seem to be missing. Contains swearing.

Michael Caine *Sir Philip Kimberly* • Laurence Olivier *Admiral Sir Gerald Scaith* • Susan George *Penny* • Robert Powell *Jamie Frazer* • Charles Gray *Sir James Chorley* • Michael Medwin *Milroy* ■ *Dir* Terence Young • *Scr* Jo Eisinger, from the novel by Dorothea Bennet

Jim Thorpe – All-American ★★ U

Sports biography 1951 · US · BW · 105mins

Jim Thorpe was often regarded as the finest all-round athlete America has ever produced. A native American Indian, he won a stack of Olympic gold medals in 1912, more than any other athlete had ever won, but was stripped of them because he had previously played professional baseball. He became a coach, a celebrity, a serial husband and a drunkard. As Thorpe, Burt Lancaster is ideally cast, but despite some fine support and an attempt not to sugar-coat the story, it's a conventional Hollywood biopic.

Burt Lancaster *Jim Thorpe* • Charles Bickford *Glenn S "Pop" Warner* • Steve Cochran *Peter Allendine* • Phyllis Thaxter *Margaret Miller* • Dick Wesson *Ed Guyac* • Jack Big Head *Little boy* ■ • *Scr* Frank Davis, Everett Freeman, from the story *Bright Path* by Douglas Morrow, Vincent X Flaherty, from a biography by Russell J Birdwell, James Thorpe

Jimmy Hollywood ★★★ 15

Comedy drama 1994 · US · Colour · 104mins

Barry Levinson divides his time between intelligent, mainstream blockbusters such as *Sleepers* and *Rain Man*, and his more personal projects that remain best typified by *Diner*. This film falls into the latter category, but it is one of the rare Levinson flops, going straight to video in Britain. It's a shame, really, because it is a likeable enough little oddity. Joe Pesci, on one of his bad-wig days, stars as a struggling actor who becomes a vigilante when a thief snatches his car radio. Despite the farcical plot, there is a deep streak of melancholy running through the piece and, for all Pesci's bluster, the film is stolen by Christian Slater, who gives a

beautifully understated performance as Pesci's slow-witted chum. Contains violence and swearing. ▭
Joe Pesci *Jimmy Alto* • Christian Slater *William* • Victoria Abril *Lorraine De La Pena* • Jason Beghe *Detective* • John Cothran Jr *Detective* ■ *Dir/Scr* Barry Levinson

Jimmy the Gent ★★
Crime comedy   1934 · US · BW · 66mins

James Cagney and Bette Davis star in this romantic comedy about rival teams of con-artists who track down legatees left fortunes in unclaimed wills. Davis, appalled at her employer Cagney's behaviour, leaves him for another firm. It's a profitable racket and the story always hovers on the edge of the gangster movie. Sharply performed by the two stars and lasting barely over an hour, it doesn't stop for lunch. Surprisingly, Warners didn't team Cagney and Davis together again until *The Bride Came C.O.D* in 1941.
James Cagney *Jimmy Corrigan* • Bette Davis *Joan Martin* • Alice White *Mabel* • Allen Jenkins *Louie* • Arthur Hohl *Joe Rector [Monty Barton]* • Alan Dinehart *James J Wallingham* ■ *Dir* Michael Curtiz • *Scr* Bertram Milhauser, from the story *Heir Chaser* by Laird Doyle, Ray Nazarro

Jimmy the Kid ★ PG
Comedy   1982 · US · Colour · 84mins

There are those who confuse acting with big movements, bulging eyes and exaggerated verbal delivery. Furthermore, noise is never a good substitute for wit. All of these irksome trifles are of no concern to Gary Coleman who plays a bored, bright rich kid enjoying his childhood in the company of his kidnappers. Clearly Walter Olkewicz, Paul LeMat and Dee Wallace hold Coleman up as a role model, since they quickly descend to his level of inanity.
Gary Coleman *Jimmy Lovejoy* • Paul LeMat *John Dortmunder* • Dee Wallace [Dee Wallace Stone] *May Dortmunder* • Don Adams *Harry Walker* • Walter Olkewicz *Andrew Kelp* • Ruth Gordon *Bernice Kelp* ■ *Dir* Gary Nelson • *Scr* Sam Bobrick, from the novel by Donald E Westlake

Jingle All the Way ★★ PG
Seasonal comedy 1996 · US · Colour · 85mins

Arnold Schwarzenegger is the overworked businesssman who promises to buy the year's hottest toy – Turbo Man – for his neglected son. Alas, the doll sold out months previously, thus sparking a frantic hunt that sees Arnie crossing swords with an obsessed postman (Sinbad) and a crooked Santa (James Belushi). Schwarzenegger acquits himself well in the slapstick action sequences – for once he is not indestructible – but he's a tad embarrassing during the cuddlier moments. Brian Levant's direction, meanwhile, could do with a harder edge. ▭
Arnold Schwarzenegger *Howard Langston* • Sinbad *Myron Larabee* • Phil Hartman *Ted Maltin* • Rita Wilson *Liz Langston* • Robert Conrad *Officer Hummell* • Martin Mull *DJ* • Jake Lloyd *Jamie Langston* • James Belushi *Mall Santa* ■ *Dir* Brian Levant • *Scr* Randy Kornfield

Jinxed! ★ 15
Black comedy   1982 · US · Colour · 98mins

It was a disaster waiting to happen when Bette Midler, brashest of song-belters, teamed with Don Siegel, briskest of action directors. Off-screen squabbles didn't help this story of a lucky gambler's girl who ropes in Reno croupier Ken Wahl to make the game of blackjack a lethal deal for her partner. Rip Torn, as the gambler, offers a token portrait of sadistic seediness, but what should have been a darkly comic take on *The Postman Always Rings Twice* is an idea that went sadly awry. The title is the best comment. Contains violence and swearing. ▭
Bette Midler *Bonita Friml* • Ken Wahl *Willie Brodax* • Rip Torn *Harold Benson* • Val Avery *Milt Hawkins* • Jack Elam *Otto* ■ *Dir* Don Siegel • *Scr* David Newman, Bert Blessing, from a story by Bert Blessing

Jit ★★★
Romantic comedy   1990 · Zim · Colour · 98mins

Director Michael Raeburn – though not himself a native Zimbabwean – has the privilege of making the nation's first wholly indigenous picture. Considering the inexperience of his largely non-professional cast, he packs this gentle love story with plenty of feel-good humour and even more foot-tapping *jit* jive. As the country boy who falls heavily for an independent city girl, Dominic Makuvachuma gives a relaxed display of charm and determination as he disregards the warnings of his hard-drinking spirit ancestor Winnie Ndemera, to seek the "bride price" required to satisfy Sibongile Nene's grasping father. Slight and shaky, but irresistibly amiable.
Dominic Makuvachuma *UK* • Sibongile Nene *Sofi* • Farai Sevenzo *Johnson* • Winnie Ndemera *Jukwa* • Oliver Mtukudzi *Oliver* • Lawrence Simbarashe *Chamba* • Kathy Kuleya *Nomsa* ■ *Dir/Scr* Michael Raeburn

Jitterbugs ★★ U
Comedy   1943 · US · BW · 74mins

Desperate for a hit after several disappointing outings, Laurel and Hardy revamped the 1933 programme filler *Arizona to Broadway*, with Ollie posing as a southern millionaire and Stan as a rich maiden aunt to help Vivian Blaine, whose mother has been swindled in a land deal. Even their devoted fans will admit that, for the most part, this is pretty feeble stuff, with the demands of the flimsy story getting in the way of the comedy. But there are bright spots, such as the pair working as a two-man orchestra in the middle of the desert, Ollie's southern blustering and newcomer Blaine's three musical numbers.
Stan Laurel *Stan* • Oliver Hardy *Ollie* • Vivian Blaine *Susan Cowan* • Bob Bailey *Chester Wright* • Douglas Fowley *Malcolm Bennett* ■ *Dir* Malcolm St Clair • *Scr* Scott Darling

Jivaro ★★
Adventure romance
1954 · US · Colour · 91mins

The *Indiana Jones* movies breathed new life into the lost treasure adventure genre, which was already in

mothballs way back in the fifties when Paramount wheeled out this lumbering yarn. Fernando Lamas and Rhonda Fleming are the adventurers seeking a cache of gold hidden in a region of the Amazon jungle populated by a tribe of headhunters, known as Jivaro. There's more life in the background foliage (shot on location) than in leads Lamas and Fleming. Much better are supporting players Lon Chaney Jr and the young Brian Keith in one of his earliest roles.
Fernando Lamas *Rio* • Rhonda Fleming *Alice Parker* • Brian Keith *Tony* • Lon Chaney Jr *Pedro* • Richard Denning *Jerry Russell* • Rita Moreno *Maroa* ■ *Dir* Edward Ludwig • *Scr* Winston Miller, from a story by David Duncan

Jo Jo Dancer, Your Life Is Calling ★★ 18
Drama   1986 · US · Colour · 96mins

Richard Pryor directs himself as comedian Jo Jo Dancer in a story that bears an uncanny resemblance to his own colourful career, both on and offstage. It tells of his early days in showbusiness and of the effects of drug use and abuse, culminating in a stay in the hospital burns unit. The cast includes singers Carmen McRae and Billy Eckstine but the results are disappointing given the dramatic possibilities offered by Pryor's life. ▭
Richard Pryor *Jo Jo Dancer/Alter Ego* • Debbie Allen *Michelle* • Art Evans *Arturo* • Fay Hauser *Grace* • Barbara Williams *Dawn* • Carmen McRae *Grandmother* • Billy Eckstine *Johnny Barnett* ■ *Dir* Richard Pryor • *Scr* Rocco Urbisci, Paul Mooney, Richard Pryor

Joan of Arc ★★ PG
Historical epic   1948 · US · Colour · 96mins

Brilliant and under-rated director Victor Fleming – *Gone with the Wind*, *The Wizard of Oz* – had a serious crush on Ingrid Bergman and, despite the fact that their affair was, shall we say, intercepted by Spencer Tracy on *Dr Jekyll and Mr Hyde*, Fleming went ahead with this costly farrago, effectively a Technicolored love letter to Bergman, who had played the role on stage. The result brought Fleming to an early grave, a comic-strip history lesson so dull and lengthy that it was trimmed down at each screening, its original 145-minute length mercifully eventually cut to around 100 minutes. Only José Ferrer as the Dauphin emerges with credit among the multi-accented supporting players. A real endurance test, this one. ▭
Ingrid Bergman *Jeanne d'Arc* • José Ferrer *Dauphin, Charles VII* • Francis L Sullivan *Pierre Cauchon* • J Carrol Naish *Count John Of Luxembourg* • Ward Bond *La Hire* • Shepperd Strudwick *Father Jean Massieu* • Gene Lockhart *Georges La Tremouille* • Leif Erickson *Jean Dunois* ■ *Dir* Victor Fleming • *Scr* Maxwell Anderson, Andrew Solt, from the play *Joan of Lorraine* by Maxwell Anderson • *Costume Designer* Dorothy Jeakins, Karinska

Joan of Arc ★★ 15
Historical biographical drama
1999 · Fr · Colour · 157mins

Kathryn Bigelow walked away from this project after refusing to cast Luc Besson's then-wife Milla Jovovich as the saint. Besson took over and cast Jovovich anyway. Sadly, she's the

biggest problem in this epic story of the peasant girl who led the French to victory over the English. OK, so she's meant to be an innocent, but her teary and naive compulsions are still unconvincing and irritating. The prologue detailing Joan's childhood is dire, but the film does kick in with the entrance of John Malkovich as Charles VII, and there are some remarkable battle scenes before Joan's downfall. Besson is a truly imaginative director, and had the film been cut to a standard two hours, it might have been a great historical masterpiece. As it stands, it is an overlong piece of directorial indulgence.
Milla Jovovich *Joan of Arc* • John Malkovich *Charles VII* • Faye Dunaway *Yolande D'Aragon* • Dustin Hoffman *The Conscience* • Tcheky Karyo *Dunois* • Gina McKee *Duchess of Bedford* ■ *Dir* Luc Besson • *Scr* Andrew Birkin, Luc Besson

Joan of Paris ★★ U
Second World War drama
1942 · US · BW · 91mins

Paul Henreid and Michèle Morgan made strong Hollywood debuts in this efficient slice of Second World War action, set in occupied France and briskly directed by Robert Stevenson. Morgan is the Joan of Paris, the brave barmaid who sidetracks Laird Cregar's Gestapo chief so that French pilot Paul Henreid and some downed RAF flyers can escape back to England. A pre-stardom Alan Ladd gains his first significant role as a wounded pilot nicknamed "Baby", while that worthy character actress May Robson, well into her eighties, makes her final screen appearance.
Paul Henreid *Paul Lavallier* • Michèle Morgan *Joan* • Thomas Mitchell *Father Antoine* • Laird Cregar *Herr Funk* • May Robson *Mlle Rosay* • Alexander Granach *Gestapo agent* • Alan Ladd *Baby* ■ *Dir* Robert Stevenson • *Scr* Charles Bennett, Ellis St Joseph, from a story by Jacques Thery, Georges Kessel

Joanna ★
Musical drama 1969 · UK · Colour · 112mins

Never was the Swinging Sixties seemed so ghastly as in this dismal "free love" fantasy from director Michael Sarne. Donald Sutherland makes the most of his passing role as a playboy who sweeps thrill-seeking art student Genevieve Waite off to North Africa before succumbing to leukaemia. Alas, the rest of the cast look uncomfortable as they contort to the music of Rod McKuen and get swept hither and thither by Waite's garish imagination. The finale, in which she is serenaded by the entire cast and crew, has to be seen to be believed.
Genevieve Waite *Joanna* • Christian Doermer *Hendrix Casson* • Calvin Lockhart *Gordon* • Donald Sutherland *Lord Peter Sanderson* • Glenna Forster-Jones *Beryl* • David Scheuer *Dominic Endersley* ■ *Dir/Scr* Michael Sarne

Jobman ★★★
Drama   1990 · SAfr · Colour · 97mins

Something of a companion piece to the powerful Australian picture by director Fred Schepisi *The Chant of Jimmie Blacksmith*, this bold, unblinkered film shows how a decent

black man is driven outside the law by the pressures of racial prejudice. One of the first films tackling bigotry and its consequences to be made and shown in apartheid South Africa, it is, sadly, deprived of pace by director Darrell Roodt. Still, Kevin Smith gives a performance of immense dignity and power as the deaf-and-dumb Jobman, while Tertius Meintjes lends solid support as his Boer childhood friend. Contains some swearing.

Kevin Smith *Jobman* • Tertius Meintjes *Karel* • Lynn Gaines *Anna* • Marcel Van Heerden *Sergeant* • Goliath Davids *Pyp* • Josephine Liedeman *Petra* ■ *Dir* Darrell Roodt [Darrell James Roodt] • *Scr* Greg Latter, from a story by Achmat Dangor

Jock of the Bushveld
★★★ **PG**

Historical adventure
1988 · SAfr · Colour · 93mins

Based on Percy Fitzpatrick's autobiographical account of life in the South African gold fields at the end of the last century, this is a stirring story that takes us from the depths of the Earth to the great outdoors, via a crocodile-infested river. The hero of the title is a sort of White Fang of the velds, an ugly dog who becomes Fitzpatrick's companion and frequently his salvation. Action-packed, yet retaining a good grasp of period, this is a solid adventure for all the family, with an undoubted star in Mfubu as the indomitable Jock. 🖭

Jonathan Rands *Percy Fitzpatrick* • Jocelyn Broderick *Lilian Cubitt* • Olivier Ngwenya *Jim Makokel* • Gordon Mulholland *Tom Barnett* • Michael Brunner *Seedling* • Marloe Scott-Wilson *Maggie Maguire* ■ *Dir* Gray Hofmeyr • *Scr* John Cundill

Jocks
★ **15**

Comedy   1986 · US · Colour · 90mins

Ever wondered when Christopher Lee's career reached its lowest point? It was probably in this comedy about college athletes, in which Lee plays the school president who is obsessed with winning, whileRichard Rountree is a long way from *Shaft* in his role as the college's tennis coach. The school's only chance of winning a championship lies in tennis player Scott Strader – if he can stop partying long enough to play a match. 🖭

Scott Strader *The Kid* • Perry Lang *Jeff* • Richard Roundtree *Chip Williams* • RG Armstrong *Coach Beetlebom* • Christopher Lee *President White* ■ *Dir* Steve Carver • *Scr* Michael Lanahan, David Oas

Joe
★★★ **15**

Drama   1970 · US · Colour · 92mins

Director John G Avildsen's violent "bigot-versus-counterculture" parable is very much a product of its conservative times, but its implausibility is tempered by strong performances. Peter Boyle became a star after playing the title character, a right-wing, blue-collar loud-mouth who forms a strange relationship with executive Dennis Patrick after the latter kills his wayward daughter's drug-pusher boyfriend. Shot on location in Greenwich Village with almost documentary-like precision, it's a creepy look at man's baser instincts,

capped with a bloody massacre. Susan Sarandon makes her film debut here as Patrick's daughter. 🖭

Peter Boyle *Joe Curran* • Susan Sarandon *Melissa Compton* • Patrick McDermott *Frank Russo* • Dennis Patrick *Bill Compton* • Audrey Caire *Joan Compton* ■ *Dir* John G Avildsen • *Scr* Norman Wexler

Joe Butterfly
★★ **U**

Comedy   1957 · US · Colour · 89mins

It takes a brave actor to invite comparison with Marlon Brando's Japanese fixer in *The Teahouse of the August Moon*. In this insipid rival comedy from Universal, Burgess Meredith does a capable job as Joe Butterfly, a wily local at the service of the American army occupying Japan. Fred Clark is splendid as a combustible colonel, but Audie Murphy is miscast as a brash photographer conducting a tentative romance with a native girl. Location filming in Japan only rubs in the falsity of the situations and the improbably cosy relationship between recent enemies.

Burgess Meredith *Joe Butterfly* • Audie Murphy *Private John Woodley* • George Nader *Sergeant Ed Kennedy* • Keenan Wynn *Henry Hathaway* • Keiko Shima *Cheiko* • Fred Clark *Colonel EE Fuller* ■ *Dir* Jesse Hibbs • *Scr* Sy Gomberg, Jack Sher, Marion Hargrove, from a play by Evan Wylie, Jack Ruge

Joe Dancer: the Big Black Pill
★★

Crime drama   1981 · US · Colour · 89mins

Remembered from films such as *In Cold Blood* and *Tell Them Willie Boy Is Here* , as well as the seventies TV series *Baretta*, Robert Blake attempted to create a new persona for himself with a trio of TV movies in the early eighties. Joe Dancer is a typical private eye in that he's always the first suspect the cops come looking for whenever crime rears its ugly head. Here he's framed for the murder of the runaway son of a prominent Beverly Hills family, whose political future depends on Dancer not uncovering the truth. JoBeth Williams, as the victim's flirtatious sister, heads a solid supporting cast, but the suspense quotient is low.

Robert Blake *Joe Dancer* • JoBeth Williams *Tiffany Farrenpour* • Neva Patterson *Eliza Farrenpour* • James Gammon *Captain Jake Jacqualone* • Veronica Cartwright *Sister Theresa* ■ *Dir* Reza S Badiyi [Reza Badiyi] • *Scr* Michael P Butler

Joe Dancer: the Big Trade
★★

Crime drama   1983 · US · Colour · 96mins

The last case for Robert Blake's LA private investigator Joe Dancer, here charged with manslaughter after accidentally driving into a terrified teenager. However, a little delving leads Dancer to suspect he's been framed by a major movie mogul keen to protect his most valuable star. Bearing in mind the ease with which the studios covered up the misdemeanours of stars like Clark Gable and Errol Flynn, this is an unusually savage, yet still flat, Tinseltown self-portrait.

Robert Blake *Joe Dancer* • Kenneth McMillan *Lieutenant Herbie Quinlan* • Joel Bailey *Judd Hampton* • William Prince *Asa Lamar* • Jane Daly *Carol Banding* • Royal Dano *Cow John* • Sondra Blake *Charley* ■ *Dir* Reza S Badiyi • *Scr* Ed Water, from an idea by Robert Blake

Joe Dancer: the Monkey Mission
★★★

Crime drama   1981 · US · Colour · 96mins

Robert Blake turns crook in the second of the teleplay trilogy featuring unconventional Los Angeles sleuth, Joe Dancer. Easily the most far-fetched of the three, it's also the most entertaining, as Blake tries to steal a looted vase from a thief-proof museum. What makes this unique is that his accomplices are an organ grinder and his monkey and a one-armed electronics wizard. Utterly preposterous, but played with great conviction by Blake and Keenan Wynn.

Robert Blake *Joe Dancer* • John Fielder *Jimmy Papadopolous* • Pepe Serna *Vito* • Clive Revill *Teabag* • Sondra Blake *Charley* • Keenan Wynn *Stump Harris* ■ *Dir* Burt Brinckerhoff • *Scr* Robert Crais

Joe Hill
★★

Biography   1971 · Swe/US · Colour · 114mins

Set in 1902 New York, this should have been a hard-hitting study of the part played by immigrants in the Industrial Workers of the World movement. But, as with *Adalen 31*, his account of a key moment in Swedish labour history, Bo Widerberg again allows imagist lyricism to detract from the authenticity of his investigation of working-class struggle. As the folk singer whose political career is curtailed by a false murder rap, Thommy Berggren occasionally unleashes the fervour of the socialist zealot. But, apart from a few shrewd insights into the American psyche, this is a disappointing picture.

Thommy Berggren *Joe Hill* • Anja Schmidt *Lucia* • Kelvin Malave *Fox* • Evert Anderson *Blackie* • Cathy Smith *Cathy* • Hasse Persson *Paul* ■ *Dir* Bo Widerberg • *Scr* Bo Widerberg, Richard Weber, Steve Hopkins

Joe Kidd
★★ **15**

Western   1972 · US · Colour · 83mins

The spaghetti western meets its classic American origins. But Clint Eastwood's potent "man with no name" persona conflicts uneasily with John Sturges's anonymous direction in this range war saga. Robert Duvall greedily dispossessing Mexican-Americans of their land is the central thread of an indifferent effort scripted by Elmore Leonard. There's little to get excited about apart from one fun highlight, completely out of keeping with the rest of the film, where gunman Eastwood drives a train through a saloon to mow down the villains. 🖭

Clint Eastwood *Joe Kidd* • Robert Duvall *Frank Harlan* • John Saxon *Luis Chama* • Don Stroud *Lamarr* • Stella Garcia *Helen Sanchez* • James Wainwright *Mingo* • Paul Koslo *Roy* ■ *Dir* John Sturges • *Scr* Elmore Leonard

The Joe Louis Story
★★ **U**

Sports biography   1953 · US · BW · 88mins

Amateur pugilist Coley Wallace plays the boxing legend who emerged from

the Chicago slums to become world champion in Robert Gordon's biography. The film follows Joe as he loses the title (and his wife) and wins it back before being crushed by Rocky Marciano in 1951. Wallace was picked because of his extraordinary physical resemblance to Louis, not for any real acting ability. On the positive side, many of the fight scenes include genuine archive footage which will delight boxing fans.

Coley Wallace *Joe Louis* • Paul Stewart *Tad McGeehan* • Hilda Simms *Marva Louis* • James Edwards *Chappie Blackburn* • John Marley *Mannie Seamon* • Dotts Johnson [Dots Johnson] *Julian Black* ■ *Dir* Robert Gordon • *Scr* Robert Sylvester

Joe Macbeth
★★★

Crime drama   1955 · UK · BW · 92mins

This interesting reworking of the "Scottish play" as gangster movie, set in the States but filmed in England, was directed with assurance at Shepperton by one of Britain's most talented film-makers, bohemian jazz freak and crime expert Ken Hughes, best known for his marvellous *Trials of Oscar Wilde*. Americans Paul Douglas and Ruth Roman were imported to play the leads, and the support cast is perfect for its period, with an American-accented Sidney James as Banky, and Bonar Colleano as his revenge-seeking son, Lennie. The Philip Yordan screenplay is terribly ambitious and, despite Douglas's powerful performance in the lead, the film was not well received in its day.

Paul Douglas *Joe Macbeth* • Ruth Roman *Lily Macbeth* • Bonar Colleano *Lennie* • Grégoire Aslan *Duca* • Sidney James *Banky* • Nicholas Stuart *Duffy* • Robert Arden *Ross* • Minerva Pious *Rosie* ■ *Dir* Ken Hughes • *Scr* Phillip Yordan, from the play *Macbeth* by William Shakespeare

Joe Panther
★★

Drama   1976 · US · Colour · 110mins

Joe (Ray Tracey), a young Seminole Indian, feels like an outcast in a white man's world until he discovers a talent for professional alligator-wrestling. This is simplistic children's stuff that labours its messages as Joe struggles to find his way in life. The acting is wooden to say the least, and the music to the alligator battle is far too reminiscent of *Jaws*.

Ray Tracey *Joe Panther* • Brian Keith *Captain Harper* • Ricardo Montalban *Turtle George* • Alan Feinstein *Rocky* • Cliff Osmond *Rance* ■ *Dir* Paul Krasny • *Scr* Dale Eunson, from the novel by Zachary Ball

Joe Smith, American
★★

Second World War drama
1942 · US · BW · 63mins

Based on a Paul Gallico story, this propaganda thriller was the first of a number of "important low-budget pictures" assigned by MGM to executive producer Dore Schary, who later headed the studio. It tells of how aircraft factory worker Robert Young is kidnapped by Nazis but refuses to give them information. Made to help persuade the USA to enter the Second World War, the film cannot help but be dated, though it is directed with plenty of pace by Richard Thorpe. Watch out for Ava Gardner in a bit part in one of her earliest movies.

Robert Young *Joe Smith* • Marsha Hunt *Mary Smith* • Harvey Stephens *Freddie Dunhill* • Darryl Hickman *Johnny Smith* • Jonathan Hale *Blake McKettrick* • Ava Gardner *Girl* ■ *Dir* Richard Thorpe • *Scr* Allen Rivkin, from a story by Paul Gallico

Joe the King ★

Drama   1999 · US · Colour · 101mins

Heavy-handed direction and a joyless script – both courtesy of actor Frank Whaley in his directorial debut – cripple this working-class melodrama about a lonely teenage boy who is coming of age. Noah Fleiss gives a sombre and vacant performance as Joe, while Val Kilmer is woefully miscast as his drunken father – the only talent he brings to this role is his ability to drink beer and chew gum at the same time. Unpleasant characters abound, including Camryn Manheim as Joe's sadistic teacher and Karen Young as his shrill mum. John Leguizamo and Ethan Hawke provide temporary relief in minor roles.

Noah Fleiss *Joe Henry* • Val Kilmer *Bob Henry* • Karen Young *Theresa* • Ethan Hawke *Len Coles* • John Leguizamo *Jorge* • Austin Pendleton *Winston* • Max Ligosh *Mike Henry* • James Costa *Ray* • Camryn Manheim *Mrs Basil* ■ *Dir/Scr* Frank Whaley

Joe versus the Volcano ★★★ **PG**

Comedy   1990 · US · Colour · 97mins

For his directorial debut, Oscar-winning *Moonstruck* screenwriter John Patrick Shanley came up with an oddity – a flawed but still entertaining comedy adventure. Tom Hanks is the downtrodden office worker who, on discovering that he has only a short time to live, accepts the proposition of a shady millionaire (Lloyd Bridges) who offers him anything he wants for 20 days, after which he must throw himself into a living volcano on a remote island. Meg Ryan pops up en route playing three different women in Hanks's life. The best bits are at the beginning with Shanley creating a *Brazil*-like portrait of the office from hell, but it runs out of steam long before Hanks reaches the volcano. Contains some swearing.

Tom Hanks *Joe Banks* • Meg Ryan *Dede/Angelica/Patricia* • Lloyd Bridges *Graynamore* • Robert Stack *Dr Ellison* • Abe Vigoda *Waponis chief* • Dan Hedaya *Mr Waturi* • Amanda Plummer *Dagmar* • Ossie Davis *Marshall* ■ *Dir/Scr* John Patrick Shanley

Joe's Apartment ★★ **12**

Comedy   1996 · US · Colour · 76mins

This was cable channel MTV's first movie production, a bid to turn the original 1992 live action/computer-animated short into a big screen hit. Jerry O'Connell (*Stand By Me*, *Jerry Maguire*) is a jobless innocent who arrives in the Big Apple and finds that life is tough. Having conned his way into a rent-controlled apartment, he finds he shares it with about 50,000 singing, dancing and (luckily) friendly cockroaches. His new-found pals come to his aid when grasping property magnate Robert Vaughn tries to kick him out in order to build a huge prison

on the site. It's faintly repulsive fun, but the laughs are fairly thin on the ground. Contains swearing.

Jerry O'Connell *Joe* • Megan Ward *Lily* • Billy West *Ralph Roach* • Reginald Hudlin *Rodney Roach* • Jim Turner *Walter* • Robert Vaughn *Senator Dougherty* • Don Ho *Alberto Bianco* ■ *Dir/Scr* John Payson

Joey ★★ **U**

Comedy drama   1985 · US · Colour · 95mins

An eighties movie, using an old-fashioned storytelling style, to put over its simple story of a music-obsessed teenager and his troubled relationship with his father. Aside from facing the usual problems of adolescence, Joey and his high school friends play in a rock 'n' roll band, and impress enough to get a once-in-a-lifetime opportunity to play at a prestigious doo-wop show. An obscure music movie memorable only because of the many original doo-wop stars making cameo appearances and singing their hits.

Neill Barry *Joey* • Elisa Heinsohn *Janie* • James Quinn *Joe Sr* • Linda Thorson *Principal O'Neill* • Ellen Hammill *Bobbie* • Rickey Ellis *John* • Dee Hourican *Bonnie* • Dan Grimaldi *Ted* • Frankie Lanz ■ *Dir/Scr* Joseph Ellison

Joey Boy ★ **PG**

Comedy   1965 · UK · BW · 87mins

Along with longtime collaborator Sidney Gilliat, Frank Launder was one of the bastions of British cinema in the forties and fifties. But his brand of comedy had passed its sell-by date by the Swinging Sixties, as this unpardonably awful film (directed and co-written by Launder) demonstrates only too well. Some of the period's top TV sitcom stars are left with egg on their faces, none more so than Harry H Corbett as the brains behind a gang of petty crooks who join the army to avoid prison. Never has Corbett's hangdog expression been worn with such justification as it has here.

Harry H Corbett *"Joey Boy" Thompson* • Stanley Baxter *Benny "the Kid" Lindowski* • Bill Fraser *Sergeant Dobbs* • Percy Herbert *"Mad George" Long* • Lance Percival *Clarence Doubleday* • Reg Varney *"Rabbit" Malone* ■ *Dir* Frank Launder • *Scr* Frank Launder, Mike Watts, from the novel by Eddie Chapman

Joey Breaker ★★★

Drama   1993 · US · Colour · 92mins

Richard Edson is New York talent agent Joey, undergoing a *Jerry Maguire*-like crisis of conscience in this less well-known industry drama. There's no Tom Cruise, of course, but Bob Marley's daughter Cedella plays Joey's girlfriend Cyan, who proves to be a much-needed humanising influence in his life. Writer/director Steven Starr obviously knows what he's talking about but, like our hero, we are left wondering why anyone would want to get involved in this amoral business in the first place.

Richard Edson *Joey Breaker* • Cedella Marley *Cyan Worthington* • Fred Fondren *Alfred Moore* • Erik King *Hip Hop Hank* • Gina Gershon *Jennie Chaser* • Philip Seymour Hoffman *Wiley McCall* • Mary Joy *Esther Trigliani* • Sam Coppola *Sid Kramer* ■ *Dir/Scr* Steven Starr

Jofroi ★★★★

Drama   1933 · Fr · BW · 55mins

The first of Marcel Pagnol's collaborations with writer Jean Giono, this featurette is an exquisite tribute to the director's beloved Provence. Filmed in his childhood home of La Treille and employing a relatively inexperienced cast, Pagnol tempered the corrosive humour of his "tragic burlesque" with rural lyricism and vibrant characterisation. Vincent Scotto is particularly memorable as the peasant who sells his land and then risks his life to prevent new owner Henri Poupon from cutting down too many trees. The passionate love for the land and wilful defiance of authority were to become recurrent themes, while the simple authenticity, anticipated neorealism. In French with English subtitles.

Vincent Scotto *Jofroi* • Henri Poupon *Fonse* • André Robert *The teacher* • Annie Toinon *Barbe* • Charles Blavette *Antonin* ■ *Dir* Marcel Pagnol • *Scr* Marcel Pagnol, from the story *Jofroi de la Maussan* by Jean Giono

John and Julie ★★ **U**

Comedy   1955 · UK · Colour · 82mins

This fantasy about the Queen's coronation arrived too late to catch the mood of national euphoria, but it's still a pleasing snapshot of fifties Britain. On the cusp of finding film fame in *The Ladykillers*, Peter Sellers plays a policeman on the trail of Colin Gibson and Lesley Dudley, two little scamps who've run away from home in order to witness the pageantry. Even with such comic dependables as Wilfrid Hyde White and Sid James among the motley characters the kids encounter, this is a pretty minor offering.

Colin Gibson *John* • Lesley Dudley *Julie* • Noelle Middleton *Miss Stokes* • Moira Lister *Dora* • Wilfrid Hyde White *Sir James* • Sidney James *Mr Pritchett* • Peter Sellers *PC Diamond* ■ *Dir/Scr* William Fairchild

John and Mary ★★

Drama   1969 · US · Colour · 92mins

A product of the Swinging Sixties, this drama of sexual mores was scripted by playwright John Mortimer and directed by Peter (*Bullitt*) Yates, but it remains conventionally stock-still in its attitudes. Icons of the time Dustin Hoffman and Mia Farrow play the eponymous couple who meet in a singles bar, make love and then spend an inordinate amount of time deciding what it all means. Not exactly compelling stuff, but the supporting cast includes Olympia Dukakis, and *Cagney and Lacey*'s Tyne Daly in her film debut.

Dustin Hoffman *John* • Mia Farrow *Mary* • Michael Tolan *James* • Sunny Griffin *Ruth* • Stanley Beck *Ernest* • Tyne Daly *Hilary* • Alix Elias *Jane* • Julie Garfield *Fran* • Olympia Dukakis *John's mother* ■ *Dir* Peter Yates • *Scr* John Mortimer, from a novel by Mervyn Jones • *Music* Quincy Jones

John and Yoko: a Love Story ★★ **15**

Biography   1985 · US · Colour · 146mins

Romanticising the love story and trivialising the politics, this is a frankly embarrassing tribute to the assassinated John Lennon and his

widow Yoko Ono. Although Mark McGann and Kim Miyori turn in passable imitations, the remainder of the casting is shambolic, with the stand-in Beatles bearing no resemblance to the originals. Tracing events from their 1966 meeting to Lennon's murder 14 years later, the action misses the disarming humour of the peace protests and glosses over the excesses of his infamous "lost weekend". Hagiographical to the point of pomposity, this sloppy TV movie at least boasts an exceptional soundtrack.

Mark McGann *John Lennon* • Kim Miyori *Yoko Ono* • Kenneth Price *Paul McCartney* • Peter Capaldi *George Harrison* • Phillip Walsh *Ringo Starr* • Richard Morant *Brian Epstein* • Rachel Laurence *Cynthia Lennon* • John Sinclair *George Martin* • Matthew Marsh *Elton John* ■ *Dir* Sandor Stern • *Scr* Sandor Stern, from a story by Sandor Stern, Edward Hume

John Carpenter's Vampires ★★★ **18**

Horror   1998 · US · Colour · 103mins

Genre auteur John Carpenter doles out the irreverent suspense and wicked splatter in a rip-roaring western horror flick leavened with agreeable humour. James Woods is wonderfully laconic as the vampire slayer on the Vatican payroll, out to destroy a 600-year-old bloodsucker before the evil creature gets his hands on an ancient relic that will enable him to appear during daylight hours. Together with arty special effects, Carpenter frames some fabulous images in welcome widescreen, and there's smart support from Sheryl Lee as the psychic link to the undead leader. A well-wrapped horror package from a master of the macabre. Contains violent scenes.

DVD

James Woods *Jack Crow* • Daniel Baldwin *Montoya* • Sheryl Lee *Katrina* • Thomas Ian Griffith *Valek* • Maximilian Schell *Cardinal Alba* • Tim Guinee *Father Adam Guiteau* • Mark Boone Junior *Catlin* • Gregory Sierra *Father Giovanni* ■ *Dir* John Carpenter • *Scr* Don Jakoby, from the novel *Vampire$* by John Steakley • *Cinematographer* Gary B Kibbe

John Goldfarb, Please Come Home ★

Comedy   1964 · US · Colour · 96mins

Scripted by William Peter Blatty – more famous for *The Exorcist* – this is a lamentably unfunny satire about American colonialism. Peter Ustinov impersonates a Middle East potentate, King Fawz, who is being courted by the US which wants to build a military base in his country. Shirley MacLaine is a journalist doing a profile of him while Richard Crenna is Goldfarb, a spy plane pilot who is shot down and then co-opted into coaching Fawz's football team. The tone is increasingly desperate while none of the film's satirical scattershot hits its target.

Shirley MacLaine *Jenny Ericson* • Peter Ustinov *King Fawz* • Richard Crenna *John Goldfarb* • Jim Backus *Miles Whitepaper* • Scott Brady *Sakalakis* • Fred Clark *Heinous Overreach* • Wilfrid Hyde White *Guz* ■ *Dir* J Lee Thompson • *Scr* William Peter Blatty

John Huston & The Dubliners ★★★
Documentary 1987 · US · Colour · 60mins

Having failed in the forties to bring *Ulysses* to the screen, John Huston finally got to adapt James Joyce in his last film, *The Dead*. Lilyan Sievernich's affectionate documentary reveals a man determined to make the most of his misfortunes – he was too ill to travel to Ireland and had to rely on Seamus Byrne's second unit to obtain the linking footage. He's seen barking orders from his wheelchair to ensure that a cast headed by his daughter, Anjelica, did justice to both the script penned by his son, Tony, and the spirit of Joyce's peerless prose.

Dir Lilyan Sievernich

John of the Fair ★★ U
Period adventure 1952 · UK · BW · 61mins

Shortly before embarking upon its series of Edgar Lustgarten true-crime cases, London production unit Merton Park made this rags-to-riches costume drama. Writer/director Michael McCarthy does a good job, on minimal resources, of re-creating the feel of an 18th-century English carnival. But once young John Charlesworth is revealed as the heir who stands between his wicked uncle and a fabulous estate, the action becomes more predictable. It's rough-and-ready fare, but rousing entertainment for youngsters prepared to use some imagination.

John Charlesworth *John Claydon* • Arthur Young *"Doc" Claydon* • Richard George *William Samuels* • Michael Mulcaster *Jasper Sly* • Hilda Barry *Ma Miggs* • Carol Wolveridge *Jill* • Sidney Bland *Gilroy* • David Garth *Sir Thomas Renton* ■ *Dir* Michael McCarthy • *Scr* Michael McCarthy, from the novel *John of the Fair* by Arthur William Groom

John Paul Jones ★ U
Biography 1959 · US · Colour · 125mins

Set during the American War of Independence, this historical drama is let down by an unappealing cast and a script which pours platitudes all over the Technirama screen. Robert Stack plays the eponymous hero, a Scottish lad who runs away to sea, becomes a captain and virtually invents the US navy. Made in Spain by producer Samuel Bronston, whose next film was the epic masterpiece *El Cid*, the film features a cameo from Bette Davis (as Catherine the Great) and a rousing score from Max Steiner. However, the result is still a plodding effort.

Robert Stack *John Paul Jones* • Marisa Pavan *Aimee DeTellison* • Charles Coburn *Benjamin Franklin* • Erin O'Brien *Dorothea Danders* • Bette Davis *Catherine the Great* ■ *Dir* John Farrow • *Scr* John Farrow, Jesse Lasky Jr, from the story *Nor'wester* by Clements Ripley

Johnnie Mae Gibson: FBI ★★★ PG
Drama based on a true story 1986 · US · Colour · 90mins

Actor Bill Duke has directed some big films – *Deep Cover* and *A Rage in Harlem* among them – and does a similarly good job with this TV movie. It's about the first black woman to become an FBI agent, overcoming poverty and institutional prejudice to do so. Lynn Whitfield gives her all as the title character, and Howard E Rollins Jr tries hard to match her. Contains violence.

Lynn Whitfield *Johnnie Mae Gibson* • Howard E Rollins Jr *TC Russell* • Richard Lawson *Adam Prentice* • William Allen Young *Marvin Gibson* • Ajuana Harrison *Johnnie aged 16* • Sandy Colton *Johnnie aged 9* ■ *Dir* Bill Duke • *Scr* James G Hirsch

Johnny Allegro ★★
Crime drama 1949 · US · BW · 80mins

In the forties, every hard-boiled crime melodrama seemed to be titled after a leading character named Johnny something-or-other. Having done a *Johnny Angel* in 1945, George Raft is now Johnny Allegro, an ex-criminal who agrees to help the Treasury Department. Their target is a villainous George Macready (did he ever play anyone nice?) who is masterminding a scheme to flood America with counterfeit money. The climax in which Raft is stalked across a private island by Macready wielding a bow and arrow, is an obvious steal from Leslie Banks's Count Zaroff hunting Joel McCrea in *The Most Dangerous Game*.

George Raft *Johnny Allegro* • Nina Foch *Glenda Chapman* • George Macready *Morgan Vallin* • Will Geer *Schultzy* • Gloria Henry *Addie* ■ *Dir* Ted Tetzlaff • *Scr* Karen DeWolf, Guy Endore, from a story by James Edward Grant

Johnny Angel ★★★★
Crime drama 1945 · US · BW · 79mins

Smoothie George Raft plays a sea captain out to find his father's killers in this tremendously entertaining melodrama, notable for a tangled flashback plot that remains wholly engrossing. The cast includes two stunning co-stars: Claire Trevor and Signe Hasso, the latter as the French girl who witnessed the murder. Hoagy Carmichael is a cab driver who rejoices in the name Celestial O'Brien; he performs his (now classic) standard *Memphis in June*. With its tense direction from Edwin L Marin and superb, moody photography from Harry J Wild, the film deserves to be much better known, although in its day it was a popular success for RKO.

George Raft *Johnny Angel* • Claire Trevor *Lilah* • Signe Hasso *Paulette* • Lowell Gilmore *Sam Jewell* • Hoagy Carmichael *Celestial O'Brien* • Marvin Miller *Gustafson* • Margaret Wycherly *Miss Drumm* ■ *Dir* Edwin L Marin • *Scr* Steve Fisher, Frank Gruber, from the novel *Mr Angel Comes Aboard* by Charles Gordon Booth

Johnny Apollo ★★★
Crime drama 1940 · US · BW · 94mins

Handsome matinée idol Tyrone Power got a chance to prove he was more than just a pretty face in this tough melodrama about the son of crooked financial scion Edward Arnold going to the bad. This is a very well acted and controlled movie, directed by talented 20th Century-Fox regular Henry Hathaway with just the right degree of understanding, and did wonders for Power's appeal at the box office. Also particularly effective is Dorothy Lamour as Ty's moll, and tough Lloyd Nolan as the rival hood for whom Power goes to work. There's a fair amount of seemingly authentic background detail that potential thriller writers would do well to note, and the whole adds up to a satisfying slice of prime studio fare.

Tyrone Power *Bob Cain/Johnny Apollo* • Dorothy Lamour *Mabel "Lucky" Dubarry* • Lloyd Nolan *Mickey Dwyer* • Edward Arnold *Robert Cain Sr* • Charley Grapewin *Judge Emmett T Brennan* • Lionel Atwill *Jim McLaughlin* • Marc Lawrence *John Bates* ■ *Dir* Henry Hathaway • *Scr* Philip Dunne, Rowland Brown, from a story by Samuel G Engel, Hal Long

Johnny Be Good ★ 15
Sports comedy 1988 · US · Colour · 87mins

It's tough believing that Brat Pack geekmeister Anthony Michael Hall can even kick a ball, let alone be America's hottest football prospect in this sub-standard teen comedy posing as a cautionary tale. Hall just can't quite decide whether to take up numerous lucrative offers from talent scouts or drop the game to attend college with his sweetheart. It's not hard to guess what happens. Disappointing directorial debut for *Flashdance* editor Bud Smith, who treats the ethics of signing gifted high school athletes as if it were merely another installment of *Porky's*. Look out for Robert Downey Jr, Jennifer Tilly and Uma Thurman in pre-star roles.

Anthony Michael Hall *Johnny Walker* • Paul Gleason *Coach Wayne Hisler* • Robert Downey Jr *Leo Wiggins* • Robert Downey Sr *NC AA Investigator* • Uma Thurman *Georgia Elkans* • Seymour Cassel *Wallace Gibson* • Steve James *Coach Sanders* • Jennifer Tilly *Connie Hisler* ■ *Dir* Bud Smith • *Scr* Jeff Buhai, Steve Zacharias, David Obst

Johnny Belinda ★★★★
Drama 1948 · US · BW · 102mins

Jane Wyman won a well-deserved best actress Academy Award for her moving portrayal of the Nova Scotia deaf-mute rape victim in this fine Warner Bros film, which in director Jean Negulesco manages to combine outright melodrama with sensitive performances. Of course, either it works for you or it doesn't; in its day, it was a mighty popular and much parodied movie, but now the censor-circumventions make the whole thing seem as phoney as its sets. The strength of the acting wins through, however, with the excellent Lew Ayres registering strongest alongside Wyman as the sympathetic accused doctor, while Jan Sterling makes her film debut as the rapist's wife.

Jane Wyman *Belinda McDonald* • Lew Ayres *Dr Robert Richardson* • Charles Bickford *Black McDonald* • Stephen McNally *Locky McCormick* • Jan Sterling *Stella McCormick* • Agnes Moorehead *Aggie McDonald* • Holmes Herbert *Judge* • Dan Seymour *Pacquet* ■ *Dir* Jean Negulesco • *Scr* Irmgard von Cube, Allen Vincent, from the play *Johnny Belinda* by Elmer Harris • *Cinematographer* Ted McCord

Johnny Bull ★★★
Drama 1986 · US · Colour · 100mins

Suzanna Hamilton plays a GI bride from London who finds America isn't the land of plenty when she moves in with her in-laws. Husband Peter MacNicol's parents live in a Pennsylvania town where the mine has run out of ore and the townspeople have run out of patience. The performances – Jason Robards, Claudia Weill, Colleen Dewhurst and MacNicol (from TV's *Ally McBeal*) — are vigorous enough to raise what could have been just another mundane TV movie into strong drama.

Jason Robards [Jason Robards Jr] *Stephan Kovacs* • Colleen Dewhurst *Marie Kovacs* • Peter MacNicol *Joe Kovacs* • Kathy Bates *Katrine Kovacs* • Suzanna Hamilton *Iris Kovacs* ■ *Dir* Claudia Weill • *Scr* Kathleen Betsko

Johnny Come Lately ★★★ U
Comedy drama 1943 · US · BW · 97mins

A strong performance from James Cagney and a fine supporting cast lift this otherwise unexceptional newspaper picture. Cagney plays a journalist who helps a widow keep her late's husband's newspaper running, despite the local politicians and businessmen who are trying to close it down. There's civic corruption, characters with shady pasts and a little romance, but mainly it's a story about integrity. The film was produced by Cagney's brother, William, as part of their bid for complete independence from the studios.

James Cagney *Tom Richards* • Grace George *Vinnie McLeod* • Marjorie Main *Gashouse Mary* • Marjorie Lord *Jane* • Hattie McDaniel *Aide* ■ *Dir* William K Howard • *Scr* John Van Druten, from the novel *McLeod's Folly* by Louis Bromfield

Johnny Concho ★★★
Western 1956 · US · BW · 85mins

Although an inexpensive western must have seemed a safe bet, it's strange that Frank Sinatra should have chosen this particular story for his producing debut. Strange because he's ideally cast as an obnoxious coward protected by his notorious gunslinger brother. After the brother is bumped off and his killers take over the town, It's predictable Sinatra should eventually summon up the courage to face them. Curiously, though, he never shakes off his odious earlier image. Sinatra's pal, former actor Don McGuire, co-wrote the script and made his directing debut with this very watchable drama.

Frank Sinatra *Johnny Concho* • Keenan Wynn *Barney Clark* • William Conrad *Tallman* • Phyllis Kirk *Mary Dark* • Wallace Ford *Albert Dark* • Dorothy Adams *Sarah Dark* ■ *Dir* Don McGuire • *Scr* David P Harmon, Don McGuire, from the story *The Man Who Owned the Town* by David P Harmon

Johnny Cool ★★★
Crime drama 1963 · US · BW · 101mins

Henry Silva plays the Sicilian hitman working overtime in America in this hugely enjoyable gangster movie. At times the picture seems to be a parody of everything Mafioso; at others, the violence is quite shocking. The supporting cast is also a bizarre mix – Rat Pack members Sammy Davis Jr and Joey Bishop, Jim Backus (the voice of Mr Magoo) and Telly Savalas – while director William Asher (the man behind all those *Beach Party* movies) cleverly mixes and matches black comedy with *Naked City* realism.

Henry Silva *Johnny Cool/Giordano* • Elizabeth Montgomery *Dare Guiness* • Richard Anderson

Correspondent • Jim Backus *Louis Murphy* • Joey Bishop *Used car salesman* • Brad Dexter *Lennart Crandall* • Telly Savalas *Mr Santangelo* • Sammy Davis Jr *"Educated"* ■ *Dir* William Asher • *Scr* Joseph Landon, from the novel *The Kingdom of Johnny Cool* by John McPartland

Johnny Dangerously ★★★ 15

Crime spoof 1984 · US · Colour · 86mins

Michael Keaton, who played for laughs in films like *Mr Mom* and *Night Shift* before donning the black cape for Tim Burton's *Batman*, here stars as a good-natured gangster whose brother is the town's crime-busting district attorney. This spoof of thirties gangster movies, from *Clueless* and *Look Who's Talking* director Amy Heckerling, is enjoyably silly stuff, peppered with some great one-liners. While there's fun support from a cast which includes Dom DeLuise and Maureen Stapleton, the film belongs to Keaton, who once again shows his comedic talents to hilarious effect. ▣

Michael Keaton *Johnny Dangerously* • Marilu Henner *Lil* • Joe Piscopo *Vermin* • Danny DeVito *Burr* • Maureen Stapleton *Mom* • Griffin Dunne *Tommy* • Peter Boyle *Dundee* • Richard Dimitri *Maroni* • Glynnis O'Connor *Sally* • Byron Thames *Young Johnny* • Dom DeLuise *Pope* • Ray Walston *Vendor* ■ *Dir* Amy Heckerling • *Scr* Norman Steinberg, Bernie Kukoff, Harry Colomby, Jeff Harris

Johnny Dark ★★ U

Action drama 1954 · US · Colour · 85mins

Aimed at younger audiences and showcasing Universal's new breed of stars, this lightweight drama requires acceptance of Tony Curtis as an engineering genius who can design and drive a new racing car. The director, western veteran George Sherman, knows how to keep a film on the move and ensures that the thrills and spills of the racing scenes, particularly the climactic drive from the Canadian border to Mexico, are forcefully put over. Piper Laurie makes a pleasant leading lady, but Don Taylor is weak as Curtis's rival in romance and on the road.

Tony Curtis *Johnny Dark* • Piper Laurie *Liz Fielding* • Don Taylor *Duke Benson* • Paul Kelly *Jim Scott* • Ilka Chase *Abbie Binns* • Sidney Blackmer *James Fielding* ■ *Dir* George Sherman • *Scr* Franklin Coen

Johnny Eager ★★★

Crime drama 1941 · US · BW · 106mins

Robert Taylor is well cast as an unscrupulous racketeer, his virtually expressionless handsome features allowing an audience to read into his character all manner of evils. This is the only film in which he co-starred with sexy Lana Turner, then 21 years old and an instantly hot on-set item with the older Taylor – so much so that Taylor's then wife Barbara Stanwyck took steps to stop Turner ever appearing opposite her husband again. Acting honours, and the Oscar, went to Van Heflin as Taylor's self-pitying alcoholic friend, whose censor-circumventing role loosely implies a homosexual bond between the two men. A crisp, clever movie, and made as glossily as only MGM knew how.

Robert Taylor (1) *Johnny Eager* • Lana Turner *Lisbeth Bard* • Edward Arnold *John Benson*

Farrell • Van Heflin *Jeff Hartnett* • Robert Sterling *Jimmy Lanthrop* • Patricia Dane *Garnet* • Glenda Farrell *Mae Blythe* ■ *Dir* Mervyn LeRoy • *Scr* John Lee Mahin, James Edward Grant, from a story by Grant

Johnny Frenchman ★★★ U

Drama 1945 · UK · BW · 111mins

Among the few faults of the films produced at Ealing were their parochialism and their tendency to patronise in their depiction of the working classes. Screenwriter TEB Clarke's third film for the studio, this tale of the rivalry between Breton and Cornish fishing communities was intended to cement the *entente cordiale* in the latter days of the Second World War. It would have been a rather forgettable affair, but for the fact that it gave British audiences a rare chance to see the sublime French actress Françoise Rosay rising well above her capable co-stars and the level of her material.

Françoise Rosay *Lanec Florrie* • Tom Walls *Nat Pomeroy* • Patricia Roc *Sue Pomeroy* • Ralph Michael *Bob Tremayne* • Paul Dupuis *Yan Kervarec* • Frederick Piper *Zacky Penrose* ■ *Dir* Charles Frend • *Scr* TEB Clarke

Johnny Got His Gun ★

Drama 1971 · US · Colour · 111mins

Screenwriter Dalton Trumbo was imprisoned during the McCarthy witch-hunts yet won two Oscars under a pseudonym – for *Roman Holiday* and *The Brave One*. With *Johnny Got His Gun* Trumbo directed his own script from his own novel about a First World War soldier who has lost his arms, legs, face, sight, smell and hearing but is kept alive for medical research and experimentation. They think he's a vegetable but he isn't. It just drags on in its excruciating, cringe-inducing, self-important way. Simply awful, but the French loved it, giving it three awards at Cannes.

Jason Robards [Jason Robards Jr] *Father* • Timothy Bottoms *Johnny/Joe Bonham* • Marsha Hunt *Mother* • Diane Varsi *Nurse* • Charles McGraw *Girl's father* ■ *Dir* Dalton Trumbo • *Scr* Dalton Trumbo, from his novel

Johnny Guitar ★★★★ PG

Cult western 1954 · US · Colour · 105mins

Although Nicholas Ray's simmering western subverts this notoriously conservative genre, the real purpose of his study in mob hysteria was to condemn the Communist witch-hunt then tearing Hollywood apart. Heavy with symbolism, Philip Yordan's script also crackles with repressed sexuality, as saloon owner Joan Crawford and cattle queen Mercedes McCambridge lock swords. Providing Crawford with one of her best roles and gloriously shot in Trucolor by Harry Stradling Jr, this baroque bonanza fascinates on so many levels that it demands to be repeatedly reviewed. ▣

Joan Crawford *Vienna* • Sterling Hayden *Johnny Guitar* • Mercedes McCambridge *Emma Small* • Scott Brady *Dancin' Kid* • Ward Bond *John McIvers* • Ben Cooper *Turkey Ralston* • John Carradine *Old Tom* • Ernest Borgnine *Bart Lonergan* ■ *Dir* Nicholas Ray • *Scr* Philip Yordan, from the novel by Ray Chanslor

Johnny Handsome ★★ 15

Crime drama 1989 · US · Colour · 89mins

One of the seemingly endless series of Mickey Rourke flops, director Walter Hill's downbeat glob of calculated nastiness shoehorns numerous genres together with scant success. Turning from latex monster to plastic surgeon's miracle, Rourke invests nil expression or thought into his role as a disfigured criminal who's given a new face in a prison hospital. Saved from total failure by a few energetically staged action sequences, this rancid movie also features a sleazy turn from Ellen Barkin, who unusually beats every bad guy in the grim violence stakes. Contains violence and swearing. ▣

Mickey Rourke *John Sedley* • Ellen Barkin *Sunny Boyd* • Elizabeth McGovern *Donna McCarty* • Morgan Freeman *Lieutenant AZ Drones* • Forest Whitaker *Dr Steven Resher* • Lance Henriksen *Rafe Garrett* ■ *Dir* Walter Hill • *Scr* Ken Friedman, from the novel *The Three Worlds of Johnny Handsome* by John Godey

Johnny Mnemonic ★ 15

Science-fiction thriller 1995 · Can/US · Colour · 92mins

Director Robert Longo's turgid sci-fi thriller, based on William Gibson's cyberpunk short story, is cyber junk. Keanu Reeves sleepwalks through the title role as a 21st-century high-tech messenger who carries top-secret information thanks to a computer chip in his brain. Empty, flashy and incredibly dull, Longo's unpleasant movie fails to generate any suspense and, worse still, is lamely tarted up with incomprehensible surf-cowboy jargon, gratuitous violence and second-rate special effects. Contains swearing, violence and nudity. ▣

Keanu Reeves *Johnny Mnemonic* • Dina Meyer *Jane* • Ice-T *J-Bone* • Takeshi Kitano *Takahashi* • Denis Akiyama *Shinji* • Dolph Lundgren *Street Preacher* • Henry Rollins *Spider* ■ *Dir* Robert Longo • *Scr* William Gibson, from his short story

Johnny Mysto ★★

Fantasy adventure 1996 · US · Colour · 87mins

Shot in Romania, this children's fantasy could have done with a sight more inspiration in both the script and special effects departments. Younger viewers will enjoy the sight of would-be magician Toran Caudell messing up his tricks, then making his sister disappear for real after sorcerer Russ Tamblyn gives him a charmed ring. But anyone familiar with Arthurian legend might well be confused by the segment in which Caudell travels back in time to help Merlin battle the wicked Malfeasor. Michael Ansara is hissably villainous, but Jeff Burr's direction is sadly short of sparkle.

Toran Caudell *Johnny Mysto* • Russ Tamblyn *Blackmoor* • Patrick Renna *Glenn* • Michael Ansara *Malfeasor* • Amber Tamblyn *Sprout* • Ian Abercrombie *Merlin* • Pat Crawford Brown *Margaret Lattamer* • Jack Donner *King Arthur* ■ *Dir* Jeff Burr • *Scr* Benjamin Carr

Johnny O'Clock ★★★

Film noir 1947 · US · BW · 95mins

Robert Rossen was that rarest of film-makers, a practising communist who

managed to write social criticism into his screenplays before he was blacklisted. This under-rated *film noir* whodunit marked his directorial debut, and is distinguished by superb Burnett Guffey photography – check out those expressionist angles – and a pleasurably sharp and knowing screenplay, as Dick Powell's tough gambler and Lee J Cobb's policeman engage in terse exchanges over who killed the hat-check girl and the cop she fancied. Rossen's next film was *Body and Soul*, and his career also included the masterpiece *The Hustler*.

Dick Powell *Johnny O'Clock* • Evelyn Keyes *Nancy Hobbs* • Lee J Cobb *Inspector Koch* • Ellen Drew *Nelle Marchettis* • Nina Foch *Harriet Hobbs* • Thomas Gomez *Pete Marchettis* • John Kellogg *Charlie* ■ *Dir* Robert Rossen • *Scr* Robert Rossen, from a story by Milton Holmes

Johnny Reno ★★

Western 1966 · US · Colour · 82mins

Dana Andrews is US marshal Johnny Reno, riding into serious trouble en route to Stone Junction. He ends up killing one would-be assassin and taking another prisoner, before coming up against Stone Junction's corrupt mayor Lyle Bettger. It's all in a day's work for a peace officer, though the story would barely fill the 30 minutes required for an episode of *Gunsmoke*. What gives the film its modest appeal is the cast – Andrews, Jane Russell, Lon Chaney, Tom Drake – who are all much too old and experienced to have to prove anything anymore.

Dana Andrews *Johnny Reno* • Jane Russell *Nona Williams* • Lon Chaney Jr *Sheriff Hodges* • John Agar *Ed Tomkins* • Lyle Bettger *Jess Yates* • Tom Drake *Joe Connors* ■ *Dir* RG Springsteen • *Scr* Steve Fisher, from a story by AC Lyles, Steve Fisher, Andrew Craddock

Johnny Skidmarks ★★★ 18

Crime thriller 1998 · US · Colour · 93mins

Sadly picked up by television network HBO in the States rather than a distributor, this film has never made it to the big screen. Peter Gallagher stars as a police photographer who's become immune to all horrors having taken pictures of every crime under the sun. Bored, he becomes involved in a criminal blackmail racket by taking photographs of prominent people in compromising positions. But when his unsavoury colleagues start turning up as corpses his worlds threaten to merge. With great support from Frances McDormand and John Lithgow, this is an above-average thriller with tension and punch. Contains scenes of violence. ▣

Peter Gallagher *Johnny Scardino* • Frances McDormand *Alice* • John Lithgow *Sergeant Larry Skovik* • John Kapelos *Walter Lippinscott* • Geoffrey Lower *Woody Washawski* • Jack Black *Jerry* ■ *Dir* John Raffo • *Scr* John Raffo, William Preston Robertson

Johnny Stecchino ★★★

Comedy 1991 · It · Colour · 121mins

Although it smashed box-office records at home, this anarchic comedy was little seen outside Roberto Benigni's native Italy. Miraculously pulling off slapstick gags that were stale even in the silent era, he coaxes you into

U = SUITABLE FOR ALL   Uc = SUITABLE FOR ALL, ESPECIALLY FOR YOUNG CHILDREN (VIDEO ONLY)   PG = PARENTAL GUIDANCE

siding with the naive bus driver who just happens to resemble a notorious Sicilian mobster. But, as with Benigni's Oscar-winning *Life Is Beautiful*, the comedy has a contentious edge, with some of the gags at the expense of the Mafia being daringly outspoken. With off-screen wife Nicoletta Braschi again winning the clown prince's heart, this frantic farce will either have you rolling on the carpet or scratching your head in puzzlement. In Italian with English subtitles.

Roberto Benigni *Dante/Johnny Stecchino* • Nicoletta Braschi *Maria* • Paolo Bonacelli *D'Agata* • Franco Volpi *Minister* • Ivano Marescotti *Dr Randazzo* • Alessandro DeSantis *Lillo* ■ *Dir* Roberto Benigni • *Scr* Roberto Benigni, Vincenzo Cerami

Johnny Stool Pigeon ★★
Crime drama 1949 · US · BW · 76mins

This capable example of the semi-documentary crime film of the late forties, which comes complete with the usual voice-over narration, stars Dan Duryea as a gangster released from prison to help detective Howard Duff round up a drug-trafficking ring. The story is overly contrived, but director William Castle extracts strong performances from his leads, who include Shelley Winters and John McIntire. Taking a prominent supporting role as a mute killer is a young contract player gaining valuable experience, Anthony (later Tony) Curtis.

Howard Duff *George Morton aka Mike Doyle/Narrator* • Shelley Winters *Terry Stewart* • Dan Duryea *Johnny Evans* • Anthony Curtis [Tony Curtis] *Joey Hyatt* • John McIntire *Nick Avery* • Gar Moore *Sam Harrison* • Leif Erickson *Pringle* ■ *Dir* William Castle • *Scr* Robert L Richards, from a story by Henry Jordan

Johnny Suede ★★★★ 15
Comedy fantasy 1991 · US · Colour · 93mins

With the rave reviews from *Thelma and Louise* still ringing in his ears, Brad Pitt further demonstrated his star quality as the bequiffed hero of this gentle tale, which marked the directorial debut of ex-cinematographer Tom DiCillo. Awash with pastel colours and dripping with style, this fantastical satire replaces the famous ruby slippers with a pair of suede shoes and the Great Oz with fifties' pop idol Ricky Nelson. DiCillo's unerring eye for both the absurd and grim is complemented by his fine pacing and the tautness of his script. Pitt is superb and is well supported by Alison Moir and Catherine Keener. 📹

Brad Pitt *Johnny Suede* • Richard Boes *Man in tuxedo* • Cheryl Costa *Woman in alley* • Michael Luciano *Mr Clepp* • Calvin Levels *Deke* • Nick Cave *Freak Storm* • Alison Moir *Darlette* • Catherine Keener *Yvonne* • Samuel L Jackson *B-Bop* ■ *Dir/Scr* Tom DiCillo • *Cinematographer* Joe DeSalvo

Johnny Tiger ★
Drama 1966 · US · Colour · 102mins

Robert Taylor's sensitive college professor goes to Florida to teach Seminole Indians, his three children in tow. However, his noble intentions are thwarted by a dying chief who wants his grandson (Chad Everett) to renounce contact with white people like Taylor and Geraldine Brooks's

local health official. The Everglades locations provide an unusual backdrop for what would otherwise be a standard western, but the lack of dramatic tension and some inadequate performances (notably Everett in the title role) prove to be fatal weaknesses in this worthy but extremely dull drama.

Robert Taylor (1) *George Dean* • Geraldine Brooks *Dr Leslie Frost* • Chad Everett *Johnny Tiger* • Brenda Scott *Barbara Dean* • Marc Lawrence *William Billie* ■ *Dir* Paul Wendkos • *Scr* Paul Crabtree, Thomas Blackburn, Philip Wylie, R John Hugh, from the story *Tiger on the Outside* by R John Hugh

Johnny Tremain ★★ U
Historical drama 1957 · US · Colour · 80mins

There's more to Disney than Mickey Mouse and Donald Duck, as this adaptation of Esther Forbes's Revolutionary War novel illustrates. Covering a well-documented chapter of American history, this is the story of Johnny, a former silversmith, who becomes committed to the revolutionary cause after being falsely accused of theft. Veteran director Robert Stevenson – probably better known for *Mary Poppins* – doesn't quite succeed in capturing the sights and sounds of the American colonial era as the kids will probably enjoy it.

Hal Stalmaster *Johnny Tremain* • Luana Patten *Cilla Lapham* • Jeff York *James Otis* • Sebastian Cabot *Jonathan Lyte* • Dick Beymer [Richard Beymer] *Rab Silsbee* • Walter Sande *Paul Revere* • Rusty Lane *Samuel Adams* • Whit Bissell *Josiah Quincy* ■ *Dir* Robert Stevenson • *Scr* Tom Blackburn, from the novel by Esther Forbes

Johnny Trouble ★★ U
Drama 1957 · US · BW · 79mins

This old-fashioned, sentimental drama marked the end of the overpowering Ethel Barrymore's career. She plays an elderly widow who stubbornly refuses to leave her apartment building after it is sold, and ends up with students for neighbours. She convinces herself that young delinquent, Johnny (Stuart Whitman) is the offspring of her own, long-absent son. The scene in which the old lady reveals the beauty of Shakespeare's sonnets to the lad is particularly risible. Both Whitman and Carolyn Jones as his girlfriend are rather good given the circumstances.

Ethel Barrymore *Mrs Chandler* • Cecil Kellaway *Tom McKay* • Carolyn Jones *Julie* • Jesse White *Parsons* • Rand Harper *Phil* • Stuart Whitman *Johnny* • Paul Wallace *Paul* • Edward Byrnes [Edd Byrnes] *Elliott* ■ *Dir* John H Auer • *Scr* Charles O'Neal, David Lord, from the story *Prodigal's Mother* by Ben Ames Williams

Johnny 2.0 ★★
Science-fiction 1998 · US · Colour

How much Jeff Fahey is too much? In this low-budget sci-fi TV movie Fahey plays Johnny Dalton, a brilliant biochemist who has invented the technology that will allow humans to make perfect clones of themselves. Surprise, surprise, the inventor clones himself and years later, his doppelgänger is sent to find him at the behest of an all-powerful corporation. It all boils down to a bunch of dumb action scenes in a grungy future and Jeff Fahey wearing a silly grey wig to simulate his older self.

Jeff Fahey *Johnny Dalton* • Tahnee Welch *Nikki Holland* • Michael Ironside *Frank* • John Neville *Bosch* • Michael Rhoades *Taylor* • Von Flores *Carlos* • Cliff Saunders *Dan-O* ■ *Dir* Neill Fearnley • *Scr* Wynne McLaughlin

Johnny's Girl ★★
Drama 1995 · US · Colour

Well-intentioned but mechanically written, this TV movie set in the sixties features Mia Kirshner as a teenager who goes to live with her smooth-talking father after her mother dies. Unprepared for his unconventional lifestyle – he runs a nightclub in Alaska – she refuses to stay until he cleans up his act. Treat Williams gives a nuanced performance as the con-artist dad but neither he nor Kirshner manage to arouse our sympathy. .

Treat Williams *Johnny Ross* • Mia Kirshner *Amy Ross* • Gloria Reuben *Monica* • Ron White *Lieutenant Jim Tesky* ■ *Dir* John Kent Harrison • *Scr* John Kent Harrison, from the novel by Kim Rich

Johns ★★★★ 18
Drama 1995 · US · Colour · 91mins

LA in all its sleazy glory is fascinatingly portrayed here by writer/director Scott Silver. David Arquette and Lukas Haas are both superb as two street hustlers determined to raise enough cash to fulfil Arquette's dream of spending Christmas Eve in a swish hotel suite. Many of the events that happen to them are based on true stories collected by Silver during his research. Very funny in places, as well as tragic and ultimately moving, this is one of those movies whose characters stay in your heart and mind for days after watching it. Contains swearing and sex scenes. 📹

Lukas Haas *Donner* • David Arquette *John* • Arliss Howard *John Cardoza* • Keith David *Homeless John* • Christopher Gartin *Eli* • Josh Schaefer [Joshua Schaefer] *David* ■ *Dir/Scr* Scott Silver

The Joke ★★★★
Drama 1968 · Cz · BW · 80mins

Jaromil Jires was the most stylistically audacious director of the Czech "new wave" of the early sixties. However, he is more restrained in this studied adaptation of Milan Kundera's scathingly satirical novel. Josef Somr gives an exceptional performance as the student who is sentenced to a spell in one of the army's brutal black units after a political joke backfires, and who subsequently seeks revenge. While the themes may be a little obscure, the hardships and humiliations Somr experiences often make excruciating viewing. In Czech with English subtitles.

Josef Somr *Ludvik* • Jana Ditetova *Helena* • Ludek Munzar *Pavel* • Evald Schorm *Kosika* • Vera Kresadlova *Brozova* ■ *Dir* Jaromil Jires • *Scr* Jaromil Jires, from the novel *The Joke* by Milan Kundera

The Joker Is Wild ★★
Biography 1957 · US · BW · 128mins

This workmanlike and overlong biography stars Frank Sinatra as comedian Joe E Lewis, whose vocal chords were seriously damaged by nightclub racketeers in the thirties –

which put paid to his original career as a singer. Lewis's stormy life and battle with alcoholism is not a lot of fun, though Jeanne Crain and Mitzi Gaynor add glamour as his two wives. Sinatra sings some good vintage numbers, and the film also features the Oscar-winning *All the Way*.

Frank Sinatra *Joe E Lewis* • Mitzi Gaynor *Martha Stewart* • Jeanne Crain *Letty Page* • Eddie Albert *Austin Mack* • Beverly Garland *Cassie Mack* • Jackie Coogan *Swifty Morgan* • Sophie Tucker ■ *Dir* Charles Vidor • *Scr* Oscar Saul, from the non-fiction book *Life of Joe E Lewis* by Art Cohn

The Jokers ★★★ U
Comedy thriller 1967 · UK · Colour · 95mins

A light-hearted romp, with Michael Crawford and Oliver Reed well cast as brothers who attempt to steal the Crown Jewels just for the heck of it. It's a quintessential "Swinging London" movie, full of nice locations and ever-so-British attitudes. The Dick Clement/Ian La Frenais screenplay was virtually director-proof and was entrusted to Michael Winner, who certainly does a decent job of it, making it seem regrettable that he ever veered away from comedy.

Michael Crawford *Michael Tremayne* • Oliver Reed *David Tremayne* • Harry Andrews *Inspector Marryatt* • James Donald *Colonel Gurney-Simms* • Daniel Massey *Riggs* • Michael Hordern *Sir Matthew* • Edward Fox *Lt Sprague* • Warren Mitchell *Lennie* • Frank Finlay *Harassed man* ■ *Dir* Michael Winner • *Scr* Dick Clement, Ian La Frenais, from a story by Michael Winner

Le Joli Mai ★★★★ U
Documentary 1962 · Fr · BW · 121mins

Indebted to Jean Rouch's *Chronicle of a Summer*, Chris Marker's fascinating documentary provides an invaluable snapshot of a city in transition. With its montage sequences, newsreel footage, narrated passages and probing interviews, it recalls the "city symphonies" made in the late silent era by the likes of Dziga Vertov, with Parisians of all classes and age groups preferring their views on everything from the nature of democracy to the state of French culture. With Yves Montand making an acerbic guide (the role is performed by Simone Signoret in the English version), this is *cinéma vérité* at its wittiest and most revealing. A French language film. 📹

Simone Signoret *Commentary* • Yves Montand *Commentary* ■ *Dir* Chris Marker • *Scr* Catherine Varlin, Chris Marker

A Jolly Bad Fellow ★
Black comedy 1964 · UK · BW · 110mins

Adapted from the novel *Down among the Dead Men*, this is an ill-advised attempt by co-screenwriter Robert Hamer to recapture the glories of his 1949 Ealing classic *Kind Hearts and Coronets*. Leo McKern has the misfortune to play a university professor who uses his new undetectable poison to liquidate those he feels have no right to live. Don Chaffey took on the directorial chores after Hamer's death, but he was beaten before he started with this tasteless comedy that aims for the macabre but hits way below mediocre.

Leo McKern *Professor Bowles-Ottery* • Janet Munro *Delia Brooks* • Maxine Audley *Clarinda Bowles-Ottery* • Duncan Macrae *Dr Brass* • Dennis Price *Professor Hughes* • Miles Malleson *Dr Woolley* • Leonard Rossiter *Dr Fisher* ■ *Dir* Don Chaffey • *Scr* Robert Hamer, Donald Taylor, from the novel *Down among the Dead Men* by CE Vulliamy

Jolson Sings Again ★★ U

Musical biography
1949 · US · Colour · 91mins

Made three years after the phenomenal success of *The Jolson Story*, this sequel suffers from the fact that the entertainer's later life was nowhere near as interesting as his rise to fame. Larry Parks produces another remarkable impersonation (backed by Jolson's own singing voice), particularly relishing the gag in which Parks (playing Jolson) meets Parks (playing himself) to discuss making the first film. Classic songs abound, but there's too little going on to give this anything but nostalgia value. 🎬

Larry Parks *Al Jolson* • Barbara Hale *Ellen Clark* • William Demarest *Steve Martin* • Ludwig Donath *Cantor Yoelson* • Bill Goodwin *Tom Baron* • Myron McCormick *Col Ralph Bryant* ■ *Dir* Henry Levin • *Scr* Sidney Buchman • *Music Director* Morris Stoloff

The Jolson Story ★★★★★ U

Musical biography
1946 · US · Colour · 124mins

One of the most popular movies ever made, and rightly so, this biopic stars Larry Parks as the entertainer with the big ego and the even bigger talent. In re-recording his greatest hits for this movie, Al Jolson proved to be in finer, more mellow timbre than ever. These versions are therefore the definitive ones, and Parks totally convinces as he mimes his way through such landmarks as *April Showers*, *My Mammy* and *Toot Toot Tootsie Goodbye*. Okay, so the blacking-up is politically unfashionable these days, the loveable Jewish characters are mere caricatures, and the tale is appallingly fancified. This is Hollywood entertainment on a grand scale, and you'll weep and cheer all the way to the uncompromising final curtain. 🎬

Larry Parks *Al Jolson* • Evelyn Keyes *Julie Benson* • William Demarest *Steve Martin* • Bill Goodwin *Tom Baron* • Ludwig Donath *Cantor Yoelson* • Tamara Shayne *Mrs Yoelson* • John Alexander *Lew Dockstader* ■ *Dir* Alfred E Green • *Scr* Stephen Longstreet, Harry Chandlee, Andrew Solt

Jonah Who Will Be 25 in the Year 2000 ★★★★

Comedy
1976 · Swi/Fr · Colour and BW · 115mins

Seen from the virtually apolitical vantage point of a new millennium, Alain Tanner's right-on comedy might seem a muddle of wishy-washy notions and impossible dreams. But political radicalism had only recently died when he paid this tribute to the indomitability of the May 1968 veterans, who may have failed in their intentions, but who still had the courage to act. A magnificent ensemble cast endures life's buffeting with equanimity, while Tanner and co-

screenwriter John Berger intertwine the diverging destinies with a dexterity that allows for revealing monochrome reveries (both brutal and fantastical). In French with English subtitles.

Jean-Luc Bideau *Max Stigny* • Myriam Boyer *Mathilde Vernier* • Rufus *Mathieu Vernier* • Miou-Miou *Marie* • Jacques Denis *Marco Perly* • Dominique Labourier *Marguerite* • Roger Jendly *Marcel Certoux* • Myriam Mézières *Madeleine* ■ *Dir* Alain Tanner • *Scr* Alain Tanner, John Berger

Jonathan Livingston Seagull ★★★ U

Fantasy
1973 · US · Colour · 94mins

Despite its title, this philosophical oddity doesn't exactly soar into comprehension. Richard Bach's bestseller is an "inspirational" parable about a seagull whose life parallels human existence – speed, contemplation, and finally redemption and resurrection. An intriguing existentialist idea, nearly flooded out by Neil Diamond's splashy score. 🎬

James Franciscus *Jonathan Livingston Seagull* • Juliet Mills *Girl* • Hal Holbrook *Elder* • Philip Ahn *Chang* • David Ladd *Fletcher* • Kelly Harmon *Kimmy* ■ *Dir* Hall Bartlett • *Scr* Hall Bartlett, Richard Bach, from the novel by Richard Bach • *Music* Neil Diamond, Lee Holdridge

Jonathan: the Boy Nobody Wanted ★★ PG

Drama based on a true story
1992 · US · Colour · 93mins

JoBeth Williams – still best known for *The Big Chill* and *Poltergeist* – stars in this rather predictable TV drama about Jonathan (Christopher Burke), a teenage boy with Down's syndrome who is rejected by his parents following their refusal to allow him to undergo possibly life-saving surgery. Williams convinces as the carer who sees more than a ray of hope in Jonathan's condition. It all ends up in court with the press swarming like flies. 🎬

Christopher Burke *Jonathan Willis* • JoBeth Williams *Ginny Moore* • Alley Mills *Carol Willis* • Tom Mason *Max Willis* • Jeffrey DeMunn *Frank Moore* ■ *Dir* George Kaczender • *Scr* Steve Lawson, Dalene Young, from a story by Steve Lawson, Dalene Young, Doris Silverton, Peter Nelson

Jory ★★★ PG

Western
1972 · US · Colour · 92mins

Unusual western, with the emphasis less on the rootin', tootin' and shootin', and more on character development. Robby Benson, in his first film role, plays a teenager who's forced to fend for himself when his father and friends are murdered. The film has points to make about manhood and maleness as Benson is rapidly compelled to cast off his boyhood. But, if that makes it all sound rather tame, there's excitement and action, too. 🎬

John Marley *Roy* • BJ Thomas *Jocko* • Robby Benson *Jory* • Brad Dexter *Jack* • Claudio Brook *Ethan* • Patricia Aspillaga *Carmelita* • Todd Martin *Barron* • Benny Baker *Mr Jordan* ■ *Dir* Jorge Fons • *Scr* Gerald Herman, Robert Irving, from a novel by Milton R Bass

Joseph Andrews ★★

Period comedy 1977 · UK · Colour · 103mins

Director Tony Richardson attempted to repeat the success of his Oscar-winning *Tom Jones* with another Fielding adaptation but falls flat on his farce. The bed-and-bawdy plot sees Peter Firth as the 18th-century footman involved in romantic adventures with the likes of Ann-Margret. It certainly looks good but Richardson fails to inject the necessary verve and pacing, opting for historical stereotypes and humour which is genteel at best.

Ann-Margret *Lady Booby* • Peter Firth *Joseph Andrews* • Michael Hordern *Parson Adams* • Beryl Reid *Mrs Slipslop* • Jim Dale *Pedlar* • Kenneth Cranham *Wicked Squire* • John Gielgud *Doctor* • Peggy Ashcroft *Lady Tattle* ■ *Dir* Tony Richardson • *Scr* Allan Scott, Chris Bryant, Tony Richardson, from the novel by Henry Fielding

Joseph in Egypt ★★★

Biblical drama
1995 · US/It /Ger · Colour · 93mins

There's nothing Technicolor about the coat in this TV-movie retelling of the Old Testament story about the dreaming Israelite who shakes off the shackles of slavery to become Pharaoh's right-hand man. *Strictly Ballroom* star Paul Mercurio plays Joseph with typical brio, particularly relishing the scenes with Ben Kingsley as the scheming Potiphar. Everywhere you look there is a familiar face, but the stand-out performance comes from Martin Landau as the elderly Jacob. Contains violence.

Paul Mercurio *Joseph* • Ben Kingsley *Potiphar* • Martin Landau *Jacob* • Lesley Ann Warren *Potiphar's wife* • Michael Angelis *Reuben* • Alice Krige *Rachel* • Dominique Sanda *Leah* ■ *Dir* Roger Young • *Scr* Lionel Chetwynd, from a TV play by James Carrington

Josephine and Men ★★ U

Comedy 1955 · UK · Colour · 88mins

Josephine (pert, husky-voiced Glynis Johns) is one of those perverse women who is always drawn to the losers in life, her interest waning when their fortunes improve. Debonair Jack Buchanan plays her suave bachelor uncle who narrates her story in flashback. Josephine leaves her wealthy fiancé (Donald Sinden) for his friend (Peter Finch), an unsuccessful playwright – until their situations are reversed. Directed by Roy Boulting, this romantic comedy is pretty lightweight and not as funny as it could have been, but the cast is likeable.

Glynis Johns *Josephine Luton* • Jack Buchanan *Uncle Charles Luton* • Peter Finch *David Hewer* • Donald Sinden *Alan Hartley* • Ronald Squire *Frederick Luton* • William Hartnell *Inspector Parsons* ■ *Dir* Roy Boulting • *Scr* Roy Boulting, Frank Harvey, Nigel Balchin, from the story by Nigel Balchin

The Josephine Baker Story ★★★ 15

Biography 1991 · UK/US · Colour · 129mins

Fine biopic of the black singer and dancer who became the toast of Paris in the twenties and thirties, but whose "uppity" personality and erotic choreography got her pilloried back home in America. Lynn Whitfield makes

the title role her own, and there's rock-solid support from Rubén Blades and David Dukes as two of the men in her life, and from Craig T Nelson as newscaster Walter Winchell. On the superficial side, but the surface is glossy and enticing. You'd never imagine it was made for TV or that it was filmed entirely in Budapest. 🎬

Lynn Whitfield *Josephine Baker* • Rubén Blades *Pepito Abatino* • David Dukes *Jo Bouillon* • Louis Gossett Jr *Sidney Williams* • Craig T Nelson *Walter Winchell* • Kene Holliday *Sidney Bechet* ■ *Dir* Brian Gibson • *Scr* Ron Hutchinson

Josette ★★

Comedy 1938 · US · BW · 70mins

This slight romantic comedy features Don Ameche and Robert Young as two brothers on a mission to rescue their philandering father from the clutches of a singer. Of course they end up falling for her themselves – problem is they've picked on the wrong girl, played by Simone Simon. Joan Davis and Bert Lahr are prominent among the supporting players. This was Simon's last picture at 20th Century-Fox, and she temporarily returned to France before proving herself in Hollywood with *Cat People*.

Don Ameche *David Brossard Jr* • Simone Simon *Renee Le Blanc* • Robert Young *Pierre Brossard* • Bert Lahr *Barney Barnaby* • Joan Davis *May Morris* • Paul Hurst *A Adolphus Heyman* • Lon Chaney Jr *Boatman* ■ *Dir* Allan Dwan • *Scr* James Edward Grant, from a play by Paul Frank, George Fraser, from a story by Ladislaus Vadnai

Josh and S.A.M. ★ 12

Adventure 1993 · US · Colour · 97mins

An unconvincing children's adventure. Brothers Josh (Jacob Tierney) and Sam (Noah Fleiss) are miserably shuttled between their divorced parents until 12-year-old Josh decides he's had enough and steals a car to embark on a road trip with his younger sibling. Sam has his own problems – Josh has convinced him that he's not a little boy but in fact a Strategically Altered Mutant (think half-boy, half-robot), and the pair are soon joined by an equally odd young woman (Martha Plimpton). It's nonsensical fare that will annoy even the youngest viewers. 🎬

Jacob Tierney *Josh* • Noah Fleiss *Sam* • Martha Plimpton *Alison* • Stephen Tobolowsky *Thom Whitney* • Joan Allen *Caroline* • Christopher Penn *Derek Baxter* ■ *Dir* Billy Weber • *Scr* Frank Deese

Joshua Then and Now ★★

Comedy drama 1985 · Can · Colour · 127mins

Just as director Ted Kotcheff's earlier film of a Mordecai Richler novel *The Apprenticeship of Duddy Kravitz* gave Richard Dreyfuss a juicy role, this one gives James Woods the chance to show his combustible talent. He plays the son of a stripper and a pugilist-turned-convict who marries into London society in 1950 and then sees his life and career turned upside down when he returns to Canada in 1977. So much happens to Woods that this engrossing, if sketchy, drama might have made a better mini-series to give it more time with its admittedly interesting story.

James Woods *Joshua Shapiro* • Gabrielle Lazure *Pauline Shapiro* • Alan Arkin *Reuben Shapiro* • Michael Sarrazin *Kevin Hornby* • Linda Sorenson *Esther Shapiro* • Alan Scarfe *Jack Trimble* ■ *Dir* Ted Kotcheff • *Scr* Mordecai Richler, from his novel

Joshua's Heart ★★★

Drama   1990 · US · Colour · 96mins

Melissa Gilbert stars in this sentimental TV movie about a woman who ditches her boyfriend only to find she can't live without his young son. Tim Matheson gives another sturdy but uninspired performance as her ruthless adversary in this emotional tug-of-war, while Lisa Eilbacher provides welcome support. Michael Pressman directs this tacky but moderately stylish tosh.

Melissa Gilbert-Brinkman [Melissa Gilbert] *Claudia Cassara* • Tim Matheson *Tom Chapman* • Matthew Lawrence *Joshua* • Lisa Eilbacher *Kit Colton* • Debra Mooney *Vera* • Jack Blessing *Nick* ■ *Dir* Michael Pressman • *Scr* Susan Cuscana

Jour de Fête ★★★★★ U

Comedy   1947 · Fr · BW and Colour · 76mins

Jacques Tati had hoped that his debut feature would be one of the first French films shot in colour, but the stock was underdeveloped during processing and the version we now have is a mainly black-and-white back-up copy. The movie is an expansion of Tati's short film, *L'Ecole des Facteurs*, and follows the comic misadventures of François the village postman as he tries to dispose of his letters at record speed, in the style of the US mail service. Sheer genius. In French with English subtitles.. ▭

Jacques Tati *François, the postman* • Guy Decomble *Roger, the showman* • Paul Frankeur *Marcel, the showman* • Maine Vallée *Jeannette* • Roger Rafal *Barber* ■ *Dir* Jacques Tati • *Scr* Jacques Tati, Henri Marquet

Le Jour se Lève ★★★★★ PG

Crime melodrama   1939 · Fr · BW · 85mins

Banned as demoralising by the Vichy government, following negative reviews, Marcel Carné's fatalistic drama is clearly symbolic of an entrapped nation awaiting its inevitable destruction. But it's also a heartrending human drama, played against Alexandre Trauner's claustrophobic, yet painterly sets. Typically outstanding as the doomed, introspective hero, Jean Gabin is the epitome of existential despair, while Jules Berry's lecherous villain is as loathsome as Arletty's showgirl is worldly wise and Jacqueline Laurent's Françoise is innocent. Told mostly in flashback, the story perfectly illustrates Carné's mastery of poetic realism and Jacques Prévert's appreciation of the lyricism of everyday speech. In French with English subtitles. ▭

Jean Gabin *François* • Jules Berry *M Valentin* • Jacqueline Laurent *Françoise* • Arletty *Clara* • René Génin *Concierge* • Mady Berry *Concierge's wife* • Bernard Blier *Gaston* • Marcel Peres *Paulo* ■ *Dir* Marcel Carné • *Scr* Jacques Prévert, Jacques Viot

Une Journée Tranquille ★★★ 15

Thriller   1999 · Fr · Colour · 71mins

This is a methodically told shaggy-dog story with a wicked twist in the tail. Written, produced and directed by Michael Jaffer, this French picture is, unusually, a thriller that seems consciously designed to stop you getting excited. Every task undertaken by birthday boy Christian Baltauss is downbeat and deliberate, whether intimidating petty crooks, setting up a major drug deal or bumping off a pimp who deals in underage innocents. However, this dour detachment somehow lends itself to a creeping fascination with both Baltauss and his fate. A moody, muted and minor work that is nevertheless quietly compelling. In French with English subtitles.

Christian Baltauss *Man* • Jean-Jacques Benhamou *Friend* • Gilles Bellomi *Associate* • Georges Vaello *Pimp* • Alexandra Bonnet *Domino* ■ *Dir/Scr* Michael Jaffer

The Journey ★★

Political drama   1959 · US/Aus · Colour · 125mins

Yul Brynner and Deborah Kerr – who co-starred in *The King and I* – are reunited in this political drama about people trying to escape the Soviet invasion of Hungary in 1956. Brynner is a Soviet officer, while Kerr plays an Englishwoman trying to smuggle dissident Jason Robards over the border into Austria. The original script was set in China, but the location was changed to Hungary to give the film some topical relevance. Alas, the dramatic impact remains negligible.

Deborah Kerr *Lady Diana Ashmore* • Yul Brynner *Major Surov* • Jason Robards Jr *Paul Kedes/Flemyng* • Robert Morley *Hugh Deverill* • EG Marshall *Harold Rhinelander* • David Kossoff *Simon Avron* ■ *Dir* Anatole Litvak • *Scr* George Tabori

Journey ★★★

Drama   1995 · US · Colour

A sensitive family TV drama, executive produced by Glenn Close and beautifully handled by Jason Robards and child actor Max Pomeranc. Eleven-year-old Journey (Pomeranc) and his sister Cat are dumped with grandparents Robards and Brenda Fricker by their irresponsible mother. Together the generations combine in their struggle to reassemble their dysfunctional family. Adapted by Patricia MacLachlan from her novel, this will while away an afternoon but is watchable for the performances alone.

Jason Robards [Jason Robards Jr] *Marcus* • Brenda Fricker *Lottie* • Max Pomeranc *Journey* • Eliza Dushku *Cat* • Meg Tilly *Min* • Sal Lopez *Boone* ■ *Dir* Tom McLoughlin • *Scr* Patricia MacLachlan, from her novel

The Journey ★★★

Drama   1997 · US · Colour · 96mins

Although it constantly runs the risk of lapsing into stereotyping and culture-clash cliché, steady direction from Harish Saluja and discerning performances give this gentle drama its charm and poignancy. As the seasoned public school teacher retiring to his doctor son's Pittsburgh home,

Roshan Seth exhibits both a reverence for tradition and stubborn insensitivity as he tries to educate his neglected granddaughter against the wishes of her American mother. Antony Zaki and Nora Bates do well on either side of the generational divide, while Carrie Preston impresses in conveying a sense of exploited hospitality.

Roshan Seth *Kishan Singh* • Saeed Jaffrey *Ashok* • Carrie Preston *Laura Singh* • Antony Zaki *Raj Singh* • Betsy Zajko *Audrey* • Nora Bates *Jenny Singh* ■ *Dir* Harish Saluja • *Scr* Harish Saluja, Lisa Kirk Puchner

Journey back to Oz ★ U

Animated fantasy 1964 · US · Colour · 85mins

Made in 1964, but not released until a decade later (you'll soon see why!), Liza Minnelli steps into her late mother's ruby slippers as the voice of Dorothy in this animated sequel to the much-loved Judy Garland classic. Barely ringing any major changes from the evergreen original, Dorothy is transported over the rainbow again by another cyclone only to end up back in the magical land of Oz surrounded by all her familiar friends. There's no wizard this time (what a swizz!) just the Wicked Witch of the West's sister (voiced by Ethel Merman) to contend with. Lacklustre songs by Sammy Cahn and Jimmy Van Heusen mark even more time and do little to keep boredom at bay or the constant thought "Why did they bother?". ▭

Liza Minnelli *Dorothy* • Mickey Rooney *Scarecrow* • Milton Berle *Cowardly Lion* • Danny Thomas *The Tin Man* • Ethel Merman *Mombi, the Bad Witch* ■ *Dir* Hal Sutherland • *Scr* Fred Ladd, Norm Prescott

Journey for Margaret ★★

Second World War drama
1942 · US · BW · 81mins

Like *Mrs Miniver*, this was one of MGM's efforts to convey to American audiences the effect of the Second World War on the British home front. In this tear-jerker, the emphasis is on homeless orphans of the Blitz for whom the best solution, it is suggested, is a new life in the United States. Robert Young plays the American journalist who befriends a young boy (William Severn) who won't talk and a small girl (Margaret O'Brien) who has retreated into a private world. Under the able coaxing of director WS Van Dyke II, it was the five-year-old O'Brien, in her first substantial role, who stole the picture in a performance capped only by her Tootie of *Meet Me in St Louis* two years later.

Margaret O'Brien *Margaret* • Robert Young *John Davis* • Laraine Day *Nora Davis* • Fay Bainter *Trudy Strauss* • Signe Hasso *Anya* • Nigel Bruce *Herbert V Allison* • William Severn *Peter Humphreys* ■ *Dir* WS Van Dyke II [WS Van Dyke] • *Scr* David Hertz, William Ludwig, from a book by William L White

Journey into Darkness: the Bruce Curtis Story ★★ 15

Drama based on a true story
1991 · Can · Colour · 89mins

Hardly a murder trial in America is allowed to pass by without Hollywood turning it into a movie. This offering focuses on the 1982 trial of a New Jersey teenager accused of killing his

mother and stepfather. Admitting one charge and denying the other, he drags an innocent friend, Bruce Curtis, into the dock beside him and into a famous case of miscarried justice. Contains some swearing. ▭

Simon Reynolds *Bruce Curtis* • Jaimz Woolvett *Scott Franz* • Bruce Boa *Al Podgis* • Dawn Greenhalgh *Rosemary Podgis* • Kenneth Welsh *Schottland* ■ *Dir* Graeme Campbell • *Scr* Keith Ross Leckie

Journey into Fear ★★★★ U

Spy drama   1942 · US · BW · 67mins

Adapted from a rousing thriller novel by Eric Ambler, this was Orson Welles's third feature film. Although Norman Foster is credited as sole director, Welles did much of the megaphone work, as well as writing the script with co-star Joseph Cotten. Logic takes something of a back seat, however, in this bewildering tale of arms smuggling in Turkey during the Second World War. Yet any narrative shortcomings are more than made up for by Welles's atmospheric camera angles and the gallery of disreputable characters. ▭

Joseph Cotten *Howard Graham* • Orson Welles *Colonel Haki* • Dolores Del Rio *Josette Martel* • Ruth Warrick *Stephanie Graham* • Agnes Moorehead *Mrs Mathews* • Everett Sloane *Kopeikin* • Jack Moss *Banat* • Jack Durant *Gogo* ■ *Dir* Norman Foster • *Scr* Joseph Cotten, Orson Welles, from a novel by Eric Ambler • *Cinematographer* Karl Struss

The Journey of August King ★★★

Period drama   1995 · US · Colour · 95mins

Jason Patric and Thandie Newton star in this period drama directed by John Duigan and based on the novel by John Ehle. Newton plays a runaway slave in 19th-century North Carolina, who is sheltered and enters into a relationship with widowed farmer August King (Patric). A beautiful looking film, co-produced by Sam Waterston (who also stars), this is severely limited by its sluggish pace and a lack of sexual tension between the two leads. Duigan's *Flirting* (which is also featured Newton, along with Nicole Kidman) is a finer piece of work but at least this is better than his *Sirens*.

Jason Patric *August King* • Thandie Newton *Annalees Williamsburg* • Larry Drake *Olaf Singletary* • Sam Waterston *Mooney Wright* • Sara-Jane Wylde *Ida Wright* • Eric Mabius *Hal Wright* ■ *Dir* John Duigan • *Scr* John Ehle, from his novel • *Cinematographer* Slawomir Idziak

Journey of Hope ★★★★ PG

Drama based on a true story
1990 · Swi · Colour · 105mins

Although Xavier Koller's uncompromising feature won an Oscar for Best Foreign Film, its power derives from its basis in reality rather than the unsentimental solidity of his direction. Accompanied by his young son, Necmettin Çobanoglu travels from southern Turkey to Switzerland more in desperation than in hope, placing himself in the hands of guides who are every bit as treacherous as the forbidding mountain terrain they must cross. The physical perils are presented with a naturalism that makes them all the more terrifying, but it's the contrast between blind faith and pitiless greed that renders the action so harrowing. In German with English subtitles. ▭

Necmettin Çobanoglu *Haydar* • Nur Srer *Meryem* • Emin Sivas *Mehmet Ali* • Erdinç Akbas *Adana* • Yaman Okay *Türkmen* • Yasar Gner *Haci Baba* ■ *Dir* Xavier Koller • *Scr* Xavier Koller, Feride Ciçekoglu, Heike Hubert

The Journey of Natty Gann
★★★ **PG**

Adventure 1985 · US · Colour · 96mins

Set during the Depression, this Disney road movie is a kind of *Homeward Bound: the Incredible Journey* with people. Meredith Salenger is so good in the role of the 14-year-old who walks 2,000 miles in search of her lumberjack father that it beggars belief that she did not go on to become a star. John Cusack impresses here as a drifter convinced the open road is no place for a girl. There's plenty of action but the film scores best for its depiction of the hardships many children were forced to face in the thirties. ▭

Meredith Salenger *Natty Gann* • John Cusack *Harry Slade* • Ray Wise *Sol Gann* • Lainie Kazan *Connie* • Scatman Crothers *Sherman* • Barry Miller *Parker* • Verna Bloom *Farm woman* ■ *Dir* Jeremy Kagan [Jeremy Paul Kagan] • *Scr* Jeanne Rosenberg

Journey of the Heart
★★

Drama 1997 · US · Colour · 120mins

A very long, slow and seemingly endless journey is taken in this dreary TV movie about a single mother (Cybill Shepherd) of a blind, autistic "musical savant" who dedicates her life to helping her son foster his talent on the piano. Chris Demetral plays the young musician with sensitive restraint and his relationship with his caring music professor (Stephen Lang) rings true. Unfortunately, dull dialogue and sappy scripting make this trite excursion a forgettable experience.

Cybill Shepherd *Janice Johnson* • Stephen Lang *Thomas DeBlois* • Chris Demetral *Tony* • Blake Heron *Ray* • Cassidy Rae *Julia* ■ *Dir* Karen Arthur • *Scr* Dalene Young

Journey through Rosebud
★★★

Drama 1972 · US · Colour · 91mins

Nothing to do with *Citizen Kane*, this is a heartfelt drama about the plight of the native American in modern society, living on reservations in conditions of Third World squalor. The message has been bottled in a rather contrived drama that seeks to draw parallels between the American Indians and the Vietnamese, with Kristoffer Tabori as the draft dodger who hides out on the Rosebud reservation in South Dakota.

Robert Forster *Frank* • Kristoffer Tabori *Danny* • Victoria Racimo *Shirley* • Eddie Little Sky *Stanley Pike* • Roy Jenson *Park Ranger* • Wright King *Indian agent* ■ *Dir* Tom Gries • *Scr* Albert Ruben

Journey to Italy
★★★

Romantic drama 1953 · It/Fr · BW · 84m

After both *Stromboli* and *Europa '51* had met with a less than rapturous critical reception this Rossellini/

Bergman collaboration saw their careers and their marriage at a low ebb. So this film about an English couple (George Sanders and Ingrid Bergman), whose marriage is in crisis, travelling by car to Naples, could be seen as semi-autobiographical. On its release, the film was attacked for being clumsily made and sentimental but those of a more romantic inclination find it beautiful. If one accepts the narrative simplicity and that the journey is both physical and spiritual, the film offers many rewards. Both English and Italian versions were filmed.

Ingrid Bergman *Katherine Joyce* • George Sanders *Alexander Joyce* • Maria Mauban *Marie* • Paul Muller *Paul Dupont* • Leslie Daniels *Tony Burton* ■ *Dir* Roberto Rossellini • *Scr* Vitaliano Brancati, Roberto Rossellini

Journey to Shiloh
★★

Adventure 1968 · US · Colour · 101mins

More interesting today for its cast than its content, this dates from the period when Universal reverted to producing programme westerns to show off young talent. Here, James Caan gets a crack at a leading role, seeking Confederate glory but discovering only the horrors of civil war alongside Michael Sarrazin and Don Stroud. The episodic, rambling narrative suggests some production interference along the way, and veteran TV director William Hale soon returned to the small screen. Keep your eyes peeled for novice Harrison Ford in an early movie role.

James Caan *Buck Burnett* • Michael Sarrazin *Miller Nalls* • Brenda Scott *Gabrielle Duprey* • Don Stroud *Todo McLean* • Paul Peterson *JC Sutton* • Michael Burns *Eubie Bell* • Michael Vincent *Little Bit Lucket* • Harrison Ford *Willie Bill Bearden* ■ *Dir* William Hale • *Scr* Gene L Coon, from a novel by Will Henry

Journey to the Beginning of the World
★★★ **U**

Road movie 1997 · Por/Fr · Colour · 94mins

Nostalgia and regret are only to be expected when an 89-year-old film-maker takes a sentimental journey around his homeland. Manoel de Oliveira's wistful odyssey is made all the more poignant, though, by the fact that it contains Marcello Mastroianni's farewell performance as the director's alter ego. However, just as the reminiscences begin to weave their spell, the emphasis shifts on to Jean-Yves Gautier trying to persuade a long-lost aunt to overcome her xenophobia and accept him as family. Touching on everything from Jesuit schooling to Bosnia, this is a highly personal film, but fascinating all the same. In French and Portuguese with English subtitles.

Marcello Mastroianni *Manoel* • Jean-Yves Gautier *Afonso* • Leonor Silveira *Judite* • Diogo Dória *Duarte* • Isabel de Castro *Maria Afonso* ■ *Dir/Scr* Manoel de Oliveira

Journey to the Center of the Earth
★★★★ **U**

Science-fiction adventure 1959 · US · Colour · 129mins

A lavish, well crafted adaptation of Jules Verne's classic tale with James Mason leading an expedition down into a volcano and finding big mushrooms, giant lizards, an underground ocean

and the lost city of Atlantis. Bernard Herrmann's fabulous music sets the mood for the spirited adventure, with the accent firmly on wholesome light-heartedness rather than vivid Verne danger. Singer Pat Boone adds his own brand of fantasy swashbuckling to the colourful proceedings, played out against some staggeringly imaginative subterranean sets. ▭

Pat Boone *Alec McEwen* • James Mason *Professor Oliver Lindenbrook* • Arlene Dahl *Carla* • Diane Baker *Jenny* • Thayer David *Count Saknussemm* • Peter Ronson *Hans* ■ *Dir* Henry Levin • *Scr* Walter Reisch, Charles Brackett, from the novel *Voyage au Centre de la Terre* by Jules Verne • *Art Director* Lyle R Wheeler, Franz Bachelin, Herman A Blumenthal • *Set Designer* Walter M Scott, Joseph Kish

Journey to the Center of the Earth
★★ **PG**

Science-fiction adventure 1986 · US · Colour · 76mins

Bearing only a passing resemblance to the Jules Verne classic, this harmless family adventure relocates the action to Hawaii where a group of teens stumbles upon an alternative world while out exploring caves. The eclectic cast includes Nicola Cowper (*Dreamchild*) and Kathy Ireland, and, although Verne purists will be disgusted, it makes for blandly enjoyable entertainment. ▭

Paul Carafotes *Richard* • Nicola Cowper *Christina* • Ilan Mitchell-Smith *Bryan* • Jeff Weston *Tola* • Jaclyn Bernstein *Sara* • Kathy Ireland *Wanda* ■ *Dir* Rusty Lemorande • *Scr* Rusty Lemorande, Debra Ricci, Regina Davis, Kitty Chalmers, from the novel *Voyage au Centre de la Terre* by Jules Verne

Journey to the Center of the Earth
★ **U**

Science-fiction adventure 1993 · US · Colour · 91mins

Once you're over the disappointment that this isn't the 1959 version starring James Mason, you'd better prepare yourself for some more bad news. This was the pilot for a TV series that never saw the light of day and when it says "based on the novel by Jules Verne", it means in the loosest possible sense. Director William Dear should surely have spotted that the script left a lot to be desired, but maybe he couldn't resist the opportunity of working with Sam Raimi, the *Evil Dead* director who here pops up in a cameo. ▭

David Dundara *Tony* • Farrah Forke *Margo* • Kim Miyori *Tesue* • John Neville *Chalmers* • Jeffrey Nordling *Chris* • Tim Russ *Briggs* • Carel Struycken *Dallas* • Fabiana Udenio *Sandy* • Justina Vail *Devin* • F Murray Abraham *Professor Harlech* ■ *Dir* William Dear • *Scr* David Mickey Evans, Robert Gunter, from the novel *Voyage au Centre de la Terre* by Jules Verne

Journey to the Far Side of the Sun
★★★

Science-fiction drama 1969 · UK · Colour · 100mins

On the other side of the sun, astronaut Roy Thinnes finds a hidden planet mirroring Earth in every exact detail. Writer/producers Gerry and Sylvia Anderson, who created the cult puppet

shows *Thunderbirds* and *Captain Scarlet*, as well as the live action series *UFO* and *Space 1999*, combine a clever concept with solid special effects. Add commendable direction from Robert Parrish and a memorable twist ending, and the result is a minor science-fiction gem.

Ian Hendry *John Kane* • Roy Thinnes *Col Glenn Ross* • Patrick Wymark *Jason Webb* • Lynn Loring *Sharon Ross* • Loni von Friedl *Lise* • Herbert Lom *Dr Hassler* ■ *Dir* Robert Parrish • *Scr* Gerry Anderson, Sylvia Anderson, Donald James

Journey Together
★★★ **U**

Second World War drama documentary 1944 · UK · BW · 95mins

Richard Attenborough and Jack Watling train for Lancaster bombing missions, though their talents take them in different directions. Later the pair are shot down and bond in a life-raft in the middle of the North Sea. Designed to show the special relationship between Britain and America – Edward G Robinson waived his fee for playing a flying instructor – the film was directed for the RAF Film Unit by John Boulting. The script is based on a story written by Terence Rattigan to exorcise the shock of losing one of his closest friends in the war.

Richard Attenborough *David Wilton* • Jack Watling *John Aynesworth* • David Tomlinson *Smith* • Edward G Robinson *Dean McWilliams* • Sid Rider *Fitter* • Hugh Wakefield *Acting Lieutenant* ■ *Dir* John Boulting • *Scr* John Boulting, from a story by Terence Rattigan

Journey's End
★★★

First World War drama 1930 · US/UK · BW · 130mins

Gods and Monsters (1998), the excellent biopic of British-born Hollywood director James Whale, cast new light on Whale's first feature, an adaptation of RC Sheriff's First World War play. Whale, who served in the trenches, shot the picture in Hollywood because British studios were not yet fully equipped for sound. The film is a valuable record of the stage production, with the same splendidly stiff-upper-lip yet touching performances from the all-male cast and "simply topping" dialogue. Colin Clive, who would play the title role in Whale's *Frankenstein* the following year, is especially good as Captain Stanhope breaking under the strain of war.

Colin Clive *Capt Stanhope* • Ian MacLaren *Lt Osborne* • David Manners *Second Lt Raleigh* • Billy Bevan *Second Lt Trotter* • Anthony Bushell *Second Lt Hibbert* • Robert A'Dair *Capt Hardy* ■ *Dir* James Whale • *Scr* Joseph Moncure March, from the play by RC Sherriff

Joy in the Morning
★★

Drama 1965 · US · Colour · 101mins

Richard Chamberlain was nearing the end of his stint as TV's Doctor Kildare when he switched professions for this drab melodrama about the financial and marital difficulties of a law student in a small mid-western town in the late twenties. Flatly directed by Alex Segal and adapted with little imagination from the novel by Betty Smith, it forces you to take sides with either workaholic Chamberlain or his neglected bride, Yvette Mimieux, neither of whom are sympathetic characters.

Richard Chamberlain *Carl Brown* • Yvette Mimieux *Annie McGairy* • Arthur Kennedy *Patrick Brown* • Oscar Homolka *Stan Pulaski* • Joan Tetzel *Beverly Karter* • Sidney Blackmer *Dean James Darwent* ■ *Dir* Alex Segal • *Scr* Sally Benson, Alfred Hayes, Norman Lessing, from the novel *Joy in the Morning* by Betty Smith

The Joy Luck Club ★★★★ 15

Drama 1993 · US · Colour · 133mins

Faithfully adapted from Amy Tan's bestselling book, director Wayne Wang's moving yet witty melodrama mixes the stories of four Chinese-born mothers with those of their American-born daughters. Murder, suicide, betrayal and love are all captured in numerous three-hanky moments, beautifully (if sentimentally) played. Tan co-wrote the script with *Rain Man* scribe Ronald Bass and if the result is a bit of a women's weepie, then at least it's an excellent one.

Kieu Chinh *Suyuan* • Tsai Chin *Lindo* • France Nuyen *Ying Ying* • Lisa Lu *An Mei* • Wen Ming-Na *June* • Tamlyn Tomita *Waverly* • Lauren Tom *Lena* ■ *Dir* Wayne Wang • *Scr* Amy Tan, Ronald Bass, from a novel by Amy Tan

Joy of Living ★★★

Comedy 1938 · US · BW · 90mins

Irene Dunne was one of the great joys of thirties Hollywood, both a talented singer (*Showboat*) and superb comedian (*The Awful Truth*). This combines her skills in a screwball comedy with songs, that's agreeable but rather pointless. As in Dunne's earlier musicals, the songs were composed by Jerome Kern and include *You Couldn't Be Cuter*. She's cast as a wealthy Broadway star who escapes from her family of spongers and discovers a new lease of life with shipping magnate Douglas Fairbanks Jr. A joyful supporting cast includes Alice Brady, Lucille Ball and Eric Blore.

Irene Dunne *Margaret* • Douglas Fairbanks Jr *Dannie* • Alice Brady *Minerva* • Guy Kibbee *Dennis* • Jean Dixon *Harrison* • Eric Blore *Potter* • Lucille Ball *Salina* ■ *Dir* Tay Garnett • *Scr* Gene Towne, Graham Baker, Allan Scott, from a story by Herbert Fields, Dorothy Fields

Joy of Sex ★ 15

Sex comedy 1984 · US · Colour · 89mins

Using just the title of Alex Comfort's bestseller, and none of its factual content, this lame teenage sex comedy gives new meaning to the words dull, vulgar and pathetic. Leslie (Michelle Meyrink) mistakenly thinks she only has a few weeks left to live and embarks on a desperate, virginity-losing campaign. Distance has lent director Martha Coolidge's soporific erotic cabaret a certain campy eighties nostalgia, but one can only lament the sad loss of John Belushi who was set to star in this unfunny feature before his untimely death.

Cameron Dye *Alan Holt* • Michelle Meyrink *Leslie Hindenberg* • Charles Van Eman *Max Holt* • Lisa Langlois *Melanie* • Colleen Camp *Liz Sampson* ■ *Dir* Martha Coolidge • *Scr* Kathleen Rowell, JJ Salter

The Joyless Street ★★★★★

Silent drama 1925 · Ger · BW · 125mins

Unique in being the only film to boast Greta Garbo and Marlene Dietrich in its cast (the latter as an uncredited extra), this silent masterpiece is also significant for its development of the technique of "seamless" editing and for pioneering the style known as "street realism". Although staged on studio sets, there's an authenticity about the Vienna depicted in this study of middle-class desperation, as both Garbo (in her last pre-Hollywood picture) and Asta Nielsen have to sell more than their souls to feed their families, while those who profiteered from the First World War indulge themselves in every vice.

Asta Nielsen *Maria Lechner* • Greta Garbo *Greta Rumfort* • Werner Krauss *Joseph Gieringer/The Butcher of Melchior Street* • Valeska Gert *Mrs Greifer* • Marlene Dietrich ■ *Dir* GW Pabst • *Scr* Willy Haas, from a novel by Hugo Bettauer • *Cinematographer* Guido Seeber, Curt Oertel, Walter Robert Lach • *Editor* Hans Sohnle

Joyride ★★ 15

Crime drama 1977 · US · Colour · 89mins

Set in Alaska, this exploitation movie looks at four teenagers who get their kicks from sex and petty crime – until things get out of hand. Made for the teen market, the film is reasonably perceptive about life on the margins and has an interesting cast, in that all four leads are the children of established movie stars (Lucille Ball, John Carradine and June Lockhart). Only Melanie Griffith (Tippi Hedren's daughter) went on to better things, however.

Desi Arnaz Jr *Scott* • Robert Carradine *John* • Melanie Griffith *Susie* • Anne Lockhart *Cindy* • Tom Ligon *Sanders* ■ *Dir* Joseph Ruben • *Scr* Joseph Ruben, Peter Rainer

Joyriders ★★ 15

Road movie 1988 · UK · Colour · 92mins

In spite of the arresting opening, in which a frustrated Dubliner dumps her kids as left luggage, and some glorious Irish scenery, this drama is soon trapped within the confines of its limited budget, Andy Smith's underdeveloped script and the overcautious approach of debut director Aisling Walsh. Patricia Kerrigan conveys something of the frustration of modern urban life, and some of her scenes with daydreaming car thief Andrew Connolly are quite touching, but the pessimism of the plot and the narrowness of approach eventually underwhelm you.

Patricia Kerrigan *Mary Flynn* • Andrew Connolly *Perky Rice* • Billie Whitelaw *Tammy O'Moore* • David Kelly *Daniel Tracey* • John Kavanagh *Hotel Manager* • Deirdre Donoghue *Dolores Flynn* • Tracy Peacock *Finbar Flynn* ■ *Dir* Aisling Walsh • *Scr* Andy Smith, from a story by Andy Smith, Aisling Walsh

Ju Dou ★★★★★ 15

Drama 1990 · Chi/Jap · Colour · 95mins

The first Chinese film to be nominated for an Oscar, this is one of the glories of recent Chinese cinema. Although superbly shot by Gu Changwei and Yang Lun, the primary credit for the

film's visual splendours belongs to principal director Zhang Yimou, himself a former cinematographer, whose command of colour and camera angle complements his assured handling of this intense tale of illicit passion set in a cloth dyer's mill sometime in the twenties. Gong Li gives a typically dynamic performance and this sly attack on China's elderly ruling elite is rightly considered by many to be Zhang's masterpiece. In Mandarin with English subtitles. Contains violence, swearing and nudity.

Li Wei *Yang Jinshan* • Gong Li *Ju Dou* • Li Baotian *Yang Tianqing* • Yi Zhang *Yang Tianbai as a child* • Jian Zheng *Yang Tianbai as a boy* ■ *Dir* Zhang Yimou, Yang Fengliang • *Scr* Liu Heng, from his story *Fuxi, Fuxi*

Juarez ★★★ U

Historical drama 1939 · US · BW · 116mins

In this epic about the French colonisation of Mexico, Paul Muni found a role that suited his stature, as Benito Pablo Juarez. Unfortunately his input resulted in the usually tight Warner Bros style becoming somewhat broken-backed and overlong. In fact, this film was made in two halves, and then edited together, and it shows. Nevertheless, there is striking work on display here: Bette Davis's Empress Carlotta going mad is a highspot, and John Garfield brings an honest heartfelt intensity to the small role of Porfirio Diaz. But Brian Aherne is a stuffy Maximilian, and the plot is tortuously slow to unwind. Thank goodness for a splendid Korngold score.

Paul Muni *Benito Juarez* • Bette Davis *Carlotta* • Brian Aherne *Maximilian* • Claude Rains *Napoleon III* • Gale Sondergaard *Empress Eugenie* • John Garfield *Porfirio Diaz* • Donald Crisp *Marechal Bazaine* ■ *Dir* William Dieterle • *Scr* John Huston, Wolfgang Reinhardt, Aeneas MacKenzie, from the play *Juarez & Maximillian* by Franz Werfel, from the novel *The Phantom Crown* by Bertita Harding

Jubal ★★★★ PG

Western drama 1956 · US · Colour · 97mins

This adaptation of Paul I Wellman's novel *Jubal Troop* is a fine work with a magnificent, grim performance from Glenn Ford in the title role. But look closer and you'll recognise plot themes and motivations – yup, it's *Othello* out west, with Ernest Borgnine's rancher as the Moor and Rod Steiger cast in the Iago role. Loner Ford is an almost-Cassio, and the suspense is stretched tightly as you long for Ford and Steiger to settle the score. *Jubal* works perfectly well if you have no knowledge of Shakespeare, but it certainly adds an extra layer of appreciation if you do. A brutal tale, well told by western maestro Delmer Daves, and magnificently photographed by Charles Lawton Jr.

Glenn Ford *Jubal Troop* • Ernest Borgnine *Shep Horgan* • Rod Steiger *Pinky* • Valerie French *Mae Horgan* • Felicia Farr *Naomi Hoktor* • Basil Ruysdael *Shem Hoktor* • Noah Beery Jr *Sam* • Charles Bronson *Reb Haislipp* ■ *Dir* Delmer Daves • *Scr* Delmer Daves, Russell S Hughes, from the novel *Jubal Troop* by Paul I Wellman

Jubilee ★★★ 18

Black comedy 1978 · UK · Colour · 100mins

Queen Elizabeth I takes a trip into the future to witness "Anarchy in the UK" in Britain's first fully fledged punk movie. Director Derek Jarman, Ken Russell's former set designer, used the 1977 Silver Jubilee to comment on the disintegration of society, crafting a fiercely inventive experimental psycho-fantasy making ample use of New Wave music (Adam Ant, Chelsea, Siouxsie and the Banshees, the Slits) and the concerns of contemporary youth culture. Always more hip King's Road than hardcore street-cred, it remains an energetic and witty time capsule. Contains violence, swearing, sex scenes and nudity.

Jenny Runacre *Bod/Queen Elizabeth I* • Little Nell *Crabs* • Toyah Willcox *Mad* • Jordan *Amyl Nitrite* • Hermine Demoriane *Chaos* • Ian Charleson *Angel* • Karl Johnson *Sphinx* • Linda Spurrier *Viv* • Neil Kennedy *Max* • Orlando *Borgia Ginz* • Wayne County *Lounge Lizard* • Richard O'Brien *John Dee* • Adam Ant *Kid* ■ *Dir/Scr* Derek Jarman

Judas Kiss ★★★

Crime thriller 1998 · US · Colour · 97mins

When a gang kidnaps a computer genius, a woman gets killed in the scrum. Turns out that she's the wife of a senator and then... well, that's just one twist in this exceedingly strange thriller. Film buffs will go wink-wink, nudge-nudge at how the director, Sebastian Gutierrez, grafts the influence of Pedro Almodóvar onto Quentin Tarantino: the first few minutes are pornography, then it's a legit thriller, then it goes all weird again, and that's before – wait for it – Emma Thompson and Alan Rickman appear as New Orleans cops. Made for cable TV, this could become a cult.

Carla Gugino *Coco Chavez* • Simon Baker-Denny *Junior Armstrong* • Gil Bellows *Lizard Browning* • Emma Thompson *Agent Sadie Hawkins* • Alan Rickman *Detective David Friedman* • Til Schweiger *Ruben Rubenbauer* • Greg Wise *Ben Dyson* ■ *Dir* Sebastian Gutierrez • *Scr* Sebastian Gutierrez, from a story by Deanna Fuller, Sebastian Gutierrez

Jude ★★★★ 15

Drama 1996 · UK · Colour and BW · 117mins

A magnificent and appropriately distressing adaptation of Thomas Hardy's final novel *Jude the Obscure*. Co-produced by the BBC, it did only fair business at British cinemas, but the presence of *Titanic* survivor Kate Winslet should now guarantee it a wide audience. The story, which involves social rejection, unrequited love, suicide and, worst of all, intellectual snobbery and religious obsession, is Hardy's bleakest. Be warned, this is not the jolliest of tales, but it is absolutely gripping and, indeed, heartbreaking, and director Michael Winterbottom and writer Hossein Amini deserve all credit for refusing to compromise the story's grimmer aspects. Contains nudity and sex scenes.

Christopher Eccleston *Jude Fawley* • Kate Winslet *Sue Bridehead* • Liam Cunningham *Phillotson* • Rachel Griffiths *Arabella* • June Whitfield *Aunt Drusilla* • Ross Colvin Turnbull *Little Jude* • James Daley *Jude as a boy* •

Berwick Kaler *Farmer Troutham* ■ *Dir* Michael Winterbottom • *Scr* Hossein Amini, from the novel *Jude the Obscure* by Thomas Hardy

Judex ★★★
Classic silent adventure
1916 · Fr · BW · 270mins

Having thrilled audiences with *Les Vampires* and *Fantôas*, Louis Feuillade was denounced for the dark and dispiriting nature of his serials, celebrating the deeds of criminals. Consequently, this 12-part adventure is less compelling than its predecessors, although Feuillade continues to make atmospheric use of his locations and René Cresté cuts a dash as the count who assumes a crimefighting disguise to avenge the death of his father.

René Cresté *Judex* • Musidora *Diana Monti/ Mlle Verdier* • Yvette Andreyor *Jacqueline* • Marcel Levesque *Cocantin* • Louis Luebas *Favraux* ■ *Dir* Louis Feuillade • *Scr* Louis Feuillade, Arthur Bernède

Judex ★★★★
Mystery adventure 1963 · Fr/It · BW · 97mins

A glorious evocation of a bygone era, French director Georges Franju's tribute to the pioneering silent serials of fantasy writer Louis Feuillade is a thrilling combination of subversive derring-do and lyrical symbolism. The convoluted plot centres around the attempts of Channing Pollock's clandestine crusade to protect banker's daughter, Edith Scob, from the machinations of the diabolical Francine Bergé. From the enchanting opening at a masked ball, the battle of wits between real-life conjurer Pollock and the chameleon Bergé is endlessly entertaining. But it's the stylised, often surreal, quality of Marcel Fradetal's atmospheric photography that proves conclusively that pulp kitsch can, occasionally, touch poetry.

Channing Pollock *Judex/Vallieres* • Francine Bergé *Diana Monti/Marie Verdier* • Edith Scob *Jacqueline Favraux* • Michel Vitold *Favraux* ■ *Dir* Georges Franju • *Scr* Francis Lacassin, Jacques Champreux, from the 1916 film • *Cinematographer* Marcel Fradetal

The Judge and Jake Wyler ★★
Comedy drama 1972 · US · Colour · 100mins

A polished TV movie with the legendary Bette Davis as a retired judge starting up a detective agency, and taking on parolees, including Doug McClure, as staff. You wouldn't be wrong in thinking that this was a pilot for a TV series that never happened, yet Davis does get some spiky dialogue from veteran TV writers and co-producers William Link and Richard Levinson. The whole is resolutely formulaic, however, and the male cast is vapid.

Bette Davis *Judge Meredith* • Doug McClure *Jake Wyler* • Eric Braeden *Anton Granicek* • Joan Van Ark *Alicia Dodd* • Gary Conway *Frank Morrison* • Lou Jacobi *Lieutenant Wolfson* ■ *Dir* David Lowell Rich • *Scr* David Shaw, Richard Levinson, William Link

Judge & Jury ★★★ 18
Action horror 1995 · US · Colour · 93mins

Following his execution, vicious murderer David Keith returns from the dead to take revenge on the two men

he blames for his wife's death – disgraced detective Paul Koslo and over-the-hill American football player Martin Kove. A barnstorming performance from the ghostly Keith drives director John Eyres's *Shocker* retread, humorously blending chills and action for a fun, fright fix. Contains violence and swearing. ⊞

David Keith *Joey* • Martin Kove *Michael Silvano* • Thomas Ian Nicholas *Alex Silvano* • Laura Johnson *Grace Silvano* • Kelly Perine *Roland* • Paul Koslo *Lockhart* • Robert Miranda *Coach Wagner* • Patricia Scanlon *Mary* ■ *Dir* John Eyres • *Scr* John Eyres, Amanda Kirpaul, John Cianetti

Judge Dredd ★★★ 15
Science-fiction action adventure
1995 · US · Colour · 91mins

Star Wars meets *Ben-Hur* in director Danny Cannon's imaginatively over-the-top science-fiction rendering of the celebrated *2000 AD* comic-strip hero. In the future, the world has formed into densely populated Mega Cities with the Cursed Earth being the uninhabitable region lying between them. Law and order is maintained by a fleet of elite officers who are judge, jury and executioner all rolled into one, and Judge Dredd (Sylvester Stallone) is the most prolific of the brigade. This is how fans like their Stallone served up best – without subtlety, monosyllabic, biceps bulging and in constant action. Judge Dredd is easily the actor's best role since *Rocky*. Always exciting, this is an under-rated fantasy, full of flash, plenty of bang and packing a considerable wallop. Contains swearing and violence. ⊞ **DVD**

Sylvester Stallone *Judge Dredd* • Armand Assante *Rico* • Rob Schneider *Fergie* • Jürgen Prochnow *Judge Griffin* • Max von Sydow *Judge Fargo* • Diane Lane *Judge Hershey* ■ *Dir* Danny Cannon • *Scr* William Wisher, Steven E de Souza, from a story by William Wisher, Michael DeLuca, from characters created by John Wagner, Carlos Ezquerra

Judge Hardy and Son ★★ U
Comedy crime 1939 · US · BW · 89mins

This is the eighth in the series that enshrines wholesome smalltown values and smothers them in comedy. This entry has Andy (Mickey Rooney) doing some serious bonding with his dad, Judge Hardy (Lewis Stone), while also trying to win the school essay competition, as well as Ann Rutherford's pretty Polly. Then pneumonia strikes Andy's mum, and the relatives gather round her with Andy offering a prayer. This family wasn't named Hardy for nothing.

Lewis Stone *Judge James K Hardy* • Mickey Rooney *Andy Hardy* • Cecilia Parker *Marian Hardy* • Fay Holden *Mrs Emily Hardy* • Ann Rutherford *Polly Benedict* • Sara Haden *Aunt Milly* ■ *Dir* George B Seitz • *Scr* Carey Wilson, from characters created by Aurania Rouverol

Judge Hardy's Children ★★
Comedy drama 1938 · US · BW · 78mins

The third film in the series and the first to have the name "Hardy" in the title. The heavy political slant to this entry – the Hardys go to Washington DC and take part in a Supreme Court investigation into public utilities – is in direct response to Roosevelt's "New Deal". Lewis Stone, as Judge Hardy,

has much to say about this but Mickey Rooney, as Andy, still gets to flirt with a succession of pretty young things, including teaching the daughter of the French ambassador how to dance.

Lewis Stone *Judge James K Hardy* • Mickey Rooney *Andy Hardy* • Cecilia Parker *Marian Hardy* • Fay Holden *Mrs Emily Hardy* • Ann Rutherford *Polly Benedict* • Betsy Ross Clarke *Aunt Milly* ■ *Dir* George B Seitz • *Scr* Kay Van Riper, from characters created by Aurania Rouverol

Judge Priest ★★★
Comedy drama 1934 · US · BW · 79mins

In the second of three films Will Rogers made for director John Ford, the folksy humorist portrays the sensible but lonely judge in 1890 Kentucky who quietly fights prejudice to see that justice is done and talks to his dead wife at her graveside. The treatment and appearance of a black character, Stepin Fetchit, accused of stealing some chickens, may seem racially offensive these days, but his character is regarded in an affectionate, if condescending, way and reflects attitudes at the time. It's a toss-up as to whether this richly humorous, often touching piece of Americana is better than Ford's own 1953 remake, *The Sun Shines Bright* (in which Jeff Poindexter repeats his role as Fetchit).

Stepin Fetchit *Jeff Poindexter* • Will Rogers *Judge William Pitman Priest* • Tom Brown *Jerome Priest* • Anita Louise *Ellie May Gillespie* • Henry B Walthall *Reverend Ashby Brand* • David Landau *Bob Gillis* • Hattie McDaniel *Aunt Dilsey* ■ *Dir* John Ford • *Scr* Dudley Nichols, Lamar Trotti, from a character created by Irvin S Cobb

The Judge Steps Out ★★★
Comedy 1949 · US · BW · 91mins

Canadian-born actor Alexander Knox was an under-rated figure in the cinema, despite receiving an Oscar nomination for his performance as Woodrow Wilson in *Wilson* (1944). In this movie he plays a man undergoing a mid-life crisis – long before the term was fashionable. Knox also co-wrote his role as a judge who leaves the rat race, becomes a short-order cook and falls for Ann Sothern. Unfortunately, this likeable movie wasn't a success, and Knox lapsed into supporting roles.

Alexander Knox *Judge Bailey* • Ann Sothern *Peggy* • George Tobias *Mike* • Sharyn Moffett *Nan* • Florence Bates *Chita* • Frieda Inescort *Evelyn Bailey* • Myrna Dell *Mrs Winthrop* ■ *Dir* Boris Ingster • *Scr* Boris Ingster, Alexander Knox, from a story by Boris Ingster

A Judgement in Stone ★ 15
Thriller 1986 · Can · Colour · 100mins

A role only a Bette Davis, at full twitch, could love: a woman is enmeshed in murderous hysteria because of the dyslexia which has plagued her all her life. But it's Rita Tushingham – admirable though she can be – who plays the "heroine" Eunice, with camp and risible results. Bullied by her father, she eventually gets a job as housemaid with a middle-class American family but goes berserk when asked to compile a shopping list. Based on a Ruth Rendell novel this is directed – barely – by Tushingham's husband Ousama Rawi. ⊞

Rita Tushingham *Eunice Parchman* • Ross Petty *George Coverdale* • Shelley Peterson *Jackie Coverdale* • Jonathan Crombie *Bobby Coverdale* • Jessica Steen *Melinda Coverdale* • Aisha Tushingham *Young Eunice* ■ *Dir* Ousama Rawi • *Scr* Elaine Waisglass, from the novel by Ruth Rendell

Judgment at Nuremberg ★★★★ PG
Drama 1961 · US · BW · 178mins

The trial of the judges who enforced Hitler's laws allowing wartime atrocities to occur might not be obvious movie material, but in the hands of brilliant producer/director Stanley Kramer this three-hour saga is mesmerising. Kramer pulled out all the dramatic stops. As producer, he secured one of the great casts of all time, headed by Spencer Tracy as Allied judge Dan Haywood, with touching cameos by Oscar-nominated Judy Garland as Irene Hoffman and Montgomery Clift as Rudolph Petersen, both victims of Nazi tyranny. The film has great dignity, exemplified by Burt Lancaster's intellectual German Ernst Janning, and an Oscar-winning performance from Maximilian Schell. Kramer has been accused of sugaring the pill, but his methods here attracted new, and notably young, audiences to this *Schindler's List* of its day. ⊞

Spencer Tracy *Judge Dan Haywood* • Burt Lancaster *Ernst Janning* • Richard Widmark *Colonel Tad Lawson* • Marlene Dietrich *Madame Bertholt* • Maximilian Schell *Hans Rolfe* • Judy Garland *Irene Hoffman* • Montgomery Clift *Rudolph Petersen* • William Shatner *Captain Harrison Byers* ■ *Dir* Stanley Kramer • *Scr* Abby Mann

Judgment Day: the John List Story ★★★ 15
Crime drama based on a true story
1993 · US · Colour · 93mins

It took a report on America's *Most Wanted* show to bring John List to justice 18 years after he murdered his mother, wife and three children, and vanished, leaving only a confession and no clues to his whereabouts. Robert Blake convinces as the New Jersey accountant whose long-repressed resentment at a childhood of abuse suddenly drives him to violent crime. Equally imposing is David Caruso as the FBI agent who refuses to be beaten by this seemingly baffling case, and this is better than most true-life TV movies. ⊞

Robert Blake *John List* • Beverly D'Angelo *Helen List* • Alice Krige *Jean Syfert* • Melinda Dillon *Eleanor* • David Caruso *Agent Bob Richland* • Carroll Baker *Alma List* ■ *Dir* Bobby Roth • *Scr* Dennis Turner

Judgment Deferred ★★
Crime thriller 1951 · UK · BW · 88mins

John Baxter forged a reputation in the early thirties for social dramas and comedies notable for their sure grasp of character and locale. This is a remake of Baxter's own 1933 feature *Dosshouse*, much admired in its day for its gritty approach to poverty at a time when most producers were churning out glib escapism. However, the intervening 18 years evidently took their toll on Baxter who, apart from some nice shots of Dorset, here

U = SUITABLE FOR ALL Uc = SUITABLE FOR ALL, ESPECIALLY FOR YOUNG CHILDREN (VIDEO ONLY) PG = PARENTAL GUIDANCE

manages only to fashion a muddled, maudlin melodrama that feels like sub-standard Frank Capra.

Hugh Sinclair *David Kennedy* • Helen Shingler *Kay Kennedy* • Abraham Sofaer *Chancellor* • Leslie Dwyer *Flowers* • Joan Collins *Lil Carter* • Harry Locke *Bert* ■ *Dir* John Baxter • *Scr* Geoffrey Orme, Barbara K Emary, Walter Meade, from a story by Herbert Ayres

Judgment in Berlin ★★PG

Courtroom drama 1988 · US · Colour · 92mins

Former Hollywood bad boy Sean Penn here proves his dramatic worth in a small part, playing the role of a key witness in the trial of two East Germans who in 1978 hijacked a Polish airliner in an attempt to escape to the west. It's an uneven but intriguing adaptation of Judge Herbert J Stern's account of the American trial of the escapees, over which he presided. Martin Sheen plays Stern with too much pomposity and Sean's father, Leon Penn, directs with cluttered symbolism. But, these flaws apart, it remains a fascinating remnant of the Cold War. Contains swearing. ▣

Martin Sheen *Herbert J Stern* • Sam Wanamaker *Bernard Hellring* • Max Gail *Judah Best* • Juergen Heinrich *Uri Andreyev* • Heinz Hoenig *Helmut Thiele* • Carl Lumbly *Edwin Palmer* • Sean Penn *Guenther X* ■ *Dir* Leo Penn • *Scr* Joshua Sinclair, Leo Penn, from the book by Herbert J Stern

Judgment Night ★★★18

Thriller 1993 · US · Colour · 105mins

This urban spin on the likes of *Deliverance* and *Southern Comfort* went straight to video here, but there are certainly far worse productions that get the big screen treatment. Stephen Hopkins, who started out on the sequel game – he directed *A Nightmare on Elm Street 5* and *Predator 2* – has fashioned a sleek action thriller that is thoroughly implausible, but an exciting ride all the same. Emilio Estevez, Cuba Gooding Jr, Jeremy Piven and Stephen Dorff are the pampered suburbanites lost in the ghetto, who find themselves on the run from a ruthless gang when they witness a murder. Denis Leary is marvellously over the top as the psychopathic gang leader. ▣

Emilio Estevez *Frank Wyatt* • Cuba Gooding Jr *Mike Peterson* • Denis Leary *Fallon* • Stephen Dorff *John Wyatt* • Jeremy Piven *Ray Cochran* • Peter Greene *Sykes* • Erik Schrody *Rhodes* ■ *Dir* Stephen Hopkins • *Scr* Lewis Colick, Jere Cunningham, Kevin Jarre, from their story

Judicial Consent ★★★18

Thriller 1995 · US · Colour · 95mins

Bonnie Bedelia takes centre stage in this above average straight-to-video thriller. She plays a judge who finds herself being drawn into a complex revenge plot designed to frame her for murder. The story defies belief but at least puts a fresh spin on the legal thriller format, and Bedelia delivers a typically gutsy performance. She is well supported by Billy Wirth, Will Patton and Dabney Coleman. Contains violence, swearing, sex scenes and nudity. ▣

Bonnie Bedelia *Gwen Warwick* • Will Patton *Alan Warwick* • Dabney Coleman *Charles Mayron* • Billy Wirth *Martin* • Lisa Blount *District Attorney* ■ *Dir/Scr* William Bindley

Judith ★

War drama 1966 · US · Colour · 109mins

On the dockside in Palestine in 1947, a cargo ship unloads its packing cases and from one of these emerges Sophia Loren, fresh as a daisy. She rushes off to Peter Finch's kibbutz as an agent of the Jewish underground organisation, Haganah, to expose her former husband Hans Verner as a Nazi war criminal and a sponsor of Arab nationalism. But mostly she's there to make us crease up with laughter. Adapted from a story by Lawrence Durrell, this is a ludicrous action thriller that also serves as anti-Arab propaganda for Israel. The location photography is by Nicolas Roeg.

Sophia Loren *Judith* • Peter Finch *Aaron Stein* • Jack Hawkins *Major Lawton* • Hans Verner *Gustav Schiller* • Zharira Charifai *Dr Rachel* • Joseph Gross *Yaneck* • Terence Alexander *Carstairs* • Zipora Peled *Hannah* ■ *Dir* Daniel Mann • *Scr* John Michael Hayes, from a story by Lawrence Durrell

Judith Krantz's Torch Song ★★15

Drama 1993 · US · Colour · 92mins

Not-quite-fading actress, Raquel Welch, plays a fading alcoholic superstar who falls for a down-to-earth fireman (Jack Scalia) she meets in a rehab centre. Oh yes, and the road to happiness is a bumpy one. Sound familiar? No it's not the Liz and Larry story but romance novelist Judith Krantz's attempt to blend sex and social issues into one trashy TV movie. It's innocuous fluff that won't do any damage. ▣

Raquel Welch *Paula Eastman* • Jack Scalia *Mike* • Alicia Silverstone *Delphine* • George Newbern *Wedge* • Laura Innes *Ronnie* ■ *Dir* Michael Miller • *Scr* Leonora Thuna, Janet Brownell, from the novel by Judith Krantz

Juggernaut ★★★PG

Thriller 1974 · UK · Colour · 105mins

A not altogether successful change of tack for director Richard Lester – much more at home with those cheeky Beatles movies – who does his best with this solemn thriller about a luxury liner threatened by a mad bomber. It's the superb editing that carries the day, creating the required amount of tension. Unfortunately, female lead Shirley Knight is given little to do, existing simply as a romantic footnote to Omar Sharif's libido, and in the male-heavy cast, Richard Harris, David Hemmings and Anthony Hopkins provide the brains and brawn to save some pretty vacuous lives. ▣

Richard Harris *Fallon* • Omar Sharif *Captain Brunel* • David Hemmings *Charlie Braddock* • Anthony Hopkins *Superintendent John McCleod* • Shirley Knight *Barbara Banister* • Ian Holm *Nicholas Porter* ■ *Dir* Richard Lester • *Scr* Richard DeKoker, Alan Plater • *Editor* Anthony Gibbs

The Juggler ★

Drama 1953 · US · BW · 85mins

A film of sledgehammer subtlety, with circus juggler Kirk Douglas as the

Holocaust survivor who makes it to Israel where he searches for the wife he knows is dead and where, too, every Israeli soldier at the refugee camp is mistaken for a Nazi. A small boy helps him escape to Egypt where Douglas has friends he believes will help him. The film's maudlin sentimentality soars right off the scale and for Douglas, who devoted months to learning how to juggle, it's possibly the worst film of his career.

Kirk Douglas *Hans Muller* • Milly Vitale *Ya'El* • Paul Stewart *Detective Karni* • Joey Walsh [Joseph Walsh] *Yehoshua Bresler* • Alf Kjellin *Daniel* • Beverly Washburn *Susy* • Charles Lane (1) *Rosenberg* ■ *Dir* Edward Dmytryk • *Scr* Michael Blankfort, from his novel

Juha ★★★

Silent drama 1999 · Fin · BW · 77mins

The rural idyll of an adoring couple is shattered by a city slicker in Aki Kaurismäki's bold attempt to turn back the cinematic clock to the monochromed silent era. Typically, the fourth adaptation of Juhani Aho's tale of corrupted innocence is easily the least conventional. But, while Kaurismäki's fully conversant with the silent style, he succumbs to the temptation to punctuate the action with intrusive background sounds. Similarly, the cast struggles to reproduce the expressive posturing that dominated silent screen acting.

Sakari Kuosmanen *Juha* • Kati Outinen *Marja* • André Wilms *Shemeikka* • Markku Peltola *Driver* ■ *Dir* Aki Kaurismäki • *Scr* Aki Kaurismaki, from a novel by Juhani Aho

Juice ★★★15

Action drama 1992 · US · Colour · 91mins

A potent, if flawed, debut from Ernest R Dickerson, who earned his director's spurs after serving as cinematographer on some of Spike Lee's most incendiary works. And you can almost hear Lee's feeling for the language of the street in this tale of four black youths and a gun. Omar Epps gets top billing, playing a confused teenager who wants to be a DJ, but finds himself inexorably drawn into the world of crime when he reluctantly joins his pals on a store heist. Epps is impressive among a then largely unknown cast, although the late rapper Tupac Shakur steals the show in one of his first films. Contains violence, swearing and sex scenes.

Omar Epps *Quincy ("Q")* • Tupac Shakur *Bishop* • Jermaine Hopkins *Steel* • Khalil Kain *Raheem* • Cindy Herron *Yolanda* • Vincent Laresca *Radames* • Samuel L Jackson *Trip* • George O Gore *Brian* ■ *Dir* Ernest R Dickerson • *Scr* Gerard Brown, Ernest R Dickerson, from a story by Ernest R Dickerson

Juke Box Rhythm ★★U

Musical 1959 · US · BW · 82mins

One of several B-movies quickly confected by producer Sam Katzman to cash in on pop stars of the day. If the thought of Johnny Otis performing *Willie and the Hand Jive* makes you misty, this is for you. Otherwise there is amiable fun in watching and hearing a very young Jack Jones (son of Allan) near the start of his career, as a singer helping an unknown designer (Hans Conried) convince a European

princess visiting New York that he should design her coronation wardrobe. All just an excuse for Otis, the Nitwits, the Treniers and the Earl Grant Trio to render the sort of sounds that were making the charts in 1959.

Jo Morrow *Princess Ann* • Jack Jones *Riff Manton* • Brian Donlevy *George Manton* • George Jessel • Hans Conried *Balenko* • Karin Booth *Leslie Anders* ■ *Dir* Arthur Dreifuss • *Scr* Mary C McCall Jr, Earl Baldwin, from a story by Lou Morheim

Jules et Jim ★★★★★PG

Period drama 1961 · Fr · BW · 101mins

Echoing the style of Jean Renoir while epitomising the exuberance of the *nouvelle vague*, this is a virtuoso technical performance from François Truffaut. He variously uses photographic stills, newsreel footage, freeze frames and undercranked, travelling and distorted imagery to capture both the era and the emotion described in Henri-Pierre Roché's semi-autobiographical tale. Embodying the complex contradictions of modern womanhood, Jeanne Moreau is enchanting, while, immune to her wilfulness, Oskar Werner and Henri Serre respond readily to her caprice. However, their failure to understand her motives and insecurities prevents them from detecting the incipient despair that will, ultimately, lead to tragedy. The masterpiece of a genius. In French with English subtitles.. ▣

Jeanne Moreau *Catherine* • Oskar Werner *Jules* • Henri Serre *Jim* • Marie Dubois *Therese* • Vanna Urbino *Gilberte* • Sabine Haudepin *Sabine* • Boris Bassiak *Albert* ■ *Dir* François Truffaut • *Scr* Jean Gruault, François Truffaut, from a novel by Henri-Pierre Roché • *Cinematographer* Raoul Coutard • *Music* Georges Delerue

Jules Verne's Rocket to the Moon ★★U

Science-fiction comedy 1967 · UK · Colour · 88mins

No prizes for guessing where the inspiration for the alternative title to this film, *Those Fantastic Flying Fools*, came from. But beware! These not-so-magnificent men in their rocketship to the moon provide strictly routine science fantasy. A fabulous cast (including ex-Bond villain Gert Fröbe and fifties' teen idol Troy Donahue) breathes life into an insipid Jules Verne concoction that has Burl Ives sending circus performers into Victorian orbit only to have them crash-land in tsarist Russia. Sadly, the comedy plummets even faster than the cheap special effects. ▣

Burl Ives *Phineas T Barnum* • Troy Donahue *Gaylord Sullivan* • Gert Frobe *Professor Von Bulow* • Hermione Gingold *Angelica* • Lionel Jeffries *Sir Charles Dillworthy* • Terry-Thomas *Captain Sir Harry Washington-smythe* • Jimmy Clitheroe *General Tom Thumb* ■ *Dir* Don Sharp • *Scr* Dave Freeman, from a story by Peter Welbeck [Harry Alan Towers], from the writings of Jules Verne

Jules Verne's Strange Holiday ★★

Adventure 1969 · Ausl · Colour · 75mins

This is a disappointingly tame attempt to film Jules Verne's adventure of boys marooned on an island, who find themselves up against some unwanted visitors. The enthusiastic performances show an abundance of youthful zest, but it's not a pleasant story, further let down by stale scripting.

Jaeme Hamilton *Briant* • Mark Healey *Doniphan* • Jaime Messang *Moco* • Van Alexander *Gordon* ■ *Dir* Mende Brown • *Scr* Mende Brown, from the novel *Deux Ans en Vacance* by Jules Verne

Julia ★★★★ 🅟🅖
Drama 1977 · US · Colour · 112mins

Lillian Hellman's memoir *Pentimento* provides the basis for Fred Zinnemann's sensitive movie about friendship, courage and the playwright's growing awareness of the Nazi menace during the early thirties. Lillian (Jane Fonda) finally makes contact with her childhood friend Julia (Vanessa Redgrave), a committed anti-fascist who has been injured in a demonstration. Later Lillian is persuaded to help smuggle money into Germany to aid in the fight against the Nazis. The film's strength lies not in complex plotting but in the excellent performances from Fonda, Oscar-winning Redgrave, and Jason Robards as author Dashiell Hammett. Meryl Streep makes her feature debut. 🖵

Jane Fonda *Lillian Hellman* • Vanessa Redgrave *Julia* • Jason Robards [Jason Robards Jr] *Dashiell Hammett* • Maximilian Schell *Johann* • Hal Holbrook *Alan Campbell* • Rosemary Murphy *Dorothy Parker* • Meryl Streep *Anne Marie* ■ *Dir* Fred Zinnemann • *Scr* Alvin Sargent, from the memoirs *Pentimento* by Lillian Hellman • *Cinematographer* Douglas Slocombe • *Music* Georges Delerue

Julia Has Two Lovers ★ 🅲🅢
Drama 1990 · US · Colour · 82mins

Lucky old Julia (Daphna Kastner, who also wrote the script), especially as one of her two lovers is *The X Files's* David Duchovny. Unfortunately, she's stuck in this tedious film, trying to decide whether to marry her boring lover (David Charles) or have an affair with the mysterious man who is attempting to seduce her over the phone. Unluckiest of all, though, is Duchovny, who has this badly-written, tritely-acted and leadenly-directed piece of soft porn still lurking somewhere on his CV. 🖵

Daphna Kastner *Julia* • David Duchovny *Daniel* • David Charles *Jack* • Tim Ray *Leo* • Martin Donovan *Freddy* • Anita Olanick *Ursula* ■ *Dir* Bashar Shbib • *Scr* Bashar Shbib, Daphna Kastner, from a story by Daphna Kastner

Julia Misbehaves ★★
Comedy 1948 · US · BW · 99mins

With her long-lost daughter's romance about to progress to the altar, actress Julia Packett (Greer Garson) decides to go back to her conventional husband. This misguided attempt to resuscitate the Oscar-winning box-office attraction of *Mrs Miniver* (1942) by re-teaming Garson and Walter Pidgeon finds them both floundering, especially Garson, who is called upon for some slapstick interludes in an attempt to enliven this flaccid romantic comedy. The heart-stoppingly lovely young Elizabeth Taylor plays the daughter and Peter Lawford is the man she really loves. MGM

wheeled out a Grade A roster of supporting players under the direction of Jack Conway, but the results are still disappointing.

Greer Garson *Julia Packett* • Walter Pidgeon *William Sylvester Packett* • Peter Lawford *Ritchie Lorgan* • Cesar Romero *Fred Gennochio* • Elizabeth Taylor *Susan Packett* • Lucile Watson *Mrs Packett* • Nigel Bruce *Col Willowbrook* ■ *Dir* Jack Conway • *Scr* William Ludwig, Harry Ruskin, Arthur Wimperis, from the novel *The Nutmeg Tree* by Margery Sharp

Julian Po ★★ 🅲🅢
Comedy drama 1997 · US · Colour · 82mins

Christian Slater stars in this superficial drama about a young wanderer drifting into a small-town community. Initially treating him as an unwelcome stranger, the locals change their tune when they discover he's there for the sole purpose of committing suicide. Cue neighbours knocking on his door to unburden their hearts, offer advice and convince him life is worth it, with everything from muffins to free haircuts. Writer/director Alan Wade handles it all with aplomb, but his characters are little more than two-dimensional sketches. Sadly, that includes mustachioed lead Slater.

Christian Slater *Julian Po* • Robin Tunney *Sarah* • Cherry Jones *Lucy* • Michael Parks *Vern* • Frankie Faison *Sheriff* • Harve Presnell *Mayor* ■ *Dir* Alan Wade • *Scr* Alan Wade, from the book *La Mort de Monsieur Golouja* by Branimir Scepanovic

Juliana ★★★
Drama 1988 · Peru · Colour · 97mins

The Peruvian film collective Grupo Chaski had already explored the topic of urban poverty in the stark docudrama, *Gregorio*. Group directors Fernando Espinoza and Alejandro Legaspi returned to the theme with this naturalistic, but often warm and amusing tale, in which a young girl (Rosa Isabel Morfino) runs away from home to escape her abusive stepfather, Guillermo Esqueche. She then encounters the even more viciously exploitative Julio Vega, when she disguises herself as a boy in order to join the band of Lima street musicians that he manages. In Spanish with English subtitles.

Rosa Isabel Morfino *Juliana* • Julio Vega *Don Pedro* • Guillermo Esqueche *Stepfather* • Edward Centeno *Clavito* • David Zuniga *Cobra* ■ *Dir* Fernando Espinoza, Alejandro Legaspi

Julie ★★★
Thriller 1956 · US · BW · 97mins

Doris Day suspects her husband Louis Jourdan is trying to kill her in director Andrew L Stone's tense thriller. Stone's speciality of filming dramas in real-life situations is put to good use here, and he certainly whips up the suspense even if the plot becomes rather implausible in places. Day is radiant and Jourdan very convincing as the baddie, while Hollywood stalwarts Barry Sullivan and Frank Lovejoy give perfectly weighted supporting performances.

Doris Day *Julie Benton* • Louis Jourdan *Lyle Benton* • Barry Sullivan *Cliff Henderson* • Frank Lovejoy *Detective Captain Pringle* • John Gallaudet *Detective Cole* • Harlan Warde *Detective Pope* ■ *Dir/Scr* Andrew L Stone

Julie and the Cadillacs ★★ 🅟🅖
Musical drama 1997 · UK · Colour · 106mins

This is less a film about making it in the pop business in the early sixties than a homage to those corny "next stop the top" movies headlining the likes of Joe Brown. Nigh on every scene is geared up to slipping in one of the 17 tunes on a soundtrack that seems to have been composed exclusively of B-side pastiches and comic ensemble routines. Despite the disappointing music, director Bryan Izzard's eagerly played film is spot-on in its tell-tale details, and provides a timely reminder that pop was once about talent, not just image.

Toyah Willcox *Barbara Gifford* • Victor Spinetti *Cyril Wise* • Peter Polycarpou *Phil Green* • Thora Hird *Julie's grandmother* • James Grout *Mr Watkins* • Mike Berry *Mac MacDonald* • Tina Russell *Julie Carr* ■ *Dir* Bryan Izzard • *Scr* John Dean • *Music/Lyrics* John Dean

julien donkey-boy ★★★★
Drama 1999 · US · Colour · 94

Considering the downbeat realism of *Gummo*, it wasn't a big step for Harmony Korine to take the Dogma vow of chastity. However, there's greater narrative contrivance in this tale of the schizophrenic who finds solace from the tyranny of his abusive father by working in a school for the blind. Visionary German director Werner Herzog startles as the perversely dysfunctional parent, while Ewen Bremner excels as the interiorised outsider. While not always repaying one's intellectual and emotional investment, this is still a challenging, technically astute and daringly inventive attempt to break the mould.

Ewen Bremner *Julien* • Chloë Sevigny *Pearl* • Werner Herzog *Father* • Evan Neumann *Chris* • Joyce Korine *Grandma* • Chrissy Kobylak *Chrissy* • Brian Fisk *Pond boy* • Alvin Law *Neighbour* ■ *Dir/Scr* Harmony Korine

Juliet of the Spirits ★★★
Fantasy drama 1965 · Fr/It/W Ger · Colour · 144mins

Having explored his own fears and failings in 8½, Federico Fellini here tries to do the same for his wife, Giulietta Masina, in this highly stylised daydream. In his first film in colour, the director employs bold hues to suggest the fantastical world in which Masina takes refuge from the even more artificial milieu into which her pretentious, philandering husband has plunged her. Determined to break from traditional storytelling techniques, Fellini strives for visual poetry, particularly during Masina's disturbing odyssey through her memories. While he succeeds in creating some memorable imagery, however, his ventures into Jungian psychology, spiritualism and astrology feel too much like dilettante dabbling. In Italian with English subtitles.

Giulietta Masina *Juliet* • Mario Pisu *Giorgio* • Sandra Milo *Susy/Fanny/Iris* • Caterina Boratto *Juliet's mother* • Luisa Della Noce *Adele* • Sylva Koscina *Sylva* ■ *Dir* Federico Fellini • *Scr* Federico Fellini, Tullio Pinelli,

Brunello Rondi, Ennio Flaiano, from a story by Federico Fellini, Tullio Pinelli • *Cinematographer* Gianni Di Venanzo

Julius Caesar ★★★★★ 🅤
Historical drama 1953 · US · BW · 116mins

Marlon Brando daringly took on the role of Mark Antony (with the help of some coaching from John Gielgud), in what was to become possibly the finest cinematic version of any of Shakespeare's plays. The cast assembled by MGM is mouthwatering. Brando is magnificent, his oration at Caesar's funeral the definitive delivery, while James Mason, as "the most noble Roman of them all" Brutus, is beautifully spoken. There's also no denying Gielgud makes a perfect "lean and hungry"-looking Cassius, Louis Calhern was clearly born to play Caesar himself, and Miklos Rosza's majestic score is mightily impressive. Director Joseph L Mankiewicz concentrates on the drama, not the spectacle, perhaps to disguise the fact that he was forced to use up the old *Quo Vadis* sets by the film's meagre budget. 🖵

James Mason *Brutus* • Marlon Brando *Mark Antony* • John Gielgud *Cassius* • Louis Calhern *Julius Caesar* • Edmond O'Brien *Casca* • Greer Garson *Calpurnia* • Deborah Kerr *Portia* • George Macready *Marullus* • Michael Pate *Flavius* • Richard Hale *Soothsayer* • Alan Napier *Cicero* ■ *Dir* Joseph L Mankiewicz • *Scr* Joseph L Mankiewicz, from the play by William Shakespeare • *Cinematographer* Joseph Ruttenberg • *Art Director* Cedric Gibbons, Edward Carfagno

Julius Caesar ★★ 🅟🅖
Historical drama 1970 · UK · Colour · 111mins

While Hollywood's Roman epics – *Ben-Hur*, for instance, or *Spartacus* – cast British actors as the villains and Americans as suffering slaves or Jews, the Shakespearean sagas have no such scheme and are much the weaker without it. This example is particularly turgid, undermined by Stuart Burge's pedestrian direction and a surprisingly weak Brutus from Jason Robards. John Gielgud, who was Cassius in the far superior 1953 version, now plays Caesar, while Charlton Heston takes his second (though not his last) stab at playing Mark Antony on film. 🖵

Charlton Heston *Mark Antony* • Jason Robards [Jason Robards Jr] *Brutus* • John Gielgud *Julius Caesar* • Richard Johnson *Cassius* • Robert Vaughn *Casca* • Richard Chamberlain *Octavius Caesar* • Diana Rigg *Portia* • Jill Bennett *Calpurnia* ■ *Dir* Stuart Burge • *Scr* Robert Furnival, from the play by William Shakespeare

Jumanji ★★★★ 🅟🅖
Fantasy adventure 1995 · US · Colour · 99mins

This was dismissed by many critics as a noisy, scary and utterly worthless excuse for some ingenious computer effects. Well, as empty experiences go, this is absolutely exhilarating. Toddlers, as well as pre-teens, have been held spellbound by the marauding wildlife that is unleashed when Kirsten Dunst and Bradley Pierce rescue Robin Williams from the sinister board game in which he's been

🅤 = SUITABLE FOR ALL   🅤🅔 = SUITABLE FOR ALL, ESPECIALLY FOR YOUNG CHILDREN (VIDEO ONLY)   🅟🅖 = PARENTAL GUIDANCE

trapped for 26 years. Any film in which the action is determined by a roll of the dice is bound to be episodic, but this hardly detracts from the enjoyment as one spectacular set piece follows another. Wonderful, escapist family entertainment. [video] DVD

Robin Williams *Alan Parrish* • Jonathan Hyde *Van Pelt/Sam Parrish* • Kirsten Dunst *Judy* • Bradley Pierce *Peter* • Bonnie Hunt *Sarah* • Bebe Neuwirth *Nora* • David Alan Grier *Bentley* • Patricia Clarkson *Carol Parrish* ■ *Dir* Joe Johnston • *Scr* Jonathan Hensleigh, Greg Taylor, Jim Strain, from a story by Greg Taylor, Jim Strain, Chris Van Allsburg, from the novel by Chris Van Allsburg

Jump the Gun ★★ 15

Drama 1996 · UK/SAfr · Colour · 108mins

This South African-set film is more concerned with ordinary people than the sociopolitical tangle in which they live. The characters British director Les Blair sets down on the streets of Johannesburg could just as easily be found ducking and diving in London's East End. The cast, particularly Lionel Newton and Michele Burgers, works hard, but we've seen wannabe singers, dreamers, hustlers and prostitutes keep company so many times before. It's only the unusual locations and the occasional piece of inspired improvisation that make this more notable than a dozen other low-budget, lowlife dramas. Contains swearing and sex scenes. [video]

Baby Cele *Gugu* • Lionel Newton *"Clint" Clinton* • Michele Burgers *Minnie* • Thulani Nyembe *Bazooka* • Rapulana Seiphemo *Thabo* • Danny Keogh *JJ* ■ *Dir/Scr* Les Blair

Jumpin' at the Boneyard ★★★ 15

Drama 1991 · US · Colour · 102mins

Tim Roth is mesmerising, both moving and effortlessly believable as a reformed smalltime crook from the Bronx. Meeting up by chance with his brother (Alexis Arquette), he uncomfortably attempts to renew family ties and ensure that his sibling won't make the same mistakes he did. Roth's turn is matched by telling performances from Arquette and a pre-fame Samuel L Jackson, even though overall it makes for grim viewing. [video]

Tim Roth *Manny* • Alexis Arquette *Danny* • Danitra Vance *Jeanette* • Kathleen Chalfant *Mom* • Samuel L Jackson *Mr Simpson* • Luis Guzman *Taxi driver* • Elizabeth Bracco *Cathy* • Jeffrey Wright *Derek* ■ *Dir/Scr* Jeff Stanzler

Jumpin' Jack Flash ★★ 15

Comedy thriller 1986 · US · Colour · 100mins

Whoopi Goldberg's first major role following her debut in *The Color Purple* is a disappointment after such an auspicious beginning to her film career. She stars as a computer operator who inadvertently gets involved in international espionage when a message for help from a spy appears on her screen. Penny Marshall (*Big*, *Awakenings*) replaced Howard Zieff in the director's chair and the script went through several writers, and this raucous comedy certainly feels at times as if there were too many cooks spoiling the broth. [video]

Whoopi Goldberg *Terry Doolittle* • Stephen Collins *Marty Phillips* • John Wood *Jeremy Talbot* • Carol Kane *Cynthia* • Annie Potts *Liz Carlson* • Peter Michael Goetz *Mr Page* • Jim Belushi [James Belushi] *Sperry repairman* • Tracey Ullman *Fiona* ■ *Dir* Penny Marshall • *Scr* David H Franzoni, JW Melville, Patricia Irving, Christopher Thompson, from a story by David H Franzoni

Jumping for Joy ★★ U

Comedy 1955 · UK · BW · 84mins

Frankie Howerd was still best known as the headliner on radio's *Variety Bandbox* when he took his first real starring role in his third film outing. His famous nuances and grimaces were not really suited to the big screen and this tepid comedy about a track dogsbody who finds himself protecting a champion greyhound from some dastardly crooks did not prove otherwise. Director John Paddy Carstairs would later guide Norman Wisdom through many of his hit comedies, but he fails to make Howerd tick here, and what fun there is comes from dependable supporting players. Titter ye will not. [video]

Frankie Howerd *Willie Joy* • Stanley Holloway *"Captain" Jack Montague* • AE Matthews *Lord Cranfield* • Tony Wright *Vincent* • Alfie Bass *Blagg* • Joan Hickson *Lady Cranfield* • Lionel Jeffries *Bert Benton* ■ *Dir* John Paddy Carstairs • *Scr* Jack Davies, Henry E Blyth

Jumping Jacks ★★ U

Comedy 1952 · US · BW · 95mins

After impressing as comedy support in the *My Friend Irma* films, Dean Martin and Jerry Lewis were given their chance to become headliners and soon established themselves as huge box-office stars. As with much of the comedy talent of the time, the pair proved particularly popular in service comedies. In this one, Martin and Lewis play up the slapstick as bumbling new recruits in a paratroop squad. Not as good as their earlier efforts.

Jerry Lewis *Hap Smith* • Dean Martin *Chick Allen* • Mona Freeman *Betty Carver* • Robert Strauss *Sgt McCluskey* ■ *Dir* Norman Taurog • *Scr* Robert Lees, Fred Rinaldo, Herbert Baker, James Allardice, Richard Weil, from a story by Brian Marlow

June Bride ★★★ U

Romantic comedy 1948 · US · BW · 96mins

Anything with Bette Davis in it is worth watching, but there are also some light, fluffy, witty moments to be savoured in this tale of two very spoilt hacks on a women's magazine who fall in love again while composing a daft feature on June weddings. Robert Montgomery is Davis's able co-star and he gives her a fair old run for her money in the scene-stealing stakes. Even if this profoundly inconsequential movie gives us little more than a few wry laughs, it does so with great style and touches of flair. Debbie Reynolds makes a fleeting film debut.

Bette Davis *Linda Gilman* • Robert Montgomery *Carey Jackson* • Fay Bainter *Paula Winthrop* • Betty Lynn *Boo Brinker* • Tom Tully *Mr Brinker* • Barbara Bates *Jeanne Brinker* • Debbie Reynolds *Boo's girl friend* ■ *Dir* Bretaigne Windust • *Scr* Ranald MacDougall, from the play *Feature for June* by Eileen Tighe, Graeme Lorimer

June Night ★★★

Drama 1940 · Swe · BW · 86mins

In the last film she made in Sweden before settling in America, Ingrid Bergman gives a performance to rival any of her early Hollywood assignments as a chemist whose affair with a sailor scandalises a quiet country town. As in so many Swedish films of the period, passions simmer beneath impassive surfaces and hypocritical citizens censure while secretly revelling in the sins of the accused. Bergman is quite captivating, whether being awoken to the joys of love, pleading the sailor's innocence when he accidentally shoots her during a suicide bid or finding fulfilment in a new life. It's melodramatic all the way, so get those hankies out. In Swedish with English subtitles..

Ingrid Bergman *Kerstin Nordback/Sara Nordana* • Marianne Lofgren *Asa* • Lill-Tollie Zellman *Jane Jacobs* • Marianne Aminoff *Nickan* ■ *Dir* Per Lindberg • *Scr* Ragnar Hylten-Cavallius, Per Lindberg, from a story by Tora Nordstrom-Bonnier

Jungle Book ★★★ U

Classic adventure
1942 · US · Colour · 101mins

Directed by Zoltan Korda, this is a starchy affair in which animal magic, preachy parable and jungle adventure have been loosely combined, missing the wisdom, drama and humour of Kipling's classic stories. Sabu stars as Mowgli, the child adopted by wolves whose friends Baloo, Hathi and Bagheera protect him as he trails man-eating tiger Shere Khan (a dog in a striped suit) and faces sundry human villains. Much of it seems rather stilted today, though the Technicolor jungle built in Los Angeles (where a panther mauled a crew member and pythons ran amok) remains a captivating fantasy world. [video]

Sabu *Mowgli* • Joseph Calleia *Buldeo* • John Qualen *Barber* • Frank Puglia *Pundit* • Rosemary De Camp *Messua* • Patricia O'Rourke *Mahala* • Ralph Byrd *Durga* • John Mather *Rao* • Faith Brook *English girl* ■ *Dir* Zoltan Korda • *Scr* Laurence Stallings, from the books by Rudyard Kipling

The Jungle Book ★★★★★ U

Classic animated adventure
1967 · US · Colour · 74mins

This outstanding family film was the last animated feature made under Walt Disney's personal supervision before his death. Based on Rudyard Kipling's *Mowgli* stories, about the man-cub among the predators, it has some wonderful set-pieces, such as Phil Harris as Baloo the Bear singing *The Bare Necessities*, and monkey-leader Louis Prima husking *I Wanna Be like You*. George Sanders is a suavely hungry tiger, while Sebastian Cabot is the caring panther. An unmissable treat for all jungle swingers! [video]

Phil Harris *Baloo the Bear* • Sebastian Cabot *Bagheera the Panther* • Louis Prima *King Louie of the Apes* • George Sanders *Shere Khan the Tiger* • Sterling Holloway *Kaa the Snake* • J Pat O'Malley *Colonel Hathi the Elephant* • Bruce Reitherman *Mowgli the Man Cub* • Verna Felton *Elephant* • Clint Howard *Elephant* • Chad Stuart *Vulture* • Lord Tim Hudson *Vulture* • John Abbott *Wolf* • Ben Wright *Wolf* • Darleen Carr *Girl* ■ *Dir* Wolfgang Reitherman • *Scr* Larry Clemmons, Ralph Wright, Ken Anderson, Vance Gerry, from the books by Rudyard Kipling

The Jungle Book: Mowgli's Story ★★

Adventure 1998 · US · Colour · 77mins

Disney revisits the Kipling tale of the boy raised by wolves more than 30 years after the animated version first delighted audiences. This new film, however, is live-action, with real animals being given voice by such talents as Eartha Kitt and Kathy Najimy. Here, unlike the disappointing *Homeward Bound: the Incredible Journey* , the result is modestly entertaining, rather than irritating. However, the often juvenile humour means parents won't enjoy this as much as their kids – and Sherman Howard's Shere Khan is just no match for George Sanders's.

Brandon Baker *Mowgli (age 12)* • Ryan Taylor *Mowgli (age 5)* • Rajan Patal *Indian soldier* • Eartha Kitt *Bagheera* • Brian Doyle-Murray *Baloo* • Kathy Najimy *Chil* • Marty Ingels *Hathi* • Stephen Tobolowsky *Tabaqui* • Sherman Howard *Voice of Shere Khan* ■ *Dir* Nick Marck • *Scr* Jose Rivera, Jim Herzfeld, from the books by Rudyard Kipling

Jungle Cat ★★★★ U

Documentary 1959 · US · Colour · 69mins

Disney's superb *True-Life Adventures* series closed with this awe-inspiring portrait of the South American jaguar. The result of over two years in the Brazilian rainforest, this is the nature documentary at its best, as a couple of jaguars meet, mate and teach their kittens about the harsh realities of life. However, it's not all encounters with crocodiles and boa constrictors, as narrator Winston Hibler guides us through a history of the cat and plenty of other Amazonian animals get their moment in the spotlight.

Winston Hibler *Narrator* ■ *Dir* James Algar

Jungle Fever ★★★ 18

Drama 1991 · US · Colour · 126mins

Spike Lee's take on inter-racial romance is typically controversial, but ultimately lacks the visceral power that he brought to *Do the Right Thing*. Successful architect Wesley Snipes falls for his white temp Annabella Sciorra and decides to leave his wife for her. However, their relationship sees them swiftly ostracised by their family and friends. Lee's direction is wonderfully fluid and, as in most of his movies, he is superbly served by the striking cinematography of Ernest Dickerson and strong lead performances. However, there is a glibness to his script, which does not delve fully into the reasons for the animosity they experience. Contains swearing, sex scenes, drug abuse and nudity. [video]

Wesley Snipes *Flipper Purify* • Annabella Sciorra *Angie Tucci* • Spike Lee *Cyrus* • Samuel L Jackson *Gator Purify* • Ossie Davis *The Good Reverend Doctor Purify* • Ruby Dee *Lucinda Purify* • Lonette McKee *Drew* • John Turturro *Paulie Carbone* • Anthony Quinn *Lou Carbone* • Frank Vincent *Mike Tucci* • Tim Robbins *Jerry* • Halle Berry *Vivian* • Brad Dourif *Leslie* ■ *Dir/Scr* Spike Lee • *Cinematographer* Ernest Dickerson

Jungle Gents ★★ U
Comedy   1954 · US · BW · 63mins

Another in the long running series of films featuring the Bowery Boys, a group of ageing New York urchins that themselves grew out of earlier film teams, namely the Dead End Kids and the East Side Kids. By 1954 the series (which had launched in 1946) was wearing thin and so were the plots. Here the gang go to Africa and overcome numerous obstacles before discovering a fortune in diamonds.

Leo Gorcey *Terrence Aloysius "Slip" Mahoney* • Huntz Hall *Horace Debussy "Sach" Jones* • Laurette Luez *Anatta* • Bernard Gorcey *Louie Dumbrowski* • David Condon [David Gorcey] *Chuck* • Bennie Bartlett *Butch* • Patrick O'Moore *Grimshaw* ■ *Dir* Edward Bernds • *Scr* Edward Bernds, Elwood Ullman

Jungle 2 Jungle ★★★ PG
Comedy adventure
1997 · US · Colour · 100mins

This junior version of *Crocodile Dundee* was another vehicle for *Home Improvement* star Tim Allen which failed to make much of dent on the UK market. Allen plays a New York financier who discovers he has a young teenage son (Sam Huntington) who has been brought up by an Amazonian tribe. The kid's arrival in New York is the cue for the usual "fish out of water" gags. It's an amiable but predictable affair, and Martin Short is wasted in a silly Russian Mafia subplot. ▭ DVD

Tim Allen *Michael* • Sam Huntington *Mimi-Siku* • JoBeth Williams *Patricia* • Lolita Davidovich *Charlotte* • Martin Short *Richard* • Valerie Mahaffey *Jan* • LeeLee Sobieski *Karen* ■ *Dir* John Pasquin • *Scr* Bruce A Evans, Raynold Gideon, from the film *Un Indien dans la ville* by Hervé Palud, Thierry Lhermitte, Igor Aptekman, Philippe Bruneau de la Salle

Junior ★★★ PG
Comedy   1994 · US · Colour · 105mins

A case of "we'll be back", as Arnold Schwarzenegger reunites with the *Twins* team of Danny DeVito and director Ivan Reitman for another comedy romp. Schwarzenegger and DeVito play struggling medical researchers working on a new fertility drug. When they lose their grant, in desperation Schwarzenegger injects himself with the experimental solution and, lo and behold, ends up pregnant. It's pretty much a one-joke concept, but Reitman milks it for all it's worth, and DeVito and Schwarzenegger look like they're having a ball. Only Emma Thompson as a fellow scientist and love interest looks out of place in an underwritten role. Contains some strong language. ▭ DVD

Arnold Schwarzenegger *Dr Alexander Hesse* • Danny DeVito *Dr Larry Arbogast* • Emma Thompson *Dr Diana Reddin* • Frank Langella *Noah Banes* • Pamela Reed *Angela* • Judy Collins *Naomi* ■ *Dir* Ivan Reitman • *Scr* Kevin Wade, Chris Conrad

Junior Bonner ★★★★ PG
Drama   1972 · US · Colour · 100mins

Sam Peckinpah was one of the most talented movie directors ever. He could be tough in *The Wild Bunch* and he could be tender in *The Ballad of Cable Hogue*. Peckinpah was happiest among

---

fellow professionals, and here he tells a tale of such a pro, the rodeo rider of the title, brilliantly played by Steve McQueen. As Junior tries to ride the unrideable, we watch his life pass by in the company of the superbly cast Robert Preston and Ida Lupino as his parents, and Joe Don Baker as his venal brother Curly. The Todd-AO widescreen compositions lose considerable impact on television, but the substance endures. ▭

Steve McQueen *Junior Bonner* • Ida Lupino *Elvira Bonner* • Robert Preston *Ace Bonner* • Joe Don Baker *Curly Bonner* • Ben Johnson *Buck Roan* • Barbara Leigh *Charmagne* • Mary Murphy *Ruth Bonner* • Bill McKinney *Red Terwiliger* ■ *Dir* Sam Peckinpah • *Scr* Jeb Rosebrook • *Cinematographer* Lucien Ballard

Junior Miss ★★★ U
Comedy   1945 · US · BW · 57mins

One of those early and distinctly jaunty generation gap family tales in which a lively teenager (Peggy Ann Garner) exhibits such wildly rebellious behaviour as staying out past nine o'clock and wearing a natty ensemble that daringly reveals her shoulders. It all looks mind-bogglingly innocent and somewhat priggish today, but Garner gives concerned dad Allyn Joslyn a few nasty turns along the way. An undemanding yet entertaining comedy derived from a hit Broadway play.

Peggy Ann Garner *Judy Graves* • Allyn Joslyn *Harry Graves* • Michael Dunne *Uncle Willis* • Faye Marlowe *Ellen Curtis* • Mona Freeman *Lois* • Sylvia Field *Grace Graves* ■ *Dir* George Seaton • *Scr* George Seaton, from the play by Jerome Chodorov, Joseph Fields

The Juniper Tree ★★★
Fantasy drama   1990 · US/Ice · BW · 80mins

This prize-winning film was inspired by a fairytale by the Brothers Grimm. For most viewers, the lure will be the chance to see Icelandic pop star, Björk, in a rare acting role. But there's a genuine fascination in the way writer/director Nietzcha Keene combines the grim realism of the desolate, monochrome landscape with the enchantment of her fantastical fable, in which Björk's sister Katla (Bryndis Petra Bragadottir) uses the witchcraft she learned from her mother to manipulate the emotions of a widowed farmer.

Björk [Björk Gudmundsdottir] *Margit* • Bryndis Petra Bragadottir *Katla* • Valdimar Örn Flygenring *Johann* • Gudrun Gisladottir *Mother* • Geirlaug Sunna Pormar *Jonas* ■ *Dir* Nietzchka Keene • *Scr* Nietzchka Keene, from a story by Wilhelm and Jacob Grimm

Junk Mail ★★★★ 15
Romantic comedy drama
1997 · Nor/Den · Colour · 80mins

With a central character who resembles a cross between Chaplin and Keaton, and deadpan humour reminiscent of Aki Kaurismäki, this comic hybrid is a delightfully offbeat accumulation of deft observations and sly coincidences. Robert Skjæestard is shambolically droll as the voyeuristic postman whose love for deaf blonde Andrine Sææther prompts him to become the scourge of the various bullies, slobs and thieves he encounters on his rounds. Pål Sletaune's debut feature is wonderfully

---

lean and controlled, restricting itself to a couple of achingly funny set-pieces. In Norwegian with English subtitles.

Robert Skjæzærstad *Roy Amundsen* • Andrine Sææether *Line Groberg* • Per Egil Aske *Georg Rheinhardsen* • Eli Anne Linnestad *Betsy* ■ *Dir* Pål Sletaune • *Scr* Pål Sletaune, Jonny Halberg

Juno and the Paycock ★★
Drama   1930 · UK · BW · 85mins

The constraints placed upon film-makers by the primitive nature of early sound recording equipment only partly explain Alfred Hitchcock's failure to transfer Sean O'Casey's celebrated play about the Irish Civil War successfully to the screen. Although an admirer of the material, which concerns an Irish family who think they have come into money, he found it stubbornly uncinematic and ended up staging the action in a calcified manner. However, Sara Allgood (who had also appeared in Hitch's *Blackmail*) excels as Juno Boyle, thus creating the mould for every forbidding Hitchcock mother to come.

Sara Allgood *Juno Boyle* • Edward Chapman *Capt John "Paycock" Boyle* • Sydney Morgan *Joxer Daly* • John Longden *Chris Bentham* • Kathleen O'Regan *Mary Boyle* • John Laurie *Johnny Boyle* ■ *Dir* Alfred Hitchcock • *Scr* Alfred Hitchcock, Alma Reville, from the play by Sean O'Casey

Junoon ★★★★ 15
Epic period drama
1978 · Ind · Colour · 121mins

This visually splendid epic drama sets a personal story of love and honour across racial and religious barriers against the historical backdrop of the Indian Mutiny. Shashi Kapoor's debut as a producer was billed as the first film to deal authentically with the Indian Mutiny. As the Pathan noble who rescues an Anglo-Indian widow (Jennifer Kendal) and her daughter (Nafisa Ali) from a terrorist attack, Kapoor gives a larger-than-life performance that somewhat undermines Shyam Benegal's otherwise naturalistic direction. But with Shabana Azmi outstanding as his betrayed wife, and the emotional melodrama intriguing both in itself and through its symbolism, this fact-based feature is always engrossing. In Urdu with English subtitles. ▭

Shashi Kapoor *Javed Khan* • Jennifer Kendal *Mariam Labadoor* • Nafisa Ali *Ruth Labadoor* • Shabana Azmi *Firdaus* • Naseeruddin Shah *Sarfraz Khan* • Kulbhushan Kharbanda *Ramjimal* • Tom Alter *Charles Labadoor* ■ *Dir/Scr* Shyam Benegal

Jupiter's Darling ★★★ U
Musical comedy   1955 · US · Colour · 96mins

An under-rated musical comedy about Hannibal and his elephants crossing the Alps to sack Rome, that's invariably confused in movie listings with Esther Williams's *Neptune's Daughter*. Williams is in her Amazonian prime here, as she lures Howard Keel's Hannibal away from the Eternal City, and the two stars are superb together. Other pleasures include George Sanders and Richard Haydn as very English patricians, and the wonderful Marge and Gower Champion,

---

who do a terrific song-and-dance number with painted elephants.

Esther Williams *Amytis* • Howard Keel *Hannibal* • Marge Champion *Meta* • Gower Champion *Varius* • George Sanders *Fabius Maximus* • Richard Haydn *Horatio* ■ *Dir* George Sidney • *Scr* Dorothy Kingsley, from the play *Road to Rome* by Robert Sherwood • *Music* David Rose • *Choreographer* Hermes Pan

Jurassic Park ★★★★★ PG
Adventure   1993 · US · Colour · 121mins

Steven Spielberg soared to new heights with this massively successful, electrifying adventure taken from Michael Crichton's bestseller. The world's ultimate theme park, featuring genetically re-created dinosaurs, is about to open and owner Richard Attenborough decides to give a sneak preview to a select few, including scientists Sam Neill and Laura Dern. However, all is not well in this new Garden of Eden and, in the jungle, the creatures are restless. T-Rex and his chums are the undoubted stars of the show and the mix of computer animation and models is truly inspiring. Spielberg orchestrates the action with effortless verve and, although it's a little too long and full of loose ends, only the most Scrooge-like viewer will fail to be transfixed by the thrilling action and the sheer scale of the director's vision. Contains strong language, and includes scenes that may be disturbing for children. ▭

Sam Neill *Dr Alan Grant* • Laura Dern *Dr Ellie Sattler* • Jeff Goldblum *Ian Malcolm* • Richard Attenborough *John Hammond* • Bob Peck *Robert Muldoon* • Martin Ferrero *Donald Gennaro* • BD Wong *Dr Wu* • Joseph Mazzello *Tim* • Ariana Richards *Lex* • Samuel L Jackson *Arnold* • Wayne Knight *Nedry* ■ *Dir* Steven Spielberg • *Scr* Michael Crichton, David Koepp, from the novel by Michael Crichton • *Cinematographer* Dean Cundey • *Visual Effects* Michael Lantieri, Dennis Muren, Phil Tippet, Stan Winston

The Juror ★★★ 18
Psychological thriller
1996 · US · Colour · 113mins

Based on the bestseller of the same name by George Dawes Green, this weak thriller has Demi Moore as the juror on a Mafia trial who is harassed, threatened and coerced by a mob henchman (Alec Baldwin) to hang the jury. Unfortunately Brian Gibson's film plods along predictably, with the only sparks of interest being the occasional utterly implausible plot twists. Still, thanks to the hilarious Baldwin, displaying more ham than a supermarket, it's marginally better than the similarly-themed *Trial by Jury* with Joanne Whalley-Kilmer, which was made two years before. ▭ DVD

Demi Moore *Annie Laird* • Alec Baldwin *The Teacher* • Joseph Gordon-Levitt *Oliver* • Anne Heche *Juliet* • James Gandolfini *Eddie* • Lindsay Crouse *Tallow* • Tony LoBianco *Louie Boffano* • Michael Constantine *Judge Weitzel* ■ *Dir* Brian Gibson • *Scr* Ted Tally, from the novel by George Dawes Green

Jury Duty ★★ 12
Comedy   1995 · US · Colour · 84mins

Pauly Shore has never enjoyed the sort of profile over here that he holds in the US, although this enjoyably crass

U = SUITABLE FOR ALL   Uc = SUITABLE FOR ALL, ESPECIALLY FOR YOUNG CHILDREN (VIDEO ONLY)   PG = PARENTAL GUIDANCE

comedy is one his better flicks. In another variation on his lazy-slacker persona, he plays a layabout who gets himself on jury service and proceeds to create havoc at a sensational murder trial. There are good supporting turns from Stanley Tucci and Brian Doyle-Murray, and director John Fortenberry has fun sending up the courtroom-drama genre. 🎦

Pauly Shore *Tommy* • Tia Carrere *Monica* • Stanley Tucci *Frank* • Brian Doyle-Murray *Harry* • Abe Vigoda *Judge Powell* • Charles Napier *Jed* • Richard Edson *Skeets* ■ *Dir* John Fortenberry • *Scr* Neil Tolkin, Barbara Williams, Samantha Adams, from a story by Barbara Williams, Samantha Adams

Just a Gigolo ★★ 15

Drama 1978 · W Ger · Colour · 88mins

Neither director David Hemmings nor a dream cast (Kim Novak, Maria Schell, Curt Jurgens) can do much with this lackadaisical look at how and why a disoriented Prussian war veteran become a gigolo in post-First World War Berlin. While this expensive West German production captures the disillusioned flavour of the era, its fragmented structure and an awkward performance from David Bowie in the lead leave much to be desired. Marlene Dietrich appears briefly to sing the title song; it was her last screen role. In English and German with subtitles. 🎦

David Bowie *Paul von Przygodsky* • Sydne Rome *Cilly* • Kim Novak *Helga* • David Hemmings *Captain Hermann Kraft* • Maria Schell *Mutti* • Curd Jürgens [Curt Jurgens] *Prince* • Marlene Dietrich *Baroness von Semering* ■ *Dir* David Hemmings • *Scr* Joshua Sinclair, Ennio De Concini

Just Another Girl on the IRT ★★★ 15

Drama 1992 · US · Colour · 97mins

Terrific slice-of-life stuff, by turns funny and sad, with Ariyan Johnson excellent as an ordinary New York high-school student who's determined to better herself, but whose plans get back-burnered when she gets pregnant. Leslie Harris directs his first feature with real sensitivity. To our knowledge, and inexplicably, he hasn't made one since. Incidentally, the film's title refers to the New York subway system.

Ariyan Johnson *Chantel* • Kevin Thigpen *Tyrone* • Ebony Jerido • Jerard Washington ■ *Dir/Scr* Leslie Harris

Just around the Corner ★★

Musical 1938 · US · BW · 70mins

Shirley Temple finds work for her architect father after befriending an eccentric old millionaire in this Depression-era fable directed by Irving Cummings. The little trouper was growing up and being given excessively mature dialogue, losing much of her bubbly charm. But she sings and dances with Bill Robinson for the fourth and last time, and that's pure magic. Joan Davis and Bert Lahr lend strong support.

Shirley Temple *Penny Hale* • Charles Farrell *Jeff Hale* • Joan Davis *Kitty* • Amanda Duff *Lola* • Bill Robinson *Corp Jones* • Bert Lahr *Gus* • Franklin Pangborn *Waters* • Cora Witherspoon *Aunt Julia Ramsby* • Claude Gillingwater Sr [Claude Gillingwater] *Samuel G*

Henshaw ■ *Dir* Irving Cummings • *Scr* Ethel Hill, JP Mcevoy, Darrell Ware, from the novel *The Lucky Penny* by Paul Gerard Smith

Just Ask for Diamond ★★★ U

Detective spoof 1988 · UK · Colour · 89mins

Perhaps alert to the criticism of product placement, the original title of Anthony Horowitz's novel, *The Falcon's Malteser*, was dropped. Pity. For it gives some clues about what this whimsical take on *The Maltese Falcon* is trying to do – have fun. With characters such as the Fat Man and Lauren Bacardi to deal with, London-based private eye Tim Diamond (Dursley McLinden) and younger brother Nick (Colin Dale) get involved in a gem-quest which is as unsophisticated as it is endearing. Susannah York is a seductively sozzled siren and cameraman Billy Williams makes it ominous enough to indulge any youngster's fancy for mystery. 🎦

Dursley McLinden *Tim Diamond* • Colin Dale *Nick Diamond* • Susannah York *Lauren Bacardi* • Patricia Hodge *Brenda Von Falkenberg* • Michael Robbins *The Fat Man* • Roy Kinnear *Jack Splendide* • Jimmy Nail *Boyle* • Bill Paterson *Chief Inspector Snape* ■ *Dir* Stephen Bayly • *Scr* Anthony Horowitz, from his novel *The Falcon's Malteser*

Just before Dawn ★★★ 18

Horror 1980 · US · Colour · 86mins

This slasher, about a group of urban hikers sharing the Oregon wilderness with machete-wielding mountain men, is very similar to *Don't Go in the Woods*, made the same year. But this is the better film, both derivative of *The Hills Have Eyes* and almost certainly an inspiration for *The Blair Witch Project*. Director Jeff Lieberman engineers a relentless build-up of suspense, culminating in an outrageous twist near the film's end. Actor Jack Lemmon's son, Chris, stars as one of the teenagers who ignore the warnings of forest ranger George Kennedy to not venture further. Haven't any of these people seen *Deliverance*? 🎦

George Kennedy *Roy McLean* • Mike Kellin *Ty* • Chris Lemmon *Jonathan* • Gregg Henry *Warren* • Deborah Benson *Constance* • Ralph Seymour *Daniel* ■ *Dir* Jeff Lieberman • *Scr* Mark Arywitz, Gregg Irving, from a story by Joseph Middleton

Just between Friends ★★★ 15

Drama 1986 · US · Colour · 106mins

Like that other sixties' TV sitcom star Sally Field, Mary Tyler Moore moved in more serious circles in the eighties and this moving drama certainly gave her a role to get her teeth into. She plays a bored California housewife, seemingly happily married to Ted Danson, whose life is turned on its head when she discovers that her husband has been cheating on her for years. Moore is good in the lead role, although the film is stolen by Christine Lahti, who is terrific as the other woman in a melodrama that packs a punch. Contains swearing. 🎦

Wendy Craig *Scilla Alexander* • Francis Matthews *Lewis McKenzie* • John Wood *John Martin* • Dennis Price *Bathroom salesman* • Miriam Karlin *Ellen Newman* • Peter Jones *Saul Alexander* • Clive Dunn *Graff Von Fischer* ■ *Dir/Scr* Robert Fuest

Mary Tyler Moore *Holly Davis* • Ted Danson *Chip Davis* • Christine Lahti *Sandy Dunlap* • Sam Waterston *Harry Crandall* • Susan Rinell *Kim Davis* ■ *Dir/Scr* Allan Burns

Just Cause ★★★ 18

Thriller 1995 · US · Colour · 97mins

Sean Connery's screen persona is now so well established that he's completely plausible as a retired lawyer seeking justice in deepest Florida. He is as charismatic as ever in a story that, though a little uneven at times, manages some pleasing twists on the usual formula. Connery is called in to help Blair Underwood, who claims he has been wrongly convicted of the murder of a young child, partly because local cop Laurence Fishburne beat a confession out of him. Director Arne Glimcher throws in enough red herrings to keep viewers guessing right to the end and makes good use of the Everglades locations. Contains swearing and violence. 🎦

Sean Connery *Paul Armstrong* • Laurence Fishburne *Tanny Brown* • Kate Capshaw *Laurie Armstrong* • Blair Underwood *Bobby Earl* • Ed Harris *Blair Sullivan* • Christopher Murray *Wilcox* • Daniel J Travanti *Warden* • Ned Beatty *McNair* ■ *Dir* Arne Glimcher • *Scr* Jeb Stuart, Peter Stone, from the novel by John Katzenbach

Just for You ★★★ U

Musical comedy 1952 · US · Colour · 104mins

Bing Crosby and Jane Wyman, who made such an agreeable duo in Frank Capra's *Here Comes the Groom* (1951), were teamed up again rather less successfully in this tale of Broadway producer Bing, who ignores his teenage children (Natalie Wood, Robert Arthur) until Jane puts him right. Ethel Barrymore is perfect as the headmistress of snooty girl's school, and Bing sings a lively Harry Warren/Leo Robin song, *Zing a Little Zong*.

Bing Crosby *Jordan Blake* • Jane Wyman *Carolina Hill* • Ethel Barrymore *Allida de Bronkhart* • Robert Arthur *Jerry Blake* • Natalie Wood *Barbara Blake* • Cora Witherspoon *Mrs Angevine* ■ *Dir* Elliott Nugent • *Scr* Robert Carson, from the novel *Famous* by Stephen Vincent Benet • *Music/Lyrics* Harry Warren, Leo Robin

Just like a Woman ★★

Comedy 1966 · UK · Colour · 89mins

With an adaptation of *Wuthering Heights*, two *Dr Phibes* horror movies and the cult TV series *The Avengers* on his résumé, director Robert Fuest can never be accused of playing safe. He made his feature debut with this sixties satire about a housewife (Wendy Craig) who rebels against her TV director husband (Francis Matthews). Craig here reveals the comic flair that enabled her to become the epitome of scatty domesticity in sitcoms like *Not in Front of the Children* and *Butterflies*. Fuest's script strives too hard to be offbeat, however, notably in the creation of a goose-stepping interior designer.

Just like a Woman ★ 15

Comedy 1992 · UK · Colour · 101mins

Julie Walters is good value, as always, but this comedy drama about transvestism is pretty worthless otherwise. Who is it aimed at? Closet cross-dressers? The prurient? Ed Wood fanatics? Hard to tell, as it lurches from frilly farce to black-lace banality with sickly sentiment piled as high as the heels. Adrian Pasdar looks as uncomfortable playing Gerald/Geraldine, as you will be watching this curious frock opera that's as emotionally fake as his falsies. 🎦

Julie Walters *Monica* • Adrian Pasdar *Gerald* • Paul Freeman *Miles Millichamp* • Susan Wooldridge *Louisa* • Gordon Kennedy *CJ* ■ *Dir* Christopher Monger • *Scr* Nick Evans, from the book *Geraldine, for the Love of a Transvestite* by Monica Jay

Just like Dad ★

Comedy drama 1996 · US · Colour · 102mins

In this sentimental made-for-TV family movie, Ben Diskin plays a boy embarrassed by his short, balding dad (Woody Allen regular Wallace Shawn, who really should know better). When the kid meets the good-looking, athletic Nick Cassavetes, he convinces him to be his surrogate father at school. You can probably guess the mushy ending.

Nick Cassavetes *Joe* • Wallace Shawn *Stan* • Ben Diskin *Charlie* • Laura Innes *Rose* • Michael Tucci *Joe* • Jarrett Lennon *Sherwood* • George Fisher *Mole* ■ *Dir* Blair Treu • *Scr* Wayne Allan Rice

Just Me and You ★★

Romantic comedy 1978 · US · Colour · 100mins

Louise Lasser is probably best known in this country for once being Mrs Woody Allen, but after her divorce from Allen she became the star of several successful American TV series, including *Mary Hartman, Mary Hartman* and *It's a Living*. Here she takes a typically kooky role in an amiable, but rather self-indulgent, TV movie. That she is perfect for the part is hardly surprising, as she scripted the story of a New Yorker who comes to re-evaluate her life en route to visiting her beloved. Lasser's loathe-at-first-sight relationship with travelling companion Charles Grodin takes a while to spark, but they play off each other nicely once they discover just how much they have in common.

Louise Lasser *Jane Alofsin* • Charles Grodin *Michael Lindsay* • Julie Bovasso *Waitress* • Paul Fix *Old man* • Michael Alldredge *Max* ■ *Dir* John Erman • *Scr* Louise Lasser

Just My Luck ★★ U

Comedy 1957 · UK · BW · 82mins

This horse-racing comedy is not a particularly distinguished Norman Wisdom movie, but a pleasant enough time-waster nonetheless. On its original release, Rank realised the film's weaknesses and shored it up with a rock 'n' roll supporting feature. Today it's a brave viewer (or a devout fan of Wisdom) who'll watch, for the star's mawkish side is virtually given free rein as he tries to win enough money to buy a gift for Jill Dixon. If you can't stand Wisdom, there are British comedy stalwarts such as Margaret Rutherford, Leslie Phillips and Joan Sims on call, and fifties nostalgia freaks will enjoy spotting Sabrina – you can't miss her! 🖵

Norman Wisdom *Norman* • Margaret Rutherford *Mrs Dooley* • Jill Dixon *Anne* • Leslie Phillips *Hon Richard Lumb* • Delphi Lawrence *Miss Daviot* • Edward Chapman *Mr Stoneway* • Marjorie Rhodes *Mrs Hackett* • Joan Sims *Phoebe* ■ *Dir* John Paddy Carstairs • *Scr* Alfred Shaughnessy, Peter Blackmore

Just One of the Girls ★ 15

Comedy   1993 · Can · Colour · 90mins

Corey Haim, who has featured in more straight-to-video movies than most actors would consider advisable, stars in this lame high-school version of *Tootsie*, also known as *Anything for Love*. To escape the bullies, Chris (Haim) dresses up as a girl and finds, to his joy, it's a game he rather enjoys – especially as it involves spending time in the girls' changing rooms. Teenage twaddle. 🖵

Corey Haim *Chris/Chrissy Calder* • Nicole Eggert *Marie Stark* • Cameron Bancroft *Kurt Stark* • Johannah Newmarch *Julie Calder* • Kevin McNulty *Louis Calder* ■ *Dir* Michael Keusch • *Scr* Raul Fernandez

Just One of the Guys ★★★ 15

Comedy   1985 · US · Colour · 96mins

Energetic comedy, sort of *Tootsie* after a sex-change, about a pretty high-school student who's convinced that her good looks have kept sexist male teachers from backing her entry in a citywide journalism competition. So she cross-dresses as a boy, and tries again at another school. The premise is slight and strained, but quirky performances elevate this above the ordinary. Watch out for small roles for Sherilyn Fenn and Arye Gross. 🖵

Joyce Hyser *Terry* • Clayton Rohner *Rick* • Billy Jacoby *Buddy* • William Zabka *Greg* • Toni Hudson *Denise* • Sherilyn Fenn *Sandy* • Deborah Goodrich *Deborah* • Arye Gross *Willie* ■ *Dir* Lisa Gottlieb • *Scr* Dennis Feldman, Jeff Franklin, from a story by Dennis Feldman

Just Tell Me What You Want ★★★

Comedy   1980 · US · Colour · 112mins

Alan King plays spoilt and strident millionaire Max Herschel in this Sidney Lumet directed comedy. Married King is dallying with his longstanding mistress Ali MacGraw but failing to commit. Not surprisingly, MacGraw seeks solace with toy boy Peter Weller, prompting King to realise that he really really wants her. Adapted by Jay Presson Allen from her novel, this is a romantic comedy with an edge. King's performance has great gusto and watch out for Myrna Loy in her last and very notable performance as his long-suffering personal assistant.

Ali MacGraw *Bones Burton* • Alan King *Max Herschel* • Myrna Loy *Stella Liberti* • Keenan Wynn *Seymour Berger* • Tony Roberts *Mike Berger* • Peter Weller *Steven Routledge* ■ *Dir* Sidney Lumet • *Scr* Jay Presson Allen, from her novel

Just the Ticket ★★ 15

Romantic comedy drama
1998 · US · Colour · 110mins

The combination of star Andy Garcia and a script from director Richard Wenk that was ten years in the making should guarantee an interesting film. But, sadly, this is a lacklustre affair. How can a tale of a ticket tout selling illegal entry to the Pope's New York visit in order to retire and save his relationship really get the juices flowing? Well, in all honesty, it can't. Garcia is all Italian-stallion charm to caterer girlfriend Andie MacDowell's southern kookiness but, acceptable performances aside, rip-roaring romantic comedy this is not. Contains swearing. 🖵

Andy Garcia *Gary Starke* • Andie MacDowell *Linda Paliski* • Richard Bradford *Benny Moran* • Fred Asparagus *Zeus* • Elizabeth Ashley *Mrs Paliski* • AndréB Blake *Casino* • Ron Leibman *Barry the Book* ■ *Dir/Scr* Richard Wenk

Just the Way You Are ★★ PG

Romantic comedy
1984 · US · Colour · 90mins

Offbeat, if a little slushy, comedy drama, in which Kristy McNichol plays a young woman who wears a leg brace following a childhood bout of polio. She hides her disability with a plaster cast on a skiing holiday in Europe and, while there, falls for Michael Ontkean (in his pre-*Twin Peaks* days), but will he still love her when he discovers that she has more than a broken leg? It could have turned out to be quite a sob story, but, although the disparate elements don't quite meld together, it's nicely played by the cast. 🖵

Kristy McNichol *Susan Berlanger* • Michael Ontkean *Peter Nichols* • Kaki Hunter *Lisa* • André Dussollier *François* • Catherine Salviat *Nicole* • Robert Carradine *Sam Carpenter* • Alexandra Paul *Bobbie* ■ *Dir* Edouard Molinaro • *Scr* Allan Burns

Just Us ★★★

Biographical drama
1986 · Ausl · Colour · 95mins

A sincere, accomplished, but distinctly one-sided look at love across the prison grill. Australian journalist Gabrielle Carey, here renamed Jessica Taylor, and nicely played by Catherine McClements, wrote the original material based on her passionately felt, but ultimately doomed, affair with long-term prisoner Terry Haley (called Billy Carter in the movie). This is a gripping, pacily written, complex tale, marred only by a naivety of intent and the whiff of whitewash covering the convicted rapist's character.

Catherine McClements *Jessica Taylor* • Scott Burgess *Billy Carter* • Merfyn Owen • Gina Riley • Jay Mannering • Kim Gyngell ■ *Dir* Gordon Glenn • *Scr* Ted Roberts from the book by Gabrielle Carey

Just William ★★ U

Comedy   1939 · UK · BW · 74mins

Richmal Crompton's tousled terror made his screen debut in the excitable form of Dicky Lupino in this hectic adventure, co-written and directed by Graham Cutts, one of Britain's finest silent directors. Although he gets up to lots of mischief, William spends too much time on the trail of a conman

and helping his father secure a seat on the council to be particularly funny. Lupino (the youngest member of that multi-talented showbiz family) hurtles around at full pelt, so it's left to Roddy McDowall to do the real acting as the hero's put-upon pal, Ginger.

Dicky Lupino *William Brown* • Fred Emney *Mr Brown* • Basil Radford *Mr Sidway* • Amy Veness *Mrs Bott* • Iris Hoey *Mrs Brown* • Roddy McDowall *Ginger* • Jenny Laird *Ethel Brown* • David Tree *Marmaduke Bott* ■ *Dir* Graham Cutts • *Scr* Doreen Montgomery, Ireland Wood, Graham Cutts, from the stories by Richmal Crompton

Just William's Luck ★★ U

Comedy   1947 · UK · BW · 92mins

Having concluded they need bikes to emulate the heroics of the Knights of the Round Table, William and his outlaws decide to marry off their older brothers and inherit their cast-off cycles. First, though, they must attend to the small matter of fur smugglers operating out of a supposedly haunted house. While William Graham captures something of the scruffy boisterousness of Richmal Crompton's timeless comic creation, director Val Guest's screenplay smoothes away the rougher edges to produce a sanitised tale of childhood mayhem.

William Graham *William Brown* • Garry Marsh *Mr Brown* • Jane Welsh *Mrs Brown* • Hugh Cross *Robert Brown* • Kathleen Stuart *Ethel Brown* • Leslie Bradley *Boss* • AE Matthews *Tramp* • Brian Roper *Ginger* • Audrey Manning *Violet Elizabeth Bott* ■ *Dir* Val Guest • *Scr* Val Guest, from the stories by Richmal Crompton

Just You and Me, Kid ★

Comedy   1979 · US · Colour · 94mins

Not even the pleasure of seeing George Burns trading wisecracks over a game of cards with fellow old-stagers Ray Bolger and Leon Ames can enliven this crass age-gap comedy. If only he'd spent more time with them and less with Brooke Shields, the runaway he discovers naked in the boot of his car after she goes on the run from a drug dealer. There is absolutely no spark between the leads, with his knowing drawl and her eager cuteness clashing in every exchange. Even less amusing is Burl Ives's demonstration of catatonia. Eminently missable.

George Burns *Bill* • Brooke Shields *Kate* • Burl Ives *Max* • Lorraine Gary *Shirl* • Nicolas Coster *Harris* • Keye Luke *Dr Device* ■ *Dir* Leonard B Stern • *Scr* Oliver Hailey, from a story by Tom Lazarus, Leonard B Stern

Juste avant la Nuit ★★★★

Thriller   1971 · Fr/It · Colour · 106mins

Claude Chabrol follows *La Femme Infidèle* and *Le Boucher* with another masterly thriller, in which Stéphane Audran (Mrs Chabrol) refuses to believe her husband – creepy Michel Bouquet – has intentionally murdered his mistress. The latter just happened to be married to their best friend; surely, Audran thinks, it was an accident? This little parable about guilt and bourgeois morality in the provinces amounts to as much or as little as you want to read into it. But few could resist the elegant way in which Chabrol tells the story or the immaculate acting of the cast. A French language film.

Michel Bouquet *Charles* • Stéphane Audran *Helen* • François Périer *François* • Dominique Zardi *Prince* • Henri Attal *Cavanna* ■ *Dir* Claude Chabrol • *Scr* Claude Chabrol, from the novel *The Thin Line* by Edouard Atiyah

Justice Denied ★★★

Drama based on a true story
1989 · Can · Colour

Restrained direction lends added force to this compelling TV dramatisation of a true-life miscarriage of justice, which resulted in a young Canadian Indian serving 11 years in prison for a murder he didn't commit. Billy Merasty does particularly well as the unjustly convicted Micmac Indian youth, while the latter's real-life parents play themselves on the screen. Filming was done in the actual Nova Scotia jail where he served time.

Billy Merasty *Donald Marshall Jr* • Thomas Peacocke *John MacIntyre* • Wayne Robson *Roy Ebsary* • Peter MacNeill *Sergeant Wheaton* • J Winston Carroll *Corporal Jim Carroll* • Steve Marshall *Maynard Chant* • Vincent Murray *John Pratico* • Ron White *Donald C MacNeil QC* • Caroline Marshall • Donald Marshall Sr ■ *Dir* Paul Cowan

Justin Case ★★ PG

Comedy thriller   1988 · US · Colour · 70mins

As his mid-life-crisis comedies continued to fall foul of the critics, Blake Edwards fared little better with this TV movie, concocted with his daughter Jennifer. The scenario, in which a ghost detective persuaded an actress to uncover his murderer, bears more than a passing resemblance to *Randall and Hopkirk (Deceased)*, which is the film's superior in every way. Whereas in the *Pink Panther* pictures the crime was almost an irrelevance, here it is crucial, but Edwards develops the plot with little guile. 🖵

Molly Hagan *Jennifer Spalding* • George Carlin *Justin Case* • Douglas Sills *David Porter* • Gordon Jump *Sheldon Wannamaker* • Timothy Stack *Detective Swan* ■ *Dir* Blake Edwards • *Scr* Blake Edwards, from a story by Blake Edwards, Jennifer Edwards

Justine ★ 15

Drama   1969 · US · Colour · 111mins

A catastrophic attempt to condense the four novels of Lawrence Durrell's celebrated *Alexandria Quartet* into a single film results in a messy farrago. Told in flashback by Justine's lover Darley (Michael York) it focuses on the influence and sexual exploits of the mysterious and beautiful Egyptian Jewess, played by French actress Anouk Aimée, who, with her banker husband, plans to send military aid to Palestine's Jews. It attempts to beef up the proceedings with sexual decadence, an international cast and some exotic atmosphere captured on location in Tunisia by cinematographer Leon Shamroy. Nothing helps, however – certainly not the inappropriate choice of George Cukor to take over the direction from Joseph Strick. 🖵

Anouk Aimée *Justine* • Dirk Bogarde *Pursewarden* • Robert Forster *Narouz* • Anna Karina *Melissa* • Philippe Noiret *Pombal* • Michael York *Darley* • George Baker *Mountolive* ■ *Dir* George Cukor • *Scr* Lawrence B Marcus, from the novels *The Alexandria Quartet* by Lawrence Durrell

K-9 ★★ 15
Crime comedy 1989 · US · Colour · 97mins

Hollywood, desperately looking for new variations on the mismatched-cops scenario, briefly lit upon the concept of the buddy-doggy movie. Fortunately for non-dog lovers, it was a genre that proved to have as much staying power as some Christmas puppies. This one, produced in the same year as the Tom Hanks comedy *Turner and Hooch*, has James Belushi as the detective who is reluctantly partnered with a surly canine in a bid to crack a drug smuggling ring. Belushi is as affable as ever, but even he looks a little embarrassed by the affair, particularly the mawkish ending. Contains swearing and violence.

James Belushi *Thomas Dooley* • Mel Harris *Tracy* • Kevin Tighe *Lyman* • Ed O'Neill *Lt Brannigan* • James Handy *Lt Byers* • Daniel Davis *Halstead* • Cotter Smith *Gilliam* • John Snyder *Freddie* ■ *Dir* Rod Daniel • *Scr* Steven Siegel, Scott Myers

K2 ★★★ 15
Drama 1991 · US · Colour · 105mins

Michael Biehn has never had the breaks he deserves, even though he remains as charismatic as ever, as this climbing epic demonstrates. Here he is perfectly cast as a brash lawyer who lives life on the edge through his passion for mountaineering. Adapted from co-writer Patrick Meyers's own play, this is largely *Boys' Own* stuff, with character development taking second place to macho heroics and bonding. However, director Franc Roddam responds by staging one exhilarating cliffside set piece after another, including a breathtaking avalanche sequence. Despite the strong performances from the cast, the spectacular snow-covered surroundings are the real stars of the show. Contains swearing and brief nudity.

Michael Biehn *Taylor Brooks* • Matt Craven *Harold Jamieson* • Raymond J Barry *Phillip Claiborne* • Hiroshi Fujioka *Takane Shimuzu* • Luca Bercovici *Dallas Woolf* • Patricia Charbonneau *Jacki Metcalfe* • Julia Nickson-Soul *Cindy* • Jamal Shah *Malik* • Annie Grindlay *Lisa* • Elena Stiteler *Tracey* ■ *Dir* Franc Roddam • *Scr* Patrick Meyers, Scott Roberts, from the play by Patrick Meyers

Kaagaz Ke Phool ★★★★ U
Drama 1959 · Ind · BW · 139mins

Echoes of *Citizen Kane* and *A Star Is Born* ring around this Bollywood classic (the subcontinent's first in CinemaScope), which flopped on its original release. Guru Dutt excels as the director whose fortunes plummet after his star discovery, Waheeda Rehman, quits to avoid hurtful gossip. In his second role as this film's director, he also imbues the drama with a visual eloquence that conveys the "neverland" atmosphere of the movies, without losing sight of the human frailty afflicting even the most successful artists. Stylishly composed by Dutt and cinematographer VK Murthy, this is a surprisingly intimate tale, considering its scale and ambition. In Hindi with English subtitles.

Guru Dutt *Suresh Sinha* • Waheeda Rehman *Shanti* • Baby Naaz *Pummy* • Johnny Walker *Brother-in-law* • Mahesh Kaul *Father-in-law* ■ *Dir* Guru Dutt • *Scr* Abrar Alvi • *Cinematographer* VK Murthy

Kabhi Kabhie ★★ U
Romantic drama
1976 · Ind · Colour · 166mins

Director Yash Chopra is famed for introducing the psychopathic hero into Indian cinema in *Darr* (1993). Here, however, he is on more traditional ground with a "masala melodrama" about arranged marriage set among the privileged classes: essentially a soap opera with a more-than-usually contrived plot and only a superficial discussion of its social and cultural themes. Amitabh Bachchan takes top billing, only to be upstaged by co-star Shashi Kapoor. In Hindi and Urdu with English subtitles. **DVD**

Amitabh Bachchan *Amit* • Raakhee Gulzar *Pooja* • Shashi Kapoor • Waheeda Rehman • Neetu Singh • Rishi Kapoor ■ *Dir* Yash Chopra • *Scr* Yash Chopra, Sagar Sarhadi

Kadosh ★★★★
Drama 1999 · Is/Fr · Colour · 116mins

As if the assault on the patriarchal nature of Hassidic Judaism wasn't controversial enough, Israeli director Amos Gitai chose an Arab (Yussef Abu Warda) to play the rabbi in this compelling Jerusalem-based drama. Indeed, Gitai compounds his audacity by viewing events from the perspective of his female protagonists. He remains studiously detached in depicting how Meital Barda refuses an arranged marriage, while her childless sister (Yael Abecassis) steps aside so her husband of ten years (Yoram Hattab) can obey the rabbinical dictate that she remarry to further his line. This is intelligently scripted, powerfully played and subtle in its subversion. In Hebrew with English subtitles.

Yael Abecassis *Rivka* • Yoram Hattab *Meir* • Meital Barda *Malka* • Uri Ran Klauzner *Yossef* • Yussef Abu Warda *Rav Shimon* • Sami Hori *Yaakov* • Lea Koenig *Elisheva* • Rivka Michaeli *Gynaecologist* ■ *Dir* Amos Gitai • *Scr* Amos Gitai, Eliette Abecassis, Jacky Cukier

Kafka ★★★ 15
Psychological thriller
1991 · US/Fr · BW and Colour · 94mins

Barely released in this country, Steven Soderbergh's follow-up to *sex, lies, and videotape* is a far cry from that auspicious debut. Yet, with its stylish references to German Expressionism and the great Universal horror films of the thirties, this fantasy on the life of the Czech insurance-clerk-turned-novellist is possibly even bolder and more imaginative. Jeremy Irons might not be everyone's first choice for the title role, but he acquits himself admirably in what is essentially a loose reworking of *The Third Man*. Alec Guinness and Ian Holm stand out in a splendid supporting cast, but the true stars are cinematographer Walt Lloyd and Gavin Bocquet's art department. Contains some violence.

Jeremy Irons *Kafka* • Theresa Russell *Gabriela Rossman* • Joel Grey *Burgel* • Ian Holm *Dr Murnau* • Jeroen Krabbé *Bizzlebek* • Armin Mueller-Stahl *Inspector Grubach* • Alec Guinness *Chief Clerk* • Brian Glover *Castle Henchman* • Keith Allen *Assistant Ludwig* ■ *Dir* Steven Soderbergh • *Scr* Lem Dobbs

Kagemusha ★★★★ PG
Period drama 1980 · Jap · Colour · 152mins

Returning to direction after a five-year lay-off, the 70-year-old Akira Kurosawa proved that none of his powers had diminished with this sprawling, almost Shakespearean tale of court intrigue. Set during the civil wars of the 16th century, this is the most expensive picture ever made in Japan and won the Palme d'Or at Cannes. Admittedly, it could stand some judicious cutting, and one or two of the set pieces smack of scale for spectacle's sake. But Tatsuya Nakadai is outstanding as the thief who becomes a puppet ruler, while Kurosawa's use of colour and his camera control are faultless. In Japanese with English subtitles.

Tatsuya Nakadai *Shingen Takeda/Kagemusha* • Tsutomu Yamazaki *Nobukado Takeda* • Kenichi Hagiwara *Katsuyori Takeda* • Kota Yui *Takemaru Takeda* • Hideji Otaki *Masakage Yamagata* ■ *Dir* Akira Kurosawa • *Scr* Akira Kurosawa, Masato Ide

Kaleidoscope ★★★ U
Crime comedy drama
1966 · UK · Colour · 102mins

This sixties' caper is so swinging it almost comes off its hinges. Warren Beatty, not exactly renowned at the time for his monkish life style, is strangely unconvincing as the cardsharp who literally marks winning cards, while hip chick Susannah York keeps his libido on the boil. The movie manages to defy its dated trendiness with the sheer esprit of performances from the villainous Eric Porter, and eccentric Clive Revill as a Scotland Yard inspector who really should be up on a charge himself – for scene-stealing. Director Jack Smight's style overcomes the lack of substance, though it's still not a patch on his *No Way to Treat a Lady* with Rod Steiger, a couple of years later.

Warren Beatty *Barney Lincoln* • Susannah York *Angel McGinnis* • Eric Porter *Harry Dominion* • Clive Revill *Inspector "Manny" McGinnis* • Murray Melvin *Aimes* • George Sewell *Billy* • Anthony Newlands *Leeds* • Jane Birkin *Exquisite Thing* ■ *Dir* Jack Smight • *Scr* Robert Carrington, Jane Howard Carrington

Kaleidoscope ★★ 15
Melodrama 1990 · US · Colour · 89mins

Although film adaptations often disappoint, Danielle Steel fans need not worry, for this tense TV movie misses none of the author's melodramatic tricks as three sisters, parted on the horrific deaths of their parents, reunite to discover they not only have little in common, but also have dark secrets to hide. Jaclyn Smith might not be Joan Crawford or Barbara Stanwyck, but she suffers in style as the sibling scarred by hardship.

Jaclyn Smith *Hilary Walker* • Perry King *John Chapman* • Patricia Kalember *Alexandra* • Claudia Christian *Meagan Kincaide* • Donald Moffat *Arthur* • Colleen Dewhurst *Margaret Gorham* ■ *Dir* Jud Taylor • *Scr* Karol Ann Hoeffner, from the novel by Danielle Steel

Kalifornia ★★ 18
Psychological thriller
1993 · US · Colour · 113mins

The X Files star David Duchovny is the writer researching serial killers for a book, and he and his photographer girlfriend unwittingly pick up two likely suspects as they travel from Kentucky to California in this so-so psycho-teen road movie. A slow start builds to an explosive climax, with Brad Pitt doing his mentally unbalanced act rather well, equally matched by Juliette Lewis as his childlike trailer-trash sweetheart. While director Dominic Sena promises much, he fails to deliver anything other than empty attitude and annoying posturing. Contains violence, swearing and sex scenes. **DVD**

Juliette Lewis *Adele Corners* • Brad Pitt *Early Grayce* • David Duchovny *Brian Kessler* • Michelle Forbes *Carrie Laughlin* • Sierra Pecheur *Mrs Musgrave* • Gregory Mars Martin *Walter Livesay* • David Milford *Driver* • Marisa Raper *Little girl* • Catherine Larson *Teenage girl* ■ *Dir* Dominic Sena • *Scr* Tim Metcalfe, from the story by Stephen Levy

Kama Sutra: a Tale of Love ★★★ 18
Erotic drama
1996 · Ind/UK/Jap/Ger · Colour · 109mins

Nothing to do with the manual depicting sexual positions, "Kama Sutra" actually translates as "love lessons", and that's what princess Sarita Choudhury and royal servant girl Indira Varma learn in director Mira Nair's lavish historical romance. Varma's "sexual treachery" with Choudhury's betrothed, Naveen Andrews, gets her banished from court and puts her on the road to erotic self-awareness in a complex story mixing the mystical with the psychological. Oddly affecting, beautifully filmed and scored, with an intense performance from Varma, Nair's emotional epic is a class act. Contains violence, swearing, sex scenes and nudity.

Naveen Andrews *Raj Singh* • Sarita Choudhury *Tara* • Ramon Tikaram *Jai Kumar* • Rekha *Rasa Devi* • Indira Varma *Maya* • Pearl Padamsee *Maham Anga* • Arundhati Rao *Annabi* ■ *Dir* Mira Nair • *Scr* Helena Kriel, Mira Nair • *Cinematographer* Declan Quinn • *Music* Mychael Danna

Kameradschaft ★★★★★
Drama 1931 · Ger/Fr · BW · 83mins

A masterpiece of studio realism and an optimistic plea for peaceful co-existence, this is one of the few social tracts of the early sound era to retain its power in this more cynical age. Based on a 1906 mining disaster (although set in the immediate aftermath of the First World War), the story of the German workers who break through artificial national boundaries to rescue their French comrades is loaded with idealistic symbolism. But, thanks to director GW Pabst's ingenious use of light and montage, it

---

12 **15** **18** = PASSED FOR PEOPLE OF THESE AGES AND OVER = RELEASED ON VIDEO **DVD** = RELEASED ON DVD

is also full of striking images designed to highlight the fragility of humanity and the futility of conflict. In German and French with English subtitles.

Alexander Granach *Kaspar* • Fritz Kampers *Wilderer* • Daniel Mendaille *Pierre* • Ernst Busch *Kaplan* • Elisabeth Wendt *Françoise* • Gustav Püttjer *Jean* • Oskar Höcker *Emile* ■ *Dir* GW Pabst • *Scr* Ladislaus Vajda, Peter Martin Lampel, Karl Otten, Fritz Eckardt, from a story by Karl Otten • *Cinematographer* Fritz Arno Wagner, Robert Baberske

Kamikaze ★★★ 15
Satirical drama   1986 · Fr · Colour · 88mins

Produced and co-written by Luc Besson (*Subway*, *The Big Blue*), this is a classic example of the style of French films dubbed *cinéma du look* on account of their flashy visuals and throwaway narratives. Directed by Besson's former assistant Didier Grousset, it boasts a wonderfully over-the-top central performance from Michel Galabru as a mad scientist who invents a death ray that can zap anyone he takes a dislike to while watching TV – without leaving a single clue as to the killer's identity. Great idea, but there is really only enough material in this satire on couch-potato culture for a razor-sharp sketch. In French with English subtitles.

Richard Bohringer *Detective Romain* • Michel Galabru *Albert* • Dominique Lavanant *Laure Frontenac* • Riton Leibman *Olive* • Kim Massee *Léa* • Harry Cleven *Patrick* • Romane Bohringer *Julie* ■ *Dir* Didier Grousset • *Scr* Luc Besson, Didier Grousset, Michèle Halberstadt

Kamikaze 1989 ★★
Fantasy thriller
1983 · W Ger · Colour · 106mins

In the last major acting role of his eclectic career, Rainer Werner Fassbinder imbues the boozy, world-weary detective Jansen with a love of the law and a loathing of its guardians. These characteristics go some way to explaining both his zealous pursuit of the bombers threatening an all-powerful media conglomerate, and his long, straggly hair and leopard-skin disco suit. Unfortunately, director Wolf Gremm is unable to create a credible world of corruption, decadence and disposable culture to complement his star's self-referential performance. In German with English subtitles.

Rainer Werner Fassbinder *Jansen* • Günther Kaufmann *Anton* • Boy Gobert *Blue Panther* • Arnold Marquis *Police chief* • Richy Muller *Nephew* • Nicole Heesters *Barbara* • Brigitte Mira *Personnel director* • Franco Nero *Weiss* ■ *Dir* Wolf Gremm • *Scr* Robert Katz, Wolf Gremm, from the novel *Murder on the 31st Floor* by Per Wahlöö

Kanal ★★★★ 12
Second World War tragedy
1957 · Pol · BW · 91mins

The second part of Andrzej Wajda's war trilogy, which won the Special Jury prize at Cannes, is a sobering re-creation of events that occurred during the 1944 Warsaw Uprising. Echoes of *Dante's Inferno* ring through the network of sewers where a resistance unit has taken refuge from the pursuing Nazis. The symbolism is occasionally overwrought, but there's no doubting the oppressive

atmosphere of the cramped tunnels, or the simple heroism of the partisans as they attempt to suppress their growing desperation. Uncompromising in its gloom, the film nevertheless has moments of quiet inspiration, such as the Chopin recital amid the ruins. In Polish with English subtitles. Contains some swearing and violence. ▭

Wieńczylaw Gliński *Lt Zadra* • Tadeusz Janczar *Korab* • Teresa Izewska *Stokrotka* • Emil Kariewicz *Madry* • Wladyslaw Sheybal [Vladek Sheybal] *Composer* • Tadeusz Gwiazdowski *Kula* ■ *Dir* Andrzej Wajda • *Scr* Jerzy Stefan Stawiński, from his short story

Kangaroo ★★
Romantic adventure
1952 · US · Colour · 84mins

Using frozen Australian earnings, 20th Century-Fox sent a full crew Down Under for this shoddy attempt to transpose a familiar western story to the outback. Australian players, even the well-known Chips Rafferty, were relegated to minor parts, as Peter Lawford poses as the long-lost son of Finlay Currie's cattle king, who reforms after falling in love with the old man's daughter, Maureen O'Hara. Director Lewis Milestone used some of Sydney's historic landmarks to advantage, but was not allowed to add an authentic local flavour to the story.

Maureen O'Hara *Dell McGuire* • Peter Lawford *Richard Connor* • Finlay Currie *Michael McGuire* • Richard Boone *Gamble* • Chips Rafferty *Trooper Leonard* • Letty Craydon *Kathleen* • Charles Tingwell *Matt* • Ron Whelan *Fenner* ■ *Dir* Lewis Milestone • *Scr* Harry Kleiner, from a story by Martin Berkeley

Kangaroo ★★★ 15
Drama   1986 · Ausl · Colour · 99mins

This fascinating and neglected Australian adaptation of DH Lawrence's semi-autobiographical novel stars the ever-excellent Judy Davis and her real-life husband Colin Friels as a couple who arrive in Sydney from Cornwall, and find themselves embroiled in an incipient socialist revolution. Literary to a point – though intelligent with it, but there is a lack of real character development. Friels, who doesn't quite have genuine star power, is very effective – charming and unsettling in equal doses – while Davis is a real treat to watch. ▭

Colin Friels *Richard Somers* • Judy Davis *Harriet Somers* • John Walton *Jack Calcott* • Julie Nihill *Vicki Calcott* • Hugh Keays-Byrne *Kangaroo* • Peter Hehir *Jaz* • Peter Cummins *Struthers* ■ *Dir* Tim Burstall • *Scr* Evan Jones, from a novel by DH Lawrence

Kangchenjunga ★★★★
Drama   1962 · Ind · Colour · 102mins

There's a foretaste of Merchant–Ivory's future preoccupations (both stylistic and thematic) in Satyajit Ray's first venture into self-scripting and colour cinematography. Fittingly, he also composed the score for what he considered his most musical work, with the cross-cutting having a beguiling rhythm that complements the oft-repeated movements of the characters around the formal gardens and winding roadways of Observatory Hill. Manipulative holidaying patriarch Chhabi Biswas meets his match in the form of Arun Mukherjee, the proud

Darjeeling local who wishes to marry his younger daughter. A true dance to the music of time, this is both sly satire and compelling drama. In Bengali with English subtitles.

Chhabi Biswas *Indranath Choudhuri* • Karuna Bannerji [Karuna Bannerjee] *Labanya* • Anil Chatterjee *Anil* • Anubha Gupta *Anima* • Subrata Sen *Shankar* • Indrani Singh *Tuklu* • Arun Mukherjee *Ashok* ■ *Dir/Scr* Satyajit Ray

Kanoon ★★★ PG
Courtroom drama   1960 · Ind · BW · 139mins

In addition to using cinema to highlight the key social, political and religious issues in Indian life, director BR Chopra also tried to introduce local audiences to the film styles popular in Hollywood. Essentially a treatise on capital punishment, this is a rare example of Indian *film noir*, with Rajendra Kumar starring as an ambitious lawyer who is forced to prosecute a thief for murder, even though he's sure the culprit is his new father-in-law – who turns out to be the judge trying the case. In Hindi with English subtitles. ▭

Ashok Kumar *Judge Badriprasad* • Nanda *Meena* • Rajendra Kumar *Public prosecutor* ■ *Dir* BR Chopra • *Scr* CJ Pavri

Kansas ★★ 15
Romantic melodrama
1988 · US · Colour · 105mins

A couple of young drifters (Matt Dillon and Andrew McCarthy) meet by chance when they steal a ride on a freight car. They become partners in crime before fate makes them bitter enemies. Australian director David Stevens follows both men's fortunes as their respective paths diverge: Dillon turns hardened ex-con, while McCarthy becomes a national hero. The detailed plot meanders, but the acting is appealing; Kyra Sedgwick is especially watchable as the trailer-trash tramp who hooks up with Dillon. ▭

Matt Dillon *Doyle Kennedy* • Andrew McCarthy *Wade Corey* • Leslie Hope *Lori Bayles* • Kyra Sedgwick *Prostitute drifter* • Arlen Dean Snyder *George Bayles* • Alan Toy *Nordquist* • Harry Northup *Governor* ■ *Dir* David Stevens • *Scr* Spencer Eastman

Kansas City ★★★ 15
Period crime drama
1995 · US/Fr · Colour · 115mins

Some isolated felicities – Harry Belafonte as a ruthless gangster, some terrific jazz – elevate Robert Altman's semi-autobiographical tribute to the town of his birth, but *Kansas City* is not as spot-on as the writer/director's more successful work. A thief's wife (Jennifer Jason Leigh) kidnaps a politician's drug-addicted spouse (Miranda Richardson) in an attempt to free her husband (Dermot Mulroney) from the clutches of a mob. The thirties' mood is beautifully evoked, but the film is too confused for its own good. Contains swearing and some violence.

Jennifer Jason Leigh *Blondie O'Hara* • Miranda Richardson *Carolyn Stilton* • Harry Belafonte *Seldom Seen* • Michael Murphy *Henry Stilton* • Dermot Mulroney *Johnny O'Hara* • Steve Buscemi *Johnny Flynn* • Brooke Smith *Babe*

Flynn • Jane Adams *Nettie Bolt* • Gina Belafonte *Hey-Hey Club hostess* ■ *Dir* Robert Altman • *Scr* Robert Altman, Frank Barhydt

Kansas City Bomber ★★★ 15
Sports drama   1972 · US · Colour · 94mins

The highs, lows and pitfalls of being a roller-derby queen are put under the spotlight in the defiantly unglamorous sleeper hit that proved Raquel Welch was a lot more than a pretty face. The former Hammer sex symbol is terrific as the roller-skating champion, juggling life as a single parent with her career when she joins an unfriendly new team. Top TV movie director Jerrold Freedman gives the picture a vital documentary feel and captures some hair-raising turns in the sporting sequences. Welch's daughter is played by a young Jodie Foster.

Raquel Welch *Diane "KC" Carr* • Kevin McCarthy *Burt Henry* • Helena Kallianiotes *Jackie Burdette* • Norman Alden *Horrible Hank Hopkins* • Jeanne Cooper *Vivien* • Mary Kay Pass *Lovey* • Martine Bartlett *Mrs Carr* • Jodie Foster *Rita* ■ *Dir* Jerrold Freedman • *Scr* Thomas Rickman, Calvin Clements, from a story by Barry Sandler

Kansas City Confidential ★★★ 12
Film noir   1952 · US · BW · 99mins

Director Phil Karlson turned out a number of commendably gritty, modestly budgeted crime films, and this is a good example. Its ingenious story has John Payne's ex-convict become a detective to unearth an ex-policeman-turned-criminal mastermind. It features the innovative touch (taken from the 1950 Brink's hold-up) of bank robbers wearing grotesque masks to conceal their identities. Someone had a sharp eye for casting, as the three accomplices are played by a young Lee Van Cleef, Jack Elam and Neville Brand. ▭

John Payne *Joe Rolfe* • Coleen Gray *Helen* • Preston Foster *Timothy Foster* • Dona Drake *Teresa* • Jack Elam *Harris* • Neville Brand *Kane* • Lee Van Cleef *Tony* • Mario Siletti *Timaso* ■ *Dir* Phil Karlson • *Scr* George Bruce, Harry Essex, from a story by Harold R Greene, Rowland Brown

Kansas Raiders ★★★
Western   1950 · US · Colour · 80mins

Audie Murphy is well cast as the young Jesse James, playing the outlaw as a tortured teenager who joins forces with the notorious Quantrill's Raiders. Murphy is tremendously sympathetic in the role, and he has an experienced co-star in Brian Donlevy as the demented William Quantrill. There are also two major stars-to-be in early roles: Tony Curtis and Richard Egan. This could be seen as a western precursor to the fifties' juvenile-delinquent cycle, but the glossy Technicolor, though a pleasure to view, softens the impact.

Audie Murphy *Jesse James* • Brian Donlevy *William Quantrill* • Marguerite Chapman *Kate Clarke* • Scott Brady *Bill Anderson* • Tony Curtis *Kit Dalton* • Richard Long *Frank James* • James Best *Cole Younger* • Dewey Martin *James Younger* • Richard Egan *First lieutenant* ■ *Dir* Ray Enright • *Scr* Robert L Richards, from his story

Kaos ★★★★

Period drama   1984 · It · Colour · 187mins

Italian siblings Paolo and Vittorio Taviani, who write and direct all their films together, have had an up-and-down career. One of their ups is this group of four folk tales by Luigi Pirandello about peasant life in Sicily at the turn of the 19th century – acted, in the main, by non-professionals. The misleading title is explained in the epilogue in which Pirandello is seen returning to his birthplace, the town of Kaos. Splendidly photographed landscapes (by Giuseppe Lanci) link the stories, which contain werewolves and ghosts and range from the tragic to the blackly comic, suiting the Tavianis' rather overcharged style. In Italian with English subtitles.

Margarita Lozano Mother • *Claudio Bigagli Batà* • *Ciccio Ingrassia Don Lollò* • *Franco Franchi Zi' Diam* • *Biagio Barone Salvatore* • *Salvatore Rossi Patriarch* • *Omero Antonutti Luigi Pirandello* • *Regina Bianchi Mother* ■ *Dir* Paolo Taviani, Vittorio Taviani • *Scr* Paolo Taviani, Vittorio Taviani, Tonino Guerra, from the short story collection *Novelle per un Anno* by Luigi Pirandello

Kapo ★★★

Second World War drama
1959 · It/Fr · BW · 117mins

Oscar-nominated for best foreign film, Gillo Pontecorvo's well-meaning drama seeks to expose and excuse the desperate measures to which people resorted in order to survive the concentration camps. The opening episode, in which orphaned Jewish teenager Susan Strasberg is saved by a kindly doctor, is plausible enough, but the surfeit of stereotypes and clichéd situations undermines the authenticity of the Polish sequences when Strasberg's promotion to "kapo" – or prison-camp guard – induces megalomania. Not even her romance with Russian Laurent Terzieff, nor a final act of self-sacrifice, can restore credibility, especially as Strasberg's performance is as hysterical as the story is sentimental. In English and Italian with subtitles.

Susan Strasberg Edith/Nicole • *Laurent Terzieff Sascha* • *Emmanuelle Riva Terese* • *Didi Perego Sofia* • *Gianni Garko German soldier* • *Annabella Besi* • *Graziella Galvani Mira Dinulovic* ■ *Dir* Gillo Pontecorvo • *Scr* Gillo Pontecorvo, Franco Solinas

The Karate Kid ★★ 15

Martial arts adventure
1984 · US · Colour · 121mins

This junior version of *Rocky* unaccountably became a massive worldwide success, spawning a series of sequels and probably ruining Ralph Macchio's career for life. Macchio has struggled ever since to shake off the image of the kid, the bullied youngster who is taught the secrets of karate by wise old Pat Morita and turns the tables on his tormentors. It's a shame, because here he rises above the trite script to deliver a sympathetic and believable performance. Morita is equally good and look out, too, for Elisabeth Shue in an early role. The best in the series, but that's not saying much. Contains some swearing and violence.

Ralph Macchio Daniel La Russo • *Noriyuki "Pat" Morita [Pat Morita] Miyagi* • *Elisabeth Shue Ali* • *Martin Kove Kreese* • *Randee Heller Lucille La Russo* • *William Zabka Johnny* • *Ron Thomas Bobby* • *Rob Garrison Tommy* ■ *Dir* John G Avildsen • *Scr* Robert Mark Kamen

The Karate Kid Part II ★★ PG

Martial arts adventure
1986 · US · Colour · 108mins

This has been a perplexingly successful film series, especially given that all the usual clichés had been exhausted well before the end of the very first film. The only interesting aspect of this dull first sequel is that the action is set largely in Japan, but that aside it is an uninspired retread of the original.

Ralph Macchio Daniel La Russo • *Noriyuki "Pat" Morita [Pat Morita] Miyagi* • *Nobu McCarthy Yukie* • *Danny Kamekona Sato* • *Yuji Okumoto Chozen* • *Tamlyn Tomita Kumiko* ■ *Dir* John G Avildsen • *Scr* Robert Mark Kamen, from characters created by Robert Mark Kamen

The Karate Kid III ★ PG

Martial arts adventure
1989 · US · Colour · 107mins

At least the first film was a reasonable mix of sentiment, fisticuffs and pace, all of which was reduced in a dire sequel. Here the "Kid" (fortunately, 27-year-old Ralph Macchio doesn't look old enough to shave) has to defend his title and tackle the bad guys, initially without the help of his mentor Miyagi. The script takes leave of reality at an early stage, and it all becomes increasingly daft and humourless with each scene. Contains swearing and violence.

Ralph Macchio Daniel La Russo • *Noriyuki "Pat" Morita [Pat Morita] Miyagi* • *Robyn Lively Jessica Andrews* • *Herbert Lom Terry Silver* • *Martin L Kove [Martin Kove] John Kreese* ■ *Dir* John G Avildsen • *Scr* Robert Mark Kamen, from characters created by Robert Mark Kamen

The Karate Killers ★★

Spy spoof   1967 · US · Colour · 92mins

In this unfunny spy spoof, Napoleon Solo and Illya Kuryakin are dispatched to prevent the formula for turning sea water into gold from falling into the hands of a memorable, but woefully underused, rogues' gallery. *Man from UNCLE* regulars Robert Vaughn, David McCallum and Leo G Carroll do battle with villains Joan Crawford, Telly Savalas, Terry-Thomas, Curt Jurgens and Herbert Lom, but director Barry Shear's clumsy slapstick approach does no credit to the TV series.

Robert Vaughn Napoleon Solo • *David McCallum Illya Kuryakin* • *Herbert Lom Randolph* • *Joan Crawford Amanda True* • *Curt Jurgens Carl von Kesser* • *Telly Savalas Count de Franzini* • *Terry-Thomas Constable* ■ *Dir* Barry Shear • *Scr* Norman Hudis, from a story by Boris Ingster

The Karen Carpenter Story ★★

Biography   1989 · US · Colour · 97mins

Given that it's produced by Karen's surviving brother Richard, it's hardly surprising that this TV movie offers a fairly sympathetic view of the seventies' chanteuse. In this version Carpenter (Cynthia Gibb) is a sweet, innocent little thing who, unfortunately, does the reverse of most music stars and revels in abstinence rather than excess (at least as far as food is concerned). The cast put on a brave face, but the end result is as sickly as some of the Carpenters' best known tracks – many of which, fans will be delighted to know, are aired here.

Cynthia Gibb Karen Carpenter • *Mitchell Anderson Richard Carpenter* • *Peter Michael Goetz Harold Carpenter* • *Louise Fletcher Agnes Carpenter* • *Michael McGuire Sherwin Bash* • *Lise Hilboldt Lucy Newman* ■ *Dir* Joseph Sargent • *Scr* Barry Morrow

Karnaval ★★★

Drama   1998 · Fr/Bel/Swi · Colour · 88mins

Expertly exploiting an atmospheric locale, Thomas Vincent makes an impressive debut with this tale of adultery and racial intolerance set against the annual Dunkirk *karnaval* (carnival). Although the action opens with Amar Ben Abdallah's decision to quit his father's garage and head for Marseilles, it's discontented wife Sylvie Testud who becomes the film's fulcrum. Trapped in a loveless marriage with boorish security guard Clovis Cornillac, her decision to romance the handsome stranger has unexpected repercussions. Yet, the most striking performance comes from Cornillac, whose drunken, prejudiced thuggery contrasts with Testud's repressed zest and the naivety of the frankly charmless Ben Abdallah. A French language film.

Clovis Cornillac Christian • *Sylvie Testud Bea* • *Amar Ben Abdallah Larbi* • *Dominique Baeyens Doriane* ■ *Dir* Thomas Vincent • *Scr* Maxime Sassier, Thomas Vincent

Kaspar Hauser ★★★ 18

Historical drama
1993 · Ger · Colour · 133mins

Where Werner Herzog explored the universal theme of corrupting civilisation in *The Enigma of Kaspar Hauser* (1974), Peter Sehr elects to speculate on the origins of the mystery man dumped in Nuremberg in 1828 after spending more than a decade of solitary confinement. Consequently, we are plunged into the politics of the Grand Duchy of Baden and left to fend for ourselves in much the same way as the sickly child who was exchanged for the Crown Prince by the Duke's scheming brother. It's a handsome film, but it only really comes to life during André Eisermann's rehabilitation under kindly professor Udo Samel. In German with English subtitles.

André Eisermann Kaspar Hauser • *Katharina Thalbach Gräfin Hochberg* • *Uwe Ochsenknecht Ludwig von Baden* • *Udo Samel Daumer* • *Jeremy Clyde Stanhope* • *Hansa Czypionka Hennenhofer* • *Hermann Beyer Anselm Ritter von Feuerbach* • *Cecile Paoli Stefanie von Baden* ■ *Dir/Scr* Peter Sehr

Katherine ★★

Drama   1975 · US · Colour · 77mins

Just after being noticed in the cult hit *Badlands* and prior to her mainstream breakthrough in *Carrie*, future Oscar-winner Sissy Spacek turned in yet another of her trademark glowing performances in this earnest TV movie. She plays the wealthy and pampered Katherine Alman, slowly galvanised by the social revolution of the sixties and transformed into a radical cause-fighting terrorist. Although the plot gets rather far-fetched, and the bumper-sticker philosophy is laughably right on, Spacek shines through all the implausibility. You simply cannot take your eyes off her.

Sissy Spacek Katherine Alman • *Art Carney Thornton Alman* • *Henry Winkler Bob Kline* • *Julie Kavner Margot* • *Jane Wyatt Emily Alman* • *Hector Elias Juan* • *Jenny Sullivan Liz Alman* ■ *Dir* Jeremy Kagan [Jeremy Paul Kagan] • *Scr* Jeremy Kagan

Katia Ismailova ★★ 18

Crime drama   1994 · Rus/Fr · Colour · 94mins

The subject of a Shostakovich opera and filmed three times previously (once by Andrzej Wajda), Nikolai Leskov's classic 19th-century novel *Lady Macbeth of the Mtensk District* has here been updated and ruthlessly reworked by writer/director Valerii Todorovsky. Putting aside any liberties taken with the text, this is still a curate's egg of a film. Combining beauty with malice, Ingeborga Dapkunaite makes a marvellous *femme-fatale*, but there's no real passion in her affair with carpenter Vladimir Mashkov or intrigue in her relationship with Yuri Kuznetsov's investigator. A bold attempt, but something of a misfire. In Russian with English subtitles. Contains violence and sex scenes.

Ingeborga Dapkunaite Katia • *Vladimir Mashkov Sergei* • *Alisa Freindlikh Irina* • *Aleksandr Feklistov Mitia* • *Yuri Kuznetsov Romanov* ■ *Dir* Valerii Todorovsky • *Scr* Alla Krinitsyna, François Gêrif, Cécile Vargaftig, from a story by Marina Sheptunova, Stanislav Govorukhin, from the novel *Lady Macbeth of the Mtensk District* by Nikolai Leskov

Katie: Portrait of a Centerfold ★★

Drama   1978 · US · Colour · 98mins

Former model Kim Basinger was well equipped – in more senses than one – to star in this slick, if utterly predictable, TV-movie exposé of the men's-magazine industry. Produced three years before her cinema debut in 1981's *Hard Country*, Basinger plays an innocent Texas beauty, lured to Hollywood and into the sleazy pin-up business before being tempted to exploit her assets for bigger bucks. It's the usual rags-to-riches morality tale, with director Robert Greenwald constrained by the made-for-TV format. An interesting supporting cast includes camp icons Dorothy Malone, Tab Hunter and Fabian.

Kim Basinger Katie McEvera • *Vivian Blaine Marietta Cutler* • *Fabian MC* • *Tab Hunter Elliot Bender* • *Don Johnson Gunther* • *Virginia Kiser Deborah Pintoff* • *Dorothy Malone Myrtle Cutler* • *Nan Martin Aunt Isabel* ■ *Dir* Robert Greenwald • *Scr* Nancy K Audley

Katok i Skrypka ★★★

Drama   1961 · USSR · Colour · 55mins

Andrei Tarkovsky's diploma film from the Soviet State School of Cinema in Moscow (VGIK), is a medium-length feature that hints at the sort of director he would become. His rich pictorial sense, the leisurely contemplation of objects and his obsession with mirrors is already evident in this fable about a little boy who gets to drive a steamroller and demonstrate his skills on the violin. The message about the unity of workers and artists is somewhat crude, but the cinematography by Vadim Yusov, the cameraman on Tarkovsky's first three features, is striking. A Russian language film.

Igor Fomchenko *Sasha* • V Zamansky *Sergey* • Marina Adzhubey *Mother* ■ *Dir* Andrei Tarkovsky • *Scr* Andrei Tarkovsky, Andrei Konchalovsky, from a story by S Bakhmetyeva

Kavik, the Wolf Dog ★★

Adventure 1980 · US/Can · Colour · 100mins

Yes, it's *Lassie* crossed with *White Fang* as loveable pooch Kavik comes to the rescue of all and sundry in this predictable tale. As well as *RoboCop's* Ronny Cox, watch out for a pre-*Uncle Buck* John Candy in a supporting role. Unfortunately, he's the sole thing of interest in this tale, which will keep only the youngest of viewers entertained.

Ronny Cox *Kurt Evans* • John Ireland *George Hunter* • Andrew Ian McMillan *Andy Evans* • Linda Sorenson *Laura Evans* • Chris Wiggins *Dr Vic Walker* • Murray Westgate *Mac* • John Candy *Pinky* • Johnny Yesno [John Yesno] *Charlie One-Eye* ■ *Dir* Peter Carter • *Scr* George Malko

Kazaam ★★ 12

Fantasy comedy adventure
1996 · US · Colour · 89mins

An early film outing for basketball legend Shaquille O'Neal, this thinly entertaining family comedy sees the athlete playing an ancient genie who is reawakened from his boom box by bullied schoolboy Francis Capra. Problem is that his potential master doesn't believe in magic, and is reluctant to take up the three wishes offer. Former *Starsky & Hutch* star Paul Michael Glaser paces it nicely as director, but ultimately this is a kids-only affair. Incidentally Capra, of *Free Willy 2* fame, wins the acting honours hands down over his adult co-star. [≣]

Shaquille O'Neal *Kazaam* • Francis Capra *Max* • Ally Walker *Alice* • Marshall Manesh *Malik* • James Acheson *Nick* • Fawn Reed *Asia Moon* • John Costelloe *Travis* ■ *Dir* Paul Michael Glaser • *Scr* Christian Ford, Roger Soffer, from a story by Paul Michael Glaser

Keaton's Cop ★ 18

Crime thriller 1990 · US · Colour · 91mins

Grouchy cop Lee Majors teams up with former mobster Abe Vigoda to investigate several assassination attempts in an obvious bid to emulate the success of *Midnight Run* and *48 HRS*. Naturally, it's hate at first sight, but this artificial attempt to generate chemistry provides neither laughs nor action. The violence at times is so bloody and ghastly, most viewers will find it hard to even think of laughing later. Those who are still in a mood to chuckle will find the attempts at humour simple-minded. [≣]

Abe Vigoda *Louie Keaton* • Lee Majors *Mike Gable* • Don Rickles *Jake Barber* • Tracy Brooks Swope *Susan Watson* ■ *Dir* Robert Burge • *Scr* Michael B Druxman

The Keep ★★★ 18

Horror 1983 · US · Colour · 91mins

In one of the weirdest Second World War movies ever made, a bunch of German soldiers bivouac in an old Romanian castle and get gruesomely dispatched by some unseen, supernatural force. By turns chilling, stylish, portentous and just plain silly, Michael Mann's second feature was a box-office bomb that temporarily wrecked his cinema career. (He went back to television and created *Miami Vice*.) However, Gabriel Byrne as an SS officer with a serious haircut, and Ian McKellen as a mad professor, are worth the price of admission alone. [≣]

Scott Glenn *Glaeken Trismegestus* • Alberta Watson *Eva* • Jürgen Prochnow *Woermann* • Robert Prosky *Father Fonescu* • Gabriel Byrne *Raempffer* • Ian McKellen *Dr Cuza* • Morgan Sheppard *Alexandru* • Royston Tickner *Tomescu* ■ *Dir* Michael Mann • *Scr* Michael Mann, from a novel by F Paul Wilson

Keep Cool ★★★★

Comedy thriller
1997 · Chi/HK · Colour · 95mins

Deprived of official funding, Zhang Yimou shot this quirky urban comedy with little formal preparation and a great deal of ingenuity. The dizzyingly mobile, hand-held technique will surprise those expecting his trademark stateliness, but the frenetic movements are totally in keeping with hip bookseller Jiang Wen's foolhardy quest to avenge himself on the club-owning mobster who not only steals his girl, but also causes him to smash passing academic Li Baotian's prized laptop. Capturing the bustle of Beijing, as well as sustaining the breathless comic pace, Zhang still finds time to comment on the growing influence of western fads and attitudes. A Mandarin language film.

Jiang Wen *Xiao Shuai* • Li Baotian *Lao Zhang* • Qu Ying *An Hong* • Ge You *The policeman* • Zhang Yimou *The peddler* ■ *Dir* Zhang Yimou • *Scr* Ping Shu

Keep 'em Flying ★★ U

Comedy musical 1941 · US · BW · 86mins

Abbott and Costello join stunt pilot Dick Foran in the Air Corps for this feeble comedy that barely manages to taxi to the runway, let alone take off. There's plenty of plot, with Foran winning the battle for Carol Bruce's affections by helping her brother over his flying phobia. But the laughs are on wartime rations, with only Martha Raye amusing as the twin waitresses who have lovestruck Costello in a spin. The runaway plane finale borrows heavily from the slapstick routines of Mack Sennett, but is nowhere near as funny.

Bud Abbott *Blackie Benson* • Lou Costello *Heathcliff* • Martha Raye *Barbara Phelps/ Gloria Phelps* • Dick Foran *Jinx Roberts* • Carol Bruce *Linda Joyce* • William Gargan *Craig Morrison* ■ *Dir* Arthur Lubin • *Scr* True Boardman, Nat Perrin, John Grant, from a story by Edmund L Hartmann

Keep Fit ★★★ U

Comedy 1937 · UK · BW · 78mins

It's hard now to imagine that a toothy-grinned, ukelele-strumming comic with a broad Lancashire accent could be a superstar – but George Formby certainly was. A huge box-office draw in Britain during the thirties and forties, Formby's saucy wit and frantic comic style proved a great tonic to wartime audiences. This movie finds the star in fine form, belting out songs and throwing himself into comedy routines, as a weedy barber forced to compete with a more athletic rival. Add a dash of romance and the unmasking of a thief and you've got all the ingredients for a first-rate Formby film. [≣]

George Formby *George Green* • Kay Walsh *Joan Allen* • Guy Middleton *Hector Kent* • Gus McNaughton *Publicity man* • Edmund Breon *Sir Augustus Marks* • George Benson *Ernie Gill* • Evelyn Roberts *Barber* • C Denier Warren *Editor* ■ *Dir* Anthony Kimmins • *Scr* Anthony Kimmins, Austin Melford

Keep It Up Downstairs ★ 18

Period comedy 1976 · UK · Colour · 90mins

In the depths of the seventies' trough, British cinema relied heavily on sitcom spin-offs and smut. Written by Hazel Adair, the creator of *Crossroads*, this dire period piece belongs firmly in the latter category. A sort of *Carry On Chatterley*, it might have been described as a costume comedy, had the cast kept its costumes on long enough. Top saucepots Françoise Pascal and Sue Longhurst team up with Diana Dors and Willie Rushton for this tale of avarice, snobbery and seduction. Just about everything's on view, but there's not a laugh in sight. Contains sex scenes and nudity. [≣]

Diana Dors *Daisy Dureneck* • Jack Wild *Peregrine Cockshute* • William Rushton *Shuttleworth* • Aimi MacDonald *Actress* • Françoise Pascal *Mimi* • Simon Brent *Rogers* • Sue Longhurst *Lady Cockshute* ■ *Dir* Robert Young [Robert M Young] • *Scr* Hazel Adair

Keep the Aspidistra Flying ★★★ PG

Period romantic comedy
1997 · UK · Colour · 96mins

In director Robert Bierman's enjoyable adaptation of George Orwell's semi-autobiographical comedy, Richard E Grant is at his angst-ridden, edgy best as an advertising man who quits his job to pursue the life of a poet. Helena Bonham Carter provides a nice contrast as his very tolerant girlfriend, who loves him despite his many faults. The sharp dialogue and gently amusing tone (Grant hasn't been this drunk since *Withnail and I*) lend appeal to a lightweight tale that's more of an appetiser than a main course. [≣]

Richard E Grant *Gordon Comstock* • Helena Bonham Carter *Rosemary* • Jim Carter *Erskine* • Harriet Walter *Julia Comstock* • Lill Roughley *Mrs Trilling* • Julian Wadham *Ravelston* • Lesley Vickerage *Hermione* • John Clegg *McKechnie* ■ *Dir* Robert Bierman • *Scr* Alan Plater, from the novel by George Orwell

Keep the Change ★★

Drama 1992 · US · Colour · 95mins

A first-rate cast including William Peterson, Jack Palance, Lolita

Davidovich and Buck Henry star in this engaging contemporary western based on the novel by Tom McGuane. Peterson plays a frustrated California painter who returns home to rescue his family's Montana homestead from a greedy rancher (Palance); there he encounters affairs of the heart, family squabbles and personal triumphs. The acting and the Montana scenery are better than the story, which unfortunately drifts into a hotch-potch of subplots and dead ends.

William Petersen *Joe Starling* • Rachel Ticotin *Astrid* • Jack Palance *Overstreet* • Buck Henry *Smitty* • Lolita Davidovich *Ellen Kelton* • Jeff Kober *Billy Kelton* ■ *Dir* Andy Tennant • *Scr* John Miglis, from the novel by Tom McGuane

Keep Your Powder Dry ★★ U

Second World War drama
1945 · US · BW · 92mins

Life in the Women's Army Corps as lived by new recruits Lana Turner, Laraine Day (locked in animosity both on screen and off) and Susan Peters, three girls from contrasting backgrounds. Directed by Edward Buzzell, it's not exactly riveting, but the supporting cast boasts Agnes Moorehead, a distinguished Oscar-nominated refugee from rather more weighty fare such as *The Magnificent Ambersons*. Sad footnote: Susan Peters was crippled in an accident after this film and never walked again.

Lana Turner *Valerie Parks* • Laraine Day *Leigh Rand* • Susan Peters *Ann Darrison* • Agnes Moorehead *Lt Col Spottiswoode* • Bill Johnson *Capt Bill Barclay* • Natalie Schafer *Harriet Corwin* • Lee Patrick *Gladys Hopkins* • Marta Linden *Capt Sanders* ■ *Dir* Edward Buzzell • *Scr* Mary C McCall Jr, George Bruce

The Keeper ★★ 15

Horror 1976 · Can · Colour · 84mins

In this rarely seen horror thriller from Canadian child-actor-turned-director Tom Drake, asylum head Christopher Lee plans to insure his inmates, murder their heirs with a hypnosis machine and use the money to conquer the world. Drake strives for dotty weirdness, but his psychic melodrama hits rock bottom with a thud every time Tell Schreiber (as detective Dick Driver) and inspector Ross Vezarian appear on screen. Their awful acting quickly grounds any hint of style or chilling ambience. [≣]

Christopher Lee *The Keeper* • Tell Schrieber *Dick Driver* • Sally Gray *Mae B Jones* • Ross Vezarian *Inspector Clarke* • Ian Tracey *The Kid* • Jack Leavy *Mr Big* • Leo Leavy *Mr Big* ■ *Dir* Tom Drake • *Scr* Tom Drake, from a story by David Curnick, Donald Wilson

The Keeper ★★

Prison drama 1995 · US · Colour · 97mins

Prison guard Giancarlo Esposito takes under his protection – and even into his home – Haitian immigrant Isaach de Bankole, who swears he's been wrongly accused of rape. But doubts set in when Esposito becomes convinced Bankole has slept with his wife and has to decide whether to take the law into his own hands or not. Director Joe Brewster, using realistic dialogue and unobtrusive direction, is clearly more interested in the

psychological aspects of the intimate piece and the contrasting value systems of each man, but blows it with the gathering soap operatics.

Giancarlo Esposito *Paul Lamont* • Regina Taylor *Angela Lamont* • Isaach de Bankole *Jean Baptiste* • Ron Brice *Ross* • OL Duke *Baker* ■ *Dir/Scr* Joe Brewster

Keeper of the City ★★ 15

Thriller 1992 · US · Colour · 91mins

The consistently under-rated Anthony LaPaglia turns in yet another brooding, complicated performance, this time as a Chicago killer targeting members of the city's mob. However, his star turn apart, this is a decidedly ho-hum effort, with actors of the calibre of Louis Gossett Jr, top-billed as the detective investigating the killings, and Peter Coyote, as a journalist on the case, sleepwalking through a perfunctory script. Contains violence, swearing and brief nudity.

Louis Gossett Jr *James Dela* • Anthony LaPaglia *Vince Benedetto* • Peter Coyote *Frank Nordhall* • Renée Soutendijk *Vickie Benedetto* • Aeryk Egan *Scotty Benedetto* • John Putch *Mitch* ■ *Dir* Bobby Roth • *Scr* Gerald DiPego, from the book by Shelly Johnson

Keeper of the Flame ★★★ U

Drama 1942 · US · BW · 96mins

This was the second of Katharine Hepburn and Spencer Tracy's nine films together and their first with director George Cukor. It's not a comedy, though, but a protracted and rather hectoring piece of wartime propaganda, kept alive by the presence of the two stars. Hepburn is the proud widow of an American hero and journalist Tracy wants to write his biography. As you would expect, the "hero" has a dark past. Tracy exudes his customary integrity and becomes a bit self-righteous as he unravels, *Citizen Kane*-like, the man's secret life. Hepburn is radiant and, from today's vantage point, she has a touch of Jackie Kennedy about her.

Spencer Tracy *Steven O'Malley* • Katharine Hepburn *Christine Forrest* • Richard Whorf *Clive Kerndon* • Margaret Wycherly *Mrs Forrest* • Donald Meek *Mr Arbuthnot* • Stephen McNally *Freddie Ridges* • Audrey Christie *Jane Harding* • Forrest Tucker *Geoffrey Midford* ■ *Dir* George Cukor • *Scr* Donald Ogden Stewart, from the novel by IAR Wylie

Keeping Secrets ★★ PG

Biographical drama
1991 · US · Colour · 89mins

Best known as Chrissy Snow in the sitcom *Three's Company*, Suzanne Somers may not be a household name in this country, but her autobiography caused quite a stir when it was released in the States. Directed by John Korty, this TV movie is caught between being a harrowing account of childhood abuse (at the hands of her alcoholic father) and a self-pitying melodrama. Curiously, the fact that Somers plays herself doesn't add to the authenticity, as it's hard to distinguish between a woman reliving painful memories and an actress playing a role.

Suzanne Somers • David Birney *Alan Hamel* • Ken Kercheval *Frank Mahoney* • Michael Learned *Marion Mahoney* ■ *Dir* John Korty • *Scr* Edmond Stevens, from the autobiography by Suzanne Somers

Keeping the Faith ★★★ 12

Romantic comedy 2000 · US · Colour · mins

A good-natured film with appealing actors, a few good laughs and some unpretentious insights into religion. First-time director Edward Norton also stars as a priest, while Ben Stiller plays his best friend, a rabbi. Their friendship is tested when they both fall in love with childhood friend Jenna Elfman. Norton's movie successfully blends romance, comedy and faith into a thoughtful and entertaining mix, which benefits from wonderful chemistry between the leads and a strong supporting cast, including Anne Bancroft as Stiller's mother.

Ben Stiller *Jake* • Edward Norton *Brian* • Jenna Elfman *Anna* • Anne Bancroft *Ruth* • Eli Wallach *Rabbi Lewis* • Ron Rifkin *Larry Friedman* • Milos Forman *Father Havel* • Holland Taylor *Bonnie Rose* • Lisa Edelstein *Ali Decker* ■ *Dir* Edward Norton • *Scr* Stuart Blumberg • *Music* Elmer Bernstein

Keeping the Promise ★★★

Period adventure 1997 · US · Colour

An exciting frontier drama, it's based on the novel *The Sign of the Beaver* and is set in mid-18th-century Massachusetts. A father (Keith Carradine) and his teenage son (Brendan Fletcher) trek to Maine to find better land and build a cabin but when the work is completed, the young man is left alone while his dad goes to fetch the rest of the family. However, a number of predicaments have to be overcome before they're reunited. Strong performances, a sensitive script and authentic costumes and locations make this TV movie a satisfying production all around.

Keith Carradine *Will Hallowell* • Annette O'Toole *Anne Hallowell* • Brendan Fletcher *Matt Hallowell* • Gordon Tootoosis *Sakniss* • Maury Chaykin *Ben* ■ *Dir* Sheldon Larry • *Scr* Gerald DiPego, from the novel *The Sign of the Beaver* by Elizabeth George Speare

Keeping Track ★★★ 15

Thriller 1986 · Can · Colour · 97mins

An interesting, suspenseful thriller with a fine pair of central performances from Michael Sarrazin and Margot Kidder as innocent bystanders who witness a major robbery and murder and find themselves thrown full pelt into saving their own necks. What lifts this film above the mundane is its concentration on the duo's burgeoning dependence on each other and issues of trust – the crash, bang, wallop come a very ordinary second. Worth catching. Contains mild swearing.

Michael Sarrazin *Daniel Hawkins* • Margot Kidder *Claire Tremayne* • Alan Scarfe *Royle Wishert* • Ken Pogue *Captain McCullough* ■ *Dir* Robin Spry • *Scr* Jamie Brown, from a story by Jamie Brown, Robin Spry

Keetje Tippel ★★★ 18

Period biographical drama
1975 · Neth · Colour · 102mins

Paul Verhoeven's third feature is based on the memoirs of a Dutch woman who was born into poverty in the 1880s, became a prostitute, married twice and met Toulouse-Lautrec in Paris. From this material, Verhoeven creates a Dickensian view of Europe – the prostitution, workhouses, squalor and the social inequality – as Keetje rises up the social ladder. Rutger Hauer, the star of Verhoeven's previous film *Turkish Delight*, has a leading role, and the cameraman is Jan de Bont, later the director of *Speed* and *The Haunting*. A Dutch language film.

Monique van de Ven *Keetje* • Rutger Hauer *Hugo* • Eddie Brugman *Andre* • Hannah De Leeuwe *Mina* • Andrea Domburg *Keetje's mother* • Jan Blaaser *Keetje's father* ■ *Dir* Paul Verhoeven • *Scr* Gerard Soeteman, from the books by Neel Doff

Kelly ★

Drama 1981 · Can · Colour · 93mins

In spite of a spirited performance from Twyla-Dawn Vokins, this town-and-country melodrama has all the momentum of a photo-story in a teenage magazine. Unhappy at living with her stepfather, the young girl sets off to join her natural father in the Alaskan backwoods, only to discover that he's as unsuited to raising a daughter as she is to living in the wild. Co-star Robert Logan also wrote the sentimental script. Only Paul van der Linden's photography is notable.

Robert Logan *Dave* • Twyla-Dawn Vokins *Kelly* • George Clutesi *Clute* • Elaine Nalee *Susan* • Doug Lennox *Beechum* ■ *Dir* Christopher Chapman • *Scr* Robert Logan

Kelly's Heroes ★★★ PG

Second World War action adventure
1970 · US/Yug · Colour · 137mins

Clint Eastwood and Telly Savalas head the cast of this enjoyable, if occasionally slightly silly, adventure yarn about a group of maverick GIs who decide to fill a lull in the war by knocking off a hoard of German bullion in occupied France. Savalas and the eccentric Donald Sutherland set to their assignment with gusto, while Eastwood remains as cool as ever as half of Europe is blowing up around him. This was never destined to win prestige prizes at foreign film festivals. Despite many flaws, though, it's not dull by any means. Contains some violence and swearing.

Clint Eastwood *Kelly* • Telly Savalas *Big Joe* • Don Rickles *Crapgame* • Donald Sutherland *Oddball* • Carroll O'Connor *General Colt* • Hal Buckley *Maitland* • Stuart Margolin *Little Joe* • Fred Pearlman *Mitchell* ■ *Dir* Brian G Hutton • *Scr* Troy Kennedy Martin

The Kennel Murder Case ★★★

Mystery 1933 · US · BW · 73mins

William Powell plays super-sleuth Philo Vance, looking into the murder of two brothers, both members of a Long Island kennel club. This doesn't faze our hero as he's also a dog fancier. At 70-odd enjoyable minutes, it's over in a flash – and so was Powell's four-film run as Vance, as Warner Bros replaced him with the serviceable Warren William. Powell then became Nick Charles in the *Thin Man* series, again with a dog in tow.

William Powell *Philo Vance* • Mary Astor *Hilda Lake* • Eugene Pallette *Sgt Heath* • Ralph Morgan *Raymond Wrede* • Jack LaRue *Eduardo Grassi* • Helen Vinson *Doris Delafield* • Paul Cavanagh *Sir Bruce MacDonald* • Robert Barrat *Archer Coe* ■ *Dir* Michael Curtiz • *Scr* Robert N Lee, Peter Milne, Robert Presnell, from the novel *The Return of Philo Vance* by SS Van Dine

The Kentuckian ★★★ PG

Western 1955 · US · Colour · 99mins

Producer/star Burt Lancaster's only film as director (although he co-directed *The Midnight Man* in the seventies) is thisa marvellously photographed outdoor adventure, based on Felix Holt's perceptive novel *The Gabriel Horn*. The main theme is Lancaster's relationship with his young son, touchingly portrayed by Donald MacDonald. The women are weakly cast, but there are a pair of prize villains: John Carradine as a travelling quack and, in his movie debut, nasty whip-wielding baddie Walter Matthau, whose main scene was hacked to ribbons by the UK censor before the film's original release. It has happily now been restored. The marvellous score is by Bernard Herrmann (*Citizen Kane*, *Psycho*) and provides another reason to enjoy this movie.

Burt Lancaster *Big Eli* • Dianne Foster *Hannah* • Diana Lynn *Susie* • John McIntire *Zack* • Una Merkel *Sophie* • Walter Matthau *Bodine* • John Carradine *Fletcher* • Donald MacDonald *Little Eli* ■ *Dir* Burt Lancaster • *Scr* Ab Guthrie Jr, from the novel *The Gabriel Horn* by Felix Holt • *Cinematographer* Ernest Lazlo

Kentucky ★★★

Romantic drama 1938 · US · Colour · 95mins

The main interest today in this hoary old 20th Century-Fox horse-racing saga resides in two things: the splendid richness of the Technicolor and the Oscar-winning performance of veteran Walter Brennan (his second of three supporting-actor Academy Awards) – a reminder of what a fine actor he could be before he was reduced to toothless characterisations in a slew of minor westerns at the end of his career. Loretta Young and Richard Greene are the impossibly good-looking young leads, and the bluegrass countryside has never looked more beguiling. The plot about feuding horse-breeding families owes as much to *Romeo and Juliet* as it does to the source novel by co-screenwriter John Taintor Foote.

Loretta Young *Sally Goodwin* • Richard Greene *Jack Dillon* • Walter Brennan *Peter Goodwin* • Douglass Dumbrille *John Dillon* • Karen Morley *Mrs Goodwin* • Moroni Olsen *John Dillon II* • Russell Hicks *Thad Goodwin Sr* • Willard Robertson *Bob Slocum* • Charles Waldron *Thad Goodwin* ■ *Dir* David Butler • *Scr* Lamar Trotti, John Taintor Foote, from the book *The Look Of Eagles* by John Taintor Foote

The Kentucky Fried Movie ★★★ 18

Comedy 1977 · US · Colour · 83mins

Director John Landis and scriptwriters Jerry Zucker, David Zucker and Jim Abrahams provide a consistently wacky collection of spoofs in a more hit-than-miss parody of TV commercials, B-movies, kung-fu adventures and porno chic. A lot more vulgar than their later movies, which included *Airplane!* and

Naked Gun, it's a bright and breezy anthology of the sketches the trio had already presented on stage. A cheap, chucklesome time-waster, which includes the star quality of Donald Sutherland and George Lazenby.

Colin Male *Spokesman* • Janice Kent *Barbara Duncan* • Michael Laurence *Frank Bowman* • Larry Curan *Tom Leclair* • Richard A Baker [Rick Baker] *Dino (AM Today)* • David Zucker *Man/second technician/Grunwald* • Lenka Novak *Linda Chambers* • George Lazenby *Architect* • Donald Sutherland *Clumsy waiter* ■ *Dir* John Landis • *Scr* David Zucker, Jim Abrahams, Jerry Zucker

Kentucky Moonshine ★★★
Musical comedy   1938 · US · BW · 87mins

The zany comedy trio The Ritz Brothers are an acquired taste but this is probably their best film, with a funny script and a good supply of risible skits. As city slickers who, hearing that a radio show is looking for genuine hayseeds, pretend to be country bumkins, they dominate the film with their frantic mixture of slapstick, tomfoolery and musical clowning. One memorable scene has them parodying *Snow White and the Seven Dwarfs* as they clean their woodland shack. Tony Martin is also on hand, playing it straight and singing the Lew Pollack–Sidney Mitchell songs.

Tony Martin *Jerry Wade* • Marjorie Weaver *Caroline* • Slim Summerville *Hank Hatfield* • John Carradine *Reef Hatfield* • Wally Vernon *Gus Bryce* ■ *Dir* David Butler • *Scr* Art Arthur, MM Musselman, from the story by MM Musselman, Jack Lait Jr, Al Ritz, Harry Ritz, Jimmy Ritz

Keoma ★★★ 15
Spaghetti western   1976 · It · Colour · 96mins

Originally despised, then admired for the elegance and poise of the camerawork, the spaghetti western is still one of the most watchable of all genres. This was released after the great days of the sixties – when scores were made – but the hero, Keoma Shannon (Franco Nero), still has plenty of the prerequisite man-alone spirit that Clint Eastwood originated. Director Enzo G Castellari attempts to fuse a popular theme – civil-rights protests – to the plot as Keoma tries to clean up his town like a liberal activist. But the ruthless action is still the element of the film that works best, which is possibly why the film's alternative title is *The Violent Breed*. Italian dialogue dubbed into English.

Franco Nero *Keoma Shannon* • Woody Strode *George* • William Berger ■ *Dir* Enzo G Castellari • *Scr* Enzo G Castellari, Mino Roli, Nico Ducci, Luigi Montefiori

Kept Husbands ★★
Drama   1931 · US · BW · 76mins

Director Lloyd Bacon's creaky early talkie was promoted by RKO with the line "every inch a man – bought body and soul by his wife". This less-than-snappy slogan did nothing to drag them in off the streets at the time, and it's still not likely to set many pulses racing. However, star Joel McCrea rarely lets the side down, and he's easily the best thing in this melodrama about a steelworker who curbs the excesses of his frivolous

wife Dorothy MacKaill, who just happens to be his boss's daughter.

Joel McCrea *Dick Brunton* • Dorothy MacKaill *Dorothy "Dot" Parker* • Robert McWade *Arthur Parker* • Florence Roberts *Mrs Henrietta Parker* • Clara Young *Mrs Post* • Mary Carr *Mrs Brunton* • Ned Sparks *Hughie* ■ *Dir* Lloyd Bacon • *Scr* Alfred Jackson, Forrest Halsey, from a story by Louis Sarecky

The Kerosene Seller's Wife ★★
Satirical drama
1989 · USSR · Colour · 101mins

Written and directed by Alexander Kaidanovsky, this is another of those *glasnost* assaults on the legacy of Stalinism. However, such is the density of the symbolism and the proliferation of dreams, flashbacks and surrealist interventions, that it's exceedingly difficult to keep up with the story of the doctor forced to become a kerosene salesman after he is betrayed to the authorities by his apparatchik twin brother. However, Alexander Bolyuev turns in a performance comparable to that of Jeremy Irons in *Dead Ringers*, while Anna Myasoedova is suitably scheming as the eponymous spouse. In Russian with English subtitles.

Vitautas Paukste *Yurgis Petravichus* • Alexander Bolyuev *Pavel Udaltsov/Sergei Udaltsov* • Anna Myasoedova *Olga* ■ *Dir/Scr* Alexander Kaidanovsky

Kes ★★★★★ PG
Drama   1969 · UK · Colour · 106mins

Ken Loach seems to acquire a surer mastery of his art with each picture, yet this, one of his earliest features, is still one of his best. Adapted from Barry Hines's "grim up North" novel, it has such a ring of authenticity that you can almost smell the chips. As ever, Loach coaxes remarkable performances, with Freddie Fletcher epitomising bullying big brotherhood and Brian Glover caricaturing every games teacher who never made it. Outstanding, however, is David Bradley as the teenager who finds solace – in a baby kestrel – from the pain of his dysfunctional family life and the torment of school.

David Bradley [Dai Bradley] *Billy Casper* • Colin Welland *Mr Farthing* • Lynne Perrie *Mrs Casper* • Freddie Fletcher *Jud* • Brian Glover *Mr Sugden* • Bob Bowes *Mr Gryce* • Trevor Hasketh *Mr Crossley* • Eric Bolderson *Farmer* ■ *Dir* Ken Loach • *Scr* Ken Loach, Tony Garnett, Barry Hines, from the novel *A Kestrel for a Knave* by Barry Hines • *Cinematographer* Chris Menges

Kevin & Perry Go Large ★★★★ 15
Comedy   2000 · UK/US · Colour · 83mins

Harry Enfield takes his finest comic creations – the hormonally charged teenage boys Kevin and Perry (played by Enfield and Kathy Burke) – and successfully expands them from a five-minute sketch into a feature-length movie. Here the spotty twosome descend on an unsuspecting Ibiza, where they hope to become top DJs and, in doing so, attract loads of ladies. Ed Bye's film zips along thanks to Burke's hilarious leering, and disgusting adventures that make

There's Something about Mary look like *Mary Poppins*. There's deliciously daft support from Rhys Ifans as a top DJ Eye, and Laura Fraser as the Essex girl who falls for Enfield's charms.

Harry Enfield *Kevin* • Kathy Burke *Perry* • Rhys Ifans *Eye Ball Paul* • Laura Fraser *Candice* • James Fleet *Dad* • Louisa Rix *Mum* • Paul Whitehouse *Bouncer* ■ *Dir* Ed Bye • *Scr* Harry Enfield, David Cummings, from characters created by Harry Enfield

The Key ★★
Political romantic drama
1934 · US · BW · 82mins

The rebellion against the British in Ireland forms the background to this drama. William Powell plays a British officer and concentrates more on his amorous career than the job in hand – namely the street fighting that one glimpses whenever the script starts to flag, based around the conflict between the Black and Tans and the Irish Revolutionaries. Colin Clive makes his mark as a British officer, and Edna Best is his wife and Powell's mistress.

William Powell *Capt Tennant* • Edna Best *Norah Kerr* • Colin Clive *Andrew Kerr* • Halliwell Hobbes *General* • Hobart Cavanaugh *Homer* • Henry O'Neill *Dan* • Donald Crisp *Conlan* ■ *Dir* Michael Curtiz • *Scr* Laird Doyle, from a play by R Gore Browne, JL Hardy

The Key ★★★
Second World War drama
1958 · UK · BW · 138mins

Playing down her usual voluptuous glamour, Sophia Loren is heartbreakingly vulnerable in this adaptation of Jan De Hartog's novel *Stella*. As the waterfront landlady who offers her favours to naval skippers, she is both a source of solace and disquiet, as few entrusted with her key survive for long. Instead of focusing on either her torment or her affair with the gruff William Holden, Carl Foreman's script spends too much time at sea. No matter how well director Carol Reed stages the action sequences, we're soon impatient for shore leave.

William Holden (1) *David Ross* • Sophia Loren *Stella* • Trevor Howard *Chris Ford* • Oscar Homolka *Captain Van Dam* • Kieron Moore *Kane* • Bernard Lee *Wadlow* • Beatrix Lehmann *Housekeeper* • Noel Purcell *Hotel porter* • Bryan Forbes *Weaver* • Michael Caine ■ *Dir* Carol Reed • *Scr* Carl Foreman, from the novel *Stella* by Jan De Hartog

The Key ★★★★
Erotic melodrama
1959 · Jap · Colour · 107mins

Kon Ichikawa's darkly comic tale of spousal obedience and sexual prowess is also a sly satire on pornography and cinematic voyeurism. Adapted from the novel by Junichiro Tanizaki, the action stems from an ageing husband's hope that his wife's infidelity with a doctor will restore his potency. However, the liaison only sparks a tragic rivalry between his liberated wife and his ultra-traditional daughter. Compromised in its content by contemporary censorship strictures, this is still a daringly subversive picture, which benefits both from the subtly coloured widescreen lensing and the exemplary performance of Machiko Kyo, as the accommodating and unexpectedly

accomplished wife. In Japanese with English subtitles.

Ganjiro Nakamura *Mr Kenmochi* • Machiko Kyo *Ikuko Kenmochi* • Tatsuya Nakadai *Kimura* • Junko Kano *Toshiko* • Tanie Kitabayashi *Hana* ■ *Dir* Kon Ichikawa • *Scr* Natto Wada, Keiji Hasebe, Kon Ichikawa, from a novel by Junichiro Tanizaki • *Cinematographer* Kazuo Miyagawa

Key Exchange ★
Romantic comedy
1985 · US · Colour · 90mins

Brooke Adams stars in a dated farce as a TV producer with an unfaithful and commitment-shy boyfriend (Ben Masters). His lawyer friend Daniel Stern, recently married to an equally unfaithful partner, upsets the apple cart by making a play for Adams and the stage is set for a typically predictable scenario. Disastrous on all counts, this should have simply remained a very successful off-Broadway play.

Ben Masters *Philip Bailey* • Brooke Adams *Lisa Simon* • Danny Aiello *Carabello* • Daniel Stern *Michael Fine* • Nancy Mette *April Fine* • Tony Roberts *David Slattery* • Seth Allen *Frank Mars* ■ *Dir* Barnet Kellman • *Scr* Kevin Scott, Paul Kurta, from the play by Kevin Wade

Key Largo ★★★ PG
Crime drama   1948 · US · BW · 101mins

A great Warner Bros cast was assembled for this screen version of Maxwell Anderson's steamy play, but, despite sterling work from movie icons Humphrey Bogart and Lauren Bacall (and, best of all, Edward G Robinson as veteran gangster Johnny Rocco), the creaky theatrical origins show through, and the climactic Florida storms are as phoney as the allegorical plot devices. Nevertheless, *Stagecoach's* Claire Trevor picked up an Oscar for playing Robinson's boozy floozy Gaye Dawn, and there's a fine feeling of postwar angst evoked by director John Huston (although frankly, this is well below Huston's best work). Although this ensemble piece doesn't really allow its stars to shine, any movie that pairs Bogey and Bacall, adds "Little Caesar" himself, and throws in Lionel Barrymore for good measure, has got to be good. **DVD**

Humphrey Bogart *Frank McCloud* • Edward G Robinson *Johnny Rocco* • Lauren Bacall *Nora Temple* • Lionel Barrymore *James Temple* • Claire Trevor *Gaye Dawn* • Thomas Gomez *Curley Hoff* • Harry Lewis *Toots Bass* • John Rodney *Deputy Clyde Sawyer* • Marc Lawrence *Ziggy* ■ *Dir* John Huston • *Scr* John Huston, Richard Brooks, from the play by Maxwell Anderson • *Cinematographer* Karl Freund

Key to the City ★★
Comedy   1950 · US · BW · 100mins

A breezy romantic comedy with Clark Gable and Loretta Young, who meet at a mayoral convention. He's the strapping ex-docker-turned-politician and she's the more classy mayor of a tiny Maine town. Set in San Francisco, where Gable has to cope with several emergencies – as well as those sorts of misunderstandings that only happen in movies – it's a neat demonstration of staying power for Gable, who was nearing the end of his career at MGM.

U = SUITABLE FOR ALL   Uc = SUITABLE FOR ALL, ESPECIALLY FOR YOUNG CHILDREN (VIDEO ONLY)   PG = PARENTAL GUIDANCE

Clark Gable *Steve Fisk* • Loretta Young *Clarissa Standish* • Frank Morgan *Fire chief Duggan* • Marilyn Maxwell *Sheila* • Raymond Burr *Les Taggart* • James Gleason *Sergeant Hogan* • Lewis Stone *Judge Silas Standish* • Raymond Walburn *Mayor Billy Butler* ■ *Dir* George Sidney • *Scr* Robert Riley Crutcher, from a story by Albert Beich

Key Witness ★★★

Crime drama 1960 · US · BW · 82mins

A group of young thugs terrorise a youth and knife him to death. Only one man – Jeffrey Hunter – is prepared to tell the police what has happened even though dozens were witnesses. The story ropes in a lot of topical social concerns – drugs, racism, bike culture – and features Dennis Hopper as the leader of the ruffians. Borrowing liberally from *The Wild One* and *Rebel without a Cause*, this teen-angst movie is tautly directed by B-movie maestro Phil Karlson, best known for *The Phenix City Story*. Though the location shooting gives the picture an up-to-the-minute urgency, the British censor banned it, mainly because of the frequent use of flick-knives.

Jeffrey Hunter *Fred Morrow* • Pat Crowley *Ann Morrow* • Dennis Hopper *"Cowboy"* • Joby Baker *"Muggles"* • Susan Harrison *Ruby* • Johnny Nash *"Apple"* • Corey Allen *"Magician"* • Frank Silvera *Detective Rafael Torno* ■ *Dir* Phil Karlson • *Scr* Alfred Brenner, Sidney Michaels, from a novel by Frank Kane

The Keys ★ PG

Drama 1992 · US · Colour · 91mins

One of those "it's our land and we're gonna fight for it" dramas, which has two brothers standing up to a local bad guy who's after their father's land for its real-estate value. Unfortunately, there's little to recommend this TV-movie adventure, which contains B-movie performances from its cast and ham-fisted direction from Richard Compton, who made the equally banal *Maniac*. Missable. ▭

Brian Bloom *Michael Bessarian* • Scott Matthew Bloom *David Bessarian* • Ben Masters *Jake Bessarian* • Geoffrey Blake *Randy* ■ *Dir* Richard Compton • *Scr* Maurice Hurley, from a story by Maurice Hurley, Joel Blasberg, Stanley J Singer

Keys ★★ 15

Thriller 1994 · US · Colour · 93mins

There's the seed of a good idea trying to take root in this botched thriller, which suffers from the usual restrictions of the TV-movie format. Marg Helgenberger plays a pathologist whose investigations into the kidnapping of a child reawaken painful memories of her own upbringing. The different strands of the film are never coherently woven together by director John Sacret Young, but he draws good performances from the eclectic cast, which includes old hands Richard Masur and Ralph Waite, plus Vondie Curtis-Hall, who has recently received critical plaudits for his directorial debut *Gridlock'd*. ▭

Marg Helgenberger *Maureen "Kick" Kickasola* • Gary Dourdan • Brett Cullen • Vondie Curtis-Hall • Richard Masur • Ralph Waite ■ *Dir/Scr* John Sacret Young

The Keys of the Kingdom ★★

Drama 1944 · US · BW · 136mins

Twentieth Century Fox must have hoped for another hit like *The Song of Bernadette* when they acquired AJ Cronin's bestseller. Gregory Peck, in only his second picture, gained a Best Actor Oscar nomination playing a saintly priest who runs a mission in 19th-century China. Directed by John M Stahl from a final script by Joseph L Mankiewicz, it's a long, talkative and rather undramatic picture (only a civil war injects much action), but its success saved Peck's career after the weak showing of his first movie, *Days of Glory*.

Gregory Peck *Father Francis Chisholm* • Thomas Mitchell *Dr Willie Tulloch* • Vincent Price *Rev Angus Mealy* • Rose Stradner *Mother Maria Veronica* • Roddy McDowall *Francis, as a boy* • Edmund Gwenn *Rev Hamish MacNabb* • Cedric Hardwicke *Monsignor Sleeth* ■ *Dir* John M Stahl • *Scr* Joseph L Mankiewicz, Nunnally Johnson, from a novel by AJ Cronin

Keys to the Kingdom ★

Drama 1991 · US · Colour

Before you get up your hopes that this is Gregory Peck with his eyes raised to heaven in the backwoods of China, this is Dick Van Dyke up to his eyes in trouble in the smarter end of Florida. It's hard to accept Van Dyke as a ruthless press baron confronted with troublesome daughters and a plot to ruin him. This TV movie is melodrama from the 900-page-novel school, but it comes pretty close to the bottom of the class.

Dick Van Dyke *Buddy Keys* • Daphne Ashbrook *Charlotte* • Kate Vernon *Diana Keys* • Angela Alvarado *Felicia Keys-Zaldivar* • Dan Futterman *Ballard Moss* ■ *Dir* Michael Fresco • *Scr* Michael Gallery

Keys to Tulsa ★★ 18

Crime drama 1996 · US · Colour · 109mins

Don't raise your hopes about the quality of this film when you see the cool cast list – James Spader, Eric Stoltz, James Coburn and Cameron Diaz (very briefly) among them – it's actually an interesting, if not exactly gripping, *film noir*. Stoltz is the prodigal son returning home to mum Mary Tyler Moore with the intention of straightening his life out. Of course, as soon as he hooks up with his old friends you know that will never happen, and it's not long before he's hip-deep in drugs, sex, blackmail and murder. Lacking in tension and hindered by rather turgid direction, this is more of a well-played character piece than a taut thriller. ▭

Eric Stoltz *Richter Boudreau* • Cameron Diaz *Trudy* • Randy Graff *Louise Brinkman* • Mary Tyler Moore *Cynthia Boudreau* • James Coburn *Harmon Shaw* • Deborah Kara Unger *Vicky Michaels Stovers* • Peter Strauss *Chip Carlson* • James Spader *Ronnie Stover* ■ *Dir* Leslie Greif • *Scr* Harley Peyton, from the novel by Brian Fair Berkey

Khartoum ★★★ PG

Historical drama
1966 · UK · Colour · 122mins

Big-budget epic about General Gordon's last stand when Sudanese

warriors, led by the Mahdi, gave the British Empire a serious jolt. As Gordon, Charlton Heston gives a finely studied performance, suggesting the complexity of the man that the script never quite comes to terms with. Heston's performance contrasts with that of Laurence Olivier – his Mahdi is all eye-rolling, lip-quivering fanaticism, like a refugee from a *Carry On* film. Intended as a rival to *Lawrence of Arabia*, this boasts a fine supporting cast – including Michael Hordern and Ralph Richardson – and is often spectacular to watch, though Basil Dearden's direction is always on the stodgy side. ▭

Charlton Heston *General Charles Gordon* • Laurence Olivier *The Mahdi* • Richard Johnson *Colonel JDH Stewart* • Ralph Richardson *Mr Gladstone* • Alexander Knox *Sir Evelyn Baring* • Johnny Sekka *Khaleel* • Nigel Green *General Wolseley* • Michael Hordern *Lord Granville* • Zia Mohyeddin *Zobeir Pasha* ■ *Dir* Basil Dearden • *Scr* Robert Ardrey

Khrustaliov, My Car! ★★

Satirical comedy drama
1998 · Rus/Fr · BW · 137mins

Alexei German ended a 16-year hiatus as a director with this long-gestating satire on Soviet society in the last days of Stalin. However, the break clearly sapped the insight and precision that made *My Friend Ivan Lapshin* so compelling. Instead, he delivers a rambling, often incoherent tale, in which the broad comedy of the opening Moscow section gives way to stylised realism inside the grim gulag to which Yuri Tsourilo's eccentric doctor is condemned after a plot against the government. However, the committed performances almost atone for the structural deficiencies. A Russian language film.

Yuri Tsourilo *General Youri Glinski* • Nina Rouslanova *Wife* • Yuri Yarvet *Swedish reporter* • M Dementiev *Son* • A Bachirov *Idiot* ■ *Dir* Alexei German • *Scr* Alexei German, Svetlana Karmalita

Khyber Patrol ★★★ U

Action drama 1954 · US · Colour · 72mins

Nicely paced and richly coloured shortish co-feature, following the trend set by Rock Hudson in *Bengal Brigade* and Tyrone Power in *King of the Khyber Rifles*. This time newcomer Richard Egan is offered a kickstart to stardom as he ruggedly romances lovely Dawn Addams and fights for the Empire on the Indian border, aided by pukka British actor Patric Knowles.

Richard Egan *Cameron* • Dawn Addams *Diana* • Raymond Burr *Ahmed* • Patric Knowles *Lieutenant Kennerly* • Paul Cavanagh *Melville* • Donald Randolph *Ishak Khan* • Philip Tonge *Colonel Rivington* • Patrick O'Moore *Brusard* • Laura Mason *Krushia* ■ *Dir* Seymour Friedman • *Scr* Jack DeWitt, from a story by Richard Schayer

Kick! ★★

Comedy drama 1979 · US · Colour

The name of Sean S Cunningham will forever be associated by horror fans with *Friday the 13th*. But just before he made that landmark in schlock horror, he was landed with this corny TV comedy that harks back to *Boys Town* and Bing Crosby's *Father O'Malley* movies such as *Going My Way*. Sadly,

this story of a football team betting stolen money on themselves to help their coach to pay his gambling debts isn't on a par with any of the above. Jim Baker is willing as the loveable loser and Malachy McCourt is an amalgam of every Irish priest you've ever seen on film. Contains mild swearing.

Jim Baker *Francis Xavier "Manny" Mansfield* • Malachy McCourt *Father Arch McCoy* • Chet Doherty *Dr Berryman* • Sel Skolnick *Mr Caputo* • Terry Vance *Amazing Grace* ■ *Dir* Sean S Cunningham • *Scr* Victor Miller, from a story by Stephen Miner

Kickboxer ★★★ 18

Martial arts action drama
1989 · US · Colour · 97mins

A key film in Jean-Claude Van Damme's career, this is the one that first gave an indication that the Muscles from Brussels could escape from straight-to-video hell and into the mainstream. Plot-wise, this is nothing special: Van Damme is the brother of an injured kickboxing champion who enters the ring seeking revenge. However, the fight sequences are staged with such élan that it is easy to ignore the hackneyed script (Van Damme had a hand in that as well) and the rather wooden performances. After this, our hero moved on to bigger and better action vehicles, but the franchise continued without him, spawning several sequels. Contains swearing, violence and nudity. ▭

Jean-Claude Van Damme *Kurt Sloane* • Dennis Alexio *Eric Sloane* • Dennis Chan *Xian Chow* • Tong Po *Tong Po* • Haskell Anderson *Winston Taylor* • Rochelle Ashana *Mylee* ■ *Dir* Mark DiSalle • *Scr* Glen Bruce, from a story by Mark DiSalle, Jean-Claude Van Damme

Kickboxer 2: the Road Back ★ 18

Martial arts adventure
1990 · US · Colour · 90mins

This explores much the same territory as its predecessor and the director is Hollywood journeyman Albert Pyun, whose name can be found on many a straight-to-video sleeve. The film stars Sasha Mitchell as the high-kicking hero who seeks revenge on the kung fu coward who killed his brother. You probably know the rest. Contains violence and swearing. ▭

Sasha Mitchell *David Sloan* • Peter Boyle *Justin Maciah* • Cary-Hiroyuki Tagawa *Mr Sangha* • Dennis Chan *Xian Chow* • Michel Qissi *Tong Po* • John Diehl *Morrison* ■ *Dir* Albert Pyun • *Scr* David S Goyer

Kickboxer III: the Art of War ★★ 18

Martial arts adventure
1992 · US · Colour · 91mins

The original *Kickboxer* helped to put Jean-Claude Van Damme on the Hollywood map; sadly, Tinseltown never really came knocking for Sasha Mitchell, who nevertheless bravely soldiered on in the role. The slimmest of plots (the hunt for a kidnapped girl) helps to link the numerous biffing sequences, which are competently, if unimaginatively, filmed. The Brazilian locations provide the only breath of fresh air. Contains violence and swearing.

Sasha Mitchell *David Sloan* • Dennis Chan *Xian Chow* • Richard Comar *Frank Lane* • Noah Verduzco *Marcos* • Ian Jacklin *Martine* ■ *Dir* Rick King • *Scr* Dennis Pratt

Kicked in the Head ★★

Black comedy thriller
1997 · US · Colour · 86mins

Self-pitying low-life Kevin Corrigan acts as a cocaine-delivery boy for his two-bit crook uncle, James Woods, but things don't go as planned and he invokes the wrath of local crime boss Burt Young. Highly derivative, and populated by truly unlikeable characters, this forced black comedy thriller is neither dark nor amusing enough to perk any interest. The screenplay is peppered with pop-culture banter in the Quentin Tarantino mode, the direction apes the *Slacker* style of Richard Linklater and the locale is clearly inspired by (executive producer) Martin Scorsese's *Mean Streets*. The result of this artistic pilfering is an artificial dud, occasionally enlivened by the performances.

Kevin Corrigan *Redmond* • Linda Fiorentino *Megan* • Michael Rapaport *Stretch* • James Woods *Uncle Sam* • Burt Young *Jack* • Lili Taylor *Happy* ■ *Dir* Matthew Harrison • *Scr* Kevin Corrigan, Matthew Harrison

Kicking and Screaming ★★★ 15

Comedy drama   1995 · US · Colour · 92mins

We're in "slacker" territory again, as a group of recent college grads (including Josh Hamilton and Olivia D'Abo) try to figure out what to do with their lives. Eric Stoltz plays the guy they don't want to become, a grad student who's been tending bar for the last ten years while he (allegedly) works on his dissertation. Everybody in this movie speaks in a painfully witty manner and it takes a while to go anywhere, but a lot of the dialogue is quite funny.

Josh Hamilton *Grover* • Olivia D'Abo *Jane* • Carlos Jacott *Otis* • Chris Eigeman *Max* • Eric Stoltz *Chet* • Jason Wiles *Skippy* • Parker Posey *Miami* • Cara Buono *Kate* • Elliott Gould *Grover's dad* • Sam Gould *Pete* ■ *Dir* Noah Baumbach • *Scr* Noah Baumbach, from a story by Oliver Berkman, Noah Baumbach

The Kid ★★★★ U

Silent comedy drama
1921 · US · BW · 68mins

Charlie Chaplin's first feature as writer, director and star was something of a watershed in his career. From now on, slapstick would slowly be replaced by more observational comedy, while an increased emphasis would be placed on both social comment and pathos. Clearly recalling his own troubled childhood in Victorian London, the film is remarkable for the chemistry between the Tramp and moppet Jackie Coogan. Chaplin may try a touch too hard for tears in places, but the scenes in which he discovers the abandoned baby and the heaven sequence show just what a gifted film-maker he was. 🎬

Charlie Chaplin [Charles Chaplin] *Tramp* • Carl Miller *Artist* • Edna Purviance *Mother* • Jackie Coogan *The Kid* • Tom Wilson *Policeman* ■ *Dir/Scr* Charles Chaplin

Kid ★★ 18

Thriller   1990 · US · Colour · 87mins

C Thomas Howell plays the Kid, a taciturn drifter in a long coat who comes back to his home town and makes out with the prettiest girl there. However, he also goes on a killing spree aimed at those who murdered his parents years before. Apart from the obvious nod to Clint Eastwood's laconic loner, Howell seems to be going for some kind of James Dean vibe here as well, but he's out of his league and the rest of the characters are mere stereotypes. Nevertheless, this violent and derivative affair does have a rather amusing death by sporting equipment. 🎬

C Thomas Howell *Kid* • R Lee Ermey *Luke Clanton* • Dale Dye *Garvey* • Sarah Trigger *Kate* • Michael Bowen *Harlan* • Brian Austin Green *Metal Louie* • Damon Martin *Pete* • Lenore Kasdorf *Alice* ■ *Dir* John Mark Robinson • *Scr* Leslie Bohem

Kid Blue ★★★

Comedy western
1971 · US · Colour · 100mins

A seriously flakey comedy western – a sort of *Easy Rider* on horseback – with Dennis Hopper as a hopeless outlaw who goes straight and is hopeless at that as well. Made at the end of the "peace and love" era, Hopper's outsider has a wayward charm, a hippy's glazed look and a talent for slapstick humour. Less a narrative than scenes glued randomly together, it's a palpable mess, albeit an entertaining one. The presence of Warren Oates, Peter Boyle, Ben Johnson and Janice Rule adds to the fun of an old genre being given the "beads and marijuana" treatment. Completed in 1971 under its original title *Dime Box*, it was kept on the shelf for two years and retitled on release.

Dennis Hopper *Bickford Waner* • Warren Oates *Reese Ford* • Peter Boyle *Preacher Bob* • Ben Johnson *Sheriff "Mean John" Simpson* • Lee Purcell *Molly Ford* • Janice Rule *Janet Conforto* • Ralph Waite *Drummer* ■ *Dir* James Frawley • *Scr* Edwin Shrake

The Kid Brother ★★★★★★ U

Silent comedy   1927 · US · BW · 82mins

The inventiveness of comedian Harold Lloyd has to be seen to be disbelieved in this comedy about the put-upon youngest of three sons and their widower father (Walter James). Ordered to close down a travelling show by his sheriff dad, Harold at last rebels against the constant bullying – because he's fallen in love with a showgirl (Jobyna Ralston) – and triumphs over parental oppression. Some of the sight gags are brilliant, including the use of a butter churn as a way of wringing and hanging out clothes. The mechanisms of laughter-making don't come much better than this, and add up to one of the comedian's best movies. 🎬

Harold Lloyd *Harold Hickory* • Jobyna Ralston *Mary Powers* • Walter James *Sheriff Jim Hickory* • Leo Willis *Leo Hickory* • Olin Francis *Olin Hickory* • Constantine Romanoff *Sardoni* • Eddie Boland *"Flash" Farrell* • Frank Lanning *Sam Hooper* ■ *Dir* Ted Wilde, JA Howe, Lewis Milestone • *Scr* John Grey, Tom Crizer, Lex Neal, Howard Green, Ted Wilde

A Kid for Two Farthings ★★★ U

Comedy fantasy   1955 · UK · Colour · 91mins

Influenced by the neo-realist fantasies of Italian director Vittorio De Sica, this is a delightful urban fairy tale set in London's East End in the harsh days after the Second World War. Adapted from his own novel by the late Wolf Mankowitz, the story – of a small boy who finds a one-horned goat, which he is convinced is a miracle-working unicorn – is handled with a wonderfully light touch by director Carol Reed, and beautifully played by a cast in which Celia Johnson, Diana Dors and little Jonathan Ashmore stand out. Yet, for all its charm and feelgood sentimentality, the blend of realism and fantasy is not always convincing.

Celia Johnson *Joanne* • Diana Dors *Sonia* • David Kossoff *Kandinsky* • Joe Robinson *Sam* • Jonathan Ashmore *Joe* • Brenda de Banzie *"Lady" Ruby* • Vera Day *Mimi* • Primo Carnera *Python Macklin* • Sidney James *Ince Berg* • Irene Handl *Mrs Abramowitz* • Alfie Bass *Alf, he Bird Man* ■ *Dir* Carol Reed • *Scr* Wolf Mankowitz, from his novel

The Kid from Brooklyn ★★★ U

Musical comedy 1946 · US · Colour · 108mins

Based on Harold Lloyd's 1936 comedy *The Milky Way*, this is one of Danny Kaye's best vehicles, allowing the versatile comedian to strut his stuff as the milkman who becomes a boxing champ. If you're not a Kaye fan, this may be the movie – along with, perhaps, *The Secret Life of Walter Mitty* – that will make you change your mind, since it's relatively free of the sentimentality that mars so much of Kaye's later work. Producer Samuel Goldwyn surrounds his star with glamour, rich forties' Technicolor and terrific character support and some super songs; the result is very pleasing. 🎬

Danny Kaye *Burleigh Sullivan* • Virginia Mayo *Polly Pringle* • Vera-Ellen *Susie Sullivan* • Walter Abel *Gabby Sloan* • Eve Arden *Ann Westley* • Steve Cochran *Speed Macfarlane* • Lionel Stander *Spider Schultz* • Fay Bainter *Mrs E Winthrop Lemoyne* ■ *Dir* Norman Z McLeod • *Scr* Don Hartman, Melville Shavelson, from the film *The Milky Way* by Grover Jones, Frank Butler, Richard Connell, from the play *The Milky Way* by Lynn Root, Harry Clork

The Kid from Left Field ★★ U

Comedy   1953 · US · BW · 80mins

Here's a cute baseball story in which Billy Chapin plays a nine-year-old kid who becomes manager of a baseball team after his advice takes it to the top of the league. In fact, it's Dan Dailey as the boy's father, a has-been player turned peanut seller, who's behind the tips. Well written by Jack Sher and directed by former editor Harmon Jones, this modest production has good support from Lloyd Bridges, Anne Bancroft and veteran Ray Collins as the club's owner.

Dan Dailey *Larry "Pop" Cooper* • Anne Bancroft *Marian* • Billy Chapin *Christy* • Lloyd Bridges *Pete Haines* • Ray Collins *Whacker* • Richard Egan *Billy Lorant* ■ *Dir* Harmon Jones • *Scr* Jack Sher

The Kid from Spain ★★★★ U

Musical comedy   1932 · US · BW · 91mins

A wonderfully insane Eddie Cantor vehicle, a wacky plot of confused identities, which climaxes when Cantor, mistaken for a great bullfighter, wears down the angry bull that his rival has arranged in place of a docile one. Famed choreographer Busby Berkeley, not quite yet in his marvellous, tasteless stride, is responsible for the production numbers. Talented Leo McCarey also directed Laurel and Hardy and the Marx Brothers, and here he's aided by the cinematography of the great Gregg Toland, who would later work on *Citizen Kane* and *Wuthering Heights*, and editor Stuart Heisler, future director of *Dallas* and *Storm Warning*. One for the video. 🎬

Eddie Cantor *Eddie Williams* • Lyda Roberti *Rosalie* • Robert Young *Ricardo* • Ruth Hall *Anita Gomez* • John Miljan *Pancho* • Noah Beery *Alonzo Gomez* • J Carrol Naish *Pedro* ■ *Dir* Leo McCarey • *Scr* William Anthony McGuire, Bert Kalmar, Harry Ruby

Kid Galahad ★★★★ PG

Sports drama   1937 · US · BW · 97mins

No, not Elvis Presley in the remake, but Wayne Morris as the chivalrous hotel porter in Warner Bros's fast-paced boxing saga, impeccably directed by *Casablanca*'s Michael Curtiz, and unforgettably teaming Edward G Robinson, Humphrey Bogart and Bette Davis. It's the mink-clad Davis, called "Fluff" who starts the action rolling, revealing sharp insights into prizefight manners and morals. Editor George Amy does a superb job in the cutting room, keeping the film on the move, and Humphrey Bogart, as a rival fight promoter, has seldom been meaner. Terrific stuff, cleverly handled and supremely entertaining. 🎬

Edward G Robinson *Nick Donati* • Bette Davis *Louise "Fluff" Phillips* • Humphrey Bogart *Turkey Morgan* • Wayne Morris *"Kid Galahad"/Ward Guisenberry* • Jane Bryan *Marie Donati* • Harry Carey *Silver Jackson* ■ *Dir* Michael Curtiz • *Scr* Seton I Miller, from the novel by Francis Wallace

Kid Galahad ★★★ PG

Musical sports drama
1962 · US · Colour · 92mins

First filmed in 1937 with Edward G Robinson and Bette Davis, this boxing tale was considerably re-fashioned for Elvis Presley, playing the title character (portrayed in the original by Wayne Morris), a fighter who would rather be a garage mechanic. Much of the plotting was jettisoned to make way for Presley's musical interludes, and the film lacks the brittle excitement of the original, but a strong supporting cast and solid direction by Gordon Douglas make this one of the singer's better movies. 🎬

Elvis Presley *Walter Gulick* • Gig Young *Willy Grogan* • Lola Albright *Dolly Fletcher* • Joan Blackman *Rose Grogan* • Charles Bronson *Lew Nyack* • Ned Glass *Lieberman* ■ *Dir* Phil Karlson • *Scr* William Fay, from the novel by Francis Wallace

Kid Glove Killer ★★★

Thriller   1942 · US · BW · 73mins

In this, director Fred Zinnemann's documentary background shines through, as police laboratory workers Van Heflin and Marsha Hunt investigate the murder of the local mayor. This was exactly the kind of movie that MGM made superbly, a B feature raised to A status with intelligent scripting, casting and direction. Heflin is impressive, as sincere and intense as always, but look closely at that stunning waitress with only two lines of dialogue – that's Ava Gardner!

Van Heflin *Gordon McKay* • Marsha Hunt *Jane Mitchell* • Lee Bowman *Gerald I Ladimer* • Samuel S Hinds *Mayor Daniels* • Cliff Clark *Captain Lynch* • Eddie Quillan *Eddie Wright* • Ava Gardner *Carhop* ■ *Dir* Fred Zinnemann • *Scr* Allen Rivkin, John C Higgins, from a story by John C Higgins

A Kid in Aladdin's Palace ★★

Fantasy adventure   1998 · US/Can · Colour · 89mins

This straight-to-video family film has an *Arabian Nights* setting, as a contemporary kid called Calvin gets whisked back to ancient Baghdad, magic-carpet style. There he encounters a bunch of story-tale characters: Aladdin, Ali Baba, Scheherazade and the like. A low budget means the film is a bit hit-and-myth, but less discriminating and younger kids should enjoy the cheesy effects of genies and magic carpets.

Thomas Ian Nicholas *Calvin* • Rhona Mitra *Scheherazade* • Nicholas Irons *Ali Baba* • James Faulkner *Luxor* • Taylor Negron *Genie* • Aharon Ipale *Aladdin* ■ *Dir* Robert L Levy • *Scr* Michael Part, Robert L Levy, from characters created by Michael Part

A Kid in King Arthur's Court ★★PG

Fantasy adventure   1995 · US · Colour · 86mins

Thomas Ian Nicholas (best known as Kevin from the comedy *American Pie*) stars as young Calvin Fuller, who is pulled from his 20th-century baseball game and brought to King Arthur's (Joss Ackland) court by Merlin (Ron Moody) to help him save Camelot. Very loosely reworked from Mark Twain's *A Connecticut Yankee in King Arthur's Court*, director Michael Gottleib (*Mr Nanny, Mannequin*) serves up a fun romp for the young and undemanding. Grown-ups will find it rather irritating due to some humungous plot holes, but may stay the distance just to catch a pre-*Titanic* Kate Winslet in a brief appearance as a princess.

Thomas Ian Nicholas *Calvin Fuller* • Joss Ackland *King Arthur* • Art Malik *Belasco* • Paloma Baeza *Katey* • Kate Winslet *Princess Sarah* • Daniel Craig *Master Kane* • Ron Moody *Merlin* ■ *Dir* Michael Gottleib • *Scr* Michael Part, Robert L Levy

Kid Millions ★★★U

Musical comedy   1934 · US · BW and Colour · 86mins

Eddie Cantor is very much an acquired taste for modern audiences, but in his day the banjo-eyed comedian was a huge stage and screen star. In this barmy vehicle canny producer Samuel Goldwyn has given him the works, including colour for a scene in an ice-cream factory, plus George Murphy and Ann Sothern singing an Irving Berlin medley. The support cast is astounding: don't miss the great Nicholas Brothers dancing team, or a young Ethel Merman as a gangster's moll; treats indeed. The plot is one for collectors of the bizarre, as Eddie is left a fortune in Egypt.

Eddie Cantor *Eddie Wilson Jr* • Ann Sothern *Joan Larrabee* • Ethel Merman *Dot Clark* • George Murphy *Jerry Lane* • Jesse Block *Ben Ali* • Eve Sully *Fanya* ■ *Dir* Roy Del Ruth, Willy Pogany • *Scr* Arthur Sheekman, Nat Perrin, Nunnally Johnson

Kid Rodelo ★U

Western adventure   1966 · US/Sp · BW · 90mins

Horse opera hokum based on a Louis L'Amour tale. Ex-con Don Murray tries to retrieve some hidden gold, while staying a jump ahead of various villains – including Broderick Crawford – and the Indians. An uneasy Spanish/US co-production, this suffers from a script crammed with clichés and fails to make the most of a good cast, which also includes Janet Leigh.

Don Murray *Kid Rodelo* • Janet Leigh *Nora* • Broderick Crawford *Joe Harbin* • Richard Carlson *Link* • Jose Nieto *Thomas Reese* ■ *Dir* Richard Carlson • *Scr* Jack Natteford, from a story by Louis L'Amour

Kid Vengeance ★★15

Western   1977 · US · Colour · 86mins

A repellent revenge western that teams genre veterans Lee Van Cleef and Jim Brown with seventies' teenage pop star Leif Garrett in some vain hope of snaring a gullible audience. Garrett plays a kid who goes after the killer of his parents (guess who?) and teams up with Brown's prospector whose gold has been stolen by the same man. Director Joseph Manduke pastes over the paucity of plot and simplicity of dialogue with violence and a number of savage deaths. Filmed in Israel, this dispiriting affair is significant only in that it marked Van Cleef's final foray into westerns.

Lee Van Cleef *McClain* • Jim Brown *Isaac* • John Marley *Jesus* • Glynnis O'Connor *Lisa* • Leif Garrett *Tom* • Matt Clark *Grover* ■ *Dir* Joseph Manduke • *Scr* Bud Robbins, Jay Telfer, from a story by Ken Globus

Kidnapped ★

Adventure   1938 · US · BW · 93mins

It might have seemed a good idea at the time to team David Copperfield (Freddie Bartholomew) and the Cisco Kid (Warner Baxter) in Robert Louis Stevenson's classic action tale, but 20th Century-Fox should have also included a higher production budget and a better director than Alfred Werker. Sticking to the original story might have helped, too. This is a decidedly cheap and murky adaptation, and Baxter as Alan Breck looks, and sounds, quite uncomfortable; far too unathletic and American.

Warner Baxter *Alan Breck* • Freddie Bartholomew *David Balfour* • Arleen Whelan *Jean MacDonald* • C Aubrey Smith *Duke of Argyle* • Reginald Owen *Captain Hoseason* • John Carradine *Gordon* • Nigel Bruce *Neil MacDonald* • Miles Mander *Ebenezer Balfour* • Ralph Forbes *James* • HB Warner *Rankeillor* ■ *Dir* Alfred Werker • *Scr* Sonya Levien, Eleanor Harris, Ernest Pascal, Edwin Blum, from the novel by Robert Louis Stevenson

Kidnapped ★U

Adventure   1948 · US · BW · 81mins

Another weak screen version of Robert Louis Stevenson's yarn about a boy who claims an inheritance from his uncle, but is grabbed and sold into slavery. He escapes and sets off to reclaim his prize. Made by dime-budget Monogram Pictures, it's associate-produced by Roddy McDowall, who stars as David Balfour, the young Scot saved by adventurer Alan Breck, played here by Dan O'Herlihy. McDowall's mother plays the wife of an innkeeper, her only film role.

Roddy McDowall *David Balfour* • Sue England *Aileen Fairlie* • Dan O'Herlihy *Alan Breck* • Roland Winters *Captain Hoseason* • Jeff Corey *Shuan* • Housley Stevenson [Houseley Stevenson] *Ebenezer* • Winefried McDowall *Innkeeper's wife* ■ *Dir* William Beaudine • *Scr* W Scott Darling, from the novel by Robert Louis Stevenson

Kidnapped ★★★U

Adventure   1960 · US · Colour · 90mins

Robert Louis Stevenson's classic yarn is given the Walt Disney treatment, with James MacArthur a sort of Steve McQueen in diapers as the disinherited David Balfour and Peter Finch as the dashing Scottish loyalist who befriends him. Filmed on beautiful Highland locations and with Peter O'Toole making an early screen appearance, this version is a decent enough romp for the bairns. It's also a nostalgia trip for those who cherish porridge-oats accents from the likes of Niall MacGinnis (who's actually Irish), John Laurie, Finlay Currie and Andrew Cruickshank, the original Dr Cameron from *Dr Finlay's Casebook.*

Peter Finch *Alan Breck* • James MacArthur *David Balfour* • Bernard Lee *Captain Hoseason* • Niall MacGinnis *Shuan* • John Laurie *Uncle Ebenezer* • Finlay Currie *Cluny MacPherson* • Peter O'Toole *Robin Oig MacGregor* • Miles Malleson *Mr Rankeillor* ■ *Dir* Robert Stevenson • *Scr* Robert Stevenson, from the novel by Robert Louis Stevenson

Kidnapped ★★★U

Adventure   1971 · UK · Colour · 102mins

Michael Caine's witty swagger, in the role of outlaw Alan Breck, stirs some otherwise rather stiff porridge into life. Robert Louis Stevenson's stories have been filmed several times before, but this version is the one that is most faithful to the source, and it contains some strong performances: Trevor Howard as the Lord Advocate and Lawrence Douglas as young David keep the narrative moving along.

Michael Caine *Alan Breck* • Trevor Howard *Lord Grant* • Jack Hawkins *Captain Hoseason* • Donald Pleasence *Ebenezer Balfour* • Gordon Jackson *Charles Stewart* • Vivien Heilbron *Catriona* • Lawrence Douglas *David Balfour* ■ *Dir* Delbert Mann • *Scr* Jack Pulman, from the novel by Robert Louis Stevenson,

Kidnapped to Mystery Island ★★

Action adventure   1964 · It/W Ger · Colour · 89mins

Although this is supposed to be an all-action adventure, it is directed by Luigi Capuano with no sense of urgency and a disregard for the basics of scene-setting, which ensures that it rarely involves or convinces. Also known as *The Mystery of Thug Island*, it is one of the many pictures made in Italy with Guy Madison after his career had come to a virtual standstill in the US. However, he can make little impression in this thickheaded tale about the rescue of an English girl who has joined the "thugee" cult that kidnapped her some 15 years earlier. Italian and German dialogue dubbed into English.

Guy Madison *Souyadhana* • Inge Schoner *Edy* • Giacomo Rossi Stuart *Tremal-Naik* • Peter Van Eyck *Captain Macpherson* • Ivan Desny *Maciadi* • Giulia Rubini *Gundali* • Nando Poggi *Kammamuri* ■ *Dir* Luigi Capuano • *Scr* Arpad De Riso, Ottavio Poggi

The Kidnappers ★★★★U

Drama   1953 · UK · BW · 89mins

Popular in its day and still charming, this drama tells the story of two Scottish orphans in turn-of-the-century Nova Scotia, who steal a baby when their stern grandfather won't let them have a dog. This slight tale is perfectly performed by two natural child actors: Jon Whiteley from *Hunted* (who went on to act in Australia) and Vincent Winter (who became a production director on major feature films); both youngsters received special Oscars as a result. Director Philip Leacock creates a realistic, almost documentary-like atmosphere of a closed-in, isolated community, and is helped by fine performances from Duncan Macrae and Jean Anderson as the grandparents.

Duncan Macrae *Granddaddy* • Jean Anderson *Grandma* • Adrienne Corri *Kirsty* • Theodore Bikel *Willem Bloem* • Jon Whiteley *Harry* • Vincent Winter *Davy* • Francis De Wolff *Jan Hooft Sr* • James Sutherland *Arron McNab* • John Rae *Andrew McCleod* ■ *Dir* Philip Leacock • *Scr* Neil Paterson

A Kidnapping in the Family ★★

Drama based on a true story   1996 · US · Colour

One of those American TV movies that takes a serious social issue and turns it into prime-time melodrama. The subject here is Satanic child abuse – a charge trumped up by Kate Jackson and levelled at her daughter, played by Tracey Gold. Soon Jackson takes the law into her own hands and plots to kidnap her hapless grandchild. Jackson – probably best known as Sabrina in *Charlie's Angels* – makes the most of her fruity role, and it's competently handled by director Colin Bucksey.

Tracey Gold *Sarah Landers* • Kate Jackson *DeDe Cooper* • Jeff Yagher *Jack Taylor* • Robert Bishop *Kyle Landers* ■ *Dir* Colin Bucksey • *Scr* David Birke

The Kidnapping of the President ★★

Thriller 1980 · Can · Colour · 113mins

Terrorists kidnap President Hal Holbrook in Toronto, bundle him into a bomb-laden, booby-trapped truck and demand a hefty ransom for his release. Secret Service agent William Shatner – having beamed down from his intergalactic day job – goes to work, leaving the White House in the hands of Vice President Van Johnson and his wife Ava Gardner. Compared to action movies like the *Die Hard* trilogy or *Air Force One*, this routine thriller is a trifling matter.

William Shatner *Jerry O'Connor* • Hal Holbrook *President Adam Scott* • Van Johnson *Vice President Ethan Richards* • Ava Gardner *Beth Richards* • Miguel Fernandes *Roberto Assanti* • Cindy Girling *Linda Steiner* ■ *Dir* George Mendeluk • *Scr* Richard Murphy, from a novel by Charles Templeton

kids ★★★★ 18

Drama 1995 · US · Colour · 86mins

Baby-faced teenager Leo Fitzpatrick is a self-styled "virgin surgeon", who spends his days beating up street trash, getting drunk and stoned and deflowering very young girls. One of his conquests (Chloë Sevigny) tries to track him down to tell him he's HIV-positive, while still dazed from her own diagnosis. Acerbically scripted by Harmony Korine and directed by influential underground photographer Larry Clark, this disturbingly explicit look at Generation X "skateboard culture" poses difficult questions and offers few easy answers. Clark's issue-raising treatise was deemed offensive exploitation by some sectors of society, but is in fact highly moral and thought provoking. Contains swearing and a violent scene. [VID]

Leo Fitzpatrick *Telly* • Justin Pierce *Casper* • Chloë Sevigny *Jennie* • Sarah Henderson *Girl* • Rosario Dawson *Ruby* • Harold Hunter *Harold* • Joseph Chan *Deli owner* ■ *Dir* Larry Clark • *Scr* Harmony Korine, from a story by Larry Clark, Jim Lewis

The Kids Are Alright ★★★ 15

Music documentary 1978 · UK · BW and Colour · 96mins

The value of this "rockumentary" trip through the highs and lows of The Who's career was increased by the death of the band's extrovert drummer Keith Moon in September 1978. However, fans will probably not want to dwell on the frankly depressing final concert footage, preferring to see Moon in classic sixties action, when his hellraising was matched by his extraordinary on-stage energy. Director Jeff Stein occasionally errs into hagiography, but there's a generous sampling of hits (and the odd miss), interviews and rare archival material, as well as guest appearances by Steve Martin, Ringo Starr, Melvyn Bragg and Jeremy Paxman. [VID] **DVD**

Dir/Scr Jeff Stein

Kids in the Hall: Brain Candy ★★ 15

Comedy 1996 · US · Colour · 84mins

Canada's answer to *Saturday Night Live* makes its first foray into the movies, although the all-male team's determination to play virtually every major role (as well as their penchant for dressing up in women's clothing) makes *Monty Python* a closer reference point. Dave Foley, Bruce McCulloch, Kevin McDonald, Mark McKinney and Scott Thompson are not in the same league as John Cleese and friends. However, this sketchy story of a young doctor who discovers a cure for depression does have its moments. [VID]

Dave Foley *Marv/Psychiatrist/Suicidal businessman/New guy/Raymond* • Bruce McCulloch *Grivo/Alice/Cisco/Cop/White-trash man/Cancer boy* • Kevin McDonald *Chris Cooper/Chris's dad/Doreen* • Mark McKinney *Don Roritor/Simon/German patient/Nina Bedford/Cabbie/White-trash woman* • Scott Thompson *Wally Terzinsky/Mrs Hurdicure/Baxter/Malek/Clemptor/The Queen* ■ *Dir* Kelly Makin • *Scr* Norm Hiscock, Bruce McCulloch, Kevin McDonald, Mark McKinney, Scott Thompson

Kids Like These ★★★ PG

Drama based on a true story 1987 · US · Colour · 92mins

Tyne Daly has never been the most subtle of actresses, but her energetic style is perfectly suited to playing the lead in this TV movie, a mother who combines bringing up her Down's syndrome son with mounting a campaign to increase public understanding of the condition. There is a good deal of insight and authenticity in Emily Perl Kingsley's script, as she went down much the same road herself. Director Georg Stanford Brown was married to Daly at the time, and he disrupts the drama slightly with his determination to do his wife justice. [VID]

Martin Balsam • Tyne Daly • Richard Crenna ■ *Dir* Georg Stanford Brown • *Scr* Emily Perl Kingsley, from her own experiences

Kids Return ★★★ 15

Crime comedy drama 1996 · Jap · Colour · 107mins

This was the first feature director Takeshi Kitano completed after he fractured his skull in a near-fatal scooter accident. With two pals forming a stand-up comedy team, there's a strong sense of autobiography about this rites-of-passage picture. But the main focus falls on Masanobu Ando and Ken Kaneko, two schoolboys who leave the education system with little option but to drift into boxing and crime respectively. Cross-cutting with typical energy and invention, Kitano persuades us to warm to these underachievers and, although the film may be less abrasive than earlier works, it still provides a bruising encounter with the hard facts of life, Kitano's trademark. In Japanese with English subtitles.

Masanobu Ando *Shinji Takagi* • Ken Kaneko *Masaru Miyawaki* • Leo Morimoto *Teacher* • Hatsuo Yamaya *Boxing club manager* • Mitsuko Oka *Coffee shop owner, Sachiko's mother* • Ryo Ishibashi *Local Yakuza chief* ■ *Dir/Scr* Takeshi Kitano

Kidz in the Wood ★★

Drama 1996 · US · Colour

Best known for co-scripting *Police Academy* and directing Tom Hanks in *Bachelor Party*, Neal Israel ventures into teenager territory with this back-to-nature made-for-TV comedy. When they get lost on an educational expedition along the Oregon trail, eight underprivileged kids (who know no fear in the urban jungle) suddenly have to draw on the wisdom of the wagon-train pioneers in order to survive. Mercifully free of the spicier sort of street language, this has enough comic incident to keep most children amused – but the patronising tone might grate on more discriminating viewers.

David Thomas [Dave Thomas (1)] *Tom Foster* • Julia Duffy *Felicia Duffy* • Tatyana M Ali [Tatyana Ali] *Rita* • Candace Cameron *Donna* • David Lascher *Sloan* ■ *Dir* Neal Israel • *Scr* Neal Israel, Robert Klane

Kika ★★ 18

Comedy 1993 · Sp · Colour · 109mins

A familiar diet of sexual deviance, rape, murder and the media from Pedro Almodóvar, the Spaniard famous for his absurd irony and outrageous imagination. A master at creating, then tying up, the most convoluted plots, this is from his lacklustre middle period (including *High Heels* and *Tie Me Up! Tie Me Down!*) and focuses on shallow make-up artist Veronica Forqué, who makes up a dead body as a favour for a serial-killing author. But the stiff of said novelist's stepson's lesbian maid's psychologically disturbed porno-star brother suddenly comes back to life – so she moves in with him! However, it's ultimately a pointless charade revealing Almodóvar on the verge of a creative breakdown. In Spanish with English subtitles. [VID]

Verónica Forqué *Kika* • Peter Coyote *Nicholas* • Victoria Abril *Andrea Caracortada* • Alex Casanovas *Ramón* • Rossy de Palma *Juana* • Santiago Lajusticia *Pablo* • Anabel Alonso *Amparo* • Bibí Andersen *Susana* ■ *Dir/Scr* Pedro Almodóvar

Kikuchi ★★★

Drama 1990 · Jap · Colour · 68mins

Disconcerting in its depiction of tedious routine, yet bristling with a sense of latent violence, this brooding study of voyeurism and the dehumanising effect of modern city life marked the directorial debut of one-time *manga* artist Kenchi Iwamoto. Considering its relatively short length, the film is so successful in conveying the stupefyingly dull nature of Jiro Yoshimura's laundry job that his obsessional pursuit of checkout girl Misa Fukuma almost becomes understandable. Almost. Often recalling Yasujiro Ozu with its use of long, immobile takes, this blend of eerie comedy and prowling thriller is guaranteed to arouse mixed emotions. In Japanese with English subtitles.

Jiro Yoshimura *Kikuchi* • Yasuhiro Oka *Man* • Misa Fukuma *Woman* ■ *Dir/Scr* Kenchi Iwamoto

Kikujiro ★★★★★ 12

Comedy drama 1999 · Jap · Colour · mins

With the violence that has characterised so many of his films toned down to slapstick socko, this is Takeshi Kitano's offbeat homage to *The Wizard of Oz*. As the amoral Yakuza who accompanies nine-year-old Yusuke Sekiguchi on a cross-country mission to find his mother, Kitano gives an inspired demonstration of muddle-headed, short-fused deadpan. The duo meanders from racetrack to fairground, encountering en route a paedophile, a rude hotel clerk and a couple of soft-centred bikers. There are no deep messages here, just dream sequences, unexpected revelations and several achingly funny set pieces. A gem from a genius. In Japanese with English subtitles.

Takeshi Kitano *Kikujiro* • Kayoko Kishimoto *Miki, Kikujiro's wife* • Yusuke Sekiguchi *Masao* • Akaji Maro *Paedophile* • Yuko Daike *Masao's mother* ■ *Dir/Scr* Takeshi Kitano

Kill! ★

Thriller 1972 · Fr/It/Sp/W Ger · Colour · 102mins

Celebrated novelist Romain Gary directs this paper-thin co-production with little demonstrable understanding of the mechanics of movie-making. By allowing his tale of drug smuggling and porn peddling to quickly sprawl out of control, he sheds vital clues to the identity of the master criminal with such abandon that the solution is apparent almost from the outset. James Mason looks glum as the man from Interpol, but beside Jean Seberg as his wife he seems exhilarated.

James Mason *Alan* • Jean Seberg *Emily* • Stephen Boyd *Killian* • Curt Jurgens *Chief* • Daniel Emilfork *Inspector* • Henri Garcin *Lawyer* ■ *Dir* Herb Shriner • *Scr* Romain Gary

Kill a Dragon ★

Martial arts action adventure 1967 · US · Colour · 97mins

Rarely seen and largely unlamented, this muddled adventure with Jack Palance finds him in China to battle crime lord Fernando Lamas. The other familiar face in the cast is screen veteran Aldo Ray, but all three leads can do little with the preposterous, haphazard plotting.

Jack Palance *Rick* • Fernando Lamas *Patrai* • Aldo Ray *Vigo* • Alizia Gur *Tisa* • Tong Kam Win Lim ■ *Dir* Michael Moore (1) • *Scr* George Schenck, William Marks

Kill and Kill Again ★★★ 15

Martial arts action 1981 · US · Colour · 94mins

James Ryan is a world-famous martial artist, recruited by Anneline Kriel to save her father – a scientist who can make fuel out of potatoes – from an evil dictator. To do this, Ryan recruits guys with names like the Fly, Gorilla and Hotdog. Probably the best karate film ever made in South Africa, though that's not much of a recommendation. Lovers of cult movies will be in seventh heaven, however. ■

James Ryan *Steve Chase* • Anneline Kriel *Kandy Kane* • Ken Gampu *Gorilla* • Norman

U = SUITABLE FOR ALL **Uc** = SUITABLE FOR ALL, ESPECIALLY FOR YOUNG CHILDREN (VIDEO ONLY) **PG** = PARENTAL GUIDANCE

Robinson *Gypsy Billy* • Stan Schmidt *The Fly* • Bill Flynn *Hotdog* • Michael Mayer *Marduk* ■ *Dir* Ivan Hall • *Scr* John Crowther

Kill and Pray ★★★ 15
Spaghetti western
1968 · It/W Ger · Colour · 102mins
Violently watchable Italian-German spaghetti western – with as many loose ends as that kind of pasta. It hides its Marxist message behind a gunsmoke-screen of shoot-outs and showdowns, as a preacher's adopted son discovers that the massacre he survived was instigated by capitalists in order to steal land from Mexican peasants. Director Carlo Lizzani must have been looking over his own shoulder with apprehension, because the great film-maker Pier Paolo Pasolini makes a guest appearance as a revolutionary priest. Not only talented, but gauntly photogenic as well. Italian dialogue dubbed into English. ▭
Lou Castel *Requiescant* • Mark Damon *Ferguson* • Barbara Frey *Princy* • Pier Paolo Pasolini *Don Juan* • Franco Citti *Burt* ■ *Dir* Carlo Lizzani

Kill Me Again ★★★ 18
Crime thriller 1989 · US · Colour · 92mins
John Dahl has emerged as a stylish *film noir* director, and hit the peak of his form with the magnificent *The Last Seduction*. Marking his directorial debut, this is far from flawless, but Dahl demonstrates an already instinctive touch for *femmes fatales* and flawed heroes in a typically convoluted story about a private detective (Val Kilmer) who is persuaded by a beautiful young woman (Joanne Whalley-Kilmer) into faking her death. Notable for providing an early psycho role for *Reservoir Dogs's* Michael Madsen, the main problem here is the two leads, who fail to convince. Still, an impressive debut from Dahl. Contains violence, swearing and sex scenes. ▭
Joanne Whalley-Kilmer [Joanne Whalley] *Fay Forrester* • Val Kilmer *Jack Andrews* • Michael Madsen *Vince Miller* • Jonathan Gries *Alan Swayzie* • Pat Mulligan *Sammy* ■ *Dir* John Dahl • *Scr* David W Warfield, John Dahl

Kill Me If You Can ★★★★
Drama based on a true story
1977 · US · Colour
In one of his most accomplished TV-movie roles, Alan Alda is riveting in the true story of Caryl Chessman, the notorious "Red Light Bandit", who served 12 years on Death Row before being executed in 1960. As the erudite Chessman, Alda veers between rage and serene determination with mesmerising power, and his performance was rewarded with an Emmy nomination. TV movies rarely come this stark or involving.
Alan Alda *Caryl Chessman* • Talia Shire *Rosalie Asher* • John Hillerman *George Davis* • Barnard Hughes *Judge Fricke* • Virginia Kiser *Virginia Gibbons* ■ *Dir* Buzz Kulik • *Scr* John Gay

Kill Me Tomorrow ★★ U
Crime drama 1957 · UK · BW · 80mins
Warner Bros rarely pushed lead roles Pat O'Brien's way. Even so, it's hard to

fathom why he crossed the Atlantic for the starring role in this far-fetched B-movie. You might expect an impoverished father trying to fund his son's eye operation to resort to some pretty desperate tactics – but confessing to a murder in order to raise the money? Hardly the behaviour of an ace reporter, although he does come to his senses in time to crack a diamond-smuggling racket. Terence Fisher directs with little enthusiasm, but it's worth hanging in there to catch the debut of Tommy Steele.
Pat O'Brien *Bart Crosbie* • Lois Maxwell *Jill Brook* • George Coulouris *Heinz Webber* • Wensley Pithey *Inspector Lane* • Freddie Mills *Waxy* • Ronald Adam *Brook* • Tommy Steele ■ *Dir* Terence Fisher • *Scr* Manning O'Brine, Robert Falconer

The Kill-Off ★★★ 18
Thriller 1989 · US · Colour · 93mins
The bleakness contained in Jim Thompson's hard-boiled novels has been a notoriously difficult tone to pull off in movie adaptations of his work, but director Maggie Greenwald's bitter little thriller does a better job than most. Loretta Gross stands out in the no-name ensemble cast as the vicious gossip-monger in a small American town, whose acid tongue is feared by every local resident. So they decide to do something to silence her, which inevitably leads to further nastiness and violence. Not a great advert for human nature, but an engaging mood piece that's both grim and grimy in an unrelentingly drab way. Contains swearing, drug abuse and nudity. ▭
Loretta Gross *Luane Devore* • Jackson Sims *Pete Pavlov* • Steve Monroe *Ralph* • Andrew Lee Barrett *Bobbie Ashton* • Cathy Haase *Danny Lee* • Jorjan Fox *Myra Pavlov* ■ *Dir* Maggie Greenwald • *Scr* Maggie Greenwald, from a novel by Jim Thompson

Kill or Cure ★ U
Comedy mystery 1962 · UK · BW · 88mins
This is the kind of comedy that could have killed off the British film industry, despite its domestic star-power and the usually reliable writing team of David Pursall and Jack Seddon. When a bumbling private detective (gap-toothed Terry-Thomas) tries to investigate a murder at a posh spa, the only interest is in seeing him lock comedy horns with Eric Sykes, Lionel Jeffries and Moira Redmond. Unfortunately, it is to little effect.
Terry-Thomas *J Barker-Rynde* • Eric Sykes *Rumbelow* • Dennis Price *Dr Crossley* • Lionel Jeffries *Inspector Hook* • Moira Redmond *Frances Reitman* • Ronnie Barker *Burton* ■ *Dir* George Pollock • *Scr* David Pursall, Jack Seddon

Killdozer ★★
Science-fiction thriller
1974 · US · Colour · 74mins
Here's a daft thriller about a bulldozer that becomes possessed by mysterious forces and becomes a death machine. Clint Walker is the leader of the construction gang under threat, while the sharp-eyed will spot a youthful Robert Urich as well as the more distinctive features of top screen heavy Neville Brand. However, in the

suspense stakes, this is a long way from *Duel*.
Clint Walker *Lloyd Kelly* • Carl Betz *Dennis Holvig* • Neville Brand *Chub Foster* • James Wainwright *Jules "Dutch" Krasner* • Robert Urich *Mack McCarthy* ■ *Dir* Jerry London • *Scr* Theodore Sturgeon, Ed Mackillop, from the novel by Theodore Sturgeon

Killer! ★★★★
Thriller 1969 · Fr/It · Colour · 110mins
Adapted from a novel by Nicholas Blake (pseudonym of former poet laureate Cecil Day Lewis), this is one of Claude Chabrol's most accomplished pictures. Starting out as a whodunit – as widower Michel Duchaussoy seeks the hit-and-run driver who killed his son – the film turns into a psychological thriller. Duchaussoy inveigles himself into the culprit's family, only to decide that his planned revenge would be inappropriate. While exploring such themes as guilt, justice and moral responsibility, Chabrol mischievously muddies the waters by allowing Jean Yanne to portray the killer as an oaf who, despite alienating his own boy, is somehow grotesquely engaging. A French language film.
Michel Duchaussoy *Charles Thenier* • Caroline Cellier *Helene Lanson* • Jean Yanne *Paul Decourt* • Anouk Ferjac *Jeanne* • Marc DiNapoli *Philippe Decourt* • Maurice Pialat *Police inspector* ■ *Dir* Claude Chabrol • *Scr* Paul Gegauff, Claude Chabrol, from the novel *The Beast Must Die* by Nicholas Blake [Cecil Day Lewis]

The Killer ★★★★ 18
Action melodrama
1989 · HK · Colour · 106mins
A Hong Kong gangster movie that's directed with such over-the-top verve by John Woo that you're transfixed by its audacity, despite several stomach-churning scenes of violence. Chow Yun-Fat is the assassin who decides to quit his profession after accidentally blinding a singer (Sally Yeh) during a hit in a nightclub. When he learns that her sight could be restored through an operation, he decides to fund it by doing just one more job. Of its amoral kind it's great bullet-dodging fun, but it's definitely not for the faint-hearted. In Cantonese with English subtitles. Contains violence and brief nudity. ▭
Chow Yun-Fat *Jeff* • Danny Lee *Inspector "Eagle" Lee* • Sally Yeh *Jennie* • Kong Chu *Sydney Fung* • Kenneth Tsang *Sergeant Randy Chung* • Chung Lam *Willie Tsang* • Shing Fui-on *Johnny Weng* ■ *Dir/Scr* John Woo

Killer ★★ 18
Crime thriller 1994 · US · Colour · 93mins
Gangland hit man Anthony LaPaglia meets his match when he's assigned *femme fatale* Mimi Rogers as his last kill; the twist in director Mark Malone's contemporary *film noir* is that Rogers knows she's due to die and intends to make the heartless killer feel as guilty as possible. Is she his saviour, or his downfall? That's the central enigma of this pretentious look at the human condition, packed with long stares, dark shadows and dialogue like "what is the meaning of meaning?". The stars deliver strong performances, but it's a lackadaisical suspense drama percolating with unfulfilled promise.

Contains swearing, sex scenes and some violence. ▭
Anthony LaPaglia *Mick* • Mimi Rogers *Fiona* • Matt Craven *Archie* • Peter Boyle *George* • Monika Schnarre *Laura* • Joseph Maher *Dr Alstricht* ■ *Dir* Mark Malone • *Scr* Gordon Melbourne, from a story by Mark Malone

Killer: a Journal of Murder ★★★ 18
Biographical prison drama
1995 · US · Colour · 87mins
This violent drama is carried along by the intensity of James Woods's performance as Carl Panzram who, having confessed to murdering 21 people, had the dubious "honour" of being America's first recognised serial killer. Robert Sean Leonard plays Henry Lesser, a liberal prison guard who sees the value in Panzram writing down his story for future reference. When the inmate slaughters a sadistic warden, however, Lesser hopes to use Panzram's journal to mount an insanity defence. An absorbing, if violent, case history that asks all the relevant moral questions. Contains swearing, violence and a sexual assault. ▭
James Woods *Carl Panzram* • Robert Sean Leonard *Henry Lesser* • Ellen Greene *Elizabeth Wyatt* • Cara Buono *Esther Lesser* • Robert John Burke [Robert Burke] *RG Greiser* • Steve Forrest *Warden Charles Casey* • Jeffrey DeMunn *Sam Lesser* ■ *Dir* Tim Metcalfe • *Scr* Tim Metcalfe, from the non-fiction book by Thomas E Gaddis, James O Long

A Killer among Friends ★★
Drama based on a true story
1992 · US · Colour · 96mins
Familiar faces, familiar terrain. The US seems to have a never-ending supply of bizarre true stories and this competent if routine drama fits the bill perfectly, neatly tying up murder, melodrama and sentimentality into a glossy package. Tiffani-Amber Thiessen is the golden girl who is shockingly murdered by a mysterious assailant. As her grieving mother Patty Duke attempts to cope with her loss, dogged detective Loretta Swit discovers disturbing clues leading to the identity of the killer. The quality cast ensures that this is always watchable, but don't expect any surprises.
Patty Duke *Jean Monroe* • Loretta Swit *Detective Staley* • Margaret Welsh *Ellen Holloway* • Tiffani-Amber Thiessen *Jenny Monroe* ■ *Dir* Charles Robert Carner • *Scr* Christopher Lofton, John Miglis, Charles Robert Carner, from a story by Christopher Lofton

A Killer among Us ★★ 15
Crime drama 1990 · US · Colour · 88mins
A banal twist on the *12 Angry Men* theme, with juror Jasmine Guy holding out on a guilty verdict on a man accused of murdering his wife, because she thinks the jury foreman may have done the dirty deed. If you believe that, you'll believe anything in this strictly routine TV movie. With credibility at a premium, director Peter Levin's drama has hardly got enough faith in itself to mount sufficient tension to keep viewers watching. ▭
Jasmine Guy *Teresa Hopkins* • Dwight Schultz *Roland Gillette* • Anna Maria Horsford *Barbara Evans* • Mykel T Williamson [Mykel T

Williamson] *Greg Hopkins* • Lisa Banes *Joanna Westrope* ■ *Dir* Peter Levin • *Scr* David Westheimer

Killer Calibre 32 ★★
Spaghetti western   1967 · It · Colour

A spaghetti western that owes more to Saturday matinée series like *The Cisco Kid* than to the grand designs of Sergio Leone. Peter Lee Lawrence stars as a dandified bounty hunter, hired to uncover the true identities of the seven masked men who have been repeatedly robbing the Carson City stagecoach. It won't take a Wyatt Earp to work out who is the mastermind behind the gang, but at least director Alfonso Brescia has the sense to realise that this has to be played tongue in cheek, and keeps the action moving at a fair lick. Italian dialogue dubbed into English.

Peter Lee Lawrence *Silver* • Cole Kitosch *Averell* • Sherill Morgan ■ *Dir* Alfonso Brescia

The Killer Elite ★★★ 18
Action thriller   1975 · US · Colour · 118mins

When the picture he wanted to make – *The Insurance Company* – was abruptly cancelled by the studio, Sam Peckinpah went straight on to direct *The Killer Elite*, which was already written, cast and ready to go. As a result, Peckinpah had nothing but contempt for this San Francisco-based thriller. *Godfather* co-stars James Caan and Robert Duvall are reunited in this tale of CIA spooks, car chases, martial artistry and bloody shoot-outs. The result is both quite exciting and instantly forgettable. ▣

James Caan *Mike Locken* • Robert Duvall *George Hansen* • Arthur Hill *Cap Collis* • Bo Hopkins *Jerome Miller* • Mako *Yuen Chung* • Burt Young *Mac* • Gig Young *Laurence Weyburn* • Tom Clancy *O'Leary* ■ *Dir* Sam Peckinpah • *Scr* Marc Norman, Stirling Silliphant, from the novel *Monkey in the Middle* by Robert Rostand

Killer Fish ★★ 15
Adventure thriller
1978 · It/Bra · Colour · 96mins

In this interestingly cast Italian-Brazilian co-production, a selected handful of near-stars enjoy an exotic Brazilian location shoot while pretending to hunt for purloined jewels in a lake full of piranha. Nice to see Margaux Hemingway and *Cabaret*'s Marisa Berenson, although there's a serious warning here to models who attempt acting careers. Interestingly, it is still the best cast director Dawson – real name Antonio Margheriti, purveyor of spaghetti western and horror – ever assembled. Watch with a six-pack. ▣

Lee Majors *Robert Lasky* • Karen Black *Kate Neville* • James Franciscus *Paul Diller* • Margaux Hemingway *Gabrielle* • Marisa Berenson *Ann* • Gary Collins *Tom* • Roy Brocksmith *Ollie* • Dan Pastorini *Hans* ■ *Dir* Anthony M Dawson [Antonio Margheriti] • *Scr* Michael Rogers

Killer Force ★★
Action thriller
1975 · Swi/Ire · Colour · 98mins

Also known as *The Diamond Mercenaries*, this action thriller concerns a plot to rob a diamond mine in South Africa. Chief of security Telly

Savalas teams up with Peter Fonda to foil the scheme. Director Val Guest's film features some impressive location footage; unfortunately, it also contains some tiresome philosophising. Maud Adams plays Fonda's girlfriend and seems bored rigid, while Christopher Lee – Adams's co-star in *The Man with the Golden Gun* – appears as a disaffected British soldier.

Telly Savalas *Harry Webb* • Peter Fonda *Mike Bradley* • Christopher Lee *Chilton* • OJ Simpson *"Bopper" Alexander* • Maud Adams *Clare Chambers* • Hugh O'Brian *Lewis* ■ *Dir* Val Guest • *Scr* Val Guest, Michael Winder, Gerald Sanford

The Killer inside Me ★★ 18
Thriller   1975 · US · Colour · 91mins

Adapted from a novel by Jim Thompson, a classy purveyor of cult pulp fiction, this never quite convinces as it attempts to show the disintegration of well-respected deputy sheriff Stacy Keach into uncontrollable mania. Keach is one of those risk-all actors who can do many things; one thing he can't do, though, is to stand up to the clunkingly obvious direction of Burt Kennedy. ▣

Stacy Keach *Lou Ford* • Susan Tyrrell *Joyce Lakeland* • Tisha Sterling *Amy Stanton* • Keenan Wynn *Chester Conway* • Don Stroud *Elmer Conway* • Charles McGraw *Howard Hendricks* • John Dehner *Bob Maples* • John Carradine *Dr Smith* ■ *Dir* Burt Kennedy • *Scr* Edward Mann, Robert Chamblee, from the novel by Jim Thompson

Killer Instinct ★★ 15
Drama   1988 · US · Colour · 94mins

This TV movie is mostly of interest for providing an early starring role for Woody Harrelson, who was then still making his name as the slow-witted barman in *Cheers*. He arrives pretty late on the scene, however, as a lawyer who defends psychiatrist Melissa Gilbert (the *Little House on the Prairie* star) after her "softly, softly" approach with dangerous patient Fernando Lopez goes murderously wrong. Directed by Waris Hussein (best known for British TV series *Edward and Mrs Simpson*), it's a solid enough piece of melodrama, but don't expect surprises. Contains violence, swearing and nudity. ▣

Melissa Gilbert *Dr Lisa DaVito* • Woody Harrelson *Charlie Daimler* • Fernando Lopez *Freddie Zamora* • Lane Smith *Dr Butler* ■ *Dir* Waris Hussein • *Scr* Conrad Bromberg

Killer Klowns from Outer Space ★★★ 15
Science-fiction horror comedy
1988 · US · Colour · 82mins

Combining inspired amateur brashness, delightful *Loony Tunes* design and a winningly bizarre unreality, this engagingly cheap affair from effects wizards Stephen and Charles Chiodo is an infantile and vicious delight. Alien clowns invade Earth in a spacecraft masquerading as a circus tent; they intend to cocoon the local population in candy floss and suck out their life juices, unless two teens and a cop can stop them. A great fairground attraction that cleverly pays homage to fifties' schlock, however with its acid custard pies,

homicidal Jack in the Boxes and malevolent Punch and Judy shows, this is definitely not for children. ▣

Grant Cramer *Mike* • Suzanne Snyder *Debbie* • John Allen Nelson *Officer Dave Hanson* • Royal Dano *Farmer Green* • John Vernon *Officer Mooney* ■ *Dir* Stephen Chiodo • *Scr* Stephen Chiodo, Charles Chiodo

Killer McCoy ★★
Sports drama   1947 · US · BW · 103mins

In this so-called "adult drama", designed to show he wasn't just able to play Andy Hardy, Mickey Rooney is cast as the son of a drunken entertainer who accidentally kills his best friend and takes over as a lightweight boxing champion. It's as implausible as only MGM can make it, and much emphasis is put on the pain that Rooney has endured to get there and keeps enduring when being punched senseless in the ring. However, audiences were still reminded of Rooney's musical talent by several vaudeville sequences.

Mickey Rooney *Tommy McCoy* • Brian Donlevy *Jim Caighn* • Ann Blyth *Sheila Carrson* • James Dunn *Brian McCoy* • Tom Tully *Cecil Y Walsh* • Sam Levene *Happy* • Walter Sande *Bill Thorne* ■ *Dir* Roy Rowland • *Scr* Frederick Hazlitt Brennan, from a screenplay (unproduced) by Thomas Lennon, George Bruce, George Oppenheimer • *Music/Lyrics* Stanley Donen

Killer Nun ★★★
Cult horror   1978 · It · Colour · 87mins

Morphine addiction, lesbianism, gore, scandal and Catholic guilt: it's all here in a gleefully demented Italian schlock cocktail that wallows in nasty sleaze while adopting an inappropriate and hilariously pious attitude. One-time European glamour queen Anita Ekberg plays a paranoid nun who isn't sure if her homicidal nightmares are the real thing or not in trash merchant Giulio Berruti's bad-taste shocker, packed with wild sex sessions and hard-edged violence. Andy Warhol icon Joe Dallesandro as a doctor and spaghetti superstar Alida Valli as the mother superior add extra cult value. In Italian with English subtitles.

Anita Ekberg *Sister Gertrud* • Joe Dallesandro *Dr Rowland* • Lou Castel *Peter* • Alida Valli *Mother superior* ■ *Dir* Giulio Berruti • *Scr* Giulio Berruti, Alberto Tarallo

Killer Party ★★ 18
Horror   1986 · US · Colour · 87mins

It's April Fool's Day in this standard dead-teens-on-campus slasher tale involving lethal fraternity hi-jinks and a vengeful killer wearing a diver's suit. After a promising start, involving a film-within-a-rock-video-within-a-film sucker-punch, and despite some creative modes of murder, this good-looking nonsense drifts into a repetitive groove of laughs and scares. However, the late cult director Paul Bartel is as delightful as always, playing a stuffy professor who gets it in the neck. ▣

Martin Hewitt *Blake* • Ralph Seymour *Martin* • Elaine Wilkes *Phoebe* • Paul Bartel *Professor Zito* ■ *Dir* William Fruet • *Scr* Barney Cohen

Killer Rules ★★ 15
Thriller   1993 · US · Colour · 88mins

An insipid, improbable TV thriller that finds two long-lost brothers (Peter Dobson and Jamey Sheridan) on the side of the police force and the Mafia, respectively, squaring up to each other while competing for a woman, the enigmatic Sela Ward. The budget extends to location shooting in Italy, which makes a change for a TV movie, but the leads lack charisma and director Robert Ellis Miller can do little with the melodramatic, hackneyed storyline. ▣

Jamey Sheridan *Marco Ponti/Mark Bridges* • Peter Dobson *Richard Guiness* • Sela Ward *Dorothy Wade* • Riccardo Garrone *John Sabatini* • Sam Wanamaker *Joe Gambon* • Anita Zagaria *Marina* ■ *Dir* Robert Ellis Miller • *Scr* Paul Monash

The Killer Shrews ★ PG
Science-fiction horror
1959 · US · BW · 68mins

Surely one of the all-time movie howlers. For sheer nerve the makers ought to have grabbed an Oscar for attempting to demonise an animal not much bigger than a mouse. However these are not just ordinary shrews, but the rampaging and flesh-eating side effects of genetic research carried out by bonkers scientist Baruch Lumet (father of noted director Sidney Lumet). Lacklustre to say the least, the film boasts inept special effects – the mutated shrews are, in reality, greyhounds sporting shaggy coats and plastic fangs – and bargain-basement production values, all factors which have contributed to its status today as a cult bad movie. Watch and enjoy, for all the wrong reasons. ▣

James Best *Thorne Sherman* • Ingrid Goude *Ann Craigis* • Baruch Lumet *Dr Craigis* • Ken Curtis *Jerry Lacer* • Gordon McLendon *Radford Baines* • Alfredo DeSoto *Mario* ■ *Dir* Ray Kellogg • *Scr* Jay Simms

Killer Tongue ★ 18
Horror   1996 · Sp/UK · Colour · 94mins

This sloppy made-in-Spain venture is a mixture of horror and humour posing as camp genre pastiche. Following her close encounter with an alien meteorite, amoral bank robber Melinda Clarke inexplicably grows an 18ft-long tongue which commits all manner of stupidly gory crimes on nuns, escaped prisoners and other lust-crazed victims. Oh, and her pet poodles turn into bitchy transvestites, too! Everything from Russ Meyer to Russ Abbot is dragged screaming into this purposely tacky collage of hammy performances (take a bow, horror icons Robert Englund and Doug Bradley) and shaky special effects. Spainful! ▣

Melinda Clarke *Candy* • Jason Durr *Johnny* • Mapi Galán *Rita* • Mabel Karr *Old nun* • Robert Englund *Chief screw* • Alicia Borrachero *Reporter* • Doug Bradley *Wig* • Michael Cule *Frank* • *Dir/Scr* Alberto Sciamma

The Killer Who Wouldn't Die ★★ 15
Crime thriller   1976 · US · Colour · 92mins

Seeking a vehicle to replace his long-running hit *Mannix*, Mike Connors headlined this pilot for a series called

Ohanian (which just happened to be his real name). However, this uninspired thriller never became a series in its own right. Quitting the force following the unsolved bomb death of his wife, Connors's detective-turned-skipper gets lured back into crime-fighting when he heads for Hawaii to investigate a friend's murder. In spite of a decent supporting cast, headed by Samantha Eggar and Patrick O'Neal, this sparkless plot refuses to catch light. ▭

Mike Connors *Kirk Ohanian* • Samantha Eggar *Anne Roland* • Grégoire Aslan *Ara* • Mariette Hartley *Heather McDougall* • Patrick O'Neal *Commissioner Pat Moore* • Clu Gulager *Harry Keller* • James Shigeta *David Lao* ■ *Dir* William Hale • *Scr* Cliff Gould

The Killers ★★★★★ PG
Classic film noir   1946 · US · BW · 98mins

One of the most powerful and influential thrillers ever made, with director Robert Siodmak's bleak and pessimistic tone virtually defining the term *film noir*. Based on a short story of remarkable power by Ernest Hemingway, the movie broadens the tale superbly with intricate flashbacks and features a stunning film debut from Burt Lancaster, all coiled anger as the fall guy, and there's also a career-defining role for Ava Gardner as the *femme fatale*. The design is clearly influenced by cult artist Edward Hopper; Miklos Rosza's superb score that was made even more memorable when it was used again for TV's *Dragnet*; and John Huston had a hand in the screenplay. The Don Siegel version with Lee Marvin and Ronald Reagan is almost as good, but don't miss this marvellous original. ▭

Edmond O'Brien *Jim Reardon* • Ava Gardner *Kitty Collins* • Burt Lancaster *Swede* • Albert Dekker *Big Jim Colfax* • Sam Levene *Lieutenant Sam Lubinsky* • Charles D Brown *Packy Robinson* • Donald MacBride *Kenyon* • Phil Brown *Nick Adams* • Charles McGraw *Al* • William Conrad *Max* ■ *Dir* Robert Siodmak • *Scr* Anthony Veiller, John Huston, from a short story by Ernest Hemingway • *Cinematographer* Elwood Bredell • *Set Designer* Jack Otterson, Martin Obzina • *Editor* Arthur Hilton • *Music* Miklos Rosza

The Killers ★★★
Thriller melodrama   1964 · US · Colour · 94mins

Ernest Hemingway's short story had already inspired a movie in 1946; this film was not a remake but a separate version of the tale. John Cassavetes is killed by hitmen Lee Marvin and Clu Gulager, who join forces when their job is done to track down the proceeds of a mail robbery the victim helped pull off. Marvin exudes his usual power and menace in a dry run for his *Point Blank* character, and Ronald Reagan makes his last screen appearance. (He later found work elsewhere.) *The Killers* was originally made for TV, but released in cinemas on account of its violence.

Lee Marvin *Charlie* • John Cassavetes *Johnny North* • Angie Dickinson *Sheila Farr* • Ronald Reagan *Browning* • Clu Gulager *Lee* • Claude Akins *Earl Sylvester* • Norman Fell *Mickey* ■ *Dir* Donald Siegel [Don Siegel] • *Scr* Gene L Coon, from a short story by Ernest Hemingway

Killer's Kiss ★★★
Drama   1955 · US · BW · 67mins

With films such as *Dr Strangelove, 2001* and *A Clockwork Orange*, Stanley Kubrick became one of the world's most famous directors and lived a reclusive, intensely private life in a stately home near St Albans. But Kubrick began with low-budget thrillers and *Killer's Kiss*, his second film and a boxing-gangland story, has that streak of fatalism and cynicism that marks his later work. There is a terrific climax, when hero and villain have a fight surrounded by mannequins, plus a spurious ballet sequence featuring Kubrick's second wife Ruth Sobotka. It's a fascinating work, albeit weakly acted and rough at the edges.

Frank Silvera *Vincent Rapallo* • Jamie Smith *Davy Gordon* • Irene Kane *Gloria Price* • Jerry Jarret *Albert* • Mike Dana *Hoodlum* • Felice Orlandi *Hoodlum* • Ralph Roberts *Hoodlum* • Phil Stevenson *Hoodlum* ■ *Dir* Stanley Kubrick • *Scr* Howard O Sackler, Stanley Kubrick, from a story by Stanley Kubrick

Killers of Kilimanjaro ★★ PG
Adventure   1960 · UK · Colour · 87mins

A typically schlocky outdoor adventure produced by Albert Broccoli, co-written by Richard Maibaum and shot by Ted Moore before they all hit gold with the Bond movies. Robert Taylor, a pricey Hollywood import, plays an engineer who is building a railroad and looking for some missing persons who may or may not have been kidnapped. Lions and natives play the part of bad guys if this is regarded as an African western, which it is. Donald Pleasence can be spotted further down the cast. ▭

Robert Taylor (1) *Robert Adamson* • Anne Aubrey *Jane Carlton* • John Dimech *Pasha* • Grégoire Aslan *Ben Ahmed* • Anthony Newley *Hooky Hook* • Donald Pleasence *Captain* ■ *Dir* Richard Thorpe • *Scr* John Gilling, Earl Felton, Richard Maibaum, Cyril Hume, from the book *African Bush Adventures* by JA Hunter, Daniel P Mannix

The Killing ★★★★ PG
Thriller   1956 · US · BW · 80mins

Stanley Kubrick's third feature is a thriller about a racetrack robbery, with Sterling Hayden, Marie Windsor, Elisha Cook Jr and other doomed criminals. Rather than tell the story straight, Kubrick scrambles the time sequence and follows separate strands of the plot towards their conclusion, detailing the planning, the robbery itself and the disastrous aftermath. Although influenced by John Huston's *The Asphalt Jungle*, as well as the French classic *Rififi*, directed by Jules Dassin, Kubrick turns a familiar story into a masterly display of technique and a moving study of desperate characters who are in thrall to fate. Kirk Douglas was so impressed by the film that he agreed to star in Kubrick's next project, *Paths of Glory*, the success of which set the seal on Kubrick's reputation. ▭

Sterling Hayden *Johnny Clay* • Coleen Gray *Fay* • Marie Windsor *Sherry Peatty* • Elisha Cook Jr *George Peatty* • Jay C Flippen *Marvin Unger* • Vince Edwards *Val Cannon* • Ted De Corsia *Randy Kennan* ■ *Dir* Stanley Kubrick • *Scr* Jim Thompson, Stanley Kubrick, from the novel *Clean Break* by Lionel White

A Killing Affair ★★★
Psychological crime thriller   1985 · US · Colour · 100mins

Based on Robert Houston's novel *Monday, Tuesday, Wednesday*, this tale of Southern intrigue concerns the murder of Kathy Baker's fickle husband and the arrival of a mysterious stranger (Peter Weller). Is he the one responsible for the deed? Directing for the first time, David Saperstein's everyday story of backward folk in the backwoods has enough surprising twists and turns to keep you guessing.

Peter Weller *Baston Morris* • Kathy Baker *Maggie Gresham* • John Glover *Maggie's brother* • Bill Smitrovich *Pink Gresham* ■ *Dir* David Saperstein • *Scr* David Saperstein, from the novel *Monday, Tuesday, Wednesday* by Robert Houston

Killing Box ★★★ 18
Horror thriller   1993 · US · Colour · 93mins

An evil African force turns massacred Civil War soldiers into bloodthirsty zombies, who then go on a cannibalistic and crucifixion rampage. This highly unusual arthouse horror is too intense for the audience it's aimed at, yet too anaemic for gore fans. Nevertheless, director George Hickenlooper's grainy, documentary-style mood piece is a skilful work of hypnotic power. The old "war is hell" message is delivered in a cool, clear and crisp fashion, while the film uses little-known tribal mythology to lend poetic weight to its effectively sparse production values. ▭

Corbin Bernsen *Colonel Nehemiah Strayn* • Adrian Pasdar *Captain John Harling* • Cynda Williams *Rebecca* • Ray Wise *Colonel George Thalman* • Martin Sheen *General Haworth* • Jefferson Mays *Martin Bradley* • Billy Bob Thornton *Langston* • David Arquette *Murphy* • Matt LeBlanc *Terhune* ■ *Dir* George Hickenlooper • *Scr* Matt Greenberg

Killing Cars ★★ 15
Mystery thriller   1986 · W Ger · Colour · 96mins

Echoes of the leaden Euro co-productions of the sixties and seventies ring flatly around this disappointing early venture from the director of *The Nasty Girl*. As soon as he patents a non-polluting automobile, inventor Jürgen Prochnow becomes the target of various international financiers and oil magnates, who fear the collapse of their empires if it's a success. A decent array of familiar faces, including William Conrad, compete for close-ups, but the camera is, understandably, more interested in Verhoeven's wife, Senta Berger. An interesting concept, but it never gets out of low gear. German dialogue dubbed into English. ▭

Jürgen Prochnow *Ralph Korda* • Senta Berger *Marie* • Agnes Soral *Violet* • Daniel Gelin *Kellermann* • William Conrad *Mahoney* ■ *Dir/Scr* Michael Verhoeven

Killing Dad ★ PG
Comedy   1989 · UK · Colour · 88mins

This singularly unimpressive British film from writer/director Michael Austin flails in its attempts at black comedy. Denholm Elliott plays a depressive drunk returning home to the wife (Anna Massey) and son (Richard E Grant) he

deserted 23 years ago. Instead of welcoming his father back with open arms, Grant, also a hopeless case, spends the remainder of the film plotting to kill him. Embarrassing for all concerned – including Julie Walters as Elliott's tarty girlfriend – this sank without a trace of laughter.

Denholm Elliott *Nathy Berg* • Julie Walters *Judith* • Richard E Grant *Alistair Berg* • Anna Massey *Edith Berg* • Laura Del Sol *Luisa* • Ann Way *Margot* • Jonathan Phillips *Terry* ■ *Dir* Michael Austin • *Scr* Michael Austin, from the novel *Berg* by Ann Quinn

Killing 'em Softly ★ 15
Romantic crime comedy   1982 · Can/US · Colour · 86mins

Considering the title, this film could be mourning for the demise of George Segal's talent, if only temporarily, in this dull thriller in which he's a down-on-his luck musician who kills a rock manager and falls for singer Irene Cara, whose boyfriend is promptly framed for the murder. Segal's usual urbanity of manner is absent, and he looks panicky – as though he's realised the mess in which he's plunged himself. ▭

George Segal *Jimmy Skinner* • Irene Cara *Janes Flores* • Clark Johnson *Michael* • Nicholas Campbell *Clifford* • Joyce Gordon *Poppy Mellinger* ■ *Dir* Max Fischer • *Scr* Leila Basen, from a story by Max Fischer, from a book by Laird Koenig

The Killing Fields ★★★★★ 15
Biographical war drama   1984 · UK · Colour · 135mins

Few feature films have captured a nation's agony more dramatically than Roland Joffé's *The Killing Fields*. It tells the story of Cambodia's Year Zero, when Pol Pot's Khmer Rouge entered the capital Phnom Penh, emptied it, turned the population into serfs and slaughtered nearly three million of them. To tell the story of this genocide, the picture has one conventional aspect – the perspective of American journalist Sidney Schanberg (Sam Waterston) – and one less so: the experiences of his Cambodian stringer Dith Pran (played by Haing S Ngor, a Cambodian doctor whose own suffering at the time was, if anything, even worse than that depicted in the film). Produced by David Puttnam and co-starring John Malkovich, the picture has scale and humanity; the evacuation of the capital is stunning, Ngor's suffering has great emotional force, while Waterston's complex mixture of shame and ambition is compelling. The music is awful, but this is still one of the greatest pictures of the eighties. Dr Ngor, who won an Oscar, was later murdered in Los Angeles. Contains violence and swearing. ▭

Sam Waterston *Sydney Schanberg* • Haing S Ngor *Dith Pran* • John Malkovich *Al Rockoff* • Julian Sands *Jon Swain* • Craig T Nelson *Military attaché* • Spalding Gray *US consul* • Bill Paterson *Dr MacEntire* • Athol Fugard *Dr Sundesval* • Graham Kennedy *Dougal* ■ *Dir* Roland Joffé • *Scr* Bruce Robinson, from the article *The Death and Life of Dith Pran* by Sydney Schanberg

The Killing Floor ★★★ PG

Historical drama
1984 · US · Colour and BW · 117mins

Bill Duke's directorial career predates Spike Lee's, but he has always seemed on the fringes of what was termed black cinema, perhaps partly because of his rather odd choice of films: the likes of *Sister Act 2* sit rather uneasily beside the explosive *Deep Cover* and this excellent debut feature. An impassioned drama of union and racial tension, it tells the story of a group of black workers fighting for their rights in a Chicago abattoir during the First World War. The then largely unknown cast – which includes Moses Gunn and Alfre Woodard – delivers believable performances, and Duke brings an air of gritty realism to the tale. Contains some violence and swearing.

Damien Leake *Frank Custer* • Alfre Woodard *Mattie Custer* • Clarence Felder *Bill Bremer* • Moses Gunn *Heavy Williams* • Jason Green *Frank Custer Jr* • Jamarr Johnson *Lionel Custer* • Micaeh Johnson *Sarah Custer* • Ernest Rayford *Thomas Joshua* • Stephen Henderson *James Cheeks* • Dennis Farina *Harry Brennan* ■ *Dir* Bill Duke • *Scr* Leslie Lee, from a story by Elsa Rassback, adapted by Ron Milner

The Killing Grounds ★★

Thriller   1997 · US · Colour · 93mins

Backpackers turn back-stabbers when they stumble on a cache of gold bullion in a nihilistic riff on *Treasure of the Sierra Madre*. Further murderous complications occur when the real "owners" of the fortune turn up and are in no mood for sharing their ill-gotten gains. The plot of *Shallow Grave* meets the style of *Deliverance* in a sadistic thriller, with many gruesome moments as the cast die one by one.

Priscilla Barnes *Della Desordo* • Rodney A Grant *Ned Stillwater* • Anthony Michael Hall *Art Styles* • Charles Rocket *Mel Delsordo* • Mike Michaud *Pilot* • Richard Brandes *Pilot number two* • James Jude Courtney *Craig* • Scott Brick *Deputy* ■ *Dir* Kurt Anderson • *Scr* Thomas Ritz, from the story by Richard Brandes, Kurt Anderson

The Killing Jar ★★ 18

Thriller   1996 · US · Colour · 97mins

This modest but not unrewarding straight-to-video chiller manages to breathe some new life into the well-worn serial-killer genre. Brett Cullen plays a winemaker who returns to his home town and witnesses a murder. Undergoing hypnosis in a bid to identify the killer, he reawakens dark memories from deep in his past – could he be a killer himself? Evan Crooke directs with some style, and there are typically wily supporting performances from Wes Studi, M Emmet Walsh, Brion James and Xander Berkeley. Contains violent scenes. ▭

Brett Cullen *Michael Sanford* • Tamlyn Tomita *Diane Sanford* • Wes Studi *Cameron* • Xander Berkeley *Danny Evans* • Edith Varen *Martha* • Jack Wallace *Dick* • John Philbin *Pete "Petey" Lawrence* • Brion James *Dr Vincent Garrett* • M Emmet Walsh *Sheriff Foley* ■ *Dir* Evan Crooke • *Scr* Mark Mullin

The Killing Kind ★★

Psychological crime drama
1973 · US · Colour · 95mins

This is a study of disturbed mother–son relationships by the director of *Planet of Blood* and *What's the Matter with Helen?*. John Savage returns home after a spell in prison for a rape he didn't commit and falls into the doting arms of his overbearing mother (Ann Sothern). Unfortunately, her loving care is so suffocating it drives him to take violent revenge on the lawyer (Ruth Roman) responsible for his incarceration and the girl whose evidence put him away. Good performances from the name cast (including Cindy Williams as a pushy lodger) elevate the familiar *Psycho* shadings in a seldom seen, lethargically paced suspense shocker.

Ann Sothern *Thelma* • John Savage *Terry* • Ruth Roman *Rhea* • Luana Anders *Librarian* • Cindy Williams *Roomer* ■ *Dir* Curtis Harrington • *Scr* Lony Crechales, George Edwards

The Killing Mind ★★ 15

Thriller   1991 · US · Colour · 94mins

Stephanie Zimbalist stars as a cop using psychiatry to solve a 20-year-old murder in this tedious and predictable thriller, which also features Tony Bill. A disappointing vehicle for Zimbalist, who surely must have felt a twinge of envy when her *Remington Steele* partner Pierce Brosnan went on to bigger and better things as James Bond. ▭

Stephanie Zimbalist *Isobel Neiman* • Tony Bill *Thomas Quinn* • Billy Beck *Digby* • Gordon Currie *Pizza boy* • Tim Dezam *Gordon Atherton* ■ *Dir* Michael Ray Rhodes • *Scr* William W Forsythe, Pat A Victor

Killing Obsession ★★

Horror thriller   1994 · US · Colour · 95mins

This by-the-numbers psycho thriller has murderer John Savage convincing the authorities that he is now a reformed character and should be let out of prison. Of course, he promptly sets off after Kimberly Chase, the grown-up daughter of his last victim. John Saxon has a supporting role, but everything about the movie screams routine. The director was Paul Leder, whose daughter Mimi followed him into the director's chair.

John Savage *Albert* • John Saxon *Dr Sachs* • Kimberly Chase *Annie* • Bernard White *Lt Jackson* ■ *Dir/Scr* Paul Leder

The Killing of a Chinese Bookie ★★★★ 15

Crime thriller   1976 · US · Colour · 104mins

A powerful performance from Ben Gazzara dominates this convoluted but compelling contemporary *film noir* by writer/director John Cassavetes. Los Angeles nightclub owner Gazzara is in debt to the mob and agrees to dispatch a troublesome bookie (Soto Joe Hugh). The overlong narrative occasionally stumbles over the improvisational techniques Cassavetes used to increase the realism of the piece, and Timothy Agoglia Carey's assassin is far too over the top. However, the convincing atmosphere of gangster menace makes this a guys-and-dolls saga that's well worth catching. ▭

Ben Gazzara *Cosmo Vitelli* • Timothy Agoglia Carey [Timothy Carey] *Flo* • Azizi Johari *Rachel* • Meade Roberts *Mr Sophistication* • Seymour Cassel *Mort Weil* • Alice Friedland *Sherry* • Donna Gordon *Margo* • Robert Phillips *Phil* • Morgan Woodward *John the boss* • Virginia Carrington *Betty the Mother* • Soto Joe Hugh [Hugh Soto] *Chinese bookie* ■ *Dir/Scr* John Cassavetes

The Killing of Angel Street ★★★

Drama   1981 · Ausl · Colour · 101mins

Loosely based on actual events, this well-intentioned drama combines populist realism with clumsy televisual clichés and corrupt stereotypes. Yet, for all its failings, Donald Crombie's film brings you onside at the outset, and keeps you rooting for Alexander Archdale and then, after his mysterious death, his feisty daughter Elizabeth Alexander. They take on an unholy alliance of gangsters, politicians, cops and property developers, with designs on their Sydney waterfront community. Particularly impressive is the way Crombie introduces elements of tension to the story that are more typical of a thriller, without losing sight of the human-interest angle. No classic, but efficient and engrossing.

Elizabeth Alexander *Jessica* • John Hargreaves *Elliot* • Alexander Archdale *BC Simmonds* • Reg Lye *Riley* • Gordon McDougall *Sir Arthur Wadham* • David Downer *Alan* • Ric Herbert *Ben* ■ *Dir* Donald Crombie • *Scr* Evan Jones, Cecil Holmes, Michael Craig, from a story by Michael Craig

The Killing of Sister George ★★★ 18

Drama   1968 · UK · Colour · 139mins

Bet Lynch wouldn't have stood for this kind of brutality when she left *Coronation Street*. An ageing actress is fired arbitrarily and her character killed off from a TV serial. She takes to the bottle as her young female friend (Susannah York) is seduced from her by a rival. Frank Marcus's touching play is not so much touched as bruised by Robert Aldrich's heavy-handed direction, which alienated the actresses during shooting and was disliked, but which still reflects the compulsive sadism he brought to bear on *What Ever Happened to Baby Jane?* A fascinating if flawed look at relationships so close they're weirdly sympathetic, especially as our loyalties swing to dominant Beryl Reid from the vapid greed of her lover. ▭

Beryl Reid *June Buckridge/"Sister George"* • Susannah York *Alice "Childie" McNaught* • Coral Browne *Mercy Croft* • Ronald Fraser *Leo Lockhart* • Patricia Medina *Betty Thaxter* • Hugh Paddick *Freddie* • Cyril Delevanti *Ted Baker* ■ *Dir* Robert Aldrich • *Scr* Lukas Heller, from the play by Frank Marcus

The Killing Secret ★★

Thriller   1997 · US · Colour

Great things were predicted for Tess Harper after she received an Oscar nomination for her performance in *Crimes of the Heart*. Just over a decade later, she's having to make do with avenging-mother roles in run-of-the-mill TV movies. Here she rises well above the material, crossing the tracks to team up with cheerleader Ari Meyers

in a bid to trap the two-timing teenager responsible for the death of her pregnant daughter. Noel Nosseck is an experienced TV-movie director, but he struggles to whip up suspense.

Ari Meyers *Nicole Voss* • Soleil Moon Frye *Emily DeCapprio* • Tess Harper *Tina DeCapprio* • Mark Krassenbaum *Greg Dunleavy* • John O'Hurley *Ted Dunleavy* • Brandon Frazier *Andy DeCapprio* • Deborah Hobart *Rachel Dunleavy* ■ *Dir* Noel Nosseck • *Scr* Rob Fresco

The Killing Time ★ 15

Crime thriller   1987 · US · Colour · 88mins

Slack morals, easy murder and brooding visuals are the very essence of classic and modern *film noir*. It's sad to see here, then, that little-known director Rick King – who was probably asked to walk west of California as a result of this effort – has made only a feeble gesture to the genre. As it is, the combination of Kiefer Sutherland, Beau Bridges, deceit and romance produces a film that comes across as too empty and confused to be of any real dramatic or entertainment value. Contains swearing and violence. ▭

Beau Bridges *Sheriff Sam Wayburn* • Kiefer Sutherland *"Brian Mars"* • Wayne Rogers *Jake Winslow* • Joe Don Baker *Sheriff Carl Cunningham* • Michael Madsen *Stu* ■ *Dir* Rick King • *Scr* • *Scr* Don Bohlinger, James Nathan, Bruce Franklin Singer

Killing Time ★ 18

Thriller   1998 · UK · Colour · 85mins

A lame attempt at transferring Quentin Tarantino-style violence to the north of England. Kendra Torgan plays a super-cool Italian hit-woman, waiting for her target to arrive at a Sunderland hotel and assassinating anyone who gets in her way. Two police inspectors, including Craig Fairbrass, arrive to survey the damage. Fairbrass, under pressure to solve the case, admits he hired Torgan himself to avenge the death of his partner. Furthermore, he cannot afford to pay her so he plans to kill her himself. An exploitative, repetitive and pointless thriller, with the occasional suspenseful moment thrown in for good measure. Contains swearing and violence. ▭

Craig Fairbrass *Bryant* • Kendra Torgan *Maria – the assassin* • Peter Harding *Madison* • Neil Armstrong *John* • Ian McLaughlin *George* • Stephen D Thirkeld *Charlie* ■ *Dir* Bharat Nalluri • *Scr* Neil Marshall, Fleur Costello, Caspar Berry

Killing Zoe ★★ 18

Crime drama   1993 · US · Colour · 91mins

Roger Avary co-wrote *Pulp Fiction* with Quentin Tarantino, and his debut feature as a director deals with many of the same themes. Eric Stoltz is a safecracker visiting his old friend Jean-Hugues Anglade in Paris; before you can say *Reservoir Dogs*, Anglade attempts to hold up a bank while high on booze and drugs. Avary gives his predictable heist tale a fresher edge than normal with some neat camerawork and a smattering of good jokes among the unflinching splatter. It's still warmed-over Tarantino at best, though Julie Delpy adds a nice twist as a good-hearted prostitute. ▭

U = SUITABLE FOR ALL   **Uc** = SUITABLE FOR ALL, ESPECIALLY FOR YOUNG CHILDREN (VIDEO ONLY)   **PG** = PARENTAL GUIDANCE

Eric Stoltz *Zed* • Julie Delpy *Zoe* • Jean-Hugues Anglade *Eric* • Tai Thai *François* • Bruce Ramsey *Ricardo* • Kario Salem *Jean* • Salvator Xuereb *Claude* • Gary Kemp *Oliver* ■ *Dir/Scr* Roger Avary

The Killing Zone ★★ 18
Thriller   1998 · UK · Colour · 87mins

Director Ian David Diaz worked miracles to get this ultra-low-budget British thriller even made, although it remains a very uneven ride. Padraig Casey is the ultra-cool, saxophone-playing professional hitman, who fancies himself as Michael Caine in his Harry Palmer period. He agrees to take one last job, but finds his enemies may be closer to him than he originally thought. It grew out of a short Diaz had made years earlier, and that is its biggest problem: it actually feels like three different films, linked together very tenuously. Still, full marks for ambition, and there are enough witty touches to suggest that he may be a director to watch in the future. ▭
Padraig Casey • Oliver Young • Mark Bowden ■ *Dir/Scr* Ian David Diaz

The Killings at Outpost Zeta ★
Science-fiction thriller
1980 · US · Colour · 92mins

Cheap science fiction gets scraped from the bottom of a very deep barrel in this unwatchable feature. Inhabitants of the planet Zeta are being found dead in the tinsel-and-plastic universe of 2002. Astronauts Gordon Devol and Jacqueline Ray discover the murders are caused by a blood-drinking rock creature. Even TV's *Lost in Space* didn't look this bad or showcase such lousy acting and not-so-special effects.
Gordon Devol • Jacqueline Ray • James A Watson Jr • Jackson Bostwick ■ *Dir* Robert Emenegger, Allan Sandler • *Scr* Peter Dawson

Kim ★★★ U
Adventure   1950 · US · Colour · 112mins

MGM put their frozen rupees to good use in filming this colourful version of the Kipling tale on the actual locations, and cast the splendidly tongue-in-cheek Errol Flynn as little Kim's idol Mahbub Ali, the swashbuckling Red Beard. A very American Dean Stockwell as the boy in question, and he does well, though British director Victor Saville's plodding pacing doesn't help the heroics. Paul Lukas is utterly ridiculous in quaint make-up as the High Lama, but Robert Douglas and Reginald Owen are suitably stiff-upper-lipped. Boys of all ages should enjoy this.
Errol Flynn *Mahbub Ali, the Red Beard* • Dean Stockwell *Kim* • Paul Lukas *Lama* • Robert Douglas *Colonel Creighton* • Thomas Gomez *Emissary* • Cecil Kellaway *Hurree Chunder* • Arnold Moss *Lurgan Sahib* • Reginald Owen *Father Victor* ■ *Dir* Victor Saville • *Scr* Leon Gordon, Richard Schayer, from the novel by Rudyard Kipling

Kim ★★★ PG
Adventure   1984 · US · Colour · 135mins

An ambitious but successful bid to adapt for television Rudyard Kipling's classic story about a youngster used by British Intelligence in colonial India.

Originally filmed in 1950 by Victor Saville with stars Errol Flynn and Dean Stockwell, this entertaining remake features Peter O'Toole, excellent as a Buddhist monk, and there's a fine debut from Ravi Sheth as Kim. ▭
Peter O'Toole *Lama* • Bryan Brown *Mahbub Ali* • Ravi Sheth *Kim* • John Rhys-Davies *Babu* • Julian Glover *Colonel Creighton* • Lee Montague *Kozelski* • Alfred Burke *Lurgan* ■ *Dir* John Davies • *Scr* James Brabazon, from the novel by Rudyard Kipling

Kind Hearts and Coronets ★★★★★ U
Classic comedy   1949 · UK · BW · 101mins

Arguably the finest of the Ealing comedies, Robert Hamer's superb *comédie noire* benefits from a deliciously witty script that slips smoothly between dastardly deaths with the ease of a self-satisfied memoir. However, the picture is elevated to greatness by the quality of its playing. Obviously, Alec Guinness, who essays the eight doomed D'Ascoynes, merits every superlative lavished on a performance of astounding versatility and virtuosity. But let's not forget Dennis Price as the ceaselessly inventive killer, and Joan Greenwood and Valerie Hobson as the vamp and the vestal in his life, who are singularly brilliant. ▭
Dennis Price *Louis Mazzini* • Valerie Hobson *Edith D'Ascoyne* • Joan Greenwood *Sibella* • Alec Guinness *Duke/Banker/Parson/General/Admiral/Young Ascoyne D'Ascoyne/Young Henry/Lady Agatha* • Audrey Fildes *Mama* • Miles Malleson *Hangman* • Clive Morton *Prison governor* • John Penrose *Lionel* • Cecil Ramage *Crown counsel* • Hugh Griffith *Lord High Steward* ■ *Dir* Robert Hamer • *Scr* Robert Hamer, John Dighton, from a novel by Roy Horniman • *Producer* Michael Balcon

Kind Lady ★★
Drama   1935 · US · BW · 77mins

That accomplished supporting actress Aline MacMahon, then in her mid-thirties, here plays the title role of a wealthy London spinster. She takes pity on a homeless artist, played with roguish charm by Basil Rathbone, only to have him invade her mansion with his cronies and seek to obtain her assets. Originally a Hugh Walpole story, then a Broadway play, this screen version is adequately directed by George B Seitz.
Aline MacMahon *Mary Herries* • Basil Rathbone *Henry Abbott* • Mary Carlisle *Phyllis* • Frank Albertson *Peter* • Dudley Digges *Mr Edwards* • Doris Lloyd *Lucy Weston* ■ *Dir* George B Seitz • *Scr* Bernard Schubert, from a play by Edward Chodorov, from the story *The Silver Casket* by Hugh Walpole

A Kind of Hush ★★★ 15
Drama   1998 · UK · Colour · 92mins

Theatre director Brian Stirner makes his screen debut with this uncompromising study of child abuse and its consequences. Refusing to shy away from either the rawest of emotions or the most brutal violence, the film is firmly rooted in the tradition of British realism so popular since the sixties. Yet, while the action deals with the revenge wrought by a bunch of teenagers on their persecutors, the story is as much about the

indomitability of the human spirit as it is about justifying vengeance. The performances of the inexperienced cast bristle with anger, but it's the wiser counsel of Roy Hudd that allows them to salvage some dignity from their indignation. Contains sexual references and swearing. ▭
Harley Smith *Stu* • Marcella Plunkett *Kathleen* • Ben Roberts *Simon* • Paul Williams *Mick* • Nathan Constance *Tony* • Peter Saunders *Wivva* • Mike Fibbens *Fish* • Roy Hudd *Chef* ■ *Dir* Brian Stirner • *Scr* Brian Stirner, from the novel *Getting Even* by Richard Johnson

A Kind of Loving ★★★★ 15
Drama   1962 · UK · BW · 107mins

Unlike the majority of other "grim up North" dramas that found critical favour during the social realist or "kitchen sink" phase of British film-making, John Schlesinger's debut feature is about making the most of life rather than carping on about the colour of the grass on the other side of the fence. Crisply adapted by Keith Waterhouse and Willis Hall from Stan Barstow's novel, the film is like a scrapbook of typical human experience, with Schlesinger's eye for detail and his persuasive storytelling style creating characters who could have lived next door to you. Alan Bates and June Ritchie are excellent, but Thora Hird is exceptional. Contains nudity. ▭
Alan Bates *Vic Brown* • June Ritchie *Ingrid Rothwell* • Thora Hird *Mrs Rothwell* • Bert Palmer *Mr Brown* • Gwen Nelson *Mrs Brown* • Malcolm Patton *Jim Brown* • Pat Keen *Christine* • David Mahlowe *David* • Jack Smethurst *Conroy* • James Bolam *Jeff* • Michael Deacon *Les* ■ *Dir* John Schlesinger • *Scr* Willis Hall, Keith Waterhouse, from the novel by Stan Barstow

Kindergarten Cop ★★★ 15
Action comedy 1990 · US · Colour · 106mins

Some day soon Arnold Schwarzenegger will have to quit action roles, and as this undemanding picture proves, the Austrian Oak can do comedy – providing he doesn't try too hard. As the cop forced to teach toddlers while searching for a crook's missing son, Arnie is at his best jousting with the little tykes (surprisingly few of whom have gone on to become major child stars). The romance with Penelope Ann Miller is less convincing, but not over-intrusive. Richard Tyson and Carroll Baker make almost pantomimic baddies, but this isn't really a children's film and parents should keep the channel-changer handy for the more violent bits. Contains some violence and swearing. ▭ *DVD*
Arnold Schwarzenegger *Detective John Kimble* • Penelope Ann Miller *Joyce* • Pamela Reed *Phoebe O'Hara* • Linda Hunt *Miss Schowski* • Richard Tyson *Cullen Crisp* • Carroll Baker *Eleanor Crisp* • Cathy Moriarty *Sylvester's mother* ■ *Dir* Ivan Reitman • *Scr* Murray Salem, Herschel Weingrod, Timothy Harris, from a story by Murray Salem

The Kindred ★ 18
Science-fiction horror thriller
1986 · US · Colour · 88mins

Once hailed as one of America's greatest actors, Rod Steiger suffered a career breakdown in the mid-eighties, appearing in straight-to-video horror

trash, of which this is fairly typical. The man who shared screen time with Brando in *On the Waterfront* is here reduced to hamming it up as a mad scientist in a fright wig, whose experiments result in the inevitable things in the cellar. Totally uninvolving from start to finish.
David Allen Brooks *John Hollins* • Amanda Pays *Melissa Leftridge* • Talia Balsam *Sharon Raymond* • Kim Hunter *Amanda Hollins* • Rod Steiger *Dr Phillip Lloyd* ■ *Dir* Jeffrey Obrow, Stephen Carpenter • *Scr* Stephen Carpenter, Jeffrey Obrow, John Penney, Earl Ghaffari, Joseph Stefano

King: a Filmed Record... Montgomery to Memphis ★★★
Biographical documentary
1970 · US · BW · 177mins

Fine documentary about Martin Luther King, co-directed by Hollywood heavyweights Joseph L Mankiewicz and Sidney Lumet. Using quality archive news footage, the film looks at the latter part of King's life, from his frontline civil rights activism of the mid-1950s, right through to his assassination in April 1968. The linking sequences are narrated by a host of film luminaries and admirers of King, including Paul Newman, Joanne Woodward, James Earl Jones and Sidney Poitier. There's no question who the real star is, though.
Paul Newman *Narrator* • Joanne Woodward *Narrator* • Ruby Dee *Narrator* • James Earl Jones *Narrator* • Clarence Williams III *Narrator* • Burt Lancaster *Narrator* • Ben Gazzara *Narrator* • Charlton Heston *Narrator* • Harry Belafonte *Narrator* • Sidney Poitier *Narrator* ■ *Dir* Sidney Lumet, Joseph L Mankiewicz

King and Country ★★★ PG
First World War drama
1964 · UK · BW · 82mins

Tom Courtenay is a hapless private who has had enough of trench warfare and walks away from his post. Naturally he's caught, and Dirk Bogarde is ordered to defend him at his court martial. As in Bogarde's earlier collaboration with director Joseph Losey, *The Servant* (1963), this moving – if sometimes pompous – tale is really an allegory about the British class system. The film also bears a striking resemblance to Stanley Kubrick's *Paths of Glory* (1957). ▭
Dirk Bogarde *Captain Hargreaves* • Tom Courtenay *Private Arthur Hamp* • Leo McKern *Captain O'Sullivan* • Barry Foster *Lieutenant Webb* • James Villiers *Captain Midgley* • Peter Copley *Colonel* • Barry Justice *Lieutenant Prescott* ■ *Dir* Joseph Losey • *Scr* Evan Jones, from the play *Hamp* by John Wilson, from a story by James Lansdale Hodson

The King and Four Queens ★★
Western   1956 · US · Colour · 83mins

The King, of course, is Clark Gable, looking vaguely lost after MGM failed to renew his contract two years earlier. He plays a drifter who wanders into a near-deserted town, Wagon Mound, inhabited by Jo Van Fleet, a woman gunfighter with four daughters-in-law (including shady Eleanor Parker) and buried loot to protect. In some respects, this weird western owes much to Nicholas Ray's offbeat cult hit *Johnny Guitar*, though Gable barely perceives the subversive opportunities and director Raoul Walsh is only interested in the tough-guy stuff. A failure, certainly, but Gable fans should watch, for this is a considerable rarity.

Clark Gable *Dan Kehoe* • Eleanor Parker *Sabina* • Jo Van Fleet *Ma McDade* • Jean Willes *Ruby* • Barbara Nichols *Birdie* • Sara Shane *Oralie* ■ *Dir* Raoul Walsh • *Scr* Margaret Fitts, Richard Simmons, from a story by Margaret Fitts

The King and I ★★★★ U

Musical 1956 · US · Colour · 127mins

A well-loved (especially in Britain) and faithful rendering of Rodgers and Hammerstein's marvellous Broadway success (originally a hit for Gertrude Lawrence) about English governess Anna Leonowens and her sexless romance with the King of Siam. The great strength of the film version is not the score (though shorn of three show tunes, it is still mightily impressive) but the casting. Yul Brynner re-created his Broadway King for posterity, picking up a best actor Oscar in the process, and this is unquestionably one of the great performances. He is magnificent and he knows it. As Mrs Anna, Deborah Kerr is both resolute and touching, with an unbilled Marni Nixon dubbing her voice for such delights as *Hello Young Lovers*. Unfortunately, 20th Century-Fox's use of its own DeLuxe Color lets down the production design severely; if ever a film needed Technicolor, it was this one. A stronger director than Walter Lang would also have been beneficial, but if you've never seen it, prepare to be enchanted. ▭

Deborah Kerr *Anna Leonowens* • Yul Brynner *The King* • Rita Moreno *Tuptim* • Martin Benson *Kralahome* • Terry Saunders *Lady Thiang* • Rex Thompson *Louis Leonowens* • Carlos Rivas *Lun Tha* • Patrick Adiarte *Prince Chulalongkorn* • Alan Mowbray *British ambassador* • Geoffrey Toone *Ramsay* ■ *Dir* Walter Lang • *Scr* Ernest Lehman, from the musical by Oscar Hammerstein Ii, Richard Rodgers, from the book *Anna and the King of Siam* by Margaret Landon • *Costume Designer* Irene Sharaff • *Cinematographer* Leon Shamroy • *Art Director* Lyle R Wheeler, John DeCuir • *Set Designer* Walter M Scott, Paul S Fox

The King and I ★★ U

Animated musical
1999 · US · Colour · 85mins

This breezy cartoon version of Rodgers and Hammerstein's musical may be no threat to Yul Brynner and Deborah Kerr in the original, but it lets youngsters in on classic tuneful delights and adds some newly invented characters. In an effort to make the complex plot more accessible to younger viewers, the film is rather dubiously enlivened by some new personalities – a black panther, a fire-breathing dragon and a chubby Master Little, forever flossing his teeth. ▭

Miranda Richardson *Anna Leonowens* • Christiane Noll *Anna Leonowens (singing)* • Martin Vidnovic *King of Siam* • Ian Richardson *Kralahome* • Darrell Hammond *Master Little* • Allen D Hong *Prince Chululongkorn* • David Burnham *Prince Chululongkorn (singing)* • Armi Arabe *Tuptim* ■ *Dir* Richard Rich • *Scr* Peter

Bakalian, David Seidler, Jacqueline Feather, Arthur Rankin, from the musical by Richard Rodgers, Oscar Hammerstein II

The King and the Chorus Girl ★★★

Comedy 1937 · US · BW · 0mins

Hollywood's pleasing Belgian import Fernand Gravet (formerly Gravey) co-stars with feisty and attractive Joan Blondell in a tale about a European aristocrat who falls madly in love with an American chorus girl from the Folies Bergère. Helping to press his cause are Jane Wyman and Edward Everett Horton. A romantic comedy, adapted by Norman Krasna and Groucho Marx from their story *Grand Passion* and efficiently produced and directed by Mervyn LeRoy, there's nothing particularly grand or passionate about the movie, but it's an inoffensive and perfectly adequate time-filler.

Fernand Gravet *Alfred* • Joan Blondell *Dorothy* • Edward Everett Horton *Count Humbert* • Alan Mowbray *Donald* • Jane Wyman *Babette* • Mary Nash *Duchess Anna* ■ *Dir* Mervyn LeRoy • *Scr* Norman Krasna, Groucho Marx, from their story *Grand Passion*

King Arthur Was a Gentleman ★★ U

Comedy 1942 · UK · BW · 94mins

It was once said that the Nazis thought they would win the Second World War because Britain's most effective men of action were nitwit comedians like Will Hay and George Formby. Over 50 years on, it's not easy to see how such tepid capers could have boosted morale. Yet this is as likeable as any flag-waving comedy, with Arthur Askey as the cheery Tommy who is convinced he has found King Arthur's sword Excalibur and is, therefore, invincible. The film could have done with fewer songs and more gags. ▭

Arthur Askey *Arthur King* • Evelyn Dall *Susan Ashley* • Anne Shelton *Gwen Duncannon* • Max Bacon *Maxie* • Jack Train *Jack* • Peter Graves (2) *Lance* ■ *Dir* Marcel Varnel • *Scr* Val Guest, Marriott Edgar

King Creole ★★★★ PG

Musical 1958 · US · BW · 110mins

This is arguably Elvis Presley's best film, and certainly his best acting performance. It's a tough New Orleans-set crime drama directed by Hollywood maestro Michael Curtiz, who invests the nightclub scenes with the kind of élan that turned the not dissimilar *Casablanca* into a classic. Elvis has tremendous support from a terrific back-up cast, notably from Walter Matthau as reptilian villain Maxie Fields, and from Carolyn Jones as the long-suffering moll. The songs are knockouts too, especially the Dixie-influenced title number and the sultry *Trouble*. This is as good as Presley gets – don't miss. ▭

Elvis Presley *Danny Fisher* • Carolyn Jones *Ronnie* • Dolores Hart *Nellie* • Dean Jagger *Mr Fisher* • Liliane Montevecchi *"Forty" Nina* • Walter Matthau *Maxie Fields* • Jan Shepard *Mimi Fisher* • Vic Morrow *Shark* ■ *Dir* Michael Curtiz • *Scr* Herbert Baker, Michael Vincente Gazzo, from the novel *A Stone for Danny Fisher* by Harold Robbins • *Music* Walter Scharf

King David ★★ PG

Biblical epic 1985 · US · Colour · 109mins

Lavish visuals and sonorous music (by Carl Davis) – both designed to match the grandeur of the subject – are badly wasted by director Bruce Beresford, who should stick to probing the Australian or American heartland and leave the Old Testament to others. In his hands, and after a promising canter through David's childhood, the spectacle quickly gets bogged down in tedious dialogue and, as the narrative begins to falter, Richard Gere (as the hero) is reduced to acting by gesture. Yet Edward Woodward, in the role of King Saul, transcends these flaws with charisma and substance. ▭

Richard Gere *David* • Edward Woodward *Saul* • Alice Krige *Bathsheba* • Denis Quilley *Samuel* • Niall Buggy *Nathan* • Cherie Lunghi *Michal* • Hurd Hatfield *Ahimilech* ■ *Dir* Bruce Beresford • *Scr* Andrew Birkin, James Costigan, from a story by James Costigan • *Cinematographer* Don McAlpine, Robin Vidgeon

A King in New York ★★★ U

Satirical comedy 1957 · UK · BW · 112mins

An embittered Charles Chaplin all but abdicates as the king of comedy for his penultimate film, mirroring the loathing he felt for the way America had treated him in real life. As the deposed monarch of Estrovia he seeks sanctuary in the United States, where he finds himself at the mercy of both the House Un-American Activities Committee and advertising executive Dawn Addams. Made in Britain (the film's New York setting is unconvincing), there are some occasionally shrewd insights, but the scenes using a young boy to mouth Chaplin's own disgust with the USA are totally embarrassing.

Charles Chaplin *King Shadhov* • Dawn Addams *Ann Kay* • Oliver Johnston *The Ambassador* • Maxine Audley *Queen Irene* • Harry Green *Lawyer Green* • Phil Brown *Headmaster* • John McLaren *Macabee Senior* • Sidney James *Mr Johnson* ■ *Dir/Scr* Charles Chaplin

King Kong ★★★★★ PG

Classic monster adventure 1933 · US · BW · 100mins

From Willis O'Brien's amazing ape animation, which has lost little of its skilful charm or ability to startle, to Fay Wray's screams atop the Empire State Building, this timeless *Beauty and the Beast* classic is one of the very few movies that will live for ever. You cannot call yourself a fantasy fan unless you've seen this exotic cornerstone thriller at least three times. Made by a team of documentary film-makers who patterned fast-talking adventurer Carl Denham (Robert Armstrong) after themselves, this is as good as mythic monster movies get. ▭

Fay Wray *Ann Darrow* • Robert Armstrong *Carl Denham* • Bruce Cabot *John Driscoll* • Frank Reicher *Capt Englehorn* • Sam Hardy *Charles Weston* • James Flavin *Second mate* • Steve Clemento *Witch king* ■ *Dir* Merian C Cooper, Ernest B Schoedsack • *Scr* James Creelman, Ruth Rose, from an idea by Merian C Cooper, Edgar Wallace • *Cinematographer* Eddie Linden, Vernon Walker, JO Taylor • *Music* Max Steiner

King Kong ★ PG

Action adventure 1976 · US · Colour · 128mins

This leaden and over-budgeted remake of the classic fantasy abandoned all the exotic mystery of the 1933 masterpiece in favour of glossy high camp and atrocious satire. A man in a monkey suit and pathetic giant models replaced the wonderful stop-motion techniques, pioneered by Willis O'Brien for the original, in this epic bomb. How Jessica Lange's career survived her debut in such a turkey ("put me down, you male chauvinist ape!") is a cinematic miracle. ▭

Jessica Lange *Dwan* • Jeff Bridges *Jack Prescott* • Charles Grodin *Fred Wilson* • John Randolph *Captain Ross* • René Auberjonois *Bagley* • Rick Baker *King Kong* ■ *Dir* John Guillermin • *Scr* Lorenzo Semple Jr, from the 1933 film • *Music* John Barry

King Kong Lives ★ PG

Fantasy adventure 1986 · US · Colour · 100mins

As if the 1976 remake wasn't bad enough, producer Dino de Laurentiis and director John Guillermin sink to even more ludicrous depths with this awful sequel. The giant ape didn't die when he fell off the World Trade Centre ten years earlier, and now Linda Hamilton leads a surgical team attempting to revive him with a giant artificial heart. Meanwhile, back in the jungle, Indiana Jones-style adventurer Brian Kerwin has discovered a female Kong – with breasts! Although there is some demented fun to be had – the transplant operation uses laughably over-sized medical props – this couldn't be worse if it tried. How did anybody keep a straight face? ▭

Brian Kerwin *Hank Mitchell* • Linda Hamilton *Amy Franklin* • Peter Elliot *King Kong* • George Yiasoumi *Lady Kong* ■ *Dir* John Guillermin • *Scr* Steven Pressfield, Ronald Shusett, from characters created by Merian C Cooper, Edgar Wallace

King Lear ★★ PG

Drama 1971 · UK/Den · BW · 131mins

If this sole attempt is anything to go by, Peter Brook's concept of filming Shakespeare was to de-emphasise the text by burying it within a phalanx of frantic camera movements and abrupt close-ups. Fortunately, Paul Scofield had the sense to contribute a performance that astonishes with its insight and intensity. Indeed, it's so good that it almost makes you forget the forbidding Danish backdrops and the directorial eccentricities. The supporting cast also strive to rescue the play from the stylised carnage, with Jack MacGowran's Fool gleefully sinister and Patrick Magee's Cornwall supplying an ambition lacking in his female cohorts. ▭

Paul Scofield *King Lear* • Irene Worth *Goneril* • Annelise Gabold *Cordelia* • Susan Engel *Regan* • Alan Webb *Duke of Gloucester* • Patrick Magee *Duke of Cornwall* • Cyril Cusack *Duke of Albany* • Jack MacGowran *The Fool* ■ *Dir* Peter Brook • *Scr* Peter Brook, from the play by William Shakespeare

King Lear – Fear and Loathing ★ 15

Experimental drama 1987 · US/Fr · Colour · 90mins

This isn't William Shakespeare's *King Lear*, or even Jean-Luc Godard's *King Lear*. It's just a self-indulgent mess about the idea of making a movie of *King Lear*. The project started out years before, scripted by Norman Mailer and starring Marlon Brando as a Mafia leader named Lear and Woody Allen as his Fool. Lee Marvin, Orson Welles and Dustin Hoffman were all involved at some point. By the time Godard got around to making it, however, he'd given up trying to make sense of it all and said it was about a Lear jet! Yet he still had the clout to lure some very impressive names, who apparently didn't mind being made to look ridiculous.

Burgess Meredith *Don Learo* • Peter Sellers *William Shakespeare Jr, the Fifth* • Molly Ringwald *Cordelia* • Jean-Luc Godard *Professor* • Woody Allen *Mr Alien* • Norman Mailer • Kate Mailer • Léos Carax *Edgar* ■ *Dir* Jean-Luc Godard • *Scr* Jean-Luc Godard, from the play *King Lear* by William Shakespeare

King of Alcatraz ★★

Comedy drama 1938 · US · BW · 55mins

J Carroll Naish escapes from Alcatraz, joins up with his old gang and hijacks a ship to Panama in a creaky old B-movie from Paramount. On board are two supposedly witty radio operators: Robert Preston (in his screen debut) and Lloyd Nolan, who gets shot early on. Luckily nurse Gail Patrick is on hand to operate following instructions from a doctor on the radio. The rest of the cast – which includes Anthony Quinn as one of Naish's cronies – might just hold your interest.

Gail Patrick *Dale Borden* • Lloyd Nolan *Raymond Grayson* • Harry Carey *Captain Glennan* • J Carrol Naish *Steve Murkil* • Robert Preston *Robert MacArthur* • Anthony Quinn *Lou Gedney* ■ *Dir* Robert Florey • *Scr* Irving Reis

King of Burlesque ★★★

Musical comedy 1936 · US · BW · 85mins

A rousing vehicle that couples two great thirties stars at differing stages of their careers: Warner Baxter, top-billed as the titular monarch, and 20th Century-Fox's newest blonde star Alice Faye, singing her way to success with such terrific numbers as *I'm Shooting High*. The plot is familiar as Baxter marries socialite Mona Barrie and finds that burlesque, Faye and Park Avenue don't mix, but who cares when it's all done with such spit and polish? There's some really sharp dialogue, but best of all is a rare appearance in features from the great Fats Waller.

Warner Baxter *Kerry Bolton* • Alice Faye *Pat Doran* • Jack Oakie *Joe Cooney* • Arline Judge *Connie* • Mona Barrie *Rosalind Cleve* • Fats Waller *Ben* ■ *Dir* Sidney Lanfield • *Scr* Gene Markey, Harry Tugend, James Seymour, from a story by Vina Delmar

The King of Comedy
★★★★ PG

Comedy drama 1983 · US · Colour · 104mins

Martin Scorsese's squirm-inducing black comedy was a commercial disaster but has developed a devoted cult following. Robert De Niro is frighteningly brilliant as the obnoxious nerd, rebounding from polite refusals to recognise his stand-up comic routine as TV-worthy with a ludicrous kidnap plot to blackmail his way on to the airwaves. Jerry Lewis is equally impressive as the Johnny Carson clone, and object of De Niro's burgeoning fanatical hatred, in an excruciatingly pungent satire on the fantasy world of show business. Contains swearing. ▭

Robert De Niro *Rupert Pupkin* • Jerry Lewis *Jerry Langford* • Diahnne Abbott *Rita* • Sandra Bernhard *Masha* • Cathy Scorsese *Dolores* • Catherine Scorsese *Mrs Pupkin* • Leslie Levinson *Roberta Posner* • Martin Scorsese *TV director* • Ed Herlihy • Liza Minnelli • Victor Borge • Tony Randall ■ *Dir* Martin Scorsese • *Scr* Paul D Zimmerman

King of Hearts ★★★★

Drama 1966 · Fr · Colour · 101mins

One of the lesser luminaries of the French New Wave, Philippe de Broca scored a cult hit with this atmospheric black comedy set during the First World War. Alan Bates is superb as the Scot who comes across a small town earmarked for blanket bombing. The satirical swipes at monarchy, patriotism and war are played down in favour of whimsical – if occasionally anarchic – comedy, as the townsfolk, each one a former asylum patient, urge Bates to become their king. The French cast is exceptional, with Pierre Brasseur, Jean-Claude Brialy and Michel Serrault outstanding. Geneviève Bujold make her name as Coquelicot. Some French and German dialogue with English subtitles.

Alan Bates *Private Charles Plumpick* • Geneviève Bujold *Coquelicot* • Jean-Claude Brialy *Duke of Clubs* • Françoise Christophe *Duchess* • Julien Guiomar *Monseigneur Marguerite* • Pierre Brasseur *General Geranium* • Michel Serrault *Crazy barber* ■ *Dir* Philippe de Broca • *Scr* Daniel Boulanger, from an idea by Maurice Bessy

The King of Jazz ★★★

Musical revue 1930 · US · Colour · 93mins

Considering the array of talent involved and the fact the film was shot in the expensive two-tone Technicolor process – including the first Technicolor animation – it's amazing that Universal entrusted this prestige project to debutant director John Murray Anderson, the only film he ever directed. However, he produces a stylish revue, showcasing the talents of songwriters Jack Yellen and Milton Ager, bandleader Paul Whiteman and first-timer Bing Crosby as a singer. Yet for all this, it was a spectacular flop, as audiences tired of the early sound era's musical boom.

John Boles • Laura La Plante • Jeanette Loff • Walter Brennan • Bing Crosby ■ *Dir* John Murray Anderson • *Scr* Charles MacArthur, Harry Ruskin, Edward T Lowe Jr • *Animation* Walter Lantz, Bill Nolan

The King of Kings ★★★★ U

Silent biblical drama 1927 · US · BW and Colour · 115mins

Complete with bookend sections in Technicolor (a lavish extravagance at the time), this is pure Cecil B DeMille. Not since his own version of *The Ten Commandments* had a biblical story been told on such a scale as this awesome retelling of the life of Christ. HB Warner might not have had the presence of Jeffrey Hunter (who would play the role in Nicholas Ray's 1961 remake), but he looks suitably spiritual, particularly during the harrowing Crucifixion scenes. Ernest Torrence impresses as Peter and Joseph Schildkraut is outstanding as Judas. Typically excessive, but truly reverential, this is a monument to the splendour of silent film. ▭

HB Warner *Jesus, the Christ* • Dorothy Cumming *Mary, the Mother* • Ernest Torrence *Peter* • Joseph Schildkraut *Judas* • James Neill *James* • Joseph Striker *John* • Robert Edeson *Matthew* • Sidney D'Albrook *Thomas* • David Imboden *Andrew* • Jacqueline Logan *Mary Magdalene* ■ *Dir* Cecil B DeMille • *Scr* Jeanie Macpherson

King of Kings ★★★★ U

Biblical epic 1961 · US · Colour · 153mins

Films in which portrayals of Jesus Christ appear generally have a bad reputation. This is an exception, despite the idiotic hype that flowed when it was made. Jeffrey Hunter, who plays Jesus, was forbidden to give interviews, his chest and armpits were shaved and the film was dubbed "I Was a Teenage Jesus", because Nicholas Ray had also directed James Dean in *Rebel without a Cause*. To compensate for some weak performances and for some lapses into high camp (notably Frank Thring's pouting Herod Antipas), there is a marvellous score, Orson Welles's narration and the lavish design that one associates with producer Samuel Bronston, who also made *El Cid* and *The Fall of the Roman Empire*. ▭

Jeffrey Hunter *Jesus Christ* • Siobhan McKenna *Mary* • Hurd Hatfield *Pontius Pilate* • Rita Gam *Herodias* • Harry Guardino *Barabbas* • Rip Torn *Judas* • Robert Ryan *John the Baptist* • Frank Thring *Herod Antipas* • Brigid Bazlen *Salome* • Grégoire Aslan *King Herod* • Orson Welles *Narrator* ■ *Dir* Nicholas Ray • *Scr* Philip Yordan • *Set Designer* Georges Wakhevitch • *Music* Miklos Rozsa

The King of Love ★★ 15

Drama 1987 · US · Colour · 90mins

The crew may have denied that this movie is loosely based on the life of *Playboy* chief Hugh Hefner, but one can't help thinking of Hef when watching this plodding drama of a tycoon's rise to power in 20th-century America. Nick Mancuso stars as a magazine publisher with the always watchable Rip Torn in this tale, which would probably have been more interesting had it been a genuine biography of the legendary entrepreneur. ▭

Nick Mancuso *Worthington Hawkes* • Rip Torn *JS Kraft* • Sela Ward *Annie Larkspur* • Michael Lerner *Nat Goldberg* • Katy Boyer *Lorna* ■ *Dir* Anthony Wilkinson • *Scr* Donald Freed

The King of Marvin Gardens ★★★★

Crime drama 1972 · US · Colour · 104mins

Jack Nicholson and director Bob Rafelson's follow-up to *Five Easy Pieces* was this often pretentious yet absorbing study of two brothers. Nicholson is a radio presenter, intellectual and withdrawn; his brother, Bruce Dern, is an aspiring property developer, brash, married to Ellen Burstyn and living in a hopeless dream world. Set in a windy, charmless Atlantic City, its original title was *The Philosopher King*, and the final title derives from the American version of Monopoly. Some rate Nicholson's performance as a career best, and his wistful monologues on the radio are indeed brilliant; others may find the cold, cerebral atmosphere easy to resist. Contains violence and swearing.

Jack Nicholson *David Staebler* • Bruce Dern *Jason Staebler* • Ellen Burstyn *Sally* • Julia Anne Robinson *Jessica* • Benjamin "Scatman" Crothers [Scatman Crothers] *Lewis* • Charles Lavine *Grandfather* ■ *Dir* Bob Rafelson • *Scr* Jacob Brackman, from a story by Jacob Brackman, Bob Rafelson

King of New York ★★★★ 18

Crime thriller 1989 · US · Colour · 99mins

A cult grew quickly around Abel Ferrara, director of those notorious "video nasties" *Driller Killer* and *Ms 45*, as well as 1992's *Bad Lieutenant* with Harvey Keitel. *King of New York* is similarly sordid and blood-soaked, the tale of a New York drug trafficker, played with appalling brilliance by the reptilian Christopher Walken. Ferrara has Sergio Leone's eye for a location – his dark, brooding view of the city is impressive – but what some viewers will regard as gripping and apocalyptic, others will just as easily find repellent. Contains violence, swearing, drug abuse and nudity. ▭ *DVD*

Christopher Walken *Frank White* • David Caruso *Dennis Gilley* • Laurence Fishburne *Jimmy Jump* • Victor Argo *Lieutenant Roy Bishop* • Wesley Snipes *Thomas Flanigan* • Janet Julian *Jennifer Poe* • Joey Chin *Larry Wong* • Giancarlo Esposito *Lance* • Paul Calderon *Joey Dalesio* • Steve Buscemi *Test Tube* ■ *Dir* Abel Ferrara • *Scr* Nicholas St John

The King of Paris ★★ 12

Romantic drama 1995 · Fr/UK · Colour · mins

A throwback to the literate films made in the thirties by the likes of Sacha Guitry, this hybrid of *All about Eve* and *A Star Is Born* is both sustained and undermined by its old-fashioned style. Expertly adopting the grand stage style, Philippe Noiret holds the piece together, even though his character's world is falling apart. Hungarian exile Veronika Varga exploits their romance to further her career before dumping him – first for his unstable son Manuel Blanc, then for Jacques Roman, a playwright who resents Noiret achieving fame through his unsung efforts. Polished, yes, but it is also ponderous and melodramatic. In French with English subtitles.

Philippe Noiret *Victor Derval* • Veronika Varga *Lisa Lanska* • Jacques Roman *Romain Coste* • Manuel Blanc *Paul Derval* • Michel Aumont *Marquis de Castellac* ■ *Dir* Dominique Maillet • *Scr* Jacques Fieschi, Jérôme Tonnerre, Bernard Minoret, Dominique Maillet

King of the Children ★★★★

Drama 1987 · Chi · Colour · 106mins

Chen Kaige explores the nature and value of education in this quietly combative inquiry into indoctrination and the unvanquishable curiosity of the individual. Set in the latter days of the Cultural Revolution, the story chronicles the conversion of Xie Yuan, a farm labourer who is ordered to supervise the local school, only for him to realise that freedom of expression and an appreciation of the world at large provide a better grounding in life than any Maoist platitude. Finding unexpected beauty in the primitive wilds of Yunan Province, this is a densely allegorical film, but it's also mesmerising and inspirational. In Mandarin with English subtitles.

Xie Yuan *Lao Gan* • Yang Xuewen *Wang Fu* • Chen Shaohua *Headmaster Chen* ■ *Dir* Chen Kaige • *Scr* Chen Kaige, Wan Zhi, from a short story by Ah Cheng

King of the Damned ★★

Prison drama   1935 · UK · BW · 81mins

Critics of the time regarded Walter Forde's film as a dry-land version of *Mutiny on the Bounty*. The setting is a prison island where the methods used by governor CM Hallard are so harsh that a rebellion ensues, led by Conrad Veidt and Noah Beery. Since the convicts can't escape, they turn the island into a collective run on communist lines. Of course, there's a spot of romance as well between Veidt and the deposed governor's daughter (Helen Vinson).

Conrad Veidt *Convict 83* • Helen Vinson *Anna Courvin* • Noah Beery *Mooche* • Cecil Ramage *Ramon Montez* • Percy Walsh *Captain Perez* • Peter Croft *"Boy" convict* • CM Hallard *Commandant Courvin* ■ *Dir* Walter Forde • *Scr* Charles Bennett, Sidney Gilliat, AR Rawlinson, from a play by John Chancellor

King of the Grizzlies ★★★ U

Adventure drama 1970 · US · Colour · 93mins

Based on *The Biography of a Grizzly* by respected author-artist Ernest Thompson Seton, this family film benefits from producer Winston Hibler's extensive experience on Disney nature pictures. With Canada standing in for the Wild West, this action-packed outdoor adventure chronicles the unusual friendship between native American John Yesno and Wahb, a bear he cares for as a cub and later encounters as a hungry 10ft menace threatening Chris Wiggins's farm. With Hibler's narration bringing an educational angle, this beautifully photographed film has some scary moments.

John Yesno *Moki* • Chris Wiggins *Col Pierson* • Hugh Webster *Shorty* • Jack Van Evera *Slim* • Winston Hibler *Narrator* ■ *Dir* Ron Kelly • *Scr* Jack Spiers, Rod Peterson, Norman Wright, from the book *The Biography of a Grizzly* by Ernest Thompson Seton • *Cinematographer* Reginald Morris

King of the Gypsies ★★★

Drama   1978 · US · Colour · 111mins

In this adaptation of Peter *Serpico* Maas's book, Sterling Hayden is the dying gypsy leader who disinherits his son in favour of his grandson who, in turn, rejects his birthright. Critics weren't quite sure whether to expect a musical like *Fiddler on the Roof* or a bloody dynastic saga like *The Godfather*. They were disappointed on

both counts – no numbers, no masterpiece – but this does offer an impressive cast, with Eric Roberts in his debut as the heir apparent, caught between loyalty to his gypsy ancestry and the attractions of a new life in the modern world. The intimidating Hayden is like a less-mannered Anthony Quinn; Susan Sarandon and Brooke Shields co-star as they did in *Pretty Baby*.

Sterling Hayden *King Zharko Stepanowicz* • Shelley Winters *Queen Rachel* • Susan Sarandon *Rose* • Judd Hirsch *Groffo* • Eric Roberts *Dave* • Brooke Shields *Tita* ■ *Dir* Frank Pierson • *Scr* Frank Pierson, from the book by Peter Maas

King of the Hill ★★★★ PG

Drama   1993 · US · Colour · 90mins

Writer/director Steven Soderbergh's richly detailed and carefully controlled coming-of-age saga follows the adventures of a 12-year-old boy left to fend for himself in a St Louis hotel during the Depression. It's a sparkling gem, wonderfully acted by Jesse Bradford as the resourceful tyke who strides with an unsentimental confidence through every real or imagined threat to his existence. A rewarding drama from the *sex, lies, and videotape* director, full of quirky characters and deeply satisfying quiet moments. Contains swearing. ▭

Jesse Bradford *Aaron* • Jeroen Krabbé *Mr Kurlander* • Lisa Eichhorn *Mrs Kurlander* • Joseph Chrest *Ben* • Spalding Gray *Mr Mungo* • Elizabeth McGovern *Lydia* • Karen Allen *Miss Mathey* • Chris Samples *Billy Thompson* ■ *Dir* Steven Soderbergh • *Scr* Steven Soderbergh, from the memoirs of AE Hotchner

King of the Khyber Rifles ★★ U

Adventure   1953 · US · Colour · 99mins

Twentieth Century-Fox lavished Technicolor and its biggest star, Tyrone Power, on this *Boys' Own* yarn set in the North-West Frontier. As a half-Indian, half-British officer who falls for the general's daughter, Power is despised by his fellow officers, but still manages to galvanise the locals against the rebels. Solid direction from Henry King and some decent heroics are let down by a weak heroine (Terry Moore) and unconvincing American locations, which stand in for Peshawar.

Tyrone Power *Captain Alan King* • Terry Moore *Susan Maitland* • Michael Rennie *Brigadier General Maitland* • Guy Rolfe *Karram Khan* • John Justin *Lieutenant Heath* • Richard Stapley *Lieutenant Baird* ■ *Dir* Henry King • *Scr* Ivan Goff, Ben Roberts, from the novel by Talbot Mundy

King of the Mountain ★★

Drama   1981 · US · Colour · 90mins

Ever wonder what came between the hippies and slackers? You'll find out in this strangely pretentious movie about Californian gearheads. Harry Hamlin plays a guy who loves to drag race along Mulholland Drive with his friends, but has to reconsider his lifestyle when he gets serious about a girl. Dennis Hopper, as a burned-out racer, steals the show by spouting lines such as "he's drunk with the greed of his youth!" and "I'm not crazy, man!", all in his own inimitable fashion.

Unfortunately, it's not enough to spare us from the clichés on parade.

Harry Hamlin *Steve* • Joseph Bottoms *Buddy* • Deborah Van Valkenburgh *Tina* • Richard Cox *Roger* • Dennis Hopper *Cal* • Dan Haggerty *Rick* ■ *Dir* Noel Nosseck • *Scr* HR Christian, from the article *Thunder Road* by David Barry

King of the Roaring 20s – the Story of Arnold Rothstein ★★

Biographical drama 1961 · US · BW · 106mins

Like its companion piece *The George Raft Story*, which was also directed by Joseph M Newman, this marks a fascinating return to the gangster era. David Janssen, of TV's *The Fugitive* fame, makes a seductively likeable Rothstein, the infamous twenties' gambler, and since audiences had barely heard of him, let alone remembered that he was fat and squat, Janssen gets away with it. The supporting cast is notable, featuring Mickey Rooney and the ever-welcome Jack Carson, plus Diana Dors near the end of her ill-advised Hollywood experience.

David Janssen *Arnold Rothstein* • Dianne Foster *Carolyn Green* • Mickey Rooney *Johnny Burke* • Jack Carson *"Big Tim" O'Brien* • Diana Dors *Madge* • Dan O'Herlihy *Phil Butler* • Keenan Wynn *Tom Fowler* ■ *Dir* Joseph M Newman • *Scr* Jo Swerling, from the book *The Big Bankroll* by Leo Katcher

King of the Turf ★★

Drama   1939 · US · BW · 88mins

This racetrack story stars Adolphe Menjou as a former horse owner who has drifted into booze and general decline. Then he meets a kid, Roger Daniel, who lifts his heart and soul and inspires him to put his life back on track. Then the boy's mother (Dolores Costello) arrives with a fateful secret... Audiences who sobbed through *The Champ* got another dose of sentimental claptrap from this one, but cynics among today's audiences will find it virtually unwatchable.

Adolphe Menjou *Jim Mason* • Roger Daniel *Goldie* • Dolores Costello *Mrs Eve Barnes* • Walter Abel *Mr Barnes* ■ *Dir* Alfred E Green • *Scr* George Bruce

King of the Underworld ★★

Crime drama   1939 · US · BW · 69mins

A remake of the 1935 melodrama *Dr Socrates*, it features Kay Francis as a female doctor out for revenge. Gangster Humphrey Bogart is the object of her retribution after he killed her surgeon husband in an earlier incident. This is just as feeble and, at times, even more risible than the original, although there is the added benefit of a snarling Bogart.

Humphrey Bogart *Joe Gurney* • Kay Francis *Dr Carol Nelson* • James Stephenson *Bill Stevens* • John Eldredge *Dr Niles Nelson* ■ *Dir* Lewis Seiler • *Scr* Vincent Sherman, George Bricker, from the story *Dr Socrates* by WR Burnett • *Costume Designer* Orry-Kelly

King of the Wind ★★★ U

Adventure   1989 · US · Colour · 101mins

This is a must-see for all keen young members of the pony set, albeit a rather dubious proposition for cynical

grown-ups who regard horse racing as a short cut to bankruptcy. Despite that, this story of a legendary Arab horse and the teenage groom (Navin Chowdhry) who accompanies him from North Africa to England has some splendid photography and is a chance to see a remarkable cast of mainly British actors. ▭

Frank Finlay *Edward Coke* • Jenny Agutter *Hannah Coke* • Nigel Hawthorne *Achmet* • Navin Chowdhry *Agba* • Ralph Bates *Leduc* • Neil Dickson *Earl of Godolphin* • Barry Foster *Mr Williams* • Jill Gascoine *Mrs Williams* • Joan Hickson *Duchess of Marlborough* • Anthony Quayle *Lord Granville* • Ian Richardson *Bey of Tunis* • Peter Vaughan *Captain* • Richard Harris *King George II* • Glenda Jackson *Queen Caroline* ■ *Dir* Peter Duffell • *Scr* Phil Frey, from the novel by Marguerite Henry, adapted by Leslie Sayle • *Cinematographer* Brian Morgan

King, Queen, Knave ★★★★

Comedy   1972 · US/W Ger · Colour · 91mins

A bold, intermittently successful attempt by Polish director Jerzy Skolimowski (*Moonlighting*, *The Shout*) to bring Vladimir Nabokov's intensely literary black comedy to the screen. Gauche orphan John Moulder-Brown goes to stay with his uncle (David Niven), only to be seduced by the latter's wife (Gina Lollobrigida) and asked to kill her husband. None of Nabokov's wordplay survives, but there are some startling moments of cold-hearted humour.

David Niven *Charles Dreyer* • Gina Lollobrigida *Martha Dreyer* • John Moulder-Brown *Frank* • Mario Adorf *Prof Ritter* ■ *Dir* Jerzy Skolimowski • *Scr* David Seltzer, David Shaw, from a novel by Vladimir Nabokov

King Ralph ★★ PG

Comedy   1991 · US · Colour · 92mins

Even the slobbish charm of *Roseanne*'s John Goodman can't save this horribly misconceived comedy of palace shenanigans. When the entire British royal family is wiped out in a freak photography accident, the unlikely successor turns out to be a Las Vegas entertainer (Goodman), who proceeds to bumble his way through the affairs of state with the assistance of adviser Peter O'Toole. The latter, and John Hurt as a scheming courtier, look to be having a hugely enjoyable time, but the talented cast is let down by writer/director David S Ward's dim script and theme-park view of British life. Contains swearing and nudity. ▭

John Goodman *Ralph Jones* • Peter O'Toole *Cedric Willingham* • John Hurt *Lord Graves* • Camille Coduri *Miranda* • Richard Griffiths *Phipps* • Leslie Phillips *Gordon* • James Villiers *Hale* • Joely Richardson *Princess Anna* • Julian Glover *King Gustav* ■ *Dir* David S Ward • *Scr* David S Ward, from the novel *Headlong* by Emlyn Williams

King Rat ★★★★ PG

Second World War prison drama
1965 · US · BW · 128mins

A bit like *Stalag 17* without the rasping humour, or *Bridge on the River Kwai* without the railway, *King Rat* is set in a Japanese PoW camp where George Segal is the opportunist and arch-manipulator, custodian of everything valuable from coffee to rats. It's a great performance; he is the sole

American amid the pukka English accents and class warfare of James Fox and Denholm Elliott. Directed by Bryan Forbes from James Clavell's novel, and shot in Hollywood (not that you'd notice), this is a gripping if overlong drama, notable also for one of John Barry's finest scores. 🖭

George Segal *Corporal King* • Patrick O'Neal *Max* • Todd Armstrong *Tex* • Sammy Reese *Kurt* • Joseph Turkel *Dino* • Michael Stroka *Miller* • William Fawcett *Steinmetz* • James Fox *Flight Lieutenant Marlowe* • Denholm Elliott *Lieutenant Colonel Denholm Larkin* • Leonard Rossiter *Major McCoy* ■ *Dir* Bryan Forbes • *Scr* Bryan Forbes, from the novel by James Clavell

King Richard and the Crusaders ★★ U

Historical epic 1954 · US · Colour · 113mins

Sir Walter Scott's novel *The Talisman* gets a Hollywood makeover courtesy of director David Butler. Rex Harrison blacks up to play the Muslim leader Saladin, who goes up against European powers led by Richard Lionheart (George Sanders). Laurence Harvey is the pretty juvenile lead, but it's Virginia Mayo who falls for sexy Saladin and gets the best line of dialogue: "War, war, that's all you think of, Dick Plantagenet!"

Rex Harrison *Saladin* • Virginia Mayo *Lady Edith* • George Sanders *King Richard I* • Laurence Harvey *Sir Kenneth* • Robert Douglas *Sir Giles Amaury* ■ *Dir* David Butler • *Scr* John Twist, from the novel *The Talisman* by Sir Walter Scott

King Solomon's Mines ★★★ U

Adventure 1937 · UK · BW · 76mins

The first of many adaptations of H Rider Haggard's tale, with Paul Robeson as the noble African who leads a party of terribly, terribly British treasure hunters across the desert and through the jungles to the mythical diamond mine. Inevitably, Robeson often breaks the journey by launching into song – great voice, pity about the loss of narrative momentum. Cedric Hardwicke plays the traditional white hunter, Roland Young offers a sense of humour, while John Loder and Anna Lee embark on a gooey romance. Aimed fair and square at the American market, it remains an old-fashioned adventure, spiced up by a certain jungle mystery. 🖭

Paul Robeson *Umbopa* • Cedric Hardwicke *Allan Quatermain* • Roland Young *Commander Good* • John Loder *Henry Curtis* • Anna Lee *Kathy O'Brien* • Sydney Fairbrother *Gagool* ■ *Dir* Robert Stevenson • *Scr* AR Rawlinson, Charles Bennett, Ralph Spence, from the novel by H Rider Haggard

King Solomon's Mines ★★★ U

Adventure 1950 · US · Colour · 102mins

Sir Henry Rider Haggard published his novel in 1885, using his own Imperial travels for background research and cashing in on the "scramble for Africa" at the time Cecil Rhodes was building his own empire and lunatic Britons were searching for the source of the Nile. The novel was an immediate success, which, curiously, was not filmed until 1937. This

remake, with Stewart Granger and Deborah Kerr, is stirring stuff, full of animal action, frenzied natives and gloopy love scenes. Compton Bennett directed the static bits, leaving Andrew Marton to handle the African exteriors. Oscars went to the colour photography and the editing.

Deborah Kerr *Elizabeth Curtis* • Stewart Granger *Allan Quatermain* • Richard Carlson *John Goode* • Hugo Haas *Van Brun* • Lowell Gilmore *Eric Masters* • Siriaque *Umbopa* • Kimursi *Khiva* ■ *Dir* Compton Bennett, Andrew Marton • *Scr* Helen Deutsch, from the novel by H Rider Haggard • *Cinematographer* Robert Surtees • *Editor* Ralph E Winters, Conrad A Nervig

King Solomon's Mines ★★ PG

Adventure 1985 · US · Colour · 95mins

Richard Chamberlain and Sharon Stone head off into the crocodile- and snake-infested jungle in search of buried treasure and something of the flair of Steven Spielberg's *Raiders of the Lost Ark*. Any similarity between their adventures and H Rider Haggard's source novel is probably accidental, but there's an old-fashioned charm to the enterprise that makes us overlook its faults. This was Sharon Stone's first starring role and it's obvious she was going places. *Allan Quatermain and the Lost City of Gold*, followed in 1987. 🖭

Richard Chamberlain *Allan Quatermain* • Sharon Stone *Jessie Huston* • Herbert Lom *Colonel Bockner* • John Rhys-Davies *Dogati* • Ken Gampu *Umbopa* ■ *Dir* J Lee Thompson • *Scr* Gene Quintano, James R Silke, from the novel by H Rider Haggard

King Solomon's Treasure ★★ PG

Adventure 1977 · Can/UK · Colour · 84mins

Allan Quatermain has been portrayed by such leading players as Cedric Hardwicke, Stewart Granger and Richard Chamberlain. John Colicos isn't exactly in their league, so any interest that this Anglo-Canadian co-production possesses lies in its teaming of ex-*Man from UNCLE* David McCallum and *Avengers* stalwart Patrick Macnee. Former Bond girl Britt Ekland co-stars as the curiously named Queen Nypeptha. 🖭

John Colicos *Allan Quatermain* • David McCallum *Sir Henry Curtis* • Patrick Macnee *Captain Good RN* • Britt Ekland *Queen Nypeptha* • Wilfrid Hyde White *Oldest club member* ■ *Dir* Alvin Rakoff • *Scr* Colin Turner, Allan Prior, from the novel *Allan Quaterman* by H Rider Haggard

The King Steps Out ★★★

Musical romance 1936 · US · BW · 85mins

Opera soprano Grace Moore shines in this adaptation of an operetta by the Marischka brothers, expertly transferred to the screen by the great director Josef von Sternberg. The plot's slight, but Moore and co-star Franchot Tone are both charming in their roles of princess and emperor. Moore was to make only three more features, her weight problem – glimpsed here but kept at bay – seriously interfering with her casting, and she died in an air crash in 1947. Watch out for veteran

character actor Herman Bing, who steals scenes as a vexed innkeeper.

Grace Moore *Cissy* • Franchot Tone *Franz Josef* • Walter Connolly *Maximilian* • Raymond Walburn *Von Kempen* • Victor Jory *Palfi* • Herman Bing *Pretzelberger* ■ *Dir* Josef von Sternberg • *Scr* Sidney Buchman, from the play *Cissy* by Gustav Hohn, Ernest Decsay, from an operetta by Ernst Marischka, Hubert Marischka

The Kingdom ★★★★ 18

Black comedy horror thriller
1994 · Den/Swe/Ger · Colour · 239mins

This lengthy but eerily engrossing movie comprises the first four episodes of Lars von Trier's 13-part Danish TV series, a supernatural soap about the bizarre doctors, nurses, patients and restless spirits in a Copenhagen hospital. Shot with a visual style that mirrors the colour of bodily fluids, and filled with an incredible gallery of eccentric characters (none of whom seems to have health care at the top of their agenda), von Trier's opus is darkly humorous and extremely creepy. After nearly four hours, though, those seeking a neat resolution might be a bit miffed. In Danish and Swedish with English subtitles. Contains some violence. 🖭

Ernst-Hugo Jaregard *Stig Helmer* • Kirsten Rolffes *Mrs Drusse* • Ghita Norby *Rigmor* • Soren Pilmark *Krogen* • Holger Juul Hansen *Dr Moesgaard* • Annevig Schelde Ebbe *Mary* • Jens Okking *Bulder* ■ *Dir* Lars von Trier • *Scr* Tomas Gislason, Lars von Trier, from a story by Lars von Trier, Niels Vorsel

Kingdom of the Spiders ★★★ PG

Horror 1977 · US · Colour · 90mins

Angered by pesticides, swarms of tarantulas attack an Arizona town in this neat low-budget chiller, directed by dependable B-movie veteran John "Bud" Cardos. William Shatner, in one of his better non-*Star Trek* roles, plays a veterinarian who joins forces with insect expert Tiffany Bolling to ascertain why nature has once more run amok in the grand tradition of *The Birds*. The creepiness is made more credible by an above-average script and some admirable staging. Arachnophobes, beware! 🖭

William Shatner *Rack Hansen* • Tiffany Bolling *Diane Ashley* • Woody Strode *Walter Colby* • Lieux Dressler *Emma Washburn* • David McLean *Sheriff Gene Smith* • Altovise Davis *Birch Colby* ■ *Dir* John "Bud" Cardos • *Scr* Richard Robinson, Alan Caillou, from a story by Jeffrey M Sneller, Stephen Lodge

Kingfish: a Story of Huey P Long ★★ 15

Biography 1995 · US · Colour · 93mins

A fine slice of American history is served up in John Goodman's dynamic portrayal of Huey P Long, the barnstorming Louisiana politician (1893–1935) who became governor and senator with his legendary persuasive powers and his zealous devotion to helping the poor and antagonising the rich. Although Goodman plays his role with remarkable insight and gusto, this TV movie races through Long's career at such a chaotic pace that viewers are

left dazed and confused. If you want better, the same subject can be visited in the 1949 multi-Oscar winning film *All the King's Men*. 🖭

John Goodman *Huey P Long Jr* • Matt Craven *Seymour Weiss* • Anne Heche *Aileen Dumont* • Ann Dowd *Rose Long* • Jeff Perry *Earl Long* • Bob Gunton *Franklin D Roosevelt* ■ *Dir* Thomas Schlamme • *Scr* Paul Monash

Kingpin ★★ 12

Sports comedy 1996 · US · Colour · 108mins

A typically vulgar tale from the Farrelly brothers, it lacks the soft centre that sweetened the taste of their later hit *There's Something about Mary*. A comedic *Color of Money* with bigger balls, it is populated by the most irredeemably unpleasant characters, yet we are expected to root for them. Humour-wise, it's a very mixed bag. Ex-bowling prodigy Woody Harrelson's detachable rubber hand is overused to the point of annoyance, but there are some very funny moments involving Randy Quaid's *Forrest Gump*-like naivety. As you would expect, Bill Murray's flamboyant villain gains the most laughs. Contains some violence and swearing. *DVD*

Woody Harrelson *Roy Munson* • Randy Quaid *Ishmael* • Vanessa Angel *Claudia* • Bill Murray *Ernie McCracken* • Chris Elliot *The Gambler* • William Jordan *Mr Boorg* • Richard Tyson *Owner of Stiffy's* ■ *Dir* Peter Farrelly, Bobby Farrelly • *Scr* Barrty Fanaro, Mort Nathan

Kings and Desperate Men ★ 15

Drama 1981 · Can · Colour · 118mins

The presence of Margaret Trudeau is the only noteworthy aspect of this sloppy kidnap drama. Here, though, the former Canadian prime minister's ex-wife has to be content with a back seat as her husband (Patrick McGoohan) is held hostage on his talk radio show by a gang of rookie terrorists, who hope to use his airtime to get a comrade off a manslaughter charge. Fleetingly, at the start of the siege, this threatens to become gripping. Soon, however, McGoohan begins chomping on the scenery, the dual ineptitude of Alexis Kanner's acting and direction becomes clear, and the picture rapidly descends into ham-fisted chaos. 🖭

Patrick McGoohan *John Kingsley* • Alexis Kanner *Lucas Miller* • Andrea Marcovicci *Girl* • Margaret Trudeau *Elizabeth Kingsley* • August Schellenberg *Aldini* ■ *Dir* Alexis Kanner • *Scr* Edmund Ward, Alexis Kanner

Kings Go Forth ★★

Second World War drama 1958 · US · BW · 110mins

In this strange blend of war adventure and racial drama, Frank Sinatra and Tony Curtis play two soldiers whose friendship is severely tested when the former falls for Natalie Wood, a girl of African descent. But it's Curtis who makes a move on Wood before dumping her, with tragic results. Delmer Daves's film is very much part of the liberalisation of Hollywood movies and American politics that took place in the mid-fifties. However, it's weighed down by plot contrivances and by its own self-importance.

Frank Sinatra *Sam Loggins* • Tony Curtis *Britt Harris* • Natalie Wood *Monique Blair* • Leora Dana *Mrs Blair* • Karl Swenson *Colonel* ■ *Dir* Delmer Daves • *Scr* Merle Miller, from the novel by Joe David Brown

Kings of the Road ★★★★ 18

Road movie   1976 · W Ger · BW · 168mins

This is an elegiac epic as much about American cultural imperialism as the forgotten border country between East and West Germany. Making evocative use of rock music and touching on topics as diverse as exile, communication and the decline of the national film industry, the action is void of contrived incident and conventional characterisation. They are barely missed, however, as Wenders demonstrates his mastery of the long take and the visual metaphor, exploiting Robbie Müller's stylish monochrome photography to locate the poetry in a seemingly desolate landscape. In German with English subtitles. ▭

Rüdiger Vogler *Bruno Winter* • Hanns Zischler *Robert Lander* • Lisa Kreuzer *Cashier* • Rudolf Schündler *Robert's father* • Marquard Bohm *Man who has lost his wife* ■ *Dir/Scr* Wim Wenders

Kings of the Sun ★★★ U

Adventure   1963 · US · Colour · 107mins

This is one of Hollywood's rare excursions into Meso-American history, with George Chakiris (*West Side Story*) looking convincingly Mayan and virile even when addressing characters with names like Ixzubin and Ah Zok. It's all faintly ridiculous, but there are some spectacular scenes in authentic Mayan sites like Chichen Itza. The Mayans were keen on human sacrifice, but don't hold that against them: according to this story, they also built the first permanent settlement in Texas.

Yul Brynner *Black Eagle* • George Chakiris *Balam* • Shirley Anne Field *Ixchel* • Brad Dexter *Ah Haleb* • Barry Morse *Ah Zok* • Armando Silvestre *Isatai* • Leo Gordon *Hunac Ceel* • Victoria Vetri *Ixzubin* ■ *Dir* J Lee Thompson • *Scr* Elliott Arnold, James R Webb, from a story by Elliott Arnold

The King's Pirate ★★ U

Swashbuckling adventure
1967 · US · Colour · 99mins

Just what the movie world didn't need in the Swinging Sixties: a low-budget remake of the Errol Flynn/Maureen O'Hara swashbuckler *Against All Flags*, with *The Virginian* TV star Doug McClure gauche and inadequate in the Flynn role. However, McClure's co-stars Jill St John and Guy Stockwell (Dean's brother), who both have some style and look comfortable in period costume, make amends. If you look closely you'll see an awful lot of the original film on display, with the new material cleverly shot around the footage by talented director Don Weis.

Doug McClure *Lt Brian Fleming* • Jill St John *Jessica Stephens* • Guy Stockwell *John Avery* • Mary Ann Mobley *Princess Patma* • Kurt Kasznar *Zucco* ■ *Dir* Don Weis • *Scr* Paul Wayne, Aeneas MacKenzie, Joseph Hoffman, from a story by Aeneas MacKenzie

King's Rhapsody ★★

Romantic drama   1955 · UK · Colour · 93mins

It was a sad sight to watch the great swashbuckler Errol Flynn in his two British movies for Herbert Wilcox. Clearly paunchy and slightly raddled, he managed to retain that twinkle in the eye but conveyed a general sense of slumming as he played opposite Mrs Wilcox, Anna Neagle. This is a sorry, tawdry affair, a Ruritanian romance that was past its sell-by date even as a play on the London stage. Flynn looks clearly the worse for drink in the many sequences where dialogue is played off him. Of course, that in itself is a reason for watching and enjoying this antiquated romp, and Flynn would restore his credibility later in character roles.

Anna Neagle *Marta Karillos* • Errol Flynn *King Richard of Laurentia* • Patrice Wymore *Princess Christiane* • Martita Hunt *Queen Mother* • Finlay Currie *King Paul* • Francis De Wolff *Prime Minister* • Joan Benham *Countess Astrid* ■ *Dir* Herbert Wilcox • *Scr* Pamela Bower, Christopher Hassall, AP Herbert, from the play by Ivor Novello

Kings Row ★★★★

Melodrama   1942 · US · BW · 126mins

Henry Bellamann's bestseller was the *Peyton Place* of its day, a steamy study of small-town mentality. Warner Bros did it full justice on the screen, subtly circumventing the censor and delivering a complex adult movie, with notable scenes and impeccable performances, offering career best opportunities to future US president Ronald Reagan (''where's the rest of me?'' he shrieks after a wanton and unnerving amputation) and Ann Sheridan as Randy Monaghan, the girl from the wrong side of the tracks. Only weak lead Robert Cummings is uncomfortably cast, but everyone else was at war. Erich Wolfgang Korngold's music is a model of its kind, his main theme superb and stunningly melodic. Strong, intelligent entertainment from a studio in its prime.

Ann Sheridan *Randy Monaghan* • Robert Cummings *Parris Mitchell* • Ronald Reagan *Drake McHugh* • Betty Field *Cassandra Tower* • Charles Coburn *Dr Henry Gordon* • Claude Rains *Dr Alexander Tower* • Judith Anderson *Mrs Harriet Gordon* • Nancy Coleman *Louise Gordon* ■ *Dir* Sam Wood • *Scr* Casey Robinson, Henry Bellamann, from a novel by Henry Bellamann

The King's Thief ★ U

Adventure   1955 · US · Colour · 78mins

David Niven is cast against type in this frightful Restoration melodrama as the villainous first minister of George Sanders (shamelessly overacting in his second turn as Charles II), intent on bumping off the enemies listed in his little black book. Among those whose wrath he has incurred is plucky Ann Blyth, who enlists the help of highwayman Edmund Purdom to help expose the nasty Niven. The ''swashbuckless'' plot limps along predictably to its Crown Jewels robbery conclusion, and the drab colour, indifferent performances and Robert Z Leonard's slack direction do nothing to make the minutes pass more easily.

David Niven *Duke of Brampton* • Ann Blyth *Lady Mary* • Edmund Purdom *Michael Dermott*

• George Sanders *Charles II* • Roger Moore *Jack* • John Dehner *Captain Herrick* • Sean Mcclory *Sheldon* • Tudor Owen *Simon* • Melville Cooper *Henry Wynch* ■ *Dir* Robert Z Leonard • *Scr* Christopher Knopf, from a story by Robert Hardy Andrews

The King's Trial ★★★

Historical drama
1990 · Fr/Por/W Ger/It · Colour

This finely crafted history lesson was a popular success on the festival circuit. The costumes and trappings of mid-17th-century Portugal have been lavishly re-created, but what makes this film stand out is its compelling tale of intrigue, lust and ambition. The overthrow of Alfonso VI by his brother Pedro and his wife Dona Maria is one of the darkest episodes in Portuguese history, and director Grilo recalls it with evident fascination and some relish. Carlos Daniel is fine as the feeble-minded king, but is outshone by Antonino Solmer and Aurelle Doazan as the ruthless schemers. In Portuguese with English subtitles.

Carlos Daniel *King Alfonso VI* • Aurelle Doazan *Dona Maria* • Gerard Hardy *Preyssac* • Antonino Solmer *Pedro II* ■ *Dir* Joao Mario Grilo • *Scr* Jean-Pierre Theilladde, Daniel Arasse, Joao Mario Grilo

The King's Whore ★★★ 15

Historical romantic drama
1990 · Fr/UK/Aus/It · Colour · 89mins

Timothy Dalton made this historical melodrama right after *Licence to Kill*, his second and final mission as James Bond. It must be said that his theatrical background serves him rather better in the role of an Italian king who takes a shine to the wife of a French count. She doesn't fancy him, however, and the king's passion leads him to declare war on France. Director Axel Corti evidently admires *Barry Lyndon* and has a clear view of what the 17th century looked, sounded and smelt like. It's a lavish movie, though there are the usual Europudding lumps: a mishmash of a cast and an uneven script written by many hands, including Frederic Raphael. ▭

Timothy Dalton *King Vittorio Amadeo* • Valeria Golino *Jeanne de Luynes* • Robin Renucci *Charles de Luynes* • Stephane Freiss *Count di Verua* • Feodor Chaliapin [Feodor Chaliapin Jr] *Scaglia* • Paul Crauchet *Duke of Luynes* • Margaret Tyzack *Dowager Countess* ■ *Dir* Axel Corti • *Scr* Axel Corti, Frederic Raphael, Daniel Vigne, from the novel *Jeanne de Luynes, comtesse de Verue* by Jacques Tournier • *Cinematographer* Gernot Roll

Kini and Adams ★★★

Drama   1997 · UK/Fr/Zim · Colour · 93mins

Burkina Faso's best-known director, Idrissa Ouedraogo, made his English-language debut with this investigation into the impact of industrialisation on rural Africa. Vusi Kunene and David Mohloki impress as the longtime buddies who fall out over the former's relationship with quarry foreman John Kani and gold-digging prostitute Netsayi Chigwendere. Although slightly muddled, this drama is still revealing in its discussion of women and their place in what is still, primarily, a patriarchal society. Made with additional backing from Switzerland and Ouedrago's home country.

Vusi Kunene *Kini* • David Mohloki *Adams* • John Kani *Ben* • Nthati Moshesh *Aida* • Netsayi Chigwendere *Binja* ■ *Dir* Idrissa Ouedraogo • *Scr* Idrissa Ouedraogo, Olivier Lorelle, Santiago Amigorena

Kinjite: Forbidden Subjects
★ 18

Crime action thriller
1989 · US · Colour · 93mins

Another Charles Bronson vehicle which you need a cast-iron gut to endure. This time the vigilante's friend plays an LA vice cop who teams up with a Japanese businessman whose daughter has been kidnapped by a gang who enslave children in the sex trade. This utterly repellent premise is handled by regular Bronson director J Lee Thompson as if it were merely an episode of *Kojak* rather than a serious subject. Bronson is decent enough, but we've seen him play the role of avenger so often he's turned into a photocopy of himself. ▭

Charles Bronson *Lieutenant Crowe* • Perry Lopez *Eddie Rios* • Juan Fernandez *Duke* • Sy Richardson *Lavonne* • Peggy Lipton *Kathleen Crowe* • Nicole Eggert *DeeDee* • Bill McKinney *Father Burke* • James Pax *Hiroshi Hada* ■ *Dir* J Lee Thompson • *Scr* Harold Nebenzal

Kipps ★★★ U

Comedy   1941 · UK · BW · 112mins

Critics were divided on the release of Carol Reed's adaptation of HG Wells's novel about the draper's clerk who discovers that, when it comes to social climbing, he has no head for heights. Some detected a certain detachment in Reed's direction, allowing Frank Launder and Sidney Gilliat's script to meander and supporting players to overact. But others claimed the film was stuffed with sly Wellsian satire, expertly staged set pieces and top-class acting from Michael Redgrave in the title role. The truth lies somewhere in between, for, while there is much to enjoy here, there are some interminable moments.

Michael Redgrave *Arthur Kipps* • Phyllis Calvert *Ann Pornick* • Diana Wynyard *Helen Walshingham* • Phillip Frost *Arthur as a boy* • Diana Calderwood *Ann as a girl* • Arthur Riscoe *Chitterlow* • Max Adrian *Chester Coote* • Helen Haye *Mrs Walshingham* • Michael Wilding *Ronnie Walshingham* ■ *Dir* Carol Reed • *Scr* Frank Launder, Sidney Gilliat, from the novel by HG Wells

The Kirlian Witness ★★

Science-fiction mystery
1978 · US · Colour · 91mins

A very odd fantasy thriller made by one-time workers in the hardcore porn industry. A plant is the sole witness to a murder and Nancy Snyder, the victim's sister, uses her telepathic powers and sensitivity to flora to unmask the killer. Kirlian photography, capturing the aura around a living object, is used to solve the case. Slow, quite moody and just plain weird.

Nancy Snyder *Rilla* • Ted Laplat *Dusty* • Joel Colodner *Robert* • Nancy Boykin *Laurie* • Lawrence Tierney *Detective* • Maia Danziger *Claire* ■ *Dir* Jonathan Sarno • *Scr* Jonathan Sarno, Lamar Sanders, from a story by Jonathan Sarno

U = SUITABLE FOR ALL   Uc = SUITABLE FOR ALL, ESPECIALLY FOR YOUNG CHILDREN (VIDEO ONLY)   PG = PARENTAL GUIDANCE

Kismet ★★★ U

Fantasy adventure
1944 · US · Colour · 99mins

Arabian Nights-style tales were seldom the stuff of A-features, least of all at opulent MGM, but this adaptation of Edward Knoblock's play about the beggar–magician who aspires to royalty gets the full gloss treatment, with top stars Ronald Colman and Marlene Dietrich looking glamorous but decidedly ill at ease in this third movie version of an oft-told tale and a hokey one at that. No surprise, then, to find that this plot would soon be turned into a musical and become a huge Broadway success. MGM then filmed the musical, and made a splendid but poorly received job of it, so the real value of this is by way of comparison. Oh, and, of course, Dietrich.

Ronald Colman *Hafiz* • Marlene Dietrich *Jamilla* • James Craig *Caliph* • Edward Arnold *Mansur the Grand Vizier* • Hugh Herbert *Feisal* • Joy Ann Page *Marsinah* • Florence Bates *Karsha* • Harry Davenport *Agha* ■ *Dir* William Dieterle • *Scr* John Meehan, from the play by Edward Knoblock

Kismet ★★★ U

Fantasy musical 1955 · US · Colour · 108mins

Maligned in its day, this *Arabian Nights* farrago has much to recommend it now, notably muscular baritone Howard Keel having the time of his life. He plays Haaj – the beggar whose daughter has fallen for a caliph – with enormous energy, filling the screen with his worthy and under-rated performance. The rest of the cast also works hard, particularly the raunchy Dolores Gray, and Ann Blyth and Vic Damone make a perfectly acceptable pair of lovebirds and get all the best songs, especially the hit *Stranger in Paradise*. ▣

Howard Keel *Haaj, the Poet* • Ann Blyth *Marsinah* • Dolores Gray *Lalume* • Vic Damone *Caliph* • Monty Woolley *Omar* • Sebastian Cabot *Wazir* • Jay C Flippen *Jawan* • Mike Mazurki *Chief policeman* • Jack Elam *Hassan-Ben* ■ *Dir* Vincente Minnelli • *Scr* Charles Lederer, Luther Davis, from the play *Kismet* by Edward Knoblock • *Music/Lyrics* George Forrest, Robert Wright

The Kiss ★★★

Silent drama 1929 · US · Colour · 64mins

In provincial France Greta Garbo is tried for the murder of her husband Anders Randolf who, in a jealous fit, tried to kill the handsome Lew Ayres, who is infatuated with her. Defence lawyer Conrad Nagel is her own former lover. This thin melodrama is elevated by the silent but eloquent presence of Garbo, starring in a silent movie for the last time. Directed by France's Jacques Feyder, imported for the occasion, it was also MGM's final silent production, and marked the impressive debut of Ayres, soon to be a star of the talkies.

Greta Garbo *Irene* • Conrad Nagel *Andre* • Anders Randolf *Guarry* • Holmes Herbert *Lassalle* • Lew Ayres *Pierre* • George Davis *Durant* ■ *Dir* Jacques Feyder • *Scr* Hans Kräly, from a story by George M Saville

The Kiss ★★ 18

Thriller 1988 · US/Can · Colour · 93mins

Zombie cats, mutilation by escalator, supernatural mumbo jumbo and African demons are just some of the delights to be found in this ludicrous chiller about an ancient witch (Joanna Pacula) who wants to pass on the secret of eternal youth via a kiss to her young niece (Meredith Salenger). Inane trash would be the best way to describe the directing debut of Pen Densham, co-writer of *Robin Hood: Prince of Thieves*. Yet for all its faults, this stilted shocker is packed with enough gratuitous incident and hokey action to rivet the viewer – despite the cheaply rendered, cat-beast succubus, which does its level best to sabotage the film at every daft turn. ▣

Joanna Pacula *Felice* • Meredith Salenger *Amy* • Mimi Kuzyk *Brenda* • Nicholas Kilbertus *Jack* • Jan Rubes *Tobin* ■ *Dir* Pen Densham • *Scr* Stephen Volk, Tom Ropelewski, from a story by Stephen Volk

Kiss and Tell ★★★

Romantic comedy 1945 · US · BW · 90mins

Once the world's biggest and smallest star, Shirley Temple was just another pretty teenage actress in the 1940s. Based on a hit Broadway comedy by F Hugh Herbert, this is one of her better later vehicles. Thought quite shocking at the time, the mildly amusing comedy had the 17-year-old Temple as Corliss Archer, pretending to be pregnant in order to divert attention from her brother's secret marriage. The film produced a sequel, *A Kiss for Corliss* in 1949, the year Temple retired from the movies.

Shirley Temple *Corliss Archer* • Jerome Courtland *Dexter Franklin* • Walter Abel *Mr Archer* • Katharine Alexander [Katherine Alexander] *Mrs Archer* • Robert Benchley *Uncle George Archer* • Porter Hall *Mr Franklin* • Virginia Welles *Mildred Pringle* • Tom Tully *Mr Pringle* • Darryl Hickman *Raymond Pringle* ■ *Dir* Richard Wallace • *Scr* F Hugh Herbert, from his play

Kiss and Tell ★★

Psychological thriller 1996 · US · Colour

Not the 1945 Shirley Temple vehicle, but a made-for-TV thriller in which Cheryl Ladd's cosy middle-class existence is shattered by a knock on the door that brings a dark warning. This is another tiresome "sleeping with the enemy" tale, given a disturbing undercurrent by the fact that Ladd's family has a history of mental instability. Never going beyond surface emotions, Ladd makes a barely plausible victim; John Terry, as the husband who seems to be plotting murder, and Francie Swift, as the mistress who tries to aid her rival, turn in somewhat better performances.

Cheryl Ladd *Jean McAvoy* • John Terry *Eric McAvoy* • Francie Swift *Kelly Krieger* • John Bedford Lloyd *Dan Turman* • Jack Gilpin *Matt Sohigan* • Caitlin Clarke *Karen Wallace* ■ *Dir* Andy Wolk • *Scr* David Birke

A Kiss before Dying ★★★

Crime drama 1956 · US · Colour · 94mins

A fine adaptation of *Rosemary's Baby* author Ira Levin's dark tale about a social climber who kills his wealthy girlfriend when her pregnancy threatens her inheritance. It stars a cast-against-type Robert Wagner, cleverly made-up as a villain and relishing the kind of role he seldom played again. This *film noir* is actually shot in bright daylight colours by cinematographer Lucien Ballard, who makes excellent use of locations. A young Joanne Woodward plays the victim and a superb Mary Astor is the wretched Wagner's mother. Interestingly, in the novel the murderer's identity is hidden; in the movie, you know who did it and watch as he's tracked down.

Robert Wagner *Bud Corliss* • Jeffrey Hunter *Gordon Grant* • Virginia Leith *Ellen Kingship* • Joanne Woodward *Dorothy Kingship* • Mary Astor *Mrs Corliss* • George Macready *Leo Kingship* ■ *Dir* Gerd Oswald • *Scr* Lawrence Roman, from the novel by Ira Levin

A Kiss before Dying ★★ 18

Thriller 1991 · US · Colour · 89mins

Despite a chilling performance from Matt Dillon, this attempt to update Ira Levin's novel (it was first filmed in 1956) for the nineties doesn't quite get there. Dillon makes for a thoroughly charming psychopath, killing his way to the top of the corporate ladder by romancing twin wealthy heiresses, both played by Sean Young, and director James Dearden stages some effective, if derivative, set pieces. He never manages to generate any real tension, however, and Young is unconvincing in her dual role. Contains violence, swearing and nudity.

Matt Dillon *Jonathan Corliss* • Sean Young *Ellen/Dorothy Carlsson* • Max von Sydow *Thor Carlsson* • Jim Fyfe *Terry Dieter* • Ben Browder *Tommy Roussell* • Diane Ladd *Mrs Corliss* • Martha Gehman *Patricia Farren* • Shane Rimmer *Commissioner Mallet* • James Russo *Dan Corelli* ■ *Dir* James Dearden • *Scr* James Dearden, from the novel by Ira Levin

Kiss Daddy Good Night ★★★ 15

Psychological crime thriller
1987 · US · Colour · 78mins

The intriguing debut of Uma Thurman is an oddball affair. Playing a precocious young vamp, she picks up wealthy men in order to rob them. Unfortunately for the young "Poison Ivy", someone then begins to stalk her. It's untidily made, but Thurman has real presence and Steve Buscemi pops up in an early role. Contains some swearing and violence. ▣

Uma Thurman *Laura* • Paul Dillon *Sid* • Paul Richards (2) *William B Tilden* • Steve Buscemi *Johnny* • Annabelle Gurwitch *Sue* • David Brisbin *Nelson Blitz* ■ *Dir* Peter Ily Huemer • *Scr* Peter Ily Huemer, Michael Gabrieli, from a story by Peter Ily Huemer

A Kiss for Corliss ★

Comedy 1949 · US · BW · 87mins

No displays of affection were shown for this limp comedy, a sad end to the phenomenal career of Shirley Temple. Four years earlier she had starred as irrepressible teenager Corliss Archer in *Kiss and Tell*. In this sequel – in which Corliss is suspected of having spent the night with a playboy (David Niven) – the same director (Richard Wallace) guided her, sometimes ill-advisedly. As the plot's implausibilities increase, even the usually reliable Niven resorts to desperate mugging.

Shirley Temple *Corliss Archer* • David Niven *Kenneth Marquis* • Tom Tully *Harry Archer* • Virginia Welles *Mildred Pringle* • Darryl Hickman *Dexter Franklin* ■ *Dir* Richard Wallace • *Scr* Howard Dimsdale, from a story by Howard Dimsdale, from characters created by F Hugh Herbert

A Kiss in the Dark ★★

Romantic comedy 1949 · US · BW · 88mins

Concert pianist David Niven inherits an apartment block and becomes involved with his disparate collection of tenants, including photographic model Jane Wyman, with whom he falls in love. Niven's flair for comedy, and the confident presence of Wyman – hardly finding this a challenge after her Oscar-winning success in the harrowing *Johnny Belinda* – only just keep this afloat. Broderick Crawford, Victor Moore and Maria Ouspenskaya also do their best for director Delmer Daves, but the flat-footed script is under-stocked with laughs.

David Niven *Eric Phillips* • Jane Wyman *Polly Haines* • Victor Moore *Horace Willoughby* • Wayne Morris *Bruce Arnold* • Broderick Crawford *Mr Botts* • Joseph Buloff *Peter Danilo* • Maria Ouspenskaya *Madame Karina* ■ *Dir* Delmer Daves • *Scr* Harry Kurnitz, from a story by Everett Freeman, Devery Freeman

Kiss Me Again ★★★

Silent comedy 1925 · US · BW

Based on a stage farce, this sophisticated romantic comedy was made by director Ernst Lubitsch during his Warner Bros days, and concerns a classic love triangle featuring a bored wife (Marie Prevost), her husband (Monte Blue), and her lover (John Roche). As handled by the masterly Lubitsch, displaying the "touch" and high style for which he would become famous at Paramount during the thirties, the simple plot is transformed into an exercise in wit, depth and intelligence. The "It" Girl, Clara Bow, features in support.

Marie Prevost *Loulou Fleury* • Monte Blue *Gaston Fleury* • John Roche *Maurice Ferriere* • Clara Bow *Grizette, Dubois's secretary* • Willard Louis *Avocat Dubois* ■ *Dir* Ernst Lubitsch • *Scr* Hans Kräly, from the play *Divorçons* by Victorien Sardou, Emile de Najac

Kiss Me Deadly ★★★★★ 12

Classic film noir 1955 · US · BW · 100mins

One of the greatest examples of *film noir*, this early feature by *Dirty Dozen* director Robert Aldrich made him a name in arty circles (the critics of the French magazine *Cahiers du Cinema* loved him and the film) and a formidable presence in cinema. He took a piece of Mickey Spillane pulp fiction and turned it into an astonishing fable, with Pandora's Box transformed into a nuclear furnace. The look is off-the-wall stylish and the tension builds to a climax that is near-apocalyptic. Everything is on the side of the unexpected, from the opening credits to the fact that Spillane's detective Mike Hammer (Ralph Meeker) is a flawed anti-hero who, after picking up a girl on the run, finds himself in over his head in events beyond his control.

Albert Dekker is a classily obnoxious villain, but it's the women you have to watch. As the title suggests, their embrace is lethal. ▢

Ralph Meeker *Mike Hammer* • Albert Dekker *Dr Soberin* • Paul Stewart *Carl Evello* • Maxine Cooper *Velda* • Gaby Rodgers *Gabrielle/Lily Carver* • Wesley Addy *Pat Chambers* • Juano Hernandez *Eddie Yeager* • Nick Dennis *Nick* • Cloris Leachman *Christina Bailey/Berga Torn* ■ *Dir* Robert Aldrich • *Scr* Al Bezzerides, from the novel by Mickey Spillane • *Cinematographer* Ernest Laszlo

Kiss Me Goodbye ★★★ PG

Romantic comedy
1982 · US · Colour · 101mins

Sally Field stars in this nicely played romantic fantasy as the widow rebuilding her life with hunky fiancé Jeff Bridges, only for her happy new existence to be complicated by the ghostly arrival of her late husband (James Caan), who is intent on stopping the wedding. Caan – whose deft comic touch has stolen the show in films like *Mickey Blue Eyes* and *Honeymoon in Vegas* – is deliciously enjoyable as the interfering apparition, while Field and Bridges have fun with their romantic roles.

Sally Field *Kay Villano* • James Caan *Jolly Villano* • Jeff Bridges *Rupert Baines* • Paul Dooley *Kendall* • Claire Trevor *Charlotte Banning* • Mildred Natwick *Mrs Reilly* • Dorothy Fielding *Emily* • William Prince *Reverend Hollis* ■ *Dir* Robert Mulligan • *Scr* Charlie Peters, from the film *Dona Flor and Her Two Husbands* by Bruno Barreto, from the novel *Dona Flor and Her Two Husbands* by Jorge Amado

Kiss Me, Guido ★★ 15

Comedy   1997 · US/UK · Colour · 85mins

Heterosexual pizza chef Nick Scotti misunderstands a Manhattan apartment want ad and moves in with gay choreographer Anthony Barrile, with the expected culture clash fall-out. When wannabe actor Scotti takes over Barrile's camp role in an off-Broadway play, things get even more farcical. Tony Vitale's first feature borders on the amateurish and indulges in increasingly strained humour as Italian-American stereotypes get pitted against obvious gay ones. Luckily, the likeable performances and classic disco soundtrack paper over the not-so-wisecracks. Contains swearing and sexual references. ▢

Nick Scotti *Frankie* • Anthony Barrile *Warren* • Anthony DeSando *Pino* • Molly Price *Meryl* • Craig Chester *Terry* • Christopher Lawford *Dakota* ■ *Dir/Scr* Tony Vitale

Kiss Me Kate ★★★★ U

Musical comedy 1953 · US · Colour · 105mins

A splendid MGM version of Cole Porter's smash-hit Broadway show, originally filmed in 3-D, hence all those shots where Ann Miller and Howard Keel chuck things at the audience, including themselves. Talented director George Sidney is completely comfortable in the world of the theatre, and utilised fabulous, and cleverly disguised, long takes in his filming of Keel, never better than as Fred Graham-cum-Petruchio, and Kathryn Grayson, playing difficult diva Lilli Vanessi, alias Shakespeare's tamed shrew Kate. Miller nearly steals the

show with *Too Darn Hot*, and straight men Keenan Wynn and James Whitmore are wonderful in composer Porter's steamy waltz *Brush Up Your Shakespeare*. A treat, but just lacking that special magic that makes a screen musical great; still, in the face of such talent, it doesn't matter. ▢

Kathryn Grayson *Lilli Vanessi, "Katherine"* • Howard Keel *Fred Graham, "Petruchio"* • Ann Miller *Lois Lane, "Bianca"* • Keenan Wynn *Lippy* • Bobby Van *"Gremio"* • Tommy Rall *Bill Calhoun, "Lucentio"* • James Whitmore *Slug* • Kurt Kasznar *"Baptista"* • Bob Fosse *"Hortensio"* • Ron Randell *Cole Porter* ■ *Dir* George Sidney • *Scr* Dorothy Kingsley, from the play by Cole Porter, Samuel Spewack, Bella Spewack, from the play *The Taming of the Shrew* by William Shakespeare

Kiss Me, Stupid ★★ PG

Comedy   1964 · US · BW · 121mins

Dean Martin is certainly an acquired taste: if he's to yours then Billy Wilder's rather obvious satire on personal ambition and sexual manipulation sees the court jester of the Rat Pack on full throttle. He's a sex-obsessed bar-room warbler, Kim Novak is the whore with a heart of lurex and Ray Walston the amateur songwriter desperate to keep Martin's greasy paws off his wife. It's Wilder, so almost by definition it's smart and sharp, but if you have a single feminist bone in your body, prepare to blow a major gasket. ▢

Dean Martin *Dino* • Kim Novak *Polly the Pistol* • Ray Walston *Orville J Spooner* • Felicia Farr *Zelda Spooner* • Cliff Osmond *Barney Millsap* • Barbara Pepper *Big Bertha* ■ *Dir* Billy Wilder • *Scr* Billy Wilder, Ial Diamond, from the play *L'Ora della Fantasia* by Anna Bonacci

Kiss of a Killer ★★★ 15

Crime thriller   1993 · US · Colour · 91mins

True-story specialist Larry Elikann has a field day with this lurid melodrama. Annette O'Toole relishes her dual roles as a schizophrenic whose other self likes to sleep around a lot, putting her in serious danger. Eva Marie Saint, Gregg Henry and Brian Wimmer offer up sterling support, and the unbelievable story will keep you hooked. ▢

Annette O'Toole *Kate* • Eva Marie Saint *Mrs Wilson* • Brian Wimmer *Gary* • Gregg Henry *Richard* • Vic Polizos *Det James* ■ *Dir* Larry Elikann • *Scr* David Warfield, from the novel *The Point of Murder* by Margaret Yorke

Kiss of a Stranger ★★

Thriller   1997 · US · Colour · 105mins

This distinctly dubious thriller actually gets off to an intriguing start. Following her light-hearted on-the-air remark that all good-looking men in Los Angeles are gay, TV gossip columnist Mariel Hemingway has a one-night stand with a handsome stranger. But no sooner has she discovered that she's pregnant than her friends become the target of a serial killer and the plot clicks into slasher autopilot. Hemingway is rather good as the self-assured journalist and there's a strong supporting cast, but Sam Irvin fails to deliver on the suspense front.

Mariel Hemingway *Nova Clarke* • Corbin Bernsen *Mason* • Matt Battaglia *Nathan Leigh* ■ *Dir/Scr* Sam Irvin

Kiss of Death ★★★★

Film noir   1947 · US · BW · 98mins

Nothing in today's Tarantino-inspired cinema of violence is as menacing as Richard Widmark's demented chuckle in this super-tough *film noir* thriller from ace director Henry Hathaway. Widmark's screen debut (he was fourth-billed as psychopath Tom Udo) has passed into screen legend, most notably for the scene in which Udo shoves an elderly lady in a wheelchair (actually stunt double Rod Amateau, who later became a director) down a flight of stairs in a fit of pique. The scene was thought too horrific for British audiences and was cut on UK release by a squeamish British censor. Shot in gritty style on authentic New York locations, the film features a surprisingly fine and sympathetic leading performance from the usually derided Victor Mature. An adult and involving crime drama with a truly tragic dimension.

Victor Mature *Nick Bianco* • Brian Donlevy *D'Angelo* • Coleen Gray *Nettie* • Richard Widmark *Tom Udo* • Karl Malden *Sergeant William Cullen* • Taylor Holmes *Earl Howser* • Howard Smith *Warden* • Anthony Ross *Williams* ■ *Dir* Henry Hathaway • *Scr* Ben Hecht, Charles Lederer, from a story by Eleazar Lipsky

Kiss of Death ★★★ 18

Crime thriller   1994 · US · Colour · 96mins

Few screen debuts were as chilling as Richard Widmark's in the 1947 original, though in this remake Nicolas Cage is agreeably nasty, with a goatee beard and bulging biceps to complement a serious streak of social irresponsibility. The plot has been thoroughly made over, though it's still about an ex-con David Caruso – formerly of *NYPD Blue* – who is determined to go straight, but is forced into becoming an informer for nasty cop Samuel L Jackson. A gripping effort, laced with black humour and directed by Barbet Schroeder with a sharp eye for the hell-holes of New York. Contains swearing, violence and some nudity. ▢

David Caruso *Jimmy Kilmartin* • Samuel L Jackson *Calvin* • Nicolas Cage *Little Junior* • Helen Hunt *Bev* • Kathryn Erbe *Rosie* • Stanley Tucci *Frank Zioli* • Michael Rapaport *Ronnie* • Ving Rhames *Omar* • Philip Baker Hall *Big Junior* ■ *Dir* Barbet Schroeder • *Scr* Richard Price, from a story by Eleazar Lipsky, from the 1947 film

Kiss of Fire ★★ U

Period romantic drama
1955 · US · Colour · 87mins

A minor costume drama, set in the 18th century, in which pretty Barbara Rush, as pretender to the Spanish throne, has to make a hazardous journey from Sante Fe to Monterey, in order to get a ship to Spain. A little excitement is engendered by a few villains, Indians on the warpath, and a bit of swashbuckling, but the direction (by Joseph M Newman) and dialogue are rather soggy. So thank goodness for the dynamic presence of Jack Palance who plays Rush's love interest, the intriguingly named El Tigre.

Jack Palance *El Tigre* • Barbara Rush *Princess Lucia* • Rex Reason *Duke of Montera* •

Martha Hyer *Felicia* • Alan Reed *Diego* • Leslie Bradley *Vega* ■ *Dir* Joseph M Newman • *Scr* Franklin Coen, Richard Collins, from the novel *The Rose and the Flame* by Jonreed Lauritzen

Kiss of the Spider Woman ★★★★ 15

Drama
1985 · US/Bra · BW and Colour · 115mins

This is not a fifties sci-fi B-movie, but an unusual, intimate tale of two very different prisoners – a flamboyant gay man (William Hurt) and a reactionary political prisoner (Raul Julia) – who share a cell in a South American jail. (The *Spider Woman* of the title refers to an old movie plot Hurt lovingly recounts to Julia.) Hector Babenco's film hinges on the believability of their relationship and the way the vast gap between their opposing beliefs and attitudes slowly begins to narrow. Fortunately, the leads are top-notch (Hurt won an Oscar for his performance), and the juxtaposition of dream-like monochrome fantasy with harsh, squalid reality is wonderfully conceived. ▢

William Hurt *Molina* • Raul Julia *Valentin* • Sonia Braga *Leni Lamaison/Marta/Spider Woman* • Jose Lewgoy *Warden* • Nuno Leal Maia *Gabriel* • Antonio Petrim *Clubfoot* ■ *Dir* Hector Babenco • *Scr* Leonard Schrader, from a novel by Manuel Puig

Kiss or Kill ★★ 18

Crime thriller   1997 · Ausl · Colour · 92mins

A disappointing Australian thriller that opens brilliantly with a crime of harrowing intensity, and then blows it all on a daftly plotted chase movie about a thieving couple pursued by cops and a sportsman from whom they've stolen an incriminating videotape. Do they simply prey on the sexual urges of men eager to bed the seductive Frances O'Connor? Or are they capable of much darker deeds? The artsy and obtrusive jump cuts are misjudged, as is the film's denouement, which hinges on a ridiculous coincidence. Contains swearing, sex scenes and some violence. ▢

Frances O'Connor *Nikki* • Matt Day *Al* • Chris Haywood *Detective Hummer* • Barry Otto *Adler Jones* • Andrew S Gilbert *Detective Crean* • Barry Langrishe *Zipper Doyle* • Max Cullen *Stan* ■ *Dir/Scr* Bill Bennett

Kiss Shot ★★ PG

Comedy drama   1989 · US · Colour · 88mins

One of those Whoopi Goldberg movies that are quickly forgotten, and you can see why. Goldberg is the single mother who ends up playing pool to raise the money she needs to pay her mortgage in a comic tale that tries hard to be a funny version of *The Hustler*, but doesn't really succeed. Oh well, at least we can see what Dennis Franz was up to before he became a big star on television with *NYPD Blue*.

Whoopi Goldberg *Sarah Collins* • Dennis Franz *Max Fleisher* • Dorian Harewood *Kevin Merrick* • Tasha Scott *Jenny Collins* • David Marciano *Rick Powell* • Teddy Wilson *Billy Tatum* ■ *Dir* Jerry London • *Scr* Carl Kleinschmitt

Kiss the Boys Goodbye ★★★ U

Musical comedy   1941 · US · BW · 84mins

Claire Boothe's Broadway satire on Hollywood's search for an actress to play Scarlett O'Hara loses its caustic edge in the transformation into a musical comedy film. The hunt is on for a southern belle to star in a New York show, and Mary Martin heads south and ropes in her aunt and uncle to help her gain an audition and become the discovery of Don Ameche's director and Oscar Levant's composer. Director Victor Schertzinger also co-wrote the songs. Not as sharp or topical as Boothe's play, but still a lot of fun.

Mary Martin *Cindy Lou Bethany* • Don Ameche *Lloyd Lloyd* • Oscar Levant *Dick Rayburn* • Virginia Dale *Gwen Abbott* • Barbara Jo Allen *Myra Stanhope* • Raymond Walburn *Top Rumson* • Elizabeth Patterson *Aunt Lilly Lou* • Jerome Cowan *Bert Fisher* ■ *Dir* Victor Schertzinger • *Scr* Harry Tugend, Dwight Taylor, from a play by Clare Boothe [Luce] • *Music Director* Victor Young

Kiss the Girls ★★★ 18

Detective thriller
1997 · US · Colour · 110mins

This screen adaptation of James Patterson's suspenseful bestseller is all surface gloss with little real substance. It gets by thanks to the atmospheric photography and great performances from Morgan Freeman and Ashley Judd. Freeman is a forensic psychologist whose niece has been abducted by a serial kidnapper known as "Casanova"; Judd is the only woman to have escaped from the villain's secret lair. Can Judd overcome her drug-induced amnesia and guide Freeman to the culprit? If all logic and credibility completely disappear as the conclusion nears, and the kidnapper's identity is relatively easy to guess, it's still a compelling enough thriller. Contains swearing, violence and sexual situations. ▦

Morgan Freeman *Alex Cross* • Ashley Judd *Kate McTiernan* • Cary Elwes *Nick Ruskin* • Alex McArthur *Sikes* • Tony Goldwyn *Will Rudolph* • Jay O Sanders *Kyle Craig* • Bill Nunn *Sampson* • Brian Cox *Chief Hatfield* ■ *Dir* Gary Fleder • *Scr* David Klass, from the novel by James Patterson

Kiss Them for Me ★★ U

Wartime comedy drama
1957 · US · Colour · 103mins

Oh dear. The combined talents of star Cary Grant and director Stanley Donen, so successful in both *Indiscreet* and *Charade*, fail miserably here, in a remake of that old perennial "three sailors on the town" plot (a veritable Donen classic), this time set in San Francisco during the Second World War and based loosely on the novel *Shore Leave*. The movie never really catches fire, and is worth viewing now only as a fifties period piece.

Cary Grant *Crewson* • Jayne Mansfield *Alice* • Suzy Parker *Gwenneth* • Leif Erickson *Eddie Turnbull* • Ray Walston *Lieutenant "Mac" McCann* • Larry Blyden *Mississip* • Nathaniel Frey *Chief Petty Officer Ruddle* • Werner Klemperer *Commander Wallace* ■ *Dir* Stanley Donen • *Scr* Julius Epstein, from the play by

Luther Davis, from the novel *Shore Leave* by Frederic Wakeman • *Music* Carroll Coates, Lionel Newman

Kiss Tomorrow Goodbye ★★★★

Crime drama   1950 · US · BW · 102mins

A terrific James Cagney vehicle, with the star playing tough and mean in his *White Heat* mode. The cracking Warner Bros pace never lets up, and there's not a key character on show who displays any kind of morals or ethics whatsoever – even the cops are bent. It's based on a novel by Horace McCoy, and director Gordon Douglas knew how to handle stuff like this in his sleep. Especially notable are Luther Adler as a phoney lawyer with a cheap line in philosophy and producer William Cagney as (surprise!) Cagney's screen brother. Seriously under-rated when it first appeared, this movie's sheer constant venality gives it a very contemporary sheen.

James Cagney *Ralph Cotter* • Barbara Payton *Holiday Carleton* • Helena Carter *Margaret Dobson* • Ward Bond *Inspector Weber* • Luther Adler *Cherokee Mandon* • William Cagney *Ralph's brother* ■ *Dir* Gordon Douglas • *Scr* Harry Brown, from the novel by Horace McCoy

Kissed ★★★ 18

Romantic drama 1996 · Can · Colour · 75mins

A controversial success on the world festival circuit, director Lynne Stopkewich's exploration of the taboo of necrophilia will divide opinion. Molly Parker plays a young woman so fascinated by death she goes to work as a mortician in a funeral parlour. There she indulges her sexual fantasies with the deceased until a living, breathing boyfriend appears. But can he measure up to the safe embraces of her former lovers? It sounds completely nauseating, but, although the script is insultingly naive in places, the subject matter is tackled with discretion and the film makes its mark, largely thanks to Parker's sensitive central performance. Odd, yet poignant and affecting. Contains some swearing and sex scenes. ▦

Molly Parker *Sandra Larson* • Peter Outerbridge *Matt* • Jay Brazeau *Mr Wallis* • Natasha Morley *Young Sandra* • Jessie Winter Mudie *Carol* • James Timmons *Jan* • Joe Maffei *Biology teacher* • Robert Thurston *Detective* ■ *Dir* Lynne Stopkewich • *Scr* Lynne Stopkewich, Angus Fraser, from the story *We So Seldom Look on Love* by Barbara Gowdy

Kisses for My President ★★ U

Comedy   1964 · US · BW · 113mins

A thunderingly mawkish pre-feminist tract, in which Polly Bergen stars as the first woman president of the United States. A lot of talent that should have known better appears alongside Bergen, including always-watchable reliables such as Fred MacMurray (as the protocol-cursed "First Man"), Arlene Dahl, Eli Wallach and Edward Andrews, but everyone seems to be struggling with the material. Director Curtis Bernhardt fails to find the right screwball tone, and the result is surprisingly witless and cloying. The sets look cheap, too.

Fred MacMurray *Thad McCloud* • Polly Bergen *Leslie McCloud* • Arlene Dahl *Doris Reid* • Edward Andrews *Senator Walsh* • Eli Wallach *Valdez* • Donald May *John O'Connor* • Harry Holcombe *Bill Richards* • Anna Capri [Ahna Capri] *Gloria McCloud* ■ *Dir* Curtis Bernhardt • *Scr* Claude Binyon, Robert G Kane

Kissin' Cousins ★★ U

Musical   1964 · US · Colour · 87mins

Most of Presley's movie vehicles arouse the suspicion that their makers thought cheapness and speed more important than quality, but this double-trouble romantic comedy is a pleasant way to pass the time. Elvis plays the two leads: a (blond!) hillbilly, resisting the US Air Force's plan to build a missile base on his family's land, as well as the lieutenant cousin whose job it is to persuade them. Plenty of gals, punch-ups and forgettable tunes ensue. ▦

Elvis Presley *Josh Morgan/Jodie Tatum* • Arthur O'Connell *Pappy Tatum* • Glenda Farrell *Ma Tatum* • Jack Albertson *Capt Robert Salbo* • Pam Austin [Pamela Austin] *Selena Tatum* • Cynthia Pepper *Midge* • Yvonne Craig *Azalea Tatum* ■ *Dir* Gene Nelson • *Scr* Gerald Drayson Adams, Gene Nelson, from a story by Gerald Drayson Adams, Gene Nelson

Kissing a Fool ★★★ 15

Romantic comedy
1998 · US · Colour · 89mins

While *Friends* actresses Courteney Cox, Jennifer Aniston and Lisa Kudrow have enjoyed screen success in *Scream*, *She's the One* and *Analyze This*, their male co-stars have found the cinematic crossover much trickier. The curse continues with this only moderately enjoyable romantic comedy, as David Schwimmer tries to shrug off his nice-guy image to play a self-centred sports journalist, who tests his girlfriend's fidelity by asking his best friend Jason Lee to seduce her. Told in flashback at the girlfriend's wedding to one of the men (but which one?), this has good performances from Lee and *Stargate*'s Mili Avital, but a miscast Schwimmer struggles to convince as the sleazy rogue. Contains swearing and sexual references. ▦

David Schwimmer *Max Abbitt* • Jason Lee *Jay Murphy* • Mili Avital *Samantha Andrews* • Bonnie Hunt *Linda* • Vanessa Angel *Natasha* • Kari Wuhrer *Dara* ■ *Dir* Doug Ellin • *Scr* Doug Ellin, James Frey, from a story by James Frey

The Kissing Bandit ★★

Musical comedy 1949 · US · Colour · 102mins

A major flop on its first release, this film became famous because its star, Frank Sinatra, would constantly joke about it being the low point of his career. The idea of casting the then-puny actor as the son of a desperado noted for his female conquests probably seemed amusing at the time, but the star is palpably uneasy, the direction by László Benedek (his first film) too stolid and the score mostly mundane.

Frank Sinatra *Ricardo* • Kathryn Grayson *Teresa* • J Carrol Naish *Chico* • Mildred Natwick *Isabella* • Ricardo Montalban *Fiesta dancer* • Ann Miller *Fiesta dancer* • Cyd Charisse *Fiesta dancer* ■ *Dir* László Benedek [Laslo Benedek] • *Scr* Isobel Lennart, John Briard Harding

Kissinger and Nixon ★★★

Historical drama   1995 · US · Colour

Riveting performances by Beau Bridges as the paranoid and prickly Nixon and Ron Silver as the ambitious Kissinger make this intense TV movie well worth watching. It recounts the 1972–3 Vietnam peace negotiations in which President Richard Nixon and his national security adviser, Henry Kissinger, were often at odds. Veteran director Daniel Petrie keeps Lionel Chetwynd's intelligent script moving briskly and produces a fascinating behind-the-scenes look at politics and power in action.

Ron Silver *Henry Kissinger* • Beau Bridges *Richard Nixon* • Matt Frewer *Alexander Haig* • Ron White *HR "Bob" Haldeman* • George Takei *Le Duc Tho* • Kenneth Welsh *James "Scotty" Reston* • Tony Rosato *Charles Colson* ■ *Dir* Daniel Petrie • *Scr* Lionel Chetwynd, from the biography *Kissinger: a Biography* by Walter Isaacson

Kit Carson ★★★ U

Western   1940 · US · BW · 96mins

There was a time when Kit Carson and Buffalo Bill were the heroes of schoolboys everywhere, with their (largely fictional) achievements celebrated in comics. This is the definitive biopic of frontier scout Carson's adventurous life, and Buffalo Bill's followed four years later with the added benefit of Technicolor. Jon Hall, the hunk from John Ford's 1937 disaster movie *The Hurricane*, makes a solid enough Carson as he tangles with expedition leader Dana Andrews for the love of Lynn Bari, but the script doesn't allow for much character depth. Since much of Carson's life was fictionalised in his own lifetime via dime novels, who could blame Hollywood for turning history into a rattling good adventure?

Jon Hall *Kit Carson* • Lynn Bari *Dolores Murphy* • Dana Andrews *Captain John C Fremont* • Harold Huber *Lopez* • Ward Bond *Ape* • Renie Riano *Miss Genevieve Pilchard* ■ *Dir* George B Seitz • *Scr* George Bruce

Kitchen ★★★ 15

Romantic drama
1997 · HK/Jap · Colour · 111mins

Banana Yoshimoto's novella had already been filmed by Japanese director Yoshimitsu Morita in 1989, but this version is infinitely superior in its exploration of deceptive appearance and unspoken emotion. Employing various distancing devices, director Ho Yim studiously chronicles the relationship between the timid Yasuko Tomita and hairdresser Jordan Chan and the impact it has on his transsexual mother, Law Kar-Ying. While this strategy occasionally makes it difficult to identify with the characters, the tone shifts deftly between tenderness and eroticism, and there is a pleasing hesitancy about the romance, which is seemingly doomed after a sudden tragedy. The result is an admirable, if not always engrossing drama. In Cantonese with English subtitles. Contains some violence, swearing and nudity.

Jordan Chan *Louie* • Yasuko Tomita *Aggie* • Law Kar-Ying *Emma* • Karen Mok *Jenny* • Lau

Siu-Ming *Mr Chiu* • Lo Koon-Lan *Chika* ■ *Dir* Ho Yim • *Scr* Ho Yim, from the novella by Banana Yoshimoto

Rosamund Marshall • *Cinematographer* Daniel L Fapp • *Music* Victor Young • *Art Director* Hans Dreier, Walter Tyler

Simpson *Garth* ■ *Dir* Terence Young • *Scr* Millard Kaufman, Samuel Fuller, from the novel by William Bradford Huie

The Kitchen Toto ★★ 15

Drama   1987 · UK · Colour · 91mins

Bob Peck gives one of his all too rare film performances as the British Chief of Police handling unrest in Kenya during the 1950s. The tale is told through the eyes of Edwin Mahinda, a young Kikuyu boy whose loyalties are torn between the Mau Mau, his tribe's rebel group – and the killers of his minister father – and the British whose service he is in. Director Harry Hook as a native Kenyan obviously has a handle on the issues here, but does a poor job in making them comprehensible to your average viewer. 🖵

Edwin Mahinda *Mwangi* • Bob Peck *John Graham* • Phyllis Logan *Janet Graham* • Nicholas Charles *Mugo* • Ronald Pirie *Edward Graham* • Robert Urquhart *DC McKinnon* • Kirsten Hughes *Mary McKinnon* • Edward Judd *Dick Luis* ■ *Dir/Scr* Harry Hook

Kitten with a Whip ★★

Thriller   1964 · US · BW · 83mins

Ann-Margret stars in this low-budget exploitation thriller about a juvenile delinquent who escapes from a detention centre and forces her way into the home of a politician (John Forsythe). Refusing to leave, she threatens to call the police and implicate him in a sex scandal. Then she calls in a pair of thugs who provide some mildly titillating thrills and purely gratuitous violence. A cross between the Roger Corman-style teen pic and *The Desperate Hours*, it veers between the sub-standard and the subversive, with Ann-Margret careering convincingly out of control.

Ann-Margret *Jody Dvorak* • John Forsythe *David Patton* • Peter Brown *Ron* • Patricia Barry *Vera* • Richard Anderson *Grant* • James Ward *Buck* • Diane Sayer *Midge* • Ann Doran *Mavis Varden* • Patrick Whyte *Philip Varden* ■ *Dir* Douglas Heyes • *Scr* Douglas Heyes, from the novel by Wade Miller

Kitty ★★★★

Period drama   1945 · US · BW · 103mins

Paulette Goddard is the cockney waif plucked from the streets of 18th-century London to be tutored for marriage into high society in this sumptuously mounted drama. Beautifully acted, well photographed and brilliantly directed (by Mitchell Leisen), this is a harsh variation of *Pygmalion* with Goddard being forced into two unsuitable marriages. Ray Milland is his dependable self as the nobleman pulling the strings, Constance Collier is a dissipated aunt and Sara Allgood a Hogarthian wreck, but the real scene-stealing is done by Reginald Owen as a lecherous old duke, whose death scene is particularly well staged.

Paulette Goddard *Kitty* • Ray Milland *Sir Hugh Marcy* • Patric Knowles *Brett Hardwood, the Earl of Carstairs* • Reginald Owen *Duke of Malmunster* • Cecil Kellaway *Thomas Gainsborough* • Constance Collier *Lady Susan Dewitt* • Dennis Hoey *Jonathan Selby* • Sara Allgood *Old Meg* ■ *Dir* Mitchell Leisen • *Scr* Darrell Ware, Karl Tunberg, from a novel by

Kitty and the Bagman ★★

Period comedy drama   1982 · Ausl · Colour · 95mins

With a rollicking blend of colourful characterisation and serio-comic drama, this Australian period picture piles mismanagement upon misjudgement. Catfights, bar-room brawls and bawdy brothel banter are the order of the day, as Donald Crombie attempts to re-create the coarse, corrupt atmosphere of 1920s Sydney. But while Liddy Clark and John Stanton turn in spirited performances as the feisty madam and bent cop caught up in a gang war, too much emphasis is placed on tone and tempo and not enough on ensuring the action has more substance than a theme-park sideshow.

Liddy Clark *Kitty O'Rourke* • John Stanton *Bagman* • Val Lehman *Lil Delaney* • Gerard Maguire *Cyril Vikkers* • Collette Mann *Doris de Salle* • Reg Evans *Chicka Delaney* • Kylie Foster *Sarah Jones* ■ *Dir* Donald Crombie • *Scr* John Burney, Philip Cornford

Kitty Foyle ★★★

Drama   1940 · US · BW · 106mins

Ginger Rogers won her best actress Oscar for this artificial melodrama, which at least proved that she had a career outside her partnership with the great Fred Astaire. What Rogers was particularly good at was portraying the common, not to say vulgar, shop girl, and that, in Christopher Morley's once-fashionable novel, is what Kitty Foyle is: a shop girl who can't make up her mind which man to choose. Unfortunately, when this film was made, all the decent Hollywood leading men had gone off to war, which makes her choice exceedingly dull: doctor James Craig or playboy Dennis Morgan? Who cares? This is hard going today, even for devout Ginger fans.

Ginger Rogers *Kitty Foyle* • Dennis Morgan *Wyn Strafford* • James Craig *Mark* • Eduardo Ciannelli *Giono* • Ernest Cossart *Pop* • Gladys Cooper *Mrs Strafford* ■ *Dir* Sam Wood • *Scr* Dalton Trumbo, Donald Ogden Stewart, from the novel by Christopher Morley

The Klansman ★★

Drama   1974 · US · Colour · 107mins

In a small southern town, sheriff Lee Marvin fails to keep the lid on simmering racial tensions between civil rights activists and active members of the Ku Klux Klan. Vilified by most American critics, this potboiler didn't do much for the careers of either Marvin or Richard Burton, here cast as a dotty landowner who spits out philosophical bubble gum and gives sanctuary to local blacks. Cult director Samuel Fuller wrote the original script as a typically forthright overhaul of American race relations. Some viewers may feel it has certain affinities with the controversial *Mandingo*.

Lee Marvin *Sheriff Bascomb* • Richard Burton *Breck Stancill* • Cameron Mitchell *Deputy Butt Cut Cates* • Lola Falana *Loretta Sykes* • Luciana Paluzzi *Trixie* • David Huddleston *Mayor Hardy* • Linda Evans *Nancy Poteet* • OJ

Kleptomania ★

Drama   1995 · US · Colour · 90mins

A kleptomaniac New York socialite (Amy Irving) crosses paths with a homeless woman (Patsy Kensit) who only shoplifts to survive. Despite having nothing in common but their thievery, they form a bond. Irving called this "the best work I've ever done", but she has to do some pretty embarrassing stuff (not least a masturbation sequence); while Kensit's character is so repulsive it's amazing she has any friends at all. Behind the camera it's strictly amateur night, with enough tilted camera angles and hand-held camera shots for ten pretentious dramas.

Amy Irving *Diana* • Patsy Kensit *Julie* • Victor Garber *Morgan* ■ *Dir/Scr* Don Boyd

Klondike Annie ★★★

Musical comedy drama   1936 · US · BW · 78mins

Even in her later pictures, Mae West refused to be tamed, provoking the usual fierce attacks from the forces of righteousness. In this picture, they objected to her being the mistress of an Oriental, a murderess who then masquerades as a missionary, and a performer of songs such as *I'm an Occidental Woman in an Oriental Mood for Love*. Mae wrote the script and typically cast as the men in her life lumpish actors – Victor McLaglen and Philip Reed – who wouldn't steal any of her limelight. Audiences loved it then, and it's still good fun.

Mae West *"The Frisco Doll"*, Rose Carlton • Victor McLaglen *Capt Bull Brackett* • Philip Reed *Inspector Jack Forrest* • Helen Jerome Eddy *Sister Annie Alden* • Harry Beresford *Brother Bowser* • Harold Huber *Chan Lo* ■ *Dir* Raoul Walsh • *Scr* Mae West

Klute ★★★★★ 18

Thriller   1971 · US · Colour · 107mins

Jane Fonda deservedly won the best actress Oscar for her remarkably cool walk on the wild side as a call girl stalked by a homicidal maniac. But Donald Sutherland is on top form, too, playing the gentle small-town detective who teaches her the difference between love and sex as he closes in on the killer. A quite exceptional adult thriller, given a striking immediacy by Alan J Pakula's highly atmospheric direction and the nail-biting suspense. Contains swearing and nudity. 🖵

Jane Fonda *Bree Daniels* • Donald Sutherland *John Klute* • Charles Cioffi *Peter Cable* • Nathan George *Lieutenant Trask* • Roy R Scheider *[Roy Scheider] Frank Ligourin* • Dorothy Tristan *Arlyn Page* • Rita Gam *Trina* • Vivian Nathan *Psychiatrist* ■ *Dir* Alan J Pakula • *Scr* Andy Lewis, Dave Lewis • *Cinematographer* Gordon Willis

The Knack... and How to Get It ★★★

Comedy   1965 · UK · BW · 84mins

Wedged between his two Beatles films, this Palme d'Or-winning comedy is an energetic example of Richard Lester's fascination with the more manic methods of the French New Wave. In opening out Ann Jellicoe's stage play, he makes dizzying use of swinging London, as timid teacher Michael Crawford wheels home the brass bed that his womanising tenant Ray Brooks has assured him will transform his romantic fortunes. Although perfectly in tune with its time, the film is now hard to watch without wincing at the incessant stream of sexist witticisms and the painfully eager performances of Crawford and Brooks.

Rita Tushingham *Nancy Jones* • Ray Brooks *Tolen* • Michael Crawford *Colin* • Donal Donnelly *Tom* • John Bluthal *Angry father* • Wensley Pithey *Teacher* • William Dexter *Dress shop owner* • Peter Copley *Picture owner* ■ *Dir* Richard Lester • *Scr* Charles Wood, from the play by Ann Jellicoe

Knave of Hearts ★★★★

Drama   1954 · Fr/UK · BW · 109mins

Gallic heart-throb Gérard Philipe was destined for a tragically early death but he made a charming philanderer in this ironic romantic drama. In the episodic story, set and shot in London (by cinematographer Oswald Morris) Philipe, though married to Valerie Hobson, still finds himself attracted to Natasha Parry. Directed and co-written by René Clément, the film offers a refreshing view of England and English women as seen through French eyes.

Gérard Philipe *Andre Ripois* • Valerie Hobson *Catherine* • Joan Greenwood *Norah* • Margaret Johnston *Anne* • Natasha Parry *Patricia* • Germaine Montero *Marcelle* • Diana Decker *Diana* • Percy Marmont *Catherine's father* ■ *Dir* René Clément • *Scr* Hugh Mills, René Clément, Hugh Queneau, from the novel *Lovers, Happy Lovers!* by Louis Hemon

Knickerbocker Holiday ★★ U

Musical comedy drama   1944 · US · BW · 85mins

Originally a heavyweight – and unappealingly heavy-handed – musical by Kurt Weill (music) and Maxwell Anderson, which flopped on Broadway where its anti-Fascist political message failed as entertainment, it now makes for a lightweight, equally unappealing, film. Stripped of most of Weill's songs (and with its politics watered down) what is left is a tedious period piece, set in New York during the Pieter Stuyvesant era, about a romance between a subversive journalist (Nelson Eddy) and the daughter (Constance Dowling) of a Dutch councillor.

Nelson Eddy *Brom Broeck* • Charles Coburn *Pieter Stuyvesant* • Constance Dowling *Tina Tienhoven* • Ernest Cossart *Tienhoven* • Johnnie "Scat" Davis *Ten Pin* • Richard Hale *Tammany* • Shelley Winters *Ulda Tienhoven* ■ *Dir* Harry Joe Brown • *Scr* David Boehm, Roland Leigh, Harold Goldman, Thomas Lennon, from a musical by Kurt Weill, Maxwell Anderson

Knife Edge ★★ 15

Thriller   1990 · US · Colour · 85mins

Brad Dourif, who made such an impact in John Huston's *Wise Blood* (1979), is seen to much less effect in this bizarre story of an artist and his sexy sister (MK Harris and Sammi Davis) who move in on the life of a reclusive parolee (Dourif), changing all their

U = SUITABLE FOR ALL   Uc = SUITABLE FOR ALL, ESPECIALLY FOR YOUNG CHILDREN (VIDEO ONLY)   PG = PARENTAL GUIDANCE

lives. Kurt Voss directs as if he knew what it all symbolised, but audiences won't really care. This was released in the UK as *Knife Edge*. 🎬

Brad Dourif *Bud Cowan* • Sammi Davis *Randi* • MK Harris *Matthew* • Vic Tayback *George Samsa* • Max Perlich *Kid* ■ *Dir* Kurt Voss • *Scr* Kurt Voss, Larry Rattner, David Birke

Knife in the Head ★★★★
Political thriller
1978 · W Ger · Colour · 112mins

Chillingly suggesting that the West Germany of the seventies was on the brink of a new form of totalitarianism, this multi-layered film is at once a socialist tract, an uncompromising thriller and a downbeat human drama. Severely wounded after he is unwittingly caught up in a police raid, scientist Bruno Ganz has to rebuild his life from scratch, inadvertently becoming a political pawn in the process. Shot with calculated detachment by director Reinhard Hauff, the action has an allegorical significance that is now primarily of historical importance. However, Ganz's quietly heroic performance remains a stirring symbol of the triumph of the individual *in extremis*. A German language film.

Bruno Ganz *Dr Berthold Hoffmann* • Angela Winkler *Ann Hoffmann* • Hans Christian Blech *Scholz* • Udo Samel *Schurig* • Eike Gallwitz *Dr Groeske* • Carla Egerer *Nurse Angelika Mueller* ■ *Dir* Reinhard Hauff • *Scr* Peter Schneider

Knife in the Water ★★★★ 🅿🄶
Drama
1962 · Pol · BW · 94mins

Nominated for the best foreign-language film Oscar, the only feature completed by Roman Polanski in his native Poland is a lean, calculated study of male posturing and the hostilities that reinforce the generation gap. Shot in a steely black and white that intensifies both the film's chilling atmosphere and the crackling charge of sexual electricity that courses between the protagonists, the action is given an unbearable tension by its claustrophobic setting on board a yacht during a weekend cruise. The cast is superb, with the non-professional Zygmunt Malanowicz judging his swaggering brio to perfection. In Polish with English subtitles..

Leon Niemczyk *Andrzej* • Jolanta Umecka *Christine* • Zygmunt Malanowicz *Young man* ■ *Dir* Roman Polanski • *Scr* Jerzy Skolimowski, Jakub Goldberg, Roman Polanski • *Cinematographer* Jerzy Lipman

A Knight in Camelot ★★
Fantasy comedy adventure 1998 · US · Colour

Whoopi Goldberg brings her wacky comic sensibilities to this updated TV-movie version of Mark Twain's *A Connecticut Yankee in King Arthur's Court*. A computer researcher accidentally transports herself back to medieval times. Taken for a witch, Goldberg is thrown into a dungeon, but her laptop computer gets her out of trouble when she's able to predict a solar eclipse – proving to King Arthur (Michael York) and the jealous wizard Merlin (Ian Richardson) that she has magical powers. Honoured as Sir Boss, she proceeds to turn Camelot upside

down. A bit preachy at times, but this Whoopi-in-armour piece is worth a look.

Whoopi Goldberg *Vivien Morgan* • Michael York *King Arthur* • Amanda Donohoe *Queen Guinevere* • Ian Richardson *Merlin* • James Coombes *Sir Lancelot* • Robert Addie *Sir Sagramour* ■ *Dir* Roger Young • *Scr* Joe Wiesenfeld, from the novel *A Connecticut Yankee in King Arthur's Court* by Mark Twain

Knight Moves ★★★ 🄸🄸
Thriller 1992 · US/Ger · Colour · 111mins

A lively thriller starring Christopher Lambert as a chess master whose bid to win a major tournament takes an unexpected turn when his lover ends up murdered. As corpses start piling up like captured pieces, cop Tom Skerritt and psychologist Diane Lane start whittling away at Lambert's defence. Solid performances, especially from the suitably intense-looking Lambert, and some decent plot twists keep the picture on the boil sufficiently to delight thriller fans as well as chess players, who are rarely given the chance to enjoy movies based on this most dramatic and violent of games. Contains swearing and violence. 🎬

Christopher Lambert *Peter Sanderson* • Diane Lane *Kathy Sheppard* • Tom Skerritt *Frank Sedman* • Daniel Baldwin *Andy Wagner* • Charles Bailey-Gates *David Willerman* • Arthur Brauss *Viktor Yurilivich* • Katherine Isobel Erica Sanderson* • Ferdinand Mayne [Ferdy Mayne] *Jeremy Edmonds* • Don Thompson *Father* ■ *Dir* Carl Schenkel • *Scr* Brad Mirman

Knight of the Plains ★★ 🅄
Western 1939 · US · BW · 62mins

Probably the most interesting fact about this B-western for viewers today is that it was co-produced by the great comedian Stan Laurel. It's a very average tale, featuring former opera singer-turned-singing cowboy Fred Scott, who's aided and abetted in his battle against villain John Merton by comic sidekick Al St John. Laurel's involvement seems to have been purely financial, and this is no different from other Scott star vehicles: it's mercifully short and has a sort of period charm.

Fred Scott *Fred "Melody" Brent* • Al St John *"Fuzzy"* • Marion Weldon *Gail Rand* • Richard Cramer *Clem Peterson* • John Merton *Dan Carson/Pedro De Cordova* • Frank Larue *JC Rand* ■ *Dir* Sam Newfield • *Scr* Fred Myton

Knight Rider – the Movie ★★ 🅿🄶
Action adventure 1982 · US · Colour · 91mins

The pilot that kicked off one of TV's most popular and durable franchises. Starting right at the beginning, David Hasselhoff is the dedicated detective who is given a new identity and a new career by mysterious millionaire Richard Basehart who provides the crimefighter with the ultimate weapon for a buddy-buddy series: a talking car (voiced here by William Daniels). Fans of the series won't be disappointed. 🎬

David Hasselhoff *Michael Knight* • Edward Mulhare *Devon* • Vince Edwards *Wilson* • Richard Basehart *Wilton* ■ *Dir* Dan Haller [Daniel Haller] • *Scr* Glen A Larson

Knight without Armour ★★★
Adventure 1937 · UK · BW · 109mins

In 1937 Marlene Dietrich, the highest paid actress in Hollywood, accepted a modest $350,000 to star in this lavish, British-made Alexander Korda production. But, when Korda couldn't raise the final $100,000, Dietrich waived the fee in return for getting her mentor Josef von Sternberg the job of directing Korda's *I Claudius*, which was to end in disaster. *Knight without Armour*, though, a story of the First World War, Russian Revolution, rebelling peasantry and espionage, became a decent critical and commercial hit. Dietrich, who looks like Garbo in *Anna Karenina*, is radiant throughout, while love interest appears in the shape of spy Robert Donat, who wears heroism on his sleeve and what looks like a dead yak on his head. The script is pure drivel, but Jacques Feyder's direction has a real sheen.

Marlene Dietrich *Alexandra Vladinoff* • Robert Donat *Ainsley Fothergill* • Irene Vanbrugh *Duchess of Zorin* • Herbert Lomas *General Gregor Vladinoff* • Austin Trevor *Colonel Adraxine* • Basil Gill *Axelstein* • John Clements *Poushkoff* ■ *Dir* Jacques Feyder • *Scr* Lajos Biró, Arthur Wimperis, Frances Marion, from the novel *Without Armour* by James Hilton

Knightriders ★★★ 🄸🄵
Drama 1981 · US · Colour · 140mins

A captivating left-field departure from zombie horror king George Romero. A travelling commune of motorcyclists try to live their lives according to the doctrine of King Arthur and the knights of the round table by organising medieval-style fairs, complete with jousting competitions. But self-styled monarch Ed Harris finds his Hell's Angels Camelot and his efforts to uphold a chivalrous code under threat from internal bickering and continual money problems. An unusual adventure fable which you will either love or hate. 🎬

Ed Harris *Billy* • Tom Savini *Morgan* • Gary Lahti *Alan* • Amy Ingersoll *Linet* • Patricia Tallman *Julie* • Christine Forrest *Angie* • Warner Shook *Pippin* • Stephen King ■ *Dir/Scr* George A Romero

Knights ★★ 🄸🄵
Science-fiction action adventure
1993 · US · Colour · 90mins

Former world kick-boxing champion Kathy Long has probably been seen by more people as a stunt double for the likes of Michelle Pfeiffer in *Batman Returns*; here, however, she gets to take centre stage in this futuristic thriller about the battle between humans and vampiric cyborgs. She throws long punches, grapples and kicks her little socks off, while Kris Kristofferson and Lance Henriksen provide a bit of class as good and bad robots, respectively. 🎬

Kris Kristofferson *Gabriel* • Lance Henriksen *Job* • Kathy Long *Nea* • Scott Paulin *Simon* • Gary Daniels *David* • Nicholas Guest *Farmer* • Clare Hoak *Mother* ■ *Dir/Scr* Albert Pyun

Knights and Emeralds ★ 🅿🄶
Comedy drama 1986 · UK · Colour · 89mins

The regional film has been one of the least successful of British genres, with only the kitchen-sink dramas of the sixties making any real impact on audiences at home, let alone abroad. This small-scale comedy is typical of the lack of ambition that blights these pictures. Set in the Midlands, it's a slight story about racism and the rivalry between black and white marching bands, from which only Warren Mitchell emerges with any credit.

Christopher Wild *Kevin Brimble* • Beverley Hills *Melissa* • Warren Mitchell *Mr Kirkpatrick* • Bill Leadbitter *Enoch* • Rachel Davies *Mrs Fontain* • Tracie Bennett *Tina* • Nadim Sawalha *Bindu* ■ *Dir/Scr* Ian Emes

Knights of the Round Table ★★★ 🅿🄶
Period adventure
1953 · US · Colour · 111mins

This fifties Hollywood retelling of the Arthurian legend finds Lancelot being given the red card by Arthur for his, shall we say, inappropriate affection for Guinevere, but galloping back to rescue the day by overcoming the wicked Mordred. Shot in Britain, as MGM's first CinemaScope movie, and starring the good-looking but passionless Robert Taylor and Ava Gardner as the doomed lovers, the finished product is long on pomp and pageantry, though sadly not as stirring as it sounds or should be. 🎬

Robert Taylor (1) *Sir Lancelot* • Ava Gardner *Queen Guinevere* • Mel Ferrer *King Arthur* • Stanley Baker *Sir Mordred* • Anne Crawford *Morgan Le Fay* • Felix Aylmer *Merlin* • Maureen Swanson *Elaine* • Robert Urquhart *Sir Gawaine* ■ *Dir* Richard Thorpe • *Scr* Talbot Jennings, Jan Lustig, Noel Langley, from the book *Le Mort d'Arthur* by Sir Thomas Mallory

Knock Off ★★ 🄸🄸
Action thriller 1998 · HK/US · Colour · 87mins

Appropriately, the counterfeit-brands – or "knock-offs" – market forms the backdrop of this Jean-Claude Van Damme vehicle, because this is another superficially authentic but ultimately fake Hong Kong thriller. True, director Tsui Hark has all the right credentials but, as with their previous project *Double Team*, this just isn't the real thing. Played more for laughs than that collaboration, this tale finds the roguish, reformed counterfeiter Van Damme and partner Rob Schneider caught up in a plot to send miniature bombs all over the world. Tsui Hark stages some imaginatively destructive action set pieces, particularly the finale. Contains swearing and violence. 🎬 **DVD**

Jean-Claude Van Damme *Marcus Ray* • Rob Schneider *Tommy Hendricks* • Lela Rochon *Karen* • Paul Sorvino *Johansson* • Carmen Lee *Ling Ho* • Wyman Wong *Eddie* • Glen Chin *Skinny* • Michael Miller *Tickler* • Steve Brettingham *Hawkeye* • Mark Haughton *Bear* ■ *Dir* Tsui Hark • *Scr* Steven E DeSouza

Knock on Any Door ★★★
Crime drama 1949 · US · BW · 99mins

Nicholas Ray's sympathy for the disadvantaged young – he would direct

Rebel without a Cause six years later – is well to the fore in this sincerely meant but now very dated drama. John Derek stars as a slum youth who turns to crime and is charged with murder, while Humphrey Bogart plays his understanding, albeit powerless, attorney. A belated sequel, *Let No Man Write My Epitaph*, followed in 1960.

Humphrey Bogart *Andrew Morton* • John Derek *Nick Romano* • George Macready *District Attorney Kerman* • Allene Roberts *Emma* • Mickey Knox *Vito* • Barry Kelley *Judge Drake* • Cara Williams *Nelly* • Jimmy Conlin *Kid Fingers* ■ *Dir* Nicholas Ray • *Scr* Daniel Taradash, John Monks Jr, from a novel by Willard Motley

Knock on Wood ★★★ U

Musical comedy 1954 · US · Colour · 103mins
Comedy writers/directors Melvin Frank and Norman Panama earned themselves a best story and screenplay Oscar nomination for this crack-a-minute showcase for the talents of Danny Kaye. The breathless delivery, facial contortions and crowded gallery of eccentric characterisations that made him one of the finest cabaret performers of his generation never fitted entirely comfortably into a film narrative, with the action too often stalling to enable him to rattle through yet another of his patter routines.

Danny Kaye *Jerry Morgan* • Mai Zetterling *Ilse Nordstrom* • Torin Thatcher *Godfrey Langston* • David Burns *Marty Brown* • Leon Askin *Gromek* • Abner Biberman *Papinek* ■ *Dir/Scr* Norman Panama, Melvin Frank

Knockin' on Heaven's Door ★★★

Road movie comedy
1997 · Ger · Colour · 100mins
Continuing the German love affair with the road movie, this odd-couple caper marked Til Schweiger's transition to superstardom. Together with fellow cancer victim Jan Josef Liefers, he refuses to wallow in institutionalised self-pity and hits the road in search of the adventure his life has been missing. However, a couple of cops and two hoods desperate to recover their stolen loot hardly make for ideal travelling companions – even if they are always one step behind the game. Thomas Jahn's compositional sense and judgement of tempo are remarkable for only a second-time director, but it's the spark between the leads that really makes the picture. A German language film.

Til Schweiger *Martin Brest* • Jan Josef Liefers *Rudi Wurlitzer* • Moritz Bleibtrau *Abdul* • Thierry Van Werveke *Henk* • Leonard Lansink *Commissar Schneider* • Ralph Herforth *Assistant Keller* ■ *Dir* Thomas Jahn • *Scr* Thomas Jahn, Til Schweiger, from a story by Thomas Jahn

Knocks at My Door ★★★

Political drama
1991 · Ven/Arg/Cub/UK · Colour · 105mins
Based on Juan Carlos Gene's acclaimed play, this Venezuelan drama was made with the backing of Channel 4. The playwright also stars as the mayor of an unnamed town who intercedes when nuns who have been sheltering a rebel soldier are brought before a military tribunal. Steadily directed by Alejandro Saderman, this earnest picture sheds some light on the uneasy relationship between church, army and state that exists in many South American countries. It might never escape its stage shackles, but it's thought-provoking and powerfully played. In Spanish with English subtitles.

Veronica Oddo *Ana* • Elba Escobar *Ursula* • Juan Carlos Gene *Mayor Cerone* • José Antonio Rodriguez *Monsignor* • Ana Castell *Severa* • Frank Spano *Pablo the Fugitive* ■ *Dir* Alejandro Saderman • *Scr* Juan Carlos Gene, Alejandro Saderman, from the play *Golpes a Mi Puerta* by Juan Carlos Gene

The Knowledge of Healing ★★★ PG

Documentary 1996 · Swi · Colour · 93mins
Swiss director Franz Reichle seeks to explore the techniques of Tibetan medicine and prove their scientific validity in this intelligent but rather airless documentary. The Dalai Lama's own doctor, Tenzin Choedrak, guides us through the complex relationship between the body's spiritual and physical energies, as well as describing the numerous natural ingredients used in his pharmacy. But while the theoretical aspects are admirably illustrated with examples from age-old scrolls, it's the doctor's encounters with his patients that prove more intriguing, particularly his treatment of a Buddhist nun, who'd been beaten in reprisal for her anti-Chinese sentiments. In Tibetan/Russian/German/Buryatian/English/Romansch with subtitles.

Dir/Scr Franz Reichle

Knute Rockne – All American ★★ U

Biography 1940 · US · BW · 97mins
In this biopic of the Norwegian-born American football coach – a national hero who died prematurely in a plane crash – Rockne himself is played by Pat O'Brien, who performs to the gallery and still seems to be wearing the dog collar from all those Cagney gangster pictures. But the movie is now more famous for Ronald Reagan in his favourite role as "The Gipper", Rockne's star player George Gipp, who died young of pneumonia. "Win one for the Gipper" is the well-known line which Reagan reprised on his presidential campaign trail, recalling not only his film role but also a vanished age of patriotic achievement.

Pat O'Brien *Knute Rockne* • Ronald Reagan *George Gipp* • Gale Page *Bonnie Skilles Rockne* • Donald Crisp *Father Callahan* • Albert Basserman *Father Julius Nieuwland* ■ *Dir* Lloyd Bacon • *Scr* Robert Buckner, from the private papers of Mrs Knute Rockne

Königsmark ★★★

Romantic drama 1935 · Fr · BW · 114mins
Silent master Maurice Tourneur (father of *Cat People's* Jacques Tourneur) directed this Ruritanian melodrama with all the visual majesty you would expect of someone who once worked as an assistant to the sculptor Auguste Rodin. It's a tantalising tale of romance and revenge, as princess Elissa Landi teams with Pierre Fresnay to avenge the murder of her husband.

Amid the lavish trappings and grand posturings Landi, in particular, gives a splendid performance, echoing the tragedy of *Hamlet* (the clear inspiration for Pierre Benoit's source novel) after she guns down a spying maid. A French language film.

Elissa Landi *Princess Aurore* • Pierre Fresnay *Raoul Vignerte* • John Lodge *Grand Duke Frederick* • Frank Vosper *Major Baron de Boise* • Marcelle Rogez *Countess Melusine* • Allan Jeayes *Grand Duke Rodolphe* • Romilly Lunge *Lieutenant de Hagen* • Cecil Humphreys *de Marçais* ■ *Dir* Maurice Tourneur • *Scr* from the novel by Pierre Benoit

Kokoda Crescent ★★

Comedy drama 1989 · Ausl · Colour · 83mins
This tale of elderly suburban commandos went straight to video in its native Australia, but the presence of TV's Alf Garnett himself, Warren Mitchell, may attract the curious over here. Mitchell, Bill Kerr and Martin Vaughan play Second World War veterans who, with their equally gung-ho wives, take on the drug dealers and corrupt coppers who have infested the Sydney estate where they live. Director Ted Robinson conveys his message in sledgehammer terms, but his emphasis is firmly on the comic. Contains violence and strong language.

Warren Mitchell *Stan* • Bill Kerr *Russ* • Ruth Cracknell *Alice* • Madge Ryan *Margaret* • Martin Vaughan *Eric* • Patrick Thompson *Brett* • Steve Jacobs *Policeman* ■ *Dir* Ted Robinson • *Scr* Patrick Cook

Kolya ★★★★ 12

Comedy drama
1996 · Cz Rep/UK/Fr · Colour · 100mins
The winner of the Oscar for best foreign film, this is a delightful odd-couple story set in Prague during the last days of Communism. The director's father, Zdenek Sverak (who also scripted), is superb as the former Philharmonic cellist who takes custody of five-year-old Andrej Chalimon after his mother (a Russian interpreter with whom the impoverished musician had contracted a marriage of convenience) flits to the west. With no political axe to grind, Jan Sverak goes for the human interest angle and produces a joyous film, which provokes more than its fair share of smiles and surreptitious dabs of the eyes. In Czech with English subtitles. Contains some strong language.

Zdenek Sverak *Frantisek Louka* • Andrej Chalimon *Kolya* • Libuse Safrankova *Klara* • Ondrej Vetchy *Mr Broz* • Stella Zazvorkova *Mother* • Ladislav Smoljak *Mr Houdek* • Irena Livanova *Nadezda* • Lilian Mankina *Aunt Tamara* ■ *Dir* Jan Sverak • *Scr* Zdenek Sverak, from a story by Pavel Taussig

Komitas ★★★★

Biographical drama
1988 · W Ger · BW and Colour · 96mins
The influence of two very different Soviet directors pervades this poetic portrait of the monk and musician who lost his reason during the onslaught that decimated the Ottoman empire's Armenian population during the period around 1915. The dramatic intensity derives from Andrei Tarkovsky, while the stylised composition owes much to Sergei Paradjanov. But it is director Don Askarian's atmospheric use of landscape and interiors that gives this episodic film its unique audiovisual lyricism. Samuel Ovasapian excels as Komitas, who spent the last 20 years of his life in various mental institutions, tormented by his memories and imaginings. A German language film.

Samuel Ovasapian *Komitas* • Onig Saadetian *Terlomesian* • Margarita Woskanjan *Pupil* • Reverend Yegishe Mangikian *Katholikos* ■ *Dir/Scr* Don Askarian

Kona Coast ★★

Adventure drama 1968 · US · Colour · 80mins
Set on Hawaii, this colourful melodrama features rugged Richard Boone, a Hollywood tough guy who never quite made it as a major movie star but always had great screen presence. Here he's a fisherman in Hawaii whose daughter is murdered, possibly by a local racketeer who has also smashed up Boone's boat. Lots of action in front of majestic scenery ensues. However, it all looks and sounds like an old studio picture from the thirties.

Richard Boone *Sam Moran* • Vera Miles *Melissa Hyde* • Joan Blondell *Kittibelle Lightfoot* • Steve Ihnat *Kryder* • Chips Rafferty *Lightfoot* • Kent Smith *Akamai* ■ *Dir* Lamont Johnson • *Scr* Gil Ralston, from the story *Bimini Gall* by John D MacDonald

Konga ★★ PG

Science-fiction horror
1960 · UK · Colour · 85mins
Michael Gough as a botanist inventing a growth serum, a ratty zip-up gorilla suit, Margo Johns as a comely housekeeper, a miniature cardboard Big Ben and pop star Jess Conrad – what more could you want in a cheap and cheerful British *King Kong* imitation originally titled *I Was a Teenage Gorilla*? With its crude horror always verging on the farcical, the entertainment value in this hilarious monkey business stems from the sheer incompetence on full view. Enjoyably terrible and filmed on location in Croydon High Street.

Michael Gough *Dr Charles Decker* • Margo Johns *Margaret* • Jess Conrad *Bob Kenton* • Claire Gordon *Sandra Banks* • Austin Trevor *Dean Foster* • Jack Watson *Superintendent Brown* ■ *Dir* John Lemont • *Scr* Herman Cohen, Aben Kandel

Korczak ★★★ PG

Historical drama
1990 · Pol/W Ger/Fr/UK · BW · 117mins
Scripted by Agnieszka Holland and shot in sombre monochrome by Robby Müller, this is an earnest attempt to portray the atrocities of the Holocaust without undue sentiment or sensationalism. Indeed, this is such a determinedly sensitive study that it's often hard to recognise it as the work of Andrzej Wajda, whose "war trilogy" was so full of anger at the loss of a generation. Tracing real-life events from 1936 to 1942, the film benefits from a dignified performance from Wojtek Pszoniak as Janusz Korczak, the doctor who ministered to the children of the Warsaw ghetto prior to his fateful train journey to Treblinka. In Polish with English subtitles.

Wojtek Pszoniak [Wojciech Pszoniak] *Dr Janusz Korczak* • Ewa Dalkowska *Stefa* • Piotr Kozlowski *Heniek* ■ *Dir* Andrzej Wajda • *Scr* Agnieszka Holland

Korea ★★★

Drama 1995 · Ire · Colour · 87mins

Eleven years after his powerful Dublin drama *Pigs*, Cathal Black returned behind the camera for this story of two wars set in the early fifties. Although the lakeside community in County Cavan is receiving electricity, the biggest sparks come between Donal Donnelly and his sworn enemy Vass Anderson, especially when it's discovered their children have fallen in love. The spectre of the Korean conflict hangs over the proceedings, which come to a head with the return in a body bag of Anderson's son. A thoughtful film, played with great conviction by a solid ensemble cast. An English/Gaelic language film.

Donal Donnelly *John Doyle* • Andrew Scott *Eamon Doyle* • Fiona Molony *Una Moran* • Vass Anderson *Ben Moran* • Christopher Callery ■ *Dir* Cathal Black • *Scr* Joe O'Byrne, from a story by John McGahern

Kotch ★★★PG

Comedy drama 1971 · US · Colour · 114mins

We always knew that Walter Matthau and Jack Lemmon had their communal heart in the right place. But here it's worn a bit too strenuously on the frayed sleeve of Matthau, as an unwanted old man who walks out on his impatient son and daughter-in-law, and befriends a pregnant teenager. Lemmon, as debut director, accords his friend a leisurely pace and some great close-ups. The film's sentimentality veers into schmaltz, but what do you expect from this wonderfully odd couple? ▭

Walter Matthau *Joseph P Kotcher* • Deborah Winters *Erica Herzenstiel* • Felicia Farr *Wilma Kotcher* • Charles Aidman *Gerald Kotcher* • Ellen Geer *Vera Kotcher* • Darrell Larson *Vincent Perrin* ■ *Dir* Jack Lemmon • *Scr* John Paxton, from the novel by Katherine Topkins

Koyaanisqatsi ★★★U

Experimental documentary
1982 · US · Colour · 85mins

An offbeat, and often off-beam, documentary-cum-meditation about the decline of western civilisation, using the difference between the untamed American wilderness and hysterical, rush-hour Manhattan as its crux. Director Godfrey Reggio shuns narration in favour of powerful, repetitive music by minimalist composer Philip Glass to match his striking visuals. Made in the early eighties when ecological warnings were starting to take hold, it was, for all its vacuity, a surprising success. The title is a Hopi Indian word meaning "life out of balance".

Dir Godfrey Reggio • *Scr* Ron Fricke, Michael Hoenig, Alton Walpole, Godfrey Reggio • *Producer* Godfrey Reggio, Francis Coppola [Francis Ford Coppola] • *Cinematographer* Ron Fricke • *Music Director* Michael Hoenig

Krakatoa, East of Java
★★PG

Disaster movie 1969 · US · Colour · 121mins

Everyone knows that the Indonesian island of Krakatoa blew its top in 1883, killing 40,000 people and creating a tidal wave of such strength that ripples were felt off Bognor Regis. Everyone knows, too, that Krakatoa lies west of Java, not east, though that would have made for a less exotic title. Problem is, as with most disaster movies, it's a long haul before nature rudely intrudes into the human dramas being enacted before back-projected images of the smoking volcano. The big bang, when it comes, is an eye-jarring explosion of cornball special effects, originally intended to be shown in Cinerama, the widest of all screen ratios. ▭ **DVD**

Maximilian Schell *Captain Chris Hanson* • Diane Baker *Laura Travis* • Barbara Werle *Charley* • Brian Keith *Connerly* • Rossano Brazzi *Giovanni Borghese* • Sal Mineo *Leoncavallo Borghese* • John Leyton *Douglas Rigby* • JD Cannon *Danzig* • Jacqui Chan *Toshi* ■ *Dir* Bernard L Kowalski • *Scr* Clifford Newton Gould, Bernard Gordon

Kramer vs Kramer ★★★★PG

Drama 1979 · US · Colour · 100mins

Winner of the Oscar for best picture and scooping best actor and supporting actress statuettes for Dustin Hoffman and Meryl Streep, this runaway success now looks a little overwrought in places, but it is still an involving, moving and discerning study of the suffering endured by all embroiled in a divorce. You could cut the courtroom sequences with a knife, but writer/director Robert Benton deserves greatest credit for the truth and restraint of the scenes in which Hoffman tries to win over six-year-old son Justin Henry, which could so easily have become false and tacky. ▭

Dustin Hoffman *Ted Kramer* • Meryl Streep *Joanna Kramer* • Jane Alexander *Margaret Phelps* • Justin Henry *Billy Kramer* • Howard Duff *John Shaunessy* • George Coe *Jim O'Connor* • JoBeth Williams *Phyllis Bernard* • Howland Chamberlain [Howland Chamberlin] *Judge Atkins* ■ *Dir* Robert Benton • *Scr* Robert Benton, from the novel by Avery Corman

The Krays ★★★★18

Crime biography 1990 · UK · Colour · 114mins

An intelligent biopic of Britain's most famous gangsters, the twin bruvvers who made life safe for East Enders when they weren't running protection rackets or inflicting gangland punishments on rival mobsters. To be fair, writer Philip Ridley and director Peter Medak largely avoid glamorising the violent world of Reggie and Ronnie, and are more interested in unravelling the complex personalities of the two brothers. They are helped by surprisingly convincing lead performances from Martin and Gary Kemp, better known from their kilt-wearing days with Spandau Ballet, although Billie Whitelaw effortlessly rises above everybody else in the star-studded cast as the boys' best friend, their mum. Contains swearing, violence and sexual references. ▭ **DVD**

Gary Kemp *Ronnie Kray* • Martin Kemp *Reggie Kray* • Billie Whitelaw *Violet Kray* • Tom Bell *Jack "The Hat" McVitie* • Susan Fleetwood *Rose* • Charlotte Cornwell *May* • Kate Hardie *Frances* • Avis Bunnage *Helen* • Gary Love *Steve* • Steven Berkoff *George Cornell* • Jimmy Jewel *"Cannonball" Lee* • Barbara Ferris *Mrs Lawson* • Victor Spinetti *Mr Lawson* ■ *Dir* Peter Medak • *Scr* Philip Ridley

The Kremlin Letter ★★18

Spy thriller 1970 · US · Colour · 115mins

The letter in question goes from Moscow to Washington and proposes the annihilation of Red China. Warren Beatty turned this Cold War saga down; the studio, 20th Century-Fox, then vetoed Robert Redford, believing the film he had just made for them, *Butch Cassidy and the Sundance Kid*, was going to flop. So director John Huston hired Patrick O'Neal and backed him up with Hollywood exiles like Orson Welles and George Sanders, here playing a transvestite. Filmed in Mexico, Finland and Italy, it's hard to follow, gimmicky and generally not worth the postage. ▭

Patrick O'Neal *Charles Rone* • Richard Boone *Ward* • Orson Welles *Bresnavitch* • Barbara Parkins *BA* • Max von Sydow *Col Kosnov* • George Sanders *"Warlock"* • Dean Jagger *"Highwayman"* • Bibi Andersson *Erika Boeck* • Ronald Radd *Potkin* ■ *Dir* John Huston • *Scr* John Huston, Gladys Hill, from a novel by Noel Behn

The Kreutzer Sonata
★★★★★15

Drama 1987 · USSR · Colour · 135mins

One of the truly great Russian films of the 1980s and a "must see" on all counts. Tolstoy's stifling, gripping tale of a dramatic, violent relationship between a man and his virtuoso musician wife is done great service by deep, multi-layered direction and the searing performance of Oleg Yankovsky, who tells his story in flashback. Yankovsky's portrayal of jealousy erupting into hate is a cinematic triumph; the movie never lets its vice-like grip on the audience's emotions slacken. In Russian with English subtitles. ▭

Oleg Yankovsky *Vasili Pozdnyshev* • Aleksandr Trofimov *Pozdnyshev's fellow traveller* • Irina Seleznyova *Lisa Pozdnyshev* • Dmitri Pokrovsky *Trukhachevsky* ■ *Dir* Mikhail Schweitzer, Sofia Milkina • *Scr* Mikhail Schweitzer, from the novel by Leo Tolstoy

Krippendorf's Tribe ★★12

Comedy 1998 · US · Colour · 90mins

One of the least enticing film titles of recent times is matched by a forgettable movie. Richard Dreyfuss plays an anthropologist whose tribe-seeking mission in New Guinea was a failure, forcing him to fabricate footage of a new tribe concocted from the names of his three kids. Not exactly a great comedy premise in the first place and it runs out of ideas (and laughs) well before the halfway mark. On this occasion, Dreyfuss's screen spark seems to have been "shorted", although Jenna Elfman (*EDtv*) has an appealingly kooky comic flair. It's hardly a movie worth seeking out, though. ▭

Richard Dreyfuss *James Krippendorf* • Jenna Elfman *Veronica Micelli* • Natasha Lyonne

Shelly • Gregory Smith *Mickey* • Carl Michael Lindner *Edmund* • Lily Tomlin *Ruth Allen* • David Ogden Stiers *Henry Spivey* ■ *Dir* Todd Holland • *Scr* Charlie Peters, from the novel by Frank Parkin

Kristin Lavransdatter ★★★

Period drama
1995 · Ger/Nor/Swe · Colour · 180mins

Adapted from Sigrid Undset's Pulitzer Prize-winning novel, Liv Ullmann's historical drama possesses all the beauty of a medieval tapestry, yet its length and inertia often make this epic seem more like a book of hours. Elizabeth Matheson's statuesque performance makes it difficult to sympathise with the landowner's daughter caught between duty and passion. However, neither she nor her less-than-gallant lover, Björn Skagestad, is given much assistance from either Ullmann's hoary script or her hesitant pacing. Fortunately, Sven Nykvist's photography is a delight and the colour, simplicity and sheer arduousness of rural life are admirably conveyed. A Norwegian language film.

Lena Endre *Eline Ormsdatter* • Erland Josephson *Broder Edvin* • Elisabeth Matheson *Kristin Lavransdatter* • Sverre Anker Ousdal *Lavrans* • Björn Skagestad *Erlend* ■ *Dir* Liv Ullmann • *Scr* Liv Ullmann, from a novel by Sigrid Undset

Kronos ★★★

Science-fiction 1957 · US · BW · 78mins

An enormous alien robot lands off the California coast and tramples on everything in sight as it advances towards Los Angeles on an energy-sucking spree. Despite its reliance on stock footage, cost-cutting special effects (mainly large-size props) and average direction – by *The Fly's* Kurt Neumann – this unusually slanted invasion thriller is a perfect example of engagingly deranged fifties B-movie-making. A minor classic with the cube-like heavy metal conqueror relieving the occasional bouts of tedium where arch scientists Jeff Morrow and Barbara Lawrence race to save the Earth from total destruction.

Jeff Morrow *Dr Leslie Gaskell* • Barbara Lawrence *Vera Hunter* • John Emery *Dr Eliot* • George O'Hanlon *Dr Arnie Culver* • Morris Ankrum *Dr Albert R Stern* • Kenneth Alton McCrary ■ *Dir* Kurt Neumann • *Scr* Lawrence Louis Goldman, from a story by Irving Block

Krull ★★★PG

Fantasy adventure
1983 · UK/US · Colour · 115mins

Engaging without ever being enthralling, this fantasy performed badly at the box office and Columbia saw little return on its $27 million investment. Yet this maligned movie has many moments to enjoy, as Ken Marshall's Prince Colwyn seeks to release princess Lysette Anthony from the clutches of the Beast. The special effects by Derek and Mark Meddings and John Evans may fall far short of spectacular, but they help to create a charming neverland and add considerably to the excitement of the quest. The acting honours go to Bernard Bresslaw as a cyclops and Freddie Jones as a gloomy seer. ▭

Ken Marshall *Prince Colwyn* • Lysette Anthony *Princess Lyssa* • Freddie Jones *Ynyr* •

Francesca Annis *Widow of the Web* • Alun Armstrong *Torquil* • David Battley *Ergo* • Bernard Bresslaw *Cyclops* • Liam Neeson *Kegan* • Todd Carty *Oswyn* • Robbie Coltrane *Rhun* • John Welsh *Seer* ■ *Dir* Peter Yates • *Scr* Stanford Sherman

Kuffs ★★ 15

Comedy drama   1991 · US · Colour · 97mins

An odd mix of comedy and action which only Christian Slater devotees will warm to. He plays the dropout whose brother – the owner of a privately funded San Francisco police franchise – is murdered in front of him. Slater is forced to shape up when he takes over the franchise in an attempt to find the killer. With Slater's smug smart-aleck asides to the camera and with silly sound effects throughout (seemingly inserted to try to spice up the banal script), this is pure trash with just enough flash to make it a mildly watchable potboiler rather than an irritating time-waster. Contains violence and swearing. 🔲

Christian Slater *George Kuffs* • Milla Jovovich *Maya Carlton* • Tony Goldwyn *Ted Bukovsky* • Bruce Boxleitner *Brad Kuffs* • Troy Evans *Captain Morino* • George De La Pena *Sam Jones* • Craig Benton *Paint store owner* • Ashley Judd *Paint store owner's wife* ■ *Dir* Bruce A Evans • *Scr* Bruce A Evans, Raynold Gideon

Kühle Wampe ★★★★ PG

Drama   1931 · Germany · BW · 68mins

Evicted from a Berlin tenement, Hertha Thiele's family makes the most of life in a camp for the dispossessed, despite the suicide of her son. Condemning big business and positing all sorts of social alternatives, Bertolt Brecht's Marxist manifesto may not sound the stuff of entertainment but the only film he didn't disown is anything but a dry political tract. Ironically recalling both Soviet montage and the work of Nazi film-maker Leni Riefenstahl, it is often riotously funny. However the over-riding impression it leaves is of a lost age of innocence and a tragically missed opportunity to create a fairer world. In German with English subtitles. 🔲

Hertha Thiele *Annie Bönike* • Ernst Busch *Fritz* • Martha Wolter ■ *Dir* Slatan Dudow • *Scr* Bertolt Brecht, Ernst Ottwald

Kull the Conqueror ★★★ 12

Fantasy action adventure
1997 · US · Colour · 91mins

Hercules star Kevin Sorbo made the switch from television to the big screen with this impressively mounted sword and sorcery epic, based on characters created by Robert E Howard of *Conan* fame. Barbarian Kull becomes King of Valusia, but his attempts to free his people put him up against shape-shifting sorceress Tia Carrere. Although dealing with the classic good-versus-evil conventions of the genre, director John (*Miami Vice*) Nicolella gives the somewhat disjointed proceedings a darker hue and edgier atmosphere than normal. Sorbo, meanwhile, fits the heroic bill perfectly. 🔲

Kevin Sorbo *Kull* • Tia Carrere *Akivasha* • Thomas Ian Griffith *Taligaro* • Litefoot *Ascalante* • Roy Brocksmith *Tu* • Harvey Fierstein *Juba* • Karina Lombard *Zareta* • Edward Tudor-Pole *Enaros* • Douglas Henshall

Ducalon ■ *Dir* John Nicolella • *Scr* Charles Edward Pogue, from the Marvel Comics character created by Robert E Howard

Kundun ★★ 12

Religious biographical drama
1997 · US · Colour · 128mins

Emerging from his usual gangster-ridden mean streets, director Martin Scorsese sets his sights higher to the wide-open Himalayan spaces for this biography of the Dalai Lama. Scorsese's epic follows the Tibetan leader from his supposed reincarnation as the son of a humble family, through his investiture and his attempts to build a working relationship with – and eventual rejection of – Chinese socialism to his exile. Trouble is, the screenplay (by Melissa Mathison, who also wrote the script for *ET*) paints too rosy a picture of Buddhism, never questioning a country in which priests and poor are set so far apart. Roger Deakin's photography, though, is as luminous as a halo. 🔲

Tenzin Tsarong Thuthob *Dalai Lama as an adult* • Tencho Gyalpo *Dalai Lama's mother* • Tsewang Migyur Khangsar *Dalai Lama's father* ■ *Dir* Martin Scorsese • *Scr* Melissa Mathison

Kung Fu ★★★

Martial arts drama
1972 · US · Colour · 87mins

No wonder Jules in *Pulp Fiction* wanted to "walk the earth" like Caine in *Kung Fu*. Jerry Thorpe's pilot for his cult TV series is a cracking blend of cowboy and "chop socky" that never for a second seems as ridiculous as it would if you stopped to think about it. David Carradine excels as the Buddhist monk who is forced to flee China for post-Civil War America after his Shaolin skills make him chief suspect in a murder case. He is well supported in this superior TV movie by half-brother Keith Carradine and veterans Keye Luke, Barry Sullivan and Philip Ahn.

David Carradine *Kwai Chang Caine* • Barry Sullivan *Dillon* • Albert Salmi *Raif* • Wayne Maunder *McKay* • Benson Fong *Han Fei* • Keye Luke *Blind Master Po* • Philip Ahn *Master Kan* • Keith Carradine *Middle Caine* ■ *Dir* Jerry Thorpe • *Scr* Edward Spielman, Howard Friedlander, from a story by Edward Spielman

Kurt & Courtney ★★★ 15

Documentary   1997 · UK · Colour · 92mins

Documentarist Nick Broomfield has always employed a blend of charm and innocence to expose the frailties of his subjects. But here that tactic somewhat backfires because the people he meets in seeking to establish the facts about the death of grunge rock star Kurt Cobain have much darker agendas than his own idle curiosity. Cobain's widow Courtney Love certainly comes across as a difficult character (an impression compounded by her campaign to block the film's screening at the Sundance festival), but at least she is devoid of the bile and envy that motivates most of the others in the film. Contains swearing. 🔲

Dir Nick Broomfield • *Editor* Mark Atkins • *Cinematographer* Joan Churchill, Alex Vendler

Kwaidan ★★★ PG

Portmanteau fantasy
1964 · Jap · Colour · 154mins

A portmanteau film of four ghost stories, perhaps best viewed as separate films – one episode was originally cut to shorten the running time. One story concerns a samurai haunted by the beauty of his first wife; another is an ingenious tale about a man who drinks not only a cup of tea but also the man reflected on the surface of the drink. Viewers expecting a compendium of horror will be disappointed, for these tales are gentle, ironic and sad. All are stunningly photographed and exquisitely designed. In Japanese with English subtitles. 🔲

Rentaro Mikuni *Samurai* • Michiyo Aratama *1st wife* • Misako Watanabe *2nd wife* • Keiko Kishi *The woman* • Tatsuya Nakadai *Minokichi* • Katsuo Nakamura *Hoichi* • Rentaro Mikuni *Samurai* ■ *Dir* Masaki Kobayashi • *Scr* Yoko Mizuki, from stories by Lafcadio Hearn

LA Confidential ★★★★★ 18

Crime drama   1997 · US · Colour · 132mins

Curtis Hanson's superlative filming of James Ellroy's complex fifties detective story fuses period authenticity, fluid direction and searing, full-blooded performances. Starting with the apparently open-and-shut case of a diner bloodbath, the sleazy scenario takes a trio of cops – ambitious rookie Guy Pearce, smooth TV adviser Kevin Spacey and punchy hard-man Russell Crowe – down a corpse-strewn path of crime, corruption and celebrity lookalikes. The roles fit the actors like tightly stitched gloves, and the film's bruising brutality is amplified by the absence of clear-cut heroes, with the police characters as morally dubious as the film's villains. Kim Basinger won an Oscar for her hard-edged vamp, as did the excellent script, but the picture really deserved a hatful. Contains swearing, violence and sex scenes. 🔲 **DVD**

Kevin Spacey *Jack Vincennes* • Russell Crowe *Bud White* • Guy Pearce *Ed Exley* • James Cromwell *Dudley Smith* • Kim Basinger *Lynn Bracken* • Danny DeVito *Sid Hudgens* • David Strathairn *Pierce Patchett* • Ron Rifkin *District Attorney Ellis Loew* • Matt McCoy *"Badge of Honor" star Brett Chase* • Paul Guilfoyle *Mickey Cohen* ■ *Dir* Curtis Hanson • *Scr* Curtis Hanson, Brian Helgeland, from the novel by James Ellroy • *Cinematographer* Dante Spinotti • *Music* Jerry Goldsmith

LA Story ★★★★ 15

Romantic comedy
1991 · US · Colour · 90mins

Following on from the success of *Roxanne*, for which he also wrote the screenplay, Steve Martin's warm-hearted salute to Los Angeles pretensions and all is another romantic comedy that boasts just enough quirkiness to comfort the old fans worried he might be selling out and abandoning his "wild and crazy" persona. He plays a weatherman who falls for visiting British journalist Victoria Tennant while undergoing a mild mid-life crisis. Martin the writer has fun sending up some of the crazier aspects of LA life and stages some lovely comic set pieces; if anything, a sniff of sentimentality is the film's failing. There are some fine supporting performances from Sarah Jessica Parker, Richard E Grant and Marilu Henner, and look out for cameos from Patrick Stewart, Chevy Chase and Rick Moranis. Contains some swearing. 🔲

Steve Martin *Harris K Telemacher* • Victoria Tennant *Sara McDowel* • Richard E Grant *Roland* • Marilu Henner *Trudi* • Sarah Jessica Parker *Sandee* • Susan Forristal *Ariel* • Kevin Pollak *Frank Swan* • Sam McMurray *Morris Frost* ■ *Dir* Mick Jackson • *Scr* Steve Martin

LA Takedown ★★★ 15

Crime drama   1989 · US · Colour · 93mins

A dedicated policeman and his team obsessively trail an equally professional thief and his crew who are preparing for one big heist. Sound familiar? Yes, this effectively is Michael Mann's full dress, made-for-TV rehearsal for *Heat*, and it shares a virtually identical plot and character names. In fact, the only real difference is that the cinema hit boasted Robert De Niro and Al Pacino; here you only have Scott Plank and Alex McArthur. Consequently, it suffers in comparison, although Mann's sleek direction and stylised design still make it compulsive viewing. Contains violence and swearing. ▣

Scott Plank *Vincent Hanna* • Alex McArthur *Patrick McClaren* • Ely Pouget *Lillian* • Vincent Guastaferro *Michael Cerrito* • Peter Dobson *Chris* • Richard J Chaves [*Richard Chaves*] *Casals* • Laura Harrington *Eady* • Daniel Baldwin *Schwartz* ■ *Dir/Scr* Michael Mann

LA without a Map ★★★ 15

Romantic comedy
1998 · UK/Fr/Fin/Lux · Colour · 107mins

Based on Richard Rayner's autobiographical cult novel *Los Angeles without a Map*, Mika Kaurismäki's film is a sharp comedy stab at Los Angeles, in which David Tennant plays the Englishman abroad – a Bradford undertaker who leaves his rain-swept, gloomy existence to track down beautiful American Vinessa Shaw to sunny Hollywood after spotting her in his local graveyard. Of course, everything which can go wrong once he gets there invariably does, but it's fun, unpredictable stuff, peppered with some fantastic supporting turns from Julie Delpy, Vincent Gallo and, playing himself in a deliciously tongue-in-cheek manner, Johnny Depp. Watch out for Margi Clarke and Amanda Plummer in cameo roles.

David Tennant *Richard Tennant* • Vinessa Shaw *Barbara* • Julie Delpy *Julie* • Vincent Gallo *Moss* • Cameron Bancroft *Patterson* • Joe Dallesandro *Michael* • Anouk Aimée • Saskia Reeves *Joy* • Johnny Depp ■ *Dir* Mika Kaurismäki • *Scr* Richard Rayner, Mika Kaurismäki, from the novel by Richard Rayner

The L-Shaped Room ★★★★ 15

Drama   1962 · UK · BW · 120mins

Adapted from Lynne Reid Banks's bestseller, this was an angry young film in its day, which comes to life under the sensitive direction of Bryan Forbes. Set in shabby bedsit land, it features Leslie Caron in an Oscar-nominated role as the unmarried, pregnant girl with a decision to make. Wonderful performances – by Tom Bell, Brock Peters, Bernard Lee and music-hall veteran Cicely Courtneidge – make the tenement in which the L-shaped abode is situated a place of vitality, concern and eventual affirmation. ▣

Leslie Caron *Jane Fosset* • Tom Bell *Toby* • Brock Peters *Johnny* • Cicely Courtneidge *Mavis* • Bernard Lee *Charlie* • Avis Bunnage *Doris* • Patricia Phoenix *Sonia* • Emlyn Williams *Dr Weaver* • Anthony Booth *Youth in street* ■ *Dir* Bryan Forbes • *Scr* Bryan Forbes, from the novel by Lynne Reid Banks • *Cinematographer* Douglas Slocombe • *Music* John Barry • *Editor* Anthony Harvey

L.627 ★★★★ 15

Crime drama   1992 · Fr · Colour · 139mins

What a wonderfully versatile director Bertrand Tavernier is. Coming between the intimate drama of *These Foolish Things* and the swashbuckling success of *D'Artagnan's Daughter*, this ultra-realistic police drama is one of his finest achievements. Witten by ex-policeman Michel Alexandre, it follows Didier Bezace's narcotics unit as it pursues a gang of drug traffickers in Paris. Whether exploring the links between drugs and racism or revealing the prejudices and inadequacies of the force, Tavernier retains an admirable objectivity, which actually adds to the steel of the picture rather than tempering it. A sobering film that should be seen. In French with English subtitles. Contains violence, swearing, drug abuse and nudity. ▣

Didier Bezace *Lucien "Lulu"Marguet* • Charlotte Kady *Marie* • Philippe Torreton *Antoine* • Nils Tavernier *Vincent* • Jean-Paul Comart *Dominique "Dodo" Cantoni* • Jean-Roger Milo *Manuel* • Lara Guirao *Cécile* ■ *Dir* Bertrand Tavernier • *Scr* Michel Alexandre

Labor of Love: the Arlette Schweitzer Story ★★ PG

Drama based on a true story
1993 · US · Colour · 89mins

Friends and foes of TV movies alike should know that it's pretty safe to assume that a film containing the word "Story" in its title is going to be a hurriedly produced, true-life embarrassment, rushed out in a bid to snare viewers while the original event is still fresh in the memory. This one stars TV-movie regular Ann Jillian as the eponymous heroine, who allowed herself to be fertilised with her son-in-law's sperm to give her daughter the baby she had always longed for. It's tabloid stuff and no amount of tearful earnestness can transform it into a life-enhancing drama. Ms Schweitzer herself has a cameo role as Ann. ▣

Ann Jillian *Arlette Schweitzer* • Tracey Gold *Christa Uchytil* • Diana Scarwid *Darlene* • Bill Smitrovich *Dan Schweitzer* • Donal Logue *Kevin Uchytil* • Frances Sternhagen *Mary Rafferty* ■ *Dir* Jerry London • *Scr* Susan Baskin

Laboratory ★

Science-fiction thriller   1980 · US · Colour

More science-fiction junk from the specialist shoestring-budget duo of directors Allan Sandler and Robert Emenegger. On a sleep-inducing par with their epic *The Killings on Outpost Zeta*, this obscurity finds humanoid aliens abducting assorted earthlings and placing them under observation in a desert research facility. And then... nothing happens! Excruciating low-grade trash.

Camille Mitchell • Corinne Michaels • Garnett Smith ■ *Dir* Allan Sandler, Robert Emenegger

Labyrinth ★★★ U

Fantasy adventure   1986 · US · Colour · 97mins

The Muppet team go into "Alice in Wonderland" territory as babysitter Jennifer Connelly wishes her younger brother into the Goblin King's clutches and has only hours to rescue him from a castle maze. With plenty of fuzzball gremlins, cute sugar plum fairies and clumsy Hoggle the dwarf to keep the children amused (adults will laugh at David Bowie's Tina Turner wig for entirely different reasons!), Jim Henson's panto *Monty Python* (written by clan member Terry Jones) is weak on suspense and thrills, but still emerges as firm fantasy fun. ▣ **DVD**

David Bowie *Jareth, King of the Goblins* • Jennifer Connelly *Sarah* • Toby Froud *Toby* • Shelley Thompson *Stepmother* • Christopher Malcolm *Father* • Natalie Finland *Fairy* • Brian Henson *Hoggle* • Michael Hordern *Wiseman* • Percy Edwards *Ambrosius* ■ *Dir* Jim Henson • *Scr* Terry Jones, from a story by Dennis Less, Jim Henson

Labyrinth ★★★

Drama documentary
1991 · Ger · Colour and BW · 86mins

A leading member of the Czech New Wave, Jaromil Jires had garnered little international attention since his 1968 adaptation of Milan Kundera's *The Joke*. This was his first feature to gain foreign distribution after the Velvet Revolution, and its blend of dramatic re-creation and archival footage reveals his powers to be undiminished. Maximilian Schell stars as a director whose research for a film on the writer is sidetracked by a sudden obsession with the historical persecution of the Jews. With Charlie Chaplin's son, Christopher, cameoing as Kafka, this is both stylish and provocative. In Czech with English subtitles.

Maximilian Schell *The Director* • Christopher Chaplin *Franz Kafka* • Milos Kopecky *Rabbi Low* • Otto Sevcik *SS Gunther* ■ *Dir* Jaromil Jires • *Scr* Jaromil Jires, Alex Koenigsmark, Hans-Jorg Weyhmuller

Labyrinth of Passion ★★★ 18

Comedy   1982 · Sp · Colour · 94mins

This was the second full-length internationally-released feature from Spanish cult director Pedro Almodóvar, and it marked the first appearance of future Hollywood superstar Antonio Banderas. A freewheeling, pop culture screwball comedy, the frenetic action revolves around numerous love affairs between nymphomaniacs, analysts, visiting royalty and Islamic extremists in bohemian Madrid. It's much the same uneven gay/bisexual mix Almódovar camp followers expect and adore, only this time with the added attraction of numerous themes that continue to recur in the director's work, especially the torch-singer mother, terrorists and a traumatic childhood. In Spanish with English subtitles. ▣

Cecilia Roth *Sexilia* • Imanol Arias *Riza Niro* • Helga Liné *Toraya* • Marta Fernandez-Muro *Queti* ■ *Dir/Scr* Pedro Almodóvar

The Lacemaker ★★★★ 15

Romantic drama   1977 · Fr · Colour · 102mins

This is an agonisingly acute study of incompatability from Swiss director Claude Goretta. Isabelle Huppert gives one of her finest performances as Pomme, the shy hairdresser whose life falls apart when her romance with student Yves Beneyton brings on a severe inferiority complex. By giving the couple's early scenes a joyous holiday feel, tinged with a sense of innocent excitement, Goretta makes the struggle to preserve their relationship all the more unbearable, although the Parisian segment strives too deliberately to achieve its effect. The final shot is one of the most gut-wrenching ever filmed. In French with English subtitles.

Isabelle Huppert *Béatrice (Pomme)* • Yves Beneyton *François Beligne* • Florence Giorgetti *Marylène Thorent* • Anne-Marie Düringer [*Annemarie Düringer*] *Pomme's mother* ■ *Dir* Claude Goretta • *Scr* Pascal Lainé, Claude Goretta, from a novel by Pascal Lainé

Lacombe Lucien ★★★★

Drama   1974 · Fr · Colour · 137mins

Louis Malle's absorbing and provocative film about the Nazi occupation of France features Pierre Blaise as the loutish young peasant who, shunned by the Resistance, joins the Gestapo and terrorises the Jewish family he moves in with. It's a moral quagmire of a movie, charting a peasant's road to fascism and redemption, though Malle's clinical depiction of torture and other crimes, and his refusal to condemn his "hero" caused the film to be vilified in some quarters in France. Beautifully made and disturbingly acted by the non-professional Blaise, it remains one of the few major films about the issue of collaboration. In French with English subtitles..

Pierre Blaise *Lucien* • Aurore Clément *France* • Holger Löwenadler *Albert Horn* • Thérèse Giehse *Bella Horn* • Stéphane Bouy *Jean Bernard* • Loumi Iacobesco *Betty Beaulieu* • René Bouloc *Faure* ■ *Dir* Louis Malle • *Scr* Louis Malle, Patrick Modiano • *Cinematographer* Tonino Delli Colli • *Music* Django Reinhardt, André Claveau, Irène de Trebert

Lacy and the Mississippi Queen ★★

Comedy western   1978 · US · Colour

Pilot for a TV series that failed to materialise, the western was already yesterday's genre by the time Kathleen Lloyd and Debra Feuer teamed up as a pair of sisters (one a tomboy, the other a belle) exchanging wisecracks while tracking down the train robbers who killed their pa. On the credit side, there's expert support from Jack Elam and an early outing for Christopher Lloyd. The script is weak, however, and, despite their energetic performances, there's not enough snap between the leads.

Kathleen Lloyd *Kate Lacy* • Debra Feuer *Queenie* • Edward Andrews *Isaac Harrison* • Jack Elam *Willie Red Fire* • Matt Clark *Reynolds* • Les Lannom *Webber* • Christopher Lloyd *Jennings* • James Keach *Parker* ■ *Dir* Robert Butler • *Scr* Kathy Donnell, Madeline DiMaggio-Wagner

The Lad ★★

Comedy   1935 · UK · BW · 72mins

Gordon Harker was such a favourite of crime writer Edgar Wallace that he frequently had material especially tailored for him. It's hardly surprising, therefore, that the actor is totally at home in this serviceable adaptation of one of Wallace's most popular thrillers.

Posing as a detective to gain entrance to a country house, Harker soon realises he's not alone in having designs on a fabled family necklace. However, unlike his horsey rivals, he's not blackmailing, embezzling or two-timing anyone. Director Henry Edwards wisely keeps the action brisk and on the light side, as the mystery is hardly baffling and the performances are painfully stiff.

Gordon Harker *Bill Shane* • Betty Stockfeld *Lady Fandon* • Jane Carr (1) *Pauline* • Gerald Barry *Lord Fandon* • Geraldine Fitzgerald *Joan* • Barbara Everest *Mrs Lorraine* • John Turnbull *Inspector Martin* ■ *Dir* Henry Edwards • *Scr* Gerard Fairlie, from the novel by Edgar Wallace

Ladder of Swords ★★ 15
Thriller   1988 · UK · Colour · 94mins

Martin Shaw was still cashing in on his brief TV celebrity when he appeared in this little-known thriller produced by Film Four. Shaw is Don Demarco, a circus performer who finds himself suspected of murder when his troubled wife (Eleanor David) disappears. Bob Peck is the policeman who doggedly pursues him through the byways and alleyways of Big Top shenanigans. Director Norman Hull conveys some of the atmosphere and imagery of the circus, but animal lovers may be distressed by the fate of Shaw's other companion – Daley the bear. ▭

Martin Shaw *Don Demarco* • Eleanor David *Denise Demarco* • Juliet Stevenson *Alice Howard* • Bob Peck *Detective Inspector Atherton* • Simon Molloy *Sergeant Bilby* • Pearce Quigley *Constable Lowe* • Anthony Benson *Grumpy Gun* ■ *Dir/Scr* Norman Hull

Ladies and Gentlemen, the Rolling Stones ★★
Music documentary
1974 · US · Colour · 82mins

How do you make the Rolling Stones look boring? Make a documentary about their 1972 US tour as dull as this one, in which Mick Jagger and company give all they've got, but the director (Rollin Binzer) can't seem to deliver. It would help if the cameras were in the right place at the right time. This is depressing stuff, especially for fans.

Dir Rollin Binzer

Ladies and Gentlemen, the Fabulous Stains ★★
Musical drama
1982 · US · Colour · 87mins

Director Lou Adler produced *The Rocky Horror Picture Show* and clearly thought he was crafting another cult item with this determinedly offbeat tale of the rise and fall, and rise again, of an all-girl punk band named the Fabulous Stains. Instead it languished on the shelf for years. What makes it worth watching is the cast: the Tubes' Fee Waybill (in a great cameo), Ray Winstone, Sex Pistols' Steve Jones and Paul Cook, and the Clash's Paul Simonon. Supposedly a music business satire, the whole concept rings hollow and wears out its initial welcome pretty quickly.

Diane Lane *Corinne Burns* • Ray Winstone *Billy* • Peter Donat *Harley Dennis* • David Clennon *Dave Robell–the Agent* • John Lehne

Stu McGrath • Cynthia Sikes *Alicia Meeker* • Laura Dern *Jessica McNeil* • Marin Kanter *Tracy Burns* • Paul Cook *Danny* • Steve Jones *Steve* • Paul Simonon *Johnny* • John "Fee" Waybill *Lou Corpse* • Christine Lahti *Aunt Linda* ■ *Dir* Lou Adler • *Scr* Rob Morton

The Ladies Club ★★★
Action drama   1986 · US · Colour · 90mins

Advertised with the tagline "Men who attack woman have two big problems. The Ladies Club is about to remove them both!" this could so easily have fallen into the trap of sick exploitation. However, director Janet Greek handles her revenge tale with an assurance that keeps such formula vigilantism at bay. There are some good, low-key performances from the largely female cast playing rape victims who band together to give justice-evading criminals their just desserts. This usually means drugging them and hacking off their testes, leading to one memorable scene where a policeman is left to ponder whether castration is assault or robbery.

Karen Austin *Joan Taylor* • Diana Scarwid *Lucy Bricker* • Christine Belford *Dr Constance Lewis* • Bruce Davison *Richard Harrison* • Shera Danese *Eva* • Beverly Todd *Georgiane* • Marilyn Kagan *Rosalie* • Kit McDonough *Carol* ■ *Dir* Janet Greek [AK Allen] • *Scr* Paul Mason, Fran Lewis Ebeling, from the novel *Sisterhood* by Betty Black, from the novel *Sisterhood* by Casey Bishop

Ladies' Day ★★ U
Romantic comedy   1943 · US · BW · 62mins

When the star pitcher of a baseball team becomes involved in a hot love affair, to the detriment of his performance on the field, his teammates, their manager, and even some of their wives set about trying to break up the romance. An occasionally diverting comedy, the movie stars Eddie Albert as the lovesick ball player and the raucous "Mexican spitfire" Lupe Velez as the girl. Leslie Goodwins directs the proceedings, squeezing what laughs he can out of the somewhat repetitive situation. It's OK entertainment for those not allergic to the singular and noisy Velez.

Lupe Velez *Pepita Zorita* • Eddie Albert *Wacky Waters* • Patsy Kelly *Hazel* • Max Baer *Hippo* • Jerome Cowan *Updyke* • Iris Adrian *Kitty* • Joan Barclay *Joan* • Cliff Clark *Dan* ■ *Dir* Leslie Goodwins • *Scr* Charles E Roberts, Dane Lussier, from a play by Robert Considine, Edward Clark Lilley, Bertrand Robinson

Ladies' House of Pleasure ★
Erotic comedy   1973 · Fr/It · Colour

After his directorial debut in 1954, film-maker and novelist Pierre Chevalier (here using the name Peter Knight) turned to skin flicks in the late sixties. This was not even up to that standard. Sandra Julien and Silvia Solar head a cast that struggles to do anything convincingly except disrobe and writhe in a tawdry tale of exploitation and rebellion. Only curio seekers need set their videos. French dialogue dubbed into English.. Contains sex scenes and nudity.

Sandra Julien *Magda* • Silvia Solar *Sylvia* • Magda Mundari *Yvette* • Olivier Mathot *Rasly* ■ *Dir* Peter Knight [Pierre Chevalier]

Ladies in Love ★★★
Romantic comedy   1936 · US · BW · 97mins

Three young lovelies (including Janet Gaynor and Loretta Young) rent a luxury apartment in Budapest in the hope of attracting their dream husbands. One of their beaux is played by Tyrone Power in a very early role that hints at his charismatic screen presence. There is no deep sub-text involved, what you see is a huge chunk of good old-fashioned entertainment. Who cares if it all seems rather chauvinistic and fey for our jaundiced modern palate? It works.

Janet Gaynor *Martha Kerenye* • Loretta Young *Susie Schmidt* • Constance Bennett *Yoli Haydn* • Simone Simon *Marie Armand* • Don Ameche *Dr Rudi Imre* • Paul Lukas *John Barta* • Tyrone Power Jr [Tyrone Power] *Karl Lanyi* ■ *Dir* Edward H Griffith • *Scr* Melville Baker, from a play by Ladislaus Bus-Fekete

Ladies in Retirement ★★★
Crime melodrama   1941 · US · BW · 91mins

Careful but compelling adaptation of a popular stage play, with Ida Lupino at her most dramatically wild-eyed. She's housekeeper to a retired actress (Isobel Elsom) who hatches a plot to help her two retarded sisters (Elsa Lanchester and Edith Barrett). With Louis Hayward as the suspicious relative who uncovers the crime, there's an artificial symmetry which betrays the film's stage origins. It transfixes you with a purposeful expertise, though, mainly because Lupino can gain your sympathy while doing the most dastardly things. She can also imbue the act of washing-up with a menace you wouldn't believe.

Ida Lupino *Ellen Creed* • Louis Hayward *Albert Feather* • Evelyn Keyes *Lucy* • Elsa Lanchester *Emily Creed* • Edith Barrett *Louisa Creed* • Isobel Elsom *Leonora Fiske* ■ *Dir* Charles Vidor • *Scr* Garrett Fort, Reginald Denham, from the play by Reginald Denham, Edward Percy

Ladies' Man ★★★ U
Drama   1931 · US · BW · 76mins

Smoothly amoral high-society man-about-town William Powell is loved by Kay Francis and lusted after by several society matrons whom he is happy to "escort" in return for their lavish tokens of gratitude. When, however, Carole Lombard, the daughter of one of his ladies, falls for him, disaster strikes. A highly sophisticated and brittle comedy of Park Avenue manners, the film boasts a sharp script by Herman J Mankiewicz that manages to combine wit with a penetrating exposé of the milieu in which it is set. Lothar Mendes directs and the classy trio of lead performers, notably Powell who specialised in well-groomed cads during the thirties, is made to measure for the material.

William Powell *Jamie Darricott* • Kay Francis *Norma Page* • Carole Lombard *Rachel Fendley* • Gilbert Emery *Horace Fendley* • Olive Tell *Mrs Fendley* • Martin Burton *Anthony Fendley* • John Holland *Peyton Waldon* • Frank Atkinson *Valet* ■ *Dir* Lothar Mendes • *Scr* Herman J Mankiewicz, from a story by Rupert Hughes

The Ladies' Man ★★★★ U
Comedy   1961 · US · Colour · 106mins

One of the most inventive and wittiest movies written, starring, and directed by Jerry Lewis, one of the great clowns in the history of cinema, and an unabashed influence on today's pre-eminent funnyman Jim Carrey. Playing a bitter jilted man in a house full of women, Lewis proves himself a master of comic cinema, playing with the medium itself in a remarkable series of spirited gags in a marvellously constructed and elaborate set. Handyman Jerry is handsomely supported by viragos Helen Traubel and Kathleen Freeman, and there is a cameo from George Raft.

Jerry Lewis *Herbert H Heebert* • Helen Traubel *Helen Welenmelon* • Pat Stanley *Fay* • Kathleen Freeman *Katie* • George Raft ■ *Dir* Jerry Lewis • *Scr* Jerry Lewis, Bill Richmond

Ladies of Leisure ★★★
Romantic drama   1930 · US · BW · 98mins

The glorious combination of director Frank Capra and leading lady Barbara Stanwyck makes this whiskered plot worth watching. Stanwyck stars as an ex-gold digger who has the misfortune to fall for would-be artist Ralph Graves, but nobody believes her capable of true lurv. Well, would you? Capra's delicate soufflé touch gives the script the bounce and pace it badly needs and, of course, Stanwyck is quite stunning. A movie object lesson in how truly exceptional talent can overcome even the direst of tales.

Barbara Stanwyck *Kay Arnold* • Ralph Graves *Jerry Strange* • Nance O'Neil *Mrs Strange* • George Fawcett *Mr Strange* • Johnnie Walker *Charlie* • Juliette Compton *Claire Collins* ■ *Dir* Frank Capra • *Scr* Jo Swerling, from the play *Ladies of the Evening* by Milton Herbert Gropper

Ladies of the Chorus ★ U
Romantic musical   1948 · US · BW · 57mins

A chorus girl in burlesque on Broadway steps out of her class, as did her mother before her, and falls in love with a smooth socialite. Directed by Phil Karlson from a monumentally feeble script, this dire but mercifully short musical programme-filler marks the less than notable first leading role for Marilyn Monroe. She is adequate to the undemanding task without giving any hint of the screen goddess she would become. Adele Jergens plays mother, and Rand Brooks the object of Monroe's affections. ▭

Adele Jergens *May Martin* • Marilyn Monroe *Peggy Martin* • Rand Brooks *Randy Carroll* • Nana Bryant *Mrs Carroll* • Eddie Carr *Billy Mackay* ■ *Dir* Phil Karlson • *Scr* Harry Sauber, Joseph Carol, from the story by Harry Sauber

Ladies Should Listen ★★
Romantic comedy   1934 · US · BW · 62mins

Cary Grant stars in this romantic comedy about a man-about-town whose switchboard operator (Frances Drake), secretly in love with him, involves herself in his affairs, business and otherwise, leading to inevitable complications. It's not surprising that this title hardly springs to mind when considering the films of the incomparable Grant. Directed by Frank

Tuttle, and with a reliable supporting cast of character players including the Edward Everett Horton, it's no more than a passing entertainment, suffering from a lazily superficial script which the stars strain to inject with some life.

Cary Grant *Julian de Lussac* • Frances Drake *Anna Mirelle* • Edward Everett Horton *Paul Vernet* • Nydia Westman *Susi Flamberg* • Clara Lou Sheridan [Ann Sheridan] *Adele* ■ *Dir* Frank Tuttle • *Scr* Guy Bolton, Claude Binyon, Frank Butler, from the play by Guy Bolton, from the play *La Demoiselle de Passy* by Alfred Savoir

Ladies They Talk About ★★★

Prison drama 1933 · US · BW · 64mins

Gang moll Barbara Stanwyck is sent to San Quentin through the efforts of powerful crime-fighting evangelist Preston Foster, who puts principle before love. Five years and several dramatic incidents later they are reunited. Entertaining crime melodrama, making a sincere attempt to portray life in a women's prison which, at times, resembles a social gathering. The highly unlikely plot is much enlivened by acid comedy (despite some Hays Office objections), and Stanwyck's cool performance. Hollywood stalwarts William Keighley and Howard Bretherton share the direction and singer Lillian (*I'll Cry Tomorrow*) Roth plays Stanwyck's prison buddy.

Barbara Stanwyck *Nan Taylor* • Preston S Foster [Preston Foster] *David Slade* • Lyle Talbot *Don* • Dorothy Burgess *Susie* • Lillian Roth *Linda* • Maude Eburne *Aunt Maggie* ■ *Dir* Howard Bretherton, William Keighley • *Scr* Brown Holmes, William McGrath, Sidney Sutherland, from the play by Dorothy Mackaye, Carlton Miles

Ladies Who Do ★★ U

Comedy 1963 · UK · BW · 81mins

A firm favourite in such TV series as *The Larkins* and *George and the Dragon*, Peggy Mount found films harder to come by. In the sixth of her ten pictures, she's joined by those other sitcom stalwarts Miriam Karlin, of *The Rag Trade* fame, and Dandy Nichols, *Till Death Us Do Part's* Else Garnett, as a trio of charladies who make a killing on the stock market through the tips they find among the office rubbish. With Harry H Corbett in support, this should have been quite amusing, but Michael Pertwee's ponderous script and the flat direction make it a one-joke bore. [video]

Peggy Mount *Mrs Cragg* • Robert Morley *Colonel Whitforth* • Harry H Corbett *James Ryder* • Miriam Karlin *Mrs Higgins* • Avril Elgar *Emily Parish* • Dandy Nichols *Mrs Merryweather* • Jon Pertwee *Mr Tait* • Nigel Davenport *Mr Strang* • Graham Stark *Foreman* • Ron Moody *Inspector* ■ *Dir* CM Pennington-Richards • *Scr* Michael Pertwee, from an idea by John Bignell

Lady and the Tramp ★★★★★ U

Animation 1955 · US · Colour · 73mins

The Disney studio's first venture into CinemaScope remains one of its most enduring favourites. Ending a sequence of fairy-tale adaptations, it returned to the animal world of *Dumbo* and *Bambi* to create a cast of charming creatures, headed by a pampered cocker spaniel called Lady and a spaghetti-munching mongrel called Tramp. In addition to voicing Lady's mistress and Siamese cats Si and Am, Peggy Lee also co-composed the unforgettable songs (with Sonny Burke), which were mystifyingly overlooked by Oscar. A joy for children and romantics alike. [video]

Peggy Lee *Darling/Peg/Si/Am* • Barbara Luddy *Lady* • Larry Roberts *Tramp* • Bill Thompson *Jock/Bull/Dachsie* • Bill Baucon *Trusty* • Stan Freberg *Beaver* • Verna Felton *Aunt Sarah* • Alan Reed *Boris* ■ *Dir* Hamilton Luske, Clyde Geronimi, Wilfred Jackson • *Scr* Erdman Penner, Joe Rinaldi, Ralph Wright, Don DaGradi, from the novel *Lady* by Ward Greene

Lady Be Good ★★★ U

Musical 1941 · US · BW · 111mins

This is a musical of two halves: a weak, badly-written and boring plot (the several acrimonious partings and tearful reconciliations of songwriting duo Robert Young and Ann Sothern), and a series of good songs, dazzling tap dancing from Eleanor Powell, and a fabulous finale staged by Busby Berkeley. The stand-out song is Jerome Kern's Oscar winner, *The Last Time I Saw Paris*, sung by Ann Sothern, and the rest of the wasted talents under Norman Z McLeod's direction include Lionel Barrymore, Red Skelton and Dan Dailey.

Eleanor Powell *Marilyn Marsh* • Ann Sothern *Dixie Donegan* • Robert Young *Eddie Crane* • Lionel Barrymore *Judge Murdock* • John Carroll *Buddy Crawford* • Red Skelton *Joe "Red" Willet* • Virginia O'Brien *Lull* • Tom Conway *Mr Blanton* • Dan Dailey Jr [Dan Dailey] *Bill Pattison* • Phil Silvers *MC* ■ *Dir* Norman Z McLeod • *Scr* Jack McGowan, Kay Van Riper, John McClain, from a story by Jack McGowan • *Choreographer* Busby Berkeley • *Costume Designer* Adrian

Lady Beware ★★ 18

Thriller 1987 · US · Colour · 103mins

The story is familiar enough, but this slick straight-to-video thriller is still worth a look. Diane Lane gives one of her best performances as a department store window dresser whose mannequin displays attract the unwelcome attentions of a disturbed secret admirer (Michael Woods, brother of James). Director Karen Arthur succeeds in generating a creepy sense of menace. [video]

Diane Lane *Katya Yarno* • Michael Woods *Jack Price* • Cotter Smith *Mac Odell* • Tyra Ferrell *Nan* • Peter Nevargic *Lionel* • Edward Penn *Thayer* ■ *Dir* Karen Arthur • *Scr* Susan Miller, Charles Zev Cohen

Lady by Choice ★★★

Comedy 1934 · US · BW · 74mins

An entertaining, if duller-edged, follow-up to Frank Capra's wonderful *Lady for a Day*, but here directed by David Burton with a rather more plodding hand. May Robson reprises a role similar to that of her scruffy fruit vendor Apple Annie (with a faint hint of *ennui*), this time given a major wash and brush-up à la *Pygmalion* by hoofer Carole Lombard. The latter, whose career was so tragically cut short, is always a joy to watch and this big-hearted, bouncy little movie shows her gift for *bons mots* to good advantage. But the overall package is a little short on pizzazz.

Carole Lombard *"Alabam" Georgia Lee* • May Robson *Patsy Patterson* • Roger Pryor *John Mills* • Walter Connolly *Judge Daly* • Arthur Hohl *Charlie Kendall* • Raymond Walburn *Front O'Malley* • James Burke *Sergeant Brannigan* • Mariska Aldrich *Lucretia* • William Faversham *Malone* • John Boyle *Walsh* ■ *Dir* David Burton • *Scr* Jo Swerling, from a story by Dwight Taylor

Lady Caroline Lamb ★★★ 15

Historical drama
1972 · UK/It · Colour · 117mins

After writing David Lean's previous three epics and *A Man for All Seasons*, Robert Bolt turned writer/director and wrote this historical drama for his wife, Sarah Miles. Lady Caroline Lamb was married to a future Prime Minister, had a celebrated affair with Lord Byron and generally scandalised Regency society. Miles plays the part to the hilt, appearing in some bizarre costumes and exploiting her own natural talent and extrovert character to advantage, being by turns ravishing, captivating, infuriating and pathetic. Olivier plays a camp Wellington with a false nose, Jon Finch is quietly authoritative as William Lamb/Lord Melbourne and Richard Chamberlain is perfectly pompous as Byron. For Bolt and Miles, Lady Caroline is a feminist pioneer so the movie has a 1970s conception but done in the rather flat style of a fifties costume drama. [video]

Sarah Miles *Lady Caroline Lamb* • Jon Finch *William Lamb* • Richard Chamberlain *Lord Byron* • John Mills *Canning* • Margaret Leighton *Lady Melbourne* • Pamela Brown *Lady Bessborough* • Ralph Richardson *The King* • Laurence Olivier *Duke of Wellington* ■ *Dir/Scr* Robert Bolt

Lady Chatterley's Lover ★ 18

Erotic drama 1981 · Fr/UK · Colour · 99mins

Sylvia Kristel's acting deficiencies were barely noticeable in the *Emmanuelle* pictures that made her name. Here, though, she is required to do more, and she is found severely wanting. Not that Nicholas Clay has anything to be proud of in his performance as the gamekeeper who exploits the disability of his master, Shane Briant, to spend more time upstairs than down. Producers Menahem Golan and Yoram Globus don't stint on the period trappings, and Robert Fraisse's photography manages to be both nostalgic and pornographic. Poor DH Lawrence scarcely gets a look-in. [video]

Sylvia Kristel *Lady Constance Chatterley* • Nicholas Clay *Oliver Mellors* • Shane Briant *Sir Clifford Chatterley* • Ann Mitchell *Mrs Bolton* • Elizabeth Spriggs *Lady Eva* • Pascale Rivault *Hilda* • Anthony Head *Anton* • Bessie Love *Flora* ■ *Dir* Just Jaeckin • *Scr* Christopher Wicking, Just Jaeckin, from the novel *Lady Chatterley's Lover* by DH Lawrence

The Lady Cop ★★★

Detective drama 1979 · Fr · Colour · 103mins

Director Yves Boisset lifts the lid on provincial life in this simmering study of injustice and iniquitous influence. Demoted for linking the mayor to a gay scandal, Parisian detective Miou-Miou soon discovers that the drama group in a small northern town is behind the staging of some less than innocent entertainments. Although there's a surfeit of sinister crime for such a backwater, this downbeat drama provides an uncompromising discussion of both moral and sexual corruption and the willingness of people to turn a blind eye. Miou-Miou is gutsily efficient, but the standout here is comedian Jean-Marc Thibault, who reveals an unexpected darker side as her boss. French dialogue dubbed into English.

Miou-Miou *Inspecteur Corinne Levasseur* • Jean-Marc Thibault *Commissaire Porel* • Leny Escudero *Diego Cortez* • Jean-Pierre Kalfon *Backmann* ■ *Dir* Yves Boisset • *Scr* Yves Boisset, Claude Veillot

The Lady Eve ★★★★★ U

Romantic comedy 1941 · US · BW · 93mins

A wonderfully witty masterpiece, written and directed by the inimitable Preston Sturges. The plot gives a couple of near career-best roles to two of Hollywood's finest players, who are perfectly cast here. Henry Fonda, a wealthy young man obsessed by snakes, lays himself wide open to the schemes of professional con artist Charles Coburn and his daughter, Barbara Stanwyck. Fonda's buddy William Demarest intervenes, but Stanwyck, undeterred, later reappears in disguise at his palatial manse and tries again. Naturally, the slick, assured sexual opportunist falls for the gauche brewer's son who has spent a year up the Amazon, resulting in a witty, sparkling combination of romance and screwball comedy that is still unequalled.

Barbara Stanwyck *Jean Harrington* • Henry Fonda *Charles Poncefort Pike* • Charles Coburn *"Colonel" Harrington* • Eugene Pallette *Mr Pike* • Eric Blore *Sir Alfred McGlennan Keith aka "Pearly"* • William Demarest *Muggsy* • Melville Cooper *Gerald* ■ *Dir* Preston Sturges • *Scr* Preston Sturges, from the story *The Faithful Heart* by Monckton Hoffe

Lady for a Day ★★★★ U

Comedy 1933 · US · BW · 95mins

A wonderful screen version of Damon Runyon's tale of Apple Annie, the Times Square fruit seller who brings so much luck to Dave the Dude that, when her daughter arrives from Europe with an aristocratic fiancé, he puts her up in a hotel and turns her into the titular madam. A fabulous cast incarnates Runyon's street characters, but none is more impressive than Australian-born May Robson in the leading role, the performance of a lifetime which rightly won her an Oscar nomination. Columbia's whiz kid Frank Capra – he also directed the 1961 remake *Pocketful of Miracles* – also secured Academy nominations for best picture and best director but his dreaded Capra corn is kept well at bay by the acerbic nature of Runyon's New York dialogue and the unsentimental performance of his superb leading lady. [video]

Warren William *Dave The Dude* • May Robson *Apple Annie* • Guy Kibbee *Judge Blake* • Glenda Farrell *Missouri Martin* • Ned Sparks *Happy McGuire* • Walter Connolly *Count Romero* • Jean Parker *Louise* • Nat Pendleton

Shakespeare • Barry Norton *Carlos* ■ *Dir* Frank Capra • *Scr* Robert Riskin, from the story *Madame la Gimp* by Damon Runyon

Lady for a Night ★★

Melodrama 1942 · US · BW · 90mins

Great idea from Republic, shame about the execution. At one of the big studios, this riverboat romantic drama could have been done properly with a decent budget and possibly colour. As it is, John Wayne is awkwardly cast alongside top-billed Joan Blondell in a murder-driven plot. There's good support, though, from Ray Middleton and the redoubtable Blanche Yurka. Director Leigh Jason wasn't the right choice to make all this back projection work, and the result is very average indeed.

Joan Blondell *Jenny Blake* • John Wayne *Jack Morgan* • Ray Middleton *Alan Alderson* • Philip Merivale *Stephen Alderson* • Blanche Yurka *Julia Alderson* • Edith Barrett *Katherine Alderson* • Leonid Kinskey *Boris* • Montagu Love *Judge* ■ *Dir* Leigh Jason • *Scr* Isabel Dawn, Boyce DeGaw, from a story by Garrett Fort

Lady from Louisiana ★★ PG

Drama 1941 · US · BW · 82mins

John Wayne considered himself too big a star to be landed with the part of a young lawyer in this bog standard Republic programmer. Certainly, there is nothing remarkable about this tale of a crooked lottery in New Orleans, and Wayne has too few opportunities to demonstrate his prowess as a man of action. Ona Munson could be forgiven for sharing her co-star's disappointment, as her own career had failed to take off in spite of a splendid performance in *Gone with the Wind*. There is little chemistry between the pair and the spectacular storm finale is all too long in coming. ▭

John Wayne *John Reynolds* • Ona Munson *Julie Mirbeau* • Ray Middleton *Blackie Williams* • Henry Stephenson *General Mirbeau* • Helen Westley *Mrs Brunot* • Jack Pennick *Cuffy* • Dorothy Dandridge *Felice* ■ *Dir* Bernard Vorhaus • *Scr* Vera Caspary, Michael Hogan, Guy Endore, from a story by Edward James, Francis Faragoh •

The Lady from Shanghai ★★★★ PG

Crime drama 1948 · US · BW · 83mins

A marvellous murky *film noir* from arguably the American cinema's greatest director, Orson Welles, though cutting his beloved Rita Hayworth's hair short and dying it platinum for her role here was perhaps not one of his better ideas. Even stranger was his decision to play his own part with a bizarre Irish accent. Nevertheless, Everett Sloane as Hayworth's disabled husband is even better than he was in *Citizen Kane*, and the climactic hall of mirrors sequence is magnificently shot, and justly famed. ▭

Rita Hayworth *Elsa Bannister* • Orson Welles *Michael O'Hara* • Everett Sloane *Arthur Bannister* • Glenn Anders *George Grisby* • Ted De Corsia *Sidney Broome* • Erskine Sanford *Judge* • Gus Schilling *Goldie* • Carl Frank *District Attorney* • Louis Merrill *Jake* • Evelyn Ellis *Bessie* ■ *Dir* Orson Welles • *Scr* Orson Welles, from the novel *If I Die Before I Wake* by Sherwood King

The Lady from the Shanghai Cinema ★★ 15

Crime drama 1987 · Bra · Colour · 116mins

The visual ambience of this Brazilian misfire is impressive, but writer/director Guilherme De Almeida Prado misses the sardonic wit and complexity of the hard-boiled *films noirs* he seeks to parody. The meeting of the dupe and the *femme fatale* is neatly achieved. But from the moment Maité Proença and her sinister husband begin reeling in boxer turned estate agent Antonio Fagundes, proceedings become bogged down with pulp tropes that are packed in merely for the sake of it. A pity, as the cast plays along with spirit, while the design and photography are impeccable. In Portuguese with English subtitles.

Antonio Fagundes *Lucas* • Maité Proença *Suzana* • Jose Lewgoy *Linus* • Jorge Doria *Velho* • José Mayer *Bolivar* • Miguel Falabella *Lana* • Paulo Villaça *Walter Desdino* • Sergio Mamberti *Stan* ■ *Dir/Scr* Guilherme De Almeida Prado

The Lady from Yesterday ★★★ PG

Drama 1985 · US · Colour · 91mins

A decent melodrama that gives a newish spin to the trauma of Vietnam by having a Vietnamese woman plus child arrive at the door of Houston businessman Wayne Rogers. Naturally, the appearance of his wartime Oriental dalliance and the son he never knew he had gives Rogers a shock, and it doesn't exactly please his wife, Bonnie Bedelia, either. Nicely performed and modestly directed by Robert Day. ▭

Wayne Rogers *Craig Weston* • Bonnie Bedelia *Janet Weston* • Pat Hingle *Jim Bartlett* • Barrie Youngfellow *Rita Bartlett* • Blue Deckert *Sam Horton* • Tina Chen *Lien* • Bryan Price *Quan* ■ *Dir* Robert Day • *Scr* Tim Maschler, Ken Pettus

The Lady Gambles ★★★

Melodrama 1949 · US · BW · 98mins

A happily married couple (Barbara Stanwyck, Robert Preston) take a trip to Las Vegas where the warm, wonderful, well-balanced wife develops a gambling addiction that drives her husband away and propels her into the most desperate of conditions. Directed by Michael Gordon, this is melodrama in capitals and italics, played for all its worth by the great Stanwyck. In her harrowing descent to the gutter she suffers with such conviction that fans both of the star and of soap opera can easily overlook the fact that this is perfunctorily written hokum and enjoy a gleeful wallow. Pity about the soft ending, though.

Barbara Stanwyck *Joan Boothe* • Robert Preston *David Boothe* • Stephen McNally *Corrigan* • Edith Barrett *Ruth Phillips* • John Hoyt *Dr Rojac* • Elliott Sullivan *Barky* • Houseley Stevenson *Pawnbroker* • Peter Leeds *Hotel Clerk* • Don Beddoe *Mr Sutherland* • Anthony Curtis [Tony Curtis] *Bellboy* ■ *Dir* Michael Gordon • *Scr* Roy Huggins, Halsted Welles, from a story by Lewis Meltzer, Oscar Saul

Lady Godiva ★ U

Historical drama 1955 · US · Colour · 89mins

Maureen O'Hara, wrapped in yards and yards of red hair to hide her nakedness, rides through 11th-century Coventry in this tedious, cardboard period piece, obviously filmed on the Universal backlot. She is the Saxon bride of Saxon nobleman George Nader, determined to thwart plans for an alliance with the Normans. Unfortunately for the actors, the director Arthur Lubin was more at home with talking mules and horses such as Francis and Mr Ed. Cast as First Saxon is 25-year-old Clint Eastwood.

Maureen O'Hara *Lady Godiva* • George Nader *Lord Leofric* • Eduard Franz *King Edward* • Leslie Bradley *Count Eustace* • Victor McLaglen *Grimald* • Torin Thatcher *Lord Godwin* • Clint Eastwood *1st Saxon* ■ *Dir* Arthur Lubin • *Scr* Oscar Brodney, Harry Ruskin, from a story by Oscar Brodney

Lady Godiva Rides Again ★★

Comedy 1951 · UK · BW · 97mins

Apart from a wonderful speech by Alastair Sim's world-weary producer about the errant ways of the British film industry, this is a hugely disappointing satire from the usually reliable pairing of Frank Launder and Sidney Gilliat. It was cruelly ironic that Pauline Stroud's real-life flirtation with movie fame should turn out to be as brief as that of the pageant queen she plays here, but she's not helped by a script so thin it wouldn't hide Godiva's blushes. Although the supporting cast reads like a who's who of fifties comedy, no one is around long enough to make much of an impact.

Dennis Price *Simon Abbott* • John McCallum *Larry Burns* • Stanley Holloway *Mr Clark* • Pauline Stroud *Marjorie Clark* • Gladys Henson *Mrs Clark* • Bernadette O'Farrell *Janie* • George Cole *Johnny* • Diana Dors *Dolores August* • Eddie Byrne *Eddie Mooney* • Kay Kendall *Sylvie* • Renee Houston *Beattie* • Dora Bryan *Publicity Woman* • Sidney James *Lew Beeson* • Joan Collins *Beauty Contestant* • Alastair Sim *Murington* ■ *Dir* Frank Launder • *Scr* Frank Lauder, Val Valentine

Lady Ice ★★

Crime drama 1973 · US · Colour · 91mins

In this not-too-sparkling caper movie Donald Sutherland rehashes his role in *Klute* as a strangely obsessive, slightly spooky insurance investigator attempting to recover stolen diamonds. Since heists and red herrings proliferate and locations change for no real reason – Miami, Chicago, the Bahamas – it's hard to follow at times, impossible at others. One is grateful for the few crumbs of enjoyment tossed at us by the cast: with Sutherland as the beautiful Jennifer O'Neill as the duplicitous heroine; Robert Duvall, briefly, as a cop you can trust; and Patrick Magee, unbearably over the top as O'Neill's daddy.

Donald Sutherland *Andy Hammond* • Jennifer O'Neill *Paula Booth* • Robert Duvall *Ford Pierce* • Patrick Magee *Paul Booth* • Eric Braeden *Peter Brinker* • Jon Cypher *Eddy Stell* ■ *Dir* Tom Gries • *Scr* Alan Trustman, Harold Clemens, from a story by Alan Trustman • *Cinematographer* Lucien Ballard

Lady in a Cage ★★★

Drama 1964 · US · BW · 93mins

This exercise in sadism and mental torture was banned outright in Britain and the fact that it stars Olivia de Havilland makes that all the more surprising. The casting of double Oscar winner de Havilland is crucial and similar to Crawford and Davis in *What Ever Happened to Baby Jane?* in that a Hollywood legend is exhumed and abused. She plays a rich invalid who is trapped in her mechanical lift – the cage of the title – and is then systematically terrorised by a drunk, a prostitute and three thugs, one of whom is played by James Caan. It's an allegory about the beast in man and woman and has a surprise twist regarding de Havilland's past life.

Olivia de Havilland *Mrs Hilyard* • Ann Sothern *Sade* • Jeff Corey *Wino* • James Caan *Randall* • Jennifer Billingsley *Elaine* • Rafael Campos *Essie* • William Swan *Malcolm Hilyard* ■ *Dir* Walter Grauman • *Scr* Luther Davis

Lady in a Jam ★★

Comedy 1942 · US · BW · 78mins

Irene Dunne is the eponymous character, a harebrained heiress who loses all her money while indulging her obsession for numerology, and whose behaviour has her kept under observation by psychiatrist Patric Knowles, posing as a chauffeur. A feeble romantic comedy that dredges the bottom of the barrel for its sprinkling of laughs, it squanders the star's superior gifts and the talent of director Gregory La Cava.

Irene Dunne *Jane Palmer* • Patric Knowles *Dr Enright* • Ralph Bellamy *Stanley Gardner* • Eugene Pallette *Billingsley* • Samuel S Hinds *Dr Brewster* • Queenie Vassar *Cactus Kate Palmer* ■ *Dir* Gregory La Cava • *Scr* Eugene Thackrey, Frank Cockrell, Otho Lovering • *Cinematographer* Hal Mohr

Lady in Cement ★★

Crime drama 1968 · US · Colour · 93mins

A great title for the second of two movies starring Frank Sinatra as world-weary private detective Tony Rome. However, the film itself is not quite as effective as the first one (*Tony Rome*, not to be confused with the much better *The Detective*). Both Sinatra himself and skilled director Gordon Douglas seem merely to be going through the paces, but there's excellent support from *Bonanza's* Hoss, Dan Blocker, and comedian Joe E Lewis, whom Sinatra once portrayed in *The Joker Is Wild*. Thick-eared and not as tough as it thinks it is, this does at least give us a glimpse of Raquel Welch in her heyday. Sinatra sure could pick 'em.

Frank Sinatra *Tony Rome* • Raquel Welch *Kit Forrest* • Richard Conte *Lieutenant Santini* • Martin Gabel *Al Mungar* • Lainie Kazan *Maria Baretto* • Pat Henry *Rubin* • Steve Peck *Paul Mungar* • Dan Blocker *Gronsky* ■ *Dir* Gordon Douglas • *Scr* Marvin H Albert, Jack Guss, from the novel by Marvin H Albert

The Lady in Question ★★★

Melodrama 1940 · US · BW · 79mins

Six years before their sensational pairing in Charles Vidor's erotically charged *Gilda* brought them stardom, a still youthful Rita Hayworth and Glenn Ford appeared in this reworking of the French classic, *Gribouille*. Brian Aherne stars as a kind-hearted French family man who, called to jury duty, takes pity on the accused (Hayworth). He gives her a job and lodging in his home, causing numerous upheavals and complications involving his wife (Irene Rich) and son (Ford). A curious, occasionally irritating, but entertaining mix of bluff domestic comedy and near tragedy that is decently acted, with Hayworth ravishingly lovely and quite touching.

Brian Aherne *AndréMorestan* • Rita Hayworth *Natalie Roguin* • Glenn Ford *Pierre Morestan* • Irene Rich *Michèle Morestan* • George Coulouris *Defense attorney* • Lloyd Corrigan *Prosecuting attorney* • Evelyn Keyes *Françoise Morestan* ■ *Dir* Charles Vidor • *Scr* Lewis Meltzer, from the film *Gribouille* by HG Lustig, Marcel Archard

The Lady in Red ★★★★ 18

Crime drama 1979 · US · Colour · 83mins

Produced on a slimline budget by Roger Corman's studio, this splendid retro gangster movie was shot in about a month by Lewis Teague from a script by John Sayles. Pamela Sue Martin plays a star-struck country girl who hopes to be a Hollywood star but gets caught up in Chicago's vice rings, working for madame Louise Fletcher and spending time in prison. On release she falls in love with gangster John Dillinger (Robert Conrad) though he claims he's just a commodities broker. In a speedy 80-plus minutes, Sayles's script does an impressive sweep of Chicago's underworld, social strata and economy in the thirties and has in Martin a fiery, attractive heroine whom the press call "the lady in red". And as it's a Corman picture, there's also a lot of sex and bullets, too. [video]

Pamela Sue Martin *Polly Franklin* • Robert Conrad *John Dillinger* • Louise Fletcher *Anna Sage* • Robert Hogan *Jake Lingle* • Laurie Heineman *Rose Shimkus* • Glenn Withrow *Eddie* • Rod Gist *Pinetop* • Peter Hobbs *Pops Geissler* • Christopher Lloyd *Frognose* ■ *Dir* Lewis Teague • *Scr* John Sayles

The Lady in the Car with Glasses and a Gun ★★

Thriller 1970 · US/Fr · Colour · 105mins

A weird little thriller, hatched by Columbia to waste some funds locked in France; it also gave a starring role to British actress Samantha Eggar, a protégée of studio boss Mike Frankovich who had cast her in *The Collector*. Eggar plays the secretary to businessman Oliver Reed; when she drives his car to Paris, various strangers claim they saw her the previous day. Is she deranged? Did she take a wrong turning at Marienbad? Or is she the victim of some dark murder plot? Some genuinely creepy moments should keep you watching, but the resolution is a bit garbled.

Samantha Eggar *Dany Lang* • Oliver Reed *Michael Caldwell* • John McEnery *Philippe* • Stéphane Audran *Anita Caldwell* • Billie Dixon *Secretary* • Bernard Fresson *Jean* ■ *Dir* Anatole Litvak • *Scr* Richard Harris, Eleanor Perry, from the novel *La Dame dans l'Auto avec des Lunettes et un Fusil* by Sébastien Japrisot • *Cinematographer* Claude Renoir

Lady in the Dark ★★★ U

Musical 1944 · US · Colour · 99mins

Fashion magazine editor Ginger Rogers, fearing for her mental health because of conflicts with three men in her life (Ray Milland, Warner Baxter, Jon Hall), consults a psychiatrist (Barry Sullivan), to whom she relates her dreams. These provide the basis for the film's production numbers, lavishly staged and extravagantly dressed. A major Broadway hit three years earlier, with a book by Moss Hart and music and lyrics by Kurt Weill and Ira Gershwin, Paramount spared no expense in bringing it to the screen with a gold-plated design and production team and Mitchell Leisen directing. The public loved it, and you might too, but it lost Danny Kaye (replaced by Mischa Auer) and much of its brilliant original score in the transfer and got a critical thumbs-down as a result. It did, however, retain *The Saga of Jenny* as the major number, and Rogers, in her first Technicolor outing, is good.

Ginger Rogers *Liza Elliott* • Ray Milland *Charley Johnson* • Jon Hall *Randy Curtis* • Warner Baxter *Kendall Nesbitt* • Barry Sullivan *Dr Brooks* • Mischa Auer *Russell Paxton* ■ *Dir* Mitchell Leisen • *Scr* Frances Goodrich, Albert Hackett, from the musical by Moss Hart, Kurt Weill, Ira Gershwin • *Costume Designer* Raoul Pene du Bois, Edith Head

Lady in the Lake ★★★★

Film noir 1947 · US · BW · 102mins

Robert Montgomery stars and directs himself as Philip Marlowe. Made only a year after Humphrey Bogart played Marlowe in *The Big Sleep*, Montgomery was looking for an offbeat approach that would surprise audiences and lessen the problems of directing himself while increasing the pressure on his co-stars. Just as Raymond Chandler's novels are written in the first person, so *Lady in the Lake* is a film in the first person: the camera is Marlowe and we only see what he would see, glimpsing Montgomery's face only in brief opening and closing sequences and when Marlowe looks in the mirror. Meanwhile, the camera smokes, gets kissed (by Audrey Totter) and punched (by various heavies). A gimmick, but it works.

Robert Montgomery *Philip Marlowe* • Lloyd Nolan *Lieutenant Degarmot* • Audrey Totter *Adrienne Fromsett* • Tom Tully *Captain Kane* • Leon Ames *Derace Kingsby* • Jayne Meadows *Mildred Havelend* • Morris Ankrum *Eugene Grayson* • Lila Leeds *Receptionist* • Richard Simmons [Dick Simmons] *Chris Lavery* ■ *Dir* Robert Montgomery • *Scr* Steve Fisher, Raymond Chandler (uncredited), from the novel by Raymond Chandler

Lady in White ★★★★ 15

Supernatural thriller
1988 · US · Colour · 108mins

Frank LaLoggia's semi-autobiographical ghost story brings a wonderful sense of magical euphoria back to the genre. This highly romanticised, sentimental chiller puts Stephen King's brand of dark and violent suspense and Frank Capra's emotional fantasy into a Norman Rockwell setting with enthralling results. Lukas Haas, the Amish boy in *Witness*, is fantastic as the key holder to a past Halloween tragedy still haunting his sleepy community, in an evocative mini-masterpiece, jam-packed with dreamy atmosphere and incandescent supernatural enchantment. Contains violence and swearing. [video]

Lukas Haas *Frankie Scarlatti* • Len Cariou *Phil* • Alex Rocco *Angelo Scarlatti* • Katherine Helmond *Amanda Harper* • Jason Presson *Gino Scarlatti* • Renata Vanni *Mama Assunta* • Angelo Bertolini *Papa Charlie* • Jared Rushton *Donald* ■ *Dir/Scr* Frank LaLoggia

The Lady Is Willing ★

Comedy 1942 · US · BW · 90mins

A glamorous stage star (Marlene Dietrich) finds an abandoned toddler in Manhattan and, in order to adopt him, undertakes a marriage of convenience with a paediatrician (Fred MacMurray). The husband, en route to actually falling in love with the wife he has thus acquired, is on hand to cure the child of a dangerous illness. Although glossily directed by Mitchell Leisen as befits Dietrich, this leaden nonsense has nothing to recommend it other than the bizarre fascination of watching its *femme fatale* star attempting to play maternal in an uneasy mix of soap opera and romantic comedy.

Marlene Dietrich *Elizabeth Madden* • Fred MacMurray *Dr Corey McBain* • Aline MacMahon *Buddy* • Stanley Ridges *Kenneth Hanline* • Arline Judge *Frances* • Roger Clark *Victor* ■ *Dir* Mitchell Leisen • *Scr* James Edward Grant, Albert McCleery, from a story by James Edward Grant

Lady Jane ★★★ PG

Historical drama
1985 · UK · Colour · 135mins

Historical biopics are notoriously difficult to do well. It's easy enough to establish the correct period look, but the action is invariably hamstrung by the need to provide background information on each character and episode. Trevor Nunn's account of the events that culminated in the brief reign of Lady Jane Grey falls into the familiar traps, with the romance between Jane and the dissolute Guildford Dudley being couched in terms more befitting a Molly Ringwald movie. However Helena Bonham Carter plays Jane with admirable earnestness and she is well supported by Patrick Stewart as her father and Jane Lapotaire as Queen Mary. [video]

Helena Bonham Carter *Lady Jane Grey* • Cary Elwes *Guilford Dudley* • John Wood *John Dudley, Duke of Northumberland* • Michael Hordern *Dr Feckenham* • Jill Bennett *Mrs Ellen* • Jane Lapotaire *Princess Mary* • Sara Kestelman *Frances Grey, Duchess of Suffolk* • Patrick Stewart *Henry Grey, Duke of Suffolk* • Warren Saire *King Edward VI* • Joss Ackland *Sir John Bridges* • Ian Hogg *Sir John Gates* ■ *Dir* Trevor Nunn • *Scr* David Edgar, from a story by Chris Bryant

Lady Killer ★★★★

Comedy thriller 1933 · US · BW · 76mins

James Cagney's rat-a-tat delivery and the film's pell-mell propulsion make this a joyous Warner Bros sideswipe at Hollywood itself. Cagney is the cinema usher who graduates to gangsterdom, ending up as a film star writing fan letters to himself. He co-stars again with Mae Clarke from *Public Enemy*, only this time he pulls her out of bed by her hair instead of filling her face with grapefruit. The legend is that it's based on the rise and rise of George Raft, but who cares? It's the fast-paced action, and Cagney's mesmeric energy which make this so worthwhile.

James Cagney *Dan Quigley* • Leslie Fenton *Duke* • Margaret Lindsay *Lois Underwood* • Henry O'Neill *Ramick* • Willard Robertson *Conroy* • Douglas Cosgrove *Jones* • Raymond Hatton *Pete* • Russell Hopton *Smiley* ■ *Dir* Roy Del Ruth • *Scr* Ben Markson, Lillie Hayward, from the story *The Finger Man* by Rosalind Keating Shaffer

Lady Killer ★★

Thriller 1995 · US · Colour · 85mins

A ho-hum variation on the *Fatal Attraction* theme, this time with the sexes reversed. Judith Light plays a woman who relieves the boredom of suburbia by starting an affair with a younger man (Jack Wagner). She sees it as a harmless fling, but Wagner has other ideas so when Light ends the romance, he comes back to haunt her. Director Steven Schachter has little success in breathing any new life into a sadly over-familiar scenario, and he is not helped by uncharismatic turns from the two main protagonists.

Judith Light *Janice Mitchell* • Tracey Gold *Sharon Mitchell* • Jack Wagner *Dr Guy Elliman* • Ben Masters *Ross Mitchell* ■ *Dir* Steven Schachter • *Scr* Michael Grace

Lady L ★★★★

Period comedy 1965 · Fr/It · Colour · 123mins

Like its writer and director, Peter Ustinov, this is an immense charmer set at the turn of the last century, about laundress Sophia Loren whose amorous adventures, told in flashback, take her downstairs and then upstairs in the class system. Though involved with anarchist Paul Newman, she still marries eccentric aristocrat David Niven. The elegant dazzle and elaborate sets may be there to blind us to the lack of real substance but with an impressive cast – and Ustinov in the small part of Prince Otto – who cares? It's a stylish diversion to make us regret that Ustinov left film-making.

Sophia Loren *Lady L* • Paul Newman *Armand* • David Niven *Lord Lendale* • Claude Dauphin *Inspector Mercier* • Philippe Noiret *Gérôme* • Michel Piccoli *Lecoeur* • Cecil Parker *Sir Percy* • Jean Wiener *Krajewski* • Daniel Emilfork *Kobeleff* • Peter Ustinov *Prince Otto* ■ *Dir* Peter Ustinov • *Scr* Peter Ustinov, from the novel by Romain Gary

Lady Liberty ★★

Comedy 1971 · It/Fr · Colour · 95mins

The original Italian title of this Sophia Loren frolic is *La Mortadella* – the name of Italy's fattest sausage, originally from Bologna and sometimes attaining a girth of 18 inches. The plot has Loren arriving in New York clutching this huge sausage, which sends the US customs officials first into a dither, and then into lip-smacking mode. Like the sausage itself, this comedy was made for the Italian market and racked up few export sales, despite the best efforts of director Mario Monicelli. The English version was written by Ring Lardner Jr, a blacklisted screenwriter who later won an Oscar for *MASH*.

Sophia Loren *Maddalena Ciarrapico* • William Devane *Jock Fenner* • Luigi Proietti *Michele Bruni* • Beeson Carroll *Dominic* • Bill Deprato *Pasquale* • Danny DeVito *Mancuso* • Susan Sarandon *Sally* ■ *Dir* Mario Monicelli • *Scr* Leonard Melfi, Suso Cecchi D'Amico, Don Carlos Dunaway, RW Spera, Mario Monicelli, Ring Lardner Jr, from a story by Leonard Melfi, from a idea by RW Spera

Lady Luck ★★
Comedy   1946 · US · BW · 97mins

Best known for playing pleasant but undeniably bland characters, Robert Young progressed to the lead in potboilers such as this RKO programme filler, in which he plays a gambler whom Barbara Hale won't marry until he breaks his habit, because her dad – loveable Frank Morgan – comes from a long line of inveterate gamblers. Films like this are pleasant enough time-wasters, but they didn't give Young box-office clout. He eventually achieved international popularity (and massive personal wealth) in two television series, *Father Knows Best* (1954-60) and *Marcus Welby, MD* (1969-76).

Robert Young *Larry Scott* • Barbara Hale *Mary Audrey* • Frank Morgan *William Audrey* • James Gleason *Sacramento Sam* • Don Rice *Eddie* • Harry Davenport *Judge Martin* ■ *Dir* Edwin L Marin • *Scr* Lynn Root, Frank Fenton, from the story by Herbert Clyde Lewis

A Lady Mislaid ★★ U
Comedy   1958 · UK · BW · 59mins

A policeman arrives at the country cottage of two spinster sisters to look for the body of the previous tenant's wife and duly unearths a skeleton in the chicken-coop. But whose skeleton is it? Phyllis Calvert and Gillian Owen play the sisters, Thorley Walters the husband under suspicion in this thriller-farce, directed by David MacDonald. A quaint idea and a decent cast make perfectly respectable entertainment out of an hour-long British programmer, but there's not much more to be said for it.

Phyllis Calvert *Esther Williams* • Alan White *Sgt Bullock* • Thorley Walters *Smith* • Gillian Owen *Jennifer Williams* • Richard Leech *George* • Constance Fraser *Mrs Small* ■ *Dir* David MacDonald • *Scr* Frederick Gotfurt, from a play by Kenneth Horne

Lady of Burlesque ★★★
Comedy mystery   1943 · US · BW · 91mins

When a chorus girl is strangled with a G-string, the show's star, Barbara Stanwyck, teams up with Michael O'Shea, the comic whose advances she has been spurning, to find the killer. Based on *The G-String Murders*, written by America's most famous stripper, Gypsy Rose Lee, the movie has the perfect star in Stanwyck, who sings and strips to a number called *Take It off the E-String, Play It on the G-String*. Directed by William A Wellman and Oscar-nominated for its music (by Arthur Lange), it's a cracking little backstage drama (released as *Striptease Lady* in the UK) that combines suspense and comedy with an authentic smell of the greasepaint.

Barbara Stanwyck *Dixie Daisy* • Michael O'Shea *Biff Brannigan* • J Edward Bromberg *SB Foss* • Iris Adrian *Gee Gee Graham* • Gloria Dickson *Dolly Baxter* • Charles Dingle

Inspector Harrigan • ■ *Dir* William A Wellman • *Scr* James Gunn, from the novel *The G-String Murders* by Gypsy Rose Lee • *Music* Arthur Lange

Lady of Deceit ★★★
Film noir   1947 · US · BW · 92mins

A smashing hard-bitten *film noir* from that great postwar period when weak men fell headlong for tough *femmes fatales*, and destiny took no hostages. Here's Lawrence Tierney – better-known today for masterminding those pesky *Reservoir Dogs* – married to pretty Audrey Long but head-over-heels in love with his divorced sister, sultry Claire Trevor; you just know no good can come of this. The surprise for today's viewers is that the director is former editor Robert Wise, responsible for *The Sound of Music* and *West Side Story*, but also one of Hollywood's most under-rated tough-guy directors – just check out *I Want to Live!* and *Odds against Tomorrow*.

Lawrence Tierney *Sam Wild* • Claire Trevor *Helen Trent* • Walter Slezak *Arnett* • Phillip Terry *Fred* • Audrey Long *Georgia Staples* • Elisha Cook Jr *Marty* • Isabel Jewell *Laury Palmer* • Esther Howard *Mrs Kraft* ■ *Dir* Robert Wise • *Scr* Richard Macaulay, Eve Green, from the novel *Deadlier Than the Male* by James Gunn

Lady of the Tropics ★★
Melodrama   1939 · US · BW · 91mins

An aimless, penniless New Yorker (Robert Taylor), cruising the Far East with his intended fiancée's wealthy family, falls in love with a girl of mixed race (Hedy Lamarr) in Saigon. He abandons everything to marry her, but with tragic consequences. The film, directed by Jack Conway, does full justice to Lamarr's fabled beauty which, together with the atmosphere and a superbly polished and sinister performance from Joseph Schildkraut as the villain of the piece, makes this nonsensical romantic melodrama very watchable. However, the moral message is dubious.

Robert Taylor (1) *Bill Carey* • Hedy Lamarr *Manon De Vargnes* • Joseph Schildkraut *Pierre Delaroch* • Gloria Franklin *Nina* • Ernest Cossart *Father Antoine* • Natalie Moorhead *Mrs Hazlitt* ■ *Dir* Jack Conway • *Scr* Ben Hecht

Lady on a Train ★★★
Crime comedy   1945 · US · BW · 94mins

With a licence to trill, opera singer Deanna Durbin's cinematic singing career was one of the most remarkable success stories of the thirties and forties. This movie backed up her vocal talents with a better story than usual when, in the style of Agatha Christie, she sees a murder being committed on a passing train – and then has to try to convince the police. Her singing of *Night And Day* is the high-note of the movie.

Deanna Durbin *Nikki Collins* • Ralph Bellamy *Jonathan* • Edward Everett Horton *Mr Haskell* • George Coulouris *Mr Saunders* • Allen Jenkins *Danny* • Dan Duryea *Arnold* ■ *Dir* Charles David • *Scr* Edmund Beloin, Robert O'Brien, from a story by Leslie Charteris • *Music* Miklos Rozsa

The Lady Pays Off ★
Comedy drama   1951 · US · BW · 80mins

"Teacher of the Year" Linda Darnell faces something of an image crisis after she runs up gambling debts of $7,000 in Stephen McNally's Reno casino. McNally gives her an ultimatum: she has to coach his daughter or face exposure in the press. That's quite a clever premise for a plot, but then things get unbelievably tacky, with Darnell faking romantic interest in McNally, only to be redeemed by the awfully cute little girl. Sirk – regarded by some critics as a master of the melodrama – once said "I have no feeling for this picture at all" and neither will most viewers.

Linda Darnell *Evelyn Warren* • Stephen McNally *Matt Braddock* • Gigi Perreau *Diana Braddock* • Virginia Field *Kay Stoddard* ■ *Dir* Douglas Sirk • *Scr* Frank Gill Jr, Albert J Cohen

Lady Sings the Blues ★★★★
Musical biography   1972 · US · Colour · 143mins

A biopic of jazz legend Billie Holliday, solely financed by Berry Gordy's Tamla Motown record label and starring Diana Ross in her screen debut. Like all Hollywood biopics, it's a typical rollercoaster ride, with Holliday suffering highs, lows, marriage, divorce, drug addiction, adulation and an early death. Ross is required to age some 20 years and gives a rich, compelling performance that only occasionally shouts "Gimme an Oscar". (She got a nomination, but lost out to Liza Minnelli in *Cabaret*). Die-hard Holliday fans may have doubts about the reworked numbers, but the thirties ambience, nightclubs and drug culture are superbly evoked.

Diana Ross *Billie Holiday* • Billy Dee Williams *Louis McKay* • Richard Pryor *"Piano Man"* • James Callahan *Reg Hanley* • Paul Hampton *Harry* • Sid Melton *Jerry* • Virginia Capers *Mama Holiday* ■ *Dir* Sidney J Furie • *Scr* Terence McCloy, Chris Clark, Suzanne De Passe, from the autobiography by Billie Holiday, William Dufty

A Lady Takes a Chance ★★★
Romantic comedy   1943 · US · BW · 85mins

A nicely packaged star vehicle for petite Jean Arthur, successfully paired with big John Wayne in a romantic comedy about a rodeo star and a city gal. Arthur's second husband, the former singer Frank Ross, was the producer and surrounded her with talent: especially watchable is funny Phil Silvers as a tour guide. Director William A Seiter was one of Hollywood's unsung craftsmen. In this slight but engaging comedy, he cleverly keeps the romance bubbling.

Jean Arthur *Mollie Truesdale* • John Wayne *Duke Hudkins* • Phil Silvers *Smiley Lambert* • Mary Field *Florrie Bendix* • Don Costello *Drunk* • Grady Sutton *Malcolm* • Grant Withers *Bob* • Hans Conried *Gregg* • Charles Winninger *Waco* ■ *Dir* William A Seiter • *Scr* Robert Ardrey, Garson Kanin (uncredited), from a story by Jo Swerling

The Lady Takes a Flyer ★★
Drama   1958 · US · Colour · 94mins

Jack Arnold, who made his name directing some of the best sci-fi pictures of the 1950s, such as *It Came from Outer Space* and *The Incredible Shrinking Man*, subsequently had an incredibly shrinking career. This predictable confection starred blonde Lana Turner and white-haired Jeff Chandler as a squabbling married couple – both are pilots – each with rivals for their affections. At least, it gave fans of the glamorous Turner a chance to see her in an action role with her hair out of place.

Lana Turner *Maggie Colby* • Jeff Chandler *Mike Dandridge* • Richard Denning *Al Reynolds* • Andra Martin *Nikki Taylor* • Chuck Connors *Phil Donahue* • Reta Shaw *Nurse Kennedy* ■ *Dir* Jack Arnold • *Scr* Danny Arnold, from the story by Edmund H North

The Lady Vanishes ★★★★★ U
Classic thriller   1938 · UK · BW · 91mins

A close second behind *The 39 Steps* as the best film of Alfred Hitchcock's British period, this sublime comedy thriller was co-scripted by Alma Reville (Mrs Hitchcock) and the dynamic duo of Frank Launder and Sidney Gilliat. There isn't a wasted frame, as Michael Redgrave and Margaret Lockwood search a Balkan express for dotty Dame May Whitty. Basil Radford and Naunton Wayne drew all the plaudits as the cricket-mad Charters and Caldicott, but the support playing of Paul Lukas, Mary Clare and Cecil Parker is also first class. Hitchcock cameo fans should keep their eyes peeled during the London station scene. ▭ **DVD**

Margaret Lockwood *Iris Henderson* • Michael Redgrave *Gilbert Redman* • Paul Lukas *Dr Hartz* • Dame May Whitty *Miss Froy* • Cecil Parker *Eric Todhunter* • Linden Travers *"Mrs"Todhunter* • Naunton Wayne *Caldicott* • Basil Radford *Charters* • Mary Clare *Baroness* • Googie Withers *Blanche* ■ *Dir* Alfred Hitchcock • *Scr* Alma Reville, Sidney Gilliat, Frank Launder, from the novel *The Wheel Spins* by Ethel Lina White

The Lady Vanishes ★★ PG
Thriller   1979 · UK · Colour · 95mins

A pointless but watchable remake of the much-loved Hitchcock classic of 1938. It's slicker than the original – gone are the amateur model shots – but it totally lacks its charm, and has none of the atmosphere of impending war that gave the Hitchcock film so much of its meaning. But Miss Froy (Angela Lansbury in high camp mode) still goes missing on a train, leaving hapless Elliott Gould and Cybill Shepherd (both miscast) flitting from one compartment to the next, where they are ruthlessly upstaged by loveable old coves Arthur Lowe and Ian Carmichael as cricket-mad Charters and Caldicott. A typical case of aiming for an American audience and running out of steam in mid-Atlantic.

Elliott Gould *Robert Condon* • Cybill Shepherd *Amanda Kelly* • Angela Lansbury *Miss Froy* • Herbert Lom *Dr Hartz* • Arthur Lowe *Charters* • Ian Carmichael *Caldicott* • Gerald Harper *Mr Todhunter* • Jean Anderson *Baroness Kisling* ■ *Dir* Anthony Page • *Scr* George Axelrod, from the film *The Lady Vanishes* (1938) by

U = SUITABLE FOR ALL   Uc = SUITABLE FOR ALL, ESPECIALLY FOR YOUNG CHILDREN (VIDEO ONLY)   PG = PARENTAL GUIDANCE

Alma Reville, Frank Launder, Sidney Gilliat, from the novel *The Wheel Spins* by Ethel Lina White

The Lady Wants Mink ★★ U

Comedy 1953 · US · Colour · 92mins

You must leave your contemporary prejudices aside to enjoy this teaming of two of the most acerbic women in Hollywood history: Ruth Hussey and the redoubtable Eve Arden, who could make any line sound witty. Hussey stars as the wife breeding minks so she can own a fur coat. Husband Dennis O'Keefe has no chance of competing with Hussey, let alone Arden, but veterans William Demarest and Gene Lockhart do what they can with the feeble material.

Dennis O'Keefe *Jim Connors* • Ruth Hussey *Nora Connors* • Eve Arden *Gladys Jones* • William Demarest *Harvey Jones* • Gene Lockhart *Mr Heggie* • Hope Emerson *Mrs Hoxie* ■ *Dir* William A Seiter • *Scr* Dane Lussier, Richard Alan Simmons, from a story by Leonard Neubauer, Lou Schor

Lady Windermere's Fan ★★★★

Silent comedy drama
1925 · US · BW · 94mins

The Lubitsch touch – the ironic, risque style of director Ernst Lubitsch – was never more blatant in the way he lightens up one of Oscar Wilde's most judgemental plays, when adventuress Mrs Erlynne intrudes on the great and the good and threatens scandal. Ronald Colman, May McAvoy and Irene Rich look aghast in one of Lubitsch's best silent movies,

Ronald Colman *Lord Darlington* • Irene Rich *Mrs Erlynne* • May McAvoy *Lady Windermere* • Bert Lytell *Lord Windermere* • Edward Martindel *Lord Augustus* ■ *Dir* Ernst Lubitsch • *Scr* Julien Josephson, from the play by Oscar Wilde

Lady with a Past ★★★★

Romantic comedy 1932 · US · BW · 70mins

The delightful Constance Bennett (older sister of Joan), briefly the highest paid female star in Hollywood in the thirties, was seen at her best in sophisticated, slightly risqué comedies. Here she is a good little rich girl, who discovers that she is much more popular with men if they think she's bad. Naturally, it all takes place in a chic and naughty Paris. Ben Lyon, once popular on British radio in *Life with the Lyons*, wittily plays Bennett's paid escort. Handsome David Manners is perfect as the young man who falls for her new self.

Constance Bennett *Venice Muir* • Ben Lyon *Guy Bryson* • David Manners *Donnie Wainwright* • Don Alvarado *The Argentine* • Albert Conti *René* ■ *Dir* Edward H Griffith • *Scr* Horace Jackson, from the story by Harriet Henry

The Lady with Red Boots ★★★

Fantasy drama
1974 · Fr /It/Sp · Colour · 92mins

Juan Buñuel, son of the legendary Spanish director, called on two of his father's best known stars, Catherine Deneuve and Fernando Rey, for this psychological thriller in which the cruel tricks played by writer Deneuve on manipulative millionaire Rey end in tragedy. Exploring the relationship between life and art, this highly stylised picture has all the hallmarks of a Buñuel film. However Juan lacks the control that characterised his father's use of satire and realism, and the outcome is more than a tad confusing. In French with English subtitles.

Catherine Deneuve *Françoise* • Fernando Rey *Perrot* • Adalberto Maria Merli *Man* • Jacques Weber *Painter* ■ *Dir* Juan Buñuel • *Scr* Juan Buñuel, Roberto Bodegas (dialogue)

The Lady with the Lamp ★★ U

Biography 1951 · UK · BW · 99mins

Having twice played Queen Victoria, Anna Neagle gave up her crown in this picture to Helena Pickard so that she could don a simple cloth cap in this reverential biopic of Florence Nightingale. Once again under the tutelage of husband Herbert Wilcox, she gives an imperious performance as the daughter of a Hampshire landowner who reformed nursing and became a national icon during the Crimean War. However, such an achievement wasn't considered sufficient for movie audiences and a disproportionate amount of time is devoted to the romance with Michael Wilding. [video]

Anna Neagle *Florence Nightingale* • Michael Wilding *Sidney Herbert* • Gladys Young *Mrs Bracebridge* • Felix Aylmer *Lord Palmerston* • Julian D'Albie *Mr Bracebridge* • Arthur Young *WE Gladstone* • Edwin Styles *Mr Nightingale* • Helen Shingler *Parthenope Nightingale* • Helena Pickard *Queen Victoria* ■ *Dir* Herbert Wilcox • *Scr* Warren Chetham Strode, from the play by Reginald Berkeley

The Lady with the Little Dog ★★★★

Drama 1960 · USSR · BW · 88mins

This remains one of the most admired film adaptations of Anton Chekhov, although the director Josef Heifitz directed two others almost as good, *In the Town of S* and *Duel*. The sensitive direction subtly evokes the prose of Chekhov's short love story, reflecting the lovers' psychology. The contrast between the seaside resort of Yalta in summer, where the two unhappily married people meet and fall in love, and Moscow in winter, is vividly portrayed. Iya Savvina (in her debut) gives a beautiful performance in the title role. In Russian with English subtitles.

Iya Savvina *Anna Sergeyevna* • Alexei Batalov *Dmitri Gurov* • Nina Alisova *Madame Gurov* ■ *Dir* Josef Heifitz • *Scr* Josef Heifitz, from the story *Dama s Sobachkoy* by Anton Chekhov

A Lady without Passport ★★★

Crime drama 1950 · US · BW · 73mins

Director Joseph H Lewis was acknowledged as the great stylist of the Hollywood B-picture, but his touch was not noticeable in this *film noir* thriller about illegal aliens – which include a glamorous Hungarian played by Hedy Lamarr – trying to enter the United States. The focus of attention is so ambigious it comes across as confused, without any of the expected thrills.

Hedy Lamarr *Marianne Lorress* • John Hodiak *Pete Karczag* • James Craig *Frank Westlake* • George Macready *Palinov* • Steven Geray *Frenchman* • Bruce Cowling *Archer Delby James* ■ *Dir* Joseph H Lewis • *Scr* Howard Dimsdale, Cyril Hume, from a story by Lawrence Taylor

Ladybird Ladybird ★★★★ 18

Drama 1994 · UK · Colour · 97mins

Stand-up comic Crissy Rock won a Silver Bear at the Berlin Film Festival for her gutsy, warts-and-all performance in this harrowing drama from Ken Loach that will leave you emotionally exhausted. She hurls herself into the part of mouthy Merseysider Maggie, whose string of abusive relationships results in her children being taken by the social services, and is simply but effectively supported by Vladimir Vega as a Paraguayan refugee who becomes her lover. By maintaining his typically low-key approach, Loach expertly prevents the endless crises from slipping into hysterical melodrama, while also managing to steer a course between the tempestuous Rock and the impassive care workers. Contains violence, swearing and nudity. [video]

Crissy Rock *Maggie* • Vladimir Vega *Jorge* • Sandie Lavelle *Mairead* • Mauricio Venegas *Adrian* • Ray Winstone *Simon* • Clare Perkins *Jill* • Jason Stracey *Sean* ■ *Dir* Ken Loach • *Scr* Rona Munro

Ladybug, Ladybug ★★★

Drama 1963 · US · BW · 81mins

This is one of the American film industry's odder responses to the Cold War and the possibility of nuclear oblivion. Made for $350,000 by the husband and wife team of Frank and Eleanor Perry – who made the disturbing psychological drama *David and Lisa* – it's set in an ordinary school in Ordinaryville, USA, and shows what happens when the head teacher has to prepare the school and its pupils for a nuclear blast. Vaguely resembling Peter Watkins's banned BBC film *The War Game*, the Perrys produce a weird blend of public information, corny melodrama and *Lord of the Flies*. It's very arty, but a relic worth watching.

June Connell *Mrs Maxton* • William H Daniels [William Daniels] *Mr Calkins* • James Frawley *Truck driver* • Richard Hamilton *JoAnn's father* • Kathryn Hays *Mrs Forbes* • Jane Hoffman *Mrs Hayworth* ■ *Dir* Frank Perry • *Scr* Eleanor Perry, from an article by Lois Dickert

Ladybugs ★★ PG

Comedy 1992 · US · Colour · 84mins

In this raucous Rodney Dangerfield comedy, the burly comic, whose abrasive style has never really found a niche in film, blusters in typical fashion as a salesman whose only chance of promotion lies in turning the company's girls' soccer team into champions. Naturally, it requires a lad in drag to act as playmaker and there is a record attempt at cramming the most locker-room gags into a single picture. Sadly the laughs are in short supply – until, that is, you see Hollywood's idea of a football match. Contains some swearing. [video]

Rodney Dangerfield *Chester Lee* • Jackée *Julie Benson* • Jonathan Brandis *Matthew/Martha* • Ilene Graff *Bess* • Vinessa Shaw *Kimberly Mullen* • Tom Parks *Dave Mullen* • Jeannetta Arnette [Jeanetta Arnette] *Glynnis Mullen* ■ *Dir* Sidney J Furie • *Scr* Curtis Burch

Ladyhawke ★★★★ PG

Fantasy adventure
1985 · US · Colour · 118mins

Michelle Pfeiffer, as the title's pretty predator, and Rutger Hauer as a legendary lycanthrope, give human poignancy to this medieval fairy tale of lovers cursed to shape-change into animals. Richard Donner, who made the first *Superman* adventure, proves to have an elegant eye for ancient as well as everyday fables, and it's all ravishingly filmed in Italy. Leo McKern dispels the dark from the Dark Ages with a comic turn as a Friar Tuck-ish priest, and Matthew Broderick makes an appealing young hero. Contains some violence. [video]

Matthew Broderick *Phillipe Gaston* • Rutger Hauer *Etienne Of Navarre* • Michelle Pfeiffer *Isabeau Of Anjou* • Leo McKern *Father Imperius* • John Wood *Bishop* • Ken Hutchison *Captain Marquet* • Alfred Molina *Cezar* ■ *Dir* Richard Donner • *Scr* Edward Khmara, Michael Thomas, Tom Mankiewicz, from a story by Edward Khmara • *Cinematographer* Vittorio Storaro

Ladykiller ★★ 15

Murder mystery 1992 · US · Colour · 87mins

A routine, tough, sexy thriller which offers yet another variation on that now familiar *Jagged Edge* scenario. Mimi Rogers is a detective who falls for the mysterious John Shea, only to suspect that he may be implicated in the deaths of two women. Director Michael Scott has assembled a classy cast, which includes Alice Krige and Tom Irwin, but fails to inject any freshness into a somewhat predictable plot. Contains violence. [video]

Mimi Rogers *Michael Madison* • John Shea *Jonathan "Jack" Packard Jr* • Tom Irwin *Vinnie* • Alice Krige *May Packard* • Bob Gunton *Wolkowski* • Bert Remsen *Medical Examiner O'Malley* • Art Kimbro *Traversy Manager* • Elizabeth Keifer *Carol Longfellow* ■ *Dir* Michael Scott • *Scr* Shelley Evans

The Ladykillers ★★★★★ U

Classic comedy 1955 · UK · Colour · 86mins

A supreme blend of the seedy and the sinister, this was Ealing's last post – indeed, the studio was shutting up shop as this film went on release. Directed with a mischievous glint by Alexander Mackendrick, the picture loses its way momentarily in the middle, when the stock scenario of a gang of ruthless thugs being stymied by a dotty innocent (the marvellous Katie Johnson as their landlady) wears a little thin. Nevertheless, this is British comedy at its best, with eccentric characters never for a second seeming out of place in the most everyday locations. Alec Guinness and his minions, among them Herbert Lom and Peter Sellers, are a marvellous collection of misfits, but they lose every scene to the Bafta-winning Johnson. [video]

Alec Guinness *Professor Marcus* • Herbert Lom *Louis* • Peter Sellers *Harry* • Cecil Parker *Major* • Danny Green *One-Round* • Katie Johnson *Mrs Wilberforce* • Jack Warner *Police superintendent* • Frankie Howerd *Barrow boy* • Philip Stainton *Police sergeant* • Kenneth Connor *Cab Driver* • Edie Martin *Lettice* ■ *Dir* Alexander Mackendrick • *Scr* William Rose, from his story

Ladykillers ★★ 15

Murder mystery 1988 · US · Colour · 95mins

The Full Monty may have focused attention on male strippers, but this tatty thriller on the same subject is neither titillating nor particularly suspenseful. Marilu Henner, a useful support in movies such as *LA Story*, is wasted in the lead role, playing the owner of the club of the title, one of whose male attractions turns up dead. The presence of Susan Blakely and Lesley-Anne Down gives the whole thing its bland made-for-TV feel, and Robert Lewis's direction plods along in uninspired fashion. ▦

Marilu Henner *Samantha Flannery* • Susan Blakely *Lilah Corbett* • Lesley-Anne Down *Morganna Ross* • William Lucking *Captain Buchholz* ■ *Dir* Robert Lewis • *Scr* Gregory S Dinallo

A Lady's Morals ★★★

Musical romance 1930 · US · BW · 86mins

The first of eight films made by talented Metropolitan Opera soprano Grace Moore before she was tragically killed in a plane crash in 1947. Moore stars as the famous opera singer Jenny Lind, the "Swedish Nightingale", in this highly fanciful treatment of what purports to be a complicated romantic relationship in Lind's life. An awesome hotch-potch of styles – it begins like a comic operetta and progresses to tragic romantic melodrama – it is nonetheless very charming and demonstrates why Moore made opera so popular. Sidney Franklin directs and Reginald Denny co-stars most winningly as Lind's persistent, volatile and self-sacrificing suitor.

Grace Moore *Jenny Lind* • Reginald Denny *Paul Brandt* • Wallace Beery *Barnum* • Gus Shy *Olaf* • Gilbert Emery *Broughm* ■ *Dir* Sidney Franklin • *Scr* Hans Kräly, Claudine West, John Meehan, Arthur Richman, from a story by Dorothy Farnum

Laguna Heat ★★ 18

Thriller 1987 · US · Colour · 104mins

Poor old Harry Hamlin hasn't made the best career decisions. First he wore a toga in *Clash of the Titans*, then he starred in the appalling misfire *Making Love*, and when he finally scored a hit in TV's *LA Law*, he decided to leave the series at the height of its success. In this made-for cable thriller, he plays an LA cop who returns to his home town, Laguna, and becomes embroiled in a series of murders. ▦

Harry Hamlin *Tom Shepherd* • Catherine Hicks *Jane Algernon* • Jason Robards *Jason Robards Jr* *Wade Shepherd* • Anne Francis *Helene Long* • Rip Torn *Joe Datilla* • James Gammon *Grimes* ■ *Dir* Simon Langton • *Scr* Pete Hamill, David Morris, David Eyre, Henry Bromell, from the novel by T Jefferson Parker

The Lair of the White Worm ★★★ 18

Horror 1988 · UK · Colour · 89mins

Nude nuns, lesbian catfights and snake-cult rituals; what else could this be but a Ken Russell fantasy sextravaganza? Based on Bram Stoker's least famous novel, and starring a then unknown Hugh Grant, this Christianity versus Paganism tract is a delirious hoot from start to finish, so serious horror fans had better look elsewhere. Those in the mood for side-splitting nonsense – the kind that has reptilian Amanda Donohoe nakedly writhing through her country mansion to snake-charming music – are on the right track. Contains violence, swearing and sex scenes. ▦

Amanda Donohoe *Lady Sylvia Marsh* • Hugh Grant *Lord James D'Ampton* • Catherine Oxenberg *Eve Trent* • Peter Capaldi *Angus Flint* • Sammi Davis *Mary Trent* • Stratford Johns *Peters* • Paul Brooke *PC Erny* • Imogen Claire *Dorothy Trent* • Chris Pitt *Kevin* • Gina McKee *Nurse Gladwell* ■ *Dir* Ken Russell • *Scr* Ken Russell, from the novel by Bram Stoker

Lake Consequence ★★ 18

Erotic melodrama 1992 · US · Colour · 86mins

9 1/2 Weeks opened up the floodgates for tales of bored women "finding themelves" through hot and sweaty encounters, and this is a typical soft-core, soft-focus example of that fornicating flurry. Joan Severance plays Irene, a repressed housewife with a loving husband and son, whose temperature is raised by free-spirited gardener Billy Zane. Rope in the latter's girlfriend (May Karasun), a diabolical script and a hot-tub built for three, and you have a top-shelf title of little distinction. Not many people thought at the time that Zane would later have third billing in *Titanic*, one of the biggest films of all time. ▦

Joan Severance *Irene* • Billy Zane *Billy* • Whip Hubley *Jim* ■ *Dir* Rafael Eisenman • *Scr* Zalman King, Melanie Finn, Henry Cobbold, from a story by MacGregor Douglas

Lake Placid ★★★ 15

Adventure thriller 1999 · US · Colour · 82mins

Writer/producer David E Kelley, of *Ally McBeal* fame, here turns his hand to a daft creature feature that will tickle fans of *The Evil Dead* and *The Relic*. There's something under the surface of Black Lake that's making monster munchies out of visitors, so warden Bill Pullman, paleontologist Bridget Fonda and nutty millionaire Oliver Platt decide to hunt down the critter before any other bits of semi-digested locals pop to the surface. Fonda and Pullman play it for laughs, but once again the show is stolen by Platt, fast becoming one of the funniest supporting actors on film.

Bill Pullman *Jack Wells* • Bridget Fonda *Kelly Scott* • Oliver Platt *Hector Cyr* • Brendan Gleeson *Sheriff Hank Keough* • Betty White *Mrs Delores Bickerman* ■ *Dir* Steve Miner • *Scr* David E Kelley

Lamb ★★★★ 15

Drama 1985 · UK · Colour · 105mins

Although the central characters are a Christian Brother and one of his unruly

students, this is one of the most sensitive "father and son" studies since *Bicycle Thieves*. Liam Neeson gives a dedicated performance as the religious teacher who finds a new vocation when he "kidnaps" epileptic Hugh O'Conor to spare him from the vindictive violence of headmaster Ian Bannen. Bernard MacLaverty adapts his own novel with care and genuine concern for his characters, without letting the action get bogged down in either spirituality or sentimentality. Director Colin Gregg makes London look disturbingly unwelcoming and handles the tragic conclusion with delicacy and truth. ▦

Liam Neeson *Brother Sebastian, Michael Lamb* • Harry Towb *Priest* • Hugh O'Conor *Owen Kane* • Frances Tomelty *Mrs Kane* • Ian Bannen *Brother Benedict* • Ronan Wilmot *Brother Fintan* • Denis Carey *Mr Lamb* ■ *Dir* Colin Gregg • *Scr* Bernard MacLaverty, from his novel

Lambada ★★ 15

Drama 1990 · US · Colour · 99mins

Remember the lambada, that dance fad that lasted about as long as an episode of *Come Dancing*? Well, this is the movie-of-the-dance as directed by Joel Silberg, who did a similar service to break-dancing in *Breakin'*. The plot is extremely unlikely (J Eddie Peck, maths teacher by day, dancer by night, teaches dropouts in the backroom of the dance club) and the dancing scenes are filmed as if they were soft porn, but Peck and his co-stars do their best with what's left.

J Eddie Peck *Kevin Laird* • Melora Hardin *Sandy* • Shabba-Doo *Raone* • Ricky Paull Goldin *Dean* • Basil Hoffman *Superintendent Leland* • Dennis Burkley *Uncle Big* • Keene Curtis *Principal Singleton* ■ *Dir* Joel Silberg • *Scr* Sheldon Renan, Joel Silberg, from a story by Joel Silberg

Lambada! The Forbidden Dance ★ 15

Drama 1990 · US · Colour · 93mins

One of two Lambada movies released at the same time to cash in on the dance craze. Here, the hip-swivelling Latin dance is merely a subplot to spice up the dire tale of a Brazilian princess who goes to America to campaign on behalf of the rainforest and ends up strutting her funky stuff on TV. A ludicrous premise if ever there was one and it's not helped by the casting of former Miss USA Laura Herring in the lead and eighties' popsters Kid Creole and the Coconuts, who supply some of the music. Watch at your peril. ▦

Laura Herring *Nisa* • Jeff James *Jason* • Sid Haig *Joa* • Richard Lynch *Benjamin Maxwell* • Barbra Brighton *Ashley* • Angela Moya *Carmen* ■ *Dir* Greydon Clark • *Scr* Roy Langsdon, John Platt

Lamerica ★★★

Drama 1994 · Fr/It · Colour · 116mins

This edgy drama is set in Albania just after the fall of communism. Two Italian capitalists aim to exploit a system in crisis by setting up a business front and intending to pocket all the proceeds. Looking for a fall guy they stumble on the wrong man, a recently liberated political prisoner. The

Italians, initially ruthless, are forced to question their values and end up suffering under Albanian reconstruction. A politically poignant and powerful examination of how a country in turmoil causes personal crises. In Italian with English subtitles.

Enrico Lo Verso *Gino* • Michele Placido *Fiore* • Carmelo Di Mazzarelli *Spiro* • Piro Milkani *Selimi* • Elida Janushi *Selimi's Cousin* ■ *Dir* Gianni Amelio • *Scr* Gianni Amelio, Andrea Porporati, Alessandro Sermoneta

The Lamp ★ 18

Horror 1987 · US · Colour · 85mins

Never released in UK cinemas, this daft horror was one of several in the last two decades to raid folklore for under-exploited evil spirits. In this case, a genie, released from its lamp, goes berserk and kills most of the young unknowns who make up the cast. The only "name" is Deborah Winters, the former child actress who starred in *The People Next Door* (1970). A promising idea, which in more creative hands could have developed into the likes of *Gremlins*, is frittered away through uninspired writing and direction. ▦

Deborah Winters *Eve Farrell* • James Huston *Dr Al Wallace* • Andra St Ivanyi *Alex Wallace* • Scott Bankston *Ted Pinson* • Mark Mitchell *Mike Daley* ■ *Dir* Tom Daley • *Scr* Warren Chaney

The Lamp Still Burns ★★

Drama 1943 · UK · BW · 90mins

Few actresses could suffer with the style and dignity of Rosamund John. In the third and last of the films she made for Leslie Howard (here producing his final picture), she plays a trainee nurse learning that gentility gets you nowhere in a crisis. Every hospital cliché has been scrubbed down and pressed into service – the cold efficient matron, the cantankerous patient and the handsome young doctor – and the wartime references give the film a home-front heroism that, while comforting for audiences of the time, now makes the whole thing seem as stiff as a starched uniform.

Rosamund John *Hilary Clarke* • Stewart Granger *Larry Rains* • Godfrey Tearle *Sir Marshall Frayne* • Sophie Stewart *Christine Morris* • John Laurie *Mr Hervey* • Margaret Vyner *Pamela Siddell* • Cathleen Nesbitt *Matron* • Eric Micklewood *Dr Trevor* • Joyce Grenfell *Dr Barratt* ■ *Dir* Maurice Elvey • *Scr* Elizabeth Baron, Roland Pertwee, Major Neilson, from the novel *One Pair of Feet* by Monica Dickens

Lana in Love ★★★

Comedy 1991 · Can · Colour · 85mins

Having been spoilt for choice in *Julia Has Two Lovers*, Daphna Kastner experiences the pain of loneliness and the uncertainty of the lonely hearts columns in this reunion with director Bashar Shbib (with whom she'd co-written *Julia*). As the journalist whose busy life has left her little room for love, Kastner convincingly veers between the excitement of attraction and the nagging paranoia of self-doubt after she begins dating the seemingly suitable Clark Gregg.

Daphna Kastner *Lana* • Clark Gregg *Marty* ■ *Dir* Bashar Shbib • *Scr* Bashar Shbib, Daphna Kastner

Lancelot and Guinevere ★★

Adventure drama
1963 · UK · Colour · 116mins

Real-life married couple Cornel Wilde and Jean Wallace play Lancelot and Guinevere, whose lingering love for each other almost destroys King Arthur's Camelot. The supporting cast is second-string British; the interiors were shot at Pinewood; Yugoslavia's army gets to dress up in medieval armour and run all over Ye Olde England. In other words, it's a cheapo that manages to look reasonably well-nourished. Wilde directs with his customary dash and sometimes startling style.

Cornel Wilde *Sir Lancelot* • Jean Wallace *Queen Guinevere* • Brian Aherne *King Arthur* • George Baker *Sir Gawaine* • Archie Duncan *Sir Lamorak* ■ *Dir* Cornel Wilde • *Scr* Richard Schayer, Jefferson Pascal, from the poem *La Morte d'Arthur* by Thomas Malory

Lancelot du Lac ★★★ PG

Historical drama
1974 · Fr/It · Colour · 79mins

Working on a shoestring budget it's remarkable that director Robert Bresson has managed to re-create the rich tapestry that is the timeworn world of King Arthur, his Knights and the Round Table code. In this reinterpretation of the legend, Lancelot (Luc Simon) returns with fellow knights after a fruitless attempt to unearth the Holy Grail. All are suffering from a tremendous loss of faith, which drives Lancelot straight back into the arms of Arthur's Guenièvre (Laura Duke Condominas). Instead of a straightforward moody swashbuckler, Bresson's skill lies in his ability here to make the film about crisis of belief and it is a fascinating study. In French with English subtitles. 🖭

Luc Simon *Lancelot du Lac* • Laura Duke Condominas *Guenièvre* • Humbert Balsan *Gawain* • Vladimir Antolek-Oresek *Artus* • Patrick Bernard *Mordred* • Arthur De Montalembert *Lionel* ■ *Dir/Scr* Robert Bresson • *Cinematographer* Pasqualino De Santis

Lancer Spy ★★★

Spy drama 1937 · US · BW · 84mins

In this atypical 20th Century-Fox thirties melodrama, the urbane George Sanders has a rare meaty double role, starring as both a Prussian baron and the British officer sent out to replace him, only to find himself enmeshed in the caresses of cabaret singer Dolores Del Rio. The first half is very exciting, with a cast full of wonderfully sinister faces, including Peter Lorre and Lionel Atwill. But Sanders's fellow expatriate, Russian director Gregory Ratoff, seems to tire of the romp, and the film grows lacklustre as it draws on, and is not nearly as swashbuckling as it ought to have been.

Dolores Del Rio *Dolores Daria* • George Sanders *Lieutenant Bruce/Baron Von Rohback* • Peter Lorre *Major Sigfried Gruning* • Virginia Field *Joan Bruce* • Sig Rumann [Sig Ruman] *Lieutenant Colonel Gottfried Hollen* • Joseph Schildkraut *Prince Ferdi Zu Schwarzwald* • Maurice Moscovich *General Von Meinhardt* •

Lionel Atwill *Colonel Fenwick* ■ *Dir* Gregory Ratoff • *Scr* Philip Dunne, from the story *Lancer Spy* by Marthe McKenna

Land and Freedom ★★★ 15

Wartime drama
1995 · UK/Sp/Ger · Colour · 104mins

In spite of some spirited performances, Ken Loach's Spanish Civil War drama too often gets bogged down in its bid for authenticity. The opening sequence in which Liverpudlian Ian Hart decides to join up rings hollow and, no matter how impassioned the discussion on the merits of collectivisation and regardless of the way in which the movie highlights the divisions that hindered the Republican cause, this still makes for dull viewing. Nevertheless, Loach manages to convey the commitment of the combatants and the chaos of the conflict, and restores some of the grim reality that was romanticised by a generation of left-wing novelists. In English, Spanish and Catalan with subtitles. 🖭

Ian Hart *David Carne* • Rosana Pastor *Blanca* • Iciar Bollain *Maite* • Tom Gilroy *Gene Lawrence* • Marc Martinez *Vidal* • Frédéric Pierrot *Bernard* • Suzanne Maddock *Kim* • Mandy Walsh *Dot* • Angela Clarke *Kitty* ■ *Dir* Ken Loach • *Scr* Jim Allen

The Land before Time ★★★★ U

Animated adventure
1988 · US · Colour · 65mins

If your little dinosaur lovers are still a bit young for *Jurassic Park*, then this charming cartoon should have them in raptures. Directed by Don Bluth, this is essentially a prehistoric reworking of his own *An American Tail*, with a displaced young brontosaurus called Littlefoot and his four dino-tot companions setting out across a strange and dangerous land in search of their families. Their adventures are pretty hair-raising as they encounter not only deadly predators, but also all manner of environmental hazards. Youngsters will love the adorable critters, while adults can admire the eerie landscape of a past age. 🖭

Fred Gwynne *Narrator* • Gabriel Damon *Littlefoot* • Helen Shaver *Littlefoot's mother* • Bill Erwin *Grandfather* • Candice Houston *Cera* • Pat Hingle *Rooter* ■ *Dir* Don Bluth • *Scr* Stu Krieger, from a story by Judy Freudberg, from Tony Geiss

The Land before Time II: the Great Valley Adventure ★★ U

Animated adventure
1994 · US · Colour · 70mins

Having struggled so heroically to reach the Great Valley, it was inevitable that Littlefoot and his friends would soon find it a less than idyllic place and, sure enough, trouble comes in the form of a couple of oviraptors, who make off into the Mysterious Beyond with an egg that simply has to be recovered. Roy Smith's direction is less assured than Don Bluth's on the original and there are some truly awful songs. But youngsters will enjoy being reunited with their prehistoric pals and meeting Chomper the baby T-rex. 🖭

Jeff Bennet *Petrie/Ozzie* • Linda Gary *Grandma* • Heather Hogan *Ducky* • Candace Hutson *Cera* • John Ingle *Narrator/Cera's father* ■ *Dir* Roy Smith • *Scr* John Loy, John Ludin, Dev Ross

The Land Girls ★★ 12

Period drama 1997 · UK/Fr · Colour · 110mins

Life on the home front is given a distinctly rosy glow in this naffly nostalgic adaptation of Angela Huth's novel. Anna Friel's randy northerner, Rachel Weisz's sheltered blue-stocking and Catherine McCormack's bourgeois prude are surely the most stereotypical volunteers in the history of the Women's Land Army. Consequently, from the moment these urban interlopers arrive at Tom Georgeson's Dorset farm, there isn't a single scene that ends unexpectedly. The performances are earnest, the scenery beautiful, but as the clichés clunk into place with deadening predictability. Contains sexual references. 🖭 ❱DVD❰

Catherine McCormack *Stella* • Rachel Weisz *Ag* • Anna Friel *Prue* • Steven Mackintosh *Joe Lawrence* • Tom Georgeson *Mr Lawrence* • Maureen O'Brien *Mrs Lawrence* ■ *Dir* David Leland • *Scr* David Leland, Keith Dewhurst, from the novel by Angela Huth

Land of the Pharaohs ★★★ U

Historical epic 1955 · US · Colour · 103mins

The stiff dialogue in parts of this Hollywood epic about pyramid-building and palace intrigue in ancient Egypt prompts the conclusion that co-writer William Faulkner would have been better off sticking to novels. But director Howard Hawks, the master storyteller, found it hard to make a bad movie and, all in all, this is a handsome and very serviceable historical melodrama, conceived and realised on the grand scale. Joan Collins is deliciously villainous as Princess Nellifer.

Jack Hawkins *Pharaoh* • Joan Collins *Princess Nellifer* • Dewey Martin *Senta* • Alexis Minotis *Hamar* • James Robertson-Justice *Vashtar* • Luisa Boni *Kyra* • Sydney Chaplin *Treneh* • James Hayter *Vashtar's servant* ■ *Dir* Howard Hawks • *Scr* William Faulkner, Harry Kurnitz, Harold Jack Bloom

Land Raiders ★★

Western 1969 · US · Colour · 101mins

An undistinguished western with a truly motley cast that makes this worth watching. Telly Savalas and *Route 66*'s George Maharis are surely the most unlikely brothers, but not quite as unlikely as the latter's Mexican accent. Also along for the bleak and dusty ride are stunning redhead Arlene Dahl and the girl Janet Landgard. Connoisseurs of the ludicrous will also enjoy finding Guy Rolfe and George Coulouris among the dross. It's sadistic, too.

Telly Savalas *Vince Carden* • George Maharis *Paul Cardenas* • Arlene Dahl *Martha Carden* • Janet Landgard *Kate Mayfield* • Jocelyn Lane *Luisa Rojas* • George Coulouris *Cardenas* ■ *Dir* Nathan H Juran [Nathan Juran] • *Scr* Ken Pettus, from a story by Ken Pettus, Jesse Lasky Jr, Pat Silver

The Land That Time Forgot ★★ PG

Fantasy adventure
1974 · UK · Colour · 86mins

The first, and worst, of the trilogy of Edgar Rice Burroughs lost world adventures produced by Amicus, despite the fact that it was co-scripted by sci-fi giant Michael Moorcock. A First World War submarine discovers an uncharted South American haven for dinosaurs, cavemen and volcanoes in director Kevin Connor's excessively fake and slipshod saga. Doug McClure is out of his depth as the heroic lead, and the puppet monsters – a phoney amalgam of prop heads and men in rubber suits dangling on wires – are just as weak. 🖭

Doug McClure *Bowen Tyler* • John McEnery *Captain Von Schoenvorts* • Susan Penhaligon *Lisa Clayton* • Keith Barron *Bradley* • Anthony Ainley *Dietz* • Godfrey James *Borg* • Bobby Farr *Ahm* • Declan Mulholland *Olson* ■ *Dir* Kevin Connor • *Scr* James Cawthorn, Michael Moorcock, from the novel by Edgar Rice Burroughs

The Land Unknown ★★

Fantasy adventure 1957 · US · BW · 78mins

A really cheesy sci-fi drama with Jock Mahoney, a TV star and one-time Tarzan, down in the frozen wastes of Antarctica where dinosaurs frolic around a hot water oasis, apparently discovered in 1947. This is *The Lost World* on ice, with an entire menagerie of monsters, including the pantomime villain T-Rex as well as the flying pterodactyl which brings down our hero's helicopter in the opening scenes. Shawn Smith adds some romantic interest as a newshound whose clothes become more sparse, while Henry Brandon is the man who's been this way before and clearly left his marbles behind.

Jock Mahoney *Commander Hal Roberts* • Shawn Smith *Margaret Hathaway* • William Reynolds *Lieutenant Jack Carmen* • Henry Brandon *Hunter* • Phil Harvey *Steve Miller* • Douglas Kennedy *Captain Burnham* ■ *Dir* Virgil Vogel [Virgil W Vogel] • *Scr* Laszlo Gorog, from a story by Charles Palmer

Land without Bread ★★★★★

Documentary 1933 · Sp · BW · 29mins

An extraordinary documentary by the great surrealist director, Luis Buñuel, about a poverty-blighted region of north Spain, hemmed in by mountains. In-breeding between inhabitants has resulted in a race of grotesque dwarfs, and the final scene of contrast is the interior of a gold-encrusted Catholic church opposed to the dreadful misery of its context. One of Buñuel's most formidable anti-clerical swipes, it's still as angry as when it was made. Its images may be hideous, but they are true. A Spanish language film.

Abel Jacquin *Narrator* ■ *Dir/Scr* Luis Buñuel

Land without Music ★★

Musical 1936 · UK · BW · 80mins

Walter Forde was a highly versatile director, but, on the evidence of this frippery, light opera was definitely not his forte. The story was typically paper-thin, as famous tenor Richard Tauber returns to his homeland to lead a melodic revolution against princess Diana Napier (Tauber's real-life wife), who has outlawed music. There's a chief of police who smuggles instruments, a couple of romances and plenty of musical interludes to keep things frothy. But, in all honesty, there are few memorable moments, and most of them are provided by Jimmy Durante, who is eminently watchable as a journalist with a song in his heart.

Richard Tauber *Mario Carlini* • Jimmy Durante *Jonah J Whistler* • Diana Napier *Princess Regent* • June Clyde *Sadie Whistler* • Derrick de Marney *Rudolpho Strozzi* • Esme Percy *Austrian Ambassador* • George Hayes *Captain Strozzi* • John Hepworth *Pedro* ■ *Dir* Walter Forde • *Scr* Rudolph Bernauer, Marian Dix, L DuGarde Peach, from a story by Fritz Koselka, Armin Robinson

Landfall ★ U
Second World War drama
1949 · UK · BW · 88mins

Fighter pilot Michael Denison, poor chap, thinks he has sunk a British submarine while patrolling the skies over the English Channel. The court thinks so, too, and he gets transferred to desk duties and unburdens his guilt to barmaid Patricia Plunkett who decides to prove he actually sunk a German sub. Love blossoms, of course, but only after Miss Plunkett is convinced that a barmaid could ever court someone so dashing and so upper class as Michael Denison without upsetting the social applecart. Laurence Harvey can also be glimpsed in this dainty item from a vanished era of British war movies.

Michael Denison *Rick* • Patricia Plunkett *Mona* • Edith Sharpe *Rick's mother* • Sebastian Shaw *Wing-Cdr Dickens* • Maurice Denham *Wing-Cdr Hewitt* • Laurence Harvey *P/O Weaver* ■ *Dir* Ken Annakin • *Scr* Talbot Jennings, Gilbert Gunn, Anne Burnaby, from the novel by Nevil Shute

The Landlord ★★★★
Comedy drama 1970 · US · Colour · 109mins

Former editor Hal Ashby made a terrific debut as director with this comedy drama, featuring a superb Beau Bridges as the wealthy scion who learns about humanity and the African-American experience in New York from his tenants. Pearl Bailey and Diana Sands shine, and there's good work too from Robert Klein and Lee Grant. Fans of Ashby's subsequent cult classic *Harold and Maude* should check this out, as there is a lot to enjoy.

Beau Bridges *Elgar Enders* • Pearl Bailey *Marge* • Marki Bey *Lanie* • Diana Sands *Fanny* • Louis Gossett [Louis Gossett Jr] *Copee* • Douglas Grant *Walter Gee* • Melvin Stewart *Professor Duboise* • Lee Grant *Mrs Enders* • Robert Klein *Peter* ■ *Dir* Hal Ashby • *Scr* William Gunn [Bill Gunn], from the novel by Kristin Hunter

Landscape after Battle ★★★★ 12
Second World War drama
1970 · Pol · Colour · 104mins

As much a treatise on Polish anti-Semitism as a denunciation of the Nazis, Andrzej Wajda's grimly stylised picture is based on the writings of Tadeusz Borowski, a Holocaust survivor who committed suicide in 1959 at the age of 29. Continuing the "generation" theme of his celebrated war trilogy, Wajda sends his restless camera in search of the grotesque ironies of life in a camp for displaced persons. Yet he also employs a lyrical expressionism to chronicle the romance between Daniel Olbrychski's writer and Stanisława Celinska's terrified refugee. Both visually and intellectually disconcerting, this is a film of brutal poetic power. A Polish language film. ▭

Daniel Olbrychski *Tadeusz* • Stanisława Celinska *Nina* • Aleksander Bardini *Professor* ■ *Dir* Andrzej Wajda • *Scr* Andrzej Brzozowski, Andrzej Wajda, from the short stories by Tadeusz Borowski

Lansky ★★
Crime drama 1999 · US · Colour · 117mins

A mumbling, whiny performance from Richard Dreyfuss undermines this cradle-to-grave biopic of gangster Meyer Lansky, associate of the equally notorious Bugsy Siegel. A Jewish immigrant, Lansky rises from the impoverished streets of New York's Lower East Side at the turn of the century and embarks on a life of crime. His "success" eventually makes him the subject of FBI probes and Congressional hearings. Emphasising dialogue rather than the usual *Godfather*-style executions, Lansky's life is unfortunately dramatised in cool, detached strokes by distinguished playwright David Mamet. Judging by the results, a contribution from Mario Puzo might have breathed some much-needed life into this less-than-satisfying TV movie.

Richard Dreyfuss *Meyer Lansky* • Eric Roberts *Ben "Bugsy" Siegel* • Anthony LaPaglia *Charles "Lucky" Luciano* • Beverly D'Angelo *Teddy Lansky* • Illeana Douglas *Anna Lansky* ■ *Dir* John McNaughton • *Scr* David Mamet, from the biography *Meyer Lansky: Mogul of the Mob* by Uri Dan, Dennis Eisenberg, Eli Landau

Lapse of Memory ★★ PG
Drama 1992 · Can/Fr · Colour · 81mins

Originally made in 1983 as the little seen *I Am the Cheese*, this is one of those repressed memory thrillers in which a sudden recollection spells danger for a previously contented amnesiac. Teenager Mathew Mackay struggles valiantly with the realisation that adoptive parents John Hurt and Marthe Keller are on the run from the mob, but there's nothing that hasn't been done better in several similar scenarios. In an unusual departure from the original picture, the part of Doctor Brint that was played by Robert Wagner is here taken by a woman, Marion Peterson. ▭

John Hurt *Conrad Farmer* • Marthe Keller *Linda Farmer* • Mathew Mackay *Bruce Farmer* • Kathleen Robertson *"Patrick"* • Marion Peterson *Dr Lauren Brint* ■ *Dir* Patrick Dewolf • *Scr* Patrick Dewolf, Philippe Le Guay, from the novel *I Am the Cheese* by Robert Cormier

Larceny, Inc ★★
Gangster spoof 1942 · US · BW · 95mins

Under cover of a smart luggage store, a gang of crooks plan to tunnel their way into the bank vault next door. However, the shop is so successful their plot is thwarted. Based on a Broadway show by husband and wife team SJ and Laura Perelman, this comedy boasts an enticing cast led by Edward G Robinson and featuring Anthony Quinn as one of the mobsters. Unfortunately, there aren't many laughs. Perhaps Warner Bros should have cast comedians as heavies rather than the other way around.

Edward G Robinson *J Chalmers "Pressure" Maxwell* • Jane Wyman *Denny Costello* • Broderick Crawford *Jug Martin* • Jack Carson *Jeff Randolph* • Anthony Quinn *Leo Dexter* • Edward S Brophy [Edward Brophy] *Weepy Davis* • Jackie Gleason *Hobart* ■ *Dir* Lloyd Bacon • *Scr* Everett Freeman, Edwin Gilbert, from the play *The Night Before Christmas* by Laura Perelman, SJ Perelman

Larger than Life ★★ PG
Comedy 1996 · US/It/Jap · Colour · 89mins

Bill Murray fans will have their allegiance tested by this extremely lightweight comedy about a motivational speaker who inherits an elephant from his estranged circus clown dad. Their cross-country journey to the animal's California destination is filled with calamitous incidents, but the laughs are spread thinly and even a supporting cast that includes Janeane Garofalo, Linda Fiorentino and Matthew McConaughey (as a conspiracy theorist trucker) can't inject much pep into this lumbering beast. This re-teaming of Murray and director Howard Franklin, who previously collaborated on the underrated *Quick Change*, just about gets by on the star's cynical charm and the innate comedy value of his jumbo-sized companion. ▭

Bill Murray *Jack Corcoran* • Janeane Garofalo *Mo* • Matthew McConaughey *Tip Tucker* • Linda Fiorentino *Terry* • Anita Gillette *Mom* ■ *Dir* Howard Franklin • *Scr* Roy Blount Jr, from the story by Pen Densham, Garry Williams

Larks on a String ★★★★
Satire 1969 · Cz · Colour · 90mins

Originally made in 1969 towards the end of the period of creativity known as the "Czech Film Miracle", this caustic comedy was banned "for ever" by the authorities and director Jirí Menzel – co-writer/director of the Oscar-winning *Closely Observed Trains* was prevented from filming for several years. Finally reaching cinema screens in 1990, after the Velvet Revolution, it justly shared the Golden Bear at the Berlin Film Festival that year. Set in a scrap-metal yard populated with discarded intellectuals and waiters, it is a sniping, eminently watchable romantic satire which, in keeping with many films of the time, sought to show how the Communist Party had failed the Czech working classes. In Czechoslovakian with English subtitles.

Jitka Zelenohorska *Jitka* • Vaclav Neckar *Pavel* • Leos Sucharipa *Public prosecutor* • Jaroslav Satoransky *Angel* ■ *Dir* Jirí Menzel • *Scr* Jirí Menzel, from a novel by Bohumil Hrabal

Larry ★★★
Drama based on a true story
1974 · US · Colour · 80mins

David Seltzer, best known for his work on *The Omen*, wrote the screenplay for this affecting TV movie. Frederic Forrest gives an inspirational performance as a man discovered to have wrongly spent the first 26 years of his life in a mental institution, trying to come to terms with life outside the place that has been both his prison and his sanctuary. Veteran TV director William A Graham ably steers the action away from mawkish sentimentality, although his fascination with Forrest means several supporting characters are reduced to cyphers.

Frederic Forrest *Larry Herman* • Tyne Daly *Nancy Hockworth* • Michael McGuire *Dr McCabe* • Robert Walden *Tom Corman* • Katherine Helmond *Maureen Whitten* ■ *Dir* William A Graham • *Scr* David Seltzer, from the novel *Larry: Case History of a Mistake* by Dr Robert McQueen

Las Vegas Shakedown ★
Crime drama 1955 · US · BW · 79mins

B-movie actor Dennis O'Keefe is in his element in this clichéd thriller about a casino owner whose life is threatened by an ex-con, played with menace and a limp by Thomas Gomez. Coleen Gray, as a demure local schoolteacher, seems carried away by all the excitement. Although set in Las Vegas, it might as well be Dodge City 70 years earlier. Director Sidney Salkow cut his teeth on the *Lone Wolf* movies, made a decent film of Jack London's *Martin Eden*, and then settled for B-westerns throughout the fifties.

Dennis O'Keefe *Joe Barnes* • Coleen Gray *Julia Rae* • Charles Winninger *Mr Raff* • Thomas Gomez *Sirago* ■ *Dir* Sidney Salkow • *Scr* Steve Fisher

The Las Vegas Story ★★
Drama 1951 · US · BW · 88mins

There's no real chemistry between Jane Russell and former flame Victor Mature in this routine RKO caper, which involves a phoney murder plot set in a patently studio-bound Las Vegas. Russell performs as though there's no tomorrow, while troupers Vincent Price and Hoagy Carmichael provide professional support, but there's no denying that this film is far from their best. Director Robert Stevenson does what he can with the resolutely substandard screenplay.

Jane Russell *Linda Rollins* • Victor Mature *Dave Andrews* • Vincent Price *Lloyd Rollins* • Hoagy Carmichael *Happy* • Brad Dexter *Thomas Hubler* • Gordon Oliver *Drucker* • Jay C Flippen *Harris* ■ *Dir* Robert Stevenson • *Scr* Earl Felton, Harry Essex, Paul Jarrico (uncredited), from a story by Jay Dratler

Laserblast ★
Science-fiction fantasy
1978 · US · Colour · 80mins

This low-budget sci-fi drama appears to have been shot in director Michael Rae's back garden and living room. When teenager Kim Milford finds a laser gun left behind by visiting aliens he decides to wreak vengeance on those who have been making his life a misery. The action seems to consist mainly of cars being blown up, leading one to surmise that Rae must have had a deal going on with a local second-hand car dealer. This isn't as interesting as it sounds and is executed with little imagination or feeling for the genre, although the

stop-motion effects are fun and Roddy McDowall makes a pleasing guest appearance.

Kim Milford *Billy Duncan* • Cheryl Smith *Kathy Farley* • Gianni Russo *Tony Craig* • Ron Masak *Sheriff* • Keenan Wynn *Colonel Farley* • Roddy McDowall *Dr Mellon* ■ *Dir* Michael Rae • *Scr* Franne Schacht, Frank Ray Perilli

The Laserman ★★★

Comedy 1988 · US/HK · Colour · 92mins

Mixing sci-fi spoof with a sermon about the proliferation of weapons, this is a hit-and-miss affair from writer/director Peter Wang, who is best known for his gentle comedy drama *A Great Wall*. Wang also appears as a New York cop, whose scientist friend Marc Hayashi gets embroiled in a sinister plot involving his laser gun project. There are some neat cultural insights and, fittingly, as Wang is on Woody Allen's Manhattan stomping ground, there is an interfering Jewish mother who makes Allen's mama from *New York Stories* look like a beginner.

Marc Hayashi *Arthur Weiss* • Maryann Urbano *Jane Cosby* • Tony Kar-Fai Leung [Tony Leung (2)] *Joey Chung* • Peter Wang *Lieutenant Lu* • Joan Copeland *Ruth Weiss* • George Bartenieff *Hanson* • David Chang *Jimmy Weiss* • Neva Small *Martha Weiss Chung* ■ *Dir/Scr* Peter Wang

Lassie ★★ U

Adventure 1994 · US · Colour · 91mins

Awesomely sentimental updating of the classic family film about the world's most intelligent canine. This time around Jon Tenney and Helen Slater are the city folk finding their feet in the country who are lucky enough to fall under the protective paw of the lovable collie. Of course, being the nineties, Lassie not only does all the usual heroic stuff but also helps a young boy come to terms with the death of his mother. Director Daniel Petrie piles on the slush but that won't bother the film's target audience a jot.

Thomas Guiry *Steve Turner* • Helen Slater *Laura Turner* • Thomas Guiry *Matt Turner* • Brittany Boyd *Jennifer Turner* • Frederic Forrest *Sam Garland* ■ *Dir* Daniel Petrie • *Scr* Matthew Jacobs, Gary Ross, Elizabeth Anderson

Lassie Come Home ★★★★★ U

Adventure 1943 · US · Colour · 88mins

This is the first and best of all those canine capers about the collie with the mostest (although Lassie was female, she was actually played by a male dog called Pal). Roddy McDowall's pet is sold to the local squire who moves to Scotland with granddaughter Elizabeth Taylor. But Lassie takes the high road back to her young master, while everyone dissolves into tears of happiness. Elizabeth Taylor never looked lovelier and Britain glowed through MGM-tinted eyes. Of its heart-warming kind this is an absolute delight. Accept no substitute or sequels.

Roddy McDowall *Joe Carraclough* • Donald Crisp *Sam Carraclough* • Edmund Gwenn *Rowlie* • Dame May Whitty *Dolly* • Nigel Bruce *Duke of Rudling* • Elsa Lanchester *Mrs*

Carraclough • Elizabeth Taylor *Priscilla* ■ *Dir* Fred M Wilcox • *Scr* Hugo Butler, from the novel by Eric Knight

Lassie's Great Adventure ★★★ U

Adventure 1963 · US · Colour · 102mins

The intrepid collie finds herself adrift in a balloon with Jon Provost in this serviceable outdoor survival story. The footage has been cobbled from four TV series episodes and the joins are all too apparent as Lassie and her master trek across the wilds, ward off a ferocious boar, negotiate raging rapids and befriend a native American trapper – all while Provost's parents await news from mountain rescue teams and Mountie patrols. The youngster's ingenuity is utterly unbelievable, but the scenery is fabulous and the dog magnificent.

June Lockhart *Ruth Martin* • Hugh Reilly *Paul Martin* • Jon Provost *Timmy* • Robert Howard *Sgt Sprague* • Will J White *Constable MacDonald* • Richard Kiel *Chinook Pete* • Walter Stocker *John Stanley* ■ *Dir* William Beaudine • *Scr* Monroe Manning, Charles O'Neal, from a story by Sumner Arthur Long

Lassiter ★★ 18

Period action adventure 1984 · US · Colour · 95mins

The modestly amiable Tom Selleck never fully recovered from the career blow of losing out on the Indiana Jones role, and this poorly conceived star vehicle did him no favours either. Set in 1934 he plays a London-based American jewel thief blackmailed by Bob Hoskins of the Yard into nabbing a cache of diamonds held in the German embassy. This is let down by an erratic script that doesn't know when to quit with the double-crosses, shaky period atmosphere and uninspired direction from Roger Young. Jane Seymour as an archetypal heroine barely registers and the usually reliable Lauren Hutton makes nothing of her vampish villainess.

Tom Selleck *Lassiter* • Jane Seymour *Sara* • Lauren Hutton *Kari* • Bob Hoskins *Becker* • Joe Regalbuto *Breeze* • Ed Lauter *Smoke* • Warren Clarke *Max Hofer* ■ *Dir* Roger Young • *Scr* David Taylor

Last Action Hero ★★★★ 15

Comedy action adventure 1993 · US · Colour · 125mins

This is a smart, funny blockbuster which gives director John McTiernan the opportunity to send up not only Arnold Schwarzenegger's heroic image, but also the action genre itself. The story centres around youngster Austin O'Brien, who finds himself sucked into the celluloid world of his biggest hero (Schwarzenegger), as he tracks bad guys Charles Dance and Anthony Quinn in his new film. Things become complicated when the fictional characters have the chance to escape into the real world. Schwarzenegger has rarely been better, and although McTiernan has fun spoofing the conventions of the action genre, he still manages to slip in some spectacular set pieces. Contains swearing and violence. ▭ **DVD**

Arnold Schwarzenegger *Jack Slater* • F Murray Abraham *John Practice* • Art Carney *Frank* •

Charles Dance *Benedict* • Frank McRae *Dekker* • Tom Noonan *Ripper* • Robert Prosky *Nick* • Anthony Quinn *Vivaldi* • Mercedes Ruehl *Mom* • Austin O'Brien *Danny Madigan* • Ian McKellen *Death* ■ *Dir* John McTiernan • *Scr* Shane Black, David Arnott, from a story by Zak Penn, Adam Leff

The Last Adventurers ★★

Romantic melodrama 1937 · UK · BW · 77mins

It's a pity there's not much entertainment value to be had from this wonderful curio about a twice-shipwrecked castaway saved by a sea captain whose daughter he then falls in love with, much to the old tar's displeasure. What is fascinating about Roy Kellino's adventure is that it was edited, with greater tautness than it deserves, by director-in-waiting David Lean. The casting is also noteworthy, with future *Carry On* star Esma Cannon in a rare glamour role, and Ballard Berkeley (who would later play the Major in *Fawlty Towers*) playing the heroic lead.

Niall MacGinnis *Jeremy Bowker* • Roy Emerton *John Arkell* • Linden Travers *Ann Arkell* • Peter Gawthorne *Fergus Arkell* • Katie Johnson *Susan Arkell* • Kay Walsh *Margaret Arkell* • Johnnie Schofield *Stalky* • Norah Howard *Mary Allen* • Ballard Berkeley *Fred Delvin* • Esma Cannon *Polly Shepherd* • Tony Wylde *Glory Be* ■ *Dir* Roy Kellino • *Scr* Denison Clift

The Last American Hero ★★★★

Drama 1973 · US · Colour · 94mins

While everyone writes about the American cinema in the early seventies in terms of hot-shot talents like Coppola, Scorsese, Bogdanovich and Friedkin, a lot of other fine movies were being made, lower-key affairs like this immensely likeable picture directed by Lamont Johnson. The excellent Jeff Bridges stars as a moonshiner's son, who begins a career in stock car racing in order to pay the legal fees of his imprisoned father. By no means an action movie or demolition derby, this is a funky character piece, written with insight and celebrating the survival of the pioneer spirit in modern America – it's based on Tom Wolfe's "New Journalism" which also produced *The Right Stuff*. Fans of Peckinpah's *Junior Bonner* should like this just as much.

Jeff Bridges *Junior Jackson* • Valerie Perrine *Marge* • Geraldine Fitzgerald *Mrs Jackson* • Ned Beatty *Hackel* • Art Lund *Elroy Jackson Sr* • Gary Busey *Wayne Jackson* • William Smith II [William Smith] *Kyle Kingman* • Ed Lauter *Burton Colt* ■ *Dir* Lamont Johnson • *Scr* William Roberts, from the works of Tom Wolfe

The Last Angry Man ★★★ U

Drama 1959 · US · BW · 99mins

Paul Muni's last Hollywood film (and his first in over a decade) gave him the kind of worthy character he relished portraying: a dedicated doctor working among the Brooklyn poor who has to choose between appearing in a live television tribute and helping a patient in trouble with the police. Muni retained the knack of letting you know you were seeing great acting, and he duly picked up his fifth Oscar nomination as best actor. (His tricks included removing his false teeth to

look haggard after a heart attack.) The character could have done with a few faults, but Muni still wins you over and his death scene is very moving.

Paul Muni *Dr Sam Abelman* • David Wayne *Woodrow Wilson Thrasher* • Betsy Palmer *Anne Thrasher* • Luther Adler *Dr Max Vogel* • Joby Baker *Myron Malkin* • Joanna Moore *Alice Taggert* • Nancy R Pollock *Sarah Abelman* • Billy Dee Williams *Josh Quincy* ■ *Dir* Daniel Mann • *Scr* Gerald Green, Richard Murphy, from the novel by Gerald Green

The Last Battle ★★★★ 15

Science-fiction 1983 · Fr · BW · 92mins

With his first feature – an arresting poetic vision of post-apocalyptic Paris after an unspecified cataclysm has reduced the earth to a desolate wasteland – director Luc Besson laid the groundwork for *The Fifth Element* and began his long relationship with actor Jean Reno. Four survivors battle for the future of mankind in this stark alternative to *Mad Max*, which conveys its raw emotions in carefully orchestrated, black-and-white visuals without any dialogue (poisonous gases having rendered the characters' vocal chords useless). It's a remarkable achievement that deals with hackneyed holocaust clichés on a compelling, humanistic and touching plane.

Pierre Jolivet *Young man* • Jean Bouise *Old doctor* • Fritz Wepper *Gang leader* • Jean Reno *Swordsman* ■ *Dir* Luc Besson • *Scr* Luc Besson, Pierre Jolivet

The Last Best Year ★★★

Drama 1990 · US · Colour · 97mins

A Mary Tyler Moore TV special with its heart in the right place, but the whiff of political correctness hangs heavy in the air. Moore is a psychologist with a few personal problems of her own, which start to leak into her work when she counsels patient Bernadette Peters, who has a terminal illness. Moore gives a performance that is by turns glossy and heart-rending, and she's matched by co-star Peters, but preaching gets in the way of the movie.

Bernadette Peters *Jane Murray* • Brian Bedford *Dr Sam Castle* • Dorothy McGuire *Anne Marcus* • Erika Alexander *Amy* • Carmen Mathews *Aunt Elizabeth* ■ *Dir* John Erman • *Scr* David W Rintels

The Last Big Thing ★

Comedy drama 1996 · US · Colour · 98mins

Written, directed by and starring Dan Zukovic – so everyone knows who to blame – this pretentious would-be comedy is a vanity home movie purportedly laying bare America's warped love affair with trashy pop culture. Zukovic decides to attack his target by interviewing C-grade celebrities for *The Next Big Thing*, a fictitious magazine. So begins a steady stream of bogus interviews with empty-headed actors, lousy rock bands, supermodels and trips to stand-up comic venues. There is a last-minute message contained in all this nonsense, but it's hardly worth wading through the whole mess to get to it.

Dan Zukovic *Simon Geist* • Susan Heimbinder *Darla* • Mark Ruffalo *Brent* • Pamela Dickerson *Tedra* • Andrew Falk *Chris* ■ *Dir/Scr* Dan Zukovic

The Last Blitzkrieg ★

Second World War drama
1958 · US · BW · 84mins

Looking around for a Hollywood actor to play the English-speaking son of a top Nazi general, producer Sam Katzman should never have settled for Van Johnson, whose lightweight presence destroys the picture. Although this was filmed in Holland and uses some local players and crew, the obvious reliance on stock battle footage further undermines credibility. The plot has Johnson leading a sabotage squad masquerading as Americans behind Allied lines.

Van Johnson *Sergeant Richardson Kroner* • Kerwin Mathews *Wilitz* • Dick York *Sergeant Ludwig* • Larry Storch *Private First Class* • Lise Bourdin *Monique* ■ *Dir* Arthur Dreifuss • *Scr* Lou Morheim

The Last Boy Scout ★★★ 18

Comedy thriller 1991 · US · Colour · 105mins

The mismatched buddy movie reaches an apotheosis of sorts here in director Tony Scott's flashy, foul-mouthed and formula no-brainer, which forsakes plot for overblown shoot-outs and endless car chases. Lifting it marginally above the thick-ear realm is the engaging chemistry between seedy gumshoe Bruce Willis and ex-footballer Damon Wayans. Both actors let humour spring effortlessly from their own personalities as well as from their screen characters, and the snappy put-downs make the epic mindlessness bearable. Contains violence, swearing, drug abuse and nudity. ▭ *DVD*

Bruce Willis *Joe Hallenbeck* • Damon Wayans *Jimmy Dix* • Chelsea Field *Sarah Hallenbeck* • Noble Willingham *Sheldon Marcone* • Taylor Negron *Milo* • Danielle Harris *Darian Hallenbeck* • Halle Berry *Cory* • Bruce McGill *Mike Matthews* • Chelcie Ross *Senator Baynard* ■ *Dir* Tony Scott • *Scr* Shane Black, from a story by Shane Black, Greg Hicks

The Last Bridge ★★★

Drama 1954 · Aus/Yug · BW · 108mins

During the 1950s, Maria Schell (elder sister to Maximilian) enjoyed great international acclaim, receiving a special mention award at the Cannes Festival for this anti-war movie, and the equivalent accolade at Venice for *Gervaise* in 1956. A rather melancholy demeanour suited her role here as a German doctor forced by Yugoslav patriots to help nurse their wounded, during the Second World War. The moral of the film is that nationality and barriers are irrelevant. Simple perhaps, but movingly told without undue histrionics. The Partisan leader is played by Bernhard Wicki, actor turned distinguished director, who died in 1999. A German language film.

Maria Schell *Helga Reinbeck* • Bernhard Wicki *Boro* • Barbara Rutting *Militza* • Carl Mohner *Sergeant Martin Berger* • Horst Haechler *Lieutenant Scherer* • Pable Mincie *Momcillo* ■ *Dir* Helmut Kautner • *Scr* Helmut Kautner, Norbert Kunze

The Last Broadcast ★★★ 18

Horror 1998 · US · Colour · 87mins

A documentary crew disappears after going into the woods to make a film about a local legend. Sounds familiar? Cheekily, though, the producers of this shoestring "mockumentary" claim to have gone into production before *The Blair Witch Project*. More formally structured than *Blair Witch*, *Broadcast* is about as scary (in other words, not very), and offers further proof of how easy it is for film-makers to manipulate fiction into a convincing form of "fact". ▭ *DVD*

David Beard *David Leigh, the filmmaker* • James Seward *Jim Suerd, the accused* • Stefan Avalos *Steven Avkast, "Fact or Fiction" host* • Lance Weiler *Locus Wheeler, "Fact or Fiction" host* ■ *Dir/Scr* Stefan Avalos, Lance Weiler • *Editor* Stefan Avalos

The Last Bus Home ★★ 15

Musical comedy drama
1997 · Ire · Colour · 90mins

Rather optimistically pitched as the punk version of *The Commitments*, this low-budget Irish effort remains an entertainingly rough and ready tale of the music business. Set at the end of the seventies, Annie Ryan and Brian F O'Byrne are the idealistic punks determined to take the music world by storm with their band Dead Patriots. But when London beckons, their music dream begins to turn sour. Slick it ain't, but maybe that was the point, and old New Wavers and punks will love the attitude and the vintage soundtrack . ▭

Annie Ryan *Reena* • Brian F O'Byrne *Jessop* • John Cronin *Petie* • Barry Comerford *Joe* • Anthony Brophy *Billy* • Gemma Craven *Reena's mother* • Donal O'Kelly *Richie* • Brendan Coyle *Steve Burkett* ■ *Dir/Scr* Johnny Gogan

The Last Butterfly ★★

Second World War drama
1990 · Fr/Cz/UK · Colour · 110mins

An obscure entry into the Holocaust genre, shot in Czechoslovakia, financed mainly in France and produced by Steven North whose father, Alex North, is the veteran Hollywood composer who provides the score here. Tom Courtenay stars as a French mime artist who is duped by the Nazis into performing at a town set aside for Jews. Only when Courtenay arrives does he tumble the fact that his act is purely to impress visiting Red Cross officials; when they are gone the Jews will be shipped to the death camps. Courtenay's mime act, a version of *Hansel and Gretel*, is the highlight in a worthy effort that never quite delivers its promised impact.

Tom Courtenay *Antoine Moreau* • Brigitte Fossey *Vera* • Ingrid Held *Michele* • Freddie Jones *Rheinberg* • Milan Knazko *Gruber* ■ *Dir* Karel Kachyna • *Scr* Karel Kachyna, Ota Hofman, from the novel *Les Enfants de Terezin* by Michael Jacot, Alex North

The Last Challenge ★★★

Western 1967 · US · Colour · 95mins

Here's a western which satisfyingly refreshes some stock characters and situations. It also has assured performances from Glenn Ford as the gunfighter turned lawman, Angie Dickinson as the saloon keeper who loves him, and Chad Everett as the young gunslinger who wants to kill him to build a reputation. On the strength of performances like the one he gives here, Everett deserved to become a big star; elsewhere, Jack Elam has a straight role as a hired gun. Richard Thorpe's slack direction lets the strong script (by John Sherry and Robert Emmett Ginna) carry the picture.

Glenn Ford *Marshal Dan Blaine* • Angie Dickinson *Lisa Denton* • Chad Everett *Lot McGuire* • Gary Merrill *Squint Calloway* • Jack Elam *Ernest Scarnes* • Delphi Lawrence *Marie Webster* ■ *Dir* Richard Thorpe • *Scr* John Sherry, Robert Emmett Ginna, from the novel *Pistolero's Progress* by John Sherry

The Last Chase ★★

Science-fiction 1981 · US · Colour · 101mins

A hymn to that most American of institutions: the car. Set in the near future, this reactionary riposte to the green movement has Lee Majors achieving heroic status when he defies the authorities by driving his banned gas-guzzler across the country. Burgess Meredith is the wily pilot detailed to stop him. Hugely funny, though for all the wrong reasons.

Lee Majors *Frank Hart* • Burgess Meredith *Captain Williams* • Chris Makepeace *Ring* • Alexandra Stewart *Eudora* ■ *Dir* Martyn Burke • *Scr* CR O'Christopher, Taylor Sutherland, Martyn Burke, from the story by CR O'Christopher

The Last Command ★★★★★

Silent drama 1928 · US · BW · 87mins

The love-hate relationship between moody actor Emil Jannings and archetypal tyrant-director Josef von Sternberg created this masterpiece – prior to another one with *The Blue Angel* (1930) – with its story of a Tsarist general (Jannings) working for peanuts as a bit-player in Hollywood. The extended flashback takes in his life in revolutionary Russia – including his seduction of a Communist actress (Evelyn Brent) – and his feud with a radical theatrical director who becomes his grudging benefactor in Tinseltown. Jannings is satisfyingly arrogant to the point of dementia, while von Sternberg's visuals have a poetic lyricism to offset the sour nature of the characters and story. A remarkable portrait of Russia and Hollywood at the height of their powers – as, indeed, were Jannings and von Sternberg themselves.

Emil Jannings *Gen Dolgorucki/Grand Duke Sergius Alexander* • Evelyn Brent *Natascha Dobrowa* • William Powell *Leo Andreiev* • Nicholas Soussanin *Adjutant* ■ *Dir* Josef von Sternberg • *Scr* John F Goodrich, Herman J mankiewicz (titles), from the story by Lajos Biró • *Cinematographer* Bert Glennon

The Last Command ★★★ PG

Historical western
1955 · US · Colour · 105mins

Remember the Alamo? No, not John Wayne's mammoth epic, but this slightly earlier account, directed by veteran Frank Lloyd on what must have been Republic Studios' highest-ever budget. The tale is well told, with star Sterling Hayden making a most impressive Jim Bowie and veteran character actor Arthur Hunnicutt portraying a grizzled and probably accurate Davy Crockett. Richard Carlson as William Barrett Travis actually makes the classic line in the sand with his sword that is curiously missing from Wayne's otherwise definitive version, and there's a healthy air of historical accuracy all around. Enjoyable, but lacking in stature, alas. ▭

Sterling Hayden *James Bowie* • Anna Maria Alberghetti *Consuela* • Richard Carlson *William Travis* • Arthur Hunnicutt *Davy Crockett* • Ernest Borgnine *Mike Radin* • J Carrol Naish *Santa Anna* ■ *Dir* Frank Lloyd • *Scr* Warren Duff, from a story by Sy Bartlett

The Last Contract ★★★

Crime drama
1998 · Swe/Nor/Fin · Colour · 114mins

The publication of John W Grow's pseudonymous novel about the murder of prime minister Olof Palme sent shockwaves through Sweden. However, Kjell Sundvall's thriller refuses to repeat the book's controversial accusations, settling instead for a flashback reconstruction of events leading up to the assassination. Echoes of *The Day of the Jackal* continuously reverberate as cop Mikael Persbrandt dogs the steps of international hit man Michael Kitchen as he leaves a trail of destruction from South Africa to Malta. A working knowledge of the conspiracy theories helps, but the action is suspenseful enough to sustain the interest. A Swedish language film.

Pernilla August *Roger's ex-wife* • Michael Kitchen *Killer* • Mikael Persbrandt *Roger* • Reine Brynolfsson *Bo Ekman* • Bjørn Floberg *Tom Nielsen* • Jacqueline Ramel *Helene Salonen* ■ *Dir* Kjell Sundvall • *Scr* Borje Hansson, Mats Aréhn, Johan Bogaeus, from the novel *Sista kontraktet* by John W Grow

Last Dance ★★★ 18

Drama 1995 · US · Colour · 98mins

Somewhat overshadowed by Tim Robbins's Oscar-winning *Dead Man Walking*, which was released a year earlier, this prison drama has Sharon Stone languishing on death row for a dozen years, condemned to die for murdering two teenagers. Rob Morrow and Randy Quaid are the parole officers who oppose capital punishment, while flashbacks gradually reveal the true nature of Stone's crime. Stone's performance as the teenage social outcast now grown up is generally impressive and Bruce Beresford's direction is typically elegant and controlled, though the ending is a bit of a cop-out. Contains swearing and violence. ▭

Sharon Stone *Cindy Liggett* • Rob Morrow *Rick Hayes* • Randy Quaid *Sam Burns* • Peter Gallagher *John Hayes* • Jack Thompson *The Governor* • Jayne Brook *Jill* • Pamela Tyson *Legal aid attorney* • Skeet Ulrich *Billy* ■ *Dir* Bruce Beresford • *Scr* Ron Koslow, from a story by Ron Koslow, Steven Haft

The Last Days ★★★★ PG

Documentary
1998 · US · Colour and BW · 87mins

Steven Spielberg's obsession with the Holocaust continues with this remarkable documentary, in which five elderly survivors of the concentration camps return to compare then with now. The *Schindler's List* director executive-produced the film with the Shoah Foundation. Such was the Nazis' hatred for the Jews that, even though they knew they were defeated, they still set out to destroy them in Hungary during the "last days" of the

Second World War. ("That's when I stopped talking to God," says one woman.) Writer/director James Moll has assembled some poignant archive material which, combined with the survivors' testimony, makes piteously compelling viewing. However, the conclusion manages to be uplifting by showing the children and grandchildren who surround the survivors in their personal last days.

Dir/Scr James Moll

The Last Days of Chez Nous ★★★ 15

Drama   1992 · Ausl · Colour · 92mins

Although she is becoming increasingly known for her costume dramas, Australian director Gillian Armstrong made her name with a series of documentaries about three working-class Adelaide women. Her experience of capturing the rhythms of everyday speech and making the most of confined spaces serves her well in this chatty character study, in which novelist Lisa Harrow reassesses her relationships with her husband Bruno Ganz and every member of her less-than-predictable family. Unfortunately, Harrow is the weakest link in a strong cast, with Kerry Fox typically arresting as the sister who makes a move on Ganz, and Bill Hunter excellent as their bluff father. ▭

Lisa Harrow *Beth* • Bruno Ganz *JP* • Kerry Fox *Vicki* • Miranda Otto *Annie* • Kiri Paramore *Tim* • Bill Hunter *Beth's father* • Lex Marinos *Angelo* ■ *Dir* Gillian Armstrong • *Scr* Helen Garner

The Last Days of Disco ★★★ 15

Comedy drama 1998 · US · Colour · 120mins

Writer/director Whit Stillman perfectly captured the lives of young upright urban New Yorkers in *Metropolitan* and American expatriates in his follow-up, *Barcelona*. Here he turns his attention – somewhat less successfully – to bright young things in the early eighties who work by day and boogie on down at night in the months before the death knell sounded for disco. Kate Beckinsale and Chloë Sevigny are overly mannered as the two girls who use the glitter-balled, strobe-lit atmosphere of an exclusive disco to meet rich kids, while Matt Keeslar and Robert Sean Leonard are among the male yuppie types who hook up with them. Unfortunately, none of the characters who populate Stillman's sharply-scripted world are remotely engaging, leaving you to wish they'd just shut up so you could sit back and enjoy the disco music. Contains some swearing and sexual references. ▭

Chloë Sevigny *Alice* • Kate Beckinsale *Charlotte* • Chris Eigeman *Des* • MacKenzie Astin *Jimmy* • Matt Keeslar *Josh* • Robert Sean Leonard *Tom* • Jennifer Beals *Nina* ■ *Dir/Scr* Whit Stillman

The Last Days of Dolwyn ★★ U

Drama   1949 · UK · BW · 95mins

Freely adapted from a historical incident, this is a classic example of how to squeeze all the life out of an intriguing situation by coating it with a thick layer of significance. The flooding of a Welsh valley, the refusal of an old woman to leave her home and the attempts of a murderer to conceal his crime should add up to a compelling drama. But writer/director/star Emlyn Williams spoils everything with a stagey approach, which sees everyone speaking in deliberate tones that owe nothing to real life. Richard Burton impresses in his debut, but the film belongs squarely to Dame Edith Evans.

Dame Edith Evans *Merri* • Emlyn Williams *Rob* • Richard Burton *Gareth* • Anthony James *Dafydd* • Barbara Couper *Lady Dolwyn* • Alan Aynesworth *Lord Lancashire* • Andrea Lea *Margaret* • Hugh Griffith *Minister* ■ *Dir/Scr* Emlyn Williams

The Last Days of Frank and Jesse James ★★★ 15

Western   1986 · US · Colour · 96mins

This compulsively watchable TV movie, with strikingly rich photography, has Johnny Cash and his fellow Nashville "outlaw" Kris Kristofferson as the Old West's two most notorious brothers. Both stars are a little portly and long-in-the-tooth for the roles, but they play well together, though the screen is hijacked by their fellow Confederate Willie Nelson as, yup, a Confederate general. Stranger casting comes with Johnny's wife, June Carter Cash, playing his, and of course Kris's, mother!

Johnny Cash *Frank James* • Kris Kristofferson *Jesse James* • Gail Youngs *Anna James* • David Allan Coe *Whiskeyhead Ryan* • Andrew Stahl *Dick Liddil* • June Carter Cash *Mother James* • Willie Nelson *General Jo Shelby* ■ *Dir* William A Graham • *Scr* Wiliam Stratton

The Last Days of Frankie the Fly ★★ 18

Crime drama 1996 · US · Colour · 91mins

Quentin Tarantino has a lot to answer for. If he hadn't cast Michael Madsen as the sadistic Mr Blonde in *Reservoir Dogs* we might never have been able to enjoy his performance as mob boss, Sal, in this black comedy/drama. Dennis Hopper is Sal's luckless henchman, Frankie, who gets bitten by the movie-making bug and an insane desire to showcase the acting talents of Daryl Hannah. A game cast try to add punchy humour to the movie satire and acerbic resonance to the violent traits but fail as *Frankie*, rather than flying high, remains depressingly grounded. Contains swearing, sexual references and violence. ▭

Dennis Hopper *Frankie* • Daryl Hannah *Margaret* • Kiefer Sutherland *Joey* • Michael Madsen *Sal* • Dayton Callie *Vic* ■ *Dir* Peter Markle • *Scr* Dayton Callie

The Last Days of Mussolini ★★★★

Second World War drama
1974 · It · Colour · 126mins

Rod Steiger contributes his own personal portrayal of the Fascist tyrant in an Italian film that allows the man to have a certain amount of vulnerability. Carlo Lizzani's drama shows him on the run – with mistress Lisa Gastoni – in the days before his own people caught him and strung him upside down from a lamp post. Steiger is tremendous as Mussolini, whom he would play again seven years later in *Lion of the Desert*.

Rod Steiger *Benito Mussolini* • Lisa Gastoni *Clara Petacci* • Henry Fonda *Cardinal Schuster* • Franco Nero *Col Valerio* • Lino Capolicchio *Pedro* ■ *Dir* Carlo Lizzani • *Scr* Carlo Lizzani, Fabio Pittorru • *Music* Ennio Morricone

Last Days of Patton ★★★ PG

Second World War drama
1986 · US · Colour · 139mins

Oscar winner George C Scott reprises his role as the arrogant four-star Second World War general, George S Patton, Jr. in this TV movie sequel. Covering the latter part of Patton's life, the opening of the movie is compelling, as it deals with Patton's conflicts with his colleagues, and his removal as military governor of Bavaria for his use of Nazi administrators and his frank anti-Soviet stance. However, the last half of the film disintegrates into a tedious medical melodrama after Patton has a car accident. Scott is obviously comfortable in the lead, and offers up a commanding performance. Eva Marie Saint is quite believable as his long-suffering wife, and Veteran Academy award-winning director Delbert Mann (*Marty*) skilfully directs both. ▭

George C Scott *General George S Patton* • Eva Marie Saint *Beatrice Patton* • Richard Dysart *General Dwight D Eisenhower* • Murray Hamilton *General Hobart Gay* • Ed Lauter *Lieutenant Colonel Paul S Hill* • Jean Gordon *Kathryn Leigh Scott* • Daniel Benzali *Colonel Glen Spurling* ■ *Dir* Delbert Mann • *Scr* William Luce

The Last Days of Pompeii ★★★

Historical drama 1935 · US · BW · 94mins

Having trashed much of Manhattan in *King Kong*, producer Merian C Cooper and director Ernest B Schoedsack here turn their attention to ancient Rome's most famous natural disaster. The film, which bears little resemblance to Sir Edward Bulwer-Lytton's novel, tells of a young blacksmith turned amoral gladiator who mends his ways when his adopted son is healed by Jesus. Then it's back to Pompeii for the big eruption, some 40 years earlier than recorded historical fact. If you can ignore the wooden performances and the religious piety, this is quite a rousing yarn, with some good arena scenes and the best special effects that 1935 could afford.

Preston Foster *Marcus* • Basil Rathbone *Pontius Pilate* • Alan Hale *Burbix* • John Wood *Flavius (as a man)* • Louis Calhern *Prefect* ■ *Dir* Ernest B Schoedsack • *Scr* Ruth Rose, Boris Ingster, from a story by James Ashmore Creelman, Melville Baker

The Last Days of Pompeii ★★

Historical adventure
1960 · It · Colour · 103mins

Steve Reeves, the uncrowned king of the muscleman epic, is gladiator Glaucus, searching downtown Pompeii for the people who murdered his father. At first it looks like the Christians but then an insurrectionist plot is traced back to the temple priests and an Egyptian princess.

During all this, Reeves poses manfully, revealing thighs as thick as the scriptwriters and biceps that bulge like shiny coconuts. Reeves bends prison bars, fights crocodiles and sundry revolutionaries and shrugs off an arrow that pierces his body. And just when things seems to get sorted, Vesuvius blows its top! A lava pallava. Italian dialogue dubbed into English.

Steve Reeves *Glaucus* • Christine Kaufmann *Ione* • Barbara Carroll *Nydia* • Anne-Marie Baumann *Julia* • Mimmo Palmara *Gallinus* • Fernando Rey *High priest* ■ *Dir* Mario Bonnard • *Scr* Ennio De Concini, Sergio Leone, Duccio Tessari, Sergio Corbucci

The Last Detail ★★★★ 18

Drama   1973 · US · Colour · 99mins

Back in the early seventies, star Jack Nicholson, writer Robert Towne and director Hal Ashby were the hippest team in Hollywood. Nicholson and Towne went on to *Chinatown* and Ashby and Towne to *Shampoo*; they could do no wrong and this earlier effort still has a combustible power. It's a story of two naval petty officers (Nicholson, Otis Young) and the pathetic young criminal (Randy Quaid) they have to escort to jail. Towne's script consists almost entirely of profanities and justifiably so, considering the characters aren't exactly choirboys.

Jack Nicholson *Billy "Bad Ass" Buddusky* • Otis Young *"Mule" Mulhall* • Randy Quaid *Larry Meadows* • Clifton James *Chief master-at-arms* • Michael Moriarty *Marine duty officer* • Carol Kane *Young whore* ■ *Dir* Hal Ashby • *Scr* Robert Towne, from the novel by Darryl Ponicsan

The Last Dragon ★★ 15

Martial arts adventure
1985 · US · Colour · 106mins

Martial arts comes to Harlem in a kung fu adventure which not surprisingly has an element of homage to Bruce Lee. With Motown guru Berry Gordy backing the project, there are plenty of musical interludes as well. Director Michael Schultz tries hard but can't quite manage to tie the varied elements of action, romance, comedy and musical video together, though, as entertainment, this is engaging enough. Contains some swearing. ▭

Taimak *Leroy Green* • Vanity *Laura Charles* • Christopher Murney *Eddie Arcadian* • Julius J Carry III *Sho'nuff* • Faith Prince *Angela* • Leo O'Brien *Richie* • Mike Starr *Rock* • Keshia Pulliam [Keshia Knight Pulliam] *Sophia* ■ *Dir* Michael Schultz • *Scr* Louis Venosta

Last Embrace ★★★★ 18

Thriller   1979 · US · Colour · 97mins

Jonathan Demme, whose fame exploded when he made *The Silence of the Lambs* 12 years after this film, was a director whose early work showed some debt to Hitchcock. As Roy Scheider convincingly plays an agent being used for target practice with a riveting mix of bleakness, determination and paranoia (his wife died in an earlier attack), Demme never loses his grip, piling on the unsettling Hitch-style claustrophobia. The suspense is aided enormously by Tak Fujimoto's atmospheric camerawork and Miklos Rosza's thoughtful, vibrant score. Contains swearing and nudity. ▣

Roy Scheider *Harry Hannan* • Janet Margolin *Ellie Fabian* • John Glover *Richard Peabody* • Sam Levene *Sam Urdell* • Charles Napier *Dave Quittle* • Christopher Walken *Eckart* • Jacqueline Brookes *Dr Coopersmith* • Mandy Patinkin *Commuter* ■ *Dir* Jonathan Demme • *Scr* David Shaber, from the novel *The Thirteenth Man* by Murray Teigh Bloom

The Last Emperor ★★★★ 15

Epic drama
1987 · It/UK/Ch · Colour · 209mins

The first western production to be allowed to film inside the Forbidden City and the winner of nine Oscars, Bernardo Bertolucci's majestic epic is one of the most visually arresting pictures of its time.The design beautifully juxtaposes the pre- and post-revolutionary Chinese worlds, and the red and yellow trappings of the simple uniforms of Mao's republic are stunningly displayed. However, the glorious images distance the viewer from the momentous events that overtook 20th-century China and, in spite of a multifaceted performance from John Lone, Emperor Pu Yi remains a stranger, even at the end of the film. ▣ *DVD*

John Lone *Aisin-Gioro "Henry" Pu Yi, as an adult* • Joan Chen *Elizabeth* • Peter O'Toole *Reginald Johnston, "RJ"* • Ying Ruocheng *Governor* • Victor Wong *Chen Pao Shen* • Dennis Dun *Big Li* • Ryuichi Sakamoto *Masahiko Amakasu* • Maggie Han *Eastern Jewel* • Ric Young *Interrogator* ■ *Dir* Bernardo Bertolucci • *Scr* Bernardo Bertolucci, Mark Peploe, Enzo Ungari • *Cinematographer* Vittorio Storaro

The Last Escape ★★ U

Second World War drama
1970 · UK · Colour · 90mins

United Artists had a pair of surprisingly big hits in the sixties with two war movies that won the hearts of moviegoers everywhere – *The Great Escape*, directed by John Sturges, and *633 Squadron*, both terrific action movies with knockout music scores. Having secured an existing audience for this type of subject, UA then worked the subject of the Second World War into the ground with films like this one, in which the director of the aforementioned *633 Squadron* deals with the same subject matter as the Sturges classic. It isn't any good, and smells of catchpenny picture-making, but Margit Saad looks nice and Stuart Whitman is amiable.

Stuart Whitman *Captain Lee Mitchell* • John Collin *Sgt Henry McBee* • Pinkas Braun *Von Heinken* • Martin Jarvis *Lt Donald Wilcox* • Günther Neutze *Major Hessel* • Margit Saad *Karen Gerhardt* • Patrick Jordan *Major Griggs* • Johnny Briggs *Corporal O'Connell* ■ *Dir* Walter E Grauman [Walter Grauman] • *Scr* Herman Hoffman, from a story by John C Champion, Barry Trivers

Last Exit to Brooklyn ★★★ 18

Drama
1989 · W Ger · Colour · 98mins

Director Uli Edel's horrendously hard-hitting adaptation of a controversial collection of short stories by Hubert Selby Jr is as depressing a film as you'll ever see. That's not to say it isn't an accomplished movie, but its

brutal early-fifties Brooklyn backdrop, plus the gallery of abusive lowlifes, make it a very uncomfortable viewing experience, especially during the climactic drunken gang bang involving prostitute Tralala (Jennifer Jason Leigh). Artistically shot and lit by cinematographer Stefan Czapsky (later to be a regular collaborator with Tim Burton), the film also benefits from some strong acting and a moody score from Mark Knopfler. But what's missing is a genuine feeling of emotional involvement with these characters Contains swearing, sex scenes, violence, nudity and drug abuse ▣ *DVD*

Stephen Lang *Harry Black* • Jennifer Jason Leigh *Tralala* • Burt Young *Big Joe* • Peter Dobson *Vinnie* • Jerry Orbach *Boyce* • Stephen Baldwin *Sal* • Jason Andrews *Tony* • Ricki Lake *Donna* • Hubert Selby Jr *Cab driver* ■ *Dir* Ulrich Edel [Uli Edel] • *Scr* Desmond Nakano, from the novel by Hubert Selby Jr • *Music* Mark Knopfler

The Last Flight ★★★

Drama
1931 · US · BW · 80mins

A fascinating early talkie, one of the few key films to deal with the legendary "lost generation", those American expatriates who found themselves in Paris or Madrid in the twenties, characters beloved by authors F Scott Fitzgerald (who coined the phrase) and Ernest Hemingway. Former silent screen matinée idol Richard Barthelmess plays a flying ace and today's audiences may find his performance a little mannered, though his face remains tenderly expressive. The paradoxical screenplay is the work of aviation expert John Monk Saunders (*Wings* and *The Dawn Patrol*), and the film marks the Hollywood debut of German émigré director Wilhelm Dieterle, later to distinguish himself with a series of Paul Muni biopics.

Richard Barthelmess *Cary Lockwood* • John Mack Brown [Johnny Mack Brown] *Bill Talbot* • Helen Chandler *Nikki* • David Manners *Shep Lambert* • Elliott Nugent *Francis* • Walter Byron *Frink* ■ *Dir* Wilhelm Dieterle [William Dieterle] • *Scr* John Monk Saunders, from the novel *Single Lady* by John Monk Saunders

The Last Flight of Noah's Ark ★★ U

Adventure
1980 · US · Colour · 93mins

Quite what Disney hoped to achieve with this anaemic adventure is anyone's guess. Director Charles Jarrott seemed to think he could thrill youngsters with a plane crash, a storm at sea, a pair of young stowaways and some scene-stealing animals, while amusing the grown-ups with the *African Queen*-like banter between pilot Elliott Gould and missionary Geneviève Bujold. Wrong! This is all at sea in every sense of the phrase and, what's more, it's little fun. Clearly there was no intention of insulting the Japanese, but the two soldiers still fighting the Second World War on a Pacific island are horrendous racist caricatures. ▣

Elliott Gould *Noah Dugan* • Geneviève Bujold *Bernadette Lafleur* • Ricky Schroder [Rick Schroder] *Bobby* • Tammy Lauren *Julie* • Vincent Gardenia *Stoney* • John Fujioka *Cleveland* • Yuki Shimoda *Hiro* • John Ryan [John P Ryan] *Coslough* ■ *Dir* Charles Jarrott

• *Scr* Steven W Carabatsos, Sandy Glass, George Arthur Bloom, from the story by Ernest K Gann

The Last Fling ★★ 15

Romantic comedy
1987 · US · Colour · 92mins

A comedy that, alas, isn't very funny. John Ritter and Connie Sellecca star in this tale of a woman who, on the eve of her marriage, decides to indulge in one last fling. Unfortunately, Sellecca – best known for her role in the eighties' TV series *Hotel* – isn't very good at comedy, so it's left to the more experienced Ritter, who found fame with the sitcom *Three's Company*, to mug his way through and provide what laughs there are. Scott Bakula from *Quantum Leap* also appears. ▣

John Ritter *Phil Reed* • Connie Sellecca *Marsha/Gloria Franklin* • Randee Heller *Mimi* • John Bennett Perry *Jason Elliott* • Paul Sand *Jack Berman* • Scott Bakula *Drew* • Shannon Tweed *Joan Preston* ■ *Dir* Corey Allen • *Scr* Mitchel Lee Katlin

The Last Frontier ★★★

Western
1955 · US · Colour · 98mins

A majestic and brooding western from director Anthony Mann, set mostly at night, that is often ignored in studies of Mann's work. In the story of three fur trappers who take jobs as cavalry scouts after losing their pelts to Indians, Mann's use of early CinemaScope is exemplary, with splendid tracking and panning shots, and there's some fascinating political commentary about the civilising of noble savage Victor Mature. Robert Preston is excellent as a single-minded military martinet, the young Anne Bancroft shows early promise as Preston's wife, but this film also marked the beginning of the decline in co-star Guy Madison's Hollywood career.

Victor Mature *Jed* • Guy Madison *Captain Riordan* • Robert Preston *Colonel Frank Marston* • James Whitmore *Gus* • Anne Bancroft *Corinna Marston* • Russell Collins *Captain Clark* • Peter Whitney *Sergeant Major Decker* • Pat Hogan *Mungo* ■ *Dir* Anthony Mann • *Scr* Philip Yordan, Russell S Hughes, from the novel *The Gilded Rooster* by Richard Emery Roberts

The Last Gangster ★★★

Crime drama
1937 · US · BW · 81mins

Edward G Robinson turns on the menace in the title role of what was among the last products of the golden age of thirties' gangster movies. Some critics rated his portrayal of a pathological hood out for revenge as highly as his famed performance seven years earlier in *Little Caesar*. Taut direction, snappy writing and a talented supporting cast, including James Stewart, add to the value of an engrossing melodrama, only let down by a soppy ending.

Edward G Robinson *Joe Krozac* • James Stewart *Paul North* • Rose Stradner *Talva Krozac* • Lionel Stander *Curly* • Douglas Scott *Paul North Jr* • John Carradine *Casper* • Sidney Blackmer *San Francisco editor* • Edward Brophy *"Fats" Garvey* ■ *Dir* Edward Ludwig • *Scr* John Lee Mahin, from a story by William A Wellman, Robert Carson

Last Gasp ★★ 18

Thriller
1995 · US · Colour · 88mins

Ruthless real estate developer Robert Patrick slaughters a tribe of Mexican Indians for their land, only to become possessed by one of their spirits. Turning into a homicidal maniac with a painted face, he will stop at nothing to guard the ancient territory. Joanna Pacula is the concerned wife of one of his victims who tries to uncover the secret behind her husband's disappearance. While Patrick brings even more sinister menace to this stark horror tale than he did as the T-1000 in the second *Terminator*, the unrelieved grimness makes it more depressing than creepy. ▣

Robert Patrick *Leslie Chase* • Joanna Pacula *Nora Weeks* • Vyto Ruginis *Ray Tattinger* • Mimi Craven *Goldie* • Alexander Enberg *Duane* ■ *Dir* Scott McGinnis • *Scr* Pierce Milestone, Stanley Isaacs, David N Twohy

The Last Gentleman ★

Comedy drama
1934 · US · BW · 78mins

Desperately dated comedy about an 80-year-old millionaire (George Arliss) who spends the whole film dying while his relatives descend like vultures waiting for him to expire. Panned by critics on release as being stagey and slow-paced, this musty old comedy will seem interminable – the constant ticking and chiming of Arliss's collection of 106 clocks don't help either. However, Arliss's dwindling army of admirers may enjoy it and the climax when the deceased Arliss reads his own will is ingenious, even vaguely amusing.

George Arliss *Cabot Barr* • Edna May Oliver *Augusta* • Janet Beecher *Helen* • Charlotte Henry *Marjorie* • Frank Albertson *Allan* • Rafaela Ottiano *Retta* • Ralph Morgan *Loring* • Edward Ellis *Claude* ■ *Dir* Sidney Lanfield • *Scr* Leonard Praskins, from the play *The Head of the Family* by Katharine Clugston

The Last Good Time ★★

Romantic drama 1994 · US · Colour · 90mins

This is a restrained romance, about an ageing violinist who starts making beautiful music with a young girl who's fleeing an abusive boyfriend. Although the film strives for the Euro feel of Louis Malle's *Atlantic City USA*, it never quite achieves it, despite sterling performances from the leads Armin Mueller-Stahl and Olivia D'Abo, and from a supporting cast that includes Maureen Stapleton, Adrian Pasdar and Lionel Stander. While it hits many of the right notes, it needs to have projected more.

Armin Mueller-Stahl *Joseph Kopple* • Olivia D'Abo *Charlotte Zwicki* • Maureen Stapleton *Ida Cutler* • Lionel Stander *Howard Singer* • Adrian Pasdar *Eddie* • Kevin Corrigan *Frank* • Zohra Lampert *Barbara* ■ *Dir* Bob Balaban • *Scr* Bob Balaban, John J McLaughlin, from the novel by Richard Bausch

The Last Great Warrior ★★★ PG

Historical adventure
1994 · US · Colour · 97mins

Swiss director Xavier Koller, who won a best foreign film Oscar for *Journey of Hope*, came to Disney to make this costume drama, which also goes under

U = SUITABLE FOR ALL   Uc = SUITABLE FOR ALL, ESPECIALLY FOR YOUNG CHILDREN (VIDEO ONLY)   PG = PARENTAL GUIDANCE

the title of *Squanto: a Warrior's Tale*. However, whereas that film was filled with grim realities, this one is far too fanciful in its description of a native American's adventures in 17th-century England. Adam Beach is suitably noble as the warrior who learns the value of life while taking sanctuary in a monastery. Younger viewers, however, will probably prefer his skirmishes with the wicked Michael Gambon to these spiritual asides. 🖭

Adam Beach *Squanto* • Irene Bedard *Nakooma* • Eric Schweig *Epenow* • Leroy Peltier *Pequod* • Michael Gambon *Sir George* • Nathaniel Parker *Thomas Dermer* • Mandy Patinkin *Brother Daniel* • Donal Donnelly *Brother Paul* ■ *Dir* Xavier Koller • *Scr* Darlene Craviotto, Bob Dolman

The Last Grenade ★★
Action drama 1970 · UK · Colour · 93mins

Stanley Baker never quite attained the heady heights his obvious talents deserved and by the seventies was the forgotten star of British cinema. Films like this only accelerated his decline, a predictable revenge drama with plenty of explosions and fights but little cranial activity. Baker plays a tough mercenary who vows retribution against a traitorous ex-colleague. Along the way he falls for the obvious charms of Honor Blackman in a ludicrous romantic subplot riddled with the kind of dialogue even soap operas would reject. A terrific supporting cast, including Richard Attenborough and a pre-*Sweeney* John Thaw, do their best, but director Gordon Flemyng misses a real chance to explore the psychology of the mercenary soldier.

Stanley Baker *Major Harry Grigsby* • Alex Cord *Kip Thompson* • Honor Blackman *Mrs Katherine Whiteley* • Richard Attenborough *General Charles Whiteley* • Rafer Johnson *Joe Jackson* • Andrew Keir *Gordon MacKenzie* • Ray Brooks *Lieutenant David Coulson* • Julian Glover *Andy Royale* • John Thaw *Terry Mitchell* ■ *Dir* Gordon Flemyng • *Scr* Kenneth Ware, John Sherlock, James Mitchell, from the novel *The Ordeal of Major Grigsby* by John Sherlock

The Last Hard Men ★
Western 1976 · US · Colour · 97mins

You expect a lot better than this violent, sadistic revenge western from a picture starring Charlton Heston and James Coburn. The latter is the villain whose plan for getting back at former lawman Heston includes kidnapping his virginal daughter (played by Barbara Hershey) and having her raped within his sight. Director Andrew V McLaglen copies Sam Peckinpah's use of slow motion for key moments but misses the relentless intensity the piece needed to be more artistically valid. It is merely nasty.

Charlton Heston *Sam Burgade* • James Coburn *Zach Provo* • Barbara Hershey *Susan Burgade* • Jorge Rivero *Cesar Menendez* • Michael Parks *Sheriff Noel Nye* • Larry Wilcox *Mike Shelby* ■ *Dir* Andrew V McLaglen • *Scr* Guerdon Trueblood, from the novel *Gun Down* by Brian Garfield

Last Holiday ★★★ Ⓤ
Comedy drama 1950 · UK · BW · 88mins

An amiable ensemble affair, Alec Guinness holds centre stage, as a stuffed shirt who, having been diagnosed with a fatal illness,

discovers all-too-late that he's been missing out on the finer things in life. It's the supporting cast, however, that gives the film the animated gentility that is so achingly British. Kay Walsh, Wilfrid Hyde White, Sid James and Ernest Thesiger stand out among the eccentrics and everyday folk who populate JB Priestley's heart-warming script. Corny, perhaps, but for all that, rather nice.

Alec Guinness *George Bird* • Beatrice Campbell *Sheila Rockingham* • Kay Walsh *Mrs Poole* • Bernard Lee *Inspector Wilton* • Wilfrid Hyde White *Chalfont* • Muriel George *Lady Oswington* • Sidney James *Joe Clarence* ■ *Dir* Henry Cass • *Scr* JB Priestley

Last House on the Left ★★★
Horror 1972 · US · Colour · 91mins

Promoted with the tagline "To avoid fainting, just keep repeating it's only a movie … it's only a movie!", this was the legendary graphic shocker which put director Wes Craven on the road to horror fame. Inspired by Ingmar Bergman's *The Virgin Spring*, and infused by a repellent Vietnam sensibility, two girls are kidnapped on the way to a rock concert by four sadistic convicts and are subjected to humiliating rape, torture and death. Their parents then mete out an equally horrific revenge when the foursome conveniently turn up on their doorstep. With hardcore violence running a grisly gamut from sodomy, urination, disembowelment and oral castration, this hard-to-watch and highly controversial cult film gains enormous power from its low-budget trappings and cinema vérité approach. A benchmark in the annals of cinematic offensiveness.

David A Hess [David Hess] *Krug* • Lucy Grantham *Phyllis* • Sandra Cassel *Mari Collingwood* • Marc Sheffler *Junior* ■ *Dir/Scr* Wes Craven

The Last Hunt ★★★★
Western 1956 · US · Colour · 108mins

Robert Taylor plays against his heroic, matinée idol image as a crazed, racist buffalo hunter who slaughters the animals, the tribesmen and anything else that comes close in an early "anti-western". Stewart Granger is another hunter, not quite in Taylor's league, who finally becomes disillusioned and steals pretty native American woman Debra Paget away from his partner. This remains a tough, unsentimental movie, with muscular direction from Richard Brooks who achieves much authenticity by staging the action in Custer State Park, South Dakota, during the annual cull of the buffalo herd.

Robert Taylor (1) *Charles Gilson* • Stewart Granger *Sandy McKenzie* • Lloyd Nolan *Woodfoot* • Debra Paget *Indian girl* • Russ Tamblyn *Jimmy* • Constance Ford *Peg* ■ *Dir* Richard Brooks • *Scr* Richard Brooks, from the novel by Milton Lott

The Last Hurrah ★★★ Ⓤ
Political drama 1958 · US · BW · 120mins

Spencer Tracy stars as Frank Skeffington, an old-time political operator standing for mayor one last time and observed with wide-eyed

approval by his nephew, Jeffrey Hunter. This is a great part for Tracy and he runs and runs with it, turning on the Irish-American blarney when it suits him, showing expediency and iron-hard calculation when he thinks no one is looking. As so often with John Ford's films, there's also a flabby sentimentality even when he's dealing with the cut-throat electoral process, but the film's optimism strangely anticipated the defeat of Nixon and the triumph of Kennedy in 1961.

Spencer Tracy *Frank Skeffington* • Jeffrey Hunter *Adam Caulfield* • Dianne Foster *Maeve Caulfield* • Pat O'Brien *John Gorman* • Basil Rathbone *Norman Cass Sr* • Donald Crisp *The Cardinal* • James Gleason *Cuke Gillen* • Edward Brophy *Ditto Boland* ■ *Dir* John Ford • *Scr* Frank Nugent, from the novel by Edwin O'Conner

Last Images of the Shipwreck ★★★ 15
Drama 1989 · Arg/Sp · Colour · 122mins

Although it passes comment on the existing political situation and provides an unflinching glimpse of Buenos Aires lowlife, Eliseo Subiela's second feature is primarily concerned with the relationship between life and art. Trapped in both his marriage and his job, insurance salesman Lorenzo Quinteros becomes convinced that he has found the subject for his much-stalled novel after he encounters prostitute Noemi Frenkel and her three bizarre brothers. The pacing is occasionally ponderous and the fantasy elements incongruous, but the performances are first-rate, with Quinteros's confusion growing apace as the lines between fact and fiction become dangerously blurred. In Spanish with English subtitles. 🖭

Lorenzo Quinteros *Roberto* • Noemi Frenkel *Estela* • Hugo Soto *Claudio* • Pablo Brichta *Jose* • Sara Benitez *Mother* • Andres Tiengo *Mario* ■ *Dir/Scr* Eliseo Subiela

The Last Innocent Man ★★★ 18
Thriller 1987 · US · Colour · 113mins

A tight coil of suspense, sustained throughout by an inventively shaped script, keeps alive the spirit of the film's source novel by American legal scribe Philip M Margolin. The palpable tension and dry heated atmosphere are helped considerably by Ed Harris in the role of a sharp criminal lawyer defending his girlfriend's estranged husband. His reliable grimace and bullet head are useful cosmetic aids in helping him to create a tangible sense of controlled thunder. 🖭

Ed Harris *Harry Nash* • Roxanne Hart *Jenny Stafford* • David Suchet *Jonathan Gault* • Bruce McGill *Bruce Mason* • Darrell Larson *Phillip Stafford* • Rose Gregorio *Monica Powers* • Clarence Williams III *DJ Johnson* ■ *Dir* Roger Spottiswoode • *Scr* Dan Bronson, from the novel by Phillip M Margolin

The Last Island ★★★★
Drama 1990 · Neth · Colour · 115mins

A superior screenplay, telling characterisation and strong ensemble acting are the qualities that make this tale about the survivors of an airline crash marooned on a desert island into an engrossing and distinctive

drama. Sharp direction by noted film-maker Marleen Gorris also helps expose the brutish realities that lie beneath the biscuit-thin veneer of what we like to think of as civilisation. With familiar faces such as Patricia Hayes and Paul Freeman in the cast, it's almost an adult version of *Lord of the Flies*. In English and Dutch with subtitles. Contains swearing.

Patricia Hayes *Mrs Godame* • Paul Freeman *Sean* • Shelagh McLeod *Joanna* • Ian Tracey *Jack* • Marc Berman *Pierre* • Kenneth Colley *Nick* • Mark Hembrow *Frank* ■ *Dir/Scr* Marleen Gorris

The Last Journey ★★★ Ⓤ
Drama 1936 · UK · BW · 62mins

By turns thrilling, ludicrous, tense and just plain naff, this British B-movie is well worth seeking out. Julian Mitchell plays a train driver who is forced into retirement and is so consumed by jealousy over his fireman's dalliance with his wife that he decides his last train journey will end in disaster. It's after he forces the fireman to stoke the engine up to dangerously high speed that panicked passenger and brain specialist, Godfrey Tearle, starts his heroic clamber along the speeding train to do his "there there, old chap, let's all have a nice cup of tea" speech. Made for peanuts, this is almost in *The Lady Vanishes* class. 🖭

Godfrey Tearle *Specialist* • Hugh Williams *Man* • Judy Gunn *Girl* • Mickey Brantford *Boy* • Julien Mitchell *Driver* • Olga Lindo *Wife* • Michael Hogan *Fireman* ■ *Dir* Bernard Vorhaus • *Scr* John Soutar, H Fowler Mear, from the story *The Last Journey* by J Jefferson Farjeon

The Last Known Address ★★★
Drama 1969 · Fr · Colour · 95mins

Written and directed by José Giovanni, this uncompromising police procedural questions whether the end ever really justifies the means. Bringing a dour purpose to the part of the veteran inspector demoted to a provincial beat after killing a murder suspect, Lino Ventura dominates proceedings as he seeks to persuade a reluctant witness to testify and, more mundanely, searches for some stolen birds. However, he's ably backed by Marlène Jobert as the assistant urging him to tone down the city methods that she deems far too ruthless for his new patch. Grittily shot by Étienne Becker, this is abrasive stuff. French dialogue dubbed into English.

Lino Ventura *Inspector* • Marlène Jobert *Assistant* • Michel Constantin *Hood* • Alain Mottet *Chief* ■ *Dir/Scr* José Giovanni • *Cinematographer* Étienne Becker

The Last Laugh ★★★★★
Classic silent drama
1924 · Ger · BW · 73mins

FW Murnau, who had made an impact with his expressionist masterpiece, *Nosferatu, a Symphony of Horrors* (1922), here moved closer to the *Kammerspielfilm* (chamber film), which dealt with ordinary people and events with an element of social criticism. The imposing Emil Jannings plays an elderly doorman at a luxury hotel, proud of his work and uniform, who is reduced to becoming a lavatory attendant. Murnau's *mise en scène* and the brilliant subjective camerawork allow the story to be told without the use of intertitles, except for one that introduces the epilogue. The happy ending, in which Jannings inherits a fortune, and which was tacked on at the insistence of the producer, can also be accepted as the man's dream.

Emil Jannings *Doorman* • Maly Delschaft *His daughter* • Max Hiller *Her fiancé* • Emilie Kurz *His aunt* • Hans Unterkircher *Hotel manager* ■ *Dir* FW Murnau • *Scr* Carl Mayer • *Cinematographer* Karl Freund

Last Light ★★★ 18

Prison drama   1993 · US · Colour · 100mins

Kiefer Sutherland made an impressive debut behind the camera with this bleak prison drama. He also takes the starring role as the brutalised prisoner on death row who forms a cautious and unlikely friendship with sensitive guard Forest Whitaker. Sutherland puts in one of his best performances, and he is matched by Whitaker, while there are also fine supporting turns from Amanda Plummer and Kathleen Quinlan. Despite its grim subject matter, this movie has a brooding power that grips.

Kiefer Sutherland *Denver Bayliss* • Forest Whitaker *Fred Whitmore* • Amanda Plummer *Lillian Burke* • Kathleen Quinlan *Kathy Rubicek* • Lynne Moody *Hope Whitmore* • Clancy Brown *Lionel McMannis* ■ *Dir* Kiefer Sutherland • *Scr* Robert Eisele

Last Lives ★ 18

Science-fiction   1997 · US · Colour · 91mins

Billy Wirth, a convict living in a parallel universe, emerges from that dimension to search for Jennifer Rubin, the earthbound soul mate to whom he is psychically connected. When he whisks her away on her wedding day, would-be groom C Thomas Howell goes in hot pursuit armed with an endless supply of life-saving magical wristbands. A poorly scripted sci-fi letdown, it sports lousy special effects and career-worst performances from practically everyone. A virtually unwatchable disaster that reaches lunatic heights with Howell mangled, burnt, blown to bits, dropped from a great height, shot and repeatedly killed so many times it becomes a bad joke.

C Thomas Howell *Aaron* • Jennifer Rubin *Adrienne* • Billy Wirth *Malakai* • Judge Reinhold *Merkhan* • Robert Pentz *Khafar* ■ *Dir* Worth Keeter • *Scr* Dan Duling

Last Man Standing ★★ 18

Western   1996 · US · Colour · 96mins

Gun-for-hire Bruce Willis arrives in a small Texas town and gets involved in a gang war over bootleg alcohol in director Walter Hill's weak Prohibition-era remake of the Japanese classic *Yojimbo* (which was also the source for *A Fistful of Dollars*). Every cliché in the Sergio Leone catalogue is dragged out and used to minor effect in this ham-fisted action thriller that's given an unattractive dusty look with uniformly weak performances to match. Willis gives his usual constipated hard-man act, but the uninspired emphasis on bloody brutality leaves what little Hill

has to say about courage and loyalty high and very dry. Contains swearing and violence. [cc] *DVD*

Bruce Willis *John Smith* • Christopher Walken *Hickey* • Alexandra Powers *Lucy Kalinski* • David Patrick Kelly *Doyle* • William Sanderson *Joe Monday* • Karina Lombard *Felina* • Ned Eisenberg *Fredo Strozzi* • Michael Imperioli *Giorgio Carmonte* ■ *Dir* Walter Hill • *Scr* Walter Hill, from a story by Akira Kurosawa, Ryuzo Kikushima

The Last Married Couple in America ★★

Comedy   1980 · US · Colour · 102mins

This last gasp of the seventies fashion for marital comedies dealing in the sexual "liberation" of middle-class couples stars Natalie Wood and George Segal. They're a husband and wife who endeavour to deal with a surfeit of divorces among their friends – which includes Segal's involvement with the inviting Valerie Harper. Despite the more than usual utterance of expletives, the competent direction of Gilbert Cates, a bunch of "swinging" couples paying for the wages of sin, and the presence of Richard Benjamin in neurotic mode, it was always superficial and is now pretty old hat.

George Segal *Jeff Thomson* • Natalie Wood *Mari Thomson* • Richard Benjamin *Marv Cooper* • Arlene Golonka *Sally Cooper* • Allan Arbus *Al Squib* • Marilyn Sokol *Alice Squib* • Dom DeLuise *Walter Holmes* • Valerie Harper *Barbara* ■ *Dir* Gilbert Cates • *Scr* John Herman Shaner

The Last Metro ★★★ PG

Wartime drama   1980 · Fr · Colour · 125mins

Considering he'd always wanted to make a film about the Occupation, François Truffaut largely ignores its hideous realities in this nostalgic tribute to the theatre. In essence, this is a backstage equivalent of *Day for Night*, with the Nazi threat replacing the impatience of the moneymen. The dynamic between the members of Jewish manager Heinz Bennent's company is well sustained, as is the mystery of whether Bennent's wife Catherine Deneuve prefers him to actor/Resistance fighter Gérard Depardieu. But the life of this enclosed ensemble is too divorced from history to make the movie anything more than just a handsomely mounted, meticulously performed fantasy. In French with English subtitles. [cc]

Catherine Deneuve *Marion Steiner* • Gérard Depardieu *Bernard Granger* • Jean Poiret *Jean-Loup Cottins* • Heinz Bennent *Lucas Steiner* • Andréa Ferréol *Arlette Guillaume* • Paulette Dubost *Germaine Fabre* • Sabine Haudepin *Nadine Marsac* • Jean-Louis Richard *Daxiat* ■ *Dir* François Truffaut • *Scr* François Truffaut, Suzanne Schiffman, Jean-Claude Grumberg, from a story by François Truffaut, Suzanne Schiffman

The Last Mile ★★

Crime drama   1959 · US · BW · 82mins

The title is the term given to the walk from a Death Row cell to the electric chair, and is also the title of the play through which Spencer Tracy and Clark Gable won Hollywood contracts. In contrast, Mickey Rooney's reputation had long been established when he took the part of a vicious convict who

organises a prison riot. The claim in the prologue that such things no longer happen in US prisons is as unconvincing as much of this clichéd but lively film.

Mickey Rooney *"Killer" John Mears* • Alan Bunce *Warden* • Frank Conroy *O'Flaherty (Guard)* • Leon Janney *Callahan (Guard)* • Frank Overton *Father O'Connors* • Clifford David *Convict Richard Walters* • Harry Millard *Convict Fred Mayor* • John McCurry *Convict Vince Jackson* • Ford Rainey *Convict "Red" Kirby* ■ *Dir* Howard W Koch • *Scr* Milton Subotsky, Seton I Miller, John Wexley

The Last Movie ★

Experimental drama
1971 · US · Colour · 107mins

After the huge success of *Easy Rider* (1969), director Dennis Hopper could have made any movie he wanted. Sadly he did just that, and the resulting fiasco is one of the all-time classics of pretentiously incomprehensible cinema. Outlining the hippy antics of a film crew in South America aiming to shoot a western, Hopper uses movie-making as a metaphor for imperialism in this mess of over-indulgent allegory and mind-numbing ranting.

Dennis Hopper *Kansas* • Stella Garcia *Maria* • Samuel Fuller *Director* • Daniel Ades *Thomas Mercado* • Tomas Milian *Priest* • Don Gordon *Neville* • Julie Adams *Mrs Anderson* • Peter Fonda *Sheriff* • Kris Kristofferson *Minstrel Wrangler* • Henry Jaglom *Minister's son* • Michelle Phillips *Banker's daughter* • Dean Stockwell *Billy* • Russ Tamblyn *Member of Billy's gang* ■ *Dir* Dennis Hopper • *Scr* Stewart Stern, from a story by Stewart Stern, Dennis Hopper

Last Night ★★★★ 15

Drama   1998 · Can/Fr · Colour · 94mins

"A small film that is really a big film" is how David Cronenberg, best known as a director but acting here, describes director Don McKellar's eclectically witty and deeply moving tale. Set against the countdown to Armageddon, this is a captivating ensemble piece that somehow makes imminent oblivion seem life-affirming. As McKellar reneges on a nostalgic family Christmas, old school pal Callum Keith Rennie completes his sexual wish-list, teacher Geneviève Bujold revisits her favourite students and Sandra Oh attempts to cross town to fulfil her suicide pact with husband Cronenberg. Lamenting both the nihilism of youth and the wistfulness of old age, this is a genuinely poignant and provocative picture. Contains swearing, sex scenes and some violence. [cc]

Don McKellar *Patrick Wheeler* • Sandra Oh *Sandra* • Callum Keith Rennie *Craig Zwiller* • Sarah Polley *Jennifer Wheeler* • David Cronenberg *Duncan* • Robin Gammell *Mr Wheeler* • Roberta Maxwell *Mrs Wheeler* • Tracy Wright *Donna* • Geneviève Bujold *Mrs Carlton* ■ *Dir/Scr* Don McKellar

The Last Ninja ★★

Martial arts drama
1983 · US · Colour · 100mins

This uninspiring TV stab at the martial arts genre looks suspiciously like a failed pilot. Michael Beck, an unlikely arts expert who also happens to be a lethal ninja warrior, is called in by the

government to track down some terrorists with similar kung fu knowledge. Sho Kosugi lends a veneer of respectability, but director William A Graham displays little understanding of the genre.

Michael Beck *Ken Sakura* • Nancy Kwan *Noriko Sakura* • Mako *Maturo Sakura* • John McMartin *Mr Cosmo* • Richard Lynch *Professor Gustave Norden* ■ *Dir* William A Graham • *Scr* Ed Spielman

The Last of England ★ 18

Drama   1987 · UK · Colour and BW · 87mins

Director Derek Jarman's angry polemic on the state of Britain in the mid-1980s is one for his die-hard fans only. Scattershot images of inner-city decay and violent paramilitaries collide with clips from Jarman's own home movies as actor Nigel Terry gives voice to concerns about the urban plight invading the collective unconsciousness. No British turn is left unstoned as Jarman experiments with technique in a boring melange of images jazzed up with deliberately confrontational material. Redundant and old-fashioned when it was made, it may serve as a relevant time capsule comment in the years to come.

Spring • Gerrard McArthur • Tilda Swinton • Nigel Terry ■ *Dir* Derek Jarman • *Music* Simon Fisher Turner • • *Scr* Derek Jarman

The Last of Mrs Cheyney ★★★

Comedy   1929 · US · BW · 94mins

MGM's favourite actress – after she married studio boss Irving Thalberg – Norma Shearer gives gloss, but not much conviction to the role of the eponymous Mrs Cheyney. Playing an adventuress let loose in English high society, she wreaks moral havoc – like a wolf among lambs – with Basil Rathbone and Hedda Hopper (who went on to be a feared gossip columnist). Adapted from an oft-filmed stage play by Frederick Lonsdale it already seemed dated at the time it was released, but its social nuances are still fascinating.

Norma Shearer *Mrs Cheyney* • Basil Rathbone *Lord Arthur Dilling* • George Barraud *Charles* • Herbert Bunston *Lord Elton* • Hedda Hopper *Lady Maria* • Moon Carroll *Joan* • Madeleine Seymour *Mrs Wynton* • Cyril Chadwick *Willie Wynton* ■ *Dir* Sidney Franklin • *Scr* Hans Krály, Claudine West, from a play by Frederick Lonsdale • *Art Director* Cedric Gibbons

The Last of Mrs Cheyney ★★★

Comedy drama   1937 · US · BW · 98mins

Revived recently on the London stage as a vehicle for Joan Collins, this Frederick Lonsdale theatrical chestnut has always attracted great female stars to its showy, creaky title role. The 1929 Norma Shearer version is rarely shown, but movie fans have the consolation of the 1951 remake called *The Law and the Lady* with a Cecil Beaton-dressed Greer Garson, and this rather slow, dated but nevertheless glossy and engaging Joan Crawford version from MGM's golden age. There's more to it than just Crawford showing off, though, with William Powell and Robert Montgomery equally

as impressive as they battle to out-suave each other in supporting roles.

Joan Crawford *Fay Cheyney* • William Powell *Charles* • Robert Montgomery *Lord Arthur Dilling* • Frank Morgan *Lord Kelton* • Jessie Ralph *Duchess* • Nigel Bruce *Sir William* • Benita Hume *Kitty* • Colleen Clare *Joan* • Ralph Forbes *Cousin John* ■ *Dir* Richard Boleslawski • *Scr* Leon Gordon, Samson Raphaelson, Monckton Hoffe, from the play by Frederick Lonsdale

The Last of Sheila ★★★★

Comedy mystery
1973 · US · Colour · 123mins

Sharing a liking for whodunits and word games, composer Stephen Sondheim and actor Anthony Perkins joined forces to write this mystery movie. Set aboard a luxury yacht, widowed Hollywood producer James Coburn gets his friends and colleagues to play a Cluedo-like game, the result of which will reveal the killer of Coburn's wife. A conceit from start to finish, it should delight connoisseurs of camp, though few critics at the time appreciated the joke. It's like *Murder on the Orient Express* rewritten by Julian Clary, but with jet-set Riviera locations and a glam cast of stars with their tongues in their cheeks.

James Coburn *Clinton* • James Mason *Philip* • Raquel Welch *Alice* • Richard Benjamin *Tom* • Joan Hackett *Lee* • Ian McShane *Anthony* • Dyan Cannon *Christine* ■ *Dir* Herbert Ross • *Scr* Anthony Perkins, Stephen Sondheim • *Production Designer* Ken Adam

Last of the Badmen ★★

Western
1957 · US · Colour · 79mins

This western has a cracking premise: a gang springs outlaws from jail, uses them for hold-ups until the price on their head increases, then turns in their corpses and collects the reward. Unfortunately, George Montgomery is wooden as the detective who goes undercover to investigate the racket, and the intriguing plotline is inadequately realised thanks to the paucity of the budget. The story was used again in 1964 as the same studio for *Gunfight at Comanche Creek* with Audie Murphy.

George Montgomery *Dan Barton* • James Best *Ted Hamilton* • Meg Randall *Lila* • Douglas Kennedy *Hawkins* • Michael Ansara *Kramer* • Keith Larsen *Roberts* • Robert Foulk *Taylor* • Willis Bouchley *Marshal Parker* ■ *Dir* Paul Landres • *Scr* Daniel B Ullman, David Chantler, from the story by Daniel B Ullman

Last of the Comanches ★★

Western
1952 · US · Colour · 85mins

Broderick Crawford is not the most charismatic of western stars but he's effectively cast as the burly cavalry sergeant fleeing across the desert from an Indian massacre with a handful of fellow soldiers. They pick up others en route and keep the Comanches at bay from an abandoned mission. The long siege is moderately suspenseful under director Andre De Toth's handling, while the excellent photography and score deserve a better picture.

Broderick Crawford *Sgt Matt Trainor* • Barbara Hale *Julia Lanning* • Johnny Stewart *Little Knife* • Lloyd Bridges *Jim Starbuck* • Mickey Shaughnessy *Rusty Potter* • George Mathews *Romany O'Rattigan* ■ *Dir* Andre De Toth • *Scr* Kenneth Gamet

Last of the Dogmen ★★ PG

Drama romance adventure
1995 · US · Colour · 112mins

Dumb modern western about a bounty hunter (Tom Berenger) on the trail of escaped convicts, who discovers a tribe of Cheyenne Indians living undisturbed in the Rocky Mountains. A pedestrian copy of *Dances With Wolves*, with native bonding and a spiky relationship between Berenger and a professor of Indian anthropology who's conveniently both female and attractive (Barbara Hershey). Throwing various other genre clichés into the soup (the bounty hunter and the sheriff have a past), this has some decent, grizzled work from Berenger, but the script isn't sharp enough to overcome the highly implausible premise. ▭

Tom Berenger *Lewis Gates* • Barbara Hershey *Professor Lillian Sloan* • Kurtwood Smith *Sheriff Deegan* • Andrew Miller *Briggs* • Steve Reevis *Yellow Wolf* • Wilford Brimley *Narrator* ■ *Dir/Scr* Tab Murphy

The Last of the Good Old Days ★★★

Comedy
1989 · Cz · Colour · 97mins

With a blend of bedroom farce and socio-political allegory that recalls Jean Renoir's *La Règle du Jeu*, this is a deliciously barbed satire on the Czech ruling elite. With aristocrats and their domestics siding against the bourgeoisie and the bureaucrats, this inter-war country house comedy bristles with class conflict as self-made slob Marian Labuda tries to keep his innocent daughter away from indolent duke Josef Abrham. Wittily scripted by Jiří Blazek and shot in autumnal hues to suggest the passage of an era, this superbly acted period piece may only be a minor effort from Jiří Menzel, but it's still hugely enjoyable. A Czech language film.

Josef Abrham *Duke Alexei* • Marian Labuda *Josef Stoklasa* • Jaromir Hanzlik *Bernard Spera, the Librarian* • Rudolf Hrusinsky *Jakub Lhota* ■ *Dir* Jiri Menzel • *Scr* Jiri Blazek, from a novel by Vladislav Vancura

Last of the High Kings ★★ 15

Comedy drama
1996 · Ire/UK/Den · Colour · 100mins

This pleasant, if unremarkable, rites of passage drama revolves around the growing pains of Dublin lad Jared Leto as he tries to cope with being a descendant of Celtic Kings. His wacky family includes an overly political mother and a virtually unseen father (Gabriel Byrne) who communicates from America in Shakespearean couplets. It's when American Christina Ricci arrives for the summer holidays that the generation gap widens further and virginity-loss becomes a top agenda item. Set in the seventies, Leto overdoes the cute confusion while the film is stolen by Stephen Rea in a small cameo as a know-it-all taxi driver. Contains some swearing and a sex scene. ▭

Catherine O'Hara *Cathleen* • Jared Leto *Frankie Griffin* • Christina Ricci *Erin* • Gabriel Byrne *Jack Griffin* • Stephen Rea *Cab driver* • Colm Meaney *Jim Davern* • Lorraine Pilkington *Jayne Wayne* • Emily Mortimer *Romy* ■ *Dir* David Keating • *Scr* David Keating, Gabriel Byrne, from the novel by Ferdia MacAnna

Last of the Mobile Hot-Shots ★★

Drama
1970 · US · Colour · 107mins

One of Sidney Lumet's lesser-known works, this trip into Tennessee Williams territory ultimately fails to live up to its promise. However, it is still worth a look for the talent alone. The script, based on Williams's play *The Seven Descents of Myrtle*, was co-written by Gore Vidal, while the interesting cast is headed up by James Coburn and Lynn Redgrave. (Released in the UK as *Blood Kin*.)

Lynn Redgrave *Myrtle* • Robert Hooks *Chicken* • Perry Hayes *George* • Reggie King *Rube* • James Coburn *Jeb* ■ *Dir* Sidney Lumet • *Scr* Gore Vidal, Mark Valenti, from the play *The Seven Descents of Myrtle* by Tennessee Williams

The Last of the Mohicans ★★★★★

Silent period adventure
1920 · US · BW

This silent adaptation of James Fenimore Cooper's famous story was the masterpiece of Maurice Tourneur, the French-born director and father of Jacques who worked for MGM until a violent disagreement made him return to Europe. One of Boris Karloff's earliest films (he plays a marauding redskin), it has visuals to die for and some of the most ferocious massacre scenes ever filmed. Yet human values are never sacrificed in this story of an Indian scout, the last survivor of the Mohican tribe, escorting two girls through perilous territory. The picture has a ruggedness to make pulses beat faster and a poignancy that touches the heart, while the ending is starkly tragic. Wallace Beery and Barbara Bedford are the stars, but it is Tourneur who makes this special – despite being forced by an accident to share directorial duties with a young Clarence Brown.

Wallace Beery *Magua* • Barbara Bedford *Cora Munro* • Albert Roscoe *Uncas* • Lillian Hall *Alice Munro* • Henry Woodward *Major Heyward* • James Gordon *Colonel Munro* • George Hackathorne *Captain Randolph* • Nelson McDowell *David Gamut* • Boris Karloff *Marauding Indian* ■ *Dir* Maurice Tourneur, Clarence Brown • *Scr* Robert A Dillon, from the novel by James Fenimore Copper

The Last of the Mohicans ★★★

Period adventure
1936 · US · BW · 91mins

Though not a patch on the 1992 epic starring Daniel Day-Lewis, this is an honest attempt at filming the James Fenimore Cooper classic. Randolph Scott makes a strapping Hawkeye, but Robert Barrat is ill-cast as Chingachgook, the native American of the title. The action sequences are remarkably well-staged by director George B Seitz, who had directed the tale in 1924 as part of a ten-part adaptation of Cooper's collected tales called *Leatherstocking*, and who would go on to make MGM's popular *Andy Hardy* series.

Randolph Scott *Hawkeye* • Binnie Barnes *Alice Munro* • Heather Angel *Cora Munro* • Hugh Buckler *Colonel Munro* • Henry Wilcoxon *Major Duncan Heyward* • Robert Barrat *Chingachgook* ■ *Dir* George B Seitz • *Scr* Philip Dunne, John Balderston, Paul Perez, Daniel Moore, from the novel by James Fenimore Cooper

The Last of the Mohicans ★★★★ 15

Period adventure
1992 · US · Colour · 107mins

This exciting mix of high adventure, romance and history lesson is wonderfully presented in a colossal, glossy package. Daniel Day-Lewis is Hawkeye, the frontiersman raised by Mohicans, who gets caught between two cultures when he falls for Madeline Stowe, a British army officer's daughter. In the ensuing and, it must be said, often confusing bloody battles involving the French, the British and American Indians (the scalpings, by the way, are very realistic) he refuses to give up his adopted tribe's cause, or his love. Directed by Michael Mann, this is one of the few war movies that has proved more popular with women than men. It's an admirable effort, but Mann should also have paid more attention to his dialogue, which often sounds too contemporary for the 1750s. However, the well staged action sequences and his grandiose sense of scale combine to produce an epic that harks back to the good old-fashioned adventure films of Hollywood's heyday. Contains violence.

Daniel Day-Lewis *Hawkeye* • Madeleine Stowe *Cora Munro* • Russell Means *Chingachgook* • Eric Schweig *Uncas* • Jodhi May *Alice Munro* • Steven Waddington *Major Duncan Heyward* • Wes Studi *Magua* • Maurice Roëves *Colonel Edmund Munro* • Patrice Chéreau *General Montcalm* ■ *Dir* Michael Mann • *Scr* Michael Mann, Christopher Crowe, from the 1936 film, from the novel by James Fenimore Cooper

Last of the Pony Riders ★ U

Western
1953 · US · BW · 59mins

This innocuous story of the last days of the Pony Express was the last of the Gene Autry B-westerns as the two-fisted warbler moved his exploits to the small screen. A declining market had led to shorter running times and fewer songs (two in this one) for his last dozen pictures, while Autry himself was looking heavier and older. It's very much business as usual here with nothing special by way of a farewell.

Gene Autry • Smiley Burnette • Kathleen Case *Katie McEwen* • Dick Jones [Dickie Jones] *Johnny Blair* • John Downey *Tom McEwen* ■ *Dir* George Archainbaud • *Scr* Ruth Woodman

The Last of the Red Hot Lovers ★★

Comedy
1972 · US · Colour · 92mins

Happily married for more than 20 years, Barney Cashman craves to have just one extra-marital affair, as if to prove his manhood and romantic worth. Neil Simon's script, based on his Broadway hit, was probably dated the day it opened and was seen mainly by out-of-town audiences up for a day on Broadway, ready to laugh at even the laziest one-liner and howl with mirth at Simon's raunchiness, even though George Axelrod had done it years before in *The Seven Year Itch*. As Cashman, Alan Arkin brings his trademark tics and seediness, and there are three beauties lined up to frustrate his longings: Sally Kellerman, Paula Prentiss and Renee Taylor.

Alan Arkin *Barney Cashman* • Sally Kellerman *Elaine* • Paula Prentiss *Bobbi Michele* • Renee Taylor *Jeanette* • Bella Bruck *Cashier* ■ *Dir* Gene Saks • *Scr* Neil Simon, from his play

The Last of the Secret Agents ★★ U

Spy comedy   1966 · US · Colour · 76mins

Matt Helm, Derek Flint, Napoleon Solo, Hollywood tried but there was no one to touch 007 in the sixties cloak-and-dagger stakes and this bumbling spy spoof was a particularly auspicious failure. US double act Marty Allen and Steve Rossi bungle their bid to be the new Abbott and Costello as recently recruited spies out to thwart international art thieves. Theo Marcuse has fun as the head of evil empire THEM, possessor of the lost arms of the Venus de Milo statue and desperate to bag the rest of her, but writer/director Norman Abbott of *Get Smart* and *The Munsters* TV fame offers us mere crumbs of comedy amid an otherwise stale series of slapstick routines.

Marty Allen *Marty Johnson* • Steve Rossi *Steve Donovan* • John Williams *J Frederick Duval* • Nancy Sinatra *Micheline* • Lou Jacobi *Papa Leo* ■ *Dir* Norman Abbott • *Scr* Mel Tolkin, from the story *Don Juan, Ole* by Norman Abbott, Mel Tolkin

The Last Outlaw ★★ 15

Western   1993 · US · Colour · 89mins

Kiwi director Geoff Murphy followed up the success of *Young Guns II* with another stab at the western genre. A ridiculously coiffeured Mickey Rourke is left for dead by his gang of outlaws, so he hooks up with the local sheriff to gain his revenge. Meanwhile, his old lieutenant (Dermot Mulroney) attempts to lead the weary crooks to safety. Rourke's performance is as outlandish as his performance, but the rest of the cast (which includes John C McGinley and Steve Buscemi) is a tad more convincing, while Murphy's no-nonsense direction keeps things bounding along at a rollicking pace. ▣

Mickey Rourke *Graff* • Dermot Mulroney *Eustis* • Ted Levine *Potts* • John C McGinley *Wills* • Steve Buscemi *Philo* • Keith David *Lovecraft* ■ *Dir* Geoff Murphy • *Scr* Eric Red

The Last Outpost ★★

First World War drama
1935 · US · BW · 70mins

This teaming of Cary Grant and Claude Rains is a far cry from their later brilliance in Hitchcock's *Notorious*, although in both films Grant is in love with Rains's wife. Set in Africa during the First World War, this earlier movie combines action scenes with amorous rivalry that drives Rains to plot Grant's murder. Gertrude Michael plays the woman in the triangle. It was originally directed by Louis Gasnier, then largely reshot by Charles Barton.

Cary Grant *Michael Andrews* • Gertrude Michael *Rosemary Haydon* • Claude Rains

John Stevenson • Margaret Swope *Nurse Rowland* • Jameson Thomas *Cullen* • Colin Tapley *Lieutenant Prescott* • Akim Tamiroff *Mirov* ■ *Dir* Louis Gasnier, Charles Barton • *Scr* Philip MacDonald, Frank Partos (adaptation), Charles Brackett (adaptation), from the short story *The Drum* by F Britten Austen

The Last Page ★★

Crime   1952 · UK · BW · 84mins

Before it latched on to horror, Hammer made a deal with a minor American outfit to co-produce thrillers in Britain with lesser Hollywood stars. This ponderous drama was the first; it also marked Terence Fisher's directorial debut at the studio. Based on a play by James Hadley Chase and scripted by Frederick Knott (the author of *Dial M for Murder*), it features stolid George Brent as the London bookshop manager who is blackmailed for a momentary indiscretion by his busty young assistant, Diana Dors, at the instigation of her evil boyfriend, Peter Reynolds. He and Dors bring some life to the picture, and she more than justifies its American title, *Man Bait*.

George Brent *John Harman* • Marguerite Chapman *Stella* • Raymond Huntley *Clive* • Peter Reynolds *Jeff* • Diana Dors *Ruby* • Eleanor Summerfield *Vi* • Meredith Edwards *Dale* • Conrad Phillips *Todd* ■ *Dir* Terence Fisher • *Scr* Frederick Knott, from a story by James Hadley Chase

The Last Party ★★★

Documentary   1993 · US · Colour · 96mins

Most definitely not your typical Robert Downey Jr film. Downey is the host for a heavily satirical documentary that takes a tongue-in-cheek look at the 1992 race for the US Presidency. And one suspects he may have used his heavy-duty Hollywood clout to rope in the famous names and faces who help him trawl his non-comprehending way through the complex workings of the Republican and Democratic conventions. Unrated and little seen, probably because America is a little sensitive to its politicians being slyly sent-up like this.

Dir Mark Benjamin, Marc Levin • *Scr* Marc Levin, Josh Richman, Donovan Leitch, Mark Benjamin

The Last Picture Show ★★★★★ 15

Classic drama   1971 · US · BW · 114mins

Beautifully adapted by director Peter Bogdanovich and Larry McMurtry (from the latter's novel), this is a masterclass in how to create fully rounded characters and then give them real lives to lead. While the nostalgic elements of this memoir of small-town Texas in the fifties are lovingly realised (a miraculous blend of John Ford and Howard Hawks), it's the re-creation of that long-lost sense of community, in which everyone knew and respected one another, that makes this such a rewarding experience. Jeff Bridges and Cybill Shepherd stand out, but it's the playing of Timothy Bottoms and Cloris Leachman that gives the film its authenticity. ▣

Timothy Bottoms *Sonny Crawford* • Jeff Bridges *Duane Jackson* • Cybill Shepherd *Jacy Farrow* • Ben Johnson *Sam the Lion* • Cloris

Leachman *Ruth Popper* • Ellen Burstyn *Lois Farrow* • Eileen Brennan *Genevieve* • Clu Gulager *Abilene* • Sam Bottoms *Billy* • Randy Quaid *Lester Marlow* ■ *Dir* Peter Bogdanovich • *Scr* Larry McMurtry, Peter Bogdanovich, from the novel by Larry McMurtry

Last Plane Out ★★

War drama   1983 · US · Colour · 92mins

Low on budget, production values and even a modicum of balance, this political thriller is mere anti-Sandinista propaganda. Produced by Jack Cox and based on his journalistic assignment to Nicaragua during the Somoza regime, it comes to something when the most sympathetic character is Somoza himself. A love affair with a Sandinista rebel (Julie Carmen) is also fashioned into this particularly unpersuasive tale. Check out *Under Fire* for a more interesting treatment of the times.

Jan-Michael Vincent *Jack Cox* • Julie Carmen *Maria Cardena* • Mary Crosby *Liz Rush* • David Huffman *Jim Corley* • William Windom *James Caldwell* • Lloyd Battista *Anastasio Somoza* ■ *Dir* David Nelson • *Scr* Ernest Tidyman

The Last Posse ★★ U

Western   1953 · US · BW · 72mins

This unusual western is more concerned with mystery and suspense, with the pieces of the sombre story told in flashbacks. What really happened to the posse that went after three men accused of theft and came back with a mortally wounded sheriff? Broderick Crawford is the lawman, and Charles Bickford co-stars as a ruthless rancher; John Derek is the latter's adopted son, while Wandra Hendrix plays his girl. Though ably directed by Alfred Werker, the film's structure becomes a little tiresome; a straightforward account might have worked better.

Broderick Crawford *Sheriff Frazier* • John Derek *Jed Clayton* • Charles Bickford *Sampson Drune* • Wanda Hendrix *Deborah Morley* • Warner Anderson *Robert Emerson* • Henry Hull *Stokely* ■ *Dir* Alfred Werker • *Scr* Seymour Bennett, Connie Lee Bennett, Kenneth Gamet, from the story by Seymour Bennett, Connie Lee Bennett

The Last Prostitute ★★ 15

Drama   1991 · US · Colour · 88mins

Brazilian soap star Sonia Braga is the best thing about this rites-of-passage drama, demonstrating the experience she has gained in a wide variety of films, most famously *Kiss of the Spider Woman* and *The Milagro Beanfield War*. The film's not as prurient as the title suggests, but veteran TV movie director Lou Antonio finds it hard to make his other characters come to life. ▣

Sonia Braga *Loah* • Wil Wheaton *Danny* • David Kaufman *Burt* • Cotter Smith *Joe* • Dennis Letts *Mr Hancock* • Woody Watson *Raleigh* ■ *Dir* Lou Antonio • *Scr* Carmen Culver, from the play *The Last Prostitute Who Took Pride in Her Work* by William Borden

The Last Rebel ★

Western   1971 · US · Colour · 90mins

Sports star Joe Namath had tried acting before, but he still appears distinctly uncomfortable swapping a football for a pistol in this post-Civil War western. A muddled script and

clumsy direction by the little-known Denys McCoy leave him looking either sheepish or grinning. At least there's polished support from Jack Elam as a friend turned enemy, Woody Strode as a black saved from lynching and Ty Hardin as a man with a badge.

Joe Namath *Burnside Hollis* • Jack Elam *Matt Graves* • Woody Strode *Duncan* • Ty Hardin *Sheriff* • Victoria George *Pearl* • Renato Romano *Virgil* ■ *Dir* Denys McCoy • *Scr* Warren Kiefer

The Last Remake of Beau Geste ★★★ PG

Comedy   1977 · US · Colour · 80mins

A scrappy but good-natured send-up of the oft-filmed desert yarn, directed by and starring the goggle-eyed, surrealist comedian Marty Feldman whose TV series and appearances in several Mel Brooks movies led to this project. As a director, Feldman is ramshackle, and there are certain Python elements in the spoof that casts him with Michael York as brothers who search the Sahara for Ann-Margret and a missing diamond. Some of it works and a lot of it doesn't, but it's worth seeing for the virtual who's who of British comedy, from anarchist Spike Milligan to silly-ass Terry-Thomas. Film buffs will especially like the liberty taken with the Universal logo, and the sudden appearance of Feldman in the 1939 version with Gary Cooper. ▣

Ann-Margret *Flavia Geste* • Marty Feldman *Digby Geste* • Michael York *Beau Geste* • Peter Ustinov *Sergeant Markov* • James Earl Jones *Sheikh Abdul* • Trevor Howard *Sir Hector Geste* • Henry Gibson *General Pecheur* • Roy Kinnear *Corporal Boldini* • Spike Milligan *Crumble* • Terry-Thomas *Prison governor* • Irene Handl *Miss Wormwood* • Sinead Cusack *Isabel Geste* ■ *Dir* Marty Feldman • *Scr* Marty Feldman, Chris Allen, from a story by Sam Bobrick, from the novel by PC Wren

The Last Ride of the Dalton Gang ★★

Western   1979 · US · Colour

The Hollywood opening of this mammoth TV movie smacks of gimmickry, though it's not as far-fetched as it seems. Emmett Dalton not only survived the Coffeyville showdown that saw off his brothers, but also made two big screen versions of it, *The Last Stand of the Dalton Boys* (1912) and *Beyond the Law* (1918). The Daltons were less glamorous than other outlaw bands and were mostly consigned to B-movies. This heavily ironic tribute does them few favours, but the raids along the Kansas-Missouri border are effectively staged by director Dan Curtis and partly atone for the mocking characterisation.

Cliff Potts *Bob Dalton* • Randy Quaid *Grat Dalton* • Larry Wilcox *Emmett Dalton* • Sharon Farrell *Flo Quick* • Jack Palance *Will Smith* • Dale Robertson *Judge Isaac Parker* ■ *Dir* Dan Curtis • *Scr* Earl W Wallace

Last Rites ★★ 15

Thriller   1988 · US · Colour · 83mins

This misfiring thriller marks one of the lowest points in Tom Berenger's roller-coaster career. He stars as an unlikely Catholic priest caught up in a totally bewildering plot revolving around

U = SUITABLE FOR ALL   Uc = SUITABLE FOR ALL, ESPECIALLY FOR YOUNG CHILDREN (VIDEO ONLY)   PG = PARENTAL GUIDANCE

murder and the Mafia. Poor writing, direction and acting must have left Berenger (Oscar-nominated for his role in Oliver Stone's *Platoon* two years earlier) wondering how he got talked into this one. Contains violence and swearing. 📼

Tom Berenger *Father Michael Pace* • Daphne Zuniga *Angela* • Chick Vennera *Nuzo* • Anne Twomey *Zena Pace* • Dane Clark *Carlo Pace* • Paul Dooley *Father Freddie* ■ *Dir/Scr* Donald P Bellisario

Last Rites ★★★ 18
Psychological thriller
1998 · US · Colour · 87mins

Randy Quaid usually gets cast as the well-meaning goofball but here he turns on the chilling charm in this smart made-for-TV thriller. He plays a killer on Death Row who survives his date with death, thanks to a timely bolt of lightning striking the prison. Awaking the next morning, he has no memory of his murderous past and it is up to shrink Embeth Davidtz to work out whether he is telling the truth and whether his newly-acquired "psychic" powers are genuine. Director Kevin Dowling has fun spinning out the mind games and the result is a gripping psychological chiller.

Randy Quaid *Jeremy Dillon* • Embeth Davidtz *Dr Lauren Riggs* • A Martinez *Matt* • Clarence Williams III *Warden Pierce* • Paul Benjamin *Fez* • Jack Coleman *Gary Blake* ■ • *Scr* Tim Frost, from a story by Richard Outten

The Last Run ★★★★ 18
Crime drama 1971 · US · Colour · 91mins

John Huston started this thriller but quit after three weeks; his meddling with the script, a natural enmity between him and George C Scott and an awful lot of booze led to him being replaced by Richard Fleischer. The result, though, is marvellous, with Scott playing a lonely, burned-out gangster who agrees to do one last job – driving Spain's most wanted man and his girlfriend to the border, with the mob and the police in pursuit. It's a riveting, Hemingway-style story with Scott playing to perfection a man staring fate straight between the eyes. The Spanish landscape is superbly captured, and the score is particularly haunting. 📼

George C Scott *Harry Garmes* • Tony Musante *Paul Ricard* • Colleen Dewhurst *Monique* ■ *Dir* Richard Fleischer • *Scr* Alan Sharp • *Cinematographer* Sven Nykvist • *Music* Jerry Goldsmith

The Last Safari ★★
Action adventure
1967 · UK · Colour · 110mins

Stewart Granger, recalling his heyday in *King Solomon's Mines*, is a former white hunter who loathes the tourists he shows around the bush. One such tourist is top-billed Kaz Garas (plucked from American TV) and his mistress, Gabriella Licudi, who discover that Stewart is haunted by the death of his best pal under the feet of an elephant. When Stewart sets off to kill the elephant, Garas and Licudi go along, leading to all sorts of sub-sub-Hemingway stuff. Shot in Kenya and full of travelogue sequences, it squanders any drama in the story,

while the location photography is undermined by some eye-jarring process shots.

Kaz Garas *Casey* • Stewart Granger *Miles Gilchrist* • Gabriella Licudi *Grant* • Johnny Sekka *Jama* • Liam Redmond *Alec Beaumont* ■ *Dir* Henry Hathaway • *Scr* John Gay, from the novel *Gilligan's Last Elephant* by Gerald Hanley

The Last Seduction ★★★★★ 18
Thriller 1993 · US · Colour · 105mins

John Dahl secured his reputation as one of the hottest directors of the nineties with this cool-as-ice, wantonly playful, bitter-and-twisted excursion into neon-shaded contemporary *film noir*. At its commanding centre is sizzling and smouldering Linda Fiorentino in a star-making role as the man-eating *femme fatale* from hell. As gorgeous go-getter Bridget Gregory, she swaps dirty talk for dirty deeds when she cons husband Bill Pullman into doing a big drug deal, only to run off with the money. Hiding out in a small town, the manipulative mantrap changes identity, gets a new job and seduces besotted insurance agent Peter Berg in carrying out her every whim. Then she sets him up as the pawn in a daring game of double-cross. This sassy and superior suspense thriller is a must-see – pulp fiction rarely comes as well appointed or as absorbingly clever. 📼

Linda Fiorentino *Bridget Gregory* • Peter Berg *Mike Swale* • Bill Pullman *Clay Gregory* • JT Walsh *Frank Griffith* • Bill Nunn *Harlan* • Herb Mitchell *Bob Trotter* • Brien Varady *Chris* • Dean Norris *Shep* • Donna Wilson *Stacy* ■ *Dir* John Dahl • *Scr* Steve Barancik

The Last Seduction 2 ★★ 18
Romantic crime thriller
1998 · UK/US · Colour · 94mins

Dull, irrelevant sequel to one of the hippest, sexiest *films noirs* of the last three decades. Joan Severance steps into Linda Fiorentino's stilettos as the murderous ice maiden, who, finding the US too hot for her, heads for Barcelona and sets her sights on violent Irish crook Con O'Neill. However, on her tail is private eye Beth Goddard who is not above using her own femine wiles to nab her prey. The cast do their best, but this only makes you wish for the marvellous 1994 original. Contains swearing, sex scenes and some violence. 📼

Joan Severance *Bridget Gregory* • Beth Goddard *Murphy* • Con O'Neill *Troy Fenton* • Rocky Taylor *Gabriel* • Dean Williamson *Earl McLaughlin* ■ *Dir* Terry Marcel • *Scr* Dave Cummings

The Last September ★★★ 15
Period drama
1999 · UK/Ire/Fr · Colour · 103mins

Theatre director Deborah Warner has rounded up a company of stellar British talent for this stylised depiction of the decline of English power in Ireland after the 1916 Easter rising. Maggie Smith and Michael Gambon are superlatively arch as aristocrats hosting relentless house parties and family gatherings despite the unrest, while Keeley Hawes plays the wayward niece whose rejection of an English soldier in favour of an Irish anarchist

ultimately leads to tragedy. Slow and studied, Warner's film debut shows flashes of inspiration despite an innate theatricality that at times appears ridiculous and unreal. Yet she also creates great emotional poignancy, typified by the unhappily married Francie (Jane Birkin), a bitter and sad shadow who floats around the estate like the ghost of happiness past.

Maggie Smith *Lady Myra* • Michael Gambon *Sir Richard Naylor* • Jane Birkin *Francie Montmorency* • Fiona Shaw *Marda Norton* • Lambert Wilson *Hugo Montmorency* • David Tennant *Captain Gerald Colthurst* • Richard Roxburgh *Daventry* • Keeley Hawes *Lois Farquar* ■ *Dir* Deborah Warner • *Scr* John Banville, from a novel by Elizabeth Bowen

The Last Shot ★★
Crime drama 1969 · Fr · Colour · 105mins

Robert Hossein plays a gangster, named after John Dillinger, who has risen to the top of the public enemy list. Yet who should be on his tail but childhood buddy Charles Aznavour, now a top-ranking drug squad cop? Having made his directorial debut at the age of 22, Sergio Gobbi shook up the popular *policier* genre with an explosively tough brand of urban action that shocked sixties cineastes. In this instance, however, he spends too much time on the romantic tug of war involving Virna Lisi. French dialogue dubbed into English.

Robert Hossein *Robert Dillinger* • Charles Aznavour *Kramer* • Virna Lisi *Stella* ■ *Dir* Sergio Gobbi • *Scr* Sergio Gobbi, André Tabet

Last Stand at Saber River ★★★ 12
Western 1997 · US · Colour · 90mins

A strong, taciturn Tom Selleck saddles up and rides into this TV-dramatisation of Elmore Leonard's novel. He's a battle-weary Confederate soldier, returning home to confront his domestic problems in the last days of the American Civil War. His Arizona homestead has been requisitioned by the Union Army, with Yankee sympathisers (Keith and David Carradine) now in charge. Then there's his embittered wife, Suzy Amis, who is still angry about being abandoned when he signed-up three years earlier. This is a thoughtful and rewarding take on America's post-Civil War trauma, which manages to avoid the usual Hollywood shoot-'em-up conventions. Look out for an early performance from *The Sixth Sense's* Haley Joel Osment. Contains some swearing and violence.

Tom Selleck *Cable* • Suzy Amis *Martha* • Rachel Duncan *Clare* • Haley Joel Osment *Davis* • Keith Carradine *Vern Kidston* • David Carradine *Duane Kidston* • Tracey Needham *Lorraine* ■ *Dir* Dick Lowry • *Scr* Ronald M Cohen, from the novel by Elmore Leonard

The Last Starfighter ★★★★ PG
Science-fiction 1984 · US · Colour · 96mins

Lance Guest's prowess at video games is monitored by emissaries from the Star League of the future, who recruit him to defend the universe from evil invaders in this glossy, space-age fairy tale. While highly derivative *Star Trek*-like aliens mix with *Star Wars*-inspired

dog-fights against a computer-graphic backdrop, the sensitive love story between Guest and Catherine Mary Stewart cuts through the cuteness and gives the intergalactic adventures a major boost. Children will love it, especially the fun moments with Guest's android double. 📼

Lance Guest *Alex Rogan* • Dan O'Herlihy *Grig* • Catherine Mary Stewart *Maggie Gordon* • Barbara Bosson *Jane Rogan* • Norman Snow *Xur* • Robert Preston *Centauri* • Kay E Kuter *Enduran* • Chris Hebert *Louis Rogan* ■ *Dir* Nick Castle • *Scr* Jonathan Betuel

Last Stop Paradise ★★★
Drama 1998 · Fr/Rom · Colour · 99mins

Romania's best-known film-maker, Lucian Pintilie, demonstrates an enviable talent for disconcerting development and quirky characterisation in this offbeat drama. Opening with a bizarre chase through Bucharest, the film settles down to concentrate on the tentative relationship between Costel Cascaval, a pig farmer about to embark on his national service, and Dorina Chiriac, a waitress engaged to the ageing owner of a mobile sausage stand. As the vodka flows and Cascaval's resentment at his family intensifies, events keep threatening to implode. Yet the impressive performances and Pintilie's unobtrusive camerawork keep the action edgy and unexpected.

Costel Cascaval *Mitou* • Dorina Chiriac *Norica* • Gheorghe Visu *Vatasescu* • Victor Rebengiuc *Grigore Cafanu* • Razvan Vasilescu *Burci* ■ *Dir* Lucian Pintilie • *Scr* Lucian Pintilie, Ravsan Popescu, Radu Aldulescu

Last Summer ★★★★
Psychological drama
1969 · US · Colour · 96mins

Unheralded for the substantial talent he was, film-maker Frank Perry will probably be best remembered for the execrable *Mommie Dearest* instead of tender, emotive movies like *David and Lisa* and this unnerving teenage odyssey. It contains some of the finest youth performances in American film. Barbara Hershey excels as the sadistic young tease, ultimately responsible for creating a jealousy with brutal and tragic consequences, and the performances Perry elicited from the boys Richard Thomas and Bruce Davison helped them to sterling careers after this movie. Oscar-nominated Catherine Burns proved harder to cast later on, but her brilliant acting illuminates this film. A brave, unsentimental, ultimately callous rites-of-passage movie, which deserves attention and respect.

Barbara Hershey *Sandy* • Richard Thomas *Peter* • Bruce Davison *Dan* • Cathy Burns [Catherine Burns] *Rhoda* • Ernesto Gonzalez *Anibal* • Ralph Waite *Peter's father* • Peter Turgeon *Mr Caudell* ■ *Dir* Frank Perry • *Scr* Eleanor Perry, from a novel by Evan Hunter

Last Summer in the Hamptons ★ 15
Comedy drama 1995 · US · Colour · 107mins

Actress diva Viveca Lindfors plays host to family and thesps for a weekend filled with discussion and double dealings in a pretentious and precious drama from director Henry Jaglom. Not caring how these folk live or who they love is hindrance enough but Jaglom's lame attempts at comedy and allegory just mute the production entirely. Contains swearing and sexual references.

Victoria Foyt *Oona Hart* • Viveca Lindfors *Helena Mora* • Jon Robin Baitz *Jake Axelrod* • Savannah Boucher *Suzanne* • Roscoe Lee Browne *Freddy* • Andre Gregory *Ivan Axelrod* • Nick Gregory *George* • Melissa Leo *Trish Axelrod* • Roddy McDowall *Thomas* • Martha Plimpton *Chloe Garfield* ■ *Dir* Henry Jaglom • *Scr* Henry Jaglom, Victoria Foyt

The Last Sunset ★★★
Western   1961 · US · Colour · 111mins

A multi-layered, superbly cast western that incorporates themes not usually found in westerns, or in many other American movies of the period, notably incest and suicide. Under the heavy hand of *Dirty Dozen* director Robert Aldrich, this Freud-on-the-range saga doesn't quite come off, but the magnificent cast ensures that the film is not just for fans of the genre – Rock Hudson and Kirk Douglas are at ease in the saddle and a joy to watch. The brunt of the movie, however, is borne by Carol Lynley, excellent as a gal brought up on a savage frontier.

Rock Hudson *Dana Stribling* • Kirk Douglas *Brendan O'Malley* • Dorothy Malone *Belle* • Joseph Cotten *John Breckenridge* • Carol Lynley *Missy* • Neville Brand *Frank Hobbs* • Regis Toomey *Milton Wing* • Rad Fulton *Julesburg Kid* ■ *Dir* Robert Aldrich • *Scr* Dalton Trumbo, from the novel *Sundown at Crazy Horse* by Howard Rigsby

The Last Supper ★★★
Religious drama
1976 · Cub · Colour · 112mins

This allegory of "Christian liberalism", as the Cuban director Tomás Gutiérrez Alea describes it, has much in common with Luis Buñuel's *Viridiana* in its context and caustic wit. A plantation owner decides to re-create the Last Supper, casting 12 of his slaves as the Apostles, but the situation turns nasty, and there is a revolt. Filmed in muted colours with a powerful black cast, the picture belabours its message in the final sequence, a symbol of the coming Socialist Cuba. In Spanish with English subtitles..

Nelson Villagra *Count* • Silvano Rey *Chaplain* • Luis Alberto Garcia *Don Manuel* • José Antonio Rodriguez *Don Gaspar* • Samuel Claxton *Sebastian* • Mario Balmaseda *Martin Sanchez* ■ *Dir* Tomás Gutiérrez Alea • *Scr* Tomás Gutiérrez Alea, Tomás Gonzalez, Maria Eugenia Haya

The Last Supper ★★15
Black comedy   1995 · US · Colour · 87mins

Five liberal students serve poisoned alcohol to a collection of bigoted extremists in a black comic stew that lacks substance. It could be an intriguing, double-edged premise – are Cameron Diaz, Ron Eldard and the rest any less twisted than their victims? – but Dan Rosen's script presents the culinary vigilantes in purely one-dimensional terms. By far the movie's strongest features are its various dinner guests, particularly racist trucker Bill Paxton (the first victim), male chauvinist Mark Harmon and

homophobic priest Charles Durning. While unquestionably unpleasant, these characters are infinitely more interesting than the ones serving the wine. Contains violence, swearing and sex scenes. ▭

Cameron Diaz *Jude* • Ron Eldard *Pete* • Annabeth Gish *Paulie* • Jonathan Penner *Marc* • Courtney B Vance *Luke* • Jason Alexander *Anti-environmentalist* • Nora Dunn *Sheriff Stanley* • Charles Durning *Reverend Gerald Hutchens* • Mark Harmon *Dominant Male* • Bill Paxton *Zack* ■ *Dir* Stacy Title • *Scr* Dan Rosen

Last Tango in Paris ★★★★★18
Drama   1972 · It/Fr · Colour · 123mins

Bernardo Bertolucci's still controversial psychodrama blazed new cinematic frontiers in the way sex was treated on screen. Artfully shot, it's the steamy and thought-provoking tale of the intense love affair that ignites between two strangers when they meet while viewing an apartment. Marlon Brando is trying to get over his wife's suicide, Maria Schneider is about to marry, and both cling to their anonymous and increasingly frank liaisons in order to separate their sexual desires from their oppressive daily realities. More existential than erotic, this brilliant study of a broken, tortured man allows Brando to deliver a devastating performance, alternately ranging between ferocity and tenderness, pathos and vulgarity. Gato Barbieri's marvellous jazz score creates a delirious atmosphere, conducive to the breaking of taboos. In French with English subtitles. ▭

Marlon Brando *Paul* • Maria Schneider *Jeanne* • Jean-Pierre Léaud *Tom* • Catherine Allégret *Catherine* ■ *Dir* Bernardo Bertolucci • *Scr* Bernardo Bertolucci, Franco Arcalli • *Cinematographer* Vittorio Storaro

The Last Temptation of Christ ★★★★18
Religious drama 1988 · US · Colour · 156mins

Ignore all the controversy and see Martin Scorsese's moving adaptation of Nikos Kazantzakis's novel for what it is – a challenging essay on the life of Jesus had he ignored his divine destiny and chosen to pursue human aims instead. Certainly neither blasphemous nor offensive, Scorsese's re-creation of the biblical milieu is highly evocative and the all-star performances are welcome modern reinterpretations of scripture stereotypes. It's slightly too long, and Scorsese does pull some punches in deference to the subject matter, but these are minor criticisms; one should take any opportunity to cut through the contention and reappraise this sincere work. ▭

Willem Dafoe *Jesus Christ* • Harvey Keitel *Judas Iscariot* • Barbara Hershey *Mary Magdalene* • Harry Dean Stanton *Saul/Paul* • David Bowie *Pontius Pilate* • Verna Bloom *Mary, Mother of Jesus* • Andre Gregory *John the Baptist* • Juliette Caton *Girl Angel* • Roberts Blossom *Aged Master* • Irvin Kershner *Zebedee* ■ *Dir* Martin Scorsese • *Scr* Paul Schrader, from the novel *The Last Temptation* by Nikos Kazantzakis

The Last Time I Committed Suicide ★★★15
Biographical drama
1996 · US · Colour · 93mins

An artful glimpse into the early life of Beat Generation figure Neal Cassady, a restless spirit who provided friendship and inspiration to cultural icons Jack Kerouac and Ken Kesey. Thomas Jane captures Cassady's cool edginess and his sharp, self-aware narration adds much spirit to the rather laid-back, low-key story. There's some well-drawn relationships with girlfriends Claire Forlani and Gretchen Mol, although the film's sticking point is the miscasting of Keanu Reeves, who is unconvincing as his persuasive, doggedly irresponsible best friend. That said, director Stephen Kay's evocative, dimly-lit ambience and the jazzy soundtrack gives the film a stylish, subdued vibe. Contains some swearing and sexual references. ▭

Thomas Jane *Neal Cassady* • Keanu Reeves *Harry* • Pat McNamara *Father Fletcher* • Kate Williamson *Nurse Waring* • Claire Forlani *Joan* • Gretchen Mol *Cherry Mary* ■ *Dir/Scr* Stephen Kay

The Last Time I Saw Archie ★★U
Comedy   1961 · US · BW · 98mins

Robert Mitchum is inveterate conman Archie Hall, who joins the army, is mistaken for a general in disguise, tricks everyone into believing his girlfriend is a Japanese agent and gets away with it. This sort of service comedy was a staple for the likes of Bob Hope and the Bilko of Phil Silvers, but Mitchum doesn't really have the light touch, though he's supported by a cast of established laughmeisters. Director Jack Webb plays Mitchum's buddy Bill Bowers – in real life, the film's screenwriter whose army career is depicted with apparent accuracy. It's worth staying the course for a nice epilogue, in which Mitchum and Webb wash up in Hollywood.

Robert Mitchum *Archie Hall* • Jack Webb *Bill Bowers* • Martha Hyer *Peggy Kramer* • France Nuyen *Cindy Hamilton* • Joe Flynn *Pvt Russell Drexel* • James Lydon *Pvt Billy Simpson* • Del Moore *Pvt Frank Ostrow* • Louis Nye *Pvt Sam Beacham* • Richard Arlen *Col Martin* • Don Knotts *Captain Little* ■ *Dir* Jack Webb • *Scr* William Bowers

The Last Time I Saw Paris ★★★U
Romantic drama
1954 · US · Colour · 115mins

In the hands of talented writer/director Richard Brooks this version of F Scott Fitzgerald's *Babylon Revisited* is remarkably faithful to the original's style and tone. It's also beautifully cast, with Elizabeth Taylor in her sublime prime as the tragic love of alcoholic writer Van Johnson. MGM bought this property from Paramount as a vehicle for Taylor and lavished the best available talent on her (photography by Joseph Ruttenberg, gowns by Helen Rose, music by Conrad Salinger). Fitzgerald's vision of Paris's "lost generation" is well captured, and, although the second half reveals the weaknesses of the original, this is still an intelligent and

glossy piece of film-making. Watch for a young Roger Moore, eight years before *The Saint*. ▭

Elizabeth Taylor *Helen Ellsworth* • Van Johnson *Charles Wills* • Walter Pidgeon *James Ellsworth* • Donna Reed *Marion Ellsworth* • Eva Gabor *Lorraine Quarl* • Kurt Kasznar *Maurice* • George Dolenz *Claude Matine* • Roger Moore *Paul* ■ *Dir* Richard Brooks • *Scr* Philip G Epstein, Julius J Epstein, Richard Brooks, from the story *Babylon Revisited* by F Scott Fitzgerald

The Last to Go ★★★15
Drama   1991 · US · Colour · 90mins

Tyne Daly of TV's *Cagney and Lacey* gives a powerhouse performance as a wife coming to terms with the fact that her husband Terry O'Quinn has left her for a much younger woman in what is otherwise a rather unoriginal and sometimes plodding drama. Director John Erman – whose highs include the moving Aids drama *An Early Frost* and whose lows embrace *Scarlett*, the dire sequel to *Gone with the Wind* – here makes a film that falls between the two: it's not that bad, but it's not that amazing, either. ▭

Tyne Daly *Mary Ellen Slattery* • Terry O'Quinn *Daniel Slattery* • Tim Ransom *Toby* • Annabeth Gish *Lydia* • Sarah Trigger *Sharon* • Amy Aquino *Ginny* ■ *Dir* John Erman • *Scr* William Hanley, from the novel by Rand Richards Cooper

The Last Train ★★
Drama   1972 · Fr · Colour

A drama set during the Nazi invasion of France, with Jean-Louis Trintignant mislaying his wife in the rush to get the last train from Paris and then helping Romy Schneider by posing as her husband. They fall in love, and then Trintignant's real wife shows up with their child. This is a solidly made story, based on a Georges Simenon novel, that trades heavily on the then commercial appeal of its two glamorous stars, especially Trintignant.

Romy Schneider *Anna* • Jean-Louis Trintignant *Julien* • Maurice Biraud *Deserter* • Regine *Large woman* • Serge Marquand *Man* ■ *Dir* Pierre Granier-Deferre • *Scr* Pascal Jardin, from a novel by Georges Simenon

Last Train from Bombay ★
Adventure   1952 · US · BW · 73mins

Jon Hall, usually to be found hanging out in Pago Pago or sailing to Tahiti, washes up in India for this B-movie, produced with every expense spared by Columbia. Hall plays an American diplomat whose friend (Douglas Kennedy) turns out to be a member of an insurrectionist group who plant bombs on trains. When the friend is bumped off, Hall becomes both a murder suspect and a target for the terrorists. Shots of India are sort of glued into the picture, as is the sense that the former British colony, liberated by the assassinated Gandhi, is in dire need of help from America to stop it slipping into anarchy.

Jon Hall *Martin Viking* • Christine Larson *Mary Anne Palmer* • Lisa Ferraday *Charlane* • Douglas Kennedy *Kevin O'Hara* • Michael Fox *Captain Tamil* • Donna Martell *Nawob's daughter* • Matthew Boulton *Col Palmer* ■ *Dir* Fred F Sears • *Scr* Robert Libott

U = SUITABLE FOR ALL   Uc = SUITABLE FOR ALL, ESPECIALLY FOR YOUNG CHILDREN (VIDEO ONLY)   PG = PARENTAL GUIDANCE

Last Train from Gun Hill ★★★★ 🄯

Western 1959 · US · Colour · 90mins

A very fine adult western, made by the same team (including director John Sturges and producer Hal Wallis) that worked on *Gunfight at the OK Corral*, with Kirk Douglas again in a starring role. Here, Douglas is at his most intense as a man seeking revenge following the rape and murder of his wife. Anthony Quinn makes a tough adversary, and the rich Technicolor and VistaVision photography is exemplary. Not a film for the squeamish but, for discerning admirers of the classic western form, this is a superior example: intelligent, finely wrought and exceptionally well cast. 🖭

Kirk Douglas *Matt Morgan* • Anthony Quinn *Craig Belden* • Carolyn Jones *Linda* • Earl Holliman *Rick Belden* • Ziva Rodann *Catherine Morgan* • Brad Dexter *Beero* • Brian Hutton *Lee* • Bing Russell *Skag* ■ *Dir* John Sturges • *Scr* James Poe, from the story *Showdown* by Les Crutchfield

The Last Train from Madrid ★★★

Period war drama 1937 · US · BW · 85mins

One of the first Hollywood movies to use the Spanish Civil War as background, it avoided taking sides, and was really an excuse to get a number of Paramount contract players together to tell various, rather feeble, stories. But for those who like train movies, an almost vanished genre, there is much to enjoy. It also offers the chance to see Dorothy Lamour in one of her few dramatic roles, heading a good cast including Lew Ayres, Gilbert Roland and hammy Lionel Atwill. Ayres was to become a conscientious objector during the war, an action which ruined his career.

Dorothy Lamour *Carmelita Castillo* • Lew Ayres *Bill Dexter* • Gilbert Roland *Eduardo De Soto* • Karen Morley *Helene Rafitte* • Lionel Atwill *Colonel Vigo* • Helen Mack *Lola* • Robert Cummings *Juan Ramos* ■ *Dir* James Hogan • *Scr* Louis Stevens, Robert Wyler, from a story by Paul Harvey Fox, Elsie Fox

The Last Tycoon ★★★★ 🄯

Drama 1976 · US · Colour · 117mins

F Scott Fitzgerald's unfinished novel about Hollywood shows a studio boss, Monroe Stahr, in love with a young actress he spots on a film set. Stahr was based on MGM's Irving Thalberg and Robert De Niro plays him with all the personality of a paper cup, only coming alive when he's talking pictures, while the girl, Ingrid Boulting, is catatonic throughout. Yet this is all deliberate, allowing director Elia Kazan and scriptwriter Harold Pinter to explore the schism between the fantasy on the screen and the void in our lives. Unfortunately for them, this approach led the film to critical and box-office doom. A pity, as it's a class act, with Robert Mitchum, Jack Nicholson, Jeanne Moreau and Tony Curtis bringing the edges of the story to vivid life. Contains swearing.

Robert De Niro *Monroe Stahr* • Tony Curtis *Rodriguez* • Robert Mitchum *Pat Brady* • Jeanne Moreau *Didi* • Jack Nicholson *Brimmer* • Donald Pleasence *Boxley* • Ingrid Boulting *Kathleen Moore* • Ray Milland *Fleishacker* •

Dana Andrews *Red Ridingwood* • Theresa Russell *Cecilia Brady* • Peter Strauss *Wylie* • John Carradine *Guide* • Anjelica Huston *Edna* ■ *Dir* Elia Kazan • *Scr* Harold Pinter, from the novel by F Scott Fitzgerald

The Last Unicorn ★★ 🄤

Animated adventure
1980 · US · Colour · 88mins

If it weren't for the lacklustre artwork, this animated fantasy might have been quite enchanting. The voices of Mia Farrow, Alan Arkin, Angela Lansbury, Christopher Lee and Jeff Bridges are topnotch and there's little wrong with Peter S Beagle's story, in which a brainy butterfly, a pirate cat, an apprentice wizard and a handsome prince join with a unicorn to help rescue her species from the underwater prison of a snarling red bull. Younger viewers will probably forgive the flat animation, but the grown-ups are going to hate Jimmy Webb's tacky songs. 🖭

Alan Arkin *Schmendrick the Magician* • Jeff Bridges *Prince Lir* • Mia Farrow *The Last Unicorn/Lady Amalthea* • Tammy Grimes *Molly Grue* • Robert Klein *The Butterfly* • Angela Lansbury *Mommy Fortuna* • Christopher Lee *King Haggard* • Keenan Wynn *Captain Cully* ■ *Dir* Arthur Rankin Jr, Jules Bass • *Scr* Peter S Beagle, from his novel

The Last Valley ★★★★ 🄯

Historical drama
1971 · UK · Colour · 119mins

A strange, ambitious and fascinating historical epic – one for the connoisseurs – in which mercenary soldier Michael Caine and scholar Omar Sharif discover a peaceful, hidden valley that's managed to avoid being ensnared in the Thirty Years War. What ensues in this Shangri-la is a debate about war, religion, the nature of the soul and the value of society – until something snaps when the swords come out to play and the stake is readied for a burning. Beautifully shot in Austria in 70mm, it contains one of Caine's very finest performances, a script that sidesteps pomposity and a marvellous score by John Barry. It flopped, of course, and is hardly ever shown today. The 1984 film *The Mission* owes much to it. 🖭

Michael Caine *The Captain* • Omar Sharif *Vogel* • Florinda Bolkan *Erica* • Nigel Davenport *Gruber* • Per Oscarsson *Father Sabastian* • Arthur O'Connell *Hoffman* • Madeline Hinde *Inge* • Yorgo Voyagis *Pirelli* • Christian Roberts *Andreas* ■ *Dir* James Clavell • *Scr* James Clavell, from the novel by JB Pick • *Cinematographer* John Wilcox

The Last Voyage ★★★

Drama 1960 · US · Colour · 91mins

Writer/director Andrew L Stone's speciality was filming on location: for this exciting melodrama, he purchased the liner *Ile de France* and put his stellar cast through its paces on her partially scuppered decks! It's very exciting and superbly shot, with no visible studio footage at all. The co-stars of *Written on the Wind*, Robert Stack and Dorothy Malone, reunite to head the cast, while George Sanders is excellent as the troubled captain. Even moppet-in-danger Tammy Marihugh doesn't offend.

Robert Stack *Cliff Henderson* • Dorothy Malone *Laurie Henderson* • George Sanders *Captain Robert Adams* • Edmond O'Brien *Second Engineer Walsh* • Woody Strode *Hank Lawson* • Jack Kruschen *Chief Engineer Pringle* • Tammy Marihugh *Jill Henderson* ■ *Dir/Scr* Andrew L Stone

The Last Wagon ★★★★

Western 1956 · US · Colour · 99mins

A smashing CinemaScope western that deserves to be better known, directed by one of the relatively unsung masters of the genre, Delmer Daves. The ever-excellent Richard Widmark plays trapper Todd, a renegade forced to help wagon train survivors through hostile Apache territory, and he hardly speaks a word for the first half-hour of the movie. The remainder of the cast is comprised of newcomers, including teen rebel Nick Adams, and the very fetching future Mrs Jack Lemmon, Felicia Farr. Daves's use of landscape is exemplary, with opening sequence crane shots that deserve to be ranked among the cinema's finest.

Richard Widmark *Todd* • Felicia Farr *Jenny* • Susan Kohner *Jolie* • Tommy Rettig *Billy* • Stephanie Griffin *Valinda* • Ray Stricklyn *Clint* • Nick Adams *Ridge* • Carl Benton Reid *General Howard* ■ • *Scr* James Edward Grant, Delmer Daves, Gwen Bagni Gielgud, from a story by Gwen Bagni Gielgud

The Last Waltz ★★★★ 🄤

Music documentary
1978 · US · Colour · 111mins

Having been one of the supervising editors of the remarkable rockumentary *Woodstock*, Martin Scorsese was the perfect choice of director for this stunning movie of the Band's farewell gig on Thanksgiving Day 1976. Taking a break from shooting *New York, New York*, he nevertheless planned this film to the last detail during rehearsals and was well served by seven cameramen, including Michael Chapman, Vilmos Zsigmond and Laszlo Kovacs, whose pinpoint shots allow you to concentrate on the performances and the brilliant music. The guests comprise a who's who of electric folk and R&B, making this not only an unmissable slice of nostalgia, but also a masterpiece of pop cinema. 🖭

Dir Martin Scorsese

The Last Wave ★★★★

Supernatural drama
1977 · Ausl · Colour · 105mins

Peter Weir was inspired to make this film after he found a piece of broken statue on a Tunisian beach. Although Richard Chamberlain is clearly out of his depth in the lead, this is a mesmerising supernatural drama, in which a dramatic change in the weather and a series of troubling dreams prompt a Sydney lawyer to venture into the city's aboriginal underworld. Aboriginal pressure groups felt Weir had debased their mythology, but David Gulpilil and the other indigenous cast members obviously felt otherwise. The spectacular final shot was borrowed from a surfing B-movie called *Crystal Voyager*.

Richard Chamberlain *David Burton* • Olivia Hamnett *Annie Burton* • Gulpilil [David Gulpilil]

Chris Lee • Frederick Parslow *Reverend Burton* • Vivean Gray *Dr Whitburn* ■ *Dir* Peter Weir • *Scr* Peter Weir, Tony Morphett, Petru Popescu

The Last Winter ★★★

Drama 1989 · Can · Colour · 115mins

An atmospheric, distinctive and picturesque film about a young country boy's coming of age in the Canadian Midwest. The prairie landscape and the punishing winters shape the mood of this semi-autobiographical work, written and directed by Aaron Kim Johnston. Joshua Murray gives a superior performance as the ten-year-old farm lad with a crush on his cousin, whose vivid fantasy life centres on a white stallion that gallops across the wintry scene.

Gérard Parkes *Grampa Jack* • Marsha Moreau *Kate* • Jillian McMillan *Susan* ■ *Dir/Scr* Aaron Kim Johnston

The Last Woman on Earth ★

Science-fiction 1960 · US · Colour · 64mins

Crooks Anthony Carbone and Ed Wain fight over Betsy Jones-Moreland when they turn out to be the only survivors of a nuclear war in Puerto Rico. Not one of cult director Roger Corman's best efforts, this sci-fi *ménage à trois* tale is cheap, dull and unappealing. "Ed Wain" is the pseudonym of future Oscar-winning screenwriter Robert Towne, who hadn't finished the script (his first) in time and was brought along to complete it on location. Ever the cost-cutter, Corman then had Towne play the second lead, even though he'd never acted before.

Antony Carbone *Harold* • Betsy Jones-Moreland *Evelyn* • Edward Wain [Robert Towne] *Martin* ■ *Dir* Roger Corman • *Scr* Edward Wain [Robert Towne]

Last Year at Marienbad ★★★★★ 🄤

Drama 1961 · Fr/It · BW · 90mins

Written by modernist novelist Alain Robbe-Grillet, this is a complex cinematic riddle without an answer. Are Delphine Seyrig and Giorgio Albertazzi really reuniting a year after their first meeting? Or was she killed by her jealous husband, Sacha Pitöeff? Does the film take place in Albertazzi's memory, or is it simply an erotic fantasy on Seyrig's part? The winner of the Golden Lion at the Venice film festival, Alain Resnais' film is a triumph of camera movement, symbolic decor, abstract structure and stylised playing. A veritable masterpiece, but beware: it is as likely to irritate as it is to mesmerise. In French with English subtitles. 🖭

Delphine Seyrig *A/Woman* • Giorgio Albertazzi *X/Stranger* • Sacha Pitöeff *M/Man/Husband or Lover* ■ *Dir* Alain Resnais • *Scr* Alain Robbe-Grillet • *Cinematographer* Sacha Vierny

The Last Yellow ★★ 🄯

Comedy drama
1999 · UK/Ger · Colour · 90mins

A promising cast – Mark Addy from *The Full Monty*, Charlie Creed-Miles from *Nil by Mouth* and rising young star Samantha Morton – can't disguise the stage origins of Julian Farino's dark comedy. The setting is Leicester, where bespectacled nerd Creed-Miles hires lodger Addy to wreak revenge on the thug who gave his brother brain damage. (The title refers to a game of snooker that turned ugly.) The relationship between the two hapless avengers is well-drawn, but the intriguing preamble eventually gives way to a disappointingly theatrical three-hander between the duo and their intended victim's trashy girlfriend (Morton). Contains swearing and violence. ▭

Mark Addy *Frank* • Charlie Creed-Miles *Kenny* • Samantha Morton *Jackie* • Kenneth Cranham *Len* • Alan Atherall *Donut* ■ *Dir* Julian Farino • *Scr* Paul Tucker, from his play

Latcho Drom ★★★★
Music documentary
1993 · Fr · Colour · 103mins

This is the second of Tony Gatlif's trilogy, which includes *Les Princes* (1982) and *Gadjo Dilo* (1997). Following the Romanies from their homelands in northern India across Africa and middle Europe to Spain, Gatlif's abstract odyssey is more a celebration of human indomitability and cultural vivacity than a protest against centuries of prejudice and injustice. What is so fascinating about this graceful musical tribute, is not just how the lyrics become increasingly bitter in countries where the persecution of the Romany peoples has been most vicious, but also how the music has both influenced and embraced the indigenous folk sound. A French/Romany language film.

Dir/Scr Tony Gatlif

Late August, Early September ★★▣
Crime
1998 · Fr · Colour · 111mins

Olivier Assayas is one of the brightest hopes of French cinema, but, in seeking to produce an adult study of art, love and friendship, he has indulged himself in verbal introspection and visual cliché. Although the circle of friends around novelist François Cluzet chatter endlessly, they fail to interest us in either their personalities or their problems. Only Jeanne Balibar's intense misery at losing noncommittal literary editor Mathieu Amalric to designer Virginie Ledoyen strikes a chord. Employing tired New Wave techniques to achieve its multi-perspective structure, this disappointingly trite picture is also guilty of some regrettable gender stereotyping. In French with English subtitles. Contains swearing and sex scenes.

Virginie Ledoyen *Anne Rosenwald* • Mathieu Amalric *Gabriel Deshays* • François Cluzet *Adrien Willer* • Jeanne Balibar *Jenny* • Alex Decas *Jérémie* ■ *Dir/Scr* Olivier Assayas

Late Autumn ★★★★
Drama
1960 · Jap · Colour · 129mins

Coming towards the end of his illustrious 35-year career, Yasujiro Ozu had a little fun at his own expense with this gently comic, petit bourgeois drama. Confounding stylistic expectations, he experiments with a variety of transitional devices while structuring the narrative around blocks of diegetically linked scenes. His third film on the subject of arranged

marriage is also one of his most slyly satirical, with the triumvirate of businessmen trying to find partners for widow Setsuko Hara and her independent daughter, Yoko Tsukasa, being ridiculed both for their insufferable interference and their smug acquiescence in postwar Japan's sociopolitical status quo. In Japanese with English subtitles.

Setsuko Hara *Akiko Miwa* • Yoko Tsukasa *Ayako* • Mariko Okada *Yuriko Sasaki* • Keiji Sada *Shotaro Goto* • Chishu Ryu *Shukichi Miwa* ■ *Dir* Yasujiro Ozu • *Scr* Yasujiro Ozu, Kogo Noda

The Late Edwina Black ★
Crime mystery
1951 · UK · BW · 82mins

Apart from questioning how closely they read the script when they were offered their parts, the first duty here is to exonerate the actors of any responsibility for this feeble Victorian whodunit. You could give director Maurice Elvey a ticking off for not trying a little harder to find ways of keeping the killer's identity a secret, but then what can he do with a story that was intent on giving the game away almost before it started? Let's lay the blame solely at the door of the long-forgotten writers of the original play and say no more about it.

David Farrar *Gregory Black* • Geraldine Fitzgerald *Elizabeth* • Roland Culver *Inspector* • Jean Cadell *Ellen the housekeeper* • Mary Merrall *Lady Southdale* • Harcourt Williams *Doctor Prendergast* ■ *Dir* Maurice Elvey • *Scr* Charles Frank, David Evans, from the play by William Dinner, William Morum

Late for Dinner ★★▣
Comedy
1991 · US · Colour · 88mins

Brian Wimmer and Peter Berg show why they are fully paid-up members of the "straight-to-video club" as two fugitives who emerge from a 29-year suspended animation experiment to find that (you'll never guess it) the world has moved on since 1962 and they are more than slightly out of place. It takes a while to warm up, but at least it predates Mel Gibson's defrost drama *Forever Young*. ▭

Brian Wimmer *Willie Husband* • Peter Berg *Frank Lovegren* • Marcia Gay Harden *Joy Husband* • Colleen Flynn *Jessica Husband* • Kyle Secor *Leland Shakes* • Michael Beach *Dr David Arrington* • Bo Brundin *Dr Dan Chilblains* • Peter Gallagher *Bob Freeman* ■ *Dir* WD Richter • *Scr* Mark Andrus

The Late George Apley ★★★
Satirical comedy
1947 · US · BW · 98mins

John P Marquand's novel in diary form about the rigidities of Boston patrician existence at the turn of the century was brought to the screen by director Joseph L Mankiewicz and contains exemplary performances from British actors Ronald Colman and Peggy Cummins. Although lacking the barbs of the book, and minus the epilogue that gives the work its title, the movie is witty and stylish. A special mention should go to Percy Waram (repeating his Broadway role) who walks away with the film, notably in a touching scene where he reminds Colman of his own thwarted young love, as Apley

seems dedicated to destroying his son's happiness in a similar manner.

Ronald Colman *George Apley* • Peggy Cummins *Eleanor Apley* • Vanessa Brown *Agnes* • Richard Haydn *Horatio Willing* • Charles Russell *Howard Boulder* • Richard Ney *John Apley* • Percy Waram *Roger Newcombe* • Mildred Natwick *Amelia Newcombe* ■ *Dir* Joseph L Mankiewicz • *Scr* Philip Dunne, from the play by John P Marquand, George S Kaufman, from the novel by John P Marquand,

The Late Liz ★★
Religious drama 1971 · US · Colour · 119mins

Hollywood veterans Anne Baxter and Steve Forrest star in this rum drama about an alcoholic who goes on the wagon when she finds religion. The film has its heart in the right place, but it's not helped by the melodramatic direction and ripe acting, which give an unintentionally kitsch air to the proceedings. Like many such "battle with the bottle" movies, one feels an overwhelming urge afterwards to head straight down to the nearest boozer.

Anne Baxter *Liz Addams Hatch* • Steve Forrest *Jim Hatch* • James Gregory *Sam Burns* • Coleen Gray *Sue Webb* • Joan Hotchkis *Sally* • Jack Albertson *Reverend Rogers* ■ *Dir* Dick Ross • *Scr* Bill Rega, from an autobiography by Gert Behanna

The Late Shift ★★★★
Comedy drama based on a true story
1996 · US · Colour · 90mins

British TV fans may not recognise the protagonists in this true-life drama about the battle of the talk show hosts, but it's interesting nonetheless just to see the behind-the-scenes intrigue of American TV, *Larry Sanders* style. When Johnny Carson, king of the late night talkshow, announced his retirement from the *Tonight Show*, a battle began for his coveted job, with David Letterman and Jay Leno (played here by dead-ringers John Michael Higgins and Daniel Roebuck, respectively) the two main contenders. It was Leno's tough-as-nails manager Helen Kushnick (Kathy Bates) who was credited with getting Leno the job, but this TV movie delves into all the political manoeuvres on both sides. Director Betty Thomas injects the fascinating story – a riveting battle of egos – with nice touches of humour.

Kathy Bates *Helen Kushnick* • John Michael Higgins *David Letterman* • Daniel Roebuck *Jay Leno* • Bob Balaban *Warren Littlefield* • Ed Begley Jr *Rod Perth* ■ *Dir* Betty Thomas • *Scr* George Armitage, from the non-fiction bestseller by Bob Carter

The Late Show ★★▣
Comedy
1977 · US · Colour · 89mins

A patchy Robert Benton-directed homage to those old homburg-and-raincoat private eye movies which flourished unabated in the forties. Art Carney and Lily Tomlin overact wildly as the curmudgeonly old PI and the neurotic object of his attentions, and the ensuing plot convolutions are so tangled as to be incomprehensible. Benton's sometimes crisp direction and a neat suburban atmosphere save the day, but overall this fails to hit the target. ▭

Art Carney *Ira Wells* • Lily Tomlin *Margo* • Bill Macy *Charlie Hatter* • Eugene Roche *Ron Birdwell* • Joanna Cassidy *Laura Birdwell* ■ *Dir/Scr* Robert Benton

Late Spring ★★★★
Drama
1949 · Jap · BW · 108mins

Yasujiro Ozu began to exhibit here the stylistic and thematic tropes that would sustain him for the remainder of his career: the "pillow shots" between scenes offering poetic digressions from the main action; the low-angle, almost static camerawork; and the preoccupation with lower-middle-class attitudes and the need to progress. Often ranked alongside *Tokyo Story*, the tale of professor Chishu Ryu's attempts to marry off Setsuko Hara, the daughter on whom he depends, remained one of the director's favourites. With its harmony of composition, tone and performance, it's easy to see why. In Japanese with English subtitles.

Chishu Ryu *Professor Shukichi Somiya* • Setsuko Hara *Noriko, Somiya's daughter* • Yumeji Tsukioka *Aya Kitagawa* • Haruko Sugimura *Masa Taguchi, Noriko's aunt* • Hohi Aoki *Katsuyochi Taguchi* ■ *Dir* Yasujiro Ozu • *Scr* Kogo Noda, from the novel *Chichi to Musume (Father and Daughter)* by Kazuo Hirotsu • *Cinematographer* Yuharu Atsuta

The Lathe of Heaven ★★★
Science-fiction drama
1979 · US · Colour · 105mins

Bruce Davison's dreams have the power to change reality in a classy adaptation of Ursula K LeGuin's popular novel. Can psychologist Kevin Conway manipulate him into dreaming a better world? Taking on lofty Kafka-esque subtexts, and using Texas landscapes to suggest the future, this subtle fantasy raises pertinent questions about individualism and the march of progress at any cost.

Bruce Davison *George Orr* • Kevin Conway *Dr William Haber* • Margaret Avery *Heather LeLache* • Peyton Park *Mannie Ahrens* • Niki Flacks *Penny Crouch* • Vandi Clark *Aunth Ethel* ■ *Dir* David Loxton, Fred Barzyk • *Scr* Roger E Swaybill, Diane English, from the novel by Ursula K LeGuin

Latin Lovers ★★▣
Musical comedy 1953 · US · Colour · 104mins

Multi-millionairess Lana Turner, on vacation in Rio and hungry to be loved for herself rather than her money, has problems deciding whether to choose rich John Lund or less rich glamorous "Latin Lover" Ricardo Montalban. Guess who wins. Hoary old romantic drivel, written by Isobel Lennart with an attempt at wit which occasionally succeeds, and directed on automatic pilot by Mervyn LeRoy (who gave Turner her first break in the rather more impressive *They Won't Forget* 16 years earlier), this leaden entertainment is periodically enlivened by a song or two, and Lana and Ricardo dancing the samba.

Lana Turner *Nora Taylor* • Ricardo Montalban *Roberto Santos* • John Lund *Paul Chevron* • Louis Calhern *Grandfather Santos* • Jean Hagen *Anne Kellwood* • Eduard Franz *Dr Lionel Y Newman* • Beulah Bondi *Analyst* ■ *Dir* Mervyn LeRoy • *Scr* Isobel Lennart

Latino ★★ 15

Drama   1985 · US · Colour · 103mins

A former Green Beret and Vietnam veteran is sent to Honduras to help the CIA-backed Contras overthrow the Marxist government of neighbouring Nicaragua. But faced with the brutality of the Contras, our hero changes sides. Directed by the gifted cinematographer Haskell Wexler, this isn't in the same league as *Under Fire* or *Salvador*. Both those films were deeply critical of US involvement in Latin America, but Wexler delivers the sort of emotionally top-heavy propaganda that once poured out of Uncle Joe Stalin's studios. It was filmed in Nicaragua with government endorsement, and back in America that well-known radical, George Lucas, co-financed it and helped with the editing. 🎞

Robert Beltran *Eddie Guerrero* • Annette Cardona *Marlena* • Tony Plana *Ruben Trevino* • Ricardo Lopez *Attila* • Luis Torrentes *Luis* ■ *Dir/Scr* Haskell Wexler

Laugh and Get Rich ★★

Comedy   1931 · US · BW · 75mins

Those who expect a witty comedy anywhere near as good as *Stage Door* (1937), also set in a boarding house and also directed by Gregory La Cava, are in for a disappointment. La Cava would go on to make funnier and faster films in the thirties than this tale of a landlady having to put up with her lazy husband's crazy get-rich-quick schemes. That they are played by horse-faced Edna May Oliver and fidgety Hugh Herbert does help matters slightly, but the title originally mooted for the film, *Room and Bored*, might have been more appropriate.

Hugh Herbert *Joe Austin* • Edna May Oliver *Sarah Austin* • Dorothy Lee *Alice Austin* • John Harron *Hepburn* • Robert Emmett Keane *Phelps* ■ *Dir* Gregory La Cava • *Scr* Gregory La Cava, Ralph Spence, from a story by Douglas MacLean

The Laughing Policeman ★★

Thriller   1973 · US · Colour · 111mins

The Laughing Policeman stars Walter Matthau as the veteran cop investigating a mass slaughter on a public bus. The trail leads to the gay underworld and a lot of closet doors. Like Eastwood's Harry Callahan, Matthau has to cut through miles of red tape that favours the criminal and makes the cops look like SS stormtroopers. San Francisco is the slightly over-familiar backdrop to all this and it ends, predictably, with a bus journey along those up-and-down, bouncy-bouncy streets.

Walter Matthau *Jake Martin* • Bruce Dern *Leo Larsen* • Lou Gossett [Louis Gossett Jr] *Larrimore* • Albert Paulsen *Camerero* • Anthony Zerbe *Lt Steiner* • Val Avery *Pappas* • Cathy Lee Crosby *Kay Butler* ■ *Dir* Stuart Rosenberg • *Scr* Thomas Rickman, from the novel by Per Wahloo, Maj Sjowall

Laughing Sinners ★★

Melodrama   1931 · US · BW · 72mins

The Joan Crawford-Clark Gable duo would have better outings than this one in which Salvation Army officer Gable saves unhappy nightclub entertainer Crawford from herself after she's dumped by the slick cad (Neil Hamilton) she worships. Nonetheless, it starts well enough, and is a must for Crawford fans who will enjoy being reminded that she was once very pretty, a good dancer, and more talented than many of her later scenery-chewing roles allowed. Director Harry Beaumont captures the authentically seedy world of travelling salesmen, one of whom is effectively played by familiar "sugar daddy" figure Guy Kibbee.

Joan Crawford *Ivy Stevens* • Neil Hamilton *Howard Palmer* • Clark Gable *Carl Loomis* • Marjorie Rambeau *Ruby* • Guy Kibbee *Cass Wheeler* • Cliff Edwards *Mike* ■ *Dir* Harry Beaumont • *Scr* Bess Meredyth, Martin Flavin, Edith Fitzgerald, from the play *Torch Song* by Kenyon Nicholson

Laughter ★★★

Comedy drama   1930 · US · BW · 85mins

This lively precursor of screwball comedy boasts ingratiating performances from Fredric March as an uninhibited composer and Nancy Carroll as his old girlfriend, who marries Frank Morgan for his money. Their conduct is shameless but great fun, as Carroll soon finds her new life empty and can't resist March's charms. Only Glenn Anders – overacting as a sourpuss romantic rival – spoils the atmosphere of sparkling jollity set up by screenwriter Donald Ogden Stewart and the talented but little remembered director, Harry D'Abbadie D'Arrast.

Fredric March *Paul Lockridge* • Nancy Carroll *Peggy Gibson* • Frank Morgan *C Mortimer Gibson* • Glenn Anders *Ralph Le Saint* • Diane Ellis *Marjorie Gibson* • Leonard Carey *Benham* • Ollie Burgoyne *Pearl* ■ *Dir* Harry d'Abbadie D'Arrast • *Scr* Donald Ogden Stewart, from a story by Harry D'Abbadie D'Arrast, Douglas Doty

Laughter in Paradise ★★★★ U

Comedy   1951 · UK · BW · 92mins

Films made up of interwoven stories are notoriously difficult to do well, as it's all too easy either to lose the threads of the difficult episodes or to become impatient with the obviously makeweight ones. That director Mario Zampi nearly brings off the trick here is down almost entirely to the fantastic performance of Alastair Sim as the henpecked thriller writer whose inheritance depends on him receiving a 28-day jail sentence. The scene in which he tries to shoplift is one of the funniest in a career overladen with choice comic moments. The other three episodes aren't bad, it's just that Sim's is exceptional. 🎞

Alastair Sim *Deniston Russell* • Fay Compton *Agnes Russell* • Beatrice Campbell *Lucille Grayson* • Veronica Hurst *Joan Webb* • Guy Middleton *Simon Russell* • George Cole *Herbert Russell* • AE Matthews *Sir Charles Robson* • Joyce Grenfell *Elizabeth Robson* • Anthony Steel *Roger Godfrey* • John Laurie *Gordon Webb* • Michael Pertwee *Stuart* • Audrey Hepburn *Cigarette girl* ■ *Dir* Mario Zampi • *Scr* Michael Pertwee, Jack Davies

Laughter in the Dark ★★★

Drama   1969 · UK · Colour · 106mins

Vladimir Nabokov's novel, set in thirties Germany, is a study in sexual psychopathy and sadism. It's about an art dealer who is blinded in a car crash and whose wife, an usherette at a cinema, gets her lover to move in with them, taunting the disabled husband until he can take no more humiliation. Updated to the London art world in the sixties, with further scenes set in Majorca, this is a gripping drama that's flawed only because everyone in it – even the blind husband – is unpleasant. As the wife-usherette, Anna Karina brings a lot of movie associations with her – she was Godard's ex-wife – but everyone is eclipsed by the powerhouse Nicol Williamson.

Nicol Williamson *Sir Edward More* • Anna Karina *Margot* • Jean-Claude Drouot *Herve Tourace* • Peter Bowles *Paul* • Sian Phillips *Lady Elizabeth More* • Sebastian Breaks *Brian* • Kate O'Toole *Amelia More* ■ *Dir* Tony Richardson • *Scr* Edward Bond, from the novel by Vladimir Nabokov

Laughterhouse ★★ PG

Comedy   1984 · UK · Colour · 88mins

A rather tame goose chase, which might have been inspired by *Red River's* classic cattle-drive. When farmer Ian Holm faces a strike by his workforce, he decides to walk his Christmas-fattened geese from Norfolk to London's Smithfield market and the slaughterhouse. Actor Brian Glover's script incorporates union-bashing and media-lashing, but can't make the human characters very likeable, although Bill Owen does appear as one of the accompanying vocal yokels. 🎞

Ian Holm *Ben Singleton* • Penelope Wilton *Alice Singleton* • Bill Owen *Amos* • Richard Hope *Hubert* • Stephen Moore *Howard* • Rosemary Martin *Continuity girl* • Patrick Drury *David Wolmer* ■ *Dir* Richard Eyre • *Scr* Brian Glover

Laura ★★★★★ U

Classic film noir   1944 · US · BW · 83mins

"I shall never forget the day that Laura died..." begins the narrator, and neither will you. This adult, sophisticated thriller encapsulates what *film noir* is all about: a taut, romantic mystery featuring New York detective Dana Andrews falling in love with an image. As good as they get, this one, with Otto Preminger's moody, stark direction greatly helped by the casting of beautiful Gene Tierney in the title role, a southern-accented Vincent Price as a smarmy gigolo and the incomparable Clifton Webb as columnist Waldo Lydecker. The David Raksin score is, quite simply, matchless. A rattling good thriller that bears watching time and time again. 🎞

Dana Andrews *Mark McPherson* • Gene Tierney *Laura Hunt* • Clifton Webb *Waldo Lydecker* • Vincent Price *Shelby Carpenter* • Judith Anderson *Ann Treadwell* • Dorothy Adams *Bessie Clary* • James Flavin *McAvity* • Clyde Fillmore *Bullitt* ■ *Dir* Otto Preminger • *Scr* Jay Dratler, Samuel Hoffenstein, Betty Reinhardt, Jerome Cady, from the novel by Vera Caspary • *Cinematographer* Joseph LaShelle

Laura Lansing Slept Here ★★★ PG

Comedy   1988 · US · Colour · 95mins

The legendary Katharine Hepburn lights up the small screen with her energy and wit in this rare television appearance. Stung by accusations that she's no longer in touch with ordinary people, wealthy novelist Hepburn accepts a bet that she can survive a week with an accountant's family. It turns out to be a learning experience all round. No one embodies eccentricity more vividly than the sparkling Miss Hepburn, and the humour she radiates makes this beguiling family comedy a treat for viewers of all ages.

Katharine Hepburn *Laura Lansing* • Karen Austin *Melody Gomphers* • Joel Higgins *Walter Gomphers* • Nicolas Surovy *Conway* • Schuyler Grant *Annette Gomphers* ■ *Dir* George Schaefer • *Scr* James Prideaux

Laurel and Hardy's Laughing 20s ★★★★ U

Comedy compilation   1965 · US · BW · 86mins

Robert Youngson's sixth Laurel and Hardy compilation was advertised with a sworn statement from a research company that promised 253 laughs, "the record for laugh content of any comedy we have measured in our 30 years of experience". This collection lives up to that hype and is a real treat for enthusiasts. The majority of the scenes are taken from Stan and Ollie's silent shorts, among them *Putting Pants on Philip*, *From Soup to Nuts*, *Wrong Again*, *The Finishing Touch* and *Liberty*. However, there is also a rare opportunity to see some of the other comics in the Hal Roach stable in action, among them the dapper Charley Chase and the scowling Edgar Kennedy. 🎞

Jay Jackson *Narrator* ■ *Dir/Scr* Robert Youngson

Lautrec ★★

Biographical drama 1998 · Fr/Sp · Colour · 127mins

Disregarding the tormented genius angle explored by John Huston in *Moulin Rouge*, director Roger Planchon aims to depict the vibrancy of the environment that inspired Impressionist painter Henri de Toulouse-Lautrec. With many tableaux consciously staged to recall posters and canvases, this superbly designed film is a joy to behold. But the endless bohemian bonhomie often feels forced as famous names come and go without adding much to the drama. Even the tempestuous relationship with Suzanne Valadon (Elsa Zylberstein) is devoid of passion. Régis Royer's portrait of Lautrec is lifelike, but the descent into absinthe and disease has all the emotional authenticity of a Hollywood biopic. In French with English subtitles.

Régis Royer *Henri de Toulouse-Lautrec* • Elsa Zylberstein *Suzanne Valadon* • Anémone *Adèle de Toulouse-Lautrec* • Claude Rich *Alphonse de Toulouse-Lautrec* ■ *Dir/Scr* Roger Planchon

The Lavender Hill Mob
★★★★★ U

Classic crime comedy
1951 · UK · BW · 77mins

While lacking the satirical edge of *The Man in the White Suit*, the other classic Ealing comedy of 1951 starring Alec Guinness, this is a superb and subtle spoof of crime films as different as the studio's own *The Blue Lamp* and the hard-boiled gangster movies produced by Hollywood in the late *film noir* era. TEB Clarke deservedly won an Oscar for his beautifully constructed story and screenplay. although Alec Guinness lost out to Gary Cooper for *High Noon* in the best actor category. The support playing is spot-on, with Alfie Bass and Sid James particularly impressive. Watch out for a couple of blink-and-miss-them walk-ons from James (billed as William) Fox and Audrey Hepburn. ▣

Alec Guinness *Henry Holland* • Stanley Holloway *Pendlebury* • Sidney James *Lackery* • Alfie Bass *Shorty* • Marjorie Fielding *Mrs Chalk* • John Gregson *Farrow* • Edie Martin *Miss Evesham* • Clive Morton *Station Sergeant* • John Salew *Parkin* • Ronald Adam *Turner* • Arthur Hambling *Wallis* • Gibb McLaughlin *Godwin* • Audrey Hepburn *Chiquita* ▪ *Dir* Charles Crichton • *Scr* TEB Clarke

LaVyrle Spencer's Home Song
★★

Drama
1996 · US · Colour

The story for this TV movie is rich in melodramatic potential but, sadly, the rather wooden cast fails to make the most of it. Lee Horsley plays a school headmaster whose life is turned on its head when a son he didn't know he had suddenly appears on the scene, stirring up much family tension. The soapy storyline exerts some attraction, but the direction is strictly by the book.

Lee Horsley *Tom Gardner* • Polly Draper *Claire Gardner* • Deborah Raffin *Monica Arins* ▪ *Dir* Nancy Malone • *Scr* Patricia K Meyer, from the novel by LaVyrle Spencer

Law and Disorder
★★★ U

Comedy
1958 · UK · BW · 72mins

This is a smashing little comedy from the *Lavender Hill Mob* pairing of director Charles Crichton and co-writer TEB Clarke. Michael Redgrave is on sparkling form as a minor league crook whose detentions at Her Majesty's pleasure are explained away to his son as missionary excursions to Africa. The plot slows slightly after the son becomes judge Robert Morley's assistant and Redgrave slips into retirement. But normal service is resumed with the smuggling episodes and the hilarious divorce trial, staged to delay Redgrave's day in court. Joan Hickson and John Le Mesurier shine in a superior supporting cast. ▣

Michael Redgrave *Percy Brand* • Robert Morley *Judge Crichton* • Ronald Squire *Colonel Masters* • Elizabeth Sellars *Gina Lasalle* • Joan Hickson *Aunt Florence* • Lionel Jeffries *Major Proudfoot* • Jeremy Burnham *Colin Brand* • Brenda Bruce *Mary Cooper* • George Coulouris *Bennie* • John Le Mesurier *Sir Humphrey Pomfret* ▪ *Dir* Charles Crichton • *Scr* Teb Clarke, Patrick Campbell, Vivienne Knight, from the novel *Smuggler's Circuit* by Denys Roberts

Law and Disorder
★★★ 18

Comedy drama
1974 · US · Colour · 97mins

Best known at home for the wonderful *Intimate Lighting*, exiled Czech director Ivan Passer's second American film was this uneven satire on the decline of neighbourhood life. When Carroll O'Connor and Ernest Borgnine set about organising a vigilante force to combat the rising tide of crime, the film is both insightful and amusing, but it never recovers from the sudden change in tone once they realise the enormity of their undertaking. Karen Black is superb as a chirpy hairdresser, while the leads have an unexpected chemistry. ▣

Carroll O'Connor *Willie* • Ernest Borgnine *Cy* • Ann Wedgeworth *Sally* • Anita Dangler *Irene* • Leslie Ackerman *Karen* • Karen Black *Gloria* • Jack Kehoe *Elliott* • David Spielberg *Bobby* ▪ *Dir* Ivan Passer • *Scr* Ivan Passer, William Richert, Kenneth Harris Fishman

The Law and Jake Wade
★★★★ U

Western
1958 · US · Colour · 86mins

A handsomely mounted MGM CinemaScope western featuring an ageing Robert Taylor and a sneering (as usual!) Richard Widmark as adversaries, and directed by a master of the genre, John Sturges (*The Magnificent Seven*, *Bad Day at Black Rock*). It's the tale of two outlaws who once rode together, but now the evil Widmark is back and trying to coerce a reformed Taylor into revealing where their ill-gotten loot is buried. The climax, an Indian attack on a ghost town, is particularly well choreographed, and veteran cameraman Robert Surtees's photography is often breathtaking, as you would expect from someone who worked on *Ben-Hur* and *King Solomon's Mines*. The clever, laconic screenplay by William Bowers tends to be under-rated as, indeed, was this fine, tense western.

Robert Taylor (1) *Jake Wade* • Richard Widmark *Clint Hollister* • Patricia Owens *Peggy Carter* • Robert Middleton *Ortero* • Henry Silva *Rennie* • DeForest Kelley *Wexler* • Burt Douglas *Lieutenant* • Eddie Firestone *Burke* ▪ *Dir* John Sturges • *Scr* William Bowers, from the novel by Marvin H Albert

Law and Order
★★★★

Western
1932 · US · BW · 70mins

Terrific version of the Wyatt Earp legend, with the names changed since some of the participants in the tale were still alive at the time of this movie. (Earp himself had only been dead four years.) Co-scripter Huston's father Walter is superb as the town-taming marshal, and the great western star Harry Carey is cleverly cast as his tortured crony. The tone is rightly sombre, and the infamous shootout at the OK Corral is quite brilliantly directed, surprising since this is the A-feature debut of Edward L Cahn, whose career plummeted hereafter, making him better known as a prolific director of dire B-grade exploitation flicks over the next three decades. Perhaps the WR Burnett original source novel has much to answer for, since these gunmen are uncompromisingly portrayed as gangsters with a badge.

Walter Huston *Frame Johnson* • Harry Carey *Ed Brant* • Raymond Hatton *Deadwood* • Russell Simpson *Judge Williams* • Russell Hopton *Luther Johnson* • Ralph Ince *Poe Northrup* • Harry Woods *Walt Northrup* • Richard Alexander *Kurt Northrup* • Walter Brennan *Lanky Smith* ▪ *Dir* Edward L Cahn • *Scr* John Huston, Tom Reed, from the story *Saint Johnson* by WR Burnett

Law and Order
★★ U

Western
1953 · US · Colour · 79mins

Town marshal Ronald Reagan plans to retire when he gets married, but, almost inevitably, is called on to fight one more battle against the bad guys. At first his brother (Alex Nicol) becomes the lawman, but soon Reagan is persuaded to rid the town of Preston Foster's criminal gang. Meanwhile, Reagan's fiancée (Dorothy Malone) prepares for imminent widowhood. The theme recalls *High Noon*, and, like Gary Cooper, Reagan is the silent, brooding type. However, that's where the comparisons end in this remake of the superior 1932 original starring Walter Huston.

Ronald Reagan *Frame Johnson* • Dorothy Malone *Jeannie Bristow* • Alex Nicol *Lute Johnson* • Preston Foster *Kurt Durling* • Russell Johnson *Jimmy Johnson* • Barry Kelley *Fin Elder* • Ruth Hampton *Maria* • Chubby Johnson *Denver Cahoon* • Dennis Weaver *Frank Durling* • Jack Kelly *Jed* ▪ *Dir* Nathan Juran • *Scr* John Bagni, Gwen Bagni, DD Beauchamp, from the novel *Saint Johnson* by WR Burnett

The Law of Desire
★★★ 18

Romantic comedy
1987 · Sp · Colour · 97mins

Released the year before *Women on the Verge of a Nervous Breakdown* catapulted Pedro Almódovar to international fame, this is a typically tangled, relationship comedy-drama centring on a homosexual love triangle between a film director and his two lovers and the film-maker's really strange family. Items that can be ticked-off on the Almodóvar checklist include early regulars Antonio Banderas and Carmen Maura (delivering a knockout performance), an off-kilter representation of romance, explicit sex, the unexpected murder of one of the central characters and truly outrageous plot twists. Not one of his very best, but still an absurdly funny and touching tale from a gifted film-maker. In Spanish with English subtitles. ▣

Eusebio Poncela *Pablo Quintero* • Carmen Maura *Tina Quintero* • Antonio Banderas *Antonio Benitez* • Miguel Molina *Juan Bermudez* ▪ *Dir/Scr* Pedro Almodóvar

Law of the Underworld
★★

Crime drama
1938 · US · BW

Two young lovers are framed for a robbery that culminates in murder in this undemanding B-movie starring Chester Morris as a gang leader with a soft centre. Anne Shirley and Richard Bond are the couple accused of the crime, their plight bringing out the best in the crook. Previously filmed as *The Pay-Off* in 1930, with writer/director Lowell Sherman impressively world weary as the self-sacrificing gangster, its fanciful but predictable course is given little vigour by Lew Landers's routine direction and the inexpressive performance of Morris.

Chester Morris *Gene Fillmore* • Anne Shirley *Annabelle* • Eduardo Ciannelli *Rockey* • Walter Abel *Rogers* • Richard Bond *Tommy* • Lee Patrick *Dorothy* • Paul Guilfoyle *Batsy* • Frank M Thomas *Capt Gargan* • Eddie Acuff *Bill* • Jack Arnold *Eddie* • Jack Carson *Johnny* ▪ *Dir* Lew Landers • *Scr* Bert Granet, Edmund L Hartmann, from the play *Crime* by John B Hymer, Samuel Shipman

The Law West of Tombstone
★★

Comedy western
1938 · US · BW · 72mins

Here's a programme filler that manages to cram into one short movie three key western plot figures, thinly-disguised caricatures of no less than Billy the Kid, Judge Roy Bean, and even ole' Ike Clanton and the boys! Film-wise, this one's quite interesting, though, as the old can be seen passing on the B-western baton to the young. In his last RKO western, Harry Carey plays the Judge, while youngster Tim Holt (son of cowboy veteran Jack Holt) makes his RKO debut out west. Cowboy comic book collectors may care to note the presence of Allan Lane and Kermit Maynard in support, but it's Harry Carey's grotesque, over-the-top performance that dominates, obviously fuelled by director Glenn Tryon's desire to make this a comedy-western.

Harry Carey *Bill Parker* • Tim Holt *The Tonto Kid* • Evelyn Brent *Clara Martinez* • Jean Rouverol *Nitta Moseby* • Clarence Kolb *Sam Kent* • Allan Lane *Danny* • Esther Muir *Mme Mustache* • Bradley Page *Doc Howard* • Kermit Maynard ▪ *Dir* Glenn Tryon • *Scr* John Twist, Clarence Upson Young, from the story by Clarence Upson Young

The Lawless
★★★

Drama
1950 · US · BW · 79mins

This pungent low-budget drama with minor stars Macdonald Carey and Gail Russell and an outstanding newcomer, Lalo Rios, was one of the best films that Joseph Losey directed in Hollywood. Gaining a sense of realism from being largely filmed on location with locals as extras, it focuses on the prejudice suffered by Mexican "fruit tramps", itinerant workers who harvested crops in California. The scenes of a manhunt and mob violence have considerable force. This kind of film-making, presenting a bad image of American society, contributed to Losey's blacklisting and flight to Europe.

Macdonald Carey *Larry Wilder* • Gail Russell *Sunny Garcia* • John Sands [Johnny Sands] *Joe Ferguson* • Lee Patrick *Jan Dawson* • John Hoyt *Ed Ferguson* • Lalo Rios *Paul Rodriguez* ▪ *Dir* Joseph Losey • *Scr* Geoffrey Homes [Daniel Mainwaring], from his novel *The Voice of Stephen Wilder*

The Lawless Breed
★★★

Western
1952 · US · Colour · 82mins

A splendidly titled biopic about notorious western outlaw John Wesley Hardin, sensitively portrayed by Rock Hudson in a star-making role that was to lift him out of the "beefcake" stakes for ever. It's directed by the grizzled veteran who first cast Hudson in a movie, the great Raoul Walsh.

Hudson excels here, eliciting sympathy for a character who was clearly no good, and the flashback structure allows an almost Hardyesque sense of a life controlled by destiny. An interesting movie, far better than the average B-feature.

Rock Hudson *John Wesley Hardin* • Julia Adams [Julie Adams] *Rosie* • Mary Castle *Jane Brown* • John McIntire *JG Hardin/John Clements* • Hugh O'Brian *Ike Hanley* • Dennis Weaver *Jim Clements* • Lee Van Cleef *Dirk Hanley* ■ *Dir* Raoul Walsh • *Scr* Bernard Gordon, from a story by William Alland

The Lawless Frontier ★ U
Western   1935 · US · BW · 47mins

Another mediocre John Wayne programme filler from that period when the Duke was trapped between *The Big Trail* (1930) and his rescue from B movies by director John Ford with the role of the "Ringo Kid" in 1939's *Stagecoach*. This has one of the most standard of all plots: Wayne is avenging the murder of his parents in under an hour's running time. George Hayes, not yet known as "Gabby", is an old-timer that the Duke rescues along the way, but there's little else of interest here to anyone other than dyed-in-the-wool fans of Wayne. ▭

John Wayne *John Tobin* • Sheila Terry *Ruby* • George "Gabby" Hayes *Dusty* • Earl Dwire *Zanti* • Yakima Canutt *Joe* ■ *Dir/Scr* Robert N Bradbury

A Lawless Street ★★ U
Western   1955 · US · Colour · 78mins

A routine Randolph Scott western, uninspiringly directed by *Gun Crazy's* Joseph H Lewis who fails to secure a satisfactory conclusion to the tale, which results in a particularly soppy ending. After this, co-producer/star Scott began his marvellous series of Budd Boetticher westerns that eschewed such sentimentality for good. Co-star Angela Lansbury was on her way up, between an MGM contract and Broadway revivalism, long before her popularity in the *Murder, She Wrote* TV series. And a darn fine western heroine she makes.

Randolph Scott *Calem Ware* • Angela Lansbury *Tally Dickinson* • Warner Anderson *Hamer Thorne* • Jean Parker *Cora Dean* • Wallace Ford *Dr Amos Wynn* • John Emery *Cody Clark* • James Bell *Asaph Dean* • Ruth Donnelly *Molly Higgins* ■ *Dir* Joseph H Lewis • *Scr* Kenneth Gamet, from the novel *Marshal of Medicine Bend* by Brad Ward

Lawman ★★ 15
Western   1971 · US · Colour · 94mins

As a producer Michael Winner is capable of assembling major players in promising material, but as a director he's no great shakes – invariably sabotaging his own films by doing his own editing and by relying too much on the zoom lens. This is an authentic-looking, tough western, filmed in situ in Durango, with a distinguished cast and a fine screenplay by Gerald Wilson, but it is totally destroyed by inept timing and a clumsy, ugly visual style. ▭

Burt Lancaster *Jered Maddox* • Robert Ryan *Cotton Ryan* • Lee J Cobb *Vincent Bronson* • Sheree North *Laura Shelby* • Joseph Wiseman

Lucas • Robert Duvall *Vernon Adams* • Albert Salmi *Harvey Stenbaugh* ■ *Dir* Michael Winner • *Scr* Gerald Wilson

Lawn Dogs ★★★★ 15
Drama   1997 · UK · Colour · 96mins

Fairy-tale themes embellish a starkly contemporary story in director John Duigan's masterful tale of helpless innocence abroad. Sam Rockwell is Trent, a lawnmower man for the exclusive Kentucky suburb Camelot Gardens, who strikes up a friendship with Devon (Mischa Barton), a new kid on the block recovering from a heart operation. How people misconstrue the relationship between the "lawn dog" and the vibrantly imaginative youngster makes for a witty and warm film, full of unexpected twists and pleasures. Duigan's visual trump card is his clever coupling of the deformed American Dream with the potent power of Eastern European fable, and his magical mystery tour through the childhood psyche is a quality diversion oozing with taste and class. The unusual climax is a stunning and heartstopping surprise. Contains violence and some swearing. ▭ *DVD*

Mischa Barton *Devon* • Sam Rockwell *Trent* • Kathleen Quinlan *Clare* • Christopher McDonald *Morton* • Bruce McGill *Nash* • Eric Mabius *Sean* • David Barry Gray *Brett* ■ *Dir* John Duigan • *Scr* Naomi Wallace

The Lawnmower Man ★★★ 15
Science-fiction thriller
1992 · UK/US · Colour · 103mins

Eye-popping special effects are the star of this science-fiction tale, vaguely based on a Stephen King short story, but otherwise notable only for crossing a variation on the Frankenstein theme with a more original attempt to probe the cinematic opportunities offered by "virtual reality". Pierce Brosnan plays a misguided scientist – is there any other kind? – who selects his simple-minded gardener as a guinea pig for his experiments with high-tech teaching aids and intelligence-boosting drugs. The film offers shades of everything from *My Fair Lady* to *Carrie* but, unlike either, also boasts cinema's first known cybersex scene. Contains violence and swearing. ▭ *DVD*

Jeff Fahey *Jobe Smith* • Pierce Brosnan *Dr Lawrence Angelo* • Jenny Wright *Marnie Burke* • Mark Bringleson *Sebastian Timms* • Geoffrey Lewis *Terry McKeen* • Jeremy Slate *Father McKeen* • Dean Norris *Director* • Colleen Coffey *Caroline Angelo* ■ *Dir* Brett Leonard • *Scr* Brett Leonard, Gimel Everett, from the short story by Stephen King

Lawnmower Man 2: Beyond Cyberspace ★ 12
Science-fiction   1995 · US · Colour · 89mins

Stephen King's name is nowhere to be seen and his original concept from the first surprise hit film has also vanished. What's left behind is a tedious slice of confusing science-fiction as Matt Frewer (Max Headroom himself) attempts to take over the world through cyberspace in director Farhad Mann's virtual unreality jumble. Scientist Patrick Bergin must stop him, but all the flashy digital effects in the

world can't disguise the incoherent plot or sketchy characterisations. ▭

Patrick Bergin *Dr Benjamin Trace* • Matt Frewer *Jobe* • Austin O'Brien *Peter* • Ely Pouget *Dr Cori Platt* • Kevin Conway *Walker* • Trevor O'Brien *Peter as a child* • Camille Cooper *Jennifer* ■ *Dir* Farhad Mann • *Scr* Farhad Mann, from a story by Michael Miner, Farhad Mann, from the film *The Lawnmower Man* by Brett Leonard, Gimel Envett

Lawrence of Arabia ★★★★★ PG
Historical epic adventure
1962 · UK · Colour · 209mins

Director David Lean's magisterial portrayal of one of Britain's most enigmatic yet charismatic heroes, TE Lawrence, whose precise role in the Arab revolt against the Turks during the First World War still perplexes military historians. Peter O'Toole's flamboyant performance hints at every aspect of Lawrence's complex character (including his masochistic tendency), while Robert Bolt and Michael Wilson's script develops into a withering satire on the ball-and-socket mentality of Lawrence's superiors, who play the Great Game of Empire by the book. Taking 15 months to shoot in Saudi Arabia, Morocco, Spain and England, Lean's obsession with the desert mirrors Lawrence's own, via some awesomely beautiful images, notably the mirage that introduced the world to a new star, Omar Sharif. Winner of seven Oscars and restored to its original version in 1989, this is movie-making on the grandest scale. ▭

Peter O'Toole *TE Lawrence* • Alec Guinness *Prince Feisal* • Anthony Quinn *Auda Abu Tayi* • Jack Hawkins *General Allenby* • José Ferrer *Turkish Bey* • Anthony Quayle *Colonel Harry Brighton* • Claude Rains *Mr Dryden* • Arthur Kennedy *Jackson Bentley* • Donald Wolfit *General Murray* • Omar Sharif *Sherif Ali Ibn El Kharish* ■ *Dir* David Lean • *Scr* Robert Bolt, Michael Wilson (uncredited), from the book *The Seven Pillars of Wisdom* by TE Lawrence • *Cinematographer* Freddie Young • *Music* Maurice Jarre • *Art Director* John Box

Laws of Gravity ★★★★ 18
Drama   1992 · US · Colour · 94mins

One of the most impressive directorial debuts of the decade, this sassily-scripted drama cost 29-year-old Nick Gomez a mere $38,000. Shot with twitchy handheld energy by documentary veteran Jean de Segonzac, the action so reeks of those familiar Brooklyn streets that, while comparisons with Martin Scorsese's *Mean Streets* are inevitable, they are in no way unflattering. Adam Trese gives a hair-trigger performance as the small-time hood whose misdemeanours bring Peter Greene's gang into dispute with gun dealer Paul Schulze. But every bit as impressive is a pre-*Sopranos* Edie Falco as Greene's feisty girlfriend. Raw, brutal and terrifyingly alive. Contains swearing and some violence. ▭

Peter Greene *Jimmy* • Edie Falco *Denise* • Paul Schulze *Frankie* • Tony Fernandez *Tommy* • James McCauley *Kenny* • Anibal Lierras *Ray* • Miguel Sierra *Vasquez* • Adam Trese *Jon* ■ *Dir/Scr* Nick Gomez

The Lawyer ★★★
Courtroom drama
1969 · US · Colour · 119mins

Sidney J Furie's moderate courtroom drama was loosely based on the true story of Dr Sam Sheppard, whose arrest in 1954 for the alleged murder of his wife attracted the kind of media storm that gathered over the OJ Simpson affair. Barry Newman plays the confident lawyer defending a client who refuses to co-operate, whose family have their doubts as to his innocence and whose notoriety looks likely to prejudice a fair hearing. Too much time is spent in the company of Newman and his screen wife Diana Muldaur, but the formula worked well enough to resurface in the TV series *Petrocelli*.

Barry Newman *Tony Petrocelli* • Harold Gould *Eric P Scott* • Diana Muldaur *Ruth Petrocelli* • Robert Colbert *Jack Harrison* • Kathleen Crowley *Alice Fiske* • Warren Kemmerling *Sergeant Moran* • Booth Colman *Judge Crawford* ■ *Dir* Sidney J Furie • *Scr* Sidney J Furie, Harold Buchman

Lawyer Man ★★★
Drama   1932 · US · BW · 72mins

William Powell stars as the lawyer of the title, a socially conscious do-gooder with a shabby office on the Lower East Side of New York, an eye for the ladies, and a devoted, wisecracking secretary (Joan Blondell). Things come unstuck when he is seduced into partnership with a smart uptown lawyer and overreaches himself. This cynical look at legal ethics and political corruption, decently played and directed, holds the attention, as does Powell, despite the loss of plot credibility about two-thirds of the way through.

William Powell *Anton Adam* • Joan Blondell *Olga Michaels* • Helen Vinson *Barbara Bentley* • Alan Dinehart *Granville Bentley* • Allen Jenkins *Issy Levine* • David Landau *John Gilmurry* • Claire Dodd *Virginia St Johns* • Sheila Terry *Flo* • Kenneth Thomson *Dr Frank Gresham* ■ *Dir* William Dieterle • *Scr* Rian James, James Seymour, from the novel by Max Trell

Laxdale Hall ★★ U
Comedy   1953 · UK · BW · 75mins

The huge success of director Alexander Mackendrick's *Whisky Galore!* meant it was inevitable that film-makers would cast around for more stories of wily Scots running rings around the stiff-necked English. However, lightning didn't strike twice and this tale of the battle between Whitehall and a tiny Hebridean island, whose inhabitants won't pay a hated road tax, lacks the magic sparkle of Mackendrick's classic. Look out for Fulton Mackay of TV sitcom *Porridge* fame in an early role.

Ronald Squire *General Matheson* • Kathleen Ryan *Catriona Matheson* • Raymond Huntley *Samuel Pettigrew MP* • Sebastian Shaw *Hugh Marvell MP* • Fulton Mackay *Andrew Flett* • Jean Colin *Lucy Pettigrew* • Jameson Clark *Roderick McLeod* • Prunella Scales *Morag McLeod* ■ *Dir* John Eldridge • *Scr* Alfred Shaughnessy, John Eldridge, from the novel by Eric Linklater

Layla Ma Raison ★★

Drama   1989 · Tun · Colour · 90mins

This film by Taieb Louhichi, the Tunisian director who made *Shadow on the Earth* about a nomadic tribe destroyed by modernity, is based on a 7th-century Arab legend about the doomed love between a poet and his beloved. The star-crossed lovers are separated by Layla's harsh father who feels his daughter has been dishonoured by the poet by enumerating her virtues in public. The biblical atmosphere and some splendid desert vistas almost overcome the weaknesses in the acting and the often obscure screenplay. In Arabic with English subtitles.

Safy Boutella *Qays* • Anca Nicola *Layla* • Abderrahmane Al Rachi *Layla's Father* ■ *Dir* Taieb Louhichi

Lazybones ★★

Romantic comedy   1935 · UK · BW · 65mins

This early studio-based, Michael Powell-directed romantic comedy casts Ian Hunter as Sir Reginald Ford, an extremely idle baronet who, along with his titled father, is also completely penniless. Seeking a solution to his lack of solvency, Ford pursues American heiress Kitty McCarthy (Claire Luce), only to discover that she's been swindled by her advisors and is overdrawn as well. Hunter changes tack and sets about recovering Kitty's fortune, falling in love with her in the process. The plot is predictable, but the film nevertheless displays the first hints of Powell's inimitable style.

Claire Luce *Kitty McCarthy* • Ian Hunter *Sir Reginald Ford* • Sara Allgood *Bridget* • Bernard Nedell *Mike McCarthy* • Michael Shepley *Hildebrand Pope* • Bobbie Comber *Kemp* • Denys Blakelock *Hugh Ford* ■ *Dir* Michael Powell • *Scr* Gerard Fairlie, from a play by Ernest Denny

Leadbelly ★★★

Musical biography
1976 · US · Colour · 126mins

Roger E Mosley stars as the famous rough 'n' tough American folk singer Huddie Ledbetter, known as Leadbelly, the traumas of whose eventful life included serving time on a chain gang. Made by Gordon Parks, the first black director of major Hollywood features (including *Shaft*), this is a straightforward biopic, technically proficient and boasting excellent cinematography from Bruce Surtees, as well as all-round excellent performances. The dozen or so of Leadbelly's songs that are featured are sung by HiTide Harris.

Roger E Mosley *Huddie "Leadbelly" Ledbetter* • Paul Benjamin *Wes Ledbetter* • Madge Sinclair *Miss Eula* • Alan Manson *Chief Prison Guard* • Albert P Hall [Albert Hall] *Dicklicker* • Art Evans *Blind Lemon Jefferson* ■ *Dir* Gordon Parks • *Scr* Ernest Kinoy

The Leading Man ★★★ 15

Romantic comedy drama
1996 · UK · Colour · 95mins

Another perceptive adult comedy-drama from director John Duigan, who made his name in the genre through *The Year My Voice Broke*, *Flirting* and *Sirens*. This time, the setting is theatrical London, for amorous encounters involving a writer, his actress-mistress, his wife and a famous Hollywood hunk who's decided to tread the boards and is happy to provide a "distraction" to the playwright's extra-marital activities. Although the thespian backdrop and central characters are a little underdeveloped, the bright, eclectic cast which includes Thandie Newton (who got her break in *Flirting*), rock star Jon Bon Jovi and French actress Anna Galiena make the romantic complications ring true. The potentially fatal opening-night performance does stretch credibility a little, though. 🖵

Jon Bon Jovi *Robin Grange* • Lambert Wilson *Felix Webb* • Anna Galiena *Elena Webb* • Thandie Newton *Hilary Rule* • Barry Humphries *Humphrey Beal* • David Warner *Tod* • Patricia Hodge *Delvene* • Diana Quick *Susan* ■ *Dir* John Duigan • *Scr* Virginia Duigan

The League of Frightened Men ★★

Murder mystery   1937 · US · BW · 71mins

A group of Harvard graduates hires detective Nero Wolfe to find out how and why three of their number have died in mysterious circumstances. Having brought Rex Stout's famously sedentary and epicurean detective to the screen the previous year, with a very well-cast Edward Arnold, Columbia seemed poised for series. However, this serviceable but static second outing, with Walter Connolly taking over the role of Wolfe, proved the last, probably because a virtually armchair-bound hero limited the possibilities for action.

Walter Connolly *Nero Wolfe* • Lionel Stander *Archie Goodwin* • Eduardo Ciannelli *Paul Chapin* • Irene Hervey *Evelyn Hibbard* • Victor Killian [Victor Kilian] *Pitney Scott* • Nana Bryant *Agnes Burton* ■ *Dir* Alfred E Green • *Scr* Eugene Solow, Guy Endore, from the novel by Rex Stout

The League of Gentlemen ★★★★ PG

Crime comedy   1960 · UK · BW · 108mins

This was the first feature from the Allied Film Makers company, with most of its founder members – producer Michael Relph, director Basil Dearden, screenwriter Bryan Forbes and actors Jack Hawkins and Richard Attenborough – making solid contributions to this rousing crime caper. Dating from a time when every third word a crook said didn't begin with an "f", this distant ancestor of such bungled heist pics as *Reservoir Dogs* gets off to a rather stodgy start, but, once Hawkins has assembled his far from magnificent seven and his intricate plan begins to unravel, the action really hots up. 🖵

Jack Hawkins *Lieutenant Colonel Hyde* • Nigel Patrick *Peter Graham Race* • Roger Livesey *Mycroft* • Richard Attenborough *Edward Lexy* • Bryan Forbes *Martin Porthill* • Kieron Moore *Stevens* • Robert Coote *Bunny Warren* • Terence Alexander *Rupert Rutland-Smith* ■ *Dir* Basil Dearden • *Scr* Bryan Forbes, from a novel by John Boland

A League of Their Own ★★★ PG

Comedy drama   1992 · US · Colour · 122mins

Before he won a couple of Oscars for more serious fare, Tom Hanks provided the laughs as the alcoholic ex-professional hired to coach a women's baseball team during the Second World War. The assembled players include Geena Davis and Lori Petty as sisters, Madonna as (of course) the team floozy and comedian Rosie O'Donnell as her best friend. Penny Marshall, who also directed Hanks in *Big*, has put together a somewhat uneven comedy, but any roughness is smoothed over by the talented cast and a great deal of charm and affection for the era. And watch out for Bill Pullman in a very small role as Davis's husband. 🖵
DVD

Tom Hanks *Jimmy Dugan* • Geena Davis *Dottie Hinson* • Lori Petty *Kit Keller* • Madonna *Mae Mordabito* • Rosie O'Donnell *Doris Murphy* • Megan Cavanagh *Marla Hooch* • Tracy Reiner *Betty Horn* • Bitty Schram *Evelyn Gardner* ■ *Dir* Penny Marshall • *Scr* Lowell Ganz, Babaloo Mandel, from a story by Kim Wilson, Kelly Candaele

Lean on Me ★★★ 15

Drama   1989 · US · Colour · 103mins

Morgan Freeman takes over as principal of a problem New Jersey high school and eventually wins the hearts of his students after a rigorous clean-up campaign. The tough-love formula works like a charm thanks to Freeman's engaging central performance, and energetic direction by John G Avildsen who brings some of the grit he displayed in *Rocky* to the true story. 🖵

Morgan Freeman *Joe Clark* • Robert Guillaume *Dr Frank Napier* • Beverly Todd *Ms Levias* • Lynne Thigpen *Leona Barrett* • Jermaine Hopkins *Thomas Sams* • Karen Malina White *Keneesha Carter* • Alan North *Mayor Don Bottman* • Ethan Phillips *Mr Rosenberg* ■ *Dir* John G Avildsen • *Scr* Michael Schiffer

Leap of Faith ★★ PG

Drama based on a true story
1988 · US · Colour · 93mins

This true-life TV melodrama directed by Stephen Gyllenhaal boasts a superior cast, there is little to distinguish it from dozens of other disease-of-the-week weepies. Anne Archer is dignified and determined as Deborah Franke Ogg, who re-ordered her world to give her immune system the best chance of combating her potentially fatal illness. Sam Neill is patience itself as her husband, but it's hard to see how such a bizarre regimen could be inspirational. 🖵

Anne Archer *Debby Franke Ogg* • Sam Neill *Oscar Ogg* • Frances Lee McCain *Susan* • Louis Giambalvo *Dr Santini* • Norman Parker *Marty* • James Hong *Mr Li* • CCH Pounder *Roberta* ■ *Dir* Stephen Gyllenhaal • *Scr* Bruce Hart

Leap of Faith ★★★ PG

Satirical drama   1992 · US · Colour · 103mins

Steve Martin takes on the role of a cynical bogus evangelist who runs a travelling gospel show in this film, which can't quite make up its mind whether it wants to be a comedy or a straight drama. When Martin and his team arrive at a poor Kansas town to fleece the residents, they find their consciences pricked as they get to know the townspeople. An interesting cast including Liam Neeson, Debra Winger, Lolita Davidovich and Meat Loaf performs well, but the film loses its way as the plot becomes tangled with miracles and saccharine twists. 🖵

Steve Martin *Jonas Nightengale* • Debra Winger *Jane* • Liam Neeson *Will* • Lolita Davidovich *Marva* • Lukas Haas *Boyd* • Meat Loaf *Hoover* • Philip Seymour Hoffman *Matt* • MC Gainey *Tiny* ■ *Dir* Richard Pearce • *Scr* Janus Cercone

The Learning Tree ★★★

Drama   1969 · US · Colour · 106mins

Best known for his film about the black private eye *Shaft*, novelist, photographer, poet, composer and film-maker Gordon Parks is a one-man cultural phenomenon. One of the godfathers of independent African-American cinema, he based his feature debut on an autobiographical novel written during a visit to Paris. While he and cinematographer Burnett Guffey lovingly re-create the look and feel of twenties' Kansas, Parks struggles to animate the inexperienced cast, led by Kyle Johnson as a young man coming to terms with the realities and prejudices of life. Historically important, but a film overly determined to be both authentic and significant. Contains strong language.

Kyle Johnson *Newt Winger* • Alex Clarke *Marcus Savage* • Estelle Evans *Sarah Winger* • Dana Elcar *Sheriff Kirky* • Mira Waters *Arcella Jefferson* • Joel Fluellen *Uncle Rob* • Malcolm Atterbury *Silas Newhall* • Richard Ward *Booker Savage* ■ *Dir* Gordon Parks • *Scr* Gordon Parks, from his novel

Lease of Life ★★★ U

Drama   1954 · UK · Colour · 90mins

Robert Donat is always unfairly overlooked in discussions of great British screen actors. An Oscar winner for *Goodbye, Mr Chips*, he fought chronic asthma throughout his life to give several moving and convincing performances, which usually belied the quality of the material. This tale of a Yorkshire vicar with only a year to live is a case in point. Thriller specialist Eric Ambler makes a mawkish mess of what is essentially a domestic drama but, through the gentle fidelity of his performance, Donat creates a decent and dignified character who sounds sincere even in his sentimental sermon to a congregation of schoolboys.

Robert Donat *William Thorne* • Kay Walsh *Vera Thorne* • Adrienne Corri *Susan Thorne* • Denholm Elliott *Martin Blake* • Walter Fitzgerald *Dean* • Cyril Raymond *Headmaster* • Reginald Beckwith *Foley* ■ *Dir* Charles Frend • *Scr* Eric Ambler, from a story by Frank Baker, Patrick Jenkins

The Leather Boys ★★★ 15

Drama   1963 · UK · BW · 107mins

Nealy 40 years on, it's almost impossible to see why this was once regarded as an unacceptably frank insight into the gay lifestyle. Colin

Campbell is so hopelessly out of his depth as the young newlywed wrestling with his sexual identity that not even the excellence of Rita Tushingham and Dudley Sutton can salvage what were intended to be powerful scenes. Sidney J Furie's film is now something of a quaint period piece, full of techniques borrowed from the French New Wave. The end result is fussy and flash rather than fresh, but the wedding and the Butlin's sequences are priceless relics of sixties' life. ▭
Rita Tushingham *Dot* • Colin Campbell *Reggie* • Dudley Sutton *Pete* • Gladys Henson *Gran* • Avice Landone *Reggie's mother* • Lockwood West *Reggie's father* • Betty Marsden *Dot's mother* ■ *Dir* Sidney J Furie • *Scr* Gillian Freeman, from the novel by Eliot George [Eliot Freeman]

Leather Jackets ★★★ 18
Crime drama 1991 · US · Colour · 90mins
English actor Cary Elwes is almost unrecognisable in this brooding, under-rated crime drama, which also provided an early starring role for Bridget Fonda. The story focuses on the complicated relationships between reformed crook DB Sweeney, his fiancée (Fonda) and his best friend (Elwes), who is on the run from Asian mobsters. Director Lee Drysdale captures the bleakness of small-town life and is rewarded with fine performances from his young leads. Look out for former porn star Ginger Lynn Allen in a small role. ▭
DB Sweeney *Mickey* • Bridget Fonda *Claudi* • Cary Elwes *Dobbs* • Christopher Penn *Big Steve* • Jon Polito *Fat Jack* • Craig Ng *Tron* • Marshall Bell *Stranger* • James LeGros *Carl* • Ginger Lynn Allen *Bree* ■ *Dir/Scr* Lee Drysdale

Leatherface: the Texas Chainsaw Massacre III ★★★
Horror 1990 · US · Colour · 85mins
Gory, graphic, gruesome and bloody hilarious, director Jeff Burr's second sequel to Tobe Hooper's classic gut-wrencher combines the suffocating atmosphere of the original with the razor-sharp black comedy of Hooper's second reworking. Kate Hodge and William Butler are the ingenuous tourists who this time take a backwoods detour and end up being prospective sausage filler thanks to Leatherface and his splatter happy family of cannibals. More provocative and taboo-busting than the first two entries in the censor-upsetting series, strong stomachs are a requirement for the tense grip this powerful charnel house of extreme horror exerts.
Kate Hodge *Michelle* • William Butler *Ryan* • Viggo Mortensen *Tex* • Ken Foree *Benny* • Joe Unger *Tinker* • Tom Everett *Alfredo* • Toni Hudson *Sara* • Miriam Byrd-Nethery *Mama* • RA Mihailoff *Leatherface* ■ *Dir* Jeff Burr • *Scr* David J Schow, from the characters by created by Kim Henkel, Tobe Hooper

The Leatherneck ★★
Drama 1929 · US · BW · 76mins
Set in the aftermath of the First World War, William Boyd is defending himslf against charges of murder and desertion. This undernourished drama with moments of romance is notable only for what became of its stars – William Boyd turned cowboy and carved

out a lucrative career as Hopalong Cassidy, while Alan Hale picked up a contract wih Warner Bros and became a character-stalwart with the studio.
William Boyd *Joseph Hanlon* • Alan Hale *Otto Schmidt* • Robert Armstrong *William Calhoun* • Fred Kohler *Heckla* ■ *Dir* Howard Higgin • *Scr* Elliott Clawson, John W Krafft

Leave All Fair ★★★
Biographical drama
1985 · NZ · Colour · 88mins
A subtle, elegantly told story about the New Zealand writer Katherine Mansfield who died in 1923 and is recalled decades later by her husband (the literary critic John Middleton Murry) while visiting a publisher in Paris. Financed in New Zealand but shot entirely in France, the film's chief virtues are the superb performances by John Gielgud as the husband and Jane Birkin (an unusual casting choice) in a dual role as Mansfield and a woman who resembles the writer. Birkin adds layers of nuance to an otherwise conventional storyline.
John Gielgud *John Middleton Murry* • Jane Birkin *Marie Taylor/Katherine Mansfield* • Feodor Atkine *Andrée Sarry* • Simon Ward *Young John* • Maurice Chevit *Alain* ■ *Dir* John Reid • *Scr* Stanley Harper, Maurice Pons, John Reid

Leave 'Em Laughing ★★★ U
Drama 1981 · US · Colour · 103mins
Mickey Rooney turns in a stand-out performance as the real-life New York comedian Jack Thum who, with wife Anne Jackson, cared for dozens of homeless youngster, despite the rigours of the comedy circuit – and cancer. A TV movie that plucks hard on the heart-strings, it's redeemed by Rooney's brisk, no-nonsense take on the situation, helped by similar direction from Jackie Cooper, whose own childhood was spent as the "little tough guy" of the *Our Gang* children's movies.
Mickey Rooney *Jack Thum* • Anne Jackson *Shirlee Thum* • Elisha Cook [Elisha Cook Jr] *Jetter* • Michael LeClair *Tom* • William Windom *Smiley Jenkins* • Red Buttons *Roland Green* ■ *Dir* Jackie Cooper • *Scr* Cynthia W Mandelberg, from a story by Peggy Chantler-Dick

Leave Her to Heaven
★★★★ U
Romantic melodrama
1945 · US · Colour · 105mins
Here's a wonderful chunk of 20th Century-Fox tosh in the most glowing Oscar-winning Technicolor you're ever likely to see. Sublimely beautiful Gene Tierney is Ellen, who drops overacting Vincent Price to go off with dull but handsome author Cornel Wilde, and lets her pretty foster sister Jeanne Crain and Wilde take the blame for murder. This is glorious melodrama that knows no bounds – cherish the sequence in which Tierney feverishly scatters ashes against the Maine horizon. ▭
Gene Tierney *Ellen Berent* • Cornel Wilde *Richard Harland* • Jeanne Crain *Ruth Berent* • Vincent Price *Russell Quinton* • Mary Phillips *[Mary Philips] Mrs Berent* • Ray Collins *Glen Robie* • Gene Lockhart *Dr Saunders* • Reed Hadley *Dr Mason* ■ *Dir* John M Stahl • *Scr* Jo

Swerling, from the novel *Leave Her to Heaven* by Ben Ames Williams • *Cinematographer* Leon Shamroy

Leave It to Beaver ★★ PG
Comedy 1997 · Colour · 84mins
No sniggering at the back, please. The popular fifties sit-com gets a modern big-screen update, but this forgettable family movie is only really of interest for fans or the easily amused. Unlike the enjoyably daft *Brady Bunch* movies, little or no concession has been made for nineties audiences, aside from mild swearing and the occasional satirical moment, like the family's therapy session. Saddled with a pedestrian script (co-written by *Flintstones* director Brian Levant), stars Janine Turner and Christopher McDonald look far from comfy in their parental roles, although young Cameron Finley has a certain cute appeal. ▭
Christopher McDonald *Ward Cleaver* • Janine Turner *June Cleaver* • Cameron Finley *Theodore "Beaver" Cleaver* • Erik Von Detten *Wally Cleaver* • Adam Zolotin *Eddie Haskell* • Barbara Billingsley *Aunt Martha* • Ken Osmond *Eddie Sr* ■ *Dir* Andy Cadiff • *Scr* Brian Levant, Lon Diamond, from the TV series by Bob Mosher, Joe Connelly

Leave of Absence ★★★ 12
Drama 1994 · US · Colour · 87mins
The ever-reliable Brian Dennehy delivers one of his most subtle and touching performances in this thoughtful drama. He plays a successful career man who falls for Jacqueline Bisset while married to Blythe Danner, then pushes his marriage to the edge by insisting on caring for Bisset when she falls victim to a terminal disease. Dennehy is more than matched in the acting stakes by Bisset, and there are equally strong turns from a supporting cast that includes Jessica Walter and Polly Bergen. It's made for TV, but it's in a different league from the usual small-screen fodder. ▭
Brian Dennehy *Sam Mercer* • Jacqueline Bisset *Nell Bergen* • Blythe Danner *Eliza Mercer* • Jessica Walter *Bess Kaufman* • Noëlle Parker *Zoey Mercer* • Polly Bergen *Janet* • Grayce Spence *Phyllis* • Tonea Stewart *Cora Winsor* ■ *Dir* Tom McLoughlin • *Scr* Betty Goldberg, from a story by Polly Bergen

Leaving Las Vegas ★★★★ 18
Drama 1995 · US · Colour · 107mins
Mike Figgis's agonising study of alcoholic self-destruction quietly impressed film-goers across the board with its uncompromising honesty and exceptional performances. Nicolas Cage won a well-deserved Oscar for his portrayal of a failed Hollywood screenwriter who goes to Vegas to drink himself to death. Just as memorable is Oscar-nominated Elisabeth Shue as the prostitute who befriends him. Shooting in Super 16mm, Figgis strips away the gaudy glamour of Nevada's temptation capital, revealing it to be nothing more than a tawdry, neon-lit tourist trap that exists solely on dashed hopes, broken promises and guilty secrets. As sobering an experience as cinema can provide, *Leaving Las Vegas* is downbeat all the way, but the sensitivity of the direction and the

authenticity of the acting also give it a curiously redemptive feel. Contains violence, swearing and drug abuse. ▭ DVD
Nicolas Cage *Ben Sanderson* • Elisabeth Shue *Sera* • Julian Sands *Yuri* • Richard Lewis *Peter* • Valeria Golino *Terri* • Steven Weber *Marc Nussbaum* • Kim Adams *Sheila* • Laurie Metcalf *Landlady* • Julian Lennon *Bartender in biker bar* ■ *Dir* Mike Figgis • *Scr* Mike Figgis, from the novel by John O'Brien

Leaving Lenin ★★★ 12
Comedy drama 1993 · UK · Colour · 89mins
What with *Hedd Wyn* receiving an Oscar nomination and this astute comedy garnering favourable reviews, 1993 was something of a glory year for Welsh cinema. A far cry from the wild things in *Twin Town*, the teens on this school trip have a comfortable life and much to look forward to. But they still have plenty to find out about themselves, and St Petersburg in the post-Communist era turns out to be the perfect scene for self-discovery. Shooting with an enthusiastic eye for the sights of the city and the naturalism of his young cast, director Endaf Emlyn makes the most of a rather contrived situation. In Welsh with English subtitles.. ▭
Sharon Morgan *Eileen* • Wyn Bowen Harries *Mostyn* • Ifan Huw Dafydd *Mervyn* • Steffan Trevor *Spike* • Catrin Mai *Rhian* • Ivan Shvedov *Sasha* • Richard Harrington *Charlie* • Shelley Rees *Sharon* ■ *Dir* Endaf Emlyn • *Scr* Endaf Emlyn, Sion Eiri

Leaving Normal ★★★ 15
Comedy drama 1992 · US · Colour · 105mins
A kind of sub-*Thelma and Louise*, with *The Big Chill*'s Meg Tilly as a bored housewife departing her second failed marriage and *Chicago Hope*'s Emmy award-winning Christine Lahti as a world-weary waitress. The two meet at a bus stop in the town of Normal, Wyoming, and decide to head for the wilds of Alaska, where Lahti has inherited a house. Sentimental stuff from director Edward Zwick that owes much to his previous TV work on the acclaimed *thirtysomething*. Contains swearing and nudity. ▭
Christine Lahti *Darly* • Meg Tilly *Marianne* • Patrika Darbo *66* • Lenny Von Dohlen *Harry* • Maury Chaykin *Leon* • Brett Cullen *Kurt* • James Gammon *Walt* • Eve Gordon *Emily* ■ *Dir* Edward Zwick • *Scr* Edward Solomon

La Lectrice ★★★★ 18
Erotic comedy 1988 · Fr · Colour · 98mins
Miou-Miou gives a beautifully judged performance as a professional reader in this wry erotic comedy from Michel Deville. This is the sort of French film that Hollywood thinks it can remake, but there's no one on the current A-list capable of reproducing Miou-Miou's subtle shifts from intellectual to companion, revolutionary to temptress, to suit the needs of her clients. Co-written by the director and his wife, Rosalinde, the script is a wonderful advertisement for books and the pleasures of reading. Full of the surprises that come with turning a page. In French with English subtitles..
Miou-Miou *Constance/Marie* • Régis Royer *Eric* • Christian Ruché *Jean/Philippe* • Charlotte Farran *Coralie* • Brigitte Catillon

Eric's mother/Jocelyne ■ *Dir* Michel Deville • *Scr* Rosalinde Deville, Michel Deville, from the novel by Raymond Jean, from a short story by Raymond Jean

The Leech Woman ★★

Horror   1960 · US · BW · 77mins

Scientist Coleen Gray goes to Africa in search of eternal youth and learns from a strange tribe that the ageing process can be reversed by drinking secretions from the pineal gland of sacrificial male victims. Her husband is the first dupe to provide the youth serum, but when it wears off she resorts to further murder to top up her supply. This is a workman-like pot-boiler, taking most of its inspiration from other modish chillers of the day although its faint feminist slant adds an extra touch.

Phillip Terry *Dr Paul Talbott* • Coleen Gray *June* • Grant Williams *Neil Foster* • Gloria Talbott *Sally* • June Van Dreelen *Bertram Garvay* ■ *Dir* Edward Dein • *Scr* David Duncan, from a story by Ben Pivar, Francis Rosenwald

The Left Hand of God ★★

Romantic wartime adventure
1955 · US · Colour · 87mins

As tacky and distasteful as its title, this 20th Century-Fox film, made in CinemaScope, has a miscast and extremely uncomfortable-looking (he was ill at the time) Humphrey Bogart posing as a priest in China in 1947, dallying with the lovely Gene Tierney and coping with warlord Lee J Cobb, complete with Hollywood oriental make-up. William E Barrett's original novel offered some provocative views on how a priest's mantle affects the man who wears it, but Bogart fails to convince as a tortured soul, and the screenplay simplifies the mental torment by using the garb as a device whereby Bogie can escape Cobb's clutches. Also along for the ride are Agnes Moorehead and EG Marshall. Edward Dmytryk directs tediously, as if overawed by the subject matter.

Humphrey Bogart *Jim Carmody* • Gene Tierney *Ann Scott* • Lee J Cobb *Mieh Yang* • Agnes Moorehead *Beryl Sigman* • EG Marshall *Dr Sigman* • Jean Porter *Mary Yin* ■ *Dir* Edward Dmytryk • *Scr* Alfred Hayes, from the novel by William E Barrett

The Left Handed Gun ★★★★ PG

Western   1958 · US · BW · 98mins

Paul Newman stepped into the role earmarked for James Dean (who would have been perfect) and delivers a brilliant, Brandoesque screen portrayal of outlaw Billy the Kid as envisaged by writer Gore Vidal, in this terrific movie debut from director Arthur Penn. Character actor John Dehner got the break of his life co-starring as Pat Garrett, and casting Hurd Hatfield (*The Picture of Dorian Gray*) as a nervous chronicler of the times was a clever touch. The film was heavily truncated on its UK cinema release, but in the complete version we can appreciate the subtlety of editor Folmar (*Rio Bravo, A Star Is Born*) Blangsted's handiwork. 🖵

Paul Newman *Billy Bonney* • Lita Milan *Celsa* • John Dehner *Pat Garrett* • Hurd Hatfield

Moultrie • James Congdon *Charlie Boudre* • James Best *Tom Folliard* ■ *Dir* Arthur Penn • *Scr* Leslie Stevens, from the teleplay *The Death of Billy the Kid* by Gore Vidal

Left Luggage ★★★ PG

Drama   1997 · Neth/Bel/US · Colour · 96mins

Set in seventies Antwerp, Jeroen Krabbé's first feature as director settles for cheap sentiment when it might have more profitably explored the challenges faced by a strict, patriarchal culture confronted with a changing world. All the characters – from David Bradley's bigoted concierge to Isabella Rossellini's dutiful Hassidic wife – are one-dimensional, with even Laura Fraser's questioning student-cum-nanny governed more by her emotions than her reason. Yet it's giving the death of Krabbé's timid son the same tragic weight as the Holocaust that most devalues this earnest but shallow film. Contains some strong language. 🖵

Isabella Rossellini *Mrs Kalman* • Maximilian Schell *Chaja's father* • Marianne Sägebrecht *Mr Apfelshnitt* • Laura Fraser *Chaja* • Jeroen Krabbé *Mr Kalman* • Adam Monty *Simcha Kalman* • David Bradley (2) *Concierge* ■ *Dir* Jeroen Krabbé • *Scr* Jeroen Krabbé, Edwin de Vries, from the novel *The Shovel and the Loom* by Carl Friedman

Left, Right and Centre ★★ U

Comedy   1959 · UK · BW · 94mins

A spoof on the effect that television has on persuading voters where to put their X. Playing another in a long line of silly asses, Ian Carmichael is spot on as the TV pundit who runs for the Conservatives in a local election. It's hardly a searing satire, but director and co-writer Sidney Gilliat scores a few points at the expense of both the media and the establishment. Stealing everyone's thunder, however, is Alastair Sim as Carmichael's impoverished uncle seeking ways to maintain his stately pile.

Ian Carmichael *Robert Wilcot* • Patricia Bredin *Stella Stoker* • Alastair Sim *Lord Wilcot* • Eric Barker *Bert Glimmer* • Richard Wattis *Harding-Pratt* • Gordon Harker *Hardy* • Jack Hedley *Bill Hemingway* • Leslie Dwyer *Alf Stoker* ■ *Dir* Sidney Gilliat • *Scr* Sidney Gilliat, from the story by Sidney Gilliat, Val Valentine

The Legacy ★★ 18

Horror   1978 · UK · Colour · 94mins

This modern variation on *The Old Dark House* formula finds Californians Katharine Ross and Sam Elliott stranded with a group of strangers – the Who's Roger Daltrey among them – in an English country mansion. As the guests are bumped off one by one, a Satanism subplot is introduced into the already unfocused proceedings to add extra suspense – it doesn't. A botched supernatural thriller with only some fiendishly clever death scenes to commend it. 🖵

Katharine Ross *Maggie Walsh* • Sam Elliott *Pete Danner* • John Standing *Jason Mountolive* • Ian Hogg *Harry* • Margaret Tyzack *Nurse Adams* • Charles Gray *Karl Liebknecht* • Lee Montague *Jacques Grandier* • Hildegard Neil *Barbara Kirstenburg* • Roger Daltrey *Clive*

Jackson ■ *Dir* Richard Marquand • *Scr* Jimmy Sangster, Patrick Tilley, Paul Wheeler, from the story by Jimmy Sangster

Legacy of Evil ★★

Supernatural thriller
1995 · US · Colour · 87mins

Stephen Lang, usually cast as the baddie, gets to play a more heroic role in this well played but unsurprisingly predictable little TV-movie chiller, supposedly based on a real-life story. He plays a man who is convinced that he has become possessed by some unseen evil spirit, a dark force that may compel him to harm his own family. *The Cosby Show's* Phylicia Rashad is one of the other familiar faces on display, but ultimately director Michael Kennedy takes the whole affair far too seriously. *The Amityville Horror* was a lot more fun.

Stephen Lang *Michael D* • Sheila McCarthy *Jenny* • Phylicia Rashad *Dr Marion Hale* • Roger Rees *Robin Banks* ■ *Dir* Michael Kennedy • *Scr* Ronald Parker

Legacy of Lies ★★★ 15

Thriller   1992 · US · Colour · 90mins

A very distinguished cast adds lustre to an otherwise ordinary story about a Chicago policeman who investigates a gangland slaying and learns that his father is corrupt and that his grandfather was a Mafia big shot. Michael Ontkean plays the suitably dumbstruck hero, ably supported by Martin Landau as his dad. 🖵

Michael Ontkean *Zack Zelnick* • Martin Landau *Abraham Zelnick* • Eli Wallach *Moses Zelnick* • Joe Morton *Samuel Flowers* • Patricia Clarkson *Pat Rafael* ■ *Dir* Bradford May • *Scr* David Black

The Legacy of Sin: the William Coit Jr Story ★★ PG

Drama based on a true story
1995 · US · Colour · 90mins

If there's one thing you can say about the character played in this TV movie by Macaulay Culkin's aunt, Bonnie Bedelia, it's that she hates to be home alone. Why else would she have married ten times? However, son Neil Patrick Harris gets to know more about his mother's life... More ludicrously sensational than the average tabloid teleplay, but the grotesque chain of events does foster a somewhat perverse fascination. 🖵

Neil Patrick Harris *William Coit Jr* • Bonnie Bedelia *Jill Coit* • Meredith Salenger *Robin Coit* • Jon Pennell *Seth Coit* ■ *Dir* Steven Schachter • *Scr* Ronald Parker, from the novel *Charmed to Death* by Stephen Singular

Legal Eagles ★★★ PG

Comedy thriller 1986 · US · Colour · 110mins

This high-gloss, Hollywood courtroom drama, which director Ivan Reitman chose to make as his next movie after the mega-hit *Ghostbusters*, features Robert Redford and Debra Winger as attorneys, at first pitted against each other but later working as a team. There's some natty dialogue, along with plenty of star appeal and sexual chemistry, but the plot (Daryl Hannah caught up in art fraud and murder) tends towards flabbiness. Harmless but not exceptional. 🖵

Robert Redford *Tom Logan* • Debra Winger *Laura Kelly* • Daryl Hannah *Chelsea Deardon* • Brian Dennehy *Cavanaugh* • Terence Stamp *Victor Taft* • Steven Hill *Bower* • David Clennon *Blanchard* • John McMartin *Forrester* ■ *Dir* Ivan Reitman • *Scr* Jim Cash, Jack Epps Jr, from a story by Jim Cash, Ivan Reitman

Legalese ★★★

Satirical courtroom drama
1998 · US · Colour · 92mins

Veteran James Garner lends his unique charm to this satirical TV drama that once again exposes the failings of the legal profession. As sleazy lawyer Norman Keane, Garner takes on the case of actress Gina Gershon, who is charged with murder. His courtroom strategy involves putting young, inexperienced attorney Edward Kerr in as his front-man, while Garner orchestrates the defence from behind the scenes. There's nothing new or shocking in this movie, but it's fun to watch old pro Garner at work, and there's good support from Kathleen Turner as a TV host.

James Garner *Norman Keane* • Kathleen Turner *Brenda Whitlass* • Gina Gershon *Angela Beale* • Mary-Louise Parker *Rica Martin* • Edward Kerr *Roy Guyton* • Brian Doyle-Murray *Harley Guyton* ■ *Dir* Glenn Jordan • *Scr* Billy Ray

Legend ★★ PG

Fantasy adventure
1985 · US · Colour · 89mins

This is probably one of the few films on director Ridley Scott's CV he would prefer to forget. It's a daft fairy tale filled with all manner of goblins, elves and pixies, as well as Tom Cruise as a young peasant who falls in love with princess Mia Sara. He takes her to see the last surviving unicorns, little knowing that the Lord of Darkness (Tim Curry) has his own evil plan for the mythical creatures. Curry prancing around with horns and yellow eyes is certainly the best thing in the film, which surprisingly did nothing to dim Cruise's rising star and it was only four short years later that he garnered an Oscar nomination for *Born on the Fourth of July*. Contains scenes that may be frightening to younger viewers. 🖵

Tom Cruise *Jack* • Tim Curry *Darkness* • Mia Sara *Lili* • David Bennent *Gump* • Alice Playten *Blix* • Billy Barty *Screwball* • Cork Hubbert *Brown Tom* • Peter O'Farrell *Pox* • Robert Picardo *Meg Mucklebones* ■ *Dir* Ridley Scott • *Scr* William Hjortsberg

The Legend of 1900 ★★★★ 15

Epic   1999 · It · Colour · 125mins

Every bit as lush, nostalgic and romantic as his *Cinema Paradiso*, director Giuseppe Tornatore's English language debut is a dreamy cross between *Life Is Beautiful* and *Titanic*. While about as plausible as the former and slightly less spectacular than the latter, this epic rumination on the human condition is still an engaging fable, delicately shot through with keen emotions and stunning visuals. It tells the strange tale of orphan Tim Roth, born on a cruise liner at the turn of the century, who becomes a star piano prodigy during the Roaring Twenties. Told in melancholy flashback by

trumpet player Pruitt Taylor Vince, this bittersweet mood piece is packed with stunning images, all choreographed to another masterly Ennio Morricone score. Unusual, adventurous and haunting, this sumptuous production is Tornatore's best work in ages.

Tim Roth *Danny Boodman TD Lemon Novecento* • Pruitt Taylor Vince *Max Tooney* • Mélanie Thierry *The girl* • Bill Nunn *Danny Boodman* • Peter Vaughan *Music shop owner* • Niall O'Brien *Plymouth harbour master* • Gabriele Lavia *Farmer* • Alberto Vásquez *Mexican stoker* ■ *Dir* Giuseppe Tornatore • *Scr* Giuseppe Tornatore, from the stage monologue *Novecento* by Alessandro Baricco • *Cinematographer* Lajos Koltai

The Legend of Billie Jean
★★ 15

Drama   1985 · US · Colour · 91mins

After making her name a year earlier with *Supergirl*, Helen Slater opted for a more modest heroic role with this well-meaning if muddled teen thriller. She plays a young girl who along with her brother and some friends inadvertently become an eighties' version of Bonnie and Clyde's gang, and icons to boot. There's no faulting the feisty performances from the youngsters or the grown-ups, but the "kids good, adults bad" message is trite and clumsily handled. ▭

Helen Slater *Billie Jean* • Christian Slater *Binx* • Keith Gordon *Lloyd* • Richard Bradford *Pyatt* • Martha Gehman *Ophelia* • Yeardley Smith *Putter* • Barry Tubb *Hubie* • Dean Stockwell *Muldaur* • Peter Coyote *Ringwald* ■ *Dir* Matthew Robbins • *Scr* Mark Rosenthal, Lawrence Konner

The Legend of Boggy Creek
★★

Horror documentary drama
1972 · US · Colour · 90mins

Long before *The Blair Witch Project* put Burkittsville on the map, this horror docu-drama featured encounters with a hairy Bigfoot-type monster supposedly prowling the environs of Fouke, Arkansas. Producer/director Charles B Pierce captures a quality of folk legend and the panic, fear and terror the fabled creature has created in the small town thanks to candid interviews with local residents who claim to have seen the mysterious beast. The obtrusive pop songs are a mistake, and so are the mocked-up monster shots, but despite the leisurely pace, it's never static enough to become arty, or slow enough to be dull.

Vern Stearman *Narration* ■ *Dir* Charles B Pierce • *Scr* Earl E Smith

The Legend of Fong Sai-Yuk I
★★★ PG

Martial arts comedy
1993 · HK · Colour · 105mins

After several outings as Wong Fei-Hong, the exciting Jet Li plays another character from Chinese legend in this hugely entertaining adventure that recalls the kind of knockabout costume dramas on which the Hong Kong film industry was founded. The lively blend of action and comedy is typified by the pantomimic contest to reach the top of a wooden tower defended by the athletic Sibelle Hu. While Li holds sway, this is also an

excellent vehicle for one of Hong Kong's top female stars, Josephine Siao. In Cantonese with English subtitles..

Jet Li *Fong Sai-Yuk* • Li Jai-Xing *Ting Ting* • Josephine Siao *Mother Fong* • Chu Kong *Father Fong* • Chan Sung-Yun *"Tiger" Lei* • Sibelle Hu *Lei Siu-Huan* ■ *Dir* Yuen Kwai • *Scr* Chai Kung-Yung, Chang Jiang-Chung, Ji Ang

The Legend of Fong Sai-Yuk II
★★ 15

Martial arts comedy
1993 · HK · Colour · 96mins

You'll remember from the first movie that, after completing his tower-climbing exertions, Jet Li sided with the Red Flower Society in its battle against the corrupt ruling dynasty. Well, this sequel concentrates on that rebellion, while providing only the briefest of history lessons to help us get by. Although director Yuen Kwai reassembles much the same cast, this has all the hallmarks of a hurried cash-in, with Jet Li allowing his temper to land him in the unlikeliest of situations, including the finale in which he fights off all comers while balancing mother Josephine Siao on a wobbling column of chairs. In Cantonese with English subtitles.

Jet Li *Fong Sai-Yuk* • Josephine Siao *Mother Fong* • Li Jai-Xing *Ting Ting* • Adam Cheng *Mr Chen* ■ *Dir* Corey Yuen [Yuen Kwai] • *Scr* Chan Kin Chung, Jay On

The Legend of Gator Face
★★

Fantasy adventure
1996 · US/Can · Colour · 99mins

Swamp dweller Paul Winfield is the weaver of tales in this undistinguished family-oriented fantasy, which has more than a little in common with *ET* as yet more well-meaning kids (in this case John White and Dan Warry-Smith) try to prevent some foolish grown-ups from doing harm to a supposedly sinister critter. The design department make the most of their meagre resources in creating the half-man, half-alligator "Gator Face" (Matt Evans), but you'll spend more time suppressing giggles than you will shedding tears.

John White *Danny* • Dan Warry-Smith *Phil* • Charlotte Sullivan *Angel* • C David Johnson *Sheriff* • Paul Winfield *Bob* • Matt Evans *Gator Face* ■ *Dir* Vic Sarin • *Scr* David Covell, Alan Mruvka, Sahara Riley

The Legend of Grizzly Adams
★★★ U

Adventure   1990 · US · Colour · 73mins

Although Dan Haggerty made the role of Grizzly Adams his own on TV, Gene Edwards stepped into the mountain man's shoes for this amiable family adventure. Plagued by shooting problems, with director Ken Kennedy replacing Don Shanks part-way through production, the film has Grizzly leave the wilderness to come to the rescue of an old banker friend. It's not much of a plot, but, as always, Grizzly's forest pets will keep the youngsters happy. The real interest, however, lies in the casting, with such B-movie troupers as Anthony Caruso, LQ Jones

and the "Venezuelan Volcano" herself, Acquanetta, in support. ▭

Gene Edwards *Grizzly Adams* • Link Wyler *Trapper* • Wayne Brennan *Horace Carson* • Red West *Bodine* • LQ Jones *Reno* • Anthony Caruso *Don Carlos* • Acquanetta *Maria* • Carla Kay Tedrow *Carla Townly* ■ *Dir* Ken Kennedy • *Scr* Ken Kennedy, from a novel by Richard Dillon

The Legend of Hell House
★★★

Horror   1973 · UK · Colour · 93mins

Richard Matheson's adaptation of his own novel is long on theory and short on terror. Dying millionaire Roland Culver offers a handsome reward to scientist Clive Revill and psychics Pamela Franklin and Roddy McDowall if they can discover the secret of the afterlife in a house with a history of violent hauntings. Although director John Hough makes atmospheric use of the suitably eerie sets, he is too content to send shivers rather than shock, and thus dilutes the efforts of a cast (including Gayle Hunnicutt as Revill's wife) that has valiantly entered into the spirit of the thing.

Pamela Franklin *Florence Tanner* • Roddy McDowall *Ben Fischer* • Clive Revill *Dr Chris Barrett* • Gayle Hunnicutt *Ann Barrett* • Roland Culver *Rudolph Deutsch* • Peter Bowles *Hanley* • Michael Gough *Corpse* ■ *Dir* John Hough • *Scr* Richard Matheson, from his novel *Hell House*

The Legend of Lylah Clare
★★★

Drama   1968 · US · Colour · 129mins

This overlong melodrama is notoriously fascinating for movie cultists, dealing as it does with a sublimely silly plot involving a long-dead movie star about to have her life story filmed by her husband. Kim Novak incarnates Lylah and her lookalike, and Peter Finch is the demonic director Lewis Zarkan. Both pull out all the stops (well, Kim pulls out her one) and the film topples over into unavoidable absurdity, a sort of wannabe *Sunset Boulevard*. Talented director Robert Aldrich may have intended something stronger, but the unique mixture of tormented sexuality and outright sadism here makes this a very peculiar experience.

Kim Novak *Lylah Clare/Elsa Brinkmann* • Peter Finch *Lewis Zarkan* • Ernest Borgnine *Barney Sheean* • Milton Selzer *Bart Langner* • Rossella Falk *Rossella* • Gabriele Tinti *Paolo* • Valentina Cortese *Countess Bozo Bedoni* • Jean Carroll *Becky Langner* ■ *Dir* Robert Aldrich • *Scr* Hugo Butler, Jean Rouverol, from the screenplay (unproduced) by Robert Thom, Edward DeBlasio

The Legend of Sleepy Hollow
★★★ U

Adventure drama
1980 · US · Colour · 104mins

A delightful, Emmy-award nominated adaptation of the Washington Irving tale, this fable stars Jeff Goldblum as Ichabod Crane, the man who meets the legendary Headless Horseman in Sleepy Hollow. Although a little tedious in places, this is still hugely enjoyable fare for anyone who likes the kind of stories you tell round a campfire at midnight. ▭

Jeff Goldblum *Ichabod Crane* • Dick Butkus *Brom Bones* • Meg Foster *Katrina Van Tassel* • Paul Sand *Frederic Dutcher* • John Sylvester White *Fritz Vanderhoof* • Laura Campbell *Thelma Vanderhoof Dumke* • James Griffith *Squire Van Tassel* • Michael Ruud *Winthrop Palmer* • Karin Isaacson *Jenny* ■ *Dir* Henning Schellerup • *Scr* Malvin Wald, Jack Jacobs, Tom Chapman, from the story by Washington Irving

The Legend of the Holy Drinker
★★★★ PG

Drama   1988 · It/Fr · Colour · 122mins

A magical, generous-of-spirit film with Rutger Hauer in one of his finest performances, as a tramp in Paris who is given a life-saving donation by a stranger on condition that he repay it to a shrine of St Theresa. But the new life the money helps him attain diverts him from his quest to pay off the debt. Italian director Ermanno Olmi has created a film from Joseph Roth's novella which, while not pressing the religious nerve too painfully, nevertheless tackles the idea of "legend" with real lyricism, evoking a magnificent Paris in the process. ▭

Rutger Hauer *Andreas Kartak* • Anthony Quayle *Distinguished gentleman* • Sandrine Dumas *Gabby* • Dominique Pinon *Woitech* • Sophie Segalen *Karoline* ■ *Dir* Ermanno Olmi • *Scr* Tullio Kezich, Ermanno Olmi, from the novella *Die Legende des beiligen Trinkers* by Joseph Roth

The Legend of the Lone Ranger
★★★ PG

Western   1981 · US · Colour · 92mins

This self-conscious attempt to bring back to the big screen the noble masked western avenger must be counted a failure largely owing to under-casting. Yet this Panavisioned retelling of the origins of the blue-clad hero and his Indian sidekick Tonto is not without a certain grandeur, and director and erstwhile cinematographer William A Fraker creates some dazzling imagery and scenic splendour, though he is terribly hampered by the plot provided. Totally unknown Klinton Spilsbury (allegedly revoiced by *Dallas* star Ken Kercheval, though some claim Stacy Keach did it) looks fine in costume, but lacks the necessary charisma and solidity that Clayton Moore brought to the role, and Michael Horse is no match for Jay Silverheels's Tonto. ▭

Klinton Spilsbury *John Reid (the Lone Ranger)* • Michael Horse *Tonto* • Christopher Lloyd *Cavendish* • Jason Robards [Jason Robards Jr] *President Grant* • Matt Clark *Sheriff Wiatt* • Juanin Clay *Amy Striker* • John Hart *Lucas Striker* • Richard Farnsworth *Wild Bill Hickok* • Ted Flicker *[Theodore Flicker]* • Buffalo Bill Cody ■ *Dir* William A Fraker • *Scr* Ivan Goff, Ben Roberts, Michael Kane, William Roberts, Jerry Berloshan, from characters created by George W Trendle

Legend of the Lost
★★ U

Adventure   1957 · US · Colour · 104mins

Big John Wayne is hard-drinking Joe January, not out West this time, but engaged as a guide by explorer Rossano Brazzi to search for Saharan treasure. Sophia Loren provides the obligatory love interest as a street girl looking for adventure. The Technirama and Technicolor Libyan locations are the main reasons for watching this turgid tosh, unless you particularly like to see major stars make major fools of themselves. Wayne's friend Henry Hathaway directed, but this languid travelogue is no *True Grit*. The premise must have seemed like fun, but unfortunately what should have been a romp is taken too seriously. ▦

John Wayne *Joe January* • Sophia Loren *Dita* • Rossano Brazzi *Paul Bonnard* • Kurt Kasznar *Prefect Dukas* • Sonia Moser *Girl* • Angela Portaluri *Girl* • Ibrahim El Hadish *Galli Galli* • *Dir* Henry Hathaway • *Scr* Robert Presnell Jr, Ben Hecht • *Cinematographer* Jack Cardiff

The Legend of the Seven Golden Vampires ★★★ 18

Martial arts horror
1974 · UK/HK · Colour · 85mins

In its waning years, Hammer tried to make imaginative changes to the old favourites and this east-meets-west tale was one of the studio's better attempts to update the vampire formula. Peter Cushing's Van Helsing treks to China to take on his long-standing enemy Dracula with the help of a martial arts clan in this highly entertaining and surprisingly thoughtful kung fu horror movie. It sounds ludicrous, but it works, mainly thanks to excellent fight choreography featuring the masked Samurai undead and rousing direction from horror veteran Roy Ward Baker. ▦

Peter Cushing *Professor Lawrence Van Helsing* • David Chiang *Hsi Ching* • Julie Ege *Vanessa Buren* • Robin Stewart *Leyland Van Helsing* • Szu Shih *Mai Kwei* • John Forbes-Robertson *Dracula* • Robert Hanna *British consul* ■ *Dir* Roy Ward Baker • *Scr* Don Houghton

The Legend of the Suram Fortress ★★★ U

Mythical drama
1984 · USSR · Colour · 83mins

After a 15-year hiatus, during which time he was twice jailed by the Soviet authorities, Sergei Paradjanov returned to directing with this beguiling allegory on the malingering disintegration of the USSR. The narrative concerns the revenge of a fortune-teller, who convinces a young man that he must be walled up inside a medieval Georgian fortress to prevent it from collapse. But such is the density of the symbolic and cultural references that western audiences would be advised simply to surrender themselves to the glorious visuals, composed with a uniquely painterly eye by Paradjanov and his star and co-director, Dodo Abashidze. In Georgian with English subtitles. ▦

Venerik'o Andzhaparidze • Dodo Abashidze ■ *Dir* Dodo Abashidze, Sergei Paradjanov • *Scr* Vazha Ghigashvili

Legend of the Werewolf ★★ 18

Horror 1974 · UK · Colour · 86mins

David Rintoul plays a lycanthropic zoo-keeper in a Paris-based slice of cod Hammer horror directed by Freddie Francis for Tyburn, his son Kevin's company. Although he offers little in the way of new ideas or situations – even the wolfman make-up is reminiscent of Oliver Reed's in *The Curse of the Werewolf* – Francis does

summon up a Gothic moodiness between the few scares. Loyal Peter Cushing fans will want to check out his usual topnotch performance as the coroner pursuing the snarling Rintoul. ▦

Peter Cushing *Paul Cataflanque* • Ron Moody *Zoo keeper* • Hugh Griffith *Maestro Pamponi* • David Rintoul *Etoile* • Stefan Gryff *Max Gerard* • Lynn Dalby *Christine* • Renee Houston *Chou-Chou* • Marjorie Yates *Madame Tellier* • Roy Castle *Photographer* • Michael Ripper *Sewerman* • Patrick Holt *Dignitary* ■ *Dir* Freddie Francis • *Scr* John Elder [Anthony Hinds]

Legend of the White Horse ★ PG

Fantasy adventure
1985 · US/Pol · Colour · 87mins

Billed as a family film, this preposterous fantasy could be a scary outing for the under-12s. Geologist father Christopher Lloyd goes to a fictitious country on an environmental "dig" and finds his plans interrupted, not to say stopped, by a white horse which turns into a dragon and several other menaces. A Polish-American production, this is a farrago hardly worth retrieving. ▦

Christopher Lloyd *Jim Martin* • Dee Wallace Stone *Alta* • Allison Balson *Jewel* ■ *Dir* Jerzy Domaradzki, Janusz Morgenstern • *Scr* Robert C Fleet

The Legend of Tom Dooley ★★★ U

Western 1959 · US · BW · 79mins

Inspired by folk group the Kingston Trio's hit song (which they perform on the soundtrack here) this Civil War western follows the lyrics all the way to their downbeat conclusion and turns out to be an unexpectedly resonant little picture. Michael Landon and Richard Rust are excellent as two of the Confederate soldiers who, not realising that the war is over, rob a Union stage and have to go on the run. Jo Morrow is good as the northern girl with whom Landon attempts to elope. Writer/producer Stan Shpetner deserves credit for an intelligent script, and director Ted Post handles his young cast well.

Michael Landon *Tom Dooley* • Jo Morrow *Laura* • Jack Hogan *Charlie Grayson* • Richard Rust *Country Boy* • Dee Pollock *Abel* • Ken Lynch *Father* • Howard Wright *Sheriff* • Ralph Moody *Doc Henry* ■ *Dir* Ted Post • *Scr* Stanley Shpetner

The Legend of Walks Far Woman ★★★

Drama 1982 · US · Colour · 120mins

A remarkable performance from Raquel Welch as a native American woman coping with all that life throws at her elevates this western adventure from the merely passable to the surprisingly affecting. Adapted by bestselling novelist Evan Hunter from Colin Stuart's book based on his boyhood memories of two women he met from the era, the sweeping tale takes in events from the Battle of the Little Bighorn to the demise of the Sioux's free-roaming ways. The whole is paraded past the camera by director Mel Damski with far too much reliance on clichés about Indian nobility and the

wicked ways of the white man. Yet, through it all, Welch endures and shows her under-rated talents as an actress with a creditable range even under masses of old-age make-up. Contains violence.

Raquel Welch *Walks Far Woman* • Bradford Dillman *Singer* • George Clutesi *Old Grandfather* • Nick Mancuso *Horses Ghost* • Eloy Phil Casados [Eloy Casados] *Feather Earrings* • Nick Ramus *Left Hand Bull* ■ *Dir* Mel Damski • *Scr* Evan Hunter, from the novel *Walks Far Woman* by Colin Stuart

The Legend of Young Dick Turpin ★★ U

Action adventure 1965 · US · Colour · 89mins

An account of one of England's most famous, home-grown outlaws. Dick Turpin didn't have the headline notoriety of, say, Jesse James, but his country-long ride still has a substantial interest. Unfortunately this movie, with David Weston and George Cole can be described as an anagram of the surname: a turnip. Lumpen and with B-picture clichés, there is little point or purpose, though the horse, Black Bess, does well enough. ▦

David Weston *Dick Turpin* • George Cole *Mr Evans* • Bernard Lee *Jeremiah* • Maurice Denham *Mr Fielding* ■ *Dir* James Neilson • *Scr* Robert Westerby

The Legends of Rita ★★★

Drama 2000 · Ger · Colour · 103mins

Bibiana Beglau and Nadja Uhl shared the best actress prize at Berlin for their work in this film which marks Volker Schlöndorff's return to the period that saw him in the vanguard of New German Cinema. Co-scripted by former DEFA stalwart, Wolfgang Kohlhaase, this memoir of life in the old East Germany eschews prejudiced western notions of repression and shortages. Yet it's undoubtedly the banality of her existence with Stasi officer Martin Wuttke that helps drive Beglau's one-time terrorist into the arms of the hard-drinking Uhl. A German language film.

Bibiana Beglau *Rita Vogt* • Martin Wuttke *Erwin Hull* • Nadja Uhl *Tatjana* • Harald Schrott *Andi* • Alexander Beyer *Jochen* ■ *Dir* Volker Schlöndorff • *Scr* Wolfgang Kohlhaase, Volker Schlöndorff

Legends of the Fall ★★★★ 15

Epic drama 1994 · US · Colour · 127mins

For someone who made his name on the small screen, *thirtysomething* creator Edward Zwick certainly has the eye for the big picture when it comes to cinema. In this fabulous throwback to the epic dramas of old, Anthony Hopkins is a stern patriarch whose disgust at the actions of his own government during the Indian Wars leads him to bring up his three sons (Brad Pitt, Aidan Quinn and Henry Thomas) on a remote ranch in the Montana mountains. However, their idyllic life is thrown into turmoil by outside events and by the arrival of the beautiful Julia Ormond. Zwick handles the various subplots with deceptive ease and fashions a poetic hymn to values of loyalty and family ties, which only occasionally slips into melodramatic cliché, while John Toll's

Oscar-winning cinematography is equally at home with the stunning beauty of the mountainous terrain and the killing fields of war-torn France. ▦
DVD

Brad Pitt *Tristan* • Anthony Hopkins *Ludlow* • Aidan Quinn *Alfred* • Julia Ormond *Susannah* • Henry Thomas *Samuel* • Karina Lombard *Isabel Two* • Tantoo Cardinal *Pet* • Gordon Tootoosis *One Stab* • Paul Desmond *Decker* • Christina Pickles *Isabel* ■ *Dir* Edward Zwick • *Scr* Susan Shilliday, Bill Wittliff, from the novella by Jim Harrison

Legion ★ 18

Science-fiction action drama
1998 · US · Colour · 93mins

Ten military prisoners sent to destroy a weapons base come up against a shape-shifting alien who exploits their weaknesses in this lamentable sci-fi appropriation of Agatha Christie's *Ten Little Indians*. *Deep Space Nine* babe Terry Farrell, erstwhile Brat Packer Corey Feldman and pop star Rick Springfield do their best to spark some life into the clichéd mess, but it's an uphill battle. This sub-standard mixture can't even cover its threadbare plot in gore thanks to its TV-movie status. Contains swearing and violence. ▦

Parker Stevenson *Aldrich* • Terry Farrell *Major Agatha Doyle* • Corey Feldman *Siegal* • Rick Springfield *Ryan* • Troy Donahue *Flemming* • Audie England *Dr Jones* ■ *Dir* Jon Hess • *Scr* Evan Spiliotopoulos

Legion of Fire: Killer Ants! ★★

Science-fiction thriller 1998 · US · Colour

Watching this in the wake of such hits as *Antz* and *A Bug's Life*, it's even harder to keep a straight face through what is already a pretty laughable concept. Eric Lutes and Mitch Pileggi are among the people trying to stop the march of some nasty South American killer ants who have ended up in a tiny town in Alaska. The direction is plodding, the performances from the anonymous cast are pretty dull, and, unless you have a phobia about ants, this TV movie is not remotely scary.

Eric Lutes *Dr Jim Conrad* • Julia Campbell *Laura Sills* • Mitch Pileggi *Sheriff Jeff Croy* • Jeremy Foley *Chad Croy* • Dallen Gettling *Bob Hazzard* ■ *Dir* Jim Charleston • *Scr* Linda Palmer, Wink Roberts

Legion of Iron ★ 18

Science-fiction action drama
1990 · US · Colour · 85mins

The story takes place deep under the surface of the earth, where the negative of this clumsy and appallingly cheap movie should be hidden. It promises ample sex and violence – male athletes are kidnapped and forced to fight gladiator-style in a secret underground arena, with sexual rewards for the victors – but fails to deliver. The director misses every opportunity to exploit the material or even place a sense of fun. ▦

Kevin T Walsh *Billy Hamilton* • Erika Nann *Diana* • Camille Carrigan *Allison* • Reggie De Morton *Lyle Wagner* ■ *Dir* Yakov Bentsvi • *Scr* Rueben Gordon, Steven Schoenberg, from a story by Edward Hunt

U = SUITABLE FOR ALL. U⒞ = SUITABLE FOR ALL, ESPECIALLY FOR YOUNG CHILDREN (VIDEO ONLY) PG = PARENTAL GUIDANCE

Legs ★★ PG
Drama 1983 · US · Colour · 95mins

John Heard, who has been superb in movies such as *Big*, *Cutter's Way* and *Heart Beat* but who has never had the success he deserves, here stars in a behind-the-scenes drama about female performers aspiring to become Rockettes, those famed dancers at New York's Radio City Music Hall. This is a cross between *Fame* and *A Chorus Line*, but without the memorable toe-tapping tunes of either. ▯

John Heard *Dan* • Sheree North *Ida* • David Marshall Grant *Lewis* • Maureen Teefy *Melissa* • Deborah Geffner *Terry* ■ Dir/Scr Jerrold Freedman

The Lemon Drop Kid ★★★
Drama 1934 · US · BW · 71m

An early adaptation of the Damon Runyon fable better known for the Bob Hope version made in 1951. This is tougher and more serious than the later version, closer in tone to Runyan's original, with Lee Tracy as the racetrack tipster who gets entangled with both the law and the underworld. Talented Tracy, a half-forgotten actor today, was a past-master at this sort of fast-talking, energetic role, and director Marshall Neilan, former co-star of Mary Pickford and a top silent era director, though in decline at the time, keeps things moving and vividly captures Runyon's world of offbeat Broadway denizens.

Lee Tracy *Wally Brooks* • Helen Mack *Alice Deering* • William Frawley *The professor* • Minna Gombell *Maizie* • Baby LeRoy *The baby* • Robert McWade *Mr Griggsby* • Henry B Walthall *Jonas Deering* • Clarence H Wilson [Clarence Wilson] *Martin Potter* ■ Dir Marshall Neilan • Scr Howard J Green, JP McEvoy, from the short story by Damon Runyon

The Lemon Drop Kid ★★
Musical comedy 1951 · US · BW · 91mins

Bob Hope was no stranger to Damon Runyon's world of idiosyncratic, kind-hearted Broadway characters, having starred in *Sorrowful Jones*, one of many versions of *Little Miss Marker*. Here, as the Lemon Drop Kid, he's a horse-racing tipster in debt to a gang boss, who has his pals dress up as Father Christmas to raise the money he needs on the pretext of collecting for elderly "dolls". Hope himself even appears in drag as an old dear. It may not be real Runyon but it has enough bright quips and inventive moments to be good Hope.

Bob Hope *Lemon Drop Kid* • Marilyn Maxwell *Brainey Baxter* • Lloyd Nolan *Charlie* • Jane Darwell *Nellie Thursday* • Andrea King *Stella* • Fred Clark *Moose Moran* • Jay C Flippen *Straight Flush* • William Frawley *Gloomy Willie* ■ Dir Sidney Lanfield • Scr Edmund Hartmann, Frank Tashlin, Robert O'Brien, from a story by Edmund Beloin, from the short story by Damon Runyon

Lemon Popsicle ★★★
Drama 1978 · Is · Colour · 95mins

One of the biggest grossing films ever made in Israel, Boaz Davidson's nostalgic comedy was more risqué than many of the rites-of-passage teen pictures being made in Hollywood at the same time. With every song on the radio echoing their adolescent pangs,

Yiftach Katzur, Jonathan Segal and Zachi Noy resort to an ageing nymphomaniac and a diseased prostitute to satiate their rampaging urges. At least until Anat Atzmon appears on the scene. Brisk, bawdy and handled with a genuine fondness for the period and the characters, it breaks every rule in the PC handbook, but spawned four sequels. In Hebrew with English subtitles.

Yiftach Katzur *Bentzi* • Anat Atzmon *Nili* • Jonathan Segal *Momo* • Zachi Noy *Yuda'leh* ■ Dir Boaz Davidson • Scr Boaz Davidson, Eli Tavor

The Lemon Sisters ★ 15
Comedy 1989 · US · Colour · 88mins

Diane Keaton dropped her name as producer from the credits of this comedy drama, which shows she recognised it as the lemon it is. The story of three Atlantic City girlfriends – Keaton, Carol Kane and Kathryn Grody – trying to put their voices together as a singing group is a series of sorry sequences that are as banal as they are boring, as the girls try to buy a nightclub to house their tuneless talents. Sourly reviewed when it first appeared, it was then shelved for a year before a brief release. ▯

Diane Keaton *Eloise Hamer* • Carol Kane *Franki D'Angelo* • Kathryn Grody *Nola Frank* • Elliott Gould *Fred Frank* • Rubén Blades *CW* • Aidan Quinn *Frankie McGuinness* • Estelle Parsons *Mrs Kupchak* • Richard Libertini *Nicholas Panas* • Sully Boyar *Baxter O'Neil* ■ Dir Joyce Chopra • Scr Jeremy Pikser

Lena: My 100 Children ★★★ U
Drama based on a true story 1987 · US · Colour · 94mins

A much-lauded TV movie, this tale is based on the true and deeply moving story of Lena Kuchler-Silberman, the extraordinary Polish Jew who risked her life to ensure a hundred Jewish children escaped from Poland to the Middle East just after the Second World War. The central role is wonderfully played by Linda Lavin who received many plaudits on the film's first transmission in 1987, the year Kuchler-Silberman died. A highly superior double hanky job. ▯

Linda Lavin *Lena Kuchler-Silberman* • Leonore Harris *Bella* • Cynthia Wilde *Rhea* • George Touliatos *Polonski* • John Evans *Sani* • Sam Malkin *Stefan* ■ Dir Ed Sherin [Edwin Sherin] • Scr Jonathan B Rintels Jr, Yabo Yablonsky, Maurice Hurley, from the non-fiction book *My Hundred Children* by Lena Kuchler-Silberman

Lena's Holiday ★★★
Comedy drama 1990 · US · Colour · 100mins

Hollywood has an unwritten law about luggage. If a suitcase gets accidentally switched, the replacement absolutely has to contain something stolen and the original's owner *must* endure all manner of dangers (comic or otherwise) before they, and their inevitable new-found love, retrieve their property and wave off the villains as they depart in a police car. But don't reach for the channel changer just yet, as this tired old tale is lifted here by some perky performances, with Felicity Waterman – a real find as an East Berliner with a mistaken bagful of

diamonds – and Chris Lemmon (son of Jack) clicking nicely as her cabby accomplice.

Felicity Waterman *Lena* • Chris Lemmon *Mike Camden* • Nick Mancuso *Corey Flynn* • Michael Sarrazin *Jan Mackenzie* • Noriyuki "Pat" Morita [Pat Morita] *Fred* ■ Dir Michael Keusch • Scr Michael Keusch, Deborah Tilton

Lenin in October ★★★
Historical drama 1937 · USSR · BW · 114mins

Completed in just three months, to mark the 20th anniversary of the October Revolution, this propagandist biopic was designed less to celebrate historical fact than to reinforce the "cult of personality" that had been erected around the Bolshevik leader, VI Lenin. Yet, even this hagiographic purpose was of secondary consequence to extolling the part played by Stalin, not only in the overthrow of Tsarism, but also in helping Lenin secure power. BV Shchukin's amazing physical impersonation was based on hours of studying agit-prop newsreels, and he reprised the role in Mikhail Romm's sequel, *Lenin in 1918*. In Russian with English subtitles.

BV Shchukin *VI Lenin* • NP Okhlopkov [Nikolai P Okhlopkov] *Vasily* • Vasili Vanin *Factory manager* ■ Dir Mikhail Romm • Scr Aleksei Kapler

Leningrad Cowboys Go America ★★★★ 15
Satirical comedy 1989 · Fin · Colour · 75mins

Proudly sporting the influence of Jim Jarmusch on his sleeve, Finnish director Aki Kaurismäki broke out of the arthouse ghetto and achieved cult status with this scattershot road movie. With their dead bassist travelling in his coffin and their Cadillac brimful of beer cans, the Leningrad Cowboys (whose hairstyles are more pointed than their winklepickers) fulfil their reputation as the world's worst rock band, as they lurch between disastrous Stateside gigs before finally landing in Mexico. Yet, this isn't a *Spinal Tap*-type of picture, as it isn't the Cowboys that are under the microscope, but the deliriously ordinary folk they meet en route. In English and Finnish with subtitles. ▯

Matti Pellonpää *Vladimir* • Kari Väänänen *Igor* • Nicky Tesco *Lost cousin* • Jim Jarmusch *Car salesman* ■ Dir/Scr Aki Kaurismäki

Leningrad Cowboys Meet Moses ★★★
Comedy 1993 · Fin/Fr/Ger · Colour · 94mins

What a busy year 1993 was for the fictional "worst rock'n'roll band in the world". In addition to this sequel to *Leningrad Cowboys Go America*, they also fronted *These Boots*, Aki Kaurismäki's five-minute history of Finland from 1950 to 1969. Unfortunately, neither film was as amusing as the original, although there are occasional laughs in this tequila-soaked trek from Mexico (where the Cowboys had enjoyed unexpected chart success), in the company of manager, Matti Pellonpää, who changes his name from Vladimir to Moses for this offbeat odyssey to the promised land of Russia. All concerned would do

much better with *Total Balalaika Show*. In Finnish with English subtitles.

Kirsi Tykkylainen *Singer* • Matti Pellonpää *Vladimir* • "Moses" • Kari Väänänen *Igor* ■ Dir/Scr Aki Kaurismäki

Lenny ★★ 18
Biographical drama 1974 · US · BW · 106mins

Dustin Hoffman plays Lenny Bruce, the provocative sixties stand-up comedian who ran the gauntlet of what was permissible, existed on drugs, married a stripper, went catatonic in public urinals, went to jail for obscenity and died young. Lenny, legendarily, had his audience in stitches and what's funny about this movie is that it isn't funny at all. You admire the technique of Hoffman's performance but he fails to make us laugh and, crucially, he fails to shock us. The laughter and the gasps come from the audience in the nightclub – that is to say, from movie extras, so the laughter is phoney. Only Valerie Perrine, as Lenny's wife, seems for real. *Lenny* is a rather creepy experience, showily directed by Bob Fosse in black-and-white and using a vaguely *Kane*-like interview-flashback structure which seems far too sophisticated for its subject. Contains swearing and nudity. ▯

Dustin Hoffman *Lenny Bruce* • Valerie Perrine *Honey Bruce* • Jan Miner *Sally Marr* • Stanley Beck *Artie Silver* • Gary Morton *Sherman Hart* ■ Dir Bob Fosse • Scr Julian Barry, from his play

Lensman ★★ PG
Animated science-fiction adventure 1984 · Jap · Colour · 107mins

Edward E "Doc" Smith's pulp sci-fi novels were among the inspirations behind *Star Wars*. This tale, set in the 25th century, features a young "lensman" who is endowed with mysterious powers to aid him in the fight against the forces of evil. Unfortunately, it's an uninspired amalgam of sci-fi clichés, redeemed only by the animation, which combines traditional hand-drawn artwork with state-of-the-art computer graphics. A real letdown after the brilliant cyber-punk energy of *Akira* did so much to put Japanese *anime* and *manga* on the international map. The American dubbed version was released in 1991. Japanese dialogue dubbed into English. ▯

Dir Yoshiaki Kawajiri, Kazuyuki Hirokawa • Scr Soji Yoshikawa, from a novel by Edward E "Doc" Smith

Leo the Last ★★
Drama 1970 · UK · Colour · 103mins

Although British director John Boorman won the best director award at Cannes for this calculatingly arty docu-fantasy. It's all too contrived for comfort as convalescent aristocrat Leo (Marcello Mastroianni) sets up home in London's Notting Hill and gets to know the poverty-stricken residents who live there and who rent his properties. As an attempt at parable, it's obviously "let's-love-everyone" propaganda and comes out looking very banal.

Marcello Mastroianni *Leo* • Billie Whitelaw *Margaret* • Calvin Lockhart *Roscoe* • Glenna Forster-Jones *Salambo* • Graham Crowden *Max* • Gwen Ffrangcon-Davies *Hilda* • David

De Keyser *David* ■ *Dir* John Boorman • *Scr* John Boorman, William Stair, from the play *The Prince* by George Tabori

Léolo ★★★★ 🔞

Comedy drama
1992 · Can/Fr · Colour · 102mins

It reveals much about this unconventional but curiously convincing take on childhood that its young hero considers himself to have been conceived during his mother's encounter with a sperm-filled Sicilian tomato. Despite this, Maxime Collin is clearly the sanest member of his family, bearing in mind the sinister antics of his father and siblings, the lasciviousness of his grandfather and the general household obsession with bowel movements. Employing expressionist tactics to give Collin's escapist and sexual fantasies a shoddy magic, Québecois director Jean-Claude Lauzon seemed a talent to be reckoned with. Tragically, he was killed in a plane crash in 1997. In French with English subtitles. 🖵
Gilbert Sicotte *Narrator* • Maxime Collin *Leo, aka Léolo* • Ginette Reno *Mother* • Julien Guiomar *Grandfather* • Pierre Bourgault *The Word Tamer* • Giudetta Del Vecchio *Bianca* • Denys Arcand *Career counsellor* ■ *Dir/Scr* Jean-Claude Lauzon

Leon ★★★★★ 🔞

Thriller   1994 · Fr · Colour · 110mins

French director Luc Besson followed his international hit *Nikita* with his first American-set movie, *Leon*, a haunting and compulsive thriller that explores the relationship between the emotionally stunted hit man of the title and his 12-year-old neighbour Mathilda. Jean Reno is reluctantly forced to befriend and protect the girl, played by Natalie Portman, after her family is wiped out in a horrific drugs operation led by Gary Oldman. Leon ends up teaching Mathilda the tricks of his trade so that she can take revenge on the deranged cop. The two masterly central performances from Reno and Portman intelligently convey how Leon's carefully constructed, reclusive existence falls apart as he lets feelings enter his life for the very first time. But it's the ultra-stylish action scenes that propel Leon into the suspense stratosphere as Besson redefines the action genre with a series of totally breathtaking set pieces. 🖵
Jean Reno *Leon* • Gary Oldman *Stansfield* • Natalie Portman *Mathilda* • Danny Aiello *Tony* • Michael Badalucco *Mathilda's father* • Peter Appel *Malky* • Ellen Greene *Mathilda's mother* ■ *Dir/Scr* Luc Besson

Léon Morin, Priest ★★★★

Second World War drama
1961 · Fr · BW · 117mins

Few French film-makers have been as forthcoming about the Occupation as Jean-Pierre Melville. If his Resistance tribute, *The Army in the Shadows*, is akin to *film noir*, this insight into the overpowering nature of love and faith irresistibly recalls the restrained character studies of Robert Bresson. Reining in his natural exuberance, Jean-Paul Belmondo is holy yet human as the small-town priest whose gentle ministrations elicit both spiritual and

sexual responses from the previously agnostic Emmanuelle Riva. Sparse yet utterly convincing in its period detail, this is a potent study of the mysteries of divine intervention. A French language film.
Jean-Paul Belmondo *Léon Morin* • Emmanuelle Riva *Barny* • Irène Tunc *Christine* • Nicole Mirel *Sabine* • Marco Behar *Edelman* ■ *Dir* Jean-Pierre Melville • *Scr* Jean-Pierre Melville, from a novel by Beatrice Beck

Leon the Pig Farmer

★★★ 🔞

Comedy   1992 · UK · Colour · 99mins

As a prime piece of crackling, this low-budget British comedy from Vadim Jean and Gary Sinyor isn't as hilarious as it thinks it is (arguably not as funny as that other porker-story, *Babe*). But, nevertheless, the story of a Jewish estate agent (Mark Frankel) discovering – shock! horror! – that his real father is a Yorkshire pig-breeder does have flashes of comic illumination to light up religious bigotry. The fantasy of a kosher pig is laboured, but there's still plenty of crisped flesh worth flossing for, especially Brian Glover as the breeder. Contains swearing. 🖵
Mark Frankel *Leon Geller* • Janet Suzman *Judith Geller* • Brian Glover *Brian Chadwick* • Connie Booth *Yvonne Chadwick* • David De Keyser *Sidney Geller* • Maryam D'Abo *Madeleine* • Gina Bellman *Lisa* • Vincenzo Ricotta *Elliot Cohen* • Jean Anderson *Mrs Samuels* • John Woodvine *Vitelli* • Annette Crosbie *Doctor Johnson* • Burt Kwouk *Art Collector* • Sean Pertwee *Keith Chadwick* ■ *Dir* Vadim Jean, Gary Sinyor • *Scr* Gary Sinyor, Michael Normand

Leonard, Part 6 ★ 🅿🅶

Comedy   1987 · US · Colour · 81mins

It's never a good sign when the star of a movie – in this case comedian Bill Cosby – warned audiences to give it a wide berth. Cosby, who also produced, is the ex-CIA man who comes out of retirement to find out why his former colleagues, counter-agents, are being assassinated by killer animals. Paul Weiland directed this lame, would-be Bond send-up, but to no great effect. Animal lovers may enjoy the irony of seeing the humans get their comeuppance. 🖵
Bill Cosby *Leonard* • Tom Courtenay *Frayn* • Joe Don Baker *Snyderburn* • Gloria Foster *Medusa* • Moses Gunn *Giorgio* • Pat Colbert *Allison* • Victoria Rowell *Joan* • David Maier *Man Ray* • Grace Zabriskie *Jefferson* • Jane Fonda ■ *Dir* Paul Weiland • *Scr* Jonathan Reynolds, from a story by Bill Cosby

The Leopard ★★★★★ 🅿🅶

Period drama   1962 · It · Colour · 185mins

Burt Lancaster is in tremendous form as the great scion of a noble Italian family, about to be brought down by a republican movement, in Luchino Visconti's contemplation of Italian history and his own role (as aristocratic Marxist) in it. The casting is splendid (Alain Delon, Claudia Cardinale) and some moments – such as the elaborate ballroom scene – sing with visual splendour. The Leopard deservedly won the Palme d'Or at Cannes. In Italian with English subtitles.

Burt Lancaster *Don Fabrizio, Prince of Salina* • Alain Delon *Tancredi, the Prince's Nephew* • Claudia Cardinale *Angelica Sedara* • Paolo Stoppa *Don Calogero Sedara* • Rina Morelli *Maria Stella, Wife Of The Prince* • Romolo Valli *Father Pirrone* • Serge Reggiani *Don Ciccio Tumeo* • Leslie French *Cavalier Chevally* • Ivo Garrani *Col Pallavicino* • Mario Girotti [Terence Hill] *Count Cavriaghi* ■ *Dir* Luchino Visconti • *Scr* Luchino Visconti, Suso Cecchi D'Amico, Pasquale Festa Campanile, Enrico Medioli, Massimo Franciosa, from the novel *Il Gattopardo* by Giuseppe Tomasi Di Lampedusa • *Cinematographer* Giuseppe Rotunno

The Leopard Man ★★★★

Thriller   1943 · US · BW · 66mins

Cornell Woolrich's novel *Black Alibi* becomes an unconventionally haunting masterpiece of "quiet horror" under B-movie auteur producer Val Lewton's watchful eye. Director Jacques Tourneur never bettered the memorable moment where a little girl's blood trickles under a locked door when she is attacked by an unseen force. That evil force is supposedly an escaped leopard, but all is not what it seems in a splendidly old-school chiller also boasting the best trapped-in-a-cemetery sequence ever.
Dennis O'Keefe *Jerry Manning* • Jean Brooks *Kiki Walker* • Margo *Clo-Clo* • Isabel Jewell *Maria* • James Bell *Dr Galbraith* • Margaret Landry *Teresa Delgado* • Abner Biberman *Charlie How-Come* ■ *Dir* Jacques Tourneur • *Scr* Ardel Wray, Edward Dein, from the novel *Black Alibi* by Cornell Woolrich

Lepke ★★★ 🔞

Biographical crime drama
1975 · US · Colour · 104mins

This crime drama was designed to cash in on the gangster boom following the success of *The Godfather* and harked back to the studio's golden age of James Cagney and Humphrey Bogart. Indeed, there's much of *The Public Enemy* in this biopic of Louis "Lepke" Buchalter, the Jewish hoodlum whose reign as the head of Murder Inc ended in the electric chair in 1944. Although he occasionally chews the scenery, Tony Curtis brings a disturbingly convincing megalomaniacal brutality to the title role, and he's well supported by Anjanette Cromer as his put-upon wife and Milton Berle, in a rare non-comic role, as his father-in-law.
Tony Curtis *Louis "Lepke" Buchalter* • Anjanette Comer *Bernice Meyer* • Michael Callan *Robert Kane* • Warren Berlinger *Gurrah Shapiro* • Gianni Russo *Albert Anastasia* • Vic Tayback *Lucky Luciano* • Mary Wilcox *Marion* • Milton Berle *Mr Meyer* ■ *Dir* Menahem Golan • *Scr* Wesley Lau, Tamar Hoffs, from a story by Wesley Lau

Leprechaun ★ 🅸🅵

Horror   1992 · US · Colour · 87mins

This tacky debasement of a charming Irish legend is too juvenile for adult tastes and too gruesome for children. Three teenagers free nasty leprechaun (Warwick Davis) who's been trapped in a crate in a farmhouse for ten years and he then goes on the gory search for his stolen pot of gold. Made up of nothing but low points – the nadir being mentally disabled Mark Holton being lacerated in the face by a silver shoe buckle – the unfunny repartee,

forced whimsicality and endless running around with characters shrieking "Gimme back my gold!" add shoddy insult to blarney injury. 🖵
Warwick Davis *The Leprechaun* • Jennifer Aniston *Tory* • Ken Olandt *Nathan* • Mark Holton *Ozzie* • Robert Gorman [Robert Hy Gorman] *Alex* • John Sanderford *JD* ■ *Dir/Scr* Mark Jones

Leprechaun 2 ★ 🔞

Horror   1994 · US · Colour · 81mins

More viciously vile shamrock shock, as the imp of Irish folklore (played again by Warwick Davis) kidnaps Los Angeles teenager Shevonne Durkin to be his bride. Her would-be boyfriend, Charlie Heath, a Hollywood Death Tour host, must search through a maze of caves to find her, in this equally uneasy mixture of kiddie fantasy and grisly gore featuring fans and coffee machines as murder weapons. 🖵
Warwick Davis *The Leprechaun* • Charlie Heath *Cody* • Shevonne Durkin *Bridget* • Sandy Baron *Morty* • Adam Biesk *Ian* • James Lancaster *William O'Day* • Jonathan R Perkins *Partner* • Tony Cox *African-American Leprechaun* • Mark Keily *Talent Agent* ■ *Dir* Rodman Flender • *Scr* Turi Meyer, Al Septien, from characters created by Mark Jones

Les Patterson Saves the World ★

Comedy   1987 · Ausl · Colour · 95mins

A prime example of TV humour getting lost in translation to the big screen. Barry Humphries makes us laugh as Dame Edna Everage and as Australia's cultural attaché Sir Les Patterson, but this cinema outing – a catalogue of misfired jokes and rock bottom tastelessness – goes way beyond Humphries's desire to shock us. The beer-swilling Patterson farts, oozes pus from scores of facial sores, stains his trousers and racks up the sort of infantile puns that even the *Carry On* team would have thrown out – an Arab called "Mustafa Toul"! The plot about international espionage implies a sort of Bond send-up but to call it racist is to dignify it. Easily a candidate for the worst movie ever made.
Barry Humphries *Sir Les Patterson/Dame Edna Everage* • Pamela Stephenson *Veronique Crudite* • Thaao Penghlis *Colonel Richard Godowni* • Andrew Clarke *Neville Thonge* • Henri Szeps *Dr Charles Herpes/Desiree* • Hugh Keays-Byrne *Inspector Farouk* • Garth Meade *Mustafa Toul* ■ *Dir* George Miller (1) • *Scr* Barry Humphries, Diane Millstead

Less than Zero ★★ 🔞

Drama   1987 · US · Colour · 94mins

The "Brat Pack" gets hedonistic in an overly glossy filming of Bret Easton Ellis's novel about rich kids living the wild life in Los Angeles. Robert Downey Jr is very convincing as a wealthy, charming cocaine addict on a slippery slope to rock bottom, and you'll struggle to find a sadder example of life imitating art. Andrew McCarthy and Jami Gertz are too lightweight for this kind of material, though, and there's a terminal lack of emotional involvement in what amounts to a pretty pop video highlighting the perils of Christmas excesses. 🖵
Andrew McCarthy *Clay* • Jami Gertz *Blair* • Robert Downey Jr *Julian* • James Spader *Rip* •

Tony Bill *Bradford Easton* • Nicholas Pryor *Benjamin Wells* • Donna Mitchell *Elaine Easton* • Michael Bowen *Hop* ■ *Dir* Marek Kanievska • *Scr* Harley Peyton, from the novel by Bret Easton Ellis

A Lesson Before Dying
★★★

Period drama 1999 · US · Colour · 101mins

Don Cheadle is the teacher attempting to restore dignity to a condemned man in this Emmy-winning TV movie set in rural 1940s Louisiana. Cheadle reluctantly visits a young African-American (Mekhi Phifer) due to be executed for a murder he did not commit. Unlike most movies in this genre, this is not about the search for an eleventh hour reprieve but rather an attempt to reconcile Phifer to his fate – however undeserved. The solid script, thoughtful direction and a first-rate cast, including veteran Cicely Tyson, make this memorable.

Don Cheadle *Grant Wiggins* • Cicely Tyson *Tante Lou* • Mekhi Phifer *Jefferson* • Irma P Hall *Miss Emma* • Brent Jennings *Reverend Ambrose* ■ *Dir* Joseph Sargent • *Scr* Ann Peacock, from the novel by Ernest J Gaines

Lesson in Love
★★★ U

Comedy 1954 · Swe · BW · 95mins

Considering it was scripted within months of Ingmar Bergman divorcing his third wife, this is a surprisingly sprightly comedy of marital manners. However, it's the performances of Gunnar Björnstrand and Eva Dahlbeck, rather than the writing, that supplies the sparkle in this story of the emotionally immature gynaecologist, who abandons a mistress to pursue his ex-wife to Copenhagen to witness her wedding to the sculptor she'd jilted at the altar once before. With carefully calculated flashbacks exploring both the tension between Björnstrand and his teenage daughter, Harriet Andersson, and the stability of his parents' marriage, this is a minor charmer. In Swedish with English subtitles..

Gunnar Björnstrand *David Erneman* • Eva Dahlbeck *Marianne Erneman* • Yvonne Lombard *Suzanne* • Harriet Andersson *Nix* ■ *Dir/Scr* Ingmar Bergman

Let 'em Have It
★

Crime drama 1935 · US · BW · 98mins

This cheap and plodding independent low-budget production was made simultaneously with James Cagney's much superior *"G" Men* in a new cycle that sought to glorify America's crime busters. Its demonstrations of the latest methods of scientific detection no longer enthral and Richard Arlen's federal agent is nowhere near as vital as Bruce Cabot's public enemy. The film's one highlight is the outcome of Cabot's use of plastic surgery to change his appearance.

Richard Arlen *Mal Stevens* • Virginia Bruce *Eleanor Spencer* • Alice Brady *Aunt Ethel* • Bruce Cabot *Joe Keefer* • Harvey Stephens *Van Rensseler* • Eric Linden *Buddy Spencer* ■ *Dir* Sam Wood • *Scr* from a story by Joseph Moncure March, Elmer Harris

Let George Do It
★★★ U

Comedy 1940 · UK · BW · 78mins

Opinion is still divided as to whether this or *I See Ice* is the best George Formby comedy. Certainly, in terms of backroom expertise this wins hands down, with Basil Dearden producing and co-scripting and Ronald Neame behind the camera. On screen, Formby is supported by Phyllis Calvert, as the homely girl who falls for his toothy charm, and Coral Browne, as a wicked seductress, as well as by every British comic's favourite stooge Garry Marsh and that villain supreme Torin Thatcher. The story sees Formby do his first bit for the war effort, as he fetches up in Bergen instead of Blackpool and finds himself on the trail of quislings and the Gestapo. The highlight is undoubtedly *Mr Wu*, but there's never a dull moment. ▭

George Formby *George* • Phyllis Calvert *Mary* • Garry Marsh *Mendez* • Romney Brent *Slim* • Bernard Lee *Nelson* • Coral Browne *Ivy* • Diana Beaumont *Greta* ■ *Dir* Marcel Varnel • *Scr* John Dighton, Austin Melford, Angus Macphail, Basil Dearden

Let Him Have It
★★★★ 15

Biographical crime drama 1991 · UK · Colour · 110mins

Director Peter Medak followed his crime biopic *The Krays* with another *cause célèbre* torn from past headlines. The Derek Bentley case remains as much a classic crusading appeal against capital punishment today as it was back in 1952 when the mentally disabled teenage epileptic stood accused of inciting the shooting of a cop after a bungled factory burglary. With drab-chic production, Christopher Eccleston's marvellous central performance and a pop nostalgia soundtrack, the odious miscarriage of justice comes vividly to life to scandalise anew those unfamiliar with the true facts. Infotainment *par excellence*. ▭ **DVD**

Chris Eccleston [Christopher Eccleston] *Derek Bentley* • Paul Reynolds *Chris Craig* • Tom Courtenay *William Bentley* • Tom Bell *Fairfax* • Eileen Atkins *Lilian Bentley* • Clare Holman *Iris Bentley* • Mark McGann *Niven Craig* • Michael Gough *Lord Goddard* • Serena Scott Thomas *Stella* • Ronald Fraser *Niven's Judge* • Michael Elphick *Jack, the warder* ■ *Dir* Peter Medak • *Scr* Neal Purvis, Robert Wade

Let It Be
★★★★ U

Musical biography 1970 · UK · Colour · 80mins

Originally arranged as rehearsals for a one-off live show, the "Get Back" sessions proved to be the most directionless and destructive of the Beatles' career. With all four already pursuing personal projects, the tensions that would cause the final split were clearly in evidence from the start. Yet, as Michael Lindsay-Hogg's *cinéma-vérité* record proves, the band was still capable of producing classical pop music, with the impromptu back-to-basics performance on the roof of the Apple building being the undoubted highlight. Astonishingly honest in its revelations, this under-rated film provides a saddening, but pointedly intentional insight into the end of a dream.

Dir Michael Lindsay-Hogg • *Executive Producer* John Lennon, Paul McCartney, George Harrison, Ringo Starr

Let It Be Me
★ 12

Romantic drama 1998 · US · Colour · 91mins

Written and directed by Eleanor Bergstein, who also wrote *Dirty Dancing*, this is another movie about dance which sadly fails to cut the rug. Campbell Scott wants to learn how to dance so he can impress his fiancée Jennifer Beals (of *Flashdance* fame). However, complications set in when both go to his dancing instructor. Leslie Caron. Elliott Gould and Patrick Stewart round out an interesting supporting cast, but their presence isn't enough to redeem this straight-to-video romance. ▭

Jennifer Beals *Emily* • Campbell Scott *Gabriel* • Jamie Goodwin *Bud* • Yancy Butler *Corinne* • Leslie Caron *Marguerite* • Patrick Stewart *John* • Elliott Gould *Sam* ■ *Dir/Scr* Eleanor Bergstein

Let It Ride
★★ 15

Comedy 1989 · US · Colour · 86mins

The National Lottery it isn't; this fickle finger of fate isn't pointing at quite so much money. But gamblers may recognise the twitches of anguish exhibited by Richard Dreyfuss as the symptoms of a compulsive chancer whose life depends on a long shot at a Florida racetrack. Others may recognise the twitches as symptoms of overacting. Those with supporting roles, such as the long-suffering Teri Garr, are more in control, but it's a very dislocated sort of movie. Screenwriter Nancy Dowd saw it, decided that all bets were off and insisted on a pseudonym: Ernest Morton. Oh, well, some you win, some you lose. ▭

Richard Dreyfuss *Joe Trotter* • Teri Garr *Pam* • David Johansen *Looney* • Jennifer Tilly *Vicki* • Allen Garfield *Greenberg* • Ed Walsh [Edward Walsh] *Marty* • Robbie Coltrane *Bookie* ■ *Dir* Joe Pytka • *Scr* Nancy Dowd, from the novel *Good Vibes* by Jay Cronley

Let No Man Write My Epitaph
★★★

Drama 1960 · US · BW · 105mins

Adapted from the novel by Willard Motley, this sturdy social drama is the sequel to the same author's *Knock on Any Door*, filmed by Nicholas Ray in 1949. Set in Chicago's deprived South Side, it stars teenage idol James Darren struggling to better himself, but getting involved with gangsters. British-born director Philip Leacock, whose Hollywood movies tackled strong themes, got powerful performances from Burl Ives as a judge, and Shelley Winters as Darren's drug-addicted mother. Jean Seberg makes a brief appearance, and Ella Fitzgerald not only gets to sing but also does a spot of acting.

Burl Ives *Judge Bruce Mallory* • Shelley Winters *Nellie Romano* • James Darren *Nick Romano* • Jean Seberg *Barbara Holloway* • Ricardo Montalban *Louie Ramponi* • Ella Fitzgerald *Flora* • Rodolfo Acosta *Max* ■ *Dir* Philip Leacock • *Scr* Robert Presnell Jr, from the novel by Willard Motley

Let the Good Times Roll
★★★★

Music documentary 1973 · US · Colour · 100mins

An exhilarating blend of archive clips, fond memories and concert footage, this will prove irresistible to anyone who's ever tied on a blue suede shoe. Directors Robert Abel and Sid Levin frequently employ split screens to contrast "then" and "now", but the acts on display have lost none of the old hunger. Easy listeners will delight in tapping along to the Five Satins and The Coasters. But hardcore rockers will be bouncing off the walls as Fats Domino, Chubby Checker, Bill Haley and Little Richard let rip. However, the highlight is Chuck Berry and Bo Diddley's rendition of *Johnny B Goode*.

Dir Sidney Levin, Robert Abel

Lethal Charm
★★ PG

Drama 1991 · US · Colour · 92mins

I Dream of Jeannie's Barbara Eden and *Melrose Place* star Heather Locklear are the two journalists who are thrown together in Washington DC in this drama. Unfortunately, the plot is just as unlikely as the casting, with the two actresses running around trying to be Woodward and Bernstein in skirts in pursuit of a great story. Unfortunately, this film gives the impression that what they are actually searching for is a hairstylist and manicurist to do a touch-up. ▭

Barbara Eden *Tess O'Brien* • Heather Locklear *Melody Shepherd* • Julie Fulton *Christine Benevent* • Stuart Wilson *Peter Chambers* • David James Elliott *Andrew O'Brien* • Jed Allen *Brad Duggan* • Jordan Charney *Bernard Robins* • Allan Miller *Allen Fairchild* ■ *Dir* Richard Michaels • *Scr* Janice Hickey, Michael Pardridge

Lethal Innocence
★★

Drama 1991 · US · Colour · 90mins

The experience of Cambodian refugees in America should have made a fascinating and emotive subject for a film, but documentary director Helen Whitney allows her feelings to get the better of her in this TV movie. Adding lashings of liberal sentimentality, Whitney turns a provocative plot into a no-holds-barred melodrama that transforms white suburbanites into humanitarian superheroes. Brenda Fricker and Blair Brown are suitably angst-ridden, but it's the young Cambodians Vanthy Rath and Vathana Biv (real-life escapees from the killing fields) who make the truest impression.

Brenda Fricker *Vinnie Moore* • Blair Brown *Sally Hatch* • Kevin Coleman *Mark Hatch* • Neil Maffin *Dave Stokely* • Gina Scianni *Laurie Hatch* ■ *Dir* Helen Whitney • *Scr* Bruce Harmon

Lethal Intent
★★

Thriller 1995 · US · Colour

Since his sensational debut in the lead of Elia Kazan's *A Face in the Crowd*, Andy Griffith has rarely been presented with suitable film opportunities, scoring more success on TV with his long-running comedy series and dramas like *Matlock*. However, he gets the chance to indulge his fondness for larger than life characterisations in this made-for-TV thriller. John Ritter finds himself on a hunting trip with a long-lost father (Griffith) who, despite initial appearances to the contrary, is hellbent on ruining his life. Griffith and Ritter joust well enough, but it's hard to take sides with either of these grizzly people and, consequently, the tension never mounts.

Andy Griffith *Jack MacGruder* • John Ritter *Clarke MacGruder* • Mary-Margaret Humes *Betsy MacGruder* • Casey Moses Wurzbach *Matthew MacGruder* • Mitchell Ryan *Oliver* ■ Dir Bradford May • Scr JB White

Lethal Weapon ★★★★ 18

Action thriller 1987 · US · Colour · 112mins

An action romp *par excellence*, with each blitzkrieg set piece becoming ever more ludicrous – implausibility is, after all, a large part of the fun here. The basic buddy-buddy situation is very familiar, but Mel Gibson, as the reckless detective whose disregard for danger reaches new heights when investigating a drugs ring, and Danny Glover, as his by-the-book, ever-fretful partner, bring a great deal of spirit and fun to the mayhem. Contains violence, swearing and nudity. ▦ *DVD*

Mel Gibson *Martin Riggs* • Danny Glover *Roger Murtaugh* • Gary Busey *Joshua* • Mitchell Ryan *General McAllister* • Tom Atkins *Michael Hunsaker* • Darlene Love *Trish Murtaugh* • Traci Wolfe *Rianne Murtaugh* • Jackie Swanson *Amanda Hunsaker* • Damon Hines *Nick Murtaugh* • Ebonie Smith *Carrie Murtaugh* • Steve Kahan *Captain Ed Murphy* ■ Dir Richard Donner • Scr Shane Black

Lethal Weapon 2 ★★ 18

Action thriller 1989 · US · Colour · 112mins

The weakest of the Mel Gibson/Danny Glover cop sagas. Let down by a tiresomely inconsistent script about South African drug runners and their crooked accountant Joe Pesci, director Richard Donner this time accents humour rather than explosive action. The mistaken result is an oddly toned cartoon-like adventure where the comedy elements make the nasty violence seem even more gratuitous. Gibson and Glover's evident rapport continues to delight, as does Pesci's fun turn, but this is bottom of the barrel formula stuff, despite its superslick sheen. Contains violence, swearing and nudity. ▦ *DVD*

Mel Gibson *Martin Riggs* • Danny Glover *Roger Murtaugh* • Joe Pesci *Leo Getz* • Joss Ackland *Arjen Rudd* • Derrick O'Connor *Pieter Vorstedt* • Patsy Kensit *Rika van den Haas* • Darlene Love *Trish Murtaugh* • Traci Wolfe *Rianne Murtaugh* • Steve Kahan *Captain Murphy* • Mark Rolston *Hans* ■ Dir Richard Donner • Scr Jeffrey Boam, from a story by Shane Black, Warren Murphy, from characters created by Shane Black

Lethal Weapon 3 ★★★ 15

Action thriller 1992 · US · Colour · 115mins

Mindless mayhem doesn't come slicker than in these action extravaganzas, and, even though by now the law of diminishing returns is starting to have an effect, the sheer scale of the set pieces will keep fans of the first two movies more than satisfied. This time around, Mel Gibson gets a girl after his own heart (cop Rene Russo with an equally impressive

collection of battle scars), soon-to-retire partner Danny Glover looks more worried than ever, and Joe Pesci finds himself the butt of the duo's jokes. Stuart Wilson, meanwhile, takes over from Joss Ackland as the obligatory imported British villain and enjoys himself immensely as the former cop turned monstrous crimelord. Disengage the brain and enjoy. Contains violence and swearing. ▦ *DVD*

Mel Gibson *Martin Riggs* • Danny Glover *Roger Murtaugh* • Joe Pesci *Leo Getz* • Rene Russo *Lorna Cole* • Stuart Wilson *Jack Travis* • Steve Kahan *Captain Murphy* • Darlene Love *Trish Murtaugh* • Traci Wolfe *Rianne Murtaugh* • Damon Hines *Nick Murtaugh* • Ebonie Smith *Carrie Murtaugh* ■ Dir Richard Donner • Scr Jeffrey Boam, Robert Mark Kamen, from a story by Jeffrey Boam, from characters created by Shane Black

Lethal Weapon 4 ★★★ 15

Action adventure 1998 · US · Colour · 120mins

The fourth instalment in the action series has a "going through the motions" feel to it all. Mel Gibson and Danny Glover continue to bicker away amicably, Joe Pesci remains the butt of most of their jokes, while the pregnant Rene Russo is stuck largely on the sidelines. Rising star Chris Rock also jumps aboard the franchise, but the most notable new addition is Jet Li, the Hong Kong action star whose awesome fighting skills leave the rest of the cast looking rather bemused. Otherwise it's business as usual, with director Richard Donner laying on the requisite destruction as Gibson and Glover track down a ruthless Triad gang that specialises in smuggling immigrants. ▦ *DVD*

Mel Gibson *Martin Riggs* • Danny Glover *Roger Murtaugh* • Joe Pesci *Leo Getz* • Rene Russo *Lorna Cole* • Chris Rock *Lee Butters* • Jet Li *Wah Sing Ku* • Steve Kahan *Captain Murphy* • Kim Chan *Uncle Benny* • Darlene Love *Trish Murtaugh* • Traci Wolfe *Rianne* ■ Dir Richard Donner • Scr Channing Gibson, from a story by Jonathan Lemkin, Alfred Gough, Miles Millar, from characters created by Shane Black

Let's Be Famous ★

Comedy 1939 · UK · BW · 83mins

The chance to see *Coronation Street's* Betty Driver as a movie heroine is the only reason to catch this piffling Ealing comedy. Caught between the ambitions of her music-hall mother and strict chorister father, she catches the eye of Jimmy O'Dea, a chirpy Irish know-all who hopes to find fame on Basil Radford's radio programme. Only in thirties Britain would anyone think that a spelling bee could be a source of hilarity. But it's a darn sight funnier than O'Dea's calamitous parachute jump or the nightmare broadcast which culminates in him getting drunk on air with Sonnie Hale.

Jimmy O'Dea *Jimmy Houlihan* • Betty Driver *Betty Pinbright* • Sonnie Hale *Finch* • Patrick Barr *Johnnie Blake* • Basil Radford *Watson* ■ Dir Walter Forde • Scr Roger MacDougal, Allan Mackinnon

Let's Dance ★★★ U

Musical comedy 1950 · US · Colour · 112mins

One of the least shown of all Fred Astaire movies, and, indeed, with

some cause, though no Astaire film is negligible. Here, after his triumph in *Blue Skies* for Paramount, maestro Fred is inexplicably second-billed to the studio's blonde bombshell Betty Hutton, and their styles simply don't mesh at all. A cowboy dance routine is particularly embarrassing, with Hutton firing on all cylinders and the suave Fred reduced to mere background. The plot's a nothing about a war widow and her son, but watch for Fred's stunning *Piano Dance* sequence, the minor Frank Loesser score and some nice Technicolor.

Betty Hutton *Kitty McNeil* • Fred Astaire *Donald Elwood* • Roland Young *Mr Edmund Pohlwhistle* • Lucile Watson *Serena Everett* • Ruth Warrick *Carola Everett* • Gregory Moffett *Richard "Richie" Everett* • Barton MacLane *Larry Channock* • Shepperd Strudwick *Timothy Bryant* • Melville Cooper *Mr Charles Wagstaffe* ■ Dir Norman Z McLeod • Scr Allan Scott, Dane Lussier, from the story *Little Boy Blue* by Maurice Zolotow

Let's Do It Again ★★★

Musical comedy 1953 · US · Colour · 94mins

Columbia indulged in a little nostalgia with this musical remake of it's 1937 hit, *The Awful Truth*. Jane Wyman and Ray Milland are no Irene Dunne and Cary Grant, however, and their gallant attempts to whip up Mary Loos and Richard Sale's script into a frothy, light confection aren't helped by Ned Washington's decidedly uninspired songs. As the couple who divorce only to discover they were never so much in love, Wyman and Milland don't quite have the necessary lightness of touch – though they're finesse itself compared with Aldo Ray, who plays his role like a bull in a china shop.

Jane Wyman *Constance Stuart* • Ray Milland *Gary Stuart* • Aldo Ray *Frank McGraw* • Leon Ames *Chet Stuart* • Valerie Bettis *Lilly Adair* ■ Dir Alexander Hall • Scr Mary Loos, Richard Sale, from the play *The Awful Truth* by Arthur Richman • Music/Lyrics Ned Washington

Let's Do It Again ★★★ U

Comedy 1975 · US · Colour · 112mins

A hysterically funny follow-up to *Uptown Saturday Night*, again teaming Sidney Poitier and Bill Cosby (under Poitier's direction) as the two lodge brothers who hypnotise a puny pugilist into becoming a dynamite boxer in order to make a quick fortune in bets. The not-very-original plot's really a series of loosely tied sketches, accompanied by a terrific Curtis Mayfield soundtrack. The third film in this series was *A Piece of the Action*, but this is easily the best, and John Amos and Calvin Lockhart give Poitier and Cosby a real run for their money as a sassy pair of New Orleans hoodlums.

Sidney Poitier *Clyde Williams* • Bill Cosby *Billy Foster* • Calvin Lockhart *Biggie Smalls* • John Amos *Kansas City Mack* • Denise Nicholas *Beth Foster* • Lee Chamberlin *Dee Dee Williams* • Mel Stewart *Ellison* ■ Dir Sidney Poitier • Scr Richard Wesley, from a story by Timothy March

Let's Face It ★★ U

Musical comedy 1943 · US · BW · 76mins

The ultimate in brassiness, when fast-talking soldier Bob Hope lines up with loud-talking Betty Hutton in a farcical comedy of cheating husbands and fed-

up wives. As a trawl of old jokes and lazy predictabilities it's the sort of cannon fodder Paramount Studios turned out for troops' relaxation. Only query is that, as it began life as a Cole Porter musical, why are so few of his songs were included?

Bob Hope *Jerry Walker* • Betty Hutton *Winnie Potter* • ZaSu Pitts *Cornelia Pidgeon* • Phyllis Povah *Nancy Collister* • Dave Willock *Barney Hilliard* • Eve Arden *Maggie Watson* ■ Dir Sidney Lanfield • Scr Harry Tugend, from the musical play by Dorothy Fields, Herbert Fields, Cole Porter, from the play *Cradle Snatchers* by Norma Mitchell, Russell G Medcraft

Let's Get Harry ★★ 18

Action adventure 1986 · US · Colour · 98mins

The name of the fictitious "Alan Smithee" on the credits alerts everyone (well, movie buffs anyway) that the real director of a film chose to have his name taken off it. In this case it was Stuart Rosenberg who quit this thriller about South American drug dealers who kidnap some US oil workers. Robert Duvall plays a mercenary hired to release the hostages when the American government refuses to negotiate. Duvall gives the movie some class while the whole theme of honour and loyalty can be ascribed to the original story by Sam Fuller who was to have directed it years before. For the most part, though, it's just a thick-ear adventure yarn that could easily have starred Chuck Norris. ▦

Robert Duvall *Norman Shrike* • Michael Schoeffling *Corey Burck* • Tom Wilson [Thomas F Wilson] *Pachowski* • Glenn Frey *Spence* • Rick Rossovich *Kurt Klein* • Ben Johnson *Mr Burck* Sr • Mark Harmon *Harry Burck* • Gary Busey *Jack* ■ Dir Alan Smithee [Stuart Rosenberg] • Scr Charles Robert Carner, from a story by Mark Feldberg, Samuel Fuller

Let's Get Laid ★★ 18

Erotic comedy 1977 · UK · Colour · 92mins

Also known as *Love Trap*, this was Robin Askwith's farewell to the world of soft-core comedy – and when you've been reduced to playing characters called Gordon Laid, it's easy to see how the novelty might have worn thin. The director is James Kenelm Clarke, whose involvement with the genre came after directing a BBC documentary on pornography; Clarke was himself rounding off a three-film collaboration with the almost inanimate *Men Only* columnist, Fiona Richmond. ▦

Fiona Richmond *Maxine Lupercal* • Robin Askwith *Gordon Laid* • Anthony Steel *Moncrieff Dovecraft* • Graham Stark *Inspector Nugent* • Linda Hayden *Gloria* ■ Dir James Kenelm Clarke • Scr Michael Robson

Let's Get Lost ★★★ 15

Documentary 1988 · US · BW · 114mins

Fashion photographer Bruce Weber produced and directed this documentary about the life and hard-drug times of jazz trumpeter Chet Baker. Because of his hard-living lifestyle Baker was described as the "James Dean of jazz". The talking-heads interviews with other musicians and lovers are interspersed with terrific jam sessions by the man whose edgy bouncy music belied his inner tribulations; this is one of the most elegant biopics of a musical world all unto itself. 🎞

Dir Bruce Weber • *Scr* Susan Stribling

Let's Get Married ★★

Comedy   1960 · US · BW · 90mins

Based on Ken Taylor's novel *Confessions of a Kept Woman*, this was a risqué (for its day) romance featuring Anthony Newley as timid trainee doctor Dickie Bird. The nervy Bird marries beautiful – but pregnant – model Anne Linton (Anne Aubrey) and finally overcomes his own lack of courage when he is called upon to deliver his baby. The main enjoyment comes from the array of British comedy talent in the supporting cast, including the likes of Lionel Jeffries, John Le Mesurier, Hermione Baddeley, Sydney Tafler, Betty Marsden, Cardew Robinson and Bernie Winters.

Anthony Newley *Dickie Bird* • Anne Aubrey *Anne Linton* • Bernie Winters *Bernie* • Hermione Baddeley *Mrs O'Grady* • James Booth *Photographer* • Lionel Jeffries *Marsh* • Diane Clare *Glad* • John Le Mesurier *Dean* • Victor Maddern *Works Manager* • Joyce Carey *Miss Finch* • Sydney Tafler *Pendle* • Betty Marsden *Miss Kaplan* • Cardew Robinson *Salesman* ■ *Dir* Peter Graham Scott • *Scr* Ken Taylor, from his novel *Confessions of a Kept Woman*

Let's Hope It's a Girl ★★★ 15

Comedy   1985 · Fr/It · Colour · 119mins

Since his comic heist movie *Big Deal On Madonna Street* in 1958, it took Italian director Mario Monicelli almost 30 years to gain another world-wide success. This rather sprawling but entertaining semi-comic family saga with feminist undertones was helped by an excellent international cast, led by Sweden's Liv Ullmann. She plays an impoverished countess struggling to keep the family's decaying property, and rules over its inhabitants, who are mostly women. When the film sags occasionally, there is always the beautiful Catherine Deneuve and the ravishing Tuscan settings to distract one. In French and Italian with English subtitles.

Liv Ullmann *Elena Leonardo* • Catherine Deneuve *Claudia* • Philippe Noiret *Count Leonardo* • Giuliana De Sio *Franca* ■ *Dir* Mario Monicelli • *Scr* Leo Benvenuti, Piero De Bernadi, Suso Cecchi D'Amico, Tullio Pinelli, Mario Monicelli

Let's Live a Little ★★

Comedy   1948 · US · BW · 85mins

This is the kind of frothy comedy that cries out for the likes of William Powell and Myrna Loy, but instead has to settle for Robert Cummings and Hedy Lamarr. Cummings seems more at home than his co-star with the endless round of misunderstandings and petty feuds, but like *Lady in the Dark* – the Ginger Rogers – musical about psychoanalysis the film suffers from a touch of the verbals whenever psychiatrist Lamarr gets to try out her couch-side manner on Cummings's neurotic advertising executive. Fatally short on pace and fun.

Hedy Lamarr *Dr JO Loring* • Robert Cummings *Duke Crawford* • Anna Sten *Michele Bennett* • Robert Shayne *Dr Richard Field* • Mary Treen *Miss Adams* • Harry Antrim *James Montgomery* ■ *Dir* Richard Wallace • *Scr* Howard Irving Young, Edmund Hartmann, Albert J Cohen, from a story by Albert J Cohen, Jack Harvey

Let's Make It Legal ★★

Comedy   1951 · US · BW · 77mins

Richard Sale directs this marital comedy about a couple (Claudette Colbert and Macdonald Carey) who decide to part after 20 years of wedded bliss. When, with divorce proceedings well under way, her old boyfriend from the distant past (Zachary Scott) turns up, her husband has second thoughts. A well-characterised screenplay and decent performances make for a proficient and mildly amusing film, in which starlet Marilyn Monroe flits through in a bathing suit. However, it's an autumnal echo of Colbert's glittering earlier outings in the genre; Carey is no Fred MacMurray, and the soufflé only rises half-way.

Claudette Colbert *Miriam* • Macdonald Carey *Hugh* • Zachary Scott *Victor* • Barbara Bates *Barbara Denham* • Robert Wagner *Jerry Denham* • Marilyn Monroe *Joyce* • Frank Cady *Ferguson* • Jim Hayward *Gardener* ■ *Dir* Richard Sale • *Scr* F Hugh Herbert, IAL Diamond, from the story by Mortimer Braus

Let's Make Love ★★★★ U

Romantic comedy   1960 · US · Colour · 113mins

Marilyn Monroe's penultimate film has always been under-rated by both critics and Monroe fans alike, but this musical actually contains some fabulous routines from the star. The lightweight plot – a trifle about a slumming billionaire – was originally created with Gregory Peck in mind. In the sophisticated hands of "woman's" director George Cukor, it becomes a fascinating study of Monroe's sexuality, helped by the fact that she and Peck's replacement, French heart-throb Yves Montand, were amorously involved in real life at the time. British import Frankie Vaughan barely gets a look-in, but don't miss the guest stars who add to the delightful streak of contemporary satire running through the film. 🎞

Marilyn Monroe *Amanda* • Yves Montand *Jean-Marc Clement* • Tony Randall *Howard Coffman* • Frankie Vaughan *Tony Danton* • Wilfrid Hyde White *John Wales* • David Burns *Oliver Burton* • Michael David *Dave Kerry* • Bing Crosby • Gene Kelly • Milton Berle ■ *Dir* George Cukor • *Scr* Norman Krasna, Hal Kanter

Let's Make Music ★★ U

Musical   1940 · US · BW · 80mins

Elderly spinster schoolteacher Elisabeth Risdon writes a song which is taken up by Bob Crosby, becomes a hit, and gives her a new lease of life as a star on the musical entertainment circuit. Leslie Goodwins directs this inane and implausible diversion, designed as a showcase for Bing's younger brother, who makes a respectable job of playing himself. What is interesting about it, however, is that novelist Nathanael West earned his dollar as the scriptwriter of this

nonsense, doubtless collecting material for his scathing view of Hollywood in *The Day of the Locust*.

Bob Crosby • Jean Rogers *Abby Adams* • Elisabeth Risdon *Malvina Adams* • Joseph Buloff *Joe Bellah* • Joyce Compton *Betty* • Bennie Bartlett *Tommy* • Louis Jean Heydt *Mr Stevens* ■ *Dir* Leslie Goodwins • *Scr* Nathanael West

Let's Scare Jessica to Death ★★★★

Horror   1971 · US · Colour · 88mins

A real nail-biting must-see. Director John Hancock cranks up the tension with a series of terrifying sequences and elicits an utterly convincing leading performance from Zohra Lampert. Jessica (Lampert) is recovering from mental illness and hopes to start over again with her husband in a seemingly quiet rural community. Alas, it isn't long before her neighbours begin to look like extras from a corny Hammer horror movie, and she discovers a young squatter staying with her resembles a Victorian girl who drowned in a nearby lake. Is what Jessica is seeing real, or is she having another breakdown? At last, a film that achieves its scare effect without resorting to gore and violence.

Zohra Lampert *Jessica* • Barton Heyman *Duncan* • Kevin O'Connor *Woody* • Gretchen Corbett *Girl* • Alan Manson *Dorker* • Mariclare Costello *Emily* ■ *Dir* John Hancock • *Scr* Norman Jonas, Ralph Rose

Let's Spend the Night Together ★★ 15

Music documentary   1982 · US · Colour · 86mins

You would not have expected Hal Ashby, the director responsible for the rich eccentricity of *Harold and Maude* and the poignancy of *Coming Home*, to have steered his career towards blandness, especially with a film about the Rolling Stones. How could Ashby have resisted making witty or punchy comments on the five highly distinctive band members? Instead, he settles for the mundane, filming the Stones playing their hits in American arenas so vast that the energy is sapped by the size. Only *Honky Tonk Woman* and a handful of helicopter shots reach across the divide. 🎞

Dir Hal Ashby

Let's Talk about Sex ★

Comedy drama   1998 · US · Colour · 82mins

A lamentable attempt at a semi-erotic "women's film" written by, directed and starring the not-so-talented Troy Beyer. Beyer, a journalist, attempts to make it into television by cutting a video in which her friends and various outspoken women discuss their sex lives and fantasies in true daytime-TV style. Somehow she manages to lose all her footage and stomps around cleaning her flat and crying on the shoulders of her two best friends. Combine the documentary-style "confessions" with a dreadful subplot about Beyer's own sex life, and you have a film for the shredder. Dire.

Troy Beyer *Jazz* • Randi Ingerman *Lena* • Paget Brewster *Michelle* • Joseph C Phillips *Michael* • Michaline Babich *Morgan* • Tina Nguyen *Drew* ■ *Dir/Scr* Troy Beyer

Let's Talk About Women ★★★

Portmanteau comedy   1964 · Fr/It · BW · 110mins

Having already forged his reputation as a screenwriter, Ettore Scola made his directorial debut with this episodic comedy, which showcased the versatility of Vittorio Gassman. He takes a different role in each of the eight vignettes, which were intended to explore the many facets of womankind. But such is his dominance of the proceedings that there's little room for co-stars of the calibre of Sylva Koscina and Antonella Lualdi to make much of an impact. It's patchy and dated, but a decent advertisement for the unfashionable portmanteau picture. An Italian language film.

Vittorio Gassman *Stranger/Practical joker/Client/Lover/Impatient lover/Waiter/Timid brother/Ragman/Prisoner* • Sylva Koscina *Reluctant girl* • Antonella Lualdi *Fiancée* • Walter Chiari *Philanderer* • Eleonora Rossi-Drago *Indolent lady* ■ *Dir* Ettore Scola • *Scr* Ettore Scola, Ruggero Maccari

The Letter ★★★

Drama   1929 · US · BW · 62mins

This is a rare chance to see the legendary Broadway star, Jeanne Eagels – the subject of the 1957 biopic with Kim Novak – who died of a drug overdose in 1929. Eagels plays the murderous middle-class wife in Malaya, who pleads self-defence to cover up her killing of a would-be lover, in the first of several adaptations of W Somerset Maugham's play. The later film starring Bette Davis may be better, but it's worth seeing this version because of the curiosity value.

Jeanne Eagels *Leslie Crosbie* • OP Heggie *Joyce* • Reginald Owen *Robert Crosbie* • Herbert Marshall *Geoffry Hammond* • Irene Browne *Mrs Joyce* ■ *Dir* Jean de Limur • *Scr* Garrett Fort, Monta Bell, Jean de Limur, from the play by W Somerset Maugham

The Letter ★★★★ PG

Drama   1940 · US · BW · 91mins

As well as its startling opening sequence, this vehicle for Bette Davis also contains one of her best performances, as murderess Leslie Crosbie. The film is superbly controlled by director William Wyler, who also guided Davis to her *Jezebel* Oscar, not to mention having an ongoing relationship with the star. The original W Somerset Maugham tale of repressed passions in Malaya is melodrama, pure and simple, but Davis uses her talent for turning tosh into art magnificently, and manages to persuade us that this is a tragedy of untold dimensions rather than a formula product of the studio system. She is aided by atmospheric photography (every blind casts a slanting shadow), an evocative and cleverly melodic score and excellent support from a sinister Gale Sondergaard. 🎞

Bette Davis *Leslie Crosbie* • Herbert Marshall *Robert Crosbie* • James Stephenson *Howard*

Joyce • Gale Sondergaard *Mrs Hammond* • Bruce Lester *John Withers* • Elizabeth Earl *Adele Ainsworth* • Victor Sen Yung *Ong Chi Seng* • Doris Lloyd *Mrs Cooper* ■ Dir William Wyler • Scr Howard Koch, from the play by W Somerset Maugham • *Cinematographer* Tony Gaudio • *Music* Max Steiner

Letter from an Unknown Woman ★★★★ U

Romantic melodrama
1948 · US · BW · 83mins

One of the most tragic romantic openings in all movie history ("By the time you finish reading this letter I'll be dead") precedes a marvellously bittersweet tale, hauntingly played by winsome Joan Fontaine and caddishly handsome Louis Jourdan, and brilliantly and economically filmed from the Stefan Zweig original by émigré director Max Ophüls, here delivering a rare product, a Hollywood art movie. For Ophüls, style was everything, but here the Zweig story harnesses his Viennese sensibility to a flawless and very real tale of an unrequited love so painful it tears at your heartstrings. Very Viennese, and very wonderful. ▣

Joan Fontaine *Lisa Berndle* • Louis Jourdan *Stefan Brand* • Mady Christians *Frau Berndle* • Marcel Journet *Johann Stauffer* • Art Smith *John* • Howard Freeman *Herr Kastner* • John Good *Lt Leopold von Kaltnegger* ■ Dir Max Ophüls • Scr Howard Koch, from the novel *Brief Einer Unbekannten* by Stefan Zweig

Letter of Introduction ★★★

Comedy drama 1938 · US · BW · 100mins

As a relief from the several "women's pictures", such as *Back Street* and *Imitation of Life*, John M Stahl was making at Universal, he produced and directed this enjoyable but slight comedy drama set in the world of theatre. It stars Adolphe Menjou as an ageing matinée idol who won't admit that aspiring young actress Andrea Leeds is actually his daughter. Adding to the pleasure are Ann Sheridan, wise-cracking Eve Arden, and ventriloquist Edgar Bergen (Candice's father) and his celebrated dummy Charlie McCarthy.

Adolphe Menjou *John Mannering* • Andrea Leeds *Kay Martin* • George Murphy *Barry Paige* • Rita Johnson *Honey* • Ann Sheridan *Lydia Hoyt* • Eve Arden *Cora* ■ Dir John M Stahl • Scr Sheridan Gibney, Leonard Spigelgass, from a story by Bernice Boone

Letter to Brezhnev

★★★★ 15

Comedy 1985 · UK · Colour · 91mins

An endearingly wayward comedy, a sort of *On the Town* reworked for Liverpool, with the Beatles replacing Leonard Bernstein and Leonid Brezhnev replacing Miss Turnstiles. Frank Clarke's ingenious starts when a Soviet ship docks in Liverpool and decants two sailors (Alfred Molina and Peter Firth) for shore leave. Two scouse girls Margi Clarke and Alexandra Pigg pick them up, have a good time and one of them falls in love, prompting the letter to the Kremlin. It's clever, vibrant, sexy and energetically performed. Contains swearing and nudity. ▣

Alfred Molina *Sergei* • Peter Firth *Peter* • Margi Clarke *Teresa King* • Alexandra Pigg

Elaine Spencer • Susan Dempsey *Girl In Yellow Pedal Pushers* • Ted Wood *Mick* • Ken Campbell *Reporter* ■ Dir Chris Bernard • Scr Frank Clarke

Letter to My Killer ★★ PG

Thriller 1995 · US · Colour · 87mins

One crime begets another in this run-of-the-mill TV movie. Mare Winningham and Rip Torn are the struggling couple who embark on an ill-advised money-making scheme following the discovery of an old letter. The writer was apparently the victim of a murder, and the couple piece together the clues and decide to blackmail the killers. Needless to say, they find that extortion is not easy and soon their lives are in danger. Not very original, but the seasoned cast make it worth tuning in. ▣

Mare Winningham *Judy Parma* • Nick Chinlund *Nick Parma* • Rip Torn *Russell Vanik* • Josef Sommer *Martin Prescott* • Eddie Jones *Wilson Hartwick* • James Murtaugh *Darryl Barnes* ■ Dir Janet Meyers • Scr Norman Strum

A Letter to Three Wives

★★★★ U

Drama 1949 · US · BW · 98mins

A witty and sophisticated, though perhaps a shade too literary, slice of entertainment from writer/director Joseph L Mankiewicz, double Oscar winner (best director, best screenplay) for this movie. Today, the clever framing device may seem a little arch, but there's no denying the strength of the central idea of three women receiving a letter from Addie Ross, the town floosie, who claims to have absconded with one of their husbands. You never see her, but her beautifully undulating voice is that of Celeste Holm. The plot carries you along in this is an intelligent, almost anti-Hollywood movie, largely filmed on location in Westchester, New York. Paul Douglas makes a fine film debut, and the other Douglas, Kirk, demonstrates his star potential. Linda Darnell looks ravishing, but the movie is stolen by clever Thelma Ritter. ▣

Jeanne Crain *Deborah Bishop* • Linda Darnell *Lora May Hollingsway* • Ann Sothern *Rita Phipps* • Kirk Douglas *George Phipps* • Paul Douglas *Porter Hollingsway* • Barbara Lawrence *Babe* • Jeffrey Lynn *Brad Bishop* • Connie Gilchrist *Mrs Finney* • Florence Bates *Mrs Manleigh* • Hobart Cavanaugh *Mr Manleigh* • Celeste Holm *Addie Ross* ■ Dir Joseph L Mankiewicz • Scr Joseph L Mankiewicz, from the adaptation by Vera Caspary of the novel by John Klempner

Letters from the East ★★

Political drama
1995 · UK/Ger/Swe/Fin · Colour · 105mins

Uncertain handling undermines intriguing material in this rare cinematic sortie into the Baltic republic of Estonia. Writer/director Andrew Grieve seeks to draw comparisons between the final days of the Nazi Occupation and the rising tide of nationalism that prompted the collapse of Communism. But, while possessing undoubted power, the flashbacks to the terror that presaged the Red Army "liberation" slot uncomfortably into his tale of the British-raised woman who discovers that the mother she thought

dead may have survived the war after all.

Ewa Fröling *Anna* • Mark Womack *Rein* • Ingeborga Dapkunaite *Marie, mother 1944* • Nicholas Le Prevost *Alan* • Rein Oja *Hans, father 1944* ■ Dir/Scr Andrew Grieve

Letters to an Unknown Lover ★★

Crime drama 1985 · UK/Fr · Colour · 101mins

This slow-burning wartime thriller was adapted from a novel by Pierre Boileau and Thomas Nacejac, the duo responsible for *Vertigo*. It was previously filmed, under its original title, *Les Louves*, by Luis Saslavsky. Yet, try as they might, Cherie Lunghi and Mathilde May can't hold a candle to their predecessors, Micheline Presle and Jeanne Moreau, largely because Peter Duffell, who had some success handling Graham Greene's *England Made Me*, struggles to recapture the brooding sense of menace that envelopes fleeing PoW Yves Beneyton as he gets sucked into a plan to defraud the sister of fellow escapee, Ralph Bates.

Cherie Lunghi *Helene* • Mathilda May *Agnes* • Yves Beneyton *Gervais* • Ralph Bates *Bernard* • Andrea Ferreol *Julia* ■ Dir Peter Duffell • Scr Pierre Boileau, Thomas Narcejac, from the novel *Les Louves* by Pierre Boileau, from the novel *Les Louves* by Thomas Narcejac

Letting Go ★★★ PG

Romantic drama 1985 · US · Colour · 91mins

Jack Bender, who directed John Ritter in an earlier TV movie, the sweet romance *In Love with an Older Woman*, here directs the comic actor once again in a comedy drama about two people coming to terms with loss who fall in love after meeting at a self-help group. Sharon Gless of TV's *Cagney and Lacey* is on form as the woman in Ritter's life, in this often funny and charming tale. ▣

John Ritter *Alex Schuster* • Sharon Gless *Kate Marshall* • Joe Cortese *Neil* ■ Dir Jack Bender • Scr Charlotte Brown, from the story Tracy Cabot, Dr Zev Wanderer

Leviathan ★★★ 18

Science-fiction 1989 · US/It · Colour · 93mins

As trashy and outstandingly stupid as this underwater *Alien* is, director George Pan Cosmatos does a great job of disguising its huge credibility gaps with a diverting fast pace and superior production design. A team of deep-sea miners discover a Russian shipwreck containing a stash of vodka laced with a genetically-mutated virus which progressively turns them into tentacled half-man, half-fish aqua-Draculas. Every shock twist from *The Fly* to *Jaws* is plumbed by Cosmatos for this enjoyable, if standard, monster scare work-out. ▣

Peter Weller *Beck* • Richard Crenna *Doc* • Amanda Pays *Willie* • Daniel Stern *Sixpack* • Ernie Hudson *Jones* • Michael Carmine *DeJesus* • Lisa Eilbacher *Bowman* • Hector Elizondo *Cobb* • Meg Foster *Martin* ■ Dir George Pan Cosmatos • Scr David Webb Peoples, Jeb Stuart, from a story by David Webb Peoples

Lewis & Clark & George

★★ 18

Road movie 1996 · US · Colour · 82mins

Two convicts go on the run and head for the Mexican border in search of the map to a gold mine. When one of them hooks up with George (Rose McGowan), who's travelling in a stolen car with a snake for company, their plans start to unravel. In a low-wattage mixture of neo-Sergio Leone western, road movie and *The Treasure of the Sierra Madre*. It's visually impressive, with energetic performances from the three leads, but it tries too hard to be hip and cool and fails embarrassingly. Contains swearing, sex scenes and violence. ▣

Salvator Xuereb *Lewis* • Dan Gunther *Clark* • Rose McGowan *George* ■ Dir/Scr Rod McCall

Une Liaison Pornographique ★★★★ 15

Romantic drama
1999 · Fr/Bel/Swi · Colour · mins

Exhibiting the combination of femininity and intelligence that has sustained her exceptional career, Nathalie Baye won the best actress prize at Venice for her work in this intriguing, intelligent study of modern sexual manners. Director Frédéric Fonteyne contrives to lock us out of the hotel room as Baye and Sergi López engage in the fantasy she outlined in a lonely hearts ad. However, as feelings begin to creep into their coupling, we are permitted to become emotional voyeurs. The linking interview sequences are a touch intrusive, but such is the veracity of the performances that the characters' inevitable parting is a source of genuine regret. In French with English subtitles.

Nathalie Baye *Her* • Sergi Lopez *Him* ■ Dir Frédéric Fonteyne • Scr Philippe Blasband

Les Liaisons Dangereuses

★★★ 15

Drama 1959 · Fr · BW · 104mins

Roger Vadim directed (and co-wrote) this updated adaptation of his compatriot Choderlos De Laclos's 18th-century epistolary novel. It coolly and poisonously exposes a very particular level of upper-class degeneracy in the sexual behaviour of Valmont and – in this version – his wife. Gérard Philipe (sadly nearing his premature death) and Jeanne Moreau co-star as the couple colluding in each other's dangerous sexual adventures, Vadim's then wife Annette Stroyberg (billed as Annette Vadim) also stars, and reveals her beautiful body. Made with a measure of restraint and a nice feeling of irony by the generally showy Vadim, it's been overtaken by the less compromising version, *Dangerous Liaisons*, with John Malkovich, Glenn Close and Michelle Pfeiffer. In French with English subtitles. ▣

Gérard Philipe *Valmont de Merteuil* • Jeanne Moreau *Juliette de Merteuil* • Jeanne Valerie *Cecile Volanges* • Annette Vadim [Annette Stroyberg] *Marianne Tourvel* • Simone Renant *Madame Volanges* • Jean-Louis Trintignant *Danceny* ■ Dir Roger Vadim • Scr Roger Vadim, Roger Vailland, Claude Brule, from the novel by Choderlos De Laclos

U = SUITABLE FOR ALL, Uc = SUITABLE FOR ALL, ESPECIALLY FOR YOUNG CHILDREN (VIDEO ONLY) PG = PARENTAL GUIDANCE

Lianna ★★ 🔞
Drama   1983 · US · Colour · 112mins

Low-key drama about the wife of a philandering university professor who returns to college to regains some confidence, and finds herself in a lesbian affair with a teacher. Ignored by her husband and generally messed about by her own lover, Lianna has so many hang-ups that it's a miracle the character, so well played by Linda Griffiths, isn't just a walking cipher. Even so, it's a mite pat, with the script turning into a bit of a shopping list of socio-sexual problems.

Linda Griffiths *Lianna* • Jane Hallaren *Ruth* • Jon DeVries *Dick* • Jo Henderson *Sandy* • Jessica Wight MacDonald *Theda* • Jesse Solomon *Spencer* • John Sayles *Jerry* • Stephen Mendillo *Bob* ■ *Dir/Scr* John Sayles

Liar ★★ 🔞
Thriller   1997 · US · Colour · 97mins

This game of psychological warfare isn't half as smart as it thinks it is. Tim Roth heads a fairly strong cast in a claustrophobic, narratively fractured tale of two cops running a polygraph test on a murder suspect. The film is intense and sharply directed by the Pate brothers, but Roth isn't credible as the twitchy, super-intelligent playboy who may be a killer, and the flurry of contrivances that eventually leads us to have suspicions about everyone are equally difficult to swallow. Contains violence and swearing 🖭

Tim Roth *Wayland* • Chris Penn [Christopher Penn] *Braxton* • Michael Rooker *Kennesaw* • Renee Zellweger *Elizabeth* • Ellen Burstyn *Mook* • Rosanna Arquette *Mrs Kennesaw* • Michael Parks *Doctor Banyard* ■ *Dir* Josh Pate, Jonas Pate • *Scr* Jonas Pate, Josh Pate

Liar Liar ★★★ 🔞
Drama   1992 · Can · Colour · 90mins

A number of films were made in the early nineties on the subject of children accusing their fathers of sexual abuse. in which the wife is torn between believing her child or the man she loves. While a tad overlong and erring on the side of melodrama, this Canadian TV movie approaches the topic with some sensitivity and insight, with Art Hindle and Vanessa King impressive as the accused and his 11-year-old daughter. Kate Nelligan provides typically solid support. 🖭

Art Hindle *Gil Farrow* • Vanessa King *Kelly Farrow* • Kate Nelligan *Susan Miori* • Rosemary Dunsmore *Mary Farrow* ■ *Dir* Jorge Montesi • *Scr* Nancy NJ Isaak

Liar Liar ★★★★ 🔞
Comedy   1997 · US · Colour · 82mins

One of Jim Carrey's funniest comedy role to date, this is not only tailor-made for his rubber-faced antics, but also gives him an opportunity to show a more human side. Carrey stars as ruthless lawyer and compulsive liar Fletcher Reede, who misses his son's birthday party and is "cursed" to tell the truth for 24 hours, with hilarious results. Carrey gives a bravura performance as the amoral attorney who hurls inadvertent insults and digs himself into an abyss as he finds it impossible to stick to his truth-bending plan in a divorce case. Carrey's

frenzied physical and vocal contortions provide several amusing comic moments, as well as a few riotous ones. Contains some violence and swearing. 🖭 *DVD*

Jim Carrey *Fletcher Reede* • Maura Tierney *Audrey Reede* • Justin Cooper *Max Reede* • Cary Elwes *Jerry* • Anne Haney *Greta* • Jennifer Tilly *Samantha Cole* • Amanda Donohoe *Miranda* • Jason Bernard *Judge Marshall Stevens* • Swoosie Kurtz *Dana Appleton* • Mitchell Ryan *Mr Allan* ■ *Dir* Tom Shadyac • *Scr* Paul Guay, Stephen Mazur

The Liar's Club ★★★
Thriller   1992 · US · Colour

Wil Wheaton has struggled to fulfil the promise he showed as a young actor in *Stand by Me*, but he excels in this above average made-for-TV thriller, which was executive produced by Roger Corman. Wheaton stars as a high-school student who faces a crisis of conscience when one of his colleagues is accused of rape, leading to his friends closing ranks. The largely unknown cast gives believable performances and director Jeffrey Porter makes some telling points about the dark side of American teenage life. Contains swearing, violence and nudity.

Wil Wheaton *David* • Brian Krause *Pat* • Michael Cudlitz *Jimbo* • Soleil Moon Frye *Gigi* • Jennifer Burns *Kim* • Bruce Weitz *Jack* ■ *Dir* Jeffrey Porter • *Scr* Jeff Yonis

Liar's Moon ★★ 🔞
Romantic drama
1982 · US · Colour · 100mins

A young Matt Dillon stars in this endearingly dumb romantic drama – crammed with clichés, woodenly acted, and generally cornier than Kansas in August, September *and* October. Dillon and Cindy Fisher play eloped newlyweds, who find their relationship haunted by a family secret from the past. As a gimmick, the film was originally released with alternative endings – one happy, one sad. Nowadays, it's usually seen with just the happy one. The movie doubtless provided Dillon with useful leading-man experience. It's sad, though, to see Hollywood veterans Yvonne De Carlo and Broderick Crawford appearing in such soapy tosh.

Matt Dillon *Jack Duncan* • Cindy Fisher *Ginny Peterson* • Christopher Connelly *Alex Peterson* • Yvonne De Carlo *Jeanene Dubois* • Hoyt Axton *Cecil Duncan* • Maggie Blye *Ellen "Babs" Duncan* • Broderick Crawford *Colonel Tubman* • Susan Tyrrell *Lora Mae Bouvier* ■ *Dir* David Fisher • *Scr* David Fisher, from the story by Janice Thompson, Billy Hanna

Libel ★★★
Drama   1959 · UK · BW · 98mins

Stagily set, despite direction by maestro Anthony Asquith, this is one of Dirk Bogarde's better movies from the fifties, with critics of the time hoisting him into the Alec Guinness class. Bringing a libel action to clear his aristocratic name against the man who doubts if he really was the prisoner of war he claims to have been, Bogarde's role is the teasing centre of a clever narrative. The context is awfully artificial, but it's Bogarde you'll be watching, not those on the sidelines. And there's always

something very compelling about courtroom scenes as drama.

Dirk Bogarde *Sir Mark Loddon/Frank Welney/ Number Fifteen* • Olivia de Havilland *Lady Maggie Loddon* • Paul Massie *Jeffrey Buckenham* • Robert Morley *Sir Wilfred* • Wilfrid Hyde White *Hubert Foxley* • Anthony Dawson *Gerald Loddon* • Richard Wattis *Judge* • Richard Dimbleby • Martin Miller *Dr Schrott* • Millicent Martin *Maisie* ■ *Dir* Anthony Asquith • *Scr* Anatole de Grunwald, Karl Tunberg, from the play by Edward Wooll

Libeled Lady ★★★★
Comedy   1936 · US · BW · 98mins

A marvellous MGM comedy, employing four great stars who play together with ease and show consummate professionalism in a wonderfully contrived farce. Spencer Tracy is the newspaper editor who can't concentrate on fiancée Jean Harlow while heiress Myrna Loy holds a libel action over him, so he uses smoothie William Powell in a counterplot. This is witty, sophisticated stuff, with the stars at their peaks. In real life, Harlow and Powell were an item, and their playing together is a joy to watch, while director Jack Conway maintains a terrific pace and the MGM gloss adds a quality finish.

William Powell *Bill Chandler* • Myrna Loy *Connie Allenbury* • Jean Harlow *Gladys Benton* • Spencer Tracy *Warren Haggerty* • Walter Connolly *James B Allenbury* • Charley Grapewin *Hollis Bane* • Cora Witherspoon *Mrs Burns-Norvell* • EE Clive *Evans* ■ *Dir* Jack Conway • *Scr* Maurine Watkins, Howard Emmett Rogers, George Oppenheimer, from a story by Wallace Sullivan

The Liberation of LB Jones ★★★★
Drama   1970 · US · Colour · 102mins

Directed by William Wyler, this story of racism in the American South tells of a black undertaker whose wife is sleeping with one of the town's racist cops. Divorce proceedings backfire, and the story ends in particularly chilling violence and little glimmer of hope. It's far more radical and disturbing than *In The Heat of the Night* – Stirling Silliphant wrote both pictures – but lacks the showy drama that turned *Heat* into an Oscar-winning smash. Despite its intensity, and a courageous performance by Lee J Cobb as the bigoted town lawyer, Wyler's movie flopped and he never made another.

Lee J Cobb *Oman Hedgepath* • Anthony Zerbe *Willie Joe Worth* • Roscoe Lee Browne *Lord Byron Jones* • Lola Falana *Emma Jones* • Lee Majors *Steve Mundine* • Barbara Hershey *Nella Mundine* • Yaphet Kotto *Sonny Boy Mosby* • Arch Johnson *Stanley Bumpas* • Chill Wills *Mr Ike* ■ *Dir* William Wyler • *Scr* Stirling Silliphant, Jesse Hill Ford, from the novel *The Liberation of Lord Byron Jones* by Jesse Hill Ford

The Liberators ★★ 🅿🄶
Historical drama based on a true story
1987 · US · Colour · 89mins

This action adventure is loosely based on the real-life character John Fairchild (played by Robert Carradine), a member of a plantation-owning family who, in the years preceding the Civil War, became involved with a Quaker group dedicated to smuggling slaves to

Canada and freedom. Made for TV by Disney, it has its heart in the right place and makes for undemanding viewing. Filmed in the tourist attraction of Upper Canada Village near Ottawa, which is historically preserved.

Robert Carradine *John Fairchild* • Larry B Scott *Bill Jackson* • Cynthia Dale *Elizabeth Giddings* • Renee Jones *Lilah* • Bumper Robinson *Adam* ■ *Dir/Scr* Kenneth Johnson

Licence to Kill ★★ 🔞
Spy adventure   1989 · US · Colour · 126mins

Without SMERSH or SPECTRE to outwit (this was the era of Mikhail Gorbachev's *glasnost*, after all), James Bond turns his attentions to big-time drug barons. Timothy Dalton phones in his performance, Desmond Llewelyn is given his biggest role to date and there's a spectacular chase with an oil tanker, but the relentless violence and lack of sexual conquests makes this more of a *Lethal Weapon* than a Bond movie. The title was to have been *Licence Revoked* until market research implied that Americans didn't know what "revoked" meant. Anyway, when 007 does get his licence revoked, he's asked to hand over his gun. "Then it's a farewell to arms," he says to "M" in the garden of Hemingway's home in Key West. A rare moment of style in a jaded effort. Contains violence and swearing. 🖭

Timothy Dalton *James Bond* • Carey Lowell *Pam Bouvier* • Robert Davi *Franz Sanchez* • Talisa Soto *Lupe Lamora* • Anthony Zerbe *Milton Krest* • Frank McRae *Sharkey* • Everett McGill *Killifer* • Wayne Newton *Professor Joe Butcher* • Desmond Llewelyn *"Q"* • David Hedison *Felix Leiter* • Robert Brown *"M"* • Caroline Bliss *Miss Moneypenny* ■ *Dir* John Glen • *Scr* Michael G Wilson, Richard Maibaum, from characters created by Ian Fleming

License to Drive ★★ 🅿🄶
Comedy   1988 · US · Colour · 86mins

Believe it or not, after their roles in Joel Schumacher's glossy vampire picture *The Lost Boys*, everyone thought Corey Haim and Corey Feldman were destined to have substantial movie careers, at least while teenage girls showed an interest in their boyish looks. A year later, they teamed up to make this dippy comedy about a teenager (Haim) who fails his driving test but continues cruising, and has no end of mishaps. There are some laughs to be had and the Coreys are fine, although it's clear that they were relying here more on their looks than their talent. Contains swearing. 🖭

Corey Haim *Les* • Corey Feldman *Dean* • Carol Kane *Les's mother* • Richard Masur *Les's father* • Heather Graham *Mercedes* • Helen Hanft *Miss Heilberg* ■ *Dir* Greg Beeman • *Scr* Neil Tolkin

License to Live ★★★
Comedy drama   1999 · Jap · Colour · 107mins

This was something of a departure for prolific Japanese director Kiyoshi Kurosawa, better known for his cult horror flicks. Yet there's a darkly comic undercurrent running through this wryly observed family drama, in which Hidetoshi Nishijima awakes from a decade-long coma to learn from gruff fish farmer Koji Yakusho that his idyllic childhood has been overtaken by dysfunction and decay. Eschewing easy gags of the *Blast from the Past* variety, and paying oblique homage to Yasujiro Ozu with his restraint, Kurosawa explores such intriging themes as identity, loyalty and mortality without ever taking himself too seriously. In Japanese with English subtitles.

Hidetoshi Nishijima *Yutaka* • Koji Yakusho *Fujimori* • Shun Sugata *Shinichiro* ■ *Dir/Scr* Kiyoshi Kurosawa

Licensed to Kill ★★
Spy spoof 1965 · UK · Colour · 96mins

Tom Adams is Charles Vine, the "Second Best Secret Agent in the Whole Wide World". Part send-up of the Bond ethos and part B-thriller, it's about a plot to assassinate some Euro-boffin who has invented an anti-gravity machine to which the British government wants exclusive rights. Vine is ordered to be the boffin's bodyguard, though problems arise when the villains produce a double. While Vine isn't in Bond's league as a Romeo, he's quite convincing in the guns and fists department. The script bursts with in-jokes and comes up with its own opening Bondian moment, when a pram-pushing nanny becomes a machine-gun wielding killer.

Tom Adams *Charles Vine* • Karel Stepanek *Henrik Jacobsen* • Veronica Hurst *Julia Lindberg* • Peter Bull *Masterman* • John Arnatt *Rockwell* • Francis De Wolff *Walter Pickering* ■ *Dir* Lindsay Shonteff • *Scr* Lindsay Shonteff, Howard Griffiths

The Lie ★★★★ 18
Drama 1992 · Fr · Colour · 92mins

Following in the footsteps of many a key figure in French film history, François Margolin worked as a critic before taking his place behind the camera. In this, his debut feature, he explores the heartbreaking plight of innocents who become infected with the HIV virus through the irresponsibility of others. It's a subject that forces the viewer into taking sides, but Margolin might have allowed a few grey areas in the interests of both drama and truth. As the victim, Nathalie Baye gives a powerful performance that switches with total credibility from shock to anger and from fear to regret. A French film with English subtitles..

Nathalie Baye *Emma* • Didier Sandre *Charles* • Hélène Lapiower *Louise* • Marc Citti *Louis* • Dominique Besnéhard *Rozenberg* ■ *Dir* François Margolin • *Scr* Denis Saada, François Margolin, from an idea by Denis Saada

Liebelei ★★★ U
Romantic drama 1932 · Ger · BW · 82mins

Max Ophüls bade farewell to his native Germany with this bittersweet confection, which, like his masterpiece, *La Ronde*, derives from a play by Arthur Schnitzler. Clearly still delighting in the novelty of sound and the gliding mobility of Franz Planer's camera, he settles for froth rather than dwelling on the text's ironic observations on the impermanence of love and the unendurable scars it leaves. Thus, the giddy whirl of imperial Viennese society is captured

with subtle effervescence, as Magda Schneider falls passionately for dashing lieutenant Wolfgang Liebeneiner. But it's not all romantic sleigh rides, as cuckolded baron Gustaf Gründgens comes seeking revenge. A German language film. 🖵

Magda Schneider *Christine* • Wolfgang Liebeneiner *Fritz* • Luise Ullrich *Mitzi* • Olga Tschechowa *Baroness* • Gustaf Gründgens *Baron Eggerdorff* ■ *Dir* Max Ophüls • *Scr* Kurt Alexander, Hans Wilhelm, from the play by Arthur Schnitzler, adapted by Felix Salten

Liebestraum ★★★ 18
Mystery drama 1991 · US · Colour · 108mins

A weirdly gripping thriller from writer/director Mike Figgis. When architectural journalist Kevin Anderson is called to the deathbed of the mother he never knew (Kim Novak), a chance encounter with an old college friend (Bill Pullman) provides an opportunity to study the site of a unique, soon-to-be-demolished department store. As passion flares between Anderson and Pullman's wife (Pamela Gidley), Novak's increasingly feverish reminiscences point to a dark secret contained within the condemned building's walls. The plot spirals out of sight, like one of the location's several staircases, but still has a dizzying compulsion, and both the direction and cinematography are relentlessly atmospheric. Contains swearing, sex scenes and nudity. 🖵

Kevin Anderson *Nick Kaminsky* • Pamela Gidley *Jane Kessler* • Bill Pullman *Paul Kessler* • Kim Novak *Mrs Anderssen* • Graham Beckel *Sheriff Ricker* • Zach Grenier *Barnett Ralston IV* • Thomas Kopache *Dr Parker* ■ *Dir/Scr* Mike Figgis

Lies ★★
Erotic drama 1999 · S Kor · Colour · 111mins

It was the political undertones that caused Jang Jung Il's novel, *Tell Me a Lie*, to be banned in South Korea, but it's the scenes of sado-masochism and coprophilia that have earned this stark study of obsession its notoriety. The film opens with non-professionals Lee Sang Hyun and Kim Tae Yeon discussing the problems of playing their roles, and director Jang Sun Woo might have more profitably pursued this line of inquiry instead of graphically depicting the beatings given to a thirtysomething sculptor by his once-innocent teenage lover. Combining hand-held and digital video footage, this may be a provocative picture, but its content rather obscures its purpose. In Korean with English subtitles.

Lee Sang Hyun *J* • Kim Tae Yeon *Y* • Jeon Hye Jin *Woori* ■ *Dir* Jang Sun Woo • *Scr* Sun Woo Jang, from the novel *Tell Me a Lie* by Jang Jung Il

Lies before Kisses ★★ 15
Thriller 1991 · US · Colour · 93mins

That doyenne of the TV movie Jaclyn Smith here plays a wealthy woman whose idyllic marriage is shattered by a blackmail plot. Yes, we're in thriller territory, which means Smith gets to look harassed for the entire film while co-stars Ben Gazzara and Greg Evigan try to keep straight faces. It's too much like a soap opera to be taken seriously, and one can't help thinking

that Smith's career peaked back in the seventies when she was one of Charlie's Angels. Contains violence and swearing. 🖵

Jaclyn Smith *Elaine Sanders* • Ben Gazzara *Grant Sanders* • Nick Mancuso *Sonny Vincent* • Greg Evigan *Ross Sanders* ■ *Dir* Lou Antonio • *Scr* Ellen Weston

Lies My Father Told Me ★★★
Period drama 1975 · Can · Colour · 102mins

This screen version of writer Ted Allan's autobiographical opus about his early childhood is sympathetically directed by Czech émigré Jan Kadar. This Canadian film benefits hugely from a wonderfully warm performance from Yiddish actor Yossi Yadin as the young hero's grandfather, while Allan himself (who wrote the script) plays old Mr Baumgarten.

Yossi Yadin *Zaida* • Len Birman *Harry Herman* • Marilyn Lightstone *Annie Herman* • Jeffrey Lynas *David Herman* • Ted Allan *Mr Baumgarten* • Barbara Chilcott *Mrs Tannenbaum* ■ *Dir* Jan Kadar • *Scr* Ted Allan, from his autobiography

Lies of the Twins ★★★ 15
Thriller 1991 · US · Colour · 88mins

Director Tim Hunter has never succeeded in recapturing the style and chilling mood he brought to the Keanu Reeves/Dennis Hopper cult movie *River's Edge*, but this classy drama shows some promising signs of recovery. Based on Joyce Carol Oates's novel, it tells the story of a strange love triangle involving identical twins (both played by Aidan Quinn) and Isabella Rossellini, who can't choose between them. The talented leads ensure this is a cut above the average made-for-television fodder. 🖵

Aidan Quinn *Jonathan/James McEwan* • Isabella Rossellini *Rachel Marks* • Iman *Elle* • Claudia Christian *Felice* • John Pleshette *Gary* • Hurd Hatfield *Gil Selwyn* • Angela Paton *Mrs Shearer* ■ *Dir* Tim Hunter • *Scr* Mel Frohman, Wally Klenhard, from the novel by Joyce Carol Oates

Lt Robin Crusoe, USN ★★ U
Comedy adventure
1966 · US · Colour · 108mins

A pretty feeble Dick Van Dyke vehicle for Disney, ostensibly a comic update of the Robinson Crusoe story, made when the studio had seemingly lost touch with contemporary audiences. Fortunately, Disney bounced back, but movies like this one, featuring a chimp from outer space, didn't help. It's nice, though, to see the screen's Suzie Wong, Nancy Kwan, as Van Dyke's love interest. 🖵

Dick Van Dyke *Lieutenant Robin Crusoe* • Nancy Kwan *Wednesday* • Akim Tamiroff *Tanamashu* • Arthur Malet *Umbrella Man* • Tyler McVey *Captain* ■ *Dir* Byron Paul • *Scr* Bill Walsh, Donald DaGradi, from a story by Retlaw Yensid

The Lieutenant Wore Skirts ★★ U
Comedy 1956 · US · Colour · 98mins

Brash but lively fun, this is one of writer/director Frank Tashlin's lesser efforts – not on a par with *The Girl Can't Help It* and *Will Success Spoil*

Rock Hunter? It's role-reversal time with glamorous Sheree North joining the Air Force and hubbie Tom Ewell reluctantly tagging along to carry out the household chores as the only civilian male at her base camp in Honolulu. His various schemes to have her discharged form the basis of the often tasteless humour. Tom Ewell parodies his performance in *The Seven Year Itch*, playing a temptation scene with Rita Moreno.

Tom Ewell *Gregory Whitcomb* • Sheree North *Katy Whitcomb* • Rita Moreno *Sandra Gaxton* • Rick Jason *Captain Barney Sloan* • Les Tremayne *Henry Gaxton* • Alice Reinheart *Captain Briggs* • Gregory Walcott *Lieutenant Sweeney* ■ *Dir* Frank Tashlin • *Scr* Albert Beich, Frank Tashlin, from a story by Albert Beich

Life ★★ 15
Prison comedy 1999 · US · Colour · 115mins

It's sad to see Eddie Murphy so completely unfunny in this cross between *The Shawshank Redemption* and *The Odd Couple*. Street-smart Eddie and bank clerk Martin Lawrence are framed by a Deep South sheriff for murder, and sent to a Mississippi jail for life. Initially racist and brutal, the regime lightens up when warden Ned Beatty takes over and makes the pair his house-servants. The necessary chemistry between chalk-and-cheese Murphy and Lawrence is absent, so their banter is simply unpleasant rather than hilarious, while the prison comes across as a holiday camp housing whimsical toughies. Contains swearing and violence. 🖵

Eddie Murphy *Rayford Gibson* • Martin Lawrence *Claude Banks* • Obba Babatundé[Obba Babatunde] *Willie Long* • Ned Beatty *Dexter Wilkins* • Bernie Mac *Jangle Leg* • Miguel A Nuñez *Biscuit* • Clarence Williams III *Winston Hancock* • Bokeem Woodbine *Can't Get Right* ■ *Dir* Ted Demme • *Scr* Robert Ramsey, Matthew Stone

The Life and Death of Colonel Blimp ★★★★★ U
Historical drama
1943 · UK · Colour · 156mins

Winston Churchill ordered this film to be banned from exportation during the Second World War for giving the wrong impression of the British fighting man. Based on the comic-strip character created by David Low, Michael Powell and Emeric Pressburger's film does indeed take a pop at the complacency of the top brass, yet, thanks to Roger Livesey's astonishing performance in the lead, it is also a tribute to the more laudable peculiarities of the British character – honour, loyalty and a genius for making the most of a bad lot. Anton Walbrook also excels as Livesey's Prussian nemesis who becomes a lifelong friend, while a young Deborah Kerr makes her mark playing the three women in Livesey's life. One of British cinema's undisputed masterpieces. 🖵

Roger Livesey *Clive Candy* • Deborah Kerr *Edith Hunter/Barbara Wyn/Johnny Cannon* • Anton Walbrook *Theo Kretschmar-Schuldorff* • James McKechnie *Spud Wilson* • Neville Mapp *Stuffy Graves* • Roland Culver *Colonel Betteridge* • David Hutcheson *Hoppy* • Spencer Trevor *Period Blimp* • AE Matthews *President Of The Tribunal* ■ *Dir/Scr* Michael Powell, Emeric Pressburger

The Life and Extraordinary Adventures of Private Ivan Chonkin ★★★ 15

Drama
1994 · U-
K/ Fr/It/Cz Rep/Rus · Colour · 110mins

Jiří Menzel, one of the key figures in the Czech film miracle of the sixties, comes rather unstuck with this rough-and-ready adaptation of Russian writer Vladimir Voinovich's cult novel. A far cry from Menzel's slyly satirical masterpiece *Closely Observed Trains*, this tale set just before the Second World War is so broad in its comedy, it often borders on farce. Paying scant regard to the themes of repression and resistance and missing the opportunity for some colourful character comedy, Menzel opts for a hectic pace and vulgar caricature. It's played with great vigour and is hugely entertaining, but it's not one of the director's best. In Czech with English subtitles.

Gennadiy Nazarov *Ivan Chonkin* • Zoya Buryak *Nyura* • Vladimir Ilyin *Golubev* • Valeriy Dubrovin *Kilin* • Alexei Zharkov *Gladyshev* • Yuriy Dubrovin *Volkov* ■ *Dir* Jiří Menzel • *Scr* Zdenek Sverak, Vladimir Voinovich, from the novel by Vladimir Voinovich

Life and Nothing But ★★★★ PG

Drama
1989 · Fr · Colour · 130mins

Philippe Noiret gives one of his most memorable performances as a major in charge of the identification of shell-shocked survivors of the First World War. As well as helping the bereaved, the authorities have charged him with the task of finding a suitable Unknown Soldier. Shot in muted colours, the film's atmosphere of loss and despair is deeply moving. Sabine Azéma and Pascale Vignal also impress as they search for lovers who went missing in action. In French with English subtitles..

Philippe Noiret *Dellaplane* • Sabine Azéma *Irène* • Pascale Vignal *Alice* • Maurice Barrier *Mercadot* • François Perrot *Perrin* ■ *Dir* Bertrand Tavernier • *Scr* Bertrand Tavernier, Jean Cosmos • *Cinematographer* Bruno De Keyzer

The Life and Times of Grizzly Adams ★★ U

Adventure 1974 · US · Colour · 93mins

Dan Haggerty had once been an animal trainer, and it was his ease with bears that won him the role of Grizzly Adams in this wilderness adventure about a fur trapper who takes to the mountains when he is accused of a crime that he did not commit. Haggerty would later reprise the part in the popular TV series and the 1982 sequel, *The Capture of Grizzly Adams*.

Dan Haggerty *James "Grizzly" Adams* • Don Shanks *Indian Brave* • Lisa Jones *Young Peg* • Marjorie Harper *Adult Peg* ■ *Dir* Richard Friedenberg • *Scr* Larry Dobkin

The Life and Times of Judge Roy Bean ★★★ 15

Comedy western
1972 · US · Colour · 118mins

Very much a vehicle for star Paul Newman, who nevertheless seems a little ill at ease as the titular Mr Bean. Despite help from a notable supporting cast, director John Huston's rambling, incident-packed movie is overlong and actually rather dull, and not a patch on William Wyler's 1940 version, called *The Westerner*, with Oscar-winning Walter Brennan as the Hanging Judge. However, its wry humour and surreal moments can't help but endear this to most audiences. A word for Ava Gardner in her late prime as the embodiment of Lily Langtry, the object of the judge's affections; casting has seldom been more appropriate. Contains violence.

Paul Newman *Judge Roy Bean* • Jacqueline Bisset *Rose Bean* • Tab Hunter *Sam Dodd* • John Huston *Grizzly Adams* • Stacy Keach *Bad Bob* • Roddy McDowall *Frank Gass* • Anthony Perkins *Reverend Lasalle* • Victoria Principal *Marie Elena* • Ned Beatty *Tector Crites* ■ *Dir* John Huston • *Scr* John Milius

The Life and Times of Rosie the Riveter ★★★

Second World War documentary
1980 · US · Colour and BW · 60mins

Forget the sham nostalgia of *Swing Shift*, as there was nothing romantic about working in America's munitions factories during the Second World War. Millions of women answered the call in 1941 and, for many of them, it was their first experience of full-time employment. Yet, rather than being welcomed with open arms by their male colleagues, they were patronised, marginalised and harassed. By shrewdly contrasting morale-boosting newsreel footage with whistleblowing personal testimonies, Connie Field is able to expose the conditions to which the "Rosies" were subjected without detracting from the scale of their achievement or their pride in it.

Dir/Scr Connie Field

Life at the Top ★★

Drama 1965 · UK · BW · 117mins

Having ridden roughshod over the citizens of Warnley in *Room at the Top*, Laurence Harvey leaves Yorkshire in search of the beautiful south in this hugely disappointing sequel. The John Braine novel on which it is based admittedly lacks the bite and insight of its predecessor, but Mordecai Richler's adaptation and Ted Kotcheff's direction capture little of the spirit of swinging London, let alone the actions and emotions of a ruthlessly ambitious "angry young man". Harvey fails to rekindle the fire of his Oscar-nominated performance in the first film, and Jean Simmons is shamefully wasted as his put-upon wife.

Laurence Harvey *Joe Lampton* • Jean Simmons *Susan Lampton* • Honor Blackman *Norah Hauxley* • Michael Craig *Mark* • Donald Wolfit *Abe Brown* • Robert Morley *Tiffield* ■ *Dir* Ted Kotcheff • *Scr* Mordecai Richler, from the novel by John Braine

Life Begins ★★

Drama 1932 · US · BW · 72mins

A drama whose content covers the events of a night in a maternity ward. Among other mothers-about-to-be is lovely Loretta Young, as a woman serving a life sentence for murder. However it's excellent character actress Aline MacMahon as the head nurse, both controlling and compassionate, who holds the rather fragmentary action together. This is a respectable little film leans towards the downbeat. Suave Gilbert Roland and spunky Glenda Farrell, both generally associated with more lively material, are in the supporting cast.

Loretta Young *Grace Sutton* • Eric Linden *Jed Sutton* • Aline MacMahon *Miss Bowers* • Glenda Farrell *Florette* • Gilbert Roland *Tony* ■ *Dir* James Flood, Elliott Nugent • *Scr* Earl Baldwin, from the play by Mary M Axelson

Life Begins at 8.30 ★★

Comedy drama 1942 · US · BW · 84mins

Emlyn Williams's play *The Light of the Heart* is adapted by Nunnally Johnson and transposed from London to New York. Ida Lupino sacrifices herself to care for her father, alcoholic actor Monty Woolley, until dashing composer Cornel Wilde arrives on cue to nurse him through a production of *King Lear*. Everything really depends on the charisma of Woolley and his ability to be actorly, grand and tragic at the same time, a man described as "a god on stage but a rat off". Woolley acquits himself reasonably well, given an overwritten script and leaden direction from Irving Pichel.

Monty Woolley *Madden Thomas* • Ida Lupino *Kathi Thomas* • Cornel Wilde *Robert* • Sara Allgood *Mrs Lothian* • Melville Cooper *Barty* • J Edward Bromberg *Gordon* • William Demarest *Officer* ■ *Dir* Irving Pichel • *Scr* Nunnally Johnson, from the play *The Light Of The Heart* by Emlyn Williams

Life Begins at 40 ★★★

Comedy 1935 · US · BW · 73mins

A charmingly folksy Will Rogers vehicle in which the garrulous movie star-cum-philosopher is given acidic lines aplenty on the American way of life, though his well-practised lazy drawl seems deliberately to remove the sting in the barbs. This is one of his best pictures, with the star as a newspaper editor (Rogers contributed to a daily newspaper column and radio broadcasts in real life) bent on clearing an innocent young man's name. Director George Marshall manages to keep the sentiment at bay, and the film, while not a major work, is still very satisfying.

Will Rogers *Kenesaw H Clark* • Rochelle Hudson *Adele Anderson* • Richard Cromwell *Lee Austin* • George Barbier *Colonel Joseph Abercrombie* • Jane Darwell *Ida Harris* • Slim Summerville *T Watterson Meriwether* • Sterling Holloway *Chris* ■ *Dir* George Marshall • *Scr* Lamar Trotti, Robert Quillen, Dudley Nichols, William M Conselman, from the novel by Walter B Pitkin

Life Begins for Andy Hardy ★★★ U

Comedy drama 1941 · US · BW · 101mins

After ten episodes, MGM decided that Andy needed to grow up a bit. His country needed him but, no, he didn't go off to Guadalcanal, he has to decide between getting a job or going to college. He has a chat with dad and decides to go and "find himself" in New York, where he meets girlfriend Judy Garland. She drops into Andyworld for the third and last time, though MGM deleted her song from the final cut. Andy gets a job on a paltry salary, and Garland decides it's time to give dad a call. Working as a smart satire on big city business ethics, this is easily one of the best of the *Andy Hardy* series.

Mickey Rooney *Andy Hardy* • Lewis Stone *Judge James K Hardy* • Judy Garland *Betsy Booth* • Fay Holden *Mrs Emily Hardy* • Ann Rutherford *Polly Benedict* • Sara Haden *Aunt Milly* • Patricia Dane *Jennitt Hicks* • Ray McDonald *Jimmy Frobisher* ■ *Dir* George B Seitz • *Scr* Agnes Christine Johnston, from characters created by Aurania Rouverol

Life Begins in College ★★★

Comedy 1937 · US · BW · 90mins

Here's a lark: Joan Davis in her pre-*I Married Joan* TV heyday, co-starring with that blandest of crooners Tony Martin, in one of those college romps where all the students look old enough to draw pensions. The zany Ritz Brothers are along for the ride, helping the college football team in much the same way the Marx Brothers did in *Horse Feathers*. If you've only seen the Marx boys, give the Ritzes a whirl: they're from the same New York background, and they're just as funny, though forgotten today. Gloria Stuart is a charming ingénue, and Nat Pendleton gets much mileage as an Indian at college, though some may find it tasteless today.

Joan Davis *Inez* • Tony Martin *Band Leader* • Gloria Stuart *Janet O'Hara* • Fred Stone *Coach O'Hara* • Nat Pendleton *George Black* • Dick Baldwin *Bob Hayner* ■ *Dir* William A Seiter • *Scr* Karl Tunberg, Don Ettlinger, Sidney Kuller, Ray Golden, Samuel Pokrass, from the stories by Darrell Ware

Life for Ruth ★★

Drama 1962 · UK · BW · 91mins

Following *Sapphire* (on racism) and *Victim* (on homosexuality), Basil Dearden turned his attention to religious conviction in another of the social realism pictures he made at the turn of the sixties. The story of a father with deep-seated religious beliefs who refuses to consent to the blood transfusion that will save his daughter's life is often too contrived to make the weighty impact that Dearden intends. The nationwide scandal whipped up by doctor Patrick McGoohan spoils the intricately developed and delicately played feud between the girl's parents (Michael Craig and Janet Munro), but if medical melodramatics are your thing, you won't be disappointed.

Michael Craig *John Harris* • Patrick McGoohan *Dr Jim Brown* • Janet Munro *Pat Harris* • Paul Rogers *Hart Jacobs* • Megs Jenkins *Mrs Gordon* • John Barrie *Mr Gordon* • Malcolm Keen *Mr Harris Sr* • Lynne Taylor *Ruth Harris* ■ *Dir* Basil Dearden • *Scr* Janet Green, John McCormick, from the play *Walk in the Shadow* by Janet Green

Life in Danger ★★

Thriller 1959 · UK · BW · 62mins

As Alfred Hitchcock repeatedly demonstrated in films such as *The Wrong Man*, there is nothing more terrifying for the innocent than finding the evidence in a murder case irrefutably piling up against them while

all attempts at establishing an alibi founder on the most unlikely caprices of fate. This is the situation confronting baby-faced Derren Nesbitt in this passable low-budget drama, this is still an effective exploration of lynch-mob mentality, made even more alarming by its picturesque country setting.

Derren Nesbitt *The Man* • Julie Hopkins *Hazel Ashley* • Howard Marion-Crawford *Major Peters* • Victor Brooks *Tom Baldwin* • Jack Allen *Jack Ashley* • Christopher Witty *Johnny Ashley* • Carmel McSharry *Mrs Ashley* • Mary Manson *Jill Shadwell* ■ *Dir* Terry Bishop • *Scr* Malcolm Hulke, Eric Paice

Life in Emergency Ward 10
★ U

Drama	1959 · UK · BW · 82mins

Two years after taking the nation by storm, ITV's soap smash made it to the big screen. And what a disappointment it must have been. The characters find themselves caught up in the round of romantic entanglements and medical emergencies that were old hat at the time of MGM's *Dr Kildare* series. Michael Craig is dreadful as the Oxbridge General new boy playing fast and loose with the hearts of his patients and a colleague's neglected wife, and even the usually reliable Wilfrid Hyde White is off colour. 💬

Michael Craig *Dr Stephen Russell* • Wilfrid Hyde White *Professor Bourne-Evans* • Dorothy Alison *Sister Janet Fraser* • Glyn Owen *Dr Paddy O'Meara* • Rosemary Miller *Nurse Pat Roberts* • Charles Tingwell *Dr Alan Dawson* • Frederick Bartman *Dr Simon Forrester* • Joan Sims *Mrs Pryor* ■ *Dir* Robert Day • *Scr* Tessa Diamond, Hazel Adair, from the TV series

A Life in the Balance ★★★

Thriller	1955 · US · BW · 71mins

After *The Big Heat* and *The Wild One*, Lee Marvin was well established as a screen heavy when he made this thriller in Mexico City, playing the only American character on view. Based on a story by Georges Simenon, it's a portrait of life in the slums, spiced up by the odd Buñuelian moment and the hunt for a serial killer with a religious fixation, played by Marvin. Ricardo Montalban plays the wrongly accused man, whose son becomes involved with Marvin; Anne Bancroft is Montalban's love interest.

Ricardo Montalban *Antonio Gomez* • Anne Bancroft *Maria Ibinia* • Lee Marvin *The Murderer* • Jose Perez *Paco Gomez* • Rodolfo Acosta *Lt Fernando* ■ *Dir* Harry Horner • *Scr* Robert Presnell Jr, Leo Townsend, from a story by Georges Simenon

A Life in the Theater★★★

Drama	1993 · US · Colour · 90mins

As the veteran actor coming to the end of his career, that consummate professional Jack Lemmon savours every line of David Mamet's inspired dialogue in Gregory Mosher's version of Mamet's acclaimed play. It speaks volumes for Matthew Broderick that he stays the distance in his role as the promising newcomer who isn't simply prepared to listen and learn. The discussions on how certain scenes should be played are fascinating, but thanks to the passion of the playing

they never become inaccessible. A touch highbrow, perhaps, but you don't often get to see acting of this calibre.

Jack Lemmon *Robert* • Matthew Broderick *John* ■ *Dir* Gregory Mosher • *Scr* David Mamet, from his play

Life Is a Bed of Roses
★★★★ PG

Fantasy	1983 · Fr · Colour · 111mins

The perfectibility of human existence is the awesome theme of director Alain Resnais's magical fable, structured in three parts. The first covers Ruggero Raimondi's pre-First World War project to create a "temple to happiness". In the second part (set in the present), a seminar examines the feasibility of creating Utopia, and emphasises the important role of the imagination in improving daily life. Finally, a medieval struggle between good and evil is played out through the imaginations of some children. Vittorio Gassman, Raimondi and Geraldine Chaplin set up the proposition with perceptive dramatic ardour, but some may find this intellectual puzzle rather heavy going. In French with English subtitles.

Vittorio Gassman *Walter Guarini* • Ruggero Raimondi *Count Michel Forbek* • Geraldine Chaplin *Nora Winkle* • Fanny Ardant *Livia Cerasquier* • Sabine Azéma *Elisabeth Rousseau* ■ *Dir* Alain Resnais • *Scr* Jean Gruault

Life Is a Circus ★★ U

Comedy	1958 · UK · BW · 91mins

The Crazy Gang were a British institution: an informal collection of comedy acts brought together to enjoy a long career of comic surrealism. Their mix of zany slapstick, wacky doubletalk and sentimental humour may seem dated now but was massively popular in its day. This movie is a late entry in their canon, and it shows. The creaky storyline has the gang coming to the aid of an ailing circus and putting it back on its feet with some help from a magic lamp. Retired Crazy Chesney Allen appears briefly to sing *Underneath the Arches* with old partner Bud Flanagan.

Bud Flanagan [Dennis O'Keefe] *Bud* • Teddy Knox *Sebastian* • Jimmy Nervo *Cecil* • Jimmy Gold *Goldie* • Charlie Naughton *Charlie* • Eddie Gray *Eddie* • Chesney Allen *Ches* • Michael Holliday *Carl Rickenbeck* • Lionel Jeffries *Genie* • Shirley Eaton *Shirley Winter* ■ *Dir* Val Guest • *Scr* Val Guest, John Warren, Len Heath

Life Is a Long Quiet River
★★★★ 15

Satirical comedy	1988 · Fr · Colour · 87mins

A breaker of box-office records and the winner of a clutch of Césars (the French Oscars), this off-beat and often hilarious debut feature seems a prime candidate for a Hollywood makeover. That it has been spared such a fate is primarily due to the subtleties underlying the blackly comic surface, which would confound even the most astute American director. These acerbic asides on class, education and parental expectations superbly complement the broader humour about mixed-at-birth babies. However, like the river of the title, the initial sparkle and freshness gives way to rather too

much meandering. In French with English subtitles. 💬

Benoît Magimel *Momo* • Valerie Lalande *Bernadette* • Tara Romer *Million* • Jérôme Floc'h *Toc-Toc* • Sylvie Cubertafon *Ghislaine* • Emmanuel Cendrier *Pierre* ■ *Dir* Etienne Chatiliez • *Scr* Florence Quentin, Etienne Chatiliez

Life Is All You Get ★★★ 18

Drama	1998 · Ger · Colour · 115mins

Incalculably indebted to Ken Loach and Mike Leigh, this slice-of-life drama is an extended metaphor for Germany in the late Kohl era. Abandoning his blood kin, Jürgen Vogel opens his house to a disparate family of dispossessed outsiders, while enduring a romantic angst that represents the difficulty of attaining unification in the face of conflicting ideologies. Similar symbols abound – Vogel works in an abattoir, fears he may be HIV-positive, met his girlfriend in a riot and is best mates with a Buddy Holly impersonator. But this gritty, often blackly comic picture is never as dense or affected as it sounds. A German language film. Contains sex scenes.

Jürgen Vogel *Jan Nebel* • Christiane Paul *Vera* • Ricky Tomlinson *Buddy* • Armin Rohde *Harri* • Martina Gedeck *Lilo Nebel* ■ *Dir* Wolfgang Becker • *Scr* Wolfgang Becker, Tom Tykwer

Life Is Beautiful ★★★★ PG

Second World War comedy drama
1997 · It · Colour · 122mins

Is *Life Is Beautiful* a glowing tribute to humanity *in extremis*, or an ill-judged trivialisation of pitiless barbarism? Both verdicts have been passed on Roberto Benigni's multi-award-winning film. However, while the sensitivities of those supporting the latter view have to be taken into account, it would be wrong to deny that there were moments of simple joy and treasurable intimacy even at the height of the Holocaust. The opening section, charting Benigni's courtship of the imperious Nicoletta Braschi, is delightful. It also serves as a poignant backdrop for the nightmare to follow, as Benigni tries to shelter his son from the bitterest of truths. The result is courageous, humanistic film-making, but only a qualified success. In Italian with English subtitles. 💬 DVD

Roberto Benigni *Guido* • Nicoletta Braschi *Dora* • Giorgio Cantarini *Giosué* • Giustino Durano *Uncle* • Sergio Bustric *Ferruccio* • Marisa Paredes *Dora's mother* • Horst Buchholz *Dr Lessing* ■ *Dir* Roberto Benigni • *Scr* Roberto Benigni, Vincenzo Cerami, from their story • *Cinematographer* Tonino Delli Colli

Life Is Cheap... but Toilet Paper Is Expensive ★★★ 18

Comedy thriller	1990 · US · Colour · 86mins

Wayne Wang, the director of such light dramas as *Dim Sum*, *The Joy Luck Club* and *Smoke*, shows the darker side of his cinematic sensibilities in an off-beat, graphically violent Hong Kong tour of some really nasty tourist sights. Wang's world is one of on-screen defecation, severed hands and dead ducks, but the nastiness is made more palatable by some humorous touches (the film's courier hero is modelled on

Clint Eastwood's "Man with No Name"). Considerably less warm and intimate than the director's American movies, this is an attention-grabbing film that deliberately sets out to shock and provoke.

Chan Kim Wan *Duck Killer* • Spencer Nakasako *Man With No Name* • Victor Wong *Blind Man* • Cheng Kwan Min *Uncle Cheng* • Cora Miao *Money* • Chung Lam *Red Guard* • Allen Fong *Taxi Driver* ■ *Dir* Wayne Wang • *Scr* Spencer Nakasako

Life Is Sweet ★★★★★ 15

Black comedy	1990 · UK · Colour · 98mins

Writer/director Mike Leigh is on top form in this superbly observed satire on late Thatcherite Britain. At once wincingly funny and socially astute, the script touches on such issues as bulimia, free enterprise and social ambition without ever labouring the point. Alison Steadman and Jim Broadbent are outstanding as the thoroughly decent working-class couple, who watch their daughters develop with a mixture of pride and regret. Jane Horrocks does Essex slacker teen with great conviction, while Claire Skinner impresses as her tomboy sister, and Timothy Spall is sweatily repellent as a wannabe restaurateur. Contains swearing, sex scenes and nudity. 💬 DVD

Alison Steadman *Wendy* • Jim Broadbent *Andy* • Jane Horrocks *Nicola* • Claire Skinner *Natalie* • Stephen Rea *Patsy* • Timothy Spall *Aubrey* • David Thewlis *Nicola's lover* • Moya Brady *Paula* • David Neilson *Steve* ■ *Dir/Scr* Mike Leigh

A Life Less Ordinary ★★ 15

Romantic fantasy	1997 · UK · Colour · 99mins

Third time unlucky for the director, producer, writer and star quartet of *Shallow Grave* and *Trainspotting*. Desperate to regain his menial job in a giant American corporation, Ewan McGregor kidnaps his former boss's daughter, rich bitch Cameron Diaz. As the two go on the run, a pair of celestial cops (miscast Holly Hunter and Delroy Lindo) embark on a quest to make the unlikely duo fall in love. A fantasy-tinged romantic road movie that comes unstuck as the feel-good whimsy gets increasingly piled on. McGregor and Diaz are on top form, but this *Life* is a lot more ordinary than it should be. 💬 DVD

Ewan McGregor *Robert* • Cameron Diaz *Celine* • Holly Hunter *O'Reilly* • Delroy Lindo *Jackson* • Dan Hedaya *Gabriel* • Ian McNeice *Mayhew* • Frank Kanig *Ted* • Mel Winkler *Frank* ■ *Dir* Danny Boyle • *Scr* John Hodge

Life, Love and Tears ★★★

Drama	1984 · USSR · Colour

A respected actor/director of stage and screen, Nikolay Gubenko played a major role in the reorganisation of the Soviet cinema in the era of *perestroika*, first as a film-maker and then as minister of culture. While not as effective as his 1981 feature *On Vacation*, this is a solid enough example of the *bytovye*, a genre of films dealing with the darker side of everyday life that would have been unthinkable in less enlightened times. Although packed with allegorical references to Mikhail Gorbachev's removal of the old Communist guard, this fascinating drama is anything but an unquestioning tribute. In Russian with English subtitles..

Zhanna Bolotova • Elena Fadeeva ■ Dir/Scr Nikolay Gubenko

The Life of Emile Zola ★★★★

Biography 1937 · US · BW · 123mins

This is one of a remarkable series of Warner Bros melodramatic biopics whose central performances were once considered prime examples of cinematic acting. Like Lon Chaney before him, Mr Paul Muni (as he like to be billed), a former Yiddish Art Theater star, was never more convincing than when disguised with make-up and wigs, and here he makes a very creditable Zola in a distinguished movie that has only dated in its earnestness. Giving Muni a run for the acting honours, and collecting a best supporting actor Oscar, is Joseph Schildkraut as Captain Alfred Dreyfus. In its courageous exposé of anti-Semitism, this film can be seen today as part of the Warners social tradition, though interestingly the word "Jew" is never spoken. Both picture and screenplay also rightly won Oscars that year.

Paul Muni *Emile Zola* • Gale Sondergaard *Lucie Dreyfus* • Joseph Schildkraut *Captain Alfred Dreyfus* • Gloria Holden *Alexandrine Zola* • Donald Crisp *Maitre Labori* • Erin O'Brien-Moore *Nana* • Robert Barrat *Major Walsin-Esterhazy* ■ Dir William Dieterle • Scr Norman Reilly Raine, Heinz Herald, Geza Herczeg

A Life of Her Own ★★

Drama 1950 · US · BW · 108mins

Lana Turner, appropriately cast as an innocent from the Midwest who becomes a top-flight fashion model, suffers nobly in this archetypal "woman's magazine" tearjerker that can hardly be called original. George Cukor directs from a script by Isobel Lennart that has Turner in love with married man Ray Milland, whose wife is crippled. The familiar territory is also inhabited by Tom Ewell as the model agency head, Louis Calhern as Milland's friend and lawyer and, best of all, Ann Dvorak as a model for whom things go badly wrong – as does the movie.

Lana Turner *Lily Brannel James* • Ray Milland *Steve Harleigh* • Tom Ewell *Tom Caraway* • Louis Calhern *Jim Leversoe* • Ann Dvorak *Mary Ashlon* • Barry Sullivan *Lee Gorrance* • Margaret Phillips *Nora Harleigh* • Jean Hagen *Maggie Collins* ■ Dir George Cukor • Scr Isobel Lennart, from the story *Abiding Vision* by Rebecca West

The Life of Oharu ★★★★★ PG

Period melodrama 1952 · Jap · BW · 130mins

One of the great works from the greatest of Japanese directors, this episodic, tragic melodrama traces the life of a woman living under the severe moral code of the Genroku era in late17th-century Japan. Played by Kinuyo Tanaka (who appeared in 11 Mizoguchi films and later became the first woman to direct a Japanese film), Oharu suffers a catalogue of injustices, most of them arbitrary and accidental,

others of her own doing. The film, which won the Silver Lion at Venice in 1952, is informed by a Buddhist view of the world that acknowledges the impermanence of everything, especially happiness. Shot in long, beautiful takes, it is more devastating than depressing. In Japanese with English subtitles..

Kinuyo Tanaka *Oharu* • Ichiro Sugai *Father* • Tsuki Matsura *Mother* • Toshiro Mifune *Katsunosuke* • Tashiaki Konoe *Lord Matsudaira* • Hisaka Yamane *Lady Matsudaira* ■ Dir Kenji Mizoguchi • Scr Yoda Yoshikata, Kenji Mizoguchi • Cinematographer Yoshimi Hirano

The Life of Stuff ★★

Drama 1997 · UK · Colour · 90mins

A strong British cast have a nasty night out, in a shallow, static study of a Glasgow criminal holding a party for select friends and colleagues to celebrate the demise of a rival boss. Jason Flemyng, Ciaran Hinds and Ewen Bremner try their hardest, but the characters aren't fleshed-out and the incidents are so meaningless that they soon lose your attention. Writer/director Simon Donald's sour story (adapted from his stage play) isn't sharp, creative or particularly interesting and aside from some fine photography, you wonder why this received a cinema conversion.

Ewen Bremner *Fraser* • Liam Cunningham *Alec* • Jason Flemyng *Dobie* • Ciaran Hinds *Arboghast* • Stuart McQuarrie *Fraser* ■ Dir Simon Donald • Scr Simon Donald, from his play

Life of the Party: the Pamela Harriman Story ★

Biographical drama 1998 · US · Colour

Ann-Margret embodies this rags-to-power story based on the book by Christopher Ogden. Recounting the tempestuous life of Pamela Digby, who seduced and married wealthy, powerful men on both sides of the Atlantic, it sees her eventually propelled into the innermost circles of Democratic party politics and a position as US Ambassador to France. Ineptly written and disjointed, this shallow TV film only serves to trivialise its subject, and even Ann-Margret's game performance fails to bring it to life.

Ann-Margret *Pamela Harriman* • Mitchell Ryan *Averell Harriman* • David Dukes *Leland Hayworth* • Joan Severance *Barbara "Babe" Paley* • Cynthia Harris *Kathleen* ■ Dir Waris Hussein • Scr Lisa Friedman Bloch, Kathy Kirtland Silverman, from the biography by Christopher Ogden

Life on a String ★★★★ PG

Drama 1991 · Chi/Ger/UK · Colour · 102mins

Alighting on such themes as spirituality and sensuality, discipline and independence, salvation and delusion, this is Chen Kaige's least regarded picture. Yet, his almost avant-garde use of the forbidding rural landscape and the haunting soundtrack delicately underscores the enigmatic story of the musician and his disciple who overcome physical blindness to master their art. As the old man clinging to his mentor's promise that his sight will be restored when he breaks the 1000th string on his sanxian, Liu Zhongyuan

displays an affecting trust that contrasts sharply with the impetuosity of Huang Lei, whose love for a village girl shatters their partnership. In Mandarin with English subtitles. 📼

Liu Zhongyuan *The Old Master* • Huang Lei *Shitou* • Xu Qing *Lanxiu* ■ Dir Chen Kaige • Scr Chen Kaige, from a short story by Shi Tiesheng

Life Stinks ★ PG

Comedy 1991 · US · Colour · 91mins

The title tells all: the film stinks, as Mel Brooks tries to be Charlie Chaplin and fails miserably. As billionaire Goddard Bolt, erecting a business monument to himself even if it means getting rid of a shantytown of vagrants, he's as callous and crass as expected. Then he succumbs to a bet that he can't live as a derelict and the plot itself falls apart while Brooks babbles for our sympathy as a put-upon everyman. The hospital scenes have enough bad-taste humour to remind us of the witty Brooks, and Lesley Ann Warren is poignant as a bag lady. Yet the film proves it takes genius to make down-and-outs comic and Chaplin wasn't available. Contains swearing and drug abuse. 📼

Mel Brooks *Goddard Bolt* • Lesley Ann Warren *Molly* • Jeffrey Tambor *Vance Crasswell* • Stuart Pankin *Pritchard* • Howard Morris *Sailor* • Rudy De Luca *J Paul Getty* • Teddy Wilson *Fumes* • Michael Ensign *Knowles* • Matthew Faison *Stevens* • Billy Barty *Willy* • Brian Thompson *Mean Victor* • Raymond O'Connor *Yo* • Carmine Caridi *Flophouse Owner* • Sammy Shore *Reverend At Wedding* ■ Dir Mel Brooks • Scr Mel Brooks, Rudy De Luca, Steve Haberman, from a story by Ron Clark, Mel Brooks, Rudy De Luca, Steve Haberman

Life with Father ★★★★

Comedy 1947 · US · Colour · 110mins

Warner Bros's movie version of the long-running Broadway hit is a rare charmer, beautifully directed by *Casablanca's* Michael Curtiz. If the whole seems slight and rather deliberately echoes MGM's 1944 hit *Meet Me in St Louis*, well, that's no bad thing, and Warners' design is every bit the equal of Metro's. Watch for star-to-be Elizabeth Taylor (on loan to Warner Bros from MGM and looking radiant) and lovely support from Edmund Gwenn and ZaSu Pitts. Author Clarence Day Jr couldn't have wished for a better screen rendering of his reminiscences of family life in late-19th century New York.

William Powell *Clarence Day Sr* • Irene Dunne *Vinnie Day* • Elizabeth Taylor *Mary* • ZaSu Pitts *Cora* • Edmund Gwenn *Rev Dr Lloyd* • Jimmy Lydon [James Lydon] *Clarence Day Jr* • Martin Milner *John* • Derek Scott *Harlan* • Johnny Calkins *Whitney* • Emma Dunn *Margaret* ■ Dir Michael Curtiz • Scr Donald Ogden Stewart, from the play by Howard Lindsay, Russel Crouse, from the book by Clarence Day Jr

Life with Mikey ★★★ PG

Comedy 1993 · US · Colour · 87mins

Released straight to video in this country as *Give Me a Break*, this is a perfect vehicle for the flustered charms of star Michael J Fox. After his experiences in *Family Ties*, he's on to every trick as the thespian who turns agent after the public stop finding him

cute. What makes his performance particularly good is the grace with which he accepts that he's been set up to lose every scene to Christina Vidal, as the little urchin he steers to stardom. While their relationship is great fun to watch, the jabs at fame and advertising are delivered without any real conviction. 📼

Michael J Fox *Michael Chapman* • Christina Vidal *Angie Vega* • Nathan Lane *Ed Chapman* • Cyndi Lauper *Geena Briganti* • David Krumholtz *Barry Corman* • Christine Baranski *Carol* ■ Dir James Lapine • Scr Marc Lawrence

Life with the Lyons ★★ U

Comedy 1953 · UK · BW · 80mins

Based on the second long-running radio show made in Britain by the American stars Ben Lyon and Bebe Daniels (after *Hi Gang!* in 1941), this is a lightweight domestic comedy whose cosy appeal has been attenuated by the passage of time. The characters familiar to millions in the mid-fifties are total strangers to most viewers now, and they lack the spark and credibility of the other film family of the time, the Huggetts. As neither star had appeared in a movie in over a decade, it is perhaps not surprising that their playing looks laboured, although the story about a reluctant landlord and the marshmallow script do not help the cause.

Bebe Daniels *Bebe* • Ben Lyon *Ben* • Barbara Lyon *Barbara* • Richard Lyon *Richard* • Horace Percival *Mr Wimple* • Molly Weir *Aggie* ■ Dir Val Guest • Scr Robert Dunbar, Val Guest, from the radio series by Bebe Daniels, Bob Block, Bill Harding

Lifeboat ★★★★ PG

Wartime drama 1944 · US · BW · 96mins

Alfred Hitchcock's tense Second World War drama has the distinction of being shot on what looks like the smallest ever film set. The action takes place exclusively on board a lifeboat after a liner is torpedoed by a Nazi sub. As so often in Hitchcock's films, the suspense lies not in the audience being kept in the dark about the identity of the villain, but in making us watch and wait while the characters find it out for themselves. Tallulah Bankhead is the pick of an exceptional cast, but it's all about Hitch's ability to create, shatter and re-create tension until our nerves are frayed. 📼

Tallulah Bankhead *Connie Porter* • William Bendix *Gus* • Walter Slezak *U-boat captain* • Mary Anderson *Alice* • John Hodiak *Kovak* • Henry Hull *Rittenhouse* • Heather Angel *Mrs Higgins* • Hume Cronyn *Stanley Garrett* • Canada Lee *Joe* ■ Dir Alfred Hitchcock • Scr Jo Swerling, from the story by John Steinbeck

Lifebreath ★★★ 18

Drama 1997 · US · Colour · 86mins

Beverly Hills 90210 star Luke Perry gives his best performance to date in this suspenseful TV movie that introduces ethical and moral dilemmas to the conventions of the "disease of the week" genre. He stars as a Manhattan schoolteacher who considers murdering estate agent Gia Carides (star of *Strictly Ballroom*) to ensure that his critically ill wife gets the lung transplant she desperately needs to prevent her from dying of cystic fibrosis. It is smartly scripted, and the very real portrayal of the symptoms of cystic fibrosis and the distress they cause packs an enormous punch, even as the clever twists and turns mount up. Contains swearing, violence and sex scenes. ⌨

Luke Perry *Marty Devoe* • Francie Swift *Chrystie Devoe* • Gia Carides *Gale Pullman* • Gary Basaraba *John* ■ *Dir* PJ Posner • *Scr* PJ Posner, Joel Posner

Lifeforce ★ 18

Science-fiction horror
1985 · US · Colour · 97mins

It's hard to believe that Tobe Hooper, director of the influential *The Texas Chain Saw Massacre*, came up with this laughably bad adaptation of Colin Wilson's *The Space Vampires*. Steve Railsback stars as the surviving astronaut from a team that discovers parasitic energy suckers on an invasion course for Earth when they investigate a strange craft lurking in the tail of Halley's Comet. A few interesting special effects help mask the appalling dialogue in the script. Rather than the homage to vintage Hammer horror that Hooper wanted to make, the daft result is more a cruel parody. Contains violence, swearing and nudity. ⌨

Steve Railsback *Colonel Tom Carlsen* • Peter Firth *Colonel Colin Caine* • Frank Finlay *Dr Hans Fallada* • Mathilda May *Space Girl* • Patrick Stewart *Dr Armstrong* • Michael Gothard *Bukovsky* • Nicholas Ball *Derebridge* ■ *Dir* Tobe Hooper • *Scr* Dan O'Bannon, Don Jakoby, from the novel *The Space Vampires* by Colin Wilson

Lifeform ★★

Science-fiction action
1996 · US · Colour · 90mins

A low-budget sci-fi movie that has its rewards, but falls just short of being a good movie. The emphasis here is not on the special effects, but an intriguing script that doesn't telegraph the plot twists. Essentially, the movie is a take on *Alien*, with an alien loose in a military compound, and the scientists and soldiers on the base trying to stop the menace. The scientists are intelligent and, for once, the military are portrayed in a sympathetic light. Much fun comes with unexpected situations forcing the viewer to reassess what he has just seen. Overall cheap production values, and a truly bad ending stop this from reaching sleeper status.

Cotter Smith *Case Montgomery* • Deirdre O'Connell *Dr Gracia Scott* • Ryan Phillippe *Private Ryan* • Raoul O'Connell *Private Jeffers* ■ *Dir/Scr* Mark H Baker

Lifeguard ★★ 15

Drama
1976 · US · Colour · 92mins

Sam Elliott is the wrong side of 30 and he's still a lifeguard on a California beach. What on earth is he gonna do when he grows up? This study of American beach culture is admittedly streets ahead of, say, the old *Beach Party* movies with Frankie Avalon and Annette Funicello, but it pales beside John Milius's *Big Wednesday*, made

the same year. Elliott is the sort of knucklehead you want to slap, though his girlfriend Anne Archer is urging him to do something really rewarding, like sell second-hand cars, which in California is almost a religious vocation. ⌨

Sam Elliott *Rick Carlson* • Anne Archer *Cathy* • Stephen Young *Larry* • Parker Stevenson *Chris* • Kathleen Quinlan *Wendy* • Steve Burns *Machine Gun* • Sharon Weber *Tina* ■ *Dir* Daniel Petrie • *Scr* Ron Koslow

Lifeline to Victory ★★★

Second World War drama 1993 · Can · Colour

Directed by Eric Till, one of Canada's leading English-language film-makers, and made to commemorate the 50th anniversary of the Battle of the Atlantic, this lavish TV movie makes light of its stock situations and over-familiar characters to pay a handsome tribute to the Royal Canadian Navy. Loosely based on actual events, the film follows the ramshackle corvette *Fireweed* and its rookie crew on their convoy escort to Scotland. The romantic interludes and feuds with the Admiralty brass are something of a disappointment after the well staged action scenes, but there's a rousing sea rescue to round things off.

Michael Riley *Paul Devereaux* • Simon Reynolds *McNaughton* • Michael Hogan *Ted Ryan* • Henry Czerny *Coxswain* • Elizabeth Marmur *Ann Conwell* • David Hemblen *Cmdr Oldbest* ■ *Dir* Eric Till • *Scr* Tony Sheer

Lifepod ★★★ 15

Science-fiction drama
1993 · US · Colour · 84mins

Inspired by Alfred Hitchcock's *Lifeboat*, actor-turned-director Ron Silver's "stranded in space" saga is a great example of stylish economical film-making. Exciting, fast-moving and containing many memorable twists, Silver uses claustrophobic tricks to great advantage in relating his tale of survivors escaping aboard an emergency spacepod when their Venusian cruiser explodes. A neat mix of Agatha Christie whodunit and *Alien* paranoia. ⌨

Ron Silver *Miles Terman* • Robert Loggia *Daniel Banks* • Adam Storke *Kane* • Jessica Tuck *Clair* • Ed Gale *Q-Three* • Kelli Williams *Rena* • Stan Shaw *Parker* • CCH Pounder *Lieutenant Janna Mayvene* ■ *Dir* Ron Silver • *Scr* M Jay Roach, Pen Densham, from a story by Jo Swerling, from the film *Lifeboat*

Lifespan ★★★ 18

Science-fiction
1975 · US/Neth · Colour · 77mins

Stitching together elements from the Faust and Frankenstein stories, this shoestring thriller posits an intriguing contrast between humanitarian hopes for the elimination of disease and the sinister medical experimentation undertaken by the Nazis. Representing enlightened science is Hiram Keller, who discovers that a dead colleague may have concocted an elixir for eternal life, while the forces of darkness summon up Klaus Kinski, as the deranged industrialist sponsoring the unnatural project. Writer/director Alexander Whitelaw makes atmospheric use of both his Amsterdam locations and the antiseptic interiors that contrast so

tellingly with the gloriously Gothic labs of expressionist horror. ⌨

Hiram Keller *Dr Ben Land* • Tina Aumont *Anna* • Klaus Kinski *Nicholas Ulrich* ■ *Dir* Alexander Whitelaw • *Scr* Alexander Whitelaw, Judith Rascoe, Alva Ruben

The Lift ★★★ 15

Science-fiction 1983 · Neth · Colour · 94mins

A lift with a mind of its own is the baffling culprit in a series of bizarre office block "accidents" in this rare example of Dutch horror exploitation. Maintenance man Huub Stapel can't find any mechanical fault and, in between soap opera interludes of domestic strife, which greatly diffuse the claustrophobic suspense, eventually uncovers the alarming – if silly – truth. But writer/director Dick Maas does extract every ounce of fear and menace in the final confrontation between man and machine, as the blackened shaft area comes into its own as a credibly frightening setting and the early longueurs are forgotten. Appalling dubbing aside, Maas does manage to shock without a single drop of blood being spilt. Dutch dialogue dubbed into English.. ⌨

Huub Stapel *Felix Adelbaar* • Willeke Van Ammelrooy *Mieke de Beer* • Josine Van Dalsum *Saskia Adelaar* • Piet Romer *Manager* ■ *Dir/Scr* Dick Maas

Lift to the Scaffold
★★★★ PG

Crime thriller 1957 · Fr · BW · 87mins

After several years as an assistant to the marine explorer and film-maker Jacques Cousteau, Louis Malle made his feature directorial debut with this assured thriller, which recalled both the poetic realism of Marcel Carné and the brooding menace of American *films noirs*. In addition to making a star of Jeanne Moreau and giving a generation a phobia about elevators, the film also had a considerable influence on the nascent French New Wave through the moody naturalism of Henri Decaë's black-and-white photography. The sublime jazz score was improvised by Miles Davis and a band of European musicians while the film played on a screen before them. In French with English subtitles. ⌨

Jeanne Moreau *Florence Carala* • Maurice Ronet *Julien Tavernier* • Georges Poujouly *Louis* • Yori Bertin *Veronique* • Jean Wall *Simon Carala* ■ *Dir* Louis Malle • *Scr* Louis Malle, from the novel *L'Ascenseur pour l'Echafaud* by Noël Calef

The Light across the Street
★★★

Drama 1956 · Fr · BW · 98mins

Brigitte Bardot was still four films away from her breakthrough in *And God Created Woman*, but she was already creating a stir on the art-house circuit with her smouldering performance in Georges Lacombe's cheerless tale of repressed passion. However, the real acting here comes from Raymond Pellegrin, as the disabled husband who is prevented from consummating the marriage and has to watch with growing indignation as his bride succumbs to the muscular charms of garage owner, Roger Pigaut. With the

fetid atmosphere recalling *The Postman Always Rings Twice*, this may be *noir lite*, but is compelling nonetheless. In French with English subtitles.

Brigitte Bardot *Olivia* • Raymond Pellegrin *Marceau* • Roger Pigaut *Pietri* • Claude Romain *Barbette* ■ *Dir* Georges Lacombe • *Scr* Louis Chavance, René Masson, René Lefèvre, from the story *La Lumière d'en Face* by Jean-Claude Aurel

The Light at the Edge of the World ★

Adventure
1971 · US/Sp/Lich · Colour · 125mins

Some movies are just so awful you wonder how they could have been conceived in the first place. This overlong adaptation of a Jules Verne novel about a lighthouse that is beset by pirates is pathetic, geared for neither adults nor children, and has grievous trouble finding both style and tone. Producer/star Kirk Douglas, villain Yul Brynner and female lead Samantha Eggar look uncomfortable, director Kevin Billington seems out of his depth, and the dubbing of the foreign supporting players rings awkwardly in the ears. Contains violence and some swearing.

Kirk Douglas *Will Denton* • Yul Brynner *Jonathan Kongre* • Samantha Eggar *Arabella* • Jean-Claude Drouot *Virgilio* • Fernando Rey *Captain Moriz* • Renato Salvatori *Montefiore* ■ *Dir* Kevin Billington • *Scr* Tom Rowe, Rachel Billington, Bertha Dominguez, from the novel by Jules Verne

The Light in the Forest
★★★ U

Period drama 1958 · US · Colour · 88mins

This intriguing period drama, which originated on Disney's *The Wonderful World of Color* series, should appeal to older children. James MacArthur stars as a white boy who, having been captured and raised by the Delaware Indians, is forced to go and live with a racist guardian under the terms of a 1764 peace treaty. Wendell Corey is utterly loathsome in an unusually unsympathetic role, while Carol Lynley makes an impressive film debut as his kindly servant. ⌨

James MacArthur *Johnny Butler/True Son* • Carol Lynley *Shenandoe* • Fess Parker *Del Hardy* • Wendell Corey *Wilse Owens* • Joanne Dru *Milly Elder* • Jessica Tandy *Myra Butler* • Joseph Calleia *Chief Cuyloga* • John McIntire *John Elder* ■ *Dir* Herschel Daugherty • *Scr* Lawrence Edward Watkin, from a novel by Conrad Richter

Light in the Piazza ★★★

Drama 1962 · US · Colour · 101mins

A splendid late MGM melodrama sumptuously produced in Europe, largely on Italian locations, by genius Arthur Freed. It's based on a novel by Elizabeth Spencer about a mother caring for her mentally disabled daughter. As the daughter, Yvette Mimeux gives a performance of great skill and subtlety under the direction of the still under-rated British cameraman-turned-director Guy Green, and Olivia de Havilland is perfectly cast as the mother. George Hamilton makes a suave suitor, but the film's delicate

tone is disrupted by the silly antics of Rossano Brazzi and Barry Sullivan.

Olivia de Havilland *Margaret Johnson* • Rossano Brazzi *Signor Naccarelli* • Yvette Mimieux *Clara Johnson* • George Hamilton *Farizio Naccarelli* • Barry Sullivan *Noel Johnson* • Isabel Dean *Miss Hawtree* ■ *Dir* Guy Green • *Scr* Julius J Epstein, from the novel by Elizabeth Spencer

Light of Day ★★ PG

Drama　　　　　1987 · US · Colour · 102mins

Writer/director Paul Schrader's attempt to graft his favourite theme of moral redemption on to a story of rock 'n' roll gets hopelessly bogged down in the sort of soul-searching and family strife one finds in Arthur Miller or Eugene O'Neill plays. To make things worse, Michael J Fox is badly miscast as a factory worker-cum-rock singer who must console a confused sister (Joan Jett), a religous mother (Gena Rowlands) and a father who has given up on all of them. Set in small-time, working-class Cleveland, the film stumbles towards that most wretched of movie clichés – the terminal disease – which provokes even more soul-searching. The title song is by Bruce Springsteen. Contains some swearing.

Michael J Fox *Joe Rasnick* • Gena Rowlands *Jeanette Rasnick* • Joan Jett *Patti Rasnick* • Michael McKean *Bu Montgomery* • Thomas G Waites *Smittie* • Cherry Jones *Cindy Montgomery* • Michael Dolan *Gene Bodine* • Paul J Harkins *Billy Tettore* • Billy Sullivan [Billy L Sullivan] *Benji Rasnick* • Jason Miller *Benjamin Rasnick* • Tom Irwin *Reverend John Ansley* ■ *Dir/Scr* Paul Schrader

Light Sleeper ★★★ 15

Thriller　　　　　1991 · US · Colour · 98mins

One of director Paul Schrader's more successful examinations of down-and-outs on society's fringe, this film features a topnotch performance from Willem Dafoe as a middle-league, middle-aged drug supplier who's come to a crossroads in his life. The "fun" era of designer drugs is over, crack and the cops have moved into his Manhattan manor, and he wants out. So, too, does his upper-class boss Susan Sarandon (equally excellent) to whom he looks to solve his career dilemma. Violent redemption awaits both well-drawn characters in Schrader's leisurely paced but ultimately rewarding study of terminal addiction in all its many forms. Contains swearing, violence, sex scenes and nudity. ▭

Willem Dafoe *John LeTour* • Susan Sarandon *Ann* • Dana Delany *Marianne* • David Clennon *Robert* • Mary Beth Hurt *Teresa Aranow* • Victor Garber *Tis* • Jane Adams *Randi* ■ *Dir/ Scr* Paul Schrader

The Light That Failed ★★★

Drama　　　　　1939 · US · BW · 87mins

Ronald Colman is impeccably cast as the former soldier-turned-artist who, going blind from a war wound, is determined to finish his masterpiece – a portrait of his turbulent cockney model (Ida Lupino). Rudyard Kipling's story had already been filmed by Pathé in 1916 and Paramount in 1923, starring Robert Edeson and Percy Marmont respectively. Under the intelligent and expert direction of

William A Wellman, an excellent supporting cast, headed by Walter Huston as Colman's friend, reflects the quality of the leading performances and Robert Carson's screenplay, to make for a moving drama, albeit one with few surprises.

Ronald Colman *Dick Heldar* • Walter Huston *Terpenhow* • Muriel Angelus *Maisie* • Ida Lupino *Bessie Broke* • Dudley Digges *The Nilghai* • Ernest Cossart *Beeton* ■ *Dir* William A Wellman • *Scr* Robert Carson, from the story by Rudyard Kipling

Light Up the Sky ★ PG

Second World War comedy drama
1960 · UK · BW · 85mins

A brief résumé should be enough to dissuade anyone from this hackneyed theatrical hand-me-down (not that it convinced the cast!). Victor Maddern heads a plane-spotting detail during the Second World War. His crew comprises Sydney Tafler who's mourning his son, Harry Locke who's short of money, lovesick Johnny Briggs and Tommy Steele, who, in addition to going AWOL to do music-hall turns with Benny Hill, has made his mistress pregnant. If that isn't enough, Maddern also has to deal with dippy NCO Ian Carmichael. Firmly in the tradition of similar plays-turned-films *Journey's End* and *Crest of the Wave*, with little to relieve the incessant chat. ▭

Ian Carmichael *Lieutenant Ogleby* • Tommy Steele *Eric McCaffey* • Benny Hill *Syd McCaffey* • Sydney Tafler *Ted Green* • Victor Maddern *Lance Bombardier Tomlinson* • Harry Locke *Roland Kenyon* • Johnny Briggs *Leslie Smith* • Cyril Smith *"Spinner" Rice* • Dick Emery *Harry The Driver* • Cardew Robinson *Compere* • Sheila Hancock *Theatre Act* ■ *Dir* Lewis Gilbert • *Scr* Vernon Harris, from the play *Touch It Light* by Robert Storey

Light Years ★★

Animated science-fiction
1988 · Fr · Colour · 83mins

This space fantasy from French director René Laloux, creator of the 1973 cult classic *Fantastic Planet*, is a disappointingly weak attempt to blend adult science-fiction with children's fables. The *Heavy Metal* magazine-inspired animation is highly stylised and stimulatingly imaginative, but this tale of a young hero defending a Utopian land from destruction is often too static and laboriously talky to engage young adults fully. Miramax's Harvey Weinstein directs this American version of the French original was scripted by none other than sci-fi literature alumnus Isaac Asimov and features such stellar voices as Christopher Plummer and Glenn Close.

Glenn Close *Ambisextra* • Christopher Plummer *Metamorphis* • Earl Hammond *Blaminhor* • Jennifer Grey *Airelle* • John Shea *Sylvain* • Bridget Fonda *Historian/Head* ■ *Dir* René Laloux • *Scr* Raphael Cluzel, Isaac Asimov (American version), from the novel *Robots Against Gandahar* by Jean-Pierre Andrevan, adapted by René Laloux

The Lighthorsemen ★★★ PG

First World War drama
1987 · Ausl · Colour · 110mins

The misuse of Australian soldiers by their British commanders during the First World War had been well chronicled by Peter Weir in *Gallipoli*.

But Simon Wincer adds a new dimension to the cannon-fodder theme by examining the horrors endured by the horses roped into service in the Middle East during the same conflict. The cavalry charge essential to Anthony Andrews's cunning plan to seize a Turkish water supply is both exhilarating and disturbing, as classical and modern warfare clash head on. As you would expect from the director of *Phar Lap* and *Free Willy*, Wincer makes the most of both animals and scenery. Contains swearing.

Peter Phelps *Dave Mitchell* • Tony Bonner *Colonel Bourchier* • Gary Sweet *Frank* • John Walton *Tas* • Tim McKenzie *Chiller* • Jon Blake *Scotty* • Sigrid Thornton *Anne* • Anthony Andrews *Major Meinertzhagen* ■ *Dir* Simon Wincer • *Scr* Ian Jones

Lightning in a Bottle ★★

Drama　　　　　1992 · US · Colour

Amnesia has always been among the film-maker's favourite standbys. Here it's exploited by director Jeff Kwitny in a TV movie designed to give Lynda Carter the opportunity to show that even Wonder Woman is capable of some good old-fashioned suffering. Devoid of recollection on awakening from a crippling car crash, Carter slowly begins to remember the events that might have made her responsible for the deaths of a man and a young boy. Kwitny leaks the information steadily and there's decent support from Dee Wallace Stone and Martin Kove, but this has been done many times (and better) elsewhere. Contains some swearing.

Lynda Carter *Charlotte Furber* • Dee Wallace Stone *Jean Markley* • Martin Kove *Duane Furber* • Matt McCoy *Troy Hoskins* • Stuart Whitman *Jonah Otterman* • Margaret Avery *Dr Sierheed* ■ *Dir* Jeff Kwitny • *Scr* Johnnie Lindsell

Lightning Jack ★★ PG

Comedy western
1994 · Ausl · Colour · 93mins

Paul Hogan was able to raise the funds to make this spoof western via the Australian Stock Exchange. If only he could have raised some laughs as well! There's very little return on the gag investment in this only moderately entertaining comedy about a legendary gunslinger teaching the tricks of his trade to mute misfit and aspiring outlaw Cuba Gooding Jr, hinting at the talents that would win him an Oscar for *Jerry Maguire*. People shoot themselves in the foot, wear specs for target practice and escape from Indians in outlandish fashion in a failed farce that boasts a guest spot from the Who lead singer Roger Daltrey. Contains some violence and swearing. ▭

Paul Hogan *Lightning Jack Kane* • Cuba Gooding Jr *Ben Doyle* • Beverly D'Angelo *Lana* • Kamala Dawson *Pilar* • Pat Hingle *Marshall Kurtz* • Richard Riehle *Reporter* • Frank McRae *Mr Doyle* • Roger Daltrey *John T Coles* • LQ Jones *Local sheriff* ■ *Dir* Simon Wincer • *Scr* Paul Hogan

Lightning Strikes Twice ★★

Mystery drama　　　　1951 · US · BW · 91mins

A turgid Warner Bros melodrama from director King Vidor, who has trouble sorting out the plot. Richard Todd, in

one of his first Hollywood movies, is cleared of murdering his wife but is still seen as guilty by his friends and neighbours, so he sets out to find the real killer with the help of new love Ruth Roman. It's neither *film noir* nor romance; Todd is excellent, as are Zachary Scott and Mercedes McCambridge, but Roman offers little in the crucial co-starring role. Interesting, but confused and ultimately rather unlikeable.

Richard Todd *Richard Trevelyan* • Ruth Roman *Shelley Carnes* • Mercedes McCambridge *Liza McStringer* • Zachary Scott *Harvey Turner* • Frank Conroy *JD Nolan* • Kathryn Givney *Myra Nolan* • Rhys Williams *Father Paul* • Darryl Hickman *String* ■ *Dir* King Vidor • *Scr* Lenore Coffee, from the novel *A Man without Friends* by Margaret Echard

Lightning the White Stallion ★ U

Adventure　　　　1986 · US · Colour · 87mins

Mickey Rooney had been in movies for 60 years when he made this glutinous family entertainment, and it's hard to believe that he ever loaned his name to a more disappointing venture. Trading on his success in such earlier horse dramas as *National Velvet* and *The Black Stallion*, Rooney trots out every scene-stealing trick in the book as the impoverished breeder who unites with a couple of kids to recover the champion who's been stolen by a disgruntled stablehand. Dripping with sentimentality and sloppily directed by William A Levey, this also marks the career low of Susan George. ▭

Mickey Rooney *Barney Ingram* • Isabel Lorca *Stephanie Ward* • Susan George *Madame Rene* • Billy Wesley *Lucas* ■ *Dir* William A Levey • *Scr* Peter Welbeck [Harry Alan Towers], Rick Marx

Lights of New York ★★

Crime drama　　　1928 · US · BW · 57mins

Billed by Warner Bros as "the first 100 per cent all-talking picture" – *The Jazz Singer* was only partly sound – they really should have spent more on voice coaching for the many vaudeville stars (Helene Costello, Cullen Landis) hired to make this gangster movie more viable and entertaining. Directed by Bryan Foy, with Gladys Brockwell as the gangster's moll and Robert Elliott as the tough detective, the story flits from small-town integrity to "Great White Way" shenanigans, with sets dwarfing everyone and very few participants knowing how to project any kind of conviction. Still, it does have a certain novelty value.

Helene Costello *Kitty Lewis* • Cullen Landis *Eddie Morgan* • Gladys Brockwell *Molly Thompson* • Mary Carr *Mrs Morgan* • Wheeler Oakman *Hawk Miller* • Eugene Pallette *Gene* • Robert Elliott *Detective Crosby* • Tom Dugan *Sam* ■ *Dir* Bryan Foy • *Scr* Hugh Herbert, Murray Roth, from a story by Charles R Gaskill

Lights of Variety ★★★★

Drama　　　　　1950 · It · BW · 94mins

Although Alberto Lattuada was credited with blocking the action for the camera, Federico Fellini's influence on the content of this "act of humility towards life" is clearly evident. Breaking with the neorealist tradition of locating characters within their environment, Fellini delights in revealing the human face behind the social mask, just as he exposes the tawdriness of the supposedly glamorous showbiz life endured by the stage-struck Carla Del Poggio until she abandons clown-manager Peppino De Filippo's itinerant band of misfits. Touching on such themes as illusion, provincial ennui and the irresistible lure of the eccentric, Fellini's debut is one to savour. In Italian with English subtitles.

Peppino De Filippo *Checco Dal Monte* • Carla Del Poggio *Liliana Antonelli* • Giulietta Masina *Melina Amour* • Folco Lulli *Adelmo Conti* • Dante Maggio *Remo* ■ *Dir* Alberto Lattuada, Federico Fellini • *Scr* Federico Fellini, Alberto Lattuada, Tullio Pinelli, Ennio Flajano, from a story by Federico Fellini

The Lightship ★★ 15

Psychological thriller
1985 · US · Colour · 84mins

After the success of films as diverse as *Mephisto* and *Out of Africa*, the Austrian actor Klaus Maria Brandauer looked set to become an international star. But he chose not wisely with this overt allegory in which Robert Duvall leads psychos aboard Captain Brandauer's rustbucket lightship. The trouble is the captain's role is as passive as his pacifism and it's Duvall who steers the action to the compass of his violence. Brandauer needed a showier showcase for his very real talents, rather than this shadow-oppressed clash of symbols. ▭

Robert Duvall *Caspary* • Klaus Maria Brandauer *Captain Miller* • Tom Bower *Coop* • Robert Costanzo *Stump* • Badja Djola *Nate* • William Forsythe *Gene* • Arliss Howard *Eddie* ■ *Dir* Jerzy Skolimowski • *Scr* William Mai, David Taylor, from the novel *Das Feuerschiff* by Siegfried Lenz

Like Father, Like Son ★★★ 15

Comedy 1987 · US · Colour · 95mins

Apart from running out of funny things for Dudley Moore and son Kirk Cameron to do once they have traded places, this first of several late eighties body-swap comedies is surprisingly good value. Giggling and scurrying for all he is worth, Moore whoops it up as the surgeon reliving his teens, and his performance is not a million miles behind the one that won Tom Hanks an Oscar nomination in *Big*. It is something of a puzzle that Cameron's career never really went anywhere, as, on the strength of this turn, he is obviously an accomplished comic. Contains swearing. ▭

Dudley Moore *Dr Jack Hammond* • Kirk Cameron *Chris Hammond* • Margaret Colin *Ginnie Armbruster* • Catherine Hicks *Dr Amy Larkin* • Patrick O'Neal *Dr Armbruster* • Sean Astin *Trigger* • Cami Cooper [Camille Cooper] *Lori Beaumont* • Micah Grant *Rick Anderson* ■ *Dir* Rod Daniel • *Scr* Lorne Cameron, Steven L Bloom, from a story by Lorne Cameron

Like Grains of Sand ★★★ 15

Drama 1995 · Jap · Colour · 123mins

Sprawling when it might have been intimate, Ryosuke Hashiguchi's second feature still has far more to say about sexual identity and the pain of adolescence than any number of

Hollywood teenage dramas. There's no holding back the emotions in this romantic triangle, yet the members of the inexperienced cast never stray into caricature or melodramatics, even though their situation initially seems more than a little contrived and becomes increasingly tortuous. Yoshinori Okada is particularly impressive as the sensitive gay student who repays the loyalty of his best friend, Kota Kusano, by trying to help him win the trust of traumatised rape victim, Ayumi Hamazaki. In Japanese with English subtitles. Contains swearing. ▭

Yoshinori Okada *Shuji Ito* • Kota Kusano *Hiroyuki Yoshida* • Koji Yamaguchi *Touru Kanbara* • Ayumi Hamazaki *Kasane Aihara* ■ *Dir/Scr* Ryosuke Hashiguchi

Like It Is ★★★ 18

Comedy drama 1997 · UK · Colour · 95mins

A young boxer from Blackpool (played by British amateur featherweight champion Steve Bell) finds love and disillusionment in London's gay clubland in first-time director Paul Oremland's refreshingly good-natured production. Ian Rose is the record producer Bell follows to Soho after a one night stand, only to face harsh realities in the big city. Roger Daltrey is Rose's predatory boss and Dani Behr Daltrey's latest singing discovery, and both see Bell as a threat. Slightly awkward, yet refusing to fall into the cliché traps that often handicap gay dramas, this is done with a light, naturalistic charm and without any preaching. Rather good of its type. Contains violence, swearing and sex scenes. ▭

Steve Bell *Craig* • Roger Daltrey *Pop mogul* • Dani Behr *Paula* • Ian Rose *Matt* ■ *Dir* Paul Oremland • *Scr* Robert Cray

Like Water for Chocolate ★★★★ 15

Romantic fantasy
1993 · Mex · Colour · 109mins

The combination of culinary art and magic realism that made Laura Esquivel's bestseller so distinctive is very much to the fore in husband Alfonso Arau's acclaimed adaptation. However, what should have been a filmic feast has been spoiled by his reluctance to beat the mixture gently before bringing the most succulent moments to the boil. Set in Mexico at the turn of the century, this epic of a forbidden love consummated only through food has a sizzling story and committed performances, but Arau's direction is naively over-emphatic, with scenes of great erotic intensity sometimes missing their mark. In English and Spanish with subtitles. ▭

Marco Leonardi *Pedro* • Lumi Cavazos *Tita* • Regina Torne *Mama Elena* • Mario Ivan Martinez *John Brown* • Ada Carrasco *Nacha* • Yareli Arizmendi *Rosaura* • Claudette Maille *Gertrudis* • Pilar Aranda *Chencha* ■ *Dir* Alfonso Arau • *Scr* Laura Esquivel, from her novel *Como Agua para Chocolate*

The Likely Lads ★★ PG

Comedy 1976 · UK · Colour · 86mins

Dating from the time when seemingly every successful British sitcom was awarded its own feature, this is a long

way short of the TV standard, with writers Dick Clement and Ian La Frenais falling into the trap of misusing film freedom to turn their material blue. However, Rodney Bewes and James Bolam are as engaging as ever as Bob and Terry, and their tour of the North East coast contains plenty of the wallowing and lamenting that gave the show its lasting appeal. ▭

Rodney Bewes *Bob Ferris* • James Bolam *Terry Collier* • Brigit Forsyth *Thelma Ferris* • Mary Tamm *Christina* • Sheila Fearn *Audrey* • Zena Walker *Laura* ■ *Dir* Michael Tuchner • *Scr* Dick Clement, Ian La Frenais

Li'l Abner ★★★★ U

Musical comedy 1959 · US · Colour · 75mins

This is a terrific adaptation of the brash and sassy Broadway show, highly stylised and superbly photographed by Daniel L Fapp (*West Side Story*) in eye-popping Technicolor and VistaVision – both sexy and witty to boot. The plot imposed on Al Capp's cartoon *Dogpatch* is classically simple: being the most worthless place in America the government wants to use it for nuclear testing. Cue for terrific songs, exhilarating dancing (choreography by Michael Kidd and Dee Dee Wood) and a wonderful cast, including Stella Stevens as Apassionata Von Climax and Julie Newmar as Stupefyin' Jones. Watch for a major uncredited star as Stupefyin's victim, and a very young Valerie (*Rhoda*) Harper in the chorus line.

Peter Palmer *Li'l Abner* • Leslie Parrish *Daisy Mae* • Stubby Kaye *Marryin' Sam* • Howard St John *General Bullmoose* • Julie Newmar *Stupefyin' Jones* • Stella Stevens *Appassionata Von Climax* • Alan Carney *Mayor Dawgmeat* • Jerry Lewis *Frank* ■ *Dir* Melvin Frank • *Scr* Norman Panama, Melvin Frank, from their musical, from characters in the comic strip *Dogpatch, created by Al Capp*

Lilac Time ★★★

Silent First World War drama
1928 · US · BW · 79mins

Misunderstandings bloom, along with the flowers, in this vastly romantic, hugely successful crowd-pleaser set in the First World War. French girl Colleen Moore endures the usual wartime romantic tribulations as she waits for dashing English pilot Gary Cooper to keep his promise to return to her. Adapted from the play by Jane Cowl and Jane Murfin, it's a theme that has survived in many guises throughout the years because it basically lives up to its optimistic alternative title of *Love Never Dies*.

Colleen Moore *Jeannine Berthelot* • Gary Cooper *Capt Philip Blythe* • Burr McIntosh *Gen Blythe* • George Cooper *Mechanic's helper* ■ *Dir* George Fitzmaurice • *Scr* Carey Wilson, Willis Goldbeck, from the play by Jane Cowl, Jane Murfin

Lilacs in the Spring ★★ U

Fantasy 1955 · UK · Colour · 99mins

Unconscious as a result of a bomb explosion during the Blitz, a young entertainer with a boyfriend dilemma dreams of herself as Nell Gwynne, as Queen Victoria and as her own actress mother, who was killed en route to a reconciliation with her famous actor husband. The girl awakes with her own problems resolved. A piece of romantic

whimsy, produced and directed in Trucolor by Herbert Wilcox as a vehicle for his wife, Anna Neagle, who acquits herself well in playing four roles and providing an opportunity for her fans to overdose on her much-loved presence. The big surprise, though, is the appearance of Errol Flynn as her mother's estranged husband.

Anna Neagle *Carole Beaumont/Lillian Grey/ Queen Victoria/Nell Gwyn* • Errol Flynn *John Beaumont* • David Farrar *Charles King/King Charles* • Kathleen Harrison *Kate* • Peter Graves (1) *Albert Gutman/Prince Albert* • Helen Haye *Lady Drayton* • Sean Connery ■ *Dir* Herbert Wilcox • *Scr* Harold Purcell, from the play *The Glorious Days* by Robert Nesbitt

Lili ★★★★ U

Romantic musical drama
1953 · US · Colour · 80mins

An absolutely charming romantic musical comedy starring gamine Leslie Caron as a waif who joins a carnival. Mel Ferrer, in his most sympathetic role as a self-pitying puppeteer, provides one of the film's most memorable moments, when Caron sings along with his puppets, a sequence which includes the lilting song *Hi-Lili, Hi-Lo* from the Oscar-winning score. There's also a marvellously rich fantasy ballet sequence featuring former dancer/ talented director Charles Walters himself, and a superb use of MGM's French village set, beautifully photographed in Technicolor by Robert Planck. Children of all ages will gasp at the magic tricks performed by Jean-Pierre Aumont and his assistant Zsa Zsa Gabor. This is a slight tale that has the potential to charm all generations.

Leslie Caron *Lili Daurier* • Mel Ferrer *Paul Berthalet* • Jean-Pierre Aumont *Marc* • Zsa Zsa Gabor *Rosalie* • Kurt Kasznar *Jacquot* • Amanda Blake *Peach Lips* ■ *Dir* Charles Walters • *Scr* Helen Deutsch, from the story by Paul Gallico • *Music* Bronislau Kaper

Lili Marleen ★★ 15

Second World War drama
1980 · W Ger · Colour · 111mins

Rainer Werner Fassbinder intended this wartime weepie to be both a homage to the Hollywood romance and an assault on the lingering influence of Nazi gloss on modern German cinema. However, his evident lack of interest in the project meant that his most expensive picture was also among his worst. Normally so reliable, Hanna Schygulla is woefully off-key as the second-rate chanteuse who risks her status within the Reich to help smuggle her Jewish beloved, composer Giancarlo Giannini, to safety. Garishly designed and lazily directed, this is so sentimental and earnest that it's often unintentionally hilarious. ▭

Hanna Schygulla *Wilkie Bunterberg* • Giancarlo Giannini *Robert Mendelssohn* • Mel Ferrer *David Mendelssohn* • Karl-Heinz von Hassel *Hans Henkel* • Erik Schumann *Von Strehlow* • Hark Bohm *Taschner* • Gottfried John *Aaron* • Udo Kier *Drewitz* ■ *Dir* Rainer Werner Fassbinder • *Scr* Manfred Purzer, Joshua Sinclair, Rainer Werner Fassbinder, from the novel *Der Himmel hat viele Farben* by Lale Andersen

Lilies ★★ 15
Drama 1996 · Can · Colour · 91mins

It's easy to spot that this tale of lingering bitterness and repressed sexuality was adapted from a play. But while the seamless shifts between past and present might have impressed on stage, they appear here as stilted as Michel Marc Bouchard's dialogue. The tactic of using theatrics to prick a hardened conscience clearly derives from *Hamlet*. But the cross-dressing teen re-enactment of the death of St Sebastian (staged by prisoner Aubert Pallascio to shame Marcel Sabourin, the schooldays nemesis who is now a prominent bishop) simply heaps artifice upon contrivance. The juvenile cast impresses, but, cinematically, this is a disappointment. 📼

Brent Carver *Countess Marie Laure de Tilly* • Marcel Sabourin *Bishop Jean Bilodeau* • Matthew Ferguson *Young Jean Bilodeau* • Danny Gilmore *Count Vallier de Tilly* • Alexander Chapman *Lydie-Anne de Rozier* • Aubert Pallascio *Old Simon Doucet* • Dir John Greyson • *Scr* Michel Marc Bouchard, from his play *Les Feluettes ou La Répétition d'un Drame Romantique*

Lilies of the Field ★★★★ U
Drama 1963 · US · BW · 94mins

Sidney Poitier won only the second Oscar for a black actor in 24 years – the first went to Hattie McDaniel in *Gone with the Wind* – for his role here as an itinerant handyman helping German nuns build a chapel on barren Arizona land. James Poe's simplistic screenplay might have become sluggishly sentimental without Ralph Nelson's discerning direction and Poitier's sharp humour, and the film also benefits from the distinguished performance of Lilia Skala as a formidable mother superior.

Sidney Poitier *Homer Smith* • Lilia Skala *Mother Maria* • Lisa Mann *Sister Gertrude* • Isa Crino *Sister Agnes* • Francesca Jarvis *Sister Albertine* • Pamela Branch *Sister Elizabeth* • Stanley Adams *Juan* • Dan Frazer *Father Murphy* • Ralph Nelson *Mr Ashton* ■ Dir Ralph Nelson • *Scr* James Poe, from the novel by William E Barrett

Lilith ★★★★
Drama 1964 · US · BW · 113mins

Lilith is a disturbing and poetic study of mental illness, with Beatty as the therapist who becomes drawn to a young woman patient, played by Jean Seberg. Shot in lustrous black and white, and the last film to be directed by Robert Rossen, this is a hypnotic experience, a movie which simmers suggestively but never comes fully to the boil. Trashed by most critics on release, and a predictable box-office bomb, the reputation of *Lilith* has grown over the years, except in the memory of Beatty himself.

Warren Beatty *Vincent Bruce* • Jean Seberg *Lilith Arthur* • Peter Fonda *Stephen Evshevsky* • Kim Hunter *Bea Brice* • Anne Meacham *Yvonne Meaghan* • James Patterson *Dr Lavrier* • Jessica Walter *Laura* • Gene Hackman *Norman* • Robert Reilly *Bob Clayfield* • René Auberjonois *Howie* ■ Dir Robert Rossen • *Scr* Robert Rossen, from the novel by JR Salamanca

Lillian Russell ★★ U
Biographical musical
1940 · US · BW · 127mins

Alice Faye takes the title role in this plodding biopic of a famous and colourful entertainer. Starting in the 1880s, the movie is lavishly mounted and costumed – it was Oscar-nominated for best interior decoration – and provides the necessary accoutrements of the genre, including a clutch of pleasingly appropriate songs. There are appearances by real-life vaudevillians Helen Westley and comedy duo Weber and Fields; while the supporting cast includes Don Ameche and Henry Fonda as two of Miss Russell's four husbands and Edward Arnold as Diamond Jim Brady. However, aside from some production number highlights, the dreary, cliché-strewn script, combined with the otherwise alluring Faye's lack of acting talent, sinks the enterprise.

Alice Faye *Lillian Russell* • Don Ameche *Edward Solomon* • Henry Fonda *Alexander Moore* • Edward Arnold *Diamond Jim Brady* • Warren William *Jesse Lewisohn* • Leo Carrillo *Tony Pastor* • Helen Westley *Grandma Leonard* • Dorothy Peterson *Cynthia Leonard* • Una O'Connor *Marie* ■ Dir Irving Cummings • *Scr* William Anthony McGuire • *Cinematographer* Leon Shamroy • *Costume Designer* Travis Banton • *Set Decorator* Thomas Little

Lily Dale ★★
Period drama 1996 · US · Colour · 98mins

A distinguished cast populates this creaky made-for-TV adaptation of the Horton Foote play. In 1910 Houston, young Tim Guinee is reunited with mother Stockard Channing and sister Mary Stuart Masterson years after being sent away to live with other relatives. On poor terms with his taciturn stepfather Sam Shepard, a mysterious illness forces them to let him stay. Another of author Foote's trademark dysfunctional-family-in-the-heartland sagas, this highly theatrical film is only redeemed by its cast's earnestness and sensitivity.

Mary Stuart Masterson *Lily Dale* • Stockard Channing *Corella* • Tim Guinee *Horace Robedaux* • Sam Shepard *Pete Davenport* • John Slattery *Will Kidder* • Jean Stapleton *Mrs Coons* ■ Dir Peter Masterson • *Scr* Horton Foote, from the play by Horton Foote

Lily in Love ★★ 15
Comedy 1985 · US · Colour · 102mins

The fanciful aspects of Ferenc Molnar's venerable play are cruelly exposed in this stodgy adaptation by Hungarian director Karoly Makk. Despite bullish performances from Christopher Plummer and Maggie Smith, the idea that a wife would not recognise her husband beneath some risibly unconvincing greasepaint, requires a suspension of disbelief that the film's smugness fails to persuade us to make. As the stage ham desperate to land the part of an Italian blonde in his screenwriter wife's new movie, Plummer sportingly debunks his own reputation. But, as the production decamps to Budapest, it's Smith who assumes centre stage. 📼

Christopher Plummer *Fitzroy Wynn* • Maggie Smith *Lily* • Elke Sommer *Alice* • Adolph

Green *Jerry Silber* • Sandor Szabo *Teodor* • Janos Dende *Gabor* ■ Dir Karoly Makk • *Scr* Frank Cucci

The Limbic Region ★★★ 18
Action thriller 1996 · US · Colour · 91mins

A dark, downbeat serial-killer thriller which, unusually, focuses on the strain facing the investigators. Told in flashback, the film boasts a grittily charismatic turn from Edward James Olmos, as the detective on the trail of a killer known as the Scorekeeper – an assignment which begins to take a toll on his personal life. George Dzundza also scores as the prime suspect, and the direction from Michael Pattinson is effective without being flashy. Contains violent scenes and swearing. 📼

Edward James Olmos *Jon Lucca* • George Dzundza *Lloyd* • Roger R Cross *Brownlee* • Gwynyth Walsh *Ann* • Don S Davis *Payne* ■ Dir Michael Pattinson • *Scr* Todd Johnson, Patrick Ranahan

Limbo ★★★
Drama 1972 · US · Colour · 111mins

While there must be dozens of movies about men fighting the war in Vietnam, this one is about being married to a soldier, waiting at home without knowing if he's dead or alive. Kate Jackson was married for only two weeks before her husband went to Vietnam and now she thinks he's dead and has fallen in love again; Kathleen Nolan has four children and believes her husband is a prisoner of the Vietcong; Katherine Justice refuses to believe her husband was killed in action. All three get flashbacks as they drive to the airport where one man is coming home. Written by two directors – Joan Micklin Silver and James Bridges – and stylishly made by the veteran Mark Robson, it soft-peddles the politics but puts its foot down for emotional impact.

Kate Jackson *Sandy Lawton* • Katherine Justice *Sharon Dornbeck* • Stuart Margolin *Phil Garrett* • Hazel Medina *Jane York* • Kathleen Nolan *Mary Kay Buell* • Russell Wiggins *Alan Weber* • Joan Murphy *Margaret Holroyd* ■ Dir Mark Robson • *Scr* Joan Micklin Silver, James Bridges

Limbo ★★ 15
Drama 1999 · US · Colour · 121mins

Pivotal indie director and mainstream screenwriter for hire, John Sayles is something of a schizophrenic film-maker. Yet in seeking to reconcile both sides of his cinematic personality, he has merely produced a jarring blend of social study and outdoor adventure. When exploring the conflicting relationships within a small Alaskan coastal community, the film brims with life. However, contrivance takes over once former fisherman David Strathairn, torch singer Mary Elizabeth Mastrantonio and her troubled teenage daughter, Vanessa Martinez, are stranded on a remote island. The ending is audacious enough, but the tragi-feel-good sense of spirituality is no substitute for the engrossing melodrama that precedes it. Contains swearing. 📼 DVD

Mary Elizabeth Mastrantonio *Donna de Angelo* • David Strathairn *Joe Gastineau* • Vanessa

Martinez *Noelle de angelo* • Kris Kristofferson *Smilin' Jack* • Casey Siemaszko *Bobby Gastineau* ■ Dir/Scr John Sayles

Limelight ★★
Musical 1936 · UK · BW · 65mins

Not to be confused with Chaplin's film of the same name, this British musical co-stars Arthur Tracy, popular on radio and record as the "Street Singer" but proving himself woefully inadequate as an actor, and Anna Neagle. Lavishly mounted by director Herbert Wilcox, the tale concerns a chorus girl (Neagle) who, in love with a busker (Tracy), helps him to success in the theatre, but complications ensue when he falls for a socialite. A syrupy and very British backstage drama, popular in its day but only the mildest of diversions now.

Anna Neagle *Marjorie Kaye* • Arthur Tracy *Bob Grant* • Jane Winton *Ray Madison* • Ellis Jeffreys *Lady Madeleine* • Muriel George *Mrs Kaye* • Alexander Field *Alf Sparkes* • Antony Holles *Impresario* • William Freshman *Joe* ■ Dir Herbert Wilcox • *Scr* Laura Whetter

Limelight ★★★★ U
Comedy drama 1952 · US · BW · 136mins

Meant as a summation of his life and art, Charles Chaplin's last American film has some stunning set pieces of vaudeville comedy – one featuring his great rival, Buster Keaton – but an inordinate degree of self-pity. As Calvero, a drunken has-been entertainer, Chaplin saves a young dancer (Claire Bloom) from suicide and nurses her to success, though his own comeback is doomed by a world which has no place for pantomime. Featuring five of his children, it's a very personal indulgence that works best as a celebration of British music hall, not as an exposé of Chaplin's own grievances. 📼

Charles Chaplin *Calvero* • Claire Bloom *Terry* • Sydney Chaplin *Neville* • Andre Eglevsky *Harlequin* • Melissa Hayden *Columbine* • Charles Chaplin Jr *Clown* • Wheeler Dryden *Clown* • Nigel Bruce *Mr Postant* • Norman Lloyd *Stage Manager* • Buster Keaton *Piano Accompanist* • Marjorie Bennett *Mrs Alsop* • Geraldine Chaplin *Street Urchin* • Michael Chaplin *Street Urchin* • Josephine Chaplin *Street Urchin* ■ Dir/Scr Charles Chaplin • *Music* Charles Chaplin

The Limey ★★★★ 18
Thriller 1999 · US · Colour · 85mins

The past lives of Terence Stamp and Peter Fonda underline and illuminate this Steven Soderbergh thriller. Stamp plays Wilson, an English ex-con out for revenge, while Fonda is Valentine, a millionaire record producer whom Wilson thinks caused the death of his daughter. The former is shown as a much younger man in flashbacks taken from Ken Loach's *Poor Cow* (1967), while Fonda is now of an age when he has to hire minders to do his dirty work for him. Soderbergh makes the film a requiem for the hard man, while Chandleresque dialogue and a machine gun resonance put it in the top flight of gangster movies. Contains violence and swearing. 📼 DVD

Terence Stamp *Wilson* • Peter Fonda *Terry Valentine* • Lesley Ann Warren *Elaine* • Melissa George *Jennifer "Jenny" Wilson* •

Luis Guzman *Ed* • Barry Newman *Jim Avery* • Joe Dallesandro *Uncle John* • Nicky Katt *Stacy* ■ *Dir* Steven Soderbergh • *Scr* Lem Dobbs

Limit Up ★★ PG

Comedy 1989 · US · Colour · 83mins

This is an uneven Faustian comedy, set against the backdrop of the modern-day stock market. Nancy Allen is the broker, continually passed over by her male colleagues, who strikes a pact with the Devil via emissary Danitra Vance but soon has second thoughts. A good supporting cast, which includes Dean Stockwell, Sally Kellerman and blues legend Ray Charles, is wasted, and the script and direction are toothless. 🔲

Nancy Allen *Casey Falls* • Brad Hall *Marty Callahan* • Rance Howard *Chuck Feeney* • Danitra Vance *Nike* • Luana Anders *Teacher* • Ray Charles *Julius* • Dean Stockwell *Peter Oak* • Sally Kellerman *Nightclub singer* ■ *Dir* Richard Martini • *Scr* Luana Anders, Richard Martini, from a story by Richard Martini

The Limping Man ★★

Crime drama 1953 · UK · BW · 76mins

Basically this is just another of those fifties British B-thrillers in which an American visitor to England finds himself up to his neck in trouble from the moment he lands. This time Lloyd Bridges is the minor Hollywood star whose casting ensured an American release. An implausible story of murder and mystery unfolds, redeemed (or not, according to taste) by a "twist" ending. Bridges had made *The Sound of Fury*, a remarkable *film noir*, in Hollywood for director Cy Endfield and here they were reunited. The blacklisted Endfield was reduced to working on films like this without credit alongside the named director, Charles de Lautour.

Lloyd Bridges *Frank Prior* • Moira Lister *Pauline* • Helene Cordet *Helene* • Leslie Phillips *Cameron* • Alan Wheatley *Inspector Braddock* • Bruce Beeby *Kendal Brown* ■ *Dir* Charles de Lautour, Cy Endfield • *Scr* Ian Stuart, Reginald Long, from a story by Anthony Verney

Linda Lovelace for President ★★

Sex comedy 1975 · US · Colour · 100mins

Infamous porn star Linda Lovelace had become a blue movie icon following her performance in *Deep Throat*, so there was no shortage of people keen to cash in on her notoriety. Director Claudio Guzmán cast the star as a version of herself in this sex fantasy in which the porn queen runs for President of the United States (representing the "Upright Party"). A broad comedy brimming with racial insults, painful double entendres and suggestive situations, this is the perfect antidote to anyone bored rigid by political campaigning.

Linda Lovelace • Fuddie Bagley *Abdul Ali Umagooma* • Val Bisoglio *Rev Billy Easter* • Jac de Leon *Captain Neldor* • Mickey Dolenz [Micky Dolenz] *Le Fenwick* ■ *Dir* Claudio Guzmán • *Scr* Jack S Margolis

The Lineup ★★★

Crime drama 1958 · US · BW · 86mins

This riveting low-budget thriller, shot on location in San Francisco, was completely overlooked on its original release, being taken for a rip-off of a TV series to which it is only loosely connected. It teams Eli Wallach (hot from *Baby Doll*) with veteran character actor Robert Keith, as two ruthless killers carrying on didactic conversations while tracking down passengers from a boat who have been unwitting heroin-carriers. Cleverly written by Stirling Silliphant (who later won an Oscar for *In the Heat of the Night*) and brilliantly staged by action director Don Siegel, the film is notable for its tense car chase along the uncompleted elevated freeway, which gave *Bullitt* and *The French Connection* something to beat.

Eli Wallach *Dancer* • Robert Keith *Julian* • Warner Anderson *Lieutenant Guthrie* • Richard Jaeckel *Sandy McLain* • Mary LaRoche *Dorothy Bradshaw* • William Leslie *Larry Warner* • Emile Meyer *Inspector Al Quine* • Marshall Reed *Inspector Fred Asher* • Raymond Bailey *Philip Dressler* ■ *Dir* Don Siegel • *Scr* Stirling Silliphant

The Linguini Incident ★★ 15

Comedy drama 1991 · US · Colour · 104mins

A designer restaurant called Dali is the setting for this bizarre and – ultimately – unsuccessful comedy. Bartender David Bowie, elegant as ever, is paired with a more quirky than usual Rosanna Arquette, who works as a waitress. Romance does blossom eventually, but not before cash-strapped Bowie has masterminded a robbery at the restaurant. Combine this with Arquette's Houdini-like desire to truss herself up in a tank full of water, and you have a plot as unappealing as a bowl of soggy pasta. The sexual chemistry between the two leads is more than a month past its sell-by date. 🔲

Rosanna Arquette *Lucy* • David Bowie *Monte* • Eszter Balint *Vivian* • Andre Gregory *Dante* • Buck Henry *Cecil* • Viveca Lindfors *Miracle* • Marlee Matlin *Jeanette* • Lewis Arquette *Texas Joe* • Iman *Dali guest* ■ *Dir* Richard Shepard • *Scr* Richard Shepard, Tamara Brott

Link ★ 15

Horror thriller 1986 · UK · Colour · 99mins

Ever wondered what a horror movie would look like made as PG Tips commercial? The answer lies here in this oddity, in which American zoologist Elisabeth Shue arrives at professor Terence Stamp's remote house-cum laboratory to work on his revolutionary simian theories. On the brink of a major breakthrough, he mysteriously disappears, and Shue is left in charge of three gifted chimpanzees. Not hard to guess what's going on as Shue's three wards gradually revert to instinctive laws of the jungle and start a campaign of ludicrous menace. 🔲

Terence Stamp *Dr Steven Phillip* • Elisabeth Shue *Jane Chase* • Steven Pinner *David* • Richard Garnett *Dennis* • David O'Hara *Tom* • Kevin Lloyd *Bailey* • Locke *Link* ■ *Dir* Richard Franklin • *Scr* Everett DeRoche, from the story by Lee Zlotoff, Tom Ackerman

The Lion ★★ U

Drama 1962 · UK · Colour · 95mins

Concocted to indulge William Holden's love of Africa and its wildlife (he had his own private game ranch and co-owned the luxurious Mount Kenya Safari Lodge), this movie also indulges its star's interest in the actress Capucine. She plays his ex-wife, now married to white hunter Trevor Howard; there is also a heavily symbolic lion named "King" who struts around and befriends Holden's daughter. It's not a movie at all, really – more an excuse for other things.

William Holden (1) *Robert Hayward* • Trevor Howard *John Bullitt* • Capucine *Christine* • Pamela Franklin *Tina* ■ *Dir* Jack Cardiff • *Scr* Louis Kamp, Irene Kamp, from a novel by Joseph Kessel

The Lion Has Wings ★★★ U

Second World War documentary drama
1939 · UK · BW · 72mins

Produced with foresight by Alexander Korda, and hustled into cinemas a mere eight weeks after it started shooting, this propagandist feature attempts to predict what would happen if war broke out, a sort of *Things to Come* meets the GPO Film Unit. The film falls into two halves. The first, brilliantly edited (by William Hornbeck) documentary section contrasts peaceful England with a Germany arming for war; the second and, frankly, ludicrous fictional section has Merle Oberon (Mrs Korda) fretting over RAF hubby Ralph Richardson. It's still interesting to see today, though. Watch for Flora Robson in an excerpt from *Fire over England* and great chunks of the air raid featurette *The Gap*. 🔲

Merle Oberon *Mrs Richardson* • Ralph Richardson *Wing Commander Richardson* • June Duprez *June* • Robert Douglas *Briefing Officer* ■ *Dir* Michael Powell, Brian Desmond Hurst, Adrian Brunel • *Scr* Adrian Brunel, EVH Emmett, from a story by Ian Dalrymple

The Lion in Winter ★★★★★ 15

Historical drama
1968 · UK · Colour · 128mins

Katharine Hepburn is on Oscar-winning form and sparring verbally with Oscar-nominated Peter O'Toole in this adaptation of James Goldman's play about Henry II and Eleanor of Aquitaine. Set mostly within the austere castle ramparts over the Christmas festival, it's a story of a family squabble that has geopolitical import, a medieval dynastic war. While the script and the performances are simply dazzling, it is notable, too, for the screen debuts of Timothy Dalton and a combustible Anthony Hopkins who, like O'Toole, was a protégé of Hepburn's. John Barry's beautiful, melancholic score won an Oscar. 🔲

Peter O'Toole *King Henry II* • Katharine Hepburn *Queen Eleanor* • Jane Merrow *Princess Alais* • John Castle *Prince Geoffrey* • Timothy Dalton *King Philip of France* • Anthony Hopkins *Prince Richard* • Nigel Stock *William Marshall* • Nigel Terry *Prince John* ■ *Dir* Anthony Harvey • *Scr* James Goldman, from his play • *Music* John Barry • *Cinematographer* Douglas Slocombe

A Lion Is in the Streets ★★★

Drama 1953 · US · Colour · 88mins

James Cagney had a few run-ins with the guardians of the Hollywood Production Code before he managed to get the green light to adapt Adria Locke Langley's novel about political corruption in the Deep South. Loosely based on the life of Louisiana governor Huey Long, the film had to depart from the ending in the book to satisfy Hollywood's vision of the American Way. Cagney and director Raoul Walsh were old sparring partners, but this picture lacks the punch and pace of earlier outings such as *The Roaring Twenties* and *White Heat*, a fact attributable to Luther Davis's pedestrian script. Barbara Hale stands out in a fine supporting cast.

James Cagney *Hank Martin* • Barbara Hale *Verity Wade* • Anne Francis *Flamingo* • Warner Anderson *Jules Bolduc* • John McIntire *Jeb Brown* • Jeanne Cagney *Jennie Brown* • Lon Chaney Jr *Spurge* • Frank McHugh *Rector* ■ *Dir* Raoul Walsh • *Scr* Luther Davis, from the novel by Adria Locke Langley

The Lion King ★★★★★ U

Animated musical
1994 · US · Colour · 84mins

This audience-devouring cartoon carnivore from the Walt Disney menagerie had enormous box-office appeal, and proved so popular that it has been adapted as a spectacular stage show. For the children there's the story of how a lion cub, exiled by his wicked uncle, achieves his destiny (Disney loves orphans); for grown-ups there's a visual feast of exciting animation work and some good Elton John songs. Voices range from Whoopi Goldberg to Rowan Atkinson, with Jeremy Irons a vocal standout as the evil uncle Scar. Generally, though, this time the beauty is in the beasts. A straight-to-video sequel, *The Lion King: Simba's Pride* followed. 🔲

Jonathan Taylor Thomas *Young Simba* • Matthew Broderick *Adult Simba* • James Earl Jones *Mufasa* • Jeremy Irons *Scar* • Moira Kelly *Adult Nala* • Niketa Calame *Young Nala* • Ernie Sabella *Pumbaa* • Nathan Lane *Timon* • Robert Guillaume *Rafiki* • Rowan Atkinson *Zazu* • Madge Sinclair *Sarabi* • Whoopi Goldberg *Shenzi the Hyena* • Richard "Cheech" Marin *Banzai the Hyena* • Jim Cummings *Ed the Hyena* ■ *Dir* Roger Allers, Rob Minkoff • *Scr* Irene Mecchi, Jonathan Roberts, Linda Woolverton

The Lion of Africa ★★ PG

Adventure 1987 · US · Colour · 104mins

This plod through Kenya, episodic from first frame to last, is boosted by the contribution of Brian Dennehy who has the natural ability to unnerve. His fleshy looks suggest that he is either mighty enough to shout the opposition into submission or kind enough to look after your kids. Here a safari guide with his mind on diamonds, he is prompted towards selflessness by a blunt lady doctor (Brooke Adams). Contains some mild swearing. 🔲

Brian Dennehy *Sam Marsh* • Brooke Adams *Grace Danet* • Josef Shiloach [Joseph Shiloach] *Valentim* • Don Warrington *Lt Henry Piggot* • Carl Andrews *Jemmy Banta* • Katharine Schofield *Cecilia* ■ *Dir* Kevin Connor • *Scr* Bruce Franklin Singer

Lion of the Desert ★★★★ 15
War adventure   1981 · UK · Colour · 156mins

Financed by Colonel Gaddafi, this paean to Libya's national hero, Omar Mukhtar, is often stirring stuff, shot in stunning desert scenery and with hordes of extras not seen since the days of *Lawrence of Arabia*. Mukhtar was a fervent nationalist and Bedouin peasant who resisted Mussolini's annexation of Libya in the thirties. Scenes in which Mukhtar's army of Arab horsemen charge the Italian tanks set the right patriotic mode and prepare us for the inevitable martyrdom. As Mukhtar, Anthony Quinn is predictable but believable; Rod Steiger is very Rod Steiger as Mussolini; while Oliver Reed is often chilling as Musso's muscle man. There's a silly love interest patched in, but overall this is a fine film that must have been a physical and logistical nightmare to make. ▣

Anthony Quinn *Omar Mukhtar* • Oliver Reed *General Rodolfo Graziani* • Irene Papas *Mabrouka* • Raf Vallone *Colonel Diodiece* • Rod Steiger *Benito Mussolini* • John Gielgud *Sharif El Gariani* • Andrew Keir *Salem* ■ *Dir* Moustapha Akkad • *Scr* HAL Craig

The Lion, the Witch and the Wardrobe ★★★ Uc
Animated fantasy
1978 · UK/US · Colour · 91mins

An animated feature, by Bill Melendez, adapted from the first of author CS Lewis's *Narnia* books. Four children discover the enchanted land of Narnia at the back of an old wardrobe and become involved in a battle between the forces of good and evil – helped by Aslan the Lion. The drawings seem too elementary for the subject, but voice-overs from the likes of June Whitfield, Arthur Lowe, Leslie Phillips and Sheila Hancock give life and lift to an idea which could have been distanced and abstract, instead of one of the most popular of contemporary children's classics. ▣

Dir Bill Melendez • *Scr* from the novel by CS Lewis

Lionheart ★★ PG
Fantasy adventure
1986 · US · Colour · 100mins

A curious drama that attempts to interest younger viewers in a little medieval history. Sadly, neither director Franklin J Schaffner nor his star Eric Stoltz has any idea how to pitch the story of a knight who interrupts his quest to join King Richard in the Holy Land to help a gang of bedraggled kids from being sold into slavery by Gabriel Byrne. The result is a sort of live-action cartoon, but with none of the charm. With a more intelligent script and some child-friendly direction, it might just have worked. ▣

Eric Stoltz *Robert Nerra* • Gabriel Byrne *Black Prince* • Nicola Cowper *Blanche* • Dexter Fletcher *Michael* • Deborah Barrymore *Mathilda* • Nicholas Clay *Charles De Montfort* • Bruce Purchase *Simon Nerra* • Neil Dickson *King Richard* • Chris Pitt *Odo* ■ *Dir* Franklin J Schaffner • *Scr* Menno Meyjes, Richard Outten, from a story by Menno Meyjes

Lions Love ★
Comedy   1969 · US · Colour · 115mins

Irritating beyond belief, *Lions Love* will be totally unwatchable and incomprehensible to anyone who wasn't around in the sixties and the American underground at that time. Directed by Agnes Varda – the wife of French New Waver Jacques Demy – it's a skew-eyed looked at Hollywood in which American indie director Shirley Clarke arrives to make a movie. She hangs out with some actors, gets turned down by a producer, nearly commits suicide in an avant garde sort of way, watches a tape of the Kennedy assassination... One of Andy Warhol's briefly shining superstars, Viva, pretty much plays herself – that was always her best role.

Viva *Harlow* • Richard Bright *Billy the Kid* • Shirley Clarke • Eddie Constantine ■ *Dir/Scr* Agnès Varda

Lip Service ★★★
Comedy drama   1988 · US · Colour · 74mins

Griffin Dunne is thoroughly objectionable in this slick movie as the smarmy television announcer who sets his sights on veteran Paul Dooley's anchorman slot. Produced by David Mamet, this was the directorial debut of actor William H Macy, who turned in a superb, Oscar-nominated performance in *Fargo*. Adapted by Howard Korder from his own play, this TV newsroom satire has a whiff of *Broadcast News* about it, but, funny as it is in places, it could have done with a touch more *Drop the Dead Donkey*-style kick. Contains swearing.

Griffin Dunne *Len Burdette* • Paul Dooley *Gil Hutchinson* ■ *Dir* WH Macy [William H Macy] • *Scr* Howard Korder, from his play

Lipstick ★★★ 18
Drama   1976 · US · Colour · 82mins

Lipstick purported to be a serious drama about the crime of rape but is actually just an up-market exploitation movie, cleverly and glossily directed by Lamont Johnson and featuring an eye-catching screen debut by Ernest Hemingway's grand-daughter, Margaux. She plays a fashion model who is raped by an apparently nice music teacher, played by Chris Sarandon. Margaux's sister, Mariel, also makes her screen debut as one of Sarandon's pupils and Anne Bancroft plays Margaux's lawyer who takes the case to court. Like the later Jodie Foster film *The Accused*, the movie argues that rape victims should come forward to prosecute their assailants, and that made the film a ground breaker in 1976. Then, having delivered its message, it hurtles towards its schlocky resolution that turns Margaux into Charles Bronson. ▣

Margaux Hemingway *Chris McCormick* • Chris Sarandon *Gordon Stuart* • Perry King *Steve Edison* • Anne Bancroft *Carla Bondi* • John Bennett Perry *Martin McCormick* • Mariel Hemingway *Kathy McCormick* • Robin Gammell *Nathan Cartwright* ■ *Dir* Lamont Johnson • *Scr* David Rayfiel

Liquid Sky ★★ 18
Science-fiction fantasy
1982 · US · Colour · 107mins

A dirty, funny, perverse and pretentiously over-long look at New York's punk-chic drug culture. An alien spacecraft lands on a Manhattan skyscraper and its inhabitants quickly get hooked on the powdered and sexual thrills indulged in by everyone populating the sordid landscape. Anne Carlisle, playing both male and female leads (don't ask, it's art!), then uses the aliens to vaporise her enemies at the height of their drug-fuelled passions. Indulgent and stylistically over the top to a distracting degree, this self-important put-on is more a fashion extravaganza than a science-fiction movie. The soundtrack is a poseur's delight, too. ▣

Anne Carlisle *Margaret/Jimmy* • Paula Sheppard *Adrian* • Bob Brady *Owen* • Susan Doukas *Sylvia* • Otto von Wernherr *Johann* • Elaine C Grove *Katherine* ■ *Dir* Slava Tsukerman • *Scr* Slava Tsukerman, Nina V Kerova, Anne Carlisle

The Liquidator ★★ PG
Spy drama   1966 · UK · Colour · 104mins

The Liquidator is one of dozens of Bond ripoffs, right down to Shirley Bassey belting out the title number. It's based on one of the novels featuring hit man and former soldier Boysie Oakes, the creation of writer John Gardner who later won the backing of Ian Fleming's estate and wrote a new series of Bond novels. Oakes – played by Aussie actor Rod Taylor – is hired by MI6, in the person of old soak Trevor Howard, to do some liquidating. Oakes, currently a waiter in a Paris bistro, sub-contracts the work out, leading to various complications, including the near assassination of Prince Philip. Very swinging sixties in tone, with jet-set locations, snazzy cartoon titles and a supporting cast of British eccentrics and willing ladies in mini-skirts. ▣

Rod Taylor *Boysie Oakes* • Trevor Howard *Mostyn* • Jill St John *Iris MacIntosh* • Wilfrid Hyde White *Chief* • David Tomlinson *Quadrant* • Eric Sykes *Griffen* • Akim Tamiroff *Sheriek* • Derek Nimmo *Fly* • Jeremy Lloyd *Young Man* ■ *Dir* Jack Cardiff • *Scr* Peter Yeldham, from the novel by John Gardner

Lisa and the Devil ★★★ 18
Horror   1976 · It · Colour · 91mins

Mario Bava's subtle and sophisticated spellbinder is his most personal movie, one putting into focus his own dark obsessions and fears of manipulation. But for years the only available version of this movie was titled *The House of Exorcism* – the jumbled concoction it became when it was extensively recut and new footage added in a post-*Exorcist* frenzy. (Hence the Mickey Lion pseudonym Bava insisted on.) Yet Elke Sommer gives one of her most endearing performances as the luckless tourist stumbling into a house filled with all manner of depravity, in this demonic possession case history. ▣

Telly Savalas *Leandro* • Elke Sommer *Lisa Reiner/Elena* • Sylva Koscina *Sophia Lehar* • Alida Valli *Max's Mother* ■ *Dir* Mickey Lion [Mario Bava] • *Scr* Alfredo Leone, Cecilio Paniagua

Lisbon ★★★ PG
Thriller   1956 · Colour · 86mins

Republic sent star/producer/director Ray Milland to Portugal to unlock frozen funds and shoot this slack but enjoyable melodrama which made early use of the studio's own variant of CinemaScope, a process called Naturama. Milland chose feisty Maureen O'Hara and suave Claude Rains as his co-stars with Francis Lederer, Percy Marmont and Yvonne Furneaux providing further very capable support. It's a pity the story – a scheming O'Hara uses Milland through Rains to "rescue" her elderly husband from behind the Iron Curtain – isn't stronger. Nelson Riddle's adaptation of a Portuguese number for the title music is catchy. ▣

Ray Milland *Captain Robert John Evans* • Maureen O'Hara *Sylvia Merrill* • Claude Rains *Aristides Mavros* • Yvonne Furneaux *Maria Maddalena Masanet* • Francis Lederer *Serafim* • Percy Marmont *Lloyd Merrill* • Jay Novello *Joao Casimiro Fonseca* ■ *Dir* R Milland [Ray Milland] • *Scr* John Tucker Battle, from a story by Martin Rackin

The List of Adrian Messenger ★★★
Murder mystery   1963 · US · BW · 97mins

John Huston's bizarre take on *Kinds Hearts and Coronets* – with stars such as Burt Lancaster, Robert Mitchum, Tony Curtis and Frank Sinatra behind make-up for cameo roles – is a gleeful black comedy for most of its running time. An unknown killer begins to eliminate 11 men who knew him as a wartime traitor, and is planning to kill the boy who is the only obstacle to his acquisition of a huge fortune. Part-way through, however, principal investigator George C Scott is at a loss and so are we, as the plot wobbles into self-indulgence, so that it becomes more of a hoot for the cast than the audience.

George C Scott *Anthony Gethryn* • Dana Wynter *Lady Jocelyn Bruttenholm* • Clive Brook *Marquis of Gleneyre* • Herbert Marshall *Sir Wilfred Lucas* • Jacques Roux *Raoul LeBorg* • Bernard Archard *Inspector Pike* • Gladys Cooper *Mrs Karoudjian* • Walter Anthony Huston [Tony Huston] *Derek* • John Merivale *Adrian Messenger* • Marcel Dalio *Max* ■ *Dir* John Huston • *Scr* Anthony Veiller, from the novel by Philip MacDonald

Listen ★★
Erotic thriller   1996 · US · Colour · 101mins

There's not been a decent phone thriller since Barbara Stanwyck was tormented in *Sorry, Wrong Number*. This kinky concoction is hardly the most complicated of whodunits, nor is the transplant of plot elements from *Bound*, *Single White Female* and *Pacific Heights* wholly successful. Yet Brooke Langton gives a spirited performance as the interior designer who suspects that the killer who's been preying on callers to an erotic chat line may live in her building. Joel Wyner provides some glamour as her hunky neighbour, but the real fireworks come from Sarah G Buxton as her one-time lesbian lover. Contains swearing, violence, sex scenes and nudity.

Brooke Langton *Sarah Ross* • Sarah G Buxton [Sarah Buxton] *Krista Barron* • Gordon Currie *Jake Taft* • Andy Romano *Detective Sam*

Steinmann • Joel Wyner *Randy Wilkes* • Evan Taylor *Detective Louis Penny* ■ Dir Gavin Wilding • *Scr* Jonas Quastel, Michael Bafaro

Listen, Darling ★★★
Musical comedy   1938 · US · BW · 72mins

A widowed mother (Mary Astor) struggling to support her children is tempted to marry a pompous, unattractive banker. Her daughter Pinkie (Judy Garland) and Pinkie's pal (Freddie Bartholomew) kidnap her in the family trailer to go in search of a more suitable match, and find two possibilities in devil-may-care Walter Pidgeon and kindly millionaire Alan Hale. Fresh and charming, this romantic/domestic comedy has a reliable adult cast and terrific performances from Garland, still evidencing puppy fat but in full voice (songs skilfully integrated into a non-musical), Bartholomew – grown from angelic child star to gawky teenager – and little Scotty Beckett as the incorrigible small brother. It evokes nostalgia for a prettier past.

Judy Garland *Pinkie Wingate* • Freddie Bartholomew *Buzz Mitchell* • Mary Astor *Dottie Wingate* • Walter Pidgeon *Richard Thurlow* • Alan Hale *JJ Slattery* • Scotty Beckett *Billie Wingate* • Barnett Parker *Abercrombie* • Gene Lockhart *Mr Drubbs* • Charles Grapewin [Charley Grapewin] *Uncle Joe* ■ Dir Edwin L Marin • *Scr* Elaine Ryan, Anne Morrison Chapin, from a story by Katherine Brush

Listen to Me ★ 15
Drama   1989 · US · Colour · 109mins

Roy Scheider oversees his bunch of squabbling students in a convoluted tale concerning a college debating competition. The final debate – on the morality of abortion – is due to be argued in front of Supreme Court judges, but this takes a back seat to the tribulations of the kids. Kirk Cameron falls for pretty swot Jami Gertz; disabled dancer Amanda Peterson turns down jock Christopher Atkins; all events that conspire to result in a a very unhappy ending for someone. Director Douglas Day Stewart fails to convey the passion and intellectual excitement of the debate and, by the end of this cliché-ridden movie, you simply won't care.

Kirk Cameron *Tucker Muldowney* • Jami Gertz *Monica Tomanski* • Roy Scheider *Charlie Nichols* • Amanda Peterson *Donna Lumis* • Tim Quill *Garson McKellar* • George Wyner *Dean Schwimmer* • Anthony Zerbe *Senator McKellar* • Christopher Atkins *Bruce Arlington* • Dan Schneider *Nathan Gore* • Yeardley Smith *Cootz* • Moon Zappa *Longnecker* • Ron Masak *Monica's Father* • Dottie Archibald *Monica's Mother* ■ Dir/Scr Douglas Day Stewart

Listen Up: the Lives of Quincy Jones ★★★ 15
Music documentary
1990 · US · Colour · 110mins

The first black composer to score mainstream Hollywood movies and the recipient of countless Grammys and six Oscar nominations, Quincy Jones has spent his career at the top. The same can't be said for his personal life. Deprived of his mother's love because of her mental illness, he has rarely enjoyed harmonious relationships with women, while he has

twice required brain surgery. Ellen Weissbrod's documentary reveals Jones as a man of regrets behind the cheery façade. But, as fascinating as he is, the film lacks focus, meandering between recollections and tributes (from the likes of Miles Davis, Steven Spielberg, Ray Charles and Ella Fitzgerald) like a musical mystery tour. Contains swearing. 🖵

Dir Ellen Weissbrod

Lisztomania ★ 18
Biographical fantasy
1975 · UK · Colour · 98mins

With *The Devils, The Music Lovers, Mahler* and *Tommy,* Ken Russell created a very powerful style that intimidated producers and divided the critics. However, he came a cropper with this ugly, migraine-inducing and mind-numbing bore. Liszt is here portrayed by pop idol Roger Daltrey of the Who; Paul Nicholas plays Richard Wagner, while Ringo Starr is a natural as the Pope. The result is a wild, kaleidoscopic romp, full of sexual symbolism, Carry On humour and Hammer horror send-ups – an epic of self-loathing, self-parody and self-destruction. 🖵

Roger Daltrey *Franz Liszt* • Sara Kestelman *Princess Carolyn* • Paul Nicholas *Richard Wagner* • Fiona Lewis *Countess Marie* • Veronica Quilligan *Cosima* • Nell Campbell *Olga* • Andrew Reilly *Hans von Bulow* • Ringo Starr *Pope* ■ Dir/Scr Ken Russell • Producer Roy Baird, David Puttnam

Little Annie Rooney ★★★
Silent comedy drama   1925 · US · BW

A characteristic Mary Pickford picture, this piece of Irish-American whimsy presents her, at age 32, as the resourceful, impish, curly-headed 12-year-old who looks after her brother and her widowed father, a cop. When the latter is killed, little Annie and her band of neighbourhood ragamuffins capture the villains, while Annie gives blood to save the life of a wounded ruffian, played by William Haines. Under William Beaudine's directorial guidance, Pickford had another hit that condemned her to remain in curls.

Mary Pickford *Little Annie Rooney* • William Haines *Joe Kelly* • Walter James *Officer Rooney* • Gordon Griffith *Tim Rooney* ■ Dir William Beaudine • *Scr* Hope Loring, Louis D Lighton, from the story by Katherine Hennessey

The Little Ark ★★★
Adventure   1972 · Neth · Colour · 85mins

James B Clark wound down his 36-year career with this arduous Dutch adventure. Something of an animal expert, having previously handled *The Sad Horse, The Dog of Flanders* and *Flipper,* Clark was the ideal choice for this adaptation of Jan de Hartog's novel, in which several barnyard animals face the perils of a rampaging flood, together with their plucky owners, Philip Frame and Genevieve Ambas. Some of the action might prove upsetting for the youngest viewers, but with Theodore Bikel grumpily amiable as the old skipper who turns his houseboat into an ark, this should appeal to the discriminating pre-teen.

Theodore Bikel *The Captain* • Philip Frame *Jan* • Genevieve Ambas *Adinda* • Max Croiset *Father Grijpma* ■ Dir James B Clark • *Scr* Joanna Crawford, from the novel by Jan De Hartog

Little Big League ★★★ PG
Sports comedy   1994 · US · Colour · 115mins

This amiable wish-fulfilment comedy is about a 12-year-old kid (Luke Edwards) who inherits a Minnesota baseball team and decides he could do a better job than their current manager. If you can accept that grown sportsman would begrudgingly take orders from a little pipsqueak, then the film will touch a few bases. Edwards conveys a real passion for the game and the script has more time for character development than your average slice of sporting life. Although aimed at both kids and adults, the two-hour running time will seriously challenge the attention span of many younger audiences. The broadcaster Wally Holland is played by John Gordon, the real-life announcer of the Minnesota Twins team. 🖵

Luke Edwards *Billy Heywood* • Timothy Busfield *Lou Collins* • John Ashton *Mac MacNally* • Ashley Crow *Jenny Heywood* • Kevin Dunn *Arthur Goslin* • Billy L Sullivan *Chuck Lobert* • Miles Feulner *Joey Smith* • Jonathan Silverman *Jim Bowers* • Dennis Farina *George O'Farrell* • Jason Robards [Jason Robards Jr] *Thomas Heywood* ■ Dir Andrew Scheinman • *Scr* Gregory K Pincus, Adam Scheinman, from a story by Gregory K Pincus

Little Big Man ★★★★ 15
Epic western   1970 · US · Colour · 133mins

Having presented an alternative view of the gangster era in *Bonnie and Clyde,* director Arthur Penn re-examined some of the most cherished myths of the old west in this sprawling, handsome and ceaselessly sly tragicomedy. While Dustin Hoffman dominates the film as the 121-year-old who claims to be the sole survivor of Custer's last stand at the Little Bighorn, the dignified, Oscar-nominated performance of Chief Dan George is equally noteworthy. One or two of Hoffman's encounters with the mavericks, hypocrites and fools of the frontier hang heavy, but this is an ambitious, offbeat and thoroughly provocative picture. 🖵

Dustin Hoffman *Jack Crabb* • Faye Dunaway *Mrs Pendrake* • Martin Balsam *Allardyce T Merriweather* • Richard Mulligan *General George A Custer* • Chief Dan George *Old Lodge Skins* • Jeff Corey *Wild Bill Hickok* • Amy Eccles [Aimee Eccles] *Sunshine* • Kelly Jean Peters *Olga* • Carol Androsky [Carole Androsky] *Caroline* ■ Dir Arthur Penn • *Scr* Calder Willingham, from the novel by Thomas Berger

Little Bigfoot ★★ PG
Fantasy adventure
1996 · US · Colour · 92mins

A cheap and cheerful cash-in on *Bigfoot and the Hendersons,* with director Art Camacho upping the cuteness stakes by making the creature a baby. Ross Malinger plays the child who makes friends with Bigfoot Jr as the pair attempt to thwart the plans of a ruthless businessman. There are some reliable supporting turns from grown-ups such as PJ Soles

and Matt McCoy, and children will love the cuddly creature. 🖵

Ross Mallinger *Payton Shoemaker* • Kenneth Tigar *Mr Largo* • Joseph Gritto *Little Bigfoot* • PJ Soles *Carolyn Shoemaker* • Caitlin Barrett *Maggie Shoemaker* ■ Dir Art Camacho • *Scr* Richard Preston Jr, Scott McAboy

Little Boy Lost ★★★ U
Drama   1953 · US · BW · 94mins

Bing Crosby acquits himself admirably in this non-musical (though he does perform a handful of songs) in one of his few dramatic roles. He plays an American news reporter who returns to France after the Second World War to find his "lost" son. Crosby is well supported by a splendid French cast, including Nicole Maurey and little Christian Fourcade, as the boy he finds in an orphanage and hopes is his son. Made in France, the film is a pleasant, but modest, tear-jerker.

Bing Crosby *Bill Wainwright* • Claude Dauphin *Pierre Verdier* • Christian Fourcade *Jean* • Gabrielle Dorziat *Mother Superior* • Nicole Maurey *Lisa Garret* • Collette Dereal *Nelly* • Georgette Anys *Madame Quilleboeuf* ■ Dir George Seaton • *Scr* George Seaton, from the novel by Marghanita Laski

Little Buddha ★★★ PG
Religious drama
1993 · Fr/UK · Colour · 117mins

In Bernardo Bertolucci's hymn to Buddhism, an American boy is chosen as the reincarnated Buddha despite the protestations of his parents (Bridget Fonda and Chris Issak). The contrast between old and new cultures is well done, with Keanu Reeves making a rather macho Siddhartha in the flashback scenes. Like Martin Scorsese did in *Kundun,* however, Bertolucci takes the religion at face value, leaving us to ponder the inadequacies of a faith that leaves its followers in abject poverty. 🖵

Keanu Reeves *Prince Siddhartha* • Ying Ruocheng *Lama Norbu* • Chris Isaak *Dean Conrad* • Bridget Fonda *Lisa Conrad* • Alex Weisendanger *Jesse Conrad* • Raju Lal *Raju* ■ Dir Bernardo Bertolucci • *Scr* Rudy Wurlitzer, Mark Peploe, from a story by Bernardo Bertolucci • *Cinematographer* Vittorio Storaro • *Music* Ryuichi Sakamoto

Little Caesar ★★★★ PG
Crime drama   1931 · US · BW · 75mins

One of the great gangster classics, the movie responsible for establishing the Edward G Robinson as the most unlikely of movie stars, in a role based on Al Capone, although the movie itself is from a novel by *The Asphalt Jungle's* WR Burnett. This tough-as-nails crime melodrama consolidated the movie-making style begun by James Cagney's *The Public Enemy* the same year at Warner Bros, the studio that specialised in such tales. Robinson's performance as Enrico Bandello is so scene-stealing that one tends to forget the excellence of the rest of the cast, particularly carefree Douglas Fairbanks Jr and caustic Glenda Farrell. But nobody will ever forget the finale: "Mother of God, is this the end of Rico?" 🖵

Edward G Robinson *Cesare Enrico Bandello* • Douglas Fairbanks Jr *Joe Massara* • Glenda Farrell *Olga Strassoff* • William Collier Jr *Tony*

Passa • Ralph Ince *Diamond Pete Montana* • George E Stone *Otero* • Thomas Jackson [Thomas E Jackson] *Lieutenant Tom Flaherty* • Stanley Fields *Sam Vettori* ■ *Dir* Mervyn LeRoy • *Scr* Francis Edward Faragoh, Robert N Lee, from the novel by WR Burnett

The Little Colonel ★★★ U

Musical drama
1935 · US · BW and Colour · 82mins

Talented moppet Shirley Temple was a huge star when this glutinous confection was made, the first of four movies she released the same year. Temple herself is the "Little Colonel" of the title, having won the heart of a regiment, and so successful was this opus that she repeated the formula with the virtually indistinguishable *The Littlest Rebel* a few months later. It's a hard heart that won't be moved by Temple bringing together crusty old Lionel Barrymore and sweet Evelyn Venable. But, for lovers of precocious talent, just watch Temple and Robinson together: the dance routines are extraordinary for one so young.

Shirley Temple *Lloyd Sherman, The Little Colonel* • Lionel Barrymore *Colonel Lloyd* • Evelyn Venable *Elizabeth Lloyd Sherman* • John Lodge *Jack Sherman* • Sidney Blackmer *Swazey* • Alden Chase *Hull* • William Burress *Dr Scott* • David O'Brien [Dave O'Brien] *Frank Randolph* • Hattie McDaniel *Mom Beck* • Geneva Williams *Maria* ■ *Dir* David Butler • *Scr* William Conselman, from the story by Annie Fellows Johnston

The Little Convict ★★ U

Animated adventure
1980 · Ausl · Colour · 76mins

Inspired by the real-life re-created location of Old Sydney Town, Australia, director Yoram Gross commissioned his *Dot and the Kangaroo* writer John Palmer to come up with this animated original. The amiable tale involves a group of convict deportees, a teenage lad and their adventures. Rolf Harris links all this, singing period songs like *Seth Davey* and *The Wild Colonial Boy*, and appears as the on-screen narrator (live, not animated). Genial stuff, and most likely to please unsophisticated males under ten years old. ▣

Rolf Harris *Grandpa* ■ *Dir* Yoram Gross • *Scr* John Palmer

Little Criminals ★★★

Crime drama
1995 · Can · Colour

A surprisingly tough-hearted drama from Canadian TV, which manages to tackle a controversial subject with some credibility. The story charts the tragic life of two young kids (Brendan Fletcher and Myles Ferguson) locked in a grim, remorseless cycle of inner city poverty and crime. The two young leads turn in electric performances, particularly newcomer Fletcher, and the unstarry cast as a whole is excellent. Dennis Foon's script is believable and moving, and director Stephen Surjik, whose previous claim to fame had been directing *Wayne's World 2*, doesn't flinch from the realities of life in the ghetto.

Brendan Fletcher *Des* • Myles Ferguson *Cory* • Adam Harrison *Mouse* • John Nguyen *Nick* ■ *Dir* Stephen Surjik • *Scr* Dennis Foon

Little Darlings ★★★ 15

Drama
1980 · US · Colour · 90mins

At summer camp, streetwise tough Kristy McNichol and rich brat Tatum O'Neal bet on which of them can lose her virginity first. McNichol sets her sights on mumbling Matt Dillon while O'Neal tries to seduce Armand Assante, one of the camp instructors. Neither really wants a sexual encounter and, as each gets into deeper romantic complications, the once firm rivals become fast friends. Director Ronald F Maxwell's teen box-office hit veers from crude humour to cute sentimentality with such breathless aplomb that it takes the edge off what could have become merely exploitative material in less dextrous hands. Worth watching for McNichol alone who is funny and sensitive. ▣

Tatum O'Neal *Ferris Whitney* • Kristy McNichol *Angel Bright* • Armand Assante *Gary Callahan* • Matt Dillon *Randy* • Krista Errickson *Cinder* ■ *Dir* Ronald F Maxwell • *Scr* Kimi Peck, Dalene Young, from a story by Kimi Peck

Little Dorrit ★★★★★ U

Period drama
1987 · UK · Colour · 343mins

Running nearly six hours, this monumental reworking of Dickens is divided into two parts – *Nobody's Fault* and *Little Dorrit's Story* – with much of the action of the first half being repeated in the second, so that we see the unfolding drama from the different perspectives of its two main protagonists, the bashful Arthur Clennam and Little Dorrit herself, who has been raised by her father in the Marshalsea debtors' prison. Christine Edzard not only directed and scripted the film, but she also made many of the costumes and, along with her husband Richard Goodwin, built the sets at the warehouse in London's Rotherhithe that is both their home and their studio. The huge cast is superb, with Derek Jacobi, Sarah Pickering and Alec Guinness outstanding. ▣

Derek Jacobi *Arthur Clennam* • Alec Guinness *William Dorrit* • Sarah Pickering *Little Dorrit* • Cyril Cusack *Frederick Dorrit* • Joan Greenwood *Mrs Clennam* • Max Wall *Flintwinch* • Patricia Hayes *Affery* • Miriam Margolyes *Flora Finching* • Roshan Seth *Mr Pancks* ■ *Dir* Christine Edzard • *Scr* Christine Edzard, from the novel by Charles Dickens

The Little Dragons ★★

Martial arts
1980 · US · Colour · 90mins

Junior martial arts action, noteworthy only for the fact that it is an early film from Curtis Hanson, later to earn much critical acclaim with *LA Confidential*. Ann Sothern is the leader of a gang who get more than they bargained for when the hold a young girl hostage. The martial arts action is mild enough for young kids although grown-ups would be hard-pressed to identify any clues of a future Oscar-winner at work.

Charles Lane (1) *JJ* • Ann Sothern *Angel* • Chris Petersen *Zack* • Pat Petersen *Woody* • Sally Boyden *Carol* • Rick Lenz *Dick Forbinger* • Sharon Weber *Ruth Forbinger* ■ *Dir* Curtis Hanson • *Scr* Harvey Applebaum, Louis G Atlee, Rudolph Borchert, Alan Ormsby

The Little Drummer Girl ★★★ 15

Spy drama
1984 · US · Colour · 124mins

Diane Keaton is still in eye-fluttering winsome mode seven years after Woody Allen's *Annie Hall*, so she never quite convinces here as Charlie, the politically-correct actress who's recruited by Israeli Intelligence to infiltrate a Palestinian terrorist group. John le Carré's bestseller, from which this is adapted, has many different character shades, but director George Roy Hill opts for broader strokes of near caricature that suit Klaus Kinski's strident performance as the Israeli agent in charge of Charlie's enrolment. There are some dramatic moments, but too much talk slows the pace from urgency to languor. ▣

Diane Keaton *Charlie* • Klaus Kinski *Kurtz* • Yorgo Voyagis *Joseph* • Sami Frey *Khalil* • David Suchet *Mesterbein* • Eli Danker *Litvak* • Ben Levine *Dimitri* • Michael Cristofer *Tayeh* • Bill Nighy *Al* • Anna Massey *Chairwoman* ■ *Dir* George Roy Hill • *Scr* Loring Mandel, from the novel by John le Carré

Little Fauss and Big Halsy ★★ 15

Action drama
1970 · US · Colour · 94mins

Robert Redford is the blondly handsome motorbike racer who swaggers sexually in tight jeans, brazenly exploits his plug-ugly mechanic Michael J Pollard (who drools at him) and gets ex-drug addict Lauren Hutton pregnant. Beyond this is a depiction of America's counter-culture of druggies, drop-outs and groupies ready for sex with the racers. Director Sidney J Furie had already made one other bike movie, *The Leather Boys*, which was Britain's answer to *The Wild One*. ▣

Robert Redford *Big Halsy* • Michael J Pollard *Little Fauss* • Lauren Hutton *Rita Nebraska* • Noah Beery Jr *Seally Fauss* • Lucille Benson *Mom Fauss* • Linda Gaye Scott *Mometh* • Ray Ballard *Photographer* ■ *Dir* Sidney J Furie • *Scr* Charles Eastman

The Little Foxes ★★★★ PG

Period drama
1941 · US · BW · 111mins

It may have been something to do with the fact that director William Wyler and star Bette Davis were romantically involved that gave their many celluloid collaborations such an exciting buzz. This is a splendid example of Davis at the height of her powers as the deeply nasty Regina, the power-hungry schemer of a once wealthy southern clan. The critics always said of Wyler that he "understood women"; they meant that he was not afraid to give a talent like Davis's full flight while also managing to contain her worst histrionic excesses. The result here is a quite magnificent movie. ▣

Bette Davis *Regina Hubbard Giddens* • Herbert Marshall *Horace Giddens* • Teresa Wright *Alexandra Giddens* • Richard Carlson *David Hewitt* • Patricia Collinge *Birdie Hubbard* • Dan Duryea *Leo Hubbard* • Charles Dingle *Ben Hubbard* • Carl Benton Reid *Oscar Hubbard* ■ *Dir* William Wyler • *Scr* Lillian Hellman, Arthur Kober, Dorothy Parker, Alan Campbell, from the play by Lillian Hellman

The Little Fugitive ★★ U

Drama
1953 · US · BW · 75mins

This independent production, winner of a Silver Lion at the Venice Film Festival, was made in New York by a team of three directors – Ray Ashley, Morris Engel, and Ruth Orkin – who were also responsible for writing, photography and editing. It's the slight story of a seven-year-old boy who is conned by his older brother into believing that he has committed a murder. The boy then runs away to savour the amusements at Coney Island. With a strong central performance by Richie Andrusco, it's pleasant enough but ultimately insubstantial.

Richie Andrusco *Joey Norton* • Rickie Brewster *Lennie Norton* • Winifred Cushing *Mother Norton* • Jay Williams *Pony Ride Man* • Will Lee *Photographer* ■ *Dir/Scr* Ray Ashley, Morris Engel, Ruth Orkin

The Little Giant ★★

Crime comedy
1933 · US · BW · 70mins

In one of the first gangster comedies, Edward G Robinson plays beer baron "Bugs" Ahearn, who at the end of Prohibition tries to establish himself as a respectable figure out west. Hiring Mary Astor's estate agent as his social adviser, he finds high society to be as full of crooks as the Chicago he left behind. Although briskly directed by Roy Del Duth, this is small beer compared to Robinson's later send-ups of his tough-guy image (*A Slight Case of Murder, Brother Orchid*).

Edward G Robinson *James Francis "Bugs" Ahearn* • Mary Astor *Ruth Wayburn* • Helen Vinson *Polly Cass* • Russell Hopton *Al Daniels* • Kenneth Thomson *John Stanley* • Shirley Grey *Edith Merriam* • Berton Churchill *Donald Hadley Cass* • Donald Dillaway *Gordon Cass* • Louise Mackintosh *Mrs Cass* ■ *Dir* Roy Del Ruth • *Scr* Wilson Mizner, Robert Lord

Little Giant ★★

Comedy
1946 · US · BW · 91mins

On this occasion, Abbott and Costello take a radical departure from their usual routine of playing pals who find themselves in all sorts of hot water. Here they perform separately rather than as a double act. Costello plays a country bumpkin who leaves for the big city to make enough money to marry his sweetheart. Abbott, in a double role, hires him on as a vacuum cleaner salesman. There's plenty of slapstick action in this film and it also features appearances from Lou's brother Pat and former Marx Brothers straight woman Margaret Dumont.

Bud Abbott *Mr EL Morrison/Tom Chandler* • Lou Costello *Benny Miller* • Brenda Joyce *Ruby* • Jacqueline de Wit *Hazel Temple* • George Cleveland *Uncle Clarence Goodring* • Elena Verdugo *Martha Hill* • Mary Gordon *Anna Miller* • Pierre Watkin *President PS Van Loon* • Margaret Dumont *Mrs Hendrickson* ■ *Dir* William A Seiter • *Scr* Walter de Leon, from a story by Paul Jarrico, from Richard Collins

Little Giants ★★ PG

Sports comedy drama
1994 · US · Colour · 101mins

Yet again, another story of misfit kids who defy all the odds to trounce the champions. The one twist this utterly predictable American football comedy has going for it is that the side has been assembled to give a girl the chance to parade her skills against some sneeringly boneheaded boys. In fairness, as the girl in question, Shawna Waldron gives a good account of herself. However, the same can't be said of Rick Moranis as her gormless dad, who only agrees to coach the team to get his own back on his doltish former football star brother, Ed O'Neill, who rejected Moranis's daughter in the first place.

Rick Moranis *Danny O'Shea* • Ed O'Neill *Kevin O'Shea* • Sam Horrigan *Spike Hammers* • Shawna Waldron *Becky O'Shea* • Mary Ellen Trainor *Karen O'Shea* • Devon Sawa *Junior Floyd* • Susanna Thompson *Patty Floyd* ■ *Dir* Duwayne Dunham, Brian Levant • *Scr* James Ferguson, Robert Shallcross, Tommy Swerdlow, Michael Goldberg, from a story by James Ferguson, Robert Shallcross

Little Girl from Hanoi ★★★
War drama 1974 · Viet · BW

Whereas American pictures made during the Vietnam War concentrated on gung-ho heroics, Nguyen Hai Ninh's Vietnamese drama focuses on the human cost of the conflict, as a 12 year-old girl goes looking for her family during the Christmas air raids on Hanoi, only to meet a kindly soldier, to whom she confides her memories of happier times. As all Vietnamese pictures were made in black and white until the mid-1980s, the action has a newsreel feel to it, which reinforces its propaganda value. In Vietnamese with English subtitles..

Dir Nguyen Hai Ninh • *Scr* Hoang Tich Chi, Nguyen Hai Ninh, Vuong Dan Hoang

The Little Girl Who Lives Down the Lane ★★★
Thriller 1976 · Can/Fr · Colour · 93mins

This chilling oddity – a psychological thriller exploring serious themes – features an intuitive performance from 13-year-old Jodie Foster that hints at what was to come. Grief-stricken Foster murders her mother when her father commits suicide and then buries both corpses in the cellar. Unfortunately, her suspicious actions arouse the curiosity of landlady Alexis Smith and – worse – the interest of her child-molesting, psychopathic son (a startling turn by Martin Sheen). This macabre fairy tale becomes a captivating experience under Nicolas Gessner's sensitive direction.

Jodie Foster *Rynn Jacobs* • Martin Sheen *Frank Hallet* • Alexis Smith *Mrs Hallet* • Mort Shuman *Officer Miglioriti* • Scott Jacoby *Mario Podesta* ■ *Dir* Nicolas Gessner • *Scr* Laird Koenig, from his novel

Little Heroes ★★★ U
Adventure 1992 · US · Colour · 87mins

A family film to melt the hardest of hearts. Eschewing excessive sentimentality, director Craig Clyde shows how even the most mean-spirited citizens can learn from a small girl and her dog. Charley (Raeanin Simpson) doesn't have the happiest of homes – her impoverished parents often bicker – but her dog is her best friend and confidant. Together they prove that there are still such things as miracles. The movie even tosses in

some nice little messages without being too preachy. This is well worth seeking out as proof that you can entertain kids without dumbing down to them.

Raeanin Simpson *Charley* • Katherine Willis *Rachael* • Reta Patterson *Mrs Evans* • Keith Christensen *Alonzo* • Craig Clyde *Virgil* • Lance Johnson *Fritz* ■ *Dir* Craig Clyde • *Scr* Craig Clyde, from a story by Vaunie Wilson Clyde

The Little Hut ★
Comedy 1957 · US · Colour · 96mins

There's nothing more tedious than Hollywood tease, as director Mark Robson attempts to film a French sex farce in the days when censorship permitted only talk and no action. Shipwrecked together on a deserted South Pacific island are Stewart Granger as a neglectful husband, Ava Gardner as his love-starved wife, David Niven as his best friend and her would-be lover, plus a puritanical Alsatian dog who guards the wife's honour whether she wants it to or not. Gardner hated the picture and only took it to be near her current beau, Walter Chiari, who turns up as the randy ship's chef.

Ava Gardner *Susan* • Stewart Granger *Sir Philip Ashlow* • David Niven *Henry Brittingham-Brett* • Walter Chiari *Mario* • Finlay Currie *Reverend Brittingham-Brett* • Jean Cadell *Mrs Brittingham-Brett* ■ *Dir* Mark Robson • *Scr* F Hugh Herbert, from a play by André Roussin, Nancy Mitford

Little Jungle Boy ★★
Adventure 1969 · Ausl · Colour · 78mins

The simple but sweet story of a young boy coming to terms with the dangers of "civilisation" after having lived in the Malayan jungle. It's very predictably mapped out by director Mende Brown, who also produced and wrote this standard Australian adventure.

Rahman Rahmin *Momman* • Mike Dorsey *Dr Mike Martin* • Niki Huen *Dr Niki Sung* • Michael Pate *Sultan* • Noel Ferrier *Father John* • Willie Fennell *Dr Barney O'Hara* ■ *Dir/Scr* Mende Brown

The Little Kidnappers ★★★ U
Drama 1990 · Can · Colour · 89mins

Charlton Heston gives one of his most creditable, robust TV-movie performances as a solitary old grouch forced to take in his two orphaned grandchildren, who promptly present him with an abandoned baby they find under a rock. This is a captivating remake of a highly praised 1953 British film, and director Donald Shebib provides just the right combination of lightness and pathos. The performances are universally excellent, but this is Heston's film, proving once again what a consistently under-rated, versatile screen actor the old charmer really is.

Charlton Heston *James MacKenzie* • Bruce Greenwood *Willem Hooft* • Patricia Gage *Grandmother MacKenzie* • Leah Pinsent *Kirsten MacKenzie* • Charles Miller *Davy MacKenzie* • Leo Wheatley *Harry MacKenzie* ■ *Dir* Donald Shebib • *Scr* Coralee Elliott Testar, from the novel *The Kidnappers* by Neil Paterson

Little Lord Fauntleroy ★★★
Silent drama 1921 · US · BW · 111mins

One of Mary Pickford's biggest box-office successes – and one of her own personal favourites – was this over-long version of Frances Hodgson Burnett's maudlin Victorian tale. As her own producer, Pickford elected to play both the widowed mother and her son, Cedric, whom she surrenders to an English castle for preparation to become the next Lord Fauntleroy. Under Alfred E Green's direction (with some help from Pickford's brother, Jack), Mary excelled both in another of her child roles, and as the mother forced to live apart from her precious son. The immaculate trick photography of the two together was quite an achievement at the time, and the vast castle set is memorable, but the story will appeal mainly to children.

Mary Pickford *Cedric, Little Lord Fauntleroy/Dearest, Cedric's mother* • Claude Gillingwater *The Earl of Dorincourt* • Joseph Dowling *Haversham, the Earl's Counsel* • James Marcus *Hobbs, the grocer* • Frances Marion *Her son, the pretender* ■ *Dir* Alfred E Green, Jack Pickford • *Scr* Bernard McConville, from the novel by Frances Hodgson Burnett • *Cinematographer* Charles Rosher

Little Lord Fauntleroy ★★★
Drama 1936 · US · BW · 98mins

David O Selznick proved the sceptics wrong when he chose this Victorian chestnut for his first independent production and had a critical and box-office success. He borrowed child star Freddie Bartholomew from MGM to portray the Brooklyn youngster who becomes a British lord and persuaded Dolores Costello to make a comeback, displaying radiant charm as the mother he calls "Dearest". Under John Cromwell's smooth direction, with C Aubrey Smith as the irritable earl who can't abide his American daughter-in-law, the sentimental story of the boy's arrival in England to take up his title is as well told as it possibly could be.

Freddie Bartholomew *Ceddie Errol* • Dolores Costello Barrymore [Dolores Costello] *"Dearest", Mrs Errol* • C Aubrey Smith *Earl of Dorincourt* • Guy Kibbee *Mr Hobbs* • Henry Stephenson *Havisham* • Mickey Rooney *Dick* ■ *Dir* John Cromwell • *Scr* Hugh Walpole, from the novel by Frances Hodgson Burnett

Little Lord Fauntleroy ★ U
Period drama 1980 · US · Colour · 98mins

Gerald Royston played him in 1914, Mary Pickford played him in 1921, then Freddie Bartholomew had a go in 1936. Now straw-thatched Ricky Schroder plays (obnoxiously) the little Lord, gallivanting about Ye Olde English countryside with old buffer Alec Guinness, who should have known better. Director Jack Gold seems content to trawl through the old story without bothering to search for contemporary parallels, so it seems even more dated than the ossified Pickford version, offering a chocolate box view of England that's treacly enough to put off even the most determined American tourist.

Ricky Schroder [Rick Schroder] *Cedric Erroll/Lord Fauntleroy* • Alec Guinness *Earl of Dorincourt* • Eric Porter *Havisham* • Colin Blakely *Hobbs* • Connie Booth *Mrs Erroll* • Rachel Kempson *Lady Lorradaile* • Gerry

Cowper *Mellon* ■ *Dir* Jack Gold • *Scr* Blanche Hanalis, from the novel by Frances Hodgson Burnett

Little Malcolm and His Struggle Against the Eunuchs ★★
Comedy drama 1974 · UK · Colour · 109mins

Beatle George Harrison began his career as a movie producer with this messily destructive political satire in which art student John Hurt forms a revolutionary group, the "Party of Dynamic Erection", and plans to launch a coup against the government. In fact, the group is a mask for Hurt's sexual incompetence and a metaphor for the fascism of the state. Lots of serious ideas go bang and whoosh in a splendid display of verbal fireworks, played up to the hilt by Hurt, John McEnery and David Warner as a novelist named Nipple. David Halliwell's play was a cult hit in the sixties but it was already something of a period piece by the time the film was made. A bit long, too.

John Hurt *Malcolm Scrawdyke* • John McEnery *Wick Blagdon* • Raymond Platt *Irwin Ingham* • Rosalind Ayres *Ann Gedge* • David Warner *Dennis Charles Nipple* ■ *Dir* Stuart Cooper • *Scr* Derek Woodward, from the play by David Halliwell

Little Man Tate ★★★★ PG
Drama 1991 · US · Colour · 95mins

Jodie Foster made an impressive directorial debut with this touching drama about a young mother (played by Foster) who is determined to get the best for her exceptionally gifted six-year-old son (an enjoyable performance from Adam Hann-Byrd). While it has its clichéd moments, you do get a feeling that Foster knows her subject matter – a child growing up too fast, and living in an adult world too soon – which, of course, she does, having worked as an actress since she was three. Moving without being cloying, the film also features some nice supporting performances, notably from Dianne Wiest as a child psychologist, and from musician/actor Harry Connick Jr. Contains some swearing.

Jodie Foster *Dede Tate* • Dianne Wiest *Dr Jane Grierson* • Adam Hann-Byrd *Fred Tate* • Harry Connick Jr *Eddie* • David Pierce [David Hyde Pierce] *Garth* • Debi Mazar *Gina* • PJ Ochlan *Damon Wells* • George Plimpton *Winston F Buckner* ■ *Dir* Jodie Foster • *Scr* Scott Frank

Little Man, What Now? ★★★
Drama 1934 · US · BW · 91mins

With poverty and unemployment rife in Germany after the First World War, newlywed Hans Pinneberg (Douglass Montgomery) loses his job, plunging himself and his pregnant wife, Lammchen (Margaret Sullavan), into a series of catastrophes. Sullavan glows at the centre of director Frank Borzage's film, rich in atmosphere and fascinating as a social document of the period. Viewed with hindsight, one is haunted by the knowledge of the Nazi regime to come. However, on the whole, this once popular and well-regarded film has dated badly, overdosing on sentimentality and with

a rather weak hero. Catherine Doucet and Alan Hale are outstanding in supporting roles as Hans's stepmother and her lover, earning a living by questionable means.

Margaret Sullavan *Emma Merceau aka Lammchen* • Douglass Montgomery *Hans Pinneberg* • Alan Hale *Holger Jachman* • Catherine Doucet *Mia Pinneberg* • DeWitt Jennings *Emil Kleinholtz* • Muriel Kirkland *Marie Kleinholz* ■ *Dir* Frank Borzage • *Scr* William Anthony McGuire, Rudolph Ditzen [Hans Fallada]

Little Men ★★ PG

Drama 1998 · US/Can · Colour · 94mins

Although this has been adapted before (by Norman Z McLeod in 1940 and Phil Rosen in 1935), this doesn't enjoy the same stature as Louisa May Alcott's much-filmed classic *Little Women*, but still makes for an intriguing companion-piece. This follows the adventures of grown-up Jo as she tries to help two young urchins who are heading into trouble. The cast isn't exactly A-list and the youngsters fare slightly better than adults but overall it's good wholesome entertainment.

Kathleen Fee *Narrator/Molly* • Michael Caloz *Nat Blake* • Mariel Hemingway *Jo Bhaer* • Ben Cook *Dan* • Ricky Mabe *Tommy Bangs* • Chris Sarandon *Fritz Bhaer* ■ *Dir* Rodney Gibbons • *Scr* Mark Evan Schwartz, from the novel by Louisa May Alcott

The Little Mermaid ★★★

Adventure 1976 · USSR · Colour · 81mins

Such was the impact of Disney's animated feature that it's difficult to approach other adaptations of Hans Christian Andersen's celebrated story with an open mind. Yet, Vladimir Bychkov's live-action version has a certain charm, reminiscent of that Eastern bloc TV classic, *The Singing Ringing Tree*. Unfussily, he extracts a little fairytale magic from the stylised backdrops against which unfolds the story of prince Valentin Nikulin, who falls in love with Vika Novikova, the mermaid who delivered him from the wiles of her singing sisters. The downbeat ending won't please everyone, but at least Bychkov has remained true to his source. A Russian language film.

Vika Novikova *The Little Mermaid* • Valentin Nikouline *Troubador* • Galina Artemova *Princess* • Yuri Senkevitch *Prince* • Galina Volchek *Witch* ■ *Dir* Vladimir Bychkov • *Scr* Victor Vitkovich, Grigory Lagfeld, from the fairy tale by Hans Christian Andersen

The Little Mermaid ★★★★★ U

Animated adventure 1989 · US · Colour · 85mins

What a splash this adventure made on its release, marking as it did the beginning of a new "golden age" of Disney animated features. The story of the plucky Ariel (who set the tone for a new generation of Disney heroines) features impressive animation and a catchy, show-stopping score by Academy Award nominated Alan Menken – including the instant hit *Under the Sea*, sung with Caribbean verve by Sebastian, composer to the court of King Triton and Ariel's reluctant minder. While some of the

scenes could possibly frighten very young children, especially those featuring the loathesome Ursula, this remains an enduring delight.

Jodi Benson *Ariel* • Samuel E Wright *Sebastian* • Christopher Daniel Barnes *Eric* • Pat Carroll *Ursula* • Edie McClurg *Carlotta* • Buddy Hackett *Scuttle* • Kenneth Mars *Triton* • Ben Wright *Grimsby* • René Auberjonois *Louis* ■ *Dir* John Musker, Ron Clements • *Scr* John Musker, Ron Clements, from the fairy tale by Hans Christian Andersen

The Little Minister ★★★

Drama 1934 · US · BW · 104mins

Adapted from a novel and play by JM Barrie, this screen incarnation of the tale (several silent versions were made) stars Katharine Hepburn as gypsy girl Babbie, an exotic outsider in a strictly religious Scottish community. Babbie's romantic relationship with new, handsome young minister John Beal causes a furore among the village congregation. Beal gives a competent portrayal of a rigid cleric gradually melting under the influence of love, while Hepburn offers one of her livelier performances under Richard Wallace's direction.

Katharine Hepburn *Babbie* • John Beal *Gavin* • Alan Hale *Rob Dow* • Donald Crisp *Dr McQueen* • Lumsden Hare *Thammas* • Andy Clyde *Wearyworld* • Beryl Mercer *Margaret* ■ *Dir* Richard Wallace • *Scr* Jane Murfin, Sarah Y Mason, Victor Heerman, Mortimer Offner, Jack Wagner, from the play by JM Barrie

Little Miss Broadway

★★★ U

Musical 1938 · US · BW · 71mins

A characteristic vehicle for the world's most famous child star phenomenon, Shirley Temple, now a veteran at ten years old and looking a mite plump. The idiotic plot is a variation on a number of other Temple vehicles in which the little moppet brings sunshine into a dozen lives and melts the stoniest of hearts – in this case mean Edna May Oliver who wants to close the hotel for stage troupers where Temple, rescued from an orphanage, lives with the family that has adopted her. With the aid of George Murphy, Jimmy Durante, Phyllis Brooks, and a host of others, the disaster is averted. The precocious child is awesome – simultaneously ghastly and irresistible.

Shirley Temple *Betsy Brown* • George Murphy *Roger Wendling* • Jimmy Durante *Jimmy Clayton* • Phyllis Brooks *Barbara Shea* • Edna May Oliver *Sarah Wendling* • George Barbier *Fiske* • Edward Ellis *Pop Shea* • Jane Darwell *Miss Hutchins* ■ *Dir* Irving Cummings • *Scr* Harry Tugend, Jack Yellen

Little Miss Marker ★★★

Comedy 1934 · US · BW · 78mins

This was the film that clinched Shirley Temple's claim to stardom. The diminutive phenomenon, six years old at the time, is utterly disarming and captivating as the moppet who is left with a bookie (Adolphe Menjou) as an IOU, and proceeds to reform the gambling fraternity with her charm. Based on a Damon Runyon story, the cast is peopled with the author's typically amusing guys and dolls. Second only to *Here Comes Mr Jordan*

in the output of variable director Alexander Hall, this is a warm and witty tale with the inestimable advantage of Temple's performance. The story was remade three times to far less effect.

Adolphe Menjou *Sorrowful Jones* • Dorothy Dell *Bangles Carson* • Charles Bickford *Big Steve* • Shirley Temple *Miss Marker* • Lynne Overman *Regret* ■ *Dir* Alexander Hall • *Scr* William R Lipman, Sam Hellman, Gladys Lehman, from the story by Damon Runyon

Little Miss Marker ★ U

Comedy 1980 · US · Colour · 97mins

Tastes change, and this remake of the Shirley Temple vehicle is so sweet it's guaranteed to give you toothache. Sara Stimson has the unenviable role of following Temple as the titular Little Miss, who is handed over by her father to Walter Matthau's bookie as the guarantee for a racing debt. Matthau soon becomes putty in her childish hands, in an unbelievable tale of a cute kid softening a grumpy old man. Throw a simpering Julie Andrews and a mincing Tony Curtis into the melting pot and you have Damon Runyon turning in his grave.

Walter Matthau *Sorrowful Jones* • Julie Andrews *Amanda* • Tony Curtis *Blackie* • Bob Newhart *Regret* • Lee Grant *The Judge* • Brian Dennehy *Herbie* • Kenneth McMillan *Brannigan* • Andrew Rubin *Carter* • Sara Stimson *The Kid* ■ *Dir* Walter Bernstein • *Scr* Walter Bernstein, from the story by Damon Runyon

Little Miss Millions ★★

Comedy 1993 · US · Colour

B-movie director Jim Wynorski takes a break from slashers and erotic thrillers for this misfiring family TV comedy. Executive produced by Roger Corman and co-written by Wynorski and longtime associate RJ Robertson, this is anything but a latter-day Shirley Temple movie, as runaway Jennifer Love Hewitt turns the tables on her wicked stepmother (Anita Morris) by teaming up with Howard Hesseman, the bounty hunter sent to find her, and going off in search of her real mother. Morris has the most fun in a Cruella De Vil sort of way, but it's Hewitt who catches the eye.

Love Hewitt [Jennifer Love Hewitt] *Heather Lofton* • Howard Hesseman *Nick Frost* • Steve Landesberg *Harvey Lipshitz* • Anita Morris *Sybil Lofton* • Terri Treas *Susan Ferris* ■ *Dir* Jim Wynorski • *Scr* Jim Wynorski, RJ Robertson

Little Monsters ★ PG

Fantasy adventure 1989 · US · Colour · 97mins

Funnyman Howie Mandel is Maurice, the wart hog-like creature who lives under Fred Savage's bed, in this adolescent *Beetle Juice* copy. Together they venture into a land of monsters and get up to all manner of childish pranks. Some of that mischief is actually quite vicious and dark so parents videoing for young children should take note. Everyone tries hard to mine the fantasy for all the quirky comedy value they can, but the clumsy script defeats even these hardened professionals. A dismal disaster.

Fred Savage *Brian* • Howie Mandel *Maurice* • Ben Savage *Eric* • Daniel Stern *Glen Stevenson* • Margaret Whitton *Holly Stevenson* ■ *Dir* Richard Alan Greenberg • *Scr* Terry Rossio, Ted Elliott

Little Moon & Jud McGraw ★

Western 1978 · US · Colour · 92mins

This comedy western was previously known by the even less appealing title *Bronco Busters*. James Caan finds himself in one of the many troughs that have characterised his rollercoaster career. He's the falsely accused Jud McGraw, trying to clear his name and track down the real villain. Leaving aside the not very original plot, you might wonder what the likes of Stefanie Powers, Sammy Davis Jr and Aldo Ray were doing in the supporting cast.

James Caan *Jud McGraw* • Aldo Ray *Nemo* • Stefanie Powers • Sammy Davis Jr ■ *Dir* Bernard Girard • *Scr* J AS McCombie, Douglas Stewart, Monroe Manning, Marcus Devian

Little Murders ★★★★

Black comedy 1971 · US · Colour · 108mins

Satiric cartoonist Jules Feiffer adapted his play for the screen under the direction of actor Alan Arkin. Elliott Gould (who also co-produced) plays a young photographer who specialises in taking pictures of excrement. As a hardened New Yorker he's blithely unconcerned about crime and violence – even when he's the victim. Into this life of apathy comes optimist Marcia Rodd who thinks he will make ideal husband material. This black comedy of Manhattan manners hasn't dated – if anything its chilling view of alienation and arbitrary violence is more relevant than when it was made. A wonderful cast, including Vincent Gardenia, Donald Sutherland (as a hippy judge) and Arkin himself make this little-known, but thought-provoking film, worth seeking out.

Elliott Gould *Alfred Chamberlain* • Marcia Rodd *Patsy Newquist* • Vincent Gardenia *Mr Newquist* • Elizabeth Wilson *Mrs Newquist* • Jon Korkes *Kenny* • John Randolph *Mr Chamberlain* • Doris Roberts *Mrs Chamberlain* • Donald Sutherland *Minister* • Alan Arkin *Detective* ■ *Dir* Alan Arkin • *Scr* Jules Feiffer, from his play

Little Nellie Kelly ★★★ U

Musical drama 1940 · US · BW · 98mins

Judy Garland was solo billed for the first time in this awkward slice of blarney, playing not only the young title character but also her dying mother! Today, some may well find this MGM adaptation of an old George M Cohan Broadway musical comedy rather mawkish, but Garland, as ever, delivers a wonderfully sincere performance, her talent shining through. George Murphy has the right surname but too bland a manner as Judy's husband/father, and Charles Winninger blusters along as usual. Once again, just watch for Garland: she's the whole movie.

Judy Garland *Nellie Kelly/Little Nellie Kelly* • George Murphy *Jerry Kelly* • Charles Winninger *Michael Noonan* • Douglas McPhail *Dennis Fogarty* • Arthur Shields *Timothy Fogarty* • Rita Page *Mary Fogarty* • Forrester Harvey *Moriarty*

• James Burke *Sergeant McGowan* ■ *Dir* Norman Taurog • *Scr* Jack McGowan, from the musical comedy by George M Cohan

Little Nemo: Adventures in Slumberland ★★★
Animated adventure
1992 · US · Colour · 85mins

This animated adaptation of Winsor McCay's pioneering comic-strip will delight young and old alike, thanks to its songs by legendary Disney stalwarts the Sherman brothers and the involvement of sci-fi maestro Ray Bradbury and French illustrator Moebius in the story. Nothing quite matches the eye-popping opening, but the twin worlds of Slumberland and Nightmareland are beautifully drawn, blending 19th-century imagination with modern graphic techniques. The story of the boy who has to rescue a kindly king after he opens a forbidden door is constantly surprising and there's a wonderfully malevolent voice-over from Mickey Rooney as the likeable con artist, Flip.

Gabriel Damon *Nemo* • Mickey Rooney *Flip* • René Auberjonois *Professor Genius* • Danny Mann *Icarus* • Laura Mooney *Princess Camille* • Bernard Erhard *King Morpheus* • William E Martin *Nightmare King* ■ *Dir* William T Hurtz, Masami Hata • *Scr* Chris Columbus, Richard Outten, from a story by Jean Moebius Giraud, Yutaka Fujioka, from the comic strip by Winsor McCay

A Little Night Music ★★★ ☑
Musical
1977 · Aus/US/W Ger · Colour · 119mins

Ingmar Bergman's 1955 film *Smiles of a Summer Night* was the inspiration for Stephen Sondheim's Broadway musical *A Little Night Music*. It's brought to the screen with glamorous Elizabeth Taylor and Diana Rigg as two of the guests at a country estate. Appropriately, Taylor is cast as an actress with a colourful past but now looking for some stability in her life. Other visitors include her current lover and his wife (Rigg) and a past beau with his new bride. Stage director Hal Prince can't replicate the pace of the Broadway show but fans of Stephen Sondheim will enjoy the music, particularly *Send in the Clowns*, and the costume design received an Oscar nomination. ▭

Elizabeth Taylor *Desiree Armfeldt* • Diana Rigg *Charlotte Mittelheim* • Len Cariou *Frederick Egerman* • Lesley-Anne Down *Anne Egerman* • Hermione Gingold *Mme Armfeldt* • Laurence Guittard *Carl-Magnus Mittelheim* • Christopher Guard *Erich Egerman* • Chloe Franks *Fredericka Armfeldt* ■ *Dir* Harold Prince • *Scr* Hugh Wheeler, from the musical by Hugh Wheeler, Stephen Sondheim, from the film *Smiles of a Summer Night* by Ingmar Bergman • *Costume Designer* Florence Klotz

Little Noises ★★ ☑
Drama
1992 · US · Colour · 87mins

A muddled, offbeat fable about greed, guilt and wanting more than you truly deserve. Struggling would-be writer Crispin Glover steals poems written by his friend Matthew Hutton who, though gifted with words, is actually mute. This unscrupulous behaviour brings Glover fame, fortune and success in the publishing world in director Jane Spencer's deliberately small-scale, character-driven opus. Fine work by Glover (who doesn't come across quite as strange as he usually does) and the unusually eclectic cast make this ambitious chamber piece worth a look – though ultimately it's a failure intellectually. ▭

Crispin Glover *Joey Kremple* • Tatum O'Neal *Stella Winslow* • John C McGinley *Stu Slovack* • Rik Mayall *Mathias Lichtenstein* • Steven Schub *Timmy Smith* • Tate Donovan *Elliott* • Nina Siemaszko *Dolores* • Matthew Hutton *Marty Slovack* • Carole Shelley *Aunt Shirley* ■ *Dir* Jane Spencer • *Scr* Jane Spencer, Jon Zeiderman, from the story by Anthony Brito, Jane Spencer

Little Odessa ★★★ ☑
Crime thriller   1994 · US · Colour · 94mins

In this intimate character study, chilly both in setting and in atmosphere, a hit man (Tim Roth) is forced to return to his old Russian-Jewish Brooklyn neighbourhood to carry out an execution. But contact with his family only serves to re-ignite old feuds. Writer/director James Gray, here making a promising debut, elicits meaty performances from Roth, Edward Furlong and Maximilian Schell. However, his tendency to swamp key moments with excessive visual stylistics does sometimes blunt this movie's dramatic edge. Contains violence, swearing and nudity. ▭

Tim Roth *Joshua Shapira* • Edward Furlong *Reuben Shapira* • Moira Kelly *Alla Shustervich* • Vanessa Redgrave *Irina Shapira* • Maximilian Schell *Arkady Shapira* • Paul Guilfoyle *Boris Volkoff* • Natasha Andreichenko *Natasha* • David Vadim *Sasha* ■ *Dir/Scr* James Gray

A Little of What You Fancy ★★★ ☑
Music documentary
1968 · UK · Colour · 79mins

A treat for anyone who laments the passing of *The Good Old Days*. Using a variety of photographs, posters, theatre bills and other memorabilia, this slickly produced documentary traces the history of British music hall from 1854 to 1968. Although much of this nostalgic wallow is occupied by a glorified *son et lumière* show, director Robert Webb tacks on an interesting finale in which he explores how the music hall tradition survived in the pubs, clubs and cabarets of the late sixties, thanks to such performers as Helen Shapiro and Barry Cryer.

Dir Robert Webb [Robert D Webb] • *Scr* Ray Mackender

Little Old New York ★★★ ☑
Comedy drama   1940 · US · BW · 100mins

The story of Robert Fulton who, back in 1807, managed to achieve his dream of building the first ever steamboat, is turned here by 20th Century-Fox into a vehicle for Alice Faye. She plays a breezy Irish saloon-keeper torn between sturdy Fred MacMurray and callow but bright Richard Greene – best remembered as TV's Robin Hood – as Fulton. Director Henry King had previously worked wonders with Faye in this kind of historical twaddle, notably *Alexander's Ragtime Band* and *In Old Chicago*, and he wisely concentrates on the boat-building sequences, which are actually rather good. But the eternal triangle plot is silly and this style of movie has dated rather badly.

Alice Faye *Pat O'Day* • Fred MacMurray *Charles Browne* • Richard Greene *Robert Fulton* • Brenda Joyce *Harriet Livingstone* • Andy Devine *Commodore* • Henry Stephenson *Chancellor Livingstone* ■ *Dir* Henry King • *Scr* Harry Tugend, from a story by John Balderson, from the play by Rita Johnson Young

The Little Prince ★★ ☑
Musical   1974 · UK · Colour · 88mins

Antoine de Saint-Exupéry's much-loved allegory on the importance of childhood becomes a ponderous musical fable with few sparkling moments under Stanley Donen's stodgy direction. Pilot Richard Kiley crashes in the Sahara desert and is discovered by the Little Prince (Steven Warner), an emissary from another planet, who proceeds to teach him the true meaning of life through surreal intergalactic flashbacks. We meet an assortment of weird characters, from Gene Wilder's Fox and Bob Fosse's Snake (a superbly slithery routine from the dance master) to Joss Ackland's King and Clive Revill's Businessman. Lumbered with pointless songs by Alan Jay Lerner and Frederick Loewe (well past their *Camelot* and *My Fair Lady* prime), Donen's inability to meld the achingly real with the strangely fantastic turns the material to heavy-handed whimsy, lacking the proper imagination it needed to really fly.

Richard Kiley *Pilot* • Steven Warner *Little Prince* • Bob Fosse *Snake* • Gene Wilder *Fox* • Joss Ackland *King* • Clive Revill *Businessman* • Victor Spinetti *Historian* • Graham Crowden *General* • Donna McKechnie *Rose* ■ *Dir* Stanley Donen • *Scr* Alan Jay Lerner, from the book *Le Petit Prince* by Antoine De Saint-Exupéry

The Little Princess ★★★★ ☑
Musical drama   1939 · US · Colour · 88mins

Made when the career of dimpled darling Shirley Temple was waning, this is now considered her best film. A lovingly produced version of Frances Hodgson Burnett's classic story of a little rich girl moved to the cold attic of her boarding school when her father is reported dead. Beautifully crafted and filmed in gorgeous Technicolor, this is a little gem. The very British Arthur Treacher accompanies the star in a delightful song and dance number, and the film's climax is appropriately tear-inducing. ▭

Shirley Temple *Sara Crewe* • Richard Greene *Geoffrey Hamilton* • Anita Louise *Rose* • Ian Hunter *Capt Crewe* • Cesar Romero *Ram Dass* • Arthur Treacher *Bertie Minchin* • Mary Nash *Amanda Minchin* • Sybil Jason *Becky* ■ *Dir* Walter Lang • *Scr* Ethel Hill, Walter Ferris, from the novel by Frances Hodgson Burnett • *Producer* Darryl F Zanuck

A Little Princess ★★★★★ ☑
Fantasy drama   1995 · Colour · 93mins

Simple for children to understand, yet sophisticated enough for adults to enjoy thoroughly too, this wonderful adaptation of the novel by Frances Hodgson Burnett (who also wrote *The Secret Garden*) is an instant classic. The importance of magic and imagination in all our lives is engagingly conveyed through the entrancing tale of a schoolgirl escaping into exotic flights of fancy after news of her father's death. Mexican director Alfonso Cuaron gives his spell-binding fable a dazzling look and an astonishing atmosphere which proves hard to resist. A little marvel you'll be enthralled by from colourful start to heart-rending finish. ▶ *DVD*

Eleanor Bron *Miss Minchin* • Liam Cunningham *Captain Crewe/Prince Rama* • Liesel Matthews *Sara Crewe* • Rusty Schwimmer *Amelia Minchin* • Arthur Malet *Charles Randolph* • Vanessa Lee Chester *Becky* • Errol Sitahal *Ram Dass* • Heather DeLoach *Ermengarde* ■ *Dir* Alfonso Cuarón • *Scr* Richard LaGravenese, Elizabeth Chandler, from the novel by Frances Hodgson Burnett

The Little Rascals ★ ☑
Comedy   1994 · US · Colour · 78mins

Launched by Hal Roach in 1922, the *Our Gang* series ran until 1944, ending its days at MGM. A decade later, around 100 of these comic shorts resurfaced on TV under the title *The Little Rascals*. Having failed the previous year to capture the magic of *The Beverly Hillbillies* on film, director Penelope Spheeris thought she'd take a crack at bringing Alfalfa, Darla and Spanky to a new audience, only to miss the target again and by a much wider margin. The members of the young cast throw themselves into the enterprise, but the antics of the He-Man Woman Haters Club belong to another age. ▭

Travis Tedford *Spanky* • Bug Hall *Alfalfa* • Brittany Ashton Holmes *Darla* • Kevin Jamal Woods *Stymie* • Zachary Mabry *Porky* • Ross Elliot Bagley *Buckwheat* • Sam Saletta *Butch* • Blake McIver Ewing *Waldo* • Mel Brooks *Mr Welling* • Whoopi Goldberg *Buckwheat's Mom* • Daryl Hannah *Miss Crabtree* • Donald Trump *Waldo's Dad* • George Wendt *Lumberyard Clerk* ■ *Dir* Penelope Spheeris • *Scr* Paul Guay, Stephen Mazur, Penelope Spheeris, from a story by Penelope Spheeris, Robert Wolterstorff, Mike Scott, Paul Guay

Little Red Monkey ★★★
Spy drama   1955 · UK · BW · 77mins

Ken Hughes honed his skills as a director of thrillers working on the Scotland Yard B-movie series. Consequently, this quota quickie has a great deal more substance and style than many of its contemporaries. In the midst of a series of scientist slayings, a top Russian boffin defects and American agent Richard Conte is called in to escort him across the Atlantic. Hughes keeps the action on the boil, while Russell Napier and Rona Anderson are fine as a Scotland Yard detective and his niece. The only drawback is Conte, who looks too old and disinterested.

Richard Conte *Bill Locklin* • Rona Anderson *Julia* • Russell Napier *Superintendent Harrington* • Colin Gordon *Martin* • Arnold Marle *Dushenko* • Sylvia Langova *Hilde* • Donald Bisset *Editor* ■ *Dir* Ken Hughes • *Scr* Ken Hughes, James Eastwood, from the TV serial *Case of the Red Monkey* by Eric Maschwitz

The Little Riders ★★★
Second World War drama
1996 · US · Colour · 96mins

A made-for-television film based on Margaretha Shemin's cute novel for children, it features the British veteran Paul Scofield, with Malcolm McDowell in prime villain mode. A Disney backed wartime drama, it centres on Joanne Hunter (Noley Thornton) who, trapped in Holland with her grandparents (Scofield and Rosemary Harris), is intent on preventing the town clock from falling into Nazi hands. McDowell is suitably nasty as Captain Kessel, the German leader set on destroying the timepiece and its ''Little Riders'' statues. It's compelling fare if tinged with Disney cuteness.

Paul Scofield *Grandpa Pieter Roden* • Malcolm McDowell *Captain Kessel* • Rosemary Harris *Grandma Juliana Roden* • Noley Thornton *Joanne Hunter* • Benedick Blythe *Lieutenant Karl Braun* ■ *Dir* Kevin Connor • *Scr* Gerald DiPego, from the novel by Margaretha Shemin

A Little Romance ★★★ PG

Romantic comedy
1979 · US/Fr · Colour · 105mins

That Laurence Olivier could ham it up with the best, or worst, of them is proved unquestionably as he takes on the role of a Maurice Chevalier-like boulevardier helping lovelorn youngsters to a happy ending. The adults (Sally Kellerman, Arthur Hill, David Dukes) are so overdrawn there's inevitable sympathy for Diane Lane, the American girl in Paris falling for Thelonious Bernard despite family pressure. Charming and entertaining fluff; watch for Broderick Crawford's abrasive cameo appearance. 📺

Laurence Olivier *Julius Edmond Santorin* • Diane Lane *Lauren King* • Thelonious Bernard *Daniel Michon* • Arthur Hill *Richard King* • Sally Kellerman *Kay King* • Broderick Crawford • David Dukes *George De Marco* • Andrew Duncan *Bob Duryea* • Claudette Sutherland *Janet Duryea* ■ *Dir* George Roy Hill • *Scr* Allan Burns, from the novel *E = MC Mon Amour* by Patrick Cauvin

A Little Sex ★★ 15

Comedy 1981 · US · Colour · 90mins

Mary Tyler Moore became a major player behind the screen when she set up MTM Enterprises, which produced such hit series as *Hill Street Blues*, *St Elsewhere* and *Lou Grant*. Their first theatrical production stayed loyal to its small screen roots, featuring Tim Matheson as a successful director of TV commercials who is also a hit with the ladies. Michael tries to commit to his live-in girlfriend Kate Capshaw but finds temptation at every turn. Capshaw, making her debut here, would later marry a certain Steven Spielberg.

Tim Matheson *Michael* • Kate Capshaw *Katherine* • Edward Herrmann *Brother* • John Glover *Walter* • Joan Copeland *Mrs Harrison* • Susanna Dalton *Nancy* ■ *Dir* Bruce Paltrow • *Scr* Robert DeLaurentiis

Little Shop of Horrors ★★★ PG

Horror comedy 1960 · US · BW · 71mins

One of cult director Roger Corman's best-loved productions, this riotous no-budget comedy horror romp was shot in three-days on a leftover set, according to Hollywood legend. Jonathan Haze is the browbeaten florist's apprentice breeding a carnivorous plant which starts

decimating the neighbourhood. Look out for Jack Nicholson, hilarious as Wilbur Force, the masochistic dental patient reading *Pain* magazine in the waiting room.

Jonathan Haze *Seymour Krelboined* • Jackie Joseph *Audrey Fulguard* • Mel Welles *Gravis Mushnik* • Myrtle Vail *Winifred Krelboined* • Leola Wendorff *Mrs Shiva* • Jack Nicholson *Wilbur Force* ■ *Dir* Roger Corman • *Scr* Charles B Griffith

Little Shop of Horrors ★★★★ PG

Musical black comedy
1986 · US · Colour · 89mins

Phil Spector cross-pollinates with Roger Corman (who directed a 1961 version). This rockery horror show is packed with great doo-wop songs, a killer line-up of stars (Steve Martin shines brightest as the sadistic dentist) and clever horticultural special effects that underline, but never swamp, the charming theatricality of the stylised whole. The Four Tops' Levi Stubbs voices the alien Venus People-Trap that causes deliciously nerdy Rick Moranis to hack up victims for plant food and impress his Monroe-inspired lover Ellen Greene, who reprises her award-winning off-Broadway role. A memorably weird musical in the grand old Hollywood tradition. Contains violence and swearing. 📺 **DVD**

Rick Moranis *Seymour Krelborn* • Ellen Greene *Audrey* • Vincent Gardenia *Mushnik* • Steve Martin *Orin Scrivello, DDS* • Tichina Arnold *Crystal* • Tisha Campbell *Chiffon* • Michelle Weeks *Ronette* • James Belushi *Patrick Martin* • John Candy *Wink Wilkinson* • Christopher Guest *First customer* • Bill Murray *Arthur Denton* • Levi Stubbs *Voice of Audrey II* ■ *Dir* Frank Oz • *Scr* Howard Ashman, from the play by Howard Ashman, from the film by Charles B Griffith

Little Spies ★★ U

Adventure 1986 · US · Colour · 88mins

Mickey Rooney plays second-string to a load of excitable Disney kids who become amateur sleuths when their dog is taken by kidnappers. It's average TV-movie adventure-romp stuff, but there's not enough action to keep most children glued to the TV. 📺

Mickey Rooney *Jimmie the Hermit* • Robert Costanzo *Bernie* • Peter Smith *Jason* • Candace Cameron *Julie* ■ *Dir* Greg Beeman • *Scr* Stephen Greenfield, Stephen Bonds, from a story by John Greg Pain, Stephen Bonds, Stephen Greenfield

The Little Theatre of Jean Renoir ★★★ U

Drama 1969 · Fr/It/W Ger · Colour · 107mins

Made for television, Jean Renoir's final feature is a delightful compendium, revisiting the humanist concerns that had preoccupied him for over forty years. In *Le Dernier Reveillon*, a homeless old couple find peace in companionship and dreams; *Le Cireuse Electrique* is a recitative denunciation of the evils of urban progress; *Quand l'Amour Se Meurt* is a musical interlude, sung by Jeanne Moreau in Belle Epoque costume; while *Le Roi d'Yvetot* centres on a cuckold forgiving both his wife and his best friend in a paean to the consoling joys of the countryside. A mixed bag,

but a master's folly. In French with English subtitles.

Nino Fornicola *Bum* • Minny Monti *Female bum* • Marguerite Cassan *Isabelle* • Jeanne Moreau *Singer* • Fernand Sardou *Duvallier* • Françoise Arnoul *Isabelle* • Jean Carmet *Feraud* • Jean Renoir *Narrator* ■ *Dir/Scr* Jean Renoir

Little Treasure ★★★ 15

Comedy adventure
1985 · US · Colour · 94mins

Margot Kidder is a loudmouthed topless dancer, summoned to Mexico for a reunion with her father, Burt Lancaster. She spends most of her time hanging out with Ted Danson and pursuing some elusive stolen cash. These are characters at the end of the line, and in some way the movie resembles a softened-up, distaff version of *Bring Me the Head of Alfredo Garcia*. This isn't really surprising since it's the directing debut of Alan Sharp, the Scottish-born scriptwriter of Robert Aldrich's *Ulzana's Raid* and Sam Peckinpah's last movie, *The Osterman Weekend*, both of which starred Lancaster. 📺

Margot Kidder *Margo* • Ted Danson *Eugene* • Burt Lancaster *Teschemacher* • Joseph Hacker *Norman Kane* • Malena Doria *Evangelina* • John Pearce *Joseph* • Gladys Holland *Sadie* ■ *Dir/Scr* Alan Sharp

Little Vegas ★★★★ 15

Comedy 1990 · US · Colour · 87mins

This small-scale comedy/drama compensates for a lack of stars with lovely ensemble playing from Anthony John Denison, Catherine O'Hara and Jerry Stiller. They're part of the community of oddballs and eccentrics who live in in a Nevada trailer park. Harvey (Bruce McGill) dreams of turning the town into a mini gambling mecca, but he's opposed by Sam (Jerry Stiller) who has seen it all before with the pioneering mobsters of the real Vegas. Directed by Perry Lang, this intriguing story has director John Sayles in a small role. 📺

Anthony John Denison *Carmine* • Catherine O'Hara *Lexie* • Anne Francis *Martha* • Michael Nouri *Frank* • Perry Lang *Steve* • Bruce McGill *Harvey* • Jerry Stiller *Sam* • John Sayles ■ *Dir/Scr* Perry Lang

Little Vera ★★★ 15

Drama 1988 · USSR · Colour · 133mins

For all its cultural significance as one of the first *glasnost* movies to present a reasonably accurate picture of everyday Soviet life, *Little Vera* is a cinematically pedestrian picture. Director Vasili Pichul never stints in his depiction of the peeling walls, the sozzled citizens and the limited opportunities, but a few astute compositions dealing with a grainy film stock and some apposite vignettes do not make a classic in themselves. What is striking, however, is the minxish performance of Natalya Negoda, who does more to convince with her desperate longings for the trappings of capitalism than Pichul does with his *cinéma vérité* posturings. In Russian with English Subtitles. Contains sex scenes and nudity.

Natalya Negoda *Vera* • Andrei Sokolov *Sergei* ■ *Dir* Vasili Pichul • *Scr* Mariya Khmelik

Little Voice ★★★★ 15

Comedy drama 1998 · UK · Colour · 92mins

Jane Horrocks reprises her stage performance as the reclusive ''LV'', whose virtuoso impersonations of the great singers – Marlene Dietrich, Judy Garland – almost disguise a complete lack of conversation. Her talents are belatedly recognised by sleazy agent Michael Caine, who's prepared to endure the attentions of her sexually predatory mother Brenda Blethyn as long as he can make some money out of that voice. The brilliance of Horrocks is slightly undermined by director Mark Herman's crude depiction of working-class life in a northern seaside town. Blethyn's strident squawking almost threatens to drown out the more subtle, Lolita-esque undertones of the story but there's good support from nightclub boss Jim Broadbent and Ewan McGregor. In any other country this would have made Horrocks a major star. Contains swearing, nudity and sexual references. 📺 **DVD**

Brenda Blethyn *Mari* • Jane Horrocks *Little Voice* • Ewan McGregor *Billy* • Philip Jackson *George* • Annette Badland *Sadie* • Michael Caine *Ray Say* • Jim Broadbent *Mr Boo* ■ *Dir* Mark Herman • *Scr* Mark Herman, from the play *The Rise and Fall of Little Voice* by Jim Cartwright

Little White Lies ★★★ U

Romantic comedy
1989 · US/Can · Colour · 89mins

Anson Williams was obviously trying to follow in the footsteps of his *Happy Days* co-stars Henry Winkler and Ron Howard when he directed this romantic comedy. While he isn't quite in the same league as Howard, this is a fair if lightweight attempt at screwball comedy. Ann Jillian and Tim Matheson are the pair who meet while on holiday in Rome but are less than honest about who they are and what they do back home in the US. Of course, they fall in love. This is amusing if not exactly ground-breaking stuff. 📺

Ann Jillian *Liz Windsor/Detective Donaldson* • Tim Matheson *Harry Wing/Dr McCrae* • Richard Coca *Claudio* • Marc McClure ■ *Dir* Anson Williams • *Scr* Janis Hirsch, Lynn Roth

Little Witches ★★ 18

Horror 1996 · US · Colour · 87mins

Forced to spend her Easter vacation at a dreary Catholic girl's school, rebellious Jamie (Sheeri Rappaport), discovers a secret passage in the church and a hidden spell book. For a lark she initiates the other girls in a naked coven and, before you can say *The Craft*, unleashes evil forces beyond her control and eventually summons up the papier-mâché Devil. Although hardly original, and often prone to bad continuity and ragged cheapness, this is a perfectly competent teen witch chiller in the sly *Buffy the Vampire Slayer* mould, with adequate acting making the most of its low-jolt factor. 📺

Mimi Reichmeister *Faith* • Jack Nance *Father Michael* • Jennifer Rubin *Sherilyn* • Sheeri Rappaport *Jamie* • Zelda Rubinstein *Mother Clodah* • Eric Pierpoint *Sheriff Gordon* ■ *Dir* Jane Simpson • *Scr* Brian DiMuccio, Dino Vindeni

Little Women ★★★★ U

Period drama 1933 · US · BW · 110mins

The first of three talkie versions of Louisa May Alcott's classic novel, starring Katharine Hepburn, Joan Bennett, Frances Dee and Jean Parker as the four sisters growing up in New England during the Civil War period. Director George Cukor had an early opportunity to show his affinity with the great female stars of the era and he apparently felt that this represented an honest picture of what America had been 60 years before. The film struck a chord with audiences at the time but lost out on the Oscars for best film and best director. This remains an entrancing film, with Hepburn perfectly cast. □

Katharine Hepburn *Jo* • Joan Bennett *Amy* • Paul Lukas *Prof Fritz Bhaer* • Edna May Oliver *Aunt March* • Jean Parker *Beth* • Frances Dee *Meg* • Henry Stephenson *Mr Laurence* • Douglass Montgomery *Laurie* • John Davis Lodge [John Lodge] *Brooke* • Spring Byington *Marmee* ■ *Dir* George Cukor • *Scr* Sarah Y Mason, Victor Heerman, from the novel by Louisa May Alcott

Little Women ★★★ U

Period drama 1949 · US · Colour · 121mins

In this lush MGM adaptation of Louisa May Alcott's novel, director Mervyn LeRoy pulls out all the stops and has the benefit of a good cast, but the studio settings and the MGM production requirements really get in the way of the storytelling. Elizabeth Taylor and Janet Leigh are far too knowing for their roles, and top-billed June Allyson is too coy (and too old) for Jo. There's charm, certainly, whenever Margaret O'Brien and Peter Lawford are around, and the whole is very pretty to look at, but the classic original demanded sterner stuff than this cotton-candy confection, which ultimately resembles an animated Christmas card.

June Allyson *Jo March* • Peter Lawford *Laurie Laurence* • Margaret O'Brien *Beth March* • Elizabeth Taylor *Amy March* • Janet Leigh *Meg March* • Rossano Brazzi *Professor Bhaer* • Mary Astor *Marmee March* • Lucile Watson *Aunt March* • C Aubrey Smith *Mr Laurence* • Elizabeth Patterson *Hannah* • Leon Ames *Mr March* ■ *Dir* Mervyn LeRoy • *Scr* Andrew Solt, Sarah Y Mason, Victor Heerman, from the novel by Louisa May Alcott

Little Women ★★★ U

Period drama 1995 · US · Colour · 113mins

Mother hen Susan Sarandon dominates this adaptation of Louisa May Alcott's much-loved novel about four impoverished sisters growing up during the American Civil War. Australian director Gillian Armstrong cuts through some of the schmaltz though Winona Ryder, superbly cast as the spirited Jo, still emotes like mad but seems to have forgotten that it was exactly that schmaltz that made the earlier versions so enjoyable. This nineties take on the tale is less cosy and therefore, despite its wonderful pedigree, less memorable. □ **DVD**

Winona Ryder *Jo March* • Susan Sarandon *Marmee March* • Gabriel Byrne *Professor Friedrich Baer* • Eric Stoltz *John Brooke* • Samantha Mathis *Amy Aged 16* • Trini Alvarado *Meg* • Kirsten Dunst *Amy Aged 12* • Claire Danes *Beth* • Christian Bale *Laurie* •

Mary Wickes *Aunt March* • Matthew Walker *Mr March* ■ *Dir* Gillian Armstrong • *Scr* Robin Swicord, from the novel by Louisa May Alcott

The Littlest Rebel ★★★ PG

Musical war drama 1935 · US · BW · 73mins

This was a quintessential vehicle for Shirley Temple, made when the incredibly talented moppet was the top box-office attraction around the world. In this Civil War tale, based on a play that had starred the later infamous Mary Miles Minter, Temple displays all the facets that made her so unique. The scene in which she pleads with President Lincoln to set her father free from a prisoner-of-war camp displays both humour and pathos, and she chirpily performs two dance duets with Bill Robinson. Only those allergic to Temple could fail to warm to this. □

Shirley Temple *Virginia "Virgie" Houston Cary* • John Boles *Confederate Capt Herbert Cary* • Jack Holt *Union Colonel Morrison* • Karen Morley *Mrs Cary* • Bill Robinson *Uncle Billy* • Guinn "Big Boy" Williams [Guinn Williams] *Sgt Dudley* • Willie Best *James Henry* • Frank McGlynn Sr *President Abraham Lincoln* • Bessie Lyle *Mammy* ■ *Dir* David Butler • *Scr* Edwin Burke, Harry Tugend, from the play by Edward Peple

Live a Little, Love a Little ★★ PG

Musical 1968 · US · Colour · 85mins

An enjoyable romp, at least by Presley standards, with several tuneful songs. Elvis plays a photographer who digs himself into a hole when he tries to shuttle between two jobs for publishers with very different editorial policies – both in the same office building. Watch out for Rudy Vallee, a singing star from an earlier era, as a publisher. Reasonably frothy, though humorist Dan Greenburg's original book, *Kiss My Firm but Pliant Lips*, sounds funnier. □

Elvis Presley *Greg* • Michele Carey *Bernice* • Don Porter *Mike Landsdown* • Rudy Vallee *Penlow* • Dick Sargent *Harry* • Sterling Holloway *Milkman* ■ *Dir* Norman Taurog • *Scr* Michael A Hoey, Dan Greenburg, from the novel *Kiss My Firm But Pliant Lips* by Dan Greenburg

Live a Little, Steal a Lot ★★ 15

Crime comedy 1974 · US · Colour · 101mins

Robert Conrad and Don Stroud play real-life heist-meisters Allan Kuhn and Jack Murphy who, when the film was made, were locked up in a Florida prison. Jumped-up beach boys in flash clothes, they specialised in fleecing Miami and Bahamian hotels and beach houses; they then went big time by removing a priceless sapphire called the Star of India from the Natural History Museum in New York. It's *Topkapi* meets *Beach Blanket Bingo*, filled with the requisite number of chases, close shaves and "characterful" performances designed to glamourise the criminals. □

Robert Conrad *Allan Kuhn* • Don Stroud *Jack Murphy* • Donna Mills *Ginny Eaton* • Robyn Millan *Sharon Kagel* • Luther Adler *Max "The Eye"* • Paul Stewart *Avery* • Burt Young *Sergeant Bemasconi* • Pepper Martin

Sergeant Terwilliger • *Dir* Marvin J Chomsky • *Scr* E Arthur Kean, from a story by Allan Dale Kuhn

Live and Let Die ★★★★ PG

Action adventure 1973 · UK · Colour · 116mins

Roger Moore's first tour of duty as James Bond, in the eighth of the licensed-to-kill series, has him up against the dark powers of voodoo in the bulky shape of Yaphet Kotto, while embracing the more curvaceous figure of tarot-reader Jane Seymour. Boasting as many cliff-hanging moments as a Saturday-matinée serial, this tale of a plan to turn everyone into drug addicts allows Bond's adversaries – among them sharks, snakes and crocodiles – to be as mechanical as is Moore himself. There are some splendid spasms of action, however, notably a speedboat leap that set a new world record, as well as the usual array of high-tech gadgetry to marvel at. □

Roger Moore *James Bond* • Yaphet Kotto *Dr Kananga* • Jane Seymour *Solitaire* • Clifton James *Sheriff Pepper* • Julius W Harris [Julius Harris] *Tee Hee* • Geoffrey Holder *Baron Samedi* • David Hedison *Felix Leiter* • Gloria Hendry *Rosie* • Bernard Lee *"M"* • Lois Maxwell *Miss Moneypenny* • Ruth Kempf *Mrs Bell* • Joie Chitwood *Charlie* ■ *Dir* Guy Hamilton • *Scr* Tom Mankiewicz, from the novel by Ian Fleming

Live Bait ★★★

Comedy 1995 · Can · BW · 84mins

Considering he was debuting as writer, director, editor and producer, Bruce Sweeney made a decent fist of this Generation X comedy, which contains echoes of both *The Graduate* and *The Pallbearer*. Overshadowed by his brother, pampered by his mother and taunted by his ambitious father, Tom Scholte has little going for him until he meets seasoned sculptress Micki Maunsell, who not only awakens his sense of self, but also becomes his sexual muse. Smart dialogue, exceptional performances and a fond nostalgia for the passing of misspent youth raise this well above the average slacker or rites-of-passage picture.

Tom Schlote *Trevor MacIntosh* • Kevin McNulty *John MacIntosh* • Babs Chula *Helen MacIntosh* • David Lovgren *Brian MacIntosh* • Micki Maunsell *Charlotte Peacock* ■ *Dir/Scr* Bruce Sweeney

Live Fast, Die Young ★★

Crime 1958 · US · BW · 82mins

Paul Henreid is best known for his part in one of cinema's great love triangles, as the man who whisks Ingrid Bergman away from Humphrey Bogart in *Casablanca*. A genuine European "Ladies' Man" (the title of his autobiography), Henreid directed several movies including this effort aimed squarely at the teen audience. It's about a young woman who gets involved in crime, and makes a bundle until her more law-abiding older sister spoils the party. Deeply moral, it stars Mary Murphy from *The Wild One* and teen heart-throb Troy Donahue.

Mary Murphy *Kim Winters* • Norma Eberhardt *Jill Winters* • Sheridan Comerate *Jerry Beckitt* • Michael Connors [Mike Connors] *Rick* • Carol Varga *Violet* • Jay Jostyn *Knox* • Peggy Maley *Sue Hawkins* • Troy Donahue *Artie* ■

Dir Paul Henreid • *Scr* Allen Rivkin, Ib Melchior, from a story by Edwin B Watson, Ib Melchior

Live Flesh ★★★★ 18

Black comedy thriller 1997 · Sp/Fr · Colour · 96mins

Excruciatingly funny, fearlessly frank and gloriously ironic, Spanish director Pedro Almodóvar's engaging take on the Ruth Rendell thriller is a deliciously twisted tale of destiny, desire and death. Using the central concept of how a single bullet fired during a botched police investigation causes a ricochet effect through the lives of five different characters, the camp iconoclast serves up a pulse-quickening cocktail of subversion and sexual tension where truth and humanity are used as clever red herrings. Featuring amazing performances from Javier Bradem and Angela Molina, this crime of passion is a must-see and easily Almodóvar's best film since *Women on the Verge of a Nervous Breakdown*. In Spanish with English subtitles. □

Francesca Neri *Elena* • Javier Bardem *David* • Jose Sancho *Sancho* • Angela Molina *Clara* • Liberto Rabal *Victor Plaza* ■ *Dir* Pedro Almodóvar • *Scr* Pedro Almodóvar, Ray Loriga, Jorge Guerricaechevarria, from the novel by Ruth Rendell

Live! From Death Row ★★ 18

Thriller 1992 · US · Colour · 92mins

Bruce Davison plays the disenchanted maverick prisoner who holds a talk show host (Joanna Cassidy) and her camera crew hostage just hours before he is due to be executed in this tough and controversial TV thriller. In spite of the occasional outbreak of tension, this turns out to be a rather shallow showdown between the psychotic prisoner and the authorities. Contains violence and swearing.

Bruce Davison *Laurence Dvorak* • Joanna Cassidy *Alana Powers* • Jason Tomlins *Director* • Michael D Roberts *Silsbee* ■ *Dir/Scr* Patrick Duncan

Live It Up ★★ U

Musical 1963 · UK · BW · 75mins

You'd hardly know that the Beatles were in the process of transforming the British pop scene from some of the sounds presented in this determinedly traditional musical. Lance Comfort was a decent director, but he was hardly cutting edge and he handles the drama as unimaginatively as he stages the songs. Icon-in-waiting David Hemmings looks distinctly uncomfortable as the Post Office messenger who defies trad dad Ed Devereux to bid for the top, prompting a hackneyed subplot about an audition tape and a big American producer.

David Hemmings *Dave Martin* • Jennifer Moss *Jill* • John Pike *Phil* • Heinz Burt *Ron* • Stephen Marriott *Ricky* • Joan Newell *Margaret Martin* • Ed Devereaux *Herbert Martin* ■ *Dir* Lance Comfort • *Scr* Lyn Fairhurst, from her story, from an idea by Harold Shampan

Live, Love and Learn ★★★

Comedy 1937 · US · BW · 78mins

Rich girl Rosalind Russell marries impoverished artist Robert Montgomery

and the two enjoy bohemian bliss in Greenwich Village until success for the artist rears its corrupting head. The two stars are delightful in the early portions of this mixture of screwball comedy and melodrama, but get little help from the script when things get tougher. The stars, the MGM polish and a sterling supporting cast – including Robert Benchley and Mickey Rooney – give the fluffy concoction enough substance to keep it watchable.

Robert Montgomery *Bob Graham* • Rosalind Russell *Julie Stoddard Graham* • Robert Benchley *Oscar* • Helen Vinson *Lily Chalmers* • Monty Woolley *Mr Charles C Bawltitude* • EE Clive *Mr Palmiston* • Mickey Rooney *Jerry Crump* ■ *Dir* George Fitzmaurice • *Scr* Charles Brackett, Cyril Hume, Richard Maibaum, from a story by Marion Parsonnet, Helen Grace Carlisle

Live Now – Pay Later ★★★★

Comedy 1962 · UK · BW · 103mins

A remarkably cynical and revealing portrait of Britain shifting from post-war austerity into rampant consumerism and the swinging sixties. Ian Hendry plays a seedy, on-the-make, door-to-door salesman who pressurises his customers – usually housewives – into bed and into hock. He runs around the council estates in a van filled with rubbish, has an illegitimate child and is himself deeply in debt. Hendry's character – Albert – is appalling, yet he is also sympathetic since he's the only character who ever does anything in a society built on inertia and the sense of defeat that only wartime victory can bring. The title song might almost be the national anthem.

Ian Hendry *Albert Argyle* • June Ritchie *Treasure* • John Gregson *Callendar* • Liz Fraser *Joyce Corby* • Geoffrey Keen *Reggie Corby* • Jeannette Sterke *Grace* • Peter Butterworth *Fred* • Nyree Dawn Porter *Marjorie Mason* • Ronald Howard *Cedric Mason* • Harold Berens *Solly Cowell* ■ *Dir* Jay Lewis • *Scr* Jack Trevor Story, from the novel *All on the Never-Never* by Jack Lindsay

Live Nude Girls ★★ 18

Comedy drama 1995 · US · Colour · 91mins

Kim Cattrall and Dana Delaney star in this stream of consciousness comedy drama from writer/director Julianna Levin. They're just two of the thirtysomething women at a reunion party, sitting around talking frankly about sex, relationships, family and friends, as people tend to do on such soul-baring occasions. You'll either get bored really fast by the group's petty, self-indulgent ramblings, or be riveted by the caring and sharing. Contains nudity and sexual references. [video]

Dana Delany *Jill* • Kim Cattrall *Jamie* • Cynthia Stevenson *Marcy* • Laila Robins *Rachel* • Lora Zane *Georgina* • Olivia D'Abo *Chris* ■ *Dir/Scr* Julianna Lavin

Live Wire ★★★ 15

Thriller 1992 · US · Colour · 81mins

After *Remington Steel* and before his James Bond debut in *Goldeneye*, Pierce Brosnan's career dipped, but this, while hardly a classic, is a step ahead of similar fare, thanks to a strong cast and an ingenious storyline. Brosnan stars as an FBI agent trying to stop the villainous Ben Cross blowing up Washington politicians. The twist here, though, is that Cross has developed a liquid explosive that gives new meaning to the phrase "don't drink the water" if you do, you effectively become a human bomb. That's the cue for some truly stunning explosive effects. Between the set pieces there are some pretty solid performances: leaving aside his dodgy American accent, Brosnan is as charismatic as ever, while there is fine support from Ron Silver, Philip Baker Hall and Lisa Eilbacher. Contains swearing, violence and brief nudity. [video]

Pierce Brosnan *Danny O'Neill* • Ron Silver *Frank Traveres* • Ben Cross *Mikhail Rashid* • Lisa Eilbacher *Terry O'Neill* • Tony Plana *Al-red* • Al Waxman *James Garvey* • Brent Jennings *Shane Rogers* • Philip Baker Hall *Senator Thyme* ■ *Dir* Christian Duguay • *Scr* Bart Baker

The Lives of a Bengal Lancer ★★★★

Action adventure 1935 · US · BW · 109mins

A fabulous chunk of "Hollywood colonial", this wonderful, rip-roaring tale was a smash hit in its day and still manages to stir the hearts of adventure lovers. Gary Cooper, in a career-defining performance, and the urbane Franchot Tone are terrific as buddies on the North-West Frontier, fighting an array of evil, turbaned character actors, and looking after new recruit Richard Cromwell, who just happens to be the son of their commanding officer, Guy Standing. Multi-Oscar nominated, this film and its attitudes have been highly influential (the *Beau Geste* series as well as *Gunga Din*) and it was virtually remade in western guise as *Geronimo* in 1939.

Gary Cooper *Lieutenant Alan McGregor* • Franchot Tone *Lieutenant "Fort" Forsythe* • C Aubrey Smith *Major Hamilton* • Richard Cromwell *Lieutenant Donald Stone* • Guy Standing *Colonel Stone* • Kathleen Burke *Tania Volkanskaya* • Douglas Dumbrille [Douglass Dumbrille] *Mohammed Khan* • Monte Blue *Hamzulla Khan* • Akim Tamiroff *Emir of Gopal* • J Carrol Naish *Grand Vizier* ■ *Dir* Henry Hathaway • *Scr* Waldemar Young, John L Balderston, Achmed Abdullah, from the novel by Major Francis Yeats-Brown, adapted by Grover Jones, Wiliam Slavens McNutt

Living Dangerously ★★

Satirical comedy 1987 · Gr · Colour · 105mins

The state of Greece is the subject of this misfiring picture that neither succeeds as thriller nor satire. Writer/director Nicos Perakis spreads his net too wide either to dissect such social evils as labour exploitation, censorship and the repression of women or to sustain our interest. Giorgos Kimoulis works hard as the phone engineer who threatens to blow the nation's phone lines unless he gets a ten-minute TV soapbox slot before a crucial football match. But, with the cops blundering around Athens harassing everyone they suspect of being his accomplice, the action gets bogged down in lengthy squabbles and political rhetoric. In Greek with English subtitles.

Giorgos Kimoulis *Karamanos* ■ *Dir/Scr* Nicos Perakis

The Living Daylights ★★★ PG

Action adventure
1987 · UK · Colour · 125mins

One of the weakest of the Bond movies, this was Timothy Dalton's debut as 007 and it was already pretty clear that he lacked the necessary ironic touch that made the credibility-straining action seem fun rather than ridiculous. Although adapted from an Ian Fleming story, the plot is merely an excuse for a little globe-trotting, as Bond tries to help Soviet general Jeroen Krabbé to defect. Maryam d'Abo's Czech cellist and Joe Don Baker's arms dealer don't help much, either. [video]

Timothy Dalton *James Bond* • Maryam D'Abo *Kara Milovy* • Jeroen Krabbé *General Georgi Koskov* • Joe Don Baker *Brad Whitaker* • John Rhys-Davies *General Leonid Pushkin* • Art Malik *Kamran Shah* • Andreas Wisniewski *Necros* • Thomas Wheatley *Saunders* • Desmond Llewelyn *"Q"* • Robert Brown *"M"* • Caroline Bliss *Miss Moneypenny* ■ *Dir* John Glen • *Scr* Richard Maibaum, Michael G Wilson, from a story by Ian Fleming

The Living Dead ★★★★

Horror thriller fantasy
1932 · Ger · BW · 98mins

Paul Wegener, the great German actor and director, notably of *The Golem* (1914 and 1920), made his talkie debut in one of the last films of the Expressionist movement. Set in a shadowy England, it was based on two Edgar Allan Poe stories and one from Robert Louis Stevenson's *The Suicide Club*. Wegener plays a crazed inventor who kills his wife accidentally and conceals her body in a wall. The film, which seems to herald incipient Nazism, contains effective scenes in a waxworks museum and in an asylum where the lunatics have taken over. In German with English subtitles.

Paul Wegener *The murderer* • Harald Paulsen *Frank Briggs* • Mary Parker *Briggs's fiancée* • Paul Henckels *Doctor* ■ *Dir* Richard Ornstein [Richard Oswald] • *Scr* Heinz Goldberg, Eugen Szatmari, from stories by Edgar Allan Poe and from a short story by Robert Louis Stevenson

The Living Desert ★★★★ U

Documentary 1953 · US · Colour · 71mins

Keen to exploit the success of the "True-Life Adventures" series, Walt Disney moved into feature documentaries with this Oscar-winning study of the wildlife that endures the climatic extremes of Death Valley, the Yuma sand dunes and the Salton Sea mud pots. Disney's regular distributor, RKO, was convinced the film would fail at the box-office and so he founded his own company, Buena Vista, to launch the phenomenally profitable picture. Critics denounced the fact that the bobcat's escape from some wild pigs was staged rather than "discovered", but with a lively commentary by Winston Hibler, it remains a classic of its kind.

Dir James Algar • *Scr* James Algar, Winston Hibler, Ted Sears, Jack Moffitt

The Living End ★★★ 18

Road movie 1992 · US · Colour · 81mins

Shot on a shoestring by Gregg Araki, the *enfant terrible* of American independent cinema, this film gleefully advertised itself as an "irresponsible" black comedy about society's attitude towards HIV-positive gay men. While Araki sometimes tries a little too hard to shock and the acting is always the wrong side of raw, this is a film that is not ashamed to make a fool of itself in order to convey its audacious mix of carefree comedy and heartfelt anger. While some might find the darkly humorous tone hard to take, others will feel that the film doesn't go far enough in its condemnation of homophobic ignorance. Contains violence, swearing and nudity. [video]

Mike Dytri *Luke* • Craig Gilmore *Jon* • Mark Finch *Doctor* • Mary Woronov *Daisy* ■ *Dir/Scr* Gregg Araki

Living Free ★★ U

Adventure 1972 · UK · Colour · 86mins

Adapted from Joy Adamson's bestseller, the sequel to the ever-popular *Born Free* follows the fate of Elsa the lioness's three cubs after she is killed. The Adamsons are determined to keep them out of the zoo, but, unfortunately, their 700-mile journey across the wilds of Kenya to the Serengeti National Park has too few moments of high drama and, try as they might, Susan Hampshire and Nigel Davenport cannot quite replace Virginia McKenna and Bill Travers as Joy and George. However, the scenery is stunning, and, of course, the cubs are as cute and cuddly as ever. [video]

Nigel Davenport *George Adamson* • Susan Hampshire *Joy Adamson* • Geoffrey Keen *John Kendall* • Edward Judd *Game Warden Weaver* ■ *Dir* Jack Couffer • *Scr* Millard Kaufman, from the books by Joy Adamson

Living in a Big Way ★★

Comedy drama 1947 · US · BW

Marrying in haste before being drafted overseas, a GI returns to repent at leisure when his wife turns out to be wealthy, pampered, intent on a good time and a totally unsuitable mate. A box-office disaster in its day and hardly seen since, this confused mix of comedy, drama, social message, and sentimentality is not without some entertainment value. Gene Kelly stars as the idealistic hero, and he dances up a storm in a handful of numbers co-choreographed with Stanley Donen. Marie "The Body" McDonald is the wife; and the experienced Gregory La Cava, while partly responsible for the inept screenplay, directs with the style you would expect.

Gene Kelly *Leo Gogarty* • Marie McDonald *Margaud Morgan* • Charles Winninger *D Rutherford Morgan* • Phyllis Thaxter *Peggy Randall* • Spring Byington *Mrs Morgan* ■ *Dir* Gregory La Cava • *Scr* Gregory La Cava, Irving Ravetch, from a story by Gregory La Cava

Living in Oblivion ★★★★ 15

Comedy 1995 · US · Colour and BW · 86mins

The trials and tribulations of low-budget independent film-making are sent up with glorious wit and economy in director Tom DiCillo's low-budget independent film. Steve Buscemi is hilarious as the harassed director contending with egomaniac lead James LeGros, inept stagehands, back-stabbing assistants, off-screen love affairs and a temperamental dwarf, all in one day of production. Packed with movie-buff in-jokes, DiCillo's incisive sparkling satire is on a par with François Truffaut's similarly themed 1973 movie *Day for Night*.

Steve Buscemi *Nick Reve* • Catherine Keener *Nicole* • Dermot Mulroney *Wolf* • Danielle Von Zerneck *Wanda* • James LeGros *Chad Palomino* ■ *Dir/Scr* Tom DiCillo

Living in Peril ★★

Thriller 1997 · US · Colour · 95mins

Seattle architect Walter Woods (Rob Lowe) goes to LA to design a mansion for wealthy businessman James Belushi, but his life quickly turns to hell. First it starts with rats in his apartment and his car being vandalised, then he wakes up with a dead body beside him. Many – and quite obvious – red herrings abound, and most viewers will have guessed the explanation before Lowe does. It's at least decently made (including an intense climax), and there is a lot of fun from the performances of supporting players Dean Stockwell, Richard Moll, and Patrick Ersgard. Lowe, however, never quite generates the sympathy his character needs.

James Belushi *Harrison/Oliver* • Rob Lowe *Walter Woods* • Dean Stockwell *William* • Dana Wheeler-Nicholson *Linda Woods* • Alex Meneses *Catherine Langtry* • Richard Moll *Fritz* ■ *Dir* Jack Ersgard • *Scr* Jack Ersgard, Patrick Ersgard, Jesper Ersgard

Living It Up ★★★ U

Musical comedy 1954 · US · Colour · 93mins

This good-natured Dean Martin and Jerry Lewis comedy is actually a remake – via a Broadway show called *Hazel Flagg* – of the 1937 black comedy movie *Nothing Sacred*. Lewis takes the Carole Lombard role as the victim of radiation poisoning, with smoothie Martin as Jerry's medic, and sexy Janet Leigh in the Fredric March part of the ambitious reporter. Highlights include Sheree North's sizzling performance of what was arguably the first rock 'n' roll number on celluloid. This movie is very funny indeed, and Jim Carrey fans should take a look at Lewis's big scene at Yankee Stadium: Jerry is funnier and did it first!

Dean Martin *Steve* • Jerry Lewis *Homer* • Janet Leigh *Wally Cook* • Edward Arnold *The Mayor* • Fred Clark *Oliver Stone* • Sheree North *Jitterbug Dancer* ■ *Dir* Norman Taurog • *Scr* Jack Rose, Melville Shavelson, from the musical *Hazel Flagg* by Ben Hecht, Jule Styne, Bob Hilliard, from a story by James Street

Living Out Loud ★★★ 15

Comedy drama 1998 · US · Colour · 95mins

Screenwriter Richard LaGravenese's directorial debut is a bittersweet comedy loosely based on two Anton Chekov stories. Holly Hunter *(The Piano)* is terrific as the chic Manhattan fortysomething trying to make it on her own after her husband of 15 years leaves her. Ensconced in her deluxe high-rise apartment, she passes the time of day with lift operator Danny DeVito and has imaginary conversations with singer Queen Latifah at a jazz bar. An interesting look at nineties' relationships and one woman's journey in particular, the film unfortunately loses its power towards the end in favour of a Hollywood-style finale, with all loose ends neatly tied up. Contains swearing. DVD

Holly Hunter *Judith* • Danny DeVito *Pat* • Queen Latifah *Liz Bailey* • Martin Donovan *Bob Nelson* • Richard Schiff *Philly* • Elias Koteas *The Kisser* • Suzanne Shepherd *Mary* • Mariangela Pino *Donna* ■ *Dir* Richard LaGravenese • *Scr* Richard LaGravenese, from stories by Anton Chekhov

Lizzie ★★★

Psychological drama 1957 · US · BW · 81mins

Eleanor Parker is very fine as the woman with three personalities: one quiet and shy, another raunchy and boisterous and the third together and caring. Psychiatric treatment from a stolidly able Richard Boone swiftly ensues. Based on Shirley Jackson's novel *The Bird's Nest*, Hugo Haas's rather humdrum and plodding movie has all the hallmarks of fifties psychiatric knowledge and practice – Ms Parker doesn't quite have leeches placed on her forehead, but it's not far off. Closely followed the same year by the vastly superior *The Three Faces of Eve* with Joanne Woodward.

Eleanor Parker *Elizabeth Richmond* • Richard Boone *Dr Neal Wright* • Joan Blondell *Aunt Morgan* • Hugo Haas *Walter Brenner* • Ric Roman *Johnny Valenzo* • Dorothy Arnold *Elizabeth's Mother* • John Reach *Robin* • Marion Ross *Ruth Seaton* • Johnny Mathis *Nightclub Singer* ■ *Dir* Hugo Haas • *Scr* Mel Dinelli, from the novel *The Bird's Nest* by Shirley Jackson

The Llano Kid ★★

Western 1939 · US · BW · 69mins

A mild little Paramount western featuring imported Latin-American crooner Tito Guizar as writer O Henry's legendary "kissing bandit", previously played by the great Gary Cooper in *The Texan*. This was made to cash in on the then-popular Cisco Kid (also an O Henry hero) style of exotic cowboy lead. Guizar has a charming though little-known Frank Loesser lullaby to sing, plus an interesting co-star in Jan Clayton, who was the original lead on Broadway in *Carousel* and is still remembered with affection as Tommy Rettig's mom in the first-ever Lassie TV series in the fifties. However, since the other woman is evil Gale Sondergaard, her co-stars barely get a look-in.

Tito Guizar *The Llano Kid* • Alan Mowbray *John Travers* • Gale Sondergaard *Lora Travers* • Jan Clayton *Lupita* • Emma Dunn *Donna Teresa* • Minor Watson *Sheriff McLane* ■ *Dir* Edward Venturini • *Scr* Wanda Tuchock, from the short story *The Double-Dyed Deceiver* by O Henry

Lloyd's of London ★★★★

Historical epic 1936 · US · BW · 115mins

No facet of history was safe from 20th Century-Fox, who managed to turn both Rothschild and Lloyd's into household names in America. The presence of the young Tyrone Power undeniably helped in the latter instance, and this is the movie that launched the matinée idol's stardom. Power's character begins, though, as an apprentice (played by top-billed Freddie Bartholomew) in the famous brokerage house. He grows up to become handsome Ty, vying with suave George Sanders for the beauteous Madeleine Carroll. It's extremely handsomely mounted and director Henry King treats it all as though it's a solid piece of Americana. It isn't, of course, and many may now be disturbed by the distinct lack of British atmosphere. Despite these minor reservations this is grand-scale entertainment from Hollywood's Golden Age.

Freddie Bartholomew *Young Jonathan Blake* • Tyrone Power *Jonathan Blake* • Madeleine Carroll *Lady Elizabeth Stacy* • Sir Guy Standing [Guy Standing] *John Julius Angerstein* • George Sanders *Lord Everett Stacy* • C Aubrey Smith *Old "Q"* • Virginia Field *Polly* • Montagu Love *Hawkins* • Una O'Connor *Widow Blake* • JM Kerrigan *Brook Watson* ■ *Dir* Henry King • *Scr* Ernest Pascal, Walter Ferris, from a story by Curtis Kenyon

Loaded ★★ 18

Psychological thriller
1994 · UK/NZ · Colour · 91mins

Anna Campion, sister of the Oscar-winning Jane, makes her directing debut with this modest, yet intriguing psychological thriller. The story focuses on a vaguely pretentious group of Generation X school-leavers (including Oliver Milburn, Thandie Newton and Catherine McCormack) who travel to the country to make a horror film. Things go pear-shaped when they collectively drop some tabs of acid one night. Campion summons up an air of quiet psychological menace, although it's hard to work up much sympathy for the self-centred characters.

Oliver Milburn *Neil* • Nick Patrick *Giles* • Catherine McCormack *Rose* • Thandie Newton *Zita* • Matthew Eggleton *Lionel* • Danny Cunningham *Lance* • Biddy Hodson *Charlotte* ■ *Dir/Scr* Anna Campion

Lobster Man from Mars ★★ PG

Science-fiction comedy
1989 · US · Colour · 78mins

Borrowing liberally from Mel Brooks's classic *The Producers*, this good-natured spoof of all those drive-in monster movies of the fifties is just about tacky and smart enough to be intermittently enjoyable. Tony Curtis stars as movie mogul JP Shelldrake who, upon being told he needs a flop for tax purposes, sets out to make the biggest howler in Hollywood history. The performances are enthusiastic and suitably ripe, but director Stanley Sheff fails to maintain the high level of inspirational parody that made *Airplane!* and *The Naked Gun* into such comedy classics.

Tony Curtis *JP Shelldrake* • Deborah Foreman *Mary* • Anthony Hickox *John* • Tommy Sledge • Dean Jacobson *Stevie Horowitz* • Fred Holiday *Colonel Ankrum* • Bobby Pickett *King of Mars, the Astrologer* • SD Nemeth *Dreaded Lobster Man* ■ *Dir* Stanley Sheff • *Scr* Bob Greenberg

Local Hero ★★★★ PG

Comedy 1983 · UK · Colour · 107mins

This comedy drama firmly established Bill Forsyth as a major British film-maker. It's a lyrical, almost mystical, tale that follows the attempts of Texas oilman Burt Lancaster and his minion Peter Riegert to buy up an isolated Scottish village in order to build an oil refinery, without bargaining on the village's integral strength of community. *Local Hero* manages to avoid the relentless whimsy of Forsyth's previous outing, *Gregory's Girl*: the scenery is gorgeous, the performances funny, ironic and moving (Lancaster, in particular, is superb), and Forsyth brings a sure directorial touch. Contains swearing.

Peter Riegert *MacIntyre* • Burt Lancaster *Happer* • Denis Lawson *Urquhart* • Peter Capaldi *Oldsen* • Fulton Mackay *Ben* • Jenny Seagrove *Marina* • Jennifer Black *Stella* • Christopher Asante *Reverend MacPherson* • Rikki Fulton *Geddes* ■ *Dir/Scr* Bill Forsyth • *Cinematographer* Chris Menges

Loch Ness ★★★ PG

Fantasy drama 1994 · UK · Colour · 96mins

There's more than a hint of *Local Hero* in this feel-good fantasy drama from director John Henderson. The script had been around for a decade before Ted Danson signed up as the scientist sent to the Highlands to disprove the existence of Nessie. Naturally, his investigation is sidetracked by romance and the self-interested schemes of the locals before he, too, becomes convinced by the legend. Although Danson is a touch bland, Joely Richardson turns in a doughty performance as the single mum whose daughter knows a thing or two about "water kelpies".

Ted Danson *Dempsey* • Joely Richardson *Laura* • Ian Holm *Water Bailiff* • Harris Yulin *Doctor Mercer* • James Frain *Adrian Foote* • Keith Allen *Gordon Shoals* • Nick Brimble *Andy Maclean* • Kirsty Graham *Isabel* • Harry Jones *Wee Wullie* • Phillip O'Brien *Doctor Abernathy* ■ *Dir* John Henderson • *Scr* John Fusco

Lock, Stock and Two Smoking Barrels ★★★★ 18

Crime comedy 1998 · UK · Colour · 102mins

Widely regarded as the best British crime movie since *The Long Good Friday*, the youthful exuberance and exaggerated modern idiom of Guy Ritchie's debut feature are truly infectious. Professional acting talent is assisted by real East End criminal faces, plus celebs such as Sting and Vinnie Jones in a well-received hard-man-with-a-heart role. The action revolves around young cardsharp Eddy, who loses £500,000 he doesn't have to gangster Hatchet Harry. With a week to come up with the shortfall, he and mates Dexter Fletcher, Jason Flemyng and Jason Statham hatch a plan involving their criminal neighbours and a local ganja farm... but things get horribly complicated very quickly. Cheerfully amoral and featuring some canny carnage, it's fun from start to finish. Contains violence and swearing. DVD

Jason Flemyng *Tom* • Dexter Fletcher *Soap* • Nick Moran *Eddy* • Jason Statham *Bacon* • Steven Mackintosh *Winston* • Nicholas Rowe *J* • Nick Marcq *Charles* • Charlie Forbes *Willie* • Vinnie Jones *Big Chris* • Lenny McLean *Barry the Baptist* • Peter McNicholl *Little Chris* • PH Moriarty *Hatchet Harry* • Stephen Marcus *Nick the Greek* • Vas Blackwood *Rory Breaker* • Sting *JD* ■ *Dir/Scr* Guy Ritchie

Lock Up ★★ 18

Prison drama 1989 · US · Colour · 104mins

Sylvester Stallone opts for some grittier material after the cartoon

840 U = SUITABLE FOR ALL Uc = SUITABLE FOR ALL, ESPECIALLY FOR YOUNG CHILDREN (VIDEO ONLY) PG = PARENTAL GUIDANCE

heroics of his Rambo and Rocky characters, in a film that proves to be almost as disastrous as his forays into comedy. He plays a nice criminal on the verge of being released, who is whisked away to a Gothic prison hell presided over by Donald Sutherland. Stallone acts moody and indulges in a spot of mud wrestling, while Darlanne Fluegel, as his girlfriend, frets at home, and it's left to Sutherland to provide the only fun as the wildly over-the-top warden. John Flynn, who directed some marvellous macho thrillers, loses his way in a flood of testosterone and prison movie clichés. Contains swearing and violence. ▢

Sylvester Stallone *Frank Leone* • Donald Sutherland *Warden Drumgoole* • John Amos *Meissner* • Tom Sizemore *Dallas* • Frank McRae *Eclipse* • Sonny Landham *Chink* • Larry Romano *First Base* • Darlanne Fluegel *Melissa* ■ *Dir* John Flynn • *Scr* Richard Smith, Jeb Stuart, Henry Rosenbaum

Lock Up Your Daughters! ★★ 15

Period comedy   1969 · UK · Colour · 97mins

The story of three sex-starved sailors on leave and at large, isn't just confined to *On the Town*, as this adaptation of an 18th-century comedy demonstrates. Derived from Henry Fielding's *Rape upon Rape* and John Vanbrugh's Restoration romp, *The Relapse*, this version of the London stage musical comes to the screen minus the songs. Despite its distinguished origins – and a cast that includes Christopher Plummer, Susannah York and Glynis Johns – it comes across as non-musical slapstick that's as loud and vulgar as a cheapjack panto. ▢

Christopher Plummer *Lord Foppington* • Susannah York *Hilaret* • Glynis Johns *Mrs Squeezum* • Ian Bannen *Ramble* • Tom Bell *Shaftoe* • Elaine Taylor *Cloris* • Jim Dale *Lusty* • Kathleen Harrison *Lady Clumsey* • Roy Kinnear *Sir Tunbelly Clumsey* • Georgia Brown *Nell* • Roy Dotrice *Gossip* • Fenella Fielding *Lady Eager* ■ *Dir* Peter Coe • *Scr* Keith Waterhouse, Willis Hall, from the musical *Lock Up Your Daughters!* by Bernard Miles, Laurie Johnson, Lionel Bart, from the play *Rape upon Rape* by Henry Fielding and the play *The Relapse* by John Vanbrugh

Locked Up: a Mother's Rage ★★ 15

Drama based on a true story
1991 · US · Colour · 89mins

Based on a true story, this is a routine drama, in which Cheryl Ladd tries to dump her glamorous image, playing a woman wrongly sent to jail who has to cope with life on the inside and the welfare of her children on the outside. Soon she's campaigning for better conditions in the prison in what is an occasionally interesting, if somewhat overwrought, tale. Co-star Angela Bassett was Oscar-nominated for her role as Tina Turner in *Tina: What's Love Got to Do with It*. Contains swearing and brief nudity. ▢

Cheryl Ladd *Annie Gallagher* • Jean Smart *Cathy* • Angela Bassett *Willie* • Joshua Harris *Shawn* • Sarah Martineck *Lisa* • Diana Muldaur *Frances* ■ *Dir* Bethany Rooney • *Scr* Selma Thompson, Robert L Freedman, from the documentary *They're Doing My Time*

The Locket ★★★

Film noir   1946 · US · BW · 85mins

A minor league *film noir*, tightly directed by John Brahm and starring Laraine Day, about a little girl who allegedly stole a locket and whose kleptomania as a woman leads to murder, suicide and nervous breakdowns for everyone around her. Every flashbacked scene is a crisis, every performance over the top. Ms Day, a devout Mormon who never smoked or drank coffee, was on loan to RKO from MGM, where getting engaged to Dr Kildare (played by Lew Ayres) had made her a star. Here she is convincingly neurotic, while Robert Mitchum gives her solid support as the first of her men to crack.

Laraine Day *Nancy* • Brian Aherne *Dr Blair* • Robert Mitchum *Norman Clyde* • Gene Raymond *John Willis* • Sharyn Moffett *Nancy, aged 10* • Ricardo Cortez *Mr Bonner* • Henry Stephenson *Lord Wyndham* ■ *Dir* John Brahm • *Scr* Sheridan Gibney

Los Locos ★★ 15

Western   1997 · US/UK · Colour · 95mins

After the overtly political *Posse*, writer/star/producer Mario Van Peebles loosens up considerably for this engaging western. This time around ace gunslinger Peebles finds himself the unwitting saviour of a group of patients at a very primitive mental asylum, after the inmates save him from death. The star is as charismatic as before and his script nods slyly towards Clint Eastwood's classic *The Outlaw Josey Wales*. Western purists may wince at some of the modern liberties that are taken, but it's always watchable. ▢

Mario Van Peebles *Chance* • René Auberjonois *Presidente* • Tom Dorfmeister *Baby Brother* • Paul Lazar *Buck* • Rusty Schwimmer *Sister Drexel* • Danny Trejo *Manuel Batista* • Melora Walters *Allison* • Eric Winzenried *Spackman* • Jean Speegle Howard *Mother Superior* ■ *Dir* Jean-Marc Vallée • *Scr* Mario Van Peebles

The Locusts ★★★ U

Drama   1997 · US · Colour · 12mins

Set in the fifties, this family melodrama appears dated, despite the up-to-the-minute casting of Vince Vaughn, Ashley Judd and Paul Rudd. Kate Capshaw stars as a sultry widow who spends her spare time bedding her farm hands to the detriment of her emotionally damaged son Jeremy Davies. Drifter Vaughn appears in town and soon becomes involved with Ashley Judd; this being Tennessee Williams territory, there are dark secrets to be revealed on the way to a suitably dramatic climax. The gothic tone and certain masterful moments transform it from bad to interesting, but it never achieves the mastery of a genuine fifties classic like *East of Eden*.

Kate Capshaw *Delilah Ashford Potts* • Jessica Capshaw *Patsy* • Vince Vaughn *Clay Hewitt* • Ashley Judd *Kitty* • Jeremy Davies *Flyboy* • Daniel Meyer *Joel* • Paul Rudd *Earl* ■ *Dir/Scr* John Patrick Kelley

The Lodger ★★★★ PG

Classic silent thriller 1926 · UK · BW · 92mins

Alfred Hitchcock once called this the first true "Hitchcock movie". In addition to being the first in which he explored his favourite theme of the innocent in danger, it also marked Hitch's debut before the camera in one of those celebrated fleeting cameos. The action is based on a potboiling novel about Jack the Ripper and played with suitable extravagance by matinée idol Ivor Novello and a truly creepy cast. Clearly reflecting the influence of German Expressionism, it showcases Hitchcock's technical virtuosity, particularly in the opening montage sequence. ▢

Ivor Novello *The Lodger/Jonathan Drew* • June *Daisy Bunting* • Marie Ault *Mrs Bunting* • Arthur Chesney *Mr Bunting* • Malcolm Keen *Joe Betts* ■ *Dir* Alfred Hitchcock • *Scr* Alfred Hitchcock, Eliot Stannard, Ivor Montagu, from the novel by Marie Belloc-Lowndes

The Lodger ★★★★

Crime drama   1944 · US · BW · 80mins

In his first big starring role, the massive young character actor Laird Cregar makes an excellent job of portraying the lodger in Victorian London who is really the notorious killer, Jack the Ripper. Merle Oberon is the singer living in the same house, George Sanders the Scotland Yard inspector. A fine script is enhanced by the striking visual sense of director John Brahm and cameraman Lucien Ballard (who later married Oberon). Sadly, Cregar's promising career ended when he died from crash-dieting after making another fine period melodrama, *Hangover Square*.

Merle Oberon *Kitty* • George Sanders *John Garrick* • Laird Cregar *The Lodger* • Sir Cedric Hardwicke [Cedric Hardwicke] *Robert Burton* • Sara Allgood *Ellen* • Aubrey Mather *Supt Sutherland* • Queenie Leonard *Daisy* • David Clyde *Sgt Bates* ■ *Dir* John Brahm • *Scr* Barré Lyndon, from the novel *The Lodger* by Marie Belloc Lowndes

Logan's Run ★★★ PG

Science-fiction thriller
1976 · US · Colour · 113mins

More of a hobble into the next millennium for Michael York and Jenny Agutter, this tale earnestly depicts a society that dooms those over the age of 30 to the myth of "renewal". Made 20 years after his *Around the World in 80 Days*, director Michael Anderson takes almost as long to make his point here, but puts on a real spurt when the runners head for the outside, only to find a wrinkled Peter Ustinov living in the ruins of what was Washington DC. Dale Hennesy and Robert De Vestel's Oscar-nominated, imaginative designs compensate for the rather cumbersome plot. Contains some violence and brief nudity. ▢

Michael York *Logan* • Jenny Agutter *Jessica* • Richard Jordan *Francis* • Roscoe Lee Browne *Box* • Farrah Fawcett-majors [Farrah Fawcett] *Holly* • Peter Ustinov *Old man* • Michael Anderson Jr *Doc* • Gary Morgan *Billy* ■ *Dir* Michael Anderson • *Scr* David Zelag Goodman, from the novel by William F Nolan, George Clayton Johnson • *Costume Designer* Bill Thomas

Lola ★★★★★ PG

Romantic comedy drama
1960 · Fr/It · BW · 83mins

Dedicated to Max Ophüls but bearing the hallmarks of a Gene Kelly musical, Jacques Demy's debut feature is a charming paean to his home town of Nantes, here given a monochrome gloss by cinematographer Raoul Coutard that evokes both the poetic realism of the thirties and the vibrancy of the *Nouvelle Vague*. Demy sweeps his camera around the port as cabaret dancer Anouk Aimée has a few affairs while awaiting the return of her daughter's absentee father. Gleefully playing games with chance and coincidence, this fond satire on movie romance remains as fresh, enchanting and deliciously superficial as it seemed on its original release. In French with English subtitles. ▢

Anouk Aimée *Lola* • Marc Michel *Roland* • Elina Labourdette *Mme Desnoyers* • Alan Scott *Frankie* • Annie Duperoux *Cecile* ■ *Dir/Scr* Jacques Demy

Lola ★★★★ 15

Black comedy
1982 · W Ger · Colour · 109mins

Coming between *The Marriage of Maria Braun* and *Veronika Voss*, and loosely based on *The Blue Angel*, the second in Rainer Werner Fassbinder's trilogy is unusual in that it has a happy ending. Or, at least as happy as possible considering that brothel chanteuse Barbara Sukowa is bedding corrupt construction boss Mario Adorf within minutes of marrying idealistic town planner Armin Mueller-Stahl. Arguing that fascism did not die with Hitler, Fassbinder mischievously makes a hero of Adorf's petty dictator by having every self-centred citizen acquiesce so compliantly in his imposed conformity. A daringly dark, yet gaudily colourful comedy. In German with English subtitles. ▢

Barbara Sukowa *Lola* • Armin Mueller-Stahl *Von Bohm* • Mario Adorf *Schuckert* • Matthias Fuchs *Esslin* • Helga Feddersen *Frau Hettich* • Karin Baal *Lola's mother* • Ivan Desny *Wittich* ■ *Dir* Rainer Werner Fassbinder • *Scr* Peter Marthesheimer, Pea Frohlich

Lola ★★★

Thriller   1986 · Sp · Colour · 106mins

Packed with moments of graphic physicality, psychological intensity and sadistic violence, Bigas Luna's three-act melodrama is sordid and compelling in equal measure. As the factory worker who escapes an abusive relationship to find all-too-brief contentment with her daughter, Angela Molina is both passionate and vulnerable, particularly in the early scenes with Feodor Atkine, the true love who reappears on the scene to investigate her seemingly respectable French husband, Patrick Bauchau. The thriller aspects are a touch overcooked, but, as so often with Bigas Luna, the excess is tempered by lavish visuals and an audacious determination to unsettle the complacent. Spanish dialogue dubbed into English.

Angela Molina *Lola* • Patrick Bauchau *Robert* • Feodor Atkine *Mario* • Assumpta Serna *Silvia* ■ *Dir* Bigas Luna • *Scr* Bigas Luna, Luis Herce, Enrique Viciano

Lola + Bilidikid ★★★ 18
Drama 1999 · Tur/Ger · Colour · 95mins

A distinct whiff of early seventies Fassbinder pervades this provocative drama, set on the fringes of Berlin's gay and Turkish communities. The style is raw and busy, in keeping with writer/director Kutlug Ataman's preoccupation with the messiness of life rather than neat fictional contrivance. The performances are also disarmingly honest, with Gandi Mukli outstanding as the drag queen ostracised from his family and pressurised by his macho lover (Erdal Yildiz) to have the sex-change operation that will legitimise their relationship. With moments of revelation and tenderness shattered by explosive violence, this study of racism and homophobia burns deep. In German and Turkish with English subtitles.

Baki Davrak *Murat* • Gandi Mukli *Lola* • Erdal Yildiz *Bili* ■ *Dir/Scr* Kutlug Ataman

Lola Montès ★★★★★
Drama 1955 · Fr/W Ger · Colour · 140mins

Max Ophüls was inspired to film this story of the rise and fall of the famous mistress of King Ludwig I and Franz Liszt by Judy Garland's nervous breakdown and Zsa Zsa Gabor's romances. Ophüls's final film, his only work in colour, transcends the trappings of a conventional historical romance by his brilliant use of the CinemaScope screen and the virtuoso camerawork. Sadly, on its initial release, the producers reduced the 140-minute film to 90 minutes. It was not until 1969, when it was shown in a restored form, that the film was recognised as the masterpiece it is. Though it can only be fully appreciated on the big screen, much of its visual quality still comes across on television. In French with English subtitles.

Martine Carol *Lola Montès* • Peter Ustinov *Circus Master* • Anton Walbrook *Ludwig I, King of Bavaria* • Ivan Desny *James* • Will Quadflieg *Liszt* • Oskar Werner *The Student* • Lise Delamare *Mrs Craigie* • Henri Guisol *Maurice* • Paulette Dubost *Joséphine* ■ *Dir* Max Ophüls • *Scr* Max Ophuls, Annette Wademant, Franz Geiger, from the novel *La Vie Extraordinaire de Lola Montès* by Cécil St Laurent, Jacques Natanson

Lolita ★★★★★ 15
Black comedy drama
1961 · UK · BW · 147mins

''How did they ever make a film of *Lolita*?'' asked the posters for this brilliant Stanley Kubrick film. Well, in Vladimir Nabokov's adaptation of his own famous novel about the professor and the 12-year-old girl, there are added layers of black comedy and only slight compromise: James Mason seems to love Sue Lyon rather than lust after her, and Lolita's age is increased to 15. As time goes by, *Lolita* gets better and funnier. Shelley Winters's hilarious and sad portrayal of Lolita's mother is American momism incarnate, while Peter Sellers as Clare Quilty is like a creepy chameleon. For economic and censorship reasons the picture was made in England, and because of this Nabokov's nightmare vision of urban America and its seedy motels is reduced to obvious back projection and even more obvious Elstree locations. This apart, a perfect movie. 🖳

James Mason *Humbert Humbert* • Sue Lyon *Lolita Haze* • Shelley Winters *Charlotte Haze* • Peter Sellers *Clare Quilty* • Diana Decker *Jean Farlow* • Jerry Stovin *John Farlow* • Gary Cockrell *Dick* • Marianne Stone *Vivian Darkbloom* ■ *Dir* Stanley Kubrick • *Scr* Vladimir Nabokov, from his novel

Lolita ★★★★
Drama 1997 · Fr/US · Colour · 137mins

Adrian Lyne's version of *Lolita* was always going to be controversial, though the delay in its release had more to do with the price being asked by its French backers than anything on screen. It is far more faithful to Vladimir Nabokov's novel than the Stanley Kubrick version of 1961 – for one thing, Lyne preserves the forties setting and shoots the film in the backroads and motels of America. The film is also more sexually explicit than its predecessor, though no more than necessary to relate the story of an older man's obsession with a pubescent girl. As Humbert Humbert, Jeremy Irons gives a credible, multi-dimensional performance that is both funny and moving. As Lolita, Dominique Swain begins as a vision of tooth-braces and ice cream sodas and becomes knowingly sensual. The tone throughout is masterly, and somewhere along those backroads Lyne discovers a new genre – screwball *noir*. 🖳

Jeremy Irons *Humbert Humbert* • Melanie Griffith *Charlotte Haze* • Frank Langella *Clare Quilty* • Dominique Swain *Lolita Haze* • Suzanne Shepherd *Miss Pratt* • Keith Reddin *Reverend Rigger* • Erin J Dean *Mona* • Joan Glover *Miss LeBone* ■ *Dir* Adrian Lyne • *Scr* Stephen Schiff, from the novel by Vladimir Nabokov

The Lolly-Madonna War ★★★
Drama 1973 · US · Colour · 105mins

Let backwoods battle commence! Rod Steiger and Robert Ryan are the heads of the feuding families – the Feathers and the Gutshalls – in this variable drama. The two sides have been brought to the brink of violence by a land dispute and matters come to a head with a bizarre case of mistaken identity involving Season Hubley as the presumed ''Lolly-Madonna''. A strong supporting cast includes Jeff Bridges, Randy Quaid and Gary Busey, and director Richard C Sarafian (*Vanishing Point*) piles a lot of enthusiasm into the mayhem. Unfortunately, the film's mood-swings make it only a superior example of Peckinpah-lite.

Rod Steiger *Laban Feather* • Robert Ryan *Pap Gutshall* • Jeff Bridges *Zack Feather* • Scott Wilson *Thrush Feather* • Katherine Squire *Mrs Feather* • Tresa Hughes *Mrs Gutshall* • Season Hubley *Roonie Gill* • Randy Quaid *Finch Feather* • Gary Busey *Seb Gutshall* ■ *Dir* Richard C Sarafian • *Scr* Rodney Carr-Smith, Sue Grafton, from the novel by Sue Grafton

London ★★★★ U
Documentary drama
1994 · UK · Colour · 81mins

After a series of shorts, documentarist Patrick Keiller made his feature debut with this unique portrait of the English capital. With its highly literate commentary from Paul Scofield, this is essentially the story of three expeditions as the narrator and his friend Robinson go in search of London's literary past as well as exploring the reasons why the city sold its soul to suburbia. However, distractions abound as contemporary events like the 1992 General Election and IRA bomb attacks intrude upon their musings. The juxtaposition of text and image is endlessly intriguing as Keiller lilts between travelogue, love letter and lament. Keiller's follow-up to this, a journey around England called *Robinson in Space*, is equally as fascinating. 🖳

Paul Scofield *Narrator* ■ *Dir/Scr* Patrick Keiller

London after Midnight
Silent mystery 1927 · US · BW

Now sadly lost, this is on the American Film Institute's ''most wanted'' list. One of the first American films to deal with vampirism, this silent classic was a memorable collaboration between Lon Chaney and that other horror genius, producer/director Tod Browning. Chaney plays multiple roles in a complex plot about a pair of actors terrorising the inhabitants of a cursed Gothic mansion into believing a vampire stalks the premises. This seminal shocker was remade as *Mark of the Vampire* in 1935. Now sadly lost, this is on the American Film Institute's ''most wanted'' list.

Lon Chaney *Burke* • Marceline Day *Lucille Balfour* • Henry B Walthall *Sir James Hamlin* • Percy Williams *Butler* • Conrad Nagel *Arthur Hibbs* ■ *Dir* Tod Browning • *Scr* Tod Browning, Waldemar Young, from a story by Tod Browning

London Belongs to Me★★★
Drama 1948 · US · BW · 112mins

Richard Attenborough as the mechanic charged with murder might be the central character in this Frank Launder and Sidney Gilliat production, but the film belongs fairly and squarely to Alastair Sim. As the fake medium desperately trying to dupe Joyce Carey into marriage, he is hilariously sinister, and the scenes can't pass quickly enough before he's back on the screen. For once, the US title, *Dulcimer Street*, is probably more apposite, as this is one of those sentimentalised ''strength in the community'' pictures that postwar British cinema was so fond of. No one in the ensemble cast puts a foot wrong, with Wylie Watson and Fay Compton particularly impressive.

Richard Attenborough *Percy Boon* • Alastair Sim *Mr Squales* • Fay Compton *Mrs Josser* • Stephen Murray *Uncle Henry* • Wylie Watson *Mr Josser* • Susan Shaw *Doris Josser* • Ivy St Helier *Connie* ■ *Dir* Sidney Gilliat • *Scr* Sidney Gilliat, JB Williams, from the novel by Norman Collins

London by Night ★★★
Crime 1937 · US · BW · 70mins

Actor/dancer and future US senator George Murphy is the star of this snappy and suspenseful thriller from MGM. A well-crafted script, with punchy dialogue, has Murphy and sassy Rita Johnson (in her film debut) on the trail of a blackmailer who fakes two murders to build his reputation. Genuine English accents were provided by London-born Virginia Field and, as a Scotland Yard detective, Manchester-born George Zucco, best known as Professor Moriarty in the Basil Rathbone *Sherlock Holmes* series.

George Murphy *Michael Denis* • Rita Johnson *Patricia Herrick* • Virginia Field *Bessie* • Leo G Carroll *Correy* • George Zucco *Inspector Jefferson* • Montagu Love *Sir Arthur Herrick* ■ *Dir* William Thiele • *Scr* George Oppenheimer, from the play *The Umbrella Man* by Will Scott

London Kills Me ★ 18
Comedy drama 1991 · UK · Colour · 102mins

A disappointing directorial debut from Hanif Kureishi, the provocative writer of *My Beautiful Laundrette* and *Sammy and Rosie Get Laid*. Clint (Justin Chadwick) is a Notting Hill drug-dealer of no fixed abode, who wants to get his life together, but needs a nice pair of shoes in order to land a waiter's job at a restaurant. Whatever Kureishi was trying to say about London criminal culture is lost amongst boring characters and a general lack of audience involvement with this meaningless story. Worse still, the film seems to be presented as a celebration of youthful abandonment.

Justin Chadwick *Clint* • Steven Mackintosh *Muffdiver* • Emer McCourt *Sylvie* • Roshan Seth *Dr Bubba* • Fiona Shaw *Headley* • Brad Dourif *Hemingway* • Tony Haygarth *Burns* • Stevan Rimkus *Tom Tom* • Eleanor David *Lily* • Alun Armstrong *Stone* • Nick Dunning *Faulkner* ■ *Dir/Scr* Hanif Kureishi

London Melody ★★
Musical romance 1937 · UK · BW · 75mins

Slight musical romance from the Anna Neagle/Herbert Wilcox partnership. Neagle, a street singer and dancer, attracts the attention of Tullio Carminati's wealthy, sophisticated diplomat who secretly pays for dancing lessons, enabling her to become a cabaret star. He even takes the blame for a mistake made by the cad (Robert Douglas) to whom she was engaged. But all turns out happily in a film completely lacking in surprises. Although started at Elstree, its one claim to fame is that it was the very first production to shoot on the sound stages of the new Pinewood Studios in September 1936.

Anna Neagle *Jacqueline* • Tullio Carminati *Marius Andreani* • Robert Douglas *Nigel Taplow* • Horace Hodges *Father Donnelly* ■ *Dir* Herbert Wilcox • *Scr* Florence Tranter, Monckton Hoffe, from a story by Ray Lewis

London Town ★ U
Musical comedy 1946 · UK · Colour · 127mins

A comedian from the provinces arrives in London for his big break, only to find he has been hired as the understudy. Thanks to the devious machinations of

his daughter, he goes on as the main comic attraction. A huge budget was lavished on this film, with American director Wesley Ruggles imported for the occasion. Unfortunately, it turned out a major disaster. The plot is unappealing, the script weak, the pace laboured and the film too long. It does have the merit of starring Sid Field, thus preserving some of the great comedian's sketches for posterity, and a cast that includes famous entertainers Sonnie Hale, Tessie O'Shea, Jerry Desmonde, the young Kay Kendall before she was famous and, co-starring as Field's daughter, Petula Clark.

Sid Field *Jerry* • Greta Gynt *Mrs Barry* • Petula Clark *Peggy* • Sonnie Hale *Charlie* • Kay Kendall *Patsy* • Jerry Desmonde *George* ■ *Dir* Wesley Ruggles • *Scr* Elliot Paul, Val Guest, Siegfried Herzig, from a story by Wesley Ruggles

The Lone Hand ★★ U
Western   1953 · US · Colour · 79mins

A routine western from Universal, with Joel McCrea posing as an outlaw to bring a criminal gang to justice. McCrea's stolid sturdiness nearly sinks the film; you keep wanting him to show more emotion, but, after all, he is in disguise, even from his own son. George Sherman's direction is undistinguished, but two subsequent TV stars make a creditable showing Barbara Hale from *Perry Mason* and *Gunsmoke*'s James Arness.

Joel McCrea *Zachary Hallock* • Barbara Hale *Sarah Jane Skaggs* • Alex Nicol *Jonah Varden* • Charles Drake *George Hadley* • Jimmy Hunt *Joshua Hallock* • Jim Arness [James Arness] *Gus Varden* ■ *Dir* George Sherman • *Scr* Joseph Hoffman, from a story by Irving Ravetch

Lone Justice ★★★
Western   1994 · Colour · 94mins

A surprisingly gritty western, made for TV but well performed by a good cast. The film opens with Ned Blessing (Daniel Baldwin) awaiting execution and looking back with not a great deal of fondness on his brutal life. There are good supporting turns from René Auberjonois and Bob Gunton, although Chris Cooper steals the show as Baldwin's fearsome father.

Daniel Baldwin *Ned Blessing* • Julia Campbell *Jilly Blue* • Luis Avalos *Crecencio* • Taylor Fry *Young Jilly Blue* • Jeff Kober *Tors Buckner* • Chris Cooper *Anthony Blessing* • René Auberjonois *Marquis* ■ *Dir* Peter Werner • *Scr* Bill Wittliff

The Lone Ranger ★★ U
Western   1956 · US · Colour · 85mins

Clayton Moore and Jay Silverheels filled a break from their long-running black-and-white TV series by starring in this deluxe Warner Bros western, still playing their usual characters of the masked avenger and his Indian cohort, Tonto. The hills of southern Utah echo to the cry of ''Hi-ho, Silver!'' as the duo carry out more brave exploits, exposing rancher Lyle Bettger as the man stirring up the Indians to break their treaty so that he can mine the silver in their sacred mountain. But what's former teenage brat Bonita Granville doing making a comeback as

Bettger's wife? Perhaps it has something to do with the fact that she was married to the producer of the *Lone Ranger* series, Jack Wrather. 🎞

Clayton Moore *Lone Ranger* • Jay Silverheels *Tonto* • Lyle Bettger *Reece Kilgore* • Bonita Granville *Welcome* • Perry Lopez *Ramirez* • Robert J Wilke *Cassidy* • John Pickard *Sheriff Kimberly* • Beverly Washburn *Lila* • Michael Ansara *Angry Horse* ■ *Dir* Stuart Heisler • *Scr* Herb Meadow, from characters created by Fran Striker, George W Trendle

The Lone Ranger and the Lost City of Gold ★★ U
Western   1958 · US · Colour · 81mins

The Lone Ranger (Clayton Moore) and his sidekick Tonto (Jay Silverheels) made a comeback after their TV series had ended to celebrate the 25th anniversary of the masked avenger's debut as a radio serial. The childish plot has hooded riders murdering Indians for medallions that, pieced together, show the location of a lost city of gold. The writers and former B-western director Lesley Selander keep the action coming, though, and kids everywhere should still enjoy it.

Clayton Moore *Lone Ranger* • Jay Silverheels *Tonto* • Douglas Kennedy *Ross Brady* • Charles Watts *Oscar Matthison* • Noreen Nash *Frances Henderson* • Lisa Montell *Paviva* • Ralph Moody *Padre Vincente Esteban* ■ *Dir* Lesley Selander • *Scr* Robert Schaefer, Eric Freiwald, from characters created by Fran Striker, George W Trendle

The Lone Rider in Ghost Town ★★ U
Western   1941 · US · BW · 55mins

Deemed the best of the 1941 *Lone Riders*, this was released first to whet the public appetite for a new cowboy hero. In 1944, however, star George Houston died of a heart attack in his mid-forties. The majority of the series was directed by the prolific Sam Newfield, and produced uncoincidentally by his brother Sigmund Neufeld, who happened to be chief of production at PRC. The series waned rapidly in popularity, and the last few were released without the words ''Lone Rider'' in the actual titles. Although there had been ''Lone Riders'' before – notably in 1930 with Buck Jones – after this PRC cheapskate series, the Lone Rider would ride no more.

George Houston *Tom Cameron* • Al St John *Fuzzy* • Alaine Brandes *Helen* • Budd Buster *Moosehide* • Frank Hagney *O'Shead* • Alden Chase *Sinclair* • Reed Howes *Gordon* • Charles King *Roberts* • George Chesebro *Jed* • Edward Peil Sr *Clark* ■ *Dir* Sam Newfield • *Scr* Joe O'Donnell

Lone Star ★★ U
Western   1952 · US · BW · 94mins

Heavy-going saga of Texas in 1845 when the big question was whether it should become part of the United States or remain a republic. Clark Gable is the rancher favouring statehood, dispatched by Andrew Jackson (Lionel Barrymore) to scupper any possible deal with the Mexicans. His main adversary is Broderick Crawford, a staunch republican senator, while Ava Gardner is the newspaperwoman caught in the

middle. Some brief but well handled action sequences aren't enough to compensate for the verbose and confused script by noted western writer Borden Chase and the dreary direction by Vincent Sherman.

Clark Gable *Devereaux Burke* • Ava Gardner *Martha Ronda* • Broderick Crawford *Thomas Craden* • Lionel Barrymore *Andrew Jackson* • Beulah Bondi *Minniver Bryan* • Ed Begley *Sen Anthony Demmett* • William Farnum *Sen Tom Crockett* • Lowell Gilmore *Capt Elliott* ■ *Dir* Vincent Sherman • *Scr* Borden Chase, from stories by Howard Estabrook, Borden Chase

Lone Star ★★★★★ 15
Mystery drama   1995 · US · Colour · 129mins

A masterpiece from John Sayles. An engrossing storyline and a superb ensemble cast make this deeply textured account of the burden of history people carry with them a graceful slow-burner. Sheriff Sam Deeds (Chris Cooper) discovers a skeleton buried in the desert outskirts of his Mexican border town and launches a murder investigation. So begins a multi-generation mosaic of family ties, local legend, interracial romance and political tinkering as he discovers the murky past of his own late father (Matthew McConaughey), also a cop. Confident direction combines with intelligent drama to craft a breathtaking and bittersweet delicacy. 🎞

Kris Kristofferson *Charlie Wade* • Chris Cooper *Sam* • Matthew McConaughey *Buddy Deeds* • Elizabeth Pena *Pilar* • Frances McDormand *Bunny* • Stephen Mendillo *Cliff* • Stephen Lang *Mickey* • Oni Faida Lampley *Celie* • Eleese Lester *Molly* • Joe Stevens *Deputy Travis* ■ *Dir/Scr* John Sayles

Lone Wolf ★★ 18
Horror science-fiction
1988 · US · Colour · 94mins

Standard horror fare about high school computer hackers and a struggling rock band tracking down a killer that's terrorising Denver, Colorado, which the police think is a wild dog. The teenagers however are convinced that the killings are due to a werewolf, while the police force bumble around getting nowhere. A quite gory, but minor, entry in The *Howling*-inspired sweepstakes. 🎞

Kevin Hart *Joel* • Jamie Newcomb *Eddie* • Ann Douglas *Deirdre* • Tom Henry *The Wolf* ■ *Dir* John Callas • *Scr* Michael Krueger, John Callas, Nancy M Gallanis

The Lone Wolf in London ★
Detective drama   1947 · US · BW · 65mins

As reformed jewel thief Michael Lanyard, Gerald Mohr had none of the sauve charm and brisk authority displayed by the late Warren William in his nine *Lone Wolf* adventures. Add the phoney image of London and a weak story about Denis Green's Scotland Yard inspector suspecting the Lone Wolf of returning to his old ways when priceless diamonds are stolen, and you have a distinctly humdrum addition to the series. But it's a pleasure to see Evelyn Ankers playing an actress of shady character.

Gerald Mohr *Michael Lanyard, ''The Lone Wolf''* • Nancy Saunders *Ann Kelmscott* • Eric Blore *Claudius Jamison* • Evelyn Ankers *Iris*

Chatham • Richard Fraser *David Woolerton* • Queenie Leonard *Lily* • Alan Napier *Monty Beresford* ■ • *Scr* Arthur E Orloff, from a story by Brenda Weisberg, Arthur E Orloff, from the character created by Louis Joseph Vance

The Lone Wolf Keeps a Date ★★★
Mystery   1941 · US · BW · 64mins

Another thoroughly entertaining adventure in the company of Warren William as troubleshooting jewel thief-turned-sleuth Michael Lanyard and the effervescent Eric Blore as his valet. This time a trip to Havana to collect a rare stamp leads to involvement in a case of stolen ransom money. Typically, slow-witted cops Thurston Hall and Fred Kelsey follow every clue to Lanyard's door before he finally comes up trumps after an ingenious dockside rescue. Frances Robinson makes a starchy heroine, but the series regulars expertly sustain interest in the merest wisp of a plot.

Warren William *Michael Lanyard, ''The Lone Wolf''* • Frances Robinson *Patricia Lawrence* • Bruce Bennett *Scotty* • Eric Blore *Jamison* • Thurston Hall *Inspector Crane* • Jed Prouty *Captain Moon* • Fred Kelsey *Dickens* ■ *Dir* Sidney Salkow • *Scr* Sidney Salkow, Earl Fenton, from the character created by Louis Joseph Vance

Lone Wolf McQuade ★★★ 18
Action adventure
1983 · US · Colour · 102mins

Probably the best movie action-man hero Chuck Norris has ever made. He's a Texas Ranger battling evil gunrunner David Carradine in this modern western, which is styled after the work of Italian maestro Sergio Leone. Barbara Carrera provides the love interest in a sticky subplot, but the thrust of director Steve Carver (another Roger Corman protégé) always remains geared towards the super-macho elements – strong, silent heroes and villains, loads of weaponry and self-styled enigmatic warriors playing rough. Contains swearing, violence and brief nudity. 🎞

Chuck Norris *JJ McQuade* • David Carradine *Rawley Wilkes* • Barbara Carrera *Lola Richardson* • Leon Isaac Kennedy *Jackson* • Robert Beltran *Kayo* • LQ Jones *Dakota* ■ *Dir* Steve Carver • *Scr* BJ Nelson, from the story by H Kaye Dyal, BJ Nelson

The Lone Wolf Spy Hunt ★★★
Mystery adventure   1939 · US · BW · 67mins

Smoothly accomplished Warren William, out of the same mould as William Powell and Melvyn Douglas, plays Michael Lanyard, alias the Lone Wolf, a gentleman jewel thief turned sleuth, in this agreeably old-fashioned comedy-thriller which finds Lanyard tangling with a ruthless international spy ring. Columbia's modestly entertaining 19-picture Lone Wolf series, based on thriller-writer Louis Joseph Vance's creation, survived from 1926 to 1949, with a five-year gap. Bert Lytell played Lanyard from 1926 to 1930; Melvyn Douglas starred in *The Lone Wolf Returns* in 1936, followed by Francis Lederer in 1938 before William took over for nine in a row. After his departure, the formula

ran out of steam and after three with the lacklustre Gerald Mohr the films ended with Ron Randell in *The Lone Wolf and His Lady*.

Warren William *Michael Lanyard, "The Lone Wolf"* • Ida Lupino *Val Carson* • Rita Hayworth *Karen* • Virginia Weidler *Patricia Lanyard* • Ralph Morgan *Spiro Gregory* • Tom Dugan *Sgt Devan* • Don Beddoe *Inspector Thomas* ■ *Dir* Peter Godfrey • *Scr* Jonathan Latimer, from the novel *The Lone Wolf's Daughter* by Louis Joseph Vance

The Lone Wolf Strikes ★★★

Mystery   1940 · US · BW · 66mins

Michael Lanyard's hopes of a retirement rearing goldfish are dashed when he is called in to retrieve a string of stolen pearls in this fast-moving series entry based on a story by Dalton Trumbo, who was jailed in 1947 for his refusal to co-operate with the Congress investigation into Communism in Hollywood. As usual, Lanyard is forced to bend the law to see justice done, indulging in a little kidnapping and posing as a fence to lure a ruthless gang on to a New York ferry for the tense finale. In their first teaming, Warren William as Lanyard and Eric Blore as his butler mix comedy and thrills with practised ease.

Warren William *Michael Lanyard, "The Lone Wolf"* • Joan Perry *Delia Jordan* • Eric Blore *Jamison* • Alan Baxter *Jim Ryder* • Astrid Allwyn *Binnie Weldon* • Montagu Love *Emil Gorlick* • Robert Wilcox *Ralph Bolton* • Don Beddoe *Conroy* ■ *Dir* Sidney Salkow • *Scr* Harry Segall, Albert Duffy, from the story by Louis Joseph Vance

The Loneliness of the Long Distance Runner ★★★★★ 15

Drama   1962 · UK · BW · 99mins

Having already scored successes with *Look Back in Anger* and *A Taste of Honey*, director Tony Richardson completed his outstanding "kitchen sink" collection with this stirring tale of the borstal boy who dares to buck the system just as it offers him a lifeline. Tom Courtenay delivers a remarkable debut performance as the embittered delinquent whose talent for running gives governor Michael Redgrave the means to raise the profile of his rundown institution. Masterfully adapted by Alan Sillitoe and unobtrusively shot by Walter Lassally, this is as powerful and relevant today as it ever was. ▭

Tom Courtenay *Colin Smith* • Michael Redgrave *Governor* • Avis Bunnage *Mrs Smith* • Peter Madden *Mr Smith* • James Bolam *Mike* • Julia Foster *Gladys* • Topsy Jane *Audrey* ■ *Dir* Tony Richardson • *Scr* Alan Sillitoe, from his story

Lonely Are the Brave
★★★★

Western   1962 · US · BW · 105mins

This moving story about a contemporary cowboy is Kirk Douglas's own favourite among his films. It highlights the dignity of the individual as Douglas's law-breaking loner is pursued across the mountains by sheriff Walter Matthau. Matthau's posse uses helicopters and mountain jeeps, making the power and speed of Douglas on his horse tragically

irrelevant. The symbolism in former blacklisted writer Dalton Trumbo's script becomes a little too obvious, especially at the end, but the location photography (by Philip Lathrop) is stunning and the cast, which includes Gena Rowlands, George Kennedy and Carroll O'Connor, is superb.

Kirk Douglas *Jack Burns* • Gena Rowlands *Jerri Bondi* • Walter Matthau *Sheriff Johnson* • Michael Kane *Paul Bondi* • Carroll O'Connor *Hinton* • William Schallert *Harry* • Karl Swenson *Reverend Hoskins* • George Kennedy *Gutierrez* ■ *Dir* David Miller • *Scr* Dalton Trumbo, from the novel *Brave Cowboy* by Edward Abbey

The Lonely Guy   ★★ 15

Comedy   1984 · US · Colour · 86mins

After the dazzling invention of his collaborations with Carl Reiner, particularly *The Man with Two Brains*, this film provided a marked and slightly awkward change of pace for Steve Martin. After he finds his girlfriend in bed with another man, Martin is escorted through the rather sad world of the "lonely guy" by a sympathetic Charles Grodin; Judith Ivey is the woman who offers him the chance of escape. It's slickly directed by Arthur Hiller and there are some genuinely funny passages. However, Martin is strangely subdued and the film is stolen from under his nose by the ever-excellent Grodin. Contains some swearing and brief nudity. ▭

Steve Martin *Larry Hubbard* • Charles Grodin *Warren Evans* • Judith Ivey *Iris* • Steve Lawrence *Jack Fenwick* • Robyn Douglass *Danielle* • Merv Griffin • Dr Joyce Brothers ■ *Dir* Arthur Hiller • *Scr* Ed Weinberger, Stan Daniels, from the novel *The Lonely Guy's Book of Life* by Bruce Jay Friedman, adapted by Neil Simon

Lonely Hearts   ★★★★ 15

Romantic comedy
1981 · Ausl · Colour · 91mins

Paul Cox delivers another of his idiosyncratic insights into the soul of the misfit in this charming tale of late-life love. As usual, Norman Kaye, harbouring fantasies that are both innocent and desperate, expertly assumes the mantle of the timid everyman, as he begins to live after years of tending to his mother. His impersonation of a blind piano teacher and his encounter with a smarmy toupee salesman are just dotty enough to come off. But it's his hesitant relationship with Wendy Hughes, who has waited until her thirties to rebel against her parents, that gives the film its heart and truth. ▭

Wendy Hughes *Patricia Curnov* • Norman Kaye *Peter Thompson* • Jon Finlayson *George* • Julia Blake *Pamela* • Jonathan Hardy *Bruce* ■ *Dir/Scr* Paul Cox

Lonely in America   ★★★

Romantic comedy
1990 · US · Colour · 96mins

We may be more used to films about the experience of the Asian community in Britain, but American examples are comparatively rare. While Mira Nair's *Mississippi Masala* played it straight, Barry Alexander Brown employs a light touch as he charts Ranjit Chowdhry's introduction to the Big Apple. Like so many recent Indian films, the story

turns on the clash between tradition and progress, as Chowdhry has to decide how much of his heritage he can jettison without alienating his family. An engaging ensemble cast, some unusual views of New York and several neat cultural asides make this an unexpected pleasure. Contains swearing and sex scenes.

Ranjit Chowdhry *Arun* • Tirlok Malik *Max* • Adelaide Miller *Faye* • Robert Kessler *Jim* • David Toney *Duncan* • Melissa Christopher *Becky* • Frankie Hughes *Carlos* ■ *Dir* Barry Alexander Brown • *Scr* Satyajit Joy Palit, Barry Alexander Brown, from a story by Tirlok Malik

The Lonely Lady   ★ 18

Drama   1983 · US · Colour · 87mins

The fact that it's based on a novel by Harold Robbins should offer a big clue as to the quality of the material. As in the equally sleazy *Showgirls*, the link between career success and sexual promiscuity is explored in the antics of aspiring screenwriter Pia Zadora. She's rescued from rapist Ray Liotta by successful writer Lloyd Bochner; they marry, suffer professional jealousies and she runs from affair to affair trying to get her material produced. Not only is it badly scripted, shot and acted but the turgid and torrid sex scenes are offensive. Possibly one of the worst films of all time. ▭

Pia Zadora *Jerilee Randall* • Lloyd Bochner *Walter Thornton* • Bibi Besch *Veronica Randall* • Joseph Cali *Vincent Dacosta* • Anthony Holland *Guy Jackson* • Jared Martin *George Ballantine* • Ray Liotta *Joe Heron* ■ *Dir* Peter Sasdy • *Scr* John Kershaw, Shawn Randall, from the novel by Harold Robbins, adapted by Ellen Shepard

The Lonely Man   ★★★

Western   1957 · US · BW · 87mins

Jack Palance and Anthony Perkins, as estranged father and son, tried to out-smoulder each other in this taut, offbeat, psychological western. Perkins, who blames his long-absent father for the death of his mother, reluctantly links up with ex-bandit Palance. It turns out that Perkins isn't the only one who has a few old scores to settle with him. Fascinating to see Perkins in this pre-*Psycho* mother-obsessed role. The supporting cast includes Lee Van Cleef and Elisha Cook Jr.

Jack Palance *Jacob Wade* • Anthony Perkins *Riley Wade* • Neville Brand *King Fisher* • Robert Middleton *Ben Ryerson* • Elaine Aiken *Ada Marshall* • Elisha Cook Jr *Willie* • Claude Akins *Blackburn* • Lee Van Cleef *Faro* • Denver Pyle *Sheriff* ■ *Dir* Henry Levin • *Scr* Harry Essex, Robert Smith

The Lonely Passion of Judith Hearne   ★★★ 15

Drama   1987 · UK · Colour · 111mins

Nobody does it better than Maggie Smith when it comes to forlorn, middle-aged Irish spinsters trying to look on the bright side, but finding the silver gleam tarnished by experience. Adapted from Brian Moore's first bestseller, director Jack Clayton counterbalances booze and religion as the most powerful passions in Judith Hearne's life, so that Bob Hoskins's flirtatious entrepreneur never really stands a chance. Too sombre for what

little it has to say, but the performances manage to redeem it. Contains swearing and nudity. ▭

Maggie Smith *Judith Hearne* • Bob Hoskins *James Madden* • Wendy Hiller *Aunt D'Arcy* • Marie Kean *Mrs Rice* • Ian McNeice *Bernard* • Alan Devlin *Father Quigley* • Rudi Davies *Mary* • Prunella Scales *Moira O'Neill* ■ *Dir* Jack Clayton • *Scr* Peter Nelson, from the novel by Brian Moore

Lonely Woman Seeks Lifetime Companion   ★★★

Romantic drama   1987 · USSR · Colour

This touching Moscow-set drama would have been unthinkable in the pre-*glasnost* era, but such *bytove* or "everyday" pictures became something of a staple of Soviet cinema in the late eighties. Desperate to escape from her midlife cul-de-sac, Irina Kupchenko sticks lonely hearts advertisements to lampposts in the hope of finding Mr Right. Homeless, alcoholic ex-acrobat Aleksandr Zbruyev is hardly what she has in mind, but love comes in all guises. Shooting in a fly-on-the-wall style, director Vyacheslav Krishtofovich makes skilful use of the drab streets and Kupchenko's cramped flat, and is rewarded with touching and totally believable performances from his leads. In Russian with English subtitles.

Irina Kupchenko *Kladvia* • Aleksandr Zbruyev *Valentin* ■ *Dir* Vyacheslav Krishtofovich • *Scr* Viktor Merezhko

Lonelyhearts   ★★

Drama   1958 · US · BW · 103mins

Fans of Nathanael West's famous 1933 novella *Miss Lonelyhearts*, which deals in the despair of Adam White, a male agony aunt columnist, will despair at this attempt to broaden and contemporise the painful story with earnest moral and political platitudes. That said, there are convincing performances from Montgomery Clift, sensitive in the title role, Robert Ryan as his hard-bitten editor, and Broadway actress Maureen Stapleton, making her screen debut (and earning an Oscar nomination) as the sexually frustrated wife of a crippled husband, who seduces the compassionate Adam. Vincent J Donehue's direction is of no consequence.

Montgomery Clift *Adam White* • Robert Ryan *William Shrike* • Myrna Loy *Florence Shrike* • Dolores Hart *Justy Sargent* • Maureen Stapleton *Fay Doyle* • Frank Maxwell *Pat Doyle* • Jackie Coogan *Gates* ■ *Dir* Vincent J Donehue • *Scr* Dore Schary, from the novella *Miss Lonelyhearts* by Nathanael West

The Loners   ★★

Crime drama   1971 · US · Colour · 79mins

A modern-day western with angst-ridden biker Dean Stockwell as a mixed-race Indian, who accidentally kills a highway patrolman and goes on the run with his best buddy Todd Susman. They pick up Julio (Pat Stich) on the way and romance, murder and mayhem ensue. Here's a film that wants to cash in on everything from biker movies like *Easy Rider* to the social banditry of *Bonnie and Clyde*, Peckinpah-style shoot-outs, and the whole counterculture thing as an expression of anti-war sentiment. All that, plus the alluring Gloria Grahame, neglected star of *noir* classics such as *The Big Heat* and *In A Lonely Place*.

Dean Stockwell *Stein* • Pat Stich [Patricia Stich] *Julio* • Todd Susman *Allan* • Scott Brady *Hearn* • Gloria Grahame *Annabelle* • Alex Dreier *Police Chief Peters* • Tim Rooney *Howie* • Ward Wood *Sheriff* ■ *Dir* Sutton Roley • *Scr* John Lawrence, Barry Sandler, from a story by John Lawrence

Lonesome Cowboys ★★★
Experimental western
1968 · US · Colour · 110mins

One of the last films to feature sixties artist Andy Warhol as director, this gay cowboy fantasy does raise the fundamental question conventional westerns have failed to address. If cowboys live, ride and die together, surely they must have sex with each other too? The plot is a thin excuse to indulge in camp and erotic posing as Warhol superstars Viva and Taylor Mead, both desperate for male company, pounce on Louis Waldon's homosexual gang when they ride into their desert town. Francis Francine is the transvestite sheriff and Tom Hompertz the object of everyone's lustful attentions. By turn boring, bizarre and hilarious, this amateur Factory film captures perfectly the decadence and ennui of sixties counterculture.

Viva *Ramona Alvarez* • Tom Hompertz *Drifter* • Louis Waldon *Mickey* • Eric Emerson *Eric* • Taylor Mead *Nurse* • Joe Dallesandro *Little Joe* • Francis Francine *Sheriff* • Julian Burroughs *Julian* ■ *Dir/Scr* Andy Warhol

The Long and the Short and the Tall ★★★ PG
Second World War drama
1960 · UK · BW · 101mins

Time hasn't been kind to this studio-bound version of a Royal Court Second World War play that originally starred Frank Finlay. The film was shatteringly powerful in its day but seems rather weak now with its lack of realistic dialogue, its palpably phoney Elstree jungle sets and the uncomfortable star performance from Richard Todd, whose well-spoken tones are overlaid with a laboured regional accent. As Bamforth, the barrack-room lawyer, an overwrought Laurence Harvey is no match for the theatre's Peter O'Toole (nor, for that matter, O'Toole's understudy, the then unknown Michael Caine), but both Richard Harris and Ronald Fraser bring a grimy realism to the work. This film was X-certificated on release, whereas the play is now a set text for schools. ▭

Richard Todd *Sergeant Mitchem* • Laurence Harvey *Private Bamforth* • Richard Harris *Corporal Johnstone* • Ronald Fraser *Lance-Corporal MacLeish* • John Meillon *Private Smith* • David McCallum *Private Whitaker* • John Rees *Private Evans* • Kenji Takaki *Tojo* ■ *Dir* Leslie Norman • *Scr* Wolf Mankowitz, Willis Hall, from the play by Willis Hall

The Long Arm ★★★ U
Police drama   1956 · UK · BW · 92mins

This rather glum insight into the policeman's lot was the final film made at Ealing Studios. Jack Hawkins wears a suitably hangdog expression as the detective faced with a series of

robberies and a rocky marriage to neglected Dorothy Alison. Far from adding to the realism of the tale, the domestic crisis is a crashing bore and it's with evident relief that director Charles Frend abandons Bromley to head back to the side streets of Covent Garden and, finally, to the Festival Hall to provide an exciting and surprising conclusion to the case. ▭

Jack Hawkins *Detective Superintendent Tom Halliday* • Dorothy Alison *Mary Halliday* • Michael Brooke Jr *Tony Halliday* • John Stratton *Sergeant Ward* • Geoffrey Keen *Superintendent Malcolm* • Newton Blick *Commander Harris* • Ralph Truman *Colonel Blenkinsop* • Joss Ambler *Cashier* • Ian Bannen *Workman* • Nicholas Parsons *Police Constable Bates* • Alec McCowen *Surgeon* ■ *Dir* Charles Frend • *Scr* Janet Green, Robert Barr, Dorothy Christie, Campbell Christie, from a story by Robert Barr

The Long Dark Hall ★
Crime thriller   1951 · UK · BW · 86mins

Off-screen spouses (at the time) Rex Harrison and Lilli Palmer star in this risible courtroom drama in which Harrison stands trial for murder, while the real killer canoodles with his wilting wife. Co-director Anthony Bushell also plays Harrison's defence lawyer, but there are no sparks in his clashes with prosecutor Denis O'Dea, and the scenes in which Anthony Dawson menaces Palmer are about as tense as snapped elastic. To add insult to boredom, there is a ridiculous final twist that makes it even harder to believe that this drivel was co-written by one of Hollywood's slickest scriptwriters, Nunnally Johnson.

Rex Harrison *Arthur Groome* • Lilli Palmer *Mary Groome* • Raymond Huntley *Chief Inspector Sullivan* • Anthony Dawson *The Man* • Denis O'Dea *Sir Charles Morton* • Anthony Bushell *Clive Bedford* ■ *Dir* Anthony Bushell, Reginald Beck • *Scr* Nunnally Johnson, William EC Fairchild, from the novel *A Case to Answer* by Edgar Lustgarten

The Long Day Closes
★★★★★ PG
Biographical drama
1992 · UK · Colour · 81mins

Anyone who has ever been lost in wonder at the magic of the movies will find that this enchanting feature strikes repeated chords. In the second of his films set in the Liverpool of his childhood, Terence Davies fondly recalls those marvellous moments at the local fleapit when the drabness of everyday life receded the instant the opening credits appeared on screen. Leigh McCormack is absolutely superb as the 11-year-old whose life revolves around film and family, and his performance lends dramatic unity to this kaleidoscopic autobiography. ▭

Marjorie Yates *Mother* • Leigh McCormack *Bud* • Anthony Watson *Kevin* • Nicholas Lamont *John* • Ayse Owens *Helen* • Tina Malone *Edna* • Jimmy Wilde *Curly* ■ *Dir/Scr* Terence Davies

The Long Day's Dying ★★
Second World War drama
1968 · UK · Colour · 93mins

Heavily allegorical war drama about three British soldiers who parachute behind enemy lines and take a German prisoner. All three are expert killers but

the drawing of straws allows their German prisoner to live and be escorted to the British HQ. Along the way there are skirmishes, debates about the morality of war, and differing degrees of psychopathy from the three men, all of whom are effectively cast against type – rather slight and delicate boys rather than a conventional heavy mob. The ending is irony writ large since everything is laid on with a trowel, including the Kensington gore which must have been bought by the barrel-load.

David Hemmings *John* • Tom Bell *Tom* • Tony Beckley *Cliff* • Alan Dobie *Helmut* ■ *Dir* Peter Collinson • *Scr* Charles Wood, from the novel by Alan White

Long Day's Journey into Night ★★★ PG
Drama   1962 · US · BW · 170mins

Set in 1912, Eugene O'Neill's epic play about a self-destructive Connecticut family is a challenge for any actor and, indeed, audience. Katharine Hepburn picked up an inevitable Oscar nomination as the morphine-addicted mother of alcoholic Jason Robards and tubercular Dean Stockwell, but the star turn here is Ralph Richardson as the miserly head of the ill-fated Tyrone clan. On asking Sidney Lumet what was required of him, the actor received a ten-minute lecture from the director. When it was over, Richardson replied: ''Ah, I think I know what you want – a little more flute, a little less cello.'' ▭

Katharine Hepburn *Mary Tyrone* • Ralph Richardson *James Tyrone Sr* • Jason Robards Jr *James Tyrone Jr* • Dean Stockwell *Edmund Tyrone* • Jeanne Barr *Cathleen* ■ *Dir* Sidney Lumet • *Scr* from the play by Eugene O'Neill

Long Day's Journey into Night ★★
Drama   1996 · Can · Colour · 174mins

Eugene O'Neill's family saga about the Tyrones, an Irish-American family raddled with alcoholism and a lifetime's worth of enmities is a challenge to any actor. This version is a filmed record of a stage production which received rave notices when first performed during the Stratford Festival in Canada. William Hutt plays James senior, the head of the household so miserable he refuses to pay for medical treatment for his sick wife (Martha Henry) and son (Tom McCamus), while Peter Donaldson is the alcholic elder son.

William Hutt *James Tyrone* • Martha Henry *Mary Tyrone* • Tom McCamus *Edward Tyrone* • Peter Donaldson *Jamie Tyrone* • Martha Burns *Cathleen* ■ *Dir* David Wellington • *Scr* from the play by Eugene O'Neill

The Long Days of Summer ★★★
Drama   1980 · US · Colour

Continuing the autobiographical odyssey that began with *When Every Day Was the Fourth of July*, director Dan Curtis shows that New England in the thirties was anything but a haven of hospitality and tolerance. Dean Jones again plays the small town Jewish lawyer with a taste for pleading confounding the odds, here

the cause of a refugee from Nazi tyranny victimised by local anti-Semites. Warm without being sentimental and provocative without being preachy, this handsome TV movie is uncompromising in its exploration of American isolationism, yet also amusing in its insights into an unconventional childhood.

Dean Jones *Ed Cooper* • Joan Hackett *Millie Cooper* • Ronnie Scribner *Daniel Cooper* • Louanne *Sarah Cooper* • Donald Moffat *Josef Kaplan* • Andrew Duggan *Sam Wiggins* ■ *Dir* Dan Curtis • *Scr* Lee Hutson, from a story by Hindi Brooks, Lee Hutson

The Long Duel ★★ U
Adventure   1966 · UK · Colour · 115mins

It's big, it's British and it's trying very hard to be spectacular. A bold bid from Rank to crack the international market, this straight-faced *Carry On Up the Khyber* was directed by Ken Annakin, an experienced hand at location shooting. He makes the twenties' Indian setting look authentic and keeps the conflict bubbling, but Yul Brynner's rebel tribal leader is prone to ranting and speechifying, police officer Trevor Howard conveys the feeling that he'd rather be in Tunbridge Wells, and the true-life story of obsessed antagonism rings false thanks to stilted dialogue and clichéd situations. Still, no movie with sixties' beauties Charlotte Rampling, Imogen Hassall and Virginia North (in her debut) is unwatchable, and keep an eye out for a young Edward Fox.

Yul Brynner *Sultan* • Trevor Howard *Freddy Young* • Harry Andrews *Stafford* • Andrew Keir *Gungaram* • Charlotte Rampling *Jane Stafford* • Virginia North *Champa* • Laurence Naismith *McDougal* • Maurice Denham *Governor* • Imogen Hassall *Tara* ■ *Dir* Ken Annakin • *Scr* Ernest Bornemann, Geoffrey Orme, Peter Yeldham, from a story by Ranveer Singh

Long Gone ★★★ 15
Comedy drama   1987 · US · Colour · 107mins

Snappy writing and nifty acting raise this diverting baseball comedy above the standard of your average made-for-cable TV movie. Martin Davidson showed his pedigree as the director of such big-screen period movies as *The Lords of Flatbush* (with Stephen F Verona) and *Eddie and the Cruisers*, and here he makes the most of an unoriginal story about a hopeless minor league baseball team bidding for success. William L Petersen, as ''Stud'' Cantrell, the team's foul-mouthed and abrasive player-manager, and Virginia Madsen, as the beautiful woman who comes into the team's life, are both impressive. Contains swearing.

William L Petersen [William Petersen] *Cecil ''Stud'' Cantrell* • Virginia Madsen *Dixie Lee Boxx* • Dermot Mulroney *Jamie Don Weeks* • Larry Riley *Joe Louis Brown* • Katy Boyer *Esther Wrenn* • Henry Gibson *Hale Buchman Sr* • Teller Lasarow *Hale Buchman Jr* • Robert Easton *Cletis Romey* ■ *Dir* Martin Davidson • *Scr* Michael Norell, from a story by Paul Hemphill

The Long Good Friday ★★★★ 18

Crime thriller 1979 · UK · Colour · 109mins

Bob Hoskins got his big break playing the East End gangster who realises his gang is being ruthlessly picked off by the IRA. Owing something to American thrillers of the forties, and rather more to *Get Carter* and TV crime shows, John Mackenzie's film remains both an explosively violent thriller and a sharp evocation of Thatcher's enterprise culture (Hoskins's dream is to build a new city in London's docklands with Mafia money). Helen Mirren offers seductive support, while Pierce Brosnan appears as an anonymous IRA hit man. ▭

Bob Hoskins *Harold* • Helen Mirren *Victoria* • Eddie Constantine *Charlie* • Dave King *Parky* • Bryan Marshall *Harris* • George Coulouris *Gus* • Derek Thompson *Jeff* • Pierce Brosnan *First Irishman* ■ *Dir* John Mackenzie • *Scr* Barrie Keefe

The Long Goodbye ★★★★★ 18

Detective drama
1973 · US · Colour · 111mins

Director Robert Altman's semi-spoof update of Raymond Chandler's novel ranks as one of the most intelligent adaptations of the celebrated thriller writer's work since *The Big Sleep*. By brilliantly deconstructing the standard private-eye thriller with irony and affection, Altman comments on the changes in American society and the American Dream to starkly satirical effect. Elliott Gould's laid-back Philip Marlowe – the catalyst in a wife-battering tale, brutally laced with blackmail, suicide and betrayal – is another sardonic masterstroke in one of the finest films of the seventies. Contains violence and swearing. ▭

Elliott Gould *Philip Marlowe* • Nina Van Pallandt *Eileen Wade* • Sterling Hayden *Roger Wade* • Mark Rydell *Marty Augustine* • Henry Gibson *Dr Verringer* • David Arkin *Harry* • Jim Bouton *Terry Lennox* • Jack Knight *Mabel* ■ *Dir* Robert Altman • *Scr* Leigh Brackett, from the novel by Raymond Chandler

The Long Gray Line ★★★ U

Drama 1955 · US · Colour · 131mins

One of director John Ford's most blarneyish and sentimental movies, this will only excite those who believe West Point Military Academy is an institution to be valued for its righteous place in the American way of life. A uniformed *Goodbye, Mr Chips*, it tells of Tyrone Power who arrives at the academy as a menial worker, becomes a cadet-instructor, marries Maureen O'Hara, and stays on teaching boys to be men, until time immemorial and a Ford-blessed sunrise. Beautifully crafted, but appallingly banal. ▭

Tyrone Power *Marty Maher* • Maureen O'Hara *Mary O'Donnell* • Robert Francis *James Sundstrom Jr* • Donald Crisp *Old Martin* • Ward Bond *Capt Herman J Koehler* • Betsy Palmer *Kitty Carter* • Phil Carey [Philip Carey] *Charles Dotson* • William Leslie *Red Sundstrom* • Harry Carey Jr *Dwight Eisenhower* • Patrick Wayne *Cherub Overton* ■ *Dir* John Ford • *Scr* Edward Hope, from the novel *Bringing up the Brass* by Marty Maher and Nardi Reeder Campion

The Long Hair of Death ★★★

Gothic horror 1964 · It · BW · 97mins

Horror queen Barbara Steele is in top form in this atmospheric slice of Italian gothic horror. Director Antonio Margheriti isn't quite up to Mario Bava standards, but serves up enough plague-riddled peasants and cobweb festooned secret passageways to keep genre fans happy. Steele plays an unfortunate 15th-century wench accused of murder and burnt as a witch who, years later, returns to torment and engineer the death of the real culprit. As with most films of this type the script wanders, the dubbing is clumsy and the pace slackens in the middle, but Steele's resurrection scene is worth staying up for on its own. Italian dialogue dubbed into English.

Giorgio Ardisson [George Ardisson] *Kurt* • Halina Zalewska *Lizabeth* • Robert Rains *Von Klage* ■ *Dir* Anthony Dawson [Antonio Margheriti] • *Scr* Robert Bohr, Julian Berry [Ernesto Gastaldi], Renato Caldonazzo (English translation)

The Long Hot Summer ★★★★ PG

Drama 1958 · US · Colour

Two short stories and a novel by William Faulkner were glued together to form the script of this torpid Deep South melodrama with a simply marvellous cast. Paul Newman is the drifter and redneck who catches the eye of Lee Remick and wins the favour of her father-in-law, local tyrant Orson Welles, who tries to pair him off with daughter Joanne Woodward. Ludicrously overheated but magnificent with it, this was the first of several pictures Newman made with Woodward; the couple married shortly after filming was completed. ▭

Paul Newman *Ben Quick* • Joanne Woodward *Clara Varner* • Orson Welles *Will Varner* • Anthony Franciosa *Jody Varner* • Lee Remick *Eula* • Richard Anderson *Alan Stewart* ■ *Dir* Martin Ritt • *Scr* Irving Ravetch, Harriet Frank Jr, from the stories *Barn Burning* , *The Spotted Horse* , and the novel *The Hamlet* by William Faulkner

The Long Journey Home ★★★ 15

Thriller 1987 · US · Colour · 88mins

Meredith Baxter stars as a wife whose life is turned upside down when her partner (played by then real-life husband David Birney), believed missing in Vietnam, reappears and drags her into a rather complicated and confusing espionage plot. Although this thriller is often ludicrous, Baxter manages to inject enough style into her performance to keep you watching, and director Rod Holcomb keeps the twists and surprises coming at a fair old pace. ▭

Meredith Baxter Birney [Meredith Baxter] *Maura Wells* • David Birney *Carter Wells* • Ray Baker *Grey Harrison* • Mike Preston *Frank Mata* ■ *Dir* Rod Holcomb • *Scr* Karen Clark

The Long Kiss Goodnight ★★★★ 18

Action thriller 1996 · US · Colour · 115mins

This vehicle for star Geena Davis is one of the loudest, sassiest and downright entertaining action blockbusters in recent years. Directed by her husband Renny Harlin, before they split up, it's wonderfully over the top in virtually every respect, from *Lethal Weapon* scriptwriter Shane Black's barmy story and even crazier characters to the non-stop reality-defying action set pieces. Davis is the nice small-town housewife who discovers that she was in fact once a ruthless assassin working for a shadowy Government agency. Samuel L Jackson is her reluctant and mainly incompetent sidekick, while there are also ripe performances from Patrick Malahide and Brian Cox, and a cheerfully villainous turn from Craig Bierko. Contains swearnig and violence. ▭ *DVD*

Geena Davis *Samantha Caine/Charly Baltimore* • Samuel L Jackson *Mitch Hennessey* • Yvonne Zima *Caitlin* • Craig Bierko *Timothy* • Tom Amandes *Hal* • Brian Cox *Nathan* • Patrick Malahide *Perkins* • David Morse *Luke/Daedalus* ■ *Dir* Renny Harlin • *Scr* Shane Black

Long Live Life ★★

Science-fiction thriller 1984 · Fr · Colour

According to Claude Lelouch, the idea for this film came to him in a dream on the day that *Edith and Marcel* opened to disastrous reviews. Critics and public alike were exhorted not to reveal the twist ending, only to deprive this psychological sci-fi puzzle of its sole talking point. The nub of the story concerns the claims of businessman Michel Piccoli and actress Evelyne Bouix that they were kidnapped by aliens and sent back to Earth to preach anti-nuclear pacifism. Piccoli's wife, Charlotte Rampling, and teacher Jean-Louis Trintignant are among the sceptics, bemused, like everyone else, by this over-elaborate hokum. In French with English subtitles..

Charlotte Rampling *Catherine Perrin* • Michel Piccoli *Michel Perrin* • Jean-Louis Trintignant *François Gaucher* • Evelyne Bouix *Sarah Gaucher* • Anouk Aimée *Anouk* • Charles Aznavour *Edouard Takvorian* ■ *Dir/Scr* Claude Lelouch

Long Live the Lady! ★★★★ 15

Comedy 1987 · It · Colour · 106mins

Six young graduates of a catering school are engaged to wait at table at a grand banquet being given in a medieval castle by a mysterious old lady. Like the bespectacled youth, through whose eyes we see the feast, the director Ermanno Olmi, whose first film this was for five years, observes, by turns fascinated and repulsed, the rituals of a strictly hierarchical, decaying society whose dominant symbol is the huge, ugly fish which the guests consume with relish. By the use of eloquent gestures, faces and looks, rather than dialogue, Olmi has created a witty and sharp satire on the haute bourgeoisie. In Italian with English subtitles..

Marco Esposito *Libenzio* • Simona Brandalise *Corinna* • Stefania Busarello *Anna* • Simone Dalla Rosa *Mao* • Lorenzo Paolini *Ciccio* • Tarcisio Tosi *Pigi* ■ *Dir/Scr* Ermanno Olmi

The Long, Long Trailer ★★ U

Comedy 1954 · US · Colour · 96mins

After mediocre cinema careers, Lucille Ball and Desi Arnaz became household names on TV in *I Love Lucy*. They returned in triumph to MGM for this episodic comedy feature which essentially preserves their small screen images of madcap wife and long-suffering husband. Playing newlyweds, Lucille persuades Desi that they should invest in a mobile home and use it for their honeymoon trip, leading to scrapes and disasters. It relies on slapstick humour rather than subtleties of characterisation but director Vincente Minnelli makes the most of the thin material.

Lucille Ball *Tacy Collini* • Desi Arnaz *Nicholas Carlos Collini* • Marjorie Main *Mrs Hittaway* • Keenan Wynn *Policeman* • Gladys Hurlbut *Mrs Bolton* • Moroni Olsen *Mr Tewitt* ■ *Dir* Vincente Minnelli • *Scr* Albert Hackett, Frances Goodrich, from the novel by Clinton Twiss

Long Lost Father ★★

Drama 1934 · US · BW · 64mins

John Barrymore was never too choosy with his later screen roles, and this was one of his lesser efforts. Barrymore, in his world-weary manner, plays a man who deserted his family many years before but finds his grown-up daughter (Helen Chandler) working in the same nightclub as he is. Naturally, he wins back her love. The director Ernest B Schoedsack, who had co-directed *King Kong* the year before, showed no feeling for the material, suggesting that action adventure was really his forte.

John Barrymore *Carl Bellairs* • Helen Chandler *Lindsey Lane* • Donald Cook *Dr Bill Strong* • Alan Mowbray *Sir Anthony Gelding* • Claude King *Inspector* • EE Clive *Spot Hawkins* • Reginald Sharland *Lord Vivyan* ■ *Dir* Ernest B Schoedsack • *Scr* Dwight Taylor, from the novel by GB Stern

The Long Memory ★★

Thriller 1952 · UK · BW · 96mins

Robert Hamer will always be remembered as the director of the classic Ealing comedy *Kind Hearts and Coronets*, but he also had an excellent eye for local detail. Here he cleverly captures the murky side of life in London's marshlands, but he is beaten from the start by the utterly predictable wrong man story. This is a quota quickie plot with a bit of money thrown at it. John Mills is badly miscast as an old lag desperate to discover who framed him for murder, while detective John McCallum is clueless in every sense.

John Mills *Davidson* • John McCallum *Detective Inspector Lowther* • Elizabeth Sellars *Fay Lowther* • Eva Bergh *Elsa* • Geoffrey Keen *Craig* • Michael Martin-Harvey *Jackson* • John Chandos *Boyd* • John Slater *Pewsey* • Thora Hird *Mrs Pewsey* ■ *Dir* Robert Hamer • *Scr* Robert Hamer, Frank Harvey, from a novel by Howard Clewes

The Long Night ★★★

Drama   1947 · US · BW · 96mins

Few movies have ever aroused as much critical fury as *The Long Night* when it was (mistakenly) believed that the producers of this remake of *Le Jour Se Lève* with Jean Gabin and Arletty had destroyed every copy of the original. Marcel Carné's great film has survived, while this effective, more socially orientated version by writer John Wexley and director Anatole Litvak is rarely revived. Henry Fonda performs sensitively as the ex-serviceman turned killer who keeps the police at bay during a long night in which he looks back on the disastrous sequence of events that have left him trapped. Barbara Bel Geddes is touching as the girl he loves, and Vincent Price suitably ominous as the sleazy magician who is murdered in the opening minutes of the film.

Henry Fonda *Joe Adams* • Barbara Bel Geddes *Jo Ann* • Vincent Price *Maximilian* • Ann Dvorak *Charlene* • Howard Freeman *Sheriff* • Moroni Olsen *Chief of Police* • Elisha Cook Jr *Frank* • Queenie Smith *Janitor's wife* ■ *Dir* Anatole Litvak • *Scr* John Wexley, from the film *Le Jour Se Lève* by Jacques Viot

Long Pants ★★★★

Silent comedy   1927 · US · BW · 60mins

This bizarre black comedy is the last of three silent features which display the full genius of baby-faced Harry Langdon, following *Tramp, Tramp, Tramp* and *The Strong Man*. Here he plays the boy who has just graduated to long pants and dreams of being a great lover. The attractions of long-time sweetheart Priscilla Bonner pale in comparison with Alma Bennett's more exciting big city vamp and our "hero" decides that drastic measures are required. Langdon's effectiveness stems from the astute direction of the young Frank Capra. When Langdon fired Capra and tried to go it alone, he wrecked his career.

Harry Langdon *The boy* • Gladys Brockwell *His mother* • Alan Roscoe *His father* • Alma Bennett *The vamp* • Priscilla Bonner *Priscilla* ■ *Dir* Frank Capra • *Scr* Robert Eddy, from a story by Arthur Ripley

The Long Ride ★★ 15

Second World War adventure
1984 · US/Hun · Colour · 88mins

In this Second World War drama, American airman John Savage is shot down over Hungary, where he joins the horsemen and resistance fighters who roam the Hortobagy plain. In civilian life, Savage is a cowboy from Wyoming, so he has no trouble fitting in, but the vast, treeless landscape Is the undoubted star of Pal Gabor's film.

John Savage *Brady* • Kelly Reno *Miki* • Ildiko Bansagi *Klara* • Laszlo Mensaros *Dr Dussek* • Ferenc Bacs *Wortmann* • Dzsoko Roszics *Csorba* • Laszlo Horvath *Moro* • Matyas Usztics *Swede* ■ *Dir* Pal Gabor • *Scr* William W Lewis, from a story by Pal Gabor

The Long Ride Home ★★★ 15

Western   1967 · US · Colour · 80mins

A Confederate soldier (George Hamilton) escapes from a Union prison and is pursued by Captain Glenn Ford whose fiancée, Inger Stevens, has been taken hostage and is then raped by Hamilton as revenge for the South's defeat. Sadly, a weak performance from Hamilton and a typically bland one from Ford diminish the story considerably, which otherwise has a startling realism and toughness in its evocation of America in the aftermath of the Civil War. Fans of ex-carpenter Harrison Ford will be eyes-akimbo for his second screen appearance. The film was begun by Roger Corman, who quit after two weeks' shooting, and Phil Karlson replaced him. Also known as *A Time for Killing*.

Glenn Ford *Major Walcott* • George Hamilton *Captain Bentley* • Inger Stevens *Emily Biddle* • Paul Petersen *Blue Lake* • Max Baer Jr *Sergeant Luther Liskell* • Todd Armstrong *Lieutenant Prudessing* • Timothy Carey *Billy Cat* ■ *Dir* Phil Karlson • *Scr* Halsted Welles, from the novel *The Southern Blade* by Nelson Wolford, Shirley Wolford

The Long Riders ★★★★ 18

Western   1980 · US · Colour · 95mins

Powerful novelty casting is a major draw in director Walter Hill's authentic-looking, grim'n'grimy western concerning the events surrounding the notorious Northfield, Minnesota, bank raid. Very reminiscent of *The Wild Bunch* in its use of slow-motion violence and flashback, the film also benefits from a superb score by guitar maestro Ry Cooder. Three of the young Carradines (David, Keith and Robert) play the Younger brothers, Stacy and James Keach are Frank and Jesse James, with the less familiar Miller boys played by Randy and Dennis Quaid, and the Fords (Bob and Charlie) are played by Nicholas and Christopher Guest. Contains mild swearing and brief nudity.

Stacy Keach *Frank James* • Dennis Quaid *Ed Miller* • David Carradine *Cole Younger* • Keith Carradine *Jim Younger* • Robert Carradine *Bob Younger* • James Keach *Jesse James* • Randy Quaid *Clell Miller* • Kevin Brophy *John Younger* • Harry Carey Jr *George Arthur* • Christopher Guest *Charlie Ford* • Nicholas Guest *Bob Ford* ■ *Dir* Walter Hill • *Scr* Bill Bryden, Steven Phillip Smith, Stacy Keach, James Keach, Ry Cooder

Long Road Home ★★ PG

Drama   1991 · Colour · 90mins

Mark Harmon stars as a husband who takes his wife and family west to California in the thirties to make a living, only to find corruption and violence at every turn when they get there. This is a nice-looking if somewhat tedious and predictable drama from director John Korty, who was also responsible for that cuddly *Star Wars* spin-off *The Ewok Adventure*.

Mark Harmon *Ertie Robertson* • Morgan Weisser *Jake Robertson* • Bianca Rose *Susie* • Sarah Lundy *Mary Ellen* ■ *Dir* John Korty • *Scr* Jane-Howard Hammerstein, from the book by Ronald B Taylor

The Long Shadow ★★ U

Drama   1992 · US/Isr/Hun · Colour · 89mins

After 35 years in America, establishing himself as one of Hollywood's finest cinematographers, Vilmos Zsigmond returned to his native Hungary to make his directorial debut. Unfortunately, even the visual aspects of this pretentious production are substandard, with the glossy style trivialising what is supposed to be an intense study of delicate feelings. As the actor son of a celebrated archaeologist, who is hired to play his father in a movie set in Israel, Michael York singularly fails to convince either as a master thespian or as a lover caught in the throes of passion for his stepmother, Liv Ullmann.

Liv Ullmann *Katherine* • Michael York *Raphael Romondy* • Teomi Oded *Johann Grabier* ■ *Dir* Vilmos Zsigmond • *Scr* Paul Salamon, Janos Edelenyi

The Long Ships ★★ PG

Historical adventure
1963 · UK/Yug · Colour · 120mins

Adapted from Frans T Bengtsson's swashbuckling novel about Vikings and Moors roaming the high seas in search of a fabulous golden bell, this eager Anglo/Yugoslavian co-production has almost everything you would expect of a lavish screen epic. There's plenty of action and more than a hint of sin, the costumes and sets are opulent, and Christopher Challis's colour photography shimmers with richness. But, while Richard Widmark plays his Viking role with pantomimic brio, Sidney Poitier chooses to play the Moorish prince as a sort of medieval civil rights activist. In other words, like many epics before and since, it's too self-indulgent for its own good. Contains violence.

Richard Widmark *Rolfe* • Sidney Poitier *El Mansuh* • Rosanna Schiaffino *Aminah* • Russ Tamblyn *Orm* • Oscar Homolka *Krok* • Lionel Jeffries *Aziz* • Edward Judd *Sven* • Beba Loncar *Gerda* • Clifford Evans *King Harald* • Colin Blakely *Rhykka* • Gordon Jackson *Vahlin* • David Lodge *Olla* ■ *Dir* Jack Cardiff • *Scr* Berkely Mather, Beverley Cross, from the novel by Frans T Bengtsson

Long Shot ★★

Drama   1978 · UK · Colour · 85mins

This unusual docu-comedy set in and around the Edinburgh Festival should be required viewing for any aspiring film-makers. Film producer and proud Scot Charles Gormley is attempting to find backers for his movie entitled *Gulf and Western*. Naturally this proves to be problematic but some farcical comedy ensues and movie buffs will enjoy spotting luminaries like Wim Wenders, Stephen Frears, John Boorman and Susannah York in the supporting cast.

Charles Gormley *Charlie* • Neville Smith *Neville* • Ann Zelda *Annie* • David Stone *Distributor* • Suzanne Danielle *Sue* • Ron Taylor (1) *American director* • Wim Wenders *Another director* • Stephen Frears *Biscuit Man* • Maurice Bulbulian *French-Canadian director* • William Forsythe *[Bill Forsyth] Billie* • Alan Bennett *Neville's doctor* • Susannah York *Actress* • John Boorman *The Director* ■ *Dir* Maurice Hatton • *Scr* Eoin McCann, Maurice Hatton

The Long Voyage Home ★★★★ PG

Drama   1940 · US · BW · 100mins

This near masterpiece from director John Ford was scripted by *Stagecoach*'s Dudley Nichols from four one-act seafaring plays by Eugene O'Neill, and it bears that satisfying streak of grim melancholy that typifies the finest work of one of America's greatest writers. Although relentlessly studio bound, the magnificent photography of Gregg Toland (*Citizen Kane*) captures the dangerous atmosphere as a freighter transports a cargo of dynamite across the Atlantic during the Second World War. Top billed is John Wayne, playing a Swedish merchant seaman, accent and all, and he's backed up by an extremely effective all-male supporting cast.

John Wayne *Ole Olsen* • Thomas Mitchell *Aloysius Driscoll* • Ian Hunter *Smitty* • Barry Fitzgerald *Cocky* • Wilfrid Lawson *Captain* • Mildred Natwick *Freda* • John Qualen *Axel Swanson* • Ward Bond *Yank* ■ *Dir* John Ford • *Scr* Dudley Nichols, from four one-act plays by Eugene O'Neill

The Long Wait ★★

Crime drama   1954 · US · BW · 94mins

What was a tasteful British film-maker like Victor Saville doing forming Parklane Productions to film the lurid crime novels of Mickey Spillane? He tried his hand at directing this one, but lacked the edgy style that Robert Aldrich brought to *Kiss Me Deadly*. Still, it has a certain seamy atmosphere as Anthony Quinn's amnesiac tries to figure out which of four sexy dames might be the one who can clear him of robbery and suspicion of murder.

Anthony Quinn *Johnny McBride* • Charles Coburn *Gardiner* • Gene Evans *Servo* • Peggie Castle *Venus* • Mary Ellen Kay *Wendy* • Shawn Smith *Carol* • Dolores Donlon *Troy* ■ *Dir* Victor Saville • *Scr* Alan Green, Lesser Samuels, from the novel by Mickey Spillane

The Long Walk Home ★★★ PG

Drama   1990 · US · Colour · 91mins

Whoopi Goldberg plays Sissy Spacek's housemaid in this convincing drama set during the early years of the Civil Rights movement. Tensions rise in Spacek's Alabama household as blacks and whites grow further apart when the blacks boycott the segregated buses and the whites up the ante with an arson attack on Martin Luther King's house. Solid acting, a no-nonsense script, a convincing fifties look and marvellous gospel music distinguish this production.

Whoopi Goldberg *Odessa Cotter* • Sissy Spacek *Miriam Thompson* • Dwight Schultz *Norman Thompson* • Ving Rhames *Herbert Cotter* • Dylan Baker *Tunker Thompson* • Erika Alexander *Selma Cotter* • Lexi Faith Randall *Mary Catherine* • Richard Habersham *Theodore Cotter* • Jason Weaver *Franklin Cotter* ■ *Dir* Richard Pearce • *Scr* John Cork

The Long Way Home ★★★★

Documentary   1996 · US · Colour · 110mins

The winner of the Oscar for Best Feature Documentary, this is a devastating exposé of the events that followed the liberation of the European concentration camps at the end of the Second World War. Narrated by Morgan Freeman and combining archive footage, stills, interviews and personal testimonies, the shameful catalogue of oversights, errors and wilful acts of neglect can only astonish those unaware that the suffering of the Holocaust survivors did not end with the defeat of the Nazis. Conducting his exhaustive research in conjunction with Rabbi Marvin Hier, Mark Jonathan Harris has produced a fitting tribute to these forgotten victims.

Morgan Freeman *Narration* ■ *Dir/Scr* Mark Jonathan Harris

The Long Way Home   ★★★

Drama   1998 · US · Colour

It's a sudsy affair, but Jack Lemmon provides an extra bit of class that lifts this TV melodrama out of the ordinary. The veteran star plays a lonely widower, staying with his son and daughter-in-law, who gets a new lease of life when his friendship with feisty young Sarah Paulson leads to a chance encounter. After the predictable formulae of movies such as *Grumpy Old Men*, Lemmon relishes the chance of a juicier role and he is well accompanied by a cast that includes *On the Town's* Betty Garrett. Director Glenn Jordan does his best to sidestep the more sugary moments.

Jack Lemmon *Tom Gerrin* • Betty Garrett *Veronica* • Sarah Paulson *Leanne Bossert* ■ • *Scr* William Hanley, from the film *Thomas Guerin, Retraite* by Louise Vincent, Patrick Jamain

Long Weekend   ★★15

Drama thriller   1977 · Ausl · Colour · 92mins

The eco-thriller is one of the coming genres of western cinema, but this is a pretty resistible early effort from Australian Colin Eggleston. The sequences of events that befall bickering marrieds John Hargreaves and Briony Behets are simply not made mysterious or shocking enough and their lack of curiosity soon rubs off on the viewer. By following each new occurrence with a renewed outburst of squabbling, Eggleston fritters away much of the suspense he has built up and reinforces the view that whatever is going to happen to this ghastly pair is more than due. ▭

John Hargreaves *Peter* • Briony Behets *Marcia* ■ *Dir* Colin Eggleston • *Scr* Everett De Roche

Longarm   ★★PG

Spoof western   1988 · US · Colour · 67mins

Based on the *Longarm* books by Tabor Evans, this was the pilot for a comic western TV series. Lawrence Kasdan's *Silverado* and Mel Brooks's *Blazing Saddles* both did this type of thing first and did it better, though director Virgil W Vogel's story of a tougher-than-nails deputy marshal with an eye for a pretty face is pleasantly amusing nonetheless. ▭

John Terlesky *Curtis "Longarm" Long* • Whitney Kershaw *Miss Barnett* • Deborah Dawn Slaboda *Tyler* • Daphne Ashbrook *Pearl Horn* • Lee DeBroux *Sheriff Jim Garrett* • Shannon Tweed *Crazy Sally* • René Auberjonois *Governor Wallace* ■ *Dir* Virgil W Vogel • *Scr* David Chisholm

The Longest Day   ★★★★PG

Second World War drama
1962 · US · BW · 168mins

A vast war movie about the D-Day landings, with an all-star cast: Henry Fonda, John Wayne and Robert Mitchum represent Uncle Sam; Kenneth More, Richard Burton and, briefly, Sean Connery represent Blighty. Burton has the best line – "I don't mind being one of the few; trouble is we keep getting fewer" – while Red Buttons has the best mini-drama, stuck on a church spire. Some production statistics: 600,000 rounds of blanks were fired, 63,000 hot meals were served on 31 locations, 9,900lb of nails were used to make the sets, 25,000 tyres were burned for the smoke effects, 22 miles of barbed wire and 1,600 members of the US Sixth Fleet went to Corsica to re-stage the Omaha Beach landing. Naturally, there were three directors, but producer Darryl F Zanuck really called the shots. Originally made in black-and-white, computer colourised versions are now usually seen. ▭

John Wayne *Colonel Benjamin Vandervoort* • Robert Mitchum *Brigadier General Norman Cota* • Henry Fonda *Brigadier General Theodore Roosevelt* • Robert Ryan *Brigadier General James Gavin* • Rod Steiger *Destroyer Commander* • Robert Wagner *US Ranger* • Richard Beymer *Schultz* • Mel Ferrer *Major General Robert Haines* • Jeffrey Hunter *Sergeant Fuller* • Paul Anka *US Ranger* • Sal Mineo *Private Martini* • Roddy McDowall *Private Morris* • Stuart Whitman *Lieutenant Sheen* • Eddie Albert *Colonel Newton* • Edmond O'Brien *General Raymond O Barton* • Fabian *Ranger* • Red Buttons *Private Steel* • Tom Tryon *Lieutenant Wilson* • Alexander Knox *Major General Walter Bedell Smith* • Richard Burton *RAF pilot* • Kenneth More *Captain Maud* • Peter Lawford *Lord Lovat* • Richard Todd *Major Howard* • Sean Connery *Private Flanagan* • Christopher Lee *Bit* ■ *Dir* Andrew Marton, Ken Annakin, Bernhard Wicki • *Scr* Cornelius Ryan, Romain Gary, James Jones, David Pursall, Jack Seddon, from the novel by Cornelius Ryan

The Longshot   ★★PG

Comedy   1986 · US · Colour · 85mins

Paul Bartel's eccentric style and off-kilter view of the world has resulted in some unusual and interesting films (*Death Race 2000*, *Eating Raoul*) but this substandard comedy isn't one of his best. Four luckless friends are conned into borrowing a fortune to bet on a "sure thing" race. Predictably it all goes horribly wrong and they find themselves pursued by the violent thugs who loaned them the money. Tim Conway and Harvey Korman enjoyed considerable success in US TV comedy – both worked on *The Carol Burnett Show* – but this big-screen outing did them no favours at all. ▭

Tim Conway *Dooley* • Harvey Korman *Lou* • Jack Weston *Elton* • Ted Wass *Stump* • Anne Meara *Madge* • Jorge Cervera [Jorge Cervera Jr] *Santiago* • Jonathan Winters *Tyler* ■ *Dir* Paul Bartel • *Scr* Tim Conway

Longtime Companion   ★★★★15

Drama   1990 · US · Colour · 95mins

The riveting, gut-wrenching account of eight friends' experiences from the day a newspaper reports "a rare cancer affecting the homosexual community" to the mounting impact Aids has on their lives and loves. Explicitly charting the way affluent gays were shocked out of their Calvin Klein lifestyles into dealing with bigotry and misunderstanding as they coped with bewildering loss, this quasi-documentary is a most accessible Aids history lesson. Oscar nominee Bruce Davison gives the stand-out performance in a powerful, courageous testament to survival, which ends on a symbol of hope and a tribute to the dearly departed. Contains swearing. ▭

Bruce Davison *David* • Campbell Scott *Willy* • Stephen Caffrey *Fuzzy* • Mark Lamos *Sean* • Patrick Cassidy *Howard* • Mary-Louise Parker *Lisa* • John Dossett *Paul* ■ *Dir* Norman René • *Scr* Craig Lucas

Look Back in Anger   ★★★★PG

Drama   1959 · UK · BW · 95mins

Richard Burton is on a whingeing streak as the ever-complaining Jimmy Porter in Tony Richardson's version of the John Osborne play, the epitome of the kitchen-sink drama that heralded the liberated Swinging Sixties. As the downtrodden, middle-class wife taking the brunt of his tirades, Mary Ure poignantly deserves better from life than a husband who believes the world owes him a living, because Burton makes the man totally unsympathetic. As an emblem of its time, though, not to be missed. ▭

Richard Burton *Jimmy Porter* • Claire Bloom *Helena Charles* • Mary Ure *Alison Porter* • Edith Evans *Mrs Tanner* • Gary Raymond *Cliff Lewis* • Glen Byam Shaw *Corporal Redfern* • Phyllis Nielson-Terry *Mrs Redfern* • Donald Pleasence *Hurst* • Jane Eccles *Miss Drury* ■ *Dir* Tony Richardson • *Scr* Nigel Kneale, John Osborne, from the play by John Osborne

Look for the Silver Lining   ★★★U

Musical biography
1949 · US · Colour · 106mins

An under-rated Warner Bros biopic of Broadway legend Marilyn Miller (after whom Marilyn Monroe was named), who is vivaciously played here by lovely June Haver. Large chunks of Miller's New York hits *Sunny* and *Sally* are re-created, with highstepping Ray Bolger as her partner Jack Donahue, the man who taught Eleanor Powell to dance. In reality, Miller married three times, the second of her husbands being Mary Pickford's brother Jack, but here she's been given a fictional husband played by Gordon MacRae. David Butler directs it all with style, and the supporting cast of Warner veterans makes this a pleasure to watch.

June Haver *Marilyn Miller* • Ray Bolger *Jack Donahue* • Gordon MacRae *Frank Carter* • Charlie Ruggles [Charles Ruggles] *Pop Miller* • Rosemary DeCamp *Mom Miller* • Lee Wilde *Claire Miller* • Lynn Wilde *Ruth Miller* • Will Rogers Jr *Will Rogers* ■ *Dir* David Butler • *Scr* Henry Ephron, Phoebe Ephron, Marian Spitzer, from the story *Life of Marilyn Miller* by Bert Kalmar, Harry Ruby

Look in Any Window   ★★

Drama   1961 · US · BW · 86mins

Pop star and composer Paul Anka had just missed a starring role in *West Side Story* when he took a risk with his image by playing a deeply disturbed teenager who gets his kicks by donning a mask and spying on the neighbours. Coming from a unhappy home, Anka is halfway to being committed to an asylum, but then so are the majority of the characters in this indie psychodrama. Anka's mother (Ruth Roman) is a nymphomaniac and his dad, played by Alex Nicol, is a drunk.

Paul Anka *Craig Fowler* • Ruth Roman *Jackie Fowler* • Alex Nicol *Jay Fowler* • Gigi Perreau *Eileen Lowell* • Carole Mathews *Betty Lowell* • George Dolenz *Carlo* • Jack Cassidy *Gareth Lowell* • Robert Sampson *Lindstrom* ■ *Dir* William Alland • *Scr* Laurence E Mascott

Look Who's Laughing   ★★U

Comedy   1941 · US · BW · 78mins

Not many people manage to become national celebrities through a radio ventriloquism act. But that's what happened to Edgar Bergen, who teams once more with his cheeky dummy Charlie McCarthy for this tolerable flag-waver. He's joined by radio regulars Fibber McGee and Molly (Jim and Marian Jordan) and Harold Peary in one of his five film ventures as the Great Gildersleeve. Lucille Ball provides a little pep as Edgar's secretary in this slight comedy about the need for everyone to pull together for the war effort.

Edgar Bergen • Jim Jordan *Fibber McGee* • Marian Jordan *Molly McGee* • Lucille Ball *Julie Patterson* • Lee Bonnell *Jerry* • Dorothy Lovett *Marge* • Harold Peary *The Great Gildersleeve* ■ *Dir* Allan Dwan • *Scr* James V Kern, Don Quinn, Leonard L Levinson, Zeno Klinker, Dorothy Kingsley

Look Who's Talking   ★★★12

Comedy   1989 · US · Colour · 91mins

A triumph of high concept from Hollywood, this is the smash-hit comedy that brought John Travolta back from the wilderness into the public eye and spawned two increasingly silly sequels. Kirstie Alley is the single mother on the lookout for the perfect husband, even though we know lowly taxi driver Travolta is the safe bet from the outset. Bruce Willis, the wisecracking voice of baby Mikey, nabs the best lines, although Travolta and Alley are an amiable pairing and there's nice support from Olympia Dukakis and George Segal. Contains swearing and some sexual references. ▭ **DVD**

John Travolta *James* • Kirstie Alley *Mollie* • Olympia Dukakis *Rosie* • George Segal *Albert* • Abe Vigoda *Grandpa* • Bruce Willis *Mikey* • Twink Caplan *Rona* ■ *Dir/Scr* Amy Heckerling

Look Who's Talking Too   ★★15

Comedy   1990 · US · Colour · 76mins

Although this sequel succeeded in reuniting the stars of the first movie, it is a pallid retread. The twist this time around is that precocious Mikey (voiced again by Bruce Willis) gets a baby sister (vocals courtesy of Roseanne Barr) but, just to be doubly sure, director Amy Heckerling throws in a couple of other big name "cameos" – Damon Wayans (the voice of Eddie) and Mel Brooks as the voice of Mr

Toilet Man. Kirstie Alley and John Travolta have very little to do, although the latter is given a dance number, and a worrying strain of sentimentality starts to seep through. Contains swearing. 🖵

John Travolta *James* • Kirstie Alley *Mollie* • Olympia Dukakis *Rosie* • Elias Koteas *Stuart* • Twink Kaplan *Rona* • Neal Israel *Mr Ross* • Bruce Willis *Mikey* • Roseanne Barr [Roseanne] *Julie* • Damon Wayans *Eddie* • Mel Brooks *Mr Toilet Man* ■ *Dir* Amy Heckerling • *Scr* Amy Heckerling, Neal Israel, from characters created by Amy Heckerling

Look Who's Talking Now! ★★ 12

Comedy   1993 · US · Colour · 91mins
The talking baby concept had been exhausted by the first two *Look Who's* films, so the makers moved on to animals for this second sequel. However, even the presence of two new big-name stars – Danny DeVito and Diane Keaton – couldn't breathe life into a tired formula. John Travolta and Kirstie Alley go through the motions again as the bickering couple, while DeVito and Keaton, providing the voices for two dogs from different sides of the tracks, snap away in similar fashion. Despite the accomplished playing of the cast, good gags are thin on the ground. 🖵

John Travolta *James Ubriacco* • Kirstie Alley *Mollie Ubriacco* • David Gallagher *Mikey Ubriacco* • Tabitha Lupien *Julie Ubriacco* • Lysette Anthony *Samantha* • Olympia Dukakis *Rosie* • Danny DeVito *Rocks* • Diane Keaton *Daphne* • George Segal *Albert* ■ *Dir* Tom Ropelewski • *Scr* Tom Ropelewski, Leslie Dixon, from characters created by Amy Heckerling

The Lookalike ★★ 15

Mystery drama   1990 · US · Colour · 88mins
This is a muddled mixture of supernatural thriller and sentimental melodrama. Far too limited to carry this sort of hokum, Melissa Gilbert-Brinkman – best known as Laura Ingalls in *Little House on the Prairie* – relies on staring, tear-stained eyes and hysterical outbursts to convey the pain and confusion of a mother who is convinced she is being hounded by the double of her daughter who died in a road accident. 🖵

Melissa Gilbert-Brinkman [Melissa Gilbert] *Gina Crandall* • Bo Brinkman *Stuart Crandall* • Diane Ladd *Mary Helen Needham* • Thaao Penghlis *Nikos Lysandros* ■ *Dir* Gary Nelson • *Scr* Linda Morrow Bergman, Martin Tahse, from a short story by Kate Wilhelm

Looker ★★★★

Science-fiction thriller
1981 · US · Colour · 93mins
Way before he cloned dinosaurs in *Jurassic Park*, writer/director Michael Crichton played with similar themes for this under-rated blend of techno horror and suspense. It's a slick science-fiction outing about subliminal advertising, in which plastic surgeon Albert Finney joins pin-up Susan Dey to investigate the deaths of his supermodel clients and their association with advertising agency chief James Coburn. Although it's confusing at times, the design is fabulous, and the time-continuum blaster gizmo is a brilliant device allowing

Crichton to indulge in some great visual effects and the acting, from Finney especially, is outstanding. 🖵

Albert Finney *Dr Larry Roberts* • James Coburn *John Reston* • Susan Dey *Cindy* • Leigh Taylor-Young *Jennifer Long* • Dorian Harewood *Lieutenant Masters* • Tim Rossovich *Moustache Man* ■ *Dir/Scr* Michael Crichton

Lookin' Italian ★★ 18

Crime drama   1994 · US · Colour · 97mins
It would have made a good plotline for *Friends* – Joey turns all Robert De Niro in a cheap cash-in on *Mean Streets*. Sadly, though, this is real life and a rather embarrassing skeleton from the future *Friends* star Matt LeBlanc's closet. His is actually a supporting one, playing the hot-headed nephew of the Mafia-connected Jay Acovone, who is attempting to begin a new peaceful life in Los Angeles. The performances are wildly over the top and Guy Magar's script is stacked with every gangster cliché in the book. 🖵 **DVD**

Jay Acovone *Vinny Pallazzo* • Matt LeBlanc *Anthony Manetti* • Stephanie Richards *Danielle* • John LaMotta *Don Dinardo* • Ralph Manza *Manza* • Lou Rawls *Willy* ■ *Dir/Scr* Guy Magar

Lookin' to Get Out ★★ 15

Comedy   1982 · US · Colour · 100mins
The title probably sums up director Hal Ashby's feelings about this dud comedy that marked the beginning of his career decline in the 1980s. Stars Jon Voight and Burt Young are the two losers who arrive in Las Vegas hoping to win back the fortune they have just managed to lose. To this end they con their way into a luxury hotel suite and – with a little help from Ann-Margret – hit the tables. There's solid character back-up from the likes of Bert Remsen but it needed more flair upfront to make it work.

Jon Voight *Alex Kovac* • Ann-Margret *Patti Warner* • Burt Young *Jerry Feldman* • Bert Remsen *Smitty* • Jude Farese *Harry* • Allen Keller *Joey* ■ *Dir* Hal Ashby • *Scr* Al Schwartz, Jon Voight

Looking for Mr Goodbar ★★★★ 18

Drama   1977 · US · Colour · 130mins
Although not the most obvious choice to play the man-hungry heroine in this adaptation of Judith Rossner's bestseller, Diane Keaton manages a wonderfully fraught performance in writer/director Richard Brooks's overcharged sexual melodrama. Keaton plays a teacher of deaf children who haunts singles bars at night, taking the sadistic rough (Richard Gere) with the decent smooth (William Atherton) until she meets a bisexual killer (Tom Berenger). Although reminiscent of the German classic *Pandora's Box*, this has a glib puritanism pervading the sleaze and, even if some aspects of the novel are glossed over, it's still very raw. Contains violence, swearing, sex scenes and drug abuse. 🖵

Diane Keaton *Theresa Dunn* • Tuesday Weld *Katherine Dunn* • Richard Gere *Tony Lopanto* • William Atherton *James Morrissey* • Richard Kiley *Mr Dunn* • Alan Feinstein *Professor Engle* • Tom Berenger *Gary Cooper White* ■ *Dir* Richard Brooks • *Scr* Richard Brooks, from the novel by Judith Rossner

Looking for Richard ★★★★ 12

Documentary drama
1996 · US · Colour · 107mins
Al Pacino's very personal and interesting tribute to Shakespeare follows his attempts to adapt *Richard III* for the screen. Part documentary (the film contains interviews with the likes of Kenneth Branagh and John Gielgud), part film adaptation of the play, Pacino discusses the work and plays out scenes with fellow Americans Kevin Spacey, Winona Ryder, Aidan Quinn and Alec Baldwin. Demonstrating a love and understanding of the Bard as well as great skill as a Shakespearean actor, Pacino provides an examination that is both compelling and original. 🖵

Alec Baldwin *Clarence* • Al Pacino *Richard III* • Kevin Spacey *Buckingham* • Winona Ryder *Lady Anne* • Aidan Quinn *Richmond* • Estelle Parsons *Margaret* ■ *Dir* Al Pacino

The Looking Glass War ★★★ 15

Spy drama   1969 · UK · Colour · 102mins
The spymasters come out best, but that's because they're played by Ralph Richardson and Paul Rogers in this John le Carré adaptation in which a Polish refugee (Christopher Jones) is persuaded to enter East Germany to verify Russian missile sites. The foot soldiers of espionage (including a young Anthony Hopkins) have a tough time of it, and its Cold War climate now seems long ago and far away. Contains violence and swearing. 🖵

Christopher Jones *Leiser* • Pia Degermark *The Girl* • Ralph Richardson *Leclerc* • Anthony Hopkins *John Avery* • Paul Rogers *Haldane* • Susan George *Susan* • Ray McAnally *Starr* ■ *Dir* Frank R Pierson [Frank Pierson] • *Scr* Frank R Pierson, from the novel by John Le Carré

Looking on the Bright Side ★★★

Musical comedy   1931 · UK · BW · 81mins
Gracie Fields hit the movie big time with this sprightly musical comedy, which was co-directed by theatre impresario Basil Dean and silent specialist Graham Cutts. As ever, she plays a spirited working lass, who keeps her wits around her, even when things are at their bleakest. Quitting her job as a manicurist, when the hairdresser she adores gets the chance to write songs for a superstar, she joins the police and not only rediscovers her self-esteem, but also arrives on stage to save her beau's flagging career. The songs have dated badly, but no one belts them out like Our Gracie.

Gracie Fields *Gracie* • Richard Dolman *Laurie* • Julian Rose *Oscar Schultz* • Wyn Richmond *Miss Joy* ■ *Dir* Basil Dean, Graham Cutts • *Scr* Basil Dean, Archie Pitt, Brock Williams

Looks and Smiles ★★★★

Drama   1981 · UK · Colour · 103mins
The rising damp of despair permeates this Ken Loach docu-drama about the effect of redundancies on teenagers living in Sheffield, South Yorkshire. One boy opts for enlistment and ends

up in Belfast; another stays at home, condemning himself to the futility of the job search and a relationship with shopgirl Carolyn Nicholson. Loach elicits marvellous performances from his three leads – Graham Greene, Nicholson and Tony Pitts – amateur actors behaving like true professionals. It's a stunning evocation of a city stricken by the vicissitudes of the free market.

Graham Greene *Mick Walsh* • Carolyn Nicholson *Karen Lodge* • Tony Pitts *Alan Wright* • Roy Haywood *Phil Adams* • Phil Askham *Mr Walsh* • Pam Darrell *Mrs Walsh* ■ *Dir* Kenneth Loach [Ken Loach] • *Scr* Barry Hines

Looney Looney Looney Bugs Bunny Movie ★★★ U

Animation   1981 · US · Colour · 69mins
Forty-one years after *A Wild Hare*, the most famous character in the Warner Bros cartoon stable returns in another greatest hits compilation. Bugs Bunny is always good value and the selection made here by Friz Freleng, one of the animators who first brought him to life (based on sketches by a story man named Bugs Hardaway, hence the name) is often very funny indeed. The highlight is *Knighty Knight Bugs*, which won the Oscar for best animated short subject in 1958. 🖵

Mel Blanc ■ *Dir* Friz Freleng, Gerry Chiniquy • *Scr* David Detiege, John W Dunn

Loophole ★★ PG

Crime drama   1980 · UK · Colour · 99mins
Albert Finney and Susannah York, together for the first time since *Tom Jones*, star in this lacklustre heist caper. Martin Sheen is the obligatory American import, whose in-depth knowledge of bank security systems and hefty overdraft make him the ideal partner for Finney's mastermind. The blag itself is pretty routine, although the action picks up slightly when the gang's escape through the London sewers is hindered by a torrential downpour. Drably directed by John Quested, not even Lalo Schifrin's score can enliven the proceedings. 🖵

Albert Finney *Mike Daniels* • Martin Sheen *Stephen Booker* • Susannah York *Dinah Booker* • Colin Blakely *Gardner* • Jonathan Pryce *Taylor* • Robert Morley *Godfrey* • Alfred Lynch *Harry* • Tony Doyle *Nolan* ■ *Dir* John Quested • *Scr* Jonathan Hales, from a novel by Robert Pollock

Loose Cannons ★ 15

Comedy   1990 · US · Colour · 90mins
Quality control has never been one of Gene Hackman's strongest suits, but this dire buddy comedy marked a new low for the excellent actor. He is the tough cop who finds himself reluctantly paired on a case with oddball detective Dan Aykroyd, who happens to suffer from a form of multiple personality disorder brought on by imminent danger. Anyone who attempts to merge *The Three Faces of Eve* with *Lethal Weapon* probably deserves some points for ambition, but this remains an almost unwatchable mess: Bob Clark's direction is lethargic, Aykroyd is spectacularly unfunny and Hackman simply looks embarrassed. Contains swearing, violence and nudity. 🖵

Gene Hackman *Mac Stern* • Dan Aykroyd *Ellis Fielding* • Dom DeLuise *Harry "The Hippo" Gutterman* • Ronny Cox *Bob Smiley* • Nancy Travis *Riva* • Robert Prosky *Curt Von Metz* ■ *Dir* Bob Clark • *Scr* Richard Christian Matheson, Richard Matheson, Bob Clark

Loose Connections ★★★ PG
Drama   1983 · UK · Colour · 95mins

This attempt by theatre director Richard Eyre to resurrect the screwball comedies of the thirties has unlikely duo Lindsay Duncan and Stephen Rea as the protagonists. Duncan plays an uptight Germaine Greer type, driving through Germany with co-"pilot" Rea as her unfortunate companion. Their inability to see eye to eye fits well with the film's general depiction of the Brits abroad. Turns from Robbie Coltrane and Gary Olsen add to the fun and the two leads carry the film with style. Eyre nearly obtains his objective with the genre – but not quite.

Stephen Rea *Harry* • Lindsay Duncan *Sally* • Carol Harrison *Kay* • Frances Low *Laurie* • Andrew De La Tour *Journalist* • David Purcell *Photographer* • Keith Allen *Keith* • Robbie Coltrane *Drunk* • Ruth Bruck *Wirtin* ■ *Dir* Richard Eyre • *Scr* Maggie Brooks

Loot ★★★★ 15
Comedy   1970 · UK · Colour · 97mins

Joe Orton's mordant play is about a bundle of stolen money hidden in a coffin that gets buried in the churchyard. The body is hidden somewhere else. It's a ruthless satire on authoritarianism as well as a send-up of the Agatha Christie-style whodunit which had kept the British theatre ticking over for decades. The play had gone from disaster to prize-winning success but the film version flopped badly. Reworked by TV writers Galton and Simpson, it's wholly faithful to Orton's surreal sense of humour and the extreme tackiness of the characters, especially Richard Attenborough who clearly delights in playing the creepiest, kinkiest detective you'll ever see. A movie of embalming fluid, garden gnomes and wallpaper that's violent enough to upstage a nuclear war. [symbol]

Richard Attenborough *Inspector Truscott* • Lee Remick *Fay* • Hywel Bennett *Dennis* • Roy Holder *Hal* • Milo O'Shea *Mr McLeavy* • Dick Emery *Mr Bateman* • Joe Lynch *Father O'Shaughnessy* • John Cater *Meadows* • Aubrey Woods *Undertaker* ■ *Dir* Silvio Narizzano • *Scr* Ray Galton, Alan Simpson, from the play by Joe Orton

The Looters ★★
Action adventure   1955 · US · BW · 87mins

Rory Calhoun and Ray Danton are two buddies who reach four survivors of a plane crash in the Rockies, only to fall out over money found on board. Calhoun is forced at gunpoint to lead the group to safety, biding his time to turn the tables. Calhoun and Danton are not particularly interesting as actors, and the plot might have worked better as a western. But Julie Adams certainly looks good playing a model, and former character actor turned director Abner Biberman does as good a job as the script allows.

Rory Calhoun *Jesse Hill* • Julie Adams *Sheryl Gregory* • Ray Danton *Pete Corder* • Thomas

Gomez *George Parkinson* • Frank Faylen *Stan Leppich* • Rod Williams *Co-pilot* • Russ Conway *Major Knowles* ■ *Dir* Abner Biberman • *Scr* Richard Alan Simmons, from a story by Paul Schneider

The Looters ★★
Crime drama   1966 · Fr/It · Colour · 102mins

Ex-criminal Frederick Stafford falls for Jean Seberg, but finds that her gangster father has other plans for him. He's recruited to crack a safe and steal some gold owned by a would-be dictator who is planning a coup – apparently no moral problems there. Despite these political undertones, the film is a straightforward crime caper which could have been livelier. However, it contains some incidental pleasures, including Serge Gainsbourg, then known in Britain largely for the classic racy song *Je t'Aime... Moi non Plus*. French and Italian dialogue dubbed into English.

Frederick Stafford *Sam Morgan* • Jean Seberg *Colleen O'Hara* • Mario Pisu *Patrick O'Hara* • Maria-Rosa Rodriguez *Estella* • Serge Gainsbourg *Clyde* ■ *Dir* Jacques Besnard • *Scr* Pierre Foucaud, Michel Lebrun

Lord Edgware Dies ★
Murder mystery   1934 · US · BW · 81mins

Agatha Christie's 13th whodunit was filmed the year after its publication. It was intended to be the start of a series of Hercule Poirot movie adventures, with Austin Trevor as the fastidious Belgian sleuth. But such was the wave of apathy that greeted this lacklustre adaptation that the plans were shelved. Trevor is wincingly bad, completely missing the trademark mannerisms of Poirot that later actors would bring to the character.

Austin Trevor *Hercule Poirot* • Jane Carr (1) *Lady Edgware* • Richard Cooper *Captain Hastings* • John Turnbull *Inspector Japp* • Michael Shepley *Captain Ronald Marsh* • Leslie Perrins *Bryan Martin* • CV France *Lord Edgware* • Esme Percy *Duke of Merton* ■ *Dir* Henry Edwards • *Scr* H Fowler Mear, from the novel by Agatha Christie

Lord Jim ★★★★ PG
Historical adventure
1965 · UK · Colour · 147mins

This is Peter O'Toole's finest performance as victim-hero after *Lawrence of Arabia*, in Joseph Conrad's story of a merchant seaman branded a coward after jumping ship during a storm. His search for salvation in South East Asia is found in action against a fanatical tyrant lording it over oppressed natives. Writer/director Richard Brooks allows the plot to meander out of control, but the presence of actors such as James Mason and Jack Hawkins provides a counterbalance to O'Toole's introspection, while Freddie Young's photography of mist-shrouded rivers and jungles emphasises the weird spirituality of Lord Jim's quest for redemption. [symbol]

Peter O'Toole *Lord Jim* • James Mason *Gentleman Brown* • Curt Jurgens *Cornelius* • Eli Wallach *The General* • Jack Hawkins *Marlow* • Paul Lukas *Stein* • Akim Tamiroff *Schomberg* • Daliah Lavi *The Girl* ■ *Dir* Richard Brooks • *Scr* Richard Brooks, from the novel by Joseph Conrad

Lord Love a Duck ★★★
Black comedy   1966 · US · BW · 105mins

George Axelrod made a notable directorial debut with this wickedly funny and beautifully acted satire on sixties California lifestyles. It is centred on a bizarre high school, where clairvoyant Roddy McDowall grants wishes for the students, notably those of Tuesday Weld as teen vamp Barbara Ann. Weld's orgasmic rummage through woollen sweaters is a surprising highlight of this film – Alicia Silverstone, eat your heart out! This is a real one-off: a wacky black comedy unfettered by taste, written and performed with great élan, with an interesting supporting cast including eccentric Ruth Gordon and Lola Albright as Weld's suicidal mom.

Roddy McDowall *Alan "Mollymauk" Musgrave* • Tuesday Weld *Barbara Ann Greene* • Lola Albright *Marie Greene* • Martin West *Bob Barnard* • Ruth Gordon *Stella Barnard* • Harvey Korman *Weldon Emmett* • Sarah Marshall *Miss Schwartz* • Hal Baylor *Jack* • Laurie Mitchell *Jack's Wife* • David Draper *Billy Gibbons* • Donald Foster *Mr Beverly* • Judith Loomis *Mrs Butch Neuhauser* • Martin Gabel *Movie producer Harry Belmont* ■ *Dir* George Axelrod • *Scr* Larry H Johnson, George Axelrod, from the novel by Al Hine

Lord of Illusions ★★ 18
Horror   1995 · US · Colour · 116mins

An unfocused and meandering dark fairy tale directed by *Hellraiser* horror novelist Clive Barker featuring his literary creation, the world-weary private eye Harry D'Amour (Scott Bakula). The troubled detective is on the trail of an evil cult spiritualist and his murder investigation takes him into the illusory world of professional theatre magicians – some of whom are the real thing awaiting the devilish return of their late leader. Barker's keen visual flair is evident throughout this gory intrigue, and it delivers a couple of genuine jolts, but there's far too much style and not enough content to fully engage the fear senses. [DVD]

Scott Bakula *Harry D'Amour* • Famke Janssen *Dorothea Swann* • Trevor Edmond *Young Butterfield* • Daniel Von Bargen *Nix* • Kevin J O'Connor *Philip Swann* • Joseph Latimore *Caspar Quaid* ■ *Dir/Scr* Clive Barker

Lord of the Flies ★★★★ PG
Drama   1963 · UK · BW · 86mins

Novelist William Golding's fierce morality tale about schoolboys marooned on a desert island and reverting to religious savagery is given the larger-than-life treatment by theatrical director Peter Brook, who can't quite cope with cinematic character, but who keeps the tension tight as a crossbow. The wider implications of the idea, as a comment on mankind's original sin (Cains versus Abels ending in murder) don't come across. But, taken as a parable limited to a bleak blueprint, it's vividly memorable. [symbol]

James Aubrey *Ralph* • Tom Chapin *Jack* • Hugh Edwards *Piggy* • Roger Elwin *Roger* • Tom Gaman *Simon* ■ *Dir* Peter Brook • *Scr* Peter Brook, from the novel by William Golding

Lord of the Flies ★★★ PG
Drama   1990 · US · Colour · 87mins

A worthy but misfired attempt to feed William Golding's classic tale to the masses. The switch from British public schoolboys to American military cadets actually works better than it sounds and, at one level, makes the boys' often savage transformation even more believable. Director Harry Hook, who made his name with another film that dealt with childhood, *The Kitchen Toto*, coaxes wonderful performances out of a young, largely unknown cast led by Balthazar Getty. However, Hook doesn't quite succeed in recapturing the dark, disturbing undercurrents of either the novel or Peter Brook's earlier film version. Contains strong language. [symbol]

Balthazar Getty *Ralph* • Chris Furrh *Jack* • Danuel Pipoly *Piggy* • Gary Rule *Roger* • Terry Wells *Andy* • Braden MacDonald *Larry* ■ *Dir* Harry Hook • *Scr* Sara Schiff, from the novel by William Golding

The Lord of the Rings ★★ PG
Animated fantasy
1978 · US · Colour · 127mins

Unlikely to satisfy fans of JRR Tolkien's novels, this animated version is also small beer compared to recent animated spectaculars. Produced by Saul Zaentz – the man behind *One Flew Over The Cuckoo's Nest* and *The English Patient* – it seems less concerned with Tolkien than the West Coast druggie culture of the mid-seventies and as a herald of New Ageism. It's also rather slow and virtually impossible to follow unless you know the source material. [symbol]

Christopher Guard *Frodo* • Michael Scholes *Samwise* • John Hurt *Aragorn "Strider"* • William Squire *Gandalf* • Simon Chandler *Merry* • Dominic Guard *Pippin* • Norman Bird *Bilbo* ■ *Dir* Ralph Bakshi • *Scr* Chris Conkling, Peter S Beagle, from the novels by JRR Tolkien

The Lords of Discipline ★★★ 15
Drama   1983 · US · Colour · 98mins

Having hanged himself in *An Officer and a Gentleman*, David Keith goes back to military school for this sinister thriller in which he combats the racist bigotry of a secret society known as "The Ten". Director Franc Roddam is every bit as comfortable with the sights and sounds of sixties Carolina as he was with the English seaside in *Quadrophenia*. But once the scene has been set he rather loses the plot, spending a disturbing amount of time on the acts of cruelty perpetrated upon the academy's first black cadet and not enough time sleuthing the culprits. Contains swearing and violence. [symbol]

David Keith *Will McClean* • Robert Prosky *Colonel "Bear" Berrineau* • GD Spradlin *General Durrell* • Barbara Babcock *Abigail* • Michael Biehn *Alexander* • Rick Rossovich *Pig* • John Lavachielli *Mark* • Judge Reinhold *Macabbee* • Bill Paxton *Gilbreath* • Jason Connery *MacKinnon* ■ *Dir* Franc Roddam • *Scr* Thomas Pope, Lloyd Fonvielle, from the novel by Pat Conroy

U = SUITABLE FOR ALL   Uc = SUITABLE FOR ALL, ESPECIALLY FOR YOUNG CHILDREN (VIDEO ONLY)   PG = PARENTAL GUIDANCE

The Lords of Flatbush
★★★★ 15

Drama 1974 · US · Colour · 80mins

Sylvester Stallone (in his first top-billed role), *Happy Days* star Henry Winkler, B-movie heart-throb Perry King and Paul Mace are members of a Brooklyn gang in this brilliant coming-of-age saga set in the late 1950s. Stallone sets the seal on his future *Rocky* success as a leather-jacketed tough-talker pushed into marriage by his pregnant girlfriend when all he really wants to do is hang out with the guys and tend his pigeons. Evoking a strong sense of time and place, the nostalgic soundtrack is the icing on a rich cake. A huge youth market sleeper, with great support from other such rising stars as Susan Blakely, Ray Sharkey and disco maestro Paul Jabara. 🔲

Perry King *Chico Tyrell* • Sylvester Stallone *Stanley Rosiello* • Henry Winkler *Butchey Weinstein* • Paul Mace *Wimpy Murgalo* • Susan Blakely *Jane Bradshaw* • Maria Smith *Frannie Malincanico* • Renee Paris *Annie Yuckamanelli* • Ray Sharkey *Student* • Paul Jabara *Crazy Cohen* ■ *Dir* Stephen Verona, Martin Davidson • *Scr* Stephen Verona, Martin Davidson, Gayle Gleckler, Sylvester Stallone

Lorenzo's Oil
★★★★ 15

Biographical drama
1992 · US · Colour · 129mins

This glossy, at times harrowing, heart-tugger is dominated by the towering performance of Susan Sarandon as the determined and bolshie Michaela Odone, who takes on the medical establishment when her young son is diagnosed with a rare and normally fatal wasting disease. But Nick Nolte is less successful as the boy's father, Augusto, sporting a bizarre Italian accent. You'll either love or loathe this intelligent, well-made wallow that's ably directed by *Mad Max* veteran George Miller. Wonderful stuff. 🔲

Nick Nolte *Augusto Odone* • Susan Sarandon *Michaela Odone* • Peter Ustinov *Professor Nikolais* • Kathleen Wilhoite *Deirdre Murphy* • Gerry Bamman *Doctor Judalon* • Margo Martindale *Wendy Gimble* • Zack O'Malley Greenburg *Lorenzo* • Laura Linney *Young teacher* ■ *Dir* George Miller (2) • *Scr* George MIller, Nick Enright

Lorna
★★ 18

Erotic drama 1964 · US · BW · 79mins

Part gothic melodrama, part sex morality play, this was the notorious Russ Meyer's first serious effort at "legitimate" film-making after a handful of nudie flicks that began with *The Immoral Mr Teas*. Certainly it's his first plot-driven movie and casts buxom Lorna Maitland as the eponymous heroine, a backwoods wife who strays from her dull husband and begins an affair with an escaped con that ultimately leads to tragedy. Meyer, with his typically flamboyant editing and direction, actually does a pretty good job of things considering the mediocre acting talent and script at his disposal. Contains sex scenes and some swearing and violence. 🔲

Lorna Maitland *Lorna* • Mark Bradley *Fugitive* • James Rucker *James* • Hal Hopper *Luther* • Doc Scortt *Jonah* • James Griffith *Prophet/Narrator* ■ *Dir* Russ Meyer • *Scr* James Griffith, from a story by R Albion Meyer

Lorna Doone
★★★ U

Period drama 1934 · UK · BW · 82mins

RD Blackmore's novel is a full-blooded melodrama set in 17th century Exmoor where two feuding families – the Doones and the Ridds – are at each other's throats. As in *Romeo and Juliet*, there is a cross-feudal romance between strappingly handsome John Ridd and pretty Lorna who, it transpires, isn't a Doone at all but a kidnapped aristocrat. The story had been immensely popular – especially with young girls – ever since its publication in 1869 and there were silent film versions in 1912 and 1920. This version stars Victoria Hopper, the wife of the producer/director Basil Dean, as Lorna. John Loder, as the hero Ridd, was always a rather wooden actor, though Margaret Lockwood, in her screen debut, is a ravishing beauty. The story still holds water, even if the acting and the techniques of 1934 may leak a bit. 🔲

Victoria Hopper *Lorna Doone* • John Loder *John Ridd* • Margaret Lockwood *Annie Ridd* • Roy Emerton *Carver Doone* • Mary Clare *Mistress Ridd* • Edward Rigby *Reuben Huckaback* • Roger Livesey *Tom Faggus* ■ *Dir* Basil Dean • *Scr* Dorothy Farnum, Miles Malleson, Gordon Wellesley, from the novel by RD Blackmore

Lorna Doone
★★ U

Drama 1951 · US · Colour · 83mins

Hollywood has a go at the classic yarn of a rustic feud, a hulking hero and a smart heroine who turns out to be a kidnapped heiress. Lorna is played by Barbara Hale, best known as Perry Mason's secretary, Della Street, over several years on TV. As the hero John Ridd, Richard Greene was also better known as ITV's Robin Hood throughout the fifties. It's made on a slimmed down budget for Columbia, though they did stomp up the dosh for Technicolor but shot it in the Yosemite National Park, California, rather than on Exmoor. B-movie director Phil Karlson treats it just like a western.

Barbara Hale *Lorna Doone* • Richard Greene *John Ridd* • Carl Benton Reid *Sir Ensor Doone* • William Bishop *Carver Doone* • Ron Randell *Tom Faggus* • Sean McClory *Charleworth Doone* • Onslow Stevens *Counsellor Doone* • Lester Matthews *King Charles II* ■ *Dir* Phil Karlson • *Scr* Jesse L Lasky Jr, Richard Schayer, from the novel by RD Blackmore

The Loser
★★★

Comedy thriller 1971 · Fr · Colour

An amusing "worm turns" story that provides an admirable showcase for Claude Brasseur. As the petty crook whose stint in the cells lands him an introduction to the big time, Brasseur milks every gag as he not only begins blackmailing the town's crooked dignitaries, but also moves in on a murdered mobster's moll (Marthe Keller). The prolific Gilles Grangier, who made over 50 features in his 30-year career, directs with a glib charm owing much to the fact that his speciality was the sort of crime drama he so gleefully spoofs here. French dialogue dubbed into English.

Claude Brasseur *Granier* • André Weber *Laigneau* • Marthe Keller *Catherine* • Pierre Tornade *Fernier* ■ *Dir* Gilles Grangier • *Scr* Albert Simonin, from a novel by Jean Stuart

Loser Takes All
★

Comedy 1990 · UK/US · Colour · 88mins

Robert Lindsay and Molly Ringwald take over from Rossano Brazzi and Glynis Johns as the British couple who are gifted a honeymoon in Monte Carlo, only for staid hubbie to become seduced by the casino. Lindsay does his best with the ploddingly predictable material but Ringwald is grievously miscast as his wife and even the presence of a distinguished supporting cast (John Gielgud, Michel Blanc, Margi Clarke) can't save it. As gambling dramas go, *National Lottery Live* is marginally more entertaining.

Robert Lindsay *Ian Bertram* • Molly Ringwald *Cary Porter* • John Gielgud *Herbert Dreuther* • Simon de la Brosse *Philippe* • Max Wall *Bowles* • Margi Clarke *Nurse* • Frances de la Tour *Mrs De Vere* ■ *Dir* James Scott • *Scr* James Scott, from the novella by Graham Greene

Losin' It
★★ 18

Comedy drama 1983 · US · Colour · 95mins

Tom Cruise, in one of his earliest roles, adds curiosity value to an unexceptional coming-of-age-tale about three teenagers heading for Tijuana to gain a broader perspective on life and lose their virginity. Strictly routine in every area, with Shelley Long of *Cheers* fame coming along for the ride as a woman hoping to get a quick divorce. 🔲

Tom Cruise *Woody* • Jackie Earle Haley *Dave* • John Stockwell *Spider* • Shelley Long *Kathy* • John P Navin Jr *Wendell the Wimp* • Henry Darrow *El Jefe, Sheriff* • Hector Elias *Chuey* ■ *Dir* Curtis Hanson • *Scr* BWL Norton, from his story

Losing Chase
★★★ 15

Drama 1996 · US · Colour · 93mins

Kevin Bacon's directorial debut is something of a family affair, with wife Kyra Sedgwick in a pivotal role and brother Michael responsible for the score. It's Helen Mirren who holds the piece together, however, as a stressed wife who emerges from a bout of depression deeply in love with the home help husband Beau Bridges had hired to lighten the load. Realising the members of his cast know what they're about, Bacon restricts himself to the odd showy moment and some very neat crosscuts that suggest he's got what it takes behind the camera as well as in front of it. Contains swearing. 🔲

Helen Mirren *Chase Philips* • Kyra Sedgwick *Elizabeth Cole* • Beau Bridges *Richard Philips* • Michael Yarmush *Little Richard* • Lucas Denton *Jason Philips* ■ *Dir* Kevin Bacon • *Scr* Anne Meredith

Losing Isaiah
★★★ 15

Drama 1995 · US · Colour · 102mins

Emotionally-charged drama about the custody battle between a young black mother (Halle Berry), who three years earlier had abandoned her baby while high on drugs, and the loving white couple (Jessica Lange and David Strathairn) who have adopted him. A strong cast – which also includes Samuel L Jackson and Cuba Gooding Jr – add dramatic weight to a "TV movie of the week" plot. The film does present a believable, well-balanced view from both sides, although Berry's successful rehabilitation from frazzled crack-head to lovely child-minder seems a little too contrived.

Jessica Lange *Margaret Lewin* • Halle Berry *Khaila Richards* • David Strathairn *Charles Lewin* • Cuba Gooding Jr *Eddie Hughes* • Daisy Eagan *Hannah Lewin* • Marc John Jeffries *Isaiah* • Samuel L Jackson *Kadar Lewis* ■ *Dir* Stephen Gyllenhaal • *Scr* Naomi Foner, from the novel by Seth J Margolis

A Loss of Innocence
★★

Drama 1996 · US · Colour

Jennie Garth is a long way from her pampered existence in *Beverly Hills 90210* in this soapy Mormon melodrama. Playing the fiancée of Mike Doyle, she causes ructions in the Mormon community when she develops a crush on his brother (Rob Estes), who has turned his back on religion. It's heated stuff if a bit daft and, while the acting leaves a lot to be desired, this TV film as a whole makes for cheesy, entertaining fun. Contains some swearing.

Jennie Garth *Chelnicia Bowen* • Rob Estes *Erik Eriksen* • Mike Doyle *Jens Eriksen* • Michael Milhoan *Ivor Eriksen* • Polly Holliday *Christine Eriksen* • Anne Sward *Ida Eriksen* ■ *Dir* Graeme Clifford • *Scr* Joyce Eliason

The Loss of Sexual Innocence
★★ 18

Drama 1999 · US/UK · Colour · 105mins

Specked with fascinating moments, this is an otherwise over-indulgent hobby horse that has been lingering in the mind of writer/director Mike Figgis since the early eighties. A fragmentary memoir of a movie producer called Nic (played variously by Jonathan Rhys-Meyers and Julian Sands), it traces his development from school bullying and love on the Tyne to marital discord and tragedy in the Sahara. Fleeting impressions, such as the airport meeting of separated twins (dual incarnations of Saffron Burrows), have a rudimentary allure. Alas, the decision to intercut the action with a mixed race re-telling of the Adam and Eve story proves calamitously self-conscious. Contains sex scenes and nudity.

Julian Sands *Nic (as an adult)* • Saffron Burrows *English twin/Italian twin* • Stefano Dionisi *Lucca* • Kelly MacDonald *Susan* • Gina McKee *Susan's Mother* • Jonathan Rhys-Meyers *Nic (age 16)* • Bernard Hill *Susan's father* ■ *Dir/Scr* Mike Figgis

Lost
★★★

Crime drama 1955 · UK · Colour · 89mins

A film that succeeds because it confronts every parent's nightmare: what happens when you suddenly look away and find your child is missing when you look back? Of course, this being a class-riddled Rank picture, it's the nanny who loses the baby, but it's pretty harrowing nonetheless, despite the casting of insipid David Knight and Julia Arnall as the parents. Granite-faced cop David Farrar is on hand to bring grit to this earnest chase movie, and not-so-hidden among the red herrings are a welter of British character players, with particularly impressive work from Thora Hird. Harry Waxman's colour location photography is superb, but the cliff-top climax is a little hard to believe in.

David Farrar *Inspector Craig* • David Knight *Lee Cochrane* • Julia Arnall *Sue Cochrane* • Anthony Oliver *Sergeant Lyel* • Thora Hird *Landlady* • Eleanor Summerfield *Sergeant Cook* • Ann Paige *Nanny* • Anna Turner *Mrs Robey* ■ *Dir* Guy Green • *Scr* Janet Green

Lost and Found ★ 15

Romantic comedy
1979 · UK/US · Colour · 100mins

Re-uniting George Segal and Glenda Jackson, the delightful duo of *A Touch of Class*, might have seemed like a good plan, but this story of a widowed American professor meeting a British divorcee on a skiing holiday, marrying, and living unhappily ever after makes us regret the very idea. The couple's incompatability degenerates into shouted slanging matches to the extent that, like a ski-run, the film heads downhill all the way. Contains swearing.

George Segal *Adam Watson* • Glenda Jackson *Patricia Brittenham* • Maureen Stapleton *Jemmy* • Hollis McLaren *Eden* • John Cunningham *Lenny* • Paul Sorvino *Reilly* • John Candy *Carpentier* • Martin Short *Engel* ■ *Dir* Melvin Frank • *Scr* Melvin Frank, Jack Rose

Lost & Found ★★ 12

Romantic comedy
1999 · US · Colour · 96mins

Dependable comic actor David Spade finally cracked the big time with his role in the US sitcom *Just Shoot Me*. His success led to a starring role in this romantic comedy in which Spade plays restaurateur Dylan Ramsey who falls in lust with his attractive French neighbour Lila Dubois (Sophie Marceau). Lila dotes on her dog, and Dylan hatches a plan to get closer to her by kidnapping the pet and then helping her search for it. But all doesn't go to plan. Spade's smarmy persona can be an acquired taste, so add a star if you're a fan, take one off if you find his bitchy asides and pointed sarcasm hard to take.

David Spade *Dylan Ramsey* • Sophie Marceau *Lila Dubois* • Patrick Bruel *Rene* • Artie Lange *Wally* • Mitchell Whitfield *Mark Glidewell* • Martin Sheen *Millstone* • Jon Lovitz *Uncle Harry* • Estelle Harris *Mrs Stubblefie* ■ *Dir* Jeff Pollack • *Scr* David Spade, Marc Meeks, JB Cook

Lost Angel ★★★ U

Drama
1943 · US · BW · 90mins

A foundling child (Margaret O'Brien), made the subject of a scientific experiment, reveals herself as a genius by the age of six, but at the cost of the normal joys of childhood. The situation is remedied when a compassionate police reporter (James Craig) takes her under his wing. Acting on Louis B Mayer's orders, Isobel Lennart wrote this specially for MGM's remarkable child star, already a veteran at the age of six. The film amply demonstrates O'Brien's talent and appeal and, although an implausible exercise in sentimentality designed to tug mercilessly at the heartstrings, its saccharine content is nicely modulated.

Margaret O'Brien *Alpha* • James Craig *Mike Regan* • Marsha Hunt *Katie Mallory* • Philip Merivale *Professor Peter Vincent* • Keenan Wynn *Packy* • Alan Napier *Dr Woodring* ■ *Dir* Roy Rowland • *Scr* Isobel Lennart, from an idea by Angna Enters

The Lost Boys ★★ 15

Horror comedy 1987 · US · Colour · 93mins

There's a nasty surprise in store for divorcee Dianne Wiest when she moves her family to the Californian coast. The local teenage gang is a pack of punk vampires with designs on her kids. A slick, noisily empty, and ultimately desperate attempt to update the undead genre for the MTV generation, *Batman and Robin* director Joel Schumacher's neon-drenched violent nightmare is an anaemic blend of Hollywood glitz and endless pop culture references. No amount of chic flash and gore makes up for the few surprises, obvious twists and witless sitcom dialogue. Contains swearing.

▷ *DVD*

Jason Patric *Michael Emerson* • Kiefer Sutherland *David* • Corey Feldman *Edgar Frog* • Corey Haim *Sam Emerson* • Dianne Wiest *Lucy Emerson* • Barnard Hughes *Grandpa* • Edward Herrmann *Max* • Jami Gertz *Star* ■ *Dir* Joel Schumacher • *Scr* Janice Fischer, James Jeremias, Jeffrey Boam, from a story by Janice Fischer, James Jeremias

The Lost Capone ★★★ 15

Crime drama 1990 · US · Colour · 88mins

An interesting morality tale about Al Capone's young brother Jimmy (Adrian Pasdar) who sought to distance himself from his gangster sibling by changing his name, moving to Nebraska and becoming a town marshal. Eric (brother of Julia) Roberts is suitably sinister and furious as Al, who understandably is a bit peeved when his little brother seeks to ruin his bootlegging business. Pasdar gives a more subtle performance as the tortured Jimmy, and his considerable screen presence makes you wonder why he isn't more of a star. An absorbing movie that provides an interesting background to the story of one of America's most notorious gangsters.

Adrian Pasdar *Jimmy Capone/Richard Hart* • Eric Roberts *Al Capone* • Ally Sheedy *Kathleen Hart* • Titus Welliver *Ralph Capone* • Anthony Crivello *Frank Capone* ■ *Dir/Scr* John Gray

The Lost Command ★★ 15

War drama 1966 · US · Colour · 124mins

French soldier Anthony Quinn gathers his old unit from the Indo-China war and heads for Algeria, ready to crush the independence movement. But his hopes to recruit another old buddy, George Segal, are dashed when he discovers that Segal has made up the rebel army. In between all this is Claudia Cardinale, looking gorgeous and changing sides according to which man she shares a scene with. Alain Delon and Maurice Ronet guaranteed the movie a huge audience in France, though it's unlikely that American audiences would even know where Algeria was or why Anthony Quinn and George Segal thought it worth the bother of their dodgy French accents.

Anthony Quinn *Lt Col Raspeguy* • Alain Delon *Capt Esclavier* • George Segal *Mahidi* • Michèle Morgan *Countess De Clairefons* • Maurice Ronet *Boisfeuras* • Claudia Cardinale *Aicha* • Grégoire Aslan *Ben Saad* • Jean Servais *General Meliès* ■ *Dir* Mark Robson • *Scr* Nelson Gidding, from the novel *Les Centurions* by Jean Lartéguy

The Lost Continent ★★

Science-fiction adventure
1968 · US · Colour · 103mins

Director Leslie Norman probably heaved a huge sigh of relief when he parted company with this Hammer stinker just a few days into production. Michael Carreras took over and immediately ran the project on to the cinematic rocks. The script (written by Carreras under the pseudonym Michael Nash) is wonderfully bizarre, with Eric Porter and his crew setting foot on an island ruled by the Spanish Inquisition. But it's the monsters that will have you shrieking with laughter, though, not terror. One of the effects wizards, Robert A Mattey, had the last laugh, however – he designed *Jaws*. Crass or classic? You choose.

Eric Porter *Captain Lansen* • Hildegarde Neff *Eva* • Suzanna Leigh *Unity* • Tony Beckley *Harry Tyler* • Nigel Stock *Dr Webster* • Neil McCallum *First Officer Hemmings* ■ *Dir* Michael Carreras • *Scr* Michael Nash [Michael Carreras], from the novel *Uncharted Seas* by Dennis Wheatley

Lost Highway ★★★★ 18

Psychological thriller fantasy
1996 · US · Colour · 128mins

Four years after the *Twin Peaks* phenomenon, David Lynch came up with this narrative-defying mystifier about a jazz saxophonist in a disturbed domestic limbo (an exemplary Bill Pullman) who suddenly and inexplicably transforms into a younger man (Balthazar Getty). Though never together in a scene, the men share what appears to be the same elusive, deceptive woman (Patricia Arquette in contrasting wigs). Its not the most accessible scenario, but the delivery is hypnotising. And while other modern films about bad people, paranoia and deceptive women get labelled *film noir*, Lynch reinvents the *form* of that genre rather than just rely on its storyline formula. Painterly, impenetrable and creepy but never consciously hip, its a painful, nightmarish vision of suffering and yearning that echoes Hitchcock's *Vertigo*, that other great work under-appreciated in its day.

Bill Pullman *Fred Madison* • Patricia Arquette *Renee Madison/Alice Wakefield* • Balthazar Getty *Pete Dayton* • Robert Blake *Mystery man* • Natasha Gregson Wagner *Sheila* • Robert Loggia *Mr Eddy/Dick Laurent* • Gary Busey *Bill Dayton* • Richard Pryor *Arnie* • Michael Massee *Andy* • Henry Rollins *Guard Henry* • Jack Nance *Phil* • Mink Stole *Forewoman* ■ *Dir* David Lynch • *Scr* David Lynch, Barry Gifford • *Cinematographer* Peter Deming

The Lost Honour of Katharina Blum ★★★★ 15

Political thriller
1975 · W Ger · Colour · 101mins

Slightly shifting the emphasis of Heinrich Böll's novel to inculcate the police, as well as the media, in the downfall of an innocent victim, Volker Schlöndorff and Margarethe von Trotta have created a chilling tale of state paranoia and tabloid sensationalism that remains a depressingly familiar tale for our times. Displaying enviable dignity in the face of provocation, Angela Winkler is harrowingly credible as the apolitical woman whose unwitting one night stand with a suspected terrorist results in the ruination of her life. Filmed with a realism that adds to its menace, this is a key example of New German Cinema.

Angela Winkler *Katharina Blum* • Mario Adorf *Beizmenne* • Dieter Laser *Werner Toetgess* • Heinz Bennent *Dr Blorna* • Hannelore Hoger *Trude Blorna* • Harald Kuhlmann *Moeding* • Karl Heinz Vosgerau *Alois Straubleder* • Jürgen Prochnow *Ludwig Götten* ■ *Dir* Volker Schlöndorff, Margarethe von Trotta • *Scr* Volker Schlöndorff, Margarethe von Trotta, from the novel by Heinrich Böll

Lost Horizon ★★★★★ U

Fantasy adventure 1937 · US · BW · 111mins

Here's one of the great dream fulfilment movies, showing there is a better place, a heaven on Earth with lasting peace and happiness, tucked away in the Himalayas. In his enthusiasm to film James Hilton's novel, Columbia's ace director Frank Capra persuaded the studio to spend a record $2.5 million. The money was well utilised to create a Shangri-la of Art Deco cleanliness and simplicity populated with unfamiliar faces – most memorably Sam Jaffe as the 250-year-old High Lama – to contrast with the typecasting of Ronald Colman, Thomas Mitchell, Edward Everett Horton and others as the outsiders. Colman ensures the film's success – his sincerity and passion make believers of us all. The largely restored version of the film runs to 132 minutes.

Ronald Colman *Robert Conway* • Jane Wyatt *Sondra* • Edward Everett Horton *Alexander P Lovett* • John Howard (1) *George Conway* • Thomas Mitchell *Henry Barnard* • Margo *Maria* • Isabel Jewell *Gloria Stone* • HB Warner *Chang* • Sam Jaffe *High Lama* ■ *Dir* Frank Capra • *Scr* Robert Riskin, from the novel by James Hilton • *Music* Dimitri Tiomkin [Dmitri Tiomkin] • *Cinematographer* Joseph Walker • *Art Director* Stephen Goosson

Lost Horizon ★ U

Musical 1973 · US · Colour · 132mins

In his 1937 adaptation, Frank Capra managed to make sense of the fanciful ideas raised in James Hilton's novel, but they are rendered risible in this ill-conceived musical remake. Aiming for the glossy sophistication he brought to his earlier projects, producer Ross Hunter presents Shangri-La as a Himalayan country club instead of a utopian sanctuary. Peter Finch, meanwhile, looks as though he's in purgatory as he exchanges trite truisms with High Lama Charles Boyer, though he's not alone in struggling with the dire ditties penned by Burt Bacharach and Hal David.

Peter Finch *Richard Conway* • Michael York *George Conway* • Liv Ullmann *Catherine* • Sally Kellerman *Sally Hughes* • George Kennedy *Sam Cornelius* • Olivia Hussey *Maria* • Bobby Van *Harry Lovett* • James Shigeta *Brother To-Lenn* • Charles Boyer *High Lama* •

John Gielgud *Chang* ■ *Dir* Charles Jarrott • *Scr* Larry Kramer, from the novel by James Hilton

The Lost Hours ★★ 🅄

Murder mystery   1952 · UK · BW · 70mins

Director David MacDonald had a chequered career, spent largely in the realms of the British B movie. This is certainly one of his least distinguished ventures, being another of the dreaded quota quickies in which a third-rate Hollywood star gets to play the lead in a threadbare crime story, notable for the cheapness of the sets, the dismal dialogue and the eagerness of the supporting cast. Mark Stevens is the luckless Yank in this ham-fisted tale about amnesia, smuggling and jealousy, which is lifted only by Jean Kent's elegance and Garry Marsh as the dogged flatfoot.

Mark Stevens *Paul Smith* • Jean Kent *Louise Parker* • Garry Marsh *Foster* • John Bentley *Clark Sutton* • Dianne Foster *Dianne Wrigley* • Jack Lambert *John Parker* • Thora Hird *Maid* ■ *Dir* David MacDonald • *Scr* Steve Fisher, John Gilling

Lost in a Harem ★★

Comedy   1944 · US · BW · 88mins

Abbott and Costello are way out east as two prop men with a travelling show touring a desert kingdom. Thrown in jail along with the show's star Marilyn Maxwell, they are freed by dispossessed prince John Conte to help him recapture his lost kingdom. This is well up to standard for the boys and there's good value from Douglass Dumbrille as the villainous Sultan Nimativ – the funnier routines involve his hypnotic rings.

Bud Abbott *Peter Johnson* • Lou Costello *Harvey Garvey* • Marilyn Maxwell *Hazel Moon* • John Conte *Prince Ramo* • Douglass Dumbrille *Nimativ* ■ *Dir* Charles Riesner • *Scr* John Grant, Harry Crane, Harry Ruskin

Lost in America ★★★ 🄵

Comedy   1985 · US · Colour · 87mins

Still best known for his sweaty but brilliant TV journalist in *Broadcast News*, Albert Brooks is one of Hollywood's most engaging, oddball talents, a sort of West Coast Woody Allen who writes, directs and stars in his own projects. In this satire, he's a nervously successful advertising executive in LA who, with wife Julie Hagerty, drops out and sets off to discover America "just like *Easy Rider*", he says. The story takes as many byways as highways and is always unpredictable and engaging, with weird characters seen through Brooks's askew lens. Maybe it lacks that extra bite – an easy ride, but always an enjoyable one. 🎞

Albert Brooks *David Howard* • Julie Hagerty *Linda Howard* • Maggie Roswell *Patty* • Michael Greene *Paul Dunn* • Tom Tarpey *Brad Tooley* • Raynold Gideon *Ray* ■ *Dir* Albert Brooks • *Scr* Albert Brooks, Monica Johnson

Lost in Siberia ★★★ 🄵

Romantic adventure drama
1991 · UK/USSR · Colour · 103mins

Among the first Russian films to consider the notorious gulags, this forceful drama may be set in the early

days of the Cold War, but the implication is that matters scarcely improved in the intervening years. In a radical departure from his *Brideshead* image, Anthony Andrews gives one his strongest performances as the Russo-British geologist, who is wrongly arrested for spying on the Persian border and consigned to a Siberian labour camp. It would have been easy for Alexander Mitta to have dwelt on the inhuman conditions, but instead he focuses on the empowerment the inmates derive from their unshakeable friendships. Two versions of this film, Russian and English, were made. 🎞

Anthony Andrews *Andrei Miller* • Yelena Mayorova *Doctor Anna* • Vladimir Ilyin *Captain Malakhov* • Ira Mikhalyova *Lilka* • Yevgeni F Mironov *Volodya* ■ *Dir* Alexander Mitta • *Scr* Alexander Mitta, Valery Fried, Yuri Korotkov, James Brabazon (English version)

Lost in Space ★★ 🄿🄶

Science-fiction adventure
1997 · US · Colour · 124mins

This big-budget screen version of Irwin Allen's cult sixties TV series is a charmless flash, bang, wallop affair under the too-straightforward direction of Stephen Hopkins. The Robinson family's Earth migration experiment is sabotaged by evil Doctor Smith (Gary Oldman) and they are forced to land on a mysterious planet where time becomes distorted and they encounter mutated monster spiders. Trying to be all things to all audiences results in the children's stuff (the loveable space monkey) annoying adults, while the "family values" sermons bore the kids rigid. The special effects, the nostalgia, the varying tone and the acting never jell in what is basically a cynical marketing exercise. 🎞 *DVD*

William Hurt *John Robinson* • Mimi Rogers *Maureen Robinson* • Heather Graham *Judy Robinson* • Lacey Chabert *Penny Robinson* • Jack Johnson *Will Robinson* • Gary Oldman *Dr Smith/Spider Smith* • Matt LeBlanc *Don West* • Jared Harris *Older Will* ■ *Dir* Stephen Hopkins • *Scr* Akiva Goldsman, from the TV series

Lost in the Stars ★★★

Musical drama   1974 · US · Colour · 114mins

This was the last musical score by *The Threepenny Opera's* Kurt Weill, an operetta that translates Alan Paton's poignant anti-apartheid novel *Cry, the Beloved Country* into ironic harmonies. There's a fine performance by Brock Peters as the black clergyman in search of his son in Johannesburg, who finds instead cruel racism and repression, and the music is memorable. Unfortunately, despite its sincerity, this "stage record" also somewhat predictable and ponderous.

Brock Peters *Stephen Kumalo* • Melba Moore *Irina* • Raymond St Jacques *John Kumalo* • Clifton Davis *Absalom* • Paul Rogers *James Jarvis* • Paulene Myers *Grace* ■ *Dir* Daniel Mann • *Scr* Alfred Hayes, from the play by Maxwell Anderson, Kurt Weill, from the novel *Cry, the Beloved Country* by Alan Paton

Lost in Yonkers ★★★ 🄿🄶

Comedy drama   1993 · US · Colour · 109mins

Richard Dreyfuss stars as a small-time gangster who returns to his childhood home in Yonkers to lie low, regaling his young nephews Brad Stoll and

Mike Damus with tall tales of his life of crime. Grandma Irene Worth rules the household with a rod of iron that has broken the spirit of Dreyfuss's sister Mercedes Ruehl. This is another of playwright Neil Simon's semi-autobiographical dramas along the lines of his *Brighton Beach Memoirs*, but, despite some wonderful acting turns, director Martha Coolidge has turned in a rather humdrum affair. 🎞

Richard Dreyfuss *Louie* • Mercedes Ruehl *Bella* • Irene Worth *Grandma* • Brad Stoll *Jay* • Mike Damus *Arty* • David Strathairn *Johnny* • Robert Guy Miranda *Hollywood Harry* ■ *Dir* Martha Coolidge • *Scr* Neil Simon, from his play

The Lost Man ★★

Drama   1969 · US · Colour · 122mins

An unofficial remake of the Carol Reed classic *Odd Man Out*, transposing that film's story about an IRA fugitive into a story set in the American South. Sidney Poitier plays a black radical who plans a robbery on a factory that only employs whites. The heist backfires and Poitier, with white love interest Joanna Shimkus, finds himself on the run. As the highly equivocal hero, partially modelled on Malcolm X, Poitier probably thought this was a brave movie to make considering his whiter-than-black image, but it's hardly a radical movie, just another caper-gone-wrong action film. There's also a twist at the end that doesn't work at all and signals a rapid descent into treacle.

Sidney Poitier *Jason Higgs* • Joanna Shimkus *Cathy Ellis* • Al Freeman Jr *Dennis Laurence* • Michael Tolan *Hamilton* • Leon Bibb *Eddie Moxy* • Richard Dysart *Barnes* ■ *Dir* Robert Alan Aurthur • *Scr* Robert Alan Aurthur, from the novel *Odd Man Out* by FL Green

The Lost Moment ★★★

Period drama   1947 · US · BW · 88mins

Henry James's novel *The Aspern Papers*, is a highly theatrical, as well as an intimate and intriguing work. The simple story concerns the quest of a publisher for the letters of a famous poet, which are now in the possession of a very old woman who lives with her spinster niece. Set in a convincing and studio-built Venice, this film version stars Robert Cummings, a superb Agnes Moorehead as the old lady and, in an unexpected piece of casting, Susan Hayward as her niece. Compelling, stylised period drama, elegantly directed by Martin Gabel, and with a surprise denouement.

Robert Cummings *Lewis Venable* • Susan Hayward *Tina* • Agnes Moorehead *Juliana* • Joan Lorring *Amelia* • John Archer *Charles* • Eduardo Ciannelli *Father Rinaldo* ■ *Dir* Martin Gabel • *Scr* Leonardo Bercovici, from the novel *The Aspern Papers* by Henry James

Lost Paradise ★★★

Drama   1997 · Jap · Colour · 119mins

As he proved in Masayuki Suo's *Shall We Dance?*, Koji Yakusho is engagingly adept at conveying the ennui of the middle-aged "salaryman". But instead of ballroom dancing, he turns here to an adulterous affair to deflect his disappointment at being passed over for promotion at the magazine to which he's given years of faithful service.

Equally impressive is Hitomi Kuroki, as the married printer who shares his reluctance to go public with their passion, for fear of losing face. Already acclaimed for *Family Game* and *Deaths in Tokimeki*, director Yoshimitsu Morita again dissects Japanese social mores with a steady hand. In Japanese with English subtitles.

Koji Yakusho *Kuki* • Hitomi Kuroki ■ *Dir* Yoshimitsu Morita • *Scr* Tomomi Tsutsui

The Lost Patrol ★★

First World War adventure
1934 · US · BW · 74mins

In the Mesopotamian desert during the First World War, a small group of lost British cavalrymen search for their comrades while being gradually decimated by Arab snipers, the scorching sun and lack of water. As directed by John Ford, it's more of a western than a war movie: the soldiers do everything but yell "Let's get the wagons into a circle, boys!", and the climactic skirmish looks like Custer's Last Stand.

Victor McLaglen *Sergeant* • Boris Karloff *Sanders* • Wallace Ford *Morelli* • Reginald Denny *Brown* • JM Kerrigan *Quincannon* • Billy Bevan *Hale* • Alan Hale *Cook* ■ *Dir* John Ford • *Scr* Dudley Nichols, Garrett Fort, from the story *Patrol* by Philip MacDonald

The Lost Son ★★ 🅈

Crime drama   1998 · UK/Fr · Colour · 102mins

This is Daniel Auteuil's first English language film, but that's not the only problem here. This deeply ambitious movie, following Auteuil as an ex-cop turned private investigator who unearths a paedophile ring while on the trail of a missing son, is sadly flawed. Aside from the interestingly bleak nature of the story and Auteuil's watchability, the casting is bizarre. Billie Whitelaw, Ciaran Hinds – whose accent is so atrocious one is left wondering where he's supposed to be from – and Nastassja Kinski all fail to convince, and just as Auteuil – trailing around London, the south east of England and Mexico – seems a bit lost, so is the audience. Worthy material this may be, but the plot and script verge on the ridiculous. Auteuil would have been well advised to stay on home territory. *DVD*

Daniel Auteuil *Xavier Lombard* • Nastassja Kinski *Deborah* • Katrin Cartlidge *Emily* • Ciaran Hinds *Carlos* • Marianne Denicourt *Nathalie* • Bruce Greenwood *Friedman* • Billie Whitelaw *Mrs Spitz* • Cyril Shaps *Mr Spitz* ■ *Dir* Chris Menges • *Scr* Eric Leclere, Margaret Leclere, Mark Mills

The Lost Squadron ★★★★

Adventure drama   1932 · US · BW

A fascinating movie that is a genuine cinematic equivalent of the great "lost generation" postwar writings of Ernest Hemingway (particularly *The Sun Also Rises*) and F Scott Fitzgerald. A group of First World War fighter pilots find themselves reduced to postwar stunt flying in the movies under the direction of demented Erich von Stroheim. The atmosphere of disillusionment is quite palpable, thanks to a knowing original story by Dick Grace, himself a stunt flyer. The acting, even from stalwarts such as Richard Dix and a young Joel

McCrea, and the plot structure may seem creaky now, but the tone is brilliantly sustained by director George Archainbaud, whose future lay in B-westerns (talk about disillusionment!). Von Stroheim's performance – lampooning himself – is a tour de force.

Richard Dix *Captain Gibson* • Mary Astor *Follette Marsh* • Erich von Stroheim *Von Furst* • Joel McCrea *Red* • Robert Armstrong *Woody* • Dorothy Jordan *The Pest* ■ *Dir* George Archainbaud • *Scr* Wallace Smith, Herman J Mankiewicz, Robert Presnell, from a story by Dick Grace

Lost Treasure of Dos Santos ★★

Action adventure drama
1997 · US · Colour · 90mins

It's a long time since Lee Majors was TV's favourite hero – the Six Million Dollar Man – and his presence here as a villain is the most notable aspect of this below-par *Indiana Jones*-style romp. David Carradine and Michele Greene star as mismatched explorers on the trail of a mythical hoard of treasure; standing in their way is Majors. It's good to see Majors cast against type, but the routine direction of Jorge Montesi does him no favours.

Michele Greene *Willa* • David Carradine *Martin Shaw* • John Wesley Shipp *Jack Owens* • Lee Majors *Roy Stark* ■ *Dir* Jorge Montesi • *Scr* Michael De Guzman, Ed Decatur

The Lost Weekend ★★★★

Drama 1945 · US · BW · 99mins

Billy Wilder's groundbreaking drama about an alcoholic writer trying to kick the bottle, won Oscars for best film, direction, screenplay and for its star, Ray Milland. Don Birnam (Milland) is the booze-afflicted antihero, suffering from writer's block and a frighteningly convincing case of DT's. Despite the grim subject matter, there are glimpses of Wilder's characteristic mordant wit – the (hidden) bottle dangling out of the apartment window and Milland's desperate mission to pawn his typewriter on a Jewish holiday. But scenes with his brother (Phillip Terry) and girlfriend (Jane Wyman) are self-centred and don't really work, making this literally a message that comes in a bottle. Wilder's location work in New York's Third Avenue district, though, is exemplary and casting the hitherto bland Milland was a stroke of genius.

Ray Milland *Don Birnam* • Jane Wyman *Helen St James* • Phillip Terry *Nick Birnam* • Howard Da Silva *Nat the bartender* • Doris Dowling *Gloria* ■ *Dir* Billy Wilder • *Scr* Charles Brackett, Billy Wilder, from the novel by Charles R Jackson • *Cinematographer* John F Seitz • *Music* Miklos Rozsa • *Special Effects* Farciot Edouart, Gordon Jennings

The Lost World ★★★ U

Silent fantasy adventure
1925 · US · BW · 107mins

Of great historical interest, this film of Arthur Conan Doyle's novel was a smash hit in 1925 because of its sensational representation of prehistoric creatures by the special effects team headed by Willis O'Brien, who later perfected his skills on *King Kong*. Wallace Beery stars as

Professor Challenger, leading an expedition to a South American plateau where an abundance of wild life previously thought extinct still lives. The spectacular finale has a huge brontosaurus, brought back to London, breaking loose and rampaging through the streets. O'Brien combined live action and stop-action animation (in which models are moved fractionally between frame exposures) to fairly convincing effect for the first time. His contribution certainly has a lot more life in it than the hackneyed work of the actors.

Bessie Love *Paula White* • Lloyd Hughes *Edward J Malone* • Lewis Stone *Sir John Roxton* • Wallace Beery *Prof Challenger* • Arthur Hoyt *Prof Summerlee* • Margaret McWade *Mrs Challenger* ■ *Dir* Harry O Hoyt • *Scr* Marion Fairfax, from the novel by Sir Arthur Conan Doyle • *Cinematographer* Arthur Edeson • *Special Effects* Willis H O'Brien

The Lost World ★★

Fantasy adventure
1960 · US · Colour · 94mins

Long before Steven Spielberg and Michael Crichton got there, the "master of disaster" Irwin Allen had already transported audiences to a lost world – author Sir Arthur Conan Doyle's South American plateau forgotten by time. In one of his later roles, Claude Rains leads the cast of lesser stars on an Amazon expedition where they confront a host of magnified pet-shop lizards with plastic fins in a glossy, if conventionally plotted, adventure with intermittent thrills. Clips from this would be a mainstay of Allen's TV fantasy series for years to come.

Michael Rennie *Lord Roxton* • Jill St John *Jennifer Holmes* • David Hedison *Ed Malone* • Claude Rains *Professor Challenger* • Fernando Lamas *Gomez* • Richard Haydn *Professor Summerlee* • Ray Stricklyn *David* • Jay Novello *Costa* ■ *Dir* Irwin Allen • *Scr* Irwin Allen, Charles Bennett, from the novel by Sir Arthur Conan Doyle

The Lost World: Jurassic Park ★★★ PG

Fantasy adventure
1997 · US · Colour · 123mins

There's another island full of genetically created dinosaurs in director Stephen Spielberg's exuberantly calculated sequel to his own *Jurassic Park*. But while the cloned prehistoric package does elicit a nagging sense of déjà vu, such feelings never get in the way of the overpowering excitement or special effects spectacle served up in deliciously scary dollops. With Richard Attenborough and Jeff Goldblum on hand once more to test the balance of nature off the coast of Costa Rica, Spielberg ensures his epic thrill-ride runs smoothly along well-oiled tracks.

Jeff Goldblum *Dr Ian Malcolm* • Julianne Moore *Dr Sarah Harding* • Pete Postlethwaite *Roland Tembo* • Arliss Howard *Peter Ludlow* • Richard Attenborough *John Hammond* • Vince Vaughn *Nick Van Owen* ■ *Dir* Steven Spielberg • *Scr* David Koepp, from the novel by Michael Crichton

Louis Armstrong: Chicago Style ★★ PG

Musical biographical drama
1976 · US · Colour · 73mins

The great Satchmo first came to the Windy City in 1922 to join King Oliver's Creole Jazz Band. He was soon recognised by his peers for his musical inventiveness, and he began to forge a reputation with the public thanks to his attractive personality and the guiding hand of his second wife, pianist Lil Hardin. But his international fame came after he received death threats from Chicago gangsters at the height of Prohibition, and it's this episode that forms the focus for this disappointing TV movie. Ben Vereen is most unpersuasive in the title role, while director Lee Philips surprisingly misses the beat of the era. ▭

Ben Vereen *Louis Armstrong* • Red Buttons *Red Cleveland* • Margaret Avery *Alma Rae* • Janet MacLachlan *Lil Hardin Armstrong* • Lee DeBroux *Jack Cherney* ■ *Dir* Lee Philips • *Scr* James Lee

Louisiana Purchase ★★★ U

Musical comedy 1941 · US · Colour · 97mins

Hard, perhaps, to whip up much enthusiasm for a musical satire on the notoriously corrupt politicians of Louisiana, but this is worth a look. For most of the way, it is unusually faithful to the Broadway hit, with veteran comedian Victor Moore reprising his role as Senator Loganberry and featuring dancer Vera Zorina and others from the original cast. The major change is bringing in Bob Hope as the fall guy for the scheming politicians, but he filibusters his way out of trouble in true *Mr Smith Goes to Washington* style. Featuring songs by Irving Berlin songs and brilliant Technicolor photography.

Bob Hope *Jim Taylor* • Vera Zorina *Marina Von Minden* • Victor Moore *Sen Oliver P Loganberry* • Irene Bordoni *Madame Bordelaise* • Dona Drake *Beatrice* • Raymond Walburn *Colonel Davis Sr* • Maxie Rosenbloom *The Shadow* • Frank Albertson *Davis Jr* ■ *Dir* Irving Cummings • *Scr* Jerome Chodorov, Joseph Fields, from the musical by Morrie Ryskind, BG "Buddy" DeSylva • *Cinematographer* Ray Rennahan, Harry Hallenberger

Louisiana Story ★★★ U

Documentary drama 1948 · US · BW · 77mins

Documentary director Robert Flaherty (*Nanook of the North*) went to the bayou country of Louisiana and recruited non-professionals to tell a simple but affecting story of a small boy, whose father ekes out a living by hunting and fishing while oil prospectors set up a floating derrick and sink a well. With sparse dialogue and a notable score by Virgil Thomson, the film has little action other than the boy's fight with an alligator. Flaherty was backed by a major oil company, which must have been delighted by the entirely favourable impression the film gives of the oil drillers and their incursion into such a striking natural habitat.

Dir Robert J Flaherty [Robert Flaherty] • *Scr* Robert J Flaherty, Frances Flaherty • *Cinematographer* Richard Leacock • *Music* Virgil Thomson

Loulou ★★★★

Drama 1980 · Fr · Colour · 105mins

Echoing both Louis Malle's *The Lovers* and Bertrand Blier's *Les Valseuses* (and not solely because the latter features both Gérard Depardieu and Isabelle Huppert), this is an unforgettable exercise in street naturalism from director Maurice Pialat. Rarely has Paris looked less inviting as it provides the backdrop for the picaresque adventures of Depardieu's blue-collar boor and the bourgeois Huppert, who abandons husband Guy Marchand out of boredom and unadulterated lust. While acknowledging the courage of the performances, however, this is much more than just an "odd couple" romance, as Pialat's accumulation of telling details exposes the soulless social and sexual state of contemporary France. In French with English subtitles. ▭

Isabelle Huppert *Nelly* • Gérard Depardieu *Loulou* • Guy Marchand *André* • Humbert Balsan *Michel* ■ *Dir* Maurice Pialat • *Scr* Arlette Langmann, Maurice Pialat, from a story by Arlette Langmann

The Lovable Cheat ★★ U

Comedy drama 1949 · US · BW · 78mins

Charles Ruggles is the bankrupt Parisian who'll stop at nothing to keep his creditors at bay in this stagey comedy/drama adapted from *Mercadet le Falseur*, by Honoré de Balzac. Claude Mercadet (Ruggles) hopes that marrying off his daughter (Peggy Ann Garner) to a suitable suitor might be the answer to his problems. A strong cast (including Buster Keaton) do their best with the material but this has nothing new going for it apart from Balzac's usual fascination with money and the way it makes both love, and the world, go round – and wrong.

Charles Ruggles *Claude Mercadet* • Peggy Ann Garner *Julie Mercadet* • Richard Ney *Jacques Minard* • Alan Mowbray *Justin* • John Wengraf *Pierquin* • Curt Bois *Count de la Brive* • Buster Keaton *Goulard* ■ *Dir* Richard Oswald • *Scr* Richard Oswald, Edward Lewis, from the play *Mercadet le Falseur* by Honoré de Balzac

Love ★★

Silent drama 1927 · US · BW · 97mins

This silent version of Tolstoy's *Anna Karenina* from MGM was a box-office hit in its day, thanks to the starring of Greta Garbo as Anna and John Gilbert as Vronsky, the lover who ruins her. Directed by Edmund Goulding, it's not uninteresting, especially for Garbo fans, but has been long superseded by the studio's much superior sound remake *Anna Karenina* (1935) in which Garbo repeats the role under Clarence Brown's direction.

Greta Garbo *Anna Karenina* • John Gilbert *Vronsky* • George Fawcett *Grand Duke* • Emily Fitzroy *Grand Duchess* • Brandon Hurst *Karenin* ■ *Dir* Edmund Goulding • *Scr* Frances Marion, Lorna Moon, from the novel *Anna Karenina* by Leo Nikolayevich Tolstoy

Love ★★★★

Drama 1971 · Hun · Colour · 88mins

Set in the twilight of the Stalinist era, and passing sly asides on the cult of personality, this adroit study of the dissemination and reception of propaganda is cleverly couched in terms of a delicate chamber drama. Handled with great finesse by Karoly Makk, there's genuine affection in the relationship between a wife who tries to assuage her bedridden mother-in-law's fears about her son by fabricating letters about his Hollywood success, while hiding her own pain at the knowledge he's in a labour camp. Both Mari Torcsik and Lili Darvas, the widow of the famous playwright, Ferenc Molnar, are superb. In Hungarian with English subtitles.

Lili Darvas *Mother* • Mari Torocsik *Luca, the wife* • Ivan Darvas *Janos, the son* ■ *Dir* Karoly Makk • *Scr* Tibor Dery, from his novella

Love Affair ★★
Romantic drama　　1932 · US · BW · 68mins

The main reason to watch this antique romantic drama is for an early performance from Humphrey Bogart. He's Jim Leonard, a reckless, handsome but impoverished aviator who attracts the attentions of an heiress who invests in the plane and then in Bogart himself. Further characters complicate the romantic situation which is resolved – naturally enough – aloft. Bogart's fans will be eager to check out his work here, but don't overlook the heroine, played by Hull-born Dorothy Mackaill, who became a Ziegfeld Girl and began acting in movies in the early twenties.

Dorothy Mackaill *Carol Owen* • Humphrey Bogart *Jim Leonard* • Jack Kennedy *Gilligan* • Barbara Leonard *Felice* • Astrid Allwyn *Linda Lee* • Bradley Page *Georgie* ■ *Dir* Thornton Freeland • *Scr* Jo Swerling, Dorothy Howell, from a story by Ursula Parrott

Love Affair ★★★★★
Romantic comedy drama
1939 · US · BW · 87mins

Charles Boyer and Irene Dunne meet on an ocean liner bound for New York and, despite their determination to avoid involvement, fall hopelessly in love. They agree to meet six months later at an appointed time at the top of the Empire State building if they still feel the same, but when the day comes, she is not there... One word suffices for Leo McCarey's film, which garnered six Academy Award nominations – perfect. Witty, sophisticated, romantic and poignant, it is extremely well-written, immaculately directed, and beautifully played by the stars and by Maria Ouspenskaya as Boyer's grandmother. It remains one of the best love stories ever to emerge from Hollywood, and McCarey remade it faithfully as *An Affair to Remember* (1957), with Cary Grant and Deborah Kerr, while Nora Ephron paid it tribute with *Sleepless in Seattle*.

Irene Dunne *Terry McKay* • Charles Boyer *Michel Marnet* • Maria Ouspenskaya *Grandmother Janou* • Lee Bowman *Kenneth Bradley* • Astrid Allwyn *Lois Clarke* • Maurice Moscovich *Maurice Cobert* • Joan Leslie *Autograph seeker* ■ *Dir* Leo McCarey • *Scr* Delmer Daves, Donald Ogden Stewart, from a story by Leo McCarey, Delmer Daves, Mildred Cram

Love Affair ★★★ 12
Romantic drama
1994 · US · Colour · 103mins

This remake of *Love Affair* and *An Affair to Remember* failed to impress the critics and never even got to cinemas In the UK. But it is an undeniably polished production and if Glenn Gordon Caron's direction is occasionally sluggish and Ennio Morricone's score is stiflingly lush, the story of the lovers who are torn apart by the cruellest twist of fate can still get the tears flowing. However, the most heartbreaking moment is the all-too-brief appearance of Katharine Hepburn, gamely fighting against the effects of Parkinson's Disease. 🎞

Warren Beatty *Mike Gambril* • Annette Bening *Terry McKay* • Katharine Hepburn *Aunt Ginny* • Garry Shandling *Kip DeMay* • Chloe Webb *Tina Wilson* • Pierce Brosnan *Ken Allen* • Kate Capshaw *Lynn Weaver* • Brenda Vaccaro *Nora Stillman* • Paul Mazursky *Herb Stillman* ■ *Dir* Glenn Gordon Caron • *Scr* Robert Towne, Warren Beatty, from the 1939 film

Love among the Ruins ★★★★
Romantic comedy
1975 · US · Colour · 72mins

An extremely classy made-for-television film from veteran director George Cukor which stars Katharine Hepburn as a dowager in the early 1900s being sued by a young upstart. Sadly her defence barrister Laurence Olivier also has it in for her as she has failed to recollect their affair from years before. Olivier thus decides to portray the poor woman as short of her marbles throughout the court case. Comic, painful and insightful, Cukor extracts excellent performances from Hepburn and Olivier and it makes for a rare televisual treat.

Katharine Hepburn *Jessica Medlicott* • Laurence Olivier *Sir Arthur Granville-Jones* • Colin Blakely *JF Devine* • Richard Pierson Druce • Joan Sims *Fanny Pratt* • Leigh Lawson *Alfred Pratt* ■ *Dir* George Cukor • *Scr* James Costigan

Love among Thieves ★★ PG
Romantic thriller　1987 · US · Colour · 89mins

The major sin this film commits is to waste the talents of Audrey Hepburn (who was combining her TV movie debut and swan song in a single outing). There are obvious echoes of Hepburn's own *Charade* and *How to Steal a Million* and her namesake Katharine's *The African Queen*, but this tale of kidnap, jewel theft and outdoor adventure isn't a patch on any of them. The presence of Robert Wagner doesn't help much, but Hepburn is always worth watching, even here. 🎞

Audrey Hepburn *Baroness Caroline DuLac* • Robert Wagner *Mike Chambers* • Jerry Orbach *Spicer* • Samantha Eggar *Solange DuLac* • Patrick Bauchau *Alan Channing* • Christopher Neame *Ian* ■ *Dir* Roger Young • *Scr* Henry Stern, Stephen Black, Sally Robinson

Love and a .45 ★★★★ 18
Thriller　　　1994 · US · Colour · 97mins

Although the Tarantino influences are clear to see, this matt-black trailer trash thriller is an impressively nasty treat. Gil Bellows is the nice-ish convenience store robber who is forced to go on the run with his devoted girlfriend (an electric early showing from Renee Zellwegger) after a raid goes horribly wrong. The body count continues to multiply as they are pursued by Bellows' s old partner in crime (Rory Cochrane) and two psycho debt collectors, along with massed ranks of law enforcement. CM Talkington's direction is hip and amoral and the performances uniformly good, particularly horror icon Jeffrey (*Re-Animator*) Combs's deranged killer and Peter Fonda's voice-boxed drugs casualty. 🎞

Gil Bellows *Watty Watts* • Renee Zellweger *Starlene Cheatham* • Rory Cochrane *Billy Mack Black* • Jeffrey Combs *Dino Bob* • Jace Alexander *Creepy Cody* • Ann Wedgeworth *Thaylene* • Peter Fonda *Vergil* ■ *Dir/Scr* CM Talkington

Love & Basketball ★★★ 12
Romantic sports drama
2000 · US · Colour · mins

Sanaa Lathan and Omar Epps are young athletes with a lifelong love of basketball and each other. The movie follows them from childhood games to professional careers, all the while contrasting the different challenges men and women face while playing the same sport. Gina Prince-Bythewood's feature debut captures the characters' passion for the game, though she struggles with scenes that take place off the court. While Lathan delivers a passionate, star-making performance, her fellow actors are hobbled by underdeveloped roles, with even Alfre Woodard fighting to rise above cliché in her role as Lathan's homemaker mom.

Sanaa Lathan *Monica Wright* • Omar Epps *Quincy McCall* • Alfre Woodard *Camille Wright* • Dennis Haysbert *Zeke McCall* • Debbi Morgan *Mona McCall* ■ *Dir/Scr* Gina Prince-Bythewood

Love and Bullets ★★ 15
Thriller　　　1978 · UK · Colour · 97mins

Charles Bronson is an FBI toughie in Switzerland, who flirts with a gangster's moll and pumps her for all the information he can get before escorting her to the nearest American witness box. Trouble is, she knows nuffink, but he pumps her all the same which makes the mobster, Rod Steiger, blow a gasket. Then she gets nixed, which makes Bronson blow a gasket as well. The movie short-changes us both on the love and the bullets; the trouble is, it isn't a comedy either, which is what it should have been, especially with Steiger in Mussolini-mode, running wild on an improvisational spree. 🎞

Charles Bronson *Charlie Congers* • Jill Ireland *Jackie Pruitt* • Rod Steiger *Joe Bomposa* • Henry Silva *Vittorio Faroni* • Strother Martin *Louis Monk* • Bradford Dillman *Brickman* ■ *Dir* Stuart Rosenberg • *Scr* Wendell Mayes, John Melson, from a story by Wendell Mayes

Love and Death ★★★★ PG
Satirical comedy　1975 · US · Colour · 81mins

You never know where Woody Allen is coming from. With homages to Sergei Eisenstein and Bob Hope – among others – this satire is located in the fatalistic Russian territory of *War and Peace* and is one of Woody Allen's early greats. In 1812 a condemned Allen looks back in bemusement at the historical events, and a hysterical Diane Keaton, that have brought him to his execution. The Grim Reaper scythes through from *The Seventh Seal*, but the jokes are strictly New York Jewish. The plotting is too desultory, but the fun comes at you from all directions, but mainly from off the wall. That's the wonder of Woody. 🎞

Woody Allen *Boris* • Diane Keaton *Sonja* • Georges Adet *Old Nehamkin* • Frank Adu *Drill Sergeant* • Edmond Ardisson *Priest* • Feodor Atkine *Mikhail* ■ *Dir/Scr* Woody Allen • *Cinematographer* Ghislain Cloquet

Love and Death on Long Island ★★★ 15
Comedy drama
1998 · UK/Can · Colour · 93mins

This mischievous, touching comedy provides John Hurt with one of his best roles of the nineties, and he doesn't miss a beat. He plays an incredibly naive, unworldly writer/scholar who becomes besotted by the American star (Jason Priestly) of *Hotpants College 2*, a low-budget teen movie he mistakenly wanders into. Hurt then travels to Long Island to meet what he thinks will be his true love. There is a sense of impending tragedy throughout but Hurt's wonderful performance ensures that it never slips into melodramatic gloom. Priestly has fun sending up his teen idol image, while Richard Kwietniowksi directs with affection. Contains swearing. 🎞

John Hurt *Giles De'Ath* • Jason Priestley *Ronnie Bostock* • Fiona Loewi *Audrey* • Sheila Hancock *Mrs Barker* • Harvey Atkin *Lou* • Gawn Grainger *Henry, Giles's agent* • Elizabeth Quinn *Mrs Reed* • Maury Chaykin *Irving Buckmuller* ■ *Dir* Richard Kwietniowski • *Scr* Richard Kwietniowski, from the novel by Gilbert Adair

Love and Human Remains ★★ 18
Drama　　　　1993 · Can · Colour · 99mins

The activities of a serial killer cast a shadow over this drama of modern relationships, as does the spectre of Aids. This was the first English language film from Québecois film-maker Denys Arcand, director of the 1989 arthouse hit *Jesus of Montreal*. Though Arcand is widely regarded as being more comfortable working in his native French, this remains a watchable drama focusing on the sexual pursuits, fears and fetishes of a bunch of adult cityfolk. 🎞

Thomas Gibson *David* • Ruth Marshall *Candy* • Cameron Bancroft *Bernie* • Mia Kirshner *Benita* • Rick Roberts *Robert* • Joanne Vannicola *Jerri* • Matthew Ferguson *Kane* ■ *Dir* Denys Arcand • *Scr* Brad Fraser, from his play *Unidentified Human Remains and the True Nature of Love*

Love and Money ★★
Thriller　　　1982 · US · Colour · 90mins

Director James Toback, presented with natural drama, doesn't know how to commit himself to his material and so turns what should be high octane into an afternoon stroll. Financier Ray Sharkey decides to inject some excitement into his life by getting

mixed up with Klaus Kinski's Latin-American business schemes. Sharkey, Ornella Muti (as his love interest) and Klaus Kinski perform adequately, but they are upstaged by an appearance from celebrated director King Vidor, who supplies the picture's one treat. This reminder of his glory days only serves to highlight the film's failings. Contains swearing.

Ray Sharkey *Byron Levin* • Ornella Muti *Catherine Stockheinz* • Klaus Kinski *Frederick Stockheinz* • Armand Assante *Lorenzo Prado* • King Vidor *Walter Klein* • Susan Heldford *Vicky* ▪ *Dir/Scr* James Toback • *Music* Aaron Copland

Love and Other Catastrophes ★★★ 15

Comedy drama 1996 · Aus · Colour · 75mins

This spirited Australian comedy is a fast-paced, incident-packed day in the life of five college students. All human life seems condensed into the 24-hour period with the protagonists experiencing unrequited love, degree worries, romantic entanglements and life-changing decisions. Reputedly shot in just 17 days, the speed of the production translates to the screen and the film whizzes by delightfully. A strong ensemble cast ensure all the characters are well rounded and believable, and the general good nature of the film makes it hard to dislike. Contains swearing and sex scenes.

Alice Garner *Alice* • Frances O'Connor *Mia* • Matthew Dyktynski *Ari* • Matt Day *Michael* • Radha Mitchell *Danni* • Suzi Dougherty *Savita* • Kim Gyngell *Professor Leach* • Suzanne Dowling *Dr Russell* ▪ *Dir* Emma-Kate Croghan • *Scr* Emma-Kate Croghan, Yael Bergman, Helen Bandis, from a story by Stavros Andonis Efthymiou

Love and Pain and the Whole Damn Thing ★★★★

Drama 1973 · US · Colour · 113mins

Alan J Pakula's political thrillers *Klute* (1971), *The Parallax View* (1974) and *All the President's Men* (1976), make him seem a social warrior, but this is an out-of-character delight with unexpected and refreshing romanticism. Maggie Smith plays a terminally ill spinster in Spain whose heartbeats click like castanets when she meets youngster Timothy Bottoms. Despite the fatal-illness undercurrent, sentimentality is kept at bay in this rare gem.

Maggie Smith *Lila Fisher* • Timothy Bottoms *Walter Elbertson* • Emiliano Redondo *Spanish gentleman* • Charles Baxter *Dr Elbertson* • Margaret Modlin *Mrs Elbertson* • May Heatherly *Melanie Elbertson* ▪ *Dir* Alan J Pakula • *Scr* Alvin Sargent

Love and Sex ★★★ 15

Romantic comedy
2000 · US · Colour · 82mins

Famke Janssen is a magazine journalist who writes a feature about love and relationships from her own past experiences – the married man, the boring boyfriend, etcetera – including a key romance with artist Jon Favreau. While writer/director Valerie Breiman doesn't cover any new ground, the combined energies of her snappy script and the two lead

performances – especially *Swingers* star Favreau – will have you nodding as you watch the pair go through all of the highs, lows and deep pitfalls of a vital relationship.

Famke Janssen *Kate Welles* • Jon Favreau *Adam* • Noah Emmerich *Eric* • Ann Magnuson *Ms Steinbacher* • Cheri Oteri *Mary* • Josh Hopkins *Joey Santino* ▪ *Dir/Scr* Valerie Breiman

Love and the Midnight Auto Supply ★★

Comedy 1977 · US · Colour · 93mins

Released, briefly, as *Midnight Auto Supply*, this is a breezy, comic cheapo about a gang of car thieves whose nocturnal activities are given an altruistic slant when they're asked to help out some impoverished farm workers. Part youth movie, part political comment on America's economic problems, it has a weird cast led by Michael Parks. Old-timers Rory Calhoun and John Ireland also appear.

Michael Parks *Duke* • Linda Cristal *Annie* • Scott Jacoby *Justin* • Bill Adler *Ramon* • Colleen Camp *Billie Jean* • Monica Gayle *Kathy* • Sedena Spivey *Violet* • George McCallister *Peter Santore* • John Ireland *Tony Santore* • Rory Calhoun *Len Thompson* ▪ *Dir/Scr* James Polakof

Love at First Bite ★★★★ 15

Horror spoof 1979 · US · Colour · 91mins

This very funny spoof on the Dracula legend has George Hamilton as the uprooted, undead Count, who's trying to adjust to life in the modern Big Apple. Former MGM heart-throb Hamilton camps it up delightfully as he clumsily romances fashion model Susan Saint James much to the chagrin of her psychiatrist lover, Richard Benjamin, who gets his vampire lore amusingly scrambled when he tries to intervene. Classic "fish out of water" sequences include the disruption of a Harlem family's mealtime, a midnight raid on a blood bank and some hypnotic disco dancing. It's fast and furious fun, superbly scripted by Robert Kaufman, and wonderfully pulled together by director Stan Dragoti. Contains some swearing.

George Hamilton *Count Dracula* • Susan Saint James *Cindy Sondheim* • Richard Benjamin *Dr Jeff Rosenberg* • Dick Shawn *Lieutenant Ferguson* • Arte Johnson *Renfield* • Sherman Hemsley *Reverend Mike* • Isabel Sanford *Judge* ▪ *Dir* Stan Dragoti • *Scr* Robert Kaufman, from a story by Robert Kaufman, from Mark Gindes

Love at Large ★★ 15

Crime drama 1990 · US · Colour · 93mins

Tom Berenger's career – so promising around the time of *Platoon*, for which he was Oscar nominated – took a downward turn with this daft, if imaginative, attempt at a light-hearted *film noir* by writer/director Alan Rudolph. A private detective, hired by a beautiful woman, ends up following the wrong man and is himself followed by a female detective. Still with us? Well, you won't be after an hour and a half of mistaken identities, tortuous plot twists and below-par acting from Anne

Archer and Elizabeth Perkins. Contains swearing.

Tom Berenger *Harry Dobbs* • Elizabeth Perkins *Stella Wynkowski* • Anne Archer *Miss Dolan* • Kate Capshaw *Ellen McGraw* • Annette O'Toole *Mrs King* ▪ *Dir/Scr* Alan Rudolph

Love at Stake ★★★ 15

Comedy drama 1987 · US · Colour · 83mins

Kelly Preston plays the town baker (Sara Lee!) in this farcical comedy set amid a colony of Puritans in 17th-century Salem. The local judge and mayor have devised a fiendish plan to steal villagers' land by accusing them of witchcraft. Very much *The Crucible* meets *The Naked Gun*, this is awash with toilet humour and screamingly bad gags. Barbara Carrera does a great turn as the only actual witch – this will keep lovers of the genre heartily amused.

Patrick Cassidy *Miles* • Kelly Preston *Sara Lee* • Bud Cort *Parson Babcock* • David Graf *Nathaniel* • Stuart Pankin *Judge Samuel John* • Dave Thomas (1) *Mayor Upton* • Barbara Carrera *Faith* ▪ *Dir* John Moffitt • *Scr* Terrence Sweeney, Lanier Laney

Love at Twenty ★★★

Portmanteau drama
1962 · Fr/It/Jap/W Ger/Pol · BW · 115mins

The most significant entry in this portmanteau picture is *Antoine et Colette*, which furthered the Antoine Doinel cycle launched by François Truffaut in *The 400 Blows*. However, there's much to enjoy elsewhere. In Renzo Rossellini's *Rome* a rich woman fights to keep her lover from a beautiful innocent, while Marcel Ophüls's *Munich* sees a photographer develop a passion for the mother of his child. A factory worker murders the student who refuses his advances in Shintaro Ishihara's *Tokyo*, while in Andrzej Wajda's intriguing *Warsaw* a man's life changes after he rescues a child from the bear pit at the zoo. In French with English subtitles.

Jean-Pierre Léaud *Antoine Doinel "Paris-Antoine et Colette"* • Marie-France Pisier *Colette* • Eleonora Rossi-Drago *Valentina* • Koji Furuhata *Hiroshi* • Nami Tamura *Fukimo* • Christian Doermer *Tonio* • Barbara Frey *Ursula* • Barbara Lass *Basia* ▪ *Dir* François Truffaut, Renzo Rossellini, Shintaro Ishihara, Marcel Ophüls, Andrzej Wajda • *Scr* François Truffaut, Yvon Samuel, Renzo Rossellini, Shintaro Ishihara, Marcel Ophüls, Jerzy Stefan Stawinski

Love before Breakfast ★★

Comedy 1936 · US · BW · 65mins

A middle-of-the-road lightweight romantic comedy given A-grade treatment in casting and production values. The title is meaningless and the flimsy plot concerns Cesar Romero and Preston Foster as suitors vying for the affections of New York socialite Carole Lombard. Foster schemes to get his rival out of the way – even out of the country – but Lombard smells a rat. Walter Lang directs what, in most circumstances, would be a waste of time, but anything starring the lovely Lombard is worth a look.

Carole Lombard *Kay Colby* • Preston Foster *Scott Miller* • Cesar Romero *Bill Wadsworth* • Janet Beecher *Mrs Colby* • Betty Lawford

Contessa Janie Campanella ▪ *Dir* Walter Lang • *Scr* Herbert Fields, from the novel *Spinster Dinner* by Faith Baldwin

The Love Bug ★★★★ U

Comedy 1969 · US · Colour · 103mins

Disney doesn't make 'em like this anymore. Here, plain good fun is at the wheel, with its foot down to the floor. Herbie, the Volkswagen with as much bottle as throttle, is a brilliant invention, and Dean Jones, as his racing driver owner, and David Tomlinson, as Jones's ruthless rival, work wonders to stop the little Beetle running away with the film. Having shown a flair for fantasy with *Mary Poppins*, director Robert Stevenson here demonstrates a sure slapstick touch. *DVD*

Dean Jones *Jim Douglas* • Michele Lee *Carole Bennett* • David Tomlinson *Peter Thorndyke* • Buddy Hackett *Tennessee Steinmetz* • Joe Flynn *Havershaw* • Benson Fong *Mr Wu* ▪ *Dir* Robert Stevenson • *Scr* Don DaGradi, Bill Walsh, from a story by Gordon Buford

The Love Bug ★★

Comedy 1997 · US · Colour · 120mins

A bevy of 1960s all-star cameos (Dean Jones, Micky Dolenz, Clarence Williams III) pepper this lemon of a remake of the 1969 Disney feature film. A down-on-his-luck mechanic (Bruce Campbell) saves VW Beetle Herbie from demolition. When the wee motorcar suddenly begins to zoom about on its rear wheels at racecar speeds, he realises the car is unique. Herbie is soon also coveted by a diabolical Scotsman (John Hannah), who schemes to possess the car at any cost. This is one old clunker which should have been left to go to the scrap heap gracefully.

Bruce Campbell *Hank Cooper* • Dean Jones *Jim Douglas* • John Hannah *Simon Moore* • Alexandra Wentworth *Alex Davis* • Kevin J O'Connor *Roddy Martel* • Dana Gould *Rupert* • Harold Gould • Micky Dolenz ▪ *Dir* Peyton Reed • *Scr* Ryan Rowe, Bill Walsh, Don DaGradi, from a story by Gordon Buford

The Love Cage ★★

Crime romance 1964 · Fr · BW · 96mins

Jane Fonda in her sex-kitten phase – that's before the leftie radical phase, the great actress phase and the mogul's wife phase. It was her first French movie, originally titled *Les Félins*. France's biggest star, Alain Delon, plays a gangster who is given refuge in a vast chateau by Fonda and her aunt, Lola Albright, whose lover, another gangster, has murdered her husband. Mobsters are banging on the door, Fonda falls for Delon who is being set up by Albright to take the fall for the lover. It's a game of sexual charades – clothes come off and then a gun goes off, spoiling all the fun. French dialogue dubbed into English.

Alain Delon *Marc* • Jane Fonda *Melinda* • Lola Albright *Barbara* • Carl Studer *Loftus* • Sorrell Booke *Harry* • André Oumansky *Vincent* • Arthur Howard *Rev Nielson* ▪ *Dir* René Clément • *Scr* René Clément, Charles Williams, Pascal Jardin, from the novel *Joy House* by Day Keene

U = SUITABLE FOR ALL   Uc = SUITABLE FOR ALL, ESPECIALLY FOR YOUNG CHILDREN (VIDEO ONLY)   PG = PARENTAL GUIDANCE

Love, Cheat & Steal ★★ 18

Erotic thriller 1994 · US · Colour · 91mins

An unpleasant modern *film noir* featuring sneering, musclebound Eric Roberts as a vengeful escaped convict who shows-up at ex-wife Mädchen Amick's house posing as her estranged brother. John Lithgow is Amick's new, rich banker husband, whose vaults full of Colombian drug money are targeted by Roberts. The latter is such an unscrupulous thug that you actually find yourself rooting for Lithgow, while the attractively elf-like, but fatally wooden, Amick goes through more skimpy costume changes than a fashion show. Things do perk up, however, in the satisfying, twist-laden robbery climax. Contains violence, swearing and sex scenes. ▭

John Lithgow *Paul Harrington* • Eric Roberts *Reno Adams* • Mädchen Amick *Lauren Harrington* • Richard Edson *Billy Quale* • Donald Moffat *Paul's father* • David Ackroyd *Tom Kerry* • Dan O'Herlihy *Hamilton Fisk* ■ *Dir/Scr* William Curran

Love Child ★★★ 18

Drama 1982 · US · Colour · 92mins

Amy Madigan made her big screen debut here as Terry Jean Moore, a condemned criminal who is initially sentenced to 15 years for robbery, increased to 20 years for starting a fire in jail. Moore campaigns for her right to keep her baby which is fathered by one of the prison guards, played by Beau Bridges. The real-life case attracted a lot of press coverage in America, turning the volatile Moore into a celebrity and feminist icon. The approach is level-headed, semi-documentary in style, and shot on the Florida locations where the events happened. ▭

Amy Madigan *Terry Jean Moore* • Beau Bridges *Jack Hansen* • Mackenzie Phillips *JJ* • Albert Salmi *Captain Ellis* • Joanna Merlin *Superintendent Sturgis* • Margaret Whitton *Jacki Steinberg* • Lewis Smith *Jesse Chaney* • Dennis Lipscomb *Arthur Brady* ■ *Dir* Larry Peerce • *Scr* Anne Gerard, Katherine Specktor, from a story by Anne Gerard

Love Crazy ★★★

Comedy 1941 · US · BW · 98mins

The favourite box-office team of William Powell and Myrna Loy (Nick and Nora Charles of the *Thin Man* series) are the beleaguered couple in this madcap farce. Instead of celebrating a wedding anniversary it looks as though they're heading for the rocks when her mother comes to stay and he meets up with an old flame. Powell cooks up several crazy schemes in response to this marital crisis, including feigning madness and disguising himself as his own sister. Directed at a rollicking pace by Jack Conway, and with top support from Florence Bates, Gail Patrick and Jack Carson, this is complete nonsense and lots of fun.

William Powell *Steven Ireland* • Myrna Loy *Susan Ireland* • Gail Patrick *Isobel Grayson* • Jack Carson *Ward Willoughby* • Florence Bates *Mrs Cooper* • Sidney Blackmer *George Hennie* • Vladimir Sokoloff *Dr Klugle* • Kathleen Lockhart *Mrs Bristol* • Sig Rumann [Sig Ruman] *Dr Wuthering* ■ *Dir* Jack Conway •

Scr William Ludwig, Charles Lederer, David Hertz, from a story by David Hertz, William Ludwig

Love Crimes ★ 18

Erotic thriller 1991 · US · Colour · 86mins

Director Lizzie Borden's unbelievable thriller has lawyer Sean Young going undercover to trap con artist Patrick Bergin, a man who preys on unsuspecting women by posing as a fashion photographer and offering them the chance of a modelling career. The ridiculous story makes little sense and wooden performances by both leads don't help much. And although the idea that Young becomes both fascinated and repelled by the serial sleazeball is intriguing, it gets royally fluffed by the supposed "feminist" director. The film had a troubled production history, and went through various edits, which might account for some of the problems. Mull on that while the excessive nudity and worse unfolds! Contains violence, swearing and nudity. ▭

Sean Young *Dana Greenway* • Patrick Bergin *David Hanover* • Arnetia Walker *Maria Johnson* • James Read *Stanton Gray* • Ron Orbach *Detective Eugene Tully* • Fern Dorsey *Colleen Dells* • Tina Hightower *Anne Winslow* ■ *Dir* Lizzie Borden • *Scr* Allan Moyle, Laurie Frank, from a story by Allan Moyle

Love etc ★★★ 15

Romantic drama 1997 · Fr · Colour · 99mins

It's not just the title and setting that director Marion Vernoux jettisons in her Gallicisation of Julian Barnes's novel *Talking It Over*. The confessional narrative style is also reined in to permit a more traditionally structured account of the romantic triangle that forms between timid executive Yvan Attal, art restorer Charlotte Gainsbourg and the indolent Charles Berling. While fitfully amusing (particularly during Berling's visually inventive pursuit of his friend's wife), this is essentially a rather sad story. However, uncertain pacing mars both the opening exposition and the resolution of what is an overly familiar and frequently flatly played scenario. In French with English subtitles. Contains swearing and sex scenes. ▭

Charlotte Gainsbourg *Marie* • Yvan Attal *Benoît* • Charles Berling *Pierre* • Thibault de Montalembert *Bernard* • Elodie Navarre *Eléonore* ■ *Dir* Marion Vernoux • *Scr* Marion Vernoux, Dodine Henry, from the novel *Talking It Over* by Julian Barnes

Love Field ★★★★ 15

Romantic drama 1992 · US · Colour · 100mins

Michelle Pfeiffer was have been nominated for an Oscar for her role in this neglected drama. She is superb as the bleach-blonde Jackie Kennedy-obsessed housewife who walks out on her husband to travel to President Kennedy's funeral, and Dennis Haysbert is equally watchable as the secretive black man travelling with his daughter, with whom she makes friends on the journey. Sixties political intrigue aside, this is a fascinating tale of innocent enthusiasm in a bigoted world. Contains violence and swearing. ▭

Michelle Pfeiffer *Lurene Hallett* • Dennis Haysbert *Paul Cater* • Stephanie McFadden *Jonell Cater* • Brian Kerwin *Ray Hallett* • Louise Latham *Mrs Enright* • Peggy Rea *Mrs Heisenbuttal* • Beth Grant *Hazel* • Rhoda Griffis *Jacqueline Kennedy* ■ *Dir* Jonathan Kaplan • *Scr* Don Roos

Love Finds Andy Hardy ★★★

Comedy drama 1938 · US · BW · 90mins

The fourth and one of the freshest films in the Andy Hardy series, with Mickey Rooney muddling dance dates and getting in a dreadful mess. Judy Garland makes the first of three appearances in the series – she sings three songs – and seems relatively natural when compared to the precocious talent of Rooney. Another star-in-waiting, Lana Turner, plays one of Rooney's girlfriends.

Mickey Rooney *Andy Hardy* • Lewis Stone *Judge James K Hardy* • Judy Garland *Betsy Booth* • Ann Rutherford *Polly Benedict* • Lana Turner *Cynthia Potter* • Cecilia Parker *Marian Hardy* • Fay Holden *Mrs Emily Hardy* • Betty Ross Clark [Betty Ross Clarke] *Aunt Milly* • Marie Blake *Augusta* ■ *Dir* George B Seitz • *Scr* William Ludwig, from stories by Vivian R Bretherton, from characters created by Aurania Rouverol

Love from a Stranger ★★★

Crime drama 1936 · UK · BW · 81mins

Having come into a fortune but quarrelled with her fiancé, an attractive young woman (Ann Harding) is swept off her feet into marriage by a man (Basil Rathbone) she barely knows. They settle in luxury in Europe, only for her to be warned that her husband murders wealthy women. Directed by Rowland V Lee, this is a neat, smooth suspense drama, based on a novel by Agatha Christie and the play by Frank Vosper. The stars give polished performances, with support from a stalwart British cast that includes Binnie Hale and Joan Hickson.

Basil Rathbone *Gerald Lovell* • Ann Harding *Carol Howard* • Binnie Hale *Kate Meadows* • Bruce Seton *Ronald Bruce* • Jean Cadell *Aunt Lou* • Bryan Powley *Dr Gribble* • Joan Hickson *Emmy* ■ *Dir* Rowland V Lee • *Scr* Frances Marion, from the play by Frank Vosper, from the novel by Agatha Christie

The Love God? ★★

Comedy 1969 · US · Colour · 103mins

Girlie magazine publisher Edmond O'Brien faces bankruptcy when a change in status means he can no longer claim cheap mailing privileges. He sees salvation in the ailing ornithological magazine edited by Abner Peacock (Don Knotts). O'Brien convinces Knott he can save the magazine, then sends him away to photograph exotic birds, while he instead turns the publication into another nudie rag. Low-octane comedy with love-him-or-hate-him star Knotts in the lead. A poor end to the career of writer/director Nat Hiken who was the genius behind the brilliant Sergeant Bilko, as creator of TV's *The Phil Silvers Show*.

Don Knotts *Abner Peacock* • Anne Francis *Lisa* • Edmond O'Brien *Osborn Tremain* • James Gregory *Hughes* • Maureen Arthur *Eleanor Tremain* ■ *Dir/Scr* Nat Hiken

The Love Goddesses ★★★★

Compilation 1965 · US · BW and Colour · 78mins

This is a marvellous compilation of clips featuring Hollywood's finest sex symbols. Trouble is, the producers were obviously constrained by availability and copyright, so where you would perhaps expect more you might get less, and vice versa. Paramount stars are favoured, but, nevertheless, many of the great ladies of the silver screen are present and correct, and the makers refreshingly cast their nets wider than the US, including Hedy Lamarr (as Hedwig Keisler), famously nude in *Ecstasy*, and that wanton Lulu, Louise Brooks, abroad in Europe. There's even a sizeable chunk of *Expresso Bongo*, one of the most daring (and under-rated) flicks of its day. Sylvia Syms a love goddess? You bet! Contains nudity.

Dir/Scr Saul J Turrell, Graeme Ferguson • *Editor* Howard Kuperman • *Music* Percy Faith

Love Happy ★★ U

Comedy 1949 · US · BW · 84mins

The Marx Brothers' last film together is a finale devoutly to be missed – unless you hanker for a glimpse of Marilyn Monroe. Harpo wrote the story and gets most of the spotlight as the shoplifting member of a penniless group of actors who unwittingly picks up a sardine can filled with diamonds. Raymond Burr is one of the villains trying to get the jewels back and Vera-Ellen plays Harpo's love interest. Groucho fans should note that his appearance is a brief one. ▭

Groucho Marx *Sam Grunion* • Chico Marx *Faustino* • Harpo Marx *Harpo* • Vera-Ellen *Maggie Phillips* • Ilona Massey *Madame Egilichi* • Marion Hutton *Bunny Dolan* • Raymond Burr *Alphonse Zoto* • Melville Cooper *Throckmorton* • Paul Valentine *Mike Johnson* • Marilyn Monroe *Grunion's client* ■ *Dir* David Miller • *Scr* Frank Tashlin, Mac Benoff, from a story by Harpo Marx

Love Has Many Faces ★

Romantic drama 1965 · US · Colour · 105mins

The title of this witless farrago is as unintentionally hilarious as its content. The many faces include Lana Turner as a millionairess in Acapulco and Cliff Robertson as her husband, a former beach lothario who married her for her money and is now lusting after Stefanie Powers. Turner has her hands full with bullfighter Jaime Bravo, and Hugh O'Brian – a gigolo on the make with both Lana and the equally wealthy Ruth Roman. This sleazy *La Ronde* comes to a bloody and melodramatic climax in a bullring. The Mexican locations look stunning, as does the star, in characteristic clothes-horse mode courtesy of Edith Head.

Lana Turner *Kit Jordan* • Cliff Robertson *Pete Jordan* • Hugh O'Brian *Hank Walker* • Ruth Roman *Margot Eliot* • Stefanie Powers *Carol Lambert* • Virginia Grey *Irene Talbot* ■ *Dir* Alexander Singer • *Scr* Marguerite Roberts

Love, Honour and Obey

★★ **18**

Comedy drama · 2000 · UK · Colour · 97mins

This is the second film from the self-styled Fugitives, a loose artists' collective centred around actors Ray Winstone, Jude Law and Sadie Frost. Jonny Lee Miller, Rhys Ifans and Denise van Outen join the trio in this tale of a courier who wheedles his way into a London crime family, only to embroil them in a deadly feud with a rival gang. The humour is laddish, lowbrow and not especially funny, while some improvised scenes should never have made the final cut. (Some of the cast are patently less adept at winging it than others.)

Ray Winstone *Ray* • Jonny Lee Miller *Jonny* • Jude Law *Jude* • Kathy Burke *Kathy* • Sadie Frost *Sadie* • Sean Pertwee *Sean* • Denise Van Outen *Denise* • Rhys Ifans *Mathew* ■ *Dir/Scr* Dominic Anciano, Ray Burdis

Love Hurts

★★ **15**

Comedy drama · 1990 · US · Colour · 102mins

Jeff Daniels's reluctant divorcee is the only believable character in this well-meaning comedy drama from veteran director Bud Yorkin. But Cloris Leachman is way over the top as our hero's zany mum, as this plodding effort attempts to look at the idea of civilised parting, what to do with the extended relatives and how to comfort the children. It's a good try, but it comes unstuck after the first reel and the inappropriately crass comedy all too often fails to hit the button. Contains violence and swearing. 🎦

Jeff Daniels *Paul Weaver* • Cynthia Sikes *Nancy Weaver* • Judith Ivey *Susan Volcheck* • John Mahoney *Boomer* • Cloris Leachman *Ruth Weaver* • Amy Wright *Karen Weaver* • Mary Griffin *Sarah Weaver* • Thomas Allen *David Weaver* ■ *Dir* Bud Yorkin • *Scr* Ron Nyswaner

Love in a Goldfish Bowl ★★

Romantic comedy
1961 · US · Colour · 88mins

Teen idols Tommy Sands and Fabian star in this unassuming romantic comedy about youthful love. Teenager Sands and his friend, fellow student Toby Michaels, decide to take an (innocent) vacation together at Sands's mother's beach house. During the holiday Michaels falls for the charms of local sailor Fabian... and this flirtation causes Tommy to – well, you know the rest. Average, but not without charm, and the leads are attractive enough.

Tommy Sands *Gordon Slide* • Fabian *Giuseppe La Barba* • Jan Sterling *Sandra Slide* • Toby Michaels *Blythe Holloway* • Edward Andrews *Senator Clyde Holloway* • John McGiver *Dr Frowley* • Majel Barrett *Alice* ■ *Dir* Jack Sher • *Scr* Jack Sher, from a story by Irene Kamp, Jack Sher

Love in Ambush

★★

Drama · 1997 · Ausl/Fr · Colour

A glossy if somewhat contrived Australian melodrama set in Cambodia prior to Pol Pot's disastrous takeover. The year is 1972 and Sigrid Thornton is the woman who returns to South East Asia to find her brother (Grant Piro), a soldier who disappeared during the conflict. Old wounds are reopened when she is reluctantly forced to call on her ex-husband and plantation owner Jacques Perrin, now a Khmer Rouge sympathiser. It looks great, but both the performances and the plotting are a touch sudsy. Contains swearing.

Sigrid Thornton *Shelley Kincaird* • Jacques Perrin *Pascal Lasalle* • Gary Sweet *Eddie Norton* • James Tolkan *Price* • Grant Piro *Lt Jon Kincaird* ■ *Dir* Carl Schultz • *Scr* Loupe Durand, David Ambrose, Christine Miller, John Howlett, Tom Hegarty

Love in Pawn

★ **U**

Comedy · 1953 · UK · BW · 70mins

Britain's popular radio (and later TV) imports from Canada, Bernard Braden and his wife Barbara Kelly, star in this indescribably puerile and unfunny comedy directed by Charles Saunders. It concerns a penniless artist who must prove his respectability in order to inherit a fortune from his wealthy uncle. His wife attempts to subvert the conditions by entertaining uncle's solicitor, to which end she pawns her husband for five pounds, setting in train a series of even more idiotic events. Best forgotten, which it was.

Bernard Braden *Roger Fox* • Barbara Kelly *Jean Fox* • Jean Carson *Amber Trusslove* • Reg Dixon *Albert Trusslove* ■ *Dir* Charles Saunders • *Scr* Guy Morgan, Frank Muir, Denis Norden, from a story by Humphrey Knight

Love in the Afternoon

★★★★★

Romantic comedy · 1957 · US · BW · 129mins

Filmed and set in Paris, Billy Wilder's romantic comedy will delight fans of his earlier *Sabrina Fair*. Audrey Hepburn again stars, this time as the daughter of a French private eye (Maurice Chevalier) who becomes obsessed by one of his targets: an American businessman and serial adulterer (Gary Cooper) who lives at the Ritz and has a gypsy band serenade his love-making sessions. Critics at the time found the crinkly Cooper much too old to romance the gorgeous Hepburn, but that's precisely the point: she humanises and energises him with her European vivacity. This first collaboration between Wilder and co-writer IAL Diamond features some lovely scenes and colourful secondary characters.

Gary Cooper *Frank Flannagan* • Audrey Hepburn *Ariane Chavasse* • Maurice Chevalier *Claude Chavasse* • John McGiver *Monsieur X* • Van Doude *Michel* • Lise Bourdin *Madame X* ■ *Dir* Billy Wilder • *Scr* Billy Wilder, Ial Diamond, from the novel *Ariane* by Claude Anet

Love in the Afternoon

★★★★ **15**

Comedy drama · 1972 · Fr · Colour · 93mins

Eric Rohmer winds up his "Six Moral Tales" series with this delightful comedy drama, also known by its American title *Chloë in the Afternoon*. Rather than exploring the doubts that beset those contemplating marriage, Rohmer here considers the temptations that take the sheen off wedded bliss. Real-life husband and wife Bernard and Françoise Verley play a well heeled couple whose contentment is jeopardised by his secret meetings with old friend Zouzou. The acting is impeccable, with Bernard Verley's shifts between happy flirtation and guilty indecision neatly judged. As ever, Rohmer's skilful use of location adds to the atmosphere and charm of the piece. A French film with English subtitles.

Zouzou *Chloë* • Bernard Verley *Frédéric* • Françoise Verley *Hélène* • Daniel Ceccaldi *Gérard* • Malvina Penne *Fabienne* • Babette Ferrier *Martine* • Frederique Hender *Madame M* ■ *Dir/Scr* Eric Rohmer

Love in the City

★★

Portmanteau comedy drama
1953 · It · BW · 110mins

In the early fifties, the Italian cinema was arguably the liveliest and most innovative in Europe, and this portmanteau movie brought together many of its major writers and directors. But, like most of these compilation films, it's a mixed blessing. The idea was to film real-life stories and real people, but Federico Fellini copped out (well, of course he would) and made a fantasy about a werewolf who uses a marriage agency because he thinks getting hitched will cure him. Michelangelo Antonioni offers some interviews with girls who attempted suicides. Other stories scour the gutter. In Italian with English subtitles.

Dir Michelangelo Antonioni, Federico Fellini, Alberto Lattuada, Carlo Lizzani, Francesco Maselli, Dino Risi, Cesare Zavattini • *Scr* Aldo Buzzi, Luigi Chiarini, Luigi Malerba, Tullio Pinelli, Vittorio Veltroni

Love in the Strangest Way

★★ **15**

Thriller · 1994 · Fr · Colour · 102mins

Seeking to break with his amiable screen image, Thierry Lhermitte plays a ruthless debt collector whose dangerous liaison with a mystery woman can only lead to one thing. Those familiar with *Fatal Attraction* (or one of its many imitations) will be at least one step ahead throughout, as Maruschka Detmers makes his life increasingly uncomfortable. Devoid of passion, suspense or social grit, this mildly salacious suspense film isn't worth waiting up for. In French with English subtitles.. Contains violence, mild swearing and nudity. 🎦

Thierry Lhermitte *Julien Bernier* • Maruschka Detmers *Anne Bernier* • Nadia Fares *Angela Galli* • Johann Martel *Charles* • Umberto Orsini *Vienne* ■ *Dir* Christopher Frank • *Scr* Christopher Frank, Jean Nachbaur, from a idea by Jean-Marc Roberts

Love Is a Ball

★★

Romantic comedy
1963 · US · Colour · 112mins

The early sixties was plagued with this kind of French Riviera tosh. Acres of bikini-clad bottoms, tinkling champagne glasses on clifftop terraces, Ferraris taking hairpin bends at ridiculous speeds and a plethora of Equity no-hopers who make the entire "We're having a jolly privileged time" premise appear more wooden than a barn door. This is a prime example of the style. Veteran Charles Boyer teams up with Glenn Ford and Hope Lange, with Ricardo Montalban, as much a fixture in these films as diamond paste, in deeply tanned attendance. Worth a giggle if you're at a very loose end.

Glenn Ford *John Davis* • Hope Lange *Millie Mehaffey* • Charles Boyer *Monsieur Etienne Pimm* • Ricardo Montalban *Gaspard* • Telly Savalas *Dr Gump* • Ruth McDevitt *Mathilda* ■ *Dir* David Swift • *Scr* David Swift, Tom Waldman, Frank Waldman, from the novel *The Grand Duke and Mr Pimm* by Lindsay Hardy

Love Is a Gun

★★★ **18**

Erotic thriller · 1994 · US · Colour · 102mins

Eric Roberts, that actor who just can't seem to say no to any script, shows better judgment with this nifty little thriller. The territory is familiar enough – police snapper Roberts becomes a murder suspect when he falls for a femme fatale – but director David Hartwell's jump-start direction and quirky eye distinguish it from other straight-to-video fodder. Roberts is less mannered than usual and is well supported by Kelly Preston and R Lee Ermey. 🎦

Eric Roberts *Jack Hart* • Kelly Preston *Jean* • Eliza Garrett *Isabel* • Joe Sirola [Joseph Sirola] *Al Kinder* • John Toles-Bey *Jay Leibowitz* • R Lee Ermey *Frank Deacon* ■ *Dir/Scr* David Hartwell

Love Is a Many-Splendored Thing

★★ **U**

Romantic drama · 1955 · US · Colour · 97mins

Despite having one of the most famous romantic titles of all time, this soap opera's distinction rests largely with its hit title ballad and director Henry King's imaginative use of early CinemaScope, which captures stars Jennifer Jones and William Holden horizontal at every possible opportunity. Trouble is, both Jones and Holden fail to convince in this occasionally trite tale of forbidden love, which is a shame, because the source book by Han Suyin is actually very moving. Alfred Newman's Oscar-winning score makes stunning use of the main theme, and will convince you that this tosh, a hugely popular success at the time, is better than it actually is. 🎦

William Holden (1) *Mark Elliot* • Jennifer Jones *Han Suyin* • Torin Thatcher *Mr Palmer-Jones* • Isobel Elsom *Adeline Palmer-Jones* • Murray Matheson *Dr Tam* • Virginia Gregg *Ann Richards* • Richard Loo *Robert Hung* • Soo Young *Nora Hung* • Philip Ahn *Third Uncle* ■ *Dir* Henry King • *Scr* John Patrick, from the book *A Many Splendored Thing* by Han Suyin

Love Is a Racket

★★★

Comedy drama · 1932 · US · BW · 72mins

Douglas Fairbanks Jr is the Broadway gossip columnist who falls for an ambitious but financially irresponsible young actress (Frances Dee). She becomes indebted to a ruthless gangster, who then meets with an untimely death. Fairbanks is terrific as the cynical reporter with sudden stardust in his eyes, and he is well supported by a cast that includes Lee Tracy, Lyle Talbot and Ann Dvorak. A pacy comedy/drama, smartly scripted and, under William Wellman's immaculate direction, offering lots of New York nightlife atmosphere.

Douglas Fairbanks Jr *Jimmy Russell* • Ann Dvorak *Sally* • Frances Dee *Mary* • Lee Tracy

Stanley Fiske • Lyle Talbot *Eddie Shaw* ■ *Dir* William A Wellman • *Scr* Courtney Terrett, from the novel by Rian James

Love Is All There Is ★

Comedy drama 1996 · US · Colour · 105mins

An oafish update of *Romeo and Juliet*, with competing catering companies as the families linked by star-crossed love. Crass, loud and a lot less funny than it thinks it is, the main interest here is an early performance from Oscar-winner Angelina Jolie as the "Juliet" character. Joseph Bologna (who also co-directed), Barbara Carrera and Paul Sorvino fill out the mid-quality cast. If food be the music of love, *don't* play on! The whizzing sound you hear isn't the caterer's Cuisinart – it's Shakespeare spinning in his grave...

Lainie Kazan *Sadie* • Paul Sorvino *Piero* • Barbara Carrera *Maria* • Joseph Bologna *Mike* • Angelina Jolie *Gina* • Nathaniel Marston *Rosario* • Renee Taylor *Mona* • William Hickey *Monsignor* • Dick Van Patten *Dr Rondino* • Abe Vigoda *Rudy* • Connie Stevens *Miss DeLuca* • Blessed Roscoe ■ *Dir/Scr* Renee Taylor, Joseph Bologna

Love Is Better Than Ever ★★ U

Romantic comedy 1951 · US · BW · 80mins

A naive dance teacher comes to New York for a dance convention and meets a slick theatrical agent. He shows her around but she misinterprets his attentiveness as honorable intentions and falls in love with him. Directed by Stanley Donen, this wisp of a forgotten romantic comedy is definitely lower-half-of-the-bill stuff, even though the girl is a young Elizabeth Taylor, glowing with loveliness despite the imminent collapse of her marriage to hotelier Nicky Hilton. Her love interest is Larry Parks, famous for playing Al Jolson, but starring in his last film before the McCarthy hearings destroyed his career.

Larry Parks *Jud Parker* • Elizabeth Taylor *Anastacia Macaboy* • Josephine Hutchinson *Mrs Macaboy* • Tom Tully *Mr Macaboy* • Ann Doran *Mrs Levoy* • Elinor Donahue *Pattie Marie Levoy* • Kathleen Freeman *Mrs Kahmey* • Doreen McCann *Albertina Kahmey* • Gene Kelly *Guest star* ■ *Dir* Stanley Donen • *Scr* Ruth Brooks Flippen

Love Is Colder than Death ★★★★

Comedy crime romance 1969 · W Ger · BW · 88mins

Clearly taking up where Jean-Luc Godard had left off in his assault on traditional cinema, Rainer Werner Fassbinder made his remarkable debut with this micro-budget deconstruction of the crime thriller. Much of the action was staged as tableaux before a doggedly static camera – indeed, one of the very few tracking shots was lifted from Jean-Marie Straub's *The Bridegroom, the Comedienne and the Pimp*, in which Fassbinder had acted. The minimalist plot is presented in fragmentary form, while lowlifes Ulli Lommel and Fassbinder (and Hannah Schygulla as the girl caught between them) scarcely exchange a word. It's almost wilfully obscure, but compelling nonetheless. In German with English subtitles.

Ulli Lommel *Bruno* • Hanna Schygulla *Johanna* • Rainer Werner Fassbinder *Franz* • Katrin Schaake *Dame im zug* • Hans Hirschmüller *Peter* ■ *Dir/Scr* Rainer Werner Fassbinder

Love Is Strange ★★ PG

Romantic drama 1998 · US · Colour · 87mins

Not even a first-rate cast that includes Kate Nelligan, Ron Silver and Julie Harris can disguise the fact that this is another disease-of-the-week TV movie. A judge, long divorced from his lawyer husband, discovers she is dying of cancer. When he learns of her condition, he provides her with emotional support and, in the process, they rekindle their love. Watching this will lead you to the conclusion that love isn't strange – just a bore. ▭

Kate Nelligan *Kathryn* • Ron Silver *Tom* • Julie Harris *Sylvia* • Bob Griggs *Frank* ■ *Dir* Annette Haywood-Carter • *Scr* Annette Haywood-Carter, Ken Carter

Love Is the Devil: Study for a Portrait of Francis Bacon ★★★ 18

Biographical drama 1998 · UK · Colour · 86mins

John Maybury's film is a highly stylised account of the painter's abrasive affair with reformed thief, George Dyer. As lovers divided by culture and class, Derek Jacobi gives a remarkable physical impersonation of Bacon, while Daniel Craig is a model of repressed anger and bemused despair. The director's use of distorting lenses, reflective surfaces, angular close-ups and split-screen devices to convey both the couple's dislocated world and the style of Bacon's paintings is bold and inspired. However, the vignette structure deprives the film of some much-needed momentum, while the dialogue is pretentiously epigrammatic. Contains nudity, sex scenes and some swearing. ▭

Derek Jacobi *Francis Bacon* • Daniel Craig *George Dyer* • Anne Lambton *Isabel Rawsthorne* • Karl Johnson *John Deakin* • Annabel Brooks *Henrietta Moraes* • Adrian Scarborough *Daniel Farson* • Tilda Swinton *Muriel Belcher* • Richard Newbold *Blonde Billy* ■ *Dir* John Maybury • *Scr* John Maybury, James Cohen, Don Jordan

Love Jones ★★★ 15

Romantic comedy
1997 · US · Colour · 104mins

Writer Theodore Witcher made his directorial debut with this funny, funky tale of love among a group of Chicago middle-class African Americans. Nia Long and Larenz Tate are the star-crossed lovers who meet, make love and then part, leading to the usual romantic complications. Portraying blacks as successful urbanites rather than the usual clichéd, downbeat characters, this features superb performances from the leads and from Isaiah Washington and *Ally McBeal's* Lisa Nicole Carson. Stylishly shot and with a snappy script, this is a knowing look at the pitfalls of love and romance in the nineties. Contains some swearing and sexual references. ▭

Larenz Tate *Darius Lovehall* • Nia Long *Nina Mosley* • Isaiah Washington *Savon Garrison* • Lisa Nicole Carson *Josie Nichols* • Bill Bellamy *Hollywood* ■ *Dir/Scr* Theodore Witcher

Love Kills ★★★ 18

Comedy 1998 · US · Colour · 90mins

Mario Van Peebles stars as the bizarrely monikered Poe Finklestein, a masseur and con artist who specialises in scamming recently widowed women in ingenious ways dreamed up by his insanely jealous girlfriend Sylvia (Loretta Devine). His new target is Evelyn Heiss (Lesley Ann Warren) who is actually broke, but whose flakey stepson (Donovan Leitch) is about to inherit jewels worth millions. Into this stew comes Daniel Baldwin as a *Columbo*-style cop who might not be what he seems. Glossily produced for indie fodder, this is worth checking out if only for Van Peebles's extraordinary dreadlocks. Look for a cameo from Mario's distinguished dad Melvin. ▭ **DVD**

Mario Van Peebles *Poe Finklestein* • Lesley Ann Warren *Evelyn Heiss* • Daniel Baldwin *Danny Tucker* • Donovan Leitch *Dominique* • Alexis Arquette *James* • Louise Fletcher *Alena Heiss* • Loretta Devine *Sylvia Finklestein* • Melvin Van Peebles *Abel* ■ *Dir/Scr* Mario Van Peebles

Love Laughs at Andy Hardy ★★ U

Comedy drama 1946 · US · BW · 93mins

This was the fifteenth and last genuine Andy Hardy movie (though there was a nostalgic straggler in 1958). Andy and his dad (Lewis Stone) had entertained America through the war years and kept alive small-town values, but Mickey Rooney couldn't conceal the fact that he was now 26-years-old. In any case, these were the days of *film noir*, romantic fatalism and venetian blinds, all of which meant curtains for the boyish Hardy. This instalment sees Rooney back from the war and crushed when his fiancée (Bonita Granville) runs off with someone else.

Mickey Rooney *Andy Hardy* • Lewis Stone *Judge James K Hardy* • Fay Holden *Mrs Emily Hardy* • Sara Haden *Aunt Milly* • Bonita Granville *Kay Wilson* ■ *Dir* Willis Goldbeck • *Scr* Harry Ruskin, William Ludwig, from a story by Howard Dimsdale, from characters created by Aurania Rouverol

Love Leads the Way ★★ U

Drama based on a true story
1984 · US · Colour · 99mins

Timothy Bottoms and Eva Marie Saint star in this incredibly sugary, truth-based tale about the people who introduced the use of guide dogs for the blind in America. Both the high-calibre cast (Patricia Neal, Ralph Bellamy, Ernest Borgnine) and director Delbert Mann (best known for *Marty*) seem unsuited to such unashamedly sentimental material (not surprisingly made by Disney), but at least the dogs are cute. ▭

Timothy Bottoms *Morris Frank* • Eva Marie Saint *Dorothy Eustis* • Arthur Hill *Mr Frank* • Patricia Neal *Mrs Frank* • Glynnis O'Connor *Lois* • Susan Dey *Beth* • Ralph Bellamy *Senator Christl* • Ernest Borgnine *Senator Brighton* ■ *Dir* Delbert Mann • *Scr* Henry Denker, from a story by Jimmy Hawkins, Henry Denker, from the book *First Lady of the Seeing Eye* by Morris Frank, Blake Clark

The Love Letter ★★

Fantasy romance 1998 · US · Colour · 99mins

The one thing that can never be said about Jennifer Jason Leigh is that she settles for safe roles. But this TV movie has got to be one of her strangest choices. Shuttling between the American Civil War era and the present day, the story traces the letter-based romance between a 19th-century woman and a man who forgets his forthcoming nuptials after he finds a 135-year-old billet-doux hidden in an antique desk. Corresponding across the chasm of time, Leigh and Campbell Scott manage to bring a semblance of credibility to what otherwise could have been preposterously sentimental twaddle.

Campbell Scott *Scotty Corrigan* • Jennifer Jason Leigh *Elizabeth Whitcomb* • Everett Reagle *David Dukes* • Estelle Parsons *Beatrice* • Daphne Ashbrook *Debra Zabriskie* • Myra Carter *Clarice* ■ *Dir* Dan Curtis • *Scr* James Hanerson, Pamela Gray, from a story by Jack Finney

The Love Letter ★★ 15

Romance 1999 · US · Colour · 82mins

This film about a divorced single mother is very much a family affair. Actress Kate Capshaw bought the rights to Cathleen Schine's novel in order to produce it for husband Steven Spielberg's DreamWorks company, while one of the Spielberg children, Sasha, has a walk-on role. As the lone parent, Capshaw finds an anonymous letter written in amorously endearing terms and thinks it's for her. Others in her group think the same, but her mother (played by Gwyneth Paltrow's mother, Blythe Danner), who's in the process of coming out as a lesbian, is convinced otherwise. Directed by Peter Ho-Sun Chan, the film's romantic focus is so unsteady and soapily blurred that the idea of love's lost chances loses a lot of its poignancy. The end result often looks as though its only real destination is video. Contains some swearing. ▭

Kate Capshaw *Helen* • Blythe Danner *Lillian* • Ellen DeGeneres *Janet* • Geraldine McEwan *Miss Scattergoods* • Julianne Nicholson *Jennifer* • Tom Everett Scott *Johnny* • Tom Selleck *George* • Gloria Stuart *Eleanor* • Jessica Capshaw *Kelly* • Sasha Spielberg *Girl with sparkler* ■ *Dir* Peter Ho-Sun Chan • *Scr* Maria Maggenti, from the novel by Cathleen Schine

Love Letters ★★★

Melodrama 1945 · US · BW · 101mins

Mogul David O Selznick loaned his protégée and future wife, Jennifer Jones, to producer Hal B Wallis and Paramount for this glitzy romantic soap opera. In Ayn (*The Fountainhead*) Rand's screenplay, Jones suffers a number of shocks, including amnesia and the traumatic discovery that her treasured collection of love letters was written not by her husband (Robert Sully) but by co-star Joseph Cotten. This stylish and enjoyable nonsense was directed by William Dieterle and received several Oscar nominations including one for Jones (as best actress).

Jennifer Jones *Singleton* • Joseph Cotten *Alan Quinton* • Ann Richards *Dilly Carson* • Anita Louise *Helen Wentworth* • Cecil Kellaway

Mack • Gladys Cooper *Beatrice Remington* • Byron Barr *Derek Quinton* • Robert Sully *Roger Morland* ■ *Dir* William Dieterle • *Scr* Ayn Rand, from the novel *Pity My Simplicity* by Chris Massie

Love Letters ★★★★ 18
Drama   1983 · US · Colour · 84mins

This hugely impressive emotional drama is beautifully played and sensitively directed by Amy Jones. The story centres on a single woman who discovers evidence of an affair among her dead mother's letters, then takes up herself with a married man. The film intelligently probes the emotions of infidelity, and its frequent justification on the grounds that it's sometimes right to do the wrong thing. The starry cast includes Jamie Lee Curtis, Amy Madigan, Bud Cort and James Keach. ▣

Jamie Lee Curtis *Anna* • James Keach *Oliver* • Amy Madigan *Wendy* • Bud Cort *Danny* • Matt Clark *Winter* • Bonnie Bartlett *Mrs Winter* ■ *Dir* Amy Jones [Amy Holden Jones] • *Scr* Amy Jones

Love, Lies and Lullabies ★★ 15
Drama   1993 · US · Colour · 89mins

After spending the eighties locked in courtroom battles in TV's *LA Law*, Susan Dey trades in her squeaky-clean image to play a cocaine addict. Her premature baby has been taken away and she faces a desperate struggle to clean up her act and get the child back. Strong stuff, with both Dey and co-star Piper Laurie giving it all they've got in this often powerful, but ultimately clichéd drama. ▣

Susan Dey *Christina Kinsey* • Piper Laurie *Margaret Kinsey* • Lorraine Toussaint *Florence Crenshaw* • DW Moffett *Gabriel* • Kathleen York *Terry* ■ *Dir* Rod Hardy • *Scr* Janet Heaney, Matthew Eisen

The Love Lottery ★★★ U
Comedy   1953 · UK · Colour · 83mins

A fizzy, old-fashioned kind of romp, shaping gentle comedy from the way of life of film stars under the strict studio system of the thirties and forties. David Niven is his usual smooth self – that man could slick his way under a locked door – and the part of a fifties celluloid heart-throb was made for him. Charles Crichton directs with his tongue well placed in his cheek. The plot is about as daft as you can possibly get – Niven agrees to be first prize in a love lottery for fans – but nobody really cares as there's just enough satire to keep the vehicle afloat. Undemanding fun.

David Niven *Rex Allerton* • Peggy Cummins *Sally* • Anne Vernon *Jane* • Herbert Lom *Amico* • Charles Victor *Jennings* • Gordon Jackson *Ralph* • Humphrey Bogart ■ *Dir* Charles Crichton • *Scr* Harry Kurnitz, from the story by Charles Neilson-Terry, Zelma Bramley-Moore

The Love Machine ★ 18
Drama   1971 · US · Colour · 103mins

Jacqueline Susann hit paydirt with this tacky adaptation of her best-selling novel. The setting is the power-crazed, sexually torrid world of television news and if you can believe John Philip Law

– that wooden artist's model from *Barbarella* – as the head honcho you will believe anything. Dyan Cannon pouts and squeezes into her cossies, Robert Ryan looks ill and bored out of his mind as a company chairman and David Hemmings plays a hyped-up photographer – a not very subtle in-joke about his role in *Blow-Up*. This machine doesn't really work at all, and lacks the really bad taste and send-up performances to make it even vaguely enjoyable. ▣

John Phillip Law *Robin Stone* • Dyan Cannon *Judith Austin* • Robert Ryan *Gregory Austin* • Jackie Cooper *Danton Miller* • David Hemmings *Jerry Nelson* ■ *Dir* Jack Haley Jr • *Scr* Samuel Taylor, from the novel by Jacqueline Susann

The Love Match ★★★ U
Comedy   1955 · UK · BW · 86mins

Although this is an admirable enough comedy, it is also one of those unforgivably patronising pictures that bourgeois British film-makers believed presented an authentic picture of working-class life. Arthur Askey stars as a football crazy railway employee whose passion for a team of no-hopers lands him in all sorts of trouble and almost costs him his job. Struggling against a shortage of genuinely funny situations, the cast does well to keep the action alive. The highlight is Askey's heckling of the referee, a wonderful moment of football hooliganism.

Arthur Askey *Bill Brown* • Thora Hird *Sal Brown* • Glenn Melvyn *Wally Binns* • Robb Wilton *Mr Muddlecombe* • James Kenney *Percy Brown* • Shirley Eaton *Rose Brown* ■ *Dir* David Paltenghi • *Scr* Geoffrey Orme, Glenn Melvyn, from the play by Glenn Melvyn

Love Matters ★★★
Drama   1993 · US · Colour · 94mins

In this study of marital fragility shows why he will be missed as a star. The convincing way in which Dunne's marriage to Annette O'Toole begins to crumble in the presence of the adulterous Tony Goldwyn and his lusty mistress Gina Gershon will have couples around the country looking questioningly at each other. Co-writer/director Eb Lottimer overdoes the sexual content, but, otherwise, has produced a provocative little picture. Contains swearing, sex scenes and nudity. ▣

Griffin Dunne *Tom* • Tony Goldwyn *Geoffrey* • Annette O'Toole *Julie* • Gina Gershon *Heather* • Kate Burton *Deborah* ■ *Dir* Eb Lottimer • *Scr* Eb Lottimer, Evan Katz

Love Me or Leave Me ★★★★
Musical drama   1955 · US · Colour · 121mins

This cracking biopic of twenties chanteuse Ruth Etting was originally intended as a vehicle for Ava Gardner, but MGM wisely brought in Doris Day, giving her a sexy new image and pairing her again, after *Starlift* and *The West Point Story*, with tough guy James Cagney, and, boy, how those sparks fly! Though censorship has diluted this tawdry saga of a kept woman and her obsessive and sexually inadequate gangster sponsor, the truth is not glossed over, despite the topnotch

production values that make the tale less squalid than it obviously actually was. Doris is a knockout, performing the title number and *Ten Cents a Dance* with great understanding, but it's the Oscar-nominated Cagney, in a great later role, as "the Gimp", who walks away with the movie.

Doris Day *Ruth Etting* • James Cagney *Martin "The Gimp" Snyder* • Cameron Mitchell *Johnny Alderman* • Robert Keith *Bernard V Loomis* • Tom Tully *Frobisher* • Harry Bellaver *Georgie* • Richard Gaines *Paul Hunter* ■ *Dir* Charles Vidor • *Scr* Daniel Fuchs, Isobel Lennart, from a story by Daniel Fuchs

Love Me Tender ★★★ PG
Western   1956 · US · BW · 85mins

When 20th Century-Fox made a cheap black-and-white CinemaScope western called *The Reno Brothers*, they couldn't possibly have foreseen how one lucky stroke of casting would bring their production costs back within the first three days of opening. For, as younger brother Clint Reno, rock 'n' roll sensation Elvis Presley made his screen debut, and the title of the movie was changed to that of its ballad, *Love Me Tender*. Elvis proved to be a natural screen presence and, although third-billed to stars Richard Egan and Debra Paget, effortlessly dominates the film. There's a marvellous mid-section where the whole plot stops to give audiences a taste of the singin' sensation in his prime, as Elvis performs *Let Me* and *Poor Boy* with that wonderful self-mocking air that distinguished his early performances. He knows he's good, and here the talent is still fresh and raw. ▣

Richard Egan *Vance* • Debra Paget *Cathy* • Elvis Presley *Clint* • Robert Middleton *Siringo* • William Campbell *Brett Reno* • Neville Brand *Mike Gavin* • Mildred Dunnock *Mother* ■ *Dir* Robert D Webb • *Scr* Robert Buckner, from a story by Maurice Geraghty

Love Me Tonight ★★★★★
Musical comedy   1932 · US · BW · 104mins

One of Hollywood's most clever and influential film musicals, with a sublime Rodgers and Hart score illuminating director Rouben Mamoulian's successful attempt at freeing the production from its staid, stage-bound forerunner. The irrepressible Maurice Chevalier is "the son-of-a-gun who's nothing but a tailor" who falls for princess Jeanette MacDonald, long before MGM put her in a straitjacket opposite the sexless Nelson Eddy. And those songs – *Mimi*, *Lover*, *Isn't It Romantic?* – and, ooh, that risqué dialogue: make a note of Myrna Loy's pre-censorship response to "Could you go for a doctor?". A real treat.

Maurice Chevalier *Maurice Courtelin* • Jeanette MacDonald *Princess Jeanette* • Myrna Loy *Countess Valentine* • Charlie Ruggles [Charles Ruggles] *Vicomte De Vareze* • C Aubrey Smith *Duke* • Charles Butterworth *Count De Savignac* • Joseph Cawthorn *Dr Armand De Fontinac* • Robert Greig *Flamond* ■ *Dir* Rouben Mamoulian • *Scr* Samuel Hoffenstein, Waldemar Young, George Marion Jr, from the play *Tailor in the Chateau* by Léopold Marchand, by Paul Armont

Love, Mother ★★ 15
Drama   1987 · Hun · Colour · 105mins

Occasionally guilty of trying to be too mischievous for his own good, Hungarian director János Rózsa has nevertheless produced a witty morality story about the dangers of lust and greed. Spied on by the young son by means of a network of periscopes dotted around the house, the affluent family at the centre of this satire is so preoccupied by upward mobility and sexual gratification that its members communicate only through chalked messages on a blackboard in the kitchen. Unfortunately, the philosophising that follows the neglected daughter's suicide bid lacks insight and sits uncomfortably amid the foolery. In Hungarian with English subtitles..

Dorottya Udvaros *Juli Kalmar* • Robert Koltai *Geza Kalmar* • Kati Lajtai *Mari Kalmar* • Simon G Gevai *Peti Kalmar* • Sandor Gáspár *Doctor* ■ *Dir* János Rózsa • *Scr* Miklos Vamos, from his story

Love, Murder & Deceit ★★ PG
Murder mystery drama
1997 · US · Colour · 92mins

British beauty Rachel Ward (remember *The Thorn Birds*?) stars as a Southern belle in a steamy tale that really lives up to its title. She plays a nurse who saves the life of a wealthy businessman Richard Cory (Terry O'Quinn) who first relentlessly woos her, and then, once they are married, ignores the poor girl. So when his handsome young son Eric (Joshua Morrow) arrives on the scene it's not long before she's taking more than a passing interest in him and the elder Cory has taken a fall. But was Morrow to blame? Some clever twists enliven a seemingly routine melodrama. ▣

Rachel Ward *Caitlin Cory* • Terry O'Quinn *Richard Cory* • Joshua Morrow *Eric Cory* • Marion Guyot *Mrs Stuart* ■ *Dir* Mary Lambert • *Scr* Ron Cutler

Love Nest ★★ U
Comedy   1951 · US · BW · 83mins

This piece of harmless fluff stars sweet and pretty June Haver in one of her rare non-musical roles. She and bland William Lundigan are a married couple who have invested their life savings in an apartment building, but a number of problems arise. One of them comes in the comely shape of Marilyn Monroe – on the eve of stardom – tossed in to create jealousy. It's difficult to believe that this ineptly contrived screenplay was written by IAL Diamond, who was to co-write some of Billy Wilder's best movies, such as *The Apartment* and *Some Like It Hot*.

June Haver *Connie Scott* • William Lundigan *Jim Scott* • Frank Fay *Charley Patterson* • Marilyn Monroe *Roberta Stevens* • Jack Paar *Ed Forbes* • Leatrice Joy *Eadie Gaynor* ■ *Dir* Joseph M Newman • *Scr* IAL Diamond, from the novel by Scott Corbett

The Love of Jeanne Ney ★★★★
Silent romance   1927 · Ger · BW · 144mins

Made in the heyday of UFA, the famed German production company, just prior to GW Pabst's best works, *Pandora's Box* and *Diary of a Lost Girl*, this epic love story deserves to be better known. A mixture of social realism and Hollywood-style romance, the rather complicated plot moves from the Crimea (studio sets) during the Russian Revolution to Paris, where sequences were shot in the streets. The lovers, portrayed by Edith Jehanne and Uno Henning, are outplayed by Fritz Rasp, a wonderfully sleazy villain, and Brigitte Helm, most famous as the robot in *Metropolis* (1926), uncharacteristically cast as a lonely blind girl.

Edith Jehanne *Jeanne Ney* • Brigitte Helm *Gabrielle Ney* • Hertha von Walther *Margot* • Uno Henning *Andreas Labov* • Fritz Rasp *Khalibiev* • Adolph Edgar Licho *Raymond Ney* • Eugen Jensen *Alfred Ney* • Hans Jaray *Emile Poitras* • Wladimir Sokoloff [Vladimir Sokoloff] *Zacharkiewitsch* ■ *Dir* GW Pabst • *Scr* Ladislao Vajda, Rudolph Leonhardt, Ilya Ehrenburg, from the novel *Die Liebe der Jeanne Ney* by Ilya Ehrenburg

The Love of Sumako the Actress ★★★
Drama 1947 · Jap · BW · 93mins

Although he had innate sympathy for geishas and others who suffered from patriarchal injustice, Kenji Mizoguchi was perhaps less astute in his handling of successful females. Consequently, although he stages this biopic of Sumako Matsui with a genuine feel for the Japanese theatre at a time when actresses and western techniques were virtually unknown, he is less certain in his presentation of the melodramatic events surrounding her affair with married director, Hogetsu Shimamura. Kinuyo Tanaka (who emerged as one of Japan's few women directors) was Mizoguchi's favourite collaborator, but even she fails to to breathe life into Hideo Nagata's play. In Japanese with English subtitles.

Kinuyo Tanaka *Sumako Matsui* • So Yamamura *Hogetsu Shimamura* • Eijiro Tono *Shoyo Tsubouchi* • Kikue Mori *Ichiko Shimamura* ■ *Dir* Kenji Mizoguchi • *Scr* Yoshikata Yoda, from a play by Hideo Nagata

Love on the Dole ★★★★ PG
Drama 1941 · UK · BW · 94mins

A major dose of the "eeh bah gooms" and dark satanic mills, starring the fragrant Deborah Kerr as a mill girl caught on the horns of a classic thirties' dilemma – become a kept woman and escape poverty or keep faith with the morality of her class. Director John Baxter has summoned all the usual slum-dwelling stereotypes, local sharp-suited bookie and sweating, cruel paterfamilias, yet the movie resonates with strong feeling for the genuine harshness and brutal truths of life in Depression Salford, and Kerr is subtly affecting in her portrayal of personal conflict. [video]

Deborah Kerr *Sally Hardcastle* • Clifford Evans *Larry Meath* • Joyce Howard *Helen Hawkins* • George Carney *Mr Hardcastle* • Mary Merrall *Mrs Hardcastle* • Geoffrey Hibbert *Harry Hardcastle* • Frank Cellier *Sam Grundy* • Martin Walker *Ned Narkey* ■ *Dir* John Baxter • *Scr* Walter Greenwood, Barbara K Emery, Rollo Gamble, from the play by Ronald Gow and the novel by Walter Greenwood

Love on the Run ★★★
Comedy 1936 · US · BW · 80mins

This is class. It may not seem very clever or original today, but it never really had to be. The stars are Joan Crawford and Clark Gable, and for many movie fans of the era that's all that matter. One of those globetrotting romances that never get off the backlot, this is whipped along ever-so-lightly by director WS Van Dyke ("One-take Woody"), an expert craftsman who knew exactly how to handle material like this: just let the stars get on with it. Franchot Tone is the other man, and in real life both he and Gable were Crawford's lovers (Tone married her) – a touch of trivia that adds extra spice to the proceedings.

Joan Crawford *Sally Parker* • Clark Gable *Michael Anthony* • Franchot Tone *Barnabas Pells* • Reginald Owen *Baron Spandermann* • Mona Barrie *Baroness* • Ivan Lebedeff *Prince Igor* ■ *Dir* WS Van Dyke • *Scr* John Lee Mahin, Manuel Seff, Gladys Hurlbut, from the story *Beauty and the Beast* by Alan Green, Julian Brodie

Love on the Run ★★★ 12
Comedy drama 1979 · Fr · Colour · 91mins

The fifth, last and least of François Truffaut's films about his alter ego Antoine Doinel, first seen in the director's debut feature, *The 400 Blows*, made 20 years earlier. This is also a nostalgic movie, with many of Antoine's former female conquests making guest appearances, some in sequences from earlier films, as he prepares to write a novel of his romantic career. It's more than a shade indulgent, and some may find Jean-Pierre Léaud a real pain as the lead. Yet it's still a funny and humane movie. A French language film. [video]

Jean-Pierre Léaud *Antoine Doinel* • Marie-France Pisier *Colette* • Claude Jade *Christine* • Dani Liliane • Dorothée *Sabine* • Dani Liliane ■ *Dir* François Truffaut • *Scr* François Truffaut, Suzanne Schiffman, Marie-France Pisier, Jean Aurel

Love or Money ★★ 15
Comedy 1990 · US · Colour · 86mins

This routine comedy, about a pushy home-seller who finds himself in a real (e)state when he faces the eternal dilemma – success in business or a shot at romantic happiness. The film stars personable Timothy Daly, later to be seen to better effect as cult leader David Koresh in the excellent *In the Line of Duty: Ambush in Waco*, plus veterans Kevin McCarthy and Elvis co-star Shelley Fabares.

Kevin McCarthy *William Reed* • Timothy Daly *Chris Murdoch* • Haviland Morris *Jennifer Reed* • Shelley Fabares *Lu Ann Reed* • David Doyle *Arthur Reed* ■ *Dir* Todd Hallowell • *Scr* Bart Davis, Elyse England, Michael Zausner

The Love Parade ★★★★
Musical comedy 1929 · US · BW · 107mins

Soprano Jeanette MacDonald, the queen of screen operetta, made her film debut as Queen Louise, being wooed by Maurice Chevalier's Count Alfred Renard in Ernst Lubitsch's first talkie. His Gallic charm and her Anglo-Saxon reserve and self-mockery

produced a seductive, piquant combination in this saucy fairy tale set in Paris and the fictional land of Sylvania. Lubitsch immediately realised that the camera and sound effects could be used with greater flexibility than hitherto, in order to counterpoint the musical scenes. With its lavish settings, songs integrated into the scenario and sexual innuendo, it set the pattern for future Hollywood musicals. Watch for Jean Harlow, in one of her first screen appearances, as an extra in the theatre audience.

Maurice Chevalier *Count Alfred Renard* • Jeanette MacDonald *Queen Louise* • Lupino Lane *Jacques* • Lillian Roth *Lulu* • Edgar Norton *Major-Domo* • Jean Harlow ■ *Dir* Ernst Lubitsch • *Scr* Ernst Vajda, Guy Bolton, from the play *The Prince Consort* by Leon Xanrof, Jules Chancel

The Love Pill ★
Erotic comedy 1971 · UK · Colour · 82mins

One of Britain's few successful hardcore directors, John Lindsay, devised the story for this instantly forgettable soft-core comedy. In the early seventies, the pill was still held responsible in many quarters for the onset of the permissive society and so this crass picture takes the argument to its illogical conclusion by having dozens of women take a tablet that transforms them into nymphomaniacs.

Henry Woolf *Libido* • Toni Sinclair *Sylvia, Libido's secretary* • David Pugh *Arnold* • Melinda Churcher *Linda* • Kenneth Waller *Professor Edwards* ■ *Dir* Kenneth Turner • *Scr* from a story by John Lindsay

Love Potion No 9 ★★ PG
Comedy 1992 · US · Colour · 92mins

Taking its plot cues from the lyrics of the famous Leiber/Stoller pop hit, this low-key fantasy romance is silly, cute and randomly amusing. Tate Donovan and Sandra Bullock are the nerdy lab assistants who discover a spray formula that makes them irresistible to the opposite sex. The expected complications ensue. Writer/director Dale Launer knows his limitations and deftly plays an unassuming feel-good factor around them. Worth seeing for Anne Bancroft's uncredited mystic gypsy cameo, Madame Ruth. [video]

Tate Donovan *Paul Matthews* • Sandra Bullock *Diane Farrow* • Mary Mara *Marisa* • Dale Midkiff *Gary Logan* • Hillary Bailey Smith *Sally* • Dylan Baker *Prince Geoffrey* • Anne Bancroft *Madame Ruth (uncredited)* ■ *Dir* Dale Launer • *Scr* Dale Launer, from a song by Jerry Leiber, Mike Stoller

Love Serenade ★★
Comedy 1996 · Ausl · Colour · 101mins

Typically quirky Australian comedy, about a top DJ who relocates to a remote Outback town. But it isn't his discs that he puts in a spin, it's the lives of the two love-hungry sisters who live next door. The storyline teeters on the edge of tastelessness, but the engagingly oddball handling and strong performances keep it just the right side of sleazy.

Miranda Otto *Dimity Hurley* • Rebecca Frith *Vicki-Ann Hurley* • George Shevtsov *Ken Sherry* • John Alansu *Albert Lee* • Jessica Napier *Deborah* • Jill McWilliam *Curler Victim* ■ *Dir/Scr* Shirley Barrett

Love Songs ★★
Drama 1984 · Fr · Colour · 109mins

The prospect of watching Christopher Lambert and Richard Anconina camp it up as wannabe rock stars will probably dissuade many from sticking with this showbiz melodrama, particularly as the ditties are hardly the finest in the Michel Legrand songbook. But the romance that develops between Lambert and record mogul Catherine Deneuve (whose husband is across the Atlantic researching a book) is not without interest, not least because of the tensions it generates within the duo as the big time finally beckons. The leads' contrasting acting styles also adds to writer/director Elie Chouraqui's otherwise pedestrian and unpersuasive picture. French dialogue dubbed into English.

Catherine Deneuve *Margaux* • Christopher Lambert *Jeremy* • Richard Anconina *Michel* • Jacques Perrin *Yves* • Dayle Haddon *Corinne* • Nick Mancuso *Peter* • Charlotte Gainsbourg *Charlotte* • Dominique Lavanant *Florence* • Lionel Rocheman *Gruber* ■ *Dir* Elie Chouraqui • *Scr* Elie Chouraqui

Love Stinks ★
Comedy 1999 · US · Colour · 93

Either writer/director Jeff Franklin made this film as revenge for a broken heart or he actually thinks this rubbish is funny. Unpleasant characters populate this story about two lovers, French Stewart and Bridgette Wilson, who torture each other with malicious pranks once their romance goes south. The film presents women as greedy, manipulative ice queens while men are seen as sex-obsessed, commitment-phobic pigs. Flat jokes and non-existent chemistry between the leads also contributes to a truly excruciating viewing experience.

French Stewart *Seth Winnick* • Bridgette Wilson *Chelsea Turner* • Bill Bellamy *Larry Garnett* • Tyra Banks *Holly Garnett* • Steve Hytner *Marty Mark* • Jason Bateman *Jesse Travis* • Tiffani-Amber Thiessen *Rebecca Melini* ■ *Dir/Scr* Jeff Franklin

Love Story ★★ U
Romantic melodrama 1944 · UK · BW · 108mins

This is one of those tragic romances in which all concerned would have been spared a lot of tears if just one of the lovers had bothered to give the other an inkling of the truth. But with former pilot Stewart Granger keeping mum about his incipient blindness and pianist Margaret Lockwood equally reticent about her terminal illness, we are guaranteed angst aplenty. Tom Walls adds to our woes with a shocking performance as a Yorkshireman sent to renovate some tin mines. This is the kind of stiff-upper-lipped hokum they don't make any more – thank heavens! [video]

Margaret Lockwood *Lissa Campbell* • Stewart Granger *Kit Firth* • Patricia Roc *Judy Martin* • Tom Walls *Tom Tanner* • Reginald Purdell *Albert* • Moira Lister *Carol* • Dorothy Bramhall *Susie* • Vincent Holman *Prospero* • Joan Rees *Ariel* ■ *Dir* Leslie Arliss • *Scr* Leslie Arliss, Doreen Montgomery, Rodney Ackland, from the story by JW Drawbell

Love Story ★★★ PG

Romantic drama 1970 · US · Colour · 95mins

A heady mixture of love and life-threatening illness, as Ali MacGraw succumbs to cancer, which was roundly condemned by critics in its day but became a massive box office hit. This has to be taken at its emotionally laden face value or not at all. Drown in the excess of it all and it's a two box of Kleenex number. This can be enormously refreshing, but bring even the remotest hint of cynicism to bear and it grates like fingernails on a blackboard. And remember, this was made at a time when everyone was drooling over Ryan O'Neal. Contains swearing and sex scenes. ▢

Ali MacGraw *Jenny Cavilleri* • Ryan O'Neal *Oliver Barrett IV* • Ray Milland *Oliver Barrett III* • Katherine Balfour *Mrs Oliver Barrett III* • John Marley *Phil Cavilleri* • Russell Nype *Dean Thompson* • Sydney Walker *Dr Shapeley* • Robert Modica *Dr Addison* • Tom Lee Jones [Tommy Lee Jones] *Hank* ■ *Dir* Arthur Hiller • *Scr* Erich Segal, from his novel

Love Streams ★★ 15

Drama 1984 · US · Colour · 134mins

Not one of John Cassavetes's better efforts, *Love Streams* casts the director's wife, Gena Rowlands, as a woman going through marital breakdown who finds solace with her alcoholic brother, played by Cassavetes. Much of the dialogue sounds like typical American psycho-babble, making the movie less of a drama and more of a confessional, "let it all hang out" therapy session. The result is intense, well-acted and more than a little tedious. ▢

Gena Rowlands *Sarah Lawson* • John Cassavetes *Robert Harmon* • Diahnne Abbott *Susan* • Seymour Cassel *Jack Lawson* • Margaret Abbott *Margarita* ■ *Dir* John Cassavetes • *Scr* John Cassavetes, Ted Allan, from a play by Ted Allan

The Love Test ★★★

Comedy 1935 · UK · BW · 63mins

This early romantic comedy from director Michael Powell features one of Bernard Miles's first appearances, as well as an early outing for Googie Withers, whom Powell claimed "brings sunshine into dull lives, makes bald hair grow". Judy Gunn stars as a laboratory overseer up against her male employees. Initially successful, Gunn has to work to outwit her adversaries, who plot to oust her by making her fall in love. Only rediscovered in the late eighties, *The Love Test* demonstrates Powell's fascination with strong women, while the glamorisation of Gunn is a definite forerunner to Sister Ruth's transformation in *Black Narcissus*.

Judy Gunn *Mary* • Louis Hayward *John* • David Hutcheson *Thompson* • Morris Harvey *President* • Googie Withers *Minnie* • Aubrey Dexter *Vice-President* • Bernard Miles *Allan* ■ *Dir* Michael Powell • *Scr* Selwyn Jepson, from a story by Jack Celestin

Love That Brute ★★★

Crime comedy 1950 · US · BW

Good-natured fun in a Runyonesque tale of a soft-hearted gangster (Paul Douglas) who falls for a naive innocent (Jean Peters). He pretends to have

children in order to hire her as a governess. The prohibition-era story was a remake of *Tall, Dark and Handsome* (1941), which starred Cesar Romero, who takes the villain's role this time round. If the earlier version was a little livelier, this one has the advantage of sterling comic players like Joan Davis and Arthur Treacher, and a fine portrayal of blustering surface toughness from Douglas, who had earlier triumphed on Broadway in a similar role in *Born Yesterday*.

Paul Douglas *Big Ed Hanley* • Jean Peters *Ruth Manning* • Cesar Romero *Pretty Willie* • Keenan Wynn *Bugs* • Joan Davis *Mamie* • Arthur Treacher *Quentin* • Peter Price *Harry* • Jay C Flippen *Biff* ■ *Dir* Alexander Hall • *Scr* Karl Tunberg, Darrell Ware, John Lee Mahin

Love Thy Neighbour ★

Comedy 1973 · UK · Colour · 84mins

The attitudes on display in this film based on the seventies TV comedy series are so dated that they are more laughable than offensive. Time, however, hasn't dimmed its spectacular unfunniness – if ever a sitcom less deserved elevation to the big screen then this was it. Watch it only to boggle at a career low point for a number of well known British faces.

Jack Smethurst *Eddie Booth* • Rudolph Walker *Bill Reynolds* • Nina Baden-Semper *Barbie* • Kate Williams *Joan Booth* • Charles Hyatt *Joe* ■ *Dir* John Robins • *Scr* Vince Powell, Harry Driver

Love to Kill ★★ 15

Comedy thriller 1997 · US · Colour · 102mins

Modestly offbeat gangster thriller, with a video-friendly cast of familiar faces. Former Taxi star Tony Danza is a gunrunner looking to go straight who gets dragged back into his old world when he and his partner (co-writer Rustam Branaman) go on a double date with girlfriend Elizabeth Barondes and her sister (Amy Locane). The latter ends up dead and the duo must then get rid of her body while avoiding rival crook Michael Madsen. It's nicely played, although it tries a little too hard for quirkiness. ▢

Tony Danza *Moe* • Elizabeth Barondes *Monica* • James Russo *Branaman* • Louise Fletcher *Gloria* • Rustam Branaman *Franco* • Amy Locane *Beth* • Michael Madsen *Donnelly* • Brian Brophy *Harry* • Richmond Arquette *Lizard* ■ *Dir* James Bruce • *Scr* Rustam Branaman, Monica Clemens

Love! Valour! Compassion! ★★★ 15

Comedy drama 1997 · US · Colour · 109mins

Joe Mantello's poignant adaptation of Terrence McNally's award-winning play explores the differing emotions and attitudes (sexual and otherwise) of eight gay men staying at a glorious country retreat. Set over three American holiday weekends, this is an involving if overly sentimental study of human relationships, with a talented ensemble cast that includes John Glover as flip-sided twins and an ultra-camp Jason Alexander providing the film's comic relief. Despite the absence of any straight characters, the film's honesty and insight into human

nature makes it accessible to all audiences. ▢

Jason Alexander *Buzz Hauser* • Randy Becker *Ramon Fornos* • Stephen Bogardus *Gregory Mitchell* • John Glover *John Jeckyll/James Jeckyll* • John Benjamin Hickey *Arthur Pape* • Justin Kirk *Bobby Brahms* • Stephen Spinella *Perry Sellars* ■ *Dir* Joe Mantello • *Scr* Terrence McNally, from his play

Love Walked In ★★ 15

Crime thriller 1997 · US/Arg · Colour · 87mins

Having won an Emmy for *Life Stories*, director Juan Jose Campanella attempted a latterday *noir* here, as struggling pianist Dennis Leary and singer wife, Aitana Sanchez-Gijon conspire with sleazy private eye, Michael Badalucco, to sting wealthy Terence Stamp with a divorce scam. But, while the thriller elements are established efficiently enough, Campanella spends too much time on staging episodes from Leary's horror scribblings, which, while revealing something of his warped mind, distract unneccesarily from the action. Contains swearing and some violence. ▢

Denis Leary *Jack Morrisey* • Aitana Sanchez-Gijon *Vicky* • Terence Stamp *Fred Moore* • Michael Badalucco *Eddie* • Gene Canfield *Joey* • Marj Dusay *Mrs Moore* • Moira Kelly *Vera* • Neal Huff *Howard* ■ *Dir* Juan Jose Campanella • *Scr* Lynn Geller, Larry Golin, Juan Jose Campanella, from the novel *Ni el Tiro del Final* by Jose Pablo Feinmann

The Love Waltz ★★★

Comedy 1930 · Ger · BW · 70mins

The operettas produced by UFA, the famed German production company, in the early sound era were so universally popular, they were often remade in foreign language versions. John Batten steps in for Willy Fritsch in this English re-working of the romance between a commoner and a princess destined for marriage to an ageing archduke. With her beautiful voice and deliciously light comic touch, London-born Lilian Harvey shows why she was one of Germany's biggest stars, but Batten lacks the charisma to justify her jilting Georg Alexander. Producer Erich Pommer provides the plushest of sets, but the going gets a little heavy towards the happy ending.

Julia Serda *Duchess of Lauenburg* • Lilian Harvey *Princess Eva* • Karl Ludwig Diehl *Court Marshal* • Lotte Spira *Archduchess Melany* • Georg Alexander *Archduke Peter Ferdinand* • Hans Junkermann *Fould* • John Batten *Bobby* • Viktor Schwannecke *Dr Lemke* • Dir Wilhelm Thiele [William Thiele], Carl Winston • *Scr* Hans Müller, Robert Liebmann

Love Will Tear Us Apart ★★

Drama 1999 · HK · Colour · 114mins

Having served as cinematographer on the uncompromisingly realistic *Xiao Wu* and *Ordinary Heroes*, Nelson Lik-Wai Yu's directorial debut more closely resembles the work of Wong Kar-Wai. With four mainland exiles trying to acclimatise to the frantic pace of Hong Kong, the picture gets off to a busy start. But there's less here than meets the eye, in spite of a touching performance from Lu Liping as the lame ex-dancing teacher now reduced to operating an elevator. Less effective are Tony Leung Kar-Fai as the manager

of a porn video shop, Wong Ning's humiliated hooker and Rolf Chow's darkly secretive eccentric. In Cantonese with English subtitles.

Tony Kar-Fai Leung [Tony Leung (2)] *Jian* • Lu Liping *Yan* • Wong Ning *Ying* • Rolf Chow *Chun* ■ *Dir/Scr* Nelson Lik-Wai Yu

Love with the Proper Stranger ★★★★

Comedy drama 1963 · US · BW · 100mins

After a one-night stand, demure Natalie Wood gets pregnant and jazz musician Steve McQueen does one of those wonderful, trademark double-takes when she tells him the news. This is a fresh and very touching drama, set against the religion and staunch family traditions of New York's Italian community. Even when the script begins to run out of ideas – you can only have so many "will she have an abortion?" scenes – the gorgeous Wood and McQueen have more than enough charisma to fill the screen without saying a single word.

Natalie Wood *Angie Rossini* • Steve McQueen *Rocky Papasano* • Edie Adams *Barbie, Barbara of Seville* • Herschel Bernardi *Dominick Rossini* • Tom Bosley *Anthony Colombo* • Harvey Lembeck *Julio Rossini* • Penny Santon *Mama Rossini* • Virginia Vincent *Anna* ■ *Dir* Robert Mulligan • *Scr* Arnold Schulman

Loved ★★ 15

Drama 1996 · US · Colour · 99mins

No doubt all the people involved in this project had their hearts and best intentions in the right place, but this drama ultimately fumbles the sensitive subject of domestic violence. Director Erin Dignam (who also wrote the script) manages to turn in an almost insulting and poorly paced drama which does its well-meaning cast a disservice. Robin Wright Penn is the woman still in love with her ex-partner despite his abuse, who is asked to testify against him by DA William Hurt, after another of the man's lovers throws herself in front of a car. Wright Penn is left with little to do other than walk around barefoot to convey her distress, while Hurt sleepwalks through his part. Look out for an extraordinary cameo from Sean Penn. Contains some swearing and nudity. ▢

William Hurt *KD Dietrickson* • Robin Wright [Robin Wright Penn] *Hedda* • Amy Madigan *Brett* • Joanna Cassidy *Elenore* • Paul Dooley *Leo* • Anthony Lucero *Defendent* • Jennifer Rubin *Debra* • Sean Penn *Michael* ■ *Dir/Scr* Erin Dignam

The Loved One ★★

Black comedy farce
1965 · US · BW · 122mins

Although he ranks among the most admired British novelists of the century, the cinema has not been kind to Evelyn Waugh. Given that this novel, set in a California pet cemetery, is overladen with scathing swipes at Hollywood and American notions of the afterlife, screenwriters Terry Southern and Christopher Isherwood (themselves acclaimed novelists) might have produced a darker, more bitingly satirical script. However, director Tony Richardson and his all-star cast make the most of their opportunities before events descend into broad farce. Rod Steiger is shudderingly awful as the mortician Mr Joyboy, but spot-on cameos from James Coburn and Lionel Stander just about compensate.

Robert Morse *Dennis Barlow* • Rod Steiger *Mr Joyboy* • Jonathan Winters *Harry Glenworthy/ Wilbur Glenworthy* • Anjanette Comer *Aimee Thanatogenos* • Dana Andrews *General Brinkman* • Milton Berle *Mr Kenton* • John Gielgud *Sir Francis Hinsley* • James Coburn *Immigration Officer* • Tab Hunter *Guide* • Liberace *Mr Starker* • Lionel Stander *Guru Brahmin* ∎ *Dir* Tony Richardson • *Scr* Terry Southern, Christopher Isherwood, from the novel by Evelyn Waugh

The Loveless ★★ 18

Drama 1981 · US · Colour · 79mins

Willem Dafoe's first major screen role was in this comatose existential biker movie co-directed by Kathryn Bigelow. Dafoe nd neo-rockabilly singer Robert Gordon are members of a rough-and-tumble biker gang who, on en route to Daytona, get stranded in a small southern town where they swagger and sneer a lot and put the narrow-minded locals' backs up. It all ends in violence but not before the bikers strike homoerotic poses and discuss the meaninglessness of life. But nothing could be more meaningless than this post-modern *The Wild One* without the charisma of a Marlon Brando to carry it on sheer star quality alone.

Willem Dafoe *Vance* • Robert Gordon *Davis* • Marin Kanter *Telena* • J Don Ferguson *Tarver* • Tina L'Hotsky *Sportster Debbie* • Lawrence Matarese *LaVille* ∎ *Dir* Monty Montgomery, Kathryn Bigelow • *Scr* Kathryn Bigelow

Lovely to Look At ★★★ U

Musical comedy 1952 · US · Colour · 101mins

Delightful to know, this is the sumptuous MGM remake of the old RKO musical hit *Roberta*, an early vehicle for Fred Astaire and Ginger Rogers who co-starred in it with Irene Dunne. The superb Jerome Kern score has been retained, and the songs, notably *Smoke Gets in Your Eyes* and *I Won't Dance*, still scintillate, especially when they're handled by such marvellous musical movie artists as Howard Keel, Ann Miller, and Marge and Gower Champion. Although the whole film is nominally directed by Mervyn LeRoy, the wonderfully Technicolored fashion show sequence was actually directed by one of the great stylists of the screen, Vincente Minnelli. Red Skelton's mugging and MGM's very Hollywood Paris may grate today, but there's no denying the talent on parade here.

Kathryn Grayson *Stephanie* • Red Skelton *Al Marsh* • Howard Keel *Tony Naylor* • Marge Champion *Clarisse* • Gower Champion *Jerry Ralby* • Ann Miller *Bubbles Cassidy* • Zsa Zsa Gabor *Zsa Zsa* ∎ *Dir* Mervyn LeRoy • *Scr* George Wells, Harry Ruby, Andrew Solt, from the musical *Roberta* by Jerome Kern, Dorothy Fields, Otto Harbach, from the novel *Roberta* by Alice Duer Miller

A Lovely Way to Go ★

Thriller 1968 · US · Colour · 103mins

This is a lifeless, excessively complicated detective story that fails to deliver suspense, wit or romance. Kirk Douglas is wasted as the ex-cop hired by Eli Wallach's wily lawyer to protect Sylva Koscina, young unfaithful wife, on trial for murdering her husband. Douglas brings his usual vitality to bear but Koscina is bland and there is no energy between them. Kenneth Haigh portrays a playboy and Ali McGraw makes her screen debut.

Kirk Douglas *Jim Schuyler* • Sylva Koscina *Rena Westabrook* • Eli Wallach *Tennessee Fredericks* • Kenneth Haigh *Jonathan Fleming* • Sharon Farrell *Carol* • Gordon Peters *Eric* • Martyn Green *Finchley* • Doris Roberts *Feeney* • Carey Nairnes *Harris* • Ralph Waite *Sean Magruder* • Ali MacGraw *Melody* ∎ *Dir* David Lowell Rich • *Scr* AJ Russell

The Lover ★★ 18

Erotic drama 1992 · Fr/UK · Colour · 110mins

Jean-Jacques Annaud raised a few eyebrows back in 1992 with this steamy tale of a girl's sexual awakening in 1920s Indo-China. Based on Marguerite Duras's novel, it did feature young star Jane March in various states of undress, but there was really nothing much to get steamed up about. March plays a 15-year-old schoolgirl who ends up losing more than her inhibitions with older man Tony Leung – cue lots of exploration in darkened rooms, a voice-over by Jeanne Moreau, and a few deep and meaningful moments which March is too out of her (acting) depth to be able to convey.

Jane March *Young Marguerite Duras* • Tony Kar-Fai Leung [Tony Leung (2)] *Chinese man* • Frédérique Meininger *Mother* • Arnaud Giovaninetti *Elder brother* • Melvil Poupaud *Younger brother* • Lisa Faulkner *Hélène Lagonelle* ∎ *Dir* Jean-Jacques Annaud • *Scr* Jean-Jacques Annaud, Gérard Brach, from the novel by Marguerite Duras

A Lover and His Lass ★★★

Comedy 1975 · Swe · Colour · 94mins

Talk about humble beginnings. This is the debut feature of Lasse Hallstrom, the Swedish director who achieved international fame with *My Life as a Dog*, before making *What's Eating Gilbert Grape* and *Something to Talk About* in Hollywood. Brasse Brännström (who also provided the story for the film) stars as a shiftless young man who is charm personified, but whose vocabulary does not include the words "fidelity" or "employment". Also known as *A Guy and His Gal*, this is a ribald, well-observed comedy, but what makes it worthwhile are the winning performances. In Swedish with English subtitles.

Brasse Brännström *Lasse* • Mariann Rudberg *Lena* • Christer Jonsson *Bosse* • Börje Ahlstedt *Lasse's Brother* • Chatarina Larsson *Ulla* ∎ *Dir* Lasse Hallström • *Scr* Lasse Hallström

Lover Come Back ★★★

Romantic comedy 1961 · US · Colour · 104mins

Another dig at the world of advertising featuring Doris Day, this time reuniting her with her *Pillow Talk* co-star Rock Hudson. This ultra-glossy romantic comedy is very much of its period, but the idea of Madison Avenue executives marketing a nonexistent product (called VIP) remains a good one, and the anti-advertising jokes are still funny. Day and Hudson get fine comic back-up from Tony Randall as the indecisive agency boss, Edie Adams as a chorus girl and Jack Kruschen as the "inventor" of the non-product. Stanley Shapiro and Paul Henning's script was Oscar-nominated, though the finale (watch and wince) is astoundingly tasteless.

Rock Hudson *Jerry Webster* • Doris Day *Carol Templeton* • Tony Randall *Peter Ramsey* • Edie Adams *Rebel Davis* • Jack Oakie *J Paxton Miller* ∎ *Dir* Delbert Mann • *Scr* Stanley Shapiro, Paul Henning • *Costume Designer* Irene

Loverboy ★★★ 15

Comedy 1989 · US · Colour · 94mins

Patrick Dempsey is the pizza delivery boy bringing more than just a deep pan with extra cheese to a somewhat silly comedy from *Crossing Delancey* director Joan Micklin Silver. Carrie Fisher, Kirstie Alley and Barbara Carrera are just three of the women falling for his charms, and Dempsey proves to be an engaging lead. Light-hearted and well played nonsense. Contains some swearing.

Patrick Dempsey *Randy Bodek* • Kate Jackson *Diane Bodek* • Kirstie Alley *Joyce Palmer* • Carrie Fisher *Monica Delancy* • Robert Ginty *Joe Bodek* • Nancy Valen *Jenny Gordon* • Charles Hunter Walsh *Jory Talbot* • Barbara Carrera *Alex Barnett* ∎ *Dir* Joan Micklin Silver • *Scr* Robin Schiff, Tom Ropelewski, Leslie Dixon, from a story by Robin Schiff

The Lovers ★★★★ 15

Drama 1958 · Fr · BW · 86mins

A *succès de scandale* on its release, Louis Malle's second feature won him the special jury prize at Venice. Although it may no longer have the power to shock, it's still got plenty to admire, first and foremost Henri Decaë's glossy black-and-white photography which helps set the film apart from most other French pictures of the New Wave era. Jeanne Moreau is also superb as the seductive socialite who seeks casual affairs to relieve the boredom of her perfect life. The celebrated 20-minute love scene she shares with Jean-Marc Bory looks a little stylised today, but it remains notable for its bold portrayal of passion and rebellion. In French with English subtitles..

Jeanne Moreau *Jeanne Tournier* • Alain Cuny *Henri Tournier* • Jean-Marc Bory *Bernard Dubois-Lambert* • Judith Magre *Maggy Thiebaut-Leroy* ∎ *Dir* Louis Malle • *Scr* Louis Malle, Louise de Vilmorin, from the novel *Point de Lendemain* by Dominique Vivant

The Lovers ★★★

Comedy 1972 · UK · Colour · 88mins

Lasting just 13 episodes on ITV in the early seventies, this popular sitcom was another stepping stone in the careers of creator Jack Rosenthal and director Michael Apted. It didn't exactly harm the prospects of Richard Beckinsale or Paula Wilcox, either, as the Mancunian couple who tiptoe towards commitment in spite of his passion for Manchester United and her refusal to entertain encounters with "Percy Filth". As Beryl, Wilcox delightfully combines prudery and bourgeois snobbery, while Beckinsale's "Geoffrey Bubbles Bon Bon" is wonderfully helpless as he veers between laddism and romance. Hardly hilarious, but rather sweet.

Paula Wilcox *Beryl* • Richard Beckinsale *Geoffrey* • Joan Scott *Beryl's mum* • Stella Moray *Geoffrey's mum* • Nikolas Simmonds *Roland* • Susan Littler *Sandra* • Anthony Naylor *Neville* • Bruce Watt *Jeremy* • John Comer *Geoffrey's dad* ∎ *Dir* Herbert Wise • *Scr* Jack Rosenthal

Lovers ★★★ 18

Erotic thriller 1991 · Sp · Colour · 104mins

Making her sixth feature for director Vicente Aranda, Victoria Abril won the Best Actress award at Berlin for her performance in this re-enactment of a true-life *crime passionnel*. Set in mid-fifties' Madrid, the film eschews any political subtext in order to concentrate on the romantic entanglements of soldier Jorge Sanz who honours fiancée Maribel Verdu's virginity by satiating his lust with landlady Abril. The action is beautifully shot but it lacks the sense of smouldering passion that might precipitate murder. Nevertheless, Abril is stunning and Verdu a picture of innocence, with only the unconvincing Sanz letting the side down. In Spanish with English subtitles. Contains violence, swearing and nudity.

Victoria Abril *Luisa* • Jorge Sanz *Paco* • Maribel Verdu *Trini* • Enrique Cerro *Commandant* • Mabel Escano *Commandant's Wife* • José Cerro *Minuta* ∎ *Dir* Vicente Aranda • *Scr* Carlos Perez Merinero, Alvaro Del Amo, Vicente Aranda • *Cinematographer* José Luis Alcaine

Lovers and Other Strangers ★★★★ 15

Comedy 1970 · US · Colour · 104mins

This caustic and very funny wedding comedy shows what happens to a couple's extended family when they decide to get married. The cast contains so many exquisite performances that it seems invidious to single out anyone in particular. Gig Young, however, is simply terrific as the father of the bride (Bonnie Bedelia.) Director Cy Howard knows when to step back and let the excellent script (based on a play by Renee Taylor and Joseph Bologna) speak for itself. Look out for Diane Keaton in her screen debut.

Bonnie Bedelia *Susan Henderson* • Gig Young *Hal Henderson* • Michael Brandon *Mike Vecchio* • Beatrice Arthur *Bea Vecchio* • Richard Castellano *Frank Vecchio* • Robert Dishy [Bob Dishy] *Jerry* • Harry Guardino *Johnny* • Diane Keaton *Joan* ∎ *Dir* Cy Howard • *Scr* Renee Taylor, Joseph Bologna, David Zelag Goodman, from a play by Renee Taylor, Joseph Bologna

Lover's Knot ★

Comedy 1995 · US · Colour · 88mins

This dire romantic comedy stars Tim Curry as a cosmic matchmaker in the service of Cupid, instructed to splice Jennifer Grey and Bill Campbell together forever. The pair, it turns out, have been karmically entwined for several lifetimes but have failed to clinch a happy ending. Curry's job is to sort them out once and for all. In a peculiar mishmash of documentary-style interviews, past life flashbacks and comments from the likes of

William Shakespeare this is, quite frankly, a terrible mess. An undo-able knot.

William Campbell [Bill Campbell] *Steve Hunter* • Jennifer Grey *Megan Forrester* • Tim Curry *Cupid Caseworker* • Adam Baldwin *John Reed* • Mark Sheppard *Nigel Bowles* • Tom McTigue *Doug Meyers* • Holly Fulger *Gwen Meyers* • Adam Ant *Marvell* ■ *Dir/Scr* Pete Shaner

Lovers Must Learn ★★★
Romantic drama
1962 · US · Colour · 118mins

Back in the sixties, teenage heart-throbs Troy Donahue and Suzanne Pleshette had their every move detailed in America's fan magazines. In this lush and soapy Warner Bros tale – a sort of *One Coin in the Fountain* – they are co-stars, though they did not marry until 1964. Librarian Pleshette is vacationing in Rome and can't choose between callow but good-looking architect Donahue, and sophisticated foreign roué Rossano Brazzi. Angie Dickinson gets all the best lines as Donahue's other woman, Max Steiner contributes one of his most romantic later scores, and director Delmer Daves knows just how far to go with his material. It's tosh on a grand scale, and very enjoyable.

Troy Donahue *Don Porter* • Angie Dickinson *Lyda* • Rossano Brazzi *Roberto Orlandi* • Suzanne Pleshette *Prudence Bell* • Constance Ford *Daisy* • Al Hirt *Al* • Chad Everett *Young man* ■ *Dir* Delmer Daves • *Scr* Delmer Daves, from the novel by Irving Fineman • *Music* Max Steiner

The Lovers of the Arctic Circle ★★★★ 15
Romantic drama 1998 · Sp · Colour · 104mins

Though not as well-known outside Spain as Pedro Almodóvar, the work of Basque director Julio Medem is just as iconoclastic and compelling. Medem gained a slew of fans with *Vacas*, *Tierra* and *The Red Squirrel*, but his latest metaphysical romance is his most inventive and accessible work to date. From the age of eight, Otto (Fele Martinez) and Ana (Najwa Nimri) know they are destined to be together. However, fate keeps intervening well into adulthood, forcing their on again/off again relationship to weather their being apart for long stretches. Will they ever be reunited? Employing an unusual narrative technique that blurs both lovers' perspectives together, and a dazzling style that confuses time periods and repeats certain key scenes, this dreamy rumination on unrequited love, chance and coincidence is a wonderfully rich and potent fable for our times. In Spanish with English subtitles. 🎬 *DVD*

Fele Martinez *Otto* • Najwa Nimri *Ana* • Nancho Novo *Alvaro* • Maru Valdivielso *Olga* ■ *Dir/Scr* Julio Medem

The Loves and Times of Scaramouche ★★
Comedy 1976 · It · Colour · 95mins

Italian director Enzo Girolami Castellari was one of the most under-rated makers of spaghetti westerns and he handles the battle sequences in this costume adventure with vigorous assurance. But he was not at his best with comedy and neither the slapstick swashbuckling nor the cod history merit more than the occasional wry smile. As the womanising scoundrel caught up in an assassination attempt on Napoleon, Michael Sarrazin hams it up so shamelessly that he barely leaves sidekick Giancarlo Prete or Ursula Andress (as an unlikely Josephine) any room to manoeuvre. An Italian film dubbed into English.

Michael Sarrazin *Scaramouche* • Ursula Andress *Josephine* • Aldo Maccione *Napoleon* • Giancarlo Prete • Michael Forest • Nico Il Grande • Romano Puppo • Massimo Vanni • Alex Togni • Damir Mejovsek • Lucia De Oliveira ■ *Dir* Enzo G Castellari • *Scr* Enzo G Castellari, Tito Carpi

Love's Labour's Lost
★★★ U
Romantic musical comedy
1999 · US/Fr/UK · Colour · 93mins

Kenneth Branagh gives his Shakespearean adaptation a lift by combining this story of four sets of lovers with a host of thirties and forties song-and-dance numbers. Adrian Lester shines in a sublime musical set piece, and Natascha McElhone again demonstrates her depth and beauty. The film is flawed, though. The environment never transcends the feel of a studio, American stars Alicia Silverstone and Matthew Lillard are clumsy and miscast, and Branagh has lost some of the play's complexity by oversimplifying the text. Though very enjoyable in places, *Love's Labour's Lost* has the feel of a West End show and displays little of Branagh's immense talent and imagination as a film-maker.

Kenneth Branagh *Berowne* • Nathan Lane *Costard, the clown* • Adrian Lester *Dumaine* • Matthew Lillard *Longaville* • Natascha McElhone *Rosaline* • Alessandro Nivola *King* • Alicia Silverstone *Princess* • Timothy Spall *Don Armado* • Richard Briers *Nathaniel* • Richard Clifford *Boyet* • Carmen Ejogo *Maria* • Daniel Hill *Mercade* • Geraldine McEwan *Holofernia* • Emily Mortimer *Katherine* ■ *Dir* Kenneth Branagh • *Scr* Kenneth Branagh, from the play by William Shakespeare

The Loves of Carmen ★★★
Drama 1948 · US · Colour · 96mins

There's no Bizet here, and hardly much of author Prosper Mérimée's great original either, as the director and stars of the immortal drama *Gilda* reunite to tell another tale of *amour fou* beneath blazing skies. Sadly, it doesn't quite gel. Not only is there no darker underside, but the forties Technicolor casts a bizarre and garish glow over the proceedings. Glenn Ford, barely out of juvenile leads and a long way from his mature roles in the fifties, is arguably the most unlikely Don Jose ever, but Hayworth looks absolutely ravishing.

Rita Hayworth *Carmen Garcia* • Glenn Ford *Don Jose* • Ron Randell *Andres* • Victor Jory *Garcia* • Luther Adler *Dancaire* • Arnold Moss *Colonel* • Joseph Buloff *Remendado* ■ *Dir* Charles Vidor • *Scr* Helen Deutsch, from the story *Carmen* by Prosper Mérimée

The Loves of Joanna Godden ★★★
Drama 1947 · UK · BW · 89mins

A classic example of how the documentary-style story (so popular with post-war British film-makers) could result in pictures as crashingly dull as they were worthy. The story centres on Edwardian farmer Googie Withers, whose determination to make good as a sheep breeder and protect her spoiled sister (Jean Kent) forces her to discard a trio of eager beaus (John McCallum, Chips Rafferty and Derek Bond). There is plenty of incident, but the realism beloved of director Charles Frend is scarcely appropriate for such ripe melodrama.

Googie Withers *Joanna Godden* • Jean Kent *Ellen Godden* • John McCallum *Arthur Alce* • Derek Bond *Martin Trevor* • Henry Mollison *Harry Trevor* • Chips Rafferty *Collard* ■ *Dir* Charles Frend • *Scr* He Bates, Angus MacPhail, from the novel *Joanna Godden* by Sheila Kaye-Smith

The Loves of Three Queens ★★
Drama 1954 · It/Fr · Colour · 90mins

Having been frustrated by the cancellation of her comeback picture, *Queen Esther and the King of Egypt*, Hedy Lamarr signed up for this project for Marc Allégret. Originally intended to be a three-hour investigation into the mysteries of womanhood, the oft-altered screenplay had Lamarr question three male friends about which historical figure she should impersonate at a masquerade ball and then appear in vignettes prompted by their answers – Helen of Troy, the Empress Josephine and Geneviève de Brabant. Instead, Edgar G. Ulmer shot some uncredited linking sequences and the picture was released to little acclaim.

Hedy Lamarr *Hedy Windsor/Helen of Troy/Empress Josephine/Geneviève de Brabant* • Gérard Oury *Napoleon Bonaparte* • Massimo Serato *Paris* • Robert Beatty *Menelaus* • Cathy O'Donnell *Oenone* • Guido Celano *Jupiter* • Rico Glori *Priamus* • Seren Michelotti *Cassandra* • Alba Arnova *Venus* ■ *Dir* Marc Allégret, Edgar G Ulmer • *Scr* Nino Novarese, Marc Allegret, Salka Viertel, from a story by Aeneas MacKenzie, Vadim Plenianikov, Marc Allégret, Hugh Gray

Lovesick ★★★ 15
Romantic comedy
1983 · US · Colour · 91mins

Long-time Woody Allen collaborator Marshall Brickman made his second outing as writer/director with this droll comedy in which psychiatrist Dudley Moore falls helplessly in love with patient Elizabeth McGovern. The unlikely pairing works a treat thanks to the coy performances and several nifty one-liners. There are also some knowing cameos from Ron Silver, Wallace Shawn and legendary director John Huston. Yet Brickman overuses the *Play It Again, Sam* device of having Alec Guinness pop up as Sigmund Freud to remind Moore of his ethical responsibilities, just as he's about to abandon himself to his emotions. Nevertheless, this is time well spent on any couch. 🎬

Dudley Moore *Saul Benjamin* • Elizabeth McGovern *Chloe Allan* • Alec Guinness *Sigmund Freud* • Renee Taylor *Mrs Mondragon* • Ron Silver *Ted Caruso* • Gene Saks *Frantic patient* • Christine Baranski *Nymphomaniac* • David Strathairn *Zuckerman* ■ *Dir/Scr* Marshall Brickman

Lovespell ★
Drama 1979 · US · Colour · 91mins

Even die-hard Wagner fans will detest this incompetent retelling of the amorous tragedy of Tristan and Isolde. Richard Burton makes a splendid king, but Kate Mulgrew (of *Star Trek: Voyager* fame) is rather too mature to play his Juliet-like bride. Filmed on lush Irish locations, the language is as parched as a desert, while Tom Donovan's direction is woefully lacking for a story that needs tender, loving care if audiences are to be convinced of its contemporary relevance.

Richard Burton *King Mark of Cornwall* • Kate Mulgrew *Iseult* • Nicholas Clay *Tristan* • Cyril Cusack • Geraldine Fitzgerald ■ *Dir* Tom Donovan

Lovestruck ★★
Romantic comedy 1997 · US · Colour

Even the terminally romantic may find this undistinguished TV-movie comedy a little hard to stomach. Costas Mandylor plays the winged matchmaker Cupid, sent to Earth to help Cynthia Gibb but shooting himself in the foot instead. Seventies pin-up Suzanne Somers pops up as Venus, with Mandylor suitably hunky as her amorous messenger, but only those with very sweet tooths should sample this sickly concoction.

Cynthia Gibb *Emily Vale* • Costas Mandylor *Cupid on Earth* • Annabelle Gurwitch *Rachel* • Suzanne Somers *Venus* • Mark Joy *Ted* • Tyler Noyes *Cupid* ■ *Dir* Larry Peerce • *Scr* Lindsay Harrison, Stephen Witkin, from a story by Stephen Witkin

Lovin' Molly ★★
Drama 1974 · US · Colour · 97mins

A misfire from director Sidney Lumet who misjudges himself after his success with *Serpico*, as if he wanted to be known for more artier things than just New York crime movies. This sprawling yarn covers 40 years – from 1925 onwards – in the lives, loves and deaths of a Texan family. Based on Larry McMurtry's novel *Leaving Cheyenne*, it needed a far more melodramatic approach — like *Giant*, say – than Lumet's more cerebral style, and the running time is inadequate to cope with the soapy story.

Anthony Perkins *Gid* • Beau Bridges *Johnny* • Blythe Danner *Molly* • Edward Binns *Mr Fry* • Susan Sarandon *Sarah* • Conrad Fowkes *Eddie* ■ *Dir* Sidney Lumet • *Scr* Stephen J Friedman, from the novel *Leaving Cheyenne* by Larry McMurtry

Loving ★★★★
Comedy drama 1970 · US · Colour · 89mins

It takes all George Segal's under-used skill to touch our sympathy here, playing a character who is well out of charm's way – an ageing commercial artist heading for mental and marital breakdown. As his emotionally devoted

but drained wife, Eva Marie Saint is outstandingly forbearing, enough to make us wonder why she married him in the first place. But then again, there is a glimmer in Segal that explains it. Contains swearing.

George Segal *Brooks Wilson* • Eva Marie Saint *Selma Wilson* • Sterling Hayden *Lepridon* • Keenan Wynn *Edward* • Nancie Phillips *Nelly* • Janis Young *Grace* • David Doyle *Will* • Paul Sparer *Marve* • Andrew Duncan *Willy* • Sherry Lansing *Susan* ■ *Dir* Irvin Kershner • *Scr* Don Devlin, from the novel *Brooks Wilson, Ltd* by JM Ryan

Loving Couples ★★
Romantic comedy
1980 · US · Colour · 97mins

Shirley MacLaine and James Coburn are the middle-aged married couple who spice up their relationship with a spot of partner-swapping with younger (and more glamorous) Susan Sarandon and Stephen Collins. While MacLaine enjoys the charms of her toyboy, Coburn looks extremely uncomfortable with a woman almost young enough to be his daughter on his arm. All the embarrassing May-September clichés are dredged up, as the oldies try not to act their age, and despite a talented cast this never gets beyond the predictable.

Shirley MacLaine *Evelyn* • James Coburn *Walter* • Susan Sarandon *Stephanie* • Stephen Collins *Gregg* • Sally Kellerman *Mrs Liggett* • Nan Martin *Walter's nurse* ■ *Dir* Jack Smight • *Scr* Martin Donovan

Loving in the Rain ★★
Romantic drama
1974 · Fr · Colour

Considering he had emerged as an actor during the auteur era and that this was the fourth of his six outings as a director, Jean-Claude Brialy invests surprisingly little personality in this understated melodrama. It's a proficient job, but pretty pictures and steady performances don't make for enthralling cinema. Experienced scenarist Jean-Claude Carrière co-wrote the script that makes only a cursory exploration of the emotions experienced by Romy Schneider and Bénédicte Boucher, as the mother and teenage daughter indulging in a holiday romance. Moreover, it gives their respective partners, Nino Castelnuovo and Alain David, next to nothing to do. Sensitive, but insubstantial. In French with English subtitles.

Romy Schneider *Elisabeth* • Nino Castelnuovo *Giovanni* • Suzanne Flon *Edith* • Bénédicte Boucher *Cecile* ■ *Dir* Jean-Claude Brialy • *Scr* Jean-Claude Brialy, Jean-Claude Carrière, from a story by Yves Simon

Loving You ★★★ U
Musical drama 1957 · US · Colour · 101mins

Elvis Presley's second movie (the first under famous producer Hal B Wallis) gives us a precious look at the King in his rock 'n' roll prime. The plot allows Presley to re-enact his rise to stardom, under the guidance here of director Hal Kanter, who studied Presley on stage beforehand for authenticity. Musical highlights include *Teddy Bear* and *Lonesome Cowboy* (the film's original title). Scorned in its day (but not by fans), this looks better by the decade, and Presley's natural screen presence

reminds us of his considerable early raw talent.

Elvis Presley *Deke Rivers* • Lizabeth Scott *Glenda Markle* • Wendell Corey *Tex Warner* • Dolores Hart *Susan Jessup* • James Gleason *Carl Meade* ■ *Dir* Hal Kanter • *Scr* Herbert Baker, Hal Kanter, from the story *A Call from Mitch Miller* by Mary Agnes Thompson • *Cinematographer* Charles Lang Jr [Charles Lang]

A Low Down Dirty Shame ★★ 18
Action spoof 1995 · US · Colour · 92mins

After scoring several direct hits with his blaxploitation spoof, *I'm Gonna Git You Sucka*, Keenen Ivory Wayans shoots high and wide with this scattergun parody of *film noir* crime pictures. Clearly spreading himself too thin, Wayans seems to be the only performer with real faith in his script, which is woefully predictable and too often settles for the easy (and occasionally offensive) gag. His direction is equally sloppy, and he fails to rein in the excessive exuberance of Jada Pinkett Smith.

Keenen Ivory Wayans *Shame* • Charles S Dutton *Rothmiller* • Jada Pinkett [Jada Pinkett Smith] *Peaches* • Salli Richardson *Angela* • Andrew Divoff *Mendoza* • Corwin Hawkins *Wayman* • Gary Cervantes *Luis* • Gregory Sierra *Captain Nunez* • Kim Wayans *Diane* ■ *Dir/Scr* Keenen Ivory Wayans

The Low Life ★★
Comedy drama 1995 · US · Colour · 98mins

Excellent central performances from a first-rate young cast can't save this clinically depressing character study. There's no life in this tale of a wannabe writer (Rory Cochrane) coming to LA only to find himself stuck in low-paying temp jobs and lumbered with a girlfriend (Kyra Sedgwick) uninterested in serious commitment. Occasionally funny and touching, ultimately this takes too long in getting nowhere in particular. Look out for a pre-*Jerry Maguire* Renee Zellweger.

Rory Cochrane *John* • Kyra Sedgwick *Bevin* • Ron Livingston *Chad* • Christian Meoli *Leonard* • Sara Melson *Suzie* • James LeGros *Mike Jr* • Sean Astin *Andrew* • JT Walsh *Mike Sr* • Renee Zellweger *Poet* ■ *Dir* George Hickenlooper • *Scr* George Hickenlooper, from the story by John Enbom

The Lower Depths ★★★
Drama 1936 · Fr · BW · 95mins

Having secured the dying Maxim Gorky's permission to rework parts of his celebrated socialist play, cinema's leading humanist, Jean Renoir, proceeded to produce his darkest film of the Popular Front period. Although there's a rapport between impoverished baron Louis Jouvet and petty thief Jean Gabin (particularly during their charming riverbank exchange), the sense of community that existed in *Le Crime de Monsieur Lange* has been replaced by a survivalist individualism, as they seek to out-manoeuvre landlord, Vladimir Sokoloff. As ever, Renoir's compositional flair is to the fore, with a strolling, deep-focus camera endlessly picking up significant expressions, gestures and details. In French with English subtitles.

Jean Gabin *Pépel* • Louis Jouvet *The baron* • Suzy Prim *Vassilissa* • Jany Holt *Nastia* • Vladimir Sokoloff *Kostyley* • André Gabriello *Commisaire Toptun* ■ *Dir* Jean Renoir • *Scr* Eugène Zamiatine, Jacques Companeez, Jean Renoir, Charles Spaak, from a play by Maxim Gorky

The Loyal 47 Ronin ★★★★
Historical epic 1941 · Jap · BW · 222mins

Threatened with closure by the government for its failure to produce enough National Policy pictures, the Shochiku studio was reprieved by Kenji Mizoguchi's offer to shoot the second part of this historical epic under its auspices. Set in the early 1700s, the action follows the revenge of Oishi and his fellow samurai on Kira, the evil warlord who had tricked their master, Asano, into committing hara-kiri. Large scale historicals were not the director's forte, but he opened out this fact-based Kabuki standard to spectacular effect. In Japanese with English subtitles.

Yoshisaburo Arashi *Takuminokami, Lord Asano* • Mantoyo Mimasu *Kozunosuke, Lord Kira* • Chojuro Kawarazaki *Kuranosuke Oishi* ■ *Dir* Kenji Mizoguchi • *Scr* Kenichiro Hara, Yoshikata Yoda

Lucas ★★★★ 15
Comedy drama 1986 · US · Colour · 95mins

Corey Haim gives an excellent performance in this sweet, simple and cliché-free study of first love. As Lucas, the serious kid whom half the school wouldn't notice unless they tripped over him, he is warm, witty and wise beyond his years, and his earnest conversations with heart's desire Kerri Green are small masterpieces of observation. But true love can never run smoothly, especially when there are sporty bozos like school football star Charlie Sheen bestriding the primrose path. Winona Ryder made her debut (as one of Lucas's schoolfriends) in this delightful comedy from writer/director David Seltzer. Contains swearing.

Corey Haim *Lucas Blye* • Kerri Green *Maggie* • Charlie Sheen *Cappie* • Courtney Thorne-Smith *Alise* • Winona Ryder *Rina* • Thomas E Hodges [Tom Hodges] *Bruno* ■ *Dir/Scr* David Seltzer

Lucia ★★ 15
Opera drama 1998 · UK · Colour · 102mins

Drawing on the old "life imitating art" formula, Don Boyd uses scenes from the opera *Lucia di Lammermoor* to comment on the doomed romance between soprano Amanda Boyd and tenor Richard Coxon. The pair are to co-star in *Lucia* just as she enters into a loveless marriage (sanctioned by her impoverished brother) to a dissolute millionaire. Essentially this is a feature-length opera video, with stylised visuals that often distract from the determinedly contemporary arrangements. Stiffly acted and archly staged, yet filmed with boundless imagination and passion, this has its rewards.

Amanda Boyd *Kate Ashton, "Lucia"* • Richard Coxon *Sam Ravensword, "Edgardo"* • Ann Taylor *Alice, "Alisa"* • John Daszak *Norman, "Normanno"* • Andrew Greenan *Raymond, "Raimondo"* • John Osborn *Oliver Hickox, "Arturo"* • Mark Holland *Hamish Ashton,*

"Enrico" • Mark Shanahan *Conductor, London Studio* ■ *Dir* Don Boyd • *Scr* Don Boyd, from the opera *Lucia Di Lammermoor* by Gaetano Donizetti, from the novel *The Bride of Lammermoor* by Sir Walter Scott

Lucie Aubrac ★★ 12
Wartime drama 1997 · Fr · Colour · 115mins

Remarkable true tale of love in adversity, with Daniel Auteuil as a French resistance worker taken prisoner by the Gestapo, and Carole Bouquet as the devoted wife who risks all to save him. Surprisingly, considering cast calibre and intrinsic drama of storyline, the film is a rather dull and plodding affair, with director Claude Berri maybe more concerned with sticking faithfully to facts rather than exploiting the story's full cinematic potential. The required territory gets covered, but there's no depth, no sense of getting under the skin of the characters and their intense love for each other. A sensational tale, but merely a solid movie.

Carole Bouquet *Lucie Bernard* • Daniel Auteuil *Raymond Samuel* • Patrice Chéreau *Max* • Eric Boucher *Serge* • Jean-Roger Milo *Maurice* • Heino Ferch *Klaus Barbie* • Jean Martin *Paul Lardanchet* • Andrzej Seweryn *Lieutenant Schlondorff* • Pascal Greggory *Hardy* ■ *Dir* Claude Berri • *Scr* Claude Berri, Arlette Langmann, from the novel *Outwitting the Gestapo (Ils Partiront dans l'Ivresse* by Lucie Aubrac, Claude Berri

Lucifer Rising ★★★
Underground 1981 · US · Colour · 29mins

Using rather startling free-association imagery, such as flying saucers hovering over the Temple of Luxor, this is one of the better Kenneth Anger "visual music" avant-garde movies (ie no plot or acting to speak of). Anger himself plays a Magus who invokes Lucifer, celebrating his rebirth with a birthday cake with Lucifer Mark VI written in pink icing. The eclectic cast includes Marianne Faithfull, director Donald Cammell, and Leslie Huggins, a hunky young Middlesbrough steel worker, in the title role. An earlier version of the film, shot in 1966, was stolen and buried in the Mojave desert by the musician Bobby Beausoleil, currently serving a life sentence for murder.

Miriam Gibril *Isis* • Donald Cammell *Osiris* • Haydn Couts *The Adept* • Kenneth Anger *The Magus* • Sir Francis Rose *Chaos* • Marianne Faithfull *Lilith* • Leslie Huggins *Lucifer* ■ *Dir* Kenneth Anger • *Scr* Kenneth Anger, from the poem *Hymn to Lucifer* by Aleister Crowley

The Luck of Ginger Coffey ★★★
Drama 1964 · US/Can · BW · 99mins

Robert Shaw and Mary Ure star as Irish immigrants in freezing Montreal, coping with his unemployment, their separation and their daughter's decision to live with her father. A slight story but an affecting one, due to the wealth of everyday detail created by writer Brian Moore and director Irvin Kershner. Shaw and Ure, a tempestuous married couple off-screen, give an immensely satisfying portrayal of a love that somehow endures.

Robert Shaw *Ginger Coffey* • Mary Ure *Vera* • Liam Redmond *MacGregor* • Tom Harvey *Joe McGlade* • Libby McClintock *Paulie* • Leo Leyden *Brott* ■ *Dir* Irvin Kershner • *Scr* Brian Moore, from his novel

Luck, Trust & Ketchup: Robert Altman in Carver
★★★ 15

Documentary   1994 · US · Colour · 89mins

Try to excuse the lousy title, for this is a highly entertaining and informative documentary about director Robert Altman, his films and his methods. Recorded during the making of *Short Cuts*, it has a day-in-the-life feel that makes it an ideal companion piece to that film, but there are also dozens of little insights that have a bearing on Altman's entire output. Co-directed by longtime colleague Mike Kaplan, this little-seen feature also contains interviews with the principal members of the *Short Cuts* cast, not all of whom present themselves in the most favourable light. Contains some swearing. ▭

Dir Mike Kaplan, John Dorr

The Luckiest Man in the World
★★

Comedy   1989 · US · Colour · 82mins

Unassuming but nicely played drama about a businessman discovering a conscience after a near death experience. Philip Bosco delivers a believable performance as the middle-aged man out to make up for past mistakes and he is ably supported by a largely unknown cast. The intelligent script and direction is from Frank D Gilroy.

Philip Bosco *Sam Posner* • Doris Belack *Mrs Posner* • Joanne Camp *Laura* • Matthew Gottlieb *Sheldon* • Arthur French *Cleveland* • Stan Lachow *Schwartz* • Moses Gunn *The Voice* ■ *Dir/Scr* Frank D Gilroy

Lucky and Zorba
★★★★

Animation   1998 · It · Colour · 75mins

This charming animation is not only uplifting in its simple message of acceptance and co-operation, but also refreshingly free of the lazy sentimentality that characterises so much commercial cartooning. The most expensive animated film ever made in Italy, Enzo D'Alo's feature chronicles the friendship between an orphan seagull named Lucky and Zorba, the cat who taught her to fly. But, spicing up the action, is Big Rat, who plans to leads a rodentine revolution by enslaving the world's cats. Beautifully drawn and touchingly entertaining, this is a delight. Italian dialogue dubbed into English.

Dir Enzo D'Alo • *Scr* Enzo D'Alo, Umberto Marino, from the story *Story of a Seagull and the Cat Who Taught Her to Fly* by Luis Sepulveda

Lucky Day
★★★

Drama   1991 · US · Colour · 93mins

Every now and then a film gets performances that it scarcely deserves. That is the case with this manipulative tear-jerker, in which a mentally disabled woman becomes the subject of a custody battle after she wins $2

million on the state lottery. Chloe Webb is totally convincing as the tug-of-war victim, whose cosy relationship with her caring sister is shattered by the return of their alcoholic mother. Carefully avoiding being too perfect, Amy Madigan is suitably selfless as the understanding sibling, while Olympia Dukakis spits bile as she tries to undo years of neglect.

Amy Madigan *Karl* • Olympia Dukakis *Katherine Campbell* • Chloe Webb *Allison* • Terence Knox *Nick* • John Beasley *Bo* • Allen Hamilton *Tom* ■ *Dir* Donald Wrye • *Scr* John Axeness, Jennifer Miller

Lucky Devils
★★★

Action adventure   1933 · US · BW · 64mins

Following on from George Cukor's successful *What Price Hollywood?* the previous year, came this pacey comedy/drama also set in Tinseltown. Based on a story by stuntman Bob Rose, who also appears in the film, this is just an excuse for stuntmen William Boyd (later Hopalong Cassidy) and William Gargan to go through their paces. Boyd also gets the girl in the person of Dorothy Wilson. Among the cast is Lon Chaney Jr, credited under his real name of Creighton Chaney. The highlights of the movie are the spectacular stunts, including a climactic ride over a waterfall in a rowing boat.

Bill Boyd [William Boyd] *Skipper* • William Gargan *Bob* • Bruce Cabot *Happy* • William Bakewell *Slugger* • Creighton Chaney [Lon Chaney Jr] *Frankie* • Bob Rose *Rusty* • Dorothy Wilson *Fran* • Sylvia Picker *Toots* ■ *Dir* Ralph Ince • *Scr* Ben Markson, Agnes Christine Johnston, from a story by Casey Robinson, Bob Rose

Lucky Jim
★★★★ U

Comedy   1957 · UK · BW · 91mins

Kingsley Amis's comic masterpiece was one of the most influential English novels of the fifties. The Boulting brothers' film adaptation misses the subtle nuances, barbed satire and deliciously sly characterisation of the book, but you will find that this makes for surprisingly agreeable entertainment. Ian Carmichael gives a good account of himself as Jim Dixon, the disaster-prone lecturer whose career in the red-bricked halls of academe gets off to the worst possible start, while those masters of comic support Hugh Griffith and Terry-Thomas are bang on form. ▭

Ian Carmichael *Jim Dixon* • Terry-Thomas *Bertrand Welch* • Hugh Griffith *Professor Welch* • Sharon Acker *Christine Callaghan* • Jean Anderson *Mrs Welch* • Maureen Connell *Margaret Peel* • Clive Morton *Sir Hector Gore-Urquhart* ■ *Dir* John Boulting • *Scr* Jeffrey Dell, Patrick Campbell, from the novel by Kingsley Amis

The Lucky Lady
★★

Silent romantic comedy   1926 · US · BW

A silent movie, directed by the admirable Raoul Walsh early in his career, in which the young Princess Antoinette (Greta Nissen) sneaks out of her convent school to see a travelling theatre show. There she meets youthful American William Collier Jr and falls in love with him. This doesn't go down well at the palace where they have lined up

lecherous Lionel Barrymore as her future husband. Set in the fictional principality of San Guido, this romantic comedy – a sort of operetta without the music – has a certain charm, but it's well past its sell-by date for all but silent movie devotees.

Greta Nissen *Antoinette* • Lionel Barrymore *Count Ferranzo* • William Collier Jr *Clarke* • Marc MacDermott *Franz Garletz* ■ *Dir* Raoul Walsh • *Scr* James T O'Donohoe, Robert Emmet Sherwood, from a story by Bertram Bloch • *Cinematographer* Victor Milner

Lucky Lady
★

Comedy   1975 · US · Colour · 118mins

Gene Hackman and Liza Minnelli were both recent Oscar-winners, and Burt Reynolds was at the peak of his stardom. Yet audiences somehow sensed *Lucky Lady* was a stinker and stayed away in droves. Since Hackman took over at the last minute from George Segal (who was ill), the romantic rivalry between the two leading men is negligible, while Minnelli never seems comfortable in her role as the nightclub singer they fall for. The plot, meanwhile – which has Hackman and Reynolds trying to smuggle bootleg liquor across the Mexican border – sinks like a stone.

Gene Hackman *Kibby* • Liza Minnelli *Claire* • Burt Reynolds *Walker* • Geoffrey Lewis *Captain Aaron Mosley* • John Hillerman *Christy McTeague* • Robby Benson *Billy Webber* • Michael Hordern *Captain Rockwell* • Anthony Holland *Mr Tully* ■ *Dir* Stanley Donen • *Scr* Willard Huyck, Gloria Katz

Lucky Luciano
★★★★ 18

Biographical crime drama
1973 · Fr/It · Colour · 105mins

Francesco Rosi's sociological melodrama, set in America and Italy, reveals the criminal network – both legal and illegal – for which Lucky Luciano was the crime kingpin. While Rod Steiger was the leading gangster in *Al Capone* (1959), here it's Gian Maria Volonté. More complex than a simple dirty-rat-tat-tat view of the world, Volonté is excellent, but Steiger's hard-man performance upstages all the political nuances by sheer power. ▭

Gian Maria Volonté *Lucky Luciano* • Rod Steiger *Gene Giannini* • Charles Siragusa • Vincent Gardenia *American colonel* ■ *Dir* Francesco Rosi • *Scr* Francesco Rosi, Tonino Guerra

Lucky Me
★★ U

Comedy musical   1954 · US · Colour · 96mins

Doris Day sings as delightfully as ever and acts with breezy gusto, but this musical about show business hopefuls – her penultimate film under her contract at Warner Bros – is substandard. Talents like Phil Silvers, Nancy Walker and Eddie Foy are wasted, and Day is saddled with an inappropriate leading man in Robert Cummings (where was Gordon MacRae?). The songs, by the *Calamity Jane* team of Sammy Fain and Paul Francis Webster, also disappoint, though *I Speak to the Stars* and *Bluebells of Broadway* had a measure of popularity. Angie Dickinson can be spotted making her screen debut as a guest in a party scene near the film's end. ▭

Doris Day *Candy Williams* • Robert Cummings *Dick Carson* • Phil Silvers *Hap Snyder* • Eddie Foy Jr *Duke McGee* • Nancy Walker *Flo Neely* • Martha Hyer *Lorraine Thayer* • Bill Goodwin *Otis Thayer* • Marcel Dalio *Anton* • Hayden Rorke *Tommy Arthur* • Angie Dickinson *Party guest* ■ *Dir* Jack Donohue • *Scr* James O'Hanlon, Robert O'Brien, Irving Elinson, from a story by James O'Hanlon

Lucky Partners
★★★ U

Comedy   1940 · US · BW · 99mins

This would-be sophisticated frothy comedy is somewhat let down by the uncomfortable pairing of its two leads. Perky Ginger Rogers, then at her professional peak, and urbane Ronald Colman fail to jell in an American remake of Sacha Guitry's 1935 French film *Bonne Chance*. It's not a bad idea, that old sweepstakes win-plus-honeymoon plot, but it seems too lightweight for Colman, under veteran Lewis Milestone's experienced, if slightly heavy-handed, direction. Still, fans of the two great stars won't want to miss.

Ginger Rogers *Jean Newton* • Ronald Colman *David Grant* • Jack Carson *Freddie* • Spring Byington *Aunt* • Cecilia Loftus *Mrs Sylvester* • Harry Davenport *Judge* • Billy Gilbert *Charles* ■ *Dir* Lewis Milestone • *Scr* Allan Scott, John Van Druten, from the film *Bonne Chance* by Sacha Guitry

The Lucky Star
★★★

Second World War drama
1980 · Can · Colour · 110mins

A Texan twist on the idea of Nazi occupation makes this Canadian family adventure original, to say the least. A young Dutch Jew (Brett Marx), fascinated by westerns, sees his parents taken away by the Germans. So he sets about kidnapping the colonel (Rod Steiger) he holds responsible. Directed by Max Fischer from a script he co-wrote with TV playwright Jack Rosenthal, it manages to say something imaginative about this emotive period of 20th-century history.

Rod Steiger *Col Gluck* • Louise Fletcher *Loes Bakker* • Lou Jacobi *Elia Goldberg* • Brett Marx *David Goldberg* • Helen Hughes *Rose Goldberg* ■ *Dir* Max Fischer • *Scr* Max Fischer, Jack Rosenthal, from a idea by Roland Topor

The Lucky Stiff
★★

Comedy drama   1949 · US · BW · 99mins

Jack Benny produced this undistinguished comedy/whodunit, but decided against appearing in it, just as top producer Leo McCarey thought about taking it on and then didn't. Leading lady Dorothy Lamour, on loan from Paramount, ended up co-starring with character actor Brian Donlevy under the direction of writer Lewis R Foster. Lamour is too pallid for her part of a shady nightclub singer (but at least it allows her to perform one number). Donlevy pursues a gang of protection racketeers, while Claire Trevor does all the scene stealing as his long-suffering secretary. Jack Benny never produced another picture.

Dorothy Lamour *Anna St Claire* • Brian Donlevy *John J Malone* • Claire Trevor *Marguerite Seaton* • Irene Hervey *Mrs Childers* • Marjorie Rambeau *Hattie Hatfield* • Robert Armstrong *Von Flanagan* • Billy Vine *Joe Di*

U = SUITABLE FOR ALL   Uc = SUITABLE FOR ALL, ESPECIALLY FOR YOUNG CHILDREN (VIDEO ONLY)   PG = PARENTAL GUIDANCE

Angelo • Warner Anderson *Eddie Britt* ■ *Dir* Lewis R Foster • *Scr* Lewis R Foster, from the novel by Craig Rice

The Lucky Texan ★ U

Western   1934 · US · BW · 54mins

One of those irritating programme fillers that mixes contemporary icons – in this case a model "T" Ford in a chase sequence – with traditional western elements. The clean-cut John Wayne provides the heroism, and Lloyd Whitlock and stuntman Yakima Canutt the villainy. But really, unless these minor movies are your cup of tea, it's not very good. ▣

John Wayne *Jerry Mason* • Barbara Sheldon *Betty* • George Hayes [George "Gabby" Hayes] *Jake Benson* • Yakima Canutt *Cole* • Gordon DeMaine *Sheriff* ■ *Dir/Scr* Robert N Bradbury

Lucky to Be a Woman ★★★

Comedy drama   1955 · It · BW · 95mins

Having established themselves as a romantic team in *Too Bad She's Bad*, Marcello Mastroianni and Sophia Loren were reunited for what is, in many ways, a dry run for *La Dolce Vita*. Oozing languid charm, Mastroianni revels in the anti-heroic antics of the scurrilous paparazzo whose cheeky snap of Loren's legs persuades lecherous aristocrat Charles Boyer to transform her into a movie star. Strewn with in-jokes and satirical pot-shots at the supposedly sophisticated worlds of film and high fashion, this polished comedy is as artificial as its target. But Alessandro Blasetti's smooth direction and the accomplished performances give it an easy charm. An Italian language film.

Sophia Loren *Antoinette* • Charles Boyer *Count Gregorio* • Marcello Mastroianni *Corrado* • Nino Besozzi *Film producer* ■ *Dir* Alessandro Blasetti • *Scr* Suso Cecchi D'Amico, Ennio Flaiano, Alessandro Continenza, Alessandro Blasetti

Lucy and Desi: before the Laughter ★★★

Biographical romantic drama 1991 · US · Colour

A well-performed TV drama based on the pre-*I Love Lucy* days of Desi Arnaz and Lucille Ball before the oddly-matched couple became a worldwide TV phenomenon. The pluses are honesty – this is no hearts-and-flowers hagiography – and Frances Fisher's performance as brittle but bubbly Ball. The forties' and fifties' period detail is impeccable, and the scenes inside a TV company as it prepares to broadcast the first *I Love Lucy* show are fascinating for media buffs. The movie fails to totally lift the lid on what we now know was a deeply troubled relationship, but it makes a welcome change from previous deifications of the Titian-haired fireball.

Frances Fisher *Lucille Ball* • Maurice Benard *Desi Arnaz* • Robin Pearson Rose *Vivian Vance* • John Wheeler *William Frawley* • Bette Ford *De-De Ball* • Edith Diaz *Mother Arnaz* ■ *Dir* Charles Jarrott • *Scr* William Luce, Cynthia A Cherbak, from a story by William Luce

Lucy Gallant ★★★ U

Drama   1955 · US · Colour · 104mins

Dressmaker Jane Wyman devotes herself to work and becomes a successful female fashion-house mogul, but the price of her independence is a rocky ride in her love life. Charlton Heston is the man involved in this particular battle of the sexes. The supporting cast includes Thelma Ritter and Claire Trevor (both irresistible) and a rare on-screen appearance from Edith Head, winner of eight Oscars, who also designed the costumes. Haute couture, VistaVision and deft direction by Robert Parrish contribute to the enjoyment of this typical 1950s "woman's picture".

Jane Wyman *Lucy Gallant* • Charlton Heston *Casey Cole* • Claire Trevor *Lady MacBeth* • Thelma Ritter *Molly Basserman* • William Demarest *Charles Madden* • Wallace Ford *Gus Basserman* • Tom Helmore *Jim Wardman* • Gloria Talbott *Laura Wilson* • Edith Head ■ *Dir* Robert Parrish • *Scr* John Lee Mahin, Winston Miller, from the novel *The Life of Lucy Gallant* by Margaret Cousins

Ludwig ★★

Historical biography 1973 · It/W Ger/Fr · Colour · 136mins

This is director Luchino Visconti's study of mad King Ludwig of Bavaria, whose obsession with Wagner's music inspired him to build a series of fairy-tale castles and lose what was already a tenuous hold on sanity before his operatic death by drowning. In the title role, Helmut Berger looks the part – pouting, wild and very pretty – and the castles themselves are stunning backdrops. Trevor Howard makes an honourable stab at Wagner and Romy Schneider is simply gorgeous as Ludwig's unhappy, sex-starved bride Empress Elizabeth. But Visconti's approach is rather too solemn, and the movie drags rather, despite being cut down from its original four hours. An Italian language film.

Helmut Berger *Ludwig* • Romy Schneider *Empress Elisabetta* • Trevor Howard *Richard Wagner* • Silvana Mangano *Cosima Von Bulow* • Gert Fröbe *Father Hoffman* • Helmut Griem *Captain Durckeim* • Isabella Telezynska *Queen Mother* • Umberto Orsini *Count Von Holstein* ■ *Dir* Luchino Visconti • *Scr* Luchino Visconti, Enrico Medioli, Suso Cecchi D'Amico

Ludwig – Requiem for a Virgin King ★★★

Historical drama 1972 · W Ger · Colour · 139mins

The inner and outer life, real and imagined, of the mad castle-building King of Bavaria is told in 28 chapters, or tableaux vivants. Cheaply made, and using a blend of theatrical techniques such as backdrops and back projections, Hans Jürgen Syberberg's collage of German history, culture and psychology – at different moments puerile, fatuous, stimulating, amusing and over-extended – says far more about Ludwig than Luchino Visconti's glossy film on the same subject. In German with English subtitles.

Harry Baer *Ludwig II of Bavaria* • Balthasar Thomas *Small Ludwig* • Peter Kern *Lackey Mayr/Hairdresser Hoppe/Röhm* • Oscar von Schab *Ludwig I/Karl May* ■ *Dir/Scr* Hans Jürgen Syberberg

Lullaby of Broadway ★★ U

Musical comedy   1951 · US · Colour · 88mins

Despite its promising title and the presence of Doris Day, this tailor-made vehicle is one of Warner Bros's least effective movies. Still, there are points in its favour: the songs though seriously underperformed and staged, are nevertheless memorable, and the amiable and talented Gene Nelson is an effective leading man. Warners veteran Gladys George brings all her experience to bear playing Day's wayward mum, and presumably taught Doris a trick or two about acting in the process, but, if ever a movie looked undirected, it's this one. ▣

Doris Day *Melinda Howard* • Gene Nelson *Tom Farnham* • SZ Sakall *Adolph Hubbell* • Billy De Wolfe *"Lefty" Mack* • Gladys George *Jessica Howard* • Florence Bates *Mrs Hubbell* • Anne Triola *Gloria Davis* ■ *Dir* David Butler • *Scr* Earl Baldwin, from his story *My Irish Molly O*

Lulu Belle ★★★

Drama musical   1948 · US · BW · 86mins

This tougher than usual melodrama marked an attempt to change Dorothy Lamour's screen image: the amoral chanteuse she plays here is as far removed from the saronged lovelies of the *Road* series that her public adored as it's possible to be. Unfortunately, such a character is hard to like, though today's more cynical audiences might be better disposed to Lulu's manner of dealing with anyone who gets in her way. Lamour's early career as a singer provides her with real insights into the role and she proves how good an actress she could be with the right material, but she's not helped by the bland performance of leading man George Montgomery and the routine direction of British-born Leslie Fenton.

Dorothy Lamour *Lulu Belle* • George Montgomery *George Davis* • Albert Dekker *Mark Brady* • Otto Kruger *Harry Randolph* • Glenda Farrell *Molly Benson* • Greg McClure *Butch Cooper* • Charlotte Wynters *Mrs Randolph* ■ *Dir* Leslie Fenton • *Scr* Everett Freeman, Karl Kamb, from the play by Charles MacArthur, Edward Sheldon • *Cinematographer* Ernest Laszlo

Lulu on the Bridge ★

Mystery drama romance 1998 · US · Colour · 103mins

What begins promisingly – Harvey Keitel is a musician starting over after ashooting ends his career – quickly takes a turn for the bizarre. He finds a mysterious glowing stone, which not only leads him to aspiring actress Mira Sorvino but also causes them to fall in love. A first-rate cast is wasted in this esoteric and monotonous film. A twist ending doesnt help clear up any of the confusion, it just makes you happy that the movies over. Writer/director Paul Auster should have spent the production budget on a good therapist and saved us all a lot of trouble.

Harvey Keitel *Izzy Maurer* • Mira Sorvino *Celia Bums* • Willem Dafoe *Dr Van Horn* • Gina Gershon *Hannah* • Mandy Patinkin *Philip Kleinman* • Vanessa Redgrave *Catherine Moore* • Don Byron *Band Member No 1* • Richard Edson *Band Member No 2* • Victor

Argo Pierre • Kevin Corrigan *Man with Gun* • Harold Perrineau *Man in Coffeehouse* ■ *Dir/Scr* Paul Auster

Lumière Noire ★★★

Crime thriller   1994 · Fr · Colour

Best known for *Sarraounia*, his portrait of the 19th-century African warrior queen who took on the might of the French colonial army, the Mauritanian director Med Hondo is one of the most politically contentious and courageous of black African film-makers. This conspiracy thriller is something of a disappointment, therefore, with its theme of asylum-seeking and deportation shunted into a subplot. However, Hondo sustains the tension admirably, as French hologram engineer Patrick Poivey seeks the illegal immigrant from Mali whose eyewitness testimony alone can prove that the state has blood on its hands after Poivey's friend is murdered. In French with English subtitles..

Patrick Poivey *Yves Guyot* • Charlie Bauer *Detective Londrin* • Gilles Ségal *Inspector Cadin* • Roland Bertin *Judge Berthier* ■ *Dir* Med Hondo • *Scr* Med Hondo, Didier Daeninckx, from the novel by Didier Daeninckx

La Luna ★★★

Drama   1979 · It · Colour · 141mins

Director Bernardo Bertolucci's deliberately artificial tale of an opera diva, her heroin-addicted son and his search for a father figure caused quite a stir on its release. In the role of the diva, Jill Clayburgh seems to be mimicking Kiri Te Kanawa as she sings her way through the Verdi back catalogue. Sadly, the other performances are wooden; as always with Bertolucci, the real star of the show is Vittorio Storaro's exquisite photography.

Jill Clayburgh *Caterina Silveri* • Matthew Barry *Joe* • Laura Betti *Ludovica* • Fred Gwynne *Douglas Winter* • Veronica Lazar *Marina* • Renato Salvatori *Communist* • Tomas Milian *Giuseppe* • Alida Valli *Giuseppe's mother* • Roberto Benigni *Upholsterer* ■ *Dir* Bernardo Bertolucci • *Scr* Bernardo Bertolucci, Giuseppe Bertolucci, Clare Peploe, George Malko, from a story by Franco Arcalli, Bernardo Bertolucci, Giuseppe Bertolucci • *Music* Ennio Morricone

The Lunatic ★★ 15

Comedy   1992 · US · Colour · 94mins

Lol Creme, founder member of the pop group 10CC and renowned rock video director, makes his feature debut with this genial oddity which boasts a low-key quirky charm. Paul Campbell is the resident idiot of a Jamaican village who has a fling with insatiable German tourist Julie T Wallace. But it's when she also starts having an affair with Rastafarian butcher Carl Bradshaw that the romantic complications begin, especially once he sucks them both into burgling a white landowner. A film of minor appeal, but reasonably beguiling all the same. ▣

Julie T Wallace *Inga* • Paul Campbell *Aloysius* • Reggie Carter *Busha/Voice of Strongheart Tree* • Carl Bradshaw *Service* • Winston Stona *Linstrom* • Linda Gambrill *Sarah* • Rosemary Murray *Widow Dawkins* • Lloyd Reckord *Judge* ■ *Dir* Lol Creme • *Scr* Anthony C Winkler, from his novel

Lunatics: a Love Story
★★★ 15

Black comedy romance
1991 · US · Colour · 83mins

The influence of Sam Raimi's *The Evil Dead* marks this bizarre comedy about the relationship between a mismatched pair of kooks. Raimi's brother Ted plays Hank, whose psychological problems include hallucinations about doctors trying to "treat" him with outsize needles, and an inability to leave his tin-foil lined apartment. The object of his affections is Nancy (Deborah Foreman), who is convinced that she causes mayhem for anyone who comes into contact with her. Eccentric, and surprisingly charming, the film puts a comedic rather than horrific spin on Ted's bizarre visions, although perhaps at the expense of developing the romance. *The Evil Dead* connection is reinforced by the presence of Sam Raimi regular Bruce Campbell in the supporting cast.

Ted Raimi *Hank* • Deborah Foreman *Nancy* • Bruce Campbell *Ray* • George Aguilar *Comet* • Brian McCree *Presto* ■ *Dir/Scr* Josh Becker

Lunch Hour
★★

Comedy
1962 · UK · BW · 73mins

A well constructed but predictable bedroom farce adapted from his own play by John Mortimer. Tired of being interrupted during their midday trysts, wallpaper executive Robert Stephens and designer Shirley Anne Field book a hotel room, but then their problems really start. Directed at a fair lick by James Hill, this lively romp is admirably played, with Kay Walsh and Nigel Davenport's supporting turns particularly worthy of note, but there's often an excess of chat between the excruciating moments.

Shirley Anne Field *Girl* • Robert Stephens *Man* • Kay Walsh *Manageress* • Hazel Hughes *Aunty* • Michael Robbins *Harris* • Nigel Davenport *Manager* ■ *Dir* James Hill • *Scr* John Mortimer, from his play

Lunch on the Grass
★★★

Romance drama
1959 · Fr · Colour · 92mins

Jean Renoir, then 65, took 21 days to shoot this late work at Les Collettes, the house of his father Auguste Renoir, in the south of France. This hymn to nature is the great film director's only direct homage to his great Impressionist painter parent. Paul Meurisse is amusing as a supercilious biology professor experimenting with artificial insemination until he gets a beautiful peasant pregnant by conventional means. The rather reactionary satire also takes a dig at nuclear weapons, space travel and a united Europe, but delivers its message too simplistically and creates mere cardboard characters. In French with English subtitles.

Paul Meurisse *Etienne* • Catherine Rouvel *Nenette* • Fernand Sardou *Nino* • Jacqueline Morane *Titine* • Jean-Pierre Granval *Ritou* ■ *Dir/Scr* Jean Renoir

Lured
★★

Crime drama
1947 · US · BW · 102mins

A preposterous and bizarrely cast would-be thriller that, alas, is over-plotted beyond redemption. It's not helped by director Douglas Sirk's ham-fisted direction of his players, particularly Cedric Hardwicke. The incredible story involves showgirl Lucille Ball being used by Scotland Yard to trap a killer in a London seemingly made up of left-over Hollywood sets. Along the way Ball falls for suspect George Sanders, while censorship stops discussion of what is obviously a prostitution racket run by evil Joseph Calleia, who abruptly vanishes from the picture. There's an astoundingly daft sequence involving Boris Karloff that has to be seen to be believed.

George Sanders *Robert Fleming* • Lucille Ball *Sandra Carpenter* • Charles Coburn *Inspector Temple* • Boris Karloff *Artist* • Alan Mowbray *Maxwell* • Cedric Hardwicke *Julian Wilde* • George Zucco *Officer Barrett* ■ *Dir* Douglas Sirk • *Scr* Leo Rosten, from the 1939 film *Pièges* by Jacques Companeez, Ernest Neuville, Simon Gantillon

Lurking Fear
★ 18

Horror
1994 · US · Colour · 74mins

Romania stands in for Massachusetts in this very loose adaptation of an HP, Lovecraft story. C Courtney Joyner's rough-and-ready chiller features the usual motley group of good guys banding together after internal, and interminable, bickering to take on undead hordes at a derelict church. An in-joke horror cast of Jeffrey (*Re-Animator*) Combs, Paul (*Robinson Crusoe on Mars*) Mantee, Ashley (*Hellraiser*) Laurence – billed here as Lauren – and Jon (*Frenzy*) Finch, stagger through the clumsily directed action. The zombie creatures vaguely resembling *The Time Machine*'s Morlocks add to its grab-bag cult appeal which is really for die-hard enthusiasts only.

Jon Finch *Bennett* • Blake Bailey *John Martense* • Ashley Lauren [Ashley Laurence] *Cathryn* • Jeffrey Combs *Doctor Haggis* • Allison Mackie *Ms Marlowe* • Paul Mantee *Father Poole* ■ *Dir* C Courtney Joyner • *Scr* C Courtney Joyner, from a story by HP Lovecraft

Lush Life
★★★ 15

Drama
1993 · US · Colour · 105mins

Having made his name playing Charlie Parker in Clint Eastwood's outstanding biopic *Bird*, Forest Whitaker blows his own trumpet in this well-above-average TV movie. Jeff Goldblum co-stars as his sax-playing partner, living life to the full around the smoky clubs of New York, until Whitaker is diagnosed as having a brain tumour and given only a month to live. But if you've gotta go, then what better way than with the mother of all jazz gigs. A little melancholic in places, but the stars make a fine team and Lennie Niehaus's music will keep your toes tapping. Contains swearing, sex scenes and drug abuse.

Jeff Goldblum *Al Gorky* • Forest Whitaker *Buddy Chester* • Kathy Baker *Janice Gorky* • Tracey Needham *Sarah* • Lois Chiles *Lucy* • Don Cheadle *Jack* ■ *Dir/Scr* Michael Elias

Lust for a Vampire
★★ 18

Gothic horror
1970 · UK · Colour · 91mins

Veteran Hammer writer/director Jimmy Sangster called it "an embarrassment" in his autobiography, and Ralph Bates regretted ever starring in something so "tasteless". Both also hated the cheesy pop song *Strange Love* (by Tracy) incongruously dubbed over the love scene in this second of Hammer's Karnstein trilogy inspired by Sheridan Le Fanu's story *Carmilla*, with gratuitous lesbianism thrown into the gore formula. A shallow performance by ex-*Golden Shot* hostess Yutte Stensgaard and some pretty ragged sets fix the lurid tone even lower as terror stalks the corridors of an exclusive girls' finishing school. Contains nudity.

Ralph Bates *Giles Barton* • Yutte Stensgaard *Mircalla/Carmilla* • Barbara Jefford *Countess Herritzen* • Suzanna Leigh *Janet Playfair* • Michael Johnson *Richard Lestrange* ■ *Dir* Jimmy Sangster • *Scr* Tudor Gates, from the novel *Carmilla* by J Sheridan Le Fanu

Lust for Life
★★★★ PG

Biographical drama
1956 · US · Colour · 117mins

A catchpenny title (from the doorstop biography by Irving Stone) for an extremely superior example of the Hollywood biopic, the tortuous tale of Vincent van Gogh. The painter is uncannily well played by Kirk Douglas, who seems to capture the very essence of the tormented artist, though it was actually Anthony Quinn's Gauguin that won the Oscar for this movie. It's lovingly crafted by brilliant director Vincente Minnelli, the superb colour and CinemaScope cinematography is by the great Freddie Young, while the authentic Arles location and a fine Miklos Rozsa score are also major plus points. This intelligent, beautifully made film was never a commercial success, but it acquired a cult following, largely owing to Minnelli's colour sense and Douglas's magnificent crystalline performance.

Kirk Douglas *Vincent van Gogh* • Anthony Quinn *Paul Gauguin* • James Donald *Theo van Gogh* • Pamela Brown *Christine* • Everett Sloane *Dr Gachet* • Niall MacGinnis *Roulin* • Noel Purcell *Anton Mauve* • Henry Daniell *Theodorus van Gogh* • Madge Kennedy *Anna Cornelia van Gogh* • Jill Bennett *Willemien* ■ *Dir* Vincente Minnelli • *Scr* Norman Corwin, from the novel by Irving Stone

Lust for Murder
★★★ 15

Thriller
1993 · US · Colour · 84mins

Two couples go on holiday together to Florida and, to begin with, it's all sun, swimsuits and smiles. But murder is on the mind of one of the wives, played by Virginia Madsen. This brisk, moderately violent TV-movie suspense thriller commendably has several unexpected twists in its plot. Madsen is joined by Richard Thomas as her husband and by Ted McGinley and Laura Harrington as the couple who experience the ultimate holiday nightmare.

Virginia Madsen *Linda Cowley* • Richard Thomas *Paul Cowley* • Ted McGinley *Brandon "Jeff" Jeffries* • Laura Harrington *Stella*

Jeffries • TE Russell *David Hill* ■ *Dir* Nathaniel Gutman • *Scr* ND Schreiner, from the novella *Linda* by John D MacDonald

Lust in the Dust
★★ 15

Comedy western 1984 · US · Colour · 80mins

Considering this lame parody of vintage American and spaghetti westerns was directed by *Eating Raoul* director Paul Bartel and features a fabulous cult cast, the end result should have been much wilder and funnier than it actually is. Greedy gunslinger Tab Hunter, fiery cantina owner Lainie Kazan, saloon singer Divine and desperado Geoffrey Lewis team up to search for gold. Their only clue to its whereabouts is a cryptic limerick and the two halves of a treasure map tattooed on the buttocks of the film's leading ladies. Overall, though, it's a lifeless and lewd lampoon.

Tab Hunter *Abel Wood* • Divine *Rosie Velez* • Lainie Kazan *Marguerita Ventura* • Geoffrey Lewis *Hard Case Williams* • Henry Silva *Bernardo* • Cesar Romero *Father Garcia* • Woody Strode *Blackman* ■ *Dir* Paul Bartel • *Scr* Philip John Taylor

Lust of the Vampire
★★★★

Horror 1956 · It · BW · 65mins

Director Riccardo Freda fought with the producers of this seminal vampire chiller, walked out, and left ace cinematographer Mario Bava to complete the undead saga in two days. The stunning result set the seal on the future of Italian horror and prompted Hammer to mine the same Gothic vein in Britain. Beautiful "vampire" Gianna Maria Canale is kept artificially young by transfusions of blood from kidnapped girls in this haunting *Grand Guignol* tale of immortal obsession given the monstrously atmospheric spark of emotion by incredible black-and-white photography and amazing in-camera special effects. One of the most influential horror movies of all time. An Italian language film.

Gianna Maria Canale *Duchess Mararethe Du Grand* • Antoine Balpêtré *Professor Julien Du Grand* • Paul Müller *Joseph Signoret* ■ *Dir* Riccardo Freda • *Scr* Piero Regnoli, Rik Sjostrom • *Cinematographer* Mario Bava

The Lusty Men
★★★ U

Western 1952 · US · BW · 95mins

This touching, realistic drama stars Robert Mitchum as the former rodeo champ forced to retire through injury, and Arthur Kennedy as the young man whom Mitchum coaches. Of course, there's also a woman – Susan Hayward, who's married to Kennedy and takes Bob's fancy. Mitchum extended his range considerably with this role, and Lee Garmes's sombre black-and-white photography mirrors the characters' drab existence. A critical and box-office failure at the time, it is now regarded as one of director Nicholas Ray's finest films.

Susan Hayward *Louise Merritt* • Robert Mitchum *Jeff McCloud* • Arthur Kennedy *Wes Merritt* • Arthur Hunnicutt *Booker Davis* • Frank Faylen *Al Dawson* • Walter Coy *Buster Burgess* • Carol Nugent *Rusty Davis* • Maria Hart *Rosemary Maddox* ■ *Dir* Nicholas Ray • *Scr* Horace McCoy, David Dortort, from a story by Claude Stanush

U = SUITABLE FOR ALL   Uc = SUITABLE FOR ALL, ESPECIALLY FOR YOUNG CHILDREN (VIDEO ONLY)   PG = PARENTAL GUIDANCE

Luther ★★★

Historical drama   1974 · US/UK · Colour · 111mins

Playwright John Osborne's vivid portrayal of the religious revolutionary who famously broke with the Roman Catholic Church gets a rather lacklustre treatment here from director Guy Green, though Stacy Keach sweats a bundle as the cleric whose heavenly aspirations were always of the earthy variety. Osborne's deliberately matey dialogue is reduced to the level of tonsured chatter by a largely underused cast that includes Patrick Magee and Hugh Griffith, although Judi Dench is a rose among all those thorny tenets of faith.

Stacy Keach *Martin Luther* • Patrick Magee *Hans* • Hugh Griffith *Tetzel* • Robert Stephens *Von Eck* • Alan Badel *Cajetan* • Judi Dench *Katherine* • Leonard Rossiter *Weinand* • Maurice Denham *Staupitz* • Julian Glover *The Knight* ■ *Dir* Guy Green • *Scr* Edward Anhalt, from the play by John Osborne

Luv ★

Sex comedy   1967 · US · Colour · 95mins

In this tasteless sex comedy, imbued with all that dated sixties liberalism, Jack Lemmon is saved from suicide by former schoolmate Peter Falk; he repays the favour by wooing and then wedding Falk's unwanted wife (Elaine May). After that, things get complicated, desperate and embarrassing for all concerned. Adapted from Murray Schisgal's successful Broadway play, this is an unmitigated disaster, not helped by the fact that Lemmon and Falk switched parts just days before shooting started.

Jack Lemmon *Harry Berlin* • Peter Falk *Milt Manville* • Elaine May *Ellen Manville* • Nina Wayne *Linda* • Eddie Mayehoff *Attorney Goodhart* ■ *Dir* Clive Donner • *Scr* Elliott Baker, from a play by Murray Schisgal

Lyddie ★★★

Drama   1995 · Can · Colour

This Canadian TV movie is one of those all-too-rare commodities in modern cinema: an intelligent film for youngsters. Set in the 1860s, it follows the fortunes of a teenage country girl as she endures life in a big-city cotton mill to pay off the debts on her father's farm and reunite her family. There's danger, tragedy, poverty and a little love along the way, as Lyddie (Tanya Allen) attempts to overcome Victorian prejudices against women and better herself. Solidly played and carefully directed this is as entertaining as it is informative.

Tanya Allen *Lyddie* • Christianne Hirt *Diana* • Simon James *Luke* • Tom Georgeson *Mr Marsden* • Pat Keen *Mrs Bedlow* ■ • *Scr* Maggie Wadey, from the novel by Katherine Paterson

Lydia ★★★ U

Romantic drama   1941 · US · BW · 94mins

Sumptuously mounted but leisurely paced, this is an unofficial Hollywood retread of the French classic *Un Carnet de Bal*, made by the same director, Julien Duvivier. Here he reworks and actively improves upon the original, working for the émigré Hungarian producer/director Alexander Korda, who provides Duvivier with a fine cast, headed by Merle Oberon (Mrs Korda), in the title role. Extravagantly romantic, and some would say overly sentimental, it nevertheless sustains a fine bittersweet tone. The marvellous score by the great Miklos Rozsa received an nomination. 🔲

Merle Oberon *Lydia MacMillan* • Edna May Oliver *Granny* • Alan Marshal *Richard Mason* • Joseph Cotten *Michael Fitzpatrick* • Hans Yaray *Frank Audry* • George Reeves *Bob Willard* • John Halliday *Fitzpatrick the Butler* • Sara Allgood *Johnny's mother* ■ *Dir* Julien Duvivier • *Scr* Ben Hecht, Samuel Hoffenstein, from a story by Julien Duvivier, Laslo Bush-Fekete

Lydia Bailey ★★ U

Adventure   1952 · US · Colour · 87mins

Kenneth Roberts's epic novel, set during Haiti's war with Napoleonic forces in the 1880s, was so simplified for this screen version that the result seems like an empty, cut-price *Gone with the Wind*, with Anne Francis and Dale Robertson pale substitutes for Leigh and Gable. The scenic splendours and Harry Jackson's gorgeous colour camerawork are the film's prime attractions. Veteran director Jean Negulesco handles the drama professionally enough, but the underpowered casting and shallow script make the film seem longer than it is.

Dale Robertson *Albion Hamlin* • Anne Francis *Lydia Bailey* • Charles Korvin *d'Autremont* • William Marshall *King Dick* • Luis Van Rooten *Gen LeClerc* • Adeline De Walt Reynolds *Madame d'Autremont* • Angos Perez *Paul* • Bob Evans *Soldier* ■ *Dir* Jean Negulesco • *Scr* Michael Blankfort, Philip Dunne, from the novel by Kenneth Roberts

M ★★★★★ PG

Classic crime drama   1931 · Ger · BW · 110mins

Peter Lorre is the most under-rated actor in the history of Hollywood. In his later years, he was content to parody the sinister snivelling that made him so compelling to watch. Here, the familiar persona has a real edge of menace, as he plays the self-loathing child murderer whose crimes are always preceded by a chilling whistle. Making his talkie debut, Fritz Lang continues to fill the screen with the atmospheric expressionist images that made him Europe's pre-eminent silent director, but his use of sound is also inspired, whether in crowd scenes or details like the clicking-open of Lorre's knife. A masterpiece. In German with English subtitles. 🔲 **DVD**

Peter Lorre *Franz Becker* • Otto Wernicke *Inspector Lohmann* • Gustav Gründgens *Safebreaker* • Theo Lingen *Conman* • Inge Landgut *Child* • Ellen Widmann *Mother* • Fritz Odemar *Cheat* • Theodore Loos [Theodor Loos] *Groeber* ■ *Dir* Fritz Lang • *Scr* Thea von Harbou, Paul Falkenberg, Karl Vash, Adolf Jansen, from an article by Egon Jacobson

M ★★★

Crime drama   1951 · US · BW · 88mins

Independent producer Seymour Nebenzal was behind this Hollywood remake of his acclaimed 1931 German production, so masterfully directed by Fritz Lang. Its basic idea of the underworld actively helping to catch a murderer of children doesn't ring true in a Los Angeles setting. Yet director Joseph Losey creates a visually powerful picture with some brilliantly chosen locations and sparingly effective use of music, while David Wayne (more noted as a light comedian) comes close to matching Peter Lorre as the pathetic murderer.

David Wayne *Martin Harrow* • Howard Da Silva *Carney* • Luther Adler *Langley* • Martin Gabel *Marshall* • Steve Brodie *Lt Becker* • Raymond Burr *Pottsy* • Glenn Anders *Riggert* • Karen Morley *Mrs Coster* • Jim Backus *Mayor* ■ *Dir* Joseph Losey • *Scr* Norman Reilly Raine, Leo Katcher, Waldo Salt, from the 1931 film, from an article by Egon Jacobson

M Butterfly ★★ 15

Drama   1993 · US · Colour · 96mins

Director David Cronenberg came horribly unstuck with this insipid adaptation of David Henry Hwang's successful Broadway play about sexual deception and espionage. Jeremy Irons is a minor French diplomat in Beijing who falls under the spell of beautiful Chinese diva Song Liling. But not only is Song a spy, she's also a man! It's not that John Lone's performance is bad, it's just that his five o'clock shadow would surely tip anyone off instantly. What worked as a stage illusion clearly doesn't in close-up and, while it's obvious why Cronenberg would be attracted to such an operatic story of blurred identity, this should be filed under "interesting failure". Contains violence, swearing and sex scenes. 🔲

Jeremy Irons *René Gallimard* • John Lone *Song Liling* • Barbara Sukowa *Jeanne Gallimard* • Ian Richardson *Ambassador Toulon* • Annabel Leventon *Frau Baden* • Richard McMillan *Embassy colleague* • Vernon Dobtcheff *Agent Etancelin* ■ *Dir* David Cronenberg • *Scr* David Henry Hwan, from his play

Ma and Pa Kettle ★★

Comedy   1949 · US · BW · 76mins

As the hillbilly couple of the 1947 hit comedy *The Egg and I*, Marjorie Main and Percy Kilbride scored so many laughs they were given a film of their own, which developed into a hugely successful annual series. Here the Kettles, facing eviction from their ramshackle abode, win a futuristic new home in which to live with their 15 offspring. Their efforts to cope with its electronic gadgets provide much of the slapstick humour.

Marjorie Main *Ma Kettle* • Percy Kilbride *Pa Kettle* • Richard Long *Tom Kettle* • Meg Randall *Kim Parker* • Patricia Alphin *Secretary* • Esther Dale *Mrs Birdie Hicks* • Barry Kelley *Mr Tomkins* • Harry Antrim *Mayor Swiggins* ■ *Dir* Charles Lamont • *Scr* Herbert Margolis, Louis Morheim, Al Lewis, from the characters created by Betty MacDonald

Ma Saison Préferée ★★ 15

Drama   1993 · Fr · Colour · 121mins

This film, which opened the 1993 Cannes Festival, comes across as a slightly stodgy drama. Daniel Auteuil and Catherine Deneuve are brother and sister brought together after many years to attend the imminent demise of their mother. The familial strife around a death-bed recalls those hothouse dramas by Tennessee Williams and Eugene O'Neill, and this effort offers few surprises. The main point of interest is the fact that Deneuve's daughter is played by her real-life daughter, Chiara, whose father was famed actor Marcello Mastroianni. In French with English subtitles. 🔲

Catherine Deneuve *Emilie* • Daniel Auteuil *Antoine* • Marthe Villalonga *Berthe* • Jean-Pierre Bouvier *Bruno* • Chiara Mastroianni *Anne* ■ *Dir* André Téchiné • *Scr* André Téchiné, Pascal Bonitzer

Ma Vie en Rose ★★★ 12

Drama   1997 · Fr/Bel/UK/Swi · Colour · 85mins

Both director Alain Berliner and his young star, Georges Du Fresne, make auspicious debuts with this bittersweet tale of sexual confusion and bourgeois prudery. Berliner's clever shifts in colour, as reality intrudes upon the boy's Barbie-doll daydreams, are inspired, while as the pre-teen convinced he'll eventually turn into a girl, Du Fresne is so disingenuously trusting that he almost atones for the film's muddled blend of social satire and whimsical fantasy. Prejudices and doubts come and go with unconvincing ease, but mother Michèle Laroque is

so delightfully sympathetic that the trite ending has just the right ring of optimism. In French with English subtitles. 🖵

Michèle Laroque *Hanna* • Jean-Philippe Écoffey *Pierre* • Hélène Vincent *Elisabeth* • Georges Du Fresne *Ludovic* • Daniel Hanssens *Albert* ∎ *Dir* Alain Berliner • *Scr* Alain Berliner, from a story by Chris Vander Stappen

Ma Vie Sexuelle ★★★ 15

Drama   1996 · Fr · Colour · 172mins

Directed with a genuine curiosity about his characters that is too rare in nineties cinema, Arnaud Desplechin's leisurely study of Parisian twentysomething angst has its moments, but too few to justify the three-hour running time. As the wannabe intellectual trapped in a dead-end teaching post, Mathieu Amalric deserves credit for creating such a introspective loser. But his relationships with neglected girlfriend Emmanuelle Devos, unhinged student Marianne Denicourt and his cousin's lover, Chiara Mastroianni, only occasionally flicker into life. With some judicious cutting and a touch more self-deprecation, this might have achieved the intimacy its epic scale disallows. In French with English subtitles. 🖵

Mathieu Amalric *Paul* • Emmanuelle Devos *Esther* • Emmanuel Salinger *Nathan* • Marianne Denicourt *Sylvia* • Chiara Mastroianni *Patricia* ∎ *Dir* Arnaud Desplechin • *Scr* Arnaud Desplechin, Emmanuel Bourdieu

Maachis ★★ 12

Drama   1996 · Ind · Colour · 159mins

The winner of numerous domestic awards, yet denounced because of its allegedly pro-terrorist stance, this is a film designed to appeal more to the emotions than to the intellect. In following a couple of lovers on their road from romance to political violence, director Gulzar is too often guilty of playing to the gallery, frequently ignoring plot and character logic if they are at odds with his explosive set pieces. Yet the performance of Om Puri, as the leader of a band of mountain rebels, does much to redeem the shortcomings of both Gulzar and the ineffectual leads, Chandrachur Singh and Tabu. In Punjabi with English subtitles. 🖵

Chandrachur Singh *Kripal* • Raj Zutshi *Jassi* • Tabu *Veeran* • Om Puri *Santan* • Ravi Gosain • Kulbushan Karband ∎ *Dir* Gulzar • *Scr* Gulzar

Mac ★★★ 18

Drama   1992 · US · Colour · 113mins

Three brothers from Queens try to set themselves up as business contractors in actor John Turturro's accomplished directing debut. But fraternal rivalry rears its ugly head in an absorbing, fifties-set ensemble piece that is brutal and warmly humorous by turns. Turturro plays Mac, the bullying perfectionist who wants to make his father proud, with a painful honesty that's both touching and believable. The result is an intimate drama of great depth and keen observation. 🖵

John Turturro *Niccolo "Mac" Vitelli* • Michael Badalucco *Vico Vitelli* • Carl Capotorto *Bruno*

Vitelli* • Katherine Borowitz *Alice Vitelli* • John Amos *Nat* • Olek Krupa *Polowski* • Ellen Barkin *Oona* ∎ *Dir* John Turturro • *Scr* John Turturro, Brandon Cole

Mac and Me ★★ U

Adventure   1988 · US · Colour · 94mins

After ET's jaunt to our planet captured the hearts of earthlings of all ages, it was only to be expected that he would be followed by a positive star fleet of cute critters from outer space. Mac was not one of the more endearing, although there are moments when his relationship with Jade Calegory (who doesn't allow spina bifida to detract from her courageous performance) is quite touching. However, director Stewart Raffill's film is otherwise an unashamed rip-off of Spielberg's classic and will only be remembered as the picture that gave product placement a bad name. 🖵

Christine Ebersole *Janet Cruise* • Jonathan Ward *Michael Cruise* • Katrina Caspary [Tina Caspary] *Courtney* • Lauren Stanley *Debbie* • Jade Calegory *Eric Cruise* • Vinnie Torrente *Mitford* • Martin West *Wickett* • Ivan Jorge Rado *Zimmerman* ∎ *Dir* Stewart Raffill • *Scr* Stewart Raffill, Steve Feke

Macabre ★★

Horror   1958 · US · BW · 71mins

The first gimmick horror movie from showman producer/director William Castle is more a mystery whodunit than a ghoulish chiller, filled with fog-shrouded cardboard graveyards and numerous surprises. Doctor William Prince has just five hours to find his daughter, who has been buried alive as part of an elaborate charade. Castle arranged a $1,000 life insurance policy with Lloyd's of London to cover audience members from "death by fright" – a successful ploy that found him mounting ever more outlandish stunts over the next decade. It still works as cheap and cheerful fun, and the closing credits are great. Theo Durrant was actually a pseudonym for 13 writers.

William Prince *Dr Rodney Barrett* • Jim Backus *Jim Tyloe* • Jacqueline Scott *Polly Baron* • Philip Tonge *Jode Wetherby* • Ellen Corby *Miss Kushins* • Susan Morrow *Sylvia Stevenson* • Christine White *Nancy Wetherby* ∎ *Dir* William Castle • *Scr* Robb White, from the novel by Theo Durrant

Macao ★★★ PG

Crime drama   1952 · US · BW · 77mins

Produced by Howard Hughes's RKO, this piece of low-budget exotica was directed by Josef von Sternberg, who was at odds with some of his cast as well as the project as a whole. Nicholas Ray, who also directed sequences for Robert Mitchum's *The Racket*, was called in to shoot some of the final scenes. Set in steamy Macao – but never straying from the RKO lot – it's a diversion, with Mitchum and Jane Russell beautifully matched. If only the story and script were on a par with them as well. 🖵

Robert Mitchum *Nick Cochran* • Jane Russell *Julie Benson* • William Bendix *Lawrence Trumble* • Thomas Gomez *Lt Sebastian* • Gloria Grahame *Margie* • Brad Dexter *Halloran* • Edward Ashley *Martin Stewart* ∎ *Dir* Josef

von Sternberg, Nicholas Ray • *Scr* Bernard C Schoenfeld, Stanley Rubin, from a story by Bob Williams

Macario ★★★★

Drama   1960 · Mex · BW · 89mins

Like the film that beat it to the Oscar for best foreign film, Ingmar Bergman's *The Virgin Spring*, this Mexican drama focuses on faith, superstition and death. But there's little optimism in Roberto Gavaldón's period fantasy, which recalls Bergman's earlier masterpiece, *The Seventh Seal*, and Fritz Lang's silent classic, *Destiny*. Evocatively shot by master cinematographer Gabriel Figueroa and drawing heavily on the magic realist tradition, the story turns on the fate of starving woodsman, Ignacio Lopez Tarso, who, having refused to share a turkey with either God or the Devil, is tricked into a pact with Death. A Spanish language film.

Ignacio Lopez Tarso *Macario* • Pina Pellicer *Macario's wife* • Enrique Lucero *Death* ∎ *Dir* Roberto Gavaldón • *Scr* Roberto Gavaldon, Emilio Carballido, from the story *The Third Guest* by Bruno Traven

Macaroni ★★★ PG

Comedy drama   1985 · It · Colour · 101mins

It sounds so improbable it could never work. Yet, in the hands of Jack Lemmon and Marcello Mastroianni, Ettore Scola's tale of the surly businessman who rediscovers the simple joys of life from an eccentric Neapolitan exercises an irresistible charm right through to its closing note of quiet optimism. Discovering that Marcello has continued writing love letters to the heartbroken sister GI Jack jilted at the end of the war, Lemmon gratefully succumbs to the companionship absent from his troubled life. But it's Mastroianni's picture: he flits between reality and illusion as if there was no dividing line between them. In English and Italian with subtitles. 🖵

Jack Lemmon *Robert Traven* • Marcello Mastroianni *Antonio* • Daria Nicolodi *Laura* • Isa Danieli *Carmelina* • Patrizia Sacchi *Virginia* • Bruno Esposito *Giulio* • Giovanna Sanfilippo *Maria* ∎ *Dir* Ettore Scola • *Scr* Ruggero Maccari, Furio Scarpelli, Ettore Scola

MacArthur ★★★ PG

Second World War biographical drama   1977 · US · Colour · 123mins

Though not in the same league as Frank McCarthy's earlier production *Patton*, this solid, old-fashioned war epic deals with a similarly controversial and complex military commander. Gregory Peck is well cast as the martinet/genius, who famously said, "I will return" after being forced to evacuate Corregidor, the last American stronghold in the Philippines. He did go back, though, defeating the Japanese and later leading the US forces in the Korean War. Amazingly, he didn't become President – though Peck's tremendous performance is presidential in every respect. 🖵

Gregory Peck *General Douglas MacArthur* • Ivan Bonar *General Sutherland* • Dan O'Herlihy *President Roosevelt* • Ward Costello *General Marshall* • Nicolas Coster *Colonel Huff* • Marj Dusay *Mrs MacArthur* • Ed Flanders *President*

Harry S Truman* • Art Fleming *The Secretary* ∎ *Dir* Joseph Sargent • *Scr* Hal Barwood, Matthew Robbins

MacArthur's Children ★★★

Second World War drama   1985 · Jap · Colour · 120mins

An ambitious Japanese film, set on the remote island of Awaji Shima at the end of the Second World War, where a large cast of characters react in different ways to defeat. There's the aggressive pupil who decides to become a gangster as a way of exorcising the military surrender; there is also an admiral who expects to be arrested and tried for war crimes. Weaving together several strands of narrative, Masahiro Shinoda's film broke new ground for Japanese cinema in confronting defeat and acknowledging America's cultural and economic colonisation. (The soundtrack includes Glenn Miller's *In the Mood*.) A Japanese language film.

Takaya Yamauchi *Ryuta Ashigara* • Yoshiyuki Omori *Saburo Masaki* • Shiori Sakura *Mume Hatano* • Masako Natsume *Komako Nakai* ∎ *Dir* Masahiro Shinoda • *Scr* Takeshi Tamura, from a novel by Yu Aku

McBain ★★ 15

Action adventure   1991 · US · Colour · 99mins

Rescued from prison on the day the Vietnam War ended, Christopher Walken vows to return the favour to his liberator, Santos. When Santos's sister calls in the debt, McBain and other Viet vets wash up in Colombia, fighting on the side of the peasants against the drug cartel-backed forces of El Presidente. Despite its violence, the movie is pitched as an updated send-up of *The Magnificent Seven*, while in other respects it resembles an episode of TV's *The A-Team*. 🖵

Christopher Walken *McBain* • Maria Conchita Alonso *Christina* • Michael Ironside *Frank Bruce* • Steve James *Eastland* • Jay Patterson *Doctor Dalton* ∎ *Dir/Scr* James Glickenhaus

Macbeth ★★★★ PG

Tragedy   1948 · US · BW · 102mins

Orson Welles's rendition of *Macbeth* may be the least of his Shakespeare adaptations but, bearing in mind the brilliance of *Chimes at Midnight* and *Othello*, this can hardly be taken as a denunciation. Admittedly, the Scottish accents are often impenetrable thanks to the indifferent sound quality, and Jeanette Nolan may not be the incarnation of merciless ambition that is most people's idea of Lady Macbeth. But Welles gives a towering performance, vacillating between ambition, indecision and conscience with supreme skill. Recalling pioneering Russian director Sergei Eisenstein's *Alexander Nevsky*, the film's design conveys an atmosphere of evil and unease far more effectively than the plush trappings of Roman Polanski's 1971 version.

Orson Welles *Macbeth* • Jeanette Nolan *Lady Macbeth* • Dan O'Herlihy *Macduff* • Roddy McDowall *Malcolm* • Edgar Barrier *Banquo* • Erskine Sanford *Duncan* • John Dierkes *Ross* • Keene Curtis *Lennox* • Peggy Webber *Lady Macduff* • Alan Napier *A Holy Father* ∎ *Dir* Orson Welles • *Scr* Orson Welles, from the play by William Shakespeare

Macbeth ★★★★ 🔞15

Tragedy 1971 · UK · Colour · 134mins

A controversial adaptation by Roman Polanski (with Kenneth Tynan advising), this sacrifices some of Shakespeare's bleak poetry in favour of great barbaric imagery. A bloody account of Macbeth (Jon Finch) and his intimidating wife (Francesca Annis) making their way to the top of the medieval heap via murder and treachery, it was Polanski's first film after the murder of his wife, Sharon Tate, and has a savagery that seems tinged with paranoia. Lady Macbeth's nude sleepwalking scene resulted in critical flak and was seen as evidence of the malign influence of production company *Playboy*. It's a film that deserves better than that jibe. 🖵

Jon Finch *Macbeth* • Francesca Annis *Lady Macbeth* • Martin Shaw *Banquo* • Nicholas Selby *Duncan* • John Stride *Ross* • Stephan Chase *Malcolm* • Paul Shelley *Donalbain* • Terence Baylor *Macduff* ∎ *Dir* Roman Polanski • *Scr* Roman Polanski, from the play by William Shakespeare • *Cinematographer* Gilbert Taylor

Macbeth ★★ 🔞12

Tragedy 1997 · UK · Colour · 142mins

Wrongly described as the first version of "the Scottish play" with indigenous accents, this doggedly low-budget affair lacks the power or cinematic imagination of earlier efforts by Orson Welles, Akira Kurosawa and Roman Polanski. As Macbeth, a role long coveted by his father, Jason Connery is suitably hesitant in his ambition, but there's a suspicion this owes more to his discomfort with the difficult dialogue than character insight. Helen Baxendale is similarly troubled as his scheming wife, so it's left to supporting players like Graham McTavish to steady the ship. Director Jeremy Freeston has some splendid locations to work with; a pity, then, he shoots much of the dialogue in suffocating close-up. 🖵

Jason Connery *Macbeth* • Helen Baxendale *Lady Macbeth* • Graham McTavish *Banquo* • Kenny Bryans *Macduff* • Kern Falconer *Seyton* • Brian Blessed *Edward the Confessor* ∎ *Dir* Jeremy Freeston • *Scr* Bob Carruthers, Jeremy Freeston, from the play by William Shakespeare

McCabe and Mrs Miller ★★★★ 🔞15

Western 1971 · US · Colour · 115mins

Before he fell from favour after making movies such as *Popeye* and *Beyond Therapy*, Robert Altman won critical acclaim for *Nashville*, *MASH* and this other early effort. Warren Beatty stars as McCabe, a gambler who sets up his girlfriend (Julie Christie) as a whorehouse madam, in a bleak western set against the backdrop of a developing town in the American North West. It's an interesting tale with all the classic elements of the genre, and the affair is given added weight by the solid performances of Beatty and Christie. A reminder of just how good Altman can be when he's on form. 🖵

Warren Beatty *John McCabe* • Julie Christie *Constance Miller* • René Auberjonois *Sheehan* • John Schuck *Smalley* • Bert Remsen *Bart Coyle* • Keith Carradine *Cowboy* • William

Devane *Lawyer* • Corey Fischer *Mr Elliott* • Shelley Duvall *Ida Coyle* ∎ *Dir* Robert Altman • *Scr* Robert Altman, Brian McKay, from the novel *McCabe* by Edmund Naughton

The McConnell Story ★★ 🔞U

Biographical drama 1955 · US · Colour · 102mins

Alan Ladd was terrified of flying, but he had no qualms about playing Captain Joseph C McConnell Jr, a real-life pilot ace of the Korean War. It's standard stuff, with Ladd putting duty first and his patient wife (June Allyson) second, though the script had to be revised when McConnell was killed testing a new type of plane shortly before production started. Allyson had scored as a grieving widow in *The Glenn Miller Story*, and she rises to the occasion here. The jingoistic embellishments are somewhat sickening, however. 🖵

Alan Ladd *Captain Joseph C "Mac" McConnell Jr* • June Allyson *"Butch"* • James Whitmore *Ty Whitman* • Frank Faylen *Sykes* • Robert Ellis *Bob* • Willis Bouchey *Newton Bass* ∎ *Dir* Gordon Douglas • *Scr* Ted Sherdeman, Sam Rolfe, from a story by Ted Sherdeman

McHale's Navy ★★★ 🔞U

War comedy 1964 · US · Colour · 92mins

McHale's Navy first aired on US TV in 1962 and was an immediate hit, showing the antics of the crew of a PT boat – the same sort of boat President John F Kennedy had commanded in the Second World War. This film version preserves the main cast and production team, giving Ernest Borgnine the plum role as Lt Comdr Quinton McHale, the least likely officer in the Pacific. Very much a product of its times, it includes some genuinely funny, even surreal moments such as a Japanese peering through his periscope and seeing a racehorse on the bows of the PT boat.

Ernest Borgnine *Lt Cmdr Quinton McHale* • Joe Flynn *Capt Wallace Burton Binghamton* • Tim Conway *Ensign Charles Parker* • Carl Ballantine *Torpedoman Lester Gruber* • Gary Vinson *QM George "Christy" Christopher* ∎ *Dir* Edward J Montagne • *Scr* Frank Gill Jr, G Carleton Brown, from a story by Si Rose

McHale's Navy ★★ 🔞PG

Comedy 1997 · US · Colour · 104mins

The world's biggest second banana, Tom Arnold, gets a shot at being first banana in this update of the sixties TV series. Lt Cmdr Quinton McHale is lured out of retirement in the Caribbean to fight the world's second most dangerous international terrorist, Tim Curry, who is trying to build his own nuclear silo and fire a missile at the Pentagon. So much attention was paid to getting an impressive cast of B-movie actors (Dean Stockwell, Bruce Campbell, Ernest Borgnine) that somebody forgot to write any jokes. Contains some swearing. 🖵

Tom Arnold *Lt Cmdr Quinton McHale* • Dean Stockwell *Capt Wallace B Binghampton* • Debra Messing *Lt Penelope Carpenter* • David Alan Grier *Ensign Charles T Parker* • Tim Curry *Major Vladikov* • Ernest Borgnine *Cobra* ∎ *Dir* Bryan Spicer • *Scr* Peter Crabbe, from a story by Andy Rose, Peter Crabbe

The Machine ★★★ 🔞18

Science-fiction horror thriller 1994 · Fr/Ger · Colour · 91mins

There are strange echoes here of *The Return of Martin Guerre*, in which Nathalie Baye wasn't quite sure if Gérard Depardieu was her husband. In this psychological thriller, Depardieu is Marc, a psychologist with a particular fascination for the criminal mind. He develops a machine that enables him to swap brains with Zyto, a man convicted of stabbing three women to death. Unfortunately, the experiment becomes permanent: Zyto's brain is in Marc's body. But does his wife, Baye, still recognise him? Grafting bits of *Frankenstein* and *The Island of Dr Moreau* on to *Dr Jekyll and Mr Hyde*, this exercise in schlock provides some effective jolts as Depardieu surfs someone else's brainwaves. A French language film. 🖵

Gérard Depardieu *Marc* • Nathalie Baye *Marie* • Didier Bourdon *Zyto* • Natalia Woerner *Marianne* • Erwan Baynaud *Leonard* ∎ *Dir* François Dupeyron • *Scr* François Dupeyron, from a novel by René Belletto

Machine Gun Kelly ★★★

Biographical crime drama 1958 · US · BW · 85mins

One of the first films to gain cult director Roger Corman international recognition and critical acclaim, a vivid and fast-moving biopic about the infamous thirties bank robber. Charles Bronson (in his first starring role) brings an edgy intensity to Kelly, the audacious gangster who – in what may be considered the greatest anticlimax in crime history – finally surrendered to the FBI rather than be killed in a shootout. Rapid-fire dialogue and effective characterisations all down the line make this a real winner.

Charles Bronson *Machine Gun Kelly* • Susan Cabot *Flo* • Morey Amsterdam *Fandango* • Jack Lambert *Howard* • Wally Campo *Maize* ∎ *Dir* Roger Corman • *Scr* R Wright Campbell

Macho Callahan ★★ 🔞15

Civil war drama 1970 · US/Sp · Colour · 94mins

Union soldier David Janssen busts out of jail and sets out to kill Lee J Cobb, murdering Jean Seberg's one-armed husband in the process. The fact that Seberg falls in love with Janssen *after* she's hired some bounty hunters to bump him off makes life complicated for all concerned. Seldom has a western shown such relish for pain and cruelty: bodies are eaten alive by insects or hung from the blades of a windmill, while Seberg has to strip off for the obligatory rape scene. The bleached look of the film gives it a certain realism, but no one's heart seems to be in it. 🖵

David Janssen *Diego "Macho" Callahan* • Jean Seberg *Alexandra Mountford* • Lee J Cobb *Duffy* • James Booth *"King Harry" Wheeler* • Pedro Armendariz Jr *Juan Fernandez* • Anne Revere *Crystal* • David Carradine *Colonel David Mountford* • Diane Ladd *Girl* ∎ *Dir* Bernard L Kowalski • *Scr* Clifford Newton Gould, from a story by Richard Carr

The Mack ★★

Blaxploitation 1973 · US · Colour · 110mins

One of the most popular of all the blaxploitation movies, this followed in the bloody wake of *Shaft* (1971) and, if anything, is even more violent. Goldie (Max Julien) is a black pimp operating out of Oakland who comes up against white cops and an evil drug lord. The morals are as sleazy as the hero, while Michael Campus directs at a pace as urgent as the slashing knives he uses.

Max Julien *Goldie* • Don Gordon *Hank* • Richard Pryor *Slim* • Carol Speed *Lulu* • Roger E Mosley *Olinga* • Dick Williams [Dick Anthony Williams] *Pretty Tony* ∎ *Dir* Michael Campus • *Scr* Robert J Poole

Mack the Knife ★★ 🔞15

Musical drama 1989 · US · Colour · 98mins

An all-star British cast – Roger Daltrey, Bill Nighy, Julie Walters – give sterling support to Raul Julia's MacHeath in this version of Bertolt Brecht and Kurt Weill's *Threepenny Opera*. However, the impressive line-up conceals an appalling travesty of a theatrical classic that's totally alien to the spirit of the original. Set in deprived Victorian London, Menahem Golan's film is a forced affair, full of turgid scenes and dialogue. It's no surprise to learn that Anthony Hopkins walked off set complaining of "creative differences"; the real mystery is why everybody else didn't follow suit. 🖵

Raul Julia *MacHeath* • Julia Migenes-Johnson *Jenny* • Richard Harris *Mr Peachum* • Julie Walters *Mrs Peachum* • Roger Daltrey *Street singer* • Rachel Robertson *Polly Peachum* • Clive Revill *Money Matthew* • Miranda Garrison *Esmerelda* ∎ *Dir* Menahem Golan • *Scr* Menahem Golan, from the musical *The Threepenny Opera* by Bertolt Brecht, Kurt Weill

Mackenna's Gold ★★★ 🔞15

Western 1969 · US · Colour · 122mins

How could this possibly fail – a western about hidden Apache gold with more stars in the cast than twists, swindles and red herrings in the plot? Yet fail it did, despite the presence of powerhouse performers like Gregory Peck, Omar Sharif and Edward G Robinson. Blame the executives at Columbia for ordering extensive re-editing, for while Carl Foreman's script might be cliché ridden, it is one of the pleasures of a cowboy movie that you know exactly what you're going to get. Here you get it in spades, thanks to J Lee Thompson's vigorous direction. 🖵

Gregory Peck *Mackenna* • Omar Sharif *Colorado* • Telly Savalas *Sergeant Tibbs* • Camilla Sparv *Inga* • Keenan Wynn *Sanchez* • Lee J Cobb *Editor* • Raymond Massey *Preacher* • Burgess Meredith *Storekeeper* • Anthony Quayle *Older Englishman* • Edward G Robinson *Old Adams* • Eli Wallach *Ben Baker* ∎ *Dir* J Lee Thompson • *Scr* Carl Foreman, from the novel by Will Henry

The McKenzie Break ★★★★ 🔞12

Second World War drama 1970 · UK · Colour · 101mins

An unusual slant on the prisoner-of-war escape movie – this time members of a German U-boat crew in a Scottish internment camp plan to make their

getaway. Brian Keith is called in as an intelligence officer and finds himself opposing fanatical Nazi Helmut Griem, who is willing to sacrifice others for the glory of the Fatherland. Directed by Lamont Johnson, this rare and interesting movie acknowledges that guards can only run such lock-ups efficiently with the tacit permission of the prisoners. Keith and Griem turn in admirable performances, but it's William Norton's tense script that ensures a nail-biting finish. ▭

Brian Keith *Captain Jack Connor* • Helmut Griem *Kapitan Schluetter* • Ian Hendry *Major Perry* • Jack Watson *General Kerr* • Patrick O'Connell *Sergeant Major Cox* • Horst Janson *Neuchl* • Alexander Allerson *Von Sperrle* • John Abineri *Kranz* ■ *Dir* Lamont Johnson • *Scr* William Norton, from the novel *The Bowmanville Break* by Sidney Shelley

The Mackintosh Man ★★15

Spy thriller 1973 · UK · Colour · 95mins

A movie with everything you would expect of a Cold War thriller – and therein lies its problem. Walter Hill has made a smooth enough job of adapting Desmond Bagley's novel *The Freedom Trap*, but John Huston handles the cleverly crafted frame-up, the ingenious escapes and the finale in Malta with little conviction. Paul Newman and James Mason seem equally distracted as, respectively, the undercover agent and the high-ranking MP who is not what he seems. A clear case of suffocation by expertise. ▭

Paul Newman *Joseph Rearden* • James Mason *Sir George Wheeler* • Dominique Sanda *Mrs Smith* • Harry Andrews *Angus Mackintosh* • Nigel Patrick *Soames-Trevelyan* • Ian Bannen *Slade* • Peter Vaughan *Brunskill* ■ *Dir* John Huston • *Scr* Walter Hill, from the novel *The Freedom Trap* by Desmond Bagley

McLintock! ★★★ U

Comedy western
1963 · US · Colour · 126mins

Rollicking John Wayne vehicle that's a real Wayne family affair – it co-stars one son, Patrick, and another, Michael, produced the movie. He also issued it in varying forms, shortened, and with different music, but the best version, is the full two hours-plus Panavisioned opus. It's basically a rewrite of *The Taming of the Shrew*, with all the pre-feminist attitudes endemic to that Shakespeare comedy; attitudes, one suspects, held by the Duke himself. Today, some viewers may not enjoy watching elegant Maureen O'Hara cascading down a mud slide or being spanked by Big John. Be warned: it's rowdy, rude and rather dated. ▭

John Wayne *George Washington McLintock* • Maureen O'Hara *Katherine McLintock* • Yvonne De Carlo *Louise Warren* • Patrick Wayne *Devlin Warren* • Stefanie Powers *Becky McLintock* • Jack Kruschen *Bimbaum* • Chill Wills *Drago* ■ *Dir* Andrew V McLaglen • *Scr* James Edward Grant

The McMasters ★★

Western 1970 · US · Colour · 97mins

A weird western, this: made in New Mexico and directed by a disciple of Ingmar Bergman, Alf Kjellin, who predictably makes the atmosphere as bleak as possible. The central theme is racial prejudice, as white rancher

Burl Ives and native American Indians, led by David Carradine, come to the aid of black soldier-turned-rancher Brock Peters, who faces hostility from other local white farmers. Add John Carradine and Jack Palance, and you get quite a combination – one of those westerns that is really a critique of the Vietnam War. Always interesting, rarely exciting. Contains violence.

Brock Peters *Benjie* • Burl Ives *Neal McMasters* • David Carradine *White Feather* • Nancy Kwan *Robin* • Jack Palance *Kolby* • Dane Clark *Spencer* • John Carradine *Preacher* • LQ Jones *Russell* ■ *Dir* Alf Kjellin • *Scr* Harold Jacob Smith

The Macomber Affair ★★★

Romantic drama 1947 · US · BW · 89mins

Based on a brilliant story by Ernest Hemingway, this is a serious – perhaps too serious – film attempt at translating the author's prose to the silver screen. Gregory Peck is handsome, if wooden, in the lead, but Robert Preston and Joan Bennett both have a rare intelligence as a sparky married couple who are on safari under Peck's wing. A hard film to like, but an easy one to admire, and a must for collectors of filmed Hemingway.

Gregory Peck *Robert Wilson* • Robert Preston *Francis Macomber* • Joan Bennett *Margaret Macomber* • Reginald Denny *Captain Smollet* • Carl Harbord *Coroner* ■ *Dir* Zoltan Korda • *Scr* Casey Robinson, Seymour Bennett, Frank Arnold, from the story *The Short Happy Life of Francis Macomber* by Ernest Hemingway

Macon County Line ★★★

Crime drama 1973 · US · Colour · 88mins

Max Baer Jr (*The Beverly Hillbillies*) wrote, produced and co-starred in this minor drive-in classic. Two footloose brothers, one of whom is about to go into the army, pick up a girl and go on one last hellraising spree in fifties Georgia, only to run foul of a redneck sheriff who hunts them down for a brutal murder they didn't commit. Supposedly based on a true story, this isn't your average "good ol' boy" flick. Although director Richard Compton has much to say about gun use and small town mores, the melodrama of the piece tends to swamp any message.

Alan Vint *Chris Dixon* • Cheryl Waters *Jenny* • Geoffrey Lewis *Hamp* • Joan Blackman *Carol Morgan* • Jesse Vint *Wayne Dixon* • Max Baer Jr *Deputy Morgan* • Sam Gilman *Deputy Bill* ■ *Dir* Richard Compton • *Scr* Max Baer Jr, Richard Compton, from a story by Max Baer Jr

McQ ★★15

Thriller 1974 · US · Colour · 106mins

John Wayne and director John Sturges are, sadly, both past their action prime in this misbegotten attempt to beat Dirty Harry at his own game. Shot entirely in Seattle by Harry Stradling Jr, the scenery and some fine minor players (Colleen Dewhurst, Eddie Albert, Clu Gulager) far outshine the Duke, whose formal blue suit and ill-fitting toupee render him more suited to a businessman's retirement home than chasing bent cops and drug dealers half his age. The finale, a car chase on the beach, is particularly poorly staged – but if you've stuck with the movie that far, this will come as no surprise. ▭

John Wayne *Detective Lt Lon McQ* • Eddie Albert *Capt Ed Kosterman* • Diana Muldaur *Lois Boyle* • Colleen Dewhurst *Myra* • Clu Gulager *Franklin Toms* • David Huddleston Edward M "Pinky" *Farrow* ■ *Dir* John Sturges • *Scr* Lawrence Roman

Macu, the Policeman's Wife ★★★

Drama based on a true story
1987 · Ven · Colour · 91mins

Born in Sweden and trained in Germany, Solveig Hoogesteijn had already explored the themes of culture and identity in a couple of pictures before adding feminist and political concerns in this disturbing melodrama. Based on actual events, the story of a policeman who murders his teenage wife's lover is told through a sequence of flashbacks which also reveal the shocking part played by young Maria Luisa Mosquera's mother in his troubled life. This complex analysis of the role of women in Venezuelan society isn't an easy watch, but its manipulation of generic convention for sociological purposes is impressive. In Spanish with English subtitles.

Daniel Alvarado *Ismael* • Maria Luisa Mosquera *Macu* • Frank Hernandez *Simon* • Tito Aponte *Willy* ■ *Dir/Scr* Solveig Hoogesteijn

McVicar ★★18

Prison drama 1980 · UK · Colour · 107mins

This is an ill-conceived account, based on his autobiography, of folk hero John McVicar's escape from Durham prison. The Who's Roger Daltrey was one of the producers and the band had a hand in the noisy, inappropriate rock score. Daltrey also attempts the role of McVicar, while another pop singer, Adam Faith, plays his mate Walter. Tom Clegg directs it all in slam-bang *Sweeney* style. You can't help feeling that British producers should leave jail-break adventures to Hollywood. ▭

Roger Daltrey *John McVicar* • Adam Faith *Walter Probyn* • Cheryl Campbell *Sheila* • Billy Murray *Joey Davis* • Georgina Hale *Kate* • Ian Hendry *Hitchens* • Steven Berkoff *Ronnie Harrison* ■ *Dir* Tom Clegg • *Scr* Tom Clegg, John McVicar, from the autobiography *McVicar by Himself* by John McVicar

Mad about Men ★★U

Fantasy 1954 · UK · Colour · 85mins

Director Ralph Thomas, so effective with the *Doctor* series, is out of his depth with this slice of outdated hokum, a cliché-ridden story that's a sequel to the first mermaid movie *Miranda*. Glynis Johns still looks good as the aquatic star, swapping roles with a sports mistress who's going on holiday, but this is certainly not the equal of the charming original.

Glynis Johns *Miranda/Caroline* • Anne Crawford *Barbara* • Donald Sinden *Jeff Saunders* • Margaret Rutherford *Nurse Cary* • Dora Bryan *Berengaria* • Nicholas Phipps *Barclay Sutton* • Peter Martyn *Ronald* • Irene Handl *Madame Blanche* ■ *Dir* Ralph Thomas • *Scr* Peter Blackmore

Mad about Music ★★★

Drama 1938 · US · BW · 98mins

In her third starring role, Deanna Durbin plays the daughter of a vain

actress (Gail Patrick) who keeps her hidden away at a Swiss school. There the parentless girl invents a romantic explorer father and regales her fellow pupils with his exploits. When her deception looks about to be revealed, she dragoons a bemused but co-operative Herbert Marshall into impersonating her fantasy. Like all of Durbin's vehicles, this is charming, delightful nonsense, with Deanna enjoying a teen romance with Jackie Moran and performing *Ave Maria* with the Vienna Boys' Choir.

Deanna Durbin *Gloria Harkinson* • Herbert Marshall *Richard Todd* • Arthur Treacher *Tripps* • Gail Patrick *Gwen Taylor* • William Frawley *Dusty Rhodes* • Jackie Moran *Tommy* • Helen Parrish *Felice* ■ *Dir* Norman Taurog • *Scr* Bruce Manning, Felix Jackson, from a story by Marcella Burke, Frederick Kohner

Mad at the Moon ★★

Horror western 1992 · US · Colour · 97mins

Fur-out blend of *The Wolf Man* and *Little House on the Prairie*, with Mary Stuart Masterson as a rancher's wife who wonders why hubby Hart Bochner keeps nipping out at night and baying at the moon. Yes, you've guessed it: he's a lycanthrope. But can beauty tame the beast before he wolfs her down for his next meal? Low on gore and long on talk and atmosphere, Martin Donovan's horror western suffered the same fate as most mixed-genre movies. Falling between two stools, it failed to find an audience.

Mary Stuart Masterson *Jenny* • Hart Bochner *Miller Brown* • Fionnula Flanagan *Jenny's mom* • Stephen Blake *James Miller* • Daphne Zuniga *Jenny's mom as a young woman* • Cec Verrell *Sally* ■ *Dir* Martin Donovan • *Scr* Martin Donovan, Richard Pelusi

Mad City ★★★★12

Crime drama 1997 · US · Colour · 110mins

John Travolta is the museum security guard who resorts to the desperate measure of holding a group of schoolkids hostage after he loses his job. In this nineties version of *Ace in the Hole*, Dustin Hoffman is the ageing newsman in need of a career break, who decides to manipulate the unsuspecting Travolta for his own ends. Surprisingly dark for a Hollywood movie, this works exceptionally well thanks to a well thought-out script, subtle direction and superb performances from Travolta, Hoffman and Alan Alda as his news rival. Ultimately, it's an interesting, thought-provoking film which has a sharp dig at the US media. Contains swearing and some violence. ▭

Dustin Hoffman *Max Brackett* • John Travolta *Sam Baily* • Alan Alda *Kevin Hollander* • Mia Kirshner *Laurie Callahan* • Ted Levine *Alvin Lemke* • Robert Prosky *Lou Potts* • Blythe Danner *Mrs Banks* • William Atherton *Dohlen* ■ *Dir* Costa-Gavras • *Scr* Tom Matthews, Eric Williams, from a story by Tom Matthews

Mad Cows ★15

Comedy 1999 · UK · Colour · 90mins

Kathy Lette's bestselling comic novel transfers to the screen with tiresomely over-the-top characters, amateurish direction and a witless script. Anna Friel nails the accent as Australian single mum Maddy, but her gamine

looks and limited thespian skills render her character utterly unconvincing. The decent British supporting cast (including Joanna Lumley and Anna Massey) make complete idiots of themselves, while a bunch of D-list British celebs have pointless cameos. If the poor performances and stupid story don't drive you mad, Sara Sugarman's heavy-handed, "wacky" camerawork should finish the job.

Anna Friel *Maddy* • Joanna Lumley *Gillian* • Anna Massey *Dwina Phelps* • Phyllida Law *Lady Drake* • Greg Wise *Alex* • John Standing *Johnny Vaguelawn* • Prunella Scales *Dr Minny Stinkler* • Mohamed Al-Fayed *Harrods doorman* • Meg Mathews *Harrods shopper* ■ *Dir* Sara Sugarman • *Scr* Sasha Hails, Sara Sugarman, from the novel by Kathy Lette

The Mad Doctor of Market Street ★★★

Drama   1942 · US · BW · 60mins

Slyly derivative of HG Wells's *The Island of Dr Moreau*, this schlocky drama stars Lionel Atwill as a deranged doctor forced to quit his plush New York surgery for indulging in strange practices. Fleeing by boat, he is shipwrecked on a desert island with a bunch of survivors who he decides to turn into zombies. Cult director Joseph H Lewis (*Gun Crazy*) keeps his tongue firmly in cheek, but his film has quite a narrative pull – and the title is terrific.

Una Merkel *Aunt Margaret* • Lionel Atwill *Dr Benson* • Nat Pendleton *"Red"* • Claire Dodd *Patricia Wentworth* ■ *Dir* Joseph H Lewis • *Scr* Al Martin

Mad Dog ★★★★🔞

Historical action drama
1976 · Ausl · Colour · 93mins

Australia, 1854, and young Morgan, partaking of opium in Chinatown, survives a massacre and is sentenced to a dozen years after stealing some clothing. Raped in jail, he gets out after six years and becomes a legendary outlaw, Mad Dog Morgan. With his boomerang-throwing, didgeridoo-playing partner, played by David Gulpilil from *Walkabout*, Morgan is every inch the social bandit, and writer/director Philippe Mora surely skews a few facts to make us regard him as a hero, like Ned Kelly or Billy the Kid. Powerfully acted by Dennis Hopper and Frank Thring (as a sadistic policeman), this is an excellent movie, superbly shot and pacily directed. 🔲

Dennis Hopper *Daniel Morgan* • Jack Thompson *Detective Manwaring* • David Gulpilil *Billy* • Frank Thring *Superintendent Cobham* • Michael Pate *Superintendent Winch* • Wallas Eaton *Macpherson* • Bill Hunter *Sergeant Smith* ■ *Dir* Philippe Mora • *Scr* Philippe Mora, from the book *Morgan the Bold Bushranger* by Margaret Carnegie

Mad Dog and Glory ★★★🔞

Romantic drama
1992 · US · Colour and BW · 97mins

An intriguing oddity from the pen of novelist and regular Martin Scorsese collaborator Richard Price. Robert De Niro is the "Mad Dog" of the title, a shy, quiet police forensics photographer who saves the life of mobster and aspiring stand-up comedian Bill Murray. In return, he

gets a present – Uma Thurman – but the arrangement becomes complicated when the mismatched duo fall in love. The direction from John McNaughton, notorious for *Henry: Portrait of a Serial Killer*, is subtle, even though he has difficulty keeping the diverse elements of the story – romance, black comedy, gangster thriller – together. He is helped, however, by an understated performance from De Niro, and a rather strange one from Murray. Contains violence, swearing and nudity. 🔲

Robert De Niro *Wayne Dobie* • Uma Thurman *Glory* • Bill Murray *Frank Milo* • David Caruso *Mike* • Mike Starr *Harold* • Tom Towles *Andrew* • Kathy Baker *Lee* ■ *Dir* John McNaughton • *Scr* Richard Price

Mad Dogs and Englishmen ★★

Music documentary
1971 · US · Colour · 111mins

An uneven record of Joe Cocker's 1970 American tour, with split-screen clips from concerts held in New York, Dallas, Minneapolis and San Francisco. The gravel-throated bluesman flails his arms through 14 of his best-loved songs, including *Delta Lady*, *With a Little Help from My Friends* and *She Came in through the Bathroom Window*. Cocker's classics make a powerful impact, but it's event organiser Leon Russell who grabs the backstage attention.

Dir Pierre Adidge • *Scr* Pierre Adidge, Harry Marks, Robert Abel

Mad Dogs and Englishmen ★🔞

Thriller   1994 · UK · Colour · 93mins

The links between drug addiction and the privileged classes form the basis of this completely misguided thriller. In an awful performance that literally has to be seen to be believed, Elizabeth Hurley plays an upper-class heroin addict who floats through stately homes surrounded by pompous twits and listless "Hooray Henriettas". Joss Ackland puts in an even worse turn as the investigating cockney policeman, while everyone else gamely tries to make sense of the dreadful dialogue. Sounds like camp fun, but it really isn't. Contains swearing, violence, drug abuse and sex scenes. 🔲

Elizabeth Hurley *Antonia Dyer* • C Thomas Howell *Mike Stone* • Joss Ackland *Inspector Sam Stringer* • Claire Bloom *Liz Stringer* • Frederick Treves *Sir Harry Dyer* • Andrew Connolly *Clive Nathan* • Jeremy Brett *Tony Vernon-Smith* ■ *Dir* Henry Cole • *Scr* Tim Sewell, from a story by Henry Cole

The Mad Game ★★★

Crime drama   1933 · US · BW · 73mins

When the former partners-in-crime of imprisoned bootlegger Edward Carson (Spencer Tracy) kidnap the children of the judge (Ralph Morgan) who put him away, Tracy is let loose to help track down the guilty men. Directed by Irving Cummings and co-starring Claire Trevor as a reporter who takes a shine to Tracy, this routine crime movie is kept very watchable by the always faultless star and lent added interest in its concern for the problematical phenomenon of kidnapping.

Spencer Tracy *Edward Carson* • Claire Trevor *Jane Lee* • Ralph Morgan *Judge Penfield* • J Carrol Naish *Chopper Allen* • John Miljan *William Bennett* ■ *Dir* Irving Cummings • *Scr* William Conselman, Henry Johnson

The Mad Genius ★★★

Drama   1931 · US · BW · 81mins

Matinée idol John Barrymore had tremendous success with the movie version of *Svengali*, and Warner Bros ordered an immediate follow-up. This virtual sequel was released later the same year, and, helped by a better director in Michael Curtiz, Barrymore is sensational. This movie does seem freer than *Svengali* in dealing with similar themes, though its plot is obviously based on the bizarre relationship between ballet impresario Diaghilev and his star dancer Nijinsky.

John Barrymore *Ivan Tzarakov* • Marian Marsh *Nana* • Donald Cook *Fedor* • Charles Butterworth *Karinsky* • Luis Alberni *Serge Bankieff* • Carmel Myers *Preskoya* • Andre Luguet *Bartag* • Frankie Darro *Fedor as a boy* • Boris Karloff *Fedor's father* ■ *Dir* Michael Curtiz • *Scr* J Grubb Alexander, Harvey Thew, from the play *The Idol* by Martin Brown

Mad Love ★★★★

Horror   1935 · US · BW · 67mins

Peter Lorre made his American debut in this, one of the all-time classic horror stories, the first sound remake of the 1925 silent shocker *The Hands of Orlac*. Colin Clive is the concert pianist given the hands of an executed killer when his own are lost in an accident. Lorre brilliantly conveys twisted compassion and obsessive madness as the surgeon who performs the operation because he loves the pianist's actress wife. A real chiller about psychological fear, made even more effective by Karl Freund's hard-edged poetic direction, way ahead of its time for atmosphere, eerie visuals and imaginative camera technique.

Peter Lorre *Doctor Gogol* • Frances Drake *Yvonne Orlac* • Colin Clive *Stephen Orlac* • Ted Healy *Reagan* • Sara Haden *Marie* • Edward Brophy *Rollo* • Henry Kolker *Prefect Rosset* • May Beatty *Françoise* ■ *Dir* Karl Freund • *Scr* Guy Endore, PJ Wolfson, John L Balderston, from the novel *Les Mains d'Orlac* by Maurice Renard • *Cinematographer* Gregg Toland, Chester Lyons

Mad Love ★★🔞

Romantic drama   1995 · US · Colour · 92mins

British director Antonia Bird made her Hollywood debut with this uninspired reworking of the tired teens-on-the-run theme. As with *Priest*, she invariably puts her foot on the emotional pedal just as the action needs to be approached with care, with the consequence that Drew Barrymore's increasingly unpredictable behaviour becomes irritating rather than harrowing. Desperately seeking depth, Paula Milne's script is a hotchpotch of half-digested clichés. Even the acting feels overly familiar, with Barrymore dusting down her *Guncrazy* mannerisms, and Chris O'Donnell seeking refuge in the abashed schoolboy expressions that served him so well in *Scent of a Woman*. 🔲

Chris O'Donnell *Matt* • Drew Barrymore *Casey* • Matthew Lillard *Eric* • Richard Chaim *Duncan*

• Robert Nadir *Coach* • Joan Allen *Margaret* • Jude Ciccolella *Richard* • Amy Sakasitz *Joanna* ■ *Dir* Antonia Bird • *Scr* Paula Milne

The Mad Magician ★★★

Horror   1954 · US · BW · 72mins

When *House of Wax* became a huge hit, Vincent Price was thrown into a quickie imitation with a similar turn-of-the-century setting, fantastic plot and lurid murders. He hams it up endearingly as a deranged illusionist who kills the rival who stole his outrageous tricks, and then assumes his identity. Wonderfully over-the-top nonsense, with Price badly dubbed each time he's in disguise, and featuring the "buzz saw trick that isn't" and the marvellous stage "crematorium". Like *House of Wax*, it was originally shot in 3-D, which explains some of the weirder effects.

Vincent Price *Gallico* • Mary Murphy *Karen Lee* • Eva Gabor *Claire* • John Emery *Rinaldi* • Donald Randolph *Ross Ormond* • Lenita Lane *Alice Prentiss* • Patrick O'Neal *Bruce Allen* ■ *Dir* John Brahm • *Scr* Crane Wilbur

Mad Max ★★★★★🔞

Futuristic action adventure
1979 · Ausl · Colour · 88mins

Though a supremely low-budget affair, Australian director George Miller's debut feature is a highly inventive, violent action picture, which became an international hit, made a star of Mel Gibson and has spawned two sequels. Gibson is at his mean and moody best as a heroic cop, one of the few who are left trying to hold together a disintegrating society in a bleak and desolate future. Perhaps the reason this vigilante fantasy cost so little was that Gibson was being paid by the word, since he, like the rest of the cast, hardly utters a syllable. What the film lacks in repartee, it makes up for in rip-roaring spectacle, marvellous chase sequences, terrific stunts and natty leather costumes, setting an early example of grunge chic. Contains violence and swearing. 🔲

Mel Gibson *Max Rockatansky* • Joanne Samuel *Jessie* • Hugh Keays-Byrne *Toecutter* • Steve Bisley *Jim Goose* • Tim Burns *Johnny the Boy* • Roger Ward *Fifi Macaffee* • Vince Gil *Nightrider* • Geoff Parry *Bubba Zanetti* ■ *Dir* George Miller (2) • *Scr* George Miller (2), James McCausland, from a story by George Miller (2), Byron Kennedy

Mad Max 2 ★★★★🔞

Futuristic action adventure
1981 · Ausl · Colour · 91mins

After the low-budget nihilism of the original movie, director George Miller moved up a gear and the result was this violent, slick and exhilarating action thriller that further helped launch Mel Gibson into superstardom. His police days now well behind him, Mel the road warrior comes to the aid of a peace-loving group that owns a valuable source of fuel and is being threatened by the voracious gangs that patrol the highways of the future. Gibson is appropriately charismatic as the introspective hero, and Miller doesn't take his foot off the accelerator for a second. Contains violence and swearing. 🔲 *DVD*

Mel Gibson *Max Rockatansky* • Bruce Spence *Gyro captain* • Vernon Wells *Wez* • Emil Minty

Feral Kid • Mike Preston *Pappagallo* • Kjell Nilsson *Humungus* • Virginia Hey *Warrior woman* • Syd Heylen *Curmudgeon* ■ *Dir* George Miller (2) • *Scr* Terry Hayes, George Miller (2), Brian Hannant

Mad Max beyond Thunderdome ★★★15

Futuristic action adventure
1985 · Ausl · Colour · 102mins

The third in Mel Gibson's sci-fi series is the weakest, but it remains a hugely entertaining futuristic spectacular. This time around Gibson finds himself a reluctant surrogate father to a lost tribe of youngsters, as well as getting mixed up with gladiatorial battles in the thunderdome of the wild city of Bartertown, ruled over by the extraordinary Tina Turner. Directors George Miller and George Ogilvie stage some exhilarating set pieces and keep the action bustling along nicely, even if there are also some daft dollops of new ageism that tend to hold up the proceedings. Gibson is effortlessly charismatic in the lead role, but you can't escape the feeling that, at this late stage in the saga, he just isn't mad enough any more. Contains violence and swearing. 🔲 *DVD*

Mel Gibson *Mad Max* • Tina Turner *Aunty Entity* • Bruce Spence *Jedediah* • Adam Cockburn *Jedediah Jr* • Frank Thring *The collector* • Angelo Rossitto *The master* • Paul Larsson *The blaster* • Angry Anderson *Ironbar* ■ *Dir* George Miller (2), George Ogilvie • *Scr* Terry Hayes, George Miller (2)

The Mad Miss Manton ★★★

Crime comedy   1938 · US · BW · 65mins

Barbara Stanwyck is a delight as the Manhattan debutante and amateur detective, and so is Henry Fonda as the obsessive but romantically rather awkward newspaper editor who finds they are both chasing the same murder story. There are borrowings from *The Thin Man* and any number of screwball comedies here, and the result is slight and completely artificial. Thanks to the appeal of its stars, who would later be reunited by Preston Sturges for *The Lady Eve*, it's also thoroughly enjoyable.

Barbara Stanwyck *Melsa Manton* • Henry Fonda *Peter Ames* • Sam Levene *Lieutenant Brent* • Frances Mercer *Helen Frayne* • Stanley Ridges *Edward Norris* • Whitney Bourne *Pat James* • Vicki Lester *Kit Beverly* ■ *Dir* Leigh Jason • *Scr* Phillip J Epstein, Hal Yates, from a story by Wilson Collison

Mad Monster Party ★★★U

Animation   1967 · US · Colour · 90mins

Baron Boris von Frankenstein (voiced by Boris Karloff) throws a retirement party and invites all his celebrity monster friends in this fun animated feature, filmed in the ''Animagic'' process using stop-motion puppets. Co-written by Harvey Kurtzman, the creator of *Mad* magazine, the film also includes contributions by Forrest J Ackerman, editor of *Famous Monsters of Filmland*. Dracula, the Creature from the Black Lagoon, Dr Jekyll and Mr Hyde, the Mummy, the Invisible Man and the Hunchback of Notre Dame all make the guest list in an enchanting blend of horror and comedy. 🔲

Boris Karloff *Baron Boris von Frankenstein* • Phyllis Diller *Frankenstein's wife* ■ *Dir* Jules Bass • *Scr* Len Korobkin, Harvey Kurtzman, Forrest J Ackerman, from a story by Arthur Rankin Jr

The Mad Room ★★

Drama   1969 · US · Colour · 92mins

In this remake of the Ida Lupino movie *Ladies in Retirement* (1941), Shelley Winters plays a rich widow whose companion and housekeeper (Stella Stevens) gets her younger brother and sister to move in with them. The problem is that the siblings are recently released mental patients who may have murdered their parents. Pitched as a whodunit, with a shock ending that's fairly easy to predict, the film needs stronger, spookier styling than TV director Bernard Girard gives it. Stevens, however – better known as a blonde comedienne – does well in a rare dramatic role.

Stella Stevens *Ellen Hardy* • Shelley Winters *Mrs Gladys Armstrong* • Skip Ward *Sam Aller* • Carol Cole *Chris* • Severn Darden *Nate* • Beverly Garland *Mrs Racine* ■ *Dir* Bernard Girard • *Scr* Bernard Girard, Az Martin, from the play *Ladies in Retirement* by Reginald Denham, Edward Percy, and the film by Reginald Denham, Garrett Ford

Mad Wednesday ★★★U

Comedy   1950 · US · BW · 76mins

This is the re-edited, re-released version of writer/director Preston Sturges's 1947 film *The Sin of of Harold Diddlebock*. The brilliant premise has elegant silent movie clown Harold Lloyd (in his final role) in a story showing what has happened to one of his earlier creations, the football hero star of *The Freshman* (1925). Thus two comic giants were united on one project and, although this is not the masterpiece it could have been, it still features some wonderful comic moments.

Harold Lloyd *Harold Diddlebock* • Frances Ramsden *Miss Otis* • Jimmy Conlin *Wormy* • Raymond Walburn *EJ Waggleberry* • Edgar Kennedy *Jake, the bartender* • Arline Judge *Manicurist* • Franklin Pangborn *Formfit Franklin* • Lionel Stander *Max* • Margaret Hamilton *Flora* ■ *Dir/Scr* Preston Sturges

Madagascar Skin ★★★15

Drama   1995 · UK · Colour · 91mins

Slow-moving and often wordless, director Chris Newby's follow-up to the enigmatic *Anchoress* is a weird and wonderful boy-meets-boy fable. Bored with the big city, John Hannah (his face covered with a birthmark in the shape of Madagascar) heads for the coast where he discovers cheeky Bernard Hill buried up to his neck in sand. When the two outcasts set up home together in a semi-derelict cottage, this strangely endearing chamber piece becomes an inventive and brave drama. Proof indeed that a film need contain neither action nor adventure, only telling little intimate moments, to be vastly enjoyable and satisfying. Contains swearing. 🔲

Bernard Hill *Flint* • John Hannah *Harry* • Mark Anthony *Adonis* • Mark Petit *Lover* • Danny Earl *Lover* • Robin Neath *Thug* • Simon Bennett *Thug* ■ *Dir/Scr* Chris Newby

Madam Satan ★

Comedy musical   1930 · US · BW · 80mins

Directed by Cecil B DeMille, this must be one of the most bizarre films ever made. It begins as a supposed comedy of manners, with socialite Kay Johnson catching on to the fact that her frivolous husband, Reginald Denny, is having an affair with good-time girl Lillian Roth. Played as a mind-numbingly unfunny and badly acted farce for the first half, it becomes a characteristic DeMille extravaganza in the second, when Roland Young throws a costume party aboard a dirigible hovering over Manhattan. There Johnson masquerades as an exotic *femme fatale*, the eponymous Madam Satan, in order to win her man back. For collectors of curiosities only.

Kay Johnson *Angela Brooks* • Reginald Denny *Bob Brooks* • Roland Young *Jimmy Wade* • Lillian Roth *Trixie* • Elsa Peterson *Martha* ■ *Dir* Cecil B DeMille • *Scr* Jeanie Macpherson, Gladys Unger, Elsie Janis

Madame ★★

Period comedy
1961 · Fr/It/Sp · Colour · 100mins

Sophia Loren plays the woman who does Napoleon's laundry, though this is before he started to own most of Europe. Gloria Swanson starred in the 1925 version of Victorien Sardou and Emile Moreau's play; there was also an Argentinian production in 1945. This version, directed by swashbuckler specialist Christian-Jaque, is a pleasantly frothy affair, with Loren falling for Robert Hossein's nobleman, marrying him and generally leading from the front in the manner of her Italian comedies. Italian dialogue dubbed into English.

Sophia Loren *Madame Sans-Gêne* • Robert Hossein *Lefevre* • Julien Bertheau *Napoleon* • Marina Berti *Elisa* • Carlo Giuffre *Jerome* ■ *Dir* Christian-Jaque • *Scr* Henri Jeanson, Ennio De Concini, Christian-Jaque, Franco Solinas, Jean Ferry, from the play *Madame Sans-Gêne* by Emile Moreau, Victorien Sardou

Madame Bovary ★★★★

Drama   1933 · Fr · BW · 101mins

What a tragedy that the producers of this fascinating adaptation of Flaubert's classic novel should have felt the need to cut over an hour from the three-hour original in the interests of commercial viability. Director Jean Renoir had attempted to translate the novel's subtle symbolism into cinematic terms and, through his pioneering use of deep-focus photography, he succeeded in visibly locating his heroine in the stifling provincial surroundings that so repressed her spirit. You'll either love or loathe Valentine Tessier's Emma Bovary, but there's no doubting the quality of Renoir's elder brother Pierre's performance as the insensitive doctor. It may not be the director's whole vision, but it's still a remarkable film. In French with English subtitles.

Valentine Tessier *Emma Bovary* • Pierre Renoir *Charles Bovary* • Fernand Fabre *Rodolphe Boulanger* • Daniel Lecourtois *Leon* • Pierre Larquey *Hippolyte* • Christiane Dor *Madame Le François* • Monette Dinay *Félicité* • Alice Tissot *Madame Bovary, Charles's mother* ■ *Dir* Jean Renoir • *Scr* Jean Renoir, from the novel by Gustave Flaubert

Madame Bovary ★★★

Drama   1949 · US · BW · 114mins

James Mason, as author Gustave Flaubert, defends his renowned tale in flashback from a Paris court in which he finds himself accused of violating contemporary morality. The story he recounts is dressed in MGM's finest forties production values, and directed by master of style Vincente Minnelli, whose wonderful ball sequence is one of the cinema's great unrecognised set pieces. Unfortunately, Jennifer Jones lacks the range for Emma Bovary, but she tries gamely, while Van Heflin and Louis Jourdan as her husband and lover respectively are both perfectly cast. This film was critically abused in its day, but now stands up well against other screen versions, including those by Jean Renoir and Claude Chabrol.

Jennifer Jones *Emma Bovary* • James Mason *Gustave Flaubert* • Van Heflin *Charles Bovary* • Louis Jourdan *Rodolphe Boulanger* • Christopher Kent [Alf Kjellin] *Leon Dupuis* • Gene Lockhart *J Homais* • Frank Allenby *L'hereux* • Gladys Cooper *Madame Dupuis* ■ *Dir* Vincente Minnelli • *Scr* Robert Ardrey, from the novel by Gustave Flaubert

Madame Bovary ★★★PG

Period romance   1991 · Fr · Colour · 136mins

Isabelle Huppert's third movie collaboration with Claude Chabrol promised much. But their resolute fidelity to Flaubert's novel makes this a less effective film than previous adaptations by Jean Renoir and Vincente Minnelli. As the doctor's wife tempted into adultery by the tedium of rural life, Huppert brilliantly conveys the stifled passions that bring about her ruin, while Chabrol uses all his skill at psychological dissection to expose the social and moral rigidity of the mid-19th century. Yet this internality and literariness prevent us from engaging with the action. In French with English subtitles. 🔲

Isabelle Huppert *Emma Bovary* • Jean-François Balmer *Charles Bovary* • Jean Yanne *Monsieur Homais, Pharmacist* • Christophe Malavoy *Rodolphe Boulanger* • Lucas Belvaux *Leon Dupuis* • Jean-Louis Maury *L'heureux* ■ *Dir* Claude Chabrol • *Scr* Claude Chabrol, from the novel by Gustave Flaubert

Madame Butterfly ★

Drama   1932 · US · BW · 86mins

Madame Butterfly started life as a novel in the late 1890s and became a play in 1900, but is now best known as an opera by Puccini. Alas, Paramount came a cropper with this film version, an updated presentation told as straight melodrama. Directed at a snail's pace by Marion Gering, with Cary Grant not at his best as Lieutenant Pinkerton, it's a turgid bore. Sylvia Sidney has the perfect face and sad soulful eyes for Butterfly, the Japanese girl whose heart is broken by Pinkerton's desertion. In the end, though, it's just not enough.

Sylvia Sidney *Cho-cho San* • Cary Grant *Lt BF Pinkerton* • Charlie Ruggles [Charles Ruggles] *Lt Barton* • Irving Pichel *Yamadori* • Helen Jerome Eddy *Cho-cho San's mother* • Edmund Breese *Cho-cho San's grandfather* • Louise Carter *Suzuki* ■ *Dir* Marion Gering • *Scr* Josephine Lovett, Joseph Moncure March, from the play by David Belasco, from the novel by John Luther Long

Madame Butterfly ★★ PG

Opera
1995 · Fr/Jap/Ger/UK · Colour · 134mins

Directed by Frédéric Mitterrand (nephew of the French president), this adaptation of Puccini's opera has the advantage of an admirable cast and some magnificent locations. But, like so many filmed operas before it, it fails to reproduce the thrill that comes from hearing the live operatic voice. Mitterrand wastes his settings either by clumping his cast together in huddled groups or by filming the important arias in tight close-up. Ying Huang gives a superb rendition of *One Fine Day* and Richard Troxell is solid as the American sailor who breaks a geisha's heart. But, in other respects, this a disappointingly unimaginative version. In Italian with English subtitles.

Huang Ying *Madame Butterfly* • Richard Troxell *Pinkerton* • Liang Ning *Suzuki* • Richard Cowan *Sharpless* • Ma Fan Jing *Goro* • Christopheren Nomura *Prince Yamadori* • Constance Hauman *Kate Pinkerton* • Yo Kusakabe *Uncle Bonze* ■ *Dir* Frédéric Mitterrand • *Scr* Frédéric Mitterrand, from the opera by Giacomo Puccini

Madame Curie ★★★ U

Biographical drama 1943 · US · BW · 124mins

Two hours of MGM gloss canonising the discoverer of radium might be a bit much for modern palates, but this thoughtful and finely-acted biopic was the epitome of taste in its day. Greer Garson and Walter Pidgeon – as Marie and Pierre Curie – X-ray themselves into dramatic bliss, with hardly a thought for the side effects (like audiences falling into a coma, for instance). Anyone who has seen Judy Garland's *Madam Crematon* take-off in *Ziegfeld Follies* will struggle to take this seriously, but it still represents worthy, educational, sincere Louis B Mayerism at its best, receiving seven Academy Award nominations.

Greer Garson *Madame Marie Curie* • Walter Pidgeon *Pierre Curie* • Robert Walker *David LeGros* • Dame May Whitty *Madame Eugene Curie* • Henry Travers *Eugene Curie* • C Aubrey Smith *Lord Kelvin* • Albert Basserman *Professor Jean Perot* • Victor Francen *President of university* ■ *Dir* Mervyn LeRoy • *Scr* Paul Osborn, Paul H Rameau, from a biography by Eve Curie

Madame de... ★★★★

Drama 1953 · Fr/It · BW · 105mins

Although Max Ophüls's penultimate film was Oscar-nominated for its costumes, it really should have brought him a direction award, as he sends his camera on a series of gliding shots around the luxurious haunts of the idle rich, revealing their every secret and laying bare their empty souls. Danielle Darrieux is the unnamed noblewoman of the title, whose precious earrings, which she has supposedly sold, return to her via husband Charles Boyer's mistress and her own lover, Vittorio De Sica. The script is witty, the performances beyond sophistication. Deliciously blending Sacha Guitry's *The Pearls of the Crown* and Ophüls's own *La Ronde*, this is just about as polished as European cinema gets. In French with English subtitles.

Danielle Darrieux *Countess Louise De...* • Charles Boyer *General André De...* • Vittorio De Sica *Baron Fabrizio Donati* • Mireille Perrey *Madame De...'s nurse* • Jean Debucourt *Monsieur Rémy, the jeweller* • Serge Lecointe *Jérome, his son* • Lia Di Léo *Lola, the general's mistress* • Jean Galland *Monsieur De Bernac* ■ *Dir* Max Ophüls • *Scr* Marcel Achard, Max Ophüls, Annette Wademant, from the novel by Louise de Vilmorin

Madame Du Barry ★★

Historical drama 1934 · US · BW · 79mins

The life and times of Louis XV's court at Versailles, seen through the eyes of his famed mistress from the time the king takes her up to her banishment when Louis XVI succeeds to the throne. Dolores Del Rio is ravishingly beautiful, as befits the legendary Du Barry. Sadly, though, she lacks the personality required to carry this lavishly mounted but disappointingly dull historical romance. Reginald Owen is the king, while the large cast impersonating the usual figures of the period includes Osgood Perkins, father of Anthony, as Cardinal Richelieu.

Delores Del Rio *Mme Du Barry* • Reginald Owen *King Louis XV* • Victor Jory *Duke D'Aiguillon* • Osgood Perkins *Richelieu* • Verree Teasdale *Duchess De Granmont* • Henry O'Neill *Duc De Choiseul* • Anita Louise *Marie Antoinette* ■ *Dir* William Dieterle • *Scr* Edward Chodorov

Madame du Barry ★★★

Historical drama 1954 · Fr/It · Colour · 110mins

Martine Carol, star of this lavish costume drama, was France's leading sex symbol and top box-office attraction in the years preceding the rise of Brigitte Bardot, and many of her greatest hits were directed by her husband Christian-Jaque. Though the director was not a favourite with the critics, the public loved his work, and it is easy to see why. This example has a typical mix of gorgeous settings, exuberant performances and an emphasis on entertainment rather than historical accuracy, and Carol complements her sex appeal with an adroit performance. Her career sadly plummeted with the rise of Bardot, and she died of a heart attack at the age of 45. A French language film.

Martine Carol *Madame Du Barry* • Andre Luguet *Louis XV* • Daniel Ivernel *Count Du Barry* • Gianna-Maria Canale *Madame Gramont* ■ *Dir* Christian-Jaque • *Scr* Christian-Jaque, Albert Valentin, Henri Jeanson

Madame Rosa ★

Drama 1977 · Fr · Colour · 105mins

Sentimental and manipulative rubbish about an Auschwitz survivor and ex-prostitute who lives out her final days in Paris cared for by an Arab youth (Samy Ben Youb). Based on a pseudonymous novel by Romain Gary, the movie is full of Arab-Israeli pieties, flashbacks to the Holocaust and a performance from Simone Signoret that was calculated to win prizes and publicity in the twilight of her career. It can be compared to Rod Steiger's deeply pretentious *The Pawnbroker*, though its badness didn't stop it winning an Oscar for best foreign film. In French with English subtitles.

Simone Signoret *Madame Rosa* • Samy Ben Youb *Mohammed, "Momo"* • Claude Dauphin *Dr Katz* • Gabriel Jabbour *Monsieur Hamil* • Michal Bat-Adam *Madame Nadine* • Costa-Gavras *Ramon* ■ *Dir* Moshe Mizrahi • *Scr* Moshe Mizrahi, from the novel *Momo* by Emile Ajar [Romain Gary]

Madame Sin ★★ PG

Spy thriller 1972 · US · Colour · 86mins

Made for television originally, but released theatrically over here, this cramped-looking melodrama offers a splendid character part to Bette Davis, who loses no opportunity to chew all the scenery in sight. Co-star Robert Wagner has little to do but observe this awesome spectacle, while director David Greene has the good sense to stand well back and let Davis queen it over a batch of English worthies (Denholm Elliott, Gordon Jackson, Roy Kinnear). The plot, by the way, is some tortuous spy stuff about flogging off a Polaris submarine. ▭

Bette Davis *Madame Sin* • Robert Wagner *Tony Lawrence* • Denholm Elliott *Malcolm* • Gordon Jackson *Commander Teddy Cavandish* • Dudley Sutton *Monk* • Catherine Schell *Barbara* • Paul Maxwell *Connors* • Roy Kinnear *Holidaymaker* ■ *Dir* David Greene • *Scr* David Greene, Barry Oringer

Madame Sousatzka ★★★ 15

Drama 1988 · UK · Colour · 115mins

John Schlesinger's careful adaptation (with Ruth Prawer Jhabvala) of Bernice Rubens's novel was rather lost in the crowd on its release. Yet it is an engaging picture that slowly draws you into the quietly tragic lives of the inhabitants of Peggy Ashcroft's rundown London house. As the imperious piano teacher of the title, Shirley MacLaine beautifully combines the wistful regret for her own disappointments with a commitment to the future of the students whom she encourages to live the artistic life to the full. Navin Chowdhry is an excellent foil as her teenage prodigy, while Twiggy and Geoffrey Bayldon do well as fellow tenants worn down by their everyday lives. Contains swearing. ▭

Shirley MacLaine *Madame Sousatzka* • Peggy Ashcroft *Lady Emily* • Twiggy *Jenny* • Navin Chowdhry *Manek Sen* • Shabana Azmi *Sushila Sen* • Leigh Lawson *Ronnie Blum* • Geoffrey Bayldon *Mr Cordle* • Lee Montague *Vincent Pick* ■ *Dir* John Schlesinger • *Scr* Ruth Prawer Jhabvala, John Schlesinger, from the novel by Bernice Rubens

Madame X ★★

Drama 1929 · US · BW · 95mins

After a romantic indiscretion, a Parisian wife is thrown out by her eminent but unbending lawyer husband. Forbidden to see her beloved son, she sinks into a life of alcoholic degradation. Based on a French play, this classic melodrama fascinated film-makers and audiences for decades, resulting in two silent films, three sound versions and a 1981 TV movie with Tuesday Weld. The title role is here played by the splendid Broadway actress Ruth Chatterton, with Lewis Stone as the husband. Both Chatterton and director Lionel Barrymore were Oscar-nominated, but the film now seems slow, mannered and stagey.

Ruth Chatterton *Jacqueline* • Lewis Stone *Floriot* • Raymond Hackett *Raymond* • Holmes Herbert *Noel* • Eugenie Besserer *Rose* ■ *Dir* Lionel Barrymore • *Scr* Willard Mack, from the play by Alexandre Bisson

Madame X ★★★★

Melodrama 1937 · US · BW · 75mins

Gladys George takes the title role in the second, and best, talkie version of the melodrama to end them all. She meets the challenge head on in a powerful performance that pulls no punches, and the film as a whole is played with a seriousness that undercuts the soap opera, at least until the sentimental histrionics of the courtroom finale. Warren William is perfectly cast as George's husband, while Henry Daniell is suitably slimy as the con man who undoes her. This treatment is much fuller than Lionel Barrymore's 1929 film, charting the various steps in the heroine's tragic descent as she travels the world, finding only despair and degradation.

Gladys George *Jacqueline Fleuriot* • John Beal *Raymond Fleuriot* • Warren William *Bernard Fleuriot* • Reginald Owen *Maurice Dourel* • Henry Daniell *Lerocle* • Jonathan Hale *Hugh Fariman Sr* • William Henry *Hugh Fariman Jr* ■ *Dir* Sam Wood • *Scr* John Meehan, from the play by Alexandre Bisson

Madame X ★★

Drama 1966 · US · Colour · 100mins

The third version of Alexandre Bisson's play about a woman on trial for murder unknowingly defended by her son. Here producer Ross Hunter casts Lana Turner in the leading role, following successes with her in *Imitation of Life* and (to a lesser degree) *Portrait in Black*. Trouble is, Turner seems to have aged suddenly since those two films, and the lame direction also does her no favours. Still, there's a super support cast, including Constance Bennett in her last screen appearance and *2001*'s Keir Dullea as the lawyer son.

Lana Turner *Holly Parker* • John Forsythe *Clay Anderson* • Ricardo Montalban *Phil Benton* • Burgess Meredith *Dan Sullivan* • Constance Bennett *Estelle* • Teddy Quinn *Clay Jr as a child* • Keir Dullea *Clay Jr as an adult* ■ *Dir* David Lowell Rich • *Scr* Jean Holloway, from the play by Alexandre Bisson

MADD: Mothers against Drunk Drivers ★★★

Drama based on a true story 1983 · US · Colour · 96mins

Mariette Hartley earned herself an Emmy nomination for her whole-hearted performance as Candy Lightner, the Californian mother who launched a national campaign after her young daughter was killed in a hit-and-run accident. To his credit, director William A Graham presents clear-headed arguments rather than scoring easy melodramatic points.

Mariette Hartley *Candy Lightner* • Paula Prentiss *Lynne Wiley* • John Rubinstein *Steve White* • Shelby Balik *Cari Lightner/Serena Lightner* • Robert Carnegie *Doug Hamilton* • Nicolas Coster *Maurice Carver* • Lee DeBroux *Officer Chesrow* • Alan Fudge *Porter* ■ *Dir* William A Graham • *Scr* Michael Braverman

The Maddening ★★ 18
Horror thriller   1995 · US · Colour · 92mins

Cassie's trip to see her sister turns nasty when she takes a short cut proposed to her by shifty gas station owner Scudder (Burt Reynolds). That's because Reynolds is a nutcase who kidnaps Cassie (Mia Sara) and her daughter Samantha to keep his own deranged wife (Angie Dickinson) and child company. This slickly produced thriller is fairly well-acted, with Burt's presence evoking memories of *Deliverance*. Alas, it's too exploitative and sordid to provide much entertainment value. 📼

Burt Reynolds *Roy Scudder* • Angie Dickinson *Georgina Scudder* • Mia Sara *Cassie Osborne* • Brian Wimmer *David Osborne* • Josh Mostel *Chicky Ross* • William Hickey *Daddy* ■ *Dir* Danny Huston • *Scr* Henry Slesar, Leslie Greif

Made for Each Other ★★★ U
Comedy drama   1939 · US · BW · 90mins

A besotted young couple who marry in indecent haste face a mounting series of travails in the form of her difficult mother-in-law (Lucile Watson), his failure to gain promotion in his law firm and, climactically, the potentially fatal illness of their baby son. James Stewart and Carole Lombard star, while Charles Coburn is terrific as the crusty law boss; the director is John Cromwell, a master of soap opera. Although certainly not one of the best of its kind (Stewart's self-deprecating persona is almost irritating here), the formula is gold-plated. 📀 *DVD*

Carole Lombard *Jane Mason* • James Stewart *Johnny Mason* • Charles Coburn *Judge Joseph Doolittle* • Lucile Watson *Mrs Mason* • Harry Davenport *Dr Healy* • Ruth Weston *Eunice Doolittle* ■ *Dir* John Cromwell • *Scr* Jo Swerling, Frank Ryan

Made in America ★★ 12
Romantic comedy   1993 · US · Colour · 106mins

The central idea of this comedy has potential – a young black teenager discovers that her biological father is white because of a mix-up at the sperm bank – and the cast just about makes it watchable. Whoopi Goldberg and Ted Danson turn in engaging performances as the unsuspecting parents, and Nia Long is entirely believable as their confused offspring, while Will Smith provides confident, film-star-in-the-making support. However, most of the creative energy seems to have gone into dreaming up the idea itself: the finished product is low on laughs and thin on content, and Richard Benjamin's direction is merely workmanlike. Contains swearing. 📼

Whoopi Goldberg *Sarah Mathews* • Ted Danson *Hal Jackson* • Nia Long *Zora Mathews* • Will Smith *Tea Cake Walters* • Paul Rodriguez *Jose* • Jennifer Tilly *Stacy* • Peggy Rea *Alberta* • Clyde Kusatsu *Bob Takashima* ■ *Scr* Richard Benjamin • *Scr* Holly Goldberg Sloan, from a story by Marcia Brandwynne, Nadine Schiff, Holly Goldberg Sloan

Made in Heaven ★★ U
Comedy   1952 · UK · Colour · 81mins

This sprightly comedy was inspired by the ancient English custom of the "Dunmow Flitch", in which married couples sought to win a sizeable side of bacon by swearing on Whit Monday to an uninterrupted year of wedded bliss. However, the chances of the ideally suited Petula Clark and David Tomlinson take a dip when they employ a pouting Hungarian maid (Sonja Ziemann). Vicar Richard Wattis and his stern sister (Athene Seyler) add considerably to the fun, which is steadily directed by John Paddy Carstairs and glossily photographed by Geoffrey Unsworth.

Petula Clark *Julie Topham* • David Tomlinson *Basil Topham* • Sonja Ziemann *Marta* • AE Matthews *Grandpa* • Charles Victor *Mr Topham* • Sophie Stewart *Mrs Topham* • Richard Wattis *Vicar* • Athene Seyler *Miss Honeycroft* ■ *Dir* John Paddy Carstairs • *Scr* William Douglas Home, George H Brown

Made in Heaven ★★ PG
Romantic fantasy   1987 · US · Colour and BW · 98mins

This quirky fantasy was cult director Alan Rudolph's conscious bid for a box-office hit. Had it been made in the Golden Age of Hollywood, it would probably have been a frothy delight, but Rudolph too often strains for effect. Timothy Hutton stars as a dead man who meets his future love (Kelly McGillis) in heaven when she's not yet been born. It looks good, like most Rudolph movies (*Choose Me*, *Trouble in Mind*), and Hutton handles the comedy with aplomb. Hutton's then wife Debra Winger gives an uncredited performance as the male administrative head of heaven. 📼

Timothy Hutton *Mike Shea/Elmo Barnett* • Kelly McGillis *Annie Packert/Ally Chandler* • Maureen Stapleton *Aunt Lisa* • Ann Wedgeworth *Annette Shea* • James Gammon *Steve Shea* • Mare Winningham *Brenda Carlucci* • Don Murray *Ben Chandler* • Timothy Daly *Tom Donnelly* ■ *Dir* Alan Rudolph • *Scr* Bruce A Evans, Raynold Gideon

Made in Hong Kong ★★★★ 15
Drama   1997 · HK · Colour · 108mins

Like Roberto Rossellini's *Rome, Open City*, Fruit Chan's searching study of a community in transition was shot on discarded scraps of film stock and makes powerful use of its authentic locations and unfamiliar performers. Prone to technical gimmickry and overdoing the political symbolism, Chan nevertheless brings an abrasive energy to this story of a triad wannabe imprisoned by both his social circumstances and fate. Endlessly exposing raw nerves, Sam Lee captures the disillusion shared by many Hong Kong youths as he tries to protect both his slow-witted mate and his dying girlfriend, while haunted by the memory of a suicide victim he never knew. In Cantonese with English subtitles. Contains swearing, violence and sexual references.

Sam Chan-Sam Lee *To Chung-Chau, "Moon"* • Neiky Hui-Chi Yim *Lam Yuk-Ping, "Ping"* • Wenbers Tung-Chuen Li *Ah-Lung, "Sylvester"* • Amy Ka-Chuen Tam *Hui Bo-San, "Susan"* ■ *Dir/Scr* Fruit Kuo Chan

Made in Paris ★★
Romantic comedy   1966 · US · Colour · 103mins

Desperately dated comedy with Ann-Margret as an American fashion buyer in Paris discovering that, like her predecessor, she is expected to wind up in bed with seductive couturier Louis Jourdan. There's a story about lopsided morals at the heart of this, but this MGM offering devotes itself to glad rags, Ann-Margret's dancing abilities and the tourist attractions of Gay Paree. There are some Burt Bacharach ditties as well, but most viewers will probably switch off.

Ann-Margret *Maggie Scott* • Louis Jourdan *Marc Fontaine* • Richard Crenna *Herb Stone* • Edie Adams *Irene Chase* • Chad Everett *Ted Barclay* • John McGiver *Roger Barclay* ■ *Dir* Boris Sagal • *Scr* Stanley Roberts • *Music/Lyrics* Burt Bacharach, Hal David

Made in USA ★★★ 18
Crime drama   1966 · Fr · Colour · 78mins

There is a story of sorts – Anna Karina on the trail of her lover's killer – but this Jean-Luc Godard movie shows the director moving inexorably and often excitingly away from conventional narrative. As a piece of sixties Pop Art, this movie takes some beating but today's viewers, largely unaware of the impact Godard made on world cinema, will soon tire of his playing with the medium, his political slogans and passing thoughts on JFK and the Algerian war. By the time the film was made, Karina and Godard were divorced; this was their final film together. A French language film. 📼

Anna Karina *Paula Nelson* • Laszlo Szabo *Richard Widmark* • Jean-Pierre Léaud *Donald Siegel* • Yves Alfonso *David Goodis* • Ernest Menzer *Edgar Typhus* ■ *Dir* Jean-Luc Godard • *Scr* Jean-Luc Godard, from the novel *The Juggler* by Richard Stark [Donald E Westlake]

Madeleine ★★ U
Drama   1949 · UK · BW · 109mins

Only two films blot David Lean's otherwise immaculate copybook (*The Passionate Friends* is the other), and both feature Ann Todd, whom he married in 1949. Todd was never the most expressive of actresses, but here she simply doesn't act at all, her face a blank and her delivery as modulated as the speaking clock. Uncomfortable with the courtroom format and confounded by the deadliness of dialogue drawn from original trial transcripts, Lean allows love to cloud his judgement, lingering too long on his wife at the expense of what might otherwise have been an intriguing tale of murder in Victorian Glasgow. 📼

Ann Todd *Madeleine Smith* • Norman Wooland *William Minnoch* • Ivan Desny *Emile l'Angelier* • Leslie Banks *James Smith* • Edward Chapman *Dr Thompson* • Barbara Everest *Mrs Smith* • André Morell *Dean* • Barry Jones *Lord Advocate* ■ *Dir* David Lean • *Scr* Stanley Haynes, Nicholas Phipps

Madeline ★★★ U
Comedy   1998 · US/Ger · Colour · 85mins

Home Alone meets *Annie* for this sweet, but not entirely successful, kids' film based on Ludwig Bemelmans's children's books. Hatty Jones is cute as the young orphan, but adults are more likely to be charmed by a warm turn from *Fargo's* Frances McDormand as the engaging Miss Clavel, who runs the orphanage and dispenses wisdom to her charges. Well-meaning entertainment for young girls, this may get overlooked in favour of funnier fare or big-budget productions. Nonetheless it will certainly hold its audience's attention on a rainy Sunday afternoon. 📼 *DVD*

Frances McDormand *Miss Clavel* • Nigel Hawthorne *Lord Covington* • Hatty Jones *Madeline* • Ben Daniels *Leopold, the tutor* • Stéphane Audran *Lady Covington* ■ *Dir* Daisy von Scherler Mayer • *Scr* Mark Levin, Jennifer Flackett, from a story by Malia Scotch Marmo, Mark Levin, Jennifer Flackett, from the books by Ludwig Bemelmans

Mademoiselle ★★★
Psychological drama   1966 · Fr/UK · BW · 102mins

Scripted by Jean Genet, the controversial French playwright, this has Jeanne Moreau in the title role as a sexually frustrated schoolmarm in a French farming community. Her secret acts of terrorism – arson, the poisoning of a well, flooding fields – lead the hatred of the village to be directed at the object of her desires, an Italian woodcutter (Ettore Manni). It has a weird compulsion, but director Tony Richardson's over-decorative style – from the first close-up shot of Mademoiselle's gloves – is too ponderous for such frail subject matter. Both French and English language versions were filmed. A French/English language film.

Jeanne Moreau *Mademoiselle* • Ettore Manni *Manou* • Keith Skinner *Bruno* • Umberto Orsini *Antonio* • Jane Beretta *Annette* • Mony Reh *Vievotte* ■ *Dir* Tony Richardson • *Scr* Jean Gênet, Bernard Frechtman

Mademoiselle Docteur ★★★★
First World War spy drama   1936 · Fr · BW · 86mins

This melodramatic account of Germany's most famous spy, Anne-Marie Lesser, is given distinction by a fine cast and the evocative direction of GW Pabst. The plotting and assignations during the First World War are vividly re-created in salons, cabarets and railway stations, while delicately beautiful Dita Parlo makes an ethereal heroine. An English language version was made similtaneously by Edmond T Gréville with Erich von Stroheim in the role played by here Louis Jouvet. The same story had been filmed by MGM in 1934 as *Stamboul Quest* with Myrna Loy, but this is by far the best version. In French with English subtitles.

Dita Parlo *Anne-Marie Lesser/Mademoiselle Docteur* • Louis Jouvet *Simonis* • Viviane Romance *Gaby* • Charles Dullin *Col Matthesius* • Pierre Fresnay *Capt Georges Carrère* • Pierre Blanchar *Gregor Courdane/Condoyan* • Jean-Louis Barrault *Crazy customer* ■ *Dir* GW Pabst • *Scr* Irma von Cube, Georges Neveux, Leo Birinski, Herman J Mankiewicz, Jacques Natanson

Madhouse ★★★ 18
Spoof horror   1974 · UK · Colour · 87mins

In the early seventies, Vincent Price came to the UK for a string of delightfully black horror comedies, among them *Theatre of Blood* and the *Dr Phibes* movies. *Madhouse* is not in the same class, but it's an entertaining enough romp all the same. The horror legend plays a distinguished actor whose return to the small screen murders. There is a sterling support cast headed by Peter Cushing, Robert Quarry and Linda Hayden, and director Jim Clark delivers enough gory chuckles to keep Price fans more than happy. Contains swearing. 📼

Vincent Price *Paul Toombes* • Peter Cushing *Herbert Flay* • Robert Quarry *Oliver Quayle* • Adrienne Corri *Faye Flay* • Natasha Pyne *Julia* • Michael Parkinson *Television interviewer* • Linda Hayden *Elizabeth Peters* ■ *Dir* Jim Clark • *Scr* Greg Morrison, Ken Levison, from the novel *Devilday* by Angus Hall

Madhouse ★★★ 15
Comedy   1990 · US · Colour · 86mins

The unwanted guest has long been a staple of cinematic comedy. The situation is taken to its extreme in this uneven farce, in which Kirstie Alley and John Larroquette find their new love nest overrun by the kind of relatives you hope you only see at weddings and funerals. The contrast between down-on-their-luck John Diehl and Jessica Lundy and wealthy wife Alison LaPlaca makes for contrived satire, but writer/director Tom Ropelewski comes up with a couple of cracking moments, the best involving a spaced-out moggie. Contains swearing. 📼

John Larroquette *Mark Bannister* • Kirstie Alley *Jessie Bannister* • Alison LaPlaca *Claudia* • John Diehl *Fred* • Jessica Lundy *Bernice* • Bradley Gregg *Jonathan* • Dennis Miller *Wes* • Robert Ginty *Dale* ■ *Dir/Scr* Tom Ropelewski

Madigan ★★★★
Action thriller   1968 · US · Colour · 100mins

Before hitting a career high with *Dirty Harry*, gifted director Don Siegel amassed a critical and cult following with such hard-boiled movies as this terrific New York-based crime drama. The superb Richard Widmark gives one of his finest performances in the title role, but the laconic Henry Fonda is more than a match for him as the troubled police commissioner. The marvellously gritty supporting cast includes Sheree North, James Whitmore and Harry Guardino, while the film contains its fair share of sex and violence. Only the cheapness of Universal's Techniscope process disappoints, though the inherent grain oddly suits the night scenes.

Richard Widmark *Det Dan Madigan* • Henry Fonda *Commissioner Anthony Russell* • Inger Stevens *Julia Madigan* • Harry Guardino *Det Rocco Bonaro* • James Whitmore *Chief Inspector Charles Kane* • Sheree North *Jonesy* ■ *Dir* Don Siegel • *Scr* Henri Simoun, Harry Kleiner, Abraham Polonsky, from the novel *The Commissioner* by Richard Dougherty

Madigan's Millions ★
Crime caper   1967 · Sp/It · Colour · 78mins

When *Midnight Cowboy* became a massive hit, two earlier films starring Dustin Hoffman and Jon Voight – *Madigan's Millions* and *Frank's Greatest Adventure* – were exhumed to cash in on the actors' newfound

success. The Hoffman film was made in Italy in 1966, before he made *The Graduate* and shot to stardom. It's a caper comedy, with Dustin playing a US tax inspector sent to Europe to look into a murdered mobster's murky accounts. Cesar Romero is seen briefly as the gangster (he replaced George Raft in the role), while Elsa Martinelli plays his daughter. An English/Spanish/Italian language film.

Dustin Hoffman *Jason Fister* • Elsa Martinelli *Vicky Shaw* • Cesar Romero *Mike Madigan* ■ *Dir* Stanley Prager, Dan Ash, Giorgio Gentili • *Scr* James Henaghan, Jose Luis Bayonas

Madison Avenue ★★★ U
Drama   1962 · US · BW · 93mins

The final feature from prolific 20th Century-Fox director H Bruce Humberstone, this is a late round-up of once major Fox stars, in a turgid but nevertheless entertaining melodrama set in the world of advertising. "Lucky" Humberstone uses the black-and-white photography very effectively, especially on those desk-bound interiors, while stars Dana Andrews, Jeanne Crain and the wonderful Eleanor Parker shine as though they knew this was going to be one of the last gasps of the once beloved Fox studio system.

Dana Andrews *Clint Lorimer* • Eleanor Parker *Anne Tremaine* • Jeanne Crain *Peggy Shannon* • Eddie Albert *Harvey Ames* • Howard St John *JD Jocelyn* • Henry Daniell *Stipe* • Kathleen Freeman *Miss Haley* • David White *Stevenson Brock* ■ *Dir* H Bruce Humberstone • *Scr* Norman Corwin, from the novel *The Build-Up Boys* by Jeremy Kirk

Madman ★
Horror   1981 · US · Colour · 88mins

Supposedly based on the legend of Madman Marz, who took an axe to his family and then escaped the local lynch mob to disappear without a trace, this derivative bore is really an insulting steal of *Friday the 13th*, with a touch of *The Texas Chain Saw Massacre* thrown in for bad measure. The Marz tale is told around a forest campfire to a group of kids the weekend before Thanksgiving. "But don't speak his name above a whisper," they are told, or else the disfigured maniac will return to answer whoever has called him. Naturally he returns, and soon the leafy glades are splattered with blood as headless corpses, strangulation victims and mutilated bodies are dragged back to the Marz shack to be meat-hooked.

Alexis Dubin *Betsy* • Tony Fish *TP* • Harriet Bass *Stacey* • Seth Jones *Dave* • Jan Claire *Ellie* ■ *Dir/Scr* Joe Giannone

The Madness of King George ★★★★★ PG
Biographical historical drama
1995 · UK · Colour · 105mins

The celebrated film of Alan Bennett's play *The Madness of George III* won Oscars for best art direction and Bennett's screenplay. Giving an inspired, funny and deeply moving performance as George is Nigel Hawthorne, unhappily married to Helen Mirren, the father of 15 children (including foppish Rupert Everett as the Prince of Wales) and the father to a nation and an empire. Problem is,

Farmer George – a nickname the king delights in – is losing his marbles, or at least that's the official diagnosis. Surgeon Ian Holm is brought in to put the king into a straitjacket, providing some of the film's most disturbing scenes. Behind the sardonic jokes and colloquialisms which are Bennett's trademark is a serious study of 18th-century politics and the monarchy, with a final scene that hints at the House of Windsor as much as that of Hanover. Immaculately directed by Nicholas Hytner, this is an unmissable treat. Contains some swearing. 📼

Nigel Hawthorne *George III* • Helen Mirren *Queen Charlotte* • Ian Holm *Willis* • Rupert Graves *Greville* • Amanda Donohoe *Lady Pembroke* • Rupert Everett *Prince of Wales* • Julian Rhind-Tutt *Duke of York* • Julian Wadham *Pitt* • Jim Carter *Fox* • Geoffrey Palmer *Warren* ■ *Dir* Nicholas Hytner • *Scr* Alan Bennett, from his play • *Production Designer* Ken Adam

Madness of the Heart ★★ PG
Drama   1949 · UK · BW · 85mins

Margaret Lockwood's career was already in terminal decline by the time she made this unpersuasive melodrama. As the London lass convinced she's been blinded by lust, she does what she can with a preposterous plot that has her marrying her French lover, Paul Dupuis, only to become the target of a mysterious assassin. The assailant's identity is obvious from the start, but this hackneyed hokum is worth sticking with for the risible showdown, in which the now-seeing Lockwood proves the attacks have not been figments of her imagination after all. Kudos to the supporting cast for keeping straight faces throughout. 📼

Margaret Lockwood *Lydia Garth* • Paul Dupuis *Paul De Vandiere* • Maxwell Reed *Joseph Rondolet* • Thora Hird *Rosa* • Kathleen Byron *Verite Faimont* • Raymond Lovell *Comte De Vandiere* • Maurice Denham *Dr Simon Blake* ■ *Dir* Charles Bennett • *Scr* Charles Bennett, from the novel by Flora Sandstrom

Mado ★★★★
Melodrama   1976 · Fr · Colour · 135mins

This scathing snapshot of France under President Giscard d'Estaing is a typically perceptive study of the country's disconcerted, middle-aged middle classes from director Claude Sautet. Shaken by the suicide of his partner, Michel Piccoli gets lured into Julien Guiomar's attempt to swindle Charles Denner. More important than the real estate McGuffin, however, are Piccoli's relationships with Ottavia Piccolo, a prostitute at the centre of the scam, and Romy Schneider, whose desperate loyalty to this confused yet undeserving man is heartbreaking. Artistically photographed by Jean Boffety and subtly played by an exemplary ensemble, this is both riveting and revealing. In French with English subtitles.

Michel Piccoli *Simon* • Ottavia Piccolo *Mado* • Jacques Dutronc *Pierre* • Romy Schneider *Helene* • Charles Denner *Manecca* • Julien Guiomar *Boss* ■ *Dir* Claude Sautet • *Scr* Claude Sautet, Claude Néron

Madonna: Innocence Lost ★
Biographical drama
1994 · US · Colour · 90mins

A bottom-of-the-barrel docudrama, loosely based on Christopher Andersen's *Madonna: Unauthorised* biography. It luridly paints the pop star as a cold-hearted, manipulative schemer, who didn't care who she destroyed on her mission to become a cultural icon. Cheaply made, with performances to match, this standard rags-to-bitches cash-in should be taken with a pinch of salt, although Madonna fans will doubtless want to watch it no matter how low it stoops. Contains swearing and sex scenes.

Terumi Matthews *Madonna* • Dean Stockwell *Tony Ciccone* • Wendie Malick *Camille Barbone* • Jeff Yagher *Paul* ■ *Dir* Bradford May • *Scr* Michael J Murray, from the biography *Madonna: Unauthorised* by Christopher Andersen

Madonna of the Seven Moons ★★★ U
Romantic drama 1944 · UK · BW · 104mins

A huge box-office success in its day, this Gainsborough costume drama divided the critics, with many denouncing it as a piece of overblown twaddle. Director Arthur Crabtree was a first-class cinematographer, and he brings a lurid glamour to the proceedings. Crabtree is all at sea, however, where plotting and pacing are concerned. Only the experience of his cast prevents the more melodramatic passages becoming even more over-the-top. 📼

Phyllis Calvert *Maddalena Lambardi/Rosanna* • Stewart Granger *Nino Barucci* • Patricia Roc *Angela Lambardi* • Peter Glenville *Sandro Barucci* • John Stuart *Giuseppi* • Jean Kent *Vittoria* • Nancy Price *Madame Barucci* • Peter Murray Hill *Logan* ■ *Dir* Arthur Crabtree • *Scr* Roland Pertwee, Brock Williams, from the novel by Margery Lawrence

La Madre Muerta ★★★★ 18
Thriller   1993 · Sp · Colour · 106mins

Exploring dark and dangerous themes, Juanma Bajo Ulloa's intense film treads a fine line between the disturbing and the distasteful with an agility remarkable for a director making only his second feature. Set in the Basque region, the film considers the controversial topic of sex and the emotionally arrested through the eyes of both a killer (who kidnaps, years later, the mute daughter of his victim to prevent her from identifying him) and his lover (whose jealousy of the girl becomes more threatening than his fear). The acting is excellent, but it's Bajo Ulloa's relentless direction that makes this so troubling. In Spanish with English subtitles. 📼

Karra Elejalde *Ismael Lopez De Matauko* • Ana Alvarez *Leire* • Lio *Maite* • Silvia Marso *Blanca* • Elena Irureta *Female director* • Ramon Barea *Nightclub owner* • Gregoria Mangas *Mrs Millas* • Marisol Sez *Mother* ■ *Dir* Juanma Bajo Ulloa • *Scr* Juanma Bajo Ulloa, Eduardo Bajo Ulloa

Madron ★★
Western   1970 · US · Colour · 93mins

Richard Boone gives one of the craggiest of his many craggy

performances in this western about a glowering gunslinger with a soft spot for the kindly nun (Leslie Caron) he's escorting through hostile Apache territory. Shot on location in Israel's Negev desert, there are shades of *The Wild Bunch* in the way the action unfolds; the occasional brutality is another thing it shares with Sam Peckinpah's film.
Richard Boone *Madron* • Leslie Caron *Sister Mary* • Paul Smith *Gabe Price* • Gabi Amrani *Angel* • Chaim Banai *Sam Red* ■ *Dir* Jerry Hopper • *Scr* Edward Chappell, Leo McMahon, from a story by Leo McMahon

The Madwoman of Chaillot ★ U
Comedy 1969 · US · Colour · 142mins
An eccentric Parisian countess (Katharine Hepburn) and her batty companions (Margaret Leighton, Giulietta Masina) foil a grotesque plan to turn the city into a giant oilfield. This wordy, repetitive and boring version of a whimsical old play by Jean Giraudoux, updated to the sixties by Edward Anhalt, is a catastrophic failure, made worse by populating it with a starry international cast. The opulent sets and costumes, reminiscent of Versailles rather than modern Paris, fails to rescue a misconceived enterprise. It's directed without flair by Bryan Forbes, and a mannered Hepburn irritatingly runs the gamut of her emotional repertoire.
Katharine Hepburn *Countess Aurelia* • Charles Boyer *The Broker* • Claude Dauphin *Dr Jadin* • Edith Evans *Josephine* • John Gavin *The Reverend* • Paul Henreid *The General* • Oscar Homolka *Commissar* • Margaret Leighton *Constance* • Giulietta Masina *Gabrielle* ■ *Dir* Bryan Forbes • *Scr* Edward Anhalt, from the novel *La Folle de Chaillot* by Jean Giraudoux

Il Maestro ★
Drama 1989 · Fr/Bel · Colour
A French-Belgian co-production, with British Malcolm McDowell and Frenchman Charles Aznavour playing Italians. Based on a story by Mario Soldati (an Italian neorealist director and novelist), it's a convoluted story about an orchestra conductor (McDowell) who gets a touch of the vapours when rehearsing *Madame Butterfly*. This leads to a flashback to an era when both McDowell and Aznavour were on the run from the Nazis. The result is a dramatic mess that rarely holds the attention.
Malcolm McDowell *Goldberg* • Charles Aznavour *Romualdi* • Andréa Ferréol *Dolores* • Francis Lemaire *Administrator* • Carmela Locantore *Paola* • Pietro Pizzuti *Father Superior* • Serge-Henri Valcke *Major Wyatt* • Chen Qilian *Margerita* ■ *Dir* Marion Hänsel • *Scr* Marion Hänsel, from the story *La Giacca Verde* by Mario Soldati

Mafia Princess ★★ 15
Drama based on a true story 1986 · US · Colour · 96mins
Susan Lucci's over-the-top characterisation anchors this fact-based TV movie that tells the story of Antoinette Giancana, the daughter of a notorious capo (charismatically played here by Tony Curtis) who told the world about life in the Mafia and struggled to establish her own identity away from

the mob. You won't find anything new or shocking here, but there's plenty of guilty fun to be had. 📼
Susan Lucci *Antoinette Giancana* • Kathleen Widdoes *Angela Giancana* • Tony Curtis *Sam Giancana* • Chuck Shamata *Louie* ■ *Dir* Robert Collins • *Scr* Robert W Lenski, from the autobiography by Antoinette Giancana, Thomas C Renner

Magee and the Lady ★★
Romantic adventure 1978 · Ausl · Colour · 92mins
Shades of *The African Queen* as skipper Tony LoBianco (so excellent in *The Honeymoon Killers* and *City of Hope*) kidnaps the daughter of the businessman who's trying to foreclose on his freighter. Sally Kellerman co-stars and, while one has a great affection for her, she's all too often at sea in her movie assignments. This feature was known Down Under by its original title *She'll Be Sweet*.
Tony LoBianco *Magee* • Sally Kellerman *Veronica* • Anne Semler *Schneider* • Rod Mullinar *Tom* • Kevin Leslie *Bos'n Shelley* • Jacqueline Kott *Clayton* • Ken Fraser *Stirling* ■ *Dir* Gene Levitt • *Scr* Colin Free

The Maggie ★★★★ U
Comedy 1953 · UK · BW · 92mins
Ostensibly, this most underestimated of Ealing comedies is a cross between *Whisky Galore!* and *The Titfield Thunderbolt*: a whimsical story about a crew of canny Clydebankers giving a brash American a torrid time after being assigned to carry his property aboard their clapped out steamer. Don't be fooled, however, by the leisurely pace, the gentle humour and the relatively good-natured conclusion. This is a wicked little satire on the mutual contempt that underlies Euro-American relations, and few could have handled it with such incisive insight as American-born Scot, Alexander Mackendrick. The film's Ealingness somewhat draws the sting, but the tone is still cruel rather than quaint.
Paul Douglas *Marshall* • Alex Mackenzie *Skipper* • James Copeland *Mate* • Abe Barker *Engineer* • Tommy Kearins *Wee Boy* • Hubert Gregg *Pusey* • Geoffrey Keen *Campbell* • Dorothy Alison *Miss Peters* ■ *Dir* Alexander Mackendrick • *Scr* William Rose, from a story by Alexander Mackendrick

Magic ★★ 15
Thriller 1978 · US · Colour · 106mins
A low-key update of the old "ventriloquist taken over by his evil dummy" theme, scripted by William Goldman. Richard Attenborough overstretches an already thin premise and deliberately minimises the horror elements by placing the emphasis on warped entertainer Anthony Hopkins's unbalanced psychological condition. The result is a sadly sentimental effort, lacking both suspense and atmosphere. Contains swearing and some violence. 📼
Anthony Hopkins *Corky/"Fats"* • Ann-Margret *Peggy Ann Snow* • Burgess Meredith *Ben Greene* • Ed Lauter *Duke* • E J Andre *Merlin* • Jerry Houser *Cab Driver* • David Ogden Stiers *George Hudson Todson* ■ *Dir* Richard Attenborough • *Scr* William Goldman, from his novel

The Magic Bow ★★ U
Biographical drama 1946 · UK · BW · 105mins
There's a temptation to suggest that Gainsborough only undertook this biopic of the violin virtuoso Niccolo Paganini in order to get more wear out of the costumes it had commissioned for its popular Regency bodice-rippers. The few facts that have been retained have been submerged in melodramatic scenes that are notable only for a certain pomposity of dialogue, while such invented details as the duel and the pawning of his Stradivarius betray the penny-dreadful imagination of the scriptwriters. Yet somehow this film still manages to get under the skin, thanks to the vigorous vulgarity of Stewart Granger's performance and Yehudi Menuhin's vibrant playing on the soundtrack.
Stewart Granger *Paganini* • Phyllis Calvert *Jeanne* • Jean Kent *Blanchi* • Dennis Price *Paul De La Roche* • Cecil Parker *Germi* • Felix Aylmer *Pasini* ■ *Dir* Bernard Knowles • *Scr* Roland Pertwee, Norman Ginsbury, from the novel by Manuel Komroff

The Magic Box ★★★★ U
Biographical drama 1951 · UK · Colour · 103mins
Produced for the Festival of Britain, this biopic of William Friese-Greene is more a piece of wishful thinking than an accurate portrait of Britain's pre-eminent cinema pioneer. So what if Friese-Greene failed in his attempt to project moving images, and who cares if he "borrowed" many of his ideas from forgotten collaborators like John Rudge and Mortimer Evans? This is charming and thoroughly entertaining myth-making, made all the more palatable by the engaging performance of Robert Donat. Yet he was just one of the array of stars John Boulting roped into this prestigious project, chief among the others being Laurence Olivier as a policeman. 📼
Robert Donat *William Friese-Greene* • Maria Schell *Helena* • Margaret Johnston *Edith Friese-Greene* • Robert Beatty *Lord Beaverbrook* • Renée Asherson *Miss Tagg* • Michael Redgrave *Mr Lege* • Richard Attenborough *Jack Carter* • Laurence Olivier *Second Holborn policeman* • Eric Portman *Arthur Collings* • Glynis Johns *May Jones* • Margaret Rutherford *Lady Pond* • Peter Ustinov *Industry man* • Stanley Holloway *Broker's man* ■ *Dir* John Boulting • *Scr* Eric Ambler, from the book *Friese-Greene, Close-up of an Inventor* by Ray Allister

The Magic Christian ★★ 15
Comedy 1969 · UK · Colour · 88mins
Admiring Terry Southern's satirical novel of 1959, Peter Sellers sent it to Stanley Kubrick who liked its humour so much he hired Southern to work on *Dr Strangelove*. Then Sellers reunited with Southern for this comedy about the richest man in the world who adopts a drop-out son, Ringo Starr, to prove his and the rest of humanity's worthlessness. A dreadful mess, very much part of the Swinging Sixties culture, this film is also unmissable for an eye-popping cast that runs all the way from Raquel Welch to Christopher Lee. 📼
Peter Sellers *Sir Guy Grand* • Ringo Starr *Youngman Grand* • Spike Milligan *Traffic Warden* • Richard Attenborough *Oxford Coach*

• Yul Brynner *Lady Singer* • Wilfrid Hyde White *Ship's Captain* • Raquel Welch *Shipboard Galley Master* • Laurence Harvey *Hamlet* • Christopher Lee *Dracula* ■ *Dir* Joseph McGrath • *Scr* Terry Southern, Joseph McGrath, Peter Sellers, from the novel by Terry Southern

The Magic Donkey ★★★ U
Fantasy 1970 · Fr · Colour · 89mins
Following their exemplary collaboration on *The Umbrellas of Cherbourg*, director Jacques Demy and composer Michel Legrand reunited for this adaptation of Charles Perrault's distinctly dubious fairy tale. Intended as a tribute to Jean Cocteau's *La Belle et la Bête* and Walt Disney's *Snow White*, the film achieves its neverland atmosphere through the enchanting decor and some glorious colour photography from Ghislain Cloquet. However, it's hard to identify with the story of a king (Jean Marais) whose promise to his dying queen that he will only marry someone of comparable beauty sets him after his daughter (Catherine Deneuve). French dialogue dubbed in English.
Catherine Deneuve *Peau d'Ane/Queen* • Jacques Perrin *Prince* • Jean Marais *King* • Delphine Seyrig *Fairy* • Fernand Ledoux *Red King* • Micheline Presle *Red Queen* ■ *Dir* Jacques Demy • *Scr* Jacques Demy, from the fairy tales *Les Contes de Ma Mère l'Oye* by Charles Perrault

Magic Fire ★★
Biographical drama 1956 · US · Colour · 112mins
Long-delayed in reaching the screen, then barely released, this biography of composer Richard Wagner proved to be too ambitious for Republic Studios. Despite a finely upholstered look and a flamboyant performance from the excellent Alan Badel, the film is scuppered by his wooden Argentinian co-star Carlos Thompson and leaden direction from veteran William Dieterle. At least the women – Yvonne De Carlo, Rita Gam, Valentina Cortese – know how to wear the period frocks. The music's not bad, either.
Alan Badel *Richard Wagner* • Yvonne De Carlo *Minna* • Carlos Thompson *Franz Liszt* • Rita Gam *Cosina* • Valentina Cortese *Mathilde* • Peter Cushing *Otto Wesendonk* • Frederick Valk *Minister von Moll* • Gerhard Riedmann *King Ludwig II* ■ *Dir* William Dieterle • *Scr* Bertita Harding, EA Dupont, David Chantler, from the novel by Bertita Harding • *Music* Erich Wolfgang Korngold

The Magic Flute ★★★ U
Opera 1974 · Swe · Colour · 134mins
Aiming both to re-create the contemporary experience of watching Mozart's final operatic masterpiece and make opera accessible to viewers of all races and ages, Ingmar Bergman's stylised staging only fitfully succeeds. A surfeit of audience reaction shots and some rather twee backstage docu-snaps interfere with the flow of the story. However, the studio re-creation of the handsome Drottningholm Theatre and its 18th-century paraphernalia is delightful, while the cast is admirable. It's certainly not dull, but Bergman is over-zealous in his determination to avoid

accusations of theatricality. In Swedish with English subtitles.

Josef Köstlinger *Tamino* • Irma Urrila *Pamina* • Hakan Hagegard *Papageno* • Elisabeth Eriksson *Papagena* • Ulrik Cold *Sarastro* ■ *Dir* Ingmar Bergman • *Scr* Ingmar Bergman

Magic Hunter ★★★

Fantasy
1994 · Hun/Swi/Fr/Can · Colour · 106mins

Executive produced by David Bowie and starring Gary Kemp and Sadie Frost, this is a surreal though beautiful treatise from director Ildiko Enyedi. Set in medieval Hungary and contemporary Budapest, the film interweaves two tales. One tells the story of a policeman (Kemp) who loses his ability to shoot on target just when he is assigned to protect a chess master from assassination. The other involves a painting of the Virgin Mary (Natalie Conde) coming to life to save a rabbit! In Hungarian with English subtitles.

Gary Kemp *Max* • Sadie Frost *Eva* • Alexander Kaidanovsky *Maxim* • Peter Vallai *Kaspar* • Mathias Gnadinger *Police chief* • Alexandra Wasscher *Lili* • Ildiko Toth *Lina* • Natalie Conde *Virgin Mary* ■ *Dir* Ildiko Enyedi • *Scr* Ildiko Enyedi, Laszlo Revesz, from the opera *Der Freischutz* by Carl Maria von Weber

Magic in the Water ★★★ PG

Fantasy adventure
1995 · Can/US · Colour · 96mins

A charming family film about a mythical water creature that helps a psychiatrist realise he's so wrapped up in his work that he's making a mess of both his life and his relationship with his kids. Rick Stevenson's film wisely goes easy on the special effects, emphasising instead the magic inherent in its basic scenario. Mark Harmon and Harley Jane Kozak star in a slice of thoroughly delightful escapism that will enchant children and their parents. 🖭

Mark Harmon *Jack Black* • Joshua Jackson *Joshua Black* • Harley Jane Kozak *Dr Wanda Bell* • Sarah Wayne *Ashley Black* • Willie Nark-Orn *Hiro* • Frank Sotonoma Salsedo [Frank Salsedo] *Uncle Kipper* ■ *Dir* Rick Stevenson • *Scr* Rick Stevenson, Icel Dobell Massey, from a story by Ninian Dunnett, Rick Stevenson, Icel Dobell Massey

Magic Island ★ PG

Fantasy drama 1995 · US · Colour · 84mins

Aside from an impressive stop-motion animation scene involving a stone statue coming to life, this children's fantasy is almost completely devoid of special effects, sets or props of any kind. An annoyingly flip Zachery Ty Bryan plays a neglected teenager who is transported to the eponymous isle, where he is pursued through the jungle by Blackbeard (Andrew Divoff) and his moronic henchmen. It's performed and directed as a live-action cartoon, right down to the sound of tweeting birds when someone is hit in the head. The result is strictly for those who haven't learned to read yet.

Zachery Ty Bryan "*Mad*" *Jack* • Edward Kerr *Prince Morgan* • Lee Armstrong *Gwya* • French Stewart *Supperstein* • Jessie-Ann Friend *Lily* • Andrew Divoff *Blackbeard* ■ *Dir* Sam Irvin • *Scr* Brent V Friedman, Neil Ruttenberg

The Magic of Lassie ★★

Drama 1978 · US · Colour · 99mins

Not even the presence of James Stewart, Mickey Rooney and Alice Faye can save this otherwise unremarkable attempt to resurrect the world's most famous collie. Director Don Chaffey (*Greyfriars Bobby*, *Jason and the Argonauts*) sticks closely to the story of the original *Lassie Come Home*, as nasty Pernell Roberts takes Lassie away from a debt-ridden family. The 1943 classic was genuinely uplifting – this is just cloyingly sentimental.

James Stewart *Clovis Mitchell* • Mickey Rooney *Gus* • Alice Faye *Alice* • Pernell Roberts *Jamison* • Stephanie Zimbalist *Kelly Mitchell* • Michael Sharrett *Chris Mitchell* ■ *Dir* Don Chaffey • *Scr* Jean Holloway, Robert B Sherman, Richard M Sherman

The Magic Sword ★★★

Fantasy 1962 · US · Colour · 80mins

This medieval fantasy never really takes off, coming across as a blunt version of *Excalibur*. Gary Lockwood plays a young knight who sets out to rescue princess Anne Helm from wicked sorcerer Basil Rathbone. The latter is magnificent, as usual, while Estelle Winwood's witch is a wonderful piece of dithery expertise. Otherwise, though, this not really cutting-edge material, despite some neat special effects by Milt Rice.

Basil Rathbone *Lodac* • Estelle Winwood *Sybil* • Gary Lockwood *St George* • Anne Helm *Princess Helene* • Leroy Johnson *Sir Ulrich* • David Cross *Sir Pedro* • Liam Sullivan *Sir Branton* ■ *Dir* Bert I Gordon • *Scr* Bernard Schoenfeld, from a story by Bert I Gordon

The Magic Sword: Quest for Camelot ★★★ U

Animated period adventure
1997 · US · Colour · 82mins

This very animated animation has the daughter of a murdered knight searching for King Arthur's magic sword, Excalibur, which has been stolen and is lost in a mythic wood. Adapted from the novel *The King's Damosel* by British writer Vera Chapman, it's hot on character but rather chilled-out on effects. There's an interesting cast of voices, from Gary Oldman to John Gielgud; the sharp-eared will recognise the smooth tones of current James Bond Pierce Brosnan as King Arthur. Contains some mild violence. 🖭 **DVD**

Cary Elwes *Garrett* • Bryan White *Garrett (singing voice)* • Jessalyn Gilsig *Kayley* • Andrea Corr *Kayley (singing voice)* • Gary Oldman *Sir Ruber* • Eric Idle *Devon* • Don Rickles *Cornwall* • Pierce Brosnan *King Arthur* • John Gielgud *Merlin* ■ *Dir* Frederik Du Chau • *Scr* Kirk De Micco, William Schiffrin, Jacqueline Feather, David Seidler, from the novel *The King's Damosel* by Vera Chapman

Magic Town ★★★ U

Comedy drama 1947 · US · BW · 103mins

An intriguing James Stewart/Jane Wyman comedy drama, deftly directed by William A Wellman, that provides a fascinating insight into small-town America. Stewart is convinced that the white picket fence haven of Grandview can be used as a cutesy statistical yardstick for the country as a whole,

while Wyman's strong, innovative newspaper editor seeks positive social change. The old and new vie for supremacy in postwar society as they actually did across the States at the time, and Wellman intelligently uses his film as a metaphor for the debate while managing to stay keenly in touch with the human story.

James Stewart *Lawrence Rip Smith* • Jane Wyman *Mary Peterman* • Kent Smith *Hoopendecker* • Ned Sparks *Ike Sloan* • Wallace Ford *Lou Dicketts* • Regis Toomey *Ed Weaver* • Ann Doran *Mrs Weaver* • Donald Meek *Mr Twiddle* ■ *Dir* William A Wellman • *Scr* Robert Riskin, from a story by Robert Riskin, Joseph Krumgold

The Magic Voyage ★★

Animated musical adventure
1992 · Ger · Colour

The handful of films made to commemorate the 500th anniversary of Columbus's discovery of America were a pretty lacklustre lot, with the serious dramas *1492: Conquest of Paradise* and *Christopher Columbus: the Discovery* too overblown for some tastes. At least this feature-length cartoon musical achieves what it sets out to do – inform and entertain its young audience with the charming story of how a woodworm helped Columbus reach the New World and how a glow-worm guided him home.

Dom DeLuise *Columbus* • Corey Feldman *Pico* • Irene Cara *Marilyn* • Samantha Eggar *Queen Isabella* • Dan Haggerty *King Ferdinand* • Mickey Rooney *Narrator* ■ *Dir* Michael Schoemann • *Scr* Scott Santoro

The Magician ★★

Detective drama 1973 · US · Colour · 78mins

Bill Bixby, of *The Incredible Hulk* fame, is the magician of the title in this feature-length pilot for the seventies TV series. Each week, Bixby had to unravel some sort of mystery, using his skills as a conjuror; here, it's the possibility that an aeroplane crash was faked. Quite why the police can't solve this without the help of a second-rate magic man is anyone's guess.

Bill Bixby *Anthony Dorian* • Keene Curtis *Max Pomeroy* • Joan Caulfield *Lulu* • Kim Hunter *Nora Coogan* • Elizabeth Ashley *Sallie Baker* • Barry Sullivan *Joseph Baker* • Allen Case *Adams* • Signe Hasso *Madame Parga* ■ *Dir* Marvin J Chomsky • *Scr* Laurence Heath, from a story by Joseph Stefano

The Magician of Lublin ★★★ 15

Drama 1979 · Is/W Ger · Colour · 108mins

Isaac Bashevis Singer's novel gets a halfway decent adaptation from, of all people, ex-Cannon boss and trash director Menahem Golan. Alan Arkin stars as Yasha, a Jewish entertainer, who becomes the toast of late 19th and early 20th-century Warsaw society thanks to his talent as an ace illusionist and escape artist. But greed, lust and his giant ego soon cause his rapid fall from grace. A good cast invest this rarefied period piece with a high-tone atmosphere and its unusual fantasy elements (Yasha believes he can fly) provide a surprising conclusion. This extraordinary portrait is the high point of Golan's shoddy career. 🖭

Alan Arkin *Yasha Mazur* • Louise Fletcher *Emilia* • Valerie Perrine *Zeftel* • Shelley Winters *Elizabeta* • Maia Danziger *Magda* • Linda Bernstein *Esther* • Lou Jacobi *Wolsky* ■ *Dir* Menahem Golan • *Scr* Irving S White, Menahem Golan, from the novel by Isaac Bashevis Singer

The Magnet ★★ U

Comedy 1950 · UK · BW · 74mins

Coming just after *Passport to Pimlico* and *The Blue Lamp*, this was one of Ealing superscribe TEB Clarke's least distinguished efforts. The story of a young boy who steals a magnet and becomes the toast of his community after his accidental heroics is understandably contrived, but it's the totally false characters that really let it down. Moreover, director Charles Frend fails to exploit the run-down urban locations. Young William Fox would later change his first name to James and become a front-rank star. 🖭

Stephen Murray *Dr Brent* • Kay Walsh *Mrs Brent* • William Fox [James Fox] *Johnny Brent* • Meredith Edwards *Harper* • Gladys Henson *Nannie* • Thora Hird *Nannie's friend* • Michael Brooke Jr *Kit* • Wylie Watson *Pickering* ■ *Dir* Charles Frend • *Scr* TEB Clarke

The Magnetic Monster ★★★

Science-fiction 1953 · US · Colour · 75mins

An excellent, low-budget slice of science-fiction about a new radioactive element, created by scientists' unauthorised experiments, that doubles its size every 12 hours by converting surrounding energy into matter. Confidently directed by Curt Siodmak with an accent on approximate authenticity, and incorporating stock footage from the 1934 German classic *Gold* to good effect, this cosmic *Frankenstein* makes full use of its interesting cast.

Richard Carlson *Dr Jeffrey Stewart* • King Donovan *Dr Dan Forbes* • Jean Byron *Connie Stewart* • Harry Ellerbe *Dr Allard* • Leo Britt *Dr Benton* • Leonard Mudie *Dr Denker* • Byron Foulger *Simon* • Michael Fox *Dr Serny* ■ *Dir* Curt Siodmak • *Scr* Curt Siodmak, Ivan Tors

The Magnetist's Fifth Winter ★★★

Period drama
1999 · Nor/Swe/Den/Fr · Colour · 119mins

Boris Karloff meets Merchant-Ivory in this stylish tale of charlatanism, superstition and the inexplicable. The action turns on the seemingly miraculous ministrations of Ole Lemmeke, an itinerant magnetist whose cure of doctor Rolf Lassgård's blind daughter, Johanna Sällström, prompts jilted physician Gard B Eidsvold to delve into the stranger's scandalous past. Possessing both an eerie spirituality and a susceptibility to temptation, Lemmeke is truly mesmerising as he seeks to exploit attitudes which, despite the 1820 setting, are positively medieval. In Swedish with English subtitles.

Rolf Lassgård *Doctor Selander* • Ole Lemmeke *Friedrich Meisner* • Johanna Sällström *Maria* • Gard B Eidsvold *Doctor Stenius* ■ *Dir* Morten Henriksen • *Scr* Morten Henriksen, Jonas Cornell, from a novel by Per Olov Enquist

---

The Magnificent Ambersons ★★★★★ U

Period drama 1942 · US · BW · 84mins

One of cinema's flawed masterpieces, this was Orson Welles's follow-up to *Citizen Kane*. Adapted from Booth Tarkington's novel, it tells the compelling story of the decline of a once-proud family in the face of sprawling industrialisation. We shall never see the director's version, as executives at RKO felt the film was too long and depressing, and so ordered over 40 minutes of cuts and tacked on a happy ending directed by production manager Freddie Fleck. Out of the country on location, Welles was powerless to do anything about it. It says much for his genius that this is still a brilliant exercise in nostalgia and film technique. ▭

Joseph Cotten *Eugene Morgan* • Agnes Moorehead *Fanny Minafer* • Dolores Costello *Isabel Amberson Minafer* • Anne Baxter *Lucy Morgan* • Tim Holt *George Amberson Minafer* • Don Dillaway *Wilbur Minafer* • Ray Collins *Jack Amberson* • Richard Bennett *Major Amberson* • Erskine Sanford *Roger Bronson* • Charles Phipps *Uncle John* • Orson Welles *Narrator* ■ *Dir* Orson Welles • *Scr* Orson Welles, from the novel *The Magnificent Ambersons* by Booth Tarkington • *Cinematographer* Stanley Cortez • *Editor* Robert Wise • *Music* Bernard Herrmann • *Costume Designer* Edward Stevenson • *Production Designer* Mark-Lee Kirk

Magnificent Doll ★★

Historical biographical drama
1946 · US · BW · 90mins

Magnificently dull, more like. One of the great romantic dramas of American history is rendered flatter than a pancake by grotesque miscasting and direction that completely fails the subject matter. Ginger Rogers is spectacularly wrong as Dolly Payne Madison, one of the White House's great ladies, in a screenplay by Irving Stone that plays fast and loose with the facts. Not that it matters, given the truly awful performance by David Niven as Aaron Burr, who apparently relinquished his bid for the presidency because of his love for Madison. Burgess Meredith, as President James Madison, brings a shred of dignity to the proceedings, but seems bored.

Ginger Rogers *Dorthea "Dolly" Payne Madison* • David Niven *Aaron Burr* • Burgess Meredith *James Madison* • Horace McNally [Stephen McNally] *John Todd* • Peggy Wood *Mrs Payne* • Frances Williams *Amy, the maid* • Grandon Rhodes *Thomas Jefferson* ■ *Dir* Frank Borzage • *Scr* Irving Stone, from his story

The Magnificent Dope ★★ U

Comedy drama 1942 · US · BW · 83mins

A minor vehicle for Henry Fonda as a lazy country hick who arrives in New York and teaches everyone how to chill out, relax and take things easy. This amazes city slicker Don Ameche and charms secretary Lynn Bari, a starlet whom 20th Century-Fox promoted as the "girl with the million dollar figure" as well as "the woo woo girl": American GIs apparently rated her second only to Betty Grable in pin-up power. Directed by future director Walter Lang and scripted by George Seaton, it's as corny as Kansas in August, but entertaining enough.

Henry Fonda *Tad Page* • Lynn Bari *Claire* • Don Ameche *Dawson* • Edward Everett Horton *Horace Hunter* • George Barbier *Barker* • Frank Orth *Messenger* • Roseanne Murray *Dawson's secretary* • Marietta Canty *Jennie* ■ *Dir* Walter Lang • *Scr* George Seaton, from a story by Joseph Schrank

The Magnificent Matador ★★

Romantic drama 1955 · US · Colour · 94mins

Anthony Quinn plays a bullfighter who falls for rich American tourist Maureen O'Hara and worries about his illegitimate son entering the arena. The director of this effort, Budd Boetticher, was a matador himself who quit the arena for a career in Hollywood – as an adviser on *Blood and Sand* (which co-starred Quinn) and director of *The Bullfighter and the Lady* and a series of cult B-westerns. Typically, there is a lot of macho posturing, snorting and hooves scratching at the sand – and that's just Anthony Quinn!

Maureen O'Hara *Karen Harrison* • Anthony Quinn *Luis Santos* • Manuel Rojas *Rafael Reyes* • Thomas Gomez *Don David* • Richard Denning *Mark Russell* • Lola Albright *Mona Wilton* • William Ching *Jody Wilton* • Eduardo Noriega *Miguel* ■ *Dir* Budd Boetticher • *Scr* Charles Lang, from a story by Budd Boetticher

Magnificent Obsession ★★★★

Melodrama 1935 · US · BW · 112mins

Directed by a master of the soap opera, Universal's John M Stahl, whose films were the inspiration for several of the studio's fifties Technicolor remakes, this romantic melodrama is the one about Bobby Merrick (Robert Taylor), a wealthy, irresponsible playboy who is partly responsible for the death of a revered doctor and, subsequently, for an accident that blinds the doctor's widow Helen (Irene Dunne), with whom he falls in love. Filled with remorse, Merrick becomes a Nobel Prize-winning brain surgeon and, years later, finds her again, hoping to redeem himself. Beautifully made and well-acted, it's a more restrained and credible version than the Douglas Sirk remake, but not half as much fun!

Irene Dunne *Helen Hudson* • Robert Taylor (1) *Bobby Merrick* • Charles Butterworth *Tommy Masterson* • Betty Furness *Joyce Hudson* • Sara Haden *Nancy Ashford* • Ralph Morgan *Randolph* • Henry Armetta *Tony* • Gilbert Emery *Dr Ramsay* ■ *Dir* John M Stahl • *Scr* George O'Neil, Sarah Y Mason, Victor Heerman, Finley Peter Dunne, from the novel by Lloyd C Douglas

Magnificent Obsession ★★★★ U

Classic melodrama
1954 · US · Colour · 107mins

Luscious, glorious Technicolor entry from Universal's memorable Ross Hunter/Douglas Sirk cycle of no-holds-barred melodramas, and the one that turned beefcake Rock Hudson into a romantic superstar. Adapted from the syrupy novel by Lloyd C Douglas, it was a box-office hit the first time around (in 1935) with Irene Dunne and Robert Taylor. This time an Oscar-nominated Jane Wyman plays the woman who loses her husband and then goes blind, partly through Hudson's irresponsibility. While she is cared for by Agnes Moorehead, he mends his ways and becomes a brilliant surgeon before seeking her out years later.

Jane Wyman *Helen Phillips* • Rock Hudson *Bob Merrick* • Barbara Rush *Joyce Phillips* • Agnes Moorehead *Nancy Ashford* • Otto Kruger *Randolph* • Gregg Palmer *Tom Masterson* ■ *Dir* Douglas Sirk • *Scr* Robert Blees, Wells Root, from the 1935 film, from the novel by Lloyd C Douglas

The Magnificent Rebel ★★ U

Biographical drama
1961 · US/W Ger · Colour · 94mins

Before Gary Oldman essayed the role in *Immortal Beloved*, Karlheinz Böhm – perhaps best known for Michael Powell's *Peeping Tom* – played a brooding and intense Ludwig van Beethoven in this Disney biography, shot in Germany to use up Walt's frozen deutschmarks. It was originally shown in two parts on American television, but released as a film elsewhere. Böhm does well, but the screenplay is poor, the direction turgid and the dubbing distracting. However, the photography and, of course, the music make this very watchable. German dialogue dubbed into English.

Karlheinz Böhm *Ludwig van Beethoven* • Giulia Rubini *Giulietta* • Ivan Desny *Lichnowsky* • Peter Arens *Amenda* • Oliver Grimm *Stefan* ■ *Dir* Georg Tressler • *Scr* Joanne Court [Joan Scott] • *Cinematographer* Göran Strindberg

The Magnificent Seven ★★★★★ PG

Classic western 1960 · US · Colour · 127mins

A massively and enduringly popular western reworking of the Japanese classic *Seven Samurai*, with one of the greatest musical themes ever written for a movie, in an altogether fine brass-led score from composer Elmer Bernstein. Under-rated director John Sturges (*The Great Escape*, *Gunfight at the OK Corral*) was extremely fortuitous in securing a near-perfect cast for this movie. Not content with forging a new iconic image for King of Siam Yul Brynner as a black-clad gunslinger, he also created key star-making roles for sixties sensations Steve McQueen, James Coburn and Charles Bronson. The use of Panavision landscape is glorious to behold, Eli Wallach is a suitably slimy villain and the action sequences are tremendously exciting. Contains violent scenes. ▭

Yul Brynner *Chris* • Steve McQueen *Vin* • Eli Wallach *Calvera* • Horst Buchholz *Chico* • Charles Bronson *O'Reilly* • Robert Vaughn *Lee* • Brad Dexter *Harry Luck* • James Coburn *Britt* • Vladimir Sokoloff *Old man* • Rosenda Monteros *Petra* ■ *Dir* John Sturges • *Scr* William Roberts, Walter Bernstein, Walter Newman (uncredited) • *Editor* Ferris Webster • *Cinematographer* Charles Lang Jr [Charles Lang]

The Magnificent Seven Ride! ★★★ PG

Western 1972 · US · Colour · 96mins

Not really, they don't. This is the fourth and last outing for the famous title, and here, as in the previous sequel, no members of the original cast are to be found. Still, Lee Van Cleef makes a perfectly acceptable substitute for Yul Brynner, and the theme remains true to the original's concept. Here the bandits kidnap Van Cleef's wife and the titular seven are rounded up to seek vengeance. Mariette Hartley and Stefanie Powers provide stronger-than-usual support, but the real star is still Elmer Bernstein's pulsating score. ▭

Lee Van Cleef *Chris* • Stefanie Powers *Laurie Gunn* • Mariette Hartley *Arilla* • Michael Callan *Noah Forbes* • Luke Askew *Skinner* • Pedro Armendariz Jr *Pepe Carral* • Ralph Waite *Jim Mackay* • William Lucking *Walt Drummond* ■ *Dir* George McCowan • *Scr* Arthur Rowe

The Magnificent Showman ★★★ U

Action adventure
1964 · US · Colour · 131mins

This enormously entertaining big-top saga features John Wayne as a circus owner whose business faces an endless variety of crises. Begun as *Circus World* by director Frank Capra, the film was then entrusted to the much more suitable Henry Hathaway, who makes the lengthy tale race by in a jiffy. On the big screen the climactic fire and the capsize of the circus ship (special effects by Alex Weldon) were amazingly effective and, even if the scale is inevitably diminished on TV, the excitement and tension remain. And what other movie features Rita Hayworth and Claudia Cardinale as mother and daughter, each trying to upstage the other? ▭

John Wayne *Matt Masters* • Rita Hayworth *Lili Alfredo* • Claudia Cardinale *Toni Alfredo* • Lloyd Nolan *Cap Carson* • Richard Conte *Aldo Alfredo* • John Smith *Steve McCabe* • Henri Dantes *Emile Schuman* • Wanda Rotha *Mrs Schuman* ■ *Dir* Henry Hathaway • *Scr* Ben Hecht, Julian Halevy [Julian Zimet], James Edward Grant, from the story by Philip Yordan, Nicholas Ray

The Magnificent Two ★★ PG

Comedy 1967 · UK · Colour · 91mins

Like most British comedians of the sixties and seventies, Morecambe and Wise failed to make it in movies because the situations that made their TV series so successful simply could not be sustained beyond an hour or the confines of a studio setting. Here Eric and Ernie do their utmost to kick-start this poor comedy of errors about travelling salesmen caught up in a South American revolution. But the plot is paper thin, the jokes aren't funny and the use of a bikini-clad army to install Margit Saad as president is unworthy of the loveable duo. ▭

Eric Morecambe *Eric* • Ernie Wise *Ernie* • Margit Saad *Carla* • Cecil Parker *British ambassador* • Virgilio Texeira *Carillo* • Isobel Black *Juanita* • Martin Benson *President Diaz* ■ *Dir* Cliff Owen • *Scr* SC Green, RM Hills, Michael Pertwee, Peter Blackmore

The Magnificent Yankee ★★★ U

Biographical drama 1950 · US · BW · 88mins

A biopic of Oliver Wendell Holmes (1841-1935), the Supreme Court judge famous for his witticisms and his espousal of liberal causes, which earned him the nickname "The Great Dissenter". The story charts Holmes's career between the presidencies of two

U = SUITABLE FOR ALL Uc = SUITABLE FOR ALL, ESPECIALLY FOR YOUNG CHILDREN (VIDEO ONLY) PG = PARENTAL GUIDANCE

Roosevelts, taking in such key historical events as the Great War, the Depression and so on. As Holmes, Louis Calhern has to age considerably, dispense justice *and* have a private life with his wife (Ann Harding). No wonder his performance earned him an Oscar nomination! A stagey, talky movie that oozes prestige.

Louis Calhern *Oliver Wendell Holmes* • Ann Harding *Fanny Bowditch Holmes* • Eduard Franz *Judge Louis Brandeis* • Philip Ober *Mr Owen Wister* • Ian Wolfe *Mr Adams* • Edith Evanson *Annie Gough* • Richard Anderson *Reynolds* ■ *Dir* John Sturges • *Scr* Emmet Lavery, from the play by Emmet Lavery, from the novel *Mr Justice Holmes* by Francis Biddle

Magnolia ★★★★★ 18

Drama 1999 · US · Colour · 188mins

Writer/director Paul Thomas Anderson (*Boogie Nights*) seals his growing reputation as one of Hollywood's most ambitious and audacious film-makers with this dark, daring and dazzling take on Robert Altman's *Short Cuts*. Boldly tossing storytelling conventions out of the window, Anderson's offbeat epic charts 24 hours in the weird and wonderful lives of a dozen San Fernando Valley inhabitants. The cast is just superb, with Tom Cruise's supremely arrogant sex guru a stand-out. But Jason Robards, Julianne Moore, Melora Walters, John C Reilly and William H Macy are also brilliant in their one-of-a-kind roles. Although the running time is a little indulgent, the film's increasingly frantic pace, manic camerawork and unpredictable scenarios command the attention, while the climactic foray into *Twilight Zone* territory will leave you gasping.

Tom Cruise *Frank TJ Mackey* • Julianne Moore *Linda Partridge* • William H Macy *Quiz Kid Donnie Smith* • Philip Seymour Hoffman *Phil Parma* • Melora Walters *Claudia Wilson Gator* • John C Reilly *Jim Kurring* • Jason Robards [Jason Robards Jr] *Earl Partridge* • Philip Baker Hall *Jimmy Gator* • Jeremy Blackman *Stanley Spector* • Melinda Dillon *Rose Gator* • April Grace *Gwenovier* ■ *Dir/Scr* Paul Thomas Anderson • *Cinematographer* Robert Elswit

Magnum Force ★★★★ 18

Crime thriller 1973 · US · Colour · 117mins

A powerful follow-up to *Dirty Harry* with a story line different enough from the original to grip the attention. Clint Eastwood is on fine form as no-nonsense cop "Dirty" Harry Callahan, yet again relying on his own instincts as he investigates the ruthless killings of prominent criminals in San Francisco. There's excellent support, too, including a pre-*Starsky and Hutch* David Soul, and the climactic chase scene is superbly staged. Contains violence and swearing.

Clint Eastwood *Harry Callahan* • Hal Holbrook *Lieutenant Briggs* • Felton Perry *Early Smith* • Mitchell Ryan *Charlie McCoy* • David Soul *Davis* • Tim Matheson *Sweet* • Robert Urich *Grimes* • Kip Niven *Astrachan* ■ *Dir* Ted Post • *Scr* John Milius, Michael Cimino, from a story by John Milius, from original material by Harry Julian Fink, RM Fink

The Magus ★

Fantasy drama 1968 · UK · Colour · 116mins

Asked whether he would do everything the same if he had to live his life all over again, Peter Sellers thought for a moment and said: "Yes. But I would not see *The Magus*." Here's a movie so pretentious, it's worth sampling a reel or two just to confirm that, yes, they *can* make them as bad as this. The producers committed a double whammy by choosing an unfilmable novel and then getting its author – John Fowles – to adapt it himself. It's about a British schoolteacher (played by Michael Caine) cast sexually and metaphysically adrift on a Greek island. Anthony Quinn is in it, naturally, along with two gorgeous women – Candice Bergen and Anna Karina.

Anthony Quinn *Maurice Conchis* • Michael Caine *Nicholas Urfe* • Candice Bergen *Lily* • Anna Karina *Anne* • Julian Glover *Anton* • Takis Emmanuel *Kapetan* ■ *Dir* Guy Green • *Scr* John Fowles, from his novel

Mahler ★★★ 15

Biographical drama
1974 · UK · Colour · 110mins

One of the more successful and less outré outings from Ken Russell, who had already directed a series of TV dramatisations of famous composers' lives. Gustav Mahler is played with some depth and subtlety by Robert Powell and there's excellent support from Georgina Hale as his self-sacrificing wife. The director here considerably tones down the cinematic excesses for which he has become notorious, and this interesting film proved a small bloom in the desert of his later career. Mahler lovers will enjoy the vast swathes of his music put to creative use by Russell.

Robert Powell *Gustav Mahler* • Georgina Hale *Alma Mahler* • Richard Morant *Max* • Lee Montague *Bernhard Mahler* • Rosalie Crutchley *Marie Mahler* • Benny Lee *Uncle Arnold* • Miriam Karlin *Aunt Rosa* • Angela Down *Justine* ■ *Dir/Scr* Ken Russell

Mahogany ★

Drama 1975 · US · Colour · 108mins

The only good thing to come out of this mess is the theme song, the Diana Ross classic *Do You Know Where You're Going To*. Ross stars as a humble Chicago secretary who becomes a fashion model called Mahogany, then a fashion designer with the help of fruitcake photographer Anthony Perkins. Pitched as a full-blooded melodrama and flitting from Chicago to Rome, it's banality has to be seen to be believed. After half the film was completed, Tony Richardson was fired as director and Berry Gordy – the founder of Tamla-Motown records and Ross's discoverer – took over.

Diana Ross *Tracy/Mahogany* • Billy Dee Williams *Brian* • Anthony Perkins *Sean* • Jean-Pierre Aumont *Christian Rosetti* • Beah Richards *Florence* • Nina Foch *Miss Evans* • Marisa Mell *Carlotta Gavina* ■ *Dir* Berry Gordy • *Scr* John Byrum, from a story by Toni Amber

The Maid ★★ PG

Romantic comedy
1991 · US/Fr · Colour · 86mins

A soft-centred romantic comedy that wastes the talents of its stars, Martin Sheen and Jacqueline Bisset. The former is a besotted businessman who poses as a servant to be with his newly discovered true love Bisset. There are some nice role-reversal moments, but the script lacks bite and there is little to work with. Supporting players Jean-Pierre Cassel and James Faulkner fare the best, but it's slim pickings all round.

Martin Sheen *Anthony Wayne* • Jacqueline Bisset *Nicole Chantrelle* • Victoria Shalet *Marie* • Jean-Pierre Cassel *CP Oliver* • James Faulkner *Laurent Leclair* • Dominique Varda *Nicole's secretary* • Gilles Gaston-Dreyfus *Pierre Meyer* • Catherine Lachens *Catherine Oliver* ■ *Dir* Ian Toynton • *Scr* Timothy Prager

Maid for Each Other ★★

Comedy thriller 1992 · US · Colour · 100mins

After making some incisive points about the class system in America (a spoiled wife goes to work as a maid following the death of her husband), this comedy thriller heads off into more predictable territory, stopping at all the expected places en route. Nonetheless, the widow's reduced circumstances and the fact that her new employer is a former pop star put a fresh spin on the utterly obvious.

Dinah Manoff *Tibby Bloom* • Nell Carter *Jasmine Jones* • Garrett Morris *Harold Brown* • Joyce Van Patten *Tibby's Mother* • Robert Costanzo *Lieutenant Jardine* ■ *Dir* Paul Schneider • *Scr* Andrew Smith, Rob Gilmer, from a story by Dinah Manoff, Les Alexander, Don Enright

Maid to Order ★★ 15

Comedy 1987 · US · Colour · 89mins

Hollywood delights in telling modern fairy stories, but does so with such little imagination that their interpretations rarely entertain as they should. This is a story of wish fulfilment, but if the majority of the cast were given the chance they would probably have wished for a sharper script than this one, in which poor little rich girl Ally Sheedy learns about life the hard way after she is erased from her father's memory. Sheedy is too nice to convince as a spoilt brat, but Valerie Perrine and Dick Shawn are good value as the vulgar wannabes who hire her as their maid.

Ally Sheedy *Jessie Montgomery* • Beverly D'Angelo *Stella* • Michael Ontkean *Nick McGuire* • Valerie Perrine *Georgette Starkey* • Dick Shawn *Stan Starkey* • Tom Skerritt *Charles Montgomery* • Merry Clayton *Audrey James* • Begona Plaza *Maria* ■ *Dir* Amy Jones [Amy Holden Jones] • *Scr* Amy Jones [Amy Holden Jones], Perry Howze, Randy Howze

The Maids ★★

Drama 1974 · UK/Can · Colour · 95mins

Dull screen version of the dreary Jean Genet play about two Parisian maids who concoct a sado-masochistic plan to murder their hated mistress, but then never actually go through with it. It's that sort of play, and film. The main interest resides in the quality acting from a top-notch British cast.

Glenda Jackson *Solange* • Susannah York *Claire* • Vivien Merchant *Madame* • Mark Burns *Monsieur* ■ *Dir* Christopher Miles • *Scr* Robert Enders, Christopher Miles, from the play *Les Bonnes* by Jean Genet

Maid's Night Out ★★★

Comedy 1938 · US · BW · 64mins

To win a bet with his self-made father, millionaire Allan Lane becomes a milkman for a month and falls for a rich girl (Joan Fontaine) whom he thinks is the maid. RKO dropped their budding star Fontaine the same year she made this jolly little film, played and directed (by Ben Holmes) with evident enjoyment; she would shortly bounce back by making *Rebecca* for Hitchcock. Gossip columnist Hedda Hopper, who began her career as an actress, is in the supporting cast.

Joan Fontaine *Sheila Harrison* • Allan Lane *Bill Norman* • Hedda Hopper *Mrs Harrison* • George Irving *Rufus Norman* • William Brisbane *Wally Martin* • Billy Gilbert *Papalapoulas* • Cecil Kellaway *Geoffrey* ■ *Dir* Ben Holmes • *Scr* Bert Granet, from a story by Willoughby Speyers

Mail Order Bride ★★★

Western 1964 · US · Colour · 83mins

In this slight but rather charming western, Buddy Ebsen tries to tame Keir Dullea, the hotheaded son of a dead friend, by making him marry Lois Nettleton, a widow with a young son. Writer/director Burt Kennedy's dialogue is splendid, and he extracts fine performances from his cast; his use of the camera could have been more dynamic, though. Warren Oates contributes some colourful work as a villain beyond reform, while Marie Windsor figures nicely as the saloon keeper who's an ideal match for Ebsen. In the UK, the film went under the title *West of Montana*.

Buddy Ebsen *Will Lane* • Keir Dullea *Lee Carey* • Lois Nettleton *Annie Boley* • Warren Oates *Jace* • Barbara Luna *Marietta* • Paul Fix *Jess Linley* • Marie Windsor *Hanna* • Denver Pyle *Preacher Pope* ■ *Dir* Burt Kennedy • *Scr* Burt Kennedy, from a story by Van Cort

The Main Event ★★ 15

Romantic comedy
1979 · US · Colour · 104mins

This is one of those self-centred films that Barbra Streisand produces, in which she takes her favourite role of sexual predator. Her target, once again, is Ryan O'Neal but the stars fail to re-create the comic success they had in *What's Up, Doc?*. Streisand plays the bankrupt owner of a perfume company whose only asset is washed-up boxer O'Neal. Sadly, director Howard Zieff's comedy falls a long way short of going the distance.

Barbra Streisand *Hillary Kramer* • Ryan O'Neal *Eddie "Kid Natural" Scanlon* • Paul Sand *David* • Whitman Sand *Percy* • Patti D'Arbanville [Patti D'Arbanville-Quinn] *Donna* • Chu Chu Malave *Luis* • Richard Lawson *Hector Mantilla* ■ *Dir* Howard Zieff • *Scr* Gail Parent, Andrew Smith

Main Street to Broadway ★★

Romantic comedy 1953 · US · BW · 101mins

The professional struggles of an aspiring young playwright (Tom Morton) and his involvement with a young actress (Mary Murphy) offer a flimsy excuse for fleeting appearances by just about every star on MGM's books. The result is a dull and uninteresting look at Broadway's backstage life, marginally enlivened by Tallulah Bankhead's guest turn. Among the few who play actual characters are Agnes Moorehead, Herb Shriner and Rosemary DeCamp.

Tom Morton *Tony Monaco* • Mary Murphy *Mary Craig* • Agnes Moorehead *Mildred Waterbury* • Herb Shriner *Frank Johnson* • Rosemary DeCamp *Mrs Craig* • Clinton Sundberg *Mr Craig* • Tallulah Bankhead • Ethel Barrymore ■ *Dir* Tay Garnett, Joel Newton • *Scr* Samson Raphaelson, from a story by Robert E Sherwood

Maisie ★★★

Comedy   1939 · US · BW · 74mins

MGM cast Ann Sothern in this programmer about a curly-headed showgirl stranded without a dime in a one-horse rodeo town. After a chapter of accidents and misunderstandings involving handsome, taciturn ranch manager Robert Young, she cons her way into a job as maid to the establishment's visiting owner (Ian Hunter) and his faithless wife (Ruth Hussey). Directed by Edwin L Marin, the success of this fresh, breezy and inconsequential film spawned a ten-picture series, making Maisie/Sothern a forties institution. Seen in our jaded age, the picture is both sociologically fascinating and enormous good fun.

Ann Sothern *Maisie Ravier* • Robert Young *Slim Martin* • Ruth Hussey *Sybil Ames* • Ian Hunter *Clifford Ames* • Cliff Edwards *Shorty* • Anthony Allan [John Hubbard] *Richard Raymond* • Art Mix *Red* • George Tobias *Rico* ■ *Dir* Edwin L Marin • *Scr* Mary C McCall Jr, from the novel *Dark Dame* by Wilson Collison

Maisie Was a Lady ★★★

Comedy   1941 · US · BW · 78mins

Maisie (Ann Sothern) loses her job as a headless woman in a carnival thanks to the antics of a wealthy, upper-class young drunk (Lew Ayres). He compensates her with a job in the family mansion, enabling her to sort out the disastrous relationships, romantic and familial, she finds there. Edwin L Marin directs, while the venerable C Aubrey Smith is enchanting as the family butler.

Ann Sothern *Maisie Ravier* • Lew Ayres *Bob Rawlston* • Maureen O'Sullivan *Abigail Rawlston* • C Aubrey Smith *Walpole* • Edward Ashley *Link Phillips* • Joan Perry *Diana Webley* ■ *Dir* Edwin L Marin • *Scr* Betty Reinhardt, Mary C McCall Jr, from a story by Betty Reinhardt, Myles Connolly, from the character created by Wilson Collison

Le Maître d'école ★★★

Comedy   1981 · Fr · Colour · 95mins

At this point in his career, Claude Berri was known for blending autobiographical incident with social satire. Yet he resorted to slapstick and sitcom for this fish-out-of-water tale of the novice supply teacher forced to deal with an uncooperative class and eccentric colleagues. Reliant on borrowed notes and his own wits, Michel Coluche rises to the challenge, without falling back on the kind of cornball feel-good that characterises such Hollywood romps as *Kindergarten Cop*. This was to be the first of a four-film collaboration between star and director, but only *Tchao Pantin* (1983) was completed before Coluche died in a motorbike accident. In French with English subtitles.

Michel Coluche *Gérard Barbier* • Josiane Balasko *Miss Joyful* • Jacques Debary *Headmaster* • Charlotte De Turckheim *Charlotte* ■ *Dir/Scr* Claude Berri

Maîtresse ★★★

Erotic black comedy
1976 · Fr · Colour · 107mins

Walking the tightrope between titillation and tact, this study of sadomasochism stars Bulle Ogier as a "mistress" or dominatrix, who inflicts pain and various sorts of humiliation upon her well-to-do clients. Coming into this secret world is petty crook Gérard Depardieu, who becomes not only Ogier's lover but also her willing assistant. At once explicit and discreet, Barbet Schroeder's film certainly looks weird enough, with Ogier's killer dog, dentists' chairs, whips and other tools dominating the imagery. Through the perversion, the purity of Ogier and Depardieu's affair emerges and, in the end, enters a surreal zone of its own. In French with English subtitles.

Gérard Depardieu *Olivier* • Bulle Ogier *Ariane* • André Rouyer *Mario* • Nathalie Keryan *Lucienne* ■ *Dir* Barbet Schroeder • *Scr* Barbet Schroeder, Paul Voujargol

The Major and the Minor ★★★U

Comedy   1942 · US · BW · 101mins

A 12-year-old girl on a train awakens the concern of an army officer (Ray Milland). She also awakens his sexual interest and that of the boys at the military academy where he's stationed. No, this is not a provocative drama from Tennessee Williams, but a romantic comedy, penned by the illustrious team of Charles Brackett and Billy Wilder, which marked Wilder's Hollywood directorial debut. The girl, of course, is not underage at all, but Ginger Rogers masquerading in order to avoid paying full fare. Famous wit and sometime character actor Robert Benchley offers support, and Ginger's real-life mother Lela plays her mom.

Ginger Rogers *Susan Applegate* • Ray Milland *Maj Kirby* • Rita Johnson *Pamela Hill* • Robert Benchley *Mr Osborne* • Diana Lynn *Lucy Hill* • Edward Fielding *Col Hill* • Frankie Thomas *Cadet Osborne* • Raymond Roe *Cadet Wigton* • Lela Rogers *Mrs Applegate* ■ *Dir* Billy Wilder • *Scr* Billy Wilder, Charles Brackett, from the play *Connie Goes Home* by Edward Childs Carpenter, from the story *Sunny Goes Home* by Fannie Kilbourne

Major Barbara ★★★★

Satirical comedy   1941 · UK · BW · 125mins

Superbly cast and acted screen adaptation of George Bernard Shaw's morality study of the Salvation Army and armaments manufacture. Wendy Hiller in the title role, Rex Harrison as her admirer and a marvellous array of British stage and screen names acquit themselves with distinction. The only flawed performance comes from Robert Morley, who mistakenly plays the key role of Hiller's capitalist father as a fool. Although direction is originally credited to the Hungarian producer Gabriel Pascal, who had acquired the sole rights to film Shaw, this was in fact an early directorial effort by the young David Lean and Harold French. Deborah Kerr looks radiant in an early appearance, and the sophistication of the comedy is perfectly balanced by Ronald Neame's photography and Vincent Korda's splendid interior sets.

Wendy Hiller *Major Barbara Undershaft* • Rex Harrison *Adolphus Cusins* • Robert Morley *Andrew Undershaft* • Emlyn Williams *Snobby Price* • Robert Newton *Bill Walker* • Sybil Thorndike *The General* • Deborah Kerr *Jenny Hill* • David Tree *Charles Lomax* ■ *Dir* Gabriel Pascal, Harold French, David Lean • *Scr* Anatole de Grunwald, George Bernard Shaw, from the play by George Bernard Shaw

Major Dundee ★★★PG

Western   1965 · US · Colour · 117mins

Sam Peckinpah's third feature stars Charlton Heston as a Union officer leading a wild bunch of Confederate prisoners, including Richard Harris, to capture an even wilder bunch of marauding Apaches. Inevitably, problems arose – the script was reportedly never really finished, let alone polished, and, while Peckinpah had in mind a dark, violent epic about the Civil War, Columbia wanted a bright and breezy cavalry and Indians adventure. When Columbia threatened to fire Peckinpah in mid-schedule, Heston backed him up and offered to return his $200,000 fee. The studio, of course, accepted this rash offer and let Peckinpah continue, though it still cut 40 minutes of footage. ▭

Charlton Heston *Major Amos Dundee* • Richard Harris *Captain Benjamin Tyreen* • Senta Berger *Teresa Santiago* • Jim Hutton *Lieutenant Graham* • James Coburn *Samuel Potts* • Michael Anderson Jr *Tim Ryan* • Mario Adorf *Sergeant Gomez* • Brock Peters *Aesop* ■ *Dir* Sam Peckinpah • *Scr* Harry Julian Fink, Oscar Saul, Sam Peckinpah, from a story by Harry Julian Fink

Major League ★★★15

Sports comedy   1989 · US · Colour · 101mins

In this amiable, if predictable sporting comedy, the players of a deadbeat baseball team, led by Tom Berenger, decide to fight back when they discover that their new boss (Margaret Whitton) is determined to see them finish bottom of the league. The misfits include the short-sighted pitcher Charlie Sheen and the hopelessly vain Corbin Bernsen. Director David S Ward, who wrote *The Sting*, allows it to get by on star power alone, while the sharp-eyed will spot the pre-stardom Rene Russo and Wesley Snipes. ▭

Tom Berenger *Jake Taylor* • Charlie Sheen *Rickie Vaughn* • Corbin Bernsen *Roger Dorn* • Margaret Whitton *Rachel Phelps* • James Gammon *Lou Brown* • Rene Russo *Lynn Wells* • Wesley Snipes *Willie Mays Hayes* ■ *Dir/Scr* David S Ward

Major League II ★★PG

Sports comedy   1994 · US · Colour · 100mins

Five years after the Cleveland Indians baseball team stepped out in *Major League*, the same sorry crew (minus Wesley Snipes and Rene Russo) reassembles for another season, with the team's original nemesis, owner Margaret Whitton, once again determined to dismantle the club. The original was nothing special, but this sequel strikes out big time. Only the occasional put-down by stadium announcer Bob Uecker relieves the tedium of the bawdy locker-room banter and the endless on-the-field foul-ups. Contains swearing. ▭

Charlie Sheen *Rick "Wild Thing" Vaughn* • Tom Berenger *Jake Taylor* • Corbin Bernsen

Roger Dorn • Dennis Haysbert *Pedro Cerrano* • James Gammon *Lou Brown* • Omar Epps *Willie Mays Hayes* • Margaret Whitton *Rachel Phelps* ■ *Dir* David S Ward • *Scr* RJ Stewart, from a story by Tom S Parker, Jim Jennewein, RJ Stewart

Major League: Back to the Minors ★★12

Sports comedy   1998 · US · Colour · 95mins

It's strike three for this comedy baseball franchise, and it's out – of ideas. Scott Bakula (*Quantum Leap*) should have been suspicious when even the non-selective Charlie Sheen declined to return for this second sequel. Slimy Corbin Bernsen is back, though, offering ex-player Bakula the job of managing the worst team in the league. There's the usual array of eccentric players and reversals of fortune, while Bakula makes a very watchable leading man. Just don't expect too many surprises. Contains some swearing. ▭

Scott Bakula *Gus Cantrell* • Corbin Bernsen *Roger Dorn* • Takaaki Ishibashi *Taka Tanakia* • Ted McGinley *Leonard Huff* • Bob Uecker *Harry Doyle* • Dennis Haysbert *Pedro Cerrano* ■ *Dir/Scr* John Warren

Major Payne ★★12

Comedy   1995 · US · Colour · 92mins

The title gives you some idea of the level of sophistication of this instantly forgettable vehicle for Damon Wayans. He plays an aggressive marine given the job of knocking the useless new junior recruits into shape at a military academy. Although no one can accuse Wayans of not giving the role his all, watching him spout abuse at a bunch of misfits is not great entertainment. Some occasionally funny dialogue and the star's enthusiastic sadism keep it just about watchable.

Damon Wayans *Major Benson Winifred Payne* • Rodney P Barnes *Weight lifter* • Ross Bickell *Colonel Braggart* • Scott "Bam Bam" Bigelow *Huge biker* • Joda Blare-Hershman *Cadet Bryan* • Orlando Brown *Cadet Tiger Dane* ■ *Dir* Nick Castle • *Scr* Damon Wayans, Dean Lorey, Gary Rosen, from the film *The Private War of Major Benson* by William Roberts, Richard Alan Simmons, from a story by Joe Connelly, Bob Mosher

A Majority of One ★U

Comedy drama   1961 · US · Colour · 153mins

The unlikely love affair between a middle-aged Jewish widow and a Japanese diplomat is the subject of this movie, adapted by Leonard Spigelgass from his hit Broadway play. The film, however, directed by Mervyn LeRoy at interminable length, falls flat on its face, due in no small part to disastrous miscasting. The blue-blooded Rosalind Russell never quite convinces as a Brooklyn mother, while Guinness, the master of disguise, substitutes inscrutability for character.

Rosalind Russell *Mrs Jacoby* • Alec Guinness *Koichi Asano* • Ray Danton *Jerome Black* • Madlyn Rhue *Alice Black* • Mae Questel *Mrs Rubin* ■ *Dir* Mervyn LeRoy • *Scr* Leonard Spigelgass, from his play

Majority Rule ★★ 🅿🅶

Drama   1992 · US · Colour · 90mins

George Washington and Dwight D Eisenhower did it, so why shouldn't Blair Brown tread the path from the battlefield to the White House? That's the premise of this TV movie in which Brown reasons that, having been the first woman to lead American troops into battle, she should also be able to exploit the fact that the majority of the electorate is female to win the highest office in the land. The whole thing is weighed down by the dopey domestic drama tacked on to prove there's no greater calling than family life. ▭

Blair Brown *General Katherine Taylor* • John Glover *Brady Mackin* • Donald Moffat *Walter Simms* • Jensen Daggett *Lucy Taylor* ■ *Dir* Gwen Arner • *Scr* David Taylor

Make Haste to Live ★★

Thriller   1954 · US · BW · 90mins

Dorothy McGuire fans need no persuading to watch this splendidly titled melodrama, in which McGuire is confronted by a neurotic criminal husband (a glowering Stephen McNally) who's come back to seek vengeance. This is a very average programme filler, from that period in McGuire's career when she was past her forties peak and before she superbly re-invented her screen image as an older, wiser woman in such hits as *Three Coins in the Fountain*, *Old Yeller* and *A Summer Place*. Director William A Seiter tries hard, but he's hamstrung by a tight budget and a short shooting schedule.

Dorothy McGuire *Crystal Benson* • Stephen McNally *Steve* • Mary Murphy *Randy Benson* • Edgar Buchanan *Sheriff* • John Howard (1) *Josh* ■ *Dir* William A Seiter • *Scr* Warren Duff, from a novel by Mildred Gordon, Gordon Gordon

Make Mine a Million ★★★ 🆄

Comedy   1959 · UK · BW · 83mins

Diminutive funster Arthur Askey had often spoofed the BBC on radio and in films and, when he made the transition from the BBC to ITV (in 1956), he likewise took the rise out of his new employers. In this satire on TV advertising, Arthur Askey is a make-up man who falls under the influence of dodgy promoter Sidney James and becomes the on-screen star of soap powder commercials. Many ITV stars of the time appear as themselves and the whole thing is a pacey romp.

Arthur Askey *Arthur Ashton* • Sidney James *Sid Gibson* • Dermot Walsh *Martin Russell* • Sally Barnes *Sally* • Olga Lindo *Mrs Burgess* • Bernard Cribbins *Jack* • Kenneth Connor *Anxious husband* ■ *Dir* Lance Comfort • *Scr* Peter Blackmore, Talbot Rothwell, Arthur Askey, from a story by Jack Francis

Make Mine Mink ★★ 🆄

Comedy   1960 · UK · BW · 100mins

This is so awash with whimsy that the comedy only occasionally manages to bob to the surface. But, while it's not an uproarious laughfest, there's still plenty to enjoy as the dependable Terry-Thomas masterminds a series of robberies for his gang of old dears in order to raise money for a children's home. Athene Seyler, Elspeth Duxbury and Hattie Jacques are good value as

the respectable rogues, and Kenneth Williams is fun as their fence. But Billie Whitelaw is less convincing as the reformed delinquent shocked by their antics.

Terry-Thomas *Major Albert Rayne* • Hattie Jacques *Nanette Parry* • Athene Seyler *Dame Beatrice Appleby* • Billie Whitelaw *Lily* • Elspeth Duxbury *Elizabeth Pinkerton* • Irene Handl *Madame Spolinski* • Jack Hedley *Jim Benham* • Kenneth Williams *Freddy Warrington* ■ *Dir* Robert Asher • *Scr* Michael Pertwee, Peter Blackmore, from the play *Breath of Spring* by Peter Coke

Make Mine Music ★★★★ 🆄

Musical animation
1946 · US · Colour · 71mins

This was Walt Disney's attempt to do for popular music what his studio's animation had achieved for classical music in *Fantasia*, but he failed to meet with similar box-office success. This beautifully-crafted film is by no means as well known as it should be. As with *Fantasia*, the crass populism of this episodic treat divided critics and delighted children, and today there's even more to enjoy, not least the glorious period Technicolor and the display of major forties talent, including the Benny Goodman Orchestra, the Andrews Sisters, Dinah Shore and Nelson Eddy. ▭

Nelson Eddy • Dinah Shore • The Andrews Sisters • Jerry Colonna • Andy Russell • Sterling Holloway ■ *Dir* Jack Kinney, Clyde Geronimi, Hamilton Luske, Robert Cormack, Joshua Meador • *Scr* Homer Brightman, Dick Huemer, Dick Kinney, John Walbridge, Tom Oreb, Dick Shaw, Eric Gurney, Sylvia Holland, T Hee, Dick Kelsey, Jesse Marsh, Roy Williams, Erdman Penner, James Bodrero, Cap Palmer, Erwin Graham

Make Way for Tomorrow ★★★★

Drama   1937 · US · BW · 91mins

There aren't many films on the painful subject of growing old and becoming a burden to one's offspring: Yasujiro Ozu's *Tokyo Story*, *Kotch* with Walter Matthau and this heartrending Leo McCarey picture, a genuine tear-jerker thanks to its acute understanding of human nature. Victor Moore and Beulah Bondi play the retired couple who lose their home and are forced to separate when none of their children will take them in. The old pair are shown realistically, being quite difficult at times, but their continuing optimism makes their plight all the worse.

Victor Moore *Barkley Cooper* • Beulah Bondi *Lucy Cooper* • Fay Bainter *Anita Cooper* • Thomas Mitchell *George Cooper* • Porter Hall *Harvey Chase* • Barbara Read *Rhoda Cooper* • Leo McCarey *Passerby/Man in overcoat/Carpet sweeper* ■ *Dir* Leo McCarey • *Scr* Vina Delmar, from the play *The Years Are So Long* by Helen Leary, Nolan Leary, from the novel by Josephine Lawrence

Make Your Own Bed ★ 🆄

Comedy   1944 · US · BW · 82mins

Private detective Jack Carson and his girlfriend Jane Wyman accept an assignment from inventor Alan Hale to move into his house as servants in order to protect him from a gang of Nazis. A witless and desperately unfunny comedy, directed by Peter Godfrey without a single idea to liven it

up. The supporting players are all drawn from the Warner Bros B-roster – George Tobias, Irene Manning and the wooden Ricardo Cortez.

Jack Carson *Jerry Curtis* • Jane Wyman *Susan Courtney* • Alan Hale *Walter Whirtle* • Irene Manning *Vivian Whirtle* • George Tobias *Boris Murphy* • Robert Shayne *Lester Knight* • Ricardo Cortez *Fritz Alten* ■ *Dir* Peter Godfrey • *Scr* Francis Swann, Edmund Joseph, Richard Weil, from a play by Harvey J O'Higgins, Harriet Ford

The Maker ★★★ 🔞

Crime drama   1997 · US · Colour · 94mins

Director Tim Hunter made his name with the startling *River's Edge*, a harrowing portrait of disaffected youth, and this sees him covering similar sort of ground. Jonathan Rhys Myers plays a teenage slacker who, along with his friends – including Fairuza Balk – fills his wasted days by hanging around malls and indulging in petty crime. Then his long-lost older brother Matthew Modine turns up out of the blue and initiates him into burglary. The thriller elements don't quite come off but Hunter still has a sharp eye for adolescent trauma. The talented supporting cast includes Michael Madsen and Mary-Louise Parker. Contains swearing, some violence and sexual references. ▭

Matthew Modine *Walter Schmeiss* • Mary-Louise Parker *Officer Emily Peck* • Jonathan Rhys Myers *Josh Minnell* • Michael Madsen *Skarney* • Fairuza Balk *Bella Sotto* • Kate McGregor-Stewart *Mother Minnell* • Lawrence Pressman *Father Minnell* ■ *Dir* Tim Hunter • *Scr* Rand Ravich

Making Contact ★★★ 🗓

Supernatural adventure
1985 · W Ger · Colour · 75mins

An early film from director Roland Emmerich, made a decade before he went big and blockbustery with *Stargate*, *Independence Day* and *Godzilla*. Emmerich brings flair and imagination to this superior kids' film about a boy whose grief at his dad's death activates previously hidden telekinetic powers. He then uses these powers to bring his favourite toys to life. After watching this, kids will have great fun trying to do likewise. ▭

Joshua Morrell *Joey* • Eva Kryll *Laura, Joey's mother* • Jan Zierold *Martin, Joey's father* • Tammy Shields *Sally* • Barbara Klein *Dr Haiden* ■ *Dir* Roland Emmerich • *Scr* Hans J Haller, Thomas Lechner

Making Love ★★ 🔞

Drama   1982 · US · Colour · 106mins

Kate Jackson gets a shock when her doctor husband Michael Ontkean confesses he is in love with another. The other happens to be a man – former *LA Law* heart-throb Harry Hamlin. Arthur Hiller's restrained account of a repressed man coming out of the closet was something of a groundbreaking film for Hollywood at the time. But because such care has been taken not to offend anyone, this never rises above the uncomplicated, routine level of a soap opera. ▭

Michael Ontkean *Zack* • Kate Jackson *Claire* • Harry Hamlin *Bart McGuire* • Wendy Hiller *Winnie Bates* • Arthur Hill *Henry* • Nancy

Olson *Christine* • John Dukakis *Tim* ■ *Dir* Arthur Hiller • *Scr* Barry Sandler, from a story by A Scott Berg

Making Mr Right ★★★ 🗓

Science-fiction satire
1987 · US · Colour · 94mins

This quirky satire was Susan Seidelman's next movie after her big hit, *Desperately Seeking Susan*. John Malkovich plays both an inventor and the android he has created, while Ann Magnuson is a wacky PR whiz hired to promote the robot but soon, wouldn't you know it, falling in love with it. Zany stuff, combining shades of vintage B-movies with punk hairstyles and post-modern imagery, but ultimately less than the sum of its rather too diverse parts. ▭

John Malkovich *Dr Jeff Peters/Ulysses* • Ann Magnuson *Frankie Stone* • Glenne Headly *Trish* • Ben Masters *Congressman Steve Marcus* • Laurie Metcalf *Sandy* • Polly Bergen *Estelle Stone* • Harsh Nayyar *Dr Ravi Ramdas* • Susan Berman *Ivy Stone* ■ *Dir* Susan Seidelman • *Scr* Floyd Byars, Laurie Frank

The Making of Maps ★★ 🗓

Drama   1995 · UK · Colour · 102mins

In *Leaving Lenin*, the Welsh film-maker Endaf Emlyn showed a group of teenagers discovering themselves during a stressful visit to St Petersburg. Set at the height of the Cuban missile crisis, his follow-up feature again contrasts adolescent trauma with the problems of a world in transition. However, this tale of a boy charting his course through the choppy waters of family life is much more personal than its predecessor, which explains the prevalence of mirror images throughout the film. It's earnestly acted, particularly by Gavin Ashcroft, but a bit too solemn. In Welsh with English subtitles.

Gavin Ashcroft *Griff* • Catherine Tregenna *Megan* • Maldwyn Pate *Robert* • Abigail Creel *Ruth* • Lara Ward *Alis* ■ *Dir/Scr* Endaf Emlyn

Making the Case for Murder: the Howard Beach Story ★★★

Crime drama based on a true story
1989 · US · Colour · 105mins

A tough step-by-step guide to an actual event in December 1986 when a black man was killed by white teens in the mainly white district of Howard Beach, New York. This TV movie has an immediate, documentary-style approach which doesn't diminish the thrill of the suspense. The sense of endemic racism is extremely strong, while Daniel J Travanti, as the battling prosecutor, brings a gritty authenticity to the role. Contains violence.

Daniel J Travanti *Joe Hynes* • William Daniels *David Slaney* • Joe Morton *Cedric Sandiford* • Dan Lauria *Doug Le Vien* • Cliff Gorman *Richard Bernstein* • Bruce Young [Bruce A Young] *Richard Mangum* ■ *Dir* Dick Lowry • *Scr* Steve Bello, from the article by Jack Newfield

Making Up ★★★★ 🗓

Romantic comedy
1992 · Ger · Colour · 54mins

It only lasts 54 minutes, but this blind date comedy was a commercial and

critical hit. Not bad for a graduation film, albeit one with a cast of TV celebrities. Man-mad nurse Nina Kronjäger and struggling cartoonist Katja Riemann have such a wonderfully knockabout relationship that it almost seems a shame to pair them off with a narcissistic hunk and his wiseacre mate. However, the star of the show is director Katja von Garnier, who manages to get extra mileage out of jokes in serious need of a retread. In German with English subtitles.

Katja Riemann *Frenzy* • Nina Kronjäger *Maischa* • Gedeon Burkhard *René* • Max Tidof *Mark* • Daniela Lunkewitz *Susa* ■ *Dir* Katja von Garnier • *Scr* Katja von Garnier, Benjamin Taylor, Hannes Jaenicke

The Makioka Sisters ★★★★
Drama 1983 · Jap · Colour and BW · 140mins

Adapted from Junichiro Tanizaki's novel, this is a sprawling study of Japanese society in the days preceding the Second World War. Bound by family wealth, but divided on everything else – from politics and progress to the role of women within an increasingly militaristic state – the four Makioka sisters take some time getting to know. But once Kon Ichikawa has established their attitudes and alliances, their ambitions, fears, romances and rivalries begin to engross. The result is impeccably played and beautifully designed and photographed. In Japanese with English subtitles.

Keiko Kishi *Tsuruko, oldest sister* • Yoshiko Sakuma *Sachiko, second oldest sister* • Sayuri Yoshinaga *Yukiko, third oldest sister* • Yuko Kotegawa *Taeko, youngest sister* • Juzo Itami *Tsuruko's husband* ■ *Dir* Kon Ichikawa • *Scr* Kon Ichikawa, Shinya Hidaki, from the novel by Junichiro Tanizaki • *Production Designer* Shinobu Muraki • *Cinematographer* Kiyoshi Hasegawa

Mal ★ 18
Drama 1999 · Por · Colour · 85mins

A gutsy performance by Pauline Cadell is the only thing to recommend this grindingly dull melodrama from Portuguese writer/director Alberto Seixas Santos, who seems more interested in flouting traditional narrative conventions than in focusing on his characters. As the respectable wife who is distracted from her bid to wean a teenager off heroin by her HIV-positive husband's revelation of his serial adultery, Cadell courageously keeps her head above the soap-operatic tide of events. But her trials – like those of the old man searching for his missing granddaughter or the junkie's relationship with his ultra-religious mother – are too clinically presented to encourage empathy. In Portuguese with English subtitles.

Pauline Cadell *Cathy* • Rui Morrisson *Pedro* • Alexandre Pinto *Daniel* • Maria Santos *Marta* • Lia Gama *Emilia* • Zita Duarte *Assunçao* ■ *Dir/Scr* Alberto Seixas Santos

Malachi's Cove ★★ U
Period adventure 1973 · UK · Colour · 85mins

Based on a story by Anthony Trollope, this period children's adventure boasts ripe, eye-rolling performances from Donald Pleasence and Peter Vaughan and a rare supporting turn from Arthur

English. Walter Lassally's photography is very attractive (the film was shot on location in Cornwall), and the children (Dai Bradley and Veronica Quilligan) are both well-cast. Henry Herbert's dilettante direction and underwritten screenplay leave much to be desired, though – which might explain why the film (also known as *The Seaweed Children*) got a limited release. ▭

Donald Pleasence *Malachi* • Dai Bradley *Barty* • Veronica Quilligan *Mally* • Peter Vaughan *Mr Gunliffe* • Lilias Walker *Mrs Gunliffe* • Arthur English *Jack Combes* ■ *Dir* Henry Herbert • *Scr* Henry Herbert, from a story by Anthony Trollope

Malaga ★ U
Crime action adventure 1954 · UK · Colour · 88mins

Tangier comes across vividly enough as the exotic setting for this British-produced thriller. Maureen O'Hara certainly looks gorgeous, but the queen of the redheads takes some swallowing as a modern Mata Hari working for the American government (armed with thigh gun and judo credentials) to expose a dope-smuggling ring. Macdonald Carey is flabby and uninspiring as her co-star. It's confusing title – given its principal setting – was changed to *Fire over Africa* in the US.

Maureen O'Hara *Joanna Dane* • Macdonald Carey *Van Logan* • Binnie Barnes *Frisco* • Guy Middleton *Soames Howard* • Hugh McDermott *Richard Farrell* • James Lilburn *Danny Boy* ■ *Dir* Richard Sale • *Scr* Robert Westerby

Malarek ★★
Biographical action drama 1989 · Can · Colour · 95mins

Crusading dramas more intent on alerting than entertaining an audience are not the sole preserve of the TV-movie industry, as this Canadian true-life action drama illustrates. The film reveals how the relatively inexperienced Montreal reporter Victor Malarek was driven to expose the abusive regime within the city's teenage detention centre after witnessing the murder of an inmate. Elias Koteas is solid enough in the title role and there's unshowy support from Michael Sarrazin. But in his determination to shatter our complacency, director Roger Cardinal fails to get us involved in his story.

Elias Koteas *Victor Malarek* • Kerrie Keane *Claire* • Al Waxman *Stern* • Michael Sarrazin *Moorcraft* • Daniel Pilon *Max Middleton* ■ *Dir* Roger Cardinal • *Scr* Avrum Jacobson, from the novel *Hey Malarek* by Victor Malarek

Malaya ★★★
Second World War adventure 1949 · US · BW · 94mins

Enjoyable tosh from MGM with an amazing cast – Spencer Tracy, James Stewart, Lionel Barrymore, Sydney Greenstreet – though in the end it's not much more than a B-movie. Tracy and Stewart play a convict and a reporter hired to smuggle rubber out of Japanese-occupied Malaya. (The fact that this was a British theatre of war doesn't seem to enter into the equation.) Greenstreet runs a bar in the jungle where Valentina Cortese sings while waiting to see which star she ends up with in the end.

Spencer Tracy *Carnahan* • James Stewart *John Royer* • Valentina Cortese *Luana* • Sydney Greenstreet *Dutchman* • John Hodiak *Keller* • Lionel Barrymore *John Manchester* • Gilbert Roland *Romano* • DeForest Kelley *Lt Glenson* ■ *Dir* Richard Thorpe • *Scr* Frank Fenton, from a story by Manchester Boddy

Malcolm ★★★ 15
Crime comedy 1986 · Ausl · Colour · 82mins

This Australian comedy tells the gently contrived story of Malcolm (Colin Friels), a simple, inarticulate man whose Heath Robinson-like constructions help his lodgers (John Hargreaves and Lindy Davies) pursue a career in remote-controlled crime. The directorial debut of Nadia Tass, whose husband, David Parker, wrote the script, it has a quaintness of observation that is never coy, and an innocence that is matched by Malcolm's own nature. ▭

Colin Friels *Malcolm* • John Hargreaves *Frank* • Lindy Davies *Judith* • Chris Haywood *Willy* • Judith Stratford *Jenny* • Beverly Phillips *Mrs T* ■ *Dir* Nadia Tass • *Scr* David Parker

Malcolm X ★★★ 15
Biographical drama 1992 · US · Colour · 193mins

To describe a film as "worthy" is to damn it with faint praise. But, as much as one admires the ambition of Spike Lee's *Malcolm X*, it is surprisingly conventional and, at times, downright dull. There are speeches, reams and reams of them, and Denzel Washington as the black militant leader of the sixties copes with them as best he can. Washington looks impressive and he has undoubted charisma, like Malcolm X himself, but he's stuck in a huge, flipside national epic that lumbers on through the decades, continents and events for over three hours. Perhaps Lee was subdued by the big budget, by the need for a white audience as well as a black one; perhaps, too, he was overawed by his subject. ▭

Denzel Washington *Malcolm X* • Angela Bassett *Betty Shabazz* • Albert Hall *Baines* • Al Freeman Jr *Elijah Muhammad* • Delroy Lindo *West Indian Archie* • Spike Lee *Shorty* • Theresa Randle *Laura* • Kate Vernon *Sophia* • Lonette McKee *Louise Little* • Tommy Hollis *Earl Little* ■ *Dir* Spike Lee • *Scr* Arnold Perl, Spike Lee, from *The Autobiography of Malcolm X, as told to Alex Haley*

Male and Female ★★★★
Silent satire 1919 · US · BW · 115mins

Before Cecil B DeMille discovered the Bible, the flamboyant producer/director explored sex in a series of enjoyably risqué comedies, six of them with Gloria Swanson. In this free adaptation of JM Barrie's *The Admirable Crichton*, Swanson plays Lady Mary, one of a group of shipwrecked aristocrats who find themselves dependent on their butler (Thomas Meighan). The director contrives to have Swanson take a bath, almost a prerequisite of a DeMille film of the time, as well as featuring a Babylonian fantasy scene in which Bebe Daniels appears as a slave girl. DeMille remade it in 1934 as *Four Frightened People*.

Thomas Meighan *Crichton* • Gloria Swanson *Lady Mary Lasenby* • Lila Lee *Tweeny* •

Theodore Roberts *Lord Loam* • Raymond Hatton *Honorable Ernest Wolley* • Mildred Reardon *Agatha Lasenby* • Bebe Daniels *The King's favourite* ■ *Dir* Cecil B DeMille • *Scr* Jeanie Macpherson, from the play *The Admirable Crichton* by JM Barrie

The Male Animal ★★★★
Comedy 1942 · US · BW · 100mins

A punchy, apposite comedy, regarded as highly sophisticated in its day, which still stands the test of time. Henry Fonda is excellent as the college professor about to lose his wife Olivia de Havilland to old flame Jack Carson, and his job, if he reads a controversial letter written by anarchists to his students. All three leads are splendid, giving great light and shade to their characters and so immediately drawing us into the complex plot. The movie has a lot to say about human relationships, particularly in the desire versus companionship arena.

Henry Fonda *Tommy Turner* • Olivia de Havilland *Ellen Turner* • Joan Leslie *Patricia Stanley* • Jack Carson *Joe Ferguson* • Eugene Pallette *Ed Keller* • Herbert Anderson *Michael Barnes* • Hattie McDaniel *Cleota* • Ivan Simpson *Dr Damon* ■ *Dir* Elliott Nugent • *Scr* Julius J Epstein, Philip G Epstein, Stephen Morehouse Avery, from the play by James Thurber, Elliott Nugent

Male Hunt ★★
Comedy 1964 · Fr/It · BW · 92mins

A sex comedy about bachelors on the run from beautiful women, directed by Edouard Molinaro who later made *La Cages aux Folles*. A big hit in France, *Male Hunt* is worth seeing only for its astonishing cast: the raffish charm of Jean-Claude Brialy is complemented by Jean-Paul Belmondo doing his trademark petty criminal act. The women are even more eye-catching and include Catherine Deneuve and her sister Françoise Dorléac, who died so tragically in a car crash in 1967. In French with English subtitles.

Jean-Paul Belmondo *Fernand* • Jean-Claude Brialy *Tony* • Bernard Blier *Mons Heurtin* • Catherine Deneuve *Denise* • Françoise Dorléac *Sandra* • Micheline Presle *Isabelle* • Claude Rich *Julien* • Marie Laforêt *Gisèle* • Bernadette Lafont *Flora* ■ *Dir* Edouard Molinaro • *Scr* France Roche, Michel Audiard, from an idea by Yvon Guezel, from stories by Albert Simonin, Michel Duran

Malice ★★★ 15
Psychological thriller 1993 · US · Colour · 102mins

Nicole Kidman (aka Mrs Tom Cruise) has surprised the cynics by forging a very individual career of her own. Here she plays the seemingly innocent young newlywed, whose life with nice-but-dim husband Bill Pullman is transformed by the arrival of charismatic surgeon Alec Baldwin. Kidman is smart and sexy as the *femme fatale* figure, while Baldwin, always better at being bad, excels as the arrogant doc. The talented support cast includes Anne Bancroft, Bebe Neuwirth, Peter Gallagher and Gwyneth Paltrow. The screenplay is a mite too tortuous, but director Harold Becker has fun piling on the red herrings. Contains violence, swearing and sex scenes. ▭

Alec Baldwin *Jed Hill* • Nicole Kidman *Tracy Safian* • Bill Pullman *Dana* • Bebe Neuwirth *Dana* • George C Scott *Dr Kessler* • Anne Bancroft *Claire Kennsinger* • Peter Gallagher *Dennis Riley* • Gwyneth Paltrow *Paula Bell* ■ *Dir* Harold Becker • *Scr* Aaron Sorkin, Scott Frank, from a story by Aaron Sorkin, Jonas McCord

Malice in Wonderland ★★ PG

Drama based on a true story
1985 · US · Colour · 90mins

A highly fictionalised, TV-movie account of how struggling actress Hedda Hopper became the arch rival of Hollywood gossip-monger Louella Parsons through movie mogul manipulation. However, what the industry never expected was that Hopper would become equally powerful and just as annoying in her own syndicated newspaper column. Solid acting by Jane Alexander and Elizabeth Taylor and a glitzy backdrop make this factually confused rumour-mill exposé an entertaining diversion.

Elizabeth Taylor *Louella Parsons* • Jane Alexander *Hedda Hopper* • Richard Dysart *Louis B Mayer* ■ *Dir* Gus Trikonis • *Scr* Jacqueline Feather, David Seidler, from the novel *Hedda and Louella* by George Eels

Malicious ★★ 18

Erotic thriller   1995 · US · Colour · 88mins

Molly Ringwald plays the woman scorned by high-school baseball star Patrick McGaw after a one-night stand, in this routine erotic thriller. It could have been called *Fatal Attraction: the College Years*, as Ringwald sets out for revenge against golden boy McGaw and his fiancée, Sarah Lassez. Ringwald is shrill rather than scary, although *Pretty in Pink* fans be warned: she does some pretty awful things to a cute cat. Contains swearing, violence and sex scenes.

Molly Ringwald *Melissa* • Patrick McGaw *Doug Gordon* • Sarah Lassez *Laura* • Ryan Michael *Mitch* • Mimi Kuzyk *Mrs Gordon* • John Vernon *Detective Pronzini* • Rick Henrickson *Rich* ■ *Dir* Ian Corson • *Scr* George Saunders

Mallrats ★★★ 18

Comedy   1995 · US · Colour · 91mins

Director Kevin Smith's follow-up to his no-budget independent hit *Clerks* was this under-rated comic look at pop Americana, junk culture and adolescent angst that gained enormously from the use of a professional cast (Shannen Doherty, Claire Forlani, Ben Affleck et al). Focusing on a pair of slackers mooching around the local shopping mall after being dumped by their girlfriends, Smith's vulgar and consistently amusing diversion is equally irreverent and desperately spot-on as its eye-opening predecessor.

Shannen Doherty *Rene* • Jeremy London *TS Quint* • Jason Lee *Brodie Bruce* • Claire Forlani *Brandi Svenning* • Ben Affleck *Shannon Hamilton* • Joey Lauren Adams *Gwen Turner* • Renee Humphrey *Tricia Jones* • Jason Mewes *Jay* • Stan Lee ■ *Dir/Scr* Kevin Smith

Malone ★★ 18

Action drama   1987 · US · Colour · 87mins

Burt Reynolds is in standard macho form as a former CIA agent on the trail of a baddie who's busy building his personal paramilitary empire. Reynolds and co-star Cliff Robertson know this all-action terrain like the backs of their hands and this is really one for the boys. Reynolds was teetering on the edge of obscurity when he shot this; he subsequently fell off, though his career took off again in the late nineties. Contains swearing.

Burt Reynolds *Malone* • Cliff Robertson *Delaney* • Cynthia Gibb *Jo Barlow* • Scott Wilson *Paul Barlow* • Kenneth McMillan *Hawkins* • Lauren Hutton *Jamie* ■ *Dir* Harley Cokliss • *Scr* Christopher Frank, from the novel *Shotgun* by William Wingate

Malpractice ★★★

Documentary drama
1989 · Ausl · Colour · 94mins

Bill Bennett is one of Australia's most accomplished documentary directors and this is a laudable experiment in having a fictional courtroom drama heard by real-life jurors. The story, about a junior doctor who mishandles a difficult birth, suffers from too many clichéd characterisations, particularly within the family who sue the hospital. But the conflicts between the exhausted junior and the arrogant consultant, and the desire of the doughty nurse to see justice done are credible enough. The dice seem loaded before the trial begins, but the verdict might spark a few debates.

Caz Lederman *Coral Davis* • Bob Baines *Doug Davis* • Ian Gilmour *Dr Frank Harrison* • Pat Thomson *Sister Margaret Beattie* • Charles Little *Dr Tom Cotterslow* • Janet Stanley *Sister Diane Shaw* • Dorothy Alison *Maureen Davis* ■ *Dir* Bill Bennett • *Scr* Jenny Ainge

The Malta Story ★★★ U

Second World War drama
1953 · UK · BW · 98mins

Intended as a cinematic tribute to the island that was awarded the George Cross for its courage during the Second World War, this is a remarkably restrained drama in comparison to other British-made accounts of wartime heroics. Blending romance and intrigue with convincing combat sequences, director Brian Desmond Hurst presents a moving human story without slipping into melodrama. Alec Guinness is perhaps overly subdued as the aerial photographer scouring the Mediterranean for enemy activity, but Flora Robson is superb as the mother whose children experience the sharply contrasting fortunes of war.

Alec Guinness *Peter Ross* • Jack Hawkins *Air Commanding Officer* • Anthony Steel *Bartlett* • Muriel Pavlow *Maria* • Flora Robson *Melita* • Renée Asherson *Joan* • Ralph Truman *Banks* • Reginald Tate *Payne* ■ *Dir* Brian Desmond Hurst • *Scr* William Fairchild, Nigel Balchin, Thorold Dickinson, Peter de Sarigny

The Maltese Bippy ★

Comedy   1969 · US · Colour · 92mins

At the height of their TV fame with *Laugh In*, comedians Dan Rowan and Dick Martin parlayed one of their catch phrases – "You bet your sweet bippy" – into a brainless, feature-length horror send-up. Rowan plays a nudie movie producer who takes his lead star, Martin, to a Long Island haunted house. Cue lots of alternative endings, none of which are remotely funny.

Dan Rowan *Sam Smith* • Dick Martin *Ernest Grey* • Carol Lynley *Robin Sherwood* • Julie Newmar *Carlotta Ravenswood* • Mildred Natwick *Molly Fletcher* • Fritz Weaver *Mr Ravenswood* • Robert Reed *Lt Tim Crane* ■ *Dir* Norman Panama • *Scr* Everett Freeman, Ray Singer, from a story by Everett Freeman

The Maltese Falcon
★★★★★ PG

Classic film noir   1941 · US · BW · 96mins

Superb cinematic entertainment, this third version of Dashiell Hammett's hard-boiled crime drama completely obliterated memories of the two perfectly fine earlier versions and created a brand new movie icon in Humphrey Bogart's cynical private detective Sam Spade. This was the beginning of a beautiful friendship between Bogie and John Huston, who was then a screenwriter making his feature debut as director, and whose tart screenplay retains most of the sharp dialogue and sleazy amorality of Hammett's original. Among the supporting cast, stage actor Sydney Greenstreet made his screen debut as Gutman, lusting after the Black Bird; Peter Lorre is the whiny, effeminate Joel Cairo; Mary Astor is cast against type as *femme fatale* supreme Brigid O'Shaughnessy: an extraordinary combination that couldn't be bettered. If you want to date *film noir*, this is where it all began. ■ **DVD**

Humphrey Bogart *Sam Spade* • Mary Astor *Brigid O'Shaughnessy* • Peter Lorre *Joel Cairo* • Sydney Greenstreet *Kasper Gutman* • Gladys George *Iva Archer* • Elisha Cook Jr *Wilmer Cook* • Barton MacLane *Det Lt Dundy* • Lee Patrick *Effie Perine* ■ *Dir* John Huston • *Scr* John Huston, from the novel by Dashiell Hammett • *Cinematographer* Arthur Edeson • *Music* Adolph Deutsch

Mamá Cumple 100 Años
★★★

Black comedy   1979 · Sp · Colour · 100mins

In *Anna and the Wolves*, Carlos Saura used Rafaela Aparicio's three sons to symbolise what he considered to be the primary evils of Franco's Spain: religion, sexual repression and authoritarian fascism. This Oscar-nominated follow-up shows the two surviving siblings joining with the rest of Aparicio's grasping family to celebrate her centenary, though they soon abandon their false bonhomie to scrap for a chunk of her fortune. The satire is ferocious, the caricatures grotesque, yet Saura is more intent on amusing than denouncing. He even resurrects Geraldine Chaplin's dead housekeeper to add a surreal touch to the already black humour. In Spanish with English subtitles.

Geraldine Chaplin *Anna* • Amparo Muñoz *Natalia* • Rafaela Aparicio *Mother* • Fernando Fernan Gomez *Fernando* • Norman Briski *Antonio* • Charo Soriano *Luchi* ■ *Dir/Scr* Carlos Saura

La Maman et la Putain
★★★★★ 18

Drama   1973 · Fr · BW · 208mins

A sprawling study of sexual politics and smug sixties intellectualism, Jean Eustache's masterpiece was the last hurrah of the French New Wave. Based on actual conversations, the screenplay was delivered verbatim by a superb cast that deserves considerable credit for making every line seem so spontaneous – particularly Françoise Lebrun, a first-time non-professional whose epic speech about the futility of sex without love is remarkable for its power and intensity. But Jean-Pierre Léaud's indolent student and his sensible girlfriend, Bernadette Lafont, are equally impressive in a brilliantly observed portrait of a moment and its attitudes that remains as compelling as it is controversial. In French with English subtitles. Contains swearing and sex scenes. ■

Bernadette Lafont *Marie* • Jean-Pierre Léaud *Alexandre* • Françoise Lebrun *Veronika* • Isabelle Weingarten *Gilberte* ■ *Dir/Scr* Jean Eustache

Mama's Dirty Girls ★

Black comedy   1974 · US · Colour · 80mins

A witless melange of attempted murders and inane seduction, this supposed black comedy was another nail in the coffin of one-time Hollywood *femme fatale* Gloria Grahame's illustrious career. She plays black widow Mama Love who, after dispatching one idiot husband, lures another allegedly rich man into marrying her. Surprise, surprise: he's just killed his wife and aims to bury Mama too. Enter Mama's well-taught daughters, Sondra Currie and Candice Rialson, and this moribund tale wends its sorry way to a yawn-inducing climax.

Gloria Grahame *Mama Love* • Paul Lambert *Harold* • Sondra Currie *Addie* • Candice Rialson *Becky* • Christopher Wines *Sheriff* ■ *Dir* John Hayes • *Scr* Gil Lasky

Mama's Going to Buy You a Mockingbird ★★★★

Drama   1988 · Can · Colour · 96mins

Canadian director Sandy Wilson, who made the critically acclaimed *My American Cousin*, here tackles a TV drama about a family coming to terms with a father's impending death from cancer. Louis Tripp is compelling as the 12-year-old son from whose perspective the story is told, while both Linda Griffiths and Geoffrey Bowes (as his mother and father) give poignant and sensitive performances that never stray into sentimentality.

Linda Griffiths *Kate Talbot* • Louis Tripp *Jeremy Talbot* • Geoff Bowes [Geoffrey Bowes] *John Talbot* • Rosa Barker Anderson *Tess* • Marsha Moreau *Sarah Talbot* ■ *Dir* Sandy Wilson • *Scr* Anna Sandor, from the novel by Jean Little

Mambo ★★

Romantic drama   1954 · US/It · BW · 93mins

This clumsy American-Italian co-production stars Silvana Mangano as a lowly shopgirl who becomes an internationally known dancer while juggling the affections of a small-time crook and a dying count. Piling agony upon agony, Robert Rossen's movie staggers from one risible scene to the next, while Michael Rennie and Shelley Winters heighten the absurdity by adopting lasagne accents.

Silvana Mangano *Giovanna Masetti* • Vittorio Gassman *Mario Rossi* • Michael Rennie *Count Enrico* • Shelley Winters *Tony Burns* •

Katherine Dunham • Mary Clare *Contessa Marisoni* • Eduardo Cianelli [Eduardo Ciannelli] *Padre di Giovanna* ■ *Dir* Robert Rossen • *Scr* Guido Piovene, Ivo Perilli, Ennio De Concini, Robert Rossen

The Mambo Kings ★★★★ 15

Musical drama
1992 · US/Fr · Colour · 99mins

Antonio Banderas made the jump from Spanish star to international hunk with this, his first big English-language movie, based on the Pulitzer Prize-winning novel by Oscar Hijuelos. Banderas and Armand Assante, the bad guy in *Judge Dredd*, star as two Cuban musicians who arrive in postwar America seeking love, fame and fortune. The film positively sizzles when the music gets going, and the mambo itself is as much a character in the movie as the actors. Debut director Arne Glimcher went on to make the Sean Connery thriller *Just Cause*. 🖭

Armand Assante *Cesar Castillo* • Antonio Banderas *Nestor Castillo* • Cathy Moriarty *Lanna Lake* • Maruschka Detmers *Delores Fuentes* • Pablo Calogero *Ramon* • Scott Cohen *Bernardito* • Mario Grillo *Mario* ■ *Dir* Arne Glimcher • *Scr* Cynthia Cidre, from the novel *The Mambo Kings Play Songs of Love* by Oscar Hijuelos

Mame ★★ PG

Musical comedy 1974 · US · Colour · 125mins

You need a better voice than Lucille Ball's to carry this dreary, predictable and almost embarrassing paean to American matriarchy at its most egocentric. Lumbered with a weak plotline and sketchy characterisation, the original show relied on one great, thumping performance to win the day, and Gene Saks's film is no different. There are plenty of musical stars who could have pulled it off, but this ageing sitcom queen is not one of them. 🖭

Lucille Ball *Mame* • Robert Preston *Beauregard* • Beatrice Arthur *Vera* • Bruce Davison *Older Patrick* • Joyce Van Patten *Sally Cato* • Don Porter *Mr Upson* • Audrey Christie *Mrs Upson* ■ *Dir* Gene Saks • *Scr* Paul Zindel, from the musical and play by Jerome Lawrence, Jerry Herman, Robert E Lee, from the novel *Auntie Mame* by Patrick Dennis

Mamma Roma ★★★★ 15

Drama 1962 · It · BW · 101mins

Following the acclaim for *Accatone*, Pier Paolo Pasolini refined his unique blend of Marxism, Catholicism, kitchen-sink naturalism, classicism and street poetry in this unforgettable portrait of a Rome that never makes the guide books. As the only professional in an outstanding cast, Anna Magnani gives a typically extrovert performance as the prostitute whose bid to prevent her beloved teenage son from being sucked into the perilous underworld of vice and crime is hamstrung by her grasping pimp. With Tonino Delli Colli's mobile camera achieving a mannerist *cinéma vérité*, this has none of the sentimentality that so clouded the neorealist vision. In Italian with English subtitles. 🖭

Anna Magnani *Mamma Roma* • Ettore Garofolo *Ettore* • Franco Citti *Carmine* • Silvana Corsini *Bruna* • Luisa Loiano *Biancofiore* • Paolo Volponi *Priest* • Luciano Gonini *Zacaria* ■ *Dir/Scr* Pier Paolo Pasolini

Mammy ★★

Musical comedy
1930 · US · BW and Colour · 83mins

A star vehicle for Al Jolson, here playing the leading light of a touring minstrel act. Unjustly accused of shooting the troupe's MC (Lowell Sherman), the two-timing fiancé of Lois Moran, Al briefly goes on the run and visits the mother he adores (Louise Dresser) before returning for the happy ending. This was a smash hit in its day, and boasts an appropriate score by Irving Berlin, but it has dated badly. The mother-son relationship, consisting of embraces more suited to lovers, is frankly embarrassing, and the comedy elements are no longer funny.

Al Jolson *Al Fuller* • Lois Moran *Nora Meadows* • Louise Dresser *Mrs Fuller* • Lowell Sherman *Westy* • Hobart Bosworth *Meadows* • Tully Marshall *Slats* ■ *Dir* Michael Curtiz • *Scr* Joseph Jackson, Gordon Rigby, from the play *Mr Bones* by Irving Berlin, James Gleason

The Man ★★★

Drama 1972 · US · Colour · 93mins

When the US president and Speaker of the House are killed in a freak accident and the Vice-President is rendered insensible by a stroke, senate leader James Earl Jones becomes the first black man to live in the White House. Based on the bestselling novel by Irving Wallace, the drama skips rather nervously over several key issues, including apartheid in South Africa. Jones, though, is impressive as the unelected president fighting for acceptance, while Jack Benny has a brief cameo as himself.

James Earl Jones *Douglas Dilman* • Martin Balsam *Jim Talley* • Burgess Meredith *Senator Watson* • Lew Ayres *Noah Calvin* • William Windom *Arthur Eaton* • Barbara Rush *Kay Eaton* • Georg Stanford Brown *Robert Wheeler* • Janet MacLachlan *Wanda* • Jack Benny ■ *Dir* Joseph Sargent • *Scr* Rod Serling, from a novel by Irving Wallace

A Man, a Woman and a Bank ★★ 15

Comedy thriller 1979 · Can · Colour · 96mins

A loopy heist movie with Donald Sutherland and Paul Mazursky plugging into their computer to a new electronic bank, hoping to transfer $4 million to their hideaway in Macao. Despite some very funny scenes and the engaging performances, including Brooke Adams as Sutherland's romantic interest, the movie is rather too ramshackle for its own good, though its predictions about computerised banking procedures seem right on the money. 🖭

Donald Sutherland *Reese Halperin* • Brooke Adams *Stacey Bishop* • Paul Mazursky *Norman Barrie* • Allan Magicovsky *Peter* • Leigh Hamilton *Marie* • Nick Rice *Gino* • Peter Erlich *Jerry* ■ *Dir* Noel Black • *Scr* Ronald Gideon, Bruce A Evans, Stuart Margolin

A Man about the House ★★ PG

Period thriller 1947 · UK · BW · 89mins

Two English spinster sisters (Margaret Johnston, Dulcie Gray) take up residence in a Neapolitan villa they have inherited and are charmed by the handsome young Italian (Kieron Moore) who is caring for the place. He marries Johnston, but slowly poisons her in order to get back the property, which once belonged to his family. A suitably brooding British-made melodrama, directed by Leslie Arliss, this seems rather drearily predictable now. 🖭

Margaret Johnston *Agnes Isit* • Dulcie Gray *Ellen Isit* • Kieron Moore *Salvatore* • Guy Middleton *Sir Benjamin Dench* • Felix Aylmer *Richard Sanctuary* • Lilian Braithwaite *Mrs Armitage* ■ *Dir* Leslie Arliss • *Scr* Leslie Arliss, JB Williams, from the play by John Perry, from the novel by Francis Brett Young

Man about the House ★★ PG

Comedy 1974 · UK · Colour · 85mins

Not the product you would normally associate with Hammer, this spin-off from the popular TV series was the kind of project the House of Horror was forced to resort to as the fright business took a down turn in the mid-seventies. The material is thinner than a bedsit wall as housemates Richard O'Sullivan, Sally Thomsett and the excellent Paula Wilcox team up with their inimitable landlords Brian Murphy and Yootha Joyce to see off unscrupulous property developers. 🖭

Richard O'Sullivan *Robin Tripp* • Paula Wilcox *Chrissy* • Sally Thomsett *Jo* • Brian Murphy *Mr Roper* • Yootha Joyce *Mrs Roper* • Doug Fisher *Larry Simmonds* • Peter Cellier *Morris Pluthero* • Patrick Newell *Sir Edmund Weir* • Arthur Lowe *Spiros* ■ *Dir* John Robins • *Scr* Johnnie Mortimer, Brian Cooke

Man about Town ★★★★

Period romantic comedy
1947 · Fr/US · BW · 89mins

René Clair's first French film for over a decade is a bittersweet, regretful look at the silent cinema in which he began his career. Maurice Chevalier plays an ageing ex-actor, now a director, who teaches his assistant (François Périer) the arts of seduction, unaware that they are both in love with the same young girl (an insipid Marcelle Derrien). The re-creation of the era is rather more convincing than the plot, but Chevalier shows a rare depth. French dialogue dubbed into English.

Maurice Chevalier *Emile* • François Périer *Jacques* • Marcelle Derrien *Madeleine* • Dany Robin *Lucette* ■ *Dir* René Clair • *Scr* René Clair, Robert Pirosh, from a story by René Clair

Man against the Mob: the Chinatown Murders ★★

Crime thriller 1989 · US · Colour · 96mins

A sequel to (surprise, surprise) *Man against the Mob*, with a crusty George Peppard detecting crime in forties' LA. Yes, we're in *Big Sleep* territory and, although Peppard is always enjoyable to watch, this material is not exactly new to the screen. There is an interesting cast, though, featuring Charles Haid from *Hill Street Blues* and original Bond girl Ursula Andress.

George Peppard *Detective Frank Doakey* • Ursula Andress *Betty Starr* • Richard Bradford *Terry O'Brien* • Charles Haid *Buddy Bunnucci* • Jason Beghe *Sammy Turner* • Julia Nickson [Julia Nickson-Soul] *Kaylie* ■ *Dir* Michael Pressman • *Scr* Michael Petryni, from a story by David J Kinghorn, from characters created by John Rester Zodrow, David J Kinghorn

A Man Alone ★★★ U

Western 1955 · US · Colour · 95mins

Ray Milland joined up with Republic as a producer, director and star, and acquitted himself well on all three counts in making this offbeat western and the melodrama *Lisbon*. Milland doesn't say a word for the first third of the film, which casts him as a mysterious loner who arrives in town, only to be accused of committing a stagecoach robbery. The house he takes refuge in belongs to sheriff Ward Bond, who's quarantined with yellow fever. Although it becomes more routine towards the end, this is still a jump ahead of most westerns of the time, especially Republic's. 🖭

Ray Milland *Wes Steele* • Mary Murphy *Nadine Corrigan* • Ward Bond *Gil Corrigan* • Raymond Burr *Stanley* • Arthur Space *Dr Mason* • Lee Van Cleef *Clantin* • Alan Hale Jr *Anderson* ■ *Dir* Ray Milland • *Scr* John Tucker Battle, from a story by Mort Briskin

A Man and a Woman ★★★★

Romantic drama
1966 · Fr · BW, Colour and Sepia · 106mins

Winner of the best foreign film Oscar and the Palme d'Or at Cannes, this teasing melodrama is one of the most famous examples of artistic triumph over adversity. The switches to sepia-tinted film stock were much applauded at the time (although they look rather flashy and trite today), but they were forced on director Claude Lelouch because he lacked the funds to shoot the picture in colour. Amid the chic cinematic trickery, Jean-Louis Trintignant and Anouk Aimée are splendid as the widowed couple teetering on the brink of romance. In French with English subtitles.

Jean-Louis Trintignant *Jean-Louis Duroc* • Anouk Aimée *Anne Gauthier* • Pierre Barouh *Pierre Gauthier* • Valérie Lagrange *Valerie Duroc* • Simone Paris *Headmistress* • Antoine Sire *Antoine Duroc* • Souad Amidou *Françoise Gauthier* • Henri Chemin *Jean-Louis's co-driver* ■ *Dir* Claude Lelouch • *Scr* Pierre Uytterhoeven, Claude Lelouch, from a story by Claude Lelouch • *Music* Francis Lai

A Man and a Woman: 20 Years Later ★★

Romance drama 1986 · Fr · Colour · 108mins

Two decades after racing driver Jean-Louis Trintignant and script girl Anouk Aimée parted, Claude Lelouch reunited them for this self-reflexive look at how film shapes life for its own ends. With Trintignant now scouting for younger talent and big-shot producer Aimée so desperate for a hit that she resorts to a musical version of her own *amour fou*, this could have been a fascinating treatise on memory and artistic and personal compromise. But Lelouch is no Alain Resnais, and this glossily empty confection is overwhelmed by a stupid subplot, gratuitous structural gimmickry and a gloating sense of cinematic significance. In French with English subtitles.

Anouk Aimée *Anne Gauthier* • Jean-Louis Trintignant *Jean-Louis Duroc* • Evelyne Bouix *Françoise* • Marie-Sophie L Pochat *Marie-Sophie* ■ *Dir* Claude Lelouch • *Scr* Claude Lelouch, Pierre Uytterhoeven, Monique Lange, Jérôme Tonnerre • *Music* Francis Lai

Man and Boy ★★ U

Western   1971 · US · Colour · 77mins

Comedian Bill Cosby launched his big-screen career as star and executive producer of this mild, old-fashioned western drama about blacks out West after the Civil War. Cosby is good as the homesteader who takes his young son in pursuit of a stolen horse, but director EW Swackhamer lets too many actors chew the scenery and stages some unconvincing shoot-outs. Yaphet Kotto plays a powerful bully, Douglas Turner Ward is a cantankerous outlaw, while Leif Erickson has the only substantial white role as a lawman.

Bill Cosby *Caleb Revers* • George Spell *Billy Revers* • Gloria Foster *Ivy Revers* • Douglas Turner Ward *Lee Christmas* • Yaphet Kotto *Nate Hodges* • Shelley Morrison *Rosita* • Leif Erickson *Sheriff Mossman* ■ *Dir* EW Swackhamer • *Scr* Harry Essex, Oscar Saul

Man and His Mate ★★ U

Science-fiction adventure
1940 · US · BW · 76mins

Hal Roach is best known as the producer who teamed Laurel and Hardy. Unfortunately, he got laughs in all the wrong places for this ambitious but ultimately preposterous prehistoric adventure. Yet the film does have a place in cinema history. This owes nothing to the story about the Rock and the Shell tribes, to the shoestring special effects, or to the grunting mime of Victor Mature, Carole Landis and Lon Chaney Jr in the principal roles. The claim to fame lies in the uncredited assistance of DW Griffith, the legendary silent director, working on his final picture after a decade in the wilderness. ▭

Victor Mature *Tumak* • Carole Landis *Loana* • Lon Chaney Jr *Akhoba* • Conrad Nagel *Archaeologist/Narrator* • John Hubbard *Ohtao* • Robert Kent *Mountain guide* • Mamo Clark *Nupondi* ■ *Dir* Hal Roach, Hal Roach Jr • *Scr* Mickell Novak, George Baker, Joseph Frickert

Man Beast ★

Adventure   1956 · US · BW · 60mins

Virginia Maynor and Lloyd Nelson mount an expedition to the Himalayas to search for her missing brother, only to uncover a dastardly plot by Abominable Snowmen to lure women into their domain. Cobbled together by cheapskate producer/director Jerry Warren from Mexican-shot location footage, with a cast full of game has-beens and men in Yeti suits, this is dumb fun in a non-scary sort of way.

Rock Madison *Lon Raynon* • Virginia Maynor *Connie Hayward* • Tom Maruzzi *Steve Cameron* • Lloyd Nelson *Trevor Hudson* • George Wells Lewis *Dr Erickson* ■ *Dir* Jerry Warren • *Scr* B Arthur Cassidy

A Man Betrayed ★

Drama   1941 · US · BW · 84mins

John Wayne became Republic's biggest asset thanks to *Stagecoach* and other good films he made elsewhere. But his home studio repeatedly let him down with feeble pictures like this, originally shown in Britain as *Citadel of Crime*, which tries to combine an exposé of crooked politics with doses of screwball comedy and fails on both counts. On the plus side, Wayne is

appealing as a crusading lawyer, Edward Ellis is forceful as a corrupt but likeable politician, while Frances Dee is unusually vivacious as the latter's daughter. The oddest element is Ward Bond's mobster, excruciatingly played as an imitation of the simple-minded Lenny from *Of Mice and Men*.

John Wayne *Lynn Hollister* • Frances Dee *Sabra Cameron* • Edward Ellis *Tom Cameron* • Wallace Ford *Casey* • Ward Bond *Floyd* ■ *Dir* John H Auer • *Scr* Isabel Dawn, Tom Kilpatrick, from a story by Jack Moffitt

The Man between ★★ U

Spy drama   1953 · UK · BW · 97mins

Set in partitioned Berlin at the height of the Cold War, this is a less than convincing return to *Third Man* territory by Carol Reed. Using some of the most outrageously oblique camera angles of his career to suggest a city out of kilter and its citizens beset by fear and doubt, Reed strains for a visual edginess that might atone for (or even distract from) the flatness of this melodramatic and, frankly, suspenseless tale. Recognising that their characters have no depth, the members of the cast fail to rouse themselves, although James Mason is as watchable as ever. ▭

James Mason *Ivo Kern* • Claire Bloom *Susanne Mallison* • Hildegarde Neff *Bettina* • Geoffrey Toone *Martin Mallison* • Aribert Waescher *Halendar* • Ernst Schroeder *Kastner* ■ *Dir* Carol Reed • *Scr* Harry Kurnitz, Eric Linklater, from the novel *Susanne in Berlin* by Walter Ebert

Man Bites Dog ★★★★ 18

Satirical black comedy
1992 · Bel · Colour · 92mins

A prize winner at Cannes, this searing satire caused a storm of protest on its original release. Were its co-directors exposing our lust for media sensationalism? Or were they merely getting away with explicit scenes of rape and slaughter in the name of social commentary? Many will bridle at the graphic imagery, while others will resent the cockiness of the approach as documentarists André Bonzel and Rémy Belvaux play an increasingly active role in the crimes of serial killer Benoît Poelvoorde. Yet this is an undeniably bold contribution to the debate on screen violence and the responsibilities of both film-makers and audiences. In French with English subtitles. ▭

Benoît Poelvoorde *Ben* • Rémy Belvaux *Reporter* • André Bonzel *Cameraman* • Jacqueline Poelvoorde-Pappaert *Ben's mother* ■ *Dir* Rémy Belvaux, André Bonzel, Benoît Poelvoorde • *Scr* Rémy Belvaux, André Bonzel, Benoît Poelvoorde, Vincent Tavier, from an idea by Rémy Belvaux

A Man Called Adam ★★

Drama   1966 · US · Colour · 103mins

Trying to yoke an allegory about race to this story of a black trumpeter (Ossie Davis) battling discrimination and feelings of inadequacy makes for a rather queasy mix. The guest stars make it enjoyable, though – Sammy Davis Jr, Louis Armstrong and Mel Tormé – while Cicely Tyson shines in a supporting role. The director is Leo Penn, father of Chris and Sean.

Sammy Davis Jr *Adam Johnson* • Ossie Davis *Nelson Davis* • Cicely Tyson *Claudia Ferguson* • Louis Armstrong *Willie "Sweet Daddy" Ferguson* • Frank Sinatra Jr *Vincent* • Peter Lawford *Manny* • Mel Tormé ■ *Dir* Leo Penn • *Scr* Tina Rome, Les Pine

The Man Called Flintstone ★★★ U

Animated comedy
1966 · US · Colour · 86mins

Feature-length spin-off from the hit TV series, which would have been called *The Flagstones* had they stuck with the title of the original pilot. Directed by creators William Hanna and Joseph Barbera and featuring original voice artists Alan Reed (Fred), Mel Blanc (Barney) and Jean Vander Pyl (Wilma), the cartoon is a spoof of all the films and TV series about spies that emerged during the sixties. Fred takes over from a lookalike secret agent to pursue the Green Goose and his evil henchmen, the men from SMIRK. The strength of the basic *Flintstones* concept just about carries this film, though there's still a feeling that what works well for 20 minutes is stretched thin across 90. ▭

Alan Reed *Fred Flintstone* • Mel Blanc *Barney Rubble* • Jean Vander Pyl *Wilma Flintstone* • Gerry Johnson *Betty Rubble* ■ *Dir* Joseph Barbera, William Hanna • *Scr* Harvey Bullock, RS Allen, from a story by Harvey Bullock, RS Allen, from material by Joseph Barbera, William Hanna, Warren Foster, Alex Lovy

A Man Called Gannon ★★

Western   1969 · US · Colour · 105mins

Quite pointless Universal remake of its own minor classic *Man without a Star*, a torrid western that benefited greatly from King Vidor's direction and the intensely masochistic presence of Kirk Douglas in the lead. Here, talented director James Goldstone does what he can, but the hyper-erotic elements of the original are missing and the cast, headed by Tony Franciosa, has little to get its teeth into.

Tony Franciosa [Anthony Franciosa] *Gannon* • Michael Sarrazin *Jess Washburn* • Judi West *Beth* • Susan Oliver *Matty* • John Anderson *Capper* • David Sheiner *Sheriff Polaski* • James Westerfield *Amos* • Gavin Macleod *Lou* ■ *Dir* James Goldstone • *Scr* Gene Kearney, Borden Chase, DD Beauchamp, from the novel by Dee Linford

A Man Called Horse ★★ 15

Western   1970 · US · Colour · 109mins

Richard Harris is an English Lord captured by Sioux Indians. A sort of *Tarzan*-style adventure, the picture was pompously pitched as an authentic account of Indian life and culture, though it's always clear who is noble and who is savage. It all builds up to the moment when Harris undergoes the Sun Vow ceremony to prove his manhood and his commitment to Sioux life. Two sequels followed. ▭

Richard Harris *Lord John Morgan* • Judith Anderson *Buffalo Cow Head* • Manu Tupou *Yellow Hand* • Jean Gascon *Batise* • Corinna Tsopei *Running Deer* • Dub Taylor *Joe* • William Jordan *Bent* ■ *Dir* Elliot Silverstein • *Scr* Jack DeWitt, from the story by Dorothy M Johnson

A Man Called Peter ★★★ U

Biographical drama
1955 · US · Colour · 119mins

Although this sounds like a biblical epic, it is an earnest and solidly mounted biopic about Peter Marshall, the Scottish cleric who began as an assistant at the Church of the Presidents and rose to become chaplain to the US Senate. Richard Todd brings dignity and zeal to the part of the Presbyterian whose uncompromising sermons did not always endear him to listeners at opposite ends of the political spectrum, while Jean Peters is quiet and loyal as his wife Catherine.

Richard Todd *Peter Marshall* • Jean Peters *Catherine Marshall* • Marjorie Rambeau *Miss Fowler* • Jill Esmond *Mrs Findlay* • Les Tremayne *Senator Harvey* • Robert Burton *Mr Peyton* • Gladys Hurlbut *Mrs Peyton* • Gloria Gordon *Barbara* ■ *Dir* Henry Koster • *Scr* Eleanore Griffin, from the memoirs by Catherine Marshall

A Man Could Get Killed ★★★ U

Spy spoof   1966 · US · Colour · 98mins

James Garner's air of suave bafflement comes in handy for this spoof thriller, in which he plays a businessman in Portugal suspected of being a secret agent. The cast is a curious mix of nationalities – Greek spitfire Melina Mercouri fizzes exotically, while Cecil Parker and Dulcie Gray keep the British end up – though a better-balanced plot would have been more to the point.

James Garner *William Beddoes* • Melina Mercouri *Aurora-Celeste da Costa* • Sandra Dee *Amy Franklin* • Tony Franciosa [Anthony Franciosa] *Steve-Antonio* • Robert Coote *Hatton-Jones* • Roland Culver *Dr Mathieson* • Grégoire Aslan *Florian* • Cecil Parker *Sir Huntley Frazier* • Dulcie Gray *Mrs Mathieson* • Jenny Agutter *Linda Frazier* ■ *Dir* Ronald Neame, Cliff Owen • *Scr* Richard Breen, T EB Clarke, from the novel *Diamonds for Danger* by David Esdaile Walker

A Man Escaped ★★★★★ U

Second World War drama
1956 · Fr · BW · 95mins

Robert Bresson's story of an imprisoned and condemned French Resistance fighter who plans an escape with his teenage cellmate is one of the great classics of European art cinema. As usual, Bresson uses non-professional actors and a technique that is utterly hypnotic despite being almost totally devoid of stylistic flourish. Many subsequent prison movies are deeply indebted to it – most notably *Birdman of Alcatraz*, *Escape from Alcatraz* and *The Shawshank Redemption*, all of which attempted to evoke the director's peculiar mood of quietitude and contemplation as the two men conduct their meticulous plan of escape. In French with English subtitles. ▭

François Leterrier *Fontaine* • Charles Le Clainche *Jost* • Roland Monod *Priest* • Jacques Ertaud *Orsini* • Maurice Beerblock *Blanchet* ■ *Dir* Robert Bresson • *Scr* Robert Bresson, from the articles by André Devigny

A Man for All Seasons
★★★★ U

Historical drama
1966 · UK · Colour · 115mins

Fred Zinnemann's Oscar-laden version of Robert Bolt's 1960 play, with Paul Scofield as Sir Thomas More who wins the moral argument but loses the more vital one, concerning custody of his head, to Henry VIII. Whereas Charles Laughton's Henry VIII made you think of Billy Bunter, Robert Shaw could not be more different. This Henry is younger, thinner, a man of formidable intelligence and political skill. Orson Welles's Cardinal Wolsey is a beached, purple whale; John Hurt (in his first major role) is eloquent in Parliament; and Leo McKern, Wendy Hiller, Susannah York and Vanessa Redgrave (as Anne Boleyn) complete the splendid cast. But it's Scofield's picture – an inspired performance of virtue with a dash of vanity. ▭

Paul Scofield *Sir Thomas More* • Wendy Hiller *Alice More* • Leo McKern *Thomas Cromwell* • Robert Shaw *King Henry VIII* • Orson Welles *Cardinal Wolsey* • Susannah York *Margaret More* • Nigel Davenport *Duke of Norfolk* • John Hurt *Richard Rich* • Corin Redgrave *William Roper* • Colin Blakely *Matthew* • Vanessa Redgrave *Anne Boleyn* ■ *Dir* Fred Zinnemann • *Scr* Robert Bolt, Constance Willis, from the play by Robert Bolt

A Man for All Seasons
★★★ PG

Historical drama
1988 · US · Colour · 148mins

A creditable television version of Robert Bolt's fine play, previously filmed by Fred Zinnemann. The director this time out, unusually, is Charlton Heston, who also plays the leading role of Sir Thomas More. Heston's creased features and distinguished tones are well suited to the part, and his innate integrity shines through. He's well served by a distinguished British support cast that includes John Gielgud, Vanessa Redgrave and, notably, Roy Kinnear. ▭

Charlton Heston *Sir Thomas More* • Vanessa Redgrave *Lady Alice More* • John Gielgud *Cardinal Wolsey* • Richard Johnson *Duke of Norfolk* • Roy Kinnear *The Common Man* • Benjamin Whitrow *Thomas Cromwell* • Adrienne Thomas *Margaret More* • Martin Chamberlain *King Henry VIII* • John Hudson *William Roper* ■ *Dir* Charlton Heston • *Scr* Robert Bolt, from his play

Man Friday
★★ PG

Drama
1975 · UK · Colour · 109mins

In revising Daniel Defoe's 1719 novel, *Robinson Crusoe*, screenwriter Adrian Mitchell clearly intended both to denounce the idea of the white man's burden and to preach a code of racial equality. Unfortunately, he has succeeded only in destroying the narrative tension of the original. Jack Gold's hesitant direction does little to rectify the situation, while Peter O'Toole and Richard Roundtree have nothing to do but mouth platitudes. Caught between satire and soapbox, this is at best misjudged, at worst embarrassing. ▭

Peter O'Toole *Robinson Crusoe* • Richard Roundtree *Friday* • Peter Cellier *Carey* • Christopher Cabot *McBain* • Sam Seabrook *Young girl* • Stanley Clay *Young boy* ■ *Dir*

Jack Gold • *Scr* Adrian Mitchell, from his play by Adrian Mitchell, from the novel *The Adventures of Robinson Crusoe* by Daniel Defoe

The Man from Bitter Ridge
★★

Western   1955 · US · Colour · 80mins

Despite the presence of distinguished cameraman Russell Metty (*Bringing Up Baby, Spartacus*), this Universal western is nothing special. Based on the 1952 novel by William MacLeod Raine, it stars former Tarzan Lex Barker as a lawman investigating stagecoach robberies. His chief suspects are Stephen McNally and John Dehner, while Mara Corday provides the glamour. Directing his first western, Jack Arnold keeps the pace up and the bullets flying.

Lex Barker *Jeff Carr* • Mara Corday *Holly Kenton* • Stephen McNally *Alec Black* • John Dehner *Ranse Jackman* • Trevor Bardette *Walter Dunham* ■ *Dir* Jack Arnold • *Scr* Lawrence Roman, Teddi Sherman, from the novel by William MacLeod Raine

The Man from Button Willow
★★ U

Animated western
1965 · US · Colour · 77mins

Set in the 1860s, this is a so-so children's animated tale about a rancher who leads a double life as a secret agent. Young children may be entertained, but it's unlikely that anyone brought up on the new generation of Disney animation that includes *The Lion King* and *Beauty and the Beast* will be too impressed with this sixties' cartoon. Dale Robertson and Howard Keel are among the actors lending their voices. ▭

Dale Robertson *Justin Eagle* • Edgar Buchanan *Sorry* • Barbara Jean Wong *Stormy* • Howard Keel ■ *Dir/Scr* David Detiege

The Man from Cairo
★ U

Crime drama   1953 · US/It · BW · 81mins

The man in question is George Raft, and he's in Algiers, not Cairo, turning the Casbah upside down in a search for Nazi gold. Along the way he meets all the usual suspects: black marketeers, shady café owners, torch singers, Arab pickpockets and shifty spies. Greek actress Irene Papas, later in *The Guns of Navarone* and *Zorba the Greek*, gets a desultory role. Raft's career was then in terminal decline due to his underworld connections, failing casinos and a flop TV series that he financed himself.

George Raft *Mike Canelli* • Gianna Maria Canale *Lorraine* • Massimo Serato *Basil Constantine* • Irene Papas *Yvonne* • Guido Celano *Emile Touchard* ■ *Dir* Ray Enright • *Scr* Eugene Ling, Janet Stevenson, Philip Stevenson, from a story by Ladislas Fodor

The Man from Colorado
★★★

Psychological western
1948 · US · Colour · 98mins

Before he adopted a crew cut for *The Blackboard Jungle* and went Method, Glenn Ford was seldom more than mildly interesting. Here, unusually, he portrays a sadistic military tyrant, appointed as judge to govern the

territory. The story by Borden Chase – author and co-screenwriter of *Red River* – can be read as an allegory of the brutalising effect the Second World War had on its returning veterans, and the insinuations are clearly there if you look for them. Ford is confronted by hero William Holden, in the type of colourless role he found himself trapped in before *Sunset Boulevard*.

Glenn Ford *Colonel Owen Devereaux* • William Holden (1) *Captain Del Stewart* • Ellen Drew *Caroline Emmett* • Ray Collins *Big Ed Carter* • Edgar Buchanan *Doc Merriam* • Jerome Courtland *Johnny Howard* • James Millican *Sergeant Jericho Howard* • Jim Bannon *Nagel* ■ *Dir* Henry Levin • *Scr* Robert D Andrews, Ben Maddow, from a story by Borden Chase

The Man from Dakota
★★★

Western   1940 · US · BW · 75mins

In this American Civil War tale a couple of Yankee soldiers escape from imprisonment in the South, become spies and hook up with a glamorous Russian refugee while they're on the run. This unlikely, not to mention fanciful, idea sounds like a Bob Hope spoof, but it's actually an action-packed period adventure. The men are Wallace Beery and John Howard; the lady is Mexican beauty Dolores Del Rio, who was to vanish from the screen until Orson Welles's *Journey into Fear* in 1942.

Wallace Beery *Sgt Barstow* • John Howard (1) *Oliver Clark* • Dolores Del Rio *Eugenia, "Jenny"* • Donald Meek *Mr Vestry* • Robert Barrat *Parson Summers* • Addison Richards *Provost Marshal* • Frederick Burton *Leader* ■ *Dir* Leslie Fenton • *Scr* Laurence Stallings, from the novel *Arouse and Beware* by MacKinlay Kantor

The Man from Down Under
★★

Drama   1943 · US · BW · 103mins

Charles Laughton stars as an Australian army sergeant who adopts two orphaned Belgian children after the Great War and takes them back with him to Oz, raising one of them to become a boxing champion. Then Laughton's old flame (Binnie Barnes) shows up… The film was produced by a certain Orville O Dull and lives up to his name. That said, Laughton's Australian accent is good for a laugh.

Charles Laughton *Jocko Wilson* • Binnie Barnes *Aggie Dawlins* • Richard Carlson *"Nipper" Wilson* • Donna Reed *Mary Wilson* • Christopher Severn *Young "Nipper"* • Clyde Cook *Ginger Gaffney* • Horace McNally [Stephen McNally] *"Dusty" Rhodes* • Arthur Shields *Father Polycarp* ■ *Dir* Robert Z Leonard • *Scr* Wells Root, Thomas Seller, from a story by Bogart Rogers, Mark Kelly

The Man from Galveston
★★

Courtroom drama   1964 · US · BW · 57mins

William Conrad was best known as the portly, gourmet detective Frank Cannon, but his career was long and varied, encompassing work as a musician, acting in films, TV and radio shows, and even production and direction. Here he went behind the camera for a TV pilot, a courtroom drama in a western setting. Jeffrey Hunter defends old pal Joanna Moore, a saloon girl accused of murder. It's

well acted and well written, but its brief running time gave the writers little room for manoeuvre.

Jeffrey Hunter *Timothy Higgins* • Preston Foster *Judge Homer Black* • James Coburn *Boyd Palmer* • Joanna Moore *Rita Dillard* • Edward Andrews *Hyde* • Kevin Hagen *John Dillard* • Martin West *Stonewall Grey* ■ *Dir* William Conrad • *Scr* Dean Riesner, Michael Zagor, from the story *Galahad of Cactus City* by Philip Lonergan

The Man from Hong Kong
★

Martial arts action
1975 · Ausl/HK · Colour · 103mins

Jimmy Wang Yu – a sort of low-rent Bruce Lee – stars in this action mess with erstwhile 007 George Lazenby, cast more for gimmick value than anything else. The tiresome Mr Wang is a Hong Kong cop who travels to Sydney to apprehend a drugs baron (Lazenby) who also happens to run a kung fu academy. To describe Lazenby as wooden is an understatement – he's an entire forestry commission.

Jimmy Wang Yu *Inspector Fang Sing-Ling* • George Lazenby *Jack Wilton* • Frank Thring *Willard* • Hugh Keays-Byrne *Morrie Grosse* ■ *Dir/Scr* Brian Trenchard-Smith

The Man from Laramie
★★★★ U

Western   1955 · US · Colour · 98mins

In partnership with director Anthony Mann, James Stewart helped change the very nature of the western. Considerably tougher than Mann's other psychological entries in the genre, this is a tale of vengeance, as Stewart seeks the man responsible for supplying the Apaches with the guns that killed his brother. The infighting between rancher Donald Crisp and sons Alex Nicol and Arthur Kennedy (one natural, one adopted) dominates the action, but the scenes in which Stewart is shot in the hand and the final shoot-out on the cliffs are the ones you'll remember. ▭

James Stewart *Will Lockhart* • Arthur Kennedy *Vic Hansbro* • Donald Crisp *Alec Waggoman* • Cathy O'Donnell *Barbara Waggoman* • Alex Nicol *Dave Waggoman* • Aline MacMahon *Kate Canaday* • Wallace Ford *Charley O'Leary* • Jack Elam *Chris Boldt* ■ *Dir* Anthony Mann • *Scr* Philip Yordan, Frank Burt, from a story by Thomas T Flynt

The Man from Left Field
★★ 15

Sports drama   1993 · US · Colour · 92mins

Burt Reynolds directs and stars in this tale of an amnesiac drifter reluctantly recruited to coach a Little League baseball team. He rallies his players and falls in love with the homespun mother of one of the kids (recording star Reba McEntire). Implausible situations and a stone-faced performance by Reynolds keep this TV movie tale of redemption from getting to first base. ▭

Burt Reynolds *Jack* • Reba McEntire *Nancy Lee Prinzi* • Kauwela Acocella *Beau* • Derek Baxter *Malcolm* • Adam Cronan *Bama* ■ *Dir* Burt Reynolds • *Scr* Wayne A Rice

The Man from Morocco ★★

Second World War adventure
1944 · UK · BW · 117mins

What should have been an intriguing drama of espionage is rendered almost unendurably tedious thanks to the moribund direction of Max Greene, better known as Herbert Wilcox's cameraman. Thankfully, this was his only film as director, although as such it does have historical value. Even the usually watchable Anton Walbrook is defeated by the film's lack of humour.

Anton Walbrook *Karel Langer* • Margaretta Scott *Manuela* • Mary Morris *Sarah Duboste* • Reginald Tate *Ricardi* • Peter Sinclair *Jock Sinclair* • David Horne *Dr Duboste* • Hartley Power *Colonel Bagley* • Sybilla Binder *Erna* ■ *Dir* Max Greene • *Scr* Edward Dryhurst, Marguerite Steen, Warwick Ward, from a story by Rudolph Cartier

The Man from Planet X ★★★

Science-fiction
1951 · US · BW · 70mins

Shot in six days by B-movie maven Edgar G Ulmer, this mini-classic was one of the first science-fiction movies to accent sombre and serious issues above gung-ho fantasy. A lonely alien seeking assistance for his freezing planet finds a similar coldness in humanity when he lands his spaceship on the Scottish moors. Ulmer's odd camera angles create a real sense of unease in this decent cosmic fable, while the extraterrestrial – a bubble-headed midget with an immobile white face and chest-plate speaker – is one of sci-fi's most haunting creations.

Robert Clarke *Lawrence* • Margaret Field *Enid Elliot* • Raymond Bond *Prof Elliot* • William Schallert *Mears* • Roy Engel *Constable* • Charles Davis *Geordie* ■ *Dir* Edgar G Ulmer • *Scr* Aubrey Wisberg, Jack Pollexfen

The Man from Snowy River ★★★ PG

Adventure
1982 · Ausl · Colour · 103mins

Based on AB ''Banjo'' Paterson's poem (known to every Australian from an early age), this epic from Down Under offers a surprising dual role to Kirk Douglas, who plays both Spur, the grizzled mountain man, and his brother, autocratic landowner Harrison. Jack Thompson has little to do in support and youthful co-star Tom Burlinson can't quite carry the picture. Behind the camera is the ''other'' George Miller, not the *Mad Max/Lorenzo's Oil* director of the same name, and he makes the most of the impressive locations in Victoria's Great Dividing Range. ⬚

Kirk Douglas *Harrison/Spur* • Tom Burlinson *Jim Craig* • Sigrid Thornton *Jessica* • Jack Thompson *Clancy* • Lorraine Bayly *Rosemary* • Chris Haywood *Curly* • Tony Bonner *Kane* • Gus Mercurio *Frew* • David Bradshaw *AB ''Banjo'' Paterson* ■ *Dir* George Miller (1) • *Scr* John Dixon, Fred Cullen, from the poem by AB ''Banjo'' Paterson

Man from Tangier ★★ U

Crime drama
1957 · UK · BW · 66mins

A barely acceptable B-thriller, made at a time when British cinemas habitually ran supporting features to give you time to buy your soft drinks and popcorn. Directed by the indefatigable

Lance Comfort, it's a forgery caper involving shifty foreigners, an international criminal mastermind, a lady without a passport and a film stuntman, played by Robert Hutton (an American actor whose Hollywood career never took off).

Robert Hutton *Chuck Collins* • Lisa Gastoni *Michele* • Martin Benson *Voss* • Leonard Sachs *Heinrich* • Robert Raglan *Inspector Meredith* • Derek Sydney *Darracq* • Jack Allen *Rex* • Richard Shaw *Johnny* ■ *Dir* Lance Comfort • *Scr* P Manning O'Brine

The Man from the Alamo ★★★ U

Western
1953 · US · Colour · 79mins

Glenn Ford is branded a coward after surviving the massacre at the Alamo, but proves himself a hero, fighting Victor Jory's band of rampaging renegades. This vigorous western has a rather perfunctory script, but director Budd Boetticher and cameraman Russell Metty stage the action scenes with some real imagination, while Julie Adams is a forceful leading lady. Both Ford and Boetticher made much better westerns later on in their careers.

Glenn Ford *John Stoud* • Julia Adams [Julie Adams] *Beth Anders* • Chill Wills *John Gage* • Victor Jory *Jess Wade* • Hugh O'Brian *Lieutenant Lamar* • Jeanne Cooper *Kate Lamar* ■ *Dir* Budd Boetticher • *Scr* Steve Fisher, DD Beauchamp, from a story by Niven Busch, Oliver Crawford

The Man from the Diner's Club ★★

Comedy
1963 · US · BW · 96mins

The author of *The Exorcist*, William Peter Blatty, wrote the script for this Danny Kaye comedy under the name Bill Blatty. Telly Savalas is a mobster, while Kaye plays the eponymous man from the Diner's Club. Both men share a physical peculiarity – one foot bigger than the other – which gives Savalas the idea of faking his own death with the help of Kaye's corpse. There's a gentle (read toothless) satire here about American capitalism, life on credit and the growing importance of computerisation. Mostly, though, it comes down to the fact that Danny Kaye – like Jerry Lewis – is very much an acquired taste.

Danny Kaye *Ernie Klenk* • Cara Williams *Sugar Pye* • Martha Hyer *Lucy* • Telly Savalas *Foots Pulardos* • Everett Sloane *Martindale* • Kay Stevens *Bea Frampton* • Howard Caine *Bassanio* • George Kennedy *George* • Harry Dean Stanton *First beatnik* ■ *Dir* Frank Tashlin • *Scr* Bill Blatty [William Peter Blatty], from a story by John Fenton Murray, Bill Blatty [William Peter Blatty]

The Man from Utah ★★ U

Western
1934 · US · BW · 51mins

A very routine example of John Wayne's B-western output, from his period at Monogram Studios. Despite the estimable Yakima Canutt as villain, the rodeo setting holds no surprises, and nor does a plot which features the Duke turning down the offer of sheriff in order to enter a horse race. There's a relatively young George ''Gabby'' Hayes to hand, and regular Archie Stout behind the camera. But this is very average fare, and typical of the seemingly endless succession of

cheap westerns in which Wayne found himself prior to his star-making role in *Stagecoach*. The fist-fight at the beginning of this one is a corker. ⬚

John Wayne *John Weston* • Polly Ann Young *Marjorie Carter* • George ''Gabby'' Hayes *George Higgins* • Yakima Canutt *Cheyenne Kent* • Edward Peil Sr *Barton* • Anita Campillo *Aurora* • Lafe McKee *Judge Carter* • George Cleveland *Sheriff* ■ *Dir* Robert N Bradbury • *Scr* Lindsley Parsons, from his story

The Man from Yesterday ★★

First World War romance
1932 · US · BW · 68mins

The ''yesterday'' of the title is more a matter of ''yesteryear'', when British officer Clive Brook married American Claudette Colbert and went off to fight in the First World War, but does not return. Years later he reappears, but when it becomes apparent that his wife loves army surgeon Charles Boyer, he bravely vanishes again. Lachrymose melodrama which strains credibility and lacks interest, despite the top-notch trio of leads.

Claudette Colbert *Sylvia Suffolk* • Clive Brook *Tony Clyde* • Charles Boyer *Rene Goudin* • Andy Devine *Steve Hand* • Alan Mowbray *Dr Waite* • Greta Meyer *Proprietress of Swiss inn* ■ *Dir* Berthold Viertel • *Scr* Oliver HP Garrett, from the play *The Wound Stripe* by Nell Blackwell, Rowland G Edwards

Man Hunt ★★★

Second World War spy drama
1941 · US · BW · 105mins

From its riveting opening, as Walter Pidgeon, perched on a ridge above Hitler's ''Eagle's Nest'' at Berchtesgaden, fixes the Führer in his rifle sight and prepares to pull the trigger, this fine adaptation of Geoffrey Household's *Rogue Male* substantially changes the tenor of the original. Screenwriter Dudley Nichols shifts the emphasis away from the central character in hiding to make a more conventional (and, for its day, prophetic) war story. Under the direction of Fritz Lang, the Germans, including svelte George Sanders and gaunt John Carradine, are genuinely chilling, but heroine Joan Bennett's English accent leaves a lot to be desired. Pidgeon was seldom better.

Walter Pidgeon *Captain Thorndike* • Joan Bennett *Jerry* • George Sanders *Quive-Smith* • John Carradine *Mr Jones* • Roddy McDowall *Vaner* • Ludwig Stossel *Doctor* • Heather Thatcher *Lady Risborough* • Frederic Worlock [Frederick Worlock] *Lord Risborough* ■ *Dir* Fritz Lang • *Scr* Dudley Nichols, from the novel *Rogue Male* by Geoffrey Household

The Man I Killed ★★★

Drama
1932 · US · BW · 77mins

Phillips Holmes is a young Frenchman who seeks out the family of a German soldier he killed during the war. Pretending he was a friend of their son's, he falls in love with the dead man's fiancée (Nancy Carroll). Though sombre and oversentimental at times, this sensitively wrought and perfectly crafted drama is, surprisingly, the work of Ernst Lubitsch, straying far from his usual territory. Critics acclaimed it, but audiences stayed away, and the great director of romantic comedy never made another serious film. It also

marked the end of Holmes and Carroll's successful on-screen partnership. Both are excellent, as are Lionel Barrymore and ZaSu Pitts.

Lionel Barrymore *Dr Holderlin* • Nancy Carroll *Elsa* • Phillips Holmes *Paul* • Tom Douglas *Walter Holderin* • ZaSu Pitts *Anna* ■ *Dir* Ernst Lubitsch • *Scr* Ernest Vajda, Samson Raphaelson, Reginald Berkeley, from the play *L'Homme Que J'ai Tué* by Maurice Rostand

The Man I Love ★★★★

Musical drama
1946 · US · BW · 96mins

This Ida Lupino/Robert Alda vehicle is a glittering, highly professional potboiler that grabs its audience by the scruff of the neck and refuses to let go. Lupino is suitably sassy as the charismatic nightclub singer relentlessly chased by Alda's feckless hood. There are more holes in the plot than in Nora Batty's tights, but who cares? Sit back and enjoy. The title song re-appeared in Martin Scorsese's 1977 tribute to golden-age musicals, *New York, New York*.

Ida Lupino *Petey Brown* • Robert Alda *Nicky Toresca* • Andrea King *Sally Otis* • Martha Vickers *Virginia Brown* • Bruce Bennett *Sam Thomas* • Alan Hale *Riley* • Dolores Moran *Gloria O'Connor* ■ *Dir* Raoul Walsh • *Scr* Catherine Turney, Jo Pagano, from the novel *Night Shift* by Maritta Wolff

The Man I Married ★★★★

Second World War drama
1940 · US · BW · 77mins

A riveting topical drama featuring Joan Bennett as the American wife of handsome Francis Lederer, who returns to Germany on holiday only to be swept up on a tide of Nazi propaganda. Oliver HP Garrett's clever screenplay is unsparing in its depiction of Hitler's prewar regime, and the plot, in which Lederer discovers that his own grandmother is Jewish, is brilliantly constructed. Twentieth Century-Fox's stark black-and-white studio look suits this film very well, and there's a marvellous supporting performance from Lloyd Nolan as an American reporter, who is asked to explain the Nazi Party machine to a pre-Pearl Harbor audience.

Joan Bennett *Carol* • Francis Lederer *Eric Hoffman* • Lloyd Nolan *Kenneth Delane* • Anna Sten *Freda Heinkel* • Otto Kruger *Heinrich Hoffman* • Maria Ouspenskaya *Frau Gerhardt* • Ludwig Stossel *Dr Hugo Gerhardt* • Johnny Russell *Ricky* ■ *Dir* Irving Pichel • *Scr* Oliver HP Garrett, from the articles *I Married a Nazi* by Oscar Schisgall

The Man in Grey ★★★ PG

Period drama
1943 · UK · BW · 88mins

A rip-roaring costume drama that thrilled war-weary audiences with its shameless depiction of the lawlessness and lasciviousness of Regency England. No longer likely to set pulses racing, this remains an excellent example of the kind of bodice-ripping escapism churned out by Gainsborough Studios. Directed with gusto by Leslie Arliss, the picture sags when the virtuous Phyllis Calvert and Stewart Granger are on screen but, from the moment Margaret Lockwood and James Mason take centre stage, the action begins to smoulder. They went one better with *The Wicked Lady* two years later. ⬚

A Man in Love ★★ 18

Romantic drama 1987 · Fr · Colour · 105mins

This French production filmed in Italy was the first mainly English-language film from Diane Kurys, the award-winning French writer/director, but it is not, unfortunately, among her finest efforts. Greta Scacchi brings her usual sensuality to some passionate scenes with Peter Coyote but, despite moments of intelligence and insight, the tale about love and adultery on a movie set in Rome ultimately outstays its welcome. In English, French and Italian with subtitles.

Greta Scacchi *Jane Steiner* • Peter Coyote *Steve Elliott* • Peter Riegert *Michael Pozner* • Claudia Cardinale *Julia Steiner* • John Berry *Harry Steiner* • Vincent Lindon *Bruno Schlosser* • Jamie Lee Curtis *Susan Elliott* ■ *Dir/Scr* Diane Kurys

Man in the Attic ★★★

Chiller 1953 · US · BW · 79mins

Marie Belloc Lowndes's novel *The Lodger*, about a man suspected of being Jack the Ripper, was filmed twice in Britain with Ivor Novello, then again in Hollywood with Laird Cregar. Fox dug out its old script, had a new writer make some unhelpful alterations and turned out this modestly budgeted thriller to exploit Jack Palance's sudden rise to villainous stardom. He's too obviously sinister and the other players are weak, but the story is virtually fool-proof and director Hugo Fregonese whips up some chilling moments and a good Victorian atmosphere.

Jack Palance *Slade* • Constance Smith *Lily Bonner* • Byron Palmer *Paul Warwick* • Frances Bavier *Helen Harley* • Rhys Williams *William Harley* ■ *Dir* Hugo Fregonese • *Scr* Robert Presnell Jr, Barre Lyndon, from the novel *The Lodger* by Marie Belloc Lowndes

The Man in the Attic ★★ 15

Drama based on a true story
1995 · US · Colour · 92mins

TV movies based on true stories are usually the preserve of worthy battles against corruption, crime or ill-health. Occasionally, however, the genre throws up an oddity. Neil Patrick Harris (*Doogie Howser MD*), stars as a humble factory worker who falls for married Anne Archer. To avoid her suspicious husband, she hides her toy boy in the attic while pretending to be the faithful wife. Harris is suitably geeky as the naive youngster, while Archer, usually cast as a devoted wife, enjoys playing against type.

Anne Archer *Krista Heldmann* • Len Cariou *Joe Heldmann* • Neil Patrick Harris *Edward Broder* • Alex Carter *Gary* • Deborah Drakeford *Amy* • Rick Roberts *Reporter* • Martha Cronyn *Mary* ■ *Dir* Graeme Campbell • *Scr* Duane Poole, Tom Swale, Norman Winski, from the book *Sex and the Criminal Mind* by Norman Winski

The Man in the Back Seat ★★★

Thriller 1961 · UK · BW · 57mins

The phrase "quota quickie" was synonymous with cheaply made, under-plotted films notable only for the ineptitude of the acting. It's a rare treat, therefore, to stumble across a British B with an intriguing idea that's been ingeniously executed. Director Vernon Sewell outdoes himself with this haunting story that obviously has its roots in the Banquo's ghost segment of *Macbeth*. Derren Nesbitt and Keith Faulkner turn in creditable performances, but you can't help wondering what it would have been like with Peter Lorre and Elisha Cook Jr.

Derren Nesbitt *Tony* • Keith Faulkner *Frank* • Carol White *Jean* • Harry Locke *Joe Carter* ■ *Dir* Vernon Sewell • *Scr* Malcolm Hulke, Eric Paice, from the novel by Edgar Wallace

The Man in the Brown Suit ★ PG

Murder mystery 1989 · US · Colour · 91mins

It's safe to assume this raucous blend of mirth, mystery and mayhem was not what Agatha Christie had in mind when she wrote the original book. The decision to shift the murder from Hyde Park tube station to Cairo Airport should give you some idea of how overblown this made-for-TV whodunit has become. However, the fact that Stephanie Zimbalist is transformed from spirited amateur sleuth into the kind of heroine Kathleen Turner played in *Romancing the Stone* is the real giveaway. Directed by Alan Grint with no feeling for the Crime Queen's unique style, this ranks among the poorest Christie adaptations.

Rue McClanahan *Suzanne Blair* • Tony Randall *Minks* • Edward Woodward *Sir Eustace Pedlar* • Stephanie Zimbalist *Anne Beddingfeld* • Ken Howard *Gordon Race* • Nickolas Grace *Guy Underhill* • Simon Dutton *Harry Lucas* ■ *Dir* Alan Grint • *Scr* Carla Jean Wagner, from the novel by Agatha Christie

Man in the Dark ★

Crime drama 1953 · US · BW · 67mins

It's nothing more than a B-feature, but this crime melodrama was dressed up with two lesser stars (Edmond O'Brien and Audrey Totter) and rush-released as one of the first features in the 3-D boom of 1953. Action director Lew Landers is out of his depth and overloads the picture with 3-D gimmicks, but at least the climactic shoot-out on a rollercoaster track has some life. Viewed without the 3-D novelty, the dreary plot becomes all the more prominent.

Edmond O'Brien *Steve Rawley/James Blake* • Audrey Totter *Peg Benedict* • Ted De Corsia *Lefty* • Horace McMahon *Arnie* • Nick Dennis *Cookie* • Dayton Lummis *Dr Marston* ■ *Dir* Lew Landers • *Scr* George Bricker, Jack Leonard, William Sackheim, from a story by Tom Van Dycke, Henry Altimus

The Man in the Glass Booth ★★

Courtroom drama
1975 · US · Colour · 117mins

Maximilian Schell stars as a rich, charming New Yorker who is suddenly bundled off to Israel, put in a glass cage in a courtroom and accused of murdering millions of Jews in a Nazi death camp. Actor Robert Shaw's play was inspired by the trial of Adolph Eichmann, whom the Israelis tried and executed in 1962. Shaw, however, was unhappy with this adaptation by playwright Edward Anhalt and had his name removed from the credits.

Maximilian Schell *Arthur Goldman* • Lois Nettleton *Miriam Rosen* • Luther Adler *Presiding Judge* • Lawrence Pressman *Charlie Cohn* • Henry Brown *Jack Arnold* • Richard Rasof *Moshe* ■ *Dir* Arthur Hiller • *Scr* Edward Anhalt, from the play by Robert Shaw

The Man in the Gray Flannel Suit ★★★

Drama 1956 · US · Colour · 152mins

An overlong, self-important yet compelling melodrama, with Gregory Peck as the appealingly flawed hero choosing between his family and a high-powered but time-consuming job. To add to his woes, his marriage to Jennifer Jones is undermined by the revelation that he fathered a child in Italy during the war. The excellent Peck and Jones, reunited after *Duel in the Sun*, are joined by the ever-reliable Fredric March and Lee J Cobb, as well as Marisa Pavan, twin sister of Pier Angeli, as Peck's Italian mistress.

Gregory Peck *Tom Rath* • Jennifer Jones *Betsy Rath* • Fredric March *Ralph Hopkins* • Marisa Pavan *Maria* • Ann Harding *Mrs Hopkins* • Lee J Cobb *Judge Bernstein* • Keenan Wynn *Caesar Gardella* • Gene Lockhart *Hawthorne* ■ *Dir* Nunnally Johnson • *Scr* Nunnally Johnson, from the novel by Sloan Wilson

The Man in the Iron Mask ★★★ U

Historical adventure
1939 · US · BW · 111mins

Louis Hayward gives a riveting performance in this adaptation of Alexandre Dumas's splendid swashbuckling tale about the twin heirs to the throne of France. Under the sympathetic direction of the great James Whale, Hayward exhibits just the right amount of baroque arrogance as Louis XIV plus a genuine feeling of romantic helplessness as the imprisoned Philippe. Warren William is fine as D'Artagnan, Philippe's guardian, but the other musketeers are blithely cast, as is Joan Bennett as Maria Theresa. Nevertheless, it's a surprising improvement on the Douglas Fairbanks silent version. Watch closely for Peter Cushing in his movie debut.

Louis Hayward *Louis XIV/Philippe* • Joan Bennett *Maria Theresa* • Warren William *D'Artagnan* • Joseph Schildkraut *Fouquet* • Alan Hale *Porthos* • Miles Mander *Aramis* • Bert Roach *Athos* • Walter Kingsford *Colbert* ■ *Dir* James Whale • *Scr* George Bruce, from the novel by Alexandre Dumas

The Man in the Iron Mask ★★★★ PG

Historical adventure
1977 · US/UK · Colour · 100mins

A sprightly adaptation of the classic Alexandre Dumas adventure, with Richard Chamberlain as the unfortunate twin of Louis XIV who's trapped in an iron mask. Money was obviously thrown at the production and it stuck: it looks good and has something of the bravura of Richard Lester's *The Three Musketeers*. There's a strong supporting cast, including Louis Jourdan, Jenny Agutter and Patrick McGoohan, plus zippy direction by Mike Newell (*Four Weddings and a Funeral*).

Richard Chamberlain *Philippe/Louis XIV* • Patrick McGoohan *Fouquet* • Louis Jourdan *D'Artagnan* • Jenny Agutter *Louise de la Vallière* • Ian Holm *Duval* • Ralph Richardson *Colbert de Voliere* • Vivien Merchant *Queen Maria Theresa* • Brenda Bruce *Anne of Austria* ■ *Dir* Mike Newell • *Scr* William Bast, from the novel by Alexandre Dumas

The Man in the Iron Mask ★★★ 12

Historical adventure
1997 · US · Colour · 126mins

Alexandre Dumas's classic warhorse rides again, though writer/director Randall Wallace can't make it as exciting and exhilarating as *Braveheart*, which he scripted. In his first film after *Titanic*, Leonardo DiCaprio has a dual role as both the wicked King Louis XIV and his mistreated twin Phillippe. The three musketeers (Jeremy Irons, John Malkovich, Gérard Depardieu) ride to the rescue, while the fourth musketeer (Gabriel Byrne) decides to support Louis, despite riots in the street and rats in the court. Great performances and the French locations are beautifully shot by cinematographer Peter Suschitzky. **DVD**

Leonardo DiCaprio *King Louis/Phillippe* • Jeremy Irons *Father Aramis* • John Malkovich *Athos* • Gérard Depardieu *Porthos* • Gabriel Byrne *D'Artagnan* • Anne Parillaud *Queen Anne* • Judith Godrèche *Christine Balfour* • Hugh Laurie *King's advisor* ■ *Dir* Randall Wallace • *Scr* Randall Wallace, from the novel by Alexandre Dumas

The Man in the Iron Mask ★★ PG

Historical adventure
1997 · US · Colour · 85mins

This probably would never have seen the light of day had a smart video label not spotted it and rushed it out just as Leonardo DiCaprio's version hit the big screen. It's faithful, cheerfully cheap stuff, with a strictly second-division cast (Timothy Bottoms, Edward Albert), and another frustratingly erratic effort from actor/director William Richert, best remembered for his Falstaffian cameo in *My Own Private Idaho*. Contains some sexual references and swearing.

Nick Richert *Philippe/King Louis XIV* • William Richert *Count Aramis* • Dennis Hayden *D'Artagnan* • Edward Albert *Athos* • Rex Ryon *Porthos* • Dan Coplan *Molière* • Dana Barron *Vallière* • Timothy Bottoms *Fouquet* ■ *Dir* William Richert • *Scr* William Richert, from the novel by Alexandre Dumas

The Man in the Middle ★★ U

Drama 1964 · US/UK · BW · 78mins

In India after the war, tensions rise between the US and Britain when an American lieutenant murders a British staff sergeant. Evidence that the American is insane and a racist is covered up, since the big brass on both sides want him executed. This is a tightly compressed drama that deals with the hangover of the war and associated moral issues. It's a rather stodgy, self-important effort, with Robert Mitchum and Trevor Howard enjoying a few rounds together before *Ryan's Daughter*. Marlon Brando's company, Pennebaker, had bought the rights to Howard Fast's original novel as a possible project about one of the actor's obsessions, the relationship between Asia and the west.

Robert Mitchum *Lt Col Barney Adams* • France Nuyen *Kate Davray* • Barry Sullivan *General Kempton* • Trevor Howard *Major Kensington* • Keenan Wynn *Lt Winston* • Sam Wanamaker *Major Kaufman* • Alexander Knox *Colonel Burton* ■ *Dir* Guy Hamilton • *Scr* Keith Waterhouse, Willis Hall, from the novel *The Winston Affair* by Howard Fast

The Man in the Mirror ★★
Fantasy comedy 1936 · UK · BW · 83mins

Lugubrious Edward Everett Horton, American master of the double-take, stars in this low-rent British fantasy as a dithering businessman whose looking-glass alter ego takes over his battles in life. Interesting more for the social assumptions of its time than for any cinematic adroitness, it was directed by Maurice Elvey, who made more than 300 forgettable features.

Edward Everett Horton *Jeremy Dike* • Genevieve Tobin *Helen* • Garry Marsh *Tarkington* • Ursula Jeans *Veronica* • Alastair Sim *Interpreter* • Aubrey Mather *Bogus of Bokhara* • Renée Gadd [Renee Gadd] *Miss Blake* ■ *Dir* Maurice Elvey • *Scr* McGrew Willis, Hugh Mills, from the novel by William Garrett

Man in the Moon ★★ U
Comedy 1960 · UK · BW · 98mins

Apart from an amiable performance by Kenneth More as the test pilot whose A1 fitness makes him the ideal candidate to become Britain's first astronaut, this British spoof on the Nasa space programme never leaves the launch pad. Seemingly stuck for ideas, writers Michael Relph and Bryan Forbes fall back on that old plot stand-by, the rival with his nose out of joint, to enliven the scenes of More's training with a few acts of unfunny sabotage. Mildly amusing.

Kenneth More *William Blood* • Shirley Anne Field *Polly* • Norman Bird *Herbert* • Michael Hordern *Dr Davidson* • John Glyn-Jones *Dr Wilmot* • John Phillips *Professor Stephens* • Charles Gray *Leo* ■ *Dir* Basil Dearden • *Scr* Michael Relph, Bryan Forbes

The Man in the Moon ★★★ PG
Drama 1991 · US · Colour · 95mins

To Kill a Mockingbird director Robert Mulligan is an old hand in dealing with coming-of-age stories. Here he lovingly re-creates the rural Americana of the fifties in this tasteful, if somewhat anachronistic drama. Reese Witherspoon, making her feature film debut, is the troubled adolescent who has a crush on an older teen equally smitten by her older sister. There are memorable performances from the youngsters, and nicely underplayed supporting turns from the likes of Sam Waterston and Tess Harper.

Sam Waterston *Matthew Trant* • Tess Harper *Abigail Trant* • Gail Strickland *Marie Foster* •

Reese Witherspoon *Dani Trant* • Jason London *Court Foster* • Emily Warfield *Maureen Trant* • Bentley Mitchum *Billy Sanders* ■ *Dir* Robert Mulligan • *Scr* Jenny Wingfield

The Man in the Net ★★
Crime mystery 1959 · US · BW · 97mins

Artist Alan Ladd is suspected of murdering his wife, an alcoholic two-timer. Hiding out in the woods, he is given sanctuary by a group of five children who help him solve the mystery. Directed by Michael Curtiz, this story has a potential that is never fully realised. Ladd has a rather haunted look as he and the children check out his dead wife's lovers, but the film remains bogged down in plot and doesn't exploit a plot that might have turned it into a New England version of *Whistle down the Wind*.

Alan Ladd *John Hamilton* • Carolyn Jones *Linda Hamilton* • Diane Brewster *Vickie Carey* • John Lupton *Brad Carey* • Charles McGraw *Steve Ritter* ■ *Dir* Michael Curtiz • *Scr* Reginald Rose, from the novel *Man in a Net* by Patrick Quentin

The Man in the Road ★★ U
Spy mystery 1957 · UK · BW · 86mins

A surprisingly fine cast was assembled for this unremarkable quickie adapted from the espionage thriller by Anthony Armstrong. Derek Farr stars as a scientist whose loss of memory alone prevents a vital secret from falling into the hands of the communists who have abducted him. Donald Wolfit was knighted the same year, but surely not on the strength of his performance here as a blustering professor.

Derek Farr *Ivan Mason* • Ella Raines *Rhona Ellison* • Donald Wolfit *Professor Cattrell* • Lisa Daniely *Mitzi* • Karel Stepanek *Dmitri Palenkov* • Cyril Cusack *Dr Kelly* • Olive Sloane *Mrs Lemming* • Bruce Beeby *Dr Manning* ■ *Dir* Lance Comfort • *Scr* Guy Morgan, from the novel *He Was Found in the Road* by Anthony Armstrong

Man in the Saddle ★★★ U
Western 1951 · US · Colour · 87mins

Excellent Randolph Scott western, with the star somewhat unusually cast in a love triangle involving Joan Leslie and Alexander Knox. Directed by the under-rated Andre De Toth, the film contains some marvellous Technicolor night scenes which, unfortunately, won't look too good on your television. John Russell, perhaps better known these days for *Rio Bravo*, is a terrific tight-lipped villain and has a great punch-up with Scott, while Ellen Drew's schoolmarm, with whom Randy holes up in the mountains, makes a very sexy other woman. Great stuff.

Randolph Scott *Owen Merritt* • Joan Leslie *Laure Bidwell* • Ellen Drew *Nan Melotte* • Alexander Knox *Will Isham* • Richard Rober *Fay Dutcher* • John Russell *Hugh Clagg* ■ *Dir* Andre De Toth • *Scr* Kenneth Gamet, from the novel by Ernest Haycox

Man in the Shadow ★★★ U
Western 1957 · US · BW · 99mins

This modern western pits new sheriff Jeff Chandler against Orson Welles as the rancher who owns everything as far as the eye can see. Chandler insists on investigating the death of a Mexican labourer and eventually

topples Welles's empire. Producer Albert Zugsmith and director Jack Arnold use Gene L Coon's script as a springboard for some action that was considered rather violent for its time, while Welles's posturing performance overwhelms both the picture and Colleen Miller, who plays his appalled daughter. The film was retitled *Pay the Devil* for its original UK release.

Jeff Chandler *Ben Sadler* • Orson Welles *Virgil Renchler* • Colleen Miller *Skippy Renchler* • Barbara Lawrence *Helen Sadler* • Ben Alexander *Ab Begley* • John Larch *Ed Yates* • Royal Dano *Aiken Clay* • James Gleason *Hank James* ■ *Dir* Jack Arnold • *Scr* Gene L Coon, from a novel by Harry Whittington

The Man in the Trunk ★
Comedy mystery drama
1942 · US · BW · 71mins

The title character is a murder victim who has been in a trunk for ten years. When the trunk is opened, his ghost appears and assists a young lawyer in capturing the murderer. A pale imitation of the popular *Topper* series, which featured murder victims returning to trap their killers, this mediocre B-movie has one saving grace, the performance of reliable Raymond Walburn as the restless spirit. But the script is poor, the romantic leads colourless and Mal St Clair's direction doggedly uninspired.

Lynne Roberts *Peggy* • George Holmes *Dick Burke* • Raymond Walburn *Jim Cheevers* • J Carrol Naish *Reginald DeWinters* • Dorothy Peterson *Lola DeWinters* • Eily Malyon *Abbie Addison* • Arthur Loft *Sam Kohler* ■ *Dir* Malcolm St Clair • *Scr* John Larkin

Man in the Trunk ★★★
Comedy drama 1973 · Fr · Colour · 100mins

Georges Lautner pulls off the tricky task of finding the lighter side of the Arab-Israeli conflict, without offending anyone's political sensibilities, in this lively spy spoof. Mireille Darc gives a customarily lively performance as the music-hall chanteuse who joins with embassy official Michel Constantin to help Israeli agent Jean-Pierre Marielle flee Tunisia during an airport strike. Considering the Bond parody had been done to death by the early seventies, Lautner does well to raise a few unexpected smiles. French dialogue dubbed into English.

Mireille Darc *Françoise* • Michel Constantin *Augier* • Jean-Pierre Marielle *Bloch* • Jean Lefebvre *Baggage controller* • Amidou *Abdul* • Raoul Saint-Yves *Ambassador* ■ *Dir* Georges Lautner • *Scr* Francis Veber

The Man in the White Suit ★★★★★ U
Classic comedy 1951 · UK · BW · 81mins

Telling the story of a scientist who is undone by the seeming perfection of his own invention, Alexander Mackendrick's astute film is the only Ealing comedy truly to bare its teeth. Capitalist greed, professional jealousy, the spectre of unemployment and a fear of progress are just some of the provocative themes explored in this razor-sharp satire that spurns the studio's customary whimsy. Alec Guinness is wonderfully unworldly as the boffin whose indestructible cloth unites the textile industry against him,

while Joan Greenwood is also impressive as the spirited daughter of mill owner Cecil Parker. ▦

Alec Guinness *Sidney Stratton* • Joan Greenwood *Daphne Birnley* • Cecil Parker *Alan Birnley* • Michael Gough *Michael Corland* • Ernest Thesiger *Sir John Kierlaw* • Vida Hope *Bertha* • Howard Marion-Crawford *Cranford* • Duncan Lamont *Harry* • Henry Mollison *Hoskins* ■ *Dir* Alexander Mackendrick • *Scr* Roger Macdougall, John Dighton, Alexander Mackendrick, from the play by Roger Macdougall • *Cinematographer* Douglas Slocombe

Man in the Wilderness ★★ PG
Adventure 1971 · US/Sp · Colour · 100mins

Richard Harris here exhibits the same sort of macho masochism he affected in *A Man Called Horse*, enduring the rigours of both nature and native American tribal rituals as a 19th-century fur trapper left to die after being mauled by a bear and vowing revenge. The resemblance is not surprising as this movie was made by the same team that saddled up *Horse*. Allegedly based on a true story, it's too much like the earlier film to be anything other than predictable. ▦

Richard Harris *Zachary Bass* • John Huston *Captain Filmore Henry* • Henry Wilcoxon *Indian Chief* • Percy Herbert *Fogarty* • Dennis Waterman *Lowrie* • Prunella Ransome *Grace* • Norman Rossington *Ferris* ■ *Dir* Richard C Sarafian • *Scr* Jack DeWitt

The Man Inside ★★★
Crime drama 1958 · UK · Colour · 96mins

Old-fashioned yarn with Nigel Patrick on the lam with a priceless diamond and Hollywood hunk Jack Palance as the private eye in hot pursuit. Made by Albert R "Cubby" Broccoli's company, Warwick, it dashes from one eye-catching European capital to the next, picking up the statuesque Anita Ekberg en route. With Anthony Newley as a Spanish cabbie, Donald Pleasence as an organ grinder and Sid James as a wideboy, the cast alone makes this worth watching, even if the plot is as old as the hills.

Jack Palance *Milo March* • Anita Ekberg *Trudie Hall* • Nigel Patrick *Sam Carter* • Anthony Newley *Ernesto* • Bonar Colleano *Martin Lomer* • Sean Kelly *Franklin* • Sidney James *Franklin* • Donald Pleasence *Organ grinder* ■ *Dir* John Gilling • *Scr* David Shaw, John Gilling, Richard Maibaum, from a novel by ME Chaber

The Man Inside ★★ 15
Thriller based on a true story
1990 · Fr/US · Colour · 94mins

This real-life tale of a German investigative journalist going undercover at a right-wing newspaper doesn't ring true. The film's main failing is that the characters seem like a work of fiction. Jürgen Prochnow's crusading Gunter Wallraff is so singleminded in his pursuit of justice, he's almost ridiculous; while Peter Coyote's alcoholic hack and Dieter Laser's aggressive editor resemble bad caricatures of people in other "paper" movies. Compared to the risky work of today's undercover journalists, this deception seems pretty tame. ▦

Jürgen Prochnow *Gunter Wallraff* • Peter Coyote *Henry Tobel* • Nathalie Baye *Christine*

• Dieter Laser *Leonard Schroeter* • Monique van de Ven *Tina Wallraff* • Philip Anglim *Rolf Gruel* ■ *Dir* Bobby Roth • *Scr* Bobby Roth, from articles by Gunter Wallraff

Man Is a Woman ★★ 15

Comedy   1998 · Fr · Colour · 99mins

A trite French reworking of Ang Lee's excellent comedy, *The Wedding Banquet*, clearly unsafe in the hands of director Jean-Jacques Zilbermann. *Eurotrash's* Antoine de Caunes stars as a gay clarinettist offered money to marry Jewish virgin Elsa Zylberstein. On their wedding night she can tell all is not well, despite her fetish for Antoine's clarinet. Zylberstein's convincing performance almost rescues the film from its poor plot, bad script and an inadequate de Caunes. In French with English subtitles.

Antoine de Caunes *Simon* • Elsa Zylberstein *Rosalie* • Gad Elmaleh *David* • Michel Aumont *Uncle Salomon* ■ *Dir* Jean-Jacques Zilbermann • *Scr* Gilles Taurand, Jean-Jacques Zilbermann, from an idea by Jean-Jacques Zilbermann, Joele Van Effenterre

Man Made Monster ★★★

Science-fiction horror
1941 · US · BW · 56mins

Lon Chaney Jr made his horror acting debut in this above-average Universal B-movie, which lacks the verve and gusto of the studio's earlier genre hits. Chaney is circus sideshow performer "Dynamo Dan, the Electric Man", and ever-reliable Lionel Atwill the mad doctor who wants to turn up his voltage and convert him into a prototype zombie killer with a lethal touch. *Frankenstein* make-up genius Jack Pierce provided Chaney's fiendish look as the natty rubber-suited "atomic monster" (the film's re-release title).

Lionel Atwill *Dr Paul Rigas* • Lon Chaney Jr *Dan McCormick* • Anne Nagel *June Lawrence* • Frank Albertson *Mark Adams* • Samuel S Hinds *Dr Lawrence* • William Davidson *District Attorney* • Ben Taggart *Detective Sergeant* • Connie Bergen *Nurse* ■ *Dir* George Waggner • *Scr* Joseph West [George Waggner], from the short story *The Electric Man* by HJ Essex, Sid Schwartz, Len Golos

The Man Next Door ★★ 15

Drama   1996 · US · Colour · 93mins

Lamont Johnson, probably best known for the controversial rape drama *Lipstick*, tackles the same subject, albeit in a less sensational manner, for this made-for-TV drama. *Twin Peaks's* Michael Ontkean plays a released rapist who decides to build a new life for himself in a small town, only to discover his past catching up with him. Ontkean is nicely cast against type and there's solid support from Pamela Reed as a sympathetic probation officer. It takes an age to get going, but the potent subject matter always makes it watchable. 🖾

Michael Ontkean *Eli Cooley* • Pamela Reed *Wanda Gilmore* • Annette O'Toole *Annie Hodges* • Sam Anderson *Dwight Cooley* • Richard Gilliland *Moe Hurley* • Vonetta McGee *Pamela* • Tracy O'Neil Heffernan *Sally Cooley* ■ *Dir* Lamont Johnson • *Scr* Susan Baskin

Man of a Thousand Faces ★★

Biographical drama 1957 · US · BW · 121mins

The life and work of silent actor and special make-up genius Lon Chaney is brought into less than sharp focus in a heavily fictionalised biopic starring the impressive James Cagney. It's a typical rags-to-riches saga of the humble boy raised by deaf-mute parents whose talent for playing grotesquely deformed screen villains made him a Hollywood legend. Cagney gets to appear in re-creations of Chaney's two most famous roles – the Phantom of the Opera and the Hunchback of Notre Dame – in a hokey but reasonably entertaining tribute.

James Cagney *Lon Chaney* • Dorothy Malone *Cleva Creighton Chaney* • Jane Greer *Hazel Bennet* • Marjorie Rambeau *Gert* • Jim Backus *Clarence Logan* • Robert Evans *Irving Thalberg* • Celia Lovsky *Mrs Chaney* • Jeanne Cagney *Carrie Chaney* ■ *Dir* Joseph Pevney • *Scr* R Wright Campbell, Ivan Goff, Ben Roberts, from a story by Ralph Wheelwright

Man of Africa ★★★ U

Documentary drama
1954 · UK · Colour · 84mins

Although this tale of the Ugandan bush was made 20 years after Robert Flaherty's seminal *Man of Aran*, it's a shade disappointing to see how little producer John Grierson had moved away from that style of drama documentary. Still, his influence is considerably more evident than that of his acolyte, Cyril Frankel. Following the migration of the Bakija and Batwa tribes, the action centres on farming couple Frederick Bijuerenda and Violet Mukabuerza as they endure everything from malaria and internecine strife to marauding elephants and pygmies.

Dir Cyril Frankel • *Scr* Montagu Slater

Man of Aran ★★★ U

Documentary   1934 · UK · BW · 73mins

Film-maker Robert Flaherty made a huge impact in the silent era with his film about Inuit life, *Nanook of the North* (1922). This account of life's daily grind on the Aran Islands (just west of Ireland) follows a similar "against the elements" theme, as the local farmers struggle to eke a living from their barren surroundings. Flaherty's films are best described as dramatised documentaries – the intention is to show life as it really is, but the method involves staging and re-staging events as necessary to fit the loose "script", and the natives are not always strictly native. Issues of authenticity aside, there's no doubt that this is a heartfelt piece of cinema, and the imagery of craggy cliffs and pounding waves is frequently breathtaking. 🖾

Dir Robert Flaherty • *Scr* John Goldman, Robert Flaherty, Frances Flaherty • *Cinematographer* John Goldman, Harces Flaherty

Man of Conquest ★★ U

Biographical western
1939 · US · BW · 98mins

Republic Pictures ventured into the bigger budget league for the first time with this popular contribution to the western cycle. The studio had so little top talent of its own that it had to borrow stars Richard Dix and Joan Fontaine, director George Nichols Jr and cameraman Joseph H August from RKO. Dix plays Sam Houston, the man who brought Texas into the Union, and the biopic includes the defeat at the Alamo and victory at San Jacinto. Stunt directors B Reeves Eason and Yakima Canutt were given a free hand with the action sequences, and together they bring some life into an otherwise static and talkative picture.

Richard Dix *Sam Houston* • Gail Patrick *Margaret Lea* • Edward Ellis *Andrew Jackson* • Joan Fontaine *Eliza Allen* • Victor Jory *William B Travis* • Robert Barrat *Davy Crockett* ■ *Dir* George Nichols Jr • *Scr* Wells Root, Ee Paramore Jr [Edward E Paramore Jr], from the story *Wagons Westward* by Wells Root, Harold Shumate

Man of Flowers ★★★ 18

Drama   1984 · Ausl · Colour · 86mins

After making his name as one of Australia's most respected photographers and documentarists, Dutch-born film-maker Paul Cox brought his distinctive, compassionate take on alienation and eccentricity to his adopted country's cinema resurgence. Here Norman Kaye is a lonely, mother-fixated bachelor who finds quiet delight in gardening and the artist's model (Alyson Best) he employs to undress for him once a week. Renowned German director Werner Herzog plays Kaye's fearsome father in the flashbacks. 🖾

Norman Kaye *Charles Bremer* • Alyson Best *Lisa* • Chris Haywood *David* • Sarah Walker *Jane* • Julia Blake *Art teacher* • Bob Ellis *Psychiatrist* • Werner Herzog *Father* ■ *Dir* Paul Cox • *Scr* Paul Cox, Bob Ellis

Man of Iron ★★★★

Drama   1981 · Pol · Colour · 152mins

The winner of the Palme d'Or at Cannes, this semi-sequel sees Krystyna Janda return to the documentary fray, this time to chart the career of her husband, a Solidarity leader and the son of her subject in *Man of Marble*. But the main focus falls on Marian Opania, a broken-down reporter whose mission to spy on the rebellious Gdansk shipworkers is undermined by his growing politicisation. Capturing history in the making and neatly weaving it into his fictional tale, Andrzej Wajda expertly manages to convey the optimism of Lech Walesa's working class heroes without losing a sense of perspective. In Polish with English subtitles.

Jerzy Radziwilowicz *Tomczyk* • Krystyna Janda *Agnieszka* • Marian Opania *Winkiel* • Irene Byrska *Anna Hulewicz's mother* ■ *Dir* Andrzej Wajda • *Scr* Aleksander Scibor-Rylski

Man of La Mancha ★ PG

Musical   1972 · US · Colour · 123mins

Jailed by the Inquisition, Cervantes sits in his cell and writes *Don Quixote*, the story of a knight who is the last living bastion of chivalry in a cynical, violent world. The Broadway show was a massive hit, but this movie bungles everything, including the big number – *The Impossible Dream* – and the moment when Peter O'Toole's knight tilts at the windmills. Arthur Hiller's film is heavy-going, tricksy and self-consciously arty, while Loren, who unwisely sings her own songs, merely makes us yearn for *El Cid*. A box-office dud. 🖾

Peter O'Toole *Miguel de Cervantes/Don Quixote/Quijana* • Sophia Loren *Aldonza/Alonso Dulcinea* • James Coco *Manservant/Sancho Panza* • Harry Andrews *Governor/Innkeeper* • John Castle *Duke/Dr Carrasco/Black Knight/Knight of the Mirrors* • Brian Blessed *Pedro* ■ *Dir* Arthur Hiller • *Scr* Dale Wasserman, from his play, from *Don Quixote* by Miguel de Cervantes

Man of Marble ★★★★ U

Drama   1977 · Pol · Colour · 153mins

Employing a "talking heads" style redolent of both *Citizen Kane* and the polemics of Jean-Luc Godard, this is a superbly controlled treatise on the power of the Party, the transience of reputation and the veracity of visual evidence. Expertly manufacturing "contemporary" newsreel footage, Andrzej Wajda turns a pseudo-documentary into a disturbing thriller as film student Krystyna Janda relentlessly investigates the part played by the Communist authorities in the tragedy of Mateusz Birkut, a Stakhanovite hero of the fifties who was destroyed when his influence became too great. In Polish with English subtitles.

Jerzy Radziwilowicz *Mateusz Birkut* • Krystyna Janda *Agnieszka* • Tadeusz Lomnicki *Jerzy Burski* • Jacek Lomnicki *Younger Burski* • Michal Tarkowski *Witek* ■ *Dir* Andrzej Wajda • *Scr* Aleksandar Sciber-Rylski

A Man of No Importance ★★★★ 15

Drama   1994 · UK/Ire · Colour · 94mins

Albert Finney gives another great performance as the eccentric Alfie, the poetry-loving Dublin bus conductor with a tenacious dream to stage Oscar Wilde's play *Salome* in the local village hall, an ambition that sets off a train of unfortunate events. One of the film's splendidly handled central themes is the painful comparison between Finney's ebullient public face and his sexually repressed, private hell. Dublin in 1963 is realistically brought to life in this major treat. 🖾

Albert Finney *Alfie Byrne* • Rufus Sewell *Robbie Fay* • Brenda Fricker *Lily Byrne* • Tara FitzGerald *Adele Rice* • Michael Gambon *Carney* • Patrick Malahide *Carson* • Anna Manahan *Mrs Grace* • Joe Pilkington *Ernie Lally* ■ *Dir* Suri Krishnamma • *Scr* Barry Devlin

Man of the House ★★ U

Comedy   1994 · US · Colour · 92mins

A vehicle more for Jonathan Taylor Thomas (TV's *Home Improvement*), than the nominal star Chevy Chase, reprising his now familiar nice-but-dim persona. In this one, well-meaning Chase moves in with girlfriend Farrah Fawcett and attempts to bond with her son (Thomas) with disastrous consequences. There's a syrupy undertone to much of the juvenile slapstick and not even *Cheers* star George Wendt can wring many laughs out of the uninspired script. 🖾

U = SUITABLE FOR ALL   Uc = SUITABLE FOR ALL, ESPECIALLY FOR YOUNG CHILDREN (VIDEO ONLY)   PG = PARENTAL GUIDANCE

Chevy Chase *Jack Sturges* • Farrah Fawcett *Sandra Archer* • Jonathan Taylor Thomas *Ben Archer* • George Wendt *Chet Bronski* • David Shiner *Lloyd Small* • Art LaFleur *Red Sweeney* ■ *Dir* James Orr • *Scr* James Orr, Jim Cruickshank, from a story by David Peckinpah, Richard Jefferies

Man of the Moment ★★★ U

Comedy	1955 · UK · BW · 84mins

Norman Wisdom is almost at the peak of his powers in this typically silly comedy, in which slapstick and sentiment jostle for centre stage. Norman is a Whitehall nobody who suddenly finds himself a target for foreign agents after he stalls the entire United Nations with his support for the island of Tarawaki. Although we usually think of Norman as a bashful bungler, he also did a nice line in cockiness, and it's surprisingly amusing to watch Whitehall and Geneva dance to his tune. Jerry Desmonde again proves to be the supreme stooge. ▭

Norman Wisdom *Norman* • Lana Morris *Penny* • Belinda Lee *Sonia* • Jerry Desmonde *Jackson* • Karel Stepanek *Lom* • Garry Marsh *British delegate* • Inia Te Wiata *Toki* • Evelyn Roberts *Sir Horace* ■ *Dir* John Paddy Carstairs • *Scr* Vernon Sylvaine, John Paddy Carstairs, from a story by Maurice Cowan

Man of the West ★★★★

Western	1958 · US · Colour · 100mins

This fine, relentlessly grim western was accorded scant critical approval on its original release. A study of choice and injustice, it stars Gary Cooper, whose haggard, ageing features lend the tale an almost biblical intensity. Director Anthony Mann's use of CinemaScope is exemplary, although the sometimes savage story suffered cuts – the rape of saloon singer Julie London, for example. The screenplay, by *12 Angry Men* writer Reginald Rose, is particularly literate, and Lee J Cobb's ferocious study in villainy is wonderful to watch. This is no ordinary Wild West tale, and may not be to everyone's taste.

Gary Cooper *Link Jones* • Julie London *Billie Ellis* • Lee J Cobb *Dock Tobin* • Arthur O'Connell *Sam Beasley* • Jack Lord *Coaley* • John Dehner *Claude* • Royal Dano *Trout* • Robert Wilke [Robert J Wilke] *Ponch* ■ *Dir* Anthony Mann • *Scr* Reginald Rose, from the novel *The Border Jumpers* by Will C Brown

Man of the World ★★★

Drama	1931 · US · BW · 71mins

A smooth, sophisticated gigolo turned blackmailer (William Powell) chooses fellow Americans in Paris as his victims. But he comes unstuck when he falls in love with one of them (Carole Lombard) and is threatened with exposure by his hard-boiled mistress (Wynne Gibson). Scripted by Herman J Mankiewicz (*Citizen Kane*), this high society drama, characteristic of the period, more than gets by thanks to its star casting. Powell is impeccable, while Lombard - his off-screen wife from 1931 to 1933 - is clearly on her way to major stardom.

William Powell *Michael Trevor* • Carole Lombard *Mary Kendall* • Wynne Gibson *Irene Hoffa* • Guy Kibbee *Harold Taylor* • Lawrence Gray *Frank Thompson* • Andre Cheron *Victor* ■ *Dir* Richard Wallace, Edward Goodman • *Scr* Herman J Mankiewicz, from his story

Man on a Tightrope ★★★

Drama based on a true story
1953 · US · BW · 103mins

A professionally made and absorbing drama, based on real-life events, about a circus troupe escaping across the border from communist Czechoslovakia to Austria. This is well acted, particularly by Fredric March and Robert Beatty, and effectively directed by Elia Kazan, but the fact that this was the movie Kazan was working on when he shamefully ''named names'' to the House Un-American Activities Committee makes the story deeply ironic. Kazan's next project would be *On the Waterfront* – a near glorification of the informer.

Fredric March *Karel Cernik* • Terry Moore *Tereza Cernik* • Gloria Grahame *Zama Cernik* • Cameron Mitchell *Joe Vosdek* • Adolphe Menjou *Fesker* • Robert Beatty *Barovic* • Alex D'Arcy *Rudolph* ■ *Dir* Elia Kazan • *Scr* Robert E Sherwood, from the story *International Incident* by Neil Peterson

Man on Fire ★ 18

Thriller	1987 · It/Fr · Colour · 87mins

Action-man heroes are generally given a decent moral side so that their outrageously violent behaviour can be justified. Here, in an often unintentionally funny mix of big-blast set pieces and patently ludicrous plot shenanigans, Scott Glenn plays a former CIA agent-turned-pacifist who becomes a Rambo-style avenger when the 12-year-old girl in his charge is kidnapped. Alongside Glenn, Jonathan Pryce, Danny Aiello and Joe Pesci are confounded by the mediocrity of the project. Contains swearing and violence. ▭

Scott Glenn *Chris Creasy* • Jade Malle *Samantha "Sam" Balletto* • Joe Pesci *David* • Brooke Adams *Jane Balletto* • Jonathan Pryce *Michael* • Paul Shenar *Ettore Balletto* • Danny Aiello *Conti* • Laura Morante *Julia* ■ *Dir* Elie Chouraqui • *Scr* Elie Chouraqui, Sergio Donati, from the novel by AJ Quinnell

A Man on the Beach ★ U

Crime drama	1955 · UK · Colour · 28mins

This obscure half-hour featurette, derived from a story by Victor Canning, has promising credentials: stars Donald Wolfit and Michael Medwin, a script by Jimmy Sangster and direction by Joseph Losey. Its somewhat bizarre plot requires Medwin to rob a French casino in drag, become wounded killing his accomplice and take refuge in the bungalow of Wolfit's retired, blind doctor. But it is notable only as the first occasion since arriving in Britain that the blacklisted Losey could put his own name on a film.

Donald Wolfit *Carter* • Michael Medwin *Max* • Michael Ripper *Chauffeur* • Edward Forsyth *Inspector Clement* ■ *Dir* Joseph Losey • *Scr* Jimmy Sangster, from a story by Victor Canning

The Man on the Eiffel Tower ★★

Detective thriller	1949 · US · Colour · 83mins

Charles Laughton stars as Inspector Maigret in a botched version of Georges Simenon's *La Tête d'un Homme*, with Franchot Tone as his fiendish and arrogant adversary.

Burgess Meredith plays an impoverished knife-grinder and directed most of the picture, filmed in Paris with some difficulty using the untried Ansco Color process. Laughton directed some scenes, including the one in which Meredith turns burglar and comes upon two women stabbed to death in the bedroom. The film has some striking touches but never builds any real suspense.

Charles Laughton *Inspector Maigret* • Franchot Tone *Johann Radek* • Burgess Meredith *Joseph Huertin* • Robert Hutton *Bill Kirby* • Jean Wallace *Edna Wallace* • Patricia Roc *Helen Kirby* • Belita *Gisella* • George Thorpe *Comelieu* • Wilfrid Hyde White *Prof Grollet* ■ *Dir* Burgess Meredith • *Scr* Harry Brown, from the novelette *La Tête d'un Homme (A Battle of Nerves)* by Georges Simenon

The Man on the Flying Trapeze ★★

Comedy	1935 · US · BW · 65mins

WC Fields, who dreamed up the storyline with Sam Hardy, is the characteristically curmudgeonly star of this misleadingly titled comedy, released more accurately in Britain as *The Memory Expert*. Fields plays a man who capitalises on his astonishing feats of memory to reduce all those around him, including his nagging wife, to gibbering submission. The sole exception is his daughter, played by Mary Brian. Clyde Bruckman directs what is essentially a showcase for a series of Fields gags.

WC Fields *Ambrose Wolfinger* • Mary Brian *Hope Wolfinger* • Kathleen Howard *Leona Wolfinger* • Grady Sutton *Claude Neselrode* • Vera Lewis *Mrs Cordelia Neselrode* • Lucien Littlefield *Mr Peabody* • Walter Brennan *''Legs'' Garnett* ■ *Dir* Clyde Bruckman • *Scr* Ray Harris, Sam Hardy, Jack Cunningham, Bobby Vernon, from a story by Sam Hardy, Charles Bogle [WC Fields]

Man on the Moon ★★★★ 15

Biographical comedy drama
1999 · US · Colour · 118mins

The non-conforming, self-destructive career of comedian Andy Kaufman (the squeaky-voiced Latka in the eighties sitcom *Taxi*) is re-created by Jim Carrey and director Milos Forman in a challenging, off-the-wall biography. Carrey *is* Kaufman in his strongest work to date, giving everything he's got to Andy's provocative, manipulative stage performances. In an audacious piece of casting, Kaufman's *Taxi* co-star Danny DeVito portrays his understanding manager, and he too is first-rate. From the bizarre credits scene onwards, Forman keeps the audience unsure of how to perceive Kaufman, prompting some critics to complain he does not allow enough insight into the off-stage Andy. That is perhaps the point: you never knew when he had stopped performing.

Jim Carrey *Andy Kaufman* • Gerry Becker *Stanley Kaufman* • Leslie Lyles *Janice Kaufman* • George Shapiro *Mr Besserman* • Danny DeVito *George Shapiro* • Courtney Love *Lynne Margulies* ■ *Dir* Milos Forman • *Scr* Scott Alexander, Larry Karaszewski

Man-Proof ★★★

Comedy drama	1937 · US · BW · 74mins

Shenanigans among the sophisticated set as an uncharacteristically predatory

Myrna Loy sets her sights on Walter Pidgeon and keeps them there, even when he marries her rival (Rosalind Russell). Rescue, however, is at hand in the shape of Franchot Tone. A mildly diverting romantic comedy drama, directed by Richard Thorpe, that holds the attention thanks to the easy expertise of the classy cast.

Myrna Loy *Mimi Swift* • Franchot Tone *Jimmy Kilmartin* • Rosalind Russell *Elizabeth Kent* • Walter Pidgeon *Alan Wythe* • Rita Johnson *Florence* • Nana Bryant *Meg Swift* • Ruth Hussey *Jane* • Leonard Penn *Bob* ■ *Dir* Richard Thorpe • *Scr* George Oppenheimer, Vincent Lawrence, Waldemar Young, from the novel *The Four Marys* by Fanny Heaslip Lea

The Man They Could Not Hang ★★★

Horror	1939 · US · BW · 64mins

While not exactly the ''holocaust of horror'' promised at the time, this incredibly prophetic sci-fi thriller is laced with enough sinister menace to get by. British bogeyman Boris Karloff plays a crazed scientist dabbling in heart transplant surgery who is sentenced to death by the medical authorities. After his execution, his own technology is used to turn him into a vengeful maniac with a mechanical ticker. As usual, kindly Karloff elevates standard fear fare with wit, grace and presence.

Boris Karloff *Dr Henryk Savaard* • Lorna Gray [Adrian Booth] *Janet Saavard* • Robert Wilcox *Scoop Foley* • Roger Pryor *District Attorney Drake* • Don Beddoe *Lt Shane* ■ *Dir* Nick Grinde • *Scr* Karl Brown, from a story by Leslie T White, George W Sayre

Man-Trap ★★

Crime drama	1961 · US · BW · 93mins

To play Jesus in *King of Kings*, Jeffrey Hunter shaved his body hair, never gave interviews and never drank or smoked. But as soon as he was through with Christ he shot this grubby exploitation movie, in which he plays the frustrated husband of drunken slut Stella Stevens, lured into a heist by war buddy David Janssen. Actor Edmond O'Brien directed this quickie after recovering from the heart attack which forced him to abandon his role as the journalist in *Lawrence of Arabia*.

Jeffrey Hunter *Matt Jameson* • David Janssen *Vince Biskay* • Stella Stevens *Nina Jameson* • Elaine Devry *Liz Adams* ■ *Dir* Edmond O'Brien • *Scr* Ed Waters, from the novella *Taint of the Tiger* by John D MacDonald

Man Trouble ★★ 15

Romantic comedy	1992 · US · Colour · 95mins

Proof that even the most talented actors – in this case, Jack Nicholson and Ellen Barkin – can make bad choices and turn in mediocre performances in a below-par film. When opera singer Barkin thinks she's being stalked, she enlists the help of oddball dog trainer Nicholson to find her an attack dog. Naturally, the pair are soon sparring along the path to true love. Of course, there are various complications to their romance, but they're too ridiculous and insignificant to mention here. ▭

Jack Nicholson *Harry Bliss* • Ellen Barkin *Joan Spruance* • Harry Dean Stanton *Redmond*

Layls • Beverly D'Angelo *Andy Ellerman* • Michael McKean *Eddy Revere* • Saul Rubinek *Laurence Moncrief* ■ *Dir* Bob Rafelson • *Scr* Carole Eastman

The Man Upstairs ★★★ PG

Drama   1958 · UK · Colour · 84mins

Le Jour Se Lève (1939) starred Jean Gabin as a killer who barricades himself in his attic flat. It was remade in 1947 as *The Long Night* with Henry Fonda, and this too is a remake, with Richard Attenborough going bonkers upstairs while the police downstairs try to calm him down. The motivation has changed (he blames himself for his fiancée's brother's death), but the dramatic set-up is identical and makes for some agreeable tension. ▭

Richard Attenborough *Peter Watson, the man* • Bernard Lee *Inspector Thompson* • Donald Houston *Sanderson* • Dorothy Alison *Mrs Barnes* • Patricia Jessel *Mrs Lawrence* • Virginia Maskell *Helen Grey* ■ *Dir* Don Chaffey • *Scr* Alun Falconer, Robert Dunbar, Don Chaffey, from a story by Alun Falconer

The Man Upstairs ★★★

Comedy drama   1992 · US · Colour · 95mins

A much awaited but ultimately disappointing appearance from a frail Katharine Hepburn, playing a rich recluse who discovers prisoner-on-the-run Ryan O'Neal hiding in her attic. Hepburn is as accomplished as ever, but the script lets her down by giving her some decidedly mawkish speeches. O'Neal, looking rather raddled, does his best with the material available.

Katharine Hepburn *Victoria Browne* • Ryan O'Neal *Moony Polaski* • Helena Carroll *Molly* • Henry Beckman *Sheriff* • Brenda Forbes *Cloris* • Lawrence King *Roy* • Tom McBeath *Priest* ■ *Dir* George Shaeffer • *Scr* James Prideaux

The Man Who Broke 1,000 Chains ★★

Drama based on a true story
1987 · US · Colour · 113mins

Val Kilmer stars in this made-for-TV prison drama as Robert Elliot Burns, the First World War veteran who found himself sentenced to hard labour in a brutal Georgia work camp after being forced to take part in an armed robbery. The same true-life story inspired the classic Paul Muni film *I Am a Fugitive from a Chain Gang* (1931); here, though, a strong supporting cast is the only bright spot in a picture whose moral is delivered with sledgehammer subtlety.

Val Kilmer *Robert Elliot Burns* • Charles Durning *Hardy* • Kyra Sedgwick *Lillian* • William Sanderson *Trump* • Sonia Braga *Emily* ■ *Dir* Daniel Mann • *Scr* Michael Campus, Wendell Mayes, David Wyles

The Man Who Broke the Bank at Monte Carlo ★★

Comedy   1935 · US · BW · 70mins

The popular song is played over the titles, but this movie is initially set in Paris where Russian émigré Ronald Colman works as a cab driver. He decides to try his luck in Monte Carlo and lands a multi-million franc windfall at the tables. Joan Bennett is the casino employee sent to woo him back and his winnings back. It was Ernst

Lubitsch who introduced this sort of sophisticated European comedy to Hollywood, but without him things tended to fall flat, as they do here under the heavy-handed direction of former stuntman Stephen Roberts.

Ronald Colman *Paul Gallard* • Joan Bennett *Helen Berkeley* • Colin Clive *Bertrand Berkeley* • Nigel Bruce *Ivan* • Montagu Love *Director* • Ferdinand Gottschalk *Office man* ■ *Dir* Stephen Roberts • *Scr* Howard Ellis Smith, Nunnally Johnson, from the play *Monsieur Alexandre, Igra, Lepy and the Gamble* by Illia Surgutchoff, Frederick Albert Swann

The Man Who Came to Dinner ★★★★ U

Comedy   1941 · US · BW · 116mins

Sparkling Warner Bros comedy based on the George S Kaufman-Moss Hart Broadway hit. Monty Woolley portrays the irascible, unwelcome house guest Sheridan Whiteside, a characterisation based on the great Algonquin wit and critic, Alexander Woollcott. While incapacitated, Woolley is visited by any number of guests in disguise, most notably the wonderful Jimmy Durante as Harpo Marx, and a louche Reginald Gardiner as Noël Coward. Despite Woolley's resolute screen-hogging, Bette Davis and Ann Sheridan get more formidable roles than the original Broadway play afforded, lending Woolley the star power he personally lacks. Splendid entertainment.

Bette Davis *Maggie Cutler* • Monty Woolley *Sheridan Whiteside* • Ann Sheridan *Lorraine Sheldon* • Richard Travis *Bert Jefferson* • Jimmy Durante *Banjo* • Reginald Gardiner *Beverly Carlton* • Billie Burke *Mrs Stanley* ■ *Dir* William Keighley • *Scr* Julius J Epstein, Philip G Epstein, from the play by George S Kaufman, Moss Hart

The Man Who Captured Eichmann ★★★★ PG

Historical drama   1996 · US · Colour · 92mins

To find a shred of humanity in the Jew-killing monster of Nazi Adolf Eichmann needs a great actor. In this made-for-cable movie, it is Robert Duvall. He portrays the bureaucrat who sent millions of people to the gas chambers as an aged, infirm exile, kidnapped in Argentina by masterspy Peter Malkin (Arliss Howard) and taken to Israel to face trial. Concentrating on the excitement of the chase, the film nevertheless carries the horror of the Holocaust across the years. Credit must also go to the restrained direction of William A Graham. ▭

Robert Duvall *Adolf Eichmann* • Arliss Howard *Peter Malkin* • Jeffrey Tambor *Isser Harel* • Jack Laufer *Uzi* • Nicolas Surovy *Hans* ■ *Dir* William A Graham • *Scr* Lionel Chetwynd, from the memoirs *Eichmann in My Hands* by Peter Malkin, Harry Stein

The Man Who Changed His Name ★★

Crime drama   1934 · UK · BW · 71mins

A millionaire causes his wife and her unscrupulous lover to think he is a notorious murderer in this above-average B-feature, based on a typically ingenious work by Edgar Wallace. Its stage origins are evident in the static, talkative development, but it's carried by Lyn Harding's characteristically powerful performance as the husband.

Betty Stockfield is adequate as the foolish wife, though Leslie Perrins is miscast as the philanderer.

Lyn Harding *Selby Clive* • Betty Stockfeld *Nita Clive* • Leslie Perrins *Frank Ryan* • Ben Welden *Jerry Muller* • Aubrey Mather *Sir Ralph Whitcomb* • Richard Dolman *John Boscombe* ■ *Dir* Henry Edwards • *Scr* H Fowler Mear, Edgar Wallace, from the play by Edgar Wallace

The Man Who Changed His Mind ★★★

Science-fiction   1936 · UK · BW · 61mins

Boris Karloff is up to his brain transference tricks again in this seldom-seen British chiller. As Dr Laurience, he's in love with lab assistant Anna Lee. Unfortunately, she's planning to marry John Loder. So Karloff plans to switch brains with him using the usual strange scientific apparatus so popular in thirties borderline sci-fi melodrama. Stereotypically cast, as so often happened, Karloff nevertheless gives one of his best performances in the matchlessly amusing leading role.

Boris Karloff *Dr Laurience* • Anna Lee *Dr Claire Wyatt* • John Loder *Dick Haslewood* • Frank Cellier *Lord Haslewood* • Donald Calthrop *Clayton* • Cecil Parker *Dr Gratton* • Lyn Harding *Professor Holloway* ■ *Dir* Robert Stevenson • *Scr* L DuGarde Peach, Sidney Gilliat, John L Balderston

The Man Who Could Cheat Death ★★

Horror   1959 · UK · Colour · 82mins

A strange Hammer horror about a 104-year-old doctor who is able to look like a 30-year-old thanks to annual glandular transplants taken from living donors. When he murders his own doctor, however, things starts to unravel. This blend of *Dorian Gray* and *Jekyll and Hyde* has its moments, but not very many. That said, it does provide a rare starring role to Anton Diffring, who usually played sadistic SS officers in war movies.

Anton Diffring *Dr Georges Bonnet* • Hazel Court *Janine* • Delphi Lawrence *Margo* • Christopher Lee *Dr Pierre Gerard* • Francis De Wolff *Inspector Legris* ■ *Dir* Terence Fisher • *Scr* Jimmy Sangster, from the play *The Man in Half Moon Street* by Barré Lyndon

The Man Who Could Work Miracles ★★ U

Fantasy comedy   1936 · UK · BW · 78mins

Having produced HG Wells's *Things to Come*, British movie mogul Alexander Korda went straight on to Wells's *The Man Who Could Work Miracles*, a rather corny fantasy about a bashful draper's assistant (Roland Young) who acquires miraculous powers when the gods look kindly upon him. The comedy soon gives way to pomposity, as Young gathers world leaders and tells them to be nice to each other. The final sequences, when Young orders time to stand still, are truly mind-boggling and, while Ralph Richardson is delightfully eccentric throughout, it's embarrassingly dated and simplistic. ▭

Roland Young *George McWhirter Fotheringay* • Ralph Richardson *Colonel Winstanley* • Edward Chapman *Major Grigsby* • Ernest Thesiger *Mr Maydig* • Joan Gardner *Ada Price* • Sophie

Stewart *Maggie Hooper* • Robert Cochran *Bill Stoker* • Lawrence Hanray *Mr Bamfylde* ■ *Dir* Lothar Mendes • *Scr* HG Wells, Lajos Biró, from the short story by HG Wells

The Man Who Cried Wolf ★★

Crime drama   1937 · US · BW · 66mins

An actor keeps making false confessions of murder to the police to avoid suspicion when he kills his wife's lover. But then, in a clever twist, he needs to persuade the police that he did commit the crime to prevent his son carrying the can. Lewis Stone does his best in the lead, while Tom Brown plays his son, but the film is content to remain an ordinary B-feature.

Lewis Stone *Lawrence Fontaine* • Tom Brown *Tommy Bradley* • Barbara Read *Nan* • Marjorie Main *Amelia Bradley* ■ *Dir* Lewis R Foster • *Scr* Charles Grayson, Sy Bartlett, from the story *Too Clever to Live* by Arthur Rohlsfel

The Man Who Fell to Earth ★★★★ 18

Cult science-fiction drama
1976 · UK · Colour · 133mins

Director Nicolas Roeg's typically eccentric and multi-dimensional movie transforms Walter Tevis's novel into an enigmatic and chilling mosaic of corporate satire and effective science-fiction. In his feature debut, David Bowie is exactly right as the Swiftian starman who becomes fabulously wealthy from his intergalactic inventions, but soon gets corrupted by such earthbound vices as alcohol, television and sex. Already an established sci-fi classic, this is a fascinating new age fairy tale, with Bowie's "fall" open to numerous allegorical interpretations. ▭

David Bowie *Thomas Jerome Newton* • Rip Torn *Nathan Bryce* • Candy Clark *Mary-Lou* • Buck Henry *Oliver Farnsworth* • Bernie Casey *Peters* • Jackson D Kane *Professor Canutti* • Rick Riccardo *Trevor* • Tony Mascia *Arthur* ■ *Dir* Nicolas Roeg • *Scr* Paul Mayersburg, from the novel by Walter Tevis

The Man Who Fell to Earth ★★ PG

Science-fiction drama
1986 · US · Colour · 93mins

No, not Nicolas Roeg's sci-fi film, but a made-for-TV remake starring Lewis Smith as the weird alien and Beverly D'Angelo as the earthling who tends to his every comfort while he absorbs our capitalist culture and looks for a way to export water to his arid planet. Intended to herald a TV series based on Walter Tevis's source novel, this inevitably pales in comparison with Roeg's visually dazzling adaptation. Contains swearing. ▭

Lewis Smith *John Dory* • Beverly D'Angelo *Eva Milton* • James Laurenson *Felix Hawthorne* • Robert Picardo *Richard Morse* • Bruce McGill *Vernon Gage* • Wil Wheaton *Billy Milton* ■ *Dir* Robert J Roth • *Scr* Richard Kletter, from the novel by Walter Tevis

The Man Who Finally Died ★

Drama   1962 · UK · BW · 100mins

Stanley Baker goes to Bavaria to find out about his long-lost German father; while there, he gets involved in espionage. A routine spy thriller based

on a TV series which plods more than it surprises, though the actors deserve some credit for delivering the deathless lines with a conviction that's way beyond the call of duty.

Stanley Baker *Joe Newman* • Peter Cushing *Dr von Brecht* • Eric Portman *Hofmeister* • Mai Zetterling *Lisa* • Niall MacGinnis *Brenner* • Nigel Green *Hirsch* • Barbara Everest *Martha* ■ *Dir* Quentin Lawrence • *Scr* Lewis Greifer, Louis Marks, from a story by Lewis Greifer

The Man Who Had Power over Women ★

Comedy 1970 · UK · Colour · 89mins

This awful, cringe-inducing story about a public relations executive and his obnoxious pop star client was filmed at the fag end of the Swinging Sixties, and it has dated very badly. Although the film toys around with the moral issue of abortion, it never achieves more than a glossy vacuity, while screenwriters Allan Scott and Chris Bryant show little of the brilliance they exhibited three years later with their work on *Don't Look Now*.

Rod Taylor *Peter Reaney* • Carol White *Jody Pringle* • James Booth *Val Pringle* • Penelope Horner *Angela Reaney* • Charles Korvin *Alfred Felix* • Alexandra Stewart *Frances* ■ *Dir* John Krish • *Scr* Allan Scott, Chris Bryant, Andrew Meredith, from the novel by Gordon M Williams

The Man Who Haunted Himself ★★★ PG

Psychological thriller
1970 · UK · Colour · 89mins

Adapted from a short story by Anthony Armstrong, this wonderfully improbable chiller affords the rare opportunity to see Roger Moore being acted off the screen — by Roger Moore! The respectable business executive whose life is transformed by a car crash is a drip of the first order, but the sinister alter ego who escapes while he is unconscious is a rip-roaring cad. Veteran director Basil Dearden just manages to sustain the eerie atmosphere and, even though the mistaken identity card is overplayed, it's very watchable.

Roger Moore *Harold Pelham* • Hildegard Neil *Eve Pelham* • Alastair Mackenzie *Michael* • Hugh Mackenzie *James* • Kevork Malikyan *Luigi* • Thorley Walters *Bellamy* • Anton Rodgers *Tony Alexander* • Olga Georges-Picot *Julie* ■ *Dir* Basil Dearden • *Scr* Basil Dearden, Michael Relph, from the short story *The Case of Mr Pelham* by Anthony Armstrong

The Man Who Knew Too Little ★★★ 12

Spy comedy 1997 · US/Ger · Colour · 89mins

As the parodic Hitchcock title suggests, this sweet-natured Bill Murray comedy is an entertaining throwback to the espionage thrillers of yesteryear. The naive Murray is visiting brother Peter Gallagher in London and unwittingly becomes entangled in an assassination plot, the inspired twist being that Murray thinks it's all part of a participatory drama group. So enjoyable to see the normally vitriolic comedian as a bumbling dimwit, even if the one-joke premise does eventually start to lose its lustre. Great support, too, from Russian hit man Alfred Molina and corrupt government agent

Richard Wilson. Contains some violence and comic sex scenes. ▭

Bill Murray *Wallace Ritchie* • Peter Gallagher *James Ritchie* • Joanne Whalley-Kilmer [Joanne Whalley] *Lori* • Alfred Molina *Boris, the Butcher* • Richard Wilson *Sir Roger Daggenhurst* • Geraldine James *Dr Ludmilla Kropotkin* ■ *Dir* Jon Amiel • *Scr* Robert Farrar, Howard Franklin, from the novel *Watch That Man* by Robert Farrar

The Man Who Knew Too Much ★★★★ U

Crime drama 1934 · UK · BW · 75mins

With a finale inspired by the 1911 Sidney Street siege, this early Hitchcock — the only film he remade — was originally devised as a case for Bulldog Drummond. A taut, twisting thriller, the film sweeps from Switzerland to London's Albert Hall as Leslie Banks and Edna Best seek to rescue kidnapped daughter Nova Pilbeam and prevent a political assassination. Laced with gallows humour, this expertly structured tale marked the English-language debut of Peter Lorre, whose delight in his own villainy is tempered with an unexpected touch of humanity. ▭ **DVD**

Leslie Banks *Bob Lawrence* • Edna Best *Jill Lawrence* • Peter Lorre *Abbott* • Frank Vosper *Ramon Levine* • Hugh Wakefield *Clive* • Nova Pilbeam *Betty Lawrence* • Pierre Fresnay *Louis Bernard* • Cicely Oates *Nurse Agnes* ■ *Dir* Alfred Hitchcock • *Scr* Edwin Greenwood, AR Rawlinson, Emlyn Williams, Charles Bennett, DB Wyndham-Lewis, from a story by DB Wyndham-Lewis

The Man Who Knew Too Much ★★★ PG

Thriller 1956 · US · Colour · 114mins

Alfred Hitchcock once told François Truffaut that his 1934 version of this exciting thriller was "the work of a talented amateur and the second was made by a professional". There's no doubt that this colour remake is technically more accomplished, while the deft tinkering with the finale adds considerably to the suspense. But not all of the additional minutes are as well spent. *Que Sera, Sera* might have won the Oscar, but its inclusion is solely to mollify Doris Day fans and the storytelling is occasionally over-deliberate. Nevertheless, James Stewart is superb, and Bernard Miles and Brenda de Banzie make admirable adversaries. ▭ **DVD**

James Stewart *Dr Ben McKenna* • Doris Day *Jo McKenna* • Bernard Miles *Mr Drayton* • Brenda de Banzie *Mrs Drayton* • Ralph Truman *Buchanan* • Daniel Gelin *Louis Bernard* • Reggie Nalder *Rien* • Mogens Wieth *Ambassador* • Alan Mowbray *Val Parnell* • Hillary Brooke *Jan Peterson* ■ *Dir* Alfred Hitchcock • *Scr* John Michael Hayes and Angus McPhail, from a story by DB Wyndham-Lewis and Charles Bennett

The Man Who Laughs ★★★★

Silent melodrama 1928 · US · BW · 110mins

The third of four moody and mysterious films German-born director Paul Leni made in Hollywood was released a year after it was made in order to add music and sound effects. Based on Victor Hugo's tale, it tells of a man whose face is distorted into a hideous

grin. Becoming a circus clown, he falls in love with a blind girl. Conrad Veidt plays the pathetic protagonist, while Mary Philbin, whose most celebrated screen role was opposite another physically damaged hero in *The Phantom of the Opera* (1925), is extremely touching as his beloved.

Conrad Veidt *Gwynplaine* • Mary Philbin *Dea* ■ *Dir* Paul Leni • *Scr* J Grubb Alexander, Charles E Whittaker, Marion Ward, May McLean, Walter Anthony (titles), from the novel *L'Homme Qui Rit* by Victor Hugo

The Man Who Liked Funerals ★★ U

Comedy 1959 · UK · BW · 59mins

Leslie Phillips landed his first starring role in this brisk B-picture. Reining in the trademark charm, he plays a printer who attempts to fill the coffers of a struggling boys' club by blackmailing the relatives of recently departed bigwigs, whose scandalous (albeit forged) memoirs he threatens to publish. However, it all goes horribly wrong when he picks on the family of a notorious gangster. The film is nothing to get excited about, but it does raise the odd smile.

Leslie Phillips *Simon Hurd* • Brian Tyler *Nutter* • Anthony Green *Tommy* • Shaun O'Riordan *Reverend Pitt* • Susan Beaumont *Stella* • Bill Fraser *Jeremy Bentham* ■ *Dir* David Eady • *Scr* Margot Bennett, from a story by C Finn, Joan O'Connor

The Man Who Lived Twice ★★★

Crime drama 1936 · US · BW · 73mins

Before Ralph Bellamy became cast as the typical "other man" — notably in 1937's *The Awful Truth* — he was known as a useful and recognisable tough lead. Here, he's excellent as a murderer who has brain and facial surgery which turns him into quite literally another person. If the plot sounds familiar, the remake is better known today: *Man in the Dark*, one of the first films to be shot in 3-D, with Edmond O'Brien in the Bellamy role. Never a big hit, this average feature has an interesting period sheen.

Ralph Bellamy *James Blake/Slick Rawley* • Marian Marsh *Janet Haydon* • Thurston Hall *Dr Schuyler* • Isabel Jewell *Peggy Russell* • Nana Bryant *Mrs Margaret Schuyler* • Ward Bond *Gloves Baker* ■ *Dir* Harry Lachman • *Scr* Tom Van Dycke, Fred Niblo Jr, Arthur Strawn, from the story by Tom Van Dycke, Henry Altimus

The Man Who Loved Cat Dancing ★★ 18

Western 1973 · US · Colour · 118mins

Rumour has it that Robert Bolt did a bit of script doctoring to improve this western, which starred his wife Sarah Miles and Burt Reynolds. Imagine how awful it must have been before he got hold of it! Directed with no sense of narrative, let alone the old West, by Richard C Sarafian, what starts out as a revenge story soon turns into a soppy romance. Lee J Cobb and Jack Warden are left cooling their heels while Reynolds and Miles make little effort to hide their obvious antipathy towards one another. ▭

Burt Reynolds *Jay Grobart* • Sarah Miles *Catherine Crocker* • Lee J Cobb *Lapchance* • Jack Warden *Dawes* • George Hamilton *Crocker* • Bo Hopkins *Billy* • Robert Donner *Dub* • Jay Silverheels *The Chief* ■ *Dir* Richard C Sarafian • *Scr* Eleanor Perry, from the novel by Marilyn Durham

The Man Who Loved Redheads ★★★

Comedy 1954 · UK · Colour · 100mins

An elegant and witty screenplay by Terence Rattigan, based on his play *Who Is Sylvia?*, helps make this extremely civilised and sophisticated entertainment. It also benefits immensely from an early Eastmancolor process and photography by the great Georges Perinal, a combination that proved ideal for showing off the titian tresses of *The Red Shoes*'s Moira Shearer. The idea is nicely bittersweet, as Shearer plays all the "other" women in the recollections of John Justin, married to Gladys Cooper in the film. The denouement is genuinely moving, and a marvellous line-up of supporting players speeds the slight tale pleasurably on its way.

Moira Shearer *Sylvia/Daphne/Olga/Colette* • John Justin *Mark St Neots* • Roland Culver *Oscar* • Gladys Cooper *Caroline* • Denholm Elliott *Denis* • Harry Andrews *Williams* • Patricia Cutts *Bubbles* • John Hart *Sergei* ■ *Dir* Harold French • *Scr* Terrence Rattigan, from his play *Who Is Sylvia?*

The Man Who Loved Women ★★★

Comedy 1977 · Fr · Colour · 118mins

Attacked for its chauvinism, François Truffaut's wry comedy is actually a shrugging admission that men are little boys who don't deserve the women who love them. As he recalls each pair of legs that has enticed him, Charles Denner emerges less of a manipulative cad and more a sad man who has missed so many opportunities to live a fuller life. Unfortunately, Truffaut turns his memoirs into a long series of flashbacks, which prevents him from exploring Denner's motives and emotions. A touch more gravitas might have made his tale more poignant. In French with English subtitles.

Charles Denner *Bertrand Morane* • Brigitte Fossey *Genevieve Bigey* • Nelly Borgeaud *Delphine Grezel* • Genevieve Fontanel *Helene* • Nathalie Baye *Martine Desdoits* • Sabine Glaser *Bernadette* • Leslie Caron *Vera* ■ *Dir* François Truffaut • *Scr* François Truffaut, Michel Fermaud, Suzanne Schiffman

The Man Who Loved Women ★★ 15

Comedy 1983 · US · Colour · 105mins

An early entrant in the American trend of adapting (and usually coarsening) a French success for the US market. Director Blake Edwards takes François Truffaut's minor film and balloons it into something grander, yet emptier. Burt Reynolds works well as a women-obsessed sculptor whose story is played out via flashbacks at his funeral. Edwards's wife and frequent star Julie Andrews is the psychiatrist to whom Reynolds confesses all. A lot of care has obviously been taken, but overall it just fails to hit the mark. ▭

Burt Reynolds *David* • Julie Andrews *Marianna* • Kim Basinger *Louise* • Marilu Henner *Agnes* • Cynthia Sikes *Courtney* • Sela Ward *Janet* ■ *Dir* Blake Edwards • *Scr* Blake Edwards, Milton Wexler, Geoffrey Edwards, from the 1977 film by François Truffaut

The Man Who Never Was ★★ U

Second World War drama
1955 · UK · Colour · 102mins

An average Second World War espionage caper about a plan to fool the Nazis into believing that the Allies had no interest in invading Sicily from North Africa. Scripted by Nigel Balchin and based on a true story, the plan hinges on a corpse, a British one, washed ashore with secret papers marking Greece as the invasion site. But the Germans aren't so easily convinced and send Irish agent Stephen Boyd to London to investigate, which naturally enough calls for the presence of a local love interest (Gloria Grahame). Stodgily directed by Ronald Neame, this is less a thriller than a game of wartime charades.

Clifton Webb *Lt Commander Ewen Montagu* • Gloria Grahame *Lucy* • Stephen Boyd *O'Reilly* • Robert Flemyng *George Acres* • Josephine Griffin *Pam* • André Morell *Sir Bernard Spilsbury* • Laurence Naismith *Admiral Cross* • Michael Hordern *General Coburn* ■ *Dir* Ronald Neame • *Scr* Nigel Balchin, from the book by Ewen Montagu

The Man Who Played God ★★★★

Drama
1932 · US · BW · 81mins

The great George Arliss, with his death's-head face, effete elegance and mannered theatrical style, might at first strike modern audiences as faintly comical. However, in this intriguing fable about love, faith and redemption, he is mesmerising as a wealthy international concert pianist who becomes an embittered recluse after going deaf from a bomb explosion. Eventually, he learns to lip-read the conversations of passers-by and uses his wealth to play God. Bette Davis made her striking Warner Bros debut as his youthful and passionate disciple, and John Adolfi directed this compelling drama with imagination and sensitivity. It was embarrassingly updated in 1955 as *Sincerely Yours*, a starring vehicle for Liberace.

George Arliss *Montgomery Royale* • Violet Heming *Mildred Miller* • Ivan Simpson *Battle* • Louise Closser Hale *Florence Royale* • Bette Davis *Grace Blair* • Andre Luguet *The King* • Donald Cook *Harold Van Adam* • Charles E Evans *The Doctor* ■ *Dir* John G Adolfi • *Scr* Julien Josephson, Maude Howell, from the play by Jules Eckert Goodman, from the short story *The Silent Voice* by Gouverneur Morris

The Man Who Shot Liberty Valance ★★★★ U

Western
1962 · US · BW · 118mins

A key late John Ford western, with James Stewart top-billed over John Wayne, and a superb Lee Marvin in support as the ironically titled Valance. The film's most famous epigram "Print the legend" effectively sums up the plot, which, told in flashback, depends on a twist that only a spoilsport would reveal. On its release, the movie was taken for granted, but with hindsight it can be reassessed as a major work, despite the awkward studio interiors, which hold it back from truly classic status. In Tom Doniphon and "Pilgrim" Ransom Stoddard, Wayne and Stewart created indelible western icons, and the film clearly shows the impact of the arrival of literacy upon an innocent, more primitive West. [video]

James Stewart *Ransom Stoddard* • John Wayne *Tom Doniphon* • Vera Miles *Hallie Stoddard* • Lee Marvin *Liberty Valance* • Edmond O'Brien *Dutton Peabody* • Andy Devine *Link Appleyard* • Woody Strode *Pompey* • Ken Murray *Doc Willoughby* • John Carradine *Major Cassius Starbuckle* ■ *Dir* John Ford • *Scr* Willis Goldbeck, James Warner Bellah, from a story by Dorothy M Johnson • *Cinematographer* William H Clothier [William Clothier]

The Man Who Understood Women ★★

Satirical drama 1959 · US · Colour · 135mins

Leslie Caron and Henry Fonda make up a May-December partnership in this overlong mix of comedy, romance and drama. Fonda is a film-maker who finds popular success by turning his new love, Caron, into a star. When she becomes involved with pilot Cesare Danova, however, Fonda gets jealous, and what could have been a hilarious satire on Hollywood turns into an unconvincing melodrama. The stars are good, but Nunnally Johnson, who writes, produces *and* directs, seems to lose his focus and his grip.

Leslie Caron *Ann Garantier* • Henry Fonda *Willie Bauche* • Cesare Danova *Marco Ranieri* • Myron McCormick *Preacher* • Marcel Dalio *Le Marne* • Conrad Nagel *GK* ■ *Dir* Nunnally Johnson • *Scr* Nunnally Johnson, from the novel *The Colors of Day* by Romain Gary

The Man Who Watched Trains Go By ★★

Mystery
1952 · UK · Colour · 78mins

Adapted from the novel by the prolific Georges Simenon, this was one of Claude Rains's rare assignments in his homeland. Notwithstanding the dreadful colour, the tale of a clerk who takes advantage of the accidental death of crooked boss Herbert Lom quickly involves, with director Harold French capturing the atmosphere of provincial France and Rains essaying the decent little man with unassuming ease. However, improbabilities tumble in on one another once the action switches to Paris and he falls into the clutches of the villainous Marta Toren.

Claude Rains *Kees Popinga* • Michael Nightingale *Clerk* • Felix Aylmer *Merkemans* • Herbert Lom *Julius de Koster Jr* • Gibb McLaughlin *Julius de Koster Sr* • Marius Goring *Lucas* • Marta Toren *Michele* ■ *Dir* Harold French • *Scr* Harold French, from the novel by Georges Simenon

The Man Who Would Be King ★★★★★ PG

Adventure
1975 · US · Colour · 123mins

Rudyard Kipling's right royal adventure set in Afghanistan in the 1880s, with Sean Connery and Michael Caine as veteran army squaddies bamboozling a remote tribe into accepting Connery's regal credentials. Greed and circumstances topple the comic elements of the tale into a serious fable about the vanity of human endeavour, in keeping with Kipling's original story and the philosophy of director John Huston's greatest movies. Huston matches character to action in masterly fashion, aided by an aloof commentary by Christopher Plummer, as Kipling himself. Contains violence and swearing. [video]

Sean Connery *Daniel Dravot* • Michael Caine *Peachy Carnehan* • Christopher Plummer *Rudyard Kipling* • Saeed Jaffrey *Billy Fish* • Karroum Ben Bouih *Kafu-Selim* • Jack May *District commissioner* • Doghmi Larbi *Ootah* • Shakira Caine *Roxanne* ■ *Dir* John Huston • *Scr* John Huston, Gladys Hill, from the story by Rudyard Kipling • *Cinematographer* Oswald Morris • *Music* Maurice Jarre

The Man Who Would Not Die ★★

Mystery thriller 1975 · US · Colour · 83mins

There's a fascinating plot struggling to get out of this muddled affair, in which Alex Sheafe investigates a series of mysterious deaths only to discover that they are tied to an elaborate robbery scam. Screen veterans Keenan Wynn, Dorothy Malone and Aldo Ray are unable to muster much enthusiasm, and director Robert Arkless seems to have less idea about what is going on than the audience.

Dorothy Malone *Paula Stafford* • Keenan Wynn *Victor Slidell* • Aldo Ray *Frank Keefer* • Alex Sheafe *Marc Rogers* • Joyce Ingalls *Pat Reagan* • Fred Scollay *Lieutenant Willetts* • James Monks *Mr Reagan* ■ *Dir* Robert Arkless • *Scr* Robert Arkless, George Chesbro, Stephen Taylor, from the novel *The Sailcloth Shroud* by Charles Williams

The Man Who Wouldn't Die ★★★ PG

Mystery
1995 · US · Colour · 88mins

Why aren't there more TV movies with the same dark sense of fun as this one? Take one crime novelist, have him meet a waitress (who is also a medium) and have her announce that the supposedly dead villain on whom he based one of his characters is not only very much alive, but is busy re-enacting the killings his monarchy-mad murderer perpetrated on the page. Cracking stuff, directed at full tilt by Bill Condon with splendidly hammy performances from Roger Moore, Malcolm McDowell and Nancy Allen. Contains violence. [video]

Roger Moore *Thomas Grace/Fullbright* • Malcolm McDowell *Drake/Morrissey* • Nancy Allen *Jesse* • Michael Puttonen *Frank* • Wendy Van Riesen *Ingrid* • Scott Bellis *Boris* • Don MacKay *Henry Graham* • Eric McCormack *Bill Sullivan* ■ *Dir* Bill Condon • *Scr* David Amann

The Man Who Wouldn't Talk ★★★

Crime drama
1940 · US · BW · 72mins

Lloyd Nolan has one of his strongest roles playing the mysterious figure who confesses to killing a businessman, yet steadfastly refuses to reveal his true identity or motive. This entertaining Fox B-feature was the second screen version of a twenties play, having previously served as the basis of Paul Muni's first film, *The Valiant* (1929). The previously tragic ending is discarded, and the film gains a topical anti-German slant when the dead man is revealed to have been an enemy spy during the First World War.

Lloyd Nolan *Joe Monday* • Jean Rogers *Alice Stetson* • Richard Clarke *Steve Phillips* • Onslow Stevens *Frederick Keller* • Eric Blore *Horace Parker* ■ *Dir* David Burton • *Scr* Robert Ellis, Helen Logan, Lester Ziffren, Edward Ettinger, from the play *The Valiant* by Holworthy Hall, Robert M Middlemass

The Man Who Wouldn't Talk ★★ U

Courtroom drama 1957 · UK · BW · 108mins

Producer/director Herbert Wilcox makes a moderately entertaining film out of this courtroom drama in which Anthony Quayle's American scientist, accused of murder, refuses to testify in his own defence. Wilcox's wife, Anna Neagle, gives another of her great lady portraits as Britain's leading Queen's Counsel, demonstrating her deductive brilliance in spotting a bullet hole in a witness's window pane and her oratorical skills in a dramatic five-minute courtroom address. She easily eclipses Zsa Zsa Gabor.

Anthony Quayle *Dr Frank Smith* • Anna Neagle *Mary Randall QC* • Zsa Zsa Gabor *Eve Trent* • Katherine Kath *Yvonne Delbeau* • Dora Bryan *Telephonist* • Patrick Allen *Kennedy* • Hugh McDermott *Bernie* ■ *Dir* Herbert Wilcox • *Scr* Edgar Lustgarten, from the book by Stanley Jackson • *Producer* Herbert Wilcox

The Man with a Cloak ★★ U

Period drama
1951 · US · BW · 80mins

In 19th-century New York, villainous housekeeper Barbara Stanwyck schemes to murder Louis Calhern and cheat innocent young Leslie Caron out of her inheritance. Mysterious stranger Joseph Cotten arrives on the scene to save the day, turning out, quite inexplicably, to be Edgar Allan Poe. A bemusing period farrago, directed by Fletcher Markle, that would deserve to sink without trace were it not for Stanwyck's characteristically uncompromising performance.

Joseph Cotten *Dupin* • Barbara Stanwyck *Lorna Bounty* • Louis Calhern *Thevenet* • Leslie Caron *Madeline Minot* • Joe De Santis *Martin* • Jim Backus *Flaherty* • Margaret Wycherly *Mrs Flynn* • Richard Hale *Durand* ■ *Dir* Fletcher Markle • *Scr* Frank Fenton, from a story by John Dickson Carr

Man with a Gun ★★ 18

Crime drama
1995 · US · Colour · 91mins

A standard contemporary *noir* tale distinguished by a better-than-average cast. Michael Madsen stars as an assassin brought in by loan shark Gary Busey to murder his wife, Jennifer Tilly, who's stolen a valuable CD-Rom – this is the nineties, after all. When Tilly reveals that she has a twin sister, the usual genre twists and turns kick in, but it's all a bit gloomy and lacking sparkle. Given the strength of the players – Madsen manages to bring a shade of sensitivity to his hired killer, Tilly has fun with her good twin/bad twin roles – this has to count as a missed opportunity. [video]

Michael Madsen *John Hardin* • Jennifer Tilly *Rena Rushton/Kathy Payne* • Gary Busey *Jack Rushton* • Robert Loggia *Philip Marquand* • Ian Tracey *Roy Burchill* • Bill Cobbs *Henry*

896

U = SUITABLE FOR ALL Uc = SUITABLE FOR ALL, ESPECIALLY FOR YOUNG CHILDREN (VIDEO ONLY) PG = PARENTAL GUIDANCE

Griggs ■ Dir David Wyles • Scr Laurie Finstad-Knizhnik, from the novel *The Shroud Society* by Hugh C Rae

Man with a Movie Camera ★★★★★

Silent experimental documentary
1929 · USSR · BW · 67mins

Dziga Vertov claimed that his purpose in making this remarkable panorama of Moscow life – the workers, shoppers, holidaymakers and machines that keep the city moving – was to film "life as it is". To achieve this, Vertov displayed all the techniques of cinema at his disposal: split-screen, dissolves, slow-motion and freeze frames. Indeed, it's the camera that is the hero of this influential documentary. Born Denis Kaufman, Vertov took his name from the Ukrainian words meaning spinning, turning or, appropriately, revolution.

Dir/Scr Dziga Vertov • *Cinematographer* Mikhail Kaufman

The Man with Bogart's Face ★★★

Comedy mystery
1980 · US · Colour · 111mins

An enjoyable, unassuming movie buff in-joke about a second-rate private eye called Sam Marlow who has plastic surgery to make him look like his role model, Humphrey Bogart. It's a neat idea, and Bogart clone Robert Sacchi could certainly be mistaken for Bogie on a darkly lit mean street. The *Maltese Falcon*-style plot involves Alexander the Great's sapphires, with Victor Buono and Herbert Lom in the Greenstreet and Lorre roles.

Robert Sacchi *Sam Marlow* • Michelle Phillips *Gena* • Franco Nero *Hakim* • Olivia Hussey *Elsa* • Victor Buono *Commodore Anastas* • Herbert Lom *Mr Zebra* • George Raft *Petey Cane* ■ *Dir* Robert Day • *Scr* Andrew J Fenady, from his novel

The Man with One Red Shoe ★★ PG

Comedy
1985 · US · Colour · 88mins

Hollywood has no qualms about trawling foreign climes for inspirational ideas and turning them into blandly inoffensive pap. This time around, however, the source is the French farce *The Tall Blond Man with One Black Shoe*, which itself limps along unfunnily in the slow lane. Unsurprisingly, so does the remake, making little use of Tom Hanks's considerable comic talents. Marooned by inanity and mistiming, he plays a violinist who is mistaken for a spy. ▭

Tom Hanks *Richard* • Dabney Coleman *Cooper* • Lori Singer *Maddy* • Charles Durning *Ross* • Carrie Fisher *Paula* • Edward Herrmann *Brown* • Jim Belushi [James Belushi] *Morris* ■ *Dir* Stan Dragoti • *Scr* Robert Klane, from the film *The Tall Blond Man with One Black Shoe* by Francis Veber, Yves Robert

The Man with the Deadly Lens ★★★ 15

Satirical conspiracy thriller
1982 · US · Colour · 113mins

This thriller finds roving TV journalist Sean Connery uncovering a hornet's nest of conspiracies and terrorist links at the heart of the US Government.

The tone is often satirical but there are so many plots, subplots and red herrings that it's hard to figure out if it's a mess or immensely sophisticated. However, Connery is an anchorman in every respect, giving the film a firm foundation and a moral centre. Writer/director Richard Brooks is better known for *Elmer Gantry* and *Cat on a Hot Tin Roof*. ▭

Sean Connery *Patrick Hale* • George Grizzard *President Lockwood* • Robert Conrad *General Wombat* • Katharine Ross *Sally Blake* • GD Spradlin *Philindros* • John Saxon *Homer Hubbard* • Henry Silva *Rafeeq* • Leslie Nielsen *Mallory* ■ *Dir* Richard Brooks • *Scr* Richard Brooks, from the novel *The Better Angels* by Charles McCarry

The Man with the Golden Arm ★★★★ 15

Drama
1955 · US · BW · 114mins

This is to drug addiction what *The Lost Weekend* was to alcoholism – a trailblazer, directed by Otto Preminger whose gloating over controversial subject matter made him the Oliver Stone of his day. From Saul Bass's opening credits to Elmer Bernstein's jazzy score, the movie boasts its modernity in its unflinching approach to the story of an aspiring musician and heroin addict. *Trainspotting* it isn't but, in the clean-cut Eisenhower era, this movie shocked audiences deeply. In any event, Frank Sinatra's Oscar-nominated performance still impresses, as do those of Eleanor Parker as his wife and Kim Novak as Sinatra's object of desire. ▭

Frank Sinatra *Frankie Machine* • Kim Novak *Molly* • Eleanor Parker *Zosch Machine* • Arnold Stang *Sparrow* • Darren McGavin *Louie* • Robert Strauss *Schwiefka* • George Mathews *Williams* • John Conte *Drunky* ■ *Dir* Otto Preminger • *Scr* Walter Newman, Lewis Meltzer, from the novel by Nelson Algren

The Man with the Golden Gun ★★★ PG

Spy adventure
1974 · UK · Colour · 119mins

This is an improvement on Ian Fleming's novel, with Christopher Lee making a fine villain, sporting a golden gun, a third nipple and a midget henchman called Nick Nack, wittily played by Herve Villechaize. Britt Ekland is funny, too, sending herself up as Bond's clueless assistant and surviving the most sexist scene in the entire 007 series: "Forgive me darling, your turn will come," Roger Moore assures her after he's dallied with Maud Adams. There are major faults as well – notably the repeat of the pre-credit scene for the climax (borrowing from Orson Welles's *The Lady from Shanghai*) and the return of redneck sheriff Clifton James from *Live and Let Die*. Thailand's Phang-Nga Bay was a stunning choice of location, though it was soon to become a tourist trap. ▭

Roger Moore *James Bond* • Christopher Lee *Scaramanga* • Britt Ekland *Mary Goodnight* • Maud Adams *Andrea* • Herve Villechaize *Nick Nack* • Clifton James *Sheriff JW Pepper* • Soon Taik Oh [Soon-Teck Oh] *Hip* • Richard Loo *Hai Fat* • Bernard Lee *"M"* • Lois Maxwell *Miss Moneypenny* • Marc Lawrence *Rodney* • Desmond Llewelyn *"Q"* ■ *Dir* Guy Hamilton • *Scr* Richard Maibaum, Tom Mankiewicz, from the novel by Ian Fleming

Man with the Gun ★★★

Western
1955 · BW · 83mins

One of Robert Mitchum's strengths was his ability to grab a western like this by its throat and turn it into a personal statement. Mitchum plays a brooding gunman who cleans up a town to try to win back his estranged wife, played by the excellent Jan Sterling. There's a fair amount of sadism on show, and the mood and tone are satisfyingly grim. It's an impressive directorial debut from former Orson Welles associate Richard Wilson. Watch for a young Angie Dickinson in an early role, and enjoy the fine photography from the great veteran Lee Garmes, who'd worked on such outstanding films as *Shanghai Express*, *Scarface* and *Duel in the Sun*.

Robert Mitchum *Clint Tollinger* • Jan Sterling *Nelly Bain* • Karen Sharpe *Stella Atkins* • Henry Hull *Marshal Sims* • Emile Meyer *Saul Atkins* • John Lupton *Jeff Castle* • Barbara Lawrence *Ann Wakefield* • Angie Dickinson *Kitty* ■ *Dir* Richard Wilson • *Scr* NB Stone Jr, Richard Wilson

The Man with the Power ★★★

Science-fiction
1977 · US · Colour

Unmomentous but diverting TV movie about a man who inherits psychokinetic powers from his father, a native of a distant planet. He is forced to call on them when he is assigned the task of guarding a beautiful Bengali princess. Persis Khambatta, is suitably decorative as the princess in peril, while Vic Morrow, who played the heavy in countless movies, turns up as a kidnapper.

Bob Neill *Eric Smith* • Tim O'Connor *Agent Walter Bloom* • Vic Morrow *Paul* • Persis Khambatta *Princess Siri* • Roger Perry *Farnsworth* • Rene Assa *Major Sajid* ■ *Dir* Nicholas Sgarro • *Scr* Allan Balter

The Man with the X-Ray Eyes ★★★★ PG

Science-fiction thriller
1963 · US · Colour · 75mins

Ray Milland plays one of his best remembered roles in Roger Corman's pocket-sized, yet highly potent, sci-fi shocker. He is scientist Dr Xavier, who experiments on himself and gains the power to see through solid materials. But as his sight gets stronger, so do the side-effects – Corman's cue to move from playful sideshow terror to mystical allegory, with plenty of engaging surreal imagery along the way. The Bible provided the inspiration for this cult classic, something clearly evident in the unforgettable revival-meeting climax. ▭

Ray Milland *Dr James Xavier* • Diana Van Der Vlis *Dr Diane Fairfax* • Harold J Stone *Dr Sam Brant* • John Hoyt *Dr Willard Benson* • Don Rickles *Crane* • Lorie Summers *Carnival owner/party dancer* • Vicki Lee *Young girl patient* • Kathryn Hart *Mrs Mart* ■ *Dir* Roger Corman • *Scr* Robert Dillon, Ray Russell, from the story by Ray Russell

The Man with Two Brains ★★★★★ 15

Comedy
1983 · US · Colour · 85mins

There have been more accomplished Steve Martin films (*Roxanne*, *LA Story*),

but this remains his finest moment: a dazzlingly inventive comedy that contains more laughs than his last half dozen movies put together. Martin is Doctor Hfuhruhurr, the brilliant brain surgeon who marries black widow Kathleen Turner but falls for a disembodied brain, voiced by Sissy Spacek. Martin gets to read his favourite poem ("Pointy Birds"), carry out a citizen's divorce and endure the world's toughest drink-driving test; and Turner hilariously sends up the *femme fatale* persona she established in *Body Heat*. David Warner co-stars as a fellow mad scientist, and there is also a surprise cameo in the form of the Elevator Killer. Sublime. ▭

Steve Martin *Dr Michael Hfuhruhurr* • Kathleen Turner *Dolores Benedict* • David Warner *Dr Necessiter* • Paul Benedict *Butler* • Richard Brestoff *Dr Pasteur* • James Cromwell *Realtor* • George Furth *Timon* • Peter Hobbs *Dr Brandon* ■ *Dir* Carl Reiner • *Scr* Steve Martin, Carl Reiner, George Gipe

The Man Within ★★★

Historical adventure
1947 · UK · BW · 87mins

Set in 19th-century Sussex, Graham Greene's first published novel tells the story of an orphaned teenager, played by Richard Attenborough, who shops his guardian (Michael Redgrave), a smuggler. Greene thought this tale of guilt, identity and moral redemption was "embarrassingly sentimental", and he dismissed Bernard Knowles's film version as a treachery, having pocketed £300 for the screen rights.

Michael Redgrave *Richard Carlyon* • Jean Kent *Lucy* • Joan Greenwood *Elizabeth* • Richard Attenborough *Francis Andrews* • Francis L Sullivan *Mr Braddock* • Felix Aylmer *Priest* • Ronald Shiner *Cockney Harry* • Basil Sydney *Sir Henry Merriman* • Ernest Thesiger *Farne* ■ *Dir* Bernard Knowles • *Scr* Muriel Box, Bernard Box, from the novel by Graham Greene

The Man without a Body ★

Horror
1957 · UK · BW · 80mins

Rock-bottom British shocker with an almost wilfully stupid story about a surgeon who revives Nostradamus's head and later grafts it on to someone else's body. (Don't ask why.) The only interesting thing is that both directors had more famous siblings: W Lee Wilder was Billy's brother, and Charles Saunders is the brother of *Mousetrap* producer Peter. Some of the same team went on to produce the similarly maniacal *Woman Eater*.

Robert Hutton *Dr Phil Merritt* • George Coulouris *Karl Brussard* • Julia Arnall *Jean Kramer* • Nadja Regin *Odette Vernet* • Sheldon Lawrence *Dr Lew Waldenhaus* • Michael Golden *Nostradamus* ■ *Dir* W Lee Wilder, Charles Saunders • *Scr* William Grote

The Man without a Face ★★★ 15

Drama
1993 · US · Colour · 109mins

Mel Gibson marked his directorial debut with this low-key, coming-of-age drama set in the late sixties. Gibson plays the horribly scarred former teacher, who lives a reclusive life away from the gossip of his small-town neighbours. He is gradually drawn out of his shell by an unhappy young boy (Nick Stahl), but their close relationship eventually comes back to haunt him. Gibson takes a back seat to his young lead, and Stahl doesn't disappoint, delivering a moving, intense performance. The supporting characters are also skilfully drawn, including Margaret Whitton as Stahl's marriage-happy mother, and although the direction sometimes errs on the side of sentimentality, it remains an assured debut. 🖵

Mel Gibson *Justin McLeod* • Margaret Whitton *Catherine* • Fay Masterson *Gloria* • Gaby Hoffman *Megan* • Geoffrey Lewis *Chief Stark* • Richard Masur *Carl* • Nick Stahl *Chuck Norstadt* • Michael DeLuise *Douglas Hall* ■ *Dir* Mel Gibson • *Scr* Malcolm MacRury, from the novel by Isabelle Holland

Man without a Star ★★★★
Western 1955 · US · Colour · 89mins

A fine Technicolor western made by King Vidor and featuring the wonderful Kirk Douglas in an all-grinning, all-snarling portrayal, the kind of role he was born to play. The tremendous sexual tension generated between Douglas and manipulative ranch owner Jeanne Crain is reminiscent of Vidor's other two studied dramas, *Duel in the Sun* and *Ruby Gentry*. The psychological slant is also cleverly integrated, as juvenile William Campbell idolises the no-good Douglas; there's also some welcome by-play from *Stagecoach's* Claire Trevor as the other woman. Remade, poorly, in 1969 as *A Man Called Gannon*.

Kirk Douglas *Dempsey Rae* • Jeanne Crain *Reed Bowman* • Claire Trevor *Idonee* • William Campbell *Jeff Jimson* • Jay C Flippen *Strap Davis* • Myrna Hansen *Tess Cassidy* • Mara Corday *Moccasin Mary* • Eddy C Waller [Eddy Waller] *Bill Cassidy* • Richard Boone *Steve Miles* ■ *Dir* King Vidor • *Scr* Borden Chase, DD Beauchamp, from the novel by Dee Linford

Man, Woman and Child
★★★ **PG**
Drama 1983 · US · Colour · 96mins

Adapting his own novel, Erich Segal teamed with David Zelag Goodman for this unashamed weepie. Every bit as sentimental as *Love Story*, it provides an unusually soft-centred role for Martin Sheen, as the happily married man who discovers that the French dalliance of a decade ago resulted in a son. But it's Blythe Danner who will have you reaching for the tissues as the wife trying to come to terms with the new member of her family. A distinct change of pace for director Dick Richards, whose previous best effort had been a reworking of *Farewell My Lovely*.

Martin Sheen *Robert Beckwith* • Blythe Danner *Sheila Beckwith* • Craig T Nelson *Bernie Ackerman* • David Hemmings *Gavin Wilson* • Nathalie Nell *Nicole Guerin* • Maureen Anderman *Margo* ■ *Dir* Dick Richards • *Scr* Erich Segal, David Zelag Goodman, from the novel by Erich Segal

The Manchu Eagle Murder Caper Mystery
★★
Spoof detective drama
1973 · US · Colour · 80mins

An eager but unsuccessful lampoon of the detective thriller genre, starring Gabriel Dell as a would-be private eye trying to find out who murdered the milkman, of all people. Writer/director

Dean Hargrove has a fine track record in TV detection, being the creative force behind *Matlock* and *Jake and the Fatman*, but his sure hand falters away from the police procedurals that made his reputation.

Gabriel Dell *Malcolm* • Will Geer *Dr Simpson* • Joyce Van Patten *Ida Mae* • Anjanette Comer *Arlevia* • Vincent Gardenia *Big Daddy* • Barbara Harris *Miss Fredericks* • Jackie Coogan *Sheriff* ■ *Dir* Dean Hargrove • *Scr* Dean Hargrove, Gabriel Dell

The Manchurian Candidate
★★★★★ **15**
Psychological thriller
1962 · US · BW · 121mins

A fearfully prophetic thriller about a political assassination. Based on Richard Condon's novel, co-written by George Axelrod and director John Frankenheimer, it stars Laurence Harvey, who's wonderfully creepy as a war hero brainwashed and programmed by Korean communists to eliminate a presidential candidate. Frank Sinatra is Harvey's ex-comrade trying to find the truth, Janet Leigh provides the sexual angle and Angela Lansbury is Harvey's utterly terrifying mother. Blackly comic and suspenseful, it ranks with Stanley Kubrick's *Dr Strangelove* as one of the toughest and most original films of the sixties. Following the assassination of JFK in 1963, Sinatra had the film withdrawn for many years. 🖵

Frank Sinatra *Bennett Marco* • Laurence Harvey *Raymond Shaw* • Janet Leigh *Rosie* • Angela Lansbury *Raymond's mother* • Henry Silva *Chunjim* • James Gregory *Senator John Iselin* • Leslie Parrish *Jocie Jordon* • John McGiver *Senator Thomas Jordon* ■ *Dir* John Frankenheimer • *Scr* George Axelrod, John Frankenheimer, from the novel by Richard Condon • *Cinematographer* Lionel Lindon • *Art Director* Richard Sylbert

Mandalay
★★
Melodrama 1934 · US · BW · 65mins

Good-time girl Kay Francis, doctor Lyle Talbot and gunrunner Ricardo Cortez are all up the Irrawaddy without a paddle in this Warner Bros melodrama. Set in a Burma that exists only on the studio backlot, Michael Curtiz's film seems to draw most of its inspiration from MGM's *Red Dust*, in which Clark Gable got all steamed up over Jean Harlow. Unfortunately, the creaky plot and arthritic performances mean that *Mandalay* is really showing its age. Shirley Temple has a small role.

Kay Francis *Tanya Borisoff/Spot White* • Ricardo Cortez *Tony Evans* • Warner Oland *Nick* • Lyle Talbot *Dr Gregory Burton* • Ruth Donnelly *Mrs Peters* • Reginald Owen *Police commissioner* • Shirley Temple *Betty Shaw* ■ *Dir* Michael Curtiz • *Scr* Austin Parker, Charles Kenyon, from a story by Paul Hervey Fox

Mandela
★★★★ **PG**
Biographical documentary
1995 · US · Colour · 143mins

Oscar-nominated, definitive documentary about the father of the new South Africa, which benefits immeasurably from having much of it fronted by Mandela himself. Afforded apparently unlimited access to the man, the film-makers trace Mandela's life from his humble village origins, through his early ANC involvement and lengthy incarceration by the white

minority government, right up to his very public distancing from troublesome second wife Winnie. Particularly moving are Mandela's returns to the village of his birth and the cell where he was imprisoned for almost three decades. 🖵

Nelson Mandela • Nomzamo Winnie Mandela ■ *Dir* Jo Menell, Angus Gibson

Mandela and de Klerk
★★★ **PG**
Political drama 1997 · US · Colour · 109mins

One of the problems of making a film about recent events is that the screenwriter has to tiptoe around the sensibilities of extant characters. Moreover, at such a short remove, the truth is never fully known. Consequently, this worthy TV movie can only tell part of the story of how Nelson Mandela and FW de Klerk jointly earned the Nobel Peace Prize for their efforts in bringing about democracy in South Africa. As the ANC leader who is thrust back into the limelight after 27 years' imprisonment, Sidney Poitier has the requisite dignity and determination. But Michael Caine's Afrikaaner president is the more grounded performance. 🖵

Sidney Poitier *Nelson Mandela* • Michael Caine *FW de Klerk* • Tina Lifford *Winnie Mandela* • Gerry Maritz *PW Botha* • Terry Norton *Marike de Klerk* ■ *Dir* Joseph Sargent • *Scr* Richard Wesley

Mandingo
★★★★ **18**
Drama 1975 · US · Colour · 120mins

From *Gone with the Wind* downwards, Hollywood always had a romantic and sanitised view of what really went on in the Old South. This full-blooded excursion into American Gothic puts the lie to all that. Plantation owner James Mason festers away in a rotten old mansion, his feet resting on a black boy so that his disease will feed from him to the child. Mason's son (Perry King) keeps a harem of women slaves, while his wife, a sweaty Susan George, has sex with one of the slaves Mason trains to be a fighter. Vilified by most critics at the time, this is a head-on examination of a culture that wasn't simply black and white, but had several shades of grey in between. It's also one of the bravest and greatest American movies of the seventies. 🖵

James Mason *Warren Maxwell* • Susan George *Blanche* • Perry King *Hammond Maxwell* • Richard Ward *Agamemnon* • Brenda Sykes *Ellen* • Ken Norton *Mede* • Lillian Hayman *Lucrezia Borgia* ■ *Dir* Richard Fleischer • *Scr* Norman Wexler, from the play by Jack Kirkland, from the novel by Kyle Onstott

Mandy
★★★★ **PG**
Drama 1952 · UK · BW · 89mins

Whisky Galore! director Alexander Mackendrick's only non-comedy during his stay at Ealing is a highly intelligent film with as much to say about the generation gap (albeit in a smaller voice) as such outspoken Hollywood teen pictures as *Rebel without a Cause*. Mandy Miller gives a performance of remarkable charm and insight as the deaf-mute child whose silent world is opened up by committed headmaster Jack Hawkins. An

unusually unsympathetic Phyllis Calvert and Terence Morgan do well as Mandy's feuding parents and there is a standout turn from Godfrey Tearle as her embittered grandfather. 🖵

Phyllis Calvert *Christine* • Jack Hawkins *Searle* • Terence Morgan *Harry* • Godfrey Tearle *Mr Garland* • Mandy Miller *Mandy* • Marjorie Fielding *Mrs Garland* • Nancy Price *Jane Ellis* • Edward Chapman *Ackland* ■ *Dir* Alexander Mackendrick • *Scr* Nigel Balchin, Jack Whittingham, from the novel *The Day is Ours* by Hilda Lewis

The Mangler
★★ **18**
Horror 1994 · US · Colour · 101mins

Stephen King-based stuff and nonsense about a possessed speed-ironing machine at a rural laundry which demands a virgin sacrifice every so often if the town's bigwigs want to remain prosperous. Horror icon Robert Englund chews the scenery in this shock-less wonder as the crotchety laundry owner, covered in old-age make-up and wearing designer leg braces, who made a pact with the Devil years before. Tobe Hooper's direction is also on crutches. 🖵

Robert Englund *Bill Gartley* • Ted Levine *John Hunton* • Daniel Matmor *Mark Jackson* • Jeremy Crutchley *Pictureman Mortician* • Vanessa Pike *Sherry Ouelette* ■ *Dir* Tobe Hooper • *Scr* Tobe Hooper, Stephen Brooks, Peter Welbeck [Harry Alan Towers], from a story by Stephen King

The Mango Tree
★★
Drama 1977 · Ausl · Colour · 105mins

A coming-of-age story set in Australia after the First World War, director Kevin James Dobson's period piece is an ambitious but fatally flawed attempt to place a small-scale drama – a troubled teenager's relationship with his aged grandmother – against a larger backdrop. All human life is here, including issues of family, society and sexuality, and there's even an action-packed hunt for a deranged preacher. But ultimately the different strands of the script fail to hang together. Geraldine Fitzgerald is excellent as the wisdom-spouting matriarch, but Christopher Pate looks ten years too old as the tentative adolescent.

Geraldine Fitzgerald *Grandma Carr* • Robert Helpmann *Professor* • Christopher Pate *Jamie Carr* • Gerard Kennedy *Preacher Jones* • Gloria Dawn *Pearl* • Carol Burns *Maudie Plover* ■ *Dir* Kevin James Dobson • *Scr* Michael Pate, from the novel by Ronald McKie

Manhattan
★★★★★ **15**
Comedy drama 1979 · US · BW · 92mins

An early masterpiece from Woody Allen, which celebrates, as ever, his beloved New York. Allen stars as Isaac, a neurotic TV writer who's taken up with 17-year-old Mariel Hemingway, but who's being diverted by fast-talking Diane Keaton and – more dangerously – by the book written about him by his lesbian ex-wife Meryl Streep. Allen and his fellow New Yorkers swan in and out of the cultural byways of the Big Apple, indulging in psychiatric therapy that's never quite the cure-all they crave. The characters could have become over-articulate bores, but Allen manages to invest them with the saving grace of humanity. This is a wonderful film, with a George Gershwin score that adds

U = SUITABLE FOR ALL **Uc** = SUITABLE FOR ALL, ESPECIALLY FOR YOUNG CHILDREN (VIDEO ONLY) **PG** = PARENTAL GUIDANCE

just the right amount of poignancy. DVD

Woody Allen *Isaac Davis* • Diane Keaton *Mary Wilke* • Meryl Streep *Jill* • Mariel Hemingway *Tracy* • Michael Murphy *Yale* • Anne Byrne *Emily* • Karen Ludwig *Connie* • Michael O'Donoghue *Dennis* ■ *Dir* Woody Allen • *Scr* Woody Allen, Marshall Brickman • *Cinematographer* Gordon Willis

Manhattan Melodrama ★★

Crime drama 1934 · US · BW · 93mins

On 22 July 1934, John Dillinger went to see *Manhattan Melodrama* at the Biograph in Chicago. He was shot dead by G-men on leaving the cinema. The film he saw is a heavily moralistic drama featuring Mickey Rooney in a childhood flashback that explains why Blackie Gallagher (Clark Gable) became a racketeer and killer. While *Manhattan Melodrama* has its wisecracking, stylish moments, it's mostly cringe-inducing – though it does mark the first teaming of William Powell and Myrna Loy, who went on to make the successful *Thin Man* films.

Clark Gable *Blackie Gallagher* • William Powell *Jim Wade* • Myrna Loy *Eleanor* • Leo Carrillo *Father Joe* • Nat Pendleton *Spud* • George Sidney *Poppa Rosen* • Mickey Rooney *Blackie as a boy* ■ *Dir* WS Van Dyke II [WS Van Dyke] • *Scr* Oliver HP Garrett, Joseph L Mankiewicz, from the story *Three Men* by Arthur Caesar

Manhattan Murder Mystery ★★★★ PG

Comedy 1993 · US · Colour · 103mins

This lightweight comedy clearly bears the hallmark of being an uncontentious romp that would keep Woody Allen occupied while he awaited his day in court with ex-partner Mia Farrow. Another couple of hours pounding away at the typewriter clearly wouldn't have gone amiss, but this is a hugely enjoyable little film that slyly mocks the pretensions of Manhattan's well-heeled intelligentsia. The role originally intended for Farrow is taken by Diane Keaton, and the ease with which she and Allen combine leaves you longing for just one more reunion.

Alan Alda *Ted* • Woody Allen *Larry Lipton* • Diane Keaton *Carol Lipton* • Anjelica Huston *Marcia Fox* • Jerry Adler *Paul House* • Joy Behar *Marilyn* • Ron Rifkin *Sy* • Lynn Cohen *Lillian House* ■ *Dir* Woody Allen • *Scr* Woody Allen, Marshall Brickman

Manhunt for Claude Dallas ★★★

Drama based on a true story 1986 · US · Colour · 93mins

A gripping drama that could only have happened in America. Matt Salinger (the son, incidentally, of *Catcher in the Rye* author JD Salinger) plays the title character, a recluse from the mountains who goes on a murderous rampage and then proceeds to run rings around his increasingly frustrated pursuers. Salinger delivers a powerful performance and is well supported by Rip Torn and Lois Nettleton.

Matt Salinger *Claude Dallas Jr* • Claude Akins *Bill Pogue* • Beau Starr *Ed Pogue* • Frederick Coffin *Frank Weston* • Lois Nettleton *Dee Pogue* • Pat Hingle *George Nielsen* • Rip Torn *Tim Nettleton* • Annette Bening *Ann Tillman* ■ *Dir* Jerry London • *Scr* John Gay, from the book *Outlaw* by Jeff Long

Manhunt: Search for the Night Stalker ★★★ 15

Drama 1989 · US · Colour · 89mins

A gripping made-for-TV drama based on the true case of the hunt for the serial killer dubbed the "Night Stalker", a burglar, rapist and murderer who terrorised California in 1985. A Martinez and Richard Jordan star as the two cops who become obsessed with catching the killer, who earned his nickname by sneaking into people's homes to commit crimes as they slept. One of the better handled and less sensational entries in the true crime genre, made all the more plausible by the performances of the two leads.

A Martinez *Gil Carrillo* • Richard Jordan *Frank Salerno* • Lisa Eilbacher *Ann Clark* • Julie Carmen *Pearl Carrillo* • Jenny Sullivan *Jane Salerno* • Max Segar *Sheriff Block* ■ *Dir* Bruce Seth Green • *Scr* Joseph Gunn

The Manhunter ★★

Thriller 1968 · US · Colour · 98mins

Well-played but often confusing hokum, with Roy Thinnes as a big-game hunter who finds man is his quarry when he's sent on the trail of a bank robber. The pursuit leads him through the Louisiana swamps and into the arms of Sandra Dee, the unlikeliest Cajun you'll ever come across. Director Don Taylor (*Escape from the Planet of the Apes*) keeps the action moving.

Sandra Dee *Mara* • Roy Thinnes *David Farrow* • Albert Salmi *Rafe Augustine* • Sorrell Booke *Carl Auscher* • David Brian *Walter Sinclair* • Royal Dano *Pa Bocock* ■ *Dir* Don Taylor • *Scr* Meyer Dolinsky, from the novel by Wade Miller

The Manhunter ★★

Crime drama 1974 · US · Colour

Ken Howard is the ex-First World War marine on the trail of some gun-toting bad guys in this TV movie, which went on to become a short-lived TV series. Director Walter Grauman, best known for the RAF drama *633 Squadron*, keeps the action going. But there's little plot to sustain the film, and the whole effort is not helped by hammy acting by co-star Stefanie Powers.

Ken Howard *Dave Barrett* • Gary Lockwood *Frank Clinger* • Tim O'Connor *Ben Marks* • James Olson *Walt Hovis* • Stefanie Powers *Ann Louise Hovis* • LQ Jones *Charles "Crutch" Shanks* ■ *Dir* Walter Grauman • *Scr* Sam H Rolfe

Manhunter ★★★★ 18

Thriller 1986 · US · Colour · 114mins

Whether or not, as some contend, this is a better movie than *The Silence of the Lambs*, the second and more celebrated film adaptation of novelist Thomas Harris's source material, it is undoubtedly a gripping psycho-chiller. William Petersen plays the former FBI whiz, hauled from retirement to help hunt a sophisticated serial murderer. Strong performances, especially from Brian Cox as Hannibal Lecktor, combine with a clever plot and top-notch direction by Michael Mann to produce an atmospheric and arresting thriller. Contains violence and swearing. DVD

William Petersen *Will Graham* • Brian Cox *Dr Hannibal Lecktor* • Dennis Farina *Jack Crawford* • Kim Greist *Molly Graham* • Stephen Lang *Freddie Lounds* • Tom Noonan *Francis Dollarhyde* • Joan Allen *Reba* • Benjamin Hendrickson *Dr Chilton* ■ *Dir* Michael Mann • *Scr* Michael Mann, from the novel *Red Dragon* by Thomas Harris

Maniac ★★★

Crime thriller 1963 · UK · BW · 87mins

This psychological horror film is a typical Hammer programme-filler of the sixties. The convoluted mystery takes ages to set up, but some of the shocks (most memorably an attempted murder by blowtorch) have stood the test of time, and the twist ending is brilliant. The Camargue setting is unusual. Kerwin Mathews plays an American artist who becomes involved with a young woman (Liliane Brousse) and her stepmother (Nadia Gray) and agrees to help them spring Brousse's father (Donald Houston) from the loony bin. Not a good idea.

Kerwin Mathews *Geoff Farrell* • Nadia Gray *Eve Beynat* • Donald Houston *Georges Beynat* • Liliane Brousse *Annette Beynat* • George Pastell *Inspector Etienne* ■ *Dir* Michael Carreras • *Scr* Jimmy Sangster

Maniac ★★★

Crime drama 1977 · US · Colour · 84mins

A solid crime drama, in which a psychotic killer starts to bump off a small town's populace before demanding a million-dollar ransom to stop. The town's richest man isn't having any of it, though, and hires a mercenary to kill the killer. Oddball but interesting casting sees the likes of Stuart Whitman and Deborah Raffin acting opposite Oliver Reed. The film has its dull spots, but it remains watchable. Contains violence.

Oliver Reed *Nick McCormick* • Deborah Raffin *Cindy Simmons* • Stuart Whitman *William Whitaker* • Jim Mitchum [James Mitchum] *Tracker* • John Ireland *Chief Haliburton* ■ *Dir* Richard Compton • *Scr* John C Broderick, Ron Silkosky

Maniac Cop ★★ 18

Action horror 1988 · US · Colour · 81mins

True to its title, this features a maniac in a policeman's uniform loose on the streets of New York City, killing any innocent people who stray into his path and giving the NYPD a bad reputation they don't deserve. (Stop laughing!) Bruce Campbell is the cop who takes the fall for the true killer and eventually hunts him down. Fairly well written (by Larry Cohen of *It's Alive* fame), but the acting can't keep up and *Evil Dead* star Campbell is given too little to do.

Tom Atkins *Lieutenant Frank McCrae* • Bruce Campbell *Jack Forrest* • Laurene Landon *Theresa Mallory* • Richard Roundtree *Commissioner Pike* • William Smith *Captain Ripley* • Robert Z'Dar *Matt Cordell* ■ *Dir* William Lustig • *Scr* Larry Cohen

Maniac Cop 2 ★★ 18

Action horror 1990 · US · Colour · 83mins

An undead ex-cop goes on another gruesome killing rampage in this sequel to *Maniac Cop*, this time in concert with a serial killer who targets strippers – presumably to get the maximum amount of skin on screen. Screenwriter Larry Cohen decides to clean up the killer's image this time: now we're told he was an honest cop who was willing to prosecute powerful people, as opposed to the first movie, in which he was well known for violating suspects' civil rights. The heroes this time are played by Robert Davi and Claudia Christian.

Robert Davi *Detective Sean McKinney* • Claudia Christian *Susan Riley* • Michael Lerner *Edward Doyle* • Bruce Campbell *Jack Forrest* • Laurene Landon *Teresa Mallory* • Robert Z'Dar *Matt Cordell* • Clarence Williams III *Blum* ■ *Dir* William Lustig • *Scr* Larry Cohen

The Manitou ★★ 15

Horror 1978 · US · Colour · 98mins

Something very nasty is growing on Susan Strasberg's neck in this preposterous *Exorcist* clone. This time around, the demon is a 400-year-old Indian witch doctor seeking reincarnation in modern-day San Francisco. Tony Curtis, as a fake medium suddenly flung into the real world of the supernatural, is always worth watching, while the monster's first appearance has a certain visceral impact. The title derives from the native Indian word for a human's spirit inhabiting all things. According to this film, that includes typewriters.

Tony Curtis *Harry Erskine* • Michael Ansara *Singing Rock* • Susan Strasberg *Karen Tandy* • Stella Stevens *Amelia Crusoe* • Jon Cedar *Dr Jack Hughes* • Ann Sothern *Mrs Karmann* ■ *Dir* William Girdler • *Scr* William Girdler, Jon Cedar, Tom Pope, from the novel by Graham Masterson

Mannequin ★★★

Drama 1937 · US · BW · 92mins

Not Kim Cattrall coming to life in a department store window, but the fabulous Joan Crawford working her way out of the Lower East Side slums and into the arms of Spencer Tracy. Crawford, whose exquisite gowns come complete with influential Adrian shoulder pads, is totally miscast as the lower-class working girl. But this is an MGM star vehicle, with all that that implies: you've never seen such glossy tenements! Director Frank Borzage seems quite at home with this corny melodrama, and audiences lapped it up at the time.

Joan Crawford *Jessie Cassidy* • Spencer Tracy *John L Hennessey* • Alan Curtis *Eddie Miller* • Ralph Morgan *Briggs* • Mary Phillips [Mary Philips] *Beryl* • Oscar O'Shea *"Pa" Cassidy* • Elisabeth Risdon *Mrs Cassidy* • Leo Gorcey *Clifford* ■ *Dir* Frank Borzage • *Scr* Lawrence Hazard, from the story *Marry For Money* by Katherine Brush • *Costume Designer* Adrian

Mannequin ★★ PG

Comedy 1987 · US · Colour · 85mins

A bewilderingly successful comedy about a sculptor (Andrew McCarthy) who falls for a shop window dummy (Kim Cattrall). To everybody else, however, Cattrall is just an ordinary mannequin, which makes for a rather tricky romance. It requires a light, frothy touch, but director Michael Gottlieb instead takes it as a cue for some helpless mugging and crude slapstick. McCarthy is even more plastic than Cattrall, Meshach Taylor is a gruesome caricature as his sympathetic co-worker, while James Spader simply looks embarrassed.

Andrew McCarthy *Jonathan Switcher* • Kim Cattrall *Emmy* • Estelle Getty *Claire Timkin* • James Spader *Richards* • GW Bailey *Felix* • Carole Davis *Roxie* • Stephen Vinovich [Steve Vinovich] *BJ Wert* • Meshach Taylor *Hollywood* ■ *Dir* Michael Gottlieb • *Scr* Edward Rugoff, Michael Gottlieb

Mannequin on the Move

★ PG

Comedy 1991 · US · Colour · 91mins

If ever a movie didn't need a sequel, it was *Mannequin*. In another story of a lovesick woman returning from the past as a shop dummy, statuesque beauty Kristy Swanson asks us to spot when she's acting and when she's deliberately being inanimate. It's not all her fault: the script is so full of old gags it must have been chiselled on stone tablets, while Stewart Raffill's direction is a prime example of how not to let the action get in the way of product placements.

Kristy Swanson *Jessie* • William Ragsdale *Jason Williamson/Prince William* • Meshach Taylor *Hollywood Montrose/Doorman* • Terry Kiser *Count Spretzle/Sorcerer* • Stuart Pankin *Mr James* ■ *Dir* Stewart Raffill • *Scr* Edward Rugoff, David Isaacs, Ken Levine, Betsy Israel, from characters created by Edward Rugoff, Michael Gottlieb

Manon des Sources ★★★ U

Drama 1952 · Fr · BW · 144mins

Even though Marcel Pagnol was working from his own screenplay (later expanded into a novel, *L'Eau des Collines*), this poetic, over-ambitious adaptation is never as captivating as Claude Berri's 1986 remake. Originally running nearly five hours, the action meanders as Pagnol places a lyrical emphasis on the beauty of the landscape at the expense of taut storytelling. His wife, Jacqueline, struggles to convince in the title role, as she seeks revenge on the Soubeyrans for the death of her hunchbacked father. However, Henri Poupon and the lovesick Rellys are more impressive as her scheming adversaries. A French language film.

Jacqueline Pagnol *Manon Cadoret* • Raymond Pellegrin *Maurice, the schoolmaster* • Rellys *Ugolin* • Robert Vattier *Monsieur Belloiseau* • Henri Poupon *Le Papet, the uncle* • Henri Vilbert *The Priest* ■ *Dir/Scr* Marcel Pagnol

Manon des Sources

★★★★ PG

Drama 1986 · Fr/It/Swi · Colour · 108mins

The conclusion of Marcel Pagnol's *The Water of the Hills* takes place 10 years after the death of Jean de Florette. Once more the photography borders on the sublime and the direction is paced to suit life under the scorching sun. The script is less convincing this time, with melodrama seeping into too many scenes and an uncomfortable number of loose ends being neatly tied up in the closing moments. Yves Montand and Daniel Auteuil maintain their quality of performance, with the latter particularly impressive as he tries to atone for the wrong done to Manon (Emmanuelle Béart) and her family. In French with English subtitles.

Yves Montand *César Soubeyran, le Papet* • Daniel Auteuil *Ugolin Soubeyran* • Emmanuelle Béart *Manon Cadoret* • Elisabeth Depardieu *Aimée Cadoret* • Hippolyte Girardot *Bernard Olivier* • Margarita Lozano *Baptistine* • Gabriel Bacquier *Victor* • Ernestine Mazurowna *Young Manon* ■ *Dir* Claude Berri • *Scr* Gérard Brach, Claude Berri, from the novel *L'Eau des Collines* by Marcel Pagnol • *Cinematographer* Bruno Nuytten

Manpower ★★★

Drama 1941 · US · BW · 102mins

Two power linesmen, Edward G Robinson and George Raft, compete for the favours of seductive café hostess Marlene Dietrich, with fatal results. A not unfamiliar tale from Warner Bros (*Slim*, for example), given heavyweight treatment thanks to the three-way star chemistry and tough direction by the experienced Raoul Walsh. It plays like a gangster movie, with some misfiring attempts at comic relief. The sassy Eve Arden is featured in support, along with Warner stalwarts Alan Hale, Frank McHugh, Barton MacLane and Ward Bond.

Edward G Robinson *Hank McHenry* • Marlene Dietrich *Fay Duval* • George Raft *Johnny Marshall* • Alan Hale *Jumbo Wells* • Frank McHugh *Omaha* • Eve Arden *Dolly* • Barton MacLane *Smiley Quinn* • Ward Bond *Eddie Adams* ■ *Dir* Raoul Walsh • *Scr* Richard Macaulay, Jerry Wald

Le Mans ★★★ U

Action drama 1971 · US · Colour · 108mins

Steve McQueen's pet project about France's 24-hour car race was started by *The Great Escape* director John Sturges, who soon clashed with the star and was replaced by TV director Lee H Katzin. Unlike John Frankenheimer's similar *Grand Prix*, (1966) there's a minimum of detail concerning the emotional lives of the drivers. Instead there's the star looking charismatic and some of the most beautiful racing footage ever filmed. For fans of McQueen and auto racing that's probably sufficient.

Steve McQueen *Michael Delaney* • Siegfried Rauch *Erich Stahler* • Elga Andersen *Lisa Belgetti* • Ronald Leigh-Hunt *David Townsend* • Fred Haltiner *Johann Ritter* • Luc Merenda *Claude Aurac* • Christopher Waite *Larry Wilson* • Louise Edlind *Anna Ritter* ■ *Dir* Lee H Katzin • *Scr* Harry Kleiner

Man's Best Friend ★★ 15

Science-fiction thriller
1993 · US · Colour · 83mins

You'd have thought Stephen King's *Cujo* was the last word on mad dogs. Not according to this sci-fi thriller, in which reporter Ally Sheedy rescues a big pooch from a laboratory, only to discover there's a reason why scientist Lance Henriksen keeps it in a cage. It's because the initially loveable canine has been genetically mutated and is now a furry killer! Daftly enjoyable for genre fans, who will spend the entire movie groaning at how the characters walk into dark rooms, open things they shouldn't open and so on.

Ally Sheedy *Lori Tanner* • Lance Henriksen *Dr Jarret* • Robert Costanzo *Detective Kovacs* • Fredric Lehne *Perry* ■ *Dir/Scr* John Lafia

Man's Castle ★★★

Romantic drama 1933 · US · BW · 66mins

A marvellously romantic view of love during the Depression, fashioned by one of Hollywood's most sensitive directors, the double Academy Award-winner Frank Borzage. His acute romanticising is sometimes hard to stomach, and Spencer Tracy's aggressively macho leading character ultimately becomes grating. But Loretta Young is genuinely charming and gives a lovely, winsome performance. On the downside, the shantytown setting looks relentlessly studio-bound, and the use of miniatures still looks phoney.

Spencer Tracy *Bill* • Loretta Young *Trina* • Glenda Farrell *Fay Larue* • Walter Connolly *Ira* • Arthur Hohl *Bragg* • Marjorie Rambeau *Flossie* • Dickie Moore *Joie* • Harvey Clark *Café manager* ■ *Dir* Frank Borzage • *Scr* Jo Swerling, from a play by Lawrence Hazard

Man's Favorite Sport?

★★★★ U

Romantic comedy
1964 · US · Colour · 119mins

One of the great under-rated American comedies, with a simple plot and layer upon layer of delicious sexual innuendo. Director Howard Hawks has fashioned a film that's the true successor to his comic masterpiece *Bringing Up Baby*. Filmed in glossy Technicolor, it features Rock Hudson as a fishing expert who can't fish: work out the sexual subtext yourself. Paula Prentiss, an unfairly overlooked actress, is simply fabulous as Hudson's nemesis, and the supporting cast, especially Norman Alden's John Screaming Eagle, is genuinely funny.

Rock Hudson *Roger Willoughby* • Paula Prentiss *Abigail Page* • Maria Perschy *Isolde "Easy" Mueller* • Charlene Holt *Tex Connors* • John McGiver *William Cadwalader* • Roscoe Karns *Major Phipps* • Forrest Lewis *Skaggs* • Norman Alden *John Screaming Eagle* ■ *Dir* Howard Hawks • *Scr* John Fenton Murray, Steve McNeil, from the story *The Girl Who Almost Got Away* by Pat Frank

Man's Hope ★★★★

War drama 1945 · Sp/Fr · BW · 72mins

Based on his novel *L'Espoir*, the only feature directed by André Malraux began shooting in Barcelona in 1938, but was interrupted when General Franco took the city. Completed in a studio in Paris, it was not shown until after the Second World War, with different editing. Malraux, who was still at the front, was not consulted; indeed, when he saw the film for the first time, he did not recognise the cutting. Nevertheless, despite the professional actors and the studio work, this semi-documentary about a small group of Republican fighters in the Spanish Civil War attempting to blow up a bridge gives the impression that the actual war is being filmed. In Spanish with English subtitles.

Andres Mejuto *Capt Munoz* • Nicolas Rodriguez *Pilot Marquez* • Jose Lado *The peasant* ■ *Dir* André Malraux • *Scr* André Malraux, from his novel *L'Espoir*

Mansfield Park ★★★★ 15

Period drama 1999 · UK · Colour · 112mins

Writer/director Patricia Rozema looks beyond Jane Austen's third novel for inspiration and uses the author's own letters and journals to beef up her cleverly constructed and lively update. Frances O'Connor dazzles as Fanny Price, plucked from poverty and sent to live with her wealthy relatives on the Mansfield Park estate. There she must choose between true love and social duty. Slave-trading, Dickensian portrayals of lower-class life and an upfront take on the sexual mores of the day all conspire to make Rozema's bracing rumination on class hypocrisy and social hierarchy a compelling revision of traditional costume drama.

Embeth Davidtz *Mary Crawford* • Jonny Lee Miller *Edmund Bertram* • Alessandro Nivola *Henry Crawford* • Frances O'Connor *Fanny Price* • Harold Pinter *Sir Thomas Bertram* • Lindsay Duncan *Lady Bertram/Frances Price* • Sheila Gish *Mrs Norris* • James Purefoy *Tom Bertram* ■ *Dir* Patricia Rozema • *Scr* Patricia Rozema, from the novel by Jane Austen

Mansion of the Doomed ★

Horror 1975 · US · Colour · 86mins

An utterly repugnant horror film that at least has the courage of its gruesome convictions. An eminent surgeon abducts victims and removes their eyes in the hope of restoring the sight of his daughter, blinded in a car wreck. Borrowing liberally from *Eyes without a Face* (1959), director Michael Pataki piles on the banality and reduces Richard Basehart and Gloria Grahame to embarrassed shells of their former selves. Squeamish viewers beware!

Richard Basehart *Dr Leonard Chaney* • Trish Stewart *Nancy Chaney* • Gloria Grahame *Katherine* • Lance Henriksen *Dr Dan Bryan* ■ *Dir* Michael Pataki • *Scr* Frank Ray Perilli

Manslaughter ★★

Drama 1930 · US · BW · 85mins

The lives of a district attorney (Fredric March) and the rich and idle society girl (Claudette Colbert) with whom he is in love are complicated when she runs over a traffic cop and kills him, forcing March to send her to jail. Written and directed by George Abbott, this updated version of a more flamboyant silent made by Cecil B DeMille in 1922 is notable mainly for Colbert's fine dramatic performance.

Claudette Colbert *Lydia Thorne* • Fredric March *Dan O'Bannon* • Emma Dunn *Miss Bennett* • Natalie Moorhead *Eleanor* • Richard Tucker *Albee* • Hilda Vaughn *Evans* • G Pat Collins *Drummond* • Gaylord Pendleton [Steve Pendleton] *Bobby* ■ *Dir* George Abbott • *Scr* George Abbott, from the story by Alice Duer Miller

Mantrap ★★★

Silent comedy drama
1926 · US · BW · 66mins

Bored to tears with her marriage to small-town businessman Ernest Torrence, sexy flapper Clara Bow falls into the arms of visiting lawyer Percy Marmont and plans to run off with him to the big city. One of Bow's more substantial vehicles, adapted for the silent screen from a novel by Sinclair Lewis and directed by her then-lover, Victor Fleming. A good example of the

screen persona that made the "It Girl" box-office dynamite in the twenties.

Ernest Torrence *Joe Easter* • Clara Bow *Alverna* • Percy Marmont *Ralph Prescott* • Eugene Pallette *E Wesson Woodbury* • Tom Kennedy *Curly Owens* • Josephine Crowell *Mrs McGavity* • William Orlamond *Mr McGavity* • Charles Stevens *Lawrence Jackfish* ■ *Dir* Victor Fleming • *Scr* Adelaide Heilbron, Ethel Doherty, George Marion Jr (titles), from a novel by Sinclair Lewis

Mantrap ★★
Thriller   1952 · UK · BW · 78mins

Paul Henreid, that oily smoothie from *Casablanca* and *Now, Voyager*, here washes up in the torrid, tawdry, cheapskate world of the British quota quickie. Lois Maxwell plays a wife who changes her name and begins a new life after her husband is convicted of murder. When he escapes, she goes to private detective Henreid for help. Maxwell later found fame as Miss Moneypenny in the Bond films.

Paul Henreid *Hugo Bishop* • Lois Maxwell *Thelma Tasman* • Kieron Moore *Mervyn Speight* • Hugh Sinclair *Maurice Jerrard* ■ *Dir* Terence Fisher • *Scr* Paul Tabori, Terence Fisher, from the novel *Queen in Danger* by Elleston Trevor

Manuela ★★
Romantic drama   1957 · UK · BW · 105mins

This unlikely shipboard romance was later gently lampooned in *Carry On Jack*. Director Guy Hamilton does a fair job of reining in Trevor Howard's natural bullishness, coming as close as anyone ever did to discovering vulnerability in his gruff make-up. Elsa Martinelli never really convinces in her boyish disguise, but it's clear to see why tipsy Captain Howard would fall for her. In truth, this frippery is beneath both Howard and the great Pedro Armendariz. It has an easy charm, however, and you suspect they are both rather enjoying it.

Trevor Howard *James Prothero* • Elsa Martinelli *Manuela* • Leslie Weston *Bleloch* • Donald Pleasence *Evans* • Jack MacGowran *Tommy* • Warren Mitchell *Moss* • Pedro Armendariz *Mario Constanza* ■ *Dir* Guy Hamilton • *Scr* William Woods, Guy Hamilton, Ivan Foxwell, from the novel by William Woods

The Manxman ★★ U
Silent drama   1929 · UK · BW · 79mins

Alfred Hitchcock's last silent film is a brooding melodrama concerning a love triangle that ends in tragedy. Anny Ondra, an early Hitchcock blonde who went on to star in *Blackmail*, is Kate Cregeen, loved by two men who are best friends – fisherman Carl Brisson and lawyer Malcolm Keen. She loves Brisson but when her father forbids marriage, he leaves the island and Keen steps in. Unfamiliar territory for present-day Hitchcock fans this is competently done and atmospheric, but too old-fashioned to be of more than limited interest. ▭

Carl Brisson *Pete Quilliam* • Malcolm Keen *Philip Christian* • Anny Ondra *Kate Cregeen* ■ *Dir* Alfred Hitchcock • *Scr* Eliot Stannard, from the novel by Sir Hall Caine

Many Rivers to Cross ★★★ U
Comedy western   1955 · US · Colour · 94mins

A good-natured buckskin-clad MGM pre-western frontier comedy, sold on the back of the similarly themed *Seven Brides for Seven Brothers*. Robert Taylor and Eleanor Parker make an attractively spunky pair, but the script lets them down badly, being neither as hilarious nor as perceptive about the female condition as it thinks it is. Under-rated director Roy Rowland does what he can, but the constant need to roister defeats him and exhausts the audience's patience. Quite funny, though, and lovely to look at.

Robert Taylor (1) *Bushrod Gentry* • Eleanor Parker *Mary Stuart Cherne* • Victor McLaglen *Cadmus Cherne* • Jeff Richards *Fremont* • Russ Tamblyn *Shields* • James Arness *Esau Hamilton* • Alan Hale Jr *Luke Radford* ■ *Dir* Roy Rowland • *Scr* Harry Brown, Guy Trosper, from a story by Steve Frazee

Map of the Human Heart ★★★★ 15
Drama   1992 · UK/Ausl/Can/Fr · Colour · 104mins

Spanning several decades and told as an elongated flashback to cartographer John Cusack, this is a rare blend of imagination and insight. Memorable moments abound, from a plane landing on the Arctic ice to Inuit Jason Scott Lee and mixed-race Anne Parillaud finally consummating their on-off affair atop a deflating barrage balloon. It would be too easy to say that it is only the stunning visuals that prevent this romantic triangle drama from lapsing into sentimental platitude. But what makes Vincent Ward's film so remarkable is that it has enough intelligence and humanity to make its tale of chance and coincidence seem like life, not fictional contrivance. ▭

Jason Scott Lee *Avik* • Robert Joamie *Young Avik* • Anne Parillaud *Albertine* • Annie Galipeau *Young Albertine* • Patrick Bergin *Walter Russell* • Clotilde Courau *Rainee* • John Cusack *Mapmaker* • Jeanne Moreau *Sister Banville* ■ *Dir* Vincent Ward • *Scr* Louis Nowra, from a story by Vincent Ward

A Map of the World ★★★★
Drama   1999 · US · Colour · 127mins

Sigourney Weaver gives what is perhaps the finest performance of her career – as a rural housewife not just on the verge of a nervous breakdown, but engulfed by it. As Alice Goodwin, she's the lone bright woman in a Wisconsin farming community. But her mundane life is disturbed when a neighbour's two-year-old daughter drowns in her care and a young local, Robbie (Marc Donato), thereafter accuses her of sexual abuse. Director Scott Elliott loses his grip in the second half, but Weaver's performance transcends the flaws.

Sigourney Weaver *Alice Goodwin* • Julianne Moore *Theresa Collins* • David Strathairn *Howard Goodwin* • Arliss Howard *Paul Reverdy* • Chloë Sevigny *Carole Mackessy* • Louise Fletcher *Nellie* • Marc Donato *Robbie* ■ *Dir* Scott Elliott • *Scr* Peter Hedges, Polly Platt, from the novel by by Jane Hamilton

Mapantsula ★★★★ 15
Crime drama   1988 · SAfr · Colour · 99mins

With its title coming from the Soweto slang for "spiv", this was one of the few South African films of the apartheid era to background the political situation and eschew fashionable caucasian liberalism. Co-scripting with white director Oliver Schmitz, Thomas Mogotlane excels as Panic, the thief who reveals unsuspected levels of determination and dignity as he endures the same sadistic brutality as the militant activists with whom he shares a cell. The township sequences teem with life, drawing additional authenticity from the fact that Panic doesn't care which side of the racial divide he operates. In Sotho, Zulu and Afrikaans with English subtitles. ▭

Thomas Mogotlane *Panic* • Marcel Van Heerden *Stander* • Thembi Mtshali *Pat* • Dolly Rathebe *Ma Mobise* • Peter Sephuma *Buma* • Darlington Michaels *Dingaan* • Eugene Majola *Sam* ■ *Dir* Oliver Schmitz • *Scr* Oliver Schmitz, Thomas Mogotlane

Maracaibo ★
Adventure drama   1958 · US · Colour · 88mins

Cornel Wilde made some fascinating adventure movies with strong environmental messages, but this is a disjointed mess. There's Wilde's half in which he struggles manfully to douse a fire in an undersea oil well in Venezuela. Then Wilde has to give his real-life wife, Jean Wallace, something to do. So a second plot is trumped up about an American woman novelist who learns about the personal tragedy of the owner of the blazing well. The two halves quickly come unglued in a welter of travelogue footage and watersports and flamenco dancing.

Cornel Wilde *Vic Scott* • Jean Wallace *Laura Kingsley* • Abbe Lane *Elena Holbrook* • Francis Lederer *Senor Miguel Orlando* • Michael Landon *Lago* • Joe E Ross *Milt Karger* ■ *Dir* Cornel Wilde • *Scr* Ted Sherdeman, from a novel by Stirling Silliphant

Marat/Sade ★★
Historical drama   1966 · UK · BW and Colour · 115mins

The Marquis de Sade (Patrick Magee) directs his insane asylum inmates in a morality play-within-a-play about the assassination of French Revolutionary leader Jean-Paul Marat (Ian Richardson). The bedlam governor (Clifford Rose) continually stops the performance to demand cuts in the polemic. Arty and worthy, with de Sade and Marat mainly shouting political rhetoric at each other, Peter Brook's hard-going film adaptation adds extra Brechtian close-up nuance to his convoluted and controversial stage hit.

Ian Richardson *Jean-Paul Marat* • Glenda Jackson *Charlotte Corday* • Patrick Magee *Marquis de Sade* • Clifford Rose *M Coulmier* • Brenda Kempner *Mme Coulmier* • Ruth Baker *Mlle Coulmier* ■ *Dir* Peter Brook • *Scr* Adrian Mitchell, from the play *The Persecution and Assassination of Jean-Paul Marat as Performed by the Inmates of the Asylum of Charenton under the Direction of the Marquis de Sade* by Peter Weiss, Geoffrey Skelton

Marathon Man ★★★★ 18
Thriller   1976 · US · Colour · 119mins

Dustin Hoffman stars as the bewildered New York student training to run an Olympic marathon who inadvertently becomes mixed up in a hunt for a haul of Nazi diamonds in director John Schlesinger's gripping thriller. Laurence Olivier is the essence of evil as the former concentration camp sadist who leaves South America to claim his legacy – the priceless gems taken from Jewish victims during the war. Also making an impact is Roy Scheider as Hoffman's secret agent older brother. Schlesinger's film is not without its flaws – it takes rather too long to get started and is too dislocated – but it's a very classy package, and one particular scene involving dentistry will leave a lasting impression. Contains violence. ▭

Dustin Hoffman *Babe Levy* • Laurence Olivier *Szell* • Roy Scheider *Doc Levy* • William Devane *Janeway* • Marthe Keller *Elsa* • Fritz Weaver *Professor Biesenthal* • Richard Bright *Karl* • Marc Lawrence *Erhard* • Allen Joseph *Babe's father* ■ *Dir* John Schlesinger • *Scr* William Goldman, from his novel

The Marauders ★★
Western   1947 · US · BW · 63mins

William Boyd, who played Hopalong Cassidy throughout the thirties and forties, here once again saddles up as the Wild West's B-movie good guy. In this tale, he tracks a gang of outlaws intent on plundering the oil under land occupied by a small town. Routine heroics are given a comedy twist by Boyd's sidekick, rasp-voiced Andy Clyde – a downmarket best-buddy.

William Boyd *Hopalong Cassidy* • Andy Clyde *California Carlson* • Rand Brooks *Lucky Jenkins* • Ian Wolfe *Black* • Dorinda Clifton *Susan* • Mary Newton *Mrs Crowell* ■ *Dir* George Archainbaud • *Scr* Charles Belden, from characters created by Clarence E Mulford

The Marauders ★★
Western   1955 · US · Colour · 81mins

A western staple, this – the powerful ranchers who hire muscle to force squatters, lowlifes and emigrants off their land. At the first skirmish the squatters win, killing the rancher and his son. But then Dan Duryea, a book-keeper who fancies himself as a military strategist and calls himself "The General", gets control of the ranch and initiates all-out range war. This is the scenario perfected first by *Shane* and then, later, by *Heaven's Gate*, though this MGM effort never rises above its B-movie station.

Dan Duryea *Mr Avery* • Jeff Richards *Corey Everett* • Keenan Wynn *Hook* • Jarma Lewis *Hannah Ferber* • John Hudson *Roy Rutherford* • Harry Shannon *John Rutherford* ■ *Dir* Gerald Mayer • *Scr* Jack Leonard, Earl Felton, from a novel by Alan Marcus

March Comes in like a Lion ★★★
Drama   1991 · Jap · Colour · 118mins

Having drawn acclaim for his intense study of lesbian infatuation, *Afternoon Breezes*, Hitoshi Yazaki tackles the even more controversial subject of incest in this laconic yet tantalisingly lyrical drama. There's also a tense undercurrent to the action, as it's only a matter of time before Cho Bang-Ho recovers his memory and realises that Yoshiko Yura, who rescued him from a Tokyo hospital, isn't just his lover, but also his sister. Imbuing the lengthy, taciturn takes with simmering eroticism and a mischievous visual sense, Yazaki avoids judging his passionate protagonists, while keeping in mind the storm gathering around their dread secret. A Japanese language film.

Yoshiko Yura *Ice* • Cho Bang-Ho *Haruo* ■ *Dir* Hitoshi Yazaki • *Scr* Hitoshi Yazaki, Hiroshi Miyazaki, Sachio Ono

The March Hare ★★★ U
Drama 1956 · UK · Colour · 84mins

This British Lion horse-racing romp gains from the fact that it was photographed in colour and CinemaScope by the great Jack Hildyard. It also has good-looking leads in handsome Terence Morgan and sultry Peggy Cummins who, together with a sly performance from Cyril Cusack, keep the whole thing a good deal more watchable than it deserves to be. Charles Hawtrey and Wilfrid Hyde White also put in appearances.

Peggy Cummins *Pat McGuire* • Terence Morgan *Sir Charles Keene* • Martita Hunt *Lady Anne* • Cyril Cusack *Lazy Mangan* • Wilfrid Hyde White *Colonel Keene* • Charles Hawtrey *Fisher* ■ *Dir* George More O'Ferrall • *Scr* Gordon Wellesley, Paul Vincent Carroll, Allan Mckinnon, from the novel *Gamblers Sometimes Win* by TH Bird

March or Die ★★ PG
Adventure 1977 · UK · Colour · 102mins

Producer Lew Grade's good intentions often led to disappointing results. So it proved in this *Beau Geste*-style tale about the French Foreign Legion. Much of the blame must lie with Terence Hill, who got by (just!) in comic westerns where his accent and lack of ability weren't too apparent. Alongside such seasoned talents as Gene Hackman and Max von Sydow, however, he is totally lost, single-handedly slowing this tough adventure's pace down to a snail's crawl. Catherine Deneuve looks radiant, though, Ian Holm is a truly fanatical El Krim, while John Alcott's photography is a real treat. ▭

Gene Hackman *Major William Sherman Foster* • Terence Hill *Marco Segrain* • Catherine Deneuve *Simone Picard* • Max von Sydow *François Marneau* • Ian Holm *El Krim* • Jack O'Halloran *Ivan* ■ *Dir* Dick Richards • *Scr* David Zelag Goodman, from a story by David Zelag Goodman, Dick Richards

Marching out of Time ★★
Science-fiction comedy 1993 · US · Colour

One of those films where the pitch was probably more interesting than the finished result. Here, it's *Home Alone* meets *Hogan's Heroes*, with a dash of *Back to the Future* thrown in and, yes, this is about as misguided as that concept sounds. Frederick Andersen is the brattish Californian teen who finds himself drawn into the Second World War when Nazis appear in the neighbourhood, courtesy of a misfiring time machine. Will he be able to stop them changing the course of history?

Frederick Andersen • Matthew Henerson • Heinrich James • Jeff Rector • Robert Z'Dar ■ *Dir/Scr* Anton Vassil

Marco ★★★
Musical 1973 · US · Colour · 109mins

The exploits of the medieval explorer Marco Polo have proved unlucky for film-makers – the sumptuous Goldwyn production starring Gary Cooper is relentlessly dull, and two versions of the tale made in the sixties were dismal failures. This little-known musical version of Marco Polo's travels is in fact the best of the lot, with the benefit of actual Oriental locations, serviceable songs and a pleasing cast. Desi Arnaz Jr has youthful exuberance as the explorer and Zero Mostel is equally scene-stealing as Kublai Khan.

Desi Arnaz Jr *Marco Polo* • Zero Mostel *Kublai Khan* • Jack Weston *Maffio Polo* • Win Cie Cie *Aigiarm* • Aimee Eccles *Kuklatoi* • Fred Sadoff *Niccolo Polo* ■ *Dir* Seymour Robbie • *Scr* Romeo Muller • *Music* Maury Laws

Mardi Gras ★★ U
Musical 1958 · US · Colour · 107mins

It must have seemed a good idea to team pop idols Pat Boone and Tommy Sands with Gary Crosby (son of Bing) as military cadets on a spree in New Orleans. Frankly, however, 20th Century-Fox could have come up with a better plot. This one's some hokum about winning a date on a raffle, which wouldn't matter too much if the songs were any good, but they're not. This empty piece of entertainment marked the downward spiral of Boone's movie career as his amiable, ingratiating smile was becoming tiresome.

Pat Boone *Pat Newell* • Christine Carère *Michelle Marton* • Tommy Sands *Barry Denton* • Sheree North *Eadie* • Gary Crosby *Tony Runkle* • Fred Clark *Curtis* • Richard Sargent [Dick Sargent] *Dick Saglon* ■ *Dir* Edmund Goulding • *Scr* Winston Miller, Hal Kanter, from a story by Curtis Harrington

Mare Nostrum ★★★
Silent First World War drama 1926 · US · BW

Directed by Rex Ingram, a master at epic romances – *The Four Horsemen of the Apocalyse* (1921), *The Prisoner of Zenda* (1922) – this tragic First World War love story touched nerves as well as hearts with its story of a German spy (Alice Terry, Ingram's wife) who falls in love with a Spanish captain (Antonio Moreno). Nowadays, of course, it feels dreadfully dated, but the film still has a narrative charge.

Alice Terry *Freya Talberg* • Antonio Moreno *Ulysses Ferragut* • Uni Apollon *The Triton* ■ *Dir* Rex Ingram • *Scr* Willis Goldbeck, from the novel by Vicente Blasco-Ibañez

Margaret Bourke-White ★★
Biographical drama 1989 · US · Colour · 91mins

This TV movie chronicles the career of one of the most famous US photographers of the thirties and forties. Farrah Fawcett takes the title role, battling against the prejudices of a male-dominated profession to become one of *Life* magazine's most respected names. Her tempestuous private life was dominated by an affair with the writer Erskine Caldwell, who

was responsible for such slices of Depression-era Americana as *Tobacco Road* and *God's Little Acre*. Fawcett and Frederic Forrest (as Caldwell) get up a fair head of steam, but the depiction of journalistic chauvinism is rather two-dimensional.

Farrah Fawcett *Margaret Bourke-White* • Frederic Forrest *Erskine Caldwell* • Mitchell Ryan *Patton* • David Huddleston *Bemis* • Jay Patterson *Henry Luce* • Robert Stanton *Lloyd-Smith* • Robert Katims *Moscowitz* ■ *Dir* Lawrence Schiller • *Scr* Marjorie David, from the biography by Vicki Goldberg

Margaret's Museum ★★★ 15
Period drama 1995 · Can/UK · Colour · 95mins

A powerful period piece, set in a Canadian coal-mining community during the forties. Helena Bonham Carter is Margaret, whose father and brother have already perished down the mines, and who is determined that the new love in her life, a bagpipe-playing, Gaelic-speaking dishwasher, won't follow suit. But times are hard, jobs are scarce and history looks bound to repeat itself. Clive Russell and Kate Nelligan offer strong support, but it's Bonham Carter's film. The precise nature of the titular museum is only explained in the closing stages. Contains sex scenes. ▭

Helena Bonham Carter *Margaret MacNeil* • Clive Russell *Neil Currie* • Craig Olejnik *Jimmy MacNeil* • Kate Nelligan *Catherine MacNeil* • Kenneth Welsh *Angus MacNeil* • Andrea Morris *Marilyn Campbell* ■ *Dir* Mort Ransen • *Scr* Mort Ransen, Gerald Wexler, from the short story *The Glace Bay Miner's Museum*

Margie ★★★★ U
Musical comedy 1946 · US · Colour · 93mins

In the wake of MGM's *Meet me in St Louis*, the other studios dusted off their songbooks and petticoats, and 20th Century-Fox produced this little Technicolored charmer, which set a style and standard that endured at the studio for well over a decade. Set in the twenties, the era of the raccoon coat and the charleston, this is a captivating work, lovingly directed by veteran Henry King, and starring Jeanne Crain in the role of her career. Completely evading the schmaltz and vulgarity that hampered later entries in the same vein (notably Fox's Betty Grable vehicles), this remains a model of wit, taste and good musical sense.

Jeanne Crain *Margie McDuff* • Glenn Langan *Professor Ralph Fontayne* • Lynn Bari *Miss Isabelle Palmer* • Alan Young *Roy Hornsdale* • Barbara Lawrence *Marybelle Tenor* • Conrad Janis *Johnny Green* • Esther Dale *Grandma McSweeney* • Hattie McDaniel *Cynthia* ■ *Dir* Henry King • *Scr* F Hugh Herbert, from a story by Ruth McKinney, Richard Bransten

Margin for Error ★★★
Comedy 1943 · US · BW · 74mins

After an unhappy start in Hollywood as a producer turned director, Otto Preminger returned to Broadway. Among the most successful plays he directed was this black comedy by Clare Boothe about the Nazi consul in Brooklyn and the Jewish policeman ordered to protect him. Preminger played the role of the arrogant Nazi himself and repeats it on screen, typecasting himself forever in the

process, while future TV comedian Milton Berle plays the cop. To improve the script Preminger hired Samuel Fuller, who worked without credit while he was on leave from the army.

Joan Bennett *Sophie Baumer* • Milton Berle *Moe Finkelstein* • Otto Preminger *Karl Baumer* • Carl Esmond *Baron Max von Alvenstor* • Howard Freeman *Otto Horst* • Poldy Dur *Frieda Schmidt* ■ *Dir* Otto Preminger • *Scr* Lillie Hayward, Samuel Fuller, from the play by Clare Boothe [Clare Boothe Luce]

Marguerite de la Nuit ★★★
Drama 1955 · Fr · Colour · 130mins

Complete with Art Deco backdrops from Max Douy and plenty of photographic tricks from Jacques Natteau, this is a stylish, if dramatically unsatisfactory updating of the Faust myth to the mid-twenties. Shifting the emphasis of Goethe's story away from the ageing doctor who signs away his soul to regain his youth, director Claude Autant-Lara concentrates instead on the relationship between the satanic Pigalle drug-dealer and Marguerite, the long-suffering object of Faust's affections. Jean-François Calvé is out of his depth, but Yves Montand and Michèle Morgan generate plenty of spark. A French language film.

Michèle Morgan *Marguerite* • Yves Montand *M Léon* • Jean-François Calvé *Georges Faust* • Massimo Girotti *Valentin* • Fernand Sardou *Le patron du café* • Palau *Dr Faust* ■ *Dir* Claude Autant-Lara • *Scr* Ghislaine Autant-Lara, Gabriel Arout, from the writings by Johann Wolfgang von Goethe

Maria Chapdelaine ★★★
Romantic drama 1982 · Can/Fr · Colour · 108mins

Louis Hémon's novel had already been adapted by Julien Duvivier (1934) and Marc Allégret (1950) before director Gilles Carle embarked on this politically-charged version. Clearly intent on commenting on Quebec's nationalist aspirations throughout the 20th century, Carle gives Carole Laure's romantic quandary an allegorical edge that intensifies the already engrossing drama. Torn between timid farmer Pierre Curzi, swarthy trapper Nick Mancuso and dapper sophisticate Donald Lautrec, Laure spiritedly personifies Québecois fervour and more than holds her own against her illustrious predecessors, Madeleine Renaud and Michèle Morgan. Pierre Mignot's images of the forbidding far north also impress. In French with English subtitles.

Carole Laure *Maria Chapdelaine* • Nick Mancuso *François Paradis* • Claude Rich *Father Cordelier* • Amulette Garneau *Laura Chapdelaine* • Yoland Guérard *Samuel Chapdelaine* • Pierre Curzi *Eutrope Gagnon* • Donald Lautrec *Lorenzo Suprenant* ■ *Dir* Gilles Carle • *Scr* Gilles Carle, Guy Fournier, from the novel by Louis Hémon

Maria Marten, or the Murder in the Red Barn ★★
Melodrama 1935 · UK · BW · 67mins

Based on a true story, this creaky melodrama tells of a rotten squire who gets a young innocent girl pregnant, then murders her. Director Milton Rosmer strives unsuccessfully for a

U = SUITABLE FOR ALL   Uc = SUITABLE FOR ALL, ESPECIALLY FOR YOUNG CHILDREN (VIDEO ONLY)   PG = PARENTAL GUIDANCE

suitably gothic air, but the cast (Eric Portman and Tod Slaughter in their movie debuts, and Sophie Stewart) has a fine time hamming things up.

Tod Slaughter *Squire William Corder* • Sophie Stewart *Maria Marten* • DJ Williams *Farmer Marten* • Clare Greet *Mrs Marten* • Eric Portman *Carlos* • Gerrard Tyrell *Tim* • Ann Trevor *Nan* • Antonia Brough *Maud Sennett* ■ *Dir* Milton Rosmer • *Scr* Randall Faye

El Mariachi ★★★ 15

Action adventure 1992 · US · Colour · 81mins
Desperado had a big-name star, Antonio Banderas, plus a Quentin Tarantino cameo, but Robert Rodriguez's debut feature is still the more endearing film. Essentially, it's a no-budget, no-frills dry run for *Desperado*, but with a much more ambivalent hero. Where Banderas was a heroic figure from the outset, Carlos Gallardo, the *mariachi* of the title, is an innocent musician mistaken for a lethal killer who's gunning for mob boss Peter Marquardt. The film's origins are clearly visible – let's just say that the acting is enthusiastic – but Rodriguez carries off the action set pieces with confidence and style. In Spanish with English subtitles. ▭

Carlos Gallardo *El Mariachi* • Consuelo Gomez *Domino* • Jaime De Hoyos *Bigoton* • Peter Marquardt *Mauricio (Moco)* • Reinol Martinez *Azul* • Ramiro Gomez *Cantinero* • Jesus Lopez *Viejo clerk* ■ *Dir/Scr* Robert Rodriguez

Marianna Ucria ★★

Period drama
1997 · It/Fr/Port · Colour · 108 mins
A stoic performance from Emmanuelle Laborit is the main asset of Roberto Faenza's otherwise pedestrian drama. As the deaf-mute teenager enduring the indignity of marriage to her lascivious uncle, she conveys a range of complex emotions without resorting to silent-style gesticulation. However, supporting stars Philippe Noiret and Laura Betti are less sure-footed. Tonino Delli Colli's lustrous photography adds to the 18th-century grandeur, but Faenza's airless direction makes this more of a bodice ripper than a literate tribute to the human spirit. An Italian language film.

Emmanuelle Laborit *Marianna Ucria* • Eva Grieco *Marianna as a child* • Roberto Herlitzka *Duke Pietro* • Philippe Noiret *Duke Signoretto* • Laura Morante *Maria* • Lorenzo Crespi *Saro* • Laura Betti *Giuseppa* ■ *Dir* Roberto Faenza • *Scr* Roberto Faenza, Sandro Petraglia, from a novel by Dacia Maraini

Marianne de Ma Jeunesse ★★★

Fantasy romantic drama
1955 · Fr · BW · 105mins
This was a huge hit with adolescent French audiences in the mid-fifties, though critics were more restrained in their enthusiasm. However, Marianne Hold is delightfully coquettish as the mysterious young girl who persuades student Pierre Vaneck (who's been locked in an eerie Bavarian castle as an initiation prank by his classmates) that she is being held captive by a pitiless ogre. Equally, there's no denying the visual fascination of Julien Duvivier's fantasy, while special effects wizard Eugen Schüfftan's trickery

enhances Léonce-Henry Burel's already atmospheric photography. A French language film.

Marianne Hold *Marianne* • Pierre Vaneck *Vincent* • Isabella Pia *Lise* • Gil Vidal *Manfred* ■ *Dir* Julien Duvivier • *Scr* Julien Duvivier, from the novel *Douloureuse Arcadie* by P De Mendelssohn

Maria's Lovers ★★★ 15

Romantic drama
1984 · US · Colour · 104mins
Traumatised Second World War veteran John Savage cannot consummate his marriage to childhood sweetheart Nastassja Kinski, so she runs off with various men, including Keith Carradine. The plot sounds a little like Tennessee Williams, but it's actually far less melodramatic than that. Indeed, the mining community setting, the Russian émigré community and the presence of Savage makes Soviet director Andrei Konchalovsky's American debut strangely reminiscent of *The Deer Hunter*. Starting with a clip from John Huston's documentary about war veterans, *Let There Be Light*, the result is tender, touching and well acted by an impressive cast. ▭

Nastassja Kinski *Maria Bosic* • John Savage *Ivan Bibic* • Robert Mitchum *Ivan's father* • Keith Carradine *Clarence Butts* • Anita Morris *Mrs Wynic* • Bud Cort *Harvey* • Karen Young *Rosie* • John Goodman *Frank* ■ *Dir* Andrei Konchalovsky • *Scr* Andrei Konchalovsky, Gérard Brach, Paul Zindel, Marjorie David

Marie: a True Story ★★★ 15

Biographical drama
1985 · US · Colour · 112mins
Sissy Spacek gives an impressive performance as Marie Ragghianti, a single mother with three kids who attempts to rid Tennessee's parole board of corruption. This utter paragon actually existed, and Roger Donaldson's well-paced biography zings with some great performances and truthful set pieces which grip from the word go. There are a few dull patches, however, largely due to the fact that Donaldson can't bear to speak ill of the dreadfully put-upon.

Sissy Spacek *Marie Ragghianti* • Jeff Daniels *Eddie Sisk* • Keith Szarabajka *Kevin McCormack* • Don Hood *Governor Ray Blanton* • Morgan Freeman *Charles Traughber* • Lisa Banes *Toni Greer* ■ *Dir* Roger Donaldson • *Scr* John Briley, from the book by Peter Maas

Marie Antoinette ★★★★

Historical romantic epic
1938 · US · BW · 160mins
This highly romanticised version of the life of France's most famous queen is, in a word, sumptuous. An Oscar-nominated Norma Shearer takes the title role, dazzlingly dressed by Adrian and lovingly photographed by William Daniels under the direction of WS Van Dyke II. Robert Morley (also Oscar-nominated) plays her husband, Tyrone Power is her self-sacrificing lover, Joseph Schildkraut makes a devious Duke of Orleans and Gladys George is the infamous Madame DuBarry. This is MGM at its most extravagant.

Norma Shearer *Marie Antoinette* • Tyrone Power *Count Axel de Fersen* • John Barrymore *King Louis XV* • Gladys George *Mme DuBarry* • Robert Morley *King Louis XVI* • Anita Louise *Princess DeLamballe* • Joseph Schildkraut

Duke of Orleans • Henry Stephenson *Count Mercey* ■ *Dir* WS Van Dyke II [WS Van Dyke], Julien Duvivier • *Scr* Claudine West, Donald Ogden Stewart, Ernest Vajda, F Scott Fitzgerald, from the book by Stefan Zweig

Marie Antoinette ★★★

Historical drama 1956 · Fr · Colour · 120mins
Tracing Marie Antoinette's life from her leave of Austria, through her affair with a dashing ambassador, to her dignified appearance before the Revolutionary Tribunal, this is a markedly less melodramatic take on the life of France's last queen than the Norma Shearer vehicle. Filmed simultaneously in French and English, Jean Delannoy's lavish biopic is strong on period detail and makes a laudable attempt to reclaim the tragic consort from the maelstrom of historical events. But, just as Michèle Morgan's regality errs towards coldness, so the screenplay tends dryly towards the academic.

Michèle Morgan *Marie Antoinette* • Richard Todd *Count Axel De Fresen* • Jacques Morel *Louis XVI* • Aimé Clariond *Louis XV* • Jeanne Boitel *Madame Campan* • Guy Tréjan *Lafayette* • Marina Berti *Comtesse de Polignac* • Madeleine Rousset *Madame de Tourzel* ■ *Dir* Jean Delannoy • *Scr* Jean Delannoy, Bernard Zimmer, Philippe Erlanger

Marie in the City ★★★

Drama 1987 · Can · Colour · 72mins
Pursuing a feminist agenda with some subtlety, Marquise LePage's French-Canadian drama drags us through Montreal's sleazy streets with abused runaway Marie (Geneviève Lenoir). Her friendship with world-weary hooker Sarah (Frédérique Collin) becomes a predictable mother-daughter set-up, but the fearsome intensity of the acting cuts through a naive situation with the serrated edge of credibility. Having made its "all gals are pals" point, though, it's a pity a bit more charity couldn't have been spared for the chaps. In French with English subtitles.

Geneviève Lenoir *Marie* • Frédérique Collin *Sarah* ■ *Dir/Scr* Marquise LePage

Marilyn and Bobby: Her Final Affair ★★

Drama 1993 · US · Colour · 95mins
Just when you thought there had been enough TV movies about the life and times of Marilyn Monroe, someone goes and makes another one. Melody Anderson stars as the screen goddess in this soapy account of the alleged relationship she had with Robert Kennedy. Unfortunately, this never quite works: there are virtually no facts to base the romance on, and the only thing Anderson has in common with Monroe is the colour of her hair.

Melody Anderson *Marilyn Monroe* • James F Kelly *Robert F Kennedy* • Jonathan Banks *Joe Scoman* • Geoffrey Blake *Carl Silberling* • Thomas Wagner *Jimmy Hoffa* • Richard Dysart *J Edgar Hoover* ■ *Dir* Bradford May • *Scr* Gerald MacDonald

Marilyn and Me ★★

Biographical drama
1991 · US · Colour · 100mins
At this rate, speculative movies about Marilyn Monroe's life will outnumber those she actually made. This one

focuses on her relationship with Robert Slatzer, a longtime confidant who claims to have been secretly married to her for three days during a trip to Mexico. Such is the curiosity value of Slatzer's much-contested story that director John Patterson gets away with a very unimaginative rendition of the tale, portraying Tinseltown as the cold, cruel place we all know it can be, and relying too much on Susan Griffiths's inconsistent impersonation of Marilyn.

Susan Griffiths *Norma Jean Baker/Marilyn Monroe* • Jesse Dabson *Robert Slatzer* • Joel Grey *Johnny Hyde* ■ *Dir* John Patterson • *Scr* Robert Boris, from a story by Robert Boris, Stu Samuels

Marilyn – The Untold Story ★★★

Biographical drama
1980 · US · Colour · 119mins
Catherine Hicks drew an Emmy nomination for her creditable impersonation of Marilyn Monroe in this otherwise unreliable account of the screen siren's tragic private life. Based on a controversial biography by Norman Mailer, this concentrates on the young Norma Jean's relationship with Johnny Hyde (Richard Basehart), the agent who helped her when she was still a struggling starlet. The Hollywood lookalikes are persuasive, but too much of the Tinseltown period is glossed over and events bear only a passing resemblance to the truth.

Catherine Hicks *Marilyn Monroe* • Richard Basehart *Johnny Hyde* • Frank Converse *Joe DiMaggio* • John Ireland *John Huston* • Viveca Lindfors *Natasha Lytess* • Jason Miller *Arthur Miller* ■ *Dir* Jack Arnold, John Flynn, Lawrence Schiller • *Scr* Dalene Young, from the book by Norman Mailer

Marine Raiders ★★

Second World War drama
1944 · US · BW · 90mins
This Second World War adventure salutes the marines who trained and then fought for the island of Guadalcanal in the South Pacific. Filmed in pseudo-documentary style, it takes a handful of marines, led by blokeish Pat O'Brien, and plonks them down in California for basic training before showing how they fare in battle. Australia serves as a halfway house, where there's time for romance for Robert Ryan and Ruth Hussey.

Robert Ryan *Capt Dan Craig* • Pat O'Brien *Major Steve Lockhard* • Ruth Hussey *Ellen Foster* • Frank McHugh *Sgt Louis Leary* • Barton MacLane *Sgt Maguire* • Richard Martin *Jimmy* • Edmund Glover *Miller* ■ *Dir* Harold Schuster • *Scr* Warren Duff, from a story by Warren Duff, Martin Rackin

Mario and the Mob ★★ PG

Comedy 1992 · US · Colour · 92mins
Sometimes you just know when a movie is going to be unbearable. Here, for example, your suspicions are aroused by the words "warm-hearted" and "gangster" in the synopsis, but their proximity to the phrase "take in five orphaned children" leaves you in no doubt that you are about to be sandbagged by a sentimental comedy of the most shamelessly tacky and unfunny kind. Even Robert Conrad and Ann Jillian don't deserve this. ▭

Robert Conrad *Mario Dante* • Ann Jillian *Alice Mooney* • Steve Cory *William Moran* • Kyle Cory *Dean Moran* • Christopher Noga *John Moran Jr* • Tammy Brady *Beth Moran* ■ *Dir* Virgil Vogel [*Virgil W Vogel*] • *Scr* Nicholas Corea

Marius ★★★★
Drama 1931 · Fr · BW · 125mins

Hungarian-born Alexander Korda directed *Marius* in France, written and produced by Marcel Pagnol. Rich in depth of characterisation and exquisitely played, it launched the famous Marseilles trilogy that continued with *Fanny* (1932), and *César* (1936). Throughout, the same actors play the principal roles: blunt but loveable café owner César (Raimu); his son, Marius (Pierre Fresnay); Fanny, Marius' sweetheart (Orane Demazis); and elderly widower Panisse (Fernand Charpin). Establishing the relationships for what is to come, Marius here pursues his dream of going to sea and joins the merchant navy, unknowingly leaving Fanny pregnant with their child. In French with English subtitles.

Pierre Fresnay *Marius* • Orane Demazis *Fanny* • Raimu *César* • Alida Rouffe *Honorine* • Fernand Charpin *Panisse* • Paul Dullac *Escartefigue* ■ *Dir* Alexander Korda • *Scr* Marcel Pagnol, from his play

Marius et Jeannette ★★★★15
Comedy drama romance
1997 · Fr · Colour · 97mins

Set in a Marseilles backwater, this kitchen sink romance resembles both Marcel Pagnol's famous *Marius* trilogy and the poetic realist films of Vigo, Renoir and René Clair. Soft-centred spitfire Ariane Ascaride is superb as the single mum struggling to provide for her kids and make sense of her relationship with taciturn nightwatchman, Gérard Meylan. Touching on everything from the failure of Communism to the overlapping doctrines of Christianity and Islam, this bristling pageant is observed with a keen eye and a wry smile by under-rated director, Robert Guédiguian. In French with English subtitles. Contains swearing, sexual references and some nudity. ▭

Ariane Ascaride *Jeannette* • Gérard Meylan *Marius* • Pascale Roberts *Caroline* • Jacques Boudet *Justin* ■ *Dir* Robert Guédiguian • *Scr* Robert Guédiguian, Jean-Louis Milesi

Marjorie Morningstar ★★
Drama 1958 · US · Colour · 123mins

A New York Jewish princess (Natalie Wood) with unconventional ambitions falls for the supposed glamour of show business, as represented by the producer of a summer stock theatrical company (Gene Kelly). Irving Rapper's film underplays the sex and Jewish angles and ends up as a rather bland "woman's picture", though Wood is very good and Kelly is fine in a non-musical role. Caire Trevor and Everett Sloane play Marjorie's middle-class parents, while Ed Wynn hams it up as her eccentric uncle.

Natalie Wood *Marjorie* • Gene Kelly *Noel Airman* • Claire Trevor *Rose* • Carolyn Jones *Marsha* • Ed Wynn *Uncle Samson* • Everett

Sloane *Arnold* • Martin Balsam *Dr David Harris* ■ *Dir* Irving Rapper • *Scr* Everett Freeman, from the novel by Herman Wouk

The Mark ★★★
Crime drama 1961 · UK · BW · 125mins

An apparently reformed paedophile starts a relationship with a young widow who has a little daughter. Things begin to unravel, however, when the press start taking an interest in his new life. Pitched as a rather sentimentalised melodrama, this is still an unusually frank and adult treatment of a serious topic, set in Britain but performed by two major Hollywood stars: an Oscar-nominated Stuart Whitman and Rod Steiger, who plays the hero's psychiatrist.

Maria Schell *Mrs Ruth Leighton* • Stuart Whitman *Jim Fuller* • Rod Steiger *Dr Edmund McNally* • Brenda de Banzie *Mrs Cartwright* • Donald Houston *Austin, reporter* • Donald Wolfit *Mr Clive* ■ *Dir* Guy Green • *Scr* Sidney Buchman, Stanley Mann, from the novel by Charles Israel

The Mark of the Hawk ★★🅄
Drama 1957 · US · Colour · 82mins

Never shown in British cinemas, this is Sidney Poitier's most obscure film: a dramatisation of black Africa's desire for self-determination that was funded by the American Presbyterian church. Poitier plays the ambitious, well-educated African workers' representative facing a choice between pursuing racial equality through terrorism, as advocated by his younger brother, or via the peaceful means urged by Juano Hernandez's pastor and John McIntire's American missionary. After Southern Rhodesia banned the film's makers, location shooting was done in eastern Nigeria. Eartha Kitt, miscast as Poitier's wife, sings one wildly inappropriate song.

Sidney Poitier *Obam* • Juano Hernandez *Amugu* • John McIntire *Craig* • Eartha Kitt *Renee* • Helen Horton *Barbara* • Marne Maitland *Sander Lal* ■ *Dir* Michael Audley, Gilbert Gunn • *Scr* H Kenn Carmichael, from a story by Lloyd Young

Mark of the Phoenix ★🅄
Thriller 1957 · UK · BW · 77mins

A dismal low-budget thriller, with a corkscrew plot involving rare metals, jewel thieves, international blackmail, the Cold War and much else. Made in 1957, it was shelved for two years until a suitably worthy main feature was found to accompany it. The mediocre cast is typical of British B-movies of the period, with the sole exception of Anton Diffring, who plays Inspector Schell. German-born Diffring built an entire career as a villain, often in the uniform of a Nazi, though his final role was as Hungarian composer and pianist Franz Liszt.

Julia Arnall *Petra* • Sheldon Lawrence *Chuck Martin* • Anton Diffring *Inspector Schell* • Eric Pohlmann *Duser* • George Margo *Emilson* • Michael Peake *Koos* • Martin Miller *Brunet* ■ *Dir* Maclean Rogers • *Scr* Norman Hudis, from a story by Desmond Cory

Mark of the Vampire ★★★
Horror 1935 · US · BW · 60mins

Bela Lugosi is on chilling form in this stylish horror from Tod Browning. It's a remake of Browning's own silent classic *London after Midnight* (which starred Lon Chaney Sr, whose death in 1930 left vacant the role of Dracula that made Lugosi a star). Lionel Barrymore is the vampire hunter, and his over-the-top performance prompted critics to acclaim the film as an astute parody. Carol Borland looks bemused as Lugosi's accomplice, which is hardly surprising since her part had been slashed after the censors detected references to incest.

Bela Lugosi *Count Mora* • Lionel Barrymore *Professor Zelen* • Lionel Atwill *Inspector Neumann* • Elizabeth Allan *Irena Borotyn* • Holmes Herbert *Sir Karell Borotyn* • Jean Hersholt *Baron Otto Von Zinden* • Carol Borland *Luna Mora* • Donald Meek *Dr Doskil* ■ *Dir* Tod Browning • *Scr* Guy Endore, Bernard Schubert

The Mark of Zorro ★★★
Silent swashbuckling adventure
1920 · US · BW · 89mins

Don Diego Vega is a sort of American-Mexican Scarlet Pimpernel who leads a double life as Zorro, a masked avenger and expert swordsman, waging war on tyranny. Combining adventure with a dash of romance and comedy, the film gave Douglas Fairbanks the first of the swashbuckling roles that earned him immortality. Directed by Fred Niblo, it co-stars Marguerite De La Motte as the woman who has no time for Don Diego, but is in love with Zorro.

Douglas Fairbanks *Don Diego Vega/Señor Zorro* • Noah Beery *Sergeant Pedro* • Charles Hill Mailes *Don Carlos Pulido* • Claire McDowell *Don Catalina, his wife* • Marguerite De La Motte *Lolita* • Robert McKim *Captain Juan Ramon* ■ *Dir* Fred Niblo • *Scr* Eugene Miller, from the short story *The Curse of Capistrano* by Johnston McCulley

The Mark of Zorro ★★★★🅄
Swashbuckling adventure
1940 · US · BW · 89mins

A wonderful definitive adaptation of the great romantic legend, with matinée idol Tyrone Power as the swashbuckling Don Diego Vega, alias the masked avenger known as Zorro. Amazingly, Ty is the equal (well, almost) of predecessor Douglas Fairbanks Sr in this lavish black-and-white 20th Century-Fox spectacular. Basil Rathbone makes a superb villain, and the sword fights are terrific. For schoolboys of all ages. ▭

Tyrone Power *Don Diego Vega* • Linda Darnell *Lolita Quintero* • Basil Rathbone *Captain Esteban Pasquale* • Gale Sondergaard *Inez Quintero* • Eugene Pallette *Fra Felipe* • J Edward Bromberg *Don Luis Quintero* • Montagu Love *Don Alejandro Vega* • Janet Beecher *Senora Isabella Vega* ■ *Dir* Rouben Mamoulian • *Scr* John Tainton Foote, Garrett Fort, Bess Meredyth, from the novel *The Curse of Capistrano* by Johnston McCulley

The Mark of Zorro ★★
Swashbuckling adventure
1974 · US · Colour · 78mins

This TV movie pales beside the 1920 silent version starring Douglas Fairbanks and the 1940 remake with

Tyrone Power. Nevertheless, Frank Langella parries and thrusts to good effect in the title role, although his adversary, Ricardo Montalban, is much more fun to watch. A young Anne Archer does little but look demure, while veterans Gilbert Roland and Yvonne De Carlo ham it up a treat.

Frank Langella *Don Diego/Zorro* • Ricardo Montalban *Captain Esteban* • Gilbert Roland *Don Alejandro Vega* • Yvonne De Carlo *Isabella Vega* • Louise Sorel *Inez Quintero* • Robert Middleton *Don Luis Quintero* • Anne Archer *Teresa* ■ *Dir* Don McDougall • *Scr* Brian Taggert, from the novel *The Curse of Capistrano* by Johnston McCulley

Mark Twain & Me ★★★🅄
Drama based on a true story
1991 · US · Colour · 89mins

This TV movie is based on the memoirs of Dorothy Quick who, in 1907 at the age of 11, befriended 72-year-old Mark Twain. Their friendship, which continued until his death, gave Dorothy a confidence she'd never known and let Twain experience a closeness he never shared with his own family. Jason Robards shines as Twain in this beautifully realised drama about a unique relationship. ▭

Jason Robards [*Jason Robards Jr*] *Mark Twain/Samuel Clemens* • Talia Shire *Jean Clemens* • RH Thomson *Albert Paine* • Amy Stewart *Dorothy Quick* • Fiona Reid *Mrs Quick* • Anna Ferguson *Arabella* ■ *Dir* Daniel Petrie • *Scr* Cynthia Whitcomb, from the book *Enchantment: a Little Girl's Friendship with Mark Twain* by Dorothy Quick

Marked for Death ★★★★18
Action thriller 1990 · US · Colour · 89mins

Steven Seagal plays a former Drug Enforcement Agency operative who gets involved in a war between local drug dealers and Jamaican Yardies when he "retires" to his home town of Chicago. Basil Wallace is wildly over the top as the bizarrely named Yardie leader Screwface, and female leads Joanna Pacula and Elizabeth Gracen are given little to do. The action sequences are superbly choreographed and it's efficiently directed by Dwight H Little. Contains violence, swearing, sex scenes and drug abuse. ▭

Steven Seagal *John Hatcher* • Basil Wallace *Screwface* • Keith David *Max* • Tom Wright *Charles* • Joanna Pacula *Leslie* • Elizabeth Gracen *Melissa* • Bette Ford *Kate Hatcher* • Danielle Harris *Tracey* ■ *Dir* Dwight H Little • *Scr* Michael Grias, Mark Victor

Marked Man ★★18
Action thriller 1996 · Can · Colour · 94mins

Former professional wrestler "Rowdy" Roddy Piper stars as a convict who witnesses corrupt prison guards killing another inmate. Forced to escape from prison when the guards frame him for the murder, he goes on the run, all the while trying to prove his innocence. There are lots of fight scenes in this by-the-numbers action thriller, though Piper is beginning to show his age. Miles O'Keeffe plays the bad guy. ▭

Roddy Piper *Frank Gibson* • Miles O'Keeffe *Vince Mallick* • Jane Wheeler *Kate Gallagher* • Alina Thompson *Sylvia Elkins* • Vlasta Vrana *Warden Jackson* • Tyrone Benskin *Boyd* ■ *Dir* Marc F Voizard • *Scr* Thomas Ritz

🅄 = SUITABLE FOR ALL   🅄c = SUITABLE FOR ALL, ESPECIALLY FOR YOUNG CHILDREN (VIDEO ONLY)   **PG** = PARENTAL GUIDANCE

The Marked One ★
Crime drama 1963 · UK · BW · 65mins

This British B-movie, barely an hour long, casts William Lucas as a truck driver and ex-con who uses his criminal contacts to help the police locate a kidnapped child. Lucas was a familiar face in threadbare capers like this one, while his co-star Zena Marshall is best remembered for her performance as the comely Miss Taro, one of James Bond's Jamaican conquests in *Dr No*.

William Lucas *Don Mason* • Zena Marshall *Kay Mason* • Patrick Jordan *Inspector Mayne* • Laurie Leigh *Maisie* • David Gregory *Ed Jones* ■ *Dir* Francis Searle • *Scr* Paul Erickson

Marked Woman ★★★★ PG
Crime drama 1937 · US · BW · 91mins

A terrific Warner Bros crime exposé melodrama, based on the real-life case of a group of prostitutes testifying against their gangland boss. No punches are pulled in this taut dramatisation, which stars Bette Davis as a battered victim of the hoodlum, and Humphrey Bogart on the right side of the law as a crusading attorney. Neither star had yet found their respective trademark style, but both display a compulsively watchable dynamic presence. Eduardo Ciannelli is particularly persuasive as the slimy hood, and the screenplay is surprisingly explicit. 🖭

Bette Davis *Mary Dwight* • Humphrey Bogart *David Graham* • Jane Bryan *Betty Strauber* • Eduardo Ciannelli *Johnny Vanning* • Isabel Jewell *Emmy Lou Egan* • Allen Jenkins *Louie* • Mayo Methot *Estelle Porter* • Lola Lane *Gabby Marvin* ■ *Dir* Lloyd Bacon • *Scr* Robert Rossen, Abem Finkel, Seton I Miller

Marlene ★★★ PG
Biographical documentary
1984 · W Ger · Colour and BW · 92mins

Mesmerising documentary from distinguished actor/director Maximilian Schell about the legendary Marlene Dietrich, based on a series of tape-recorded interviews. (She wouldn't let him point the camera at her, but had no objection to the sound rolling.) Although the image is necessarily blunted, Dietrich's comments are utterly revelatory, and Schell utilises film clips and archive material to flesh out his unseen subject. The style palls after a while, but this is still essential viewing for film students and quite unmissable for fans. An English and German language film. 🖭

Marlene Dietrich • Maximilian Schell ■ *Dir* Maximilian Schell • *Scr* Maximilian Schell, Meir Dohnal

Marlowe ★★★★
Mystery thriller 1969 · US · Colour · 95mins

Raymond Chandler always preferred Dick Powell to Humphrey Bogart as his great private eye, but he might well have liked James Garner's quizzical, slightly bemused charm, which even Bruce Lee's martial arts – to update the idea for the sixties – cannot faze. In taking on a missing-person case, chivalrous Marlowe is once more saddened to find that everyone's as false as the Hollywood in which the story is set. Gayle Hunnicutt and Rita

Moreno are the glamour girls, easy on the eye but hard on morality.

James Garner *Philip Marlowe* • Gayle Hunnicutt *Mavis Wald* • Carroll O'Connor *Lt Christy French* • Rita Moreno *Dolores Gonzales* • Sharon Farrell *Orfamay Quest* • William Daniels *Crowell* • Jackie Coogan *Grant W Hicks* • Bruce Lee *Winslow Wong* ■ *Dir* Paul Bogart • *Scr* Sterling Silliphant, from the novel *The Little Sister* by Raymond Chandler

Marnie ★★★★ 15
Psychological drama
1964 · US · Colour · 124mins

Rumours abounded that Grace Kelly would be making a comeback before this adaptation of Winston Graham's novel went into production. Her icy aloofness would have been perfect for this tale of kleptomania, frigidity, fetishism and suppressed anxiety, and Tippi Hedren was considered no substitute by contemporary critics. Hindsight has established this as one of Hitchcock's more interesting misfires. Some of the conspicuously artificial set design and back projection may not suit all tastes, but watch for Robert Burks's suave colour photography and the mental duel between a man (Sean Connery) turned on by crime and a woman who steals to forget. 🖭

Tippi Hedren *Marnie* • Sean Connery *Mark Rutland* • Diane Baker *Lil Mainwaring* • Martin Gabel *Sidney Strutt* • Louise Latham *Bernice Edgar* • Bob Sweeney *Cousin Bob* • Alan Napier *Mr Rutland* • S John Launer *Sam Ward* ■ *Dir* Alfred Hitchcock • *Scr* Jay Presson Allen, from the novel by Winston Graham.

Maroc 7 ★★
Crime drama 1967 · UK · Colour · 91mins

The heavily insured, flashing pins of Cyd Charisse are on display in this lacklustre crime caper about an international jewel thief and a priceless medallion, with a support cast that includes such acting luminaries as Elsa Martinelli and Leslie Phillips. It makes you wonder why someone in the production line didn't cry out "Stop, abandon ship".

Gene Barry *Simon Grant* • Cyd Charisse *Louise Henderson* • Elsa Martinelli *Claudia* • Leslie Phillips *Raymond Lowe* • Denholm Elliott *Inspector Barrada* • Alexandra Stewart *Michele Craig* ■ *Dir* Gerry O'Hara • *Scr* David Osborn, from his story

Marooned ★★★ U
Science-fiction adventure
1969 · US · Colour · 123mins

Winner of the Oscar for best special visual effects, this astute blend of science fact and fiction eerily anticipated the kind of lost-in-space crisis that would actually occur during the *Apollo 13* mission. Gene Hackman, Richard Crenna and James Franciscus successfully combine public confidence with private misgivings as the stranded crew, while Gregory Peck heads the Nasa operation with typical reserve. But although he makes the most of his space hardware, director John Sturges never gets the domestic drama off the ground, with Lee Grant and the other wives being reduced to little more than cardboard cut-outs. 🖭

Gregory Peck *Charles Keith* • Richard Crenna *Jim Pruett* • David Janssen *Ted Dougherty* • James Franciscus *Clayton Stone* • Gene

Hackman *Buzz Lloyd* • Lee Grant *Celia Pruett* • Nancy Kovack *Teresa Stone* • Mariette Hartley *Betty Lloyd* ■ *Dir* John Sturges • *Scr* Mayo Simon, from the novel by Martin Caidin • *Special Effects* Lawrence Butler, Donald C Glouner, Robie Robinson

Marquis ★★★ 18
Historical fantasy satire
1989 · Bel/Fr · Colour · 79mins

It's hard to know whether to applaud this for its sheer audacity or to decry its many misfiring ideas. Certainly, director Henri Xhonneux and his designer Roland Topor can't be accused of taking a traditional approach to the Marquis de Sade's last days in the Bastille, as scenes from his books are presented as claymation diversions, while their much-maligned author spends most of the time in earnest conversation with his penis, an extended, human-faced member named Colin. All the cast wear symbolic animal heads, while the dialogue could have come from a bawdy pantomime. In French with English subtitles. 🖭

François Marthouret *Marquis/Dog* • Valérie Kling *Colin/Colin's Sex* • Michel Robin *Ambert/Rat* • Isabelle Canet-Wolfe *Justine/Cow* ■ *Dir* Henri Xhonneux • *Scr* Roland Topor, Henry Xhonneux, from the novel *Justine* by the Marquis de Sade

Marquise ★★ 15
Historical romance
1997 · Fr/It/Swi/Sp · Colour · 110mins

Meticulously re-creating the 17th-century theatrical milieu, this handsome film still has all the vigour of a waxwork tableau. Véra Belmont's directorial inexperience conspicuously counts against her, as the action veers between novelettish melodrama and am-dram classicism. As the dancer thrust into the rivalry between Molière (Bernard Giraudeau) and Racine (Lambert Wilson), Sophie Marceau pouts persuasively as she hops between the playwrights' beds. But her rendition of *Andromaque* is anything but the work of a great tragedienne. Pompous dialogue equally hampers the normally accomplished supporting cast. In French with English subtitles. Contains sex scenes and nudity. 🖭

Sophie Marceau *Marquise* • Bernard Giraudeau *Molière* • Lambert Wilson *Jean Racine* • Thierry Lhermitte *Louis XIV* ■ *Dir* Véra Belmont • *Scr* Jean-François Josselin, Véra Belmont, Marcel Beaulieu

The Marquise of O ★★★★
Period drama
1976 · W Ger/Fr · Colour · 102mins

One of Eric Rohmer's extremely rare departures from France and the present, this elegant version of Heinrich von Kleist's classic novella is set during the Franco-Prussian War. It concerns a virtuous widow who is drugged, then raped by an officer in the invading Russian army. When she finds herself pregnant, she marries the man, not realising it was he who raped her. Shooting in Germany, with members of Peter Stein's Berlin theatre, Rohmer seems perfectly at ease with the ironic nuances of the delicate story. Rohmer and his cinematographer Nestor Almendros were inspired by German Romantic

painters and bathe the neo-classical interiors in an unearthly light. In German with English subtitles.

Edith Clever *Marquise* • Bruno Ganz *Count* • Peter Lühr *Marquise's father* • Edda Seippel *Marquise's mother* • Otto Sander *Marquise's brother* • Ruth Drexel *Midwife* ■ *Dir* Eric Rohmer • *Scr* Eric Rohmer, from a novella by Heinrich von Kleist

The Marriage Circle ★★★★★
Silent comedy 1924 · US · BW · 90mins

The first, and perhaps best, of the six silent films Ernst Lubitsch made at Warner Bros is a daring and sophisticated comedy of manners. Set in Vienna, the scenario tells of the intricate intrigues between two married couples and their suspicions of infidelity, both justified and unjustified. What distinguishes the "Lubitsch touch" is the way he works by suggestion rather than direct statement, coupled with casually significant close-ups of objects. The playing, notably by Florence Vidor (recently separated from director King Vidor), Marie Prevost and Adolphe Menjou, is particularly subtle.

Florence Vidor *Charlotte Braun* • Monte Blue *Dr Franz Braun* • Marie Prevost *Mizzie Stock* • Creighton Hale *Dr Gustav Mueller* • Adolphe Menjou *Prof Josef Stock* ■ *Dir* Ernst Lubitsch • *Scr* Paul Bern

The Marriage Fool ★★★
Comedy drama 1998 · US · Colour · 86mins

The chemistry between Walter Matthau and Carol Burnett is irresistible in this TV movie. A recently widowed man is ready to enter into a new romantic relationship, only to have his conservative, immature son (John Stamos) get in the way. The son finally perceives his own fear of commitment and his father's desire for happiness when he falls in love with a divorcee himself. Matthau's director son Charles displays a fine hand at comedy in this poignant ode to love.

Walter Matthau *Frank Walsh* • Carol Burnett *Florence* • John Stamos *Rupert Walsh* • Teri Polo *Susan Prescot* ■ *Dir* Charles Matthau • *Scr* Richard Vetere, from the play by Richard Vetere

The Marriage-Go-Round ★★
Romantic comedy
1960 · US · Colour · 98 mins

The marriage of James Mason and Susan Hayward is upset when Swedish beauty Julie Newmar comes to stay. Newmar decides that the brains of brilliant anthropology professor Mason, combined with her physical attributes, would make for the perfect child. In adapting his play for the screen, Leslie Stevens mislays the laugh quotient, resulting in a faintly embarrassing comedy that falls flat on its face. Mason is suitably bemused and Newmar overacts, yet Hayward rises above the situation to give a terrific performance as the unfortunate wife.

Susan Hayward *Content Delville* • James Mason *Paul Delville* • Julie Newmar *Katrin Sveg* • Robert Paige *Dr Ross Barnett* • June Clayworth *Flo Granger* • Joe Kirkwood Jr *Henry* • Mary Patton *Mamie* ■ *Dir* Walter Lang • *Scr* Leslie Stevens, from his play

Marriage Is a Private Affair ★★★

Romantic comedy 1944 · US · BW · 116mins

A spoilt but insecure New York beauty (Lana Turner), fearful of following in the footsteps of her shallow, much-married mother, makes a hasty wartime marriage to a stuffed-shirt air force officer (John Hodiak) and has a baby. Tempted to commit infidelity with an old flame (James Craig), she finally grows up and finds herself. Under Robert Z Leonard's direction, the inexperienced Turner does well in this intelligent drama, slightly marred by extraneous and silly excesses.

Lana Turner *Theo Scofield West* • James Craig *Captain Miles Lancing* • John Hodiak *Lieutenant Tom West* • Frances Gifford *Sissy Mortimer* • Hugh Marlowe *Joseph I Murdock* • Keenan Wynn *Major Bob Wilton* ■ *Dir* Robert Z Leonard • *Scr* David Hertz, Lenore Coffee, from the novel by Judith Kelly

Marriage – Italian Style ★★12

Comedy drama 1964 · Fr/It · Colour · 95mins

The director and stars of the hit comedy *Yesterday, Today and Tomorrow* immediately reunited for another Neapolitan sex comedy, but with less success. Businessman Marcello Mastroianni hires a prostitute to double as his live-in lover and his aged mother's nursemaid. Years later, she traps him into marriage by pretending she's terminally ill; in fact, she's hiding three children, one of whom may be Mastroianni's. Male chauvinist pigs may admire Mastroianni's behaviour, while feminists will revel in Loren's sly scheming. Few will laugh, though. An Italian language film. 🎞

Sophia Loren *Filomena Marturano* • Marcello Mastroianni *Domenico Soriano* • Aldo Puglisi *Alfredo* • Tecla Scarano *Rosalie* • Marilu Tolo *Diane* ■ *Dir* Vittorio De Sica • *Scr* Eduardo De Filippo, Renato Castellani, Tonino Guerra, Leo Benvenuti, Piero De Bernardi, from the play *Filumena Marturano* by Eduardo DeFilippo

The Marriage of a Young Stockbroker ★★

Comedy drama 1971 · US · Colour · 94mins

Lawrence Turman, producer of *The Graduate*, here directs another Charles Webb novel. Richard Benjamin and Joanna Shimkus are trapped in an unhappy marriage: he just likes to eye young girls, so she moves in with her sister and plans to divorce. What follows is certainly in the satirical vein of *The Graduate*, as well as *Bob & Carol & Ted & Alice* and a dozen other comedies aimed at mildly shocking the middle-aged, middle-class audience.

Richard Benjamin *William Alren* • Joanna Shimkus *Lisa Alren* • Elizabeth Ashley *Nan* • Adam West *Chester* • Patricia Barry *Psychiatrist* • Tiffany Bolling *Girl in the rain* ■ *Dir* Lawrence Turman • *Scr* Lorenzo Semple Jr, from the novel by Charles Webb

The Marriage of Maria Braun ★★★★15

Romantic drama 1978 · W Ger · Colour · 114mins

Hanna Schygulla won the best actress prize at Berlin for her work in Rainer Werner Fassbinder's most avowedly commercial film. The first instalment of his celebrated postwar trilogy, it owes much to the glossy fifties melodramas of Douglas Sirk and works just as well as soap opera as socio-political treatise. The choices Maria makes for survival during her husband's prolonged absences clearly reflect those made by Germany in the post-Hitler era, and Fassbinder evidently disapproves of Maria's (and the nation's) notion of paradise postponed. Accessible, yet also complex and ambiguous. In German with English subtitles. 🎞

Hanna Schygulla *Maria Braun* • Klaus Löwitsch *Hermann Braun* • Ivan Desny *Karl Oswald* • Gottfried John *Willi Klenze* ■ *Dir* Rainer Werner Fassbinder • *Scr* Peter Marthesheimer, Pea Fröhlich, Rainer Werner Fassbinder, from a story by Rainer Werner Fassbinder

Marriage on the Rocks ★★

Comedy 1965 · US · Colour · 109mins

An unfunny and tasteless farrago that looks like an attempt by Frank Sinatra and Dean Martin to have a holiday on location in Mexico away from fellow clan members, while dragging along an awkwardly cast Deborah Kerr. There's a moderately entertaining turn from Cesar Romero, plus a motley collection of supporting players including Hermione Baddeley and Trini Lopez, not to mention Sinatra's daughter Nancy. Beautifully photographed by Garbo's cameraman William H Daniels, who also gets a producer credit, it's not entirely without interest either. Yet it's surprisingly underdirected by one-time dance supremo, Jack Donohue.

Frank Sinatra *Dan Edwards* • Deborah Kerr *Valerie Edwards* • Dean Martin *Ernie Brewer* • Cesar Romero *Miguel Santos* • Hermione Baddeley *Jeannie MacPherson* • Tony Bill *Jim Blake* • John McGiver *Shad Nathan* • Nancy Sinatra *Tracy Edwards* • Trini Lopez ■ *Dir* Jack Donohue • *Scr* Cy Howard

The Marriage Playground ★★★

Drama 1929 · US · BW · 70mins

This was the fourth of five films made in 1929 by the undeservedly neglected German director, Lothar Mendes. Elegantly adapted from an Edith Wharton novel, it also confirmed Broadway actor Fredric March as a Hollywood fixture. As the wealthy American touring Italy, he comes to the rescue of young Mary Brian, who has been left by her pleasure-loving parents (Huntley Gordon and Lilyan Tashman) to care for her siblings. As ever in Wharton's fiction, social convention (in the form of March's fiancée) momentarily threatens the happy ending.

Fredric March *Martin Boyne* • Mary Brian *Judith Wheater* • Lilyan Tashman *Joyce Wheater* • Huntley Gordon *Cliffe Wheater* • Kay Francis *Zinnia La Crosse* ■ *Dir* Lothar Mendes • *Scr* J Walter Ruben, Doris Anderson, from the novel *The Children* by Edith Wharton

Married for Murder ★★★

Thriller based on a true story 1992 · Colour · 93mins

An absorbing thriller based on a true story about insurance fraud and murder. Treat Williams turns in another fine performance as the devious protagonist who specialises in bumping off assorted friends and relatives and collecting on their life policies. It's not quite in the same class as *Double Indemnity*, but not at all bad for its kind. Contains violence.

Treat Williams *Alan Palliko* • Arliss Howard *Vince Bugliosi* • Rebecca Jenkins *Sandra Stockton* • Embeth Davidtz *Katherine Palliko* • JE Freeman *Robert Guy* • Pruitt Taylor Vince *Michael Brockington* • Valerie Mahaffey *Gail Bugliosi* ■ *Dir* Yves Simoneau • *Scr* Philip Rosenberg, from the book *Till Death Us Do Part* by Vincent Bugliosi, Ken Hurwitz

Married People, Single Sex ★★18

Erotic psychological drama 1993 · US · Colour and BW · 91mins

Despite the straight-to-camera "confessions" and the mix of black-and-white and colour photography, this is little different from a standard straight-to-video erotic feature. Director Mike Sedan may have intended this as an exploration of grown-up sexuality and marriage, but he lingers (usually in colour) too long on the various couples' coupling for this to stand any serious analysis. A dismal sequel followed in 1995. 🎞

Josef Pilato [Joseph Pilato] *Artie* • Chase Masterson *Beth* • Shelley Michelle *Carol* • Darla Slavens *Fran* • Teri Thompson *Meg* • Bob Rudd *Mike* ■ *Dir* Mike Sedan • *Scr* Catherine Tavel

Married to a Stranger ★★

Drama 1997 · US · Colour · 97mins

Jaclyn Smith, queen of the TV movie, here uses every available emotion to play a mother struck down with amnesia who doesn't remember her husband and daughter. Regressing back to her teenage years, she's about to leave for Europe to pursue a career in art. Unlike Smith, audiences will recall they have seen this story more than a few times before – usually done better – and when Smith starts frolicking like a teenager you yearn for Kathleen Turner's far better turn in *Peggy Sue Got Married*. A bit of a comedown for director Sidney J Furie.

Jaclyn Smith *Megan Potter* • Robert Clohessy *David Potter* • Kim Coates *Dr Jesse Bethan* • Ed Lauter *Megan's father* • Louise Fletcher *Nana* ■ *Dir* Sidney J Furie • *Scr* Susan Black

Married to It ★★15

Romantic comedy drama 1991 · US · Colour · 107mins

Shot in 1991 but unreleased until 1993, this marital comedy from Arthur Hiller (*Love Story*) tries hard to raise a laugh but instead suffocates us in sugar. Harking back to the golden days of the sixties and sexual liberation, it's about the tribulations of three married New York couples and looks like out-takes from various sitcoms glued together. The members of the cast are good, though (Beau Bridges, Stockard Channing, Ron Silver and Cybill Shepherd among them), and they do their best with the substandard material. Contains swearing. 🎞

Beau Bridges *John Morden* • Stockard Channing *Iris Morden* • Robert Sean Leonard *Chuck Bishop* • Mary Stuart Masterson *Nina Bishop* • Cybill Shepherd *Claire Laurent* • Ron Silver *Leo Rothenberg* ■ *Dir* Arthur Hiller • *Scr* Janet Kovalcik

Married to the Mob ★★★★15

Comedy thriller 1988 · US · Colour · 99mins

Michelle Pfeiffer proves she's a deft hand at light-hearted fare in Jonathan Demme's gangster comedy thriller. Pfeiffer plays the widow of a mobster (Alec Baldwin) who decides to make a new life for herself and her child, unaware that the FBI (including the inept Matthew Modine) and the mob (in the form of lust-driven Dean Stockwell) are both keeping an eye on her. The cast is superb, especially Mercedes Ruehl in over-the-top mode as Stockwell's brassy, jealous wife, and Demme keeps both the action and the laughs perfectly tuned. 🎞

Michelle Pfeiffer *Angela De Marco* • Matthew Modine *Mike Downey* • Dean Stockwell *Tony "The Tiger" Russo* • Alec Baldwin *Frank "The Cucumber" De Marco* • Mercedes Ruehl *Connie Russo* • Joan Cusack *Rose Boyle* ■ *Dir* Jonathan Demme • *Scr* Barry Strugatz, Mark R Burns

The Married Woman ★★★★

Drama 1964 · Fr · BW · 98mins

Jean-Luc Godard's movie gained immediate notoriety for its sex scenes, and no less a personage than General De Gaulle objected to the morality of its heroine. Macha Méril is married to a pilot, has an affair with an actor and seems to fill her head with glamorous images from magazines. As with all Godard movies, this is like a scrapbook of bits and pieces that, glued together, reveal the impact of the consumer society. In French with English subtitles.

Macha Méril *Charlotte Giraud* • Bernard Noël *Robert, the lover* • Philippe Leroy *Pierre, the husband* • Roger Leenhardt • Rita Maiden *Madame Celine* ■ *Dir/Scr* Jean-Luc Godard

Marry Me! ★★

Romantic comedy 1949 · UK · BW · 97mins

The story of four couples introduced by a matrimonial agency run by two spinster sisters, this Gainsborough Picture languishes in obscurity through its lack of major stars and poor reputation. Inevitably, it's a hit-and-miss affair with Susan Shaw and Patrick Holt faring best in the most serious relationship as an ill-matched dance hall hostess and country parson. But Guy Middleton brings a deft lighter touch as the aristocrat who fancies the schoolteacher introduced to his manservant.

Derek Bond *Andrew* • Susan Shaw *Pat* • Patrick Holt *Martin* • Carol Marsh *Doris* • David Tomlinson *David Haig* • Zena Marshall *Marcelle* • Guy Middleton *Sir Gordon Blake* ■ *Dir* Terence Fisher • *Scr* Denis Waldock, Lewis Gilbert

Marry Me Again ★★

Comedy 1953 · US · BW · 73mins

Writer/director Frank Tashlin's cartooning experience intermittently livens up this tame satire in which garage hand Robert Cummings leaves blonde scatterbrain Marie Wilson at the altar to become a Korean War

🅄 = SUITABLE FOR ALL   🅄ᴄ = SUITABLE FOR ALL, ESPECIALLY FOR YOUNG CHILDREN (VIDEO ONLY)   🅿🅶 = PARENTAL GUIDANCE

hero, then won't marry her because she's inherited a fortune. Tashlin, who married supporting player Mary Costa at the end of shooting, has mild fun with nutty psychiatrists, empty shoes and the vogue for 3-D movies, but it's a far cry from his best work.

Robert Cummings *Bill* • Marie Wilson *Doris* • Ray Walker *Mac* • Mary Costa *Joan* • Jess Barker *Jenkins* • Lloyd Corrigan *Mr Taylor* • June Vincent *Miss Craig* • Richard Gaines *Dr Pepperdine* ■ Dir Frank Tashlin • Scr Frank Tashlin, from a story by Alex Gottlieb

Marry Me! Marry Me! ★★★

Comedy drama   1968 · Fr · Colour · 89mins

Years before his tragic rural masterpieces, *Jean de Florette* and *Manon des Sources* (both 1986), writer/producer/director Claude Berri allowed himself a little levity with this inconsequential trifle about Parisienne love and marriage. Berri stars as an encyclopedia salesman torn between two women. A French language film.

Claude Berri *Claude* • Elisabeth Wiener *Isabelle Schmoll* • Luisa Colpeyn [Louisa Colpeyn] *Madame Schmoll* • Grégoire Aslan *Monsieur Schmoll* • Regine *Marthe Schmoll* • Prudence Harrington *Helen* ■ Dir/Scr Claude Berri

The Marrying Kind ★★★★

Comedy drama   1952 · US · BW · 92mins

A post office worker (Aldo Ray) and his ex-secretary wife (Judy Holliday) are on the brink of divorce. As they tell their story to an understanding judge (one-time silent screen star Madge Kennedy), we watch their relationship in flashback, from first meeting through marriage and children. Well directed by George Cukor, this is a perfect vehicle for the quirky, brilliant Holliday, following her success in *Born Yesterday*. Overlaid with incisive wit and beautifully played by both stars, this combination of domestic drama and comedy is a winner all the way.

Judy Holliday *Florence Keefer* • Aldo Ray *Chet Keefer* • Madge Kennedy *Judge Carroll* • Sheila Bond *Joan Shipley* • John Alexander *Howard Shipley* • Rex Williams *George Bastian* • Phyllis Povah *Mrs Derringer* • Peggy Cass *Emily Bundy* ■ Dir George Cukor • Scr Ruth Gordon, Garson Kanin

Mars ★ 18

Science-fiction action drama
1996 · US · Colour · 86mins

Another grungy future, another nameless corporation running everything... didn't we cover this in *Blade Runner*? This time around, Olivier Gruner is a police officer (a "keeper") who's investigating the death of his brother on Mars. It's tough to stay interested in the film: Gruner, who's rarely animated, is not being paid enough here to change facial expression, or even use his own voice. The sloppily edited fights hardly make up for the plodding script and wooden acting. Contains sex scenes, violence and some swearing. 📺

Olivier Gruner *Caution Templar* • Shari Belafonte *Doc Halliday* • Gabriel Dell Jr *Buckskin Greenberg* • Alex Hyde-White *Phillip Clement* • Scott Valentine *Pete the Hermit* • Lindsey Lee Ginter *Ike Ringo* ■ Dir Jon Hess • Scr Patrick Highsmith, Steven Hartov, from a story by Patrick Highsmith

Mars Attacks! ★★★ 12

Satirical science-fiction
1996 · US · Colour · 101mins

Little green men from the angry red planet launch a flying-saucer attack on Earth in director Tim Burton's uneven space oddity, based on a bubble-gum card storyline from the sixties. Both a tribute to and a spoof of fifties' B-movies, Burton stumbles as many times as he succeeds in playing with the back catalogue of lurid pulp sci-fi references. But once the computer-generated bug-eyed Martians strut their evil stuff, this daffy *Independence Day* lampoon comes alive. Among an amazing cast, Pierce Brosnan is hilarious as a presidential adviser and Lisa Marie is weirdly creepy as an alien temptress. 📺 **DVD**

Jack Nicholson *President James Dale/Art Land* • Glenn Close *Marsha Dale* • Annette Bening *Barbara Land* • Pierce Brosnan *Donald Kessler* • Danny DeVito *Rude gambler* • Martin Short *Jerry Ross* • Sarah Jessica Parker *Nathalie Lake* • Michael J Fox *Jason Stone* • Rod Steiger *General Decker* • Tom Jones • Lisa Marie *Martian girl* ■ Dir Tim Burton • Scr Jonathan Gems, from his story, from the illustrated card series by the Topps Company

La Marseillaise ★★★ U

Historical drama   1938 · Fr · BW · 116mins

Sponsored by the trades union movement, this is the "official" film of the French Revolution, filmed some time after the actual event. It's not one of Renoir's greatest films: he seems torn between the need to make a big populist epic and his own instinct to produce a humane document, in which both the doomed aristocracy and the revolting peasantry are accorded a sympathetic hearing. Thus the king has toothache and worries about his wig; the approaching army has foot sores; and, when the national anthem is first heard, someone says how awful it is. In French with English subtitles.

Pierre Renoir *Louis XVI* • Lise Delamare *Marie Antoinette* • Léon Larive *Picard* • William Aguet *La Rochefoucald-Liancourt* • Louis Jouvet *Roederer* ■ Dir Jean Renoir • Scr Jean Renoir, Carl Koch, N Martel Dreyfus, Mme Jean-Paul Dreyfus

The Marseilles Contract ★★

Thriller   1974 · UK/Fr · Colour · 89 mins

Despite an endearing performance from Michael Caine as a hit man, this carefree slice of mayhem involving drug smuggling, an assassination attempt and executive double-crosses never quite gets into top gear. Only the presence of Anthony Quinn and James Mason, along with some eye-catching Paris and Marseilles locations, adds any interest to the stereotypical characters and overly familiar plot.

Michael Caine *Deray* • Anthony Quinn *Steve Ventura* • James Mason *Brizard* • Maureen Kerwin *Lucianne* • Marcel Bozzuffi *Calmet* • Catherine Rouvel *Brizard's mistress* • Maurice Ronet *Inspector Briac* • André Oumansky *Marsac* • Alexandra Stewart *Rita* ■ Dir Robert Parrish • Scr Judd Bernard, from his story *What Are Friends For?*

Marshal Law ★★ 18

Action thriller   1996 · US · Colour · 92mins

When is a disaster movie just a disaster? Jimmy Smits is a loveable construction worker who's just about to go home after overseeing the building of a posh apartment complex when an earthquake hits. If that weren't bad enough, an escaped convict and his band of punk desperadoes arrive on the scene, looking to take advantage of the chaos. Kristy Swanson co-stars, while Jimmy's kids are tossed in for pathos. Contains swearing and violence. 📺

Jimmy Smits *Jack Coleman* • Ethan Peck *Josh Coleman* • Kristy Swanson *Betty* • Camilla Belle *Boot Coleman* • Vonte Sweet *Weathers* • James LeGros *Cougar* ■ Dir Stephen Cornwell • Scr Stephen Cornwall, Nick Gregory

Martha ★★★ 15

Thriller   1973 · W Ger · Colour · 111mins

Updating the story of *Effi Briest*, Rainer Werner Fassbinder laid waste the "woman's picture" with this highly stylised study of the dark desires that lurk behind even the most respectable façades. Sunny, naturalistic compositions take on unexpectedly sinister aspects, as Karlheinz Böhm dominates and then destroys Margit Carstensen, the thirtysomething virgin whose yearning for romance contributes to her own downfall. Littering the Hollywood-style melodrama with Freudian dream symbols and allusions to Germany's fascist past, Fassbinder also encourages a florid performance from Carstensen, reinforcing the film's debt to the camp weepies of Douglas Sirk. A German language film. 📺

Margit Carstensen *Martha* • Karlheinz Böhm *Helmut Salomon* • Barbara Valentin *Marianne* • Peter Chatel *Kaiser* • Gisela Fackeldey *Mother* ■ Dir/Scr Rainer Werner Fassbinder

Martha and Ethel ★★★★

Documentary   1993 · US · Colour · 80mins

Although they are both genuinely fond of their nannies (Martha Kneifel and Ethel Edwards), it's clear that both director Jyll Johnstone and producer Barbara Ettinger resent the way in which their parents parcelled them off while they got on with their own lives. But then there is an uncomfortable tension underpinning nearly all of the relationships here. Johnstone's respect for Martha, for example, is tempered by mixed memories of the German immigrant's clinical methods, while Ettinger's mother still seems to see the African-American Ethel as some sort of servant. Full of knowing asides, this is a real curio.

Dir Jyll Johnstone • Scr Alysha Cohen, Barbara Ettinger, Christina Houlihan, Jyll Johnstone, Frank Ortega, Sharon Woods

Martha and I ★★★★

Drama   1990 · W Ger/It/Fr · Colour · 107mins

Fifty-one years after he made his classic documentary, *The Rape of Czechoslovakia*, 77-year-old Jiri Weiss returned to the eve of the Second World War for this moving and unforced plea for tolerance. Defying conventional wisdom about class, race and physical appearance, Michel

Piccoli married the family's portly maid (Marianne Sägebrecht) and found a contentment that young Ondrej Vetchy immediately appreciates when he is sent to stay with his uncle by his haughty parents in the hope that he will be cured of a similar obsession. In German with English subtitles.

Marianne Sägebrecht *Martha* • Michel Piccoli *Dr Ernst Fuchs* • Vaclav Chalupa *Emil as a teenager* • Ondrej Vetchy *Emil as an adult* ■ Dir/Scr Jiri Weiss

Martha – Meet Frank, Daniel and Laurence ★★★ 15

Romantic comedy drama
1997 · UK · Colour · 83mins

Three hapless British chaps (Rufus Sewell, Joseph Fiennes and Tom Hollander) fall for gorgeous American Monica Potter when she arrives in London hoping to start a new life. There's the odd rough patch, but the witty script uses coincidence as a springboard for plot, rather than something to avoid, and shows that a British movie can be both romantic and funny. Potter, despite appearing in some dreadful films (*Patch Adams* for one), proves to be an adept comedian, though the film suffered from being released around the same time as the Gwyneth Paltrow hit *Sliding Doors*. Despite its dreadful title, this deserved better. Contains swearing and sexual references. 📺 **DVD**

Monica Potter *Martha* • Rufus Sewell *Frank* • Tom Hollander *Daniel* • Joseph Fiennes *Laurence* • Ray Winstone *Pedersen* ■ Dir Nick Hamm • Scr Peter Morgan

Martha, Ruth and Edie ★★

Drama   1988 · Can · Colour · 98mins

The three protagonists of the title gather at a women's self-help conference to indulge in the kind of emotional regurgitation that gives barroom chauvinists their best ammunition. The three actresses (Jennifer Dale, Andrea Martin and Lois Maxwell, aka Miss Moneypenny) nobly attempt to rise above this TV movie's basic premise ("better out than in"). But they cannot stop the screenplay from presenting the complexities of individual psychology in uncomfortably graphic detail.

Jennifer Dale *Martha* • Andrea Martin *Ruth* • Lois Maxwell *Edie* ■ Dir Norma Bailey, Danièle J Suissa, Deepa Mehta Saltzman [Deepa Mehta] • Scr Anna Sandor, Barbara O'Kelly, Janet Maclean

Martial Outlaw ★★ 18

Martial arts action
1993 · US · Colour · 85mins

Martial arts star Jeff Wincott gives a truly horrendous performance as a Drug Enforcement Agency agent investigating the Russian mafia. Gary Hudson is not much better as Wincott's brother, a dirty cop who sabotages his efforts. In fact, the real stars here are several unbelievably long and sadistic fight sequences, where the participants not only use martial arts, but everything else they can get their hands on. 📺

Jeff Wincott *Kevin White* • Gary Hudson *Jack White* • Vladimir Skomarovsky *Niko* • Krista

Errickson *Lori White* • Liliana Komorowska *Marina* • Richard Jaeckel *Mr White* ■ *Dir* Kurt Anderson • *Scr* Thomas Ritz, Pierre David, John Bryant, George Saunders

Martin ★★★★ 18

Horror   1978 · US · Colour and BW · 93mins

A neglected minor masterpiece from cult horror director George A Romero. Is teenager John Amplas a sexually repressed oddball with a Dracula fixation, or an octogenarian kept youthful by blood? Romero doesn't give the game away easily, instead telling his highly intelligent story with overdoses of atmosphere, gore and jet-black humour. The film also features a splendid central performance from Amplas, who stalks suburbia killing frenziedly with razor blades instead of the traditional fangs. Not everyone's cup of tea (or blood), this is well worth a look for horror addicts with a craving for the offbeat and strange. ▣

John Amplas *Martin* • Lincoln Maazel *Tati Cuda* • Christine Forrest *Christina* • Elayne Nadeau *Mrs Santini* • Tom Savini *Arthur* • George A Romero *Father Howard* ■ *Dir/Scr* George A Romero

Martin Roumagnac ★★

Crime drama   1946 · Fr · BW · 88mins

Directed by Georges Lacombe, this French drama concerns an affair between Jean Gabin, a provincial builder, and Marlene Dietrich, a sophisticated new arrival from the city for whom he is building a house. On discovering that she is a high-class whore, Gabin murders her. The potentially erotic pairing of Dietrich and Gabin promises much. Sadly, it delivers little more than a run-of-the-mill courtroom drama, with the story of the affair told in flashback.

Marlene Dietrich *Blanche Ferrand* • Jean Gabin *Martin Roumagnac* • Margo Lion *Martin's sister* • Marcel Herrand *Consul* • Jean d'Yd *Blanche's uncle* ■ *Dir* Georges Lacombe • *Scr* Pierre Véry, from a novel by Pierre-René Wolf

Martin's Day ★★ 15

Drama   1984 · Can · Colour · 94mins

A Canadian drama which managed to attract a notable cast (Richard Harris, Linday Wagner, James Coburn, Karen Black) but little attention. Director Alan Gibson struggles with the emotionally driven material, which revolves around an escaped convict and his adventures with his young hostage, and he doesn't manage to get even half the performance out of Justin Henry that Robert Benton did in *Kramer vs Kramer* five years earlier.

Richard Harris *Martin Steckert* • Lindsay Wagner *Dr Mennen* • James Coburn *Lieutenant Lardner* • Justin Henry *Martin* • Karen Black *Karen* • John Ireland *Brewer* ■ *Dir* Alan Gibson • *Scr* Allan Scott, Chris Bryant

Marty ★★★★★ U

Drama   1955 · US · BW · 86mins

''Whaddya wanna do tonight, Marty?'' ''I dunno, Angie, what do you wanna do tonight?'' This Paddy Chayefsky original began life as one of the great live television dramas; it went on to become part of the fabric of the fifties and win a fistful of Oscars, including

best picture and best actor. Ernest Borgnine was never better as the Bronx butcher with low self-esteem, though vulnerable Betsy Blair is equally good as the ''dog'' he falls in love with. This tender, moving film was a major triumph for its uncredited producer Burt Lancaster, who allegedly made the picture as a tax loss. ▣

Ernest Borgnine *Marty* • Betsy Blair *Clara* • Esther Minciotti *Mrs Pilletti* • Joe Mantell *Angie* • Augusta Ciolli *Catherine* • Karen Steele *Virginia* • Jerry Paris *Thomas* • Frank Sutton *Ralph* ■ *Dir* Delbert Mann • *Scr* Paddy Chayefsky, from his TV play

Marvin and Tige ★

Drama   1983 · US · Colour · 104mins

An eminently missable tear-jerker, this stars John Cassavetes as a middle-aged dropout reduced to earning a little cash by collecting the deposits on discarded bottles. For company he ties up with 11-year-old Tige, a street urchin whom he saves from committing suicide. And then, when the kid gets ill and goes to hospital, Cassavetes goes in search of Tige's father. Working like one of the corniest, most manipulative products of the Depression era, this has a banality that is hard to credit.

John Cassavetes *Marvin Stewart* • Billy Dee Williams *Richard Davis* • Denise Nicholas-Hill [Denise Nicholas] *Vanessa Jackson* • Gibran Brown *Tige Jackson* • Fay Hauser *Brenda Davis* ■ *Dir* Eric Weston • *Scr* Wanda Dell, Eric Weston, from a novel by Frankcina Glass

Marvin's Room ★★★★ 12

Comedy drama   1996 · US · Colour · 94mins

Scott McPherson adapted his play for the screen before dying of an Aids-related illness, and this drama never quite escapes its theatrical roots. Nevertheless, this character-driven tale benefits from a clutch of restrained and impressive performances, including one from a pre-*Titanic* Leonardo DiCaprio. Bessie (Diane Keaton), who has been looking after her bedridden father for years, is forced to ask her estranged sister Lee (Meryl Streep) for help after she is told she has leukaemia. Streep arrives with her two sons – Hal Scardino and DiCaprio – and a stubbornness that makes you realise why the sisters have stayed apart for so long. ▣

Meryl Streep *Lee* • Leonardo DiCaprio *Hank* • Diane Keaton *Bessie* • Robert De Niro *Dr Wally* • Hume Cronyn *Marvin* • Gwen Verdon *Ruth* • Hal Scardino *Charlie* • Dan Hedaya *Bob* ■ *Dir* Jerry Zaks • *Scr* Scott McPherson, from his play

Marx Brothers Go West ★★ U

Comedy   1940 · US · BW · 80mins

The fourth film the Marx Brothers made for MGM is one of their weakest vehicles, with too much time being spent in the company of John Carroll and Diana Lewis. Sorely missing the stately presence of Margaret Dumont and saddled with a mediocre script, they are forced to plunder that Buster Keaton masterpiece *The General* for the best scene in the picture, in which they strip a train for fuel. There are a couple of other worthwhile routines, notably the opening sequence in which Groucho fails to dupe Chico and Harpo

out of ten dollars and the safe-cracking sketch, but it's all rather hit and miss.

Groucho Marx *S Quentin Quale* • Chico Marx *Joe Panello* • Harpo Marx *''Rusty''* • John Carroll *Terry Turner* • Diana Lewis *Eve Wilson* • Walter Woolf King *Beecher* ■ *Dir* Edward Buzzell • *Scr* Irving Brecher

Mary Higgins Clark's Moonlight Becomes You ★★

Thriller   1998 · US · Colour

Yet another TV potboiler from the author of such runaway bestsellers as *Stillwatch* that recalls the thrillers of Agatha Christie, but with a much darker tone. Sadly, it lacks the ingenuity of Christie's classic whodunits, so it won't take you long to detect who was responsible for the bizarre country-house murder of Donna Mills's stepmother. It takes a while to get used to seeing Mills as a sleuth. However, she does a solid job in disproving police theories and establishing that a twisted criminal mastermind is at work.

Donna Mills *Maggie Holloway* • Frances Hyland *Nuala Moore* • Helen Hughes *Greta* ■ *Dir* Bill Corcoran • *Scr* David Kinghorn, from the novel by Mary Higgins Clark

Mary, Mary ★★

Comedy   1963 · US · Colour · 126mins

After an illustrious early career, director Mervyn LeRoy turned his attention to Broadway successes. *Gypsy* and *No Time for Sergeants* were notable hits, but the same was not true of *A Majority of One* or this rather dour comedy based on the play by Jean Kerr (whose own life was filmed as *Please Don't Eat the Daisies*) about a divorced couple bent on destroying each other's future happiness. Brash Debbie Reynolds is miscast, and the men in her life – amiable Barry Nelson and gaunt Michael Rennie – are colourless. LeRoy, meanwhile, fails to disguise the obvious theatrical origins.

Debbie Reynolds *Mary McKellaway* • Barry Nelson *Bob McKellaway* • Michael Rennie *Dirk Winston* • Diane McBain *Tiffany Richards* • Hiram Sherman *Oscar Nelson* ■ *Dir* Mervyn LeRoy • *Scr* Richard Breen, from the play by Jean Kerr

Mary of Scotland ★★★ U

Historical drama   1936 · US · BW · 122mins

Despite sterling work by Katharine Hepburn in the title role, and moody, shadowy photography by the great Joseph H August, director John Ford fails to make this screen version of the Maxwell Anderson play very cinematic. Fredric March (as the Earl of Bothwell) and Mrs Fredric March, Florence Eldridge (as Queen Elizabeth I), are too contemporary and therefore feel miscast, though John Carradine and Donald Crisp – the only member of the cast with a genuine Scottish accent – seem quite at home at court. ▣

Katharine Hepburn *Mary Stuart* • Fredric March *Bothwell* • Florence Eldridge *Elizabeth Tudor* • Douglas Walton *Darnley* • John Carradine *Rizzio* • Robert Barrat *Morton* • Gavin Muir *Leicester* • Donald Crisp *Huntley* ■ *Dir* John Ford • *Scr* Dudley Nichols, from the play by Maxwell Anderson

Mary Poppins ★★★★★ U

Classic musical fantasy   1964 · US · Colour · 133mins

Easily the best of Disney's experiments in combining animation and live action, this is one of the studio's best-loved films. The last feature compiled by Walt Disney before his death, it was nominated for 13 Oscars and scooped five, including best actress for Julie Andrews on her screen debut. She is splendid as the prim nanny who transforms the lives of her young charges through their visits to her charming fantasy world. Quite why Dick Van Dyke was not even nominated for his performance as Bert the chimney sweep remains a mystery, as his energy is one of the picture's main assets (though his cockney accent does leave something to be desired). Packed with unforgettable sequences, adorable cartoon characters and timeless songs, it's supercalifragilisticexpialidocious. ▣

DVD

Julie Andrews *Mary Poppins* • Dick Van Dyke *Bert/Mr Dawes Sr* • David Tomlinson *Mr Banks* • Glynis Johns *Mrs Banks* • Hermione Baddeley *Ellen* • Karen Dotrice *Jane Banks* • Matthew Garber *Michael Banks* • Reta Shaw *Mrs Brill* ■ *Dir* Robert Stevenson • *Scr* Bill Walsh, Don DaGradi, from the *Mary Poppins* books by PL Travers • *Costume Designer* Tony Walton • *Music/Lyrics* Richard M Sherman, Robert B Sherman

Mary, Queen of Scots ★★★★

Historical drama   1971 · UK · Colour · 126mins

A film that tends to separate the girls from the boys, in that the former usually adore it and the latter nod off after 20 minutes. The great Tudor power play is laid out like a richly embroidered carpet with, in the blue corner, Glenda Jackson as Elizabeth I and, in the red corner, Vanessa Redgrave as her deeply principled cousin Mary Stuart. In short, two of Britain's finest actresses shine in tailor-made roles. There are a few liberties taken with historical fact, but who cares? This is a splendid costume drama with the stars ably assisted by the likes of Ian Holm, Nigel Davenport and Trevor Howard. Wonderful stuff.

Vanessa Redgrave *Mary, Queen of Scots* • Glenda Jackson *Queen Elizabeth I* • Patrick McGoohan *James Stuart* • Timothy Dalton *Henry, Lord Darnley* • Nigel Davenport *Lord Bothwell* • Trevor Howard *William Cecil* • Ian Holm *David Riccio* • Daniel Massey *Robert Dudley, Earl of Leicester* ■ *Dir* Charles Jarrott • *Scr* John Hale

Mary Reilly ★★★ 15

Psychological horror   1995 · US · Colour · 103mins

A clever twist on that evergreen tale of *Dr Jekyll and Mr Hyde*, as seen through the eyes of his housemaid, played by a totally miscast but oddly touching Julia Roberts. As the famous schizophrenic, John Malkovich gives a typically complex and powerful performance and Stephen Frears's lavish, black-bricked and gaslit production is satisfying both as a meditation on a literary classic and as an old-fashioned Victorian horror story. But this was a jinxed

U = SUITABLE FOR ALL   Uc = SUITABLE FOR ALL, ESPECIALLY FOR YOUNG CHILDREN (VIDEO ONLY)   PG = PARENTAL GUIDANCE

production, virtually disowned by the studio that financed it. ▣ **DVD**

Julia Roberts *Mary Reilly* • John Malkovich *Dr Jekyll/Mr Hyde* • George Cole *Mr Poole* • Michael Gambon *Mary's father* • Kathy Staff *Mrs Kent* • Glenn Close *Mrs Farraday* • Michael Sheen *Bradshaw* • Bronagh Gallagher *Annie* ▪ Dir Stephen Frears • Scr Christopher Hampton, from the novel by Valerie Martin, from the story *The Strange Case of Dr Jekyll and Mr Hyde* by Robert Louis Stevenson

Mary Shelley's Frankenstein   ★★ 🔳

Horror   1994 · US · Colour · 118mins

Kenneth Branagh's version of the much-filmed story is as pompous as it is perverse in the way it wastes not only his own talents (as Victor Frankenstein), but also those of Robert De Niro (who boasts a few moving moments as the man-made monster) and Helena Bonham Carter. The creation of the creature is undoubtedly spectacular, but the rest of the movie is not a fraction as frightening or funny as the 1931 classic with Boris Karloff. In attempting to keep faith with the original novel, Branagh concentrates too much on design and content, and loses the heart and soul of the story in the process. Contains violence, sex scenes and nudity. ▣ **DVD**

Robert De Niro *Creature/Sharp-featured man* • Kenneth Branagh *Victor Frankenstein* • Tom Hulce *Henry* • Helena Bonham Carter *Elizabeth* • Aidan Quinn *Captain Walton* • Ian Holm *Victor's father* • Richard Briers *Grandfather* • John Cleese *Professor Waldman* ▪ Dir Kenneth Branagh • Scr Steph Lady, Frank Darabont, from the novel by Mary Shelley

Maryland   ★★★ 🅄

Drama   1940 · US · Colour · 91mins

One of a seemingly unending series of 20th Century-Fox horse-racing sagas, superbly photographed in breathtaking Technicolor. Veteran director Henry King extracts the maximum drama from an awkward plot about a mother who won't let her son ride because that's how his father died. As vapid John Payne plays the son, however, who really cares? Fay Bainter and Walter Brennan, Oscar winners both, ride out the grimmer moments and prove to be more than a match for the scenery.

Walter Brennan *William Stewart* • Fay Bainter *Charlotte Danfield* • Brenda Joyce *Linda* • John Payne *Lee Danfield* • Charles Ruggles *Dick Piper* • Hattie McDaniel *Hattie* • Marjorie Weaver *Georgie Tomlin* • Sidney Blackmer *Spencer Danfield* ▪ Dir Henry King • Scr Ethel Hill, Jack Andrews • Cinematographer George Barnes, Ray Rennahan

Masala   ★★★ 🔳

Comedy drama 1991 · Can · Colour · 105mins

Srinivas Krishna makes an impressive debut with this deceptively serious study of the problems facing Asians settling in the New World. Besides the black comedy and the pastiches of Bollywood's trademark musical sequences, what gives the film its appeal is the superb characterisation, whether it's Krishna himself as the outsider who scandalises his adoptive family with his attitude to sex and drugs; Zohra Segal, who uses her VCR to communicate with the gods; or Saeed Jaffrey as both Krishna's

grasping uncle and the impoverished father of the girl he loves. Quirky, inventive and socially astute.

Saeed Jaffrey *Lallu Bhai Solanki/Mr Tikkoo/Lord Krishna* • Zohra Segal *Grandma Tikkoo* • Srinivas Krishna *Krishna* • Sakina Jaffrey *Rita Tikkoo* ▪ Dir/Scr Srinivas Krishna

Mascara   ★★ 🔳

Psychological thriller
1987 · Bel/Neth/Fr/US · Colour · 94mins

An unabashed exploitation movie, with oodles of sex and swearing, about a kinky relationship between a brother and his sister. Charlotte Rampling and Michael Sarrazin star in a film that one suspects doesn't exactly hold pride of place on their respective CVs. Lurid and rather nasty, the best thing that can be said about Patrick Conrad's thriller is that, unlike its title, it didn't run and run. ▣

Charlotte Rampling *Gaby Hart* • Michael Sarrazin *Bert Sanders* • Derek De Lint *Chris Brine* • Jappe Claes *Colonel March* • Herbert Flack *David Hyde* ▪ Scr Hugo Claus, Pierre Drouot, Patrick Conrad, from an idea by Patrick Conrad

La Maschera   ★★

Period romance   1988 · It · Colour · 90mins

With landscapes as picturesque as a Claude Lorrain painting, Fiorella Infascelli's feature debut is a visual delight. Striking masks and costumes add to the lustre of this 18th-century romance between a dissolute Italian aristocrat and a fiery actress. Credibility is somewhat strained by her inability to see through the various masks he wears in a bid to atone for his boorish behaviour. But what really undermines the production is that too little takes place beneath the surface, with Michael Maloney and Helena Bonham Carter unable to overcome the two-dimensionality of their characters. In Italian with English subtitles.

Helena Bonham Carter *Iris* • Michael Maloney *Leonardo* • Roberto Herlitzka *Elia* • Alberto Cracco *Viola* • Valentina Lainati *Maria* ▪ Dir Fiorella Infascelli • Scr Fiorella Infascelli, Adriano Apra

Masculine Feminine   ★★★

Romantic comedy drama
1966 · Fr/Swe · Colour · 104mins

Jean-Pierre Léaud is best known for playing Antoine Doinel, the shambolic but incurable romantic in a series of Truffaut films. In this, his first of many films for Jean-Luc Godard, Léaud plays a more politicised Doinel: demobbed from the army, dallying with several girls and dabbling with radical politics. Fans at the time hailed this as a vital Godard masterpiece about sixties youth; his detractors saw it as yet another self-indulgent, puerile mess.

Jean-Pierre Léaud *Paul* • Chantal Goya *Madeleine* • Marlène Jobert *Elisabeth* • Michel Debord *Robert* • Catherine-Isabelle Duport [Catherine Duport] *Catherine* • Brigitte Bardot ▪ Dir Jean-Luc Godard • Scr Jean-Luc Godard, from the short stories *La Femme de Paul* and *Le Signe* by Guy de Maupassant

The Masculine Mystique   ★★★

Documentary drama
1984 · Can · Colour · 87mins

This intriguing example of docudrama, by Canadian film-makers John N Smith and Giles Walker, has a style and structure that has rarely been pursued since. Four men discuss the impact of women's lib on their attitudes, re-enacting situations to echo those reactions. These days TV does this sort of thing better, and it's easy to dismiss it all as glib. But the intention is sincere, the technique is skilful, and the witty quartet manage to save the picture from pretentiousness.

Stefan Wodoslawsky *Blue* • Char Davies *Amurie* • Sam Grana *Alex* • Eleanor MacKinnon *Shelley* • Mort Ransen *Mort* • Annebet Zwartsenberg *Bet* • Ashley Murray *Ashley* ▪ Dir John N Smith, Giles Walker • Scr John N Smith, Giles Walker, David Wilson

MASH   ★★★★★ 🔳

Wartime black comedy
1969 · US · Colour · 110mins

The quality of Robert Altman's acerbic study of life in a Korean War field hospital has been too often overlooked because of the popularity of the TV series it spawned. It takes a while to get used to Donald Sutherland in the role of Hawkeye that Alan Alda later made his own; similarly, you keep expecting Loretta Swit and not Sally Kellerman whenever "Hot Lips" is mentioned. But the glorious wit of Ring Lardner Jr's Oscar-winning script soon has you under its spell. Altman and Kellerman were both rewarded with Oscar nominations, only to lose out to Franklin J Schaffner and Helen Hayes, while the film lost – in a bitterly ironic twist – to the Second World War biopic *Patton*. Contains some violence and swearing. ▣

Donald Sutherland *Hawkeye Pierce* • Elliott Gould *Trapper John McIntyre* • Tom Skerritt *Duke Forrest* • Sally Kellerman *Major "Hot Lips" Houlihan* • Robert Duvall *Major Frank Burns* • Jo Ann Pflug *Lieutenant Dish* • René Auberjonois *Dago Red* • Roger Bowen *Colonel Henry Blake* • Gary Burghoff *Radar O'Reilly* ▪ Dir Robert Altman • Scr Ring Lardner Jr, from the novel by Richard Hooker

The Mask   ★

Horror 1961 · Can · BW and Colour · 79mins

In this Canadian gimmick picture, donning a cursed sacrificial mask causes the wearer to commit atrocities under the spell of hallucinatory visions. Audiences at the time donned 3-D glasses so they could witness colour segments of hooded satanists, a ghoul rowing a coffin through a sea of mist and mouldering corpses jumping into view in "thrilling depth dimension". Without that extra incentive, this cult revival flick is a weakly-acted bore.

Paul Stevens *Dr Allan Barnes* • Claudette Nevins *Pamela Albright* • Bill Walker *Lt Martin* • Anne Collings *Jill Goodrich* • Martin Lavut *Michael Randin* ▪ Dir Julian Roffman, Slavko Vorkapich • Scr Frank Taubes, Sandy Haber, Slavko Vorkapich

Mask   ★★★★ 🔳

Biographical drama
1985 · US · Colour · 114mins

This film features what is perhaps Cher's finest role as the mother of Rocky Dennis (Eric Stoltz), a teenager trying to cope with disfigurement caused by a rare bone disease and the prospect of imminent death. Peter Bogdanovich's direction shrewdly reveals the strengths and weaknesses of both mother and son as she tries to give him the confidence he lacks and encourage him to follow her example and live life to the full. The end result is both an enormously moving and life-affirming experience. ▣

Cher *Rusty Dennis* • Eric Stoltz *Rocky Dennis* • Sam Elliott *Gar* • Estelle Getty *Evelyn* • Richard Dysart *Abe* • Laura Dern *Diana* • Micole Mercurio *Babe* • Harry Carey Jr *Red* • Dennis Burkley *Dozer* ▪ Dir Peter Bogdanovich • Scr Anna Hamilton Phelan

The Mask   ★★★★ 🅿🅶

Comedy   1994 · US · Colour · 97mins

Jim Carrey consolidated his "Ace Ventura" position as America's most successful comedian with this stunning tribute to the zany style of Tex Avery and other Warner Bros animators from the golden age of cartoons. Amazing computer-generated special effects drive this slick showcase for Carrey's explosively unpredictable talents, as he plays a mild-mannered banker who turns into a wild and crazy superhero when he finds a magical ancient mask. Highlights include the Bugs Bunny-style *Cuban Pete* routine, Carrey's pet dog donning the mask and gorgeous Cameron Diaz as the star's love interest. But mainly it's an excuse for Carrey to move with whirlwind speed, pop his eyeballs and swap parts of his anatomy for the cartoon equivalents in hysterically funny and tremendously imaginative ways. ▣ **DVD**

Jim Carrey *Stanley Ipkiss/The Mask* • Cameron Diaz *Tina Carlyle* • Peter Riegert *Lieutenant Mitch Kellaway* • Peter Greene *Dorian* • Amy Yasbeck *Peggy Brandt* • Richard Jeni *Charlie Schumaker* • Orestes Matacena *Niko* • Timothy Bagley *Irv* ▪ Dir Charles Russell [Chuck Russell] • Scr Mike Werb, from a story by Michael Fallon, Mark Verheiden, from characters in the *Dark Horse, comics*

The Mask of Dimitrios   ★★★★

Spy drama   1944 · US · BW · 95mins

Peter Lorre and Sidney Greenstreet, those beloved character actors best known for *Casablanca* and *The Maltese Falcon*, co-star in this marvellous *film noir*. Terrifically directed by *Johnny Belinda*'s Jean Negulesco, it's a scorching adaptation of Eric Ambler's novel that provides a fine example of Warner Bros literacy at work. Dimitrios himself is played by Zachary Scott in his screen debut – his acting ability would later earn him the nickname "The Eyebrow".

Sydney Greenstreet *Mr Peters* • Zachary Scott *Dimitrios* • Faye Emerson *Irana Preveza* • Peter Lorre *Cornelius Latimer Leyden* • George Tobias *Fedor Muishkin* ▪ Dir Jean Negulesco • Scr Frank Gruber, from the novel *A Coffin for Dimitrios* by Eric Ambler

Mask of Dust ★

Sports drama   1954 · UK · BW · 68mins

In this cheap action drama from Hammer's pre-horror days, its American partner imposed a Hollywood scriptwriter and sent over not one, but two minor stars to ensure appeal to US audiences. British racing drivers such as Stirling Moss appear as themselves and double for lead Richard Conte and other players in this cliché-ridden tale of the tracks. The intercut footage of real races shows up the artificiality of the studio work.

Richard Conte *Peter Wells* • Mari Aldon *Pat Wells* • George Coulouris *Dallapiccola* • Peter Illing *Bellario* • Alec Mango *Guido Rizetti* • Meredith Edwards *Lawrence* • Jimmy Copeland *[James Copeland] Johnny* • Jeremy Hawk *Martin* ■ *Dir* Terence Fisher • *Scr* Richard Landau, Paul Tabori, from a novel by Jon Manchip White

The Mask of Fu Manchu
★★★

Horror melodrama   1932 · US · BW · 72mins

Boris Karloff only played Sax Rohmer's ruthless Asian madman once, but the result is a wonderfully outrageous exercise in campy exotica. Forget the story – something about stealing Genghis Khan's ceremonial mask and sword to take over the world. Just marvel at the fabulous sets and costumes artfully and stylishly employed to disguise the thin content. A death ray, the Room of the Golden Peacock, crocodile pits, dungeons and assorted torture devices provide this classic "Yellow Peril" adventure with enough colourful incident to pack an entire thirties serial.

Boris Karloff *Dr Fu Manchu* • Lewis Stone *Nayland Smith* • Karen Morley *Sheila Barton* • Charles Starrett *Terence Granville* • Myrna Loy *Fah Lo See* • Jean Hersholt *Professor Von Berg* • Lawrence Grant *Sir Lionel Barton* ■ *Dir* King Vidor, Charles Brabin • *Scr* Irene Kuhn, Edgar Allen Woolf, John Willard, from the novel by Sax Rohmer

The Mask of Satan
★★★★ 15

Horror   1960 · It · BW · 83mins

For his directing debut, Italian cinematographer Mario Bava cast British starlet Barbara Steele as the soul-snatching witch Asa and shot the whole grisly tale of vengeance from beyond the grave in stunning black and white. He created an instant horror classic that established his cutting-edge reputation, confirmed over the next two decades. A masterpiece of the macabre, it had censors worldwide up in arms over its still powerful opening torture sequence, in which a mask of nails is hammered onto Steele's screaming face. Steele launched an entire career playing vamps, vampires and victims on the strength of her impact in this atmospheric stunner. Italian dialogue dubbed in English. ▭

Barbara Steele *Katia/Asa* • John Richardson *Andrej* • Ivo Garrani *Prince Vajda* • Andrea Checchi *Dr Kruvajan* • Arturo Dominici *Javutich* • Clara Bindi *Inn keeper* • Enrico Olivieri *Constantine* • Mario Passante *Nikita* ■ *Dir* Mario Bava • *Scr* Mario Bava, Marcello Coscia, Ennio De Concini, Mario Serandrei, from the story *The Vij* by Nikolai Gogol

The Mask of Zorro ★★★★ PG

Swashbuckling action adventure
1998 · US · Colour · 131mins

Zorro may wear a mask, but there's no disguising the fact that this is an absolutely splendid swashbuckler. Anthony Hopkins is the original righter of wrongs who hands over his rapier, and his mission, to a younger man (Antonio Banderas). Catherine Zeta-Jones is a heroine to die for, while the dramatic swordplay and climactic mine explosions show that director Martin Campbell (*GoldenEye*) can still make movies like they used to. Contains some violence. ▭ *DVD*

Antonio Banderas *Alejandro Murrieta/Zorro* • Anthony Hopkins *Zorro/Don Diego de la Vega* • Stuart Wilson *Don Rafael Montero* • Catherine Zeta-Jones *Elena* • Matt Letscher *Captain Harrison Love* • Maury Chaykin *Prison warden* • LQ Jones *Three-Fingered Jack* ■ *Dir* Martin Campbell • *Scr* John Eskow, Ted Elliott, Terry Rossio, from a story by Randall Johnson, from characters created by Johnston McCulley

Le Masque de Fer   ★★★

Historical swashbuckling adventure
1962 · Fr/It · Colour · 127mins

In his efforts to install Louis XIV's identical brother on the throne, D'Artagnan proves invincible with a sword but perilously susceptible to feminine wiles in this rousing adventure. It has little but a title in common with Richard Pottier's 1954 version of Dumas's *The Man in the Iron Mask* – opting instead for swashbuckling fun. The period trappings and historical characters are therefore just an exotic backdrop against which Jean Marais can demonstrate his dashing athleticism and irresistibility to Claudine Auger and Sylva Koscina. A French language film.

Jean Marais *D'Artagnan* • Jean-François Poron *Louis XIV/Henri* • Germaine Montero *Anne d'Autriche* • Claudine Auger *Isabelle de Saint-Mars* • Jean Rochefort *Lastreaumont* • Jean Davy *Marchal de Turenne* • Sylva Koscina *Marion* ■ *Dir* Henri Decoin • *Scr* Cecil Saint-Laurent, Gerard Devries, from the novel *The Man in the Iron Mask* by Alexandre Dumas

The Masque of the Red Death   ★★★★ 18

Horror   1964 · UK/US · Colour · 89mins

Easily the finest of director Roger Corman's Edgar Allan Poe adaptations, with Vincent Price the very essence of evil as the sadistic devil-worshipper trying to keep the plague at bay in 12th-century Italy by indulging in degenerate revels. While there are touches of deliciously wicked humour, the aura of terror comes from the doom-laden tone Corman creates by reaching as much into sombre Ingmar Bergman territory (the poignant tableaux showing crimson-robed Death stalking through fog-shrouded woods) as atmospheric Hammer shock. Shot in England by Nicolas Roeg, who went on to direct *Don't Look Now* among others. ▭

Vincent Price *Prince Prospero* • Hazel Court *Juliana* • Jane Asher *Francesca* • David Weston *Gino* • Patrick Magee *Alfredo* • Nigel Green *Ludovico* • Skip Martin *Hop Toad* ■ *Dir* Roger Corman • *Scr* Charles Beaumont, R Wright Campbell, from the short stories by Edgar Allan Poe

Masquerade   ★★ U

Comedy adventure
1965 · UK · Colour · 99mins

This slack send-up of British imperialism and James Bondism has Jack Hawkins and Cliff Robertson as British and American agents involved in the kidnapping of an Arab oil sheik. The plot is sometimes impossible to follow, so one is left half-smiling at the familiar turns from the likes of Bill Fraser, John Le Mesurier and Charles Gray. Robertson, who was brought in at the last minute to replace Rex Harrison, enlisted screenwriter William Goldman to rewrite his scenes.

Cliff Robertson *David Frazer* • Jack Hawkins *Col Drexel* • Marisa Mell *Sophie* • Michel Piccoli *Sarrasin* • Bill Fraser *Dunwoody* • Charles Gray *Benson* • John Le Mesurier *Sir Robert* ■ *Dir* Basil Dearden • *Scr* Michael Relph, William Goldman, from the novel *Castle Minerva* by Victor Canning

Masquerade   ★★ 18

Thriller   1988 · US · Colour · 87mins

Director Bob Swaim's misfiring attempt at a Hitchcock-style thriller set among the Long Island yachting fraternity has the advantage of good performances by Rob Lowe and Meg Tilly. Otherwise, it's a rather dumb and violent affair as timid heiress Tilly is married to gigolo Lowe as part of a long-term plot to kill her and get their millions. Sleek boats and beautiful beaches give it the glossy look of a holiday commerical, but out-of-the-blue character changes make it totally implausible. ▭

Rob Lowe *Tim Whalan* • Meg Tilly *Olivia Lawrence* • Kim Cattrall *Brooke Morrison* • Doug Savant *Mike McGill* • John Glover *Tony Gateworth* • Dana Delany *Anne Briscoe* • Erik Holland *Chief of police* • Brian Davies *Granger Morrison* ■ *Dir* Bob Swaim • *Scr* Dick Wolf

The Masquerader   ★★★ PG

Drama   1933 · US · BW · 73mins

Suave Ronald Colman essays a dual role in a virtual rehearsal for *The Prisoner of Zenda* four years later. He plays a drug-addicted MP who hires his cousin to impersonate him and make a major speech in parliament. Of course, this has a knock-on effect on his love life (can the lovely Elissa Landi tell them apart?) and his conniving butler (brilliant Halliwell Hobbes). Intelligent stuff, though a little creaky. ▭

Ronald Colman *Sir John Chilcote/John Loder* • Elissa Landi *Eve Chilcote* • Juliette Compton *Lady Joyce* • Halliwell Hobbes *Brock* • David Torrence *Fraser* • Creighton Hale *Lakely* ■ *Dir* Richard Wallace • *Scr* Howard Estabrook, from the play by John Hunter Booth, from the novel by Katherine Cecil Thurston

Masques   ★★★★ 15

Thriller   1987 · Fr · Colour · 100mins

The name of Alfred Hitchcock is often bandied around during the discussion of suspense thrillers, but French director Claude Chabrol has consistently demonstrated a near-understanding of the master's style and preoccupations. This isn't Chabrol at his best, but the teasing tale of writer Robin Renucci trying to uncover the guilty secret of game show host Philippe Noiret's country chateau is endlessly entertaining. It's flashy rather than fulfilling, but littered with delicious Hitchcockian moments. In French with English subtitles.

Philippe Noiret *Christian Legagneur* • Robin Renucci *Roland Wolf* • Bernadette Lafont *Patricia Marquet* • Monique Chaumette *Colette* • Anne Brochet *Catherine* • Roger Dumas *Manuel Marquet* ■ *Dir* Claude Chabrol • *Scr* Odile Barski, Claude Chabrol

Mass Appeal   ★★★ 15

Comedy drama   1984 · US · Colour · 95mins

Not quite as funny as *The Apartment*, this is another film comedy with a theatrical feel and Jack Lemmon in the lead. Directed by Glenn Jordan, it's an enjoyable screen adaptation of Bill C Davis's hit Broadway play, in which a live wire theology student (Zeljko Ivanek) challenges an easy-going, affable priest (played by the ever-excellent Lemmon). The picture has appeal, though not necessarily of the mass variety. ▭

Jack Lemmon *Father Farley* • Zeljko Ivanek *Mark Dolson* • Charles Durning *Monsignor Burke* • Louise Latham *Margaret* • Alice Hirson *Mrs Hart* • Helene Heigh *Mrs Hart's mother* • Sharee Gregory *Marion Hart* ■ *Dir* Glenn Jordan • *Scr* Bill C Davis, from his play

Massacre in Rome   ★ 15

Wartime drama based on a true story
1973 · It/Fr · Colour · 95mins

Based on a true story, this stars Richard Burton as the German commandant in Rome, and Marcello Mastroianni as a priest trying to prevent mass executions in retaliation for the death of German troops at the hands of the partisans. The two fine actors have to gargle with some awful dialogue, and the pace would make a snail itch with impatience. A resounding flop everywhere except Italy, the film made headline news when a niece of Pope Pius XII sued the author of the novel, director George Pan Cosmatos and producer Carlo Ponti for claiming her uncle was a Nazi collaborator. She won the case, but they never served their jail terms. ▭

Richard Burton *Col Kappler* • Marcello Mastroianni *Father Pietro Antonelli* • Leo McKern *General Kurt Maelzer* • John Steiner *Colonel Dollmann* • Delia Boccardo *Elena* ■ *Dir* George Pan Cosmatos • *Scr* George Pan Cosmatos, Robert Katz, from the book *Death in Rome* by Robert Katz

The Master   ★★ 18

Martial arts action
1992 · HK · Colour · 88mins

Jet Li enjoyed moderate Hong Kong success via a series of period martial arts movies that highlighted his balletic prowess. In this modern action thriller Li plays a martial arts student in America who contacts his old teacher and gets caught up in a local gang war. A flop at first, it was re-released in 1992 to cash in on the success of *Once upon a Time in China*. Lovers of kung fu set pieces will enjoy the stunning final fight. In Cantonese with English subtitles. Contains violence and some swearing. ▭

Jet Li *Jet* • Wah Yuen *Uncle Tak* • Crystal Hwoh *May* • Jerry Trimble *Jonny* ■ *Dir* Tsui Hark • *Scr* Lam Hee To, Lau Tai Mo, from a story by Tsui Hark

The Master Gunfighter ★

Western 1975 · US · Colour · 110mins

This sloppy western is credited to Frank Laughlin, the nine-year-old son of real director and star Tom Laughlin. That family in-joke sets the tone for a painfully self-indulgent mess. Following the trend set by *The Magnificent Seven* and *A Fistful of Dollars*, the film is based on a Japanese samurai movie, with Laughlin as the gun expert pitted against a Mexican warlord. There are obvious nods to Vietnam, the peace movement and native American consciousness amid the clumsily shot bloodletting. Contains violence.

Tom Laughlin *Finley McCloud* • Ron O'Neal *Paulo* • Lincoln Kilpatrick *Jacques St Charles* • Geo Anne Sosa *Chorika* • Barbara Carrera *Eula* • Victor Campos *Maltese* • Hector Elias *Juan* ■ *Dir* Frank Laughlin [Tom Laughlin] • *Scr* Harold Lapland, from the film *Goyokin* by Kei Tasaka, Hideo Gosha

The Master of Ballantrae ★★★ U

Historical swashbuckling adventure 1953 · US/UK · Colour · 88mins

Errol Flynn was beginning to look old and tired when he made this colourful adaptation of the Robert Louis Stevenson story (changed almost beyond recognition) in Europe. Nevertheless, with the help of Warner Bros veteran William Keighley, who'd co-directed *The Adventures of Robin Hood*, 15 years earlier, the ailing star revived enough to make his mark in a movie that's not entirely without charm. There's a fine British cast and a lovely, now forgotten, leading lady called Beatrice Campbell. Those familiar with the 1948 film *Bonnie Prince Charlie* should be able to spot a lot of footage from that production.

Errol Flynn *James Durrisdeer* • Roger Livesey *Colonel Francis Burke* • Anthony Steel *Henry Durrisdeer* • Beatrice Campbell *Lady Alison* • Yvonne Furneaux *Jessie Brown* • Jacques Berthier *Arnaud* • Felix Aylmer *Lord Durrisdeer* • Mervyn Johns *MacKellar* • Gillian Lynne *Marianne* ■ *Dir* William Keighley • *Scr* Herb Meadow, Harold Medford, from the novel by Robert Louis Stevenson

The Master of Bankdam ★★★

Drama 1947 · UK · BW · 105mins

Adapted from a novel that apes the family sagas of Arnold Bennett and John Galsworthy, this is a thunderingly good melodrama spanning virtually the entire Victorian era. For once repressing his mischievous twinkle, Tom Walls is all accent and folly as the mill-owning head of a northern family who entrusts the business to the wrong son. But the feud between swaggering Stephen Murray and his gritty brother Dennis Price is nothing compared to the rivalry between the foppish David Tomlinson and the down-to-earth Jimmy Hanley. Walter Forde keeps the brew simmering nicely.

Anne Crawford *Annie Pickersgill* • Dennis Price *Joshua Crowther* • Tom Walls *Simeon Crowther Sr* • Stephen Murray *Zebediah Crowther* • Linden Travers *Clara Baker* • Jimmy Hanley *Simeon Crowther Jr* • Nancy Price *Lydia Crowther* • David Tomlinson *Lancelot Handel Crowther* ■ *Dir* Walter Forde

• *Scr* Edward Dryhurst, Moie Charles, from the novel *The Crowthers of Bankdam* by Thomas Armstrong

Master of the House ★★★★★

Silent romantic drama 1925 · Den · BW · 107mins

This domestic tragicomedy with a feminist slant was Danish director Carl Theodor Dreyer's seventh feature and anticipates his greatest films. The deceptively simple story tells of a husband whose disregard for his wife's feelings causes her to become ill. When she is sent away to recuperate, his old nanny moves in and teaches him to mend his ways. Dreyer filmed in an exact replica of a real two-roomed flat built in a studio, using its limitations to his advantage. A film of close-ups and gestures, it contains a wonderful performance from Mathilde Nielsen as the nanny.

Johannes Meyer *John/Victor Frandsen* • Astrid Holm *Ida, his wife* • Karin Nellemose *Kathleen/Karen Frandsen* • Mathilde Nielsen *Nana Marsh/Mads* ■ *Dir* Carl Theodor Dreyer • *Scr* Carl Theodor Dreyer, Svend Rindom, from the play *Tyrannens Fald (The Fall of a Tyrant)* by Svend Rindom

Master of the Islands ★

Historical drama 1970 · US · Colour · 133mins

Also known as *The Hawaiians*, this is still remembered for the huge cardboard cut-out of star Charlton Heston that stood outside the London Pavilion in the days of its UK premiere. Today, that cardboard figure seems to symbolise the movie. Producer Walter Mirisch had bought the rights to James A Michener's doorstop novel *Hawaii*, and filmed most of it in the 1966 movie of that title. This is the rest, unenlivened by location shooting and the reuniting of the star and director of the classic western *Will Penny*.

Charlton Heston *Whip Hoxworth* • Geraldine Chaplin *Purity Hoxworth* • John Phillip Law *Noel Hoxworth* • Tina Chen *Nyuk Tsin* • Alec McCowen *Micah Hale* • Mako *Mun Ki* • Don Knight *Milton Overpeck* ■ *Dir* Tom Gries • *Scr* James R Webb, from the novel *Hawaii* by James A Michener

Master of the World ★★ U

Fantasy adventure 1961 · US · Colour · 98mins

An uneven mixture of two Jules Verne novels to make one highly moralistic anti-war fable. Vincent Price plays a 19th-century inventor planning to destroy all of mankind's weapons from a flying airship with his usual suave and sinister panache. Spiced up with stock battle footage taken from other costume epics (the reason why the Globe theatre suddenly appears in Victorian London), it's a cheap and cheerful fantasy, reuniting Charles Bronson with Price for the first time since *House of Wax*.

Vincent Price *Robur* • Charles Bronson *Strock* • Henry Hull *Prudent* • Mary Webster *Dorothy* • David Frankham *Philip* • Richard Harrison *Alistair* • Vito Scotti *Topage* ■ *Dir* William Witney • *Scr* Richard Matheson, from the novels *Master of the World* and *Robur, the Conqueror* by Jules Verne

The Master Plan ★★★ U

Spy drama 1954 · UK · BW · 77mins

Blacklisted in Hollywood during the communist witch-hunt, South African-born Cy Endfield worked uncredited on three British thrillers with Charles De Lautour. This was his first solo venture in exile, made under the pseudonym Hugh Raker (Raker being his middle name). It is an above-average quota quickie, with war hero and B-movie stalwart Wayne Morris as a government troubleshooter fighting against both mental blackouts and the double agent who is leaking secrets to the enemy. Endfield injects an urgency and credibility not usually associated with British fillers.

Wayne Morris *Major Brent* • Tilda Thamar *Helen* • Norman Wooland *Colonel Cleaver* • Mary Mackenzie *Miss Gray* • Arnold Bell *General Goulding* • Marjorie Stewart *Yvonne* • Laurie Main *Johnny Orwell* • Frederick Schrecker *Dr Morgan Stern* ■ *Dir* Hugh Raker [Cy Endfield] • *Scr* Hugh Raker [Cy Endfield], Donald Bull, from the TV play *Operation North Star* by Harold Bratt

The Master Race ★★

Second World War drama 1944 · US · BW · 101mins

A bizarre wartime curio about a Nazi officer who hides out in Belgium and tries to keep the fascist fires burning by causing dissent among the newly liberated countries. Made promptly after the D-Day landings, it's a heavy slice of peace propaganda, with George Coulouris deeply sinister as the villain. Director Herbert J Biberman, blacklisted in 1948 as a result of his communist sympathies, was one of the original Hollywood Ten. He later made *Salt of the Earth*, one of the most left-wing films ever made in America.

George Coulouris *Von Beck* • Stanley Ridges *Phil Carson* • Osa Massen *Helena* • Carl Esmond *Andrei* • Nancy Gates *Nina* • Morris Carnovsky *Old Man Bartoc* • Lloyd Bridges *Frank* ■ *Dir* Herbert J Biberman • *Scr* Herbert J Biberman, Anne Froelick, Rowland Leigh, from a story by Herbert J Biberman

Master Spy ★ U

Spy drama 1964 · UK · BW · 70mins

There isn't an atom of suspense in Montgomery Tully's tepid thriller about spying scientists. Indeed, the most exciting moments are the games of chess during which defector Stephen Murray passes vital secrets to communist squire, Alan Wheatley. There's a valiant attempt to put a sting in the tail, but only lab assistant June Thorburn fails to see through the slenderest web of deception.

Stephen Murray *Boris Turganev* • June Thorburn *Leila* • Alan Wheatley *Paul Skelton* • John Carson *Richard Colman* • John Brown *John Baxter* • Jack Watson *Captain Foster* ■ *Dir* Montgomery Tully • *Scr* Maurice J Wilson, from the story *They Also Serve* by Gerald Anstruther, Paul White

Mastermind ★★★

Spoof detective drama 1976 · US · Colour · 131mins

Shot in 1969 and left on the shelf for seven years, this curiosity is worth seeking out. It's a Charlie Chan parody, with Zero Mostel as a bumbling oriental detective, and a

sterling supporting cast including a last appearance from *On the Town's* Jules Munshin. Plus there's a knockout car chase and some voluble slapstick, too.

Zero Mostel *Inspector Hoku* • Bradford Dillman *Jabez Link* • Keiko Kishi *Nikki Kono* • Gawn Grainger *Nigel Crouchback* • Jules Munshin *Israeli agent* ■ *Dir* Alex March • *Scr* Terence Klein, Ian McLellan Hunter, from a story by Terence Klein

Masterminds ★ 12

Action adventure 1997 · US · Colour · 100mins

Patrick Stewart must have had a boat payment due; it's the only way to explain his presence in this odious adventure movie. Stewart's character poses as a security expert, installing surveillance systems at a posh private school in order to hold a small number of the wealthiest kids in the world hostage. He expects to receive a hefty ransom for their return, but doesn't count on the school's biggest troublemaker, who has the school rigged for his own mischievous ends. Contains violence. 🖭

Patrick Stewart *Rafe Bentley* • Vincent Kartheiser *Ozzie* • Brenda Fricker *Principal Claire Maloney* • Brad Whitford [Bradley Whitford] *Miles Lawrence* • Matt Craven *Jake Paxton* ■ *Dir* Roger Christian • *Scr* Floyd Byars, from a story by Alex Siskin, Chris Black, Floyd Byars

The Masterpiece of Murder ★★

Detective drama 1986 · US · Colour

Bob Hope took on his first starring role in 14 years with this TV movie shot in Canada. He plays a private eye who teams up with retired crook Don Ameche to track down an art thief with a penchant for murder. Ameche is sprightly and the supporting cast adds some glitter, but the script is never more than mediocre. Hope is game, but painfully past his glorious prime.

Bob Hope *Dan Dolan* • Don Ameche *Frank Aherne* • Jayne Meadows *Matilda Hussey* • Claudia Christian *Julia Forsythe* • Yvonne De Carlo *Mrs Murphy* • Anne Francis *Ruth Beekman* • Frank Gorshin *Pierre Rudin* • Kevin McCarthy *Jonathan Hire* • Stella Stevens *Della Vance/Deb Potts* ■ *Dir* Charles S Dubin • *Scr* Andrew J Fenady, Terry Nation, from a story by Andrew J Fenady

The Masters ★★★

Mystery drama 1975 · It · Colour

A naive schoolmistress (Jennifer O'Neill), newly arrived in a tiny Sicilian town, is insulted by a local peasant who is then murdered by the local Mafia. It's all to do with the corrupt police, but the teacher takes a long time to figure out exactly what's going on. Director Luigi Zampa gives the mystery more credibility than it deserves, while James Mason supplies a menacing turn. Italian dialogue dubbed into English.

James Mason *Antonio Bellocampo* • Franco Nero *Prof Belcore* • Jennifer O'Neill *Elena Bardi* • Orazio Orlando • Claudio Gora ■ *Dir* Luigi Zampa • *Scr* Piero Bernardi, from the novel by Giuseppe Fava

Masters of Menace ★ 15

Comedy   1990 · US · Colour · 93mins

David Rasche is a Hell's Angel-style gang leader and Catherine Bach is his pregnant wife in this juvenile comedy from director Daniel Raskov, who seems to think the dumber the gag, the funnier it is. Adding embarrassing support to a farcical fiasco with very questionable undertones are slumming jokers Dan Aykroyd, John Candy and James Belushi. Contains violence, swearing and drug abuse. 🖵

David Rasche *Buddy* • Catherine Bach *Kitty* • Lance Kinsey *Wallace* • Teri Copley *Sunny* • Ray Baker *Hoover* • Malcolm Smith *Schouweiller* • George "Buck" Flower *Sheriff Julip* ■ *Dir* Daniel Raskov • *Scr* Tino Insana

Masters of the Universe ★★ PG

Fantasy adventure
1987 · US · Colour · 101mins

It is difficult to make convincing live-action versions of cult cartoon strips, and this big-screen version of the momentarily popular TV series is one of the least successful attempts. Dolph Lundgren has the necessary physique for He-Man, and Frank Langella has been splendidly made-up for the role of Skeletor. But the story – about a cosmic key that will enable its holder to become master of the universe – is uninspired, while the effects look painfully cheap. 🖵

Dolph Lundgren *He-Man* • Frank Langella *Skeletor* • Meg Foster *Evil-Lyn* • Billy Barty *Gwildor* • Courteney Cox *Julie Winston* • Robert Duncan McNeill *Kevin* ■ *Dir* Gary Goddard • *Scr* David Odell

Mata Hari ★★★

Spy melodrama   1931 · US · BW · 91mins

Greta Garbo as spy Mata Hari sounds like ideal casting, but in truth this was one of Garbo's lesser vehicles. Under-produced by MGM, and desperately in need of atmosphere – either a better score or more thought to the sound effects – it's directed at a snail's pace by silent screen specialist George Fitzmaurice (*Son of the Sheik*). As her lovers, Ramon Novarro is stilted and Lionel Barrymore is arch, but Garbo is Garbo and, for that reason alone, this is worth watching – especially for her exotic dance around a statue.

Greta Garbo *Mata Hari* • Ramon Novarro *Lieutenant Alexis Rosanoff* • Lionel Barrymore *General Serge Shubin* • Lewis Stone *Andriani* • C Henry Gordon *Dubois* • Karen Morley *Carlotta* • Alec B Francis *Caron* • Blanche Frederici *Sister Angelica* ■ *Dir* George Fitzmaurice • *Scr* Benjamin Glazer, Leo Birinski, Doris Anderson, Gilbert Emery

Mata Hari ★ 18

Spy drama   1985 · US · Colour · 103mins

This soft-core sex version of the old World War One yarn has Sylvia Kristel (*Emmanuelle*) as the French spy, taking off her clothes at the drop of a proverbial hat. Handsome Christopher Cazenove is her opposite number in Germany – the spy who loved her. Director Curtis Harrington may have intended a satire – he's a horror aficionado and all-round film buff – but the producers certainly wanted a bit of hot stuff. It's really no different in

approach from the earlier spy dramas with Garbo and Dietrich, which were also pitched as erotica rather than espionage stories. 🖵

Sylvia Kristel *Mata Hari* • Christopher Cazenove *Karl Von Byerling* • Oliver Tobias *Captain Ladoux* • Gaye Brown *Fraulein Doktor* • William Fox *Maitre Clunet* ■ *Dir* Curtis Harrington • *Scr* Joel Ziskin

Matador ★★★ 18

Black comedy   1986 · Sp · Colour · 101mins

Flashy, trashy and vibrantly colourful, Pedro Almodóvar's film echoes the stylised melodramatics of such fifties' directors as Douglas Sirk to explore the links between eroticism and violence in this typically flamboyant outing. Antonio Banderas gives a courageous performance as the trainee bullfighter whose overpowering fantasies and his own sexual misdemeanours prompt him to confess to a series of kinky killings. Assumpta Serna, Nacho Martinez and Carmen Maura do well in the face of some laughably pretentious dialogue. Almodóvar's emphasis on voyeuristic titillation and cheap black comedy comes at the expense of developing some interesting themes. In Spanish with English subtitles. Contains violence and nudity. 🖵

Assumpta Serna *Maria Cardenal* • Antonio Banderas *Angel Giminez* • Nacho Martinez *Diego Montes* • Eva Cobo *Eva* • Julieta Serrano *Berta* • Chus Lampreave *Pilar* • Carmen Maura *Julia* • Eusebio Poncela *Police inspector* ■ *Dir* Pedro Almodóvar • *Scr* Pedro Almodóvar, Jesus Ferrero, from a story by Pedro Almodóvar

The Match ★★★ 15

Comedy drama
1999 · UK/US/Ire · Colour · 96mins

Apparently an attempt at reviving the spirit of the Ealing comedy, this tells the story of a young Scottish villager, milkman Wullie (Max Beesley), looking forward to the return of girlfriend Rosemary (Laura Fraser) from university. Despite Wullie's physical disadvantages, he finds himself involved in a soccer match-cum-feud between two local watering holes. An amiable movie with no great pretensions, this presents a host of familiar British faces and plenty of cosy characters. Contains swearing. 🖵

Max Beesley *Wullie Smith* • Isla Blair *Sheila Bailey* • James Cosmo *Billy Bailey* • Laura Fraser *Rosemary Bailey* • Richard E Grant *Gorgeous Gus* • Ian Holm *Big Tam* • Tom Sizemore *Buffalo* • Pierce Brosnan *John McGee* ■ *Dir/Scr* Mick Davis

The Match Factory Girl ★★★ 15

Drama   1990 · Fin/Swe · Colour · 65mins

Finnish film-maker Aki Kaurismäki claimed that this picture was intended to make Robert Bresson seem like the director of epic action movies. While it certainly shares the French master's minimalist style, the story of a plain Jane who defies the harshest of odds, finally to take control of her life, lacks the compassion that characterised even the bleakest Bresson scenario. But Kati Outinen is superb in the title role, overcoming the odd improbable

plot twist to convince you that she is one of the countless Eleanor Rigbys totally dependent on dreams to sweeten their bitter reality. In Finnish with English subtitles. 🖵

Kati Outinen *Iris* • Elina Salo *Mother* • Esko Nikkari *Stepfather* • Vesa Vierikko *Aarne* • Reijjo Taipale *Singer* • Silu Seppala *Brother* • Outi Maenpaa *Workmate* • Marja Packalen *Doctor* ■ *Dir/Scr* Aki Kaurismäki

The Matchmaker ★★★ U

Period comedy   1958 · US · BW · 102mins

This is *Hello, Dolly!* without the tunes or, indeed, Barbra Streisand. Shirley Booth is Dolly Levi, the widowed, interfering busybody who arranges marriages like flowers in a vase. In her own sights is Paul Ford's merchant; getting tangled up in her plans are Shirley MacLaine and Anthony Perkins. The performances are perfectly attuned to the 1880s ambience, which is nicely enhanced when the actors address the camera directly. This was a technique adopted by the trendy New Wave, though here it's more of a Broadway convention.

Shirley Booth *Dolly Levi* • Anthony Perkins *Cornelius* • Shirley MacLaine *Irene Molloy* • Paul Ford *Horace Vandergelder* • Robert Morse *Barnaby Tucker* • Wallace Ford *Malachi Stack* • Perry Wilson *Minnie Fay* ■ *Dir* Joseph Anthony • *Scr* John Michael Hayes, from the play by Thornton Wilder

The Matchmaker ★★★ 15

Romantic comedy
1997 · Ire/UK/US · Colour · 97mins

The under-rated Janeane Garofalo gets to flex her acting muscles as Marcy, dispatched to the Emerald Isle to round up a US senator's ancestors. Inadvertently she finds herself at a matchmaking festival, where sparks are soon flying between her and gauche barman David O'Hara. Matchmaker Milo O'Shea bets he can get them together and sends them on a wild goose chase to the Aran islands. It's unfortunate that the movie begins and ends in America, but what's in between has all the charm that Ireland can offer.

Janeane Garofalo *Marcy Tizard* • David O'Hara *Sean Kelly* • Milo O'Shea *Dermot O'Brien* • Jay O Sanders *Senator John McGlory* • Denis Leary *Nick* ■ *Dir* Mark Joffe • *Scr* Karen Janszen, Louis Nowra, Graham Linehan, from a screenplay by Greg Dinner

Maternal Instincts ★★ 15

Thriller   1996 · US · Colour · 88mins

This TV movie, about a woman obsessed with the idea of having a baby, is a (literally) brooding revenge thriller. When Delta Burke's motherhood plans are destroyed following an emergency hysterectomy, she sets out to destroy the doctor who did the op. Melodramatic and over-ripe, the film is dodgily acted by TV regulars Burke (*Designing Women*), Beth Broderick (*Sabrina, the Teenage Witch*) and Garwin Sanford. 🖵

Delta Burke *Tracy Patterson* • Beth Broderick *Dr Eva Warden* • Garwin Sanford *Gary Warden* • Sandra Nelson *Sabrina Crane* • Gillian Barber *Julie Taft* • Kevin McNulty *Joe Reilly* ■ *Dir* George Kaczender • *Scr* Lisa Friedman Block, Kathy Kirtland Silverman

Matewan ★★★★ 15

Historical drama
1987 · US · Colour · 127mins

When the local coal company cuts the pay of its mainly white workforce and begins using blacks and Italian immigrants at cheaper rates, tensions run high in the West Virginian mining town of Matewan. Union organiser Joe Kenehan (Chris Cooper) arrives to sort out the increasingly violent confrontation. Set in the twenties, this resembles a western: the good, the bad and the ugly characters are clearly delineated, even if writer/director John Sayles often gives them speeches instead of dialogue. Films about the American labour movement are rare, so this uncompromising, fact-based drama is to be savoured. The glowing cinematography is by Haskell Wexler. Contains swearing. 🖵

Chris Cooper *Joe Kenehan* • James Earl Jones "Few Clothes" *Johnson* • Will Oldham *Danny Radnor* • Jace Alexander *Hillard* • Ken Jenkins *Sephus Purcell* • Bob Gunton *CE Lively* • Gary McCleery *Ludie* • Kevin Tighe *Hickey* ■ *Dir/Scr* John Sayles

Matilda ★★ U

Sports comedy   1978 · US · Colour · 87mins

Screen version of the Paul Gallico book, about a boxing kangaroo and the small-time theatrical agent who becomes the marsupial's manager. The budget obviously didn't stretch to special effects, so the kangaroo is played by a man in a costume. This cute comedy looks a little dated these days, but kids might want to hop along to see it. Elliott Gould and Robert Mitchum head the humans, while Gary Morgan is the guy in the suit.

Elliott Gould *Bernie Bonnelli* • Robert Mitchum *Duke Parkhurst* • Harry Guardino *Uncle Nono* • Clive Revill *Billy Baker/Narration* • Lionel Stander *Pinky Schwab* • Karen Carlson *Kathleen Smith* • Gary Morgan ■ *Dir* Daniel Mann • *Scr* Albert S Ruddy, Timothy Galfas, from the novel by Paul Gallico

Matilda ★★★★ PG

Comedy fantasy   1996 · US · Colour · 94mins

Director Danny DeVito revels in the black comedy of this typically dark Roald Dahl story, in which monstrous adults consider children as inconvenient accessories. DeVito – who also stars as Matilda's boorish dad – cleverly emphasises the point by shooting much of the film from a child's-eye view, making people and buildings alike look forbidding and cold. *Miracle on 34th Street*'s Mara Wilson is excellent in the lead, while Embeth Davidtz prevents beloved teacher Miss Honey from being too sickly sweet. Stealing the acting honours, however, is *Darling Buds of May* star Pam Ferris, who brings vicious headmistress Miss Trunchbull to terrifying life. 🖵 **DVD**

Mara Wilson *Matilda* • Danny DeVito *Harry Wormwood* • Rhea Perlman *Zinnia Wormwood* • Embeth Davidtz *Miss Honey* • Pam Ferris *Agatha Trunchbull* • Paul Reubens *FBI agent* ■ *Dir* Danny DeVito • *Scr* Nicholas Kazan, Robin Swicord, from the novel by Roald Dahl

U = SUITABLE FOR ALL   Uc = SUITABLE FOR ALL, ESPECIALLY FOR YOUNG CHILDREN (VIDEO ONLY)   PG = PARENTAL GUIDANCE

Matinee ★★★★ PG
Comedy drama 1993 · US · Colour · 94mins

A glorious mix of *American Graffiti*, *Stand by Me* and *The Fly*, this super coming-of-age saga from Joe Dante (director of *Gremlins* and *Small Soldiers*) is a tender paean to growing up in the early sixties, using the twin backdrops of nuclear bomb paranoia and "Atom Age" monster flicks. It's also a loving tribute to legendary producer/director William Castle, the schlock showman responsible for gimmick B-movies such as *The Tingler* and *House on Haunted Hill*. Charming John Goodman is the Castle clone launching his new giant insect horror film *Mant* in Key West during the Cuban missile crisis, and it's the contrast between fake movie scares and real-life ones that makes Dante's nostalgic inferno so engaging. 📼

John Goodman *Lawrence Woolsey* • Cathy Moriarty *Ruth Corday/Carole* • Simon Fenton *Gene Loomis* • Omri Katz *Stan* • Lisa Jakub *Sandra* • Kellie Martin *Sherry* • Jesse Lee *Dennis Loomis* • Lucinda Jenney *Anne Loomis* ■ *Dir* Joe Dante • *Scr* Charlie Haas, from a story by Jerico Haas

The Matinee Idol ★★
Silent comedy 1928 · US · BW · 60mins

A Broadway star catches a Civil War drama performed by a theatrical troupe out in the boondocks. It's so badly done that he takes it to the city as a comedy and has a hit. Bessie Love is the appealing star of this silent, the second to be directed for Columbia by their future financial saviour, Frank Capra. (Romance blossoms between Love and the actor who plays a black soldier and only declares his affection when rain washes off his make-up.) Although Capra could have given more weight to the fact that the actors have been made fools of, the film is frequently very funny.

Bessie Love *Ginger Bolivar* • Johnnie Walker *Don Wilson/Harry Mann* • Lionel Belmore *Col Jasper Bolivar* ■ *Dir* Frank Capra • *Scr* Peter Milne, Elmer Harris, from the story *Come Back to Aaron* by Robert Lord

The Mating Game ★★★★ U
Comedy 1959 · US · Colour · 96mins

The Darling Buds of May is better known here as the popular TV series which introduced us to Catherine Zeta-Jones. But this MGM version of HE Bates's novel is actually much funnier and more faithful to the spirit of the original. The cast is also much classier: Paul Douglas is a truly estimable father to Debbie Reynolds, the farm girl who falls for taxman Tony Randall, while director George Marshall keeps it all zipping along.

Debbie Reynolds *Mariette Larkin* • Tony Randall *Lorenzo Charlton* • Paul Douglas *Pop Larkin* • Fred Clark *Oliver Kelsey* • Una Merkel *Ma Larkin* ■ *Dir* George Marshall • *Scr* William Roberts, from the novel *The Darling Buds of May* by HE Bates

The Mating Season ★★ U
Comedy 1951 · US · BW · 101mins

A working man (John Lund) ascends the social ladder through marriage to the beautiful daughter (Gene Tierney) of an ambassador, whose family is unaware of his humble origins. His mother (Thelma Ritter) pretends to be a servant and comes to work for the newlyweds. In the face of his somewhat lifeless co-stars and a workmanlike but uninspired script, director Mitchell Leisen wisely allowed Thelma Ritter to walk away with this domestic comedy. Her performance earned her the second of her record six Oscar nominations for best supporting actress.

Gene Tierney *Maggie Carleton* • John Lund *Van McNulty* • Miriam Hopkins *Fran Carleton* • Thelma Ritter *Ellen McNulty* • Jan Sterling *Betsy* • Larry Keating *Mr Kallinger Sr* • James Lorimer *George C Kallinger Jr* ■ *Dir* Mitchell Leisen • *Scr* Charles Brackett, Walter Reisch, Richard Breen

The Matrix ★★★★★ 15
Science-fiction action thriller 1999 · US · Colour · 136mins

Keanu Reeves reclaims his action hero crown in the Wachowski Brothers' super-smart science fiction action adventure set across two dimensions. Thematically complex, yet intelligently integrating Eastern philosophy, Lewis Carroll and ancient mysticism, the film has Reeves as Neo, a reclusive computer hacker who may just be the one to save the world from the evils of cyberspace slavery. Taking a quantum leap beyond anything the fantasy sensation seeker has seen before in the special effects department, this mixes ultra-cool visuals, vertigo-inducing kung fu and a deliciously paranoid scenario for an adrenalin-pumping roller coaster ride of extraordinary vision and power. Contains violence. 📼 DVD

Keanu Reeves *Neo* • Carrie-Anne Moss *Trinity* • Laurence Fishburne *Morpheus* • Hugo Weaving *Agent Smith* • Joe Pantoliano *Cypher* • Gloria Foster *Oracle* • Marcus Chong *Tank* ■ *Dir/Scr* Larry Wachowski, Andy Wachowski

A Matter of Life and Death ★★★★★ U
Romantic fantasy 1946 · UK · BW and Colour · 99mins

The theatrical stylisation of Michael Powell and Emeric Pressburger sometimes deflected their thematic purpose, but in this dazzling fantasy they succeed in marrying the two to perfection. Although the film was intended to celebrate the Anglo-American alliance that had prevailed in the Second World War, the Archers production company instead delivered a barbed allegory that called into question not only the strength of the ties between the Allies, but also Britain's continued status as a world power. Its political outspokenness, visual audacity and mannered playing now make it one of the most fondly recalled British movies. 📼 DVD

David Niven *Squadron Leader Peter Carter* • Kim Hunter *June* • Roger Livesey *Dr Reeves* • Robert Coote *Bob Trubshawe* • Marius Goring *Conductor 71* • Raymond Massey *Abraham Farlan* • Kathleen Byron *Angel* • Richard Attenborough *English pilot* • Bonar Colleano *American pilot* • Joan Maude *Chief recorder* ■ *Dir/Scr* Michael Powell, Emeric Pressburger • *Cinematographer* Jack Cardiff • *Production Designer* Alfred Junge

A Matter of Time ★ PG
Drama 1976 · It/US · Colour · 99mins

A newly emerged movie star (Liza Minnelli) recalls her encounters with an aged contessa (Ingrid Bergman) whose rambling tales of her life inspired the young girl. Made up of a series of utterly confusing flashbacks-within-flashbacks, this maudlin rubbish is not helped by Minnelli's undisciplined, characteristically edgy performance – or that of Bergman, done up as a dessicated crone. Vincente Minnelli subsequently disclaimed responsibility for the finished film. Isabella Rossellini, looking the way we like to remember her mother, has a cameo as the old contessa's nurse. 📼

Liza Minnelli *Nina* • Ingrid Bergman *Contessa Sanziani* • Charles Boyer *Count* • Spiros Andros *Mario* • Tina Aumont *Valentina* • Gabriele Ferzetti *Antonio Vicari* • Isabella Rossellini *Sister Pia* ■ *Dir* Vincente Minnelli • *Scr* John Gay, from the novel *The Film of Memory* by Maurice Druon

A Matter of Wife...and Death ★★
Thriller 1976 · US · Colour · 74mins

Rod Taylor attempts to emulate Burt Reynolds's 1973 cinema success as private eye Shamus McCoy, who this time around gets caught up in a gambling racket. But the gamble failed to pay off for the producers of this TV pilot, as the planned series never materialised. The cast includes *Wonder Woman*'s Lynda Carter and Anne Archer, who would later find her niche playing the faithful but long-suffering wife in such films as *Fatal Attraction* and *Patriot Games*.

Rod Taylor *Shamus McCoy* • Joe Santos *Lieutenant Vincent Promuto* • Eddie Firestone *Blinky* • Luke Askew *Snell* • John Colicos *Joe Ruby* • Anne Archer *Carol* • Lynda Carter *Zelda* ■ *Dir* Marvin J Chomsky • *Scr* Don Ingalls, from characters created by Barry Beckerman

Matters of the Heart ★★ PG
Romantic drama 1990 · US · Colour · 89mins

Geoffrey Lewis is now perhaps better known as the father of Juliette Lewis than as a performer in his own right. Here he gets to chew a little scenery as a heavy-handed father who disapproves of his promising pianist son's romantic entanglement with an older woman held in low esteem by the musical establishment. Jane Seymour lacks the edge that made Jacqueline Bisset such a bad influence in *Class*, but she manages to convey some of the bitterness and passion of her character. Contains swearing. 📼

Jane Seymour *Hadley Norman* • Christopher Gartin *Steven Harper* • James Stacy *Glen Harper* • Geoffrey Lewis *Frank Harper* • Katherine Cannon *Hope Harper* • Samantha Jordan *Sally* ■ *Dir* Michael Ray Rhodes • *Scr* Martin Tahse, Linda Bergman, from the book *The Country of the Heart* by Barbara Wersba

Maurice ★★★ 15
Period drama 1987 · UK · Colour · 140mins

EM Forster's autobiographical novel about homosexuals at Cambridge was written in 1914, but withheld from publication until after his death in 1970. From its opening scenes, in which Simon Callow campily tells the young Maurice what great things he can expect from his body, James Ivory's film skips rather gingerly around the subject matter. The older Maurice, now played by James Wilby, goes up to Cambridge where Hugh Grant awaits; eventually, though, he ends up with a bit of rough trade, played by Rupert Graves. As with all Merchant-Ivory films, it's impeccably mounted, prim and a tad dull. DVD

James Wilby *Maurice Hall* • Hugh Grant *Clive Durham* • Denholm Elliott *Dr Barry* • Simon Callow *Mr Ducie* • Billie Whitelaw *Mrs Hall* • Ben Kingsley *Lasker-Jones* • Judy Parfitt *Mrs Durham* • Rupert Graves *Alec Scudder* ■ *Dir* James Ivory • *Scr* Kit Hesketh-Harvey, James Ivory, from the novel by EM Forster

Mausoleum ★ 18
Horror 1983 · US · Colour · 92mins

Self-styled sleaze starlet Bobbie Bresee plays a housewife who, due to a family curse, becomes possessed by a demon that turns her into a ritually homicidal nymphomaniac. Bresee dances around topless a lot and, in the film's only fun moment, reveals her breasts have teeth. Otherwise the special effects are cheesy (Bresee sports glowing green eyes when feeling lustful), the acting amateurish and the dialogue dreadful. 📼

Marjoe Gortner *Oliver Farrell* • Bobbie Bresee *Susan Farrell* • Norman Burton *Dr Simon Andrews* • Maurice Sherbanee *Ben, the gardener* • LaWanda Page *Elsie* ■ *Dir* Michael Dugan • *Scr* Robert Madero, Robert Barich, from a story by Katherine Rosenwink

Maverick ★★★ PG
Comedy western 1994 · US · Colour · 121mins

This comedy western written by script doctor supreme William Goldman was clearly in need of a little attention itself. Goldman has produced a gentle tribute to the hit TV series, but misses a golden opportunity for a razor-sharp spoof. There's no doubt the stars had a ball, though, with Mel Gibson and Jodie Foster sparking nicely as the eponymous gambler and the con artist who is more than his match. But it's left to James Garner (the original Bret Maverick) to demonstrate what comic acting is really all about. Contains violence. 📼 DVD

Mel Gibson *Bret Maverick* • Jodie Foster *Annabelle Bransford* • James Garner *Zane Cooper* • Graham Greene *Joseph* • Alfred Molina *Angel* • James Coburn *Commodore Duval* • Dub Taylor *Room clerk* • Geoffrey Lewis *Matthew Wicker* ■ *Dir* Richard Donner • *Scr* William Goldman, from the TV series by Roy Huggins

The Maverick Queen ★★ U
Western 1955 · US · Colour · 86mins

Barbara Stanwyck stars in a cheaply-made, lurid western that vaguely resembles Republic's far more successful *Johnny Guitar*. Stanwyck plays an outlaw who gives young studs the runaround before falling in love with Barry Sullivan, a Pinkerton agent on the trail of the Sundance Kid. This was directed by Republic workhorse Joseph Kane and shot in the studio's widescreen process, Naturama. 📼

Barbara Stanwyck *Kit Banion* • Barry Sullivan *Jeff* • Scott Brady *Sundance* • Mary Murphy

Lucy Lee • Wallace Ford *Jamie* • Howard Petrie *Butch Cassidy* ■ *Dir* Joseph Kane • *Scr* Kenneth Gamet, DeVallon Scott, from the novel by Zane Grey, Romer Grey

Max ★★★

Drama   1994 · Can · Colour · 94mins

This intelligent and involving drama takes an occasionally bitter look at how the ideals of the sixties have been sold out by the nineties. The film follows a family's bid to escape the tensions and dangers of the city by settling in the desert, only to discover that their new environment brings new problems. RH Thomson and Denise Crosby head a credible cast.

RH Thomson *Andy Blake* • Denise Crosby *Jayne Blake* • Walter Dalton *Jayne's Dad* • Garwin Sanford *Doctor Kaye* • Don Davis [Don S Davis] *Earl* ■ *Dir/Scr* Charles Wilkinson

Max and Helen ★★★ 15

Drama based on a true story
1990 · US/Hun · Colour · 90mins

A topnotch cast breathes much-needed life into a grim, plodding storyline about two lovers who meet up 20 years after they were separated during the Second World War. Martin Landau, Jodhi May and Alice Krige lend an impressive level of depth and dignity to their roles in a movie that often comes perilously close to pomposity. It's based on Simon Wiesenthal's award-winning book (he is played by Landau) and director Philip Saville struggles to keep to the heart of the text, with only partial success. ▭

Treat Williams *Max Rosenberg* • Alice Krige *Helen Weiss* • Martin Landau *Simon Wiesenthal* • Jonathan Phillips *Werner Schultze* • Adam Kotz *Peter* • Jodhi May *Miriam Weiss* • Lulee Fisher *Judith* ■ *Dir* Philip Saville • *Scr* Corey Blechman, from the memoirs *Max and Helen: a Remarkable True Love Story* by Simon Wiesenthal

Max Dugan Returns ★★★ PG

Comedy   1983 · US · Colour · 93mins

A Neil Simon comedy starring his then wife, Marsha Mason, as a widow struggling against the foibles of modern life to bring up her 15-year-old son (Matthew Broderick). Just as we get to know them and their world – a world in which every domestic appliance is against them – Jason Robards shows up as Mason's father. He abandoned her when she was nine; now he's terminally ill and stinking rich. Easy on the eye and the mind, with a very attractive cast. ▭

Marsha Mason *Nora* • Jason Robards [Jason Robards Jr] *Max Dugan* • Donald Sutherland *Brian* • Matthew Broderick *Michael* • Dody Goodman *Mrs Litke* • Sal Viscuso *Coach* • Panchito Gomez *Luis* • Kiefer Sutherland *Bill* ■ *Dir* Herbert Ross • *Scr* Neil Simon

Max Mon Amour ★★ 18

Black comedy   1986 · Fr/US · Colour · 97mins

A clever idea from director Nagisa Oshima who obviously tries to follow in Luis Buñuel's surreal footsteps by taking apart the hypocrisies of the French bourgeoisie. Charlotte Rampling is the diplomat's deeply bored wife in Paris who takes a chimpanzee as a lover, and Anthony Higgins is her non-plussed husband who is determined to take it on the stiff upper lip and chin.

The satire fails to bite, however, owing to a pair of stultifying performances from the main stars, though Max the chimp is actually rather good. In French and English with subtitles.

Charlotte Rampling *Margaret Jones* • Anthony Higgins *Peter Jones* • Bernard-Pierre Donnadieu *Archibald* • Victoria Abril *Maria* • Anne-Marie Besse *Suzanne* • Nicole Calfan *Hélène* ■ *Dir* Nagisa Oshima • *Scr* Nagisa Oshima, Jean-Claude Carrière, from an idea by Jean-Claude Carrière

Maxie ★★★ PG

Comedy fantasy   1985 · US · Colour · 93mins

An old-fashioned fantasy, with Glenn Close as the bishop's secretary whose body is taken over by a free spirit from the twenties called Maxie Malone. Close has fun with the dual role of the conservative working wife and the jazz-age flapper, but it is *Chicago Hope's* Mandy Patinkin who, as Close's husband, comes across as most at home with the light romantic comedy. Slight but enjoyable. ▭

Glenn Close *Jan/Maxie* • Mandy Patinkin *Nick* • Ruth Gordon *Mrs Lavin* • Barnard Hughes *Bishop Campbell* • Valerie Curtin *Miss Sheffer* • Googy Gress *Father Jerome* ■ *Dir* Paul Aaron • *Scr* Patricia Resnick, from the novel *Marion's Wall* by Jack Finney

Maximum Overdrive ★★ 18

Horror   1986 · US · Colour · 93mins

…but minimum credibility, as horror writer Stephen King decided his neon-lit prose needed his neon-lit direction. It's a courageous debut, with the machinery in a North Carolina small town coming to lethal life and besieging a group headed by Emilio Estevez and Pat Hingle. The trouble is that writer King should have explained to director King that you must not outpace your audience's interest, however well-managed the action. Contains violence and swearing. ▭

Emilio Estevez *Bill Robinson* • Pat Hingle *Hendershot* • Laura Harrington *Brett* • Yeardley Smith *Connie* • John Short *Curt* • Ellen McElduff *Wanda June* ■ *Dir* Stephen King • *Scr* Stephen King, from his story.

Maximum Risk ★★ 18

Action thriller   1996 · US · Colour · 96mins

In *Double Impact*, we suffered the agony of two Jean-Claude Van Dammes for the entire movie. Here, thankfully, his twin gets bumped off in the opening few minutes. It's still hard work, but at least in the hands of Hong Kong director Ringo Lam (*City on Fire*) there are plenty of tremendous action set pieces to relish as Van Damme takes on the might of the Russian Mafia with the help of his late sibling's girlfriend (Natasha Henstridge from *Species*). French stars Jean-Hugues Anglade and Stéphane Audran are largely wasted, however. ▭ *DVD*

Jean-Claude Van Damme *Alain/Mikhail* • Natasha Henstridge *Alex* • Jean-Hugues Anglade *Sebastien* • Zach Grenier *Ivan* • Stéphane Audran *Chantal Moreau* ■ *Dir* Ringo Lam • *Scr* Larry Ferguson

May Wine ★★★ 15

Romantic comedy
1990 · Fr/US · Colour · 80mins

Lara Flynn Boyle is on good form here as a troublesome daughter whose refusal to dump an unsuitable boyfriend prompts mother Joanna Cassidy to sweep her off to Paris. No sooner have they arrived than they both fall for the same doctor, Guy Marchand. Cassidy (*Blade Runner, Who Framed Roger Rabbit*), is one of Hollywood's more under-rated actresses, while Marchand is among French cinema's most accomplished supporting players. Consequently, the cast brings out the best in director Carol Wiseman's frothy script. Contains swearing and nudity. ▭

Joanna Cassidy *Lorraine* • Lara Flynn Boyle *Camille* • Guy Marchand *Dr Paul Charmant* • Paul Freeman *Tom* • Andre Penvern *Concierge* • Emmanuel Fouquet *Porter* ■ *Dir* Carol Wiseman • *Scr* Carol Wiseman, from a screenplay by Peter Lefcourt

Maya ★★★ 15

Drama   1992 · Ind/UK · Colour · 121mins

Ketan Mehta emerged as one of India's foremost directors with *Mirch Masala* and he further enhanced his reputation with this imaginative adaptation of Flaubert's *Madame Bovary*. Set in the days following independence from Britain, Mehta manages to be faithful to the spirit of the novel while also developing his own themes, using Maya's passionate fantasies and unrewarding affairs to highlight the mood of the Indian people in 1949, torn between the notion of nationhood and nostalgia for the Raj. Deepa Sahi is impressive in the lead. In Hindi with English subtitles.

Deepa Sahi *Maya* • Farooque Sheikh *Charudatta Das* • Raj Babbar *Rudrapratap Singh* • Shah Rukh Khan *Lalit Kumar* • Satyadev Dubey *Old interrogator* • Shrivallabh Vyas *Young interrogator* • Dr Shree Ram Lagoo *Maya's father* ■ *Dir* Ketan Mehta • *Scr* Sitanshu Yashashchandra, Ketan Mehta

Maybe Baby ★ 15

Romantic comedy
1999 · UK · Colour · 104mins

Debut writer/director, Ben Elton tries – and fails – to step into the winning comedy shoes of erstwhile *Black Adder* partner Richard Curtis (*Four Weddings and a Funeral, Notting Hill*). Revolving around Hugh Laurie and Joely Richardson's attempts to have a child, this clichéd, caricatured and dreadfully acted tale has all the wit, sparkle and profundity of a seventies *Confessions* movie. Elton's direction is bland and colourless, and even gratuitous cameos from chums Rowan Atkinson, Emma Thompson and Dawn French fail to disperse the odour of turkey.

Hugh Laurie *Sam Bell* • Joely Richardson *Lucy Bell* • Adrian Lester *George* • James Purefoy *Carl Phipps* • Tom Hollander *Ewan Proclaimer* • Joanna Lumley *Sheila* • Emma Thompson *Druscilla* • Rowan Atkinson *Mr James* • Dawn French *Charlene* ■ *Dir/Scr* Ben Elton

Mayerling ★★★★

Historical romance   1936 · Fr · BW · 96mins

An exquisite French account of one of history's most famous and poignant love affairs: that of Crown Prince

Rudolph, heir to the Austro-Hungarian throne, and the youthful Marie Vetsera, a well-born commoner. Denied a release from his loveless marriage, Rudolph and Marie escape for a 24-hour idyll to Mayerling, his hunting lodge, at the end of which he shoots her and then himself in a suicide pact. Charles Boyer and Danielle Darrieux are faultlessly cast as the ill-fated lovers under Anatole Litvak's stylish and sensitive direction. The film led to a Hollywood contract for Litvak and made an international heart-throb of Boyer. A French language film.

Charles Boyer *Archduke Rudolph of Austria* • Danielle Darrieux *Marie Vetsera* • Suzy Prim *Countess Larisch* • Jean Dax *Emperor Franz Joseph* • Gabrielle Dorziat *Empress Elizabeth* • Jean Debucourt *Count Taafe* • Marthe Régnier *Baroness Helene/Helene* ■ *Dir* Anatole Litvak • *Scr* Joseph Kessel, Irma Von Cube, from the novel by Claude Anet

Mayerling ★★ PG

Historical romance
1968 · Fr/UK · Colour · 132mins

Omar Sharif is Crown Prince Rudolf of Austria, helplessly in love with young Marie Vetsera (Catherine Deneuve). Unable to free himself from his marriage, he enters a suicide pact with his lover. After spending 24 idyllic hours together at Mayerling, his country retreat, he shoots her and then himself. This love story was definitively filmed in France in 1936 by Anatole Litvak. Terence Young's version is overblown, unmoving and overlong, with the presence of James Mason, Ava Gardner and Genevieve Page adding only surface gloss. ▭

Omar Sharif *Crown Prince Rudolf* • Catherine Deneuve *Baroness Maria Vetsera* • James Mason *Emperor Franz Josef* • Ava Gardner *Empress Elizabeth* • James Robertson-Justice *Edward, Prince of Wales* • Genevieve Page *Countess Larisch* ■ *Dir* Terence Young • *Scr* Terence Young, Denis Cannan, Joseph Kessel, from the novel by Claude Anet and the novel *The Archduke* by Michael Arnold

Mayflower Madam ★★ 18

Drama based on a true story
1987 · US · Colour · 92mins

A fact-based TV movie that wastes the talents of lead actress Candice Bergen. She plays Sydney Biddle Barrows, a debutante descended from America's founding fathers (and mothers) and so thought of as an aristocrat, who ended up running a high-class "escort service of fantasy girls" and made headlines for over a year in the eighties. The real-life Barrows turns up in a cameo role, but there's little else of interest.

Candice Bergen *Sydney Biddle Barrows* • Chris Sarandon *Matt Whittington* • Caitlin Clarke *Virginia* • Jim Antonio *Frank Gullett* • Debra Rogers *Tammy* • Leslie Hardy *Hilary* • Sydney Biddle Barrows *Peggy Eaton* ■ *Dir* Lou Antonio • *Scr* Elizabeth Gill, Charles Israel

The Mayor of Hell ★★

Crime drama   1933 · US · BW · 85mins

A typical Warner Bros social melodrama, with James Cagney as a racketeer who suddenly takes an interest in a reform school and the conditions of the youngsters inside. Will he corrupt them or does he become a do-gooder? Despite

U = SUITABLE FOR ALL   Uc = SUITABLE FOR ALL, ESPECIALLY FOR YOUNG CHILDREN (VIDEO ONLY)   PG = PARENTAL GUIDANCE

Cagney's energy, the picture is hopelessly dated, full of mawkish moments, dire knockabout humour and bouts of violence as Cagney carries on with his profession.

James Cagney *Patsy Gargan* • Madge Evans *Dorothy Griffith* • Allen Jenkins *Mike* • Dudley Digges *Mr Thompson* • Frankie Darro *Jimmy Smith* • Farina *Smoke* • Dorothy Peterson *Mrs Smith* ■ *Dir* Archie Mayo • *Scr* Edward Chodorov, from a story by Islin Auster

Maytime ★★★★ U
Romantic musical 1937 · US · BW · 131mins
Singing duo Jeanette MacDonald and Nelson Eddy were in their prime in this splendid version of Rida Johnson Young and Sigmund Romberg's melancholy operetta, and the theme song *Will You Remember?* became for ever identified with them. The classy MGM production is particularly lavish, and director Robert Z Leonard manages a marvellous tragic tone, unusual for this type of mainstream light entertainment. The film is further enhanced by the presence of the great John Barrymore, in one of his last worthwhile roles. A superb showcase for the silver screen's most popular singing team.

Jeanette MacDonald *Marcia Morney/Miss Morrison* • Nelson Eddy *Paul Allison* • John Barrymore *Nicolai Nazaroff* • Herman Bing *August Archipenko* • Tom Brown *Kip Stuart* • Lynne Carver *Barbara Roberts* • Rafaela Ottiano *Ellen* ■ *Dir* Robert Z Leonard • *Scr* Noel Langley, from the operetta by Rida Johnson Young, Sigmund Romberg

Maytime in Mayfair ★★★ U
Romantic musical 1949 · UK · Colour · 98mins
This is virtually a remake of the previous year's Anna Neagle/Michael Wilding smash hit *Spring in Park Lane*. The plot resembles an earlier Neagle movie, *Irene*, with its dress-shop rivalry, once so fashionable and today so dated. Neagle looks rather too old and staid to partner the charming Wilding, but a hard-working supporting cast, including Tom Walls, Nicholas Phipps, Peter Graves and Thora Hird, keeps the fun bubbling.

Anna Neagle *Eileen Grahame* • Michael Wilding *Michael Gore-Brown* • Peter Graves (2) *D'Arcy Davenport* • Nicholas Phipps *Sir Henry Hazelrigg* • Thora Hird *Janet* • Michael Shepley *Shepherd* • Tom Walls *Inspector* ■ *Dir* Herbert Wilcox • *Scr* Nicholas Phipps

Me and My Gal ★★★
Comedy drama 1932 · US · BW · 78mins
A charming but creaky 20th Century-Fox comedy drama that's given a lift by its tart dialogue and the naturalistic playing of stars Spencer Tracy and Joan Bennett. The bulk of the plot turns out to be some nonsense about Bennett's sister falling for a gangster, with Tracy playing a cop who's keen on Bennett. Director Raoul Walsh tries to keep sentimentality at bay, but the whole turns out to be rather ramshackle, if short and sweet.

Spencer Tracy *Dan Dolan* • Joan Bennett *Helen Riley* • Marion Burns *Kate Riley* • George Walsh *Duke Castege* • J Farrell MacDonald *Pat "Pop" Riley* • Noel Madison *Baby Face Castenega* • Henry B Walthall

Sergeant Collins • Bert Hanlon *Jake the Tailor* ■ *Dir* Raoul Walsh • *Scr* Arthur Kober, from a story by Barry Connors, Phillip Klein

Me and the Colonel ★★★ U
Second World War comedy 1958 · US · BW · 105mins
Danny Kaye gained new admirers with his subdued performance and altered appearance in this serious comedy, playing one half of an odd couple: a self-effacing, resourceful Jew fleeing the German occupation of Paris in 1940. Joining the journey of escape is an arrogant, aristocratic Polish colonel, played by Curt Jurgens, who ultimately overcomes his anti-Semitism. Director Peter Glenville draws finely judged performances from his leads, and there are some expert supporting performances, particularly from Martita Hunt as a mother superior. 📼

Danny Kaye *SL Jacobowsky* • Curt Jurgens *Colonel Tadeusz Boleslav Prokoszny* • Nicole Maurey *Suzanne Roualet* • Françoise Rosay *Madame Bouffier* • Akim Tamiroff *Szabuniewicz* • Martita Hunt *Mother Superior* • Alexander Scourby *Major Von Bergen* ■ *Dir* Peter Glenville • *Scr* George Froeschel, SN Behrman, from the play *Jacobowsky and the Colonel* by Franz Werfel

Me and the Kid ★★
Comedy crime drama 1993 · US · Colour · 97mins
In this plodding semi-comedy, bungling burglars break into a rich man's home, find the safe empty and decide to kidnap the rich guy's neglected kid instead. The thieves fall out when one decides to return the boy, only to find that he prefers his new life and doesn't want to go back. Poor pacing makes the film heavy going for a high-calibre cast of character actors, including Danny Aiello, Cathy Moriarty and Joe Pantoliano. Contains swearing.

Danny Aiello *Harry* • Alex Zuckerman *Gary Feldman* • Joe Pantoliano *Roy* • Cathy Moriarty *Rose* • David Dukes *Victor Feldman* • Anita Morris *Mrs Feldman* ■ *Dir* Dan Curtis • *Scr* Richard Tannenbaum, from the novel *Taking Gary Feldman* by Stanley Cohen

Me and the Mob ★★
Crime comedy 1992 · US · Colour · 86mins
Corny crime caper with James Lorinz as an author suffering from writer's block who joins the mob to get some background information for his next book. An insignificant release at the time, this energetic but inane comedy has more resonance now due to the presence of Sandra Bullock, albeit in a small role. There's also a fleeting appearance from Steve Buscemi, whose career would shortly take off thanks to cult hit *Reservoir Dogs*.

James Lorinz *Jimmy Corona* • Stephen Lee *Bobby Blitzer* • Sandra Bullock *Lori* • Tony Darrow *Tony Bando* • Vinny Pastore [Vincent Pastore] *"Fixer" Giachetti* • John Costelloe *"Bink-Bink" Borelli* • Steve Buscemi *Conspiracy nut* ■ *Dir* Frank Rainone • *Scr* Rocco Simonelli, James Lorinz, Frank Rainone

Me, Myself and I ★★
Romantic comedy 1992 · US · Colour · 94mins
The subject of multiple personality disorder provides a seemingly

irresistible lure for the makers of movie comedies. Here JoBeth Williams, so memorable in *Poltergeist*, gives her absolute best as the schizophrenic romancing George Segal, but she simply doesn't have the screen presence to carry the film. Director Pablo Ferro made his name designing the titles for such classic movies as *Dr Strangelove* and *Bullitt*; after this ill-advised foray into the major league, he returned to his former profession.

George Segal *Buddy Arnett* • JoBeth Williams *Diane* • Shelley Hack *Jennifer* • Don Calfa *Irving* • Betsy Lynn George *Jailbait* • Bill Macy *Sydney* ■ *Dir* Pablo Ferro • *Scr* Julian Barry

Me Myself I ★★★★ 15
Romantic comedy fantasy 1999 · Fr/Ausl · Colour · 104mins
Rachel Griffiths delivers an engaging performance as a single thirtysomething journalist in this comedy drama which asks the often-posed question: "what if?" In Griffiths's case, she wonders what would have happened if she had married her former sweetheart David Roberts and settled down to the life of a housewife and mother. After a freak (and never explained) occurrence, she wakes up to discover that her old life has disappeared and she is *that* woman, complete with annoying kids and a sexless marriage. Brilliantly written and directed by Pip Karmel, this realistically presents the pros and cons of both lives, while Griffiths proves she has a deft comic touch.

Rachel Griffiths *Pamela* • David Roberts *Robert* • Sandy Winton *Ben* • Yael Stone *Stacey* • Shaun Loseby *Douglas* • Trent Sullivan *Rupert* • Rebecca Frith *Terri* • Felix Williamson *Geoff* ■ *Dir/Scr* Pip Karmel

Mean Dog Blues ★★ 18
Prison drama 1978 · US · Colour · 104mins
After a hit-and-run incident, musician Gregg Henry (*Payback*) ends up in prison and comes up against guard George Kennedy (a *Naked Gun* regular). Prison is predictably hell – especially in a chain gang. Director Mel Stuart has had a varied career that encompasses the Oscar-winning Kennedy documentary *Four Days in November* and *Willy Wonka and the Chocolate Factory*. Despite his efforts, this is basically a B-movie with slim production values. 📼

Gregg Henry *Paul Ramsey* • Kay Lenz *Linda Ramsey* • Scatman Crothers *Mudcat* • Tina Louise *Donna Lacey* • Felton Perry *Jake Turner* • Gregory Sierra *Jesus Gonzales* • James Wainwright *Sergeant Hubbell Wacker* • George Kennedy *Captain Omar Kinsman* ■ *Dir* Mel Stuart • *Scr* George Lefferts

Mean Guns ★★★ 18
Crime action 1996 · US · Colour · 93mins
Highlander star Christopher Lambert and rapper Ice-T strut their lethal stuff in this blood-soaked and slightly surreal action thriller. Ice-T is a sinister gangster who invites scores of criminal honchos, including troubled hit man Lambert, to an empty prison to atone for their sins against the syndicate. There they must fight each other to the death, with the last three survivors emerging with $10 million so they can retire from crime forever. Set-bound

but stylish, it is one of the better films from director Albert Pyun. 📼

Christopher Lambert *Lou* • Ice-T *Vincent Moon* • Michael Halsey *Marcus* • Deborah Van Valkenburgh *Cam* • Tina Cote *Barbie* • Yuji Okumoto *Hoss* ■ *Dir* Albert Pyun • *Scr* Andrew Witham, Nat Whitcomb

The Mean Machine ★★★★
Action comedy 1974 · US · Colour · 121mins
Released in the States as *The Longest Yard*, this is the film that fixed Burt Reynolds's "good old boy" image in the minds of audiences everywhere and helped propel him to superstardom. Reynolds exudes star quality as an imprisoned football pro who's forced to organise a team of convicts for a match against their guards. Full of references to *The Dirty Dozen* (director Robert Aldrich's earlier feature about prisoners being hand-picked for a suicidal assignment) and the corrupt regime of President Nixon, it's a little heavy-handed as a political satire. But as a boisterous comedy, with a few choice asides on dignity, loyalty and liberty, it's hard to beat.

Burt Reynolds *Paul Crewe* • Eddie Albert *Warden Hazen* • Ed Lauter *Captain Knauer* • Michael Conrad *Nate Scarboro* • Jim Hampton [James Hampton] *Caretaker* • Harry Caesar *Granville* • John Steadman *Pop* • Charles Tyner *Unger* ■ *Dir* Robert Aldrich • *Scr* Tracy Keenan Wynn, from a story by Albert S Ruddy

The Mean Season ★★★ 15
Thriller 1985 · US · Colour · 99mins
This is a cracker of a thriller, marred only by some seriously duff moments, most notably supplied by poor old Mariel Hemingway, who is saddled with the weak "girlfriend under threat from a psychopath" role. Her boyfriend is cynical journalist Kurt Russell, who gives a mesmerising performance as a man who finds himself dragged further into his latest crime story than is comfortable for kith and kin. A taut, atmospheric and potentially distressing movie, with the odd dull spell.

Kurt Russell *Malcolm Anderson* • Mariel Hemingway *Christine Connelly* • Richard Jordan *Alan Delour* • Richard Masur *Bill Nolan* • Joe Pantoliano *Andy Porter* • Richard Bradford *Phil Wilson* • Andy Garcia *Ray Martinez* ■ *Dir* Phillip Borsos • *Scr* Leon Piedmont, from the novel *In the Heat of the Summer* by John Katzenbach

Mean Streets ★★★★ 18
Drama 1973 · US · Colour · 107mins
Catholic rituals are at the heart of this passion-driven, excitable film, which established Martin Scorsese's reputation and set up Robert De Niro and Harvey Keitel as the men to take over where Marlon Brando and Rod Steiger left off. The virtually plotless story of the hangers-on at Tony's Bar in New York's Little Italy – Keitel's spiritually aspiring Charlie, De Niro's anarchic Johnny Boy – elevates low-down realism into a tragic vision of no-hopers with violent destinies, which not even the suffering of Charlie's epileptic girlfriend (Amy Robinson) can redeem. Contains violence and swearing. 📼

Harvey Keitel *Charlie* • Robert De Niro *Johnny Boy* • David Proval *Tony* • Amy Robinson *Teresa* • Richard Romanus *Michael* • Cesare

Danova *Giovanni* • Vic Argo [Victor Argo] *Mario* • Robert Carradine *Assassin* ■ *Dir* Martin Scorsese • *Scr* Martin Scorsese, Mardik Martin, from a story by Martin Scorsese

The Meanest Man in the World ★★★ U

Comedy   1943 · US · BW · 57mins

This is a cracking vehicle for the inimitable partnership of Jack Benny and Eddie "Rochester" Anderson. Few comics could milk a gag as well as Benny, whose expression, as he steals a lollipop from a child in an effort to prove to both his prospective father-in-law and millionaire Edmund Gwenn that he is a lawyer to be reckoned with, is priceless. Priscilla Lane is under-used as Benny's fiancée, but Anne Revere is splendid as his wavering secretary.

Jack Benny *Richard Clark* • Priscilla Lane *Janie Brown* • Eddie "Rochester" Anderson *Shufro* • Edmund Gwenn *Frederick P Leggitt* • Matt Briggs *Mr Brown* • Anne Revere *Kitty Crockett* • Margaret Seddon *Mrs Leggitt* • Harry Hayden *Mr Chambers* ■ *Dir* Sidney Lanfield • *Scr* George Seaton, Allan House, from a play by Augustin MacHugh, George M Cohan

Meatballs ★★ 15

Comedy   1979 · Can · Colour · 89mins

This early collaboration for *Ghostbusters* director Ivan Reitman and Bill Murray is solely dependent on its star for laughs, and there aren't that many of those. Murray plays a goofy counsellor at a Canadian summer camp who acts like an idiot. But he has a softer side, too, which comes to the fore when he takes a young loner under his wing. No better or worse than dozens of other similarly-plotted comedies, although Reitman has the good sense to get Murray on screen as often as possible. ▣

Bill Murray *Tripper* • Harvey Atkin *Morty* • Kate Lynch *Roxanne* • Russ Banham *Crockett* • Kristine DeBell *AL* • Sarah Torgov *Candace* • Jack Blum *Spaz* • Keith Knight *Fink* ■ *Dir* Ivan Reitman • *Scr* Len Blum, Dan Goldberg, Janis Allen, Harold Ramis

Meatballs 2 ★ 15

Comedy   1984 · US · Colour · 83mins

Quite why it took five years to come up with this sequel is a mystery, since they seem to be making it up as they go along. This time, the plot revolves around a big boxing match (rather than the predecessor's athletics event), but Richard Mulligan (from TV's *Soap*) is no Bill Murray. The only bright spots come from the weirdness of Paul Reubens, aka Pee-wee Herman. ▣

Archie Hahn *Jamie* • John Mengatti *Flash* • Tammy Taylor *Nancy* • Kim Richards *Cheryl* • Ralph Seymour *Eddie* • Richard Mulligan *Giddy* • Hamilton Camp *Hershey* • John Larroquette *Foxglove* • Paul Reubens *Albert* ■ *Dir* Ken Wiederhorn • *Scr* Bruce Singer, from a story by Martin Kitrosser, Carol Watson

Meatballs III: Summer Job ★★ 18

Comedy   1987 · US · Colour · 89mins

The original *Meatballs* was notable only for the fact that it gave an early starring role to Bill Murray. Two sequels on, this mix of smut and slapstick looks very dated indeed.

Patrick Dempsey plays a randy young teen at summer camp desperate to lose his virginity and receiving unexpected help from a ghostly porn queen (Sally Kellerman), who has been instructed to perform one good deed before she can enter heaven. Contains swearing and sex scenes. ▣

Sally Kellerman *Roxy Du Jour* • Patrick Dempsey *Rudy Gerner* • Al Waxman *Saint Peter* • Isabelle Mejias *Wendy* • Shannon Tweed *The Love Goddess* • Jan Taylor *Rita* • George Buza *Mean Gene* ■ *Dir* George Mendeluk • *Scr* Michael Paseornek, Bradley Kesden, from a story by Chuck Workman

The Mechanic ★★★ 15

Action thriller   1972 · US · Colour · 95mins

No-frills direction from Michael Winner creates the right tone of seething disquiet for star Charles Bronson in this forerunner to *Death Wish*. No one is better at suggesting silent menace than Bronson, who here plays a hit man capable of making his messy work look accidental and training a young pretender to the throne. Winner, though sometimes disrupting the action with unnecessary gloss, keeps his film tight, suspenseful and violent. ▣

Charles Bronson *Arthur Bishop* • Jan-Michael Vincent *Steve McKenna* • Keenan Wynn *Harry McKenna* • Jill Ireland *Prostitute* • Linda Ridgeway *Louise* • Frank De Kova *Syndicate head* • Lindsay Crosby *Policeman* ■ *Dir* Michael Winner • *Scr* Lewis John Carlino

A Medal for Benny ★★★ U

Satire   1945 · US · BW · 80mins

Though Benny himself is never seen, his trouble-making has got him evicted from the small town on the California coast, home to Mexican immigrants. Then his shamed family and the townspeople learn he's a war hero, having killed 100 Japanese single-handed before being killed himself. Interesting, untypical casting and a semi-satirical script that manages (just) to veer off easy sentimentality make this little-known picture well worth a look. The story, partly by John Steinbeck, was Oscar-nominated.

Dorothy Lamour *Lolita Sierra* • Arturo De Cordova *Joe Morales* • J Carrol Naish *Charley Martin* • Mikhail Rasumny *Raphael Catalina* • Fernando Alvarado *Chito Sierra* • Charles Dingle *Zach Mibbe* • Frank McHugh *Edgar Lovekin* • Douglas Dumbrille [Douglass Dumbrille] *General* ■ *Dir* Irving Pichel • *Scr* Frank Butler, Jack Wagner, from a story by Jack Wagner, John Steinbeck

Medea ★★★ PG

Drama   1970 · It/Fr/W Ger · Colour · 105mins

Following this 1967 adaptation of Sophocles's *Oedipus Rex*, this was Pier Paolo Pasolini's second venture into Greek mythology. But this version of Euripides's play suffers as much from miscasting as it does from lacklustre direction. Opera legend Maria Callas is stripped of much of her power by the fact that her voice is dubbed, while Giuseppe Gentile brings little but physique to the part of Jason. The locations have been exploited to the full, but Pasolini's overambitious mix of myth, Marxism and psychology makes for heavy going. In Italian with English subtitles. ▣

Maria Callas *Medea* • Giuseppe Gentile *Jason* • Massimo Girotti *Creon* • Laurent Terzieff *Centaur* • Margareth Clementi *Glauce* ■ *Dir* Pier Paolo Pasolini • *Scr* Pier Paolo Pasolini, from the play by Euripides

Medicine Man ★★★ PG

Drama   1992 · US · Colour · 100mins

An eco-movie that would have been swiftly forgotten if not for an effortlessly charismatic performance from Sean Connery, who manages to overcome an unfocused script and an even worse ponytail. He plays a grumpy scientist who has discovered a cure for cancer deep in the heart of the South American rainforest, but is now unable to reproduce it. He also has to cope with the twin threats of rampant developers out to destroy the forest and Lorraine Bracco (badly miscast), who has been sent to supervise him. *Die Hard* director John McTiernan makes the most of the spectacular setting, but looks a little lost away from his trademark action and explosions. ▣

Sean Connery *Dr Robert Campbell* • Lorraine Bracco *Dr Rae Crane* • José Wilker *Dr Miguel Ornega* • Rodolfo De Alexandre *Tanaki* • Francisco Tsirene Tsere Rereme *Jahausa* • Elias Monteiro Da Silva *Palala* • Edinei Maria Serrio Dos Santos *Kalana* ■ *Dir* John McTiernan • *Scr* Tom Schulman, Sally Robinson

Medicine River ★★★

Romantic comedy   1992 · Can · Colour

An actor with dozens of supporting credits to his name, Stuart Margolin turned director in the late seventies. He finally struck gold with this Canadian romantic comedy starring Graham Greene (*Dances with Wolves*). Greene plays a photographer whose return home for his mother's funeral leads to some highly unexpected misadventures in the company of the rascally Tom Jackson. Neatly steering clear of any cloying moments as Greene rediscovers his Blackfoot heritage, this rousing romp should prove a pleasant surprise.

Graham Greene *Will* • Sheila Tousey *Louise* • Tom Jackson *Harlen Bigbear* • Janet-Laine Green *Will's girlfriend* ■ *Dir* Stuart Margolin

Mediterraneo ★★★★ 15

Comedy drama   1991 · It · Colour · 86mins

As with so many recent winners of the Oscar for best foreign language film, this is an undemanding picture closer to the Hollywood brand of light entertainment than to arthouse *gravitas*. Set in a largely forgotten theatre of the Second World War, the action centres on eight Italian soldiers sent to guard the strategically negligible Greek island of Kastellorizo. The interaction between the mismatched squad and its increasingly amicable relationship with the islanders throws up few novel situations, but everything is done with such sleepy good humour that it makes for easy watching. In Italian with English subtitles. ▣

Diego Abatantuono *Sergeant Lo Russo* • Claudio Bigalli *Lieutenant Montini* • Giuseppe Cederna *Farina* • Claudio Bisio *Noventa* • Gigio Alberti *Strazzabosco* • Ugo Conti *Colosanti* • Memo Dini *Felice Munaron* •

Vasco Mirondola *Libero Munaron* ■ *Dir* Gabriele Salvatores • *Scr* Vincenzo Monteleone

The Medium ★★

Opera   1951 · US · BW · 80mins

A fake medium is driven to murder by her paranoiac fear of a resentful spirit world in Gian-Carlo Menotti's adaptation of his own one-act opera. It might have made for an atmospheric night at the theatre, but it falls prey to staginess and bombast when subjected to the unforgiving gaze of the camera. Both opera lovers and film fans will find this a frustrating experience, despite a spirited performance from Marie Powers.

Marie Powers *Mme Flora* • Anna Maria Alberghetti *Monica* • Leo Coleman *Toby* • Belva Kibler *Mrs Nolan* • Beverly Dame *Mrs Gobineau* • Donald Morgan *Mr Gobineau* ■ *Dir* Gian-Carlo Menotti • *Scr* Gian-Carlo Menotti, from his opera

Medium Cool ★★★★★

Drama   1969 · US · Colour · 110mins

The Oscar-winning cameraman Haskell Wexler turned director with this semi-documentary study of America's political temperature in the turbulent late-sixties. Robert Forster plays a TV news cameraman who covers various major events, notably the riots at the Democratic Convention in Chicago, while trying to prevent his personal life from falling apart. Much of the movie's thrust derives from media pundit Marshall McLuhan's dictum that "the medium is the message" – in other words, that TV itself is more important than anything shown on it. The film's flaws are obvious, but never mind: this is a provocative and hugely influential movie that ends on a note of deep pessimism with the famous chant, "The whole world is watching".

Robert Forster *John Cassellis* • Verna Bloom *Eileen Horton* • Peter Bonerz *Gus* • Marianna Hill *Ruth* • Harold Blankenship *Harold Horton* • Sid McCoy *Frank Baker* ■ *Dir* Haskell Wexler • *Scr* Haskell Wexler, from the novel *The Concrete Wilderness* by Jack Couffer • *Cinematographer* Haskell Wexler

The Medusa Touch ★★★ PG

Supernatural thriller   1978 · UK/Fr · Colour · 104mins

Written by John Briley (*Gandhi, Cry Freedom*), this is a quietly effective thriller that combines the kinetic thrills of a disaster movie with *Omen*-style shocks. Richard Burton is a novelist driven to the brink of insanity by his murderous mental powers, while Lee Remick is the psychiatrist attempting to piece together the puzzle. Director Jack Gold keeps this amiable tosh ticking along, aided by some spectacular disaster footage (a cathedral crashing around the heads of its parishioners, a jumbo jet hitting a tower block) and an impressive roster of British support players. ▣

Richard Burton *John Morlar* • Lee Remick *Dr Zonfeld* • Lino Ventura *Detective Inspector Brunel* • Harry Andrews *Assistant Commissioner* • Marie-Christine Barrault *Patricia* • Michael Hordern *Atropos* • Gordon Jackson *Dr Johnson* • Derek Jacobi *Townley* ■ *Dir* Jack Gold • *Scr* John Briley, Jack Gold, from a novel by Peter Van Greenaway

U = SUITABLE FOR ALL   Uc = SUITABLE FOR ALL, ESPECIALLY FOR YOUNG CHILDREN (VIDEO ONLY)   PG = PARENTAL GUIDANCE

Meet Danny Wilson ★★★

Musical drama 1952 · US · BW · 86mins

Frank Sinatra is Danny Wilson, a crooner who rises to the top through his ultimately disastrous association with a racketeering thug (Raymond Burr). Playing a role that, in the context of the star's own life, is pretty close to the bone, Ol' Blue Eyes does justice to his twin talents as actor and singer in a tight drama, directed by Joseph Pevney and generously laced with some of Frank's best-loved standards (*I've Got a Crush on You* and *That Old Black Magic* among them). Shelley Winters is the girl caught between Sinatra and his best friend, Alex Nicol.

Frank Sinatra *Danny Wilson* • Shelley Winters *Joy Carroll* • Alex Nicol *Mike Ryan* • Raymond Burr *Nick Driscoll* • Tommy Farrell *Tommy Wells* • Vaughn Taylor *TW Hatcher* • Donald MacBride *Sergeant* • Barbara Knudsen *Marie* • Tony Curtis *Man in nightclub* ■ *Dir* Joseph Pevney • *Scr* Don McGuire, from his story

Meet Joe Black ★★ 12

Romantic fantasy drama
1998 · US · Colour · 172mins

The thirties classic *Death Takes a Holiday* remade as a cross-generational tear-jerker, with youthful Brad Pitt and venerable Anthony Hopkins. Hopkins is William Parrish, a powerful media magnate whose end is nigh. Enter the Grim Reaper (an enigmatic Pitt), who gives Parrish an offer he can't refuse – extra life, provided Death can spend a few days living among mortals. However, no one is more startled by Pitt's arrival than Parrish's beautiful daughter Susan (Claire Forlani). That's because Death (''Joe Black'') has taken over the body of the handsome youth she met in a coffee shop earlier! Nicely played but ridiculously overlong. Contains a mild sex scene and some swearing. ▭ *DVD*

Brad Pitt *Joe Black/Young man in coffee shop* • Anthony Hopkins *William Parrish* • Claire Forlani *Susan Parrish* • Jake Weber *Drew* • Marcia Gay Harden *Allison* • Jeffrey Tambor *Quince* ■ *Dir* Martin Brest • *Scr* Ron Osborn, Jeff Reno, Kevin Wade, Bo Goldman, from the film *Death Takes a Holiday* by Maxwell Anderson, Gladys Lehman, Walter Ferris, from the play *Death Takes a Holiday* by Alberto Casella

Meet John Doe ★★ U

Drama 1941 · US · BW · 122mins

This sombre populist fantasy from self-appointed social commentator Frank Capra starts off interesting. By the end, though, it's almost unwatchable. Capra failed to solve the film's structural problems and allegedly shot five different endings. Gary Cooper and Barbara Stanwyck head a fine cast of character actors, but Capra provides no colour in the characters, no fire in the belly and far too much worthy dialogue. ''John Doe'' is American slang for Everyman, usually tagged to an unidentified corpse. Here, though, it is the signature on a powerful letter from a mystery man promising to commit suicide by Christmas and atone for the sins of the world. Any scriptwriter would agree that's an intellectual notion virtually impossible to convey in a popular movie.

Gary Cooper *John Doe/Long John Willoughby* • Barbara Stanwyck *Ann Mitchell* • Edward

Arnold *DB Norton* • Walter Brennan *Colonel* • James Gleason *Henry Connell* • Spring Byington *Mrs Mitchell* • Gene Lockhart *Mayor Lovett* ■ *Dir* Frank Capra • *Scr* Robert Riskin, from the story *The Life and Death of John Doe* by Robert Presnell, Richard Connell

Meet Me after the Show ★★ U

Musical comedy 1951 · US · Colour · 86mins

A feeble Betty Grable vehicle with precious little to recommend it. A perfunctory plot and appallingly static direction from Richard Sale battle in vain to hold the attention, though Grable's co-stars Macdonald Carey and Rory Calhoun are likeable. More of the healthy vulgarity that characterised Grable's other Fox features would have helped, and the faked amnesia plot is strictly for the birds. Still, Eddie Albert and Fred Clark are always welcome in support, and the film is mercifully short – though it doesn't seem so.

Betty Grable *Delilah* • Macdonald Carey *Jeff* • Rory Calhoun *David Hemingway* • Eddie Albert *Christopher Leeds* • Fred Clark *Tim* • Lois Andrews *Gloria Carstairs* ■ *Dir* Richard Sale • *Scr* Mary Loos, Richard Sale, from a story by Erna Lazarus, W Scott Darling

Meet Me at Dawn ★★

Romantic comedy 1946 · UK · BW · 98mins

After making his name with *Flying down to Rio*, this was something of a crash-landing for American director Thornton Freeland. His understanding of the peculiarities of British humour seems to have deserted him after his wartime sojourn in Hollywood, for he misses every laughter cue (and goodness knows there are precious few) in this feeble comedy. His fellow Yank in exile, William Eythe, looks increasingly uncomfortable as this tale of duelling and duplicity develops, confounding even such troupers as Margaret Rutherford and Stanley Holloway.

William Eythe *Charles Morton* • Stanley Holloway *Emile* • Hazel Court *Gabrielle Vermorel* • George Thorpe *Senator Philipe Renault* • Irene Browne *Madame Renault* • Beatrice Campbell *Margot* • Basil Sydney *Georges Vermorel* • Margaret Rutherford *Madame Vermorel* ■ *Dir* Thornton Freeland, Peter Cresswell • *Scr* Lesley Storm, James Seymour, from the play *La Tueur* by Marcel Achard, Anatole Litvak

Meet Me at the Fair ★★★ U

Musical romantic drama
1952 · US · Colour · 87mins

When a travelling show's medicine man (Dan Dailey) takes in an orphan boy (Chet Allen) who has run away from a cruel institution, he is accused of kidnapping and must battle with a politician's social worker fiancée (Diana Lynn). No prizes for guessing how things are resolved in this amiable, folksy musical, which combines a dose of drama with romance and features some pleasing numbers performed by Dailey, Allen, Scatman Crothers and Carole Mathews. Director Douglas Sirk is better known for such Technicolor melodramas as *Magnificent Obsession* and *Imitation of Life*.

Dan Dailey *''Doc'' Tilbee* • Diana Lynn *Zerelda Wing* • Chet Allen *''Tad'' Bayliss* • Scatman Crothers *Enoch Jones* • Hugh O'Brian *Chilton Corr* • Carole Mathews *Clara Brink* • Rhys

Williams *Pete McCoy* ■ *Dir* Douglas Sirk • *Scr* Irving Wallace, Martin Berkeley, from the novel *The Great Companions* by Gene Markey

Meet Me in Las Vegas ★★★★ U

Musical 1956 · US · Colour · 112mins

Better known here by its British title *Viva Las Vegas!* (and not to be confused with the Elvis Presley vehicle), this late MGM musical is a delight. A showcase for Vegas itself, the negligible plot (every time Dan Dailey holds Cyd Charisse's hand he comes up trumps) serves as a framing device for a whole slew of talent: here are on-screen numbers from Lena Horne and Frankie Laine, and uncredited guest slots from some of the biggest stars of the day, including Frank Sinatra. Charisse dances up a storm, but the sizzle is stolen by Cara Williams, who lights up the screen. Cyd has her day, though, with a superb retelling of the *Frankie and Johnny* story as a ballet for the film's climax.

Dan Dailey *Chuck Rodwell* • Cyd Charisse *Maria Corvier* • Agnes Moorehead *Miss Hattie* • Lili Darvas *Sari Hatvani* • Jim Backus *Tom Culdane* • Oscar Karlweis *Loisi* • Liliane Montevecchi *Lilli* • Cara Williams *Kelly Donavan* • George Kerris *Young groom* ■ *Dir* Roy Rowland • *Scr* Isobel Lennart

Meet Me in St Louis ★★★★★ U

Musical 1944 · US · Colour · 108mins

Its portrayal of a perfect American family was too sugary for some critical tastes at the time, but this is still a vintage MGM musical. Whatever the film's minor flaws, they are more than made up for by some dazzling musical numbers such as *Have Yourself a Merry Little Christmas* and *Skip to My Lou* enhanced by the masterly direction of Vincente Minnelli at the top of his form. Providing a romanticised but still uplifting depiction of life in turn-of-the-century St Louis, with Mary Astor as mom and Judy Garland as one of four daughters, this is a tale that only works against the backdrop of a more innocent age. Too good to miss. ▭

Judy Garland *Esther Smith* • Margaret O'Brien *''Tootie'' Smith* • Mary Astor *Anna Smith* • Lucille Bremer *Rose Smith* • Tom Drake *John Truett* • Marjorie Main *Katie* • Leon Ames *Alonzo Smith* • Harry Davenport *Grandpa* • June Lockhart *Lucille Ballard* • Henry H Daniels Jr *Lon Smith Jr* ■ *Dir* Vincente Minnelli • *Scr* Irving Brecher, Fred F Finklehoffe • *Costume Designer* Irene • *Cinematographer* George Folsey

Meet Me Tonight ★★ PG

Portmanteau comedy
1952 · UK · Colour · 80mins

A poor portmanteau picture comprising three one-act plays written by Noël Coward. There are too few examples of the urbane Coward wit to atone for the banality of the stories, while the observations on the types produced by the British class system are shallow to the point of platitude. However, the performances stand up rather well, with Ted Ray and Kay Walsh cheerfully hurling insults as the unhappy music-hall marrieds in *Red Peppers*; Stanley Holloway dour and determined as the worm who turns in *Fumed Oak*; and,

best of all, Valerie Hobson and Nigel Patrick brimming with charm as Riviera fraudsters confronted by burglar Jack Warner in *Ways and Means*. ▭

Kay Walsh *Lily Pepper* • Ted Ray *George Pepper* • Stanley Holloway *Henry Gow* • Betty Ann Davies *Doris Gow* • Valerie Hobson *Stella Cartwright* • Nigel Patrick *Toby Cartwright* • Jack Warner *Murdoch* ■ *Dir* Anthony Pelissier • *Scr* Noël Coward, from his plays

Meet Mr Lucifer ★★ U

Fantasy comedy 1953 · UK · BW · 82mins

For every Ealing comedy gem there is at least one poor imitation, packed with cosy caricatures and devoid of the usual satirical bite. This tepid assault on television is loosely based on the play *Beggar My Neighbour* by Arnold Ridley (Godfrey in *Dad's Army*). Stanley Holloway is a pantomime demon who is sent as an emissary from hell to ensure that TV sets throughout the nation bring nothing but misery. Thanks to any station that chooses to air this sorry offering, his mission is close to being accomplished.

Stanley Holloway *Sam Hollingsworth/Mr Lucifer* • Peggy Cummins *Kitty Norton* • Jack Watling *Jim Norton* • Barbara Murray *Patricia Pedelty* • Joseph Tomelty *Mr Pedelty* • Kay Kendall *Lonely hearts singer* • Gordon Jackson *Hector McPhee* ■ *Dir* Anthony Pelissier • *Scr* Monja Danischewsky, Peter Myers, Alec Graham, from the play *Beggar My Neighbour* by Arnold Ridley

Meet Nero Wolfe ★★★ U

Mystery 1936 · US · BW · 71mins

Edward Arnold plays the corpulent gourmet and orchid cultivator Nero Wolfe, who solves most of his cases from the comfort of his own home. Directed by Herbert Biberman with Lionel Stander, Victor Jory and Rita Cansino (later Hayworth) in the cast, this neat little thriller finds the sleuth connecting and solving the murders of a college president and a mechanic. Columbia intended to build a series around Rex Stout's popular detective, but there was just one more picture, *League of Frightened Men* (1937).

Edward Arnold *Nero Wolfe* • Joan Perry *Ellen Barstow* • Lionel Stander *Archie Goodwin* • Victor Jory *Claude Roberts* • Nana Bryant *Sarah Barstow* • Dennie Moore *Mazie Gray* • Rita Cansino [Rita Hayworth] *Maria Maringola* ■ *Dir* Herbert Biberman [Herbert J Biberman] • *Scr* Howard J Green, Bruce Manning, Joseph Anthony, from the novel *Fer de Lance* by Rex Stout

Meet Simon Cherry ★

Detective drama 1949 · UK · BW · 66mins

An early Hammer B-feature based on *Meet the Rev*, a popular radio series about a parson turned detective. Its star, Hugh Moxey, made his screen debut in this feeble story in which the Reverend Simon Cherry tries to take a much-needed holiday. Of course, his car breaks down and an overnight stay at the nearest manor produces a corpse by morning.

Zena Marshall *Lisa Colville* • John Bailey *Henry Dantry* • Hugh Moxey *Rev Simon Cherry* • Anthony Forwood *Alan Colville* ■ *Dir* Godfrey Grayson • *Scr* Gale Pedrick, Godfrey Grayson, AR Rawlinson, from the radio series *Meet the Rev* by Gale Pedrick

Meet the Applegates
★★★★ 15

Satire   1991 · US · Colour · 86mins

A surreal send-up of fifties monster insect flicks, environmental issues and life in semi-detached suburbia. *Heathers* director Michael Lehmann's stinging satire on brainless pop culture and trashy Americana is a hilarious eco-comedy. Giant insects take on human form and move to Ohio from the Amazon rainforest to take revenge on humanity for destroying their home. But while their creepy-crawly spirits are willing, their flesh-and-blood disguises are weak and soon they succumb to human nature: sex (*Entomology* magazine's page 3), drugs (''pass the roach'') and drink (''grasshopper cocktail, anyone?''). Great fun. ▣

Ed Begley Jr *Dick Applegate* • Stockard Channing *Jane Applegate* • Dabney Coleman *Aunt Bea* • Bobby Jacoby *Johnny Applegate* • Cami Cooper *Camille Cooper)* Sally Applegate • Glenn Shadix *Greg Samson* • Susan Barnes *Opal Withers* • Adam Biesk *Vince Samson* ▪ *Dir* Michael Lehmann • *Scr* Redbeard Simmons, Michael Lehmann

Meet the Deedles
★ PG

Comedy   1998 · US · Colour · 90mins

This downmarket cousin to *Bill & Ted's Excellent Adventure* has two surf bum twins (Paul Walker and Steve Van Wormer) accidentally becoming rangers in Yellowstone National Park. There they are given the task of thwarting former employee Dennis Hopper, who plans to sabotage the landscape with help from a pack of prairie dogs. Only for teenagers who have absolutely nothing better to do. Contains some swearing and sexual references. ▣

Steve Van Wormer *Stew Deedle* • Paul Walker *Phil Deedle* • AJ Langer *Jesse Ryan* • John Ashton *Captain Douglas Pine* • Dennis Hopper *Frank Slater* • Eric Braeden *Elton Deedle* • Robert Englund *Nemo* ▪ *Dir* Steve Boyum • *Scr* Jim Herzfeld, Dale Pollock

Meet the Feebles
★★★ 18

Comedy   1989 · NZ · Colour · 92mins

In the sickest and most deliberately offensive puppet movie ever made, Peter Jackson presents his madcap Muppets as violent, perverted and just plain unpleasant. Taking the form of an animal backstage musical, the unhinged creatures and debauched behaviour are often amusing, but mainly because you can't believe someone made a fluffy animal movie this twisted. It might be that Jackson is satirising the idea that all celebrities have both a public and a private side. We doubt it, though. ▣

Dir Peter Jackson • *Scr* Peter Jackson, Frances Walsh, Stephen Sinclair, Daniel Mulheron

Meet the People
★★★ U

Musical comedy   1944 · US · BW · 100mins

Masquerading as a minor MGM musical, this is a delight, featuring such period entertainers as frozen-faced Virginia O'Brien, crooner Vaughn Monroe and vaudevillian (and Cowardly Lion) Bert Lahr. The plot is extraordinarily liberal, with committed activist Dick Powell causing Broadway star Lucille Ball to abandon show

business and work as a riveter in the shipyards. Well, it was wartime, but even so, this is pre-McCarthy era political dynamite. Despite their respective fame elsewhere, both leads were hardly used again by MGM.

Lucille Ball *Julie Hampton* • Dick Powell *William "Swanee" Swanson* • Virginia O'Brien "*Woodpecker*" *Peg* • Bert Lahr *Commander* • Rags Ragland *Mr Smith* • June Allyson *Annie* ▪ *Dir* Charles Reisner • *Scr* SM Herzig, Fred Saidy, from a story by Sol Barzman, Ben Barzman, Louis Lantz

Meet Wally Sparks
★★ 15

Comedy   1997 · US · Colour · 101mins

Both a satire of sensationalistic US talk shows and a vehicle for Rodney Dangerfield's brand of crude one-liners, this begins amusingly but gets sillier as it goes along. Feigning paralysis after trashing a governor's party, Dangerfield makes life hell for his unwilling host, eventually presenting the most manic outside broadcast in TV history. Although certainly energetic, the repetitive slapstick destruction is little compensation for a distinct lack of plot. Contains swearing and sexual references. ▣

Rodney Dangerfield *Wally Sparks* • Burt Reynolds *Lenny Spencer* • Debi Mazar *Sandy Gallo* • David Ogden Stiers *Governor Floyd Preston* • Cindy Williams *Emily Preston* • Alan Rachins *Judge Williams* ▪ *Dir* Peter Baldwin • *Scr* Harry Basil, Rodney Dangerfield

Meeting Venus
★★★ 15

Romantic comedy
1990 · UK · Colour · 114mins

Kiri Te Kanawa provides the arias for Glenn Close's Swedish high-diva in director István Szabó's upmarket romantic comedy. Close clearly has fun as the man-eating prima donna whose infamous temperament threatens the career-enhancing project of young conductor Niels Arestrup. Wagner's music ponderously matches the melodrama, as hardline politics are exposed along with naked ambition. Szabó keeps it all mostly under control as the backstage passions flare, and if you can't stand the tantrums, the soundtrack is marvellous. ▣

Glenn Close *Karin Anderson* • Niels Arestrup *Zoltan Szanto* • Marian Labuda *Von Schneider* • Maite Nahyr *Maria Krawiecki* • Victor Poletti *Stefano Del Sarto* • Jay O Sanders *Stephen Taylor* ▪ *Dir/Scr* István Szabó

Meetings with Remarkable Men
★★ U

Biographical drama
1979 · UK · Colour · 102mins

With Gilbert Taylor's camera rejoicing in the beauty of the Afghan mountainscapes, this is an uncomfortable combination of the gloriously cinematic and the doggedly theatrical. In electing to employ his famous technique of ''forced improvisation'' to adapt the memoirs of GI Gurdjieff, Peter Brook conveys something of the assiduity of the mystic's lifelong search for enlightenment. But neither his ideas nor his unique methods of meditation make for riveting viewing, especially when espoused by the singularly charmless Dragan Maksimovic. ▣

Dragan Maksimovic *Gurdjieff* • Terence Stamp *Prince Lubovedsky* • Athol Fugard *Professor Skridlov* • Warren Mitchell *Gurdjieff's father* • Natasha Parry *Vitvitskaia* ▪ *Dir* Peter Brook • *Scr* Peter Brook, Jeanne DeSalzmann, from the book by GI Gurdjieff

Mélo
★★★★ PG

Romantic drama   1986 · Fr · Colour · 109mins

Alain Resnais easily surpasses his predecessors with this fourth screen incarnation of Henri Bernstein's 1929 play. Surprisingly opting for a traditionally linear (and rather theatrical) approach, Resnais explores his perennial theme of memory by peeling away the sophisticated veneer to reveal the genuine pain felt by the Sabine Azéma, the adulterous wife of violinist Pierre Arditi, who is driven to suicide by the loyalty of his more celebrated virtuoso friend, André Dussolier. Impeccably played and outwardly old-fashioned, this is a deceptively powerful study of ruthless decency and emotional anguish. In French with English subtitles.

Sabine Azéma *Romaine Belcroix* • Pierre Arditi *Pierre Belcroix* • André Dussollier *Marcel Blanc* • Fanny Ardant *Christiane Levesque* • Jacques Dacqmine *Dr Remy* • Catherine Arditi *Yvonne* ▪ *Dir* Alain Resnais • *Scr* Alain Resnais, from the play by Henri Bernstein

Melody
★★ PG

Drama   1971 · UK · Colour · 106mins

David Puttnam's first production – from Alan Parker's first script – was retitled *S.W.A.L.K.*, as in *Sealed with a Loving Kiss*. Puttnam had bought the rights to a handful of songs by the Bee Gees which had to be incorporated into a story. So Parker came up with this tale of two kids at a south London comprehensive whose friendship is tested when a pretty girl comes into their social orbit. The boys (played by *Oliver!* stars Jack Wild and Mark Lester) can be seen as mirror images of Puttnam and Parker.

Jack Wild *Ornshaw* • Mark Lester (1) *Daniel* • Tracy Hyde *Melody* • Colin Barrie *Chambers* • Billy Franks *Burgess* • Ashley Knight *Stacey* • Craig Marriott *Dadds* ▪ *Dir* Waris Hussein • *Scr* Alan Parker, Andrew Birkin

Melody Cruise
★★

Musical comedy   1933 · US · BW · 76mins

Phil Harris – the voice of Disney favourites Baloo the bear and O'Malley the alley cat – stars as a millionaire pursued by a shipful of gold diggers in this likeable musical comedy. Stealing the show, however, is flustered *farceur* Charles Ruggles as the minder hired to keep Harris on the straight and narrow. Mark Sandrich overdoes the camera trickery, but he handles the song and dance routines with some flair.

Charles Ruggles *Pete Wells* • Phil Harris *Alan Chandler* • Greta Nissen *Ann* • Helen Mack *Laurie Marlowe* • Chick Chandler *Steward* • Betty Grable *Stewardess* ▪ *Dir* Mark Sandrich • *Scr* Mark Sandrich, Ben Holmes, Allen Rivkin, RG Wolfson, from a story by Mark Sandrich, Ben Holmes

Melody Time
★★ U

Animation   1948 · US · Colour · 75mins

Hit-and-miss Disney short story collection with each tale inspired by a popular tune. Whereas *Fantasia* was

founded on established pieces from the classical repertoire, this relies on numbers that have not stood the test of time, and younger viewers may struggle to identify with the songs. Best of the bunch is *Little Toot* about a mischievous tugboat, and *Bumble Boogie*, a jazz variation on *The Flight of the Bumble Bee*. A Donald Duck samba and the stories of Johnny Appleseed and how Texas became the Lone Star state are less memorable, however. ▣

Dir Clyde Geronimi, Hamilton Luske, Jack Kinney, Wilfred Jackson

Melvin and Howard
★★★★

Comedy drama   1980 · US · Colour · 94mins

In 1976, hard-up, much-married Melvin Dummar learned he had been left $156 million in the will of a man he barely knew. And all, according to this delightful film from Jonathan Demme, because Melvin treated the reclusive tycoon Howard Hughes to a slice of real life just when he needed it most. Jason Robards is typically bluff as the bedraggled eccentric, while Paul LeMat is so good as the amiable everyman it's hard to fathom why his career has never really taken off. But then, Mary Steenburgen's Oscar for best supporting actress didn't exactly land her on the A-list, either.

Paul LeMat *Melvin Dummar* • Jason Robards [Jason Robards Jr] *Howard Hughes* • Mary Steenburgen *Lynda Dummar* • Elizabeth Cheshire *Darcy Dummar* • Chip Taylor *Clark Taylor* • Michael J Pollard *Little Red* • Denise Galik *Lucy* • Gloria Grahame *Mrs Sisk* ▪ *Dir* Jonathan Demme • *Scr* Bo Goldman

The Member of the Wedding
★★★

Drama   1952 · US · BW · 89mins

This interesting, emotive family drama would have been wonderful if it had shifted up a gear. Carson McCullers's highly intelligent novel and stage play are transferred delicately to the screen and directed with some flair by Fred Zinnemann. Julie Harris is sublime as the unworldly child forced to face reality as the arrangements for her brother's wedding gather steam – it was her film debut, and she was nominated for an Oscar. Well worth catching for the beautifully rendered, claustrophobic atmosphere.

Ethel Waters *Berenice Sadie Brown* • Julie Harris *Frankie Addams* • Brandon de Wilde *John Henry* • Arthur Franz *Jarvis* • Nancy Gates *Janice* • William Hansen *Mr Addams* • James Edwards *Honey Camden Brown* ▪ *Dir* Fred Zinnemann • *Scr* Edna Anhalt, Edward Anhalt, from the novel and play by Carson McCullers

The Member of the Wedding
★★★

Drama   1997 · US · Colour · 93mins

Carson McCullers's novel is vividly brought to life by Oscar-winner Anna Paquin (*The Piano*). In Georgia during the summer of 1944, a feisty, 12-year-old tomboy comes of age with the guidance of family housekeeper Alfre Woodard, who offers wisdom and solace. As her family prepare for the girl's beloved older brother's wedding, she must cope with her feelings of abandonment and jealousy. David

U = SUITABLE FOR ALL   **Uc** = SUITABLE FOR ALL, ESPECIALLY FOR YOUNG CHILDREN (VIDEO ONLY)   **PG** = PARENTAL GUIDANCE

Rintels's script and Fielder Cook's direction are more straightforward and perfunctory than the 1952 film version, but this timeless material retains enough magic to charm all ages.

Alfre Woodard *Berenice Sadie Brown* • Anna Paquin *Frankie Addams* • Enrico Colantoni *Mr Addams* • Matt McGrath *Jarvis* • Pat Hingle *Officer Wyle* • Joanne Pankow *Mrs Wray* ■ *Dir* Fielder Cook • *Scr* David W Rintels, from the novel and play by Carson McCullers

Memoirs of an Invisible Man ★★★ PG

Comedy thriller 1992 · US · Colour · 94mins

Director John Carpenter returned to the Hollywood mainstream with this flawed thriller. While Carpenter ensures that the action whips along at a cracking pace and the effects are stunning, the main problem is the uncertainty of tone. Chevy Chase, the innocent man who inadvertently becomes invisible, looks at home with the comic elements but is less convincing as a straightforward action hero, and it's left to Sam Neill, as the scheming spy who wants Chase's invisibility kept secret, and Stephen Tobolowsky to take the acting honours. ▣

Chevy Chase *Nick Halloway* • Daryl Hannah *Alice Monroe* • Sam Neill *David Jenkins* • Michael McKean *George Talbot* • Stephen Tobolowsky *Warren Singleton* • Jim Norton *Dr Bernard Wachs* • Pat Skipper *Morrissey* • Paul Perri *Gomez* ■ *Dir* John Carpenter • *Scr* Robert Collector, Dana Olsen, William Goldman, from the novel by HF Saint

Memories of Me ★ 15

Comedy drama 1988 · US · Colour · 98mins

When funny man Billy Crystal is good, he's very good, but when he's bad, he's terrible. This mawkish comedy drama falls in the latter category, as doctor Abbie Polin (Crystal) tries to put his life in order after a mind-altering heart attack. This means searching out his estranged father – the cue for even more sickly sentiment and some hopelessly artificial, angst-ridden emotion. The laughs are certainly there, but they're mostly unintentional. ▣

Billy Crystal *Dr Abbie Polin* • Alan King *Abe Polin* • JoBeth Williams *Lisa McConnell* • Sean Connery • Janet Carroll *Dorothy Davis* • David Ackroyd *First Assistant Director* ■ *Dir* Henry Winkler • *Scr* Eric Roth, Billy Crystal

Memories of Murder ★★

Thriller 1990 · US · Colour · 104mins

A strictly routine TV thriller, shot in Canada, and resurrecting that old plot device in which the central character suffers from amnesia. Nancy Allen is the woman who has lost her memory – she doesn't even recognise her daughter and husband – who finds things going from bad to worse when she realises that she is also the target of a killer. Allen does her best, but the script holds few surprises.

Nancy Allen *Jennifer Gordon* • Robin Thomas *Michael Gordon* • Vanity *Carmen* • Olivia Brown *Brenda* • Robyn Simons *Amy Gordon* • Veena Soud *Dr Kahn* • Peter Yunker *Ronnie Fields* • Don Davis [Don S Davis] *Detective Silk* ■ *Dir* Robert Lewis • *Scr* John Harrison, Kevin Schreiner, from a story by John Harrison

Memories of Underdevelopment ★★★★

Political drama 1968 · Cuba · BW · 97mins

Already acclaimed for *Death of a Bureaucrat*, Cuban director Tomas Gutierrez Alea came of age with this scathing satire, in which bourgeois intellectual Sergio Corrieri refuses the chance to flee to Miami. Instead he finds himself caught between his socialist ideals, European aspirations and the comfortable trappings of his rarified lifestyle as he tries to sustain a new love affair and assimilate to the new regime. Slotting newsreel footage into the already exhilarating visuals, this shrewd insight into a society still struggling to come to terms with both its post-colonial identity and the Cold War is Alea's most personal and accomplished achievement. In Spanish with English subtitles.

Sergio Corrieri *Sergio* • Daisy Granados *Elena* ■ *Dir* Tomás Gutiérrez Alea • *Scr* Tomas Gutierrez Alea, Edmundo Desnoes, from a novel by Edmundo Desnoes

The Memory of Eva Ryker ★★

Mystery 1980 · US · Colour · 92mins

Having already produced one sinking ship drama, *The Poseidon Adventure*, Irwin Allen tried the same trick with this made-for-TV effort about a luxury ocean liner hit by a torpedo during the Second World War. Not nearly as starry as Allen's cinema disasters, this lumbering affair features a double dose of Natalie Wood as both mother and daughter, thus facilitating a major case of flashback syndrome.

Natalie Wood *Eva Ryker/Claire Ryker* • Robert Foxworth *Norman Hall* • Roddy McDowall *MacFarland* • Bradford Dillman *Jason Eddington* • Jean-Pierre Aumont *Inspector Laurier* • Peter Graves (1) *Rogers* • Mel Ferrer *Dr Sanford* • Ralph Bellamy *William Ryker* ■ *Dir* Walter Grauman • *Scr* Laurence Heath, from the novel by Donald A Stanwood

Memory Run ★★ 18

Science-fiction action thriller 1995 · US · Colour · 89mins

An unnecessarily complicated slice of sci-fi which sees Karen Duffy going on the run from an evil corporate empire after she discovers that its executives have been literally playing with her mind. Saul Rubinek and Matt McCoy add respectability, but this one is really for genre fans only. ▣

Karen Duffy *Celeste/Josette* • Saul Rubinek *Dr Munger* • Matt McCoy *Gabriel* • Chris Makepeace *Andre Fuller* ■ *Dir* Allan A Goldstein • *Scr* David Gottlieb, Dale Hildebrand, from the novel *Season of the Witch* by Hank Stine

Memphis ★★ 15

Drama 1992 · US · Colour · 88mins

Set around the time of the civil rights movement, this plodding thriller stars Cybill Shepherd as a woman who plans the kidnapping of the son of a wealthy black family, assuming the police won't intervene. Of course, things don't always turn out the way they're planned, and it's not long before the boy's grandfather is staging a rescue mission. This would be silly if it wasn't so tedious and, although Shepherd is

good, even she can't drag it out of the ordinary. ▣

Cybill Shepherd *Reeny Purdew* • John Laughlin *Rufus Hutton* • JE Freeman *Podjo Harris* • Richard Brooks *Eben Kinship* • Moses Gunn *Tio Wiggins* • Vanessa Bell Calloway *Martha Kinship* • Martin C Gardner *Teddy Kinship* ■ *Dir* Yves Simoneau • *Scr* Larry McMurty, Cybill Shepherd, Susan Rhinehart, from the novel *September, September* by Shelby Foote

Memphis Belle ★★★★ U

Second World War documentary 1943 · US/UK · Colour · 39mins

This is one of the finest combat documentaries of the Second World War. The Flying Fortress *Memphis Belle* had flown 24 successful missions and this daylight bombing raid was to be its last. Director William Wyler's pulsating short film uses diagrams to explain the mission and then takes us on board as the crew encounters flak and enemy fighters before hitting its targets. Footage from the film was used in the 1990 feature of the same name, which was co-produced by Wyler's daughter, Catherine.

Eugene Kern *Narrator* • Corp John Beal *Narrator* ■ *Dir* Lt Col William Wyler [William Wyler] • *Scr* Capt Edwin Gilbert, Tech Sgt Lester Koenig • *Cinematographer* Major William Clothier [William Clothier], Lt Col William Wyler [William Wyler], Lt Harold Tannenbaum [Harold Tannenbaum]

Memphis Belle ★★★ PG

Historical war drama 1990 · UK · Colour · 102mins

Co-producer David Puttnam was the force behind this moving and nostalgic trip back to the Second World War. The focus is upon the crew of a B-17 bomber bidding to complete its final mission. It's all a bit too predictable – the usual "will they make it back or not" heroics – but the characters, all slickly played by a strong cast including Matthew Modine and Eric Stoltz, are endearing and the crew's final flight is grippingly filmed. Most of the plaudits, though, must go to the real heroes of this true-life story. ▣

Matthew Modine *Dennis Dearborn* • John Lithgow *Colonel Bruce Derringer* • Eric Stoltz *Danny Daly* • Sean Astin *Richard "Rascal" Moore* • Harry Connick Jr *Clay Busby* • Tate Donovan *Luke Sinclair* • DB Sweeney *Phil Rosenthal* • Billy Zane *Val Kozlowski* • Jane Horrocks *Faith* ■ *Dir* Michael Caton-Jones • *Scr* Monte Merrick

The Men ★★★★ PG

Drama 1950 · US · BW · 86mins

This film is now remembered for the remarkable screen debut of Marlon Brando, who changed the very nature of screen acting with a mesmerising, naturalistic, self-pitying performance. The title is ironic, since these "men" are paraplegic war veterans, having lost all feeling below the waist. The sexual aspect of the tale is superbly circumvented (made necessary by the censors) in Carl Foreman's sensitive screenplay. Brando first appears after the notable opening address by doctor Everett Sloane, a clever ploy used by director Fred Zinnemann to set the tone and prepare the audience for what follows. It may all seem dated today, but at the time this was ground-breaking stuff. ▣

Marlon Brando *Ken "Bud" Wilozek* • Teresa Wright *Ellen* • Everett Sloane *Dr Brock* • Jack Webb *Norm Butler* • Richard Erdman *Leo* • Arthur Jurado *Angel* • Virginia Farmer *Nurse Robbins* ■ *Dir* Fred Zinnemann • *Scr* Carl Foreman, from his story

Men... ★★★ 15

Comedy 1985 · W Ger · Colour · 99mins

Originally made for German television, this is an astute satire on the emotional immaturity of the average male. As the womanising businessman who moves in with his wife's bohemian lover in a bid to turn him into an equally unregenerate cad, Heiner Lauterbach gives a wonderfully sleazy display of bitter insecurity. Yet Doris Dörrie shrewdly presents this behaviour as only marginally more heinous than the lazy charm of artist Uwe Ochsenknecht and the disillusioned self-absorption of Ulrike Kreiner. Although straining credibility in places, this is still an amusing skirmish in cinema's ongoing battle of the sexes. A German language film.

Heiner Lauterbach *Julius Armbrust* • Uwe Ochsenknecht *Stefan Lachner* • Ulrike Kriener *Paula Armbrust* • Janna Marangosoff *Angelika* ■ *Dir/Scr* Doris Dörrie

Men Are Not Gods ★★ U

Drama 1936 · UK · BW · 90mins

A chance to see a youthful Rex Harrison in a supporting role in this languid luvvie yarn about an actor (Sebastian Shaw) playing Othello, who takes his work too seriously and attempts to strangle his wife Gertrude Lawrence (who's playing Desdemona) because he's fallen for Miriam Hopkins. Essentially an excuse to look at the incestuous antics within a theatre company, this is daft from its portentous title onwards. ▣

Miriam Hopkins *Ann Williams* • Gertrude Lawrence *Barbara Halford* • Sebastian Shaw *Edmund Davey* • Rex Harrison *Tommy Stapleton* • AE Matthews *Skeates* • Val Gielgud *Producer* • Laura Smithson *Katherine* ■ *Dir* Walter Reisch • *Scr* GB Stern, Iris Wright, Walter Reisch

Men at Work ★★ 15

Comedy thriller 1990 · US · Colour · 94mins

Emilio Estevez wrote and directed this comedy action tale about two dustbin men (played by Estevez and his brother Charlie Sheen) who uncover a corpse on their daily clean-up route. Together with a nutty Vietnam vet (Keith David), they attempt to solve the crime and keep their community clean. Unsurprisingly, Sheen and Estevez have a chemistry which charms, though the subject matter and genre require you to watch *sans* brain. ▣

Charlie Sheen *Carl Taylor* • Emilio Estevez *James St James* • Leslie Hope *Susan Wilkins* • Keith David *Louis Fedders* • Dean Cameron *Pizza man* • John Getz *Maxwell Potterdam III* ■ *Dir/Scr* Emilio Estevez

Men Don't Leave ★★★★ 15

Drama 1990 · US · Colour · 109mins

Jessica Lange gives another powerful performance as a mother coping with starting life anew after the death of her husband. Trying to pay off mounting debts and reduced to living in a small apartment with her sons (Charlie Korsmo and Chris O'Donnell, in one of his first roles), she also tries to begin a new relationship while battling against depression. Honest and absorbing, this confirms Lange as one of the best actresses of her generation. Watch out, too, for strong supporting turns from the excellent Joan Cusack and Kathy Bates. Contains violence and swearing. 🖵

Jessica Lange *Beth Macauley* • Chris O'Donnell *Chris Macauley* • Charlie Korsmo *Matt Macauley* • Arliss Howard *Charles Simon* • Tom Mason *John Macauley* • Joan Cusack *Jody* • Kathy Bates *Lisa Coleman* ■ *Dir* Paul Brickman • *Scr* Barbara Benedek, Paul Brickman, from a story by Barbara Benedek, suggested by the film *La Vie Continue*

Men in Black ★★★★ 🅿🅶
Science-fiction adventure
1997 · US · Colour · 93mins

The smash-hit science-fiction comedy based on a short-lived eighties comic strip, with secret agent Tommy Lee Jones and new recruit Will Smith as part of a top secret agency responsible for regulating all alien activity on Earth. While investigating an alien sighting the pair become involved in the search for a missing galaxy to appease an interstellar force and avert the Earth's destruction. Great special effects, inventive alien designs and Smith and Jones's hip, hilarious double act make director Barry Sonnenfeld's bug-eyed *Lethal Weapon*-style buddy picture a fast-paced pleasure. 🖵

Tommy Lee Jones *K* • Will Smith *J* • Linda Fiorentino *Laurel* • Vincent D'Onofrio *Edgar* • Rip Torn *Zed* • Tony Shalhoub *Jeebs* ■ *Dir* Barry Sonnenfeld • *Scr* Ed Solomon, from the comic book by Lowell Cunningham

The Men in Her Life ★★
Drama
1941 · US · BW · 89mins

An ambitious former circus performer rises to become a famous ballerina and has several romances, at the cost of her relationship with her daughter. A trite and unconvincing melodrama, with the lovely but totally miscast Loretta Young at the centre. The under-characterised men in her life are Dean Jagger, John Shepperd (a pseudonym for Shepperd Strudwick) and Conrad Veidt as the strict ballet master who helps her to the top. Gregory Ratoff directs more stylishly than one might expect in the circumstances.

Loretta Young *Lina Varasvina/Polly Varley* • Conrad Veidt *Stanislas Rosing* • Dean Jagger *David Gibson* • Eugenie Leontovich *Marie* • John Shepperd [Shepperd Strudwick] *Sir Roger Chevis* • Otto Kruger *Victor* • Ann Todd [Ann E Todd] *Rose* ■ *Dir* Gregory Ratoff • *Scr* Frederick Kohner, Michael Wilson, Paul Trivers, from the novel *Ballerina* by Lady Eleanor Smith

Men in War ★★★
War drama
1957 · US · BW · 102mins

One of those minor war movies that were thick on the ground in the fifties. But this account of a US infantry platoon in Korea is given distinction by Philip Yordan's intelligent script and Anthony Mann's in-your-face direction, while the music by Elmer Bernstein is also a bonus. Robert Ryan's battle-exhausted lieutenant is a character whose attitude says more about war's futility than many a major epic.

Robert Ryan *Lieutenant Benson* • Aldo Ray *Montana* • Robert Keith *Colonel* • Phillip Pine *Riordan* • Vic Morrow *Zwickley* • Nehemiah Persoff *Lewis* • LQ Jones *Editor* ■ *Dir* Anthony Mann • *Scr* Philip Yordan, from the novel *Combat* by Van Van Praag

Men in White ★★★
Drama
1934 · US · BW · 80mins

Clark Gable is a brilliant and dedicated young intern who is chosen to work with veteran physician Jean Hersholt – Hollywood's resident kindly doctor – to the distress of his socialite fiancée Myrna Loy. This modest, decently-made drama is a flag-waver for the medical profession. Gable's tragic involvement with a student nurse (marvellously played by Elizabeth Allan) strays into unconvincing melodrama, but the rest is believable and absorbing.

Clark Gable *Dr Ferguson* • Myrna Loy *Laura* • Jean Hersholt *Dr Hochberg* • Elizabeth Allan *Barbara* • Otto Kruger *Dr Levine* ■ *Dir* Richard Boleslawski • *Scr* Waldemar Young, from the play by Sidney Kingsley

Men o' War ★★★★ 🅄
Comedy
1929 · US · BW · 19mins

One of 100-plus movie appearances for beloved comedy double act Laurel and Hardy, this 20-minute short is one of the team's best talkies. It's especially important for being the film that demonstrated that the duo could succeed with sound, following their previous effort, the clumsy *Berth Marks* (1929), which was their first all-talking movie. In *Men o' War*, the boys play sailors on leave enjoying a series of comic encounters – in a park, at an ice cream parlour and on a lake in a rowing boat. 🖵

Stan Laurel *Stan* • Oliver Hardy *Ollie* • James Finlayson *Soda jerk* ■ *Dir* Lewis R Foster • *Scr* HM Walker

Men of Boys Town ★
Drama
1941 · US · BW · 106mins

Unspeakably yucky farrago, with Spencer Tracy reprising his Oscar-winning role as Father Edward J Flanagan, first seen in *Boys' Town*, who seems to think there's a saint in every delinquent. At one point, Tracy even employs a pet pooch to help win over the kids. Tracy's rehabilitation of cute little Mickey Rooney from an unforgiving reform school will probably leave today's audiences nauseous.

Spencer Tracy *Father Flanagan* • Mickey Rooney *Whitey Marsh* • Bobs Watson *Pee Wee* • Larry Nunn *Ted Martley* • Darryl Hickman *Flip* • Henry O'Neill *Mr Maitland* • Lee J Cobb *Dave Morris* ■ *Dir* Norman Taurog • *Scr* James Kevin McGuinness

Men of Respect ★★ 🔞
Crime drama
1990 · US · Colour · 108mins

The idea of translating William Shakespeare's "Scottish play" to the Mafia underworld is a good one but this film, like *Joe Macbeth*, fails to capitalise on the high concept. This has all the makings of a cult classic, as writer/director William Reilly's dialogue teeters between the clever and the unintentionally hysterical. As the hood who becomes head of the mob by bumping off his rivals, John Turturro is occasionally very sinister,

and Katherine Borowitz (as his wife) eggs him on with sadistic glee. But there are just too many sniggers for a tough crime drama. Contains violence and swearing. 🖵

John Turturro *Mike Battaglia* • Katherine Borowitz *Ruthie Battaglia* • Rod Steiger *Charlie D'Amico* • Peter Boyle *Duffy* • Dennis Farina *Bankie Como* • Stanley Tucci *Mal* ■ *Dir* William Reilly • *Scr* William Reilly, from the play *Macbeth* by William Shakespeare

Men of Sherwood Forest ★★ 🅄
Adventure
1954 · UK · Colour · 77mins

A cheap and cheerful Hammer outing to Sherwood. Although he strives hard to reproduce the derring-do of Errol Flynn (the screen's finest Robin Hood), American nobody Don Taylor lacks both the dash and the devilment to convince as he leads his Merrie Men on a mission to aid Richard the Lionheart. Leonard Sachs similarly makes a lightweight Sheriff of Nottingham, while Eileen Moore provides some rather soppy love interest. Val Guest directs with little feel for the boisterous action.

Don Taylor *Robin Hood* • Reginald Beckwith *Friar Tuck* • Eileen Moore *Lady Alys* • David King-Wood *Sir Guy Belton* • Patrick Holt *King Richard* • John Van Eyssen *Will Scarlett* • Leonard Sachs *Sheriff of Nottingham* ■ *Dir* Val Guest • *Scr* Allan MacKinnon

Men of Texas ★★★ 🅄
Western
1942 · US · BW · 82mins

Chicago reporter Robert Stack is sent to investigate the aftermath of the Civil War in Texas and confronts Broderick Crawford, who refuses to admit defeat. The interesting interplay between the characters suggests that the pen is mightier than the sword, a strange concept to be advocating in the dark days of the Second World War. This is a good-looking western, pacily directed by Ray Enright. Anne Gwynne makes a very attractive leading lady, while Leo Carrillo supplies the humour as Stack's photographer sidekick.

Robert Stack *Barry Conovan* • Broderick Crawford *Henry Clay Jackson* • Jackie Cooper *Robert Houston Scott* • Anne Gwynne *Jane Baxter Scott* • Ralph Bellamy *Major Lamphere* • Leo Carrillo *Sam Sawyer* ■ *Dir* Ray Enright • *Scr* Harold Shumate, Richard Brooks, from the story *Frontier* by Harold Shumate • *Cinematographer* Milton Krasner

Men of the Fighting Lady ★
War drama
1954 · US · Colour · 79mins

A commie-bashing Korean war yarn about a US aircraft carrier, *The Fighting Lady*, and the brave men who fly her bombers, aim their rockets at the enemy's railway network, then return to base to exchange some of the corniest dialogue ever to emerge from the MGM studio. The sort of movie that makes a British effort like *The Dam Busters* seem positively Shakespearean in philosophical and poetic import. Louis Calhern plays author James A Michener, whose reports in *The Saturday Evening Post* formed the basis for the script.

Van Johnson *Lieutenant Howard Thayer* • Walter Pidgeon *Commander Kent Dowling* • Louis Calhern *James A Michener* • Dewey Martin *Ensign Kenneth Schechter* • Keenan

Wynn *Lieutenant Commander Ted Dodson* • Frank Lovejoy *Lieutenant Commander Paul Grayson* • Robert Horton *Ensign Neil Conovan* • Bert Freed *Lieutenant Andrew Szymanski* ■ *Dir* Andrew Marton • *Scr* Art Cohn, from the stories *The Forgotten Heroes of Korea* by James A Michener and *The Case of the Blind Pilot* by Commander Harry A Burns

Men of Two Worlds ★
Drama
1946 · UK · Colour · 107mins

A well-intentioned but terribly tedious attempt to portray the beneficial side of British colonialism in helping the indigenous population achieve social and economic progress. Robert Adams is the educated black musician who overcomes the superstitious powers of Orlando Martins's witch doctor to persuade a tribe to move away from an area infected with tsetse fly. Almost all the extensive Technicolor footage filmed in Tanganyika had to be re-shot at Denham, ruining the semi-documentary approach taken by director Thorold Dickinson.

Eric Portman *District Commissioner Randall* • Phyllis Calvert *Dr Caroline Munro* • Robert Adams *Kisenga* • Orlando Martins *Magole* • Arnold Marle *Professor Gollner* • Cathleen Nesbitt *Mrs Upjohn* • Sam Blake *Chief Raki* ■ *Dir* Thorold Dickinson • *Scr* Thorold Dickinson, Herbert W Victor, from a story by E Arnot Robertson, Joyce Cary

Men of War ★★★ 🔞
Action drama
1995 · US · Colour · 98mins

Although the testosterone-laden action is plentiful in this jungle-island war drama, the script (partially written by John Sayles) is startlingly good. A group of mercenaries sent to the island is charged with convincing the natives to sign over the mineral rights, but some of the group find themselves siding with the natives. Despite the fact that this has all the makings of a bad commando movie, it's probably the best film of Lundgren's career. 🖵

Dolph Lundgren *Nick* • Charlotte Lewis *Loki* • BD Wong *Po* • Anthony John Denison *Jimmy* • Don Harvey *Nolan* • Tom "Tiny" Lister Jr *Blades* • Kevin Tighe *Merrick* ■ *Dir* Perry Lang • *Scr* John Sayles, Ethan Reiff, Cyrus Voris, from a story by Stan Rogow

Men with Guns ★★★★★ 🄸🄵
Drama
1997 · US · Colour · 127mins

John Sayles, one of America's most impressive and enterprising independent film-makers, makes this Spanish-language film a socially significant fable about tyranny. An elderly doctor (Federico Luppi) goes to visit former students working in poor Latin American villages, only to find they've been killed by the dictatorial regime. Made with a feeling and sincerity that is never undermined by sentimentality, it's a poignant reminder of how we all turn a blind eye to that which would inconvenience us. In Spanish with English subtitles.

Federico Luppi *Doctor Humberto Fuentes* • Damian Alcazar *Padre Portillo, the priest* • Tania Cruz *Graciela, the mute girl* • Mandy Patinkin *Andrew* ■ *Dir* John Sayles • *Scr* John Sayles, inspired by a character in *The Long Night of White Chickens* by Francisco Goldman

🅄 = SUITABLE FOR ALL   🅄꜀ = SUITABLE FOR ALL, ESPECIALLY FOR YOUNG CHILDREN (VIDEO ONLY)   🅿🅶 = PARENTAL GUIDANCE

Men with Wings ★★

Drama   1938 · US · Colour · 105mins

Starting with a re-enactment of the Wright Brothers' first manned flight in 1903, this flying epic from *Wings* director William ''Wild Bill'' Wellman isn't nearly exciting enough. Childhood buddies Fred MacMurray and Ray Milland grow up to become aerial obsessives, building and inventing planes, fighting in the wars and having a protracted and rather dull dogfight over Louise Campbell. The end result was an expensive flop for all concerned. Donald O'Connor, who plays MacMurray as a child, would later turned into the all-singing, all-dancing genius of *Singin' in the Rain*.

Fred MacMurray *Pat Falconer* • Ray Milland *Scott Barnes* • Louise Campbell *Peggy Ranson* • Andy Devine *Joe Gibbs* • Lynne Overman *Hank Rinebow* • Walter Abel *Nick Ranson* • Porter Hall *Hiram F Jenkins* • Donald O'Connor *Pat Falconer, aged 10* ■ *Dir* William A Wellman • *Scr* Robert Carson

Men without Women ★★★

Drama   1930 · US · BW · 77mins

Filmed as an early talkie but apparently surviving only in the alternative silent version, director John Ford's first collaboration with writer Dudley Nichols is the compelling drama of the attempts to rescue the crew of a crippled American submarine from the floor of the China Sea. John Wayne has a bit part as a sailor relaying messages with earphones and mouthpiece, but he did more to impress Ford with some dangerous underwater stuntwork. Kenneth MacKenna and Frank Albertson are the stars, but it's Ford masterly direction that is the film's main attraction now.

Kenneth MacKenna *Chief Torpedoman Burke* • Frank Albertson *Ens Price* • Paul Page *Handsome* • Walter McGrail *Cobb* • Warren Hymer *Kaufman* • John Wayne ■ *Dir* John Ford • *Scr* Dudley Nichols, from a story by John Ford, James Kevin McGuiness

Men, Women: a User's Manual ★★★ 12

Satire   1996 · Fr · Colour · 122mins

Disregard the title. Look instead to the subtitle, *An Inhuman Comedy*, to find a clue to this wry tale about a cruel practical joke. The perpetrator is doctor Alessandra Martines, whose long-harboured lover's grudge prompts her to inform oversexed tycoon Bernard Tapie that he is terminally ill, while telling dying cop Fabrice Luchini the opposite. In spite of the plot's preposterous contrivance, you are still drawn to director Claude Lelouch's rather resistible characters, although the subplots are less successful. In French with English subtitles. 🖭

Bernard Tapie *Benoît Blanc* • Fabrice Luchini *Fabio Lini* • Alessandra Martines *Doctor Nitez* • Pierre Arditi *Dr Pierre Lerner* • Caroline Cellier *Madame Blanc* • Ophélie Winter *Pretty blonde of Crillon* • Anouk Aimée *The widow* ■ *Dir* Claude Lelouch • *Scr* Claude Lelouch, René Bonnell, Jean-Phillipe Chatrier

Menace II Society ★★★ 18

Drama   1993 · US · Colour · 92mins

A searing, if bleak portrait of life in the 'hood from Allen and Albert Hughes,

twins who were just 20 at the time it was made. Tyrin Turner is the surly adolescent, the son of a junkie mother and a drug-pushing dad, who's torn between nice single mom Jada Pinkett or a life of drive-by shootings and petty crime. There's no denying the visceral power of the Hughes brothers' vision, but – with the exception of Pinkett – it's hard to have sympathy for any of the characters. 🖭 **DVD**

Jada Pinkett [Jada Pinkett Smith] *Ronnie* • Tyrin Turner *Caine* • Larenz Tate *O-Dog* • Charles S Dutton *Mr Butler* • Bill Duke *Detective* • Samuel L Jackson *Tat Lawson* ■ *Dir* Allen Hughes, Albert Hughes • *Scr* Tyger Williams, Allen Hughes, Albert Hughes, from their story

The Men's Club ★ 18

Drama   1986 · US · Colour · 96mins

A static and stagey bore about seven men who meet up to swap sexual stories, throw knives at a wall and howl like wolves before heading off to the weirdest brothel in the US. One-dimensional, misogynistic garbage, with flat direction from Peter Medak (*The Krays*) and unengaging performances from Roy Scheider, Frank Langella, Harvey Keitel and Treat Williams. The second half is plain embarrassing, though Jennifer Jason Leigh shines as an enthusiastic prostitute. 🖭

David Dukes *Phillip* • Richard Jordan *Kramer* • Harvey Keitel *Solly Berliner* • Frank Langella *Harold Canterbury* • Roy Scheider *Cavanaugh* • Craig Wasson *Paul* • Treat Williams *Terry* • Stockard Channing *Nancy* • Jennifer Jason Leigh *Teensy* ■ *Dir* Peter Medak • *Scr* Leonard Michaels, from his novel

Menu for Murder ★★★ PG

Comedy murder mystery
1990 · US · Colour · 89mins

What with poisoned sandwiches and a murderous mum on the rampage, this whodunit is definitely from the old school. There are more laughs than clues in the amiable script, but there's still plenty of fun to be had from figuring out who killed a domineering parent/teacher association president, as well as several of the prime suspects. Julia Duffy, Morgan Fairchild and Cindy Williams head a cast that shamelessly camps it up. 🖭

Cindy Williams *Connie Mann* • Morgan Fairchild *Paula Preston* • Julia Duffy *Susan Henshaw* • Ed Marinaro *Det Joe Russo* • Joan Van Ark *Julia Alberts* • Edie McClurg *Patsy Webber* ■ *Dir* Larry Peerce • *Scr* Duane Poole, Tom Swale, from the novel *Murder at the PTA Luncheon* by Valerie Wolzien

Mephisto ★★★★★ 15

Drama   1981 · Hun · Colour · 138mins

Winner of the Oscar for best foreign film, this was the first of István Szabó's loose trilogy on the theme of treachery and ambition. As in the subsequent *Colonel Redl* and *Hanussen*, Klaus Maria Brandauer plays a character who sells his soul for power, here as an actor who blithely ignores the implications of Nazi patronage to achieve stardom. Klaus Mann's source novel is essentially a revision of the Faust legend, but Szabó never loses a sense of historical perspective and delineates the seductive allure of fascism with chilling

detachment to make its evil tenets all the more hideous. Brandauer is majestic and this is a masterpiece. In German with English subtitles. 🖭

Klaus Maria Brandauer *Hendrik Höfgen* • Ildiko Bansagi *Nicoletta von Niebuhr* • Rolf Hoppe *General* • Gyorgy Cserhalmi *Hans Miklas* • Peter Andorai *Otto Ulrichs* • Karin Boyd *Juliette Martens* • Christine Harbort *Lotte Lindenthal* ■ *Dir* István Szabó • *Scr* Peter Dobai, István Szabó, Klaus Mann

The Mephisto Waltz ★★★

Horror drama   1971 · US · Colour · 108mins

An under-rated occult thriller blending the urban Gothic trappings of *Rosemary's Baby* with the psychological insights of *The Innocents*. Dying concert pianist Curt Jurgens uses black magic to possess journalist Alan Alda's body in this unnerving shocker. It's when Alda's wife, Jacqueline Bisset, finds out what's going on that things start getting really scary. Director Paul Wendkos uses soap-opera clichés and dazzling psychedelic colours to distort the boundary between reality and fantasy in this diabolical tale of enigmatic paranoia.

Alan Alda *Myles Clarkson* • Jacqueline Bisset *Paula Clarkson* • Barbara Parkins *Roxanne* • Curt Jurgens *Duncan Ely* • Brad Dillman [Bradford Dillman] *Bill* • William Windom *Dr West* • Kathleen Widdoes *Maggie West* • Pamelyn Ferdin *Abby Clarkson* ■ *Dir* Paul Wendkos • *Scr* Ben Maddow, from the novel by Fred Mustard Stewart

Le Mépris ★★★ 15

Satire   1963 · Fr/It · Colour · 102mins

Jean-Luc Godard's weird satire on Hollywood's invasion of Europe stars Jack Palance as the American producer who says: ''When I hear the word culture I reach for my cheque book.'' Fritz Lang plays the director of an intended version of Homer's *Odyssey*, while the sex interest is provided by – who else? – Brigitte Bardot. It sounds relatively straightforward, and probably would be if Godard didn't veer off at tangents in a desperate attempt not to be swamped by his biggest budget and cast to date. In English and French with subtitles.

Brigitte Bardot *Camille Javal* • Michel Piccoli *Paul Javal* • Jack Palance *Jeremy Prokosh* • Fritz Lang • Giorgia Moll *Francesca Vanini* ■ *Dir/Scr* Jean-Luc Godard

Mercenary ★★ 18

Action thriller   1997 · US · Colour · 98mins

Serviceable action fare, with Olivier Gruner as a killer for hire recruited by a vengeance-seeking millionaire (John Ritter). The villains are a sadistic bunch of Islamic terrorists, in keeping with nineties trends, and there's a variety of graphic deaths on display as Gruner and team hack, shoot and kick their way through the enemy. Some decent use of Israeli locations and plenty of combat are the film's virtues, though Gruner is a shockingly charmless hero, even by genre standards. A sequel, *Mercenary II: Thick and Thin*, was released on video in 1999. Contains violence, some swearing and a sex scene. 🖭

Olivier Gruner *Captain Carl May* • John Ritter *Jonas Ambler* • Ed Lauter *Cochran* • Robert

Culp *McClean* • Michael Zelniker *Bailey* • Martin Kove *Phoenix* • Lara Harris *Joanna Ambler* ■ *Dir* Avi Nesher • *Scr* Patrick Highsmith, Steven Hartov

The Merchant of Four Seasons ★★★★

Drama   1971 · W Ger · Colour · 88mins

Recalling the fate of his own uncle, Rainer Werner Fassbinder explores the emotional tyranny of women in this archly realist melodrama. Having failed in the Foreign Legion and the police, been neglected by his mother, jilted by his romantic ideal and humiliated by his jealous wife, greengrocer Hans Hirschmüller has become trapped in an irrelevant, drink-sodden existence. Demonstrating how social oppression leads to irreversible ennui, Fassbinder employs a series of perfectly judged flashbacks to piece together this life just as it's falling apart. What results is both a sympathetic portrait of a far from blameless nobody and a pessimistic vision of everyday life. In German with English subtitles.

Hans Hirschmüller *Hans Epp* • Irm Hermann *Irmgard Epp* • Hanna Schygulla *Anna* • Andrea Schober *Renate Epp* ■ *Dir/Scr* Rainer Werner Fassbinder

Merci la Vie ★★★ 18

Surreal fantasy drama
1991 · Fr · Colour and BW · 113mins

Writer/director Bertrand Blier's at times dazzling film is a cross between a teenage *Thelma and Louise* and Blier's controversial *Les Valseuses*. But, while it teems with ideas, it too often finds itself at a loss with what to do with them. Charlotte Gainsbourg and Anouk Grinberg give spellbinding performances as the social misfits confronted with a mélange of maladjusted males, including doctor Gérard Depardieu and Nazi officer Jean-Louis Trintignant. It's a challenging, violent and often outrageously funny movie, though even Blier seems unsure whether the action is real, a dream or simply a filmed record of either or both. In French with English subtitles. Contains violence, swearing and sex scenes. 🖭

Charlotte Gainsbourg *Camille* • Anouk Grinberg *Joëlle* • Gérard Depardieu *Marc Antoine* • Michel Blanc *Young father* • Jean Carmet *Old father* • Catherine Jacob *Young mother* • Thierry Fremont *François* • François Perrot *Director* • Jean-Louis Trintignant *Officer* ■ *Dir/Scr* Bertrand Blier

Mercury Rising ★★ 15

Action thriller   1998 · US · Colour · 106mins

Prior to *The Sixth Sense*, Bruce Willis was paired with another young lead in this minor thriller. Willis plays a renegade government operative who becomes protector of an autistic child (Miko Hughes) who has cracked the supposedly impenetrable Mercury security code; Alec Baldwin is the crooked national security man determined to hunt them down. Director Harold Becker manages to impart a little depth to the relationship between Willis and Hughes – in between the chases and shootouts – but the psychological backdrop is too contrived. Contains swearing and violence. 🖭 **DVD**

Bruce Willis *Art Jeffries* • Alec Baldwin *Nicholas Kudrow* • Miko Hughes *Simon Lynch* • Chi McBride *Tommy B Jordan* • Kim Dickens *Stacey* • Robert Stanton *Dean Crandell* ■ *Dir* Harold Becker • *Scr* Lawrence Konner, Mark Rosenthal, from the novel *Simple Simon* by Ryne Douglas Pearson

Mercy Mission: the Rescue of Flight 771 ★★

Drama based on a true story
1993 · US · Colour

Having played count the celebs in the *Airport* blockbusters and wept with laughter at the *Airplane!* spoofs, it's pretty hard to get excited about a routine plane-in-crisis TV movie like this one. Every scenario has been exhausted and every cockpit cliché done to death. Scott Bakula has the misfortune to be at the controls of this particular lame duck, but he's lucky to have Robert Loggia not only to rescue his plane, but also to salvage some credibility for the film.

Robert Loggia *Captain Gordon Vette* • Scott Bakula *Jay Pearman* • Rebecca Rigg *Ellen* • Michael Bishop *First Officer Mann* • Kit Taylor *Captain Warren Banks* • Alan Fletcher *Frank* ■ *Dir* Roger Young • *Scr* George Rubino, from a story by Robert Benedetti

Mercy or Murder? ★★★ PG

Drama based on a true story
1987 · US · Colour · 92mins

Abandoning his *Marcus Welby* bedside manner, Robert Young stars in this TV movie as a Florida man who killed his terminally ill wife (Frances Reid) and was prosecuted for murder. Young vividly conveys the agony of Roswell Gilbert's gut-wrenching decision to kill the woman he loved, and his subsequent painful estrangement from daughter Michael Learned (*The Waltons*). Still topical, writer/director Steven Gethers's script makes Roswell a figure of great dignity. 🎞

Robert Young *Roswell Gilbert* • Frances Reid *Emily Gilbert* • Michael Learned *Skipper* • Eddie Albert *Joe Varon* ■ *Dir/Scr* Steven Gethers

Merlin and the Sword ★★ PG

Fantasy   1982 · US · Colour · 89mins

A bizarre and muddled attempt from director Clive Donner to combine Arthurian legend with a dash of *Alice in Wonderland* and a generous pinch of the supposed origins of Stonehenge. Dyan Cannon is the unfortunate soul who first falls down the rabbit hole, swiftly followed by the script and the likes of Candice Bergen, Liam Neeson and Rupert Everett, most of whom at least look shamefaced about it. One of those clunkers that provides some unintentional laughs, the movie had a chequered transmission history, finally being shown in America under the title *Arthur the King* . 🎞

Malcolm McDowell *Arthur* • Candice Bergen *Morgan Le Fey* • Edward Woodward *Merlin* • Dyan Cannon *Katherine* • Lucy Gutteridge *Niniane* • Joseph Blatchley *Mordred* • Rupert Everett *Lancelot* • Rosalyn Landor *Guinevere* • Liam Neeson *Grak* • Patrick Ryecart *Gawain* ■ *Dir* Clive Donner • *Scr* J David Wyles

Mermaids ★★★★ 15

Romantic comedy
1990 · US · Colour · 105mins

Richard Benjamin has forged a career in quirky comedies, despite the occasional return to acting. In this gentle romantic comedy, he coaxes a deft performance from Winona Ryder as a confused sixties teen, caught between her lust for a local handyman (Michael Schoeffling) and her desire to be a nun. Surrounded by an eccentric mother (Cher) who's romantically involved with a local shopkeeper (Bob Hoskins), and a younger sister (Christina Ricci) who practises being a swimmer by holding her breath in the bath, it's not surprising she finds life so perplexing. A curious, light-hearted tale, with Ryder the greatest surprise as the young girl who's experiencing all kinds of pubescent angst. Contains some swearing. 🎞

Cher *Mrs Flax* • Bob Hoskins *Lou Landsky* • Winona Ryder *Charlotte Flax* • Michael Schoeffling *Joe Peretti* • Christina Ricci *Kate Flax* • Caroline McWilliams *Carrie* • Jan Miner *Mother Superior* • Betsey Townsend *Mary O'Brien* ■ *Dir* Richard Benjamin • *Scr* June Roberts, from the novel by Patty Dann

Merrill's Marauders
★★★★ U

Wartime drama   1962 · US · Colour · 94mins

Grey-haired Jeff Chandler never made it to the top rung of Hollywood stardom, and this, his last and finest movie, makes us wonder why. As Brigadier General Frank Merrill, he's a vivid and boisterous leader of a top US Army unit in 1942 Burma. What marks it out from other battle movies is William Clothier's dramatic photography and director Samuel Fuller's understanding of soldiers in action. He knows that war is hell but that the heat of action can strengthen character. 🎞

Jeff Chandler *Brigadier General Frank Merrill* • Ty Hardin *Lieutenant Lee Stockton* • Peter Brown *Bullseye* • Andrew Duggan *Major "Doc" Nemeny* • Will Hutchins *Chowhound* • Claude Akins *Sergeant Kolowicz* • Luz Valdez *Burmese girl* • John Hoyt *General Stilwell* • Charles Briggs *Muley* ■ *Dir* Samuel Fuller • *Scr* Samuel Fuller, Milton Sperling, from the novel by Charlton Ogburn Jr

Merrily We Go to Hell ★★★

Comedy   1932 · US · BW · 78mins

Sylvia Sidney once commented that she had been "paid by the tear", and her on-screen suffering was indeed relentless. At least this melodrama allowed her to leave the milieu of poverty and crime in which she was so often placed. Here she plays an heiress whose marriage to attractive writer Fredric March disintegrates as a result of his alcoholism and womanising. Deft direction and the strong presence of the stars rescue a plot that, despite incident, is short on substance. Look out for Cary Grant in a bit part.

Sylvia Sidney *Joan Prentice* • Fredric March *Jerry Corbett* • Adrianne Allen *Claire Hempstead* • Richard "Skeets" Gallagher *Buck* • Cary Grant *Charlie Baxter* ■ *Dir* Dorothy Arzner • *Scr* Edwin Justus Mayer, from the story *I, Jerry, Take Thee, Joan* by Cleo Lucas

Merrily We Live ★★★

Comedy   1938 · US · BW · 90mins

This delightful screwball comedy might be better known if the plot were not so similar to *My Man Godfrey*, made only two years earlier. The earlier film had a crazy rich family employing as a butler an educated bum who tames the spoilt daughter, while this has a crazy family (headed by Billie Burke) employing as a chauffeur an educated bum (Brian Aherne) who tames the spoilt daughter (Constance Bennett). The pacing is a little off, but the timing of the cast cannot be faulted.

Constance Bennett *Jerry Kilbourne* • Brian Aherne *Wade Rawlins* • Billie Burke *Mrs Emily Kilbourne* • Alan Mowbray *Grosvenor* • Patsy Kelly *Cook* • Ann Dvorak *Minerva Harlan* • Tom Brown *Kane Kilbourne* • Bonita Granville *Marion Kilbourne* ■ *Dir* Norman Z McLeod • *Scr* Eddie Noran, Jack Jevne

Merry Andrew ★★ U

Musical romantic comedy
1958 · US · Colour · 102mins

Directed and choreographed by Michael Kidd, this is by no means the funniest Danny Kaye vehicle, but it is energetic and good-humoured. Kaye is a teacher at a stuffy boys' school in England who sets out on an archaeological dig but ends up joining a circus, where he falls in love with Pier Angeli. Saul Chaplin and Johnny Mercer's score includes *The Square on the Hypotenuse* and *Salud*, the latter given a spirited production number with some dazzling dancing by Tommy Rall.

Danny Kaye *Andrew Larabee* • Pier Angeli *Selena* • Salvatore Baccaloni *Antonio Gallini* • Robert Coote *Dudley Larabee* • Noel Purcell *Matthew Larabee* • Patricia Cutts *Letitia Fairchild* • Rex Evans *Gregory Larabee* • Tommy Rall ■ *Dir* Michael Kidd • *Scr* Isobel Lennart, Ial Diamond, from the story *The Romance of Henry Menafee* by Paul Gallico

Merry Christmas Mr Lawrence ★★★★ 15

Second World War drama
1982 · UK/Jap · Colour · 118mins

Nagisa Oshima, the most controversial director of the Japanese New Wave, made his English-language debut with this affecting story set in a PoW camp during the Second World War. Tom Conti stars as a bilingual prisoner who is forced to act as intermediary between commandant Ryuichi Sakamoto and his sadistic number two Takeshi "Beat" Kitano, and the blustering British CO Jack Thompson. Treading carefully in matters of duty and culpability, Oshima creates credible and complex characters, played with distinction by his international cast. Contains some swearing. 🎞

David Bowie *Major Jack "Straffer" Celliers* • Tom Conti *Colonel John Lawrence* • Ryuichi Sakamoto *Captain Yonoi* • Takeshi [Takeshi Kitano] *Sergeant Gengo Hara* • Jack Thompson *Group Captain Hicksley* • Johnny Okura *Kanemoto* • Alistair Browning *De Jong* • Chris Broun *Celliers, aged 12* ■ *Dir* Nagisa Oshima • *Scr* Nagisa Oshima, Paul Mayersberg, from the novel *The Seed and the Sower* and the stories *A Bar of Shadow* and *The Sword and the Doll* by Laurens van der Post

Merry-Go-Round ★★★

Romance   1956 · Hun · BW · 100mins

Zoltan Fabri emerged as a leading figure in Hungarian "New Course" cinema with this rural *Romeo and Juliet* fable. Although the film's main purpose was to extol the virtues of collective farming, the romance between Béla Barsi and the debuting Mari Törőcsik is full of touching moments, particularly during their whirlwind fairground courtship. Yet, in spite of the vivacious performances, Fábri's direction is stickily sentimental, a failing he would correct in his next picture, *Professor Hannibal*, an expressionist assault on totalitarianism that was banned by the government. In Hungarian with English subtitles.

Mari Torocsik *Pataki Mari* • Imre Soós *Mate* • Béla Barsi *Pataki Istvan* ■ *Dir* Zoltan Fabri • *Scr* Zoltan Fabri, from a novel by Imre Sarkadi

The Merry Widow ★★★★

Silent romantic drama
1925 · US · BW · 110mins

Erich von Stroheim transformed the Ruritanian romance of Franz Lehar's operetta into an erotic black comedy that carries with it a whiff of decay. Von Stroheim dwells on the lechery of Prince Danilo (John Gilbert) before he is sent to Paris to woo a wealthy American widow (Mae Murray) and thereby save his bankrupt country. Despite the fact that von Stroheim and Murray fought throughout the shooting, she gave one of her best performances, and the lavish pre-sound musical was a great success with both the public and the critics.

Mae Murray *Sally O'Hara* • John Gilbert *Prince Danilo* • Roy D'Arcy *Crown Prince Mirko* • Tully Marshall *Baron Sadoja* ■ *Dir* Erich von Stroheim • *Scr* Erich von Stroheim, Benjamin Glazer, from the operetta *Die Lustige Witwe* by Victor Leon, Leo Stein, Franz Lehar

The Merry Widow ★★★★

Musical comedy   1934 · US · BW · 99mins

A scintillating version of Franz Lehar's operetta, with all the favourite tunes included and a fabulous pairing of the great Maurice Chevalier (as Danilo) and Jeanette MacDonald (as the widow). If you only know MacDonald for the films she made with Nelson Eddy, you'll find she's a revelation here – a very merry widow indeed! The film's wit, style and polish is down to the talents of brilliant director Ernst Lubitsch, whose risqué "touch" is apparent in every scene. This is a real pleasure, dated only in its fashions and its view of a long-gone Europe.

Maurice Chevalier *Prince Danilo* • Jeanette MacDonald *Sonia* • Edward Everett Horton *Ambassador Popoff* • Una Merkel *Queen Dolores* • George Barbier *King Achmed* • Minna Gombell *Marcelle* • Ruth Channing *Lulu* • Sterling Holloway *Mischka* ■ *Dir* Ernst Lubitsch • *Scr* Samson Raphaelson, Ernest Vajda, from the operetta *Die Lustige Witwe* by Victor Leon, Leo Stein, Franz Lehar

Mesmer ★★

Biographical drama
1994 · UK/Ger · Colour · 107mins

This biography of Franz Anton Mesmer, the 18th-century psychiatrist and father of mesmerism, is a classic Europudding. Alan Rickman stars in a

U = SUITABLE FOR ALL   Uc = SUITABLE FOR ALL, ESPECIALLY FOR YOUNG CHILDREN (VIDEO ONLY)   PG = PARENTAL GUIDANCE

film which chronicles both Mesmer's unorthodox healing practices, based on a theory of ''animal magnetism'', and his affair with a blind pianist, which so scandalised Viennese society that he was booted out of the city. Roger Spottiswoode directs from a screenplay by Dennis Potter.

Alan Rickman *Franz Anton Mesmer* • Amanda Ooms *Maria Teresa Paradies* • Gillian Barge *Mrs Mesmer* • David Hemblen *Dr Inginhousz* • Jan Rubes *Professor Stoerk* • Anna Thalbach *Francisca* • Simon McBurney *Franz* • Beatie Edney *Marie Antoinette* ■ *Dir* Roger Spottiswoode • *Scr* Dennis Potter

Mesmerized ★★15

Period drama
1984 · Ausl/NZ/UK · Colour · 94mins

This sluggish and visually uninspired film pales into insignificance compared to Jane Campion's far superior, if similarly themed *The Piano* (1993). Here, too, an innocent girl (Jodie Foster) is forced into marrying an older man (John Lithgow) in 19th-century New Zealand. Unable to tolerate his sexual peccadilloes, Foster kills him in self-defence and has to stand trial as a result. Foster delivers a strong performance, but this is not one of her better efforts.

Jodie Foster *Victoria* • John Lithgow *Oliver Thompson* • Michael Murphy *Reverend Wilson* • Harry Andrews *Old Thompson* • Dan Shor *George Thompson* • Philip Holder *Dr Finch* • Reg Evans *Mr Simmons* • Beryl Te Wiata *Mrs Simmons* ■ *Dir* Michael Laughlin • *Scr* Michael Laughlin, from a treatment by Jerzy Skolimowski

The Message ★★PG

Religious epic
1976 · Leb/UK · Colour · 170mins

Also known as *Mohammed, Messenger of God*, this three-hour epic re-creates the feudal life and times of the seventh-century leader of the religious movement that became known as Islam. Whatever sense of drama director Moustapha Akkad might have intended to create is undercut by the decision – as with early films of Christ – not to show the prophet himself, but instead have Anthony Quinn, as his uncle Hamza, a honoured warrior, take centre stage. Nonetheless the film caused an uproar among the faithful for daring to tell the tale at all. Non-believers may well find it sprawling and reverentially tedious.

Anthony Quinn *Hamza* • Irene Papas *Hind* • Michael Ansara *Abu-Sofyan* • Johnny Sekka *Bilal* • Michael Forest *Khalid* • Damien Thomas *Zaid* • Garrick Hagon *Ammar* ■ *Dir* Moustapha Akkad • *Scr* HAL Craig, AB Jawdat Al-Sahhar, Tawfik Al-Hakim, AB Rahman Al-Sharkawi, Mohammad Ali Maher

A Message from Holly ★★PG

Drama
1992 · US · Colour · 90mins

It's *Beaches* all over again, as best pals Lindsay Wagner and Shelley Long learn to laugh, cry, love and generally get all gooey in the face of heart-rending trauma. There's a fine line between poignant drama and sickly melodrama, and here that line is unfortunately crossed. Both Wagner and Long do well with their respective roles, but there is only so much hugging one movie can take.

Shelley Long *Kate Barnes* • Lindsay Wagner *Holly* • Molly Orr *Jenny* • Macdonald Carey *Judge Caufield* • Tony Colitti *Tomas* • Raphael Sbarge *Guy Weks* • Adilah Barnes *Miss Gregory* ■ *Dir* Rod Holcomb • *Scr* Dalene Young, from a story by Beth Polson

Message in a Bottle ★★★12

Romantic drama
1998 · US · Colour · 125mins

Kevin Costner is back on romantic form as the strong, silent and sensitive boat-builder, tracked down by newspaper researcher Robin Wright Penn after she finds a love letter to his late wife in a bottle on the seashore. She softens as she decides to learn more about the man and his solitary life. Although the inevitable happens, the beauty of director Luis Mandoki's tear-jerker is how all the emotions ring believably true. A rewarding tribute to the human spirit, this is warm-hearted stuff, with an absolutely brilliant scene-stealing performance from Paul Newman as Costner's grizzled father. Contains a sex scene. ▭ *DVD*

Robin Wright Penn *Theresa Osborne* • Paul Newman *Dodge Blake* • John Savage *Johnny Land* • Illeana Douglas *Lina Paul* • Robbie Coltrane *Charlie Toschi* • Jesse James *Jason Osborne* ■ *Dir* Luis Mandoki • *Scr* Gerald DiPego, from the novel by Nicholas Sparks

A Message to Garcia ★★

Historical adventure 1936 · US · BW · 77mins

It's the Hollywood version of the Spanish-American war, as army envoy John Boles goes in search of the titular general, surrounded by a cast of fine character actors, all of whom, alas, look quite out of place in the phoney Cuban setting. Unfortunately, George Marshall's direction lacks the vitality this type of film really needs, but it's entertaining enough. Rogue Wallace Beery and Barbara Stanwyck are the leads helping bland Boles deliver that message.

Wallace Beery *Sergeant Dory* • Barbara Stanwyck *Raphaelita Maderos* • John Boles *Lieutenant Andrew Rowan* • Herbert Mundin *Henry Piper* • Martin Garralaga *Rodriquez* • Juan Torena *Luis Maderos* • Alan Hale *Dr Krug* • Enrique Acosta *General Garcia* ■ *Dir* George Marshall • *Scr* WP Lipscomb, Gene Fowler, Sam Hellman, Gladys Lehman, from the non-fiction book by Lieutenant Andrew S Rowan and an essay by Elbert Hubbard

Messenger of Death ★★★18

Crime thriller 1988 · US · Colour · 92mins

The title promises the usual Charles Bronson bloodfest. But the script is by Paul Jarrico, a mild-mannered intellectual who was blacklisted and then produced the provocative, Union-financed *Salt of the Earth*. Bronson plays a Denver crime reporter whose snooping into a multiple killing leads him into Mormon society and a family who seem to be ritualistically following the examples of Cain and Abel. Director J Lee Thompson juggles the various elements – mystery, biblical allegory, bloody thriller – with great assurance. ▭

Charles Bronson *Garret Smith* • Trish Van Devere *Jastra Watson* • Laurence Luckinbill *Homer Foxx* • Daniel Benzali *Chief Barney Doyle* • Marilyn Hassett *Josephine Fabrizio* •

Charles Dierkop *Orville Beecham* ■ *Dir* J Lee Thompson • *Scr* Paul Jarrico, from the novel *The Avenging Angel* by Rex Burns

Messidor ★★★

Crime drama 1978 · Swi/Fr · Colour · 122mins

A key link in the chain connecting *Bonnie and Clyde* and *Thelma and Louise*, Alain Tanner's road movie caused a stir not just because of the amorality of its hitchhiking heroines, but also because of its unflattering portrait of his native Switzerland. From the moment student Clémentine Amouroux and shop assistant Catherine Rétor decide to embark on a robbery spree, Tanner is less concerned with the nature of their crimes or their impact upon the women themselves than with the response of this unrepentantly capitalist country. In French with English subtitles.

Clémentine Amouroux *Jeanne* • Catherine Rétoré *Marie* ■ *Dir/Scr* Alain Tanner

Metal Beast ★★18

Science-fiction horror
1995 · US · Colour · 83mins

A daft monster movie that tries ringing a few changes on the werewolf myth with little success. A werewolf is discovered in 1970s Hungary by deranged agent Barry Bostwick, who uses its blood for top secret government experiments and then puts it in suspended animation. Twenty years later, biology expert Kim Delaney defrosts it to carry on synthetic skin tests and turns the lycanthrope into something resembling a mutated gorilla before it goes on the rampage through the research facility. Bad special make-up effects and laughable genre riffs fail to promote interest. Contains violence and swearing. ▭

Kim Delaney *Anne De Carlo* • John Marzilli *Donald Butler* • Barry Bostwick *Pete Miller* • Musetta Vander *Debbie* ■ *Dir* Alessandro DeGaetano • *Scr* Alessandro DeGaetano, Timothy E Sabo

Meteor ★★PG

Disaster movie 1979 · US · Colour · 102mins

Wrapping up the spate of seventies blockbuster disaster movies, director Ronald Neame here places the planet on star-studded collision course with a gigantic asteroid. Spectacle has never looked cheaper or more pathetic than the tidal waves, avalanches and mud-slides on view in this celluloid catastrophe. Reaching an apex of absurdity when America (Sean Connery) and Russia (Natalie Wood) bury the hatchet to nuke the big rock, this mega-flop was initiated, amazingly, by Anthony Burgess (of *A Clockwork Orange* fame) who left for reasons that won't need an explanation. ▭

Sean Connery *Dr Paul Bradley* • Natalie Wood *Tatiana Donskaya* • Karl Malden *Harry Sherwood* • Brian Keith *Dr Dubov* • Martin Landau *General Adlon* • Trevor Howard *Sir Michael Hughes* • Richard Dysart *Secretary of Defense* • Henry Fonda *President* ■ *Dir* Ronald Neame • *Scr* Stanley Mann, Edmund H North, from a story by Edmund H North

The Meteor Man ★★PG

Comedy 1993 · US · Colour · 95mins

After *Hollywood Shuffle* and *The Five Heartbeats*, this was third time unlucky for young, gifted and black actor/ writer/director Robert Townsend. It's certainly about time we had more non-Caucasian superheroes, but there's something a little too fallible about this emerald-clad warrior whose powers have a nasty habit of waning at crucial moments. Similarly, although tackling the neighbourhood drug barons is a worthy mission, the heavy-handed social commentary provides surprisingly few laughs or thrills. ▭

Robert Townsend *Jefferson Reed* • Marla Gibbs *Mrs Reed* • Eddie Griffin *Michael* • Robert Guillaume *Mr Reed* • James Earl Jones *Mr Moses* • Roy Fegan *Simon* • Bill Cosby *Marvin* ■ *Dir/Scr* Robert Townsend

Meteorites! ★PG

Disaster thriller 1998 · US · Colour · 85mins

Tom Wopat (*The Dukes of Hazzard*) and Roxanne Hart (*Chicago Hope*) struggle under the debris of this derivative disaster TV movie. When a meteorite shower wreaks havoc, the people of an Arizona desert town must band together to survive in this lame effort that leaves a vast, empty crater where the drama should be. Contains some swearing and violence. ▭

Tom Wopat *Tom Johnson* • Roxanne Hart *Cath Johnson* • Pato Hoffmann *John Whitehorse* • Amiel Daemion *Crystal Cassidy* • Darrin Klimek *Mac Johnson* • Leo Taylor *Filbo* ■ *Dir* Chris Thomson • *Scr* Bart Baker

Metro ★★18

Action thriller 1997 · US · Colour · 112mins

Eddie Murphy returns to the genre that made him a star with this misfiring action vehicle. It has a harder centre than usual as negotiator Murphy uses his motormouth talents to haggle with hostage takers. However, his persuasive charms are sorely tested when he comes up against psychotic jewel thief Michael Wincott. The highlight set piece is a car chase involving a runaway tram, but otherwise director Thomas Carter, who cut his teeth on such TV series as *Miami Vice* and *Equal Justice*, displays little flair in the action department. ▭ *DVD*

Eddie Murphy *Scott Roper* • Michael Rapaport *Kevin McCall* • Kim Miyori *Detective Kimura* • James Carpenter *Officer Forbes* • Art Evans *Lieutenant Sam Baffert* • Michael Wincott *Michael Korda* ■ *Dir* Thomas Carter • *Scr* Randy Feldman

Metroland ★★18

Drama 1997 · UK/Fr/Sp · Colour · 96mins

Commuting is the slow way to death, according to this dull meditation on suburbia from former TV director Philip Saville. Based on Julian Barnes's novel, it's about an advertising executive who starts to question his family life when an old friend from his bachelor days in Paris turns up to rekindle memories of a past romance. Christian Bale, Lee Ross and Emily Watson try to make it all worthwhile, but Adrian Hodges's script works against it. Contains sex scenes and swearing. ▭

Christian Bale *Chris Lloyd* • Emily Watson *Marion Lloyd* • Lee Ross *Toni* • Elsa Zylberstein *Annick* • Rufus *Henri* ■ *Dir* Philip Saville • *Scr* Adrian Hodges, from the novel by Julian Barnes

Metropolis ★★★★★ PG

Silent science-fiction fantasy
1926 · Ger/US · BW · 138mins

Fritz Lang's futuristic landmark of the silent era got a Hi-NRG overhaul in 1984 when Giorgio Moroder added an electronic score and songs by Freddie Mercury, Bonnie Tyler and Adam Ant. Re-edited with some forgotten footage, colour-tinted and with the special effects segments optically enhanced, the result is a fabulous reminder of how truly great this twenties *Star Wars* is. A contrived and simplistic parable in retrospect, it still contains unforgettable images of the 21st century that have been mercilessly plagiarised ever since. ▭ *DVD*

Alfred Abel *John Fredersen* • Gustav Frolich *Freder* • Rudolf Klein-Rogge *Rotwang* • Brigitte Helm *Maria/Robot* • Fritz Rasp *Slim* • Theodor Loos *Josaphat/Joseph* ■ *Dir* Fritz Lang • *Scr* Fritz Lang, Thea von Harbou, from the novel by Thea von Harbou • *Cinematographer* Karl Freund, Gunther Rittau

Metropolitan ★★★ 15

Comedy 1990 · US · Colour · 94mins

Director Whit Stillman sold his Manhattan apartment to raise the budget for his debut movie. Using a cast of unknowns, it tells the story of a group of young, privileged New Yorkers who call themselves the SFRP (Sally Fowler Rat Pack, named after a party hostess) and do little other than spend the Christmas season attending debutante balls, having party postmortems, swapping *bons mots* and courting each other. It's the world of F Scott Fitzgerald caught in a time warp, complete with social interloper. Stillman's witty, sophisticated screenplay was Oscar-nominated. ▭

Edward Clements *Tom Townsend* • Carolyn Farina *Audrey Rouget* • Christopher Eigeman [Chris Eigeman] *Nick Smith* • Taylor Nichols *Charlie Black* • Allison Rutledge-Parisi *Jane Clarke* • Dylan Hundley *Sally Fowler* • Isabel Gillies *Cynthia McLean* ■ *Dir/Scr* Whit Stillman

Mexican Bus Ride ★★★★

Comedy drama 1951 · Mex · BW · 85mins

Esteban Marquez plays a young man dragged away on his wedding night by his avaricious elder brothers, who need his endorsement of their dying mother's will. A perilous and incident-packed mountain bus trip ensues, during which a woman gives birth and Marquez has to fend off the attentions of the local tart. From Spain's great Luis Buñuel, who based this deftly-made film on a real journey made by his poet friend Altolaguirre, it's one of the director's lightest works, but doesn't neglect the weightier issues of life, love and death. In Spanish with English subtitles.

Lilia Prado *Raquel* • Carmelita Gonzalez *Oliviero's wife* • Esteban Marquez *Oliviero* • Manuel Donde *Eladio Gonzales* • Roberto Cobo *Juan* • Luis Acevez Castañeda *Silvestre* ■ *Dir* Luis Buñuel • *Scr* Manuel Altolaguirre, Luis Buñuel, Juan De La Cabada

Mexican Spitfire ★★ U

Comedy 1940 · US · BW · 67mins

The spitfire of the title is Lupe Velez, married to Donald Woods's advertising executive and fighting off efforts by his disapproving aunt (Elisabeth Risdon) and jealous ex-fiancée (Linda Hayes) to break them up. Based on characters introduced in *The Girl from Mexico*, this cleverly orchestrated, lowbrow farce has Leon Errol as both a benevolent uncle and a visiting English whisky baron called Lord Epping. The pie-throwing finale recalls Mack Sennett in his prime. The film spawned a series.

Lupe Velez *Carmelita Lindsay* • Leon Errol *Uncle Matt Lindsay/Lord Basil Epping* • Donald Woods *Dennis Lindsay* • Linda Hayes *Elizabeth* • Cecil Kellaway *Chumley* • Elisabeth Risdon *Aunt Della Lindsay* ■ *Dir* Leslie Goodwins • *Scr* Joseph Fields, Charles E Roberts, from a story by Joseph Fields

Mi Vida Loca ★★★ 15

Drama 1993 · US · Colour · 91mins

Allison Anders's third feature is a much tougher picture than her poignantly moving *Gas, Food, Lodging*, being closer to the uncompromising portrait of inner city life presented in the films of the African-American new wave. Although some of the dialogue recalls the work of longtime friend Quentin Tarantino, their concerns could not be more diverse, with Anders showing how religion and pulp romance sustain Hispanic teenage girls in a world where violence and loss are commonplace. The use of real street gangsters adds to the urgency and authenticity, although the dramatic quality suffers. Contains swearing and substance abuse. ▭

Angel Aviles *Sad girl* • Seidy Lopez *Mousie* • Jacob Vargas *Ernesto* • Marlo Marron *Giggles* • Jesse Borrego *El Duran* • Magali Alvarado *La Blue Eyes* ■ *Dir/Scr* Allison Anders

Miami Blues ★★★★ 18

Crime thriller 1990 · US · Colour · 92mins

Alec Baldwin has never been better than as a vicious ex-con who takes up with naive hooker Jennifer Jason Leigh in Miami. Things get complicated when he steals investigating cop Fred Ward's gun, badge and false teeth and sets about robbing and shooting just about everyone in his path, while masquerading as a police officer. An absorbing, gripping (and often very violent) battle of wits, this has some wonderfully dark comic moments and superb performances. ▭

Fred Ward *Sergeant Hoke Moseley* • Alec Baldwin *Frederick J Frenger Jr* • Jennifer Jason Leigh *Susie Waggoner* • Cecilia Perez-Cervera *Stewardess* • Georgie Cranford *Little boy* • Edward Saxon *Krishna Ravindra* ■ *Dir* George Armitage • *Scr* George Armitage, from the novel by Charles Willeford

Miami Rhapsody ★★★ 15

Romantic comedy
1995 · US · Colour · 91mins

You could be forgiven here for thinking that you are watching a Woody Allen comedy. The setting may be Miami, not Manhattan, but there is the central character (Sarah Jessica Parker) bemoaning her lot, a dysfunctional family and Mia Farrow in a co-starring role as Parker's mother. But as the

action develops, it's clear that writer/director David Frankel is more of a Woody wannabe than a genuine pretender to the throne. The unravelling strands of romance are neatly established as Parker, newly engaged to Gil Bellows, discovers that just about everyone she knows is cheating on their partners. If this lacks the deft touches that make Allen's work so uniquely enjoyable, it's still a clever and satisfying counterfeit. ▭

Sarah Jessica Parker *Gwyn Marcus* • Gil Bellows *Matt* • Antonio Banderas *Antonio* • Mia Farrow *Nina Marcus* • Paul Mazursky *Vic Marcus* • Kevin Pollak *Jordan Marcus* • Barbara Garrick *Terri* • Naomi Campbell *Kaia* ■ *Dir/Scr* David Frankel

Micha ★★★

Drama 1992 · Ire/Rus · Colour · 97mins

Having worked in St Petersburg for several years, Irish director Gerard Michael MacCarthy was almost on home soil for this debut feature. His rite-of-passage drama is a heady cocktail of visual styles which echoes the many different facets of the city. It also captures the conflicting emotions of 11-year-old Genya Korhin as he wanders between his strict school, the spartan flat he shares with his mum and the TV location where he hangs out with the star of a cop show (Igor Kostolevsky). Ambitiously stylised yet movingly authentic. In Russian with English subtitles.

Genya Korhin *Micha* • Victoria Korhina *Julia, Micha's mother* • Igor Kostolevsky ■ *Dir/Scr* Gerard Michael MacCarthy

Michael ★★★ PG

Fantasy comedy 1996 · US · Colour · 100mins

John Travolta revisits *Phenomenon* territory for this Nora Ephron fantasy, in which he stars as an angel living in backwoods Iowa. Even though he comes with feathers on his back, he's close to being white trash, but when some journalists arrive to write a story about him Travolta turns their hardboiled hearts into slush. This formed part of Travolta's campaign to win the family audience and, up to a point, he's been successful. William Hurt is trademark strange and often very funny as one of the hacks, but Bob Hoskins is embarrassing as Hurt's editor and Andie MacDowell fails to make her mark as the female lead. Contains some swearing. ▭

John Travolta *Michael* • Andie MacDowell *Dorothy Winters* • William Hurt *Frank Quinlan* • Bob Hoskins *Vartan Malt* • Robert Pastorelli *Huey Driscoll* • Jean Stapleton *Pansy Milbank* • Teri Garr *Judge Esther Newberg* • Wallace Langham *Bruce Craddock* ■ *Dir* Nora Ephron • *Scr* Nora Ephron, Delia Ephron, Pete Dexter, Jim Quinlan, from a story by Pete Dexter, Jim Quinlan

Michael Collins ★★★★ 15

Biographical drama
1996 · US/UK · Colour · 126mins

Neil Jordan's screen biography of the founder of the IRA, an intellectual who virtually invented urban terrorism and bombed his way to talks in Downing Street before being assassinated by his own side in 1922. The movie begins with an impressively filmed Easter uprising, in which Jordan

appears to demolish Dublin, yet there's also an even-handedness when it comes to depicting and simplifying the political struggle for Irish independence. As Collins, Liam Neeson is both charming and menacing, while Alan Rickman is superbly cast as Eamon De Valera. Julia Roberts, however, looks hopelessly lost. Contains swearing and violence. ▭ *DVD*

Liam Neeson *Michael Collins* • Ian Hart *Joe O'Reilly* • Julia Roberts *Kitty Kiernan* • Stephen Rea *Ned Broy* • Aidan Quinn *Harry Boland* • John Kenny *Patrick Pearse* • Alan Rickman *Eamon De Valera* • Charles Dance *Soames* ■ *Dir/Scr* Neil Jordan

Michael Shayne, Private Detective ★★

Crime mystery 1940 · US · BW · 76mins

The first in an interesting series of programme fillers from 20th Century-Fox, important today because it featured a tough, resilient and self-reliant private eye before the popularity of those moody Humphrey Bogart movies later on in the decade. Shayne was incarnated on screen by the excellent Lloyd Nolan, an actor whose very persona suggested he brooked no nonsense. This pilot movie is abrasive, sexy and eminently watchable within its B-budget confines.

Lloyd Nolan *Michael Shayne* • Marjorie Weaver *Phyllis Brighton* • Joan Valerie *Marsha Gordon* • Walter Abel *Elliott Thomas* • Elizabeth Patterson *Aunt Olivia* • Donald MacBride *Chief Painter* • Douglass Dumbrille *Gordon* ■ *Dir* Eugene Forde • *Scr* Stanley Rauh, Manning O'Connor, from a novel by Brett Halliday

The Michelle Apartments ★★

Black comedy 1995 · Can · Colour · 91mins

Canadian director John Pozer followed his admired but little-seen *The Grocer's Wife* with this offbeat TV thriller, billed as "a toxic love story". Henry Czerny holds the piece together as a tax auditor sent to investigate the dealings of a chemical company. Naturally, his investigations open up a whole can of worms and bring him into contact with the eccentric inhabitants of the eponymous apartment block. Pozer captures the one-horse town atmosphere rather well, but he over-relies on the quirkiness of his minor characters when the pace flags. Contains violence and sex scenes.

Henry Czerny *Alex Hartwell* • Nancy Beatty *Mrs Haggerty* • Mary Elizabeth Rubens [Mary Beth Rubens] *Madeleine* • Peter Outerbridge *Jules* • Daniel Kash *Dean* • David Calderisi *Mr Turnbull* • Ian D Clark *Abernathy* ■ *Dir* John Pozer • *Scr* Ross Weber

Mickey Blue Eyes ★★★ 15

Comedy 1999 · US/UK · Colour · 98mins

Hugh Grant is sublimely ridiculous as an English auctioneer in New York, who learns that marrying sweetheart Jeanne Tripplehorn means getting spliced to the mob. Tripplehorn's father, James Caan, is the local don and Grant quickly finds himself up to his neck in linguine as he fakes the identity of out-of-town mobster "Mickey Blue Eyes". How the couple extricate themselves from a life of crime involves an inadvertent murder and a

U = SUITABLE FOR ALL, **Uc** = SUITABLE FOR ALL, ESPECIALLY FOR YOUNG CHILDREN (VIDEO ONLY), **PG** = PARENTAL GUIDANCE

dire impression of Don Corleone from Hugh. Gently entertaining fodder. Contains swearing and violence. 🎬

Hugh Grant *Michael Felgate* • James Caan *Frank Vitale* • Jeanne Tripplehorn *Gina Vitale* • Burt Young *Vito Graziosi* • James Fox *Philip Cromwell* • Joe Viterelli *Vinnie* • Gerry Becker *Agent Connell* • Maddie Corman *Carol* ■ *Dir* Kelly Makin • *Scr* Mark Lawrence, Adam Scheinmann, Robert Kuhn

Mickey One ★★★
Crime drama   1965 · US · BW · 92mins

Warren Beatty made *Mickey One* right after *Lilith* and the result was another flop. It's easy to see why. Essentially a thriller about a nightclub comic, the plot fragments into a psychological drama about the mob. The style, though, is something else. This is an American art movie, incredibly flash and tricksy, with a melodramatic Hurd Hatfield as a homosexual club owner and oblique references to the Kennedy assassination and Jack Ruby. It's a fascinating mess from which one clear masterpiece emerged: Beatty teamed up again with director Arthur Penn for *Bonnie and Clyde*.

Warren Beatty *Mickey One* • Alexandra Stewart *Jenny* • Hurd Hatfield *Castle* • Franchot Tone *Ruby Lopp* • Teddy Hart *Berson* • Jeff Corey *Fryer* • Kamatari Fujiwara *Artist* ■ *Dir* Arthur Penn • *Scr* Alan M Surgal

Mickey Spillane's Mike Hammer: Murder Takes All ★★
Detective drama   1989 · US · Colour · 92mins

Mickey Spillane's sullen, monosyllabic but resolute gumshoe has provided Stacy Keach with almost his only source of work in recent years. Keach is so conversant with the unemotional crimebuster that he often looks asleep, even when in the thick of gun-happy action. The convoluted plot of this TV movie further contributes to the sense of exhaustion, while even a fairly startling opening can't stop the script drowning in clichés. Look out for Jim Carrey in a supporting role.

Stacy Keach *Mike Hammer* • Lynda Carter *Helen Durant* • Lindsay Bloom *Velda* • Don Stroud *Captain Pat Chambers* • Ed Winter [Edward Winter] *Johnny Roman* • Michelle Phillips *Leora* • Jim Carrey *Brad Peterson* ■ *Dir* John Nicolella • *Scr* Mark Edward Edens, from a story by Mark Edward Edens, Rudy Day

Micki & Maude ★★ 🄿🄶
Comedy   1984 · US · Colour · 112mins

Dudley Moore's cinematic career reached its height with the movies *10* and *Arthur*, but by the time this weak Blake Edwards comedy was made in 1984 it was in a trough as deep as the Grand Canyon. Needless to say, this farcical tale of a man who wants to marry his pregnant mistress while still remaining married to his equally expectant wife didn't help matters, and the blame has to be laid at the feet of the similarly out-of-luck Edwards. 🎬

Dudley Moore *Rob Salinger* • Amy Irving *Maude Guillory* • Ann Reinking *Micki Salinger* • Richard Mulligan *Leo Brody* • George Gaynes *Dr Eugene Glztski* • Wallace Shawn *Dr Elliot Fibel* • John Pleshette *Editor* • HB Haggerty *Barkhas Guillory* ■ *Dir* Blake Edwards • *Scr* Jonathan Reynolds

Microcosmos ★★★★ 🅄
Documentary   1996 · Fr/Swi/It · Colour · 72mins

Directors Claude Nuridsany and Marie Pérennou redefine the boundaries of the nature documentary with this astounding look at the insect life in a French meadow. Filmed over three years using revolutionary camera and sound equipment, it presents a bug's-eye view of the world in a series of visually amazing close-ups highlighting a stag beetle battle, an ant colony hatching and the deliberate movement of a caterpillar. The soundtrack contains the startling noises of the insects themselves and an eclectic array of music, and the result is an overpowering experience. 🎬

Kristin Scott Thomas *Narrator* ■ *Dir* Claude Nuridsany, Marie Pérennou

Midaq Alley ★★ 🄸🄵
Melodrama   1995 · Mex · Colour · 138mins

Apparently, this film has won 45 international film awards, yet it would undoubtedly have remained buried if it wasn't for the presence of one Salma Hayek. Unreleased on video until 1999, it was made when she was largely unknown outside her native Mexico. Hayek is the young innocent who is plunged into the world of prostitution in one of three loosely linked stories, which take place over the same time period but are viewed from different perspectives. In Spanish with English subtitles. 🎬

Ernesto Gomez Cruz *Don Rutilio* • Maria Rojo *Doña Cata* • Salma Hayek *Alma* • Bruno Bichir *Abel* ■ *Dir* Jorge Fons • *Scr* Vicente Leñero, from the novel by Naguib Mahfouz

Midas Run ★★
Crime mystery   1969 · US · Colour · 106mins

Swedish actor/director Alf Kjellin – so memorable in *Torment* (1944), a tale of troubled adolescence – comes a cropper with this Hollywood hokum about an elderly spymaster determined to steal a load of gold bullion. (Hence the alternative title, *A Run On Gold*.) It has a splendid job-lot of class actors: Fred Astaire, Richard Crenna, Ralph Richardson, Cesar Romero. They don't help much, though.

Richard Crenna *Mike Warden* • Anne Heywood *Sylvia Giroux* • Fred Astaire *John Pedley* • Roddy McDowall *Wister* • Ralph Richardson *Henshaw* • Cesar Romero *Dodero* • Adolfo Celi *Aldo Ferranti* • Maurice Denham *Crittenden* • John Le Mesurier *Wells* ■ *Dir* Alf Kjellin • *Scr* James Buchanan, Ronald Austin, Berne Giler, from a story by Berne Giler

Middle Age Crazy ★★★
Comedy drama   1980 · Can · Colour · 91mins

Bruce Dern has a midlife crisis, though his gangling frame, thinning hair, buck teeth and country hick voice make him look a little unhinged to begin with. He's a Texan architect – nothing fancy, just fast food stands – who has just clocked 40. So when his dad dies, he buys a Porsche, dresses like JR Ewing, leaves his wife (played by the wittily voluptuous Ann-Margret) and runs off with sexy Deborah Wakeham. All the clichés of a movie marriage on the rocks fall into place, but it's none the worse for that.

Bruce Dern *Bobby Lee* • Ann-Margret *Sue Ann* • Graham Jarvis *JD* • Eric Christmas *Tommy* • Helen Hughes *Ruth* • Geoffrey Bowes *Greg* • Deborah Wakeham *Nancy* ■ *Dir* John Trent • *Scr* Carl Kleinschmitt, from the song by Jerry Lee Lewis

Middle of the Night ★★
Drama   1959 · US · BW · 117mins

A typically overwrought drama from Paddy Chayefsky about life and love in the garment industry. The factory is run by unhappily married Albert Dekker and lonely widower Fredric March, who suddenly falls for pretty secretary Kim Novak. Emotions start to fray, and the shadow of *Death of a Salesman* looms large. As usual with these wordy, liberal dramas, characters make speeches and there's a dollop of psychobabble to make us understand them better. A strong cast, though.

Kim Novak *Betty Preisser* • Fredric March *Jerry Kingsley* • Lee Philips *George* • Glenda Farrell *Mrs Mueller* • Albert Dekker *Lockman* • Martin Balsam *Jack* • Lee Grant *Marilyn* • Edith Meiser *Evelyn Kingsley* ■ *Dir* Delbert Mann • *Scr* Paddy Chayefsky, from his play

The Middleman ★★★★
Satirical drama   1975 · Ind · BW · 122mins

More acerbic than its fellows, this knowing satire from Satyajit Ray on the corruption that grips all aspects of Indian commerce completes the Calcutta trilogy that began with *The Adversary* and *Company Limited*. Providing an unflattering picture of both the middle classes and inner-city life, the film focuses on the shady dealings of a university graduate as he searches for an escort for an important client. Deftly switching between comedy and social comment, Ray draws a fine performance from Pradip Mukherjee as the ambitious twentysomething who has been reduced to behaving like the Arthur Daley of Calcutta. In Bengali with English subtitles.

Pradip Mukherjee *Somnath Bannerji* • Satya Bannerji [Satya Bannerjee] *Somnath's father* • Dipankar Dey *Bhombol* • Lily Chakravarty *Kamala* • Aparna Sen *Somnath's girlfriend* • Goutam Chakravarti *Sukumar, Somnath's friend* • Utpal Dutt *Bishuda, broker* ■ *Dir* Satyajit Ray • *Scr* Satyajit Ray, from the novel by Shankar

Middleton's Changeling ★ 🄸🄸
Tragedy   1997 · UK · Colour · 95mins

Based on the classic Jacobean tragedy about doomed love, betrayal and madness, director Marcus Thompson's film is a total bore. His interpretation involves much poetic license with the text (now containing a liberal sprinkling of four-letter words) and period (heroine Amanda Ray-King wears sneakers under her petticoats). Although such gimmickry is shrouded in visually arresting images, the film remains an infuriating curiosity. Contains sex scenes and violence.

Ian Dury *De Flores* • Amanda Ray-King *Beatrice Joanna* • Colm O Maonlai *Alsemero* • Billy Connolly *Alibius* • Campbell Morrison *Lollio* • Moya Brady *Isabella* • Richard Mayes *Vermandero* ■ *Dir* Marcus Thompson • *Scr* Marcus Thompson, from the play by Thomas Middleton, William Rowley

Midnight ★★
Drama   1934 · US · BW · 68mins

A crime of passion repeats itself: just as a jury foreman announces the guilty verdict that sends a woman to the electric chair, his daughter shoots her lover to stop him going away. The daughter is Sidney Fox, and the lover is a racketeer played by the young Humphrey Bogart. The film is rather pretentious, and Bogart is quite unremarkable in his small role – though that didn't stop an American distributor reissuing it in 1947 as *Call It Murder*, billing Bogie as the star.

Humphrey Bogart *Gar Boni* • Henry Hull *Bob Nolan* • Sidney Fox *Stella Weldon* • OP Heggie *Edward Weldon* • Richard Whorf *Arthur Weldon* • Lynne Overman *Joe "Leroy" Biggers* • Granville Bates *Henry McGrath* • Margaret Wycherly *Mrs Weldon* ■ *Dir* Chester Erskine • *Scr* Chester Erskine, from a play by Paul Sifton, Claire Sifton

Midnight ★★★★★
Romantic comedy   1939 · US · BW · 94mins

Written by the incomparable team of Charles Brackett and Billy Wilder, starring Claudette Colbert, Don Ameche and John Barrymore (in one of his best late roles), this is right up there with *Ninotchka*, another Wilder and Brackett classic. Add Mary Astor and Francis Lederer in support, Hedda Hopper in a featured role and expert direction from Mitchell Leisen, and the result is one of the most stylish and enduring romantic comedies of the era. The story involves an American girl (Colbert) who arrives penniless in Paris at midnight. After catching the eye of a Hungarian taxi driver (Ameche), she finds herself masquerading as a wealthy baroness, hired by a wealthy man (Barrymore) to lure away his wife's lover. Sophisticated and hilarious, it sparkles, sizzles and is an absolute delight.

Claudette Colbert *Eve Peabody/"Baroness Czerny"* • Don Ameche *Tibor Czerny* • John Barrymore *George Flammarion* • Francis Lederer *Jacques Picot* • Mary Astor *Helene Flammarion* • Elaine Barrie *Simone* • Hedda Hopper *Stephanie* • Rex O'Malley *Marcel* • Monty Woolley *Judge* ■ *Dir* Mitchell Leisen • *Scr* Charles Brackett, Billy Wilder, from a story by Edwin Justus Mayer, Franz Shulz

Midnight ★★ 🄸🄸
Horror thriller   1980 · US · Colour · 90mins

Occasionally scary, but too often pedestrian, this cheap horror movie marked the directorial debut of John A Russo, who wrote *Night of the Living Dead* and adapted this film from his own novel. It has the feel of a George A Romero classic, crossed with *The Texas Chain Saw Massacre*. Melanie Verlin flees from her wicked stepfather (forties star Lawrence Tierney, apparently down on his luck) only to be captured by satanists in need of a human sacrifice. The horrid theme is weighed down by reams of dialogue and too many scenes of driving, walking or singing. 🎬

Lawrence Tierney *Bert Johnson* • Melanie Verliin *Nancy Johnson* • John Hall *Tom* • Charles Jackson *Hank* • Doris Hackney *Harriet Johnson* • John Amplas *Abraham* ■ *Dir* John A Russo • *Scr* John A Russo, from his novel

Midnight ★★
Satire 1989 · US · Colour · 84mins

In recent years, Lynn Redgrave has been enjoying something of an Indian summer with triumphant performances in *Shine* and *Gods and Monsters*, for which she was Oscar-nominated. Hard to believe, then, that back in the late eighties she was suffering the indignity of appearing in low-grade horror rubbish like this lame lampoon on showbiz. Lynn plays an Elvira-style TV horror hostess, complete with frizzy wig and gothic costume, whose entourage is being killed off. There's good support from Tony Curtis as her greedy network boss and Frank Gorshin as a double-crossing agent, but director Norman Thaddeus Vane generates no suspense whatsoever.

Lynn Redgrave *Midnight (Vera)* • Tony Curtis *Mr B* • Steve Parrish *Mickey Modine* • Rita Gam *Heidi* • Gustav Vintas *Siegfried* • Karen Witter *Mitty* • Frank Gorshin *Ron* ■ *Dir/Scr* Norman Thaddeus Vane

Midnight ★★★
Drama 1998 · Bra/Fr · Colour · 76mins

Walter Salles's follow-up to *Central Station* may be set on Millennium Eve, but by the time an escaped prisoner and an abandoned teacher meet on a Rio rooftop, it's clear this is no nostalgic paean to the passing century or expression of hope for the future. Instead it's a grim reminder that, for all the high-minded resolutions of the international establishment, life will continue to grind on for those ordinary people caught in time's relentless mechanism. Co-directed by Daniela Thomas, this offers none of the resigned bathos of Don McKellar's *Last Night* in putting Y2K in its sobering historical context. In Portuguese with English subtitles.

Fernanda Torres *Maria* • Luis Carlos Vasconcellos *Joao* • Carlos Vereza *Pedro* ■ *Dir* Walter Salles, Daniela Thomas • *Scr* Daniela Thomas, José de Carvalho, Walter Salles, Joao Emanuel Carneiro

Midnight at Madame Tussaud's ★★
Chiller 1936 · UK · BW · 66mins

Made at Highbury studios, this creaky old chiller benefits from some superb sets, but the story, about a famous explorer who hopes to reduce his debts by betting he can spend the night in the famous Chamber of Horrors, is pretty limp. Not even a subplot involving his daughter's shady love life can pep it up. Bernard Miles is good value as the ghoulish sculptor delighting in the crimes of his waxworks, but James Carew as the explorer is less animated than the exhibits. One of Britain's best silent directors, George Pearson, struggles with the dialogue, but the atmosphere is truly eerie.

James Carew *Sir Clive Cheyne* • Lucille Lisle *Carol Cheyne* • Charles Oliver *Harry Newton* • Kim Peacock *Nick Frome* • Patrick Barr *Gerry Melville* • William Hartnell *Stubbs* • Lydia Sherwood *Brenda* • Bernard Miles *Modeller* ■ *Dir* George Pearson • *Scr* Kim Peacock, Roger MacDougall, from a story by James S Edwards, Roger MacDougall

Midnight Blue ★★ 🔞
Erotic thriller 1996 · US · Colour · 90mins

Another glossy erotic thriller from the *Playboy* stable, in which a strong cast more than makes up for the ropey storyline. Damian Chapa is the banker who falls for prostitute, Annabel Schofield, only to discover that she is the wife of his boss. Or is she? It's actually rather tame, but likeable enough, and the talented supporting players, including Dean Stockwell and Harry Dean Stanton, add an extra bit of class. Contains swearing, violence, sex scenes.

Annabel Schofield *Martine/Georgine* • Damian Chapa *Martin* • Dean Stockwell *Katz* • Harry Dean Stanton *Eric* • Steve Kanaly *Collier* • Jennifer Jostyn *Barbara* • Collin Bernsen *Cab driver* • Steve Ford [Steven Ford] *Detective Dobbin* ■ *Dir* Skott Snider • *Scr* Douglas Brode

A Midnight Clear ★★★★ 🔞
Second World War drama
1991 · US · Colour · 103mins

The shifting group dynamics of a Second World War infantry squad are put under the psychological microscope, in director Keith Gordon's gripping morality play about the personal price exacted by battle. It's when the GIs meet some German soldiers, just back from the disastrous campaign on the Russian front, that the main thrust of this insightful drama snaps into focus. Former actor Gordon gives his able young ensemble cast (including Peter Berg, Kevin Dillon, Ethan Hawke, Gary Sinise, Frank Whaley and Arye Gross) a chance to shine in a powerful tragedy full of surprises and visual style. 🖵

Peter Berg *Bud Miller* • Kevin Dillon *Mel Avakian* • Arye Gross *Stan Shutzer* • Ethan Hawke *Will Knott* • Gary Sinise "Mother" *Wilkins* • Frank Whaley "Father" *Mundy* • John C McGinley *Major Griffin* • Larry Joshua *Lieutenant Ware* ■ *Dir* Keith Gordon • *Scr* Keith Gordon, from the novel by William Wharton

Midnight Cop ★★★ 🔞
Thriller 1988 · W Ger · Colour · 92mins

This passable police thriller benefits enormously from Armin Mueller-Stahl's strong central performance as an eccentric, ageing Berlin cop hunting down a vicious serial killer. Director Peter Patzak works wonders with a meandering storyline and deserves a medal for the sheer temerity of casting TV soap bimbette Morgan Fairchild as a call girl who acts as a decoy to trap the killer. Journeymen Frank Stallone and Michael York, before his career got an *Austin Powers* makeover, also star. Stahl later went on to appear in several American movies, notably *Jakob the Liar* and *Shine*. 🖵

Armin Mueller-Stahl *Inspector Alex Glas* • Morgan Fairchild *Lisa* • Michael York *Karstens* • Frank Stallone *Jack Miskowski* • Julia Kent *Shirley* ■ *Dir* Peter Patzak • *Scr* Julia Kent, Paul Nicholas, Peter Patzak

Midnight Cowboy ★★★★★ 🔞
Drama 1969 · US · Colour · 108mins

This tawdry, strident yet deeply affecting tale of a naive Texas stud striking up a relationship with a tubercular con man deservedly won several Oscars. British John Schlesinger was the perfect director to cast an alien eye on Manhattan's sexual permissiveness and Warhol weirdness and, with scalpel-sharp precision, expose the jaundiced strata below the hip surface. Jon Voight and Dustin Hoffman are a perfectly matched odd couple adrift on the sea of amorality in a warped buddy picture cleverly walking a fine line between warmth and cruelty. Contains brief nudity. 🖵 *DVD*

Dustin Hoffman *Ratso Rizzo* • Jon Voight *Joe Buck* • Sylvia Miles *Cass* • Brenda Vaccaro *Shirley* • John McGiver *Mr O'Daniel* • Barnard Hughes *Towny* • Ruth White *Sally Buck* • Jennifer Salt *Annie* • Gil Rankin *Woodsy Niles* ■ *Dir* John Schlesinger • *Scr* Waldo Salt, from the novel by James Leo Herlihy • *Music* John Barry

Midnight Crossing ★★ 🔞
Thriller 1988 · US · Colour · 92mins

It doesn't seem that long ago that Faye Dunaway was giving impressive performances in such classics as *Bonnie and Clyde*, *Chinatown* and *Network*. But *Midnight Crossing* shows that even the most illustrious career can suffer a nose dive. *Hill Street Blues's* Daniel J Travanti takes blind wife Dunaway on a Caribbean holiday; unbeknown to her, though, he's actually there to recover some stolen money. The plot gets seriously twisted as everyone starts crossing and double-crossing each other, but the script and the performances don't generate much interest. 🖵

Faye Dunaway *Helen Barton* • Daniel J Travanti *Morely Barton* • Kim Cattrall *Alexa Schubb* • Ned Beatty *Ellis* • John Laughlin *Jeffrey Schubb* • Pedro De Pool *Capt Mendoza* • Doug Weiser *Miller* ■ *Dir* Roger Holzberg • *Scr* Roger Holzberg, Doug Weiser, from a story by Roger Holzberg

Midnight Dancers ★★★ 🔞
Drama 1994 · Phil · Colour · 122mins

Directed in almost documentary style by Mel Chionglo, this is an uncompromising insight into the risks and realities faced by the "macho dancers" of Manila. Ricky Lee's script focuses on three brothers forced on to the street in order to survive. Although the emphasis is firmly on the youngest and his transvestite lover as they cruise the city's clubs and bars, the attention regularly switches to the eldest, as he juggles his wife and gay lover, and to the middle boy, who lives for the danger of street hustling. Revealing, provocative and often deeply disturbing. In English and Tagalog with subtitles. 🖵

Axel Del Rosario • Grandong Cervantes • Lawrence David • Luis Cortez ■ *Dir* Mel Chionglo • *Scr* Ricky Lee

Midnight Express ★★★★★ 🔞
Biographical drama
1978 · UK/US · Colour · 115mins

It's hard to counter some of the criticisms about the sympathetic depiction of drug traffickers, the pitiless violence, the stereotypical representation of the Turkish jailers and the over-simplistic approach to the key issues raised that greeted this film on its release. Yet it is still a superbly staged drama, which exploits its excesses to force the viewer into considering the broader moral and humanitarian themes, as well as the harrowing events on the screen. Scripted by Oliver Stone from the memoirs of Billy Hayes, it is directed with power and intelligence by Alan Parker, while Brad Davis is outstanding in the lead. 🖵 *DVD*

Brad Davis *Billy Hayes* • Randy Quaid *Jimmy Booth* • John Hurt *Max* • Irene Miracle *Susan* • Bo Hopkins *Tex* • Paolo Bonacelli *Rifki* • Paul Smith *Hamidou* • Norbert Weisser *Erich* ■ *Dir* Alan Parker • *Scr* Oliver Stone, from the non-fiction book by Billy Hayes, William Hoffer

Midnight Fear ★★ 🔞
Thriller 1990 · US · Colour · 89mins

This is a clumsy thriller from director Bill Crain, highlighted by the fact that it ruins the plot with a red herring so inept that it's almost laughable. David Carradine, who has a fine track record playing tough guys, is a saving grace as the booze-loving sheriff trying to solve the mystery of a grim murder. Even though we have no idea what led the sheriff to the bottle, Carradine gives a believable performance. 🖵

Craig Wasson *Paul Prexton* • David Carradine *Sheriff Steve Hanley* • August West *Jenny* • Page Fletcher *John* • Evan Richards *David* ■ *Dir* Bill Crain • *Scr* Bill Crain, Craig Hughes, Craig Wasson

Midnight Heat ★★
Detective drama 1994 · US · Colour

American football provides the backdrop for this TV-movie mystery, but the result is a strictly pedestrian affair. A football star becomes the prime suspect when his team's boss is murdered; just to compound his misery, the detective investigating the case turns out to be an old school rival. Mimi Craven smoulders as the female interest, but despite sterling work by the performers, the plotting and direction offer no surprises. Contains swearing and sex scenes.

Tim Matheson *Tyler Grey* • Stephen Mendel *Travis Handy* • Mimi Craven *Allison Miller* • Kathrin Nicholson *Vivian Grey* • David Fredricks *Coleman Miller* • Garvin Cross *Carl Wurtly* • Paul Jarrett *Mel* ■ *Dir* Harvey Frost • *Scr* Meredith Preston

Midnight in St Petersburg ★★ 🔞
Thriller 1995 · UK/Can/Rus · Colour · 85mins

Harry Palmer really should have stayed in retirement, but Michael Caine was persuaded to resurrect the bespectacled spy character that made his name back in the sixties for two new adventures, shot back-to-back on location in Russia. However, his heart doesn't really seem in it and the result is the worst sort of Europudding. This is the second of the two films (following *Bullet to Beijing*), with Harry running a security firm in Moscow. When the ballerina girlfriend of one of his employees (Jason Connery) is kidnapped in St Petersburg, Harry finds himself drawn into a conspiracy involving art fraud and the theft of a large quantity of plutonium. 🖵

Michael Caine *Harry Palmer* • Jason Connery *Nick* • Michael Sarrazin *Craig* • Michael Gambon *Alex Alexovich* • Michelle Rene

Thomas [Michelle Burke] *Brandy* • Tanya Jackson *Tatiana* • Yuri Limonty *Circus clown* • Michael Scherer *Mafioso* ■ *Dir* Doug Jackson • *Scr* Peter Welbeck [Harry Alan Towers], from the novel by Len Deighton

Midnight in the Garden of Good and Evil ★★★★ 15

Crime drama 1997 · US · Colour · 148mins

John Berendt's bestseller was an audacious blend of travel journalism and true-life crime that gave a tremendous boost to the tourist industry of Savannah, Georgia. Clint Eastwood's long and leisurely adaptation seems so seduced by the town's sultry, seedy atmosphere – those overstuffed mansions and steamy streets with oak trees draped with Spanish Moss – that the plot sometimes seems incidental. John Cusack is the naive New York journalist who stumbles into Savannah's sinister underbelly, meeting Kevin Spacey's wealthy antique's dealer and getting lost in a demimonde of soirées, rent boys and murder. Underrated by most critics, this grows in stature and lingers long in the memory. Contains some swearing and violence. [video] DVD

Kevin Spacey *Jim Williams* • John Cusack *John Kelso* • Jack Thompson *Sonny Seiler* • Irma P Hall *Minerva* • Jude Law *Billy Hanson* • Alison Eastwood *Mandy Nichols* • Paul Hipp *Joe Odom* • The Lady Chablis [Frank "Chablis" Devau] *Chablis Deveau* ■ *Dir* Clint Eastwood • *Scr* John Lee Hancock, from the novel by John Berendt

Midnight Lace ★★

Psychological thriller
1960 · US · Colour · 107mins

With Doris Day and Rex Harrison, one expects a comedy. But this is a thriller in which Day, married to businessman Harrison, is stalked, receives abusive phone calls and is nearly pushed under a bus. The police think she's fibbing; Harrison claims she losing her marbles. What on earth is going on? Well, it's not too hard to figure out. Set in London and filmed entirely in Hollywood, the supporting cast of such veterans as Myrna Loy and Herbert Marshall, plus the inimitable John Williams as the man from Scotland Yard, are distinct bonuses.

Doris Day *Kit Preston* • Rex Harrison *Tony Preston* • John Gavin *Brian Younger* • Myrna Loy *Aunt Bea* • Roddy McDowall *Malcolm* • Herbert Marshall *Charles Manning* • Natasha Parry *Peggy Thompson* • John Williams *Inspector Byrnes* • Hermione Baddeley *Dora* ■ *Dir* David Miller • *Scr* Ivan Goff, Ben Roberts, from the play *Matilda Shouted Fire* by Janet Green • *Costume Designer* Irene

The Midnight Man ★★

Mystery 1974 · US · Colour · 118mins

Burt Lancaster stars as a former cop, jailed for the murder of his wife's lover, who investigates another murder on the university campus where he now works as a janitor. Set in South Carolina, this is never more than a routine murder mystery; Lancaster later admitted he made it as a favour to his longtime buddy and partner, Roland Kibbee, who badly needed the money and got a co-writer and co-director credit. Susan Clark, who appeared alongside Burt in the earlier *Valdez Is Coming*, plays Lancaster's parole officer and romantic interest.

Burt Lancaster *Jim Slade* • Susan Clark *Linda* • Cameron Mitchell *Quartz* • Morgan Woodward *Clayborn* • Harris Yulin *Sheriff Casey* • Joan Lorring *Judy* ■ *Dir* Roland Kibbee, Burt Lancaster • *Scr* Roland Kibbee, Burt Lancaster, from the novel *The Midnight Lady and the Mourning Man* by David Anthony

Midnight Man ★★★ 18

Action thriller 1998 · US · Colour · 87mins

A middling action romp, based on a Jack Higgins bestseller, this is as watchable as Higgins's books are readable. Rob Lowe is curiously cast as a former terrorist brought in by the British government to help foil a planned attack on the Royal Family. While the action scenes are good, the bits in between drag a little. The mostly British cast includes Kenneth Cranham and Deborah Moore, daughter of Roger. [video]

Rob Lowe *Sean Dillon* • Kenneth Cranham *Brigadier Charles Ferguson* • Deborah Moore *Hannah Bernstein* • Daphne Cheung *Su Yin* • Hannes Jaenicke *John Engel* • Michael Sarrazin *Mr Tayi* ■ *Dir* Lawrence Gordon-Clark • *Scr* Jurgen Wolff, from the novel *Eye of the Storm* by Jack Higgins

Midnight Movie Massacre ★

Science-fiction comedy horror
1987 · US · Colour · 86mins

An alien monster closes in on a movie theatre packed with fifties teens watching a sci-fi double bill, in this cobbled-together mess of lame nostalgia, nerd humour, real trailers and bad re-creations of black-and-white serials that use unreleased footage from shelved projects. The idea of hack producer Wade Williams, who shoehorns his uncompleted production of *Space Patrol* (starring Ann Robinson of *The War of the Worlds*) into director Mark Stock's *Animal House*-style antics, the result is a gory but completely nonsensical farrago.

Ann Robinson *Dr Van Buren* • Robert Clarke *Colonel Carlyle* ■ *Dir/Scr* Mark Stock

Midnight Run ★★★★ 18

Comedy thriller 1988 · US · Colour · 120mins

An action picture with a twist: Robert De Niro played it for laughs and, as a result, had his first hit in years. Made by the director of the original *Beverly Hills Cop*, Martin Brest, it's a variant on the odd-couple theme, as De Niro's bounty hunter goes on the run with an accountant who has embezzled $15 million from the Mob. The accountant is Charles Grodin, whose underplaying is an absolute joy: he looks like a puppy that's lost its poop tray. As with all the best road movies – and this is one of the best – the picture really moves, as a simple air trip from New York to LA turns into a saga of trains and automobiles, car crashes and skirmishes with the FBI and a dozen other interested parties. Contains swearing and violence. [video] DVD

Robert De Niro *Jack Walsh* • Charles Grodin *Jonathan Mardukas* • Yaphet Kotto *Alonzo Mosely* • John Ashton *Marvin Dorfler* • Dennis Farina *Jimmy Serrano* • Joe Pantoliano *Eddie Moscone* • Richard Foronjy *Tony Darvo* ■ *Dir* Martin Brest • *Scr* George Gallo

Midnight Sting ★★★ 15

Sports drama 1992 · US · Colour · 93mins

This sparky comedy drama – also known as *Diggstown* – packs such a punch, that it's hard to believe it sank without trace on its British cinema release. Adapted from Leonard Wise's novel, this boxing variation on *The Sting* bristles with sassy dialogue, dynamic fight sequences and truly dastardly villainy (provided by the ever-hissable Bruce Dern). As the cons who hope to clean up with a boxing scam in a small rural backwater, James Woods, Louis Gossett Jr and Oliver Platt are bang on form, but director Michael Ritchie lets the side down by wasting time on a tiresome romantic interlude and a sentimental subplot. [video]

James Woods *Gabriel Caine* • Louis Gossett Jr *"Honey" Roy Palmer* • Bruce Dern *John Gillon* • Oliver Platt *Fitz* • Heather Graham *Emily Forrester* • Randall "Tex" Cobb *Wolf Forrester* • Thomas Wilson Brown *Robby Gillon* • Duane Davis *Hambone Busby* ■ *Dir* Michael Ritchie • *Scr* Steven McKay, from the novel *The Diggstown Ringers* by Leonard Wise

The Midnight Story ★★★

Crime mystery 1957 · US · BW · 90mins

Traffic cop Tony Curtis is refused a transfer to homicide, so he resigns from the force in order to investigate the murder of his best friend, the Catholic priest who raised him as an orphan. Curtis's main quarry is restaurateur Gilbert Roland, who invites him to lodge at his house. Set in the Italian community of San Francisco, it's as much about Curtis's need for a family, a faith and a sense of belonging as it is a whodunit. Unpretentious, compelling and with a neat twist at the end, the movie gives Curtis an excellent dramatic role.

Tony Curtis *Joe Martini* • Marisa Pavan *Anna Malatesta* • Gilbert Roland *Sylvio Malatesta* • Jay C Flippen *Sergeant Jack Gillen* • Argentina Brunetti *Mama Malatesta* • Ted De Corsia *Lieutenant Kilrain* ■ *Dir* Joseph Pevney • *Scr* John Robinson, Edwin Blum, from a story by Edwin Blum

Midnight Tease ★ 18

Erotic thriller 1994 · US · Colour · 77mins

If you like your sex with plenty of violence, then *Midnight Tease* will be right up your street. Squeezed between sequences of exotic dancers plying their trade are some bits of dialogue that might lead you to believe there's a murderer on the loose who's going around killing strippers. One of their number has dreams about the murders and becomes the prime suspect. Yet she still finds time to sleep with her therapist, who is treating her for emotional problems linked to child abuse. You won't have much trouble guessing the "twist" ending. [video]

Cassandra Leigh [Lisa Boyle] *Samantha* • Rachel Reed *Amy* • Edmund Halley *Dr Saul* • Ashlie Rhey *Mantra* • Todd Joseph *J J* • Bob McFarland *Sergeant Gates* ■ *Dir* Scott Levy • *Scr* Daniella Purcell

Midnight Witness ★★ 18

Action thriller 1993 · US · Colour · 86mins

Don't be fooled by the title and the early shower scene: *Midnight Witness* isn't an erotic thriller. It's actually an "innocent people on the run from corrupt authorities" movie. Paul Johansson, a feckless artist, witnesses and videotapes Los Angeles police officers beating a suspect to death. Unfortunately for Johansson, the cops spot him and proceed to frame him and his girlfriend, Karen Moncrieff, for the murder, making it look like a drug deal gone bad. Jan-Michael Vincent plays a murderous psychopath the couple just happen to hitch a ride with on their quest to prove their innocence. [video]

Paul Johansson *Paul Harrison* • Karen Moncrieff *Katy* • Maxwell Caulfield *Garland* • Jan-Michael Vincent *Lance* • Mark Pellegrino *Patterson* ■ *Dir/Scr* Peter Foldy

Midnight's Child ★★ 15

Chiller 1992 · US · Colour · 85mins

Want to know what happened to Victoria Principal post-*Dallas*? She formed a production company that churned out derivative tosh like this schlocky blend of *Rosemary's Baby* and *The Hand That Rocks the Cradle*. Olivia D'Abo is the satanic "nanny from hell", who picks an LA couple's daughter to be the Devil's next bride. She even has a red crystal pendant that gives her mind-control powers in this hopelessly old-fashioned chiller, with surprises that even Pam Ewing could have figured out. [video]

Marcy Walker *Kate Cowan* • Cotter Smith *Nick Cowan* • Olivia D'Abo *Anna* • Pierrette Grace *Christina* • Jeff Nowinski *Bob* • Jake Jacobs *Medical examiner* ■ *Dir* Colin Bucksey • *Scr* David Chaskin, from a story by David N Gottlieb, Jeff Myrow, David Chaskin

A Midsummer Night's Dream ★★★★ U

Romantic comedy 1935 · US · BW · 139mins

One of the pottiest movies ever made in Hollywood – a loose rendition of Shakespeare's play, set amid lavish and fantastical woodland sets and with some extraordinary performances from James Cagney as Bottom, Olivia de Havilland as Hermia, Dick Powell as Lysander and Mickey Rooney as Puck. Rooney broke his leg during production and was moved around the set on a bicycle. Warner Bros gave theatre maestro Max Reinhardt carte blanche to create a masterwork and, when he set too slow a pace and got into a muddle, decided to give him a co-director, studio hack William Dieterle. From the mess came two Oscars, the debut of a movie composer Erich Wolfgang Korngold, and a breathtaking, if kitsch classic.

James Cagney *Bottom* • Dick Powell *Lysander* • Mickey Rooney *Puck* • Joe E Brown *Flute* • Jean Muir *Helena* • Hugh Herbert *Snout* • Ian Hunter *Theseus* • Frank McHugh *Quince* • Victor Jory *Oberon* • Anita Louise *Titania* • Olivia de Havilland *Hermia* • Ross Alexander *Demetrius* ■ *Dir* Max Reinhardt, William Dieterle • *Scr* Charles Kenyon, Mary McCall Jr, from the play by William Shakespeare • *Cinematographer* Hal Mohr, Ernest Haller • *Art Director* Anton Grot

A Midsummer Night's Dream ★★★★

Animated romantic comedy
1961 · Cz · Colour · 76mins

Three years in the making, Jiri Trnka's masterpiece seeks to dispense with the Shakespearean text and tell the still-enchanting story by means of pantomimic puppetry and dance. Trnka and his co-animator, Bretislav Pojar, lavished considerable care on both the costumes and the forest settings. For all the richness of the visual detail, though, there was still room for the simple exhilaration created by Puck and the mechanicals. The balletic quality of the action left international audiences confused, however, and a voiceover quoting from and commenting on the Bard's play was added against Trnka's wishes.

Richard Burton *Narrator* • Tom Criddle *Lysander* • Ann Bell *Hermia* • Michael Meacham *Demetrius* • John Warner *Egeus* • Barbara Leigh-Hunt *Helena* • Hugh Manning *Theseus* • Joss Ackland *Quince* • Alec McCowen *Bottom* • Stephen Moore *Flute* • Barbara Jefford *Titania* • Jack Gwillim *Oberon* ■ *Dir* Jiri Trnka, Howard Sackler • *Scr* Jiri Trnka, Jiri Brdecka, Howard Sackler, from the play by William Shakespeare

A Midsummer Night's Dream ★★ 🆄

Romantic comedy
1969 · UK · Colour · 119mins

Sir Peter Hall's early attempt at translating this Shakespearean classic from stage to screen is too close to the original RSC production to achieve a new lease of life on film. Diana Rigg, Helen Mirren, Judi Dench and Ian Richardson star in this tale of four lovers and a "rude mechanical", lost in the forest and at the mercy of mischievous fairies. Hall, an opera and theatre veteran, betrays his lack of film experience by making some very strange editing and sound choices.

Derek Godfrey *Theseus* • Barbara Jefford *Hippolyta* • Hugh Sullivan *Philostrate* • Nicholas Selby *Egeus* • David Warner *Lysander* • Michael Jayston *Demetrius* • Diana Rigg *Helena* • Helen Mirren *Hermia* • Ian Richardson *Oberon* • Judi Dench *Titania* • Ian Holm *Puck* ■ *Dir* Peter Hall • *Scr* from the play by William Shakespeare

A Midsummer Night's Dream ★★ 🅿🅶

Romantic comedy
1996 · UK · Colour · 99mins

The great tragedy of this screen version of director Adrian Noble's Royal Shakespeare Company production is that, on stage, it would be absolutely electrifying. The hanging lightbulbs that comprise the Athenian forest, the stylised costumes and the glittery make-up help convey some of the play's magic. But the fairies in glowing wigs and the tacky conceit of having the whole thing dreamed by a Christopher Robin-like boy are ghastly misjudgements. The leaden camera movements are matched only by the clumsiness of the editing, while none of the cast takes the trouble to rein in their stage grandiloquence. 🖵

Lindsay Duncan *Hippolyta/Titania* • Alex Jennings *Theseus/Oberon* • Desmond Barrit *Nick Bottom* • Barry Lynch *Puck/Philostrate* • Monica Dolan *Hermia* • Kevin Doyle *Demetrius* • Daniel Evans *Lysander* • Emily Raymond *Helena* ■ *Dir* Adrian Noble • *Scr* Adrian Noble, from the play by William Shakespeare

A Midsummer Night's Sex Comedy ★★★★ 🆕

Comedy   1982 · US · Colour · 84mins

Woody Allen pays homage to Ingmar Bergman in this re-vamp of *Smiles of a Summer Night*, in which six characters gather at a turn-of-the-century farmhouse in search of sexual satisfaction. José Ferrer is the pedantic scholar engaged to Mia Farrow; Allen is the stockbroker trying to bed his frigid wife, Mary Steenburgen. The jokes come thin and slow for a Woody movie, with the result that Allen's oddball inventions (which include a flying bicycle) are at least as interesting as the oddball people. Gordon Willis's photography is exquisite, however, and one suspects Bergman would not be displeased. 🖵

Woody Allen *Andrew* • Mia Farrow *Ariel* • José Ferrer *Leopold* • Julie Hagerty *Dulcy* • Tony Roberts *Maxwell* • Mary Steenburgen *Adrian* • Michael Higgins *Reynolds* • Adam Redfield *Student Foxx* ■ *Dir/Scr* Woody Allen

Midwest Obsession ★★ 🆕

Thriller   1995 · US · Colour · 91mins

A tame, but watchable variation on the *Fatal Attraction* theme and supposedly based on a real-life story. *Ally McBeal* regular Courtney Thorne-Smith is the beauty queen who reveals a distinctly sinister side when she attempts to wrest Kyle Secor, probably best known as one of the stars of the under-rated TV series *Homicide: Life on the Street*, from his longtime girlfriend (Tracey Gold). The protagonists are bland, but director William A Graham (billed here as Billy) wrings a fair amount of suspense from the familiar story. Contains violence and swearing. 🖵

Courtney Thorne-Smith *Cheryl Davis* • Kyle Secor *Kevin Reese* • Tracey Gold *Beth McKinnis* ■ *Dir* Billy Graham [William A Graham] • *Scr* Duane Poole

Mifune ★★★ 🆕

Romantic comedy drama
1999 · Swe/Den · Colour · 101mins

Less abrasive than earlier Dogma outings, this surprisingly traditional comedy is similar in storyline and tone to the 1998 Dutch film *The Polish Bride*. Spurning the shock tactics and hand-held camera style of *Festen* and *The Idiots*, director Søren Kragh-Jacobsen uses the beautiful Lolland light to bring a pleasing rusticity to the piece. The tale centres on the romance between prostitute Iben Hjejle and Anders W Berthelsen, a newly married yuppie who hides his country origins in much the same way that Toshiro Mifune's character did in *Seven Samurai*. A predictable but rather pleasing little film. In Danish with English subtitles. Contains swearing and sexual references.

Anders W Berthelsen *Kresten* • Jesper Asholt *Rud* • Iben Hjejle *Liva Psilander* • Sofie Gråbøl *Claire* • Emil Tarding *Bjarke Psilander* ■ *Dir* Søren Kragh-Jacobsen • *Scr* Søren Kragh-Jacobsen, Anders Thomas Jensen

The Mighty ★★★★ 🅿🅶

Fantasy drama   1998 · US · Colour · 96mins

Get the tissues ready for this moving, wonderfully-played tale of childhood and the heroism inside all of us.

Lumbering outcast Elden Henson doesn't fit in with the other kids in school, but he finally finds a friend when Kieran Culkin is instructed to tutor him. Culkin is a disabled hunchback, but he is also a lover of stories who introduces Henson to an imaginary life outside their own depressing existence. Both boys are superb, and they are ably supported by a cast which includes Sharon Stone, Gena Rowlands, Gillian Anderson and Harry Dean Stanton. 🖵

Sharon Stone *Gwen Dillon* • Harry Dean Stanton *Grim* • Gena Rowlands *Gram* • Kieran Culkin *Kevin Dillon* • Gillian Anderson *Loretta Lee* • Elden Henson *Maxwell Kane* • Meat Loaf Aday [Meat Loaf] *Iggy* ■ *Dir* Peter Chelsom • *Scr* Charles Leavitt, from the novel *Freak the Mighty* by Rodman Philbrick

Mighty Aphrodite ★★★ 🆕

Comedy   1995 · US · Colour · 90mins

It's all Greek (myth) to Woody Allen in this story of a sportswriter (Allen) who, with his gallery-owner wife (Helena Bonham Carter), adopts a baby boy. When Allen decides to seek out the boy's birth mother, he finds she's a hooker (the Oscar-winning Mira Sorvino) and becomes entangled in a web of convoluted plot twists that not even an occasional and rather boring Greek chorus can explain. Too self-conscious, the never-ending radio-play dialogue needs gagging rather than more gags. 🖵

Woody Allen *Lenny* • Helena Bonham Carter *Amanda* • Mira Sorvino *Linda* • F Murray Abraham *Chorus leader* • Claire Bloom *Amanda's mother* • Olympia Dukakis *Jocasta* • Michael Rapaport *Kevin* • David Ogden Stiers *Laius* ■ *Dir/Scr* Woody Allen

The Mighty Barnum ★★★

Biographical drama   1934 · US · BW · 87mins

Before Michael Crawford and Jim Dale did in the theatre what Barnum would have called "standing room only business", Wallace Beery made Phineas T Barnum his own, in this breezy 20th Century-Fox biography of the self-styled greatest showman of them all. Beery seemed born to espouse Barnum's phrases and philosophy, such as "There's one born every minute", and if the plot errs a little on the fanciful side, that would have been just dandy for old Phineas. Adolphe Menjou makes an unlikely reluctant partner, hardly ideal casting for one of the two faces conjured up by advertisements for Barnum and Bailey's immortal three-ring circus. In women, though, headed by Virginia Bruce as the "Swedish Nightingale" Jenny Lind, are lovely.

Wallace Beery *Phineas T Barnum* • Adolphe Menjou *Mr Bailey Walsh* • Virginia Bruce *Jenny Lind* • Rochelle Hudson *Ellen* • Janet Beecher *Nancy Barnum* • Tammany Young *Todd* • Lucille La Verne *Joyce Heth* • George Brasno *General Tom Thumb* ■ *Dir* Walter Lang • *Scr* Gene Fowler, Bess Meredyth

The Mighty Ducks ★★ 🅿🅶

Sports comedy   1992 · US · Colour · 99mins

As a disgraced lawyer coaching the world's worst ice-hockey team as part of his community service, former Brat Packer Emilio Estevez makes the best of what, at the ice apart, could hardly be

called a cool assignment. This is *The Bad News Bears* with skates on, and you know from the first face-off how it's going to end. But director Stephen Herek pitches every gag and moment of melodrama at just the right level. Released here as *Champions*, this film inspired Disney to form its own pro-league club, called, not surprisingly, the Mighty Ducks. 🖵 *DVD*

Emilio Estevez *Gordon Bombay* • Joss Ackland *Hans* • Lane Smith *Coach Reilly* • Heidi Kling *Casey* • Josef Sommer *Gerald Ducksworth* • Joshua Jackson *Charlie Conroy* • Elden Ratliff *Fulton Reed* • Shaun Weiss *Goldberg* ■ *Dir* Stephen Herek • *Scr* Steven Brill

Mighty Joe Young ★★★★ 🆄

Fantasy adventure   1949 · US · BW · 93mins

As an emasculated *King Kong*, this variation on the monster theme is, nevertheless, entertaining enough. Terry Moore is persuaded to bring her enormous pet gorilla from Africa to America to become part of a nightclub act which includes, in superlatively kitsch style, her playing *Beautiful Dreamer* while being held aloft by the gorilla. Directed by Ernest B Schoedsack, who co-directed *King Kong*, with special effects by *King Kong* originator Willis O'Brien and, among others, Ray Harryhausen, it's excruciatingly schmaltzy but keeps its innocence intact.

Terry Moore *Jill Young* • Robert Armstrong *Max O'Hara* • Ben Johnson *Gregg Ford* • Frank McHugh *Press agent* • Douglas Fowley *Jones* ■ *Dir* Ernest B Schoedsack • *Scr* Ruth Rose, from a story by Merian C Cooper

Mighty Joe Young ★★★ 🅿🅶

Fantasy adventure
1998 · US · Colour · 109mins

This entertaining remake of the 1949 family drama has beautiful Charlize Theron as the woman who befriends a colossal, but cute, gorilla hidden in the deepest jungle. Of course, Joe doesn't remain concealed for long after explorer Bill Paxton discovers him, and he's soon pursued by nasty hunters who want to capture him for some rich collector's amusement. It's a fun romp with some impressive ape effects and luscious scenery, though really young viewers may be slightly disturbed by the later scenes that show the cuddly King Kong under attack from the bad guys. 🖵 *DVD*

Charlize Theron *Jill Young* • Bill Paxton *Gregg O'Hara* • Rade Serbedzija *Strasser* • Peter Firth *Garth* • David Paymer *Harry Ruben* • Regina King *Cecily Banks* • Robert Wisdom *Kweli* • Naveen Andrews *Pindi* ■ *Dir* Ron Underwood • *Scr* Mark Rosenthal, Lawrence Konner, from the 1949 film

Mighty Morphin Power Rangers: the Movie ★★★ 🅿🅶

Science-fiction adventure
1995 · US · Colour · 91mins

Remember them? A few years ago these superheroes in vinyl tights were the hottest thing around. Now the tie-in toys are about as fashionable as Cabbage Patch dolls. Here the Power Rangers battle their old enemy Rita Repulsa, fight off slime creatures and squash the world domination plans of evil Ivan Ooze. If your children are feeling nostalgic, then this colourful

junk will while away a couple of very mindless hours. Go, go, Power Rangers. And they did!

Karan Ashley *Aisha/Yellow Ranger* • Johnny Yong Bosch *Adam/Black Ranger* • Stephen Antonio Cardenas *Rocky/Red Ranger* • Jason David Frank *Tommy/White Ranger* • Amy Jo Johnson *Kimberly/Pink Ranger* • David Harold Yost *Billy/Blue Ranger* • Paul Schrier *Bulk* • Paul Freeman *Ivan Ooze* • Julia Cortez *Rita Repulsa* ■ *Dir* Bryan Spicer • *Scr* Arne Olsen, from a story by John Kamps, Arne Olsen

The Mighty Quinn ★★★ 15

Detective drama 1989 · US · Colour · 94mins

Denzel Washington hasn't made many wrong moves in his movie career, but he nearly came a cropper with this lightweight Caribbean thriller. He is his usual charismatic self as the determined police chief on a small former colony who gets mixed up in murder and political corruption, and there is a solid enough supporting cast – James Fox, Robert Townsend, Mimi Rogers and Art Evans. But director Carl Schenkel seems to have been seduced by the beautiful locations and laid-back lifestyle, as there is little in the way of suspense. Contains swearing.

Denzel Washington *Xavier Quinn* • James Fox *Elgin* • Mimi Rogers *Hadley* • Robert Townsend *Maubee* • M Emmet Walsh *Miller* • Sheryl Lee Ralph *Lola* • Art Evans *Jump* • Esther Rolle *Ubu Pearl* ■ *Dir* Carl Schenkel • *Scr* Hampton Fancher, from the novel *Finding Maubee* by AHZ Carr

Mignon Has Left ★★★ 12

Drama 1988 · It/Fr · Colour · 98mins

Italian director Francesca Archibugi made a considerable impact with this, her debut feature. Ostensibly a tale of two cities, the story focuses on Mignon (Céline Beauvallet) a chic Parisian teen who is sent to stay with working-class relatives in Rome when her father is jailed. Mignon's abrupt awakening and her bashful cousin's achingly true-to-life crush are delicately handled, but it's the upward struggle of her put-upon aunt (the excellent Stefania Sandrelli) that gives this drama its poignancy and credibility. In Italian with English subtitles.

Stefania Sandrelli *Mama* • Jean-Pierre Duriez *Federico* • Leonardo Ruta *Giorgio* • Céline Beauvallet *Mignon* • Francesca Antonelli *Chiara* • Lorenzo De Pasqua *Cacio* • Eleonora Sambiagio *Antonella* • Daniele Zaccaria *Tommaso* ■ *Dir* Francesca Archibugi • *Scr* Francesca Archibugi, Gloria Malatesta, Claudia Sbarigia

The Mikado ★★★

Operetta 1939 · UK · Colour · 93mins

A lavish, British production of the famed Gilbert and Sullivan Savoy operetta, faithfully directed by imported American Victor Schertzinger, a composer himself and best known for a pair of Bing Crosby/Bob Hope *Road* movies. Also imported from the States was chubby-faced radio crooner Kenny Baker to star as Nanki-Poo, and he seems decidedly ill-at-ease among the D'Oyly Carte players, notably Martyn Green as Ko-Ko and Sydney Granville as Pooh-Bah, playing as if born to their roles. The marvellous use of early Technicolor makes this rather dull adaptation very watchable today, and the score is remarkably, and unusually,

complete, and superbly played by the now-defunct Royal Symphony Orchestra.

Kenny Baker (2) *Nanki-Poo* • Martyn Green *Ko-Ko* • Sydney Granville *Pooh-Bah* • John Barclay *The Mikado* • Gregory Stroud *Pish-Tush* • Jean Collin *Yum-Yum* • Constance Willis *Katisha* • Elizabeth Paynter *Pitti-Sing* ■ *Dir* Victor Schertzinger • *Scr* Geoffrey Toye, from the operetta by WS Gilbert, Arthur Sullivan • *Cinematographer* William Skall [William V Skall], Bernard Knowles

Mike's Murder ★★ 18

Thriller 1984 · US · Colour · 104mins

Long-delayed and barely released, this murky thriller reunites Debra Winger with her *Urban Cowboy* director, James Bridges. Nothing Winger does or says (isn't that the throatiest voice this side of June Allyson?) is without interest, but sometimes her choice of material leaves a lot to be desired. Here she's sleuthing over a drug deal that went wrong – though not half as wrong as the movie itself, which spent a couple of years being edited, restructured, cut again and then finally dubbed in England. Legend has it Bridges asked for some odd sound effects: listen hard to those car doors closing and you'll hear gunshots. Still, there's a clever cameo from Paul Winfield as a blasé record producer, while Joe Jackson provides sterling support on the soundtrack. Contains swearing.

Debra Winger *Betty Parrish* • Mark Keyloun *Mike* • Paul Winfield *Phillip* • Darrell Larson *Pete* • Brooke Alderson *Patty* • Robert Crosson *Sam* ■ *Dir/Scr* James Bridges

Mikey and Nicky ★★ 15

Drama 1976 · US · Colour · 101mins

Some people make such idiosyncratic movies, it's impossible to imagine how the films would turn out in other hands. Elaine May is one of those people. Perhaps most infamous for huge money-loser *Ishtar*, she is also the director of a handful of odd comedies that are virtually two-handers. This one is a gangland tale of cross and double-cross. Nicky (John Cassavetes) is a holed-up and scared gangster, Mikey (Peter Falk) is his supposed friend who may or may not be setting him up for a hit. An uncomfortable, often painfully funny film is wrought from this premise.

Peter Falk *Mikey* • John Cassavetes *Nicky* • Ned Beatty *Kinney* • Rose Arrick *Annie* • Carol Grace *Nell* • William Hickey *Sid Fine* • Sanford Meisner *Dave Resnick* • M Emmet Walsh *Bus driver* ■ *Dir/Scr* Elaine May

The Milagro Beanfield War ★★★★ 15

Drama 1988 · US · Colour · 112mins

With *Quiz Show* and *Ordinary People*, former heart-throb Robert Redford revealed himself to be one of America's finest directors of actors. Here he proves adept at handling a large ensemble cast in this adaptation of John Nichols's whimsical novel about a New Mexican farmer (Chick Vennera), who deflects water from a housing development to start his own beanfield. Watch out for Melanie Griffith, John Heard and Christopher Walken, enjoy Dave Grusin's Oscar-

winning score, and don't be put off by that title. Contains swearing.

Rubén Blades *Sheriff Bernabe Montoya* • Richard Bradford *Ladd Devine* • Sonia Braga *Ruby Archuleta* • Julie Carmen *Nancy Mondragon* • James Gammon *Horsethief Shorty* • Melanie Griffith *Flossie Devine* • John Heard *Charlie Bloom* • Christopher Walken *Kyril Montana* ■ *Dir* Robert Redford • *Scr* David Ward, John Nichols, from the novel by John Nichols

Mildred Pierce ★★★★★ PG

Film noir 1945 · US · BW · 106mins

Although it will forever be known as the movie that relaunched Joan Crawford's flagging career, there is much more to this classic "woman's picture" than an Oscar-winning performance. While it reworks the original plot, Ranald MacDougall's script retains the sharp edge of James M Cain's novel (this is as much *film noir* as soap opera), while Michael Curtiz's cool direction keeps the action moving and Crawford, Ann Blyth and Zachary Scott away from caricature. Ernest Haller's moody photography and Anton Grot's sets (which, at a glance, convey Mildred's changing social status) are also outstanding. Screen suffering was never so sophisticated.

Joan Crawford *Mildred Pierce* • Jack Carson *Wally Fay* • Zachary Scott *Monte Beragon* • Eve Arden *Ida Corwin* • Ann Blyth *Veda Pierce* • Bruce Bennett *Bert Pierce* • Lee Patrick *Mrs Maggie Biederhof* • Moroni Olsen *Inspector Peterson* • Veda Ann Borg *Miriam Ellis* ■ *Dir* Michael Curtiz • *Scr* Ranald MacDougall, from the novel by James M Cain • *Music* Max Steiner

Milena ★★★

Biographical drama 1990 · Can/Fr/W Ger · Colour · 139mins

Those familiar with Valérie Kaprisky solely as Richard Gere's co-star in *Breathless* will be overwhelmed by the way she comports herself in this biography of Milena Jesenka, the communist confidante of Franz Kafka whose outspoken journalism resulted in her incarceration by the Nazis in Ravensbruck concentration camp. For all its evident admiration for its subject, however, Véra Belmont's film spends too much time gazing on the gorgeous costumes and conducting intellectual debates that neither engross nor provoke. The sequences in Vienna, where Milena lived with music critic Ernst Pollack, are particularly decorative, but the later politicised scenes have more passion.

Valérie Kaprisky *Milena Jesenka* • Philip Anglim *Franz Kafka* • Peter Gallagher *Polak* • Gudrun Landgrebe *Olga* • Stacy Keach *Jesenski* • Nick Mancuso *Jaromir* ■ *Dir/Scr* Véra Belmont

Miles from Home ★★★ 15

Drama 1988 · US · Colour · 103mins

Richard Gere, whose career was somewhat in the doldrums at the time, made a stab for credibility with this worthy, if uneven, rural drama. Gere is the farmer whose property is in danger of being seized by the banks, forcing him into increasingly drastic action. Gary Sinise (more familiar as an actor in *Forrest Gump* and *Apollo 13*) directs ably, but it is the playing that really makes the picture; if Gere is not

entirely convincing in the leading role, Kevin Anderson, as his younger brother, is terrific, while the supporting turns from the likes of Laurie Metcalf, John Malkovich and Brian Dennehy more than compensate for the weaknesses in the script. Contains violence, swearing and drug abuse.

Richard Gere *Frank Roberts Jr* • Kevin Anderson *Terry Roberts* • Brian Dennehy *Frank Roberts Sr* • Jason Campbell *Young Frank* • Austin Bamgarner *Young Terry* • Larry Poling *Nikita Khrushchev* • Laurie Metcalf *Ellen* • John Malkovich *Barry Maxwell* ■ *Dir* Gary Sinise • *Scr* Chris Gerolmo

Miles from Nowhere ★★ PG

Drama 1992 · US · Colour · 86mins

Diabetics beware – the sugar content in this melodrama is excessive, even for the made-for-TV movie genre. Rick Schroder plays a top-class student who embraces unconventional methods in a bid to stir his badly injured brother (Shawn Phelan) from a coma; James Farentino is the unforgiving, disapproving father. Director Buzz Kulik is an old hand when it comes to TV – he was responsible for the mini-series remake of *From Here to Eternity* – and he shamelessly milks the material for all its worth.

Rick Schroder *Frank Reilly* • James Farentino *John Reilly* • Marlyn Mason *Barbara Reilly* • Shawn Phelan *Emmett Reilly* • Melora Hardin *Teresa* • Tom Schanley *Bill Reilly* • Kaj-Erik Eriksen *Patrick Reilly* • Johannah Newmarch *Susan Reilly* ■ *Dir* Buzz Kulik • *Scr* Steve McGraw, Janet Ward, Jeff Andrus, from a story by Steve McGraw

Miles to Go ★★★ 15

Drama 1986 · US · Colour · 93mins

Jill Clayburgh was so good in films like *Gable and Lombard* and *An Unmarried Woman* that her place among American cinema's elite seemed assured. But Hollywood has always had problems accommodating intelligent actresses and the roles she deserved simply didn't come her way. She's easily the best thing in this TV movie, playing a dying woman trying to find a replacement wife and mother for her family. Prolific TV-movie director David Greene, who made the screen version of the hit musical *Godspell*, directs with a sensitive touch.

Jill Clayburgh *Moira Browning* • Tom Skerritt *Stuart Browning* • Mimi Kuzyk *Suzanne* • Rosemary Dunsmore *Cynthia* • Cyndy Preston *Jani Browning* • Andrew Bednarski *Brad Browning* • Peter Dvorsky *Dr Michael Kosberg* • Caroline Arnold *Centre woman* ■ *Dir* David Greene • *Scr* Beverly Levitt, Stuart Fischoff, from a story by Beverly Levitt

Military Policeman ★★ U

Comedy 1953 · US · Colour · 90mins

The Bob Hope style of wise-cracking comedy was showing some strain by the time of this effort, and 1953 was the last year in which he figured in the top ten box-office stars. His teaming with the exuberant Mickey Rooney does not always gel, either, but there are sufficient laughs in the Hal Kanter/Jack Sher script to make this a pleasant enough time-passer. Eddie Mayehoff shines as a military policeman who despairs at the ineptitude of Hope, playing a boxer's manager unwittingly stuck with a term in the army. Marilyn Maxwell, Hope's longtime girlfriend, is the leading lady.

Bob Hope *Wally Hogan* • Mickey Rooney *Herbert Tuttle* • Marilyn Maxwell *Connie Curtis* • Eddie Mayehoff *Karl Danzig* • Stanley Clements *Bullet Bradley* • Jack Dempsey • *Dir* George Marshall • *Scr* Hal Kanter, Jack Sher, from a story by Hal Kanter

Milk and Honey ★★
Drama　　　　1988 · Can · Colour · 89mins

Directed by Rebecca Yates and Glen Salzman, this is a didactic and dull attempt to educate the viewer about the immigration of Jamaican nannies to Canada. Josette Simon stars as a woman who leaves her son at home, while seeking opportunity in Toronto. Sadly, she discovers repression and racism which soon make her desperate to return. Shot in a pseudo-documentary style that is deathly and uninspired, this is more cornflour than oatmeal; in other words, very bland.

Josette Simon *Johanna* • Lyman Ward *Adam* • Richard Mills *David* • Djanet Sears *Del* ■ *Dir* Rebecca Yates, Glen Salzman

Milk Money ★★★☒
Romantic comedy
1994 · US · Colour · 104mins

Four years after *Pretty Woman* came *Milk Money*, another implausible "prostitute finds love with a nice man" romantic comedy, this time from *My Stepmother Is an Alien* director, Richard Benjamin. It is more warm-hearted than the successful Julia Roberts film, with Melanie Griffith sexy and down-to-earth as the hooker brought home by a young boy as a prospective wife for his lonely dad (Ed Harris). Both Harris and Griffith give nice, unshowy performances, while Malcolm McDowell is convincingly nasty as the pimp who's after Griffith. Utterly preposterous, but thoroughly enjoyable entertainment. ▭

Melanie Griffith *V* • Ed Harris *Tom Wheeler* • Michael Patrick Carter *Frank Wheeler* • Malcolm McDowell *Waltzer* • Anne Heche *Betty* • Casey Siemaszko *Cash* • Philip Bosco *Jerry the Pope* • Brian Christopher *Kevin Clean* ■ *Dir* Richard Benjamin • *Scr* John Mattson

The Milky Way ★★★★
Sports comedy　　1936 · US · BW · 89mins

Perhaps the last great Harold Lloyd comedy classic (this was later remade as *The Kid from Brooklyn* with Danny Kaye, becoming blandly pasteurised in the process). Lloyd plays a mild-mannered milkman who, mistaken for a potential world boxing champion, gets caught up with a gang of crooked fixers. Adolphe Menjou, Helen Mack and Lionel Stander provide wonderful back-up for his endeavours.

Harold Lloyd *Burleigh "Tiger" Sullivan* • Adolphe Menjou *Gabby Sloan* • Verree Teasdale *Ann Westley* • Helen Mack *Mae Sullivan* • William Gargan *Elwood "Speed" MacFarland* • George Barbier *Wilbur Austin* • Dorothy Wilson *Polly Pringle* • Lionel Stander *Spider Schultz* ■ *Dir* Leo McCarey • *Scr* Grover Jones, Frank Butler, Richard Connell, from a play by Lynn Root, Harry Clork

The Milky Way ★★★★★☒
Drama　　　　1968 · Fr/It · Colour · 97mins

A pilgrim's regress by the great surrealist master Luis Buñuel, which, while being among his most anti-clerical and enigmatic movies, is still marvellously accessible even for those not in tune with Catholic concerns. His two tramps, progressing from Paris to a shrine in Spain, slip through time to encounter the Devil, the Virgin Mary and many zealots. They conclude, on their road to religious ruin, that intolerance is next to godliness. Buñuel, who was always on the side of the heretics, makes his points with sarcastic compassion. In French with English subtitles. ▭

Laurent Terzieff *Jean* • Paul Frankeur *Pierre* • Delphine Seyrig *Prostitute* • Edith Scob *Virgin Mary* • Bernard Verley *Jesus* • Georges Marchal *Jesuit* • Jean Piat *Jansenist* • Pierre Clémenti *The Devil* ■ *Dir* Luis Buñuel • *Scr* Luis Buñuel, Jean-Claude Carrière

The Mill on the Floss ★★
Drama　　　　1937 · UK · BW · 82mins

Director, Tim Whelan was also one of four writers attempting to adapt George Eliot's famous novel about the tragic feud between the Tullivers and the Wakems, and the resulting Victorian period piece is to be recommended for its polished British cast. Geraldine Fitzgerald stars as Maggie Tulliver, in love with Frank Lawton, son of her father's arch-enemy Felix Aylmer, but fatally compromised by Lawton's friend Griffith Jones. James Mason is Tom Tulliver, Fay Compton Mrs Tulliver – and that's all you really need to know.

Geraldine Fitzgerald *Maggie Tulliver* • James Mason *Tom Tulliver* • Felix Aylmer *Mr Wakem* • Frank Lawton *Philip Wakem* • Fay Compton *Mrs Tulliver* • Griffith Jones *Stephen Guest* • Mary Clare *Mrs Moss* • Victoria Hopper *Lucy Deane* ■ *Dir* Tim Whelan • *Scr* Tim Whelan, John Drinkwater, Garnett Weston, Austin Melford, from the novel by George Eliot

Millennium ★★☒
Science-fiction drama
1989 · US · Colour · 101mins

Although based upon an interesting short story called *Air Raid* by John Varley, who also wrote the script, this doesn't have enough meat on it for a feature and it's a struggle to stay watching to the end. Kris Kristofferson is the investigator trying to work out what happened after an air disaster, who discovers that the passengers were whisked off by time traveller Cheryl Ladd before the crash. Her intention? To take the survivors to a disease-ridden planet of the future and save the human race. Unfortunately, a promising premise gets lost among the clichés and B-movie performances. For hardened sci-fi fans only. ▭

Kris Kristofferson *Bill Smith* • Cheryl Ladd *Louise Baltimore* • Daniel J Travanti *Arnold Mayer* • Robert Joy *Sherman* • Lloyd Bochner *Walters* • Brent Carver *Coventry* • David McIlwraith *Tom Stanley* • Maury Chaykin *Roger Keane* ■ *Dir* Michael Anderson • *Scr* John Varley, from the short story *Air Raid* by John Varley

Miller's Crossing ★★★★☒
Crime drama　　1990 · US · Colour · 110mins

The Coen brothers' sublime Prohibition-era gangster saga is a magnificent display of compelling acting, spellbinding storytelling and fine film-making. A dark-hued, richly operatic mood piece, with machine gun-fire dialogue and twisted meaty substance to spare, it focuses on the friendship between politician Albert Finney and Gabriel Byrne, the power behind his throne, and the bloody mob war that erupts when they fall in love with the same woman, Marcia Gay Harden. The title refers to a lonely, leafy glade where somebody's murder will take place. Byrne is simply outstanding as the cool, calculating catalyst around whom the whole vivid spectacle revolves. Contains violence, swearing, sex scenes and nudity. ▭

Gabriel Byrne *Tom Reagan* • Marcia Gay Harden *Verna* • John Turturro *Bernie Bernbaum* • Jon Polito *Johnny Caspar* • JE Freeman *Eddie Dane* • Albert Finney *Leo* • Mike Starr *Frankie* • Al Mancini *Tic-Tac* • Steve Buscemi *Mink* ■ *Dir* Joel Coen • *Scr* Joel Coen, Ethan Coen • *Cinematographer* Barry Sonnenfeld

The Miller's Wife ★
Period comedy　　1955 · It · Colour · 95mins

The governor of Naples (Vittorio De Sica), lusting after the sexy wife (Sophia Loren) of the local miller (Marcello Mastroianni), has the man arrested on a trumped-up charge, then offers the wife her husband's release in return for her favours. A melodramatic plot is the basis for a vulgar and unfunny Neapolitan farce, directed without a trace of inspiration by Mario Camerini, which heaps indignity on two of Italy's most distinguished actors while revealing Loren's limitations as a comedienne. An Italian language film.

Vittorio De Sica *The Governor* • Marcello Mastroianni *Luca, the miller* • Sophia Loren *Carmela* • Paolo Stoppa *Gardunia* ■ *Dir* Mario Camerini • *Scr* Mario Camerini, Ennio De Concini, Augusto Camerini, Alessandro Continenza, Ivo Perilli, from the play by Pedro DeAlacon

Le Million ★★★★
Comedy　　　　1931 · Fr · BW · 85mins

René Lefèvre stars as a poor painter who wins a fortune on the lottery, only to discover that the ticket is in the pocket of an old jacket that's been stolen. His chase across Paris to recover it, which lands him on the stage of the opera house, forms the delightfully funny substance of this famously charming, innovative and influential early sound film from French director René Clair. The lovely Annabella and the fluent camera of future cinematographic ace Georges Périnal contribute to the overall stylishness. A French language film.

Annabella *Beatrice* • René Lefèbvre *Michel* • Paul Olivier "Father Tulipe" *Crochard, a gangster* • Louis Allibert *Prosper* ■ *Dir* René Clair • *Scr* René Clair, from the musical by Georges Berr, M Guillemaud

Million Dollar Baby ★★
Romantic comedy　1941 · US · BW · 100mins

This modest little comedy was one of eight movies in which Warner Bros paired sparky and wholesome Priscilla Lane with handsome Jeffrey Lynn. The plot has Lane inheriting a million dollars from crotchety May Robson, only to arrive at the unrealistic conclusion that money doesn't bring happiness. Along the way she dallies with Ronald Reagan, improbably cast as a concert pianist.

Priscilla Lane *Pamela McAllister* • Jeffrey Lynn *James Amory* • Ronald Reagan *Peter Rowan* • May Robson *Cornelia Wheelwright* • Lee Patrick *Josie LaRue* • Helen Westley *Mrs Galloway* ■ *Dir* Curtis Bernhardt • *Scr* Casey Robinson, Richard Macaulay, Jerry Wald, from the story *Miss Wheelwright Discovers America* by Leonard Spigelgass

The Million Dollar Duck ★★★☒
Comedy　　　　1971 · US · Colour · 92mins

Disney's unofficial remake of the Douglas Fairbanks Jr vehicle, *Mr Drake's Duck*, provides yet another twist on the nutty professor story. Dean Jones is a scientist whose experiments on the behaviour of ducks go haywire when his prize specimen, Charley, dips his beak into some radioactive apple sauce and begins laying golden eggs. From then on, it's the familiar tale of bungling baddies and government agents seeking to snatch the remarkable bird from the prof and his young friends. Most youngsters will probably think it's quackers. ▭

Dean Jones *Professor Albert Dooley* • Sandy Duncan *Katie Dooley* • Joe Flynn *Finley Hooper* • Tony Roberts *Fred Hines* • James Gregory *Rutledge* • Lee Harcourt Montgomery [Lee Montgomery] *Jimmy Dooley* • Jack Kruschen *Dr Gottlieb* ■ *Dir* Vincent McEveety • *Scr* Roswell Rogers, from a story by Ted Key

The Million Dollar Hotel ★☒
Comedy drama
1999 · Ger/US · Colour · 121mins

Director Wim Wenders applies his arty Euro-touch to this tale of an FBI agent investigating a suspicious death at a bizarre, bohemian hotel. Kept simple, it could have worked; unfortunately, Wenders cloaks everything in needless complexity and wilful obscurity. Mel Gibson, whose Icon company produced the film, plays the agent and winds up looking considerably less than a million dollars. Others involved include Milla Jovovich, Jeremy Davies, Amanda Plummer and Julian Sands.

Jeremy Davies *Tom Tom* • Milla Jovovich *Eloise* • Mel Gibson *Skinner* • Jimmy Smits *Geronimo* • Peter Stormare *Dixie* • Amanda Plummer *Vivien* • Bud Cort *Shorty* • Julian Sands *Terence Scopey* • Tim Roth *Izzy Goldkiss* ■ *Dir* Wim Wenders • *Scr* Nicholas Klein, from a story by Bono, Nicholas Klein

Million Dollar Legs ★
Comedy　　　　1932 · US · BW · 64mins

As the President of Klopstokia, a mythical principality that's bankrupt, WC Fields plays very much second fiddle to Jack Oakie in this nonsensical slapstick farce. Oakie is a visiting American brush salesman, who falls in love with the President's daughter and comes up with the money-making scheme of entering Klopstokia in the Los Angeles Olympics. Directed by Edward Cline, it plays like a tenth-rate version of a Marx Brothers excursion into silliness, with pratfalls, non-sequiturs and really terrible gags.

Jack Oakie *Migg Tweeny* • WC Fields *The President of Klopstokia* • Andy Clyde *The Major-domo* • Lyda Roberti *Mata Machree* • Susan Fleming *Angela* ■ *Dir* Edward Cline • *Scr* Henry Myers, Nick Barrows, from a story by Joseph L Mankiewicz

Million Dollar Legs ★★ U

Comedy   1939 · US · BW · 64mins

A lightweight programme-filler about a college student who takes up a collection and bets the money on a horse named Million Dollar Legs, thus raising the cash to buy badly needed equipment for the college rowing team. One of many now forgotten films that the studios made to try out young talent, this is most interesting for a cast that includes future stars Betty Grable, 14-year-old Donald O'Connor and William Holden, in a two-word bit part. Also cast were Larry "Buster" Crabbe, famous as Flash Gordon, and Jackie Coogan, the real-life husband of Grable whose period of stardom had ended with his coming of age.

Betty Grable *Carol Parker* • John Hartley *Greg Melton* • Donald O'Connor *Sticky Boone* • Jackie Coogan *Russ Simpson* • Larry Crabbe [Larry Crabbe] *Coach Baxter* ■ *Dir* Nick Grinde • *Scr* Lewis R Foster, Richard English, from a story by Lewis R Foster

Million Dollar Mermaid ★★★ U

Biographical drama
1952 · US · Colour · 115mins

Who else but the divine water-goddess of MGM, Esther Williams, this time afloat in a highly-fictionalised biopic of her predecessor, silent screen sensation Annette Kellerman? Of course, this being MGM, the plot is just an excuse for some wonderfully ornate Busby Berkeley routines, which today seem hilarious or camp. No wonder Victor Mature looks ill-at-ease. Despite the period sense being virtually nonexistent, Williams is as radiant as ever.

Esther Williams *Annette Kellerman* • Victor Mature *James Sullivan* • Walter Pidgeon *Frederick Kellerman* • David Brian *Alfred Harper* • Donna Corcoran *Annette, aged ten* • Jesse White *Doc Cronnel* • Maria Tallchief *Pavlova* • Howard Freeman *Aldrich* ■ *Dir* Mervyn LeRoy • *Scr* Everett Freeman

The Million Dollar Rip-off ★★

Crime caper   1976 · US · Colour · 73mins

A TV movie based on an unproduced screenplay written by actors William Devane and John Pleshette, yet neither features in this forgettable heist caper, which offered Freddie Prinze his one and only film role. While never totally at home as the electronics wizard who blags a fortune from the Chicago Transit Authority, Prinze clearly enjoys the company of his four female accomplices. More convincing is Allen Garfield as the gastrically bedevilled cop who always finds himself one step behind his target. Director Alexander

Singer can't disguise the shortcomings of either script or star.

Freddie Prinze *Muff Kovak* • Allen Garfield *Lieutenant Ralph Fogherty* • Christine Belford *Lil* • Linda Scruggs Bogart *Helene* • Joanna Devorana *Jessie* • Brooke Mills *Kitty* ■ *Dir* Alexander Singer • *Scr* Andrew P Marin, from a screenplay by William Devane, John Pleshette

The Million Pound Note ★★★★ U

Classic satire   1953 · UK · Colour · 84mins

A lovely comedy, with Gregory Peck as a bankrupt American abroad, who is given the title bank note and told to keep it intact for a month. As the butt of a joke between two rich gamblers, Peck has problems at first, but then finds the note means he never has to spend a penny because his credit rating is so good. Set in Edwardian London, the picture has a lot of charm and humour, owing to Peck's evident delight in the role and to Neame's unobtrusive direction. The witty script, based on the story by Mark Twain, was written by Jill Craigie, the film-maker wife of Michael Foot. ▭

Gregory Peck *Henry Adams* • Jane Griffiths *Portia Lansdowne* • Ronald Squire *Oliver Montpelier* • Wilfrid Hyde White *Roderick Montpelier* • Joyce Grenfell *Duchess of Cromarty* • Reginald Beckwith *Rock* • Hartley Power *Hastings* • Brian Oulton *Lloyd* ■ *Dir* Ronald Neame • *Scr* Jill Craigie, from the story by Mark Twain

A Million to Juan ★★★

Comedy   1994 · US · Colour · 97mins

Also shown as *A Million to One*, this is a Hispanic reworking of that old Gregory Peck favourite, *The Million Pound Note*. Loosely based on the story by Mark Twain, the film marked the directorial debut of comedian Paul Rodriguez, who also stars as the hard-working father who is given a cheque for a million dollars by a stranger. A reward is promised, providing he does good with the money without actually spending it. There are cameos from such luminaries as Cheech Marin, Ruben Blades and Edward James Olmos, and, if Rodriguez occasionally gets a little tacky, he still does enough to raise a smile.

Paul Rodriguez *Juan Lopez* • Polly Draper *Olivia Smith* • Gerardo *Flaco* • Jonathan Hernandez *Alejandro Lopez* • Edward James Olmos *Mr Angel* • Victor Rivers *Hector Delgado* • Bert Rosario *Alvaro* • Pepe Serna *Jorge/Mr Ortiz* ■ *Dir* Paul Rodriguez • *Scr* Robert Grasmere, Francisca Matos, Paul Rodriguez, from the story *The Million Pound Note* by Mark Twain

A Million to One ★★★

Drama   1937 · US · BW · 59mins

One of the main functions of film is as a recording medium, and this artless, fictionalised true story is of real value as a social record, featuring 1932 Olympic shot-putter Herman Brix as an athlete preparing for an Olympic decathlon. If Brix looks vaguely familiar, it's because he did actually become a film star, initially as Tarzan, and latterly changing his name to Bruce Bennett. A young Joan Fontaine rather sweetly plays a society lass who falls for Brix, and the film has a overall charm, despite static direction and a

pace which may well deter all but the hardiest of Olympic fans.

Herman Brix [Bruce Bennett] *Johnny Kent* • Joan Fontaine *Joan Stevens* • Reed Howes *Duke Hale* • Monte Blue *John Kent Sr* • Kenneth Harlan *William Stevens* • Suzanne Kaaren *Pat Stanley* • Ed Piel *Mac* • Ben Hall *Joe* ■ *Dir* Lynn Shores • *Scr* John T Neville

A Millionaire for Christy ★★★★ U

Romantic comedy   1951 · US · BW · 91mins

A good old-fashioned madcap comedy has always been a pleasing way to pass the time and this latter-day screwball provides more than its fair share of laughs. Fred MacMurray gives a droll performance as a folksy radio celebrity who becomes the target of legal secretary Eleanor Parker after he unexpectedly becomes a millionaire. Adding to the fun is MacMurray's on/off wedding with Kay Buckley and his chaotic pursuit of absconded best man Richard Carlson. Ken Englund's script brings plenty of verbal wit to the breezy situations, while director George Marshall outdoes himself with the hilarious beach scene.

Fred MacMurray *Peter Ulysses Lockwood* • Eleanor Parker *Christy Sloane* • Richard Carlson *Dr Roland Cook* • Kay Buckley *June Chandler* • Una Merkel *Patsy* • Douglass Dumbrille *AK Thompson* • Raymond Greenleaf *Benjamin Chandler* • Nestor Paiva *Mr Rapello* ■ *Dir* George Marshall • *Scr* Ken Englund, from a story by Robert Harari

The Millionairess ★★★ U

Comedy   1960 · UK · Colour · 86mins

An important film for British comedy actor Peter Sellers, this would give him his first real international audience. Sophia Loren was already a Sellers fan and was happy to have him play the Indian doctor opposite her spoiled heiress, in this adaptation of the George Bernard Shaw play. Sellers brings a gentle charm to his character and avoids taking the easy route to laughter by racial caricature. Loren is stunning and excels at the light comedy. Romance blossomed on set between the two and perhaps helped to make plausible the unlikely on-screen romance between the mismatched couple. ▭

Sophia Loren *Epifania Parerga* • Peter Sellers *Dr Ahmed el Kabir* • Vittorio De Sica *Joe* • Alastair Sim *Sagamore* • Dennis Price *Dr Adrian Bond* • Gary Raymond *Alastair* • Alfie Bass *Fish Curer* • Miriam Karlin *Mrs Joe* ■ *Dir* Anthony Asquith • *Scr* Wolf Mankowitz, Riccardo Aragno, from the play by George Bernard Shaw

Millions ★★ 18

Satirical thriller   1991 · It · Colour · 106mins

Director Carlo Vanzina is very much the Michael Winner of Italy. All his pictures contain elements of frothy camp, and this vague *Theorem* re-fit has more than most. Greedy Billy Zane (*Titanic*), tries to take over his sick uncle's industrial empire with the help of his equally grasping relatives, then proceeds to sleep with everyone to gain full control. Lauren Hutton and Vanzina regular Carol Alt, both ex-models, betray the thrust of this *Hello*-style piece. A typical Italian sex

comedy from a master of the genre that's silly, glossy entertainment. ▭

Billy Zane *Maurizio Ferretti* • Lauren Hutton *Cristina* • Carol Alt *Betta* • Jean Sorel *Leo Ferretti* • Catherine Hickland *Connie* • Alexandra Paul *Giulia* • Donald Pleasence *Ripa* ■ *Dir* Carlo Vanzina • *Scr* Carlo Vanzina, Enrico Vanzina, from a novel by Renzo Barbieri

Millions like Us ★★★★ U

Second World War drama
1943 · UK · Colour · 103mins

Although they're best known for comedies, the partnership of Frank Launder and Sidney Gilliat produced here one of the finest home-front dramas of the Second World War. Adopting the docu-dramatic approach that characterised many British flag-wavers, the directors present a nation pulling together in spite of class differences. The sequences in the factory and at the workers' dormitory are particularly fascinating for the way in which they depict the emergence of both a new kind of woman and a new social order. Patricia Roc and Eric Portman stand out in an excellent ensemble cast.

Eric Portman *Charlie Forbes* • Patricia Roc *Celia Crowson* • Gordon Jackson *Fred Blake* • Anne Crawford *Jennifer Knowles* • Joy Shelton *Phyllis Crowson* • Megs Jenkins *Gwen Price* • Terry Randall *Annie Earnshaw* • Basil Radford *Charters* • Naunton Wayne *Caldicott* ■ *Dir/Scr* Frank Launder, Sidney Gilliat

Milou en Mai ★★★ 15

Black comedy   1989 · Fr · Colour · 102mins

Recalling Jean Renoir's *La Règle du Jeu* and Bertrand Tavernier's *Sunday in the Country*, Louis Malle's final French film may not stand comparison with his earlier classics, but it is still a polished piece from a director whose willingness to tackle the more controversial aspects of France's recent past established him as one of the most fascinating artists to emerge from the New Wave era of the early sixties. He handles the family flirting and bickering with typical assurance, but uncharacteristically fumbles the serious and satirical political themes. Only Michel Piccoli's mischievous performance sustains the interest. In French with English subtitles. ▭

Michel Piccoli *Milou* • Miou-Miou *Camille* • Michel Duchaussoy *Georges* • Dominique Blanc *Claire* • Harriet Walter *Lily* • Bruno Carette *Grimaldi* • François Berléand *Daniel* • Martine Gautier *Adèle* ■ *Dir* Louis Malle • *Scr* Louis Malle, Jean-Claude Carrière • *Music* Stéphane Grappelli

Mimic ★★★ 15

Science-fiction horror
1997 · US · Colour · 101mins

In the same vein as *The Relic* and all those other movies about creepy-crawlies that go crunch in the night, this horror movie stars Mira Sorvino as an entomologist determined to find out exactly what has invaded the New York subway system. It's preposterous stuff, but the tale of oversized insects (a genetically enhanced species developed to eradicate an epidemic-spreading breed of cockroaches) is suitably gruesome and atmospheric thanks to *Cronos* director Guillermo del Toro's dark direction. Sorvino is believably tough, too, and smartly

supported by Jeremy Northam, Charles S Dutton and Josh Brolin as potential monster munchies. Yummy. Contains violence and swearing. ▭
Mira Sorvino *Dr Susan Tyler* • Jeremy Northam *Dr Peter Mann* • Josh Brolin *Josh Maslow* • Giancarlo Giannini *Manny* • Alexander Goodwin *Chuy* • Alix Koromzay *Remy* • F Murray Abraham *Doctor Gates* • Charles S Dutton *Leo* ■ *Dir* Guillermo Del Toro • *Scr* Matthew Robbins, Guillermo Del Toro, from a story by Matthew Robbins, Guillermo Del Toro, Donald A Wollheim

Min and Bill ★★★
Comedy drama 1930 · US · BW · 66mins

Dated but of considerable historical interest, this comedy drama was MGM's biggest hit of 1930 and won Marie Dressler an Academy Award for best actress. Dressler was an inimitable character performer, best remembered for *Anna Christie* and *Dinner at Eight*; she died of cancer in 1934. Here she portrays the hard-boiled owner of a ramshackle waterfront hotel who kills to protect the waif she has raised (Dorothy Jordan). Cast as her fisherman sweetheart, Wallace Beery registered so well opposite her that they were teamed in another smash hit, *Tugboat Annie*.
Marie Dressler *Min Divot* • Wallace Beery *Bill* • Dorothy Jordan *Nancy Smith* • Marjorie Rambeau *Bella Pringle* • Donald Dillaway *Dick Cameron* • DeWitt Jennings *Groot* ■ *Dir* George Hill • *Scr* Frances Marion, Marion Jackson, from the novel *Dark Star* by Lorna Moon

Mina Tannenbaum ★★★★ 🄸🄸
Drama 1993 · Fr/Bel/Neth · Colour · 123mins

Martine Dugowson made her directorial debut with this tragicomic rites-of-passage story. Tackling such diverse topics as heredity, conformity, compatibility, Jewishness and the nature of friendship in a competitive world, the film employs an impressive range of cinematic devices, including jump cuts, speeches direct to camera, Truffaut-like movie references and trick photography. Romane Bohringer and Elsa Zylberstein are superb as the lifelong friends, while Jean-Philippe Ecoffey stands out among the dreadful men they encounter over the years. Dugowson's humanity and perception are as noteworthy as her technical mastery and control over such a sprawling tale. In French with English subtitles. Contains swearing. ▭
Romane Bohringer *Mina Tannenbaum* • Elsa Zylberstein *Ethel Bénégui* • Nils Tavernier *François* • Stéphane Slima *Didier* • Florence Thomassin *The cousin* • Chantal Krief *Daisy* • Jany Gastaldi *Gisèle* • Jean-Philippe Ecoffey *Jacques Dana* ■ *Dir/Scr* Martine Dugowson

Minbo – or the Gentle Art of Japanese Extortion ★★★
Comedy 1992 · US/Jap · Colour · 123mins

Director Juzo Itami specialises in sly satires on Japanese society like *The Funeral* and *Tampopo*. However, in this darkly humorous thriller, he turns his attention to the underworld and the grip it exerts on all aspects of life. Nobuko Miyamoto, Itami's wife and the star of *A Taxing Woman*, plays a crusading lawyer who helps the management of a hotel resist a gang

of extortionists. Smartly spoofing the stylised violence and downbeat toughness of the cult *yakuza eiga* or gangster pictures, the film earned notoriety when Itami was slashed across the face by three hoods as punishment for mocking gangland. In Japanese with English subtitles.
Nobuko Miyamoto *Mahiru Inoue* • Akira Takarada *Kobayashi* • Masahiro Murata *Takehiro Murata* • Yasuo Daichi *Yuki Suzuki* • Hideji Otaki *Hotel owner* • Noboru Mitani *Gang boss* • Shiro Ito *Iriuchijima* • Akira Nakao *Ibagi* ■ *Dir/Scr* Juzo Itami

The Mind Benders ★★
Science-fiction drama
1963 · UK · BW · 113mins

Ahead of its time in 1963 and now hopelessly dated, this melodrama about spying, brainwashing and Oxford dons was ill-fated from the start. Dirk Bogarde is just one of the scientists who spends a few hours in an isolation tank and ends up even more unpleasant than he was before. The film boasts some fine performances – not to mention the screen debut of Edward Fox – but Basil Dearden's direction is far too straightforward for such a bizarre story. It cries out for a Michael Powell or a Hitchcock.
Dirk Bogarde *Dr Henry Longman* • Mary Ure *Oonagh Longman* • John Clements *Major Hall* • Michael Bryant *Dr Tate* • Wendy Craig *Annabelle* • Harold Goldblatt *Professor Sharpey* • Geoffrey Keen *Calder* • Terry Palmer *Norman* • Edward Fox *Stewart* ■ *Dir* Basil Dearden • *Scr* James Kennaway

Mind Breakers ★
Science-fiction thriller
1996 · US · Colour · 92mins

Cult director-turned-producer Roger Corman ruthlessly plunders his extensive back catalogue for a cobbled-together tale about dying aliens looking to mankind for ways to sustain their race. This incredibly cheap trash takes its special effects scenes from *Battle beyond the Stars* and other Corman classics, and wastes the talents of actors such as Adam Baldwin and Robert Englund in nonsensical roles. A real stinker.
Adam Baldwin *Lee* • Robert Englund *Father O'Neill* • Kate Rodger *Susan* • Duane Davis *Charles* • Gretchen Palmer *Carrie* ■ *Dir/Scr* Fred Gallo

Mind of a Killer ★★★ 🄸🄵
Psychological thriller
1993 · US · Colour · 86mins

Tim Matheson ditches his light leading-man image for a more intense role in this above average made-for-TV thriller. Matheson plays a troubled psychiatrist who is drawn into a perplexing mystery in which a seemingly respectable businesswoman has murdered her husband for no apparent reason. Director John Patterson pulls no major surprises out of the hat, but manages to build up a reasonable amount of suspense, and he is assisted by a solid performance from his leading man. There's also a nice supporting turn from Giancarlo Esposito as an ambiguous private detective, and a slinky cameo from Claudia Christian. ▭

Tim Matheson *Dr Peter Hellman* • Alberta Watson *Ellen Giancola* • Giancarlo Esposito *Arthur Sistrunk* • Claudia Christian *Lee Ann* • Kurt Fuller *Dahlberg* • Nancy Sorel *Natalie* • Christine Jansen *Annette* • Pierre Epstein *Gersh* ■ *Dir* John Patterson • *Scr* Ken Solarz, Jacob Epstein

Mind over Murder ★★ 🄸🄸
Chiller 1979 · US · Colour · 91mins

As well as being a top model, Suzy (Deborah Raffin) is a psychic whose life is thrown into turmoil when she senses a bomber is about to kill her. Though competently made for TV by veteran TV-movie director Ivan Nagy, this pseudo-psychological thriller arouses the suspicion that it was originally intended as a pilot for a series that never happened. ▭
Deborah Raffin *Suzy* • David Ackroyd *Ben* • Bruce Davison *Jason* • Andrew Prine *Bald man* • Christopher Cary *John Povey* • Robert Englund *Ted* • Penelope Willis *Pierce* ■ *Dir* Ivan Nagy • *Scr* Robert Carrington

Mindwalk ★
Drama 1990 · US · Colour · 112 mins

A group of ecologists talk at length about environmental philosophy in the medieval French town of St Michel, in director Bernt Capra's tortuous adaptation of his brother Fritjof's New Age bestseller. With virtually no action, drama or narrative, this deathly dull variation on *My Dinner with Andre* is a vanity production of epic proportions. Despite the presence of Liv Ullman and Sam Waterston, it's a film that gives conversation a bad name.
Liv Ullmann *Sonia Hoffman* • Sam Waterston *Jack Edwards* • John Heard *Thomas Harriman* • Ione Skye *Kit Hoffman* • Emmanuel Montes *Romain* ■ *Dir* Bernt Capra • *Scr* Fritjof Capra, Floyd Byars, from a story by Bernt Capra, from the non-fiction book *The Turning Point* by Fritjof Capra

Mindwarp ★★ 🄸🄸
Science-fiction horror
1992 · US · Colour · 91mins

Marta Alicia is a young woman in a society where everybody spends their lives hooked into virtual reality fantasies. When she shows the ability to leap into other people's fantasies, however, she is banished to the real world: a post-apocalyptic wasteland crawling with cannibals and violent, fanatical despots. Despite the presence of B-movie stalwart Bruce Campbell, *Mindwarp* is too slow, grimy and serious to be fun. ▭
Bruce Campbell *Stover* • Marta Alicia *Judy* • Elizabeth Kent *Cornelia* • Angus Scrimm *Seer* • Wendy Sandow *Claude* • Mary Becker *Mom* ■ *Dir* Steve Barnett • *Scr* Henry Dominic, Michael Ferris

Mine Own Executioner ★★★
Psychological drama
1947 · UK · BW · 110mins

A nerve-shattered former prisoner of war, who has tried to kill the wife he loves, is treated by a lay psychiatrist with problems of his own. This is a brave and intelligent piece of film-making, which allowed Nigel Balchin to adapt his novel with almost no box-office concessions. The psychiatrist becomes Canadian to suit American

actor Burgess Meredith, but he plays the part brilliantly. Under the direction of Anthony Kimmins, Kieron Moore is also excellent as the disturbed war veteran. The climax on the ledge of a high building will make your feet tingle.
Burgess Meredith *Felix Milne* • Dulcie Gray *Patricia Milne* • Kieron Moore *Adam Lucian* • Barbara White *Molly Lucian* • Christine Norden *Barbara Edge* • John Laurie *Dr James Garsten* • Michael Shepley *Peter Edge* • Lawrence Hanray *Dr Lefage* ■ *Dir* Anthony Kimmins • *Scr* Nigel Balchin, from his novel

The Minion ★ 🄸🄵
Supernatural thriller
1998 · US/Can · Colour · 91mins

Fallen star Dolph Lundgren reaches rock bottom in this absurdly expensive straight-to-video movie that frequently looks worse than films made for a third or less of its $12 million budget. The muddled storyline has something to do with a spirit that travels from body to body, searching for a holy door that will release evil on earth if opened. Lundgren plays a preacher intent on stopping it; this he does by punching possessed people in the back of their heads with a spiked glove. ▭
Dolph Lundgren *Lukas* • Francoise Robertson *Karen Goodleaf* • Roc Lafortune *David Schulman* ■ *Dir* Jean-Marc Piche • *Scr* Matt Roe

Ministry of Fear ★★★
Spy drama 1945 · US · BW · 86mins

Paramount snapped up the rights to Graham Greene's novel because they liked the title. The plot that came with it was largely disposable, and the book was turned into a pursuit thriller starring Ray Milland as a mental patient who has spent two years in an insane asylum for murdering his wife. Fritz Lang turns this into a creepily effective work, full of bravura set pieces and subtle suggestions and somehow creating, in Hollywood, an impression of the London Blitz.
Ray Milland *Stephen Neale* • Marjorie Reynolds *Carla Hilfe* • Carl Esmond *Willi Hilfe* • Hillary Brooke *Mrs Bellane* • Percy Waram *Inspector Prentice* • Dan Duryea *Cost/Travers* • Alan Napier *Dr Forrester* • Erskine Sanford *Mr Rennit* ■ *Dir* Fritz Lang • *Scr* Seton I Miller, from the novel by Graham Greene

The Miniver Story ★ 🄸
Drama 1950 · UK/US · BW · 104mins

MGM's *Mrs Miniver* (1942) won six Oscars and remains a famous beacon of patriotic light in the darkest days of the Second World War. This disastrously ill-judged sequel brings back the stars: Greer Garson wasting away with a mysterious fatal disease, and Walter Pidgeon wanting to escape blitzed-out London for new pastures in Brazil. A new cast plays the now grown-up Miniver children, with daughter Cathy O'Donnell in love with middle-aged Leo Genn, while her mother extricates herself from an involvement with American serviceman John Hodiak. Directed by HC Potter, this irrelevant follow-up is a second-rate soap opera, bleak and depressing.
Greer Garson *Kay Miniver* • Walter Pidgeon *Clem Miniver* • John Hodiak *Spike Romway* • Leo Genn *Steve Brunswick* • Cathy O'Donnell *Judy Miniver* • Reginald Owen *Mr Foley* •

Anthony Bushell *Dr Kanesley* • Peter Finch *Polish officer* ■ Dir HC Potter • Scr Ronald Millar, George Froeschel, from characters created by Jan Struther

Minnie and Moskowitz ★★★

Comedy drama 1971 · US · Colour · 114mins

Two sad and lonely people meet and fall in love against the hectic, heedless backdrop of the big city. Minnie (Gena Rowlands) works in a museum; Moskowitz (Seymour Cassel) is a car park attendant. The setting, Los Angeles, is important, since the movie is about the ribbon of dreams that people tie up their lives with. As always with Cassavetes, the film goes out of its way to show how different it is from conventional Hollywood fare.

Gena Rowlands *Minnie Moore* • Seymour Cassel *Seymour Moskowitz* • Val Avery *Zelmo* • Timothy Carey *Morgan* • Katherine Cassavetes *Sheba Moskowitz* • Elizabeth Deering *Girl* • Elsie Ames *Florence* • Lady Rowlands *Georgia Moore* ■ Dir/Scr John Cassavetes

The Minus Man ★★★★

Psychological thriller
1999 · US · Colour · 115mins

Written and directed by Hampton Fancher (co-writer of *Blade Runner*), this low-key, minor masterpiece is a tension-builder of the unbearable kind. The pleasant boy-next-door manner of drifter Owen Wilson hides the fact that he's a serial killer. It's when he lodges with troubled marrieds Brian Cox and Mercedes Ruehl that fate selects his next mark, and his precarious union with postal worker Janeane Garofalo suggests his poisoning days might be numbered. A very creepy, jet-black psychological thriller, this adaptation of Lew McCreary's novel is made more unsettling by having Wilson meditate on his actions in comically-toned voice-over and his actions dogged by imaginary cops. A true original.

Owen Wilson *Vann Siegert* • Janeane Garofalo *Ferrin* • Brian Cox *Doug* • Mercedes Ruehl *Jane* • Dwight Yoakam *Blair* • Dennis Haysbert *Graves* • Sheryl Crow *Caspar* • Eric Mabius *Gene* ■ Dir Hampton Fancher • Scr Hampton Fancher, from the novel by Lew McCreary

The Miracle ★★★ 📟

Historical drama
1959 · US · Colour · 121mins

Carroll Baker, who played the nymphet in *Baby Doll* and received the condemnation of the Catholic Legion of Decency for her trouble, plays a Spanish novice who falls for British dragoon Roger Moore as he drifts across Spain towards the battle of Waterloo. Lavish, wooden and ridiculous, with bullfights, duels, droughts, plagues and an astonishing rainstorm at the end, this kitsch clunker was inspired by Max Reinhard's stage production of Karl Vollmoeller's play. Hilariously awful, it is, without doubt, one of the most ill-conceived movies ever made.

Carroll Baker *Teresa* • Roger Moore *Captain Michael Stuart* • Walter Slezak *Flaco* • Vittorio Gassman *Guido* • Katina Paxinou *La Roca* • Gustavo Rojo *Cordoba* ■ Dir Irving Rapper • Scr Frank Butler, Jean Rouverol (uncredited), from the play by Karl Vollmoeller

The Miracle ★★★★ 🔞

Drama 1990 · UK · Colour · 92mins

Set in a small Irish seaside town, Neil Jordan's wonderful drama is often overlooked. Teenagers Lorraine Pilkington and Niall Byrne spend most of their time imagining the secret lives of their neighbours. Then, one day, a glamorous actress (Beverly D'Angelo) turns up and pulls them into a real world of romance and mystery. Deliciously romantic and affecting, this was a small-scale comeback for Jordan after a couple of American disasters (*High Spirits*, *We're No Angels*). 📟

Beverly D'Angelo *Renee* • Donal McCann *Sam* • Niall Byrne *Jimmy* • Lorraine Pilkington *Rose* • JG Devlin *Mr Beausang* • Cathleen Delaney *Miss Strange* ■ Dir/Scr Neil Jordan

Miracle at Midnight ★★★

Wartime drama based on a true story
1998 · US · Colour · 90mins

A painful subject is given a gripping treatment in this *Diary of Anne Frank*-style true story. As Nazi forces begin to deport Copenhagen's Jews, gentile doctor Sam Waterston and his initially fearful wife (Mia Farrow) stash healthy Jewish "patients" in various hospital wards, then arrange transport on fishing boats. This fast-paced TV movie speeds past its few wartime clichés, its fine script and cast concentrating instead on the characters' perilous decision to risk imprisonment or death for their fellow human beings.

Sam Waterston *Dr Koster* • Mia Farrow *Doris Koster* • Justin Whalin *Hendrik Koster* • Patrick Malahide *Georg Ferdinand Duckwitz* • Daisy Beaumont *Hannah* ■ Dir Ken Cameron • Scr Chris Bryant, Monte Merrick

Miracle in Milan ★★★ 🔞

Fantasy drama 1950 · It · BW · 91mins

Vittorio De Sica's follow-up to the internationally acclaimed *Bicycle Thieves* is a modern biblical parable that begins with the words, "Once upon a time". Abandoned in a cabbage patch, the hero, Toto, is brought up by a kindly old lady. The boy grows up to become one of life's saints, and the poverty that surrounds him in the shanty town outside Milan only sharpens his faith in human nature. Then his guardian angel descends from heaven and gives him the ability to perform miracles. Like a piece of 16th-century Renaissance art seen through a neorealist lens, this will probably seem very corny and simplistic to modern audiences. In 1950, though, it was widely admired and shared the Grand Prix at Cannes with Alf Sjöberg's *Miss Julie*. In Italian with English subtitles. 📟

Branduani Gianni *Little Toto, aged 11* • Francesco Golisano *Good Toto* • Paolo Stoppa *Bad Rappi* • Emma Gramatica *Old Lolatta* • Guglielmo Barnabo *Mobbi the rich man* ■ Dir Vittorio De Sica • Scr Cesare Zavattini, Vittorio De Sica, Suso Cecchi D'Amico, Mario Chiari, Adolfo Franci, from the story *Toto Il Buono* by Cesare Zavattini

Miracle in Soho ★★ 🔞

Drama 1957 · UK · Colour · 97mins

Emeric Pressburger's screenwriting outings in Britain, without Michael Powell, were few and far between and this dour little drama might go some way to explaining why. Pressburger's script aims for the sort of semi-documentary tone that had become fashionable at the time, but this romance between a roadsweeper and an Italian girl needed a little local colour to buck it up, not grey sociological pronouncements. Christopher Challis's grim images of Soho have a certain historical value, but neither John Gregson nor Belinda Lee comes close to convincing.

John Gregson *Michael Morgan* • Belinda Lee *Julia Gozzi* • Cyril Cusack *Sam Bishop* • Rosalie Crutchley *Mafalda Gozzi* • Peter Illing *Papa Gozzi* • Marie Burke *Mama Gozzi* • Ian Bannen *Filippo Gozzi* • Brian Bedford *Johnny* ■ Dir Julian Amyes • Scr Emeric Pressburger

Miracle in the Rain ★★ 🔞

Romantic drama 1956 · US · BW · 107mins

Fine performances from stars Jane Wyman (as a timid office girl) and the ever-dependable Van Johnson (as an extrovert soldier) keep this soapy melodrama watchable, but its ending takes an awful lot of swallowing. Director Rudolph Maté sketches in an all-too-credible working class New York, unusual for a period in American cinema when gloss ruled. There are some touching support performances, particularly from comedian Alan King as a soldier nuts about his new bride, a deeply untalented cabaret artiste lovingly portrayed by the under-rated Barbara Nichols. Warner Bros pulled all the stops out and the film is certainly well made, but it comes across as either very moving or rather tacky.

Jane Wyman *Ruth Wood* • Van Johnson *Arthur Hugenon* • Peggie Castle *Millie Kranz* • Fred Clark *Stephen Jalonkik* • Eileen Heckart *Grace Ullman* • Josephine Hutchinson *Agnes Wood* • Alan King *Sgt Gil Parker* • Barbara Nichols *Arleene* ■ Dir Rudolph Maté • Scr Ben Hecht, from a novel by Ben Hecht

Miracle in the Wilderness ★★★ 🅿🅶

Seasonal western drama
1991 · US · Colour · 84mins

Based on a short story by Paul Gallico, this sentimental, but nonetheless watchable, TV movie brings a touch of christmas to the Wild West. Kris Kristofferson and Liverpool-born Kim Cattrall are the members of a frontier family kidnapped by a tribe of native Americans, who head for Canada with the US cavalry in hot pursuit. Unfortunately, an excess of talk rather slows down the action, and not everyone will approve of the "white man's burden" theme as the hostages teach their captors the Nativity story. However, the breathtaking scenery does compensate somewhat for the lack of pace. 📟

Kris Kristofferson *Jericho Adams* • Kim Cattrall *Dora Adams* • Rino Thunder *Chief Washakie* • John Dennis Johnston *Sam Webster* • Peter Alan Morris *Asher Adams* • David Oliver *Lieutenant Reid* • Sheldon Peters Wolfchild *Many Horses* • Steve Reevis *Grey Eyes* ■ Dir Kevin James Dobson • Scr Michael Michaelian, Jim Byrnes, from the novella *The Snow Goose* by Paul Gallico

Miracle Landing ★★★ 🅿🅶

Drama based on a true story
1990 · US · Colour · 84mins

This fact-based story involves a commercial flight to Honolulu which, somehow, avoided tragedy after the plane's roof vanished at 24,000 feet. Made long after disaster movies had stopped being fashionable, this TV movie is not hindered by too much implausible plot and hysterical action, as films of this type often are. This example is sufficiently buoyed up by well-coiled thrills and a sustained sense of danger and unease. 📟

Wayne Rogers *Bob Schornstheimer* • Connie Sellecca *Mimi Tompkins* • Ana-Alicia [Ana Alicia] *Michelle Honda* • Nancy Kwan *CB Lansing* • Jay Thomas *Ed Meyer* • James Cromwell *BJ Cocker* • Will Nipper *David Kornberg* ■ Dir Dick Lowry • Scr Garner Simmons

The Miracle Maker ★★★ 🔞

Biblical animation
1999 · UK/Rus · Colour · 91mins

This Russian/Welsh co-production uses clay puppets and Wallace and Gromit-style techniques to tell the tale of Christ's life, his eventual crucifixion, resurrection and ascension. The puppets are beautifully carved, if a tad creepy, while the stop-motion animation is state-of-the-art, especially during crowd scenes that feature dozens of little figures pootling about. Like many things religious, *The Miracle Maker* is on the dull and reverential side, but younger audiences may be enthralled. Ralph Fiennes, Richard E Grant, William Hurt and Julie Christie are among the voice providers.

Ralph Fiennes *Jesus* • Michael Bryant *God/ The Doctor* • Julie Christie *Rachel* • Richard E Grant *John the Baptist* • Ian Holm *Pilate* • William Hurt *Jairus* • Bob Peck *Joseph of Arimathea* • Miranda Richardson *Mary Magdalene* • Antony Sher *Ben Azra* • David Thewlis *Judas* ■ Dir Derek Hayes, Stanislav Sokolov • Scr Murray Watts

The Miracle of Fatima ★★★ 🔞

Religious drama 1952 · US · Colour · 102mins

Never approaching the Oscar-winning standard of *The Song of Bernadette*, this is, nevertheless, a sincere account of the 1917 apparition of the Virgin Mary to the Cova de Iria outside the Portuguese village of Fatima. The trio, who claim to have heard prophecies from a "lady in the sky" on the 13th of six consecutive months, are played by Susan Whitney, Sherry Jackson and Sammy Ogg. But even through director John Brahm makes such moments as the cure of the lame and blind truly inspirational, the reverential approach will be harder to take for many than the episode's religious implications.

Gilbert Roland *Hugo Da Silva* • Susan Whitney *Lucia Dos Santos* • Sherry Jackson *Jacinta Marto* • Sammy Ogg *Francisco Marto* • Angela Clark *Maria Rosa* • Frank Silvera *Arturo Dos Santos* • Jay Novello *Antonio* • Richard Hale *Father Ferreira* ■ Dir John Brahm • Scr Cran Wilbur, James O'Hanlon

---

The Miracle of Morgan's Creek ★★★★★

Classic comedy   1944 · US · BW · 98mins

With its controversial (at the time) subject matter, the real miracle was that this film was allowed to be made in the first place. Writer/director Preston Sturges thumbed his nose at the Hays Office (administrators of the film censorship code) delivering a fast-paced story of a girl (Betty Hutton) who finds herself pregnant after attending a GI party and has no idea of the identity of the father from the men present. Sturges was the great Hollywood satirist of the forties and he made a slew of trailblazing films that remain some of the period's finest. This is a blistering comedy with marvellous moments all the way through and terrific interplay between the leads.

Eddie Bracken *Norval Jones* • Betty Hutton *Trudy Kockenlocker* • Diana Lynn *Emmy Kockenlocker* • Brian Donlevy *Governor McGinty* • Akim Tamiroff *Boss* • William Demarest *Officer Kockenlocker* • Porter Hall *Justice of the Peace* ■ *Dir/Scr* Preston Sturges • *Cinematographer* John F Seitz

The Miracle of the Bells ★★

Drama   1948 · US · BW · 119mins

Definitely one for those who like religious themes tied up in a neat parcel and featuring bearded men on fluffy clouds. Frank Sinatra, Fred MacMurray and Alida Valli star in an undemanding slice of whimsy, in which movie star Valli is laid to rest in her mining home town to rather dramatic effect. It's all a shade too sugary and daft, with stereotypes firmly in place, but there is an inherent charm about the screenplay that rescues the proceedings from total overkill.

Fred MacMurray *Bill Dunnigan* • Alida Valli *Olga Treskovna* • Frank Sinatra *Father Paul* • Lee J Cobb *Marcus Harris* • Jim Nolan *Ted Jones* • Veronika Pataky *Anna Klovna* • Philip Ahn *Ming Gow* • Harold Vermilyea *Nick Orloff* ■ *Dir* Irving Pichel • *Scr* Ben Hecht, Quentin Reynolds, DeWitt Bodeen, from the novel by Russell Janney

Miracle of the White Stallions ★★★ U

Wartime adventure based on a true story
1963 · US · Colour · 89mins

An adventure drama in which the famous white Lippizaner stallions of the Spanish Riding School in Vienna are evacuated to the countryside during the final days of the war. The head of the School leads the horses to safety and puts on a show for General Patton, thus securing American protection from the advancing Russians. The Disney brand might induce a certain cynicism and lead one to expect something akin to *One Hundred and One Dalmatians*, but mercifully the studio resisted this and produced a fairly sugar-free yarn. 🎬

Robert Taylor (1) *Colonel Podhajsky* • Lilli Palmer *Verena Podhajsky* • Curt Jurgens *General Tellheim* • Eddie Albert *Rider Otto* • James Franciscus *Major Hoffman* • John Larch *General Patton* ■ *Dir* Arthur Hiller • *Scr* Aj Carothers, from the non-fiction book *The Dancing White Stallions of Vienna* by Colonel Alois Podhajsky

Miracle on Main Street ★★★

Seasonal drama   1940 · US · BW · 76mins

It reads like the plot of the previous year's *Bachelor Mother*, only this time it's dance-hall girl Margo, not sales girl Ginger Rogers, who finds an abandoned baby on Christmas Eve in a Los Angeles alley. A tight little Columbia programme filler, inexplicably neglected today, this derives great strength from the performance of Margo herself, perhaps better known today for 1943's *The Leopard Man* and for being married to actor Eddie Albert. Hungarian-born director Steve Sekely, keeps sentiment at bay, and Jane Darwell and Veda Ann Borg provide potent cameos. The musical arranger was Hans J Salter, later to achieve fame as a great composer of horror scores for Universal.

Margo *Maria Porter* • Walter Abel *Jim Forman* • William Collier Sr *Doctor Miles* • Jane Darwell *Mrs Herman* • Lyle Talbot *Dick Porter* • Wynne Gibson *Sade "Coochie" Blake* • Veda Ann Borg *Flo* • Pat Flaherty *Detective* ■ *Dir* Steve Sekely • *Scr* Frederick Jackson, from a story by Samuel Ornitz, Boris Ingster

Miracle on 34th Street ★★★★★ U

Christmas fantasy   1947 · US · BW · 92mins

Not the benign remake with Richard Attenborough, but the marvellous original first shown in the UK as *The Big Heart*. Natalie Wood is a jaded youngster who knows there's no such thing as Father Christmas because her mother, Maureen O'Hara, organises a New York department store's yearly parade, and Wood has always seen Santa played by drunken old men. The great plot was rightly awarded Oscars for best screenplay and original story, while Edmund Gwenn also won as best supporting actor. Indeed, Gwenn became so identified with the role of Kris Kringle that every holiday he found himself hired to hand out presents at the houses of such Hollywood notables as Louis B Mayer. 🎬

Maureen O'Hara *Doris Walker* • John Payne *Fred Gailey* • Edmund Gwenn *Kris Kringle* • Gene Lockhart *Judge Henry X Harper* • Natalie Wood *Susan Walker* • Porter Hall *Mr Sawyer* • William Frawley *Charles Halloran* • Jerome Cowan *Thomas Mara* • Philip Tonge *Mr Shellhammer* • James Seay *Dr Pierce* ■ *Dir* George Seaton • *Scr* George Seaton, from a story by Valentine Davies

Miracle on 34th Street ★★★ U

Christmas fantasy
1994 · US · Colour · 109mins

Richard Attenborough plays Kriss Kringle in this remake of the classic 1947 fantasy. In the original, Edmund Gwenn won an Oscar for his portrayal of the elderly gent, whose behaviour while working as a department-store Santa suggests that he believes he is really is Father Christmas. Here Attenborough positively twinkles in the role in an attempt to convince moppet Mara Wilson and, the audience, that he is a living legend. Yet, although the film as a whole is a much more glamorous affair, and Wilson and Elizabeth Perkins as her mother are

undoubtedly charming, it does lack some of the magic of the original. 🎬

Richard Attenborough *Kriss Kringle* • Elizabeth Perkins *Dorey Walker* • Dylan McDermott *Bryan Bedford* • JT Walsh *Ed Collins* • James Remar *Jack Duff* • Jane Leeves *Alberta Leonard* • Simon Jones *Shellhammer* • Mara Wilson *Susan Walker* ■ *Dir* Les Mayfield • *Scr* John Hughes, from the 1947 film, from a story by Valentine Davies

The Miracle Woman ★★★

Drama   1931 · US · BW · 90mins

A rarely-seen, extraordinary early work from director Frank Capra. Its theme of fake evangelism made it a controversial film in its day, based as it was on a play featuring a thinly disguised portrait of popular evangelist Aimée Semple McPherson. McPherson is incarnated here by Barbara Stanwyck in a remarkable performance, combining rare delicacy with great strength of purpose. Interestingly, this movie was produced in the days before the Hays Code censored such dialogue and sequences dealing with religious issues. Only a few years later such content would not be deemed fit material for US audiences.

Barbara Stanwyck *Florence "Faith" Fallon* • David Manners *John Carson* • Sam Hardy *Bob Hornsby* • Beryl Mercer *Mrs Higgins* • Russell Hopton *Sam Welford* • Charles Middleton *Simpson* • Eddie Boland *Collins* • Thelma Hill *Gussie* ■ *Dir* Frank R Capra [Frank Capra] • *Scr* Dorothy Howell, Jo Swerling, from the play *Bless You Sister* by John Meehan

The Miracle Worker ★★★★ PG

Biographical drama 1962 · US · BW · 102mins

Marvellously moving biopic about the youth of deaf, dumb and blind Helen Keller, and her remarkable teacher Annie Sullivan. There are outstanding Oscar-winning performances from Anne Bancroft as Sullivan and Patty Duke as Keller – both had played the roles on Broadway. Arthur Penn's direction is superb, remaining solidly unsentimental throughout. Unsettling and thought-provoking, this is a fine American humanitarian work, brilliantly photographed in harsh black and white by Ernesto Caparros. Incidentally, a grown-up Duke later played the Sullivan role in a 1979 TV movie remake. 🎬

Anne Bancroft *Annie Sullivan* • Patty Duke *Helen Keller* • Victor Jory *Captain Keller* • Inga Swenson *Kate Keller* • Andrew Prine *James Keller* • Kathleen Comegys *Aunt Ev* • Beah Richards *Viney* ■ *Dir* Arthur Penn • *Scr* William Gibson, from the non-fiction book *The Story of My Life* by Helen Keller

Miracles ★★ PG

Comedy   1985 · US · Colour · 83mins

Those of a nervous disposition may find Teri Garr's constant high-pitched squealing rather trying in this predictable, frantic caper, in which Garr and her ex-husband (Tom Conti) suffer various indignities in the South American desert. Conti gives us his floppy-haired, shyly charming act, while Garr, a passably talented actress on occasion, is once again handed a script requiring little more than constant hysterics. If you're in a tolerant mood, this piece of visual chewing gum may amuse. 🎬

Tom Conti *Roger* • Teri Garr *Jean* • Christopher Lloyd *Harry* • Paul Rodriguez *Juan* • Adalberto Martinez *Kayum, witch doctor* • Jorge Russek *Judge* • Paco Morayta *Sgt Gomez* ■ *Dir/Scr* Jim Kouf

Miracles for Sale ★★

Murder mystery   1939 · US · BW · 71mins

A change of pace for director Tod Browning, best known for controversial cult favourite *Freaks*, with a story about a magician (Robert Young) who gets involved in some supernatural murders. Browning plays it fairly straight in his final film but builds the tension nicely, aided by the capable performances of his cast.

Robert Young *Michael Morgan* • Florence Rice *Judy Barclay* • Frank Craven *Dad Morgan* • Henry Hull *Dave Duvallo* • Lee Bowman *La Clair* • Cliff Clark *Inspector Gavigan* • Astrid Allwyn *Zelma La Clair* • Walter Kingsford *Colonel Watrous* ■ *Dir* Tod Browning • *Scr* Harry Ruskin, Marion Parsonnet, James Edward Grant, from the novel *Death from a Top Hat* by Clayton Rawston

Mirage ★★★★

Mystery thriller   1965 · US · Colour · 108mins

Corkscrew plots come no screwier than in this corker from the screenwriter of *Charade*. The plot is unfathomable, and it's not certain whether that's deliberate or simply a symptom of poor film-making. Gregory Peck stars as an amnesiac who finds himself in a variety of tense situations, aided, abetted and threatened by a fine supporting cast of spooks that includes George Kennedy and Walter Matthau (both of whom were in *Charade*). One could regard this paranoid nightmare as a reflection of director Edward Dmytryk's experience of the Hollywood blacklist.

Gregory Peck *David Stillwell* • Diane Baker *Sheila* • Walter Matthau *Ted Caselle* • Kevin McCarthy *Josephson* • Jack Weston *Lester* • Leif Erickson *Major Crawford* • Walter Abel *Charles Calvin* • George Kennedy *Willard* ■ *Dir* Edward Dmytryk • *Scr* Peter Stone, from the novel *Fallen Angel* by Walter Ericson

Mirage ★★ 18

Erotic thriller   1995 · US · Colour · 87mins

Edward James Olmos is a down on his luck ex-cop, hired by a wealthy Californian land developer to protect his wife, Sean Young. The twist is that she has multiple personalities, including one that is a stripper. Olmos and Young begin an affair, but it's cut short when she is murdered. Or is she really alive? If that isn't enough to keep you interested, Sean Young's attempt to do an Irish accent will keep you amused. Contains violence, swearing and drug abuse. 🎬

Edward James Olmos *Matteo Juarez* • Sean Young *Jennifer Gale/Shannon* • Paul Williams *Donald Gale* • James Andronica *Lt Richie Randazzo* ■ *Dir* Paul Williams • *Scr* James Andronica

Miranda ★★★

Comedy fantasy   1947 · UK · BW · 79mins

Glynis Johns gives one of the best performances of her career as Miranda the mermaid, in this fishy tale that had more than a passing influence on the Ron Howard hit *Splash*. Griffith Jones is something of a stuffed shirt as the

doctor who pulls her out of the sea and gives her the run of his bathroom, but Googie Withers is good value as his suspicious wife and David Tomlinson makes a suitably silly-ass suitor. Yet no one can compare with the marvellous Margaret Rutherford as the local nurse. Slickly handled by Ken Annakin, it's never exactly funny, but it's highly enjoyable all the same.

Glynis Johns *Miranda* • Googie Withers *Clare Marten* • Griffith Jones *Dr Paul Marten* • John McCallum *Nigel Hood* • Margaret Rutherford *Nurse Cary* • David Tomlinson *Charles* • Yvonne Owen *Betty* • Sonia Holm *Isobel* ■ *Dir* Ken Annakin • *Scr* Peter Blackmore, Denis Waldock, from the play by Peter Blackmore

Mirch Masala ★★★ 15
Drama 1987 · Ind · Colour · 119mins

Although it loses track of its intellectual purpose and ends up being a rather bland melodrama, this political allegory made the international reputation of Indian director Ketan Mehta. Naseeruddin Shah plays the Raj-obsessed tax collector, or subedar, whose passion for Smita Patil is drawn with considerable ferocity. Om Puri is also impressive as the sage watchman who protects the frightened Patil in an otherwise all-female spice factory. It's beautifully photographed, but much of the symbolism will lack significance for western audiences. In Hindi with English subtitles.

Naseeruddin Shah *Subedar* • Smita Patil *Sonbai* • Suresh Oberoi *Mukhi* • Om Puri ■ *Dir* Ketan Mehta

Mirror ★★★★ U
Lyrical drama 1974 · USSR · Colour and BW · 101mins

Cinema doesn't get much more personal than this. Casting his mother as the old woman and using his famous father, Arseni Tarkovsky's poetry on the soundtrack, director Andrei Tarkovsky draws on childhood memories, artistic fantasies and actual events to explore the ways in which the history of his country impinged on the lives of three generations of his family. It's a bewildering blend of documentary footage and stylised imagery, that can only be described as cinematic poetry. Some of the references are decidedly obscure and it takes considerable concentration to keep in step. An awesome achievement, nevertheless. In Russian with English subtitles. 📺

Margarita Terekhova *Alexei's mother/Natalia* • Fillip Yankovsky *Alexei, aged five* • Ignat Daniltsev *Ignat/Alexei, aged 12* • Oleg Yankovsky *Father* ■ *Dir* Andrei Tarkovsky • *Scr* Andrei Tarkovsky, Aleksandr Misharin

The Mirror Crack'd ★★ PG
Mystery 1980 · UK · Colour · 101mins

Adapted from Agatha Christie's *The Mirror Crack'd from Side to Side*, this mediocre mystery gave Angela Lansbury the chance to rehearse her role as *Murder She Wrote's* crime-solving novelist Jessica Fletcher, by taking up the prized knitting needles of Miss Marple. Unfortunately, we are now all too familiar with her subsequent persona for this to seem new, and frankly, with the clash of the titans going on between Elizabeth

Taylor and Kim Novak, nobody else really gets a look in. That includes Tony Curtis and Rock Hudson (in his penultimate picture). 📺

Angela Lansbury *Miss Marple* • Geraldine Chaplin *Ella Zielinsky* • Tony Curtis *Marty N Fenn* • Edward Fox *Inspector Craddock* • Rock Hudson *Jason Rudd* • Kim Novak *Lola Brewster* • Elizabeth Taylor *Marina Rudd* ■ *Dir* Guy Hamilton • *Scr* Jonathan Hales, Barry Sandler, from the novel by Agatha Christie

The Mirror Has Two Faces ★★★ 15
Romantic comedy 1996 · US · Colour · 121mins

Barbra Streisand directs and stars in this so-so romantic comedy, packed with numerous scenes of the singing/ acting/directing diva, shot in the most flattering light. She plays a dowdy professor who agrees to have a purely platonic relationship with Jeff Bridges, which is his solution to years of empty sexual romances. Of course, Babs secretly fancies the pants off him, so she decides to turn herself into a sensual swan and seduce him. While Streisand and Bridges fumble with their roles, the movie is stolen out from under them by supporting cast members Mimi Rogers, as Barbra's glamour-puss sister, and Lauren Bacall as her critical mother. 📺 DVD

Barbra Streisand *Rose Morgan* • Jeff Bridges *Gregory Larkin* • Lauren Bacall *Hannah Morgan* • George Segal *Henry Fine* • Mimi Rogers *Claire* • Pierce Brosnan *Alex* • Brenda Vaccaro *Doris* • Austin Pendleton *Barry* • Elle Macpherson *Candy* ■ *Dir* Barbra Streisand • *Scr* Richard LaGravenese, from his story, from the film *Le Miroir A Deux Faces* by André Cayatte, Gérard Oury • *Music* Marvin Hamlisch • *Cinematographer* Dante Spinotti

Mirror Images ★ 18
Erotic thriller 1991 · US · Colour · 93mins

What happens when the makers of porn films decide to make ''serious'' movies? You end up with something like *Mirror Images*. Delia Sheppard is the trophy wife of a smarmy political consultant. She just wants ''one night to be myself'', which – happily for male viewers – involves her undressing in front of mirrors every ten minutes or so. To escape her loveless marriage, Sheppard begins impersonating her slutty twin sister, Shauna (also played by Sheppard). The plot is non-existent and the acting is awful, but there are a couple of amusing parodies of political campaign ads. 📺

Delia Sheppard *Kaitlin/Shauna* • Jeff Conaway *Jeffrey* • Julie Strain *Gina Kaye* • Nels Van Patten *Joey Zoom* • Korey Mall *Gil* • Richard Arbolino *Carter Sayles* ■ *Dir* Gregory Hippolyte • *Scr* Rick Marx

Mirror Images II ★★ 18
Erotic thriller 1994 · US · Colour · 88mins

Erotic thriller queen Shannon Whirry followed *Animal Instincts* with this splendidly trashy slice of soft-core suspense. And because she's playing twin sisters – one good, the other very bad – she gets her kit off twice as much! Things start to get complicated when the bad girl starts impersonating the nice one. Naturally, the performances and script are risible.

Given the limitations of the genre, though, it's actually rather good. 📺

Shannon Whirry *Carrie/Terrie* • Luca Bercovici *Clete Dyker* • Tom Reilly *Jake* • Sara Suzanne Brown *Prostitute* ■ *Dir* Gregory Hippolyte • *Scr* Daryl Haney

Mirrors ★★ 15
Romantic drama 1985 · US · Colour · 94mins

Romance or performance? That's the choice starry-eyed Marguerite Hickey must make after arriving in New York to follow her prima ballerina dreams. Harry Winer, director of the popular TV movie *Single Bars, Single Women*, does nothing with this average stage door melodrama except throw in pointed references to far better examples of the genre (*The Turning Point, Fame, A Chorus Line*). However, it's the cast that counts, and veterans Keenan Wynn, Patricia Morison and one-time Garbo pretender Signe Hasso are always watchable.

Marguerite Hickey *Karin Bradley* • Timothy Daly *Chris Philips* • Shanna Reed *Diane* • Antony Hamilton *Gino* • Nicholas Gunn *Terry* • Ron Field *Sonny* • Signe Hasso *Madame Eugenia* • Keenan Wynn *Reverend Dahlstrom* • Patricia Morison *Mrs Rome* ■ *Dir* Harry Winer • *Scr* James Lipton, from his novel

The Misadventures of Margaret ★★ 15
Romantic comedy 1998 · Fr/UK/US · Colour · 88mins

The art of screwball comedy was dead long before writer/director Brian Skeet banged this nail into its coffin. Alluding to everything from *Bringing up Baby* to *The More the Merrier*, this is a film in search of a laugh. As she attempts valiantly to impersonate Katharine Hepburn, star Parker Posey succeeds only in being irritatingly overeager in the role of the novelist whose marriage, to genial academic Jeremy Northam, begins to unravel as she researches her latest book. The bodice-ripping fantasy sequences are excruciating, but Posey's scenes with sister Elizabeth McGovern and her chum Brooke Shields manage a cosy charm where the rest of the movie fails. Despite a few clever touches and its strong cast, this is a misadventure from start to finish. Contains swearing and sex scenes.

Parker Posey *Margaret Nathan* • Jeremy Northam *Edward Nathan* • Craig Chester *Richard Lane* • Elizabeth McGovern *Till Turner* • Brooke Shields *Lily* • Corbin Bernsen *Art Turner* ■ *Dir* Brian Skeet • *Scr* Brian Skeet, from the novel *Rameau's Niece* by Cathleen Schine

The Misadventures of Merlin Jones ★★
Comedy 1964 · US · Colour · 88mins

A pleasant, undemanding Disney comedy from the director of *The Absent-Minded Professor*. A college genius accidentally develops a means of reading minds. Turning this new ability to good use – in contrast to the way some of us might be tempted to exploit it – he tries to solve crimes, but winds up in court himself. The characters returned in a 1965 sequel, *The Monkey's Uncle*. 📺

Tommy Kirk *Merlin Jones* • Annette Funicello *Jennifer* • Leon Ames *Judge Holmby* • Stuart

Erwin *Police Capt Loomis* • Alan Hewitt *Prof Shattuck* • Connie Gilchrist *Mrs Gossett* ■ *Dir* Robert Stevenson • *Scr* Tom August [Alfred Lewis Levitt], Helen August [Helen Levitt], from a story by Bill Walsh

Misbegotten ★★ 18
Thriller 1998 · US · Colour · 92mins

This is a nasty stalker movie, vaguely in *The Hand That Rocks the Cradle* vein. Kevin Dillon plays a sociopath who's desperate to father a child, but who has a less than winning way with women. (The problem is he has a tendency to kill them.) When he donates his sperm, it's used by a couple who can't have children. Soon he's terrorising the twosome in a bid to become the hand that rocks the cradle. Dillon, younger brother of Matt, is undeniably good as the psycho-dad, but the film leaves an unpleasant taste. Nick Mancuso and Britain's Lysette Anthony co-star as the hapless couple. Contains swearing, violence, sex scene. 📺

Kevin Dillon *Billy Crapshoot* • Nick Mancuso *Paul Bourke* • Lysette Anthony *Caitlin Bourke* • Robert Lewis (2) *Detective Cross* • Matthew Walker *Dr Dotterweigh* • Stefan Arngrim *Conan Cornelius* ■ *Dir* Mark L Lester • *Scr* Larry Cohen, from the novel by James Gabriel Berman

Mischief ★★
Crime thriller 1983 · W Ger · Colour · 98mins

We hear so much about the decline of the British film industry, but that is nothing in comparison to the collapse of the German cinema. The situation is unlikely to improve if directors of the calibre of Peter Fleischmann can find nothing better than this quirky murder mystery. (It's as if Alan Parker had been hired to direct an episode of *Taggart*.) Fleischmann also stars as a workaholic cop who postpones a holiday to investigate the death of a child. The friction between the policeman and Angelika Stute, the child's mother and chief murder suspect, generates the odd spark, but otherwise there are too few surprises. German dialogue dubbed into English.

Peter Fleischmann *Detective Inspector Lohmann* • Angelika Stute *Annette* • Isolde Barth *Gilla* • Balduin Baas *Dürkheimer* • Horst Kummeth *Vesselitz* ■ *Dir* Peter Fleischmann • *Scr* Peter Fleischmann, Jacques Rozier, Werner Sommer

Mischief ★★ 15
Comedy 1985 · US · Colour · 92mins

Predictable teen comedy, set in the fifties, that tries to be a cross between *Porky's* and *American Graffiti* – a daft combination if ever there was one. Doug McKeon and Catherine Mary Stewart are two of the youngsters trying to find love and a decent plot in a cast that includes Jami Gertz and Kelly Preston, now better known as Mrs John Travolta. Contains swearing, violence, nudity. 📺

Doug McKeon *Jonathan* • Catherine Mary Stewart *Bunny* • Kelly Preston *Marilyn* • Chris Nash *Gene* • DW Brown *Kenny* • Jami Gertz *Rosalie* • Maggie Blye *Claire Miller* ■ *Dir* Mel Damski • *Scr* Noel Black

Les Misérables ★★★★★

Historical epic 1934 · Fr · BW · 305mins

Since 1909, there have been nearly two dozen film versions of Victor Hugo's vast novel. The story is trifling yet monumental. After serving a massive prison sentence for petty theft, Jean Valjean's spiritual transformation into a pillar of society is undermined by Javert, the policeman who obsessively pursues him. Add to this an epic panorama of French Revolutionary history and a doomed love affair, and you have a humanist masterpiece that works on a multitude of levels. Raymond Bernard's epic version of 1934 might be compared to Abel Gance's *Napoleon* (it shares the same cameraman, Jules Kruger): it's slow, unfailingly faithful to the source, and contains towering performances by Harry Bauer and Charles Vanel. In French with English subtitles.

Harry Baur *Jean Valjean* • Charles Vanel *Javert* • Henry Krauss *Monseignor Myriel* • Odette Florelle [Florelle] *Fantine* ■ *Dir* Raymond Bernard • *Scr* Raymond Bernard, Andre Lang, from the novel by Victor Hugo • *Cinematographer* Jules Kruger • *Music* Arthur Honneger

Les Misérables ★★★★

Historical epic 1935 · US · BW · 111mins

Victor Hugo's classic novel, popularly known as "The Glums", had been filmed several times in the silent era, and there was an impressive French version in 1934. Despite the guillotine taken to the text, however, this lavish 20th Century-Fox production (which imported MGM talent for the occasion) is generally considered to be the best. Fredric March, as condemned criminal Jean Valjean, gives a solid and noble performance, but the film is dominated by Charles Laughton as the policeman Javert, a magnificent portrayal of dark obsession. The film's emotional and ironic climax was regarded by Laughton as "the finest thing I have ever been able to accomplish on the screen".

Fredric March *Jean Valjean* • Charles Laughton *Javert* • Cedric Hardwicke *Bishop Bienvenu* • Rochelle Hudson *Big Cosette* • Marilyn Knowlden *Little Cosette* • Frances Drake *Eponine* • John Beal *Marius* • Jessie Ralph *Madame Magloire* ■ *Dir* Richard Boleslawski • *Scr* WP Lipscomb, from the novel by Victor Hugo • *Cinematographer* Gregg Toland

Les Misérables ★★

Historical drama 1946 · It · BW · 120mins

An Italian version of the Victor Hugo story, with the emphasis not, as one would expect, on Jean Valjean (Gino Cervi) and Inspector Javert (Hans Hinrich), but on Valentina Cortese, who plays both Fantine and her daughter Cosette. Original versions played in two parts – *Manhunt* and *Storm Over Paris* – of 90 minutes each. A foreign version, with lamentable English dubbing, was released in 1952 at 140 minutes; it was later cut to two hours. Italian dialogue dubbed into English.

Valentina Cortese *Fantine/Cosette* • Gino Cervi *Jean Valjean* • Hans Hinrich *Inspector Javert* • Aldo Nicodemi *Marius* ■ *Dir* Riccardo Freda • *Scr* Riccardo Freda, Mario Monicelli, Stefano Vanzina, from the novel by Victor Hugo • *Cinematographer* Rodolfo Lombardi

Les Misérables ★★★ U

Historical epic 1952 · US · BW · 105mins

Lewis Milestone's film is a faithful but undeniably pedestrian version of Victor Hugo's masterpiece. Michael Rennie makes a decent Valjean, but he comes in some way behind Harry Baur, Fredric March and Jean Gabin, all of whom invested the part with considerably more truth and emotion. Robert Newton plays Javert as an eye-rolling villain whose fanaticism is at odds with Milestone's contention that personality has no part to play in the enforcement of the law. Edmund Gwenn alone captures the novel's humanity as a benevolent bishop.

Michael Rennie *Jean Valjean* • Robert Newton *Javert* • Debra Paget *Cosette* • Edmund Gwenn *Bishop* • Sylvia Sidney *Fantine* • Cameron Mitchell *Marius* • Elsa Lanchester *Madame Magloire* • James Robertson-Justice *Robert* ■ *Dir* Lewis Milestone • *Scr* Richard Murphy, from the novel by Victor Hugo

Les Misérables ★★

Historical epic
1957 · E Ger/It/Fr · Colour · 210mins

Despite the presence of France's greatest screen actor, Jean Gabin, this version of Victor Hugo's classic is likely to lose many viewers during the course of its three-and-a-half hours. Gabin's performance as the petty criminal turned saintly hero Jean Valjean is perfectly adequate, and Bernard Blier is also good as Javert, the cop who obsessively haunts him. The problem lies in the stolid direction by former Resistance fighter Jean-Paul Le Chanois, while filming in the state-run studios of communist East Germany benefited only the budget. In French with English subtitles.

Jean Gabin *Jean Valjean* • Bernard Blier *Javert* • Bourvil *Thenardier* • Danièle Delorme *Fantine* • Fernand Ledoux *Myriel* • Béatrice Altariba *Cosette* • Gianni Esposito *Marius* • Silvia Montfort *Eponine* ■ *Dir* Jean-Paul Le Chanois • *Scr* Jean-Paul Le Chanois, Michel Audiard, René Barjavel, from the novel by Victor Hugo,

Les Misérables ★★★ PG

Historical drama
1978 · US · Colour · 137mins

Richard Jordan and Anthony Perkins take on the challenging roles of Valjean (the hunted) and Javert (the hunter) respectively in Victor Hugo's classic tale, investing this impressive TV movie with intelligence and depth. Director Glenn Jordan, a TV movie specialist whose early career was in the theatre, gives a luxurious (and thus ironic) feel to the claustrophobic world of Hugo's characters, providing plenty of room for his stars to shine.

Richard Jordan *Jean Valjean* • Anthony Perkins *Inspector Javert* • Cyril Cusack *Fauchelevent* • Claude Dauphin *Bishop Myriel* • John Gielgud *Gillenormand* • Ian Holm *Thenardier* • Celia Johnson *Sister Simplice* • Flora Robson *Prioress* ■ *Dir* Glenn Jordan • *Scr* John Gay, from the novel by Victor Hugo

Les Misérables ★★★

Historical epic 1982 · Fr · Colour · 180mins

A middling *Misérables*, better than the 1957 version with Jean Gabin, but not in the same league as the 1934 and 1935 versions or Claude Lelouch's radical update of 1995. Made for French TV and shown in six 50-minute episodes (a cinema version of three hours was shown first), Hossein's exhaustive and exhausting effort boasts an excellent Valjean and Javert in the charismatic, Bogart-like Lino Ventura and the creepy Michel Bouquet. It's a bit like a primer for French lit students, but some of it is spectacular to look at, with marvellous use of the medieval town of Sarlat. In French with English subtitles.

Lino Ventura *Jean Valjean* • Michel Bouquet *Inspector Javert* • Jean Carmet *Thenardier* • Françoise Seigner *La Thenardier* • Evelyne Bouix *Fantine* • Christine Jean *Cosette* • Frank David *Marius* • Candice Patou *Eponine* ■ *Dir* Robert Hossein • *Scr* Robert Hossein, Alain Decaux, from the novel by Victor Hugo

Les Misérables ★★★★ 12

Historical drama 1995 · Fr · Colour · 167mins

Director Claude Lelouch makes an ambitious attempt to update Victor Hugo's tale to the present century. Although he provides a provocative portrait of France under the Nazi occupation, this sprawling epic is very much a picaresque adventure, with Jean-Paul Belmondo outstanding as the former boxer for whom the task of keeping a Jewish family out of the clutches of the Nazis is no less daunting than completing Hugo's mammoth tome. Brimming with incident and with excellent support from Annie Girardot, this is an exhilarating and moving experience. In French with English subtitles.

Jean-Paul Belmondo *Henri Fortin/Jean Valjean* • Michel Boujenah *André Ziman* • Alessandra Martines *Elise Ziman* • Salomé [Salomé Lelouch] *Salomé Ziman* • Annie Giradot *Théardière farmer woman* ■ *Dir* Claude Lelouch • *Scr* Claude Lelouch, from the novel by Victor Hugo

Les Misérables ★★ 12

Historical epic 1997 · US · Colour · 127mins

Liam Neeson stars as the reformed criminal, Jean Valjean; Geoffrey Rush is the obsessive detective, Javert; while Uma Thurman and Claire Danes play the women Valjean cares for. On paper, this is an impressive cast; on screen, though, the performances are distinctly underwhelming. Bille August's production, mostly shot in Prague, looks like a TV mini-series that's been hacked down for cinema release; the rhythm is all wrong, and what is one of the shorter *Les Misérables* often seems the longest. Contains some swearing and violence.

Liam Neeson *Jean Valjean* • Geoffrey Rush *Javert* • Uma Thurman *Fantine* • Claire Danes *Cosette* • Hans Matheson *Marius* • Reine Brynolfsson *Captain Beauvais* • Peter Vaughan *Bishop* ■ *Dir* Bille August • *Scr* Rafael Yglesias, from the novel by Victor Hugo

Misery ★★★★ 18

Chiller 1990 · US · Colour · 103mins

Director Rob Reiner's superb adaptation of Stephen King's bestseller deals with the trappings of celebrity, fanatical devotion, artistic dilemmas and the worthiness of commercial fiction within a psychological suspense context. Kathy Bates deservedly won an Oscar for her monstrously scary performance as novelist James Caan's "Number One Fan", turning from caring nurse to insane "Baby Jane" torturer after learning he's killed off her favourite literary character. While not a true-blue horror movie, Reiner's adept exercise in chilling claustrophobia nevertheless contains numerous jolts, with the sledgehammer "hobbling" scene certain to evoke screams of revulsion. Contains violence and swearing.

James Caan *Paul Sheldon* • Kathy Bates *Annie Wilkes* • Richard Farnsworth *Buster, Sheriff* • Frances Sternhagen *Virginia* • Lauren Bacall *Marcia Sindell* • Graham Jarvis *Libby* • Jerry Potter *Pete* ■ *Dir* Rob Reiner • *Scr* William Goldman, from the novel by Stephen King • *Cinematographer* Barry Sonnenfeld

The Misfits ★★★★ PG

Drama 1961 · US · BW · 119mins

The last film of both Marilyn Monroe and Clark Gable, and some might say containing the last real performance by Montgomery Clift, John Huston's *The Misfits* is more of a mausoleum than a movie, going from box-office flop to cult status within the space of a year. Written by Monroe's then husband, Arthur Miller, it's a grey, solemn and at times pretentious piece about three drifters who hunt horses destined to become pet food. Somehow the flat, arid Nevada landscape mirrors the characters' bleak existence and sets the overall mood of despair and depression. Dogged by various production problems (Monroe's emotional upheavals, Clift's substance abuse, United Artists freezing the budget), it's a film that's easy to admire but hard to enjoy fully.

Clark Gable *Gay Langland* • Marilyn Monroe *Roslyn Taber* • Montgomery Clift *Perce Howland* • Eli Wallach *Guido* • Thelma Ritter *Isabelle Steers* • James Barton *Old man in bar* • Estelle Winwood *Church lady* • Kevin McCarthy *Raymond Taber* ■ *Dir* John Huston • *Scr* Arthur Miller

Mishima ★★★★ 15

Biographical drama
1985 · US/Jap · Colour and BW · 115mins

This is an astonishing account by Paul Schrader of the life and works of Yukio Mishima, the Japanese literary icon who committed *seppuku* (ritual suicide) on 25 November 1970. Audaciously cutting between the events of that day, monochrome flashbacks and stylised excerpts from Mishima's writings, Schrader produces a film of exemplary control and penetrating insight – a feat made all the more impressive by the fact that Mishima's widow forbade any explicit reference to her late husband's sexuality and controversial politics. Exquisitely designed by Eiko Ishioka, the scenes from *Temple of the Golden Pavilion*, *Kyoko's House* and *Runaway Horses* are not only mesmerisingly beautiful, but also shed as much light on the workings of Mishima's mind as any of his actions. In English and Japanese with subtitles.

Ken Ogata *Yukio Mishima* • Masayuki Shionoya *Morita* • Junkichi Orimoto *General Mashita* • Naoko Otani *Mother* • Go Riju *Mishima, aged 18-19* • Masato Aizawa *Mishima, aged 9-14* • Yuki Nagahara *Mishima, aged 5* • Haruko Kato *Grandmother* ■ *Dir* Paul Schrader • *Scr* Leonard Schrader, Paul Schrader, Chieko Schrader, from various literary works by Yukio Mishima

936

U = SUITABLE FOR ALL Uc = SUITABLE FOR ALL, ESPECIALLY FOR YOUNG CHILDREN (VIDEO ONLY) PG = PARENTAL GUIDANCE

Misplaced ★★★
Drama   1989 · US · Colour · 98mins

The feature debut of Polish-born Louis Yansen was barely seen outside the film festival circuit, but this intelligent exploration of coming to terms with an entirely new way of life deserved a wider audience. The melting-pot theme has been a Hollywood standby since Charlie Chaplin's *The Immigrant* in 1917, but this is one of the few films to focus on the struggles of an exile whose life has been ruined. An English and Polish language film.

John Cameron Mitchell *Jacek Nowak* • Viveca Lindfors *Zofia* • Elzbieta Czyzewska *Halina Nowak* • Drew Snyder *Bill* • Deirdre O'Connell *Ela* • Debralee Scott *Mrs Padway* • John Christopher Jones *David* • Tico Wells *Clayton* ■ *Dir* Louis Yansen • *Scr* Louis Yansen, Lonnie Carter, Thomas De Wolfe, from a story by Louis Yansen

Miss Amerigua ★★★
Political satire
1994 · Chil/Swe · Colour · 97mins

Chilean director Luis R Vera is currently based in Sweden, but he returns to his homeland for this stylish tale of love and revenge. Neatly plotted by Vera and his fellow scriptwriter Andras Colman, the story follows a young revolutionary as he returns to avenge his father's murder just as the town is gripped by a beauty contest, in which the three favourites are his sister, his beloved and the daughter of his father's killer. Forget the complex political allegory, this is a sizzling melodrama in the tradition of *Chronicle of a Death Foretold*. In Spanish with English subtitles.

Hector Silva *Evaristo* • Sonia Marchewka *Maria Desamparo* • Jesus Perez *Colonel Banderas* • Jorge Baez *Inocencio Periodista* • Carlos Cristaldo *Reencarnacion* ■ *Dir* Luis R Vera • *Scr* Andras Colman, Luis R Vera

Miss Annie Rooney ★★
Drama   1942 · US · BW · 86mins

At the age of 14, former childhood sweetheart Shirley Temple was having trouble sustaining her popularity, and this is one of the mild vehicles she found herself in after leaving Fox. The star sings and jitterbugs, but its chief selling point was the fact that Temple received her first screen kiss (though it's little more than a peck on the cheek). It was given by another former child star Dickie Moore (later married to Jane Powell), who would state that the kiss was a first for him too. Moore couldn't dance, so those scenes were performed by Roland Dupree, wearing a moulded rubber face-mask in the image of his co-star.

Shirley Temple *Annie Rooney* • William Gargan *Tim Rooney* • Guy Kibbee *Grandpop Rooney* • Dickie Moore *Marty White* • Peggy Ryan *Myrtle* • Roland DuPree *Joey* • Jonathan Hale *Mr White* • Gloria Holden *Mrs White* ■ *Dir* Edwin L Marin • *Scr* George Bruce

Miss Evers' Boys ★★★★
Period drama   1997 · US · Colour · 118mins

Based on the play by David Feldshuh, this Emmy-award-winning true story brilliantly dramatises a dark and shameful chapter in America's recent past. Alfre Woodard stars as a caring nurse who tries to alleviate her

patients' suffering while working on a federal health project in thirties Alabama. The study, intended to monitor and treat syphilis among poor African-American men, instead lapses into a heartless experiment on patients deteriorating into madness from the untreated disease. Writer Walter Bernstein's sensitive adaptation, Joseph Sargent's direction and a distinguished cast make this TV movie a drama of rare power and eloquence.

Alfre Woodard *Eunice Evers* • Laurence Fishburne *Caleb Humphries* • Craig Sheffer *Dr Douglas* • Joe Morton *Dr Brodus* • Ossie Davis *Mr Evers* • EG Marshall *Senate chairman* ■ *Dir* Joseph Sargent • *Scr* Walter Bernstein, from the play by David Feldshuh

Miss Firecracker ★★★ PG
Comedy drama   1989 · US · Colour · 98mins

Dazzling Holly Hunter is full of energetic snap, crackle and pop as she re-creates the part she made her own on stage in the play by Beth Henley, writer of *Crimes of the Heart*. It's Hunter's dream to win the Yazoo City beauty contest, and the tale of how she makes it to the finals against all the odds is beautifully told by director Thomas Schlamme. A gentle comedy, filled with Southern eccentrics deliciously brought to scene-stealing life by the likes of Mary Steenburgen, Alfre Woodard and Tim Robbins. 📼

Holly Hunter *Carnelle Scott* • Mary Steenburgen *Elain Rutledge* • Tim Robbins *Delmount Williams* • Alfre Woodard *Popeye Jackson* • Scott Glenn *Mac Sam* • Veanne Cox *Tessy Mahoney* • Ann Wedgeworth *Miss Blue* ■ *Dir* Thomas Schlamme • *Scr* Beth Henley, from her play

Miss Grant Takes Richmond ★★★ U
Crime comedy   1949 · US · BW · 88mins

An archetypal dumb blonde takes a job as a secretary in a real-estate office, unaware that it's a fake outfit fronting a crooked betting syndicate. When she concerns herself with the problems of the homeless, her boss finds himself organising a low-cost housing scheme as a way of paying off his bad gambling debts. A lightweight comedy, directed with a suitably light touch by Lloyd Bacon, the movie's main attraction is Lucille Ball in a role tailor-made for her kooky talents. She's ably supported by a personable William Holden as her bemused boss.

Lucille Ball *Ellen Grant* • William Holden (1) *Dick Richmond* • Janis Carter *Peggy Donato* • James Gleason *J Hobart Gleason* • Gloria Henry *Helen White* • Frank McHugh *Kilcoyne* ■ *Dir* Lloyd Bacon • *Scr* Nat Perrin, Devery Freeman, Frank Tashlin, from the story by Everett Freeman

Miss Julie ★★★★
Drama   1951 · Swe · BW · 90mins

Considered shocking in its day for the eroticism of its exchanges, Alf Sjöberg's adaptation of August Stringberg's one-act play shared the Grand Prix at Cannes with Vittorio De Sica's *Miracle in Milan*. Defying her inexperience, Anita Björk gives a wickedly wilful performance as the spoilt daughter who takes out the resentment she feels towards her ex-fiancé (and men in general) by goading

the family's misanthropic valet, Ulf Palme, into seducing her. Though the flashback/flash forward structure dissipates the intensity of their confrontations, it enables Sjöberg to explore the attitudes Björk inherited from her mother, and the price she pays for her cruelty. A Swedish language film.

Anita Björk *Miss Julie* • Ulf Palme *Jean* • Inger Norberg *Miss Julie as a child* • Jan Hagerman *Jean as a child* ■ *Dir* Alf Sjöberg • *Scr* Alf Sjöberg, from the play by August Strindberg

Miss Julie ★★★ 15
Drama   1999 · US · Colour · mins

Mike Figgis directs this fourth screen adaptation of August Strindberg's play as a vehicle for the statuesque Saffron Burrows. She plays the eponymous Julie, the spoilt daughter of a wealthy family, whose nocturnal dalliance with footman Jean (Peter Mullan) threatens to bring destruction down on both their heads. Claustrophobically filmed on a single set, this virtual two-hander (the third main character, played by Maria Doyle Kennedy, sleeps through most of the action) suffers from a marked height imbalance between the leads, which renders much of their interaction faintly ludicrous. Mullan, however, brings an intensity and rage to the upstart Jean that can be compared favourably with his sterling work in Ken Loach's *My Name Is Joe*. Contains swearing and a sex scene.

Saffron Burrows *Miss Julie* • Peter Mullan *Jean* • Maria Doyle Kennedy *Christine* ■ *Dir* Mike Figgis • *Scr* Helen Cooper, from the play by August Strindberg

Miss London Ltd ★★★
Musical comedy   1943 · UK · BW · 99mins

This was the first feature film directed by Val Guest, who had written several scripts for comics Will Hay and Arthur Askey. For this lively musical, Guest also co-wrote the script and provided the lyrics for the eight Manning Sherwin melodies. The story – perky blonde Evelyn Dall inherits half of a rundown escort agency and sets out to make it a success with partner Askey – is an excuse for songs and lots of comic business. Guest keeps the whole jolly affair ticking along nicely.

Arthur Askey *Arthur Bowman* • Evelyn Dall *Terry Arden* • Anne Shelton *Gail Martin* • Richard Hearne *Commodore* • Max Bacon *Romeo* • Jack Train *Joe Nelson* • Peter Graves (2) *Capt Rory O'More* ■ *Dir* Val Guest • *Scr* Val Guest, Marriott Edgar

Miss Mary ★★★ 15
Drama   1986 · Arg/US · Colour · 95mins

One of those strange but all too vacuous roles that the highly politicised Julie Christie took on during the eighties. She plays a sexually repressed but simmering governess, employed by an aristocratic Argentinian family in the late thirties. And that's your lot, really, as the pot never boils over sufficiently to make it interesting. Christie looks great in high-cut, flouncy collars and the scenery is spectacular, but one has an irresistible urge to tell her to stop dithering. Some dialogue in Spanish with English subtitles. Contains some swearing. 📼

Julie Christie *Mary Mulligan* • Nacha Guevara *Mecha* • Luisina Brando *Perla* • Eduardo Pavlovsky *Alfredo* • Gerardo Romano *Ernesto* • Iris Marga *Grandmother* • Guillermo Battaglia *Grandfather* ■ *Dir* Maria Luisa Bemberg • *Scr* Maria Luisa Bemberg, Jorge Goldenberg

Miss Nobody ★★★
Drama   1997 · Pol · Colour · 103mins

Adapted from a novel by Tomek Tryzna, this is one of Andrzej Wajda's lesser achievements. Few of his films have focused solely on female protagonists, and an uncertainty of tone undermines the account of rural teenager Anna Wielgucka's tempestuous relationships with the girls at her Warsaw school. These include New Age devotee Anna Mucha and Anna Powierza, whose brusque cynicism arouses unexpectedly rebellious emotions. Overstressing the allegorical undertones and uncomfortable with both the philosophical and sexual aspects of the story, Wajda nevertheless coaxes persuasive performances from his young cast. A Polish language film.

Anna Wielgucka *Marysia Kawaczak* • Anna Mucha *Kasia* • Anna Powierza *Ewa* • Stanislawa Celinska *Marysia's mother* ■ *Dir* Andrzej Wajda • *Scr* Radoslaw Piwowarski, from a novel by Tomek Tryzna

Miss Oyu ★★★
Drama   1951 · Jap · Colour · 95mins

Kenji Mizoguchi's first collaboration with cinematographer Kazuo Miyagawa disappointed the critics and the director alike. However, this had little to do with the long, fluid takes, nor the intensity of the performances. The problem lies with Junichiro Tanizaki's source novel, which offered Mizoguchi little chance to explore his usual social and gynocentric themes. The film stars Kinuyo Tanaka as the respectable widow who persuades her younger sister, Nobuko Otowa, to marry the wealthy Yuji Hori so that she can continue their affair while protecting her son's inheritance. A Japanese language film.

Kinuyo Tanaka *Oyu Kayukawa* • Nobuko Otowa *Shizu* • Yuji Hori *Shinnosuke Seribashi* • Kiyoko Hirai *Osumi* ■ *Dir* Kenji Mizoguchi • *Scr* Yoshikata Yoda, from a novel by Junichiro Tanizaki • *Cinematographer* Kazuo Miyagawa

Miss Robin Hood ★★ U
Comedy   1952 · UK · BW · 76mins

Coming between her acclaimed supporting roles in *The Importance of Being Earnest* and *Innocents in Paris*, this disappointing comedy gave the much-loved and ever-reliable Margaret Rutherford a rare chance to star. Considering the infectious enthusiasm of her performance as the mischievous Miss Honey, she deserved better material than this slight skirmish with a gang of crooks over a valuable whisky recipe. There are solid turns from such stalwarts as Sid James and James Robertson-Justice, but writers Val Valentine and Patrick Campbell (of *Call My Bluff* fame) have over-diluted the mixture for most tastes.

Margaret Rutherford *Miss Honey* • Richard Hearne *Henry Wrigley* • Michael Medwin *Ernest* • Peter Jones *Lidstone* • James Robertson-Justice *McAllister* • Sidney James

Sidney • Dora Bryan *Pearl* ■ *Dir* John Guillermin • *Scr* Val Valentine, Patrick Campbell, from a story by Reed de Rouen

Miss Rose White ★★★★

Drama   1992 · US · Colour · 95mins

Kyra Sedgwick made her debut as a Polish Jew in the little-seen 1985 feature *War and Love*, and she plays a similiar character in this TV movie. Adapted from Barbara Lebow's much-praised play *A Shayna Maidel*, this is the moving story of two sisters exiled in New York – one who escaped the Holocaust and one who survived it. Describing their terrifying experiences with heartrending conviction, Amanda Plummer will surprise those used to seeing her in more manic roles, while Maximilian Schell and Maureen Stapleton provide solid support.

Kyra Sedgwick *Rayzell Weiss/Rose White* • Amanda Plummer *Lusia* • Penny Fuller *Miss Ryan* • Maureen Stapleton *Tanta Perla* • Maximilian Schell *Mordechai* • DB Sweeney *Dan* • Milton Selzer *Shimon* • Gina Gershon *Angie* ■ *Dir* Joseph Sargent • *Scr* Anna Sandor, from the play *A Shayna Maidel* by Barbara Lebow

Miss Sadie Thompson ★★★

Drama   1953 · US · Colour · 90mins

It's Somerset Maugham's *Rain* again, this time with sexy Rita Hayworth in the title role as the hooker who floors a religious fanatic. Originally this movie was made in 3-D and composed for widescreen, so on TV you see too many floors and ceilings and a lot of room above the actors' heads in close-up. Try to ignore all that, and enjoy instead an over-the-top performance from the smitten José Ferrer. Watch out, too, for a young Charles Bronson.

Rita Hayworth *Sadie Thompson* • José Ferrer *Alfred Davidson* • Aldo Ray *Sergeant Phil O'Hara* • Russell Collins *Dr Robert MacPhail* • Diosa Costello *Ameena Horn* • Harry Bellaver *Joe Horn* • Wilton Graff *Governor* • Charles Bronson *Edwards* ■ *Dir* Curtis Bernhardt • *Scr* Harry Kleiner, from the short story *Rain* by W Somerset Maugham

Miss Susie Slagle's ★★★

Period drama   1945 · US · BW · 87mins

Lillian Gish runs a boarding house in Baltimore for medical students training at the famed John Hopkins institution and keeps a motherly eye on their concerns and love affairs. Under the direction of John Berry, a newcomer to film but an alumnus of Orson Welles and John Houseman's Mercury Theatre company, those involved include Veronica Lake, Joan Caulfield, Sonny Tufts and Lloyd Bridges, father of Jeff and Beau. A charming and gentle period piece, set in 1910 and illumined, as always, by the presence of Gish. She'd been in film for three decades, and had another four to go.

Veronica Lake *Nan Rogers* • Sonny Tufts *Pug Prentiss* • Joan Caulfield *Margaretta Howe* • Ray Collins *Dr Elijah Howe* • Billy De Wolfe *Ben Mead* • Lillian Gish *Miss Susie Slagle* • Lloyd Bridges *Silas Holmes* ■ *Dir* John Berry • *Scr* Anne Froelick, Hugo Butler, Theodore Strauss, Adrian Scott, from the novel by Augusta Tucker

Miss Tatlock's Millions ★★★★ Ⓤ

Comedy   1948 · US · BW · 100mins

One of the brighter comedies of the late forties, this verges perilously close to bad taste, with lead John Lund pretending to be an idiot for most of the picture. Hired to attend the reading of a will, Lund continues the deception after the lunatic he is portraying unexpectedly becomes co-heir to a fortune. Character actor Richard Haydn proves an astute choice of director, milking the situations for all their worth as the avaricious family endure Lund's outrageous behaviour to remain in favour. Billed as Richard Rancyd, Haydn also appears as an eccentric lawyer. John Lund and writers Charles Brackett and Richard Breen had developed their feel for acerbic comedy on Billy Wilder's *A Foreign Affair*.

John Lund *Burke* • Wanda Hendrix *Nan Tatlock* • Barry Fitzgerald *Denno Noonan* • Monty Woolley *Miles Tatlock* • Ilka Chase *Cassie Van Alen* • Robert Stack *Nickey Van Alen* • Ray Milland • Richard Rancyd [Richard Haydn] *Fergel* ■ *Dir* Richard Haydn • *Scr* Charles Brackett, Richard Breen, from the play *Oh – Brother* by Jacques Deval

Missing ★★★★ ⑮

Drama based on a true story
1981 · US · Colour · 117mins

The US State Department denounced Costa-Gavras's uncompromising human drama when it was first released because of possible political repercussions. But then the director of *Z* and *State of Siege* was used to causing controversy, and this riveting true saga proved to be his most accessible Kafkaesque nightmare. What happened to American writer Charles Horman, who disappeared during the military coup that overthrew the Allende government of Chile in 1973? That's what his liberal wife Sissy Spacek and staunchly conservative father Jack Lemmon try to find out in a compelling moral tale. Contains swearing and nudity. ▦

Jack Lemmon *Ed Horman* • Sissy Spacek *Beth Horman* • Melanie Mayron *Terry Simon* • John Shea *Charles Horman* • Charles Cioffi *Captain Ray Tower* • David Clennon *Consul Phil Putnam* • Richard Venture *US Ambassador* • Jerry Hardin *Colonel Sean Patrick* ■ *Dir* Costa-Gavras • *Scr* Costa-Gavras, Donald Stewart, from a non-fiction book by Thomas Hauser • *Music* Vangelis

Missing in Action ★★ ⑮

Action thriller   1984 · US · Colour · 97mins

Chuck Norris is Colonel Braddock, an American soldier who was held illegally in a Vietnamese PoW camp for seven years after the war ended. Now he returns to Vietnam to prove that other Americans are still being held. When diplomatic means fail, Braddock arms himself and goes on a one-man commando mission to liberate the GIs. Stupid, simplistic and often racist, *Missing in Action* helped kick off the cycle of films in which Americans fought the Vietnam War again – only this time, they won. Lots of action and posturing by Norris. ▦

Chuck Norris *Colonel Braddock* • M Emmet Walsh *Tuck* • David Tress *Senator Porter* • Lenore Kasdorf *Ann* • James Hong *General Tran* ■ *Dir* Joseph Zito • *Scr* James Bruner,

from a story by John Crowther, Lance Hool, from characters created by Arthur Silver, Larry Levinson, Steve Bing

Missing in Action 2: the Beginning ★★ ⑱

Action adventure   1985 · US · Colour · 91mins

"You may not give a damn about the Geneva Convention, but some day you will be held accountable," Chuck Norris warns the commander of the camp in which he is being held. If only we could hold Norris accountable for this movie, which is even more blockheaded than the first. The subtitle should clue you in to the fact that this prequel shows us the origins of Colonel Braddock, Norris's self-righteous, gun-toting patriot. His adventures among the scheming commanders, brutal guards and their sadistic torture methods will make you beg for mercy long before he does. A second sequel, *Braddock: Missing in Action III* followed in 1988. ▦

Chuck Norris *Colonel Braddock* • Soon-Teck Oh *Colonel Yin* • Cosie Costa *Mazilli* • Steven Williams *Captain David Nester* • David Chung *Dou Chou* • Joe Michael Terry *Opelka* ■ *Dir* Lance Hool • *Scr* Arthur Silver, Larry Levinson, Steve Bing

Missing Link ★★ ⓅⒼ

Prehistoric documentary drama
1989 · US · Colour · 87mins

The travails of the last apeman, doomed to extinction by Man's invention of the axe circa one million years BC, provide the basis for this odd, non-dialogue "mockumentary". Gifted mime artist Peter Elliott, who choreographed the primates in *Greystoke*, brings a savage wistfulness to a prehistory lesson resembling the "Dawn of Man" prologue from *2001* in both look and tone. Shot on stunning Namibian locations, it contains unsubtle ecological messages and dire warnings, but fans of nature shows will love the wildlife footage. ▦

Peter Elliott *Apeman* • Michael Gambon *Narrator* ■ *Dir/Scr* David Hughes, Carol Hughes • *Cinematographer* David Hughes, Carol Hughes

Missing Pieces ★★★ ⑮

Thriller   1983 · US · Colour · 96mins

Not the misfiring Eric Idle comedy of the same name, but an entertaining made-for-TV thriller starring former *Bewitched* actress Elizabeth Montgomery. Directing his first film since 1980's camp sci-fi fantasy *Flash Gordon*, Mike Hodges makes a solid job of bringing Karl Alexander's source novel *A Private Investigation* to the screen. Hodges generates plenty of suspense as a widow turns sleuth to find the murderer of her husband. Montgomery is perfectly cast and she's matched by Ron Karabatsos as a cynical private eye. ▦

Elizabeth Montgomery *Sara Scott* • Ron Karabatsos *Claude Papazian* • John Reilly *Sam* • Louanne *Valerie Scott* • Robin Gammell *Lawrence Conrad* • Julius Harris *Spencer Harris* • David Haskell *Andy Scott* • Daniel Pilon *Jorge Martinez* ■ *Dir* Mike Hodges • *Scr* Mike Hodges, from the novel *A Private Investigation* by Karl Alexander

Missing Pieces ★★ ⓅⒼ

Comedy thriller   1991 · US · Colour · 88mins

Unlike Messrs Cleese and Palin, ex-Monty Python member Eric Idle hasn't had much success in movies. In this mongrel of a comedy, he plays a man who, fired by a greetings card company, teams up with unemployed cellist Robert Wuhl. What follows is a detective mystery about an inheritance that leads our heroes to Los Angeles and up several blind alleys. Blending *The Maltese Falcon* with *The Odd Couple*, this comedy falls flat in most departments, though there is a decent *femme fatale* in Lauren Hutton. Contains some swearing. ▦

Eric Idle *Wendel Dickens* • Robert Wuhl *Lou Wimpole* • Lauren Hutton *Jennifer* • Bob Gunton *Mr Gabor* • Richard Belzer *Baldesari* • Bernie Kopell *Dr Gutman* • Kim Lankford *Sally* ■ *Dir* Leonard Stern [Leonard B Stern] • *Scr* Leonard Stern [Leonard B Stern]

The Mission ★★★ ⓅⒼ

Historical drama
1986 · UK · Colour · 119mins

Winner of the Palme d'Or at Cannes, but given a mixed critical reception on release, this is a studied, elegant and, ultimately, very moving historical drama set in 1750s South America. There's no denying the existence of longueurs in Robert Bolt's script, a certain flabbiness in Roland Joffé's direction and a distinctly detached contribution from a curiously cast Robert De Niro. However, Jeremy Irons more than makes amends with a performance of great sincerity as the head of a Jesuit mission under threat from the greed of Iberian slavers and the whim of cardinal Ray McAnally. Chris Menges's Oscar-winning photography is glorious, while Ennio Morricone's score sends shivers down the spine. Contains violence and some nudity. ▦

Robert De Niro *Mendoza* • Jeremy Irons *Father Gabriel* • Ray McAnally *Altamirano* • Aidan Quinn *Felipe* • Cherie Lunghi *Carlotta* • Ronald Pickup *Hontar* • Liam Neeson *Fielding* • Chuck Low *Cabeza* ■ *Dir* Roland Joffé • *Scr* Robert Bolt, from his story

Mission: Impossible ★★★★ ⓅⒼ

Action spy thriller
1996 · US · Colour · 105mins

Superstar Tom Cruise and director Brian De Palma join forces for this thrilling extravaganza of jaw-dropping special effects and amazing stunts. Based on the cult sixties TV series about a covert strike force designing situations villains believe to be real, it's best to forget the complicated plot – something about Cruise clearing his name and proving to the CIA he's not a treacherous mole – and simply enjoy the epic roller coaster ride that De Palma brings to life with his customary brilliance. The burglary of a guarded vault and the Channel Tunnel helicopter pursuit alone put other thrillers in intensive care. ▦ **DVD**

Tom Cruise *Ethan Hunt* • Jon Voight *Jim Phelps* • Emmanuelle Béart *Claire* • Henry Czerny *Kittridge* • Jean Reno *Krieger* • Ving Rhames *Luther* • Kristin Scott Thomas *Sarah Davies* • Vanessa Redgrave *Max* • Dale Dye *Frank Barnes* • Marcel Iures *Golitsyn* ■ *Dir*

Brian De Palma • *Scr* David Koepp, Robert Towne, from a story by David Koepp, Steven Zaillian, from the TV series by Bruce Geller

Mission: Impossible 2 ★★★★ 15

Action spy thriller
1999 · US · Colour · 123mins

By junking the tired spy shenanigans of the original TV series and replacing them with the slick, slo-mo mayhem that has become his trademark, John Woo creates a sequel very different from the first *Mission: Impossible*. Admittedly, there's a distinct shortage of pulse-quickening, slam-bang action in the first hour, which finds Tom Cruise's pumped-up agent Ethan Hunt wooing voluptuous lady thief Thandie Newton before heading Down Under to stop bad guy Dougray Scott holding the world to ransom with a new killer virus. Around the halfway mark, though, Woo cranks the pace up a gear and bombards the viewer with high-tech lab raids, jaw-dropping motorbike stunts and balletic martial arts moves. If it's adrenalin you're after, look no further.

Tom Cruise *Ethan Hunt* • Dougray Scott *Sean Ambrose* • Thandie Newton *Nyah Hall* • Ving Rhames *Luther Stickell* • Richard Roxburgh *Hugh Stamp* • John Polson *Billy Baird* • Anthony Hopkins *Mission Commander Swanbeck* ■ *Dir* John Woo • *Scr* Robert Towne, Ronald D Moore, from the TV series by Bruce Geller • *Cinematographer* Jeffrey L Kimball

Mission of Justice ★★ 18

Martial arts action
1992 · US · Colour · 94mins

Brigitte Nielsen's presence is the first sign that the proceedings here are unlikely to be taken too seriously. As mayoral candidate Rachel K Larkin, she runs the titular mission, a training centre for ersatz Guardian Angels, though she is already secretly executing her sinister plans. Jeff Wincott, stiff as ever, is the cop who goes undercover to expose her. Cheerfully mindless, this excuse for action delivers a number of well-executed fight sequences as well as some welcome mirth. 🖭

Jeff Wincott *Kurt Harris* • Brigitte Nielsen *Rachel K Larkin* • Tony Burton *Cedric Williams* • Luca Bercovici *Roger Stockwell* • Matthias Hues *Titus Larkin* • Karen Sheperd *Lynn Steele* • Cyndi Pass *Erin Miller* ■ *Dir* Steve Barnett • *Scr* George Saunders, John Bryant Hedberg, from a story by Pierre David

Mission of the Shark ★★★ PG

Second World War drama
1991 · US · Colour · 93mins

Featuring scenes that equal those in *Jaws* for tension, this tale of military incompetence and deceit comes straight from official war records. When the USS *Indianapolis* (a carrier for parts of the atom bomb that was used on Hiroshima) is struck by torpedoes from a Japanese submarine, Captain Charles McVay (played by Stacy Keach) orders his crew to abandon ship and face the shark-infested waters of the Pacific. But it is not until 15 years after the event that the full story of the sinking emerges. Keach gives an impressive performance as the beleaguered commanding officer, and

he gets solid support from Richard Thomas and David Caruso.

Stacy Keach *Captain Charles McVay* • Richard Thomas *Lt Cmdr Steven Scott* • David Caruso *Marine Captain Gerald Wilkes* • Robert Cicchini *Lt Gary DiAngelo* • Don Harvey *Petty Officer Charles Kinderman* • William Jordan *Commodore William Hathaway* • Cary Hiroyuki-Tagawa *Lt Cmdr Mochitsura Hashimoto* ■ *Dir* Robert Iscove • *Scr* Alan Sharp

Mission to Mars ★★★ PG

Science-fiction 1999 · US · Colour · 113mins

Brian De Palma slums it with his first science-fiction melodrama, which comes loaded with sentiment, camp moments and risible dialogue. However, while there's nothing new in this red planet space opera (mostly lifted from *2001: a Space Odyssey* and *Close Encounters of the Third Kind*) the *Carrie* director covers its drawbacks with pristine craftsmanship, trademark suspense sequences and a full quota of sharp computer visuals. The age-old question "Is there life on Mars?" is answered by NASA astronauts Gary Sinise and Tim Robbins when they embark on a rescue mission to the planet and make an extraordinary discovery. It may be an overbaked *Mission: Improbable*, but De Palma's outer space adventure is still a highly affecting warp drive.

Gary Sinise *Jim McConnell* • Don Cheadle *Mission Commander Luke Graham* • Connie Nielsen *Mars Rescue Mission specialist Dr Terri Fisher* • Tim Robbins *Commander Woody Blake* • Jerry O'Connell *Mission Specialist Phil Ohlmyer* • Armin Mueller-Stahl *Ray Beck* ■ *Dir* Brian De Palma • *Scr* John Thomas, Jim Thomas, Graham Yost, from a story by John Thomas, Jim Thomas, Lowell Cannon

Mission to Moscow ★★★★ U

Drama 1943 · US · BW · 121mins

This prestigious Warner Bros epic is based on US ambassador Joseph E Davies's bestseller about his pre-Second World War years in the Soviet Union, and is introduced by Davies himself. What lends it particular piquancy today is its documentary-style depiction of a pre-Cold War, pre-Red Scare Russia, filmed at an impressive pace by director Michael Curtiz. Walter Huston is ideally cast as the avuncular Davies, and it's sobering to realise that in subsequent years the film was denounced as pro-Communist propaganda because of its view of Stalin as a benevolent ruler.

Walter Huston *Ambassador Joseph E Davies* • Ann Harding *Mrs Davies* • Oscar Homolka *Maxim Litvinov* • George Tobias *Freddie* • Gene Lockhart *Vyacheslav Molotov* • Frieda Inescort *Madame Molotov* • Eleanor Parker *Emlen Davies* • Richard Travis *Paul Grosjean* ■ *Dir* Michael Curtiz • *Scr* Howard Koch, from the non-fiction book by Joseph E Davies

Mission Top Secret ★★

Adventure 1990 · Ausl · Colour

Lightweight children's adventure about an intrepid group of teenagers jetting around the world to foil a gang of baddies who have stolen some valuable middle-eastern artefacts. It's an episodic affair that probably would be better as a TV series. But locations are suitably exotic, and Shane Briant, British veteran of horror movies such

as *Cassandra* and *Frankenstein and the Monster from Hell*, has fun as the evil super-criminal.

Miguel Ayesa *Pedro* • Rachel Friend *Annette* • Beth Buchanan *Danielle* • Brian Rooney *Jim* • Jason Phillips *Prince Hassan* • Fedja Nijhold *Marco* • Shane Briant *Savage* ■ *Dir* Howard Rubie • *Scr* David Phillips

The Missionary ★★★ 15

Comedy 1982 · UK · Colour · 77mins

In his first solo film venture away from the Pythons, Michael Palin came up with a sort of saucy Ealing comedy, in which the characters seem like refugees from a bawdy version of PG Wodehouse's timeless neverland of toffs and twits. Palin is pleasing enough as an innocent abroad in the crinoline jungle of Edwardian prostitution, but it's the supporting cast that has all the fun, with Maggie Smith in fine fettle as a frustrated aristocrat. Palin struggles to sustain the comedy throughout this bodice-ripping yarn, but Richard Loncraine lashes on the period style to good effect. Contains swearing. 🖭

Michael Palin *Reverend Charles Fortescue* • Maggie Smith *Lady Ames* • Trevor Howard *Lord Ames* • Denholm Elliott *The Bishop* • Michael Hordern *Slatterthwaite* • Graham Crowden *Reverend Fitzbanks* • Phoebe Nicholls *Deborah* • Tricia George *Ada* ■ *Dir* Richard Loncraine • *Scr* Michael Palin

Mississippi ★★

Musical comedy 1935 · US · BW · 80mins

To escape accusations of cowardice, a creamy-voiced Southerner joins a showboat on the Mississippi, finds true love and rescues his reputation. Directed by A Edward Sutherland as a vehicle for Bing Crosby, this rambling period musical is partly redeemed by several Rodgers and Hart numbers, while WC Fields is splendid as the boat's captain. (In one memorable scene, he draws five aces in a poker game.) Joan Bennett provides the romantic interest.

Bing Crosby *Tom Grayson/Col Steele* • WC Fields *Commodore Orlando Jackson* • Joan Bennett *Lucy Rumford* • Queenie Smith *Alabam'* • Gail Patrick *Elvira Rumford* ■ *Dir* A Edward Sutherland • *Scr* Francis Martin, Jack Cunningham, Claude Binyon, Herbert Fields, from the play *Magnolia* by Booth Tarkington

Mississippi Burning ★★★★ 18

Drama based on a true story
1988 · US · Colour · 121mins

Arguably Alan Parker's most powerful film to date, in which Gene Hackman gives a mesmerising performance as a Southern States FBI agent fighting racism with local knowledge and canny psychology, teamed with an equally impressive, if more restrained Willem Dafoe as his rule-obsessed Ivy League partner. Parker's wonderful creation crackles with dramatic tension and simmering violence which often reaches boiling point. Loosely based on a true story and shot with great visual flair (Peter Biziou won the Oscar for best cinematography), this is a gripping evocation of the early days of the civil rights movement. 🖭

Gene Hackman *Rupert Anderson* • Willem Dafoe *Alan Ward* • Frances McDormand *Mrs*

Pell • Brad Dourif *Deputy Pell* • R Lee Ermey *Mayor Tilman* • Gailard Sartain *Sheriff Stuckey* • Michael Rooker *Frank Bailey* • Pruitt Taylor Vince *Lester Cowens* ■ *Dir* Alan Parker • *Scr* Chris Gerolmo

The Mississippi Gambler ★★★ U

Adventure 1953 · US · Colour · 98mins

This film comes from an awkward stage in the career of matinée idol Tyrone Power, when his shrewd agent Ted Richmond set up independent deals at various studios to capitalise on Power's star appeal before it waned, or before Power lost his looks, whichever occurred the sooner. As it happened, Power matured nicely, but tragically didn't live long enough to progress to character roles. Here he is at Universal playing a handsome and honest riverboat gambler, forced to jump ship with partner John McIntire to chase comely Piper Laurie in New Orleans. The studio sets and location photography look superb, but the leads are dull and the plot unnecessarily complicated. Despite its flaws, however, the film proved popular.

Tyrone Power *Mark Fallon* • Piper Laurie *Angelique Duroux* • Julia Adams [Julie Adams] *Ann Conant* • John McIntire *Kansas John Polly* • William Reynolds *Pierre* • Paul Cavanagh *Edmund Duroux* • John Baer *Laurent Duroux* ■ *Dir* Rudolph Maté • *Scr* Seton I Miller

Mississippi Masala ★★★★ 15

Romantic drama
1991 · US · Colour · 112mins

A "masala" is a culinary collection of hot and colourful spices used in curry dishes. Here, though, it's a good word to describe the Mississippi community where black American Denzel Washington falls in love with Asian woman Sarita Choudhury, causing tension between their families. As a mix of romance and racism, Mira Nair's follow-up to *Salaam Bombay!* (1988) ends on an ingenuously optimistic note. Roshan Seth is powerfully credible as Choudhury's bigoted father, however. 🖭

Denzel Washington *Demetrius* • Sarita Choudhury *Mina* • Roshan Seth *Jay* • Sharmila Tagore *Kinnu* • Charles S Dutton *Tyrone* • Joe Seneca *Williben* • Ranjit Chowdhry *Anil* ■ *Dir* Mira Nair • *Scr* Sooni Taraporevala

Mississippi Mermaid ★★

Mystery 1969 · Fr/It · Colour · 108mins

Catherine Deneuve arrives on the island of Réunion to marry plantation owner Jean-Paul Belmondo in this adaptation of a Cornell Woolrich novel, transformed by Truffaut into a lavish study of obsessive love (what the French call *l'amour fou*). Things turn decidedly darker when the tropics give way to winter in the French Alps and romance turns to murder. This was the director's first major flop, only released abroad in a slightly cut and badly dubbed version that rendered the dialogue utterly risible. The stars have an undeniable glamour, and the first half-hour is superb. However, most audiences will find the whole thing pretty silly. A French language film.

Jean-Paul Belmondo *Louis Mahe* • Catherine Deneuve *Marion/Julie Roussel* • Michel

Bouquet *Comolli* • Nelly Borgeaud *Berthe Roussel* • Marcel Bozzufi *Jardine* ■ Dir François Truffaut • *Scr* François Truffaut, from the novel *Waltz into Darkness* by William Irish [Cornell Woolrich]

The Missouri Breaks
★★★★ 15

Western   1976 · US · Colour · 121mins

As a clash of titans, this film – despite a shambles of a plot – is exciting stuff because of the ego battle between Marlon Brando and Jack Nicholson. Brando's a hired bounty hunter, pitting his wits against horse-thief Nicholson amid the conflict between Montana ranchers and rustlers, and both actors twitch their way through an upstaging duel that is mesmerising in its brazen arrogance. Director Arthur Penn seems to stand back from the proceedings, bemused, though his view of pioneer days is still so fascinatingly uncluttered and fresh that you can almost smell the raw wood of log cabins. Never mind the quality, though, feel the vanity. Contains some violence. ▭

Marlon Brando *Lee Clayton* • Jack Nicholson *Tom Logan* • Randy Quaid *Little Tod* • Kathleen Lloyd *Jane Braxton* • Frederic Forrest *Cary* • Harry Dean Stanton *Calvin* • John McLiam *David Braxton* ■ Dir Arthur Penn • *Scr* Thomas McGuane • *Music* John Williams

The Missouri Traveler ★★ U

Drama   1958 · US · Colour · 100mins

This pleasant but overlong slice of Americana has something of John Ford about it. Ford's son, Patrick, is the producer; the superb Technicolor photography is by one of the director's favourite cameramen, Winton Hoch; while the epic fight at the end recalls the one in *The Quiet Man*. However, Jerry Hopper's direction is hardly in the Ford class. Brandon de Wilde, the boy in *Shane*, stars as the friendly 15-year-old runaway who stops in a small Missouri town and falls foul of Lee Marvin's surly farmer. Marvin's not entirely a heavy, though, and this role helped to demonstrate that he could be more than a one-dimensional villain.

Brandon de Wilde *Brian Turner* • Lee Marvin *Tobias Brown* • Gary Merrill *Doyle Magee* • Paul Ford *Finas Daugherty* • Mary Hosford *Anna Love Price* • Ken Curtis *Fred Mueller* ■ Dir Jerry Hopper • *Scr* Norman S Hall, from the novel by John Burress

Mr and Mrs Bridge ★★★ PG

Drama   1990 · UK · Colour · 125mins

The winning Merchant/Ivory partnership is off target in this pretty but ultimately disappointing vehicle for Paul Newman and his wife Joanne Woodward. It's another of director James Ivory's polite studies of emotional repression, but the rambling, episodic tale of American family life in the thirties and forties lacks cohesion. However, the two stars are superb as the eponymous married couple: Newman all starched conservatism as the stiff-necked lawyer, stubbornly resisting the changes around him; and Woodward the devoted wife attempting in her own quiet way to open his eyes. ▭

Paul Newman *Walter Bridge* • Joanne Woodward *India Bridge* • Robert Sean Leonard *Douglas Bridge* • Margaret Welsh *Carolyn Bridge* • Kyra Sedgwick *Ruth Bridge* • Blythe

Danner *Grace Barron* • Simon Callow *Dr Alex Sauer* ■ Dir James Ivory • *Scr* Ruth Prawer Jhabvala, from the novels *Mr Bridge* and *Mrs Bridge* by Evan S Connell

Mr and Mrs '55 ★★★★ U

Satirical comedy   1955 · Ind · BW · 129mins

Even Busby Berkeley would have been proud of the musical numbers in this classic Bollywood masala from actor/director Guru Dutt. Ostensibly a satire at the expense of the urban upper echelons, this is also a delightfully romantic comedy, in which Dutt is hired as a groom by heiress Madhubala for the wedding of convenience that will fulfil the terms of her father's will. But, while aunt Lalita Pawar makes arrangements for the agreed quickie divorce, the couple fall in love. Don't look for any plot sophistication, simply sit back and revel in the joyous performances of the leads and the wholly cinematic, endlessly inventive song-and-dance routines. A Hindi language film. ▭

Guru Dutt *Preetam Kumar* • Madhubala *Anita* • Lalita Pawar *Seeta Devi* • Johnny Walker *Johnny* • Tuntun *Lily D'Silva* ■ Dir Guru Dutt • *Scr* Abrar Alvi, Majrooh Sultanpuri

Mr and Mrs Loving ★★★

Drama based on a true story
1993 · US · Colour · 104mins

After his Oscar-winning performance in *Ordinary People* (1980), Timothy Hutton made few memorable movies until *Beautiful Girls* and *Playing God* in the late nineties. A little before his successful comeback, he starred in this powerful civil rights drama, set in the fifties and based on a true story. Hutton and Lela Rochon play a couple in breach of local laws following their inter-racial marriage. The resulting benchmark trial by the Supreme Court is given the right degree of gravitas by director Richard Friedenberg.

Timothy Hutton *Richard Loving* • Lela Rochon *Mildred "Bean" Jeter* • Ruby Dee *Sophia* • Bill Nunn *Leonard* • Corey Parker *Bernie Cohen* • Isaiah Washington *Blue* • Lawrence Dane *Sheriff* ■ Dir/Scr Richard Friedenberg

Mr and Mrs North ★★

Comedy mystery   1941 · US · BW · 66mins

Gracie Allen (minus George Burns on this occasion) is Mrs North, the wife of William Post Jr, in this comedy suspense drama from MGM's programmer department. The couple return home from a weekend trip to find a dead body in a cupboard in their apartment. Instead of leaving it to the cops, they decide to play detective and line up their friends as suspects. A moderately amusing, even occasionally tense spoof, this is competently directed by Robert B Sinclair. But it's really held together by Allen, who bears the major burden of the wordy script.

Gracie Allen *Pamela North* • William Post Jr *Gerald P North* • Paul Kelly *Lt Weigand* • Rose Hobart *Carol Brent* • Virginia Grey *Jane Wilson* • Tom Conway *Louis Berex* ■ Dir Robert B Sinclair • *Scr* SK Lauren, from a story by Richard Lockridge, Frances Lockridge, from the play by Owen Davis

Mr and Mrs Smith ★★★ U

Romantic comedy   1941 · US · BW · 90mins

Carole Lombard had always wanted to star in an Alfred Hitchcock film and, although situation comedy was far from Hitchcock's forte, he agreed to take the assignment as a favour for a friend. The result is a patchy farce in which Lombard (in her penultimate picture) and Robert Montgomery discover that their marriage is invalid and set about trying to outdo each other in their pleasure at being single. Even a screwball maestro like Howard Hawks would have been pushed to do much with Norman Krasna's clunky script, and Hitch's lack of interest is apparent. Lombard took over the director's chair for Hitch's obligatory cameo in which he plays a drunk asking Montgomery for money. ▭

Carole Lombard *Ann* • Robert Montgomery *David Smith* • Gene Raymond *Jeff* • Jack Carson *Chuck* • Philip Merivale *Mr Custer* • Lucile Watson *Mrs Custer* • William Tracy *Sammy* • Charles Halton *Mr Deever* ■ Dir Alfred Hitchcock • *Scr* Norman Krasna

Mr Baseball ★★ 15

Comedy   1992 · US · Colour · 103mins

Tom Selleck was never much of an actor for detail and here paints his has-been hero with too broad a brush. Even though his character, a faded baseball player transferred to Japan, is meant to be annoying the locals because of his tendency for arrogance, Selleck just can't resist letting his natural charm wash over the screen. Director Fred Schepisi should have known better than to build the action round Selleck's personality, reducing the pace to a tepid canter. The film went straight to video in the UK. Contains swearing. ▭

Tom Selleck *Jack Elliot* • Ken Takakura *Uchiyama* • Aya Takanashi *Hiroko Uchiyama* • Dennis Haysbert *Max "Hammer" Dubois* • Toshi Shioya *Yoji Nishimura* • Kosuke Toyohara *Toshi Yamashita* • Toshizo Fujiwara *Ryoh Mukai* ■ Dir Fred Schepisi • *Scr* Gary Ross, Kevin Wade, Monte Merrick, Theo Pelletier, John Junkerman

Mr Belvedere Goes to College ★★ U

Comedy   1949 · US · BW · 82mins

Clifton Webb had made a spectacular success playing the egocentric genius Lynn Belvedere in the previous year's *Sitting Pretty*, and this was the first of two sequels in which he played the same character. Proposing to earn a four-year degree in one year, he enters college; alas, his escapades are too predictable to generate the amusement intended. Shirley Temple, nearing the end of her film career, and Tom Drake, the "boy next door" from *Meet Me in St Louis*, provide romance.

Clifton Webb *Lynn Belvedere* • Shirley Temple *Ellen Baker* • Tom Drake *Bill Chase* • Alan Young *Avery Brubaker* • Jessie Royce Landis *Mrs Chase* • Kathleen Hughes *Kay Nelson* ■ Dir Elliott Nugent • *Scr* Richard Sale, Mary Loos, Mary McCall Jr, from the character created by Gwen Davenport

Mr Belvedere Rings the Bell ★★★ U

Comedy   1951 · US · BW · 87mins

Former Broadway musical star Clifton Webb (and his infamous mother, who went with him everywhere) had been around since the silent days, but it took his portrayal of the sour-tongued misanthrope Belvedere in 1948's *Sitting Pretty* to actually endear him to movie audiences. In this light-hearted nonsense, the second sequel to *Sitting Pretty*, Belvedere takes up residence in an old people's home to prove age is no barrier to living a full life.

Clifton Webb *Lynn Belvedere/Oliver Erwenter* • Joanne Dru *Miss Tripp* • Hugh Marlowe *Reverend Watson* • Zero Mostel *Emmett* • William Lynn *Mr Beebe* • Doro Merande *Mrs Hammer* • Frances Brandt *Miss Hoadley* ■ Dir Henry Koster • *Scr* Ranald MacDougall, from the play *The Silver Whistle* by Robert C McEnroe and the character created by Gwen Davenport

Mr Billion ★★ PG

Drama   1977 · US · Colour · 88mins

As Terence Hill, the Italian actor Mario Girotti starred in several spaghetti westerns and seemed unhealthily fixated on Clint Eastwood. *Mr Billion* was Hill's Hollywood debut, a chase thriller clearly modelled on Hitchcock but with a little bit of social moralising thrown in. Hill plays an Italian who inherits a fortune and must travel to San Francisco to claim it; Valerie Perrine is the double agent who gets in his way. ▭

Terence Hill *Guido Falcone* • Valerie Perrine *Rosi Jones* • Jackie Gleason *John Cutler* • Slim Pickens *Duane Hawkins* • William Redfield *Leopold Lacy* • Chill Wills *Colonel Clayton T Winkle* • Dick Miller *Bernie* • RG Armstrong *Sheriff TC Bishop* ■ Dir Jonathan Kaplan • *Scr* Ken Friedman, Jonathan Kaplan

Mr Blandings Builds His Dream House ★★★★

Comedy   1948 · US · BW · 92mins

Married couple Cary Grant and Myrna Loy move to the countryside and do, quite literally, what the title states – except they get conned by every cowboy builder along the way. Many viewers will identify with their still relevant plight in this sublime comedy. The film was remade in the mid-eighties as *The Money Pit*, but it was not as funny or stylish as this original, as neither Tom Hanks nor Shelley Long can compete with Grant and Loy at their best – just watch Loy recite her proposed colour scheme!

Cary Grant *Jim Blandings* • Myrna Loy *Muriel Blandings* • Melvyn Douglas *Bill Cole* • Sharyn Moffett *Joan Blandings* • Connie Marshall *Betsy Blandings* • Louise Beavers *Gussie* • Harry Shannon *Mr Tesander* ■ Dir HC Potter • *Scr* Norman Panama, Melvin Frank, from the novel by Eric Hodgins

Mister Buddwing ★★

Drama   1966 · US · BW · 96mins

This is what can happen when a Hollywood director sees the work of French New Wave folk like Godard and Resnais and thinks: "Hey, I can do that!" *Mister Buddwing* is *Last Year at Marienbad* relocated to New York, with James Garner waking up in Central

U = SUITABLE FOR ALL   Uc = SUITABLE FOR ALL, ESPECIALLY FOR YOUNG CHILDREN (VIDEO ONLY)   PG = PARENTAL GUIDANCE

Park not knowing who is is or where he's from. Three beautiful women – Jean Simmons, Suzanne Pleshette and Katharine Ross – are seen in the multiple flashbacks. With its first-person camera, jump cuts and other "look at me" devices, it's rather tedious, despite Garner's efforts.

James Garner *Mister Buddwing* • Jean Simmons *The blonde* • Suzanne Pleshette *Fiddle* • Katharine Ross *Janet* • Angela Lansbury *Gloria* • Jack Gilford *Mr Schwartz* ■ *Dir* Delbert Mann • *Scr* Dale Wasserman, from the novel *Buddwing* by Evan Hunter

Mr Corbett's Ghost ★★
Fantasy drama 1986 · UK · Colour · 60mins

Directed by Danny Huston (John Huston's son) this is a slapdash adaptation of Leon Garfield's superb story about transferred identities and eerie disappearances. Starring Paul Scofield, it was supervised by John Huston – who also acted in it – but its period atmosphere is TV-fustian and it never takes on the book's elaborate tension. That is probably why it was never theatrically released.

Paul Scofield *Mr Corbett* • John Huston *Soul collector* • Burgess Meredith *Mad Tom* • Mark Farmer *Benjamin Partridge* ■ *Dir* Danny Huston • *Scr* Terry Wilson, from the novel by Leon Garfield

Mister Cory ★★★
Drama 1957 · US · Colour · 92mins

Tony Curtis emerges from the slums of Chicago, becomes a dishwasher at a swish country club, teams up with gambler Charles Bickford and ends up owning a casino. It's pure Americana, a rags-to-riches tale close to Curtis's heart and which helped move him out of the matinée idol, sword-and-sandal ghetto. As written by Blake Edwards – this was also his third directing stint – the story is shot through with a certain cynicism as Curtis is clearly on the make, moving through various layers of social class and wealth. The use of CinemaScope and colour, though, tends to blunt the film's sharp edge.

Tony Curtis *Cory* • Martha Hyer *Abby Vollard* • Charles Bickford *Biloxi* • Kathryn Grant *Jen Vollard* • William Reynolds *Alex Wyncott* • Henry Daniell *Earnshaw* • Russ Morgan *Ruby Matrobe* ■ *Dir* Blake Edwards • *Scr* Blake Edwards, from a story by Leo Rosten

Mr Death: the Rise and Fall of Fred A Leuchter Jr ★★★★
Documentary 1999 · US · Colour · 90mins

Errol Morris has always fed on obsessional outsiders, but none has been so dangerously deluded as Fred A Leuchter, the American executioner whose vanity led to his becoming a reviled apologist for Holocaust denial. This is certainly an ironic portrait of a man who takes pride in his work and pleasure at his expertise. But Morris avoids mockery, as he demonstrates Leuchter's commitment to bringing humanity and efficiency to the various death penalty procedures, before following him to Auschwitz, where he spent his honeymoon illicitly and inexpertly collecting evidence to support scientifically Ernst Zündel's theories denying the existence of the gas chambers. Chilling and compelling.

Dir Errol Morris • *Cinematographer* Peter Donohue, Robert Richardson

Mr Deeds Goes to Town ★★★★ U
Comedy 1936 · US · BW · 110mins

A popular and critical success in its day, this slight morality tale won an Oscar for director Frank Capra, but today's more cynical audience might find it too full of Capra-corn. Lanky Gary Cooper is wonderful as Longfellow Deeds, the tuba-playing "Cinderella Man" who inherits a small fortune. But the character of the investigative reporter played by Jean Arthur rings false, as do the myriad minor roles, although many are well cast. 🖭

Gary Cooper *Longfellow Deeds* • Jean Arthur *Babe Bennett* • George Bancroft *MacWade* • Lionel Stander *Cornelius Cobb* • Douglass Dumbrille *John Cedar* • Raymond Walburn *Walter* • Margaret Matzenauer *Madame Pomponi* • HB Warner *Judge Walker* • Warren Hymer *Bodyguard* ■ *Dir* Frank Capra • *Scr* Robert Riskin, from the story *Opera Hat* by Clarence Budington Kelland

Mr Denning Drives North ★★★
Comedy thriller 1951 · UK · BW · 93mins

John Mills looked thoroughly brooding in the startling red-and-black poster for this film, and audiences might have found themselves somewhat disappointed by this resolutely genteel drama. Mills is excellent as the father who accidentally bumps off his daughter's devious lover, but acting honours are stolen by Sam Wanamaker as the truth-seeking boyfriend, and there's one of those excellent supporting casts of stalwarts (this time including Bernard Lee, Wilfrid Hyde White and Herbert Lom) that makes films of this era so watchable.

John Mills *Tom Denning* • Phyllis Calvert *Kay Denning* • Sam Wanamaker *Chick Eddowes* • Herbert Lom *Mados* • Eileen Moore *Liz Denning* • Raymond Huntley *Wright* • Bernard Lee *Inspector Dodds* • Wilfrid Hyde White *Woods* ■ *Dir* Anthony Kimmins • *Scr* Alec Coppel, from his novel

Mr Destiny ★★ PG
Comedy drama 1990 · US · Colour · 105mins

You might expect this fantasy to live up to its wistful plotline, as Michael Caine's bartender dispenses what-if potions to a baseball fan (James Belushi) who regrets the day all those years ago when he missed a home run. Yet as Belushi lives his life again, more successful but wishing he was still married to Linda Hamilton rather than his new wife (Rene Russo), it's hard not to see him as a tedious slob who can't make up his mind. 🖭

James Belushi *Larry Burrows* • Linda Hamilton *Ellen Burrows* • Michael Caine *Mike* • Jon Lovitz *Clip Metzler* • Hart Bochner *Niles Pender* • Bill McCutcheon *Leo Hansen* • Rene Russo *Cindy Jo* • Jay O Sanders *Jackie Earle* • Maury Chaykin *Guzelman* ■ *Dir* James Orr • *Scr* James Orr, Jim Cruickshank

Mr Drake's Duck ★★★ U
Comedy 1950 · UK · BW · 85mins

A bright, breezy comedy from British writer/director Val Guest about a duck that lays uranium eggs, filmed in an innocent postwar era when the long-term effects of radiation poisoning were still unknown. Mrs Guest, the blonde and perky Yolande Donlan, plays Mrs Drake, who's married to suave Douglas Fairbanks Jr and who, together with her husband, breeds ducks on their Sussex farm, one of which turns out to be a source of possible riches. Very enjoyable, and deservedly popular in its day.

Douglas Fairbanks Jr *Don Drake* • Yolande Donlan *Penny Drake* • Howard Marion-Crawford *Major Travers* • Reginald Beckwith *Mr Boothby* • Wilfrid Hyde White *Mr May* • John Boxer *Sergeant* • Jon Pertwee *Reuben* • Peter Butterworth *Higgins* ■ *Dir* Val Guest • *Scr* Val Guest, from the play by Ian Messiter

Mister 880 ★★★ U
Comedy drama 1950 · US · BW · 89mins

Amazingly based on a true story, this is a delightful light comedy about an old codger who has forged dollar bills for years and bewilderingly left the authorities in his wake. Loveable Edmund Gwenn, everybody's favourite Santa, is the junk collector with his own printing press, and Burt Lancaster, on the cusp of stardom, is all teeth and shoulders as the federal agent chasing him. It'll come as no surprise to find that Lancaster finds it jolly difficult to prosecute his amiable prey.

Burt Lancaster *Steve Buchanan* • Dorothy McGuire *Ann Winslow* • Edmund Gwenn *Skipper Miller* • Millard Mitchell *Mac* • Minor Watson *Judge O'Neil* • Howard St John *Chief* • Hugh Sanders *Thad Mitchell* • James Millican *Olie Johnson* ■ *Dir* Edmund Goulding • *Scr* Robert Riskin, from the *New Yorker* article *Old Eight Eighty* by St Clair McKelway

Mister Frost ★★ 15
Horror 1990 · Fr/UK · Colour · 99mins

Jeff Goldblum makes an unlikely Satan in this psychological thriller about a mass murderer whose countryside estate is littered with mutilated victims. Arrested and sent to a mental institution, he confides to psychiatrist Kathy Baker that he is in fact the Devil. His mission is simple: to get her to kill him… Policeman Alan Bates is also involved, making for an overly earnest and rather ridiculous film. Try *The Devil's Advocate* instead. 🖭

Jeff Goldblum *Mister Frost* • Alan Bates *Felix Detweiler* • Kathy Baker *Dr Sarah Day* • Roland Giraud *Raymond Reynhardt* • François Négret *Christophe Kovac* • Jean-Pierre Cassel *Inspector Correlli* ■ *Dir* Philippe Setbon • *Scr* Philippe Setbon, Brad Lynch

Mr Hobbs Takes a Vacation ★★★ U
Comedy 1962 · US · Colour · 114mins

James Stewart made some amiable movies during the sixties, lightweight fluff that warmed the heart without stretching the brain. Here he's married to the lovely Maureen O'Hara, and the slight plot is encapsulated in the title. Contemporary heart-throbs Fabian and John Saxon add to the period charm, and the ingénue is Cliff Richard's flame from *Summer Holiday*, Lauri Peters. (Whatever happened to her?) It's all rather endearing in a ramshackle kind of way.

James Stewart *Mr Hobbs* • Maureen O'Hara *Peggy Hobbs* • Fabian *Joe* • Lauri Peters *Katey* • Lili Gentle *Janie* • John Saxon *Byron* • John McGiver *Martin Turner* • Marie Wilson *Emily Turner* ■ *Dir* Henry Koster • *Scr* Nunnally Johnson, from the novel *Hobb's Vacation* by Edward Streeter

Mr Holland's Opus ★★★★ PG
Drama 1995 · US · Colour · 136mins

Richard Dreyfuss strikes just the right note of sentiment and truth as music teacher Glenn Holland, who wonders if 30 years at the high school chalkface have been worthwhile, especially as he sacrificed his ambitions to be a composer. A shrewd mix of *Goodbye Mr Chips* and *It's a Wonderful Life*, it adds harsher ingredients including Mr Holland's neglect of his wife and hearing-impaired son to further the education of his students. The way Richard Dreyfuss lightens up his character, for example incorporating jazz in the syllabus, makes the film satisfyingly accessible to young and old. Contains some swearing. 🖭

Richard Dreyfuss *Glenn Holland* • Glenne Headly *Iris Holland* • Jay Thomas *Bill Meister* • Olympia Dukakis *Principal Jacobs* • William H Macy *Vice Principal Wolters* • Alicia Witt *Gertrude Lang* • Terrence Howard *Louis Russ* • Damon Whitaker *Bobby Tidd* ■ *Dir* Stephen Herek • *Scr* Patrick Sheane Duncan

Mr Imperium ★ U
Drama 1951 · US · Colour · 86mins

A glamorous vocalist with a cowboy quartet (Lana Turner) and a European prince (Ezio Pinza) meet and fall in love. When he inherits the throne, though, he can't consort with a commoner. Marking the screen debut of Metropolitan Opera star Pinza, this cardboard drivel was so disastrous that MGM released his second film, *Strictly Dishonorable*, first. Both bombed. This one, directed by Don Hartman, boasts good-looking locations and sumptuous clothes for Lana; Pinza is in good voice on the rare occasions he's permitted to sing.

Lana Turner *Fredda Barlo* • Ezio Pinza *Mr Imperium* • Marjorie Main *Mrs Cabot* • Barry Sullivan *Paul Hunter* • Cedric Hardwicke *Prime Minister Bernand* • Keenan Wynn *Motor cop* • Debbie Reynolds *Gwen* ■ *Dir* Don Hartman • *Scr* Don Hartman, Edwin H Knopf, from a play by Edwin H Knopf

Mr India ★★★ U
Drama 1986 · Ind · Colour · 133mins

An entertaining Hindi fantasy about the clash between good and evil which was hugely successful on its release in India. There's a rousing portrait of villainy from Amrish Puri, while Anil Kapoor plays his nemesis, a scientist's son who has discovered the secret of invisibility. It's stylishly directed by Shekhar Kapur, who went on to direct *Bandit Queen*. In Hindi with English subtitles. 🖭

Amrish Puri *Mugambo* • Anil Kapoor *Arun* ■ *Dir* Shekhar Kapur

Mr Inside/Mr Outside ★★ PG
Crime drama 1973 · US · Colour · 73mins

The annals of TV moviedom are littered with feature-length pilots for series that failed to get the go-ahead. Even with the gimmick that one of the heroes has lost an arm, this one was heading

for the out tray almost from the start. However, teleplay stalwart William A Graham makes the most of a moderate script, which sends maverick cops Tony LoBianco and Hal Linden inside a foreign embassy in a bid to thwart a gang of ruthless criminals. Despite a couple of bruising confrontations, the action spends too much time indoors and barely registers on the suspense scale.

Tony LoBianco *Detective Rick Massi* • Hal Linden *Detective Lou Isaacs* • Paul Benjamin *Lieutenant Valentine* • Marcia Jean Kurtz *Renee Isaacs* • Stefan Schnabel *Luber* • Philip Bruns *Brack* ■ *Dir* William A Graham • *Scr* Jerome Coopersmith

Mr Jealousy ★★★

Romantic comedy
1997 · US · Colour · 105mins

Eric Stolz plays the mister of the title, a guy permanently obsessed about his dates' fidelity. His latest flame is Ramona (Annabella Sciorra), but his relentless stalking and green-eyed psychology work against him. Director Noah Baumbach is sadly too concerned with "clever" pastiches of Truffaut and Woody Allen to create a focused film. His script is good, as is his depiction of a generation of 30-year-olds refusing to grow old gracefully, but the end result is mixed.

Eric Stoltz *Lester Grimm* • Annabella Sciorra *Ramona Ray* • Chris Eigeman *Dashiell Frank* • Carlos Jacott *Vince* • Marianne Jean-Baptiste *Lucretia* • Brian Kerwin *Stephen* • Peter Bogdanovich *Dr Poke* • Bridget Fonda *Irene* ■ *Dir/Scr* Noah Baumbach

Mister Jerico ★★ U

Comedy adventure
1969 · US · Colour · 85mins

A run-of-the-mill comedy adventure, chiefly of interest today for fans of Patrick Macnee, better known even then as John Steed in *The Avengers*. The usual ingredients of diamonds, crooks and blonde sirens can't make up for the lack of plot, although Herbert Lom is on hand to remind viewers of the *Pink Panther* capers.

Patrick Macnee *Dudley Jerico* • Connie Stevens *Susan* • Herbert Lom *Victor Russo* • Marty Allen *Wally* • Leonardo Pieroni *Angelo* ■ *Dir* Sidney Hayers • *Scr* Philip Levene, from an idea by David T Chantler

Mister Johnson ★★★ PG

Period drama   1991 · US · Colour · 96mins

Following on from *Driving Miss Daisy*, Bruce Beresford returned to the idea of a white master and a black servant, possibly hoping to garner the best director Oscar he didn't get the year before. It's colonial West Africa in the twenties, and Mr Johnson (Maynard Eziashi) is the clerk of English administrator Harry Rudbeck (a pre-James Bond Pierce Brosnan). Unfortunately, this slight film has none of the depth of the Joyce Cary novel upon which it is based, and much of the blame can be laid at the director's door. Although Beresford peppers the movie with beautiful landscapes, there is not enough characterisation to really engage the viewer.

Pierce Brosnan *Harry Rudbeck* • Maynard Eziashi *Mister Johnson* • Edward Woodward *Sargy Gollup* • Beatie Edney *Celia Rudbeck* ■

Denis Quilley *Bulteen* • Nick Reding *Tring* ■ *Dir* Bruce Beresford • *Scr* William Boyd, Bruce Beresford, from the novel by Joyce Cary

Mr Jones ★★ 18

Romantic drama
1993 · US · Colour · 109mins

Here's one Jones that audiences won't want to keep up with, as manic-depressive Richard Gere suffers a Freudian slip-up by having an affair with his psychiatrist, Lena Olin. Gere's mood-swinging hero displays surprising energy and verve, which was probably not the original intention: studio executives ordered extensive recutting in order to lighten up what was by all accounts a rather sombre movie, and the result makes uncomfortable viewing. Director Mike Figgis has since found Oscar-nominated success with 1995's *Leaving Las Vegas*. Contains swearing. ▣ **DVD**

Richard Gere *Mr Jones* • Lena Olin *Dr Libbie Bowen* • Anne Bancroft *Dr Catherine Holland* • Tom Irwin *Patrick* • Delroy Lindo *Howard* • Bill Pullman *Construction site foreman* ■ *Dir* Mike Figgis • *Scr* Eric Roth, Michael Cristofer, from a story by Eric Roth

Mr Kingstreet's War ★★★

Adventure drama 1970 · US · Colour · 92mins

Former Alfred Hitchcock leading lady Tippi Hedren became a lady with a cause after marrying African safari ecologist Noel Marshall, and made a worthy series of movies espousing wildlife campaigns. This film, not thought good enough for a cinema release in the UK, is an unusual and fascinating study of pre-Second World War Africa, where, despite the encroachment of the opposing Italian and British forces, the wildlife sanctuaries are preserved by a determined couple. In spite of its amateur origins, the casting of former heart-throbs John Saxon and Rossano Brazzi keeps the movie watchable.

John Saxon *Jim Kingstreet* • Tippi Hedren *Mary Kingstreet* • Rossano Brazzi *Count Ugo Bernadelli* • Brian O'Shaughnessy *Morgan* ■ *Dir* Percival Rubens

Mr Klein ★★★★ 12

Second World War thriller
1976 · Fr · Colour · 118mins

Set in Paris during the Nazi occupation, this thriller by director Joseph Losey is one of his most poignant and Kafkaesque. Alain Delon is the Roman Catholic antiques dealer who fleeces Jews desperate to flee France. His world starts to unravel when he is mistaken for another Robert Klein, a Jew who is using his identity as a cover for subversive activities. Delon gives one of his greatest performances in this undervalued drama. French dialogue dubbed into English. ▣

Alain Delon *Mr Klein* • Jeanne Moreau *Florence* • Suzanne Flon *Concierge* • Michel Lonsdale *Pierre* • Juliet Berto *Janine* ■ *Dir* Joseph Losey • *Scr* Franco Solinas

Mr Love ★★★ 15

Comedy   1985 · UK · Colour · 87mins

A very satisfying British gem, originally intended for Channel 4's *First Love* series, but made as a feature and

awarded a short-lived theatrical outing. With a better-known cast, this might have been a real winner. As it stands, though, it's a cleverly made minor item, with the virtually unknown Barry Jackson as a sort of British version of François Truffaut's "Man Who Loved Women". Excellent though Jackson is, the role really requires an Alec Guinness or a Peter Sellers, and they don't grow on trees. The casting of the women in his life also leaves a little to be desired, but persevere if you will: this works better on TV, is very rewarding and contains a knock-out send-up of *Casablanca*. ▣

Barry Jackson *Donald Lovelace* • Maurice Denham *Theo* • Margaret Tyzack *"Pink Lady"* • Linda Marlowe *Barbara* • Christina Collier *Esther* • Helen Cotterill *Lucy Nuttall* • Julia Deakin *Melanie* ■ *Dir* Roy Battersby • *Scr* Kenneth Eastaugh

Mr Lucky ★★★ U

Comedy   1943 · US · BW · 95mins

Cary Grant stars as a cynical professional gambler who romances heiress Laraine Day. Having cheated the American War Relief Society, he redeems himself by turning his gambling ship into a vessel laden with medical supplies. It sounds tacky, and it is a bit, but the movie was a big hit in 1943 and Grant always rated it as one of his favourites "because the character I played was more like the real Cary Grant than any before". First-time screenwriter Milton Holmes was in fact a pro at the Beverly Hills Tennis Club who pitched the idea to Grant in the parking lot. ▣

Cary Grant *Joe Adams* • Laraine Day *Dorothy Bryant* • Charles Bickford *Hard Swede* • Gladys Cooper *Capt Steadman* • Alan Carney *Crunk* • Henry Stephenson *Mr Bryant* • Paul Stewart *Zepp* ■ *Dir* HC Potter • *Scr* Milton Holmes, Adrian Scott, from the story *Bundles for Freedom* by Milton Holmes

Mr Magoo ★ PG

Comedy   1997 · US · Colour · 83mins

The main joke of the original cartoon was the myopia of its hero, the lugubrious Magoo. In a squirm-inducing sop to political correctness, a title at the end of this live-action feature points out that short-sighted people are not being ridiculed – which, of course, they are. As Magoo, Leslie Nielsen shows his limitations as a comedian: he barely raises a smile, let alone a laugh. The plot, about the chase for a stolen jewel, is pathetic. Did no one predict this would be a turkey? That's real short-sightedness. Contains some violence. ▣ **DVD**

Leslie Nielsen *Mr Magoo* • Kelly Lynch *Luanne* • Matt Keeslar *Waldo* • Nick Chinlund *Bob Morgan* • Stephen Tobolowsky *Agent Chuck Stupak* • Ernie Hudson *Agent Gus Anders* • Jennifer Garner *Stacey* • Malcolm McDowell *Austin Cloquet* ■ *Dir* Stanley Tong • *Scr* Pat Proft, Tom Sherohman

Mr Majestyk ★★ 18

Action thriller 1974 · US · Colour · 99mins

Wanna know what happens if you touch Charles Bronson's melons? He gets mad, that's what, in this unpleasantly violent action tale about a peaceful farmer forced to turn tough to protect his harvest. It's sort of *Death*

Wish with pitchforks, directed with gut-wrenching skill by *Fantastic Voyage's* Richard Fleischer from an Elmore Leonard screenplay, and rightly certified X by the squeamish British censor. (In the UK it originally played double-billed with another violent Fleischer action movie, *The Spikes Gang*.) Contains violence and swearing. ▣

Charles Bronson *Vince Majestyk* • Al Lettieri *Frank Renda* • Linda Cristal *Nancy Chavez* • Lee Purcell *Wiley* • Paul Koslo *Bobby Kopas* • Taylor Lacher *Gene Lundy* • Frank Maxwell *Det Lt McAllen* • Alejandro Rey *Larry Mendoza* ■ *Dir* Richard Fleischer • *Scr* Elmore Leonard

Mr Mom ★★ PG

Comedy drama 1983 · US · Colour · 91mins

Role-reversal comedy about a dad who gets fired from his high-powered job and winds up as a househusband while his wife goes out to work. The basic concept was probably something of a novelty back in 1983. Nowadays, though, the tendency would be to tell "Mr Mom" to stop flapping and start coping. Michael Keaton and Teri Garr star, with support from Christopher Lloyd and Martin Mull, and they're all likeable enough. But the film takes the easy options, plumping for farce and slapstick when something more subtle might have been better.

Michael Keaton *Jack Butler* • Teri Garr *Caroline Butler* • Frederick Koehler *Alex Butler* • Taliesin Jaffe *Kenny Butler* • Courtney White *Megan Butler* • Brittany White *Megan Butler* • Martin Mull *Ron Richardson* • Christopher Lloyd *Larry* ■ *Dir* Stan Dragoti • *Scr* John Hughes

Mister Moses ★★ U

Adventure   1965 · US · Colour · 126mins

Following *Lawrence of Arabia*, Hollywood was keen for David Lean to direct this preposterous African adventure, though the job eventually went to Lean's former associate, Ronald Neame. Robert Mitchum plays a diamond smuggler who gets the name of Moses when he leads the population of an African village out of harm's way, parting the waters of a vast dam which will drown the village. Irritants on the journey include a mobile menagerie, magic spells cast by the witch doctor, a dull missionary and his sexy, sweaty daughter (Carroll Baker). The film never allows us to forget its biblical parallels, though the stars share some witty repartee.

Robert Mitchum *Joe Moses* • Carroll Baker *Julie Anderson* • Ian Bannen *Robert* • Alexander Knox *Reverend Anderson* • Raymond St Jacques *Ubi* • Orlando Martins *Chief* ■ *Dir* Ronald Neame • *Scr* Charles Beaumont, Monja Danischewsky, from the novel by Max Catto

Mr Moto in Danger Island ★★★

Detective drama 1939 · US · BW · 63mins

The last filmed of the *Mr Moto* series, although it was released before *Mr Moto Takes a Vacation*. Beginning to look bored with the part of the wily Japanese troubleshooter, Peter Lorre finds himself in Puerto Rico, where he loads the evidence against himself in order to lure a gang of murderous diamond smugglers into the open.

U = SUITABLE FOR ALL   Uc = SUITABLE FOR ALL, ESPECIALLY FOR YOUNG CHILDREN (VIDEO ONLY)   PG = PARENTAL GUIDANCE

Although there is more frantic action than usual, it's hardly the most complex of mysteries, which makes the writing credits seem all the more ridiculously congested.

Peter Lorre *Mr Moto* • Jean Hersholt *Sutter* • Amanda Duff *Joan Castle* • Warren Hymer *Twister McGurk* • Richard Lane *Commissioner Gordon* • Leon Ames *Commissioner Madero* • Douglass Dumbrille *Commander La Costa* ∎ *Dir* Herbert I Leeds • *Scr* Peter Milne, from ideas by John Reinhardt, George Bricker, from the novel *Murder in Trinidad* by John W Vandercook, from the character created by JP Marquand

Mr Moto Takes a Chance ★★

Detective drama 1938 · US · BW · 63mins

Inspired by JP Marquand's stories, the *Mr Moto* movies are hardly known for the clarity of their storylines. This one, though, is virtually impenetrable. On his fourth outing as the Japanese detective, Peter Lorre finds himself in Cambodia in order to discover the secret of the caverns beneath a ruined temple. Notwithstanding the machinations of the plot and the abundance of incidental characters, the identity of the villain is as obvious as one of Moto's disguises. J Edward Bromberg has a ball as the chieftain whose throne is under threat.

Peter Lorre *Mr Moto* • Rochelle Hudson *Victoria Mason* • Robert Kent *Marty Weston* • J Edward Bromberg *Rajah Ali* • Chick Chandler *Chick Davis* • George Regas *Boker, High Priest* ∎ *Dir* Norman Foster • *Scr* Lou Breslow, John Patrick, from a story by Willis Cooper, Norman Foster, from the character created by JP Marquand

Mr Moto Takes a Vacation ★★★

Detective drama 1939 · US · BW · 65mins

One of the last entries in the *Mr Moto* series; by the end of 1939, with Japan flexing its military muscles in South East Asia, the character was considered unsuitably heroic. This time, JP Marquand's master meddler is asked to protect an ancient African crown before it falls into the hands of a collector who has already nabbed some of the crown jewels. Slumming it just two years after winning an Oscar for *The Life of Emile Zola*, Joseph Schildkraut revels in his villainy.

Peter Lorre *Mr Moto* • Joseph Schildkraut *Hendrik Manderson* • Lionel Atwill *Professor Hildebrand* • Virginia Field *Eleanor Kirke* • John King *Howard Stevens* • Iva Stewart *Susan French* ∎ *Dir* Norman Foster • *Scr* Norman Foster, Philip MacDonald, from the character created by JP Marquand

Mr Moto's Gamble ★★★

Detective drama 1938 · US · BW · 71mins

Returning for the third time to the role of the wily Japanese detective, Peter Lorre cruises through this undemanding boxing mystery, originally intended as a case for Charlie Chan. However, Keye Luke, who played Chan's "Number One Son", puts in a welcome appearance alongside Maxie Rosenbloom as a trainee sleuth. The latter helps Moto discover how poison got on the gloves of contender Dick Baldwin during a bout on which gangster Douglas Fowley had placed a

sizeable bet. Lynn Bari and Jayne Regan show up well as the women squabbling over Baldwin, but the picture belongs to Luke and Rosenbloom, whose bungling eagerness is hugely entertaining.

Peter Lorre *Mr Moto* • Keye Luke *Lee Chan* • Dick Baldwin *Bill Steele* • Lynn Bari *Penny Kendall* • Douglas Fowley *Nick Crowder* • Jayne Regan *Linda Benton* ∎ *Dir* James Tinling • *Scr* Charles Belden, Jerry Cady, from the character created by JP Marquand

Mr Moto's Last Warning ★★★

Detective drama 1939 · US · BW · 71mins

The sixth in the series featuring Peter Lorre as JP Marquand's Japanese sleuth sees Mr Moto in the Middle East, doing battle with spies intent on sabotaging French ships in the Suez canal and blaming it on the British. The formula is B-movie basic, with lots of rat-a-tat chat, plenty of plot twists and a scarcity of clues. The supporting cast is premier-league calibre, though, with George Sanders, John Carradine, Ricardo Cortez and Robert Coote all on devilish form. Virginia Field struggles to hold her own in such august company.

Peter Lorre *Mr Moto* • Ricardo Cortez *Fabian* • Virginia Field *Connie Porter* • John Carradine *Danforth* • George Sanders *Eric Norvel* • Joan Carol *Mary Delacour* • Robert Coote *Rollo Venables* ∎ *Dir* Norman Foster • *Scr* Philip MacDonald, Norman Foster, from the character created by JP Marquand

Mr Muggs Rides Again ★★U

Comedy 1945 · US · BW · 63mins

Not even the presence of Leo Gorcey as Muggs could endear this weak entry in the East Side Kids series to its fans, and the following year the kids were disbanded, to resurface as the Bowery Boys. Gorcey is typecast as a jockey who gets suspended from racing owing to some alleged dirty doings. Unfortunately, it's neither very funny nor remotely fast-moving. ▭

Leo Gorcey *Ethelbert Aloysius "Muggs" McGinnis* • Huntz Hall *Glimpy* • Billy Benedict *Skinny* • Johnny Duncan *Squeegie Robinson* • Bud Gorman *Danny* • Mende Koenig *Sam* • Minerva Urecal *Nora "Ma" Brown* • Bernard B Brown *Gaby O'Neill* • George Meeker *Dollar Davis* ∎ *Dir* Wallace Fox • *Scr* Harvey H Gates

Mr Murder ★★15

Thriller
1998 · US/Ger/Neth · Colour · 126mins

Though based on a book by horror maestro Dean R Koontz, this thriller places the emphasis on action rather than chills. Stephen Baldwin plays a writer of bizarre murder mysteries who becomes embroiled in a deadly real-life game, when a mix-up involving blood samples during a shady genetics experiment results in the creation of Baldwin's evil clone. The supporting cast – including Julie Warner and James Coburn – adds a touch of class and the end result is enjoyable, if a tad unbelievable. Contains violence, swearing and nudity. ▭

Stephen Baldwin *Marty Stillwater/Alfie* • Julie Warner *Paige Stillwater* • Bill Smitrovich *Lieutenant Lowbock* • James Coburn *Drew*

Oslett Sr • Thomas Haden Church *Drew Oslett Jr* ∎ *Dir* Dick Lowry • *Scr* Stephen Tolkin, from a novel by Dean R Koontz

Mr Music ★★★U

Musical 1950 · US · Colour · 114mins

This agreeable musical remake of 1935's *Accent on Youth*, itself based on a play, was tailor-made for the easy-going talents of Bing Crosby. Bing, who plays a middle-aged songwriter who would rather play golf than write songs, gets to sing several lively Burke/Van Heusen numbers. However, the film – under the direction of prissy comic actor Richard Haydn, best known for his role as the impresario Max Detweiler in *The Sound of Music* – is even more laid-back than its star. It's also far too long for its flimsy subject matter. The guest stars, including Peggy Lee and Groucho Marx, perk things up considerably.

Bing Crosby *Paul Merrick* • Nancy Olson *Katherine Holbrook* • Charles Coburn *Alex Conway* • Ruth Hussey *Lorna* • Robert Stack *Jefferson* • Ida Moore *Aunt Amy* • Tom Ewell *Haggerty* ∎ *Dir* Richard Haydn • *Scr* Arthur Sheekman, from the play *Accent on Youth* by Samson Raphaelson

Mr Nanny ★★PG

Comedy 1992 · US · Colour · 80mins

This is the one where "Hulk" Hogan gets to dress up like a ballerina and aims to entertain what one assumes is his main fan base: young children. In a variation on the concept of youngsters inflicting humiliation on grown-ups, Hogan plays a former wrestler who winds up as bodyguard-cum-nanny to two troublesome brats, whose father is under threat because he has invented a super microchip. Hogan draws on his wrestling training to make the most of his many pratfalls. Contains swearing and violence. ▭

Terry "Hulk" Hogan [Hulk Hogan] *Sean Armstrong* • Sherman Hemsley *Bert Wilson* • Austin Pendleton *Alex Mason Sr* • Robert Gorman *Robert Hy Gorman] Alex Mason Jr* • Madeline Zima *Kate Mason* • Raymond O'Connor *Frank Olsen* • Mother Love *Corinne* ∎ *Dir* Michael Gottlieb • *Scr* Edward Rugoff, Michael Gottlieb

Mr Nice Guy ★★15

Martial arts action comedy
1996 · HK · Colour · 84mins

This Melbourne-set vehicle for Hong Kong action star Jackie Chan may have been shot in English, but something definitely got lost in the translation. Chan plays a TV chef who gets mixed up with journalist Gabrielle Fitzpatrick's investigation into a drugs ring led by Richard Norton (himself a martial arts favourite of the eighties). The fight sequences are as inventive and imaginative as ever, but all the performances border on the hysterical. It's directed by Sammo Hung, the star of TV's *Martial Law*. ▭ **DVD**

Jackie Chan *Jackie* • Richard Norton *Giancarlo "The Saint" Lucchetti* • Miki Lee *Miki* • Karen McLymont *Lakeisha* • Gabrielle Fitzpatrick *Diana* • Vince Poletto *Romeo Baggio* ∎ *Dir* Sammo Hung • *Scr* Edward Tang, Fibe Ma

Mr North ★★★PG

Comedy drama 1988 · US · Colour · 88mins

An exceptional amalgam of American greats – Robert Mitchum, Lauren Bacall, a script co-written by John Huston – adds much to this gently amusing tale. A young man (Anthony Edwards of *ER* fame) performs healing miracles amongst the Newport elite in the twenties and finds himself going head to head with the local doctor. Very much a family affair – executive produced by Huston, the film stars his daughter Anjelica and is directed by his son Danny – this is a quality period fare and well worth watching. ▭

Anthony Edwards *Theophilus North* • Robert Mitchum *James McHenry Bosworth* • Lauren Bacall *Mrs Amelia Cranston* • Harry Dean Stanton *Henry Simmons* • Anjelica Huston *Persis Bosworth-Tennyson* • Mary Stuart Masterson *Elspeth Skeel* • Virginia Madsen *Sally Boffin* • David Warner *Dr McPherson* ∎ *Dir* Danny Huston • *Scr* Janet Roach, John Huston, James Costigan, from the novel *Theophilus North* by Thornton Wilder

Mr Peabody and the Mermaid ★★★U

Comedy fantasy 1948 · US · BW · 89mins

A year after *Miranda* and long before *Splash*, this gentle and now-forgotten romantic comedy was the first mermaid movie to make postwar movie censors tremble. Not that there is much to worry about, since lovely Ann Blyth is a most provocative, but totally covered-up, former denizen of the deep. William Powell catches her while fishing, and his urbanity makes this Nunnally Johnson-scripted tosh acceptable, though it would have benefited from a stronger director than Irving Pichel. The film became a great favourite with American teenagers and featured in several comic books of its day, continuing the tale in cartoon-strip form through to the mid-fifties.

William Powell *Mr Peabody* • Ann Blyth *Mermaid* • Irene Hervey *Polly Peabody* • Andrea King *Cathy Livingston* • Clinton Sundberg *Mike Fitzgerald* • Art Smith *Dr Harvey* ∎ *Dir* Irving Pichel • *Scr* Nunnally Johnson, from the novel *Peabody's Mermaid* by Guy Jones, Constance Jones

Mr Perrin and Mr Traill ★★★

Drama 1948 · UK · BW · 91mins

Hugh Walpole's novel becomes a well-performed but obvious drama of life in a boys' public school. Marius Goring plays the stuffy, frustrated, ageing house master, while David Farrar is the virile and popular new games teacher. The problems start when they clash disastrously over Greta Gynt's glamorous school nurse. Lacking the subtlety of the later, rather similar *The Browning Version*, this swaps any sense of tragedy for melodrama, with a climax that makes use of the school's location on a Cornish clifftop.

Marius Goring *Vincent Perrin* • David Farrar *David Traill* • Greta Gynt *Isobel Lester* • Raymond Huntley *Moy-Thompson* • Edward Chapman *Birkland* • Mary Jerrold *Mrs Perrin* • Ralph Truman *Comber* • Finlay Currie *Sir Joshua Varley* ∎ *Dir* Lawrence Huntington • *Scr* LAG Strong, TJ Morrison, from the novel by Hugh Walpole

Mister Quilp ★★ U

Musical　1975 · UK · Colour · 122mins

Anthony Newley, who first came to prominence as the Artful Dodger in David Lean's *Oliver Twist*, plays the mean-spirited, hunchbacked money-lender Quilp in this film version of Charles Dickens's *The Old Curiosity Shop*. The star also composed the songs in the manner of Lionel Bart's *Oliver!*. Co-financed by the Readers' Digest organisation, this is principally a sanitised, Americanised, family-orientated affair that nevertheless preserves some of the darker elements of the original. The performances, particularly Newley's, put the emphasis on grotesquerie.

Anthony Newley *Daniel Quilp* • David Hemmings *Richard Swiveller* • David Warner *Sampson Brass* • Michael Hordern *Grandfather/Edward Trent* • Paul Rogers *Single gent/Henry Trent* • Jill Bennett *Sally Brass* • Mona Washbourne *Mrs Jarley* ■ *Dir* Michael Tuchner • *Scr* Louis Kamp, Irene Kamp, from the novel *The Old Curiosity Shop* by Charles Dickens

Mr Reliable ★★★★ 15

Comedy drama 1996 · Ausl · Colour · 108mins

The team behind that quirky gem *Malcolm* – star Colin Friels and director Nadia Tass – are reunited for another utterly charming slice of offbeat Australiana. Incredibly, it's based on a true story: Down Under in the late sixties, dim-witted crook Friels and his new girlfriend, single mum Jacqueline McKenzie, scare off an irritating policeman with a shotgun, sparking a full-scale hostage crisis. However, much to the embarrassment of the local Establishment, the fair dinkum general public are firmly on the lovestruck couple's side. Friels and McKenzie are terrific as the dopey heroes, but the characters are fleshed out with great affection, even the bumbling bureaucrats and policeman. In a word, beaut. Contains swearing, violence and some sex scenes. ▭

Colin Friels *Wally Mellish* • Jacqueline McKenzie *Beryl Muddle* • Paul Sonkkila *Norman Allan* • Fred Gallacher *Don Fergusson* • Lisa Hensley *Penny Wilberforce* ■ *Dir* Nadia Tass • *Scr* Don Catchlove, Terry Hayes

Mister Roberts ★★★★★ U

Comedy　1955 · US · Colour · 115mins

A magnificent adaptation of the hit Broadway comedy, with Henry Fonda returning to the screen after a long absence to re-create his stage role, as a supply-ship officer who longs to be part of the action during the Second World War. Fonda clashed with original director John Ford over how to play the part, which led to director Mervyn LeRoy taking over, but the transfer was seamless and the qualities of the play were retained. The film has a cast to die for: James Cagney as the captain, William Powell (making his last movie appearance) as the wise old doc, and young Jack Lemmon, winning his first Oscar as the brash, irresistible and irrepressible Ensign Pulver. ▭

Henry Fonda *Lieutenant Doug Roberts* • James Cagney *Captain* • Jack Lemmon *Ensign Frank Thurlowe Pulver* • William Powell *Doc* • Betsy Palmer *Lieutenant Ann Girard* • Ward Bond *Chief Petty Officer Dowdy* • Phil Carey *[Philip Carey] Mannion* ■ *Dir* John Ford,

Mervyn LeRoy • *Scr* Joshua Logan, Frank S Nugent, from the play by Joshua Logan, Thomas Heggen, from the novel by Thomas Heggen

Mr Sardonicus ★★★ 12

Horror　1961 · US · BW · 86mins

Director William Castle worked overtime on this unofficial reworking of the 1928 chiller *The Man Who Laughs*. Having personally introduced the picture, Castle concluded proceedings with a Punishment Poll, in which the audience decided the fate of Guy Rolfe as Sardonicus, the 19th-century aristocrat who kidnaps Audrey Dalton to compel her surgeon sweetheart, Ronald Lewis, to operate on his face, which was frozen in childhood into a hideous grin. Eerily shot by Burnett Guffey with a surprisingly literate script from Ray Russell, all is primed for Oscar Homolka to steal the show as Rolfe's embittered servant. ▭

Ronald Lewis *Sir Robert Cargrave* • Audrey Dalton *Maude Sardonicus* • Guy Rolfe *Sardonicus* • Oscar Homolka *Krull* • Vladimir Sokoloff *Father* ■ *Dir* William Castle • *Scr* Ray Russell, from a short story by Ray Russell

Mr Saturday Night ★★★ 15

Comedy drama 1992 · US · Colour · 114mins

Billy Crystal builds on a character he developed during his early stand-up days for this affectionate, fictional biopic. Crystal's Buddy Young Jr is a stand-up comedian whose career spans more than 50 years; however, he is less successful with personal relationships, notably with his brother and manager David Paymer. The best bits are the scenes of his initial bids for success on stage; the dramatic elements are less successfully incorporated into the picture. However, it's a role tailor-made for Crystal and there's a talented supporting cast, including Helen Hunt, Ron Silver and Jerry Orbach, plus a cameo from Jerry Lewis. Contains swearing. ▭

Billy Crystal *Buddy Young Jr* • David Paymer *Stan Yankelman* • Julie Warner *Elaine* • Helen Hunt *Annie* • Mary Mara *Susan* • Jerry Orbach *Phil Gussman* • Ron Silver *Larry Meyerson* • Jerry Lewis ■ *Dir* Billy Crystal • *Scr* Billy Crystal, Lowell Ganz, Babaloo Mandel

Mr Skeffington ★★★★

Melodrama　1944 · US · BW · 116mins

Narcissistic, selfish, faithless and rich society woman marries loyal, dignified, adoring businessman to protect her feckless brother's reputation, and treats him like dirt. Retribution arrives when diptheria ravages her looks, redemption when he returns blind from a Nazi concentration camp... This is vintage Warner Bros melodrama, well directed by Vincent Sherman in opulent sets, a Franz Waxman score emphasising the drama and, above all, Bette Davis and Claude Rains, both Oscar-nominated and at the height of their powers. Davis delivers a paradigm synthesis of the vain bitch roles she made uniquely her own; Rains, dignified and sincere, is the perfect foil. The plot, spanning the years from 1914 to 1940, is archetypal drivel, yet absolutely irresistible.

Bette Davis *Fanny Trellis* • Claude Rains *Job Skeffington* • Walter Abel *George Trellis* •

Richard Waring *Trippy Trellis* • George Coulouris *Dr Byles* • Marjorie Riordan *Young Fanny* • Robert Shayne *MacMahon* ■ *Dir* Vincent Sherman • *Scr* Philip G Epstein, Julius J Epstein, James Leicester, from the novel by "Elizabeth" [Mary Annette Beauchamp Russell] • *Art Director* Robert Haas

Mr Smith Goes to Washington ★★★★★ U

Political comedy drama
1939 · US · BW · 124mins

This superb discourse on corruption in American politics is one of Hollywood's finest achievements. Director Frank Capra resolutely and remarkably (for him) keeps sentimentality at bay in his film of Lewis R Foster's Oscar-winning original story (adapted by Sidney Buchman) about an idealistic young senator who finally realises that he is not his own man. Washington hated this movie, but the public flocked to see James Stewart in, arguably, his finest hour. Few movies are as well cast. The bell-voiced Jean Arthur is wonderful as a super-cynical secretary, but veteran western star Harry Carey is quite magnificent as the vice president, one of the greatest supporting roles in all cinema, and alone a reason for viewing. ▭

James Stewart *Jefferson Smith* • Jean Arthur *Saunders* • Claude Rains *Senator Joseph Paine* • Edward Arnold *Jim Taylor* • Guy Kibbee *Governor Hubert Hopper* • Thomas Mitchell *Diz Moore* • Harry Carey *Vice President* • Beulah Bondi *Ma Smith* ■ *Dir* Frank Capra • *Scr* Sidney Buchman, from the book *The Gentleman from Montana* by Lewis R Foster

Mr Sycamore ★ PG

Comedy drama 1974 · US · Colour · 84mins

They don't make them like this anymore, with good reason. A fine cast is ill-used in this whimsical comedy about one man's attempt to escape the rat race. A mild-mannered postman (Jason Robards), under the heel of his overbearing wife, decides to become a tree. Luckily for Robards, his cinema career perked up shortly afterwards with an Oscar-winning role in *All the President's Men*. ▭

Jerome Thor *Higgins* • Jason Robards [Jason Robards Jr] *John Gwilt* • Sandy Dennis *Jane Gwilt* • Jean Simmons *Estelle Benbow* • Robert Easton *Fred Staines* • Brenda Smith *Daisy* ■ *Dir* Pancho Kohner • *Scr* Pancho Kohner, Ketti Frings, from a story by Robert Ayre, from a play by Ketti Frings

Mister Ten Per Cent ★★ U

Comedy　1967 · UK · Colour · 85mins

For all his success on TV, Charlie Drake has failed to make an impact on the big screen, with only four movies in 13 years before this flop. Co-scripted by Drake and Norman Hudis, it's a comedy about the deliberate staging of a box-office bomb to claim the insurance, which predated Mel Brooks's similarly themed *The Producers* by a year. In spite of an accomplished cast, it is killed stone dead by Drake himself, who was so hurt by its failure that he went into temporary retirement. ▭

Charlie Drake *Percy Pointer* • Derek Nimmo *Tony* • Wanda Ventham *Kathy* • John Le Mesurier *Jocelyn Macauley* • Anthony Nicholls

Casey • Noel Dyson *Mrs Gorman* • John Hewer *Townsend* ■ *Dir* Peter Graham Scott • *Scr* Norman Hudis, Charlie Drake

Mr Topaze ★★ U

Comedy　1961 · UK · Colour · 96mins

Peter Sellers directed himself in this adaptation of a Marcel Pagnol play, so he has only himself to blame. He plays an ex-schoolmaster in a small French town who falls among thieves and comes up wealthy. Beset by the likes of Herbert Lom, Leo McKern and Nadia Gray, Sellers makes an endearing innocent at large. Alas, his direction lacks the edge the idea needed.

Peter Sellers *Mr Topaze* • Nadia Gray *Suzy* • Herbert Lom *Castel Benac* • Leo McKern *Muche* • Martita Hunt *Baroness* • John Neville *Roger* • Billie Whitelaw *Ernestine* • Michael Gough *Tamise* • Joan Sims *Colette* ■ *Dir* Peter Sellers • *Scr* Pierre Rouve, from the play *Topaze* by Marcel Pagnol

Mr Vampire ★★★★ 15

Comedy　1986 · HK · Colour · 93mins

Slapstick comedy, mystic martial arts and astonishing gore appear in the first of a long line of popular, and much copied, period Chinese horror films. Lam Ching Ying is the voodoo priest hired by a prominent merchant to exorcise his bouncing bloodsucker father. Complications arise thanks to Ching Ying's two over-enthusiastic apprentices, lured by lonely ghosts into exhausting nights of spectral passion, and the eight zombies left in his undertaking care. With flying heads, fang filing and all manner of unusual contributions to western undead mythology (holding the breath makes one invisible, sticky rice is a vampire deterrent), this is oriental knockabout horror at its most entertaining. In Cantonese with English subtitles. ▭

Ricky Hui *Man Chor* • Moon Lee *Ting Ting* • Lam Ching Ying *Master* • Pauline Wong *Jade Ah Wai* • Anthony Chan *Brother* ■ *Dir* Wai Lau Kun • *Scr* Wong Ching, Szeto Cheuk Hon

Mr Winkle Goes to War ★

Second World War drama
1944 · US · BW · 79mins

One of the crassest wartime propaganda movies ever made, with Edward G Robinson as a meek little bank clerk who's bullied by his wife (Ruth Warrick) – until he's drafted, that is. This same little man becomes a hero when he fetches up on a Pacific island and drives a bulldozer straight through the Japanese defences. Give that man a medal and watch his wife dissolve with pride. The manipulative calculation of this movie has to be seen to be believed. Released as *Arms and the Woman* in the UK.

Edward G Robinson *Wilbert George Winkle* • Ruth Warrick *Amy Winkle* • Ted Donaldson *Barry* • Bob Haymes *Jack Pettigrew* • Richard Lane *Sgt "Alphabet"* • Robert Mitchum *Corporal* ■ *Dir* Alfred E Green • *Scr* Waldo Salt, George Corey, Louis Solomon, from a novel by Theodore Pratt

Mr Wonderful ★★★★ 15

Romantic drama 1992 · US · Colour · 95mins

Following the highly acclaimed *Truly Madly Deeply* but before his multi-Oscar-nominated film *The English*

Patient, director Anthony Minghella made his American debut with this quaint comedy that scores so heavily on the performance level that you can forgive it its contrived plot and odd lapses in logic. Matt Dillon's plans to open a bowling alley depend entirely on cutting the alimony paid to ex-wife Annabella Sciorra, but she's dating married academic William Hurt and has no plans to tie the knot. It's blatantly obvious Dillon's schemes to find her a new husband will rekindle his own passion, but what really matters is that romantics will not be disappointed. ▨

Matt Dillon *Gus* • Annabella Sciorra *Lee* • Mary-Louise Parker *Rita* • William Hurt *Tom* • Vincent D'Onofrio *Dominic* • David Barry Gray *Pope* • Dan Hedaya *Harvey* ■ *Dir* Anthony Minghella • *Scr* Anthony Minghella, from a screenplay by Amy Schor, Vicki Polon

Mr Wrong ★★★ 15
Chiller   1985 · NZ · Colour · 88mins

A New Zealand-made thriller, based on a story by Elizabeth Jane Howard about a woman who buys a Jaguar car that turns out to be haunted. Hitchcock himself once showed interest in filming the tale, while *Christine*, Stephen King's novel about a possessed car, was filmed just two years before. None of that stops this being a skilful and enjoyable feature debut by former documentary maker Gaylene Preston.

Heather Bolton *Meg* • David Letch *Mr Wrong* • Margaret Umbers *Samantha* • Suzanne Lee *Val* • Gary Stalker *Bruce* • Danny Mulheron *Wayne* ■ *Dir* Gaylene Preston • *Scr* Gaylene Preston, Geoff Murphy, Graeme Tetley, from a story by Elizabeth Jane Howard

Mr Wrong ★ 12
Romantic comedy   1996 · US · Colour · 92mins

You will discover how truly unfunny a comedy can be if you subject yourself to this unfortunate fare, made as a big-screen vehicle for TV star Ellen DeGeneres. She's the lonely single woman who meets Bill Pullman and discovers, too late, what a loser he really is – by which point she can't seem to get rid of him. Unfortunately, director Nick Castle (who made the equally unamusing *Major Payne*) lets this tedious tale amble along, and DeGeneres, Pullman and Joan Cusack can't save it. Contains some swearing and sexual references. ▨

Ellen DeGeneres *Martha* • Bill Pullman *Whitman* • Joan Cusack *Inga* • Dean Stockwell *Jack Tramonte* • Joan Plowright *Mrs Crawford* • John Livingston *Walter* • Robert Goulet *Dick Braxton* • Ellen Cleghorne *Jane* • Hope Davis *Annie* ■ *Dir* Nick Castle • *Scr* Chris Matheson, Kerry Ehrin, Craig Munson

Mistress ★★ 15
Drama   1987 · US · Colour · 93mins

A soppy made-for-TV tear-jerker featuring *Dallas* stalwart Victoria Principal, who desperately attempts to prove she can act. She plays the contented mistress of a rich man who is forced to re-evaluate her life when her lover suddenly dies. It's a potentially interesting story, but one that requires subtlety, and that's the one thing lacking from both the performances and Michael Tuchner's cliché-ridden direction. ▨

Victoria Principal *Rae Colton* • Don Murray *Wyn* • Kerrie Keane *Margo* • Joanna Kerns *Stephanie* • Michael Prince *Frank* ■ *Dir* Michael Tuchner • *Scr* Joyce Eliason

Mistress ★★
Satirical comedy   1992 · US · Colour · 109mins

Demonstrating the thin line between a power-player and a no-hoper, this Tinseltown comedy keeps threatening to blow the lid off the whole movie-making business. Yet, while the script wickedly captures the nitty-gritty of wheeler-dealing, the story lacks originality and direction. It's the quality of the performances, however, that finally scuppers the debuting director Barry Primus's satirical intents. As the trio willing to back Robert Wuhl's film (providing there are starring roles available for their mistresses), Eli Wallach, Danny Aiello and Robert De Niro (who also co-produced) are hugely disappointing, although Martin Landau shines as a grubbing producer. ▨

Robert Wuhl *Marvin Landisman* • Martin Landau *Jack Roth* • Jace Alexander *Stuart Stratland Jr* • Robert De Niro *Evan M Wright* • Laurie Metcalf *Rachel Landisman* • Eli Wallach *George Lieberhoff* • Danny Aiello *Carmine Rasso* • Christopher Walken *Warren Zell* ■ *Dir* Barry Primus • *Scr* Barry Primus, JF Lawton, from a story by Barry Primus

Mistrial ★★ 15
Courtroom drama   1996 · US · Colour · 88mins

Bill Pullman stars in this vigilante fantasy, executive-produced by Renny Harlin and Geena Davis. When a cop killer is acquitted, a dedicated New York City detective goes ballistic, takes the courtroom hostage at gunpoint and retries the case. This slow-moving, self-righteous endurance test plays like a rejected episode from *LA Law*, while a good cast fails to keep it from being a total misfire. Contains some swearing and violence. ▨

Bill Pullman *Steve Donohue* • Robert Loggia *Captain Lou Unger* • Blair Underwood *Lieutenant C Hodges* • Jon Seda *Eddie Rios* • James Rebhorn *Mayor Taylor* ■ *Dir/Scr* Heywood Gould

Misunderstood ★★ PG
Drama   1984 · US · Colour · 90mins

Gene Hackman is an industrialist living in some splendour in Tunisia. Recently widowed and consumed by grief, he has to raise two young boys, the older of whom is played by Henry Thomas, then basking in worldwide fame as the young hero of *ET*. Hackman and young Thomas are complete strangers who slowly start to understand each other, a process heightened when the latter is seriously hurt in an accident. This is a serious, sometimes sombre study of human relationships, though director Jerry Schatzberg – who made *Scarecrow* with Hackman in 1973 – disowned the cop-out, freeze-frame ending added by the producers. ▨

Gene Hackman *Ned* • Henry Thomas *Andrew* • Rip Torn *Will* • Huckleberry Fox *Miles* • Maureen Kerwin *Kate* • Susan Anspach *Lilly* • June Brown *Mrs Paley* • Nadim Sawalha *Ahmed* ■ *Dir* Jerry Schatzberg • *Scr* Barra Grant, from a novel by Florence Montgomery

Mitchell ★★
Crime action drama   1975 · US · Colour · 96mins

Following hard on the heels of *Dirty Harry* and *The French Connection*, *Mitchell* stars Joe Don Baker as the bull-headed cop on the trail of two big-time drug dealers, played by Martin Balsam and John Saxon. Trawling through the sewer of life, Baker finds a tart-with-heart (Linda Evans) and a whole range of pimps, bent cops, Bel Air socialites and mob members. Baker certainly has a physical presence but here he lacks the material that made his sheriff hero of *Walking Tall*, or his hit man in *Charley Varrick*, such compelling screen characters.

Joe Don Baker *Mitchell* • Martin Balsam *James Arthur Cummins* • John Saxon *Walter Deaney* • Linda Evans *Greta* • Merlin Olsen *Benton* ■ *Dir* Andrew V McLaglen • *Scr* Ian Kennedy Martin

Mitsou ★★★
Romantic drama   1957 · Fr · Colour · 98mins

Delighting in toying with the scruples of the hypocritical, this adaptation of Colette's short novel was, in its day, considered risqué both in its frank imagery and its bold approach to love. Viewed from afar, it seems a perfect specimen of the "tradition of quality" so despised by the young bucks of the Nouvelle Vague. For all the occasional starchiness of the dialogue, though, this is a charmingly coquettish picture, with Danièle Delorme radiantly naive as the music-hall singer who turns to ageing roué Fernand Gravey for a crash course in the refinements that will turn the head of priggish soldier François Guérin. A French language film.

Danièle Delorme *Mitsou* • Fernand Gravey [Fernand Gravet] *Pierre Duroy-Lelong* • François Guérin *Lieutenant Bleu* • Claude Rich *Lieutenant Kaki* • Odette Laure *Petite Chose* ■ *Dir* Jacqueline Audry • *Scr* Pierre Laroche, from a novel by Colette

Mixed Blood ★★★
Black comedy drama   1984 · US/Fr · Colour · 99mins

There's shades of *Bloody Mama* in this violent tale of gang warfare in New York's Alphabet City. The focus is on the Brazilian immigrant "Maceteros", a group of teenage hoodlums dominated by matriarch Rita La Punta (Marilia Pêra), who become involved in an escalating conflict with their Puerto Rican opposite numbers. Written and directed by Warhol acolyte Paul Morrissey, this meanders in tone between the trashy arthouse realism of *Flesh* and the gross-out parody of *Blood for Dracula*. But it deserves some marks for at least attempting to challenge, and Pera is barnstorming.

Marilia Pêra *Rita La Punta* • Richard Ulacia *Thiago* • Linda Kerridge *Carol* • Geraldine Smith *Toni* • Angel David *Juan the Bullet* • Ulrich Berr *The German* • Marcelino Rivera *Hector* ■ *Dir* Paul Morrissey • *Scr* Paul Morrissey, Alan Browne

Mixed Company ★★
Comedy drama   1974 · US · Colour · 108mins

A mildly entertaining but overly simplistic look at what happens when a couple adopt a string of ethnic children and naively introduce them

into their secretly bigoted neighbourhood. It's an honourable attempt by director Melville Shavelson and stars Barbara Harris and Joseph Bologna to treat an important subject with some lightness of touch, and not the worst film on racial prejudice ever made by any means, but its overall effect is sadly one of sporadically relieved tedium. Contains some swearing and nudity.

Barbara Harris *Kathy* • Joseph Bologna *Pete* • Lisa Gerritsen *Liz* • Ariane Heller *Mary* • Stephen Honanie *Joe* • Haywood Nelson *Freddie* • Eric Olson *Rob* • Jina Tan *Quan* • Tom Bosley *Al* ■ *Dir* Melville Shavelson • *Scr* Melville Shavelson, Mort Lachman

Mixed Nuts ★★ 12
Comedy   1995 · US · Colour · 93mins

An off-form Steve Martin stars as the manager of a struggling telephone help-line that's about to be disconnected in this California-set adaptation of French comedy *Le Père Noël est une Ordure*. It's so tasteless you'd scarcely believe it's by Nora Ephron, director of that eminently inoffensive romantic comedy *Sleepless in Seattle*. There's also little to warm the heart in the bleak Christmas context. Contains swearing. ▨

Steve Martin *Philip* • Rita Wilson *Catherine* • Madeline Kahn *Mrs Munchnik* • Robert Klein *Mr Lobel* • Anthony LaPaglia *Felix* • Juliette Lewis *Gracie* • Rob Reiner *Dr Kinsky* • Garry Shandling *Stanley* • Adam Sandler *Louie* • Liev Schreiber *Chris* ■ *Dir* Nora Ephron • *Scr* Nora Ephron, Delia Ephron, from the 1982 film *Le Père Noël est une Ordure*

Mixing Nia ★★★
Romantic comedy   1998 · US · Colour · 92mins

Bermuda-born documentarist Alison Swan made her feature debut as the writer/director of this perky romantic comedy drama, a reworking of 1949's *Pinky* in which Jeanne Crain starred as an African-American whose skin colour was pale enough to pass as white. Here Karyn Parsons gives a truly vibrant performance as the yuppy daughter of a mixed-race marriage who quits her copywriting job and embarks on a voyage of self-discovery. Swan gets a little carried away with the recurrent fantasy sequences, but she handles her themes with care.

Karyn Parsons *Nia* • Eric Thal *Matt* • Isaiah Washington *Lewis* • Diego Serrano *Joe* • Rosalyn Coleman *Renee* • Heidi Schanz *Jen* ■ *Dir/Scr* Alison Swan

Mo' Better Blues ★★★ 15
Drama   1990 · US · Colour · 123mins

Spike Lee suffers under the weight of his own ambition here, trying to cram his film with so many ideas (the nature of obsession, the avoidance of reality, the conflict between art and life) that it comes unglued at an early stage, especially as there's not enough plot to shore it up. Yet Denzel Washington, as a single-minded trumpeter, gingerly steps over the cracks to provide plenty of powerful scenes. He is helped by Wesley Snipes and Lee himself, and the lack of coherence is offset by vigorous, stylish camerawork and a killer jazz score. Contains violence, swearing, sex scenes and nudity. ▨

Denzel Washington *Bleek Gilliam* • Spike Lee *Giant* • Wesley Snipes *Shadow Henderson* • Joie Lee *Indigo Downes* • Cynda Williams *Clarke Bentancourt* • Dick Anthony Williams *Big Stop Gilliam* • Giancarlo Esposito *Left Hand Lacey* ■ *Dir/Scr* Spike Lee

Mo' Money ★★ 15
Action comedy 1992 · US · Colour · 85mins

Written and executive produced by its star, Damon Wayans, this is a ridiculous and gratuitously violent action movie which, sadly, also professes to be a comedy. Wayans plays an Eddie Murphy-style idiot who tries to impress his girlfriend (Stacey Dash) by getting a lowly job at the credit card company where she works. In no time at all, he's up to his neck in blackmail and fraud. A poorly scripted attempt to elevate his career, *Mo' Money* does Wayans few favours. ▭

Damon Wayans *Johnny Stewart* • Stacey Dash *Amber Evans* • Joe Santos *Lieutenant Raymond Walsh* • John Diehl *Keith Heading* • Harry J Lennix *Tom Dilton* • Marlon Wayans *Seymour Stewart* ■ *Dir* Peter MacDonald • *Scr* Damon Wayans

Moana ★★★★
Silent documentary 1926 · US · BW · 77mins

Because of the success of Robert Flaherty's first feature, *Nanook of the North* (1922), Paramount asked the ethnological director to make a "Nanook of the South Seas". So, with an unlimited budget, Flaherty spent two years in the Samoan islands making *Moana*. He returned with a lyrical, beautifully photographed, idealised picture of an island paradise where noble savages hunt, fish and cook. Although it did not as successful as the earlier film, it inspired British film producer John Grierson to coin the word "documentary".

Dir Robert Flaherty • *Scr* Robert Flaherty, Julian Johnson (titles) • *Cinematographer* Robert Flaherty

The Mob ★★★
Crime drama 1951 · US · BW · 86mins

When talented, under-rated director Robert Parrish worked as an editor, he managed to help pull together the shambles that was *All the King's Men*, not only winning himself an Oscar nomination (with Al Clark), but securing the best picture award and the best actor statuette for star Broderick Crawford. Crawford paid back the debt by lending his considerable (and bulky) presence to this, Parrish's second film as a director. Crawford brings great credibility to the role of a cop passing for a thug, and is especially good at the sexy repartee with forgotten actress Lynne Baggett.

Broderick Crawford *Johnny Damico* • Betty Buehler *Mary Kiernan* • Richard Kiley *Thomas Clancy* • Otto Hulett *Lieutenant Banks* • Matt Crowley *Smoothie* • Neville Brand *Gunner* • Ernest Borgnine *Joe Castro* • Charles Buchinski [Charles Bronson] *Jack* ■ *Dir* Robert Parrish • *Scr* William Bowers, from the novel *Waterfront* by Ferguson Findley

The Mobster ★★
Crime drama 1958 · US · BW · 79mins

After gaining critical attention with *Machine Gun Kelly*, director Roger

Corman quickly followed up that historical gangster thriller with one set in the modern era. Told in flashback to a Senate investigating committee, it charts the rise and fall of gangland leader Joe Sante (Steve Cochran), from his lowly slum beginnings working a numbers racket and dealing drugs to becoming head of the syndicate. While the script is nowhere near as strong as *Kelly*, Corman expertly captures the grimy criminal atmosphere in credible broad strokes and with swift action pacing. Lili St Cyr sings a song in a rare screen appearance.

Steve Cochran *Joe Sante* • Lita Milan *Teresa Porter* • Robert Strauss *Black Frankie* • Celia Lovsky *Mrs Sante* • Lili St Cyr • John Brinkley *Ernie Porter* • Yvette Vickers *Blonde* • Grant Withers *Joe Moran* ■ *Dir* Roger Corman • *Scr* Steve Fisher, from the novel *I, Mobster* by Joseph Hilton Smyth

Mobsters ★★ 18
Crime thriller 1991 · US · Colour · 115mins

It is extraordinary that, with gangster-era America providing such a natural source of drama, director Michael Karbelnikoff should turn gritty reality into such an empty tale. Hampered by inanity and a tortuous plot, Christian Slater (as "Lucky" Luciano), Patrick Dempsey (Meyer Lansky) and Richard Grieco ("Bugsy" Siegel) still manage to look reasonably credible in period suits, while Anthony Quinn and Michael Gambon, as two hard-nut mobsters, supply the flair and fire. Contains swearing, violence, sex and nudity. ▭

Christian Slater *Charlie "Lucky" Luciano* • Patrick Dempsey *Meyer Lansky* • Richard Grieco *Benjamin "Bugsy" Siegel* • Costas Mandylor *Frank Costello* • Anthony Quinn *Don Masseria* • F Murray Abraham *Arnold Rothstein* • Michael Gambon *Don Faranzano* • Lara Flynn Boyle *Mara Motes* ■ *Dir* Michael Karbelnikoff • *Scr* Michael Mahern, Nicholas Kazan, from a story by Michael Mahern

Moby Dick ★★
Adventure drama 1930 · US · BW · 75mins

A bowdlerised version of Herman Melville's classic novel, this has Captain Ahab (John Barrymore) losing his leg to a whale as a result of being pushed overboard by an evil stepbrother who is after the preacher's daughter (Joan Bennett) Ahab loves. Directed by Lloyd Bacon, the sequences where Ahab hunts the whale are let down by the clumsily obvious model of the predator. Barrymore, who had already played a silent-screen Ahab in the 1926 version of the tale, *The Sea Beast*, almost holds the nonsensically melodramatic plot together with a fine performance.

John Barrymore *Captain Ahab* • Joan Bennett *Faith* • Lloyd Hughes *Derek* • May Boley *Whale Oil Rosie* • Walter Long *Stubbs* • Tom O'Brien *Starbuck* • Nigel De Brulier *Elijah* ■ *Dir* Lloyd Bacon • *Scr* J Grubb Alexander, from the novel by Herman Melville

Moby Dick ★★★ PG
Adventure drama 1956 · UK/US · Colour · 110mins

John Huston's long-cherished adaptation of Herman Melville's novel has some wonderful scenes but must be counted as a noble failure. The great white whale always looks phoney; it performed badly in high seas off the

coasts of Ireland and the Canaries, pushing the budget through the roof. Gregory Peck, as Captain Ahab, is fatally miscast, completely lacking the required demonic presence. Wags at the time joked that Orson Welles, who plays Father Mapple, should have played the whale, while Peck himself thought that Huston should have played Ahab. Now, in the age of digital effects, there have been persistent rumours of a remake by Roland Joffé or Hugh Hudson with Sean Connery as the obsessed captain. ▭

Gregory Peck *Captain Ahab* • Richard Basehart *Ishmael* • Leo Genn *Starbuck* • Orson Welles *Father Mapple* • Friedrich Ledebur *Queequeg* • Harry Andrews *Stubb* • Bernard Miles *Manxman* • James Robertson-Justice *Captain Boomer* ■ *Dir* John Huston • *Scr* John Huston, Ray Bradbury, from the novel by Herman Melville • *Cinematographer* Oswald Morris, Freddie Francis

The Mod Squad ★ 15
Action crime drama 1999 · US · Colour · 94mins

This moody remake of the popular sixties TV cop show spends 40 minutes establishing the hipness of its trio of main characters before getting to the plot. Even then, the movie's a lot more about atmosphere and twentysomething angst than it is about what happens to three former criminals who become undercover cops. Although Omar Epps is somewhat intriguing as Linc, Claire Danes is merely present in her role as Julie, and Giovanni Ribisi is by turns annoying and embarrassing as Pete. A good example of how not to make a movie. Contains swearing and violence. ▭

Claire Danes *Julie Barnes* • Giovanni Ribisi *Pete Cochrane* • Omar Epps *Linc Hayes* • Josh Brolin *Billy Waites* • Dennis Farina *Captain Adam Greer* • Steve Harris *Detective Briggs* ■ *Dir* Scott Silver • *Scr* Scott Silver, Stephen Kay, Kate Lanier, from characters created by Buddy Ruskin

The Model and the Marriage Broker ★★★
Comedy drama 1951 · US · BW · 103mins

A minor but charming movie from "women's director" George Cukor, here slightly overdependent on the undoubted talents and weather-beaten features of character actress and notorious scene-stealer Thelma Ritter. Ritter is marvellous, trying to pair friend Jeanne Crain with handsome radiographer Scott Brady, while trying not to let Crain know matchmaking is her real profession. Others in the marriage market include a pre-blacklist Zero Mostel. "It will walk into your hearts," promised the advertising. For once, you won't be let down.

Jeanne Crain *Kitty Bennett* • Scott Brady *Matt Hornbeck* • Thelma Ritter *Mae Swazey* • Zero Mostel *Wixted* • Michael O'Shea *Doberman* • Helen Ford *Emmy Swazey* • Frank Fontaine *Johannson* ■ *Dir* George Cukor • *Scr* Charles Brackett, Walter Reisch, Richard Breen

Model by Day ★★★
Comedy thriller 1994 · US/Can · Colour · 100mins

Before making her name as a bad girl in the Bond film *GoldenEye*, Famke Janssen displayed her fighting prowess in this above-average thriller. She

takes the role of Lady X, a fashion model turned high-kicking vigilante, who sets out to find the people responsible for the beating of her flatmate. The eclectic support cast includes Shannon Tweed and Sean Young, and it's directed with some style by Christian Duguay. Contains violence, swearing and nudity.

Famke Janssen *Lex/Lady X* • Stephen Shellen *Eddie Walker* • Traci Lind *Jae* • Shannon Tweed *Shannon* • Sean Young *Mercedes* ■ *Dir* Christian Duguay • *Scr* Joseph Loeb III, Matthew Weisman

Model Shop ★
Drama 1969 · US/Fr · Colour · 95mins

Jacques Demy made some fine films in France, but his Hollywood debut was a mistake from start to finish. Made in LA during the time of anti-Vietnam demos, the counterculture and the sexual revolution, it's a frivolous thing about fashion design and photography. Gary Lockwood, who played one of the astronauts in *2001*, has all the personality of a paper cup, while Anouk Aimée, who revives her 1960 character of Lola, does little but stare vacantly into the middle distance.

Anouk Aimée *Lola* • Gary Lockwood *George Matthews* • Alexandra Hay *Gloria* • Carol Cole *Barbara* • Severn Darden *Portly man* • Tom Fielding *Gerry* ■ *Dir* Jacques Demy • *Scr* Jacques Demy, Adrien Joyce

Modern Love ★★ 15
Romantic comedy 1990 · US · Colour · 104mins

A lame, hackneyed look at the problems of modern relationships and the family that adds nothing new to the great American middle income debate. Director/writer/star Robby Benson co-opted his real-life wife, Karla DeVito, and their own daughter to play his family, which gives the whole plodding affair a smug, incestuous air. Benson cobbled this one together as part of a university film course – proof that he should have listened to the old maxim "those who can, do; those who can't, teach".

Robby Benson *Greg* • Karla DeVito *Dr Billie Parker* • Burt Reynolds *Colonel Frank Parker* • Debra Port *Annabell* • Cliff Bemis *Dirk Martin* • Rue McClanahan *Evelyn* • Frankie Valli *Mr Hoskins* ■ *Dir/Scr* Robby Benson

Modern Problems ★
Comedy 1981 · US · Colour · 90mins

Stressed-out air traffic controller Chevy Chase is driving along the freeway when a truck carrying nuclear waste springs a leak, drenching our hero in radioactive slime. Instead of making him grow an extra head or simply killing him, the incident causes Chase to develop telekinetic powers. These help him sort out the problems in his life and enable him to take sweet revenge on his enemies. Mostly this involves sub-Stephen King stuff and some flying vomit à la *The Exorcist*. An idea that might have occupied a five-minute sketch on a TV show is stretched to feature-film length and shows that, without the Griswold clan, Chase can't carry a picture.

Chevy Chase *Max* • Patti D'Arbanville [Patti D'Arbanville-Quinn] *Darcy* • Mary Kay Place *Lorraine* • Nell Carter *Dorita* • Brian Doyle-

Murray *Brian* • Dabney Coleman *Mark* • Mitch Kreindel *Barry* ■ *Dir* Ken Shapiro • *Scr* Ken Shapiro, Tom Sherohman, Arthur Sellers

Modern Romance ★★★ 15
Romantic comedy
1981 · US · Colour · 89mins

A neglected and totally original comedy from co-writer/director/star Albert Brooks. He plays a film editor, and the sequences involving the cutting process are insightful and truthful, as he and the excellent Bruno Kirby go to work on a sci-fi flick with the mercilessly hamming George Kennedy as space leader Zeron. The man behind the camera for the schlock movie is played by real-life director James L Brooks, who would later offer Albert (no relation) the role of his career in *Broadcast News*. The plot's slight, but the film is enjoyable and interesting, especially for movie buffs. Contains swearing. 🎞

Albert Brooks *Robert Cole* • Kathryn Harrold *Mary Harvard* • Tyann Means *Waitress* • Bruno Kirby *Jay* • Jane Hallaren *Ellen* • Karen Chandler *Neighbour* • James L Brooks *David* • George Kennedy *Zeron* ■ *Dir* Albert Brooks • *Scr* Albert Brooks, Monica Johnson

Modern Times ★★★★★ U
Comedy
1936 · US · Colour · 86mins

Charles Chaplin's ridiculing of an increasingly mechanised and mechanical society is an inspired assembly line of gags, similar to *A Nous la Liberté* by the French director René Clair, who declared he had always been inspired by Chaplin so was honoured if "the master" had been inspired by him. As machines chew up our hero and spit him out, Charlie finds solace in the love of Paulette Goddard and a sunset stroll into a happy-ever-after. Naive this may be, but what else could Chaplin do? He was in the business of redemption and this was the only way out he could find in increasingly darkening days. 🎞

Charlie Chaplin [Charles Chaplin] *Factory worker* • Paulette Goddard *Gamine* • Henry Bergman *Café owner* • Stanley J Sanford [Stanley] *Big Bill/Worker* • Chester Conklin *Mechanic* ■ *Dir* Charlie Chaplin [Charles Chaplin] • *Scr* Charles Chaplin • *Cinematographer* Rollie Totheroh, Ira Morgan

The Moderns ★★★ 15
Period drama
1988 · US · Colour and BW · 121mins

Alan Rudolph's wry study of the cabal that gathered itself around Ernest Hemingway in twenties Paris is short on drama, but stuffed with arch academic allusions. As convincingly fake as the pictures Keith Carradine is commissioned to paint, the neverland of bons mots and chic cafés is superbly sustained by the brilliance of the screenplay and Rudolph's lightness of touch, which enables his cast to shine without dazzling. With Wallace Shawn impressive as the journalist feeding off the "lost generation" and Linda Fiorentino as Carradine's ex-wife, this is both ambitious and accessible. Contains nudity. 🎞

Keith Carradine *Nick Hart* • Linda Fiorentino *Rachel Stone* • Geneviève Bujold *Libby Valentin* • Geraldine Chaplin *Nathalie de Ville* • Wallace Shawn *Oiseau* • John Lone *Bertram Stone* • Kevin J O'Connor *Ernest Hemingway* •

Elsa Raven *Gertrude Stein* • Ali Giron *Alice B Toklas* ■ *Dir* Alan Rudolph • *Scr* Alan Rudolph, John Bradshaw

Modesty Blaise ★★ PG
Spy spoof
1966 · UK · Colour · 114mins

With its dizzy set designs and flamboyant costumes, Joseph Losey's misguided screen adaptation of Peter O'Donnell's seminal cartoon strip is a paean to the excesses of the mid-sixties. The years have not been kind, however, and the film now exists in a pop art time-bubble of its own making – unlike, say, the Bond movies it hopelessly apes. In a plot that makes virtually no sense, Monica Vitti is miscast as the sexy female spy, a sort of earthbound Barberella out to thwart effete arch fiend Dirk Bogarde. The latter has a ball in his silver wig and sunglasses, while Terence Stamp turns up somewhere as Modesty's bed-hopping accomplice. Camper than a lift full of Graham Nortons, this was deservedly lambasted upon release, though that hasn't quelled repeated rumours of a possible remake. 🎞

Monica Vitti *Modesty Blaise* • Dirk Bogarde *Gabriel* • Terence Stamp *Willie Garvin* • Michael Craig *Paul Hagan* • Harry Andrews *Sir Gerald Tarrant* • Rossella Falk *Mrs Fothergill* • Scilla Gabel *Melina* • Clive Revill *McWhirter/Sheik Abu Tahir* • Joe Melia *Crevier* ■ *Dir* Joseph Losey • *Scr* Evan Jones, from a story by Peter O'Donnell, Stanley Dubens, from the comic strip by Peter O'Donnell, Jim Holdaway

Mogambo ★★★
Romantic adventure
1953 · US · Colour · 115mins

In 1932, Clark Gable made a picture for MGM called *Red Dust*, and very steamy it was too. A story of lust set in the jungles of south-east Asia, it featured Gable as a rubber planter choosing between temptress Jean Harlow and demure Mary Astor. *Mogambo*, directed by John Ford, is the remake, transposed to Africa with Gable again, plus Ava Gardner and Grace Kelly. Gone is the steaminess of the original: this is a Technicolor adventure romp fit for the postwar Eisenhower era of healthy living, with a supporting cast of monkeys, lions, elephants and rhinos. Freddie Young shot the African exteriors; Robert Surtees did the interiors in Hollywood.

Clark Gable *Victor Marswell* • Ava Gardner *Eloise Y Kelly* • Grace Kelly *Linda Nordley* • Donald Sinden *Donald Nordley* • Philip Stainton *John Brown Pryce* • Eric Pohlmann *Leon Boltchak* • Laurence Naismith *Skipper* ■ *Dir* John Ford • *Scr* John Lee Mahin, from the play *Red Dust* by Wilson Collison

Mohawk ★★ U
Western
1956 · US · Colour · 79mins

Splendidly camp stuff, as a quintessential bevy of fifties movie icons throw themselves at devil-may-care artist Scott Brady (Joan Crawford's outlaw lover in *Johnny Guitar*). Brady's love interest in this movie is Rita Gam as a squaw, but that doesn't stop him dallying with Lori Nelson and Allison Hayes. Director Kurt Neumann made this co-feature between *Carnival Story* and *The Fly*, but it's probably for the star-making *Son of Ali Baba* that he'll be remembered, if at all. Certainly his

baroque style was way ahead of contemporary audiences' tastes.

Scott Brady *Jonathan Adams* • Rita Gam *Onida* • Neville Brand *Rokhawah* • Lori Nelson *Cynthia Stanhope* • Allison Hayes *Greta* • John Hoyt *Butler* • Vera Vague [Barbara Jo Allen] *Aunt Agatha* ■ *Dir* Kurt Neumann • *Scr* Maurice Geraghty, Milton Krims

Mojave Moon ★★
Romantic comedy
1996 · US · Colour · 85mins

This determinedly "difficult" indie movie has a decent cast trying desperately to make sense of a wilfully wacky script and coping manfully with indifferent direction. Danny Aiello plays a lovelorn LA car salesman who drives a young woman back to her Mojave desert home. There, he's drawn into the weird world of the girl's mom and her paranoid boyfriend. The super cast also includes Anne Archer, Michael Biehn and, in an early screen appearance, Angelina Jolie. Contains violence, nudity, swearing, drug abuse and sexual situations.

Danny Aiello *Al* • Angelina Jolie *Ellie* • Anne Archer *Julie* • Jack Noseworthy *Kaiser* • Alfred Molina *Sal* • Michael Biehn *Boyd* ■ *Dir* Kevin Dowling • *Scr* Leonard Glasser

Mojo ★★ 15
Drama
1998 · UK · Colour · 92mins

Revealing the dark underside of London in the late fifties, this brutal Soho-set drama by Jez Butterworth was a big hit at London's Royal Court theatre. But, in spite of a nervously energetic camera and diverse directorial flourishes, this adaptation remains a stubbornly theatrical experience. There's a laudable eagerness about the performances, as ambitious henchman Ian Hart gets embroiled in Harold Pinter's scheme to move in on a singing sensation at Ricky Tomlinson's seedy club. In the end, however, the self-consciously stylised sets and the rather mannered dialogue afflict too many scenes for this to really work on screen. Contains swearing and violence.

Ian Hart *Mickey* • Ewen Bremner *Skinny Luke* • Aidan Gillen *Baby* • Martin Gwynn Jones *Sweets* • Hans Matheson *Silver Johnny* • Andy Serkis *Sid Potts* • Ricky Tomlinson *Ezra* • Harold Pinter *Sam Ross* ■ *Dir* Jez Butterworth • *Scr* Jez Butterworth, Tom Butterworth, from the play by Jez Butterworth

Moll Flanders ★★★ 12
Period drama
1995 · US · Colour · 117mins

Daniel Defoe's story of the hard-edged young woman with dubious virtues gets the Hollywood treatment in a classy, if sometimes yawn-inducing reworking of the 18th-century romp. Robin Wright (*Forrest Gump*) is well cast as Moll, whose sad, eventful life is recounted to her abandoned daughter (Aisling Corcoran) by manservant Hibble (Morgan Freeman). Far grittier than you would expect from a Tinseltown interpretation, director Pen Densham's convincing period evocation is bolstered by Wright's terrific work as the abused heroine. Contains some swearing and sexual situations. 🎞

Robin Wright [Robin Wright Penn] *Moll Flanders* • Morgan Freeman *Hibble* • Stockard Channing *Mrs Allworthy* • John Lynch *Fielding*

• Brenda Fricker *Mrs Mazzawatti* • Geraldine James *Edna* • Aisling Corcoran *Flora* ■ *Dir* Pen Densham • *Scr* Pen Densham, from the novel by Daniel Defoe

Molly ★ 15
Drama
1999 · US · Colour · 98mins

Allegedly based on fact, this syrupy drama has an uncanny similarity to Daniel Keyes's short story, *Flowers For Algernon*. Elisabeth Shue plays a 28-year-old autistic woman who undergoes an operation that brings her out of her shell. Unfortunately, the changed persona does little to improve the star's performance, which is so over-the-top it's embarrassing to watch. Neither she nor the makers of the movie seem to have had any idea of how autistic people function when they made this drivel; worse still are their attempts to punctuate the drama with various kinds of humour, which are not only unfunny but also offensive. 🎞

Elisabeth Shue *Molly McKay* • Aaron Eckhart *Buck McKay* • Thomas Jane *Sam* • Jill Hennessy *Susan Brookes* • DW Moffett *Mark Cottrell* • Elizabeth Mitchell *Beverly Trehare* ■ *Dir* John Duigan • *Scr* Dick Christie

Molly and Lawless John ★★★
Western
1972 · US · Colour · 97mins

There's a ingenious storyline and a distinct feminist slant to this undiscovered western, directed by TV-movie expert Gary Nelson. Vera Miles plays the unhappy, fortysomething wife of staid local sheriff John Anderson who has blond and dashing young outlaw Sam Elliott in his jail. Elliott persuades Miles to organise his escape and they elope together, though it's not long before Miles begins to despise her new man.

Vera Miles *Molly Parker* • Sam Elliott *Johnny Lawler* • Clu Gulager *Deputy* • John Anderson *Sheriff Parker* • Cynthia Myers *Dolly* ■ *Dir* Gary Nelson • *Scr* Terry Kingsley-Smith

Molly and Me ★★★
Musical comedy
1945 · US · BW · 76mins

Following their charming pairing in *Holy Matrimony* in 1943, Gracie Fields and Monty Woolley were reunited for this slight but engaging variation on the *Pollyanna* story, in which Our Gracie and a bunch of "resting" entertainers transform Woolley's staid existence while working as his servants. Brightly directed by Lewis Seiler, the film is as interesting for its supporting cast as it is for its leads. Rada-trained veteran Reginald Gardiner is magnificent as Peabody the butler, Doris Lloyd is suitably grasping as Woolley's ex-wife and Roddy McDowall is agonisingly twee as his gone-astray son.

Gracie Fields *Molly* • Monty Woolley *Graham* • Roddy McDowall *Jimmy Graham* • Reginald Gardiner *Peabody* • Natalie Schafer *Kitty* • Edith Barrett *Julia* • Clifford Brooke *Pops* • Aminta Dyne *Musette* • Queenie Leonard *Lily* • Doris Lloyd *Mrs Graham* ■ *Dir* Lewis Seiler • *Scr* Leonard Praskins, Roger Burford, from the novel by Frances Marion

The Molly Maguires ★★ PG
Drama
1970 · US · Colour · 119mins

With a cast that featured Sean Connery as a rebellious coalminer,

Richard Harris as a mining company *agent provocateur* and Samantha Eggar as Harris's above-the-ground love interest, it was sad that the end result proved so disappointing. All the effort here has gone into the depiction of mining conditions in 19th-century Pennsylvania, but the script seems to have been written by a mechanical digger. Every scene rams home some kind of message, and Martin Ritt directs from a soapbox. Contains violence and swearing. 🎬

Richard Harris *James McParlan/McKenna* • Sean Connery *Jack Kehoe* • Samantha Eggar *Mary Raines* • Frank Finlay *Captain Davies* • Anthony Zerbe *Dougherty* • Bethel Leslie *Mrs Kehoe* • Art Lund *Frazier* ■ *Dir* Martin Ritt • *Scr* Walter Bernstein, from the novel *Lament for the Molly Maguires* by H Arthur Lewis

Moloch ★★★
Historical drama
1999 · Rus/Ger/Fr · Colour · 108mins

Owing the same visual debt to the German Romantic artist, Caspar David Friedrich, as his previous outing, *Mother and Son*, Alexander Sokurov's Berchtesgaden dissertation on the nature of power also nods, occasionally, in the direction of the Reich's official film-maker, Leni Riefenstahl. However, instead of presenting a revealing portrait of the Führer through the eyes of his long-suffering mistress, Eva Braun, Sokurov succeeds only in presenting an illustrated digest of the table talk of Adolf Hitler. He also suggests that he knew little of the Final Solution and was merely the short-fused, deluded dupe of such supposed sidekicks as his propaganda chief, Goebbels. A German language film.

Leonid Mosgovoi *Adolf Hitler* • Elena Rufanova *Eva Braun* • Leonid Sokol *Josef Goebbels* • Elena Spiridonova *Magda Goebbels* • Vladimir Bogdanov *Martin Bormann* ■ *Dir* Alexander Sokurov • *Scr* Yuri Arabov, Marina Koreneva

Mom and Dad Save the World ★ 🅿🅶
Science-fiction comedy
1992 · US · Colour · 86mins

This infantile comedy, which pokes broad fun at those creaky old *Flash Gordon* serials, hails from the same writers as the *Bill and Ted* movies – and don't it show! When middle-class parents Teri Garr and the wonderful Jeffrey Jones are spirited away to a far distant planet whose ruler intends making Garr his bride, Jones is forced into warrior mode to oust the tyrant and put rightful heir Eric Idle onto the throne. With its tasteless sets and rubber-suited monsters, the film's modest budget is flaunted as if it were a selling point. Yet director Greg Beeman can't disguise the lamentable script which, despite the best efforts of a likeable cast, falls flat. 🎬

Teri Garr *Marge Nelson* • Jeffrey Jones *Dick Nelson* • Jon Lovitz *Tod Spengo* • Dwier Brown *Sirk* • Kathy Ireland *Semage* • Thalmus Rasulala *General Afir* • Wallace Shawn *Sibor* • Eric Idle *Raff* ■ *Dir* Greg Beeman • *Scr* Ed Solomon, Chris Matheson

A Mom for Christmas ★★★ 🆄
Fantasy drama 1990 · US · Colour · 88mins

A sweet, seasonal Disney tale about a young girl who wishes she had a mother. Her wish comes true when a department store mannequin comes to life. Much more watchable than the similar 1987 film *Mannequin*, this also marks a welcome return to the screen for Olivia Newton-John, who never really cashed in on the success of *Grease* back in 1978. 🎬

Olivia Newton-John *Amy* • Doug Sheehan *Jim Slocum* • Juliet Sorcey *Jessica Slocum* • Doris Roberts *Philomena* • James Piddock *Wilkins* • Aubrey Morris *Santa/Nicholas* ■ *Dir* George Miller (1) • *Scr* Gerald DiPego, from the novel *A Mom by Magic* by Barbara Dillon

Moment by Moment ★
Romantic comedy
1978 · US · Colour · 93mins

Jane Wagner writes and directs this embarrassing romance, a vehicle for her longtime companion and collaborator, Lily Tomlin. The latter stars as Trisha, a bored Malibu housewife whose juices are stirred by a post-*Saturday Night Fever* John Travolta, playing a drifter with the hilarious name of Strip. Alas, audiences showed little interest in their May-December relationship.

Lily Tomlin *Trisha Rawlings* • John Travolta *Strip* • Andra Akers *Naomi* • Bert Kramer *Stu Rawlings* • Shelley R Bonus *Peg* • Debra Feuer *Stacie* ■ *Dir/Scr* Jane Wagner

Moment of Danger ★★
Crime drama 1960 · UK · BW · 97mins

Meek little locksmith and cuckolded husband Trevor Howard is recruited by debonair Edmund Purdom to rob a Mayfair jewellers'. After the robbery, Purdom vanishes with all the swag so Howard pursues him to Spain with Purdom's jilted girlfriend, Dorothy Dandridge. Part thriller, part romantic tangle, this is produced by Douglas Fairbanks Jr and directed by Laslo Benedek, best known for *The Wild One*. The British critics accused workaholic Howard of slumming so, upset by the notices, he issued a statement: "You can't do anything better if there's nothing better to do."

Trevor Howard *John Bain* • Dorothy Dandridge *Gianna* • Edmund Purdom *Peter Carran* • Michael Hordern *Inspector Farrell* • Paul Stassino *Juan Montoya* ■ *Dir* Laslo Benedek • *Scr* David Osborn, Donald Ogden Stewart, from the novel *The Scent of Danger* by Donald MacKenzie

A Moment of Innocence ★★★
Comedy drama
1996 · Iran/Fr/Swi · Colour · 77mins

Iranian cinema's preoccupation with the mechanics of movie-making once again comes to the fore in this teasing treatise on idealism, love, coincidence and the selectivity of memory. Recalling an incident from the days of the Shah when he stabbed a policeman, Moshen Makhmalbaf cross-cuts between this moment of revolutionary zeal and the production of a film re-creating the event. With the actual cop, Ali Bakhsi, playing himself

and coaching his young alter ego, the action challenges you to question the motives of the participants and the relevance of distinguishing between fact and fiction. Superbly controlled and stylishly self-reflexive, it is also genuinely intriguing. In Farsi with English subtitles.

Mirhadi Tayebi • Ali Bakhshi • Ammar Tafti • Mohsen Makhmalbaf ■ *Dir/Scr* Mohsen Makhmalbaf

Moment to Moment ★★
Thriller 1966 · US · Colour · 107mins

A psychiatrist's wife, left alone on the French Riviera during her husband's frequent absences, becomes involved with a young officer who is later shot and left for dead. The result is a ludicrous brew of adultery and attempted murder, directed by Mervyn LeRoy, dressed by Yves Saint-Laurent and photographed by Harry Stradling. Alas, the overlay of gloss and glamour fails to disguise the dreadful script or the inert performances from Jean Seberg (the wife), Sean Garrison (the lover) and Arthur Hill (the cuckolded husband). Only Honor Blackman, as Seberg's helpful neighbour, breathes life into the proceedings.

Jean Seberg *Kay Stanton* • Honor Blackman *Daphne Fields* • Sean Garrison *Mark Dominic* • Arthur Hill *Neil Stanton* • Peter Robbins *Timmy Stanton* • Grégoire Aslan *Edward DeFargo* • Donald Woods *Mr Singer* • Walter Reed *Hendricks* ■ *Dir* Mervyn LeRoy • *Scr* John Lee Mahin, Alec Coppel, from the short story *Laughs With a Stranger* by Alec Coppel

Mommie Dearest ★★★★ 🆖
Biographical drama
1981 · US · Colour · 122mins

An absolutely riveting melodrama about Joan Crawford, based on her daughter Christina's vengeful memoir. Faye Dunaway is astonishing as Crawford, risen from rags to bitches, who still scrubs the floors, runs rings around studio bosses and creates a living hell for her daughter (brilliantly played by young Mara Hobel and, later, Diana Scarwid). As Tinseltown exposés go, this one is lavish and pretty accurate as far as Hollywood lore is concerned. Contains swearing. 🎬

Faye Dunaway *Joan Crawford* • Diana Scarwid *Christina Crawford* • Steve Forrest *Gret Savitt* • Howard Da Silva *Louis B Mayer* • Mara Hobel *Christina as a child* • Rutanya Alda *Carol Ann* • Harry Goz *Al Steele* ■ *Dir* Frank Perry • *Scr* Frank Yablans, Frank Perry, Tracy Hotchner, Robert Getchell, from the memoirs by Christina Crawford

Mom's Army ★★★
Comedy 1989 · US · Colour · 100mins

Anson Williams (Potsie in *Happy Days*) directed this *Private Benjamin*-style comedy about a mother who joins the army to keep her newly recruited son from getting killed. *I Dream of Jeannie's* Barbara Eden is on form as the ditzy mom of the title, and she's ably supported by Hector Elizondo (of *Chicago Hope* and *Pretty Woman* fame) as the obligatory grumpy sergeant.

Barbara Eden *Brenda Anderson* • Hector Elizondo *Sgt Charlie Burke* • David Kaufman *Jimmy Anderson* • Meagan Fay *Edie Winchell* • Maria O'Brien *Carla* • Conchata Ferrell

Mononaghee ■ *Dir* Anson Williams • *Scr* Susan Hunter, April Kelly from a story by Susan Hunter, Kelly Novodor, Bill Novodor

Mon Homme ★★★ 🅸🅸
Drama 1996 · Fr · Colour · 95mins

A typically outrageous and undisciplined effort from Bertrand Blier, with Anouk Grinberg as the proverbial tart with a heart who decides to rescue the homeless man (Gérard Lanvin) living in the garbage dump of her apartment block. After she cooks for him and sleeps with him, he becomes her pimp. There are snatches here of Jean Renoir's 1932 classic *Boudu, Saved from Drowning*, as well as Billy Wilder's *Irma la Douce*. Buried beneath the sexual frolics, however, there lies a chaste tale of redemption. In French with English subtitles. 🎬

Anouk Grinberg *Marie* • Gérard Lanvin *Jeannot* • Valeria Bruni Tedeschi *Sanguine* • Olivier Martinez *Jean-François* • Sabine Azéma *Bérangère* • Mathieu Kassovitz *Client* • Jean-Pierre Léaud *Claude* ■ *Dir/Scr* Bertrand Blier

Mon Oncle ★★★★★ 🆄
Comedy 1958 · Fr · Colour · 103mins

Jacques Tati revived Monsieur Hulot for this typically gentle yet incisive satire on the mechanised madness of the modern world. Although shot in widescreen for the maximum democracy of viewing and patterned with plenty of symbolic colour, Hulot's baffled encounter with his sister's soulless, state-of-the-art residence depends as much on the meticulously constructed soundtrack as the visual humour for its comic impact. Belying hours of puntilious preparation, each gag seems positively spontaneous as Tati puts progress in its place by extolling the virtues of human contact. A French language film. 🎬

Jacques Tati *Monsieur Hulot* • Jean-Pierre Zola *Monsieur Arpel* • Adrienne Servantie *Madame Arpel* • Alain Bécourt *Gérard* • Lucien Frégis *Monsieur Pichard* • Dominique Marie *Neighbour* ■ *Dir* Jacques Tati • *Scr* Jacques Tati, Jacques Lagrange, Jean L'Hote

Mon Oncle d'Amérique ★
Drama 1980 · Fr · Colour · 123mins

We all know that life is a rat race. To underline the point, though, Alain Resnais uses the staggeringly original device of actually filming rats scurrying about! He also indulges animal behaviourist Dr Henri Laborit as he laboriously passes comment on the three main characters: a suicidal middle manager (Gérard Depardieu), an actress (Nicole Garcia) and a TV executive (Roger Pierre). For a director with the back catalogue and the sophistication of Resnais, this satire on modern life is a complete waste of time. A French language film.

Gérard Depardieu *Rene Ragueneau* • Nicole Garcia *Janine Garnier* • Roger Pierre *Jean Le Gall* • Marie Dubois *Therese Ragueneau* • Nelly Borgeaud *Arlette Le Gall* • Henri Laborit ■ *Dir* Alain Resnais • *Scr* Jean Gruault, from the works of Henri Laborit

🆄 = SUITABLE FOR ALL   🆖 = SUITABLE FOR ALL, ESPECIALLY FOR YOUNG CHILDREN (VIDEO ONLY)   🅿🅶 = PARENTAL GUIDANCE

Mon Père Ce Héros ★★★★ PG

Romantic comedy 1991 · Fr · Colour · 99mins

There are moments in this boisterous French comedy that will cause many politically correct brows to knit in disapproval. However, without ever atoning for its lapses, Gérard Lauzier's one-joke comedy rather creeps up on you, almost solely on account of the performance of Gérard Depardieu as the indulgent father who becomes the talk of a holiday hotel when his 14-year-old daughter tells all and sundry he is her lover. Marie Gillain bristles with coquettish charm, but the pace dips when Depardieu is off screen. Consequently, he was the obvious choice for the 1994 Hollywood remake, *My Father the Hero*. In French with English subtitles. ▭

Gérard Depardieu *André* • Marie Gillain *Véronique* • Patrick Mille *Benjamin* • Catherine Jacob *Christelle* • Charlotte De Turckheim *Irina* • Jean-François Rangasamy *Pablo* • Koomaren Chetty *Karim* ■ *Dir/Scr* Gérard Lauzier

Mona Lisa ★★★★ 18

Crime drama 1986 · UK · Colour · 99mins

A haunting, if often disturbing, London-set thriller, in which Bob Hoskins manages to convey some deeper emotion than his more usual thuggery. As the gangster's chauffeur madly in love with Cathy Tyson's detached, emotionally bruised prostitute, Hoskins brings rich pathos to a plot not overloaded with such feelings. Neil Jordan directs with great flair and insightful wisdom, and the photography lingers long in the mind. A movie that seems to sum up a certain eighties soullessness, this is still a thought-provoking gem. Contains violence, swearing, sex scenes and nudity. ▭

Bob Hoskins *George* • Cathy Tyson *Simone* • Michael Caine *Mortwell* • Robbie Coltrane *Thomas* • Clarke Peters *Anderson* • Kate Hardie *Cathy* • Zoe Nathenson *Jeannie* • Sammi Davis *May* • Joe Brown (2) *Dudley* ■ *Dir* Neil Jordan • *Scr* Neil Jordan, David Leland • *Cinematographer* Roger Pratt

Le Monde du Silence ★★★★

Documentary 1956 · Fr · Colour · 82mins

The first feature of Jacques-Yves Cousteau, the famous French oceanographer, diver and documentary film-maker, is an exploration of the fascinating fauna and flora of the ocean's depths. Cousteau, and his underwater cameramen, went beyond the bounds of a scientific documentary by capturing the poetry of the "silent world". Cousteau's co-director was 24-year-old Louis Malle, getting his first director's credit. His work on the film caused him ear problems for the rest of his life. A French language film.

Dir Jacques-Yves Cousteau, Louis Malle • *Scr* James Dugan (commentary)

Mondo Cane ★

Documentary 1962 · It · Colour · 91mins

The British censor initially banned this "shockumentary", which looks at the weirdest, freakiest and least pleasant aspects of life in a way that defines prurience. Examples include irradiated creatures on Bikini Atoll; religious self-flagellation; restaurants which serve dogs, insects or crocodile; street kids polishing the skulls of their Roman ancestors; islanders taking hideous revenge on sharks; and "stone age" Papuans making an air strip, then waiting for the plane that never comes. An unedifying experience for all concerned. An Italian language film.

Stefano Sibaldi *Narrator* ■ *Dir* Gualtiero Jacopetti, Franco Prosperi • *Scr* Gualtiero Jacopetti, Paolo Cavara, Franco Prosperi,

Mondo Trasho ★★

Underground satirical melodrama
1970 · US · BW · 94mins

The first widely-seen feature from John Waters, the "Pope of Trash", was made on a shoestring budget of $2,000 with no synchronised sound. An engagingly overwrought porn parody, it details a single day in the lives of hit-and-run driver Divine and her tormented victim, Mary Vivian Pearce. Foot fetishism, fifties rock 'n' roll, visions of the Virgin Mary and a tacky homage to Tod Browning's controversial horror film *Freaks* are thrown around with typical gay abandon in this Fellini-esque lampoon.

Mary Vivian Pearce *Girl* • John Leisenring *Shrimper* • Sharon Sandrock *Stepsister* • Berenica Cipcus *Stepsister/Nurse* • Divine *Hit-and-run driver* • Margie Skidmore *Madonna* • Mink Stole *Tapdancer* • David Lochary *Dr Coathanger* ■ *Dir/Scr* John Waters

Money for Nothing ★★ 15

Black comedy based on a true story
1993 · US · Colour · 96mins

The problem with this black comedy is that it's based on actual events that are anything but amusing. Joey Coyle's decision to keep the $1.2 million he found after it fell out of a casino security van was the worst he ever made. Not only did he have to resort to a plea of temporary insanity to escape jail, but he committed suicide shortly before Ramon Menendez's film was released. John Cusack has the unenviable task of playing the docker who fell in with the mob to safeguard his windfall, but not even his geniality can save this frantic misfire. Contains swearing. ▭

John Cusack *Joey Coyle* • Debi Mazar *Monica Russo* • Michael Madsen *Detective Pat Laurenzi* • Benicio Del Toro *Dino Palladino* • Michael Rapaport *Kenny Kozlowski* • Maury Chaykin *Vincente Goldoni* • James Gandolfini *Billy Coyle* • Fionnula Flanagan *Mrs Coyle* ■ *Dir* Ramon Menendez • *Scr* Ramon Menendez, Tom Musca, Carol Sobieski

Money from Home ★★ U

Comedy 1953 · US · Colour · 100mins

Dean Martin and Jerry Lewis meet Damon Runyon in this rather weak entry in the Paramount canon, its combination of racetrack high-jinks and comic Arabs defeating even Martin and Lewis. It certainly seemed funnier and more convincing in its original 3-D format, but it was shown "flat" on release in the UK. The comic duo began well in the *Irma* flicks and made some super pictures with director Frank Tashlin, but frankly this largely uninspired and rather juvenile romp is really just fan fodder.

Dean Martin *"Honey Talk" Nelson* • Jerry Lewis *Virgil Yokum* • Marjie Millar *Phyllis Leigh* • Pat Crowley *Autumn Claypool* • Richard Haydn *Bertie Searles* • Robert Strauss *Seldom Seen Kid* ■ *Dir* George Marshall • *Scr* Hal Kanter, James Allardice, from a story by Damon Runyon

Money Mania ★ U

Comedy 1987 · US · Colour · 90mins

"Greed is good," said Gordon Gekko in *Wall Street*, attempting to give credence to eighties acquisitiveness. This truly abysmal picture tried to cash in on the get-rich-quick ethos by offering its audience a prize of one million dollars if anyone could find the money while the characters rushed around losing it. A sort of board game turned into a movie, it was titled *Million Dollar Mystery* on its brief American release. Expecting to fork out millions in prizes, executive producer Dino De Laurentiis saved money on stars (well, have you heard of Eddie Deezen or Wendy Sherman?) though somehow got veteran director Richard Fleischer to call the shots. ▭

Royce D Applegate *Tugger* • Pam Matteson *Dotty* • Rich Hall *Slaughter* • Eddie Deezen *Rollie* • Wendy Sherman *Lollie* • Rick Overton *Stuart Briggs* • Mona Lyden *Barbara Briggs* • Tom Bosley *Sidney Preston* ■ *Dir* Richard Fleischer • *Scr* Tim Metcalfe, Miguel Tejada-Flores, Rudy De Luca

Money Movers ★★★

Thriller 1978 · Ausl · Colour · 94mins

A fast, furious and tough Australian heist movie, which writer/director Bruce Beresford has paced with all the agility of a kangaroo stampede. Apart from Bryan Brown, best known now for those Citroën car commercials, the cast is largely unknown, but the theme of corruption among police and crooks is one that keeps the cynicism as well as the adrenalin on the boil.

Terence Donovan *Eric Jackson* • Ed Devereaux *Dick Martin* • Bryan Brown *Brian Jackson* • Tony Bonner *Leo Bassett* • Lucky Grills *Robert Conway* ■ *Dir* Bruce Beresford • *Scr* Bruce Beresford, from the novel by Devon Minchin

The Money Pit ★★★ 15

Comedy 1985 · US · Colour · 87mins

There are belly laughs aplenty in this unofficial remake of *Mr Blandings Builds His Dream House*, but director Richard Benjamin runs out of inspiration after an hour and the film ends up being more in need of renovation than Tom Hanks and Shelley Long's new home. However, Hanks does enough to remind us of what we've been missing since he made his mark in serious drama, while Long's perfect timing leaves you wondering why she has never quite made the transition from sitcom to cinema. Joe Mantegna and Philip Bosco have sly cameos as shiftless contractors, and Alexander Godunov is fine as Long's smarmy conductor ex-husband. Contains some swearing. ▭

Tom Hanks *Walter Fielding* • Shelley Long *Anna Crowley* • Alexander Godunov *Max Beissart* • Maureen Stapleton *Estelle* • Joe Mantegna *Art Shirk* • Philip Bosco *Curly* • Josh Mostel *Jack Schnittman* ■ *Dir* Richard Benjamin • *Scr* David Giler

Money Plays ★★

Thriller 1997 · US · Colour · 92mins

An agreeably quirky crime caper that offers up a juicy role for the now rarely-seen Roy Scheider. He plays a Vietnam vet barely making a living at a Las Vegas casino, who strikes up a friendship with prostitute Sonia Braga. When one of her punters, carrying half a million in cash, dies suddenly, she persuades Scheider that they should take the money and gamble on a new life for themselves. Writer/director Frank D Gilroy neatly blends black humour with more straightforward action and is rewarded with engaging performances from his two leads.

Roy Scheider *Johnny Tobin* • Sonia Braga *Irene* • Elisabeth Lund *Stacy* ■ *Dir/Scr* Frank D Gilroy

Money, Power, Murder ★★ 15

Mystery 1989 · US · Colour · 90mins

It's tough for performers like Kevin Dobson, better known as Kojak's sidekick, who for years are merely a familiar face on primetime TV without anybody actually knowing who they are. Then, when the series ends, they are presented with leads in instantly forgettable TV movies like this one. Dobson plays a cable news reporter on the trail of a missing newsreader. The story is hardly shrouded in mystery and the only selling point is Dobson's vainglorious attempt to make the character seem worthy of a series of his own.

Kevin Dobson *Peter Finley* • Blythe Danner *Jeannie* • Josef Sommer *Jack Finley* • John Cullum *Reverend Endicott* • Paul McCrane *Billy Lynn* • Julianne Moore *Peggy Lynn Brady* ■ *Dir* Lee Philips • *Scr* Mike Lupica, from the novel *Dead Air* by Mike Lupica

Money Talks ★★ 18

Action comedy 1997 · US · Colour · 91mins

A mediocre action comedy with complete opposites Chris Tucker and Charlie Sheen forced to rely on each other when the former, a small-time crook, crosses a gang of jewel thieves. Sheen is a TV reporter who sees the unfolding story as a way to save his ailing career. Endless explosions, tedious car chases and brainless shoot-outs punctuate a drearily crass plot whose appeal wholly depends on one's reaction to helium-voiced comedian Tucker. If you like him, you'll like this. If you don't – well, there's always Heather Locklear as Sheen's wife-to-be. Contains swearing, violence and sexual references. ▭

Chris Tucker *Franklin Hatchett* • Charlie Sheen *James Russell* • Heather Locklear *Grace Cipriani* • Paul Sorvino *Guy Cipriani* • Veronica Cartwright *Connie Cipriani* ■ *Dir* Brett Ratner • *Scr* Joel Cohen, Alec Sokolow

Money Train ★★ 18

Comedy thriller 1995 · US · Colour · 105mins

Die Hard meets *Speed*, but with the brakes on, as transport cop Wesley Snipes tries to stop his flaky foster brother Woody Harrelson robbing the New York subway transit system. Lightning doesn't strike twice for the *White Men Can't Jump* dynamic duo, and director Joseph Ruben's recycling

of exhausted gags is lacklustre in the extreme. The last third, set on an out-of-control express train, is packed with eye-popping crashes and sterling stunt work, but it all comes far too late to save a vehicle that is so reliant on the good-natured double act both striking the funny bone and quickening the pulse. On the plus side, Jennifer Lopez is dynamite as the Hispanic rookie cop completing the culturally balanced trio. Contains swearing, violence and sex scenes. ▭ **DVD**

Wesley Snipes *John* • Woody Harrelson *Charlie* • Robert Blake *Patterson* • Jennifer Lopez *Grace Santiago* • Robert Blake *Patterson* • Chris Cooper *Torch* ■ *Dir* Joseph Ruben • *Scr* Doug Richardson, David Loughery, from a story by Doug Richardson

The Money Trap ★★
Crime drama　　1966 · US · BW · 92mins

This dull thriller is based on a novel by Lionel White. who also wrote the source novel for Kubrick's *The Killing*. Glenn Ford plays a cop, married to pretty rich gal Elke Sommer and stretched financially as a result. When the opportunity arises, Ford crosses over to the wrong side of the law, with predictable results. What wouldn't pass muster as a 10-minute subplot on *Kojak* is here turned into a dusty showcase for a distinctly secondhand Ford. Adding to the aura of faded glamour is Rita Hayworth, playing a drug dealer's widow and a former flame of Ford's, and recalling the couple's great partnership in *Gilda*.

Glenn Ford *Joe Baron* • Elke Sommer *Lisa Baron* • Rita Hayworth *Rosalie Kenny* • Joseph Cotten *Dr Horace Van Tilden* • Ricardo Montalban *Pete Delanos* • Tom Reese *Matthews* • James Mitchum *Detective Wolski* ■ *Dir* Burt Kennedy • *Scr* Walter Bernstein, from the novel by Lionel White

Money, Women and Guns
★★ **U**
Western　　1958 · US · Colour · 80mins

A negligible western programme filler from Universal, given distinction by the casting of Kim Hunter, who'd won a best supporting actress Oscar for *A Streetcar Named Desire*, opposite former stuntman Jock Mahoney. The script concerning the investigation into the murder of an old prospector is clever but feebly executed, although the photography is impressive.

Jock Mahoney *Hogan* • Kim Hunter *Mary Kingman* • Tim Hovey *Davey Kingman* • Gene Evans *Sheriff Crowley* • Tom Drake *Jess Ryerson* • Lon Chaney Jr *Art Birdwell* ■ *Dir* Richard Bartlett • *Scr* Montgomery Pittman • *Cinematographer* Philip Lathrop

The Mongols ★★
Historical drama
1961 · Fr/It · Colour · 105mins

Jack Palance stars as Ogotai, son of Genghis Khan, who invades Europe in AD 1240 and gets as far as Cracow, Poland, where the local bigwig, Franco Silva, tries to negotiate peace. Also in the invasion party is the absurdly statuesque Anita Ekberg who, like her beloved Ogotai, leads from the front. Palance goes from one outlandish act of cruelty to the next, grinning madly and dressed in the height of Mongol fashion. Such sadism, though, doesn't

quite prepare us for the masochism of the climax. Made in Italy by no less than three directors, it has the usual hilarious dubbing. Italian dialogue dubbed into English.

Jack Palance *Ogotai* • Anita Ekberg *Huluna* • Antonella Lualdi *Amina* • Franco Silva *Stephen* • Gianni Garko *Henry* • Roldano Lupi *Genghis Khan* ■ *Dir* Andre De Toth, Leopoldo Savona • *Scr* Ugo Guerra, Luciano Martino, Ottavio Alessi, Alessandro Ferrau

The Monk ★★★
Gothic drama
1990 · UK/Sp · Colour · 106mins

A curious British/Spanish co-production, starring Paul McGann as the brother in brown whose quiet life begins to unravel spectacularly when a young woman with designs on him disguises herself and slips into his monastery. The source novel by MG Lewis caused a sensation on its publication at the end of the 18th century, but here writer/director Paco Lara eschews the gothic delights of the book in favour of a more ironic approach, shooting on stylised sets that seem to parody their Hammer counterparts from the sixties.

Paul McGann *Father Lorenzo* • Sophie Ward *Juan/Matilda* • Isla Blair *Mother Agueda* • Freda Dowie *Sister Ursula* • Aitana Sanchez-Gijon *Sister Ines* ■ *Dir* Paco Lara • *Scr* Paco Lara, from the novel by MG Lewis

Monk Dawson ★★ **18**
Religious drama 1997 · UK · Colour · 107mins

Mildly entertaining tale of a monk who rapidly falls into bad habits when he quits cloistered monastery life and re-enters the real world. John Michie makes an engaging hero, and there's strong support from *EastEnders* star Martin Kemp. The film's "real" world never convinces, however, and the tone is wildly inconsistent. It's as if debut director Tom Waller wasn't really sure what sort of movie he wanted to make. Contains some swearing and sex scenes. ▭

John Michie *Eddie Dawson* • Ben Taylor *Bobby Winterman* • Paula Hamilton *Jenny Stanten* • Martin Kemp *David Allenby* • Rupert Vansittart *Father Timothy* • Frances Tomelty *Mrs Carter* ■ *Dir* Tom Waller • *Scr* James Magrane, from a novel by Piers Paul Read

Monkey Business ★★★★ **U**
Comedy　　1931 · US · BW · 74mins

This is the one in which Groucho Marx dances the tango (with Thelma Todd) and the little-seen Zeppo gets tough with a gangster. One of the funniest early Marx Brothers comedies, it was the first to be written for the screen (by SJ Perelman among others) instead of being adapted from their stage routines. As stowaways on an ocean liner, the brothers have to keep on the move from cabin to cabin to avoid being clapped in irons. Harpo works in a Punch and Judy show, while Chico tickles the ivories – gentle competition for Groucho's acerbic one-liners. ▭

Groucho Marx *Groucho* • Harpo Marx *Harpo* • Chico Marx *Chicago* • Zeppo Marx *Zeppo* • Thelma Todd *Lucille* • Tom Kennedy *Gibson* • Ruth Hall *Mary Helton* • Rockliffe Fellowes *Joe Helton* ■ *Dir* Norman Z McLeod • *Scr* Arthur Sheekman, from a story by SJ Perelman, WB Johnstone, Roland Pertwee

Monkey Business ★★★★★ **U**
Comedy　　1952 · US · BW · 92mins

Not the Marx Brothers Paramount classic, but one of the funniest, smartest and most under-rated Hollywood comedies ever made. It's a movie that has never secured the reputation it deserves, considering its pedigree. It was made by, arguably, Hollywood's greatest ever studio director, Howard Hawks, who was also responsible for the scatty *Bringing Up Baby* and dynamic *His Girl Friday*. Hawks is reunited there with his star from those films, Cary Grant, in a sublime performance as a man reduced to juvenility for arcane plot reasons too complex to divulge. Ginger Rogers is a great foil, but it's Marilyn Monroe who steals the movie. ▭

Cary Grant *Professor Barnaby Fulton* • Ginger Rogers *Edwina Fulton* • Charles Coburn *Mr Oliver Oxley* • Marilyn Monroe *Lois Laurel* • Hugh Marlowe *Harvey Entwhistle* • Henri Letondal *Dr Siegfried Kitzel* ■ *Dir* Howard Hawks • *Scr* Ben Hecht, Charles Lederer, IAL Diamond, from a story by Harry Segall

Monkey Grip ★★ **18**
Drama　　1983 · Ausl · Colour · 101mins

Based on a prize-winning novel and highly praised by local critics, *Monkey Grip* takes a look at life on the margins in Melbourne. Noni Hazlehurst stars as a divorcee with a ten-year-old daughter who leaves her regular boyfriend for a struggling actor, initially unaware that's he's a junkie. The drug and rock scene has a certain authenticity, but the project seems dated and contrived.

Noni Hazlehurst *Nora* • Colin Friels *Javo* • Alice Garner *Gracie* • Harold Hopkins *Willie* • Candy Raymond *Lillian* • Michael Caton *Clive* ■ *Dir* Ken Cameron • *Scr* Ken Cameron, Helen Garner, from the novel by Helen Garner

Monkey Shines ★★★★ **18**
Horror　　1988 · US · Colour · 108mins

Dr Jekyll and Mr Hyde goes ape in a provocative shocker from *Night of the Living Dead* director George A Romero that contains some of his finest and most disturbing visions. Jason Beghe is the wheelchair-bound student who gradually realises the genetically brain-altered monkey trained to assist him is acting out his darkest desires and revenge impulses. Intense yet surprisingly tender, Romero's confident chiller is an intelligent nail-biter that takes a highly unusual look at the warped laws of the jungle one man must combat to survive. ▭

Jason Beghe *Allan Mann* • John Pankow *Geoffrey Fisher* • Kate McNeil *Melanie Parker* • Joyce Van Patten *Dorothy Mann* • Christine Forrest *Maryanne Hodges* • Stephen Root *Dean Burbage* • Stanley Tucci *Dr John Wiseman* • Janine Turner *Linda Aikman* ■ *Dir* George A Romero • *Scr* George A Romero, from the novel by Michael Stewart

Monkey Trouble ★★★ **U**
Action comedy　　1994 · US · Colour · 92mins

A cute family film from director Franco Amurri, this stars accomplished child actress Thora Birch (*Hocus Pocus*, *Alaska*) as the young girl who finds and adopts a capuchin monkey, unaware the creature is actually a trained jewel thief belonging to petty criminal Harvey Keitel. Quite what the hard-as-nails

star of *Reservoir Dogs* and *The Bad Lieutenant* is doing in this comedy adventure is anyone's guess, but his performance will delight adults as much as the monkey business will enchant young children. ▭

Harvey Keitel *Azro* • Mimi Rogers *Amy* • Thora Birch *Eva* • Christopher McDonald *Tom* • Adrian Johnson *Jack* ■ *Dir* Franco Amurri • *Scr* Franco Amurri, Stu Krieger

Monkeys, Go Home! ★★ **U**
Comedy　　1967 · US · Colour · 86mins

Maurice Chevalier bade movies farewell with this Disney offering that will have animal activists reaching for their placards. The sight of four chimps being trained to harvest olives might have delighted youngsters in the mid-sixties, but it's doubtful whether it will have quite the same quaint impact today. The studio spared no expense to re-create Provence in its backyard, even planting its own olive grove. But the story of Dean Jones's contretemps with his disgruntled French neighbours is less than gripping. The Sherman brothers composed *Joie de Vivre* for Chevalier's swan song, but that is exactly what the film is lacking. ▭

Maurice Chevalier *Father Sylvain* • Dean Jones *Hank Dussard* • Yvette Mimieux *Maria Riserau* • Bernard Woringer *Marcel Cartucci* • Clément Harari *Emile Paraulis* ■ *Dir* Andrew V McLaglen • *Scr* Maurice Tombragel, from the short story *The Monkeys* by GK Wilkinson

A Monkey's Tale ★ **PG**
Animated adventure
2000 · Fr/UK/Ger/Hun · Colour · 78mins

This European attempt to board the Disney bandwagon boasts a hackneyed plot, a clutch of dreadful songs and some ghastly animation that actually makes *Pokémon* look good. A tree-dwelling ape falls to earth and takes up residence with his clothes-wearing, "civilised" brethren, though it's not long before he becomes embroiled in a plot to usurp the monkey throne. John Hurt, Michael York and Rik Mayall lend their distinctive tones to the cast of simian characters, but don't be duped: your little ones won't thank you for putting them through this.

Matt Hill *Kom* • John Hurt *Chancellor Sebastian* • Michael York *The King* • Sally Ann Marsh *Gina* • Rik Mayall *Gerard* • Michael Gambon *Master Martin* • Shirley Anne Field *Governess* • French Tickner *Korkonak* ■ *Dir* Jean-François Laguionie • *Scr* Norman Hudis, Jean-François Laguionie

The Monkey's Uncle ★★ **U**
Comedy　　1965 · US · Colour · 86mins

A chimpanzee called Stanley is the real star of this droopy Disney sequel to *The Adventures of Merlin Jones*, in which young inventor Tommy Kirk helps two kids pass a test and constructs a bike-powered flying machine. The chimp gets the best of it, spending most of the movie in the arms Annette Funicello. The latter dropped her surname on the billing, but it didn't help her acting much. ▭

Tommy Kirk *Merlin Jones* • Annette [Annette Funicello] *Jennifer* • Leon Ames *Judge Holmsby* • Frank Faylen *Mr Dearborne* • Arthur O'Connell *Darius Green III* • Leon Tyler *Leon* •

U = SUITABLE FOR ALL　**Uc** = SUITABLE FOR ALL, ESPECIALLY FOR YOUNG CHILDREN (VIDEO ONLY)　**PG** = PARENTAL GUIDANCE

Norman Grabowski *Norman* ■ *Dir* Robert Stevenson • *Scr* Tom August [Alfred Lewis Levitt], Helen August [Helen Levitt]

Monolith ★★ 18
Science-fiction adventure
1993 · US · Colour · 90mins

Police detectives Bill Paxton and Lindsay Frost stumble onto a secret government plot to exploit an ancient and evil alien creature, while John Hurt sounds like he's fighting a case of laryngitis in his role as the conspiracy's wispy-voiced mastermind. Snappy patter and competent acting makes up for some rough editing, but the film-makers have a tough time deciding whether they're making a police procedural or a sci-fi thriller. 🖭

Bill Paxton *Tucker* • Lindsay Frost *Terri Flynn* • John Hurt *Villano* • Louis Gossett Jr *Capt MacCandless* • Paul Ganus *Connor* ■ *Dir* John Eyres • *Scr* Steven Lister

The Monolith Monsters ★★★
Science-fiction 1957 · US · Colour · 77mins

Meteor fragments land on earth, absorb moisture and grow to epic proportions. After a rainstorm, they start covering the world like living skyscrapers. An effective minor entry from sci-fi's golden era, based on a story by fifties icon Jack Arnold (*The Incredible Shrinking Man*, *Creature from the Black Lagoon*) and set in his favourite small-town desert locale.

Grant Williams *Dave Miller* • Lola Albright *Cathy Barrett* • Les Tremayne *Martin Cochrane* • Trevor Bardette *Arthur Flanders* • Phil Harvey *Ben Gilbert* • William Flaherty *Police Chief Dan Corey* ■ *Dir* John Sherwood • *Scr* Norman Jolley, Robert M Fresco, from a story by Jack Arnold, Robert M Fresco

Monsieur Beaucaire ★★★
Comedy 1946 · US · BW · 93mins

Made at the peak of Bob Hope's popularity, this remake of a Rudolph Valentino silent (based on a novel by Booth Tarkington) is played strictly for laughs as Bob, a barber at the court of Louis XV, is forced to masquerade as a great lover and swordsman. Joan Caulfield makes a colourless leading lady (she was Bing Crosby's girlfriend at the time, so the studio were favouring her), but those scene-stealing stalwarts Joseph Schildkraut and Constance Collier add to the fun. Comedy specialist George Marshall directed, but the climactic swordfight was filmed by Frank Tashlin.

Bob Hope *Mons Beaucaire* • Joan Caulfield *Mimi* • Patric Knowles *Duc de Chandre* • Marjorie Reynolds *Princess Maria of Spain* • Cecil Kellaway *Count D'Armand* • Joseph Schildkraut *Don Francisco* • Reginald Owen *King Louis XV of France* • Constance Collier *The Queen* ■ *Dir* George Marshall • *Scr* Melvin Frank, Norman Panama, from the novel by Booth Tarkington

Monsieur Hire ★★★★★ 15
Thriller 1989 · Fr · Colour · 75mins

Previously filmed by Julien Duvivier as *Panique*, Georges Simenon's chilling tale of murder and obsession has been turned into a tender and compelling love story by Patrice Leconte. The director's insight,

restraint and humanity is reinforced by Michael Nyman's achingly beautiful score and echoed in the superb performances. Never has the pain of loneliness been more truthfully depicted on screen than by Michel Blanc as the timid little man who willingly sacrifices all to assist his stunning neighbour, Sandrine Bonnaire. In French with English subtitles. 🖭

Michel Blanc *Monsieur Hire* • Sandrine Bonnaire *Alice* • Luc Thuillier *Emile* • André Wilms *Inspector* ■ *Dir* Patrice Leconte • *Scr* Patrice Leconte, Patrick Dewolf, from the novel *Les Fiançailles de M Hire* by Georges Simenon

Monsieur Hulot's Holiday ★★★★★ U
Comedy 1953 · Fr · BW · 88mins

Inspired by the sophisticated silent clowning of Max Linder and Buster Keaton, Jacques Tati's masterpiece is a sublime blend of satire, slapstick and character comedy that was itself a key influence on the *nouvelle vague*. With the genial Hulot invariably at its centre, much of the hilarious seaside action was filmed in long shot – not only to allow the gags to develop in their own time and space, but also to enable audiences to discover for themselves Tati's intuitive use of the film frame, his acute understanding of human behaviour, and his gently mocking appreciation of the absurdities of the modern world.

Jacques Tati *Monsieur Hulot* • Nathalie Pascaud *Martine* • Louis Perraud *Fred* • Michelle Rolla *Aunt* ■ *Dir* Jacques Tati • *Scr* Jacques Tati, Jacques LaGrange, Henri Marquet

Monsieur Verdoux ★★★★★ PG
Black comedy 1947 · US · BW · 123mins

The greatest of the latter-day sound movies by Charles Chaplin, this is a chilling black comedy in which a bank clerk (watch him riffling through those bank-notes!) turns to killing wealthy women. Sentiment sneaks in with the appearance of the waifish Marilyn Nash, but it's soon dispelled by the vulgarity of Martha Raye as an intended victim. There's a fastidious cruelty about it all, reflecting Chaplin's deep-seated contempt for the middle-class, and the final speech allies the bank clerk's Bluebeard tendencies with the activities of the major political powers. Adapted from an idea by Orson Welles, this is an unmissable, astringent treat. 🖭

Charles Chaplin *Henri Verdoux/Varney/ Bonheur/Floray/Narrator* • Mady Correll *Mona Verdoux* • Allison Roddan *Peter Verdoux* • Robert Lewis (1) *Maurice Bottello* • Martha Raye *Annabella* ■ *Dir* Charles Chaplin • *Scr* Charles Chaplin, from an idea by Orson Welles • *Cinematographer* Rollie Rotheroh

Monsignor ★★★ 15
Drama 1982 · US · Colour · 116mins

Having turned Joan Crawford's life into a dizzying, hilarious melodrama in *Mommie Dearest*, producer Frank Yablans and director Frank Perry here do the same for the Catholic Church. Christopher Reeve stars as an ambitious young priest who greases his way up the Vatican's slippery pole

and faces various temptations along the way, including lusty nuns and Mafia gangsters. The film rests on a knife edge between schlock and solemnity – when *The Exorcist*'s Jason Miller pops up, you start wondering when the green vomit will start flying – but it's not a patch on Otto Preminger's *The Cardinal* (1963). 🖭

Christopher Reeve *Flaherty* • Geneviève Bujold *Clara* • Fernando Rey *Santoni* • Jason Miller *Appolini* • Joe Cortese *Varese* • Adolfo Celi *Vinci* • Leonardo Cimino *Pope* ■ *Dir* Frank Perry • *Scr* Abraham Polonsky, Wendell Mayes, from the novel by Jack Alain Leger

The Monster ★★★
Silent horror comedy
1925 · US · BW · 71mins

One of Lon Chaney's more tongue-in-cheek horror films, this is a delight, if less memorable than *The Unholy Three* and *The Phantom of the Opera*, released in the same year. Here he's without elaborate make-up as the dapper Dr Ziska, a mad surgeon who arranges car accidents on a lonely road, thereby subjecting those who survive to his experiments to discover the secret of life. Director Roland West handles the story with considerable humour.

Lon Chaney *Dr Ziska* • Johnny Arthur *Under clerk* • Gertrude Olmsted *Betty Watson* • Hallam Cooley *Watson's head clerk* • Charles A Sellon [Charles Sellon] *Constable* ■ *Dir* Roland West • *Scr* Willard Mack, Albert Kenyon, from a play by Crane Wilbur • *Cinematographer* Hal Mohr

Monster ★★★ 18
Horror comedy 1980 · US · Colour · 80mins

Pollution-spawned creatures go on a carnal rampage in a lively update of the concepts Roger Corman adeptly used for his own cult films of the fifties. Director Barbara Peeters complained producer Corman spliced in the sensationalised rape scenes after she had finished with the project, but they only add to the lurid, lip-smacking sleaze of the whole enjoyably tacky enterprise. Doug McClure and Ann Turkel finish off the sex-mad bimbo hunters after they've torn a carnival apart in a zestful guilty pleasure that has not a single dull moment. Also known as *Humanoids from the Deep*. 🖭

Doug McClure *Jim Hill* • Ann Turkel *Dr Susan Drake* • Vic Morrow *Hank Slattery* • Cindy Weintraub *Carol Hill* • Anthony Penya *Johnny Eagle* • Denise Galik *Linda Beale* ■ *Dir* Barbara Peeters • *Scr* Frederick James, from a story by Frank Arnold, Martin B Cohen

The Monster Club ★★★ 15
Horror 1980 · UK · Colour · 93mins

John Carradine (as famed horror writer R Chetwynd-Hayes) travels to a Transylvanian disco where bloodsucker Vincent Price (playing a vampire for the first and only time) relates three macabre stories of varying quality in a shaky anthology based on Chetwynd-Hayes's tales of terror and complicated ghoul genealogy. Included in the pseudo-hip monster mash is a Shadmock whose silent whistle is fatal to mortals, a band of Mafia-type undead chasers with stakes in their violin cases, and the Humgoos who wreak havoc on a film director looking for a creepy location. Worth watching

for the all-star cast alone, and for appearances by the Pretty Things and UB40. Contains brief nudity. 🖭

Vincent Price *Erasmus* • John Carradine *R Chetwynd-Hayes* • Anthony Steel *Lintom Busotsky* • Barbara Kellerman *Angela* • Simon Ward *George* • James Laurenson *Raven* • Geoffrey Bayldon *Psychiatrist* • Donald Pleasence *Pickering* • Richard Johnson *Father* • Britt Ekland *Mother* ■ *Dir* Roy Ward Baker • *Scr* Edward Abraham, Valerie Abraham, from the short story collection by R Chetwynd-Hayes

Monster from Green Hell ★★ PG
Science-fiction 1958 · US · BW · 67mins

Future *Dallas* star Jim Davis leads an expedition of scientists through the African jungle, courtesy of stock footage from *Stanley and Livingstone* (1939) and some cheap backlot trimmings. He's looking for a crashed space probe and its cargo of radioactively enlarged wasps, but he needn't have bothered: after going on a weakly rendered trail of destruction, the inept wasps eventually stumble into an erupting volcano. Although just as ridiculous as producer Al Zimbalist's infamous clinker *Robot Monster*, this thick-witted trek through fifties clichés is by far the more enjoyable bet.

Jim Davis *Quent Brady* • Robert E Griffin [Robert Griffin] *Dan Morgan* • Barbara Turner *Lorna Lorentz* • Eduardo Ciannelli *Mahri* • Vladimir Sokoloff *Dr Lorentz* • Joel Fluellen *Arobi* ■ *Dir* Kenneth Crane • *Scr* Louis Vittes, Endre Boehm

Monster in a Box ★★★
Biographical documentary
1991 · US · Colour · 90mins

Following the success of *Swimming to Cambodia*, writer/actor Spalding Gray embarked upon a second one-man show. The film tells of the interruptions Gray experienced while writing his autobiographical novel, *Impossible Vacation*, including an account of a trip to the Soviet Union along with several Hollywood stars for a Soviet film festival. Shot in London by Nick Broomfield, this country's master documentarist, the film suffers from audience laughter intruding into the soundtrack. Contains swearing.

Dir Nick Broomfield • *Scr* Spalding Gray

Monster in the Closet ★★ 15
Horror comedy 1983 · US · Colour · 85mins

Released by Troma (though produced independently), this amusing update of fifties horror movies works because its earnest cast deliver their absurd dialogue in a relatively straight fashion. Across the land, people are being killed by a monster (Kevin Peter Hall) who pops out of their closets. Rookie reporter Donald Grant pounds the streets for an answer and helps save the day when the monster comes out into the open. Lots of cameo appearances – Paul Dooley, Stella Stevens, John Carradine – add to the nostalgic feel. 🖭

Donald Grant *Richard Clark* • Denise DuBarry *Diane Bennett* • Claude Akins *Sheriff Ketchum* • Howard Duff *Father Finnegan* • Henry Gibson *Dr Pennyworth* • Donald Moffat *General Turnbull* • Paul Dooley *Roy Crane* • Stella Stevens *Margo Crane* • John Carradine *Old*

Joe • Kevin Peter Hall *Monster* ■ *Dir* Bob Dahlin • *Scr* Bob Dahlin, from a story by Peter Bergquist, Bob Dahlin

The Monster Maker ★

Horror   1944 · US · BW · 62mins

This repellent horror movie – more closely allied to surgical fiction than imaginative fantasy – casts J Carrol Naish (later to play Charlie Chan on TV) as a mad scientist who infects his enemies with distorting bacteria. Directed by Sam Newfield and co-starring Ralph Morgan and Wanda McKay, it has little to recommend it apart from its freak-show novelty and an audience-pulling title.

J Carrol Naish *Dr Igor Markoff* • Ralph Morgan *Lawrence* • Tala Birell *Maxine* • Wanda McKay *Patricia Lawrence* • Terry Frost *Blake* • Glenn Strange *Giant* ■ *Dir* Sam Newfield • *Scr* Pierre Gendron, Martin Mooney, from a story by Lawrence Williams

The Monster of Highgate Ponds ★★ Ⓤ

Fantasy adventure   1961 · UK · BW · 58mins

Although Michael Balcon usually gets all the credit for the creative stature of Ealing Studios, the director Alberto Cavalcanti was the major force, pouring oil on troubled waters and encouraging brilliance from the film-makers. This is a lacklustre example of his work in decline, a children's film set in north London and featuring Roy Vincente and Ronald Howard. Although it includes some neat touches, which show the talent that Cavalcanti was, it's too obviously aimed at its target audience of youngsters.

Roy Vincente *The monster* • Ronald Howard *Uncle Dick* • Rachel Clay *Sophie* • Michael Wade *David* • Terry Raven *Chris* • Frederick Piper *Sam* • Michael Balfour *Bert* ■ *Dir* Alberto Cavalcanti • *Scr* Mary Cathcart Borer, from a story by Joy Batchelor

Monster on the Campus ★★

Science-fiction   1958 · US · BW · 76mins

This typically wacky fifties monster movie might have scared the pants off teen audiences back in the days of drive-ins, but will probably send today's youngsters straight to sleep. Still, there's much to enjoy in this corny tale of a fossilised fish whose blood transforms everything it touches into snarling monsters. A dog becomes a sabre-toothed beast, while poor old professor Arthur Franz turns into a Neanderthal apeman with a bad attitude. The effects are quaint, but the stilted script makes this perhaps the least interesting of Jack Arnold's genre efforts. Leading lady Joanna Moore later married Ryan O'Neal.

Arthur Franz *Donald Blake* • Joanna Moore *Madeline Howard* • Judson Pratt *Mike Stevens* • Nancy Walters *Sylvia Lockwood* • Troy Donahue *Jimmy Flanders* • Phil Harvey *Sergeant Powell* • Helen Westcott *Molly Riordan* ■ *Dir* Jack Arnold • *Scr* David Duncan

The Monster Squad ★★★★ 15

Comedy horror   1987 · US · Colour · 78mins

A horror movie for older teenagers that manages to scare just enough and amuse quite a lot without getting its audience into an unnecessary lather. A

well-cast Duncan Regehr is Count Dracula, journeying to suburban America to search for a mysterious amulet with the help of Frankenstein's monster and the Wolf Man. But he reckons without a group of excitable children who are soon rustling up a few stakes in woodwork class. 🖵

André Gower *Sean Crenshaw* • Robby Kiger *Patrick* • Stephen Macht *Del Crenshaw* • Duncan Regehr *Count Dracula* • Tom Noonan *Frankenstein's monster* • Brent Chalem *Horace* • Ryan Lambert *Rudy* ■ *Dir* Fred Dekker • *Scr* Shane Black, Fred Dekker

The Monster That Challenged the World ★★★

Science-fiction horror
1957 · US · BW · 84mins

A fun, low-budget sci-fi horror movie, in which the eggs of an extinct sea monster are released during an earthquake and hatch as giant snail-like creatures that kill humans for their blood and water. Tim Holt, former cowboy star and occasional actor of note (*The Magnificent Ambersons*, *The Treasure of the Sierra Madre*), came out of retirement to play the naval officer teaming up with Hans Conried's boffin to prevent the monsters breeding and spreading. An effective piece of film-making results from the good script by Pat Fielder (based on a story by David Duncan), suspenseful direction by Arnold Laven and convincing monsters by Augie Lohman.

Tim Holt *Lieutenant Commander John Twillinger* • Audrey Dalton *Gail MacKenzie* • Hans Conried *Dr Jess Rogers* • Harlan Warde *Lieutenant Bob Clemens* • Casey Adams [Max Showalter] *Tad Johns* ■ *Dir* Arnold Laven • *Scr* Pat Fielder, from a story by David Duncan

Montana ★★ PG

Western   1950 · US · Colour · 73mins

A routine western in glorious Technicolor, this stars an amiable Errol Flynn as the sheepherder daring to seek grazing land in cattle country. Directed by Ray Enright, the film lacks any real bite, suffering in particular from the absence of an authoritative villain. Douglas Kennedy does his best, but it is the redheaded cattle queen played by Alexis Smith who wants to shoot it out with him at the end. To fill in time, Flynn plays guitar and sings a mediocre number called *I Reckon I'm Falling in Love*. 🖵

Errol Flynn *Morgan Lane* • Alexis Smith *Maria Singleton* • SZ "Cuddles" Sakall [SZ Sakall] *Poppa Schultz* • Douglas Kennedy *Rodney Ackroyd* • James Brown (2) *Tex Coyne* • Ian MacDonald *Slim Reeves* • Paul E Burns *Tecumseh Burke* ■ *Dir* Ray Enright • *Scr* James R Webb, Borden Chase, Charles O'Neal, from a story by Ernest Haycox

Montana ★★★ PG

Western   1990 · US · Colour · 86mins

Set in one of America's most beautiful states, this is an interesting family drama about a husband and wife (Richard Crenna and Gena Rowlands) who have to decide whether to sell their ailing ranch to a coal developer or try to keep it going. Although slow-moving, this is an often affecting, character-driven film, given extra weight by the performances of Crenna, Rowlands and the supporting cast,

which includes *Caroline in the City's* Lea Thompson. Contains swearing, sex scenes and brief nudity.

Gena Rowlands *Bess* • Richard Crenna *Hoyce* • Lea Thompson *Peg* • Justin Deas *Clyde* • Elizabeth Berridge *Lavetta* ■ *Dir* William A Graham • *Scr* Larry McMurtry

Montana ★★

Crime drama   1997 · US · Colour · 96mins

Though directed by a woman (Jennifer Leitzes) and centering around a female assassin (Kyra Sedgwick) framed and pursued by gun-wielding mobsters, this crime drama doesn't have any ambitions to offer a feminist perspective. The focus is definitely more on dialogue and characters than violence, though, which makes the bloody shoot-outs seem slightly out of place. The best and most original parts of the movie are its bizarre flashes of humour, while the cast is certainly worth a look (Robbie Coltrane, John Ritter, Philip Seymour Hoffman).

Kyra Sedgwick *Claire* • Stanley Tucci *Nick* • Robin Tunney *Kitty* • John Ritter *Dr Wexler* • Robbie Coltrane *The Boss* • Philip Seymour Hoffman *Duncan* ■ *Dir* Jennifer Leitzes • *Scr* John Hoeber, Erich Hoeber

Montana Trap ★★

Western   1976 · W Ger · Colour · 96mins

Originally released in a cut version called *Potato Fritz*, this German-made western stars Hardy Krüger as the potato farmer who settles in Indian territory, shows his good intentions by hanging his gun on a flag-pole and dreams of eating bratwurst and mash. Other settlers are played by Stephen Boyd – slumming it after *Ben-Hur* and other big-budget epics – and director Peter Schamoni who plays the Reverend. Filmed in Yugoslavia, with bought-in footage of Montana buffalos. A German language film.

Hardy Krüger *Potato Fritz* • Stephen Boyd *Bill Addison* • Anton Diffring *Lieutenant Slade* • Paul Breitner *Sergeant Black* • Christiane Gött *Jane Antrim* • Arthur Brauss *James Wesley* • Peter Schamoni *Reverend Cavenham* ■ *Dir* Peter Schamoni • *Scr* Paul Hengge

Monte Carlo ★★★ PG

Musical comedy   1930 · US · BW · 184mins

On the French Riviera, a count (Jack Buchanan) poses as a hairdresser and woos a countess (Jeanette MacDonald) in this feather-light musical romance from Ernst Lubitsch. What follows is enjoyable and characteristically stylish, though not as good as those to come (*One Hour With You*, *The Merry Widow*) which paired MacDonald with Maurice Chevalier. English stage star Buchanan is witty and appealing but lacks Chevalier's Gallic charm. Memorable for the sequence in which MacDonald sings *Beyond the Blue Horizon*. 🖵

Jack Buchanan *Count Rudolph Falliere* • Jeanette MacDonald *Countess Vera von Conti* • ZaSu Pitts *Maria, Vera's maid* • Claude Allister [Claud Allister] *Prince Otto von Seibenheim* • Lionel Belmore *Duke Gustave von Seibenheim, his father* • Tyler Brooke *Armand, Rudolph's friend* ■ *Dir* Ernst Lubitsch • *Scr* Ernest Vajda, Vincent Lawrence, from the play *The Blue Coast* by Hans Muller and the novel *Monsieur Beaucaire* by Booth Tarkington

Monte Carlo or Bust ★★ PG

Comedy   1969 · Fr/UK/ It · Colour · 119mins

A well-intentioned sequel to the massively popular *Those Magnificent Men in Their Flying Machines* from the same director, Ken Annakin, and with many of the same cast, only this time it's about a 1,500-mile car race. It's a long haul, but star Tony Curtis makes the most of the journey and there's a rare opportunity to see Peter Cook and Dudley Moore in the same movie, plus accomplished turns from Terry-Thomas and Eric Sykes. What Jack Hawkins is doing in this farrago is hard to fathom, however. 🖵

Tony Curtis *Chester Schofield* • Peter Cook *Major Dawlish* • Terry-Thomas *Sir Cuthbert* • Dudley Moore *Lt Barrington* • Eric Sykes *Perkins* • Hattie Jacques *Lady journalist* • Susan Hampshire *Betty* • Jack Hawkins *Count Levinovitch* • Bourvil *Monsieur Dupont* ■ *Dir* Ken Annakin, Sam Itzkovich • *Scr* Ken Annakin, Jack Davis

The Monte Carlo Story ★★ Ⓤ

Comedy drama
1957 · It/US · Colour · 101mins

Italian count Vittorio De Sica, bankrupted by gambling, looks for a rich woman to finance his "system" at the tables. He falls in love with Marlene Dietrich, but they part when he discovers she is also penniless. Writer/director Samuel Taylor trespasses into Lubitsch territory with this well-worn tale, but he lacks the latter's gift for transforming this kind of story and setting into witty and romantic magic. The result is a desperately overplotted affair, more arch than amusing, that squanders the charisma of his stars.

Marlene Dietrich *Marquise Maria de Crevecoeur* • Vittorio De Sica *Count Dino della Fiaba* • Arthur O'Connell *Mr Hinkley* • Jane Rose *Mrs Freeman* • Clelia Matania *Sophia* • Alberto Rabagliati *Albert* • Mischa Auer *Hector* ■ *Dir* Sam Taylor • *Scr* Samuel Taylor, from a story by Marcello Girosi, Dino Risi

Monte Walsh ★★★ PG

Western   1970 · US · Colour · 94mins

An evocative, painterly and melancholy western, the directing debut of William A Fraker, the cameraman on *Bullitt* and *Paint Your Wagon*. It was the star of the latter, Lee Marvin, who enabled Fraker to make this movie about two cowboy friends, Marvin and Jack Palance, who see their way of life ending yet find their attempts to forge domesticated lives also doomed. This is a dying west of unemployment, exploitation, market forces and illness (the tuberculosis that afflicts Marvin's mistress, Jeanne Moreau), a west faded to a mere carnival sideshow. A pity that Fraker's directing career all but fizzled out after this striking, beautifully cast first feature. Contains some violence. 🖵

Lee Marvin *Monte Walsh* • Jack Palance *Chet Rollins* • Jeanne Moreau *Martine Bernard* • Mitch Ryan [Mitchell Ryan] *Shorty Austin* • Jim Davis *Cal Brennan* • John Hudkins *Sonny Jacobs* • Raymond Guth *Sunfish Perkins* • John McKee *Petey Williams* ■ *Dir* William A Fraker • *Scr* David Z Goodman, Lukas Heller, from the novel by Jack Warner Schaefer

Ⓤ = SUITABLE FOR ALL   Ⓤc = SUITABLE FOR ALL, ESPECIALLY FOR YOUNG CHILDREN (VIDEO ONLY)   PG = PARENTAL GUIDANCE

Montenegro ★★ 18

Surreal comedy
1981 · Swe/UK · Colour · 92mins

It's not often that a scene involving a toy tank and a stripper provides the most arresting moment in a film, but that's the case with this comedy, also known as *Pigs and Pearls*. Serbian director Dusan Makavejev coaxes a vibrant performance out of Susan Anspach as the bored housewife who gets to sample the wild side of life after missing a flight. But chauvinistic husband Erland Josephson is less impressive, and the symbolism is much too heavy-handed. Contains swearing, sex scenes and nudity. 📼

Susan Anspach *Marilyn Jordan* • Erland Josephson *Martin Jordan* • Jamie Marsh *Jimmy* • Per Oscarsson *Dr Pazardjian* • Bora Todorovic *Alex* • Marianne Jacobi *Cookie* ■ *Dir/Scr* Dusan Makavejev

Monterey Pop ★★★

Music documentary
1968 · US · Colour · 79mins

This breakthrough concert movie, which paved the way for *Woodstock* with its groundbreaking, *cinéma vérité* style, was directed by DA Pennebaker, who made the Bob Dylan documentary *Don't Look Back* one year earlier. Over 45 hours of 16mm film was shot at the 1967 Monterey International Pop Festival and edited into the first major rock festival documentary, capturing some of the greatest music legends of the hippy era. In between shots of sexy chicks, arrays of sleeping bags and queues for the toilets, Janis Joplin wails her way through *Ball and Chain*, The Who trash sound equipment to *My Generation*, Otis Redding warbles *I've Been Loving You Too Long* and Jimi Hendrix sets his guitar aflame to *Wild Thing* – the still talked-about highlight.

Dir/Scr DA Pennebaker

A Month by the Lake ★★★ PG

Period drama 1994 · UK/US · Colour · 87mins

John Irvin's period drama is a *ménage à quatre* set on the shores of Italy's Lake Como on the eve of the Second World War. Middle-aged Miss Bentley (Vanessa Redgrave) falls for an English major (Edward Fox), but loses him to an American nanny (Uma Thurman). Then along comes an Italian youth (Alessandro Gassman) who has a taste for older women. Gently, Miss Bentley – you never know what will happen! Nothing of any emotional importance, though it's luscious to look at. 📼

Vanessa Redgrave *Miss Bentley* • Edward Fox *Major Wilshaw* • Uma Thurman *Miss Beaumont* • Alida Valli *Signora Fascioli* • Alessandro Gassman *Vittorio Balsari* • Carlo Cartier *Mr Bonizzoni* • Paolo Lombardi *Enrico* • Riccardo Rossi *Guido* • Sonia Martinelli *Maria* ■ *Dir* John Irvin • *Scr* Trevor Bentham, from the novella by HE Bates

A Month in the Country ★★★★ PG

Drama 1987 · UK · Colour · 87mins

This moving and sensitive meditation on the aftereffects of the First World War shows shell-shocked survivors Colin Firth and Kenneth Branagh learning to live with each other's idiosyncracies and quirks of sexual nature while preserving and restoring relics from a bygone age. Working from Simon Gray's adaptation of JL Carr's book, director Pat O'Connor (*Circle of Friends*) fashions a small and poignant gem, with a finale that brings one close to tears. 📼

Colin Firth *Tom Birkin* • Kenneth Branagh *Charles Moon* • Natasha Richardson *Alice Keach* • Patrick Malahide *Reverend Keach* • Jim Carter *Ellerbeck* • Richard Vernon *Colonel Hebron* ■ *Dir* Pat O'Connor • *Scr* Simon Gray, from the novel by JL Carr

Montparnasses 19 ★★★

Biographical drama
1958 · Fr/It · BW · 110mins

What an ill-fated film! Having developed the project, Max Ophüls died before shooting, while both his replacement, Jacques Becker, and star, Gérard Philipe, would be dead within three years. Philipe was only 36 when he died, one year older than Amedeo Modigliani, the reckless artist he portrays in this colourfully tragic biography. The film revels in both his various addictions and the cutthroat nature of bohemian Paris in the early 1900s, but Becker leaves too little room for drama by refusing to stray from the facts. The script (co-written by Ophüls) also covers the Italian's relationships with dissipated novelist Lilli Palmer and Anouk Aimée, the pregnant mistress who committed suicide within days of his death. In French with English subtitles.

Gérard Philipe *Amedeo Modigliani* • Lilli Palmer *Béatrice Hastings* • Anouk Aimée *Jeanne Hébuterne* • Lea Padovani *Rosalie* • Gérard Séty *Zborowski* • Lino Ventura *Morel* ■ *Dir* Jacques Becker • *Scr* Jacques Becker, Max Opüls, Henri Jeanson, from the novel *Les Montparnos* by Georges-Michel Michel

Monty Python and the Holy Grail ★★★★ 15

Comedy 1975 · UK · Colour · 85mins

Complete with some inspired digressions and shorn of some of the weaker sketches, the soundtrack album of the Pythons' first story-based feature is even funnier than the film itself. Yet this remains a wonderfully inventive comedy, brilliantly debunking the Dark Ages and the legends of chivalry through King Arthur's encounters with an anarcho-syndicalist commune, the Black Knight, God (courtesy of Terry Gilliam) and the "knights who say ni". The *Camelot* and *Sir Robin* songs also get beneath the visor, but the highlights are the trial of Connie Booth's witch and the Holy Hand Grenade of Antioch sequence. Contains swearing, some violence and nudity. 📼

Graham Chapman *King Arthur* • John Cleese *Black Knight/Sir Lancelot* • Terry Gilliam *Patsy/Green Knight* • Eric Idle *Sir Robin/ Brother Maynard* • Michael Palin *Dennis/ Sir Galahad* • Connie Booth *Witch* ■ *Dir* Terry Gilliam, Terry Jones • *Scr* Graham Chapman, John Cleese, Terry Gilliam, Eric Idle, Terry Jones, Michael Palin • *Music/Lyrics* Neil Innes

Monty Python Live at the Hollywood Bowl ★★★ 15

Comedy 1982 · UK · Colour · 77mins

Suffering from writer's block during the scripting on *Monty Python's The Meaning of Life*, the Pythons decided to play the famous open-air Hollywood Bowl to revive their creative spirits. Under-rehearsed and prone to fits of giggles, the team still ran through such favourites as the *The Ministry of Silly Walks*, the *Bruces*, the *Four Yorkshiremen* and the *Lumberjack Song*. It's a mixed bag but, because HandMade decided to cut parts of the show for the film version, it's all over far too soon. Contains swearing. 📼

Graham Chapman • John Cleese • Terry Gilliam • Eric Idle • Terry Jones • Michael Palin • Neil Innes • Carol Cleveland ■ *Dir* Terry Hughes, Ian MacNaughton • *Scr* Graham Chapman, John Cleese, Terry Gilliam, Eric Idle, Terry Jones, Michael Palin

Monty Python's Life of Brian ★★★★ 15

Comedy 1979 · UK · Colour · 89mins

The controversy that surrounded this inspired send-up of religious epics overshadows the fact that this is the Monty Python team's most assured work. Graham Chapman ("he's not the Messiah, he's just a naughty boy") is the Judaean whose life bears some resemblance to a certain carpenter's around the same time, although the shambling story serves mainly as an excuse for the assembled Pythons to take pot shots at some of their favourite targets and serve up some joyfully juvenile gags. Michael Palin gets some memorable roles, notably the Roman governor with a speech impediment ("Welease Wodewick"); Spike Milligan makes a very funny and quite irrelevant cameo. Contains violence, swearing and nudity. 📼

Terry Jones • Graham Chapman • Michael Palin • John Cleese • Eric Idle • Terry Gilliam ■ *Dir* Terry Jones • *Scr* Graham Chapman, John Cleese, Terry Gilliam, Eric Idle, Terry Jones, Michael Palin

Monty Python's The Meaning of Life ★★★ 18

Comedy 1983 · UK · Colour · 86mins

A pick 'n' mix selection of comedy sketches by the anarchic, surrealistic team of John Cleese, Terry Gilliam, Eric Idle, Terry Jones, Michael Palin and Graham Chapman. Exploring the stages of human existence, ranging from conception to death, this is British humour at its most tasteless and occasionally brilliant – the sequence in which a financial institution is boarded by swashbuckling pirates is superb, while the one in which a glutton explosively overeats is wholly nasty. An acquired taste. Contains swearing and brief nudity. 📼

Graham Chapman • John Cleese • Terry Gilliam • Eric Idle • Terry Jones • Michael Palin ■ *Dir* Terry Jones • *Scr* Terry Jones (HYF), Graham Chapman, John Cleese, Terry Gilliam, Eric Idle, Michael Palin

The Moon and Sixpence ★★★

Melodrama
1942 · US · BW and Colour · 88mins

George Sanders stars as a London stockbroker who becomes a painter in Paris, goes all Bohemian and then drops out in the South Seas. Somerset Maugham's novel was partly inspired by Gauguin and his sojourn in the Marquesas Islands, but Sanders's performance is more Oscar Wilde than Maugham. (It's certainly far removed from Anthony Quinn's piratical Gauguin in *Lust for Life*.) Don't look for luscious location photography either; this is an effete, studio-bound exploration of artistic temperament.

George Sanders *Charles Strickland* • Herbert Marshall *Geoffrey Wolfe* • Steve Geray [Steven Geray] *Dirk Stroeve* • Doris Dudley *Blanche Stroeve* • Eric Blore *Captain Nichols* • Albert Basserman *Doctor Coutras* • Molly Lamont *Mrs Strickland* ■ *Dir* Albert Lewin • *Scr* Albert Lewin, from the novel by W Somerset Maugham

Moon 44 ★★ 15

Science-fiction action drama
1990 · W Ger/US · Colour · 95mins

Before his Hollywood success with *Universal Soldier, Independence Day* and *Godzilla*, Roland Emmerich directed this German-financed sci-fi thriller about a cop (Michael Paré) going undercover as a convict on an industrial planet to investigate ongoing sabotage. Over-plotted, cliché-ridden and highly derivative, this mining mess certainly benefits from Emmerich's gift for getting every dollar on screen, and both the effects and production values belie its origins. But so little of it makes any sense – particularly an unpleasant rape subplot. 📼

Michael Paré *Felix Stone* • Lisa Eichhorn *Terry Morgan* • Dean Devlin *Tyler* • Malcolm McDowell *Major Lee* • Brian Thompson *Jake O'Neal* • Stephen Geoffreys *Cookie* ■ *Dir* Roland Emmerich • *Scr* Dean Heyde, Oliver Eberle, from a story by Dean Heyde, Eberle, Roland Emmerich, PJ Mitchell

The Moon in the Gutter ★★★ 18

Mystery romance
1983 · Fr/It · Colour · 132mins

Critically panned and reviled by even its star, Gérard Depardieu, director Jean-Jacques Beneix's follow-up to *Diva* is another glittering visual delight that suffers from a cumbersome and pretentious plot. Depardieu is a poor stevedore searching for the man who raped his sister. While on his traumatic odyssey, he ends up pursuing rich Nastassja Kinski who is, literally, the girl of his dreams. Deliriously obscure and dazzlingly superficial by turns, this curiosity contains the most erotic images of Kinski, Depardieu and Victoria Abril ever captured on film. In French with English subtitles. 📼

Gérard Depardieu *Gerard* • Nastassja Kinski *Loretta* • Victoria Abril *Bella* • Vittorio Mezzogiorno *Newton Channing* • Dominique Pinon *Frank* • Bertice Reading *Lola* ■ *Dir* Jean-Jacques Beineix • *Scr* Jean-Jacques Beineix, Olivier Mergault, from the novel by David Goodis

The Moon Is Blue ★★★ PG
Comedy   1953 · US · BW · 95mins

William Holden meets actress Maggie McNamara on top of the Empire State Building, only for McNamara to be pursued by older man David Niven. This mildly amusing comedy of romantic errors was a huge box-office success when director Otto Preminger defied the censor and released the film with dialogue that was considered extreme for its day. This adaptation of F Hugh Herbert's Broadway play was a two-pronged act of defiance by the tyrannically single-minded Preminger; he also gave an enormously appreciated boost to Niven's career simply by casting him. Niven had broken with a vindictive Sam Goldwyn and was described by this film's production company, United Artists, as "all washed up". Given the chance to prove himself once again, Niven rose to the challenge brilliantly. ▣

William Holden (1) *Donald Gresham* • David Niven *David Slater* • Maggie McNamara *Patty O'Neill* • Tom Tully *Michael O'Neill* • Dawn Addams *Cynthia Slater* ■ *Dir* Otto Preminger • *Scr* F Hugh Herbert, from his play

The Moon Is Down ★★
Second World War drama
1943 · US · BW · 90mins

Adapted from the novel by John Steinbeck, this clumsy piece of wartime propaganda sees some plucky Norwegians overcome the might of the Nazis. Doubtless such acts of selfless heroism occurred throughout the Second World War, but Hollywood (particularly its European exiles) could never resist setting them in fairy-tale towns populated entirely by quaint characters whom you could always trust to come up with a schnitzel when you were down on your luck. Cedric Hardwicke credits his Nazi commander with having some intelligence, but he's no match for Henry Travers, who's armed to the teeth with decency and a whimsical love of liberty.

Cedric Hardwicke *Colonel Lanser* • Henry Travers *Mayor Orden* • Lee J Cobb *Dr Winter* • Dorris Bowdon *Molly Morden* • Margaret Wycherly *Madame Orden* • Peter Van Eyck *Lieutenant Tonder* • Irving Pichel *Innkeeper* ■ *Dir* Irving Pichel • *Scr* Nunnally Johnson, from the novel by John Steinbeck

Moon over Miami ★★★ U
Musical   1941 · US · Colour · 87mins

One of the very best of the 20th Century-Fox Technicolor Betty Grable vehicles: a pleasingly bright, garish and utterly unsophisticated version of Fox's great stand-by plot about money-hungry gals on a spree (*Three Blind Mice*, *Three Little Girls in Blue*, *How to Marry a Millionaire*). There's some fun dancing here from Jack Cole and the Condos Brothers, and some nice songs, such as *You Started Something* and the title tune. Easy on the eye and ear, with a strong cast including Don Ameche, this is prime viewing for nostalgists. ▣

Don Ameche *Phil O'Neil* • Betty Grable *Kay Latimer* • Robert Cummings *Jack Bolton* • Charlotte Greenwood *Aunt Susie Latimer* • Jack Haley *Jack O'Hara* • Carole Landis *Barbara Latimer* • Cobina Jr Wright *Connie Fentress* ■ *Dir* Walter Lang • *Scr* Vincent

Lawrence, Brown Holmes, George Seaton, Lynn Starling, from the play *Three Blind Mice* by Stephen Powys

Moon over Parador ★★ 15
Comedy   1988 · US · Colour · 99mins

Director Paul Mazursky, whose instinct for comic manners and mores is usually razor-sharp, resorts to a lazy trawl through a decent comedy idea, blunting the edges of any comic potential in the process. However, Richard Dreyfuss puts plenty of energy into his scenes as a frustrated actor turned South American despot, using his nervy tics and schoolboy charm to advantage, and there are a handful of pointed barbs at the expense of dictatorship. Contains swearing. ▣

Richard Dreyfuss *Jack Noah* • Raul Julia *Roberto Strausmann* • Sonia Braga *Madonna* • Jonathan Winters *Ralph* • Fernando Rey *Alejandro* • Sammy Davis Jr • Michael Greene *Clint* • Charo *Madame Loop* ■ *Dir* Paul Mazursky • *Scr* Leon Capetanos, Paul Mazursky, from a story by Charles G Booth

Moon Pilot ★★★ U
Science-fiction comedy
1962 · US · Colour · 98mins

One of the better Disney live-action pictures, in which Tom Tryon is selected to become the first man in space by a test-flight chimpanzee. The unwilling Tryon's resolve to remain on Earth is reinforced when he falls for Dany Saval, but when he discovers that she is a visitor from another planet, his feelings about outer space quickly change. Solidly supported by Brian Keith and Edmond O'Brien, Tryon and Saval make an engaging couple, and there are plenty of smart jokes at the expense of Nasa. ▣

Tom Tryon *Captain Richmond Talbot* • Brian Keith *Major General John Vanneman* • Edmond O'Brien *McClosky* • Dany Saval *Lyrae* • Bob Sweeney *Senator McGuire* ■ *Dir* James Neilson • *Scr* Maurice Tombragel, from a novel by Robert Buckner

The Moon-Spinners ★★★ U
Mystery   1964 · US/UK · Colour · 113mins

Walt Disney fashioned numerous star vehicles for young Hayley Mills, and here she's involved (along with the wonderfully husky-voiced Joan Greenwood) in some likeable nonsense about jewel thieves in Crete. But it's the supporting cast that makes this worth watching: silent screen vamp Pola Negri came out of retirement to play the mysterious Madame Habib, only to be upstaged by the evil Eli Wallach and Greek star Irene Papas as his sister. Unfortunately, it doesn't come off as a Hitchcock-style mystery, and Mary Stewart's original novel should have been reworked.

Hayley Mills *Nikky Ferris* • Eli Wallach *Stratos* • Pola Negri *Madame Habib* • Peter McEnery *Mark Camford* • Joan Greenwood *Aunt Frances* • Irene Papas *Sophia* • Sheila Hancock *Cynthia Gamble* • John Le Mesurier *Anthony Chelmscott Gamble* ■ *Dir* James Neilson • *Scr* Michael Dyne, from the novel by Mary Stewart

Moon Zero Two ★★ U
Science-fiction 1969 · UK · Colour · 100mins

In an effort to diversify, Hammer attempted this "U" certificate space

western, in which James Olson and Ori Levy do battle with the bad guys for prospecting rights on a somewhat bleak-looking moon. It's exactly what you might expect from a western set on the moon, complete with shoot-outs, ambushes and dancing girls. The plot and dialogue are terrible, though there are a few thrills for the kids.

James Olson *Bill Kemp* • Catherina von Schell [Catherine Schell] *Clementine Taplin* • Warren Mitchell *JJ Hubbard* • Adrienne Corri *Liz Murphy* • Ori Levy *Karminski* • Dudley Foster *Whitsun* • Bernard Bresslaw *Harry* • Carol Cleveland *Hostess* ■ *Dir* Roy Ward Baker • *Scr* Michael Carreras, from a story by Gavin Lyall, Frank Hardman, Martin Davison

Moondance ★★
Romantic drama
1995 · Ger/Ire/UK · Colour · 92mins

Two eccentric young brothers are torn apart when a beautiful woman enters their lives. The Irish scenery is gorgeous, as is German actress Julia Brendler, but the two brothers (Ian Shaw and Ruaidhri Conroy) are so eccentric they're hardly believable. The characters' motivations are obscure, and the movie often leaves the viewer behind. Since this story has been told better many times before, it's tough to recommend this version. An English/German language film.

Ruaidhri Conroy *Dominic* • Ian Shaw *Patrick* • Julia Brendler *Anya* • Marianne Faithfull *Mother* ■ *Dir* Dagmar Hirtz • *Scr* Mark Watters, Bert Weinshanker, from the novel *The White Hare* by Francis Stuart

Moonfleet ★★★
Historical adventure
1955 · US · Colour · 86mins

While a long way from being the best film on director Fritz Lang's illustrious CV, this adaptation of J Meade Falkner's swashbuckling classic still makes for rousing entertainment. Set in Dorset in the 1770s, this fast-moving tale of smuggling and secret identities provides Stewart Granger with the chance to add a touch of devilment to the expected romantic dash and derring-do. George Sanders gives his usual performance of silky smooth malevolence in this solid piece of old-fashioned escapism.

Stewart Granger *Jeremy Fox* • Joan Greenwood *Lady Ashwood* • George Sanders *Lord Ashwood* • Viveca Lindfors *Mrs Minton* • Liliane Montevecchi *Gypsy* ■ *Dir* Fritz Lang • *Scr* Jan Lustig, Margaret Fitts, from the novel by J Meade Falkner

Moonlight ★★ 15
Crime drama   1982 · US · Colour · 71mins

It's not often that Alan Smithee, the prolific pseudonymous director, pops up in TV circles, and it's an indication of the quality of this failed TV-movie pilot. The charisma-free Robert Desiderio is the takeaway food worker who bizarrely ends up battling international baddies when he falls in with a secret US government agency. Michelle Phillips is the only recognisable face in the cast and neither Rod Holcomb nor Jackie Cooper, who both took a crack at direction, succeed in generating any semblance of thrills or suspense. ▣

Robert Desiderio *Lenny Barbella* • Michelle Phillips *Meredith Tyne* • William Prince *Mr White/Bibb* • Antony Ponzini *Victor Barbella* • Carmine Mitore "Pop" *Barbella* • Penny Santon *Josephine Barbella* ■ *Dir* Allan Smithee [Jackie Cooper], Allan Smithee [Rod Holcomb] • *Scr* David H Chase

Moonlight and Valentino ★★★ 15
Drama   1995 · US · Colour · 99mins

A talky but well-acted adaptation of Ellen Simon's stage play about the struggles of a young widow to cope with life without her husband. Elizabeth Perkins's moving performance as the widow is the centrepiece of this beautifully shot, intimately detailed drama, but the supporting cast is equally praiseworthy, with special mention for star-in-the-making Gwyneth Paltrow as Perkins's eccentric sister. The sluggish, grief-drenched first half is pretty heavy going, though the tone is lightened by the introduction of charismatic rock star turned actor Jon Bon Jovi, who helps to re-awaken Perkins. Contains some sex scenes and swearing. ▣

Elizabeth Perkins *Rebecca Trager Lott* • Whoopi Goldberg *Sylvie Morrow* • Gwyneth Paltrow *Lucy Trager* • Kathleen Turner *Alberta Russell* • Jon Bon Jovi *The painter* • Peter Coyote *Paul* ■ *Dir* David Anspaugh • *Scr* Ellen Simon, from her play

Moonlight Sonata ★★
Romantic drama 1937 · UK · BW · 86mins

A plane makes a forced landing in the grounds of a Swedish country house owned by the music-loving Baroness Lindenborg (Marie Tempest). The passengers needing refuge include a fortune-hunting cad (Eric Portman), who temporarily sweeps the baroness's granddaughter off her feet. This British film exists only as an excuse for the great pianist Ignace Jan Paderewski to make his screen debut at the age of 77 as one of the passengers. ▣

Ignace Jan Paderewski • Charles Farrell *Eric Molander* • Marie Tempest *Baroness Lindenborg* • Barbara Greene *Ingrid* • Eric Portman *Mario de la Costa* • Graham Browne *Dr Broman* • Queenie Leonard *Margit, his niece* • Lawrence Hanray *Bishop* ■ *Dir* Lothar Mendes • *Scr* Edward Knoblock, EM Delafield, from a story by Hans Rameau

The Moonlighter ★★
Western   1953 · US · BW · 77mins

Barbara Stanwyck and Fred MacMurray, the doomed lovers from the classic *Double Indemnity*, are reunited in a western that was originally released in 3-D. Niven Busch – the writer of *Duel in the Sun* and the deeply Freudian western *The Furies* – came up with the weird plot of a cattle rustler (MacMurray) who escapes a lynch mob and robs a bank. He is then pursued by his girlfriend (Stanwyck), who also happens to be the sheriff. The title derives from western lore that says rustlers work only in moonlight.

Barbara Stanwyck *Rela* • Fred MacMurray *Wes Anderson* • Ward Bond *Cole* • William Ching *Tom Anderson* • John Dierkes *Sheriff Daws* • Morris Ankrum *Prince* • Jack Elam *Strawboss* ■ *Dir* Roy Rowland • *Scr* Niven Busch

Moonlighting ★★★★ 15

Political drama 1982 · UK · Colour · 93mins

Directed with vigour and assurance by the exiled Polish director Jerzy Skolimowski, this razor-sharp satire brilliantly equates the experiences of a crew of moonlighting Polish builders in Thatcherite London with the plight of the workers in the Gdansk shipyard at the height of the Solidarity uprising. As the leader of the gang, Jeremy Irons gives one of the finest performances of his career as he imposes curfews and news blackouts to prevent his idle, excitable colleagues learning of the momentous events back home before the job is done. The shoplifting sequence is the highlight of an enthralling and intelligent picture. ▭

Jeremy Irons *Nowak* • Eugene Lipinski *Banaszak* • Jiri Stanislaw *Wolski* • Eugeniusz Haczkiewicz *Kudaj* ■ *Dir/Scr* Jerzy Skolimowski

The Moonraker ★★★ U

Historical adventure
1957 · UK · Colour · 78mins

Lacking the budget and the stars to pack the same punch as recent historical costume dramas such as *Shakespeare in Love* and *Plunkett and Macleane*, *The Moonraker* is still an enjoyable romp. George Baker is the Cavalier who keeps the future Charles II out of the clutches of Oliver Cromwell (portrayed with visible relish by John Le Mesurier). Sylvia Syms provides the glamour and *Doctor Who* fans will recognise Patrick Troughton, who played the time-traveller in his second incarnation. ▭

George Baker *Earl Anthony of Dawlish, "The Moonraker"* • Sylvia Syms *Anne Wyndham* • Peter Arne *Edmund Tyler* • Marius Goring *Colonel Beaumont* • Clive Morton *Lord Harcourt* • Gary Raymond *Prince Charles Stuart* • John Le Mesurier *Oliver Cromwell* • Patrick Troughton *Captain Wilcox* ■ *Dir* David MacDonald • *Scr* Robert Hall, Wilfrid Eades, Alistair Bell, from the play by Arthur Watkyn

Moonraker ★★ PG

Spy adventure 1979 · UK · Colour · 121mins

The 11th Bond movie jettisons Ian Fleming's marvellous novel and sends 007 into space. Weighed down by its often clunky special effects and non-existent plotting, the movie seems to be merely an attempt to update Bond in the wake of *Star Wars*. Roger Moore smirks throughout, Michael Lonsdale makes a lacklustre master criminal and Jaws, the towering sub-villain from *The Spy Who Loved Me*, makes a return appearance. Venice and Rio are also part of the package, but too much of the budget was wasted in overblown spectacle, without enough attention being given to the basics. ▭

Roger Moore *James Bond* • Lois Chiles *Holly Goodhead* • Michael Lonsdale *[Michel Lonsdale] Hugo Drax* • Richard Kiel *Jaws* • Corinne Cléry *Corinne Dufour* • Bernard Lee *"M"* • Desmond Llewelyn *"Q"* • Lois Maxwell *Miss Moneypenny* ■ *Dir* Lewis Gilbert • *Scr* Christopher Wood, from the novel by Ian Fleming • *Music* John Barry

Moonrise ★★★★ PG

Film noir 1948 · US · BW · 86mins

This sombre but compelling rural drama is a tribute to the skill of director Frank Borzage, a fine example of his tender feelings for young lovers in adversity. Dane Clark gives his best performance as the murderer's son who kills one of his tormentors, while Gail Russell brings her fragile beauty to the part of the girl who believes in him. Though tracked by the sheriff and his posse, his biggest enemy is himself. The film is a visual treat, and a true mood piece. ▭

Dane Clark *Danny Hawkins* • Gail Russell *Gilly Johnson* • Ethel Barrymore *Grandma* • Allyn Joslyn *Clem Otis* • Henry Morgan [Harry Morgan] *Billy Scripture* • Rex Ingram *Mose* ■ *Dir* Frank Borzage • *Scr* Charles Haas, from the novel by Theodore Strauss

The Moon's Our Home ★★★

Romantic comedy 1936 · US · BW · 80mins

The major attraction of this romantic comedy is the pairing of Margaret Sullavan and Henry Fonda, two of Hollywood's most attractive and gifted stars of the thirties, who were married in real life for a stormy couple of years from 1931 to 1933. She plays a movie star, he's a writer and explorer; they fly in the face of temperamental incompatibility and marry. The rest of the film, directed by William Seiter from a witty script that includes contributions from Dorothy Parker, is concerned with how they sort out their differences. It's all done with warmth and charm, though Sullavan tends to overplay the comic tantrums.

Margaret Sullavan *Sarah Brown/Cherry Chester* • Henry Fonda *John Smith/Anthony Amberton* • Charles Butterworth *Horace Van Steedan* • Beulah Bondi *Mrs Boyce Medford* • Margaret Hamilton *Mitty Simpson* • Henrietta Crosman *Lucy Van Steedan* ■ *Dir* William A Seiter • *Scr* Isabel Dawn, Boyce DeGaw, Dorothy Parker, Alan Campbell, from the story by Faith Baldwin

Moonshine County Express ★★

Action crime drama
1977 · US · Colour · 95mins

A hillbilly is murdered and his three daughters decide to sell his ocean of illicit whiskey, thereby incurring the wrath of local moonshine big shot William Conrad. This sort of slipshod, sour mash jape is a macho affair usually, but *Moonshine County Express* has performed a sex-change op on the old genre, with Susan Howard, Claudia Jennings and Maureen McCormick as the three hoochettes. John Saxon works for Conrad but fancies Howard, which adds a dash of morality and romance to the original recipe of car chases and banjo music.

John Saxon *JB Johnson* • Susan Howard *Dot Hammer* • William Conrad *Jack Starkey* • Morgan Woodward *Sweetwater* • Claudia Jennings *Betty Hammer* • Jeff Corey *Preacher Hagen* • Dub Taylor *Uncle Bill* • Maureen McCormick *Sissy Hammer* ■ *Dir* Gus Trikonis • *Scr* Hubert Smith, Daniel Ansley

The Moonstone ★★

Mystery 1934 · US · BW · 62mins

Wilkie Collins's novel has always been a hard nut for film-makers to crack, so it comes as no surprise to learn that there have been no film versions since this one (although there have been some made-for-TV efforts). David

Manners, better known today as the juvenile lead in the Bela Lugosi *Dracula* (1931), makes a stiff and unappealing hero, though the result does have some historical interest. Collins fared much better with Warner Bros's 1948 version of *The Woman in White*, which came complete with all the requisite Gothic trimmings.

David Manners *Franklin Blake* • Phyllis Barry *Anne Verinder* • Jameson Thomas *Godfrey Ablewhite, rare book dealer* • Gustav von Seyffertitz *Septimus Lucker, money-lender* • Herbert Bunston *Sir John Verinder* ■ *Dir* Reginald Barker • *Scr* Adele Buffington, from the novel by Wilkie Collins

Moonstruck ★★★★ PG

Romantic comedy
1987 · US · Colour · 97mins

An unashamedly romantic comedy that established once and for all that Cher could act. She gives an Oscar-winning performance as a widow who looks set for a safe marriage with Danny Aiello, but falls instead for his moody younger brother Nicolas Cage. John Patrick Shanley, who won an Oscar for best original screenplay, paints a warm and affectionate picture of Italian-American life, and there are enough quirky touches to prevent it from toppling into treacle. Norman Jewison directs subtly and unobtrusively, allowing the splendid cast to make the most of Shanley's fine writing; the film is stolen by the wonderful Olympia Dukakis and Vincent Gardenia. ▭

Cher *Loretta Castorini* • Nicolas Cage *Ronny Cammareri* • Olympia Dukakis *Rose Castorini* • Vincent Gardenia *Cosmo Castorini* • Danny Aiello *Mr Johnny Cammareri* • Julie Bovasso *Rita Cappomaggi* • John Mahoney *Perry* ■ *Dir* Norman Jewison • *Scr* John Patrick Shanley

Moontide ★★★

Drama 1942 · US · BW · 94mins

Jean Gabin is a heavy-drinking, rootless Frenchman who wanders from job to job in dockside towns supporting "buddy" Thomas Mitchell, who has a hold over him and clings like a leech. Gabin saves Ida Lupino from suicide, setting in motion a chain of dramatic events. A modest, grittily effective and absorbing drama, with French idol Gabin impressive and Lupino appealing. Mitchell is excellent as the weak and scummy villain, while Claude Rains is unlikely but sympathetic as an educated night watchman. Archie Mayo's direction is uneven, but there are some fine sequences of brooding tension – doubtless explained by the fact that an uncredited Fritz Lang directed some of the film.

Jean Gabin *Bobo* • Ida Lupino *Anna* • Thomas Mitchell *Tiny* • Claude Rains *Nutsy* • Jerome Cowan *Dr Frank Brothers* • Helene Reynolds *Woman on boat* • Ralph Byrd *Rev Wilson* ■ *Dir* Archie Mayo, Fritz Lang • *Scr* John O'Hara, from the novel by Willard Robertson

Moonwalker ★★★ PG

Musical fantasy 1988 · US · Colour · 89mins

Made when Michael Jackson was still the biggest pop star in the world, this is, unfortunately, a bit of a mess. However, fans will still love the music and the innovative pop promo interludes, while some older viewers might enjoy the discomfort of Joe Pesci as the evil Mr Big. Look out for Sean

Lennon as one of Jackson's chums. Contains violent scenes.

Michael Jackson *Michael* • Joe Pesci *Mr Big* • Sean Lennon *Sean* • Kellie Parker *Katie* • Brandon Adams *Zeke/"Baby Bad" Michael* ■ *Dir* Colin Chilvers, Jerry Kramer • *Scr* David Newman, from a story by Michael Jackson

More ★

Drama 1969 · Lux /Fr · Colour · 110mins

The fag end of the Swinging Sixties, as seen by debutant director Barbet Schroeder (previously Eric Rohmer's producer). More soft-core porn than social comment, it's about a German lad who hitchhikes across Europe, gets into drugs and ends up in Ibiza with Mimsy Farmer. This is the full druggie nightmare, complete with acid trips, skinny-dipping, hippy speak and a music score by Pink Floyd.

Mimsy Farmer *Estelle* • Klaus Grunberg *Stefan* • Heinz Engelmann *Wolf* • Michel Chanderli *Charlie* • Louise Wink *Cathy* • Henry Wolf *Henry* ■ *Dir* Barbet Schroeder • *Scr* Paul Gegauff, Barbet Schroeder, from a story by Barbet Schroeder

More American Graffiti ★★

Comedy drama 1979 · US · Colour · 110mins

How do you follow a modern masterpiece like *American Graffiti*? Not with this plodding, inferior sequel, which catches up with the Class of 1962 as they live through the Vietnam-dominated, hippy sixties. The only saving grace is yet another brilliant soundtrack, featuring golden oldies from the Supremes, Mary Wells, the Byrds, Bob Dylan and Cream. Wolfman Jack and Country Joe and the Fish also make appearances in this failure, aimlessly directed by Bill L Norton.

Candy Clark *Debbie Dunham* • Bo Hopkins *Little Joe* • Ron Howard *Steve Bolander* • Paul LeMat *John Milner* • Mackenzie Phillips *Carol Rainbow* • Charles Martin Smith *Terry the Toad* • Cindy Williams *Laurie Bolander* • Harrison Ford *Motorcycle cop* ■ *Dir* BWL Norton [Bill L Norton] • *Scr* BWL Norton, from characters created by George Lucas, Gloria Katz, Willard Huyck

More Dead than Alive ★★

Western 1969 · US · Colour · 100mins

A potentially interesting western, obviously influenced by Sergio Leone's *Dollars* trilogy and starring TV hunk Clint Walker as a hired gun readjusting to life after 18 years in jail. Unemployable and harassed by former enemies, Walker gets a job in a Wild West show owned by kindly impresario Vincent Price. It's only now that the real plot emerges – Price has hired Walker to replace another crack shot who proceeds to turn psychotic. There're bags of potential here for an off-kilter drama, but Walker has all the charisma of a sack of concrete.

Clint Walker *"Killer" Cain* • Vincent Price *Dan Ruffalo* • Anne Francis *Monica Alton* • Paul Hampton *Billy Eager* • Mike Henry *Luke Santee* • Craig Littler *Rafe Karma* ■ *Dir* Robert Sparr • *Scr* George Schenck

More than a Miracle ★★★ U

Fantasy romantic drama
1967 · It/Fr · Colour · 103mins

Sophia Loren and Omar Sharif are paired in this Italian film, directed by

Francesco Rosi, about a Spanish aristocrat who falls in love with a peasant girl. The path of true love, however, runs anything but smoothly. Despite being weakened by a running time that's a little too long to support the tale, this is a charming mix of romance, social comment and whimsy, directed and played with a suitably light touch and photographed in the style of an illustrated fairy tale. Italian dialogue dubbed into English.

Sophia Loren *Isabella* • Omar Sharif *Prince Ramon* • Dolores Del Rio *Queen Mother* • Georges Wilson *Monzu* • Leslie French *Brother Joseph of Copertino* • Carlo Pisacane *Witch* • Marina Malfatti *Devout princess* ■ *Dir* Francesco Rosi • *Scr* Francesco Rosi, Tonino Guerra, Raffaele La Capria, Giuseppe Patroni Griffi • *Cinematographer* Pasquale De Santis

The More the Merrier ★★★★ U

Comedy 1943 · US · BW · 99mins

The wartime housing shortage in Washington DC forces government employee Jean Arthur and Joel McCrea to share an apartment with kindly businessman Charles Coburn. Part screwball comedy, part message movie about the need to pull together, it's a piece of fluff effortlessly carried by the charm of its stars and by George Stevens's elegant direction. A scene on the steps of the apartment, when McCrea makes a pass at Arthur, aroused a good deal of comment at the time for being shockingly sexy. There was a 1966 remake, *Walk, Don't Run*, set in Tokyo with Cary Grant in the Coburn role.

Jean Arthur *Connie Milligan* • Joel McCrea *Joe Carter* • Charles Coburn *Benjamin Dingle* • Richard Gaines *Charles J Pendergast* • Bruce Bennett *Evans* • Frank Sully *Pike* • Clyde Fillmore *Senator Noonan* ■ *Dir* George Stevens • *Scr* Robert Russell, Frank Ross, Richard Flournoy, Lewis R Foster, from a story by Robert Russell, Frank Ross, Garson Kanin

The More Things Change ★★★ PG

Comedy drama 1985 · Aust · Colour · 90mins

Robyn Nevin was already one of Australia's most respected theatrical directors when she embarked on this, her debut as a film director. She is evidently more at home with coaching her cast than she is with moving a camera and creating dramatic tension through editing, but the strength of the story carries the day. Judy Morris and Barry Otto impress as the Melbourne couple whose relationship becomes strained when he drops out of city life to renovate a run-down farm. The points made about role reversal are deftly handled, but the melodramatic subplot involving their pregnant teenage nanny gets in the way.

Judy Morris *Connie* • Barry Otto *Lex* • Victoria Longley *Geraldine* • Lewis Fitz-Gerald *Barry* • Peter Carroll *Roley* • Louise Le Nay *Lydia* • Owen Johnson *Nicholas* • Brenda Addie *Angela* ■ *Dir* Robyn Nevin • *Scr* Moya Wood

Morgan – a Suitable Case for Treatment ★★★ PG

Comedy drama 1966 · UK · Colour · 92mins

Angry young men were abundant in the British cinema of the sixties, but they were never so irate as working-class artist David Warner, who tries to sabotage the second marriage of his middle-class ex-wife Vanessa Redgrave to art dealer Robert Stephens by rewiring their house and dressing in a gorilla suit. Adapted from David Mercer's television play, it's really a fable about the class society. Yet its dream sequences and surreal touches make it more odd than meaningful, and it now feels dreadfully dated.

Vanessa Redgrave *Leonie Delt* • David Warner *Morgan Delt* • Robert Stephens *Charles Napier* • Irene Handl *Mrs Delt* • Newton Blick *Mr Henderson* • Nan Munro *Mrs Henderson* • Bernard Bresslaw *Policeman* ■ *Dir* Karel Reisz • *Scr* David Mercer, from his TV play *A Suitable Case for Treatment*

Morgan the Pirate ★★ U

Swashbuckling adventure
1960 · It/Fr · Colour · 95mins

In this swashbuckler co-directed by Andre De Toth, bodybuilder Steve Reeves shakes off the loincloth of his usual Greek heroes and dons the costume of legendary pirate Henry Morgan, the Robin Hood of the high seas (or so the legend goes). Reeves sticks in the craw of the Spanish, launches a raid on Panama and sweeps the governor's daughter off her feet. His performance is fairly gormless but he's got a bigger chest than his leading ladies and a jawline that would make a crocodile shed tears.

Steve Reeves *Sir Henry Morgan* • Valérie Lagrange *Dona Inez* • Lydia Alfonsi *Dona Maria* • Chelo Alonso *Concepcion* • Armand Mestral *L'Olannais* • Ivo Garrani *Governor* ■ *Dir* Andre De Toth, Primo Zeglio • *Scr* Andre De Toth, Primo Zeglio, Filippo Sanjust

The Morning After ★★★ 15

Thriller 1986 · US · Colour · 102mins

Sidney Lumet is best known for his New York stories of civic crime and corruption. This, though, was the first film Lumet directed that was set in LA and he gives it an abstract gloss (like a Hockney painting) and uses some bizarre locations, including a Gaudi-esque house that hides away behind Rodeo Drive. The plot is rather more ordinary: Jane Fonda wakes up next to a man with a knife through his chest. An alcoholic actress, she hasn't a clue what happened, so ex-cop Jeff Bridges helps her out. There are false trails, red herrings and Raul Julia as Fonda's hairdresser husband, but, for Lumet, it's a rare exercise in style and mood. Contains swearing and violence.

Jane Fonda *Alex Sternbergen* • Jeff Bridges *Turner Kendall* • Raul Julia *Joaquin "Jacky" Manero* • Diane Salinger *Isabel Harding* • Richard Foronjy *Sergeant Greenbaum* • Geoffrey Scott *Bobby Korshack* ■ *Dir* Sidney Lumet • *Scr* James Hicks

Morning Departure ★★★

Drama 1950 · UK · BW · 102mins

An atmospheric "confined space" drama, with John Mills in one of his best roles as the commander of a submarine, holed by a mine and plunging to the sea bed. Twelve crew members survive the initial impact, but only eight will be able to use the escape equipment. A spot of bother, in other words, but everyone makes you proud to be British, apart from Richard Attenborough, playing a weak-willed stoker with his trademark intensity.

John Mills *Lieutenant Commander Armstrong* • Helen Cherry *Helen* • Richard Attenborough *Stoker Snipe* • Lana Morris *Rose Snipe* • Nigel Patrick *Lieutenant Harry Manson* • Andrew Crawford *Warrant Officer McFee* • Michael Brennan *Chief Petty Officer Barlow* ■ *Dir* Roy Baker [Roy Ward Baker] • *Scr* WEC Fairchild, from the play by Kenneth Woollard

Morning Glory ★★★

Drama 1933 · US · BW · 74mins

"The calla lillies are in bloom again" in Katharine Hepburn's stunningly mannered performance, which won her the first of her unequalled (and likely to remain so) four best actress Oscars. Cast as young Broadway hopeful Eva Lovelace, she's all angles and angst in this adaptation of Zoe Akins's play about a starry-eyed Cinderella. Despite Hepburn's worthy co-stars, who include Adolphe Menjou as a lecherous producer and Douglas Fairbanks Jr as an earnest playwright, the movie belongs totally to Kate.

Katharine Hepburn *Eva Lovelace* • Douglas Fairbanks Jr *Joseph Sheridan* • Adolphe Menjou *Louis Easton* • Mary Duncan *Rita Vernon* • C Aubrey Smith *Robert Harley Hedges* ■ *Dir* Lowell Sherman • *Scr* Howard J Green, from the play by Zoe Akins

Morning Glory ★★

Romantic drama 1993 · US · Colour · 90mins

A romantic drama with Deborah Raffin as a widow in thirties Georgia who marries ex-con Christopher Reeve and then has to prove him innocent when he is accused of murdering a sheriff's girlfriend. It's all rather predictable, but Raffin (who co-wrote the screenplay) makes it worth watching. JT Walsh plays the bereaved sheriff.

Christopher Reeve *Will Parker* • Deborah Raffin *Elly Dinsmore* • Lloyd Bochner *Bob Collins* • Nina Foch *Miss Beasley* • Helen Shaver *Lula Peaks* • JT Walsh *Sheriff Reese Goodloe* ■ *Dir* Steven Hilliard Stern • *Scr* Charles Jarrott, Deborah Raffin, from the novel by LaVyrle Spencer

Morocco ★★★★★

Romance 1930 · US · BW · 90mins

Screen goddess Marlene Dietrich's first American-made movie, sumptuously directed by her *Blue Angel* mentor Josef von Sternberg and ravishingly photographed by the great Lee Garmes and Lucien Ballard. Dietrich's romantic partner is the impossibly young and handsome foreign legionnaire Gary Cooper, and the audience is left wondering whether she'll choose between him or dapper, worldly Adolphe Menjou. Dietrich makes something very real and touching out of her displaced cabaret chanteuse, and her first appearance in the Moroccan nightclub is an ultra-sophisticated piece of staging (apparently suggested by Howard Hawks) that is as ornate as it is outrageous. This movie set the seal on Dietrich's image for ever, and its potent blend of romance and high gloss also helped consolidate the Paramount style of the thirties.

Marlene Dietrich *Amy Jolly* • Gary Cooper *Tom Brown* • Adolphe Menjou *Le Bessier* • Ullrich Haupt *Adjutant Caesar* • Juliette Compton *Anna Dolores* • Francis McDonald *Cpl Tatoche* ■ *Dir* Josef von Sternberg • *Scr* Jules Furthman, from the novel *Amy Jolly* by Benno Vigny • *Art Director* Hans Dreier

Morons from Outer Space ★ PG

Science-fiction comedy
1985 · UK · Colour · 86mins

Moronic isn't the word! Mel Smith and Griff Rhys Jones's lamentable lampoon is a shambling spoof of *2001*, *Star Wars* and *Close Encounters*, with little wit or wisdom on display. Directed by Mike Hodges, who really should have known better, the pathetic story concerns aliens from the planet Blob crash-landing on Earth and forming a glam-rock band. But the end result wouldn't have made the grade during the Oxbridge duo's student rag week. If sneezing in an astronaut suit, aliens mistaking a dustbin for a human and a spaceship trailing a caravan sound funny, then you may find this miserable farce on the cheap and cheerful side. Otherwise, alas Smith and Jones indeed. Contains some swearing.

Mel Smith *Bernard* • Griff Rhys Jones *Graham Sweetley* • James B Sikking *Col Laribee* • Dinsdale Landen *Cdr Matteson* • Jimmy Nail *Desmond* • Joanne Pearce *Sandra* • Paul Bown *Julian* ■ *Dir* Mike Hodges • *Scr* Mel Smith, Griff Rhys Jones, Bob Mercer

The Morrison Murders ★★★

Mystery drama based on a true story
1997 · US · Colour · 89mins

Whereas so many TV movies based on actual events are presented with almost tabloid sensationalism, this admirably restrained tale of murder and sinister secrets shows how a true-life story can provide compelling entertainment instead of melodramatic excess. John Corbett and Jonathan Scarfe work well together as the siblings whose pursuit of the killer of their parents and younger brother results in a shocking revelation and a unique police operation. Contains some violence and brief nudity.

John Corbett *Walker Morrison* • Jonathan Scarfe *Luke Morrison* • Gordon Clapp *Sheriff Byron Calhoun* • Maya McLaughlin *Patti Morrison* • Tanya Allen *Kimberly* • Alex Carter *Deputy George Pettygrew* • Barry Flatman *Donald Fraser* • Patricia Gage *Aunt Clare* ■ *Dir* Chris Thomson • *Scr* Keith Ross Leckie

Mortal Fear ★★ 12

Medical drama 1994 · US · Colour · 86mins

A medical thriller based on the novel by Robin Cook that bears a remarkable similarity to his earlier bestseller, *Coma*, which was turned into a feature film by director Michael Crichton. This time Joanna Kerns is the high-flying medic who begins to suspect something is not quite right when her hospital begins to lose patients at a rate even an overworked junior doctor might notice. With the exception of Robert Englund minus his Freddy Krueger make-up, you've seen it all many times before.

Joanna Kerns *Dr Jennifer Kessler* • Gregory Harrison *Philip Montgomery* • Robert Englund *Dr Ralph Wanakmaker* • Max Gail *Det Michael Curran* • Rebecca Schull *Dr Danforth* ■ *Dir* Larry Shaw • *Scr* Rob Gilmer, Roger Young, from the novel by Robin Cook

956
U = SUITABLE FOR ALL Uc = SUITABLE FOR ALL, ESPECIALLY FOR YOUNG CHILDREN (VIDEO ONLY) PG = PARENTAL GUIDANCE

Mortal Kombat ★★★ 🔞

Martial arts action adventure
1995 · US · Colour · 97mins

At the time this film was made, *Mortal Kombat* was the world's biggest-selling game franchise, so it was a natural choice for a Hollywood makeover. And unlike other games-inspired turkeys (*Super Mario Bros*, *Street Fighter*), this one actually works, thanks mainly to director Paul Anderson's single-minded dedication to nonstop, expertly choreographed martial arts action. Christopher Lambert is the nominal star, but the best work comes from Cary-Hiroyuki Tagawa, who steals the show with a typically charismatic performance. Contains violence and some swearing. ▭ *DVD*

Christopher Lambert *Lord Rayden* • Bridgette Wilson *Sonya Blade* • Linden Ashby *Johnny Cage* • Talisa Soto *Princess Kitana* • Cary-Hiroyuki Tagawa *Shang Tsung* ■ *Dir* Paul Anderson • *Scr* Kevin Droney, from the video game by Ed Boon, John Tobias

Mortal Kombat: Annihilation ★★

Martial arts action adventure
1997 · US · Colour · 91mins

The martial arts arcade game spawns a second movie incarnation that offers even bigger helpings of action and special effects than the original. Robin Shou is back from the first outing, though Christopher Lambert's role is now taken by James Remar (*48 HRS*). Evil warlords from the sinister Outworld are bent on dominating Earth again, and the elder gods are powerless to intervene. Only a handful of fearless heroes can save the day with their amazing fighting skills and superhuman abilities. Undemanding fun, even if there is only slightly more plot than appeared in the original computer game. ▭ *DVD*

Robin Shou *Liu Kang* • Talisa Soto *Princess Kitana* • James Remar *Rayden* • Sandra Hess *Sonya Blade* ■ *Dir* John R Leonetti • *Scr* Brent V Friedman, Bryce Zabel, from a story by John Tobias, Lawrence Kasanoff, Joshua Wexler, from the video game by Ed Boon, John Tobias

Mortal Passions ★★ 🔞

Black comedy thriller
1989 · US · Colour · 91mins

David Warner adds a little bit of class to this otherwise routine erotic thriller, which went straight to video over here. Krista Errickson is the *femme fatale* who leads innocent husband Zach Galligan (best known as the teen lead of *Gremlins*) into a web of sexual and murderous intrigue. Warner plays the psychiatrist who is Galligan's only confidante. Director Andrew Lane throws in plenty of sex and nudity, but is less sure when it comes to the unnecessarily complicated plotting. Contains violence and swearing. ▭

Zach Galligan *Todd* • David Warner *Dr Powers* • Krista Errickson *Emily* • Sheila Kelley *Adele* • Michael Bowen *Berke* • Luca Bercovici *Darcy* ■ *Dir* Andrew Lane • *Scr* Alan Moskowitz

Mortal Sins ★★

Detective drama 1989 · US · Colour · 90mins

Private investigator Brian Benben is hired by a local TV evangelist to investigate the death of an associate, and he is approached shortly afterwards by the reverend's daughter on another matter. Signs point to a competing televangelist as the culprit, but Benben discovers that little is as it seems and the stern righteousness displayed by the fundamentalist church leaders may be no more than a veneer. Benben has some funny moments, but there's a lot of melodrama slowing things down.

Brian Benben *Nathan* • Debrah Farentino *Laura Rollins* • Anthony LaPaglia *Vito* • James Harper *Malcolm Rollins* • Brick Hartney *Billy Beau Backus* • James Saito *Park Sung* ■ *Dir* Yuri Sivo • *Scr* Allen Blumberg

Mortal Sins ★★ 🔞

Thriller 1992 · US · Colour · 88mins

Swapping his Superman cape for a cassock, Christopher Reeve plays a priest out to trap the serial killer he encounters in his confessional. An over-ambitious mix of Hitchcock's *I Confess*, *Death Wish* and the TV series *Father Dowling Investigates*, it still has a few twists to keep you intrigued. Contains some violence. ▭

Christopher Reeve *Father Thomas Cusack* • Roxann Biggs *Maria Croce* • Francis Guinan *Father Donald Simmons* • Weston McMillan *Paul Kaye* • Phillip R Allen *Lieutenant Benjamin Williams* ■ *Dir* Bradford May • *Scr* Greg Martinelli, Dennis Paoli

The Mortal Storm ★★★

Drama 1940 · US · BW · 100mins

This version of Phyllis Bottome's novel was daring in its time for alerting American audiences to the dangers of Nazism, though the horror is softened by the casting of resolutely all-American types as Germans and by a very Culver City Reich. Director Frank Borzage does not keep sentimentality at bay, but his drama is nevertheless moving and tragic by turns. It also reunites the marvellous Margaret Sullavan and the lanky but loveable James Stewart, who made *The Shop around the Corner* the same year. Frank Morgan (*The Wizard of Oz*) is genuinely touching as the father who watches his family disintegrate, and there's a chilling early cameo from later dance master Dan Dailey.

Margaret Sullavan *Freya Roth* • James Stewart *Martin Brietner* • Robert Young *Fritz Marlberg* • Frank Morgan *Professor Roth* • Robert Stack *Otto Von Rohn* • Bonita Granville *Elsa* • Irene Rich *Mrs Roth* • William T Orr *Erich Von Rohn* ■ *Dir* Frank Borzage • *Scr* Claudine West, Anderson Ellis, George Froeschel, from the novel by Phyllis Bottome

Mortal Thoughts ★★★ 🔞

Thriller 1991 · US · Colour · 98mins

Considered somewhat bleak and cold by many critics when it was released at the cinema, this drama (co-produced by star Demi Moore) actually works much better on the small screen. Told in flashback, the film follows two women friends (Moore and Glenne Headly) who are both unhappy in their marriages, and who end up being linked with the murder of Headly's husband (Bruce Willis). The acting from the three protagonists, and Harvey Keitel as the investigating detective, is superb, lifting what could have been a depressing tale into an intriguing mystery. Contains swearing and violence. ▭ *DVD*

Demi Moore *Cynthia Kellogg* • Glenne Headly *Joyce Urbanski* • Bruce Willis *James Urbanski* • John Pankow *Arthur Kellogg* • Harvey Keitel *Detective John Woods* • Billie Neal *Linda Nealon* • Frank Vincent *Dominic Marino* • Karen Shallo *Gloria Urbanski* • Crystal Field *Jeanette Marino* ■ *Dir* Alan Rudolph • *Scr* William Reilly, Claude Kerven

Mortgage ★★★

Documentary drama
1989 · Ausl · Colour · 92mins

Former documentary director Bill Bennett was the pioneer of the docudrama in which real-life professionals played themselves in situations built around a couple of fictional characters. This often engrossing film recalls the Cary Grant-Myrna Loy comedy *Mr Blandings Builds His Dream House*, only without the laughs, as the string of setbacks that beset this couple are staged to arouse the anger of any viewer who has ever applied for a mortgage, sought planning permission or been ripped off by cowboy builders.

Brian Vriends *Dave Dodd* • Doris Younane *Tina Dodd* • Bruce Venables *George Shooks* • Andrew Gilbert [Andrew S Gilbert] *Kevin Grant* • Paul Coolahan *Jack Napper* ■ *Dir/Scr* Bill Bennett

Moscow Distrusts Tears ★★★

Romantic comedy drama
1979 · USSR · Colour · 147mins

A surprise winner of the Oscar for best foreign film, Vladimir Menshov's "that was then, this is now" melodrama harks back to the ensemble "women's pictures" made in Hollywood in the fifties. Beginning in a Moscow factory hostel in the Khrushchev era, the action jumps forward 20 years to see how socially ambitious Irina Muravyova, conservative Raisa Ryazanova and ditzy Vera Alentova made out. Despite the broken marriages, illegitimate births, compromises and disappointments, the trio remain inseparable. For all the energetic performances and politicised setting, however, there's nothing remarkable about the characters or their situations. In Russian with English subtitles.

Vera Alentova *Katya* • Alexei Batalov *Goscha* • Irina Muravyova *Ludmilla* • Raisa Ryazanova *Antonia* • Yuri Vasilyev *Rudolf* ■ *Dir* Vladimir Menshov • *Scr* Valentin Chernykh

Moscow Nights ★★

Drama 1935 · UK · BW · 100mins

The daughter of impoverished Russian aristocrats (a colourless Penelope Dudley-Ward), forced into marriage with a boorish but wealthy tradesman (Harry Baur), really loves a handsome army officer (Laurence Olivier). In debt to her husband after losing a card game, the officer's efforts to pay up lead him into the spy game and a charge of treason. Directed by Anthony Asquith, this tangled and creaky brouhaha offers good performances from Olivier and the splendid French actor Baur, repeating the role he played in the French version of the same tale made one year earlier. For all that, the movie is curiously uninteresting.

Harry Baur *Brioukow* • Laurence Olivier *Capt Ignatoff* • Penelope Dudley Ward *Natasha* • Robert Cochran *Polonsky* • Morton Selten *Kovrin* • Athene Seyler *Mme Sabline* ■ *Dir* Anthony Asquith • *Scr* Anthony Asquith, Erich Seipmann, from the novel *Les Nuits de Moscou* by Pierre Benoit

Moscow on the Hudson ★★★ 🔞

Comedy drama 1984 · US · Colour · 112mins

There's a gentle, sweet-natured core to Robin Williams's screen personality that is too often camouflaged by the hysteria that forms the basis of his performances. This rather melancholy comedy lets that attractive side surface to good effect, with Williams playing a Soviet circus musician who defects while shopping in New York. He then finds, once he's part of the immigrant experience, that life is as racist and rancid as back home, with freedom as a meagre bonus. Director Paul Mazursky gallops off in too many directions at once, but Williams's performance is a real treat. Contains swearing, violence and nudity. ▭

Robin Williams *Vladimir Ivanoff* • Maria Conchita Alonso *Lucia Lombardo* • Cleavant Derricks *Lionel Witherspoon* • Alejandro Rey *Orlando Ramirez* • Savely Kramarov *Boris* • Oleg Rudnik *Yury* ■ *Dir* Paul Mazursky • *Scr* Paul Mazursky, Leon Capetanos

Moses ★★ 🔞

Biblical epic 1975 · UK/It · Colour · 135mins

Burt Lancaster does everything you'd expect as Moses: he orders up plagues, leads his people out of Egypt, parts the Red Sea, climbs Mount Sinai and comes back down with the Ten Commandments. This Lew Grade production was originally a six-hour mini-series, partly written by Anthony Burgess; the latter also composed his own music score, but it was rejected in favour of one from Ennio Morricone. However, where Cecil DeMille's 1956 version was a ponderous but occasionally juicy religious epic, this is more of a dreary historical drama that breaks the 11th commandment: "Thou Shalt Not Bore." ▭

Burt Lancaster *Moses* • Anthony Quayle *Aaron* • Ingrid Thulin *Miriam* • Irene Papas *Zipporah* • Mariangela Melato *Princess Bithia* • William Lancaster *Young Moses* ■ *Dir* Gianfranco de Bosio • *Scr* Anthony Burgess, Victorio Bonicelli, Gianfranco de Bosio

Mosquito ★★

Science-fiction horror
1995 · US · Colour · 92mins

If you ever wondered what Leatherface, the killing machine from *The Texas Chain Saw Massacre*, really looked like behind that mask, then here's your chance, as Gunnar Hansen does battle with a swarm of pesky mozzies that have mutated into insects the size of a Spitfire. A throwback to such fifties sci-fi B-movies as *Them!*, Gary Jones's bargain-basement schlocker is clearly aimed at the seven-pints-and-a-takeaway market, and has enough gore, cheapo effects and wincingly bad dialogue to amuse down to the last mouthful. Seekers of truth and beauty

should look elsewhere. Contains violence and swearing.

Gunnar Hansen *Earl* • Ron Asheton *Hendricks* • Steve Dixon *Parks* ■ *Dir* Gary Jones • *Scr* Steve Hodge, Tom Chaney, Gary Jones, from a story by Gary Jones

The Mosquito Coast
★★★★ PG

Drama   1986 · US · Colour · 113mins

Harrison Ford is usually cast as a straight as an arrow, regular guy. However, this absorbing journey into the heart of darkness provided him with probably the most unsympathetic character of his film career. Ford plays an idealistic, obsessive inventor who begins a slow slide into madness when he moves his family to Central America in a doomed attempt to bring ice to the jungle. Paul Schrader intelligently adapts Paul Theroux's source novel and, if director Peter Weir loses his way a little, the performances are uniformly superb. Ford is surprisingly convincing as the outwardly charming control freak, while River Phoenix gives a portrayal beyond his years as his troubled son. Contains some mild violence. [CC]

Harrison Ford *Allie Fox* • Helen Mirren *Mother* • River Phoenix *Charlie* • Jadrien Steele *Jerry* • Hilary Gordon *April* • Rebecca Gordon *Clover* • Jason Alexander *Clerk* • Martha Plimpton *Emily Spellgood* ■ *Dir* Peter Weir • *Scr* Paul Schrader, from the novel by Paul Theroux

Mosquito Squadron
★★ U

Second World War adventure
1968 · UK · Colour · 86mins

What do you do when the Nazis' top secret weapon is being developed in the same building as some of your own captured comrades? Invent an even more secret weapon, of course, and use it to win the day. Hurrah! David McCallum heads a cast of familiar faces you can't quite put a name to, as our intrepid fliers try out the bouncing bomb that they hope will destroy the V3 rocket, an even more explosive successor to the V2. McCallum makes light of his awful name (Quint Munroe), but only the typically mellifluous support of Charles Gray passes muster. [CC]

David McCallum *Quint Munroe* • Suzanne Neve *Beth Scott* • David Buck *Squadron Leader David Scott* • David Dundas *Flight Lieutenant Douglas Shelton* • Dinsdale Landen *Wing Commander Penrose* • Charles Gray *Air Commodore Hufford* • Michael Anthony *Father Bellague* ■ *Dir* Boris Sagal • *Scr* Donald S Sanford, Joyce Perry

Moss Rose
★★

Period detective drama
1947 · US · BW · 81mins

Who is murdering Victor Mature's lovers and leaving behind the clue of a bible marked with a dried moss rose? No prizes for guessing in a pleasant murder mystery which drew Vincent Price's Fox contract to a close. He plays the sly detective in charge of the cryptic case, proving he could be just as convincing on the right side of the law as he would soon be on the wrong. Mature isn't interesting or enigmatic enough in this muddled whodunit, but solid trouping by a good supporting cast gives it a much needed lift.

Peggy Cummins *Belle Adair* • Victor Mature *Sir Alexander Sterling* • Ethel Barrymore *Lady Sterling* • Vincent Price *Inspector Clinner* • Margo Woode *Daisy Arrow* • George Zucco *Craxton* • Patricia Medina *Audrey Ashton* • Felippa Rock *Liza* ■ *Dir* Gregory Ratoff • *Scr* Jules Furthman, Tom Reed, Niven Busch, from the novel by Joseph Shearing

The Most Dangerous Man Alive
★

Science-fiction   1961 · US · Colour · 80mins

Escaped convict Ron Randell is accidentally exposed to radiation by a cobalt bomb explosion and becomes an unstoppable superman, hell-bent on revenge against the gangsters who framed him. The last film directed by silent pioneer Allan Dwan is an over-familiar, poverty-row mix of science-fiction thriller and mob melodrama, with only the halting exploration of Randell's post-holocaust sex life adding spin to the proceedings.

Ron Randell *Eddie Candell* • Debra Paget *Linda Marlow* • Elaine Stewart *Carla Angelo* • Anthony Caruso *Andy Damron* • Gregg Palmer *Lt Fisher* ■ *Dir* Allan Dwan • *Scr* James Leicester, Phillip Rock, from the story *The Steel Monster* by Michael Pate, Phillip Rock

The Most Desired Man
★★★ 18

Romantic comedy
1994 · Ger · Colour · 90mins

Highly rated by those who know their German movies, *The Most Desired Man* is proof that the phrase "German comedy" isn't always an oxymoron. The film concerns a heterosexual man and incorrigible womaniser who, having been booted out of his girlfriend's flat, moves in with a gay friend. When the girlfriend discovers she's pregnant, she sets out to get him back, ignorant of the circle he now moves in. The German title is *Der Bewegte Mann*, which sounds better somehow. In German with English subtitles. [CC]

Til Schweiger *Axel Feldheim* • Katja Riemann *Doro Feldheim* • Joachim Król *Norbert Brommer* • Antonia Lang *Elke Schmitt* ■ *Dir* Sönke Wortmann • *Scr* Sönke Wortmann, from the comic books *Der Bewegte Mann* and *Pretty Baby* by Ralf König

The Most Terrible Time in My Life
★★

Detective drama   1993 · Jap · BW · 92mins

Neither *Circus Boys* director Kaizo Hayashi nor actor Masatoshi Nagase, best known here for his roles in Jim Jarmusch's *Mystery Train* and Fridrik Thor Fridrikson's Jarmusch-like *Cold Fever*, come close to reproducing their best work in this Japanese crime comedy, a yakuza spoof that is simply too knowing for its own good. Hayashi is too intent on pace and pastiche to make the plot intelligible, while the flashy camerawork is dizzying rather than dazzling. Indeed, the director is so pleased with his efforts that he even tacks on a cod trailer for Nagase's return as private eye Maiku Hama (get it?). In Japanese with English subtitles. Contains violence.

Masatoshi Nagase *Maiku Hama* • Shiro Sano *Kanno* • Kiyotaka Nanbara *Hoshino* • Yang Haitin *Yang Hai Tin* • Hou De Jian *De Jian* •

Akaji Maro *Lt Nakayama* • Shinya Tsukamoto *Yamaguchi* ■ *Dir* Kaizo Hayashi • *Scr* Daisuke Tengan, Kaizo Hayashi

Most Wanted
★★★ 15

Action adventure   1997 · US · Colour · 94mins

In the conspiracy thriller stakes, this is minor league stuff, but very entertaining nonetheless. In a more serious role than usual, writer/star Keenen Ivory Wayans plays a former army sniper recruited into a shadowy government organisation, only to find himself framed for the murder of the First Lady. The political machinations don't bear close scrutiny, but director David Glenn Hogan stages some immaculate action set pieces and the cast is top quality, with Jon Voight staging a dress rehearsal for his role in *Enemy of the State*. Contains some swearing and violence. [CC] *DVD*

Keenen Ivory Wayans *James Dunn* • Jon Voight *Casey/General Woodward* • Jill Hennessy *Dr Victoria Constantini* • Paul Sorvino *CIA Deputy Director Kenny Rackmill* • Robert Culp *Donald Bickhart* ■ *Dir* David Glenn Hogan [David Hogan] • *Scr* Keenen Ivory Wayans

Mother
★★★★★

Silent drama   1926 · USSR · BW · 106mins

Vsevolod Pudovkin's first feature is one of the classics of the golden age of Russian cinema. The tightly constructed narrative, adapted from Maxim Gorky's rambling novel, concerns a mother (the extraordinary Vera Baranovskaya) who, at the time of the abortive revolution of 1905, accidentally gives up her communist son to the police. The superb cast is made up of members of the Moscow Arts Theatre, with Pudovkin himself playing the interrogating officer. By an ingenious juxtaposition of images, the director has managed to create an illusion of sound, and the emotional impact has not diminished with time.

Vera Baranovskaya *Pelageya Vlasova, the mother* • A Tchistyakova *Vlasov, her husband* • Nikolai Batalov *Pavel, her son* • Vsevolod I Pudovkin *Police officer* ■ *Dir* Vsevolod I Pudovkin • *Scr* Nathan Zarkhi, Vsevolod Pudovkin, from the novel *Mat* by Maxim Gorky

Mother
★

Horror   1995 · US · Colour · 90 mins.

In his first two movies, *Fear No Evil* and *Lady in White*, director Frank LaLoggia revealed a flair for horror and the ability to evoke a tangible sense of unease from pretty standard fear fare. None of those gifts are on show in this dire psycho-thriller, with the accent on *Psycho*. A doting mother (Diane Ladd) murders any relatives, friends or neighbours who suggest to her son (Morgan Weisser) that it's time for him to leave home and make his own way in the world. Limp slaughter matches the lame script in a forgettable bust from a one-time horror hopeful.

Diane Ladd *Olivia Hendrix* • Olympia Dukakis *Mrs Jay* • Morgan Weisser *Tom* • Ele Keats *Audrey* • Matt Clark *Ben Wilson* ■ *Dir* Frank LaLoggia • *Scr* Michael Angelella

Mother
★★★ 12

Comedy   1996 · US · Colour · 103mins

Albert Brooks writes, directs and stars in this uneven but intermittently hilarious ode to mothers. He plays a writer who returns to his childhood home when his relationship and career go down the pan, only to be driven over the edge by his mom (hilariously played by Debbie Reynolds) and her sly, sarcastic comments. Brooks gives a nice performance, while the cast includes *Northern Exposure*'s Rob Morrow and Lisa Kudrow from *Friends*. But this is Reynolds's film. Making the most of a terrific part, she steals every scene she's in.

Albert Brooks *John Henderson* • Debbie Reynolds *Beatrice Henderson* • Rob Morrow *Jeff* • Lisa Kudrow *Linda* • John C McGinley *Carl* • Paul Collins *Lawyer* • Laura Weekes *Karen Henderson* ■ *Dir* Albert Brooks • *Scr* Albert Brooks, Monica Johnson

Mother and Son
★★★★ U

Drama   1997 · Ger/Rus · Colour · 70mins

The agony of seeing a loved one draw close to death is presented in such intimate detail in this meticulous Russian drama, that watching it feels like an intrusion on the grief of the ailing mother and her devoted son. Considering neither Gudrun Geyer nor Alexei Ananishnov are professionals, they give performances of remarkable power and simplicity as they explore their mutual dependence. Rarely has silence been so poignant as director Alexander Sokurov fashions images that draw as heavily on the romantic art of Caspar David Friedrich as they do on the cinema of Vsevolod Pudovkin and Andrei Tarkovsky. Intense, moving and memorable. In Russian with English subtitles.

Gudrun Geyer *Mother* • Alexei Ananishnov *Son* ■ *Dir* Alexander Sokurov • *Scr* Yuri Arabov

Mother Goose Rock 'n' Rhyme
★★ U

Musical fantasy   1990 · US · Colour · 77mins

This is a delightful, imaginative family TV movie, especially for younger viewers, which is populated by an all-star cast, including Shelley Duvall, Jean Stapleton, Teri Garr and pop star Cyndi Lauper. In this contemporary musical based on the well-known nursery rhymes, Mother Goose's son, Gordon Goose, teams up with Little Bo Peep and travels through Rhymeland in search of his missing mum. This is really for the little ones, but adults will be entertained too, thanks to the talented cast. [CC]

Shelley Duvall *Little Bo Peep* • Jean Stapleton *Mother Goose* • Teri Garr *Jill* • Art Garfunkel *Bartender* • Garry Shandling *Jack* • Elayne Boosler *Mother Hubbard* • Cyndi Lauper *Mary* • Paul Simon *Simple Simon* • Dan Gilroy *Gordon Goose* • Jeff Stein • *Scr* Mark Curtiss, Rod Ash, from a story by Hilary Hinkle, Linda Engelsiepen

Mother India
★★★★ U

Drama   1957 · Ind · Colour · 159mins

Regarded by some as Bollywood's *Gone with the Wind*, Mehboob Khan's colour remake of his 1940 film, *Aurat*, alters the original storyline by having the heartbroken mother win the

support of her neighbours instead of suffering in isolation, thus becoming a symbol of national pain and perseverance. Recalling the rural lyricism of the great Soviet director, Alexander Dovzhenko, the action is told as an extended flashback, as Nargis remembers the hardships that ultimately drove her to kill her own rebellious son, Sunil Dutt (Nargis's future husband). Sacrificing realism for epic spectacle, the film was nominated for the best foreign film Oscar. In Hindi with English subtitles.

Nargis *Radha* • Sunil Dutt *Birju* • Rajendra Kumar *Ramu* • Raaj Kumar *Shamoo* ■ *Dir* Mehboob Khan • *Scr* S Ali Raza, Vajahat Mirza, Mehboob Khan

Mother Is a Freshman ★★★
Comedy   1949 · US · Colour · 81mins

An utterly charming Loretta Young vehicle, with a very silly plot but so ravishingly filmed in that rich and garish forties Technicolor that it hardly matters if mother Loretta or daughter Betty Lynn ends up with charmer Van Johnson. Veteran director Lloyd Bacon, responsible for *42nd Street*, just lets the laughs fall where they may, and there's a nice supporting turn from the one-time king of the megaphone, former heart-throb Rudy Vallee.

Loretta Young *Abigail "Abby" Fortitude Abbott* • Van Johnson *Professor Richard Michaels* • Rudy Vallee *John Heaslip* • Barbara Lawrence *Louise Sharpe* • Robert Arthur *Beaumont Jackson* • Betty Lynn *Susan Abbott* ■ *Dir* Lloyd Bacon • *Scr* Mary Loos, Richard Sale, from a story by Raphael Blau

Mother, Jugs & Speed ★★★ 15
Black comedy   1976 · US · Colour · 98mins

Guess who's who in the title roles as Bill Cosby, Harvey Keitel and Raquel Welch charge around as private ambulance drivers in this dark comedy with slapstick moments from *Bullitt* director Peter Yates. The cast acquits itself well, and there's an especially funny pre-JR Larry Hagman playing a randy driver, but the whole enterprise really comes to a halt thanks to the lack of narrative. It's a fun ride while it lasts, though definitely not for fans of *Casualty*. Contains some violence, swearing and drug abuse.

Bill Cosby *Mother* • Raquel Welch *Jugs* • Harvey Keitel *Speed* • Allen Garfield *Harry Fishbine* • LQ Jones *Davey* • Bruce Davison *Leroy* • Dick Butkus *Rodeo* • Larry Hagman *Murdoch* ■ *Dir* Peter Yates • *Scr* Tom Mankiewicz, from a story by Stephen Manes, Tom Mankiewicz

Mother Küsters Goes to Heaven ★★★★
Drama   1975 · W Ger · Colour · 108mins

Banned from the Berlin Film Festival for its scathing exposé of the self-seeking agendas of both political activists and the press, Rainer Werner Fassbinder's bitterly ironic fable was filmed in a remarkable 20 days. Widowed after her working-class husband kills both his boss and himself, Brigitte Mira is cast into isolation before being besieged by new exploitative "friends". That she emerges having discovered both herself and her fate owes much to

Mira's astute performance and to Fassbinder's world-weary cynicism. In German with English subtitles.

Brigitte Mira *Mother Küsters* • Ingrid Caven *Corinna Corinne* • Armin Meier *Ernst* • Irm Hermann *Helene* • Gottfried John *Journalist* • Karlheinz Böhm *Thalmann* • Margit Carstensen *Mrs Thalmann* ■ *Dir* Rainer Werner Fassbinder • *Scr* Rainer Werner Fassbinder, Kurt Raab, from a story by Heinrich Zille

Mother Lode ★★ PG
Adventure   1982 · US · Colour · 98mins

Kim Basinger and Nick Mancuso fly into the Canadian wilderness in the hope of finding gold. But all they find is Charlton Heston, a wild man of the forest with a weird Scottish accent and a twin brother. Written and produced by Chuck's son, Fraser, and financed outside the studio system, this is almost a Heston home movie; what drew them to make it, however, remains buried underground. The usual things happen – Basinger and Mancuso's plane crashes on landing, leaving them stranded – but there's little to enjoy here except some spectacular scenery.

Charlton Heston *Silas McGee/Ian McGee* • Nick Mancuso *Jean Dupre* • Kim Basinger *Andrea Spalding* • John Marley *Elijah* • Dale Wilson *Gerard Elliot* • Ricky Zantolas *George Patterson* ■ *Dir* Charlton Heston • *Scr* Fraser Clarke Heston

Mother Night ★★★ 15
Historical drama
1996 · US · Colour and BW · 109mins

Kurt Vonnegut's source novel about a Nazi war criminal – a sort of Lord Haw-Haw figure – standing trial in Israel, whose memoirs claim he was in fact an American spy, proves a hard nut to crack. It's a diffuse story told in flashback that stretches over five decades and also deals with racism in Harlem in the fifties. Director Keith Gordon's film is brave and ambitious but not completely successful, though Nick Nolte is excellent in an especially demanding central role, and there is strong support from John Goodman and Alan Arkin.

Nick Nolte *Howard Campbell* • Sheryl Lee *Helga Noth/Resi Noth* • Alan Arkin *George Kraft* • John Goodman *Major Frank Wirtanen* • Kirsten Dunst *Young Resi Noth* • Arye Gross *Abraham Epstein* ■ *Dir* Keith Gordon • *Scr* Robert B Weide, from the novel by Kurt Vonnegut Jr

Mother of the Bride ★★
Comedy   1993 · US · Colour · 74mins

This fitfully amusing TV movie concludes the sprightly trilogy that saw Rue McClanahan first defy her disapproving kids and marry a younger man, and then have another baby. Now it's tetchy daughter Kristy McNichol's turn to tie the knot, but just as the big day dawns her long-lost father (Paul Dooley) turns up after 20 years to throw the whole family into turmoil. A little more strained than its predecessors, this is closer to your typical domestic melodrama, with angst, tears and soul-searching replacing the wry humour that made the earlier instalments such fun.

Rue McClanahan *Margret Becker* • Kristy McNichol *Mary Becker* • Ted Shackelford *John Hix* • Anne Bobby *Anne Becker* • Paul Dooley *Richard Becker* • Conor O'Farrell *Andrew Becker* ■ *Dir* Charles Correll • *Scr* Bart Baker

Mother Wore Tights ★★★ U
Musical   1947 · US · Colour · 106mins

An immensely popular Betty Grable musical, in which she's teamed with the likeable and talented Dan Dailey as 20th Century-Fox tells the story of the early days of vaudeville in garish Technicolor. Neither clever nor sophisticated, this effortlessly whiles away the time. It also has the benefit of a superb Oscar-winning Alfred Newman/Charles Henderson score, and contains a rare opportunity to see the great ventriloquist Senor Wences on celluloid. The story itself, however, which is held together by off-screen narration from Anne Baxter, rambles rather and lacks any real climax.

Betty Grable *Myrtle McKinley Burt* • Dan Dailey *Frank Burt* • Mona Freeman *Iris Burt* • Connie Marshall *Mikie Burt* • Vanessa Brown *Bessie* • Robert Arthur *Bob Clarkman* • Sara Allgood *Grandmother McKinley* • William Frawley *Mr Schneider* • Anne Baxter *Narrator* ■ *Dir* Walter Lang • *Scr* Lamar Trotti, from the novel by Miriam Young

Motherhood ★★★ 15
Black comedy   1993 · US · Colour · 86mins

There's equal parts gore and guffaw in this spirited horror romp, notable for a cast that includes the cream of America's wackier character actors. Tombstone-toothed Steve Buscemi plays a mummy's boy who'll do anything to bring his dearly departed back from the dead. Trouble is, anything works and back mum comes. But now she's dead different, her new appetite for insects being a particular bugbear. John Glover, Ned Beatty and Miriam Margolyes join in the fun.

Steve Buscemi *Ed Chilton* • Miriam Margolyes *Mother* • Ned Beatty *Uncle Benny* • John Glover *AJ Pattie* • Sam Jenkins *Storm Reynolds* ■ *Dir* Jonathan Wacks • *Scr* Chuck Hughes

Mother's Boys ★★ 15
Thriller   1993 · US · Colour · 91mins

After the mistress, nanny and teenager from hell, it was inevitable that sooner or later we would get around to psycho-mums. Jamie Lee Curtis is the disturbed ex-wife of Peter Gallagher, and she doesn't like the way his new partner, Joanne Whalley-Kilmer, has taken over her former role. Curtis, who made her name as a teen scream queen in *Halloween*, relishes the chance to do a bit of stalking herself, and there is also dignified support from Vanessa Redgrave. Yves Simoneau's direction is competent, but it's not really nasty enough to please ardent chiller fans and the ending is daft. Contains swearing, violence and brief nudity.

Jamie Lee Curtis *Jude* • Peter Gallagher *Robert* • Joanne Whalley-Kilmer [Joanne Whalley] *Callie* • Vanessa Redgrave *Lydia* • Luke Edwards *Kes* • Colin Ward *Michael* • Joey Zimmerman *Ben* • Joss Ackland *Lansing* • Paul Guilfoyle *Mark Kaplan* ■ *Dir* Yves Simoneau • *Scr* Barry Schneider, Richard Hawley, from the novel by Bernard Taylor

Mother's Day on Waltons Mountain ★★
Drama   1982 · US · Colour · 97mins

The syrupy, homespun wisdom of the much-loved Depression-set TV series *The Waltons* has been a regular Sunday morning fixture on Channel 4, and fans will no doubt look forward to this feature-length spin-off. Grandpa and grandma have gone, as has John Boy, but nearly everyone else is present and correct, including mum Michael Learned, who had bowed out of the TV series before its conclusion in 1981. Here she leaves her sick bed in a TB sanitarium when Mary Ellen is injured on her honeymoon. Treacly stuff, and the absence of Richard Thomas as John Boy is keenly felt.

Ralph Waite *John Walton* • Michael Learned *Olivia Walton* • Jon Walmsley *Jason Walton* • Judy Norton-Taylor *Mary Ellen Walton* • Mary Beth McDonough *Erin Walton* • Eric Scott *Ben Walton* • David W Harper *Jim-Bob Walton* • Kami Cotler *Elizabeth Walton* ■ *Dir* Gwen Arner • *Scr* Juliet Packer

Mothra ★★★
Science-fiction   1962 · Jap · Colour · 90mins

This introduction to one of Japan's most famous radioactive monsters was one of Toho Studios' best efforts, boasting colourful photography, a more ambitious story and good special effects. Surprisingly, Mothra here stays in egg or caterpillar form for most of the movie before finally growing wings, leaving less time than usual for monster mayhem. Much of the movie instead concerns Mothra's guardians – two tiny twin girls – and the greedy businessman who covets them. This is cute, though a sober reminder of the increased campiness that would later give the genre a bad name. Japanese dialogue dubbed into English.

Frankie Sakai *Reporter* • Hiroshi Koizumi *Photographer* • Kyoko Kagawa *Showman* • Emi Ito *Twin* • Yumi Ito *Twin* ■ *Dir* Inoshiro Honda • *Scr* Shinichi Sekizawa, Robert Myerson (English dialogue), from a story by Shinichiro Nakamura, Takehiko Fukunaga, Yoshie Hotta

Motor Psycho ★★ 18
Crime drama   1965 · US · BW · 72mins

In this slightly more tasteful companion to sexploitation director Russ Meyer's legendary *Faster, Pussycat! Kill! Kill!*, a three-man gang of bikers led by deranged Vietnam veteran Stephen Oliver bring terror, rape and mayhem to a small town. Country vet Alex Rocco teams up with Meyer regular Haji to take revenge on the hoodlums. Not as wild or as sordid as your typical Meyer melodrama, this homage to *The Wild One* is one of the mammary maestro's less memorable offerings. Contains violence, sexual situations and some swearing.

Haji *Ruby Bonner* • Alex Rocco *Cory Maddox* • Stephen Oliver *Brahmin* • Holle K Winters *Gail Maddox* • Joseph Cellini *Dante* ■ *Dir* Russ Meyer • *Scr* William E Sprague, Russ Meyer, from a story by Russ Meyer, James Griffith, Hal Hopper • *Cinematographer* Russ Meyer

Motorcycle Gang ★

Drama   1957 · US · BW · 77mins

Four years after Marlon Brando terrorised a town in *The Wild One*, this film breezed into drive-in cinemas, double-billed with Roger Corman's *Sorority Girl*. Compared to the Brando picture, this is a pink Lambretta with a puncture – a daft, woodenly acted and underwritten saga about teenagers and a police-organised bikers' club. A town gets trashed, the jails fill up and the girls look vacant. Jack Nicholson isn't in it, Corman didn't direct it and you probably won't watch it to the end. Contains violence and swearing.

Anne Neyland *Terry* • Steven Terrell *Randy* • John Ashley *Nick* • Carl Switzer *Speed* • Raymond Hatton *Uncle Ed* • Russ Bender *Joe* • Jean Moorhead *Marilyn* ■ *Dir* Edward L Cahn • *Scr* Lou Rusoff

Motorcycle Gang ★★★ 18

Action drama   1994 · US · Colour · 80mins

Director John Milius relaxes and keeps his tongue firmly in his cheek with this slight but affectionate biker tale, part of *The Young and the Restless* series of remakes of classic drive-in movies from the fifties. Jake Busey (looking and sounding uncannily like Gary) is the leader of a gang of bikers who torment Gerald McRaney's family as they make their way to California to start a new life. Milius stays pretty faithful to the original blueprint, right down to the uplifting moral messages, but throws in a bit more nastiness than the original director, Edward L Cahn, was allowed to include. Contains violence and swearing.

Gerald McRaney *Cal* • Elan Oberon *Jean* • Carla Gugino *Leann* • Jake Busey *Sonny* • Richard Edson *Volker* • John Cassini *Crab* • Pete Antico *Road pig* ■ *Dir* John Milius • *Scr* Kent Anderson, Laurie McQuillan, from a story by Laurie McQuillan

Mouchette ★★★★

Tragedy   1966 · Fr · BW · 81mins

Bresson's intense, typically pared-down study of a Provençal village girl who's a bit like the donkey hero of Bresson's previous film, *Au Hasard, Balthazar*. Poor backward Mouchette is systematically abused, exploited and ignored; with nothing to live for, she quietly drowns herself. That, of course, is her liberation and a sacrifice with powerful religious connotations. Bresson's admirers regard this as one of his greatest masterpieces, but beware: film critic Pauline Kael once suggested seeing a Bresson film is "like taking a whipping and watching every stroke coming". In French with English subtitles.

Nadine Nortier *Mouchette* • Marie Cardinal *Mother* • Paul Hébert *Father* • Jean Vimenet *Mathieu* • Jean-Claude Guilbert *Arsène* ■ *Dir* Robert Bresson • *Scr* Robert Bresson, from the novel *Nouvelle Histoire de Mouchette* by Georges Bernanos

Moulin Rouge ★★

Silent melodrama   1928 · UK · BW

Using German production facilities and creative personnel and opening with a long portrait of Paris by night, this silent drama – one of the costliest ever made in Britain – turns into a melodrama about a stripper whose aristocratic boyfriend plans to marry her own daughter, then decides to kill himself in his racing car. The film was was heavily cut between its European and American premieres; when the original version was restored, it was given a jazz soundtrack specially composed by Mike Westbrook and performed by the Matrix Ensemble.

Olga Tschechowa *Parysia* • Eve Grey *Margaret, her daughter* • Jean Bradin *Andre* • Georges Treville *Father* ■ *Dir/Scr* EA Dupont

Moulin Rouge ★★★★ PG

Biographical drama
1952 · US/UK · Colour · 114mins

The first 20 minutes of this movie are truly exhilarating, with cancan dancers, amazing lookalike re-creations of period characters and a magnificent sense of the vibrancy of 1880s Paris. This segment is one of director John Huston's finest achievements, and rightly helped the film win its Oscars for best art direction and best costume design. The film then goes on to tell the morbid tale of artist Henri de Toulouse-Lautrec, memorably played by José Ferrer, much of it on his knees (though a dwarf was used for some long shots). Ferrer is brilliant, seeking not a shred of sympathy as he fleshes out the disabled artist's weaknesses. The women in his life are particularly well cast, notably an unusually credible Zsa Zsa Gabor as Jane Avril, but the real co-star is Georges Auric's lovely main theme, recorded by both Percy Faith and Mantovani.

José Ferrer *Henri de Toulouse-Lautrec/Comte de Toulouse-Lautrec* • Colette Marchand *Marie Charlet* • Suzanne Flon *Myriamme Hayem* • Zsa Zsa Gabor *Jane Avril* • Katherine Kath *La Goulue* • Claude Nollier *Countess de Toulouse-Lautrec* ■ *Dir* John Huston • *Scr* Anthony Veiller, John Huston, from the novel by Pierre La Mure • *Cinematographer* Oswald Morris • *Art Director* Paul Sheriff, Marcel Vertes • *Costume Designer* Marcel Vertes

The Mountain ★★★ U

Drama   1956 · US · Colour · 104mins

When a plane crashes on top of a mountain, vile wastrel Robert Wagner plans to loot it with the help of his older brother, Spencer Tracy. What follows is a well-made, heavily symbolic drama about greed and the nature of heroism, further complicated by the fact that one person survives the plane crash. The survivor, an Indian girl, is played by Anna Kashfi, who was chosen for the part because she was skinny, and therefore less of a burden for Tracy to carry down the mountain. Shortly afterwards Kashfi became Mrs Marlon Brando, though the marriage was short-lived.

Spencer Tracy *Zachary Teller* • Robert Wagner *Chris Teller* • Claire Trevor *Marie* • William Demarest *Father Belacchi* • Barbara Darrow *Simone* • Richard Arlen *Rivial* • EG Marshall *Solange* • Anna Kashfi *Hindu girl* ■ *Dir* Edward Dmytryk • *Scr* Ranald MacDougall, from the novel by Henri Troyat

Mountain Family Robinson ★★ Uc

Adventure   1979 · US · Colour · 95mins

Updated spin on the *Swiss Family Robinson* story, about a couple with kids who've swapped big-city crime and grime for a back-to-nature life in the spectacular Rocky Mountains. Predictably, they discover mountain life also has its ups and downs, just different ones. Corny but fun family film, the third in a series.

Robert Logan *Skip* • Susan Damante Shaw *Pat* • Heather Rattray *Jenny* • Ham Larsen *Toby* ■ *Dir* John Cotter • *Scr* Arthur R Dubs

The Mountain Men ★★ 15

Period adventure 1980 · US · Colour · 95mins

Charlton Heston and Brian Keith play fur trappers hounded by Indians in the 1830s in this Disney-style wilderness adventure, albeit with considerably more violence. The script is by Heston's son, Fraser, who apparently lived with Alaskan Indians as a "part-time 20th-century mountain man". Yet the story also chimes with Heston's public political posturings on the freedom of the individual and the right to bear arms (and chest). Nice scenery, but Richard Lang's western is not a patch on *Jeremiah Johnson*.

Charlton Heston *Bill Tyler* • Brian Keith *Henry Frapp* • Victoria Racimo *Running Moon* • Stephen Macht *Heavy Eagle* • John Glover *Nathan Wyeth* • Seymour Cassel *La Bont* • David Ackroyd *Medicine Wolf* ■ *Dir* Richard Lang • *Scr* Fraser Clarke Heston

The Mountain Road ★★ U

Second World War drama
1960 · US · BW · 102mins

The great James Stewart is always worth watching, but even he could be defeated by weak material and feeble direction. Although he does what he can here, this overlong war drama set in a very Hollywood-backlot China as the Second World War nears its end remains one of his weaker vehicles. Director Daniel Mann was strong on theatrical adaptations (*Butterfield 8*) and comedy (*Our Man Flint*), but has problems with the tone here, and Stewart looks uncomfortable throughout. A stronger supporting cast and colour might have helped.

James Stewart *Major Baldwin* • Lisa Lu *Madame Sue-Mei Hung* • Glenn Corbett *Collins* • Harry Morgan *Michaelson* • Frank Silvera *General Kwan* • James Best *Niergaard* ■ *Dir* Daniel Mann • *Scr* Alfred Hayes, from the novel by Theodore White

Mountains of the Moon ★★★ 15

Historical adventure
1989 · US · Colour · 129mins

Five Easy Pieces director Bob Rafelson is not perhaps the first film-maker you would associate with a tale of Victorian explorers bonding manfully in the search for the source of the Nile. Yet he turned this long-cherished project into a stirring, offbeat and often compelling adventure. Patrick Bergin as the adventurer Richard Burton and Iain Glen as the aristocratic John Hanning Speke are both excellent, and there are neat turns from Richard E Grant and Bernard Hill as Dr Livingstone. Contains violence and nudity.

Patrick Bergin *Richard Burton* • Iain Glen *John Hanning Speke* • Richard E Grant *Laurence Oliphant* • Fiona Shaw *Isabel Arundell* • John Savident *Lord Murchison* • James Villiers *Lord Oliphant* • Adrian Rawlins *Edward* • Peter Vaughan *Lord Houghton* • Delroy Lindo *Mabruki* • Bernard Hill *Dr Livingstone* ■ *Dir* Bob Rafelson • *Scr* William Harrison, Bob Rafelson, from the novel by William Harrison and the journals by Richard Burton, John Hanning Speke

Mourning Becomes Electra ★★★

Melodrama   1947 · US · BW · 159mins

A heavy-duty adaptation of Eugene O'Neill's Civil War play based on Aeschylus's *Oresteia*. It's an impressive but over-ambitious and terribly stagey attempt from director Dudley Nichols, best known as the screenwriter of such movie classics as *Stagecoach* and *For Whom the Bell Tolls*. Rosalind Russell is seriously miscast in the lead, having neither the range nor the intensity for Lavinia, and the mix 'n' match gathering of distinguished US and European thespians (Michael Redgrave, Katina Paxinou, Leo Genn, Kirk Douglas) doesn't gel, but there's no denying that, for Hollywood, getting this made at all ranked as a major achievement.

Rosalind Russell *Lavinia Mannon* • Michael Redgrave *Orin Mannon* • Raymond Massey *Ezra Mannon* • Katina Paxinou *Christine Mannon* • Leo Genn *Adam Brent* • Kirk Douglas *Peter Niles* • Nancy Coleman *Hazel Niles* • Henry Hull *Seth Beckwith* ■ *Dir* Dudley Nichols • *Scr* Dudley Nichols, from the play by Eugene O'Neill

The Mouse and His Child ★★ U

Animation   1977 · US · Colour · 80mins

Animation is at its best when propelled by imaginative action. But American animators Charles Swenson and Fred Wolf, perhaps worshipping at the shrine of British costume drama, overdo the chitchat in this feature-length cartoon about two toy mice and their attempts to become self-winding. There are some sequences which border on the lively, though, like the opening toyshop scene where the protagonists are introduced. The distinctive vocal intelligence of Peter Ustinov also freshens up the character of Manny the rat.

Peter Ustinov *Manny* • Cloris Leachman *Euterpe* • Sally Kellerman *Seal* • Andy Devine *Frog* • Alan Barzman *Mouse* • Marcy Swenson *Mouse child* ■ *Dir* Fred Wolf, Chuck Swenson [Charles Swenson] • *Scr* Carol Mon Pere, from the novel by Russell Hoban

The Mouse on the Moon ★★ U

Comedy   1963 · UK · Colour · 86mins

The combination of a witty Michael Pertwee script, the exuberant direction of Richard Lester and the unique talents of Margaret Rutherford would normally have been enough to guarantee comic gold. But, perhaps because Peter Sellers in a triple role was a hard act to follow, this sequel to *The Mouse That Roared* never gets off the ground – a not inconsiderable handicap since its topic is the space race. Once again the tiny duchy of Grand Fenwick takes on the superpowers, this time using a rocket fuelled by the local wine. Fitfully amusing, it wastes a splendid cast.

U = SUITABLE FOR ALL   Uc = SUITABLE FOR ALL, ESPECIALLY FOR YOUNG CHILDREN (VIDEO ONLY)   PG = PARENTAL GUIDANCE

Margaret Rutherford *The Grand Duchess Gloriana* • Ron Moody *Mountjoy* • Bernard Cribbins *Vincent* • David Kossoff *Kokintz* • Terry-Thomas *Spender* • June Ritchie *Cynthia* • John Le Mesurier *British delegate* ■ *Dir* Richard Lester • *Scr* Michael Pertwee, from the novel by Leonard Wibberley

The Mouse That Roared
★★★ U

Comedy　　　　1959 · UK · Colour · 79mins

Adapted from Leonard Wibberley's novel *The Wrath of Grapes*, this wry little comedy opens brightly, but quickly loses direction as its one joke is stretched to breaking point. The idea of a tiny country declaring war on America to benefit from aid in defeat is a lovely one, but not even Peter Sellers in three widely differing roles can compensate for the longueurs that occupy the film's final hour. Jean Seberg (whose next picture, Jean-Luc Godard's *A Bout de Souffle*, would make her an international star) is wasted in decorous support, along with David Kossoff and William Hartnell. ▣

Peter Sellers *Tully Bascombe/Grand Duchess Gloriana XII/PM Count Mountjoy* • Jean Seberg *Helen* • David Kossoff *Professor Kokintz* • William Hartnell *Will* • Leo McKern *Benter* • Macdonald Parke *Snippet* • Timothy Bateson *Roger* ■ *Dir* Jack Arnold • *Scr* Roger MacDougall, Stanley Mann, from the novel *The Wrath of Grapes* by Leonard Wibberley

Mousehunt
★★★★ PG

Comedy　　　　1997 · US · Colour · 93mins

An energetic and highly inventive comedy, as hapless brothers Nathan Lane and Lee Evans inherit a valuable old house but find it is already occupied by a pesky rodent. There's stacks of Laurel and Hardy-style visual comedy as the pair wreak havoc in their bid to rid themselves of the furry fiend, though adults may prefer Christopher Walken's hilarious turn as an exterminator to the more obvious sight gags. The darker touches might upset younger children and, with over 60 mice used for the animal stunts, the film is definitely not for viewers with a phobia of rodents. But for sheer verve, this family entertainment is hard to beat. Contains some swearing. ▣

Nathan Lane *Ernie Smuntz* • Lee Evans *Lars Smuntz* • Vicki Lewis *April Smuntz* • Maury Chaykin *Alexander Falko* • Eric Christmas *The Lawyer* • Christopher Walken *Caesar* • William Hickey *Rudolf Smuntz* ■ *Dir* Gore Verbinski • *Scr* Adam Rifkin

The Mouth Agape
★★★★

Drama　　　　1974 · Fr · Colour · 82mins

Director Maurice Pialat's first three features (of which this was the third) have been embraced as a loosely autobiographical trilogy. Shot in a series of intense long takes, this movingly natural drama explores the effect the news that she has terminal cancer has on 50-year-old Monique Mélinand's philandering husband and impotent son. Exploring the connection between sex and death and the inextricable bonds that somehow keep unhappy couples together, Pialat's analysis of physical and emotional pain is never moralistic or sentimental. In French with English subtitles.

Monique Mélinand *Mother* • Hubert Deschamps *Father* • Philippe Léotard *Philippe* • Nathalie Baye *Nathalie* ■ *Dir/Scr* Maurice Pialat

Mouth to Mouth
★★★

Black comedy thriller
1995 · Sp · Colour · 97mins

A screwball Spanish comedy about an actor (Javier Bardem) who, after a spell of unemployment, devotes his talent to a phone sex company. Unfortunately, his most regular callers are all male! When Aitana Sanchez-Gijon suggests a rendezvous, he jumps at the opportunity – and walks straight into a ploy to enrage her unfaithful husband. Director Manuel Gomez Pereira gives his Spanish peer Almodóvar a real run for his money with a compelling, cheeky and genuinely funny film that knocks spots off Spike Lee's American equivalent, *Girl 6*. In Spanish with English subtitles.

Javier Bardem *Victor Ventura* • Jose Maria Flotats *Ricardo/Bill* • Aitana Sanchez-Gijon *Amanda* • Maria Barranco *Angela* • Myriam Mezieres *Sheila* • Fernando Guillen-Cuervo *Raul* ■ *Dir* Manuel Gomez Pereira • *Scr* Manuel Gomez Pereira, Joaquin Oristrell, Juan Luis Iborra, Naomi Wise

Move Over, Darling
★★★★ U

Comedy　　　　1963 · US · Colour · 99mins

A Doris Day classic – a remake of 1940's *My Favorite Wife* – in which the seriously correct blonde stars as a woman who returns from a desert island to find that her husband James Garner has remarried. Providing perfect support for Day and Garner are Polly Bergen as the "other woman" and Chuck Connors as the hunk who was marooned with Day. Stealing the show, however, is the wonderful Thelma Ritter as Day's outspoken mother-in-law. Day's popularity suffered from the onset of the sexual revolution in the mid-sixties when her wholesome image seemed out of step with the time, but this film shows how her great talent has endured. Slick, utterly professional and without a wasted scene, this is sheer delight from start to finish. ▣

Doris Day *Ellen Wagstaff Arden* • James Garner *Nicholas Arden* • Polly Bergen *Bianca Steele Arden* • Chuck Connors *Stephen "Adam" Burkett* • Thelma Ritter *Grace Arden* • Fred Clark *Codd* • Don Knotts *Shoe salesman* ■ *Dir* Michael Gordon • *Scr* Hal Kanter, Jack Sher, from the film *My Favorite Wife* by Bella Spewack, Samuel Spewack, from a story by Leo McCarey, Samuel Spewack, Bella Spewack

Movers and Shakers
★ 15

Comedy　　　　1985 · US · Colour · 76mins

Charles Grodin is undoubtedly a superb comic actor who never really gets the material worthy of his talents. With this woeful comedy, however, he really only has himself to blame, as he wrote and co-produced it. A wonderful cast (Walter Matthau, Steve Martin, Gilda Radner, Vincent Gardenia) is reduced to mugging furiously in a supposedly satirical look at the movie business. Contains swearing. ▣

Walter Matthau *Joe Mulholland* • Charles Grodin *Herb Derman* • Vincent Gardenia *Saul Gritz* • Tyne Daly *Nancy Derman* • Steve

Martin *Fabio Longio* • Bill Macy *Sid Spokane* • Gilda Radner *Livia Machado* ■ *Dir* William Asher • *Scr* Charles Grodin

Movie Crazy
★★★ U

Comedy　　　　1932 · US · BW · 79mins

One of the great silent film clowns, Harold Lloyd was a master of physical comedy whose exploits delighted and thrilled early audiences. *Movie Crazy*, made later in his career, is undoubtably his best talkie. Lloyd plays Harold Hall, an unassuming type who yearns to be in the movies and gets his break when he meets starlet Mary Sears (Constance Cummings). The brilliant set pieces include the famous sequence in which Lloyd wears a magician's suit to a swanky ball, only to find it contains more than he bargained for. ▣

Harold Lloyd *Harold Hall* • Constance Cummings *Mary Sears* • Kenneth Thomson *Vance, a gentleman heavy* ■ *Dir* Clyde Bruckman • *Scr* Agnes Christine Johnston, John Grey, Felix Adler, Vincent Lawrence

Movie Movie
★★★ PG

Comedy 1978 · US · BW and Colour · 101mins

Stanley Donen's attempt to recapture the spirit of thirties double-bills is in the form of two B-movies – a boxing melodrama, *Dynamite Hands*, and a backstage musical, *Baxter's Beauties of 1933*. Donen even offers a trailer in the middle. It's a smart idea which all film buffs will warm to, even if the execution doesn't quite do justice to the concept. It was one of several movies at the time – such as *Nickelodeon* and *Silent Movie* – that cashed in on the perceived nostalgia for old movies, but all that *Movie Movie* inspired was some bad jokes from critics – "Lousy, Lousy", for instance. It's actually better than that and the musical sequence – as one would expect of Donen – has some delectable moments. ▣

George C Scott *Gloves Malloy/Spats Baxter* • Trish Van Devere *Betsy McGuire/Isobel Stewart* • Barbara Harris *Trixie Lane* ■ *Dir* Stanley Donen • *Scr* Larry Gelbart, Sheldon Keller

Moving
★ 15

Comedy　　　　1988 · US · Colour · 85mins

Director Alan Metter appears perfectly content to replace bona fide comedy with Richard Pryor's exaggerated racket in this lame suburban farce. Showing off is no substitute for acting, and letting Pryor roam free is a big mistake. Desperation sinks its jaws into this mediocrity at an early stage, as director and star latch on to anything in the vain hope of laughter. Children, removal men and Randy Quaid (playing a lawn-trimming slob) are all pushed into service, to meagre effect. Contains swearing. ▣

Richard Pryor *Arlo Pear* • Beverly Todd *Monica Pear* • Dave Thomas (1) *Gary Marcus* • Dana Carvey *Brad Williams* • Randy Quaid *Frank/ Cornell Crawford* • Stacey Dash *Casey Pear* • Raphael Harris *Marshall Pear* • Ishmael Harris *Randy Pear* ■ *Dir* Alan Metter • *Scr* Andy Breckman

The Moving Target
★★★★

Thriller　　　　1966 · US · Colour · 121mins

Also known as *Harper*, this features an early script by screenwriting guru William Goldman, who went on to win Oscars for *Butch Cassidy and the Sundance Kid* and *All the President's Men*. Paul Newman is a Chandleresque private eye in the missing persons business, and Lauren Bacall the wealthy client who hires him to find her spouse. From the moment private eye Harper recycles coffee for his breakfast beverage, we know the territory: a detective, with only honour to sustain him, up against the idle rich with time on their hands and murder on their minds. Even if you do guess the ending, Goldman's pungent adaptation of Ross MacDonald's novel, Jack Smight's pacy direction and Newman's confident portrayal of the LA gumshoe make this a classy and enjoyable thriller. A sequel, *The Drowning Pool*, followed nine years later.

Paul Newman *Lew Harper* • Lauren Bacall *Mrs Sampson* • Julie Harris *Betty Fraley* • Arthur Hill *Albert Graves* • Janet Leigh *Susan Harper* • Pamela Tiffin *Miranda Sampson* • Robert Wagner *Alan Taggert* • Robert Webber *Dwight Troy* • Shelley Winters *Fay Estabrook* ■ *Dir* Jack Smight • *Scr* William Goldman, from the novel by Ross MacDonald

Moving Target
★★★ 15

Thriller　　　　1988 · US · Colour · 89mins

If you returned from holiday to discover that your entire family, including the pets, had moved house, you might wonder what you'd done to upset them. This being an American TV movie, the brave young hero (Jason Bateman) immediately assumes that a hideous crime has taken place and sets off to track them down, only to find villains on his tail. Watch out for *Alien* star Tom Skerritt and Chynna Phillips, of singing group Wilson Phillips, further down the cast of this intriguing, well-paced thriller. ▣

Jason Bateman *Toby Kellogg* • Tom Skerritt *John Kellogg* • Jack Wagner *Sutcliff* • John Glover *Dobbins* • Chynna Phillips *Megan* • Richard Dysart *Cambridge* • Robert Downey Sr *Weinberg* ■ *Dir* Chris Thomson • *Scr* Andy Tennant, from a story by Edward Hunsaker, Neil Roach

Moving Violations
★ 15

Comedy　　　　1985 · US · Colour · 85mins

It takes some skill to aim even more downmarket than *Police Academy*, but this dire cash-in certainly succeeds in that respect. The story revolves around the usual loveable collection of anarchic misfits who run rings around the establishment when they are sentenced to traffic school. James Keach (*The Long Riders*), Sally Kellerman (*MASH*) and Jennifer Tilly (*Bullets over Broadway*) have doubtless erased this from their CVs. Contains swearing. ▣

John Murray *Dana Cannon* • Jennifer Tilly *Amy Hopkins* • James Keach *Deputy Halik* • Sally Kellerman *Judge Nedra Henderson* • Brian Backer *Scott Greeber* • Ned Eisenberg *Wink Barnes* • Clara Peller *Emma Jean* ■ *Dir* Neal Israel • *Scr* Neal Israel, Pat Proft, from a story by Paul Boorstin, Sharon Boorstin

Mrs 'arris Goes to Paris ★★★

Comedy   1992 · US · Colour · 97mins

This is one of those projects that spent decades doing the Hollywood rounds before finally being made as a TV movie. *Murder, She Wrote* star Angela Lansbury is the housekeeper who saves and saves so she can fulfil her lifelong dream of going to Paris and buying a Christian Dior dress. (Didn't anyone tell her she could have just popped along to her local department store?) Lightweight stuff indeed, but Lansbury and co-stars Diana Rigg and Omar Sharif all seem to be having so much fun you can't help but laugh along with them.

Angela Lansbury *Mrs Harris* • Omar Sharif *Marquis DeChassange* • Diana Rigg *Madame Colbert* • Lothaire Bluteau *André* • John Savident *Armand* • Lila Kaye *Mrs Butterfield* • Tamara Gorski *Natasha* ■ *Dir* Anthony Shaw • *Scr* John Hawkesworth, from the novella *Mrs 'arris Goes to Paris* by Paul Gallico

Mrs Brown ★★★★★ PG

Period drama
1997 · UK/US/Ire · Colour · 100mins

Judi Dench and Billy Connolly are a wonderfully regal double-act in this perceptive blend of fact and fiction. The story examines the relationship between Queen Victoria and her Scottish gillie John Brown, who audaciously dispelled her gloom after the death of Prince Albert and with whom she became so close that gossips gave her his name. The Oscar-nominated Dench provides a wonderfully dignified counter-balance to comedian Connolly, whose forthright bluntness causes consternation among her tradition-bound household staff. Director John Madden and scriptwriter Jeremy Brock have created an engrossing account of an attachment that might have fulfilled itself romantically had it not been for the repressive conventions of the time. An impeccable portrait.

Judi Dench *Queen Victoria* • Billy Connolly *John Brown* • Antony Sher *Benjamin Disraeli* • Geoffrey Palmer *Henry Ponsonby* • Richard Pasco *Doctor Jenner* • David Westhead *Bertie, Prince of Wales* • Bridget McConnel *Lady Ely* • Georgie Glen *Lady Churchill* ■ *Dir* John Madden • *Scr* Jeremy Brock, from an idea by George Rosie

Mrs Cage ★★★

Crime drama   1992 · US · Colour

The wonderful Anne Bancroft, still best remembered as seductress Mrs Robinson in *The Graduate*, growls her way through another mesmerising performance in this TV movie. She plays Mrs Cage, a respectable lady who walks into a police station and confesses to a murder. Of course, all is not what it seems. As the truth unravels, both Bancroft and Hector Elizondo keep the drama tightly wound. Contains swearing.

Anne Bancroft *Mrs Cage* • Hector Elizondo *Lieutenant Angel* • Stanley Grover *Martin Cage* • Steve Hornyack *The detective* • Amy Morton *Elizabeth Cage* ■ *Dir* Robert Allan Ackerman • *Scr* Nancy Barr

Mrs Dalloway ★★★ PG

Period drama
1997 · US/UK/Neth · Colour · 93mins

A day in the life of Clarissa Dalloway (Vanessa Redgrave), the emotionally troubled wife of an MP, and Septimus Smith (Rupert Graves), a shell-shocked war veteran. They never meet, but fate still brings them together at the end of a series of flashbacks that sketch in Clarissa's early life and feature Natascha McElhone as Redgrave's younger self. Adapting Virginia Woolf's intricate novel, Eileen Atkins juggles time and emotional choices with skill, while the performances are uniformly excellent. Yet it's also a rather smug production, trapped in an ivory tower of its own making. Marleen Gorris directs. Contains brief nudity. ▣

Vanessa Redgrave *Mrs Clarissa Dalloway* • Natascha McElhone *Young Clarissa Dalloway* • Rupert Graves *Septimus Warren Smith* • Michael Kitchen *Peter Walsh* • Alan Cox *Young Peter Walsh* • Sarah Badel *Lady Rosseter* • Lena Headey *Young Sally* • John Standing *Richard Dalloway* ■ *Dir* Marleen Gorris • *Scr* Eileen Atkins, from the novel by Virginia Woolf

Mrs Delafield Wants to Marry ★★★★

Romantic comedy
1986 · US · Colour · 94mins

This delightful romantic comedy features the incomparable Katharine Hepburn as a rich, high society widow who scandalises her friends and family when she decides to marry her divorced, Jewish doctor (Harold Gould). As usual, Hepburn is eminently watchable in a role created expressly for her by Broadway playwright James Prideaux. The premise is hardly original (in essence, it's a geriatric *Guess Who's Coming to Dinner*), but the execution is deft and the underlying issues of race and class bigotry are dealt with in an entertaining way.

Katharine Hepburn *Mrs Delafield* • Harold Gould *Dr Marvin Elias* • Denholm Elliott *George Parker* • Brenda Forbes *Gladys Parker* • David Ogden Stiers *Horton* ■ *Dir* George Schaefer • *Scr* James Prideaux

Mrs Doubtfire ★★★★ PG

Comedy drama   1993 · US · Colour · 120mins

This knowing blend of comedy and common sense is family entertainment *par excellence*. Aided by Oscar-winning make-up, Robin Williams gives one of the performances of his career as an actor who disguises himself as a Scottish nanny to be close to his kids after he splits with wife Sally Field. Director Chris Columbus reins in the Williams exuberance, while retaining enough of his quick-fire personality to ensure that just about every gag hits its target. Pierce Brosnan also does well as the late-thirtysomething looking for a ready-made family, but Sally Field overdoes the exasperation at times. Cracking set pieces like the make-up experiments and the series of table-hopping quick changes make up for the slightly protracted running time. Contains swearing. ▣

Robin Williams *Daniel Hillard/Mrs Doubtfire* • Sally Field *Miranda Hillard* • Pierce Brosnan *Stu* • Harvey Fierstein *Frank* • Polly Holliday *Gloria* • Lisa Jakub *Lydia Hillard* • Matthew Lawrence *Chris Hillard* • Mara Wilson *Natalie Hillard* ■ *Dir* Chris Columbus • *Scr* Randi

Mayem Singer, Leslie Dixon, from the novel *Alias Mrs Doubtfire* by Anne Fine • *Make-up* Ve Neill, Greg Cannon, Yolanda Toussieng

Mrs Lambert Remembers Love ★★★ PG

Drama   1991 · US · Colour · 89mins

This heart-felt TV movie explores the strains placed on the bonds of family by Alzheimer's disease. Ellen Burstyn stars as a grandmother who flees from the authorities rather than be separated from her nine-year-old orphaned grandson. The performances of Burstyn and co-star Walter Matthau, as her close friend, elevate what could have been a mawkish melodrama, and it's capably directed by Matthau's son, Charles. ▣

Walter Matthau *Clifford* • Ellen Burstyn *Lil Lambert* • Ryan Todd *Jared Lambert* • William Schallert *Sheriff Pomeroy* • Kathleen Garrett *Darlene* • Sherry Hursey *Etta Crue* ■ *Scr* Charles Matthau • *Scr* Janet Heaney

Mrs Mike ★★

Romantic drama   1949 · US · BW · 98mins

At the end of the 19th century, Boston girl Kathy O'Fallon (Evelyn Keyes) ventures to the rugged north-west of Canada, where she meets and falls in love with mountie Mike Flanagan (Dick Powell). They marry, and our heroine sets about adjusting to an unfamiliar way of life. Louis King directs this sentimental drama that's neither memorable nor absorbing, but does feature believable performances.

Dick Powell *Sergeant Mike Flannigan* • Evelyn Keyes *Kathy O'Fallon* • JM Kerrigan *Uncle John* • Angela Clarke *Sarah Carpentier* • John Miljan *Mr Howard* • Nan Boardman *Georgette Beauclaire* • Will Wright *Dr McIntosh* ■ *Dir* Louis King • *Scr* Alfred Lewis Levitt, DeWitt Bodeen, from the novel by Benedict Freedman, Nancy Freedman

Mrs Miniver ★★★★★ U

Classic wartime drama
1942 · US · BW · 128mins

A superb wartime melodrama, which, said Winston Churchill, was "more valuable than the combined efforts of six army divisions". Greer Garson and Walter Pidgeon are the British couple suffering in the Second World War, bringing this country's plight to the American public, and today this MGM production is best viewed in that propagandist light. The film won six Oscars, including best picture, best actress and best direction for William Wyler, and it's easy to understand why. Trivia buffs might like to note that Garson's real-life lover at the time was her son in this movie, Richard Ney, whom she married the following year. A sequel, *The Miniver Story*, filmed in England eight years later, is nowhere near as good. ▣

Greer Garson *Mrs Miniver* • Walter Pidgeon *Clem Miniver* • Teresa Wright *Carol Beldon* • Dame May Whitty *Lady Beldon* • Reginald Owen *Foley* • Henry Travers *Mr Ballard* • Richard Ney *Vin Miniver* • Henry Wilcoxon *Vicar* • Christopher Severn *Toby Miniver* ■ *Dir* William Wyler • *Scr* Arthur Wimperis, George Froeschel, James Hilton, Claudine West, from the novel by Jan Struther • *Cinematographer* Joseph Ruttenberg

Mrs Munck ★★★

Drama   1995 · US · Colour · 99mins

Diane Ladd (*Wild at Heart*) wrote the script (based on the novel by Ella Leffland), directed and starred in this drama about a newly widowed woman who takes revenge on the secret lover she had in her youth, who is now disabled. Smartly paced, this is most interesting for the cast, which includes Ladd's ex-husband Bruce Dern (father of their child Laura Dern), Shelley Winters and Kelly Preston. Not surprisingly, Ladd steals the show in the title role. Contains violence, swearing, sex scenes and nudity.

Diane Ladd *Mrs Rose Munck* • Bruce Dern *Patrick Leary* • Kelly Preston *Young Rose Munck* • Shelley Winters *Aunt Monica* • Scott Fisher *Felix* ■ *Dir* Diane Ladd • *Scr* Diane Ladd, from the novel by Ella Leffland

Mrs Parker and the Vicious Circle ★★★★ 15

Biographical drama
1994 · US · BW and Colour · 119mins

Love or loathe Jennifer Jason Leigh's mannered performance as Dorothy Parker (the brilliant wit of the twenties and thirties), she is still a constant delight of looks and language. Director Alan Rudolph celebrates the story of members of the Algonquin hotel's Round Table, which consisted of writers and celebrities who gathered around Parker. Her affair with Charles MacArthur (the co-writer of *The Front Page*, played here by Matthew Broderick) and her subsequent affairs and fractured marriage chime a note of doom and despair that counters the show-off cleverness of the rest. By the end, you can't help but like as well as admire her. ▣

Jennifer Jason Leigh *Dorothy Parker* • Campbell Scott *Robert Benchley* • Matthew Broderick *Charles MacArthur* • Andrew McCarthy *Eddie Parker* • Tom McGowan *Alexander Woollcott* • Nick Cassavetes *Robert Sherwood* ■ *Dir* Alan Rudolph • *Scr* Alan Rudolph, Randy Sue Coburn

Mrs Parkington ★★

Drama   1944 · US · BW · 123mins

One of the weakest of the eight films in which Walter Pidgeon supported Greer Garson, this drama gained the actress an Oscar nomination more deserved by the make-up department. She starts the picture as an octagenarian widow and matriarch who suffers from flashback disease, thereby revealing her early life as the brash mining-town girl who married Pidgeon's millionaire and became a society figure. Garson learned card tricks for the film, but the lumbering script deprives director Tay Garnett of a winning hand. In the original American version, Edward, Prince of Wales (played by Cecil Kellaway) is entranced by Garson, but British audiences were given Hugo Haas as a Balkan monarch to avoid offending Buckingham Palace.

Greer Garson *Susie Parkington* • Walter Pidgeon *Maj Augustus Parkington* • Edward Arnold *Amory Stilham* • Frances Rafferty *Jane Stilham* • Agnes Moorehead *Aspasia Conti* • Selena Royle *Mattie Trounsen* • Gladys Cooper *Alice, Duchess de Brancourt* • Lee Patrick *Madeleine* • Dan Duryea *Jack Stilham*

   U = SUITABLE FOR ALL   Uc = SUITABLE FOR ALL, ESPECIALLY FOR YOUNG CHILDREN (VIDEO ONLY)   PG = PARENTAL GUIDANCE

■ *Dir* Tay Garnett • *Scr* Robert Thoeren, Polly James, from the novel by Louis Bromfield • *Costume Designer* Irene

Mrs Pollifax – Spy ★

Spy parody   1970 · US · Colour · 110mins

This unfunny comedy adventure brought Rosalind Russell's big screen career to an end. She had only herself and husband Frederick Brisson to blame, though, since she wrote it pseudonymously and he produced it and employed the undistinguished Leslie Martinson to direct. Russell plays a middle-aged woman who joins the CIA and embarks on a series of unlikely and over-energetic adventures. (As she was over 60 at the time, stunt doubles are much in evidence.)

Rosalind Russell *Emily Pollifax* • Darren McGavin *Johnny Farrell* • Nehemiah Persoff *General Berisha* • Harold Gould *Colonel Nexdhet* • Albert Paulsen *General Perdido* • John Beck *Sgt Lulash* ■ *Dir* Leslie Martinson [Leslie H Martinson] • *Scr* CA McKnight [Rosalind Russell], from the novel *The Unexpected Mrs Pollifax* by Dorothy Gilman

Mrs R's Daughter ★★★

Drama based on a true story
1979 · US · Colour

Cloris Leachman brings her Oscar-winning talents to the small screen to give a hard-hitting performance in this challenging TV movie. It's based on the true story of a woman who takes on the US legal system in a lone and exasperating battle to bring the man who raped her daughter to justice. A vivid screenplay and restrained direction by Dan Curtis give an important subject an intelligent and engrossing treatment.

Cloris Leachman *Ruth Randell* • Season Hubley *Ellie Pruitt* • Donald Moffat *Frank Randell* • John McIntire *Attorney Paul Underwood* ■ *Dir* Dan Curtis • *Scr* George Rubino

Mrs Soffel ★★★PG

Biographical drama
1984 · US · Colour · 106mins

Based on the true story of a prison warden's wife who fell in love with an inmate and plotted his escape, this turn-of-the-century costume romance is too dour for its own good. Australia's Gillian Armstrong directs the potentially passionate content with a cool detachment that mirrors the wintry landscapes across which the lovers flee, while Diane Keaton's contemporary style is also at odds with the piece. But there's plenty of appeal in the young Mel Gibson, appropriately seductive as the convicted murderer, and Matthew Modine is nicely cast as his dimwit brother. ▭

Diane Keaton *Kate Soffel* • Mel Gibson *Ed Biddle* • Matthew Modine *Jack Biddle* • Edward Herrmann *Peter Soffel* • Trini Alvarado *Irene Soffel* • Jennie Dundas *Margaret Soffel* • Danny Corkill *Eddie Soffel* ■ *Dir* Gillian Armstrong • *Scr* Ron Nyswaner

Mrs Wiggs of the Cabbage Patch ★★

Melodrama   1934 · US · BW · 80mins

Director Norman Taurog's film recounts the poverty-stricken but incident-packed existence of Mrs Wiggs (Pauline Lord) and her five children, whose father has disappeared without trace. Always cheerful in the face of struggle, the family is helped by a local rich girl (Evelyn Venable). At times Dickensian in flavour, at others Chaplinesque, it's at its best in the second half when Mr C Ensworth Stubbins (WC Fields) arrives on the scene and courts the Wiggs' family friend Miss Tabitha Hazy (ZaSu Pitts). Fields and Pitts are hilarious, and this remains overall the best version of a once-popular novel, filmed as a silent in 1919 and again in 1942, with Fay Bainter as Mrs Wiggs.

Pauline Lord *Mrs Elvira Wiggs* • WC Fields *Mr C Ensworth Stubbins* • ZaSu Pitts *Miss Tabitha Hazy* • Evelyn Venable *Lucy Olcott* • Kent Taylor *Bob Redding* • Charles Middleton *Mr Bagby* • Donald Meek *Mr Hiram Wiggs* • Clara Lou Sheridan [Ann Sheridan] *Girl* ■ *Dir* Norman Taurog • *Scr* William Slavens McNutt, Jane Storm, from the play by Anne Crawford Flexner, from the novel by Alice Hegan Rice

Mrs Winterbourne ★★★12

Comedy drama   1995 · US · Colour · 101mins

This comic remake of the far more serious *No Man of Her Own* stars US talk-show queen Ricki Lake as Connie, a young girl with a baby on the way who, following a train crash, adopts the identity of the late Patricia Winterbourne. She is promptly whisked off to meet the rich Winterbourne family, who had never met their dead son's bride. Shirley MacLaine steals the show, naturally, as the *grande dame* of the family, but Lake holds her own and there is nice support from Brendan Fraser as the brother-in-law with whom she falls in love. Contains swearing and sexual references. ▭

Shirley MacLaine *Grace Winterbourne* • Ricki Lake *Connie Doyle* • Brendan Fraser *Bill Winterbourne/Hugh Winterbourne* • Miguel Sandoval *Paco* • Loren Dean *Steve DeCunzo* • Peter Gerety *Father Brian* • Jane Krakowski *Christine* ■ *Dir* Richard Benjamin • *Scr* Phoef Sutton, Lisa-Marie Radano, from the novel *I Married a Dead Man* by Cornell Woolrich

Ms 45 ★★★18

Crime drama   1981 · US · Colour · 76mins

Abel Ferrara was once Public Enemy No 1 as far as the UK censors were concerned: his first two movies ended up on the banned list. The notorious *Driller Killer* was the first; *Ms 45* was the second, and it's a far more accomplished affair. Zoe Tamerlis plays a mute woman who, after being raped twice in one day, decides to get her own back on mankind. It was billed as a feminist *Death Wish*, but it's a lot more disturbing than that, even if Ferrara and his regular scriptwriter Nicholas St John once again go overboard on the religious guilt. It was eventually approved for release, with a few minor cuts. ▭

Zoe Tamerlis *Thana* • Bogey *Phil* • Albert Sinkys *Albert* • Darlene Stuto *Laurie* • Jimmy Laine [Abel Ferrara] *First rapist* • Peter Yellen *Second rapist* ■ *Dir* Abel Ferrara • *Scr* Nicholas St John

Ms Scrooge ★★U

Fantasy drama   1997 · US · Colour · 83mins

In this racially updated, gender-bending retelling of Charles Dickens's *A Christmas Carol*, Emmy award-winner Cicely Tyson stars as modern-day banker and miser, Ebenita Scrooge. The plot's the same, though, with Scrooge being visited by the ghosts of Christmas past, present and future so she can learn valuable life lessons and mend her greedy ways. Sadly, this uneven modern version doesn't have the makings of a holiday classic, as it wanders aimlessly from the spirit of the original. ▭

Cicely Tyson *Ebenita Scrooge* • Katherine Helmond *Maude Marley* • Michael Beach *Reverend Luke* • John Bourgeois *Bob Cratchit* ■ *Dir* John Korty • *Scr* John McGreevey, from the story *A Christmas Carol* by Charles Dickens

Much Ado about Nothing ★★★★PG

Comedy drama   1993 · UK · Colour · 106mins

A real luvvies outing this one, as Ken and Em (Branagh and Thompson, before their much publicised marriage break-up) decamp to Tuscany with pals to film an exciting, joyful and rollicking version of Shakespeare's tale of frenetic wooing. Branagh, who stars and directs, gives the story enormous energy and is aided by a fine supporting cast that includes Thompson's mother Phyllida Law, Imelda Staunton, Ben Elton, Keanu Reeves and Denzel Washington. Contains brief nudity. ▭ **DVD**

Kenneth Branagh *Benedick* • Richard Briers *Leonato* • Michael Keaton *Dogberry* • Denzel Washington *Don Pedro* • Robert Sean Leonard *Claudio* • Keanu Reeves *Don John* • Emma Thompson *Beatrice* • Kate Beckinsale *Hero* • Imelda Staunton *Margaret* • Phyllida Law *Ursula* • Ben Elton *Verges* ■ *Dir* Kenneth Branagh • *Scr* Kenneth Branagh, from the play by William Shakespeare

Much Too Shy ★★U

Comedy   1942 · UK · BW · 95mins

Although he was still Britain's biggest box-office attraction, George Formby was already showing signs of the novelty fatigue that would result in the collapse of his screen career four years later. Too bashful to paint anything below the neck, he gets into hot water when his portraits of three village matrons end up in a soap advertisement attached to nude torsos. The cheeky wit that informed so many of Formby's songs is foregrounded in this contrived comedy, but the storyline about the handyman with aspirations to become an artist simply isn't strong enough to sustain so much smutty innuendo.

George Formby *George Andy* • Kathleen Harrison *Amelia Peabody* • Hilda Bayley *Lady Driscoll* • Eileen Bennett *Jackie Somers* • Joss Ambler *Sir George Driscoll* ■ *Dir* Marcel Varnel • *Scr* Ronald Frankau

Muddy River ★★★★PG

Drama   1981 · Jap · BW · 103mins

Adapted from a novel by Teru Miyamoto, yet clearly inspired by Yasujiro Ozu's delightful studies of childhood friendship, Kohei Oguri's Oscar-nominated debut makes striking use of its black-and-white imagery to evoke a sense of both nostalgic innocence and the grinding poverty that so many Japanese experienced, even at the height of the fifties boom. As the nine-year-old son of comfortable restaurateurs, Nobutaka Asahara is touchingly awestruck as he learns some harsh lessons about class and sex from the widow who works as a prostitute on the houseboat she shares with her kids. Dramatically satisfying, visually authentic and beautifully played. In Japanese with English subtitles.

Nobutaka Asahara *Nobuo* • Takahiro Tamura *Shinpei* • Yumiko Fujita *Nobuo's mother* • Minoru Sakurai *Kiichi* ■ *Dir* Kohei Oguri • *Scr* Takako Shigemuri, from the novel by Teru Miyamoto

Mudhoney ★★★★18

Melodrama   1965 · US · BW · 92mins

This early film by soft porn maestro Russ Meyer has been hailed as an undiscovered masterpiece, and it's easy to see why. Apart from some brief glimpses of nudity, this Southern melodrama, set in the Prohibition era, could easily have been made by any of Hollywood's all-time greats. The plot (desperate men feuding over sex and power on a farm) is straight out of a dime novel, but the action builds to a rivetingly horrible denouement, while the high standard of photography and performances has rarely been equalled in low-budget exploitation. One of the best of its kind. ▭

Hal Hopper *Sidney Brenshaw* • Lorna Maitland *Clara Belle* • Antoinette Cristiani *Hannah Brenshaw* • John Furlong *Calif McKinney* • Stuart Lancaster *Lute Wade* ■ *Dir* Russ Meyer • *Scr* Raymond Friday Locke, William E Sprague

The Mudlark ★★★U

Drama   1950 · UK · BW · 99mins

A first-class British movie from 20th Century-Fox, which in its day achieved minor notoriety for its relatively daring casting, with noted Hollywood *grande dame* Irene Dunne playing Queen Victoria to Alec Guinness's elegant Disraeli. Dunne acquits herself well enough, and Guinness is superb, particularly in a long speech that seems to be uninterrupted by cutting: bravura screen acting indeed. The story is about one of those Oliver Twist-like foundlings, played here by Andrew Ray, and the sentimental plot is hard to take seriously. The young romantic leads are Anthony Steel and the lovely Beatrice Campbell, and they're much more interesting.

Irene Dunne *Queen Victoria* • Alec Guinness *Benjamin Disraeli* • Andrew Ray *Wheeler, the mudlark* • Beatrice Campbell *Lady Emily Prior* • Finlay Currie *John Brown* • Anthony Steel *Lieutenant Charles McHatten* • Raymond Lovell *Sergeant Footman Naseby* ■ *Dir* Jean Negulesco • *Scr* Nunnally Johnson, from the novel by Theodore Bonnet

Mulan ★★★★U

Animated musical adventure
1998 · US · Colour · 87mins

Set in ancient China, this recounts the adventures of the eponymous heroine who dons man's clothing and goes to war to save her family honour, because her father's health is failing. Some splendid action set pieces, the inevitable love between Mulan and her brave captain, and the often uproarious presence of a snappy little dragon (voiced by Eddie Murphy) are the highlights. Aspects of the story go a bit over young children's heads, but it's an enthralling narrative for everyone else and there's plenty of slapstick fun to keep youngsters happy. A startling addition to the Disney studio's catalogue. ▣ **DVD**

Wen Ming-Na *Mulan* • Eddie Murphy *Mushu* • Lea Salonga *Mulan* • BD Wong *Shang* • Donny Osmond *Shang* • Miguel Ferrer *Shan-Yu* • Harvey Fierstein *Yao* • Miriam Margolyes *Matchmaker* • Pat Morita *Emperor* • George Takei *First ancestor* ■ *Dir* Barry Cook, Tony Bancroft • *Scr* Rita Hsiao, Christopher Sanders, Philip Lazebnik, Raymond Singer, Eugenia Bostwick-Singer, from a story by Robert D San Souci

Mule Train ★★ U
Western   1950 · US · Sepia · 70mins

The song of the title was a million-selling pop hit for Frankie Laine, and this Gene Autry programme filler was made quickly to capitalise on the song's success. But threading a plot around the lyrics wasn't easy and resulted in this loose thriller about the construction of a dam and, bizarrely, cement claim jumping. The popular Autry is his usual likeable self, but Robert Livingston's evil freight shipper is actually far more interesting than the bland hero. The movie was originally filmed in the now forgotten screen process of Sepiatone, which gave an attractive burnish to William Bradford's photography.

Gene Autry • Pat Buttram *Smokey Argyle* • Sheila Ryan *Carol Bannister* • Robert Livingston *Sam Brady* • Frank Jacquet *Clayton Hodges* • Vince Barnett *Barber Mulkey* • Syd Saylor *Skeeter* • Sandy Sanders *Bud* ■ *Dir* John English • *Scr* Gerald Geraghty, from a story by Alan James

Mulholland Falls ★★★ 18
Thriller   1996 · US · Colour · 102mins

A flawed bid to re-create the sleazy glamour of postwar Los Angeles, an era that would be stunningly evoked a year later by the Oscar-winning *LA Confidential*. Nick Nolte heads a very starry cast, playing the hard-nosed head of the Hat Squad – a group of detectives prepared to take the law into their own hands to deal with mobsters. Nolte becomes entangled in a political conspiracy when investigating the death of a beautiful woman (Jennifer Connelly) who had been his lover. Director Lee Tamahori stylishly evokes the period and elicits excellent performances from a cast that also includes John Malkovich, Melanie Griffith, Treat Williams and Christopher Penn. However, all are let down by the muddled script that fails to flesh out the intriguing premise. Contains violence, swearing, nudity and sex scenes. ▣

Nick Nolte *Hoover* • Melanie Griffith *Katherine* • Chazz Palminteri *Coolidge* • Michael Madsen *Eddie Hall* • Christopher Penn *Arthur* • Treat Williams *Fitzgerald* • Jennifer Connelly *Allison Pond* • John Malkovich *Timms* • Bruce Dern *The Chief* • William Petersen *Mobster* ■ *Dir* Lee Tamahori • *Scr* Pete Dexter, from a story by Floyd Mutrux, Pete Dexter

Multiple Maniacs ★★ 18
Underground satirical melodrama
1970 · US · BW · 90mins

John Waters, the self-styled "Sovereign of Sleaze", dubbed this early work a

"celluloid atrocity", while its title is a homage to the 1964 gorefest *2000 Maniacs*. Waters's most overtly Catholic tale to date centres on "Lady Divine's Cavalcade of Perversions", a travelling freak show that pitches its tent in Baltimore and offers such lurid sights as homosexuals kissing, heroin addicts going cold turkey, puke-eating and bicycle seat-sniffing to curious heterosexuals. The moral is that the world at large contains far worse horrors than those featured in Divine's ghoulish gallery. An eye-opening gutter parable that comes complete with the Infant of Prague (Michael Renner Jr) and ends with Divine being raped by a gigantic lobster. ▣

Divine *Lady Divine* • David Lochary *Mr David* • Mary Vivian Pearce *Bonnie* • Mink Stole • Cookie Mueller *Cookie* • Paul Swift *Steve* • Rick Morrow *Ricky* • Michael Renner Jr *Infant of Prague* ■ *Dir/Scr* John Waters

Multiplicity ★★★ 12
Fantasy comedy 1996 · US · Colour · 112mins

Michael Keaton finds his time stretched to the limit between his wife, career and family, until he meets a scientist who offers to clone him, in director Harold Ramis's inventive comedy. Of course, one clone ends up not being enough and soon he has an attic full of them – all played by Keaton and each with a different personality – while his unsuspecting wife (Andie MacDowell) wonders what is going on. Not as eye-wateringly funny as Ramis's *Groundhog Day*, this is nonetheless a sprightly romp that benefits from very funny multiple performances by Keaton. ▣ **DVD**

Michael Keaton *Doug Kinney* • Andie MacDowell *Laura Kinney* • Zack Duhame *Zack Kinney* • Katie Schlossberg *Jennifer Kinney* • Harris Yulin *Dr Leeds* • Richard Masur *Del King* • Eugene Levy *Vic* • Ann Cusack *Noreen* ■ *Dir* Harold Ramis • *Scr* Chris Miller, Mary Hale, Lowell Ganz, Babaloo Mandel, from a short story by Chris Miller

Mumford ★★ 15
Comedy drama
1999 · US · Colour and BW · 111mins

Though advertised as a riotous comedy, this story of a small town psychiatrist with a deep secret and his wondrous effect on the locals is really more of a light-hearted drama. While never boring, and filled with moments both touching and humorous, it moves at a snail's pace. Relieved of its multiple subplots, the film might have felt less congested. Even then, some unexplained changes in the characters – particularly Martin Short's – would remain. Contains drug abuse, sex scenes, nudity and some swearing.

Loren Dean *Mumford* • Hope Davis *Sofie Crisp* • Jason Lee *Skip Skipperton* • Alfre Woodard *Lily* • Mary McDonnell *Althea Brockett* • Pruitt Taylor Vince *Henry Follett* • Zooey Deschanel *Nessa Watkins* • Martin Short *Lionel Dillard* • Ted Danson *Jeremy Brockett* • Robert Stack ■ *Dir/Scr* Lawrence Kasdan

The Mummy ★★★★ 15
Classic horror   1932 · US · BW · 72mins

Boris Karloff's next film after *Frankenstein* shows what an intensely subtle actor he was compared with the walking-dead performances of the supporting cast. He plays the ancient

Egyptian Im-Ho-Tep who has been buried alive for trying to restore life to his beloved princess. Brought back to life in the present day, he pursues his lost love, believing her to be reincarnated as the fiancée of a member of an archaeological expedition. Master photographer Karl Freund directs without shock tactics, apart from the burying alive scene, but with images of death and decay worthy of Edgar Allan Poe. ▣

Boris Karloff *Im-Ho-Tep/Ardeth Bey* • Zita Johann *Helen Grosvenor/Princess Anck-es-en-Amon* • David Manners *Frank Whemple* • Edward Van Sloan *Muller* • Arthur Byron *Sir Joseph Whemple* • Bramwell Fletcher *Norton* • Eddie Kane *Doctor* ■ *Dir* Karl Freund • *Scr* John L Balderston, from a story by Nina Wilcox Putnam, Richard Schayer

The Mummy ★★★ PG
Horror   1959 · UK · Colour · 84mins

After its huge success with Dracula and Frankenstein, Hammer turned to another vintage Universal monster for its scream dream team of Peter Cushing, Christopher Lee and director Terence Fisher. Although rather talky and undemanding plot-wise, Cushing is marvellously crisp as the tomb-desecrating archaeologist, fending off the malevolent attentions of gauze-wrapped Lee. And, unlike your usual shambling mummy, Lee really does capture the murderously powerful, fast-moving ferocity of the bandaged reincarnation as he stomps through foggy London. ▣

Peter Cushing *John Banning* • Christopher Lee *Kharis, the mummy* • Yvonne Furneaux *Isobel Banning/Princess Ananka* • Eddie Byrne *Inspector Mulrooney* • Felix Aylmer *Stephen Banning* • Raymond Huntley *Joseph Whemple* ■ *Dir* Terence Fisher • *Scr* Jimmy Sangster, from the 1932 film

The Mummy ★★★ 12
Horror adventure
1999 · US · Colour · 124mins

In the good old days, the Mummy merely met Abbott and Costello. Now, thanks to the wizards of the special effects industry, this digitally manipulated variation on a classic theme can meet his adversaries on a roller coaster ride of vibrant action and epic adventure. Screenwriter/director Stephen Sommers has embroidered the original story to excess at times, with flesh-eating beetles and battling zombie slaves just two of the gruesome modern additions. Yet Brendan Fraser does his goofy macho best as an Indiana Jones clone romancing prim librarian Rachel Weisz, and Arnold Vosloo has the perfect bone-structure for the brooding menace returned from the dead. ▣ **DVD**

Brendan Fraser *Rick O'Connell* • Rachel Weisz *Evelyn* • John Hannah *Jonathan* • Kevin J O'Connor *Beni* • Arnold Vosloo *Imhotep* • Jonathan Hyde *Egyptologist* ■ *Dir* Stephen Sommers, from a story by LLoyd Fonvielle, Kevin Jarre, Stephen Sommers

The Mummy's Shroud ★★
Horror   1966 · UK · Colour · 90mins

Hammer could never resist dabbling with the dark forces of ancient Egypt, but this third descent into the mummy's tomb was one of the studio's least accomplished horrors.

After dwelling a bit too long in the land of the pharaohs, the action shifts to 1920 as André Morell's expedition ventures into the vault. We know it's doomed because a) it's sponsored by treasure-seeking rogue John Phillips and b) local malcontent Roger Delgado knows the spell to revive the avenging mummy. There are some particularly grisly murders and a terrific finale, but it's mostly dry as dust.

André Morell *Sir Basil Walden* • John Phillips *Stanley Preston* • David Buck *Paul Preston* • Elizabeth Sellars *Barbara Preston* • Maggie Kimberley *Claire De Sangre* • Michael Ripper *Longbarrow* • Roger Delgado *Hasmid Ali* ■ *Dir* John Gilling • *Scr* John Gilling, from a story by John Elder [Anthony Hinds]

Mumsy, Nanny, Sonny & Girly ★
Horror thriller   1970 · UK · Colour · 101mins

The title promises rubbish, and the film readily obliges. Michael Bryant falls prey to a weird gang – comprising a mother, two children and a maid – who kidnap men, play with them and then kill them. Neither comedy or horror, this is merely a mess. The director is Freddie Francis, a former house cameraman for Hammer Films who would later collaborate with David Lynch on *Dune* and *The Elephant Man*.

Michael Bryant *New friend* • Ursula Howells *Mumsy* • Pat Heywood *Nanny* • Howard Trevor *Sonny* • Vanessa Howard *Girly* ■ *Dir* Freddie Francis • *Scr* Brian Comport, from the play *The Happy Family* by Maisie Mosco

Munchie ★ PG
Fantasy comedy   1992 · US · Colour · 77mins

A magical furry creature (voiced by Dom DeLuise) befriends a precocious young boy struggling to adjust at his new school. Munchie's appearance may actually frighten kids, especially since the puppetry is so poor that his lip movements rarely match DeLuise's voice. Loni Anderson plays the kid's mom, but it rather looks as if she's doing a favour for pal DeLuise. It's no surprise that the executive producer was Roger Corman. Watch for a young Jennifer Love Hewitt as the obligatory "cute girl". Contains drug abuse. ▣

Loni Anderson *Cathy* • Dom DeLuise *Munchie* • Andrew Stevens *Elliott* • Jaime McEnnan *Gage Dobson* • Arte Johnson *Professor Cruikshank* • Mike Simmrin *Leon* • Scott Ferguson *Ashton* • Love Hewitt [Jennifer Love Hewitt] *Andrea* ■ *Dir* Jim Wynorski • *Scr* Jim Wynorski, RJ Robertson

Munchies ★ PG
Comedy horror   1987 · US · Colour · 78mins

What's worse than a rip-off of *Gremlins*? A rip-off of *Gremlins* with Harvey Korman in multiple roles, of course. Alien-hunter Korman thinks he's found definitive proof in the form of Arnold, a cute little creature who eats junk food. His evil brother (Korman again) gets hold of the little guy and, before you know it, there are scads of them, causing trouble for everyone. ▣

Harvey Korman *Cecil/Simon Waterman* • Charles Stratton *Paul* • Nadine Van Der Velde *Cindy* • Alix Elias *Melvis* • Charlie Phillips *Eddie* • Hardy Rawls *Big Ed* • Jon Stafford *Dude* • Robert Picardo *Bob Marvelle* ■ *Dir* Bettina Hirsch • *Scr* Lance Smith

U = SUITABLE FOR ALL   Uc = SUITABLE FOR ALL, ESPECIALLY FOR YOUNG CHILDREN (VIDEO ONLY)   PG = PARENTAL GUIDANCE

Munimji ★★★ U
Drama 1955 · Ind · BW · 149mins

Subodh Mukherjee made his directorial debut with this typically tangled Hindi tale. At the centre of events are Pran and Dev Anand as half-brothers who were switched at birth and now find themselves on opposite sides of the law, yet in love with the same girl. However, for all these melodramatic machinations, the film's main interest lies in the fact that it provided the prolific Nirupa Roy, who would go on to become the most famous mother figure in Indian cinema, with her first maternal role. Indeed, fans used to seeing her play goddesses might be a little shocked to see the way she schemes here. In Hindi with English subtitles. ▣

Dev Anand *Amar* • Pran *Ratan* • Nirupa Roy *Malati* • Nalini Jaywant *Roopa* ■ *Dir* Subodh Mukherjee • *Scr* Subodh Mukherjee, Ranjan, from a story by Ranjan

Munster, Go Home! ★★★
Comedy 1966 · US · Colour · 96mins

Popular sitcoms rarely make the grade when they are extended to feature-film length. Here's one of the few exceptions, originally made for television but deemed good enough for theatrical release. The family inherits an English estate that is being used by their nefarious relatives as the centre of a counterfeiting ring. When they turn up to inspect Munster Hall, their aristocratic next-of-kin (under the deliciously plummy command of Hermione Gingold) try and scare them away with fake apparitions and musty scares. Of course, such spookiness only makes the Munsters feel even more at home. Terry-Thomas and genre veteran John Carradine enter into the spirit of a charming, colourful and funny affair that ends with a wild car chase through the countryside.

Fred Gwynne *Herman* • Yvonne De Carlo *Lily* • Al Lewis *Grandpa* • Butch Patrick *Eddie* • Debbie Watson *Marilyn* • Terry-Thomas *Freddie* • Hermione Gingold *Lady Effigie* • Robert Pine *Roger* • John Carradine *Cruikshank* ■ *Dir* Earl Bellamy • *Scr* George Tibbles, Joe Connelly, Bob Mosher, from the TV series *The Munsters*

The Muppet Christmas Carol ★★★★ U
Comedy drama 1992 · US · Colour · 85mins

With Michael Caine as Scrooge, Kermit and Miss Piggy as the Cratchits, and Gonzo as Dickens, this is quite simply corking Christmas entertainment. Although the story has been Muppetised (with Fozzie Bear as Fozziwig, the owner of a rubber chicken factory), no attempt has been made to water down the story, and the poignance of the moral tale is as affecting as ever. Caine hasn't been this good in years, and his scenes with those hecklers supreme Statler and Waldorf, as the Marley brothers, are the highlight of the film. ▣

Michael Caine *Scrooge* • Steve Whitmire *Bob Cratchit (Kermit)/Rizzo/Beaker/Bean Bunny/Belinda Cratchit* • Frank Oz *Emily Cratchit (Miss Piggy)/Sam Eagle/Animal/Fozziwig (Fozzie Bear)* • Dave Goelz *Charles Dickens (The Great Gonzo)/Bunsen Honeydew/Waldorf/Zoot/Betina Cratchit* • David Rudman *Peter Cratchit/Swedish Chef/Old Joe* • Jerry

Nelson *Statler/Floyd/Ma Bear/Tiny Tim/The Ghost of Christmas Present* ■ *Dir* Brian Henson • *Scr* Jerry Juhl, from the story by Charles Dickens

The Muppet Movie ★★★★ U
Comedy adventure 1979 · US · Colour · 94mins

Jim Henson's beloved, zany puppets made their feature film debut in this entertaining adventure relating Kermit the Frog's inspirational journey from Georgia swamp tadpole to Hollywood star. Comedy director James Frawley imposes pleasing order on the charming proceedings while Henson and his long-time associate Frank Oz delightfully dominate as the manipulators and voices of Kermit and Miss Piggy. An indication of how big the Muppets were at the time is the more than a dozen silly star cameos (Orson Welles, Steve Martin, Bob Hope and James Coburn among them). The only let-down is Paul Williams and Kenny Ascher's disappointingly forgettable song score. ▣

Jim Henson *Kermit the Frog/Rowlf/Dr Teeth/Waldorf* • Frank Oz *Miss Piggy/Fozzie Bear/Animal/Sam the Eagle* • Jerry Nelson *Floyd Pepper/Crazy Harry/Robin the Frog/Lew Zealand* • Richard Hunt *Scooter/Statler/Janice/Sweetums/Beaker* • Dave Goelz *Gonzo/Zoot/Dr Bunsen Honeydew* ■ *Dir* James Frawley • *Scr* Jerry Juhl, Jack Burns

Muppet Treasure Island ★★★★ U
Comedy adventure 1996 · US · Colour · 95mins

The Muppets take on Robert Louis Stevenson in their inimitable way for a rollicking musical version of the pirate saga. Using the bare bones of the classic story as a framework, director Brian Henson press-gangs the likes of Billy Connolly, Jennifer Saunders and Tim Curry into service for a series of hilarious cameos, accompanied by some rousing songs and the now customary "romance" of Miss Piggy and Kermit. Children will love it. ▣

Steve Whitmire *Captain Abraham Smollet (Kermit the Frog)/Rizzo the Rat* • Frank Oz *Benjamina Gunn (Miss Piggy)* • Tim Curry *Long John Silver* • Kevin Bishop *Jim Hawkins* • Billy Connolly *Billy Bones* • Jennifer Saunders *Mrs Bluveridge* • David Goelz *The Great Gonzo* ■ *Dir* Brian Henson • *Scr* Jerry Juhl, Kirk R Thatcher, James V Hart

Muppets from Space ★★★★ U
Science-fiction comedy adventure 1999 · UK/US · Colour · 85mins

Nasally challenged Gonzo believes his long-lost family are aliens and that they're coming to take him home. Aspiring TV reporter Miss Piggy and assorted government agents, led by Jeffrey Tambor, want to abduct him for their own ends. Although more earthbound than the title suggests, this boasts a relatively coherent storyline and the incessant gags achieving a high chuckle factor. Although Fozzie Bear still doesn't get the starring role he deserves, movies from *Close Encounters* to *The Shawshank Redemption* are wickedly parodied, while F Murray Abraham, Ray Liotta and Andie MacDowell seem to be having a great time. ▣ **DVD**

Frank Oz *Miss Piggy/Fozzie Bear/Animal/Sam Eagle* • Dave Goelz *Gonzo/Bunsen Honeydew/Waldorf/The Birdman* • Steve Whitmire *Kermit the Frog/Rizzo the Rat/Beaker/Cosmic Fish No 1* • Bill Barretta *Pepe the Prawn/Bobo as Rentro/Bubba the Rat/Johnny Fiama/Cosmic Fish No 2* • F Murray Abraham *Noah* • Ray Liotta *Gate guard* • Andie MacDowell *Shelley Snipes* ■ *Dir* Tim Hill • *Scr* Jerry Juhl, Joseph Mazzarino, Ken Kaufman

The Muppets Take Manhattan ★★★ U
Comedy 1984 · US · Colour · 93mins

The third big-screen outing for Jim Henson's puppets has playwright Kermit frog-marching his pals to New York to stage his college show on Broadway. Alas, he finds that biting the Big Apple can leave a sour taste in the mouth. It's not quite up to the standards of the two earlier outings, *The Muppet Movie* and *The Great Muppet Caper*, but the bouncy songs and clever use of Manhattan locations are bonuses. Muppet movies always feature a vast array of guest stars: watch out here for cameos from Liza Minnelli, Brooke Shields, Joan Rivers and Gregory Hines, among others. ▣

Jim Henson *Kermit the Frog/Rowlf/Dr Teeth/Ernie/Muppet newsman/Swedish chef/Waldorf* • Frank Oz *Miss Piggy/Fozzie Bear/Animal/Sam the Eagle/Bert/Cookie Monster* • Dave Goelz *Gonzo/Chester Rat/Bill the Frog/Dr Bunsen Honeydew/Zoot* • Steve Whitmire *Rizzo the Rat/Gil the Frog* ■ *Dir* Frank Oz • *Scr* Frank Oz, Tom Patchett, Jay Tarses, from a story by Tom Patchett, Jay Tarses

Murder ★★★ PG
Mystery 1930 · UK · BW · 99mins

Alfred Hitchcock's third talkie is a creaky murder mystery, co-adapted by Hitch's wife Alma Reville from a novel and a play by Clemence Dane and Helen Simpson. Herbert Marshall does well in only his second sound film as a juror who conducts his own inquiries after he suspects an actress isn't a killer. Without giving too much away, the denouement was considered rather daring in its day, as was the use of a stream-of-consciousness voice-over, which established Hitchcock as one of the most inventive of sound directors. The acting now seems rather stagey and the whodunit isn't particularly taxing, but it's still a fascinating exercise. ▣

Herbert Marshall *Sir John Menier* • Norah Baring *Diana Baring* • Phyllis Konstam *Dulcie Markham* • Edward Chapman *Ted Markham* • Miles Mander *Gordon Druce* • Esme Percy *Handel Fane* ■ *Dir* Alfred Hitchcock • *Scr* Alma Reville, Walter C Mycroft, Alfred Hitchcock, from the novel and play *Enter Sir John* by Clemence Dane, Helen Simpson

Murder Ahoy ★★★ U
Murder mystery 1964 · UK · BW · 88mins

The last entry in Margaret Rutherford's Miss Marple casebook is the only one not reworked from a story by Agatha Christie. While David Pursall and Jack Seddon's original screenplay has all the characteristics of a Christie whodunit, closer scrutiny reveals too many offbeat characters, a glut of inconsequential chat and more comedy (mostly for the benefit of an overcooked Lionel Jeffries) than you'd ever find in a well-stocked shelf of the

great Dame's marvellous mysteries. Having said that, it's neatly staged and the solution is neither blatantly obvious nor buried under a mass of barely perceptible clues. ▣

Margaret Rutherford *Miss Marple* • Lionel Jeffries *Captain Rhumstone* • Charles Tingwell *Detective Inspector Craddock* • William Mervyn *Breeze-Connington* • Joan Benham *Matron Alice Fanbraid* • Stringer Davis *Mr Stringer* • Nicholas Parsons *Dr Crump* • Derek Nimmo *Humbert* ■ *Dir* George Pollock • *Scr* David Pursall, Jack Seddon, from the character created by Agatha Christie

Murder at My Door ★★ 15
Thriller 1996 · US · Colour · 90mins

A grimmer-than-usual TV-movie chiller that focuses on a seemingly ordinary American family's dark secrets. Judith Light plays a mother still grieving following the death of her son and worrying about his surviving twin (played by *Roseanne* star Johnny Galecki), who is developing some rather morbid pastimes. Meanwhile, a serial killer is stalking the town's students. There are few surprises in the script, but director Eric Till manages to generate a fair amount of suspense. Contains violence. ▣

Judith Light *Irene McNair* • RH Thomson *Ed McNair* • Johnny Galecki *Teddy McNair* ■ *Dir* Eric Till • *Scr* Patti Sullivan, Chris Canaan

Murder at 1600 ★★ 15
Political thriller 1997 · US · Colour · 102mins

Wesley Snipes delivers another of his one-note tough guys in an uninspired, cliché-ridden action thriller about a Washington DC cop called in to investigate a murder at the White House. As he delves deeper into the crime with the help of Secret Service agent Diane Lane, he uncovers a conspiracy which may reach all the way to the President himself. Unfolding like a cheap novel, director Dwight Little's routine mystery generates little suspense and even less interest as the sloppy scenario keeps falling apart, adding further implausibility to a yarn that's already hard to swallow. Contains violence, some swearing and a sex scene. ▣ **DVD**

Wesley Snipes *Detective Harlan Regis* • Diane Lane *Nina Chance* • Alan Alda *Alvin Jordan* • Daniel Benzali *Nick Spikings* • Dennis Miller *Detective Stengel* • Ronny Cox *President Jack Neil* • Diane Baker *Kitty Neil* ■ *Dir* Dwight H Little • *Scr* Wayne Beach, David Hodgin

Murder at the Gallop ★★★ U
Murder mystery 1963 · UK · BW · 77mins

Robert Morley and Flora Robson add a touch of class to the list of suspects as Miss Marple investigates the murder of a rich recluse. While detective Charles Tingwell scratches his head in bewilderment, the divine Miss M lures the killer into a trap using herself as bait. Director George Pollock effortlessly blends clues and comedy in Margaret Rutherford's second outing as the doyenne of St Mary Mead, but the most striking thing about this irresistible whodunit is that it was inspired by the novel *After the Funeral*, in which the case was actually solved by Hercule Poirot! ▣

Margaret Rutherford *Miss Marple* • Robert Morley *Hector Enderby* • Flora Robson *Miss Gilchrist* • Charles Tingwell *Det Insp Craddock* • Stringer Davis *Mr Stringer* • Duncan Lamont *Hillman* • James Villiers *Michael Shane* ■ *Dir* George Pollock • *Scr* James P Cavanagh, David Pursall, Jack Seddon, from the novel *After The Funeral* by Agatha Christie

Murder at the Mardi Gras

★★

Crime thriller 1978 · US · Colour

Britain's Ken Annakin was in the twilight of a patchy career when he made his TV movie debut with this unconvincing blend of comedy and thrills. The film was made in the glow of Didi Conn's performance as Frenchie in *Grease*, but the actress demonstrates none of that exuberance in this tale of a featherbrained Philadelphia waitress who arrives in New Orleans looking for romance and ends up witnessing a murder.

Didi Conn *Julie Evans* • Bill Daily *Jack Murphy* • David Groh *Harry Benson* • Gregg Henry *Randy Brian* • Harry Morgan *Jim-Bob Jackson* • Ron Silver *Larry Cook* • Joyce Van Patten *Janet Murphy* • David Wayne *Mickey Mills* • Wolfman Jack ■ *Dir* Kenneth C Annakin [Ken Annakin] • *Scr* Stanley Ralph Ross

Murder at the Vanities

★★★

Thriller 1934 · US · BW · 95mins

A rare breed, this – a musical thriller set inside the famous Vanities vaudeville theatre and opening with a dance routine that features nude ladies inside huge models of powder compacts. There's also a near-Hitchcock moment when one of the girls finds blood dripping from the catwalk on to her shoulder. Director Mitchell Leisen's biographer, David Chierichetti, claimed the film "pushed the limits of bawdiness and nudity farther than they would go in any American film until the 1960s".

Victor McLaglen *Bill Murdock* • Carl Brisson *Eric Lander* • Jack Oakie *Jack Ellery* • Kitty Carlisle *Ann Ware* • Gertrude Michael *Rita Ross* • Jessie Ralph *Mrs Smith* • Gail Patrick *Sadie Evans* • Charles B Middleton [Charles Middleton] *Homer* • Clara Lou Sheridan [Ann Sheridan] *Lou* ■ *Dir* Mitchell Leisen • *Scr* Carey Wilson, Joseph Gollomb, Sam Hellman, from the play by Earl Carroll, Rufus King

Murder at the Windmill ★★

Musical 1949 · UK · BW · 70mins

Comic policemen Garry Marsh and Jon Pertwee investigate a murder at London's Windmill theatre, famous for its nude tableaux and the fact that it remained open throughout the Second World War. Partly filmed *in situ*, with performers and staff playing themselves, this creaky whodunit is a valuable record, within the bounds of the strict censorship of the day, of the lowbrow songs and sketches that made the theatre famous. Jimmy Edwards's spot, dreadful now, was thought hilarious at the time, and won the whiskery comic his part in radio's celebrated *Take It From Here*.

Garry Marsh *Detective Inspector* • Jon Pertwee *Sergeant* • Jack Livesey *Vivian Van Damm* • Eliot Makeham *Gimpy* • Jimmy Edwards *Jimmy* • Diana Decker *Frankie* • Donald Clive *Donald* • Jill Anstey *Patsy* ■ *Dir/Scr* Val Guest

Murder at the World Series

★★ PG

Thriller 1977 · US · Colour · 96mins

Janet Leigh stars in this baseball thriller about a kidnapping plot involving five women during the last two games of the World Series in Houston. A rather trite and predictable TV movie directed by Andrew V McLaglen who was more at home with westerns. It has some interesting moments of atmosphere, but not much more to recommend it.

Janet Leigh *Karen Weese* • Lynda Day George *Margot Mannering* • Murray Hamilton *Harvey Murkison* • Bruce Boxleitner *Cisco* • Karen Valentine *Lois Marshall* • Gerald O'Loughlin [Gerald S O'Loughlin] *Moe Gold* • Michael Parks *Larry Marshall* ■ *Dir* Andrew V McLaglen • *Scr* Cy Cermak

Murder between Friends

★★★ 15

Comedy drama 1994 · US · Colour · 91mins

Alfred Hitchcock couldn't have put together a more intriguing plot for this story of a perplexing murder in Louisiana, actually based on true events. Stephen Lang (*The Hard Way*) and Martin Kemp (*The Krays*) play friends who are spotted leaving the house where Lang's wife has been beaten to death; both then insist the other is guilty of the murder, and it's left to assistant DA Timothy Busfield to unravel the mystery. It borders on the melodramatic, but Lang and Kemp deliver chilling performances, and there are solid supporting turns from Nicholas Pryor and Lisa Blount.

Timothy Busfield *Assistant DA John Thorn* • Stephen Lang *Kerry Meyers* • Martin Kemp *Bill Fontanille* • Lisa Blount *Janet Myers* • O'Neal Compton *Detective Easby* • Alex Courtney *Rene Legallais* ■ *Dir* Waris Hussein • *Scr* Philip Rosenberg

Murder by Contract ★★★

Thriller 1958 · US · BW · 80mins

Here's a real gem and total justification for the existence of the B-movie. X-certificated in the UK on release, this darkly sinister plot masks a deeply original screenplay proffering philosophical insights into what makes hit man Vince Edwards (long before his role as TV doctor Ben Casey) tick. Ostensibly he wants more cash on discovering that his victim is female, but really he begins to ruminate on himself and his ambitions. Stunningly directed by Irving Lerner and cleverly produced on a shoestring, this is original, clever and absorbing.

Vince Edwards *Claude* • Phillip Pine *Marc* • Herschel Bernardi *George* • Michael Granger *Moon* • Caprice Toriel *Billie Williams* ■ *Dir* Irving Lerner • *Scr* Ben Simcoe

Murder by Death ★★ PG

Detective spoof 1976 · US · Colour · 90mins

A bizarre hotchpotch of greats, also-rans and has-beens combine to pay the mortgage in one of those whodunits in a big house. Truman Capote has gathered together the world's top sleuths to present them with a slaying due to take place at midnight, and only Maggie Smith is worth watching as the hands creep round. This one belongs firmly in the genre that maintains that as long as you can get enough famous names on the poster the public will accept anything. Not true.

Peter Sellers *Sidney Wang* • Peter Falk *Sam Diamond* • David Niven *Dick Charleston* • Maggie Smith *Dora Charleston* • Alec Guinness *Butler Bensonumum* • Truman Capote *Lionel Twain* • Eileen Brennan *Tess Skeffington* • James Coco *Milo Perrier* • Elsa Lanchester *Jessica Marbles* ■ *Dir* Robert Moore • *Scr* Neil Simon

Murder by Decree ★★ 15

Detective drama
1978 · Can/UK · Colour · 118mins

Rather than having Holmes and Watson plod wearily around London, director Bob Clark gives them a surprisingly imaginative lift. Following a similar course to Stephen Knight's book, *The Final Solution*, the film proposes politicians, freemasons and royalty as links to the Jack the Ripper murders. Such speculation is made with a fair degree of gothic credibility, even though the flabby plot wanders off up too many byways. Also, Donald Sutherland is not the best choice as a fruitcake visionary. Still, even during moments of slack, Christopher Plummer and James Mason interpret their roles as Holmes and Watson with plenty of heart.

Christopher Plummer *Sherlock Holmes* • James Mason *Dr Watson* • David Hemmings *Inspector Foxborough* • Anthony Quayle *Sir Charles Warren* • Geneviève Bujold *Annie Crook* • Frank Finlay *Inspector Lestrade* • John Gielgud *Prime Minister* • Donald Sutherland *Robert Lees* ■ *Dir* Bob Clark • *Scr* John Hopkins, from a story by Bob Clark, from characters created by Sir Arthur Conan Doyle

Murder by Night ★★ 15

Crime thriller 1989 · US · Colour · 89mins

That king of the TV movie, Robert Urich, here stars in a so-so thriller about a man, found unconscious at a murder scene, who has lost his memory and is suspected by the police of either being the killer or a witness to the crime. Urich is his usual reliable self, and he is ably supported by Michael Ironside, best known as the bad guy in *Total Recall*, but they both lose the fight against a plodding script and predictable plot.

Robert Urich *Allan Strong* • Kay Lenz *Karen Hicks* • Michael Ironside *Carl Madsen* • Jim Metzler *Kevin Carlisle* • Sandra P Grant *Nurse* • Geoffrey Bowes *Doctor* ■ *Dir* Paul Lynch • *Scr* Alan B McElroy

Murder by Phone ★★ 15

Chiller 1982 · Can · Colour · 89mins

If you answer the phone in this picture you end up dead. The killer has devised a system that sends an electric pulse down the line, which sends the brain into immediate meltdown. The room you are in also gets a makeover. (This might sound familiar to fans of thirties B-movies as a similar idea was used in a prescient 1935 film *Murder by Television*.) Richard Chamberlain is the science lecturer investigating the death of a student, John Houseman is a glorified telephone engineer and Sara Botsford an artist who taps into phone company files to trap the killer.

Richard Chamberlain *Nat Bridger* • John Houseman *Dr Stanley Markowitz* • Sara Botsford *Ridley Taylor* • Robin Gammell *Noah Clayton* • Gary Reineke *Detective Meara* • Barry Morse *Fred Waits* ■ *Dir* Michael Anderson • *Scr* Michael Butler, Dennis Shryack, John Kent Harrison

Murder by Rope ★★

Thriller 1936 · UK · BW · 64mins

A man who laughed in the dock at his death sentence appears to return from the gallows to take revenge on the people involved in his trial and execution. This dramatic set-up is frittered away in a cheap British B-feature which helped fulfil Paramount's quota obligations as a distributor. After a judge dies at a country house gathering, DA Clarke-Smith's handwriting expert interrogates the usual suspects. The explanation is delightfully preposterous.

Constance Godridge *Daphne Farrow* • DA Clarke-Smith *Hanson* • Sunday Wilshin *Lucille Davine* • Wilfrid Hyde White *Alastair Dane* • Donald Read *Peter Paxton* • Daphne Courtney *Flora* ■ *Dir* George Pearson • *Scr* Ralph Neale

Murder by the Book ★★ PG

Crime drama 1986 · US · Colour · 90mins

Robert Hays, whose career never took off after his starring role in *Airplane!*, here plays a mystery writer involved in a real crime in a *Murder, She Wrote*-style thriller. Catherine Mary Stewart is the moll he's trying to rescue, but maybe he should have spent more time trying to save the script, which never rises above the mediocre. Only worth watching to see old-timers Fred Gwynne from *The Munsters* and *High Society's* Celeste Holm.

Robert Hays *Hank Mercer* • Catherine Mary Stewart *Merissa Winfield* • Fred Gwynne *Victor Greville* • Celeste Holm *Claire Mercer* ■ *Dir* Mel Damski • *Scr* Michael Norell, from the novel *Alter Ego* by Mel Arrighi

Murder COD ★★

Thriller 1990 · US · Colour · 96mins

This could be seen as being loosely based on Alfred Hitchcock's *Rear Window*, with the story reversed. This time it's the villain, a self-appointed hit man, who's the eavesdropper, using a formidable array of surveillance equipment to select his victims. Patrick Duffy is the detective trying to discover a common thread and the killer is played by William Devane, best remembered for his charming villain in Hitchcock's *Family Plot*. Despite some effectively macabre scenes, though, it all seems rather predictable.

William Devane *Alex Brandt* • Patrick Duffy *Steve Murtaugh* • Chelsea Field *Ellie Murtaugh* • Mariette Hartley *Sally Kramer* • Charles Robinson *Lieutenant Silk* • Walt Hoppert *Arthur Kramer* • Allan Miller *Leon Walsh* ■ *Dir* Alan Metzger • *Scr* Andrew Peter Martin, from the novel *Kill Fee* by Barbara Paul

Murder, He Says ★★★

Comedy 1945 · US · BW · 94mins

This slapstick comedy is one of the most bizarre pictures made in Hollywood, a kind of *Arsenic and Old Lace* in hillbilly country that's either very funny or totally unendurable, depending on your point of view. Fred MacMurray stars as the insurance

966 U = SUITABLE FOR ALL Uc = SUITABLE FOR ALL, ESPECIALLY FOR YOUNG CHILDREN (VIDEO ONLY) PG = PARENTAL GUIDANCE

investigator who runs into Marjorie Main's mad brood in a house where poisoned food glows in the dark (along with anyone foolish enough to eat it) and secret passages lead to hidden treasure. The film was shot chronologically by veteran director George Marshall, who claimed to have made it up as he went along with the help of writer Lou Breslow and suggestions from the cast.

Fred MacMurray *Pete Marshall* • Helen Walker *Claire Mathews* • Marjorie Main *Marnie Johnson* • Jean Heather *Elany Fleagle* • Porter Hall *Mr Johnson* • Peter Whitney *Mert Fleagle/ Bert Fleagle* ■ *Dir* George Marshall • *Scr* Lou Breslow, from a story by Jack Moffitt

Murder in a College Town

★★ 15

Drama based on a true story
1997 · US · Colour · 87mins

Kate Jackson could have used some help from her old *Charlie's Angels* castmates in this run-of-the-mill TV movie. In 1990, a blue-collar Pittsburgh mother (Jackson) sends her favourite son off to college, where he goes missing after becoming entangled with a wealthy frat boy and an older, alluring con woman. Mom teams up with a private investigator to discover the sordid truth. The pacing is slow, the casting uninspired, while Jackson phones in her role as the distraught mother turned sleuth. Contains some swearing and violence.

Kate Jackson *Rose Earl* • Kristian Alfonso *Chelsea Coates* • Matthew Settle *Tom Stahl* • Drew Ebersole *Bobby Earl* ■ *Dir* Bradley Wigor • *Scr* Joseph Maurer

Murder in Black & White

★★★

Thriller   1990 · US · Colour

Richard Crenna and Cliff Gorman are paired once again for this sequel to the mini-series *Doubletake* and *Internal Affairs* (which were based on detective novelist William Bayer's thrillers). This time the detectives find themselves investigating the death of the black police commissioner in New York. As with the previous two tales, this is grittier than the usual made-for-TV police fare and Crenna is excellent in the lead role. The reliable supporting cast includes Diahann Carroll, Philip Bosco and Herman Munster himself, Fred Gwynne.

Richard Crenna *Lieutenant Frank Janek* • Diahann Carroll *Margo Stover* • Keith David *Martin Stover* • Fred Gwynne *Brannigan* • Cliff Gorman *Aaron Greenberg* • Philip Bosco *Captain John Wyckoff* ■ *Dir* Robert Iscove • *Scr* Gordon Cotler

Murder in High Places ★★

Crime adventure   1991 · US · Colour · 97mins

A rather ludicrous buddy thriller, with Adam Baldwin (no relation to Alec, William et al) as the cop who teams up with mayor Ted Levine (who played Buffalo Bill in *The Silence of the Lambs*) to investigate the murder of Levine's ex-wife. And what a murder: the high point (pardon the pun) of this run-of-the-mill tale is when Levine's ex-spouse drops in (literally) to a party from about 30,000 feet. Shame the rest of John Byrum's film couldn't live up to its early promise.

Ted Levine *Carson Russell* • Adam Baldwin *Stoney Ptak* • Judith Hoag *Meg Faithorn* • Miguel Ferrer *Dick Wilhoite* • Richard Edson *Noogie Feliz* • Dana Wheeler-Nicholson *Natalie* • James Keach *Ronald Levering* • Traci Lords *Diane Cody* ■ *Dir/Scr* John Byrum

Murder in Mind   ★★★ 18

Psychological thriller
1996 · US/UK · Colour · 84mins

Nigel Hawthorne leads an impressive cast as a respected psychiatrist who uses hypnosis to question a disturbed Mary-Louise Parker, the prime suspect in the murder of her husband. As the mind games are played out, the lines between victim, suspect and investigator become blurred. It's a claustrophobic, sometimes erratic affair, but there are striking supporting turns from Jimmy Smits and Jason Scott Lee. Rather surprisingly, it went straight to video over here. Contains violence, swearing and brief nudity.

Nigel Hawthorne *Dr Ellis* • Mary Louise Parker [Mary-Louise Parker] *Caroline* • Jimmy Smits *Peter* • Jason Scott Lee *Holloway* • Gailard Sartain *Charlie* • Jon Cedar *Superior officer* ■ *Dir* Andrew Morahan • *Scr* Michael Cooney, from his play

Murder in Mississippi

★★★★ 15

Drama   1990 · US · Colour · 92mins

A US TV movie made just two years after Alan Parker's Oscar-nominated *Mississippi Burning*. However, while Parker's movie was only loosely based on truth, this small-screen flick sticks more closely to the known facts about the murder of three civil rights activists by the Ku Klux Klan in the Deep South. Parker's movie was a hard act to follow yet, thanks to a strong narrative, superior acting and a mournful score, this powerful and violent second stab at the story makes almost equally compelling viewing.

Tom Hulce *Mickey Schwerner* • Blair Underwood *James Chaney* • Josh Charles *Andrew Goodman* • Jennifer Grey *Rita Schwerner* • Eugene Byrd *Ben Chaney Jr* • Donzaleigh Abernathy *Sue Brown* • CCH Pounder *Fannie Lee Chaney* ■ *Dir* Roger Young • *Scr* Stanley Weiser, from an article by Ben Stein • *Music* Mason Daring

Murder in My Mind   ★ 15

Thriller   1997 · US · Colour · 87mins

A lacklustre sci-fi thriller with a sleepwalking script to match. Soap opera icon Nicollette Sheridan is the sexy FBI agent assigned to an apparently unsolvable case of a serial killer who preys on beautiful blondes. Her scientist husband is experimenting with memory transplants among rats and, in an attempt to break the investigative deadlock, she ill-advisedly decides to take on the memory of one of the killer's victims who is in a coma. Bad idea. Contains violence and some swearing.

Nicollette Sheridan *Agent Callain Peterson* • Stacy Keach *Agent Cargill* • Peter Outerbridge *Jack Bolinas* • Peter Coyote *Dr Arthur Lefcourt* ■ *Dir* Robert Iscove • *Scr* Tom Swale

Murder in New Hampshire

★★ 15

Crime drama based on a true story
1991 · US · Colour · 89mins

A TV movie based on an infamous real-life case in which a small-town schoolteacher plans to murder her husband with the help of her student lover. Not the most obvious role for Oscar winner Helen Hunt, but she attacks it with gusto and, even though the whole farrago has a rather "filming by numbers" feel, it still packs a generous punch. Definitely made on the cheap as soon as the ink was dry on the riveting court case.

Helen Hunt *Pamela Smart* • Chad Allen *Billy Flynn* • Michael Learned *Judy Smart* • Ken Howard *Bill Smart* • Howard Hesseman *DA Paul Maggiotto* • Larry Drake *Mark Sisti* ■ *Dir* Joyce Chopra • *Scr* William Wood, Joe Cacaci

Murder in Paradise   ★★

Crime drama   1990 · US · Colour · 96mins

An off-the-peg thriller, made for TV, with Kevin Kilner as a New York cop whose wife is murdered by a serial killer. Unable to solve the case he says goodbye to the dirt of New York City and hello to Hawaii, where he hopes for a quieter life. But guess what? The Aloha State turns out to be just as dangerous when a murder there proves to be exactly like his last case. A reasonable yarn, with a twist or two and lots of sunshine.

Kevin Kilner *Charlie Raski* • Maggie Han *Dr Diane Mahona* • Mako *Captain Kilalo* • James Sutorius *Dave Craft* • James Pax *Jim Ishita* • Yuji Okumoto *Jackie Lo* • Manu Tupou *Willy Kua* • John Pleshette *Wagner Thorne* • Barbara Carrera *Emma Danton* ■ *Dir* Fred Walton • *Scr* Gerald DiPego, from a story by Bill McCutchen, Hanania Baer

Murder in the Cathedral

★★ U

Religious drama   1952 · UK · BW · 145mins

TS Eliot's play about Thomas à Becket and the political and theosophical complexities surrounding his murder by Henry II's henchmen was first performed in 1935. Negligible as a piece of cinema, this film version preserves Eliot's text and allows us to see National Theatre actors like Leo McKern much as theatre audiences would have seen them. We hear Eliot himself, as the "Fourth tempter", goading Henry into killing his Archbishop. The director, George Hoellering, was a Hungarian émigré who was known mainly as the proprietor of the Academy, for years London's leading arthouse cinema.

John Groser *Thomas à Becket* • Alexander Gauge *King Henry II* • David Ward *First tempter* • George Woodbridge *Second tempter* • Basil Burton *Third tempter* • TS Eliot *Fourth tempter* • Donald Bisset *First priest* • Clement McCallin *Second priest* • Leo McKern *Third knight* ■ *Dir* George Hoellering • *Scr* George Hoellering, from the play by TS Eliot

Murder in the City of Angels   ★★

Crime thriller   1988 · US · Colour

White-haired *A-Team* star George Peppard plays a cop who takes on the mob in this "one man against the world" TV thriller. Peppard is his usual grizzled self, and he's certainly the best thing in what is otherwise a rather banal tale. It's the sort of thing that would only take up a 45-minute slot in an episode of *Starsky and Hutch*.

George Peppard *Frank Doakey* • Kathryn Harrold *Marilyn Butler* • Max Gail *Vernon "Rusty" Kitchens* • Barry Corbin *Roy "Big Mac" McCleary* • Stella Stevens *Joey Day* • Fredric Lehne *Sammy Turner* ■ *Dir* Steven Hilliard Stern • *Scr* David J Kinghorn

Murder in the First

★★★★ 15

Drama based on a true story
1994 · US · Colour · 117mins

Kevin Bacon gives the performance of his career in this sensational assault on the prison system. Based on the actual experiences of Henri Young, Marc Rocco's uncompromising picture alternates between Alcatraz and a forbidding courtroom, as lawyer Christian Slater tries to pin Bacon's murder of a fellow inmate on the regime that maltreated him to the verge of madness. A little over-intense at times, this is essentially a showcase for its two leads, although Gary Oldman is terrifyingly sinister as the nasty Warden Glenn. Exhausting but enthralling. Contains swearing, violence and a sex scene.

Christian Slater *James Stamphill* • Kevin Bacon *Henri Young* • Gary Oldman *Associate Warden Glenn* • Embeth Davidtz *Mary McCasslin* • Bill Macy [William H Macy] *William McNeil* • Stephen Tobolowsky *Mr Henkin* • Brad Dourif *Byron Stamphill* • R Lee Ermey *Judge Clawson* ■ *Dir* Marc Rocco • *Scr* Dan Gordon

Murder in the Music Hall

★★

Mystery   1946 · US · BW · 87mins

Former Olympic skater Vera Hruba Ralston donned her blades for this hammy hogwash from the biggest studio on Hollywood's "poverty row", Republic. The skating sequences rather slow down the action in a fair-to-middlin' whodunit which, in typical B-movie style, is taken at such a lick that it's next to impossible to follow what's going on. Ann Rutherford, Julie Bishop and Helen Walker are on cop William Gargan's list of suspects, but where is the blind man who is the key to the mystery?

Vera Hruba Ralston *Lila* • William Marshall *Don* • Helen Walker *Millicent* • Nancy Kelly *Mrs Morgan* • William Gargan *Inspector Wilson* • Ann Rutherford *Gracie* • Julie Bishop *Diane* ■ *Dir* John English • *Scr* Frances Hyland, Laszlo Gorog, from a story by Arnold Phillips, Maria Matray

Murder, Inc   ★★★★

Crime drama   1951 · US · BW · 84mins

Released in America as *The Enforcer* with an X certificate, this terrific Warner Bros crime drama features Humphrey Bogart on the right side of the law for once, closing in on a gang of professional killers with the help of key witnesses, including Zero Mostel in one of his last movie roles before he was blacklisted during the communist witch-hunt. Bretaigne Windust takes the credit as director, though most of the film was actually directed by the uncredited Raoul Walsh (*The Roaring*

Twenties, *High Sierra*). Crimebusting US senator Estes Kefauver supplies the earnest on-screen prologue, and, unusually, there's no romance to slow down the action as it moves to a riveting, suspense-laden finale.

Humphrey Bogart *Martin Ferguson* • Zero Mostel *''Big Babe'' Lazich* • Ted De Corsia *Joseph Rico* • Everett Sloane *Albert Mendoza* • Roy Roberts *Captain Frank Nelson* • Lawrence Tolan *''Duke'' Tiano* • King Donovan *Sergeant Whitlow* • Robert Steele [Bob Steele] *Herman* ■ *Dir* Bretaigne Windust, Raoul Walsh • *Scr* Martin Rackin

Murder, Inc ★★

Crime drama   1960 · US · BW · 103mins

A mob movie about the Depression-era gang headed by Albert Anastasia and Louis ''Lepke'' Buchalter, whose hit men later went freelance and rubbed out to order. Set in thirties New York, it stars Stuart Whitman and May Britt as nightclub performers caught up in a spiral of blackmail and extortion. What should have been an 80-minute firecracker is extended in a futile stab at social significance and gets hopelessly bogged down in plot and subplot. Peter Falk overacts hilariously as a hissable, cartoon-strip killer, though jazz fans will welcome the appearance by Sarah Vaughn.

Stuart Whitman *Joey* • May Britt *Eadie* • Henry Morgan *Turkus* • Peter Falk *Reles* • David J Stewart *Lepke* • Simon Oakland *Tobin* • Warren Fennerty *Bug* • Sarah Vaughn • Howard I Smith [Howard Smith] *Albert Anastasia* ■ *Dir* Burt Balaban, Stuart Rosenberg • *Scr* Irv Tunick, Mel Barr, Sid Feder, from the non-fiction book by Burton Turkus

Murder Man ★★★

Crime drama   1935 · US · BW · 70mins

From a time when newspapermen were the folk heroes that psychiatrists and counter-agents became in later years, comes this low-budget but gutsy crime drama. Spencer Tracy is the boozy reporter who plots the perfect revenge for the crooks who ruined his father and caused the suicide of his estranged wife, while Virginia Bruce is the girl who loves him and tends his hangovers. The great Lionel Atwill articulates authority with every word, while a briefly-glimpsed James Stewart is starting to drawl his way to stardom.

Spencer Tracy *Steve Gray* • Virginia Bruce *Mary Shannon* • Lionel Atwill *Capt Cole* • Harvey Stephens *Henry Mander* • Robert Barrat *Robbins* • James Stewart *Shorty* • William Collier Sr *Pop Gray* • William Demarest *Rod McGuire* ■ *Dir* Tim Whelan • *Scr* Tim Whelan, John C Higgins, from a story by Tim Whelan, Guy Bolton

Murder Most Foul ★★★ ▣U

Murder mystery   1964 · UK · BW · 86mins

Margaret Rutherford dons the tweed twinset of Miss Marple for the third time after *Murder at the Gallop* and *Murder Ahoy* in this rather contrived adaptation of *Mrs McGinty's Dead*, the second Hercule Poirot case to be reworked as a vehicle for Agatha Christie's spinster sleuth. Having hung a jury during a murder trial, Miss M treads the boards with a shambolic theatre company to find the real culprit. Ron Moody is over the top as a temperamental thesp, but director

George Pollock sustains the suspense and there is solid support from series regulars Charles Tingwell and Rutherford's real-life husband, Stringer Davis. ▣

Margaret Rutherford *Miss Marple* • Ron Moody *Driffold Cosgood* • Charles Tingwell *Detective Inspector Craddock* • Andrew Cruickshank *Justice Crosby* • Megs Jenkins *Mrs Thomas* • Ralph Michael *Ralph Summers* • James Bolam *Bill Hanson* • Stringer Davis *Mr Stringer* • Francesca Annis *Sheila Upward* ■ *Dir* George Pollock • *Scr* David Pursall, Jack Seddon, from the novel *Mrs McGinty's Dead* by Agatha Christie

A Murder of Crows ★★★

Action thriller   1998 · US · Colour · 101mins

A slick if barely credible suspense yarn, with Cuba Gooding Jr as a disbarred lawyer turned writer who appropriates a dead man's unpublished novel and passes it off as his own. The novel's a huge hit. But Cuba is hauled up on homicide charges when killings in the book are found to mirror real-life murders and include details that only the killer himself could have known. The film hinges on a daft piece of deception, and some of the dialogue, especially Gooding Jr's voice-over narration, tries too hard to sound hardboiled. But it's stylishly made and well-acted by a quality cast that includes Tom Berenger, Eric Stoltz and Marianne Jean-Baptiste (*Secret & Lies*).

Cuba Gooding Jr *Russell Lawson* • Eric Stoltz *Thurman Parks III* • Tom Berenger *Clifford Dubose* • Marianne Jean-Baptiste *Elisabeth Pope* • Ashley Lauren [Ashley Laurence] *Janine DeVrie* • Doug Wert *Billy Ray* • Carmen Argenziano *Judge Bon* ■ *Dir/Scr* Rowdy Herrington

Murder of Innocence ★★ ▣18

Crime drama based on a true story 1993 · US · Colour · 94mins

Judging by the glut of American TV movies on the subject, there must be a neighbourhood eccentric around every corner in the USA. Based on the inevitable true story, this tells the tale of a seemingly normal housewife whose increasingly oddball behaviour begins to deeply concern her husband. It soon becomes clear that his worries are tragically justified. Stars Valerie Bertinelli and Stephen Caffrey are helped by a competent enough supporting cast, but there are few surprises in either the script or the direction. ▣

Valerie Bertinelli *Laurie Wade* • Stephen Caffrey *Matthew Wade* • Graham Beckel *Frank Kendall* • Jerry Hardin *Mort Webber* • Millie Perkins *Edna Webber* ■ *Dir* Tom McLoughlin • *Scr* Philip Rosenberg, from the book by Joel Kaplan, George Papajohn, Eric Zorn

Murder on a Bridle Path ★★

Comedy mystery   1936 · US · BW · 63mins

It took two directors and four writers to fashion this fourth entry in the Hildegarde Withers RKO series. This time Helen Broderick (Broderick Crawford's mum) took over as the sleuthing schoolmarm from the redoubtable Edna May Oliver, but to lesser effect. James Gleason is still aboard as cigar-chomping cop Oscar Piper, but unfortunately is lumbered here with some very silly dialogue. That

and the slowish pace make this a weaker entry in the generally excellent series, although the finale is great fun.

James Gleason *Inspector Oscar Piper* • Helen Broderick *Hildegarde Withers* • Louise Latimer *Barbara Foley* • Owen Davis Jr *Eddie Fry* • John Arledge *Joey* ■ *Dir* William Hamilton, Edward Killy • *Scr* Dorothy Yost, Thomas Lennon, Edmund H North, James Gow, from the novel by Stuart Palmer

Murder on a Honeymoon ★★★

Mystery   1935 · US · BW · 94mins

The third film in RKO's splendid series featuring schoolteacher sleuth Hildegarde Withers (played by Edna May Oliver in her last appearance in the role) and detective partner Oscar Piper (James Gleason). Wittily co-scripted by famed humourist Robert Benchley, it has the distinction of actually being filmed on location on Catalina Island off the coast of California. Very enjoyable indeed.

Edna May Oliver *Hildegarde Withers* • James Gleason *Inspector Oscar Piper* • Lola Lane *Phyllis La Font* • Chick Chandler *Pilot French* • George Meeker *Kelsey* • Dorothy Libaire *Kay Deving* • Harry Ellerbe *Marvin Deving* ■ *Dir* Lloyd Corrigan • *Scr* Seton I Miller, Robert Benchley, from the novel *Puzzle of the Pepper Tree* by Stuart Palmer

Murder on the Blackboard ★★

Mystery   1934 · US · BW · 71mins

In the second of RKO's series based on Stuart Palmer's stories, Edna May Oliver and James Gleason as Hildegarde Withers and Oscar Piper investigate the death of a schoolteacher. Also returning from the first film is delightful character actor Edgar Kennedy, as one of Gleason's colleagues. Thinking about marriage at the end of the first film, Withers and Piper are single here, presumably to make the drama more interesting. Not as good as the original, but fun if you're in the mood.

Edna May Oliver *Hildegarde Withers* • James Gleason *Inspector Oscar Piper* • Bruce Cabot *Asst principal Addison Stevens* • Gertrude Michael *Janey Davis* • Regis Toomey *Smiley* • Edgar Kennedy *Detective Donahue* • Tully Marshall *MacFarland* • Jackie Searle *Leland Jones* ■ *Dir* George Archainbaud • *Scr* Willis Goldbeck, from the story by Stuart Palmer

Murder on the Iditarod Trail ★★★

Adventure   1995 · US · Colour · 97mins

Long an admirer of Sue Henry's novel, Kate Jackson finally brought this outdoor adventure to American TV screens under the title *The Cold Heart of a Killer*. Rolling back the years to her *Charlie's Angels* days, she turns in a gutsy performance as a contestant in a gruelling dogsled race, who quickly realises that she's more in peril from one of her fellow competitors than the icy wastes of Alaska. With Corbin Bernsen heading a weather-beaten supporting cast and director Paul Schneider setting a cracking pace, this is proof positive that actresses can handle action roles. Contains some violence and swearing.

Kate Jackson *Jessie Arnold* • Corbin Bernsen *Alex Jensen* • Kevin Zegers *Matthew Arnold* •

Nick Allan *Dave Haggerty* ■ *Dir* Paul Schneider • *Scr* Mimi Rothman Schapiro, Bill Wells, Colley Cibber, from the novel by Sue Henry

Murder on the Orient Express ★★★★ ▣PG

Murder mystery 1974 · UK · Colour · 122mins

Easily the best screen adaptation of an Agatha Christie whodunit and, for those unfamiliar with either book or film, the solution will take your breath away. Albert Finney earned an Oscar nomination for his wonderful performance as Hercule Poirot, which makes the fussy Belgian detective seem every bit as preposterous as Christie intended, yet without relying on the oversize mannerisms of Peter Ustinov. The supporting cast does everything that is expected of it, with Ingrid Bergman's Oscar-winning turn just about the pick of a stellar selection. Praise should also go to director Sidney Lumet for keeping you guessing right to the end. Contains some swearing. ▣

Albert Finney *Hercule Poirot* • Lauren Bacall *Mrs Hubbard* • Martin Balsam *Bianchi* • Ingrid Bergman *Greta Ohlsson* • Jacqueline Bisset *Countess Andrenyi* • Jean-Pierre Cassel *Pierre Paul Michel* • Sean Connery *Colonel Arbuthnot* • John Gielgud *Beddoes* • Wendy Hiller *Princess Dragomiroff* • Anthony Perkins *Hector McQueen* • Vanessa Redgrave *Mary Debenham* • Rachel Roberts *Hildegarde Schmidt* • Richard Widmark *Ratchett* • Michael York *Count Andrenyi* • Colin Blakely *Hardman* ■ *Dir* Sidney Lumet • *Scr* Paul Dehn, from the novel by Agatha Christie

Murder on the Rio Grande ★★

Thriller   1993 · US · Colour · 100mins

It may predate the similarly plotted *The River Wild*, but this TV movie suffers in comparison with its big-budget Hollywood companion. Nevertheless, Victoria Principal gives a spirited performance as a woman who goes on a seemingly idyllic rafting trip only to find herself pursued by a gang of villains. Principal apart, the rest of the cast is rather anonymous while the direction of TV veteran Robert Iscove is proficient rather than exhilarating. Contains violence.

Victoria Principal *Maggie Keene* • Peter Onorati *Kim* • Sean Murray *Matthew* • David R Beecroft [David Beecroft] *Eric* • Gary Grubbs *CW Hardgrave* • Ari Meyers *Nancy* ■ *Dir* Robert Iscove • *Scr* Michael Norell

Murder 101 ★★★ ▣15

Crime thriller   1991 · US · Colour · 88mins

While the title suggests an elementary effort, you'll be pleasantly surprised by what turns out to be a rather sophisticated assignment. A pre-James Bond Pierce Brosnan stars as a college English professor teaching a mystery writing class, who challenges his pupils to write the perfect crime story and then finds himself the patsy in someone's murder scheme. Brosnan turns in a sparkling and engaging performance, while the plot's twists and turns take the audience on a fun ride. Co-writer/director Bill Condon (*Gods and Monsters*) does well with his clever, inventive and intelligent script, placing this original TV-movie mystery at the top of its class. 🖭

Pierce Brosnan *Professor Charles Lattimore* • Dey Young *Professor Laura Lattimore* • Antoni Corone *Mike Dowling* • Raphael Sbarge *Robert Miner* • Mark L Taylor *Henry Potter* • Kim Thomson *Francesca Lavin* ■ *Dir* Bill Condon • *Scr* Bill Condon, Roy Johansen

Murder or Memory? ★★ 15
Psychological drama
1994 · US · Colour · 86mins

This TV drama with a theme of "confession under hypnosis" doesn't really make for compulsive viewing. Based on a true story, the tale concerns a teenager owning up to a murder after a game of strip poker goes wrong. However, his parents are convinced of his innocence and are determined to fight the legal system over what they claim is a bogus confession. Leigh Taylor-Young takes the lead role as the battling mum, but the direction from Christopher Leitch is plodding. Contains swearing. 🖭

Leigh Taylor-Young *Barbara Hansen* • Michael Brandon *Arnie Hansen* • Karl David-Djerf *Chris Hansen* • Rebecca Budig *Kathy Hansen* ■ *Dir* Christopher Leitch • *Scr* Dan Levine, from a story by Anthony Adams, Christina Adams

Murder She Said ★★ PG
Murder mystery
1961 · UK · BW · 83mins

Through the window of a passing train, Miss Marple (Margaret Rutherford) spots a woman being murdered. When no corpse can be found, however, her suspicions are dismissed as the ravings of an eccentric elderly spinster. Determined to solve the mystery, she takes a job as a maid at the estate of James Robertson-Justice... The first screen adaptation to star Rutherford as Agatha Christie's amateur sleuth only holds the interest now because of its star's unique persona and comic timing. Thanks to her, this otherwise uninteresting film found popularity and spawned three sequels. 🖭

Margaret Rutherford *Miss Marple* • Arthur Kennedy *Dr Quimper* • Muriel Pavlow *Emma Ackenthorpe* • James Robertson-Justice *Mr Ackenthorpe* • Charles Tingwell *Inspector Craddock* • Thorley Walters *Cedric Ackenthorpe* • Joan Hickson *Mrs Kidder* ■ *Dir* George Pollock • *Scr* David Pursall, Jack Seddon, David Osborn, from the novel *4.50 from Paddington* by Agatha Christie

Murder So Sweet ★★ PG
Mystery
1993 · US · Colour · 89mins

LA Law hunk Harry Hamlin should have stayed on the right side of the law if this mediocre TV movie from *Wired* director Larry Peerce is anything to go by. He's the lady-killer who may actually be killing ladies for real, or so his ex-wife Helen Shaver believes. It's all very predictable, and worth viewing only for the acting talents of Terence Knox, star of the television series *Tour of Duty*, who would be exciting to watch even if he was reading the Yellow Pages. 🖭

Harry Hamlin *Steve Catlin* • Helen Shaver *Edie Ballew* • KT Oslin *Candy* • Terence Knox *Bobby Ballew* • Ed Lauter *Glen Emory* • Frances Lee McCain *Bea Emory* • Daphne Ashbrook *Dyna Emory* ■ *Dir* Larry Peerce • *Scr* Caliope K Brattlestreet, Stephen Glantz

Murder Times Seven ★★★
Thriller
1990 · US · Colour · 97mins

Another entry in the occasional series featuring dogged cops Richard Crenna and Cliff Gorman. Here the focus is on a nasty multiple homicide that has left five people dead, one of whom happens to be Crenna's former sidekick. Crenna is believable in the lead role and he is well supported by Gorman, Susan Blakely and Moses Gunn. Jud Taylor's direction is a touch pedestrian, but it remains a better than average TV movie.

Richard Crenna *Lieutenant Frank Janek* • Cliff Gorman *Aaron Greenberg* • Moses Gunn *Inspector Paxton* • Susan Blakely *Gert* • Caroline Kava *Jean* • James McDaniel *Fred* ■ *Dir* Jud Taylor • *Scr* Monte Stettin, from a story by William Bayer

Murder without Crime ★★
Crime thriller
1950 · UK · BW · 78mins

Director J Lee Thompson – best known for *The Guns of Navarone* and the original *Cape Fear* – was also a playwright, and this is his own adaptation of his play, *Double Error*. It's basically a four-hander about a marriage, a murder and a third party who sees an opportunity for blackmail. The result is a film of modest budget and ambition with a nice performance by Dennis Price, as suave and duplicitous as ever.

Derek Farr *Stephen* • Dennis Price *Matthew* • Patricia Plunkett *Jan* • Joan Dowling *Grena* ■ *Dir* J Lee Thompson • *Scr* J Lee Thompson, from his play *Double Error*

Murder without Motive ★★ PG
Drama based on a true story
1992 · US · Colour · 91mins

This TV movie, based on a real-life incident, looks into the death of promising academic Edmund Perry, played by Curtis McClarin. Was he killed by accident or was he the victim of police racism? Expertly presenting the problem of 'hood loyalty facing many upwardly mobile African-American youths, director Kevin Hooks makes the most of his Harlem locations and pulls no punches in depicting the problems with crime and drugs. 🖭

Curtis L McClarin *Edmund Perry* • Anna Maria Horsford *Veronica Perry* • Carla Gugino *Allison Connors* • Christopher Daniel Barnes *Sean* • Taurean Blacque *Jonah Perry Sr* • Guy Killum *Jonah Perry* • Dakin Matthews *Howards* • Cuba Gooding Jr *Tyree* ■ *Dir* Kevin Hooks • *Scr* Richard Wesley, from the novel *Best Intentions* by Robert Sam Anson

The Murderers Are amongst Us ★★★
Drama
1946 · W Ger · BW · 87mins

This was one of the earliest German films to examine the notion of collective guilt in the Nazi era. A sombre, well-intentioned film shot in a style reminiscent of the expressionist films of the twenties, it concerns a doctor tormented by the terrible things he witnessed in a concentration camp. His anguish is accentuated by the presence of a man, responsible for mass executions, living a comfortable, untroubled life nearby. There is also an important early role for Hildegarde Neff

who subsequently became a Hollywood leading lady and one of Europe's greatest cabaret singers. In German with English subtitles.

Hildegarde Knef [Hildegarde Neff] *Susanna Wallner* • Ernst Borchert *Dr Hans Mertens* • Arno Paulsen *Capt Bruckner* • Erna Sellner *Frau Bruckner* ■ *Dir/Scr* Wolfgang Staudte

Murderers' Row ★★
Spy spoof
1966 · US · Colour · 108mins

In this sequel to *The Silencers*, Dean Martin returns as secret agent Matt Helm to save Washington from dastardly Karl Malden and his "Helio Beam". Martin's "morning after the night before" performance has a certain louche appeal, but, like any self-respecting Bond rip-off, Harry Levin's film has problems spoofing a spoof. (Indeed, the plot is remarkably similar to *Thunderball*.) The decor is hard on the eye, while Ann-Margret's disco gyrations are cringeworthy.

Dean Martin *Matt Helm* • Ann-Margret *Suzie Solaris* • Karl Malden *Julian Wall* • Camilla Sparv *Coco Duquette* • James Gregory *MacDonald* • Beverly Adams *Lovey Kravezit* • Richard Eastman *Dr Norman Solaris* ■ *Dir* Henry Levin • *Scr* Herbert Baker, from the novel by Donald Hamilton

A Murderous Affair ★★ 15
Drama based on a true story
1992 · US · Colour · 89mins

Virginia Madsen is probably best known for being terrorised by the Candyman and for having a Reservoir Dog for a brother (Michael). In this TV movie she plays another in a long line of *femmes fatales*. The Carolyn Warmus case made headline news in the States, as a seemingly respectable teacher not only had an affair with a married man, but also murdered his wife. The frankly sensational events have been toned down from their tabloid origins for TV consumption. William H Macy also appears. 🖭

Virginia Madsen *Carolyn Warmus* • Chris Sarandon *Paul Solomon* • Ned Eisenberg *Richard Freeman* • Tom Mason *Mike McCormick* • Robert Picardo *David Lewis* • William H Macy *Sean Hammel* • Olivia Burnette *Kristan Solomon* ■ *Dir* Martin Davidson • *Scr* Earl Wallace, Pamela Wallace, Martin Davidson

Murderous Intent ★★ 12
Drama based on a true story
1995 · US · Colour · 88mins

A typically far-fetched true story, which at least benefits from an above-average cast. Corbin Bernsen and Lesley Ann Warren are the couple who are driven to desperate measures after being relentlessly stalked by Bernsen's obsessed ex-wife. It's completely barmy, of course, and the two leads have a ball with the melodramatic material. Contains some violence. 🖭

Corbin Bernsen *Brice Talbot* • Lesley Ann Warren *Gayle Bernish* • Tushka Bergen *Colleen Bernish* • Dash Mihok *Kevin Bernish* • Sean Bridgers *Dennis Knapp* • John Finn *Detective Hewitt* • Michael Goodwin *Detective Imholte* ■ *Dir* Gregory Goodell • *Scr* Jeffrey Jur

Murders in the Rue Morgue ★★★
Horror
1932 · US · BW · 60mins

Vintage *Grand Guignol* as director Robert Florey plunders German expressionism and atmospheric shocks while allowing plenty of room for Bela Lugosi to enjoy his Dr Caligari-esque mad scientist role. As Dr Mirakle, Lugosi runs an offbeat carnival attraction featuring a giant gorilla by day. By night, however, he's engaged in diabolical blood transfusion experiments involving apes and beautiful virgins. Although far removed from its Edgar Allan Poe inspiration, the lurid overtones of the pulp plot are handled with surprising candour.

Bela Lugosi *Dr Mirakle* • Sidney Fox *Camille* • Leon Waycoff [Leon Ames] *Pierre Dupin* • Bert Roach *Paul* • Brandon Hurst *Prefect of Police* • Noble Johnson *Janos* ■ *Dir* Robert Florey • *Scr* Tom Reed, Dale Van Every, John Huston, from the story by Edgar Allan Poe

Murders in the Rue Morgue ★★★
Horror
1971 · US · Colour · 87mins

Director Gordon Hessler's fourth collaboration with Hammer scriptwriter Christopher Wicking is one of the most undervalued horror movies of the seventies. A superb Eurotrash cast populate this clever revenge story, in which a series of grisly murders strike members of Jason Robards's *Grand Guignol* theatre company while they are presenting a stage version of the Edgar Allan Poe classic. Brilliantly blending fantasy and reality, Hessler's suspense shocker is packed with sophisticated insight, surrealistic poetry and a nightmarish delirium.

Jason Robards [Jason Robards Jr] *Cesar Charron* • Herbert Lom *Marot* • Christine Kaufmann *Madeleine* • Adolfo Celi *Vidocq* • Lilli Palmer *Madeleine's mother* • Maria Perschy *Genevre* ■ *Dir* Gordon Hessler • *Scr* Christopher Wicking, Henry Slesar, from the story by Edgar Allan Poe

The Murders in the Rue Morgue ★★ 15
Chiller
1986 · US · Colour · 88mins

George C Scott puts in another tour-de-force performance playing Edgar Allan Poe's 19th-century French detective Auguste Dupin, who comes out of retirement to solve two bloody murders and prove his daughter's fiancé is not guilty of the hideous crimes. The fifth film version of the classic mystery is well produced (the atmospheric Paris locations are cleverly used), but Jeannot Szwarc's direction is rather plodding and fails to match the incandescence of his charismatic star. Good support from Val Kilmer and Rebecca De Mornay.

George C Scott *Inspector Auguste Dupin* • Rebecca De Mornay *Claire Dupin* • Ian McShane *Prefect of Police* • Neil Dickson *Adolphe Le Bon* • Val Kilmer *Philippe Huron* ■ *Dir* Jeannot Szwarc • *Scr* David Epstein, from the story by Edgar Allan Poe

Murders in the Zoo ★★
Horror
1933 · US · BW · 66mins

Lionel Atwill overacts a storm as a sadistic zookeeper using the animals in his care to kill anyone who so much

as looks at his gorgeous wife, Kathleen Burke. Lions, snakes and alligators are called on to do their worst by the insanely jealous warden, but it's the moment where he sews up the mouth of one paramour which provides the most chills. Randolph Scott is the hero and Charles Ruggles provides the comic relief in a menacing melodrama considered highly shocking and tasteless in its day.

Charles Ruggles *Peter Yates* • Lionel Atwill *Eric Gorman* • Gail Patrick *Jerry Evans* • Randolph Scott *Dr Woodford* • John Lodge *Roger Hewitt* • Kathleen Burke *Evelyn Gorman* • Harry Beresford *Professor Evans* ■ *Dir* Edward Sutherland [A Edward Sutherland] • *Scr* Phillip Wylie, Seton I Miller

Muriel ★★★★
Drama   1963 · Fr/It · Colour · 115mins

With her stepson (Jean-Baptiste Thierrée) home from army service in Algeria, a middle-aged woman (Delphine Seyrig) invites her erstwhile lover (Jean-Pierre Kérien), together with his niece (Nita Klein), to visit her in Boulogne. The son is haunted by memories of a dead girl called Muriel, while the ex-lovers are similarly caught in memories of their past. From the unique poetic and metaphysical imagination of French director Alain Resnais, who launched the exquisite Seyrig with *Last Year at Marienbad* (1961), this shares its opaque mix of memory and imagination, past and present. Faultlessly assembled, acted and photographed, it's certainly intriguing and generally regarded as one of Resnais's masterworks. A French language film.

Delphine Seyrig *Helene Aughain* • Jean-Pierre Kérien *Alphonse Noyard* • Nita Klein *Françoise* • Jean-Baptiste Thierrée *Bernard* • Laurence Badie *Claudie* • Martine Vatel *Marie-Dominique* ■ *Dir* Alain Resnais • *Scr* Jean Cayrol, from his story

Muriel's Wedding ★★★★ 15
Comedy drama 1994 · Ausl · Colour · 101mins

The Ugly Duckling is given a delightful Down-Under spin in this congenial comedy. Flabby Muriel Heslop lives in a frothy fantasy world of Abba songs, husband-shopping and wedding-dress dreams. It's when she leaves her small-minded home town of Porpoise Spit under a cloud to flat-share with an old acquaintance from school, Rhonda (snappily played by Rachel Griffiths), that the initially hilarious humour begins to turn a shade more poignant. Breezily directed by PJ Hogan (*My Best Friend's Wedding*), the film features a tremendously affecting Toni Collette as the mousey no-mark who spends her life flicking through bridal catalogues. Contains swearing and nudity. ▭
DVD

Toni Collette *Muriel Heslop* • Bill Hunter *Bill Heslop* • Rachel Griffiths *Rhonda* • Jeanie Drynan *Betty Heslop* • Gennie Nevinson *Deidre* • Matt Day *Brice* ■ *Dir* PJ Hogan • *Scr* PJ Hogan, from a story by PJ Hogan, Jocelyn Moorhouse

Murphy's Law ★★ 18
Action thriller 1986 · US · Colour · 96mins

The Defiant Ones meets *Death Wish* in a formula Charles Bronson crime thriller, which casts him as an

alcoholic cop framed for murdering his estranged wife by a psychopathic criminal with a grudge. There's lots of shouting and shooting, as Bronson escapes arrest handcuffed to a female offender, but not much in the way of gripping suspense. However, while the plot lurches from one tiresome cliché to another, director J Lee Thompson still keeps the violent mayhem moving smartly along. ▭

Charles Bronson *Jack Murphy* • Kathleen Wilhoite *Arabella McGee* • Carrie Snodgress *Joan Freeman* • Robert F Lyons *Art Penney* • Richard Romanus *Frank Vincenzo* • Bill Henderson *Ben Wilcove* ■ *Dir* J Lee Thompson • *Scr* Gail Morgan Hickman

Murphy's Romance ★★★ 15
Drama   1985 · US · Colour · 103mins

Six years after she won the best actress Oscar for *Norma Rae*, Sally Field teamed up with director Martin Ritt again for this easy-going comedy about a *May to December*-style romance between an ambitious horse trainer and a widowed pharmacist. The result? Her rugged love interest, twinkle-eyed James Garner, gained a first-time nomination instead. Quite why is the question; while eager to please, this is flimsy stuff that lacks the director's usual hard edge. ▭

James Garner *Murphy Jones* • Sally Field *Emma Moriarty* • Brian Kerwin *Bobby Jack Moriarty* • Corey Haim *Jake Moriarty* • Dennis Burkley *Freeman Coverly* • Georgann Johnson *Margaret* • Carole King *Tillie* ■ *Dir* Martin Ritt • *Scr* Harriet Frank Jr, Irving Ravetch, from the novella by Max Schott

Murphy's War ★★★
Second World War action adventure 1971 · UK · Colour · 106mins

This trifle has hints of *The African Queen*, with Peter O'Toole as a manic Irish seaman teaming up with a Quaker missionary (O'Toole's then wife, Sian Phillips) and a French oil engineer, convincingly played by Philippe Noiret. O'Toole's scheme is to repair an old plane and use it to sink a German U-boat down on the Orinoco delta. Shot in the jungles of Venezuela, the film is a blend of whimsy and battle, skilfully handled by director Peter Yates, who was riding high on the success of *Bullitt*. Contains some swearing.

Peter O'Toole *Murphy* • Sian Phillips *Dr Hayden* • Philippe Noiret *Louis Brezan* • Horst Janson *Kapitan Lauchs* • John Hallam *Lieutenant Ellis* • Ingo Mogendorf *Lieutenant Voght* ■ *Dir* Peter Yates • *Scr* Stirling Silliphant, from the novel by Max Catto

Murrow ★★
Biographical drama 1986 · US/UK · Colour · 105mins

Daniel J Travanti (*Hill Street Blues*) stars in this well-crafted biography about the life of legendary newsman Edward R Murrow. Beginning as a Second World War radio correspondent, Murrow later became a TV journalist at CBS, using his formidable skills to battle the evils of McCarthyism. Concentrating more on political issues than getting under Murrow's skin, Travanti's subdued performance fails to convey what made him one of the most provocative newsmen of his day. A strong supporting cast, including Dabney

Coleman and Edward Herrmann, help bolster this disappointing TV movie.

Daniel J Travanti *Edward R Murrow* • Dabney Coleman *William S Paley* • Edward Herrmann *Fred Friendly* • David Suchet *William L Shirer* • John McMartin *Frank Stanton* • Robert Vaughn *Franklin Delano Roosevelt* ■ *Dir* Jack Gold • *Scr* Ernest Kinoy

Musashi Miyamoto ★★★ PG
Drama   1944 · Jap · BW · 93mins

This was the first film made by Kenji Mizoguchi after his wife, Chieko, was declared insane and committed to the asylum where she was to spend the rest of her life. Yet his lack of interest in the project owes as much to the fact that he had little empathy for either the samurai genre or the nationalist sentiments that lay behind it. Mizoguchi was incapable of making an unwatchable film, however, and so it proves here. The story shows how Kinuyo Tanaka and Kigoro Ikushima's determination to avenge the murder of their father leads to a showdown between two legendary swordsmen. A Japanese language film.

Chojuro Kawarazaki *Musashi Miyamoto* • Kanemon Nakamura *Kojiro Sasaki* • Kinuyo Tanaka *Shinobu Nonomiya* • Kigoro Ikushima *Genichiro Nonomiya* ■ *Dir* Kenji Mizoguchi • *Scr* Matsutaro Kawaguchi

Muscle Beach Party ★★
Musical   1964 · US · Colour · 94mins

This one is so dated that it practically has cobwebs hanging off it. The quiffed crooner Frankie Avalon starred in a plethora of these jivin' beach party movies, in which everyone hops around in shorts shaking their heads wildly to truly terrible music. The original *Beach Party* was a big teen success, so the producers came up with this lacklustre sequel. Avalon warbles horribly, Annette Funicello dances as if she has a live octopus attached to her derrière, and the major plotline of clashing teenage rivals makes *West Side Story* look like *Assault on Precinct 13*.

Frankie Avalon *Frankie* • Annette Funicello *Dee Dee* • Luciana Paluzzi *Julie* • John Ashley *Johnny* • Don Rickles *Jack Fanny* • Peter Turgeon *Theodore* • Jody McCrea *Deadhead* • Little Stevie Wonder [Stevie Wonder] • Peter Lorre *Mr Strangdour* ■ *Dir* William Asher • *Scr* Robert Dillon, from a story by Robert Dillon, William Asher

The Muse ★★★ PG
Satirical comedy 1999 · US · Colour · 96mins

American satirist Albert Brooks casts his waspish eye over the film business, writing, directing and starring in this tale of a screenwriter who has lost his touch. Though he is sceptical when successful writer chum Jeff Bridges claims to be inspired by a real-life muse, Brooks nonetheless woos the temperamental Sarah (Sharon Stone), only to find her turning his life with wife Andie MacDowell upside down. Despite Brooks's ever-present cynicism about life, his film is full of lovely, gentle humour, while film fans will love the cameos from Stone's other "clients", among them James Cameron and Martin Scorsese.

Albert Brooks *Steven Phillips* • Sharon Stone *Sarah Liddle/Christine* • Andie MacDowell *Laura Phillips* • Jeff Bridges *Jack Warrick* •

Mark Feuerstein *Josh Martin* • Steven Wright *Stan Spielberg* ■ *Dir* Albert Brooks • *Scr* Albert Brooks, Monica Johnson

Mushrooms ★★
Comedy   1995 · Ausl · Colour · 93mins

Writer/director Alan Madden clearly intended this curio to be a quaintly black comedy, but what he ended up with is a fine showcase for his elderly co-stars and a ragbag of decidedly dubious gags. Julia Blake and Lynette Curran are most engaging as the sixtysomethings who decide to take in lodgers, only to find themselves needing to dispose of a new tenant's body. One of Australia's finest character actresses, Blake has a ball as she twitters around the shop that's below the widows' home, but you never feel Madden is totally in control. Contains violence and swearing.

Julia Blake *Flo* • Lynette Curran *Minnie* • Simon Chilvers *Instep* • Brandon Burke *Lynch* • Boris Brkic *Grubb* ■ *Dir/Scr* Alan Madden

The Music Box ★★★★★ U
Classic comedy 1932 · US · BW · 28mins

A legend in its own laugh-time as those wonderful chumps Laurel and Hardy try to deliver a player-piano to an address at the top of a huge flight of steps. A nurse is kicked "right in the middle of my daily duties", Ollie is dunked in an ornamental pond, and the great Billy Gilbert takes an axe to everything. Fabulously inventive. ▭

Stan Laurel *Stan* • Oliver Hardy *Ollie* • Billy Gilbert *Professor Theodore von Schwarzenhoffen* • William Gillespie *Piano salesman* • Charlie Hall *Postman* ■ *Dir* James Parrott • *Scr* HM Walker

Music Box ★★★★ 15
Drama   1989 · US · Colour · 120mins

This political melodrama raises more questions than it answers. But, despite Costa-Gavras's detached direction, the acting intensity of Jessica Lange and Armin Mueller-Stahl still manages to confront issues affecting a universal conscience, as lawyer/daughter Lange defends her blue-collar Hungarian father (Mueller-Stahl) from the charge of being leader of an SS-run death squad. Courtroom battles are always compulsive, this one more than most as we are kept on a knife-edge of suspense wondering if the now kindly veteran could have been a hideous monster in his past. Contains swearing. ▭

Jessica Lange *Ann Talbot* • Armin Mueller-Stahl *Mike Laszlo* • Frederic Forrest *Jack Burke* • Donald Moffat *Harry Talbot* • Lukas Haas *Mikey Talbot* • Cheryl Lynn Bruce *Georgine Wheeler* ■ *Dir* Costa-Gavras • *Scr* Joe Eszterhas

Music for Millions ★★★
Musical drama 1945 · US · BW · 117mins

Child prodigy Margaret O'Brien co-stars with June Allyson in this family entertainment from MGM that mixes wartime sentiments and tear-jerking sentimentality with comedy, songs and classical music. O'Brien is the younger sister dispensing comfort to pregnant older sibling Allyson, a cellist with José Iturbi's orchestra whose husband is away fighting in the Pacific. Pianist

Iturbi supplies outpourings of Debussy, Tchaikovsky, Dvorak and Grieg, while Jimmy Durante (as the maestro's manager) leavens the mix with a couple of characteristic numbers.

Margaret O'Brien *"Mike"* • José Iturbi • Jimmy Durante *Andrews* • June Allyson *Barbara Ainsworth* • Marsha Hunt *Rosalind* • Hugh Herbert *Uncle Ferdinand* • ■ *Dir* Henry Koster • *Scr* Myles Connolly • *Costume Designer* Irene

The Music Freelancers ★★★

Drama 1998 · Fr · Colour · 90mins

Exploring the perils of liberty, the temperament of the artiste and the sheer pleasure that music can bring, this is a delightful ensemble comedy from writer/director Denis Dercourt. Amid all the instrumental rivalries and personality clashes that occur as a freelance chamber orchestra rehearses for a one-off concert, a baby is born, a mournful maestro dies and a petty thief reforms. (Well, almost.) Despite this, these disparate *cachetonneurs* still manage to make beautiful music. Taken at a pleasingly relaxed tempo, the humour flows from the situations without a hint of contrivance. In French with English subtitles.

Pierre Lacan *Roberto* • Marc Citti *Lionel* • Philippe Clay *The aristocrat* • Henri Garcin *Svarowski* • Marie-Christine Laurent *Therese* ■ *Dir/Scr* Denis Dercourt

Music Hath Charms ★

Musical 1935 · UK · BW · 70mins

Henry Hall merits his place in musical legend for that all-time children's classic *The Teddy Bears' Picnic*. However, he goes down in cinematic infamy for this dismal collection of sketches in which people around the world have their cares soothed away by the soporific melodies of Henry and his orchestra. So, if you're facing a revolt in Africa, lost up a mountain, embroiled in a breach of promise case or heading for the marital rocks on a luxury cruise, tune in to Henry the universal panacea and all will be well.

Henry Hall (2) • WH Berry *Basil Turner* • Carol Goodner *Mrs Norbray* • Arthur Margetson *Alan Sterling* • Lorna Hubbard *Marjorie Turner* • Antoinette Cellier *Joan* • Billy Milton *Jack Lawton* • Aubrey Mallalieu *Judge* ■ *Dir* Thomas Bentley, Alexander Esway, Walter Summers, Arthur Woods [Arthur B Woods] • *Scr* Jack Davies, Courtney Terrett, from a story by L DuGarde Peach

Music in Manhattan ★★

Musical comedy 1944 · US · BW · 80mins

Song-and-dance hopeful Anne Shirley is mistaken for war hero Phillip Terry's bride when she visits Washington to promote her act with Dennis Day in this professionally produced, albeit lacklustre musical comedy. There are lots of songs, but few are any good, though it's a pleasant enough period piece that includes a rare appearance by Charlie Barnet and his band.

Anne Shirley *Frankie* • Dennis Day *Stanley* • Phillip Terry *Johnny* • Raymond Walburn *Professor* • Jane Darwell *Mrs Pearson* • Patti Brill *Gladys* ■ *Dir* John H Auer • *Scr* Lawrence Kimble, from a story by Maurice Tombragel, Hal Smith, Jack Scholl

Music in My Heart ★★

Musical 1940 · US · BW · 69mins

Someone once described Tony Martin as a "singing tuxedo". Although he was rather a stiff actor, he was handsome and charming, with a winning, dimpled smile and, most importantly, a mellifluous tenor voice. In the silly paper-thin plot of this low-budget musical, Martin plays a foreign singer fighting deportation from the US. He's given a few pleasant songs and a lovely partner in Rita Hayworth, in her first musical for Columbia. Hayworth would go on to gain real stardom within a year.

Tony Martin *Robert Gregory* • Rita Hayworth *Patricia O'Malley* • Edith Fellows *Mary O'Malley* • Alan Mowbray *Charles Gardner* • Eric Blore *Griggs* • George Tobias *Sascha* ■ *Dir* Joseph Santley • *Scr* James Edward Grant, from his story *Passport to Happiness*

The Music Lovers ★★ 18

Historical drama 1970 · UK · Colour · 118mins

Overwrought to the point of muddled confusion, Ken Russell's "biography" of Tchaikovsky is a crescendo of images which portray the Russian composer as a homosexual whose wife (Glenda Jackson) is so appalled by his lack of loving that she goes mad. Russell keeps up a shrill note of hysteria throughout, though Richard Chamberlain does at least attempt to understand the workings of a tortured soul. Outrageous in its time, it is now almost charmingly quaint, while its account of the *1812 Overture* is so over the top as to be risible. 📼

Richard Chamberlain *Tchaikovsky* • Glenda Jackson *Nina Milyukova* • Max Adrian *Nicholas Rubenstein* • Christopher Gable *Chiluvsky* • Isabella Telezynska *Madame Von Meck* • Kenneth Colley *Modeste Tchaikovsky* ■ *Dir* Ken Russell • *Scr* Melvyn Bragg, from the novel *Beloved Friend* by Catherine Drinker Bowen, Barbara von Meck

The Music Man ★★★★ U

Musical comedy 1962 · US · Colour · 144mins

Morton DaCosta, who directed Meredith Willson's hit musical on Broadway, was given carte blanche by Jack Warner to re-create it on the screen. He did so with the aid of his Broadway leading man, the dynamic Robert Preston, and came up with an Oscar-winning blockbuster. Preston plays the energetic, charming and silver-tongued con man who charms the elders of River City, Iowa, to finance a band. Also involved are Buddy Hackett, Hermione Gingold and Shirley Jones, the romantic interest and subject of the song *Marian the Librarian*. Onna White's electric choreography and a score that includes *Till There Was You* and *76 Trombones* contribute to an invigorating two-and-a-half hours. 📼

Robert Preston *Harold Hill* • Shirley Jones *Marian Paroo* • Buddy Hackett *Marcellus Washburn* • Hermione Gingold *Eulalie Mackechnie Shinn* • Paul Ford *Mayor Shinn* • Pert Kelton *Mrs Paroo* • Timmy Everett *Tommy Djilas* ■ *Dir* Morton Da Costa • *Scr* Marion Hargrove, from the musical by Meredith Willson, Franklin Lacey

The Music of Chance ★★★ 15

Drama 1993 · US · Colour · 94mins

This is a beguiling adaptation of Paul Auster's disquieting novel from ex-documentary director Philip Haas, who extracts every ounce of intelligence, wit and insight from a slight tale without ever straining for effect. He is excellently served by some exceptional performances, notably from James Spader and Mandy Patinkin as the gamblers forced to build a medieval stone wall to pay off a debt. Notwithstanding a disappointing conclusion, this neglected curio is well worth watching, and more successful than Haas's 1996 effort, *Angels and Insects*. Contains swearing. 📼

James Spader *Jack Pozzi* • Mandy Patinkin *James Nashe* • Charles Durning *Bill Flower* • Joel Grey *Willie Stone* • M Emmet Walsh *Calvin Murks* • Samantha Mathis *Tiffany* • Christopher Penn *Floyd* • Pearl Jones *Louise* ■ *Dir* Philip Haas • *Scr* Philip Haas, Belinda Haas, from the novel by Paul Auster

Music of the Heart ★★ PG

Biographical drama 1999 · US · Colour · 118mins

Horror maestro Wes Craven's first non-fantasy is a bland bust. The true story of violin teacher Roberta Guaspari (Meryl Streep), who brought music and hope to the school kids of East Harlem, gets nothing more than a vacuous telemovie treatment under Craven's restrained direction. Streep merely plays a parody of herself in this mix of *Fame* and *Dangerous Minds*, while salsa superstar Gloria Estefan couldn't have made a more ineffectual feature debut. The reasonably rousing finale aside – a fundraiser at Carnegie Hall with Isaac Stern and Itzhak Perelman accompanying the students – this emotional concerto has too many flat notes to soar. 📼

Meryl Streep *Roberta* • Angela Bassett *Janet* • Aidan Quinn *Brian* • Cloris Leachman *Assunta* • Gloria Estefan *Isabel* • Jane Leeves *Dorothea* • Itzhak Perelman • Isaac Stern ■ *Dir* Wes Craven • *Scr* Pamela Gray, from the documentary *Small Wonders*

The Music Room ★★★ U

Drama 1958 · Ind · BW · 100mins

In addition to scripting the majority of his pictures, Bengali director Satyajit Ray also regularly composed the soundtracks. Few films better showcased his command of Indian music than this poignant tale of an aristocrat who spends everything he has on a concert to serenade a passing age. There is much to admire in Chhabi Biswas's mournful performance and the way in which Ray maintains the delicate balance between progress and decay. But you really need an ear for Indian classical music to fully appreciate this. In Hindi with English subtitles.

Chhabi Biswas *Bishwambar Roy* • Padmadevi *Roy's wife* • Pinaki Sengupta *Khoka* • Tulsi Lahiri *Manager of Roy's estate* ■ *Dir* Satyajit Ray • *Scr* Satyajit Ray, from a short story by Tarashankar Bannerjee

The Music Teacher ★★ U

Drama 1988 · Bel · Colour · 93mins

The director Gérard Corbiau has received an Oscar nomination each time he has ventured into the world of opera. However, his later film *Farinelli il Castrato* is far superior to this confection, though there's still much here for the eye and ear to enjoy. Snippets from Verdi, Mozart, Schubert and Bellini pop up like selections from a classical jukebox, as retiring tenor José Van Dam pits his pickpocketing protégé against bisexual prince Patrick Bauchau's toyboy baritone. The action often teeters between the pretentious and the preposterous, but the art direction and cinematography look good enough to eat. In French with English subtitles. 📼

José Van Dam *Joachim Dallayrac* • Anne Roussel *Sophie* • Philippe Volter *Jean* • Sylvie Fennec *Estelle* • Patrick Bauchau *Prince Scotti* • Johan Leysen *François* ■ *Dir* Gérard Corbiau • *Scr* Gérard Corbiau, André Corbiau, from a story by Luc Jabon, Gérard Corbiau • *Cinematographer* Walther van den Ende

The Musketeers of Pig Alley ★★★★

Silent drama 1912 · US · BW · 17mins

Advertised as "a depiction of the gangster evil", the finest of DW Griffith's short films is also one of the first gangster pictures. Lillian Gish, in only her third film, shines as a young wife who becomes the object of a hoodlum's attentions. This realistic drama, which reflected the director's increased interest in social concerns, was shot in authentic locations and is of lasting historical interest as a picture of New York's slums in 1912.

Lillian Gish *Little Lady* • Elmer Booth *Snapper Kid, "Chief of the Musketeers"* • Walter Miller *A musician* • Harry Carey ■ *Dir* DW Griffith • *Scr* DW Griffiths, Anita Loos

Mustang Country ★★ U

Western 1976 · US · Colour · 79mins

There's more than a little biographical irony in this solidly crafted western. The action is set in 1925, around the time that a young hopeful named Joel McCrea was working as a movie stuntman and horse wrangler. Here, 51 years on, McCrea is making his final appearance in a distinguished screen career, playing a retired rodeo star and rancher who helps a native American lad track down and tame a wild horse in time for a big meet.

Joel McCrea *Dan Treego* • Nika Mina *Nika* • Robert Fuller *Griff* • Patrick Wayne *Tee Jay* ■ *Dir/Scr* John Champion

Mutant ★★ 18

Science-fiction horror 1984 · US · Colour · 95mins

A small midwestern town is menaced by zombie mutants who have been contaminated by a toxic waste spill. As usual, the local corporation is trying to cover up the scandal that has endangered the whole community. Although the zombies do little more than lunge at people with outstretched arms, the movie is well-paced. Yet it lacks the tension and relentless suspense of the *Living Dead*

landmarks director John "Bud" Cardos is so clearly trying to copy. ▭

Wings Hauser *Josh Cameron* • Bo Hopkins *Sheriff Will Stewart* • Jody Medford *Holly Pierce* • Lee Montgomery *Mike Cameron* • Marc Clement *Albert* • Cary Guffey *Billy* • Jennifer Warren *Dr Myra Tate* ■ *Dir* John "Bud" Cardos • *Scr* Peter Orton, Michael Jones, from a story by John Kruize

The Mutations ★★

Horror 1973 · UK · Colour · 92mins

Frankenstein meets *Freaks* in veteran cinematographer-turned-director Jack Cardiff's mind-boggling mad scientist extravaganza, which triumphantly embraces bad taste to provide queasy frissons rarely witnessed in British horror. Demented biologist Donald Pleasence crosses humans with plants and sends his gruesome failures to Michael Dunn, a dwarf who runs a circus sideshow. His most successful hybrid is a man-sized Venus fly trap (Scott Antony) which ingests a tramp before traumatising Jill Haworth and Julie Ege. Mixing genuinely deformed performers with made-up actors, the discomfiting template may be that of *Freaks*, but its prurient atmosphere is rooted in seventies British sleaze.

Donald Pleasence *Dr Nolter* • Tom Baker *Lynch* • Brad Harris *Brian* • Julie Ege *Hedi* • Michael Dunn *Burns* • Scott Antony *Tony* • Jill Haworth *Lauren* ■ *Dir* Jack Cardiff • *Scr* Robert D Weinbach, Edward Mann

Mute Witness ★★★★ 18

Thriller 1995 · UK/Ger · Colour · 92mins

A mute special-effects make-up artist accidentally sees a "snuff" movie being filmed in a Moscow studio, then spends the rest of this viciously super-cool thriller running for her life. Reminiscent of early Brian De Palma shockers, Anthony Waller's witty fright stuff revitalises the "woman in peril" genre with jet-black humour, tons of superbly controlled style, grisly corkscrew twists and the sinister appearance of Alec Guinness as "the Reaper". The Russian locations only add to the edge-of-your-seat atmosphere. Contains violence, swearing, sex scenes and nudity. ▭

Marina Sudina *Billie Hughes* • Fay Ripley *Karen Hughes* • Evan Richards *Andy Clarke* • Oleg Jankowskij [Oleg Jankowski] *Larsen* • Igor Volkov *Arkadi* • Sergej Karlenkov *Lyosha* • Alexander Buriev *Strohbecker* • Alec Guinness "The Reaper" ■ *Dir/Scr* Anthony Waller

Mutiny ★★★ U

Historical drama 1999 · US · Colour

Actor Morgan Freeman (*Driving Miss Daisy*) produced this made-for-TV true historical drama illuminating a dark episode in American history. In 1944, a segregated unit of black seamen, who are poorly trained and ill-equipped, are forced by belittling, racist officers to load dangerous munitions at a navy base in California. After an explosion kills more than 300 men, 50 black sailors take a stand and refuse to work. Although conventionally told, the film is full of convincing period detail and powerfully conveys the anger of a group of men determined to seek justice. A compelling film that will leave you outraged, yet satisfied.

Michael Jai White *Ben Cooper* • Duane Martin *BJ Teach* • David Ramsey *Vernon Nettles* • Adrian Pasdar *Lieutenant Maravich* • Joe Morton *Thurgood Marshall* • Matthew Glave *Lieutenant Kirby* • James B Sikking *Lieutenant Commander Tynan* ■ *Dir* Kevin Hooks • *Scr* James Henerson

Mutiny on the Bounty ★★★★

Classic adventure 1935 · US · BW · 132mins

Clark Gable squirmed at the idea of wearing a pigtail, knickerbockers and shoes with silver buckles to play the part of Fletcher Christian, in what was to be his first costume movie. But he and Charles Laughton (as Captain Bligh) teamed to bracing effect in this lavish and stirring adventure on the high seas, based, of course, on the famous real-life mutiny. Director Frank Lloyd won best director Oscars for *The Divine Lady* and *Cavalcade*, but this may be his best movie of all. The Academy certainly thought so: they voted it best picture.

Charles Laughton *Captain William Bligh* • Clark Gable *Fletcher Christian* • Franchot Tone *Roger Byam* • Herbert Mundin *Smith* • Eddie Quillan *Ellison* • Dudley Digges *Bacchus* • Donald Crisp *Burkitt* • Henry Stephenson *Sir Joseph Banks* • James Cagney • David Niven ■ *Dir* Frank Lloyd • *Scr* Talbot Jennings, Jules Furthman, Carey Wilson, from the novels *Mutiny on the Bounty* and *Men against the Sea* by Charles Nordhoff, James Norman Hall

Mutiny on the Bounty ★★★★ 15

Historical adventure
1962 · US · Colour · 177mins

Marlon Brando should walk the plank for the strangulated English accent he adopts as Fletcher Christian, at odds with Trevor Howard's sadistic Captain Bligh. But Lewis Milestone's take on the 19th-century maritime tale is a memorable successor to the Oscar-winning 1935 version. Milestone is to be especially congratulated for surviving laborious re-shoots and difficulties caused by Brando's temperament. "I was as near nervous breakdown as I've ever been," said the great director of *All Quiet on the Western Front*. Nevertheless, Brando is impressive as he moves from arrogant fop to gallant hero. ▭

Marlon Brando *Fletcher Christian* • Trevor Howard *Captain William Bligh* • Richard Harris *John Mills* • Hugh Griffith *Alexander Smith* • Richard Haydn *William Brown* • Tarita *Maimiti* • Tim Seely *Edward Young* • Percy Herbert *Matthew Quintal* • Gordon Jackson *Edward Birkett* ■ *Dir* Lewis Milestone • *Scr* Charles Lederer, Eric Ambler, William L Driscoll, Borden Chase, John Gay, Ben Hecht, from the novel by Charles Nordhoff, James Norman Hall

Mutiny on the Buses ★ PG

Comedy 1972 · UK · Colour · 84mins

Fangs weren't what they used to be down at Hammer when they resorted to big-screen TV spin-offs such as this woefully unfunny comedy based on the popular ITV series. Windsor Safari Park must also have been desperate for custom to allow its animals to be subjected to the pathetic gags cracked by a cast clearly going through the motions. You'd have thought there was simply no more mileage left in the jokes about Blakey's schedules, Olive

and Arthur's marriage and Stan and Jack's allergy to work, but they managed to squeeze out a third movie the following year. Atrocious. ▭

Reg Varney *Stan Butler* • Doris Hare *Mrs Butler* • Anna Karen *Olive* • Michael Robbins *Arthur* • Bob Grant *Jack* • Stephen Lewis *Inspector Blake* ■ *Dir* Harry Booth • *Scr* Ronald Wolfe, Ronald Chesney

My Ain Folk ★★★★ PG

Biographical drama 1973 · UK · BW · 52mins

The second part of Bill Douglas's autobiographical trilogy owes more to the style of the Soviet cinema of the twenties and thirties than the others in the series. Extreme close-ups leave us nowhere to hide from the misery Stephen Archibald experiences as he goes to stay with his father's parents after his maternal grandma dies and his half-brother is packed off to a home. Such is the loveless nature of the relationship between his grandparents and the bitterness they feel towards the boy's mother that you are left with that uncomfortable feeling you get when you hear the neighbours having a blazing row. ▭

Stephen Archibald *Jamie* • Hughie Restorick *Tommy* • Jean Taylor-Smith *Grandmother* • Bernard McKenna *Tommy's father* • Mr Munro *Jamie's grandfather* • Paul Kermack *Jamie's father* ■ *Dir/Scr* Bill Douglas

My American Cousin ★★★ PG

Comedy drama 1985 · Can · Colour · 85mins

A delightful coming-of-age tale made and set in Canada. It's the summer of 1959, and all there is to do is some cherry picking until a pre-teen girl's Californian cousin rides into town in his red Cadillac and sets everyone's hearts a-flutter. The film won six Genies (the Canadian equivalent of the Oscar), and it's easy to see why, thanks to the charming script and enjoyable performances by a relatively unknown cast. ▭

Margaret Langrick *Sandy* • John Wildman *Butch Walker* • Richard Donat *Major Wilcox* • Jane Mortifee *Kitty Wilcox* • TJ Scott *Lenny McPhee* • Camille Henderson *Shirley Darling* ■ *Dir/Scr* Sandy Wilson

My Antonia ★★★ PG

Romantic drama 1995 · US · Colour · 93mins

A leisurely, beautifully shot period piece, from the novel by Willa Cather, about a teenager coming of age at the turn of the century in Nebraska. Neil Patrick Harris plays the orphaned youngster from a farming family who falls for a poor immigrant girl, much to his grandparents' disapproval. Harris is impressive in a weightier role than usual, it's good to see Eva Marie Saint back on the screen, and the direction from Joseph Sargent is nicely understated. All in all, solid family entertainment. ▭

Jason Robards [Jason Robards Jr] *Grandfather Burden* • Eva Marie Saint *Grandmother Burden* • Neil Patrick Harris *Jimmy Burden* • Elina Lowensohn *Antonia Shimerda* • Norbert Weisser *Otto* ■ *Dir* Joseph Sargent • *Scr* Victoria Riskin, from the novel by Willa Cather

My Beautiful Laundrette ★★★★★ 15

Drama 1985 · UK · Colour · 93mins

A seminal eighties movie which launched a plethora of now distinguished careers, including those of director Stephen Frears and Daniel Day-Lewis. The latter shines here in his first major role as the scabrous punk and friend to Gordon Warnecke's entrepreneurial Asian, who dreams of creating the most glittering laundrette in London. The movie's undoubted importance lies in the way it takes many of the decade's Thatcherite characteristics – grafting in the free market, the desire for material acquisitions, the establishment of stability – and turns everything on its head with a merciful lack of polemic. A marvellously played film. Contains violence and sex scenes. ▭ *DVD*

Daniel Day-Lewis *Johnny* • Gordon Warnecke *Omar* • Saeed Jaffrey *Nasser* • Roshan Seth *Papa* • Derrick Branche *Salim* • Shirley Anne Field *Rachel* • Rita Wolf *Tania* ■ *Dir* Stephen Frears • *Scr* Hanif Kureishi

My Best Fiend ★★★

Documentary
1999 · Ger/UK · Colour and BW · 90mins

Even though the tensions that existed between them bordered on genuine hatred, director Werner Herzog and actor Klaus Kinski made five quite remarkable films together. Yet, as Herzog recalls in this bittersweet documentary memoir, he only prevented the native Indians from killing his star on the Amazonian set of *Fitzcarraldo* because he needed him for a few more scenes. Almost fondly philosophical about the tantrums and abuse, Herzog recalls them at length, and he virtually regards the infrequent ceasefires as wasted opportunities. This is clearly only one side of the story, but it's a fascinating one nonetheless. A German language film.

Werner Herzog *Narrator* ■ *Dir* Werner Herzog

My Best Friend's Wedding ★★★★ 12

Romantic comedy
1997 · US · Colour · 100mins

This sparkling comedy proved to be a career-resurrecting movie for Julia Roberts, and for once she plays someone who may not get the guy. When she hears her best friend and former lover (Dermot Mulroney) is getting married to Cameron Diaz, Roberts realises she wants to be more than just friends after all. What makes this film – from *Muriel's Wedding* director PJ Hogan – work so well is that it's not just *The Julia Roberts Show*. While she does the bumbling, adorable stuff she's best at, the stunning Diaz and superb Rupert Everett (as Roberts's gay friend and accomplice) battle it out for best supporting performance. (They both win.) Terrific stuff. ▭ *DVD*

Julia Roberts *Julianne Potter* • Dermot Mulroney *Michael O'Neal* • Cameron Diaz *Kimmy Wallace* • Rupert Everett *George Downes* • Philip Bosco *Walter Wallace* • M Emmet Walsh *Joe O'Neal* • Rachel Griffiths *Samantha Newhouse* ■ *Dir* PJ Hogan • *Scr* Ronald Bass

U = SUITABLE FOR ALL Uc = SUITABLE FOR ALL, ESPECIALLY FOR YOUNG CHILDREN (VIDEO ONLY) PG = PARENTAL GUIDANCE

My Best Girl ★★★ U

Silent romantic comedy
1927 · US · BW · 66mins

Made for her own production company under the auspices of United Artists, which she co-founded with Douglas Fairbanks, Charlie Chaplin and DW Griffith, this was one of Mary Pickford's last silent films. As the only normal member of a hopelessly irresponsible family, Pickford works in a Five-and-Dime and becomes romantically involved with the new clerk (Charles "Buddy" Rogers), who is really the boss's son. Other than asking us to believe that the 34-year-old "Little Mary" is 18, Sam Taylor's movie is sweetly pleasing, if inconsequential.

Mary Pickford *Maggie Johnson* • Charles "Buddy" Rogers *Joe Grant* • Sunshine Hart *Ma Johnson* • Lucien Littlefield *Pa Johnson* • Carmelita Geraghty *Liz Johnson* ■ *Dir* Sam Taylor • *Scr* Hope Loring, Allen McNeil, Tim Whelan, from a story by Kathleen Norris

My Blue Heaven ★★★ U

Musical comedy 1950 · US · Colour · 95mins

No, not the 1990 Steve Martin/Rick Moranis comedy, but yet another teaming of Betty Grable and Dan Dailey from 20th Century-Fox following the surprise success of 1947's *Mother Wore Tights*. This isn't bad, but its plot about vaudevillians wanting to adopt a child may seem a little tasteless, and, frankly, it's hard to accept Grable drooling over a baby and admitting that she wants to wash nappies! Co-stars Mitzi Gaynor and David Wayne give Grable and Dailey a run for their money, and it wouldn't be long before they themselves became top-billed.

Betty Grable *Molly Moran* • Dan Dailey *Jack Moran* • David Wayne *Walter Pringle* • Jane Wyatt *Janet Pringle* • Mitzi Gaynor *Gloria Adams* • Una Merkel *Miss Gilbert* • Louise Beavers *Selma* ■ *Dir* Henry Koster • *Scr* Lamar Trotti, Claude Binyon, from the story *Storks Don't Bring Babies* by SK Lauren

My Blue Heaven ★★★ PG

Comedy 1990 · US · Colour · 91mins

With Steve Martin and Rick Moranis in the leads and a script by Nora Ephron, this satire on suburban America promises much. Sadly, it delivers very little, largely because the supply of gags runs out too quickly and Martin rather overdoes it in a hoked version away near San Diego prior to testifying in a mob murder trial. Moranis's FBI agent won't be the only one not to see the funny side as Martin commits a few crimes for old time's sake. However, the underused Joan Cusack amuses as the humourless DA determined to put Martin away. Contains swearing and violence. ▭

Steve Martin *Vinnie Antonelli* • Rick Moranis *Barney Coopersmith* • Joan Cusack *Hannah Stubbs* • Melanie Mayron *Crystal Rybak* • William Irwin [Bill Irwin] *Kirby* • Carol Kane *Shaldeen* • William Hickey *Billy Sparrow* • Deborah Rush *Linda* ■ *Dir* Herbert Ross • *Scr* Nora Ephron

My Body, My Child ★★★

Drama based on a true story
1982 · US · Colour · 100mins

Based on a true story, this "moral dilemma of the week" TV movie may not have the most original premise in

the world, but it is well told and directed by Marvin J Chomsky. Vanessa Redgrave gives one of her strongest recent performances as a middle-aged Catholic schoolteacher who must wrestle with the mother of all decisions when she finds herself pregnant with what may be a deformed foetus. Joseph Campanella convinces as Redgrave's equally confused husband, while Jack Albertson won a posthumous Emmy for his final performance as her invalid dad.

Vanessa Redgrave *Leenie Cabrezi* • Joseph Campanella *Joe Cabrezi* • Stephen Elliott *Dr Gallagher* • James Naughton *Dr Dan Berenson* • Gail Strickland *Adele* • Jack Albertson *Poppa MacMahon* • Sarah Jessica Parker *Katy* ■ *Dir* Marvin J Chomsky • *Scr* Louisa Burns-Bisogno

My Bodyguard ★★★ PG

Drama 1980 · US · Colour · 92mins

School bully Matt Dillon persecutes rich kid Chris Makepeace, who retaliates by attempting to hire the morose and overgrown Adam Baldwin as his personal bodyguard. First-time director Tony Bill creates a believable atmosphere at this Chicago school while gradually shifting attention away from Makepeace's plight to Baldwin's troubled past. Cameos from oldsters Ruth Gordon and John Houseman, plus the screen debut of Joan Cusack, are bonuses. ▭

Chris Makepeace *Clifford* • Adam Baldwin *Linderman* • Matt Dillon *Moody* • Paul Quandt *Carson* • Joan Cusack *Shelley* • Dean R Miller *Hightower* • Richard Bradley *Dubrow* • Ruth Gordon *Gramma* • John Houseman *Dobbs* ■ *Dir* Tony Bill • *Scr* Alan Ormsby

My Boyfriend's Back ★★★★

Comedy drama 1989 · US · Colour · 96mins

Sandy Duncan, Judith Light and Jill Eikenberry star as the members of a sixties trio who reunite 25 years on for a television concert of sixties music, in this TV movie that does more than just skate across the surface of events. The three leads give carefully layered performances, personal and social insights abound, real emotion is built into every frame and drama is fused seamlessly with wit. Actual pop stars of the sixties appear, including Mary Wells, Gary Puckett and the Penguins.

Sandy Duncan *Chris Henry* • Jill Eikenberry *Deborah McGuire* • Judith Light *Vicki Vine* • John Sanderford *Harry Simons* • Stephen Macht *Joseph, Deborah's boyfriend* ■ *Dir* Paul Schneider • *Scr* Lindsay Harrison, from a story by April Campbell, Bruce Jones

My Boyfriend's Back ★ 15

Comedy 1993 · US · Colour · 81mins

As naff and dreadful as the title suggests, this gross comedy regurgitates that old chestnut about the high school geek who woos the prettiest girl in school. Andrew Lowery is the bespectacled teen who gets shot just before his dream prom date with Traci Lind. In absolute absurdist style, he returns from the dead and goes to the ball regardless. Things go from bad to worse when his body parts start dropping off, with cannibalism and necrophilia following on. ▭

Andrew Lowery *Johnny Dingle* • Traci Lind *Missy McCloud* • Danny Zorn *Eddie* • Edward Herrmann *Mr Dingle* • Mary Beth Hurt *Mrs*

Dingle • Jay O Sanders *Sheriff McCloud* • Libby Villari *Camille McCloud* • Matthew Fox *Buck* ■ *Dir* Bob Balaban • *Scr* Dean Lorey

My Breast ★★★ PG

Drama based on a true story
1994 · US · Colour · 92mins

The title and the words "based on a true story" would normally set the alarm bells ringing, but this isn't your average "disease of the week" TV movie. For a start, it was written by Joyce Wadler, a sassy New York journalist with a neat turn of phrase, and directed by Betty Thomas, who made her directing name with the hilarious *Brady Bunch Movie*. Meredith Baxter, the star of so many humdrum teleplays, also outdoes herself as Wadler, never allowing self-pity or false courage to colour her performance. Interesting rather than inspirational, but honest and intelligent. ▭

Meredith Baxter *Joyce Wadler* • Jamey Sheridan *Nick Distefano* • James Sutorius *Herb Levine* • Barbara Barrie *Milly* • Sara Botsford *Eve* ■ *Dir* Betty Thomas • *Scr* Joyce Wadler, from her book

My Brilliant Career ★★★★ U

Period drama 1979 · Ausl · Colour · 100mins

A key film in the Australian film renaissance of the seventies, this sensitive story of a fiercely independent young woman with aspirations to be a writer in male-dominated turn-of-the-century Australia made international reputations for director Gillian Armstrong and her remarkably assured 23-year-old star Judy Davis. With Sam Neill and Wendy Hughes providing attractive support, the one drawback is being expected to believe any woman in her right mind would turn down Neill's charming, wealthy suitor. That said, this is based on a true story.

Judy Davis *Sybylla Melvyn* • Sam Neill *Harry Beecham* • Wendy Hughes *Aunt Helen* • Robert Grubb *Frank Hawdon* • Max Cullen *Mr McSwat* • Patricia Kennedy *Aunt Gussie* ■ *Dir* Gillian Armstrong • *Scr* Eleanor Witcombe, from the novel by Miles Franklin

My Brother Jonathan ★★ U

Drama 1947 · UK · BW · 103mins

Time has not been kind to the films featuring husband and wife Michael Denison and Dulcie Gray. Yet Denison's clipped tones and stiff acting style and Gray's mousey loyalty turned this into a respectable hit 50 years ago. Based on the bestseller by Francis Brett Young, it follows the fortunes of Black Country doctor Denison, whose ambitions to become a surgeon are thwarted by family ties. Harold French directs steadily, but without a feel for small-town life. ▭

Michael Denison *Jonathan Dakers* • Dulcie Gray *Rachel Hammond* • Stephen Murray *Doctor Craig* • Ronald Howard *Harold Dakers* • Mary Clare *Mrs Dakers* • Finlay Currie *Doctor Hammond* • James Robertson-Justice *Eugene Dakers* ■ *Dir* Harold French • *Scr* Leslie Landau, Adrian Alington, from the novel by Francis Brett Young

My Brother Talks to Horses ★★★ U

Comedy 1946 · US · BW · 92mins

An MGM co-feature that served to show off the burgeoning talent of director Fred Zinnemann, who would later make such Oscar-winning classics as *High Noon*, *From Here to Eternity* and *A Man for All Seasons*. There's not much sign of the promise to come in this silly but charming picture, however, which is succinctly summed up by its title. Young Jackie "Butch" Jenkins plays the original horse whisperer, and there's interesting period support from Peter Lawford and veterans Edward Arnold, Spring Byington and Charlie Ruggles, but the central gimmick becomes tiresome and the plot has nowhere to go.

"Butch" Jenkins [Jackie "Butch" Jenkins] *Lewis Penrose* • Peter Lawford *John S Penrose* • Spring Byington *Mrs Penrose* • Beverly Tyler *Martha* • Edward Arnold *Mr Bledsoe* • Charlie Ruggles [Charles Ruggles] *Richard Pennington Roeder* ■ *Dir* Fred Zinnemann • *Scr* Morton Thompson

My Brother's Keeper ★★

Drama 1948 · UK · BW · 86mins

Although best known in the forties for its lavish costume dramas, Gainsborough was also capable of turning out gritty contemporary fare. A decade before Tony Curtis and Sydney Poitier played *The Defiant Ones*, Jack Warner and George Cole star as a couple of convicts whose escape is hindered by the fact that they are handcuffed together. Replacing the racial theme is the neat twist that only one of the runaways is guilty. Under the direction of Alfred Roome and Roy Rich, however, their perils and predicaments are often predictable.

Jack Warner *George Martin* • George Cole *Willie Stannard* • Jane Hylton *Nora Lawrence* • David Tomlinson *Ronnie Waring* • Bill Owen *Syd Evans* • Yvonne Owen *Margaret "Meg" Waring* • Raymond Lovell *Bill Wainwright* ■ *Dir* Alfred Roome, Roy Rich • *Scr* Frank Harvey, from a story by Maurice Wiltshire

My Brother's Wife ★

Romantic comedy
1989 · US · Colour · 96mins

Comic star John Ritter is still in search of a good script, and, unfortunately, he doesn't find it here. He's a man in love with his sister-in-law (played by *thirtysomething's* Mel Harris), but he bumbles about so much you can quite understand why she ignores him. Which is exactly what you should do with this film. Contains swearing.

John Ritter *Barney Rusher* • Mel Harris *Eleanor Gilbert-Rusher* • Polly Bergen *Myra Gilbert* • Dakin Matthews *Barney's father* • David Byron *Billy Rusher* ■ *Dir* Jack Bender • *Scr* Percy Granger, from a play by AR Gurney

My Chauffeur ★★ 15

Comedy 1986 · US · Colour · 97mins

Feisty Deborah Foreman stars as a girl who makes it in the predominantly male profession of limousine driving. Picking up a depressed and drunk millionaire's son, she is dismissed when he wakes up the next day on her couch. The pair are thrown together yet again when Foreman's car breaks down with the same chap in the back, and this acts as a device for their relationship to develop further. An inconsequential attempt at screwball comedy and farce, with a truly terrible combination of bad jokes thrown in for good measure. 📺

Deborah Foreman *Casey Meadows* • Sam J Jones [Sam Jones] *Battle Witherspoon* • Sean McClory *O'Brien* • Howard Hesseman *McBride* • EG Marshall *Witherspoon* • Penn Jillette *Bone* • Teller *Abdul* ■ *Dir/Scr* David Beaird

My Childhood ★★★ PG

Biographical drama 1972 · UK · BW · 44mins

Costing some £40,000 to make and lasting less than an hour, this is the first part of director Bill Douglas's autobiographical trilogy, one of the most painful evocations of childhood ever brought to the screen. Set in a run-down Scottish mining village, the film explores the strained relationships between an eight-year-old boy, his half-brother, his uncompromising grandmother and a kindly German prisoner of war. Stephen Archibald gives a remarkable performance as Douglas's alter ego, while Jean Taylor-Smith sends shivers as the very antithesis of a loving granny. 📺

Stephen Archibald *Jamie* • Hughie Restorick *Tommy* • Jean Taylor-Smith *Grandmother* • Karl Fieseler *Helmuth* • Bernard McKenna *Tommy's father* • Paul Kermack *Jamie's father* ■ *Dir/Scr* Bill Douglas

My Cousin Rachel ★★★ PG

Romantic mystery 1952 · US · BW · 176mins

Based on Daphne du Maurier's novel, this overwrought melodrama has Richard Burton first detesting, then obsessively loving Olivia de Havilland, who married and may have murdered his beloved cousin. Set on the clifftops of 19th-century Cornwall, it puts the story of *Rebecca* into reverse gear and delivers great dollops of emotion. The dashingly handsome, brooding Burton picked up the first of his seven unsuccessful Oscar nominations for his first Hollywood role. 📺

Olivia de Havilland *Rachel Ashley* • Richard Burton *Philip Ashley* • Audrey Dalton *Louise* • Ronald Squire *Nick Kendall* • George Dolenz *Rainaldi, Rachel's lawyer* • John Sutton *Ambrose Ashley* • Tudor Owen *Seecombe* ■ *Dir* Henry Koster • *Scr* Nunnally Johnson, from the novel by Daphne du Maurier

My Cousin Vinny ★★★★ 15

Comedy 1992 · US · Colour · 114mins

Joe Pesci is the Vinny of the title, an extremely inept lawyer who comes to the rescue of his young cousin (Ralph Macchio) when the lad runs into a bit of trouble with the law in the Deep South. Pesci has great fun with his role, but the biggest surprise is Marisa Tomei, who plays his coarse Brooklyn girlfriend. Although she's great in what was her first real role, there was widespread surprise when she won the best supporting actress Oscar, beating three British nominees, including Miranda Richardson for her role in *Damage*. Contains swearing. 📺

Joe Pesci *Vinny Gambini* • Marisa Tomei *Mona Lisa Vito* • Ralph Macchio *Bill Gambini* • Mitchell Whitfield *Stan Rothenstein* • Fred Gwynne *Judge Chamberlain Haller* • Lane

Smith *Jim Trotter IIII* • Austin Pendleton *John Gibbons* • Bruce McGill *Sheriff Farley* ■ *Dir* Jonathan Lynn • *Scr* Dale Launer

My Darling Clementine ★★★★★ U

Classic western 1946 · US · BW · 92mins

A classic western, with Henry Fonda as Wyatt Earp and Victor Mature as Doc Holliday, both heading for that close shave at the OK Corral. Owing rather less to historical accuracy than more recent movies – *Tombstone* and Kevin Costner's *Wyatt Earp* – this John Ford picture boasts some fine sequences, especially a dance in an unfinished church, a fine symbol of the "garden being fashioned from the wilderness" by the strong-arm methods of Fonda's self-righteous lawman. Filmed in expressive black-and-white against Monument Valley backdrops, the picture combines both the grandeur and the folksiness so typical of its director. 📺

Henry Fonda *Wyatt Earp* • Victor Mature *Doc Holliday* • Linda Darnell *Chihuahua* • Walter Brennan *Old Man Clanton* • Cathy Downs *Clementine* • Tim Holt *Virgil Earp* • Ward Bond *Morgan Earp* • John Ireland *Billy Clanton* ■ *Dir* John Ford • *Scr* Samuel G Engel, Winston Miller, from a story by Sam Hellman, from the novel *Wyatt Earp, Frontier Marshal* by Stuart N Lake • *Cinematographer* Joe MacDonald

My Date with the President's Daughter ★★★

Comedy 1998 · US · Colour · 93mins

In this high-spirited kids' caper, a shy teen is goaded by his pals into asking an attractive girl he sees in the mall to go with him to the prom – unaware that she is the daughter of the US President. Problems start when they conspire to ditch her Secret Service escorts. This is harmless, family fun, enlivened by gruff Dabney Coleman as the Commander-in-Chief and Will Friedle, who shines as he strives to win the hand of First Daughter Elisabeth Harnois. Director Alex Zamm keeps the pace brisk.

Dabney Coleman *President Richmond* • Will Friedle *Duncan* • Elisabeth Harnois *Hallie Richmond* • Jay Thomas *Charles Fletcher* • Mimi Kuzyk *Carol Richmond* • Wanda Cannon *Rita Fletcher* ■ *Dir* Alex Zamm • *Scr* Alex Zamm, William Robertson

My Dear Secretary ★★★

Romantic comedy 1948 · US · BW · 94mins

Bestselling novelist Kirk Douglas, who suffers from an irresistible drive to make passes at his secretaries, gets more than he bargained for when he hires Laraine Day. He ends up marrying her – whereupon she becomes jealous of her replacement. This mindless variant on the familiar wife-versus-secretary idea, directed by Charles Martin from his own thin script, is made thinner still by Douglas's patent lack of comic flair. What laughs there are come from Keenan Wynn and Rudy Vallee.

Laraine Day *Stephanie Gaylord* • Kirk Douglas *Owen Waterbury* • Keenan Wynn *Ronnie Hastings* • Helen Walker *Elsie* • Rudy Vallee *Charles Harris* • Florence Bates *Mrs Reeves* ■ *Dir/Scr* Charles Martin

My Demon Lover ★★ 15

Horror comedy 1987 · US · Colour · 83mins

A typical eighties horror comedy, enlivened by an enthusiastic cast and some good make-up effects. Brat Pack wannabe Scott Valentine is subject to an ancient curse that turns him into a whole managerie of monsters whenever he is sexually aroused. Shot on location in New York, one wonders if director Charles Loventhal has ever been there, especially when he places a huge gothic castle straight out of a Bela Lugosi movie slap-bang in the middle of Central Park. 📺

Scott Valentine *Kaz* • Michelle Little *Denny* • Arnold Johnson *Fixer* • Robert Trebor *Charles* • Alan Fudge *Captain Phil Janus* ■ *Dir* Charles Loventhal • *Scr* Leslie Ray

My Dinner with Andre ★★★

Drama 1981 · US · Colour · 111mins

Few films polarise critical opinion more than this love it or loathe it chat-fest from director Louis Malle. Your response to the film depends entirely on whether you consider avant-garde theatre director Andre Gregory to be a man of charm, imagination and questing intellect, or a pompous narcissist in love with the sound of his own voice. Wallace Shawn is altogether easier to take as Gregory's straight man with a nice line in barbed quippery. Drawn from the pair's actual conversations, the adventures and ideas Gregory relates range from the fascinating to the preposterous.

Wallace Shawn *Wally* • Andre Gregory *Andre* • Jean Lenauer *Waiter* ■ *Dir* Louis Malle • *Scr* Wallace Shawn, Andre Gregory

My Dream Is Yours ★★★

Musical 1949 · US · Colour · 99mins

This Warner Bros remake of its own 1934 Dick Powell/Ginger Rogers musical comedy *Twenty Million Sweethearts* gives Doris Day the chance to rework that film's biggest hit, the lovely *I'll String along with You*. The film is an extremely pleasant, if very gentle satire on radio, in which Day and co-star Jack Carson clown and croon sweetly under Michael Curtiz's competent direction. Scene-stealing honours go to Bugs Bunny, who appears in a super dream sequence.

Jack Carson *Doug Blake* • Doris Day *Martha Gibson* • Lee Bowman *Gary Mitchell* • Adolphe Menjou *Thomas Hutchins* • Eve Arden *Vivian Martin* • SZ Sakall *Felix Hofer* • Selena Royle *Freda Hofer* • Edgar Kennedy *Uncle Charlie* ■ *Dir* Michael Curtiz • *Scr* Harry Kurnitz, Dane Lussier, Allen Rivkin, Laura Kerr, from the story *Hot Air* by Jerry Wald, Paul Moss

My English Grandfather ★★★

Comedy 1986 · USSR · BW and Colour · 76mins

This is an engagingly offbeat story about a British communications engineer who seeks refuge from the events of the Russian Revolution and its aftermath by camping out on the three metres he claims for England at the foot of a recently erected telegraph pole. Slyly exploring the adverse effects of communism on a previously contented community, Nana Dzhordzhadze's film has all the energy

and inventiveness of *glasnost* cinema. If the conversations and confrontations of the revolutionary era are not entertaining enough, the latter-day search for the man's murderer by his Georgian lover is quite compelling. In Georgian with English subtitles.

Zhanri Lolashvili *Hughes* ■ *Dir* Nana Dzhordzhadze • *Scr* Irakly Kvirikadze

My Fair Lady ★★★★★ U

Classic musical 1964 · US · Colour · 171mins

This sumptuous record of Lerner and Loewe's smash Broadway version of George Bernard Shaw's play *Pygmalion* won eight well-deserved Oscars. It boasts superb performances from Rex Harrison repeating his stage success as Henry Higgins and Stanley Holloway as Alfred P Doolittle. At the time, there was criticism that Julie Andrews didn't re-create her original Broadway role, but Audrey Hepburn is still quite wonderful as Eliza. If not coarse enough for the Covent Garden flower girl, nobody, but nobody, could ever blossom as beautifully as Hepburn does in the Cecil Beaton costumes later on, and, despite being dubbed in the songs by Marni Nixon, her portrayal is funny and heart-warming in equal doses. A more visually inspired director might have brought a little more élan to the work, but George Cukor rightly preserves the theatricality of the enterprise and provides a film to savour again and again. 📺 *DVD*

Audrey Hepburn *Eliza Doolittle* • Rex Harrison *Professor Henry Higgins* • Stanley Holloway *Alfred P Doolittle* • Wilfrid Hyde White *Colonel Hugh Pickering* • Gladys Cooper *Mrs Higgins* • Jeremy Brett *Freddy Eynsford-Hill* • Theodore Bikel *Zoltan Karpathy* • Isobel Elsom *Mrs Eynsford-Hill* • Mona Washbourne *Mrs Pearce* ■ *Dir* George Cukor • *Scr* Alan Jay Lerner, from the musical by Alan Jay Lerner, Frederick Loewe, from the play *Pygmalion* by George Bernard Shaw • *Cinematographer* Harry Stradling • *Art Director* Cecil Beaton, Gene Allen • *Music Director* Andre Previn

My Family ★★★★ 15

Drama 1994 · US · Colour · 126mins

Writer/director Gregory Nava's drama charts the trials, triumphs and tribulations of a family of Mexican immigrants in Los Angeles over three generations. What sets this picture apart from other such films are the striking performances from the cast, which includes Jimmy Smits, Esai Morales and Edward James Olmos, plus an admirable lack of sentimentality from Nava. Both moving and funny, this is an unexpected treat.

Jimmy Smits *Jimmy Sanchez* • Esai Morales *Chucho* • Edward James Olmos *Paco* • Eduardo Lopez Rojas *Jose Sanchez* • Jenny Gago *Maria Sanchez* • Elpidia Carrillo *Isabel Magana* ■ *Dir* Gregory Nava • *Scr* Gregory Nava, Anna Thomas

My Father Is Coming ★★★ 18

Comedy drama 1991 · US/Ger · Colour · 80mins

Considering the sadomasochism of *Seduction: The Cruel Woman* (1985) and the frank eroticism of *Virgin Machine* (1988), this is a surprisingly restrained mainstream comedy from Monika Treut. Caught in the oh-so-

U = SUITABLE FOR ALL   **Uc** = SUITABLE FOR ALL, ESPECIALLY FOR YOUNG CHILDREN (VIDEO ONLY)   **PG** = PARENTAL GUIDANCE

familiar fib of telling the folks back home that all is going swimmingly, waitress Shelley Kästner is torn between a lesbian affair and a mysterious male when her strait-laced German father (Alfred Edel) arrives in New York to see his "stage star" daughter in action. Enlivening the usual round of farcical deceptions is real-life porn star Annie Sprinkle, who keeps Edel mind-bogglingly occupied while Käster ponders her future.

Shelley Kästner *Vicky* • Alfred Edel *Hans* • Mary-Lou Graulau *Lisa* • Dominique Gaspar *Christa* • Flora Gaspar *Dora* • David Bronstein *Ben* • Annie Sprinkle *Annie* ■ *Dir* Monika Treut • *Scr* Bruce Benderson, Monika Treut

My Father, My Son ★★ 15

Drama based on a true story
1988 · US · Colour · 88mins

The tragic consequences of duty versus family give terrific power to this true story of a US Navy admiral whose order to use toxic defoliant "Agent Orange" in Vietnam apparently caused his own son's subsequent cancer. The fine, unsentimental script by Jacqueline Feather and David Seidler, Jeff Bleckner's sensitive direction and strong performances by Karl Malden and Keith Carradine make this unusual story of guilt and love between father and son seem vividly real. ▦

Karl Malden *Admiral Elmo R Zumwalt* • Keith Carradine *Lt Elmo R Zumwalt Jr* • Margaret Klonk *Kathy Zumwalt* • Michael Horton *Martin* • Dirk Blocker *Nairmore* • Grace Zabriskie *Mouza Zumwalt* ■ *Dir* Jeff Bleckner • *Scr* Jacqueline Feather, David Seidler

My Father, the Hero ★★★ PG

Comedy drama 1994 · US · Colour · 86mins

If you enjoyed the French original, *Mon Père Ce Héros*, then steer well clear of this Hollywood remake. However, if you are coming to the film with an open mind, there's every chance you will glean some enjoyment from this frivolous comedy in which Katherine Heigl tries to impress the admiring Dalton James by pretending that her father, Gérard Depardieu, is really her sugar daddy. The film has the distinction of being the only American remake of a Gallic hit to retain the original star, but Depardieu is obviously aware of the gulf between the two pictures. ▦

Gérard Depardieu *André* • Katherine Heigl *Nicole* • Dalton James *Ben* • Lauren Hutton *Megan* • Faith Prince *Diana* • Stephen Tobolowsky *Mike* • Ann Hearn *Stella* ■ *Dir* Steve Miner • *Scr* Francis Veber, Charlie Peters, from the film *Mon Père Ce Héros* by Gérard Lauzier

My Favorite Blonde ★★★★

Comedy 1942 · US · BW · 78mins

Vaudeville entertainer Bob Hope meets gorgeous blonde Madeleine Carroll who, it turns out, is a British spy being pursued by Nazi villains, notably the sinister duo of George Zucco and glamorous Gale Sondergaard. It's Bob to the rescue in one of his best vehicles. Directed at a laugh a minute and a thrilling pace by Sidney Lanfield, this is a glorious spoof on the espionage-chase films so beloved of Alfred Hitchcock.

Bob Hope *Larry Haines* • Madeleine Carroll *Karen Bentley* • Gale Sondergaard *Mme Stephanie Runick* • George Zucco *Dr Hugo Streger* • Lionel Royce *Karl* • Walter Kingsford *Dr Faber* • Bing Crosby *Man giving directions* ■ *Dir* Sidney Lanfield • *Scr* Don Hartman, Frank Butler, from a story by Melvin Frank, Norman Panama

My Favorite Brunette ★★★ PG

Comedy mystery 1947 · US · BW · 86mins

Bob Hope (starring in the first film for his own production company, which made him richer than ever) plays a guy who, mistaken for a Philip Marlowe-type private eye, decides to live out the role in order to help mysterious Dorothy Lamour, who's in a spot of bother involving gangsters. Only moderately successful as a spoof of the Raymond Chandler school of thriller, it's amusing enough, with Peter Lorre and Lon Chaney Jr lining up for director Elliott Nugent, and Bob's crony Bing Crosby in a guest cameo as the executioner at San Quentin prison. ▦

Bob Hope *Ronnie Jackson* • Dorothy Lamour *Carlotta Montay* • Peter Lorre *Kismet* • Lon Chaney Jr *Willy* • Charles Dingle *Major Simon Montague* • John Hoyt *Dr Lundau* • Reginald Denny *James Collins* • Jack LaRue *Tony* • Alan Ladd *Sam McCloud* ■ *Dir* Elliott Nugent • *Scr* Edmund Beloin, Jack Rose

My Favorite Martian ★ PG

Science-fiction comedy
1999 · US · Colour · 93mins

A numbing headache in movie disguise, this special-effects farce is a pointless farrago that's nowhere near as fun as the cult sixties TV show that inspired it. Unemployed TV news producer Jeff Daniels hides crash-landed alien Christopher Lloyd in his car as the manic shape-shifter searches for spaceship spare parts. A highly talented cast drown in a mass of bad quips, slapstick pratfalls and shameless mugging clearly tailored as a youngster's *Men in Black*. ▦ **DVD**

Jeff Daniels *Tim O'Hara* • Christopher Lloyd *Uncle Martin* • Elizabeth Hurley *Brace Channing* • Daryl Hannah *Lizzie* • Christine Ebersole *Mrs Lorelei Brown* • Wallace Shawn *Coleye* • Michael Lerner *Mr Channing* • Jeremy Hotz *Billy* • Ray Walston ■ *Dir* Donald Petrie • *Scr* Deanna Oliver, Sherri Stoner, from the TV series by John L Greene

My Favorite Spy ★ U

Musical comedy 1942 · US · BW · 85mins

Bandleader/comedian Kay Kyser is an aquired taste, and though some of his films prove ingenuous fun, this is the weakest of the five films he made for RKO in the early forties. Produced by former silent star Harold Lloyd with too much reliance on Kyser's minimal flare for comedy, it has surprisingly lifeless direction by Tay Garnett, who had been a gagman for Hal Roach and Mack Sennett in the twenties. Pleasant songs by Jimmy Van Heusen and Johnny Burke provide some respite from the antics of Kyser as a bandleader chosen by Army Intelligence to infiltrate a spy ring.

Kay Kyser • Jane Wyman *Connie* • Ellen Drew *Terry Kyser* • Robert Armstrong *Harry Robinson* • Helen Westley *Aunt Jessie* • Una

O'Connor *Cora* ■ *Dir* Tay Garnett • *Scr* William Bowers, Sig Herzig, from a story by M Coates Webster

My Favorite Spy ★★★

Comedy 1951 · US · BW · 93mins

Not to be confused with a feeble RKO comedy of the same title made in 1942, this is Bob Hope's third *My Favorite* outing, directed this time by Norman Z McLeod, and with the stunningly beautiful Hedy Lamarr following in the footsteps of Madeleine Carroll and Dorothy Lamour as the comedian's co-star. The nonsensical plot has Hope as a minor-league vaudeville comic being persuaded to take the place of an agent in Tangier and foil a conspiracy. Less funny than its predecessors but offering some adroit slapstick, fans will enjoy it.

Bob Hope *Peanuts White/Eric Augustine* • Hedy Lamarr *Lily Dalbray* • Francis L Sullivan *Karl Brubaker* • Arnold Moss *Tasso* • John Archer *Henderson* • Luis Van Rooten *Hoenig* • Stephen Chase *Donald Bailey* ■ *Dir* Norman Z McLeod • *Scr* Edmund Hartmann, Jack Sher, Edmund Beloin, Lou Breslow, Hal Kanter, from a story by Edmund Beloin, Lou Breslow

My Favorite Wife ★★★★ U

Comedy 1940 · US · BW · 84mins

Irene Dunne, having disappeared seven years earlier in a shipwreck, shows up alive and well just as her husband, Cary Grant, is about to remarry. With a screenplay (by Sam and Bella Spewack) that burns brightly for most of the way and a cast that scintillates to the last, this hit romantic comedy of 1940 remains a delight. Producer Leo McCarey had directed the 1937 Dunne-Grant smash hit *The Awful Truth* and was due to direct this one, but had to let Garson Kanin take over after being involved in a serious car crash. It was remade in 1963 as *Move Over, Darling*, with Doris Day and James Garner. ▦

Cary Grant *Nick Arden* • Irene Dunne *Ellen Arden* • Randolph Scott *Stephen Burkett* • Gail Patrick *Bianca* • Ann Shoemaker *Ma* • Mary Lou Harrington *Chinch Arden* ■ *Dir* Garson Kanin • *Scr* Sam Spewack, Bella Spewack, from a story by Sam Spewack, Bella Spewack, Leo McCarey

My Favorite Year ★★★★ PG

Comedy 1982 · US · Colour · 88mins

Peter O'Toole's deliciously unbalanced portrayal of a legendary Hollywood star falling off the wagon is one of the joys of this farcical excursion to the relatively early days (1954) of American TV. Lots of echoes here, with naive writer Mark Linn-Baker trying to keep the Errol Flynn-like hero sober for a television interview in the way Budd Schulberg was minder for F Scott Fitzgerald, while the show's despotic boss, Joseph Bologna, has more than a touch or two of comedian Sid Caesar. Contains swearing. ▦

Peter O'Toole *Alan Swann* • Mark Linn-Baker *Benjy Stone* • Jessica Harper *KC Downing* • Joseph Bologna *King Kaiser* • Bill Macy *Sy Benson* • Lainie Kazan *Belle Carroca* • Anne DeSalvo *Alice Miller* • Basil Hoffman *Herb Lee* • Lou Jacobi *Uncle Morty* ■ *Dir* Richard Benjamin • *Scr* Norman Steinberg, Dennis Palumbo, from a story by Dennis Palumbo

My Fellow Americans ★★★ 12

Satirical comedy 1996 · US · Colour · 96mins

In this clever twist on the *Odd Couple* format, two grouchy ex-Presidents – one Democrat, the other Republican – hit the road pursued by the secret service. Old-timers Jack Lemmon and James Garner fight over this juicy lump of meat like a pair of bloodhounds, but this showcase for their talents is also a gentle satire on US politics and middle America. Dan Aykroyd plays the current President, John Heard the Vice President, while Lauren Bacall makes one hell of an ex-First Lady. Contains sexual references and swearing. ▦

Jack Lemmon *Russell P Kramer* • James Garner *Matt Douglas* • John Heard *Ted Matthews* • Dan Aykroyd *William Haney* • Sela Ward *Kaye Griffin* • Wilford Brimley *Joe Hollis* • Lauren Bacall *Margaret Kramer* ■ *Dir* Peter Segal • *Scr* E Jack Kaplan, Richard Chapman, Peter Tolan

My First Love ★★★

Romantic comedy
1988 · US · Colour · 90mins

A slight but good-natured comedy drama, which gives *Golden Girls* star Beatrice Arthur a chance to stretch her acting muscle a little. She plays a cranky widow who is drawn out of her shell when she meets up again with her school boyfriend Richard Kiley. The playing of the two veterans is exemplary, and there's good support from Joan Van Ark (*Knots Landing*). Director Gilbert Cates wisely sits back and lets the stars get on with it. Contains swearing.

Beatrice Arthur *Jean Miller* • Richard Kiley *Sam Morrissey* • Joan Van Ark *Claire* ■ *Dir* Gilbert Cates • *Scr* Ed Kaplan

My First Wife ★★★★ 15

Drama 1984 · Ausl · Colour · 97mins

This frankly autobiographical tale from writer/director Paul Cox is a harrowing and highly personal account of marital break-up. Memories and emotions tumble over each other as DJ/composer John Hargreaves learns that not only is his father dying, but his wife is also having an affair. As Hargreaves resorts to increasingly desperate measures to keep his family together, it would have been easy for Cox to turn Wendy Hughes's character into a callous bitch. However, such is the honesty and intensity of this curiously poetic treatise on desire we are too shattered to take sides.

John Hargreaves *John* • Wendy Hughes *Helen* • Lucy Angwin *Lucy* • David Cameron *Tom* ■ *Dir* Paul Cox • *Scr* Paul Cox, Bob Ellis

My Foolish Heart ★★★ U

Romantic drama 1949 · US · BW · 94mins

Forties favourite Susan Hayward could turn on the tears like a tap, and here gives one of her least mechanical performances as the wife and mother unhappily married to Kent Smith and remembering past moments with pilot Dana Andrews. Written by Julius J and Philip G Epstein (co-scripters with Howard Koch of *Casablanca*) from a JD Salinger short story, this weepie has the customary gloss associated with its producer, Samuel Goldwyn, but the

direction (by Mark Robson) never really achieves the emotional depth required. Sadly, Salinger was so unhappy with this adaptation that he decided against agreeing to any further films of his work. *The Catcher in the Rye* was published two years later. 🔲

Dana Andrews *Walt Dreiser* • Susan Hayward *Eloise Winters* • Kent Smith *Lew Wengler* • Lois Wheeler *Mary Jane* • Jessie Royce Landis *Martha Winters* • Robert Keith *Henry Winters* ■ *Dir* Mark Robson • *Scr* Julius J Epstein, Philip G Epstein, from the short story *Uncle Wiggily in Connecticut* by JD Salinger

My Forbidden Past ★★
Drama 1951 · US · BW · 80mins
With the starry line-up of beautiful Ava Gardner, cool Robert Mitchum and debonair Melvyn Douglas, you'd assume this RKO feature would be well nigh unmissable. Actually it's a Deep South potboiler of staggering banality, not even raised above its own low level by the stars. The director is the usually excellent Robert Stevenson, who has to be held partly responsible for the slow pace and lack of action. The casual attitude accorded this New Orleans-set melodrama is indicated by the fact that nobody, not even Lucile Watson as Gardner's aunt, or Gardner herself who came from North Carolina, attempts a southern accent.

Robert Mitchum *Dr Mark Lucas* • Ava Gardner *Barbara Beaurevel* • Melvyn Douglas *Paul Beaurevel* • Lucile Watson *Aunt Eula* • Janis Carter *Corinne* • Gordon Oliver *Clay Duchesne* ■ *Dir* Robert Stevenson • *Scr* Marion Parsonnet, Leopold Atlas, from the novel *Carriage Entrance* by Polan Banks

My Friend Flicka ★★★★ U
Drama 1943 · US · Colour · 88mins
Adapted from the novel by Mary O'Hara, this is one of those films for all the family carelessly referred to by hardened hacks as heart-warming. But it really is. Roddy McDowall is the lonely son of Rocky Mountain rancher Preston Foster, whose dearest wish comes true when he is entrusted with raising his own horse. The story is simply irresistible, the photography glows and the scenes in which the delightful McDowall trains the animal and nurses it through sickness put the film up among the best of its kind.

Roddy McDowall *Ken McLaughlin* • Preston Foster *Rob McLaughlin* • Rita Johnson *Nell* • James Bell *Gus* • Jeff Corey *Tim Murphy* • Diana Hale *Hildy* • Arthur Loft *Charley Sargent* ■ *Dir* Harold Schuster • *Scr* Lillie Hayward, Frances Edwards Faragoh

My Friend Irma ★★
Comedy 1949 · US · BW · 102mins
Based on a hit radio show starring Marie Wilson as the ultimate dumb blonde (a characterisation exceedingly sexist by today's standards), this mild comedy is notable only for marking the screen debut of Dean Martin and Jerry Lewis. They raise more laughs than Wilson, whose predictably daffy reactions as she tries to help her larcenous boyfriend (John Lund) in his money-making schemes lack the sublimely convoluted logic of the more endearingly eccentric Gracie Allen. Character actor Felix Bressart died during production and was replaced by

Hans Conried, though the former can still be glimpsed in long shots.

John Lund *Al* • Diana Lynn *Jane Stacey* • Don DeFore *Richard Rhinelander* • Marie Wilson *Irma Peterson* • Dean Martin *Steve Baird* • Jerry Lewis *Seymour* • Hans Conried *Prof Kropotkin* • Kathryn Givney *Mrs Rhinelander* ■ *Dir* George Marshall • *Scr* Cy Howard, Parke Levy, from a radio series by Cy Howard

My Friend Irma Goes West ★★
Comedy 1950 · US · BW · 90mins
This sequel to *My Friend Irma* (1949) has dumb blonde Irma (Marie Wilson) heading for California with her friends to try their luck in movies. It is marginally superior to its predecessor, due mainly to the extra time given to the comedy team of Dean Martin and Jerry Lewis, who had received an enthusiastic response from audiences with their debut in the earlier film. Martin is given French actress Corinne Calvet as love interest, while Lewis has some classic comic moments, including some inventive business with a plate of spaghetti and a scene where he imitates a chimpanzee.

John Lund *Al* • Marie Wilson *Irma Peterson* • Diana Lynn *Jane Stacey* • Dean Martin *Steve Baird* • Jerry Lewis *Seymour* • Corinne Calvet *Yvonne Yvonne* • Lloyd Corrigan *Sharpie* ■ *Dir* Hal Walker • *Scr* Cy Howard, Parke Levy, from a radio series by Cy Howard

My Friend Ivan Lapshin ★★★★ 15
Period drama 1982 · USSR · Colour and BW · 98mins
Adapted from his father Yuri's stories, Alexei Gherman's third feature is a compelling, understated portrait of Soviet provincial life in the days before the Stalinist purges. Opening in colour, the action flashes back into atmospheric monochrome to follow police chief Andrei Boltnev as he divides his time between tracking down an unscrupulous gang and pursuing actress Nina Ruslanova. Even the subplots, focusing on his relationships with a recently widowed friend and a neighbour and his nine-year-old son, are packed with acute observations that not only evoke the everyday, but also suggest the carnage to come. In Russian with English subtitles.

Andrei Boltnev *Ivan Lapshin* • Nina Ruslanova *Natasha Adashova* • Andrei Mironov *Khanin* • Z Adamovich *Patrikeyevna* ■ *Dir* Alexei German • *Scr* Eduard Volodarsky, from stories by Yuri Gherman

My Gal Sal ★★★ U
Biographical musical drama 1942 · US · Colour · 103mins
They really don't make 'em like this anymore: a musical, set in the 1890s, that bounces along on enough high-octane energy to run the National Grid for a week. Rita Hayworth is at her most luscious and appealing as the chanteuse love object of Victor Mature, playing popular songwriter Paul Dresser, whose wonderful old songs give this warm, engaging movie its fuel. Watch out for great performances from Carole Landis and a pre-*Bilko* Phil Silvers who make up the movie's feel-good ingredients is the sublime choreography of Hermes Pan, the man

partly responsible for Fred Astaire's legendary routines, and Val Raset.

Rita Hayworth *Sally Elliott* • Victor Mature *Paul Dresser* • John Sutton *Fred Haviland* • Carole Landis *Mae Collins* • James Gleason *Pat Hawley* • Phil Silvers *Wiley* ■ *Dir* Irving Cummings • *Scr* Seton I Miller, Darrell Ware, Karl Tunberg, from the biography *My Brother Paul* by Theodore Dreiser

My Geisha ★★
Romantic comedy 1962 · US · Colour · 119mins
When a movie director (Yves Montand) refuses to cast his wife (Shirley MacLaine) in his film of *Madame Butterfly*, she disguises herself as a geisha girl in order to change his mind. Produced in Japan by Steve Parker as a vehicle for his powerhouse wife MacLaine, and directed by Oscar-winning cinematographer Jack Cardiff, the film looks gorgeous. The mildly amusing idea fails to take fire, however, and what should have been a sprightly comedy becomes a big yawn.

Shirley MacLaine *Lucy Dell/Yoko Mori* • Yves Montand *Paul Robaix* • Edward G Robinson *Sam Lewis* • Bob Cummings [Robert Cummings] *Bob Moore* ■ *Dir* Jack Cardiff • *Scr* Norman Krasna

My Giant ★★ PG
Comedy 1998 · US · Colour · 99mins
The fluctuating fortunes of Billy Crystal's career continue with this one-joke comedy, which mixes elements of *Broadway Danny Rose* and *Twins* to less than scintillating effect. Crystal plays Sammy, a second-rate talent agent who, while in Romania to visit his latest signing, has a close encounter with a seven-foot-seven giant (basketball player Gheorghe Muresan). Crystal sees potential in this soft-hearted titan and promptly whisks him off to America, promising to reunite him with his childhood sweetheart. What follows is the kind of mawkish family flick for which a free sickbag should be handed out with every ticket sold – quite appropriate for a film whose biggest "laugh" involves a drunken Muresan splattering a precocious star with projectile vomit. Contains some swearing. 🔲

Billy Crystal *Sammy* • Kathleen Quinlan *Serena* • Gheorghe Muresan *Max* • Joanna Pacula *Lillianna* • Zane Carney *Nick* • Jere Burns *Weller* • Harold Gould *Milt* • Dan Castellaneta *Partlow* ■ *Dir* Michael Lehmann • *Scr* David Seltzer, from a story by Billy Crystal, David Seltzer

My Girl ★★ PG
Drama 1991 · US · Colour · 98mins
Macaulay Culkin may have his name high up on the credits, but luckily he doesn't have enough screen time to spoil this occasionally charming tale. The title character is a young tomboy (Anna Chlumsky) who is trying to come to terms with life and the fact that her mortician father (Dan Aykroyd) is starting a relationship with the woman (Jamie Lee Curtis) who makes up the bodies at his funeral parlour. One for the not-too-cynical members of the audience, although younger viewers may find some of the unhappier moments somewhat distressing. Contains swearing. 🔲

Dan Aykroyd *Harry Sultenfuss* • Jamie Lee Curtis *Shelly Devoto* • Macaulay Culkin *Thomas J Sennett* • Anna Chlumsky *Vada Sultenfuss* • Richard Masur *Phil Sultenfuss* • Griffin Dunne *Mr Bixler* ■ *Dir* Howard Zieff • *Scr* Laurice Elehwany

My Girl 2 ★★ PG
Romance 1994 · US · Colour · 94mins
Unthreatening, absolutely redundant sequel, in which the now adolescent Anna Chlumsky treks off to Los Angeles to find out what her real mother (who died during childbirth) was like. The nominal adult leads (Dan Aykroyd and Jamie Lee Curtis) are left stuck at home with little to do but wring their hands with concern, while not even the appearance of seventies celebs such as Richard Masur and John David Souther succeeds in enlivening the proceedings. 🔲

Dan Aykroyd *Harry Sultenfuss* • Jamie Lee Curtis *Shelly Sultenfuss* • Anna Chlumsky *Vada Sultenfuss* • Austin O'Brien *Nick Zsigmond* • Richard Masur *Phil Sultenfuss* • John David Souther [JD Souther] *Jeffrey Pommeroy* ■ *Dir* Howard Zieff • *Scr* Janet Kovalcik

My Girl Tisa ★★★ U
Drama 1948 · US · Colour · 95mins
A starring vehicle for Lilli Palmer, an actress who successfully combined beauty, intelligence and acting ability. She plays a young immigrant trying to bring her father to America, a role which must have had many resonances for Palmer, who herself grew up in Germany, the daughter of a Jewish surgeon, fled with her sister Irene to Paris to avoid the persecution of the Jews by the Nazis, and eventually found her way to England. Here she co-stars with other noted refugees Sam Wanamaker, Akim Tamiroff and Hugo Haas in a deeply committed movie that doesn't quite reach the heights of social realism to which it aspires.

Lilli Palmer *Tisa Kepes* • Sam Wanamaker *Mark Denek* • Akim Tamiroff *Mr Grumbach* • Alan Hale *Dugan* • Hugo Haas *Tescu* • Gale Robbins *Jenny Kepes* • Stella Adler *Mrs Faludi* ■ *Dir* Elliott Nugent • *Scr* Allen Boretz, from the play *Ever the Beginning* by Lucille S Prumbs, Sara B Smith

My Girlfriend's Boyfriend ★★★★ PG
Comedy drama 1987 · Fr · Colour · 99mins
Concluding his "Comedies and Proverbs" series, Eric Rohmer effortlessly blends the old and the new in this typically deft study of the inconsequential love lives of his youthful, self-obsessed protagonists. Inspired by the social wit of the 18th-century playwright Marivaux, yet set against the futuristic landscape of the antiseptic Parisian suburb of Cergy-Pontoise, the focus falls on Emmanuelle Chaulet, who finds herself irresistibly drawn to her best friend's swain, Eric Viellard. While the characters endlessly analyse emotions which seem as artificial as their surroundings, Rohmer experiments with colour and language as he explores the nature of fidelity and friendship. A delight. In French with English subtitles. 🔲

U = SUITABLE FOR ALL Uc = SUITABLE FOR ALL, ESPECIALLY FOR YOUNG CHILDREN (VIDEO ONLY) PG = PARENTAL GUIDANCE

Emmanuelle Chaulet *Blanche* • Sophie Renoir *Léa* • Anne-Laure Meury *Adrienne* • Eric Viellard *Fabien* • François-Eric Gendron *Alexandre* ■ *Dir/Scr* Eric Rohmer

My Heroes Have Always Been Cowboys ★★★

Western   1991 · US · Colour · 106mins

It would be all too easy to write off Stuart Rosenberg's film as a pale imitation of Sam Peckinpah's rodeo classic, *Junior Bonner*. But that would be unfair to a fine ensemble cast that rises above a formulaic screenplay to create some highly credible characters. There's a real air of disappointment about Scott Glenn's battle-scarred rider, while Kate Capshaw makes light of the clichés as a woman torn between the thrill of love and the pain of bitter experience. But stealing the show is Ben Johnson as Glenn's contrarily cantankerous father. Contains violence and swearing.

Scott Glenn *HD Dalton* • Kate Capshaw *Jolie Meadows* • Ben Johnson *Jesse Dalton* • Tess Harper *Cheryl Hornby* • Paul Balthazar Getty *[Balthazar Getty] Jud Meadows* • Gary Busey *Clint Hornby* • Mickey Rooney *Junior* • Clarence Williams III *Virgil* • Dub Taylor *Gimme Cap* ■ *Dir* Stuart Rosenberg • *Scr* Joel Don Humphreys

My Husband's Secret Life ★ 12

Drama   1998 · US · Colour · 89mins

Preposterous situations and cardboard characters handcuff this story of a widow coming into her own. The wife of a slain cop discovers that her husband died in the arms of the hostess of a "social club" frequented by members of the police department. She teams up with the mistress to uncover a web of high-level police corruption. A good cast (Anne Archer, Maria Conchita Alonso) is totally wasted by the pat and shallow script and opaque direction. Contains some swearing, violence and sexual situations.

Anne Archer *Theresa "Sissy" Sullivan* • James Russo *Sal Bianculli* • Maria Conchita Alonso *Toni Diaz* • Gerard Plunkett *Mike McClary* ■ *Dir* Graeme Clifford • *Scr* Georgia Jeffries, from the novel *Tin Wife* by Joe Flaherty

My Hustler ★★

Drama   1965 · US · BW · 79mins

This was one of 18 films Andy Warhol made in 1965, the year he also made *Empire*, his epic, one-shot movie of the Empire State Building. *My Hustler* offers slightly more dramatic interest and even, unusually for Warhol, some sort of plot. The latter concerns a young hustler, hired for the weekend through "Dial-a-Hustler", who bronzes himself on Fire Island beach while a trio of admirers bitch and banter about who will seduce him first. Be advised that the sexually explicit film also contains lengthy shots of men shaving.

Paul America *Young hustler* • Ed Hood *The "John"* • Joseph Campbell *Sugar Plum Fairy* • John MacDermott *Houseboy* ■ *Dir* Andy Warhol • *Scr* Chuck Wein

My Learned Friend ★★★★ U

Comedy   1943 · UK · BW · 73mins

Will Hay's last film is a devilishly black comedy in which he not only stars, but also co-directs with Basil Dearden. Reduced to writing begging letters after he's disbarred, shyster lawyer Hay joins forces with bungling barrister Claude Hulbert to end the reign of terror being waged by Mervyn Johns, an ex-jailbird bent on taking murderous revenge on all who convicted him for forgery. Hay is on tip-top form, Johns indulges himself as the eye-rolling maniac, and the Big Ben finale skilfully marries Hitchcock and Harold Lloyd.

Will Hay *William Fitch* • Claude Hulbert *Claude Babbington* • Mervyn Johns *Grimshaw* • Laurence Hanray *Sir Norman* • Aubrey Mallalieu *Magistrate* • Charles Victor *"Safety" Wilson* ■ *Dir* Will Hay, Basil Dearden • *Scr* John Dighton, Angus Macphail

My Left Foot ★★★★★ 15

Biographical drama
1989 · UK/Ire · Colour · 98mins

A superb movie chronicling the life of writer and artist Christy Brown, who was born with cerebral palsy, portrayed with astonishing passion and sensitivity by Daniel Day-Lewis. All concerned were rightly showered with praise and plaudits at the time, including Oscars for Day-Lewis and ex-*Casualty* staff nurse Brenda Fricker as Christy's stoical mum. There were some low rumblings that Day-Lewis's role should have been given to a disabled actor, a view which won some sympathy, but nothing can be taken away from this all-round great movie. It's also notable for the penultimate screen appearance of the marvellous Ray McAnally. Contains swearing.

Daniel Day-Lewis *Christy Brown* • Ray McAnally *Mr Brown* • Brenda Fricker *Mrs Brown* • Ruth McCabe *Mary Carr* • Fiona Shaw *Dr Eileen Cole* • Eanna MacLiam *Benny* • Alison Whelan *Sheila* • Hugh O'Conor *Younger Christy* ■ *Dir* Jim Sheridan • *Scr* Shane Connaughton, Jim Sheridan, from the autobiography by Christy Brown • *Music* Elmer Bernstein

My Life ★★★ 15

Drama   1993 · US · Colour · 112mins

The directorial debut of screenwriter Bruce Joel Rubin, who won an Oscar for his screenplay for *Ghost*, and a passable effort it is too. Michael Keaton is very effective as the hotshot public relations executive given only months to live, and Nicole Kidman is nicely sparky as his newly pregnant wife. Rubin keeps everything just the right side of pathos until the final reel, when he jettisons all semblance of reality. The film is at its most endearing and revealing, however, when Keaton, talking to camera, videotapes messages to leave to his unborn child. Contains swearing.

Michael Keaton *Bob Jones* • Nicole Kidman *Gail Jones* • Bradley Whitford *Paul* • Queen Latifah *Theresa* • Michael Constantine *Bill* • Rebecca Schull *Rose* • Mark Lowenthal *Doctor Mills* • Lee Garlington *Carol Sandman* • Haing S Ngor *Mr Ho* ■ *Dir/Scr* Bruce Joel Rubin

My Life as a Dog ★★★★★ PG

Comedy drama 1985 · Swe · Colour · 101mins

Over the last decade, Scandinavian cinema has proved itself equal (if not superior) to Hollywood in the depiction of childhood. Oscar-nominated Lasse Hallström invests this delightful rites-of-passage picture with as many autobiographical references as he does incidents from Reidar Jonsson's popular novel to produce a film of great warmth and wit. He shows the keenest appreciation of the workings of a young mind in the quality of the performance he elicits from 12-year-old Anton Glanzelius, who is wonderfully natural whether getting into mischief, experiencing misery or taking on all comers. In Swedish with English subtitles. Contains some swearing and nudity.

Anton Glanzelius *Ingemar Johansson* • Anki Liden *Ingemar's mother* • Tomas von Brömssen *Uncle Gunnar* • Manfred Serner *Erik Johansson* ■ *Dir* Lasse Hallström • *Scr* Lasse Hallström, Brasse Brannstrom, Pelle Berglund, Reidar Jonsson

My Life So Far ★★★ 12

Drama   1999 · UK/US · Colour · 98mins

This offering from *Chariots of Fire* director Hugh Hudson is a small, intimate portait of one eccentric family in the Scottish highlands of the twenties. Seen from the perspective of the family's ten-year-old son, the movie follows the traumatic events of one tumultuous year as the boy's madcap inventor dad (Colin Firth) has a fling with a visiting uncle's French fiancée (Irène Jacob). Crammed with quirkily memorable characters, the film's subject matter may be too twee for some tastes, though others will appreciate its fine evocation of an era long gone. The fine cast also includes Mary Elizabeth Mastrantonio, Rosemary Harris and Malcolm McDowell.

Colin Firth *Edward Pettigrew* • Rosemary Harris *Gamma Macintosh* • Irène Jacob *Heloise* • Tcheky Karyo *Gabriel Chenoux* • Mary Elizabeth Mastrantonio *Moira Pettigrew* • Malcolm McDowell *Uncle Morris Macintosh* • Kelly MacDonald *Elspeth Pettigrew* • Robert Norman *Fraser Pettigrew* ■ *Dir* Hugh Hudson • *Scr* Simon Donald, from the memoir *Son of Adam* by Sir Denis Forman

My Life with Caroline ★★

Comedy   1941 · US · BW · 80mins

When his wife (British actress Anna Lee in her Hollywood debut) decides that she might be better off married to either Reginald Gardiner or Gilbert Roland, Ronald Colman must constantly woo her to retain her affections. Considering the talents involved – playwright John Van Druten wrote it, Lewis Milestone directs – this idiotic romantic comedy is remarkably devoid of amusement. It's always a pleasure, though, to watch and listen to the elegant Colman.

Ronald Colman *Anthony Mason* • Anna Lee *Caroline Mason* • Charles Winninger *Bliss* • Reginald Gardiner *Paul Martindale* • Gilbert Roland *Paco Del Valle* • Katherine Leslie *Helen* ■ *Dir* Lewis Milestone • *Scr* John Van Druten, Arnold Belgard, from the play *Train to Venice* by Louis Verneuil, Georges Berr

My Little Chickadee ★★★

Comedy western 1940 · US · BW · 83mins

The teaming of WC Fields and Mae West should have resulted in one of the funniest wisecracking movies of all time, but this spoof western never came close to hilarity and ended up as merely rollicking fun. Returning to the screen after two years, West (aided by Fields) penned a script that suited her style of precisely timed innuendo, but which also reined in Fields's unique brand of off-the-cuff rambling. There are some memorable moments, such as their wedding night, the crooked poker game and the scene in which they trade catchphrases, but the linking narrative is ponderous.

WC Fields *Cuthbert J Twillie* • Mae West *Flower Belle Lee* • Joseph Calleia *Jeff Badger, the masked bandit* • Dick Foran *Wayne Carter, editor* • Donald Meek *Amos Budge, cardsharp* • Margaret Hamilton *Mrs Gideon* ■ *Dir* Edward Cline • *Scr* Mae West, WC Fields

My Little Girl ★★★ 15

Drama   1986 · US · Colour · 112mins

A little contrived and a tad sentimental, this well-meaning melodrama marked Connie Kaiserman's directorial debut. As the poor little rich girl spending her summer in a hostel for underprivileged kids, Mary Stuart Masterson conveys something of a teenager's confusion at coming face to face with the real world. She's well supported by Erika Alexander, as the girl who'd rather go on the lam than be separated from her sister, and James Earl Jones, who adds some down-to-earth dignity to the proceedings as the hostel's director. Contains violence and swearing.

James Earl Jones *Ike Bailey* • Geraldine Page *Molly* • Mary Stuart Masterson *Franny Bettinger* • Anne Meara *Mrs Shopper* • Pamela Payton-Wright *Cordelia "Delly" Bettinger* • Peter Michael Goetz *Norman Bettinger* ■ *Dir* Connie Kaiserman • *Scr* Connie Kaiserman, Nan Mason

My Little Pony ★★ U

Animated adventure
1986 · US · Colour · 89mins

A children's favourite from those bygone days when Pokémons and Power Rangers were still mere twinkles in their merchandisers' eyes, and when collectibles were altogether softer, more cuddly things. A feature-length spin-off from the TV series and toy range, *My Little Pony* was indifferently animated in Japan and voiced rather better than it deserved to be by Danny DeVito, Cloris Leachman and Rhea Perlman. The plot has the rainbow-maned denizens of Ponyland fighting hoof and nail against a wicked witch with a living lava weapon.

Danny DeVito *Grundle King* • Madeline Kahn *Draggle* • Cloris Leachman *Hydia* • Rhea Perlman *Reeka* ■ *Dir* Michael Joens • *Scr* George Arthur Bloom, from characters created by Hasbro

My Love Has Been Burning ★★★★

Political drama   1949 · Jap · BW · 96mins

Made quickly and cheaply, yet anticipating the director's mature style, this *film à clef* was based on the autobiography of the 19th-century women's rights campaigner, Hideko Kageyama. As played by Kinuyo Tanaka, Eiko is a typical Kenji Mizoguchi heroine: she sees her school closed down on account of her political views, suffers imprisonment and then marries a prominent liberal who refuses to support her demand for female suffrage. The action, inspired by the abrasive postwar art of Picasso, is unexpectedly violent. In Japanese with English subtitles.

Kinuyo Tanaka *Eiko Hirayama* • Mitsuko Mito *Chiyo* • Eitaro Ozawa *Hayase* • Ichiro Sugai *Kentaro Omoi* • Kuniko Miyake *Toshiko Kishida* ■ *Dir* Kenji Mizoguchi • *Scr* Yoshikata Yoda, Kaneto Shindo, from the autobiography *Warawa no Hanshogai (My Half Life)* by Hideko Kageyama

My Lucky Star ★★★

Musical 1938 · US · BW and Tinted · 63mins

Minor but by no means negligible Sonja Henie vehicle, with a nice Mack Gordon-Harry Revel score and a daft plot that gives the dimpled skater plenty of opportunity to strut her stuff. Henie plays a department store clerk who catches the eye of the boss's son, Cesar Romero; the latter's wife is played by Louise Hovick, better known as Gypsy Rose Lee. The rest of the supporting cast is way above par – look for character veterans Buddy Ebsen, Arthur Treacher and Elisha Cook Jr – though leading man Richard Greene is a bland foil for spunky Sonja. The *Alice in Wonderland* ice ballet was originally tinted pink.

Sonja Henie *Kristina Nielson* • Richard Greene *Larry Taylor* • Joan Davis *Mary Boop* • Cesar Romero *George Cabot Jr* • Buddy Ebsen *Buddy* • Arthur Treacher *Whipple* • George Barbier *George Cabot Sr* • Louise Hovick [Gypsy Rose Lee] *Marcelle* • Billy Gilbert *Nick* ■ *Dir* Roy Del Ruth • *Scr* Harry Tugend, Jack Yellen, from the story *They Met in Chicago* by Karl Tunberg, Don Ettlinger

My Man Adam ★★🅸🅵

Comedy 1985 · US · Colour · 83mins

Page Hannah (sister of Daryl) is the object of Raphael Sbarge's fantasies in this weak comedy about a high school student who finds his daydreams aren't nearly as exciting as real life when he inadvertently becomes involved in a murderous crime. A very slight comedy which goes some way to explain why Page's career didn't take off like her sister's. ▭

Raphael Sbarge *Adam Swit* • Page Hannah *Sabrina McKay* • Veronica Cartwright *Elaine Swit* • Dave Thomas (1) *Jerry Swit* • Charlie Bennett *Leroy* • Larry B Scott *Donald* • John Kapelos *Mr Rangle* ■ *Dir* Roger L Simon • *Scr* Roger L Simon, Renee Missel

My Man Godfrey ★★★★🅸

Comedy 1936 · US · BW · 89mins

A derelict (William Powell) finds himself rescued by a wealthy Park Avenue family's irrepressible younger daughter (Carole Lombard) and installed as the latest in an endless succession of butlers. Who he really is, and how he withstands the pressure of the family's insane antics, is the stuff of this classic Universal comedy. It would be faultless if the family's farcical behaviour didn't strain credibility. Yet it's no surprise that both stars, director Gregory La Cava and the screenplay he co-wrote were all nominated for Oscars, as were Alice Brady for her portrayal of the featherbrained mother of the clan and Mischa Auer for his performance as the latter's posturing protégé. ▭

William Powell *Godfrey Parke* • Carole Lombard *Irene Bullock* • Alice Brady *Angelica Bullock* • Eugene Pallette *Alexander Bullock* •

Gail Patrick *Cornelia Bullock* • Alan Mowbray *Tommy Gray* • Jean Dixon *Molly* • Mischa Auer *Carlo* ■ *Dir* Gregory La Cava • *Scr* Morrie Ryskind, Eric Hatch, Gregory La Cava, from the novel *1101 Park Avenue* by Eric Hatch

My Man Godfrey ★★🅸

Comedy 1957 · US · Colour · 91mins

Perhaps it was a mistake to try to recapture the atmosphere of the well-loved original, a classic thirties screwball comedy that starred William Powell and Carole Lombard. But Universal did try gamely here, casting David Niven and June Allyson and throwing in the dubious benefits of colour and CinemaScope. To be fair, if you've never seen the 1936 movie, this may pass the time well enough, especially if you're a fan of either star. Trouble is, director Henry Koster helped neither of them. Niven is too often reduced to eyebrow-raising double takes, while Allyson seems, as ever, outclassed by her leading man.

David Niven *Godfrey* • June Allyson *Irene* • Jessie Royce Landis *Angelica* • Robert Keith *Mr Bullock* • Eva Gabor *Francesca* • Jay Robinson *Vincent* • Martha Hyer *Cordelia* • Herbert Anderson *Hubert* ■ *Dir* Henry Koster • *Scr* Everett Freeman, Peter Berneis, William Bowers, from the 1936 film, from the novel *1101 Park Avenue* by Eric Hatch

My Mother's Courage
★★★★🅸

Wartime biography
1995 · Ger/UK/Aus · Colour · 90mins

A powerful, moving and decidedly different telling of a true Holocaust tale about the deportation of 4,000 Hungarian Jews from Budapest to Auschwitz in 1944. Told in flashback, the film focuses on the narrator's mother (Pauline Collins), who survived due to a mix of coincidence, courage and help from a most unexpected quarter. Director Michael Verhoeven also made *The Nasty Girl*, and there are similar touches of surrealism here.

Pauline Collins *Elsa Tabori* • Ulrich Tukur *SS officer* • Heribert Sasse *Kelemen* • Natalie Morse *Maria* • Robert Giggenbach *Cornelius Tabori* • Günter Bothur *"Moustache"* • Simon Verhoeven *Young SS man* ■ *Dir* Michael Verhoeven • *Scr* Michael Verhoeven, from the novel by George Tabori

My Name Is Bill W ★★★★

Drama based on a true story
1989 · US · Colour · 100mins

A generally impressive drama about the founding of Alcoholics Anonymous. Few of the familiar Hollywood clichés about drunks are present in the script, and Daniel Petrie's direction is sensitive and well tuned to the remarkable actors. James Woods is compelling as Bill Wilson, living and drinking himself to an early grave until he meets Dr Bob Smith, another alcoholic, played by the excellent James Garner. Together they put the cork in the bottle and start the famous meetings. There's splendid support, too, from JoBeth Williams, Fritz Weaver and Gary Sinise (*Forrest Gump*).

James Woods *Bill Wilson* • JoBeth Williams *Lois Wilson* • James Garner *Dr Bob Smith* • Gary Sinise *Ebby Thatcher* • George Coe *Frank Shaw* • Fritz Weaver *Dr Burnham* ■ *Dir* Daniel Petrie • *Scr* William G Borchert

My Name Is Joe ★★★★🅸

Drama
1998 · UK/Ger/Fr/It/Sp · Colour · 100mins

Ken Loach's trawl through the Glaswegian underworld tells the story of Peter Mullan, a recovering alcoholic who falls in love with social worker Louise Goodall. However, his past comes back to haunt him when he vainly tries to help a young friend and his junkie wife who are being threatened by local gangsters. Downbeat and buoyant by turns, Loach's poignant drama boasts laugh-out-loud moments and a host of splendid performances. Mullan was named best actor at Cannes. Contains swearing and violence. ▭ **DVD**

Peter Mullan *Joe* • Louise Goodall *Sarah* • Gary Lewis *Shanks* • Lorraine McIntosh *Maggie* • David McKay *Liam* • Annemarie Kennedy *Sabine* • Scott Hannah *Scott* ■ *Dir* Ken Loach • *Scr* Paul Laverty

My Name is Julia Ross
★★★

Film noir 1945 · US · BW BW · 64mins

With unusual acumen, the bosses of Columbia realised that they had a rather good little thriller on their hands and gave this a major launch, earning some rave reviews despite the lack of box-office names. Nina Foch takes the principal role of the secretary who is given a new identity against her will and imprisoned in a remote mansion. Dame May Whitty plays against type as the villainess, supported by the ever-sinister George Macready as her murderous son. The setting is Hollywood's idea of England, but it's still an entertaining, commendably brief picture that helped director Joseph H Lewis climb out of the B-feature ranks.

Nina Foch *Julia Ross* • May Whitty [Dame May Whitty] *Mrs Williamson Hughes* • George Macready *Ralph Hughes* • Roland Varno *Dennis Bruce* • Anita Bolster *Sparkes* • Doris Lloyd *Mrs Mackie* ■ *Dir* Joseph H Lewis • *Scr* Muriel Roy Bolton, from the novel *The Woman in Red* by Anthony Gilbert

My Name Is Kate ★★★🅸

Drama 1994 · US · Colour · 90mins

Donna Mills attempts to ditch her glamorous *Knots Landing* image for this worthy, occasionally sentimental drama about alcoholism. She plays a successful career woman and wife whose life begins to fall apart when she develops an unhealthy interest in the demon drink. Daniel J Travanti is her caring, sharing husband who, along with the rest of the family, tries to lead her back on to the straight and narrow. There's good support from Eileen Brennan, but it's Mills's movie. Contains swearing. ▭

Donna Mills *Kate Bannister* • Daniel J Travanti *Hal Bannister* • Nia Peeples *Annie* • Ryan Reynolds *Kevin* • Deanna Milligan *Carrie* • Babz Chula [Babs Chula] *Nora* • Linda Darlow *Suzanne* • Eileen Brennan *Barbara Mannix* ■ *Dir* Rod Hardy • *Scr* George Eckstein

My Name Is Nobody ★★★🅸

Spaghetti western
1973 · It/Fr/W Ger · Colour · 115mins

Sergio Leone produced this spaghetti western and once again cast Henry Fonda, the star of *Once upon a Time in the*

West, as a notorious gunfighter who plans to take an ocean liner from New Orleans and retire in Europe. Terence Hill plays "Nobody", who idolises Fonda and seduces him into one last, ultimate showdown. The story certainly has epic pretensions, but the knockabout mood is poorly judged, while Hill is no substitute for Clint Eastwood. Leone's involvement is clear from the gunfights, huge close-ups and Ennio Morricone score. Some dialogue dubbed into English. ▭

Henry Fonda *Jack Beauregard* • Terence Hill *Nobody* • Jean Martin *Sullivan* • Leo Gordon *Red* • RG Armstrong *Honest John* ■ *Dir* Tonino Valerii • *Scr* Ernesto Gastaldi, from a story by Fulvio Morsella, Ernesto Gastaldi, from an idea by Sergio Leone

My New Gun ★★★🅸

Black comedy 1992 · US · Colour · 94mins

A charming, eccentric slice of Americana that provides Diane Lane with probably her best role to date, playing an ordinary suburban housewife who strikes up a curious relationship with wild neighbour James LeGros. When LeGros steals the gun Lane's husband Stephen Collins bought her for protection, a series of events unfolds that changes her life for ever. Writer/director Stacy Cochran, in her first feature, pokes some wry fun at the American obsession with weaponry, and there are winning performances from Lane, LeGros, Tess Harper and the cast-against-type Collins. Contains swearing. ▭

Diane Lane *Debbie Bender* • James LeGros *Skippy* • Stephen Collins *Gerald Bender* • Tess Harper *Kimmy Hayes* • Bill Raymond *Andrew* • Bruce Altman *Irwin* • Maddie Corman *Myra* ■ *Dir/Scr* Stacy Cochran

My Night with Maud ★★★★

Drama 1969 · Fr · BW · 110mins

Oscar-nominated for best foreign language film, this was released as the fourth of Eric Rohmer's "Six Moral Tales". One of the director's few films to boast a star-studded cast, it is an engrossing study of temptation and moral rectitude, with a delicious twist in which Rohmer questions the validity of religious and philosophical conviction in the face of human caprice. As the staunchly Catholic engineer, Jean-Louis Trintignant gives one of his finest performances as he resists the seduction of sophisticated divorcée Françoise Fabian out of fidelity to Marie-Christine Barrault, a woman he adores silently from afar. In French with English subtitles.

Jean-Louis Trintignant *Jean-Louis/Narrator* • Françoise Fabian *Maud* • Marie-Christine Barrault *Françoise* • Antoine Vitez *Vidal* • Leonide Kogan *Concert violinist* ■ *Dir/Scr* Eric Rohmer • *Cinematographer* Nestor Almendros

My Own Private Idaho
★★★★🅸

Drama 1991 · US · Colour · 99mins

A narcoleptic rent boy's doomed quest to find his mother is all the story director Gus Van Sant needs to explore the meaning of "home" and "family" in this unsettling tone poem. Using hallucinatory dream sequences, *cinéma vérité* confessions with male

🅰 = SUITABLE FOR ALL, 🅰🅴 = SUITABLE FOR ALL, ESPECIALLY FOR YOUNG CHILDREN (VIDEO ONLY) 🅿🅶 = PARENTAL GUIDANCE

hustlers, artful sexual posing and impressionistic effects to hammer home the disturbed state of River Phoenix's mind, Van Sant also manages to extract a mould-breaking performance from Keanu Reeves (playing the object of Phoenix's affections). Audacious, controversial, directional, important and totally unique, you'll either love it or hate it. But see it! Contains swearing, sex scenes, drug abuse and nudity. ▭

River Phoenix *Mike Waters* • Keanu Reeves *Scott Favor* • James Russo *Richard Waters* • William Richert *Bob Pigeon* • Rodney Harvey *Gary* • Chiara Caselli *Carmella* • Michael Parker *Digger* • Jessie Thomas *Denise* • Grace Zabriskie *Alena* ■ *Dir* Gus Van Sant • *Scr* Gus Van Sant, with additional dialogue by William Shakespeare

My Pal Gus ★★
Comedy drama   1952 · US · BW · 83mins
Somewhat glib and predictable, this comedy drama features Richard Widmark as a divorced businessman; George Winslow as his neglected, misbehaving son; Joanne Dru as the schoolteacher who takes the youngster in hand; and Audrey Totter as the ex-wife who comes back to cause trouble. It's nice to see Winslow, the boy with the foghorn voice from *Gentlemen Prefer Blondes*, in a meatier role, but the film could have done with a lighter touch. Both Widmark and director Robert Parrish were far more comfortable with straight drama.

Richard Widmark *Dave Jennings* • Joanne Dru *Lydia Marble* • Audrey Totter *Joyce* • George Winslow *Gus Jennings* • Joan Banks *Ivy Tolliver* • Regis Toomey *Farley Norris* ■ *Dir* Robert Parrish • *Scr* Fay Kanin, Michael Kanin

My Pal Trigger ★★ U
Western   1946 · US · BW · 79mins
Roy Rogers declared this a favourite among his westerns, though it's hard to see why – except for the fact that it gives Trigger more prominence than usual. Horse breeding is central to a rather dramatic storyline, which sees one champion steed shot dead, Rogers accused of the crime, and a mare being fatally injured by a mountain lion while protecting her offspring. Former star Jack Holt plays the lead heavy, with the familiar faces of Roy Barcroft, LeRoy Mason and Kenne Duncan backing him up.

Roy Rogers • George "Gabby" Hayes *Gabby Kendrick* • Dale Evans *Susan* • Jack Holt *Brett Scoville* • LeRoy Mason *Carson* • Roy Barcroft *Hunter* • Kenne Duncan *Croupier* ■ *Dir* Frank McDonald • *Scr* Jack Townley, John K Butler, from a story by Paul Gangelin

My Pleasure Is My Business ★★
Erotic comedy   1974 · Can · Colour · 94mins
This sex comedy was designed to exploit celebrity prostitute Xaviera Hollander, who achieved notoriety as author of *The Happy Hooker*. Here she plays Gabrielle, a promiscuous movie star who's deported from the US and takes her sexually liberated views to the small country of Gestalt. Via a mix of orgies, lesbian flings and plain old-fashioned fornication, Hollander scandalises the authorities and thwarts the corrupt Prime Minister.

Recommended for only the most undemanding porn fans.

Xaviera Hollander *Gabrielle* • Henry Ramer *Prime Minister* • Kenneth Lynch *Alfie, Porno King* • Colin Fox *Freddy* • Don Cullen *Shagnoss* • Jayne Eastwood *Isabella* ■ *Dir* Albert S Waxman • *Scr* Alvin Boretz

My Reputation ★★
Melodrama   1946 · US · BW · 92mins
A typical Barbara Stanwyck vehicle in which she plays a widow who creates a scandal by dating too soon after her husband's death (hence the title). She's got two suitors, one of whom is George Brent, playing against type as a womaniser, and there are no real surprises, except for the fact that Stanwyck fairly drips with furs and jewellery when rolling bandages for the local Red Cross. Eve Arden as Stanwyck's best friend steals the movie, but it's petty larceny.

Barbara Stanwyck *Jessica Drummond* • George Brent *Major Scott Landis* • Warner Anderson *Frank Everett* • Lucile Watson *Mrs Kimball* • John Ridgely *Cary Abbott* • Eve Arden *Ginna Abbott* • Jerome Cowan *George Van Orman* ■ *Dir* Curtis Bernhardt • *Scr* Catherine Turney, from the novel *Instruct My Sorrows* by Clare Jaynes

My Science Project ★★ 15
Science-fiction adventure
1985 · US · Colour · 90mins
This laugh-free comedy typifies the problems that the Disney studios have always had in producing films for kids who've outgrown their cartoons. The plot is OK: high school students get their hands on an extra-terrestrial gizmo that lets them summon up objects from the past and future. But its development, especially the emphasis on clumsily portrayed and badly integrated adolescent sex, leaves a nasty taste in the mouth. You'll spot some familiar faces in the cast (Fisher Stevens, Barry Corbin, Richard Masur), while Dennis Hopper is truly funny as an ageing hippy science teacher.

John Stockwell *Michael Harlan* • Danielle Von Zerneck *Ellie Sawyer* • Fisher Stevens *Vince Latello* • Raphael Sbarge *Sherman* • Dennis Hopper *Bob Roberts* • Barry Corbin *Lew Harlan* • Richard Masur *Detective Isadore Nulty* ■ *Dir/Scr* Jonathan Betuel

My Side of the Mountain ★★★ U
Adventure   1969 · Can/US · Colour · 100mins
A touching celebration of nature, this children's film is about a highly intelligent 13-year-old who, after a family trip to the country is called off, runs away from home and manages to survive in the Montana wilds. It's attractively photographed, well-acted (particularly by Teddy Eccles in the lead) and thankfully unsentimental.

Teddy Eccles *Sam Gribley* • Theodore Bikel *Bando* • Tudi Wiggins *Miss Turner* • Frank Perry *Mr Gribley* • Peggi Loder *Mrs Gribley* ■ *Dir* James B Clark • *Scr* Ted Sherdeman, Jane Klove, Joanna Crawford, from the novel by Jean Craighead George

My Sister Eileen ★★★ U
Comedy   1942 · US · BW · 96mins
This film version of the hit play was a great success in its day, though it seems somewhat forced and strident now. Yet Rosalind Russell's expert comic timing is a joy to behold in her role as aspiring writer Ruth, trying her luck in Manhattan and finding opportunity comes more easily to her beautiful sister (Janet Blair). Russell won an Oscar nomination for her performance, which she re-created to enormous acclaim in the stage musical *Wonderful Town*. Columbia, however, who owned the rights to the original play, made a completely different musical of the property in 1955.

Rosalind Russell *Ruth Sherwood* • Brian Aherne *Robert Baker* • Janet Blair *Eileen Sherwood* • George Tobias *Landlord Appopolous* • Allyn Joslyn *Chick Clark* • Richard Quine *Frank Lippincott* ■ *Dir* Alexander Hall • *Scr* Joseph Fields, Jerome Chodorov, from their play, from the stories by Ruth McKenney

My Sister Eileen ★★★ U
Musical comedy   1955 · US · Colour · 96mins
This charming musical remake of the 1942 comedy details the adventures of two girls from the Ohio backwoods getting to grips with the fleshpots of New York. Starring a whole host of early fifties faces – Janet Leigh, Jack Lemmon, Bob Fosse (who also choreographs) – the whole enterprise zings with an amiable kookiness. Betty Garrett in particular shines as the plain older sister with a heart of fractured gold. Based on the same material as the Broadway hit *Wonderful Town*.

Janet Leigh *Eileen Sherwood* • Betty Garrett *Ruth Sherwood* • Jack Lemmon *Bob Baker* • Robert Fosse [Bob Fosse] *Frank Lippencott* • Kurt Kasznar *Appopolous* • Richard York [Dick York] *"Wreck"* • Lucy Marlow *Helen* • Tommy Rall *Chick Clark* ■ *Dir* Richard Quine • *Scr* Blake Edwards, Richard Quine, from the play by Joseph Fields, Jerome Chodorov, from the stories by Ruth McKenney

My Six Convicts ★★
Prison drama   1952 · US · BW · 104mins
John Beal plays a psychologist who enters Harbour State Prison to interview a variety of prisoners, including a safecracker, an embezzler and a killer. Based on Donald Powell Wilson's bestselling novel, this quasi-documentary was produced by message movie maestro Stanley Kramer and was intended to give convicts a human face, even a sense of humour. Some scenes were shot inside the actual San Quentin prison, using real convicts as extras.

Millard Mitchell *James Connie* • Gilbert Roland *Punch Pinero* • John Beal *Doc* • Marshall Thompson *Blivens Scott* • Alf Kjellin *Clem Randall* • Henry Morgan [Harry Morgan] *Dawson* • Jay Adler *Steve Kopac* • Regis Toomey *Doctor Gordon* • Charles Buchinski [Charles Bronson] *Jocko* ■ *Dir* Hugo Fregonese • *Scr* Michael Blankfort, from a novel by Donald Powell Wilson

My Six Loves ★★★ U
Comedy   1962 · US · Colour · 100mins
As a film director, ace choreographer Gower Champion never achieved the heights he reached on Broadway. Nor

did he equal his popularity as half of the dance team of Marge and Gower Champion who appeared in a series of superbly entertaining MGM features. Here he reunites with another MGM alumnus, Debbie Reynolds, in a likeable tale of theatrical folk. This is either mawkish or genuinely sentimental, according to taste, but there's no denying the sheer professionalism of all involved.

Debbie Reynolds *Janice Courtney* • Cliff Robertson *Reverend Jim Larkin* • David Janssen *Martin Bliss* • Jim Backus *The Sheriff* • Eileen Heckart *Ethel Swenson* • Hans Conried *Kingsley Cross* • Alice Pearce *Bus driver* ■ *Dir* Gower Champion • *Scr* John Fante, Joseph Calvelli, William Wood, from a story by Peter VK Funk

My Son Is Innocent ★★★
Courtroom drama   1996 · US · Colour
Is there any topic in America that doesn't get made into a worthy TV movie? This is another predictable stroll down familiar TV-movie lanes, with Marilu Henner getting her teeth into the chunky role of a mother trying to clear son Nick Stahl of a rape charge. It's nice to see Andrew Robinson, the psycho from *Dirty Harry*, back on the screen, but this is really one for fans of the genre only. Contains violence and swearing.

Marilu Henner *Maggie Sutter* • Nick Stahl *Eric Sutter* • Andrew Robinson *David* ■ *Dir* Larry Elikann • *Scr* Robert Inman, Philip Rosenberg

My Son John ★ U
Drama   1952 · US · BW · 121mins
A heavily religious, flag-wavingly patriotic American family goes into shock when they learn their beloved son is a communist. All is forgiven when he recants and dies. An abysmal anti-Red movie, directed by Leo McCarey of all people, who one can only assume was temporarily deranged by the prevailing hysteria of the McCarthy witch-hunts. Helen Hayes returned to the screen after a long absence to play the mother, while Robert Walker died before the film's completion, forcing the production to fill in the gaps with footage from *Strangers on a Train*. To the astonishment of many, McCarey was Oscar-nominated for his original story.

Helen Hayes *Lucille Jefferson* • Van Heflin *Stedman of the FBI* • Robert Walker *John Jefferson* • Dean Jagger *Dan Jefferson* • Minor Watson *Dr Carver* • Frank McHugh *Father O'Dowd* • Richard Jaeckel *Chuck Jefferson* • James Young *Ben Jefferson* ■ *Dir* Leo McCarey • *Scr* Myles Connolly, Leo McCarey, John Lee Mahin, from a story by Leo McCarey

My Son Johnny ★★★ 15
Drama based on a true story
1991 · US · Colour · 89mins
Another drama based on a true story, this time with *Knots Landing's* Michele Lee as a harassed mother forced to testify in court after her son is charged with murdering his own brother. Rick Schroder – cute as a child star (when he was Ricky) but now seemingly typecast as a TV-movie loner – gives a solid and decidedly non-cute performance as the nasty one of the twosome, who goads his sibling (a believably desperate Corin Nemec) into retaliating. Rip Torn appears in a

supporting role in what is a genuinely intriguing and well-handled tale. ▢

Michele Lee *Marianne Cortino* • Rick Schroder *Johnny Cortino* • Corin Nemec *Anthony Cortino* • Rip Torn *Brian Stansbury* • Mariangela Pino *Rhoda Cortino* • Stephen Dimopoulos *Louie Cortino* • Ken Pogue *Judge Burke* ■ *Dir* Peter Levin • *Scr* Peter Nelson

My Son, My Son ★★★★
First World War drama
1940 · US · BW · 116mins

A solid and stellar cast, under Charles Vidor's sober and well-judged direction, brings Howard Spring's powerful bestseller to life. The always attractive Brian Aherne plays William Essex who, born into a poverty-stricken background, has pulled himself up by the bootstraps to become a successful novelist. He dotes on his son (Louis Hayward), but the latter grows into cruel, unfeeling manhood, mocking his father, destroying his own childhood sweetheart (Laraine Day) and attempting to seduce the woman his father loves (Madeleine Carroll). An absorbing drama of the highest order.

Madeleine Carroll *Livia Vaynol* • Brian Aherne *William Essex* • Louis Hayward *Oliver Essex* • Laraine Day *Maeve O'Riorden* • Henry Hull *Dermot O'Riorden* • Josephine Hutchinson *Nellie Essex* • Sophie Stewart *Sheila O'Riorden* • Bruce Lester *Rory O'Riorden* ■ *Dir* Charles Vidor • *Scr* Leonore Coffee, from the novel by Howard Spring

My Son the Fanatic ★★★15
Drama   1997 · UK · Colour · 86mins

Caricature and cliché come close to scuppering this Yorkshire-based drama from screenwriter Hanif Kureishi. But such is the excellence of leads Om Puri and Rachel Griffiths that this study of religious intolerance, class snobbery and the seeming impossibility of social integration never makes for less than absorbing viewing. As the immigrant cab driver whose hopes for acceptance are dashed by his son's involvement with a strict Islamic sect, Puri strikes up a rapport with Griffiths's harassed prostitute and thus deepens his crisis. Steadily directed by Udayan Prasad, the sometimes comic drama steers clear of outright controversy, but still touches on some pretty contentious issues. Contains swearing, sex scenes and drug abuse.

Om Puri *Parvez* • Rachel Griffiths *Bettina* • Stellan Skarsgård *Schitz* • Akbar Kurtha *Farid* • Gopi Desai *Minoo* • Harish Patel *Fizzy* • Bhasker Patel [Bhasker] *The Maulvi* • Sarah Jane Potts *Madelaine* ■ *Dir* Udayan Prasad • *Scr* Hanif Kureishi, from his short story

My Stepmother Is an Alien ★★★15
Science-fiction comedy
1988 · US · Colour · 103mins

''Barbarella Goes Shopping'' is the premise of this clunky cosmic satire, saved by Kim Basinger's untapped flair for light comedy. She plays a gorgeous ET who shacks up with scientist slob Dan Aykroyd to save her planet from destruction. Forget the plot, just settle down and watch a series of goofy culture-clash sketches revolving around Basinger coping with suburban life on Earth armed only with her talking alien handbag. Fine moments of inspired

lunacy jostle with predictably slight comic relief, but Basinger's eager-to-please freshness and verve make this intergalactic muddle impossible to dislike. Contains swearing. ▢

Dan Aykroyd *Dr Steven Mills* • Kim Basinger *Celeste Martin* • Jon Lovitz *Ron Mills* • Alyson Hannigan *Jessie Mills* • Joseph Maher *Dr Lucas Budlong* • Seth Green *Fred Glass* • Wesley Mann *Grady* • Adrian Sparks *Dr Morosini* ■ *Dir* Richard Benjamin • *Scr* Jerico Weingrod, Herschel Weingrod, Timothy Harris, Jonathan Reynolds

My Summer Story ★ PG
Comedy   1994 · US · Colour · 81mins

Despite the return of writer/narrator Jean Shepherd and director Bob Clark, this continuation of *A Christmas Story* (1983) is a big letdown. Though it's understandable that different actors had to be cast in the roles, the new additions have no sparkle, while Charles Grodin is grossly miscast as the Old Man. While the various vignettes (white trash neighbours, a movie theatre promotion) were hilarious in Shepherd's books, they come across as flat and extremely rushed on the screen. What this movie really lacks is warmth and love for the characters and the period. ▢

Charles Grodin *Old Man* • Kieran Culkin *Ralphie Parker* • Mary Steenburgen *Mom* • Christian Culkin *Randy Parker* • Al Mancini *Zudoc* • Troy Evans *Gertz* ■ *Dir* Bob Clark • *Scr* Jean Shepherd, Leigh Brown, Bob Clark, from the novels *In God We Trust, All Others Pay Cash* and *Wanda Hickey's Night of Golden Memories and Other Disasters* by Jean Shepherd

My Sweet Little Village ★★★ PG
Comedy   1986 · Cz · Colour · 99mins

Touching obliquely on bureaucratic corruption, the underdevelopment of the countryside and the shortage of decent housing, this is one of Jiří Menzel's mildest political allegories. It's a benign gaze that falls upon the villagers of a muddle-along collective, where the doctor is accident-prone, a bashful student becomes besotted with his teacher, a young wife strays from nuptial bliss and a truck driver and his doltish assistant fall out over repeated bungling. It all makes for amiable entertainment, with Menzel slyly idealising the sense of rural community while gleaning some Laurel and Hardy-style pathos from Marian Labuda and Janos Ban. A Czech language film.

Janos Ban *Otik Rakosnik* • Marian Labuda *Pavek* • Rudolf Hrusinsky *Dr Skruzny* • Petr Cepek *Turek* ■ *Dir* Jiří Menzel • *Scr* Zdenek Sverak

My Teenage Daughter ★
Drama   1956 · UK · BW · 102mins

Anna Neagle stars in this ludicrous and staggeringly awful melodrama about the problems of motherhood in the fiifties. Neagle plays a magazine editor whose teenage daughter (Sylvia Syms) gets a new boyfriend and ends up in jail for manslaughter. The villain of the piece is jive dancing, while everyone speaks with Mayfair accents and seems to think they're making a statement about the youth of today.

Anna Neagle *Valerie Carr* • Sylvia Syms *Janet Carr* • Wilfrid Hyde White *Sir Joseph* • Norman Wooland *Hugh Manning* • Kenneth Haigh *Tony Ward Black* • Julia Lockwood *Poppet Carr* • Helen Haye *Aunt Louisa* ■ *Dir* Herbert Wilcox • *Scr* Felicity Douglas

My 20th Century ★★
Surreal comedy drama
1988 · Hun/Can · BW · 104mins

Winner of the Caméra d'Or at Cannes for best first feature, Ildiko Enyedi's period comedy is illuminated by the triple performance of Dorotha Segda as a mother and her twins. The latter unsuspectingly come together 20 years after they were orphaned as passengers on the Orient Express. One is now the coquettish mistress of a powerful man; the other is a radical activist with a bagful of bombs. This might have made for an amusing comedy of errors; instead, Enyedi insists on interspersing the sisters' adventures with surreal diversions and references to the dehumanising advance of progress. A Hungarian language film.

Dorotha Segda *Dora/Lili/Mother* • Oleg Jankowski *Z* • Peter Andorai *Thomas Alva Edison* • Gabor Mathe *X* • Paulus Manker *Weininger* ■ *Dir/Scr* Ildiko Enyedi

My Two Loves ★★★
Drama   1986 · US · Colour · 100mins

Widowed Mariette Hartley is forced to confront her sexuality when she adds an affair with a female co-worker to that with her late husband's male business partner. The drama benefits from a first-rate script by Reginald Rose and Rita Mae Brown, plus forceful direction from Noel Black that elicits fine and sympathetic performances from the likes of Sada Thompson, Barry Newman and Lynn Redgrave. Yet there's still a contrived feel to the whole thing.

Mariette Hartley *Gail Springer* • Lynn Redgrave *Marjorie Lloyd* • Barry Newman *Ben Taylor* • Sada Thompson *Dorothea* • Sarah Inglis *Amy Springer* ■ *Dir* Noel Black • *Scr* Reginald Rose, Rita Mae Brown

My Uncle Antoine ★★★
Drama   1971 · Can · Colour · 110mins

This small-scale, forties-set rural drama is sometimes regarded as the best Canadian film ever made. Dealing with life and death in a Quebec village, it gently juggles a gallery of characters, focusing on teenage Benoit and his uncle, the local undertaker. Director Claude Jutra has a small role as the town clerk, but his career was tragically cut short by Alzheimer's disease. In 1986, he vanished; a year later, his decomposed body was found in the frozen St Lawrence river with a note to identify himself. In French with English subtitles.

Jacques Gagnon *Benoit* • Lyne Champagne *Carmen* • Jean Duceppe *Antoine* • Monique Mercure *Alexandrine* • Lionel Villeneuve *Joseph Poulin* • Olivette Thibault *Cecile* • Claude Jutra *Fernand* ■ *Dir* Claude Jutra • *Scr* Clement Perron, Claude Jutra, from a story by Clement Perron

My Uncle the Alien ★★
Drama   1996 · US · Colour · 90mins

There aren't any American princesses to have *Roman Holiday*-style adventures, so it's up to the President's young daughter to slip her secret service minders and go walkabout in downtown Los Angeles. But, in trying to raise some money for a struggling shelter for the homeless, Kelly Sullivan (played by Hayley Foster) doesn't have to rely solely on her own devices, as she's joined on her mission by guardian alien Joshua Paddock. With lashings of yuletide sentimentality coating the already sugary asides on patriotism and the duties of the privileged, this corny fantasy comedy should amuse youngsters, but will leave grown-ups feeling slightly sickly.

Hayley Foster *Kelly Sullivan* • Joshua Paddock [Josh Paddock] *Zig* • Ace Ross *Ratt* • Wendi Wesbrook *Lois Sullivan* • Dink O'Neal *President Patrick J Sullivan* ■ *Dir* Henry Charr [Henri Charr] • *Scr* Robert Newcastle, from a story by Henry Charr [Henri Charr], Jess Mancilla

My Very Best Friend ★★ PG
Drama   1996 · US · Colour · 88mins

Jaclyn Smith leaves *Charlie's Angels* behind to star as a murderous psychopath in this muddled TV movie. Afer her spouse's death, an ex-model goes to stay with her best friend. There the devious widow showers affection on her pal's husband and daughter, causing jealousy and mistrust. Perfunctory performances by Smith and Jill Eikenberry (*LA Law*) and indifferent direction from Joyce Chopra make this houseguest-from-hell tale every viewer's worst nightmare.

Jaclyn Smith *Dana Griffin* • Jill Eikenberry *Barbara Wilkins* • Tom Mason *Ted Marshall* • Mary Kay Place *Molly Butler* ■ *Dir* Joyce Chopra • *Scr* Lindsay Harrison

My Way Home ★★★★15
Biographical drama 1978 · UK · BW · 68mins

Having endured endless poverty and rejection, Stephen Archibald emerges from the dark tunnel of his childhood in the concluding part of Bill Douglas's magnificent film autobiography. After all the pain of family life, it is, unsurprisingly, a stranger whom Archibald meets on National Service in Egypt who transforms the boy's life. It is no accident either that one of the books that sustains his ambition to become an artist is by the Russian author Gorky, as the series has clearly been influenced by Mark Donskoy's classic ''Gorky Trilogy'' of the thirties. Taken together, Douglas's trilogy is one of the finest achievements in British cinema history. ▢

Stephen Archibald *Jamie* • Paul Kermack *Jamie's father* • Jessie Combe *Father's wife* • William Carrol *Archie* • Morag McNee *Father's girlfriend* • Lennox Milne *Grandmother* ■ *Dir/Scr* Bill Douglas

My Wild Irish Rose ★★ U
Biographical musical
1947 · US · Colour · 100mins

The subject of this rather feeble biopic is Chauncey Olcott, an Irish-American tenor who co-wrote the title song,

U = SUITABLE FOR ALL   Uc = SUITABLE FOR ALL, ESPECIALLY FOR YOUNG CHILDREN (VIDEO ONLY)   PG = PARENTAL GUIDANCE

Mother Machree and *When Irish Eyes Are Smiling*. The songs are well sung by charming Dennis Morgan, who plays the composer with a wobbly Irish brogue. If the film is to be believed (and it isn't), Olcott was enamoured with glamorous singer Lillian Russell (Andrea King) before settling down with his wife. The latter is portrayed by beautiful redhead Arlene Dahl.

Dennis Morgan *Chauncey Olcott/Jack Chancellor* • Arlene Dahl *Rose Donovan* • Andrea King *Lillian Russell* • Alan Hale *John Donovan* • George Tobias *Nick Popolis* • George O'Brien *William "Duke" Muldoon* • Sara Allgood *Mrs Brennan* ■ *Dir* David Butler • *Scr* Peter Milne, Edwin Gilbert, Sidney Fields, from the story *Song in His Heart* by Rita Olcott

Myra Breckinridge ★★★ 18

Comedy   1970 · US · Colour · 89mins

Time has tempered the scandalised revulsion that initially greeted director Michael Sarne's ultra-melodramatic adaptation of Gore Vidal's transsexual satire. Clouded by the controversy, contemporary critics failed to see it as a rather sly essay on gender, all-American movie-star stereotypes and vintage Hollywood nostalgia. Despite Mae West's barnstorming comeback after a 27-year absence from the big screen to play a triple-entendre "talent agent", the movie belongs to Raquel Welch in her most under-rated role. Contains swearing and nudity. ▭

Mae West *Leticia* • John Huston *Buck Loner* • Raquel Welch *Myra Breckinridge* • Rex Reed *Young man* • Farrah Fawcett *Mary Ann* • Roger C Carmel *Dr Montag* • Jim Backus *Doctor* • John Carradine *Surgeon* • Andy Devine *Coyote Bill* • Tom Selleck *Stud* ■ *Dir* Michael Sarne • *Scr* Michael Sarne, David Giler, from the novel by Gore Vidal

The Mysteries of Paris ★★★ U

Period adventure   1962 · Fr · Colour · 95mins

This lavish production was adapted from Eugene Sue's celebrated story of kidnap and murder, set during the reign of Louis Philippe. The novel's sociopolitical themes have been excised to leave a lively adventure in which master of disguise Rodolphe sweeps through the Paris underworld avenging evil and rewarding good. Packed with reformed crooks, vile urchins, mischievous artists and gullible do-gooders, André Hunebelle's film blends thrills and laughs to good effect, while the statuesque Jean Marais is suitably mysterious amid the splendid period trappings. French dialogue dubbed into English.

Jean Marais *Rodolphe De Sambreuil* • Dany Robin *Irene* • Raymond Pellegrin *Baron De Lansignac* • Jill Haworth *Marie* • Pierre Mondy *Le Chourineur* • Renée Gardes *"The Witch"* ■ *Dir* André Hunebelle • *Scr* Jean Halain, Pierre Foucaud, Diego Fabbri, from a novel by Eugene Sue

Mysterious Island ★★★ U

Science-fiction adventure
1961 · UK/US · Colour · 96mins

Based on Jules Verne's sequel to *20,000 Leagues under the Sea*, this enjoyable British production blends Sinbad-style giant monster thrills, pirates, volcanic eruptions and, of course, Captain Nemo (not James Mason this time, but Herbert Lom). As

ever, stop-frame animation maestro Ray Harryhausen's monstrous menagerie provides most of the film's highlights, as oversized bees and colossal crabs threaten the health of Michael Craig, Joan Greenwood and their companions. Although the rather colourless cast doesn't do much to raise excitement levels, Harryhausen's fine work and Bernard Herrman's atmospheric score make this fantasy island worth an excursion. ▭

Michael Craig *Captain Cyrus Harding* • Joan Greenwood *Lady Mary Fairchild* • Michael Callan *Herbert Brown* • Gary Merrill *Gideon Spilett* • Herbert Lom *Captain Nemo* • Beth Rogan *Elena* ■ *Dir* Cy Endfield • *Scr* John Prebble, Daniel Ullman, Crane Wilbur, from the novel *L'Ile Mysterieuse* by Jules Verne

The Mysterious Lady ★★

Silent romantic drama   1928 · US · BW

In her sixth Hollywood film, Greta Garbo stars as a Russian spy who has an affair with Austrian officer Conrad Nagel in order to steal some secret documents. But she falls in love with him for real, eventually betraying her masters. Competently directed by Fred Niblo to capitalise on the camera's love affair with Garbo, it's actually the most risible nonsense, only good for a giggle and an opportunity for her fans to gaze upon her beauty and savour her mysterious persona.

Greta Garbo *Tania* • Conrad Nagel *Karl von Heinersdorff* • Gustav von Seyffertitz *General Alexandroff* • Albert Pollet *Max* ■ *Dir* Fred Niblo • *Scr* Bess Meredyth, Marian Ainslee (titles), Ruth Cummings (titles), from the novel *Der Krieg im Dunkel* by Ludwig Wolff

Mysterious Mr Moto ★★★

Detective drama   1938 · US · BW · 62mins

Master of disguise and intrepid meddler in other people's business, Mr Moto sweeps from Scotland Yard to Devil's Island in pursuit of an international crime ring in one of the weaker entries in 20th Century-Fox's amiable B-movie series. The production has an all-expenses-spared feel about it and the plot is hardly out of the top drawer. Such is the pace of Norman Foster's direction, though, that you barely have time to notice. Apart from Leon Ames and Erik Rhodes, the supporting line-up is third-rate, but Peter Lorre more than atones.

Peter Lorre *Mr Moto* • Mary Maguire *Ann Richman* • Henry Wilcoxon *Anton Darvak* • Erik Rhodes *David Scott-Frensham* • Harold Huber *Ernst Litmar* • Leon Ames *Paul Brissac* ■ *Dir* Norman Foster • *Scr* Norman Foster, Philip MacDonald, from the character created by JP Marquand

Mystery, Alaska ★★★ 15

Sports drama   1999 · US · Colour · 118mins

Ice hockey forms the backbone of this likeable comedy. The remote town of Mystery makes the headlines thanks to its passion for the game, prompting a sports network to arrange a challenge between the locals and a major league New York team. There's laughs enough, but the tale loses its way under a welter of characters and subplots; it's no surprise to find that one of the writers is David E Kelley, creator of TV's *Ally McBeal*. Compensation comes courtesy of the

excellent cast, headed by Russell Crowe and featuring the likes of Burt Reynolds and Maury Chaykin in support. There's even a cameo from Mike Myers as a TV commentator.

Russell Crowe *John Biebe* • Hank Azaria *Charles Danner* • Mary McCormack *Donna Biebe* • Burt Reynolds *Judge Walter Burns* • Colm Meaney *Mayor Scott Pitcher* • Lolita Davidovich *Mary Jane Pitcher* • Maury Chaykin *Bailey Pruitt* • Mike Myers *Donnie Shulzhoffer* • Little Richard ■ *Dir* Jay Roach • *Scr* David E Kelley, Sean O'Byrne

Mystery Date ★★ 15

Comedy thriller   1991 · US · Colour · 93mins

What's the real reason behind Ethan Hawke's shady older brother organising a blind date for him with the sexy next door neighbour? Could it have something to do with the corpse in his car? A wildly uneven, but nonetheless fun black comedy with many surprising touches, not least how endearing Hawke proves to be in a thankless role. For optimum enjoyment, Jonathan Wacks's film should be viewed as a teenage *After Hours*. Contains some swearing and violence. ▭

Ethan Hawke *Tom McHugh* • Teri Polo *Geena Matthews* • Brian McNamara *Craig McHugh* • Fisher Stevens *Dwight* • BD Wong *James Lew* • Tony Rosato *Sharpie* ■ *Dir* Jonathan Wacks • *Scr* Terry Runte, Parker Bennett

Mystery in Mexico ★

Crime drama   1948 · US · Colour · 65mins

RKO made this B-feature as a cost-cutting experiment at the Churubusco Studios in Mexico City which it half-owned. Little money was saved and even with a talented director, Robert Wise, it was no spicier than the average B because of weak stars and a by-the-numbers script that has insurance investigator William Lundigan flying to Mexico City to find a missing colleague with the help of the man's sister, Jacqueline White.

William Lundigan *Steve Hastings* • Jacqueline White *Victoria Ames* • Ricardo Cortez *Norcross* • Tony Barrett *Carlos* • Jacqueline Dalya *Dolores* • Walter Reed *Glenn Ames* ■ *Dir* Robert Wise • *Scr* Lawrence Kimble, from a story by Muriel Roy Bolton

Mystery Men ★★★ PG

Comedy action adventure
1999 · US · Colour · 116mins

An eclectic cast adds a quality sheen to this mildly diverting superhero spoof, based on the Dark Horse comic. The gimmick is that these saviours of Champion City possess abilities that are of no use whatsoever – fork-throwing expertise, shovel-wielding skills, noxious bodily odours and so on. At a shade over two hours, Kinka Usher's film is much too long to sustain the script's slender humour quotient. However, with actors of the calibre of William H Macy, Greg Kinnear, Ben Stiller, Wes Studi and Geoffrey Rush, it's never short of quirky appeal. ▭ *DVD*

Hank Azaria *The Blue Raja* • Janeane Garofalo *The Bowler* • William H Macy *The Shoveler* • Kel Mitchell *Invisible Boy* • Paul Reubens *The Spleen* • Ben Stiller *Mr Furious* • Wes Studi *The Sphinx* • Greg Kinnear *Captain Amazing/Lance* ■ *Dir* Kinka Usher • *Scr* Neil Cuthbert, from the comic book by Bob Burden

The Mystery of Edwin Drood ★★★

Mystery   1935 · US · BW · 87mins

Faced with the unenviable prospect of concocting a credible finale to the tale Charles Dickens left unfinished at his death, John L Balderston and his fellow screenwriters wisely place the emphasis on character in this atmospheric adaptation of the novelist's most sinister opus. The exceptional cast thrives under Stuart Walker's generous direction, with Claude Rains responding particularly well as John Jasper, the opium-addled chorister whose love for Heather Angel spells disaster for her fiancé, David Manners. Albert S D'Agostino's stylised Gothic sets add to the overall sense of unease, but the wildly melodramatic ending undermines an otherwise effective production.

Claude Rains *John Jasper* • Douglass Montgomery *Neville Landless* • Heather Angel *Rosa Bud* • David Manners *Edwin Drood* • Valerie Hobson *Helena Landless* • Francis L Sullivan *Mr Crisparkle* • Walter Kingsford *Hiram Grewigious* • EE Clive *Thomas Sapsea* ■ *Dir* Stuart Walker • *Scr* John L Balderston, Gladys Unger, Leopold Atlas, Bradley King, from the novel by Charles Dickens

The Mystery of Edwin Drood ★ 15

Mystery   1993 · UK · Colour · 97mins

Filming Charles Dickens's unfinished novel presents two distinct, but equally difficult challenges: to capture the style of what is a decidedly atypical tome, and to devise a feasible finale. Sadly, despite having the original Rochester settings at his disposal, Timothy Forder fails to come close on either count, shooting the opening section with stuffy reverence with a stubbornly static camera before launching into a hand-held Hammer pastiche that lacks both imagination and credibility. With his fellow cast members seemingly unable to rouse themselves from their lethargy, Robert Powell's sinister performance takes on an unfortunate pantomimic quality. ▭

Robert Powell *John Jasper* • Nanette Newman *Mrs Crisparkle* • Gemma Craven *Miss Twinkleton* • Rosemary Leach *Mrs Tope* • Finty Williams *Rosa* • Glyn Houston *Grewgious* • Ronald Fraser *Dean* ■ *Dir* Timothy Forder • *Scr* Timothy Forder, from the novel by Charles Dickens

Mystery of the Wax Museum ★★★★ PG

Horror   1933 · US · Colour · 74mins

A golden era fright classic, with Lionel Atwill as the mad sculptor re-populating his burnt-down museum with wax-covered murder victims. Fay Wray supplies the screams (as she did so memorably in *King Kong* in the same year), plus the magic moment where she cracks Atwill's false face to reveal the scars beneath, and Glenda Farrell shines as a wise-cracking reporter. The inspiration for the later *House of Wax*, this *Grand Guignol* outing boasts fabulous sets, zippy pacing, surprising frankness and marvellously evocative early two-strip Technicolor. ▭

Lionel Atwill *Ivan Igor* • Fay Wray *Charlotte Duncan* • Glenda Farrell *Florence Dempsey* • Frank McHugh *Jim* • Gavin Gordon *Harold*

Winton • Edwin Maxwell *Joe Worth* ■ *Dir* Michael Curtiz • *Scr* Don Mullally, Carl Erickson, from a play by Charles S Belden • *Art Director* Anton F Grot [Anton Grot]

Mystery Science Theater 3000: The Movie ★★★ PG

Science-fiction comedy
1996 · US · Colour · 70mins

In this big-screen version of the long-running American cable TV series, we watch Michael J Nelson and his two robot friends (voiced by Trace Beaulieu and Kevin Murphy) watch the fifties sci-fi movie *This Island Earth*. Mike and the droids are adept at poking fun at the bad movies they're forced to watch by evil scientist Dr Forrester (also played by Beaulieu), though *This Island Earth* is cut above the vast majority of films featured on the original TV show. ▭

Trace Beaulieu *Dr Clayton Forrester/Crow T Robot* • Michael J Nelson *Mike Nelson* • Jim Mallon *Gypsy* • Kevin Murphy *Tom Servo* • John Brady *Benkitnorf* ■ *Dir* Jim Mallon • *Scr* Michael J Nelson, Trace Beaulieu, Jim Mallon, Kevin Wagner Murphy [Kevin Murphy], Mary Jo Pehl, Paul Chaplin, Bridget Jones, from the TV series by Joel Hodgson

Mystery Street ★★★

Crime thriller   1950 · US · Colour · 92mins

MGM's B-movies were quite unlike any other studio's: they had a professional, glossy look to them and often featured players who would be quite at home in costlier fare. This is a rattlingly good example: a tight little caper tale expertly directed by John Sturges, who over the next decade-and-a-half would be producing such heavyweight movies as *Gunfight at the OK Corral*, *The Magnificent Seven* and *The Great Escape*. Sturges does well by the Boston setting, and he's helped by an expert cast headed by the versatile Ricardo Montalban.

Ricardo Montalban *Lieutenant Peter Moralas* • Sally Forrest *Grace Shanway* • Bruce Bennett *Dr McAdoo* • Elsa Lanchester *Mrs Smerrling* • Marshall Thompson *Henry Shanway* • Jan Sterling *Vivian Heldon* ■ *Dir* John Sturges • *Scr* Sydney Boehm, Richard Brooks, from a story by Leonard Spiegelgass

Mystery Submarine ★ U

Spy drama   1950 · US · BW · 78mins

Of interest only to close observers of the career of its director, Douglas Sirk, this minor work was his first as a contract director at Universal, long before the delirious delights of *Written on the Wind* and others. The extravagant plot has Robert Douglas's U-boat captain, who has survived the Second World War in South America along with his vessel, kidnapping a German atomic scientist and offering him for sale to a foreign power. Fortunately, Macdonald Carey's US agent has infiltrated the crew.

Macdonald Carey *Dr Brett Young* • Marta Toren *Madeline Brenner* • Robert Douglas *Comdr Eric Von Molter* • Carl Esmond *Lt Heldman* • Ludwig Donath *Dr Adolph Guernitz* ■ *Dir* Douglas Sirk • *Scr* George W George, George F Slavin, from a story by George W George, George F Slavin, Ralph Dietrich

Mystery Train ★★★★ 15

Comedy drama
1989 · US/Jap · Colour · 105mins

Demonstrating his customary, quirky genius for character, director Jim Jarmusch effortlessly weaves together three stories set in a moth-eaten Memphis hotel, which is little more than a seedy shrine to Elvis Presley, whose spirit pervades the entire picture. The scenes involving Japanese rock pilgrims Masatoshi Nagase and Youki Kudoh are a delight, while the postmortem into Joe Strummer and Steve Buscemi's bungled robbery is tantamount to a Tarantino prototype. Capping the lot are the exchanges between night clerk Screamin' Jay Hawkins and bellboy Cinque Lee. In English and Japanese with subtitles. Contains violence, swearing, nudity and drug abuse. ▭

Masatoshi Nagase *Jun* • Youki Kudoh *Mitzuko* • Screamin' Jay Hawkins *Night clerk* • Cinque Lee *Bellboy* • Nicoletta Braschi *Luisa* • Elizabeth Bracco *Dee Dee* • Joe Strummer *Johnny* • Steve Buscemi *Charlie* • Tom Waits *Voice of radio DJ* ■ *Dir/Scr* Jim Jarmusch

Mystic Pizza ★★★★ 15

Romantic comedy
1988 · US · Colour · 103mins

One of "pretty woman" Julia Roberts's first major roles and still one of her best, this romantic comedy has Julia, pal Lili Taylor and sister Annabeth Gish getting into trouble with love while working at a pizza parlour in their home town of Mystic, Connecticut. Donald Petrie serves up a splendid coming-of-age tale, successfully interlacing the story of the girls' problems of the heart with some delightfully comic moments and astute observations about romance. Contains swearing and sex scenes. ▭

Julia Roberts *Daisy Araujo* • Annabeth Gish *Kat Araujo* • Lili Taylor *Jojo Barboza* • Vincent Phillip D'Onofrio [Vincent D'Onofrio] *Bill Montijo* • William R Moses *Tim Travers* • Adam Storke *Charles Gordon Winsor* • Conchata Ferrell *Leona Valsouano* ■ *Dir* Donald Petrie • *Scr* Amy Jones [Amy Holden Jones], Perry Howze, Randy Howze, Alfred Uhry, from a story by Amy Jones [Amy Holden Jones]

The Myth of Fingerprints ★★★★ 15

Drama   1996 · US · Colour · 86mins

Julianne Moore and *ER*'s Noah Wyle are two of four grown-up siblings who return to their New England home for the traditional Thanksgiving dinner. Cue the airing of family grudges, secrets and emotions in this sly and subdued drama from writer/director Bart Freundlich. Blythe Danner and Roy Scheider stand out as the overwrought parents, but what is most attractive about the film is that it offers no jaw-dropping revelations or happily-ever-after resolutions. Instead it allows us to draw our own conclusions. Contains swearing and sex scenes. ▭

Roy Scheider *Hal* • Julianne Moore *Mia* • Blythe Danner *Lena* • Noah Wyle *Warren* • Hope Davis *Margaret* • James LeGros *Cezanne* • Brian Kerwin *Elliot* • Laurel Holloman *Leigh* ■ *Dir/Scr* Bart Freundlich

The Myth of the Male Orgasm ★★

Comedy   1993 · Can · Colour · 90mins

Now there's a title guaranteed to send a fair proportion of the population scouting the other channels for viewing alternatives. Director John Hamilton made his debut with this satire that was barely seen outside his native Canada. Bruce Dinsmore stars as a college professor who is so bewildered by his failure to attract the opposite sex that he agrees to be a guinea pig for a study of male attitudes being conducted by a group of feminist psychologists. There are one or two amusing moments, but that's about it. Contains swearing.

Bruce Dinsmore *Jimmy Ruvinsky* • Miranda de Pencier *Jane Doe* • Mark Camacho *Tim* • Burke Lawrence *Sean* • Ruth Marshall *Mimi* • Macha Grenon *Paula* ■ *Dir* John Hamilton • *Scr* John Hamilton, David Reckziegel

Nada ★★★★ 18

Political crime drama
1974 · Fr/It · Colour · 106mins

Claude Chabrol here adopts the style of the exciting political thrillers of Costa-Gavras, though he adds his special brand of cynicism and black humour and refuses to take sides. Nada, the Spanish for "nothing", is the name of a group of anarchists who decide to kidnap the American ambassador in Paris during his weekly visit to a high-class bordello. Conflicts grow within the group and among the police, who are viewed as the flip side of the same coin. This rather overlong film came as a surprise after Chabrol's series of domestic murder stories featuring his wife, Stéphane Audran. In French with English subtitles. ▭

Fabio Testi *Buenaventura Diaz* • Michel Duchaussoy *Marcel Treufais* • Maurice Garrel *André Epaulard* • Michel Aumont *Goémond* • Lou Castel *D'Arey* ■ *Dir* Claude Chabrol • *Scr* Claude Chabrol, Jean-Patrick Manchette, from a novel by Jean-Patrick Manchette

Nadine ★★ PG

Comedy thriller   1987 · US · Colour · 79mins

Director Robert Benton scores something of a misfire with this well-intentioned but uneven comedy. The story of a manicurist who witnesses a murder and teams up with her soon-to-be ex-husband to solve the crime has its moments. But the problems lie mainly with Kim Basinger and Jeff Bridges, neither of whom is adept enough to make this broad comedy work. An interesting and mildly amusing diversion nonetheless. Contains violence and swearing. ▭

Jeff Bridges *Vernon Hightower* • Kim Basinger *Nadine Hightower* • Rip Torn *Buford Pope* • Gwen Verdon *Vera* • Glenne Headly *Renee* • Jerry Stiller *Raymond Escobar* • Jay Patterson *Dwight Estes* ■ *Dir/Scr* Robert Benton

Nadja ★★★★ 15

Horror   1995 · US · BW · 88mins

David Lynch (who pops up in a cameo as a mortuary attendant) executive-produced this erotic vampire thriller, stylishly shot in black and white. Elina Lowensohn is the Nadja of the title, an enthusiastic creature of the night who just happens to be the daughter of Dracula. She prowls the clubs of New York for her prey, but vampire-hunter Van Helsing (Peter Fonda) is on her trail. It's a bizarre update of the vampire legend by independent film-maker Michael Almereyda, a deft hand at powerful visual images. ▭

Elina Lowensohn *Nadja* • Suzy Amis *Cassandra* • Peter Fonda *Dracula/Dr Van*

Helsing • Martin Donovan *Jim* • Galaxy Craze *Lucy* • Karl Geary *Renfield* • Jared Harris *Edgar* ■ *Dir/Scr* Michael Almereyda

Nails ★★ 15

Crime thriller   1992 · US · Colour · 96mins

A hard-nosed, maverick cop plays by his own rules as he seeks to avenge the death of his beloved partner at the hands of drug-smuggling Cuban hitmen. Veteran actor Dennis Hopper gives a characteristically intense performance as a man treading the edge between insanity and legality. However, this tale of relentless cop versus drug smugglers squanders good support from Anne Archer and sharp production values with a trite and painfully obvious story. ☐

Dennis Hopper *Harry "Nails" Niles* • Anne Archer *Mary Niles* • Tomas Milian *Pedro Herrera* • Keith David *Noah Owens* ■ *Dir* John Flynn • *Scr* Larry Ferguson

Nairobi Affair ★★

Adventure drama   1984 · US · Colour · 95mins

Pretty African locations do nothing to enhance this turgid father-son melodrama. Charlton Heston plays a big game hunter turned tour guide whose relationship with stepson John Savage is sorely tested when the latter learns his ex-girlfriend is romantically involved with Chuck. Despite the efforts of veteran director Marvin J Chomsky, this hackneyed tale of rivalry and forbidden love never strays from the well-worn path of predictability.

Charlton Heston *Lee Cahill* • John Savage *Rick Cahill* • Maud Adams *Anne Malone* • John Rhys-Davies *Simon* • Connie Booth *Mrs Gardner* • Shane Rimmer *Mr Gardner* ■ *Dir* Marvin J Chomsky • *Scr* David Epstein

Naked ★★★★ 18

Drama   1993 · UK · Colour · 125mins

Mike Leigh prowls new working class territory with this grim tale about a Mancunian misfit who turns up at his ex-girlfriend's London flat and proceeds to tell the naked truth regarding the city's uncaring society by lashing out unmercifully at everyone he meets. David Thewlis is outstanding as a deeply nasty nineties version of Alfie, and Leigh's bravura mix of comedy, tragedy, violence and warmth marks this uncompromising exposé as British film-making at its finest. Contains swearing, drug abuse and nudity. ☐

David Thewlis *Johnny* • Lesley Sharp *Louise* • Katrin Cartlidge *Sophie* • Greg Cruttwell *Jeremy* • Claire Skinner *Sandra* • Peter Wight *Brian* • Ewen Bremner *Archie* • Susan Vidler *Maggie* ■ *Dir/Scr* Mike Leigh

Naked Alibi ★★

Crime drama   1954 · US · BW · 85mins

After he is dismissed for harrassing a suburban baker (Gene Barry) whom he's convinced is a violent killer, a senior cop Sterling Hayden continues to hunt his quarry. When he finds himself in trouble in a Mexican bordertown, he is helped by Barry's girlfriend Gloria Grahame. Directed by Jerry Hopper, this mix of detective thriller, gangster movie and *film noir* starts promisingly enough but degenerates about a third of the way through as a result of a derivative

screenplay and some unconvincing characterisation.

Sterling Hayden *Joseph Conroy* • Gloria Grahame *Marianna* • Gene Barry *Al Willis* • Marcia Henderson *Helen Willis* • Casey Adams [Max Showalter] *Lieutenant Parks* • Billy Chapin *Petey* • Chuck Connors *Captain Owen Kincaide* ■ *Dir* Jerry Hopper • *Scr* Lawrence Roman, from the story *Cry Copper* by J Robert Breen, Gladys Atwater

The Naked and the Dead ★★★ PG

Second World War drama
1958 · US · Colour · 130mins

Since it was clearly impossible to film the vigorous intensity, not to mention the language, of Norman Mailer's superb anti-war first novel, director Raoul Walsh opted for a virtual remake of his 1955 Warners hit *Battle Cry*, although this time the characters are not realistic enough. *Battle Cry* veteran Aldo Ray is Mailer's sadistic Sergeant Croft, handling most of the diatribes and virtually holding the long movie together by himself. The battle scenes are fine, and shot (by cameraman Joseph LaShelle) through a green night filter, so don't fiddle with the colour controls on your TV set. ☐

Aldo Ray *Croft* • Cliff Robertson *Hearn* • Raymond Massey *General Cummings* • Lili St Cyr *Lily* • Barbara Nichols *Mildred* • William Campbell *Brown* • Richard Jaeckel *Gallagher* • James Best *Ridges* • Joey Bishop *Roth* ■ *Dir* Raoul Walsh • *Scr* Denis Sanders, Terry Sanders, from the novel by Norman Mailer

The Naked City ★★★★

Crime drama   1948 · US · BW · 95mins

Hugely influential, thanks to its innovative documentary-style and character-driven treatment, of an otherwise conventional cop drama (murdered blonde in bathtub, homicide squad gets moving). The movie is hard-hitting, gripping and a hymn to the excitement of New York City, where it was shot entirely on location. Narrated by its producer, former crime reporter Mark Hellinger, it stars Barry Fitzgerald as the police lieutenant heading the murder investigation. There were Oscars for cinematography and editing, and the voice-over proclaiming "there are eight million stories in the naked city" passed into popular culture, thanks to the long-running TV series.

Barry Fitzgerald *Lt Dan Muldoon* • Howard Duff *Frank Niles* • Dorothy Hart *Ruth Morrison* • Don Taylor *Jimmy Halloran* • Ted De Corsia *Garzah* • House Jameson *Dr Stoneman* • Mark Hellinger *Narrator* ■ *Dir* Jules Dassin • *Scr* Albert Maltz, Malvin Wald, from a story by Malvin Wald • *Music* Miklos Rozsa, Frank Skinner • *Cinematographer* William H Daniels [William Daniels] • *Editor* Paul Weatherwax

Naked City: a Killer Christmas ★★★ 15

Crime drama   1998 · US · Colour · 92mins

In this slick update of the 1948 classic, NYPD detectives hunt for a Yuletide serial killer who manipulates both law enforcement and news media to throw them off the scent. When a ratings-obsessed TV anchorwoman broadcasts exclusive information about the killer, the cops themselves become the killer's targets. Fine performances by Scott Glenn and

Courtney B Vance, a solid script and taut direction by Peter Bogdanovich skilfully convey the dedication of New York's finest. Contains some violence and swearing. ☐

Scott Glenn *Sergeant Dan Muldoon* • Courtney B Vance *Officer Jimmy Halloran* • Laura Leighton *Gerry Millar* • Barbara Williams *Eva* • Nigel Bennett *Soloff* • Lisa Vidal *Lori Halloran* ■ *Dir* Peter Bogdanovich • *Scr* Jeff Freilich, Christopher Trumbo, from characters created by Albert Maltz, Malvin Wald

The Naked Country ★★★ 18

Thriller   1985 · Ausl · Colour · 87mins

Set in the Australian outback, this is a gripping outdoors thriller from Tim Burstall, one of the key directors of the seventies "new wave". Based on the novel by Morris West, it's about a ranch owner who gets caught up in a bitter struggle with an unruly tribe of Aborigines. Burstall (*Alvin Purple*, *Kangaroo*) conjures up a taut, well-paced drama that builds up nicely to a tense chase climax. ☐

John Stanton *Lance Dillon* • Rebecca Gilling *Mary Dillon* • Ivar Kants *Sergeant Neil Adams* • Tommy Lewis *Mundaru* • Simon Chilvers *Inspector Poole* • John Jarratt *Mick Conrad* ■ *Dir* Tim Burstall • *Scr* Ross Dimsey, Tim Burstall, from the novel by Morris West

The Naked Dawn ★★★

Crime drama   1955 · US · Colour · 82mins

Arthur Kennedy plays the likeable Mexican bandit whose booty tempts the impoverished farmer he befriends, and whose way of life appeals to the farmer's dissatisfied young wife. This character study was made on a shoestring in Mexico by the low-budget maestro Edgar G Ulmer, who shapes the material into a moving study of salvation. It could have been an intense, brooding piece, but it's shot in colour and displays a generosity of spirit that is ultimately moving.

Arthur Kennedy *Santiago* • Betta St John *Maria* • Eugene Iglesias *Manuel* • Charlita *Tita* • Roy Engel *Guntz* ■ *Dir* Edgar G Ulmer • *Scr* Nina Schneider, Herman Schneider (fronts for Julian Zimet)

The Naked Earth ★★

Adventure   1958 · UK · BW · 96mins

The husky-voiced French singer Juliette Greco, protégée of studio boss Darryl F Zanuck, livens up this slow-paced, British-made saga with her volatile personality and offbeat looks. She plays the former whore who teams up with Richard Todd's penniless Irishman and helps him grow tobacco in Uganda in 1895. When they fail to harvest the crop, he takes up shooting crocodiles for their skins, but they're so obviously phoney there's no need to shed any tears. Milton Holmes's intelligent script deserved a more interesting lead and a less plodding director.

Richard Todd *Danny* • Juliette Greco *Maria* • John Kitzmiller *David* • Finlay Currie *Father Verity* • Laurence Naismith *Skin trader* ■ *Dir* Vincent Sherman • *Scr* Milton Holmes, Harold Buchman (uncredited)

The Naked Edge ★★

Mystery thriller   1961 · UK · BW · 103mins

This bleak and undistinguished thriller, about an American businessman

based in London whose wife (Deborah Kerr) comes to suspect him of murder, marked a most unfitting end to Gary Cooper's illustrious career. The actor died shortly after giving one last wooden performance and floundering among the plot's multiple red herrings. Director Michael Anderson's excellent cast includes Eric Portman, Diane Cilento and Peter Cushing, but neither they nor an accomplished Kerr can hide the deficiencies.

Gary Cooper *George Radcliffe* • Deborah Kerr *Martha Radcliffe* • Eric Portman *Jeremy Clay* • Diane Cilento *Mrs Heath* • Hermione Gingold *Lilly Harris* • Peter Cushing *Mr Wrack* • Michael Wilding *Morris Brooke* • Ray McAnally *Donald Heath* ■ *Dir* Michael Anderson • *Scr* Joseph Stefano, from the novel *First Train to Babylon* by Max Ehrlich

The Naked Face ★★ 18

Crime thriller   1984 · US · Colour · 100mins

Psychiatrist Roger Moore is the prime suspect when one of his patients is murdered in director Bryan Forbes's tepid adaptation of an early Sidney Sheldon bestseller. When it becomes clear he's the next target, he takes the law into his own hands to unmask the killer, despite the suspicions of cops Rod Steiger and Elliott Gould. Reasonably well-acted, the complex plot has too many red herrings to be completely satisfying. Contains swearing, violence and brief nudity. ☐

Roger Moore *Dr Judd Stevens* • Rod Steiger *Lieutenant McGreavy* • Elliott Gould *Angeli* • Art Carney *Morgens* • Anne Archer *Ann Blake* • David Hedison *Dr Hadley* • Deanna Dunagan *Mrs Hadley* ■ *Dir* Bryan Forbes • *Scr* Bryan Forbes, from the novel by Sidney Sheldon

Naked Fury ★ U

Crime drama   1959 · UK · BW · 64mins

As with many other crime capers of the late fifties, this gives the impression of being a routine TV episode that has had a bit of money thrown at it. Given the utterly misleading title of *The Pleasure Lovers* in the USA, this is a sordid little tale about a gang of safe-crackers who are forced to kill a night watchman and kidnap his daughter to make good their escape. Journeyman director Charles Saunders and his willing cast are left high and dry by Brock Williams's desperate script.

Kenneth Cope *Johnny* • Reed De Rouen *Eddy* • Leigh Madison *Carol* • Arthur Lovegrove *Syd* • Thomas Eytle *Steve* • Alexander Field *Vic* ■ *Dir* Charles Saunders • *Scr* Brock Williams, from a story by Guido Coen

The Naked Gun ★★★★★ 15

Comedy   1988 · US · Colour · 81mins

The team behind *Airplane!* first turned their wicked talents on to the police force with the short-lived cult TV series *Police Squad!*, but it took this feature-length version to make Leslie Nielsen's inspired Frank Drebin a worldwide star. He remains wonderfully stone-faced as he proceeds to wreak havoc in Los Angeles while investigating the shooting of a colleague around the time of a visit by the Queen. The supporting players – George Kennedy as his captain, Priscilla Presley as the equally clumsy love interest and OJ Simpson as the wounded colleague – are delightfully

deadpan, and the juvenile gags never stop flowing. Contains swearing. ▣

Leslie Nielsen *Lieutenant Frank Drebin* • Priscilla Presley *Jane Spencer* • Ricardo Montalban *Vincent Ludwig* • George Kennedy *Captain Ed Hocken* • OJ Simpson *Nordberg* • Nancy Marchand *Mayor* ■ *Dir* David Zucker • *Scr* Jerry Zucker, Jim Abrahams, David Zucker, Pat Proft, from the TV series *Police Squad!* by David Zucker, Jerry Zucker, Jim Abrahams

The Naked Gun 2 ½: the Smell of Fear ★★★★15

Comedy   1991 · US · Colour · 81mins

Billed on release as the latest film from the brother of the man who directed *Ghost* (and complete with a wonderful send-up of the pottery scene from that film), this second instalment from the files of *Police Squad* is a deliriously funny delight. Leslie Nielsen, as the steadfastly stupid Frank Drebin, starts off by wrecking a White House reception, then proceeds to blunder his way through an investigation into a group of corrupt businessmen plotting to stave off radical new changes to the energy industry. Many of the original cast (George Kennedy, Priscilla Presley and the infamous OJ Simpson) return for this sequel, and there's also strong support from villain Robert Goulet, Lloyd Bochner and wonderful British actor Richard Griffiths. It's not quite up to the standard set by the first film, but Nielsen's inspired playing still makes this an unmissable treat. Contains swearing. ▣

Leslie Nielsen *Lieutenant Frank Drebin* • Priscilla Presley *Jane Spencer* • George Kennedy *Ed Hocken* • Robert Goulet *Quentin Hapsburg* • Richard Griffiths *Dr Meinheimer/Earl Hacker* • OJ Simpson *Nordberg* • Anthony James *Hector Savage* • Lloyd Bochner *Baggett* • Tim O'Connor *Fenzwick* ■ *Dir* David Zucker • *Scr* David Zucker, Pat Proft, from the TV series *Police Squad!* by David Zucker, Jerry Zucker, Jim Abrahams

Naked Gun 33⅓: the Final Insult ★★★★12

Comedy   1994 · US · Colour · 79mins

The first two *Naked Guns* were comedy classics, but this is only very, very funny. Leslie Nielsen and the team return for another endearingly silly, gag-filled spoof in which house-husband Frank Drebin comes out of retirement to catch a lethal bomber. Although it trades a little too casually on the jokes and slapstick of the first two, Nielsen delivers another wonderfully deadpan performance, and there are a host of neat cameos (Pia Zadora, Fred Ward). ▣

Leslie Nielsen *Lieutenant Frank Drebin* • Priscilla Presley *Jane Spencer* • George Kennedy *Ed Hocken* • OJ Simpson *Nordberg* • Fred Ward *Rocco* • Kathleen Freeman *Muriel* • Anna Nicole Smith *Tanya* • Ellen Greene *Louise* ■ *Dir* Peter Segal • *Scr* David Zucker, Pat Proft, Robert LoCash, from the TV series *Police Squad!* by David Zucker, Jerry Zucker, Jim Abrahams

Naked in New York ★★★15

Romantic comedy
1994 · US · Colour · 87mins

An autobiographical first feature by Daniel Algrant, who got Martin Scorsese to executive produce – in other words, help raise the money and

encourage some big names to guest star. The story is slight enough: Eric Stoltz grows up without a dad, decides to be a playwright and becomes a magnet to women. But it's the guest appearances that make the most impact – Tony Curtis, Timothy Dalton and Kathleen Turner, camping it up as a Broadway star. ▣

Eric Stoltz *Jake Briggs* • Mary-Louise Parker *Joanne White* • Ralph Macchio *Chris* • Jill Clayburgh *Shirley Briggs* • Tony Curtis *Carl Fisher* • Timothy Dalton *Elliot Price* • Kathleen Turner *Dana Coles* • Whoopi Goldberg *Tragedy Mask* • Quentin Crisp ■ *Dir* Dan Algrant • *Scr* Dan Algrant [Daniel Algrant], John Warren

The Naked Jungle ★★★★

Adventure drama 1953 · US · Colour · 93mins

Charlton Heston is the South American plantation owner battling both his red-haired wife (Eleanor Parker) and a plague of red ants, which provides a spectacular climax to this riveting tale directed by Byron Haskin (*The War of the Worlds*). Both an adventure and a thought-provoking drama, the movie is beautifully photographed by Ernest Laszlo and remains one of Heston's most interesting early films.

Eleanor Parker *Joanna Leiningen* • Charlton Heston *Christopher Leiningen* • William Conrad *Commissioner* • Romo Vincent *Boat captain* • Douglas Fowley *Medicine man* • John Dierkes *Gruber* • Leonard Strong *Kutina* ■ *Dir* Byron Haskin • *Scr* Philip Yordan, Ranald MacDougall, from the story *Leiningen Versus the Ants* by Carl Stephenson

The Naked Kiss ★★★★18

Melodrama   1964 · US · BW · 86mins

A typically bleak and brutal tale from maverick American independent Sam Fuller, who this time turns his cynical eye to the corrupt values lurking beneath small-town life. Constance Towers gives a dignified performance, especially considering the circumstances, as a former prostitute who attempts to build a new life in a new town, but finds her past coming back to haunt her when she tries to establish a relationship with the local leading citizen. The storyline is pure melodrama, but the harsh black-and-white photography and the startling images make this a cult classic.

Constance Towers *Kelly* • Anthony Eisley *Griff* • Michael Dante *Grant* • Virginia Grey *Candy* • Patsy Kelly *Mac* • Betty Bronson *Miss Josephine* • Marie Devereux *Buff* • Karen Conrad *Dusty* ■ *Dir/Scr* Samuel Fuller • *Cinematographer* Stanley Cortez

Naked Lie ★★18

Drama   1989 · US · Colour · 93mins

Former *Dallas* soap queen Victoria Principal dons a power suit for her role as a successful district attorney who gets caught up in political intrigue and murder in this so-so drama. James Farentino co-stars as her lover – a judge who is not all he seems. Of course it's pretty predictable stuff, but both leads are pleasing to watch. Contains violence, swearing and sex scenes. ▣

Victoria Principal *Joanne Dawson* • James Farentino *Jonathan Morris* • Glenn Withrow *Andy Fencik* • William Lucking *Bob Webster* ■ *Dir* Richard Colla [Richard A Colla] • *Scr*

Timothy Wurtz, Glenn M Benest, John Robert Bensink, from a story by Timothy Wurtz, Glenn M Benest

Naked Lies ★★18

Thriller   1997 · US · Colour · 89mins

Formulaic, straight-to-video fare, spiced up with bit of sex and nudity. Shannon Tweed plays a tough FBI agent who is suspended from duty when she accidentally kills a child during a drugs bust. With her career at a crossroads, she finds herself falling for an international counterfeiter. Steven Bauer appears briefly as Tweed's supervisor and must surely be wondering where it all went wrong. Contains violence, swearing, sex scenes and nudity. ▣

Shannon Tweed *Cara Landry* • Fernando Allende *Damian Medina* • Steven Bauer *Kevin Dowd* • Hugo Stiglitz *Santiago* ■ *Dir* Ralph Portillo • *Scr* D Alvelo

Naked Lunch ★★★18

Fantasy drama
1991 · UK/Can · Colour · 110mins

Only David Cronenberg could have filmed William S Burroughs's notorious cult novel as an intellectual paranoid acid trip through the creative writing process. Deftly exploring new shock corridors of outrageous disgust, Cronenberg underlines Burroughs's autobiographical concerns over abuses of power (metaphorically disguised as fantasy drug addiction and surreal sexual acts), crafting a uniquely slanted mind-blower with more than a hint of highbrow inaccessibility. Contains violence, swearing, sex scenes, drug abuse and nudity. ▣

Peter Weller *William Lee* • Judy Davis *Joan Frost/Joan Lee* • Ian Holm *Tom Frost* • Julian Sands *Yves Cloquet* • Roy Scheider *Dr Benway* • Monique Mercure *Fadela* • Nicholas Campbell *Hank* • Michael Zelniker *Martin* ■ *Dir* David Cronenberg • *Scr* David Cronenberg, from the novel by William S Burroughs

The Naked Maja ★★

Biography   1959 · US/It · Colour · 111mins

Despite the title, there's nothing particularly revelatory in this account of the life of the Spanish painter Goya (Anthony Franciosa), who grew from peasant stock to become a painter of royalty. The script revolves around Goya's scandalous nude portrait of a duchess (Ava Gardner), but director Henry Koster gives no more than a surface gloss to the proceedings. Movies about artists were all the rage at the time, but this one is a still life in more ways than one.

Ava Gardner *Duchess of Alba* • Anthony Franciosa *Francisco Goya* • Amedeo Nazzari *Manuel Godoy* • Gino Cervi *King Carlos IV* • Lea Padovani *Queen Maria Luisa* ■ *Dir* Henry Koster, Mario Russo • *Scr* Norman Corwin, Giorgio Prosperi, from a story by Oscar Saul, Talbot Jennings

The Naked Prey ★★★PG

Adventure   1966 · US · Colour · 91mins

Filmed entirely in South Africa, this offbeat adventure was directed by ex-matinée idol Cornel Wilde, who also stars as a 19th-century white hunter whose safari expedition is captured and tortured by tribesmen. Set free in

a skimpy loincloth that would make even Johnny Weissmuller blush, Wilde is then relentlessly hunted down like prey. Bolstered by a documentary-style realism, if dated in its African stereotypes, this remains a riveting tale of survival against the odds. Wilde gives a fine performance, despite being ill for much of the filming. ▣

Cornel Wilde *Man* • Gert Van Den Bergh *Second man* • Ken Gampu *Warrior leader* • Patrick Mynhardt *Safari overseer* ■ *Dir* Cornel Wilde • *Scr* Clint Johnston, Don Peters

The Naked Runner ★★PG

Spy drama   1967 · UK · Colour · 99mins

Was it official policy in the sixties to make every "serious" spy movie duller than dishwater in a motorway café? This Stanley Mann-scripted slice of Cold War shenanigans is blander than most, thanks to unappealing characters and a far-fetched narrative. Frank Sinatra stars as a wartime crack shot reluctantly reactivated for an assassination plot in East Germany; Edward Fox and Peter Vaughan represent British intelligence. Sidney J Furie's gimmicky direction is jarring on the eye, while Sinatra can do nothing with a monotonous role that merely requires him to be shunted around like a pawn on a chessboard. ▣

Frank Sinatra *Sam Laker* • Peter Vaughan *Martin Slattery* • Derren Nesbitt *Colonel Hartmann* • Nadia Gray *Karen Gisevius* • Toby Robins *Ruth* • Inger Stratton *Anna* • Cyril Luckham *Cabinet minister* • Edward Fox *Ritchie Jackson* ■ *Dir* Sidney J Furie • *Scr* Stanley Mann, from the novel by Francis Clifford

Naked Souls ★18

Erotic science-fiction thriller
1995 · US · Colour · 81mins

Pamela Anderson's main assets unsurprisingly play a prominent role in this daft erotic science-fiction thriller. The pneumatic former *Baywatch* babe portrays an artist – don't laugh – whose geeky scientist boyfriend (Brian Krause) gets into trouble when he starts playing around with the memories of dead serial killers and messing with sinister rival David Warner. As Anderson's art consists of pouring gloop over naked female models, the nudity is fairly evenly shared, which will no doubt please the lads. Contains violence, swearing, sex scenes and nudity. ▣

Pamela Anderson Lee [Pamela Anderson] *Britanny "Brit" Clark* • Brian Krause *Edward Adams* • David Warner *Everett Longstreet* • Dean Stockwell *Duncan Ellis* ■ *Dir* Lyndon Chubbuck • *Scr* Frank Dietz

The Naked Spur ★★★

Western   1953 · US · Colour · 91mins

James Stewart stars as a neurotic bounty hunter on the trail of Robert Ryan, hoping to make enough money to buy a ranch in California, but threatened by madness. The third of the great collaborations between Stewart and director Anthony Mann, this melodramatic western aspires to Greek or Shakespearean tragedy and, set in the truly Olympian Rocky Mountains of Colorado, the characters look suitably puny and pitiful, the playthings of the Gods. Janet Leigh,

U = SUITABLE FOR ALL   Uc = SUITABLE FOR ALL, ESPECIALLY FOR YOUNG CHILDREN (VIDEO ONLY)   PG = PARENTAL GUIDANCE

though, looks gorgeous, straight from the soda fountains of fifties America.

James Stewart *Howard Kemp* • Robert Ryan *Ben Vandergroat* • Janet Leigh *Lina Patch* • Ralph Meeker *Roy Anderson* • Millard Mitchell *Jesse Tate* ■ *Dir* Anthony Mann • *Scr* Sam Rolfe, Harold Jack Bloom

The Naked Street ★★
Crime drama   1955 · US · BW · 84mins

In this lurid melodrama, Anthony Quinn is the racketeer who, not unlike Paul Muni in *Scarface*, has an almost unhealthy fixation with his sister, played by Anne Bancroft. When she becomes pregnant by Farley Granger's two-bit hood, Quinn gets him off a murder rap and tries in vain to make him go straight. Writer/director Maxwell Shane draws effective performances from his three lead players but the contrived plot deprives the film of any tragic force.

Farley Granger *Nicky Bradna* • Anthony Quinn *Phil Regal* • Anne Bancroft *Rosalie Regalzyk* • Peter Graves (1) *Joe McFarland* • Else Neft *Mrs Regalzyk* • Jerry Paris *Latzi Franks* • Frank Sully *Nutsy* • John Dennis *Big Eddie* ■ *Dir* Maxwell Shane • *Scr* Maxwell Shane, from a story by Leo Katcher

Naked Tango ★★ 18
Erotic thriller   1990 · US · Colour · 88mins

An overheated and rather silly melodrama set in Argentina in the days when Rudolph Valentino was "tango-ing" a swooning female audience. Mathilda May is the young wife en route to South America who takes on a new identity and ends up being fought over by gangster Esai Morales and "dirty dancer" Vincent D'Onofrio. It's beautifully designed, and the much put-upon May delivers a sensual performance. Unfortunately, there are *Come Dancing* contestants with more charisma than D'Onofrio – the victim in *The Player* – and writer/director Leonard Schrader's script is dripping with pretension. Contains swearing, violence, sex scenes and nudity. ▭

Vincent D'Onofrio *Cholo* • Mathilda May *Stephanie/Alba* • Esai Morales *Zico Borenstein* • Fernando Rey *Judge Torres* • Josh Mostel *Bertoni the jeweller* ■ *Dir* Leonard Schrader • *Scr* Leonard Schrader, from the works of Manuel Puig

The Naked Truth ★★★★ U
Black comedy   1957 · UK · BW · 88mins

An early Peter Sellers comedy that supplied him with some of his funniest and finest material. He plays a crowd-pleasing TV host who's being blackmailed by smarmy Dennis Price, editor of a muck-raking magazine. Terry-Thomas (who would work with Sellers on *tom thumb* the following year) and Peggy Mount are among the victims who gang up against their persecutor. Based on class and sex, as the best British humour often is, it's satisfyingly scripted by Michael Pertwee and directed with superb timing by Mario Zampi. ▭

Peter Sellers *Sonny MacGregor* • Terry-Thomas *Lord Mayley* • Peggy Mount *Flora Ransom* • Dennis Price *Michael Dennis* • Shirley Eaton *Belinda Wright* • Georgina Cookson *Lady Mayley* • Joan Sims *Ethel Ransom* ■ *Dir* Mario Zampi • *Scr* Michael Pertwee

Naked Werewolf Woman
★★ 18
Erotic horror   1976 · It · Colour · 89mins

Annik Borel believes she's the reincarnation of a wolf creature from two centuries ago in this delightfully silly sex, sleaze and horror outing. But it's only her sexual drive that's causing fur to grow all over her body as she runs around foaming at the mouth and killing people in nasty ways. Graphic blood-letting, obligatory lesbian and rape scenes, virtually nonexistent direction from Rino Di Silvestro and hilariously hairy special effects make this lyncanthropic loser a schlock treat. Italian dialogue dubbed into English. Contains violence, sex scenes and nudity. ▭

Annik Borel *Daniela Messeri* • Frederick Stafford *Police inspector* • Tino Carraro *Count Messeri* ■ *Dir* Rino Di Silvestro • *Scr* Rino Di Silvestro, Howard Ross

The Naked Zoo ★
Crime drama   1970 · US · Colour · 78mins

Starring former screen goddess Rita Hayworth in her penultimate movie, this was directed by B-movie meister William Grefe, whose CV includes films with such tell-all titles as *The Wild Rebels*, *Death Curse of Tartu* and *The Jaws of Death*. One suspects this sleazy drama set in Miami, which justly had only a limited release, wasn't exactly a highlight of Rita's career.

Rita Hayworth *Mrs Golden* • Stephen Oliver *Terry Shaw* • Ford Rainey *Mr Golden* • Fay Spain *Golden's daughter* • Fleurette Carter *Black woman* ■ *Dir* William Grefe • *Scr* William Grefe, Ray Preston, from a story by Ray Preston

The Name of the Rose
★★★★ 18
Medieval thriller
1986 · It/W Ger/Fr · Colour · 123mins

Sean Connery is in majestic form as the Franciscan friar who, with novice Christian Slater, investigates a series of murders in a remote 14th-century abbey, incurring the wrath of vicious inquisitor F Murray Abraham in the process. Director Jean-Jacques Annaud has decoded Umberto Eco's cryptic bestseller with an eye-blinkingly ornate visual style. While the inhabitants of the abbey are mostly as grotesque as gargoyles, the Holmesian figure of Connery dominates and elucidates with the kind of deductive brilliance that Conan Doyle's sleuth was to display centuries later. Contains violence, nudity and a sex scene. ▭

Sean Connery *William of Baskerville* • F Murray Abraham *Bernardo Gui* • Christian Slater *Adso of Melk* • Elya Baskin *Severinus* • Feodor Chaliapin Jr *Jorge de Burgos* • William Hickey *Ubertino de Casale* • Michael Lonsdale [Michel Lonsdale] *Abbot* • Ron Perlman *Salvatore* ■ *Dir* Jean-Jacques Annaud • *Scr* Andrew Birkin, Gerard Brach, Howard Franklin, Alain Godard, from the novel *Il Nome Della Rosa* by Umberto Eco

Namu, the Killer Whale
★★★ U
Adventure based on a true story
1966 · US · Colour · 88mins

Hungarian director Laslo Benedek made his name with *Death of a*

Salesman and the Marlon Brando teen pic *The Wild One*, but his career meandered somewhat before he found himself behind the camera for this factually-based drama that focuses on a very different kind of wild life. Superbly photographed on location in Puget Sound off the Washington coast, the film follows the struggle of marine biologist Robert Lansing to prevent local fishermen from killing the trapped whale which is threatening their livelihood. The story can't fail to stir the emotions, but Benedek deserves credit for presenting the case for both sides with admirable fairness.

Robert Lansing *Hank Donner* • John Anderson *Joe Clausen* • Robin Mattson *Lisa Rand* • Richard Erdman *Deke* • Lee Meriwether *Kate Rand* ■ *Dir* Laslo Benedek • *Scr* Arthur Weiss

Nana ★★★ PG
Romantic melodrama
1934 · US · BW · 83mins

Dorothy Arzner was one of the few women directors working in Hollywood during its Golden Age. Her films have recently been given a feminist slant, but it is hard to see this loose adaptation of Emile Zola's novel as anything other than pure melodrama. In place of Zola's gritty naturalism is producer Samuel Goldwyn's glossy sensationalism, as waif Anna Sten plunges into the seedy world of the French music hall and finds herself torn between amorous brothers Lionel Atwill and Phillips Holmes. ▭

Anna Sten *Nana* • Phillips Holmes *Lieutenant George Muffat* • Lionel Atwill *Colonel André Muffat* • Richard Bennett *Gaston Greiner* • Mae Clarke *Satin* • Muriel Kirkland *Mimi* ■ *Dir* Dorothy Arzner • *Scr* Willard Mack, Harry Wagstaff Gribble, from the novel by Emile Zola

Nana ★★
Period drama   1955 · Fr · Colour · 122mins

Emile Zola's gritty realism is virtually dispensed with altogether in favour of Second Empire opulence in this glossy adaptation of the ninth *Rougon-Macquart* novel. Never the most cerebral of directors, Christian-Jaque has produced an undemanding melodrama that spends a disproportionate amount of time eavesdropping on romantic trysts, at the expense of savouring the sights and sounds of the Parisian theatre and exploring the motives and emotions of Zola's complex characters. The director's passion for his then-wife, Martine Carol, is clearly evident. But the excellent Charles Boyer outshines her as the rich man she betrays. French dialogue dubbed into English.

Charles Boyer *Count Muffat* • Martine Carol *Nana* • Walter Chiari *Fontane* • Jacques Castelot *Count Vandeuvres* • Noel Rocquevert *Steiner* • Paul Frankeur *Bordenave* • Jean Debucourt *Napoleon II* ■ *Dir* Christian-Jaque • *Scr* Christian-Jaque, Henson Henson, Albert Valentin, Jean Ferry, from the novel by Emile Zola

Nancy Goes to Rio ★★★ U
Musical   1950 · US · Colour · 99mins

MGM's resident soubrette, pert and pretty Jane Powell, was the true successor to Deanna Durbin, as underlined by this remake of Durbin's *It's a Date* (1940). This time around,

instead of a trip to Hawaii and black and white, Powell and her actress mother (Ann Sothern) are on a luxury liner on their way to Rio in glorious Technicolor. There are some good numbers, especially *Shine on Harvest Moon*, sung by Powell, Sothern and (unexpectedly) Louis Calhern.

Jane Powell *Nancy Barklay* • Ann Sothern *Frances Elliott* • Barry Sullivan *Paul Berten* • Carmen Miranda *Marina Rodriguez* • Louis Calhern *Gregory Elliott* ■ *Dir* Robert Z Leonard • *Scr* Sidney Sheldon, from a story by Jane Hall, Frederick Kohner, Ralph Block

Nancy Steele Is Missing
★★★
Drama   1937 · US · BW · 84mins

Lindbergh baby kidnapper Bruno Hauptmann had been sent to the electric chair the year before this film opened, so the timing could not have been entirely coincidental. Nunnally Johnson's rambling production confronts the Hays Office head on by using loveable, gruff Victor McLaglen as a sympathetic abductor who eventually ends up as a gardener after reuniting his victim with her real father. George Marshall's direction is on the slow side, but McLaglen, caught mid-career between *The Informer* and *Gunga Din*, keeps it watchable.

Victor McLaglen *Dannie O'Neill* • Walter Connolly *Michael Steele* • Peter Lorre *Professor Sturm* • June Lang *Sheila O'Neill/Nancy Steele* • Robert Kent *Jimmie Wilson* • Shirley Deane *Nancy* • John Carradine *Harry Wilkins* ■ *Dir* George Marshall • *Scr* Hal Long, Gene Fowler, from the story *Ransom* by Charles Francis Coe

Nang Nak ★★★
Supernatural period drama
1999 · Thai · Colour · 99mins

A much retold tale and a huge box-office hit in its native Thailand, this mixture of folklore, gore fest and love story will either affect with its intensity or alienate with its minimalist approach and stylised acting. Set in the 1860s, the story centres on Winai Kraibutr, a young bride who lingers in ghostly form beside the Prakanong canal after dying in childbirth while her husband, Intira Jaroenpura, is away at war. The tenderness of their romance contrasts sharply with her violent assaults on those who challenge her ethereal idyll, including a Buddhist ghostbuster hired by the terrified villagers. In Thai with English subtitles.

Intira Jaroenpura *Mak* • Winai Kraibutr *Nak* ■ *Dir* Nonzee Nimibutr • *Scr* Wisid Sartsanatieng

The Nanny ★★★ 15
Thriller   1965 · UK · BW · 89mins

The first of two movies Bette Davis made for Britain's Hammer films is a genuinely chilling horror tale, with a clever plot written by Hammer regular Jimmy Sangster from an Evelyn Piper novel. However, some purists may well object to the fact that the flashbacks reveal incidents that never actually happened, completely undermining and consequently manipulating the expectations of the audience. Despite valiant work from Davis and director Seth Holt, the narrative weaknesses and the general unpleasantness of the piece spoil what could have been an interesting addition to the genre. 🖵

Bette Davis *Nanny* • Wendy Craig *Virgie Fane* • Jill Bennett *Pen* • James Villiers *Bill Fane* • William Dix *Joey* • Pamela Franklin *Bobby* • Jack Watling *Dr Medman* • Alfred Burke *Dr Wills* • Maurice Denham *Dr Beamaster* ■ *Dir* Seth Holt • *Scr* Jimmy Sangster from a novel by Evelyn Piper

Nanook of the North
★★★ U

Classic silent documentary
1922 · US · BW · 49mins

Sponsored by furriers Revillon Frères, shot in the frozen wastes of Hudson Bay and re-edited in 1948 with commentary and music added, this remains a historic, ground-breaking work by the great pioneering documentarist Robert Flaherty. According to his subject matter the dignity it deserves, Flaherty recorded, with insight and touches of humour, the life of Eskimo Nanook, his wife Nyla and their family and their harsh daily struggle for survival. A truthful, unembellished account of Eskimo life – building an igloo, capturing a seal, fishing in ice for food – the film looks undeniably primitive by today's standards, but present-day documentarists owe it a debt.

Dir Robert Flaherty • *Scr* Robert Flaherty, Carl Stearns Clancy (titles), Robert Flaherty (titles) • *Cinematographer* Robert Flaherty

Nanou
★★ 15

Drama 1986 · UK/Fr · Colour · 110mins

Writer/director Conny Templeman's only feature to date displays the characteristic urge of eighties British cinema to fuse the personal with the political. In this instance English teenager Imogen Stubbs's pre-college trip to Europe results in a liaison with French activist Jean-Philippe Ecoffey, who is intent on making his feelings about local unemployment heard. The opening act is well played, with a light, surprisingly humorous touch, but Stubbs shows considerable talent, but as the demands of Ecoffey and his cronies become increasingly extreme, so credibility is stretched. In English and French with subtitles.

Imogen Stubbs *Nanou* • Jean-Philippe Ecoffey *Luc* • Christophe Lidon *Charles* • Valentine Pelka *Jacques* • Roger Ibanez *Michel* • Nathalie Becue *Chantal* • Daniel Day-Lewis *Max* ■ *Dir* Conny Templeman • *Scr* Conny Templeman, Antione Lacomblez

Napoléon
★★★★★

Silent historical drama
1927 · Fr · BW · 234mins

Intended as the first instalment of a six-part biography, Abel Gance's factitious account of Bonaparte's life from military school to the Italian campaign originally ran for over five hours. Achieving his audacious movements by variously attaching the camera to a galloping horse's back, a pendulum and a flying football, Gance pushed the technology of silent cinema to its limits, even shooting several scenes in a triptych process called Polyvision. His energetic metaphorical editing was also endlessly innovative, at one point filling the screen with 16 superimposed images. Albert

Dieudonné gives a spirited performance in the title role, but the accolades all belong to the director.

Albert Dieudonné *Napoleon Bonaparte* • Gina Manès *Josephine de Beauharnais* • Vladimir Roudenko *Young Napoleon* • Alexandre Koubitzky *Georges Jacques Danton* • Antonin Artaud *Jean-Paul Marat* • Abel Gance *Louis Saint-Just* ■ *Dir/Scr* Abel Gance

Napoléon
★★★★

Biography 1955 · Fr · Colour · 190mins

One of the most entertaining of Sacha Guitry's witty all-star extravaganzas, it featured the 70-year-old actor/writer/director as Talleyrand, recounting a series of anecdotes about the life and loves of Napoleon Bonaparte (played first by Daniel Gélin and then Raymond Pellegrin). The film, which cost $1.8 million, a then record for a French film, was shot at the Parc des Expositions because no studio was large enough to accommodate the sets. Yet the three-hour film has an intimate feel as Guitry holds court, introducing a mouth-watering cast that includes Michèle Morgan as Josephine, Erich von Stroheim as Beethoven and Orson Welles as Napoleon's jailer, Hudson Lowe. In French with English subtitles.

Jean-Pierre Aumont *Renault de Saint-Jean d'Angely* • Pierre Brasseur *Barras* • Danielle Darrieux *Eleonore Denuelle* • Jean Gabin *Marshal Lannes* • Daniel Gélin *Bonaparte* • Sacha Guitry *Talleyrand* • Jean Marais *Count de Montholon* • Yves Montand *Marshal Lefebvre* • Michèle Morgan *Joséphine de Beauharnais* • Raymond Pellegrin *Napoléon* • Serge Reggiani *Lucien Bonaparte* • Maria Schell *Marie-Louis d'Autriche* • Erich von Stroheim *Beethoven* • Orson Welles *Hudson Lowe* ■ *Dir/Scr* Sacha Guitry

Napoleon and Samantha
★★★ U

Adventure 1972 · US · Colour · 91mins

Just think how much it would cost to team Michael Douglas and Jodie Foster today. Back in 1972, Disney had to shell out next to nothing to land the relatively unknown Douglas and the debuting Foster for this amiable adventure about a couple of runaway kids and their pet lion. Fans of such cross-country films as *The Incredible Journey* will lap this up, and no one will be able to resist Major, the retired circus lion who was also a veteran of several movies and TV episodes opposite Ron Ely's Tarzan.

Michael Douglas *Danny* • Will Geer *Grandpa* • Arch Johnson *Chief of Police* • Johnny Whitaker *Napoleon Wilson* • Jodie Foster *Samantha* • Henry Jones *Mr Gutteridge* ■ *Dir* Bernard McEveety • *Scr* Stewart Raffill

The Narrow Margin
★★★★ PG

Crime drama 1952 · US · BW · 71mins

Rattlingly good (literally!) train thriller epitomising the very best of the style now known and recognised as *film noir*, directed with a wonderful sense of the claustrophobic by Richard Fleischer and terrifically performed by tough guy Charles McGraw. He's the cop taking floozy Marie Windsor to testify to the grand jury, with evidence that will send a mobster gang to the chair. Naturally enough, they don't want her to squeal. The suspense is

acute, nobody is quite who they seem to be, and the action is riveting. A classic B-movie. 🖵

Charles McGraw *Walter Brown* • Marie Windsor *Mrs Neil* • Jacqueline White *Ann Sinclair* • Gordon Gebert *Tommy Sinclair* • Queenie Leonard *Mrs Troll* • David Clarke *Kemp* • Peter Virgo *Densel* ■ *Dir* Richard Fleischer • *Scr* Earl Fenton, from a story by Martin Goldsmith, Jack Leonard

Narrow Margin
★★★ 15

Thriller 1990 · US · Colour · 92mins

Efficient remake of Richard Fleischer's cracking 1952 B-movie, with the ever-reliable Gene Hackman as the assistant district attorney who faces a nightmarish train journey when he escorts a key witness (Anne Archer) to a mob trial. Action specialist Peter Hyams doesn't bring anything particularly new or innovative to this update, but the cat-and-mouse games between Hackman and chief assassin James B Sikking (*Hill Street Blues*) are a delight, and the action sequences on the roof of the speeding train are exhilaratingly shot. Look out for those veritable scene stealers JT Walsh and M Emmet Walsh in small cameos. 🖵

Gene Hackman *Robert Caulfield* • Anne Archer *Carol Hunnicut* • James B Sikking *Nelson* • JT Walsh *Michael Tarlow* • M Emmet Walsh *Sergeant Dominick Benti* • Susan Hogan *Kathryn Weller* ■ *Dir* Peter Hyams • *Scr* Peter Hyams, from the 1952 film

Nashville
★★★★★

Comedy drama 1975 · US · Colour · 160mins

Produced in time for the American bicentennial, *Nashville* is Robert Altman's magnum opus, perhaps not as fully realised as *The Long Goodbye*, *California Split* or *The Player*, but breathtaking in its scope and ambition. Set in Nashville, it is less a story than a mosaic with two dozen characters who connect, disconnect and reflect aspects of America, notably its music and politics. Ronee Blakley is one of the principal characters, supported by, among others, Geraldine Chaplin, Shelley Duvall and Ned Beatty, with cameos from Elliott Gould and Julie Christie. Its blend of country and western music, comedy and tragedy is never less than dazzling, and represents a major technical achievement for its visual and sound editors. Contains some violence, swearing and nudity.

David Arkin *Norman* • Barbara Baxley *Lady Pearl* • Ned Beatty *Delbert Reese* • Karen Black *Connie White* • Ronee Blakley *Barbara Jean* • Timothy Brown *Tommy Brown* • Keith Carradine *Tom Frank* • Geraldine Chaplin *Opal* • Robert DoQui *Wade* • Shelley Duvall *LA Joan* • Allen Garfield *Barnett* • Henry Gibson *Haven Hamilton* • Lily Tomlin *Linnea Reese* • Jeff Goldblum *Tricycle man* ■ *Dir* Robert Altman • *Scr* Joan Tewkesbury

The Nasty Girl
★★★★ PG

Drama based on a true story
1990 · W Ger · Colour and BW · 92mins

Barely seen in this country on its original release, this bitingly brilliant film is a searing study of the way in which modern Germany has assuaged its conscience following the Nazi era. Writer/director Michael Verhoeven based his script on the experiences of Anja Rosmus, whose rummaging into

the history of her own town led to her becoming a social outcast. The style is clearly influenced by Hans Jürgen Syberberg's remarkable *Hitler, a Film from Germany*, with the dazzling use of back projection and the unexpected transitions between scenes giving the film a vibrancy that both invigorates and disturbs. In German with English subtitles. Contains some violence. 🖵

Lena Stolze *Sonja* • Monika Baumgartner *Maria* • Michael Garr *Paul Rosenberger* • Fred Stillkrauth *Uncle* • Elisabeth Bertram *Grandmother* ■ *Dir/Scr* Michael Verhoeven

Nasty Habits
★★ PG

Comedy 1976 · US/UK · Colour · 87mins

An appropriate title for a mildly sacrilegious comedy, based on the novel *The Abbess of Crewe* by Muriel Spark, about nuns who smoke, drink, swear and cheat. As the nuns attempt to rig the election of a new abbess, it gradually becomes apparent that the events are those of the Watergate scandal transferred to a Philadelphia convent. Today, though, few people will appreciate the political references. Glenda Jackson seems to have little interest in the proceedings, but Sandy Dennis is very funny as the raucous Sister Winifred. 🖵

Glenda Jackson *Sister Alexandra* • Melina Mercouri *Sister Gertrude* • Geraldine Page *Sister Walburga* • Sandy Dennis *Sister Winifred* • Anne Jackson *Sister Mildred* • Anne Meara *Sister Geraldine* • Susan Penhaligon *Sister Felicity* ■ *Dir* Michael Lindsay-Hogg • *Scr* Robert Enders, from the novel *The Abbess of Crewe* by Muriel Spark

The National Health
★★★

Comedy 1973 · UK · Colour · 97mins

This adaptation of Peter Nichols's play shows the United Kingdom in intensive care. The setting is a rundown, ramshackle hospital, where the grisly reality of life on a men's ward contrasts with the slippery fiction of a TV soap opera entitled *Nurse Norton's Affair*. Director Jack Gold assembles some sprightly set pieces and fine actors (Donald Sinden, Lynn Redgrave, Jim Dale) who give real clout to Nichols's sometimes contrived satire.

Lynn Redgrave *Nurse Sweet/Petty* • Donald Sinden *Mr Carr/Dr Boyd* • Jim Dale *Barnet/Neil* • Eleanor Bron *Nurse McFee/Sister Mary* • Colin Blakely *Loach* • Clive Swift *Ash* • Bob Hoskins *Foster* ■ *Dir* Jack Gold • *Scr* Peter Nichols, from his play

National Lampoon's Animal House
★★★★ 15

Comedy 1978 · US · Colour · 105mins

It spawned a number of puerile spin-offs, but this cheerfully vulgar offering deserves the status of comedy classic. As well as providing John Belushi with his best ever role, it also helped launch the career of a number of rising young actors (Kevin Bacon, Tom Hulce, Peter Riegert), not to mention director John Landis and co-writer Harold Ramis. There's not much of a plot to speak of: at a US college in the early sixties, dean John Vernon plots to remove the depraved Delta House fraternity from the campus; Belushi and his fellow students decide to fight back. Everyone remembers the food fight, but the film is crammed with

smart sight gags and one-liners. Contains some swearing. 🖭 📀

John Belushi *John "Bluto" Blutarsky* • Tim Matheson *Eric "Otter" Stratton* • John Vernon *Dean Vernon Wormer* • Verna Bloom *Marion Wormer* • Thomas Hulce [Tom Hulce] *Larry "Pinto" Kroger* • Peter Riegert *Donald "Boon" Schoenstein* • Stephen Furst *Kent "Flounder" Dorfman* • Kevin Bacon *Chip Diller* ■ *Dir* John Landis • *Scr* Harold Ramis, Douglas Kenney, Chris Miller • *Music* Elmer Bernstein

National Lampoon's Christmas Vacation ★★ PG

Comedy   1989 · US · Colour · 92mins

One suspects actress Juliette Lewis leaves this one off her CV, as might director Jeremiah Chechik, who went on to make the infinitely more enjoyable *Benny and Joon*. The plot here revolves around the Griswold family, led by Chevy Chase and Beverly D'Angelo. This time, after destroying an American theme park and most of Europe in the previous movies, the family stays at home, and, of course, is beset by a series of disasters during the Christmas holiday. Silly in the extreme, and only saved by Randy Quaid's performance as an obnoxious relative. Contains swearing. 🖭

Chevy Chase *Clark W Griswold Jr* • Beverly D'Angelo *Ellen Griswold* • Randy Quaid *Cousin Eddie* • Miriam Flynn *Catherine, Eddie's wife* • Johnny Galecki *Rusty Griswold* • Juliette Lewis *Audrey Griswold* • John Randolph *Clark W Griswold Sr* • Diane Ladd *Nora Griswold* • EG Marshall *Art, Ellen's father* ■ *Dir* Jeremiah Chechik • *Scr* John Hughes

National Lampoon's Class Reunion ★ 18

Comedy horror   1982 · US · Colour · 81mins

An appalling comedy horror, this has a bunch of obnoxious ex-students locked in at their class reunion and stalked by a psychotic killer. The script is so inept, repulsive and agonisingly humour-free that it's hard to believe it was written by the usually dependable John Hughes. The cast, including *Animal House*'s Stephen Furst, wander aimlessly from room to room, while we cross our fingers hoping that the maniac will butcher them all. It's hard to isolate a low point, but the demonic possession gags come close. One of the worst comedies ever made. 🖭

Gerrit Graham *Bob Spinnaker* • Michael Lerner *Dr Robert Young* • Fred McCarren *Gary Nash* • Miriam Flynn *Bunny Packard* • Stephen Furst *Hubert Downs* • Marya Small *Iris Augen* ■ *Dir* Michael Miller • *Scr* John Hughes

National Lampoon's Dad's Week Off ★★ 12

Comedy   1997 · US · Colour · 95mins

In this reversal of the usual vacation theme, stressed-out computer executive Jack (Henry Winkler) looks forward to being "home alone" when his family leave him to his own devices and go camping. But temptation arrives in the shape of a free-spirited, liberated girl (Olivia D'Abo) whose openly sexual nature arouses desires Jack can't control. The result is harmlessly lecherous, late-night fun for adolescents and their envious fathers. Contains some swearing and sexual references. 🖭

Henry Winkler *Jack* • Olivia D'Abo *Cherice* • Richard Jeni *Bernie* • Justin Louis *Chip* • Ken Pogue *Emmett Sharpel* ■ *Dir* Neal Israel • *Scr* Neal Israel, from a story by Robert Kosberg

National Lampoon's European Vacation ★★★ 15

Comedy   1985 · US · Colour · 90mins

Co-scripted by John Hughes, Amy Heckerling's politically incorrect comedy should be dismissed without hesitation. But there is something endearing about the Griswold family, and Chevy Chase and Beverly D'Angelo's infectious enthusiasm manages to sweep you along on this cliché-ridden package tour. Every conceivable national stereotype is pressed into service, as polite British cyclists, rude French waiters, aggressive Germans in lederhosen and Mafia hit men are trotted out with soothing predictability. Contains swearing. 🖭

Chevy Chase *Clark W Griswold* • Beverly D'Angelo *Ellen Griswold* • Dana Hill *Audrey Griswold* • Jason Lively *Rusty Griswold* • John Astin *Quiz host* • Eric Idle *Bike rider* • Mel Smith *Hotel manager* • Robbie Coltrane *Man in bathroom* • Maureen Lipman *Lady In bed* ■ *Dir* Amy Heckerling • *Scr* John Hughes, Robert Klane, from a story by John Hughes

National Lampoon's Golf Punks ★★ U

Comedy   1998 · US · Colour · 88mins

National Lampoon's trademark silliness sets out for a day on the links in this lightweight entry in the series. Desperate for money, ex-golf pro Tom Arnold (Roseanne's ex-husband) agrees to teach a group of misfit kids to play golf. The star's highly-strung performance and the formulaic script neither helps nor hinders this pleasant, *Mighty Ducks*-style comedy. The sport may be different, but everything else stays the same in a family-oriented tale that's par for the course. 🖭

Tom Arnold *Al Oliver* • James Kirk *Peter* • Rene Tardif *Allistair McGrath* • Rhys Huber *Billy* • Greg Thriloway *Bo* ■ *Dir* F Harvey Frost [Harvey Frost] • *Scr* Jill Mazursky

National Lampoon's Last Resort ★★

Comedy   1994 · US · Colour · 91mins

Although energetic and with the usual hedonistic shenanigans, this is a far cry from *Animal House* and not as much fun as vacationing with the Griswolds. The simplistic plot has Sam (Corey Feldman) and Dave (Corey Haim) rushing to the aid of Sam's uncle Rex (Geoffrey Lewis) on a Caribbean resort. The two pose as CIA agents-cum-scuba instructors and thwart the villain of the piece (Robert Mandan), who's out to swindle Rex.

Corey Haim *Dave* • Corey Feldman *Sam* • Geoffrey Lewis *Uncle Rex* • Robert Mandan *Hemlock* • Demeta Hampton *Alex* • Maureen Flannigan *Sonja* ■ *Dir* Rafal Zielinski • *Scr* Damian Lee, Patrick Labyorteaux

National Lampoon's Loaded Weapon 1 ★★★ PG

Comedy   1993 · US · Colour · 79mins

The National Lampoon team's bid to cash in with some *Naked Gun*-style spoofery lacks the brainless invention of the latter films but still manages to score quite a few laughs. The *Lethal Weapon* series is its main target, with Emilio Estevez taking over the Mel Gibson role and Samuel L Jackson standing in for Danny Glover; a badly miscast William Shatner and Tim Curry are the villains of the piece. As well as *Lethal Weapon*, the movie also takes some pot shots at *The Silence of the Lambs* (F Murray Abraham in the Hannibal Lecter role) and *Basic Instinct*, but often the targets and gags are far too obvious. There's more fun to be had in watching out for the cameos, with appearances from the likes of Denis Leary, Charlie Sheen and JT Walsh, as well as James Doohan (*Star Trek*'s Scotty) and the *CHiPs* pair of Larry Wilcox and Erik Estrada. Contains some swearing. 🖭

Emilio Estevez *Jack Colt* • Samuel L Jackson *Wes Luger* • Tim Curry *Jigsaw* • Jon Lovitz *Becker* • Kathy Ireland *Destiny Demeanor* • William Shatner *General Mortars* • Frank McRae *Captain Doyle* • F Murray Abraham *Harold Leacher* ■ *Dir* Gene Quintano • *Scr* Don Holley, Gene Quintano, from a story by Don Holley, Tori Tellem

National Lampoon's Men in White ★★★ PG

Science-fiction comedy
1998 · US · Colour · 83mins

This National Lampoon send-up of sci-fi smash *Men in Black* is more in the tradition of *The Naked Gun* and *Airplane!* than the more usual misadventures of the Griswold family. Karim Prince and Thomas F Wilson (*Back to the Future*) play a pair of klutzy dustmen whose lives are changed when they are abducted by aliens. Back on this planet, they turn their dustcart into a space-going attack vehicle to tackle a menace from another galaxy. The sight gags come thick and fast.

Tom Wilson [Thomas F Wilson] *Ed Klingbottom* • Karim Prince *Roy DuBro* • Barry Bostwick *President Robert "Bud" Smith* ■ *Dir* Scott Levy • *Scr* Rob Kerchner, Scott Sandin

National Lampoon's Movie Madness ★ 15

Comedy   1981 · US · Colour · 85mins

Aside from *Animal House* and the first *Vacation*, the *National Lampoon* brand is best taken with an "avoid at all costs" warning. This is one of their worst films: a bloated, desperately unfunny trilogy of mini-spoofs which unforgivably wastes the talents of an exceptional cast, which ranges from such proven comedy performers as Christopher Lloyd, Julie Kavner and Olympia Dukakis through to movie legends Richard Widmark and Elisha Cook Jr. Personal growth films, cop movies and soaps are the predictable targets; a fourth segment on disaster movies never saw the light of day. 🖭

Christopher Lloyd *Samuel Starkman* • Robby Benson *Brent Falcone* • Richard Widmark *Stan Nagurski* • Barry Diamond *Junkie* • Elisha Cook Jr *Mousy* • Julie Kavner *Mrs Falcone* •

Robert Culp *Paul Everest* • Olympia Dukakis *Helena Naxos* • Peter Riegert *Jason Cooper* • Diane Lane *Liza* ■ *Dir* Henry Jaglom, Bob Giraldi • *Scr* Tod Carroll, Shary Slenniken

National Lampoon's Senior Trip ★ 15

Comedy   1995 · US · Colour · 87mins

Each successive entry in this once hilariously irreverent series is denounced as its nadir, but this risible comedy has stronger claims than most. Every character is a walking cliché, while every gag is designed to be cheap, and often offensive, rather than funny. Satire is at a premium as a gang of high school students write to the President lamenting the state of the nation and receive an invitation to the White House. Naturally, there's a corrupt senator on hand who tries to exploit them, and Lawrence Dane's pantomimic villainy is the sole reason for tuning in to this inept twaddle. Contains some swearing and sexual references. 🖭

Matt Frewer *Principal Moss* • Valerie Mahaffey *Miss Tracy Milford* • Lawrence Dane *Senator John Lerman* • Tommy Chong *Red* • Jeremy Renner *Mark "Dags" D'Agostino* • Rob Moore *Reggie* ■ *Dir* Kelly Makin • *Scr* Roger Kumble, I Marlene King

National Lampoon's The Don's Analyst ★★ 15

Crime comedy   1997 · US · Colour · 99mins

While this comedy predates both *Analyze This* and *The Sopranos*, it only goes to show that being first doesn't always count. Robert Loggia plays a mob boss suffering from depression who announces that he is retiring from the Mafia business. His sons then hire hapless shrink Kevin Pollak to bring him back to his old criminal ways. There a few nice jibes at the gangster genre, but David Hurwitz's script fails to build on its fascinating premise. Contains swearing. 🖭

Robert Loggia *Don Vito Leoni* • Kevin Pollak *Julian Riceputo* • Joseph Bologna *Vincent DeMarco* • Sherilyn Fenn *Isabella* • Angie Dickinson *Victoria Leoni* ■ *Dir* David Jablin • *Scr* David Hurwitz

National Lampoon's Vacation ★★★ 15

Comedy   1983 · US · Colour · 94mins

National Lampoon's first outing (1978's *Animal House*) is still the funniest by far, but this is a decent effort. Chevy Chase is the put-upon dad who sets off to take his family across America to an amusement park, encountering numerous mishaps and disasters along the way. Director Harold Ramis, who went on to make the comedy *Groundhog Day*, keeps the silliness coming fast and furious, and he is ably abetted by a supporting cast that includes Beverly D'Angelo, Randy Quaid and John Candy. Contains swearing and nudity. 🖭 📀

Chevy Chase *Clark Griswold* • Beverly D'Angelo *Ellen Griswold* • Imogene Coca *Aunt Edna* • Randy Quaid *Cousin Eddie* • Anthony Michael Hall *Rusty Griswold* • Dana Barron *Audrey Griswold* • Eddie Bracken *Roy Walley* • James Keach *Motorcycle cop* • John Candy *Lasky* • Christie Brinkley *Girl in red Ferrari* ■ *Dir* Harold Ramis • *Scr* John Hughes

National Velvet ★★★★ U

Classic drama   1944 · US · Colour · 118mins

One of the best-remembered of all movies, featuring a star-making role for 12-year-old Elizabeth Taylor, whose violet eyes have seldom since been seen to greater advantage. Enid Bagnold's original tale about a young girl racing her horse in the Grand National has to be taken with a large pinch of salt, but *The Yearling* director Clarence Brown knows how to pull all the right heartstrings. Thanks to a strong performance from Mickey Rooney, an Oscar-winning one from Anne Revere as Velvet's mother and the appeal of Taylor as Velvet herself, this is a richly satisfying movie. ▣

Mickey Rooney *Mi Taylor* • Elizabeth Taylor *Velvet Brown* • Donald Crisp *Mr Brown* • Anne Revere *Mrs Brown* • Angela Lansbury *Edwina Brown* • Jackie Jenkins [Jackie "Butch" Jenkins] *Donald Brown* • Juanita Quigley *Malvolia Brown* • Reginald Owen *Farmer Ede* ■ *Dir* Clarence Brown • *Scr* Theodore Reeves, Helen Deutsch, from the novel by Enid Bagnold

Native Son ★★

Crime drama   1951 · US/Arg · BW · 91mins

The work of American author Richard Wright probably offers the harshest portrait of the South ever published. Shortly after he exiled himself to Paris in 1950, Wright was persuaded by director Pierre Chenal to star in his own adaptation of his most famous novel, about a boy from the slums who gets a job as a chauffeur to a white family. When the daughter of the family gets drunk, the youngster tries to keep her quiet and accidentally kills her. Sadly, Wright was no actor and he was twice the age of his protagonist, Bigger Thomas, so this tame version of his work failed.

Richard Wright *Bigger Thomas* • Jean Wallace *Mary Dalton* • Nicholas Joy *Mr Dalton* • Gloria Madison *Bessie Mears* ■ *Dir* Pierre Chenal • *Scr* Pierre Chenal, Richard Wright, from the novel by Richard Wright

Native Son ★★★ 15

Drama   1986 · US · Colour · 106mins

Native Son has an impressive pedigree. It began as a 1940 novel by Richard Wright about a maladjusted, malcontented black youth, Bigger Thomas, who is taken for a night out by his employer's pretty daughter and her boyfriend. Both are active communists who make a show of equality. Later he accidentally murders the girl, incinerates the body and gets sentenced to death. This 1986 adaptation is pitched as a full-blooded melodrama and is worth seeing for its splendid cast: Carroll Baker as the blind mother, Elizabeth McGovern and Matt Dillon as the young communists, Victor Love as the central character and Oprah Winfrey in a cringe-making final scene. ▣

Carroll Baker *Mrs Dalton* • Akosua Busia *Bessie* • Matt Dillon *Jan* • Art Evans *Doc* • John Karlen *Max* • Victor Love *Bigger Thomas* • Elizabeth McGovern *Mary Dalton* • John McMartin *Mr Dalton* • Geraldine Page *Peggy* • Oprah Winfrey *Mrs Thomas* ■ *Dir* Jerrold Freedman • *Scr* Richard Wesley, from the novel by Richard Wright

The Natural ★★★★ PG

Sports drama   1984 · US · Colour · 116mins

Based on Bernard Malamud's 1952 novel, this is a wistful and often memorable look at the world of baseball by director Barry Levinson. Robert Redford is at his beautiful best as the player who experiences the highs and lows of the game in a film that's more *Field of Dreams* than *Bull Durham*. Baseball here is seen as something magical – Redford has a mystical bat named "Wonderboy", which he fashioned from a tree struck by lightning – rather than merely a sport. If you can suspend disbelief, you'll be rewarded with an emotional and heart-warming experience. Contains swearing.

Robert Redford *Roy Hobbs* • Robert Duvall *Max Mercy* • Glenn Close *Iris* • Kim Basinger *Memo Paris* • Wilford Brimley *Pop Fisher* • Barbara Hershey *Harriet Bird* • Robert Prosky *The Judge* • Richard Farnsworth *Red Blow* • Joe Don Baker *The Whammer* ■ *Dir* Barry Levinson • *Scr* Roger Towne, Phil Dusenberry, from the novel by Bernard Malamud

Natural Born Killers ★★★★ 18

Satirical crime drama
1994 · US · Colour and BW · 114mins

Woody Harrelson and Juliette Lewis are serial killers turned into folk heroes by media excesses in this striking movie, criticised by original story author Quentin Tarantino after being largely rewritten by director Oliver Stone and others. Ambitious, unrelenting and inventive, Stone's controversial landmark movie excites the intellect while bludgeoning the senses, blending naturalistic violence with stylised visuals, and commandeering every available cinematic trick to put across its searing message. A dazzling display of technique underscoring the media's obsession with violent crime, this is the most provocative addition to the debate since *A Clockwork Orange*. Contains violence, swearing, sex scenes and nudity. ▣

Woody Harrelson *Mickey Knox* • Juliette Lewis *Mallory Knox* • Robert Downey Jr *Wayne Gale* • Tommy Lee Jones *Dwight McClusky* • Tom Sizemore *Jack Scagnetti* • Rodney Dangerfield *Mallory's dad* ■ *Dir* Oliver Stone • *Scr* David Veloz, Richard Rutowski, Oliver Stone, from a story by Quentin Tarantino

Natural Enemy ★★ 18

Thriller   1996 · US · Colour · 87mins

Wall Street meets *Fatal Attraction* in this far-fetched straight-to-video thriller. William McNamara is the young stockbroker who is literally making a killing on the financial markets. However, it is not until he inveigles his way into the family home of his boss (Donald Sutherland) that things start to get really nasty. This is sloppily plotted, but McNamara is good value and the experienced supporting cast (Lesley Ann Warren, Joe Pantoliano, Tia Carrere) ensures that it is always watchable. Contains violence, swearing and sex scenes. ▣

Donald Sutherland *Ted* • William McNamara *Jeremy* • Lesley Ann Warren *Sandy* • Joe Pantoliano *Stuart* • Tia Carrere *Christina D'Amelio* ■ *Dir* Douglas Jackson • *Scr* Kevin Bernhardt

Natural Selection ★★★ 15

Science-fiction thriller
1994 · US · Colour · 87mins

The old good twin/bad twin routine is given a science-fiction twist in this superior suspense thriller from director Jack Sholder (*The Hidden*). Computer expert C Thomas Howell discovers he's really the end result of a high-tech cloning experiment, and that his dead ringer brother is planning to eradicate, then replace him. Sholder resourcefully tweaks the deliberate mistaken identity ploys to great cumulative effect. ▣

C Thomas Howell *Ben Braden/Alex Connelly* • Lisa Zane *Elizabeth Braden* • Cameron Dye *Craig* • Jenna Cole *Carol* • Ethan Phillips *Henry* • Miko Hughes *Nick* • Joanna Miles *Claudia* • Brenda Varda *Donna* ■ *Dir* Jack Sholder • *Scr* Todd Slavkin, Darren Swimmer

Naughty but Nice ★★★ U

Musical   1939 · US · BW · 89mins

Crooner Dick Powell's last movie under his Warner Bros contract is an amiable lightweight tale, in which Powell – courtesy of some demon rum – plays a Jekyll-and-Hyde music professor. This loose satire on Tin Pan Alley is really a vehicle for top-billed Ann Sheridan, the lovely and talented Texas sophisticate who Warners tagged the "Oomph Girl". But even she can't salvage this silly movie, in which the only satirical content is a look at how popular songs always steal from the classics. Look out for an early appearance from a callow Ronald Reagan.

Ann Sheridan *Zelda Manion* • Dick Powell *Professor Hardwick* • Gale Page *Linda McKay* • Helen Broderick *Aunt Martha* • Allen Jenkins *Joe Dirk* • ZaSu Pitts *Aunt Penelope* • Ronald Reagan *Ed Clark* ■ *Dir* Ray Enright • *Scr* Richard Macaulay, Jerry Wald, from their story *Always Leave Them Laughing*

Naughty Marietta ★★★

Musical   1935 · US · BW · 103mins

This was the first movie to team "America's Sweethearts", Jeanette MacDonald and Nelson Eddy. The somewhat sickly mixture of Nelson as a lecherous rake and Jeanette as a maligned loose woman might seem old hat today, but there's no denying the sheer panache of the production, and the undoubted pleasure (if you like that sort of thing) of a Victor Herbert score that includes *Tramp, Tramp, Tramp* and *Ah, Sweet Mystery of Life*. Louis B Mayer liked it so much that he willed MacDonald to sing *Sweet Mystery* at his funeral. She did.

Jeanette MacDonald *Princess Marie de Namours de la Bonfain/"Marietta Franini"* • Nelson Eddy *Captain Richard Warrington* • Frank Morgan *Governor Gaspard d'Annard* • Elsa Lanchester *Madame d'Annard* • Douglass Dumbrille *Prince de Namours de la Bonfain* ■ *Dir* WS Van Dyke II [WS Van Dyke] • *Scr* John Lee Mahin, Frances Goodrich, Albert Hackett, from the operetta by Victor Herbert, Rida Johnson Young

Navajo Joe ★★

Spaghetti western
1966 · It/Sp · Colour · 90mins

Burt Reynolds made this spaghetti western shortly after he saw his friend Clint Eastwood in *A Fistful of Dollars*. "They'll love you in Italy," Eastwood told Reynolds. "You're quarter Indian, you can ride a horse like no one I know and you like to hug people." Reynolds plays a Navajo Indian who sees his entire tribe murdered, including his wife, and in revenge kills a lot of people. That's all there is to it. Italian dialogue dubbed into English.

Burt Reynolds *Joe* • Aldo Sambrell *Marvin "Vee" Duncan* • Nicoletta Machiavelli *Estella* • Tanya Lopert *Maria* • Fernando Rey *Rattigan* ■ *Dir* Sergio Corbucci • *Scr* Dean Craig [Mario Pierotti], Fernando Di Leo, from a story by Ugo Pirro

The Navigator ★★★★ U

Classic silent comedy
1924 · US · BW · 57mins

A gorgeous Buster Keaton comedy set aboard a real ocean liner – the SS *Buford*, which was destined for the scrapyard before Keaton turned it into a marvellous prop. The story has Keaton playing Rollo Treadway – "heir to the Treadway fortune and and living proof that every family tree must have its sap" – who becomes adrift on the ship with his girlfriend. There are encounters with cannibals, an impromptu duel between swordfish, and an extraordinary underwater sequence with Keaton in full frogman's gear, filmed in 20 feet of water in Lake Tahoe, Nevada. ▣

Buster Keaton *Rollo Treadway* • Kathryn McGuire *Girl* • Frederick Vroom *Girl's father* • Noble Johnson *Cannibal chief* ■ *Dir* Donald Crisp, Buster Keaton • *Scr* Clyde Bruckman, Joseph Mitchell, Jean Havez

The Navigator – a Medieval Odyssey ★★★★ PG

Fantasy adventure
1988 · Ausl/NZ · Colour and BW · 87mins

An outstanding fable from New Zealand director Vincent Ward, which switches in time between Cumbria in the Middle Ages and the Antipodes of today. A medieval village threatened by the plague sends a group on a journey to find a miraculous church located on the other side of the world. The intrepid miners, however, burrow through the earth and end up in 20th-century New Zealand. The story could have been the basis for a knockabout time-travel comedy; indeed, there are some nice gags. Yet Ward is more interested in creating a mythical tale that subtly alludes to the Aids crisis and the nuclear apocalypse. ▣

Bruce Lyons *Connor* • Hamish McFarlane *Griffin* • Noel Appleby *Ulf* • Marshall Napier *Searle* • Chris Haywood *Arno* • Paul Livingston *Martin* ■ *Dir/Scr* Vincent Ward

Navy Blue and Gold ★★ U

Drama   1937 · US · BW · 93mins

One of dozens of movies set in the naval training academy of Annapolis. There's an important football game coming up against the army, and a question mark hangs over James Stewart's vital participation. It seems he slipped into Annapolis under an assumed name, because his father, also a navy man, had a major blemish on his career. Can Stewart redeem his family name and get to the game on time? The supporting cast comes straight out of the MGM commissary, as did Jimmy himself, still moving up the ranks to genuine stardom.

U = SUITABLE FOR ALL   Uc = SUITABLE FOR ALL, ESPECIALLY FOR YOUNG CHILDREN (VIDEO ONLY)   PG = PARENTAL GUIDANCE

Robert Young *Roger Ash* • James Stewart *John "Truck" Cross* • Lionel Barrymore *Capt "Skinny" Dawes* • Florence Rice *Patricia Gates* • Billie Burke *Mrs Alyce Gates* • Tom Brown *Richard Arnold Gates Jr* • Samuel S Hinds *Richard A Gates Sr* ■ *Dir* Sam Wood • *Scr* George Bruce, from his novel

The Navy Comes Through
★★ U

Second World War drama
1942 · US · BW · 81mins

During the war, Hollywood rolled out patriotic flag-wavers by the yard. Whether you want to see this one depends on your tolerance of leading actors Pat O'Brien and George Murphy, neither of whom are exactly blessed with screen magnetism. There's a convoy heading across the ocean, and it's O'Brien's job to sink the enemy subs, shoot the fighters out of the sky and keep Murphy guessing about his promotion prospects. That's because Murphy has been having an affair with O'Brien's sister (Jane Wyatt), who also happens to be aboard. The action scenes mainly comprise stock footage from a dozen other RKO efforts.

Pat O'Brien *Mallory* • George Murphy *Sands* • Jane Wyatt *Myra* • Jackie Cooper *Babe* • Carl Esmond *Kroner* • Max Baer *Berringer* • Desi Arnaz *Tarriba* ■ *Dir* A Edward Sutherland • *Scr* Earl Baldwin, Roy Chanslor, John Twist, Aeneas MacKenzie, from the story *Pay to Learn* by Borden Chase

The Navy Lark
★ U

Comedy　　　1959 · UK · BW · 82mins
The Navy Lark was a BBC Home Service comedy show that tickled people pink throughout the fifties. Filmed in CinemaScope and running three times its normal length, it's a nostalgia trip for those who remember and a completely baffling experience for those who don't. The idea was to show naval life as a jolly jape, so the plot deals with life aboard a mine sweeper whose skipper invents an outbreak of yellow fever. What follows is wrapped up in *Carry On*-style puns and saucy seaside postcard situations.

Cecil Parker *Commander Stanton* • Ronald Shiner *CPO Banyard* • Leslie Phillips *Lieutenant Pouter* • Elvi Hale *Leading Wren Heather* • Nicholas Phipps *Captain Povey* • Cardew Robinson *Lieutenant Binns* • Gordon Jackson *Leading Seaman Johnson* • Hattie Jacques *Fortune teller* ■ *Dir* Gordon Parry • *Scr* Sid Colin, Laurie Wyman, from the radio series by Laurie Wyman

Navy SEALS
★★ 15

Thriller　　1990 · US · Colour · 108mins
Charlie Sheen has proved to be more convincing sending up action heroes (namely in the *Hot Shots!* films) than playing it straight, and this uninspired adventure yarn is a perfect case in point. Sheen is the slightly crazy crack commando who, with colleagues such as Michael Biehn and Rick Rossovich, sets out to rid the world of baddies. Director Lewis Teague lets off the requisite amount of explosions, but the script is riddled with clichés and Sheen is hardly a charismatic lead. Contains swearing and violence. 📺

Charlie Sheen *Lieutenant Dale Hawkins* • Michael Biehn *Lieutenant Commander James Curran* • Joanne Whalley-Kilmer [Joanne

Whalley] *Claire Verens* • Rick Rossovich *Leary* • Bill Paxton *Dane* ■ *Dir* Lewis Teague • *Scr* Chuck Pfarrer, Gary Goldman

The Navy Steps Out
★★★ U

Comedy　　　1941 · US · BW · 90mins
Produced by the great silent comedian Harold Lloyd, this lightweight farce starts merrily enough as stenographer Lucille Ball and her wacky family and friends show stuffed-shirt tycoon Edmond O'Brien how to get some fun out of life. The rapid pace and slapstick situations keep the fun bubbling until the last reel, in which Lucille finally chooses between O'Brien and sailor George Murphy. Worth a look, if only to see Ball displaying the assurance and talent that Hollywood took so long to acknowledge.

Lucille Ball *Dot Duncan* • George Murphy *Coffee Cup* • Edmond O'Brien *Stephen Herrick* • George Cleveland *Pokey* • Henry Travers *Abel Martin* • Franklin Pangborn *Pet shop owner* • Kathleen Howard *Jawme* ■ *Dir* Richard Wallace • *Scr* Bert Granet, Frank Ryan, from a story by Grover Jones

The Navy vs the Night Monsters
★★ 12

Science-fiction drama
1966 · US · Colour · 85mins

Antarctic vegetable samples replanted on an island naval base grow into acid-bleeding, walking trees and terrorise the inhabitants of a South Seas navy base. But most of the cast are too busy ogling fifties blonde bombshell Mamie Van Doren to even notice, in this kiddie version of *The Day of the Triffids*. A terrible script, awful direction and ham acting from an eclectic bunch of Z-movie celebrities make this mind-boggling misfire a camp must-see. 📺

Mamie Van Doren *Lt Nora Hall* • Anthony Eisley *Lt Charles Brown* • Pamela Mason *Maria, a scientist* • Billy Gray *Petty Officer Fred Twining* • Bobby Van *Ens Rutherford Chandler* ■ *Dir* Michael A Hoey • *Scr* Michael A Hoey, from the novel *Monster from Earth's End* by Murray Leinster

Naya Daur
★★★ U

Drama　　　1957 · Ind · BW · 172mins
Directed by BR Chopra, this is a solid example of the politically conscious movie known as the "masala social". Just about every problem besetting the inhabitants of India's outlying rural communities comes under the microscope in this relentless melodrama, in which the arrival of new technology blows the lid off a long-simmering class and caste crisis. As if this wasn't enough to be getting on with, there is also a romantic triangle, a villain out to exploit the villagers and a handful of those extravagant song-and-dance routines that make Indian cinema so unique. Polished stuff. In Hindi with English subtitles. 📺

Jeevan *Kundan* • Dilip Kumar *Shankar* • Ajit *Krishna* • Nasir Hussain *Seth Maganlal* ■ *Dir* BR Chopra • *Scr* Akhtar Mirza

Nazarín
★★★★

Religious drama　1958 · Mex · BW · 94mins
Rejecting the chance to adapt *The House of Bernarda Alba*, Luis Buñuel instead chose to direct this distressing odyssey through rural Mexico, which is

sufficiently ambiguous to be claimed as both a scathing attack on the Catholic Church and a humanist lament at the impossibility of evangelising a determinedly secular world. Recalling Claude Laydu in Robert Bresson's *Diary of a Country Priest*, Francisco Rabal wears an increasingly haunted look as his journey (which frequently echoes events from the Gospels) reveals the virtual irrelevance of religion, even to people beset by plague and poverty. A Spanish language film.

Francisco Rabal *Nazarín* • Marga Lopez *Beatriz* • Rita Macedo *Andara* • Jesus Fernandez *Ujo, the dwarf* ■ *Dir* Luis Buñuel • *Scr* Luis Buñuel, Julio Alejandro, from a novel by Benito Perez Galdos

Nazi Hunter: the Beate Klarsfeld Story
★★★

Drama based on a true story
1986 · US · Colour · 120 mins

Every now and then a star pulls out a performance that leaves you dumbfounded because you simply didn't think they had it in them. Farrah Fawcett is the performer working wonders here, in the title role of this genuinely affecting TV movie about the capture of the Butcher of Lyons, Klaus Barbie, who, at the end of the war, had fled into exile in Bolivia. Director Michael Lindsay-Hogg also draws expert performances from Tom Conti as Fawcett's devoted husband, and Geraldine Page as a camp survivor whose testimony helps nail the fugitive. It's just a shame it dips too frequently into melodrama.

Farrah Fawcett *Beate Klarsfeld* • Tom Conti *Serge Klarsfeld* • Geraldine Page *Itta Halaunbrenner* • Catherine Allégret *Madame Simone Lagrange* • Feodor Atkine *Luc Pleyel* • Helene Vallier *Raissa Klarsfeld* • Vincent Gauthier *Barbie in 1944* ■ *Dir* Michael Lindsay-Hogg • *Scr* Frederic Hunter

Near Dark
★★★★ 18

Horror　　　1987 · US · Colour · 89mins
An undead revamp of *Bonnie and Clyde*, director Kathryn Bigelow's tense road movie combines the western and horror genres in one visually stunning and frightening package. Adrian Pasdar is the luckless farm boy inducted by tarty Jenny Wright into her itinerant family of gangster bloodsuckers as they manage to keep one step ahead of the law and daylight. Bigelow spins a genuinely scary tale, slickly examining the violent lifestyle of the outlaw gang, with Lance Henriksen and Bill Paxton giving stand-out degenerate performances. Contains violence and swearing. 📺

Adrian Pasdar *Caleb Colton* • Jenny Wright *Mae* • Lance Henriksen *Jesse* • Bill Paxton *Severen* • Jenette Goldstein *Diamondback* • Joshua Miller *Homer* • Marcie Leeds *Sarah Colton* • Tim Thomerson *Loy Colton* ■ *Dir* Kathryn Bigelow • *Scr* Eric Red, Kathryn Bigelow

Near Mrs
★★ 15

Romantic comedy
1990 · Fr/US · Colour · 89mins

Also known as *Near Misses* and *Toujours les Femmes*, this Franco-American comedy has more titles than laughs. Judge Reinhold strains every

sinew to amuse as the high-tech executive whose bigamous double life is exposed when he persuades doltish Casey Siemaszko to stand in for him on the annual Army Reserve fortnight while he romances his latest mistress. The farce that follows Siemaszko's kidnap by the Soviets is hopelessly laboured, in spite of the frantic pace. Contains swearing. 📺

Judge Reinhold *Claude Jobert* • Casey Siemaszko *Colin Phipps* • Cecile Paoli *Molly* • Rebecca Pauly *Maggie* • Muriel Combeau *Toni* • Katarzyna Figura *Sasha* ■ *Dir* Baz Taylor • *Scr* Peter I Baloff, David W Wollert

The Near Room
★★ 18

Thriller　　1995 · UK · Colour · 85mins
The third feature from actor/director David Heyman (*Silent Scream*, *The Hawk*) is a rather grim thriller about a gutter-press journalist (Adrian Dunbar) on the trail of his long-lost teenage daughter. The search takes him through child sex rackets, pornography rings and other underworld horrors. Shot in Glasgow, the film fuses the urban landscape of *Trainspotting* with that old chestnut, *The Searchers*. However, many viewers will find the relentless squalor, thick accents and foul language hard to take. 📺

Adrian Dunbar *Charlie Colquhoun* • David O'Hara *Harris Hill* • David Hayman *Dougie Patterson* • Julie Graham *Elise Grey* ■ *Dir* David Hayman • *Scr* Robert Murphy

Nearest and Dearest
★★

Comedy　　1972 · UK · Colour · 84mins
Responsible for some of Hammer's most grisly horrors, Michael Carreras was perhaps a surprise choice to produce this spin-off from the long-running ITV comedy series. Released the year before this fondly remembered sitcom departed our screens, it provides a worthy record of the word-mangling sniping between Hylda Baker and Jimmy Jewel as they try to suppress their sibling rivalry and make a go of their father's pickle factory. With Baker trotting out catchphrases like "You big girl's blouse" and Yootha Joyce joining the usual supporting cast, this may be bawdy, music hall entertainment, but it's also good, old-fashioned fun.

Hylda Baker *Nellie Pledge* • Jimmy Jewel *Eli Pledge* • Eddie Malin *Walter* • Madge Hindle *Lily* • Joe Gladwin *Stan* • Norman Mitchell *Vernon Smallpiece* • Pat Ashton *Freda* • Yootha Joyce *Mrs Rowbottom* ■ *Dir* John Robins • *Scr* Tom Brennan, Roy Bottomley, from the TV series

Nearly a Nasty Accident
★★★ U

Comedy　　　1961 · UK · BW · 89mins
Taking a break from his TV duties in *Whack-O!*, Jimmy Edwards teamed with Kenneth Connor (himself on sabbatical from the *Carry Ons*) for this old-fashioned blend of slapstick and bluster. Although Edwards, his handlebar moustache bristling with indignation, is the nominal star as the RAF officer whose cushy lifestyle is shattered by the arrival of an accident-prone mechanic, it's Connor's talent for timidity and catastrophe that makes this catalogue of disasters so amusing. Don Chaffey directs with

undue fuss, and there's practised support from such stalwarts as Richard Wattis and Shirley Eaton.

Jimmy Edwards *Group Captain Kingsley* • Kenneth Connor *AC2 Alexander Wood* • Shirley Eaton *Jean Briggs* • Ronnie Stevens *Fl Lt Pocock* • Richard Wattis *Wagstaffe* • Jon Pertwee *General Birkenshaw* • Eric Barker *Minister* • Peter Jones *Fl Lt Winters* ■ *Dir* Don Chaffey • *Scr* Jack Davies, Hugh Woodhouse, from the play *Touch Wood* by David Stringer

'Neath the Arizona Skies ★★ U

Western   1934 · US · BW · 51mins

There's little to get excited about here in a very routine John Wayne Monogram programme filler, except for a spectacular, waterlogged fistfight between the Duke and stuntman Yakima Canutt at the climax. The rest of the tiresome tale is flimsily plotted around a far-fetched case of mistaken identity. Wayne must have wondered if it was his destiny to play in these cheap B-movies for ever, but, fortunately, five years later director John Ford cast him in the career-changing *Stagecoach*. ▭

John Wayne *Chris Morrell* • Sheila Terry *Clara Moore* • Jay Wilsey [Buffalo Bill Jr] *Jim Moore* • Shirley Ricketts [Shirley Jane Ricketts] *Nina* • George "Gabby" Hayes *Matt Downing* • Yakima Canutt *Sam Black* ■ *Dir* Harry Fraser • *Scr* Burl Tuttle, from his story

Necessary Roughness ★★ 15

Comedy   1991 · US · Colour · 103mins

An American football comedy which replays all the situations and clichés from the baseball saga *Major League*, but with a minor-league cast and clumsy direction from Stan Dragoti. Scott Bakula is the hero, a mature college student and member of the team that must clear itself of a reputation for foul play. Marginal amusement can be had from the team's coach, played by Hector Elizondo, best known on the big screen as the hotel manager in *Pretty Woman*. But really, this is eminently missable. Contains swearing. ▭

Scott Bakula *Paul Blake* • Robert Loggia *Wally Riggendorf* • Hector Elizondo *Ed Gennero* • Harley Jane Kozak *Suzanne Carter* • Sinbad *Andre Krimm* • Larry Miller *Dean Elias* ■ *Dir* Stan Dragoti • *Scr* Rick Natkin, David Fuller

Necessity ★★ PG

Crime drama   1988 · US · Colour · 92mins

A very average made-for-TV thriller, based on a script by Brian Garfield, who is better known to paperback buyers and film fans as author and progenitor of the dreaded *Death Wish*. This TV movie stars the ex-Mrs Burt Reynolds, Loni Anderson, as a menaced fashion model threatened by the mob (which is run by her husband, of course) and trying to keep her baby out of trouble. That quick resumé gives a fair indication of the tale's lack of resemblance to reality. ▭

Loni Anderson *Lauren LaSalle* • John Heard *Charlie* • James Naughton *Rick LaSalle* ■ *Dir* Michael Miller • *Scr* Michael Anemann, Brian Garfield

Necronomicon ★★ 18

Horror   1993 · US · Colour · 92mins

Pacts with sea devils, mad scientists searching for eternal life and alien sacrifices are the themes of this Brian Yuzna, Christophe Gans and Shu Kaneko-directed trilogy of terror based on the works of HP Lovecraft. Nothing too remarkable is on offer here, although the gothic lyricism of Gans's episode *The Drowned* is noteworthy and the gruesome Edgar Allan Poe poetry of Kaneko's *The Cold* gets a lift from the manic performance of David Warner. Yuzna's *Whispers* is the goriest and daftest of the three horrors, which are held together by Jeffrey Combs, of *Re-Animator* fame, who plays Lovecraft himself. ▭

Jeffrey Combs *HP Lovecraft* • Tony Azito *Librarian* • Brian Yuzna *Cabbie* • Bruce Payne *Edward de la Poer* • Richard Lynch *Jethro de la Poer* • David Warner *Dr Madden* ■ *Dir* Christophe Gans, Shu Kaneko [Shusuke Kaneko], Brian Yuzna • *Scr* Brent V Friedman, Christophe Gans, Kazunori Ito, from stories by HP Lovecraft

Ned Kelly ★★ 15

Biographical drama
1970 · UK · Colour · 99mins

One of the unfortunate temptations of hiring a rock star to carry a film is for the director to rely rather lazily on that star's in-built charisma instead of trying to mould him into a character. Witness Mick Jagger, here cast as Australia's most memorable outlaw, who is so similar to his stage image that you half expect him to start shrieking, "It's great to be Down Under!" or "Thank you, you've been a great audience!". Realistically, though, the blame has to be laid at the door of director Tony Richardson, whose handling sometimes obscures the message and buries the drama. Contains swearing. ▭

Mick Jagger *Ned Kelly* • Allen Bickford *Dan Kelly* • Geoff Gilmour *Steve Hart* • Mark McManus *Joe Byrne* • Serge Lazareff *Wild Wright* • Peter Sumner *Tom Lloyd* • Ken Shorter *Aaron Sherritt* • James Elliott *Pat O'Donnell* ■ *Dir* Tony Richardson • *Scr* Tony Richardson, Ian Jones

Needful Things ★★ 15

Horror   1993 · US · Colour · 115mins

The Devil arrives in the sleepy coastal town of Castle Rock to open a curiosity shop selling bric-a-brac with nasty surprises attached in director Fraser C Heston's overlong, if mechanically efficient adaptation of a Stephen King tale. Because the script can't make up its mind whether to mine the humour or the horror, the result is by schizophrenic turn a colourful cartoon and a grisly chiller with awkward doses of black comedy dropped in. Despite capable performances, this "Antiques Creepshow" fails to generate any sympathy for its characters, and the episodic format is annoying. Contains swearing, violence and nudity. ▭

Max von Sydow *Leland Gaunt* • Ed Harris *Sheriff Alan Pangborn* • Bonnie Bedelia *Polly Chalmers* • Amanda Plummer *Nettie Cobb* • JT Walsh *Danforth Keeton III* • Ray McKinnon *Deputy Norris Ridgewick* • Duncan Fraser *Hugh Priest* ■ *Dir* Fraser C Heston • *Scr* WD Richter, from the novel by Stephen King

Nefertite, Queen of the Nile ★★★

Historical epic   1961 · It · Colour · 97mins

Part of a deal made by 20th Century-Fox with Italian studios, this is a negligible trip to Ancient Egypt. Contract player Edmund Purdom is the sculptor who falls for the high priest's daughter (Jeanne Crain) and is sentenced to death. She's meant to be a bride of the new pharaoh so it's a case of "less majesty" if she loses her virginity. There are some cherishable lines, but otherwise it's a very dull excursion to the past. Italian dialogue dubbed into English.

Jeanne Crain *Tanit/Nefertite* • Vincent Price *Benakon* • Edmund Purdom *Tumos* • Amedeo Nazzari *Amenophis IV* • Liana Orfei *Merith* ■ *Dir* Fernando Cerchio • *Scr* John Byrne, Ottavio Poggi, Fernando Cerchio

The Negotiator ★★★★ 15

Action drama
1998 · US/Ger · Colour · 133mins

Cluttered with clichés from other thrillers, this is still efficiently exciting cinema because of the electrifying chemistry between Samuel L Jackson and Kevin Spacey as Chicago police negotiators – cops skilled at talking hostage-takers out of the dead ends into which they put themselves. Jackson, as Danny Roman, has just persuaded a madman from killing his daughter when he's accused of stealing from police funds. So he takes captives until his name is cleared, and Chris Sabian (Spacey) has the job of "talking him down". It's that stand-off that director F Gary Gray makes such a cunningly dramatic centrepiece. Contains swearing and violence. ▭ **DVD**

Samuel L Jackson *Danny Roman* • Kevin Spacey *Chris Sabian* • David Morse *Commander Adam Beck* • Ron Rifkin *Commander Grant Frost* • John Spencer *Chief Al Travis* • JT Walsh *Terence Niebaum* • Siobahn Fallon *Maggie* ■ *Dir* F Gary Gray • *Scr* James DeMonaco, Kevin Fox

Neighbors ★★★ 15

Comedy   1981 · US · Colour · 91mins

This swan song of the John Belushi/ Dan Aykroyd partnership is a flawed but fascinating stab by the comedians at breaking away from their traditional knockabout slapstick. The two stars even swap their usual comic personae, with Belushi playing a geeky, mild-mannered suburbanite who is slowly being driven mad by his crazy neighbours (Aykroyd and Cathy Moriarty). Director John G Avildsen shows little affinity for the material, but Aykroyd and especially Belushi are excellent and make it worth a look. Contains swearing. ▭

John Belushi *Earl Keese* • Dan Aykroyd *Vic* • Kathryn Walker *Enid Keese* • Cathy Moriarty *Ramona* • Igors Gavon *Chic* ■ *Dir* John G Avildsen • *Scr* Larry Gelbart, from the novel by Thomas Berger

Neil Simon's Jake's Women ★★

Comedy   1996 · US · Colour

Neil Simon translates his stage play into this creaky TV movie. New York writer Alan Alda, in the throes of a trial

separation from wife Anne Archer, conjures up apparitions of the women in his life: his late first wife (Mira Sorvino), his analyst and his annoying sister. Talky and lacking action, this ambitious examination of the relationships between men and women moves along at a snail's pace, despite an impressive cast. If you're looking for Simon's wit and wisdom, wait for the next showing of *The Odd Couple*.

Alan Alda *Jake* • Anne Archer *Maggie* • Lolita Davidovich *Sheila* • Julie Kavner *Karen* • Joyce Van Patten *Edith* • Mira Sorvino *Julie* ■ *Dir* Glenn Jordan • *Scr* Neil Simon, from his play

Neil Simon's London Suite ★★

Comedy   1996 · US · Colour

Kelsey Grammer from *Frasier* and *Seinfeld*'s Michael Richards and Julia Louis-Dreyfus are among the guests who check in at a swish London hotel for this TV version of Neil Simon's follow-up to *Plaza Suite* and *California Suite*, both of which were released at the cinema. Madeline Kahn and Julie Hagerty also feature in the plot in which Americans lose their luggage, their husbands and their tickets to Wimbledon. Jay Sandrich's direction, however, is resolutely studio-bound. Contains some swearing.

Kelsey Grammer *Sidney Nichols* • Patricia Clarkson *Diana Nichols* • Julia Louis-Dreyfus *Debra Dolby* • Michael Richards *Mark Ferris* • Jonathan Silverman *Paul Dolby* • Madeline Kahn *Sharon Semple* • Jane Carr (2) *Mrs Sitwood* • Richard Mulligan *Dennis Cummings* • Julie Hagerty *Anne Ferris* ■ *Dir* Jay Sandrich • *Scr* Neil Simon, from his play

Neither the Sea nor the Sand ★★

Fantasy drama   1972 · UK · Colour · 95mins

Based on the novel by one-time newsreader Gordon Honeycombe, this romantic ghost story is a genuine oddity that was sadly overlooked at the time. Susan Hampshire retreats to Jersey where she meets and falls in love with lighthouse keeper Michael Petrovitch. When he dies, her friends and family (including Anthony Booth, Cherie's dad) are dismayed to find that death is no barrier to their love.

Susan Hampshire *Anna Robinson* • Michael Petrovitch *Hugh Dabernon* • Frank Finlay *George Dabernon* • Michael Craze *Collie* • Jack Lambert *Dr Irving* • David Garth *Mr Mackay* • Betty Duncan *Mrs Mackay* • Anthony Booth *Delamare* ■ *Dir* Fred Burnley • *Scr* Gordon Honeycombe, Rosemary Davies, from the novel by Gordon Honeycombe

Nell ★★★ 12

Drama   1994 · US · Colour · 108mins

This variation on the "wild child" scenario gave Jodie Foster a very juicy role to sink her teeth into and the double Oscar-winning actress doesn't miss a trick. She plays a young woman living in the North Carolina woods who has never seen the outside world and speaks a strange indecipherable language. Psychologist Natasha Richardson wants to take her into psychiatric care for research; sympathetic local doctor Liam Neeson believes she should be left alone. Although Foster is perhaps a little too showy in the title role (and was again

Oscar-nominated for her pains), she still delivers a marvellous performance, and director Michael Apted, making the most of the stunning locations, keeps the syrup at bay. Contains some swearing and brief nudity. ▭

Jodie Foster *Nell* • Liam Neeson *Jerome Lovell* • Natasha Richardson *Paula Olsen* • Richard Libertini *Alexander Paley* • Nick Searcy *Todd Peterson* • Robin Mullins *Mary Peterson* • Jeremy Davies *Billy Fisher* ■ *Dir* Michael Apted • *Scr* William Nicholson, Mark Handley, from the play *Idioglossia* by Mark Handley

Nell Gwyn ★★★
Historical drama   1934 · UK · BW · 85mins

The American censors were appalled when Herbert Wilcox's bawdy historical drama about Charles II's mistress was presented to them. In addition to 35 cuts, they suggested that a much more suitable ending would be to have Nell marry the king! A box-office smash in this country, the film benefits from a script by Miles Malleson (who also appears) that took much of its dialogue from Samuel Pepys's famous diary. Cedric Hardwicke has a rare old time as Charles, but Anna Neagle is just a touch too refined as Nell and comes off second best in her court intrigues with Jeanne de Casalis.

Anna Neagle *Nell Gwyn* • Cedric Hardwicke *King Charles II* • Miles Malleson *Chiffinch* • Esme Percy *Samuel Pepys* • Jeanne de Casalis *Duchess of Portsmouth* • Lawrence Anderson *Duke of York* • Helena Pickard *Mrs Pepys* ■ *Dir* Herbert Wilcox • *Scr* Miles Malleson, from the diaries of Samuel Pepys

Nelly & Monsieur Arnaud ★★★★PG
Drama   1995 · Fr/It /Ger · Colour · 102mins

Director Claude Sautet's distinctively cool style is wonderfully suited to this melancholy study of a young woman (Emmanuelle Béart) who becomes involved in a fragile, unfulfilled relationship with the elderly businessman (Michel Serrault) to whom she's secretary. There are more emotional insights than in many a so-called romantic movie – looks that are loaded with meaning, touches that bruise with the suggestion of passion – while the tale of obsession is told so discreetly it makes the film all the more haunting. In French with English subtitles. ▭

Emmanuelle Béart *Nelly* • Michel Serrault *Monsieur Arnaud* • Jean-Hugues Anglade *Vincent* • Claire Nadeau *Jacqueline* • Françoise Brion *Lucie* ■ *Dir* Claude Sautet • *Scr* Claude Sautet, Jacques Fieschi

Nemesis ★ 18
Science-fiction action
1993 · US · Colour · 91mins

Schlockmeister Albert Pyun isn't just content with ripping off *The Terminator* in this sci-fi cheapie; he also steals from *Escape from New York*. Cyborg ex-cop Olivier Gruner is forced by police chief Tim Thomerson into stopping a band of techno-terrorists planning to disrupt a summit meeting. If he refuses, he'll die from a bomb implanted in his body. Pyun has had a long fascination with futuristic stories involving cyborgs, but this effort is just as threadbare and unconvincing as all his other attempts. ▭ **DVD**

Olivier Gruner *Alex Rain* • Tim Thomerson *Farnsworth* • Deborah Shelton *Julian* • Marjorie Monaghan *Jared* • Merele Kennedy *Max Impact* • Cary-Hiroyuki Tagawa *Angie Liv* ■ *Dir* Albert Pyun • *Scr* Rebecca Charles

Nemesis 2 – Nebula ★ 15
Science-fiction action
1995 · US · Colour · 81mins

The *Nemesis* series's emulation of *The Terminator* is most blatant in this entry, with a future world enslaved by cyborgs sending one back in time to terminate Sue Price, a genetically enhanced woman warrior living in the African desert who offers hope for mankind. Director Albert Pyun makes this entry more action-oriented than the original, but the strident, frenzied tone numbs the viewer as much as the desolate landscape (actually filmed in the American southwest). ▭

Sue Price *Alex* • Chad Staholaki *Nebula* • Tina Cote *Emily* • Earl White *Po* • Jahi JJ Zuri *Zumi* ■ *Dir/Scr* Albert Pyun

Nemesis 3 – Time Lapse ★ 18
Science-fiction action
1996 · US · Colour · 90mins

The third entry in the *Nemesis* series plays less like a rip-off than the previous two entries, though that's mainly because of a storyline that's both incoherent and unfinished, leaving the viewer hanging for the inevitable *Nemesis 4*. Assuming viewers have seen the first two parts, the story starts shortly after the previous film, with Sue Price waking up with amnesia and trying to retrace her steps in the midst of very familiar danger. ▭

Sue Price *Alex* • Norbert Weisser *Edson* • Xavier Declie *Johnny* ■ *Dir/Scr* Albert Pyun

The Neon Bible ★★★ 15
Drama   1995 · UK · Colour · 87mins

Adapted from the novel by John Kennedy Toole, this measured, beautifully photographed but harrowing study of family angst in Georgia around the time of the Second World War marked the American debut of director Terence Davies. Although far from his Liverpool home, Davies revisits much of the territory covered in his acclaimed *Distant Voices, Still Lives* and *The Long Day Closes*. Yet he manages to breathe some new life into the familiar small-town formula, thanks to his keen eye for detail and a supremely assured performance from Gena Rowlands as the nightclub singer aunt who shakes up the lives of ten-year-old Drake Bell and his parents Diana Scarwid and Denis Leary. Contains violence and swearing. ▭

Gena Rowlands *Aunt Mae* • Diana Scarwid *Sarah* • Denis Leary *Frank* • Jacob Tierney *David aged 15* • Leo Burmester *Bobbie Lee Taylor* • Frances Conroy *Miss Scover* • Peter McRobbie *Reverend Watkins* • Joan Glover *Flora* • Drake Bell *David aged ten* ■ *Dir* Terence Davies • *Scr* Terence Davies, from the novel by John Kennedy Toole

The Neon Empire ★★★
Thriller   1989 · US · Colour

Las Vegas's mobster connections have long fascinated movie-makers. This TV movie explores the early days of the gambling capital of America and details Ray Sharkey and Gary Busey's battle for control. It's a tad predictable and suffers in comparison to *Bugsy*, which dealt with a similar subject. On the plus side, there is a classy, very watchable supporting cast that includes Martin Landau, Julie Carmen, Dylan McDermott and Linda Fiorentino. Released on video in the UK as *The Las Vegas Story*. Contains swearing, violence and a sex scene.

Ray Sharkey *Junior Moloff* • Linda Fiorentino *Lucy Jordan* • Gary Busey *Frank Weston* • Martin Landau *Max* • Julie Carmen *Miranda* • Harry Guardino *Nick* • Dylan McDermott *Vic Rothman* • Andreas Katsulas *Vito Carnesecca* ■ *Dir* Larry Peerce • *Scr* Pete Hamill, Edward Anhalt, from a story by Pete Hamill

The Nephew ★★ 12
Drama   1997 · Ire · Colour · 104mins

Yet another Irish rural saga – this time about a young American man who returns to the village from which his deceased mother came, sending the residents into a turmoil. Sounds familiar? The only twist in the tale is that the young Irish-American man is black, and the man who runs the local pub is played by James Bond himself, Pierce Brosnan, who's also one of the producers. Unfortunately, that's not enough to keep you entertained through this well-meaning but cliché-ridden tale. Contains some violence and sexual references.

Donal McCann *Tony Egan* • Pierce Brosnan *Joe Brady* • Sinead Cusack *Brenda O'Boyce* • Aislin McGuckin *Aislin Brady* • Niall Toibin *Sean Post* ■ *Dir* Eugene Brady • *Scr* Jacqueline O'Neill, Sean P Steele, from a story by Eugene Brady, Douglas Mayfield, Jacqueline O'Neill

The Neptune Factor ★ U
Science-fiction adventure
1973 · Can · Colour · 98mins

''The most fantastic undersea odyssey ever filmed,'' bragged the poster. Hardly – the producers should have been done under the trades description act for this feeble slice of aquatic sci-fi. Ben Gazzara and Ernest Borgnine are in charge of a mini-submarine, which offers the only chance of rescuing the crew of a sea-lab trapped by an earthquake on the ocean floor. Daniel Petrie brings zero excitement to a talky first half largely set in the cramped confines of the sub, while the sea monsters the crew later encounter are a huge let-down.

Ben Gazzara *Commander Adrian Blake* • Yvette Mimieux *Leah Jansen* • Walter Pidgeon *Dr Samuel Andrews* • Ernest Borgnine ''Mack'' MacKay • Chris Wiggins *Captain Williams* ■ *Dir* Daniel Petrie • *Scr* Jack DeWitt

Neptune's Daughter ★★★ U
Musical comedy   1949 · US · Colour · 92mins

Super-fun all-star MGM Technicolor musical, as good-natured as they come, and emphatically not to be confused with the period romp *Jupiter's Darling*, though both star Metro's aqua-queen Esther Williams. Here, along with co-stars Red Skelton, Ricardo Montalban and the ever-wonderful Betty Garrett, she gets to sing one of the nicest numbers ever to win the Academy Award for best song, Frank Loesser's catchy *Baby, It's Cold Outside*. The mistaken-identity plot is purely functional, but keep a beady eye out for a rare appearance on screen of the great Mel Blanc, the voice of all the Warner Bros cartoon characters.

Esther Williams *Eve Barrett* • Red Skelton *Jack Spratt* • Ricardo Montalban *Jose O'Rourke* • Betty Garrett *Betty Barrett* • Keenan Wynn *Joe Backett* • Xavier Cugat • Mike Mazurki *Mac Mozolla* • Mel Blanc *Julio* ■ *Dir* Edward Buzzell • *Scr* Dorothy Kingsley, Ray Singer, Dick Chevillat

The Nesting ★ 18
Horror   1981 · US · Colour · 99mins

Tame ghost story about an author (Robin Groves) who moves to an old, dark house, unaware that it is full of vengeful ghosts (two of whom are played by veterans John Carradine and Gloria Grahame). It all looks terribly cheap, while the attempts at special effects appear desperate. Another example of a porno director failing to cross to the mainstream. ▭

Robin Groves *Lauren Cochran* • Christopher Loomis *Mark Felton* • Michael David Lally *Daniel Griffith* • John Carradine *Colonel LeBrun* • Gloria Grahame *Florinda Costello* • Bill Rowley *Frank Beasley* ■ *Dir* Armand Weston • *Scr* Daria Price, Armand Weston

The Net ★★ U
Drama   1953 · UK · BW · 82mins

Nothing to do with Sandra Bullock or computer crime, but a tepid thriller that might have enjoyed more box-office success under its American title, *Project M7*. Although best known for his literary adaptations, director Anthony Asquith was no stranger to suspense movies but, having just scored a major hit with *The Importance of Being Earnest*, you can hardly blame him for plodding through John Pudney's novel about aviation espionage with little enthusiasm. The surprisingly strong cast probably deserved better, and only Herbert Lom manages to give a good account of himself. ▭

Phyllis Calvert *Lydia Heathley* • James Donald *Michael Heathley* • Robert Beatty *Sam Seagram* • Herbert Lom *Alex Leon* • Muriel Pavlow *Caroline Cartier* • Noel Willman *Dr Dennis Bord* • Walter Fitzgerald *Sir Charles Cruddock* • Patric Doonan *Brian Jackson* • Maurice Denham *Carrington* • Marjorie Fielding *Mama* ■ *Dir* Anthony Asquith • *Scr* William Fairchild, from the novel by John Pudney

The Net ★★ 12
Thriller   1995 · US · Colour · 109mins

The star charisma of Sandra Bullock raises this mediocre computer-age paranoia fantasy to the level of watchable entertainment. The *Speed* heroine goes on-line as a lonely hacker receiving a floppy disc that helps her uncover a criminal conspiracy. How she copes with the threat of cyberspace annihilation from an unknown assassin turns an already slow-moving thriller into a predictable game of hide-and-seek relying on major lapses in logic and coincidence for a happy ending. Contrived and confusing direction by Irwin Winkler doesn't help. Contains some violence and swearing. ▭ **DVD**

Sandra Bullock *Angela Bennett* • Jeremy Northam *Jack Devlin* • Dennis Miller *Dr Alan Champion* • Diane Baker *Mrs Bennett* •

Wendy Gazelle *Imposter* • Ken Howard *Bergstrom* • Ray McKinnon *Dale* ■ *Dir* Irwin Winkler • *Scr* John Brancato, Michael Ferris

Network ★★★★ 15

Drama 1976 · US · Colour · 116mins

A thunderous, strangely eerie swansong for Peter Finch as the bilious and increasingly demented TV anchorman who rants on air against his powerlessness. This is a bravura performance from Finch, who was awarded a posthumous Oscar, given full flight by Paddy Chayefsky's daring, sumptuously satirical script, which throws a continuous hail of barbs at the electronic eye. Sidney Lumet directs with wild aplomb, allowing Finch free rein and keeping up a furious pace. Criticised by some at the time for a certain naivety and lack of subtlety, this still remains one of the most devastating condemnations of the media's urge to exploit. Contains swearing, and a sex scene. ▭

Peter Finch *Howard Beale* • Faye Dunaway *Diana Christensen* • William Holden (1) *Max Schumacher* • Robert Duvall *Frank Hackett* • Wesley Addy *Nelson Chaney* • Ned Beatty *Arthur Jensen* • Beatrice Straight *Louise Schumacher* ■ *Dir* Sidney Lumet • *Scr* Paddy Chayefsky

Neutral Port ★★

Second World War drama
1940 · UK · BW · 92mins

A wartime romp, with Will Fyffe as the irrepressible skipper who decides to replace his torpedoed cargo vessel with a brand new German ship. He plans to steal one from a neutral port, much to the horror of the British consul (Leslie Banks). As directed by Marcel Varnel, who made the Will Hay classic *Oh, Mr Porter!*, it has the mood of a French movie; you keep looking round for a glimpse of Raimu or Michel Simon. Watch for the screen debut of Hugh Griffith, who went on to win an Academy Award for *Ben-Hur*.

Will Fyffe *Capt Ferguson* • Leslie Banks *George Carter* • Yvonne Arnaud *Rosa Pirenti* • Phyllis Calvert *Helen Carter* • Hugh McDermott *Jim Grey* • Hugh Griffith ■ *Dir* Marcel Varnel • *Scr* JB Williams, TJ Morrison

Nevada Smith ★★★ 15

Western 1966 · US · Colour · 125mins

An epic western with a fascinating premise – a young man tracks down the outlaws who killed his white father and Indian mother – is suffocated by lethargic direction from veteran Henry Hathaway, though the film is redeemed by Lucien Ballard's lush photography and an outstanding supporting cast. Playing a younger version of the character played by Alan Ladd in *The Carpetbaggers*, a miscast Steve McQueen brings star presence to a film that was backed by his own production company, Solar, and became a major hit in its day. ▭

Steve McQueen *Nevada Smith/Max Sand* • Karl Malden *Tom Fitch* • Brian Keith *Jonas Cord* • Arthur Kennedy *Bill Bowdre* • Suzanne Pleshette *Pilar* • Raf Vallone *Father Zaccardi* • Janet Margolin *Neesa* • Pat Hingle *Big Foot* • Howard Da Silva *Warden* • Martin Landau *Jesse Coe* ■ *Dir* Henry Hathaway • *Scr* John Michael Hayes, from characters created by Harold Robbins

Never a Dull Moment ★★★ U

Comedy 1950 · US · BW · 89mins

A Manhattan lady songwriter and a widowed farmer meet at a charity show and fall in love. Transplanted to his rustic ranch, she has to cope with her precocious stepdaughters as well as the living conditions, the horses and the local characters. Irene Dunne and Fred MacMurray co-star in this good-natured, sometimes near-farcical romantic comedy; both stars had built careers on better material, but it's still a lot of fun and didn't deserve the scathing critical reception it received upon release.

Irene Dunne *Kay* • Fred MacMurray *Chris* • William Demarest *Mears* • Andy Devine *Orvie* • Gigi Perreau *Tina* • Natalie Wood *Nan* • Philip Ober *Jed* • Jack Kirkwood *Papa Dude* ■ *Dir* George Marshall • *Scr* Lou Breslow, Doris Anderson, from the novel *Who Could Ask for Anything More* by Kay Swift

Never a Dull Moment ★★ U

Crime comedy 1968 · US · Colour · 84mins

In fact, there are too many dull moments in this formula comedy. Starring Dick Van Dyke and directed by Jerry Paris (who cut his directorial teeth on Van Dyke's TV show), it's a caper story, with our hero as a TV actor who is mistaken for a professional hit man and tries to prevent art fancier and mobster Edward G Robinson from stealing a priceless masterpiece. Robinson was known to be one of Hollywood's great connoisseurs of fine art, which is presumably why he took on the role. But Dorothy Provine, as the mobster's moll, gives the most spirited performance. ▭

Dick Van Dyke *Jack Albany* • Edward G Robinson *Leo Joseph Smooth* • Dorothy Provine *Sally Inwood* • Henry Silva *Frank Boley* • Joanna Moore *Melanie Smooth* • Tony Bill *Florian* • Slim Pickens *Cowboy Schaeffer* • Jack Elam *Ace Williams* ■ *Dir* Jerry Paris • *Scr* AJ Carothers, from the novel *A Thrill a Minute with Jack Albany* by John Godey

Never Been Kissed ★★★ 12

Romantic comedy
1999 · US · Colour · 107mins

Drew Barrymore does what she does best – cute, funny romance – in this simple teen comedy about a bumbling young copy editor on the *Chicago Sun-Times* who gets a chance to prove herself as a reporter when she is sent undercover to a high school to find out just what sort of nefarious things students get up to nowadays. It also gives her the chance to rewrite her own painful school memories – she was the class nerd – and get that first, memorable kiss she never had. Thanks to Barrymore's infectious performance and a fun turn from David Arquette as her older brother, this is enjoyably sweet first-date fare. ■ *DVD*

Drew Barrymore *Josie Geller* • David Arquette *Rob Geller* • Michael Vartan *Sam Coulson* • Molly Shannon *Anita* • John C Reilly *Gus* • Garry Marshall *Rigfort* • LeeLee Sobieski *Aldys* ■ *Dir* Raja Gosnell • *Scr* Abby Kohn, Marc Silverstein, Jenny Bicks

Never Cry Wolf ★★★ PG

Adventure based on a true story
1983 · US · Colour · 100mins

After his directorial debut with the superb *Black Stallion*, Carroll Ballard spent two years on location in British Columbia making this captivating adaptation of Farley Mowat's autobiographical account of his time spent with a pack of wolves. With the help of the Inuit who saved his life, he not only learns all about the frozen wilderness and the people who live there, but also discovers who is responsible for ravaging the local caribou herds. As you'd expect of Ballard, a cameraman on *Star Wars*, the photography is awesome. ▭

Charles Martin Smith *Tyler* • Brian Dennehy *Rosie* • Zachary Ittimangnaq *Ootek* • Samson Jorah *Mike* • Hugh Webster *Drunk* ■ *Dir* Carroll Ballard • *Scr* Curtis Hanson, Sam Hamm, Richard Kletter, Charles Martin Smith, Eugene Corr, Christina Luescher, from the non-fiction book by Farley Mowat

Never Forget ★★★

Drama based on a true story
1991 · US · Colour · 94mins

Every now and then a film focuses on a subject of such significance that it is almost impossible to judge it on its cinematic merits. *Never Forget* is one of those pictures. It tells the true story of death-camp survivor Mel Mermelstein's battle in the US courts to disprove a neo-Nazi organisation's claim that the Holocaust was Allied propaganda designed to discredit the Third Reich. It's hard to believe such a case could ever be tried, and the hearings were charged with emotion. Unfortunately, this TV movie only hints at the drama of the courtroom events, in spite of a courageous performance from Leonard Nimoy.

Leonard Nimoy *Mel Mermelstein* • Blythe Danner *Jane Mermelstein* • Dabney Coleman *William Cox* • Paul Hampton *Richard Fusilier* • Jason Presson *Bernie Mermelstein* • Juliet Sorcey *Edie Mermelstein* ■ *Dir* Joseph Sargent • *Scr* Ronald Rubin

Never Give a Sucker an Even Break ★★★★ U

Comedy 1941 · US · BW · 70mins

Although only credited (as Otis Criblecoblis) with devising the story, WC Fields actually scripted his final feature because director Edward Cline felt the rewrite imposed by the Universal front office was abysmal. In addition to being a dart directed at the empty heart of Hollywood, this is also a joyously anarchic assault on the sort of film narrative that Tinseltown held dear. By linking a series of bizarre, unrelated incidents and by blurring the line between reality and fantasy, Fields was way ahead of his time. A blistering parting gesture to an industry that failed to appreciate his genius.

WC Fields *The Great Man* • Gloria Jean *His niece* • Leon Errol *His rival* • Billy Lenhart *Butch* • Kenneth Brown *Buddy* • Margaret Dumont *Mrs Hemogloben* • Susan Miller *Ouliotta Hemogloben* • Anne Nagel *Madame Gorgeous* ■ *Dir* Edward Cline • *Scr* John T Neville, Prescott Chaplin, from a story by Otis Criblecoblis [WC Fields]

Never Give an Inch ★★★ 15

Drama 1971 · US · Colour · 109mins

Set in Oregon, Paul Newman's film of Ken Kesey's gargantuan novel, *Sometimes a Great Notion*, tells of a family of lumberjacks – no Python jokes, please – who have no truck with the striking loggers' union. However, it's the family itself, led by Henry Fonda, that offers the meatiest bits of the drama, resulting in scenes that vaguely recall Newman's earlier fim, *Hud*. A strong cast and fine location work make this a gripping, if rather solemn effort. Newman took over from director Richard A Colla halfway through shooting. ▭

Paul Newman *Hank Stamper* • Henry Fonda *Henry Stamper* • Lee Remick *Viv Stamper* • Michael Sarrazin *Leeland Stamper* • Richard Jaeckel *Joe Ben Stamper* • Linda Lawson *Jan Stamper* ■ *Dir* Paul Newman • *Scr* John Gay, from the novel *Sometimes a Great Notion* by Ken Kesey

Never Let Go ★★

Crime drama 1960 · UK · BW · 91mins

What was intended to be a gritty insight into the brutality of the underworld ends up being a tatty melodrama in this mid-budget misfire from director John Guillermin. Peter Sellers is cast against type as the leader of a stolen car racket, whose ruthless methods prompt victim Richard Todd and street punk Adam Faith to forge an unlikely alliance against him. Alun Falconer's script does nobody any favours, with Sellers reduced to embarrassing histrionics in the bid to shed his comic image.

Richard Todd *John Cummings* • Peter Sellers *Lionel Meadows* • Elizabeth Sellars *Anne Cummings* • Adam Faith *Tommy Towers* • Carol White *Jackie* • Mervyn Johns *Alfie Barnes* • Peter Jones *Alec Berger* • John Le Mesurier *Pennington* ■ *Dir* John Guillermin • *Scr* Alun Falconer, from a story by John Guillermin, Peter De Sarigny

Never Let Me Go ★★★ U

Romantic adventure
1953 · US/UK · BW · 93mins

An American news reporter in Russia falls in love with a ballerina and marries her, only for him to be deported by the authorities. A middle-aged Clark Gable and the glamorous Gene Tierney are the stars in this love story, which turns into a rescue drama halfway through. Directed by Delmer Daves, it was made by MGM's British arm, which explains the presence of Kenneth More, Bernard Miles and Frederick Valk in the cast. No surprises, but respectably escapist.

Clark Gable *Philip Sutherland* • Gene Tierney *Marya Lamarkina* • Richard Haydn *Christopher Wellington St John Denny* • Bernard Miles *Joe Brooks* • Belita *Valentina Alexandrovna* • Kenneth More *Steve Quillan* • Karel Stepanek *Commissar* • Theodore Bikel *Lieutenant* • Frederick Valk *Kuragin* ■ *Dir* Delmer Daves • *Scr* Ronald Millar, George Froeschel, from the novel *Came the Dawn* by Roger Bax

Never Love a Stranger ★★ PG

Crime drama 1958 · US · BW · 87mins

Novelist Harold Robbins produced and adapted his own potboiler about the Catholic orphan (John Drew Barrymore)

who discovers he's actually Jewish and becomes a mobster, the leader of one of New York's crime syndicates. Covering over 20 years, from 1900 to the Depression, this proves to be a distinctly tacky exercise with schmaltzy stuff about orphanages (*Dead End Kids*-style) mixed up with the events surrounding an internecine war between rival protection rackets. The only reason to watch it today is for Steve McQueen (billed as Steven) in his first significant screen role. ▣

Steven McQueen [Steve McQueen] *Martin Cabell* • John Drew Barrymore *Frank Kane* • Lita Milan *Julie* • Robert Bray *"Silk" Fennelli* • Salem Ludwig *Moishe Moscowitz* • Douglas Rodgers *Brother Bernard* ■ *Dir* Robert Stevens • *Scr* Harold Robbins, Richard Day, from the novel by Harold Robbins

Never on Sunday ★★★
Comedy drama   1960 · Gr · BW · 92mins

Melina Mercouri won the best actress prize at Cannes for her boisterous performance in this rarified romp that owes more than a little to the Pygmalion myth. As the waterfront prostitute who receives a cultural crash course from a besotted American professor, she gleefully casts restraint to the winds, much to the approval of her director, co-star and future husband, Jules Dassin. Although Dassin successfully soaks up the local atmosphere, his derivative script too often errs on the side of laboured bons mots and intellectual snobbery. Manos Hadjidakis's bouzouki music is also an acquired taste, although his theme song landed him an Oscar.

Melina Mercouri *Ilya* • Jules Dassin *Homer* • George Foundas *Tonio* • Titos Vandis *Jorgo* ■ *Dir/Scr* Jules Dassin

Never on Tuesday ★★15
Comedy   1988 · US · Colour · 86mins

Writer/director Adam Rifkin was barely in his twenties when he made this slight but amiable "stranded on the road" movie following the template of Rob Reiner's infinitely superior *The Sure Thing*. Andrew Lauer and a very youthful Peter Berg are the jocks stranded in the desert after a car collision with Claudia Christian, fantasising about getting lucky while an assortment of characters – including some celebrity cameos – fail to get them up and running again. ▣

Andrew Lauer *Matt* • Peter Berg *Eddie* • Claudia Christian *Tuesday* • Charlie Sheen *Thief* • Judd Nelson *Motorcycle cop* • Emilio Estevez *Tow-truck driver* • Gilbert Gottfried *Lucky Larry Lupin* • Nicolas Cage *Man in red sports car* • Cary Elwes *Tow-truck driver* ■ *Dir/Scr* Adam Rifkin

Never Say Die ★★
Comedy   1939 · US · BW · 80mins

A lesser effort for Bob Hope, playing an eccentric millionaire who, believing he has only weeks to live, marries a girl (Martha Raye) so that she can inherit his money. Though the script (co-written by Preston Sturges) has its fair share of gags, too much of the film is silly rather than funny and Raye, who sings *The Tra La La and the Oom Pah Pah*, tries to compensate with a surfeit of mugging. Alan Mowbray provides some of the best moments

with his droll underplaying of a disagreeable prince.

Martha Raye *Mickey Hawkins* • Bob Hope *John Kidley* • Andy Devine *Henry Munch* • Alan Mowbray *Prince Smirnov* • Gale Sondergaard *Juno* • Sig Rumann [Sig Ruman] *Poppa Ingleborg* • Ernest Cossart *Jeepers* • Paul Harvey *Jasper Hawkins* ■ *Dir* Elliott Nugent • *Scr* Don Hartman, Frank Butler, Preston Sturges, from a play by William H Post

Never Say Goodbye ★★
Romantic comedy   1946 · US · BW · 97mins

The small daughter (Patti Brady) of a devil-may-care commercial artist (Errol Flynn) and a Park Avenue mother (Eleanor Parker) must live alternately with each of her recently divorced parents who, of course, still really love each other. Directed by James V Kern, this romantic comedy, while admittedly a collection of recycled clichés devoid of substance and populated by stereotypes, is nonetheless an entertainingly breezy affair, cute and often funny.

Patti Brady *Phillippa "Flip" Gayley* • Errol Flynn *Phil Gayley* • Eleanor Parker *Ellen Gayley* • Lucile Watson *Mrs Hamilton* • SZ Sakall *Luigi, restaurateur* • Forrest Tucker *Cpl Fenwick Lonkowski* • Donald Woods *Rex DeVallon* • Peggy Knudsen *Nancy Graham* • Hattie McDaniel *Cozy* ■ *Dir* James V Kern • *Scr* James V Kern, Ial Diamond, Lewis R Foster, from the story *Don't Ever Leave Me* by Ben Barzman, Norma Barzman

Never Say Goodbye ★★U
Romantic drama   1955 · US · Colour · 95mins

American doctor Rock Hudson marries Cornell Borchers in Europe, but later walks out on her, taking their small daughter with him. Reconciliation is prevented by her incarceration in a Russian labour camp, but he runs into her ten years later in America... A shameless attempt by Universal to recycle the hit formula of their five-handkerchief weepie *Magnificent Obsession*, right down to Hudson operating on Borchers after she is hit by a truck in Chicago! The result is a cornucopia of wilted clichés, with the German Miss Borchers no match for Jane Wyman, and a plot lifted from *This Love of Ours* (1945).

Rock Hudson *Dr Michael Parker* • Cornell Borchers *Lisa Gosting/Dorian Kent* • George Sanders *Victor* • Ray Collins *Dr Bailey* • David Janssen *Dave* • Shelley Fabares *Suzy Parker* ■ *Dir* Jerry Hopper, Douglas Sirk • *Scr* Charles Hoffman, from the film *This Love of Ours* by Bruce Manning, John Klorer, Leonard Lee, from the play *Come Prima Meglio de Prima* by Luigi Pirandello

Never Say Never Again ★★★★PG
Spy adventure   1983 · UK · Colour · 128mins

Even though the Bond genre had long been steeped in self-parody, aided hugely by the smirking frivolity of Roger Moore, it was down to Sean Connery, returning to the role after 12 years, to balance the comic hysteria with action-man authenticity. Connery, ever-aware that he's at the centre of a big, expensive joke, still makes you believe that he's heroic to the core. His well-groomed presence holds the screen with ease, but he is flanked by three charismatic ne'er-do-wells, Klaus Maria Brandauer, Max von Sydow and

Barbara Carrera. The plot, which owes much to *Thunderball*, lurches badly at times, but the wild action set pieces, decked out in gals (Kim Basinger among them), gadgets and glib lines, are there to be cherished. ▣

Sean Connery *James Bond* • Klaus Maria Brandauer *Largo* • Max von Sydow *Blofeld* • Barbara Carrera *Fatima Blush* • Kim Basinger *Domino* • Bernie Casey *Felix Leiter* • Alec McCowen *"Q"/Algy* • Edward Fox *"M"* • Pamela Salem *Miss Moneypenny* ■ *Dir* Irvin Kershner • *Scr* Lorenzo Semple Jr, from a story by Kevin McClory, Jack Whittingham, Ian Fleming

Never So Few ★★
Second World War drama
1959 · US · Colour · 124mins

This MGM drama about wartime activity in Burma was clearly influenced by *The Bridge on the River Kwai*, and is notable mainly for its use of Ceylon locations; the discussion of key moral issues is quickly discarded for the sake of a hot romance between Frank Sinatra and the immaculate Gina Lollobrigida. Today, this film is a fascinating relic of a studio in decline, combining those on the way up (Steve McQueen, Charles Bronson) with those in the twilight of their careers (Paul Henreid, Brian Donlevy) in a story undimmed by the star casting of Sinatra, who had yet to acquire the image that would undermine his credibility in such roles forever. ▣

Frank Sinatra *Captain Tom C Reynolds* • Gina Lollobrigida *Carla Vesari* • Peter Lawford *Captain Grey Travis* • Steve McQueen *Bill Ringa* • Richard Johnson *Captain Danny de Mortimer* • Paul Henreid *Nikko Regas* • Brian Donlevy *General Sloane* • Dean Jones *Sergeant Jim Norby* • Charles Bronson *Sergeant John Danforth* ■ *Dir* John Sturges • *Scr* Millard Kaufman, from the novel by Tom T Chamales

Never Steal Anything Small ★★★★
Musical crime drama
1959 · US · Colour · 94mins

Terrific if little-known semi-musical starring James Cagney, based on a play about trade unionism that never made it to Broadway. This is colourful and funny stuff, classily shot in CinemaScope and with some knockout production numbers, especially from moll Cara Williams. Cagney shines throughout, though, in truth, he's a mite old for the role. Shirley Jones is just a little too sweet to be Cagney's other half, but there's super character work from the likes of Nehemiah Persoff and Royal Dano.

James Cagney *Jake MacIllaney* • Shirley Jones *Linda Cabot* • Roger Smith *Dan Cabot* • Cara Williams *Winnipeg* • Nehemiah Persoff *Pinelli* • Royal Dano *Words Cannon* • Anthony Caruso *Lieutenant Tevis* • Horace McMahon *OK Merritt* ■ *Dir* Charles Lederer • *Scr* Charles Lederer, from the play *The Devil's Hornpipe* by Maxwell Anderson, Rouben Mamoulian

Never Take No for an Answer ★★★U
Drama   1951 · UK/It · BW · 83mins

Awash with sentimentality, yet rejoicing in the innocence and faith of its young hero, Paul Gallico's novel, *The Small Miracle*, is given a light coating of neo-realism by its joint directors, Maurice

Cloche and Ralph Smart. As Peppino, the seven-year-old war orphan convinced that his ailing donkey will be cured if they visit the tomb of St Francis, the patron saint of animals, Vittorio Manunta is miraculously natural, whether bantering with priest Denis O'Dea, or touring the Vatican while seeking the Pope's permission to enter the shrine. However, stealing even more scenes is Violetta, the donkey with the happy smile.

Vittorio Manunta *Peppino* • Denis O'Dea *Father Damico* • Guido Celano *Strotti* • Nerio Bernardi *Father Superior* ■ *Dir* Maurice Cloche, Ralph Smart • *Scr* Paul Gallico, Pauline Gallico, Maurice Cloche, Ralph Smart, from the novel *The Small Miracle* by Paul Gallico

Never Take Sweets from a Stranger ★★★
Drama   1960 · UK · BW · 91mins

An extremely audacious film for its time, dealing with the problem of paedophilia and building towards a surprisingly grim and disturbing climax. The story concerns an English family who emigrate to a small town in Canada. The father, Patrick Allen, takes up the post of headmaster at a school, but then his nine-year-old daughter is sexually abused by a local bigwig, played by Felix Aylmer. When Allen takes Aylmer to court he runs into a wall of antipathy from the townspeople and the case is lost, allowing Aylmer to go from bad to worse. It's made by Hammer Films, so the movie walks a tightrope between seriousness and sensation.

Gwen Watford *Sally Carter* • Patrick Allen *Peter Carter* • Felix Aylmer *Clarence Olderberry Sr* • Niall MacGinnis *Defense counsel* • Alison Leggatt *Martha* • Bill Nagy *Clarence Olderberry Jr* ■ *Dir* Cyril Frankel • *Scr* John Hunter, from the play *The Pony Cart* by Roger Garis

Never Talk to Strangers ★★18
Erotic thriller
1995 · US/Can · Colour · 82mins

One of Peter Hall's spasmodic and invariably failed forays into the cinema, this rehash of *Fatal Attraction* stars Rebecca De Mornay as a criminal psychologist who picks up Antonio Banderas in a supermarket and virtually rapes him. Kinkiness is continued at his place where a steel cage surrounds his bed. But when De Mornay's pet cat and a neighbour are killed, she finally flips. Boasting a butt-naked Banderas, this may make his army of female fans afraid to close their eyes, but the rest of us can safely nod off. ▣ DVD

Rebecca De Mornay *Dr Sarah Taylor* • Antonio Banderas *Tony Ramirez* • Dennis Miller *Cliff Raddison* • Len Cariou *Henry Taylor* • Harry Dean Stanton *Max Cheski* • Eugene Lipinski *Dudakoff* • Martha Burns *Maura* ■ *Dir* Peter Hall • *Scr* Jordan Rush, Lewis Green

Never Too Late ★★★
Comedy   1965 · US · Colour · 103mins

Adapting his own Broadway hit, Sumner Arthur Long succeeds better than most in opening out a play for the big screen. He's helped in no small measure by Paul Ford and Maureen O'Sullivan, who expertly reprise their stage roles as the not exactly youthful couple whose ordered existence is thrown into turmoil by an unexpected pregnancy. Less effective, however, are Connie Stevens and Jim Hutton as their self-obsessed daughter and incompetent son-in-law, who milk the gags that their elders time to perfection. A firmer hand from director Bud Yorkin might have helped.

Paul Ford *Harry Lambert* • Connie Stevens *Kate Clinton* • Maureen O'Sullivan *Edith Lambert* • Jim Hutton *Charlie Clinton* • Jane Wyatt *Grace Kimbrough* • Henry Jones *Doctor Kimbrough* ■ *Dir* Bud Yorkin • *Scr* Sumner Arthur Long, from his play

Never Too Young to Rock ★★ U

Musical   1975 · UK · Colour · 101mins

Fans of *TOTP2* won't want to miss this crucial guide to mid-seventies glam rock, featuring the tinsel tonsils of the Rubettes, Mud and the Glitter Band. Sixties heart-throb Peter Noone (of Herman's Hermits) bridges the generation gap in the daftest plot imaginable. But the whole point to this sequined extravaganza is hearing such jukebox jives as *Angel Face*, *Tiger Feet* and the classic *Sugar Baby Love* again.

Peter Denyer *Hero* • Freddie Jones *Mr Rockbottom* • Sheila Steafel *Café proprietress* • Joe Lynch *Russian soldier* • John Clive *Bandsman* • Peter Noone *Army captain* ■ *Dir* Dennis Abey • *Scr* Ron Inkpen, Dennis Abey

Never Wave at a WAC ★★★

Comedy   1952 · US · BW · 87mins

Delightful, light-hearted farce in which a divorced Washington hostess joins the Women's Army Corps in order to get to Paris and meet her boyfriend. Rosalind Russell has fun playing the unworldly heroine – when she goes to sign up, she takes her secretary with her to fill in the forms – and when not in uniform she wears a succession of eye-catching James Galanos gowns. When the script flags, the top-flight cast keeps things bubbling.

Rosalind Russell *Jo McBain* • Paul Douglas *Andrew McBain* • Marie Wilson *Clara Schneiderman* • William Ching *Lt Col Schuyler Fairchild* • Leif Erickson *Sgt Noisy Jackson* • Arleen Whelan *Sgt Toni Wayne* • Charles Dingle *Senator Tom Reynolds* • Lurene Tuttle *Capt Murchison* ■ *Dir* Norman Z McLeod • *Scr* Ken Englund, from the story *The Private Wore Skirts* by Frederick Kohner, Fred Brady

The NeverEnding Story ★★★★ U

Fantasy adventure
1984 · W Ger · Colour · 89mins

German director Wolfgang Petersen is now perhaps best known for such taut thrillers as *Shattered* and *In the Line of Fire*, but in his first English-language movie he proves to be equally at home in the world of fantasy. Barret Oliver is the young boy drawn by a magical book into a wondrous alternative world that is threatened by evil forces. The story is a touch simplistic, but Petersen's direction is assured and children will be dazzled by the imaginative effects and stunning sets.

Noah Hathaway *Atreyu* • Barret Oliver *Bastian* • Tami Stronach *Childlike empress* • Moses Gunn *Cairon* • Patricia Hayes *Urgl* • Gerald McRaney *Bastian's father* • Thomas Hill

Koreander ■ *Dir* Wolfgang Petersen • *Scr* Wolfgang Petersen, Herman Weigel, from the novel by Michael Ende

The NeverEnding Story II: the Next Chapter ★★ U

Fantasy adventure
1991 · Ger/US · Colour · 85mins

Bastian returns (albeit in a different guise) for another adventure in the imaginary land of Fantasia in this frankly disappointing sequel to Wolfgang Petersen's English-language debut. Australian director George Miller (not the *Mad Max* one) assumes the storyteller's chair only to find that, for all its empresses, towers and enchanted creatures, he's been given a rather dull tale to relate. He does what he can with some engaging special effects, but Jonathan Brandis is too feeble a hero to get especially excited about. The memory-snatching Xayide is a different matter, however, particularly as she is played with such pantomime gusto by Clarissa Burt.

Jonathan Brandis *Bastian* • Kenny Morrison *Atreyu* • Clarissa Burt *Xayide* • Alexandra Johnes *Childlike empress* • Martin Umbach *Nimbly* • John Wesley Shipp *Barney Bux* ■ *Dir* George Miller (1) • *Scr* Karin Howard, from the novel *The NeverEnding Story* by Michael Ende

The NeverEnding Story III ★★ U

Fantasy   1994 · Ger · Colour · 91mins

By now the *NeverEnding Story* franchise was, well, heading towards an end. This one is more firmly anchored in real life, possibly to its detriment, with young Bastian being badly bullied at school by a bunch of no-gooders called the ''Nasties''. His only sanctuary is the library where he can escape to the world of Fantasia via the *NeverEnding Story* book. Almost inevitably, the Nasties steal the volume and, in order to save his fantasy world, Bastian must return the book. Jason James Richter from the *Free Willy* films is Bastian.

Jason James Richter *Bastian Bux* • Melody Kay *Nicole* • Freddie Jones *Mr Coreander/Old Man of Wandering Mountain* • Jack Black *Slip* • Ryan Bollman *Dog* • Carole Finn *Mookie* ■ *Dir* Peter MacDonald • *Scr* Jeff Lieberman, from a story by Karin Howard, from characters created by Michael Ende

The New Adventures of Pippi Longstocking ★ U

Adventure   1988 · US · Colour · 96mins

There was absolutely no point whatsoever in Americanising the popular creation of Swedish children's novelist Astrid Lindgren, whose character had already featured in several home-grown film versions. Despite a much publicised quest to find a new Pippi, this new movie barely saw the light of day, and was never shown at cinemas in the UK. Sad to report, under the leaden direction of the once-reliable Ken Annakin, this is unwatchable for anyone over five, and an insult to anyone under.

Tami Erin *Pippi Longstocking* • David Seaman Jr *Tommy* • Cory Crow *Annika* • Eileen Brennan *Miss Bannister* • Dennis Dugan *Mr Settigren* • Dianne Hull *Mrs Settigren* ■ *Dir* Ken Annakin • *Scr* Ken Annakin, from the books by Astrid Lindgren

The New Adventures of Tarzan ★★★ U

Adventure   1935 · US · BW · 74mins

The jungle swinger from Edgar Rice Burroughs's famous yarns goes to Guatemala to rescue an old friend and encounters a dangerous cult religion. Also known as *Tarzan and the Lost Goddess*, this B-picture was originally a Saturday matinée serial, but was later released as a feature. It lacks any kind of sophistication, but is mildly compelling all the same. Tarzan is played by Herman Brix, who later changed his name to Bruce Bennett.

Herman Brix [Bruce Bennett] *Tarzan* • Frank Baker *Major Martling, archaeologist* • Dale Walsh *Alice Martling* • Harry Ernest *Gordon Hamilton* • Lewis Sargent *George* • Ula Holt *Ula Vale* • Don Castello *Raglan* ■ *Dir* Edward Kull, WF McGaugh • *Scr* Edwin Blum, Charles Francis Royal, from the novels by Edgar Rice Burroughs

The New Age ★★ 18

Satire   1994 · US · Colour · 107mins

Since arriving in Hollywood from Australia in the early nineties, Judy Davis has all too rarely been given the chance to show what she can do. Given that it was written and directed by *The Player* screenwriter Michael Tolkin, this should have been the perfect vehicle. Yet, as with *The Rapture*, his earlier film about the search for spiritual solace in a soulless consumer society, Tolkin infuriatingly misses the target. Davis and *RoboCop* star Peter Weller are splendid as the downwardly spiralling couple, but what should have been a savage satire emerges merely as a collection of clever ideas.

Peter Weller *Peter Witner* • Judy Davis *Katherine Witner* • Patrick Bauchau *Jean Levy* • Rachel Rosenthal *Sarah Friedberg* • Adam West *Jeff Winter* • Paula Marshall *Alison Gale* ■ *Dir/Scr* Michael Tolkin

The New Babylon ★★★ U

Silent political drama
1929 · USSR · BW · 76mins

Babylon is a fashionable Paris department store where a salesgirl (Elena Kuzmina) works for the capitalist bourgeoisie. A significant silent film from the influential Soviet partnership of Grigori Kozintsev and Leonid Trauberg, this utilises the montage techniques that characterised the films of Eisenstein. Satirical, cynical and inventive, the film is also episodic and emblematic – capitalists are cowardly and greedy, the workers patriotic and brave – as it observes the devastating effects of the Franco-Prussian war and the collapse of the people's commune of 1871 through a devotedly Marxist/Stalinist eye.

Elena Kuzmina *Louise Poirier* • Pyotr Sobolevsky *Jean, a soldier* • David Gutman *Grasselin* • Sophie Magarill *An actress* • Sergei Gerasimov *Lutro, journalist* ■ *Dir/Scr* Grigori Kozintsev, Leonid Trauberg

New Eden ★★ PG

Science-fiction adventure
1994 · US · Colour · 85mins

Yes, it's *Mad Max* time again, although without the style or black humour. Stephen Baldwin and Michael Bowen

are among a group of convicts dumped on a barren, futuristic prison planet who are not expected to live long enough to apply for parole. While Bowen looks for supremacy among the criminals of the desert, Baldwin fights off the bad guys while helping struggling Lisa Bonet and her tribe. Turgidly directed by Alan Metzger, this will sorely test the patience of even the most dedicated fan of post-apocalypse adventures. Contains violence, swearing and nudity.

Stephen Baldwin *Adams* • Lisa Bonet *Lily* • Michael Bowen *Kyne* • Tobin Bell *Ares* • Janet Hubert-Whitten *Queen Ashtarte* • MC Gainey *Thor* • Abraham Verduzco *Luke* ■ *Dir* Alan Metzger • *Scr* Dan Gordon

New Face in Hell ★★

Crime thriller   1968 · US · Colour · 108mins

Wealthy tycoon William Orbison (Raymond Burr) suspects that his wife is trying to murder his mistress, so he hires shabby private eye PJ Detweiler (George Peppard) to be her bodyguard. Making his first Hollywood movie, British director John Guillermin pays passing nods to all the old Bogart movies. However, this is essentially an essay in late sixties graphic violence and James Bond-style glamour. (At one point, the location suddenly switches to the Bahamas.) It's dated badly, but Peppard looks convincingly haggard while Gayle Hunnicutt is radiantly beautiful as Burr's mistress.

George Peppard *PJ Detweiler* • Raymond Burr *William Orbison* • Gayle Hunnicutt *Maureen Preble* • Coleen Gray *Betty Orbison* • Susan Saint James *Linette Orbison* • Wilfrid Hyde White *Billings-Browne* • Brock Peters *Police Chief Waterpark* ■ *Dir* John Guillermin • *Scr* Philip Reisman Jr, from a story by Philip Reisman Jr, Edward Montagne Jr [Edward J Montagne]

New Faces ★★★

Musical comedy revue
1954 · US · Colour · 98mins

No attempt was made to open out this hit-and-miss filmed record of the popular Broadway revue, and CinemaScope only enhanced the feeling of a proscenium arch. Yet it's interesting to see a cast of talented newcomers headed by the incomparable Eartha Kitt, who sings (or rather purrs) five wittily sexy songs including *C'est Si Bon* and *Monotonous*. Comedienne Alice Ghostley has an ironic number called *Boston Beguine*, while Carol Lawrence sings and dances. Mel Brooks was among the writers.

Ronny Graham • Eartha Kitt • Robert Clary • Carol Lawrence • Alice Ghostley • June Carroll • Paul Lynde ■ *Dir* Harry Horner • *Scr* Melvin Brooks [Mel Brooks], Ronny Graham, Paul Lynde, Luther Davis, John Cleveland, from the revue *New Faces of 1952* by Leonard Sillman

New Faces of 1937 ★★ U

Musical   1937 · US · BW · 98mins

A theatrical producer sells 85 per cent of a show to four backers, then tries to make sure it's a flop so he can pocket the surplus. Yes, it's the plot of *The Producers* some 30 years earlier, though this version lacks both the wit and the flair of the Mel Brooks classic, with even the great Milton Berle straining to compensate for poor

material. An undistinguished score is no help, but musical fans will find it watchable for the array of variety acts.

Joe Penner *Seymore Semor* • Milton Berle *Wellington Wedge* • Parkyakarkus *Parky* • Harriet Hilliard *Patricia* • William Brady *Jimmy* • Jerome Cowan *Robert Hunt* • Thelma Leeds *Elaine* • Lorraine Krueger *Suzy* • Ann Miller ■ *Dir* Leigh Jason • *Scr* Nat Perrin, Philip G Epstein, Irving S Brecher, Harold Kusell, Harry Clork, Howard J Green, David Freedman, from the story *Shoestring* by George Bradshaw

The New Gulliver ★★★★
Fantasy   1935 · USSR · BW · 85mins

Russian special effects expert Alexander Ptushko chose Jonathan Swift's satire *Gulliver's Travels* as the basis for the world's first feature-length puppet film. The laborious process – it took Ptushko almost three years to complete – also made it one of the last of the genre. Effective use is made of tiny, grotesque wax puppets, created in conjunction with an actor playing Gulliver, while the tale itself was adapted to fit the Soviet ideology of the time. Updated episodes from the book included a newsreel cameraman filming Gulliver being hauled into the Lilliputian capital, modern engineering techniques deployed to feed Gulliver, and the hero helping the oppressed in the class war. In Russian with English subtitles.

Vladimir Konstantinov *Gulliver* ■ *Dir* Alexander Ptushko • *Scr* Alexander Ptushko, Grigori Roshal, from the novel *Gulliver's Travels* by Jonathan Swift • *Puppet Maker* Sarra Mokil

The New Interns ★★
Medical melodrama
1964 · US · BW · 122mins

The sequel to the 1962 hit *The Interns* again turns the medical profession into racy melodrama, as if *Dr Kildare* and *Carry On Doctor* had been joint organ donors. Original cast members Michael Callan, Telly Savalas and Stefanie Powers remain in post while George Segal and Dean Jones are the new surgeons on the block, along with a bevy of young Hollywood hopefuls. Several separate stories are interwoven, notably Jones's low sperm count and Segal's background as a juvenile delinquent.

Michael Callan *Dr Alec Considine* • Dean Jones *Dr Lew Worship* • Telly Savalas *Dr Riccio* • Stefanie Powers *Gloria Worship* • Barbara Eden *Laura Rogers* • Kay Stevens *Didi Loomis* • Inger Stevens *Nancy Terman* • George Segal *Dr Tony Parelli* ■ *Dir* John Rich • *Scr* Wilton Schiller, from characters created by Richard Frede

New Jack City ★★★★ 18
Action drama   1991 · US · Colour · 96mins

Turning the minuscule budget to his advantage, Mario Van Peebles made his directorial debut with this hard-hitting mix of crime thriller and social drama, which is equally indebted to the urban realism of Spike Lee and such gangster movies as Brian De Palma's *Scarface*. Based on actual events, the film suggests that the problems facing black inner-city kids are caused as much by exploitative drug barons as they are by racial discrimination. Wesley Snipes achieves a chilling mix of arrogance and malevolence as crime kingpin Nino

Brown, while Van Peebles and fellow cops Ice-T and Judd Nelson successfully convey a sense of crusade rather than mere law enforcement. Contains swearing, violence and sex scenes. ▭ **DVD**

Wesley Snipes *Nino Brown* • Ice-T *Scotty Appleton* • Allen Payne *Gee Money* • Chris Rock *Pookie* • Mario Van Peebles *Detective Stone* • Michael Michele *Selina* • Bill Nunn *Duh Duh Duh Man* • Judd Nelson *Officer Nick Peretti* ■ *Dir* Mario Van Peebles • *Scr* Barry Michael Cooper, Thomas Lee Wright, from a story by Thomas Lee Wright

New Jersey Drive ★★★ 18
Drama   1995 · US · Colour · 93mins

Director Nick Gomez returns to the themes of his debut feature *Laws of Gravity* for this exploration of disillusioned urban youth set in Newark, "the car theft capital of the world". It has grit, attitude and pseudo-documentary realism to spare as it adds new insightful twists to the time-honoured tale of youths up to no good. Sharron Corley and Gabriel Casseus are excellent as the petty criminal joyriders hounded relentlessly by sadistic racist cop Saul Stein. A deliberately dark and potently disturbing look at inner-city issues and the moral ambiguities of life on the mean streets. Contains violence, swearing and drug abuse. ▭

Sharron Corley *Jason Petty* • Gabriel Casseus *Midget* • Saul Stein *Roscoe* • Gwen McGee *Renee Petty* • Andre Moore *Ritchie* • Donald Adeosun Faison *Tiny Dime* • Michele Morgan *Coreen* • Samantha Brown *Jackie Petty* ■ *Dir* Nick Gomez • *Scr* Nick Gomez, from a story by Michel Marriott, Nick Gomez

A New Kind of Love ★★
Comedy   1963 · US · Colour · 110mins

Paul Newman has had his moments as a screen comedian, but this is not one of them. In this undistinguished battle of the sexes, he plays a struggling writer who makes his name penning a newspaper column based on the romantic exploits of a smart Parisienne, unaware that she is the tomboy fashion designer he met on the plane. While not in the screwball class of a Katharine Hepburn or a Jean Arthur, Joanne Woodward is nevertheless highly engaging as both the dippy career girl and the fibbing socialite. Writer/director Melville Shavelson is no Preston Sturges either, but he coaxes a few smiles.

Paul Newman *Steve Sherman* • Joanne Woodward *Samantha Blake* • Thelma Ritter *Lena O'Connor* • Eva Gabor *Felicianne Courbeau* • George Tobias *Joseph Bergner* ■ *Dir/Scr* Melville Shavelson

The New Land ★★★★
Adventure drama
1972 · Swe · Colour · 160mins

Having survived the perilous passage depicted in *The Emigrants*, Swedish farmer Max von Sydow and his wife, Liv Ullmann, endeavour to make their mark upon the unrelenting plains of Minnesota in this concluding part of Jan Troell's epic adaptation of Vilhelm Moberg's literary saga. As before, Troell's refusal to romanticise either the landscape or the daily grind heightens the authenticity of the struggle, as well as its dramatic

intensity. Proud but vulnerable, von Sydow is superb as he tries to comprehend both his kinsmen's lust for gold and the complex politics that will plunge his adopted nation into civil war. In Swedish with English subtitles.

Max von Sydow *Karl Oskar* • Liv Ullmann *Kristina* • Eddie Axberg *Robert* • Hans Alfredson *Jonas Petter* • Halvar Bjork *Anders Mansson* • Allan Edwall *Danjel* ■ *Dir* Jan Troell • *Scr* Bengt Forslund, Jan Troell, from the novel *The Emigrants* by Vilhelm Moberg

A New Leaf ★★★★ U
Black comedy   1971 · US · Colour · 101mins

Sophisticated, cynical black comedy from writer/director/star Elaine May about a middle-aged playboy (Walter Matthau) who, lacking the resources to sustain his extravagant lifestyle, decides to marry wealthy wallflower May to keep himself in the luxury to which he's accustomed. Matthau intends to bump his new bride off, only to find himself afflicted by a guilty conscience. A Manhattan fairy tale with a wonderfully mordant edge.

Walter Matthau *Henry Graham* • Elaine May *Henrietta Lowell* • Jack Weston *Andrew McPherson* • George Rose *Harold* • William Redfield *Beckett* • James Coco *Uncle Harry* ■ *Dir* Elaine May • *Scr* Elaine May, from the short story *The Green Heart* by Jack Ritchie

A New Life ★★★ 15
Comedy drama   1988 · US · Colour · 99mins

Alan Alda, still trying to break free from his *M*A*S*H* TV image, here takes control of his career by writing and directing, as well as starring in, this comedy drama. He and his screen wife Ann-Margret divorce after more than 20 years, leaving Alda to drink and wisecrack his way through a series of one-night stands before both he and Ann-Margret start up relationships with younger people (Veronica Hamel and John Shea). It's all sub-Woody Allen stuff, but the performances are amiable. Contains swearing. ▭

Alan Alda *Steve Giardino* • Ann-Margret *Jackie Giardino* • Hal Linden *Mel Arons* • Veronica Hamel *Dr Kay Hutton* • John Shea *Doc* • Mary Kay Place *Donna* ■ *Dir/Scr* Alan Alda

The New Love Boat ★★
Romantic drama   1977 · US · Colour · 74mins

The familiar cast of the series had pretty much come together for this amiable voyage into "all at sea" clichés, the third pilot of the TV show. The formulaic storyline involving the crew dealing with a new captain and passenger guest stars coping with romantic problems is also present and correct, with Phil Silvers among the celebrities here.

Gavin MacLeod *Captain Merrill Stubing* • Bernie Kopell *Dr Adam Bricker* • Fred Grandy *Burl Smith* • Ted Lange *Isaac Washington* • Lauren Tewes *Julie McCoy* • Georgia Engel *Cleo* • Gary Frank *Stanley Adams* • Phil Silvers *Morris Beckman* • Stella Stevens *Leonara Klopman* ■ *Dir* Richard Kinon • *Scr* Brad Buckner, Rick Hawkins, Liz Sage, Michael Norell from the book *The Love Boats* by Jeraldine Saunders

New Moon ★★★ U
Musical   1940 · US · BW · 104mins

A splendid and popular Jeanette MacDonald/Nelson Eddy version of Sigmund Romberg's operetta, which was filmed a decade earlier with Metropolitan Opera stars Grace Moore and Lawrence Tibbett. MGM changed the setting from pre-revolutionary Russia to a very anti-British New Orleans, but it makes no difference. The terrific score includes *Softly as in a Morning Sunrise*, *Lover Come Back* and *One Kiss*, all with marvellous Oscar Hammerstein lyrics.

Jeanette MacDonald *Marianne de Beaumanoir* • Nelson Eddy *Charles Mission/Duc de Villiers* • Mary Boland *Valerie de Rossac* • George Zucco *Vicomte de Ribaud* • HB Warner *Father Michel* • Richard Purcell *[Dick Purcell]* *Alexander* • Stanley Fields *Tambour* • Bunty Cutler *Julie the maid* ■ *Dir* Robert Z Leonard • *Scr* Jacques Deval, Robert Arthur, from the operetta by Sigmund Romberg, Oscar Hammerstein II, Frank Mandel, Lawrence Schwab

New Rose Hotel ★
Science-fiction drama
1998 · US · Colour · 92mins

Based on a William Gibson short story, cult director Abel Ferrara's cyberpunk *Pygmalion* is an incomprehensible mess. It's an arrogantly arty sci-fi reverie about Willem Dafoe's life unravelling as the dirty deals he's involved in finally catch up with him and he anguishes over the true meaning of love. Throughout the murkily-shot action which recycles the same images over and over, Dafoe and Christopher Walken give creditable performances as the two retro Cold War pawns in a geo-political millennium chess game. Otherwise Ferrara's pretentious drone is a boring insult to the intelligence.

Christopher Walken *Fox* • Willem Dafoe *X* • Asia Argento *Sandii* • Yoshitaka Amano *Hiroshi* • Annabella Sciorra *Madame Rosa* ■ *Dir* Abel Ferrara • *Scr* Christi Zois, Abel Ferrara, from a short story by William Gibson

The New Swiss Family Robinson ★★
Adventure   1999 · US · Colour · 90mins

Jane Seymour and her real-life husband James Keach star in this updated adventure yarn. The Robinsons, having set sail from Australia to Singapore, are attacked by pirates, who have secretly planted treasure in their boat's hull. Shipwrecked on a deserted tropical island, the family turn it into their home. Then the pirates return... Some classics should be left alone, and Johann David Wyss's tale looks preposterous in the age of global-positioning satellites, cell phones and the internet. The leering, jet ski-riding pirates hardly make credible adversaries for the stalwart family, who end up playing second fiddle to an enterprising monkey.

Jane Seymour *Anna Robinson* • James Keach *Jack Robinson* • David Carradine *Sheldon Blake* • John Asher *[John Mallory Asher]* *Shane Robinson* • Blake Bashoff *Todd Robinson* • Jamie Renee Smith *Elizabeth Robinson* ■ *Dir* Stewart Raffill • *Scr* Stewart Raffill, from the novel *The Swiss Family Robinson* by Johann David Wyss

New Tales of the Taira Clan ★★★ U

Historical drama
1955 · Jap · Colour · 102mins

Working in colour for only the second time, Kenji Mizoguchi hired his old art teacher, Mitsuzo Wada, as the visual consultant on this bellicose tale of historical intrigue. But his heart was clearly not in what was to be his penultimate picture. Set in a turbulent 12th-century Japan, when Buddhist monks, backed by the indolent nobility, took up arms against the rebellious samurai, the action is efficiently staged in the manner of John Ford. However, the rise of Raizo Ichikawa and his Taira kinsmen at the expense of the tyrannical Minamoto clan lacked the character complexity in which Mizoguchi revelled. In Japanese with English subtitles. ▣

Raizo Ichikawa *Taira no Kiyomori* • Yoshiko Kuga *Tokiko* • Michiyo Kogure *Yasuko* • Ichijiro Oya *Taira no Tadamori* ■ *Dir* Kenji Mizoguchi • *Scr* Yoshikata Yoda, Masashige Narusawa, from the novel by Eiji Yoshikawa

New York Confidential ★★★

Crime drama   1955 · US · BW · 87mins

This gangster thriller, a precursor to *The Godfather*, was among the first to show the Mafia as a business linked as much by blood as bloodiness. Written by Clarence Greene and Russell Rouse, who also directs, it marked the end of an era for Warner Bros, and the beginning of a new one. Broderick Crawford is the godfather, Anne Bancroft portrays his daughter, while Richard Conte plays the assassin he takes under his wing.

Broderick Crawford *Charlie Lupo* • Richard Conte *Nick Magellan* • Marilyn Maxwell *Iris Palmer* • Anne Bancroft *Kathy Lupo* • J Carrol Naish *Ben Dagajanian* ■ *Dir* Russell Rouse • *Scr* Clarence Greene, Russell Rouse, from a book by Jack Lait, Lee Mortimer

New York Cop ★ 18

Police drama 1995 · US/Jap · Colour · 84mins

A Japanese-American co-production that's as bland and generic as its title, despite being supposedly based on a true story. An attempt to emulate US cop movies, complete with sporadic action sequences, it lacks their energy and even a basic understanding of their conventions, while its treatment of African-Americans will be considered by many to be offensive. Toru Nakamura brings nothing to his character except an accent that makes much of his dialogue hard to understand. ▣

Toru Nakamura *Toshi* • Chad McQueen *Hawk* • Andreas Katsulas *Ferrara* • Conan Lee *Konen Li* • Mira Sorvino *Maria* • Tony Sirico *Mr C* ■ *Dir* Toru Murakawa • *Scr* Hiroshi Kashiwabara, from the non-fiction book *New York Undercover Cop* by Jiro Ueno

New York Mounted ★★

Action adventure 1991 · US · Colour

This unusual tale of a rodeo cowboy turned mounted policeman is all rather far-fetched and unbelievable, but the action sequences really keep the movie rolling. Although the popular TV series *Due South* now manages to give a similar idea a much classier

treatment, the numerous adventures of our provincial friend in the Big Apple are entertaining enough. They're helped along by the lively relationship between him and his city cop partner, played by the estimable Dennis Franz.

Dennis Franz *Anthony Tony Spampatta* • Dan Gauthier *Lonnie Lucky Wellington* • Cliff De Young *Captain Smithers* • Roxann Biggs *Lieutenant Torres* ■ *Dir* Sam Weisman, Mark Tinker • *Scr* Patrick Hasburgh, Alfonse Ruggerio Jr, from their story

New York, New York ★★★★ PG

Musical drama   1977 · US · Colour · 156mins

A neglected gem from Martin Scorsese, tracing the love-hate relationship of saxophonist Robert De Niro and singer Liza Minnelli. The action fairly swings along from the couple's first meeting on VJ Day, through De Niro's rise to bandleader and the birth of their baby, to Minnelli's big break in the movies. Although the tempo drops occasionally, Scorsese's re-creation of the postwar era is faultless, and he handles the musical numbers with considerable aplomb. De Niro packs plenty of swaggering sax appeal, but the effervescent Minnelli steals the spotlight with a series of show stoppers. Contains swearing. ▣

Robert De Niro *Jimmy Doyle* • Liza Minnelli *Francine Evans* • Lionel Stander *Tony Harwell* • Mary Kay Place *Bernice* • George Memmoli *Nicky* • Murray Moston *Horace Morris* • Barry Primus *Paul Wilson* • Georgie Auld *Frankie Harte* ■ *Dir* Martin Scorsese • *Scr* Earl MacRauch, Mardik Martin, from a story by Earl MacRauch

New York Stories ★★★ 15

Portmanteau   1989 · US · Colour · 119mins

A word to the wise. As soon as Martin Scorsese's *Life Lessons* episode ends, you have 33 minutes to yourself – unless, of course, you feel you really have to sit through Francis Coppola's atrocious aberration *Life without Zoe*. Scorsese's contribution, on the other hand, is a superbly controlled drama focusing on artist Nick Nolte's relationship with his muse, Rosanna Arquette. But the real showstopper comes from Woody Allen, whose *Oedipus Wrecks* is one of the funniest things he's ever done, thanks largely to a monstrous performance from mother-from-hell Mae Questel. Contains swearing. ▣

Nick Nolte *Lionel Dobie* • Rosanna Arquette *Paulette* • Steve Buscemi *Gregory Stark* • Peter Gabriel • Heather McComb *Zoe* • Talia Shire *Charlotte* • Giancarlo Giannini *Claudio* • Woody Allen *Sheldon Mills* • Mia Farrow *Lisa* • Julie Kavner *Treva* • Mae Questel *Sadie Millstein* ■ *Dir* Martin Scorsese, Francis Coppola [Francis Ford Coppola], Woody Allen • *Scr* Richard Price, Francis Coppola [Francis Ford Coppola], Sophia Coppola, Woody Allen

Newman's Law ★★

Police drama   1974 · US · Colour · 98mins

George Peppard stars in this suitably dour and predictable cop movie. Squaring up against big city politics and corrupt police colleagues, he's framed and then suspended for getting too close to a drug kingpin. Director Richard T Heffron deals efficiently with

the requisite physical action and bolsters the routine good cop/bad cop plot with diverting insights into bureaucratic police methods.

George Peppard *Vince Newman* • Roger Robinson *Garry* • Eugene Roche *Reardon* • Gordon Pinsent *Eastman* • Abe Vigoda *Dellanzia* • Louis Zorich *Falcone* • Michael Lerner *Frank Acker* • Victor Campos *Jimenez* ■ *Dir* Richard T Heffron • *Scr* Anthony Wilson

News at Eleven ★★★ 15

Drama   1986 · US · Colour · 90mins

Martin Sheen heads the cast as a local television news reporter who breaks the story of an alleged sexual involvement between a high school teacher and a student. Mike Robe's film provides a timely showcase for the issues of media intrusion into privacy and journalistic hyping of facts. Sheen's acting is, as usual, top quality, but the rest of the players find it hard to match his high standard. ▣

Martin Sheen *Frank Kenley* • Peter Riegert *Eric Ross* • Barbara Babcock *Joanne Steckler* • David Sheiner *David Kogan* • Christopher Allport *Gene Silas* ■ *Dir/Scr* Mike Robe

The News Boys ★★ PG

Musical   1992 · US · Colour · 116mins

This is a Disney concoction about the Manhattan newsboys' strike of 1899, which *Variety* shrewdly described as "a strange cross between *Oliver!* and Samuel Fuller's *Park Row*". Yes, it's a musical, directed by choreographer Kenny Ortega in traditional – rather than MTV – style. Christian Bale leads the strike against Robert Duvall as miserly publisher Joseph Pulitzer, who gave his name to the prize. ▣

Christian Bale *Jack Kelly/Frances Sullivan* • Bill Pullman *Bryan Denton* • Ann-Margret *Medda Larkson* • Robert Duvall *Joseph Pulitzer* ■ *Dir* Kenny Ortega • *Scr* Bob Tzudiker, Noni White

News from the Good Lord ★★★

Black comedy
1996 · Fr/Swi/Por · Colour · 100mins

Demanding a willingness to surrender to its logic, Didier Le Pêcheur's debut rewards patient attention with a surfeit of audaciously original thinking and some bravura performances. Convinced they are characters in a badly-written celestial novel, Christian Charmetant and his passionate sister, Marie Trintignant, set off in search of God to query his literary prowess. However, the idea that moral responsibility lies with one's creator is somewhat sidetracked by the designer violence of a road-movie crime spree. The encounters with a spiritualist, a doubting priest, the widow of their favourite author and God himself are much more intriguing.

Marie Trintignant *Evangila* • Maria de Medeiros *Karenina* • Christian Charmetant *North* • Mathieu Kassovitz • Jean Yanne *God* ■ *Dir/Scr* Didier Le Pêcheur

Newsfront ★★★★

Drama 1978 · Ausl · Colour and BW · 110mins

Set during the forties and fifties, this is a humane, witty and affectionate tribute to Australia's cinema newsreel cameramen. It beautifully conveys the

mood of a nation, still tied emotionally and politically to Britain, and details both domestic crises and national disasters such as the Maitland floods. Clever use of black-and-white archive footage and a strong central performance from the burly, no-nonsense Bill Hunter distinguishes this fine movie from other first features. It's the movie directing debut of Phillip Noyce, who has since rather squandered his talent on Hollywood action blockbusters such as *Patriot Games* and *The Saint*.

John Dease *Ken* • Wendy Hughes *Amy McKenzie* • Gerard Kennedy *Frank Maguire* • John Ewart *Charlie* • Angela Punch McGregor *Fay Maguire* • Bryan Brown *Geoff* • Bill Hunter *Len Maguire* ■ *Dir* Phillip Noyce • *Scr* Phillip Noyce, Bob Ellis, from an idea by David Elfick, Philippe Mora

The Newton Boys ★★★ 15

Western   1998 · US · Colour · 117mins

In the early twenties, the four Texan-born Newton brothers were the most successful bank robbers in history. *Slacker* director Richard Linklater gives this little-known piece of Americana a pumped-up modern spin and crafts a well constructed, highly entertaining romantic adventure. Matthew McConaughey, Skeet Ulrich, Ethan Hawke and Vincent D'Onofrio make the boys a personable bunch with their differing traits, and Dwight Yoakam's portrayal of a nervous explosives expert is a blast. ▣

Matthew McConaughey *Willis Newton* • Skeet Ulrich *Joe Newton* • Ethan Hawke *Jess Newton* • Gail Cronauer *Ma Newton* • Vincent D'Onofrio *Dock Newton* • Julianna Margulies *Louise Brown* • Dwight Yoakam *Brentwood Glasscock* • Bo Hopkins *KP Aldrich* ■ *Dir* Richard Linklater • *Scr* Richard Linklater, Claude Stanush, Clark Lee Walker, from a story by Willis Newton, Joe Newton, from the book *The Newton Boys: Portrait of an Outlaw Gang* by Claude Stanush, David Middleton

The Next Best Thing ★★ 12

Comedy drama 2000 · US · Colour · 107mins

After the atypical blip that was *Evita*, Madonna is back in bad-movie mode with this humdrum romantic weepie. The material girl plays an LA yoga instructor whose life takes a dramatic turn when she sleeps with her gay best friend (Rupert Everett) and ends up pregnant. The couple set up house together for the good of their son, but problems arise when she falls for hunky Benjamin Bratt and Everett sues for custody. Veteran British director John Schlesinger handles his stars with kid gloves, and both deliver self-conscious performances that feel false and hollow throughout.

Madonna *Abbie* • Rupert Everett *Robert* • Illeana Douglas *Elizabeth Ryder* • Michael Vartan *Kevin* • Josef Sommer *Richard Whittaker* • Malcolm Stumpf *Sam* • Lynn Redgrave *Helen Whittaker* • Benjamin Bratt *Ben Cooper* • Neil Patrick Harris *David* ■ *Dir* John Schlesinger • *Scr* Thomas Ropelewski, Leslie Dixon, Rupert Everett, Mel Bordeaux

Next Door ★★★ 15

Drama   1994 · US · Colour · 90mins

Between his usually heavy and sinister assignments such as *Nixon*, the tremendous James Woods notched up this wry drama in which he gets

U = SUITABLE FOR ALL   **Uc** = SUITABLE FOR ALL, ESPECIALLY FOR YOUNG CHILDREN (VIDEO ONLY)   **PG** = PARENTAL GUIDANCE

cheesed off with his neighbours. What starts as a dispute over a sprinkler gets, well, out of hand. Directed by Tony Bill (one of Hollywood's most invisible movers and shakers), it's a made-for-video sitcom with an unusually impressive cast – Kate Capshaw as Woods's wife and Randy Quaid as the slobbish neighbour. Contains swearing and violence. [cc]

James Woods *Matt Coler* • Randy Quaid *Lenny Benedetti* • Kate Capshaw *Karen Coler* • Lucinda Jenney *Marci Benedetti* ■ Dir Tony Bill • Scr Barney Cohen

Next Friday ★★ 15

Comedy 1999 · US · Colour · 97mins

Rapper turned actor Ice Cube grabs writing, producing and performing credits for this follow-up to his hit US comedy *Friday*. Just as lowbrow in its laughs, but sadly lacking the original's darkish hue, *Next Friday* has Cube's street-savvy character hiding out in an affluent LA suburb where, thanks to a lottery win, his uncle is the richest man on the block. Add "comic" gangsters, a curvy señorita and a doped-up dog, and you have the recipe for some undemanding hokum.

Ice Cube *Craig Jones* • Mike Epps *Day-Day* • Justin Pierce *Roach* • John Witherspoon *Mr Jones* • Don "DC" Curry *Uncle Elroy* ■ Dir Steve Carr • Scr Ice Cube, from characters created by Ice Cube, DJ Pooh

The Next Karate Kid ★★ PG

Action drama 1994 · US · Colour · 102mins

Ralph Macchio may have departed, but at least the fourth instalment in this singularly unremarkable series could still call on the services of Pat Morita. Even he must have questioned his loyalty during shooting, however, as a sense of *déjà vu* wafted over him. Essentially, this is a case of same stunts, different sex, as future Oscar-winner Hilary Swank becomes Morita's prize pupil in the wake of her parents' death in a car crash. A few pre-prom dance lessons are the only significant departure from the tried and trusted chop-socky formula, although Michael Ironside is good value as Swank's sinister gym teacher.

Noriyuki "Pat" Morita [Pat Morita] *Mr Miyagi* • Hilary Swank *Julie Pierce* • Michael Ironside *Colonel Dugan* • Constance Towers *Louisa* • Chris Conrad *Eric* • Arsenio "Sonny" Trinidad *Abbot Monk* • Michael Cavalieri *Ned* ■ Dir Christopher Cain • Scr Mark Lee, from characters created by Robert Mark Kamen

The Next Man ★★ 15

Thriller 1976 · US · Colour · 99mins

Even in the seventies, Sean Connery was exercising an eccentric choice in film roles. This confused thriller is a long way from his best, while the plot certainly takes a lot of swallowing. A hired killer (Cornelia Sharpe) is sent to murder a high-flying Arab diplomat (Connery), but finds herself falling for his charms. However, Connery is charismatic even when sleepwalking through a role, the locations are certainly exotic, and there's even an appearance from Adolfo Celi, the villain from *Thunderball*. [cc]

Sean Connery *Khalil Abdul Muhsen* • Cornelia Sharpe *Nicole Scott* • Albert Paulsen *Hamid* • Adolfo Celi *Al Sharif* • Marco St John *Justin* ■

Dir Richard C Sarafian • Scr Mort Fine, Alan Trustman, David M Wolf, Richard C Sarafian, from a story by Martin Bregman, Alan Trustman

Next of Kin ★★ 15

Crime drama 1989 · US · Colour · 103mins

From the days when Liam Neeson was serving his Hollywood apprenticeship, this sleazy muddle of a movie at least gives him a chance to show his presence as the hillbilly brother of Chicago cop Patrick Swayze. They unite in vengeance when another brother is wiped out by the mob. British director John Irvin seems to have little idea of movie momentum or the way characters are developed. But these weaknesses may also be the fault of the banal script. Contains swearing and violence. [cc]

Patrick Swayze *Truman Gates* • Liam Neeson *Briar Gates* • Adam Baldwin *Joey Rossellini* • Helen Hunt *Jessie Gates* • Andreas Katsulas *John Isabella* • Bill Paxton *Gerald Gates* • Ben Stiller *Lawrence Isabella* ■ Dir John Irvin • Scr Michael Jenning, Jeb Stuart

Next One ★

Science-fiction fantasy drama 1984 · US · Colour · 105mins

This is a tedious fantasy with quasi-religious overtones from Greek hack director Nico Mastorakis, producer of *The Greek Tycoon*. Adrienne Barbeau and her son Jeremy Licht are living on the island of Mykonos when stranger Keir Dullea washes ashore. It turns out he's a Jesus Christ figure from the future. As well as being totally ludicrous, this is slow-paced from the start. If the Greeks don't have a word for it, they should – pathetic, dull...

Keir Dullea *Glenn/The Next One* • Adrienne Barbeau *Andrea Johnson* • Jeremy Licht *Timmy* ■ Dir/Scr Nico Mastorakis

Next Stop, Greenwich Village ★★★

Comedy crime 1976 · US · Colour · 111mins

Set in New York in 1953, aspiring actor Lenny Baker has finally escaped his momma, Shelley Winters. Or so he thinks, for Winters shows up to steal a scene and to give her son some maternal advice and clean underwear. That makes the movie funny, but the evocation of bohemian New York is also splendidly realised. Of course, it's autobiographical since writer/director Paul Mazursky lived this life himself, brushed up against Brando, Strasberg and Actors' Studio types and finally went to Hollywood to play in Stanley Kubrick's first film, *Fear and Desire*.

Lenny Baker *Larry Lapinsky* • Shelley Winters *Mrs Lapinsky* • Ellen Greene *Sarah* • Lois Smith *Anita* • Christopher Walken *Robert* • Dori Brenner *Connie* • Antonio Fargas *Bernstein* ■ Dir/Scr Paul Mazursky

Next Stop Wonderland ★★★★

Romantic comedy 1998 · US · Colour · 111mins

Terrific romantic comedy, all the more laudable for being the first feature from up-and-coming indie director Brad Anderson. Hope Davis plays Erin, a Boston night-shift nurse who swears off men after she's dumped by her

boyfriend. Her mother, though, has other ideas and places a personal ad on her daughter's behalf. The film then chronicles Erin's reluctant return to the meet market. Philip Seymour Hoffman (*Happiness*) is the best-known face among the supporting cast.

Hope Davis *Erin Castleton* • Alan Gelfant *Alan Monteiro* • Victor Argo *Frank* • Jon Benjamin *Eric* • Cara Buono *Julie* • Larry Gilliard Jr *Brett* • Philip Seymour Hoffman *Sean* ■ Dir Brad Anderson • Scr Brad Anderson, Lyn Vaus

Next Time We Love ★★★

Romantic melodrama 1936 · US · BW · 86mins

The marriage between a Broadway actress and a news correspondent suffers from a conflict in career interests. A top-billed Margaret Sullavan co-stars with James Stewart in his first important role, while Ray Milland plays a stalwart friend of the couple who nurses an unrequited love for the wife. Beautifully mounted and superbly cast, this has all the makings of a first-class movie. Under Edward H Griffith's direction, though, it just plods along, just about held together by the polish and personality of the stars.

Margaret Sullavan *Cicely Tyler* • James Stewart *Christopher Tyler* • Ray Milland *Tommy Abbott* • Grant Mitchell *Michael Jennings* • Robert McWade *Frank Carteret* ■ Dir Edward H Griffith • Scr Melville Baker, Preston Sturges, from the novel *Say Goodbye Again* by Ursula Parrott

Next to No Time ★★★ U

Comedy 1958 · UK · Colour · 92mins

Based on the Paul Gallico short story *The Enchanted Hour*, this whimsical comedy was something of a disappointment considering it marked the reunion of director Henry Cornelius with his *Genevieve* star Kenneth More. Sadly, it proved to be Cornelius's last picture before his tragically early death the same year during the production of *Law and Disorder*. More is curiously out of sorts as an engineer who uses a voyage on the *Queen Elizabeth* to persuade wealthy Roland Culver to back his latest project. His romantic interest is provided by Betsy Drake, who was then married to Cary Grant.

Kenneth More *David Webb* • Betsy Drake *Georgie Brant* • Harry Green *Saul* • Patrick Barr *Jerry* • Maureen Connell *Mary* • Bessie Love *Becky* • Reginald Beckwith *Warren* • Roland Culver *Sir Godfrey Cowan* ■ Dir Henry Cornelius • Scr Henry Cornelius, from the story *The Enchanted Hour* by Paul Gallico

The Next Voice You Hear ★★★

Drama 1950 · US · BW · 82mins

MGM's new studio head Dore Schary had made some interesting, relevant, and mildly liberal (by MGM standards) programme fillers during his tenure at RKO, and attempted to raise the thought and quality content at Metro, with varying degrees of success. This oddity, produced by Schary himself, concerns the effects on an allegorical US town when no less than the voice of God is heard over the radio. It's a fascinating idea, but action director William A Wellman handles it like a tub of molasses. Interesting today to

watch Nancy Reagan, then Davis, in among all those liberals.

James Whitmore *Joe Smith* • Nancy Davis *Mary Smith* • Gary Gray *Johnny Smith* • Lillian Bronson *Aunt Ethel* • Art Smith *Mr Brannan* • Tom D'Andrea *Hap Magee* • Jeff Corey *Freddie* ■ Dir William A Wellman • Scr Charles Schnee, from a story by George Sumner Albee

Ngati ★★★

Drama 1987 · NZ · Colour · 88mins

Made by a predominantly Maori cast and crew, this was the first feature produced anywhere by an indigenous community resident within a primarily white country. Set in 1948 and tackling the age-old theme of tradition versus progress, Barry Barclay's drama demonstrates the importance of ethnic unity by linking three distinct plot strands, concerning a dying child, an obsolete meat-freezing depot and an Australian doctor making a pilgrimage to the place of his birth. With incidents drawn from screenwriter Tama Poata's own childhood lending authentic weight, this may be rough around the edges, but the political points are soundly made.

Michael Tibble *Tione* • Oliver Jones *Ropata* • Judy McIntosh *Jenny Bennett* • Ross Girven *Greg Shaw* • Wi Kuki Kaa *Iwi, Ropata's father* ■ Dir Barry Barclay • Scr Tama Poata

Niagara ★★★★ PG

Thriller 1953 · US · Colour · 85mins

If ever a film poster could be said to have created a star's image, it was the one for this movie: Marilyn Monroe draped across said falls with a certain look in her eye and a come-on caption to match her décolletage: "A raging torrent of emotion that even nature can't control!" Director Henry Hathaway clearly knew what he had in front of his lens, with the 20th Century-Fox Technicolor seldom better deployed. The film itself is a sordid melodrama, daft and clever by turns, with a fine performance from Joseph Cotten and some interesting location shots of the falls. But this is Monroe's star-making movie and, boy, does she know it. [cc]

Marilyn Monroe *Rose Loomis* • Joseph Cotten *George Loomis* • Jean Peters *Polly Cutler* • Casey Adams [Max Showalter] *Ray Cutler* • Dennis O'Dea *Inspector Sharkey* • Richard Allen *Patrick* • Don Wilson *Mr Kettering* • Lurene Tuttle *Mrs Kettering* ■ Dir Henry Hathaway • Scr Charles Brackett, Walter Reisch, Richard Breen

Niagara Niagara ★★ 15

Romantic drama 1997 · US · Colour · 82mins

Playing a victim of Tourette syndrome, Robin Tunney won the best actress prize at Venice for her convincing outbursts and involuntary acts of violence. But there are too many echoes of such road movies as *Mad Love* to elevate Bob Gosse's film above the crowd. Travelling with the taciturn Henry Thomas, it's only a matter of time before Tunney's lack of medication renders her increasingly unpredictable and the pair turn to crime. There's a brief moment of respite as they shelter with a kindly tow-trucker, but there's only one way this earnest drama is going to end once the couple reach the Falls. [cc]

Robin Tunney *Marcy* • Henry Thomas *Seth* • Stephen Lang *Pharmacist* • John MacKay *Seth's father* • Michael Parks *Walter* ■ *Dir* Bob Gosse • *Scr* Matthew Weiss

The Nibelungen ★★★★

Silent fantasy epic 1924 · Ger · BW · 249mins

Fritz Lang's adaptation of the 13th-century German saga is a superb example of the craftsmanship at the UFA studios. Paul Richter is Siegfried, married to Margarete Schön; together the two journey from Iceland to Burgundy and become the bride of Theodor Loos. Adventures, magical and otherwise, death and revenge all ensue. The stylised sets create a mysterious beauty, especially the misty forest (constructed in a Zeppelin hangar) and the romantic castles. There is also a wonderful dragon that the hero slays early in Part I (*Siegfried*) and a massively staged battle to end Part II (*Kriemhild's Revenge*). The characters are deliberately one-dimensional as befits the epic mode.

Paul Richter *Siegfried* • Margarete Schön *Kriemhild* • Theodor Loos *King Gunther* • Hanna Ralph *Brunhild* ■ *Dir* Fritz Lang • *Scr* Fritz Lang, Thea von Harbou, from the anonymous 13th-century German poem *Das Nibelungenlied,and various Norse legends*

Nice Girl? ★★★ U

Musical comedy 1941 · US · BW · 97mins

Nice Deanna Durbin was at her most charming as a headstrong small-town girl who falls for a much older man (36-year-old Franchot Tone), a New York roué, because the boy next door (Robert Stack) is more interested in cars than in her. The situation, redolent with sexual possibilities, is rendered as innocently as possible, making the question mark in the title unnecessary. Durbin had already received her first screen kiss two years earlier from Robert Stack in *First Love*, amid much newspaper ballyhoo. Among the pleasures here are the casting of humorist Robert Benchley as Deanna's father and Walter Brennan as a lovesick postman.

Deanna Durbin *Jane Dana* • Franchot Tone *Richard Calvert* • Walter Brennan *Hector Titus* • Robert Stack *Don Webb* • Robert Benchley *Oliver Dana* • Helen Broderick *Cora Foster* • Ann Gillis *Nancy Dana* ■ *Dir* William A Seiter • *Scr* Richard Connell, Gladys Lehman, from the play by Phyllis Duganne

A Nice Girl Like Me ★

Comedy 1969 · UK · Colour · 90mins

An abysmal comedy in which Barbara Ferris goes to France and Italy and comes back pregnant both times. If you want to see it as an allegory about Britain's thwarted desire to join the Common Market, the film has significance and irony; but seen as a comedy its ability to send its audience into a deep sleep is unrivalled. As the liberated young woman, proud of her right to choose her mate, Ferris is a real pain, while the supporting cast suggests an amateur rep production.

Barbara Ferris *Candida* • Harry Andrews *Savage, caretaker* • Gladys Cooper *Aunt Mary* • Bill Hinnant *Ed* • James Villiers *Freddie* • Joyce Carey *Aunt Celia* • Christopher Guinee

Pierre ■ *Dir* Desmond Davis • *Scr* Anne Piper, Desmond Davis, from the novel *Marry at Leisure* by Anne Piper

Nice Girls Don't Explode ★★ PG

Horror spoof 1987 · US · Colour · 78mins

April (Michelle Meyrink) is a girl who can make things explode, usually whenever she gets amorous – a curse she's inherited from her mother (Barbara Harris). With its unabashed lifts from *Carrie*, this peculiar hybrid is rarely amusing and only distinguished by the presence of Harris, a delightfully quirky actress who is perhaps best remembered as the phoney medium in Alfred Hitchcock's *Family Plot*. ▭

Barbara Harris *Mom* • Michelle Meyrink *April* • William O'Leary *Andy* • Wallace Shawn *Ellen* ■ *Dir* Chuck Martinez • *Scr* Paul Harris

A Nice Little Bank That Should Be Robbed ★★ U

Crime comedy 1958 · US · BW · 87mins

Despite its whimsical title, a script by one of Fox's star writers (Sydney Boehm) and the presence of Mickey Rooney and Tom Ewell, this is a rather pathetic attempt at heist comedy. Two incompetent crooks rob a small-town bank, then buy a racehorse that is just as much of a loser as they are. Henry Levin directs with little of the flair such a subject needs, while the stars seem to know they're in a stinker.

Tom Ewell *Max Rutgers* • Mickey Rooney *Gus Harris* • Mickey Shaughnessy *Harold "Rocky" Baker* • Dina Merrill *Margie Solitaire* • Madge Kennedy *Grace Havens* ■ *Dir* Henry Levin • *Scr* Sydney Boehm, from an article by Evan Wylie

Nicholas and Alexandra ★★★ PG

Historical drama 1971 · UK · Colour · 164mins

This sumptuous, if overlong epic about the last days of the Russian Romanov dynasty, before the Bolsheviks executed Tsar Nicholas II and his family, shows the stretchmarks of too much padding, though Michael Jayston and Janet Suzman, as the Tsar and Tsarina, are a poignant reminder that a royal marriage can be both faithful and true. Adapted from the book by Robert K Massie, it overwhelms us with its detail, though Tom Baker is a lot of fun as the leering mystic Rasputin, and there are cameo appearances from Timothy West, Laurence Olivier and Michael Redgrave among others. ▭

Michael Jayston *Tsar Nicholas II* • Janet Suzman *Empress Alexandra* • Fiona Fullerton *Princess Anastasia* • Tom Baker *Rasputin* • Candace Glendenning *Princess Marie* • Lynne Frederick *Princess Tatiana* • Ania Marson *Princess Olga* • Roderic Noble *Prince Alexis* • John McEnery *Kerensky* ■ *Dir* Franklin Schaffner [Franklin J Schaffner] • *Scr* James Goldman, Edward Bond, from a non-fiction book by Robert K Massie

Nicholas' Gift ★★ PG

Drama based on a true story 1998 · It/US · Colour · 86mins

As true weepies go, this TV movie is definitely in the premier league, if only for the top quality cast. Jamie Lee Curtis and Alan Bates play tourists on

holiday in Italy whose young son is seriously wounded when they are attacked by jewel thieves. With the child given no chance of surviving, the grieving couple agree to donate his organs. Unbeknown to them, though, Italy has an appalling record in this area of medicine, and they come up against a brick wall of bureaucracy. Sentimentality runs riot. ▭

Jamie Lee Curtis *Maggie Green* • Alan Bates *Reginald Green* • Gene Wexler *Nicholas Green* • Hallie Kate Eisenberg *Eleanor Green* ■ *Dir* Robert Markowitz • *Scr* Christine Berardo

Nicholas Nickleby ★★★★ U

Drama 1947 · UK · BW · 102mins

Alberto Cavalcanti was the Brazilian-born film-maker who joined Michael Balcon's famous team of Ealing directors after helping to develop the documentary movement at the GPO Film Unit. One of his infrequent outings as a director, this was to be overshadowed by David Lean's *Oliver Twist* and *Great Expectations*, but it still deserves attention as a screen version of a Dickens fable that has relevance today. Derek Bond is hopelessly wooden as Nicholas, but Alfred Drayton is suitably loathsome as the head of Dotheboys Hall and Cedric Hardwicke is an Uncle Ralph of diabolical villainy. ▭

Derek Bond *Nicholas Nickleby* • Cedric Hardwicke *Ralph Nickleby* • Stanley Holloway *Vincent Crummles* • Alfred Drayton *Wackford Squeers* • Cyril Fletcher *Alfred Mantalini* • Bernard Miles *Newman Noggs* • Sally Ann Howes *Kate Nickleby* • Mary Merrall *Mrs Nickleby* • Sybil Thorndike *Mrs Squeers* ■ *Dir* Alberto Cavalcanti • *Scr* John Dighton, from the novel by Charles Dickens

Nicholas Nickleby ★★★ U

Animation 1985 · Ausl · Colour · 72mins

Live-action adaptations of the world's literary classics are hard enough to do well, but producing successful animated versions is almost impossible, especially on the kind of budget allocated to this project. However, this is a laudable attempt to bring Dickens to a younger audience. Naturally, the narrative has been simplified and some of the characters have been omitted. But the story of Nicholas and the unfortunate Smike remains as tragic as ever. ▭

Dir Warwick Gilbert • *Scr* Rob Mowbray, from the novel by Charles Dickens

Nick and Jane ★★★ 15

Romantic comedy 1996 · US · Colour · 88mins

This is a watchable enough romantic comedy that includes all the staple elements of the genre. Dana Wheeler-Nicholson is businesswoman Jane who, after catching her unfaithful boyfriend *in flagrante*, dives into a getaway cab driven by – you've guessed it – Nick (James McCaffrey). Chalk and cheese, the two are attracted to each other and, at the same time, repelled. Inevitably, they spend the rest of the movie getting together. ▭

Dana Wheeler-Nicholson *Jane* • James McCaffrey *Nick* • Gedde Watanabe *Enzo* • David Johansen *Carter* • George Coe *Mr*

Morgan ■ *Dir* Richard Mauro • *Scr* Richard Mauro, Neil Alumkal, Peter Quigley, from a story by Richard Mauro

Nick Carter, Master Detective ★★

Detective spy drama 1939 · US · BW · 60mins

This polished MGM B-feature was the first of three films in which Walter Pidgeon played the screen incarnation of a popular dime-novel sleuth. The topical story has Carter preventing blueprints of a new high-speed plane falling into the hands of spies. The film gives director Jacques Tourneur little chance to display the skill he would later bring to *Cat People* and *I Walked with a Zombie*, but it moves briskly and painlessly through its brief duration.

Walter Pidgeon *Nick Carter/Robert Chalmers* • Rita Johnson *Lou Farnsby* • Henry Hull *John A Keller* • Stanley C Ridges [Stanley Ridges] *Dr Frankton* • Donald Meek *Bartholomew* ■ *Dir* Jacques Tourneur • *Scr* Bertram Millhauser, from a story by Bertram Millhauser, Harold Buckley

Nick Knight ★

Police drama 1989 · US · Colour

Plodding direction, uninspired performances and a fatuous story about a cop who just happens to be a vampire make it surprising that this American TV-movie pilot ever spun off into the proposed series (called *Forever Knight*). Part comedy, part police thriller, part vampire movie, this finally falls between all stools and ends up in a heap on the floor.

Rick Springfield *Nick Knight* • Richard Fancy *Brunetti* • John Kapelos *Schanke* • Robert Harper *Dr Brittington* • Michael Nader *Lacroix* • Laura Johnson *Alyce Hunter* ■ *Dir* Farhad Mann • *Scr* James D Parriott, from a story by Barney Cohen

Nick of Time ★★ 15

Action thriller 1995 · US · Colour · 85mins

Accountant Johnny Depp is told he has 90 minutes, and six bullets, to murder the governor of California or his daughter will be killed, in director John Badham's weak suspense thriller. Supposedly playing out his shock predicament in real-time, with lots of close-ups of clocks, Badham fluffs the tension by accenting the preposterous plot contrivances rather than creating any real emotional empathy with the plight of the characters. Even the usually engaging Depp can't help this turkey fly. ▭

Johnny Depp *Gene Watson* • Christopher Walken *Mr Smith* • Courtney Chase *Lynn Watson* • Charles S Dutton *Huey* • Roma Maffia *Ms Jones* • Marsha Mason *Governor Eleanor Grant* • Peter Strauss *Brendan Grant* • Gloria Reuben *Krista Brooks* ■ *Dir* John Badham • *Scr* Patrick Sheane Duncan

Nickel & Dime ★★ PG

Action comedy 1991 · US · Colour · 91mins

Small-time heir hunter Jack Stone (C Thomas Howell) is down on his luck, but he thinks if he can just make that one big case, everything will turn around. Too bad he's been saddled with a by-the-book certified public accountant Everett (Wallace Shawn). The middle portion of the film drags terribly, but if you're a fan of Shawn's

unique acting style, you may want to check it out. ▭

C Thomas Howell *Jack Stone* • Wallace Shawn *Everett Willis* • Lise Cutter *Cathleen Markson* • Roy Brocksmith *Sammy Thornton* • Lynn Danielson *Destiny Charm* • Kathleen Freeman *Judge Lechter* ■ *Dir* Ben Moses • *Scr* Eddy Pollon, Seth Front

Nickelodeon ★★★ U
Comedy   1976 · US · Colour · 116mins

Peter Bogdanovich intended this tribute to the early days of film-making to be his masterwork, but it turned out to be one of his biggest flops. Ryan O'Neal plays the director, Burt Reynolds the handsome star, Stella Stevens a vamp and Brian Keith a fledgling movie mogul. Slaughtered by the critics, it was a commercial disaster. It's no masterpiece, but still a charmer, with nice performances and impeccable period atmosphere. ▭

Ryan O'Neal *Leo Harrigan* • Burt Reynolds *Buck Greenway* • Tatum O'Neal *Alice Forsyte* • Brian Keith *HH Cobb* • Stella Stevens *Marty Reeves* • John Ritter *Franklin Frank* • Jane Hitchcock *Kathleen Cooke* • Harry Carey Jr *Dobie* ■ *Dir* Peter Bogdanovich • *Scr* Peter Bogdanovich, WD Richter

Nico ★★ 18
Martial arts action
1988 · US · Colour · 94mins

Released in the US as *Above the Law*, this was Steven Seagal's action debut. Despite his obvious limitations as an actor, Seagal's rock-fisted martial arts style made this a massive video hit and paved the way for his lengthy career in similar biff-em-ups for the next ten years. He's a cop whose massive drug bust is suddenly stolen from under his nose by pushy FBI men for complex, and possibly criminal, reasons. Providing the actual acting talent are rejuvenated blaxploitation star Pam Grier, Sharon Stone and villainous Henry Silva. Contains swearing and violence. ▭ **DVD**

Steven Seagal *Nico Toscani* • Pam Grier *Delores Jackson* • Sharon Stone *Sara Toscani* • Daniel Faraldo *Salvano* • Henry Silva *Zagon* ■ *Dir* Andrew Davis • *Scr* Steven Pressfield, Ronald Shusett, Andrew Davis, from a story by Steven Seagal, Andrew Davis

Nico the Unicorn ★★★
Fantasy drama 1998 · Can · Colour · 90mins

A Canadian gem based on the Frank Sacks novel that allows both children and adults to share something magical. Julie Hastings (Anne Archer) moves house after her husband is killed and her son (Kevin Zegers) is crippled in the same accident. Feeling alone and somewhat bitter, the son visits a nearby circus and cajoles his mother into buying a neglected pony. When it gives birth to a unicorn, both their lives take a turn for the better.

Anne Archer *Julie Hastings* • Kevin Zegers *Billy Hastings* • Michael Ontkean *Tom Gentry* ■ *Dir* Graeme Campbell • *Scr* Frank Sacks, from his novel

Night after Night ★★
Comedy drama 1932 · US · BW · 70mins

An ex-prizefighter (George Raft), looking to make something of his life, buys a ritzy nightclub, mingles with the smart set and falls in love with a socialite. Constance Cummings and Alison Skipworth co-star in this small-scale drama, which is long on Prohibition-era atmosphere but short on interesting content. The film is remembered, however, for promoting Raft to leading man status, and is unforgettable for marking the screen debut of Mae West. "Goodness, what diamonds!" remarks a hat-check girl as she makes her entrance. "Goodness had nothing to do with it, dearie," Mae replies.

George Raft *Joe Anton* • Constance Cummings *Jerry Healy* • Wynne Gibson *Iris Dawn* • Mae West *Maudie Triplett* • Alison Skipworth *Mrs Mabel Jellyman* ■ *Dir* Archie Mayo • *Scr* Vincent Lawrence, Kathryn Scola, Mae West, from the novel *Single Night* by Louis Bromfield

Night and Day ★★★ U
Musical biography
1946 · US · Colour · 122mins

Mawkish yet mesmerising Warner Bros musical biopic, whose casting of Cary Grant as Cole Porter completely eliminated any suggestion of Porter's homosexuality and reduced his tragic riding accident (Porter eventually lost a leg) to Grant using a walking stick to get around. But the truth doesn't matter much in this kind of movie, and director Michael Curtiz does a smashing job, helped by ravishing Technicolor and a marvellous cast including Mary Martin performing *My Heart Belongs to Daddy*.

Cary Grant *Cole Porter* • Alexis Smith *Linda Lee Porter* • Monty Woolley • Ginny Simms *Carole Hill* • Jane Wyman *Gracie Harris* • Eve Arden *Gabrielle* • Victor Francen *Anatole Giron* • Alan Hale *Leon Dowling* • Dorothy Malone *Nancy* • Tom D'Andrea *Bernie* ■ *Dir* Michael Curtiz • *Scr* Charles Hoffman, Leo Townsend, William Bowers, from a biography by Jack Moffit

Night and Day ★★★★ 15
Romantic drama
1991 · Bel/Fr/Swi · Colour · 95mins

Bearing the influence of François Truffaut (to whom the film is dedicated), Chantal Akerman's delicately-played morality tale continues her fascination with the way emotion reveals itself through the banalities of everyday life. Radiant in the atmospheric nocturnal photography, Guilaine Londez gives a disarmingly truthful performance as the provincial girl whose love for cabby Thomas Langmann is supplanted by a passion for François Négret, who drives the same taxi on the day shift. Thanks to Akerman's genuine interest in her characters, the dialogue is as authentic as the resolution. In French with English subtitles.

Guilaine Londez *Julie* • Thomas Langmann *Jack* • François Négret *Joseph* • Nicole Colchat *Jack's mother* • Pierre Laroche *Jack's father* ■ *Dir* Chantal Akerman • *Scr* Chantal Akerman, Pascal Bonitzer

Night and the City ★★★★
Crime drama 1950 · UK/US · BW · 95mins

Here's a really interesting crime drama, a genuine 20th Century-Fox *film noir* set and filmed entirely in London, with imported American stars and a British supporting cast. Surprisingly, it works, largely because of star Richard Widmark's brilliant, desperate portrayal of a hustler on the edge, and skilled director Jules Dassin's cleverly atmospheric use of London locations, plus expertly controlled pacing. The plot hangs on a wrestling fix, and is both adult and original. Especially impressive is the gross Francis L Sullivan as a sweaty nightclub owner, and faces like Googie Withers and Herbert Lom add authenticity.

Richard Widmark *Harry Fabian* • Gene Tierney *Mary Bristol* • Googie Withers *Helen Nosseross* • Hugh Marlowe *Adam Dunn* • Francis L Sullivan *Phil Nosseross* • Herbert Lom *Kristo* • Stanley Zbyszko [Stanislaus Zbyszko] *Gregorius* • Mike Mazurki *Strangler* ■ *Dir* Jules Dassin • *Scr* Jo Eisinger, from the novel by Gerald Kersh

Night and the City ★★★ 15
Drama 1992 · US · Colour · 103mins

A respectful update of Jules Dassin's 1950 classic, with the setting switched from London to New York. Robert De Niro takes the Richard Widmark role of the small-time promoter desperately trying to hustle his way to the big time, while Jessica Lange is the woman who gets too close to his dreams. Irwin Winkler's direction is functional, but he is smart enough to surround himself with an impressive array of talent. The two stars are joined by a wonderful supporting cast (comedian Alan King in particular), while the deft script comes from Richard Price (*Sea of Love*). Contains violence and swearing. ▭

Robert De Niro *Harry Fabian* • Jessica Lange *Helen* • Cliff Gorman *Phil* • Alan King *"Boom Boom" Grossman* • Jack Warden *Al Grossman* • Eli Wallach *Peck* • Barry Primus *Tommy Tessler* • Gene Kirkwood *Resnick* • Pedro Sanchez *Cuda Sanchez* ■ *Dir* Irwin Winkler • *Scr* Richard Price, from the 1950 film

A Night at the Opera ★★★★★ U
Comedy 1935 · US · BW · 87mins

At Paramount, the Marx Brothers had specialised in zany, freewheeling comedies that owed much to the anarchic antics of their vaudeville shows. This first outing for MGM was also honed on the stage, but producer Irving Thalberg used the three-week pre-production tour to chip away at the rough edges that made their humour so unique. Nevertheless, this remained Groucho's favourite picture and there are several classic routines to atone for the ghastly interludes featuring soppy lovers Allan Jones and Kitty Carlisle, the best being Groucho's schmoozing of Margaret Dumont, the Groucho-Chico contract sketch and the slapstick ruination of *Il Trovatore*. ▭

Groucho Marx *Otis B Driftwood* • Chico Marx *Fiorello* • Harpo Marx *Tomasso* • Margaret Dumont *Mrs Claypool* • Allan Jones *Riccardo Baroni* • Kitty Carlisle *Rosa Castaldi* • Siegfried "Sig" Rumann [Sig Ruman] *Herman Gottlieb* ■ *Dir* Sam Wood • *Scr* George S Kaufman, Morrie Ryskind, Al Boasberg, Bert Kalmar, Harry Ruby, from a story by James Kevin McGuinness

A Night at the Roxbury ★ 15
Comedy 1998 · US · Colour · 81mins

Beware movies based on comedy sketches as, with very few exceptions (*Wayne's World* being one), they are rarely very good. This tale, based on a *Saturday Night Live* skit about two dumber-than-dumb, sexist brothers trying to get into the coolest clubs in LA, is utterly devoid of any redeeming features. The actors (Will Ferrell, Chris Kattan) are irritating, the script is humourless, and at under an hour-and-a-half it is still 80 minutes too long. Contains sexual references and some swearing. ▭

Will Ferrell *Steve Butabi* • Chris Kattan *Doug Butabi* • Richard Grieco • Loni Anderson *Barbara Butabi* • Dan Hedaya *Kameh! Butabi* ■ *Dir* John Fortenberry • *Scr* Steven Koren, Will Ferrell, Chris Kattan

Night Beat ★★
Crime drama 1948 · UK · BW · 102mins

A reliably bad British crime drama set in an unreal Soho underworld of spivs and nightclubs. It's a compendium of clichés as two army friends end up on opposite sides of the law – one a policeman, the other a black-market racketeer who marries a good girl but dallies with a glamorous cabaret singer. Particularly enjoyable are Maxwell Reed as the swaggering villain, Christine Norden as the vicious blonde vamp, and Michael Medwin in a spot of light relief as an indignant pickpocket. Benjamin Frankel's score is better than the film deserves.

Maxwell Reed *Felix Fenton* • Ronald Howard *Andy Kendall* • Anne Crawford *Julie Kendall* • Christine Norden *Jackie* • Michael Medwin *Spider* ■ *Dir* Harold Huth • *Scr* Guy Morgan, TJ Morrison, Robert Westerby, Roland Pertwee, from a story by Guy Morgan

The Night Before ★ 15
Comedy 1988 · US · Colour · 86mins

Keanu Reeves's first starring vehicle was understandably shelved for two years before its minuscule release. The future star of *The Matrix* shows no charisma as he stumbles through this *After Hours* for the adolescent crowd, playing a prom-bound teenager who retraces his steps after he wakes up in an alley with no car, no date and no memory of how he got there. The surreal touches are self-conscious and distracting and do not blend well with the movie's comic tone. ▭

Keanu Reeves *Winston Connelly* • Lori Loughlin *Tara Mitchell* • Theresa Saldana *Rhonda* • Trinidad Silva *Tito* • Suzanne Snyder *Lisa* • Morgan Lofting *Mom* • Gwil Richards *Dad* ■ *Dir* Thom Eberhardt • *Scr* Gregory Scherick, Thom Eberhardt, from a story by Gregory Scherick

Night Boat to Dublin ★★
Second World War spy drama
1946 · UK · BW · 91mins

This B-thriller is worth seeing for its treatment of a topical theme – atomic weapons – and the performance of Robert Newton, then on the cusp of stardom. (He was shortly to play a chilling Bill Sikes in David Lean's *Oliver Twist*.) Newton plays a British secret service agent who travels to Dublin, where a Swedish scientist is giving atomic secrets to the Nazis. Hitchcock also realised the dramatic potential of the A-bomb in *Notorious*, but this isn't in the same league.

Robert Newton *Captain David Grant* • Raymond Lovell *Paul Faber* • Guy Middleton *Captain Tony Hunter* • Muriel Pavlow *Marion*

Decker • Herbert Lom *Keitel* • John Ruddock *Bowman* • Martin Miller *Professor Hansen* • Marius Goring *Frederick Jannings* ■ *Dir* Lawrence Huntington • *Scr* Robert Hall, Lawrence Huntington

The Night Caller ★★

Science-fiction thriller
1965 · UK · BW · 83mins

You are an alien sent to Earth to find women to help re-populate your planet. How would you go about recruiting them? A wanted advert in *Bikini Girl* magazine, of course. That is the premise behind this cheerful piece of nonsense from cheapie specialist John Gilling. Playing along with it are John Saxon as the earnest American scientist who is called in to investigate the arrival of a mysterious pod, and Alfred Burke as the copper unable to explain a spate of disappearances of young women. The undoubted highlight is the TV interview spoof in which Warren Mitchell plays an anxious parent discussing the generation gap.

John Saxon *Jack Costain* • Maurice Denham *Professor Morley* • Patricia Haines *Ann Barlow* • Alfred Burke *Superintendent Hartley* • Jack Carson *Major* • Jack Watson *Sergeant Hawkins* • Warren Mitchell *Lilburn* ■ *Dir* John Gilling • *Scr* Jim O'Connolly, from the novel *The Night Callers* by Frank Crisp

The Night Caller ★★ 18

Thriller
1998 · US · Colour · 89mins

Beth (Tracy Nelson) is a loser who has delusions that a radio psychologist, Dr Lindsay Roland (Shanna Reed), is talking directly to her. Beth subsequently acquires a new job as Lindsay's babysitter and keeps it by killing anyone who threatens her happiness. While the premise is derivative and the treatment surprisingly violent, Nelson does an effective job at keeping the demented Beth sympathetic. ▭

Shanna Reed *Dr Lindsay Roland* • Tracy Nelson *Beth Needham* • Mary Crosby *Nikki Rogers* • Cyndi Pass *Marge Hampton* • Eve Sigall *Mama* • Howard Miller *Lee Dixon* ■ *Dir* Robert Malenfant • *Scr* Mark Bomback, Frank Rehwaldt, from a story by George Saunders

Night Comes Too Soon ★★

Supernatural drama 1949 · UK · BW · 57mins

While Valentine Dyall became famous for radio shows like *The Man in Black* and *Appointment with Fear*, he never quite made his mark on the big screen. However, his mellifluous tones add considerably to this tricksy chiller, in which he plays a "paranormalist" called in by newlyweds to remove the curse from their dream home. With only meagre resources to play with, most of the eerie effects are achieved by lighting changes and good old-fashioned dissolves. That said, the ghostly visions are effective and the ending is wonderfully corny.

Valentine Dyall *Dr Clinton* • Anne Howard *Phyllis* • Alec Faversham *John* • Beatrice Marsden *Mrs Paxton* • Howard Douglas • Anthony Baird *Lionel Waddell* • Arthur Brander • Frank Dunlop ■ *Dir* Denis Kavanagh • *Scr* Pat Dixon, from the play *The Haunted and the Haunters* by Lord Lytton [Lord Edward George Bulwer-Lytton]

Night Crossing ★★★ PG

Adventure based on a true story
1981 · UK/US · Colour · 102mins

An attempt to impose Disney cuteness on a true Cold War story about two East German families who float perilously over the border to western life, liberty and the pursuit of capitalism in a home-made balloon. Children make it a brat-pack escape, as you'd expect from a Disney movie, but director Delbert Mann conveys little of the truth of what must have been a strange and terrifying business. John Hurt, Jane Alexander and Beau Bridges give their all, but ultimately it is so much hot air. ▭

John Hurt *Peter Strelzyk* • Jane Alexander *Doris Strelzyk* • Doug McKeon *Frank Strelzyk* • Keith McKeon *Fitscher Strelzyk* • Beau Bridges *Gunter Wetzel* • Glynnis O'Connor *Petra Wetzel* ■ *Dir* Delbert Mann • *Scr* John McGreevey

Night Eyes ★★ 18

Erotic thriller 1990 · US · Colour · 94mins

Andrew Stevens has carved himself a nice little niche in that reliable video genre the erotic thriller, both in front of and behind the camera. This is the first in what has turned out to be a very profitable franchise, already spawning three very similar sequels. Stevens plays a security guard called in to protect Tanya Roberts, but whose voyeuristic tendencies get the better of him. The sex and thrills are strictly soft-core, the performances little more than adequate. Contains violence, swearing and nudity. ▭

Andrew Stevens *Will* • Tanya Roberts *Nikki* • Cooper Huckabee *Ernie* • Veronica Henson-Phillips *Lauretta* • Stephen Meadows *Michael Vincent* • Karen Elise Baldwin *Ellen* • Warwick Sims *Brian Walker* ■ *Dir* Jag Mundhra • *Scr* Tom Citrano, Andrew Stevens

Night Falls on Manhattan ★★ 15

Crime drama 1997 · US · Colour · 108mins

A big-time drug dealer and cop killer is sent down, and rookie prosecutor Andy Garcia finds himself elected New York's chief law enforcement officer. Then a skeleton is hauled out of the river, opening a hornet's nest of corruption. Despite some good performances this is really just another drive around the block for Sidney Lumet: he not only lets the pace slacken, but also sanctions a corny romance between Garcia and legal rival Lena Olin that turns the gritty realism into soapy melodrama. ▭

Andy Garcia *Sean Casey* • Richard Dreyfuss *Sam Vigoda* • Lena Olin *Peggy Lindstrom* • Ian Holm *Liam Casey* • James Gandolfini *Joey Allegretto* ■ *Dir* Sidney Lumet • *Scr* Sidney Lumet, from the novel *Tainted Evidence* by Robert Daley

Night Fire ★★ 18

Erotic thriller 1994 · US · Colour · 91mins

Video favourite Shannon Tweed stars as a rich businesswoman whose plans for a lovey-dovey weekend with her husband are thwarted by the arrival of an odd couple at their remote country home. The plot is full of the sort of twists and turns – some sexy, some murderous – that you can see several

miles away without binoculars. It's entertaining all the same, in a best-watched-on-video sort of way. ▭

Shannon Tweed *Lydia* • John Laughlin *Barry* • Rochelle Swanson *Gwen* • Martin Hewitt *Cal* • Alma Beltran *Maria* ■ *Dir* Mike Sedan, Eric Davies • *Scr* Catherine Tavel, Helen Haxton, from a story by Mike Sedan

Night Flight ★★

Adventure 1933 · US · BW · 84mins

MGM wheeled out a lot of stars for this flying yarn – two Barrymores, Clark Gable, Robert Montgomery and two fine leading ladies, Myrna Loy and Helen Hayes. The story is about the setting up of a company that delivers mail across the high Andes. In the air, it's all turbulence, fog and mountain peaks; on the ground, it's all macho posturing and romantic clinches. The box-office success of the movie spawned a whole series of imitators, including RKO's *Flight from Glory* and, best of all, Howard Hawks's *Only Angels Have Wings*.

John Barrymore *Riviere* • Helen Hayes *Mme Fabian* • Clark Gable *Jules* • Lionel Barrymore *Robineau* • Robert Montgomery *Auguste Pellerin* • Myrna Loy *Brazilian pilot's wife* ■ *Dir* Clarence Brown • *Scr* Oliver HP Garrett, from the story by Antoine de Saint-Exupéry

A Night Full of Rain ★★

Drama 1978 · It/US · Colour · 104mins

The first in a four-picture deal with Warners, *The End of the World in Our Usual Bed in a Night Full of Rain* – to give it its full title – turned out to be the only film controversial Italian director Lina Wertmuller made in the States. Despite working once more with her favourite star, Giancarlo Giannini, Wertmuller lets herself be weighed down by polemic in this talkative confrontation between old-world machismo and self-assertive feminism. The observations are worth making, but the flashback structure does little to make things more accessible, as communist journalist Giannini's ten-year marriage to photographer Candice Bergen descends into a full-scale slanging match. Contains swearing.

Giancarlo Giannini *Paolo* • Candice Bergen *Lizzy* • Anne Byrne *Friend* • Flora Carabella *Friend* • Mario Scarpeta *Friend* ■ *Dir/Scr* Lina Wertmuller

Night Gallery ★★★

Supernatural horror
1969 · US · Colour · 95mins

The clever and inventive three-part pilot anthology that launched Rod Serling's cult television series is now more famous for containing the first directorial assignment of Steven Spielberg. In his segment, blind Joan Crawford buys a beggar's eyes for an operation to regain her sight, but when she does it's during a New York blackout. The other two episodes feature Roddy McDowall speeding along the death of an uncle to inherit his money, and Nazi war criminal Richard Kiley haunted by a museum painting. Good creepy fun, introduced by Serling in his art gallery.

Joan Crawford *Claudia Menlo* • Ossie Davis *Osmond Portifoy* • Richard Kiley *Joseph Strobe* • Roddy McDowall *Jeremy* • Barry Sullivan

Doctor Frank Hetherton • Tom Bosley *Resnick* • Sam Jaffe *Bleum* • George Macready *Hendricks* ■ *Dir* Boris Sagal, Steven Spielberg, Barry Shear • *Scr* Rod Serling

Night Game ★★ 18

Thriller 1989 · US · Colour · 91mins

Over-familiar story of a Texas police chief trying to track down a serial lady-killer before he can claim his next victim. The reliable Roy Scheider and Karen Young deliver good performances, but their efforts are wasted on mediocre material. It's sad to think that, back in the seventies, Scheider was riding high in such hits as *The French Connection, Jaws* and *Klute*. He's never come close to recapturing that success. ▭

Roy Scheider *Seaver* • Karen Young *Roxy* • Richard Bradford *Nelson* • Carlin Glynn *Alma* ■ *Dir* Peter Masterson • *Scr* Spencer Eastman, Anthony Palmer, from a story by Spencer Eastman

Night Games ★ 18

Erotic thriller 1979 · US · Colour · 101mins

Risible soft-core erotica from Roger Vadim, the man who "discovered", then married Brigitte Bardot and Jane Fonda (though not at the same time). Vadim's protégée, Cindy Pickett, isn't bad in her feature debut, playing a Beverly Hills housewife terrified of sexual contact due to a traumatic childhood incident. When she's reduced to having sex with a man dressed as a bird, though, it's fatally unclear whether Vadim is being mocking or serious. ▭

Cindy Pickett *Valerie St John* • Joanna Cassidy *Julie Miller* • Barry Primus *Jason St John* • Paul Jenkins *Sean Daniels* • Gene Davis *Timothy* • Juliet Fabriga *Alicia* • Clem Parsons *Jun* • Mark Hanks *"The Phantom"* ■ *Dir* Roger Vadim • *Scr* Anton Diether, Clarke Reynolds, from a story by Barth Jules Sussman, Anton Diether

Night Has a Thousand Eyes ★★

Mystery 1948 · US · BW · 81mins

The assumption that a vaudeville show clairvoyant (Edward G Robinson) is a fake turns out to be unfounded when he proves he really can foretell the future. John Farrow directs this minor entry in Robinson's filmography, which bears a strong resemblance to the 1934 Claude Rains film, *The Clairvoyant*. Efficiently made but rather bland entertainment, it co-stars Gail Russell, John Lund, Virginia Bruce and William Demarest.

Edward G Robinson *John Triton* • Gail Russell *Jean Courtland* • John Lund *Elliott Carson* • Virginia Bruce *Jenny* • William Demarest *Lt Shawn* • Richard Webb *Peter Vinson* ■ *Dir* John Farrow • *Scr* Barre Lyndon, Jonathan Latimer, from a novel by Cornell Woolrich

The Night Has Eyes ★★

Thriller 1942 · UK · BW · 79mins

The saturnine side of James Mason's screen persona was exploited to the full in this studio-bound melodrama, set on the Yorkshire moors. Mason plays a reclusive composer and wounded veteran of the Spanish Civil War who is subject to fits. He could well be a threat to Joyce Howard, one

U = SUITABLE FOR ALL   **Uc** = SUITABLE FOR ALL, ESPECIALLY FOR YOUNG CHILDREN (VIDEO ONLY)   **PG** = PARENTAL GUIDANCE

of two female teachers taking refuge from a storm. On the other hand, there's something not quite right about Wilfrid Lawson and Mary Clare, the couple who run the house... Director Leslie Arliss develops the sinister atmosphere with some skill.

James Mason *Stephen Deremid* • Joyce Howard *Marian Ives* • Wilfrid Lawson *Sturrock* • Mary Clare *Mrs Ranger* • Tucker McGuire *Doris* • John Fernald *Dr Barry Randall* ◾ *Dir* Leslie Arliss • *Scr* John Argyle, Leslie Arliss, Alan Kennington, from a story by Alan Kennington

The Night Holds Terror ★★

Crime drama   1955 · US · BW · 85mins

Watch this and you'll spend the night checking all locks and doors three times over. One of those post-*film noir* movies where everything is shadow and promised substance, but you get little more than a lot of characters with their mouths hanging open and jauntily angled fedoras. Here, a family is held to ransom by crooks John Cassavetes (in only his second minor role), Vince Edwards and David Cross. Quite exciting for the first 20 minutes, and immensely tedious thereafter.

Jack Kelly *Gene Courtier* • Hildy Parks *Doris Courtier* • Vince Edwards *Victor Gosset* • John Cassavetes *Robert Batsford* • David Cross *Luther Logan* • Edward Marr [Eddie Marr] *Captain Cole* ◾ *Dir* Andrew Stone [Andrew L Stone] • *Scr* Andrew Stone

Night Hunter ★★ 🔞

Martial arts horror
1995 · US · Colour · 90mins

One-time world kickboxing champion Don ''The Dragon'' Wilson has – since hanging up his feet – become something of a cult video action star, but he's never quite managed to cross over into mainstream pictures in the same way as Jean-Claude Van Damme. Here he plays the last in a long line of vampire hunters (a sort of Rambo meets Professor Van Helsing) whose attempt to avenge his family's death ends up with him being chased around modern-day Los Angeles by both bloodsuckers and police.

Don ''The Dragon'' Wilson *Jack Cutter* • Melanie Smith *Raimy Baker* • Nicholas Guest *Bruno Fischer* ◾ *Dir* Rick Jacobson • *Scr* William C Martell

A Night in Casablanca
★★★ 🆄

Comedy   1946 · US · BW · 84mins

While it has none of the sustained genius of their earlier outings, the Marx Brothers' penultimate picture has enough moments of inspired lunacy to merit a place on most viewers' ''must see'' lists. Although freed from the constraints placed upon them by MGM, the trio (ending a five-year screen exile) are forced to play second fiddle to a contrived plot about spies and buried treasure, which was supposed to invite cheeky comparisons with the classic Bogart/Bergman drama. Groucho goes into one-liner overdrive to compensate for the absence of Margaret Dumont, but Harpo has the best gag in the opening minutes. 📼

Groucho Marx *Ronald Kornblow* • Harpo Marx *Rusty* • Chico Marx *Corbaccio* • Lisette Verea *Beatrice Reiner* • Charles Drake *Pierre* • Lois

Collier *Annette* • Dan Seymour *Captain Brizzard* • Sig Rumann [Sig Ruman] *Count Pfefferman* ◾ *Dir* Archie Mayo • *Scr* Joseph Fields, Roland Kibbee

A Night in Havana: Dizzy
Gillespie in Cuba ★★★

Music documentary
1988 · US · Colour · 84mins

An intriguing account of the great jazz trumpeter's 1985 tour of Cuba, a country which had particular relevence to him since for 40 years he had been pioneering the use of Afro-Cuban rhythms within American music. Educational as well as entertaining, the affable bebopper is shown performing full-length versions of *A Night in Tunisia* and *Manteca*, cracking jokes, relating anecdotes and offering illuminating historical and musical analyses of Cuban rhythms.

Dizzy Gillespie • Allen Honigberg *Interviewer* ◾ *Dir* John Holland

A Night in Heaven ★★ 🔞

Romantic drama   1983 · US · Colour · 79mins

College professor Lesley Ann Warren goes to a male strip club and finds that the featured dancer is Christopher Atkins (*The Blue Lagoon*), who happens to be one of her more problematical students. A contrived May-December romantic drama, this coasts along thanks mainly to Warren's captivating turn and ''Heaven'', the Chippendales-style locale. Watch out for Andy Garcia in his first screen role. 📼

Christopher Atkins *Rick* • Lesley Ann Warren *Faye* • Robert Logan *Whitney* • Deborah Rush *Patsy* • Deney Terrio *Tony* • Sandra Beall *Slick* • Alix Elias *Shirley* • Carrie Snodgress *Mrs Johnson* • Amy Levine *Eve* • Andy Garcia *TJ* ◾ *Dir* John G Avildsen • *Scr* Joan Tewkesbury

A Night in the Life of
Jimmy Reardon ★★★ 🔞

Drama   1988 · US · Colour · 88mins

River Phoenix strayed from his usual thoughtful pubescent role to play a romeo teenager with a gravity-defying hairdo in this hit-and-miss comedy. Although Phoenix is as engaging as he was in *Running on Empty* and *Stand by Me*, he seems ill at ease playing such an extrovert character. Nonetheless, the movie has its moments, notably Phoenix's assignations with older woman Ann Magnuson. Contains swearing. 📼

River Phoenix *Jimmy Reardon* • Meredith Salenger *Lisa* • Matthew L Perry [Matthew Perry] *Fred* • Ione Skye *Denise* • Ann Magnuson *Joyce* • Louanne *Suzie* • Paul Koslo *Mr Reardon* • Jane Hallaren *Mrs Reardon* ◾ *Dir* William Richert • *Scr* William Richert, from his novel *Aren't You Even Gonna Kiss Me Goodbye?*

Night Is My Future ★★★

Drama   1948 · Swe · BW · 87mins

Adapted by Dagmar Edqvist from her own novel, Ingmar Bergman's fourth feature was the first to turn a profit. His mentor, producer Lorens Marmstedt, insisted he adhered closely to the storyline, even though it was awash with sentimentality: from the fact that Birger Malmsten is blinded while trying to rescue a puppy

from a firing range, to the final reunion with a radiantly waifish Mai Zetterling. However, there's a persuasive poetic realism about the picture, with the hallucinatory dream sequence allowing Bergman to break out of the film's melodramatic straitjacket. A Swedish language film.

Mai Zetterling *Ingrid Olofsdotter* • Birger Malmsten *Bengt* • Bengt Eklund *Ebbe* ◾ *Dir* Ingmar Bergman • *Scr* Dagmar Edqvist, from her novel

The Night Is Young ★★★ 🔞

Romantic thriller 1986 · Fr · Colour · 114mins

For all his visual flair, director Léos Carax's storytelling skills leave a lot to be desired. There's a carelessly pulpy quality about this futuristic thriller, in which Denis Lavant's commitment to the theft of a serum that cures a fatal disease afflicting only the romantically insincere is diminished by his growing obsession with Juliette Binoche, the mistress of fellow gang member, Michel Piccoli. Away from the plot's comic-book sensibilities, however, the compositions irresistibly recall the pictorial genius of film-makers as different as Fritz Lang and Jean-Luc Godard. A fascinating yet frustrating experience. In French with English subtitles. 📼

Denis Lavant *Alex* • Juliette Binoche *Anna* • Michel Piccoli *Marc* • Hans Meyer *Hans* • Julie Delpy *Lise* • Carroll Brooks *The American* • Hugo Pratt *Boris* • Serge Reggiani *Charlie* ◾ *Dir/Scr* Léos Carax

Night Mail ★★★★★ 🆄

Documentary   1936 · UK · BW · 23mins

The jewel of British cinema in the thirties was the documentary movement presided over by John Grierson (the man who coined the term ''documentary'' for factual films). Grierson and Stuart Legg provide the commentary for this evocative short, directed by Harry Watt and Basil Wright for the GPO Film Unit. Never have the dry statistics about the operation of the London-Glasgow mail train been presented with such flair. The beautiful shots of steaming engines, Benjamin Britten's pulsing score and WH Auden's adroit verses combine to form a film poem that delights both the ear and the eye.

Dir Harry Watt, Basil Wright • *Scr* WH Auden, Basil Wright, Harry Watt

'Night, Mother ★★★★ 🔞

Drama   1986 · US · Colour · 92mins

Sissy Spacek, who won an Oscar six years earlier for her performance in *Coal Miner's Daughter*, tells her mother she's going to commit suicide in this drama based on Marsha Norman's Pulitzer Prize-winning play. Both Spacek and Anne Bancroft (an Academy Award-winner herself for *The Miracle Worker*) are excellent, and though this character-driven piece sometimes feels a bit stagey, the performances are mesmerising enough to keep you riveted. 📼

Sissy Spacek *Jessie Cates* • Anne Bancroft *Thelma Cates* • Ed Berke *Dawson Cates* • Carol Robbins *Loretta Cates* • Jennifer Roosendahl *Melodie Cates* • Michael Kenworthy *Kenny Cates* ◾ *Dir* Tom Moore • *Scr* Marsha Norman, from her play

Night Moves ★★★★ 🔞

Mystery thriller 1975 · US · Colour · 95mins

Despite its title, this brilliantly self-conscious gumshoe movie by director Arthur Penn from Alan Sharp's sparkling script lights up a time of post-Watergate confusion, when bloodshot private eye Gene Hackman seeks a client's lost daughter and his own lost honour. It's a bleak, pointless quest, encapsulated by the final shot of a boat going round in meaningless circles, but there's a sour wit that can mock other directors. An enigmatic masterpiece whose pleasures are allusive and cinematic. Contains some violence and swearing. 📼

Gene Hackman *Harry Moseby* • Susan Clark *Ellen* • Jennifer Warren *Paula* • Edward Binns *Ziegler* • James Woods *Quentin* • Melanie Griffith *Delly Grastner* • Harris Yulin *Marty Heller* • Kenneth Mars *Nick* ◾ *Dir* Arthur Penn • *Scr* Alan Sharp

Night Must Fall ★★★★

Thriller   1937 · US · BW · 116mins

Emlyn Williams's famous shocker has had many incarnations, but this MGM version is very good indeed, largely due to the casting against type of the totally plausible Robert Montgomery as the suspected killer, and a marvellous performance from Rosalind Russell as the woman who slowly but surely discovers the killer's identity for herself. Several of the cast MGM employed had played their parts on stage in both London and New York, and the film is especially notable for the appearance of May Whitty, in one of her first talking roles, as a foolish, isolated old woman.

Robert Montgomery *Danny* • Rosalind Russell *Olivia* • May Whitty [Dame May Whitty] *Mrs Bransom* • Alan Marshal *Justin* • Merle Tottenham *Dora* • Kathleen Harrison *Mrs Terence* ◾ *Dir* Richard Thorpe • *Scr* John van Druten, from the play by Emlyn Williams

Night Must Fall ★★★

Thriller   1964 · UK · BW · 104mins

Emlyn Williams's popular, if shakily plotted, stage thriller was originally filmed by Richard Thorpe in 1937, with Robert Montgomery and Rosalind Russell in the leads. In this flashy remake, Susan Hampshire steps into the shoes of the woman who gradually comes to realise who is responsible for a series of countryside killings. Director Karel Reisz's attempts to explore the murderer's mental instability through camera movements and cross-cuts (recalling the vigorous unpredictability of the French New Wave) are undone by the staginess of the dialogue. Yet Freddie Francis's photography is highly atmospheric and Albert Finney's performance is occasionally electrifying.

Albert Finney *Danny* • Susan Hampshire *Olivia* • Mona Washbourne *Mrs Bramson* • Sheila Hancock *Dora* • Michael Medwin *Derek* • Joe Gladwin *Dodge* ◾ *Dir* Karel Reisz • *Scr* Clive Exton, from the play by Emlyn Williams

The Night My Number
Came Up ★★★

Drama   1955 · UK · BW · 94mins

This intriguing film bears more than a passing resemblance to the James

Stewart airplane melodrama *No Highway*. Similarly held together by a first-rate central performance, the film features Michael Redgrave intent on grounding his flight to Tokyo as events alarmingly begin to resemble those in one of his nightmares. Exploring with a keen intelligence the coincidences and implausibilities generated by fear, RC Sherriff's tense screenplay is full of unsympathetic, self-obsessed characters, played to a nicety by a model supporting cast.

Michael Redgrave *Air Marshal John Hardie* • Sheila Sim *Mary Campbell* • Alexander Knox *Owen Robertson* • Denholm Elliott *Flight Lieutenant McKenzie* • Ursula Jeans *Mrs Robertson* • Michael Hordern *Commander Lindsay* • Ralph Truman *Lord Wainwright* ■ *Dir* Leslie Norman • *Scr* RC Sherriff, from an article by Air Marshal Sir Victor Goddard

Night Nurse ★★★
Crime drama   1931 · US · BW · 72mins

A fast-moving melodrama with a great cast headed by Barbara Stanwyck and Joan Blondell, who were accused by contemporary critics of boosting the film's audiences by spending an inordinate amount of screen time dressing and undressing. Ben Lyon is the co-star, but the screen is well and truly stolen by a young actor in the supporting role of sadistic chauffeur: a clean-shaven Clark Gable on the road to stardom. This kind of tough, sexy drama vanished with the coming of the restrictive Hays Code, and it's always interesting to see what Hollywood could get away with before it was introduced.

Barbara Stanwyck *Lora Hart* • Ben Lyon *Mortie* • Joan Blondell *Maloney* • Charles Winninger *Dr Arthur Bell* • Charlotte Merriam *Mrs Ritchey* • Edward Nugent *Eagan* • Blanche Frederici *Mrs Maxwell* ■ *Dir* William A Wellman • *Scr* Oliver HP Garrett, Charles Kenyon, from the novel by Dora Macy [Grace Perkins Oursler]

The Night of Counting the Years ★★★★
Historical drama
1969 · Egy · Colour · 102mins

Recalling the actual theft by members of the Horrabat tribe of artefacts from a tomb in Thebes in 1881, this stunningly photographed picture considers whether an impoverished people should sell its antiquities to survive or resist the export of its heritage. Shadi Abdelsalam's background in art direction is evident in his hypnotic selection of deep-focus shots and his control of light and contrasting colours. Yet he also manages to keep this slow-moving story absorbing throughout. In Arabic with English subtitles.

Ahmed Marei *Wanniss* • Zouzou El Hakim *Mother* • Ahmad Hegazi *Brother* • Nadia Loutfy *Zeena* • Gaby Karraz *Maspero* ■ *Dir/Scr* Shadi Abdelsalam

Night of Courage ★★★ 15
Drama   1987 · US · Colour · 92mins

A toughish made-for-TV drama about a Hispanic school pupil (David Hernandez) who is supposedly denied refuge by an elderly man (Barnard Hughes) before being murdered in a racial attack. Daniel Hugh-Kelly plays the school teacher who is determined

to find out what really happened. Originally a play, the drama has been effectively opened out on grim Chicago locations and also features a rare TV-movie role for Hollywood veteran Geraldine Fitzgerald as Hughes's terminally ill wife. 🎞

Barnard Hughes *Abner Abelsen* • Daniel Hugh-Kelly *Paul Forrest* • David Hernandez *Angel Ortiz* • Geraldine Fitzgerald *Abby Abelsen* • Holly Fulger *Karen* • Alba Oms *Carla Gonzalez* ■ *Dir* Elliot Silverstein • *Scr* Bryan Williams, from his play *In This Fallen City*

Night of Dark Shadows ★★
Horror   1971 · US · Colour · 93mins

The presence of Jonathan Frid as Barnabas the vampire is greatly missed in this second film sequel to the cult TV daytime serial *Dark Shadows*. The tale of the haunting of a newlywed couple who have recently moved in to their infamous ancestral home unfolds in extremely haphazard fashion. Barking more than terrifying, this will be best enjoyed by fans of the soap opera and its misbegotten nineties update. Watch for Kate Jackson in a very early role.

David Selby *Quentin/Charles Collins* • Lara Parker *Angelique* • Kate Jackson *Tracy Collins* • Grayson Hall *Carlotta Drake* • John Karlen *Alex Jenkins* • Nancy Barrett *Claire Jenkins* ■ *Dir* Dan Curtis • *Scr* Sam Hall, from a story by Sam Hall, Dan Curtis

The Night of San Lorenzo ★★★★ 12
Second World War drama
1981 · It · Colour · 102mins

Told as an extended flashback by a woman who was just six when Tuscany was liberated by the Allies, this pacifist drama draws on both the Taviani brothers' own memories of the summer of 1944 and their cinematic influences to create an unforgettable, neorealist fairy tale. Against the visual poetry, small instances of surreal fantasy and warm moments of simple humanity, however, is set the horror of war, as the Nazis and their Italian collaborators deal peremptorily with the partisans undermining their defence of San Martino. Thus the film's glowing romanticism lies less in the hard-won victory than in the people's unity and indomitability. In Italian with English subtitles. 🎞

Omero Antonutti *Galvano* • Margarita Lozano *Concetta* • Claudio Bigagli *Corrado* • Massimo Bonetti *Nicola* • Norma Martelli *Ivana* ■ *Dir* Paolo Taviani, Vittorio Taviani • *Scr* Paolo Taviani, Vittorio Taviani, Giuliani G De Negri, Tonino Guerra

Night of the Big Heat ★★
Science-fiction horror
1967 · UK · Colour · 92mins

The ever-reliable team of Peter Cushing and Christopher Lee put a crisp British cast through its paces as mystified islanders are plagued by a winter heatwave caused by energy-starved aliens. Most of the action takes place at a local inn, where the helpless survivors get on each other's nerves. You'll soon know how they feel! However, the final arrival of the monsters signals a few tepid thrills, even if they do resemble badly fried

eggs with tinned spaghetti innards. Contains some violence.

Christopher Lee *Hanson* • Peter Cushing *Dr Stone* • Patrick Allen *Jeff Callum* • Sarah Lawson *Frankie Callum* • Jane Merrow *Angela Roberts* • William Lucas *Ken Stanley* • Kenneth Cope *Tinker Mason* ■ *Dir* Terence Fisher • *Scr* Ronald Liles, Pip Baker, Jane Baker, from the novel by John Lymington

Night of the Comet ★★★ 15
Science-fiction   1984 · US · Colour · 94mins

Full of fun scares, gleeful unease and touching warmth, director Thom Eberhardt's tongue-in-cheek cult item pastes together numerous ideas from other science-fiction flicks and takes them the full distance. The same comet that wiped out the dinosaurs reappears to make most of mankind extinct this time. Catherine Mary Stewart and Kelli Maroney are two tough talking Valley girls who survive to take on the remaining flesh-eating zombies, marauding punks and sinister scientists in this upbeat and funky metaphor for maturity. 🎞

Catherine Mary Stewart *Regina* • Robert Beltran *Hector* • Kelli Maroney *Samantha* • Geoffrey Lewis *Carter* • Mary Woronov *Audrey* ■ *Dir/Scr* Thom Eberhardt

Night of the Demon ★★★★
Horror   1957 · UK · BW · 95mins

A remarkably well-constructed essay on the realm of the supernatural, *Cat People* director Jacques Tourneur's classic devil-cult chiller is a superb adaptation of the MR James short story *Casting the Runes*. Pitting rational scientist Dana Andrews against sinister mystic Niall MacGinnis, this topnotch suspense drama works marvellously well, despite studio interference insisting that the scary demon Tourneur wanted to avoid showing be included at the last minute. Edge-of-the-seat stuff, with a truly memorable climax.

Dana Andrews *John Holden* • Peggy Cummins *Joanna Harrington* • Niall MacGinnis *Dr Karswell* • Maurice Denham *Professor Harrington* • Athene Seyler *Mrs Karswell* • Liam Redmond *Mark O'Brien* • Reginald Beckwith *Mr Meek* • Ewan Roberts *Lloyd Williamson* ■ *Dir* Jacques Tourneur • *Scr* Charles Bennett, Hal E Chester, from the story *Casting the Runes* by MR James

Night of the Demons ★★ 18
Horror   1988 · US · Colour · 85mins

A high schoolers' Halloween party at the local spook house goes predictably wrong in this goofy eighties horror film. Think *The Breakfast Club* crossed with *The Evil Dead* and you'll get the basic idea. Sadly, it's nowhere near as funny as the first, or as scary as the second. Scream queen Linnea Quigley provides most of the requisite nudity, while Steve Johnson (Quigley's future husband) supplies the gore. There are a few bright moments, but mostly it's the same old schtick. 🎞

Lance Fenton *Jay* • Cathy Podewell *Judy* • Alvin Alexis *Roger* • Hal Havins *Stooge* • Amelia Kinkade *Angela* • Linnea Quigley *Suzanne* ■ *Dir* Kevin S Tenney • *Scr* Joe Augustyn • *Special Effects* Steve Johnson

Night of the Demons 2 ★★★ 18
Horror   1994 · US · Colour · 96mins

This belated follow-up to the 1988 cult horror is actually a more imaginative and outrageous ride, despite the clichéd plot about a group of brattish students holding a Halloween bash in a creepy old house. Director Brian Trenchard-Smith plays it for laughs at every opportunity and throws a smidgen of gratuitous nudity and gore into the teen-slasher brew. There are some truly inspired moments, such as when a nun saves the day (think *The Sound of Music* meets *Rambo*) using holy water in a squirt gun Uzi. A third instalment followed in 1997. 🎞

Cristi Harris *Bibi* • Bobby Jacoby *Perry* • Merle Kennedy *Mouse* • Amelia Kinkade *Angela* • Rod McCary *Father Bob* • Johnny Moran *Johnny* • Rick Peters *Rick* ■ *Dir* Brian Trenchard-Smith • *Scr* Joe Augustyn, from a story by James Penzi, Joe Augustyn

Night of the Eagle ★★★ 15
Horror   1961 · UK · BW · 83mins

A woman uses witchcraft to further her husband's career in this nifty adaptation of Fritz Leiber Jr's classic tale *Conjure Wife*, which had already been made into a movie in 1944 (Lon Chaney Jr's *Weird Woman*). Despite being over-melodramatic at times, Sidney Hayers's solid direction creates a great deal of terror out of the unseen to make it above average in the spine-tingling department. You'll still be unnerved even though you can glimpse the wires on the stone eagle as it comes to life in the eerie coda. 🎞

Peter Wyngarde *Norman Taylor* • Janet Blair *Tansy Taylor* • Margaret Johnston *Flora Carr* • Anthony Nicholls *Harvey Sawtelle* • Colin Gordon *Professor Lindsay Carr* • Kathleen Byron *Evelyn Sawtelle* • Reginald Beckwith *Harold Gunnison* ■ *Dir* Sidney Hayers • *Scr* Charles Beaumont, Richard Matheson, George Baxt, from the novel *Conjure Wife* by Fritz Leiber Jr

The Night of the Following Day ★★ 18
Crime thriller 1968 · UK/US · Colour · 89mins

Marlon Brando wears a blonde wig and a black T-shirt to show off his shockingly lithe figure in this deservedly obscure thriller, shot in Normandy under conditions of considerable chaos and tension, not least due to Brando's on-off relationship with co-star Rita Moreno. British actress Pamela Franklin is kidnapped by drug addict Moreno, tough cookie Richard Boone and chauffeur Brando, though the latter has a Damascan conversion halfway through. It's around this point that the movie becomes extremely arty in a way that suggests the director had been watching too much Godard. 🎞

Marlon Brando *Bud the chauffeur* • Richard Boone *Leer* • Rita Moreno • Pamela Franklin *Girl* • Jess Hahn *Wally* ■ *Dir* Hubert Cornfield • *Scr* Hubert Cornfield, Robert Phippeny, from the novel *The Snatchers* by Lionel White

The Night of the Generals

★★★ **15**

Second World War drama
1966 · UK/Fr · Colour · 137mins

Three Nazi generals are the prime suspects following a series of Jack the Ripper-style murders in this lurid Second World War drama. Omar Sharif heads the inquiry while Peter O'Toole is top-billed as one of the officers under investigation. Director Anatole Litvak gives up on the whodunit element early on and the plot just about muddles through, with Tom Courtenay representing the powerless ordinary soldier wondering why one mass murderer should stand out among so many. ▭

Peter O'Toole *General Tanz* • Omar Sharif *Major Grau* • Tom Courtenay *Corporal Hartmann* • Donald Pleasence *General Kahlenberge* • Joanna Pettet *Ulrike von Seidlitz-Gabler* • Philippe Noiret *Inspector Morand* • Charles Gray *General von Seidlitz-Gabler* • Coral Browne *Eleanore von Seidlitz-Gabler* ▪ *Dir* Anatole Litvak • *Scr* Joseph Kessel, Paul Dehn, from the novels *Die Nacht der Generale* by Hans Helmut Kirst and *The Wary Transgressor* by James Hadley Chase

Night of the Ghouls

★ **PG**

Horror
1960 · US · BW · 66mins

Even by the standards of Edward D Wood Jr, generally acknowledged as the worst director ever, this is woeful stuff. In this sequel of sorts to *Bride of the Monster*, Kenne Duncan, in a role originally written for Bela Lugosi, plays a fake medium who unwittingly resurrects the dead; while the opening shot of Wood regular Criswell arising from his coffin to warn the audience of things that go bump in the night is funnier than every Abbott and Costello film put together. ▭

Criswell • Kenne Duncan *Dr Acula* • Maila Nurmi *Black ghost* • Tor Johnson *Lobo* • Valda Hansen *Fake ghost* • Lon Chaney Jr ▪ *Dir/Scr* Edward D Wood Jr

The Night of the Grizzly

★★ **PG**

Western
1966 · US · Colour · 97mins

TV star Clint Walker is a homesteader who arrives on his slice of Wyoming with his wife and family. Almost at once he runs into opposition from the locals, but there is also a greedy grizzly bear that seems to single Walker out for special treatment, slaughtering Walker's valuable herd and bringing about the mortgaging of the property. Part *Jaws*, part *Shane*, it's really a children's film that relies on its bear and some attractive mountain photography. ▭

Clint Walker *Jim Cole* • Martha Hyer *Angela Cole* • Keenan Wynn *Jed Curry* • Nancy Kulp *Wilhelmina Peterson* • Kevin Brodie *Charlie Cole* • Ellen Corby *Hazel Squires* • Jack Elam *Hank* • Ron Ely *Tad Curry* ▪ *Dir* Joseph Pevney • *Scr* Warren Douglas

The Night of the Hunter

★★★★★ **12**

Classic thriller
1955 · US · BW · 88mins

Charles Laughton's only film as a director is one of the great masterpieces of American cinema, a movie so strangely repellent, so poetic and so utterly hypnotic that it sadly never found an audience. Based on a novel by Davis Grubb, it features Robert Mitchum's finest screen performance as a bogus priest and psychopath who has ''love'' and ''hate'' tattooed on his knuckles. Mitchum's always imposing, menacing presence is heightened by Laughton to an extraordinary degree, a stunning collaboration enhanced by Lillian Gish's portrayal of a gun-toting spinster. Set during the Depression in a rural backwater where the riverbanks are alive with croaking frogs, this is a fairy tale turned into a dark night of the soul. ▭

Robert Mitchum *Preacher Harry Powell* • Shelley Winters *Willa Harper* • Lillian Gish *Rachel* • Evelyn Varden *Icey Spoon* • Peter Graves (1) *Ben Harper* • Billy Chapin *John* • Sally Jane Bruce *Pearl* • James Gleason *Birdie* ▪ *Dir* Charles Laughton • *Scr* James Agee, from the novel by Davis Grubb • *Cinematographer* Stanley Cortez

Night of the Hunter

★★ **PG**

Thriller
1991 · US · Colour · 91mins

Before you get excited, this isn't the classic 1955 Robert Mitchum movie, but an unnecessary remake with Richard Chamberlain trying to look mean and moody as the self-styled preacher who has the words ''love'' and ''hate'' tattooed on his knuckles. Unfortunately, it was Mitchum with his brooding looks and booming voice who made the original so scary. Without his presence or the atmospheric black-and-white photography, this is simply a so-so update that – horror of horrors – even has a different ending. ▭

Richard Chamberlain *Preacher* • Diana Scarwid *Willa Harper* • Reid Binion *John Harper* • Amy Bebout *Pearl Harper* • Burgess Meredith *Birdy* ▪ *Dir* David Greene • *Scr* Edmond Stevens, from the novel by Davis Grubb

The Night of the Iguana

★★★ **12**

Drama
1964 · US · Colour · 112mins

It says much for the quality of the performances here that, from a cast that includes Richard Burton, Ava Gardner and Deborah Kerr, it was the little-known Grayson Hall who was nominated for an Oscar. As you would expect of a Tennessee Williams play, every performer has something to sink their teeth into. Yet Burton's defrocked cleric, Gardner's hotelier and Kerr's artist owe more to polished technique than flesh and blood. This may have something to do with director John Huston viewing this steamy story from his own laconic perspective. ▭

Richard Burton *Rev T Lawrence Shannon* • Ava Gardner *Maxine Faulk* • Deborah Kerr *Hannah Jelkes* • Sue Lyon *Charlotte Goodall* • James Ward *Hank Prosner* • Grayson Hall *Judith Fellowes* • Cyril Delevanti *Nonno* ▪ *Dir* John Huston • *Scr* Anthony Veiller, John Huston, from the play by Tennessee Williams

Night of the Juggler

★★ **18**

Action thriller
1980 · US · Colour · 96mins

Despite its title, this has nothing to do with nocturnal clowns practising with their balls. Instead it's an overblown urban thriller that achieves the rare feat of making New York look even uglier than it is in real life. When his daughter is mistakenly kidnapped by a candidate for ''psycho of the month'', ex-cop James Brolin trashes the city looking for her. Director Robert Butler brings undoubted technical craft to the numerous scenes of car crashes, but he seems rather less interested in the human beings in the cast. ▭

James Brolin *Sean Boyd* • Cliff Gorman *Gus Soltic* • Richard Castellano *Lieutenant Tonelli* • Abby Bluestone *Kathy Boyd* • Dan Hedaya *Sergeant Otis Barnes* • Julie Carmen *Marie* • Mandy Patinkin *Cabbie* ▪ *Dir* Robert Butler • *Scr* William Norton Sr, Rick Natkin, from the novel by William P McGivern

Night of the Living Dead

★★★★★ **18**

Horror
1968 · US · BW · 95mins

Director George Romero's seminal classic redefined the meaning of horror for fear-sated audiences in the sixties. It starts suddenly, without rhyme or reason, with a jolting attack in a cemetery and relentlessly continues on a downward spiral of frantic despair as terrified people take fragile shelter in a secluded house to fight off an army of cannibalistic zombies. Conveying visceral terror through an unrelieved black-and-white documentary atmosphere, Romero's graphic cult chiller no longer scares the daylights out of viewers because of its countless imitations. But his radical style and lethal wit still impress. ▭

Judith O'Dea *Barbara* • Russell Streiner *Johnny* • Duane Jones *Ben* • Karl Hardman *Harry Cooper* • Keith Wayne *Tom* ▪ *Dir* George A Romero • *Scr* John A Russo, from a story by George A Romero

Night of the Living Dead

★★★★ **18**

Horror
1990 · US · Colour · 84mins

Familiarity breeds content, not the expected contempt, in gore-meister director Tom Savini's highly acceptable remake of George A Romero's 1968 zombie classic. Staying close to the ingrained terror events of the original while keeping the viewer off-guard with fresh slants is Romero (who wrote the script) and Savini's joint masterstroke. Shot in atmospheric muted colours and well-acted by Patricia Tallman and Tom Towles in particular, Savini's sure hand underscores the flair, intelligence and imagination with which he's tackled such a thankless task. Laced with great zombie effects and gripping suspense, this is one remake that's better than anyone had a right to expect. ▭

Tony Todd *Ben* • Patricia Tallman *Barbara* • Tom Towles *Harry* • McKee Anderson *Helen* • William Butler *Tom* • Katie Finneran *Judy Rose* • Bill Mosley [Bill Moseley] *Johnnie* ▪ *Dir* Tom Savini • *Scr* George A Romero, from the 1968 film

Night of the Party

★★

Detective drama
1934 · UK · BW · 60mins

In this typical thirties murder mystery, a press magnate with many enemies seems to have invited them all to the same party. He is shot during a murder game with the lights out and anyone could have done it. The film's surviving interest is as one of the earliest extant works of Michael Powell, still in his twenties at the time. The project offered little artistic challenge, but he directs fluently enough and seems to have cut short the lengthy courtroom denouement in favour of a lively, if implausible, interruption by the culprit.

Leslie Banks *Sir John Holland* • Ian Hunter *Guy Kennington* • Jane Baxter *Peggy Studholme* • Ernest Thesiger *Chiddiatt* ▪ *Dir* Michael Powell • *Scr* Ralph Smart, from a play by Roland Pertwee, John Hastings Turner

The Night of the Prowler ★

Crime drama
1962 · UK · BW · 60mins

British director Francis Searle had the distinction of making only one bill-topping feature in his entire 27-film career, the daft comedy *A Girl in a Million*. The remainder of his output consisted of B-movies in every sense of the term, including this offering. Devotees of laughably bad low-budget crime movies should set their videos for a tawdry little tale of ambition, murder and deceit, set in the apparently cutthroat world of the motor trade! Patrick Holt stars, while John Horsley puts together the pieces in yet another of his dogged Scotland Yard support roles.

Patrick Holt *Robert Langton* • Colette Wilde *Marie Langton* • Paul Conrad • Mitzi Rogers *Jacky Reed* • John Horsley *Inspector Cameron* • Marianne Stone *Mrs Cross* ▪ *Dir* Francis Searle • *Scr* Paul Erickson

Night of the Running Man

★★★ **18**

Thriller
1994 · US · Colour · 88mins

Following in the footsteps of Laurence Harvey and Arnold Schwarzenegger, Andrew McCarthy takes on the mantle of the ''running man'' in this decent enough crime thriller. Reuniting with Mark L Lester, his director on the previous year's *Extreme Justice*, Scott Glenn plays a hit man sent to wipe out cabby McCarthy after he absconds with a cool million stolen from a Las Vegas casino. Lester is no stranger to this kind of action tale, but he too often allows the pace to drop to a canter. Contains violence, swearing and sex scenes.

Andrew McCarthy *Jerry Logan* • Scott Glenn *David Eckhart* • Janet Gunn *Chris Altman* • John Glover *Derek Mills* • Kim Lankford *Waitress* ▪ *Dir* Mark L Lester • *Scr* Rodney Vaccaro, from the novel by Lee Wells

Night of the Scarecrow

★★ **18**

Horror
1995 · US · Colour · 80mins

The spirit of a buried 17th-century warlock is transferred by lightning into a cornfield scarecrow, which then goes on a murderous rampage with various farm vehicles and implements in this rural version of *Friday the 13th*. With scant attention paid to the script or the cast (including an almost unrecognisable Gary Lockwood from *2001: a Space Odyssey*) by director Jeff Burr, the ludicrous story only exists to highlight every conceivable way guts can splatter over the camera lens. One for gore hounds only. Contains swearing and violence. ▭

Howard Swain *The Scarecrow* • Elizabeth Barondes *Claire Goodman* • John Mese *Dillon* • Gary Lockwood *William* • John Hawkes *Danny Thompson* • Stephen Root *Frank* ▪ *Dir* Jeff Burr • *Scr* Dan Mazur, Reed Steiner

Night of the Strangler ★

Thriller   1975 · US · Colour · 88mins

The sight of ex-Monkee Micky Dolenz investigating the mysterious deaths of a white woman and her black lover is the only noteworthy aspect of this violent thriller. Lots of nudity and a racism subplot do little to perk the interest in an awkwardly acted programme filler, set in New Orleans and directed by Joy N Houck Jr. Dolenz's far from prestigious acting career includes appearances in *Linda Lovelace for President* and *Deadfall*.

Mickey Dolenz [Micky Dolenz] *Vance* • Chuck Patterson *Priest* • James Ralston *Dan* ■ *Dir* Joy N Houck Jr

The Night of the Twisters ★★

Action adventure 1996 · US · Colour · 92mins

A shameless TV cash-in on the blockbusting success of the Jan De Bont hit *Twister*. OK, this one focuses on the impact a series of dangerous tornados has on a small rural town rather than the scientists chasing them, but if *Twister* hadn't been released, it is very likely that this would have vanished without trace. Unsurprisingly, the effects aren't up to much, and the subplot about the attempts of a father (played by *Dukes of Hazzard* star John Schneider) to patch up his relationship with his teenage stepson (Devon Sawa) just slows everything down.

John Schneider *Jack Hatch* • Devon Sawa *Dan Hatch* • Lori Hallier *Laura Hatch* • Thomas Lastewka *Ryan Hatch* • Alex Lastewka *Ryan Hatch* ■ *Dir* Tim Bond [Timothy Bond] • *Scr* Sam Graham, Chris Hubbell, Christopher Canaan, from the novel by Ivy Ruckman

Night on Earth ★★★ 🔞

Comedy drama 1992 · US · Colour · 123mins

Five taxi rides take place on the same night in Los Angeles, New York, Paris, Rome and Helsinki. In each cab, a moving, scatty or weird story about life's little ironies unfolds. While the two American-based tales in Jim Jarmusch's highly accessible compendium fall flat, the European segments – Roberto Benigni confessing all to his priest-passenger, blind Béatrice Dalle teaching her cabbie a thing or two – hit the right note of quirkiness that has become the arthouse director's trademark. Well worth watching. In English, French, Finnish and Italian with subtitles. ▭

Winona Ryder *Corky* • Gena Rowlands *Victoria Snelling* • Giancarlo Esposito *Yoyo* • Armin Mueller-Stahl *Helmut Grokenberger* • Rosie Perez *Angela* • Isaach de Bankole *Driver* • Béatrice Dalle *Blind woman* • Roberto Benigni *Gino* ■ *Dir/Scr* Jim Jarmusch

A Night on the Town ★★★ 🔞

Comedy   1987 · US · Colour · 102mins

Released in America as *Adventures in Babysitting*, this is one of the lightweight comedies Chris Columbus made before he directed the blockbusting hit *Home Alone*. It's a daft but fun teen movie with Elisabeth Shue as a girl who has a series of ridiculous adventures on the streets of Chicago one night with the children

she's supposed to be babysitting. The film also features a range of crazed performances from the likes of Penelope Ann Miller, Keith Coogan and Vincent D'Onofrio (at that time billed as Vincent Phillip D'Onofrio). Contains some violence and swearing. ▭

Elisabeth Shue *Chris Parker* • Maia Brewton *Sara Anderson* • Keith Coogan *Brad Anderson* • Anthony Rapp *Daryl Coopersmith* • Calvin Levels *Joe Gipp* • Vincent Phillip D'Onofrio [Vincent D'Onofrio] *Dawson* • Penelope Ann Miller *Brenda* ■ *Dir* Chris Columbus • *Scr* David Simkins

Night Owl ★★ 🔞

Supernatural thriller
1993 · US · Colour · 75mins

There are creepy goings-on down the airwaves in this so-so chiller. Jennifer Beals is the damsel in distress who discovers that a mysterious voice being broadcast on the radio is driving men to murder, and her husband James Wilder happens to be an avid listener. The largely unfamiliar cast does its best, but director Matthew Patrick struggles to bring any real suspense or danger to the piece. Contains some violence. ▭

Jennifer Beals *Julia Kuffner* • James Wilder *Harry Kuffner* • Justin Louis *Alex* • Allison Hossack *Jackie* • Jackie Burroughs *Dr Matthews* • Real Andrews *Ivan* ■ *Dir* Matthew Patrick • *Scr* Rose Schacht, Ann Powell

Night Passage ★★ 🔵

Western   1957 · US · Colour · 90mins

James Stewart, director Anthony Mann and writer Borden Chase already had a whole string of hit westerns under their belt when they started work on *Night Passage*. But Mann quit after a few days, sensing that the script wasn't quite ready, and made way for TV director James Neilson. Stewart plays a former railroad man who comes up against his own brother, a train robber played by Audie Murphy, when he is hired to deliver a payroll. Though beautifully shot in Technirama, it rather dawdles along, indulging Stewart's singing and accordion-playing skills before the climactic shoot-out.

James Stewart *Grant McLaine* • Audie Murphy *Utica Kid* • Dan Duryea *Whitey Harbin* • Dianne Foster *Charlotte Drew* • Elaine Stewart *Verna Kimball* • Brandon de Wilde *Joey Adams* ■ *Dir* James Neilson • *Scr* Borden Chase, from a story by Norman A Fox

Night People ★★

Spy drama   1954 · US · Colour · 92mins

Gregory Peck plays an American intelligence officer who flies to Berlin to secure the release of a US soldier kidnapped by the communists. There he runs into a giant conspiracy involving the young man's father, an influential magnate (Broderick Crawford), and the failed assassination plot against Hitler. This blend of Cold War jitters and Nazi hangover makes for a moderately gripping thriller that uses the real bombed-out city as its location, though gritty black and white might have served the story better than touristy Technicolor.

Gregory Peck *Colonel Van Dyke* • Broderick Crawford *Leatherby* • Anita Björk *Hoffy* • Rita Gam *Miss Cates* • Buddy Ebsen *Sergeant*

McColloch • Walter Abel *Foster* ■ *Dir* Nunnally Johnson • *Scr* Nunnally Johnson, from a story by Jed Harris, Thomas Reed

The Night Porter ★★★ 🔞

Drama   1973 · It · Colour · 112mins

What happens when former SS officer Dirk Bogarde and concentration camp inmate Charlotte Rampling meet years later and pick up their sadomasochistic sexual relationship more or less where they left off? Not quite the examination of the Nazi legacy in political and allegorical terms that director Liliana Cavani probably hoped for; hence the reason why her celebration of self-disgust and degradation so preoccupied the censors. Mere sexploitation or a serious analysis of guilty repression? The debate still rages. Contains violence and nudity. ▭

Dirk Bogarde *Max* • Charlotte Rampling *Lucia* • Philippe Leroy *Klaus* • Gabriele Ferzetti *Hans* • Giuseppe Addobbati *Stumm* • Isa Miranda *Countess Stein* ■ *Dir* Liliana Cavani • *Scr* Liliana Cavani, Italo Moscati, from a story by Liliana Cavani, Barbara Alberti, Amedeo Pagani

Night Ride Home ★★★

Drama   1999 · US · Colour

Rebecca De Mornay and Keith Carradine star as a couple whose life is ripped apart when their 17-year-old son is killed in a riding accident. Plagued by grief and guilt, the family struggle to heal their wounds. Thora Birch as angst-ridden daughter Clea and Ellen Burstyn as the caring grandmother round out this powerful drama, subtly directed by Glenn Jordan. Among this TV movie's most praiseworthy aspects are the fine performances of De Mornay and Carradine, who endow their actions with a truth that goes beyond melodramatics.

Rebecca De Mornay *Nora Mahler* • Keith Carradine *Neal Mahler* • Ellen Burstyn *Maggie* • Jordan Brower *Simon Mahler* • Thora Birch *Clea Mahler* • Lynne Thigpen *Fran* • Ryan Merriman *Justin* ■ *Dir* Glenn Jordan • *Scr* Ronald Parker, Darrah Cloud, from the novel by Barbara Esstman

The Night Runner ★★★

Film noir   1957 · US · BW · 78mins

Ray Danton, who went on to play the title role in *The Rise and Fall of Legs Diamond* (1960), is well-cast in this short, sharp shocker about a schizophrenic mental patient who takes up with Colleen Miller, much to the displeasure of her father. Abner Biberman directs with occasional flashes of insight, but the film never lets Danton show off his acting skills.

Ray Danton *Roy Turner* • Colleen Miller *Susan Mayes* • Merry Anders *Amy Hansen* • Willis Bouchey *Loren Mayes* • Harry Jackson *Hank Hansen* • Robert Anderson *Ed Wallace* ■ *Dir* Abner Biberman • *Scr* Gene Levitt, from a story by Owen Cameron

Night Shift ★★★★ 🔞

Comedy   1982 · US · Colour · 101mins

It was intended as a vehicle for director Ron Howard's old *Happy Days* chum Henry "the Fonz" Winkler, but future Batman Michael Keaton steals the show in this breezy comedy.

Winkler is the shy mortuary attendant who gets involved in a call-girl operation run from the morgue by sharp-talking Keaton. The broad script doesn't attempt to milk the black opportunities in the scenario, but it is still very funny, and the film is remarkably free of the earnestness that has marred Howard's subsequent hits. As well as providing a showcase for Keaton's talents, it also gave early exposure to a number of other future stars, including Kevin Costner and Shannen Doherty. Contains violence, swearing and nudity. ▭

Henry Winkler *Chuck Lumley* • Michael Keaton *Bill Blazejowski* • Shelley Long *Belinda Keaton* • Gina Hecht *Charlotte Koogle* • Pat Corley *Edward Koogle* • Clint Howard *Jefferey* • Kevin Costner *Frat boy* • Shannen Doherty *Bluebird* ■ *Dir* Ron Howard • *Scr* Lowell Ganz, Babaloo Mandel

Night Song ★★★ 🔵

Romantic drama   1947 · US · BW · 102mins

Merle Oberon gets to weep buckets in this sudsy melodrama in which she poses as a blind young woman to help her sightless protégé Dana Andrews fulfil his potential as a composer. Director John Cromwell could churn out this kind of sentimental nonsense in his sleep, and he knows just when to play on the heartstrings or lighten the atmosphere through the knowing performances of Ethel Barrymore and Hoagy Carmichael. The best part is watching Artur Rubinstein and the New York Philharmonic treating Andrews's lousy tune as a classical masterpiece.

Dana Andrews *Dan* • Merle Oberon *Cathy* • Ethel Barrymore *Miss Willey* • Hoagy Carmichael *Chick* • Artur Rubinstein • Jacqueline White *Connie* ■ *Dir* John Cromwell • *Scr* DeWitt Bodeen, Frank Fenton, Dick Irving Hyland, from a story by Dick Irving Hyland

The Night Stalker ★★★ 🅿🅖

Horror thriller 1971 · US · Colour · 74mins

Insouciant reporter Carl Kolchak (Darren McGavin) cannot convince his editor (Simon Oakland) that there is a supernatural connection to the murders of Las Vegas showgirls. Noted science-fiction writer Richard Matheson builds the mystery expertly, but the comedy now appears strained. The film, however, is more entertaining than many of the genre made for the big screen. Contains some violence and swearing. ▭

Darren McGavin *Carl Kolchak* • Carol Lynley *Gail Foster* • Simon Oakland *Tony Vincenzo* • Ralph Meeker *Bernie Jenks* • Claude Akins *Sheriff Warren Butcher* • Barry Atwater *Janos Skorzeny* • Elisha Cook Jr *Mickey Crawford* ■ *Dir* John Llewellyn Moxey • *Scr* Richard Matheson, from a story by Jeff Rice

The Night Stalker ★★★ 🔞

Thriller   1985 · US · Colour · 89mins

In this neatly compact B-thriller, Charles Napier – usually cast in supporting roles in such films as *The Blues Brothers* and *The Grifters* – is outstanding as a cop on skid row in pursuit of a serial killer who targets prostitutes. Directed by Max Kleven, it has some gripping moments, but the pace slackens about halfway through.

Charles Napier *Sergeant JJ Striker* • Michelle Reese *Rene* • Katherine Kelly Lang *Denise* • Robert Viharo *Charlie Garrett* • Joseph Gian *Buddy Brown* • Robert Z'Dar *Sommers* ■ *Dir* Max Kleven • *Scr* John Goff, Don Edmonds

The Night Strangler ★★★ 12

Horror thriller   1973 · US · Colour · 90mins

Producer Dan Curtis doubles as director on this sequel to *The Night Stalker*, which some prefer to the original. Screenwriter Richard Matheson begins with the same premise as before – a reporter investigates a series of murders (this time in Seattle) – but then develops the story with more surprising twists and turns; the climax has a flavour of *The Phantom of the Opera*. There is also the bonus of three legends of the genre – John Carradine, Margaret Hamilton and Al Lewis. ▭

Darren McGavin *Carl Kolchak* • Jo Ann Pflug *Louise Harper* • Simon Oakland *Tony Vincenzo* • Scott Brady *Captain Roscoe Schubert* • Wally Cox *Titus Berry* • Margaret Hamilton *Prof Hester Crabwell* • John Carradine *Llewellyn Crossbinder* • Al Lewis *Tramp* ■ *Dir* Dan Curtis • *Scr* Richard Matheson, from characters created by Jeff Rice

Night Sun ★★★ 15

Historical drama
1990 · It/Fr/W Ger · Colour · 107mins

Tolstoy's story, *Father Sergius*, is translated to 18th-century Italy in this handsome yet minimalist study of asceticism, idealism and the perils of pride and fame. Quitting the Neapolitan court on discovering that his bride-to-be, Nastassja Kinski, was once the king's mistress, ennobled trooper Julian Sands embraces desert monasticism, only to be beset by worldly temptation (in the form of the minxish Charlotte Gainsbourg) after he's hailed as a miracle worker by pilgrims to Mount Petra. Paolo and Vittorio Taviani again demonstrate their ability to tell absorbing stories by combining deceptive visual simplicity with thematic depth. In Italian with English subtitles. ▭

Julian Sands *Sergio Giuramondo* • Charlotte Gainsbourg *Matilda* • Nastassja Kinski *Cristina* • Massimo Bonetti *Prince Santobuono* • Margarita Lozano *Sergio's mother* • Patricia Millardet *Aurelia* ■ *Dir* Paolo Taviani, Vittorio Taviani • *Scr* Paolo Taviani, Vittorio Taviani, Tonino Guerra, from the story *Father Sergius* by Leo Tolstoy

The Night that Panicked America ★★★

Drama based on a true story
1975 · US · Colour · 100mins

On October 30 1938, Orson Welles and his company broadcast a version of HG Wells's *The War Of The Worlds* on the radio – and millions took it seriously as a warning of alien invasion. Director Joseph Sargent's made-for-TV docudrama shows how some people fled to the hills, while others prayed in the streets; it was as near to a state of emergency as America has ever seen. Paul Shenar, Vic Morrow and Eileen Brennan poignantly fictionalise some of the real-life stories that unfolded that night.

Paul Shenar *Orson Welles* • Vic Morrow *Hank Muldoon* • Cliff De Young *Stefan Grubowski* • Michael Constantine *Jess Wingate* • Walter

McGinn *Paul Stewart* • Eileen Brennan *Ann Muldoon* • Meredith Baxter *Linda Davis* • Tom Bosley *Norman Smith* ■ *Dir* Joseph Sargent • *Scr* Nicholas Meyer, Anthony Wilson

The Night the Lights Went Out in Georgia ★ 15

Drama   1981 · US · Colour · 107mins

Appealing performances by Dennis Quaid and Kristy McNichol can't save this barely credible road movie. They play sibling country and western singers. McNichol is trying to invest her rowdy brother with some of her Nashville ambition, but he's more interested in the women he gets to meet backstage – although this often gets him into scrapes with their jealous boyfriends. Meanwhile, she is having a dead-end affair with Mark Hamill. Stereotypical situations, barely functional dialogue and directional incompetence doesn't give the fine cast any chance at all. ▭

Kristy McNichol *Amanda Child* • Dennis Quaid *Travis Child* • Mark Hamill *Conrad* • Don Stroud *Seth* • Arlen Dean Snyder *Andy* ■ *Dir* Ronald F Maxwell • *Scr* Bob Bonney, from the song by Bobby Russell

The Night They Raided Minsky's ★★★

Comedy   1968 · US · Colour · 98mins

An amiably eccentric story of America's burlesque theatre with Norman Wisdom (yes, our Norm!) upstaging everyone, including Jason Robards. It's an atmospheric comedy with Britt Ekland as the Amish girl who eventually rebels against her father and takes off her clothes on a commercial basis. The scatter-shot narrative never quite gets its act together, but director William Friedkin injects enough enthusiasm to make it enjoyable, if boisterous viewing. Contains brief nudity.

Jason Robards [Jason Robards Jr] *Raymond Paine* • Britt Ekland *Rachel Schpitendavel* • Norman Wisdom *Chick Williams* • Forrest Tucker *Trim Houlihan* • Harry Andrews *Jacob Schpitendavel* • Joseph Wiseman *Louis Minsky* • Denholm Elliott *Vance Fowler* • Elliott Gould *Billy Minsky* ■ *Dir* William Friedkin • *Scr* Arnold Schulman, Sidney Michaels, Norman Lear, from the novel by Rowland Barber

The Night They Saved Christmas ★★ U

Fantasy drama   1984 · US · Colour · 89mins

A fanciful yet environmentally correct Yuletide TV movie, directed by Jackie Cooper and starring Jaclyn Smith of *Charlie's Angels* fame. The story centres on a nasty old oil company planning to drill near Santa's home. One of Santa's elves enlists the help of a mother and her young children to try and save the North Pole, and Christmas. Singer/songwriter Paul Williams plays the elf, while Art Carney delights as Santa. ▭

Jaclyn Smith *Claudia Baldwin* • Art Carney *Santa Claus* • Paul LeMat *Michael Baldwin* • Mason Adams *Sumner Murdock* • June Lockhart *Mrs Claus* • Paul Williams *Ed* • Scott Grimes *David Baldwin* ■ *Dir* Jackie Cooper • *Scr* James C Moloney, David Niven Jr

The Night They Took Miss Beautiful ★★

Thriller   1977 · US · Colour

The Rifleman (Chuck Connors), *Dallas's* Pam Ewing (Victoria Principal) and Sergeant Bilko (Phil Silvers) are among those who join forces for this ludicrous made-for-TV hijacking caper involving beauty contestants, an aeroplane and some deadly microbes engineered for biological warfare. But the question is, are the baddies after the germs, or the Carmen rollers?

Gary Collins *Paul Fabiani* • Chuck Connors *Mike O'Toole* • Henry Gibson *Rolly Royce* • Peter Haskell *Damon Faulkner* • Karen Lamm *Cindy Lou Barrett* • Sheree North *Layla Burden* • Victoria Principal *Reba Bar Lev* • Phil Silvers *Marv Barker* • Stella Stevens *Kate Malloy* ■ *Dir* Robert Michael Lewis [Robert Lewis] • *Scr* George Lefferts

Night Tide ★★ PG

Thriller drama   1961 · US · BW · 86mins

Avant-garde film-maker Curtis Harrington made his feature debut with this strange story of a sailor who meets a mysterious woman who may or may not be a mermaid. The principal setting is the Californian amusement pier where the woman works under the care of her guardian, who claims she was found on a Greek island. The sailor, played by Dennis Hopper, is thoroughly smitten despite being warned that she brought death to two previous admirers. One for Hopper completists only. ▭

Dennis Hopper *Johnny Drake* • Linda Lawson *Mora* • Gavin Muir *Capt Murdock* • Luana Anders *Ellen Sands* • Marjorie Eaton *Madame Romanovitch* ■ *Dir/Scr* Curtis Harrington

A Night to Remember ★★★ PG

Comedy thriller   1942 · US · BW · 88mins

Not the 1958 Rank film of the same name about the sinking of the *Titanic*, but a witty and clever mystery tale with Brian Aherne and Loretta Young well cast as a husband and wife trying to solve a murder. He is an author of whodunits who knows he has a romantic novel in him; she is simply radiant and for some will be the whole reason for watching this sub-*Thin Man* opus. Editor turned director Richard Wallace lacks the requisite style to bring anything special to the mix, but he lets the stars shine and marshals a fine supporting cast of suspects, including "Charlie Chan" Sidney Toler. ▭

Loretta Young *Nancy Troy* • Brian Aherne *Jeff Troy* • Jeff Donnell *Ann Carstairs* • William Wright *Scott Carstairs* • Sidney Toler *William Wright* • Gale Sondergaard *Mrs Devoe* • Lee Patrick *Polly Franklin* ■ *Dir* Richard Wallace • *Scr* Richard Flournoy, Jack Henley, from the story by Kelly Roos

A Night to Remember ★★★★ PG

Drama   1958 · UK · BW · 117mins

While this drama about the sinking of the *Titanic* can't compete in terms of spectacle with James Cameron's multi-million-dollar blockbuster, it still manages to present the facts of the disaster in a deeply moving and compelling manner. Basing his film on

Walter Lord's meticulously researched book (adapted by Eric Ambler), director Roy Baker opts for a documentary style that focuses on the human interest angle without recourse to melodramatics. The result is a gripping account of the tragedy, impeccably acted by a sterling British cast, with Kenneth More excelling as heroic second officer Herbert Lightoller, from whose perspective we see events unfolding. ▭ *DVD*

Kenneth More *Herbert Lightoller* • Ronald Allen *Clarke* • Robert Ayres *Peuchen* • Honor Blackman *Mrs Lucas* • Anthony Bushell *Captain Rostron* • John Cairney *Murphy* • Jill Dixon *Mrs Clarke* • David McCallum *Bride* • Sean Connery ■ *Dir* Roy Baker [Roy Ward Baker] • *Scr* Eric Ambler, from the book by Walter Lord

Night Train ★★ 15

Romantic drama   1998 · Ire · Colour · 93mins

If John Lynch's debut feature is to be believed, the key to a girl's heart is not to be found at the florist or the jewellery store. No, fellas – if you really want to impress her, buy a train set. Brenda Blethyn plays a timid spinster who strikes up a friendship with ex-con John Hurt when he rents a room in her house. Hurt, who's on the run from some nasty gangsters, has a passion for model trains and uses them to worm his way into Blethyn's heart. The two stars make a fine duo, but this uneasy mix of crime thriller and middle-aged romance takes some swallowing.

John Hurt *Michael Poole* • Brenda Blethyn *Alice Mooney* • Pauline Flanagan *Mrs Mooney* • Lorcan Cranitch *Billy* ■ *Dir* John Lynch • *Scr* Aodhan Madden

Night Train to Munich ★★★★

Spy thriller   1940 · UK · BW · 90mins

Witty and suspenseful, Frank Launder and Sidney Gilliat's screenplay about a missing Czech scientist bears an uncanny resemblance to the earlier classic they had a hand in, Alfred Hitchcock's *The Lady Vanishes*. Reinforcing the link is the reappearance of Basil Radford and Naunton Wayne as the cricket-mad eccentrics Charters and Caldicott. The dashing Rex Harrison evidently enjoys himself as the bemused British spy and Margaret Lockwood as the scientist's daughter does well to keep up with him. It's fast, furious and funny but, even with that master of atmosphere Carol Reed as director, it could have done with a couple of fresh tricks to keep us guessing.

Margaret Lockwood *Anna Bomasch* • Rex Harrison *Gus Bennett* • Paul Henreid *Karl Marsen* • Basil Radford *Charters* • Naunton Wayne *Caldicott* • James Harcourt *Axel Bomasch* ■ *Dir* Carol Reed • *Scr* Sidney Gilliat, Frank Launder, from a story by Gordon Wellesley

Night Train to Venice ★ 18

Thriller   1993 · Ger · Colour · 94mins

Journalist and neo-Nazi expert Martin Gamil (Hugh Grant) is victimised by skinheads during his train trip from Munich to Venice and spends the rest of the film agonising over his plight. Malcolm McDowell is "the stranger" who looks on with smug delight. Of course, the skinheads aren't finished with him just yet... Erratically edited and incoherently directed, this is as repulsive as it sounds. ▣

Hugh Grant *Martin Gamil* • Tahnee Welch *Vera Cortese* • Malcolm McDowell *Stranger* • Samy Langs *Pedro* ■ *Dir* Carlo U Quinterio • *Scr* Leo Tichat, Toni Hirtreiter

Night unto Night ★★

Romantic drama   1949 · US · BW · 92mins

Directed by Don Siegel, this obviously well-intended movie emerges as verbose, portentous claptrap that criminally wastes the gifts of the beautiful and talented Swedish-born actress Viveca Lindfors (Siegel's wife from 1949–53). She stars as a woman locked in grief over the death of her husband, whose suffering is temporarily relieved by a lot of introspective talk with a troubled epileptic scientist she meets somewhere on the Florida coast. He is played by Ronald Reagan, whose earnest, well-meaning performance goes some way to explaining why he was successful in politics.

Ronald Reagan *John* • Viveca Lindfors *Ann* • Broderick Crawford *Shawn* • Rosemary De Camp *Thalia* • Osa Massen *Lisa* • Craig Stevens *Tony* ■ *Dir* Don Siegel • *Scr* Kathryn Scola, from the novel by Philip Wylie

Night Visions ★ 15

Thriller   1990 · US · Colour · 91mins

In this tepid TV movie, predictability hamstrings yet another ''crime-fighting makes strange bedfellows'' tale. Alcoholic cop James Remar and traumatised psychic Loryn Locklin team up to capture a psychotic serial killer loose in Los Angeles. You know the ending before it begins, and neither the serviceable cast nor the direction by horror specialist Wes Craven can make this anything more than a weak exercise in banality. ▣

Loryn Locklin *Sally Powers* • James Remar *Detective Tom Mackey* • Jon Tenney *Martin* • Mitch Pileggi *Keller* ■ *Dir* Wes Craven • *Scr* Wes Craven, Thomas Baum

The Night Visitor ★★★

Chiller   1970 · Swe/US · Colour · 101mins

Very odd and rarely shown, this intriguing, arty horror movie was shot in Sweden by Hungarian director Laslo Benedek and stars a handful of Ingmar Bergman's repertory company of actors – Max von Sydow, Liv Ullmann, Per Oscarsson. Von Sydow is a farmer accused of murder he didn't commit, who ingeniously escapes from his insane asylum prison nightly to kill the people who put him there. This spooky gothic thriller has a compelling atmosphere that's most unusual.

Max von Sydow *Salem* • Trevor Howard *Inspector* • Liv Ullmann *Esther Jenks* • Per Oscarsson *Dr Anton Jenks* • Rupert Davies *Clemens, the attorney* • Andrew Keir *Dr Kemp* ■ *Dir* Laslo Benedek • *Scr* Guy Elmes, from the short story *Salem Came to Supper* by Samuel Roecca

Night Visitor ★★

Horror   1989 · US · Colour · 93mins

Strange that a film boasting satanists, hookers, ritual butchery and voyeurism should prove such a dull watch. Yet

this proves to be the case with Rupert Hitzig's uninspired slant on the boy-who-cried-wolf story. Derek Rydall stars as a school kid given to outrageous lies who witnesses the murder of a neighbourhood prostitute. The police, in the shape of Richard Roundtree (*Shaft*), don't believe him, so Rydall turns to retired cop Elliott Gould for help. The awkward blend of thrills and cheap laughs is further marred by too many tedious subplots, but Allen Garfield and the puckish Michael J Pollard enjoy themselves as bungling devil worshippers.

Elliott Gould *Ron Devereaux* • Richard Roundtree *Captain Crane* • Allen Garfield *Zachary Willard* • Michael J Pollard *Stanley Willard* • Derek Rydall *Billy Colton* • Teresa Van Der Woude *Kelly Fremont* • Shannon Tweed *Lisa Grace* ■ *Dir* Rupert Hitzig • *Scr* Randal Viscovich

Night Visitors ★ 15

Science-fiction thriller
1996 · US · Colour · 90mins

Graduate student Faith Ford is pursued by secret agents after her brother is killed for stealing a box containing alien remains. With the help of journalist boyfriend Thomas Gibson, she struggles to survive and expose the conspiracy. This is a race to see who is the dumbest: the crash-prone aliens, the inept spies or the spunky but clueless heroine. The grand prize, however, goes to the makers of this derivative TV movie, who should have known better than to inflict this on an unsuspecting planet. ▣

Faith Ford *Kelly Wells* • Thomas Gibson *Ross Williams* • Stephen Tobolowsky *Taylor* • Todd Allen *David Wells* • Eric McCormack *Andy Robinson* • Charles S Dutton *Dr Eldon James* ■ *Dir* Jorge Montesi • *Scr* D Brent Mote

Night Walk ★★ 15

Thriller   1989 · US · Colour · 89mins

As television becomes ever more greedy for material, this is just the sort of hand-me-down thriller which is made by the batch to fill the schedules. So as not to frighten you with any sign of novelty, this concerns a woman (Lesley-Anne Down) who has witnessed a murder but can't convince the police. Gosh! Busy TV director Jerrold Freedman slackens his grip on the suspense just once too often, yet actor Robert Urich still manages to convey the right kind of gritty authenticity. ▣

Robert Urich *Jake Simon* • Lesley-Anne Down *Geneva Miller* • Mark Joy *Jerry Miller* • Michael Alldredge *Brody* • Lawrence P Casey *Shooter* • Richie Devaney *Brian* • Ryan Urich *Matt* ■ *Dir* Jerrold Freedman • *Scr* Harry Longstreet, Renée Longstreet

The Night Walker ★★

Horror thriller   1964 · US · BW · 85mins

Barbara Stanwyck's last theatrical feature is a lame *Psycho* imitation from producer/director William Castle, who lit up the fifties with such ingenious gimmick flicks as *Homicidal* and *The Tingler*. Starring with her real-life ex-husband Robert Taylor, Stanwyck is a widow suffering from recurring dreams about her dead spouse (Hayden Rorke). Written by Robert Bloch, who wrote the book on which *Psycho* was based, this is a tepid chiller with

laughable special effects. Stanwyck is great value, though.

Barbara Stanwyck *Irene Trent* • Robert Taylor (1) *Barry Morland* • Hayden Rorke *Howard Trent* • Lloyd Bochner *The man in the dream* • Judith Meredith [Judi Meredith] *Joyce* • Rochelle Hudson *Hilda* • Ted Durant *Narrator* ■ *Dir* William Castle • *Scr* Robert Bloch, from the story *Witches' Friday* by Elizabeth Kata

Night Warning ★

Horror   1982 · US · Colour · 96mins

Bo Svenson's sour and homophobic cop character gets in the way of making this horror mystery funnier than it already is. Investigating the death of a gay TV repairman, Svenson sees Jimmy McNichol as the chief suspect. Actually, it was McNichol's aunt (Susan Tyrrell) who did it in a rage of fury when the guy wouldn't have sex with her. Tyrrell's acting makes this film a must for bad movie fans. Not content to chew the scenery, she tears it up, digests it and asks for seconds.

Jimmy McNichol *Billy* • Susan Tyrrell *Aunt Cheryl* • Bo Svenson *Detective Carlson* ■ *Dir* William Asher • *Scr* Stephen Breimer, Boon Collins, Alan Jay Glueckman

Night Was Our Friend ★★

Psychological drama 1951 · UK · BW · 61mins

Michael Gough is best known now for playing butler Alfred in the *Batman* movies. But this dowdy little drama from his dim and distant past is one picture he'd probably prefer to forget. Long believed to have perished in the Brazilian jungle, he returns to haunt wife Elizabeth Sellars and her new beau Ronald Howard. Adapted by Michael Pertwee from his own play, this was one of director Michael Anderson's earliest features: within five years he would have *The Dam Busters*, *1984* and *Around the World in 80 Days* under his belt.

Michael Gough *Martin Raynor* • Elizabeth Sellars *Sally Raynor* • Ronald Howard *Dr John Harper* • Marie Ney *Emily Raynor* • Edward Lexy *Arthur Glanville* • Nora Gordon *Kate* • Felix Felton *Jury foreman* ■ *Dir* Michael Anderson • *Scr* Michael Pertwee, from his play

Night Watch ★★★ 15

Mystery thriller   1973 · UK · Colour · 98mins

Reminiscent of *Gaslight*, this thriller stars Elizabeth Taylor as a woman recovering from a nervous breakdown who thinks she sees a corpse outside her window. Could it be the work of her husband (Laurence Harvey in his final film), who may or may not be having an affair with her best friend (Billie Whitelaw)? The actors give the tired plot all they've got, but director Brian G Hutton is more concerned with action than atmosphere, abbreviating tension where it should be given time to accumulate. ▣

Elizabeth Taylor *Ellen Wheeler* • Laurence Harvey *John Wheeler* • Billie Whitelaw *Sarah Cooke* • Robert Lang *Appleby* • Tony Britton *Tony* • Bill Dean *Inspector Walker* ■ *Dir* Brian G Hutton • *Scr* Tony Williamson, Evan Jones, from a play by Lucille Fletcher

Night Watch ★★★ 15

Crime thriller 1995 · UK/US · Colour · 94mins

Inspired by the work of Alistair MacLean, this leaden caper is forced

by budgetary constraint to serve up an uninvolving combination of high-tech gadgetry and bruising stuntwork. Not to be confused with the Elizabeth Taylor thriller or either of the two versions of Ole Bornedal's morgue chiller, this sub-007 adventure was Pierce Brosnan's last assignment before his debut as James Bond. Reprising the role of Mike Graham that he had previously played in *Death Train*, Brosnan turns art detective in a bid to recover a Rembrandt painting before it falls into the hands of a Hong Kong crime lord. Contains violence and swearing. ▣

Pierce Brosnan *Mike Graham* • Alexandra Paul *Sabrina Carver* • William Devane *Nick Caldwell* • Michael J Shannon *Martin Schrader* • Lim Kay Siu *Mao Yixin* • Irene Ng *Myra Tang* ■ *Dir* David S Jackson [David Jackson] • *Scr* David S Jackson, from the novel by Alistair MacLean

The Night We Dropped a Clanger ★★ U

Second World War comedy
1959 · UK · BW · 84mins

An identity switch picture set during the Second World War that tends to stretch its comic notions to breaking point. More disciplined comic timing would have provided an effective cure for the problem. However, farce king Brian Rix is a sensible choice for this wartime foolishness and he switches convincingly from military rigour (in one guise) to gormlessness (in the other).

Brian Rix *Arthur Atwood/Wing Commander Blenkinsop* • Cecil Parker *Sir Bertram* • William Hartnell *Sergeant Bright* • Leslie Phillips *Squadron Leader Thomas* • Leo Franklyn *Sergeant Belling* • John Welsh *Squadron Leader Grant* • Toby Perkins *Flight Lieutenant Spendal* • Liz Fraser *Lulu* ■ *Dir* Darcy Conyers • *Scr* John Chapman

The Night We Got the Bird ★

Comedy   1960 · UK · BW · 88mins

Your heart will go out to the splendid cast that found itself lumbered with this turkey. Ronald Shiner has the most luck, as he at least gets to spend much of the picture as a reincarnated parrot, thus leaving doltish egghead Brian Rix to carry the can for his misdemeanours as an antiques forger. With bedroom mix-ups, courtroom chaos, St Trinian's-style aggro and a break-in at a top secret space lab, there's enough going on, but it's all so dismally unfunny, even though practised *farceur* Ray Cooney had a hand in the script.

Brian Rix *Bertie Skidmore* • Dora Bryan *Julie Skidmore* • Leo Franklyn *Victor* • Irene Handl *Ma* • Liz Fraser *Fay* • John Slater *Wolfie Green* • Reginald Beckwith *Chippendale Charlie* • Robertson Hare *Dr Vincent* • John Le Mesurier *Court clerk* • Ronald Shiner *Cecil Gibson* • Terry Scott *PC Lovejoy* ■ *Dir* Darcy Conyers • *Scr* Ray Cooney, Tony Hilton, Darcy Conyers, from the play *The Love Birds* by Basil Thomas

The Night We Never Met ★★★★ 15

Romantic comedy
1993 · US · Colour · 94mins

A sharp and cute study of young New Yorkers sharing a studio apartment on an alternate-days rota. Writer/director Warren Leight tinges the light comedy with a touch of Woody Allen-style angst, but whenever the story gets down-hearted his three leads (Kevin Anderson, yuppie slob; Annabella Sciorra, bored housewife; Matthew Broderick, dumped nice guy) perk it up with ensemble acting that dovetails perfectly. Love among the skyscrapers has rarely been such a delight. Contains swearing and nudity. ▭

Matthew Broderick *Sam Lester* • Annabella Sciorra *Ellen Holder* • Kevin Anderson *Brian McVeigh* • Justine Bateman *Janet Beehan* • Jeanne Tripplehorn *Pastel* • Michael Mantell *Aaron Holder* • Christine Baranski *Lucy* ■ Dir/Scr Warren Leight

Night without Stars ★★★ U

Crime drama 1951 · UK · BW · 82mins

David Farrar is virtually blind and retires to the Riviera where he falls in love with Nadia Gray. Then he tangles with murderers, blackmailers and forgers when he discovers she is the widow of a resistance fighter. He's pushed off a cliff which forces him to get his sight restored and – very smart this – return to the Riviera still claiming to be blind so that he can trap the dirty rotters. Winston Graham adapted his own novel for this enjoyable little thriller. ▭

David Farrar *Giles Gordon* • Nadia Gray *Alix Delaisse* • Maurice Teynac *Louis Malinay* • Gilles Queant *Deffand* • Gerard Landry *Pierre Chaval* • June Clyde *Claire* • Robert Ayres *Walter* ■ Dir Anthony Pelissier • Scr Winston Graham, from his novel

Nightbreaker ★★★ 15

Historical drama 1989 · US · Colour · 94mins

After such hits as *Stakeout* and *Young Guns*, Emilio Estevez opted for a change of pace and appeared alongside his father Martin Sheen in this modest, worthy drama. The subject matter concerns the postwar nuclear tests in the Nevada desert and the tragic consequences for the unwitting soldiers forced to witness them. Estevez plays the naive young doctor who gets involved in the test programme, with Sheen playing the same character in the eighties. It's a tad overwrought at times, but the two leads are excellent. ▭

Martin Sheen *Dr Alexander Brown (present)* • Emilio Estevez *Dr Alexander Brown (past)* • Lea Thompson *Sally Matthews* • Melinda Dillon *Paula Brown* • Joe Pantoliano *Jack Russell* • Nicholas Pryor *Colonel William Devereau* ■ Dir Peter Markle • Scr TS Cook, from the novel *Atomic Soldiers* by Howard Rosenberg

Nightbreed ★★★ 18

Horror 1990 · US · Colour · 97mins

Hellraiser established Clive Barker as a major force in modern horror, but nothing he's done since has ever quite matched its unique visceral power. The trump up Barker's sleeve this time is the casting of cult horror director David Cronenberg as a malevolent shrink. He dupes a patient into believing that he's a serial killer and then tracks him down to the netherworld of Midian, a secret sanctuary for mutants and freaks. While this is certainly self-indulgent – Barker directs and adapted the screenplay from his own novel *Cabal* – the imagination on view certainly impresses. ▭

Craig Sheffer *Boone* • Charles Haid *Captain Eigerman* • David Cronenberg *Dr Decker* • Anne Bobby *Lori* • Hugh Quarshie *Detective Joyce* ■ Dir Clive Barker • Scr Clive Barker, from his novel *Cabal*

The Nightcomers ★★ 18

Thriller 1972 · UK · Colour · 92mins

Marlon Brando is at his most loutishly sexual, tearing the clothes off Stephanie Beacham in this prequel to Henry James's *The Turn of the Screw*. Filmed at a Gothic manse near Cambridge, it's a cod-Freudian exercise in sadomasochism, with Brando playing the groundsman and Beacham the governess to the two children destined to see ghosts later. Filmed with a distinct lack of subtlety and stretching early seventies permissiveness to the limit, it was the last picture Brando made before he revived his flagging fortunes with *The Godfather* and *Last Tango in Paris*. It's trashily enjoyable, though, which is as good as any Michael Winner movie gets. Contains sex scenes, some swearing and violence. ▭

Marlon Brando *Quint* • Stephanie Beacham *Miss Jessel* • Thora Hird *Mrs Grose* • Verna Harvey *Flora* • Christopher Ellis *Miles* • Harry Andrews *Master of the house* ■ Dir Michael Winner • Scr Michael Hastings, from characters created by Henry James

Nightfall ★★★

Crime drama 1956 · US · BW

Aldo Ray was a briefly glimpsed star who burned himself out all too quickly, but he was a formidable presence even as the "wronged man" in this pacey thriller by *noir*-meister Jacques Tourneur. It's an early outing for scriptwriter Stirling Silliphant from a cult-pulp by David Goodis, and he's fashioned a bleak morality tale about a man who thinks he can't win after being framed for murder and robbery, but then discovers gleams of hope. Anne Bancroft is particularly good as the ambiguous figure of salvation.

Aldo Ray *James Vanning* • Brian Keith *John* • Anne Bancroft *Marie Gardner* • Jocelyn Brando *Laura Fraser* • James Gregory *Ben Fraser* • Frank Albertson *Dr Edward Gurston* ■ Dir Jacques Tourneur • Scr Stirling Silliphant, from a novel by David Goodis

Nightfall ★★★ 18

Drama 1999 · Ger/Por/Neth · Colour · 146mins

If *Fate* and *Frost* hadn't already established Fred Kelemen among Europe's offbeat elite, then this unremittingly bleak study of the contemporary human condition surely will. Emasculated by unemployment, Wolfgang Michael wanders his desolate town in a impenetrable torpor that finally drives his girlfriend, Verena Jasch, out of his life and into prostitution. But their everyday tragedy pales beside the Tarkovsky-esque encounter with an eccentric bellmaker, the sight of some paedophiles bidding for a small child and the discovery of her body in the river. The technical accomplishment somewhat undermines the nihilism of the action, but this is still a sobering experience. In German with English subtitles.

Wolfgang Michael *Anton* • Verena Jasch *Leni* • Isa Hochgerner *Nina* • Adolfo Assor *Bell founder* ■ Dir/Scr Fred Kelemen

Nightflyers ★ 18

Science-fiction 1987 · US · Colour · 85mins

Adapted from a novella by George RR Martin, this futuristic tale had potential, but lacked the budget and the expertise to capitalise on it. (The production had a troubled history, while a major re-edit by the producers made director Robert Collector opt for the pseudonym TC Blake.) The fog machine works overtime to hide the substandard sets as the motley crew of a decrepit spaceship goes in search of an alien race. The cast includes Catherine Mary Stewart and Michael Des Barres; they've both done better work elsewhere. ▭

Catherine Mary Stewart *Miranda* • John Standing *D'Branin* • Michael Praed *Royd* • Lisa Blount *Audrey* • Michael Des Barres *Jon Winderman* ■ Dir TC Blake [Robert Collector] • Scr Robert Jaffe, from a novella by George RR Martin

Nighthawks ★★★ 18

Action thriller 1981 · US · Colour · 94mins

At this stage in his career Sylvester Stallone was not known as an action star, and in some ways this is his first real stab at the genre with which he is now most closely associated. And it certainly is a belter. Stallone and Billy Dee Williams play two New York cops who are sent scampering all over the Big Apple on the trail of a vicious international terrorist (Rutger Hauer, making an electrifying Hollywood debut). The able supporting cast includes Lindsay Wagner and British actor Nigel Davenport, and director Bruce Malmuth keeps the action zipping along at a pleasing pace. Contains swearing and violence. ▭

Sylvester Stallone *Deke Dasilva* • Billy Dee Williams *Matthew Fox* • Lindsay Wagner *Irene* • Persis Khambatta *Shakka* • Nigel Davenport *Peter Hartman* • Rutger Hauer *Wulfgar* • Hilarie Thompson *Pam* ■ Dir Bruce Malmuth • Scr David Shaber, from a story by David Shaber, Paul Sylbert

A Nightingale Sang in Berkeley Square ★★★ PG

Comedy thriller 1979 · UK · Colour · 105mins

This pleasing, if predictable, heist caper boasts an extraordinary cast. Giving one of the better performances of his twilight years, David Niven plays a criminal mastermind who blackmails old lag Richard Jordan into joining his audacious assault on a swanky bank. Making his first film in five years, director Ralph Thomas fails to impose himself on the familiar sequence of events, but coaxes a splendid performance from Gloria Grahame. ▭

Richard Jordan *Pinky Green* • David Niven *Ivan the Terrible* • Oliver Tobias *Foxy* • Gloria Grahame *Ma* • Elke Sommer *Miss Pelham* • Richard Johnson *Inspector Watford* • Joss Ackland *Governor* • Michael Angelis *Pealer Bell* ■ Dir Ralph Thomas • Scr Guy Elmes

Nightlife ★★ 15

Comedy horror 1989 · US · Colour · 89mins

It must have sounded like a bundle of laughs at the time. A female vampire

(Maryam d'Abo) pitches up in modern-day Mexico City and falls in love with a blood-bank doctor, but her centuries-old ex-lover (Ben Cross) can't let go. Like many good wheezes, however, this one gets a stake through the heart from reel one, and the sheer absence of any discernible class or wit is painfully evident. There is a decent comedy in here somewhere struggling to get out, but the reality is less than impressive. Contains violence. ▭

Ben Cross *Vlad* • Maryam D'Abo *Angelique* • Keith Szarabajka *Dr David Zuckerman* • Jesse Corti *Jose* • Glenn Shadix *Jose* ■ Dir Daniel Taplitz • Scr Anne Beatts

The Nightman ★★★

Thriller 1992 · US · Colour · 96mins

Charles Haid (*Hill Street Blues*), goes behind the camera for this above-average TV thriller. Ted Marcoux plays a Vietnam soldier who finds himself caught up in a love triangle with Joanna Kerns, the owner of a decrepit hotel, and her teenage daughter Jenny Robertson, with tragic consequences. Years later, Robertson attempts to piece together the truth about the affair. It won't win many points for originality, but there are attractive performances from the largely unknown cast. Contains violence, swearing and nudity.

Joanna Kerns *Eve Rhodes* • Jenny Robertson *Dr Margaret Rhodes* • Ted Marcoux *Tom Wolfe* • Lou Walker *Willie* • Latanya Richardson *Emily* • Benji Wilhoite *Billy* ■ Dir Charles Haid • Scr John Wells, Lucille Fletcher, James Poe

Nightmare ★★★★

Crime drama 1956 · US · BW · 89mins

Director Maxwell Shane remade his 1947 film *Fear in the Night* to produce a much better movie from Cornell Woolrich's original story. Kevin McCarthy gives a good performance as the musician who becomes convinced he's a murderer, but Edward G Robinson is better as the detective who sees the flaw in what appears to be an open-and-shut case. Cameraman Joseph Biroc's moody, black-and-white photography adds real menace to the disturbing idea, and there's a jazz score by Herschel Burke Gilbert that's as jumpy as a neurotic's bad dream.

Edward G Robinson *Rene Bressard* • Kevin McCarthy *Stan Grayson* • Connie Russell *Gina* • Virginia Christine *Sue* • Rhys Williams *Torrence* • Gage Clarke *Belknap* ■ Dir Maxwell Shane • Scr Maxwell Shane, from the short story by William Irish [Cornell Woolrich]

Nightmare ★★★

Horror 1964 · UK · BW · 82mins

Ace cameraman Freddie Francis directs this Hammer-financed production, with English rose Jennie Linden having terrible nightmares about being tossed into a loony bin. The poor dear is taken to one of those dark, foreboding country houses where things go bump in the night. Is Jennie really mad or is there some diabolical plot afoot? It isn't too long before the knives come out and everyone starts screaming. Brimming with sexual imagery and the odd reference to Henry James's *The Turn of the Screw*, this is let down by a pallid hero (David Knight) but pulls off quite a few decent shocks.

David Knight *Henry Baxter* • Moira Redmond *Grace* • Brenda Bruce *Mary* • Jennie Linden *Janet* • George A Cooper *John* ■ *Dir* Freddie Francis • *Scr* Jimmy Sangster

Nightmare ★★
Thriller   1991 · US · Colour · 95mins

Look who's stalking? In brutally topical and lurid fashion, this rather tacky TV movie follows a young mother (Victoria Principal) trying to save her daughter from a molester (Jonathan Banks) who is now out on bail and threatening to return to the scene of his previous crimes. The scenario is scary enough, but the film really needs a more in-depth approach than this.

Victoria Principal *Linda Hemmings* • Jonathan Banks *Eddie Ryter* • Paul Sorvino *Lieutenant Jake Willman* • Danielle Harris *Dana Hemmings* • Christopher Wynne *Officer Haggerty* • Christine Healy *Susan Fisher* ■ *Dir* John Pasquin • *Scr* John Bensink, Rick Husky, from a novel by Marjorie Dorner

Nightmare Alley ★★★
Horror   1947 · US · BW · 111mins

Tyrone Power, 20th Century-Fox's most bankable and romantic leading man at the time, gave his image a jolt with this bizarre study of mental breakdown, in which he was reunited with his *Razor's Edge* director, Edmund Goulding. Power is a bogus mind-reader in a small-time carnival who revives Joan Blondell and Ian Keith's long forgotten act as a means to get rich, with tragic results. The script, by Jules Furthman, is based on a novel by William Lindsay Gresham, a writer obsessed by the emotional nakedness of circus performance who eventually committed suicide.

Tyrone Power *Stanton Carlisle* • Joan Blondell *Zeena* • Coleen Gray *Molly* • Helen Walker *Dr Lilith Ritter* • Taylor Holmes *Ezra Grindle* • Mike Mazurki *Bruno* • Ian Keith *Pete* • Julia Dean *Mrs Peabody* ■ *Dir* Edmund Goulding • *Scr* Jules Furthman, from the novel by William Lindsay Gresham

Nightmare at Bitter Creek ★★15
Thriller   1988 · US · Colour · 88mins

It's *Deliverance* for the gals, as Lindsay Wagner, Joanna Cassidy and their friends go wandering through the wilderness with alcoholic guide Tom Skerritt and end up coming face to face with a group of psychotic killers. Unfortunately, director Tim Burstall doesn't inject anywhere near as much tension into his drama as there was in John Boorman's superior white-knuckler, and you spend more time worrying about how the girls are managing without their hairstylists and make-up bags than about whether or not they will survive. Contains violence and swearing. ▭

Lindsay Wagner *Nita* • Tom Skerritt *Ding Harris* • Joanna Cassidy *Allison* • Constance McCashin *Connie* ■ *Dir* Tim Burstall • *Scr* Scott Swanton, Greg McCarty

Nightmare Come True ★★
Psychological thriller   1996 · US · Colour

A reasonable TV-movie thriller that opts for psychological chills rather than

---

standard suspense. Katy Boyer is the newly trained nurse who moves back in with her parents (Gerald McRaney and Shelley Fabares) and discovers that their constant bickering provokes some unpleasant childhood memories. It's well played by the cast and director Christopher Leitch, best known so far for family films such as *Courage Mountain* and *Teen Wolf Too*, handles the proceedings with aplomb. Contains violence and swearing.

Gerald McRaney *Don Zarn* • Katy Boyer *Sarah Zarn* • Shelley Fabares *Lily Zarn* ■ *Dir* Christopher Leitch • *Scr* Gerald Dipego, Nevin Schriner

Nightmare in Big Sky Country ★★
Drama based on a true story   1998 · US · Colour

America's continuing struggle with radical fringe groups provides the background to this true story of one woman's determination to do the right thing. Single mother and local court judge Marty Bethel (*thirtysomething*'s Patricia Wettig) finds her life turns into a nightmare when Montana freeman M Emmet Walsh refuses to pay overdue traffic fines and begins terrorising her. Solid, restrained performances from Wettig and Walsh, the lack of false heroics and authentic locations lend believability and interest to this TV movie exploring the darker aspects of American life.

Patricia Wettig *Marty Bethel* • Matt McCoy *Joe* • M Emmet Walsh *Marshall Jim Phillip* • Anne Archer ■ *Dir* Alan Metzger • *Scr* Sharon Elizabeth Doyle

Nightmare in Chicago ★★★★
Crime drama   1968 · US · Colour · 80mins

Robert Altman was working in television when he directed this tale of a psychotic murderer known to the police and press as the Georgie Porgie killer. Featuring Philip Abbott, Ted Knight and Charles McGraw, it was shot entirely on location in Chicago and has the creepy atmosphere of an authentic bad dream. TV movies don't come much better than this.

Charles McGraw *Georgie Porgie* • Robert Ridgely • Ted Knight • Philip Abbott ■ *Dir* Robert Altman • *Scr* David Moessinger, from the novel *Killer on the Turnpike* by William P McGivern

A Nightmare in the Daylight ★★
Thriller   1992 · US · Colour · 120mins

Superman star Christopher Reeve and TV movie queen Jaclyn Smith head the cast of this thriller about a married woman who discovers she and her family are being followed by a man (Reeve) who claims she is his long-lost wife. It's interesting to see Reeve in a meaty bad guy role as opposed to the do-gooder parts we're used to, but, unfortunately, he can't raise this predictable tale above the ordinary. However, the big puzzle is how come ex-Charlie's Angel Smith doesn't just do one of her high kicks and get rid of him once and for all.

Jaclyn Smith *Megan Lambert* • Christopher Reeve *Sean Farrell* • Tom Mason *Peter*

Lambert • Christina Pickles *Sarah Jenner* • Glynnis O'Connor *Sloan Evans* ■ *Dir* Lou Antonio • *Scr* Frederic Hunter

Nightmare in the Sun ★★
Crime drama   1964 · US · Colour · 81mins

This innocent-on-the-run thriller finds the sexy wife (Ursula Andress) of a rich ranch owner picking up a hitchhiker (John Derek, her then real-life husband) and bringing him home. The hitchhiker decides to leave, but in a fit of rage the ranch boss kills Andress, leaving the drifter blamed for her murder by a corrupt, blackmailing sheriff. Less suspenseful than it sounds, but there are some early walk-ons from the likes of Robert Duvall and Richard Jaeckel.

Ursula Andress *Marsha* • John Derek *Hitchhiker* • Aldo Ray *Sheriff* • Arthur O'Connell *Sam Wilson* • Sammy Davis Jr *Truckdriver* • Allyn Joslyn *Junk dealer* • Keenan Wynn *Song-and-dance misfit* • Chick Chandler *Tavern owner* • Richard Jaeckel *Motorcyclist* • Robert Duvall *Motorcyclist* ■ *Dir* Marc Lawrence • *Scr* Ted Thomas, Fanya Lawrence, from a story by Marc Lawrence, Fanya Lawrence, George Fass

A Nightmare on Elm Street ★★★★18
Horror   1984 · US · Colour · 87mins

Scream director Wes Craven's exciting and pioneering fright flick led to six sequels and a TV series. Four teens experience identical nightmares haunted by the shockingly popular supernatural fiend Freddy Krueger (known here as Fred). Only Heather Langenkamp can save her friends from violent death by staying awake and keeping the razor-fingered maniac at bay. Craven's ingenious merging of dreams with reality gives a markedly different horror jolt. Bloody special effects and suspenseful murders disguise a somewhat weak script, but the engaging performances (look for Johnny Depp in his screen debut) and Craven's command of the chilling concept make it a classic. ▭

Robert Englund *Fred Krueger* • John Saxon *Lt Thompson* • Ronee Blakely *Marge Thompson* • Heather Langenkamp *Nancy Thompson* • Amanda Wyss *Tina Gray* • Johnny Depp *Glen Lantz* ■ *Dir/Scr* Wes Craven

A Nightmare on Elm Street 2: Freddy's Revenge ★18
Horror   1985 · US · Colour · 81mins

Mark Patton moves into the sinister Elm Street house with his family, and Freddy Krueger just as quickly moves into his dreams in this damp squib of a sequel. Melting furniture, eyes peering out from mouths and an exploding budgerigar are director Jack Sholder's poor substitutes for the meaty terror creator Wes Craven provided the first time around. Surprisingly homo-erotic in content, Sholder's sub-standard shocker replaces clever dream imagery with the more conventional theme of possession. Patton contributes a one-expression performance. That the series completely recovered from this bust is a miracle. ▭

Mark Patton *Jesse Walsh* • Kim Myers *Lisa Webber* • Robert Rusler *Ron Grady* • Clu Gulager *Mr Walsh* • Hope Lange *Mrs Walsh* •

Robert Englund *Freddy Krueger* ■ *Dir* Jack Sholder • *Scr* David Chaskin, from a character created by Wes Craven

A Nightmare on Elm Street 3: Dream Warriors ★★★★18
Horror   1987 · US · Colour · 92mins

Anything can happen, and always does, in this imaginative sequel, which stretches the boundaries of eighties horror to new limits with wildly inventive and brilliantly executed mayhem. Thanks to the psychic ability of Patricia Arquette, a group of youngsters terrorised by Freddy Krueger take part in a controlled experiment where they enter each other's nightmares on a time-share basis to exorcise his malevolent spirit from the shock corridors of their dream psyches. Full of great special effects (a Freddy snake, a possessed TV set, a bondage victim lashed to a bed by human tongues), this is a roller-coaster ride from the opening Edgar Allan Poe quotation to the final Ray Harryhausen homage. ▭

Heather Langenkamp *Nancy Thompson* • Patricia Arquette *Kristen Parker* • Larry Fishburne [Laurence Fishburne] *Max* • Priscilla Pointer *Dr Elizabeth Simms* • Craig Wasson *Dr Neil Goldman* • Robert Englund *Freddy Krueger* ■ *Dir* Chuck Russell • *Scr* Wes Craven, Bruce Wagner, Chuck Russell, Frank Darabont, from a story by Wes Craven, Bruce Wagner, from characters created by Wes Craven

A Nightmare on Elm Street 4: The Dream Master ★★★★18
Horror   1988 · US · Colour · 88mins

Alice (Lisa Wilcox) goes through the blood-stained looking glass in one of the best Freddy Krueger episodes, given a wonderfully different European art-horror feel by future blockbuster director Renny Harlin. Winning Wilcox takes on the talents of her deceased friends to become the Dream Master, the ancient guardian of positive scenarios, poised to counterattack Freddy's negative nightmares in this beautifully photographed redefinition of the pop-culture formula. Harlin puts a fresh spin on the recurring nightmare cliché and there's a marvellous scene where Wilcox is flung into the on-screen action from a cinema balcony. A better symbol of the effectiveness of this particular segment would be hard to find. ▭

Robert Englund *Freddy Krueger* • Lisa Wilcox *Alice* • Rodney Eastman *Joey* • Danny Hassel *Danny* • Andras Jones *Rick* • Tuesday Knight *Kristen Parker* ■ *Dir* Renny Harlin • *Scr* Brian Helgeland, Scott Pierce, from a story by Ken Wykowski... William Kotzwinkle, Brian Helgeland, from a character created by Wes Craven

A Nightmare on Elm Street 5: The Dream Child ★★18
Horror   1989 · US · Colour · 86mins

Psycho child molester Freddy Krueger again survives through thick and thin – mostly thin – in this unimaginative body counter. Lisa Wilcox thinks she's banished "the bastard son of a thousand maniacs" from her life until she's made pregnant by college jock Danny Hassel. Because, according to the jumbled script, a foetus can dream a few days after conception, and

 = SUITABLE FOR ALL   Uc = SUITABLE FOR ALL, ESPECIALLY FOR YOUNG CHILDREN (VIDEO ONLY)   PG = PARENTAL GUIDANCE

Freddy seizes this chance to enter her subconscious once more and finger-blade her unbelieving friends to death. Director Stephen Hopkins valiantly tries to paper over the huge cracks in the derivative low-energy thrills by replacing vapid gore with furious pacing, sudden shock cuts and rock video-style cartoonish imagery, but the womb with a view concept never puts it on a convincingly empathetic footing.

Robert Englund *Freddy Krueger* • Lisa Wilcox *Alice Johnson* • Danny Hassel *Dan* • Kelly Jo Minter *Yvonne* • Erika Anderson *Greta* • Joe Seely *Mark* ■ *Dir* Stephen Hopkins • *Scr* Leslie Bohem, from a story by John Skip, Craig Spector, Leslie Bohem, from a character created by Wes Craven

Nightmare Street ★★

Mystery thriller   1998 · US · Colour

A successful film career was predicted for Sherilyn Fenn following her starring role in David Lynch's TV series *Twin Peaks*, but so far she has failed to live up to expectations. In this Lynch-like TV-movie thriller, she plays a mother who wakes up in hospital to discover that her world has been turned on its head: not only does everybody insist that she is someone else, but this "other person" is also the prime suspect following the disappearance of her daughter. Apart from Fenn, the cast is short of familiar faces, but this is an adequate time-filler.

Sherilyn Fenn *Joanna Burke/Sarah Randolph* • Thomas Gibson *Dr Matt Westbrook* • Rena Sofer *Penny* • Steve Harris *Detective Miller* ■ *Dir* Colin Bucksey • *Scr* Rama Laurie Stagner, Dan Witt, Margaret Tabor

Nightmares ★★ 15

Science-fiction horror
1983 · US · Colour · 94mins

Originally the pilot for an intended TV series in *The Twilight Zone* tradition, this uneven four-part anthology is more miss than hit. A housewife under murderous threat, a deadly video game obsessing Emilio Estevez, a priest losing faith on the eve of battling a possessed truck, and a giant rat terrorising a suburban family jostle for attention in a workmanlike collection accenting substandard eeriness and few scares. While the first two tales are OK, the other two are dire.

Emilio Estevez *JJ Cooney* • Cristina Raines *Lisa* • Joe Lambie *Phil* • Anthony James *Clerk* • Clare Nono *Newswoman* • Raleigh Bond *Neighbour* • Robert Phelps *Newsman* • Dixie Lynn Royce *Little girl* ■ *Dir* Joseph Sargent • *Scr* Christopher Crowe, Jeffrey Bloom

Nights of Cabiria ★★★★★ 15

Drama   1957 · It · BW · 106mins

Often dismissed as grating and sentimental, this is one of Federico Fellini's most accessible films, which harks back to his days as a screenwriter during Italy's neorealist phase. The winner of the 1957 Oscar for best foreign film, it boasts a bravura performance from the director's wife, Giulietta Masina, as the child-like prostitute who is misused by everyone she encounters, yet still has the sense of self-worth to come bouncing back. Every bit as vulnerable as Shirley MacLaine in the Hollywood musical remake, *Sweet Charity*,

Masina eschews sentiment to meet fate with enviable grace. An Italian language film.

Giulietta Masina *Cabiria* • François Périer *Oscar D'Onofrio, accountant* • Amedeo Nazzari *Alberto Lazzari, movie star* • Aldo Silvani *Hypnotist* ■ *Dir* Federico Fellini • *Scr* Federico Fellini, Ennio Flaiano, Tullio Pinelli, Pier Paolo Pasolini (additional dialogue) • *Music* Nino Rota • *Art Director* Piero Gherardi

Nightscream ★★

Mystery thriller   1997 · Can · Colour

Is Candace Cameron Bure really the reincarnation of a popular teenager who died in a murder that shocked a small Oregon town? Teri Garr, the girl's grieving mother, wants to think so, but the community and, especially, the killer don't want old scandals and clues raked up again. Despite its superficial gloss, this strange supernatural TV mystery thriller is very average indeed, and both the direction and performances are bland.

Candace Cameron Bure *Drew Summers/Laura Fairgate* • Casper Van Dien *Teddie* • Denis Arndt *Ray Ordwell* • Teri Garr *Julie Ordwell* • Ned Vaughn *Charles Pendelton* • Bobby Hosea *RJ Turnage* ■ *Dir* Noel Nosseck • *Scr* Eugenia Bostwick-Singer, Raymond Singer, Gary Tieche, from the novel *The Soul of Betty Fairchild* by Robert Specht

Nightwatch ★★★★ 18

Chiller   1994 · Den · Colour · 102mins

A young student becomes night watchman at a mortuary where sinister things are happening and, before long, he's suspected of being a serial killer. Danish director Ole Bornedal's tense chiller is a quality genre item full of slow-burning suspense and high shock value. Everything good about this nerve-wracking original was dumbed down for the American remake. In Danish with English subtitles.

Nikolaj Coster Waldau *Martin Bork* • Sofie Gråbøl *Kalinka Martens* • Kim Bodnia *Jens Arnkiel* ■ *Dir/Scr* Ole Bornedal

Nightwatch ★★ 18

Horror thriller   1997 · US · Colour · 96mins

Just as Dutch film-maker George Sluizer ruined his own film *The Vanishing* in Hollywood, so director Ole Bornedal takes his original 1994 Danish terror masterpiece *Nattevagten* – about a rookie morgue night watchman suspected of being a serial killer – and replaces the scary terrors with formula gruesome shocks. The artful blend of hairy humour and creepy horror that graced the original doesn't quite survive in this good-looking poor relation, and both Nick Nolte and Patricia Arquette sleepwalk through their familiar roles. But Ewan McGregor acquits himself well, despite a wavering accent. Contains swearing, violence and sexual references.

Ewan McGregor *Martin* • Nick Nolte *Inspector Thomas Cray* • Patricia Arquette *Katherine* • Josh Brolin *James* • Lauren Graham *Marie* • Brad Dourif *Duty doctor* ■ *Dir* Ole Bornedal • *Scr* Steven Soderbergh, Ole Bornedal, from the 1994 film

Nightwing ★★ 15

Horror   1979 · US · Colour · 100mins

The native Americans of New Mexico are in an uproar thanks to nightly raids by swarms of vampire bats that leave their cattle dead and their people horribly mutilated. Time to call in bat biologist David Warner, who's had it in for the migratory beasts ever since they ate his father. The initial promise of a penetrating look at the plight of American Indians as they struggle to be recognised by their white political representatives is soon dropped in favour of one unconvincing bat attack after another. Arthur Hiller's uninspired direction and the absurd fake bats (built by Carlo Rambaldi of *ET* fame) doom this laughable version of Martin Cruz Smith's bestseller.

Nick Mancuso *Youngman Duran* • David Warner *Phillip Payne* • Kathryn Harrold *Anne Dillon* • Stephen Macht *Walker Chee* • Strother Martin *Selwyn* ■ *Dir* Arthur Hiller • *Scr* Steve Shagan, Bud Shrake, Martin Cruz Smith, from the novel by Martin Cruz Smith

Nijinsky ★★★★ 15

Biographical drama
1980 · UK · Colour · 119mins

Originally a Ken Russell project, this biopic of the tormented Russian ballet dancer has enough sex, angst and controversy to keep it boiling. Based on Nijinsky's diaries and Mrs Nijinsky's memoirs, it stars George De La Pena as the dancer and Alan Bates as his jilted inamorata, the impresario Diaghilev. As a study of life, art and ego, it's often close to Powell and Pressburger's *The Red Shoes* – powerfully acted and convincingly staged, with wonderful music. But the details of Nijinsky's final years of mental collapse are somewhat skated over.

Alan Bates *Sergei Diaghilev* • George De La Pena *Vaslav Nijinsky* • Leslie Browne *Romola DePulsky* • Alan Badel *Baron De Gunzberg* • Carla Fracci *Tamara Karsavina* • Colin Blakely *Vassili* • Ronald Pickup *Igor Stravinsky* • Ronald Lacey *Leon Bakst* ■ *Dir* Herbert Ross • *Scr* Hugh Wheeler, from the memoirs by Romola Nijinsky and the diary by Vaslav Nijinsky

Nikita ★★★★ 18

Thriller   1990 · Fr/It · Colour · 112mins

After being involved in a robbery, vicious junkie Anne Parillaud is reprogrammed as an assassin for a secret government agency in French director Luc Besson's extremely exciting thriller with a feminist slant. In paying homage to American action movies, Besson goes one better than his clear inspirations, to craft a beautifully stylised, enthralling and very violent comic strip. Parillaud (married to Besson at the time) is tremendous as the unscrupulous hit woman and Jeanne Moreau's Charm Teacher cameo is a gem. But it's Besson's boldly modern approach to traditional *film noir* material that makes this elemental mind-blower so striking. In French with English subtitles. Contains violence.

Anne Parillaud *Nikita* • Jean-Hugues Anglade *Marco* • Tcheky Karyo *Bob* • Jeanne Moreau *Amande* • Jean Reno *Victor the cleaner* • Marc Duret *Rico* • Philippe Leroy-Beaulieu *Grossman* ■ *Dir/Scr* Luc Besson

Nil by Mouth ★★★★★ 18

Drama   1997 · UK/US · Colour · 128mins

A harrowing directorial debut by actor Gary Oldman, this centres on violence and alcoholism within a working-class south London family. Although the film is not specifically autobiographical, Oldman has drawn from his own background to create a portrait of dysfunctional domestic life that is both convincing and compelling. Ray Winstone hulks brilliantly in the central role as the alienated husband and father trapped in a descending spiral of drunken rage. Kathy Burke matches Winstone's intensity – and won the best actress award at Cannes – for her performance as the brutalised wife. *Nil by Mouth* tempers its bleakness with tender understanding and wounding insight. Contains swearing, sexual references and violence.

Ray Winstone *Raymond* • Kathy Burke *Valerie* • Charlie Creed-Miles *Billy* • Laila Morse *Janet* • Edna Doré *Kath* • Chrissie Cotterill *Paula* ■ *Dir/Scr* Gary Oldman

Nina Takes a Lover ★★ 18

Romantic comedy
1993 · US · Colour · 93mins

This initially intriguing romantic comedy has *sex, lies, and videotape*'s Laura San Giacomo as a young married woman who decides to have an affair with a photographer (played by Welsh actor Paul Rhys) while her husband is away. The story is related in flashbacks with San Giacomo relating the tale of her now-over fling to a journalist, and it soon becomes clear that things are not quite as they seem. But the main weakness of this run-of-the-mill movie is the fact that all the characters come across as so self-absorbed.

Laura San Giacomo *Nina* • Paul Rhys *Photographer* • Michael O'Keefe *Journalist* • Fisher Stevens *Paulie* ■ *Dir/Scr* Alan Jacobs

Nine ½ Weeks ★★ 18

Erotic drama   1985 · US · Colour · 94mins

Despite the high production values and a starry cast, this remains mild, soft-core entertainment. Kim Basinger is the successful career woman who falls under the spell of the mysterious Mickey Rourke and finds herself being led into dangerous sexual waters. It's complete tosh, of course, and the storyline is so slim that it just becomes a series of beautifully composed nude encounters. However, Adrian Lyne's flashy direction gives the material a glossy surface sheen that it barely deserves. Contains sex scenes, violence and swearing.

Mickey Rourke *John* • Kim Basinger *Elizabeth* • Margaret Whitton *Molly* • David Margulies *Harvey* • Christine Baranski *Thea* • Karen Young *Sue* • William De Acutis *Ted* • Dwight Weist *Mathew Farnsworth* ■ *Dir* Adrian Lyne • *Scr* Patricia Knop, Zalman King, Sarah Kernochan, from the novel by Elizabeth McNeill

9 Deaths of the Ninja ★ 18

Martial arts spoof
1985 · US · Colour · 89mins

The makers of this abysmal martial arts adventure would have you believe it's a spoof, but there is little evidence

to support what looks like a claim hurriedly made after the ghastly truth became all too clear. The story follows the adventures of an elite anti-terrorist force's attempts to free hostages imprisoned deep in the Philippines jungle. Star Sho Kosugi brings a meagre amount of credibility and dignity to the proceedings, but Brent Huff, then being groomed as a possible successor to Chuck Norris, is devoid of charisma. You have been warned! Contains violence. ▭

Sho Kosugi *Spike Shinobi* • Brent Huff *Steve Gordon* • Emilia Lesniak *Jennifer Barnes* • Blackie Dammett *Alby the cruel* • Regina Richardson *Honey Hump* • Vijay Amritraj *Rankin* ■ *Dir/Scr* Emmett Alston

Nine Hours to Rama ★★
Historical drama
1963 · UK/US · Colour · 125mins

While David Lean tried but gave up and Richard Attenborough battled for 20 years to make biopics of Gandhi, this melodrama about the assassination simply cut through all the red tape. German actor Horst Buchholz is rather good as the Hindu extremist, Naturam Godse, who believed that Gandhi should die, though Robert Morley in Indian make-up lacks credibility, and some of the lesser characters fail to come to life. There's some fine location work, yet in the end the best thing in the entire picture is Saul Bass's fine credit titles.

Horst Buchholz *Naturam Godse* • José Ferrer *Superintendent Gopal Das* • Valerie Gearon *Rani Mehta* • Don Borisenko *Naryan Apte* • Robert Morley *PK Mussadi* • Diane Baker *Sheila* • Harry Andrews *General Singh* ■ *Dir* Mark Robson • *Scr* Nelson Gidding, from the novel by Stanley Wolpert

The Nine Lives of Fritz the Cat ★ 18
Animated erotic comedy
1974 · US · Colour · 73mins

This uninspired sequel to *Fritz the Cat* finds the stoned feline imagining his other lives in the past and future. The astute social comment of both Robert Crumb's original strips and the first film directed by Ralph Bakshi is mostly gone, and instead the animators seem more intent on creating psychedelic effects for the benefit of substance abusers at midnight matinées. ▭

Skip Hinnant *Fritz* • Reva Rose *Fritz's old lady* ■ *Dir* Robert Taylor • *Scr* Fred Halliday, Eric Monte, Robert Taylor

Nine Months ★★★
Comedy
1994 · Fr · Colour · 107mins

Just as *Trois Hommes et un Couffin* surpasses *Three Men and a Baby*, so this French comedy is infinitely superior to its Hollywood remake. Primarily, this is because it is less coy in its depiction of the sexual and gynaecological aspects of pregnancy than Chris Columbus's film. It is therefore able to develop its relationships and shifting attitudes on more than a superficially comic level. Similarly, Patrick Braoudé is less mannered than Hugh Grant and genuinely appears to be perturbed by the prospect of fatherhood, despite the advice of family and friends and the

assurances of long-suffering wife, Philippine Leroy-Beaulieu.

Philippine Leroy-Beaulieu *Mathilde* • Catherine Jacob *Dominique* • Patrick Braoudé *Samuel* • Daniel Russo *Georges* • Patrick Bouchitey *Marc* ■ *Dir/Scr* Patrick Braoudé

Nine Months ★★ 12
Comedy
1995 · US · Colour · 98mins

This attempt to cement Hugh Grant's reputation as the Cary Grant of the nineties following the massive international success of *Four Weddings and a Funeral* collapses under sentimental crudity, as child psychologist Grant tries to come to terms with his fear of impending fatherhood when long-term girlfriend Julianne Moore announces she is pregnant. In fact, the movie's better known for Grant's off-screen performance with a Hollywood prostitute shortly before its release, which gave the film more publicity than it warranted. Contains swearing. ▭

Hugh Grant *Samuel Faulkner* • Julianne Moore *Rebecca Dwyer* • Tom Arnold *Marty Dwyer* • Joan Cusack *Gail Dwyer* • Jeff Goldblum *Sean Fletcher* • Robin Williams *Dr Kosevich* ■ *Dir* Chris Columbus • *Scr* Chris Columbus, from the 1994 film by Patrick Braoudé

976-EVIL ★ 18
Horror
1988 · US · Colour · 94mins

Nerdy Stephen Geoffreys calls a "horrorscope" hot line and obtains supernatural powers that enable him to take revenge on his tormentors. A confusing mess directed by horror icon Robert Englund who, not surprisingly, falls back on Freddy Krueger wisecracks and other lifts from *A Nightmare on Elm Street* to beef up his demonic disaster. Sandy Dennis as Geoffreys's kooky religious aunt makes this stale tale almost worthwhile. ▭

Patrick O'Bryan *Spike* • Sandy Dennis *Aunt Lucy* • Stephen Geoffreys *Hoax* • Jim Metzler *Marty Palmer* • Maria Rubell *Angella Martinez* • Lezlie Deane *Suzie* ■ *Dir* Robert Englund • *Scr* Rhet Topham, Brian Helgeland

976-EVIL 2 ★ 18
Horror
1992 · US · Colour · 86mins

In this awful sequel to the 1988 original, a serial killer is revealed to be a rotting zombie who murders via astral projection. Completely devoid of imagination, apart from one sequence where a victim is trapped in a black-and-white mix of *Night of the Living Dead* and *It's a Wonderful Life*, this horror cheapie is royally fouled up by director Jim Wynorski, a protégé of Roger Corman's. ▭

Patrick O'Bryan *Spike* • Rene Assa *Professor Grubeck* • Debbie James *Robin* • Brigitte Nielsen ■ *Dir* Jim Wynorski • *Scr* Erik Anjou

9/30/55 ★★★
Drama
1977 · US · Colour · 107mins

The title is the date on which James Dean crashed his Porsche and turned himself into a legend. This film's hero, Richard Thomas, is a Dean-obsessed student in Arkansas, who hears the news of his idol's death and with other students stages an elaborate pagan-style ceremony which ends in a terrible accident to one of his friends. Moodily shot by Gordon Willis and scored by

veteran Leonard Rosenman (who began his career by scoring the Dean classics *East of Eden* and *Rebel Without a Cause*), this is an effective meditation on the power of celebrity and its impact on youth culture.

Richard Thomas *Jimmy J* • Susan Tyrrell *Melba Lou* • Deborah Benson *Charlotte* • Lisa Blount *Billie Jean* • Tom Hulce *Hanley* • Dennis Quaid *Frank* • Mary Kai Clark *Pat* • Dennis Christopher *Eugene* ■ *Dir/Scr* James Bridges

Nine to Five ★★★ 15
Comedy
1980 · US · Colour · 104mins

Dolly Parton makes her movie debut and, while she's at it, belts the Oscar-nominated title song in this cheery comedy, which went on to spawn a sitcom series of the same name. Parton, Lily Tomlin and Jane Fonda play three office colleagues who scheme revenge on their chauvinist boss. It was Fonda who came up with the idea of making a Hollywood version of a feminist comedy. But it is Tomlin, as the junior manager overlooked for promotion, and Parton as a personal secretary whose performances impress the most. ▭

Jane Fonda *Judy Bernly* • Lily Tomlin *Violet Newstead* • Dolly Parton *Doralee Rhodes* • Dabney Coleman *Franklin Hart Jr* • Sterling Hayden *Russell Tinsworthy* • Elizabeth Wilson *Roz Keith* • Henry Jones *Hinkle* ■ *Dir* Colin Higgins • *Scr* Colin Higgins, Patricia Resnick, from a story by Patricia Resnick

1918 ★★★
Period drama
1985 · US · Colour · 91mins

A fact-based period drama, set in rural Texas, this chronicles the death and despair brought to one small town by the killer flu epidemic that swept much of the US in the year of the title. Adapted from a Horton Foote play and shown on TV as part of the American Playhouse series, the film seems understandably stagey at times. Nonetheless, the innate strength of story and some powerful performances carry it through. Look out for an early screen appearance by a young Matthew Broderick.

William Converse-Roberts *Horace Robedaux* • Hallie Foote *Elizabeth Robedaux* • Rochelle Oliver *Mrs Vaughn* • Matthew Broderick *Brother* • Jeannie McCarthy *Bessie* • Bill McGhee *Sam* • Horton Foote Jr *Jessie* ■ *Dir* Ken Harrison • *Scr* Horton Foote, from his play

1984 ★★★
Futuristic drama
1955 · UK · BW · 89mins

The 1955 version of George Orwell's dystopian novel is set in a futuristic 1984, while the 1984 version of *1984* was set in the grim, postwar era in which Orwell lived and wrote. All of which proves that Orwell's book was at once timely and timeless. Michael Anderson's adaptation is reasonably faithful to its source, concentrating on the possibility of love and humanity in a totalitarian state ruled by a powerful bureaucratic elite, a world of "Big Brother", "Thought Police" and "Doublethink". It's every bit the equal of Michael Radford's remake, but both pale beside the chilling, authentically Orwellian vision of *Brazil*.

Edmond O'Brien *Winston Smith* • Michael Redgrave *O'Connor* • Jan Sterling *Julia* • David

Kossoff *Charrington* • Mervyn Johns *Jones* • Donald Pleasence *Parsons* ■ *Dir* Michael Anderson • *Scr* William P Templeton, Ralph Bettinson, from the novel by George Orwell

Nineteen Eighty-Four ★★★★ 15
Futuristic drama
1984 · UK · Colour · 108mins

Inspired less by Soviet tyranny than the paranoia induced by British wartime censorship and propaganda, George Orwell's study of a dystopian future has lost none of its pessimism and dread. Much bleaker than the 1955 version, Michael Radford's superbly designed return to Oceania holds out little hope that the human spirit will be able to withstand the onset of totalitarianism. John Hurt is perfectly cast as the government cog who enters into a relationship with co-worker Suzanna Hamilton as an act of rebellion. But it's his encounter with Richard Burton, as the personification of "Big Brother's" omnipresence, that provides the dramatic highlight. ▭

John Hurt *Winston Smith* • Richard Burton *O'Brien* • Suzanna Hamilton *Julia* • Cyril Cusack *Charrington* • Gregor Fisher *Parsons* • James Walker *Syme* • Andrew Wilde *Tillotson* • Phyllis Logan *Telescreen announcer* • Roger Lloyd Pack *Waiter* ■ *Dir* Michael Radford • *Scr* Michael Radford, Jonathan Gems, from the novel by George Orwell

1941 ★★★ PG
Comedy
1979 · US · Colour · 113mins

Widely regarded as the one Steven Spielberg disaster, this sprawling comedy never deserved all the flak that was thrown at it. True, it's a messy, hysterical affair and many of the gags are strictly puerile. However, the sentimentality that mars many of Spielberg's more acclaimed works is nowhere to be seen, and there is a mischievous, anarchic edge to the story of how LA collapsed into chaos over fear of Japanese invasion following Pearl Harbor. There is also a winning lunacy to the sheer scale of the slapstick and Spielberg even finds time to send up the opening sequence of *Jaws*. Contains swearing. ▭

Dan Aykroyd *Sergeant Tree* • Ned Beatty *Ward Douglas* • John Belushi *Wild Bill Kelso* • Lorraine Gary *Joan Douglas* • Murray Hamilton *Claude* • Christopher Lee *Von Kleinschmidt* • Tim Matheson *Birkhead* • Toshiro Mifune *Commander Mitamura* • Warren Oates *Maddox* • Robert Stack *General Stilwell* • Treat Williams *Sitarski* • Nancy Allen *Donna* • John Candy *Foley* • Elisha Cook [Elisha Cook Jr] *Patron* • Slim Pickens *Hollis Wood* • Sam Fuller [Samuel Fuller] *Interceptor commander* • John Landis *Mizerany* • Mickey Rourke *Reese* ■ *Dir* Steven Spielberg • *Scr* Robert Zemeckis, Bob Gale, from a story by Robert Zemeckis, Bob Gale, John Milius

1942: a Love Story ★★★ 12
Drama
1994 · Ind · Colour · 151mins

As the Quit India movement gathered momentum at the height of the Second World War, the British response to the growing unrest (much of which came in the form of the passive resistance advocated by Gandhi) was often swift and brutal. Packed with songs that topped the Indian charts, this Romeo and Juliet story stars Anil Kapoor and Munisha Koirala as a Himalayan

U = SUITABLE FOR ALL   **Uc** = SUITABLE FOR ALL, ESPECIALLY FOR YOUNG CHILDREN (VIDEO ONLY)   **PG** = PARENTAL GUIDANCE

couple whose fathers are on opposite sides in the conflict. Director Vidhu Vinod Chopra admirably combines the human and the historical elements of the story and draws committed performances from his cast. In Hindi with English subtitles. 📺

Anil Kapoor *Nandu* • Munisha Koirala *Rajjo* • Brian Glover *General Douglas* ■ *Dir* Vidhu Vinod Chopra • *Scr* Kamna, Chandra, Shiv Subrahmanyam, Vidhu Vinod Chopra

1900 ★★★★★ 18

Period drama 1976 · It · Colour · 244mins

Italian director Bernardo Bertolucci's flawed masterpiece is an epic about an Italian family surviving under fascism, then communism. It's a fanfare for the uncommon man, with Burt Lancaster and Robert De Niro as the macho elements in a story that is otherwise dominated by women. The film towers when it should really soar, though its visual look is stunning thanks to Bertolucci's regular cinematographer, Vittorio Storaro. In Italian with English subtitles. 📺

Burt Lancaster *Alfredo Sr* • Robert De Niro *Alfredo Jr* • Gérard Depardieu *Olmo* • Donald Sutherland *Attila* • Dominique Sanda *Ada* • Sterling Hayden *Leo Dalco* • Stefania Sandrelli *Anita* • Alida Valli *Signora Pioppi* • Laura Betti *Regina* ■ *Dir* Bernardo Bertolucci • *Scr* Bernardo Bertolucci, Franco Arcalli, Giuseppe Bertolucci • *Music* Ennio Morricone

1919 ★★★

Period drama 1983 · Sp · Colour · 85mins

Despite its visual lustre, this is a markedly less nostalgic picture than its predecessor, *Valentina*. Again recounted by a Republican PoW at the end of the Spanish Civil War, the story has now moved on to 1919, with Miguel Molina assuming the role of the young poet, Pepe. The hero is still devoted to his childhood sweetheart, Emma Suarez, but his passion is compromised by an encounter with Cristina Marsillach, the domestic he meets while studying in Zaragoza following the collapse of the family fortune. As before, his outlook is shaped by a kindly mentor, though anarchist Walter Vidarte's ideas are based on social reality and not romanticised ideals. In Spanish with English subtitles.

Anthony Quinn *Mosen Joaquin* • Miguel Molina *Pepe* • Cristina Marsillach *Isabelita* • Saturno Cerra *Don Jose* • Conchita Leza *Doña Luisa* • Walter Vidarte *Checa* • Emma Suarez *Valentina* ■ *Dir* Antonio Jose Betancor • *Scr* Lautaro Murúa, Antonio José Betancor, Carlos Escobedo, Javier Moro, from the novel *Crónica del Alba (Days Of Dawn)* by Ramón J Sender

Nineteen Nineteen ★★ 15

Drama 1985 · UK · Colour · 98mins

If this starred Rock Hudson and Doris Day, it would have been called *Two on a Couch*. But it stars Paul Scofield and Maria Schell, and laughs are few and far between. In fact, this is a very solemn movie about Freudian analysis, with Scofield and Schell meeting up in Vienna and recalling their separate consultations with Dr Freud, given voice (but not a physical presence) by Frank Finlay. Scofield remembers the war, his marriage and his impossible

love objects; Schell relives her lesbian relationship, marriage and divorce.

Maria Schell *Sophie Ruben* • Paul Scofield *Alexander Scherbatov* • Frank Finlay *Dr Freud* • Diana Quick • Clare Higgins • Colin Firth ■ *Dir* Hugh Brody • *Scr* Hugh Brody, Michael Ignatieff

1991: The Year Punk Broke ★

Music documentary 1992 · US · Colour · 99mins

A documentary record of Sonic Youth's 1991 European tour as they moved from small club venues to the much bigger outdoor festival circuit. Nicely shot and edited, but rather dull overall; other bands featured include Nirvana, Dinosaur Jr and the Ramones. Gumball and Babes in Toyland also appear, but neither group show the talent or class of Sonic Youth, despite front man Thurston Moore failing to live up to his legendary image as a vicious wit.

Dir Dave Markey

1969 ★★★ 15

Drama 1988 · US · Colour · 91mins

An effective and often moving portrayal of life in America at the end of the sixties, with Kiefer Sutherland and Robert Downey Jr as two friends who find themselves on opposite sides of US involvement in Vietnam. Downey takes a moral and social stance; Sutherland loses himself in drink and drugs while waiting for his number to come up on Nixon's Vietnam draft lottery. Although clichéd in places, and definitely slow towards the middle, it's an interesting and alternative look at the war that never should have been. There's strong support, too, from Joanna Cassidy and Mariette Hartley as the boys' distraught mothers, Bruce Dern as Sutherland's over-the-top father, and a young Winona Ryder as the sister torn between her brother and his best friend. Contains some violence, swearing and nudity. 📺

Robert Downey Jr *Ralph Carr* • Kiefer Sutherland *Scott Denny* • Bruce Dern *Cliff Denny* • Mariette Hartley *Jessie Denny* • Winona Ryder *Beth Carr* • Joanna Cassidy *Ev Carr* ■ *Dir/Scr* Ernest Thompson

90 Days ★★★ 15

Romantic comedy 1986 · Can · Colour · 99mins

Cute little comedy, shot in mock documentary style, about a Canadian who invites his Korean penpal to come and be his wife. The film amusingly explores the consequent clash of cultures as east and west not only meet but mate – or, at least, try to. Director Giles Walker would explore broadly similar culture clashes seven years later in the equally good *Ordinary Magic*, about an Indian orphan sent to live with his Canadian aunt.

Stefan Wodoslawsky *Blue* • Christine Pak *Hyang-Sook* • Sam Grana *Alex* • Fernanda Tavares *Laura* ■ *Dir* Giles Walker • *Scr* David Wilson, Giles Walker

99 and 44/100% Dead ★★ 15

Crime comedy 1974 · US · Colour · 97mins

Arguably cinema's first pop-art gangster movie, this offbeat black comedy matches up to the strangeness of its title. In a role meant for Robert Mitchum, the always superb Richard Harris plays a hit man who is hired by a gang leader struggling for supremacy over a criminal colleague. A below-par John Frankenheimer brings a comic-book feel to the various bloody shoot-outs and keeps the action moving at a fair clip, but he seems to get lost amid the nonsense. It's not without some lovely touches, such as Harris using an alligator-infested sewer as a short cut to a mob's hideout and a sea bed that's littered with the corpses of gangsters, their feet encased in concrete. 📺

Richard Harris *Harry Crown* • Edmond O'Brien *Uncle Frank* • Bradford Dillman *Big Eddie* • Ann Turkel *Buffy* • Constance Ford *Dolly* • David Hall *Tony* • Katherine Baumann *Baby* • Chuck Connors *Marvin "Claw" Zuckerman* ■ *Dir* John Frankenheimer • *Scr* Robert Dillon

92 Grosvenor Street ★★ PG

Spy drama 1985 · US · Colour · 91mins

Also known as *Behind Enemy Lines*, this was the pilot for a proposed TV series. Several character stalwarts got their call-up for this Second World War adventure, including Patricia Hodge and Ian Lavender, in a much more senior position than in *Dad's Army*. But the focus falls firmly on Hal Holbrook as the academic-turned-spy who is kept on the straight and narrow by dogged brass-hat David McCallum as the duo are sent to Norway to rescue scientist Julian Glover. Contains swearing, violence and nudity. 📺

Hal Holbrook *Colonel Calvin Turner* • David McCallum *Lt Col Shelley Flynn* • Ray Sharkey *Master Sergeant Max Zierman* • Anne Twomey *Dr Helen Isaacs* • Maryam D'Abo *Claudie Debrille* • Lucy Hornack *Peggy Whitmore* • Julian Glover *Prof Thoresen* ■ *Dir* Sheldon Larry • *Scr* Stephen McPherson

92 in the Shade ★★★

Drama 1975 · US/UK · Colour · 83mins

Although he found fame in *Easy Rider*, Peter Fonda was too much of an easy rider himself to consolidate celebrity as his father, Henry, and his sister, Jane, did. So he's happy enough in this amiable coast-along playing a fishing guide in Florida's Key West at odds with the captain of another boat, especially as he's in the company of such specialists in eccentricity as Warren Oates, Margot Kidder, Burgess Meredith and Harry Dean Stanton. Written and directed by Thomas McGuane, it makes up in atmosphere what it lacks in suspense.

Peter Fonda *Tom Skelton* • Warren Oates *Nichol Dance* • Margot Kidder *Miranda* • Burgess Meredith *Goldsboro* • Harry Dean Stanton *Carter* • Sylvia Miles *Bella* • Elizabeth Ashley *Jeannie Carter* • William Hickey *Mr Skelton* ■ *Dir* Thomas McGuane • *Scr* Thomas McGuane, from his novel

Ninotchka ★★★★★ U

Comedy 1939 · US · BW · 105mins

This is without doubt one of the funniest, most original screen comedies ever made, and from the greatest year in Hollywood's history. Director Ernst Lubitsch brings his magic touch to bear on this inspired tale of a Russian emissary (the great Greta Garbo in a startling change of image) sent to Paris to retrieve three errant communists who have fallen in love with the ways of the west. Of course, it's just a matter of time before Garbo melts and falls in love, in her case with debonair count Melvyn Douglas. Witty, sophisticated, immaculately cast and superbly performed, this film was advertised in its day simply as "Garbo laughs!". That she does, and so will you, long and loud, especially at the utterly charming café scene. 📺

Greta Garbo *Ninotchka* • Melvyn Douglas *Count Leon D'Algout* • Ina Claire *Grand Duchess Swana* • Sig Rumann [Sig Ruman] *Michael Iranoff* • Felix Bressart *Buljanoff* • Alexander Granach *Kopalski* • Bela Lugosi *Commissar Razinin* • Gregory Gaye *Count Alexis Rakonin* ■ *Dir* Ernst Lubitsch • *Scr* Charles Brackett, Billy Wilder, Walter Reisch, from a story by Melchior Lengyel • *Cinematographer* William H Daniels [William Daniels] • *Costume Designer* Adrian

The Ninth Configuration ★★★ 15

Psychological thriller 1979 · US · Colour · 117mins

Produced, directed and scripted (from his own novel *Twinkle, Twinkle, Killer Kane*) by *The Exorcist* creator William Peter Blatty, this surreal exercise in Freudian vaudeville stars Stacy Keach as a psychiatrist who provides radical therapy to possibly insane military veterans in a remote Gothic mansion. Of course, Keach has a gruesome secret and is going through his own apocalyptic catharsis. At times absolutely bewildering (the title refers to a speech about God and molecular structure), at others completely gripping and harrowing, this overly literate and obtuse thriller has become the thinking man's cult classic. You'll either love it and praise its meaningful symbolism, or hate it for being a pretentious and shallow endurance test. Contains swearing and violence.

Stacy Keach *Colonel Hudson Kane* • Scott Wilson *Captain Cutshaw* • Jason Miller *Lieutenant Reno* • Ed Flanders *Colonel Fell* • Neville Brand *Major Groper* • Moses Gunn *Major Nammack* • Robert Loggia *Lieutenant Bennish* ■ *Dir* William Peter Blatty • *Scr* William Peter Blatty, from the novel *Twinkle, Twinkle, Killer Kane* by William Peter Blatty

The Ninth Gate ★★★★★ 15

Supernatural thriller 2000 · Fr/Sp/US · Colour · 133mins

A triumphant return to the horror genre by Roman Polanski, crammed with sardonic wit, subtle suspense tricks and razor-sharp irony. Johnny Depp is a rare books expert hired by billionaire Frank Langella to track down three ancient tomes written in conjunction with the Devil. When the nine illustrations drawn by Lucifer are combined at a predestined location, the Prince of Darkness will appear.

This rich and satisfying Gothic chiller has moody atmosphere and sinister unease to spare as it leads the gripped viewer up numerous garden paths to a brilliant, burnished and hallucinatory climax. Easily one of the best satanic spectaculars since Hammer's *The Devil Rides Out*, Polanski's carefully-crafted visual knock-out is on a par with *Rosemary's Baby*, while Wojciech Kilar's stunning score complements every creepy moment with insouciant élan.

Johnny Depp *Dean Corso* • Frank Langella *Boris Balkan* • Lena Olin *Liana Telfer* • Emmanuelle Seigner *The girl* • Barbara Jefford *Baroness Kessler* • Jack Taylor *Victor Fargas* • James Russo *Bernie* ■ *Dir* Roman Polanski • *Scr* Enrique Urbizu, John Brownjohn, Roman Polanski, from the novel *El Club Dumas* by Arturo Pérez-Reverte • *Cinematographer* Darius Khondji

Nirvana ★★★★★

Science-fiction thriller
1996 · It/Fr · Colour · 112mins

A stunning cyber-fantasy, rich in design and innovative ideas, that intellectually engages the mind while always remaining enjoyable on the purest pulp levels. Superstar video game inventor Christopher Lambert creates a new game called *Nirvana*, then realises his virtual reality hero (Italian matinée idol Diego Abatantuono) has a human consciousness. How he tries to erase the game before its mass-market Christmas release, which would condemn Abatantuono to a never-ending existence, pits Lambert against a ruthless multi-national corporation and takes him through the seedy underworlds of a future metropolis known as the Northern Agglomerate. An Italian language film.

Christopher Lambert *Jimi* • Diego Abatantuono *Solo* • Sergio Rubini *Joystick* • Emmanuelle Seigner *Lisa* • Stefania Rocca *Naima* ■ *Dir* Gabriele Salvatores • *Scr* Gabriele Salvatores, Gloria Corica, Pino Cacucci

Nirvana Street Murder ★★★

Black comedy   1990 · Ausl · Colour · 75mins

Mark Little is best known in this country as a comedian and one-time presenter of *The Big Breakfast*. But he proves himself a more than capable actor in this uncompromising black comedy that anticipates the mix of violence and dark humour now so common in American independent cinema. Any film in which someone attempts murder by drowning the victim in a waterbed has got to be worth seeing, but director Aleksi Vellis also has some shrewd points to make about Australia's multifarious clashing cultures. Ben Mendelsohn co-stars as Little's brother.

Mark Little *Boady* • Ben Mendelsohn *Luke* • Mary Coustas *Helen* • Tamara Saulwick *Penny* • Sheila Florance *Molly* • Roberto Micale *Hector* ■ *Dir/Scr* Aleksi Vellis

Nitti: the Enforcer ★★★

Crime drama   1988 · US · Colour · 96mins

The memorable villain from Brian De Palma's *The Untouchables* (played in that film by Billy Drago as a smirking sadist) gets his own starring role in this better-than-average TV movie. The always watchable Anthony LaPaglia

offers a rounded, thoughtful portrayal of Frank Nitti, the chief enforcer for Al Capone who rose to power when Capone was imprisoned. The talented supporting cast includes Trini Alvarado and Michael Moriarty, while director Michael Switzer demonstrates a flair for period detail.

Anthony LaPaglia *Frank Nitti* • Vincent Guastaferro *Al Capone* • Trini Alvarado *Anna* • Michael Moriarty *Hugh Kelly* ■ *Dir* Michael Switzer • *Scr* Lee David Zlotoff

Nixon ★★★★ 15

Biographical drama
1995 · US · Colour · 182mins

Near the end of *Nixon*, the disgraced President gazes at a painting of John Kennedy and says, "When people look at you, they see what they want to see. When they look at me, they see what they are." That's a great line, the key to Oliver Stone's movie, which, like his earlier *JFK*, is three hours of brilliance, provocation and information overload. Stone sees Nixon as a paranoid, haunted by the spectre of two dead Kennedys and by his own dead brothers, yet devoted to his wife, a role beautifully played by Joan Allen. The movie makes great demands on the viewer and on Anthony Hopkins, whose brave performance is more than an impression than an impersonation. At one point Paul Sorvino's sinister Henry Kissinger says, "He had greatness within his grasp but he had the defects of his qualities." Much the same can be said of this mesmerising, infuriating movie. Contains swearing. ▨

Anthony Hopkins *Richard Milhous Nixon* • Joan Allen *Pat Nixon* • Powers Boothe *Alexander Haig* • Ed Harris *E Howard Hunt* • Bob Hoskins *J Edgar Hoover* • EG Marshall *John Mitchell* • David Paymer *Ron Ziegler* • David Hyde Pierce *John Dean* • Paul Sorvino *Henry Kissinger* • Mary Steenburgen *Hannah Nixon* • JT Walsh *John Ehrlichman* • James Woods *HR Haldeman* ■ *Dir* Oliver Stone • *Scr* Stephen J Rivele, Christopher Wilkinson, Oliver Stone

Nô ★★ 15

Comedy drama
1998 · Can · Colour and BW · 84mins

Adapted by Robert Lepage from his own epic stage show, *The Seven Streams of the River Ota*, this ambitious study in cultural and national dualism unsuccessfully seeks to combine high politics and low farce as it alternates between a monochrome Montreal and a vividly hued Osaka. Departing drastically from the stylised psychodramatics of *The Confessional* and *The Polygraph*, Lepage raises the occasional smile and makes some pertinent political points. However, he fails to rein in an over-exuberant cast, with Anne-Marie Cadieux particularly voluble as the pregnant actress fretting over the activities of her terrorist lover (Alexis Martin). In French with English subtitles. Contains swearing, nudity and drug abuse.

Anne-Marie Cadieux *Sophie* • Alexis Martin *Michel* • Marie Brassard *Hanako* • Richard Fréchette *Walter* • Marie Gignac *Patricia* ■ *Dir* Robert Lepage • *Scr* Robert Lepage, André Morency, from the play *The Seven Streams of the River Ota* by Robert Lepage

No Big Deal ★ PG

Drama   1983 · US · Colour · 86mins

The key to the great teen movies from *Rebel without a Cause* through John Hughes's "Brat Pack" dramas to the recent *Boyz n the Hood* and *Kids* is that they present a credible portrait of the everyday world of their adolescent audiences without patronising them. Overstrain to be hip or hammer home the social message, and you'll have even the least discerning couch potato reaching for the remote. This lifeless tale of a troubled misfit at a strictly-run school commits all the cardinal errors. Movies in which the system sucks need charismatic rebels, but all Kevin Dillon can do is sulk. ▨

Kevin Dillon *Arnold Borberry* • Christopher Gartin *Michael Parker* • Mary Joan Negro *Jennifer Kirkpatrick* • Sylvia Miles *Principal* ■ *Dir* Robert Charlton • *Scr* Jeff Kindley, from the novel *Would You Settle for Improbable* by PJ Petersen

No Code of Conduct ★★ 18

Action crime   1998 · US · Colour · 85mins

Martin and Charlie Sheen are together again for the first time since *Wall Street* (if one overlooks their brief reunion in *Hot Shots! Part Deux*, that is). This time around, Charlie plays a maverick cop who's prepared to use any means necessary to bust a gigantic heroin ring, while Martin is a police executive waging his own war against high-level corruption. Expect the body count to mount rapidly. ▨

Martin Sheen *Bill Petersen* • Charlie Sheen *Jake Peterson* • Bret Michaels *Shane* • Mark Dacascos *Paul DeLucca* • Joe Lando *Willdog* • Meredith Salenger *Rebecca Peterson* ■ *Dir* Bret Michaels • *Scr* Bill Gucwa, Ed Masterson, Bret Michaels, Charlie Sheen, Shane Stanley

No Contest ★ 18

Martial arts action drama
1995 · US · Colour · 94mins

Considering all the various rip-offs of *Die Hard*, it was probably only a matter of time before somebody replayed the action at a beauty pageant. What a perfect excuse to have guns and chicks in one movie! The biggest problem is that, despite establishing early on that hostess Sharon Bell (Shannon Tweed) is a martial artist, no one fights back for the first half of the picture. Instead, director Paul Lynch wastes time having the gunmen (who include Andrew Dice Clay and ex-wrestler "Rowdy" Roddy Piper) terrorise the contestants. ▨

Robert Davi *Crane* • Andrew Clay [Andrew Dice Clay] *Oz* • Shannon Tweed *Sharon Bell* • Roddy Piper *Ice* • Nicholas Campbell *Vic* ■ *Dir* Paul Lynch • *Scr* Robert Cooper

No Deposit No Return ★★ U

Comedy   1976 · US · Colour · 106mins

There were times, before the company's recent renaissance, when the plots of Disney's live-action pictures seemed pretty second-rate. But the story here is basically fine, with a couple of kids co-operating in their own kidnap in an attempt to avoid spending the summer with their uncaring grandfather. But it takes much more than a car chase, a pet skunk and David Niven hanging upside

down by his heels to persuade a busy child that it's worth sitting through what is a fairly long film. Darren McGavin and Don Knotts do their darndest as the dim-witted kidnappers, but the result isn't up to much. ▨

David Niven *JW Osborne* • Darren McGavin *Duke* • Don Knotts *Bert* • Herschel Bernardi *Sergeant Turner* • Barbara Feldon *Carolyn* • Kim Richards *Tracy* • Brad Savage *Jay* • John Williams *Jameson* ■ *Dir* Norman Tokar • *Scr* Arthur Alsberg, Don Nelson, from a story by Joe L McEveety

No Dessert Dad, Till You Mow the Lawn ★

Comedy   1994 · US · Colour · 89mins

This rare foray by producer Roger Corman into PG territory is a surprisingly reprehensible family film. When a brother/sister duo accidentally discover they can manipulate the self-hypnosis tapes of their parents (Robert Hays and Joanna Kerns), they use this knowledge to get everything they want. The movie is never able to justify this pseudo-rape of the mind, even when the siblings' tape manipulation becomes unselfish (at least as far as they're concerned). Though the premise may not bother children, they might share their parents' discomfort, not just at the film's cold tone, but also its attempts to find humour in cat faeces and cracks about incest.

Robert Hays *Ken Cochran* • Joanna Kerns *Carol Cochran* • Richard Moll • Lyman Ward • Larry Linville *JJ* ■ *Dir* Howard McCain • *Scr* Cathy Moran, Martha Moran

No Down Payment ★★★

Drama   1957 · US · BW · 105mins

Four couples who seek upward mobility by buying homes in a suburban housing estate must face the reality of paying the mortgage and cope with the dramas that arise as their lives intersect. Some commentators consider the movie sociologically significant as an accurate picture of fifties suburban Americana; as entertainment, it's a reasonable enough compendium of soap opera clichés. It showcased the talents of several Fox contract players. Only Joanne Woodward and Tony Randall made it to major stardom, however.

Joanne Woodward *Leola Boone* • Sheree North *Isabelle Flagg* • Tony Randall *Jerry Flagg* • Jeffrey Hunter *David Martin* • Cameron Mitchell *Troy Boone* • Patricia Owens *Jean Martin* • Barbara Rush *Betty Kreitzer* • Pat Hingle *Herman Kreitzer* ■ *Dir* Martin Ritt • *Scr* Philip Yordan, from the novel by John McPartland

No Drums, No Bugles ★★★

Drama   1971 · US · Colour · 86mins

A fascinating, low-budget movie in which Martin Sheen plays a Civil War soldier who, sickened by the killing, deserts and goes to live in the depths of the West Virginian forests. Vowing never to kill a living thing, Sheen turns into a mountain man with flowers in his hair and eco-awareness in his veins. This Vietnam allegory is artfully made – Sheen is the only real character, although others are briefly glimpsed or heard – and probably influenced by the Oscar-winning 1963 short, *Incident at Owl Creek*.

U = SUITABLE FOR ALL   Uc = SUITABLE FOR ALL, ESPECIALLY FOR YOUNG CHILDREN (VIDEO ONLY)   PG = PARENTAL GUIDANCE

Martin Sheen *Ashby Gatrell* • Davey Davison *Callie Gatrell* • Rod McCary *Lieutenant* • Denine Terry *Sarah* ■ *Dir/Scr* Clyde Ware

No End ★★★ 18
Drama　1984 · Pol · Colour · 107mins

Watched by the ghost of lawyer Jerzy Radziwilowicz (symbolising the helpless spirit of Poland under martial law), both his widow, Grazyna Szapolowska, and his trade unionist client, Artur Barcis, face impossible moral dilemmas. She agonises over dishonouring his memory through physical need, while he debates whether to compromise his principles for freedom or become a martyr for the cause of liberty. Made in 1984, director Krzysztof Kieslowski's first collaboration with screenwriter Krzysztof Piesiewicz was withheld from international release because of its pro-Solidarity sentiments. It emerged two years later as a subdued treatise on political and personal allegiance and the pain of living with missed opportunity. A Polish language film.

Grazyna Szapolowska *Ula Zyro* • Maria Pakulnis *Joan* • Aleksander Bardini *Labrador* • Jerzy Radziwilowicz *Antoni Zyro* • Artur Barcis ■ *Dir* Krzysztof Kieslowski • *Scr* Krzysztof Kieslowski, Krzysztof Piesiewicz

No Escape ★★★ 15
Futuristic action thriller
1994 · US · Colour · 118mins

Try as he might, Ray Liotta is never going to make a hero. Nevertheless, he gives it his best shot in this cheerfully trashy futuristic thriller from British director Martin Campbell. In the 21st century, Liotta finds himself imprisoned on an isolated island where the convicts have split, *Lord of the Flies*-style, into caring hippies and warmongering tribesmen, and he has to choose between them. Lance Henriksen and Stuart Wilson ham it up for all they're worth as the leaders of the rival factions and, although his direction is a little erratic, Campbell delivers some satisfying set pieces. Contains swearing and violence. 📼

Ray Liotta *Robbins* • Lance Henriksen *The Father* • Stuart Wilson *Marek* • Kevin Dillon *Casey* • Kevin J O'Connor *Stephano* • Don Henderson *Killian* • Ian McNeice *King* • Jack Shepherd *Dysart* • Michael Lerner *Warden* ■ *Dir* Martin Campbell • *Scr* Michael Gaylin, Joel Gross, from the novel *The Penal Colony* by Richard Herley

No Escape, No Return ★ 18
Action crime drama
1994 · US · Colour · 91mins

Three childhood friends grow up to be renegade cops who just can't work on teams. Of course, that means the police department end up assigning them all to the same team, working "deep undercover, no backup" to bust a drug ring. Each member of this unlikeable two-man, one-woman team has his (or her) own speciality and each will, of course, come into play as they get themselves into trouble with the drug lords and – when things go wrong – their fellow cops. 📼

Maxwell Caulfield *William Robert Sloan* • Michael Nouri *Dante* • Dustin Nguyen *Tommy Cuff* • John Saxon *James Mitchell* ■ *Dir/Scr* Charles T Kanganis

No Exit ★★
Drama　1954 · Fr · BW · 95mins

Jacqueline Audry usually approached her text with great reverence, but here she was revisionist to the point of destruction. Quite why screenwriter Pierre Laroche felt it necessary to emasculate Jean-Paul Sartre's existential masterpiece remains a mystery. Yet it's plain to see what a disservice his decision to add extra characters and incorporate other-worldly flashbacks does to the relentless intensity of the original drama, in which a recently deceased trio discover the bitter truth that "hell is other people". However, Arletty imparts some much-needed class as the ageing lesbian desperately trying to dissuade flirty Gaby Sylvia from hitting on homosexual Frank Villard. A French language film.

Arletty *Inès* • Gaby Sylvia *Estelle* • Frank Villard *Garcin* ■ *Dir* Jacqueline Audry • *Scr* Pierre Laroche, from the play *Huis Clos* by Jean-Paul Sartre

No Greater Glory ★★★ U
Thriller　1934 · US · BW · 73mins

A frail young boy (George Breakston) gains courage, confidence and happiness when he is allowed into a gang, but his life is cut tragically short. No, this is not a juvenile crime movie, but a poignant, sensitive portrait of courage and love. Based on an autobiographical novel by Hungarian-born playwright Ferenc Molnar, Frank Borzage's film is acutely scripted by Jo Swerling and makes for a compelling, if sentimental, little drama.

George Breakston *Nemecsek* • Jimmy Butler *Boka* • Jackie Searl [Jackie Searle] *Gereb* • Frankie Darro *Feri Ats* • Donald Haines *Csonakos* • Rolf Ernest *Ferdie Pasztor* ■ *Dir* Frank Borzage • *Scr* Jo Swerling, from the novel *The Paul Street Boys* by Ferenc Molnar

No Highway ★★★ U
Thriller　1951 · UK · BW · 98mins

James Stewart is in his best absent-minded professor mode as a scientist whose obstinacy prevents a series of flying disasters in this watchable thriller, based on Nevil Shute's novel. It's about a boffin (Stewart) who can't find his own front door, but who confidently predicts metal fatigue in a new type of British aircraft. Naturally, he's branded a loony. Marlene Dietrich has an inflated part as a film star who believes in him, along with Glynis Johns as a friendly stewardess and Janette Scott as his daughter. Directed by Henry Koster, this is much better than the family comedies he later made with Stewart in Hollywood.

James Stewart *Theodore Honey* • Marlene Dietrich *Monica Teasdale* • Glynis Johns *Marjorie Corder* • Jack Hawkins *Dennis Scott* • Ronald Squire *Sir John* • Janette Scott *Elspeth Honey* ■ *Dir* Henry Koster • *Scr* RC Sherriff, Oscar Millard, Alec Coppel, from the novel by Nevil Shute

No Holds Barred ★ 15
Action comedy　1989 · US · Colour · 88mins

Rip (Hulk Hogan) is the world's most beloved wrestler. He's also a man of his word. His morals won't let him take on a lucrative contract for an upstart network mogul, and this sets him up for a fight with the mogul's anointed hero Zeus (Tom "Tiny" Lister). If you think that pro wrestlers are actors, Hogan's performance will probably convince you otherwise, and the script is so simplistic that you'll yearn for the relative sophistication of cable grappling shows. Amusingly, in the real world, Hogan sold out to Ted Turner's World Championship Wrestling league at the first opportunity. 📼

Hulk Hogan *Rip* • Kurt Fuller *Brell* • Joan Severance *Samantha Moore* • Tom "Tiny" Lister [Tom "Tiny" Lister Jr] *Zeus* • Mark Pellegrino *Randy* • David Palmer *Unger* ■ *Dir* Thomas J Wright • *Scr* Dennis Hackin

No Kidding ★★ PG
Comedy　1960 · UK · BW · 82mins

The *Carry On* team of producer Peter Rogers and director Gerald Thomas are responsible for this wallow in whimsy in which a couple inherit a large house and convert it into a holiday home for rich kids. As the house fills with the offspring of oil sheikhs, royals and sundry millionaires, the locals speak up for the underprivileged kids in the area. Leslie Phillips and Geraldine McEwan play the couple who kick off the plot, Joan Hickson is their conspiratorial busybody, while Irene Handl is the local busybody. 📼

Leslie Phillips *David Robinson* • Geraldine McEwan *Catherine Robinson* • Julia Lockwood *Vanilla* • Noel Purcell *Tandy* • Irene Handl *Mrs Spicer* • Joan Hickson *Cook* • Francesca Annis ■ *Dir* Gerald Thomas • *Scr* Norman Hudis, Robin Estridge, from the novel *Beware of Children* by Verily Anderson

No Laughing Matter ★★ 12
Drama　1998 · US · Colour · 85mins

Pat situations and shallow characters serve to trivialise the enduring problem of alcohol addiction in the made-for-TV movie. In her grief, policeman's widow Suzanne Somers comes to rely on booze. When her teenage son (Chad Christ) learns his girlfriend is pregnant, he decides to help his mother pull her life back together. Considering that Somers is the real-life child of alcoholics, this is an example of missed opportunities, with its easily dried-out heroine and quick resolution. You'd be much better served by the fine *My Name Is Bill W* or *The Lost Weekend*. 📼

Suzanne Somers *Emma* • Robert Desiderio *Richard Warren* • Chad Christ *Charlie* • Selma Blair *Lauren* • Frank Gerrish *George* ■ *Dir* Michael Elias • *Scr* Ted Kristian, Michael Elias, from a story by Ted Kristian

No Limit ★★ PG
Comedy　1935 · UK · BW · 77mins

Based on a story by Walter Greenwood, author of the Depression classic, *Love on the Dole*, produced by influential British movie entrepreneur Basil Dean and directed by Gracie Fields's husband Monty Banks, this was George Formby's debut for Associated Talking Pictures. Unfortunately, the on-screen activity never quite lives up to this impressive roll call, with Formby struggling to impose his inimitable personality on a plot that resembles an episode of the *Wacky Races* cartoon series.

Sabotaged throughout the Isle of Man's famous TT Races, George eventually wins the day, thanks to the love of Florence Desmond and the assistance of a donkey. 📼

George Formby *George Shuttleworth* • Florence Desmond *Florrie Dibney* • Howard Douglas *Turner* • Beatrix Fielden-Kaye *Mrs Horrocks* • Peter Gawthorne *Mr Higgins* • Alf Goddard *Norton* • Florence Gregson *Mrs Shuttleworth* • Jack Hobbs *Bert Tyldesley* ■ *Dir* Monty Banks • *Scr* Tom Geraghty, Fred Thompson, from a story by Walter Greenwood

No Looking Back ★★
Romantic comedy drama
1998 · US · Colour · 96 mins.

As with writer/director Edward Burns's previous movies (*The Brothers McMullen* and *She's the One*), this is about a bunch of beautiful people who talk endlessly about who is Mr or Mrs Right. On this occasion, waitress Lauren Holly must decide between safe and dependable mechanic boyfriend Jon Bon Jovi, or her ex-lover, an exciting but unreliable drifter (played by Burns). Although the stars have charm to spare, this is painfully bland and risk-free. The script and performances aren't bad – it's just difficult to distinguish it from hundreds of similar movies.

Lauren Holly *Claudia* • Edward Burns *Charlie* • Jon Bon Jovi *Michael* • Connie Britton *Kelly* • Nick Sandow *Goldie* • Kaili Vernoff *Alice* • Shari Albert *Shari* • Blythe Danner *Claudia's mother* ■ *Dir/Scr* Edward Burns

No Love for Johnnie ★★★★
Political drama　1960 · UK · BW · 110mins

Labour win the general election but Peter Finch MP is overlooked for the cabinet post he was expecting. Instead, his communist wife leaves him, he falls in with shifty communist-leaning MP Donald Pleasence and has a passionate affair with Mary Peach, a fashion model. Based on a novel by a Labour MP, this resembles *Room at the Top* in Westminster. It seemed to prefigure the Profumo affair with its then outspoken blend of sex and politics and remains eminently watchable and wholly plausible, due mainly to Finch's totally believable, award-winning portrayal of the ambitious politician with more libido than principle.

Peter Finch *Johnnie Byrne* • Stanley Holloway *Fred Andrews* • Mary Peach *Pauline West* • Donald Pleasence *Roger Renfrew* • Billie Whitelaw *Mary* • Dennis Price *Flagg* • Hugh Burden *Tim Maxwell* • Rosalie Crutchley *Alice Byrne* ■ *Dir* Ralph Thomas • *Scr* Nicholas Phipps, Mordecai Richler, from the novel by Wilfred Fienburgh

No Man of Her Own ★★
Comedy drama　1932 · US · BW · 80mins

Clark Gable, on loan to Paramount from MGM, co-stars with Carole Lombard in this tale of romance between a shady New York gambler and a librarian in the small town where he hides out. Wesley Ruggles directs an essentially routine script, elevated by the personalities of the attractive stars and their evident chemistry. (They would marry a few years later.) Dorothy Mackaill is the jealous woman whose threats to destroy Gable have a beneficial outcome.

Clark Gable *Jerry "Babe" Stewart* • Carole Lombard *Connie Randall* • Dorothy Mackaill *Kay Everly* • Grant Mitchell *Charlie Vane* • George Barbier *Mr Randall* • Elizabeth Patterson *Mrs Randall* ■ *Dir* Wesley Ruggles • *Scr* Maurine Watkins, Milton Gropper, from a story by Edmund Goulding, Benjamin Glazer

No Man of Her Own ★★★

Melodrama   1950 · US · BW · 97mins

Barbara Stanwyck fires on all cylinders as the unmarried mother-to-be who adopts the identity of an also pregnant but much wealthier woman after the latter dies in a train crash. Just as she's enjoying her new life of deception, her baby's father shows up and starts blackmailing her. Given that the story is complete and utter tosh (it's based on a story written by *Rear Window* author Cornell Woolrich), and that John Lund is a lummox as Stanwyck's new beau, this *film noir* is gripping stuff – full of shadows, furtive looks and an opening that drifts comfortably into a doom-laden flashback.

Barbara Stanwyck *Helen Ferguson* • John Lund *Bill Harkness* • Jane Cowl *Mrs Harkness* • Phyllis Thaxter *Patrice Harkness* • Lyle Bettger *Stephen Morley* • Henry O'Neill *Mr Harkness* • Richard Denning *Hugh Harkness* ■ *Dir* Mitchell Leisen • *Scr* Sally Benson, Catherine Turney, from the novel *I Married a Dead Man* by William Irish [Cornell Woodrich]

No Man's Land ★★★🔟

Thriller   1987 · US · Colour · 100mins

Welcome to the "chop shop", a scrap yard where stolen cars are broken up and reassembled as new. It was the arena of conflict for the 1994 thriller *Kiss of Death*, but this earlier, stylish use of the locale has rookie cop DB Sweeney going undercover in a Porsche garage. He becomes a close friend of crooked proprietor Charlie Sheen, a fast-lane traveller who dazzles our hero not only with his lifestyle, but also with his sister (Lara Harris). A low-budget thriller that nevertheless makes a big impact. Contains swearing and violence. ▭

Charlie Sheen *Ted Varrick* • DB Sweeney *Benjy Taylor* • Randy Quaid *Lieutenant Vincent Bracey* • Lara Harris *Ann Varrick* • Bill Duke *Malcolm* • M Emmet Walsh *Captain Haun* ■ *Dir* Peter Werner • *Scr* Dick Wolf

No Margin for Error ★★★

Crime thriller   1978 · US · Colour · 97mins

Paul Tulley, Christopher Connelly and James Farentino star in a crime thriller that deals with the touchy subject of when a policeman should fire his gun. Unlike Dirty Harry, who seemed to shoot first and ask questions later, these cops come under investigation for every incident, especially when one accidentally guns down an innocent bystander. Serious stuff, but interesting just the same.

Paul Tulley *Parker* • Christopher Connelly *Bakalayan* • James Farentino *Anderson* • Ron Mask *Onorato* • Glenn Ford *Deputy Chief Hayes* • Harry Guardino *Lieutenant Bramlett* ■ *Dir* Virgil Vogel [Virgil W Vogel] • *Scr* Mark Rodgers

No Mercy ★★★ 18

Thriller   1986 · US · Colour · 103mins

Richard Gere stars to real effect in the first film that made critics note how much greyer, older and better he was. There's a lot to age him in this swampland thriller, in which he plays a Chicago cop seeking vengeance in New Orleans following the death of his partner. Jeroen Krabbé is his crimelord target and Kim Basinger is the reluctant gangster's moll, with whom Gere takes off into the Louisiana bayous for the rousing action finale. It's predictable hokum, but director Richard Pearce spins an artful story, helped by Gere's slick performance. Contains swearing and violence. ▭

Richard Gere *Eddie Jillette* • Kim Basinger *Michel Duval* • Jeroen Krabbé *Losado* • George Dzundza *Capt Stemkowski* • Gary Basaraba *Joe Collins* • Ray Sharkey *Angles Ryan* • William Atherton *Allan Deveneux* • Terry Kinney *Paul Deveneux* ■ *Dir* Richard Pearce • *Scr* Jim Carabatsos

No Mercy ★★

Drama   1994 · Peru/Mex/Fr · Colour · 117mins

In transferring the action of Dostoyevsky's *Crime and Punishment* to modern day Lima, Francisco José Lombardi clearly seeks to link the central character's torment with the problems facing Peruvian society. However, such is the narrowness of his approach to both murderous student Diego Bertie's soul-crushing guilt and devout prostitute Adriana Davila's guileless promise of redemption that there's little room left to explore the squalor and exploitation that drove Bertie to kill his landlady and steal her cash. The melodramatic tone of the romance further dissipates the novel's intensity, as does the plodding investigation conducted by pitiless cop, Jorge Chiarella. In Spanish with English subtitles.

Diego Bertie *Ramon Romano* • Adriana Davila *Sonia Martinez* • Jorge Chiarella *Mayor Portillo* • Hernan Romero *Alejandro Velaochaga* • Marcello Rivera *Julian Razuri* • Mariella Trejos *Senora Aliaga* • Ricardo Fernandez *Leandro Martinez* ■ *Dir* Francisco José Lombardi • *Scr* Augusto Cabada, from the novel *Crime and Punishment* by Fyodor Dostoyevsky

No Minor Vices ★★★

Comedy   1948 · US · BW · 95mins

This is a slight piece about an eccentric artist who attempts to separate a stuffy paediatrician from his wife. The doctor is Dana Andrews, the artist is dashing foreigner Louis Jourdan, and the lady in question is the charming Lilli Palmer. Oh, and Jane Wyatt's in there, too, as Andrews's devoted assistant. This type of time-wasting tosh needs a far lighter touch than that provided by veteran Lewis Milestone, better remembered for a stark series of uncompromising war classics than for the fact that he once won the first ever Academy Award for comedy direction.

Dana Andrews *Dr Perry Aswell* • Lilli Palmer *April Aswell* • Louis Jourdan *Otavio Quaglini* • Jane Wyatt *Miss Darlington* • Norman Lloyd *Dr Sturdivant* • Bernard Gorcey *Mr Zitzfleisch* ■ *Dir* Lewis Milestone • *Scr* Arnold Manoff

No My Darling Daughter ★★ U

Romantic comedy   1961 · UK · BW · 96mins

The quality cast deserves something far better than this tepid British comedy from producer Betty Box. Juliet Mills does a feisty turn as the tomboy daughter of businessman Michael Redgrave, whose romance with an American student leads to scandal. Both Redgrave and Roger Livesey are totally wasted as director Ralph Thomas squeezes all the fun out of a screwball plot that would have been meat and drink to even the most plodding Hollywood hack.

Michael Redgrave *Sir Matthew Carr* • Michael Craig *Thomas Barclay* • Juliet Mills *Tansy Carr* • Roger Livesey *General Henry Barclay* • Rad Fulton *Cornelius Allingham* • Renee Houston *Miss Yardley* • Joan Sims *Second typist* • Peter Barkworth *Charles* ■ *Dir* Ralph Thomas • *Scr* Frank Harvey, from the play *Handful of Tansy* by Harold Brooke, Kay Bannerman

No Name on the Bullet ★★★

Western   1959 · US · Colour · 77mins

One of the very best of Universal's series of westerns starring baby-faced Second World War hero Audie Murphy. Mean and mustachioed, he's brilliantly cast in this study in paranoia as a gunman on the prowl, threatening a collection of victims, all of whose roles are cleverly written. So potent is his evil power that a wheelchair-bound judge even tries to rise up in order to mow him down. Director Jack Arnold keeps the tension taut, while the supporting cast is excellent.

Audie Murphy *John Gant* • Joan Evans *Ann* • Charles Drake *Doctor Luke Canfield* • RG Armstrong *Asa Canfield* • Virginia Grey *Mrs Fraden* • Warren Stevens *Lou Fraden* • Whit Bissell *Thad Pierce* • Karl Swenson *Earl Sticker* ■ *Dir* Jack Arnold • *Scr* Gene L Coon, from a story by Howard Amacker

No, No, Nanette ★★ U

Musical   1940 · US · BW · 96mins

In the early forties, British producer/director Herbert Wilcox and Anna Neagle (who married in 1943) landed a contract with RKO, but their combined career in Hollywood was short-lived. Not surprising given this second filming of the 1925 Broadway musical, in which the best things were songs such as *Tea for Two* and *I Want to Be Happy*. Unwisely, Wilcox relegated the score to the background at the expense of the silly plot about a young woman who helps her uncle out of his financial and amorous difficulties.

Anna Neagle *Nanette* • Richard Carlson *Tom* • Victor Mature *William* • Roland Young *Mr Smith* • Helen Broderick *Mrs Smith* • ZaSu Pitts *Pauline* • Eve Arden *Winnie* • Tamara Sonya • Billy Gilbert *Styles* ■ *Dir* Herbert Wilcox • *Scr* Ken Englund, from the musical by Frank Mandel, Otto Harbach, Emil Nyitray, Vincent Youmans

No, Not Yet ★★

Drama   1993 · Jap · Colour · 134mins

A meditation on death, and the final film directed by famed Japanese director Akira Kurosawa, then aged 83. The film's hero is a university professor who decides to give up teaching for writing. The setting, though, is the Second World War and its aftermath, during which the professor and his wife lose their home in a bombing raid, though most drama comes from the heartache caused by a missing cat. It's a long, philosophical and very talkative movie that may entrance the director's admirers but will test the patience of more casual viewers. A Japanese language film.

Hisashi Igawa *Takayama* • Kyoko Kagawa *Professor's wife* • Tatsuo Matsumura *Professor Hyakken Uehida* • George Tokoro *Amaki* ■ *Dir/Scr* Akira Kurosawa

No Nukes ★★

Concert documentary
1980 · US · Colour · 103mins

Over five nights at Madison Square Garden in September 1979, and at an outdoor rally in Battery Park, a socially conscious group of rockers got together for pro-solar energy, anti-nuclear benefit concerts. Despite an impressive list of artists – including Bruce Springsteen, Carly Simon, Bonnie Raitt, Jackson Browne – this well-intentioned rockumentary is a thinly stretched effort, with only Bruce Springsteen shaking any life into the "right on" blandness.

Dir Julian Schlossberg, Danny Goldberg [Dan Goldberg], Anthony Potenza

No One Could Protect Her ★★★ 18

Thriller   1996 · US · Colour · 87mins

A superior slice of TV-movie suspense, which almost inevitably is based on true events. Joanna Kerns plays a victim recruited by the police to draw out a rapist/killer who has been stalking a quiet, respectable neighbourhood. The familiar faces in the cast include cop Dan Lauria, best known for his role in *The Wonder Years*, and Anthony John Denison, the baddie from Michael Mann's stylish cop series *Crime Story*. Contains some violence and swearing. ▭

Joanna Kerns *Jessica Rayner* • Anthony John Denison *Dan Rayner* • Dan Lauria *Detective Greg Corning* • Christina Cox *Detective Elizabeth Jordan* • Dan Lett *Nick Foster* ■ *Dir* Larry Shaw • *Scr* • *Scr* Bruce Miller

No One Man ★

Drama   1932 · US · BW · 71mins

A wealthy Florida divorcee (Carole Lombard), eager to snare a new husband, is torn between two contenders – Ricardo Cortez, handsome and oozing charm but a feckless creature of questionable character, and the less dazzling but decent and dependable Paul Lukas, an Austrian physician. How Lombard, her natural charms dulled under the weight of a trivial, unconvincing and boring script, makes her choice takes up the thankfully short running time of Lloyd Corrigan's pointless film.

Carole Lombard *Penelope Newbold* • Ricardo Cortez *Bill Hanaway* • Paul Lukas *Dr Karl Bemis* • Juliette Compton *Sue Folsom* • George Barbier *Alfred Newbold* • Virginia Hammond *Mrs Newbold* ■ *Dir* Lloyd Corrigan • *Scr* Sidney Buchman, Agnes Brand Leahy, Percy Heath, from the novel by Rupert Hughes

U = SUITABLE FOR ALL   Uc = SUITABLE FOR ALL, ESPECIALLY FOR YOUNG CHILDREN (VIDEO ONLY)   PG = PARENTAL GUIDANCE

No One Would Tell ★★

Drama   1996 · US · Colour

Fred Savage will forever be stamped on our memories as the worldly wise sixties child from *The Wonder Years*. Here he attempts to dump the cute image, playing a bullying, obnoxious teenager who proceeds to make his girlfriend Candace Cameron's life hell. The two leads deliver convincing performances, but even an appearance by talk-show host Sally Jessy Raphael can't rescue this from the rigid conventions of true-life TV movies.

Fred Savage *Bobby Tennyson* • Candace Cameron *Stacy Collins* • Heather McComb • Season Hubley • Sally Jessy Raphael *Judge* ■ *Dir* Noel Nosseck • *Scr* Steven Loring

No One Writes to the Colonel ★★★

Period drama
1999 · Mex/Sp/Fr · Colour · 118mins

While this compassionate study of love in a time of adversity is restrained by his usual baroque standards, Mexican director Arturo Ripstein still overcooks this adaptation of Gabriel Garcia Marquez's novel. Driven to the brink of despair by the murder of his son, Fernando Lujan's melancholic optimist invests heavily in his cock-fighting dreams and the overdue military pension that his asthmatic wife, Marisa Paredes, knows will never come. The acting is impeccable, while Ripstein expertly captures the ambience of their forties coastal town. Yet the director allows inconsequential subplots and slack pacing to dissipate the story's dramatic intensity. A Spanish language film.

Fernando Lujan *The Colonel* • Salma Hayek *Julia* • Marisa Paredes *Lola* • Ernesto Yanez *Don Sabas* • Rafael Inclan *Father Angel* ■ *Dir* Arturo Ripstein • *Scr* Paz Alicia Garciadiego, from the novel by Gabriel Garcia Marquez

No Ordinary Summer ★★15

Drama   1994 · US · Colour · 107mins

A decent coming-of-age story about a black New York teenager spending the summer of 1976 with wealthy relatives in snooty Martha's Vineyard. The characters are a shade underwritten, and less is made of the clash of cultures than might have been. But the seventies fashions are fun to look at, and there are decent performances from the cast of rising black stars. Contains nudity, sex scenes, drug abuse and swearing. [video]

Larenz Tate *Drew Tate* • Joe Morton *Kenny Tate* • Suzzanne Douglas *Brenda Tate* • Glynn Turman *Spencer Phillips* • Vanessa Bell Calloway *Frances Phillips* ■ *Dir* Matty Rich • *Scr* Trey Ellis, Paris Qualles

No Place for Jennifer ★★

Drama   1949 · UK · BW · 91mins

It's hard to believe that this tosh was one of the biggest box-office hits of 1949. Eleven-year-old Janette Scott (daughter of Thora Hird) plays the tormented girl whose vanishing act brings about a change of heart in divorcing parents Leo Genn and Rosamund John. Scriptwriter J Lee Thompson (the future director of the startling *Cape Fear*) obviously had little enthusiasm for the task of adapting

Phyllis Hambledon's penny-dreadful *No Difference to Me*, while director Henry Cass fails to inject any sense of agony or urgency into the search.

Leo Genn *William* • Rosamund John *Rachel Kershaw* • Beatrice Campbell *Paula* • Guy Middleton *Brian Stewart* • Janette Scott *Jennifer* • Anthony Nicholls *Baxter* ■ *Dir* Henry Cass • *Scr* J Lee Thompson, from the novel *No Difference to Me* by Phyllis Hambledon

No Place like Home ★★★★PG

Drama   1989 · US · Colour · 90mins

Christine Lahti always brings heat to a performance, but is careful never to overcook it. Here, in one of her most rounded roles to date, she puts fire in the soul of a blue-collar American who finds herself on the street along with her family. Director Lee Grant paints a biting portrait of how easy it is to end up struggling in limbo, while writers Sam Blackwell and Ara Watson view the family's plight through the dark prism of irony. Punchy, pithy and emotionally charged. [video]

Jeff Daniels *Mike Cooper* • Christine Lahti *Zan Cooper* • Lantz Landry *David* • Kyndra Joy Casper *Tina* • Scott Marlowe *Eddie* • Kathy Bates *Bonnie Cooper* ■ *Dir* Lee Grant • *Scr* Ara Watson, Sam Blackwell

No Place to Hide ★★★18

Thriller   1992 · US · Colour · 92mins

Some critics claim that Kris Kristofferson is so wooden, you can get splinters just watching him. But that's unfair. The country singer may not be the most dynamic of actors, but he boasts a certain screen presence which is evident in this fast-moving thriller, where his gruff manliness is in nice contrast to Drew Barrymore's precocious chirpiness. He's a rough, tough cop; she's a kid hunted by a murderer who's already slaughtered her sister. Thrown together, they have to stay alive long enough for Kris to give the killer his comeuppance. [video]

Kris Kristofferson *Joe Garvey* • Drew Barrymore *Tinsel Hanley* • Martin Landau *Frank McCay* • OJ Simpson *Allie Wheeler* • Dey Young *Karen* • Bruce Weitz *Captain Nelson Silva* ■ *Dir/Scr* Richard Danus

No Problem! ★★★

Comedy   1975 · Fr · Colour

Proof positive that French cinema isn't all angst and ennui, this rousing romp tosses slapstick and farce into the road movie formula to produce an hilarious and surprisingly sophisticated chase comedy. Heading for a Swiss rendezvous, Jean Lefebvre's womanising innocent is blissfully unaware of the corpse his son (Bernard Menez) has stashed in the boot of his car. The son sets off in hot pursuit with the stranger (Miou-Miou) who had asked him to dispose of the body. Maintaining a cracking pace, director Georges Lautner keeps the gag count high without sacrificing too much character depth. French dialogue dubbed into English.

Miou-Miou *Anita* • Jean Lefebvre *Michalon* • Bernard Menez *Jean-Pierre* • Henri Guybet *Daniel* • Anny Duperey *Janis* ■ *Dir* Georges Lautner • *Scr* Jean-Marie Poire

No Regrets for Our Youth ★★★★

Political drama based on a true story
1946 · Jap · BW · 110mins

Even though its critical reception was decidedly mixed, Akira Kurosawa's sixth feature marked his breakthrough as a major film-maker. Political subjects were never to be his strong point, but his conviction that postwar Japanese society needed to rediscover its self-respect drew him to the fact-based story of the young city sophisticate (played with a mix of romantic innocence and indomitable spirit by Setsuko Hara) who found the will to survive while slaving as a peasant after her father was dismissed from his university post for his communist views and her lover was executed as a spy. In Japanese with English subtitles.

Denjiro Okochi *Professor Yagihara* • Eiko Miyoshi *Madame Yagihara, his wife* • Setsuko Hara *Yukie Yagihara, his daughter* • Susumu Fujita *Ryukichi Noge* ■ *Dir* Akira Kurosawa • *Scr* Eijirō Hisaita, Akira Kurosawa

No Retreat, No Surrender ★★15

Martial arts action drama
1986 · US/HK · Colour · 79mins

With a plot reminiscent of *The Karate Kid*, this has Kurt McKinney as a martial arts-enthusiast kid. New in Seattle, he is victimised by his peers until he acquires an unexpected ally – the ghost of Bruce Lee. Almost charming in its silliness, the movie gets close to the so-bad-it's-good level but too often takes itself too seriously. This is most noteworthy as Jean-Claude Van Damme's first real role, though his unspeaking character is introduced only so that McKinney has someone to fight in the inevitable final tournament. [video]

Kurt McKinney *Jason Stillwell* • Jean-Claude Van Damme *Karl Brezdin/Ivan the Russian* • JW Fails *RJ Madison* • Kathie Sileno *Kelly Reilly* • Kent Lipham *Scott* ■ *Dir* Corey Yuen • *Scr* Keith Strandberg, from a story by Ng See Yuen, Corey Yuen

No Road Back ★★

Crime melodrama   1957 · UK · BW · 62mins

Sean Connery had been a lifeguard and a coffin polisher before he began acting. He must have doubted the wisdom of giving up the day job after his first experience of film-making, as this is almost an identikit "quota quickie". The lead is a skid-row American star (Skip Homeier), the plot is a threadbare crime caper, the sets are cheap and much of the action takes place in dank inner city backstreets. Crooks Connery and Alfie Bass are convincing enough, with their botched robbery causing Homeier to question the honesty of his blind and deaf, club-owning ma.

Skip Homeier *John Railton* • Paul Carpenter *Clem Hayes* • Patricia Dainton *Beth* • Norman Wooland *Inspector Harris* • Margaret Rawlings *Mrs Railton* • Alfie Bass *Rudge Haven* • Sean Connery *Spike* ■ *Dir* Montgomery Tully • *Scr* Charles Leeds, Montgomery Tully, from the play *Madame Tictac* by Falkland D Cary, Philip Weathers

No Room for the Groom ★★

Comedy   1952 · US · BW · 82mins

Piper Laurie is the young wife of a GI who moves in with her family while he is off on duty. When her husband (Tony Curtis) returns, he finds himself surrounded by her relatives, including Spring Byington as the mother trying to marry her off to someone else (Don DeFore). The breezy and attractive young leads help to keep this idiotic, frenzied and only mildly amusing comedy alive for director Douglas Sirk, whose reputation rests on rather better material than this.

Tony Curtis *Alvah Morrell* • Piper Laurie *Lee Kingshead* • Don DeFore *Herman Strouple* • Spring Byington *Mamma Kingshead* • Jack Kelly *Will Stubbins* ■ *Dir* Douglas Sirk • *Scr* Joseph Hoffman, from the novel *My True Love* by Darwin L Teilhet

No Room to Run ★★

Thriller   1978 · Ausl · Colour · 101mins

Richard Benjamin, a rising star in the late sixties, was reduced to taking roles in substandard TV movies by 1978. Judging by this hotchpotch of pop music, thirtysomething romance and indifferent political intrigue, his decision to switch to directing in 1982 was long overdue. In Sydney to set up a rock tour, Benjamin becomes a fugitive after the airport assassination of politician Ray Barrett. As the courier helping to clear his name, Paula Prentiss (Benjamin's real-life wife) tries to pep things up, but the hackneyed plot gets the performances it deserves.

Richard Benjamin *Nick Loomis* • Paula Prentiss *Terry McKenna* • Noel Ferrier *Ralph Fleming* • Barry Sullivan *Garth Kingswood* • Ray Barrett *Jack Deakin* • Anne Haddy *Julie Deakin* ■ *Dir* Robert Michael Lewis [Robert Lewis] • *Scr* George Kirgo

No Sad Songs for Me ★★★

Melodrama   1950 · US · BW · 88mins

The wistful Margaret Sullavan was a rare and special talent, and this was her last film, a Columbia melodrama about a dying woman preparing her family for her untimely but inevitable death. Sullavan makes this trite material unbearably moving, and there is real truth in her portrayal: tragic but uplifting, sad yet inspirational. Wendell Corey and Natalie Wood play the rest of the family, and Viveca Lindfors is admirable in support, but the film belongs totally to Sullavan.

Margaret Sullavan *Mary Scott* • Wendell Corey *Brad Scott* • Viveca Lindfors *Chris Radna* • Natalie Wood *Polly Scott* • John McIntire *Dr Ralph Frene* • Ann Doran *Louise Spears* • Richard Quine *Brownie* • Jeanette Nolan *Mona Frene* ■ *Dir* Rudolph Maté • *Scr* Howard Koch, from a story by Ruth Southard

No Secrets ★

Comedy   1982 · UK/US · Colour · 95mins

This would-be comedy stars Oliver Reed as a bumbling US Army officer and Peter Cushing as a British commissioner who attempt to recover an American spaceship that's being held for ransom by an African emperor. While it's pleasant to see both stars tackling comedy for once, the humour is so strained as to be sieved of all fun. Character names such as

President P Nutts and Miss Funnypenny set the tone to which the rest of the film aspires. Contains violence and swearing.

Oliver Reed *Captain Nelson* • Sylvaine Charlet *Natasha* • Keenan Wynn *General Spelvin* • Edwin Manda *Emperor Sumumba* • Fred Carter *President P Nutts* • Hilary Pritchard *Miss Funnypenny* • Wilfrid Hyde White *M1* ■ *Dir* Peter Curran • *Scr* Alfred Shaughnessy

No Sex Please, We're British ★★ PG

Comedy 1973 · UK · Colour · 87mins

One of the West End's longest-ever running comic farces arrived on the screen virtually intact, but with a significantly different leading man. Whereas Michael Crawford had consolidated both career and image by instigating the gauche lead on stage, in the film the role went to the diminutive British comedian Ronnie Corbett, changing the nature of the part to fit a precreated comic persona. Corbett does well by the hackneyed plot, and under-rated director Cliff Owen keeps up the pace. There's sterling support from the likes of Arthur Lowe and the wonderful Beryl Reid. ▣

Ronnie Corbett *Brian Runnicles* • Beryl Reid *Bertha* • Arthur Lowe *Mr Bromley* • Ian Ogilvy *David Hunter* • Susan Penhaligon *Penny Hunter* • David Swift *Inspector Paul* • Cheryl Hall *Daphne* • Michael Bates *Needham* ■ *Dir* Cliff Owen • *Scr* Anthony Marriott, Johnnie Mortimer, Brian Cooke, from the play by Anthony Marriott, Alistair Foot

No Small Affair ★★ 15

Romantic comedy 1984 · US · Colour · 98mins

A teenage photographer develops an obsessive crush for an up-and-coming rock singer and goes to stalker-like lengths to get her to like him. This patchy tale has its clever and funny moments, but it also has its stupid ones, and the overall impression isn't improved by the basic unlikeability of the characters. The film could earn a third star for the calibre of its cast which, in addition to Jon Cryer and Demi Moore, also features early appearances by Tim Robbins and Jennifer Tilly. ▣

Jon Cryer *Charles Cummings* • Demi Moore *Laura Victor* • George Wendt *Jake* • Peter Frechette *Leonard* • Elizabeth Daily *Susan* • Ann Wedgeworth *Joan Cummings* • Jeffrey Tambor *Ken* • Tim Robbins *Nelson* • Jennifer Tilly *Mona* ■ *Dir* Jerry Schatzberg • *Scr* Charles Bolt, Terrence Mulcahy, Craig Bolotin, from a story by Charles Bolt

No Smoking ★ U

Comedy 1954 · UK · BW · 72mins

A small-town boffin comes up with a swallowable version of the nicotine patch, and then wonders why the tobacco giants will stop at nothing to put a stop to his discovery. Notable only for its anti-smoking theme in a period where no one bothered about puffing away on a cigarette, this gentle comedy ends up a wasted opportunity, though the cast give their all.

Reg Dixon *Reg Bates* • Belinda Lee *Miss Tonkins* • Lionel Jeffries *George Pogson* • Myrtle Rowe *Milly* • Ruth Trouncer *Joyce* •

Peter Martyn *Hal* ■ *Dir* Henry Cass • *Scr* Kenneth R Hayles, Phil Park, from a TV play by Rex Rientis, George Moresby-White

No Surrender ★ 15

Black comedy 1986 · UK · Colour · 99mins

This offensive little tale purports to be black comedy but verges on the tasteless. A Liverpool nightclub owner plays host to a party of Irish OAPs with entertainment provided by, among others, Elvis Costello (in a cameo role). Problem is, they're a warring bunch of Catholics and Protestants, and the evening threatens to be explosive. Alan Bleasdale's script isn't bad as much as misdirected – as are the talents of Joanne Whalley. ▣

Michael Angelis *Mike Moriarty* • Avis Bunnage *Martha Gorman* • JG Devlin *George Corman* • James Ellis *Paddy Burke* • Tom Georgeson *Mr Ross* • Bernard Hill *Bernard* • Ray McAnally *Billy McRacken* • Joanne Whalley *Cheryl* • Elvis Costello *Rosco De Ville* ■ *Dir* Peter K Smith • *Scr* Alan Bleasdale

No Time for Comedy ★★★

Comedy drama 1940 · US · BW · 92mins

One of those romantic comedies set in the cosy world of Broadway theatreland, this stars James Stewart as a playwright who's down in the dumps because of a mid-life crisis that has leaked into his work. Rosalind Russell co-stars as his acerbic but uncomplaining wife. It's directed by William Keighley with the same smooth-paced energy that he brought to many Warner Bros gangster movies. Although it has similarities to Preston Sturges's *Sullivan's Travels*, it goes for the heart rather than the jugular.

James Stewart *Gaylord Esterbrook* • Rosalind Russell *Linda Esterbrook* • Charlie Ruggles [Charles Ruggles] *Philo Swift* • Genevieve Tobin *Amanda Swift* • Allyn Joslyn *Morgan Carrel, theatrical director* • Clarence Kolb *Richard Benson* ■ *Dir* William Keighley • *Scr* Julius J Epstein, Philip G Epstein, from the play by SN Behrman

No Time for Love ★★★ U

Romantic comedy 1943 · US · BW · 83mins

Claudette Colbert and Fred MacMurray star in yet another romantic comedy that revolves around hostility which is really true love. This time around, she's a professional photographer and he's the foreman of a tunnel-digging crew who becomes her assistant, inevitably leading to complications. The snappy screenplay, tailor-made for the two attractive stars, veers slightly more towards slapstick than sophistication, but is lent gloss by Paramount's first-rung production values and direction from the stylish and experienced Mitchell Leisen.

Claudette Colbert *Katherine Grant* • Fred MacMurray *Jim Ryan* • Ilka Chase *Hoppy Grant* • Richard Haydn *Roger, composer* • Paul McGrath *Henry Fulton, magazine publisher* • June Havoc *Darlene, chorus girl* • Marjorie Gateson *Sophie* ■ *Dir* Mitchell Leisen • *Scr* Claude Binyon, Warren Duff, from a story by Robert Lees

No Time for Sergeants ★★★ U

Comedy 1958 · US · BW · 114mins

Andy Griffith starred in the long-running Broadway play and in this screen adaptation, using his Carolina drawl to good effect as the simple-minded hillbilly drafted into the air force. He teams up with Nick Adams and they both manage to fall out of their plane and then attend their own military funeral. Directed by the veteran Mervyn LeRoy, there's more than a touch of Laurel and Hardy, as well as the Marx Brothers' brand of irreverence, about this comic caper. ▣

Andy Griffith *Will Stockdale* • Myron McCormick *Sergeant King* • Nick Adams *Ben Whitledge* • Murray Hamilton *Irvin Blanchard* • Howard Smith *General Bush* • Will Hutchins *Lieutenant Bridges* • Don Knotts *Manual Dexterity Corporal* ■ *Dir* Mervyn LeRoy • *Scr* John Lee Mahin, from the play by Ira Levin, from the novel by Mac Hyman

No Time for Tears ★★ U

Medical drama 1957 · UK · Colour · 85mins

What else could you call a film whose sole intention is to have you blubbing your eyes out from the off? Anna Neagle stars in this mawkish account of life in a children's hospital. If the triumphs and tragedies of the kiddies don't have you reaching for tissues, then the torrid love life of nurse Sylvia Syms certainly will. When else could you end a weepie like this but at Christmas? The members of the cast work minor miracles despite the string of clichés, with Flora Robson and Anthony Quayle particularly impressive.

Anna Neagle *Matron Eleanor Hammond* • George Baker *Nigel Barnes* • Sylvia Syms *Margaret* • Anthony Quayle *Dr Seagrave* • Flora Robson *Sister Birch* • Alan White *Dr Hugh Storey* • Joan Sims *Sister O'Malley* ■ *Dir* Cyril Frankel • *Scr* Anne Burnaby

No Time to Die ★★ U

Second World War drama 1958 · UK · Colour · 104mins

The team behind *Dr No* and *From Russia With Love* – producer Albert R "Cubby" Broccoli, director Terence Young, writer Richard Maibaum, cameraman Ted Moore – were all present and correct for this war drama about the campaign in the Libyan desert. American hunk Victor Mature was imported to play an American who serves as a sergeant in the British army. He organises an escape from an Italian PoW camp and is then captured and tortured by a shifty sheikh in league with the Nazis. Every racial stereotype in the book stands to attention as Mature lurches from one heroic deed to the next, culminating in a joust with a Panzer tank.

Victor Mature *Sgt David Thatcher* • Leo Genn *Sgt Kendall* • Anthony Newley *Tiger Noakes* • Bonar Colleano *Pole* • Luciana Paluzzi *Carola* • Anne Aubrey *Italian girl* ■ *Dir* Terence Young • *Scr* Richard Maibaum, Terence Young

No Trace ★★★

Crime thriller 1950 · UK · BW · 75mins

A better-than-average "quota quickie" from writer/director John Gilling, in which crime writer Hugh Sinclair tries to cover his tracks (and delude

snooping cop John Laurie) after he kills a blackmailer from his gangland past. As we know from the outset that he won't get away with it, the fun lies in watching him make the slips that give him away to secretary Dinah Sheridan and her flatfoot admirer, Barry Morse. In spite of the plot transparencies and a smug leading performance, this holds the attention rather effectively.

Hugh Sinclair *Robert Southley* • Dinah Sheridan *Linda* • John Laurie *Inspector MacDougall* • Barry Morse *Harrison* • Dora Bryan *Maisie* ■ *Dir/Scr* John Gilling

No Trees in the Street ★★ PG

Drama 1958 · UK · BW · 92mins

Although a stalwart of stage and TV, screenwriter Ted Willis worked less in movies and it rather shows in this ludicrously sentimental adaptation of his own play. It was unlucky enough to be released in the same year that British cinema entered its great "kitchen sink" phase, but this thin-cut slice of street life could never feel anything but stale. Herbert Lom tries to inject a little menace as a small-time hoodlum, but, confronted with sickly sweet Sylvia Syms and teen tearaway Melvyn Hayes, he succumbs to the mediocrity all around him. ▣

Sylvia Syms *Hetty* • Herbert Lom *Wilkie* • Ronald Howard *Frank* • Stanley Holloway *Kipper* • Joan Miller *Jess* • Melvyn Hayes *Tommy* ■ *Dir* J Lee Thompson • *Scr* Ted Willis, from his play

No Way Back ★ 18

Crime thriller 1996 · US · Colour · 87mins

This movie should have just been titled "No Way", in keeping with its utter preposterousness. Russell Crowe plays an FBI agent who, after a sting operation goes wrong in the most unbelievable manner, tries to bring a Yakuza boss (Etsushi Toyokawa) back with him from New York to Los Angeles on a commercial flight. The boss gets loose and forces the plane down on a small field in the mountains. Yet somehow he, the FBI agent and a stewardess (Helen Slater at her most annoying) end up pushing a broken car around the desert.

Russell Crowe *Zack Grant* • Helen Slater *Mary* • Etsushi Toyokawa *Yuji* • Michael Lerner *Frank Serlano* • Kyusaku Shimada *Tetsuro* • Kristopher Logan *Mr Contingency* ■ *Dir/Scr* Frank Cappello

No Way Home ★★★ 18

Crime drama 1996 · US · Colour · 96mins

A grim yet uplifting story of rehabilitation and redemption, shot through with a dynamic tone and moody atmosphere by independent director Buddy Giovinazzo. Fresh out of prison, Tim Roth moves in with his older brother (James Russo) in an anxious attempt to go straight. Alas, he's soon sucked back into the criminal life. Almost Pinteresque in the way silences convey as much heart-rending truth as the succinct dialogue, this touching moral tale is an uncompromising character study given an unusually poignant level of honesty. Deborah Kara Unger steals the picture as Roth's suspicious sister-in-law. ▣

U = SUITABLE FOR ALL, Uc = SUITABLE FOR ALL, ESPECIALLY FOR YOUNG CHILDREN (VIDEO ONLY) PG = PARENTAL GUIDANCE

Tim Roth *Joey* • James Russo *Tommy* • Deborah Kara Unger *Lorraine* • Bernadette Penotti *Ronnie* • Larry Romano *Carter* ■ *Dir/Scr* Buddy Giovinazzo

No Way Out ★★★

Drama   1950 · US · BW · 101mins

Joseph L Mankiewicz's drama about racial prejudice stars Sidney Poitier, launching his career as a persecuted doctor at a metropolitan hospital. The head of Fox, Darryl F Zanuck, said the picture would be as "real as sweat, dealing with the absolute blood and guts of negro hating." Mankiewicz said it was "the first time racial violence was shown on the screen except for *Birth of a Nation* in modern times." Both were rather overblown statements, and so is the picture, not least because of Richard Widmark's snarling, racist villain and the contrived, if ironic conclusion.

Richard Widmark *Ray Biddle* • Linda Darnell *Edie* • Stephen McNally *Dr Wharton* • Sidney Poitier *Dr Luther Brooks* • Mildred Joanne Smith *Cora* • Harry Bellaver *George Biddle* ■ *Dir* Joseph L Mankiewicz • *Scr* Joseph L Mankiewicz, Lesser Samuels

No Way Out ★★★★ 15

Thriller   1986 · US · Colour · 109mins

Famous for its limousine sex scene, this Kevin Costner spy thriller provides a gripping insight into the corridors of US power. Based on the novel *The Big Clock* by Kenneth Fearing, this is a highly intelligent, intriguing movie containing some wonderful performances, most notably that of Gene Hackman as an icily manipulative politician. For once, Costner's tendency to stay emotionally removed from his character pays dividends as we are left guessing about the man right up to the final reel. Contains swearing, violence and nudity. 🖳

Kevin Costner *Lieutenant Commander Tom Farrell* • Gene Hackman *David Brice* • Sean Young *Susan Atwell* • Will Patton *Scott Pritchard* • Howard Duff *Senator Willy Duvall* • George Dzundza *Dr Sam Hesselman* • Jason Bernard *Major Donovan* • Iman *Nina Beka* ■ *Dir* Roger Donaldson • *Scr* Robert Garland, from the novel *The Big Clock* by Kenneth Fearing

No Way to Treat a Lady ★★★★

Black comedy   1968 · US · Colour · 107mins

Romantic comedies don't come much blacker than this immensely enjoyable tale of a serial strangler, incarnated in several guises by Rod Steiger. George Segal plays Jewish cop Morris "Mo" Brummel, hysterically henpecked by his mother (Eileen Heckart), while co-star Lee Remick has never looked lovelier as the sophisticated Lincoln Center guide who graduates from witness to intended victim. New York's the star, too, thanks to Jack Priestley's glossy photography, which includes interiors in both Joe Allen's and Sardi's.

Rod Steiger *Christopher Gill* • Lee Remick *Kate Palmer* • George Segal *Morris Brummel* • Eileen Heckart *Mrs Brummel* • Murray Hamilton *Inspector Haines* • Michael Dunn *Mr Kupperman* ■ *Dir* Jack Smight • *Scr* John Gay, from the novel by William Goldman

No Worries ★★★

Drama   1993 · Ausl/UK · Colour

In his third feature, director David Elfick tries to do too much. Initially set in the heart of Australian sheep-rearing country, his earnest TV drama explores the impact of a slump in the wool market and a cruel drought on a close-knit community. However, having involved us deeply in this courageous struggle against overwhelming odds, Elfick suddenly transports the family to the city, where the emphasis shifts to the hostility of townies towards their country cousins. The performances are fine, but the story sprawls out of control and the ending is a letdown.

Amy Terelinck *Matilda Bell* • Geoff Morrell *Ben Bell* • Susan Lyons *Ellen Bell* • Geraldine James *Anne O'Dwyer* • John Hargreaves *Clive Ryan* • Harold Hopkins *Burke* ■ *Dir* David Elfick • *Scr* David Holman

Noah ★★★

Fantasy drama   1998 · US · Colour · 120 mins

Humorous situations float this modern telling of a very old tale. A heavenly messenger directs sceptical, corner-cutting contractor Tony Danza to build an immense ark from ancient blueprints. His kids and co-workers think he is crazy – until they are saved from the devastating flood that inevitably follows. A sharp script and energetic playing by Danza and Wallace Shawn make this TV-movie update of the Bible story a pleasing affair.

Tony Danza *Norman Waters* • Wallace Shawn *Zack* • Jane Sibbett *Angela* • John Marshall Jones *Ernie* ■ *Dir* Ken Kwapis • *Scr* Juliet Aires, Keith Giglio, Charles Bohl

Noah's Ark ★★ U

Biblical epic   1928 · US · BW · 135mins

This early Warner Bros epic parallels a First World War story with the flooding of the temple in the Old Testament; the cast, headed by George O'Brien and Dolores Costello, play roles in both periods. Some of the flood water was for real and reputedly cost the lives of three extras, though the miniatures of a crumbling city are rather obvious. Silent and sound versions were issued, the latter adding contrived banter in the trenches.

Dolores Costello *Mary/Miriam* • George O'Brien *Travis/Japheth* • Noah Beery *Nickoloff/King Nephilim* • Louise Fazenda *Hilda/Tavern maid* • Guinn "Big Boy" Williams [Guinn Williams] *Al/Ham* • Paul McAllister *Minister/Noah* • Myrna Loy *Dancer/Slave girl* ■ *Dir* Michael Curtiz • *Scr* Anthony Coldeway, from a story by Darryl F Zanuck

Nob Hill ★★

Musical   1945 · US · Colour · 95mins

Nob Hill is where the nobs used to live in San Francisco, an area now the preserve of the city's swishest hotels. But this brash Fox musical is pretty downmarket, starring George Raft as the saloon owner who jilts torch singer Vivian Blaine for socialite Joan Bennett. The songs are strictly B-sides and Henry Hathaway's direction doesn't have the necessary light touch. Another drawback is Raft, never a convincing leading man, though he once laid claim to being the world's fastest Charleston dancer.

George Raft *Johnny Angelo* • Joan Bennett *Harriet Carruthers* • Vivian Blaine *Sally Templeton* • Peggy Ann Garner *Katie Flanagan* • Falstaff Openshaw [Alan Reed] *Dapper Jack Harrigan* • BS Pully *Joe the bartender* • Emil Coleman *Pianist* ■ *Dir* Henry Hathaway • *Scr* Wanda Tuchock, Norman Reilly Raine, from a story by Eleanore Griffin

Nobody Lives Forever ★★★

Romantic drama   1946 · US · BW · 99mins

Before method acting, John Garfield was doing it for real with a tough-talking style that seemed ad-libbed. It's that hard-bitten personality which saves this romance from sentimental stickiness. The star plays a con man who swindles rich widow Geraldine Fitzgerald, only to fall in love with his victim. Mills and Boon stuff, though Garfield transforms it into near-credible drama. Walter Brennan co-stars.

John Garfield *Nick Blake* • Geraldine Fitzgerald *Gladys Halvorsen* • Walter Brennan *Pop Gruber* • Faye Emerson *Toni* • George Coulouris *Doc Ganson* • George Tobias *Al Doyle* ■ *Dir* Jean Negulesco • *Scr WR* Burnett, from his story *I Wasn't Born Yesterday*

Nobody Runs Forever ★★ PG

Thriller   1968 · UK · Colour · 97mins

But the audience did, in droves. Rank threw together a motley array of B-list actors, plus Rod Taylor and Christopher Plummer, and let them fight it out among themselves with scant direction for this over-complicated yet weakly scripted thriller, based on Jon Cleary's novel *The High Commissioner*. The thrills are in distinctly short supply as an Australian cop is sent to London to arrest a dastardly diplomat for murder. 🖳

Rod Taylor *Scobie Malone* • Christopher Plummer *Sir James Quentin* • Lilli Palmer *Sheila Quentin* • Camilla Sparv *Lisa Pretorius* • Daliah Lavi *Madame Cholon* • Franchot Tone *Ambassador Townsend* • Clive Revill *Joseph* ■ *Dir* Ralph Thomas • *Scr* Wilfred Greatorex, from the novel *The High Commissioner* by Jon Cleary

Nobody Waved Goodbye ★★★

Drama   1964 · Can · BW · 84mins

This Canadian drama ventures into the mental jungle of the alienated teenager, dealing with youngster Peter Kastner and his problems with his parents and girlfriend (Julie Briggs). Keen insights and good acting make this a whole lot more pleasurable than others of the genre, while director Don Owen makes the adolescents comic and not merely self-absorbed.

Peter Kastner *Peter* • Julie Biggs *Julie* • Claude Rae *Father* • Toby Tarnow *Sister* • Charmion King *Mother* ■ *Dir/Scr* Don Owen

Nobody's Child ★★★★

Drama based on a true story
1986 · US · Colour · 100mins

The haunting isolation of mental illness is made vividly personal by the breathtaking performance of Marlo Thomas in this true story of Marie Balter, a woman who spent 20 harrowing years in a mental hospital until a compassionate doctor helped her regain her sanity. The first-rate script by Mary Gallagher and Ara

Watson, sensitive direction by Lee Grant and Thomas's single-minded commitment to telling the story make this a memorable and moving drama.

Marlo Thomas *Marie Balter* • Ray Baker *Joe Balter* • Caroline Kava *Dr Blackwell* • Kathy Baker *Lucy* • Blanche Baker *Shari* ■ *Dir* Lee Grant • *Scr* Mary Gallagher, Ara Watson

Nobody's Children ★★ 12

Drama based on a true story
1994 · US · Colour · 91mins

One couple's longing for children forms the basis of this tear-jerking TV movie. Detroit housewife Ann-Margret and her husband Jay O Sanders travel to Romania to adopt two babies. Enlisting the aid of dedicated French doctor Dominique Sanda, they battle self-serving bureaucrats to save abandoned babies from certain death in squalid, state-run orphanages. Henry Winkler put on his producing cap for this true story, which benefits from its grim Romanian locations and the earnestness of its stars. 🖳

Ann-Margret *Carol Stevens* • Dominique Sanda *Dr Stephanie Green* • Jay O Sanders *Joe Stevens* • Clive Owen *Bratu* ■ *Dir* David Wheatley • *Scr* Petru Popescu, Iris Friedman

Nobody's Fool ★★★ 15

Romantic comedy
1986 · US · Colour · 102mins

A modest portrait of Arizona small-town life, with Rosanna Arquette as a waitress, aspiring actress and local "celebrity" learning to live with her chequered past. As she searches for love and redemption, Arquette's performance becomes a three-ring circus – funny here, touching there, veering off balance elsewhere. Sharply written by Beth Henley (who also co-wrote *True Stories* and penned *Crimes of the Heart*), and co-starring Oscar-winner Louise Fletcher, it's a pleasing diversion, if lacking in real surprises and dramatic fireworks. Contains swearing.

Rosanna Arquette *Cassie* • Eric Roberts *Riley* • Mare Winningham *Pat* • Jim Youngs *Billy* • Louise Fletcher *Pearl* • Gwen Welles *Shirley* • Stephen Tobolowsky *Kirk* • Lewis Arquette *Mr Fry* ■ *Dir* Evelyn Purcell • *Scr* Beth Henley

Nobody's Fool ★★★★ 15

Drama   1994 · US · Colour · 105mins

The crumpled charisma of Paul Newman effortlessly carries this pleasing, low-key drama. Now content to take on less sympathetic roles, this finds Newman playing a grouchy town rogue who is forced to face up to his family responsibilities when his long-neglected son turns up for Thanksgiving. Director Robert Benton (*Kramer vs Kramer*) is an old hand at this kind of heart-warming fare, and doesn't swamp it with sentimentality. He is also well-served by an exceptionally starry cast in which the likes of Bruce Willis and Melanie Griffith line up with venerable character actors such as Jessica Tandy and Josef Sommer. Contains swearing and brief nudity. 🖳

Paul Newman *Donald Sullivan* • Jessica Tandy *Miss Beryl* • Bruce Willis *Carl Roebuck* • Melanie Griffith *Toby Roebuck* • Dylan Walsh *Peter* • Pruitt Taylor Vince *Rub Squeers* •

Gene Saks *Wirf* • Josef Sommer *Clive Peoples Jr* ■ *Dir* Robert Benton • *Scr* Robert Benton, from the novel by Richard Russo

Nobody's Perfect ★★ U

Comedy   1968 · US · Colour · 102mins

In a break between filming *The Virginian* TV series, blond action man Doug McClure teamed with Nancy Kwan to star in this lame nautical comedy about exploits on board the USS *Bustard* stationed in the Pacific during the Second World War. Though amiable enough, the leads are seriously lightweight and struggle to bring this rather uninspired and unamusing movie to life.

Doug McClure *Doc Willoughby* • Nancy Kwan *Tomiko Momoyama* • James Whitmore *Capt Mike Riley* • James Shigeta *Toshi O'Hara* • Gary Vinson *Walt Purdy* • David Hartman *Boats McCafferty* ■ *Dir* Alan Rafkin • *Scr* John DF Black, from the novel *The Crows of Edwina Hill* by Allan R Bosworth

Noce Blanche ★★ 15

Drama   1989 · Fr · Colour · 88mins

Films featuring pop stars can usually be labelled "For Fans Only", and this pouting piece of self-publicity thinly disguised as a tale of hopeless passion is a case in point. Aware that the camera loves her, French singing sensation Vanessa Paradis struts her stuff like a true pop video veteran, but doesn't display an ounce of emotion as a girl who suffers enough domestic strife to keep the social services busy for months. Bruno Cremer is slyly effective as the older man she stalks, but this is risible stuff. In French with English subtitles. Contains nudity. ▭

Bruno Cremer *François Hainaut* • Vanessa Paradis *Mathilde Tessier* • Ludmila Mikael *Catherine Hainaut* • François Negret *Carpentier* • Véronique Silver *Academic adviser* • Jean Dasté *Concierge* ■ *Dir/Scr* Jean-Claude Brisseau

Les Noces Rouges ★★★

Drama based on a true story
1973 · Fr/It · Colour · 90mins

Another variation on Claude Chabrol's pet theme of infidelity leading to murder, *Les Noces Rouges* was part of the cycle of films in which Stéphane Audran, Chabrol's then-wife, added spice by playing either the victim or cause of the crime. Chabrol based his own screenplay on a newspaper account of a *crime passionnel*, which got the film banned for a while as it concerned a real murder case. The film is as elegant, cool and blackly humorous as one would expect, while the playing of the unsympathetic characters is impeccable. In French with English subtitles.

Michel Piccoli *Pierre Maury* • Stéphane Audran *Lucienne Delamare* • Claude Piéplu *Paul Delamare* • Eliana De Santis *Hélène* • Pipo Merisi *Berthier* ■ *Dir/Scr* Claude Chabrol

Nocturne ★★★

Crime drama   1946 · US · BW · 88mins

A wealthy, cold-blooded composer is shot, bringing a verdict of suicide. Detective George Raft sets out to investigate further and comes to suspect glamorous starlet Lynn Bari of killing him. This glossy *film noir*, slickly

directed by Edwin L Marin, offers an appealing performance from Raft in cultivated good-guy mode; it also features a catch of well-played red herrings, led by Virginia Huston, Joseph Pevney and Diana Dors lookalike Myrna Dell. The nocturne of the title, composed by Leigh Harline, features heavily in the plot.

George Raft *Lt Joe Warne* • Lynn Bari *Frances Ransom* • Virginia Huston *Carol Page* • Joseph Pevney *Fingers* • Myrna Dell *Susan* ■ *Dir* Edwin L Marin • *Scr* Jonathan Latimer, from a story by Frank Fenton, Rowland Brown

Noi Tre ★★★ PG

Biographical comedy drama
1984 · It · Colour · 85mins

As Milos Forman showed us in his Oscar-winning biopic *Amadeus*, the young Mozart didn't have much of a childhood, what with having to impress all the crowned heads of Europe before he had his first shave. In this interesting, but inconsistent, Italian feature, director Pupi Avati tries to create an adolescence for the budding genius by following the course of a summer stay with a country aristocrat and his mischievous teenage kin. Although it impressively conveys a sense of the crushing level of expectation placed on Mozart's shoulders, the film falls down in its portrayal of the youthful brawls and pranks, and the romantic stirrings that could have made it more engaging. An Italian language film. ▭

Christopher Davidson *Wolfgang Amadeus Mozart* • Lino Capolicchio *Leopoldo* • Gianni Cavina *Cousin* • Carlo Delle Piane *Count Pallovicini* • Ida DiBenedetto *Maria Caterino* • Dario Parisini *Giuseppe* • Barbara Rebeschini *Antonia-Leda* ■ *Dir* Pupi Avati • *Scr* Pupi Avati, Antonio Avati, Cesare Bornazzini

Noir et Blanc ★★★ 18

Drama   1986 · Fr · BW · 80mins

Claire Devers won the Camera d'Or at Cannes for this debut feature. Shooting in monochrome, Devers explores the grey area between pain and pleasure as she chronicles the increasingly abrasive relationship between timid health centre accountant Francis Frappat and muscular masseur Jacques Martial. A study in sensuality without the sensationalism, this is an admirably controlled film, in which Devers dispassionately depicts both the unspoken emotion and the sadomasochistic desire that fuels the dangerous liaison. Yet this tale of fatal attraction is also interspersed with moments of gentle humour and humanity. A French language film. ▭

Francis Frappat *Antoine* • Jacques Martial *Dominique* • Josephine Fresson *Josy* • Marc Berman *Monsieur Roland* ■ *Dir* Claire Devers • *Scr* Claire Devers, Alain Bergala, from the story *Desire and the Black Masseur* by Tennessee Williams

Noises Off ★★★★ 15

Comedy   1992 · US · Colour · 99mins

Robbed of its essentially theatrical device (the comic contrast between off-stage chaos and on-stage calculation), this American adaptation of Michael Frayn's West End play provides more than enough laughs to skim over the

potholes of improbability. Peter Bogdanovich's quick-fire direction is matched and aided by some wondrously staccato performances, notably from Carol Burnett, Michael Caine and Christopher Reeve. Luvvies at play have never been so pompously vulnerable or so sympathetic. ▭

Carol Burnett *Dotty Otley/Mrs Clackett* • Michael Caine *Lloyd Fellowes* • Denholm Elliott *Selsdon Mowbray/Burglar* • Julie Hagerty *Poppy Taylor* • Marilu Henner *Belinda Blair/Flavia Brent* • Mark Linn-Baker *Tim Allgood* • Christopher Reeve *Frederick Dallas/ Philip Brent* ■ *Dir* Peter Bogdanovich • *Scr* Marty Kaplan, from the play by Michael Frayn

Nomads ★★★ 18

Supernatural thriller
1985 · US · Colour · 88mins

A fascinating and ambitious directorial debut from John McTiernan that bypasses the eighties fad for excessive gore and sex and focuses instead on atmosphere and dramatic visual scares. Pierce Brosnan gives a restrained performance as a French anthropologist working in Los Angeles drawn to a disparate gang of street punks, led by one-time pop idol Adam Ant, who are in reality nomadic demons roaming the earth. McTiernan apparently based his tale on Eskimo legends, though his intriguing supernatural chiller might perhaps have worked better as a shorter, made-for-TV movie. ▭

Pierce Brosnan *Pommier* • Lesley-Anne Down *Dr Flax* • Anna Maria Montecelli *Niki* • Adam Ant *Number One* • Hector Mercado *Ponytail* • Josie Cotton *Silver Ring* • Frank Doubleday *Razor* ■ *Dir/Scr* John McTiernan

None but the Brave ★★

Second World War drama
1965 · US/Jap · Colour · 105mins

You'd think Frank Sinatra might have chosen a better project for his only foray into direction than this wartime morality chestnut about enemy US and Japanese troops forced to co-exist on a remote Pacific island. As director, Sinatra manages to succeed moderately well, but the proceedings lose credibility during his occasional moments on screen as a pharmacist forced to amputate a Japanese soldier's leg. Several of Sinatra's friends and family turn up in the cast: there's his son-in-law Tommy Sands, Brad Dexter (who saved him from drowning) and protégé Tony Bill, Sinatra's brother in *Come Blow Your Horn*. ▭

Frank Sinatra *Chief Pharmacist's Mate Maloney* • Clint Walker *Captain Dennis Bourke* • Tommy Sands *Second Lieutenant Blair* • Brad Dexter *Sergeant Bleeker* • Tony Bill *Air Crewman Keller* • Tatsuya Mihashi *Lieutenant Kuroki* • Dir Frank Sinatra • *Scr* John Twist, Katsuya Susaki, from a story by Kikumaru Okuda • *Producer* Frank Sinatra

None but the Lonely Heart ★★ U

Melodrama   1944 · US · BW · 108mins

The great Cary Grant was surprisingly nominated for an Oscar for this pretentious drama, in which he's hopelessly miscast as author Richard Llewellyn's cockney drifter Ernie Mott, a punk philosopher who drifts easily into crime because of the poverty of

his circumstances. The star found an affinity between Mott and his own upbringing and insisted the left-wing playwright Clifford Odets be hired as director; however, the result is relentlessly turgid and grimly earnest. Many will find it unwatchable today, interesting only as a curio. ▭

Cary Grant *Ernie Mott* • Ethel Barrymore *Ma Mott* • Barry Fitzgerald *Twite* • June Duprez *Ada* • Jane Wyatt *Aggie Hunter* • George Coulouris *Jim Mordiney* • Dan Duryea *Lew Tate* ■ *Dir* Clifford Odets • *Scr* Clifford Odets, from the novel by Richard Llewellyn

None Shall Escape ★★★

Drama   1944 · US · BW · 85mins

A very interesting and extremely clever movie, which examines in depth the career of a high-ranking Nazi during his trial for war crimes. What lends this plot value is that the film, though set after the First World War, was made and released before the end of the Second World War, and proved to be extraordinarily prescient. Director Andre De Toth keeps the story suspenseful and elicits excellent performances from Marsha Hunt and Henry Travers.

Marsha Hunt *Marja Pacierkowski* • Alexander Knox *Wilhelm Grimm* • Henry Travers *Father Warecki* • Erik Rolf *Karl Grimm* • Richard Crane *Willie Grimm as a man* • Dorothy Morris *Janina* • Richard Hale *Rabbi Levin* ■ *Dir* Andre De Toth • *Scr* Lester Cole, from a story by Alfred Neumann, Joseph Than

Noon Wine ★★

Drama   1985 · US · Colour · 90mins

Executive-produced by costume drama maestros Ishmail Merchant and James Ivory, this is an interesting and unsettling tale of how a Texan family's life in the thirties is changed by the arrival of a mysterious stranger. Based on the story by Katherine Ann Porter, this is well-played by a cast that includes Fred Ward and Pat Hingle. Yet it pales in comparison to other Merchant-Ivory fare, having been constrained by a TV-movie budget.

Fred Ward *Earle Thompson* • Stellan Skarsgård *Olaf Helton* • Lise Hilboldt *Ellie Thompson* • Pat Hingle *Homer T Hatch* • Enrique Brown *Young Herbert* • James Gammon *Sheriff* ■ *Dir* Michael Fields • *Scr* Michael Fields, from the story by Katherine Ann Porter

Noose ★★★

Crime thriller   1948 · UK · BW · 95mins

Based on Richard Llewellyn's stage play, *The Silk Noose*, this is a sterling slice of British *film noir*, starring American sex symbol Carole Landis. As the fashion journalist who gets mixed up in the murky underworld of London's black market, Landis bravely goes up against spivs and wide-boy racketeers in this surprisingly well-made little thriller. The film is stolen by the performance of Nigel Patrick as a fast-talking, charismatic villain. On a sad note, blonde bombshell Landis commited suicide shortly after completing the film. She was 29.

Carole Landis *Linda Medbury* • Joseph Calleia *Sugiani* • Derek Farr *Captain Jumbo Hoyle* • Stanley Holloway *Inspector Rendall* • Nigel Patrick *Bar Gorman* ■ *Dir* Edmond T Gréville • *Scr* Richard Llewellyn, Richard Dryhurst, from the play *The Silk Noose* by Richard Llewellyn

   U = SUITABLE FOR ALL, Uc = SUITABLE FOR ALL, ESPECIALLY FOR YOUNG CHILDREN (VIDEO ONLY), PG = PARENTAL GUIDANCE

Noose ★★★ 18
Crime drama 1997 · US · Colour · 89mins

Mystifyingly straight-to-video here, this brutish tale of "boys from the O'Hood" is a cracking tale of bullets and blarney, carried along by a good cast. Set in Boston, it stars Denis Leary as the small-time car thief who is forced to examine his loyalty to local crime boss Colm Meaney when one of his relatives (Billy Crudup) falls foul of the gangster. With the supporting players including Famke Janssen, Ian Hart, Martin Sheen and Jeanne Tripplehorn, this is a classy affair directed with some sympathy by Ted Demme. Contains swearing, some violence and sexual references. ▣

Denis Leary *Bobby O'Grady* • Jason Barry *Seamus* • Billy Crudup *Teddy* • Ian Hart *Moose Murphy* • Famke Janssen *Katy O'Connor* • Colm Meaney *Jackie O'Hara* • Martin Sheen *Hanolon* • Jeanne Tripplehorn *Annie* ■ *Dir* Ted Demme • *Scr* Mike Armstrong

The Noose Hangs High ★★ U
Comedy 1948 · US · BW · 76mins

Just when the fortunes of comedians Bud Abbott and Lou Costello seemed at their lowest, director Charles Barton brought in Leon Errol as guest star: a balding ditherer from countless B-pictures whose take on the double take was something to behold. Errol was the kind of trouper one could rely on, and he certainly raised the laughs in this predictable yarn about window cleaners mistaken for gamblers.

Bud Abbott *Ted Higgins* • Lou Costello *Homer Hinchcliffe* • Cathy Downs *Carol Scott* • Joseph Calleia *Mike Craig* • Leon Errol *Julius Caesar McBride* • Mike Mazurki *Chuck* ■ *Dir* Charles Barton • *Scr* John Grant, Howard Harris, from a story by Daniel Taradash, Julian Blaustein, Bernard Feins

Nor the Moon by Night ★★ U
Adventure 1958 · UK · Colour · 92mins

Guy Elmes was one of the busiest British screenwriters of the fifties and sixties. In addition to penning several "sword and sandal" adventures in Italy, he also adapted the Graham Greene short story *The Stranger's Hand* for producer John Stafford, with whom he reunited for this rather scrappy melodrama. There's little to be said in defence of either the acting or the story, in which the warden of an African game reserve finally meets his pen pal only to discover she's not the person he expected her to be.

Belinda Lee *Alice Lang* • Michael Craig *Rusty Miller* • Patrick McGoohan *Andrew Miller* • Anna Gaylor *Thea Boryslawski* • Eric Pohlmann *Anton Boryslawski* • Pamela Stirling *Mrs Boryslawski* ■ *Dir* Ken Annakin • *Scr* Guy Elmes, from the novel by Joy Packer

Nora ★★ 15
Biographical drama
1999 · UK/Ire/Ger/It · Colour · 106mins

Director Pat Murphy's exploration of James Joyce's relationship with his wife, Nora Barnacle, boasts a tour de force performance from Susan Lynch in the title role. The Irish actress excels as a passionate woman rebelling against a repressive existence while struggling to understand her selfish, obsessive, literary genius of a husband. Telling Joyce's story from Nora's point of view is a clever stroke, but the movie is let down by Ewan McGregor's risible portrait of the artist as a young man. Slow and unbalanced, the result falls well short of the mark.

Ewan McGregor *James Joyce* • Susan Lynch *Nora Barnacle* • Peter McDonald *Stanislas Joyce* • Roberto Citran *Roberto Prezioso* • Andrew Scott *Michael Bodkin* • Vincent McCabe *Uncle Tommy* • Veronica Duffy *Annie Barnacle* ■ *Dir* Pat Murphy • *Scr* Pat Murphy, Gerard Stembridge, from the biography by Brenda Maddox

Nora Prentiss ★★★
Crime melodrama 1947 · US · BW · 111mins

In the trade, this kind of glossy Warner Bros melodrama used to be known as a "women's picture", a generic term dismissively implying that a woman's story could only be enjoyed by female audiences. However, this romp can be enjoyed by all – if you leave your brains behind, that is. Sexy nightclub chanteuse Ann Sheridan ruins doctor Kent Smith when he falls for her and assumes the identity of a dead patient. Allegedly based on an actual insurance scandal, this is high-camp entertainment, with a technical crew of the very best to ensure that every ludicrous moment seems credible. It's a little overlong for its plot, but don't miss Sheridan's two solos.

Ann Sheridan *Nora Prentiss* • Kent Smith *Dr Richard Talbot* • Bruce Bennett *Dr Joel Merriam* • Robert Alda *Phil McDade* • Rosemary DeCamp *Lucy Talbot* • John Ridgely *Walter Bailey* • Robert Arthur *Gregory Talbot* ■ *Dir* Vincent Sherman • *Scr* N Richard Nash, Philip McDonald, from the story *The Man Who Died Twice* by Paul Webster, Jack Sobell

Norma Jean & Marilyn ★★
Biography 1996 · US · Colour · 129mins

The rise and fall of a 20th-century legend forms the basis of yet another TV-movie biography, which charts the life of Marilyn Monroe from her poor, rootless childhood as Norma Jean Baker, to her makeover as a blonde bombshell, to her final, tragic failure to resist her private demons. The unusual approach of having two actresses – Ashley Judd and Mira Sorvino – play the same character fails to overcome the fact that this a leering, pointless fantasy on the life of one of Hollywood's most discussed yet least understood icons.

Ashley Judd *Norma Jean Baker* • Mira Sorvino *Marilyn Monroe* • David Dukes *Arthur Miller* • Josh Charles *Eddie Jordan* • Ron Rifkin *Johnny Hyde* • Peter Dobson *Joe DiMaggio* • Taylor Nichols *Fred Karger* • John Rubinstein *Darryl Zanuck* ■ *Dir* Tim Fywell • *Scr* Jill Isaacs

Norma Rae ★★★★ PG
Drama 1979 · US · Colour · 109mins

Director Martin Ritt's last important film is typical of his best work. Based on the true story of a reluctant real-life heroine, this sincere drama with a social conscience makes its union cause authentic, heartfelt and grittily entertaining. Determinedly shedding her image as a perennially cute, bubbly comedian, Sally Field deservedly won her first Oscar for her committed performance as the widowed Southern textile worker who nervously allies herself with New York labour organiser Ron Leibman to fight appalling conditions and, with growing gumption, takes on the mill owners. There are fine performances all around, including Beau Bridges as her boorish man, but it's Field's triumph. ▣

Sally Field *Norma Rae* • Beau Bridges *Sonny Webster* • Ron Leibman *Reuben* • Pat Hingle *Vernon* • Barbara Baxley *Leona* • Gail Strickland *Bonnie Mae* • Morgan Paull *Wayne Billings* • Robert Broyles *Sam Bolen* ■ *Dir* Martin Ritt • *Scr* Irving Ravetch, Harriet Frank Jr

Normal Life ★★ 18
Crime drama 1995 · US · Colour · 102mins

Director John McNaughton, of *Henry: Portrait of a Serial Killer* and *Wild Things* fame, here delivers a sub-*Badlands*, "true crime" drama whose ending is obvious even before the opening credits have finished. Straight-laced cop Chris (Luke Perry) finds his world unravelling after he falls for wild child Pam (Ashley Judd) and gets caught up in credit card fraud and bank robbery. It all ends up like an over-dramatic TV movie, with Perry proving why he hasn't got much work outside *Beverly Hills 90210*.

Ashley Judd *Pam Anderson* • Luke Perry *Chris Anderson* • Bruce Young [Bruce A Young] *Agent Parker* • Jim True *Mike Anderson* • Dawn Maxey *Eva* • Tom Towles *Frank Anderson* ■ *Dir* John McNaughton • *Scr* Peg Haller, Bob Schneider

Norman... Is That You? ★★
Comedy drama 1976 · US · Colour · 91mins

Veteran black comedian Redd Foxx become a huge TV star via the sitcom *Sandford and Son* (based on the UK's *Steptoe and Son*) and made this movie while still on the show. Foxx plays Ben Chambers who, after discovering his wife's infidelity with his own brother, travels to LA to share his troubles with his son, Norman (Michael Warren). Upon arrival, he discovers his son's live-in male lover and vows to straighten his boy out. Although pleasingly acerbic in places, the film is unable to shake off its theatrical origins and, like many cutting-edge comedies of the time, now feels simplistic and occasionally offensive.

Redd Foxx *Ben Chambers* • Pearl Bailey *Beatrice Chambers* • Dennis Dugan *Garson Hobart* • Michael Warren *Norman Chambers* • Tamara Dobson *Audrey* • Vernée Watson *Melody* ■ *Dir* George Schlatter • *Scr* Ron Clark, Sam Bobrick, George Schlatter, from the play by Ron Clark, Sam Bobrick

Norman Loves Rose ★★★
Comedy 1982 · Ausl · Colour · 97mins

Typically offbeat Australian comedy about a lovestruck teenager (Tony Owen) who becomes enamoured of his sexy sister-in-law (Carol Kane). When the latter gets pregnant, it's less a case of how's-your-father than who's-the-father. The unsavoury-sounding plot actually raises more than its fair share of laughs – Aussies are good at handling this sort of quirky material – while Warren Mitchell, TV's Alf Garnett, shines in a supporting role.

Carol Kane *Rose* • Tony Owen *Norman* • Warren Mitchell *Morris* • Myra De Groot *Norman's mother* • David Downer *Michael* ■ *Dir/Scr* Henri Safran

Norman Rockwell's Breaking Home Ties ★★★
Melodrama 1987 · US · Colour · 95mins

Jason Robards and Eva Marie Saint head a strong cast in a moving TV movie, inspired by the work of the great American folk painter Norman Rockwell and, like the best of Rockwell's paintings, set in the mid-fifties. Doug McKeon, who played the young boy in *On Golden Pond*, does well as the farm boy off to college and adulthood, while equally fine performances by Robards and Saint save the film from becoming a clichéd melodrama.

Jason Robards [Jason Robards Jr] *Lloyd Welles* • Eva Marie Saint *Emma Welles* • Claire Trevor *Grace Porter* • Doug McKeon *Lonnie Welles* • Erin Gray *Carol Sheldrake* ■ *Dir/Scr* John Wilder

The Norseman ★ PG
Historical adventure
1978 · US · Colour · 86mins

A pathetic would-be historical adventure, with Lee Majors as a Viking named Thorvald who goes overseas looking for his lost father (played by Mel Ferrer). This is the sort of movie where men wear horns on their heads and say "Vrolop thar, gravad lax" to each other before hacking their enemies to pieces. The violence is of the slo-mo variety, the budget clearly nonexistent. Charles B Pierce writes, directs and produces at the sort of crass level that makes *Erik the Viking* look like a masterpiece. ▣

Lee Majors *Thorvald Helge* • Cornel Wilde *Ragnar* • Mel Ferrer *King Eurich* • Jack Elam *Death Dreamer* • Chris Connelly [Christopher Connelly] *Rolf* • Deacon Jones *Thrall* ■ *Dir/Scr* Charles B Pierce

El Norte ★★★★ 15
Drama 1983 · US · Colour · 140mins

Hailed as the "first American independent epic", Gregory Nava's compassionate film eschews political sermonising to concentrate on the human aspect of the arduous trek undertaken by so many Latinos to that pitiless promised land to the north. Adeptly using a docudramatic style to ward off overt sentimentality, Nava draws wondrously naturalistic performances from David Villalpando and Zaide Silvia Gutierrez. They play a brother and sister who, following the murder of their peasant father, experience both the despair of the refugee and the optimism of the immigrant after quitting their remote Guatamalan village. A sobering glimpse of reality, this is also an irresistibly involving drama. In English and Spanish with subtitles.

Ernesto Gomez Cruz *Arturo Xuncax* • David Villalpando *Enrique Xuncax* • Zaide Silvia Gutierrez *Rosa Xuncax* • Alicia del Lago *Lupe Xuncax* ■ *Dir* Gregory Nava • *Scr* Gregory Nava, Anna Thomas

North ★★ PG
Comedy drama 1994 · US · Colour · 83mins

Tired of saving the world, Bruce Willis is out to save the soul of 11-year-old North (Elijah Wood). However, the casting of Willis as a guardian angel dressed as a pink bunny rabbit is laughably typical of the misjudgements in Rob Reiner's fantastical extravaganza. North "divorces" his selfish parents and sets out on a worldwide odyssey to audition possible alternatives. Meanwhile, the school swot has set up a youngsters-versus-adults political power base on the strength of North's revolution. An interesting idea, clumsily carried through by Reiner. Contains some violence and swearing. ▭

Elijah Wood *North* • Bruce Willis *Narrator* • Jason Alexander *North's dad* • Julia Louis-Dreyfus *North's mom* • Mathew McCurley *Winchell* • Jon Lovitz *Arthur Belt* • Alan Arkin *Judge Buckle* • Dan Aykroyd *Pa Tex* ■ *Dir* Rob Reiner • *Scr* Alan Zweibel, Andrew Scheinman, from the novel by Alan Zweibel

North Beach and Rawhide
★★
Drama 1985 · US · Colour · 93mins

Star Trek's William Shatner beams down into this TV-movie as the idealistic director of a juvenile corrections ranch threatened by wealthy landowner James Olson, who schemes to buy the land and close the place down. Despite a colourful supporting cast (Tate Donovan, Ron O'Neal, Conchata Ferrell), this dull melodrama gives delinquency a bad name with its "we can save the world by saving the kids" message.

William Shatner *Rawhide MacGregor* • Tate Donovan *Sean Connelly* • James Olson *Bill Cassidy* • Ron O'Neal *Kyle Weston* • Lori Loughlin *Candy Cassidy* • Conchata Ferrell *Doc Norman* • GW Bailey *Sheriff* • Grace Zabriskie *Hearings Officer* ■ *Dir* Harry Falk • *Scr* Jimmy Sangster, John Beaird, George Yanok, from a story by John Beaird

North by Northwest
★★★★★ PG
Classic spy thriller
1959 · US · Colour · 130mins

A Hitchcock classic containing extra-generous helpings of the ingredients that make his films so unmissable. Action, intrigue, romance and comedy are blended throughout with consummate skill; the attack by the crop-dusting plane and the finale on Mount Rushmore are simply the icing on the cake. Rarely did Hitchcock have as much fun with his favourite "innocent in peril" theme or make such inventive use of famous landmarks. In his fourth and final collaboration with the "Master of Suspense", Cary Grant is the personification of suavity as he tackles a nest of enemy agents, led by a rather disengaged James Mason. ▭

Cary Grant *Roger Thornhill* • Eva Marie Saint *Eve Kendall* • James Mason *Phillip Vandamm* • Jessie Royce Landis *Clara Thornhill* • Leo G Carroll *Professor* • Philip Ober *Lester Townsend* • Martin Landau *Leonard* • Adam Williams *Valerian* ■ *Dir* Alfred Hitchcock • *Scr* Ernest Lehman • *Cinematographer* Robert Burks • *Music* Bernard Herrmann

North Dallas Forty ★★★ 18
Sports drama 1979 · US · Colour · 113mins

An all-American sports saga, with Nick Nolte looking every foot the part of the professional American football player, now almost over the hill, and wanting to escape the steroid culture and corruption surrounding the game. Since the National Football League declined to assist in the production, action footage is minimal until the climax, but this turns the spotlight on the characters involved and, it must be said, the clichés about heroism, role models and the girls on the sidelines. Contains swearing and nudity. ▭

Nick Nolte *Phillip Elliott* • Mac Davis *Maxwell* • Charles Durning *Coach Johnson* • Dayle Haddon *Charlotte* • Bo Svenson *Jo Bob Priddy* • Steve Forrest *Conrad Hunter* • Dabney Coleman *Emmett* ■ *Dir* Ted Kotcheff • *Scr* Frank Yablans, Ted Kotcheff, Peter Gent, from the novel by Peter Gent

North Sea Hijack ★★ 15
Action adventure 1979 · UK · Colour · 95mins

Presumably because it was assumed that American audiences might not know where the North Sea is, this action caper was retitled *Ffolkes* for the US market. In view of the age of the stars, they might have gone the whole hog and titled it *Old Ffolkes Home*. Roger Moore is the frogman hero, James Mason is an admiral and Anthony Perkins is planning to hijack a North Sea oil rig. It's sub-Bond, sub-Forsyth, even sub-Alistair MacLean, and tailored to the British market by cashing in on Britain's oil bonanza and by casting Faith Brook as the resident of 10 Downing Street. Ffeeble. Contains swearing and violence. ▭

Roger Moore *Rufus Excalibur Ffolkes* • James Mason *Admiral Sir Francis Brinsden* • Anthony Perkins *Lou Kramer* • Michael Parks *Shulman* • David Hedison *King* • Jack Watson *Olafsen* • Faith Brook *Prime Minister* ■ *Dir* Andrew V McLaglen • *Scr* Jack Davies, from his novel *Esther, Ruth and Jennifer*

North Shore ★★ PG
Action drama 1987 · US · Colour · 91mins

An extremely daft attempt to construct a youth-oriented surfer movie while straining to maintain an Elvis Presley-style innocence. The result? Anodyne nonsense. Matt Adler is the top surfer in Arizona (not much competition there, methinks) who hitches to Hawaii to do battle with the famous Oahu waves. Matt falls in love, but his inamorata's family is not too keen on the oval-eyed interloper. The script stinks, but the screen comes alive once surf's up. ▭

Matt Adler *Rick Kane* • Gregory Harrison *Chandler* • Nia Peeples *Kiani* • John Philbin *Turtle* • Gerry Lopez *Vince* ■ *Dir* William Phelps • *Scr* William Phelps, Tim McCanlies, from a story by William Phelps, Randall Kleiser

North Shore Fish ★★
Comedy drama 1997 · US · Colour · 93mins

A fine cast flounders in this TV adaptation of Israel Horovitz's stage play. The camaraderie in a seaside fish-packing plant helps the employees cope with the monotony of their work, especially when they're pressured to increase output. Complicating matters is a new health inspector, whose

investigations may shut the plant down if it does not meet government standards. Mercedes Ruehl, Peter Riegert and Tony Danza are wasted as an eccentric cross-section of whiny New Englanders, trapped in lives they'd rather not be living.

Mercedes Ruehl *Florence* • Peter Riegert *Porker* • Tony Danza *Sal* • Wendie Malick *Shimma* • Carroll Baker *Arlyne* • Cordelia Richards *Ruthie* ■ *Dir* Steve Zuckerman • *Scr* Israel Horovitz, from his play *North Shore Fish*

The North Star ★★★ PG
Second World War drama
1943 · US · BW · 99mins

A Second World War drama that's lifted above the mundane by a fine Lillian Hellman script (from her own story) and some strong playing from Walter Huston as a Ukrainian village doctor and Erich von Stroheim as his urbane Nazi counterpart. When the action is concentrated on the battle of words, this is a multi-layered, complex film which throws up some insights on the struggle against oppression. But there are far too many lengthy and tedious scenes of combat, which, although terrible at the time, make this movie appear almost as protracted as the real-life conflict. ▭

Anne Baxter *Marina* • Farley Granger *Damian* • Jane Withers *Claudia* • Eric Roberts *Grisha* • Dana Andrews *Kolya* • Walter Brennan *Karp* • Walter Huston *Dr Kurin* • Erich von Stroheim *Dr Otto Von Harden* ■ *Dir* Lewis Milestone • *Scr* Lillian Hellman, from her story

North Star ★ 15
Period adventure
1996 · Fr/It/Nor/UK · Colour · 84mins

During the 1899 Alaskan Gold Rush, prospector James Caan (*Misery*) battles Indian Christopher Lambert (*Highlander*) for land and the love of his girlfriend, played by Catherine McCormack of *Braveheart* fame. Directed by the Norwegian Nils Gaup, this contrived action adventure is weak on both plot and logic, resulting in a freeze-dried potboiler with little to recommend it apart from some spectacular locations. ▭

Christopher Lambert *Hudson Ipsehawk* • James Caan *Sean McLennon* • Catherine McCormack *Sarah* • Jacques François *Colonel Johnson* • Burt Young *Reno* ■ *Dir* Nils Gaup • *Scr* Sergio Donati, Lorenzo Donati, Paul Ohl, from a story by Gilles Behat, Philippe Schwartz, from the novel by Heck Allen [Will Henry]

North to Alaska ★★★★ U
Comedy adventure
1960 · US · Colour · 116mins

Johnny Horton's theme song for this marvellous roistering action film went to number four in the US charts, creating massive public awareness and popularity for this splendid comedy adventure with a sparkling cast. John Wayne is Big Sam, and the always under-rated Stewart Granger is his wily partner. The eclectic casting also includes teen idol Fabian as Granger's unlikely sibling, and the acerbic Ernie Kovacs as a confidence trickster. Director Henry Hathaway keeps up the pace and humour, and the movie contains one of the wackiest barroom brawls in Hollywood history. ▭

John Wayne *Sam McCord* • Stewart Granger *George Pratt* • Ernie Kovacs *Frankie Canon* • Fabian *Billy Pratt* • Capucine *Michelle, "Angel"* • Mickey Shaughnessy *Peter Boggs* ■ *Dir* Henry Hathaway • *Scr* John Lee Mahin, Martin Rackin, Claude Binyon, Wendell Mayes, from an idea by John Kafka and the play *Birthday Gift* by Laszlo Fodor

North West Frontier ★★★ U
Adventure 1959 · UK · Colour · 124mins

A cracking adventure, directed with great pace and precision by J Lee Thompson, which proves that an old-fashioned, all-action drama can still keep you on the edge of your seat without the benefit of flashy special effects. It could almost be called an eastern, transplanting the old western plot of a railroad journey through hostile territory to turn-of-the-century India. Kenneth More gives an assured performance as the soldier entrusted with the safety of a Hindu prince, and he is given able support by Lauren Bacall and Wilfrid Hyde White. ▭

Kenneth More *Captain Scott* • Lauren Bacall *Catherine Wyatt* • Herbert Lom *Van Leyden* • Wilfrid Hyde White *Bridie* • IS Johar *Gupta* • Ursula Jeans *Lady Windham* • Eugene Deckers *Peters* • Ian Hunter *Sir John Windham* • Jack Gwillim *Brigadier Ames* ■ *Dir* J Lee Thompson • *Scr* John Estridge

Northern Lights ★★ PG
Drama 1997 · US/Can · Colour · 86mins

Diane Keaton stars in this humorous drama of love and redemption as a neurotic single woman who arrives in a small New England town to collect her inheritance. Appalled to learn that her estranged late brother has left her custody of his nine-year-old son (Joseph Cross), she's humbled when events conspire to teach her life lessons. Keaton trod the same territory in *Baby Boom*, but her engaging and quirky personality does manage to enliven this otherwise poorly-mounted made-for-TV production. ▭

Diane Keaton *Roberta* • Joseph Cross *Jack* • Maury Chaykin *Ben* • John Robert Hoffman *Joe* • Crystal Verge *Aggie* ■ *Dir* Linda Yellen • *Scr* John Robert Hoffman [John Hoffman], Kevin Kane, from the play by John Robert Hoffman [John Hoffman]

Northern Pursuit ★★
Second World War adventure
1943 · US · BW · 93mins

The idea of Nazi saboteurs secretly entering Canada had been cleverly explored in the British film *49th Parallel*, but here it gets a juvenile treatment by Warner Bros. Errol Flynn is the Mountie of German descent who goes undercover, foiling a German scheme to assemble a bomber and attack the Panama Canal. Helmut Dantine is a Nazi heavy again after his teaming with Flynn in the far superior *Edge of Darkness*. Made just after Flynn's acquittal on charges of rape, the film goes lightly on the romance with Julie Bishop.

Errol Flynn *Steve Wagner* • Julie Bishop *Laura McBain* • Helmut Dantine *Von Keller* • John Ridgely *Jim Austin* • Gene Lockhart *Ernst* • Tom Tully *Inspector Barnett* ■ *Dir* Raoul Walsh • *Scr* Frank Gruber, Alvah Bessie, from the story *Five Thousand Trojan Horses* by Leslie T White

U = SUITABLE FOR ALL   Uc = SUITABLE FOR ALL, ESPECIALLY FOR YOUNG CHILDREN (VIDEO ONLY)   PG = PARENTAL GUIDANCE

The Northerners ★★★★ 15

Surreal comedy drama
1992 · Neth · Colour · 102mins

Director Alex van Warmerdam first came to the attention of British audiences with his 1986 black comedy *Abel*. This is an equally offbeat offering, which presents a surreal and, ultimately, macabre portrait of life on an incomplete Dutch housing estate in 1960. Among the eccentric inhabitants are a sexually frustrated butcher and his saintly wife, a short-sighted forest ranger with delusions of grandeur, a couple of travelling missionaries and a postman (played by the director himself) who hides away in the forest to read people's mail. In Dutch with English subtitles.

Leonard Lucieer *Thomas* • Jack Wouterse *Jacob the butcher* • Rudolf Lucieer *Anton the ranger* • Alex van Warmerdam *Simon the postman* • Annet Malherbe *Martha* ■ *Dir* Alex van Warmerdam • *Scr* Alex Van Warmerdam, Aat Ceelen

Northwest Mounted Police
★★

Period adventure
1940 · US · Colour · 125mins

Cecil B DeMille's flat-footed tribute to the Mounties has Gary Cooper as the Texas Ranger turned Mountie who, in the 1880s, helps suppress a 15-year revolt by settlers, many of whom are of mixed race. Madeleine Carroll and Paulette Goddard provide Cooper and buddy Robert Preston with additional motivation. From these historical skirmishes, DeMille suggests, came the Mounties' motto of always getting their man (or woman). A box-office blockbuster, this was shot on sound stages and in Oregon when DeMille's preferred location in the Canadian Rockies proved to be too expensive.

Gary Cooper *Dusty Rivers* • Madeleine Carroll *April Logan* • Paulette Goddard *Louvette Corbeau* • Preston Foster *Sgt Jim Brett* • Robert Preston *Constable Ronnie Logan* • George Bancroft *Jacques Corbeau* • Lynne Overman *Tod McDuff* • Akim Tamiroff *Dan Duroc* ■ *Dir* Cecil B DeMille • *Scr* Alan LeMay, Jesse Lasky Jr, C Gardner Sullivan, from the book *Royal Canadian Mounted Police* by RC Fetherston-Haugh

Northwest Outpost ★★

Western musical 1947 · US · BW · 91mins

After Nelson Eddy was reduced to working at Republic he had nowhere to go and this musical, with a weak score by Rudolf Friml, was his last. Eddy is the American captain at a Russian outpost in California in the 1830s who falls for Ilona Massey (in her third film with Eddy), who is the wife of Joseph Schildkraut's disgraced Count. The script is quite lively and Allan Dwan directs with a light touch, but it's never more than pleasant, old-fashioned fluff.

Nelson Eddy *Capt James Laurence* • Ilona Massey *Natalia Alanova* • Joseph Schildkraut *Count Igor Savin* • Hugo Haas *Prince Nickolai Balinin* • Elsa Lanchester *Princess "Tanya" Tatiana* ■ *Dir* Allan Dwan • *Scr* Elizabeth Meehan, Laird Doyle, Richard Sale, from a story by Angela Stuart

Northwest Passage ★★★ PG

Epic adventure 1940 · US · Colour · 121mins

A richly textured, beautifully shot adventure tale from MGM, which bears the subtitle *Book One: Rogers' Rangers*, creating the impression that a second film to complete the tale was on the way, but a sequel never actually materialised. No matter: this is pretty sturdy stuff on its own, featuring a rugged Spencer Tracy as Robert Rogers himself, setting out to find the passage of the title. Director King Vidor spares nothing, with the river sequences particularly well-filmed, and there is a genuinely epic feel to the whole endeavour. The ending (shot by uncredited director Jack Conway) certainly leaves you wanting more, but all that followed was a feeble TV series in the late fifties.

Spencer Tracy *Major Robert Rogers* • Robert Young *Langdon Towne* • Walter Brennan *Hunk Marriner* • Ruth Hussey *Elizabeth Browne* • Nat Pendleton *Captain Huff* • Louis Hector *Reverend Browne* • Robert Barrat *Humphrey Towne* • Lumsden Hare *General Amherst* • Donald MacBride *Sergeant McNott* ■ *Dir* King Vidor • *Scr* Laurence Stallings, Talbot Jennings, from the novel by Kenneth Roberts

Northwest Stampede ★★ U

Western 1948 · US · Colour · 75mins

James Craig was an ineffective but handsome substitute for Clark Gable and Robert Taylor while those two estimable stars fought for their country in the Second World War. On their return, MGM downgraded Craig and loaned him out on films like this, co-starring former Warner Bros ingénue Joan Leslie. Essentially, it's a romantic western with Leslie as a rancher who's trying to make rodeo-rider Craig settle down. Both Craig and Leslie were tormented by alcoholism during this period.

Joan Leslie *Chris Johnson* • James Craig *Dan Bennett* • Jack Oakie *Mike Kirby* • Chill Wills *Mileaway* • Victor Kilian *Mel Saunders* ■ *Dir* Albert S Rogell • *Scr* Art Arthur, Lillie Hayward, from the *Saturday Evening Post* story *Wild Horse Roundup* by Jean Muir

Nosferatu, a Symphony of Horrors ★★★★ PG

Classic silent horror
1922 · Ger · Tinted and BW · 79mins

Celebrated German director FW Murnau plundered Bram Stoker's *Dracula* without permission for this 1922 ground-breaker, and was successfully sued by Stoker's wife – all prints were ordered to be destroyed, but a few survived. The result is the most frightening incarnation of the vampire count in horror history. With his grasping claws, pointed fangs, bald pate and white cadaverous features, Count Orlock, played by the hideous Max Schreck, creeps through Murnau's archetypal silent imagery with a mesmerising authority that retains a surprising amount of tension. The chilling finale, highlighted by Schreck's terrifying shadow outside his victim's door, packs a powerful punch even by today's standards. **DVD**

Max Schreck *Count Orlock, Nosferatu* • Alexander Granach *Knock, an estate agent* • Gustav von Wangenheim *Hutter, his employee* • Greta Schroeder *Ellen, his wife* • GH Schnell *Harding, ship owner* • Ruth Landshoff *Annie,*

his wife ■ *Dir* Friedrich W Murnau [FW Murnau] • *Scr* Henrik Galeen, from the novel *Dracula* by Bram Stoker

Nosferatu, the Vampire ★★

Horror 1979 · Fr/W Ger · Colour · 107mins

Director Werner Herzog's all-too literal remake of FW Murnau's 1922 silent horror classic is a beautiful-looking bore. Murnau's pirated version of *Dracula* becomes a plodding exercise in image re-creation – with exactly the same sets, lighting effects and Klaus Kinski's replication of Max Schreck's Count Orlock – that one wonders why Herzog even bothered. Leisurely paced, and coming too close to parody for its own good, this redundant labour of love is a sometimes haunting yet mostly magnificent misfire. In German with English subtitles.

Klaus Kinski *Count Dracula* • Isabelle Adjani *Lucy Harker* • Bruno Ganz *Jonathan Harker* • Roland Topor *Renfield* • Walter Ladengast *Dr Van Helsing* • Dan Van Husen *Warden* ■ *Dir* Werner Herzog • *Scr* Werner Herzog, from the 1922 film by Henrik Galeen, from the novel *Dracula* by Bram Stoker

Nostalgia ★★★★ 15

Drama
1983 · USSR/It · Colour and BW · 120mins

Andrei Tarkovsky's first non-Soviet picture is clearly the work of an exile who can never regain his lost past. Yet, in rejecting a possible affair and his intellectual researches to undertake the eternal quest for enlightenment, Oleg Yankovsky finds redemption of sorts as he rises to the symbolic challenge of carrying a lighted candle across a sulphurous spa – a challenge posed by Erland Josephson, the apocalypse-obsessed resident of a Tuscan shrine town. Contrasting monochrome flashbacks with desaturated colour landscapes, Tarkovsky poetically employs langorous takes which not only convey Yankovsky's fragile mental and spiritual condition, but also heighten the mesmerising mysticism of this metaphysical allegory. In Italian with English subtitles.

Oleg Yankovsky *Andrei Gorchakov* • Erland Josephson *Domenico* • Domiziana Giordano *Eugenia* • Patrizia Terreno *Gorchakov's wife* ■ *Dir* Andrei Tarkovsky • *Scr* Andrei Tarkovsky, Tonino Guerra

Nostradamus ★★★ 15

Biographical drama
1993 · UK/Ger · Colour · 114mins

A semi-fantasy biopic tracing the life and predictions of the most famous soothsayer in history, Michel de Notredame (Nostradamus is his Latinised name). Director Roger Christian paints the charismatic 16th-century rebel doctor as a person shaken by the relevance of his dreams, but whose reputation for accuracy eventually attracts the patronage of French queen Catherine de'Medici. Using bursts of newsreel footage depicting African famine, atomic bomb testing, re-creations of the Second World War and space travel to visualise Notredame's most important predictions, Christian's po-faced venture is a singular oddity.

Tcheky Karyo *Nostradamus* • F Murray Abraham *Scalinger* • Rutger Hauer *Mystic*

Monk • Amanda Plummer *Catherine de'Medici* • Julia Ormond *Marie* • Assumpta Serna *Anne* • Anthony Higgins *King Henry II* • Diana Quick *Diane de Portier* ■ *Dir* Roger Christian • *Scr* Kurt Boeser, from a story by Piers Ashworth, Roger Christian

Not as a Stranger ★★★

Medical drama 1955 · US · BW · 136mins

After producing many key films, notably *High Noon*, *The Wild One* and *The Caine Mutiny*, Stanley Kramer turned director with this melodrama. It's about impoverished medical student Robert Mitchum, who marries Swedish nurse Olivia de Havilland because she can pay his tuition fees. Then Mitchum steps out with Gloria Grahame. Based on a 700-page bestseller by Morton Thompson, and containing lots of lurid detail about surgical procedures, this lumpen effort won't exactly leave you in stitches, but the high-powered cast is always worth watching.

Olivia de Havilland *Kristina Hedvigson* • Robert Mitchum *Lucas Marsh* • Frank Sinatra *Alfred Boone* • Gloria Grahame *Harriet Lang* • Broderick Crawford *Dr Aarons* • Charles Bickford *Dr Runkleman* • Myron McCormick *Dr Snider* • Lon Chaney Jr *Job Marsh* • Lee Marvin *Brundage* ■ *Dir* Stanley Kramer • *Scr* Edna Anhalt, Edward Anhalt, from the novel by Morton Thompson

Not for Publication ★★★ 15

Comedy 1984 · US · Colour · 83mins

Lois Thorndyke (Nancy Allen) works for *The Informer*, at one time a crusading newspaper run by her father, but now a sleazy scandal sheet. Sent to interview the mayor of New York (Laurence Luckinbill), Lois finds his campaign plans in a mess and agrees to help out – without revealing her links to the muckraking *Informer*. A romantic subplot links Lois to photographer Barry Denver (David Naughton). This eighties attempt to capture the flavour and style of a forties screwball comedy never quite comes off, but delivers plenty of fun along the way.

Nancy Allen *Lois Thorndyke* • Laurence Luckinbill *Mayor Claude Franklyn* • David Naughton *Barry Denver* • Alice Ghostley *Doris* • Don Peoples *Cy Katz* • Richard Blackburn *Jim* • Cork Hubbert *Odo* ■ *Dir* Paul Bartel • *Scr* Paul Bartel, John Meyer

Not in This Town ★★ 12

Drama based on a true story
1997 · US · Colour · 90mins

A well-intentioned but dull TV movie, based on the true story of Tammy Schnitzer, a Jewish woman who fought to save her family and Montana town from the bullying tactics of a white supremacist hate group. Kathy Baker plays the idealistic housewife, while Adam Arkin does his best in the thinly-written role of her cautious husband. At times the script bangs you over the head with lectures on social injustice; unfortunately, these fail to evoke feelings of outrage or indignation. Contains some swearing.

Kathy Baker *Tammy Schnitzer* • Adam Arkin *Brian Schnitzer* • Ed Begley Jr *Henry Whitcomb* • Max Gail Jr [Max Gail] *Wayne Inman* ■ *Dir* Donald Wrye • *Scr* Adam Gilad

Not My Kid ★★★ 🔟5
Drama   1985 · US · Colour · 91mins

Superficially, this is just another "trauma of the week" TV movie, with Hollywood dependables George Segal and Stockard Channing as parents who discover that their teenage daughter is hooked on drugs. But superior scripting and a non-sensationalised approach to the general subject of adolescent drug abuse elevates this significantly above the norm. 🖵

George Segal *Frank Bower* • Stockard Channing *Helen Bower* • Viveka Davis *Susan Bower* • Andrew Robinson *Dr Royce* • Gary Bayer *Dr Gramley* • Christa Denton *Kelly Bower* • Nancy Cartwright *Jean* • Tate Donovan *Ricky* ■ *Dir* Michael Tuchner • *Scr* Christopher Knopf

Not Now, Comrade ★
Comedy   1976 · UK · Colour · 89mins

It's hard to envisage anyone wanting to film any British stage farce. Yet what is so unforgivable about this woeful farrago is that it has been done in such a visually uninteresting way that it comes over as little more than illustrated radio. The fault lies squarely with Ray Cooney, who not only wrote and co-directed, but also co-stars in this horrid comedy of errors about a defecting Russian ballet dancer hiding in the country house of a top secret service bod. Let's draw a discreet Iron Curtain over the whole charade.

Leslie Phillips *Commander Rimmington* • Roy Kinnear *Hoskins* • Windsor Davies *Constable Pulford* • Don Estelle *Bobby Hargreaves* • Michele Dotrice *Nancy Rimmington* • Ray Cooney *Mr Laver* • June Whitfield *Janet Rimmington* ■ *Dir* Ray Cooney, Harold Snoad • *Scr* Ray Cooney

Not Now Darling ★★ 🄿🄶
Comedy   1972 · UK · Colour · 89mins

What an appalling waste of a remarkable cast that provides a comic link between the golden age of music hall and the *Carry Ons*. Popular thirties husband-and-wife team Jack Hulbert and Cicely Courtneidge were reunited on screen for the first time in 12 years for this clumsy version of Ray Cooney's long-running West End farce. But it's Leslie Phillips who holds this threadbare piece together, as the furrier up to his neck in girlfriends and cheap minks. Joan Sims and Barbara Windsor do what they can, but it's all rather tatty. 🖵

Leslie Phillips *Gilbert Bodley* • Ray Cooney *Arnold* • Moira Lister *Maude Bodley* • Julie Ege *Janie* • Joan Sims *Miss Tipdale* • Derren Nesbitt *Harry* • Barbara Windsor *Sue* • Jack Hulbert • Cicely Courtneidge ■ *Dir* Ray Cooney, David Croft • *Scr* John Chapman, from the play by Ray Cooney

Not of This Earth ★★★
Science-fiction horror
1956 · US · BW · 67mins

Cult director Roger Corman mixes science-fiction, horror and humour in his classic alien invasion quickie with vampiric overtones. Paul Birch is a visitor from the planet Davanna on the trail of human blood because his own race is facing extinction from nuclear anaemia. Death rays are generated whenever he removes his black sunglasses. Corman's elegantly styled,

fast-paced gem was the first of his prolific output to successfully lace comedy with suspense, inspiring him to continue in the same vein. The flying, head-crushing bat monster is a fine example of pure fifties pulp sci-fi.

Paul Birch *Paul Johnson* • Beverly Garland *Nadine Story* • Morgan Jones *Harry Sherbourne* • William Roerick *Dr Rochelle* • Jonathan Haze *Jeremy Perrin* • Richard Miller [Dick Miller] *Joe Piper* ■ *Dir* Roger Corman • *Scr* Charles Griffith, Mark Hanna

Not of This Earth ★ 🔟8
Science-fiction horror
1988 · US · Colour · 77mins

Ex-porn queen Traci Lords tried to go respectable in this dire remake of Roger Corman's 1956 cult favourite. After opening, for no apparent reason, with numerous clips from the New World Pictures back catalogue – *Piranha*, *Galaxy of Terror* and *Humanoids from the Deep*, a segment of which is also intercut into the main narrative – director Jim Wynorski's laughably cheap effort tells exactly the same story as the original (a vampire from outer space checks out earthlings' blood types for possible invasion purposes). Trash with no flash, dash or cash. 🖵

Traci Lords *Nadine Story* • Arthur Roberts *Mr Johnson* • Lenny Juliano *Jeremy* • Ace Mask *Dr Rochelle* • Roger Lodge *Harry* • Michael Delano *Vacuum cleaner salesman* • Rebecca Perle *Davanna Girl* ■ *Dir* Jim Wynorski • *Scr* Jim Wynorski, RJ Robertson, from the 1956 film

Not of This World ★★★
Drama   1998 · It · Colour · 100mins

Giuseppe Piccioni has become known as the "Italian Truffaut" for his humanity and eye for telling detail. He provides a clear-sighted analysis of the dehumanising effect of urban life in this moving drama, in which novice nun Margherita Buy's ordered world is thrown into turmoil on meeting miserly dry-cleaning boss Silvio Orlando, the presumed father of an abandoned baby thrust into her care by a passing jogger. As Buy struggles with her suppressed maternal instincts and a growing fondness for the misunderstood Orlando, Piccioni still has time for Carolina Freschi, the mother racked by a guilt intensified by her desperate domestic situation. In Italian with English subtitles.

Margherita Buy *Caterina* • Silvio Orlando *Ernesto* • Carolina Freschi *Teresa* • Maria Cristina Minerva *Esmeralda* ■ *Dir* Giuseppe Piccioni • *Scr* Giuseppe Piccioni, Gualtiero Rosella, Lucia Zei

Not One Less ★★★★ 🄄
Comedy drama   1999 · Chi · Colour · 106mins

Shades of *The Story of Qiu Ju* colour this sentimental but engaging drama from Zhang Yimou. Wryly humanist but politically outspoken, the winner of the Golden Lion at Venice starts out by castigating the shoddiness of the Chinese education system, especially in the desperately poor rural regions. However, once 13-year-old stand-in teacher Wei Minzhi sets off to retrieve the runaway student who can deprive her of a bonus for keeping all 28 charges in class, the focus of protest

switches to the exploitation of child labour on the urban black market. In Mandarin with English subtitles.

Wei Minzhi • Zhang Huike • Tian Zhenda *Village chief* • Gao Enman *Teacher Gao* ■ *Dir* Zhang Yimou • *Scr* Xiangsheng Shi

Not Our Son ★★★ 🄿🄶
Drama   1995 · US · Colour · 83mins

In this gripping fact-based story, Neal Patrick Harris (*Doogie Howser, MD*) effectively portrays the troubled son of a middle-class family. His parents are shocked to discover that he is a crazed arsonist, responsible for at least 76 devastating fires and his father must decide whether to help the police by setting a trap for his son. Gerald McRaney (*Major Dad*) brings depth to the role of an anguished parent faced with a troubling moral dilemma. What could have been a generic movie of the week is, in fact, an intense psychological portrait of a damaged young man and the family that loves him. 🖵

Neil Patrick Harris *Paul Keller* • Gerald McRaney *George Keller* • Cindy Pickett *Margaret Keller* • Ari Meyers *Ruth Keller* • Tom Verica *Randy Litchfield* • Scott Allan Campbell *Dane Whetsel* ■ *Dir* Michael Ray Rhodes • *Scr* Scott Swanton

Not Quite Human ★ 🄄
Fantasy comedy   1987 · US · Colour · 87mins

Not quite funny or entertaining either. A super-intelligent android is programmed never to tell a lie, leading to a series of "embarrassing" situations in this dire Disney comedy. Probably the most embarrassing thing is the script, which lacks both originality and humour, as well as a decent plot. But the most horrible thing to contemplate is the fact that there was actually a sequel made two years later, in which the android gets to attend college. 🖵

Alan Thicke *Dr Jonas Carson* • Jay Underwood *Chip Carson* • Robyn Lively *Becky Carson* • Joseph Bologna *Gordon Vogel* ■ *Dir* Steven Hilliard Stern • *Scr* Alan Ormsby, from characters created by Seth McAvoy

Not Quite Human II ★ 🄄
Comedy   1989 · US · Colour · 91mins

This comedy repeats the theme of the 1987 original, with teenage humans and androids having lots of predictable "fun" as the android continues his education. It contains eccentric, stupid or horrified adults, one or two near-villains and a complete lack of dramatic tension. Nearer the bottom of the Disney pile than the top. 🖵

Alan Thicke *Dr Jonas Carson* • Greg Mullavey *Dr Phil Masters* • Robyn Lively *Becky Carson* • Jay Underwood *Chip Carson* • Dey Young *Professor Victoria Gray* ■ *Dir* Eric Luke • *Scr* Eric Luke, from characters created by Seth McAvoy

Not Quite Jerusalem ★★ 🔟5
Comedy drama   1985 · UK · Colour · 109mins

Old-fashioned romance from Lewis Gilbert, director of *Alfie, Educating Rita* and *Shirley Valentine*. This film isn't quite up to those august standards, but it's a pleasant enough yarn about multinational volunteers working on an Israeli kibbutz and the budding

relationship that develops between young American Sam Robards and local girl Joanna Pacula. The pacing is a little pedestrian, but it's still the sort of low-key love story that very easy to get lost in. 🖵

Joanna Pacula *Gila* • Sam Robards *Mike* • Kevin McNally *Pete* • Todd Graff *Rothwell T Schwartz* • Selina Cadell *Carrie* • Bernard Strother *Dave* ■ *Dir* Lewis Gilbert • *Scr* Paul Kember, from his play

Not Reconciled, or Only Violence Helps Where Violence Rules ★★★★
Classic experimental drama
1965 · W Ger · BW · 53mins

With this debut feature, a deconstruction of Heinrich Böll's novel, *Billiards at Half-Past Nine*, Jean-Marie Straub and his wife Danièle Huillet, who has a role in the film, immediately established themselves as among the most interesting film-makers in Germany at the time, helping herald the New German Cinema movement. In less than an hour, the film deals with three generations of a middle-class German family, against the background of the anti-communism of 1910s to the Nazism of the thirties to the revolutionary politics of the sixties. In German with English subtitles.

Heinrich Hargesheimer *Heinrich Fähmel at 80* • Carlheinz Hargesheimer *Heinrich Fähmel at 35* • Martha Ständner *Johanna Fähmel at 70* • Danièle Straub [Danièle Huillet] *Johanna Fähmel as a young woman* • Henning Harmssen *Robert Fähmel at 40* • Ulrich Hopmann *Robert Fähmel at 18* ■ *Dir* Jean-Marie Straub • *Scr* Jean-Marie Straub, Danièle Huillet, from the novel *Billiards at Half-Past Nine* by Heinrich Böll

Not Wanted on Voyage ★ 🄄
Comedy   1957 · UK · BW · 87mins

A story about a luxury liner and a stolen necklace – sounds familiar? The script of *Titanic* might not be poetry, but it's a darn sight better than the drivel that passes for dialogue in this dismal comedy. Co-screenwriter Michael Pertwee enjoyed considerable success both before and after making a contribution to this venture, which is so unfunny that even gallant troupers Ronald Shiner and Brian Rix cannot conceal their dismay.

Ronald Shiner *Steward Albert Higgins* • Brian Rix *Steward Cecil Hollebone* • Griffith Jones *Guy Harding* • Catherine Boyle *Julie Haines* • Fabia Drake *Mrs Brough* • Michael Brennan *Chief Steward* ■ *Dir* Maclean Rogers • *Scr* Michael Pertwee, Evadne Price, Roland Pertwee, Jack Marks, from a screenplay by Dudley Sturrock, from the play *Wanted On Voyage* by Evadne Price, Ken Attiwill

Not with My Wife, You Don't! ★★★
Comedy   1966 · US · Colour · 118mins

George C Scott, usually associated with heavyweight drama rather than lightweight fluff, here proves his comic strength when he muscles in on the uneasy marriage of US Air Force aide Tony Curtis and Virna Lisi, intent on carrying off the woman for whom he and Curtis once vied when they were Korean War comrades. Comic director Norman Panama and co-writers Larry Gelbart and Peter Barnes make the

🄄 = SUITABLE FOR ALL   🄄c = SUITABLE FOR ALL, ESPECIALLY FOR YOUNG CHILDREN (VIDEO ONLY)   🄿🄶 = PARENTAL GUIDANCE

non-stop contrivance of the situation appear seamless.

Tony Curtis *Tom Ferris* • Virna Lisi *Julie Fisher* • George C Scott *"Tank" Martin* • Carroll O'Connor *General Parker* • Richard Eastham *General Walters* • Eddie Ryder *Sergeant Gilroy* • George Tyne *Sergeant Dogerty* ■ *Dir* Norman Panama • *Scr* Norman Panama, Larry Gelbart, Peter Barnes, from a story by Norman Panama, Melvyn Frank

Not without My Daughter ★★ 🔟

Biographical drama
1990 · US · Colour · 111mins

A real-life nightmare is turned, unfortunately, into an overwrought soap. Betty Mahmoody, played by Sally Field, went to Iran with her doctor husband and their daughter, only to find him becoming a violent tyrant and all rights being taken from her. It took an underground chain of helpers to aid her and her daughter's escape, but sympathy for Field's character is distanced by her hysterical performance, and not even the usually impressive Alfred Molina can believably convey the husband's personality switch. Contains some violence and swearing. 🔲

Sally Field *Betty Mahmoody* • Alfred Molina *Moody* • Sheila Rosenthal *Mahtob* • Roshan Seth *Houssein* • Sarah Badel *Nicole* • Mony Rey *Ameh Bozorg* • Georges Corraface *Mohsen* ■ *Dir* Brian Gilbert • *Scr* David W Rintels, from the non-fiction book by Betty Mahmoody, William Hoffer

Notebook on Cities and Clothes ★★ 🔟

Documentary 1989 · W Ger · Colour · 81mins

Although this is not as engaging, amusing or as insightful as the somewhat similar *Unzipped*, this documentary by German director Wim Wenders nonetheless provides an astute look at the work and creative process of innovative Japanese fashion designer Yohji Yamamoto. We see him contemplating the relationship between cities, identity and the future of cinema in the digital age. The film culminates in a Paris spring catwalk show at the Louvre and the way in which Wenders draws comparisons between his own work and Yamamoto's high-chic designs is a fascinating exercise. An English language version was also released. A German language film.

Wim Wenders *Narrator* ■ *Dir* Wim Wenders • *Scr* Wim Wenders, from an idea by François Burkhardt

Nothing but a Man ★★★

Drama 1964 · US · BW · 91mins

This engrossing drama stars Ivan Dixon as the black railroad worker in a small Southern town who takes on racist bully-boys so that he can stand tall in front of his wife and family. By making the dilemma small and intimate instead of loud and declamatory, director Michael Roemer ensures the issues involved are relevant to all.

Ivan Dixon *Duff Anderson* • Abbey Lincoln *Josie Dawson* • Gloria Foster *Lee* • Julius Harris *Will Anderson* • Yaphet Kotto *Jocko* ■ *Dir* Michael Roemer • *Scr* Michael Roemer, Robert Young

Nothing but the Best ★★★★

Black comedy 1964 · UK · Colour · 97mins

Scripted by Frederic Raphael, photographed by Nicolas Roeg and directed by Clive Donner, this has all the credentials to be one of the best British big-screen satires. There's no denying it's a very funny film, a sort of *School for Scoundrels* in a *Room at the Top*, but the brushstrokes are so broad that there is no room for the finer detail that would have made it a classic. Alan Bates is splendid as a working-class wannabe, but Denholm Elliott steals every scene as an indolent aristocrat who tutors him in the delicate art of being a cad.

Alan Bates *Jimmy Brewster* • Denholm Elliott *Charlie Prince* • Harry Andrews *Mr Horton* • Millicent Martin *Ann Horton* • Pauline Delany *Mrs March* • Godfrey Quigley *Coates* ■ *Dir* Clive Donner • *Scr* Frederic Raphael, from the short story *The Best of Everything* by Stanley Ellin

Nothing but the Night ★★

Supernatural murder mystery
1972 · UK · Colour · 90mins

The first and last production from Christopher Lee's own company, Charlemagne, is a silly, supernatural variant on *Village of the Damned*. The brooding atmosphere of John Blackburn's pre-*Exorcist* possession novel goes awry under horror stalwart Peter Sasdy's confusing direction, leading to a complete absence of menace or suspense. Despite Lee making great claims for the innate intelligence of his misunderstood "masterpiece", it's a patchy affair with little to recommend it.

Christopher Lee *Colonel Bingham* • Peter Cushing *Sir Mark Ashley* • Diana Dors *Anna Harb* • Georgia Brown *Joan Foster* • Keith Barron *Dr Haynes* • Gwyneth Strong *Mary Valley* • Fulton Mackay *Cameron* • John Robinson *Lord Fawnlee* • Michael Gambon *Inspector Grant* ■ *Dir* Peter Sasdy • *Scr* Brian Hayles, from a novel by John Blackburn

Nothing but the Truth ★★★

Comedy 1941 · US · BW · 90mins

Based on a play filmed twice before, in 1920 and 1929, this has a sure-fire plot in its story of a young man who vows to tell the absolute truth for 24 hours. Though slow to start, it pays off in the second half during a party on a yacht at which the hero's dilemma becomes increasingly farcical. Bob Hope was a master at this sort of thing and the vivacious Paulette Goddard always teamed well with him – this was their third film together.

Bob Hope *Steve Bennett* • Paulette Goddard *Gwen Saunders* • Edward Arnold *TT Ralston* • Leif Erickson *Tommy Van Deusen* • Willie Best *Samuel* • Glenn Anders *Dick Donnelly* • Clarence Kolb *Mr James P Van Deusen* ■ *Dir* Elliott Nugent • *Scr* Don Hartman, Ken Englund, from the play by James Montgomery, from the novel by Frederic S Isham

Nothing but the Truth ★★ 🔟

Thriller 1995 · US · Colour

thirtysomething co-stars and real-life husband and wife Patricia Wettig and Ken Olin star in this run-of-the-mill thriller. She's a lie-detector specialist who finds herself torn between love

and the truth when an old flame (Olin) turns up in town, then quickly becomes a suspect in a murder case. Directed in a workmanlike way by Michael Switzer, this TV movie follows predictable lines, with the game of "is he or isn't he?" being played out with far too little tension. We're all familiar with this sort of scenario and there's nothing to make the pulse quicken.

Patricia Wettig *Jill Ross* • Ken Olin *Peter Clayman* • Tia Carrere *Simone Gideon* ■ *Dir* Michael Switzer • *Scr* Matt Dorff

Nothing but Trouble ★★ 🇺

Comedy 1944 · US · BW · 66mins

A mawkish late entry from Laurel and Hardy working for a studio (MGM) which didn't understand their needs, so straitjacketed them into an oddly unlikeable story. Stan and Ollie are descendants of a long line of butlers and chefs whose own culinary disasters make them pariahs. They befriend the boy king Christopher (David Leland), who is in peril from his uncle, Prince Saul (Philip Merivale). The attempted murder puts the glooms on Stan and Ollie's light-hearted spirits. 🔲

Stan Laurel *Stan* • Oliver Hardy *Ollie* • Henry O'Neill *Basil Hawkley* • Mary Boland *Mrs Elvira Hawkley* • David Leland *King Christopher* • John Warburton *Ronetz* • Philip Merivale *Prince Saul* ■ *Dir* Sam Taylor • *Scr* Russell Rouse, Ray Golden, Bradford Ropes, Margaret Gruen

Nothing but Trouble ★ 🔟

Fantasy comedy 1991 · US · Colour · 89mins

"Wasn't Worth the Trouble" might have been a more suitable title for a lousy comedy that quite blatantly rips off the premise of Peter Weir's cult classic, *The Cars That Ate Paris*. Dan Aykroyd wrote and directed this cinematic calamity, in which he also stars as a sadistic judge who delights in tormenting unsuspecting motorists. Chevy Chase and Demi Moore deserve no sympathy: they read the script before they signed their contracts. John Candy rescued many pictures with his engaging cameos, but even in drag he is unable to salvage anything from the wreckage. 🔲

Chevy Chase *Chris Thorne* • Dan Aykroyd *"JP"/Bobo* • John Candy *Dennis/Eldona* • Demi Moore *Diane Lightston* • Taylor Negron *Fausto* • Bertila Damas *Renalda* ■ *Dir* Dan Aykroyd • *Scr* Dan Aykroyd, from a story by Peter Aykroyd

Nothing in Common ★★ 🔟

Drama 1986 · US · Colour · 113mins

It's not usually the done thing to quote another film critic, but Pauline Kael was spot-on when she said that this mawkish mess was tantamount to a sitcom version of Arthur Miller's *Death of a Salesman*. Once the king of American TV comedy, Jackie Gleason stars as the washed-up rag trader who foists himself on his yuppy son (Tom Hanks) after his wife of 36 years, Eva Marie Saint, walks out on him. Director Garry Marshall treats the veteran Gleason with far too much respect, allowing him to get away with a hugely self-indulgent performance. Even Hanks is below his usually sparkling best. Contains swearing. 🔲

Tom Hanks *David Basner* • Jackie Gleason *Max Basner* • Eva Marie Saint *Lorraine Basner* • Hector Elizondo *Charlie Gargas* • Barry Corbin *Andrew Woolridge* • Bess Armstrong *Donna Mildred Martin* • Sela Ward *Cheryl Ann Wayne* ■ *Dir* Garry Marshall • *Scr* Rick Podell, Michael Preminger

Nothing Lasts Forever ★★★ 🔟

Comedy 1984 · US · Colour and BW · 155mins

A rather bizarre but entertaining comedy shot in colour and black and white, with Zach Galligan of *Gremlins* fame as an artist experiencing life in the New York of the future. Most notable for its quirky cast including Dan Aykroyd, Imogene Coca, Eddie Fisher and Bill Murray. this was produced by *Saturday Night Live*'s Lorne Michaels, but is far stranger than anything which appeared on that innovative show. Not to everyone's taste, but worth a look. 🔲

Zach Galligan *Adam Beckett* • Lauren Tom *Ely* • Apollonia Van Ravenstein *Mara Hofmeier* • Dan Aykroyd *Buck Heller* • Imogene Coca *Daisy Schackman* • Eddie Fisher • Mort Sahl *Uncle Mort* • Bill Murray ■ *Dir* Tom Schiller • *Scr* Tom Schiller

Nothing Personal ★ 🔟

Comedy 1980 · US/Can · Colour · 96mins

Donald Sutherland is a college professor who teams up with hot-shot Harvard law graduate Suzanne Somers to prevent the slaughter of baby seals on the Arctic Circle. In the course of their campaign, they lobby Washington and tackle the big bosses. This serious environmental issue sits rather uncomfortably in what is really a screwball comedy romance between Sutherland and Somers. It all ends up, predictably, with a chase across the ice. But long before that, the fate of the cuddly little seals has been sealed – they are simply the McGuffins. 🔲

Donald Sutherland *Roger Keller* • Suzanne Somers *Abigail Adams* • Lawrence Dane *Robert Ralston* • Roscoe Lee Browne *Mr Paxton* • Dabney Coleman *Tom Dickerson* • Saul Rubinek *Peter Braden* ■ *Dir* George Bloomfield • *Scr* Robert Kaufman

Nothing Personal ★★★ 🔟

Drama 1995 · UK/Ire · Colour · 81mins

In striving for balance, Thaddeus O'Sullivan's pre-Irish peace process drama fails to deliver its intended statement and ends up merely reinforcing the clichés and stereotypes that exist on either side of the divide. Adapted by Daniel Mornin from his own novel, *All Our Fault*, the story is over-reliant on cross-denominational coincidence to truly convince, while its murderous conclusion is cheaply manipulative. John Lynch is too familiar as the father who finds himself on the front line, while Ian Hart is wildly over-the-top as a trigger-happy bigot. Yet the solid work of Michael Gambon and James Frain, makes it worth watching. Contains violence and swearing. 🔲

Ian Hart *Ginger* • John Lynch *Liam* • James Frain *Kenny* • Michael Gambon *Leonard* • Gary Lydon *Eddie* • Ruaidhri Conroy *Tommy* ■ *Dir* Thaddeus O'Sullivan • *Scr* Daniel Mornin, from his novel *All Our Fault*

Nothing Sacred ★★★ U

Satirical comedy 1937 · US · Colour · 73mins

A cynical black comedy from the acid pen of former journalist Ben Hecht, based on a *Strand* magazine short story, terrifically acted by the dashing Fredric March as a tabloid reporter and Carole Lombard as a Vermont girl whose last wish before she dies of radium poisoning is to see New York in all its glory. Of course, she isn't really dying, but that doesn't stop March from exploiting her case to the hilt, and affording writer Hecht the opportunity to take swipes at his former profession. Tasteless, certainly, and not quite as funny as it thinks it is in the hands of director William A Wellman, best known for his aerial epics and gangster pictures.

Carole Lombard *Hazel Flagg* • Fredric March *Wally Cook* • Charles Winninger *Dr Downer* • Walter Connolly *Stone* • Sig Rumann [Sig Ruman] *Dr Eggelhoffer* • Frank Fay *Master of Ceremonies* • Maxie Rosenbloom *Max Levinsky* • Hattie McDaniel *Mrs Walker* • Hedda Hopper *Dowager* ■ *Dir* William Wellman [William A Wellman] • *Scr* Ben Hecht, Ring Lardner Jr, Budd Schulberg, from the story *Letter to the Editor* by James H Street

Nothing to Lose ★★ 18

Action comedy 1997 · US · Colour · 92mins

After such heavyweight message flicks as *The Shawshank Redemption* and *Dead Man Walking*, Tim Robbins has a comic breather in this glossy but empty-headed buddy movie. Robbins plays a stressed-out exec who thinks his wife (Kelly Preston) is having an affair with his boss (Michael McKean). Seeking revenge, he finds an unlikely ally in petty thief Martin Lawrence. The two stars do their best with the comic crumbs they are handed, but both they and writer/director Steve Oedekerk are hampered by the fact that this is an action comedy where nothing really happens. ▭ *DVD*

Martin Lawrence *T Paul* • Tim Robbins *Nick Beam* • John C McGinley *Davis "Rig" Lanlow* • Giancarlo Esposito *Charlie Dunt* • Kelly Preston *Ann* • Michael McKean *Phillip Barrow* ■ *Dir/Scr* Steve Oedekerk

Notorious ★★★★★ U

Classic romantic thriller
1946 · US · BW · 100mins

Originally to be a story about Nazi training camps in the South American jungle, *Notorious* caused some disquiet on its release by dealing with uranium at a time when it was still supposed to be top secret. While not as thematically complex or technically audacious as some of Hitchcock's later classics, this is the finest of his "entertainments". He allowed himself one moment of technical virtuosity (the stunning crane shot swooping in on a key), but mostly confines his yarn to spinning with customary skill. Ingrid Bergman and Cary Grant strike sparks off each other, while Claude Rains excels as the villain. ▭

Ingrid Bergman *Alicia Huberman* • Cary Grant *Devlin* • Claude Rains *Alexander Sebastian* • Louis Calhern *Paul Prescott* • Madame Konstantin [Leopoldine Konstantin] *Madame Sebastian* • Reinhold Schunzel *Dr Anderson* ■ *Dir* Alfred Hitchcock • *Scr* Ben Hecht

Notorious ★★ 15

Thriller 1992 · US · Colour · 95mins

Remaking films by revered directors at best smacks of bravery. Remaking Hitchcock is more akin to jumping off a cliff. Yet director Colin Bucksey, who is still waiting to be fished out of the water, not only offers us his own tepid style but an update to boot, wherein nasty Nazis are replaced by Soviet spies. The question "why?" has yet to be answered. ▭

John Shea *Devlin* • Jenny Robertson *Alicia Velorus* • Jean-Pierre Cassel *Alex Sebastian* • Marisa Berenson *Katarina Sebastian* • Paul Guilfoyle *Norman Prescott* • Ronald Guttman *Joseph* ■ *Dir* Colin Bucksey • *Scr* Douglas Lloyd McIntosh, from the 1946 film

The Notorious Landlady ★★★

Comedy mystery 1962 · US · BW · 126mins

An eccentric comedy mystery set principally in London with a sparkling cast led by Jack Lemmon, Kim Novak and, briefly, Fred Astaire as the American ambassador. Lemmon plays a newly arrived diplomat whose landlady, Miss Novak, is suspected of murdering her husband who has vanished. When the husband does appear, Novak promptly shoots him. After that twist the plot thickens – so much, in fact, that Lemmon admitted that he didn't have a clue what was going on. London was created entirely on studio sets, giving the film an arch theatricality, like a blend of *Arsenic and Old Lace*, a Gilbert and Sullivan operetta and Agatha Christie.

Kim Novak *Carlye Hardwicke* • Jack Lemmon *William Gridley* • Fred Astaire *Franklyn Ambruster* • Lionel Jeffries *Inspector Oliphant* • Estelle Winwood *Mrs Dunhill* • Maxwell Reed *Miles Hardwicke* • Philippa Bevans *Mrs Brown* ■ *Dir* Richard Quine • *Scr* Larry Gelbart, Blake Edwards, from a story by Margery Sharp

La Notte ★★★★★

Drama 1961 · Fr/It · BW · 121mins

Antonioni's famous study of a marriage on the rocks stars Marcello Mastroianni as a novelist who blames his wife, Jeanne Moreau, for his lack of inspiration. She, in turn, feels ignored and patronised. After visiting a friend in hospital, Mastroianni and Moreau have an argument and separate. She spends the night wandering through the ugly bits of Milan; he goes to a party and pursues a virtually catatonic Monica Vitti. Mastroianni and Moreau loathed their parts, their director and the favouritism that he showed to Vitti, who was then his mistress. Yet this is, first and foremost, a director's film: rigidly controlled, very slow and with dazzling shots of the modern city that seem to infect the characters' despair and alienation. Dated it may be, but *La Notte* remains a mesmeric movie that cracks open the shell of the human soul. An Italian language film.

Marcello Mastroianni *Giovanni Pontano* • Jeanne Moreau *Lidia Pontano* • Monica Vitti *Valentina Gherardini* • Bernhard Wicki *Tommaso* ■ *Dir* Michelangelo Antonioni • *Scr* Michelangelo Antonioni, Ennio Flaiano, Tonino Guerra, from a story by Michelangelo Antonioni

Notting Hill ★★★★★ 15

Romantic comedy
1999 · US/UK · Colour · 123mins

The *Four Weddings* team produced another smash with this charming tale of bumbling bookshop owner Hugh Grant falling for "most famous actress in the world" Julia Roberts. Inevitably, the course of true love is a bumpy road, with friends, family and flatmates getting in the way, but that's the cue for a series of screamingly funny scenarios. Saturated with wit and well directed by Roger Michell, the film was bashed by sceptics for its fluffiness and lack of realism (for a racially mixed area of London, there's not a black face to be seen). But, if you can accept the context as 100 per cent white middle class, it's an intensely enjoyable experience. ▭ *DVD*

Julia Roberts *Anna Scott* • Hugh Grant *William Thacker* • Hugh Bonneville *Bernie* • Emma Chambers *Honey* • James Dreyfus *Martin* • Rhys Ifans *Spike* • Tim McInnerny *Max* • Gina McKee *Bella* • Richard McCabe *Tony* ■ *Dir* Roger Michell • *Scr* Richard Curtis

La Nouvelle Eve ★★★ 18

Romantic drama 1999 · Fr · Colour · 94mins

A lifeguard with a fierce sense of independence may sound like an unlikely *femme fatale*, but that's exactly what Karin Viard plays in this quirky romantic comedy, set in the new Eden of nineties Paris. However, in ambitiously updating notions of the stock literary heroine, director Catherine Corsini tempers Viard's aggressive pursuit of a balding, politically active family man (Pierre-Loup Rajot) by adopting the rather rosy view that everyone's soul mate is out there somewhere. In French with English subtitles.

Karin Viard *Camille* • Pierre-Loup Rajot *Alexis* • Catherine Frot *Isabelle* • Sergi Lopez *Ben* • Laurent Lucas *Emile* • Mireille Roussel *Louise* • Nozha Khouadra *Solveig* • Valentine Vidal *Sophie* ■ *Dir* Catherine Corsini • *Scr* Catherine Corsini, Marc Syrigas, Emmanuel Bourdieu, Denyse Rodriguez-Tome

Nouvelle Vague ★★★

Drama 1990 · Swi/Fr · Colour · 89mins

Seducing us with some lustrous visuals before disarming our expectations with a melodramatic storyline and dialogue taken from a range of literary, philosophical and cinematic sources, this is something of a curate's egg from Jean-Luc Godard. Despite his dual involvement, Alain Delon looks curiously detached from the proceedings as he returns to wreak his revenge on murderous aristocrat Domiziana Giordano. Everything from sociopolitical allegory to morality tale is there if you can be bothered to scour the stylised imagery, but few critics were. A French language film.

Alain Delon *Roger Lennox/Richard Lennox* • Domiziana Giordano *Countess Elena Torlato-Favrini* • Roland Amstutz *Jules the gardener* ■ *Dir/Scr* Jean-Luc Godard

The November Conspiracy ★★

Political action thriller
1995 · US · Colour · 103mins

As ambitious journalist Paige Turco tries to interview Democratic presidential candidate George Segal, the latter twice becomes the target of attempts on his life. When Turner's boyfriend Dirk Benedict turns out to be a secret agent who seems responsible for the second bid, Turner becomes the hunted party with only her knowledge of self-defence to protect her. This agreeable junk thriller displays a canny appreciation of its limitations, resulting in a loose, spirited B-movie political suspenser.

Paige Turco *Jennifer Barron* • Dirk Benedict *John Mackie* • Conrad Janis *Frank* • Bo Hopkins *Captain Brogan* • George Segal *Senator Ashton* • Elliott Gould *Kahn* ■ *Dir* Conrad Janis • *Scr* Maria Grimm

The November Men ★★ 15

Spoof political thriller
1993 · US · Colour · 95mins

An intriguing concept doesn't quite come off in this sluggishly paced drama about a politically obsessed film-maker who enlists a handful of actors for an improvised movie about the fake assassination of President Bush. There's a fair share of twists and turns, as almost everybody involved in the guerrilla film-making is suspected as being a real assassin using the film as a cover. However, all the characters – particularly the Secret Service agents – are phoney and implausible. ▭

James Andronica *Duggo* • Leslie Bevis *Elizabeth* • Beau Starr *Chief Agent Granger* • Paul Williams *Arthur Gwenlyn* • Coralissa Gines *Lorina* • Rod Ellis *Special Agent Eric Clancy* • Shanda Cunningham *Waitress* ■ *Dir* Paul Williams • *Scr* James Andronica

Now about These Women ★★

Satire 1964 · Swe · Colour · 79mins

Coming between *The Silence* and *Persona*, Ingmar Bergman's first production in colour is one of his few miscalculations. Co-written with actor Erland Josephson, this clumsy costume comedy seeks both to explore the elusive nature of genius and decry the parasitic insolence of critics, whose only acts of creation depend entirely on the destruction of another's work. Although there are flashes of Mack Sennett, Jacques Tati and Federico Fellini in the humour, biographer Jarl Kulle's encounters with a cellist's female entourage are resolutely unfunny. The harder Bergman and his splendid cast try, the more stilted the action becomes. In Swedish with English subtitles.

Jarl Kulle *Cornelius* • Bibi Andersson *Humlan* • Harriet Andersson *Isolde* • Eva Dahlbeck *Adelaide* ■ *Dir* Ingmar Bergman • *Scr* Erland Josephson, Ingmar Bergman

Now and Forever ★★

Comedy drama 1934 · US · BW · 81mins

Gary Cooper steals some jewellery from wealthy Charlotte Granville and hides it in the teddy bear belonging to his small daughter. When they're

U = SUITABLE FOR ALL   Uc = SUITABLE FOR ALL, ESPECIALLY FOR YOUNG CHILDREN (VIDEO ONLY)   PG = PARENTAL GUIDANCE

discovered, his mistress, Carole Lombard, takes the blame, and Cooper allows the owner of the gems to adopt his child. Marking director Henry Hathaway's move away from minor westerns to big-league features, this comedy drama is nonetheless a run-of-the-mill affair, with neither star shining too brightly. Its main attraction, then and now, is the appearance of six-year-old Shirley Temple as Coop's daughter.

Gary Cooper *Jerry Day* • Carole Lombard *Toni Carstairs* • Shirley Temple *Penelope Day* • Guy Standing *Felix Evans* • Charlotte Granville *Mrs JHP Crane* • Gilbert Emery *James Higginson* ■ *Dir* Henry Hathaway • *Scr* Vincent Lawrence, Sylvia Thalberg, from the story *Honor Bright* by Jack Kirkland, Melville Baker

Now and Forever ★★ 15
Melodrama 1983 · Ausl · Colour · 88mins

Based on the Danielle Steel book, this routine "trauma of the week" movie stars Cheryl Ladd as a chic boutique owner who returns from a clothes-buying trip abroad to find her philandering hubby has been had up on rape charges. Not surprisingly, the accusation puts strain on their marriage. Decent performances make this ideal for fans of Mills & Boon-type melodramas. ▱

Cheryl Ladd *Jessie Clarke* • Robert Coleby *Ian Clarke* • Carmen Duncan *Astrid Bonner* • Christine Amor *Margaret Burton* ■ *Dir* Adrian Carr • *Scr* Richard Cassidy, from the novel by Danielle Steel

Now and Then ★★★ PG
Drama 1995 · US · Colour · 102mins

Demi Moore co-produced this female version of *Stand by Me*, which follows four young girls (Gaby Hoffmann, Christina Ricci, Thora Birch, Ashleigh Aston Moore) in 1970 as they attempt to solve the mystery of the death of a local boy. It's a simple, small-town story, bookended by the present-day revelations of the girls, now grown up into Moore, Melanie Griffith, Rita Wilson (Mrs Tom Hanks) and Rosie O'Donnell. Lesli Linka Glatter delivers a sweet, girlie film that should strike a chord with anyone who believes that life was better in the seventies. Fans of Brendan Fraser should keep an eye out for his brief, uncredited performance. Contains some swearing and nudity. ▱

Demi Moore *Samantha Albertson* • Melanie Griffith *Teeny* • Rosie O'Donnell *Roberta Martin* • Rita Wilson *Chrissy* • Christina Ricci *Young Roberta* • Thora Birch *Young Teeny* • Gaby Hoffmann *Young Samantha* • Ashleigh Aston Moore *Young Chrissy* ■ *Dir* Lesli Linka Glatter • *Scr* I Marlene King

Now Barabbas Was a Robber ★★★
Prison drama 1949 · UK · BW · 84mins

"Elsie's Dad is inside again" reads the chalk message on a prison wall, one of several humorous touches in an otherwise sombre story of prison life. The assorted inmates include a bigamist, an embezzler, an Irish terrorist (strikingly portrayed by Richard Burton in his second screen role) and a well-mannered murderer about to be executed (a likeable performance by Richard Greene). Ably directed by Gordon Parry, this film version of

William Douglas Home's play argues against the death penalty, but had the development of a homosexual relationship cut by the censor.

Richard Greene *Tufnell* • Cedric Hardwicke *Governor* • Kathleen Harrison *Mrs Brown* • Ronald Howard *Roberts, bank cashier* • Stephen Murray *Chaplain* • William Hartnell *Warder Jackson* • Beatrice Campbell *Kitty* • Richard Burton *Paddy* • Kenneth More *Spencer* • Dora Bryan *Winnie* • *Dir* Gordon Parry • *Scr* Gordon Parry, from the play by William Douglas Home

Now or Never ★★
Drama 1986 · W Ger · Colour · 55mins

A less than inspired German melodrama that attempts to enliven its proceedings by falling back on that most trustworthy of novelettish devices, the dark secret. As a woman rekindling her passion for a long-discarded lover, Eva Mattes does a tolerable job of safeguarding said skeleton in the cupboard, but the looks of anguish and the pregnant pauses each time a raw nerve is touched soon become tiresome. Christel Buschmann snoops on the tensions between the reunited lovers and their new partners like a nosy neighbour rather than an insightful director. German dialogue dubbed into English.

Eva Mattes *Mo* • Werner Stocker *Tom* • Teo Gostischa *Benjamin* • Silke Wülfing *Sarah* • August Zirner *Paul* • Eva Zlonitzky *Mutter* ■ *Dir/Scr* Christel Buschmann

Now, Voyager ★★★★★ PG
Classic romantic melodrama 1942 · US · BW · 113mins

One of the all-time great weepies, with a consummate performance from Bette Davis as the lifelong spinster emerging from her confining chrysalis into the arms of Paul Henreid. A lush, beautifully acted movie, which has gone down in the annals of cinema history for Henreid's lighting of two cigarettes scene and a tear-jerking speech from Davis, at her best in front of a moonlit sky. Irving Rapper directs with suitably grand aplomb and cinematographer Sol Polito lights everything with an almost magical touch. A movie in which all the elements came together in perfect harmony to give a hackneyed theme the imprint of greatness. ▱

Bette Davis *Charlotte Vale* • Paul Henreid *Jerry Durrance* • Claude Rains *Dr Jaquith* • Bonita Granville *June Vale* • Ilka Chase *Lisa Vale* • Gladys Cooper *Mrs Henry Windle Vale* ■ *Dir* Irving Rapper • *Scr* Casey Robinson, from the novel by Olive Higgins Prouty • *Music* Max Steiner

Now You See Him, Now You Don't ★★ U
Comedy adventure 1972 · US · Colour · 88mins

Kurt Russell returns in this follow-up to *The Computer Wore Tennis Shoes* (1969), this time using a revolutionary new invisibility serum to save his school from financial ruin. The Disney studio's trick is to cast squeaky-clean Russell against such old-time pros as Cesar Romero and Jim Backus, thus luring both teen and mature audiences to this undemanding mix of golf, bank

robbery and car chases. Lightweight stuff, though Robert Butler's comedy boasts ingenious special effects. ▱

Kurt Russell *Dexter Riley* • Cesar Romero *AJ Arno* • Joe Flynn *Dean Higgins* • Jim Backus *Timothy Forsythe* • William Windom *Professor Lufkin* • Michael McGreevey *Richard Schuyler* ■ *Dir* Robert Butler • *Scr* Joseph McEveety, from a story by Robert L King

Nowhere ★★★ 18
Experimental comedy drama 1997 · US/Fr · Colour · 78mins

Gregg Araki (*The Doom Generation*) is certainly a film-making original, expressing teenage disillusionment through an otherwordly Los Angeles populated by surreal characters, trippy production design (the pop-art decor echoes each teen's inner psyche) and relentless, pounding music. Like a David Lynch flick with a sense of humour, *Nowhere* charts a day in the lives of the young, the restless and the really disturbed. The attractive cast is a who's who of teen talent, including Mena Suvari (*American Beauty*) and Heather Graham (*Boogie Nights*). Contains violence, sex scenes and drug abuse. ▱

James Duval *Dark* • Rachel True *Mel* • Nathan Bexton *Montgomery* • Chiara Mastroianni *Kriss* • Debi Mazar *Kozy* • Kathleen Robertson *Lucifer* • Heather Graham *Lilith* • Mena Suvari *Zoe* ■ *Dir/Scr* Gregg Araki

Nowhere to Go ★★ U
Crime drama 1958 · UK · BW · 103mins

Don't be fooled by the label "Made at Ealing": this is nothing more than a low-budget programme filler. Co-written by director Seth Holt and critic Kenneth Tynan, it is a routine crime drama in which thief George Nader goes into partnership with unscrupulous Bernard Lee. Neither the central round of robberies and escapes nor the finale in the Brecon Beacons are presented with any imagination. Only Maggie Smith, making her film debut, rises above the material. The title says it all.

George Nader *Paul Gregory* • Maggie Smith *Bridget Howard* • Bernard Lee *Vic Sloane* • Bessie Love *Harriet Jefferson* • Geoffrey Keen *Inspector Scott* • Andrée Melly *Rosa* • Howard Marion-Crawford *Cameron* ■ *Dir* Seth Holt • *Scr* Seth Holt, Kenneth Tynan, from the novel by Donald MacKenzie

Nowhere to Hide ★★ 15
Action thriller 1987 · Can · Colour · 90mins

This Canadian action thriller boasts some surprisingly good performances, particularly from Amy Madigan as an ex-marine who flees into hiding with her son when crooked defence contractors kill her husband. Michael Ironside also does well as the survivalist who shelters her and helps her fight back. Though made for cinemas, the film has the dark look, tone and slow pacing of a typical, low-budget Canadian TV drama. ▱

Amy Madigan *Barbara Cutter* • Michael Ironside *Ben* • John Colicos *General Howard* • Daniel Hugh-Kelly *Rob Cutter* • Robin MacEachern *Johnny Cutter* ■ *Dir* Mario Azzopardi • *Scr* Alex Rebar, George Goldsmith, from a story by Alex Rebar

Nowhere to Hide ★★★ PG
Crime thriller 1994 · US · Colour · 87mins

What sounds like a generic, woman-in-jeopardy TV movie turns out to be a suspense thriller with some unexpected twists and turns. Rosanna Arquette stars as a wealthy divorcee who believes she is entering the federal government's witness-protection programme when her life is threatened by her mob-connected ex-husband. She falls in love with the agent (Scott Bakula) assigned to protect her, but soon discovers he is not who he seems to be. Savvy direction by veteran Bobby Roth keeps the pace brisk and edgy. ▱

Rosanna Arquette *Sarah Blake* • Scott Bakula *Kevin Nicholas* • Max Pomeranc *Sam Blake* ■ *Dir* Bobby Roth • *Scr* Dan Gordon

Nowhere to Run ★★ 15
Romantic action adventure 1992 · US · Colour · 90mins

The problem with Jean-Claude Van Damme is that he seems intent on broadening his acting range. Give him a simple plot, cartoonish characters and a legion of bad guys to duff up, and he's fine. However, the "Muscles from Brussels" comes unstuck when he attempts to show his more sensitive side. In this soft-centred action thriller, Van Damme plays a convict on the run who holes up with a pretty young widow (Rosanna Arquette) and her kids. Bad guy Joss Ackland is trying to evict Arquette from her land, but Van Damme comes to her rescue. Director Robert Harmon looks to have been aiming for some sort of modern-day *Shane*, but Van Damme is no Alan Ladd; to make matters worse, the fighting sequences are a letdown. Contains swearing, violence and nudity. ▱ **DVD**

Jean-Claude Van Damme *Sam* • Rosanna Arquette *Clydie* • Kieran Culkin *Mookie* • Ted Levine *Mr Dunston* • Tiffany Taubman *Bree* • Edward Blatchford *Lonnie* • Anthony Starke *Billy* • Joss Ackland *Franklin Hale* ■ *Dir* Robert Harmon • *Scr* Joe Eszterhas, Leslie Bohem, Randy Feldman

The Nude Bomb ★ PG
Spoof spy drama 1980 · US · Colour · 89mins

This feature-length adaptation of the sixties TV spy spoof *Get Smart* has agent Maxwell Smart (Don Adams) called in to stop a madman who is threatening to destroy all the clothing in the world. One has to wonder why the film-makers bothered to get the rights to the show, considering Smart here bears little resemblance to the character in the TV series. In addition, none of the show's supporting players return – the most missed being Barbara Feldon, whose relatively normal character made the humour seem funnier. This plays like a lame, expanded sitcom that's missing its laughter track. ▱

Don Adams *Maxwell Smart/Agent 86* • Sylvia Kristel *Agent 34* • Vittorio Gassman *Nino Salvatore Sebastiani/Norman Saint Sauvage* • Rhonda Fleming *Edith Von Secondberg* • Dana Elcar *Chief* ■ *Dir* Clive Donner • *Scr* Arne Sultan, Bill Dana, Leonard Stern, from characters created by Mel Brooks, Buck Henry

Nude on the Moon ★

Cult science-fiction drama
1961 · US · Colour · 83mins

''You're acting like a schoolboy. Don't forget we're rocket scientists,'' says an ageing doctor to a multi-millionaire playboy as they lift off in this weird space oddity from bargain-basement cult director Doris Wishman. Their journey ends, as the title suggests, with the discovery of topless models on the Moon. This pitiful production contains Nasa stock footage and is decorated with toy spaceships, funny-coloured tights and star-covered astronaut boots. It also features the songs *Moon Doll* and *I'm Mooning over You*. Wishman went on to give the world Chesty Morgan and her 73-inch bust in *Deadly Weapons*.

Marietta *Cathy/Moon Goddess* ■ *Dir/Scr* Doris Wishman

La Nuit de Varennes ★★ 12

Historical drama 1983 · Fr · Colour · 144mins

A historical conceit in which various notables arrive by coach at Varennes where the fugitive king Louis XVI and Marie Antoinette were captured. Thus Casanova (Marcello Mastroianni), political theorist Tom Paine (Harvey Keitel) and an Austrian countess (Hanna Schygulla) gather to discuss politics, sex, art, history and everything that can be crammed into almost two and a half hours. An excellent supporting cast should delight followers of European cinema, but Ettore Scola's film is neither as witty nor clever as it thinks it is. In French with English subtitles. 🖭

Marcello Mastroianni *Casanova* • Hanna Schygulla *Countess Sophie de la Borde* • Jean-Louis Barrault *Nicolas Edme Restif* • Harvey Keitel *Thomas Paine* • Michel Piccoli *King Louis XVI* • Eléonore Hirt *Queen Marie-Antoinette* • Jean-Louis Trintignant *M Sauce* • Jean-Claude Brialy *M Jacob* ■ *Dir* Ettore Scola • *Scr* Ettore Scola, Sergio Amidei

Nuit et Brouillard ★★★★★ 15

Documentary
1955 · Fr · Colour and BW · 30mins

Exploring his perennial themes of time and memory, Alain Resnais described this documentary as a ''warning siren'' to those who believed that the horrors of Auschwitz were now consigned to history. Transposing hideous monochrome images of the camp in wartime with prowling takes capturing the melancholic calm that descended in the ensuing decade, the footage is often as unbearable to watch as the crimes are impossible to comprehend. Former deportee Jean Cayrol contributes a commentary that, for all its poignancy, makes several incontrovertible points, which prompted François Truffaut to declare this the greatest film ever made. It's certainly the most powerful. In French with English subtitles. 🖭

Michel Bouquet *Narrator* ■ *Dir* Alain Resnais • *Scr* Jean Cayrol

La Nuit Fantastique ★★★★

Comedy fantasy 1942 · Fr · BW · 103mins

The most widely known of Marcel L'Herbier's sound films was one of the great successes of the French cinema during the occupation. Although this atmospheric comedy fantasy has a dark side, the film catered to a population that needed escapist entertainment. It tells of a student who continually dreams of a woman in white, whom he then meets. He and the woman have a series of fantastic adventures, so that he is still not sure whether he's dreaming or not. Fernand Gravey was soon to join the French Resistance movement, while co-star Micheline Presle continued to work under the Nazi occupation. A French language film.

Micheline Presle *Irène* • Fernand Gravey [Fernand Gravet] *Denis* • Saturnin Fabre *Thalès* • Jean Paredes *Cadet* • Bernard Blier *Lucien* • Christiane Néré *Nina* • Charles Granval *Adalbert* • Michel Vitold *Boris* ■ *Dir* Marcel L'Herbier • *Scr* Louis Chavance, Maurice Henry, Marcel L'Herbier, Henri Jeanson, from a story by Louis Chavance

Les Nuits Fauves ★★★★

Biographical drama
1992 · Fr · Colour · 126mins

This brutally honest insight into the mind of an HIV-positive man was written and directed by its bisexual star, Cyril Collard, who succumbed to an Aids-related illness just three days before the film's triumph at the Césars. Also released under its English title *Savage Nights*, this uncompromising picture is made particularly compelling by the credibility of its characters. So what if Collard's actions are reckless, or if teenage waif Romane Bohringer's decision to have unprotected sex with him is incomprehensible? These are the failings and irrationalities of real people, and film-makers should be encouraged to show such truths far more often. In French with English subtitles. Contains violence, swearing, sex scenes, drug abuse and nudity.

Cyril Collard *Jean* • Romane Bohringer *Laura* • Carlos Lopez *Samy* • Corine Blue *Laura's mother* • Claude Winter *Jean's mother* • René-Marc Bini *Marc* • Maria Schneider *Noria* ■ *Dir* Cyril Collard • *Scr* Cyril Collard, Jacques Fieschi, from the novel by Cyril Collard

Nukie ★ U

Science-fiction 1992 · SAfr · Colour · 95mins

This has got to be the worst *ET* rip-off ever made, and that's against some stiff competition (*Mac and Me*, **batteries not included*). Nukie, who looks like a char-broiled Tinky Winky, lands in Africa and befriends two twins from a rural village. He enlists their help to find his brother, who is the subject of cruel tests by the ''Space Foundation'' in Florida. Incoherent and frustrating, you have to wonder why anyone bothered. 🖭

Glynis Johns *Sister Anne* • Steve Railsback *Dr Eric Harvey* • Ronald France • Fats Dibeco • Michael McCabe • Kurtis Kent • Janice Honeyman ■ *Dir* Sias Odendal • *Scr* Benjamin Taylor, from a story by Sias Odendal

Number One ★★

Drama 1969 · US · Colour · 104mins

Seldom have actor and director shown such mutual understanding first time out as Charlton Heston and Tom Gries in the masterly western *Will Penny*. This contemporary version, about an ageing quarterback player with the New Orleans Saints, followed almost immediately, but *Number One* turned out to be a complete failure. Heston is relatively convincing, albeit no football player, and the setting is interesting, but few scenes really work and the script and direction are slovenly. The supporting cast does its best, but this movie is for collectors only.

Charlton Heston *Ron ''Cat'' Catlan* • Jessica Walter *Julie Catlan* • Bruce Dern *Richie Fowler* • John Randolph *Coach Jim Southerd* • Diana Muldaur *Ann Marley* • GD Spradlin *Dr Tristler* • Richard Elkins *Kelly Williams* ■ *Dir* Tom Gries • *Scr* David Moessinger

Number One ★★ 15

Drama 1984 · UK · Colour · 98mins

This British crime drama boasts the presence of two legendary pop stars – Bob Geldof in the lead role and Ian Dury. They put in admirable performances, Geldof as a snooker hustler and Dury as an ineffectual hold-up man. But they and the rest of the cast are let down by wayward direction and an unfocused script, which borrows too blatantly from films such as *The Cincinnati Kid*. 🖭

Bob Geldof *Harry ''Flash'' Gordon* • Mel Smith *Billy Evans* • Alison Steadman *Doreen* • PH Moriarty *Mike the Throat* • Phil Daniels *Terry the Boxer* • Alfred Molina *Constable Rogers* • Ian Dury *Teddy Bryant* ■ *Dir* Les Blair • *Scr* GF Newman

Number One Fan ★

Erotic thriller 1994 · US · Colour · 89mins

Aside from delicious cameos from cult icons Paul Bartel, Mary Woronov and Dick Miller, this would-be erotic thriller exhibits a lack of quality typical of the genre. Chad McQueen plays an actor about to be wed to Catherine Mary Stewart, who is in turn seduced by beautiful but psychotic Renee Ammann. Director Jane Simpson brings no insights or twists to the turgid plot, and ultimately this is sleazy, soft-core trash masquerading as something more interesting. Contains violence, sex scenes, nudity and swearing.

Chad McQueen *Zane Barry* • Renee Ammann *Blair Madsen* • Catherine Mary Stewart *Holly Newman* • Paul Bartel *Director* • Eric Da Re *Randall McSwain* • Charles Matthau *Scotty Youngman* • Hoyt Axton *Lt Joe Halsey* ■ *Dir* Jane Simpson • *Scr* Anthony Laurence Greene

Number One with a Bullet ★★ 15

Action thriller 1986 · US · Colour · 96mins

This standard action pic, which cleanly apes the buddy cop formula of *Lethal Weapon*, marks something of a climb-down for Jack Smight, director of *Airport 1975* and *Battle of Midway*. Here the veteran can do little with the hackneyed cops-versus-drug lord plotline. He does at least manage to wring a few laughs out of the mismatched pairing of Billy Dee Williams, a smooth and urbane cop, and Robert Carradine. Known for his unorthodox police tactics, Carradine is obsessed with bringing down the Mr Big of the Los Angeles drug scene. *Mission: Impossible*'s Peter Graves is also on board; he must have wished that this lame affair had self-destructed in five seconds. 🖭

Robert Carradine *Berzak* • Billy Dee Williams *Hazeltine* • Valerie Bertinelli *Teresa Berzak* • Peter Graves (1) *Captain Ferris* • Doris Roberts *Mrs Berzak* ■ *Dir* Jack Smight • *Scr* Gail Morgan Hickman, Andrew Kurtzman, Rob Riley, James Belushi, from a story by Gail Morgan Hickman

Number Seventeen ★★★

Crime comedy 1932 · UK · BW · 64mins

A girl member (Anne Grey) of a gang of criminals falls for the gentlemanly detective (John Stuart) who is investigating their nefarious activities and helps bring her former colleagues to justice. Little-seen and largely forgotten, this is an Alfred Hitchcock film of minor entertainment value but superb technical expertise. It's especially notable for a climactic chase sequence involving a train. Trains, of course, became one of the director's favourite locations, used most memorably during his early British period in *The 39 Steps* (1935) and *The Lady Vanishes* (1938).

Leon M Lion *Ben* • Anne Grey *The girl* • John Stuart *Detective* • Garry Marsh *Sheldrake* • Ann Casson *Miss Ackroyd* • Henry Caine *Mr Ackroyd* ■ *Dir* Alfred Hitchcock • *Scr* Alma Reville, Alfred Hitchcock, Rodney Ackland, from a play by J Jefferson Farjeon

Number Two ★★

Experimental drama
1975 · Fr · Colour · 88mins

Absent from film-making for three years due to a motorcycle crash, influential French director Jean-Luc Godard returned with this dour tale of an ordinary family coping with the problems and pressures of modern life. However, Godard seems most preoccupied by the husband's impotence and the wife's constipation. But it's the style of the film that is most striking – Godard shot it all on video and uses a variety of split-screen effects. A French language film.

Sandrine Battistella *Wife* • Pierre Oudry *Husband* • Alexandre Rignault *Grandpa* • Rachel Stefanopoli *Grandma* • Jean-Luc Godard ■ *Dir* Jean-Luc Godard • *Scr* Anne-Marie Miéville, Jean-Luc Godard

The Nun and the Bandit ★★

Crime drama 1992 · Ausl · Colour · 92mins

It's a truism that nuns don't fare too well on the screen (unless played by Deborah Kerr) since they are often the objects of menace. That's true here in Paul Cox's rather odd dramatic thriller. Sister Lucy is the frightened and none-too-worldly aunt of a kidnapped child who is being held for ransom in the Australian outback. The film is adapted from a novel set in the thirties, but the story has been somewhat updated.

Gosia Dobrowolska *Sister Lucy* • Chris Haywood *Michael Shanley* • Victoria Eagger *Maureen* • Charlotte Hughes Haywood *Julie* • Norman Kaye *George Shanley* • Tom E Lewis [Tommy Lewis] *Bert Shanley* ■ *Dir* Paul Cox • *Scr* Paul Cox, from a novel by EL Grant Watson

Nuns on the Run ★★★ 15

Comedy 1990 · UK · Colour · 88mins

Writer/director Jonathan Lynn, one half of the team behind the scorching wit of *Yes, Minister*, has been swimming rather more lazily in the mainstream in

recent years. Here, by trying to squeeze a whole film from the single joke of Robbie Coltrane and Eric Idle decked out as nuns, he was in danger of veering towards a comic dud. Yet there is a natural spark between the two performers that saves many a scene and, when the genial proceedings are not burdened by the full weight of cliché, they do begin to catch fire. Contains violence. 🎞

Eric Idle *Brian Hope* • Robbie Coltrane *Charlie McManus* • Camille Coduri *Faith* • Janet Suzman *Sister Superior* • Doris Hare *Sister Mary of the Sacred Heart* • Lila Kaye *Sister Mary of the Annunciation* • Robert Patterson *"Case" Casey* ■ *Dir/Scr* Jonathan Lynn

The Nun's Story ★★★★★ 🅿🅶

Drama   1959 · US · Colour · 145mins

Kathryn C Hulme's popular autobiographical novel makes a magnificent vehicle for the luminous Audrey Hepburn, battling with her conscience and wondering if, indeed, she is truly cut out for her calling. Hepburn is a marvel to behold, whether flirting with passion in the Congo (in the guise of Peter Finch, terrific as an agnostic doctor) or discovering that some nuns (Dames Edith Evans and Peggy Ashcroft) are only human after all. This is arguably director Fred Zinnemann's finest movie, and won eight nominations, but no Oscars, in the year of *Ben-Hur*. Unjust, really, as you watch Franz Planer's superb photography, listen to Franz Waxman's haunting score and wonder to what greater heights popular cinema can aspire. 🎞

Audrey Hepburn *Sister Luke* • Peter Finch *Dr Fortunati* • Edith Evans *Mother Emmanuel* • Peggy Ashcroft *Mother Mathilde* • Dean Jagger *Dr Van Der Mal* • Mildred Dunnock *Sister Margarita* • Beatrice Straight *Mother Christophe* • Rosalie Crutchley *Sister Eleanor* ■ *Dir* Fred Zinnemann • *Scr* Robert Anderson, from the novel by Kathryn C Hulme

Nurse Edith Cavell ★★ 🅤

First World War drama
1939 · US · BW · 96mins

English producer/director Herbert Wilcox's first Hollywood film is an account of Nurse Edith Cavell, the brave and self-sacrificing heroine of the First World War who smuggled English soldiers out of German-occupied Belgium and was executed as a spy for her pains. Anna Neagle (Wilcox's wife), an actress not noted for her dramatic range, makes do with her natural regal dignity in a film that is sober, competent and dull, yet nevertheless quite affecting.

Anna Neagle *Nurse Edith Cavell* • George Sanders *Captain Heinrichs* • Edna May Oliver *Countess de Mavon* • May Robson *Mme Rappard* • ZaSu Pitts *Mme Moulin* • Sophie Stewart *Sister Watkins* ■ *Dir* Herbert Wilcox • *Scr* Michael Hogan, from his novel

Nurse on Wheels ★★★ 🅤

Comedy   1963 · UK · BW · 82mins

Peter Rogers and his wife Betty Box seem to have had an obsession with medical matters. She produced the popular *Doctor* series, while he was responsible for four hospital-based *Carry Ons* and this charming comedy that reunited him with Juliet Mills, who had played a nurse in the previous

year's *Twice round the Daffodils*. As it was scripted by Norman Hudis and directed by Gerald Thomas, both of whom were *Carry On* regulars, it has its moments of broad humour, but old-fashioned family fun is to the fore as district nurse Mills encounters a range of eccentrics in a farming village. 🎞

Juliet Mills *Joanna Jones* • Ronald Lewis *Henry Edwards* • Joan Sims *Deborah Walcott* • Athene Seyler *Miss Farthingale* • Norman Rossington *George Judd* • Barbara Everest *Nurse Merrick* • Ronald Howard *Dr Harold Golfrey* • Joan Hickson *Mrs Wood* ■ *Dir* Gerald Thomas • *Scr* Norman Hudis, from the novel *Nurse Is a Neighbour* by Joanna Jones

Nurses on the Line ★★ 🅿🅶

Drama   1993 · US · Colour · 88mins

This is actually a plane-crash drama. A group of doctors and nurses, including mini-series queen Lindsay Wagner and *Jagged Edge's* Robert Loggia, fight for survival after their aircraft comes down in the jungle en route to a Mexican village. Although this is an interesting story, one can't help but think that its ingredients are all rather too familiar. This sort of thing has been handled better in bigger-budget movies such as *Fearless* and *Alive*. 🎞

Lindsay Wagner *Elizabeth Hahn* • Robert Loggia *Dr Daniel Perrin* • David Clennon *Dr Ruland Beesley* • Hilary Edson *Danae Hahn* • Farrah Forke *Fran* • Gary Frank *Len* • Tom Irwin *Eddie* • Jennifer Lopez *Rosie* ■ *Dir* Larry Shaw • *Scr* Andrew Laskos, Norman Morrill, from a story by Norman Morrill

Nutcracker ★★ 🔞

Drama   1982 · UK · Colour · 96mins

When Russian ballerina Finola Hughes defects and joins an international ballet company, she soon realises she is being used by its owner (Joan Collins) as a high-class call girl to local politicians. Meanwhile, photojournalist Paul Nicholas goes to extraordinary lengths to snap a scoop picture of Collins's new star dancer in action. A thin plot full of soap-opera theatrics and soft-core erotica is played out against intensely cheap sets, resulting in a film which does little to engage the interest. Collins, decked out in Lycra and legwarmers, almost saves the day, giving another full-blooded variation on her rich-bitch persona. 🎞

Joan Collins *Mme Carrere* • Carol White *Margaux Lasselle* • Paul Nicholas *Mike McCann* • Finola Hughes *Nadia* • William Franklyn *Sir Arthur Cartwright* ■ *Dir* Anwar Kawadri • *Scr* Raymond Christodoulou

Nutcracker ★ 🅤

Ballet   1986 · US · Colour · 81mins

Yet another version of the Christmas classic, this time performed by the Pacific Northwest Ballet. Despite inspired design by Maurice Sendak and direction by Carroll Ballard (*The Black Stallion*), this never transcends its stage origins, regardless of Ballard's attempts to create a fourth wall. Similarly, his overly tricky, close-up shots of dancers' limbs in action give the film the feel of a pop promo. If you want to see how it should be done, watch *The Red Shoes*. 🎞

Hugh Bigney *Herr Drosselmeier* • Vanessa Sharp *Young Clara* • Patricia Barker *Dream Clara/Ballerina Doll* • Wade Walthall

Nutcracker • Maia Rosal *Frau Stahlbaum/Peacock* • Carey Homme *Dr Stahlbaum/Moor* • Martha Boyle *Mother* ■ *Dir* Carroll Ballard • *Scr* Maurice Sendak, Kent Stowell, from the ballet by Peter Ilich Tchaikovsky, from the fairy tale *The Nutcracker and the Mouse King* by ETA Hoffman

The Nutcracker Prince ★★ 🅤

Animated fantasy
1990 · Can · Colour · 70mins

Canada has a proud tradition of ground-breaking animation, but this lowbrow, low-budget offering is something of an embarrassment. Based on *The Nutcracker and the Mouse King* by the German fabler ETA Hoffman, the story sees a young girl shrink to the size of her toys to help her model soldiers overcome a tyrannical rodent. Kiefer Sutherland and Peter O'Toole provide effective voice-overs, and there's Tchaikovsky's music on the soundtrack. But the artwork looks shoddy and Paul Schibli's direction is anything but magical. 🎞

Peter O'Toole *Pantaloon* • Kiefer Sutherland *Nutcracker/Hans* • Megan Follows *Clara* • Michael Macdonald *Mouse King* ■ *Dir* Paul Schibli • *Scr* Patricia Watson, from the fairy tale *The Nutcracker and the Mouse King* by ETA Hoffman

Nuts ★★★ 🔞

Drama   1987 · US · Colour · 110mins

You can imagine Tom Topor's play about a prostitute proving her sanity so that she can stand trial for manslaughter making for a cracking night at the theatre. That it is marginally less compelling as a film is down to director Martin Ritt's decision to reveal key facts via clumsily staged flashbacks rather than as courtroom testimony, as this considerably diminishes their impact. Even though the outcome is inevitable, this is still an involving drama thanks to the bullish performances of Barbra Streisand as the hooker and Richard Dreyfuss as her attorney. Eli Wallach and Robert Webber stand out in an accomplished supporting cast. 🎞

Barbra Streisand *Claudia Draper* • Richard Dreyfuss *Aaron Levinsky* • Maureen Stapleton *Rose Kirk* • Eli Wallach *Dr Herbert A Morrison* • Karl Malden *Arthur Kirk* • Robert Webber *Francis MacMillan* ■ *Dir* Martin Ritt • *Scr* Alvin Sargent, Darryl Ponicsan, Tom Topor, from the play by Tom Topor

The Nutty Professor ★★★★ 🅿🅶

Comedy   1963 · US · Colour · 102mins

In spite of almost universal criticism, this immensely accomplished comedy remains actor/co-writer/director Jerry Lewis's best and funniest screen work. It's really "Doctor Jerry and Mister Love" (the film's French title translated), as Lewis plays nerdish chemistry professor Julius Kelp who is hooked on lovely student Stella Stevens. Lewis makes and takes a potion that turns him into Buddy Love, singing lounge lizard *par excellence*. The witty design and the use of fabulously rich Paramount Technicolor are major bonuses, and this clever movie remains extremely funny. 🎞

Jerry Lewis *Professor Julius Kelp/Buddy Love* • Stella Stevens *Stella Purdy* • Del Moore *Dr Hamius R Warfield* • Kathleen Freeman *Millie Lemmon* ■ *Dir* Jerry Lewis • *Scr* Jerry Lewis, Bill Richmond, from a story by Jerry Lewis

The Nutty Professor ★★★★ 🅵🅸🅴

Comedy   1996 · US · Colour · 91mins

This reworking of the 1963 Jerry Lewis comedy finds Eddie Murphy back on form as Sherman Klump, a sweet-natured, obese science whiz who perfects a potion that turns him into a sexy, skinny love machine. Of course, the potion wears off at the most unfortunate of times, which affects his attempts at romance with attractive teaching assistant Jada Pinkett. Murphy plays the professor to poignant perfection; thanks to the genius of the Oscar-winning make-up and computer graphics departments, he also portrays three generations of his family at the same dinner table. Snappily directed, this isn't quite as daft as the mad original. It is, though, a thoroughly enjoyable laughfest that provides plenty of rib-tickling moments. 🎞
DVD

Eddie Murphy *Sherman Klump/Buddy Love* • Jada Pinkett [Jada Pinkett Smith] *Carla Purty* • Larry Miller *Dean Richmond* • Dave Chappelle *Reggie Warrington* • John Ales *Jason* • Patricia Wilson *Dean's secretary* • James Coburn *Harlan Hartley* ■ *Dir* Tom Shadyac • *Scr* David Sheffield, Barry W Blaustein, Tom Shadyac, Steve Oederderk, from the 1963 film

O Brother, Where Art Thou? ★★★★ 12

Crime drama   2000 · US · Colour · mins

The eighth collaborative effort produced and directed by brothers Ethan and Joel Coen concerns the attempts of escaped convict Ulysses Everett McGill (George Clooney, nicely self-mocking) to get back to his wife Penny (Holly Hunter in almost a cameo role), and the picaresque adventures he has on the way. The title derives from Preston Sturges' *Sullivan's Travels* (1941), whose comic spirit hangs over the Coens' episodic comedy. Apart from the Sturges film, it contrives to encapsulate every con-on-the-run picture one has ever seen, as well as Southern period crime dramas. Yet again, the Coens' alchemy has worked.

George Clooney *Ulysses Everett McGill* • John Turturro *Pete* • Tim Blake Nelson *Delmar* • Charles Durning *Pappy O'Daniel* • John Goodman *Big Dan Teague* • Michael Badalucco *George Nelson* • Holly Hunter *Penny* ■ *Dir* Joel Coen • *Scr* Ethan Coen, Joel Coen, from the poem *The Odyssey* by Homer

OC and Stiggs ★★ 15

Comedy   1987 · US · Colour · 105mins

Before returning to fine, focused form with *The Player*, director Robert Altman barked up several wrong trees in the preceding years. This film was one of them: a meandering, stop-start sprawl, with a tone too blunt for satire. The eponymous characters are a couple of teen clowns who get up to all kinds of merry japes. There are, however, some semi-inspired moments of Altman strangeness, like Dennis Hopper's Vietnam vet with a taste for guns and drugs. ▦

Daniel H Jenkins [Daniel Jenkins] *OC Ogilvey* • Neill Barry *Mark Stiggs* • Jane Curtin *Elinore Schwab* • Paul Dooley *Randall Schwab* • Jon Cryer *Randall Schwab Jr* • Laura Urstein *Lenore Schwab* • Victor Ho *Frankie Tang* • Dennis Hopper *Sponson* ■ *Dir* Robert Altman • *Scr* Donald Cantrell, Ted Mann, from a story by Tod Carroll, Ted Mann, from a story in *National Lampoon,magazine*

O Henry's Full House ★★★ U

Portmanteau comedy drama
1952 · US · BW · 117mins

This compendium of five short stories by a genius of the form is beautifully adapted, well cast and directed. The most deeply moving tale is *The Last Leaf*, with Anne Baxter as a dying woman saved by self-sacrificing artist Gregory Ratoff. Charles Laughton stars as a tramp trying to get arrested in the cruelly ironic *The Cop and the Anthem*, in which Marilyn Monroe appears as a streetwalker; Dale Robertson is a cop who must arrest his good friend Richard Widmark in the tough-minded *The Clarion Call*; while *The Ransom of Red Chief* has kidnappers offering to pay the parents of the ghastly child they've nabbed to take him back. However, perhaps the most fondly remembered is the painfully tender *Gift of the Magi*, with Jeanne Crain and Farley Granger as the poverty-stricken young couple who each sacrifice a treasured possession to buy the other a Christmas gift.

Jeanne Crain *Della* • Farley Granger *Jim* • Sig Rumann [Sig Ruman] *Menkie* • Anne Baxter *Joanna* • Jean Peters *Susan* • Gregory Ratoff *Behrman* • Charles Laughton *Soapy* • Marilyn Monroe *Streetwalker* • Dale Robertson *Barney Woods* • Richard Widmark *Johnny Kernan* • Fred Allen *Sam* • Oscar Levant *Bill* • John Steinbeck *Narrator* ■ *Dir* Henry Hathaway, Henry Koster, Henry King, Howard Hawks, Jean Negulesco • *Scr* Lamar Trotti, Richard L Breen, Ben Roberts, Ivan Goff, Walter Bullock, Nunnally Johnson, from stories by O Henry

The OJ Simpson Story ★★ 12

Biographical drama
1995 · US · Colour · 86mins

Such is the unquenchable thirst for real-life stories, this biopic was rushed out before the infamous verdict was actually delivered. So anyone expecting the full story behind the murder case may be disappointed: the film opens with Simpson (played by Bobby Hosea) talking to the police following the discovery of his former wife's body, but the majority of the footage is taken up with his rise to fame and his troubled relationship with the unfortunate Nicole. It's competently put together and Hosea makes a good fist of playing Simpson, but there is an unfinished feeling to whole project. Contains some violence. ▦

Bobby Hosea *OJ Simpson* • Jessica Tuck *Nicole Brown Simpson* • Bruce Weitz *Robert Shapiro* • David Roberson *AC Cowlings* • Kimberly Russell *Marguerite* • James Handy *Detective Vannatter* • Paul Witten *Ronald Goldman* ■ *Dir* Alan Smithee [Jerrold Freedman] • *Scr* Stephen Harrigan

O Lucky Man! ★★★ 15

Satirical fantasy 1973 · UK · Colour · 169mins

There always was less to director Lindsay Anderson than met the eye, but this irreligious, updated *Pilgrim's Progress* through society remains a determined attempt to irritate, incite and entertain. The fine cast is led by Anderson's regular collaborator Malcolm McDowell, who plays an everyman adrift in a surreal landscape littered with British character actors such as Ralph Richardson, Rachel Roberts and Arthur Lowe, all playing multiple parts. The title is not so much ironic as downright sarcastic and, despite the jarring clash of symbols, it's a provocative fable not to be missed, even if it is now somewhat dated. Alan Price's energetic score is a bonus. Contains sex scenes. ▦

Malcolm McDowell *Mick Travis* • Ralph Richardson *Monty/Sir James Burgess* • Rachel Roberts *Gloria/Mme Paillard/Mrs Richards* • Arthur Lowe *Mr Duff/Charlie Johnson/Dr Munda* • Helen Mirren *Patricia Burgess* • Dandy Nichols *Tea lady/Neighbour*
■ *Dir* Lindsay Anderson • *Scr* David Sherwin, from an idea by Malcolm McDowell • *Music/Lyrics* Alan Price

O Pioneers! ★★★ PG

Period drama   1992 · US · Colour · 94mins

A classy period piece that finds Jessica Lange in a rare made-for-television movie role. Based on the novel by Willa Cather, this tells the story of a farming family at the turn of the century who are riven apart when the unmarried daughter (Lange) inherits the land from her father. Director Glenn Jordan is a tad too respectful of the material, but the film is carried by the performances of Lange, David Strathairn and Tom Aldredge. ▦

Jessica Lange *Alexandra Bergson* • David Strathairn *Carl Linstrum* • Tom Aldredge *Ivar* • Reed Diamond *Emil Bergson* • Heather Graham *Young Alexandra* • Josh Hamilton *Young Carl* • Anne Heche *Marie Shabata* • Leigh Lawson *Frank Shabata* ■ *Dir* Glenn Jordan • *Scr* Robert W Lenski, from the novel by Willa Cather

OSS ★★★

Spy drama   1946 · US · BW · 105mins

Paramount's resident tough guy Alan Ladd finds himself spying in France during the Second World War in the dark days before D-Day. It's pretty routine action material for the studio, but it's given dignity by the strength of the star's performance. As the movie is so obviously a Ladd vehicle, there are no other stellar names in support; Geraldine Fitzgerald is an attractive though unexciting heroine, and Patric Knowles is as wooden as ever. Ladd was making roughly three films a year at this time, and it was films like this that helped create his image and consolidate his stardom. Contains violence.

Alan Ladd *John Martin* • Geraldine Fitzgerald *Ellen Rogers* • Patric Knowles *Commander Brady* • John Hoyt *Colonel Meister* • Gloria Saunders *Mary "Sparks" Kenny* • Richard Benedict *Bernay* ■ *Dir* Irving Pichel • *Scr* Richard Maibaum

The Oberwald Mystery ★★★

Drama   1980 · It/W Ger · Colour · 128mins

Sixteen years after *The Red Desert*, Michelangelo Antonioni and his muse, Monica Vitti, reunited for this flawed but fascinating reworking of Jean Cocteau's courtly melodrama, *The Eagle Has Two Heads*. As the royal widow roused from a decade of mourning by the intrusion of anarchist poet Franco Branciaroli, Vitti is both vulnerable and tragic. However, Antonioni's attempt to fuse Cocteau's escapist flamboyance with his own coolly detached style was dramatically ill-conceived. Similarly, his scheme to shoot on video and then transfer the footage to 35mm proved visually unsatisfactory. An Italian language film.

Monica Vitti *The Queen* • Luigi Diberti *Willenstein* • Paolo Bonacelli *Count of Foehn* • Franco Branciaroli *Sebastian* ■ *Dir* Michelangelo Antonioni • *Scr* Michelangelo Antonioni, Tonino Guerra, from the play *The Eagle Has Two Heads* by Jean Cocteau

The Object of Beauty ★★★ 15

Comedy drama
1991 · US/UK · Colour · 98mins

This is still a pleasingly deft comedy of crooked manners. As the Americans who live on their wits and other people's money, Andie MacDowell and John Malkovich make an unexpectedly good team, with their on-screen limitations actually contributing to the credibility of their characters. Indeed, the insurance scam involving a Henry Moore sculpture rather gets in the way of their bantering, as it shifts the focus on to the deaf-mute maid who has purloined it. Smoothly directed by Michael Lindsay-Hogg, this may not be a masterpiece, but it has undeniable curio value. ▦

John Malkovich *Jake* • Andie MacDowell *Tina* • Lolita Davidovich *Joan* • Rudi Davis *Jenny* • Joss Ackland *Mr Mercer* • Bill Paterson *Victor Swayle* • Ricci Harnett *Steve* • Peter Riegert *Larry* • Jack Shepherd *Mr Slaughter* • Rosemary Martin *Mrs Doughty* ■ *Dir/Scr* Michael Lindsay-Hogg

The Object of My Affection ★★★ 15

Romantic comedy
1998 · US · Colour · 106mins

Jennifer Aniston tries to escape her *Friends* persona in this uneven romantic comedy, surprisingly directed by Nicholas Hytner (*The Madness of King George*). Aniston plays a girl who gets pregnant by her oafish ex-boyfriend (Paul Rudd) but decides to ask her gay friend (Paul Rudd) to be the baby's father. She falls in love with him, of course, but the resulting mess it makes of both their lives is more sad than humorous, while the ending is contrived and unbelievable. Well-meaning, with some nice performances from co-stars Alan Alda and Nigel Hawthorne, but ultimately unsuccessful. Contains swearing and a sex scene. ▦

Jennifer Aniston *Nina Borowski* • Paul Rudd *George Hanson* • John Pankow *Vince McBride* • Alan Alda *Sidney Miller* • Tim Daly [Timothy Daly] *Dr Robert Joley* • Nigel Hawthorne *Rodney Fraser* ■ *Dir* Nicholas Hytner • *Scr* Wendy Wasserstein, from the novel by Stephen McCauley

Object of Obsession ★ 18

Erotic thriller   1995 · US · Colour · 92mins

A dumb slice of mild erotica. Wanting to experience new sexual thrills, divorced Erika Anderson picks up mysterious Scott Valentine who takes her hostage and holds her against her will. Trying to have its cake and eat it, Gregory Hippolyte's sexploitation thriller is more soap than sleaze. It indulges in male fantasies before half-heartedly reasserting its supposedly politically correct credentials and introducing a stupidly feminist revenge motive. Contains swearing and sex scenes. ▦

Scott Valentine *Blaze* • Erika Anderson *Margaret* • Liza Whitcraft *Christy* • Robert Keith *Harvey* ■ *Dir* Gregory Hippolyte • *Scr* Brad Marlowe

Objective, Burma! ★★★ PG

Second World War drama
1945 · US · BW · 135mins

A rousing Second World War drama, with Errol Flynn parachuting into the Burmese jungle with a company of paratroopers to destroy a Japanese radio station. It went unshown in Britain for seven years because it made no mention of the fact that the British played the major role in Burma. For some reason, action director Raoul Walsh stretches things out for over two hours – with John Wayne as star he could have mopped things up in an hour and a half. But, despite its frequent longueurs, it's exciting stuff, with Flynn bringing all his swashbuckling swagger to his role as the scourge of Southeast Asia. ▣

Errol Flynn Major Nelson • James Brown (2) Sergeant Treacy • William Prince Lieutenant Jacobs • George Tobias Gabby Gordon • Henry Hull Mark Williams • Warner Anderson Colonel Carter • John Alvin Hogan ■ Dir Raoul Walsh • Scr Ranald MacDougall, Lester Cole, from a story by Alvah Bessie

Oblivion ★★

Science-fiction western
1993 · US · Colour · 94mins

Some critics called Star Wars a western in space. That probably inspired low-budget guru Charles Band to try setting a literal western on an alien planet. The cast of characters are amusingly eccentric, including reluctant sheriff Richard Joseph Paul (who, as an empathic psychic, feels the pain of anybody he kills), saloon owner Julie Newmar; and George Takei as Doc Valentine, who speaks in Star Trek puns. It probably looked a lot funnier on paper, but the resulting film is rather flat.

Richard Joseph Paul Zack Stone • Jackie Swanson Mattie Chase • Andrew Divoff Redeye • Meg Foster Stell Barr • Jimmie Skaggs [Jimmie F Skaggs] Buteo • George Takei Doc Valentine • Julie Newmar Miss Kitty • Isaac Hayes Buster ■ Dir Sam Irvin • Scr Peter David, from a story by Charles Band

Oblomov ★★★★ U

Satire
1980 · USSR · Colour · 140mins

Covering only half of Ivan Goncharov's sprawling novel, this two-part period piece dissects the dissolute charm of the aristocracy. Transfixed by ennui, corpulent thirtysomething Oleg Tabakov cannot be roused from his lethargy by a series of idyllic flashbacks prompted by his best friend, Yuri Bogatyrev. But the reformist zeal of Elena Solovei is another matter altogether. Criticised for a lack of incident and its stately pace, Nikita Mikhalkov's film is both intelligently faithful to the spirit of its source and meticulous in its blend of satire and sentimentality. Superbly photographed by Pavel Lebeshev, it's also slyly subversive in its stance on progress. A Russian language film.

Oleg Tabakov Oblomov • Yuri Bogatyrev Stoltz • Yelena Solovey [Elena Solovei] Olga ■ Dir Nikita Mikhalkov • Scr Nikita Mikhalkov, Aleksander Adabashyan, from the novel by Ivan Goncharov • Cinematographer Pavel Lebeshev

The Oblong Box ★★★ 15

Horror
1969 · UK · Colour · 87mins

Hitchcock protégé Gordon Hessler took over the direction of this obvious shocker when Michael Reeves committed suicide after planning it as his follow-up to Witchfinder General. A deranged and disfigured voodoo victim is buried alive by his brother, Vincent Price, only to return from the grave to wreak gory vengeance in a story tenuously connected to Edgar Allan Poe. A pervasive aura of evil is summoned up in a well-mounted period piece containing occasional flashes of Hessler's trademark visual flair. Yet, while Price is well used, but this is almost incidental, adding enormous weight to the clichéd dialogue, Christopher Lee in a blond wig is wasted.

Vincent Price Julian Markham • Christopher Lee Dr Neuhartt • Alistair Williamson Sir Edward Markham • Hilary Dwyer Elizabeth Markham • Peter Arne Samuel Trench • Harry Baird N Galo • Carl Rigg Mark Norton • Maxwell Shaw Tom Hackett • Michael Balfour Ruddock ■ Dir Gordon Hessler • Scr Lawrence Huntingdon, Christopher Wicking, from the story by Edgar Allan Poe

Obsessed ★★ 15

Thriller
1989 · Can · Colour · 99mins

An emotive and topical subject is sensitively handled by experienced Canadian documentary director Robin Spry. Kerrie Keane movingly portrays the mother whose grief increasingly turns to anger as the law fails to deal with the hit-and-run driver responsible for her young son's death. ▣

Kerrie Keane Dinah Middleton • Saul Rubinek Owen Hughs • Daniel Pilon Max Middleton ■ Dir Robin Spry • Scr Douglas Bowie, from a story by Douglas Bowie, Robin Spry, from the novel Hit and Run by Tom Alderman

Obsessed ★★ 15

Thriller
1992 · US · Colour · 87mins

Shannen Doherty had established herself as a teenage terror supreme in films such as Heathers and with off-screen antics while starring in Beverly Hills 90210 when she made this rather less exalted TV project, a sort of junior Fatal Attraction. Doherty plays an impressionable youngster who falls rather badly for the much older William Devane and, when she is finally rejected by him, proceeds to make his life hell. The story is a tad improbable, but the two stars give it all they've got. ▣

Shannen Doherty Lorie Brindel • William Devane Ed Bledsoe • Clare Carey Andie Bledsoe • James Handy Jerry • Lois Chiles Louise • Lisa Poggi Tina Hamilton ■ Dir Jonathan Sanger • Scr David Peckinpah

Obsession ★★★ PG

Thriller
1948 · UK · BW · 93mins

Blacklisted by the McCarthy witch-hunts for being a communist, Hollywood director Edward Dmytryk came to Britain and made three films, including this suspenseful "perfect murder" thriller. Robert Newton over-acts as the doctor who plans the murder of his wife's American lover. Keeping the man alive and locked in a room, he plans to dissolve him in acid when the police call off the search.

The movie is based on a play called A Man about a Dog, and a dog is indeed crucial to the story.

Robert Newton Dr Clive Riordan • Sally Gray Storm Riordan • Naunton Wayne Superintendent Finsbury • Phil Brown Bill Kronin • Olga Lindo Mrs Humphreys • Ronald Adam Clubman • James Harcourt Aitkin ■ Dir Edward Dmytryk • Scr Alec Coppel, from his novel A Man about a Dog

Obsession ★★

Crime drama
1954 · Fr/It · Colour · 105mins

Making her first film in colour, Michèle Morgan is the only reason to invest time in this hackneyed big-top melodrama. The sets are as woefully artificial as the performances, while the storyline feels like something from the silent era. Director Jean Delannoy tries to give it some atmosphere by borrowing the central conceit from Alfred Hitchcock's Suspicion (a genial husband might be responsible for the death of his friend). Despite Morgan's affecting timorousness, however, Delannoy never makes us care whether trapeze artist Raf Vallone or dog trainer Olivier Hussenot is a killer. In French with English subtitles.

Michèle Morgan Hélène Giovanni • Raf Vallone Aldo Giovanni • Marthe Mercadier Arlette Bernardin • Jean Gaven Alex • Robert Dalbin Inspector Chardin ■ Dir Jean Delannoy • Scr Jean Delannoy, Roland Laudenbach, Antoine Blondin, from short stories by William Irish [Cornell Woolrich]

Obsession ★★★ 15

Thriller
1976 · US · Colour · 93mins

Director Brian De Palma made a brave stab at a homage to his idol Alfred Hitchcock with this sexy thriller in which Paul Schrader's screenplay offers more than one nod to Vertigo. Further echoes of Hitch are supplied in the Oscar-nominated score by Psycho composer Bernard Herrmann. Geneviève Bujold is particularly fetching as Cliff Robertson's dead wife and her double, but John Lithgow in his second movie steals the acting honours as Robertson's suspicious business partner. Star Wars editor Paul Hirsch consolidated his reputation on this movie, which is nearly, but not quite, as clever as it thinks it is. ▣

Cliff Robertson Michael Courtland • Geneviève Bujold Elizabeth Courtland/Sandra Portinari • John Lithgow Robert Lasalle • Sylvia "Kuumba" Williams Judy • Wanda Blackman Amy Courtland • J Patrick McNamara Kidnapper • Stanley J Reyes Inspector Brie ■ Dir Brian De Palma • Scr Paul Schrader, from a story by Brian De Palma, Paul Schrader

An Occasional Hell ★★ 18

Mystery thriller
1996 · US · Colour · 88mins

Tom Berenger stars as a former cop-turned-professor who enlists the help of his forensics class to find out who killed Valeria Golino's husband. The plot is muddled and the ending not entirely satisfactory, but Berenger gives his character an intriguing shady background. Unfortunately, Berenger's gritty performance isn't enough to lift this thriller out of the ordinary. Contains swearing, violence, sex scenes, drug abuse and nudity. ▣

Tom Berenger Doctor Ernest Dewalt • Kari Wuhrer Jeri Gillen • Valeria Golino Elizabeth

Laughton • Robert Davi Trooper Abbott • Stephen Lang Alex Laughton ■ Dir Salome Breziner • Scr Randall Silvis, from his book

Ocean's Eleven ★★★★ PG

Crime caper
1960 · US · Colour · 122mins

One of the great (and one of the most critically under-rated) caper movies, this story was discovered by Clan member Peter Lawford and brought to Clan head Frank Sinatra, who effectively produced the movie. He cast himself as former sergeant Danny Ocean, who calls on his old wartime pals to help him in a raid on Las Vegas. The League of Gentlemen had a similar plot, but this is altogether sleeker and more audacious, and superbly cast. It's directed by veteran Lewis Milestone, who keeps a tight lid on the Rat Pack's antics. The ending, if rather derivative, is still utterly brilliant.

Frank Sinatra Danny Ocean • Dean Martin Sam Harmon • Sammy Davis Jr Josh Howard • Peter Lawford Jimmy Foster • Angie Dickinson Beatrice Ocean • Richard Conte Anthony Bergdorf • Cesar Romero Duke Santos • Patrice Wymore Adele Ekstrom • Joey Bishop "Mushy" O'Conners • Akim Tamiroff Spyros Acebos ■ Dir Lewis Milestone • Scr Harry Brown, Charles Lederer, from a story by George Clayton Johnson, Jack Golden

Oceans of Fire ★★ PG

Action adventure
1986 · US · Colour · 90mins

The tough guys are shipped in for this "battle against the sea" adventure about oil riggers. Former boxing champions Ken Norton and Ray "Boom Boom" Mancini are joined by ex-American football star Lyle Alzado for this macho-men outing. Strictly for those who like watching brawn without having to use the brain. ▣

Gregory Harrison Ben Laforche • Billy Dee Williams Jim McKinley • David Carradine JC Busch • Lyle Alzado Witkowski • Tony Burton Clay • Ray "Boom Boom" Mancini [Ray Mancini] Romano • Ken Norton Chief • Lee Ving Pembroke ■ Dir Steve Carver • Scr Walter Halsey Davis

The Octagon ★★ 18

Martial arts action
1980 · US · Colour · 98mins

With his penchant for martial art butt-kicking and monosyllabic, mahogany-table acting, Chuck Norris was probably the precursor to the likes of Van Damme and Schwarzenegger. Here he plays a retired kung fu champ hired as a bodyguard for a wealthy woman against attack by sinister ninja types. As chop-socky movies go, this is better than most, but still devoid of a single brain cell. You have to pity poor old Lee Van Cleef, roped in as a mercenary soldier.

Chuck Norris Scott James • Karen Carlson Justine • Lee Van Cleef McCarn • Art Hindle A J • Carol Bagdasarian Aura ■ Dir Eric Karson • Scr Leigh Chapman, from a story by Paul Aaron, Leigh Chapman

October ★★★★ PG

Silent historical epic
1928 · USSR · Colour · 99mins

Despite being made to celebrate the tenth anniversary of the overthrow of Kerensky's provisional government, this impersonal tribute to the

proletariat found little official or critical favour in the Soviet Union. Bitingly satirical and overtly political, it marked Sergei Eisenstein's most ambitious experiment in intellectual montage. However, despite such memorable set pieces as the assault on the Winter Palace, the raising of the bridge and the toppling of Alexander III's statue, the obscurity of some of its imagery and the uncomfortable blend of symbolism and realism rendered it less dramatically unified, thematically consistent and emotionally overwhelming than its predecessor, *The Battleship Potemkin.*

Nikandrof *Lenin* • N Popov *Kerensky* • Boris Livanov *Minister* ■ *Dir* Sergei Eisenstein, Grigori V Aleksandrov • *Scr* Sergei Eisenstein, Grigori Alexandrov • *Cinematographer* Edouard Tissé

The October Man ★★★★ PG

Murder mystery 1947 · UK · BW · 91mins

Sturdily scripted from his own novel by Eric Ambler, cannily directed by Roy Baker and atmospherically photographed by Erwin Hillier, this is one of British cinema's best stabs at *film noir*. John Mills gives a highly accomplished performance as the amnesiac who, having been responsible for an accidental death, now has to prove to himself and the authorities that he didn't kill fellow boarding-house tenant Kay Walsh. But what really makes this seedy thriller so compelling is the support playing of Joan Greenwood, Joyce Carey and Edward Chapman. Keep an eye out for a six-year-old Juliet Mills, making her third screen appearance.

John Mills *Jim Ackland* • Joan Greenwood *Jenny Carden* • Edward Chapman *Mr Peachey* • Kay Walsh *Molly* • Joyce Carey *Mrs Vinton* • Catherine Lacey *Miss Selby* • Frederick Piper *Godby* • Felix Aylmer *Dr Martin* ■ *Dir* Roy Baker [Roy Ward Baker] • *Scr* Eric Ambler, from his novel

October Sky ★★★★ PG

Drama 1999 · US · Colour · 102mins

Joe Johnston, director of *Honey, I Shrunk the Kids*, reins himself in with this charming true story of pluck and determination in fifties West Virginia. Although his dad (Chris Cooper) is superintendent of the town mine, schoolboy Jake Gyllenhaal is determined to avoid a life underground. With Sputnik launching the space age, he gathers a group of friends together to build their own rockets. Encouraged by teacher Laura Dern, the lads hope to enter the state science fair. Droll, touching and awe-inspiring in turn, this is an engrossing tale, even if it does contain too much sentimental father-son bonding in its closing stages.

DVD

Jake Gyllenhaal *Homer Hickam* • Chris Cooper *John Hickman* • Laura Dern *Miss Riley* • Chris Owen *Quentin* • William Lee Scott *Roy Lee* • Chad Lindberg *O'Dell* ■ *Dir* Joe Johnston • *Scr* Lewis Colick, from the autobiography *Rocket Boys* by Homer Hickam Jr

Octopussy ★★★ PG

Spy adventure 1983 · UK · Colour · 125mins

Adapted from the Ian Fleming stories *Octopussy* and *The Property of a Lady*, this was the 13th Bond movie and is possibly the most frivolous (and certainly the most careless) to date. The plot meanders more than the Ganges as Roger Moore follows Maud Adams and renegade Soviet general Steven Berkoff across India and Central Europe. All the usual paraphernalia are on view (although the gadgets aren't quite up to Q's customary standard), but director John Glen (who'd been editor and second unit director on several earlier entries) never quite seems in control, either of the breathless action or the overly glib dialogue.

Roger Moore *James Bond* • Maud Adams *Octopussy* • Louis Jourdan *Kamal* • Kristina Wayborn *Magda* • Kabir Bedi *Gobinda* • Steven Berkoff *General Orlov* • David Meyer *One of twins* • Tony Meyer *One of twins* • Vijay Amritraj *Vijay* • Desmond Llewelyn *"Q"* • Robert Brown *"M"* • Walter Gotell *Gogol* • Geoffrey Keen *Minister of Defence* • Lois Maxwell *Miss Moneypenny* ■ *Dir* John Glen • *Scr* George MacDonald Fraser, Richard Maibaum, Michael G Wilson, from the stories *Octopussy* and *The Property of a Lady* by Ian Fleming

The Odd Angry Shot ★★★ 15

War comedy drama
1979 · Ausl · Colour · 87mins

This Vietnam war movie fired off a barrage of controversy in its native Australia, with its story of a group of Aussie professional soldiers, bitterly complaining about a conflict they don't think is any of their business and feeling danger has been foisted on them by back-home politicians. John Hargreaves and Bryan Brown are outstanding, despite having to play stereotypical boozing and brawling comrades, while director Tom Jeffrey catches the claustrophobia of the occasion as much as the violent action.

Graham Kennedy *Harry* • John Hargreaves *Bung* • John Jarratt *Bill* • Bryan Brown *Rogers* • Graeme Blundell *Dawson* • Richard Moir *Medic* • Brandon Burke *Isaacs* • Ian Gilmour *Scott* ■ *Dir* Tom Jeffrey • *Scr* Tom Jeffrey, from a novel by William Nagle

Odd Birds ★

Drama 1985 · US · Colour · 90mins

This tale of a Chinese immigrant girl in sixties San Francisco is a no-hoper. Ming Lew gives a convincing performance as a teen who is told she can't be an actress by her mother. Having sought advice and found solace in a friendship with priest Michael Moriarty she decides to, at least, have a go. Cue an audition and the ultimate "You could make it kid" scene. Lew has a voice, but the dubbing and feel of the film dumbs down any attempts by the performers to make it work. The ending is ridiculous.

Michael Moriarty *Brother TS Murphy* • Donna Lai Ming Lew *Joy Chan* • Nancy Yee *Mrs Chan* • Bruce Gray *Gower Champion* • Scott Crawford *Eric* ■ *Dir/Scr* Jeanne Collachia

The Odd Couple ★★★★ PG

Comedy 1968 · US · Colour · 101mins

Jack Lemmon, devastated by the break-up of his marriage, packs his sinuses and his nervous tics and moves in with happily divorced Walter Matthau. While Lemmon is the finicky housewife (crustless sandwiches, coasters for drinks, nifty hoover technique), Matthau is the arch slob (brimming ashtrays, unmade bed, linguini on the walls), and they inevitably drive each other nuts. Apart from a cringe-making scene with two English girls, Neil Simon's comedy has weathered well, bristling with one-liners timed to perfection by the two leads.

Jack Lemmon *Felix Ungar* • Walter Matthau *Oscar Madison* • John Fiedler *Vinnie* • Herbert Edelman *Murray* • David Sheiner *Roy* • Larry Haines *Speed* • Monica Evans *Cecily* • Carole Shelley *Gwendolyn* ■ *Dir* Gene Saks • *Scr* Neil Simon, from his play

The Odd Couple II ★★★ 15

Comedy 1998 · US · Colour · 92mins

Although coming 30 years after the original, this belated sequel would have us believe it's really only 17 years since Jack Lemmon and Walter Matthau shared an apartment. The 78-year-old Matthau has retired to Florida to play poker with rich widows, but the impending marriage of his son to Jack's daughter brings the bickering pair together again. Scripted by original author Neil Simon, it's rarely more than a contrivance and a pension enhancement for all concerned, but Lemmon and Matthau are still eminently watchable and it's hard to resist the film's lazy charm. Contains some swearing.

Jack Lemmon *Felix Ungar* • Walter Matthau *Oscar Madison* • Richard Riehle *Detective* • Jonathan Silverman *Brucey Madison* • Lisa Waltz *Hannah Ungar* • Mary Beth Peil *Felice* • Christine Baranski *Thelma* • Jean Smart *Holly* • Barnard Hughes *Beaumont* ■ *Dir* Howard Deutch • *Scr* Neil Simon

The Odd Couple: Together Again ★★

Comedy 1993 · US · Colour

This sequel to the TV series based on Neil Simon's play and film will leave those looking for a good chuckle disappointed. The plot revolves around fussy Tony Randall's moving back in temporarily with his old messy roommate Jack Klugman. The sparks fly as Randall helps his depressed friend rehabilitate from throat cancer surgery (which actor Klugman actually had). Thankfully, the arrival of old-timers such as Penny Marshall helps add a sprinkle of humour to this overly sentimental script.

Jack Klugman *Oscar Madison* • Tony Randall *Felix Ungar* • Barbara Barrie *Gloria* • Jim Haynie *Mr Gil Sutton* • Toni Kalem *Edna* • Jerry Adler *Murray the Cop* • Penny Marshall *Myrna* ■ *Dir* Robert Klane • *Scr* Robert Klane, from characters created by Neil Simon

The Odd Job ★★ 15

Comedy 1978 · UK · Colour · 84mins

A key member of the *Monty Python* team, Graham Chapman seemed lost without a little help from his friends in his solo ventures. The cast he gathered around him in this off-colour black comedy tries its hardest to tune into the cockeyed humour at which he excelled, but only David Jason, as the hit man hired by the heartbroken Chapman to kill him, and Bill Paterson, as a pompous flatfoot, come close. It's a one-joke movie, with Jason making a number of bizarre murder attempts unaware that Chapman has changed his mind. There are laughs, but too few.

Graham Chapman *Arthur Harris* • David Jason *Odd Job Man* • Diana Quick *Fiona Harris* • Simon Williams *Tony Sloane* • Edward Hardwicke *Inspector Black* • Bill Paterson *Sergeant Mull* • Michael Elphick *Raymonde* • Stewart Harwood *Bernard* ■ *Dir* Peter Medak • *Scr* Graham Chapman, Bernard McKenna, from a TV play by Bernard McKenna

Odd Jobs ★★ 15

Comedy 1986 · US · Colour · 84mins

Paul Reiser is takes top billing in this broad comedy, but in name only, for, like his 1982 hit, *Diner*, this is essentially an ensemble piece. Indeed, Robert Townsend has the best lines, as he and Reiser join a group of college friends spending their summer working as removal men with a little help from the Mob. Directed without a hint of subtlety by Mark Story, this is a crude compendium of obvious sight gags, and it's to the cast's credit that this is occasionally quite funny. Contains swearing.

Paul Reiser *Max* • Robert Townsend *Dwight* • Scott McGinnis *Woody* • Rick Overton *Roy* • Paul Provenza *Bryon* • Leo Burmester *Wylie D Daiken* • Thomas Quinn *Frankie* • Savannah Smith Boucher *Loretta/Lynette* • Richard Dean Anderson *Spud* • Richard Foronjy *Manny* • Eleanor Mondale *Mandy* • Julianne Phillips *Sally* ■ *Dir* Mark Story • *Scr* Robert Conte, Peter Martin Wortmann

Odd Man Out ★★★★★

Drama 1946 · UK · BW · 116mins

As agonising a piece of cinema as you are ever likely to see. James Mason gives the performance of a lifetime as an IRA man on the run in the backwaters of Belfast after he is fatally wounded during a robbery. Mason conveys his pain and isolation with consummate skill, but his desperate plight is made unbearable by Carol Reed's masterly direction exploiting the unforgiving landscape with outrageous camera angles and photographic distortions and Robert Krasker's chillingly atmospheric photography, to fashion a city that is at once forbiddingly cold and worth dying for.

James Mason *Johnny* • Robert Newton *Lukey* • Kathleen Ryan *Kathleen* • Robert Beatty *Dennis* • FJ McCormick *Shell* • Kitty Kirwan *Granny* • Fay Compton *Rosie* • Cyril Cusack *Pat* ■ *Dir* Carol Reed • *Scr* FL Green, RC Sherriff, from the novel by FL Green

Oddball Hall ★ PG

Comedy 1990 · US · Colour · 83mins

Written and directed by Jackson Hunsicker, it's a smug joke at the expense of the developing world that no amount of spin could reposition as a satire on western civilisation. The mugging of Don Ameche and BurgessMeredith is as embarrassing as the plotline, which casts them as a couple of jewel thieves who are mistaken for members of a charitable fraternity with the magical powers to end a drought. Oh yes, very funny!

Don Ameche *G Paul Siebriese* • Burgess Meredith *Ingersol* • Bill Maynard *Copperthwaite* • Tullio Moneta *"Goose" Linguine* • Tiny Skefile *Meetoo-U* ■ *Dir/Scr* Jackson Hunsicker

1030

U = SUITABLE FOR ALL Uc = SUITABLE FOR ALL, ESPECIALLY FOR YOUNG CHILDREN (VIDEO ONLY) PG = PARENTAL GUIDANCE

Odds against Tomorrow
★★★★

Crime drama   1959 · US · BW · 96mins

A terrific heist movie, grimly told and well performed, with a prescient and tough racist subtext that makes for compulsive viewing. Executive produced by Harry Belafonte and directed by master craftsman Robert Wise, it benefits from a high octane cast, headed by Belafonte himself, with Robert Ryan as the bigoted ex-con at his throat. There's also fine nervy back-up from Shelley Winters as Ryan's wife, Gloria Grahame as his mistress and Ed Begley, as the disgraced ex-cop who has the idea for the robbery. While the cast vividly brings William P McGivern's dime novel to life, it's two technical credits that help make the movie memorable; the edgy score is by Modern Jazz Quartet pianist John Lewis, and the film is the first major production for editor Dede Allen, who would later work on *The Hustler* and *Bonnie and Clyde*.

Harry Belafonte *Johnny Ingram* • Robert Ryan *Earl Slater* • Shelley Winters *Lorry* • Ed Begley *Dave Burke* • Gloria Grahame *Helen* • Will Kuluva *Bacco* ■ *Dir* Robert Wise • *Scr* John O Killens [Abraham Polonsky], Nelson Gidding, from the novel by William P McGivern

Ode to Billy Joe
★★★★ 15

Drama   1976 · US · Colour · 101mins

The heartache of teenage love has rarely been so sensitively caught as in this romantic tragedy set in a Mississippi backwater, dramatising Bobby Gentry's 1967 hit-song lyric. Robby Benson is Billy Joe McAllister and Glynnis O'Connor the schoolgirl Bobbie Lee Hartley, while the Tallahatchie Bridge looms as the predestined doom for a traumatised Billy Joe. Although the ending is overly sentimental, the achievement of director Max Baer Jr and writer Herman Raucher is to mingle small-town behaviour with small-scale romance and show that there is a dramatic poignancy to both.

Robby Benson *Billy Joe McAllister* • Glynnis O'Connor *Bobbie Lee Hartley* • Joan Hotchkis *Mrs Hartley* • Sandy McPeak *Mr Hartley* • James Best *Dewey Barksdale* ■ *Dir* Max Baer Jr • *Scr* Herman Racher, from the song by Bobbie Gentry

The Odessa File
★★★ PG

Thriller   1974 · UK · Colour · 123mins

A terrific Frederick Forsyth plot and impressive production values make this thriller eminently watchable, but unfortunately veteran director Ronald Neame lets the pace drag, and the length feels excessive for what should be a taut thriller. However, the often undervalued Jon Voight is superb as the journalist tracking down a concentration camp commandant, his quest hindered at every turn by members of the sinister Odessa organisation. There are splendid moments along the way, notably a nasty grilling of Voight by slimy Noel Willman, but Derek Jacobi is wasted, and female lead Mary Tamm inadequate. Also, Maximilian Schell is far too sympathetic for the villain, and the Andrew Lloyd Webber score really

doesn't help. Contains violence and swearing. ▭

Jon Voight *Peter Miller* • Maximilian Schell *Eduard Roschmann* • Maria Schell *Frau Miller* • Mary Tamm *Sigi* • Derek Jacobi *Klaus Wenzer* • Peter Jeffrey *David Porath* • Klaus Lowitsch [Klaus Löwitsch] *Gustav Mackensen* • Kurt Meisel *Alfred Oster* ■ *Dir* Ronald Neame • *Scr* George Markstein, Kenneth Ross, from the novel by Frederick Forsyth

Odette
★★★ PG

Second World War drama
1950 · UK · BW · 112mins

There is an inescapable predictability about wartime exploits movies, even though there is no denying the magnitude of the achievements of people such as Odette Churchill who survived Nazi torture while working for the French Resistance. Director Herbert Wilcox has little new to offer in his depiction of underground activities and pulls his punches during Odette's interrogation by suitably sadistic Gestapo types. Anna Neagle suggests a certain stiffness in the upper lip region, but she is not at her best. ▭

Anna Neagle *Odette* • Trevor Howard *Captain Peter Churchill* • Marius Goring *Henri* • Peter Ustinov *Arnaud* • Bernard Lee *Jack* • Marie Burke *Mme Glière* • Gilles Queant *Jacques* • Alfred Shieske *Commandant* • Marianne Waller *Wardress* ■ *Dir* Herbert Wilcox • *Scr* Warren Chetham-Strode, from the book by Jerrard Tickell

The Odyssey
★★★ 12

Epic fantasy
1997 · Ger/It/US · Colour · 172mins

Whittled down from a mini-series, this lavish dramatisation of Homer's epic poem has some breathtaking Mediterranean scenery, including the ruins of Troy that lend unrivalled authenticity to the famous Trojan Horse episode. Armand Assante is suitably heroic as the King of Ithaca, who encountered the Cyclops, the treacherous Eurymachus and the bewitching Circe and Calypso during his 20-year adventure. Andrei Konchalovsky directs with a judicious blend of mythical spectacle and philosophical insight, and expertly handles a stellar cast that includes Isabella Rossellini and Greta Scacchi.

Armand Assante *Odysseus* • Greta Scacchi *Penelope* • Isabella Rossellini *Athene* • Bernadette Peters *Circe* • Eric Roberts *Eurymachus* • Irene Papas *Anticlea* • Jeroen Krabbé *King Alcinous* • Geraldine Chaplin *Eurycleia* ■ *Dir* Andrei Konchalovsky • *Scr* Andrei Konchalovsky, Christopher Solimine, from the poem by Homer

Oedipus Rex
★★★ 15

Tragedy   1967 · It · Colour · 100mins

Remembering Pier Paolo Pasolini's own problems with paternal authority, there's a distinctly autobiographical element to his rendition of the infamous story of the son who murders his father and marries his mother. Working from his own translation, Pasolini sought to emphasise the continued universality of Sophocles's tragedy by book-ending the action with episodes set in modern-day Bologna. He also imparts additional atmosphere by staging the play in the dramatic setting of a 15th-century adobe city

deep in the Moroccan desert, and by employing a primordially powerful soundtrack. For all its impressive qualities, though, it's a strangely dispassionate picture. An Italian language film. ▭

Franco Citti *Oedipus Rex* • Silvana Mangano *Jocasta* • Carmelo Bene *Creon* • Julian Beck *Tiresias* • Ninetto Davoli *Messenger* • Pier Paolo Pasolini *High Priest* ■ *Dir* Pier Paolo Pasolini • *Scr* Pier Paolo Pasolini, from the play by Sophocles

Oedipus the King
★★

Tragedy   1968 · UK · Colour · 94mins

Neither a full-blooded epic nor an engrossing art-house tale, *Oedipus the King* goes to show that even with a decent cast and with Sophocles as your source you can still come a cropper. As Oedipus, Christopher Plummer is far less compelling than he was as Commodus in *The Fall of the Roman Empire*, despite the fact that he murders his father, marries his mother and then takes out his own eyes. This should be juicy stuff, but it just fails to ignite and even Orson Welles comes across as just the town bore.

Christopher Plummer *Oedipus* • Lilli Palmer *Jocasta* • Richard Johnson *Creon* • Orson Welles *Tiresias* • Cyril Cusack *Messenger* • Roger Livesey *Shepherd* • Donald Sutherland *Chorus leader* ■ *Dir* Philip Saville • *Scr* Philip Saville, Michael Luke, from the play by Paul Roche, from the play by Sophocles

Of a Thousand Delights
★★★

Psychological drama   1965 · It · BW · 100mins

Also known as *Sandra*, Visconti's operatic tale of guilt, betrayal and incest, derived from the Electra myth, is pretty unconvincing. But it boasts fine black-and-white photography by Armando Nannuzzi, and powerful performances from Marie Bell and Claudia Cardinale as a mother and daughter in conflict while commemorating their husband and father respectively, a Jewish scientist killed by the Nazis. An Italian language film.

Claudia Cardinale *Sandra* • Jean Sorel *Gianni* • Michael Craig *Andrew* • Renzo Ricci *Gilardini* ■ *Dir* Luchino Visconti • *Scr* Suso Cecchi D'Amico, Enrico Medioli, Luchino Visconti

Of Freaks and Men
★★★ 18

Drama   1998 · Rus · BW/Sepia · 92mins

Alexei Balabanov's sojourn in the sinful backwaters of 1900s St Petersburg could not be any more different from his bruisingly realistic *Brother*. However, the swaggering disregard for political correctness is again to the fore as widows, virgins and Siamese twins are exploited by immigrant pornographer Sergei Makovetsky. Such shock tactics are not employed to titillate, but to expose the corruption inherent in Russian society throughout the last century. Littered with references to the nation's cinematic heritage, this is an eccentric, enigmatic yet always enthralling allegory. In Russian with English subtitles.

Sergei Makovetsky *Johan* • Dinara Drukarova *Liza* • Lika Nevolina *Ekaterina Kirillovna* • Viktor Sukhorukov *Victor Ivanovich* ■ *Dir/Scr* Alexei Balabanov

Of Human Bondage
★★★ PG

Drama   1934 · US · BW · 82mins

The first, and best, screen version of Somerset Maugham's famous novel. Leslie Howard is sensitive and polished as Philip Carey, the gentlemanly artist turned medical student who almost ruins his life over his obsessive infatuation with a vindictive teashop waitress. Bette Davis proves her credentials in this latter role, offering a nuanced portrayal that rises above her cockney accent. There is excellent support, too, from Reginalds Denny and Owen, Frances Dee and Kay Johnson. Above all, however, plaudits must go to John Cromwell's tightly controlled and atmospheric direction. ▭

Leslie Howard *Philip Carey* • Bette Davis *Mildred Rogers* • Frances Dee *Sally Athelny* • Reginald Owen *Thorpe Athelny* • Reginald Denny *Harry Griffiths* • Kay Johnson *Norah* • Alan Hale *Emil Miller* • Reginald Sheffield *Dunsford* ■ *Dir* John Cromwell • *Scr* Lester Cohen, from the novel by W Somerset Maugham

Of Human Bondage
★★

Drama   1946 · US · BW · 105mins

This miscast effort stars Paul Henreid and Eleanor Parker: he too sophisticated and uncomfortably wooden, she doing her best to convince as a cockney. The film is solid and respectable, but ends up dull and unconvincing. For all its intrinsic deficiencies, however, one keeps watching, buoyed by a good supporting cast that includes Alexis Smith and Edmund Gwenn.

Eleanor Parker *Mildred Rogers* • Paul Henreid *Philip Carey* • Alexis Smith *Nora Nesbitt* • Edmund Gwenn *Athelny* • Janis Paige *Sally Athelny* • Patric Knowles *Griffiths* • Henry Stephenson *Dr Tyrell* • Marten Lamont *Dunsford* ■ *Dir* Edmund Goulding • *Scr* Catherine Turney, from the novel by W Somerset Maugham

Of Human Bondage
★★

Drama   1964 · UK · BW · 98mins

An unnecessary third version of W Somerset Maugham's tale of a doctor besotted with a floozy, with both leads so miscast that it took three directors (Henry Hathaway, Bryan Forbes and the credited Ken Hughes) to get something almost credible on screen. Kim Novak is far too bright and intelligent a person to cope with cockney Mildred's idiocies, and it's anyone's guess what Laurence Harvey thought he was up to. There is a compulsive watchability factor built into movies like this, but it's sad that the once-mighty MGM let this British-made tosh reach the screen in such a half-baked form. ▭

Kim Novak *Mildred Rogers* • Laurence Harvey *Philip Carey* • Robert Morley *Dr Jacobs* • Siobhan McKenna *Norah Nesbitt* • Roger Livesey *Thorpe Athelny* • Jack Hedley *Griffiths* • Nanette Newman *Sally Athelny* ■ *Dir* Ken Hughes, Henry Hathaway, Bryan Forbes • *Scr* Bryan Forbes, from the novel by W Somerset Maugham

Of Human Hearts ★★★ U

Period drama 1938 · US · BW · 103mins

A period family drama, played out in rural surroundings and focusing on the conflict between a heavily religious paterfamilias (Walter Huston), his rebellious son (James Stewart) who wishes to break away and become a surgeon, and the lad's mother (Beulah Bondi, Oscar-nominated), caught in the middle and making sacrifices to help him. Beautifully directed by Clarence Brown, with top-class production values and impeccable acting from a cast that includes stage actor Charles Coburn, virtually a newcomer to films at age 61, John Gilbert's daughter Leatrice Joy Gilbert and John Carradine as Abraham Lincoln.

James Stewart *Jason Wilkins* • Walter Huston *Rev Ethan Wilkins* • Beulah Bondi *Mary Wilkins* • Guy Kibbee *Mr George Ames* • Charles Coburn *Dr Charles Shingle* • John Carradine *President Lincoln* • Ann Rutherford *Annie Hawks* • Charley Grapewin *Jim Meeker* • Leatrice Joy Gilbert *Annie Hawks at age 10* • *Dir* Clarence Brown • *Scr* Bradbury Foote, from the novel *Benefits Forgot* by Honoré Morrow

Of Love and Desire ★★

Drama 1963 · US · Colour · 96mins

Nobody comes off particularly well in this lurid melodrama set in Mexico about a lustful woman (Merle Oberon) who seduces an engineer and subsequently falls for him, to her great surprise. In her confused state, she is raped by one of her old flames, then tries to kill herself. Adult themes – loveless sex, nymphomania and incest – are in large supply and while it's worth seeing as a wild curio, the general air of depravity undermines the positive ending.

Merle Oberon *Katherine Beckman* • Steve Cochran *Steve Corey* • Curt Jurgens *Paul Beckman* • John Agar *Gus Cole* • Steve Brodie *Bill Maxton* • Eduardo Noriega *Mr Dominguez* • Elsa Cardenas *Mrs Dominguez* ■ *Dir* Richard Rush • *Scr* Laslo Gorog, Richard Rush, from a story by Victor Stoloff, Jacqueline Delessert

Of Love and Shadows ★ 18

Romantic political drama 1994 · Sp/Arg · Colour · 103mins

Antonio Banderas and Jennifer Connolly star as the lovers whose relationship is set against a backdrop of corruption in Chile. Connelly is unconvincing as a naive journalist, unfamiliar with Chile's criminal underbelly. Banderas is a photographer trying to expose the fact that her fiancé is a fascist involved in official torture and the corruption at the heart of government. Notable for appalling direction and dialogue, the film jolts from one dysfunctional scene to another. Banderas deserves better than this. 🔲

Antonio Banderas *Francisco* • Jennifer Connelly *Irene* • Stefania Sandrelli *Beatriz* • Diego Wallraff *Jose* • Camillo Gallardo *Gustavo* • Patricio Contreras *Mario* ■ *Dir* Betty Kaplan • *Scr* Donald Freed, from the novel by Isabel Allende

Of Mice and Men ★★★★

Drama 1939 · US · BW · 106mins

The aptly named Lewis Milestone created a little Hollywood history with this adaptation of John Steinbeck's best-loved novel, by commencing the action before the opening credits. However, it's the astute performances and Aaron Copland's superb score on which its reputation really rests. Burgess Meredith and Lon Chaney Jr excel as the wiry drifter and genial giant wandering the west seeking refuge from the Depression. But every bit as effective is B-Western star Bob Steele, who casts off his matinée idol persona to bring genuine menace to the part of the ranch owner's sadistic son, whose inability to control enticing wife Betty Field leads to tragedy.

Burgess Meredith *George* • Betty Field *Mae* • Lon Chaney Jr *Lennie* • Charles Bickford *Slim* • Roman Bohnen *Candy* • Bob Steele *Curley* • Noah Beery Jr *Whit* ■ *Dir* Lewis Milestone • *Scr* Eugene Solow, from the novel and by John Steinbeck • *Music* Aaron Copland

Of Mice and Men ★★★★ PG

Drama 1992 · US · Colour · 106mins

Twelve years after they first played George and Lennie on stage at Chicago's Steppenwolf Theater, Gary Sinise and John Malkovich reprised their roles in this sensitive screen adaptation of John Steinbeck's classic novel. Blending tenderness and confusion with temper and power, Malkovich is quite superb as the simple-minded hulk whose titanic strength brings the pair untold trouble. On the directorial side, Sinise acquits himself remarkably well, at times even managing to improve on the excellent 1939 Lewis Milestone version. Contains violence and swearing. 🔲

John Malkovich *Lennie* • Gary Sinise *George* • Ray Walston *Candy* • Casey Siemaszko *Curley* • Sherilyn Fenn *Curley's wife* • John Terry *Slim* • Richard Riehle *Carlson* • Alexis Arquette *Whitt* • Joe Morton *Crooks* • Noble Willingham *The boss* ■ *Dir* Gary Sinise • *Scr* Horton Foote, from the novel and play by John Steinbeck

Of Pure Blood ★ 15

Drama 1986 · US · Colour · 89mins

In a laughably overwrought melodrama, cornily scripted and implausibly plotted, Lee Remick is the mother whose investigation of her son's violent death in Germany leads to her stumbling on some cornball conspiracy involving neo-Nazis and the genetic breeding of a new Aryan master race. This mediocre made-for-TV movie squanders the talents of Remick and co-star Patrick McGoohan. 🔲

Lee Remick *Alicia Browning* • Patrick McGoohan *Dr Felix Neumann* • Gottfried John *Paul Bergmann* • Richard Munch *Dr Gregor Bamberg* • Katharina Bohm *Ursula Schiller* ■ *Dir* Joseph Sargent • *Scr* Michael Zagor, from a story by Del Coleman, Michael Zagor, from the book *Au Nom de la Race* by Marc Hillel, Clarissa Henry

Of Unknown Origin ★★★★ 15

Horror 1983 · Can · Colour · 85mins

A minor gem insightfully outlining the psychological breakdown of a high-powered business executive which manifests itself in the form of a larger-than-life rat. Director George Pan Cosmatos wrings every ounce of terror and suspense from this simple premise, as Peter Weller believably fights for his sanity in a battle of wits with the vicious rodent when it moves into his Manhattan brownstone. Seat-edged tension is evoked by giving out horrendous facts concerning the very real threat rats are to our society and through nerve-racking dream sequences, which cleverly trade on universal phobias. 🔲

Peter Weller *Bart Hughes* • Jennifer Dale *Lorrie Wells* • Lawrence Dane *Eliot Riverton* • Kenneth Welsh *James Hall* • Shannon Tweed *Meg Hughes* • Maury Chaykin *Dan* ■ *Dir* George Pan Cosmatos • *Scr* Brian Taggert, from the novel *The Visitor* by Chauncey G Parker III

Off and Running ★★ 15

Comedy 1991 · US · Colour · 86mins

It's obvious why this wannabe screwball comedy only premiered on cable five years after it was made. As the "resting" actress who is forced to work as a mermaid at a Miami hotel, Cyndi Lauper soon outstays her welcome. But, because she's now being pursued by the crooks who killed her boyfriend, we feel obliged to stick with her as she and failed golf pro David Keith encounter a kidnapped child and a nobbled racehorse. Too nasty to be romantic and too unfunny to be a comedy. Contains violence, swearing, nudity and drug abuse 🔲

Cyndi Lauper *Cyd* • David Keith *Jack* • Johnny Pinto *Pompey* • David Thornton *Reese* • Richard Belzer *Milt Zoloth* ■ *Dir* Edward Bianchi • *Scr* Mitch Glazer

Off Beat ★★ PG

Comedy 1986 · US · Colour · 88mins

Judge Reinhold – best known as the gormless LA detective in the *Beverly Hills Cop* trilogy – tries (and fails) to be a leading man in this below-average comedy about a librarian who poses as a police officer and ends up falling in love with unsuspecting policewoman Meg Tilly. Worth watching just to spot John Turturro and Harvey Keitel in roles they'd now rather forget. 🔲

Judge Reinhold *Joe Gower* • Meg Tilly *Rachel Wareham* • Cleavant Derricks *Abe Washington* • Joe Mantegna *Pete Peterson* • Jacques d'Amboise *August* • Amy Wright *Mary Ellen Gruenwald* • John Turturro *Neil Pepper* • Fred Gwynne *Commissioner* • Harvey Keitel *Mickey* ■ *Dir* Michael Dinner • *Scr* Mark Medoff, from a story by Dezso Magyar

Off Limits ★★

Comedy 1953 · US · BW · 89mins

The Bob Hope style of wise-cracking was showing some strain by the time of this comedy, and 1953 was the last year in which he figured in the top ten box-office stars. His teaming with the exuberant Mickey Rooney does not always gell, but there are sufficient laughs in the Hal Kanter/Jack Sher script to make this a pleasant enough time-passer. Eddie Mayehoff shines as a military policeman who despairs at the ineptitude of Hope, a boxer's manager stuck with a term in the army. Marilyn Maxwell, who often appeared with Hope in his shows for American servicemen, is the leading lady and, for fight fans, there is an appearance by the legendary boxer Jack Dempsey.

Bob Hope *Wally Hogan* • Mickey Rooney *Herbert Tuttle* • Marilyn Maxwell *Connie Curtis* • Eddie Mayehoff *Karl Danzig* • Stanley Clements *Bullet Bradley* • Jack Dempsey ■ *Dir* George Marshall • *Scr* Hal Kanter, Jack Sher, from a story by Hal Kanter

Off the Minnesota Strip ★★★

Drama 1980 · US · Colour · 104mins

An often impressive TV drama, with Mare Winningham as the country girl-turned-New York prostitute who returns home hoping to lead a normal life again, except that her parents can't cope with the shame she brings to them. A decent performance from Winningham and another from the dependable Hal Holbrook make for some dramatic fireworks. Lamont Johnson's direction does a first-class job in capturing the moral climate of the Midwest.

Hal Holbrook *Budd Johansen* • Michael Learned *Hughlene Johansen* • Mare Winningham *Michele Johansen* • Heather McAdam *Danielle Johansen* ■ *Dir* Lamont Johnson • *Scr* David H Chase

Offbeat ★★

Crime drama 1960 · UK · BW · 72mins

Best known for his collaborations with Morecambe and Wise and seventies' sitcom spin-offs, Cliff Owen made his directorial debut with this rather forced thriller, which is also known as *The Devil Inside*. William Sylvester gives a good account of himself as the undercover cop who finds the life of crime to his liking, but Mai Zetterling is somewhat wasted as the gang widow for whom he falls. Given the budgetary restraints, it's not too bad, but, with the exception of the leads, the characters are a clichéd bunch, and the finale is far too convenient.

William Sylvester *Steve Layton/Steve Ross* • Mai Zetterling *Ruth Lombard* • John Meillon *Johnny Remick* • Anthony Dawson *James Dawson* • Neil McCarthy *Leo Farrell* • Harry Baird *Gill Hall* • John Phillips *Superintendent Gault* ■ *Dir* Cliff Owen • *Scr* Peter Barnes

The Offence ★★★ 18

Psychological drama 1972 · UK · Colour · 107mins

Gritty police programmes are now so much a part of the TV landscape that it is hard to realise that a feature like *The Offence* once packed quite a punch. Adapted by former *Z Cars* scriptwriter John Hopkins from his own play, this sordid study of evil and human weakness lacks the intensity of the stage production and suffers from director Sidney Lumet's uncharacteristically shaky handling of local colour and atmosphere. Yet, Sean Connery as the brutal, world-weary copper and Ian Bannen as the lowlife he suspects of child molesting still give compelling performances. Contains violence and swearing. 🔲

Sean Connery *Detective Sergeant Johnson* • Trevor Howard *Lieutenant Cartwright* • Vivien Merchant *Maureen Johnson* • Ian Bannen *Baxter* • Derek Newark *Jessard* • John Hallam *Panton* • Peter Bowles *Cameron* ■ *Dir* Sidney Lumet • *Scr* John Hopkins, from his play *This Story of Yours*

U = SUITABLE FOR ALL   Uc = SUITABLE FOR ALL, ESPECIALLY FOR YOUNG CHILDREN (VIDEO ONLY)   PG = PARENTAL GUIDANCE

Office Space ★★★ 15

Comedy   1999 · US · Colour · 89mins

This unconventional satire of work relationships and office politics comes courtesy of Mike Judge, one of the creators of the far from subtle *Beavis and Butt-head*. The relatively unknown cast is boosted by support from waitress Jennifer Aniston and dreary boss Gary Cole, while the offbeat jokes range from droll references to singer Michael Bolton and *Superman III*, to swipes at restaurant etiquette and office technology. It's not for all tastes, though, and the final third is disappointingly mundane. Contains swearing and sexual references. ▣

Ron Livingston *Peter Gibbons* • Jennifer Aniston *Joanna* • David Herman *Michael Bolton* • Ajay Naidu *Samir* • Diedrich Bader *Lawrence* • Stephen Root *Milton Waddams* • Gary Cole *Bill Lumbergh* ■ *Dir/Scr* Mike Judge

An Officer and a Gentleman ★★★ 15

Romantic drama
1982 · US · Colour · 118mins

Hugely popular in its day, appealing to the incurable, brainless romantic in all of us, this is a highly manipulative mixture of boot camp is good for you and every girl loves a uniform. More sophisticated thoughts on human relationships form no part of Taylor Hackford's glossy hymn to overcoming a trailer-park background. Richard Gere looks a treat in his pristine white togs, and gives a performance more wooden than a wardrobe. Not even the combined talents of Debra Winger and Louis Gossett Jr can turn this one into a great movie, but if you're in the mood for a wallow, it's perfect. Contains some violence, swearing, sex scenes and nudity. ▣

Richard Gere *Zack Mayo* • Debra Winger *Paula Pokrifki* • David Keith *Sid Worley* • Robert Loggia *Byron Mayo* • Lisa Blount *Lynette Pomeroy* • Lisa Eilbacher *Casey Seeger* • Louis Gossett Jr *Sergeant Emil Foley* • David Caruso *Topper Daniels* • Grace Zabriskie *Esther Pokrifki* ■ *Dir* Taylor Hackford • *Scr* Douglas Day Stewart

Official Denial ★★ PG

Science-fiction thriller
1993 · US · Colour · 83mins

Erin Gray made her name as Buck Rogers's sidekick in the TV series of the same name. Here she is grounded on Earth in this better than average sci-fi chiller about the possibilities of alien life. Parker Stevenson is the victim of an alien kidnapping who is pressed into service by the military when they capture their own ET. It is directed with some intelligence and perception by Brian Trenchard-Smith. ▣

Parker Stevenson *Paul Corliss* • Holly Brisley *Dos A* • Serena Dean *Dos B* • Chad Everett *General Kenneth Spalding* • Dirk Benedict *Lt Col Dan Lerner* • Erin Gray *Annie Corliss* • Michael Pate *Wisdomkeeper* • Christopher Pate *Sam Fools Crow* ■ *Dir* Brian Trenchard-Smith • *Scr* Bryce Zabel

The Official Version ★★★★ 15

Drama   1985 · Arg · Colour · 109mins

The winner of the Oscar for best foreign film, this is the compelling story of a history teacher whose acquiescence in the military regime in Argentina is shaken when she begins to suspect she has adopted the child of a "disappeared" couple. It's an impressive effort from Luis Puenzo, who made his name directing commercials, that uses Norma Aleandro's credible conversion and the dignified determination of the ever-vigilant women of the Plaza del Mayo to make its political points. As much a treatise on the sacred trust of motherhood as a plea for human rights, this subtly impassioned drama is both persuasive and uplifting. In Spanish with English subtitles. ▣

Hector Alterio *Roberto* • Norma Aleandro *Alicia* • Chela Ruiz *Sara* • Chunchuna Villafane *Ana* ■ *Dir* Luis Puenzo • *Scr* Aida Bortnik, Luis Puenzo

Oh Dad, Poor Dad, Mama's Hung You in the Closet and I'm Feelin' So Sad ★

Comedy   1967 · US · Colour · 86mins

Rosalind Russell plays the horrendously awful, dominating mother of Robert Morse who is a worthless, emasculated creep. Morse's father, Jonathan Winters, is dead, murdered by Russell and stored in a coffin, but his ghost emerges on occasion to narrate the story. Barbara Harris is a sort of sex maniac who drives Morse so crazy with desire that he turns into Norman Bates. With its touches of *Psycho* and *Lolita*, this black comedy about all-American "momism" is very much a product of its time, though it bombed in 1967.

Rosalind Russell *Madame Rosepettle* • Robert Morse *Jonathan* • Barbara Harris *Rosalie* • Hugh Griffith *Commodore Roseabove* • Jonathan Winters *Dad/Narrator* • Lionel Jeffries *Airport commander* ■ *Dir* Richard Quine, Alexander Mackendrick • *Scr* Ian Bernard, Pat McCormick, Herbert Baker, from the play by Arthur L Kopit

Oh Daddy! ★★

Comedy drama   1935 · UK · BW · 77mins

Stage star Leslie Henson takes the title role in this cheeky farce, which typifies the kind of bawdy music-hall humour producer Michael Balcon brought to so many of his screen comedies. Henson is a puritanical toff whose conservative values are put to the test during a night in London, but the inimitable Robertson Hare (as his shockable sidekick) wins several scenes on points. A touch of seedy glamour is provided by Frances Day as Henson's showgirl stepdaughter, but Austin Melford's script is very tame by today's standards.

Leslie Henson *Lord Pye* • Frances Day *Benita de Lys* • Robertson Hare *Rupert Boddy* • Barry MacKay *Jimmy Ellison* • Marie Lohr *Lady Pye* • Alfred Drayton *Uncle Samson* ■ *Dir* Graham Cutts, Austin Melford • *Scr* Austin Melford, from his play

Oh, God! ★★★★ PG

Comedy   1977 · US · Colour · 93mins

A very, very funny original, which, together with *The Sunshine Boys*, revitalised the career of cigar-chomping veteran comedian George Burns. He plays the Almighty, visiting Earth to seek a messenger to convey to an indifferent world that He is still around, and choosing a supermarket assistant manager for the task (the perfectly cast country singer John Denver). Skilled comedy director Carl Reiner works wonders with this material, which in other hands could have turned out extremely tasteless. Teri Garr and Ralph Bellamy provide wonderful support, and the whole has a marvellous feelgood quality to it. ▣

George Burns *God* • John Denver *Jerry Landers* • Teri Garr *Bobbie Landers* • Donald Pleasence *Dr Harmon* • Ralph Bellamy *Sam Raven* • William Daniels *George Summers* ■ *Dir* Carl Reiner • *Scr* Larry Gelbart, from the novel by Avery Corman

Oh, God! You Devil ★★ 15

Comedy   1984 · US · Colour · 91mins

A third heavenly outing for veteran vaudevillian George Burns, here playing both the Almighty and his Satanic counterpart, the Devil. The *Faust*-like plot reveals a lack of ideas and John Doolittle is not as affable a leading man as John Denver in the first of the series, but Burns is, nevertheless, remarkably watchable. Contains swearing. ▣

George Burns *God/The Devil* • Ted Wass *Bobby Shelton* • Ron Silver *Gary Frantz* • Roxanne Hart *Wendy Shelton* • Eugene Roche *Charlie Gray* • Robert Desiderio *Billy Wayne* ■ *Dir* Paul Bogart • *Scr* Andrew Bergman

Oh God! Book II ★ PG

Comedy   1980 · US · Colour · 89mins

Directed with cloying sentimentality by Gilbert Cates, this vulgar follow-up should have spawned a new aphorism – never work with children or deities. The combination of George Burns growling out street-preacher wisdom and Louanne burbling kiddie banalities is enough to drive saints to sin. It's a neat idea to have God ask a troubled schoolgirl to spearhead an advertising campaign to prove He's alive and well. The script needs to contain more wit and insight, however, if such a slender concept is going to amuse and inspire. ▣

George Burns *God* • Suzanne Pleshette *Paula* • David Birney *Don* • Louanne *Tracy* • John Louie *Shingo* • Conrad Janis *Mr Benson* • Dr Joyce Brothers • Wilfrid Hyde White *Judge Miller* ■ *Dir* Gilbert Cates • *Scr* Josh Greenfeld, Hal Goldman, Fred S Fox, Seaman Jacobs, Melissa Miller, from a story by Josh Greenfeld

Oh, Heavenly Dog! ★★ PG

Comedy   1980 · US · Colour · 98mins

Silly comedy, with Chevy Chase as a private investigator who's murdered, then comes back as a dog to sniff out his killer. If the plot gives you paws for thought, ponder this too: canine lead Benji was already a dog star in his own right, with two other films under his collar. Oddly, this film was shot in England, with a "local" support cast

that includes Jane Seymour, Robert Morley and Omar Sharif. Kids will like the cute stuff, whereas grown-ups will find it all rather tiresome. ▣

Chevy Chase *Benjamin Browning* • Jane Seymour *Jackie Howard* • Omar Sharif *Malcolm Bart* • Robert Morley *Bernie* • Alan Sues *Freddie* • Donnelly Rhodes *Montanero* • Barbara Leigh-Hunt *Margaret* ■ *Dir* Joe Camp • *Scr* Rob Browning, Joe Camp

Oh, Men! Oh, Women! ★★★ U

Comedy   1957 · US · Colour · 90mins

David Niven stars in this slightly farcical comedy but it's successful Broadway actor Tony Randall, making his screen debut, who runs away with director/writer Nunnally Johnson's movie. Niven is a psychiatrist about to be married to screwball Barbara Rush, who's proud of how he manages to keep his personal and professional lives completely separate. Then he learns that Dan Dailey, the husband of his patient Ginger Rogers, is making a play for his fiancée, a situation topped by another patient (Randall), when he reveals his current amour as the same girl. Adapted from a successful play by Edward Chodorov (blacklisted under McCarthy and uncredited), the movie has its longueurs, but takes enough sideswipes at psychiatrists to provide a modicum of fun.

Ginger Rogers *Mildred Turner* • David Niven *Dr Alan Coles* • Dan Dailey *Arthur Turner* • Barbara Rush *Myra Hagerman* • Tony Randall *Cobbler* ■ *Dir* Nunnally Johnson • *Scr* Nunnally Johnson, from the play by Edward Chodorov

Oh, Mr Porter! ★★★★ U

Comedy   1937 · UK · BW · 80mins

This is easily the funniest film Will Hay made with his willing stooges Moore Marriott and Graham Moffatt. As the incompetent master of a tumbledown Irish railway station, Hay is at his blustering best, whether trying to bring the facilities into the 20th century or curtailing the scrounging schemes of his cohorts. In addition to the endlessly inventive comic quips, there is also plenty of action, as the trio takes on a gang of gunrunners, with the final chase particularly entertaining. ▣

Will Hay *William Porter* • Moore Marriott *Jeremiah Harbottle* • Graham Moffatt *Albert Brown* • Sebastian Smith *Charles Trimbletow* • Agnes Lauchlan *Mrs Trimbletow* ■ *Dir* Marcel Varnel • *Scr* JOC Orton, Val Guest, Marriott Edgar, from a story by Frank Launder

Oh, Rosalinda!! ★★★★ U

Musical   1955 · UK · Colour · 100mins

A splendidly original British musical, an update of the Strauss opera *Die Fledermaus*, set in postwar Vienna, though clearly based at Elstree Studios, with a marvellous international cast obviously enjoying itself under co-directors Michael Powell and Emeric Pressburger. Time has been kind to this stylish exercise, which was derided on its first release. Michael Redgrave and Ludmilla Tcherina are the stars, with support from Anton Walbrook and Mel Ferrer, and if you watch closely you might spot

director John Schlesinger in uniform in a jeep.

Michael Redgrave *Colonel Eisenstein* • Ludmilla Tcherina *Rosalinda* • Anton Walbrook *Dr Falke* • Mel Ferrer *Captain Westerman* • Dennis Price *Major Frank* • Anthony Quayle *General Orlofsky* ■ *Dir* Michael Powell, Emeric Pressburger • *Scr* Michael Powell, Emeric Pressburger, from the opera *Die Fledermaus* by Johann Strauss

Oh! What a Lovely War ★★★★ PG

First World War musical satire
1969 · UK · Colour · 136mins

Based on Joan Littlewood's stage production, Richard Attenborough's first film as a director is a stylised, satirical and ultimately moving tribute to the soldiers who answered their country's call and fought in the Great War. An all-star cast perform the original's jingoistic music hall songs, which Attenborough cleverly stages in the Brighton Pavilion and on the old pier. While there was animosity behind the scenes – Len Deighton refused screen credit as the film's writer – this remains a distinctive piece of work and by far the most audacious film Attenborough has ever made. ▭

Dirk Bogarde *Stephen* • Phyllis Calvert *Lady Haig* • Jean-Pierre Cassel *French Colonel* • John Clements *General Von Molke* • John Gielgud *Count Berchtold* • Jack Hawkins *Emperor Franz Joseph* • Kenneth More *Kaiser Wilhelm II* • Laurence Olivier *Field Marshal Sir John French* • Michael Redgrave *General Sir Henry Wilson* • Vanessa Redgrave *Sylvia Pankhurst* • Ralph Richardson *Sir Edward Grey* • Maggie Smith *Music hall star* • Susannah York *Eleanor* • John Mills *Sir Douglas Haig* • Ian Holm *President Poincaré* • Paul Daneman *Tsar Nicholas II* • Joe Melia *Photographer* • Mary Wimbush *Mary Smith* • Wendy Allnutt *Flo Smith* • Corin Redgrave *Bertie Smith* • Maurice Roëves *George Smith* • Angela Thorne *Betty Smith* ■ *Dir* Richard Attenborough • *Scr* Len Deighton (uncredited), from the stage musical, from the play *The Long, Long Trail* by Charles Chilton

Oh, What a Night ★★★ 15

Romantic comedy
1992 · Can · Colour · 87mins

This is a familiar enough rites-of-passage tale: at the end of the fifties, Corey Haim is a troubled teenager who moves to the country with his father and stepmother and begins an affair with an older woman (Barbara Williams). Although director Eric Till overdoes the golden hue shots of the countryside, he brings a rare perception and wry sense of humour to the action. Our own Robbie Coltrane pops up as Haim's confidant, and there's a great soundtrack. Contains brief nudity. ▭

Corey Haim *Eric* • Robbie Coltrane *Todd* • Barbara Williams *Vera* • Keir Dullea *Thorvald* • Geneviève Bujold *Eva* ■ *Dir* Eric Till • *Scr* Richard Nielsen

O'Hara's Wife ★★

Fantasy drama 1982 · US · Colour · 87mins

This comedy drama, one of a string of reassuring family movies Ed Asner made after TV's *Lou Grant* was axed, features a care-worn widower whose life, particularly his relationship with his children, improves after his dead wife comes back to haunt him.

Undemanding, with a warm message and plenty of familiar faces in the cast, including Jodie Foster and Tom Bosley from *Happy Days*.

Edward Asner [Ed Asner] *Bob O'Hara* • Mariette Hartley *Harry O'Hara* • Jodie Foster *Barbara O'Hara* • Tom Bosley *Fred O'Hara* • Perry Lang *Rob O'Hara* ■ *Dir* William S Bartman • *Scr* James Nasella, William S Bartman, from a story by William S Bartman, Joseph Scott Kierland

Oh, You Beautiful Doll ★★★ U

Musical biography
1949 · US · Colour · 93mins

Broadway star, and later one of America's favourite raconteurs, George Jessel achieved some success later in his career as a producer of a series of colourful vaudeville-based light musicals at 20th Century-Fox. This is a typical example of what were superbly glossy star vehicles: a treasure trove of popular songs, in what is the alleged biography of little-known popular composer Fred Fisher. Fisher is not portrayed by the star of this movie, Mark Stevens, but by the wonderful character actor SZ "Cuddles" Sakall, whose delightful hamming is always watchable.

June Haver *Doris Breitenbach* • Mark Stevens *Larry Kelly* • SZ Sakall *Fred Fisher* • Charlotte Greenwood *Anna Breitenbach* • Gale Robbins *Marie Carle* • Jay C Flippen *Lippy Brannigan* ■ *Dir* John M Stahl • *Scr* Albert Lewis, Arthur Lewis

Oil for the Lamps of China ★★★

Drama 1935 · US · Colour · 104mins

A minor, but still very watchable, example of the sort of social message melodrama in which Warner Bros specialised in the early thirties. Although he delivers his lines with the finesse and intonation of a cattle auctioneer, Pat O'Brien gives a fair impression of the little man who is prepared to sacrifice everything for a company that has given him nothing in return. Hampered by the patchiness of the script, director Mervyn LeRoy still maintains the cracking pace appropriate to O'Brien's lung-busting style.

Pat O'Brien *Stephen Chase* • Josephine Hutchinson *Hester Chase* • Jean Muir *Alice Wellman* • John Eldredge *Don Wellman* • Lyle Talbot *Jim* • Arthur Byron *Ross* • Henry O'Neill *Hartford* • Donald Crisp *MacCargar* ■ *Dir* Mervyn LeRoy • *Scr* Laird Doyle, from the novel by Alice Tisdale Hobart

O-Kay for Sound ★★★

Comedy 1937 · UK · BW · 86mins

The much-loved Crazy Gang wreak their own particular brand of chaos in this breathless comedy in which they play extras who are mistaken for movie moguls and bring production to a grinding halt. Unsurprisingly, it's Flanagan and Allen who catch the eye, but the Gang's other troublesome twosomes, Nervo and Knox and Naughton and Gold, chip in to good effect. Will Hay's regular backroom staff, writers Marriott Edgar and Val Guest, provide the ammunition, while director Marcel Varnel keeps the gags

coming thick and fast. It has worn a little thin, but it's fun all the same.

Jimmy Nervo • Bud Flanagan [Dennis O'Keefe] • Chesney Allen • Teddy Knox • Charlie Naughton • Jimmy Gold ■ *Dir* Marcel Varnel • *Scr* Marriott Edgar, Val Guest

Oklahoma! ★★★★ U

Musical 1955 · US · Colour · 145mins

The film version of the massively influential and, in its day, revolutionary Rodgers and Hammerstein Broadway musical preserves both the magnificent songs and the key Agnes DeMille choreography. Heading the notable cast is the under-rated Gordon MacRae as a finely shaded romantic Curly, while Shirley Jones, in her film debut, is superb as Laurey. If Rod Steiger is a shade morose and out of kilter, well, so is his character Jud Fry. Trouble is, director Fred Zinnemann can't quite manage the pizzazz the movie really needs, and seriously messes up the stirring title number. Nevertheless, there's much to be thankful for. ▭

Gordon MacRae *Curly* • Shirley Jones *Laurey* • Rod Steiger *Jud Fry* • Gloria Grahame *Ado Annie* • Gene Nelson *Will Parker* • Eddie Albert *Ali Hakim* • James Whitmore *Carnes* • Barbara Lawrence *Gertie* • Jay C Flippen *Skidmore* ■ *Dir* Fred Zinnemann • *Scr* Sonya Levien, William Ludwig, from the musical by Richard Rodgers, Oscar Hammerstein Ii, from the play *Green Grow the Lilacs* by Lynn Riggs

Oklahoma Crude ★★

Drama 1973 · US · Colour · 112mins

If ever a movie ran out of steam it's this one. Sumptuously produced and directed by Stanley Kramer on a high budget, it boasts terrific production values (though weak special effects work) and a fine cast led by Faye Dunaway and George C Scott at their respective ripsnorting bests. But once the oil gushers have gushed there's precious little plot or characterisation left, only the vicious Jack Palance, determined to wrest Faye's lone oil well from her.

George C Scott *Noble "Mase" Mason* • Faye Dunaway *Lena Doyle* • John Mills *Cleon Doyle* • Jack Palance *Hellman* • William Lucking *Marion* • Harvey Jason *Wilcox* ■ *Dir* Stanley Kramer • *Scr* Marc Norman

The Oklahoma Kid ★★★ U

Western 1939 · US · BW · 77mins

Warner Bros achieved hit-and-miss results with its thirties westerns, often making cowboy versions of its gangster movies. This film is no exception and no less effective for its unbelievable casting because the outlaw hero is played by none other than New York's own James Cagney, strapping on his six-guns and singing like the best of them. The villain is snarling Humphrey Bogart, and there's a lot of pleasure to be had from watching Bogie and Cagney out west. The plot is that old western stand-by about trying to find out who was responsible for the death of the hero's father, but the two knockout leads certainly make it fun. ▭

James Cagney *Jim Kincaid/"Oklahoma Kid"* • Humphrey Bogart *Whip McCord* • Rosemary Lane *Jane Hardwick* • Donald Crisp *Judge Hardwick* • Harvey Stephens *Ned Kincaid* • Hugh Sothern *John Kincaid* • Charles

Middleton *Alec Martin* ■ *Dir* Lloyd Bacon • *Scr* Warren Duff, Robert Buckner, Edward E Paramore, from a story by Edward E Paramore, Wally Klein

The Oklahoma Woman ★★

Western 1956 · US · BW · 71mins

Roger Corman will always be remembered for his cult horror films, but the B-movie maestro was also prepared to dabble in other genres and this was one of four low-budget westerns he made for the drive-in market. Richard Denning is the reformed gunfighter who lines up against an old flame, the villainous Peggie Castle, when he falls for nice girl Cathy Downs. Corman assembles his usual eclectic cast but he shows little feel for the western genre and the lack of production money doesn't help.

Richard Denning *Steve Ward* • Peggie Castle *Marie "Oklahoma" Saunders* • Cathy Downs *Susan Grant* • Tudor Owen *Ed Grant* ■ *Dir* Roger Corman • *Scr* Lou Rusoff

The Oklahoman ★★ U

Western 1957 · US · Colour · 79mins

This minor western features a too-old Joel McCrea in the lead and next to nothing spent on a wardrobe for leading lady Barbara Hale (Della Street from TV's *Perry Mason*). The screenplay's nothing either, as McCrea befriends an Indian (Australian actor Michael Pate from *Hondo*) and upsets some townies. Director Francis D Lyon was a superb editor (*Rembrandt, Things to Come, Body and Soul*) but turned into a truly mediocre director.

Joel McCrea *Dr John Brighton* • Barbara Hale *Anne Barnes* • Brad Dexter *Cass Dobie* • Gloria Talbott *Maria Smith* • Verna Felton *Mrs Waynebrook* • Douglas Dick *Mel Dobie* • Michael Pate *Charlie Smith* ■ *Dir* Francis D Lyon • *Scr* Daniel B Ullman

Okoge ★★★

Drama 1992 · Jap · Colour · 120mins

With its title deriving from the Japanese for "fag hag" and the inclusion of a drag queen chorus, this refreshingly non-judgemental, gay variation on *The Apartment* caused uproar on its original release because of its frank discussion of a still-taboo topic and its provocatively graphic eroticism. Combining acerbic social commentary with camp comedy, director Takehiro Nakajima slickly establishes the unconventional menage constituted when Misha Shimizu offers the use of her bed to Takehiro Murata and his married salaryman lover. However, when outsiders intrude upon their idyll, the plot spirals out of control and the resolution is messily unsatisfactory. A Japanese language film.

Misa Shimizu *Sayoko* • Takehiro Murata *Goh* • Takeo Nakahara *Tochi* ■ *Dir/Scr* Takehiro Nakajima

Old Acquaintance ★★★

Drama 1943 · US · BW · 110mins

One of the great Bette Davis Warner Bros melodramas, reteaming her with Miriam Hopkins. The two stars battle it out as a pair of childhood friends who become lifelong literary rivals – art starts to imitate life and the

resonances are plain to see, and enjoy, on screen. The unsympathetic Hopkins has a tough time holding the screen against Davis, but director Vincent Sherman ensures that the scenery chewing is kept to a minimum. The subplot involving Hopkins's grown-up offspring Dolores Moran is less than intriguing, but thankfully the rivals return to a verbal slanging match at the end.

Bette Davis *Kitty Marlowe* • Miriam Hopkins *Millie Drake* • Gig Young *Rudd Kendall* • John Loder *Preston Drake* • Dolores Moran *Deirdre* • Philip Reed *Lucian Grant* ■ *Dir* Vincent Sherman • *Scr* John Van Druten, Lenore Coffee, from the play by John Van Druten

Old Bones of the River
★★ PG

Comedy	1938 · UK · BW · 86mins

This muddled lampoon at the expense of the colonial service completed a decidedly disappointing 1938 for Will Hay. Although the film reunited him with regular stooges Moore Marriott and Graham Moffatt, it was a rather uninspired spoof of the old Edgar Wallace story *Sanders of the River*, with the scriptwriters struggling to combine a worthwhile storyline with the endless stream of music-hall gags, some of which were so old they'd failed to amuse Queen Victoria. However, they are infinitely more preferable to the racist remarks, which are simply unacceptable today. ▭

Will Hay *Prof Benjamin Tibbetts* • Moore Marriott *Jerry Harbottle* • Graham Moffatt *Albert* • Robert Adams *Bosambo* • Jack Livesey *Capt Hamilton* • Jack London *M'Bapi* • Wyndham Goldie *Commissioner Sanders* ■ *Dir* Marcel Varnel • *Scr* Marriott Edgar, Val Guest, JOC Orton, from the stories by Edgar Wallace

Old Boyfriends
★★

Comedy drama	1979 · US · Colour · 102mins

It should have worked, but somehow it doesn't. Talia Shire plays a clinical psychologist who, after a botched suicide attempt, goes on the trail of her past relationships. John Belushi and Keith Carradine are just two of the old beaux she meets up with in this lukewarm comedy drama. It marked the feature debut of Joan Tewkesbury, writer of *Nashville*, and was scripted by Paul and Leonard Schrader – which only goes to show that good pedigrees do not always a great movie make.

Talia Shire *Diane Cruise* • Richard Jordan *Jeff Turrin* • John Belushi *Eric Katz* • Keith Carradine *Wayne Van Til* • John Houseman *Dr Hoffman* • Buck Henry *Art Kopple* • Bethel Leslie *Mrs Van Til* • Joan Hotchkis *Pamela Shaw* ■ *Dir* Joan Tewkesbury • *Scr* Paul Schrader, Leonard Schrader

The Old Curiosity Shop
★★★ U

Drama	1934 · UK · BW · 91mins

A maligned adaptation of Dickens's tale of the destitute storekeeper and his granddaughter, Little Nell, who are forced to endure the hardship of the road after being terrorised by the monstrous money-lender, Quilp. Director Thomas Bentley was a former Dickens impersonator on the stage and had already filmed several silent versions of his novels. Here he does a

commendable job of condensing the sprawling story, although his direction is occasionally lacklustre. Ben Webster and Elaine Benson make tolerably troubled Trents, but the film belongs to Hay Petrie, whose Quilp is the embodiment of evil. ▭

Ben Webster *Grandfather Trent* • Elaine Benson *Nell Trent* • Hay Petrie *Quilp* • Beatrix Thompson *Mrs Quilp* • Gibb McLaughlin *Sampson Brass* • Lily Long *Sally Brass* • Reginald Purdell *Dick Swiveller* • Polly Ward *Marchioness* • James Harcourt *Single gentleman* ■ *Dir* Thomas Bentley • *Scr* Margaret Kennedy, Ralph Neale, from the novel by Charles Dickens

The Old Dark House
★★★★ PG

Comedy horror	1932 · US · BW · 69mins

Splendidly screwball ghoulish nonsense based on JB Priestley's *Benighted*, played in a high style by a cast to die for. It's directed by that master of camp horror, James Whale. British actors Charles Laughton and Boris Karloff are magnificent, and Melvyn Douglas is both suitably suave and alternately puzzled. Gloria Stuart is the young female lead, while Ernest Thesiger and Raymond Massey add to the fun. ▭

Boris Karloff *Morgan* • Melvyn Douglas *Roger Penderel* • Charles Laughton *Sir William Porterhouse* • Gloria Stuart *Margaret Waverton* • Lillian Bond *Gladys Ducane* • Ernest Thesiger *Horace Femm* • Eva Moore *Rebecca Femm* • Raymond Massey *Philip Waverton* • Brember Wills *Saul Femm* • John Dudgeon [Elspeth Dudgeon] *Sir Roderick Femm* ■ *Dir* James Whale • *Scr* Benn W Levy, RC Sherriff, from the novel *Benighted* by JB Priestley

Old Enough
★★ PG

Drama	1984 · US · Colour · 91mins

The sort of film that Jodie Foster would have been perfect in (before she grew up, that is) stars Rainbow Harvest (were her parents hippies, do you think?) and Sarah Boyd as two young girls from the opposite ends of the social scale who strike up an unlikely friendship. Harvest is the girl from the wrong side of the tracks; Boyd is a rich, 12-year-old New Yorker.

Sarah Boyd *Lonnie Sloan* • Rainbow Harvest *Karen Bruckner* • Neill Barry *Johnny* • Danny Aiello *Bruckner* ■ *Dir/Scr* Marisa Silver

The Old-Fashioned Way
★★★★ U

Comedy	1934 · US · BW · 71mins

In one of WC Fields's greatest comedies, based on his own story, he appears as the one and only Great McGonigle. He's an impecunious impresario heading a travelling vaudeville troupe, outwitting landladies and writ-servers, putting on a full performance of the wheezy vintage melodrama *The Drunkard* and even finding time for his juggling routines. In addition, he conducts a running battle with Baby LeRoy – with the nipper inflicting the most damage. William Beaudine's direction gives it a more polished look than many of Fields's other comedies.

WC Fields *The Great McGonigle* • Judith Allen *Betty McGonigle* • Joe Morrison *Wally Livingston* • Jan Duggan *Cleopatra Pepperday* • Nora Cecil *Mrs Wendelschaffer* • Baby

LeRoy *Albert Wendelschaffer* • Jack Mulhall *Dick Bronson* • Tammany Young *Marmaduke Gump* ■ *Dir* William Beaudine • *Scr* Garnett Weston, Jack Cunningham, from a story by Charles Bogle [WC Fields]

Old Gringo
★★★ 15

Historical drama
1989 · US · Colour · 115mins

This adaptation of Carlos Fuentes's acclaimed novel is meticulously staged, played with great conviction and studiously faithful to the psychological and historical complexities of the original. The only problem is that it is just a tad dull. Set in Mexico at the time of Pancho Villa's uprising, it skirts around the political issues and takes the easy way out by concentrating on the romance that develops between Jane Fonda's wayward traveller and Jimmy Smits's revolutionary leader. Gregory Peck steals every scene he's in as the American journalist and author Ambrose Bierce. Contains swearing. ▭

Jane Fonda *Harriet Winslow* • Gregory Peck *Ambrose Bierce* • Jimmy Smits *Arroyo* • Patricio Contreras *Colonel Frutos Garcia* • Jenny Gago *La Garduna* • Jim Metzler *Ron* • Gabriela Roel *La Luna* • Anne Pitoniak *Mrs Winslow* • Pedro Armendariz Jr *Pancho Villa* ■ *Dir* Luis Puenzo • *Scr* Aida Bortnik, Luis Puenzo, from the novel *Gringo Viejo* by Carlos Fuentes

The Old Lady Who Walked in the Sea
★★★ 18

Comedy	1991 · Fr · Colour · 90mins

As the haughty con artist seeking to pass on the tricks of her trade, that *grande dame* of French cinema, Jeanne Moreau, gives a much better performance than this slight comedy really deserves. Although Michel Serrault stooges selflessly as her loyal partner, Moreau is badly let down by the feebleness of Luc Thuillier, as the beach baby she nominates as her protégé. However, Moreau's ebullience carries much of the action, whether she is trading curses with Serrault, fawning on the young Thuillier or delighting in the ingenuity of her scams, and she thoroughly merited her César award. In French with English subtitles. Contains swearing, sex scenes and nudity. ▭

Jeanne Moreau *Lady M* • Michel Serrault *Pompilius* • Luc Thuillier *Lambert* • Géraldine Danon *Noémie* • Marie-Dominique Aumont *Muriel* ■ *Dir* Laurent Heynemann • *Scr* Dominique Roulet, from the novel *La Vieille Qui Marchait dans la Mer* by San Antonio

Old Louisiana
★

Historical adventure drama
1938 · US · BW · 63mins

Former western hero Tom Keene starred in a series of short historical adventures made on a shoestring budget, of which this is a particularly poor specimen. Keene stars as an American living in Louisiana when it was still a Spanish colony. Rejecting outright rebellion against iniquitous taxes, he seeks a peaceful solution, leading to the colony's purchase by the United States. An actress called Rita Cansino plays the daughter of the Spanish governor; after she became famous as Rita Hayworth, the film was

relaunched as *Louisiana Gal*, giving her top billing under her new name.

Tom Keene [Richard Powers] • Rita Cansino [Rita Hayworth] *Dona Angela Gonzalez* • Will Morgan *Steve* • Robert Fiske *Luke E Gilmore* ■ *Dir* Irvin Willat • *Scr* Mary Ireland, from a story by John T Neville

The Old Maid
★★★★ U

Drama	1939 · US · BW · 90mins

A wonderful slice of melodramatic soap opera that froths and crackles with gloriously histrionic performances. This is Bette Davis at her best as an unmarried mother whose unsuspecting daughter prefers the company of Davis's deeply Machiavellian sister Miriam Hopkins. Davis and Hopkins spar like a pair of theatrical prizefighters rising from the last knock-out punch to reel around the set, shake the sweat from their brows and come back for more. The period setting provides the perfect costumes to accompany all the trouncing and flouncing. Never a dull moment. ▭

Bette Davis *Charlotte Lovell* • Miriam Hopkins *Delia Lovell Ralston* • George Brent *Clem Spender* • Jane Bryan *Tina* • Donald Crisp *Dr Lanskell* ■ *Dir* Edmund Goulding • *Scr* Casey Robinson, from the play by Zoë Akins, from the novel by Edith Wharton

The Old Man and the Sea
★★★ U

Drama	1958 · US · Colour · 86mins

Spencer Tracy is Ernest Hemingway's obsessed angler, riding the Caribbean with macho rubbish in his head and a giant marlin on the line. Inconsistent use of back projection and a certain monotony to the fishing sequences are serious drawbacks, but Tracy is tremendous, capturing the simple humanity and heroism of the central character and nearly capturing an Oscar as well. Director John Sturges, who took over the project after Fred Zinnemann had laboured for months on it, was later to retire from picture-making and live Hemingway's idealised life for real, sailing his fishing sloop between Mexico and Hawaii until his death in 1992.

Spencer Tracy *Old Man* • Felipe Pazos *Boy* • Harry Bellaver *Martin* ■ *Dir* John Sturges • *Scr* Peter Viertel, from the novella by Ernest Hemingway

The Old Man and the Sea
★★

Drama	1990 · UK · Colour · 93mins

This is a well-intentioned but mediocre adaptation of Ernest Hemingway's Pulitzer Prize-winning novella about a Cuban fisherman who finally lands a mighty marlin. Anthony Quinn gives a layered performance as the embattled protagonist despite the difficult-to-film subject matter. Quinn's family members populate this remake of the 1958 film, which starred Spencer Tracy (a hard act to follow).

Anthony Quinn *Santiago* • Patricia Clarkson *Mary* • Gary Cole *Tom* • Francesco Quinn *Santiago as a young man* • Valentina Quinn *Angela* • Joe Santos *Innkeeper* ■ *Dir* Jud Taylor • *Scr* Roger Hirson, from the novella by Ernest Hemingway

Old Man Rhythm ★★★ U
Musical comedy   1935 · US · BW · 74mins

It's as lightweight as tissue paper but music buffs and film collectors still shouldn't miss this treat, which features a very young Betty Grable, and a rare appearance by the great songwriter Johnny Mercer as a college boy (he's the one on the train, with the southern accent). Watch out, too, for Lucille Ball. The plot, surprisingly, does have some relevance to its title, as George Barbier plays a businessman who goes back to college to keep a stern paternal eye on his playboy son, Charles "Buddy" Rogers, who is way too old for the part. None of this matters, though: the songs are excellent and the college lads and girls are charming. ●

Charles "Buddy" Rogers *Johnny Roberts* • George Barbier *John Roberts Sr* • Barbara Kent *Edith* • Grace Bradley *Marion* • Betty Grable *Sylvia* • Eric Blore *Phillips* • Johnny Mercer *Colonel* • Lucille Ball *College girl* ■ *Dir* Edward Ludwig • *Scr* Sig Herzig, Ernest Pagano, HW Hanemann, from a story by Lewis Gensler, Sidg Herzig, Don Hartman • *Music/Lyrics* Johnny Mercer, Lewis Gensler

Old Mother Riley in Paris ★★ U
Comedy   1938 · UK · BW · 78mins

Arthur Lucan first created the part of Old Mother Riley on the music hall stage with his own wife Kitty McShane in the part of the dotty dame's daughter. Here they find themselves in Paris in order to rescue Kitty's fiancé who has become involved with a spy ring after fleeing to avoid his future mother-in-law. There are jokes about steak puddings, hospital wards, planes, parachutes, illegal entries and the French language that were antiques even back in 1938, although the scene in which the befrocked Lucan beats up a male dancer has its moments. ●

Arthur Lucan *Mrs Riley* • Kitty McShane *Kitty Riley* • Jerry Verno *Joe* • Magda Kun *Mme Zero* ■ *Dir* Oswald Mitchell • *Scr* Con West

Old Scores ★★★
Sports drama 1991 · UK/NZ · Colour · 93mins

Co-produced by HTV Wales and New Zealand's South Pacific Pictures, this odd little rugby drama is a well played, if rather preachy, look at the re-match of a Wales–All Blacks game discovered to have been fixed 25 years previously. The players have long since scattered between God, drink and all points in between, but Windsor Davies and Glyn Houston round them up and add some necessary gravitas. Lots of famous rugby faces, including Phil Bennett and Gareth Edwards, are also featured. ●

Robert Pugh *Bleddyn Morgan* • Glyn Houston *Aneurin Morgan* • Alison Bruce *Ngaire Morgan* • Clayton Spence *Dai Morgan* • Dafydd Emyr *Owen Llewellyn* • John Francis *David Llewellyn* • Beth Morris *Bronwen Llewellyn* • Windsor Davies *Evan Price* ■ *Dir* Alan Clayton • *Scr* Dean Parker, Greg McGee

An Old Spanish Custom ★★
Comedy   1935 · UK · BW · 61mins

Working with British director Adrian Brunel, this comedy was an incongruous flop for Buster Keaton.

The star of *The General* and *The Navigator* plays Leander Proudfoot, a wealthy yachtsman who sails to Spain. While there, he falls under the spell of scheming siren Lupita Tovar. Pretty miserable stuff, especially when one remembers what the stone-faced genius was capable of when he really put his mind to it.

Buster Keaton *Leander Proudfoot* • Lupita Tovar *Lupita Malez* • Esme Percy *Jose* • Lyn Harding *Gonzalo Gonzalez* • Webster Booth *Serenader* ■ *Dir* Adrian Brunel • *Scr* Edwin Greenwood

Old Yeller ★★★★ U
Drama   1957 · US · Colour · 80mins

A sort of movie equivalent of the country classic *Old Shep*, this epic about man's best friend will not leave a dry eye in the house. This was Walt Disney's first boy-and-his-dog adventure, based on Fred Gipson's homespun bestseller, and despite all the *Savage Sams* and *Big Reds* that followed remains resolutely the best, largely because of sensitive direction from British-born Robert Stevenson. Dorothy McGuire and Fess Parker make an upstanding and sympathetic Texas couple, and the frontier atmosphere is well-recreated, though Tommy Kirk and Kevin Corcoran behave more like 20th- than 19th-century kids. ▭

Dorothy McGuire *Katie Coates* • Fess Parker *Jim Coates* • Tommy Kirk *Travis Coates* • Kevin Corcoran *Arliss Coates* • Jeff York *Bud Searcy* • Beverly Washburn *Lisbeth Searcy* • Chuck Connors *Burn Sanderson* ■ *Dir* Robert Stevenson • *Scr* Fred Gipson, William Tunberg, from the novel by Fred Gipson

The Oldest Profession ★★
Comedy drama
1967 · Fr/It/W Ger · Colour · 97mins

Six vignettes exploring prostitution through the ages, yet only one has cinematic merit. Set in the then distant Y2K, Jean-Luc Godard's encounter between space traveller Jacques Charrier and Anna Karina was intended to be a bold experiment with colour, but the print undermined his efforts by daubing the pre-kiss sequences with a jaundiced yellow. Passing from prehistoric and Roman times to revolutionary and *fin de siècle* France, the other episodes are uninspiring, with Claude Autant-Lara loitering in an ambulance in the Bois de Boulogne, while Philippe de Broca and Michael Pfleghar succeed in making Jeanne Moreau and Raquel Welch seem dull. A French language film.

Michèle Mercier *Brit* • Enrico Maria Salerno *Braque* • Elsa Martinelli *Empress* • Jeanne Moreau *Mimi* • Jean-Claude Brialy *Philibert* • Raquel Welch *Nini* • Nadia Gray *Nadia* • Anna Karina *Miss Conversation* • Jean-Pierre Léaud *Bellboy* ■ *Dir* Franco Indovina, Mauro Bolognini, Philippe de Broca, Michael Pfleghar, Claude Autant-Lara, Jean-Luc Godard • *Scr* Ennio Flaiano, Daniel Boulanger, Georges Tabet, André Tabet, Jean Aurenche, Jean-Luc Godard

Oleanna ★★
Drama   1994 · US/UK · Colour

Exploring the theme of inter-gender power-plays long before Michael Crichton dabbled with it in *Disclosure*, David Mamet's play enraged nearly all

who saw it by forcing them to declare exactly where they stood on the subjects of sexual harassment and political correctness. Even though Mamet opts for a straight filmed record of the stage show, the screen version has markedly less impact, because the intensity of the theatrical experience cannot possibly be re-created, in spite of the spirited performances of William H Macy and Debra Eisenstadt. A work better suited to the stage than the screen, Mamet's film lacks analysis of the issues raised and, for the most part, it fails to involve its audience. Contains violence and swearing.

William H Macy *John* • Debra Eisenstadt *Carol* ■ *Dir* David Mamet • *Scr* David Mamet, from his play

Oliver! ★★★★ U
Musical   1968 · UK · Colour · 139mins

Curiously charmless but immensely popular film version of Lionel Bart's sanitised musical of Charles Dickens's classic novel *Oliver Twist*. Fagin is played by the splendidly cast Ron Moody, top-billed and Oscar-nominated, who brings a certain magnificence to the role he had created on stage. The film collected six Oscars, including best picture and best director (Carol Reed), and there's no denying that the Academy recognition for sound and art direction is well and truly justified. Today, the film works well as a child's introduction to Dickens and adults can enjoy Shani Wallis's Nancy, Onna White's brisk Broadway choreography and the inimitable Harry Secombe's Mr Bumble. ▭

Ron Moody *Fagin* • Oliver Reed *Bill Sikes* • Mark Lester (1) *Oliver* • Harry Secombe *Mr Bumble* • Shani Wallis *Nancy* • Jack Wild *Artful Dodger* • Hugh Griffith *Magistrate* • Sheila White *Bet* • Joseph O'Conor *Mr Brownlow* • Peggy Mount *Widow Corney* • Leonard Rossiter *Mr Sowerberry* • Hylda Baker *Mrs Sowerberry* ■ *Dir* Carol Reed • *Scr* Vernon Harris, from the musical play by Lionel Bart , from the novel *Oliver Twist* by Charles Dickens • *Cinematographer* Oswald Morris • *Production Designer* John Box • *Music/Lyrics* Lionel Bart • *Choreographer* Onna White

Oliver & Company ★★★ U
Animated drama 1988 · US · Colour · 70mins

Disney gives Oliver a new Twist with a Dickens of an animation job. A cute orphan kittycat is drafted into a doggy pack of streetwise New York pickpockets whose human master, Fagin, is up to his ears in debt to Sykes, the city's sinister kingpin of crime. Bette Midler, Billy Joel, Richard "Cheech" Marin, Dom DeLuise and Robert Loggia provide the voices for a nicely told tale that, though a little lacking in Disney's customary charm, still provides fine family entertainment. Don't know what Dickens would have made of it, though. ▭

Joey Lawrence *Oliver* • Bette Midler *Georgette* • Billy Joel *Dodger* • Richard "Cheech" Marin *Tito* • Richard Mulligan *Einstein* • Roscoe Lee Browne *Francis* • Sheryl Lee Ralph *Rita* • Dom DeLuise *Fagin* • Robert Loggia *Sykes* ■ *Dir* George Scribner • *Scr* Jim Cox, Timothy J Disney, James Mangold, suggested by the novel *Oliver Twist* by Charles Dickens

Oliver the Eighth ★★★ U
Comedy   1934 · US · BW · 26mins

Typical Laurel and Hardy high-jinks in this short in which the great double act play a pair of barbers who both write to a rich widow who is advertising for a husband. However, Ollie neglects to post Stan's letter, planning to woo the widow by himself. She has, however, already seen off seven husbands and intends Ollie to be her eighth victim. In some territories the prefix "The Private Life of" was added to the title to mirror that of a hugely successful British film of the period, *The Private Life of Henry VIII* (1933). ▭

Stan Laurel *Stan* • Oliver Hardy *Ollie* • Mae Busch *Eccentric widow at Box 204J* • Jack Barty *Jitters, the butler* ■ *Dir* Lloyd French

Oliver Twist ★★
Silent drama   1922 · US · BW · 74mins

Wonderful lighting and production design, which beautifully evoke Dickensian London, are the saving grace of this otherwise disappointing silent transcription of the classic novel. Lon Chaney is surprisingly ineffectual as Fagin – one of his few performances which fails to satisfy. Jackie Coogan, who plays the title role, had become a phenomenal success the previous year starring with Chaplin in *The Kid* and this was one of the first films he made under a million-dollar contract with MGM. He confessed later that he found Chaney cold and distant, and there is little rapport between them.

Jackie Coogan *Oliver Twist* • Lon Chaney *Fagin* • Gladys Brockwell *Nancy Sikes* • George Siegmann *Bill Sikes* • Edouard Trebaol *Artful Dodger* • Lionel Belmore *Mr Brownlow* • Carl Stockdale *Monks* • Eddie Boland *Toby Crackit* ■ *Dir* Frank Lloyd • *Scr* Frank Lloyd, Harry Weil, Walter Anthony (titles), from the novel by Charles Dickens • *Art Director* Stephen Goosson • *Lighting* Lewis Johnson

Oliver Twist ★★★★★ U
Classic drama   1948 · UK · BW · 110mins

David Lean's masterly adaptation of the Dickens novel brims with unforgettable scenes and performances, notably Alec Guinness's Fagin and Robert Newton's genuinely frightening Bill Sikes. From the opening, with Oliver's mother struggling to the workhouse to give birth, to the climax on the roofs of Docklands, the picture brings the novel vividly to life. The movie caused riots in Germany and was initially banned and then heavily cut in America for its alleged anti-Semitism. ▭ **DVD**

Alec Guinness *Fagin* • Robert Newton *Bill Sikes* • John Howard Davies *Oliver Twist* • Kay Walsh *Nancy* • Anthony Newley *Artful Dodger* • Ralph Truman *Monks* • Francis L Sullivan *Mr Bumble* • Henry Stephenson *Mr Brownlow* • Josephine Stuart *Oliver's mother* • Henry Edwards *Police official* • Diana Dors *Charlotte* • Maurice Denham *Chief of police* ■ *Dir* David Lean • *Scr* David Lean, Stanley Haynes, from the novel by Charles Dickens • *Cinematographer* Guy Green • *Art Director* John Bryan

Oliver Twist ★★★ PG
Drama   1982 · US · Colour · 98mins

Made for American television but released theatrically outside the

States, this umpteenth version of Charles Dickens's famous tale poses no threat to David Lean's definitive British version. It does, however, boast a rumbunctious rasping Fagin played by George C Scott. He alone provides positive reason for viewing. However, director Clive Donner also gets value for money out of a slew of British thespians, notably the perfectly cast Tim Curry, Michael Hordern and Cherie Lunghi, and the screenplay by James Goldman is adult and respectful. English literature the easy way. ▭

George C Scott *Fagin* • Richard Charles *Oliver Twist* • Tim Curry *Bill Sikes* • Michael Hordern *George Brownlow* • Timothy West *Mr Bumble* • Eileen Atkins *Mrs Mann* • Cherie Lunghi *Nancy* • Oliver Cotton *Monks* • Martin Tempest *Artful Dodger* ■ *Dir* Clive Donner • *Scr* James Goldman, from the novel by Charles Dickens

Oliver's Story ★★★
Romantic drama   1978 · US · Colour

The less than successful sequel to schmaltzy *Love Story* has Ryan O'Neal trying to get his life together. The original was a complete one-off which should never have been revisited but even so director John Korty makes a game fist of dealing with the complexities of dating after your loved one's death. O'Neal looks a trifle jaded as well he might (his own personal life was going through several shades of hell at the time) but if you adored the blockbusting first picture you will be fascinated by this.

Ryan O'Neal *Oliver Barrett IV* • Candice Bergen *Marcie Bonwit* • Nicola Pagett *Joanna Stone* • Edward Binns *Phil Cavilleri* • Benson Fong *John Hsiang* • Charles Haid *Stephen Simpson* • Kenneth McMillan *James Francis* • Ray Milland *Mr Barrett* • Josef Sommer *Dr Dienhart* • Swoosie Kurtz *Gwen Simpson* ■ *Dir* John Korty • *Scr* Erich Segal, John Korty, from the novel by Erich Segal

Olivier Olivier ★★★★ 15
Drama   1991 · Fr · Colour · 104mins

Anyone who enjoyed *The Return of Martin Guerre* and its Hollywood remake *Sommersby* will find themselves on familiar ground with this puzzling true-life tale of a runaway who returns. Is Grégoire Colin really the long-lost son of François Cluzet and the mollycoddling Brigitte Roüan, or is he, as his older sister Marina Golovine suspects, an imposter? Set in a rural idyll usually associated with innocence, this is both a mystery story and a disturbingly dark dissection of the modern family. Polish director Agnieszka Holland's persistent prying and the totally credible performances of the dysfunctional foursome make this compelling viewing.

François Cluzet *Serge* • Brigitte Roüan *Elisabeth* • Jean-François Stévenin *Druot* • Grégoire Colin *Olivier* • Marina Golovine *Nadine* ■ *Dir/Scr* Agnieszka Holland

Los Olvidados ★★★★★
Drama   1950 · Mex · BW · 88mins

Luis Buñuel restored his critical reputation with this harsh, almost neorealist, study of street poverty that earned him the best director prize at Cannes in 1951. Shot in only 21 days and brimming with shrewd humanity, this keenly observed film is not without its surreal moments. But for all its political awareness, this is not a blindly liberal portrait of the pitiless crime, sexual corruption and cruel intimidation that is part and parcel of slum life. Society may be culpable for their plight, but Roberto Cobo and Alfonso Mejia, as the two leaders of a gang of boys who wreak havoc on their home town, are by no means saints. In Spanish with English subtitles.

Estela Inda *Mother* • Alfonso Mejia *Pedro* • Roberto Cobo *Jaibo* ■ *Dir* Luis Buñuel • *Scr* Luis Buñuel, Luis Alcoriza • *Cinematographer* Gabriel Figueroa

Olympiad ★★★★
Documentary   1938 · Ger · BW · 225mins

After *Triumph of the Will* (1935), the documentary of the Nuremberg Rally, Leni Riefenstahl was commissioned by Hitler to film the 1936 Berlin Olympics "as a song of praise to the ideals of National Socialism". With over 30 cameramen as well as planes and airships at her disposal, Riefenstahl provided a two-part, near four-hour epic that links the Olympic ideal with that of the Third Reich. But even Riefenstahl couldn't avoid showing the victories of the black American Jesse Owens. Despite the bad taste it leaves in the mouth, one cannot be blind to the exceptional technique and beauty of the film, which many consider one of the greatest documentaries ever made. A German language film.

Dir/Scr Leni Riefenstahl

Omar Khayyam ★★
Period adventure   1957 · US · Colour

There's only a slight inkling in this childish *Arabian Nights* adventure that Omar Khayyam was actually the medieval Persian poet of love and indolence and also a brilliant mathematician and astronomer. First and foremost he's a muscle-flexing, scimitar-swishing Cornel Wilde intent on saving Shah Raymond Massey from murderous foes while hazardously romancing his leader's beloved Debra Paget. Now so preposterously cute, this costume romp is watchably camp.

Cornel Wilde *Omar Khayyam* • Michael Rennie *Hasani* • Debra Paget *Sharain* • John Derek *Prince Malik* • Raymond Massey *Shah of Persia* • Sebastian Cabot *Nizam* • Yma Sumac *Karina* • Margaret Hayes *Zarada* • Joan Taylor *Yaffa* ■ *Dir* William Dieterle • *Scr* Barré Lyndon

Omega Doom ★ 15
Science-fiction thriller   1996 · US · Colour · 80mins

Those familiar with director Albert Pyun's movies will not be surprised by the poor quality of this, or the fact it reworks the premise of a better-known film. This time, Pyun borrows from *Yojimbo* and *A Fistful of Dollars*, updating the basic story to a post-apocalypse future. Rutger Hauer sleepwalks through his role as a mysterious robot who arrives in a ruined amusement park occupied by two robot groups. Dark and dreary, the movie's action sequences are both sporadic and so poorly directed as to be incomprehensible. Contains violence. ▭

Rutger Hauer *Omega Doom* • Shannon Whirry *Zed* • Tina Cote *Blackheart* • Anna Katarina *Bartender* • Norbert Weisser *The Head* • Jill Pierce *Zinc* • Simon Pollard *Zed Too* • Cynthia Ireland *Ironface* ■ *Dir* Albert Pyun • *Scr* Albert Pyun, Ed Naha, from a story by Albert Pyun

The Omega Man ★★★★ PG
Science-fiction thriller   1971 · US · Colour · 93mins

If you're hooked on sci-fi, this is for you – a weirdly engrossing futuristic tale about the world after a viral apocalypse. The conflict between "normals" (led by Charlton Heston) and light-sensitive mutants (led by Anthony Zerbe) is one of science against superstition, and, while lacking the vampiristic teeth of Richard Matheson's novel, it still has an eerie topicality. One of two great science-fiction allegories starring Heston, the other being *Soylent Green*. Contains violence, swearing and brief nudity. ▭

Charlton Heston *Robert Neville* • Anthony Zerbe *Matthias* • Rosalind Cash *Lisa* • Paul Koslo *Dutch* • Lincoln Kilpatrick *Zachary* • Eric Laneuville *Richie* ■ *Dir* Boris Sagal • *Scr* John William Corrington, Joyce H Corrington, from the novel *I Am Legend* by Richard Matheson

The Omen ★★★★ 18
Horror   1976 · US · Colour · 106mins

A big-budget horror blockbuster given class by a distinguished cast (Gregory Peck battling the Antichrist? Whatever next!) and an unsettling atmosphere created by director Richard Donner. Cleverly borrowing a prophecy from the Book of Revelation about Armageddon, scriptwriter David Seltzer fashioned a supernatural terror tale of religious epic proportions. This carries its suspenseful premise with great uneasiness and David Warner's grisly beheading is only one of several remarkably imaginative ghastly deaths. The music, by Jerry Goldsmith, was awarded an Oscar. Contains violence and swearing. ▭

Gregory Peck *Robert Thorn* • Lee Remick *Katherine Thorn* • David Warner *Jennings* • Billie Whitelaw *Mrs Baylock* • Harvey Stevens *Damien* • Leo McKern *Bugenhagen* • Patrick Troughton *Father Brennan* • Martin Benson *Father Spiletto* • Anthony Nichols *Dr Becker* • John Stride *Psychiatrist* ■ *Dir* Richard Donner • *Scr* David Seltzer

Omen IV: the Awakening ★ 15
Horror   1991 · US · Colour · 93mins

A desperate, irrelevant attempt to revive the successful horror series, with an adopted young girl this time attracting death and destruction, much to the worry of her step-parents. The likes of Faye Grant and Michael Lerner do their best with the tired material, but the absence of Damien means this late entry is doomed to failure from the start, and the fact that it was originally made for horror-shy American TV means there is also very little for gore fans to sink their teeth into. ▭

Faye Grant *Karen York* • Michael Woods *Gene York* • Michael Lerner *Earl Knight* • Madison Mason *Dr Hastings* • Ann Hearn *Jo Thueson* • Jim Byrnes *Noah* • Don S Davis *Jake Madison* • Asia Vieira *Delia* • Megan Leitch *Sister Yvonne/Felicity* • Joy Coghill *Sister Francesca* ■ *Dir* Jorge Montesi, Dominique Othenin-Girard • *Scr* Brian Taggert, from a story by Harvey Bernhard, from a story by Brian Taggert, from characters created by David Seltzer

On a Clear Day You Can See Forever ★★★ U
Musical   1970 · US · Colour · 124mins

A great libretto from Alan Jay Lerner is delivered with gusty force by Barbra Streisand as the Brooklyn "goil" who regresses to the 19th century while being hypnotised to stop smoking. Vincente Minnelli could direct these musical heart-twangers with his eyes closed, and it does, indeed, look like he has done just that in some wayward scenes. Yet it is hard to dislike a movie that combines so much talent at full throttle, and features the likes of Yves Montand, Bob Newhart and Jack Nicholson. It is all a bit long-winded, but Minnelli's awesome gifts are deployed in full, especially in the gloriously shot opening sequences. ▭

Barbra Streisand *Daisy Gamble* • Yves Montand *Dr Marc Chabot* • Bob Newhart *Dr Mason Hume* • Larry Blyden *Warren Pratt* • Simon Oakland *Dr Conrad Fuller* • Jack Nicholson *Tad Pringle* • John Richardson *Robert Tentrees* • Pamela Brown *Mrs Fitzherbert* • Irene Handl *Winnie Wainwhisle* • Roy Kinnear *Prince Regent* • John Le Mesurier *Pelham* ■ *Dir* Vincente Minnelli • *Scr* Alan Jay Lerner, from the musical play by Alan Jay Lerner, Burton Lane

On an Island with You ★★★ U
Musical   1948 · US · Colour · 103mins

Former Olympic swimmer Esther Williams proved that not only was she a superb athlete, but with her robust good humour and innate sexiness she was a major musical star. Trouble was, the inevitable swimming sequences placed ridiculous strictures on Esther's plots. Here she plays a movie star, on location in Hawaii, torn between dashing Ricardo Montalban and stalwart Peter Lawford. The production numbers are the thing, though, and, as ever in these musicals, the use of Technicolor is exquisite. Williams made better films either side of this one, but here's much pleasure to be gained from watching this movie.

Esther Williams *Rosalind Reynolds* • Peter Lawford *Lt Larry Kingslee* • Ricardo Montalban *Ricardo Montez* • Jimmy Durante *Buckley* • Cyd Charisse *Yvonne* • Leon Ames *Commander Harrison* • Kathryn Beaumont *Penelope Peabody* • Dick Simmons *George Blaine* ■ *Dir* Richard Thorpe • *Scr* Dorothy Kingsley, Charles Martin, Hans Wilhelm, from a story by Charles Martin, Hans Wilhelm

On Any Sunday ★★★★ U
Documentary   1971 · US · Colour · 82mins

Steve McQueen's love of motorsport existed off screen as well as in films such as *The Great Escape*. So, it's appropriate there should be so much footage of him in this lyrical documentary that celebrates being on two wheels with no speed limit. There are crashes galore – though not for ace Mert Lawwill – and director Bruce Brown, who made the fine surfing movie *The Endless Summer*, clearly exhibits his fascination for motorbiking, showing that road-surfing is just as much fun. And there are no Hell's Angels to bother the eye, even if the

country-and-western soundtrack irritates the ear. It's the speedtrack that's irresistible, though.

Dir Bruce Brown

On Connaît la Chanson ★★★ PG

Musical comedy 1997 · Fr · Colour · 117mins

Versed in the tradition of René Clair and Jacques Demy, Alain Resnais's enjoyable comedy owes its biggest debt to Dennis Potter, as its characters burst into lip-synched song at the least provocation. Polished, sophisticated, yet occasionally obvious, it will most intrigue those with a sound knowledge of French pop music, as the uninitiated not only miss out on the thrill of hearing familiar tunes, but they are also deprived of any socio-cultural significance they possess. However, what fatally undermines the conceit is the slightness of the satire into which the tunes are inserted, as various self-obsessed bourgeois types fall prey to their passions. In French with English subtitles. 🖦

Pierre Arditi *Claude* • Sabine Azéma *Odile Lalande* • Jean-Pierre Bacri *Nicolas* • André Dussollier *Simon* • Agnès Jaoui *Camille Lalande* • Lambert Wilson *Marc Duveyrier* • Jane Birkin *Jane* ■ *Dir* Alain Resnais • *Scr* Agnès Jaoui, Jean-Pierre Bacri

On Dangerous Ground ★★

Drama 1951 · US · BW

Like many a major director, cult auteur Nicholas Ray often did minor work, but even his lesser movies are of interest. This RKO semi-*noir* begins terrifically with a manhunt led by tough cop Robert Ryan displaying a totally unsympathetic, even sadistic, temperament, but then he falls for blind Ida Lupino and goes all gooey against cheap studio backdrops. Nevertheless, the mood is well maintained, boosted by a remarkable score by composer Bernard Herrmann, allegedly his own favourite. Trouble is, it's not nearly grim enough for its subject matter, and ultimately it's all rather silly and boring.

Robert Ryan *Jim Wilson* • Ida Lupino *Mary Malden* • Ward Bond *Walter Brent* • Charles Kemper *Bill Daly* • Anthony Ross *Pete Santos* • Ed Begley *Captain Brawley* ■ *Dir* Nicholas Ray • *Scr* Al Bezzerides, Nicholas Ray, from the novel *Mad with Much Heart* by Gerald Butler • *Music* Bernard Herrmann

On Dangerous Ground ★★ PG

Thriller 1986 · US · Colour · 91mins

If you catch this bizarrely plotted piece of hokum in the right mood, you might find much to enjoy in it. All-American Stephen Collins plays a physicist who takes on an evil industrialist illegally dumping nuclear waste. Using the handy appearance of Halley's Comet, Collins hopes to convert sound waves into a more environmentally friendly source of energy. Filmed on location in Utah by former actor and stunt co-ordinator Chuck Bail, it's not surprising its limited dramatic appeal is significantly broadened by plentiful action and some dazzling aerial sequences. Only the sloppy editing disappoints. 🖦

Stephen Collins *David Lowell* • Janet Julian *Vanessa Pilgrim* • Lance Henriksen *Brook Alistair* • Bo Svenson *Captain* • Victoria Racimo *Rachel* • Nicholas Pryor *John Pilgrim* ■ *Dir* Chuck Bail • *Scr* Sheila Goldberg, Ovidio G Assonitis, Alfonso Brescia, Steve Luotto

On Deadly Ground ★★★ 15

Action adventure 1994 · US · Colour · 96mins

Action star Steven Seagal has always brought a vaguely liberal slant to his no-brain thrillers and his directorial debut is admirably politically correct. It's just a shame that the caring, sharing eco-friendly message tends to overpower what Seagal does best – kicking the stuffing out of bad guys. Here he's a troubleshooter who goes into battle with oil tycoon Michael Caine – hammily over the top and with a scary hairdo to boot – who is about to pollute virtually all of Alaska. Seagal the director shows that he has picked up the odd trick or two from the action specialists who made his name, but his impassioned green speeches will have viewers reaching for the remote control. Contains swearing, violence and nudity. 🖦 **DVD**

Steven Seagal *Forrest Taft* • Michael Caine *Michael Jennings* • Joan Chen *Masu* • John C McGinley *MacGruder* • R Lee Ermey *Stone* • Shari Shattuck *Liles* • Billy Bob Thornton *Homer Carlton* • Richard Hamilton *Hugh Palmer* ■ *Dir* Steven Seagal • *Scr* Ed Horowitz, Robin U Russin

On Fire ★★ 15

Drama 1987 · US · Colour · 83mins

This family drama about an arson investigator who's angry at having to take early retirement (hence the awful pun of the title) is saved only by the convincing performances of John Forsythe (miles from *Dynasty*) and Carroll Baker (light years from *Baby Doll*) as his wife, both of whom make the couple's frustrations eminently believable. A better script? A stronger director? Hey, it's a TV movie, and it does its clearly defined job well enough. 🖦

John Forsythe *Joe Leary* • Carroll Baker *Maureen Leary* • Gordon Jump *Chief Heller* • Michael Bowen *Joe Jr* • Brian McNamara *Richie* • Woody Strode *Woody* ■ *Dir* Robert Greenwald • *Scr* John Herzfeld

On Golden Pond ★★★★ PG

Drama 1981 · US · Colour · 104mins

Nominated for ten Oscars, this old-fashioned family melodrama won three best adapted screenplay for Ernest Thompson and, more notably, Katharine Hepburn's fourth award for best actress and Henry Fonda's first as best actor. Considering neither was in the best of health, their performances are remarkable. The quiet authority of their acting is all the more apparent in their scenes with Jane Fonda, who overdoes the angst, particularly when opposite the father with whom she occasionally disagreed in real life. Complementing the subtle shades of performance are cinematographer Billy Williams's superb images, using to dramatic effect the changing light of the countryside in summer. 🖦

Henry Fonda *Norman Thayer Jr* • Katharine Hepburn *Ethel Thayer* • Jane Fonda *Chelsea Thayer Wayne* • Doug McKeon *Billy Ray* •

Dabney Coleman *Bill Ray* • William Lanteau *Charlie Martin* • Chris Rydell [Christopher Rydell] *Sumner Todd* ■ *Dir* Mark Rydell • *Scr* Ernest Thompson, from his play

On Her Majesty's Secret Service ★★★ PG

Spy adventure 1969 · UK · Colour · 127mins

This is the James Bond everyone forgets, mainly because it stars the Australian actor George Lazenby, who went from chocolate commercial to big-screen disaster. Wittily written (by Richard Maibaum and Simon Raven) and pacily directed (by Peter Hunt), it has excitement galore. Yet the chemistry between Diana Rigg and Lazenby is nonexistent – garlic-chewing did not endear the one to the other. Louis Armstrong is around to sing *We Have All the Time in the World*, which is some compensation. 🖦

George Lazenby *James Bond* • Diana Rigg *Tracy* • Telly Savalas *Blofeld* • Ilse Steppat *Irma Bunt* • Gabriele Ferzetti *Draco* • Yuri Borienko *Gruenther* • Bernard Horsfall *Campbell* • George Baker *Sir Hilary Bray* • Bernard Lee *"M"* • Lois Maxwell *Miss Moneypenny* • Desmond Llewelyn *"Q"* ■ *Dir* Peter Hunt • *Scr* Richard Maibaum, Simon Raven, from the novel by Ian Fleming • *Music* John Barry • *Editor* John Glen

On Moonlight Bay ★★★ U

Musical comedy 1951 · US · Colour · 91mins

A charming and delightful Warner Bros riposte to MGM's *Meet Me in St Louis*, featuring an almost identical family – Leon Ames plays the father in both films. Doris Day shines as the tomboyish heroine, and she's surrounded by warm-hearted character players like Mary Wickes and Rosemary DeCamp in this elegantly designed but slight movie that beautifully evokes its turn-of-the-century period. Based on stories by Booth Tarkington (*The Magnificent Ambersons*), this was so popular that the same cast was reunited two years later for an equally perky sequel, *By the Light of the Silvery Moon*. 🖦

Doris Day *Marjorie Winfield* • Gordon MacRae *William Sherman* • Jack Smith *Hubert Wakeley* • Leon Ames *George Winfield* • Rosemary DeCamp *Mrs Winfield* • Mary Wickes *Stella* • Ellen Corby *Miss Stevens* • Billy Gray *Wesley Winfield* ■ *Dir* Roy Del Ruth • *Scr* Jack Rose, Melville Shavelson, from stories by Booth Tarkington

On My Own ★★★

Drama 1992 · It/Can/Aus · Colour · 97mins

Australian actress Judy Davis proves once more that she is one of the most remarkable actresses around in this thoughtful drama from director Antonio Tibaldi. As a schizophrenic whose outbursts and shameless behaviour intrude upon the already troubled life of her adolescent son, she erupts on to the screen and lurches between reason and recklessness with a power that shocks with its intensity. Unfortunately, we get too little of her and the burden of carrying the action falls on Matthew Ferguson as her 15-year-old son, who adequately conveys the confusions that cost him his school goalkeeping record and disrupt his relationships with his friends. Contains swearing and nudity.

Judy Davis *Mother* • Matthew Ferguson *Simon Henderson* • David McIlwraith *John Henderson* • Jan Rubes *The Colonel* • Michele Melega *Shammas* ■ *Dir* Antonio Tibaldi • *Scr* Antonio Tibaldi, Gill Dennis, John Frizzell

On My Way to the Crusades, I Met a Girl Who... ★

Farce 1967 · It/US · Colour · 110mins

Also known as *The Chastity Belt* and left waiting for two years on the shelf, this sex comedy stars Tony Curtis as a Middle Ages knight who keeps gamekeeper's daughter Monica Vitti securely locked up in order to preserve her "reputation". The bawdiness of the story owes something to the success of *Tom Jones* (Hugh Griffith has a supporting role) and to the Italian comedies with Marcello Mastroianni and Sophia Loren. Curtis remembered it mainly for Vitti's unwillingness to be photographed from any angle except head-on. He's quoted as saying, "She had a big nose and would never turn in profile."

Tony Curtis *Guerrando Da Montone* • Monica Vitti *Boccadoro* • Hugh Griffith *Sultan of Bari* • John Richardson *Dragone* ■ *Dir* Pasquale Festa Campanile • *Scr* Luigi Magni, Larry Gelbart, from a story by Ugo Liberatore

On Our Merry Way ★★ U

Portmanteau comedy drama 1948 · US · BW · 107mins

A mediocre and unconvincing portmanteau movie, directed by (among others) the illustrious King Vidor on a bad day, this links its several episodic stories by means of a newspaper ad salesman (Burgess Meredith) who dreams of being an investigative journalist. He fibs to his new wife (Paulette Goddard, Meredith's then real-life wife) that he is the reporter responsible for a series of stories and then must make good the lie. The cast does include some notable names, with Henry Fonda and James Stewart teamed as jazz musicians in the best segment, which was actually directed – uncredited – by John Huston and George Stevens.

Burgess Meredith *Oliver Pease* • Paulette Goddard *Martha Pease* • Fred MacMurray *Al* • Hugh Herbert *Elisha Hobbs* • James Stewart *Slim* • Dorothy Lamour *Gloria Manners* • Victor Moore *Ashton Carrington* • Eilene Janssen *Peggy Thorndyke* • Henry Fonda *Lank* • William Demarest *Floyd* • Dorothy Ford *Lola* ■ *Dir* King Vidor, Leslie Fenton • *Scr* Laurence Stallings, Lou Breslow, from a story by John O'Hara, Arch Oboler

On the Air Live with Captain Midnight ★★ PG

Drama 1979 · US · Colour · 79mins

Very much a family project for the Sebastians with Ferd and Beverly sharing duties behind the camera and son Tracy taking the lead role. Nevertheless, it is still a shambolic affair about a young man who comes out of his shell with his anarchic pirate radio show. The budget constraints hardly help and the whole theme was better handled in the later *Pump Up the Volume*. The Sebastians are probably better known for the dubious exploitation film *'Gator Bait*. 🖦

U = SUITABLE FOR ALL   Uc = SUITABLE FOR ALL, ESPECIALLY FOR YOUNG CHILDREN (VIDEO ONLY)   PG = PARENTAL GUIDANCE

Tracy Sebastian • John Ireland • Dena Dietrich • Ted Gehring • Mia Kovacs ■ *Dir/Scr* Beverly Sebastian, Ferd Sebastian

On the Avenue ★★★ U
Musical comedy   1937 · US · BW · 88mins

A host of classic Irving Berlin songs cut a swathe through this bright, cliché-free musical like gold in rock. Director Roy Del Ruth was well known for extracting thoughtful, multi-layered performances from his stars, and Dick Powell as the showbiz charmer and Madeleine Carroll as the lovestruck uptown lady are both stunning. The movie has much to say on the nature of love and passion, serving it up with enormous verve and incisive wit. The jaunty pace tends to slacken in the middle but this is a minor criticism of such an, on the whole, upbeat entertainment.

Dick Powell *Gary Blake* • Madeleine Carroll *Mimi Caraway* • Alice Faye *Mona Merrick* • George Barbier *Commodore Caraway* • Alan Mowbray *Frederick Sims* • Cora Witherspoon *Aunt Fritz Peters* • Walter Catlett *Jake Dribble* • Douglas Fowley *Eddie Eads* • Joan Davis *Miss Katz* ■ *Dir* Roy Del Ruth • *Scr* Gene Markey, William Conselman

On the Beach ★★★
Drama   1959 · US · BW · 134mins

An atomic submarine boldly goes where no atomic sub has gone before: to survey a nuclear-wasted Earth. The few survivors suffer from contamination by cliché, a sickness of conversational banality. Stanley Kramer's film of Nevil Shute's bestseller means well, and Gregory Peck, Ava Gardner and Anthony Perkins certainly try their best, but it lacks any apocalyptic excitement to go with its appalling premise. Dreary solemnity may well be the way it might happen in real life. However, as it's fiction, let's go out with a bang, not a whimper.

Gregory Peck *Dwight Towers* • Ava Gardner *Moira Davidson* • Fred Astaire *Julian Osborn* • Anthony Perkins *Peter Holmes* • Donna Anderson *Mary Holmes* • John Tate *Admiral Bridie* • Lola Brooks *Lieutenant Hosgood* ■ *Dir* Stanley Kramer • *Scr* John Paxton, James Lee Barrett, from the novel by Nevil Shute

On the Beat ★★ U
Comedy   1962 · UK · BW · 101mins

A fairly average Norman Wisdom vehicle, casting his alter ego Norman Pitkin as a would-be policeman who is reduced to being a Scotland Yard car park attendant because he's not tall enough to be a bobby. Then it turns out that he's the spitting image of a criminal – well, you've guessed the rest. Wisdom is funny enough, Jennifer Jayne is a moderately pert leading lady, and a host of British character actors go through the motions. But the formula was beginning to wear thin by now and this is pretty simplistic stuff. For Wisdom fans only.

Norman Wisdom *Norman Pitkin/Giulio Napolitani* • Jennifer Jayne *Rosanna* • Raymond Huntley *Sir Ronald Ackroyd* • David Lodge *Superintendent Hobson* • Esma Cannon *Mrs Stammers* • Eric Barker *Doctor* ■ *Dir* Robert Asher • *Scr* Jack Davies, Norman Wisdom, Eddie Leslie

On the Black Hill ★★★ 15
Drama   1987 · UK · Colour · 110mins

Adapted from Bruce Chatwin's bestseller, this charming film balances its realism and whimsy with such a light hand. Director Andrew Grieve's careful storytelling is rewarded with some lovely performances, notably from Bob Peck and Gemma Jones as a farming couple enduring the hardships and grasping the fleeting joys of life in the Welsh Marches. Mike and Robert Gwilym do well as the twins at the centre of the story, although their acting inexperience occasionally shows through during the weightier scenes. Beautifully shot by Thaddeus O'Sullivan.

Mike Gwilym *Benjamin Jones* • Robert Gwilym *Lewis Jones* • Bob Peck *Amos Jones* • Gemma Jones *Mary Jones* • Jack Walters *Sam Jones* • Nesta Harris *Hannah Jones* ■ *Dir* Andrew Grieve • *Scr* Andrew Grieve, from the novel by Bruce Chatwin • *Cinematographer* Thaddeus O'Sullivan

On the Buses ★ PG
Comedy   1971 · UK · Colour · 84mins

This spin-off from a popular ITV comedy series was a box-office hit back in 1971. Nostalgia masochists and those too full of the holiday spirit to find the remote control should account for the bulk of those tuning in to this atrocious film, in which women drivers are taken on at Blakey's depot, much to the frustration of the ''loveable'' misogynists Stan (Reg Varney) and Jack (Bob Grant).

Reg Varney *Stan Butler* • Doris Hare *Mrs Butler* • Anna Karen *Olive* • Michael Robbins *Arthur* • Stephen Lewis *Inspector Blake* • Bob Grant *Jack* ■ *Dir* Harry Booth • *Scr* Ronald Chesney, Ronald Wolfe

On the Double ★★
Comedy   1961 · UK · Colour · 93mins

Danny Kaye plays a dual role as a soldier-mimic and the general he resembles in this comedy with echoes of Kaye's earlier *On the Riviera* and the true-life war adventure *I Was Monty's Double*, but alas this is not as funny as the former or as exciting as the latter. Most Kaye movies have their moments, and there are a few good laughs, notably a quick-change sequence in which Kaye does a breath-taking set of imitations (including Marlene Dietrich), and Diana Dors perks things up as a German spy, but the script and direction are below par.

Danny Kaye *PFC Ernest Williams/Gen Sir Lawrence Mackenzie-Smith* • Dana Wynter *Lady Margaret Mackenzie-Smith* • Wilfrid Hyde White *Colonel Somerset* • Margaret Rutherford *Lady Vivian* • Diana Dors *Sergeant Bridget Stanhope* • Allan Cuthbertson *Captain Patterson* ■ *Dir* Melville Shavelson • *Scr* Jack Rose, Melville Shavelson

On the Edge ★★★ 15
Drama   1985 · US · Colour · 82mins

One of the most overlooked of American actors, Bruce Dern typically shines as a middle-aged runner on the fast track to redemption after previous sporting indiscretions. Along the way he teams up with his one-time coach John Marley and ex-lover Pam Grier. Exciting sports footage (Dern himself is a keen amateur runner) and solid

camerawork is undermined by the all-too familiar formula and inaccessible characters. Ultimately Rob Nilsson's film falls short between art-house pretension and mainstream acceptance.

Bruce Dern *Wes Holman* • Pam Grier *Cora* • Bill Bailey *Flash Holman* • Jim Haynie *Owen Riley* • John Marley *Elmo* ■ *Dir/Scr* Rob Nilsson

On the Fiddle ★★
Comedy   1961 · UK · BW · 96mins

Amazingly, in his role here as dim-witted gypsy Pedlar Pascoe, Sean Connery was only a year away from becoming an international superstar as James Bond in *Dr No*. He's forced to play second fiddle to Alfred Lynch in this hit-and-miss comedy. Known as *Operation Snafu* in the States, it's meant to be a minor variation on the Bilko theme, but it feels more like one of those wartime morale boosters featuring a couple of fading music-hall comics. There's a fine supporting cast, but the gags mostly lack smartness and pace.

Alfred Lynch *Horace Pope* • Sean Connery *Pedlar Pascoe* • Cecil Parker *Group Captain Bascombe* • Stanley Holloway *Mr Cooksley* • Alan King *T/Sergeant Buzzer* • Eric Barker *Doctor* • Wilfrid Hyde White *Trowbridge* • Kathleen Harrison *Mrs Cooksley* • Eleanor Summerfield *Flora McNaughton* ■ *Dir* Cyril Frankel • *Scr* Harold Buchman, from the novel *Stop at a Winner* by RF Delderfield

On the Line ★★
Police crime drama
1998 · US · Colour · 96mins

In this tepid cop story, Linda Hamilton plays an embattled single mother and LAPD detective, who transfers from the sex crimes unit to robbery homicide, where she is the only woman in the group. While tracking a gang of murderous teenage bank robbers, she must also contend with her colleagues' misogynistic behaviour. Linda Hamilton trades on her *Terminator* toughness, but fails to evoke much empathy for her rather one-dimensional character. Contains violence.

Linda Hamilton *Detective Jean Martin* • Jeff Fahey *Detective Dan Collins* • Jay Acovone *Captain Unander* • Coolio *Lieutenant Gil Suggs* • Dan Ferro *W Featherhill* ■ *Dir* Elodie Keene • *Scr* Walter Halsey Davis, Vickie Patik

On the Nickel ★★★
Drama   1979 · US · Colour · 96mins

This gloomy drama drowns in a splurge of sentimentality, but it has the power to move because of its autobiographical edge. Ralph Waite, a former alcoholic and the actor who played Daddy in the squeaky-clean TV series *The Waltons*, has retraced his own long night's journey into day, as a boozed down-and-out in Los Angeles. With Donald Moffat co-starring, Waite's film competently establishes the despair and the destitution of the characters' existences. Most of the cast were drawn from his own LA theatre company, which is why it comes across as therapy.

Donald Moffat *Sam* • Ralph Waite *CG* • Hal Williams *Paul* • Penelope Allen *Rose* • Jack Kehoe *Bad Mood* ■ *Dir/Scr* Ralph Waite

On the Right Track ★★
Comedy   1981 · US · Colour · 97mins

Child star Gary Coleman was a hit with US TV audiences as one of a pair of black kids in *Diff'rent Strokes* (1978-86). Due to a congenital kidney complaint, Coleman looked much younger than his age and would play child roles for many years. This, his feature film debut, mined the same sentimental and gently humorous vein as the TV show, with Coleman playing a 10-year-old shoeshine boy who lives out of a locker at a train station. When word gets round that the boy has an uncanny knack at picking out winning horses, he becomes a local celebrity.

Gary Coleman *Lester* • Michael Lembeck *Frank* • Lisa Eilbacher *Jill* • Maureen Stapleton *Mary* • Norman Fell *Mayor* • Herbert Edelman *Sam* ■ *Dir* Lee Philips • *Scr* Tina Pine, Avery Buddy, Richard Moses

On the Riviera ★★★
Musical comedy   1951 · US · Colour · 88mins

'' Here, Danny Kaye deserts his mentor Samuel Goldwyn for 20th Century-Fox, and a remake of one of the company's main plotlines – the dual identity stand-by used in *That Night in Rio* and *Folies Bergère*. As both musical star and military hero, Kaye makes the film very much his own, aided by glossy Technicolor and support from his two comely co-stars Gene Tierney and Corinne Calvet, the latter lending the requisite soupçon of authentic Gallic flavour. Buffs and connoisseurs should watch out for, in the chorus, Mrs Bob Fosse-to-be, *Damn Yankees'* Gwen Verdon.

Danny Kaye *Henri Duran/Jack Martin* • Gene Tierney *Lilli* • Corinne Calvet *Colette* • Marcel Dalio *Philippe Lebrix* • Jean Murat *Periton* • Henri Letondal *Louis Forel* • Clinton Sundberg *Antoine* • Sig Rumann *[Sig Ruman] Gapeaux* • Gwyneth Verdon *[Gwen Verdon] Specialty dancer* ■ *Dir* Walter Lang • *Scr* Valentine Davies, Phoebe Ephron, Henry Ephron, from a play by Rudolph Lothar, Hans Adler

On the Run ★★
Action drama   1983 · Ausl · Colour · 101mins

Rod Taylor returned to his native Australia for this routine thriller. Playing against type, he turns in a menacing performance as the respected, multi-lingual farmer who also masquerades as a calculating hitman, nicknamed ''The Dingo''. Director Mende Brown makes good use of the Sydney conurbation, as Taylor pursues the witnesses to his latest crime, who just happen to be his nephew and a fugitive from his past. But, while Paul Winfield bonds well with his young charge, Beau Cox, the action is derivative and predictable.

Paul Winfield *Harry* • Rod Taylor *Payette* • Beau Cox *Paul* ■ *Dir* Mende Brown • *Scr* Michael Fisher

On the 2nd Day of Christmas ★★
Seasonal comedy drama
1997 · US · Colour · 120 mins

In this sweet seasonal romance, the charming Mary Stuart Masterson turns in a winning performance as a professional pickpocket who, along with her adopted six-year-old niece, gets nabbed on Christmas Eve. Luckily for the larcenous pair, they are caught by a sympathetic department store security guard (Mark Ruffalo), who is given the task of watching the lawbreakers over the holidays and takes them into his home. As holiday specials go, this one is heart-warming, as it should be; although no new ground is broken, Masterson's charisma and that of her young co-star carry the day.

Mary Stuart Masterson *Trish* • Mark Ruffalo *Bert* • Lauren Suzanne Pratt *Patsy* • David Hewlett *Mel* • James Purcell *Bill* • Lawrence Dane *Mr Limber* • Howard Hesseman *David* ■ *Dir* James Frawley • *Scr* Brian Hohlfeld

On the Streets of LA ★★★

Crime drama   1991 · US · Colour

Louis Gossett Jr will always be remembered as the drill sergeant who gave Richard Gere seven shades of hell in *An Officer and a Gentleman*. Here he shows again what a fine actor he is, lifting this rather hammy, albeit hard-hitting, TV prison drama above the average, providing you can forgive the plot inconsistencies in the otherwise decently written script. There's also a good supporting performance from Blair Underwood as Gossett's delinquent son. Contains some swearing.

Louis Gossett Jr *Leonard Clay* • Blair Underwood *Jared Williams* • Rae Dawn Chong *Yvonne James* • Tony Plana *Enrique Torres* • David Harris *Mario* • Clarence Williams III *Raymond* ■ *Dir* Georg Stanford Brown • *Scr* Walter Halsey Davis

On the Third Day Arrived the Crow ★★

Spaghetti western   1973 · It · Colour

Nothing to do with the ill-fated Brandon Lee vehicle, this is a very average spaghetti western about the hunt for a mysterious gunman nicknamed "The Crow". Director Gianni Crea displays some neat stylistic touches, but the clichéd story and indifferent dubbing eventually sink the project. Italian dialogue dubbed into English.

Lincoln Tate • William Berger ■ *Dir* Gianni Crea

On the Town ★★★★ U

Musical   1949 · US · Colour · 93mins

This utterly exhilarating landmark movie musical gave Gene Kelly and choreographer Stanley Donen their directing break. The opening sequence is magnificent, as three sailors (Kelly, Frank Sinatra and Jules Munshin) hail the delights of *New York, New York* in Manhattan itself – it was unusual for MGM to leave its Hollywood lot. There are flaws: the substitution of dancers for Sinatra and Munshin in the ballet and a third act that's not nearly as funny or as pithy as it should be. But the rest – the exuberance of the title number, Ann Miller extolling the virtues of *Prehistoric Man*, Alice Pearce as Lucy Shmeeler, Sinatra and Betty Garrett, the delights of *Main Street* – is a joy. ▭

Gene Kelly *Gabey* • Frank Sinatra *Chip* • Vera-Ellen *Ivy Smith* • Jules Munshin *Ozzie* • Betty Garrett *Brunhilde Esterhazy* • Ann Miller *Claire Huddesen* • Florence Bates *Madame*

Dilyovska • Alice Pearce *Lucy Shmeeler* • George Meader *Professor* ■ *Dir* Stanley Donen, Gene Kelly • *Scr* Adolph Green, Betty Comden, from the musical play by Adolph Green, Betty Comden, Leonard Bernstein, from the ballet *Fancy Free* by Jerome Robbins • *Cinematographer* Harold Rosson • *Music Director* Lennie Hayton • *Music* Roger Edens, Adolph Green, Betty Comden, Leonard Bernstein • *Choreographer* Gene Kelly, Stanley Donen

On the Waterfront

★★★★★ PG

Classic crime drama
1954 · US · BW · 103mins

Asked to nominate the greatest ever male performance in cinema, some might plump for Marlon Brando as Terry Malloy in this searing, unforgettable seminal American classic. Rightly awarded the Oscar for best actor (the youngest ever at the time), Brando plays a none-too-bright longshoreman, a brooding misfit among the rampant corruption of the New York docks. The movie works on several levels. On the surface it's an extremely well-crafted and entertaining drama, but peel away some layers and you'll discover an apologia for informing. Fascinating, then, to discover the superb direction is by Elia Kazan, who himself "named names" in McCarthyite America. Mix in Leonard Bernstein's Oscar-nominated score, memorable dialogue from screenwriter Budd Schulberg ("I coulda been a contender, Charley") and truly great performances from screen newcomers Eva Marie Saint and Rod Steiger – if ever a movie deserved its eight Oscars, it was this one. ▭

Marlon Brando *Terry Malloy* • Karl Malden *Father Barry* • Lee J Cobb *Johnny Friendly* • Rod Steiger *Charley Malloy* • Pat Henning "*Kayo*"*Dugan* • Eva Marie Saint *Edie Doyle* • Leif Erickson *Glover* • James Westerfield *Big Mac* • Marty Balsam [Martin Balsam] *Gillette* • Fred Gwynne *Slim* ■ *Dir* Elia Kazan • *Scr* Budd Schulberg, from a series of articles by Malcolm Johnson • *Cinematographer* Boris Kaufman • *Music* Leonard Bernstein • *Art Director* Richard Day

On the Yard ★★★ 15

Prison drama   1978 · US · Colour · 96mins

A rare return to the style of Warner Bros dramas of the thirties, this prison-set tale is good at evoking the conflicts and conversation of convicts milling around the vast exercise yard into which they're released for daily recreation. But it's not so good at establishing a story and revealing the character of the four inmates who are at the centre of the narrative. John Heard is the wife-killer at violent odds with inmate leader Thomas Waites. Director Raphael D Silver efficiently summons up the atmosphere of a volatile community. Silver's wife, Joan Micklin Silver, produced the movie, though they had swapped roles successfully in *Hester Street* and *Between the Lines*. ▭

John Heard *Juleson* • Thomas Waites [Thomas G Waites] *Chilly* • Mike Kellin *Red* • Richard Bright *Nunn* • Joe Grifasi *Morris* • Lane Smith *Captain Blake* • Richard Hayes *Stick* ■ *Dir* Raphael D Silver • *Scr* Malcolm Braly, from his novel

On Top of Old Smoky ★★ U

Western   1953 · US · BW · 58mins

It's amazing that "Public Cowboy No 1" Gene Autry actually found time to churn out series movies like this one, since by the fifties his many careers as radio station owner, publishing magnate, composer and recording artiste had turned him into one of the hardest working and richest businessmen in America. His fans, though, expected film after film in which he practised his cowboy code – no hitting anyone smaller than him, no shooting men in the back, no gambling, drinking or smoking, and, especially, no kissing.

Gene Autry • Smiley Burnette • Gail Davis *Jen Larrabee* • Grandon Rhodes "*Doc*" *Judson* • Sheila Ryan *Lila Maryland* • Kenne Duncan *McQuaid* ■ *Dir* George Archainbaud • *Scr* Gerald Geraghty, from his story

On Your Toes ★★ U

Musical comedy   1939 · US · BW · 94mins

Richard Rodgers, Lorenz Hart and George Abbott's smash-hit Broadway musical came to the screen in a dispiritingly pale shadow of the original. The delightfully nonsensical tale of misunderstandings between an American composer-dancer and a visiting Russian ballet company, notably its ballerina, is worked over into a lacklustre screenplay and the gorgeous score denied its due. Eddie Albert and Vera Zorina star, but the real high point of the movie is the *Slaughter on Tenth Avenue* ballet, choreographed by George Balanchine.

Eddie Albert *Phil Dolan Jr* • Zorina [Vera Zorina] *Vera Barnova* • Alan Hale *Sergei Alexandrovitch* • Frank McHugh *Paddy Reilly* • James Gleason *Phil Dolan Sr* • Donald O'Connor *Phil, as a boy* • Leonid Kinsky *Ivan Boultonoff* • Erik Rhodes *Constantine Morrisine* ■ *Dir* Ray Enright • *Scr* Jerry Wald, Richard Macaulay, Sig Herzig, Lawrence Riley, from the musical by Richard Rodgers, by Lorenz Hart, George Abbott

Once a Jolly Swagman ★★ U

Drama   1948 · UK · BW · 98mins

This is an improbably melodramatic tale of love, honour and speedway. Set in the thirties, it scores with its realistic portrait of track life (courtesy of director Jack Lee's documentary background), but the wheels come off during the studio-bound sequences, in which ex-factory worker Dirk Bogarde is dazzled both by his new-found fame and the radiance of socialite Moira Lister. Bill Owen and Renée Asherson provide dependable support, but Bogarde never gets out of first gear. ▭

Dirk Bogarde *Bill Fox* • Bonar Colleano *Tommy Possey* • Renée Asherson *Pat Gibbon* • Bill Owen *Lag Gibbon* • Cyril Cusack *Duggie Lewis* • Thora Hird *Ma Fox* • James Hayter *Pa Fox* • Pauline Jameson *Mrs Lewis* • Stuart Lindsell *Mr Yates* • Moira Lister *Dotty Liz* ■ *Dir* Jack Lee • *Scr* Jack Lee, William Rose, Cliff Gordon, from a novel by Montagu Slater

Once a Thief ★★

Crime drama   1965 · US · BW · 106mins

This routine cops and robbers melodrama was French star Alain

Delon's first American feature and he looks unusually awkward and out of place as an ex-con trying to go straight while being harassed by a vengeful cop and becoming a pawn in his brother's plans for a million-dollar heist. Director Ralph Nelson assembles an able support cast (Ann-Margret, Van Heflin and Jack Palance) but the strength of his semi-documentary approach and the pre-*Bullitt* San Francisco locations are undercut by a cliché-ridden script. The Lalo Schifrin score is a mighty plus.

Alain Delon *Eddie Pedak* • Ann-Margret *Kristine Pedak* • Van Heflin *Mike Vido* • Jack Palance *Walter Pedak* • John Davis Chandler *James Sargatanas* • Jeff Corey *Lt Kebner* • Tony Musante *Cleve Shoenstein* ■ *Dir* Ralph Nelson • *Scr* Zekial Marko, from his novel *Scratch a Thief*

Once a Thief ★★★ 15

Romantic action comedy
1991 · HK · Colour · 103mins

John Woo remade this five years later for TV, yet wasn't able to touch this light-hearted caper movie, atypical for him. Beginning in France, three crooks (Chow Yun-Fat, Leslie Cheung, and Cherie Chung), who were raised as thieves after each being orphaned in their childhood, plan one last caper to steal a valuable painting... but things don't work out smoothly, both with the plan and with the affection both men feel for their female member. Woo goes for comedy and less violent action in this effort, and the result is alternately charming and hilarious, frequently simultaneously. Those expecting the standard grandiose Woo shoot-outs will be disappointed – until the surprisingly violent climax. A Cantonese language film.

Chow Yun-Fat *Joe* • Leslie Cheung *Jim* • Cherie Chung *Cherie* ■ *Dir* John Woo • *Scr* John Woo, Clifton Ko, Janet Chung

Once a Thief ★★★ 15

Action drama
1996 · Can/US · Colour · 96mins

Before hitting pay dirt in Hollywood with *Face/Off*, film-maker John Woo made this loose reworking of one of his old Hong Kong films of the same name, and considerably different from the highly stylised melodrama of his best-known action thrillers. The story follows three quick-witted criminals who find themselves on opposite sides of the law when two of them are recruited into a special police unit investigating the underworld. There are plenty of characteristic touches to keep Woo's fans happy: lots of gun battles, slow motion set pieces and spectacular explosions. Intended as a pilot for a series, it was released on video in the UK as *Violent Tradition*. ▭

Sandrine Holt *Li Ann Tsei* • Ivan Sergei *Mac Ramsey* • Nicholas Lea *Victor Mansfield* • Michael Wong *Michael Tang* • Jennifer Dale *The Director* ■ *Dir* John Woo • *Scr* Glenn Davis, William Laurin

Once Around ★★★ 15

Romantic comedy
1991 · US · Colour · 110mins

Some of the best talent Hollywood could muster graces this often affecting story of a repressed little rich

girl, the excellent Holly Hunter, who falls madly in love with a garrulous salesman, a rather caricatured performance from Richard Dreyfuss, much to his family's chagrin. The tightly packed, occasionally lyrical script by Malia Scotch Marmo gives each character suitable depth and emotional history, but almost imperceptibly goes off the boil as the movie progresses. Watching such actors as Gena Rowlands, Danny Aiello and, of course, Dreyfuss and Hunter perform together is a rich experience, but somehow all this class and effort results in an oddly flat movie. Contains swearing. ▭

Holly Hunter *Renata Bella* • Richard Dreyfuss *Sam Sharpe* • Danny Aiello *Joe Bella* • Gena Rowlands *Marilyn Bella* • Laura San Giacomo *Jan* • Roxanne Hart *Gail Bella* • Danton Stone *Tony Bella* • Tim Guinee *Peter Hedges* ■ *Dir* Lasse Hallström • *Scr* Malia Scotch Marmo, Lasse Hallström

Once Before I Die ★★

Second World War drama
1965 · US · Colour · 97 mins

What on earth is Ursula Andress doing in the middle of the jungle and in the thick of the war in the Philippines? Well, appearing in husband John Derek's movie is the answer. Viewers may find it difficult to fathom whether Derek wanted to deck a dull war movie out with glam shots of his wife, or vice versa. Either way, this is a blatant vanity project, made purely to show what amazingly beautiful people John and Ursula are, or were. Richard Jaeckel co-stars as a certain Lt Custer and plays him as a psychotic sadist who loves killing the Japanese.

Ursula Andress *Alex* • John Derek *Maj Bailey* • Rod Lauren *Captain* • Richard Jaeckel *Lt Custer* • Ron Ely ■ *Dir* John Derek • *Scr* Vance Skarstedt, from the story *Quit for the Next* by Anthony March

Once Bitten ★★ 15

Horror comedy 1985 · US · Colour · 88mins

This is a dumb teenage sex comedy with supernatural overtones and a very hit-and-miss gags quotient. Countess Lauren Hutton is a 400-year-old vampire looking for virgin blood in Los Angeles. Supplies are short until she picks up a student nerd (future superstar Jim Carrey) who hasn't managed to get his girlfriend Karen Kopins into bed. As he takes on more undead qualities, Carrey gets amusingly cooler but ultimately turns his back on the complete vampire lifestyle. Cleavon Little as Hutton's gay manservant has some funny moments, but eventually the one-joke premise screeches to a halt under Howard Storm's lifeless direction. ▭

Lauren Hutton *Countess* • Jim Carrey *Mark Kendall* • Karen Kopins *Robin Pierce* • Cleavon Little *Sebastian* • Thomas Ballatore *Jamie* • Skip Lackey *Russ* ■ *Dir* Howard Storm • *Scr* David Hines, Jeffrey Hause, Jonathan Roberts, from a story by Dimitri Villard

Once in Paris ★★★

Drama 1978 · US · Colour · 100mins

Writer/director Frank D Gilroy drew on his own experiences of writing *The Only Game in Town* to piece together this warm, character-driven look at

friendship and love. Wayne Rogers plays a screenwriter who is drafted to Paris to salvage a script. His chauffeur there is Jack Lenoir (Gilroy's real-life driver) against whom Rogers is warned, but despite finding out about his dodgy past, decides to keep him on and they become friends. All is hunky-dory until Moore meets Gayle Hunnicutt, a British aristocrat who has the room next to his and they fall in love. A sympathetic and adult film.

Wayne Rogers *Michael Moore* • Gayle Hunnicutt *Susan Townsend* • Jack Lenoir *Jean-Paul Barbet* • Philippe March *Marcel Thery* • Clément Harari *Abe Wiley* • Tanya Lopert *Eve Carling* ■ *Dir/Scr* Frank D Gilroy

Once Is Not Enough ★★

Melodrama 1975 · US · Colour · 121 mins

Some unkind people may comment that once is quite enough, thank you. Adapted from Jacqueline Susann's potboiler novel, this is a forerunner of the *Dallas* and *Dynasty* soap operas, peppered with starry names and an appallingly camp plotline. Kirk Douglas plays a past-it producer and doting dad to Deborah Raffin. He is so keen to keep his darling daughter in the best that money can buy that he marries Alexis Smith – a rich, bisexual woman, who is still involved with her lesbian lover, Melina Mercouri. Brenda Vaccaro won a Golden Globe for her supporting role as a man-mad fashion editor. So bad it is almost good, but not quite.

Kirk Douglas *Mike Wayne* • Alexis Smith *Deidre Milford Granger* • David Janssen *Tom Colt* • George Hamilton *David Milford* • Melina Mercouri *Karla* • Gary Conway *Hugh* • Brenda Vaccaro *Linda* • Deborah Raffin *January Wayne* ■ *Dir* Guy Green • *Scr* Julius J Epstein, from the novel by Jacqueline Susann

Once More, My Darling ★★

Comedy 1949 · US · BW · 92mins

Robert Montgomery, past the peak of his stardom, directs himself in this romantic comedy about an actor turned lawyer who is hired by the army to romance lovely young heiress Ann Blyth and find out how she came by some stolen Nazi jewellery. Needless to say, true love conquers all. The stars play well together, and Montgomery's direction is competent, but the end result is forgettable and unconvincing.

Robert Montgomery *Collier Laing* • Ann Blyth *Marita Connell* • Lillian Randolph *Mamie the maid* • Jane Cowl *Mrs Laing* • Steven Geray *Kalzac* ■ *Dir* Robert Montgomery • *Scr* Robert Carson, Oscar Saul, from the story *Come Be My Love* by Robert Carson

Once More, with Feeling ★★

Comedy 1959 · UK · Colour · 92 mins

Yul Brynner is Victor Fabian, a flamboyant and hot-headed conductor who enjoys a volatile relationship with his wife, Dolly, who is getting fed up with his egotistic excesses. This is a heavy-handed comedy (based on a stage play) with Brynner uncomfortable in the role and unable to milk laughs from the script. The piece is rescued from being totally worthless by the presence of Kay Kendall as Dolly who turns in a performance way above the standard of the production. Kendall died from leukaemia in 1959, and this,

her last film, was shelved for some months.

Yul Brynner *Victor Fabian* • Kay Kendall *Dolly Fabian* • Gregory Ratoff *Maxwell Archer* • Geoffrey Toone *Dr Hilliard* • Maxwell Shaw *Jascha Gendel/Grisha Gendel* • Mervyn Johns *Mr Wilbur Jr* • *Dir* Stanley Donen • *Scr* Harry Kurnitz, from his play

Once upon a Crime ★ PG

Comedy 1992 · US · Colour · 90mins

The comic genius of John Candy is there for all to see in this dismal crime caper. Only someone of his immense talent could raise a laugh out of material this bad. All around him flounder, particularly Richard Lewis and Sean Young as the couple who become embroiled in a trans-European murder mystery after finding a valuable dachshund. It would be too easy to blame debuting director Eugene Levy for the chaotic structure and the bellowing performances. Any film with seven scriptwriters is likely to be a mishmash, but the unfortunate coincidence of so much ineptitude renders this almost unwatchable. Contains swearing. ▭

John Candy *Augie Morosco* • James Belushi *Neil Schwary* • Cybill Shepherd *Marilyn Schwary* • Sean Young *Phoebe* • Richard Lewis *Julian Peters* • Ornella Muti *Elena Morosco* • Giancarlo Giannini *Inspector Bonnard* • George Hamilton *Alfonso de la Pena* • Roberto Sbaratto *Detective Toussaint* • Joss Ackland *Hercules Popodopoulos* ■ *Dir* Eugene Levy • *Scr* Charles Shyer, Nancy Meyers, Steve Kluger, from a screenplay (unproduced) by Rodolfo Sonego, Giorgio Arlorio, Stefano Strucchi, Luciano Vincenzoni

Once upon a Family ★★

Drama 1980 · US · Colour · 94mins

In the eighties, Barry Bostwick was the king of TV movies and mini-series, and this is a suitably glossy, sentimental example of the tear-jerkers he is best known for. In this one, nice-guy Bostwick is forced to reassess his life when his wife Maureen Anderman leaves and he is left literally holding the babies. Alvin Sapinsley's screenplay leaves no cliché unturned while director Richard Michaels ensures no grittiness scratches the surface sheen. Worth a wallow if you're in the mood, but you're probably better off with *Kramer vs Kramer*.

Barry Bostwick *Henry Demerjian* • Maureen Anderman *Janet Demerjian* • Lee Chamberlin *Mrs Grace* • Jonathan Goldsmith *George Conway* • James Licht *Dw Demerjian* • Nancy Marchand *Mrs Demerjian* • Lara Parker *Maggie Conway* ■ *Dir* Richard Michaels • *Scr* Alvin Sapinsley

Once upon a Forest ★★ U

Musical animation
1992 · US · Colour · 67mins

Whether children will take on board the eco message contained in this feature-length musical animation is open to debate, especially as the tone of the politically correct tale is often rather preachy. But the "furlings" who venture out into the big bad world to find the herbs needed to save one of their sickly playmates are cute and courageous, and their encounters with some unthinking humans and menacing machines should keep youngsters on the edge of their seats.

As with so many non-Disney cartoons, the standard of the songs is poor and the animation lacks magic. ▭

Michael Crawford *Cornelius, the Badger* • Ben Vereen *Phineas* • Ellen Blain *Abigail* • Ben Gregory [Benjamin Gregory] *Edgar* • Paige Gosney *Russell* • Elisabeth Moss *Michelle* ■ *Dir* Charles Grosvenor • *Scr* Mark Young, Kelly Ward, from the story by Rae Lambert

Once upon a Honeymoon ★★ PG

Wartime comedy 1942 · US · BW · 114mins

A lengthy and astoundingly tasteless comedy drama, revealing how little America knew about the Nazis back in 1942 when this was made. The sequences involving Cary Grant and Ginger Rogers being mistaken for Jews and shipped off to a concentration leave a strange taste in the mouth. In later years, director Leo McCarey actually disowned the film. Grant is his usual self, while still managing to convey that the whole exercise is beneath him. It's well made, however, and contemporary audiences simply accepted what was on screen; time has rendered that no longer possible. ▭

Ginger Rogers *Katie O'Tara* • Cary Grant *Pat O'Toole* • Walter Slezak *Baron Von Luber* • Albert Dekker *LeBlanc* • Albert Basserman *General Borelski* • Ferike Boros *Elsa* • Harry Shannon *Cumberland* ■ *Dir* Leo McCarey • *Scr* Sheridan Gibney, from a story by Sheridan Gibney, Leo McCarey

Once Upon a Scoundrel ★★★

Comedy 1973 · US · Colour · 90mins

A morality tale directed by veteran US TV director George Schaefer and starring that bundle of explosive humour, Zero Mostel. He plays a duplicitous landowner who gets the fiancé of a girl he desires out of the way by having him thrown into prison. To teach Mostel a lesson, the girl and her aunt get together and contrive a ruse where they treat him as if he is dead. When this scheme is put into motion, Mostel gradually comes round to believing he really has died and become a ghost. Clever idea, fairly well executed and with a smattering of amusing scenes.

Zero Mostel *Carlos del Refugio* • Katy Jurado *Aunt Delfina* • Titos Vandis *Dr Fernandez* • Priscilla Garcia *Alicia* • A Martinez *Luis* ■ *Dir* George Schaefer • *Scr* Rip Van Ronkel

Once upon a Spy ★★★ PG

Spy adventure 1980 · US · Colour · 91mins

Christopher Lee chews the scenery again as a paralysed mad scientist who invents a shrinking machine in a whimsical spy spoof that hits the 007 targets dead on, especially in the Bond theme department. Jimmy Sangster, another Hammer veteran, scripted this glitzy tale of unbelievable derring-do – or rather don't – in star Ted Danson's case which moves along at a bright and breezy pace, thanks to some engagingly quirky humour. ▭

Ted Danson *Jack Chenault* • Mary Louise Weller *Paige Tannehill* • Christopher Lee *Marcus Velorium* • Eleanor Parker *The Lady* • Leonard Stone *Dr Charlie Webster* ■ *Dir* Ivan Nagy • *Scr* Jimmy Sangster, from a story by Jimmy Sangster, Lemuel Pitkin

Once upon a Texas Train
★★★ U

Western 1988 · US · Colour · 86mins

An entertaining TV movie with a splendid cast headed by Texas Ranger Richard Widmark and ageing outlaw Willie Nelson, who find that youngster Shaun Cassidy is about to disrupt their unlawful business by intercepting some ill-gotten loot. Veteran writer/producer/ director Burt Kennedy has assembled a fine supporting cast of western stalwarts, including Angie Dickinson, Stuart Whitman, Jack Elam, Royal Dano and Chuck Connors. The lighthearted tone might offend western purists, but others will enjoy this rollicking entertainment. ▭

Willie Nelson *John Henry Lee* • Richard Widmark *Captain Oren Hayes* • Angie Dickinson *Maggie Hayes* • Shaun Cassidy *Cotton* • Chuck Connors *Nash Crawford* • Jack Elam *Jason Fitch* • Ken Curtis *Kelly Sutton* • Royal Dano *Nitro Jones* • Kevin McCarthy *Governor* ▪ *Dir/Scr* Burt Kennedy

Once upon a Time ★★★ U

Comedy 1944 · US · BW · 88mins

This amazing piece of whimsy is about impecunious theatre producer Cary Grant promoting a dancing caterpillar. Thanks to the deceptive skill of the ever-dependable Grant and the quiet cleverness of the screenplay, it works. Director Alexander Hall was skilled at this kind of fantasy and casts the quizzical James Gleason and Janet Blair, supporting the debonair Grant with some style. Slight and trivial in the extreme, but supremely watchable in its daffy, good-natured way.

Cary Grant *Jerry Flynn* • Janet Blair *Jeannie Thompson* • James Gleason *The Moke* • Ted Donaldson *Pinky Thompson* • Howard Freeman *McKenzie* • William Demarest *Brandt* ▪ *Dir* Alexander Hall • *Scr* Lewis Meltzer, Oscar Saul, Irving Fineman, from the radio play *My Client Curly* by Norman Corwin, Lucille Fletcher Herrmann

Once upon a Time in the West
★★★★★ 15

Spaghetti western
1968 · It/US · Colour · 158mins

In seeking to paint "a fresco on the birth of a great nation", Sergio Leone turned to the Hollywood western for his inspiration. Set at the time when the dollar replaced the bullet as the currency of the frontier, this breathtaking tale of progress, greed and revenge. The story focuses on Henry Fonda, a brutish gunfighter who dreams of becoming a tycoon, but who is still prepared to resort to trusted methods to drive widow Claudia Cardinale off the land coveted by a ruthless railroad company. However, Frank must also deal with the mysterious harmonica player (Charles Bronson), as well as sympathetic outlaw Jason Robards, if he is to achieve his goal. Much of the action was improvised around the mood of the score, which Ennio Morricone had composed in advance. No wonder many critics described the film as an operatic masterpiece. ▭

Henry Fonda *Frank* • Claudia Cardinale *Jill McBain* • Jason Robards [Jason Robards Jr] *Cheyenne* • Charles Bronson *Harmonica* • Frank Wolff *Brett McBain* • Gabriele Ferzetti

Morton • Keenan Wynn *Sheriff* ▪ *Dir* Sergio Leone • *Scr* Sergio Leone, Sergio Donati, from a story by Sergio Leone, Dario Argento, Bernardo Bertolucci • *Music* Ennio Morricone • *Cinematographer* Tonino Delli Colli

Once upon a Time in America
★★★★★ 18

Crime drama 1984 · US · Colour · 217mins

Sergio Leone's final film is an extraordinary crime drama which runs for nearly four hours in its full length-version and chronicles the lives of two New York gangsters, Noodles and Max, played by Robert De Niro and James Woods. Four decades roll past in flashback, underpinned by a great Ennio Morricone score. The plotting is often arbitrary but, unlike *The Godfather*, Leone and his fine actors never try to win our sympathy: these are nasty people and there are two rape scenes, involving Tuesday Weld and Elizabeth McGovern, that may be among the most shocking ever filmed. But just gasp at the scale, at the immaculate period reconstruction and at that incredible opening with its endlessly ringing phone. A resounding flop on its US release, it was heavily cut by its panicked distributors. It fared better in Europe, where it was hailed as a masterpiece of eighties cinema. Contains violence, swearing and nudity. ▭

Robert De Niro *Noodles* • James Woods *Max* • Elizabeth McGovern *Deborah* • Treat Williams *Jimmy O'Donnell* • Tuesday Weld *Carol* • Burt Young *Joe* • Joe Pesci *Frankie* • Danny Aiello *Police chief* • Bill Forsythe [William Forsythe] *Cockeye* ▪ *Dir* Sergio Leone • *Scr* Leonardo Benvenuti, Piero De Bernardi, Enrico Medioli, Franco Arcalli, Franco Ferrini, Sergio Leone, Stuart Kaminsky, from the novel *The Hoods* by Harry Grey • *Cinematographer* Tonino Delli Colli • *Music* Ennio Morricone

Once upon a Time in China
★★★★ 15

Martial arts action drama
1991 · HK · Colour · 128mins

Wong Fei-Hung (1847-1924) was one of the undisputed masters of such kung fu techniques as the no-shadow kick and drunken boxing. He was already a cult figure in pulp fiction before his exploits finally reached the screen in the late forties. Tsui Hark revitalised the legend with this box-office smash, which itself launched a whole new series of adventures that made a superstar of Jet Li. Notable for its stance against foreign influences, this is an explosive picture, with breakneck action sequences – the best featuring Li, a dozen baddies and an umbrella. In Cantonese with English subtitles. Contains violence. ▭

Jet Li *Wong Fei-Hung* • Yuen Biao *Leung Foon* • Jacky Cheung *Buck Teeth Sol* ▪ *Dir* Tsui Hark • *Scr* Tsui Hark, Yuen Kai-Chi, Leung Yiu-Ming

Once upon a Time in China II
★★★ 15

Martial arts action drama
1992 · HK · Colour · 107mins

The explosive combination of Tsui Hark and Jet Li as Wong Fei-Hung ensured a sequel to the smash hit *Once Upon a Time in China* and the result is another extravagant action pic. More sequels

followed, culminating (so far) in *Once Upon a Time in China and America* (aka *Once Upon a Time in China VI*), directed by Hong Kong superstar Sammo Hung. Jet Li bowed out after episode three in the series but returned triumphantly for the most recent adventure. All of these films (even the non-Li ones) have their moments and deliver some great cinematic action sequences. In Cantonese with English subtitles. Contains violence. ▭

Jet Li *Wong Fei-Hung* • Rosamund Chi-Lam Kwan *Aunt Yee* • Donnie Chi Tan Yen *Lan* • David Chiang *Luke* • Max Siu Chung Mok *Leung Fu* ▪ *Dir* Tsui Hark • *Scr* Tsui Hark, Hanson Chan [Chan Tin Suen], Cheung Tan

Once Were Warriors
★★★★★ 18

Drama 1994 · NZ · Colour · 98mins

Told in a bold, unflinching manner, director Lee Tamahori's drama grips and fascinates as it lifts the lid on ghetto Maori life. Rena Owen is drainingly moving as the put-upon housewife, pushed physically and mentally to the brink while trying to hold her family together, bearing the brunt of her unemployed husband's drink-fuelled frustrations. Tamahori's bleak film is raw, brutal cinema with a unique voice, showing a people adrift from their cultural roots and trapped in an urban nightmare of cheap housing and gangland controlled precincts. One of the most pertinent and important works to emerge from Down Under in years. Contains violence and swearing. ▭ *DVD*

Rena Owen *Beth Heke* • Temuera Morrison *Jake Heke* • Mamaengaroa Kerr-Bell *Grace Heke* • Julian Arahanga *Nig Heke* • Taungaroa Emile *Boogie Heke* • Rachael Morris Jr *Polly Heke* • Joseph Kairau *Huata Heke* ▪ *Dir* Lee Tamahori • *Scr* Riwia Brown, from the novel by Alan Duff

Once You Kiss a Stranger
★★

Drama 1969 · US · Colour · 105mins

This is a loose remake of Alfred Hitchcock's classic *Strangers on a Train* or, perhaps more accurately, it's another telling of the same source novel by Patricia Highsmith. Carol Lynley takes on the original, sinister Robert Walker role, meeting golf pro Paul Burke and offering to murder his rival if he, Burke, will murder Lynley's psychiatrist in return. When Burke's rival winds up dead, he finds himself blackmailed. Panned by most critics, it's only worth seeing to compare with the Hitchcock version.

Paul Burke *Jerry* • Carol Lynley *Diana* • Martha Hyer *Lee* • Peter Lind Hayes *Peter* • Philip Carey *Mike* • Stephen McNally *Lieutenant Gavin* ▪ *Dir* Robert Sparr • *Scr* Frank Tarloff, Norman Katkov, from the novel by Patricia Highsmith

Once You Meet a Stranger
★★

Thriller 1996 · US · Colour · 95mins

This is an unnecessary role-reversed remake of the Hitchcock classic *Strangers on a Train*. As the fading star determined to see the back of her ex-husband, Jacqueline Bisset loses

out in every scene she shares with Theresa Russell, who is in *Black Widow* form as the deranged fellow traveller who suggests a murderous pact to get rid of her overbearing mother. Director Tommy Lee Wallace brings nothing new to this adaptation of Patricia Highsmith's novel. Contains violence.

Jacqueline Bisset *Sheila Gaines* • Theresa Russell *Margo Anthony* • Robert Desiderio *Andy Stahl* • Celeste Holm *Clara* • Nick Mancuso *Aaron* • Matthew Thomas Carey *Barnaby* ▪ *Dir* Tommy Lee Wallace • *Scr* Tommy Lee Wallace, from the film *Strangers on a Train* by Czenzi Ormonde, Raymond Chandler, Whitfield Cook, from the novel by Patricia Highsmith

One after the Other ★★

Spaghetti western
1968 · It/Sp · Colour · 105mins

Since his arrival in Italy in the late fifties, American muscleman Richard Harrison had tried his hand at "sword and sandal" epics, spy spoofs and gangster movies. So it was only logical that he should also have a bash at Italian cinema's most celebrated export – the spaghetti western. However, the "spaghetti" label is no guarantee of quality and he was unfortunate in his choice of this unremarkable Italo-Spanish co-production in which an unholy duo go in search of the thieves who have snatched the gold from the Canyon City bank. Italian dialogue dubbed into English..

Richard Harrison *Stan Ross* • Pamela Tudor *Sabine* • Paul Stevens [Paolo Stevens] *Glenn* • José Bódalo *Jefferson* ▪ *Dir* Nick Howard [Nick Nostro] • *Scr* Nick Nostro, Carlos E Rodriquez, from a story by Simon O'Neill [Giovanni Simonelli]

One against the Wind
★★★★ PG

Drama based on a true story
1991 · US · Colour · 95mins

An excellent wartime drama, shot in Luxembourg and based on the real-life exploits of Mary Lindell, a British woman who used her Paris home as a halfway house for Allied soldiers trapped behind enemy lines. The story is tense and emotive, mainly because of the array of talent on display: Judy Davis, one of the greatest and least "starry" actresses around, plays Lindell and brings the same sensivity that she brought to her roles in *A Passage to India* and Woody Allen's *Husbands and Wives*. There is also fine support from Sam Neill, Anthony Higgins, Kate Beckinsale and the always dependable Denholm Elliott in one of his final screen appearances. ▭

Judy Davis *Mary Lindell* • Sam Neill *Captain James Leggatt* • Denholm Elliott *Father LeBlanc* • Christien Anholt *Maurice* • Kate Beckinsale *Barbe* • Anthony Higgins *Herman Gruber* ▪ *Dir* Larry Elikann • *Scr* Chris Bryant

The One and Only ★★★

Comedy drama 1978 · US · Colour · 97mins

Henry Winkler plays Andy Schmidt, a man whose huge ego is only matched by his determination to become an acting star. Convinced he knows better than anyone else, he alienates would-

▭ = SUITABLE FOR ALL   ▭ = SUITABLE FOR ALL, ESPECIALLY FOR YOUNG CHILDREN (VIDEO ONLY)   PG = PARENTAL GUIDANCE

be employers by his insistence on changing lines and suggesting alterations in his roles. However he does make a success as a wrestler, relishing in the opportunity to use his acting talent in the ring, although his long-suffering wife and her parents are less enamoured with this new career. TV's Fonzie here found a decent vehicle for his comedic talents and a sparkling script ensured plenty of fine moments.

Henry Winkler *Andy Schmidt* • Kim Darby *Mary Crawford* • Gene Saks *Sidney Seltzer* • William Daniels *Mr Crawford* • Harold Gould *Hector Moses* • Polly Holliday *Mrs Crawford* • Herve Villechaize *Milton Miller* • Ed Begley Jr *Arnold the King* ■ *Dir* Carl Reiner • *Scr* Steve Gordon

The One and Only, Genuine, Original Family Band ★★
Musical drama 1968 · US · Colour · 110mins

This Disney family drama is notable only for the fact that it has a young Kurt Russell and Goldie Hawn (credited as Goldie Jeanne Hawn) appearing on screen together for the first time. Set during the 1888 presidential campaign, the film follows the efforts of Walter Brennan to win the right for his family band to perform in the face of both political opposition and domestic discord. Adapted from an autobiographical novel, the story has too few hooks for modern audiences and the Sherman brothers' songs are of little interest. ▭

Walter Brennan *Granpa Bower* • Buddy Ebsen *Calvin Bower* • John Davidson *Joe Carder* • Lesley Ann Warren *Alice Bower* • Janet Blair *Katie Bower* • Kurt Russell *Sidney Bower* • Steve Harmon *Ernie Stubbins* • Goldie Jeanne Hawn [Goldie Hawn] *Giggly girl* ■ *Dir* Michael O'Herlihy • *Scr* Lowell S Hawley, from the autobiography *Nebraska 1888* by Laura Bower Van Nuys

One Born Every Minute ★★★★
Comedy 1967 · US · Colour · 104 mins

Also called *The Flim-Flam Man*, this is one of the choicest comedies in which George C Scott has starred. He's Mordecai, an elderly con-man of epic proportions, who takes on Michael Sarrazin as his apprentice, until the youngster falls in love and starts to reconsider his chosen path. Written by William Rose (*Genevieve*, *The Ladykillers*), it's directed by Irvin Kershner with panache, helped by his second unit director and stunt man, the legendary Yakima Canutt.

George C Scott *Mordecai* • Sue Lyon *Bonnie Lee Packard* • Michael Sarrazin *Curley* • Harry Morgan *Sheriff Slade* • Jack Albertson *Mr Packard* • Alice Ghostley *Mrs Packard* • Albert Salmi *Deputy Meshaw* • Slim Pickens *Jarvis Bates* ■ *Dir* Irvin Kershner • *Scr* William Rose, from the story *The Ballad of the Flim Flam Man* by Guy Owen

One Christmas ★★★
Drama 1994 · US · Colour · 96mins

A festive tale with a nasty bite, even if its teeth are extracted for a happy ending. Based on Truman Capote's story, this thirties' drama follows the adventures of a young country boy who is expecting the perfect Christmas with his estranged father (Henry Winkler)

when he visits him in New Orleans. However, Dad is not only an alcoholic but also a gigolo who sees his son as just another means to fleece wealthy widows. Director Tony Bill provides a sharp and witty dissection of the Christmas experience, and Winkler is unexpectedly good cast against type, but he is upstaged by the top-billed Katharine Hepburn and an experienced supporting cast, which includes Swoosie Kurtz, and Julie Harris.

Katharine Hepburn *Cornelia Beaumont* • Henry Winkler *Dad* • Swoosie Kurtz *Emily Yarbrough* • TJ Lowther *Buddy* • Julie Harris *Sook* ■ *Dir* Tony Bill • *Scr* Duane Poole, from the story by Truman Capote

One Crazy Night ★★★ 15
Drama 1993 · Ausl · Colour · 92mins

Reminiscent of *The Breakfast Club*, this is about five Aussie teens who are stuck overnight in the basement of a hotel in which the touring Beatles are staying. The film focuses not on the Fab Four, but on the fab conversations the five have – about hopes, fears, sexual fantasies and hero worship. Bittersweet but often funny, it benefits from good direction and a fresh cast, the best known of whom are Noah Taylor from *Shine* and Kylie Minogue's little sister Dannii. ▭

Noah Taylor *Randolph* • Beth Champion *Emily* • Dannii Minogue *Didi* • Malcolm Kennard *Danny* • Willa O'Neill *Vicki* ■ *Dir* Michael Pattinson • *Scr* Jan Sardi

One Crazy Summer ★★ PG
Comedy 1986 · US · Colour · 89mins

There are youthful appearances by John Cusack and Demi Moore in this offbeat comedy about a college wannabe who has to learn about love on holiday in Nantucket before he goes off to the educational institution of his choice. It's filmed in a cartoon-style with some fun sight gags, witty dialogue and even a handful of well-integrated animation sequences, but there's little connective tissue. ▭

John Cusack *Hoops McCann* • Demi Moore *Cassandra* • Curtis Armstrong *Ack Ack Raymond* • Joel Murray *George Calamari* • Joe Flaherty *General Raymond* • Bobcat Goldthwait *Egg Stork* • Mark Metcalf *Aguilla Beckersted* • William Hickey *Old Man Beckersted* ■ *Dir/Scr* Savage Steve Holland

One Damned Day at Dawn… Django Meets Sartana ★★
Spaghetti western 1971 · It · Colour · 90mins

An intriguing title hides a very undistinguished spaghetti western. More imagination seems to have gone into the names of characters like the Vicious Mexican and Joe "the Worm" Smith than into the plot, which is a routine affair about a sheriff teaming up with a bounty hunter to confound gun-runners. Hunt Powers is a poor Sartana, but Fabio Testi is a scowling substitute for Franco Nero as Django, "the Man in Black". Directing under the pseudonym Miles Deem, Demofilo Fidani ensures there is just enough bruising action to keep you awake. Italian dialogue dubbed into English.

Hunt Powers *Sheriff Ronson/Sartana* • Fabio Testi *The Man in Black/Django* • Dean

Stratford *Bud Wheeler* • Dennis Colt *Sanchez* • Lucky McMurray *Joe "the Worm" Smith* ■ *Dir* Miles Deem [Demofilo Fidani]

One Dangerous Night ★
Crime mystery 1943 · US · BW · 76mins

Warren William makes his eighth appearance as reformed jewel thief Michael Lanyard, known as the "Lone Wolf". Here he is suspected of involvement in the death of a gangster who is blackmailing three women and had planned to elope with another. This low-life character is played by Gerald Mohr, who three years later took over the Lone Wolf role. These potboilers were a training ground for new talent: Ann Savage, later the femme fatale in *Detour*, makes her debut, while director Michael Gordon went on to make major features such as the 1950 version of *Cyrano de Bergerac*.

Warren William *Michael Lanyard, "The Lone Wolf"* • Marguerite Chapman *Eve Andrews* • Eric Blore *Jamison* • Mona Barrie *Jane Merrick* • Tala Birell *Sonia* • Margaret Hayes *Patricia* • Ann Savage *Vivian* • Gerald Mohr *Harry Cooper* ■ *Dir* Michael Gordon • *Scr* Donald Davis, from a story by Arnold Phillips, Max Nosseck, from characters created by Louis Joseph Vance

One Dark Night ★★ 15
Supernatural horror 1982 · US · Colour · 88mins

Even by the early eighties the teens-in-peril scenario was well past its sell-by-date. In her first leading role a young Meg Tilly, sister of Jennifer, is forced to spend the night in a creepy mausoleum as part of a gang initiation test unaware that its recently interned occupant is about to wake up! Director Tom McLoughlin manages to muster not one ounce of tension and the gore count is fatally low. At least cult heroes Adam (*Batman*) West and Kevin Peter Hall, the man behind the Predator's prosthetics, make welcome appearances and the climax is adequately staged with the requisite floating apparitions and SFX light show.

Meg Tilly *Julie* • Robin Evans *Carol* • Leslie Speights *Kitty* • Elizabeth Daily *Leslie* • Adam West *Allan* • Melissa Newman *Olivia* • Donald Hotton *Dockstader* • Kevin Peter Hall *Eddie* ■ *Dir* Tom McLoughlin • *Scr* Tom McLoughlin, Michael Hawes

One Day in September ★★★★ 15
Documentary 1999 · UK · Colour · 94mins

The protests of the victims' relatives have somewhat tarnished the sheen of Kevin Macdonald's Oscar-winning documentary. But it remains a revelatory account of the terrorist atrocity that turned the 1972 Munich Olympics into the "Games of Shame". Narrated by Michael Douglas and seamlessly linking news footage, interviews and graphics, this meticulously researched exposé of the hideously bungled German security operation simply beggars belief. Examples of poor communication, military inexpertise and governmental dithering almost overshadow the horror of the Black September action, which left 11 Israeli Olympians, five Palestinians and one policeman dead.

A damning indictment of political violence and bureaucratic arrogance.

Michael Douglas *Narrator* ■ *Dir* Kevin Macdonald

One Day in the Life of Ivan Denisovich ★★★
Prison drama 1971 · UK/Nor · Colour · 108mins

Although meticulously adapted by Ronald Harwood from Alexander Solzhenitsyn's celebrated novel, this Anglo-Norwegian co-production only hints at the appalling conditions inside a Soviet labour camp in the late-Stalinist era, and the dignity and ingenuity with which Ivan survived them. Admittedly, it is a difficult novel to film, even when photographed by a genius like Sven Nykvist and interpreted with such intelligence by Tom Courtenay. But director Casper Wrede has turned it into the wrong sort of ordeal – overwhelmed by the political and literary significance of his material, he has missed both art and life.

Tom Courtenay *Ivan Denisovich* • Espen Skjonberg *Tiurin* • James Maxwell *Captain Buinovsky* • Alfred Burke *Alyosha* • Eric Thompson *Tsezar* • John Cording *Pavlo* • Mathew Guinness *Kilgas* ■ *Dir* Caspar Wrede [Casper Wrede] • *Scr* Ronald Harwood, from the novel by Alexander Solzhenitsyn

One Deadly Summer ★★★★ 18
Drama 1983 · Fr · Colour · 127mins

Exploiting her beauty to disarming effect, Isabelle Adjani won a César for her smouldering performance in this deceptively complex thriller. Working from his own novel, Sébastien Japrisot fashions a script that consistently disconcerts the viewer as the narrative focus shifts between Adjani's vengeful temptress and her besotted husband, Alain Souchon. Similarly director Jean Becker refuses to mislead us simply with appearances, as what seems to be a study of provincial boorishness is overtaken by more sinister events. Atmospherically photographed with a roving camera by Etienne Becker, this meticulously paced picture is a tad overlong, but it's undeniably dark, daring and disturbing. In French with English subtitles. ▭

Isabelle Adjani *Eliane/Elle* • Alain Souchon *Florimond/Pin Pon* • Suzanne Flon *Cognata* • Jenny Clève *Pin Pon's mother* • Michel Galabru *Gabriel Devigne* • François Cluzet *Mickey* • Manuel Gélin *Boubou* ■ *Dir* Jean Becker • *Scr* Sébastien Japrisot, from his novel • *Cinematographer* Etienne Becker

One Desire ★★
Period drama 1955 · US · Colour · 94mins

One of producer Ross Hunter's least interesting "women's pictures" of the fifties, this stars Anne Baxter as the proprietor of an oil town's notorious gambling saloon whose big desire is to settle down and live a respectable life with Rock Hudson's handsome but carefree croupier. Rich bitch Julie Adams gets in the way but the scriptwriters come up with a drastic method of eliminating her. Baxter is too hard-as-nails to elicit much sympathy or tears while Hudson seems to be somewhere else.

Anne Baxter *Tacey Cromwell* • Rock Hudson *Clint Saunders* • Julie Adams *Judith Watrous* • Carl Benton Reid *Senator Watrous* • Natalie Wood *Seely* • William Hooper *MacBain* ■ *Dir* Jerry Hopper • *Scr* Lawrence Roman, Robert Blees, from the novel *Tacey Cromwell* by Conrad Richter

One Eight Seven ★★ 15

Drama 1997 · US · Colour · 114mins

Samuel L Jackson's typically intense work is the sole merit of this over-directed, uninvolving school drama from *Waterworld*'s Kevin Reynolds. He plays a New York teacher physically and psychologically scarred after a vicious knife assault from a student, who transfers to a new school in Los Angeles to rebuild his life, only to find equally violent conditions. Shot in a distracting MTV pop video style, Jackson's sincere performance is wasted on such clichéd, one-dimensional fare and the movie's climactic descent into full-on melodrama provokes giggles rather than shudders. Contains swearing, violence and some nudity.

Samuel L Jackson *Trevor Garfield* • John Heard *Dave Childress* • Kelly Rowan *Ellen Henry* • Clifton Gonzalez Gonzalez *Cesar* • Karina Arroyave *Rita* • Jonah Rooney *Stevie Middleton* • Lobo Sebastian *Benny* • Jack Kehler *Hyland* ■ *Dir* Kevin Reynolds • *Scr* Scott Yagemann

One-Eyed Jacks ★★★★ PG

Western 1961 · US · Colour · 135mins

This stunning and deeply satisfying psychological western is the only film Marlon Brando directed, but Paramount had reason to regret indulging its star – not only does the movie contain levels of sadism and perversity that made it unique for a Hollywood studio film of the period, but it also failed to recoup its $6 million outlay in the States. With a story that is loosely based on the legend of Billy the Kid and Pat Garrett, it reunites the stars of *A Streetcar Named Desire* and *On the Waterfront*, as Brando seeks revenge on his devious partner Karl Malden. It's a fine, adult work, with the Monterey seascapes (magnificently photographed by Charles Lang Jr) making an unusual setting for a western. Incidentally, Brando took over from Stanley Kubrick, who left to direct *Spartacus*.

Marlon Brando *Rio* • Karl Malden *Dad Longworth* • Katy Jurado *Maria* • Pina Pellicer *Louisa* • Slim Pickens *Lon* • Ben Johnson *Bob Amory* ■ *Dir* Marlon Brando • *Scr* Guy Trosper, Calder Willingham, from the novel *The Authentic Death of Hendry Jones* by Charles Neider • *Cinematographer* Charles Lang Jr [Charles Lang] • *Music* Hugo Friedhofer

One False Move ★★★★ 18

Crime drama 1992 · US · Colour · 101mins

A mesmerising slice of modern *film noir*, in which director Carl Franklin skilfully steers past the usual clichés to deliver a thoughtful, ultimately tragic tale. A trio of criminals sets off on a murderous cross-country journey, fleeing Los Angeles with the takings from a brutal drugs heist. LA cops Jim Metzler and Earl Billings are convinced the criminals will head for the tiny southern town where one of their number (Cynda Williams) used to live, and lie in wait with the naive local cop (the ever excellent Bill Paxton). It's a gripping affair, punctuated with isolated splashes of shocking violence, and is superbly acted by the largely unknown cast. Contains swearing and drug abuse.

Cynda Williams *Fantasia/Lila* • Bill Paxton *Dale "Hurricane" Dixon* • Billy Bob Thornton *Ray Malcolm* • Jim Metzler *Dud Cole* • Michael Beach *Pluto* • Earl Billings *McFeely* • Natalie Canerday *Cheryl Ann* • Robert Ginnaven *Charlie* • Robert Anthony Bell *Byron* • Kevin Hunter *Ronnie* ■ *Dir* Carl Franklin • *Scr* Billy Bob Thornton, Tom Epperson

One Fine Day ★★★ PG

Romantic comedy
1996 · US · Colour · 104mins

In this warm-hearted but underwritten romantic comedy, George Clooney stars as a newspaper columnist saddled with parental responsibilities when he's forced to look after his five-year-old daughter while his ex-wife is on honeymoon. Into his life comes Michelle Pfeiffer, who's struggling to hold down a job and bring up a child, and the couple reluctantly agree to help each other out – only to find that what can go wrong naturally does. Clooney, Pfeiffer and Mae Whitman (as Clooney's daughter) are suitably charming, but they are all let down by a very bratty and irritating performance from Alex D Linz as Pfeiffer's hideous son, and some uninspired direction from Michael Hoffman.

Michelle Pfeiffer *Melanie Parker* • George Clooney *Jack Taylor* • Mae Whitman *Maggie Taylor* • Alex D Linz *Sammy Parker* • Charles Durning *Lew* • Jon Robin Baitz *Yates Jr* • Ellen Greene *Elaine Lieberman* • Joe Grifasi *Manny Feldstein* ■ *Dir* Michael Hoffman • *Scr* Terrel Seltzer, Ellen Simon

One Flew over the Cuckoo's Nest ★★★★★ 18

Drama 1975 · US · Colour · 128mins

Adapted from Ken Kesey's novel, this film is one the classic movies of the seventies, thanks in no small measure to the talents of director Milos Forman, who propelled the comic antics to a horrifyingly poignant finale and resounding critical and commercial success; it became one of the few to be awarded all the major Oscars, winning for best picture, director, screenplay, actor (Jack Nicholson) and actress (Louise Fletcher). Nicholson's performance as McMurphy, a free spirit at loose in a state mental home, is one of his greatest characterisations, as he stirs up rebellion against the oppressive regime of Fletcher's ward sister, in which drugs make patients' decisions. And among those patients are such then almost unknowns as Danny DeVito, Brad Dourif and Christopher Lloyd. Contains swearing and some violence. DVD

Jack Nicholson *Randle P McMurphy* • Louise Fletcher *Nurse Mildred Ratched* • William Redfield *Harding* • Will Sampson *Chief Bromden* • Brad Dourif *Billy Bibbit* • Sydney Lassick *Charlie Cheswick* • Christopher Lloyd *Taber* • Danny DeVito *Martini* • Sherman "Scatman" Crothers [Scatman Crothers] *Turkle* ■ *Dir* Milos Forman • *Scr* Lawrence Hauben, Bo Goldman, from the play by Dale Wasserman, from the novel by Ken Kesey • *Cinematographer* Haskell Wexler

One Foot in Heaven ★★★ U

Biographical drama 1941 · US · BW · 107mins

The illustrious Fredric March is at the centre of this Oscar-nominated, pleasingly old-fashioned movie about William Spence, a Methodist minister who, at the turn of the 20th century, takes his message from parish to parish, and must grapple with the changes in society that conflict with his beliefs. Adapted from a once popular biography of his father by Hartzell Spence, this is a loving, if slighty mawkish, piece, peddling piety but not sanctimoniousness. March is well-supported by, among others, Martha Scott, Beulah Bondi and Gene Lockhart, while Irving Rapper directs with a nice sense of period (and a generous supply of sentimentality).

Fredric March *William Spence* • Martha Scott *Hope Morris Spence* • Beulah Bondi *Mrs Lydia Sandow* • Gene Lockhart *Preston Thurston* • Grant Mitchell *Clayton Potter* • Moroni Olsen *Dr John Romer* • Harry Davenport *Elias Samson* • Elisabeth Fraser *Eileen Spence, aged 17* • Frankie Thomas *Hartzell Spence, aged 18* • Laura Hope Crews *Mrs Thurston* ■ *Dir* Irving Rapper • *Scr* Casey Robinson, from the biography by Hartzell Spence

One Foot in Hell ★★★

Western 1960 · US · Colour · 89mins

As an argument for America to introduce a National Health Service, this western takes some beating. Alan Ladd is the Civil War soldier whose wife dies in Arizona because he doesn't have the money to buy her medicine. Nevertheless, he becomes sheriff and plots revenge by robbing the bank and killing everyone he can. Giving a novel twist to the western formula, this has some fresh characters and doesn't readily cop out in the end. Producer and co-writer Sydney Boehm wrote some cult movies such as *When Worlds Collide* and *The Big Heat* while the other writer, Aaron Spelling, later became the most famous producer in American TV, responsible for *Dynasty*, *Beverly Hills 90210* and a host of other hit shows.

Alan Ladd *Mitch Barrett* • Don Murray *Dan Keats* • Dan O'Herlihy *Harry Ivers* • Dolores Michaels *Julie Reynolds* • Barry Coe *Stu Christian* • Larry Gates *Doc Seltzer* • Karl Swenson *Sheriff Olson* ■ *Dir* James B Clark • *Scr* Aaron Spelling, Sydney Boehm, from the story by Aaron Spelling

One from the Heart ★★ 15

Musical romance
1982 · US · Colour · 102mins

Feeling the need to lighten up after *Apocalypse Now*, Francis Ford Coppola concocted this featherweight, Fellini-esque romantic fantasy about two sets of lovers in Las Vegas. Of rather more interest to Coppola was the idea of staging the whole thing in his Los Angeles studio – even a re-creation of Vegas's airport – and shooting it with new video techniques. Coppola thought this was the way of the future, a simplified system, but the budget soared and the movie was barely released, virtually bankrupting its director. Pauline Kael quipped, "This movie isn't from the heart, or from the head, either; it's from the lab." As far as Hollywood's grand follies go, this goes further than most.

Frederic Forrest *Hank* • Teri Garr *Frannie* • Nastassja Kinski *Leila* • Raul Julia *Ray* • Lainie Kazan *Maggie* • Harry Dean Stanton *Moe* • Allen Goorwitz [Allen Garfield] *Restaurant owner* ■ *Dir* Francis Ford Coppola • *Scr* Armyan Bernstein, Francis Ford Coppola, from a story by Armyan Bernstein • *Cinematographer* Vittorio Storaro • *Music* Tom Waits • *Art Director* Dean Tavoularis

One Full Moon ★★★ 15

Drama 1991 · UK · Colour · 97mins

Adapted from a novel by Caradog Prichard (which had been a favourite of director Endaf Emlyn since his teens), this poetic exercise in rural realism shifts between the fifties and the twenties, as Dyfan Roberts revisits the slate-mining community where he was raised by his mother. The relationship between Betsan Llwyd and young Tudor Roberts is both touching and unfeigned, as they put on a united front against the harshness of their existence and the censoriousness of the local preacher. But the nostalgic humour dissipates after Llwyd is assaulted by a travelling tinker and their grim idyll begins to unravel. In Welsh with English subtitles.

Dyfan Roberts *Man* • Tudor Roberts *Boy* • Betsan Llwyd *Mother* • Delyth Einir *Jini* • Cian Ciaran *Huw* • Dilwyn Vaughn Thomas *Moi* ■ *Dir* Endaf Emlyn • *Scr* Gwenlyn Parry, Endaf Emlyn, from the novel by Caradog Prichard

One Good Cop ★★★ 15

Drama 1991 · US · Colour · 100mins

A smoothly orchestrated movie, veering unapologetically between shameless sentimentality and violent melodrama, which is given a gritty reality by Michael Keaton's performance as a decent cop planning to adopt his murdered partner's three children. How he blots his record after robbing a local drug baron is a wrenching tale, skilfully told by writer/director Heywood Gould, whose true-life experiences were the basis of *Cocktail*. An under-rated look at the personal and professional conflicts faced by the police force. Contains violence and some swearing.

Michael Keaton *Artie Lewis* • Rene Russo *Rita Lewis* • Anthony LaPaglia *Stevie Diroma* • Kevin Conway *Lieutenant Danny Quinn* • Rachel Ticotin *Grace* • Tony Plana *Beniamino* • Benjamin Bratt *Felix* ■ *Dir/Scr* Heywood Gould

One Good Turn ★★★ U

Comedy 1954 · UK · BW · 90mins

This is the cleverly constructed follow-up to Norman Wisdom's smash-hit debut *Trouble in Store*. Arguably the best of his vehicles, it features the bumbling star as a handyman trying to save the orphanage that employs him from collapse. His money-raising schemes are invariably hilarious, while his sequences with leading ladies Joan Rice and Australian zither girl Shirley Abicair are charming. Of course, the film is overly sentimental, but sentiment was part of Wisdom's stock-in-trade, and today we can look beyond the home-grown schmaltz and recognise the rare quality of a true cinematic clown.

Norman Wisdom *Norman* • Joan Rice *Iris* • Shirley Abicair *Mary* • Thora Hird *Cook* • William Russell *Alec* • Richard Caldicot *Bigley*

• Marjorie Fender *Tuppeny* ■ *Dir* John Paddy Carstairs • *Scr* Maurice Cowan, John Paddy Carstairs, Ted Willis, from a story by Dorothy Whipple, Sid Colin, Talbot Rothwell

One Good Turn ★★ 18

Thriller   1996 · US · Colour · 88mins

A whole lot of setup for very little payoff. Lenny Von Dohlen is a successful software designer who spots James Remar living as a vagrant on the streets of LA. Since Remar had saved Von Dohlen's life years before when they were in the army together, he offers him a job, and then spends the next hour or so of screen time ignoring glaringly obvious clues that Remar has some insane agenda of his own. The complicated back story is just a smoke screen obscuring the fact that this is little more than an average psycho-stalker movie. ▭

James Remar *Simon* • Suzy Amis *Laura* • Lenny Von Dohlen *Matt* • Richard Minchenberg *John* • Audie England *Kristen* • Rowena Guinness *Kim* • John Savage *Santapietro* ■ *Dir* Tony Randel • *Scr* Jim Piddock

One Heavenly Night ★★ U

Romantic musical
1931 · US · Colour · 76mins

A flower-seller in Budapest (Evelyn Laye) is persuaded by musical hall star Lilyan Tashman to take her place in her absence, in which guise Laye finds romance with handsome count John Boles. Complications ensue when Tashman reveals the masquerade. English star Laye was spirited away from the London stage by Samuel Goldwyn, who had this operetta especially written for her Hollywood debut. She is charming, pretty and graceful, and George Fitzmaurice's direction fine. However, the film founders on a silly and inadequate script and, when it lost money, Goldwyn dropped his new protégée. After four more Hollywood films, Laye returned to a long and successful career on the British stage. ▭

Evelyn Laye *Lilli* • John Boles *Count Mirko Tibor* • Leon Errol *Otto* • Lilyan Tashman *Fritzi Vyez* • Hugh Cameron *Janos* • Marian Lord [Marion Lord] *Liska* • Lionel Belmore *Zagen* ■ *Dir* George Fitzmaurice • *Scr* Sidney Howard, from a story by Louis Bromfield

One Hour with You ★★★

Musical romantic comedy
1932 · US · BW · 78mins

Parisian doctor Maurice Chevalier and his wife Jeanette MacDonald are still utterly devoted to each other after three years of marriage. But their harmony is disrupted when her devious, man-eating best friend Genevieve Tobin gets her clutches into Chevalier, and his best friend Charles Ruggles declares his passion for MacDonald. Paramount's master of sophistication, Ernst Lubitsch, remakes his 1924 silent hit, *The Marriage Circle*, as a vehicle for Chevalier and MacDonald, beautifully orchestrating an experimental mix of verse, song and soliloquies delivered straight to camera by Chevalier. The result is a frothy, sophisticated and risqué comedy of manners.

Maurice Chevalier *Dr André Bertier* • Jeanette MacDonald *Colette Bertier* • Genevieve Tobin *Mitzi Olivier* • Charlie Ruggles [Charles Ruggles] *Adolph* • Roland Young *Professor Olivier* • George Barbier *Police commissioner* ■ *Dir* Ernst Lubitsch, George Cukor • *Scr* Samson Raphaelson, from the play *Nur ein Traum, Lustspiel in 3 Akten (Only a Dream)* by Lothar Schmidt [Lothar Goldschmidt] • *Cinematographer* Victor Milner

One Hundred and One Dalmatians ★★★★★ U

Animated comedy drama
1960 · US · Colour · 77mins

The perennially popular Disney animation, from a novel by Dodie Smith, goes to prove that a dog's life can be as adventurous and unnerving as any James Bond story. The fifteen Dalmatian puppies of Pong and Perdita are stolen by the grotesque henchmen of monstrous villainess Cruela De Vil, who wants to add them to her collection to create a fabulous fur coat. So the canine couple rally a force – including a cat called Sergeant Tibs and the Colonel, a pompous sheepdog – to mount a rescue operation on Cruella's Hell Hall. This is great fun, with the necessary tinge of real terror, and features a voice cast, headed by Rod Taylor. ▭

Rod Taylor *Pongo* • Ben Wright *Roger Radcliff* • J Pat O'Malley *Colonel/Jasper Badun* • Cate Bauer *Perdita* • Betty Lou Gerson *Cruella De Vil/Miss Birdwell* • Dave Frankham *[David Frankham] Sergeant Tibs* • Martha Wentworth *Nanny/Queenie/Lucy* • Frederick Worlock *Horace Badun/Inspector Craven* • Lisa Davis *Anita Radcliff* ■ *Dir* Wolfgang Reitherman, Hamilton S Luske [Hamilton Luske], Clyde Geronimi • *Scr* Bill Peet, from the novel by Dodie Smith

101 Dalmatians ★★★ U

Comedy drama   1996 · US · Colour · 98mins

Disney updates its classic animated tale with this live-action version starring a deliciously over-the-top Glenn Close as infamous villain Cruella De Vil, the rich bitch who wants to turn loads of cuddly little Dalmatian puppies into a fur coat. Jeff Daniels and Joely Richardson (as the couple trying to stop her) are slightly more subdued, but enjoyable to watch nonetheless. The only complaint for older viewers (and those sentimental about the original) is that live dogs lack the variety of expression – and the vocals – of their animated counterparts. That said, little ones will love it . ▭

Glenn Close *Cruella De Vil* • Jeff Daniels *Roger* • Joely Richardson *Anita* • Joan Plowright *Nanny* • Hugh Laurie *Jasper* • Mark Williams *Horace* • John Shrapnel *Skinner* • Tim McInnerny *Alonzo* • Hugh Fraser *Frederick* ■ *Dir* Stephen Herek • *Scr* John Hughes, from the novel by Dodie Smith

One Hundred Men and a Girl ★★★★

Musical   1937 · US · BW · 85mins

Deanna Durbin, the devoted daughter of a classical trombonist Adolphe Menjou, seeks the assistance of famous conductor Leopold Stokowski (playing himself) to form an Orchestra of the Unemployed. The result is a quintessential feel-good movie, played with precocious zest by Universal Studios' meal ticket and a splendid supporting cast that includes Mischa Auer and bombastic fat man Eugene Pallette. All one needs in order to enjoy this nonsense is the ability to surrender to its fairy-tale sweetness and enjoy the classical music under Stokowski's baton.

Deanna Durbin *Patricia ''Patsy'' Cardwell* • Adolphe Menjou *John Cardwell* • Leopold Stokowski • Alice Brady *Mrs Frost* • Eugene Pallette *John R Frost* • Mischa Auer *Michael Borodoff* • Billy Gilbert *Garage owner* • Alma Kruger *Mrs Tyler* ■ *Dir* Henry Koster • *Scr* Bruce Manning, Charles Kenyon, James Mulhauser

100 Rifles ★★ 15

Western   1969 · US · Colour · 104mins

A below-par western, filmed in Spain and directed by Tom Gries, who made the elegiac *Will Penny* with Charlton Heston. This is a breezier and more routine affair, with muscular black actor and former football star Jim Brown as a lawman in search of Burt Reynolds, a half-breed Mexican who has robbed a bank in order to build an arsenal for a revolution. Raquel Welch is the glamorous and scantily clad senorita of the piece who gets into bed with Brown, a startling scene for 1969. People sweat profusely, say ''Hey, gringo'', and generally use up a lot of ammunition. ▭

Jim Brown *Lyedecker* • Raquel Welch *Sarita* • Burt Reynolds *Yaqui Joe* • Fernando Lamas *Verdugo* • Dan O'Herlihy *Grimes* • Hans Gudegast [Eric Braeden] *Von Klemme* • Michael Forest *Humara* ■ *Dir* Tom Gries • *Scr* Clair Huffaker, Tom Gries, from the novel *The Californio* by Robert MacLeod

One in a Million ★★★ U

Romantic musical comedy
1936 · US · BW · 94mins

Norwegian ice skating star Sonja Henie's first American film was a smash hit which resulted in a 20th Century-Fox contract and top international screen stardom. Viewed today it is probably her best vehicle; there's a winsome topicality attached to this film, dealing as it did with the pre-war Winter Olympics, where the blonde cutie wins the gold and is schlepped to Madison Square Garden by manager Adolphe Menjou. There she meets likeable Don Ameche. There are real treats on show here, so, even if you're not a fan of the pert ice star, give this fun flick a try.

Sonja Henie *Greta Muller* • Adolphe Menjou *Thadeus ''Tad'' Spencer* • Jean Hersholt *Heinrich Muller* • Ned Sparks *Danny Simpson* • Don Ameche *Bob Harris* • Arline Judge *Billie Spencer* • Borrah Minevitch *Adolphe* • Dixie Dunbar *Goldie* • Montagu Love *Ratoffsky alias Sir Frederick Brooks* ■ *Dir* Sidney Lanfield • *Scr* Leonard Praskins, Mark Kelly, from a story by Leonard Praskins

One Is a Lonely Number ★★★ 15

Drama   1972 · US · Colour · 93mins

In this seventies women's movie, Trish Van Devere plays a wife who grapples with the aftermath of divorce, travelling the emotional rollercoaster with the help of Hollywood stalwarts Melvyn Douglas, who plays a lonely shopkeeper, and Janet Leigh, an acerbic president of a group for divorced women. Though a little lightweight at times, it has been treated perhaps more harshly than it deserves – at one point, the title was considered so downbeat, they even tried to rename it *Two Is a Happy Number!* ▭

Trish Van Devere *Amy Brower* • Monte Markham *Howard Carpenter* • Janet Leigh *Gert Meredith* • Melvyn Douglas *Joseph Provo* • Jane Elliott *Madge Frazier* ■ *Dir* Mel Stuart • *Scr* David Seltzer, from the story *The Good Humor Man* by Rebecca Morris

One Little Indian ★★ U

Western comedy drama
1973 · US · Colour · 86mins

At the time when books such as *Bury My Heart at Wounded Knee* and films such as *Little Big Man* were re-evaluating the history of the American Indian, or Native American, the Disney studio offered its own saccharine and sentimentalised slant on the new political correctness. James Garner plays a cavalryman who tries to save the Indians during a massacre and is sentenced to hang. His neck and everyone else's conscience is saved by a white boy who has been brought up by Indians. Aimed firmly at the family audience, it boasts a Jerry Goldsmith score, the familiar backdrops of Utah's deserts and buttes, and an early appearance by a young Jodie Foster.

James Garner *Clint Keyes* • Vera Miles *Doris* • Pat Hingle *Captain Stewart* • Morgan Woodward *Sergeant Raines* • John Doucette *Sergeant Waller* • Clay O'Brien *Mark* • Robert Pine *Lieutenant Cummins* • Bruce Glover *Schrader* • Jodie Foster *Martha* ■ *Dir* Bernard McEveety • *Scr* Harry Spalding • *Music* Jerry Goldsmith

One Magic Christmas ★★ U

Seasonal drama   1985 · US · Colour · 85mins

One suspects that the intention here was to put a modern slant on Dickens's tale *A Christmas Carol*. But quite how her husband's redundancy, impending homelessness and bankruptcy are supposed to rekindle the Christmas spirit in housewife Mary Steenburgen is anybody's guess. It takes a huge leap of faith for anyone to believe that an angel with an uncanny resemblance to Harry Dean Stanton can do much to rectify the situation, but this is Disney, so prepare for take off. Earnestly played, but far too downbeat for the festive season. ▭

Mary Steenburgen *Ginnie Grainger* • Gary Basaraba *Jack Grainger* • Elisabeth Harnois *Abbie Grainger* • Arthur Hill *Caleb* • Wayne Robson *Harry Dickens* • Harry Dean Stanton *Gideon* • Jan Rubes *Santa Claus* • Elias Koteas *Eddie* ■ *Dir* Phillip Borsos • *Scr* Thomas Meehan, from a story by Thomas Meehan, Phillip Borsos, Barry Healey

One Man Force ★★ 18

Action thriller   1989 · US · Colour · 85mins

Former professional American football player John ''the Tooz'' Matuszak plays Jake Swan, who is a cop on the edge following the murder of his partner. He investigates the kidnapping of a singer, which then leads him on a tour of LA's nightclubs. This is somehow connected with a money-laundering scheme and naturally gives Jake the chance to get revenge for his partner. The Tooz isn't much of an actor, and this limp star vehicle doesn't even have very good action scenes. ▭

John Matuszak *Jake Swan* • Ronny Cox *Lieutenant McCoy* • Charles Napier *Dante* • Sharon Farrell *Shirley* • Robert Tessier *Wilson* ■ *Dir/Scr* Dale Trevillion

One Man Jury ★

Action crime drama
1978 · US · Colour · 98 mins

It seems like a B-movie dream: Jack Palance as a Dirty Harry-like cop who goes even further than Eastwood did, killing various street scum in cold blood. But despite the premise, the slow proceedings are actually rather tame. Palance's performance is half-hearted, as if he's being distracted by some personal issue, and his character does more complaining than fighting, while the cheesy look of the enterprise resembles a seventies Aaron Spelling TV show.

Jack Palance *Wade* • Christopher Mitchum *Blake* • Pamela Shoop *Wendy* • Angel Tompkins *Kitty* • Joe Spinell *Mike* • Cara Williams *Nancy* • Alexandra Hay *Tessie* • Jeff McCracken *Billy Joe* ■ *Dir/Scr* Charles Martin

One Man's Justice ★★ 18

Action thriller 1996 · US · Colour · 101mins

Army drill sergeant and hand-to-hand combat expert Brian Bosworth wakes from a coma only to recall that his wife and daughter were murdered by punks in a convenience store. Of course, the punks were connected to a corrupt cop who runs guns for the local crime lord, played by rapper MC Hammer in one of his more amusing career diversions. Bosworth bulls his way through this by-the-numbers production, and it's tough to imagine what he hopes to gain from all this, but in these films it's impolite to question the hero's motives. ▭

Brian Bosworth *John North* • DeJuan Guy *Mikey* • Bruce Payne *Karl Savak* • Jeff Kober *Marcus* • MC Hammer *Dexter Kane* • Rachel Duncan *Marianne* • Neal McDonough *Agent Ward* • Robert Kotecki *Agent Klark* ■ *Dir* Kurt Wimmer • *Scr* Steven Selling

One Man's Way ★★ U

Biographical drama 1964 · US · BW · 104mins

After *Invasion of the Bee Girls* (1973) the only way for director Denis Sanders to go was up – to this devout biopic about Norman Vincent Peale, a reporter who became one of those aspirational Dale Carnegie-types in American pop culture. Don Murray gives a sympathetically sanitised performance, but memories of Sanders's wonderful Oscar-awarded short *A Time Out of War* – made with brother Terry – haunt this decline into good taste.

Don Murray *Norman Vincent Peale* • Diana Hyland *Ruth Peale* • William Windom *Rev Clifford Peale* • Virginia Christine *Anna Peale* • Carol Ohmart *Evelyn* • Veronica Cartwright *Mary* ■ *Dir* Denis Sanders • *Scr* Eleanore Griffin, John W Bloch, from the biography *Norman Vincent Peale: Minister to Millions* by Arthur Gordon

One Million Years BC ★★★ PG

Adventure 1966 · US/UK · Colour · 96mins

A long, long time ago, women looked like Raquel Welch and got to wear furry bikinis as they roamed the wilderness. Welch has a stunning physique but no dialogue, merely some grunts and a furrowed brow that puts Shakespearean actors into the shade. Made by Hammer, this is an absolute hoot, a sort of Jurassic lark, as it describes the war between the Rock People and the Shell People, as well as some wobbly prehistoric monsters, courtesy of genre maestro Ray Harryhausen. It should have co-starred Kenneth Williams and been called *Carry On Caveman*. ▭

Raquel Welch *Loana* • John Richardson *Tumak* • Percy Herbert *Sakana* • Robert Brown *Akhoba* • Martine Beswick *Nupondi* • Jean Wladon *Ahot* • Lisa Thomas *Sura* ■ *Dir* Don Chaffey • *Scr* Michael Carreras, from the film *Man and His Mate (One Million BC)* by Mickell Novak, George Baker, Joseph Frickert

One Minute to Zero ★

Drama 1952 · US · BW · 105mins

Robert Mitchum goes into action during the Korean War, here teaming up with Ann Blyth who represents the United Nations and provides the love interest. Their romance comes under strain when Mitchum mows down some innocent refugees but, hey, they soon get together for a syrupy song called *Tell Me Golden Moon*. Despite the pains taken with the battle scenes, this is a pretty dismal job, designed to show how the UN was deep inside Uncle Sam's pocket.

Robert Mitchum *Colonel Steve Janowksi* • Ann Blyth *Linda Day* • William Talman *Colonel Parker* • Charles McGraw *Sgt Baker* • Margaret Sheridan *Mary Parker* • Richard Egan *Captain Ralston* ■ *Dir* Tay Garnett • *Scr* Milton Krims, William Wister Haines

One More Kiss ★★★★ 12

Drama 1999 · UK · Colour · 98mins

What would you do if you only had a few months to live? When she discovers she has terminal cancer, single-minded Valerie Edmond returns from New York to her home town of Berwick-upon-Tweed to patch things up with her dad (James Cosmo). She's also keen to spend time with old flame Gerard Butler – always assuming his wife doesn't mind! Using only available light, director Vadim Jean has created a beautiful movie that manages to be moving without being too sentimental. Thanks to some sterling performances, particularly from Cosmo, this is an uplifting, rewarding film that, while occasionally harrowing, is also full of gutsy humour. ▭

Gerard Butler *Sam* • James Cosmo *Frank* • Valerie Edmond *Sarah* • Valerie Gogan *Charlotte* • Carl Proctor *Barry* • Danny Nussbaum *Jude* • Dilys Miller *Mary* • Ron Guthrie *Robin* ■ *Dir* Vadim Jean • *Scr* Suzie Halewood

One More River ★★★

Drama 1934 · US · BW · 90mins

Looking fearfully dated today, this once prestigious Universal feature is based upon the last novel in John Galsworthy's *The Forsyte Saga*. Despite being directed by the talented expatriate Englishman James Whale, this Hollywood, England, study of a divorce remains relentlessly theatrical, although Diana Wynyard is sublime as the wife accused by Colin Clive of committing adultery with young Frank Lawton. Watch for distinguished Brits Mrs Patrick Campbell and C Aubrey Smith, and also the screen debut of lovely Jane Wyatt.

Diana Wynyard *Clare Corven* • Frank Lawton *Tony Croom* • Mrs Patrick Campbell *Lady Mont* • Jane Wyatt *Dinny Cherrell* • Colin Clive *Sir Gerald Corven* • Reginald Denny *David Dornford* • C Aubrey Smith *General Charwell* • Henry Stephenson *Sir Lawrence Mont* • Lionel Atwill *Brough* • Alan Mowbray *Forsyte* ■ *Dir* James Whale • *Scr* RC Sherriff, from the novel by John Galsworthy

One More Time ★★

Comedy 1970 · UK · Colour · 95mins

Salt and Pepper, a lacklustre British-made comedy vehicle for Sinatra clan cronies Sammy Davis Jr and Peter Lawford, rather surprisingly spawned this even weaker sequel, in which the buddies are again Soho club-owners involved in crime. This time Lawford plays identical twin brothers; the death of one leads to attempts on the life of the other in a Scottish castle. Interesting (for a while) is the way director Jerry Lewis, who doesn't appear, transfers his zany persona to Davis and interpolates typical Lewis setups and sentimentality.

Sammy Davis Jr *Charlie Salt* • Peter Lawford *Chris Pepper/Lord Sydney Pepper* • Maggie Wright *Miss Tomkins* • Leslie Sands *Inspector Crook* • John Wood *Figg* • Sydney Arnold *Tombs* • Edward Evans *Gordon* • Percy Herbert *Mander* • Christopher Lee • Peter Cushing ■ *Dir* Jerry Lewis • *Scr* Michael Pertwee

One More Train to Rob ★★

Western 1971 · US · Colour · 108mins

A breezy western with George Peppard as a train robber who tries to settle down with his girl and ends up in jail, only then realising that he has been set up by his partner in crime, John Vernon. Directed by Andrew V McLaglen, it's very much a post-*Butch Cassidy* picture, rarely more than a jolly jape, and Peppard makes for a pleasingly laconic hero.

George Peppard *Harker Fleet* • Diana Muldaur *Katy* • John Vernon *Timothy X Nolan* • France Nuyen *Ah Toy* • Steve Sandor *Jim Gant* • Soon-Teck Oh *Yung* ■ *Dir* Andrew V McLaglen • *Scr* Don Tait, Dick Nelson, from a story by William Roberts

One Night at the Music Hall ★★

Musical 1956 · Fr · Colour · 104mins

Rarely sending critics or public into raptures, Henri Decoin was known as a dependable commercial director throughout his 30-year career. This is a typically steady offering, with Eddie Constantine (taking a break from the Lemmy Caution series that made him a huge star) as an American in Paris whose marriage seems to be heading for the final curtain after his wife, Zizi Jeanmaire, eclipses his singing celebrity. A kind of *A Star Is Born* without the tragedy, the film is most notable for Constantine's growling performance and a handful of ridiculous showstoppers. French dialogue dubbed into English.

Eddie Constantine *Bob Hardie* • Zizi Jeanmaire *Claudie* • Yves Robert *Jeff* • Nadia Gray *Suzy Morgan* • Jacques Morel *Director* • Jacques Castelot *Philippe Loiselet* ■ *Dir* Henri Decoin • *Scr* Henri Decoin, Jacques Companeez, Georges Tabet, AndréTabet

One Night of Love ★★★★ U

Musical 1934 · US · BW · 83mins

This is the hit musical that made a movie star out of the diva Grace Moore, and brought opera to a wide film-going public. Somewhat mirroring her own career, it told of an American soprano who studies in Italy and wins fame at the Met. After being turned down by MGM for *The Merry Widow* (1934), because she was considered too fat, Moore slimmed down and was signed with Columbia for this first (and best) of five deliriously silly, well-mounted and tuneful operettas she made for the studio. (Moore was killed in a plane crash in 1947.) The director Victor Schertzinger, an accomplished musician, co-wrote the title song.

Grace Moore *Mary Barrett* • Tullio Carminati *Giulio Monteverdi* • Lyle Talbot *Bill Houston* • Mona Barrie *Lally* • Jessie Ralph *Angelina* • Luis Alberni *Giovanni* ■ *Dir* Victor Schertzinger • *Scr* SK Lauren, James Gow, Edmund North, from a play by Dorothy Speare, Charles Beahan

One Night Stand ★ 15

Drama 1984 · Ausl · Colour · 89mins

Directed by John Duigan, this Australian apocalypse movie concerns four disparate characters holed up in the Sydney Opera House on a New Year's Eve that may well be their last. A radio broadcast announces that nuclear bombs have been dropped in Europe, North America and Australia and advises people to stay where they are. Two terrified teenagers are joined in the Opera House by an AWOL soldier and a janitor. These four explore the building and each other and engage in strip poker (as you do) to pass the time before morning comes and they find out whether or not they have a future. Good on the claustrophobia and characters but overall a little thin. ▭

Tyler Coppin *Sam* • Cassandra Delaney *Sharon* • Jay Hackett *Brendan* • Saskia Post *Eva* ■ *Dir/Scr* John Duigan

One Night Stand ★★

Psychological thriller 1994 · US · Colour · 92mins

Francis Ford Coppola's actress sister Talia Shire takes a creditable stab at directing with this brooding stew of steamy psychodrama. Ally Sheedy is the lonely divorcee who becomes romantically involved with tall, dark and handsome A Martinez, only to discover that her new lover may well have murdered his first wife. Sheedy takes her acting duties seriously and delivers an engaging, if at times rather earnest performance. Frederic Forrest contributes a psychotic turn as Martinez's father-in-law that brings to mind his neo-Nazi store-holder from *Falling Down*, but otherwise this erotic thriller sticks to increasingly familiar territory as it progresses to its inevitable twist ending.

Ally Sheedy *Michelle Sanderson* • A Martinez *Jack Gillman* • Frederic Forrest *Michael Joslyn*

U = SUITABLE FOR ALL   Uc = SUITABLE FOR ALL, ESPECIALLY FOR YOUNG CHILDREN (VIDEO ONLY)   PG = PARENTAL GUIDANCE

• Diane Salinger *Barbara Joslyn* • Don Novello *Warren Miller* • Gina Hecht *Cy Watson* ■ *Dir* Talia Shire • *Scr* Marty Casella

One Night Stand ★★18

Romantic drama 1997 · US · Colour · 98mins

After the superb *Leaving Las Vegas*, director Mike Figgis took a misstep with this annoying drama about nineties relationships and how one indiscretion can change the course of your life forever. Unfortunately, the characters who swap beds and partners (Wesley Snipes, Nastassja Kinski, Kyle MacLachlan and Wen Ming-Na) are all thoroughly unlikeable and annoying. Only Robert Downey Jr – as Snipes' Aids-stricken friend – emerges unscathed, delivering a believable and meaningful performance. Empty fare indeed. Contains swearing and sex scenes.

Wesley Snipes *Max Carlyle* • Nastassja Kinski *Karen* • Kyle MacLachlan *Vernon* • Wen Ming-Na *Mimi Carlyle* • Robert Downey Jr *Charlie* ■ *Dir/Scr* Mike Figgis

One of Her Own ★★12

Drama based on a true story 1994 · US · Colour · 87mins

A made-for-TV police drama, based on a true story, in which a rookie woman officer (Lori Loughlin) is raped by a colleague (Greg Evigan), wrecking her career and turning her from victim into "villain" when she reports the incident. Martin Sheen adds some gravitas as the local Assistant DA and *Die Hard* fans will recognise Bruce Willis's ally Reginald VelJohnson. Contains violence.

Lori Loughlin *Toni Shroud* • Martin Sheen *Assistant DA Pete Maresca* • Greg Evigan *Charlie Lloyd* • Reginald VelJohnson *Detective Bob Hymes* • Valerie Landsburg *Stacy Schoep* ■ *Dir* Armand Mastroianni • *Scr* Valerie West

One of Our Aircraft Is Missing ★★★ U

Second World War drama 1942 · UK · BW · 102mins

This is an exciting enough Second World War adventure, as the crew of a crashed Wellington bomber attempts to evade Nazi patrols and reach home. Directors Michael Powell (who also has a cameo role) and Emeric Pressburger are more successful at re-creating the bomber raid and its spectacular crash than they are at capturing an authentic Dutch atmosphere. It's a classic example of the way in which fictional stories were given a documentary style in order to increase their propaganda impact, and Powell and Pressburger's script received an Oscar nomination. There are sterling supporting turns from Peter Ustinov and Hay Petrie, but the film looks rather dated now.

Godfrey Tearle *Sir George Corbett* • Eric Portman *Tom Earnshaw* • Hugh Williams *Frank Shelley* • Bernard Miles *Geoff Hickman* • Hugh Burden *John Glyn Haggard* • Emrys Jones *Bob Ashley* • Pamela Brown *Els Meertens* • Googie Withers *Jo De Vries* ■ *Dir/Scr* Michael Powell, Emeric Pressburger

One of Our Dinosaurs Is Missing ★★★ U

Comedy 1975 · US · Colour · 94mins

Youngsters who like their prehistoric monsters to rampage around theme parks aren't going to be particularly impressed by this offering from Disney, in which a top secret formula is hidden by aristocrat Derek Nimmo inside the skeleton of a dinosaur at the Natural History Museum in London. There's not even a sniff of a velociraptor, but there is Peter Ustinov as a Chinese agent and Helen Hayes leading a gang of nannies that even Mary Poppins would be hard-pressed to join. A couple of kung-fu fights, a very silly car chase and some wildly over-the-top acting help liven things up.

Peter Ustinov *Hnup Wan* • Helen Hayes *Hettie* • Clive Revill *Quon* • Derek Nimmo *Lord Southmere* • Joan Sims *Emily* • Bernard Bresslaw *Fan Choy* • Natasha Pyne *Susan* • Roy Kinnear *Superintendent Grubbs* • Joss Ackland *BJ Spence* ■ *Dir* Robert Stevenson • *Scr* Bill Walsh, from the novel *The Great Dinosaur Robbery* by David Forrest

One of Our Own ★★

Drama 1975 · US · Colour

When a top doctor is wrongly diagnosed by an incompetent colleague, only neurosurgeon George Peppard can save him as well as solving 101 other problems at the same time. Over a decade after *Breakfast at Tiffany's* and still seven years away from playing Hannibal Smith in *The A-Team*, Peppard hoped that this pilot would lead to a successful TV series. In the event, *Doctors' Hospital* only ran for a couple of seasons and it's easy to see why. Pitched somewhere between *Dr Kildare* and *ER*, this is very tame fare indeed.

George Peppard *Dr Jake Goodwin* • William Daniels *Dr Moresby* • Louise Sorel *Carole Simon* • Strother Martin *Leroy Atkins* ■ *Dir* Richard C Sarafian • *Scr* Jack Laird

One of Our Spies Is Missing ★★★ U

Spy adventure 1966 · US · Colour · 91mins

The Man from UNCLE was a TV series that began as a spoof of James Bond but took off with a life – albeit a mechanical one – of its own. This is one of the classier feature outings, with Robert Vaughn as indomitable Napoleon Solo and David McCallum as impassive Illya Kuryakin in an adventure that lives up to its title and to the series' hallmarks of well-groomed suspense and jingly music. Nostalgia buffs should have a ball with all those buffant hairdos and the snappy stylised editing.

Robert Vaughn *Napoleon Solo* • David McCallum *Illya Kuryakin* • Leo G Carroll *Mr Waverly* • Vera Miles *Madame de Sala* • Maurice Evans *Sir Norman Swickert* • Ann Elder *Joanna Sweet* • Bernard Fox *Jordin* • Dolores Faith *Lorelei Lancer* • Anna Capri [Ahna Capri] *Do Do* • Harry Davis *Alexander Gritsky* • Yvonne Craig *Wanda* ■ *Dir* E Darrell Hallenbeck • *Scr* Howard Rodman, from a story by Henry Slesar

One of Those Things ★★

Thriller 1970 · Den · Colour · 86mins

Bearing an uncanny resemblance to both *The Bonfire of the Vanities* and *Disclosure*, this bitter little film has little or nothing to say, and spends almost an hour and a half saying it. Ostensibly, it's a grim parable on how easily a cosy middle-class existence can be reduced to rubble by forces which it doesn't understand and can't control. Roy Dotrice gives a nice impression of the smug businessman whose vulnerability is cruelly exposed by scheming Judy Geeson after he covers up a hit-and-run accident. By shocking rather than pricking the bourgeois conscience, Danish director Erik Balling fails to unsettle and succeeds only in leaving a nasty taste.

Roy Dotrice *Henrik Vinther* • Judy Geeson *Susanne Strauss* • Zena Walker *Berit Vinther* • Frederick Jaeger *Melchior* • Ann Firbank *Sonja Melchior* • Geoffrey Chater *Falck* • Henry Okawa *Kawasaki* • Yvette Dotrice *Charlotte Vinther* ■ *Dir* Erik Balling • *Scr* Erik Balling, Anders Bodelsen, from the novel *Hit and Run, Run, Run.* by Anders Bodelsen

One of Us ★★★★ U

Drama 1989 · Is · Colour · 110mins

Scripted by Benny Barbash from his stage play and directed by his brother Uri, this perceptive insight into the Middle East conflict brings home with some force the realisation that, for all the efforts of the politicians, peace depends on the actions of committed men whose convictions and loyalties do not always coincide with the greater good. Sharon Alexander gives an impressive performance as the army investigator who discovers that those suspected of the murder of an Arab are brothers in arms, his dilemma made all the more credible by the persuasive playing of Alon Aboutboul as the friend he must betray. In Hebrew with English subtitles. Contains violence and some nudity.

Alon Aboutboul *Yotam* • Sharon Alexander *Rafa* • Dan Toren *Amir* • Dahlia Shimko *Tamar* • Amon Tzadok *The Colonel* ■ *Dir* Uri Barbash • *Scr* Benny Barbash, from his play

One on One ★★15

Sports drama 1977 · US · Colour · 93mins

Having acted since the age of three, Robby Benson was twenty when he co-wrote and starred in this saga about college basketball, playing the blue-eyed nerd who – in Rocky style – becomes the champ. Two students fall head over heels in love with him – Annette O'Toole and Gail Strickland – and there's also Melanie Griffith in a minor supporting role. Drama is provided by the college coach who drives his athletes like a sadist – he's played by GD Spradlin whom some may remember as the corrupt Senator Geary who is caught with his pants down in *The Godfather Part II*.

Robby Benson *Henry Steele* • Annette O'Toole *Janet Hays* • GD Spradlin *Coach Moreland Smith* • Gail Strickland *BJ Rudolph* • Melanie Griffith *Hitchhiker* • James G Richardson *Malcolm* • Hector Morales *Gonzales* ■ *Dir* Lamont Johnson • *Scr* Robby Benson, Jerry Segal

One Plus One ★★

Experimental documentary drama 1968 · UK · Colour · 99mins

Intended for large audiences because of the presence of the Rolling Stones, this turned out to be one of Jean-Luc Godard's most cryptic, fragmentary and irritating works. The Stones rehearsing their song *Sympathy for the Devil* in a recording studio is intercut with shots of a black man reading anticolonial texts, as well as a girl (Anne Wiazemsky, for whom Godard had left his wife Anna Karina) contemplating suicide when her boyfriend joins the Black Panther movement. After Iain Quarrier, one of the performers in the film, added a complete recording of the Stones' number at the end, he was physically attacked by the director at the 1968 London Film Festival.

Anne Wiazemsky *Eve Democracy* • Iain Quarrier *Bookman* • Frankie Dymon Jr *Black Power militant* • Sean Lynch *Narrator* ■ *Dir/Scr* Jean-Luc Godard

One Potato, Two Potato ★★★

Drama 1964 · US · BW · 89mins

This drama could have been quite a hot potato, made at a time of racial unrest in America and telling a story of a mixed romance that leads to marriage. The relationship is treated as utterly normal until the woman's former husband enters the frame, inciting a bitter dispute over the custody of their child. While a starry cast might have paid dividends at the box-office, the unknowns give this liberal film added authenticity, even though the Oscar-nominated script sometimes lapses into sentimentality. It was shot in Ohio by debutant director Larry Peerce for a reported $250,000.

Barbara Barrie *Julie Cullen Richards* • Bernie Hamilton *Frank Richards* • Richard Mulligan *Joe Cullen* • Harry Bellaver *Judge Powell* • Marti Mericka *Ellen Mary* ■ *Dir* Larry Peerce • *Scr* Raphael Hayes, Orville H Hampton, from a story by Orville H Hampton

One Rainy Afternoon ★★★ U

Comedy 1936 · US · BW · 80mins

A typical thirties romance which bears as much relevance to "real lurv" as Ida Lupino to your average gal. But it works, with a deft combination of slick script, daft idea cleverly executed and wonderful light performances from all concerned. An innocuous kiss causes a major stir in Paris and sets the assembled company on a helter-skelter ride of rearranged lives. Lupino has a luminous screen presence, and those unfamiliar with her output should take a look.

Francis Lederer *Philippe Martin* • Ida Lupino *Monique Pelerin* • Hugh Herbert *Toto* • Roland Young *Maillot* • Erik Rhodes *Count Alfredo Donstelli* • Joseph Cawthorn *M Pelerin* • Countess Liev de Maigret *Yvonne* • Donald Meek *Judge* ■ *Dir* Rowland V Lee • *Scr* Stephen Morehouse Avery, Maurice Hanline, from the film *Monsieur Sans-Gêne* by Emeric Pressburger, from the film by René Pujal

One Romantic Night ★

Romantic drama 1930 · US · BW · 73mins

Lillian Gish made her talking picture debut in this stumbling adaptation of *The Swan*, Ferenc Molnár's creaky play about a young aristocratic girl being groomed for marriage to a prince. The film, which co-stars a wooden Rod La Rocque, a ridiculously mannered Conrad Nagel and Marie Dressler doing battle with the script, went through three directors – George Fitzmaurice, Harry D'Abbadie D'Arrast and Paul L Stein (the only one credited) – and much re-shooting, only to emerge as a stilted bore.

Lillian Gish *Alexandra* • Rod La Rocque *Prince Albert* • Conrad Nagel *Dr Nicholas Haller* • Marie Dressler *Princess Beatrice* • OP Heggie *Father Benedict* • Albert Conti *Count Lutzen* • Edgar Norton *Col Wunderlich* ■ *Dir* Paul L Stein • *Scr* Melville Baker, from the play *The Swan* by Ferenc Molnár

One Single Night ★★★

Drama 1939 · Swe · BW · 90mins

Reunited with Gustaf Molander, the director who had done so much to make her a star in films such as *Intermezzo*, Ingrid Bergman gives a polished performance in this mildly shocking drama of illegitimacy and pre-marital sex. Bergman plays the ward of an aristocrat who has just discovered that he has an illegitimate son who has been raised by circus folk. The problem facing son Edvin Adolphson is whether to opt for romance with the well heeled Bergman or stay true to circus owner Aino Taube. The cross-class themes and the romantic interludes are handled with a sure touch by Molander. In Swedish with English subtitles.

Ingrid Bergman *Eva Beckman* • Edvin Adolphson *Valdemar Moreaux* • Aino Taube *Helga Martenson* • Olof Sandborg *Colonel Magnus Von Brede* • Erik Berglund *Hagberg* ■ *Dir* Gustaf Molander • *Scr* Gosta Stevens, from the story *En Eneste Natt* by Harald Tandrup

One Sings, the Other Doesn't ★★★

Drama 1976 · Fr/Bel/Cur · Colour · 120mins

Agnès Varda found few takers for this chronicle of an unconventional friendship. Meeting in 1962, when student Valérie Mairesse helps single mother-of-two Thérèse Liotard terminate an unwanted pregnancy, the pair reunite a decade later to discover the former is fronting a radical all-girl band (awful songs!), while the latter works in a family planning clinic. By their final encounter, Mairesse has abandoned her Iranian husband and is raising her kids alone, while Liotard has married a doctor. As the shifting emotional and political attitudes suggest, this is an impartial film designed for the common woman – not critics and feminists, who detested it. In French with English subtitles.

Valérie Mairesse *Pauline "Pomme"* • Thérèse Liotard *Suzanne* • Ali Raffi *Darius* • Jean-Pierre Pellegrin *Dr Pierre Aubanel* • Robert Dadies *Jerome* ■ *Dir/Scr* Agnès Varda

One Spy Too Many ★★

Spy adventure 1966 · US · Colour · 101mins

One of five features spun-off from the hit TV series *The Man from UNCLE* to be released in 1966, this lazy effort comprises situations from previously aired episodes and the result is most unsatisfactory. As Napoleon Solo and Illya Kuryakin, Robert Vaughn and David McCallum have the film stolen from under their noses by the excellent Rip Torn, who throws restraint to the winds. There are some hilarious dices with death along the way, but it's far too long for a cut-and-paste job.

Robert Vaughn *Napoleon Solo* • David McCallum *Illya Kuryakin* • Rip Torn *Alexander* • Dorothy Provine *Tracey Alexander* • Leo G Carroll *Mr Waverly* • Yvonne Craig *Maude Waverly* ■ *Dir* Joseph Sargent • *Scr* Dean Hargrove

One Summer Love ★ 15

Romantic drama 1975 · US · Colour · 93mins

Also known as *Dragonfly*, this is a stinker under any name; stars Susan Sarandon and Beau Bridges probably wish it could be erased from their CVs. Gilbert Cates directs this worn-out romantic tale about the relationship between a man recently released from a mental asylum and a young woman who works at a cinema. Despite Bridges and Sarandon giving it their all, this never engages, enthralls or amuses at any point in the proceedings. It's really only worth watching if you're a die-hard Sarandon fan who is interested in seeing a clunker from early on in her acting career.

Beau Bridges *Jesse Arlington* • Susan Sarandon *Chloe* • Mildred Dunnock *Mrs Barrow* • Michael B Miller *Gabriel Arlington* • Linda Miller *Willa Arlington* • Martin Burke *Lonnie Arlington* • James Otis *Clifford* • James Noble *Dr Leo Cooper* ■ *Dir* Gilbert Cates • *Scr* N Richard Nash

The One That Got Away ★★★ U

Second World War drama 1957 · UK · BW · 115mins

Just 12 years after the end of the Second World War, this action-packed feature shows that not everything the Allies attempted resulted in success. A swaggering Hardy Kruger is excellent as Franz von Werra, the Luftwaffe pilot who not only escaped from several camps in this country, but who also absconded from Canada and crossed America in his bid to rejoin his outfit. Directed at a fair clip by Roy Baker, this true-life tale is more notable for its fair-minded approach than for its thrills, but still delivers the occasional exciting moment.

Hardy Kruger *Franz von Werra* • Colin Gordon *Army interrogator* • Michael Goodliffe *RAF interrogator* • Terence Alexander *RAF intelligence officer* • Jack Gwillim *Commandant at Grizedale* • Alec McCowen *Duty Officer Hucknall* ■ *Dir* Roy Baker [Roy Ward Baker] • *Scr* Howard Clewes, from a book by Kendal Burt, James Leasor

One Touch of Venus ★★★ U

Comedy fantasy 1948 · US · BW · 81mins

The 1987 romantic comedy *Mannequin* stole this plot, and Columbia did something similar in 1947 with *Down to Earth* starring Rita Hayworth, but this is the movie where the love goddess herself, Ava Gardner plays *the* love goddess, Venus, and comes to life for 24 hours on a window dresser's kiss. Gardner is fabulous: sexy, alluring, warm and womanly, and more than a match for feeble, miscast Robert Walker. Originally, this was a novel by F Anstey, and it came to the screen via a Broadway show, thankfully retaining some of the songs from that incarnation, including the lovely *Speak Low* by Kurt Weill and Ogden Nash, magically performed by the great Dick Haymes.

Ava Gardner *Venus* • Robert Walker *Eddie Hatch* • Dick Haymes *Joe Grant* • Eve Arden *Molly* • Olga San Juan *Gloria* • Tom Conway *Whitfield Savory* ■ *Dir* William A Seiter • *Scr* Harry Kurnitz, Frank Tashlin, from the musical play by Kurt Weill, SJ Perelman, Ogden Nash, from the novel *The Tinted Venus* by F Anstey

One Tough Cop ★

Police drama 1998 · US · Colour · 90mins

A clunky crime drama "inspired" by the life of renegade NYPD cop Bo Dietl, as played with Neanderthal stoicism by Stephen Baldwin. Together with his heavy-gambling partner Duke Finnerty (Chris Penn), Dietl busts up an ethnic hostage crisis and uses his mob connections to investigate the murder of a nun. (It was the latter brand of controversial policing that led to Bietl's enforced retirement at 35.) Cliché-ridden and generic to a fault, this is a humourless rehash of the buddy cop format served up by Brazilian director Bruno Barreto without any narrative punch or real thrills.

Stephen Baldwin *Bo Dietl* • Chris Penn [Christopher Penn] *Duke Finnerty* • Mike McGlone *Rickie La Cassa* • Gina Gershon *Joey O'Hara* • Christopher Bregman *Gang Banger No 1* • Mike Santana *Gang Banger No 2* • Amy Irving *FBI Agent Jean Devlin* ■ *Dir* Bruno Barreto • *Scr* Jeremy Iacone, from the book *One Tough Cop: The Bo Dietl Story* by Bo Dietl, Ken Gross

One-Trick Pony ★★★

Musical drama 1980 · US · Colour · 98mins

Paul Simon stars as the failing rock singer Jonah Levine, facing up to an uncertain future after 14 years on the road, in this unusually harsh look at the realities of being a pop performer. Semi-autobiographical in the way it clearly reflects his post Simon and Garfunkel feelings, Simon fans will relish the ten new songs written for his vanity production even if they don't like his caustic screenplay. Cameos from Rip Torn, Lou Reed and Tiny Tim, plus vintage sets from Sam and Dave, the Lovin' Spoonful and the B52s, make this bitter pill easier to swallow. Contains swearing and nudity.

Paul Simon *Jonah* • Blair Brown *Marion* • Rip Torn *Walter Fox* • Joan Hackett *Lonnie Fox* • Allen Goorwitz [Allen Garfield] *Cal Van Damp* • Mare Winningham *Modeena Dandridge* • Michael Pearlman *Matty Levin* • Lou Reed *Steve Kunelian* ■ *Dir* Robert M Young • *Scr* Paul Simon

One True Thing ★★★ 15

Drama 1998 · US · Colour · 122mins

Get those hankies out for this family weepie, which earned Meryl Streep an Oscar nomination. She's the cancer-stricken mum whom daughter Renee Zellweger comes home to look after, even though the pair have never got along. Rounding out the family are William Hurt, as Renee's revered father, and Tom Everett Scott as her brother, but it is Streep who steals every scene and wrings tears you didn't know you had out of you. An assured adaptation of the Anna Quindlen novel, this is subtly handled by actor-turned-director Carl Franklin, but nonetheless remains one for the girls. ▭ DVD

Meryl Streep *Kate Gulden* • Renee Zellweger *Ellen Gulden* • William Hurt *George Gulden* • Tom Everett Scott *Brian Gulden* • Lauren Graham *Jules* • Nicky Katt *Jordan Belzer* • James Eckhouse *District attorney* • Patrick Breen *Mr Tweedy* ■ *Dir* Carl Franklin • *Scr* Karen Croner, from the novel by Anna Quindlen

One, Two, Three ★★★★ U

Political comedy 1961 · US · BW · 103mins

If you count the punchlines per minute, this has to be one of the fastest, talkiest comedies ever made. Billy Wilder's satire never lets up and gives James Cagney his finest role for many years. Cagney plays a combustible Coca-Cola executive in West Berlin, desperate to improve sales at any cost, while his boss's visiting daughter falls for a communist named Piffl, played by Horst Buchholz. While some may find Wilder's scattershot approach a trifle obvious – capitalism and communism are both subjected to ridicule – it remains, like *Dr Strangelove*, a key product of the Cold War, when some things were just too serious to take seriously. ▭

James Cagney *CR MacNamara* • Horst Buchholz *Otto Ludwig Piffl* • Pamela Tiffin *Scarlett Hazeltine* • Arlene Francis *Phyllis MacNamara* • Lilo Pulver [Liselotte Pulver] *Ingeborg* • Howard St John *Hazeltine* • Hanns Lothar *Schlemmer* • Lois Bolton *Mrs Hazeltine* • Leon Askin *Peripetchikoff* • Peter Capell *Mishkin* • Ralf Wolter *Borodenko* ■ *Dir* Billy Wilder • *Scr* Billy Wilder, Ial Diamond, from the play *Egy, Ketto, Harom* by Ferenc Molnár

One Way Out ★ U

Thriller 1955 · UK · BW · 61mins

This unassuming B-thriller was made for its time and went out in support of the Norman Wisdom comedy *Man of the Moment*. All these years later, it hardly bears looking at. John Chandos plays the ruthless jewel thief who blackmails Eddie Byrne's veteran police superintendent into dropping his investigations by implicating the cop's daughter, Jill Adams, in a robbery. Lyndon Brook is prominent as a flashy young crook. The weak writing, acting and staging combine to deprive the final confrontation of cop and master criminal of any real impact.

Jill Adams *Shirley Harcourt* • Eddie Byrne *Superintendent Harcourt* • Lyndon Brook *Leslie Parrish* • John Chandos *Danvers* • Arthur Lowe *Sam* ■ *Dir* Francis Searle • *Scr* Jonathan Roche, from story by John Temple-Smith, Jean Scott-Rogers

One Way Passage ★★★★

Romantic drama 1932 · US · BW · 68mins

Aboard an ocean liner homeward bound for the United States, William

U = SUITABLE FOR ALL   Uc = SUITABLE FOR ALL, ESPECIALLY FOR YOUNG CHILDREN (VIDEO ONLY)   PG = PARENTAL GUIDANCE

Powell (returning to face a murder charge) and Kay Francis (suffering from an incurable illness) enjoy a necessarily short-lived love affair. Very short, poignantly sweet, and discreetly directed by Tay Garnett, this is the kind of romantic drama redolent of thirties Hollywood which, at its best, is involving and effective. Enhanced by Frank McHugh and Aline MacMahon as a pair of confidence tricksters (apparently an obligatory feature of Hollywood passenger lists), the movie won the Oscar for Robert Lord's original story.

William Powell *Dan Hardesty* • Kay Francis *Joan Ames* • Frank McHugh *Skippy* • Aline MacMahon *Betty the countess* • Warren Hymer *Steve Burke* • Frederick Burton *Doctor* ■ *Dir* Tay Garnett • *Scr* Wilson Mizner, Joseph Jackson, from a story by Robert Lord

One Way Pendulum ★★★ U

Comedy   1965 · UK · BW · 85mins

While Mr Groomkirby (Eric Sykes) constructs a model of the Old Bailey in the living room, his son Kirby (Jonathan Miller) teaches his collection of I-Speak-Your-Weight machines to sing. The rest of the family are equally strange in this movie adaptation of NF Simpson's surreal stage play, which climaxes in a do-it-yourself murder trial organised by Mr Groomkirby. The theatre production was a triumph of bizarre nonsense but the film never quite captures the spirit of the original. Although deemed a failure on release, it now benefits from a certain period charm which adds to its overall allure, as does its outstanding cast.

Eric Sykes *Mr Groomkirby* • George Cole *Defense Counsel/Friend* • Julia Foster *Sylvia* • Jonathan Miller *Kirby* • Peggy Mount *Mrs Gantry* • Alison Leggatt *Mrs Groomkirby* • Mona Washbourne *Aunt Mildred* ■ *Dir* Peter Yates • *Scr* NF Simpson, from his play

One Way Street ★★

Crime drama   1950 · US · BW · 79mins

A curious attempt to create a fatalistic crime drama is made all the more pretentious by the casting of the saturnine James Mason as the disillusioned doctor who double-crosses Dan Duryea's gang boss. He tries to make a new life in a primitive Mexican village but, of course, can't escape his past. Swedish actress Marta Toren plays the gangster's lover who deserts him for Mason. Besides Duryea, the supporting cast includes such stalwarts as William Conrad and Jack Elam.

James Mason *Doc Matson* • Marta Toren *Laura* • Dan Duryea *Wheeler* • William Conrad *Ollie* • King Donovan *Grieder* • Jack Elam *Arnie* • Tito Renaldo *Hank Torres* • Rock Hudson *Truck driver* ■ *Dir* Hugo Fregonese • *Scr* Lawrence Kimble, from his story *Death on a Side Street*

One Week ★★★★ U

Silent comedy   1920 · US · Colour · 17mins

Blissful mayhem for Buster Keaton fans as honeymooners Keaton and Sybil Sealey are given a home to assemble, only to watch it go cock-eyed because a rival to Buster has changed the numbers on the home components. The result is a lop-sided structure which gets swept away by an

oncoming train. A tad mechanical, but it has some groundbreaking gags, most of which are still used by comedians today. ▭

Buster Keaton *Man* • Sybil Sealey *Wife* ■ *Dir* Buster Keaton, Eddie Cline [Edward Cline] • *Scr* Buster Keaton and Eddie Cline

One Woman's Courage ★★★ 15

Thriller   1994 · US · Colour · 86mins

The excellent Patty Duke stars in a laudable attempt to combine adultery, alcoholism, stalking and grievous bodily harm in one woman's rather hectic life. Margot Kidder appears in a cast which also includes the usually reliable James Farentino. If there is a *soupçon* too much going on – make a cup of tea and you are, quite frankly, done for – it is at least a movie which tries to cover up any slack in the script. ▭

Patty Duke *Grace McKenna* • James Farentino *Police Lieutenant Bill Lawson* • Keith Szarabajka *Wallace Bremer* • Margot Kidder *Stella Jenson* • Dennis Farina *Craig McKenna* ■ *Dir* Charles Robert Carner • *Scr* John Steven Owen

Onegin ★★★ 12

Period romantic drama
1999 · UK/US · Colour · 106mins

Ralph Fiennes is directed by his sister Martha in this ponderous adaptation of Pushkin's classic. Fiennes is well cast as Evgeny Onegin, a decadent, dissipated aristocrat who moves to his recently deceased uncle's estate in rural Russia. There he proceeds to devastate the lives of all around him, rejecting the advances of the luscious Liv Tyler and driving bumpkin Toby Stephens into a deadly duel. Years later, he encounters Tyler again and falls hopelessly in love – but this realisation comes too late. Though beautifully shot, *Onegin* desperately needs pace, and the endless shots of Ralph's face show more sisterly devotion than emotion. Contains a violent scene.

Ralph Fiennes *Evgeny Onegin* • Liv Tyler *Tatyana Larin* • Toby Stephens *Vladimir Lensky* • Lena Headey *Olga Larin* • Martin Donovan *Prince Nikitin* • Alun Armstrong *Zaretsky* • Harriet Walter *Madame Larina* • Irene Worth *Princess Alina* ■ *Dir* Martha Fiennes • *Scr* Peter Ettedgui, Michael Ignatieff, from the novel *Eugene Onegin* by Alexander Pushkin

Onibaba ★★★ 15

Horror   1964 · Jap · BW · 98mins

Set during the 16th-century Japanese civil wars, this cult favourite focuses on the tensions that arise when widow Jitsuko Yoshimura defies mother-in-law Nobuko Otowa by flirting with a neighbour and jeopardising their livelihood – the sale of armour stripped from murdered samurai. This is a frankly erotic and often hysterically acted tale, which director Kaneto Shindo clearly intended as an allegory on the modern world. However, it works best as a disturbing study of ruthless survivalism and supernatural punishment, which makes atmospheric use of the swaying swamp reeds and a terrifying mask. In Japanese with English subtitles. ▭

Nobuko Otowa *Mother* • Jitsuko Yoshimura *Daughter-in-law* • Kei Sato *Hachi, farmer* • Jukichi Uno *Warrior* ■ *Dir/Scr* Kaneto Shindo

The Onion Field ★★★ 18

Police drama   1979 · US · Colour · 121mins

Cop-turned novelist-Joseph Wambaugh was so upset by the way *The Choirboys* was turned into a movie, he had complete control over this script based on a real-life case in 1963 when two small-time hoods kidnap two cops and murder one of them in an onion field. As a documentary-style record of police procedure and the fallibility of the legal system this is a gripping and disturbing movie, powerfully acted by John Savage as the surviving cop who quits the force to become a gardener and by Franklyn Seales and the combustible James Woods as the killers. ▭

John Savage *Karl Hettinger* • James Woods *Gregory Powell* • Franklyn Seales *Jimmy Smith* • Ted Danson *Ian Campbell* • Priscilla Pointer *Chrissie Campbell* • Ronny Cox *Pierce Brooks* • David Huffman *DA Phil Halpin* • Christopher Lloyd *Jailhouse lawyer* ■ *Dir* Harold Becker • *Scr* Joseph Wambaugh, from his novel

Onionhead ★★

Comedy   1958 · US · BW · 96mins

Following the box-office success of *No Time for Sergeants*, Warner Bros pushed Andy Griffith into military service again, casting him as a cook, third class, aboard the USS *Periwinkle*, docked at Boston. On the run from one love affair, Griffith drops anchor with a decidedly promiscuous barfly, Felicia Farr, and jousts regularly with the ship's chief cook, a permanently sozzled Walter Matthau, who is the best thing in the movie.

Andy Griffith *Al Woods* • Felicia Farr *Stella* • Walter Matthau *"Red" Wildoe* • Erin O'Brien [Erin O'Brien-Moore] *Jo Hill* • Joe Mantell *"Doc" O'Neal* • Ray Danton *Ensign Dennis Higgins* • James Gregory *"The Skipper"* • Joey Bishop *Gutsell* ■ *Dir* Norman Taurog • *Scr* Nelson Gidding, from the novel by Weldon Hill

Only Angels Have Wings ★★★★★ U

Drama   1939 · US · BW · 115mins

One of the greatest films from the most memorable year in cinema history, overlooked at the time as a simple action adventure but now recognised as a superb study of grace under pressure. This Howard Hawks movie about a civil airline taking mail and freight over the treacherous Andes contains all of producer/director Hawks's key themes and some of his finest sequences, and boasts a splendid cast headed by hard-bitten Cary Grant and chirpy Jean Arthur. They are superbly backed by Rita Hayworth as a vamp and Richard Barthelmess as a disgraced flier. This is great cinema: supremely entertaining, mature storytelling. ▭

Cary Grant *Geoff Carter* • Jean Arthur *Bonnie Lee* • Richard Barthelmess *Bat McPherson* • Rita Hayworth *Judith McPherson* • Thomas Mitchell *Kid Dabb* • Sig Rumann [Sig Ruman] *Dutchman* • Victor Killian [Victor Kilian] *Sparks* ■ *Dir* Howard Hawks • *Scr* Jules Furthman, from a story by Howard Hawks

The Only Game in Town ★★★

Drama   1970 · US · Colour · 113mins

And that game is love, if you can believe a word of this rather talky story of the love affair between chorus girl Elizabeth Taylor and gambling piano player Warren Beatty. The actors give it all they've got, and director George Stevens, making his last film, convincingly sets up the Las Vegas location as a place of glamour and sleaze, but it never quite involves as it should.

Elizabeth Taylor *Fran Walker* • Warren Beatty *Joe Grady* • Charles Braswell *Thomas Lockwood* • Hank Henry *Tony* • Olga Valery *Woman with purple wig* ■ *Dir* George Stevens • *Scr* Frank D Gilroy, from his play

The Only Son ★★★★

Drama   1936 · Jap · BW · 103mins

Having demonstrated an intuitive mastery of silent technique, Yasujiro Ozu proved his sound credentials with this delicate, character-driven entry in the *shomin-geki* genre of lower middle-class dramas that would become his speciality. Chishu Ryu (an Ozu regular) is outstanding as the Tokyo teacher, who borrows a small fortune so he can prove to his doting small-town mother that the sacrifices she made for his education had all been worthwhile. Ozu would rework the material as a father-daughter tale in *There Was a Father* (1942), to show how ordinary people were coping with the war. In Japanese with English subtitles.

Choko Iida *Otsune Nonomiya* • Shinichi Himori *Ryosuke, Otsune's son* • Masao Hayama *Ryosuke as a child* • Yoshiko Tsubouchi *Sugiko, Ryosuke's wife* ■ *Dir* Yasujiro Ozu • *Scr* Tadao Ikeda, Masao Arata, from a story by James Maki [Yasujiro Ozu]

Only the Brave ★★★ 15

Drama   1994 · Ausl · Colour · 58mins

In keeping with many of the pictures produced in Australia during this period, Ana Kokkinos's coming-of-age drama deals with the frustrations experienced by an alienated urban youth. However, this featurette also has a lesbian agenda, as it traces the gradual disintegration of a close friendship after one of the girls realises the true nature of her feelings. Elena Mandalis cleverly conveys the confusions caused by the crushes on both her friend and her teacher, but the film is not always convincing in its portrayal either of Greek ethnicity or teenage disillusion.

Elena Mandalis *Alex* • Dora Kaskanis *Vicki* • Maude Davey *Kate Groves* • Helen Athanasiadis *Maria* • Tina Zerella *Sylvie* ■ *Dir* Ana Kokkinos • *Scr* Ana Kokkinos, Mira Robertson

Only the Lonely ★★★ 15

Romantic comedy
1991 · US · Colour · 100mins

Director Chris Columbus took a break from the juvenile slapstick of the *Home Alone* series to make this understated little gem. It's a sweet, rather old-fashioned comedy about a shy policeman, John Candy, who falls for equally bashful mortician Ally Sheedy, much to the dismay of his overbearing

mother, Maureen O'Hara. Although it occasionally lapses into sentimentality, it is sympathetically written and there are winning performances from the two leads. However, the film is all but stolen by O'Hara, returning to the big screen after a lengthy absence, and that other wily old veteran, Anthony Quinn. Look out, too, for a brief cameo from Macaulay Culkin. Contains swearing. ▭

John Candy *Danny Muldoon* • Maureen O'Hara *Rose Muldoon* • Ally Sheedy *Theresa Luna* • Kevin Dunn *Patrick Muldoon* • Milo O'Shea *Doyle Ryan* • Bert Remsen *Spats Shannon* • Anthony Quinn *Nick Acropolis* • James Belushi *Sal Buonarte* • Macaulay Culkin *Billy* ■ Dir/Scr Chris Columbus

Only the Strong ★★ 🄫
Martial arts action drama
1993 · US · Colour · 92mins

An OK action thriller, this has martial arts hero Mark Dacascos encouraged by his former teacher Geoffrey Lewis to instruct students in how to acquire self-discipline and battle the drug dealers infesting the high-school campus. The gimmick here is that Dacascos is a master of the Brazilian fighting skill *capoeira* – a sort of cross between kung-fu and the lambada. Mild violence and samba music makes this one an easy-listening no-brainer. Contains violence and some swearing. ▭

Mark Dacascos *Louis Stevens* • Stacey Travis *Dianna* • Geoffrey Lewis *Kerrigan* • Paco Christian Prieto *Silverio* • Todd Susman *Cochran* ■ Dir Sheldon Lettich • Scr Sheldon Lettich, Luis Esteban

Only the Valiant ★★ 🄿🄶
Western
1950 · US · BW · 104mins

Gregory Peck plays the cavalry commander whose harsh methods make him less than popular with his men, though everyone pulls together heroically when the Apaches gather at the mountain pass. A traditional, no-nonsense western, influenced by earlier westerns, most notably *Red River* and *Fort Apache*. Peck has a decent role as the martinet, and the supporting cast includes such familiar faces as Ward Bond and Jeff Corey. ▭

Gregory Peck *Capt Richard Lance* • Barbara Payton *Cathy Eversham* • Ward Bond *Cpl Timothy Gilchrist* • Gig Young *Lt William Holloway* • Lon Chaney Jr *Trooper Kebussyan* • Neville Brand *Sgt Ben Murdock* • Jeff Corey *Joe Harmony* ■ Dir Gordon Douglas • Scr Edmund H North, Harry Brown, from the novel by Charles Marquis Warren

Only Two Can Play★★★★🄿🄶
Comedy
1962 · UK · BW · 101mins

A misleading title because the players in this story of a would-be adulterous Welsh librarian (Peter Sellers) and his wannabe mistress (Mai Zetterling) also include Virginia Maskell as his dispirited wife and Richard Attenborough as the poet she flirts with. Adapted by Bryan Forbes from Kingsley Amis's *That Uncertain Feeling*, this small-town drama is played out as farce and makes its satirical points with comic deftness. That may be because Sellers is more than usually restrained and believable. ▭

Peter Sellers *John Lewis* • Mai Zetterling *Elizabeth Gruffydd-Williams* • Virginia Maskell *Jean Lewis* • Richard Attenborough *Gareth Probert* • Kenneth Griffith *Ieuen Jenkins* • Maudie Edwards *Mrs Davies* • Frederick Piper *Davies* • Graham Stark *Hyman* • John Arnatt *Bill* • Sheila Manahan *Mrs Jenkins* • John Le Mesurier *Salter* ■ Dir Sidney Gilliat • Scr Bryan Forbes, from the novel *That Uncertain Feeling* by Kingsley Amis

The Only Way Out ★★
Thriller
1993 · US · Colour

Two actors better known for their comedy roles – John Ritter and Henry Winkler – have a stab at grittier material with mixed results in this made-for-TV thriller. Ritter plays a successful architect drawn into a dangerous cat-and-mouse game with his ex-wife's new boyfriend Winkler. Both leads do their best to dispel memories of their lightweight personae, but the rest of the cast does little to help their cause. Rod Hardy's direction is competent enough, but he fails to provide the requisite menace.

John Ritter *Jeremy Carlisle* • Henry Winkler *Tony* • Stephanie Faracy *Lynn Carlisle* • Julianne Phillips *Susannah* • Sam Mancuso *Edward* ■ Dir Rod Hardy • Scr Jerome Kass, from a screenplay (unproduced) by Mick Ford

The Only Way Out Is Dead ★★ 🄤
Science-fiction thriller
1970 · Can · Colour · 88mins

Sandy Dennis and Stuart Whitman play surgeons who suddenly discover that their secret medical research facility is, in fact, an unending source of heart donors for their benefactor (Burl Ives), a bedridden billionaire who craves immortality like a villain in a Bond movie. This cleverly plotted but rather flashily directed drama was made three years after the world's first heart transplant operation, giving it a topicality unusual for the genre.

Stuart Whitman *McCarter Purvis* • Sandy Dennis *Enid* • Burl Ives *TM Trask* • Tom Harvey *McBride* • Robert Goodier *Morton* ■ Dir John Trent • Scr Henry Denker

Only When I Larf ★★★
Comedy
1968 · UK · Colour · 103mins

A jolly comedy, based on a novel by Len Deighton, the *Ipcress File* man, about three confidence tricksters (Richard Attenborough, David Hemmings, Alexandra Stewart) who begin plotting against each other. The succession of scams, disguises and surprises is very entertaining and builds to a quadruple-cross (multiple double-crossing was very popular at the time). The production, in several glamorous locations, is amusingly trendy, in Swinging Sixties style, and Attenborough gives one of his most uninhibited comedy performances.

Richard Attenborough *Silas* • David Hemmings *Bob* • Alexandra Stewart *Liz* • Nicholas Pennell *Spencer* • Melissa Stribling *Diana* • Terence Alexander *Gee Gee Gray* • Edric Connor *Awana* • Clifton Jones *General Sakut* ■ Dir Basil Dearden • Scr John Salmon, from the novel by Len Deighton

Only When I Laugh ★★★ 🄫
Comedy drama
1981 · US · Colour · 114mins

This is a bittersweet Neil Simon comedy about a brilliant but boozy and self-destructive actress (Marsha Mason) striving to strike up a relationship with her teenage daughter (Kristy McNichol). Fine performances from the two leading ladies, and from support stars James Coco and Joan Hackett, as a failed gay actor and an ageing New York society beauty, respectively. ▭

Marsha Mason *Georgia Hines* • Kristy McNichol *Polly* • James Coco *Jimmy Perino* • Joan Hackett *Toby Landau* • David Dukes *David Lowe* ■ Dir Glenn Jordan • Scr Neil Simon, from his play *The Gingerbread Lady*

Only Yesterday ★★★★
Romantic drama
1933 · US · BW · 106mins

During the First World War, innocent young Margaret Sullavan and a handsome lieutenant John Boles meet at a dance in Virginia and fall in love, but he is shipped to France before they can meet again. Pregnant with his child, she goes to live with her feminist aunt Billie Burke in New York, but when Boles returns he has forgotten her. Romantic soap opera to be sure but, as directed by genre specialist John M Stahl, of a superior kind. The film, which opens on the day of the Wall Street crash and unfolds the beginning of the affair in flashback, wonderfully evokes the temper of the times and Sullavan, as ever, suffers with poignant dignity.

Margaret Sullavan *Mary Lane* • John Boles *James Stanton Emerson* • Billie Burke *Julia Warren* • Reginald Denny *Bob* • Jimmy Butler *Jim* • Edna May Oliver *Leona* • Benita Hume *Phyllis Emerson* • George Meeker *Dave Reynolds* • June Clyde *Deborah* • Marie Prevost *Amy* ■ Dir John M Stahl • Scr William Hurlbut, Arthur Richman, George O'Neill Allen, from the book by Frederick Lewis and the novel *Letter to an Unknown Woman* by Stefan Zweig

Only You ★★★ 🄫
Romantic comedy
1992 · US · Colour · 87mins

This romantic comedy features *St Elmo's Fire* brat-packer Andrew McCarthy as the shy bloke who finds himself lucking out when he falls for two different women – glamorous Kelly Preston and the more sensible, studious Helen Hunt. This is sweetly enjoyable, thanks to a witty script and nice performances from the cast. Contains nudity and sexual situations. ▭

Andrew McCarthy *Clifford Godfrey* • Kelly Preston *Amanda* • Helen Hunt *Claire* ■ Dir Betty Thomas • Scr Wayne Allan Rice

Only You ★★★★ 🄿🄶
Romantic comedy
1994 · US · Colour · 103mins

Moonstruck director Norman Jewison successfully mines the same territory with this delicious "Cinderella Italian-style" romantic comedy. Following the prophecy of a childhood Ouija game, Pittsburgh schoolteacher Marisa Tomei runs out on her wedding and goes to Rome to find the man of her dreams. There she meets shoe salesman Robert Downey Jr, who may or may not

fit the bill. The pairing of Tomei and Downey Jr works like a charm: both inject scintillating substance into an unashamedly lightweight affair through their winning chemistry. Billy Zane is also on hand to provide a neat twist in the tale, and the lush Italian scenery will have you changing your holiday plans to head for the idyllic town of Positano. ⬮ *DVD*

Marisa Tomei *Faith Corvatch* • Robert Downey Jr *Peter Wright* • Bonnie Hunt *Kate* • Joaquim de Almeida *Giovanni* • Fisher Stevens *Larry* • Billy Zane *The false Damon Bradley* • Adam LeFevre *Damon Bradley* • John Benjamin Hickey *Dwayne* • Siobhan Fallon *Leslie* ■ Dir Norman Jewison • Scr Diane Drake

Ooh... You Are Awful ★★ 🄿🄶
Comedy
1972 · UK · Colour · 92mins

No prizes will be handed out for guessing that this is a vehicle for the late, great iDick Emery. When Emery discovers his freshly dead accountant has left the number of a safety deposit account tattooed to the derriere of several young models, he sets to with gusto. This is a McGill seaside postcard come to boozy, nudge-nudge, wink-wink, "mine's a large one" life, and if that's to your taste then it belts along like a runaway Blackpool tram. ▭

Dick Emery *Charlie Tully* • Derren Nesbitt *Sid Sabbath* • Ronald Fraser *Reggie Campbell Peek* • Pat Coombs *Libby Niven* • William Franklyn *Arnold Van Cleef* • Cheryl Kennedy *Jo Mason* • Norman Bird *Warder Burke* • Roland Curram *Vivian* • Liza Goddard *Liza Missenden Green* ■ Dir Cliff Owen • Scr John Warren, John Singer

Op Center ★★★ 🄿🄶
Thriller
1995 · US · Colour · 113mins

Tom Clancy's Jack Ryan novels – *The Hunt for Red October*, *Patriot Games*, *Clear and Present Danger* – have already hit big-screen paydirt. This made-for-TV adaptation tries to do the same for one of his lesser known characters, with mixed results. Harry Hamlin takes the lead role, playing the head of a secret government agency that swings into action when a former KGB officer seizes control of a trio of nuclear warheads. There is a strong supporting cast, but director Lewis Teague struggles at times to keep the dense, sprawling plot under control. ▭

Harry Hamlin *Paul Hood* • Lindsay Frost *Pamela Bluestone* • Wilford Brimley *Admiral Troy Davis* • Kim Cattrall *Jane Hood* • Carl Weathers *General Mike Rodgers* • Bo Hopkins *Darrell McCaskey* • John Savage *Bob Ebert* • Ken Howard *President* • Deidre Hall *Kate Michaels* • Rod Steiger *Boroda* ■ Dir Lewis Teague • Scr Steve Sohmer, from a story by Tom Clancy, Steve Pieczenik Alan, Otino Caso

Open All Night ★★
Drama
1934 · UK · BW · 61mins

An unusually ambitious little British "quota quickie", this gives Frank Vosper the kind of role associated with the German silent film tragedian Emil Jannings. As an elderly former Russian Grand Duke reduced to being night manager of a hotel, Vosper is given notice rather than the promotion he expected. Adding a dash of *Grand Hotel* melodrama, he sorts out some of the guests' problems on his final

🄤 = SUITABLE FOR ALL   🄤🄲 = SUITABLE FOR ALL, ESPECIALLY FOR YOUNG CHILDREN (VIDEO ONLY)   🄿🄶 = PARENTAL GUIDANCE

night. Scripted by Gerard Fairlie from a play by John Chancellor, this is one of the better late works of pioneer director George Pearson.

Frank Vosper *Anton* • Margaret Vines *Elsie Warren* • Gillian Lind *Maysie* • Lewis Shaw *Bill Warren* • Leslie Perrins *Ranger* ■ *Dir* George Pearson • *Scr* Gerard Fairlie, from a play by John Chancellor

Open Doors ★★★★

Crime drama   1990 · It · Colour · 108mins

Adapted from Leonardo Sciascia's account of an actual court case that was heard in Sicily in the thirties, Gianni Amelio's solemnly paced study of the quality of justice under the Fascist regime makes few dramatic concessions. However, impeccable performances and an oppressive sense of period ensure that it makes for compelling viewing. Realising that, far from being the "monster of Palermo", dedicated union official Ennio Fantastichini was driven to rape and multiple murder by his humiliating dismissal, liberal judge Gian Maria Volonté obdurately battles to save a victim of corruption and expediency from his self-willed fate. In Italian with English subtitles.

Gian Maria Volonté *Vito Di Francesco* • Ennio Fantastichini *Tommaso Scalia* • Renzo Giovampietro *Judge Sanna* • Renato Carpentieri *Giovanni Consolo* • Tuccio Musumeci *Spadafora* ■ *Dir* Gianni Amelio • *Scr* Gianni Amelio, Vincenzo Cerami, from the novel by Leonardo Sciascia

Open Fire ★ 18

Action drama   1995 · US · Colour · 88mins

Yet another entry in the competition to be the most shameless rip-off of *Die Hard*, *Open Fire* sets the well-worn plot in a chemical plant. Our hero is played by Jeff Wincott – he's an ex-FBI agent who works in manual labour because he was traumatised by a hostage situation that went horribly wrong. The movie tends towards kung fu fights to maintain its action quotient, which is a shame because Wincott is a terrible martial artist. ▣

Jeff Wincott *Alec McNeil* • Patrick Kilpatrick *Kruger* • Mimi Craven • Arthur Taxier • Leo Lee • Lee DeBroux • Brenda Swanson • Michael Shaner • Yuji Kumoto ■ *Dir* Kurt Anderson • *Scr* Thomas Ritz

Open Season ★

Action   1974 · US/Sp · Colour · 106mins

Three Vietnam vets kidnap a man and a woman, force them to act as servants at the remote cabin, sexually abuse the woman, then hunt them down like game. Full of psychological baloney to justify its story, this exploitation effort makes some cheap shots about American democracy and justice before getting down to the nitty-gritty of gratuitous sex and violence. Peter Fonda, John Phillip Law and Richard Lynch are convincingly psychotic as the heavies, but for the most part this is a ham-fisted *Deliverance* rip-off. There is a twist at the end involving the great William Holden, though his fans would do well to mentally erase him from this rubbish.

Peter Fonda *Ken* • Cornelia Sharpe *Nancy* • John Phillip Law *Greg* • Richard Lynch *Art* •

Albert Mendoza [Alberto de Mendoza] *Martin* • William Holden (1) *Wolkowski* ■ *Dir* Peter Collinson • *Scr* David Osborn, Liz Charles-Williams

Open Season ★★★

Comedy satire   1995 · US · Colour · 97mins

A sharp-edged satire on contemporary television in which a foul-up in the ratings mistakenly suggests that US viewers are giving dumb dross the thumbs down, and tuning in to shows of culture and intellect instead. Predictably, the very idea puts programmers in a tizz. Robert Wuhl stars, writes and directs, while Rod Taylor, Helen Shaver and Gailard Sartain co-star. A spot-on comedy, that retains its relevance.

Robert Wuhl *Stuart Sain* • Rod Taylor *Billy Patrick* • Gailard Sartain *George Plunkett* • Helen Shaver *Rachel Rowen* • Maggie Han *Cary Sain* • Dina Merrill *Doris Hays-Britton* • Saul Rubinek *Eric Schlockmeister* ■ *Dir/Scr* Robert Wuhl

Open Your Eyes ★★★★ 15

Psychological thriller
1997 · Sp · Colour · 119mins

This is a dazzling second feature from young Spanish film-maker Alejandro Amenábar. As the pampered playboy whose life begins to unravel after a disfiguring car crash, Eduardo Noriega conveys both resentment and vulnerability as he strives to make sense of a relentless sequence of increasingly disconcerting events. Criss-crossing genres and referencing such films as *Vertigo* and *Eyes without a Face*, this delirious treatise on appearance and reality, dreams and disappointments requires total concentration, right through to its dissatisfyingly glib denouement. A Spanish language film.

Eduardo Noriega *César* • Penelope Cruz *Sofia* • Chete Lera *Antonio* • Fele Martinez *Pelayo* • Najwa Nimri *Nuria* ■ *Dir* Alejandro Amenábar • *Scr* Alejandro Amenábar, Mateo Gil

Opening Night ★★★★ 15

Drama   1977 · US · Colour · 138mins

In addition to his own talent and daring as actor/writer/director, John Cassavetes was blessed in his wife and regular collaborator, Gena Rowlands, for whom this is a tour de force. Rowlands is spellbinding as the star experiencing an intense emotional and spiritual crisis before the first performance of her new play. A truthful testament to the self-absorption, fragility and art of actors, it's hard-going if you're not keen on Cassavetes's uncompromising, unconventional style. But the acting is suitably rivetting: Cassavetes is compelling as Rowlands's leading man, and veteran Joan Blondell is on splendid form as her author friend. ▣

Gena Rowlands *Myrtle Gordon* • John Cassavetes *Maurice Aarons* • Ben Gazzara *Manny Victor* • Joan Blondell *Sarah Goode* • Paul Stewart *David Samuels* • Zohra Lampert *Dorothy Victor* ■ *Dir/Scr* John Cassavetes

Opera ★★★

Horror   1987 · It · Colour · 107mins

There's no phantom in Italian horror maestro Dario Argento's masterwork;

just a mentally deranged maniac obsessed with ingénue singer Cristina Marsillach as she rehearses Verdi's *Macbeth*. But this aria of savage beauty contains Argento's single most potent and self-revelatory image: Marsillach, forced to watch orchestrated murders, is unable to close her eyes due to needles taped under the lids. Argento's relentless search for the outer limits of hardcore gore takes an autopsy-turvy turn with the knife-through-the-throat shot, and his glides from the opera house roof to the auditorium are stunning. It doesn't make much sense, but it's bravura cinema at its shock-inducing best. An Italian language film.

Cristina Marsillach *Betty* • Urbano Barberini *Inspector Santini* • Daria Nicolodi *Mira* • Ian Charleson *Marco* ■ *Dir* Dario Argento • *Scr* Dario Argento, Franco Ferrini

Opera do Malandro ★★★★ 15

Musical fantasy
1986 · Bra · Colour · 107mins

Adapted from the Chico Buarque play, which was itself inspired by Bertolt Brecht and Kurt Weill's *Threepenny Opera*, this is less a stylised snapshot of Brazil on the eve of war than a tribute to the musical extravaganzas of MGM (although Arthur Freed never envisaged flamenco cat fights or production numbers set in the Gents!). Directing with visual and visceral panache, Ruy Guerra allows his camera to prowl around Rio's seedy bars and crumbling slums, as small-time racketeer Edson Celulari's plan to corrupt the daughter of his deadly, pro-Nazi rival calamitously backfires. It's sensual, surreal and subversive, and throbs with life. In Portuguese with English subtitles.

Edson Celulari *Max* • Claudia Ohana *Ludmila* • Elba Ramalho *Margot* ■ *Dir* Ruy Guerra • *Scr* Chico Buarque, Orlando Senna, Ruy Guerra

The Operation ★★★

Thriller   1990 · US · Colour · 100mins

This surprisingly effective TV movie blends medical melodrama, marital mayhem and murder mystery in a potent prescription that may well have adverse side-effects for some, but should prove to be just what the doctor ordered for those in need of an undemanding watch. Mercifully avoiding the histrionics typical of so many US teleplays, the film benefits from the measured performance of Kathleen Quinlan as the wife attempting to wrestle doctor/husband Joe Penny's gynaecological practice away from him at the same time he's fighting a malpractice suit.

Joe Penny *Dr Ed Betters* • Lisa Hartman *Laura Parks* • Kathleen Quinlan *Dr Ginnie Betters* • Jason Beghe *John Kopiak* • John Santucci *Lieutenant Harry Gold* ■ *Dir* Thomas J Wright • *Scr* Douglas Stefen Borghi

Operation Amsterdam ★★★ U

Second World War drama
1958 · UK · BW · 104mins

It might seem like double Dutch these days, but director Michael McCarthy's final film (he died the following year) was convincing enough on its release –

a British pseudo-documentary, set in 1940, about a bunch of spies sent into Holland to recover a hoard of industrial diamonds before the Nazis get to them. Diamond expert Alexander Knox looks grave and concerned, and Peter Finch is dashing and daring. There's also a note of interest in seeing Eva Bartok, who starred in gossip columns more often than movies.

Peter Finch *Jan Smit* • Eva Bartok *Anna* • Tony Britton *Major Dillon* • Alexander Knox *Walter Keyser* • Malcolm Keen *Johann Smit* • Christopher Rhodes *Alex* • Tim Turner *Lieutenant* • John Horsley *Commander Bowerman* ■ *Dir* Michael McCarthy • *Scr* Michael McCarthy, John Eldridge, from the book *Adventure in Diamonds* by David E Walker

Operation Bullshine ★★ U

Comedy   1959 · UK · Colour · 83mins

It's just feasible that this feeble comedy might have raised a smile in the darkest days of the Second World War, but more than a decade after the event there was simply no excuse for the tired collection of jokes that aren't worth a smutty snigger. This is a clear case of too much bull and not enough shine. Donald Sinden and Barbara Murray could do this sort of marital misunderstanding material in their sleep, and it's to their credit that they try to give it some pep, as does the splendid supporting cast.

Donald Sinden *Lieutenant Gordon Brown* • Barbara Murray *Private Betty Brown* • Carole Lesley *Private Marge White* • Ronald Shiner *Gunner Slocum* • Naunton Wayne *Major Pym* • Dora Bryan *Private Cox* • John Cairney *Gunner Willie Ross* • Fabia Drake *Junior Commander Maddox, Ats* • Joan Rice *Private Finch* • Daniel Massey *Bombardier Palmer* ■ *Dir* Gilbert Gunn • *Scr* Anne Burnaby, Rupert Lang, Gilbert Gunn

Operation CIA ★★★

Spy action thriller   1965 · US · BW · 90mins

This nifty spy thriller sees agent Burt Reynolds (in one of his earliest roles) sent to Saigon during the Vietnam conflict to try to prevent an assassination. Not totally American propaganda, the film maintains a detached stance on the differing values of the goodies and the baddies, while director Christian Nyby keeps it all very lively.

Burt Reynolds *Mark Andrews* • Kieu Chinh *Kim-chinh* • Danielle Aubry *Denise, French agent* • John Hoyt *Wells* • Cyril Collick *Withers* • Vic Diaz *Prof Yen* • William Catching *Frank Decker* ■ *Dir* Christian Nyby • *Scr* Peer J Oppenheimer, Bill S Ballinger, from a story by Peer J Oppenheimer

Operation Condor: the Armour of God II ★★★★ 15

Martial arts adventure
1990 · HK · Colour · 102mins

Here, Hong Kong superstar Jackie Chan plays an Indiana Jones-style secret agent (codenamed Condor) searching for a stash of Nazi gold in the Sahara. Cue some wonderfully choreographed kung-fu fights with militant desert rats, hugely entertaining action-hero parodies and silly slapstick for which Chan has the perfect timing. There are even fun out-takes under the final credits. Cantonese dialogue

dubbed into English. Contains violence.
▭

Jackie Chan *Jackie* • Carol Cheng *Ada* • Eva Cobo de Garcia [Eva Cobo] *Elsa* • Shoko Ikeda *Momoko* • Alfredo Brel Sanchez *Adolf* ■ *Dir* Jackie Chan • *Scr* Jackie Chan, Edward Tang, Szeto Chuek-Hun, Ken Lowe, John Sheppard, from a story by Barry Wong

Operation Crossbow ★★★ PG
Second World War drama
1965 · It/US/UK · Colour · 111mins
The credits are impressive, the plot intriguing and the production values impeccable, but they only add up to an average wartime thriller. In common with many blockbuster writers, Emeric Pressburger (co-writing here under the pseudonym Richard Imrie) and his colleagues were confounded by the dual task of telling a ripping yarn and finding enough to do for a big-name cast. As a result, the mission to replace German V-2 rocket scientists with Allied boffins is often of secondary interest to the stargazing. However, there is plenty of derring-do, although director Michael Anderson struggles to find a workable balance between action and chat. ▭

George Peppard *Lieutenant John Curtis* • Sophia Loren *Nora* • Trevor Howard *Professor Lindemann* • John Mills *General Boyd* • Richard Johnson *Duncan Sandys* • Tom Courtenay *Robert Henshaw* • Jeremy Kemp *Phil Bradley* • Anthony Quayle *Bamford* • Lilli Palmer *Frieda* • Paul Henreid *General Ziemann* ■ *Dir* Michael Anderson • *Scr* Richard Imrie [Emeric Pressurger], Derry Quinn, Ray Rigby, from a story by Duilio Coletti, Vittoriano Petrilli

Operation Daybreak ★★★ 15
Second World War thriller
1975 · US/UK · Colour · 114mins
A grimly exciting war drama about the Czech resistance's assassination of Reinhard Heydrich, deputy chief of the Gestapo and better known as "Hitler's Hangman". This is drily, if expertly, directed by veteran Lewis Gilbert, and features a motley cast including American Tim Bottoms and a particularly excellent Anthony Andrews as Czech patriots. That this film convinces is a tribute to the story, and today, when the village of Lidice, which was razed by the Nazis in reprisal for the assassination, is hardly remembered, its telling is still timely. ▭

Timothy Bottoms *Jan Kubis* • Martin Shaw *Karel Curda* • Joss Ackland *Janak* • Nicola Pagett *Anna* • Anthony Andrews *Joseph Gabcik* • Anton Diffring *Reinhard Heydrich* • Diana Coupland *Aunt Marie* • Cyril Shaps *Father Petrek* • Ray Smith *Hajek* • Timothy West *Vaclav* ■ *Dir* Lewis Gilbert • *Scr* Ronald Harwood, from the novel *Seven Men at Daybreak* by Alan Burgess

Operation Dead End ★★
Thriller 1986 · W Ger · Colour · 95mins
This passable thriller from focuses on three strangers who volunteer for an experiment to monitor stress levels in the wake of a nuclear holocaust. However, 72 days in close confinement on a deserted island, and the discovery that the experiment is not all that it seems, cause tempers to fray. The claustrophobic shelter sequences are essentially chat-bound, but the pace picks up once the trio begins to

investigate what the sinister scientists are really up to. German dialogue dubbed into English.

Hannes Jaenicke *Leslie* • Uwe Oxenknecht *Boris* • Isabelle Willer *Kim* • Anton Diffring *Professor Lang* ■ *Dir* Nikolai Müllerschön • *Scr* Stanislav Barabas, Nikolai Mullerschon

Operation Delta Force ★★ 15
Action drama 1996 · US · Colour · 89mins
Jeff Fahey is the unlikely lead in this standard action film, in which he plays the commander of a special military unit that is charged with retrieving a super-virus from Afrikaaner terrorists. The action scenes take place on trains, boats, bridges and in tunnels. The movie is fairly slickly made, but occasionally low-budget touches shine through the gloss: during a shoot-out in a train car, there are four or five people emptying machine guns at each other, yet the furnishing of the train never show the slightest damage! Contains violence and some swearing. ▭

Jeff Fahey *Lang* • Ernie Hudson *Tipton* • Rob Stewart *Sparks* • Frank Zagarino *McKinney* • Joe Lara *Nash* • Todd Jensen *Hutch* • Natasha Sutherland *Marie* • Hal Holbrook *Henshaw* ■ *Dir* Sam Firstenberg • *Scr* David Sparling

Operation Dumbo Drop ★★★ PG
Comedy adventure
1995 · US · Colour · 103mins
Good Morning, Vietnam meets *The Incredible Journey* in an amiable family comedy with more than a fair share of surprisingly adult-orientated jokes. Director Simon Wincer's harmless allegory stars Danny Glover and Ray Liotta as the leaders of a group of Green Beret soldiers who promise to deliver an elephant to a Vietnamese village. The problems they face in order to carry out their pledge triggers off lots of fun escapades and leads to a winning climax with the pachyderm plummeting from a plane. ▭ DVD

Danny Glover *Captain Sam Cahill* • Ray Liotta *Captain Doyle* • Denis Leary *David Poole* • Doug E Doug *Harvey Ashford* • Corin Nemec *Lawrence Farley* • Tcheky Karyo *Goddard* ■ *Dir* Simon Wincer • *Scr* Gene Quintano, Jim Kouf, from a story by Jim Morris

Operation Golden Phoenix ★★
Martial arts adventure
1994 · Can/Leb · Colour · 91mins
Notable mainly for being the first and only Canadian/Lebanese martial arts movie, this was obviously a labour of love for producer/director/star Jalal Merhi. The mainly nonsensical story revolves around the hunt for some long-lost treasure, which at least gives Merhi the chance to film in some unfamiliar locations. The fight sequences aren't too bad, but things drag badly away from the action set pieces. Contains violence and swearing.

Jalal Merhi *Mark Assante* • James Hong *Chang* • Loren Avedon *Ivan Jones* • Joseph Nano *Professor Amid* • Karen Sheperd *Princess Tara* • Guylaine St Onge *Princess*

Angelique • Al Waxman *Chief Gordon* ■ *Dir* Jalal Merhi • *Scr* J Stephen Maunder, Kevin Ward, from a story by Samir Ghouseine

Operation Mad Ball ★★★ U
Comedy 1957 · US · BW · 104mins
After his Oscar-winning turn in *Mister Roberts*, Jack Lemmon enlisted in the army for this breakneck comedy, co-written by Blake Edwards and directed by Richard Quine, both of whom would work with Lemmon later in his career. It's set in Normandy in 1945 where the low-ranking soldiers in a military hospital stage a "mad ball" in order to fraternise with the otherwise off-limits high-ranking nurses. Lemmon is in sparkling form as the "Mr Fixit" and Mickey Rooney's performance will either reduce you to hysterics or set your teeth on edge. Despite the setting, it's really a comedy about American sexual mores in the fifties – sort of like *The Seven Year Itch* in army fatigues.

Jack Lemmon *Private Hogan* • Kathryn Grant *Lieutenant Betty Bixby* • Ernie Kovacs *Captain Paul Locke* • Arthur O'Connell *Colonel Rousch* • Mickey Rooney *Yancy Skibo* • Dick York *Corporal Bohun* • James Darren *Private Widowskas* ■ *Dir* Richard Quine • *Scr* Arthur Carter, Jed Harris, Blake Edwards, from the play by Arthur Carter

Operation Madonna ★★
Thriller 1987 · Neth/W Ger · Colour · 83mins
Dutch star Renée Soutendjik and versatile French character actor Michel Lonsdale (here billed as Michael) add a touch of unmerited class to this humdrum thriller, in which a forged painting, a case of mistaken identity and a pair of identical twins singularly fail to raise the pulse rate. Director Hans-Christoph Blumenberg captures some of Hamburg's tawdry ambience, but he plods through the plot's predictable twists with little enthusiasm or imagination. In Dutch and German with English subtitles.

Marius Müller-Westernhagen *Martin Graves* • Renée Soutendjik *Juliane Mundt* • Michael Lonsdale [Michel Lonsdale] *Tanzmann* • Heinrich Schweiger *Arthur/Otto Wiegand* • Ingrid Van Bergen *Charly* • Nina Hoger *Monika* • Peter Kraus *Schirmer* ■ *Dir* Hans-Christoph Blumenberg • *Scr* Jonathan Thornhill, Hans-Christoph Blumenberg

Operation Pacific ★★ U
Second World War drama
1951 · US · BW · 104mins
Like most of Wayne's war pictures, *Operation Pacific* is gung-ho, action-packed and grossly sentimental – the plot leans in homeless children, dewy-eyed nuns, a batch of dud torpedoes and marital difficulties. Wayne, of course, takes everything in his stride, scuppering the Japanese fleet, playing daddy to the youngsters and winning back the hand of Patricia Neal. The navy liked this one so much it held regular screenings at all its bases. ▭

John Wayne *"Duke" Gifford* • Patricia Neal *Mary Stuart* • Ward Bond *"Pop" Perry* • Scott Forbes *Larry* • Philip Carey *Bob Perry* • Paul Picerni *Jonesy* • William Campbell *Talker* • Kathryn Givney *Commander Steele* • Martin Milner *Caldwell* • Jack Pennick *Chief* ■ *Dir/Scr* George Waggner

Operation Petticoat ★★★★ U
Comedy 1959 · US · Colour · 120mins
This wonderfully wacky wartime comedy teams those two great *farceurs* Cary Grant and Tony Curtis in their only movie together; ironically (or intentionally, since Grant produced), it was made immediately following Curtis's take-off of Grant in *Some Like It Hot*. Here Grant is a submarine commander trying to keep his ropey old vessel in the water with the help of wheeler-dealer junior officer Curtis. Complications arise as the sub takes on board a number of unorthodox passengers, among them a group of sexy nurses. Grant is brilliant, with every reaction immaculately timed. *Pink Panther* director Blake Edwards ensures no gag is missed, and the whole is a deliciously tasteless joy. ▭

Cary Grant *Admiral Matt Sherman* • Tony Curtis *Lt Nick Holden* • Joan O'Brien *Lt Dolores Crandall* • Dina Merrill *Lt Barbara Duran* • Gene Evans *Molumphrey* • Arthur O'Connell *Sam Tostin* • Richard Sargent [Dick Sargent] *Stovall* ■ *Dir* Blake Edwards • *Scr* Stanley Shapiro, Maurice Richlin, from a story by Paul King, Joseph Stone

Ophélia ★★
Drama 1962 · Fr · BW · 103mins
The textual influence may be Shakespeare, but the atmospheric sire of this dramatic curio from Claude Chabrol is clearly Franz Kafka. With Jean Rabier's camera prowling around the shabby grandeur of a murky mansion, the familiar story of the grieving son who becomes convinced that his mother and lecherous uncle were responsible for his father's death is laced with juvenile humour and melodramatic excess. Alida Valli and Claude Cerval enjoy themselves as the murder suspects, but André Jocelyn is out of his depth as the angst-ridden avenger. Even as a modern dress parody of Olivier's *Hamlet* , this is a disappointing misfire. In French with English subtitles.

André Jocelyn *Yvan Lesurf* • Alida Valli *Claudia* • Juliette Mayniel *Lucie* • Claude Cerval *Adrien Lesurf* • Robert Burnier *André Lagrange* • Jean-Louis Maury *Sparkos* ■ *Dir* Claude Chabrol • *Scr* Claude Chabrol, Martial Matthieu [Paul Gégauff]

Opportunity Knocks ★★ 15
Comedy 1990 · US · Colour · 96mins
Made two years before he struck paydirt as Garth in *Wayne's World*, Dana Carvey takes the lead in this fumbled comedy of errors. Trotting out the full repertoire of silly voices he made famous on *Saturday Night Live*, Carvey just about carries the story of a con man who wins the confidence of a wealthy plumbing family while on the run from a gangster. Robert Loggia contributes some assured support, but it's the script that lets the side down. ▭

Dana Carvey *Eddie Farrell* • Robert Loggia *Milt Malkin* • Todd Graff *Lou Pasquino* • Julia Campbell *Annie Malkin* • Milo O'Shea *Max* • James Tolkan *Sal Nichols* ■ *Dir* Donald Petrie • *Scr* Mitchel Katlin, Nat Bernstein

U = SUITABLE FOR ALL **Uc** = SUITABLE FOR ALL, ESPECIALLY FOR YOUNG CHILDREN (VIDEO ONLY) **PG** = PARENTAL GUIDANCE

Opposing Force ★★★

Action drama   1986 · US · Colour · 97mins

This exploitation action flick, unusually for the genre, carries a strong moral message, focusing on the overzealous nature of military training techniques. Tom Skerritt is his usual solid self as an army major who enrolls in a special military camp run by the slightly unhinged Anthony Zerbe, who's not averse to using physical and psychological torture on his soldiers. The film pulls few punches in its depiction of gruelling war games and pitches the question of just how closely training can mirror actual combat conditions. Alas, what suspense the film manages to build up is thrown away in the formulaic shoot-out finale.

Tom Skerritt *Major Logan* • Lisa Eichhorn *Lieutenant Casey* • Anthony Zerbe *Becker* • Richard Roundtree *Sergeant Stafford* • Robert Wightman *Gen McGowan* • John Considine *Gen MacDonald* • George Kee Cheung [George Cheung] *Tuan* ■ *Dir* Eric Karson • *Scr* Gil Cowan, Linda Cowgill, Hugh Corcoran

The Opposite of Sex ★★★★ 18

Comedy   1998 · US · Colour · 96mins

Former screenwriter Don Roos cuts through the thicket of political correctness with rapier wit and rude humour in his eye-opening feature directing debut about contemporary sexual values and lifestyles. Christina Ricci is deadly funny as the white-trash teenager who steals her gay half-brother's boyfriend so she can have an instant father for the child she's carrying. With Lisa Kudrow from *Friends* also giving a spot-on turn as a self-righteous old maid, Roos's bitchy oddball comedy is hilarious, and even manages a touching ending. Contains swearing, and some violence and sexual references. ▭ 𝐃𝐕𝐃

Christina Ricci *Dedee Truitt* • Martin Donovan *Bill Truitt* • Lisa Kudrow *Lucia Dalury* • Lyle Lovett *Sheriff Carl Tippett* • Johnny Galecki *Jason Bock* • William Lee Scott *Randy* ■ *Dir/ Scr* Don Roos

The Opposite Sex ★★★

Musical comedy 1956 · US · Colour · 116mins

A musical remake of *The Women*, but while that MGM classic featured no men in its cast, this film makes the mistake of allowing the pretty dreary Jeff Richards and a young Leslie Nielsen to appear opposite female stars Joan Collins, Dolores Gray, Ann Sheridan, Ann Miller (not on screen enough) and Joan Blondell. The only fly in the ointment is top-billed June Allyson, who seems neither sophisticated nor brittle enough for the shenanigans. There's also strong support from Barbara Jo Allen, Agnes Moorehead and Charlotte Greenwood, and good use of early CinemaScope. It's sexy, witty and glamorous, and if you can forget the original, it's a lot of fun.

June Allyson *Kay Hilliard* • Joan Collins *Crystal Allen* • Dolores Gray *Sylvia Fowler* • Ann Sheridan *Amanda Penrose* • Ann Miller *Gloria Dell* • Leslie Nielsen *Steve Hilliard* • Jeff Richards *Buck Winston* • Agnes Moorehead

Countess Lavaliere • ■ *Dir* David Miller • *Scr* Fay Kanin, Michael Kanin, from the play by Clare Boothe Luce

The Opposite Sex and How to Live with Them ★★ 15

Romantic comedy
1993 · US · Colour · 82mins

An amiable but hardly ground-breaking romantic comedy. *Friends* star Courteney Cox plays the daughter of conservative parents who endures a mismatched, up-and-down relationship with Arye Gross. The two leads are fine, but, as is often the case, the best performances and lines go to their respective best friends, Julie Brown and Kevin Pollak. Director Matthew Meshekoff attempts to spice up the formula with some raunchy scenes and characters talking directly to the camera, but it isn't in the same league as *When Harry Met Sally...*, which it obviously aspires to be. ▭

Arye Gross *David* • Courteney Cox *Carrie* • Kevin Pollak *Eli* • Julie Brown *Zoe* • Jack Carter *Rabbi* • Kimber Sissons *Tracy* • Mitchell Ryan *Kenneth Davenport* ■ *Dir* Matthew Meshekoff • *Scr* Noah Stern

Opposites Attract ★★

Romantic comedy
1990 · US · Colour · 96mins

Clint Eastwood and Sonny Bono are among the Hollywood stars who have tried their hand at civic office, and that's the theme explored in this lightweight but genial romantic comedy. Former *Dynasty* star John Forsythe plays a big-name actor who decides to enter local politics as a protest and finds himself pitted against Barbara Eden, with predictable consequences. The two stars are old hands when it comes to this sort of inconsequential fluff, and director Noel Nosseck supplies a bland, glossy sheen. Contains some strong language.

John Forsythe *Rex Roper* • Barbara Eden *Charlene McKeon* • Dori Brenner *Jane Conyers* ■ *Dir* Noel Nosseck • *Scr* Susan Rice

The Optimists of Nine Elms ★★★ PG

Drama   1973 · UK · Colour · 106mins

This was originally to have been a vehicle for Danny Kaye, but it's hard to see how his energetic style would have been suitable for the part of Sam the busker, who has little to sustain him apart from his music-hall memories and his faithful dog. Resisting the temptation for pathos, Peter Sellers gives a surprisingly sensitive and somewhat overlooked performance, made even more memorable by his generous encouragement of his young co-stars. Lionel Bart's songs aren't among his best, but Simmons's musings on freedom and the family, poverty and community spirit, are nicely expressed. ▭

Peter Sellers *Sam* • Donna Mullane *Liz* • John Chaffey *Mark* • David Daker *Bob Ellis* • Marjorie Yates *Chrissie Ellis* ■ *Dir* Anthony Simmons • *Scr* Anthony Simmons, Tudor Gates, from the novel by Anthony Simmons

The Oracle ★ U

Fantasy comedy   1952 · UK · BW · 85mins

Gilbert Harding voices the oracle at the bottom of a well in this piffling comedy in which whimsy is heaped on to make up for the absence of genuine humour. Ordinarily, Harding dispenses his wisdom to the inhabitants of a small Irish island. But then journalist Robert Beatty begins using him to predict horse races and other momentous events until the British mainland is reduced to chaos. Celebrated at the time as the rudest man on TV, Harding comes over today as an irascible prig and there is too little in the threadbare story to compensate for his blustering.

Robert Beatty *Bob Jefferson* • Joseph Tomelty *Terry Roche* • Michael Medwin *Timothy Blake* • Mervyn Johns *Tom Mitchum* • Virginia McKenna *Shelagh* • Gillian Lind *Jane Bond* • Ursula Howells *Peggy* • Gilbert Harding *Oracle's voice* ■ *Dir* CM Pennington-Richards • *Scr* Patrick Campbell, from the radio play *To Tell You the Truth* by Robert Barr

Orbit ★★ 15

Action adventure thriller
1996 · US · Colour · 79mins

An ambitious but unnecessary complicated conspiracy thriller, which centres on an abortive attempt to sabotage a US shuttle mission via a virus in the computer system. Unfolded in flashback at a subsequent court case, the story stirs in right-wing American terrorists and even alien life forms into an already overheated brew and, for all the intriguing ideas on show, budgetary restraints means it's largely a static, earth-bound affair. Contains swearing. ▭

Casper Van Dien • Bentley Mitchum • Kelly Ann Sweeney • Joe Estevez • Carrie Mitchum • Nick Wilder • Jan-Michael Vincent • Chris Mitchum [Christopher Mitchum] • Ulli Lommel *Max Braun* ■ *Dir* Mario Van Cleef [Ulli Lommel] • *Scr* Budd Garrison

Orca ★★ PG

Action thriller   1977 · US · Colour · 88mins

Although Richard Harris's acting chews up the scenery, Bo Derek simply gets chewed up in this man-versus-beast story, made before current ecological concerns. Harris is the shark-hunting macho man who incurs the wrath of Orca, a super-intelligent killer whale, because he's slaughtered its pregnant mate. Scientist Charlotte Rampling strikes a lot of poses, but not even some remarkable underwater photography can make up for a narrative that's dumber than a shoal of kippers. ▭

Richard Harris *Captain Nolan* • Charlotte Rampling *Rachel Bedford* • Will Sampson *Umilak* • Bo Derek *Annie* • Keenan Wynn *Novak* • Scott Walker *Swain* • Robert Carradine *Ken* • Peter Hooten *Paul* ■ *Dir* Michael Anderson • *Scr* Luciano Vincenzoni, Sergio Donati

Orchestra Rehearsal ★★★ PG

Drama   1978 · It/Fr/W Ger · Colour · 69mins

Prompted by the murder of ex-Prime Minister Aldo Moro, yet also clearly a swipe at the strikers who had disrupted the production of *Amarcord* and *Casanova*, Fellini's microcosmic

burlesque on the shortcomings of both anarchy and authoritarianism was originally made for Italian television. Dismissed as a one-gag vignette, it's actually a revealing snapshot of late seventies socio-political attitudes and an unconscious rebellion against the cult of auteurism. With Nino Rota's playfully banal score (sadly, one of his last) and Dante Ferretti's symbolically crumbling edifice reinforcing the satire, this allegory allegretto may be Fellini in a minor key, but it's still wryly amusing. In Italian with English subtitles. ▭

Balduin Baas *Conductor* • Clara Colosimo *Harpist* • Elisabeth Labi *Pianist* ■ *Dir* Federico Fellini • *Scr* Federico Fellini, Brunello Rondi

Orchestra Wives ★★★ PG

Musical   1942 · US · BW · 93mins

Life on the road as lived by a touring swing orchestra and, more particularly the musicians' wives, with the new wife (Ann Rutherford) of trumpeter George Montgomery having to cope with the female rivalry and backbiting. The mediocre script and second-rung cast, however, are secondary to the delights of the Mack Gordon-Harry Warren score, the Glenn Miller Orchestra, which had huge hits with *I've Got a Gal in Kalamazoo* and *At Last*, vocalists Tex Beneke and Marion Hutton and the Modernaires, and dazzling tap-dancing team the Nicholas Brothers. Archie Mayo directed. ▭

George Montgomery *Bill Abbott* • Ann Rutherford *Connie* • Glenn Miller *Gene Morrison* • Cesar Romero *Sinjin* • Lynn Bari *Jaynie* • Carole Landis *Natalie* • Virginia Gilmore *Elsie* • Jackie Gleason *Beck* • Nicholas Brothers *Specialty* • Tex Beneke • Marion Hutton ■ *Dir* Archie Mayo • *Scr* Karl Tunberg, Darrel Ware, from a story by James Prindle • *Music* Mack Gordon, Harry Warren

Ordeal by Innocence ★★ 15

Detective drama
1984 · UK · Colour and BW · 86mins

Mediocre screen version of an Agatha Christie potboiler, about an explorer returning to England after two years in the Antarctic to find a man he knew on a murder rap from which he might have saved him. Donald Sutherland, Christopher Plummer, Faye Dunaway, Sarah Miles and Ian McShane head the bi-national cast. All act on autopilot, especially Sutherland, who looks as bemused as the audience about what an amateur American sleuth is doing in a Devon village. Equally out of place is Dave Brubeck's jazzy score. ▭

Donald Sutherland *Dr Arthur Calgary* • Faye Dunaway *Rachel Argyle* • Ian McShane *Philip Durrant* • Sarah Miles *Mary Durrant* • Christopher Plummer *Leo Argyle* • Diana Quick *Gwenda Vaughan* • Annette Crosbie *Kirsten Lindstrom* • Michael Elphick *Inspector Huish* ■ *Dir* Desmond Davis • *Scr* Alexander Stuart, from the novel by Agatha Christie

Ordeal in the Arctic ★★★ PG

Drama based on a true story
1993 · US/Can · Colour · 89mins

While not as gripping as the Andes plane-crash drama *Alive*, this TV movie still has enough action and suspense to keep you hooked. Based on a real-life incident, when a Canadian transport plane, with 18 people on board, crashed into a glacier 500 miles from the North Pole, the film focuses on both the rescue bid and the plight of the survivors as they try to cope with their injuries and a savage blizzard. Richard Chamberlain is perfectly cast as the heroic captain, while there's sterling support from Melanie Mayron and Catherine Mary Stewart. ▣

Richard Chamberlain *Captain John Couch* • Catherine Mary Stewart *Captain Wilma DeGroot* • Melanie Mayron *Sue Hillier* • Scott Hylands *Fred Ritchie* • Page Fletcher *Joe Bales* ■ *Dir* Mark Sobel • *Scr* Paul Edwards, from the non-fiction book *Death and Deliverance* by Robert Mason Lee

The Ordeal of Bill Carney
★★★

Drama based on a true story
1981 · US · Colour · 100mins

An often moving drama, based on a true story, about a quadriplegic father (Ray Sharkey) who fights in court for the custody of his children with the aid of his paraplegic lawyer (Richard Crenna). Sharkey is impressive in what could have been a one-note role, and he is given able support from Betty Buckley and Ana Alicia. Competently and sensitively made by *Shogun* director Jerry London.

Richard Crenna *Mason Rose* • Ray Sharkey *Bill Carney* • Betty Buckley *Barbara Slaner* • Ana Alicia *Lisa Saldonna* • Jeremy Licht *Willie Carney* ■ *Dir* Jerry London • *Scr* Tom Lazarus

Order of Death
★★★⑱

Thriller   1983 · It · Colour · 96mins

A genre-twisting spaghetti thriller featuring Harvey Keitel in an early vicious role and Sex Pistol John Lydon (aka Johnny Rotten) as his sociopathic confessor. Lydon shows up at detective Keitel's secret Central Park apartment, paid for by drug dealers' backhanders, and admits he's the serial killer responsible for slaughtering numerous narcotics division cops. Is he telling the truth and what is Keitel going to do now the punk has seen his illicit apartment? Thus begins a sadistic game of cat-and-mouse psychology in which the captor and victim are interchangeable. A cleverly crafted, homoerotic minuet of strong wills. ▣

Harvey Keitel *Lt Fred O'Connor* • John Lydon *Leo Smith* • Nicole Garcia *Lenore Carvo* • Leonard Mann *Bob Carvo* • Sylvia Sidney *Margaret Smith* ■ *Dir* Roberto Faenza • *Scr* Ennio De Concini, Hugh Fleetwood, Roberto Faenza, from the novel by Hugh Fleetwood

Orders Are Orders
★★Ⓤ

Comedy   1954 · UK · BW · 74mins

A play from the thirties was dug up to provide the basis for this army comedy, which pokes fun at American producers coming to Britain to make cheap science-fiction movies. The film is chiefly of interest today because of the amount of radio talent involved. Brian Reece, who had just finished a long run as PC49, stars, and up-and-coming Peter Sellers and Tony Hancock lend support, while even Eric Sykes was brought in to pep up the corny old script. ▣

Peter Sellers *Private Goffin* • Sidney James *Ed Waggermeyer* • Brian Reece *Capt Harper* •

Margot Grahame *Wanda Sinclair* • Raymond Huntley *Col Bellamy* • Tony Hancock *Lt Wilfrid Cartroad* • Clive Morton *Gen Grahame-Fox* • June Thorburn *Veronica Bellamy* • Bill Fraser *Private Slee* • Donald Pleasence *Lance Cpl Martin* • Eric Sykes *Private Waterhouse* ■ *Dir* David Paltenghi • *Scr* Donald Taylor, Eric Sykes, Geoffrey Orme, from the play by Ian Hay, Anthony Armstrong

Orders to Kill
★★★★

Second World War drama
1958 · UK · BW · 110mins

A forgotten gem of the British cinema, this wartime drama sends a French-speaking American bomber pilot, Paul Massie, to Paris to liquidate a double agent. However, when Massie meets his target and finds him to be friendly and mild-mannered, he questions the man's guilt. But orders are orders and after the deed is done, Massie steals the victim's money and blows it all on booze. After that comes a succession of major ironies and a complex moral argument, tightly directed by Anthony Asquith and co-written by Paul Dehn.

Eddie Albert *Major MacMahon* • Paul Massie *Gene Summers* • Lillian Gish *Mrs Summers* • James Robertson-Justice *Naval commander* • Irene Worth *Leonie* • Leslie French *Marcel Lafitte* • John Crawford *Kimball* • Lionel Jeffries *Interrogator* ■ *Dir* Anthony Asquith • *Scr* Paul Dehn, George St George, from a story by Donald C Downes

Ordet
★★★★★⑫

Religious drama   1955 · Den · BW · 119mins

Thirty-five years after he first saw Kaj Munk's play (by which time it had already been filmed by Gustav Molander), Carl Theodor Dreyer finally brought this much-cherished project to the screen and won the Golden Lion at Venice. His only feature of the 1950s is filled with sharp contrasts – lively faith and dour dogma, optimism and fatalism, youth and age, cynical sanity and mystical madness – which are further highlighted by the authentic starkness of the Jutland setting and the deceptive simplicity of the long mobile takes. This establishes the atmosphere in which a family feud is resolved by a miraculous resurrection. It's simply a masterpiece. In Danish with English subtitles. ▣

Henrik Malberg *Morten Borgen* • Emil Hass Christensen *Mikkel Borgen* • Preben Lerdorff Rye *Johannes Borgen* • Cay Kristiansen *Anders Borgen* • Birgitte Federspiel *Inger, Mikkel's wife* ■ *Dir* Carl Theodor Dreyer • *Scr* Carl Theodor Dreyer, from the play by Kaj Munk

Ordinary Decent Criminal
★★★⑮

Crime caper
1999 · UK/Ger/Ire · Colour · 93mins

A thinly veiled attempt to retell the story of real-life Irish criminal Martin Cahill, the subject of John Boorman's critically acclaimed *The General*. This time Kevin Spacey plays Cahill (here renamed Michael Lynch), the cocky Dublin gangster who spent his days robbing the rich, annoying the police and falling foul of the IRA. Director Thaddeus O'Sullivan gives his star every possible moment of screen time, which is no bad thing for Spacey fans. However, anyone who has seen *The General* or knows about the man on

whom Michael is based will bristle at his transformation into a loveable rogue who likes nothing better than flashing his naked bum at nasty, irritating policemen. This is worth seeing thanks to another powerhouse performance from Spacey (dodgy accent notwithstanding).

Kevin Spacey *Michael Lynch* • Linda Fiorentino *Christine Lynch* • Peter Mullan *Stevie* • Stephen Dillane *Noel Quigley* • Helen Baxendale *Lisa* • David Hayman *Tony Brady* • Patrick Malahide *Commissioner Daly* ■ *Dir* Thaddeus O'Sullivan • *Scr* Gerry Stembridge [Gerard Stembridge]

Ordinary Magic
★

Drama   1993 · Can · Colour · 104mins

A Canadian film notable for the appearance of Paul Anka, one-time pop star from the fifties and early sixties. Jeffrey (nicknamed Ganesh) is a 15-year-old boy brought up in India by his strong social activist parents. When they die, he is shipped off to his aunt in Canada (Glenne Headly) where he tries to find some common ground between his eastern upbringing and his western counterparts. When his aunt is unfairly evicted by a property developer (Anka), he puts into practice everything he has learned in India to right the wrong. An interesting if unsatisfying attempt to portray both alienation and Hindu ideals.

Glenne Headly *Charlotte* • Ryan Reynolds *Ganesh* • David Fox *Father/Warren* • Heath Lamberts *Mayor* • Paul Anka *Joey Dean* ■ *Dir* Giles Walker • *Scr* Jefferson Lewis, from a novel by Malcolm Bosse

Ordinary People
★★★★⑮

Drama   1980 · US · Colour · 118mins

A critically acclaimed blockbuster in its time, *Ordinary People* won four Oscars, including best film and best director for Robert Redford, stepping behind the camera for the first time. There is one truly great performance from Mary Tyler Moore as the thin, elegant, golfing and social-mixing mother strung tighter than a piano wire, and she is ably assisted by Donald Sutherland and Timothy Hutton, who won a best supporting actor Oscar. Even though there is something very pat about Redford's exposition of the seemingly cosy middle-class family simmering with unconscious angst after the death of a son, and the movie has appeared more banal and obvious with the passage of time, this is still an auspicious directorial debut that stands as one of the first films to deal intelligently with the role of therapy. Contains swearing. ▣

Donald Sutherland *Calvin* • Mary Tyler Moore *Beth* • Judd Hirsch *Berger* • Timothy Hutton *Conrad* • M Emmet Walsh *Swimming Coach* • Elizabeth McGovern *Jeannine* • Dinah Manoff *Karen* • Fredric Lehne *Lazenby* • James B Sikking *Ray* ■ *Dir* Robert Redford • *Scr* Alvin Sargent, from the novel by Judith Guest

The Oregon Trail
★★Ⓤ

Western   1959 · US · Colour · 85mins

Fred MacMurray plays a New York reporter who gets kidnapped by Indians while investigating a story about the army's harsh treatment of the hostiles. Directed by Gene Fowler Jr, this atypical offering has a serious plot that

gets positively controversial when MacMurray goes all dewy-eyed over a Indian maiden and marries her. There's even a song or two.

Fred MacMurray *Neal Harris* • William Bishop *Captain George Wayne* • Nina Shipman *Prudence Cooper* • Gloria Talbott *Shona Hastings* • Henry Hull *Seton* • John Carradine *Zachariah Garrison* ■ *Dir* Gene Fowler Jr • *Scr* Louis Vittes, Gene Fowler Jr, from a story by Louis Vittes

The Oregon Trail
★★

Western   1976 · US · Colour · 110mins

This was the pilot for a TV series that was dropped almost as soon as its run began. A popular lead in the sixties, Rod Taylor was somewhat slumming it here, but he nevertheless gives a committed performance as the head of a pioneering family who ups sticks and treks 2,000 miles across unknown territory in search of free land. Although not a patch on such wagon-train classics as *Red River* or *Bend of the River*, this is a well-mounted adventure, with Blair Brown and David Huddleston backing Taylor to the hilt.

Rod Taylor *Evan Thorpe* • Blair Brown *Jessica Thorpe* • David Huddleston *Painted Face Kelly* • Douglas V Fowley [Douglas Fowley] *Eli Thorpe* • Andrew Stevens *Andrew Thorpe* • Tony Becker *William Thorpe* • Gina Maria Smika *Rachel Thorpe* ■ *Dir* Boris Sagal • *Scr* Michael Gleason

The Organization
★★★★

Crime drama   1971 · US · Colour · 107mins

Sidney Poitier embarks on his third tour of duty as San Francisco homicide cop Virgil Tibbs – first seen in 1967's *In the Heat of the Night* – and, surprisingly, there's still life left in his character. This story is neatly linked to the emerging youth culture of the time as Tibbs sets out to smash a drug syndicate with the help of young vigilantes out to get the organisation for what it's done to their family and friends. Director Don Medford keeps this moving in a convincingly tense manner and Poitier doesn't need to play the superhero to still come out on top. Contains violence and swearing.

Sidney Poitier *Lieutenant Virgil Tibbs* • Barbara McNair *Valerie Tibbs* • Gerald S O'Loughlin *Lieutenant Jack Pecora* • Sheree North *Gloria Morgan* • Fred Beir *Bob Alford* • Allen Garfield *Benjy* • Bernie Hamilton *Lieutenant Jessop* • Raul Julia *Juan Mendoza* • Ron O'Neal *Joe Peralez* • James A Watson Jr *Stacy Baker* ■ *Dir* Don Medford • *Scr* James R Webb, from characters created by John Ball

The Organizer
★★★★

Period drama
1963 · Fr/It/Yug · BW · 126mins

In Turin in the 1890s textile workers stage a massive and bitter strike and are organised by a radical intellectual played by Marcello Mastroianni. The government send in strikebreakers and then the army. Released when Italy was in the grip of industrial action, Monicelli's film, almost a black comedy, aroused considerable controversy. Mastroianni – hiding behind a beard and glasses – gives a superb performance, consolidating his position as Italy's pre-eminent actor. He thought the film was "stupendous... really one of the

Ⓤ = SUITABLE FOR ALL   Ⓤⓒ = SUITABLE FOR ALL, ESPECIALLY FOR YOUNG CHILDREN (VIDEO ONLY)   ℙ𝔾 = PARENTAL GUIDANCE

postwar classics of Italian cinema." In Italian with English subtitles.

Orgazmo

Comedy ★★ 18

1997 · US · Colour · 88mins

The characters may be real-life actors rather than crudely drawn caricatures, but this second full-length feature from Desiderio rediscovers his Sicilian roots when his young son is kidnapped. TV-movie queen Ann Jillian gets to do supporting player in this overly melodramatic story, in which Robert Parker, admirably continues to flout all things tasteful, politically correct and sophisticated. Director Parker plays a naive Mormon actor doing the rounds of LA who finds himself cast as the lead player in a porn movie. He intends to use the $20,000 salary for his impending marriage to his devoted fiancée back in Utah. However, the evil porn baron is reluctant to let his new star ("Joe Hung") retire. Oddly enough, it's not quite as offensive as *South Park*, but sensitive souls will still be outraged by the relentless flow of lavatorial laughs and vulgarity. Contains swearing and comic scenes of sex and violence. **DVD**

Trey Parker Joe Young · Dian Bachar Ben Chapleski · Robyn Lynne Raab Lisa · Michael Dean Jacobs Maxx Orbison · Ron Jeremy Clark · Andrew W Kemler Rodgers · David Dunn A-Cup · Matt Stone Dave the lighting guy · Dir/Scr Trey Parker

Original Gangstas

Crime drama ★★★ 18

1996 · US · Colour · 98mins

Attention all blaxploitation fanatics! Five seventies icons — Pam Grier, Fred Williamson, Jim Brown, Ron O'Neal and Richard Roundtree — team up to teach a Gary, Indiana, ghetto gang a tough-guy lesson in veteran B-movie director Larry Cohen's hip, black badass action update. Exciting and thought-provoking (should fire be fought with fire?), it's both a contemporary morality tale and an affectionately nostalgic look back at the *Shaft* and *Foxy Brown* era. **DVD**

Fred Williamson John Bookman · Jim Brown Jake Trevor · Pam Grier Laurie Thompson · Paul Winfield Reverend Marshall Dorsey · Ron O'Neal Bubba · Richard Roundtree Slick · Isabel Sanford Gracie Bookman · Dir Larry Cohen · Scr Aubrey Rattan

Original Sin

Thriller ★★ 15

1989 · US · Colour · 95mins

Charlton Heston is really only a supporting player in this overly melodramatic story, in which Robert Desiderio's revelations. Hardly a classic, but Heston is always worth watching, even when he's a shade below par. Contains violence and swearing.

Ann Jillian Sharon Richards · Charlton Heston Louis Mancini · Robert Desiderio John Richards · Lou Liberatore Chris · Richard Portnow Vincent · Dir Ron Satlof · Scr Philip F Messina

Orlando

Historical fantasy ★★★ PG

1992 · UK/Rus/Fr/It/Neth · Colour · 89mins

Director Sally Potter achieves the near-impossible task of bringing Virginia Woolf's complex tale to the screen in a series of burnished and glittering images that dazzle the eye. The film tells the story of young nobleman Orlando who lives for 400 years and mysteriously changes into a woman during the 18th century. As the hero/heroine, Tilda Swinton moves passively through the romantic, dramatic and intriguing events that befall Orlando, and there's an excellent supporting cast that includes Billy Zane. Lothaire Bluteau and, best of all, Quentin Crisp as Elizabeth I. The film, like the novel, is sometimes puzzling, sometimes boring, but it's unforgettably sumptuous and atmospheric. **[ ]**

Tilda Swinton Orlando · Billy Zane Shelmerdine · John Wood Archduke Harry · Lothaire Bluteau The Khan · Charlotte Valandrey Sasha · Heathcote Williams Nick Greene/Publisher · Quentin Crisp Queen Elizabeth I · Dudley Sutton King James I · Thom Hoffman King William of Orange · Anna Healy Euphrosyne · Ned Sherrin Mr Addison · Dir of Moray · Simon Russell Beale Earl of Moray · Rosemary Stevenson Sheila Flynn · Frank Gallagher Tanga · Alex Norton Hanson · Dir/Scr Sally Potter, from the novel by Virginia Woolf

Original Sins

Psychological thriller ★★★ 18

1995 · US · Colour · 103mins

Echoes of *Play Misty for Me* and *Talk Radio* reverberate around this TV movie. Mark Harmon proves a dependable small-screen stalwart, and the momentum here with a bravura performance as the Pittsburgh radio chat-show host who not only falls in love with one of his callers, but also has to deal with a murderer confessing live on air. Director Jan Egleson clearly isn't in the same class as Clint Eastwood or Oliver Stone, but turns in a decent enough thriller all the same. Contains violence and swearing. **[ ]**

Mark Harmon Jonathan Frayme · Julianne Phillips Becka Sharp · David Clennon Jimbo · Ron Perlman Chas Bradley · Gustave Johnson Detective Mark Kanin · Dir Jan Egleson · Scr John Pielmeier

Orion's Belt

Thriller ★★★ 87

1985 · Nor · Colour · 87mins

Starting out as an arresting, almost docu-dramatic insight into how a trio of opportunist North Sea boatmen supplement their meagre earnings by ferrying tourists, this big-budget Norwegian production slickly transforms itself into a sinister mystery, as the group seeks shelter on a remote Arctic outpost only to discover that it is actually the home of a Soviet spy station. But once he's past the spectacular helicopter sequence, director Ola Solun begins to run out of ideas and resorts to the stereotypes of the average Cold War thriller, with exposition and ideology replacing the stunning seascapes and ballistic action. In Norwegian with English subtitles. **[ ]**

Helge Jordal Tom Jansen · Sverre Anker Ousdal Larse · Hans Ola Sonle Sverre · Kjersti Holmen Eva Jelseth · Dir Ola Solun · Scr Richard Harris (Harald Paalgard, Ola Solun), from the novel by Jon Michelet

Orphans

Black comedy drama ★★★ 15

1998 · UK · Colour · 97mins

Peter Mullan, weighed down with awards for his appearance in Ken Loach's *My Name Is Joe*, takes a turn behind the camera (having already won critical acclaim for short films including *Fridge*) to write and direct this black comedy-drama about four siblings and the long night they experience before burying their dearly departed mum. Star-in-the-making Douglas Henshall is the brother who ends up being stabbed following a bar brawl, Gary Lewis is the oldest of the four who gets caught up in religious ritual, Stephen McCole is out for revenge tooling about Henshall's injury, while Rosemarie Stevenson — as sister Sheila who has cerebral palsy — gets stranded in an alley when her electric wheelchair breaks down. Unusual and quirky stuff indeed, yet Mullan deftly manages to mix humour with pathos. Contains swearing and violence.

Douglas Henshall Michael Flynn · Gary Lewis Thomas Flynn · Stephen McCole John Flynn · Rosemarie Stevenson Sheila Flynn · Frank Gallagher Tanga · Alex Norton Hanson · Dir/Scr Peter Mullan

Orphans

Drama ★★★ 15

1987 · US · Colour · 110mins

Albert Finney had played the drunken kidnap victim on stage in 1986 at the Hampstead Theatre Club, received rave reviews and filmed it a year later with Matthew Modine and Kevin Anderson as his kidnappers. Influenced by Harold Pinter, Lyle Kessler's play is a dark fable about domination that recalls *The Caretaker* as well as old-time gangster movies. Director Alan J Pakula respects the source material, eschews the sort of visual flourishes that distinguished his other films like *Klute* and *The Parallax View*, and puts his camera at the service of the actors. In other words, it's stagey, but the great Finney. Contains swearing.

Albert Finney Harold · Matthew Modine Treat · Kevin Anderson Phillip · John Kellogg Barney · Anthony Heald Man in Park · Novella Nelson Mattie · Dir Alan J Pakula · Scr Lyle Kessler, from his play

Orphan Train

Historical drama ★★

1979 · US · Colour · 150mins

Jill Eikenberry and Kevin Dobson star in this well-meaning TV drama set in the 19th century, about a social worker and a photographer who take orphaned children from the ghettos of New York on a railroad journey to a fresh start in the West. Directed by William A Graham, this is an enjoyable period tale, also worth watching to catch Glenn Close in a very early role. Contains violence.

Jill Eikenberry Emma Symms · Kevin Dobson Frank Carlin · Linda Manz Sarah · Graham Fletcher-Cook Liverpool · Melissa Michaelsen JP · Glenn Close Jessica Graham · Scr Millard Lampell, from a story by Dorothea G Petrie

Orphée

Fantasy ★★★★★ PG

1950 · Fr · BW · 90mins

Jean Cocteau's updating of the Orpheus myth to post-Liberation Paris is one of the cinema's great artistic masterpieces, a piece of Méliès-like magic that is intensely powerful and moving even at its most bewildering. Jean Marais is the poet who falls in love with Death (Maria Casarès); her assistant, the angel Heurtebise (François Périer), snatches the poet's wife and forces him to enter the underworld to get her back. The use of images, especially the looking-glass which turn into water, is still daring and — it might be said — rich in gay iconography. In 1959, Cocteau made a sequel, *Le Testament d'Orphée*. In French with English subtitles. **[ ]**

Jean Marais Orphée · François Périer Heurtebise · Maria Casarès Princess · Marie Déa Eurydice · Jacques Varennes First Judge · Pierre Bertin The Inspector · Juliette Greco Aglaonice · Edouard Dermit Cégeste · Jean Cocteau The Voice · Dir/Scr Jean Cocteau

Orpheus Descending

Drama ★★

1990 · US · Colour · 117mins

Originally an unsuccessful piece called *Battle of Angels*, this Tennessee Williams play enjoyed limited success when the reworked version opened in the States in 1957. Regarded as one of the playwright's minor works, it is here given an over-earnest treatment by British stage director Peter Hall, whose ventures into film-making have been mixed, to say the least. This tale of lust in the dust of the Deep South tests the patience with its inflated

Orphans of the Storm

★★★ ★

Silent historical melodrama

1921 · US · BW · 125mins

Following on *Broken Blossoms* in 1919 and *Way Down East* in 1920, DW Griffith, writing under the name of Gaston de Tolignac, transposed a play to the French Revolution, Paris on 14 acres at his Mamaroneck studios, and had his luminous star, Lillian Gish, and her sister, Dorothy, play the orphaned sisters caught up in the bloody events. The plot, bursting with colourful and melodramatic incident, has Lillian, the carer of her blind sister, sent to the guillotine for harbouring her aristocrat lover (the splendid Joseph Schildkraut), only to be saved at the last minute by the intervention of Danton (Monte Blue). Not quite a silent masterpiece, it's heavily sentimental and marred by Griffith's taste for unsubtle and inappropriate comedy, but is, nonetheless, visually spectacular and largely absorbing.

Lillian Gish Henriette Girard · Dorothy Gish Louise · Joseph Schildkraut Chevalier de Vaudrey · Frank Losee Count de Linières · Katherine Emmett Director · Monte Blue Danton · Dir DW Griffith · Scr Marquis Gaston de Tolignac (DW Griffith), from the play Les Deux Orphelines by Adolphe Philippe Dennery, Eugène Cormon, adapted by N Hart Jackson, Albert Marshman Palmer, from the novel A Tale of Two Cities by Charles Dickens, from the non-fiction book The French Revolution by Thomas Carlyle · Cinematographer Hendrik Sartov, Paul Allen, GW Bitzer [Billy Bitzer]

sense of importance, although there is no denying that Vanessa Redgrave and Kevin Anderson are thoroughly committed to their roles.

Vanessa Redgrave *Lady Torrance* • Kevin Anderson *Val Xavier* • Anne Twomey *Carol Cutrere* • Miriam Margolyes *Vee Talbot* • Sloane Shelton *Beulah Binnings* • Patricia Allison *Dolly Hamma* • Peg Small *Sister Temple* • Marlene Cameron *Eva Temple* ■ Dir Peter Hall • Scr Peter Hall, from the play by Tennessee Williams

Osaka Elegy ★★★★★
Drama 1936 · Jap · BW · 71mins

Inspired by the sacrifices made by his own geisha sister, Kenji Mizoguchi's masterly drama marked the beginning of his longtime collaboration with screenwriter Yoshikata Yoda. Scrupulously avoiding sensationalism, it charts the descent into prostitution of a young telephonist, who becomes her boss's mistress in a bid to repay her embezzling father's debts and fund her brother's education. Mizoguchi regular Isuzu Yamada contributes a superb display of abused decency, but it's the director's astute visual sense that gives the picture its power, with the stylised realism of his claustrophobic compositions suggesting the exploitative repression of a corrupt patriarchal society. A Japanese language film.

Isuzu Yamada *Ayako Murai* • Kensaku Hara *Susumu Nishimura* • Benkei Shiganoya *Sonosuke* • Yoko Umemura *Sonosuke's wife* ■ Dir Kenji Mizoguchi • Scr Yoshikata Yoda, from the story *Mieko* by Saburo Okada

The Oscar ★★★
Drama 1966 · US · Colour · 120mins

Stephen Boyd was great as the villainous Messala in *Ben-Hur* and makes a fair fist of villainy here as actor Frank Fane who has been nominated for an Oscar and sits in the Shrine Auditorium waiting for the envelope to be opened. As he waits the flashback starts, showing how this slimeball walked over countless people to be a major movie star. It's hugely, trashily enjoyable – sort of like *The Bad and the Beautiful* meets Harold Robbins – and filled with a lot of in-jokes and bursting with cameos, from Bob Hope, Frank and Nancy Sinatra, Merle Oberon and Edith Head, the legendary costume designer.

Stephen Boyd *Frank Fane* • Elke Sommer *Kay Bergdahl* • Milton Berle *Kappy Kapstetter* • Eleanor Parker *Sophie Cantaro* • Joseph Cotten *Kenneth H Regan* • Jill St John *Laurel Scott* • Tony Bennett *Hymie Kelly* • Edie Adams *Trina Yale* • Ernest Borgnine *Barney Yale* • Ed Begley *Grobard* • Walter Brennan *Orrin C Quentin* • Broderick Crawford *Sheriff* • Peter Lawford *Steve Marks* • Edith Head • Bob Hope • Merle Oberon • Frank Sinatra • Nancy Sinatra • Hedda Hopper ■ Dir Russell Rouse • Scr Harlan Ellison, Russell Rouse, Clarence Greene, from the novel by Richard Sale

Oscar ★★★ PG
Comedy 1991 · US · Colour · 105mins

The decline of John Landis is one of the cruellest blows to strike Hollywood comedy in recent years. However, he manages a semblance of form with this gangster farce based on a French play that had already been filmed in 1967. Sylvester Stallone strives a touch too hard for laughs as the mobster whose plans to quit the rackets are confounded by a series of domestic crises and that old standby, the "mixed-up bags" routine. The main interest lies in the sly cameos of Kirk Douglas, Don Ameche, Yvonne De Carlo and Eddie Bracken, with Peter Riegert and Chazz Palminteri the standouts in the supporting cast. Contains mild swearing.

Sylvester Stallone *Angelo "Snaps" Provolone* • Ornella Muti *Sofia Provolone* • Peter Riegert *Aldo* • Vincent Spano *Anthony Rossano* • Marisa Tomei *Lisa Provolone* • Elizabeth Barondes *Theresa* • Kirk Douglas *Eduardo Provolone* • Art LaFleur *Officer Quinn* • Ken Howard *Kirkwood* • Don Ameche *Father Clemente* • Chazz Palminteri *Connie* • Tim Curry *Dr Thornton Poole* ■ Dir John Landis • Scr Michael Barrie, Jim Mulholland, from the play by Claude Magnier

Oscar and Lucinda ★★ 15
Romantic drama 1997 · US/Ausl · Colour · 126mins

Adapted from Peter Carey's Booker Prize-winning novel, this story about two Victorian eccentrics with a passion for gambling was never going to be an easy choice to make into a film. Director Gillian Armstrong was undaunted, but unfortunately the end result is an irritating and generally incomprehensible art movie. Anglican minister Ralph Fiennes's wager that he can transport a glass chapel across the Australian outback is reminiscent of Klaus Kinski hauling a boat overland in director Werner Herzog's *Fitzcarraldo*, but this is far stranger and much less spectacular. This is very pretentious, if not total, twaddle. Contains swearing, and some violence and sex scenes.

Ralph Fiennes *Oscar Hopkins/Oscar's great grandson* • Cate Blanchett *Lucinda Leplastrier* • Ciarán Hinds *Reverend Dennis Hasset* • Tom Wilkinson *Hugh Stratton* • Richard Roxburgh *Mr Jeffris* • Clive Russell *Theophilus* ■ Dir Gillian Armstrong • Scr Laura Jones, from the novel by Peter Carey

Oscar Wilde ★★★
Biographical drama 1959 · UK · BW · 96mins

Emboldened by the Government's Wolfenden Report, British film-makers at the turn of the sixties began to deal frankly with homosexual themes. Unfortunately two film companies hit on the same idea, an Oscar Wilde biopic, at the same time, and this modest production, directed by Russian actor Gregory Ratoff, who died months after the premiere, had its thunder stolen by the more ambitious *The Trials of Oscar Wilde*. Nevertheless it is well worth seeing, with Sir Ralph Richardson and Alexander Knox sparring in a grippingly staged courtroom scene, and Robert Morley, although too old, revealing hidden depths in the title role.

Robert Morley *Oscar Wilde* • Phyllis Calvert *Constance Wilde* • John Neville *Lord Alfred Douglas* • Ralph Richardson *Sir Edward Carson* • Dennis Price *Robert Ross* • Alexander Knox *Sir Edward Clarke* • Edward Chapman *Marquis of Queensbury* • Martin Benson *George Alexander* ■ Dir Gregory Ratoff • Scr Jo Eisinger, from a play by Leslie Stokes, Sewell Stokes

Ossessione ★★★ PG
Drama 1942 · It · BW · 134mins

A drifter gets a job at a roadside café and has a torrid affair with the owner's wife who then asks her lover to murder her fat, loutish husband. Yes, this is the Italian version of *The Postman Always Rings Twice*, and it marked the directing debut of the Marxist aristocrat, Luchino Visconti. There had already been a French version of James M Cain's classic novel, but this transposition to the flat marshland of the Po Valley, with its working class characters, drab settings and base morality, was banned by Mussolini's censors for its depiction of working-class life. The Fascists burned the negative, but Visconti managed to save a print. It was later credited with starting a new movement in Italian cinema called neorealism. In Italian with English subtitles.

Clara Calamai *Giovanna* • Massimo Girotti *Gino* • Juan de Landa *The husband* • Elia Marcuzzo *Giuseppe Favolato, "The Spaniard"* • Dhia Cristani *Anita* • Vittorio Duse *The lorry driver* ■ Dir Luchino Visconti • Scr Mario Alicata, Antonio Pietrangeli, Gianni Puccini, Giuseppe De Santis, Luchino Visconti, from the novel *The Postman Always Rings Twice* by James M Cain

The Osterman Weekend ★★★ 18
Thriller 1983 · US · Colour · 97mins

Sam Peckinpah's final film is not a western but a thriller, an adaptation of the Robert Ludlum bestseller that displays a notable absence of the director's trademark slow-motion violence. Burt Lancaster is the CIA chief with presidential ambitions, who for his own murky reasons gets operative John Hurt to persuade TV journalist Rutger Hauer that there are Soviet agents among the guests assembled for a weekend get-together. Video gadgets push the atmosphere of post-Watergate paranoia to breaking point, but the confusion experienced by the characters is as nothing compared with the audience's bafflement at the convoluted plot. Contains violence, swearing and brief nudity.

Rutger Hauer *John Tanner* • John Hurt *Lawrence Fassett* • Craig T Nelson *Bernard Osterman* • Dennis Hopper *Richard Tremayne* • Chris Sarandon *Joseph Cardone* • Burt Lancaster *Maxwell Danforth* • Meg Foster *Ali Tanner* • Helen Shaver *Virginia Tremayne* ■ Dir Sam Peckinpah • Scr Ian Sharp, Ian Masters, from the novel by Robert Ludlum

Otello ★★★★ U
Opera 1986 · It · Colour · 117mins

Franco Zeffirelli transposes Verdi's classic version of Shakespeare's tragedy into sweeping big-screen melodrama. Plácido Domingo is magnificent as the jealous Moor, whose corruption by Iago crucifies his marriage to the gentle Desdemona. Domingo looks relaxed on screen, with Zeffirelli managing to remove the static tendencies of stage-bound singers to make a fluid and compelling film drama. Katia Ricciarelli is a delicate Desdemona, Justino Díaz a demonic Iago and Urbano Barberini a Cassio worthy of arousing crippling infidelity anxiety. One of the best films of opera ever made. In Italian with English subtitles.

Plácido Domingo *Otello* • Katia Ricciarelli *Desdemona* • Justino Díaz *Iago* • Petra Malakova *Emilia* • Urbano Barberini *Cassio* ■ Dir Franco Zeffirelli • Scr Franco Zeffirelli, from the libretto by Arrigo Boito for the opera by Giuseppe Verdi

Othello ★★★★★ U
Tragedy 1952 · US/Fr/Mor/It · Colour · 89mins

Orson Welles found filming Shakespeare's tale about the Moor far from straightforward – most disruptively, he had to close production down three times so he could go away and earn the money to continue. But it's testimony to the master film-maker's tremendous talent that he continually turned the many setbacks to his advantage. When the costumes failed to arrive, he improvised one of the movie's finest scenes, the murder in the Turkish bath; and he compensates for the lack of purpose-built sets by making inspired use of the north African architecture to sculpt a world of shadows and treachery. With all this, plus a script that slashes the Bard's original over-three-hour text down to 90 minutes, Welles creates far more than a filmed version of the play – more like the most cinematic Shakespeare adaptation ever.

Orson Welles *Othello* • Michael MacLiammóir *Iago* • Suzanne Cloutier *Desdemona* • Robert Coote *Rodrigo* • Hilton Edwards *Brabantio* • Michael Lawrence *Cassio* • Fay Compton *Emilia* ■ Dir Orson Welles • Scr Orson Welles, from the play by William Shakespeare

Othello ★★★ U
Tragedy 1955 · USSR · Colour · 103mins

Having striven for 20 years to make this film, Sergei Yutkevitch got his just desserts by being made Best Director at Cannes. Working from a free translation by the novelist Boris Pasternak, and employing a symbolic palette to emphasise the play's physical and temperamental contrasts, Yutkevitch played down the Moor's rage to concentrate on the corruption of his nobility by the scheming Iago. Despite being unable to impose himself in quite the manner of his screen predecessors, director-in-waiting Sergei Bondarchuk still manages to acquit himself admirably as Othello opposite his future wife, Irina Skobtseva, as the wrongfully accused Desdemona. Russian dialogue dubbed into English.

Sergei Bondarchuk *Othello* • Irina Skobtseva *Desdemona* • Andrei Popov *Iago* • Vladimir Soshalsky *Cassio* • E Vesnik *Rodrigo* • Antonina Maximova *Emilia* ■ Dir Sergei Yutkevitch • Scr Sergei Yutkevitch, from a translation by Boris Pasternak of the play by William Shakespeare

Othello ★★★ PG
Tragedy 1965 · UK · Colour · 158mins

Stagebound and elegantly lit by cinematographer Geoffrey Unsworth, this is a stunning transfer of Laurence Olivier's legendary National Theatre production to film. While it does not

have the cinematic fireworks of Orson Welles's version, it is an indispensable record of Olivier's titanic, vigorously African performance as the Moor of Venice who ''loved not wisely but too well''. This also has the distinction of being the only Shakespearean film for which all four principals received Oscar nominations (Olivier, Maggie Smith as wronged Desdemona, Frank Finlay as scheming Iago and Joyce Redman as loyal Emilia) and features the screen debut of a young Derek Jacobi as Cassio. ▣

Laurence Olivier *Othello* • Maggie Smith *Desdemona* • Frank Finlay *Iago* • Joyce Redman *Emilia* • Derek Jacobi *Cassio* • Robert Lang *Roderigo* • Kenneth Mackintosh *Lodovico* • Anthony Nicholls *Brabantio* • Sheila Reid *Bianca* ■ *Dir* Stuart Burge • *Scr* Margaret Unsworth, from the stage production by John Dexter of the play by William Shakespeare

Othello ★★★ 12

Tragedy   1995 · UK · Colour · 118mins

Laurence Fishburne follows in the footsteps of Orson Welles and Laurence Olivier. Young, gifted and appropriately black, he plays the title role as a sensual, bald and tattooed soldier, and is joined by Irène Jacob as Desdemona and Kenneth Branagh as a magnificently seething Iago. Shakespeare's tragedy has been hacked roughly in half by director Oliver Parker whose choice of locations is a plus but whose scaling down is generally a minus. ▣

Laurence Fishburne *Othello* • Irène Jacob *Desdemona* • Kenneth Branagh *Iago* • Nathaniel Parker *Cassio* • Michael Maloney *Roderigo* • Anna Patrick *Emilia* • Nicholas Farrell *Montano* • Indra Ove *Bianca* • Michael Sheen *Lodovico* • André Oumansky *Gratiano* ■ *Dir* Oliver Parker • *Scr* Oliver Parker, from the play by William Shakespeare

The Other ★★★★

Horror   1972 · US · Colour · 99mins

A commercial flop, with no stars, too ''arty'' for popular taste, this highly atmospheric spook drama is much admired by aficionados. It is the only horror film from distinguished director Robert Mulligan, who adds beautiful visual touches to former actor Tom (here credited as Thomas) Tryon's screenplay, an adaptation of his own first novel. Set in 1935, the slow-moving but increasingly disturbing tale concerns a 10-year-old boy (a wonderful performance by Chris Udvarnoky) who claims that a series of murders are the work of his dead identical twin. The twins' grandmother is played by noted drama teacher Uta Hagen. Be prepared for a shocking climax. Contains swearing.

Uta Hagen *Ada* • Chris Udvarnoky *Niles Perry* • Martin Udvarnoky *Holland Perry* • Diana Muldaur *Alexandra Perry* • Norma Connolly *Aunt Vee* • Victor French *Angelini* • Loretta Leversee *Winnie* • Lou Frizzell *Uncle George* • John Ritter *Rider* ■ *Dir* Robert Mulligan • *Scr* Thomas [Tom] Tryon, from his novel

Other Halves ★★ 15

Drama   1984 · NZ · Colour · 104mins

Touching drama about the romance between two people who meet in a mental hospital. Lisa Harrow is a white woman who's recovering from a

nervous breakdown; Tug is a Maori teenager who's undergoing drug rehab. As soon as they're discharged, the pair move in together, but gradually find their relationship threatened by a clash of cultures and outlooks. There's a nice performance from Lisa Harrow but a slightly wooden one from Mark Pilisi, who was found after a nationwide star-search across New Zealand.

Lisa Harrow *Liz* • Mark Pilisi *Tug* • Fraser Stephen-Smith *Michael* • Paul Gittins *Ken* • Emma Piper *Audrey* ■ *Dir* John Laing • *Scr* Sue McCanley, from her novel

The Other Love ★★ PG

Romantic drama   1947 · US · BW · 88mins

This larded, treacly plot comes firmly under the heading of Nonsense. Barbara Stanwyck is dying, as only a cinema diva can, but instead of taking the advice of devoted doctor David Niven, she hightails it with wild gambler Richard Conte. Niven pines, Conte leers, Stanwyck over-eggs the pudding alarmingly with every gripe and twinge. ▣

Barbara Stanwyck *Karen Duncan* • David Niven *Dr Anthony Stanton* • Richard Conte *Paul Clermont* • Gilbert Roland *Croupier* • Joan Lorring *Celestine* • Richard Hale *Professor Linnaker* ■ *Dir* Andre De Toth • *Scr* Ladislas Fodor, Harry Brown, from the short story *Beyond* by Erich Maria Remarque

Other Men's Women ★★★★

Melodrama   1931 · US · BW · 69mins

Basically a conventional love-triangle story, this early talkie is given tremendous power and resonance by the vigorous direction of William A Wellman and the tight editing that was a trademark of the Warner Bros studio in the thirties. Called *The Steel Highway* while in production (a reference to its railroad milieu) and enacted in nocturnal, sometimes rainswept settings, it provides riveting viewing. In a typically audacious sequence, James Cagney, playing a minor role in his third film but clearly a star in the making, walks into a dance hall and breaks into an impromptu tap routine. A remarkable moment in a constantly inventive movie.

Grant Withers *Bill* • Mary Astor *Lily* • Regis Toomey *Jack* • James Cagney *Ed* • Fred Kohler *Haley* • J Farrell MacDonald *Pegleg* • Joan Blondell *Marie* • Walter Long *Bixby* ■ *Dir* William A Wellman • *Scr* William K Wells, Maude Fulton, from a story by Maude Fulton

The Other Mother ★★ PG

Drama based on a true story
1995 · US · Colour · 86mins

Part of the American TV-movie series *Moment of Truth*, this drama offers Frances Fisher as Carol Schaefer, the mother who devoted herself to searching for the son she had given up for adoption 18 years earlier. Adapted by Steven Loring from Schaefer's own book, this is your typical tear-jerking story, with director Bethany Rooney pressing all the right melodrama buttons at the appropriate time. A little long, but involving enough to keep you watching. ▣

Frances Fisher *Carol Schaefer* • Deborah May *Kate* • Corrie Clark *Young Carol* • Cameron Bancroft *Jack* • Joy Coghill *Sister Vincent* •

Gwynyth Walsh *Barbara* ■ *Dir* Bethany Rooney • *Scr* Steven Loring, from the book by Carol Schaefer

Other People's Money ★★★ 15

Comedy drama   1991 · US · Colour · 96mins

Danny DeVito plays Larry the Liquidator, whose asset-stripping gaze falls upon the old-fashioned New England company run by stubborn Gregory Peck. However, the battle becomes complicated when he falls for the company's lawyer, Penelope Ann Miller, who is leading the fight against him. DeVito is charmingly sleazy as the ruthless corporate raider and Peck is the embodiment of the honourable liberal capitalist. Director Norman Jewison tries a little too hard to make DeVito look human, but his direction is smooth and he is well served by cinematographer Haskell Wexler, who neatly contrasts the glossy superficiality of Wall Street with the blue-collar grit of the threatened community. Contains swearing. ▣

Danny DeVito *Lawrence Garfield* • Gregory Peck *Andrew Jorgenson* • Penelope Ann Miller *Kate Sullivan* • Piper Laurie *Bea Sullivan* • Dean Jones *Bill Coles* • RD Call *Arthur* • Mo Gaffney *Harriet* • Bette Henritze *Emma* • Tom Aldredge *Ozzie* ■ *Dir* Norman Jewison • *Scr* Alvin Sargent, from the play by Jerry Sterner

The Other Side of Midnight ★★★ 18

Melodrama   1977 · US · Colour · 158mins

Based on a airport blockbuster novel by Sidney Sheldon, this huge melodrama runs for nearly three hours, covers the whole of the Second World War and its aftermath, and flits between the continents without pausing for breath. It has the courage of its clichés, so sometimes we laugh as the characters bump into each other across the years, tears and oceans. Maybe major stars would have deflected from the story, but Marie-France Pisier, John Beck and Raf Vallone are more than adequate, as is Susan Sarandon in an early role. ▣

Marie-France Pisier *Noelle Page* • John Beck *Larry Douglas* • Susan Sarandon *Catherine Douglas* • Raf Vallone *Constantin Demeris* • Clu Gulager *Bill Fraser* • Christian Marquand *Armand Gautier* • Michael Lerner *Barbet* ■ *Dir* Charles Jarrott • *Scr* Herman Raucher, Daniel Taradash, from the novel by Sidney Sheldon

The Other Side of Murder ★★★

Drama   1991 · US · Colour · 100mins

A mother and her teenage son witness an armed robbery and suffer the ghastly consequences in this gripping drama based on a true story. Michael Learned and Denis Heames give convincing performances, while Richard Chamberlain brings considerable depth to his role as the father whose attachment to his family is tested to the limit by events beyond his control. Director Glenn Jordan proves expert at highlighting key moments and characters. Contains violence.

Richard Chamberlain *Ross Colburn* • Michael Learned *Irene Colburn* • Zeljko Ivanek *Matt Colburn* • Doug Savant *Jeff Colburn* • Denis Heames *Terry Colburn* • Lisanne Falk

Gretchen Colburn ■ *Dir* Glenn Jordan • *Scr* Gregory J Goodell, from the book *Victim* by Gary Kinder

The Other Side of Sunday ★★★

Comedy drama   1996 · Nor · Colour · 103mins

Nominated for the best foreign film Oscar, this charming drama unassumingly captures the curiosity and contumacy of a strictly raised small-town teenager. But what sets it apart is a take on religion that unmistakably echoes that of the great Danish film-maker, Carl Theodor Dreyer. Ending with a freeze-frame reminiscent of Truffaut's *The 400 Blows*, this tragicomic study of repression and rebellion adroitly avoids both melodrama and the clichés of the rites-of-passage picture. But, thanks to Maria Theisen's spirited performance, there is also subtle power in Berit Nesheim's attack on the patriarchal nature of both church and state. In Norwegian with English subtitles..

Marie Theisen *Maria* • Bjorn Sundquist *Father* • Sylvia Salvesen *Mother* • Hildegunn Riise *Fru Tunheim* ■ *Dir* Berit Nesheim • *Scr* Berit Nesheim, Lasse Glomm, from the novel *Søndag (Sunday)* by Reidun Nortvedt

The Other Side of the Mountain ★★★

Biographical drama
1975 · US · Colour · 99mins

Superior and heart-wrenching biopic about Jill Kinmont, an Olympic-standard skier whose career hit the skids when a fall left her paralysed. Marilyn Hassett makes an impressive film debut as Kinmont, portraying her as a fighter whose gutsiness initially arouses expectations of recovery that were destined to be unfulfilled. The film's modest success prompted a sequel three years later.

Marilyn Hassett *Jill Kinmont* • Beau Bridges *Dick Buek* • Belinda J Montgomery *Audra-Jo* • Nan Martin *June Kinmont* • William Bryant *Bill Kinmont* • Dabney Coleman *Dave McCoy* ■ *Dir* Larry Peerce • *Scr* David Seltzer, from the biography *A Long Way Up* by EG Valens

The Other Side of the Mountain – Part 2 ★★

Biographical romantic drama
1978 · US · Colour · 105mins

Tear-jerking sequel to the 1975 movie based on the real-life story of Jill Kinmont. The film opens with Jill (again played by Marilyn Hassett) recovering from yet another emotional body blow with the death of the man who helped her overcome her paraplegia, before continuing with her burgeoning romance with a truck driver played by Timothy Bottoms, whose real-life father James also appears in the film.

Marilyn Hassett *Jill Kinmont* • Timothy Bottoms *John Boothe* • Nan Martin *June Kinmont* • Belinda J Montgomery *Audra-Jo* • Gretchen Corbett *Linda* • William Bryant *Bill Kinmont* • James A Bottoms *Mr Boothe* • June Dayton *Mrs Boothe* ■ *Dir* Larry Peerce • *Scr* Douglas Day Stewart

The Other Sister ★★ 15
Romantic drama
1999 · US · Colour · 130mins

It needs a sure and delicate touch to use a mental disability as a dramatic device; otherwise, it's a tasteless gimmick to move the plot along. Sadly, despite a fine performance from Juliette Lewis, this would-be weepie is both clumsy and manipulative. Lewis is a rich San Francisco teenager fresh out of a mental institution. She wants to be a vet's assistant; despite the approval of father Tom Skerritt, however, she has to fight mother Diane Keaton every step of the way. There's a good story here, but it's buried under a load of cute and unconvincing dialogue. Contains sexual references. 🖵

Diane Keaton *Elizabeth* • Juliette Lewis *Carla Tate* • Tom Skerritt *Radley Tate* • Giovanni Ribisi *Danny* • Poppy Montgomery *Caroline* • Sarah Paulson *Heather* • Linda Thorson *Drew* • Joe Flanigan *Jeff* • Juliet Mills *Winnie* ■ *Dir* Garry Marshall • *Scr* Garry Marshall, Bob Brunner, from a story by Alexandra Rose, Blair Richwood

The Other Victim ★★★
Drama
1981 · US · Colour · 96mins

Director Noel Black began his movie career on a high with the quirky Anthony Perkins film, *Pretty Poison*, but lost his way in Hollywood after that, returning to form with this well-crafted TV movie about a construction site foreman whose outlook on life changes substantially after his wife has been raped at knifepoint. Richard DeRoy's teleplay provides meaty dramatic roles for Jennifer O'Neill and William Devane as the wife and her husband, with the undervalued Devane again demonstrating just how good he is at conveying suppressed anger.

William Devane *Harry Langford* • Jennifer O'Neill *Nancy Langford* • James Blendick *Mack Fisher* • Charles Hallahan *Jack Berger* • Todd Susman *Tim McQuire* ■ *Dir* Noel Black • *Scr* Richard DeRoy

Other Voices, Other Rooms ★★ 12
Period drama 1995 · US/UK · Colour · 98mins

After producing a handful of enterprising documentaries, British director David Rocksavage made an inauspicious start to his feature career with this achingly dull adaptation of Truman Capote's debut novel. Trotting out all those tired Deep South Gothic clichés, Rocksavage seems uncertain whether to concentrate on atmosphere, plot or character, and ends up fudging all three. David Speck works hard as the teenager sent to live with his suspiciously infirm father. As his deeply disturbed cousins, however, Anna Thomson is twitchily timid, while Lothaire Bluteau's effete aesthete is embarrassingly melodramatic.

Lothaire Bluteau *Randolph Skully* • Anna Thomson [Anna Levine] *Amy Skully* • David Speck *Joel Sansom* • April Turner *Zoo* • Frank Taylor *Edward "Ed" R Sansom* ■ *Dir* David Rocksavage • *Scr* Sara Flanigan, David Rocksavage, from the novel by Truman Capote

The Other Woman ★★ PG
Drama
1994 · US · Colour · 88mins

This is an unashamedly sentimental melodrama, in which bitter enmity turns to friendship in the face of terminal illness. As the finally reconciled women, *LA Law's* Jill Eikenberry and *Melrose Place's* Laura Leighton make the most of a glutinous script in a movie that really does have to be seen to be believed. 🖵

Jill Eikenberry *Tessa* • Laura Leighton *Carolyn* • Lloyd Bridges *Jacob* • James Read *Michael* ■ *Dir* Gabrielle Beaumont • *Scr* Nancey Silvers

Other Women's Children ★★ PG
Drama
1993 · Can · Colour · 90mins

Melanie Mayron stars in this manipulative, densely plotted "women's" movie, which deals with the modern working woman's dilemma – how to balance career and family. Mayron plays a pediatrician whose professional life comes into conflict with the needs of her child and the desires of her husband. As she tries to cope with the pressure, her mental health becomes increasingly fragile. While many women will relate to Mayron's situation, they'll be disappointed with the overly simplistic ending that mars an otherwise well-intentioned film. 🖵

Melanie Mayron *Amelia Stewart* • Geraint Wyn Davies *Matt Stewart* • Eric Pospisil *Alexander Stewart* • Ja'net DuBois *Roberta* ■ *Dir* Anne Wheeler • *Scr* Rama Laurie Stagner, from the novel by Perri Klass

Otley ★★★ PG
Spy spoof
1968 · UK · Colour · 87mins

Even when it was released in 1968, this London-set Swinging Sixties spy spoof looked dreadfully old-fashioned. Indeed, without the comic genius of writers Dick Clement and Ian La Frenais it might have been a disaster. Forget about the labyrinthine plot that soon becomes impossible to follow and concentrate instead on the delightful performance of Tom Courtenay as the hapless Gerald Otley, a very petty criminal caught up in the slick world of spy Romy Schneider. There's marvellous support, too, from the likes of Alan Badel, Leonard Rossiter, Freddie Jones and Likely Lad James Bolam. DJs Jimmy Young and Pete Murray pop up as themselves. 🖵

Tom Courtenay *Gerald Arthur Otley* • Romy Schneider *Imogen* • Alan Badel *Hadrian* • James Villiers *Hendrickson* • Leonard Rossiter *Johnston* • James Bolam *Albert* • Fiona Lewis *Lin* • Freddie Jones *Proudfoot* ■ *Dir* Dick Clement • *Scr* Ian La Frenais, Dick Clement, from the novel by Martin Waddell

Our Betters ★★★
Comedy
1933 · US · BW · 79mins

RKO producer David O Selznick deployed the polished gifts of director George Cukor and actress Constance Bennett for this now dated screen version of W Somerset Maugham's equally dated but far from uninteresting play. An acid and brittle comedy of manners exposing the amorality of the English upper classes, it focuses on an American heiress (Bennett) who marries an English aristocrat (Alan Mowbray), only to realise that her money was what attracted her. When he fails to give up his mistress, she wreaks cold revenge on his London social circle. A polished and sophisticated film about unappealing people, with a meticulous performance from the gifted, intelligent and elegant Bennett.

Constance Bennett *Lady Pearl Grayston* • Gilbert Roland *Pepi D'Costa* • Anita Louise Bessie • Hugh Sinclair *Lord Bleane* • Alan Mowbray *Lord George Grayston* • Grant Mitchell *Thornton Clay* • Charles Starrett *Fleming Harvey* • Phoebe Foster *Princess* ■ *Dir* George Cukor • *Scr* Jane Murfin, Harry Wagstaff Gribble, from the play by W Somerset Maugham

Our Daily Bread ★★
Drama
1934 · US · BW · 75mins

A young couple (Karen Morley and Tom Keene), victims of the Depression, leave the city for a derelict farm they've inherited. They form a farming co-operative with Depression-hit unemployed and work to reclaim the land, coping with a series of setbacks before the hopeful climax. Revisiting the socially conscious territory of *The Crowd*, his 1928 silent masterpiece about the Depression, master director King Vidor picks up the same protagonists (played by different actors), to make a film of admirable and serious intentions, though lacking in pace and clarity. However, the piece as a whole disappoints audience expectations. The film's failure drove Vidor, who was accused of "pinko" politics by the Hearst newspapers, back to the commercial cinema.

Karen Morley *Mary Sims* • Tom Keene [Richard Powers] *John Sims* • John Qualen *Chris* • Barbara Pepper *Sally* • Addison Richards *Louie* • Harry Holman *Uncle Anthony* ■ *Dir* King Vidor • *Scr* King Vidor, Elizabeth Hill, Joseph L Mankiewicz

Our Dancing Daughters ★★★
Silent romantic drama
1928 · US · BW · 86mins

A melodrama reflecting the morals and mores of the jazz age, this is the movie that catapulted Joan Crawford to major stardom. She plays a wild-living, hard-drinking, man-eating socialite who pulls herself out of the fast lane in the nick of time, settling for true love with John Mack Brown. Some of her friends are less fortunate. It's directed with an accurate sense of its milieu by Harry Beaumont, who went on to make several more films with Crawford.

Joan Crawford *Diana Medford* • John Mack Brown [Johnny Mack Brown] *Ben Blaine* • Nils Asther *Norman* • Dorothy Sebastian *Beatrice* • Anita Page *Ann* • Kathlyn Williams *Ann's mother* • Edward Nugent *Freddie* • Dorothy Cumming *Diana's mother* ■ *Dir* Harry Beaumont • *Scr* Josephine Lovett, Marion Ainslee (titles), Ruth Cummings (titles), from a story by Josephine Lovett

Our Girl Friday ★ U
Comedy
1953 · UK · Colour · 79mins

This is one of those films that you think you've seen before until you realise that all the oh-so-familiar scenes have come from many different pictures. The story of amorous castaways competing for a single woman was told in *The Little Hut*; Joan Collins was shipwrecked again in *Sea Wife*; Kenneth More proved a dab hand at desert island life in *The Admirable Crichton*; and so on. The problem is all of the above were better than this one-joke movie, although George Cole and Robertson Hare are amusing as the no-hopers tilting their caps at Collins's sexy Sadie.

Joan Collins *Sadie* • Kenneth More *Pat* • George Cole *Jimmy Carroll* • Robertson Hare *Gibble* • Hermione Gingold *Spinster* • Walter Fitzgerald *Captain* • Hattie Jacques *Mrs Patch* • Lionel Murton *Barman* ■ *Dir/Scr* Noel Langley

Our Guys: Outrage in Glen Ridge ★★★
Crime drama
1999 · US · Colour · 97mins

This is an affecting fact-based TV drama with a solid cast, in which a group of affluent high-school jocks sexually assault a mildly retarded 17-year-old girl (Heather Matarazzo). Determined detective Ally Sheedy faces a conspiracy of silence from the community, the school board and the police who are intent on protecting the winning athletes. Matarazzo, although at times unsympathetic, gives a stand-out performance, while Eric Stoltz, as the prosecutor, invokes the moral outrage of his uphill battle for justice.

Ally Sheedy *Detective Kelly Brooks* • Heather Matarazzo *Leslie Faber* • Sara Botsford *Mrs Faber* • Eric Stoltz *Robert Laurino* • Scott Vickaryous *Paul Archer* ■ *Dir* Guy Ferland • *Scr* Paul Brown, from the book *Our Guys* by Bernard Lefkowitz

Our Hospitality ★★★★ U
Silent comedy
1923 · US · BW · 65mins

A feudin' and fussin' masterpiece for Buster Keaton – which he co-directed with John Blystone – in which Buster is William, the last of the McKays, returning to Rockville to inherit his father's estate and falling foul of the vengeful Canfields, whose daughter (Natalie Talmadge) he's fallen in love with. Buster's beloved trains supply a hilarious track of running gags and there is some astonishing stuntwork, all of which Buster did himself. It's one of his few films in which he puts on drag – to escape the Canfields – and there's a sequence with a waterfall that is brilliant in its audacity. Three generations of Keatons are featured, from Joseph the elder to Buster's own son, while the period detail is at once comic and – believe it – totally accurate. 🖵

Buster Keaton *William McKay* • Natalie Talmadge *Virginia Canfield* • Buster Keaton Jr *William McKay as a baby* • Joseph Keaton [Joe Keaton] *Lem Doolittle* ■ *Dir* Buster Keaton, John Blystone [John G Blystone] • *Scr* Jean Havez, Joseph Mitchell, Clyde Bruckman

Our Little Girl ★★
Drama
1935 · US · BW · 65mins

In this typical Shirley Temple vehicle, the star runs away to the circus while conspiring to reunite her estranged parents (Joel McCrea and Rosemary Ames) by driving the wolf (Lyle Talbot) from the door. Made at the peak of Temple's popularity, between *The Little*

U = SUITABLE FOR ALL   Uc = SUITABLE FOR ALL, ESPECIALLY FOR YOUNG CHILDREN (VIDEO ONLY)   PG = PARENTAL GUIDANCE

Colonel and *Curly Top*, this was her weakest film of the period, an under-developed, slow-moving and predictable tale. The star is as charming as ever, particularly in her scenes with Poodles Hanneford as a clown, but only her keenest admirers should sample.

Shirley Temple *Molly Middleton* • Rosemary Ames *Elsa Middleton* • Joel McCrea *Dr Donald Middleton* • Lyle Talbot *Rolfe Brent* • Erin O'Brien-Moore *Sarah Boynton* • Poodles Hanneford *Circus performer* ■ *Dir* John S Robertson • *Scr* Stephen Avery, Allen Rivkin, Jack Yellen, from the story *Heaven's Gate* by Florence Leighton Pfalzgraf

Our Man Flint ★★★ 🅿🅶

Spy spoof 1966 · US · Colour · 102mins

As superspy Derek Flint, granite-faced James Coburn is equipped with the standard-issue suave mannerisms and harem of girls, plus one particular accessory that James Bond would have throttled Q for: a cigarette lighter with 83 uses (two-way radio, blowtorch and so on). No wonder ZOWIE (Zonal Organisation on World Intelligence Espionage) chooses Coburn to assassinate three villains who want to take over the world (so what else is new?). Incredible action, credibly packaged if only Coburn weren't so smug! 🖭

James Coburn *Derek Flint* • Lee J Cobb *Cramden* • Gila Golan *Gila* • Edward Mulhare *Malcolm Rodney* • Benson Fong *Dr Schneider* • Shelby Grant *Leslie* • Sigrid Valdis *Anna* • Gianna Serra *Gina* • Helen Funai *Sakito* ■ *Dir* Daniel Mann • *Scr* Hal Fimberg, Ben Starr, from a story by Hal Fimberg

Our Man in Havana ★★★

Comedy drama 1959 · UK · BW · 110mins

What a different film this would have been if Graham Greene had been able to overcome his antipathy towards Alfred Hitchcock. Instead, he offered the film rights to his amusing spy spoof to longtime collaborator Carol Reed and Hitch went off to make *Psycho*. Reed drew deft performances from his superb cast, with Alec Guinness in fine fettle as the vacuum cleaner salesman-turned-agent. But he seemed uncertain how dark to make the action once the joke took its sinister turn. He wasn't helped by Greene's occasionally pedestrian script, but what the film really needed was a mischievous hand at the helm.

Alec Guinness *Jim Wormold* • Burl Ives *Doctor Hasselbacher* • Maureen O'Hara *Beatrice Severn* • Ernie Kovacs *Captain Segura* • Noël Coward *Hawthorne* • Ralph Richardson *"C"* • Jo Morrow *Milly Wormold* ■ *Dir* Carol Reed • *Scr* Graham Greene, from his novel

Our Man in Marrakesh ★★ 🅄

Spy spoof 1966 · UK · Colour · 93mins

Producer Harry Alan Towers has an eye for an exotic location, and here he casts the excellent Tony Randall as an American tourist caught up in spy antics in Morocco. The scenery is fabulous and the second-rung supporting cast fun to watch, but the script and production budget would defeat the hardiest director. Still, veteran professionals such as Herbert Lom, Wilfrid Hyde White and Terry-Thomas do what they can with the material, and Klaus Kinski and John Le

Mesurier turn up, too. It's all summed up far better by its banal US title, *Bang! Bang! You're Dead!*

Tony Randall *Andrew Jessel* • Senta Berger *Kyra Stanovy* • Terry-Thomas *El Caid* • Herbert Lom *Mr Casimir* • Wilfrid Hyde White *Arthur Fairbrother* • Grégoire Aslan *Achmed* • John Le Mesurier *George Lillywhite* • Klaus Kinski *Jonquil* ■ *Dir* Don Sharp • *Scr* Peter Yeldham, from a story by Peter Welbeck [Harry Alan Towers]

Our Miss Fred ★★ 🅿🅶

Second World War comedy 1972 · UK · Colour · 91mins

Danny La Rue, Britain's most popular female impersonator during the seventies, seems terribly constricted in his one major film, an old-fashioned wartime comedy written by distinguished playwright Hugh Leonard. Soldier La Rue is playing a woman on stage in France when the Germans invade. He escapes, wearing his costume, and, somewhat implausibly, remains in drag as he evades the enemy for the rest of the film. Some of the daft situations may raise a smile and the photography is quite pretty, which is more than can be said for La Rue, already somewhat matronly. 🖭

Danny La Rue *Fred Wimbush* • Alfred Marks *General Brincker* • Lance Percival *Smallpiece* • Frances de la Tour *Miss Lockhart* ■ *Dir* Bob Kellett • *Scr* Hugh Leonard

Our Modern Maidens ★★

Silent drama 1929 · US · BW · 75mins

Capitalising on the success of *Our Dancing Daughters* (1928), MGM again starred Joan Crawford as a socialite in this follow-up romance, which was also released as a talkie. Anita Page returns as well for a second outing, and is joined by Rod La Rocque. But the main focus of the movie was the on-screen love affair between Crawford (dressed by Adrian, as she would be for many years) and Douglas Fairbanks Jr; they were the hot gossip item in Hollywood at the time and would soon be married in real life. The general formula was recycled again in *Our Blushing Brides* (1930).

Joan Crawford *Billie* • Rod La Rocque *Abbott* • Douglas Fairbanks Jr *Gil* • Anita Page *Kentucky* • Edward Nugent *Reg* • Josephine Dunn *Ginger* ■ *Dir* Jack Conway • *Scr* Josephine Lovett, Marian Ainslee, Ruth Cummings, from a story by Josephine Lovett • *Costume Designer* Adrian

Our Mother's House ★★★

Drama 1967 · UK/US · Colour · 105mins

A weird and often chilling horror story about some children (including a pre-*Oliver!* Mark Lester) who bury their mother's dead body in the garden and carry on as if she were still alive. Then shifty cockney Dirk Bogarde shows up, claiming to be their errant father. Set in a derelict house in Croydon, it's like a rehash of Henry James's *The Turn of the Screw*, which director Jack Clayton had previously filmed in 1961 as *The Innocents*. Bogarde and Clayton believed they had failed honourably, but Italian director Luchino Visconti thought it was a "beautiful" film and hired Bogarde for *The Damned* and *Death in Venice* on the strength of it.

Dirk Bogarde *Charlie Hook* • Margaret Brooks *Elsa Hook* • Pamela Franklin *Diana Hook* • Louis Sheldon Williams *Hubert Hook* • John Gugolka *Dunstan Hook* • Mark Lester (1) *Jiminee Hook* • Sarah Nicholls *Gerty Hook* • Gustav Henry *Willy Hook* ■ *Dir* Jack Clayton • *Scr* Jeremy Brooks, Haya Harareet, from the novel by Julian Gloag

Our Relations ★★★ 🅄

Comedy 1936 · US · BW · 64mins

In *Our Relations* masterful double act Laurel and Hardy turn in four great comic performances for the price of two. Comic mayhem is assured when family men Laurel and Hardy encounter their long lost identical twin brothers, a pair of jolly sailors who are enjoying shore leave. The inevitable mistaken identity occurs and our heroes find themselves up to their armpits in misunderstandings and sophisticated slapstick. Just over an hour of delightful, sometimes hilarious shenanigans. 🖭

Stan Laurel *Stan/Alfie Laurel* • Oliver Hardy *Ollie/Bert Hardy* • Sidney Toler *Captain of the SS Periwinkle* • Alan Hale *Joe Groagan, waiter* • Daphne Pollard *Mrs Daphne Hardy* • Betty Healy *Mrs Betty Laurel* ■ *Dir* Harry Lachman • *Scr* Richard Connell, Felix Adler, Charles Rogers, Jack Jevne, from the short story *The Money Box* by WW Jacobs

Our Sons ★★

Drama 1991 · US · Colour · 96mins

A tear-sodden, dramatically sagging piece of manipulation in which Julie Andrews (in her TV-movie debut) is the career woman who tries to persuade Arkansas barmaid Ann-Margret to become reconciled with the son (Zeljko Ivanek) who's dying from an Aids-related illness. Ivanek plays the partner of Andrews's son, Hugh Grant, whose gay lifestyle she has tolerated. Grant's performance is almost convincing, but not quite, undermined like so much of the acting by the total contrivance of the plot.

Julie Andrews *Audrey Grant* • Ann-Margret *Luanne Barnes* • Hugh Grant *James Grant* • Zeljko Ivanek *Donald Barnes* ■ *Dir* John Erman • *Scr* Micki Dickoff, William Hanley

Our Town ★★

Drama 1940 · US · BW · 89mins

An exercise in Hollywood bathos, based on Thornton Wilder's play about a small village in New Hampshire where a boy and girl's childhood friendship leads to adolescent romance, marriage and a tragic ending, which Hollywood tinkered with. An on-screen narrator – local pharmacist Frank Craven – guides us through the town and the 1901, 1904 and 1913 settings, but mostly we have William Holden and Martha Scott as the lovers. Hollywood constantly tried to capture this "lost America" of small towns, porch philosophy and pure love – and did so most notably in *Meet Me in St Louis*. However, this attempt is often like wading through an ocean of the stickiest maple syrup. Holden and Scott have youthful appeal, though, and the Oscar-nominated music is by Aaron Copland.

Frank Craven *Mr Morgan, the narrator* • William Holden (1) *George Gibbs* • Martha Scott *Emily Webb* • Fay Bainter *Mrs Gibbs* • Beulah Bondi *Mrs Webb* • Thomas Mitchell *Dr*

Gibbs • Guy Kibbee *Editor Webb* ■ *Dir* Sam Wood • *Scr* Thornton Wilder, Frank Craven, Harry Chandlee, from the play by Thornton Wilder • *Music* Aaron Copland

Our Very Own ★★ 🅄

Drama 1950 · US · BW · 88mins

Whenever producer Samuel Goldwyn announced a serious drama about a socially significant subject, you could bet your bottom dollar that you were in for a cosy domestic melodrama with just the vaguest whiff of controversy about it. That's certainly what you get here in this underwritten and overplayed saga, in which spoiled teenager Ann Blyth snubs parents Jane Wyatt and Donald Cook on learning that she's been adopted. No prizes for guessing either the response of her natural mother or the sentimental denouement. Farley Granger and Natalie Wood do their best in support, but you'll soon be as bored as director David Miller obviously was. 🖭

Ann Blyth *Gail* • Jane Wyatt *Lois Macaulay* • Donald Cook *Fred Macaulay* • Farley Granger *Chuck* • Joan Evans *Joan* • Ann Dvorak *Mrs Lynch* • Phyllis Kirk *Zaza* • Jessie Grayson *Violet* ■ *Dir* David Miller • *Scr* F Hugh Herbert • *Cinematographer* Lee Garmes

Our Vines Have Tender Grapes ★★★★ 🅄

Drama 1945 · US · BW · 105mins

This warm-hearted MGM drama contains a simply superb performance from Edward G Robinson as the Norwegian dad of lovable little Margaret O'Brien, set against a Wisconsin (though largely studio) background. There's not a lot of plot as incident follows incident: the barn burns down, the floods come, there's a quarrel over some roller skates, the circus passes through town... There's a boring romance, too, but don't be put off: this is a movie of great charm, well directed by the under-rated Roy Rowland, from a great studio in a great period.

Edward G Robinson *Martinius Jacobson* • Margaret O'Brien *Selma Jacobson* • James Craig *Nels Halverson* • Agnes Moorehead *Bruna Jacobson* • Jackie "Butch" Jenkins *Arnold Hanson* • Morris Carnovsky *Bjorn Bjornson* ■ *Dir* Roy Rowland • *Scr* Dalton Trumbo, from the novel by George Victor Martin

Our Wife ★★

Romantic comedy 1941 · US · BW · 92mins

A divorced classical trumpeter Melvyn Douglas, happily engaged to marry the supportive and inspirational young Ruth Hussey, finds himself caught in a no-holds barred battle for his affections when his ex-wife Ellen Drew decides she wants him back. A run-of-the-mill romantic triangle, with the polished Douglas reduced to a blank excuse for the women's rivalry. Neither actress has the high style necessary for the material, directed by John M Stahl in a manner more suited to heavy drama than light comedy.

Melvyn Douglas *Jerry Marvin* • Ruth Hussey *Susan Drake* • Ellen Drew *Babe Marvin* • Charles Coburn *Prof Drake* • John Hubbard *Tom Drake* • Harvey Stephens *Dr Cassell* • Theresa Harris *Hattie* ■ *Dir* John M Stahl •

Scr PJ Wolfson, from the play by Lillian Day, Lyon Mearson • *Cinematographer* Franz F Planer

Out Cold ★ 15

Black comedy 1989 · US · Colour · 87mins

Malcolm Mowbray made a beautifully funny directing debut, *A Private Function*, from Alan Bennett's script about a black market pig. Mowbray then went to Hollywood and came a real cropper with this second meaty comedy. Originally titled *Stiffs*, it lay on a marble slab for two years before it was released as *Out Cold*. It's a tale of two butchers, with the long-suffering John Lithgow thinking he has killed his loathsome partner, Bruce McGill, by locking him in the freezer. In fact, McGill's wife, Teri Garr, has done the deed after hiring private eye Randy Quaid. Macabre is the word for it and like tripe, it's an acquired taste. ▣

Teri Garr *Sunny Cannald* • John Lithgow *Dave Geary* • Randy Quaid *Lester Atlas* • Bruce McGill *Ernie Cannald* • Lisa Blount *Phyllis* • Alan Blumenfeld *Lew* ■ *Dir* Malcolm Mowbray • *Scr* Leonard Glasser, George Malko, from a story by Leonard Glasser

Out for Justice ★★ 18

Action crime drama
1991 · US · Colour · 87mins

Steven Seagal gets more dialogue than in all his other movies put together, in this lukewarm attempt to give him a lot more heart and soul. He plays a Brooklyn cop with the comedic name of Gino Felino, who comes up against old neighbourhood foe William Forsythe, resulting in much retaliatory violence. Frankly, Seagal is no actor and his career has been founded upon his ability to look cool in combat situations, rather than convey the sort of softly spoken sadness he's aiming for here. There are plenty of adequate action scenes, but stabs at characterisation are a big mistake under the circumstances. Contains swearing and violence. ▣ **DVD**

Steven Seagal *Gino Felino* • William Forsythe *Richie Madano* • Jerry Orbach *Detective Ronnie Donziger* • Jo Champa *Vicky Felino* • Sal Richards *Frankie* • Gina Gershon *Patti Madano* ■ *Dir* John Flynn • *Scr* David Lee Henry, Steven Seagal

Out of Africa ★★★★ PG

Biographical drama
1985 · US · Colour · 154mins

Or "Afreeka" as Meryl Streep would have it, with a bizarre Danish accent that manages to overshadow her entire performance as awkward, free-spirited writer and Kenyan farmer Karen Blixen. A multiple Oscar-winner, this is a beautifully filmed movie, with director Sydney Pollack propelling the camera across lush wide-angled country teeming with all manner of exotic beasts. The other exotic beasts – Streep, Klaus Maria Brandauer as her husband and Robert Redford as her adventurer/lover – overact on a level to match the magnificence of the backdrop, but with this cast it is still eminently watchable stuff. What the movie loses in emotional realism, it gains in sheer epic audacity. ▣

Meryl Streep *Karen* • Robert Redford *Denys Finch Hatton* • Klaus Maria Brandauer *Baron/Hans* • Michael Kitchen *Berkeley Cole* •

Malick Bowens *Farah* • Joseph Thiaka *Kamante* • Stephen Kinyanjui *Kinanjui* • Michael Gough *Lord Delamere* • Suzanna Hamilton *Felicity* • Rachel Kempson *Lady Belfield* ■ *Dir* Sydney Pollack • *Scr* Kurt Luedtke, from the autobiographical books by Isak Dinesen [Karen Blixen], from *Isak Dinesen: the Life of a Storyteller* by Judith Thurman, from *Silence Will Speak* by Errol Trzebinski • *Cinematographer* David Watkin • *Production Designer* Stephen Grimes • *Music* John Barry

Out of Annie's Past ★★ 15

Drama 1995 · US · Colour · 86mins

Catherine Mary Stewart had a chance to break out of the TV-movie rut in such features as *Weekend at Bernie's* and *The Last Starfighter*, but here returns to the genre that has been her bread and butter for the last decade or so. It's a fairly predictable drama about a young woman whose past returns to haunt her (doesn't it always in these films?). Scott Valentine and Dennis Farina give Stewart able support, but the rest of the cast are merely going through the motions. Director Stuart Cooper keeps up the pace as this moves effortlessly to its rather obvious conclusion. Contains some violence. ▣

Catherine Mary Stewart *Annie Carver* • Scott Valentine *Michael Carver* • Dennis Farina *Charlie Ingle* • Carsten Norgaard *Lev Petrovich* • Carlos Gomez *Detective Mendoza* ■ *Dir* Stuart Cooper • *Scr* Pablo F Fenjves

Out of Darkness ★★★

Biographical drama
1990 · US · Colour · 89mins

Alternatively called *The Light in the Jungle*, as well as *Schweitzer and Lambarene*, this clumsy biopic rather dims the brightness of its subject, Albert Schweitzer, musician, intellectual, missionary and Nobel Peace Prize winner, who rejected European acclaim to minister to disease-ridden natives in the African jungle as a kind of male Mother Teresa. It's not a whitewash – according to this he ran his deliberately run-down hospital like a tyrant – but its simplistic plot doesn't do the man justice. However, Malcolm McDowell is at the top of a form that wasn't even suggested by his starring role in *If…* over 20 years previously. Contains some violence and nudity.

Malcolm McDowell *Dr Albert Schweitzer* • Susan Strasberg *Helene Schweitzer* • Andrew Davis *Lionel Curtis* • Helen Jessop *Amanda Hampton* • John Carson *Horton Herschel* • Henry Cele *Onganga* ■ *Dir* Gray Hofmyer [Gray Hofmeyr] • *Scr* Michel Potts, Patrick Lee

Out of Darkness ★★ 15

Drama 1994 · US · Colour · 87mins

Given her impressive performance in the Billie Holliday biopic *Lady Sings the Blues*, it's surprising that soul diva Diana Ross hasn't appeared more on the screen. With this, her TV-movie debut, she gets her chance to sink her teeth into a good meaty role as a woman suffering from schizophrenia, who, after years of being a recluse, is coaxed back into normal society. Lindsay Crouse is the only other "face" in the cast but this is Ross's show and she makes the most of it,

even if the direction of Larry Elikann is a touch on the bland side. ▣

Diana Ross *Paulie Cooper* • Beah Richards *Mrs Cooper* • Lindsay Crouse *Kim Donaldson* • Carl Lumbly *Addison Haig* • Ann Weldon *Virginia Cooper* • Rhonda Stubbins White *Zoe Price* ■ *Dir* Larry Elikann • *Scr* Barbara Turner

Out of Order ★★★ 15

Thriller 1984 · W Ger · Colour · 83mins

Playing fast and loose with the conventions of existential drama and the disaster movie, German director Carl Schenkel mischievously takes Jean-Paul Sartre's contention that hell is other people and twists it by trapping his protagonists in a lift, with only some fraying cables keeping them from a 300-ft plunge. Naturally, there's not much to recommend about executive Götz George, mistress Renée Soutendijk, punk Hannes Jaenicke and embezzling accountant Wolfgang Kieling in the first place. But, as the tension mounts, their foibles and prejudices become voyeuristically irresisitible, even though the quartet eventually descends into caricature as the storyline becomes increasingly strained. In German with English subtitles. ▣

Götz George *Jörg* • Renée Soutendijk *Marion* • Wolfgang Kieling *Gössmann* • Hannes Jaenicke *Pit* ■ *Dir/Scr* Carl Schenkel

Out of Season ★★ 18

Drama 1975 · UK · Colour · 86mins

This stagey, moody, ambiguous love triangle, played in and around a holiday hotel in winter, will either intrigue or irritate, depending on one's predilection. The plot, such as it is, consists of the sex/power games played by three people: a middle-aged woman (Vanessa Redgrave), her teenage daughter (Susan George) and an American (Cliff Robertson) who enters their lives 20 years after his affair with the older woman. Director Alan Bridges cleverly teases suspense from the conflict, but although the performances are excellent, the female roles are, by today's standards, sexual stereotypes. ▣

Vanessa Redgrave *Ann* • Cliff Robertson *Joe* • Susan George *Joanna* ■ *Dir* Alan Bridges • *Scr* Eric Bercovici, Reuben Bercovitch

Out of Sight ★★★★ 15

Romantic crime comedy
1998 · US · Colour · 117mins

George Clooney and Jennifer Lopez simply sizzle in director Steven Soderbergh's sexy, sly and snappy crime caper, which neatly combines its seventies heist-picture roots with sparkling romantic comedy. The Elmore Leonard plot gets a classy and playful screen makeover as the stars on opposite sides of the law fighting their instant attraction when robber Clooney escapes from prison and cop Lopez vows to bring him to justice. Using intricate flashbacks and a keen visual style, Soderbergh takes a sharp script from Scott Frank – who also wrote *Get Shorty* – and weaves it into an ambitious and accomplished work. Suspenseful, sophisticated and brimming with good humour and bright dialogue. Contains swearing, violence and sexual references. ▣ **DVD**

George Clooney *Jack Foley* • Jennifer Lopez *Karen Sisco* • Ving Rhames *Buddy Bragg* • Don Cheadle *Maurice (Snoopy) Miller* • Dennis Farina *Marshall Sisco* • Albert Brooks *Richard Ripley* • Michael Keaton *Ray Nicolette* • Samuel L Jackson *Hejira* ■ *Dir* Steven Soderbergh • *Scr* Scott Frank, from the novel by Elmore Leonard

Out of Sync ★

Action crime drama
1995 · US · Colour · 105mins

Strangely, rapper LL Cool J doesn't once here get a chance to rap on screen or on the soundtrack, despite his hero character being an underground club DJ. The proceedings are a confusing mix of typical action in the 'hood and forties *film noir*, with the hero led astray by a *femme fatale* who persuades him to assist in the robbery of his mobster boss. It's no wonder LL gets lost in the clash of styles and is unable to provoke any sympathy for his character.

LL Cool J *Jason "The Saint"* St Julian • Victoria Dillard *Monica Collins* • Ramy Zada *Danny Simon* • Howard Hesseman *Detective Caldwell* • Yaphet Kotto • Isaac Hayes • Aries Spears • Debbie Allen *Manicurist* ■ *Dir* Debbie Allen • *Scr* Robert Dorn

Out of the Blue ★★

Comedy 1947 · US · BW · 84mins

Displaying an unexpected flair for comedy, George Brent is a Greenwich Village resident, married to Carole Landis and feuding with his exotic artist neighbour (Turhan Bey). With Landis away, Brent invites interior designer Ann Dvorak in for a drink; already pretty loaded, she passes out. He thinks she's dead and dumps her body on Bey's porch… The plot might signal *film noir*, but what you actually get, under Leigh Jason's direction, is a chaotic mix of black farce, slapstick and screwball comedy. The laughs don't always come off, but the wry Dvorak is terrific.

George Brent *Arthur Earthleigh* • Virginia Mayo *Deborah Tyler* • Turhan Bey *David Gelleo* • Ann Dvorak *Olive Jensen* • Carole Landis *Mae Earthleigh* ■ *Dir* Leigh Jason • *Scr* Vera Caspary, Walter Bullock, Edward Eliscu, from a story by Vera Caspary

Out of the Blue ★★

Drama 1980 · US/Can · Colour · 93mins

Dysfunctional family relationships are examined in a typically downbeat fashion by director Dennis Hopper. He also plays the ex-con whose return to his put-upon wife (Sharon Farrell) and rebellious teenage daughter (an exceptional Linda Manz) leads to intense conflict and inevitable tragedy. While not a pretty picture, it is one that occasionally resonates with honest emotion and truthful situations.

Linda Manz *Cindy "CeBe" Barnes* • Sharon Farrell *Kathy Barnes* • Dennis Hopper *Don Barnes* • Raymond Burr *Dr Brean* ■ *Dir* Dennis Hopper • *Scr* Leonard Yakir, Gary Jules Jouvenat, Brenda Nielson

Out of the Body ★ 18

Horror 1988 · Ausl · Colour · 87mins

Journeyman Australian genre director Brian Trenchard-Smith comes unstuck in this reheated chiller inelegantly poised between slaughter and laughter. A supernatural monster is killing women in Sydney, Australia, and removing their eyes. Musician Mark Hembrow foresees the murders but the police think he's responsible for the crimes. Soon they realise their only hope of catching the fiend is to trust in his strange psychic link to the being. Tedious tried-and-tested terror. ▄

Mark Hembrow *David Gaze* • Tessa Humphries *Neva St Clair* • Carrie Zivetz *Dr Lydia Langton* • Linda Newton *Carla Dupré* • John Clayton *Detective Sergeant Whitaker* • John Ley *Sergeant Delgano* ■ *Dir* Brian Trenchard-Smith • *Scr* Kenneth Ross

Out of the Clouds ★★ U

Drama 1954 · UK · Colour · 87mins

The last and least in the series of compendium dramas made for Ealing Studios by director Basil Dearden and producer Michael Relph. This time, the newly expanded London Airport forms the backdrop for vignettes that put passengers and pilots alike through their clichéd paces. The documentary-style glimpses into the day-to-day running of the airport are fascinating, but the performances are no more than adequate, although James Robertson-Justice makes an imposing captain who, even in the fog, has a better sense of direction than Dearden. Not one of Ealing's finest hours.

Anthony Steel *Gus Randall* • Robert Beatty *Nick Milbourne* • David Knight *Bill Steiner* • Margo Lorenz *Leah Roche* • James Robertson-Justice *Captain Brent* • Eunice Gayson *Penny Henson* • Isabel Dean *Mrs Malcolm* • Michael Howard *Purvis* • Gordon Harker *Taxi driver* ■ *Dir* Basil Dearden • *Scr* John Eldridge, Michael Relph, Rex Rienits, from the novel *The Springboard* by John Fores

Out of the Dark ★★★ 18

Thriller 1988 · US · Colour · 83mins

An original take on the serial-killer genre in which a murderer in a clown mask kills staff members of a phone-sex service one by one. Director Michael Schroeder lays on the visual agony, while Cameron Dye and Lynn Danielson emote strenuously, but the real hysteria comes from actors such as Paul Bartel (a Roger Corman alumnus) and Divine, cast here a police detective! ▄

Cameron Dye *Kevin/Bobo* • Karen Black *Ruth* • Lynn Danielson *Kristi* • Karen Witter *Jo Ann* • Starr Andreeff *Camille* • Karen Mayo-Chandler *Barbara* • Bud Cort *Stringer* • Divine *Detective Langella* • Paul Bartel *Motel clerk* • Tab Hunter *Driver* • Lainie Kazan *Hooker Nancy* ■ *Dir* Michael Schroeder • *Scr* Zane W Levitt, J Gregory DeFelice

Out of the Darkness ★★★

Crime thriller based on a true story
1985 · US · Colour · 96mins

A strong central role attracted big name Martin Sheen, and he doesn't let anybody down. He is superb as detective Ed Zigo, who helped to solve the "Son of Sam" murders in the late seventies, and he is almost matched by stage actor Robert Trebor as the killer. Sheen's son Charlie, later a major star in his own right, makes a brief appearance on screen with his father.

Martin Sheen *Ed Zigo* • Hector Elizondo *Father George* • Matt Clark *John Hubbard* • Jennifer

Salt *Ann Zigo* • Eddie Egan *Tom Duncan* • Robert Trebor *David Berkowitz* • Charlie Sheen ■ *Dir* Jud Taylor • *Scr* Thomas S Cook

Out of the Fog ★★★

Crime drama 1941 · US · BW · 84mins

A Brooklyn tailor and a short-order chef enjoy their little fishing trips around the bay, until a minor league gangster moves in, offering them protection and offering the tailor's daughter something else. A plot is hatched to dispense with the Mafioso's services. More of a character study than a thriller, it spins on a surprising twist and then goes on to become a sentimental tale about exploitation. A good cast, though, and a subtle opening out of Irwin Shaw's play which was presented on Broadway by Lee Strasberg's left-wing Group Theatre.

Ida Lupino *Stella Goodwin* • John Garfield *Harold Goff* • Eddie Albert *George Watkins* • Thomas Mitchell *Jonah Goodwin* • John Qualen *Olaf Johnson* • George Tobias *Igor Propotkin* • Aline MacMahon *Florence Goodwin* ■ *Dir* Anatole Litvak • *Scr* Robert Rossen, Jerry Wald, Richard Macaulay, from the play *The Gentle People* by Irwin Shaw

Out of the Present ★★★★ U

Documentary
1995 · Ger/Fr/Bel/Rus · Colour · 99mins

After ten months in orbit, Sergei Krikalev returned to a homeland very different from the one he had left in May 1991. Yet, according to Andrei Ujica's documentary, the transition from Gorbachev's Soviet Union to Yeltsin's Russia was almost as painless as a change of crew on board the Mir space station. Combining grainy video footage with glossier imagery recorded with Krikalev's own camera, this account of the longest-ever space flight fascinates on a technical, political and human level. The immense silence, the awkward camaraderie and the fragility of the craft make a huge impression. But the spectacular views of Earth will live longest in the memory. In Russian with English subtitles.

Dir/Scr Andrei Ujica

Out of the Rain ★★

Thriller 1991 · US · Colour · 91mins

Why do so many mediocre movies begin with someone coming home for the funeral of a loved one? That's the device that kicks off this particular opus, as black sheep Michael O'Keefe attends the service of his brother, who apparently committed suicide. A bit of detective work reveals that it probably wasn't suicide after all, and a few talks with the locals (including dead brother's girlfriend Bridget Fonda, with whom he develops a relationship, naturally) reveal that the culprit may be close to home. Vaguely intriguing but a bit too dialogue-heavy.

Bridget Fonda *Jolene* • Michael O'Keefe *Frank Reade* • John O'Keefe *Sheriff Norris* • Al Shannon *Drew* • John Seitz *Nat Reade* ■ *Dir* Gary Winick • *Scr* Shem Bitterman, from his play

Out of This World ★★★

Musical 1945 · US · BW · 96mins

Bing Crosby is heard but not seen in this amusingly satirical look at fame and pop fans, forties-style. Eddie Bracken is the small-town telegram boy who sings like Crosby and is taken to New York by Diana Lynn, the leader of a girls' band. Crosby dubbed the songs, including the enduring title number by Harold Arlen and Johnny Mercer. Lynn has a rare chance to show her considerable skills at the piano with a version of the *Minute Waltz* (played in exactly one minute), and Crosby's four sons can be seen as part of Bracken's adoring audience.

Eddie Bracken *Herbie Fenton* • Veronica Lake *Dorothy Dodge* • Diana Lynn *Betty Miller* • Cass Daley *Fanny the Drummer* • Parkyakarkus *Gus Palukas* • Don Wilson *Radio announcer* • Bing Crosby *Herbie Fenton* ■ *Dir* Hal Walker • *Scr* Walter DeLeon, Arthur Phillips, from stories by Elizabeth Meehan, Sam Coslow

The Out of Towners ★★★★ U

Comedy 1970 · US · Colour · 97mins

Playwright Neil Simon blends comedy with pain in his first solo original screenplay, directed by Arthur Hiller. Jack Lemmon stars as the Ohio businessman who decides to combine a job interview in New York with a night on the town in the company of his wife Sandy Dennis. However, their excursion turns into a nightmare as they become increasingly bothered and bewildered by the Big Apple's ruthless manners. Lemmon takes it all with despairing aplomb, but Dennis seems less able to deal with the mounting calamities, leaving us to wonder whether comedy should be so serious.

Jack Lemmon *George Kellerman* • Sandy Dennis *Gwen Kellerman* • Milt Kamen *Counterman* • Sandy Baron *TV man* • Anne Meara *Woman in police station* • Robert Nichols *Man in aeroplane* • Ann Prentiss *Airline stewardess* • Ron Carey *Boston cab driver* • Phil Bruns *Officer Meyers* ■ *Dir* Arthur Hiller • *Scr* Neil Simon

The Out-of-Towners ★★ 12

Comedy 1999 · US · Colour · 92mins

A listless, pointless remake of Neil Simon's 1970 comedy that reunites Steve Martin and Goldie Hawn, who scored a hit together in 1992 with *HouseSitter*. They play a couple from the sticks who fly to New York for a job interview. No sooner have they left the ground than everything that could possibly go wrong (getting mugged, having their credit cards cancelled and so on), does. The two stars do their best, but they lack the desperation that Jack Lemmon and Sandy Dennis brought to the roles, while John Cleese's Basil Fawlty reprise is faintly embarrassing. Contains some sexual references.

Goldie Hawn *Nancy Clark* • Steve Martin *Henry Clark* • John Cleese *Mr Mersault* • Mark McKinney *Greg* • Oliver Hudson *Alan* • Valerie Perri *Stewardess* • Rudolph Giuliani *Mayor* ■ *Dir* Sam Weisman • *Scr* Marc Lawrence, from the 1970 film

Out on a Limb ★ PG

Comedy 1992 · US · Colour · 79mins

Turning his back on a $140 million business deal, yuppie Matthew Broderick heads for Buzzsaw, California, to save his sister from the clutches of a villain, played by Jeffrey Jones. The fact that Jones is a twin confuses things and makes this movie even less watchable than it already is. Indeed, this stinker was barely released on video, let alone in cinemas, and went through various versions and alternative titles before it was left to die alone. French director Francis Veber came to the project having directed *A Pain in the A...!* and co-written *La Cage aux Folles*. Contains some swearing. ▄

Matthew Broderick *Bill Campbell* • Jeffrey Jones *Matt/Peter* • Heidi Kling *Sally* • John C Reilly *Jim Jr* • Marian Mercer *Ann* • Larry Hankin *Darren* • David Margulies *Buchenwald* ■ *Dir* Francis Veber • *Scr* Joshua Goldin, Daniel Goldin

Out on the Edge ★★★

Drama 1989 · US · Colour · 96mins

Rick Schroder, after his early success in *The Champ*, has made a useful contribution to countless TV movies. Playing a lost Californian teenager, he certainly doesn't blot his copybook here, even when events begin to break free of credibility. Schroder homes in convincingly on the inner life of a sun-kissed youth whose looks and demeanour are an effective cover for his angst. Only his friendship with a psychiatric counsellor threatens to edge into melodrama.

Rick Schroder *Danny Evetts* • Mary Kay Place *Sondra Evetts* • Dakin Matthews *Dr Cutler* • Richard Jenkins *Paul Evetts* • Maya Lebenzon *Kerri* • Patricia Allison *Miss Fox* • Grand L Bush *Quinn* ■ *Dir* John Pasquin • *Scr* Rene Balcer, from a story by Rene Balcer, AL Martinez

Out 1: Spectre ★★★★

Experimental mystery
1973 · Fr · Colour · 260mins

Never one to worry about length, Jacques Rivette allowed *Out 1* to run to over 12 hours. When it was reduced to this 4 hour 20 minute version, out of necessity, Rivette thought it was a mere ghost of the original, and changed the title. But, as the film doesn't seek to reach any conclusion, it could have gone on forever. A mystery story partly concerning a man and a woman who used to live together, separately rehearsing two plays by Aeschylus, this haunting film creates an unsettling atmosphere. The cast, including François Truffaut favourite Jean-Pierre Léaud, is brilliant considering Rivette had virtually no shooting script. A French language film.

Pierre Baillot *Quentin* • Juliet Berto *Frédérique* • Jacques Doniol-Valcroze *Etienne* • Françoise Fabian *Lucie* • Bernadette Lafont *Sarah* • Jean-Pierre Léaud *Colin* • Michel Lonsdale *Thomas* • Bulle Ogier *Pauline/Emilie* ■ *Dir* Jacques Rivette • *Scr* Jacques Rivette, Suzanne Schiffman, from the story *L'Histoire des Treize* by Honoré de Balzac

Out There ★★★

Science-fiction comedy
1995 · US · Colour · 98mins

Bill Campbell headlines this irreverent, at times tongue-in-cheek, sci-fi TV movie. Trouble ensues when a down-on-his-luck Pulitzer Prize-winning photographer buys an old Brownie camera with undeveloped film inside. When he develops the prints, he sees what appear to be snapshots of the alien abduction of two deer hunters. When he is dismissed by the military as a phoney, he searches for the truth, aided by the daughter (Wendy Schaal) of one of the victims. Fresh direction by Sam Irvin makes the unconventional subject matter amusingly believable.

Bill Campbell *Delbert Mosley* • Wendy Schaal *Paige Davis* • Rod Steiger *Colonel Buck Gunner* • Jill St John *Bunny Wells* • Bill Cobbs *Lyman Weeks* • Paul Dooley *Emmett Davis* • Bobcat Goldthwait *Cobb* • Billy Bob Thornton *Biker* • June Lockhart *Donna* ■ *Dir* Sam Irvin • *Scr* Thomas Strelich, Alison Nigh

Out to Sea ★★ 12

Comedy 1997 · US · Colour · 102mins

Jack Lemmon and Walter Matthau are brothers-in-law working as dance partners for singles aboard a cruise ship. Lemmon and Matthau's schtick – they were brothers-in-law in their first joint outing, *The Fortune Cookie* – had a strange revival in the nineties, as if adding wrinkles to the recipe might create a great new dish for moviegoers who regard Tom Cruise as middle-aged. This high-concept, low development movie has its moments (well, one or two) but a poor screenplay means it's more embarrassing than it is funny. Contains strong language and some sexual references. ▣

Jack Lemmon *Herb* • Walter Matthau *Charlie* • Dyan Cannon *Liz* • Gloria DeHaven *Vivian* • Brent Spiner *Gil Godwyn* • Elaine Stritch *Mavis* • Hal Linden *Mac* • Donald O'Connor *Jonathan* ■ *Dir* Martha Coolidge • *Scr* Robert Nelson Jacobs

Out West with the Hardys ★★ U

Comedy drama 1938 · US · BW · 83mins

Judge Hardy and family take a vacation on a dude ranch for this fifth in the series. While Lewis Stone gives his legal advice to the ranch owner, daughter Cecilia Parker runs off with the foreman and Mickey Rooney's ego is punctured by 11 year-old ranch temptress Virginia Weidler who steals the show something rotten. It's all quite witty and charming.

Lewis Stone *Judge James K Hardy* • Mickey Rooney *Andy Hardy* • Fay Holden *Mrs Emily Hardy* • Cecilia Parker *Marian Hardy* • Ann Rutherford *Polly Benedict* • Sara Haden *Aunt Milly* • Don Castle *Dennis Hunt* • Virginia Weidler *"Jake" Holt* ■ *Dir* George B Seitz • *Scr* Kay Van Riper, Agnes Christine Johnston, William Ludwig, from characters created by Aurania Rouverol

Outback Bound ★★ PG

Romantic adventure
1988 · US · Colour · 89mins

Knots Landing star Donna Mills forgoes the hairsprayed hairdos she is known for to play a Beverly Hills woman who ends up taking on an old opal mine in Australia when she is made penniless. Essentially, this made-for-TV movie is *Crocodile Dundee* in reverse and without the laughs as Mills goes native and gets involved with John Schneider (so this is what happened to him after *The Dukes of Hazzard*). Not bad, but, on the other hand, not good either. ▣

Donna Mills *Samantha Hollings* • Andrew Clarke *Bill* • John Meillon *Nobby* • Collette Mann *Edith* • John Schneider *Jim Tully* ■ *Dir* John Llewellyn Moxey • *Scr* Elizabeth Comici, Luciano Comici

Outbreak ★★★★ 15

Thriller 1995 · US · Colour · 122mins

An exciting eco-thriller, with army medic Dustin Hoffman trying to save the world from a lethal virus imported into America from Africa. You could read this as an Aids allegory, but it also works well as a regular against-the-clock jeopardy thriller with almost mandatory conspiracy cover-up overtones. Director Wolfgang Petersen marshals the effects superbly and there's terrific support from the likes of Morgan Freeman, Kevin Spacey and a particularly nasty Donald Sutherland. If Hoffman lacks the requisite heroic quality needed for the lead, you certainly feel you could put your trust in him. Contains violence and swearing. ▣ *DVD*

Dustin Hoffman *Col Sam Daniels* • Rene Russo *Dr Roberta "Robby" Keough* • Morgan Freeman *General Billy Ford* • Cuba Gooding Jr *Major Salt* • Kevin Spacey *Major Casey Schuler* • Patrick Dempsey *Jimbo Scott* • Donald Sutherland *General Donald McClintock* ■ *Dir* Wolfgang Petersen • *Scr* Laurence Dworet, Robert Roy Pool

The Outcast ★★

Western 1954 · US · Colour · 90mins

One of Republic's better-written routine westerns of the fifties, this stars a virile John Derek as the youngster who comes back to claim land stolen by his uncle, played by Jim Davis. The film teeters on bedroom farce at one point when Davis insists on entering the hotel room of his fiancée, Catherine McLeod, while she's sheltering his wounded nephew, but director William Witney, a veteran of Republic serials and B-features, stages the numerous outdoor action scenes with commendable vigour.

John Derek *Jet Cosgrave* • Joan Evans *Judy Polsen* • Jim Davis *Major Cosgrave* • Catherine McLeod *Alice Austin* • Ben Cooper *The Kid* • Taylor Holmes *Andrew Devlin* • Nana Bryant *Mrs Banner* • Slim Pickens *Boone Polsen* ■ *Dir* William Witney • *Scr* John K Butler, Richard Wormser, from a story by Todhunter Ballard

Outcast of the Islands ★★★ PG

Drama 1951 · UK · BW · 95mins

Joseph Conrad's bustling, disquieting tale about a self-seeking wastrel's calamitous impact on a group of Far Eastern islands has, sadly, been turned into a loud, disjointed and rather disagreeable picture by Carol Reed. Such is the haphazard nature of the script that incidents come and go at an alarming rate, leaving the usually poised Reed powerless to tie them into a cohesive narrative. There are compensations, however, notably the atmospheric use of exotic locations and the controlled performances of Ralph Richardson and Robert Morley, who show up to much better advantage than the excitable top-billed Trevor Howard. ▣

Trevor Howard *Willems* • Ralph Richardson *Lingard* • Robert Morley *Almayer* • Kerima *Aissa* • Wendy Hiller *Mrs Almayer* • George Coulouris *Babalatchi* • Betty Ann Davies *Mrs Williams* • Peter Illing *Alagappan* • James Kenney *Ramsey* • Dharma Emmanuel *Ali* ■ *Dir* Carol Reed • *Scr* William Fairchild, from the novel by Joseph Conrad

The Outfit ★★★★ 15

Thriller 1973 · US · Colour · 98mins

In this brutish but compulsive thriller, taken from the novel by Richard Stark (a pseudonym for Donald E Westlake), bank robber Robert Duvall leaves prison determined to find out who murdered his brother; the trail leads to ageing mobster Robert Ryan. Duvall is excellent in an all-too-rare starring role, and there's a terrific supporting cast that includes Joe Don Baker, Richard Jaeckel and Elisha Cook Jr. The under-rated writer/director John Flynn lets the story unfold in a simple, unflashy way, but stages some marvellous, if extremely violent, set pieces. Contains violence and swearing. ▣

Robert Duvall *Earl Macklin* • Joe Don Baker *Cody* • Robert Ryan *Mailer* • Karen Black *Bett* • Timothy Carey *Jake Menner* • Richard Jaeckel *Chemey* • Sheree North *Buck's wife* • Marie Windsor *Madge Coyle* • Jane Greer *Alma* • Henry Jones *Doctor* • Joanna Cassidy *Rita* • Elisha Cook Jr *Carl* ■ *Dir* John Flynn • *Scr* John Flynn, from the novel by Richard Stark [Donald E Westlake]

The Outfit ★★ 18

Crime drama 1993 · US · Colour · 88mins

A charmless gangster flick that went straight-to-video in the States, this plays fast and loose with both historical setting and attention to period detail in its vain attempt to sustain interest. Despite naming his characters after "real" gangsters, director/co-writer J Christian Ingvordsen is in fact merely trotting out the clichés of the genre to dress up a sub-standard action movie, as maverick FBI agent Bone Conn (played by John Christian – Ingvordsen again) goes undercover to infiltrate the Mob, with predictable results. ▣

Lance Henriksen *Dutch Schultz* • Billy Drago *Lucky Luciano* • Martin Kove *Agent Baker* • Josh Mosby *Legs Diamond* • John Christian [J Christian Ingvordsen] *Bone Conn* • Rick Washburn *Red* • Jeffrey Howard *Max* • J Gregory Smith *Jimmy* ■ *Dir* J Christian Ingvordsen • *Scr* Steven Kaman, J Christian Ingvordsen, Whitney Ransick

Outland ★★ 15

Science-fiction action adventure
1981 · UK/US · Colour · 104mins

It's *High Noon* in outer space as mining colony marshal Sean Connery confronts the pushers peddling lethal drugs to Jupiter moon workers so they'll produce more ore. This bleak dramatisation of final frontier contamination comes complete with *Alien*-inspired decor and smooth direction by Peter Hyams. But eschewing the cleverness of his *Capricorn One* for a doggedly one-dimensional approach to both plot and character, Hyams sinks this far-flung fantasy with cheap scare tactics, illogical science and B-movie western-style laser gun battles that scupper credibility. And why does Connery never call for back up? Contains violence and swearing. ▣ *DVD*

Sean Connery *O'Niel* • Peter Boyle *Sheppard* • Frances Sternhagen *Lazarus* • James B Sikking *Montone* • Kika Markham *Carol* • Clarke Peters *Ballard* • Steven Berkoff *Sagan* • John Ratzenberger *Tarlow* • Nicholas Barnes *Paul O'Niel* ■ *Dir/Scr* Peter Hyams

The Outlaw ★★★ U

Western 1943 · US · BW · 115mins

"Mean, moody, magnificent" was the advertising tag for this infamous movie, and it didn't refer to the outlaw of the title – Billy the Kid – but to Doc Holliday's delectable mistress Rio, played so memorably here by Howard Hughes's exciting discovery, Jane Russell. Censorship and reshooting led to a three-year release delay for this languorous western, originally directed by the estimable Howard Hawks, which contrives strange fictional relationships between Billy (colourless newcomer Jack Buetel), Pat Garrett (Thomas Mitchell) and Holliday (the superb Walter Huston). Best remembered today for Russell's cleavage – she never quite lived down the attendant publicity – there's also salty dialogue from Hawks's regular collaborator, Jules Furthman. ▣

Jack Buetel *Billy the Kid* • Jane Russell *Rio* • Thomas Mitchell *Pat Garrett* • Walter Huston *Doc Holliday* • Mimi Aguglia *Aunt Guadelupe* • Joseph Sawyer [Joe Sawyer] *Woodruff* • Gene Rizzi *Stranger* • Frank Darien *Shorty* ■ *Dir* Howard Hughes • *Scr* Jules Furthman

Outlaw Blues ★★★ 15

Comedy drama 1977 · US · Colour · 96mins

If you can cope with Peter Fonda singing country and western ditties, then you might just find yourself having a good time with this scattergun mixture of comedy, musical and road movie. Fonda is clearly enjoying himself as a convict who breaks parole to get even with shyster singer James Callahan who has stolen his song. Michael Lerner and Susan Saint James also score as the unscrupulous duo who turn Fonda into Public Enemy Number One to boost his career. Director Richard T Heffron overdoes the motor mayhem, but does well to keep his cast at full throttle. ▣

Peter Fonda *Bobby Ogden* • Susan Saint James *Tina Waters* • John Crawford *Chief Cavenaugh* • James Callahan *Garland Dupree* • Michael Lerner *Hatch* ■ *Dir* Richard T Heffron • *Scr* BWL Norton

Outlaw Force ★ 18

Action adventure 1988 · US · Colour · 90mins

Surely one of the biggest vanity productions to date, with David Heavener not only starring, but taking the directing, writing, and producing reins, and also writing and singing seven of the eleven songs on the soundtrack. Only his singing gets a passing mark. Playing a dyed-in-the-wool modern day cowboy, Heavener

U = SUITABLE FOR ALL   Uc = SUITABLE FOR ALL, ESPECIALLY FOR YOUNG CHILDREN (VIDEO ONLY)   PG = PARENTAL GUIDANCE

straps on his six guns and heads to the big city after the scum who raped and killed his wife, and kidnap his young daughter. Even if one disregards the blurred photography, dim lighting, and sound that makes some dialogue hard to make out, the movie is still ponderously slow and lacking action, with a hero who is about as expressive as Chuck Norris. ▭

David Heavener *Billy Ray Dalton* • Paul L Smith *[Paul Smith] Inspector Wainwright* • Frank Stallone *Grady* • Robert Bjorklund *Washington* • Devin Dunsworth *Jesse* • Stephanie Cicero *Holly Dalton* • Warren Berlinger *Captain Morgan* ■ *Dir/Scr* David Heavener

The Outlaw Josey Wales
★★★★ 18

Western   1976 · US · Colour · 130mins

Clint Eastwood seized the directorial reins from Phil Kaufman and fashioned this tough, sprawling post-Civil War western epic, about a wronged farmer bent on revenge, into something approaching a personal testament. The film consists more of a series of vignettes compared with the tightness of structure that so distinguishes the later *Unforgiven*. But there's much power derived from the iconographic value of Eastwood the star, and through Josey's eyes we begin to understand the importance of the community in American life. Jerry Fielding's fine score and Chief Dan George's drily humorous Lone Watie are major pluses. Contains violence, some swearing and brief nudity. ▭

DVD

Clint Eastwood *Josey Wales* • Sondra Locke *Laura Lee* • Chief Dan George *Lone Watie* • Bill McKinney *Terrill* • John Vernon *Fletcher* • Paula Trueman *Grandma Sarah* • Sam Bottoms *Jamie* • Geraldine Keams *Little Moonlight* • Dir Clint Eastwood • *Scr* Phil Kaufman, Sonia Chernus, from the novel *Gone to Texas* by Forrest Carter

Outlaw Justice
★★

Western   1999 · US · Colour · 94mins

A posse of country-and-western music stars thunders across the sagebrush in this amusing drama. Ageing gunslingers Willie Nelson and Kris Kristofferson reunite to avenge the murder of a member of their old gang. Joined by the victim's strait-laced son, and another of their outlaw buddies, they talk fast and drink hard while riding toward a final, fatal showdown. The solid support of Waylon Jennings and Travis Tritt make this a serviceable, if conventional addition to the genre, though the absence of singing from some of Nashville's brightest lights may disappoint country-and-western fans.

Willie Nelson *Lee* • Kris Kristofferson *Torrance* • Travis Tritt *Dalton* • Waylon Jennings *Tobey Naylor* • Chad Willett *Bryce Naylor* • Danny Sullivan *Mr Preble* • Jonathan Banks *Sheriff Conklin* ■ *Dir* Bill Corcoran • *Scr* Gene Quintano

The Outlaws Is Coming
★★★ U

Comedy western   1965 · US · BW · 88mins

Hardworking comedy team the Three Stooges appeared in nearly 200 shorts and over 20 feature films in their long career and this western spoof marks their last big-screen appearance together. Loved by millions, loathed by many, the Stooges never strayed far from their comic roots as violent exponents of lightning-paced slapstick. Here those skills honed over the years are used to good effect in a story of the boys taking on gunslingers and other assorted villains.

Moe Howard • Larry Fine • Joe De Rita • Adam West *Kenneth Cabot* • Nancy Kovack *Annie Oakley* • Mort Mills *Trigger Mortis* • Don Lamond *Rance Roden* ■ *Dir* Norman Maurer • *Scr* Elwood Ullman, from a story by Norman Maurer

Outrage
★★

Drama   1950 · US · BW · 74mins

It took a female director, Ida Lupino, to make a film centred directly on the provocative subject of rape (although the word itself could not be used). Lupino's main concern is with the aftermath – the victim, well played by newcomer Mala Powers, feels so "dirty" that she runs away to start a new life. As the co-writer as well as director, Lupino avoids obvious sensationalism. However, Tod Andrews's preacher, who helps the young woman overcome her trauma, seems too good to be true and the film is overly concentrated on a single issue.

Mala Powers *Ann Walton* • Tod Andrews *Ferguson* • Robert Clarke *Jim Owens* • Raymond Bond *Mr Walton* • Lilian Hamilton *Mrs Walton* • Rita Lupino *Stella Carter* ■ *Dir* Ida Lupino • *Scr* Ida Lupino, Malvin Wald, Collier Young

The Outrage
★★★

Western   1964 · US · BW · 95mins

Having successfully remade Akira Kurosawa's *Seven Samurai* as *The Magnificent Seven*, Hollywood turned its sights on Kurosawa's earlier classic *Rashomon*, the story of a rape and a murder told by four different people with differing perspectives. Transposed to the Wild West, Paul Newman plays the killer, a Mexican outlaw, Claire Bloom and Laurence Harvey are the victims, and Edward G Robinson plays a con man. It's a starry cast (William Shatner is in it as well) and worth watching for that reason alone, though Martin Ritt's direction labours every point and totally lacks the intensity of the original film.

Paul Newman *Juan Carrasco* • Laurence Harvey *Husband* • Claire Bloom *Wife* • Edward G Robinson *Con Man* • William Shatner *Preacher* • Howard Da Silva *Prospector* • Albert Salmi *Sheriff* • Thomas Chalmers *Judge* ■ *Dir* Martin Ritt • *Scr* Michael Kanin, from the stories by Ryunosuke Akutagawa, from the film *Rashomon* by Akira Kurosawa, Shinobu Hashimoto, and from the play *Rashomon* by Michael Kanin, Fay Kanin

Outrage
★★

Drama   1993 · Sp/It · Colour · 108mins

Francesca Neri's exotic circus artiste, an accomplished sharpshooter, hunts down the thugs who gang-raped. Seasoned director Carlos Saura disappointingly undermines his powerful message with some gratuitous nudity and by romanticising her pitiless spree in having it viewed through the eyes of besotted journalist Antonio Banderas. The result, while staged with sophistication, is less shocking and provocative than Tony Garnett's similarly themed *Handgun*. In Spanish with English subtitles. Contains violence and nudity.

Antonio Banderas *Marcos Vallez* • Francesca Neri *Ana* • Walter Vidarte *Manuel* • Eulalia Ramón *Mother* • Chema Manzo *Father* • Archero Manas *Mario* ■ *Dir* Carlos Saura • *Scr* Carlos Saura, Enzo Monteleone, from the story *Spara Che Ti Pasa* by Giorgio Scerbanenco

Outrage
★

Thriller   1998 · US · Colour · 96mins

Predictable situations hobble this tale of urban revenge and survival. A trio of prep school students vandalise the car of New York insurance agent Rob Lowe and his pregnant wife, Jennifer Grey. The vandals are caught, but quickly released, and set about terrorising the couple. Attractive couple Lowe and Grey can't rise above the inane dialogue and repellent violence, which inevitably reduce this TV movie to a clumsy, pandering exercise in wish-fulfilment.

Rob Lowe *Tom Casey* • Jennifer Grey *Sally Casey* • Eric Michael Cole *Jeffrey* • Kathryn Harrold *Deena* ■ *Dir* Robert Allan Ackerman • *Scr* Ellen Weston

Outrage!
★★★ PG

Courtroom drama 1986 · US · Colour · 94mins

In a head-reeling performance, Robert Preston is a father who admits to killing the man who raped and killed his daughter. It's a TV-movie that has more power than most, particularly when lawyer Beau Bridges takes on the man's defence and in doing so manages to indict the American judicial system. This is not so much a depiction of a trial as of a series of show-off turns by lawyers, but the grandstanding onslaught seems very controversial – and is dramatically very entertaining.

Robert Preston *Dennis Riordan* • Beau Bridges *Brad Grodan* • Burgess Meredith *Judge Aaron Klein* • Linda Purl *Arlene Robbins* • Mel Ferrer *Judge Michael Lengel* • Anthony Newley *Victor Coles* ■ *Dir* Walter Grauman • *Scr* Henry Denker, from his novel

Outrageous!
★★★

Drama   1977 · Can · Colour · 96mins

The hilarious and touching story of overweight Toronto hairdresser Craig Russell whose dream is to dazzle the world as a top-class female impersonator. His best friend, Hollis McLaren, is a certified schizophrenic who's pregnant. How director Richard Benner shows these misfits sticking two fingers up at society as they liberate their fantasies makes a sympathetic, uncompromising and well-acted feel-good gay movie. Divisions within the gay community itself are also touched on with unsentimental candour (macho denim fags versus satin drag queens) for a well-rounded view of the way it was in the heady disco days, pre-Aids.

Craig Russell *Robin Turner* • Hollis McLaren *Liza Connors* • Richert Easley *Perry* • Allan Moyle *Martin* • David McIlwraith *Bob* • Gerry Salzberg *Jason* • Andrée Pelletier *Anne* •

Helen Shaver *Jo* ■ *Dir* Richard Benner • *Scr* Richard Benner, from the story *Butterfly Ward* by Margaret Gibson

Outrageous Fortune
★★★ 15

Action comedy   1987 · US · Colour · 95mins

Bette Midler and *Cheers* star Shelley Long team up for this buddy-buddy comedy to play two women from different sides of the tracks who find they have the same two-timing boyfriend (Peter Coyote, in a serious piece of miscasting – it's hard to believe one woman would be after him, let alone two). Director Arthur Hiller manages to keep the action and comedy rolling along at a fairly boisterous rate, and he is helped considerably by the assured performances of Midler and Long, who refuse to let the humour lapse for a second. Contains swearing. ▭

Bette Midler *Sandy Brozinsky* • Shelley Long *Lauren Ames* • Peter Coyote *Michael Sanchez* • Robert Prosky *Stanislav Korzenowski* • John Schuck *Atkins* • George Carlin *Frank* • Anthony Heald *Weldon* ■ *Dir* Arthur Hiller • *Scr* Leslie Dixon

The Outriders
★★ U

Western   1950 · US · Colour · 93mins

A very average Technicolor western from MGM with a seemingly uninterested Joel McCrea getting involved with Quantrill's Raiders and redhead Arlene Dahl. It's given some distinction by the studio's high production values and excellent location photography; the plot, though, is disappointingly routine. Director Roy Rowland manages an excellent and suspenseful river crossing, but the movie badly needs a grittier lead.

Joel McCrea *Will Owen* • Arlene Dahl *Jen Gort* • Barry Sullivan *Jesse Wallace* • Claude Jarman Jr *Roy Gort* • James Whitmore *Clint Priest* • Ramon Novarro *Don Antonio Chaves* • Jeff Corey *Keeley* ■ *Dir* Roy Rowland • *Scr* Irving Ravetch

Outside Providence
★★ 15

Comedy   1999 · US · Colour · 91mins

The sensitive side of the Farrelly brothers (*Dumb and Dumber*, *There's Something about Mary*) may be pushing it a little, but this is certainly a lot more tasteful than their usual fare. Set in the seventies and based on Peter Farrelly's novel, this stars Shawn Hatosy as a working class youth constantly battling his dad who causes even more trouble when he is sent to a snobby prep school. The performances from the strong cast are appealing, although it takes in no real new ground. ▭

Alec Baldwin *Old Man Dunphy* • Shawn Hatosy *Tim Dunphy* • George Wendt *Joey* • Tommy Bone *Jackie Dunphy* • Samantha Lavigne *"Clops"* • Jonathan Brandis *Mousy* • Adam Lavorgna *Tommy the Wire* • Jesse Leach *Decenz* ■ *Dir* Michael Corrente • *Scr* Peter Farrelly, Michael Corrente, Bobby Farrelly, from a novel by Peter Farrelly

The Outside Woman
★★★

Drama   1989 · US · Colour · 100mins

Implausible, despite its claim of being based on a true story, this mindlessly enjoyable romantic drama has bored do-gooder Sharon Gless hijacking a

helicopter to free Scott Glenn from a maximum security prison. The moment that Gless shows up in jail with a throaty church choir in tow, the picture goes off the rails. Yet, with *Cagney and Lacey's* Gless being her usual gutsy self, the final result still manages to be entertaining hokum.

Sharon Gless *Joyce Mattox* • Scott Glenn *Jesse Smith* • Max Gail *Billy Ballew* • Kyle Secor *Jimmy Leonard* ■ *Dir* Lou Antonio • *Scr* William Blinn

The Outsider ★★★

Biography   1961 · US · BW · 108mins

One of the seminal images of the Second World War showed a group of US marines raising the flag at Iwo Jima; it was a photograph first, then a memorial in Washington. This ambitious biography tells the story of Ira Hamilton Hayes, a native American who volunteers for the navy and suffers from racial hostility, yet ends up a part of that famous photograph. After the war he becomes a celebrity, but alcoholism turns his life into a tragedy. A committed performance from Tony Curtis helps glide over the stickier parts of the script, resulting in a moving account of a tragic hero.

Tony Curtis *Ira Hamilton Hayes* • James Franciscus *Jim Sorenson* • Gregory Walcott *Sgt Kiley* • Bruce Bennett *General Bridges* • Vivian Nathan *Mrs Nancy Hayes* ■ *Dir* Delbert Mann • *Scr* Stewart Stern

The Outsider ★★★

Political thriller
1979 · US/Neth · Colour · 127mins

Irish-American Vietnam vet Craig Wasson is welcomed by the IRA who send him to Belfast, knowing that if he's killed he will become a martyr in America, aiding the organisation's fund-raising. Wasson's journey turns out to be through minefields of cross and double-cross and generations of hate. The whole film is somewhat partisan in its approach – the British security forces are depicted as the oppressors who are not above a little torture, something which got the film a lot of flak on its limited release. But as a thriller, it has tension and some superb location work. Blink and you'll miss Gabriel Byrne's screen debut.

Craig Wasson *Michael Flaherty* • Sterling Hayden *Seamus Flaherty* • Patricia Quinn *Siobhan* • Niall O'Brien *Emmet Donovan* • TP McKenna *John Russell* • Niall Tiobin *Farmer* • Frank Grimes *Tony Coyle* • Elizabeth Begley *Mrs Cochran* • Gabriel Byrne ■ *Dir* Tony Luraschi • *Scr* Tony Luraschi, from the novel *The Heritage of Michael Flaherty* by Cohn Leinster

The Outsiders ★★★ PG

Drama   1983 · US · Colour · 87mins

Adapted from the cult teen novel by SE Hinton (who crops up in a cameo), this was a conscious attempt by Francis Ford Coppola to do a small film after the excesses of *Apocalypse Now*. Unfortunately, his re-creation of the sights and sounds of sixties Tulsa is more than a little ham-fisted, a situation not helped by some stilted dialogue and a ludicrously over-the-top score by his father Carmine. If you think the rivalry between the gangs looks authentic, it was because

Coppola pampered the Socs and persecuted the Greasers throughout the shoot so that a genuine resentment built up between them. Contains violence and swearing. ▣

Matt Dillon *Dallas Winston* • Ralph Macchio *Johnny Cade* • C Thomas Howell *Ponyboy Curtis* • Patrick Swayze *Darrel Curtis* • Rob Lowe *Sodapop Curtis* • Emilio Estevez *Two-bit Matthews* • Tom Cruise *Steve Randle* • Glenn Withrow *Tim Shepherd* • Diane Lane *Cherry Valance* • Leif Garrett *Bob Sheldon* • Darren Dalton *Randy Anderson* • Tom Waits *Buck Merrill* ■ *Dir* Francis Ford Coppola • *Scr* Kathleen Knutsen Rowell, from the novel by SE Hinton

Outward Bound ★★

Drama   1930 · US · BW · 82mins

The first film version of Sutton Vane's once celebrated and controversial play concerns the passengers on an ocean liner who come to realise they are dead and drifting between heaven and hell. As an early talkie made by the director of the stage version, Robert Milton, with many members of the Broadway cast, it's extremely creaky with all the players – even Leslie Howard – overdoing their performances. Nevertheless, it's an intriguing historical curiosity that initiated Howard's Hollywood film career.

Leslie Howard *Tom Prior* • Douglas Fairbanks Jr *Henry* • Helen Chandler *Ann* • Beryl Mercer *Mrs Midget* • Alec B Francis *Scrubby* • Alison Skipworth *Mrs Cliveden-Banks* • Lyonel Watts *Rev William Duke* • Montagu Love *Mr Lingley* • Dudley Digges *Thompson, the Examiner* ■ *Dir* Robert Milton • *Scr* J Grubb Alexander, from the play by Sutton Vane

Over Her Dead Body ★★★ 15

Black comedy   1990 · US · Colour · 97mins

For some reason, at the tail end of the eighties, there was a mini-vogue for body-disposal comedies. *Weekend at Bernie's* may be the most recognisable title, but this jet-black comedy is the funniest of the lot – that is, if you like your humour in bad taste and served as macabre as possible. The under-rated Elizabeth Perkins shines as the woman who accidentally kills her much-hated sister after being caught in bed with the latter's cop husband. How she tries to elude discovery and bury the body gives rise to some very rewarding slapstick and laughter-inducing grossness. Contains violence and swearing. ▣

Elizabeth Perkins *June* • Judge Reinhold *Harry* • Jeffrey Jones *Floyd* • Maureen Mueller *Enid Purley* • Rhea Perlman *Mavis* • Brion James *Trucker* • Charles Tyner *Man at Indian burial site* • Henry Jones *Old man* • Michael J Pollard *Hotel manager* ■ *Dir* Maurice Phillips • *Scr* AJ Tipping, James Whaley, Maurice Phillips

Over She Goes ★★★

Musical comedy   1937 · UK · BW · 77mins

One of the better films featuring British musical comedy star Stanley Lupino, father of actress/director Ida. This was a stage success for Stanley, and the film version manages to transfer all its unsubtleties intact. The hopelessly dated blackmail plot involves three girls quite literally falling for three men, one of whom is the likeable Lupino. To be fair, the girls – Claire Luce, Sally

Gray and Gina Malo – are lovely, but the triple wedding idea is daft.

John Wood *Lord Drewsden* • Claire Luce *Pamela* • Laddie Cliff *Billy Bowler* • Sally Gray *Kitty* • Stanley Lupino *Tommy Teacher* • Gina Malo *Dolly Jordan* • Judy Kelly *Alice Mayhill* • Max Baer *Silas Morner* • Syd Walker *Inspector Giffnock* • Richard Murdoch *Sergeant Oliver* ■ *Dir* Graham Cutts • *Scr* Elizabeth Meehan, Hugh Brooke, from the play *Over She Goes* by Stanley Lupino

Over the Brooklyn Bridge ★★★ 15

Romantic comedy
1983 · US · Colour · 101mins

Elliott Gould is the owner of a Brooklyn nosherie who dreams of running a big-time Manhattan restaurant and is in love with a Catholic girl, played by Margaux Hemingway. This romance irks Gould's traditional Jewish relatives, especially Uncle Benjamin, who makes ladies underwear for a living. Though it's set in the eighties, this is the kind of film that could have been made 50 years earlier. Shelley Winters does her usual schtick as a Jewish momma, but it's Sid Caesar as Uncle Benjamin who steals the show – a great movie comeback for the TV legend. ▣

Elliott Gould *Alby Sherman* • Margaux Hemingway *Elizabeth Anderson* • Sid Caesar *Uncle Benjamin* • Burt Young *Phil Romano* • Shelley Winters *Becky Sherman* • Carol Kane *Cheryl Goodman* ■ *Dir* Menahem Golan • *Scr* Arnold Somkin

Over the Edge ★★★★ 18

Drama   1979 · US · Colour · 90mins

Matt Dillon's first film – and a humdinger of a debut it is, too. Dillon plays a disaffected teenager in a sterile planned community that is more concerned with attracting big business than it is with providing amenities for its kids. Bored out of their skulls, and fuelled on drugs and drink, the kids start running riot and laying siege to the place. Jonathan Kaplan directs a genuinely powerful portrayal of alienated youth, with Dillon excellent in the causeless-rebel. Even the soundtrack is a stunner. ▣

Michael Kramer *Carl* • Pamela Ludwig *Cory* • Matt Dillon *Richie* • Vincent Spano *Mark* • Tom Fergus *Claude* • Harry Northup *Doberman* • Andy Romano *Fred Willat* • Ellen Geer *Sandra Willat* ■ *Dir* Jonathan Kaplan • *Scr* Charles Haas, Tim Hunter

Over the Hill ★★★ PG

Drama   1992 · Ausl · Colour · 97mins

A highly sentimental look at ageing, directed by the other Australian George Miller (not the one who directed *Mad Max* and produced *Babe*) in which Olympia Dukakis sets out on ''a journey of personal odyssey'' to prove to her selfish, chilly family that she is not, in fact, over the hill. Dukakis, an accomplished, always watchable actress, gives the rather hackneyed material a lift, and watch out for Bill Kerr and Derek Fowlds, who provide polished performances in supporting roles. A film that's more noble in intent than in execution. Contains swearing and brief nudity. ▣

Olympia Dukakis *Alma Harris* • Sigrid Thornton *Elizabeth* • Derek Fowlds *Dutch* • Bill Kerr *Maurio* • Steve Bisley *Benedict* • Martin

Jacobs *Alan Forbes* ■ *Dir* George Miller (1) • *Scr* Robert Caswell, from the book *Alone in the Australian Wilderness* by Gladys Taylor

Over the Moon ★★ U

Romantic comedy
1937 · UK · Colour · 75mins

This was one of two early Technicolor movies set up by Alexander Korda for Merle Oberon – the other was *The Divorce of Lady X* – and her frozen-faced acting does little for the role of a sudden heiress who is helped in squandering her money by Ursula Jeans among others. Rex Harrison, as a village doctor, doesn't help much, either, though it is interesting to see him in a non-cad role. There's usually a quaint charm about this sort of dated attempt at British sophistication, but it's not much in evidence here. This was only released two years after being made. ▣

Merle Oberon *June Benson* • Rex Harrison *Dr Freddie Jarvis* • Ursula Jeans *Lady Millie Parsmill* • Robert Douglas *John Flight* • Louis Borell *Count Pietro d'Altamura* • Zena Dare *Julie Deethorpe* • Peter Haddon *Lord Petcliffe* • Elisabeth Welch *Cabaret singer* ■ *Dir* Thornton Freeland • *Scr* Anthony Pelissier, Alec Coppel, Arthur Wimperis, from a story by Robert E Sherwood, from a story by Lajos Bíró • *Cinematographer* Harry Stradling, Robert Krasker

Over the Top ★★ PG

Drama   1987 · US · Colour · 89mins

Dating from the post-*Rambo* period when Sylvester Stallone's career was in the doldrums, this is a tacky action adventure with its roots in that old Wallace Beery classic *The Champ*. Here boxing is replaced by everybody's favourite spectator sport, arm wrestling, as trucker Sly tries to chill out his military academy-trained son on a make-up or break trek across the States. The grapple scenes are so devoid of thrills that you long to return to the mushy melodramatics. You expect more from a script co-written by Stallone and Stirling Silliphant, who won an Oscar for his work on *In the Heat of the Night*. Contains some violence and strong language. ▣

Sylvester Stallone *Lincoln Hawk* • Robert Loggia *Jason Cutler* • Susan Blakely *Christina Hawk* • Rick Zumwalt *Bob ''Bull'' Hurley* • David Mendenhall *Michael Cutler* • Chris McCarty *Tim Salanger* • Terry Funk *Ruker* ■ *Dir* Menahem Golan • *Scr* Stirling Silliphant, Sylvester Stallone, from a story by Gary Conway, David C Engelbach

Over 21 ★★

Second World War comedy
1945 · US · BW · 104mins

Successful writer Irene Dunne and her editor husband Alexander Knox move out of town, where the nearby army base attracts him to go for officer training. He leaves her to cope with wartime domestic difficulties, and his boss Charles Coburn to manage the newspaper without him. This adaptation of actress/writer Ruth Gordon's first play is kept afloat by Dunne's immaculate screen presence, Gordon's wit and Charles Vidor's sharp direction. Yet it remains essentially theatrical, Knox is dull, and the film hasn't much of interest to say.

Irene Dunne *Paula Wharton* • Alexander Knox *Max Wharton* • Charles Coburn *Robert Gow* • Jeff Donnell *Jan Lupton* • Loren Tindall *Roy Lupton* ■ *Dir* Charles Vidor • *Scr* Sidney Buchman, from the play by Ruth Gordon

Overboard ★★★★ PG

Romantic comedy
1987 · US · Colour · 107mins

A charming throwback to the screwball comedies of the thirties and one of the better vehicles designed for Goldie Hawn. She plays the pampered heiress to a fortune, who suffers amnesia after falling off her luxury yacht. Carpenter Kurt Russell, who had clashed with her earlier, sees the chance for revenge, and convinces her that she is his wife. There is a real chemistry between the two stars (a couple in real life), complemented by the performances of an experienced support cast that includes Katherine Helmond, Roddy McDowall and Edward Herrmann. The entire package is slickly directed by Garry Marshall, who juggles the sharp repartee and slapstick with ease.

Goldie Hawn *Joanna Stayton/Annie* • Kurt Russell *Dean Proffitt* • Edward Herrmann *Grant Stayton III* • Katherine Helmond *Edith Mintz* • Michael Hagerty [Michael G Hagerty] *Billy Pratt* • Roddy McDowall *Andrew* • Jared Rushton *Charlie* • Jeffrey Wiseman *Joey* ■ *Dir* Garry Marshall • *Scr* Leslie Dixon

Overdrive ★

Action thriller 1997 · US · Colour · 92mins

Executive-produced by Roger Corman, this missable action thriller has ex-*Police Academy* star Steve Guttenberg as a racing driver who gets into trouble when he becomes involved with betrayed secret agent Kaela Dobkin. It's rather dull for a film featuring racing cars, and Guttenberg is upstaged by veteran Robert Wagner, who manages to look cooler than his co-star. Contains swearing and violence.

Steve Guttenberg *Matt Stricker* • Robert Wagner *Freddie* • Kaela Dobkin *Wendy Sheehan* • Stephen Meadows *Cray* • Richard Arquette *Harding* ■ *Dir* Lev L Spiro • *Scr* Malcolm Stephens

Overexposed ★★★ 15

Drama 1992 · US · Colour · 89mins

Marcy Walker plays the wife who, thinking her husband is having an affair, is tricked into playing away from home herself in this drama that is short on originality but strong on star-quality performances. Walker is joined by Dan Lauria of TV's *The Wonder Years* as her husband, while *Tour of Duty's* Terence Knox is suitably sinister as the man who leads her astray. If you don't take it too seriously, this film (executive produced by Oprah Winfrey) is a fun diversion.

Marcy Walker *Ann Demski* • Dan Lauria *Norm Demski* • Jeri Lynn Ryan [Jeri Ryan] *Holly Evans* • Terence Knox *Nick Kasten* • Taylor Miller *Gayle Sabitt* • Rod Sell *Stan* • Howard Platt *King* • Mike Nussbaum *Bob Davis* ■ *Dir* Robert Markowitz • *Scr* Christine Berardo, Harlan Woods, Adam Greenman

Overkill: the Aileen Wuornos Story ★★★ 15

Crime drama 1992 · US · Colour · 93mins

A formulaic yet gripping true story that focuses on America's first female serial killer, Aileen Wuornos. Jean Smart is electrifying as the hooker who turns on her clients and there is also fine support from reliable character actor Brion James. Director Peter Levin, who was responsible for the equally controversial true story *Rape and Marriage: the Rideout Case*, works wonders within the made-for-TV format and manages to avoid the most sensationalistic aspects of the story. Contains swearing.

Jean Smart *Aileen Wuornos* • Park Overall *Tyria Moore* • Tim Grimm *Captain Steve Binegar* • Brion James *Bruce Munster* • Ernie Lively *Major Dan Henry* ■ *Dir* Peter Levin • *Scr* Fred Mills

Overland Stage Raiders ★★ U

Western 1938 · US · BW · 54mins

This up-to-date Republic B-western features hold-ups not of stagecoaches but of motor coaches. The gang then rob a plane carrying gold in mid-flight, handing the passengers parachutes and booting them out. Its plot is of serial-like simplicity but it's directed by George Sherman with positive vigour. John Wayne is the upright leader of the "Three Mesquiteers" and the luminous silent star Louise Brooks (in her very last film role) displays a relaxed radiance and good humour sparked in part by her appreciation of Wayne as "the hero of all mythology miraculously brought to life… a purely beautiful being".

John Wayne *Stony Brooke* • Louise Brooks *Beth Hoyt* • Ray Corrigan *Tuscon Smith* • Max Terhune *Lullaby Joslin* • Anthony Marsh *Ned Hoyt* • Gordon Hart *Mullins* • Roy James *Harmon* ■ *Dir* George Sherman • *Scr* Luci Ward, from a story by Bernard McConville, Edmond Kelso, from characters created by William Colt McDonald

The Overlanders ★★★ U

Second World War drama
1946 · UK · BW · 91mins

A very impressive re-creation of a spectacular event that took place in Australia during the Second World War the moving to safety of 500,000 head of cattle (reduced in the movie to a mere thousand), made necessary by the prospect of a Japanese invasion of the Northern Territory. This was one of Ealing's first Australian-made movies, and mightily effective it is under the direction of documentary film-maker Harry Watt. Trouble is, Watt also wrote the screenplay, and the clichés come thick and fast. Nevertheless, the action is very exciting, Australian lead Chips Rafferty is convincing, and the finale manages to be very moving.

Chips Rafferty *Dan McAlpine* • John Nugent Hayward *Bill Parsons* • Daphne Campbell *Mary Parsons* • Jean Blue *Mrs Parsons* • Helen Grieve *Helen Parsons* • John Fernside *Corky* ■ *Dir/Scr* Harry Watt

The Owl ★★

Crime drama 1991 · US · Colour

In this above-average pilot for a series that never saw the light of day, Adrian

Overlord ★★

Second World War drama
1975 · UK · BW · 82mins

Made with the co-operation of the Imperial War Museum, this account of the D-Day landings attempts to convey the grim reality of the soldier's lot by combining newsreel footage with dramatic re-enactments. Unfortunately, too much time was spent rooting out clips and not enough on the script, which is a collection of clichéd ideas and utterances. Director Stuart Cooper seems content to allow his cast to remain inanimate, while his presentation of the combat sequences comes dangerously close to suggesting war may be hell, but is also grotesquely beautiful. A bold venture, but poorly executed.

Brian Stirner *Tom* • Davyd Harries *Jack* • Nicholas Ball *Arthur* • Julie Neesam *Girl* ■ *Dir* Stuart Cooper • *Scr* Stuart Cooper, Christopher Hudson

Overnight Delivery ★★ 15

Romantic comedy
1997 · US · Colour · 84mins

With *Pleasantville*, *Cruel Intentions* and *Election*, Reese Witherspoon was on a roll. This could be regarded as one of her misfires, though it's an entertaining enough teen romp. Paul Rudd plays a frustrated student who drowns his sorrow with a stripper (Witherspoon) when he discovers that his virginal girlfriend is apparently stepping out with a jock. Having sent compromising "evidence" of his sexual prowess through the post to his girlfriend, he is horrified to discover that she has been with a dog rather than a fellow student. He and Witherspoon then have 24 hours to intercept the post. The two leads spark off each other quite nicely, but it's slight affair. Contains mild swearing and sexual references.

Reese Witherspoon *Ivy Miller* • Paul Rudd *Wyatt Trips* • Larry Drake *Hal Ipswich* • Christine Taylor *Kimberly* • Tobin Bell *John Dwayne Beezly* ■ *Dir* Jason Bloom • *Scr* Marc Sedaka, Steven L Bloom

Owd Bob ★★★ U

Drama 1938 · UK · BW · 75mins

Prepare to shed a tear at this shamelessly sentimental sheepdog drama set in the Lake District. The tale turns on the rift ageing shepherd Will Fyffe and his new neighbour, John Loder, when the latter's dog – the Owd Bob of the title – upstages Fyffe's prized Black Wull at the local trials. With flavoursome support coming from the likes of Moore Marriott and Graham Moffatt, there's barely room for Margaret Lockwood to make an impression as Loder's love interest.

Will Fyffe *Adam McAdam* • John Loder *David Moore* • Margaret Lockwood *Jeannie* • Graham Moffatt *Tammas* • Moore Marriott *Samuel* • Wilfred Walter *Thwaites* ■ *Dir* Robert Stevenson • *Scr* Michael Hogan, JB Williams, from the novel *Bob, Son of Battle* by Alfred Ollivant

Paul plays Alex L'Hiboux, a ruthless mercenary-cum-vigilante, also known as "the Owl" because of chronic insomnia brought on by a combination of a medical disorder and recurring nightmares of his wife and daughter's murder. When he's approached by a young girl to find her missing father, the standard revenge plot kicks in. If you don't take too many expectations, it should prove reasonably entertaining.

Adrian Paul *The Owl* • Patricia Charbonneau *Danny Santerre* • Brian Thompson *Norbert* • Erika Flores *Lisa* • Jacques Apollo Bolton *Cool Ice* • David Anthony Marshall *Bobby B* • Billy "Sly" Williams *Gullett* ■ *Dir* Allan Smithee [Tom Holland] • *Scr* Allan Smithee [Tom Holland], from the novel *The Owl* by Robert Forward

The Owl and the Pussycat ★★★ 15

Romantic comedy
1970 · US · Colour · 92mins

Barbra Streisand plays against type, as well as actually letting co-star George Segal get a word in edgeways, in this slick adaptation of Bill Manhoff's Broadway hit. She's an eccentric hooker who moves in with bookish neighbour Segal who had her evicted from her own flat in this Neil Simon-esque comedy. Director Herbert Ross and scriptwriter Buck Henry give the raucous original an extra glow of warmth and Streisand and Segal are so good together you wonder why they never did a sequel.

Barbra Streisand *Doris* • George Segal *Felix* • Robert Klein *Barney* • Allan Goorwitz [Allen Garfield] *Dress shop proprietor* • Roz Kelly *Eleanor* • Jacques Sandulescu *Rapzinsky* • Jack Manning *Mr Weyderhaus* • Grace Carney *Mrs Weyderhaus* • Barbara Anson *Ann Weyderhaus* ■ *Dir* Herbert Ross • *Scr* Buck Henry, from the play by Bill Manhoff

The Ox ★★★ 15

Period drama based on a true story
1991 · Swe · Colour · 88mins

Sven Nykvist, best known for his work as a cinematographer with Ingmar Bergman, here directs a heart-rending true-life drama set in 19th-century rural Sweden. Bergman regulars Liv Ullmann, Erland Josephson and Max von Sydow turn in polished support performances, but the action is carried by the excellent Stellan Skarsgård and Ewa Froling as the couple driven to desperate measures to survive a merciless famine. While Nykvist occasionally allows the pace to drop, he maintains an atmosphere worthy of his mentor and in the village dance creates a scene of great cinematic simplicity and power. In Swedish with English subtitles.

Stellan Skarsgård *Helge* • Ewa Froling *Elfrida* • Lennart Hjulstrom *Svenning* • Max von Sydow *Pastor* • Liv Ullmann *Maria* • Erland Josephson *Silver* ■ *Dir* Sven Nykvist • *Scr* Sven Nykvist, Lasse Summanen

The Ox-Bow Incident ★★★★★

Western drama 1943 · US · BW · 75mins

Here's claustrophobic bigotry in the western's wide-open spaces. William A Wellman directs this low-budget picture, which confronts the lynch-mob mentality head-on by revealing the characters who hang three innocent men for a rancher's alleged murder.

The lynchers include a woman (Jane Darwell) who's for the moral majority, and a sham major (Frank Conroy) who wants his son ''to be a man'', while Henry Fonda is the voice of reason. A mite preachy towards the end, but there's a savage tension throughout which makes it almost unbearable. Francis Ford, who plays the senile victim, was the brother of John Ford, who would have been proud.

Henry Fonda *Gil Carter* • Dana Andrews *Donald Martin* • Mary Beth Hughes *Rose Mapen* • Anthony Quinn *The Mexican* • William Eythe *Gerald Tetley* • Henry Morgan [Harry Morgan] *Art Croft* • Jane Darwell *Ma Grier* • Matt Briggs *Judge Daniel Tyler* • Francis Ford *''Dad'' Hardwick* ■ *Dir* William A Wellman • *Scr* Lamar Trotti, from the novel by Walter Van Tilburg Clark

Oxford Blues ★ 15

Drama 1984 · US · Colour · 93mins

It's easy to see why this brat-pack version of *A Yank at Oxford* was delayed for two years before being released in the UK. It's familiar teen territory all the way as Rob Lowe finances an Oxford education via gambling, but fails to impress titled debutante Amanda Pays. With the bias towards bland travelogue footage, a major point of interest is noting how many actors in the student bit parts have now become stars. Contains swearing. ▣

Rob Lowe *Nick Di Angelo* • Ally Sheedy *Rona* • Amanda Pays *Lady Victoria* • Julian Firth *Geordie* • Alan Howard *Simon* • Gail Strickland *Las Vegas Lady* • Michael Gough *Dr Ambrose* • Aubrey Morris *Dr Boggs* • Cary Elwes *Lionel* ■ *Dir/Scr* Robert Boris

Oxygen ★★★

Psychological crime thriller
1999 · US · Colour · 92mins

Adrien Brody is a psycho obsessed with the feats of Harry Houdini, so he kidnaps a millionaire's wife and buries her alive in the middle of the woods. Naturally he's caught, but as only he knows where the woman is buried, he plays a high-stakes game of cat and mouse with the police. Most of the time he psychologically tortures cop Maura Tierney, who has all kinds of problems of her own. Not particularly original, but at least this one doesn't wimp out at the climax.

Maura Tierney *Madeline* • Adrien Brody *Harry* • Terry Kinney *Tim* • Dylan Baker *Jackson* • Paul Calderon *Jessie* • James Naughton *Hannon* ■ *Dir/Scr* Richard Shepard

The Oyster Princess ★★★★

Silent romantic drama
1919 · Ger · BW · 65mins

Satirising Prussian militarism, American materialism and fadism, and snobbery in general, this was the first comedy that former slapstick clown Ernst Lubitsch felt demononstrated ''the Lubitsch touch'' of sly sophistication that would become his trademark. Combining visual opulence with narrative intricacy, the tale of the nouveau riche heiress and the impoverished prince, who are matchmade in the pursuit of dynastic and fiscal legitimacy, is packed with mistaken identities, unlikely developments and inspired resolutions. In short, it's a delight, with Ossi

Oswalda radiantly capricious in the title role and Victor Janson wonderfully debauched as her self-made father.

Ossi Oswalda *The Princess, daughter of the Oyster King* • Victor Janson *Quaker, the Oyster King* • Julius Falkenstein *Josef, servant of Nuki* • Harry Liedtke *Prince Nuki* ■ *Dir* Ernst Lubitsch • *Scr* Hans Kräly, Ernst Lubitsch • *Cinematographer* Theodor Sparkuhl

PK and the Kid ★★★

Drama 1982 · US · Colour · 90mins

Already bursting with potential, Molly Ringwald made her second screen appearance in this arm-wrestling melodrama, which languished on the shelf for five years before it was dusted down following the release of Sylvester Stallone's *Over the Top*. As in *Melvin and Howard*, Paul LeMat's decision to pick up a hitcher brings untold trouble, this time in the form of Alex Rocco, the abusive partner of runaway Ringwald's mom. It's tacky, teen wish-fulfilment, but director Lou Lombardo develops the unlikely friendship without prurient undertones, although he overdoes the arm-wrestling bouts that LeMat hopes will deliver him from the factory grind.

Paul LeMat *Kid Kane* • Molly Ringwald *PK Bayette* • Alex Rocco *Les* • Charles Hallahan *Bazooka* • John Di Santi *Benny* • Leigh Hamilton *Louise* • Esther Rolle *Mim* ■ *Dir* Lou Lombardo • *Scr* Neal Barbera

POW the Escape ★★ 15

War action adventure
1986 · US · Colour · 85mins

Yet another gung ho American Vietnam War movie that attempts to rewrite the history books while also apeing the *Rambo* movies. Shot in the Philippines, like so many of its type, it stars David Carradine, who plays a high-ranking Vietcong prisoner determined to lead his comrades to freedom in the last days before the fall of Saigon. Oriental-for-hire Mako plays the camp commandant as if he's been cast as Ming the Merciless. Director Gideon Amir brings an impressive physicality to the fistful of action sequences, but this is strictly second division war heroics. ▣

David Carradine *Colonel Jim Cooper* • Charles R Floyd *Sparks* • Mako *Captain Vinh* • Steve James *Jonston* • Phil Brock *Adams* ■ *Dir* Gideon Amir • *Scr* Jeremy Lipp, James Bruner, Malcolm Barbour, John Langley, from a story by Avi Kleinberger, Gideon Amir

PT 109 ★★★ U

Biographical Second World War drama
1963 · US · Colour · 134mins

During his war service, John F Kennedy's torpedo boat was blown in half by the Japanese. Towing a wounded shipmate for three miles by swimming with the wounded man's life belt clamped in his jaws, JFK landed on an uninhabited Pacific island and was rescued some days later. This folkloric story was a natural for Hollywood and Cliff Robertson makes a fine pre-president, though the build-up to the incident is rather slow. But as a piece of hero worship and political propaganda, released just after the

Cuban missile crisis, the movie is a fascinating relic from a less cynical age. ▣

Cliff Robertson *Lieutenant John F Kennedy* • Ty Hardin *Ensign Leonard J Thom* • James Gregory *Commander CR Ritchie* • Robert Culp *Ensign ''Barney'' Ross* • Grant Williams *Lieutenant Alvin Cluster* • Lew Gallo *Yeoman Rogers* • Errol John *Benjamin Kevu* • Michael Pate *Lieutenant Reginald Evans* • Robert Blake *''Bucky'' Harris* ■ *Dir* Leslie H Martinson • *Scr* Richard L Breen, Howard Sheehan, Vincent X Flaherty, from the non-fiction book *PT 109, John F Kennedy in World War II* by Robert J Donovan

Pacific Heights ★★★ 15

Thriller 1990 · US · Colour · 98mins

Michael Keaton enjoys himself immensely as the tenant from hell, turning the life of nice yuppie couple Matthew Modine and Melanie Griffith into a nightmare. It's a little hard to summon up much sympathy for a landlord, and it must be said that the story just gets sillier as the film progresses. However, director John Schlesinger is an old hand when it comes to this sort of thing and Keaton delivers a genuinely creepy performance. There is also strong support from Laurie Metcalf, and Griffith's mother Tippi Hedren has a minor role. Contains swearing, violence and nudity. ▣

Melanie Griffith *Patty Palmer* • Matthew Modine *Drake Goodman* • Michael Keaton *Carter Hayes* • Mako *Toshio Watanabe* • Nobu McCarthy *Mira Watanabe* • Laurie Metcalf *Stephanie MacDonald* • Carl Lumbly *Lou Baker* • Dorian Harewood *Dennis Reed* • Luca Bercovici *Greg* • Tippi Hedren *Florence Peters* ■ *Dir* John Schlesinger • *Scr* Daniel Pyne

Pacific Inferno ★ 15

Second World War adventure
1979 · US/Phil · Colour · 85mins

Bottom of the barrel Second World War action hokum produced by and starring Jim Brown as the leader of a team of captured American Navy divers. Brown and his men are forced by the Japanese to recover $16 million in silver pesos that General MacArthur ordered dumped in Manila Bay to avoid them falling into enemy hands. Shot in 1977 on location in the Philippines, it didn't see daylight until a belated video release in the mid-eighties. And it's not difficult to see why, as this is desperate stuff indeed. ▣

Jim Brown *Clyde Preston* • Richard Jaeckel *Dealer* • Tim Brown [Timothy Brown] *Zoe* • Tad Horino *Yamada* • Dindo Fernando *Totoy* • Wilma Reading *Tita* • Rik Van Nutter *Dennis* ■ *Dir/Scr* Rolf Bayer

The Pack ★★★ 15

Horror 1977 · US · Colour · 94mins

Snarlingly effective horror movie in which marine biologist Joe Don Baker is sent in to stop a bunch of ferocious dogs tearing and ravaging holidaymakers on a remote island. Although the idea is drawn from Alfred Hitchcock's *The Birds*, this film doesn't have the same terrifying sense of nature arbitrarily fighting back, but it comes across as an intriguing adventure nonetheless. Director Robert Clouse brings the same kind of energy

U = SUITABLE FOR ALL   Uc = SUITABLE FOR ALL, ESPECIALLY FOR YOUNG CHILDREN (VIDEO ONLY)   PG = PARENTAL GUIDANCE

to the canine castaways that he did to his kung fu movies. 🎬

Joe Don Baker *Jerry* • Hope Alexander-Willis *Millie* • Richard B Shull *Hardiman* • RG Armstrong *Cobb* • Ned Wertimer *Walker* • Bibi Besch *Marge* • Delos V Smith Jr *McMinnimee* • Richard O'Brien *Dodge* ■ *Dir* Robert Clouse • *Scr* Robert Clouse, from a novel by Dave Fisher

Pack of Lies ★★★ 🅿🅶

Drama 1987 · US · Colour · 100mins

Ellen Burstyn heads an impressive cast in this TV drama based on the play by Hugh Whitemore. Loosely based on a true story, the tale is set in London in the sixties, when a couple allow British Intelligence agents to use their home to spy on their Canadian neighbours who are suspected of being KGB agents. Interesting stuff, especially for paranoiacs, helped by the performances of Burstyn, Teri Garr, Alan Bates and Ronald Hines. 🎬

Ellen Burstyn *Barbara Jackson* • Teri Garr *Helen Schaefer* • Alan Bates *Stewart* • Ronald Hines *Bob Jackson* • Daniel Benzali *Peter Schaefer* • Sammi Davis *Julie Jackson* ■ *Dir* Anthony Page • *Scr* Ralph Gallup, from the play by Hugh Whitemore

Pack Up Your Troubles
★★★★★ 🆄
Comedy 1932 · US · BW · 64mins

Seldom seen intact since it was made, this Laurel and Hardy delight has gone through the mincing machine of distributors' cuts but still remains one of their best movies for producer Hal Roach. After a disastrous wartime service, Stan and Ollie try to keep their promise to a dying buddy that they would look after his little girl (Jacquie Lyn). The usual L and H ins-and-outs follow as they try to reunite her with her grandparents. It touches the nerves of comedy and pathos with just the right amount of pressure and also has a vivid portrayal of a revenge-crazed army cook by George Marshall, the film's co-director. 🎬

Stan Laurel *Stan* • Oliver Hardy *Ollie* • Tom Kennedy *Recruiting sergeant* • Jacquie Lyn *Eddie's baby* • Grady Sutton *Eddie, the silly groom* • Donald Dillaway *The boys' nephew, Eddie Smith* • Mary Carr *Woman who delivers Nan's letters to Eddie* • Billy Gilbert *Mr Hathaway, nearly nervous father of the bride* • James Finlayson *The general* ■ *Dir* George Marshall, Raymond McCarey • *Scr* HM Walker

Pack Up Your Troubles
★★★ 🆄
Comedy 1939 · US · BW · 75mins

Produced by Sol M Wurtzel, who headed Fox's B-movie division, this is a very funny vehicle for the comedy team the Ritz Brothers, even though Harry was heard to say after the premiere, ''Boys, we've gone from bad to Wurtzel.'' Jane Withers, the child star who memorably bullied Shirley Temple in *Bright Eyes*, here makes a successful transition to adolescent actress. The brothers play First World War soldiers mistaken for the enemy who escape in a balloon and find themselves actually in Germany. The team are an acquired taste but this is one of their best.

Al Ritz • Jimmy Ritz *Jim Ritz* • Harry Ritz • Jane Withers *Colette* • Lynn Bari *Yvonne* •

Joseph Schildkraut *Hugo Ludwig* • Stanley Fields *Sergeant ''Angel Face'' Walker* • Fritz Leiber *Pierre Ferrand* • Dir H Bruce Humberstone • *Scr* Lou Breslow, Owen Francis, from their story

The Package ★★ 🄵

Political thriller 1989 · US · Colour · 103mins

Despite a lookalike President Gorbachev and Gene Hackman acting as though back on *The French Connection*, this post-Cold War thriller comes apart like a package damaged in the post. In fact, ''the package'' is Tommy Lee Jones, whom sergeant Hackman has to escort to America from Berlin, but the complications and coincidences are so formidable that not even the participants seem to know what's going on. Director Andrew Davis is used to working with action men such as Chuck Norris and Steven Seagal, so perhaps working with Hackman went to his head. Contains swearing. 🎬 **DVD**

Gene Hackman *Sergeant Johnny Gallagher* • Tommy Lee Jones *Thomas Boyette* • Joanna Cassidy *Lieutenant Colonel Eileen Gallagher* • John Heard *Colonel Glen Whitacre* • Kevin Crowley *Walter Henke* • Chelcie Ross *General Thomas Hopkins* • Joe Greco *General Robert Carlson* • Dennis Franz *Milan Delich* • Pam Grier *Ruth Butler* ■ *Dir* Andrew Davis • *Scr* John Bishop, from a story by Dennis Haggerty, John Bishop

Packin' It In ★★

Drama 1983 · US · Colour · 92mins

Richard Benjamin here stars with his real-life wife Paula Prentiss. They play a couple who decide to leave the rat race behind and move their family to the great outdoors. Yes, it's *Lost in America* crossed with *The Adventures of the Wilderness Family*, but twice as predictable and half as funny. Perhaps Benjamin should continue to stay behind the camera.

Richard Benjamin *Gary Webber* • Paula Prentiss *Diana Webber* • Tony Roberts *Charlie Baumgarten* • Andrea Marcovicci *Rita Baumgarten* • Molly Ringwald *Melissa Webber* ■ *Dir* Jud Taylor • *Scr* Patricia Jones, Donald Reiker

Paco ★★

Comedy adventure
1975 · Col · Colour · 100mins

Puerto Rican-born José Ferrer is the star of this Colombian kidpic, a crime adventure in which eager kids lock horns with pantomimic villains. Combining Dickensian melodrama with a somewhat romanticised view of urban street poverty, Robert Vincent O'Neil's film will seem old-fashioned to modern youngsters, in spite of a willing performance from Panchito Gómez, as the orphan who is forced to leave the family farm and head for the big city, where he discovers that his uncle is the Fagin-like brains behind a juvenile jewellery racket.

JoséFerrer *Fermin Flores* • Allen Garfield *Padre* • Inês Elvira Cortês *Susana* • Panchito Gómez *Paco* ■ *Dir* Robert Vincent O'Neil • *Scr* Andrew Davis, Andre Marquis, Robert Vincent O'Neil

The Pad (and How to Use It) ★★

Comedy 1966 · US · Colour · 85mins

In days of yore, ''the pad'' is what student types called their bedsits, flats or apartments. In this relic from the sixties, based on a play by Peter Shaffer, shy, virginal Brian Bedford shares his bedsit with his hi-fi gear and really loves his music. Then he meet the smashing Julie Sommars and asks his lothario friend for advice on how to romance her. Less innovative than Richard Lester's iconic *The Knack... and How to Get It* but barking up the same tree, this is probably now way beyond being merely dated and more in the realms of the historical comedy. The soundtrack features the Knickbockers. Groovy!

Brian Bedford *Bob Handman* • Julie Sommars *Doreen Marshall* • James Farentino *Ted* • Edy Williams *Lavinia* ■ *Dir* Brian G Hutton • *Scr* Thomas C Ryan, Ben Starr, from the play *The Private Ear* by Peter Shaffer

Padre Nuestro ★★

Comedy drama 1985 · Sp · Colour · 104mins

Francisco Regueiro aspired to Buñuelian heights with this seedy study of the shameless hypocrisy of those adhering to Catholicism and Marxism. But there's little of the master in this overblown melodrama, which its star, Fernando Rey (a four-time Buñuel collaborator), opted to omit from his official filmography. Ignoring a papal appeal, the dying Cardinal Rey leaves the Vatican for the first time in 30 years to settle the affairs of his family's vineyard, in spite of the interference of his atheist doctor brother, Francisco Rabal, his illegitimate, prostitute daughter, Victoria Abril, and the grandchild he never knew he had. A Spanish language film.

Fernando Rey *Cardinal* • Francisco Rabal *Abel* • Victoria Abril *Cardenala* • Emma Penella *Maria* • Amelia de la Torre *Valentina* • Rafaela Aparicio *Jerónima* • Lina Canalejas *Blanca* • Jose Vivo *El Papa* ■ *Dir* Francisco Regueiro • *Scr* Francisco Regueiro, Angel Fernandez Santos

Padre Padrone ★★★★ 🄵

Drama 1977 · It · Colour · 108mins

Brothers Paolo and Vittorio Taviani had their first international success with this portrayal of primitive patriarchal Sardinian life in the late forties after the film won the Palme d'Or at Cannes. Based on a true story, it tells of how a peasant father sends his small son to the mountains to look after the sheep all by himself for years. Deprived of company and language, the young man struggles to adapt when he re-enters society. Perhaps if the sibling directors had approached the tale in a more sober and detached manner, the film might have been even more moving. But it remains a fascinating subject and many of the pastoral images are stunning. In Italian with English subtitles. 🎬

Omero Antonutti *Efisio Ledda, Gavino's father* • Saverio Marconi *Gavino Ledda* • Marcella Michelangeli *Gavino's mother* ■ *Dir* Paolo Taviani, Vittorio Taviani • *Scr* Paolo Taviani,

Vittorio Taviani, from the autobiographical novel *Padre Padrone: l'Educazione di un Pastore* by Gavino Ledda

Page Miss Glory ★★ 🆄

Comedy 1935 · US · BW · 94mins

Promoter Pat O'Brien, something of a chancer, sends in a composite photograph of a girl for a beauty contest, wins, and then has to find a real girl to live up to the illustrated ideal. She comes along in the shape of Marion Davies, starring in the first of four pictures at Warner Bros under a deal made by her lover, William Randolph Hearst, for his Cosmopolitan Pictures. Mervyn LeRoy directed what is a pleasing if oh-so-lightweight comedy in which Davies, a better comedian than straight actress, is fine, propped up by familiar who include Dick Powell and Mary Astor.

Marion Davies *Loretta Dalrymple/''Dawn Glory''* • Pat O'Brien *Dan ''Click'' Wiley* • Dick Powell *Bingo Nelson* • Mary Astor *Gladys Russell* • Frank McHugh *Ed Olsen* ■ *Dir* Mervyn LeRoy • *Scr* Delmer Daves, Robert Lord, from the play by Joseph Schrank, Philip Dunning

A Page of Madness ★★★★★

Silent melodrama 1926 · Jap · BW · 60mins

Director Teinosuke Kinugasa, who made his name with a series of samurai movies, came across this lost silent masterpiece in his storeroom in the early seventies, and released it with a music soundtrack. Relying on its eloquent images without the need for intertitles, the film tells of how an elderly man, working in a mental hospital where his wife is confined, hopes to set her free. Kinugasa, who would study with Sergei Eisenstein after this film, displays a remarkable range of cinematic techniques to give the impression of madness, in between the sane flashbacks to the wife's pre-asylum days. Acted brilliantly by an avant-garde theatre group, the film is closer to German Expressionism than any Japanese tradition of film-making.

Masao Inoue *Custodian* • Yoshie Nakagawa *Wife* • Ayako Iijima *Daughter* ■ *Dir* Teinosuke Kinugasa • *Scr* Yasunari Kawabata, Teinosuke Kinugasa • *Cinematographer* Kohei Sugiyama

The Pagemaster ★★★ 🆄

Adventure 1994 · US · Colour · 72mins

Macaulay Culkin takes refuge in a library during a thunderstorm, turns into a two-dimensional cartoon (no comment!) and is transported into an animated world where classic literature comes to life, in this so-so merging of *The Wizard of Oz* with *The Neverending Story*. Although the homilies ''There's no place like home'' and ''Books are worth reading'' are repeated continuously, the dull story and crude animation sabotage any well-intentioned message. None of the segments show any real imagination or artistry, and the incredible Culk always takes centre stage. Young children may enjoy it, but not even the voices of Whoopi Goldberg and Leonard Nimoy can put this on the bestseller list.

Macaulay Culkin *Richard Tyler* • Ed Begley Jr *Alan Tyler* • Mel Harris *Claire Tyler* •

Christopher Lloyd *Mr Dewey/Pagemaster* • Patrick Stewart *Adventure* • Whoopi Goldberg *Fantasy* • Frank Welker *Horror* • Leonard Nimoy *Dr Jekyll/Mr Hyde* ■ *Dir* Joe Johnston, Maurice Hunt • *Scr* David Casci, David Kirschner, Ernie Contreras, from a story by David Casci, David Kirschner

Pagliacci ★★

Musical 1936 · UK · BW and Colour · 92mins

While known for his glossy visuals, the Austrian director Karl Grune never really came to terms with sound (making him a rather odd choice for a musical) and this clumsy adaptation of Ruggiero Leoncavallo's masterpiece was to be his final film. His fellow countryman Richard Tauber gives a solid rendition of the insanely jealous Canio, while Steffi Duna makes a spirited Nedda. Grune is not the only film-maker to be confounded by opera, but he is the most pedestrian.

Richard Tauber *Canio Tonini* • Steffi Duna *Nedda Tonini* • Diana Napier *Trina* • Arthur Margetson *Tonio* • Esmond Knight *Silvio* ■ *Dir* Karl Grune • *Scr* Monckton Hoffe, John Drinkwater, Roger Burford, Ernest Betts, from the opera *I Pagliacci* by Ruggiero Leoncavallo

Pagliacci ★★★

Opera 1948 · It · BW · 80mins

Fresh from completing his version of *Don Giovanni*, Mario Costa embarked on this Calabrian-set adaptation of Ruggiero Leoncavallo's one-act opera about the lachrymose clown whose act of charity towards a homeless waif is repaid by treachery and heartache. Although the star of the show is, nominally, the celebrated baritone, Tito Gobbi, Costa was more interested in showcasing the talents of his "discovery", Gina Lollobrigida, who had already appeared in his earlier outing, *Mad about Opera*. Even though her singing voice was dubbed, "La Lollo" made sufficient impression to be prised away from her mentor by Lux Films, where stardom beckoned. An Italian language film.

Tito Gobbi *Tonio/Silvio* • Gina Lollobrigida *Nedda* • Onelia Fineschi *Nedda (singing voice)* • Afro Poli *Canio* • Galliano Masini *Canio* ■ *Dir* Mario Costa • *Scr* from the opera by Ruggiero Leoncavallo

A Pain in the A...! ★★★★

Comedy crime drama
1973 · Fr/It · Colour · 84mins

A very funny ebony-hued comedy with Lino Ventura as the hit man trying to carry out a murder contract, who's constantly hindered by the suicidal Jacques Brel. The contrast between the implacable Ventura and Brel's walking nervous breakdown is a constant source of laughs. Edouard Molinaro directs this adaptation of Francis Veber's stage success, later remade by Billy Wilder as *Buddy Buddy*. This is the original and the best version. A French language film.

Jacques Brel *Pignon* • Lino Ventura *Ralph* • Caroline Cellier *Louise* • Nino Castelnuovo *Bellhop* • Jean-Pierre Darras *Fuchs* ■ *Dir* Edouard Molinaro • *Scr* Edouard Molinaro, Francis Veber, from the play *Le Contrat* by Francis Veber • *Music* Jacques Brel • *Cinematographer* Raoul Coutard

Paint It Black ★★★ 18

Thriller 1989 · US · Colour · 96mins

A strange little psychodrama from Tim Hunter, the director who'd burst so promisingly on the independent movie scene two years earlier with quirky teen-murder tale *River's Edge*. *Paint It Black* isn't quite in the same class, but it's impressive enough, with a strong performance from Rick Rossovich as an up-and-coming sculptor who's artistically and emotionally tied to unscrupulous art gallery owner Sally Kirkland. Things get a little weird when he also falls under the influence of an oddball art collector. 🔲

Sally Kirkland *Marion Easton* • Rick Rossovich *Jonathan Dunbar* • Doug Savant *Eric* • Julie Carmen *Gina Hayworth* • Martin Landau *Daniel Lambert* • Jason Bernard *Lt Wilder* ■ *Dir* Tim Hunter • *Scr* AH Zacharias [Timothy Harris], Michael Drexier [Herschel Weingrod]

Paint Your Wagon ★★★ PG

Musical comedy western
1969 · US · Colour · 153mins

Alan Jay Lerner invented a new "adult" plot, quite unnecessarily, for this screen version of his own Broadway show, in which Lee Marvin and Clint Eastwood share Jean Seberg in a *ménage à trois*. Joshua Logan directs with the heaviest of hands, and only Harve Presnell as Rotten Luck Willie emerges with credit, but then he does have all the best songs, even though Marvin topped the UK charts with *Wandrin' Star*. Clint uses his own singing voice charmingly, too, and there's some of the finest chorale work (directed by Roger Wagner) ever heard in a film musical. This overlong screen adaptation almost works. 🔲

Lee Marvin *Ben Rumson* • Clint Eastwood *Pardner* • Jean Seberg *Elizabeth* • Harve Presnell *Rotten Luck Willie* • Ray Walston *Mad Jack Duncan* • Tom Ligon *Horton Fenty* • Alan Dexter *Parson* • William O'Connell *Horace Tabor* ■ *Dir* Joshua Logan • *Scr* Alan Jay Lerner, Paddy Chayefsky, from the musical play by Alan Jay Lerner, Frederick Loewe • *Cinematographer* William A Fraker

Painted Angels ★★ 15

Western drama
1997 · Can/UK · Colour · 109mins

Brenda Fricker and Kelly McGillis star in this tedious western about a prairie-town bordello in the 1870s, the whores who work there and the pragmatic madam who runs the place. The use of period lighting gives the film a murky, washed-out look, while director Jon Sanders taxes the patience with lengthy static takes where people just sit around, saying nothing and doing even less. There's potential in a drama about the Wild West's women; this, though, is like watching painted angels dry. Contains swearing and a sex scene.

Brenda Fricker *Annie Ryan* • Kelly McGillis *Nettie* • Meret Becker *Katya* • Bronagh Gallagher *Eileen* • Lisa Jakub *Georgie* • Anna Mottram *Ada* ■ *Dir* Jon Sanders • *Scr* Anna Mottram, Jon Sanders

The Painted Desert ★★ U

Western 1931 · US · BW · 83mins

A western about two miners whose discovery of a six-month-old baby in the wilderness results in a long and bitter feud. Doubtless very creaky by modern standards, well worth seeing for its cast. The heroine is played by Helen Twelvetrees, a beautiful New York-born actress whose career collapsed in 1938. The hero is played by William Boyd, four years before he hit paydirt as Hopalong Cassidy. And then there's a certain Mr Clark Gable, in the supporting cast, playing his first speaking role.

Bill Boyd [William Boyd] *Bill Holbrook* • Helen Twelvetrees *Mary Ellen Cameron* • William Farnum *Cash Holbrook* • J Farrell MacDonald *Jeff Cameron* • Clark Gable *Rance Brett* ■ *Dir* Howard Higgin • *Scr* Howard Higgin, Tom Buckingham

Painted Desert ★

Western 1938 · US · BW · 58mins

George O'Brien was the star of two of the most famous silent movies ever made – John Ford's *The Iron Horse* and Murnau's *Sunrise* – but here he's slumming in a B-minus western. The plot is about a land deal and crams in the expected gunfights and chases, as well as three musical numbers performed by singing cowboy Ray Whitley, before the hour is up.

George O'Brien *Bob McVey* • Laraine Johnson [Laraine Day] *Carol Banning* • Ray Whitley *Steve* • Fred Kohler *Fawcett* • Maude Allen *Yukon Kate* ■ *Dir* David Howard • *Scr* John Rathmell, Oliver Drake, from a story by Jack Cunningham

Painted Heart ★★ 15

Thriller 1992 · US · Colour · 86mins

A complex thriller about a woman in love with two men. One's the painter next door, the other's her hubby, the painter's boss. Torn apart emotionally, she finds she could also wind up torn apart physically, because one of the men is a serial killer. The plot actually plays better than it reads, with the quality cast of Will Patton, Bebe Neuwirth and Robert Pastorelli creating credence out of confusion. 🔲

Will Patton *Wesley* • Bebe Neuwirth *Margaret* • Robert Pastorelli *Willie* • Casey Siemaszko *Cal* ■ *Dir/Scr* Michael Taav

The Painted Smile ★

Crime drama 1961 · UK · BW · 61mins

This dreadfully dull British B movie makes its brief running time seem like an eternity. From the moment that Liz Fraser's partner-in-crime is murdered, fugitive Kenneth Griffith tries desperately to avoid the finger of suspicion pointing at him. The cast members do what they can with the script, but they clearly received little encouragement from director Lance Comfort.

Liz Fraser *Jo Lake* • Kenneth Griffith *Kleinie* • Peter Reynolds *Mark Davies* • Tony Wickert *Tom* • Craig Douglas *Nightclub Singer* • Nanette Newman *Mary* • Ray Smith *Glynn* • David Hemmings *Roy* ■ *Dir* Lance Comfort • *Scr* Pip Baker, Jane Baker, from an idea by Brock Williams

The Painted Veil ★★★

Drama 1934 · US · BW · 84mins

Greta Garbo, the newlywed wife of doctor Herbert Marshall, accompanies her husband to China, where his work leads to his frequent absence, and his absence to her affair with married diplomat George Brent. Several dramatic upheavals later, including a cholera epidemic, all ends happily. Unadulterated melodramatic hokum, glitzed up with Cedric Gibbons's oriental sets, Adrian's costumes and William H Daniels's photography, and given committed direction by Richard Boleslawski, the movie offers Garbo at her loveliest in her familiar "noble suffering" mode.

Greta Garbo *Katherine Koerber Fane* • Herbert Marshall *Dr Walter Fane* • George Brent *Jack Townsend* • Warner Oland *General Yu* • Jean Hersholt *Prof Koerber* • Beulah Bondi *Frau Koerber* • Katherine Alexander *Mrs Townsend* • Cecilia Parker *Olga* ■ *Dir* Richard Boleslawski • *Scr* John Meehan, Salka Viertel, Edith Fitzgerald, from the novel by W Somerset Maugham • *Cinematographer* William H Daniels [William Daniels]

Painting the Clouds with Sunshine ★★★ U

Musical 1951 · US · Colour · 86mins

Here Warner Bros reworked its highly successful *Gold Diggers* format, updated to take in Las Vegas and dressed in glowing fifties' Technicolor. Nothing to shout about, but this pleasant film does feature a cast of bright young performers (bland top-billed Dennis Morgan is the exception) entertaining us with recognisable songs and dances in glamorous settings. Worth watching for hoofer Gene Nelson – best known today for his "Kansas City" routine in *Oklahoma!* – alone, but keep an eye out for George Sanders's brother, the suave Tom Conway.

Dennis Morgan *Vince Nichols* • Virginia Mayo *Carol* • Gene Nelson *Ted Lansing* • Lucille Norman *Abby* • Tom Conway *Bennington* ■ *Dir* David Butler • *Scr* Harry Clark, Roland Kibbee, Peter Milne, from the play *Gold Diggers of Broadway* by Avery Hopward

Pair of Aces ★★ 15

Western 1990 · US · Colour · 93mins

A tolerable modern-day western, in which Willie Nelson and Kris Kristofferson are thrown together in the search for a killer on the loose. Nelson's safecracker is supposed to be a loveable rogue in the mould of Walter Brennan, but he simply hasn't the finesse to carry it off. Kristofferson (who also started out as a singer) is much more at home as the gruff Texas Ranger, and there are capable support performances from Rip Torn and Helen Shaver. 🔲

Willie Nelson *Billy Roy Barker* • Kris Kristofferson *Rip Metcalf* • Rip Torn *Captain Jack Parsons* • Helen Shaver *Rose* ■ *Dir* Aaron Lipstadt • *Scr* Bud Shrake, Gary Cartwright

A Pair of Briefs ★★

Comedy 1961 · UK · BW · 90mins

This tepid comedy falls flat for the simple reason that feuding barristers Michael Craig and Mary Peach just don't click. They were clearly supposed to be reproducing the sparks created by Spencer Tracy and Katharine Hepburn as the husband-and-wife lawyers in the similarly themed *Adam's Rib*. Yet not only is the romantic banter

U = SUITABLE FOR ALL, Uc = SUITABLE FOR ALL, ESPECIALLY FOR YOUNG CHILDREN (VIDEO ONLY), PG = PARENTAL GUIDANCE

very poor, but there is also none of the knowing courtroom comedy that made the Boulting brothers' *Brothers in Law* so enjoyable. James Robertson-Justice contributes some typically bullish support, but thanks to the highly suspect leads the jury can only bring in a ''Not Funny'' verdict.

Michael Craig *Tony Stevens* • Mary Peach *Frances Pilbright* • Brenda de Banzie *Gladys Pudney* • James Robertson-Justice *Justice Hadden* • Roland Culver *Sir John Pilbright* • Liz Fraser *Pearly Girl* • Ron Moody *Sid Pudney* • Jameson Clark *George Lockwood* ■ *Dir* Ralph Thomas • *Scr* Nicholas Phipps, from the play *How Say You?* by Harold Brooke, Kay Bannerman

Paisà ★★★ PG
Second World War drama
1946 · It · BW · 120mins

Following *Rome, Open City*, Roberto Rossellini moved on from the dramas of resistance workers to the Allied invasion of Sicily to the declaration of victory. The film, using entirely unknown and largely non-professional actors, focuses on a series of individual encounters – one between a black American soldier and an Italian urchin, for example – as well as showing the arrest and execution of partisans. Not as good as its predecessor, but the documentary style and flavour make for a realistic, involving, and significant film, despite some awkwardness of dialogue and performance. In Italian with English subtitles. ▭

Carmela Sazio *Carmela* • Robert Van Loon *Joe* • Alfonsino Pasca *Boy* • Harriet White *Harriet* • Dots Johnson *MP* • William Tubbs *Capt Bill Martin* ■ *Dir* Roberto Rossellini • *Scr* Sergio Amidei, Federico Fellini, Roberto Rossellini, Annalena Limentani (English dialogue), from a story by Klaus Mann

The Pajama Game ★★★★ U
Musical   1957 · US · Colour · 96mins

Workers' demands for a seven-and-a-half per cent pay rise in a pajama factory is the unlikely subject for this bouncy, infectious musical. However, it provided an exuberant Doris Day with several terrific songs and one of her best roles as the head of the workers' grievance committee who falls in love with the foreman (John Raitt). Co-directors Stanley Donen and George Abbott demonstrated that it was possible to remain true to a stage original, in this case the Broadway hit, while using creative camerawork and editing. A good example is the *Once-a Year-Day* number, enhanced by Bob Fosse's robust and witty choreography, in which the worker-dancers cavort at a picnic. ▭

Doris Day *Katie ''Babe'' Williams* • John Raitt *Sid Sorokin* • Carol Haney *Gladys Hotchkiss* • Eddie Foy Jr *Vernon Hines* • Reta Shaw *Mabel Mae* • Barbara Nichols *Poopsie* • Thelma Pelish *Mae* • Jack Straw *Prez* ■ *Dir* George Abbott, Stanley Donen • *Scr* George Abbott, Richard Bissell, from their musical, from the novel *Seven and a Half Cents* by Richard Bissell • *Music/Lyrics* Richard Adler, Jerry Ross • *Choreographer* Bob Fosse

Pajama Party ★ U
Comedy   1964 · US · Colour · 84mins

One of those terribly kitsch movies so rooted in sixties Californian beach

parties that it erupts into hilarious entertainment. This is part of a teen culture series which began with *Beach Party* and was slowly strangled to death by awful scripts. In this one, ''star'' Tommy Kirk plays a Martian who drops in on the high jinks with suitably nonplussed results. It is meant to be gently amusing but is unintentionally gut-wrenchingly funny, despite the presence of such greats as Buster Keaton and Dorothy Lamour.

Tommy Kirk *Go-Go* • Annette Funicello *Connie* • Elsa Lanchester *Aunt Wendy* • Harvey Lembeck *Eric Von Zipper* • Jesse White *J Sinister Hulk* • Buster Keaton *Chief Rotten Eagle* • Dorothy Lamour *Head saleslady* • Don Rickles • Frankie Avalon ■ *Dir* Don Weis • *Scr* Louis M Heyward

Pakeezah ★★★★ PG
Romantic drama
1971 · Ind · Colour · 145mins

Determined to showcase the talents of his alcoholic wife, Meena Kumari (who died shortly after the picture wrapped), director Kamal Amrohi finally made this project some 13 years after he came up with its concept. Production started in 1964, but marital strife, money problems and Kumari's precarious health prevented the completion of this richly coloured, romantic period melodrama, which became an instant box-office hit. As both the abused courtesan rejected by her husband's snobbish Lucknow family and the daughter kept from her father and her beloved, the doe-eyed Kumari gives a career-best performance that makes her hopeless plight all the more distressing. In Urdu with English subtitles. ▭

Ashok Kumar *Shahab* • Meena Kumari *Sahebjaan* • Raaj Kumar *Salam Ahmed Khan* ■ *Dir/Scr* Kamal Amrohi

Pal Joey ★★★ PG
Musical comedy 1957 · US · Colour · 104mins

Frank Sinatra's Exocet delivery of some great Richard Rodgers/Lorenz Hart songs, which include *The Lady Is a Tramp* and *My Funny Valentine*, more than makes up for the whitewash here of the black-hearted hero from the stage version. Joey is now a crooner, not a hoofer as on stage, and his rapacious greed for bed (on the make for fading star Rita Hayworth, but really loving Kim Novak) and bright lights has been toned down to give it a happy ending that has nothing to do with being bewitched, bothered and bewildered. The heel proves to have a soul, which is rather a pity as novelist John O'Hara's original Broadway exposé deserved a more sarcastic treatment. ▭

Rita Hayworth *Vera Simpson* • Frank Sinatra *Joey Evans* • Kim Novak *Linda English* • Barbara Nichols *Gladys* • Bobby Sherwood *Ned Galvin* • Hank Henry *Mike Miggins* • Elizabeth Patterson *Mrs Casey* ■ *Dir* George Sidney • *Scr* Dorothy Kingsley, from the musical play by John O'Hara, Richard Rodgers, Lorenz Hart, from stories in the New Yorker, magazine by John O'Hara

Palais Royale ★★ 15
Crime comedy drama
1988 · Can · Colour · 87mins

The gangster movie gets a Canadian spin in this Toronto-shot *film noir*, set

in the late fifties, and starring Matt Craven as an adman whose unbridled ambition embroils him in a world of gunmen and goons. Dean Stockwell and Kim Cattrall provide sturdy support. But there's nothing really to distinguish this formulaic flick from a hundred other Canadian thrillers. ▭

Kim Cattrall *Odessa* • Matt Craven *Gerald* • Kim Coates *Tony* • Dean Stockwell *Dattalico* • Brian George *Gus* • Michael Hogan *Sergeant Leonard* ■ *Dir* Martin Lavut • *Scr* Hugh Graham, David Daniels, Zachary Zack, Jo Ann McIntyre

Pale Rider ★★ 15
Western   1985 · US · Colour · 110mins

A huge disappointment from director and star Clint Eastwood, virtually a reworking of the classic western *Shane*, but filmed in such a welter of underlit interiors and riddled with ridiculously complicated attempts to be simultaneously mystical and mythical that it really doesn't succeed at any level. As the Preacher, Eastwood relies too much on his own iconic image, but without the resonances he brought to his two classics, *The Outlaw Josey Wales* and the magnificent *Unforgiven*. Slow and violent as well as dull, this is really for die-hard Eastwood fans only. Contains swearing. ▭ **DVD**

Clint Eastwood *Preacher* • Michael Moriarty *Hull Barret* • Carrie Snodgress *Sarah Wheeler* • Christopher Penn *Josh Lahood* • Richard Dysart *Coy Lahood* • Sydney Penny *Megan Wheeler* • Richard Kiel *Club* • Doug McGrath *Spider Conway* ■ *Dir* Clint Eastwood • *Scr* Michael Butler, Dennis Shryack

The Paleface ★★★★★ U
Silent comedy   1921 · US · Colour · 20mins

Although Buster Keaton's movie is in a comedy class of its own, containing gags that have survived through the years. In his quest to catch butterflies, a collector innocently wanders into an Indian encampment and becomes involved in a war between rival tribes with hilarious results. In one great sequence, Keaton is tied to a stake, then uproots it and walks away. In another, he is locked in an embrace with a pretty Indian squaw; a title-card flashes up saying, ''Two years later!'' When it cuts back, they are still kissing. ▭

Buster Keaton • Eddie Cline [Edward Cline] • Joe Roberts ■ *Dir* Buster Keaton, Eddie Cline [Edward Cline]

The Paleface ★★★ U
Comedy western 1948 · US · Colour · 91mins

One of Bob Hope's most popular films in which he plays a correspondence school-qualified dentist meeting up with sharpshooter Jane Russell (as Calamity Jane) out west. At the time known primarily for the scandal surrounding her film *The Outlaw*, Russell proved here that she could handle droll comedy, and Hope provides a lively mix of wisecracks and slapstick. The film has fun spoofing the western genre and includes the Oscar-winning song by Jay Livingston and Ray Evans, *Buttons and Bows*. Hope's biggest box-office hit and very entertaining, though it is one of the rare cases where the sequel *Son of*

Paleface, made in 1952, is even better. ▭

Bob Hope *''Painless'' Peter Potter* • Jane Russell *Calamity Jane* • Robert Armstrong *Terris* • Iris Adrian *Pepper* • Robert Watson [Bobby Watson] *Toby Preston* • Jack Searl [Jackie Searle] *Jasper Martin* • Joseph Vitale *Indian Scout* • Charles Trowbridge *Governor Johnson* ■ *Dir* Norman Z McLeod • *Scr* Edmund Hartman, Frank Tashlin, Jack Rose

The Pallbearer ★★ 12
Romantic comedy
1996 · US · Colour · 93mins

David Schwimmer attempted to leave his TV *Friends* persona behind with this movie, but instead ended up playing an even more annoying version of his well-known character Ross. He gets himself into a pickle when he is asked to be a pallbearer at the funeral of a schoolfriend he doesn't remember by the deceased's mother (Barbara Hershey). You can see the young-man-older-woman *Graduate*-style seduction coming a mile off, and Schwimmer is so whiny it's hard to imagine that any woman would want him in the first place. Only worth enduring for the performances of the luminous Gwyneth Paltrow (as the girl Schwimmer had always dreamed of) and talented Michael Rapaport as Brad. ▭

David Schwimmer *Tom Thompson* • Gwyneth Paltrow *Julie DeMarco* • Michael Rapaport *Brad Schorr* • Toni Collette *Cynthia* • Carol Kane *Tom's Mom* • Bitty Schram *Lauren* • Barbara Hershey *Ruth Abernathy* ■ *Dir* Matt Reeves • *Scr* Jason Katims, Matt Reeves

The Palm Beach Story ★★★★ U
Comedy   1942 · US · BW · 82mins

Made by the brilliant writer/director of satirical comedy Preston Sturges, *The Palm Beach Story* stars Claudette Colbert who, by the early forties, had become firmly established as Hollywood's queen of romantic comedy. Watching her antics and listening to her way with a witty line in the face of this film's ever-escalating absurdities, it's easy to see why. Teamed with Joel McCrea (star of Sturges's famed *Sullivan's Travels*), Colbert is the young wife who decides that her poverty-stricken husband would be better off without her. So she leaves for Florida to seek a divorce and a rich man. How she gets there, the consequences of her meeting with a prissy, eccentric bachelor billionaire (Rudy Vallee) and McCrea's response to the situation supply the action.

Claudette Colbert *Gerry Jeffers* • Joel McCrea *Tom Jeffers* • Mary Astor *Princess Centimillia* • Rudy Vallee *JD Hackensacker III* ■ *Dir/Scr* Preston Sturges • *Costume Designer* Irene

Palm Springs Weekend ★★
Comedy drama 1963 · US · Colour · 100mins

Long before *The Waltons*, Earl Hamner Jr penned this moderately entertaining beach comedy. Various teens follow the spring exodus to Palm Springs, Florida, where grim police chief Dixon (Andrew Duggan) tries to keep order. One of them, Troy Donahue, is interested in Stefanie Powers, who unfortunately for him is the chief's daughter. Fans of TV''s *Lost in Space* will easily spot Will Robinson (Billy Mumy) as Boom Boom. ▣

Troy Donahue *Jim Munroe* • Connie Stevens *Gail Lewis* • Ty Hardin *Stretch Fortune* • Stefanie Powers *Bunny Dixon* • Robert Conrad *Eric Dean* • Andrew Duggan *Chief Dixon* • Jack Weston *Coach Campbell* • Billy Mumy [Bill Mumy] *Boom Boom* ▪ *Dir* Norman Taurog • *Scr* Earl Hamner Jr

Palmer's Pick-Up ★★

Comedy 1999 · US · Colour · 106mins

Offered a lot of money to drive a crate to Florida in time for the millennium New Year, LA package delivery duo Robert Carradine and Richard Hillman hit the highway and rub hard shoulders with a gay ex-con, a nymphomaniac trucker (Rosanna Arquette) and an androgynous mob boss. A quirky road movie that's the sum of its often camp and hilarious parts more than being an overall long-haul success. Disco diva Grace Jones adds a further level of kitsch to another entry from the multi-talented Coppola family.

Robert Carradine *Bruce Palmer* • Richard Hillman *Pearl* • Patrick Kilpatrick *Bo* • Neil Giuntoli *Mac* • Rosanna Arquette *Dawn* • Alice Ghostley *Mrs Eleanor Palmer* • Grace Jones *Ms Remo* • Piper Laurie *Radio Evangelist* ▪ *Dir* Christopher Coppola • *Scr* Christopher Coppola, Nick Johnson

Palmetto ★★ 15

Crime thriller
1998 · US/Ger · Colour · 109mins

Like many German directors before him, Volker Schlöndorff is clearly intrigued by *film noir*. But this update of James Hadley Chase's 1961 novel *Just Another Sucker* to contemporary Florida is fudged and fuzzy. Ex-con Woody Harrelson returns home to the title town to get suckered into a fake kidnapping scam by a dying millionaire's trophy wife, Elisabeth Shue. Although at times an artful blend of atmosphere and sharp dialogue, Schlöndorff's low energy suspense film fails because Harrelson's pivotal role is so unremittingly stupid and unsympathetic it's hard to care what happens to him. Contains swearing, some violence and sexual references. ▣

Woody Harrelson *Harry Barber* • Elisabeth Shue *Rhea Malroux* • Gina Gershon *Nina* • Rolf Hoppe *Felix Malroux* • Michael Rapaport *Donnelly* • Chloë Sevigny *Odette Malroux* • Tom Wright *John Renick* • Marc Macaulay *Miles Meadows* ▪ *Dir* Volker Schlöndorff • *Scr* E Max Frye, from the novel *Just Another Sucker* by James Hadley Chase

Palmy Days ★★★ U

Musical comedy 1931 · US · BW · 73mins

An Eddie Cantor vehicle in which the banjo-eyed comedian frenetically gets involved with a gang of crooks masquerading as fortune tellers: one of them is a young George Raft. There's some funny stuff in a bakery involving high-kicking Charlotte Greenwood, but the credited ace choreographer Busby Berkeley was still a fair way from finding the unique style that made him a household name at Warner Bros. Despite the somewhat perfunctory work of director A Edward Sutherland, Cantor is genuinely amusing – he's a fine example of a

unique talent captured in his prime. ▣

Eddie Cantor *Eddie Simpson* • Charlotte Greenwood *Helen Martin* • Spencer Charters *Ab Clark* • Barbara Weeks *Joan Clark* • George Raft *Joe the Frog* • Paul Page *Steve Clayton* • Harry Woods *Plug Moynihan* ▪ *Dir* A Edward Sutherland • *Scr* Morrie Ryskind, Eddie Cantor, from a story by Morrie Ryskind, Keene Thompson, David Freedman, David Freedman, Eddie Cantor

Palomino ★★ PG

Romantic drama 1991 · US · Colour · 91mins

There's enough corn to fill you up for a lifetime in this adaptation of Danielle Steel's romantic novel. Lindsay Frost plays the photographer who retreats to a ranch after her marriage ends, and subsequently falls in love with a rough and ready ranch hand Lee Horsley, from the wrong side of the tracks. This also features Eva Marie Saint and Rod Taylor, both of whom should have known better. ▣

Lindsay Frost *Samantha Taylor* • Lee Horsley *Tate* • Eva Marie Saint *Caroline* • Rod Taylor *Bill* • Beau Gravitte *Charlie* • Michael Greene *Josh* • Daniel Davis *Dr Feld* • Ryan Todd *Timmie* • Peter Bergman *Warren Taylor* ▪ *Dir* Michael Miller • *Scr* Karol Ann Hoefner, from the novel by Danielle Steel

Palooka ★★★★

Comedy 1934 · US · BW · 87mins

Hey, youse guys this is the bee's knees! Promoter Knobby Walsh (the great Jimmy Durante) has plucked a comer (hick Stu Erwin) from the streets, and is grooming him for the big fight, only the Palooka doesn't know what's (about to) hit him. Fabulous stuff, with the Schnoz on top form. Heck of a support cast, too: watch for sexy Lupe Velez, tragic Thelma Todd, and James Cagney's spitting image brother, William. A Joe Palooka B series followed, with Joe Kirkwood Jr as Ham Fisher's chump champ.

Jimmy Durante *Knobby Walsh* • Lupe Velez *Nina Madero* • Stuart Erwin *Joe Palooka* • Marjorie Rambeau *Mayme Palooka* • Robert Armstrong *Pete Palooka* • Mary Carlisle *Anne* • William Cagney *Al Mcswatt* • Thelma Todd *Trixie* ▪ *Dir* Benjamin Stoloff • *Scr* Ben Ryan, Murray Roth, Gertrude Purcell, Jack Jevne, Arthur Kober, from the comic strip by Ham Fisher

Palookaville ★★★★ 15

Comedy crime 1995 · US · Colour · 88mins

Strong on character, and with a keen ear for sharp, witty dialogue, this is a low-key delight. Inspired by the works of Italian author Italo Calvino, three dead-end New Jersey buddies turn to a life of petty crime to ease their boredom with remarkably unspectacular results. The story events are incidental to the superbly nuanced interplay between the uniformly excellent William Forsythe, Vincent Gallo and Adam Trese as they go about their daily grind. Frances McDormand lends winning support as the local hooker. Clever, richly atmospheric and perfectly pitched. ▣

Adam Trese *Jerry* • Vincent Gallo *Russ* • William Forsythe *Sid* • Frances McDormand *June* • Gareth Williams *Ed* ▪ *Dir* Alan Taylor • *Scr* David Epstein

Pals ★★★ PG

Comedy 1986 · US · Colour · 86mins

This slight but amiable affair is distinguished by delightful performances from veterans George C Scott and Don Ameche. The duo play bored pensioners who discover a fortune in drugs money and decide to keep it. Scott and Ameche spark off each other superbly, there is a fine supporting performance from another old trouper, Sylvia Sidney, and director Lou Antonio keeps the action moving along briskly. ▣

George C Scott *Jack Stobbs* • Don Ameche *Art Riddle* • Sylvia Sidney *Fern* • James Greene *Leek* • Lenka Peterson *Betty* • Richard Hamilton *Herman* ▪ *Dir* Lou Antonio • *Scr* Michael Norell

Pan-Americana ★

Romantic comedy 1945 · US · BW · 84mins

The editor of a magazine (Eve Arden), her foreign editor (Robert Benchley), their girl reporter (Audrey Long) and a photographer (Philip Terry), make a whistle-stop tour of several South and Central American countries to research a feature on Latin America. Each venue is a cue to showcase an act, which might be Rosario and Antonio, or Harold and Lola with their exotic snake dance, or Nestor Amaral and his Samba Band – the list goes on. Unfurled in flashback and "narrated" by Benchley, this pathetic excuse for a musical exhibition piece tacks on a feeble romantic sideline in which Long dithers over whether she loves Terry or her Rio-based fiancé Marc Cramer.

Phillip Terry *Dan Jordan* • Audrey Long *Jo Anne Benson* • Robert Benchley *Charlie Corker* • Eve Arden *Helen "Hoppy" Hopkins* • Ernest Truex *Uncle Rudy* • Marc Cramer *Jerry Bruce* ▪ *Dir* John H Auer • *Scr* Lawrence Kimble, from a story by Frederick Kohner, John H Auer

Pancho Villa ★★

Western 1971 · Sp · Colour · 91mins

Hammy *Kojak* star Telly Savalas might not be ideally cast as Mexico's saviour (but were Wallace Beery or Yul Brynner?), yet this is still an interesting example of a Spanish western. Against a background of arid landscapes, a watchable cast of Hollywood veterans – Anne Francis, Clint Walker as a gunrunner, and Chuck Connor as a polo-playing officer. Director Eugenio Martin had a clever knack for handling train sequences and both here and in the following year's *Horror Express* used the same locomotives. Stay awake to the end and watch them crash head-on!

Telly Savalas *Pancho Villa* • Clint Walker *Scotty* • Anne Francis *Flo* • Chuck Connors *Colonel Wilcox* • Angel Del Pozo *Lieutenant Eager* • Jose Maria Prada *Luis* ▪ *Dir* Gene Martin [Eugenio Martin] • *Scr* Julian Halevy [Julian Zimet], from a story by Gene Martin [Eugenio Martin]

Pandora and the Flying Dutchman ★★★★

Romantic drama
1951 · UK · Colour · 123mins

Albert Lewin was in some ways Hollywood's answer to Michael Powell and Emeric Pressburger, as a maker of weird, exotic and often slightly barmy

Technicolor fantasies. This bizarre British-made effort stars the ravishing Ava Gardner as a woman incapable of returning the love of her men, and James Mason as the sailor of legend, condemned to roam the seas for eternity until he meets a woman willing to give up her life for him. Set in Spain, its flights of romantic fantasy are heightened by the work of Powell and Pressburger's regular cinematographer, Jack Cardiff. An acquired taste, perhaps, but Lewin was a genuine maverick talent.

James Mason *Hendrick van der Zee* • Ava Gardner *Pandora Reynolds* • Nigel Patrick *Stephen Cameron* • Sheila Sim *Janet Fielding* • Harold Warrender *Geoffrey Fielding* • Mario Cabre *Juan Montalvo* • John Laurie *Angus* • Pamela Kellino *Jenny Ford* • Patricia Raine *Peggy Ford* • Margarita D'Alvarez *Senora Montalvo* ▪ *Dir/Scr* Albert Lewin

The Pandora Project ★ 15

Action thriller 1998 · US · Colour · 86mins

Daniel Baldwin specialises in straight-to-video stinkers like this dull thriller about a CIA agent on the trail of muscley madman Richard Tyson, who has acquired an unpleasant and very deadly new weapon. It's as flat and formulaic as they come – hero and villain have sneering contests, Baldwin's sexy girlfriend Erika Eleniak is kidnapped by Tyson and there's a climactic punch-up in a moving vehicle. ▣

Daniel Baldwin *John Lacy* • Erika Eleniak *Wendy Lane* • Richard Tyson *Bill Stenwick* ▪ *Dir* Jim Wynorski, John Terlesky • *Scr* John Terlesky

Pandora's Box ★★★★★ PG

Silent drama 1929 · Ger · BW · 104mins

American-born Louise Brooks is devastating as Lulu, the insatiable *femme fatale* who murders her husband and tangos with a lesbian countess before falling victim herself to Jack the Ripper. Screenwriter Ladislaus Vajda makes a superb job of condensing Frank Wedekind's two Lulu plays, but it's the visual imagination of director GW Pabst that most fully conveys the story's brooding sexual tension and all-pervading atmosphere of latent violence. A masterly mix of Expressionism and street realism, this ranks among the undisputed masterpieces of German silent cinema. ▣

Louise Brooks *Lulu* • Fritz Kortner *Dr Peter Schön* • Franz Lederer [Francis Lederer] *Alwa Schön* • Carl Götz *Schigolch* • Alice Roberts *Countess Anna Geschwitz* ▪ *Dir* GW Pabst • *Scr* Ladislaus Vajda, from the plays *Erdgeist/ Die Büchse der Pandora* by Frank Wedekind • *Cinematographer* Günther Krampf

Panhandle Calibre 38 ★★

Spaghetti western 1972 · It · Colour · 90mins

The plot twists may be signposted and the humour might have been laid on with a trowel, but this is a lively enough spaghetti western with a tough edge from director Toni Secchi. Keenan Wynn plays a has-been gunslinger hired to take a Confederate gold shipment across treacherous terrain in the company of his city slicker son, Scott Holden (son of William Holden and Brenda Marshall).

Delia Boccardo (posing as a schoolteacher) leads the shiftless shower hot on their trail that includes a French con artist, a fake preacher, a Mexican bandit and an Indian.

Keenan Wynn *Billy Bronson* • Delia Boccardo *Connie* • Scott Holden *Bobo* ■ *Dir* Antonio Secchi [Toni Secchi] • *Scr* Mario Mendola, Massimo Franciosa, Louisa Montagnana

Panic Button ★★

Comedy 1964 · US · BW · 90mins

Michael Connors is the producer looking to make a flop as a tax write-off who hires forgotten movie star Maurice Chevalier – completely unsuited to the role – to play Romeo, and professional tart Jayne Mansfield as Juliet, for a TV pilot of Shakespeare's play. For good measure, he gets a Akim Tamiroff as a director who is only too happy to give him the garbage he wants. Barely released, this minor but quite appealing comedy directed by George Sherman is an unusual vehicle for Chevalier and a credit to the sweet personality and comedic talents of Mansfield.

Maurice Chevalier *Philippe Fontaine* • Jayne Mansfield *Angela* • Michael Connors [Mike Connors] *Frank Pagano* • Eleanor Parker *Louise Harris* • Akim Tamiroff *Pandowski* ■ *Dir* George Sherman • *Scr* Hal Biller, from a story by Mort Friedman, Ron Gorton

The Panic in Needle Park ★★★★ 18

Drama 1971 · US · Colour · 103mins

Drug abuse movies can be hard to take, but this compelling drama has a superior screenplay (by Joan Didion and her husband John Gregory Dunne) and sensational performances from young Al Pacino and Kitty Winn. He's the cheeky bad boy and she the nice, sweet girl irresistibly drawn to him, and together their youthful dabbling in drugs drags them down into addiction and a harrowing spiral of squalor and loathing. Pacino's electrifying presence here convinced Francis Ford Coppola to fight enormous studio resistance to cast him as Michael Corleone in *The Godfather*. ▭

Al Pacino *Bobby* • Kitty Winn *Helen* • Alan Vint *Hotchner* • Richard Bright *Hank* • Angie Ortega *Irene* • Marcia Jean Kurtz *Marcie* • Raul Julia *Marco* • Kiel Martin *Chico* • Paul Sorvino *Samuels* ■ *Dir* Jerry Schatzberg • *Scr* Joan Didion, John Gregory Dunne, from a novel by James Mills

Panic in the City ★★★ U

Thriller 1968 · US · Colour · 91mins

One of those all-too-possible thrillers, common in the sixties, about the threat of Armageddon in which a revolutionary group try to start a Third World War ("The human race has been given its chance – and failed"). This particular group plan to explode an atomic bomb in Los Angeles in the hope that the US will blame the Soviet Union. Howard Duff tries to stop it all from happening but he cannot impede the banality of an idea which required more money and a better director.

Nehemiah Persoff *August Best* • Anne Jeffreys *Myra Pryor* • Howard Duff *Dave Pomeroy* • Linda Cristal *Dr Paula Stevens* • Stephen

McNally *James Kincade* • Dennis Hopper *Goff* ■ *Dir* Eddie Davis • *Scr* Eddie Davis, Charles E Savage

Panic in the Skies! ★★

Thriller 1996 · US · Colour · 90mins

After *Airplane!*, it's astonishing that anyone would make a film about an aircraft heading for disaster. Even more amazing would be one in which the pilots are dead and an inexperienced passenger and a stewardess have to navigate it to safety, while officials on the ground are gradually made aware of new and deadly information. But here it is, a splendidly straight-faced return to the disaster movie, with Kate Jackson as the heroine of the hour and Ed Marinaro as her hunky partner. Shame there wasn't a part for a singing nun, though.

Kate Jackson *Laurie Ann* • Ed Marinaro *Brett Young* • Erik Estrada *Ethan Walker* • Maureen McCormick *Tukey* • Robert Guillaume *Rob Barnes* ■ *Dir* Paul Ziller • *Scr* Robert Hamilton, from a story by Rick Rosner, Rod Parkhurst

Panic in the Streets ★★★★

Drama 1950 · US · BW · 94mins

Shot on location in New Orleans, this tense drama might have seemed an unusual choice for director Elia Kazan. Yet the killing of an illegal immigrant and the mood that prevailed at the time that foreigners were a plague infesting the United States are themes very much in keeping with Kazan's preoccupation with racism. Richard Widmark gives one of his more restrained performances as the health inspector teaming up with cop Paul Douglas to apprehend a couple of plague-infected murderers, compellingly played by Jack Palance and Zero Mostel, who was himself hounded during the Communist witch-hunt the following year.

Richard Widmark *Clinton Reed* • Paul Douglas *Police Captain Tom Warren* • Barbara Bel Geddes *Nancy Reed* • Walter Jack Palance [Jack Palance] *Blackie* • Zero Mostel *Raymond Fitch* • Dan Riss *Neff* ■ *Dir* Elia Kazan • *Scr* Richard Murphy, Daniel Fuchs, from the stories *Quarantine* and *Some Like 'Em Cold* by Edna Anhalt, Edward Anholt

Panic in Year Zero ★★★★

Science-fiction drama
1962 · US · BW · 91mins

Ray Milland directs and stars in this story about a nuclear war and the breakdown of society that follows. Milland's direction is plain, even nondescript, which sometimes makes the film even more chilling as survivors take the law into their own hands and head for the hills, through a traffic jam of surreal proportions. It's as if *Fail-Safe* had been grafted on to Marlon Brando's biker movie *The Wild One*, with Milland as the boring, everyday Joe who holds up a store, takes his wife and family to live in a cave and kills the thugs who threaten them. There's a lot going on in this movie, with much to think about, and there's Frankie Avalon, too!

Ray Milland *Harry Baldwin* • Jean Hagen *Ann Baldwin* • Frankie Avalon *Rick Baldwin* • Mary Mitchell *Karen Baldwin* • Joan Freeman

Marilyn Hayes • Richard Garland *Mr Johnson* ■ *Dir* Ray Milland • *Scr* Jay Simms, John Morton, from a story by Jay Simms

Panther ★★★ 15

Political drama 1995 · US · Colour · 124mins

The troubled rise of the Black Panther group, from their formation in Oakland, California, to their media hounding by J Edgar Hoover, is put under the spotlight by director Mario Van Peebles in a "factional" account of an important chapter in American race politics. Although densely plotted, with a huge host of characters, the director's use of extreme close-ups and energetic flashy visuals keep the attention riveted. Highly controversial – the FBI collaborating with the Mafia to flood the ghettos with cheap heroin to quell the activism – *Panther* is a thought-provoking film that works on a number of levels. ▭

Kadeem Hardison *Judge* • Bokeem Woodbine *Tyrone* • Joe Don Baker *Brimmer* • Courtney B Vance *Bobby Seale* • Tyrin Turner *Cy* • Marcus Chong *Huey Newton* • Anthony Griffith *Eldridge Cleaver* • Bobby Brown *Rose* ■ *Dir* Mario Van Peebles • *Scr* Melvin Van Peebles, from his novel

Papa's Delicate Condition ★★★ U

Comedy 1963 · US · Colour · 97mins

Jackie Gleason has a touch of the staggers which, considering his size, is a risky lurch to be in the way of. It's a totter brought about by too many nips of liquor, an ailment his loving household in their turn-of-the-century Texas small town has to deal with or avoid. Based on memoirs by silent screen star Corinne Griffith and with an Oscar-winner of a song *Call Me Irresponsible*, by James Van Heusen and Sammy Cahn, it's the kind of eulogy to old-time family values which has gone out of fashion, if not favour.

Jackie Gleason *Jack "Papa" Griffith* • Glynis Johns *Ambolyn Griffith* • Charles Ruggles *Grandpa Anthony Ghio* • Laurel Goodwin *Augusta Griffith* • Linda Bruhl *Corinne Griffith* ■ *Dir* George Marshall • *Scr* Jack Rose, from the non-fiction book by Corinne Griffith

The Paper ★★★★ 15

Comedy drama 1994 · US · Colour · 106mins

Stop press: here's a funny, frothy fourth estate fling. Michael Keaton heads a formidable cast as a city editor on the New York *Sun* in a highly engaging and absorbing look at 24 hours in the life of an ailing tabloid. As he faces another day of decisions, deadlines and compromises both job-wise (he's being head-hunted by rival editor Spalding Gray) and personally (his pregnant wife, Marisa Tomei, is feeling neglected) director Ron Howard deftly ties the numerous story strands together with some vibrantly snappy dialogue. Although Keaton provides the narrative focus, this is very much an ensemble film, with everyone getting a headline moment of their own. Robert Duvall is superb as the editor who has sacrificed his life for the paper, while Glenn Close cleverly shows the difficulties of being a woman with power over men. Contains swearing. ▭

Michael Keaton *Henry Hackett* • Glenn Close *Alicia Clark* • Robert Duvall *Bernie White* • Marisa Tomei *Martha Hackett* • Randy Quaid *McDougal* • Jason Robards [Jason Robards Jr] *Graham Keighley* • Jason Alexander *Marion Sandusky* • Catherine O'Hara *Susan* • Lynne Thigpen *Janet* ■ *Dir* Ron Howard • *Scr* David Koepp, Stephen Koepp

The Paper Chase ★★★★

Comedy drama 1973 · US · Colour · 111mins

After years as one of America's most important producers (*They Live By Night*, *The Bad and the Beautiful*) and as an occasional actor, the 71-year-old John Houseman won a best supporting actor Oscar for his unforgettable portrayal of a Harvard law professor in this fine drama from writer/director James Bridges. While the central, intellectual duel between Houseman, an absolute stickler for excellence, and Timothy Bottoms as his rather obnoxious student makes for bracing entertainment, Bridges also tosses in some melodramatic and contrived subplots, including a rather gooey romance between Bottoms and Houseman's daughter (Lindsay Wagner). Houseman repeated his role in the TV series that followed.

Timothy Bottoms *Hart* • Lindsay Wagner *Susan* • John Houseman *Kingsfield* • Graham Beckel *Ford* • Edward Herrmann *Anderson* • Bob Lydiard *O'Connor* • Craig Richard Nelson *Bell* ■ *Dir* James Bridges • *Scr* James Bridges, from the novel *The Paper Chase* by John Jay Osborn Jr

Paper Hearts ★★★

Drama 1993 · US · Colour · 90mins

Sally Kirkland is a good 'ole Southern gal, dutifully married to wandering Lothario James Brolin with two grown-up daughters (Renée Estevez and Pamela Gidley) and a patient, biding-his-time cowboy boyfriend (Kris Kristofferson). It's an intelligent, grown-up movie that is both resonant and affecting, if a little pat. Jenny has two things on her mind. One is that her beloved ancestral homestead is facing foreclosure through errant Henry's incompetence. The other is the wedding of her younger daughter, an event that brings crisis and resolution for the three women and a come-uppance for Henry. It's a reassuringly old-fashioned heart-tugger.

Sally Kirkland *Jenny* • James Brolin *Henry* • Kris Kristofferson *Tom* • Pamela Gidley *Samantha* • Laura Johnson *Patsy* • Michael (4) Moore *Bill* • Renée Estevez *Kat* • Mickey Cottrell *Brady* ■ *Dir/Scr* Rod McCall

Paper Lion ★★★

Comedy drama based on a true story
1968 · US · Colour

Engagingly good-tempered "mockumentary" from sports writer George Plimpton's bestseller about his time as quarterback for the Detroit Lions American football team. Technical knowledge of the game is unnecessary because Alan Alda, in his first starring role, interprets for us through his naive, amateurish actions, while Lauren Hutton is a pleasure to watch as Alda's secretary. There are also cameos from middleweight boxing champion Sugar Ray Robinson, and other American sporting heroes. Contains swearing.

Alan Alda *George Plimpton* • Lauren Hutton *Kate* • David Doyle *Oscar* • Ann Turkel *Susan* ■ *Dir* Alex March • *Scr* Lawrence Roman, from the book by George Plimpton

Paper Marriage ★★15

Romantic comedy drama
1991 · UK/Pol · Colour · 84mins

A Polish woman arrives in Newcastle to marry a British man, but discovers he's decided against it. Reluctant to return to home, she blindly suggests marriage to the astonished Gary Kemp, hoping she can then get to stay in the country. As the down-on-his-luck artist desperately needs money, he goes along with her indecent proposal in this perfectly crafted small-scale version of *Green Card*. Strong on characterisation and humour, low on plausibility, but shot through with engaging pathos, ex-Spandau Ballet pop star Kemp cuts an immensely likeable figure. ▭

Gary Kemp *Aiden Carey* • Joanna Trzepiecinska *Alicja Stralkowska* • Rita Tushingham *Lou* • Richard Hawley *Red* • William Ilkley *Jack* • Gary Whelan *Boss* • Ann Mitchell *Phyllida* • Fred Pearson *Officer Crane* ■ *Dir* Krzysztof Lang • *Scr* Krzysztof Lang, Marek Kreutz, Debbie Horsfield

Paper Mask ★★★15

Thriller   1990 · UK · Colour · 100mins

The stories you occasionally read in the papers about people who somehow manage to pass themselves off as medics are the inspiration for this dark tale. It stars Paul McGann as the hospital porter-turned-bogus doctor and Amanda Donohoe as the casualty department nurse who becomes involved in his deception. Director Christopher Morahan turns in a spookily plausible and engrossing thriller. Contains some violence and nudity. ▭

Paul McGann *Matthew Harris* • Amanda Donohoe *Christine Taylor* • Frederick Treves *Dr Mumford* • Tom Wilkinson *Dr Thorn* • Barbara Leigh-Hunt *Celia Mumford* • Jimmy Yuill *Alec Moran* ■ *Dir* Christopher Morahan • *Scr* John Collee

Paper Moon ★★★★

Comedy drama   1973 · US · BW · 102mins

The wandering star of Peter Bogdanovich's directorial talent brilliantly lights up this cynical charmer of a story – set during the Depression – of a Bible-toting con man (Ryan O'Neal) forming a bizarre partnership with the brattish nine-year-old (real-life daughter Tatum O'Neal) who may or may not be his child. Laszlo Kovacs's outstanding monochromatic photography lends an affectionate sheen to a quest through the Kansas dustbowl in which the girl gradually becomes mother to the man. With this, *Targets*, and *The Last Picture Show*, Bogdanovich looked set to be one of Hollywood's finest but, seems to have been a flash in the pan.

Ryan O'Neal *Moses Pray* • Tatum O'Neal *Addie Loggins* • Madeline Kahn *Trixie Delight* • John Hillerman *Sheriff Hardin/Jess Hardin* • PJ Johnson *Imogene* ■ *Dir* Peter Bogdanovich • *Scr* Alvin Sargent, from the novel *Addie Pray* by Joe David Brown

Paper Tiger ★★★PG

Comedy adventure
1974 · UK · Colour · 95mins

David Niven portrayed himself as a buffoon in his autobiography *The Moon's a Balloon*. In fact, he was a fine actor, at his best when playing life-cashiered failures, as in *Separate Tables* for which he won an Oscar, and in this otherwise tedious effort, as the tutor to a Japanese child who finds he has to live up to the Walter Mitty-ish fantasies with which he's entertained the boy when both are kidnapped by terrorists. His performance as a man trying to make up for a loser's lifetime is at once noble and sad, but it lifts this rather leaden idea to heights to which it might never have aspired. ▭

David Niven *Walter Bradbury* • Toshiro Mifune *Ambassador Kagoyama* • Hardy Kruger *Muller* • Ando *Koichi Kagoyama* • Ivan Desny *Foreign minister* • Irene Tsu *Talah* • Ronald Fraser *Forster* ■ *Dir* Ken Annakin • *Scr* Jack Davies

A Paper Wedding ★★★

Drama   1989 · Can · Colour · 90mins

Released around the same time as *Green Card*, this Canadian drama also focuses on a marriage of convenience, only without the laughs. Although normally outspoken in his political views, director Michel Brault resists the temptation to soapbox about either the conditions in Chile at the time or the illogicalities of the Canadian immigration system. Consequently, what emerges is a film that argues its case without distracting from the human drama that unfolds when college professor Geneviève Bujold is given just three days to dispose of her married lover and get to know exiled Chilean dissident Manuel Aranguiz. Imaginatively structured, this is both engaging and eminently cinematic. In French with English subtitles.

Geneviève Bujold *Claire* • Manuel Aranguiz *Pablo* • Dorothée Berryman *Annie* • Monique Lepage *Gaby* • Teo Spychalski *Milosh* ■ *Dir* Michel Brault • *Scr* Jefferson Lewis, Andrée Pelletier, with the collaboration of Sylvain Brault

Paperback Hero ★★★

Drama   1972 · Can · Colour · 93mins

Keir Dullea plays a small-town hockey hero and ladies' man who leads a double life as the town's gunfighter. In his daydreams, anyway. Nicely acted by a cast which also includes Elizabeth Ashley, the film holds interest but never quite scales the same heights of escapist excellence as *The Secret Life of Walter Mitty*.

Keir Dullea *Rick Dillon* • Elizabeth Ashley *Loretta* • John Beck *Pov* • Dayle Haddon *Joanna* • Franz Russell *Big Ed* ■ *Dir* Peter Pearson • *Scr* Les Rose, Barry Pearson

Paperback Hero ★★★15

Romantic comedy
1998 · Ausl · Colour · 96mins

The karaoke love duet should be the nail in any film's coffin. Yet this outback-set romantic comedy survives reasonably intact thanks to the amiable performances of Hugh Jackman, as a handsome trucker who secretly pens period romances, and Claudia Karvan, as the feisty crop-

dusting mate he persuades to front his popular novel on a PR campaign so that she can afford to marry the local vet. Writer/director Antony J Bowman clearly intended a nineties variation on battle-of-the-sexes screwball, but ends up with a frothy concoction that might be dubbed a ''Crocodile Mills and Boon''. With sharp support from Angie Milliken as a Sydney-based publishing executive and Andrew S Gilbert as Karvan's faithful fiancé, this is pleasing but utterly predictable entertainment. ▭

Claudia Karvan *Ruby Vale* • Hugh Jackman *Jack Willis* • Angie Milliken *Ziggy Keane* • Andrew S Gilbert *Hamish* • Jeanie Drynan *Suzie* • Bruce Venables *Artie* • Barry Rugless *Mad Pete* • Barry Lea *Policeman* ■ *Dir/Scr* Antony J Bowman

Paperback Romance ★★

Romantic comedy
1994 · Ausl · Colour · 93mins

A romantic comedy from Australia that comes close to being offensive. Gia Carides is a writer of steamily erotic romances, living out in her imagination what she lacks in real life. Embarrassed by a paralysed leg (a result of childhood polio), she rejects the advances of Anthony LaPaglia, a handsome, slighty dodgy jewellery dealer, with a jealous fiancée. Then Carides breaks her leg and uses the cast to hide her disability. Carides and LaPaglia (a real-life couple) do their best to elevate director Ben Lewin's poor taste burlesque into something with more chemistry but their efforts are not helped by unnecessary sex scenes.

Gia Carides *Sophie* • Anthony LaPaglia *Eddie* • Rebecca Gibney *Gloria* • Robyn Nevin *Anne-Marie LePine* • Marshall Napier *George LePine* ■ *Dir/Scr* Ben Lewin

The Paperboy ★★18

Thriller   1994 · Can · Colour · 89mins

The infrequently used but unoriginal killer child plotline is given a boost here, in part because of competent acting and fleshed-out characters. Newly arrived single mother Alexandra Paul makes friends with the neighbourhood's lonely paperboy (Marc Marut), but soon discovers a dangerous side to him, especially when suitor William Katt enters her life. The movie manages the difficult task of plausibly explaining Marut's dementia, even making him somewhat sympathetic, though it's unable to tidy things up completely at the end. ▭

Alexandra Paul *Melissa Thorpe* • William Katt *Brian* • Marc Marut *Johnny* • Krista Errickson *Diana* • Brigid Tierney *Cammie* • Frances Bay *Mrs Rosemont* • Karen Dwyer *Brenda* ■ *Dir* Douglas Jackson • *Scr* David Peckinpah

Paperhouse ★★★15

Fantasy horror   1988 · UK · Colour · 88mins

Loosely based on Catherine Storr's novel *Marianne Dreams* (too loosely for some of the book's fans), this is a highly intelligent horror, in which the terror comes from the exploration of the subconscious rather than from banal schlock set pieces. Neglected by busy father Ben Cross and at loggerheads with (miscast) mother Glenne Headly, Charlotte Burke is the

11-year-old who enters a threatening world shaped by her dreams and the drawings in her notebook. Contains some swearing. ▭

Charlotte Burke *Anna Madden* • Elliott Spiers *Marc* • Glenne Headly *Kate* • Ben Cross *Dad* • Gemma Jones *Dr Sarah Nichols* • Sarah Newbold *Karen* • Samantha Cahill *Sharon* ■ *Dir* Bernard Rose • *Scr* Matthew Jacobs, from the novel *Marianne Dreams* by Catherine Storr

Papillon ★★★★18

Biographical prison drama
1973 · US · Colour · 144mins

On its original release, the critics had few good words to say about Franklin J Schaffner's adaptation of Henri Charrière's autobiographical account of his escape from Devil's Island. They sighed dejectedly at the stately pace and the careful development of the forbidding prison atmosphere. None could find any merit in Steve McQueen's performance as the convict bent on breaking free and even blamed him for bringing Dustin Hoffman down to his level. But this harrowing study of confinement and single-mindedness has been criminally hard done by. Occasionally McQueen is perhaps a little too enigmatic for his own good, but Hoffman's depiction of cunning corruption is splendid. Contains violence and some swearing. ▭

Steve McQueen *Henri Charrière, Papillon* • Dustin Hoffman *Louis Dega* • Victor Jory *Indian Chief* • Don Gordon *Julot* • Anthony Zerbe *Toussaint, Leper Colony Chief* • Robert Deman *Maturette* • Woodrow Parfrey *Clusoit* • Bill Mumy *Lariot* • George Coulouris *Dr Chatal* ■ *Dir* Franklin J Schaffner • *Scr* Dalton Trumbo, Lorenzo Semple Jr, from the novel by Henri Charrière

Paracelsus ★★★

Historical drama   1943 · Ger · BW · 107mins

Produced to celebrate the 400th birthday of the famous physician and philosopher, this is one of the most controversial films from the great impressionist director GW Pabst. Made for the Nazi regime, and starring the favourite actor of both Pabst and the Third Reich, Werner Krauss, the film transforms its hero, who rescues a city from the plague only to have its inhabitants turn on him, into a surrogate Furher, a poor-boy-made-good and a genius ahead of his time. Excessively talky, episodic and blatantly tendentious, it has been condemned by some as an example of a great talent reduced to studio hack, but at least one astounding sequence mid-way into the film, an abandoned dance of death followed by a procession of flagellants, displays the director's celebrated pictorial imagination and flair. In German with English subtitles.

Werner Krauss *Paracelsus* • Mathias Wieman *Ulrich von Hutten* • Harald Kreutzberg *Fliegenbein* • Martin Urtel *Johannes* • Harry Langewisch *Hans Pfefferkorn* • Annelies Reinhold *Renata Pfefferkorn, his daughter* • Fritz Rasp *The master* ■ *Dir* GW Pabst • *Scr* Kurt Heuser • *Cinematographer* Herbert Stephan

U = SUITABLE FOR ALL   Uc = SUITABLE FOR ALL, ESPECIALLY FOR YOUNG CHILDREN (VIDEO ONLY)   PG = PARENTAL GUIDANCE

Parade ★ U

Comedy documentary
1974 · Fr/Swe · Colour · 69mins

This Swedish TV co-production filmed in a circus tent in Sweden using video techniques was sadly Jacques Tati's last film. Basically, the film records a series of dismal repetitive provincial circus acts in between Tati's own appearance, doing the musical mimes of sportsmen with which he had started his career. As director, Tati attempts to demonstrate his whimsical philosophy that everyone's a clown by showing members of the audience. There are few more depressing experiences in the cinema than watching admired comedians in stuff far below their talent.

Dir/Scr Jacques Tati · *Cinematographer* Jean Badal, Gunnar Fischer

The Parade ★★★★ PG

Drama
1984 · US · Colour · 91mins

Directed with considerable care by Peter Hunt, this compelling drama is set in a small Kansas town on the eve of the annual Fourth of July parade. The story focuses on the impact on three women of the return of a recently released prisoner. Frederic Forrest gives one of his best performances, inspiring solid work from his co-stars in the process. ▭

Michael Learned *Rachel Kirby* • Frederic Forrest *Matt Kirby* • Rosanna Arquette *Tilda Kirby* • Maxwell Caulfield *Jeff* • James Olson *Andy Janacek* • Geraldine Page *Sarah* ■ *Dir* Peter H Hunt • *Scr* N Richard Nash, Emily Tracy, from the story by N Richard Nash

The Paradine Case ★★★ U

Crime drama
1947 · US · BW · 114mins

This is one of those pictures that no amount of professional polish could save. Producer David O Selznick and director Alfred Hitchcock disagreed over the script, the shooting style and the leads (Hitchcock wanting Laurence Olivier and Greta Garbo for the roles filled by Peck and Alida Valli, in her US film debut), and the discord shows on screen. Peck has never looked so uncomfortable as the lawyer who jeopardises his career and his marriage (to Ann Todd) to help Valli, who's accused of murdering her wealthy husband and is keeping secret her affair with Louis Jourdan. Hitchcock is always watchable, but this should have been so much better. ▭

Gregory Peck *Anthony Keane* • Alida Valli *Maddalena Paradine* • Ann Todd *Gay Keane* • Charles Laughton *Lord Horfield* • Charles Coburn *Sir Simon Flaquer* • Ethel Barrymore *Lady Sophie Horfield* • Louis Jourdan *AndréLatour* ■ *Dir* Alfred Hitchcock • *Scr* David O Selznick, Alma Reville, James Bridie, from the novel by Robert Hichens

Paradise ★★ 15

Period romantic adventure
1982 · US · Colour · 89mins

Daft period piece, sort of a *Blue Lagoon* without the water, with Phoebe Cates and Willie Aames as two 19th-century teenagers travelling by caravan from Baghdad to Damascus. But it's harem-scarum time when Miss Cates attracts the unwanted attentions of a desert rogue. There's plenty of flesh on display as the two abandoned teens find love in the sand. ▭

Willie Aames *David* • Phoebe Cates *Sarah* • Richard Curnock *Geoffrey* • Tuvia Tavi *The Jackal* • Neil Vipond *Reverend* ■ *Dir/Scr* Stuart Gillard

Paradise ★★★ PG

Drama
1991 · US · Colour · 106mins

Melanie Griffith and Don Johnson strip themselves of Hollywood glamour for this remake of the French film *Le Grand Chemin*, playing a married couple at war over the loss of a child. Elijah Wood is the ten-year-old from Manhattan who comes to stay with them and makes friends with girl-next-door Thora Birch. It's less lurid and more convincing than its Gallic predecessor, and first-time director Mary Agnes Donoghue joins the rare ranks of current US mainstream film-makers who can cope with people, not just special effects. Surprisingly, considering some of their work, both Johnson and Griffith deliver honest and effective performances. Contains swearing and nudity. ▭

Melanie Griffith *Lily Reed* • Don Johnson *Ben Reed* • Elijah Wood *Willard Young* • Thora Birch *Billie Pike* • Sheila McCarthy *Sally Pike* • Eve Gordon *Rosemary Young* • Louise Latham *Catherine Reston Lee* ■ *Dir* Mary Agnes Donoghue • *Scr* Mary Agnes Donoghue, from the film *Le Grand Chemin* by Jean-Loup Hubert

Paradise Alley ★★ 15

Comedy drama
1978 · US · Colour · 102mins

Having scripted *Rocky* and *FIST*, Sylvester Stallone made his debut as a writer/director with this sentimental story of three brothers trying to claw their way out of the poverty trap of Hell's Kitchen in the forties. When one brother, Lee Canalito, becomes a successful wrestler – shades of *Rocky* – the others climb aboard his bandwagon. As writer/director, Stallone's approach is strong on period atmosphere, with a tendency to overcook the dialogue, recalling the heyday of Clifford Odets and movies like *Golden Boy*. ▭

Sylvester Stallone *Cosmo Carboni* • Lee Canalito *Victor "Kid Salami" Carboni* • Armand Assante *Lenny Carboni* • Frank McRae *Big Glory* • Anne Archer *Annie O'Sherlock* • Kevin Conway *"Stitch" Mahon* • Terry Funk *"Franky The Thumper"* • Joyce Ingalls *Bunchie* ■ *Dir/Scr* Sylvester Stallone

Paradise Canyon ★★ U

Western
1935 · US · BW · 52mins

Another of John Wayne's many films for poverty row studio Monogram, so like all the others that it's virtually impossible to tell them apart. Once again stunt specialist Yakima Canutt plays the baddie and the Duke's undercover agent has to call on the help of suspicious locals to bring him to book. It hardly matters that Canutt is running a counterfeiting operation out of a cave on the Mexican border. What matters is that there are plenty of scenes of horses galloping across the brush and a few fist fights – on this count director Carl Pierson more than delivers the goods. ▭

John Wayne *John Wyatt* • Marion Burns *Linda Carter* • Earle Hodgins *Dr Carter* • Yakima Canutt *Curly Joe Gale* • Reed Howes *Trigger* ■ *Dir* Carl Pierson • *Scr* Lindsley Parsons, Robert Tansey [Robert Emmett], from a story by Lindsley Parsons

Paradise for Three ★★★

Comedy
1938 · US · BW · 75mins

The delightful Mary Astor sues American millionaire soap-manufacturer Frank Morgan for breach of promise in this romantic comedy. Set in the German Alps on the eve of the Second World War, there are some thoughtful undertones, as Morgan's character tries to assimilate himself with the German people to understand their way of life. Eddie Buzzell directs with a light touch, and the supporting cast includes the indomitable Edna May Oliver as Morgan's bossy housekeeper.

Frank Morgan *Rudolph Tobler aka Edward Schultze* • Robert Young *Fritz Hagedorn* • Mary Astor *Mrs Mallebre* • Edna May Oliver *Aunt Julia Kunkel* • Florence Rice *Hilde Tobler* • Reginald Owen *Johann Kesselhut* • Henry Hull *Sepp* ■ *Dir* Edward Buzzell • *Scr* George Oppenheimer, Harry Ruskin, from the novel *Three Men in the Snow* by Erich Kästner

Paradise, Hawaiian Style ★★ U

Musical
1966 · US · Colour · 86mins

Elvis Presley struck box-office gold with the massive hit *Blue Hawaii* back in 1961, and the combination of sun, surf, girls and song was too good to let rest. Unfortunately, this time out, the formula looks decidedly shopworn, and this movie formed part of the downward spiral that would eventually destroy the on-screen credibility of the King of rock 'n' roll. Elvis himself reveals a disarmingly charming persona, but the thin plot and naff sequences with children, plus the unmemorable songs, undermine all his best efforts. ▭

Elvis Presley *Rick Richards* • Suzanna Leigh *Judy Hudson* • James Shigeta *Danny Kohana* • Donna Butterworth *Jan Kohana* • Marianna Hill *Lani* • Irene Tsu *Pua* • Linda Wong *Lehua* ■ *Dir* Michael Moore (1) • *Scr* Allan Weiss, Anthony Lawrence, from a story by Allan Weiss

Paradise Road ★★ 15

Second World War prison drama
1997 · Ausl/US · Colour · 116mins

Director Bruce Beresford's drama about a Japanese PoW camp for women in hot and sticky Sumatra, covers similar physical and emotional terrain as the eighties BBC series *Tenko*. Unfortunately it has some glaring weaknesses – everyone is too well-nourished and too neatly made-up for one thing – and it threatens to become syrupy when the women form themselves into a vocal ensemble in order to pass the time and raise morale. But the movie has an undeniable integrity and an outstandingly good cast. Contains violence. ▭

Glenn Close *Adrienne Pargiter* • Frances McDormand *Doctor Verstak* • Pauline Collins *Margaret Drummond* • Cate Blanchett *Susan Macarthy* • Jennifer Ehle *Rosemary Leighton-Jones* • Julianna Margulies *Topsy Merritt* • Wendy Hughes *Mrs Dickson* • Elizabeth Spriggs *Mrs Roberts* ■ *Dir* Bruce Beresford • *Scr* Bruce Beresford, from a story by David Giles, Martin Meader, from the non-fiction book *White Coolies* by Betty Jeffrey

Paradisio ★

Spy spoof 1962 · UK · BW and Tinted · 90mins

Long before the advent of Alan Smithee (the American director credit used when film-makers disown their films), a director who was so ashamed of the way his picture turned out or who resented constant studio interference had to release the offending work anonymously. No one has ever owned up to directing this silly comedy (which in its original version included some 3-D sequences) and it's easy to see why. Arthur Howard (brother of the more famous Leslie) struggles valiantly as a dotty professor whose discovery of a pair of x-ray sunglasses makes him the target for spies and the bane of women everywhere. Downright odd. Contains nudity.

Arthur Howard *Professor Sims* • Eva Waegner *Lisa Hinkle* ■ *Scr* Lawrence Zeitlin, Henri Haile, Jacques Henrici

The Parallax View ★★★★ 15

Political thriller 1974 · US · Colour · 97mins

Two years before *All the President's Men*, Alan J Pakula directed this equally potent and startlingly similar conspiracy thriller. Investigating a political assassination, reporter Warren Beatty uncovers evidence of a sinister agency called the Parallax Corporation, which recruits its marksmen from the dregs of disillusioned society. With an excellent script, stunning photography, and acted to perfection, the story of Beatty's infiltration of the society and his attempt to foil yet another killing is riveting, fascinating and nerve-racking. The definitive suspense/spy/paranoia thriller. Contains swearing. ▭

Warren Beatty *Joe Frady* • Paula Prentiss *Lee Carter* • William Daniels *Austin Tucker* • Walter McGinn *Jack Younger* • Hume Cronyn *Rintels* • Kelly Thordsen *LD* • Chuck Waters *Assassin* • Earl Hindman *Red* ■ *Dir* Alan J Pakula • *Scr* David Giler, Lorenzo Semple Jr, from the novel by Loren Singer • *Cinematographer* Gordon Willis

Parallel Lives ★★★ 15

Drama
1994 · US · Colour · 100mins

A sequel of sorts to Linda Yellen's *Chantilly Lace*, this largely improvised drama boasts one of the finest casts ever assembled for a TV movie. And what a mix of acting styles there is, too, with Method men like Ben Gazzara jousting with such old-fashioned idols as Robert Wagner and improvisation legends like Gena Rowlands rubbing shoulders with such rising stars as Mira Sorvino. Yet, in the end, this rambling, unfocused tale of a college reunion (which concludes with a totally unnecessary murder mystery) is unexpectedly hijacked by the less vaunted talents of Liza Minnelli, James Belushi and Helen Slater. Contains swearing and sex scenes. ▭

James Belushi *Nick Dimas* • Ben Gazzara *Charlie Duke* • Gena Rowlands *Francie Pomerantz* • JoBeth Williams *Winnie Winslow* • Liza Minnelli *Stevie Merrill* • Paul Sorvino *Ed Starling* • Mira Sorvino *Mattie DeRosa* • Dudley Moore *Stanley/President Andrews* • Treat Williams *Peter Barnum* • Robert Wagner *Sheriff* • Jill Eikenberry *Lula Sparks* • Ally Sheedy *Louise* • Helen Slater *Elsa Freedman* • LeVar Burton *Dr Franklin Carter* ■ *Dir* Linda Yellen • *Scr* Gisela Bernice

Paramount on Parade ★★
Musical revue
1930 · US · BW and Colour · 102mins

One of the earliest but not one of the best of a seemingly endless supply of studio revues designed to show off a roster of contract stars. In later years the formula occasionally had some flimsy excuse for a plot attached to it, but this overstuffed rag-bag, utilising the services of 11 directors, including Dorothy Arzner and Ernst Lubitsch, offers no such distraction. Sometimes tedious, sometimes ill-judged in matching the players to the material, this is nonetheless a collector's piece, with Maurice Chevalier's three sparkling turns, directed by Lubitsch, standing the test of time. Vaudeville veteran Elsie Janis supervised the production, which includes a couple of elaborate production numbers and some Technicolor sequences.

Jean Arthur • Mischa Auer • Clara Bow • Clive Brook • Nancy Carroll • Ruth Chatterton • Maurice Chevalier • Gary Cooper • Mitzi Green • Helen Kane • Fredric March • Nino Martini • Jack Oakie • Eugene Pallette • William Powell • Lillian Roth • Fay Wray ■ *Dir* Dorothy Arzner, Otto Brower, Edmund Goulding, Victor Heerman, Edwin H Knopf, Rowland V Lee, Ernst Lubitsch, Lothar Mendes, Victor Schertzinger, Edward Sutherland [A Edward Sutherland], Frank Tuttle

Paranoiac ★★★
Horror
1963 · UK · BW · 80mins

This is one of the best of a cycle of psychological horror films Hammer made in the sixties. Heiress Janette Scott and her crazy brother Oliver Reed are confronted by Alexander Davion, who claims to be their long-lost sibling. The plot is reminiscent of *The Case of the Frightened Lady* (1940) and the devices (organ played in the middle of the night, car brakes tampered with) now seem very hackneyed. But this was the *Scream* of its day, very popular with rebellious teens, and the twist ending is still not easily guessable.

Janette Scott *Eleanor Ashby* • Oliver Reed *Simon Ashby* • Liliane Brousse *Francoise* • Alexander Davion *Tony Ashby* • Sheila Burrell *Aunt Harriet* • Maurice Denham *John Kossett* • John Bonney *Keith Kossett* ■ *Dir* Freddie Francis • *Scr* Jimmy Sangster

Parasite ★ 18
Science-fiction horror
1982 · US · Colour · 84mins

In a post-holocaust future, where paramilitary forces and mutant punks clash continuously, scientist Robert Glaudini creates a parasitic monster that burrows into its victims and eats them from the inside. This is a crummy *Alien* meets *Mad Max* exploitation movie, directed by straight-to-video maven Charles Band, which wastes the talents of musical star Vivian Blaine, ex-Runaways singer Cherie Currie and fledgling superstar Demi Moore. Its one feature of note is that it cashed in on the early eighties 3-D revival frenzy and so cinema audiences got to experience the slimy creature leaping out of abdomens at them with eye-straining effect. Without that gimmick, it's a nothing piece of junk. ▭

Robert Glaudini *Dr Paul Dean* • Demi Moore *Patricia Welles* • Luca Bercovici *Ricus* • James

Davidson *Merchant* • Al Fann *Collins* • Tom Villard *Zeke* • Cherie Currie *Dana* ■ *Dir* Charles Band • *Scr* Michael Shoob, Frank Levering, Alan Adler [Alan J Adler]

Pardners ★★
Musical western spoof
1956 · US · Colour · 90mins

Dean Martin and Jerry Lewis, making a last-ditch stand before splitting up their partnership, star as a ranch foreman and the well-intentioned but inept city greenhorn who helps him fend off a bunch of cattle raiders. Stomping about in buckskins and ten-gallon hats, six-shooters to the ready, the pair burlesques every cliché of the western tradition, but the one-dimensional screenplay yields insufficient hilarity. The supporting cast offers a few surprises, though, with the appearances of Agnes Moorehead, Lee Van Cleef and Lon Chaney Jr.

Dean Martin *Slim Mosely Sr/Slim Mosely Jr* • Jerry Lewis *Wade Kingsley Sr/Wade Kingsley Jr* • Lori Nelson *Carol Kingsley* • Jeff Morrow *Rio* • Jackie Loughery *Dolly Riley* • John Baragrey *Dan Hollis* • Agnes Moorehead *Mrs Kingsley* • Lon Chaney Jr *Whitey* • Lee Van Cleef *Gus* ■ *Dir* Norman Taurog • *Scr* Sidney Sheldon, Jerry David, from the story *Rhythm on the Range* by Marvin J Houser

Pardon Mon Affaire ★★
Comedy
1976 · Fr · Colour · 108mins

If you think Yves Robert's sex comedy looks familiar, that's probably because it borrows heavily from *The Seven Year Itch* and was remade as *The Woman in Red*. However, neither Tom Ewell nor Gene Wilder can hold a candle to the comic ingenuity of Jean Rochefort, whose deliciously restrained performance atones for the slightness of the story, in which he risks his happy marriage to Danièle Delorme to pursue poster girl Anny Duperey. There's also much enjoyment to be had from the misadventures of his maladroit buddies, Claude Brasseur, Guy Bedos and Victor Lanoux. French dialogue dubbed into English.

Jean Rochefort *Etienne* • Claude Brasseur *Daniel* • Guy Bedos *Simon* • Victor Lanoux *Bouly* • Danièle Delorme *Marthe* • Anny Duperey *Charlotte* ■ *Dir* Yves Robert • *Scr* Jean-Loup Dabadie, Yves Robert

Pardon My Past ★★★
Comedy
1945 · US · BW · 88mins

While demobbed GI Fred MacMurray is on his way to start a mink farm with his pal William Demarest, he is hauled in by a gambler (Akim Tamiroff) who believes he is Francis Pemberton (also MacMurray), a playboy idler who owes Tamiroff money. MacMurray is appealing in his dual role, trying to deal with the complications that arise before this neat little comedy of mistaken identity resolves itself and he gets the girl (Marguerite Chapman). Director Leslie Fenton keeps an effective grip on the proceedings.

Fred MacMurray *Eddie York/Francis Pemberton* • Marguerite Chapman *Joan* • Akim Tamiroff *Jim Arnold* • William Demarest *Chuck Gibson* • Rita Johnson *Mary Pemberton* • Harry Davenport *Grandpa Pemberton* • Douglass Dumbrille *Uncle Wills* ■ *Dir* Leslie Fenton • *Scr* Earl Felton, Karl Kamb, from a story by Patterson McNutt, Harlan Ware

Pardon My Sarong ★★ U
Comedy
1942 · US · BW · 84mins

Ten years after his chilling version of HG Wells's *The Island Of Dr Moreau* – *The Island of Lost Souls* with Charles Laughton – director Erle C Kenton found himself in another pocket of tropical isolation when cast adrift with comedians Bud Abbott and Lou Costello. Made to cash in on the South Seas bubble of the time – Dorothy Lamour's sarong was much in vogue – the duo are bus drivers who find themselves all at sea with a jewel thief, the sinister Lionel Atwill from Universal's horror stable. Speciality acts such as the Four Ink Spots and Tip, Tap, Toe fill in the gaps, of which there are quite a few.

Bud Abbott *Algy Shaw* • Lou Costello *Wellington Phlug* • Virginia Bruce *Joan Marshall* • Robert Paige *Tommy Layton* • Lionel Atwill *Dr Varnoff* • Leif Erickson *Whaba* • William Demarest *Detective Kendall* ■ *Dir* Erle C Kenton • *Scr* True Boardman, Nat Perrin, John Grant

Pardon Us ★★★ U
Prison comedy
1931 · US · BW · 64mins

In this parody of the 1930 prison melodrama, *The Big House*, Laurel and Hardy play unintentional bootleggers who are imprisoned with two of their old faithfuls: spluttering James Finlayson and two-fisted hard man Walter Long. Some scenes are far from politically correct – the boys don blackface at one point to avoid recapture – but Ollie warbles an attractive tenor, while Stan's loose tooth means it's raspberries all round. ▭

Stan Laurel *Stan* • Oliver Hardy *Ollie* • June Marlowe *Warden's daughter* • Wilfred Lucas *Warden* • James Finlayson *Instructor* • Walter Long *Tiger* • Stanley J Sandford *Officer LeRoy Shields* ■ *Dir* James Parrott • *Scr* HM Walker • *Cinematographer* Jack Stevens

The Parent Trap ★★★ U
Comedy
1961 · US · Colour · 121mins

Remade in 1998 by Disney, here's a chance to see the studio's popular original. Hayley Mills stars in the dual role as twins trying to reunite their divorced parents, played by Maureen O'Hara and Brian Keith. Like many Disney films of the period, it's overlong, drawn out by the interminable section at a summer camp. But David Swift's direction is adroit and Lucien Ballard's Technicolor photography is particularly fetching. ▭

Hayley Mills *Sharon/Susan* • Maureen O'Hara *Maggie McKendrick* • Brian Keith *Mitch* • Charlie Ruggles [Charles Ruggles] *Charles McKendrick* • Una Merkel *Verbena* • Leo G Carroll *Rev Mosby* • Joanna Barnes *Vicky Robinson* • Cathleen Nesbitt *Louise McKendrick* ■ *Dir* David Swift • *Scr* David Swift, from the novel *Das Doppelte Lottchen* by Erich Kastner

The Parent Trap ★★★ PG
Comedy drama
1998 · US · Colour · 122mins

Freckle-faced Lindsay Lohan is the American youngster who steps into Hayley Mills's shoes for this update of the 1961 original. Lohan plays twins separated not long after birth, one growing up with British wedding-gown

designer Natasha Richardson, the other with her ex-husband, American vineyard owner Dennis Quaid. Meeting by chance at an American summer camp, the twins plot to bring their parents back together. Thanks to modern technology, it's impossible to tell there aren't really two Lohans, and this unashamedly sentimental comedy will delight its target audience of young girls. ▭ *DVD*

Lindsay Lohan *Hallie Parker/Annie James* • Dennis Quaid *Nick Parker* • Natasha Richardson *Elizabeth James* • Elaine Hendrix *Meredith Blake* • Lisa Ann Walter *Chessy* • Simon Kunz *Martin* ■ *Dir* Nancy Meyers • *Scr* Nancy Meyers, Charles Shyer, David Swift, from the novel *Das Doppelte Lottchen* by Erich Kastner

Parent Trap II ★★ U
Comedy
1986 · US · Colour · 81mins

A belated sequel to Disney's 1961 film about identical siblings, with a grown-up Hayley Mills again playing twin roles. This time Mills's daughter and her friend are the scheming ones, trying to kindle romance between the adults in the cast, including widower Tom Skerritt. Amiable entertainment, made for TV, with technological advances allowing Mills to be beside herself more convincingly than she had been 25 years earlier. ▭

Hayley Mills *Sharon Ferris/Susan Corey* • Tom Skerritt *Bill Grand* • Carrie Kei Heim *Nikki Ferris* • Bridgette Andersen *Mary Grand* • Alex Harvey *Brian Corey* • Gloria Cromwell *Florence* ■ *Dir* Ronald F Maxwell • *Scr* Stuart Krieger

Parent Trap Hawaiian Honeymoon ★★ U
Comedy
1989 · US · Colour · 86mins

Another TV-movie sequel to Disney's 1961 original about lookalike siblings, with Hayley Mills once again picking up two pay packets. This time out, the sisters plus their families (including teenage girl triplets) relocate to Hawaii to take over a rundown holiday resort. The realisation that the twin thing was wearing thin led Disney to shut its *Trap*, until 1998's cute and glossy remake of the original film. ▭

Hayley Mills *Susan Evers/Sharon Evers* • Barry Bostwick *Jeffrey Wyatt* • Leanna Creel *Lisa Wyatt* • Monica Creel *Jessie Wyatt* • Joy Creel *Megan Wyatt* ■ *Dir* Mollie Miller

Parenthood ★★★★ 15
Comedy
1989 · US · Colour · 118mins

Director Ron Howard's feel-good family ensemble piece just manages to stay the right side of sentimentality, and the result is an affectionate, leisurely comedy about the joys (and otherwise) of bringing up children. Steve Martin grabs the comic honours as the elder son of a family headed up by crotchety Jason Robards, although there are fine performances, too, from a star-studded cast which includes Dianne Wiest, Rick Moranis, Mary Steenburgen, Martha Plimpton and Keanu Reeves. Howard handles the large number of different story strands adeptly and, while it gets a little soppy at times, he makes the most of the sharp script and some neat set pieces, notably Martin's cowboy turn at his son's birthday party. Contains swearing and sex scenes. ▭ *DVD*

U = SUITABLE FOR ALL   Uc = SUITABLE FOR ALL, ESPECIALLY FOR YOUNG CHILDREN (VIDEO ONLY)   PG = PARENTAL GUIDANCE

Steve Martin *Gil Buckman* • Mary Steenburgen *Karen Buckman* • Dianne Wiest *Helen* • Jason Robards [Jason Robards Jr] *Frank* • Rick Moranis *Nathan* • Tom Hulce *Larry* • Keanu Reeves *Tod* • Martha Plimpton *Julie* • Harley Kozak *Susan* • Leaf Phoenix [Joaquin Phoenix] *Garry* ■ *Dir* Ron Howard • *Scr* Lowell Ganz, Babaloo Mandel, from a story by Lowell Ganz, Babaloo Mandel, Ron Howard

Parents ★★★★ 18
Horror comedy 1988 · US · Colour · 78mins

If the BSE scare didn't put you off eating meat, then Bob Balaban's grim horror comedy certainly will. Could young Michael's suburban parents really be the cannibals he thinks they are? Or is he just a disturbed child suffering from juvenile hallucinations brought on by the atom-age anxieties of the Eisenhower fifties? Set firmly in *Blue Velvet* territory, with a spot-on big band Muzak soundtrack, this disquieting explosion of the nuclear family unit will have you screaming with both laughter and revulsion. Contains swearing. ▦

Randy Quaid *Nick Laemle* • Mary Beth Hurt *Lily Laemle* • Sandy Dennis *Millie Dew* • Bryan Madorsky *Michael Laemle* • Juno Mills-Cockell *Sheila Zellner* • Kathryn Grody *Miss Baxter* • Deborah Rush *Mrs Zellner* • Graham Jarvis *Mr Zellner* ■ *Dir* Bob Balaban • *Scr* Christopher Hawthorne • *Music* Angelo Badalamenti

Les Parents Terribles ★★★★★
Drama 1948 · Fr · BW · 102mins

Making few alterations to his original text, Jean Cocteau proved with this tragi-comic tale of dysfunction and sexual frustration that it was possible to adapt a play and be inventively cinematic at the same time. The credits may roll over a stage curtain, the acts may be divided by captions and the action may be confined to two stylised sets, but through judicious use of telephoto lenses, rigid framing and punctilious editing, Cocteau was able to register every twisted emotion and treacherous expression as the skeletons tumble out of the closet and domineering matriarch Yvonne de Bray's world slowly falls apart. A French language film.

Jean Marais *Michel* • Yvonne de Bray *Yvonne* • Gabrielle Dorziat *Aunt Léo* • Marcel André *Georges* • Josette Day *Madeleine* • Jean Cocteau *Narrator* ■ *Dir* Jean Cocteau • *Scr* Jean Cocteau, from his play ■ *Cinematographer* Michel Kelber

Le Parfum d'Yvonne ★★★ 18
Drama 1994 · Fr · Colour · 85mins

Patrice Leconte always manages to create a world in which reality and fantasy happily co-exist. However, here he overdoes the unlikely to the extent that this charming but flimsy study of daydreaming and delusion has so little substance to support adequately its more serious undercurrents. Hippolyte Girardot, in Swiss exile to avoid Algerian War service, and Sandra Majani, as the girl dreaming of movie stardom, are as dull as Jean-Pierre Marielle is outrageously camp. Too much perfume is often overpowering, but here the fragrance is so subtle that it's been carried away on the wind before we can truly savour it. In French

with English subtitles. Contains sex scenes and nudity. ▦

Jean-Pierre Marielle *René Meinthe* • Hippolyte Girardot *Victor Chmara* • Sandra Majani *Yvonne* • Richard Bohringer *Uncle Roland* • Paul Guers *Daniel Hendrickx* • Corinne Marchand *Tilleuls Patron* • Philippe Magnan *Pulli* ■ *Dir* Patrice Leconte • *Scr* Patrice Leconte, from the novel *Villa Triste* by Patrick Modiano

Paris after Dark ★★
Second World War drama
1943 · US · BW · 84mins

France's resolve to continue resisting the German occupation is reaffirmed by the story of Philip Dorn's sick and defeated Frenchman, released from captivity by the Germans. He suspects his wife Brenda Marshall of having an affair with her employer, a doctor played by George Sanders, but they turn out to be stalwarts of the Resistance who inspire him to stand up for the cause of freedom. Of all the Hollywood studios, 20th Century-Fox made the biggest effort to employ displaced European film-makers and here gave director Léonide Moguy and producer André Daven their first Hollywood picture.

George Sanders *Dr André Marbel* • Philip Dorn *Jean Blanchard* • Brenda Marshall *Yvonne Blanchard* • Madeleine Lebeau *Collette* • Marcel Dalio *Michel* • Robert Lewis (1) *Col Pirosh* • Peter Lawford ■ *Dir* Léonide Moguy • *Scr* Harold Buchman, from a story by George Kessel

Paris Blues ★★★★ 12
Romantic drama 1961 · US · BW · 94mins

Handsome buddies Paul Newman and Sidney Poitier click as footloose, free-spirited American jazzmen Ram and Eddie on the razzle in Paris, where pretty, comparatively square tourists Joanne Woodward and Diahann Carroll are understandably captivated by the charismatic musicians. The sensational Duke Ellington score provides the film's highlight; ageing like a fine wine – even with its vintage "Ya dig, baby?" lingo – this offbeat affair from one of Newman's favourite directors, Martin Ritt, is also one of the most delightful jazz movies ever made. Contains some violence. ▦

Paul Newman *Ram Bowen* • Joanne Woodward *Lillian Corning* • Sidney Poitier *Eddie Cook* • Louis Armstrong *Wild Man Moore* • Diahann Carroll *Connie Lampson* • Serge Reggiani *Michel Duvigne* ■ *Dir* Martin Ritt • *Scr* Jack Sher, Irene Kamp, Walter Bernstein, Lulla Adler, from the novel by Harold Flender • *Music* Duke Ellington

Paris by Night ★★★ 15
Drama 1988 · UK · Colour · 99mins

Film noir meets allegorical Thatcherite morality as the problems pile up for Conservative Euro MP Charlotte Rampling. Her marriage to alcoholic Michael Gambon is on the rocks and she's convinced she's being blackmailed. While in Paris for political talks, she is surprised by her suspected blackmailer and murders him. But can she avoid the consequences of her deed with the same steely efficiency? Utilising brittle dialogue, wilful obscurity and nightmarish visuals, writer/director David Hare conjures up a symbolic and

often devastating fable about warped British values in the yuppie eighties. ▦

Charlotte Rampling *Clara Paige* • Michael Gambon *Gerald Paige* • Robert Hardy *Adam Gillvray* • Iain Glen *Wallace Sharp* • Jane Asher *Pauline* • Andrew Ray *Michael Swanton* • Niamh Cusack *Jenny Swanton* ■ *Dir/Scr* David Hare

Paris Calling ★★
Second World War drama
1941 · US · BW · 95mins

Elisabeth Bergner's sole stab at a Hollywood career came with this routine wartime melodrama about underground resistance after the Germans capture Paris. She plays the wealthy Parisienne who joins the fight for freedom, with intrepid Randolph Scott as a downed RAF pilot and heinous Basil Rathbone as a French politician turned collaborator. Add Lee J Cobb as the top Nazi, and you have a cast that makes the proceedings just about watchable.

Elizabeth Bergner [Elisabeth Bergner] *Marianne* • Randolph Scott *Nick* • Basil Rathbone *Benoit* • Gale Sondergaard *Colette* • Lee J Cobb *Schwabe* • Charles Arnt *Lantz* ■ *Dir* Edwin L Marin • *Scr* Benjamin Glazer, Charles S Kaufman, from a story by John S Toldy

Paris France ★★ 18
Erotic drama
1993 · Can · Colour and BW · 112mins

Director Gérard Ciccoritti's intention here was obviously to make an erotic drama about the connection between the sexual and the creative urge. He certainly packs his picture with passionate encounters, but the pronouncements that he hoped would have the audience nodding sagely had them rolling in the aisles, such is their pompous absurdity. Leslie Hope plays a novelist married to a publisher who is living life to the full after he believes that he has received an answerphone message from John Lennon telling him he's only got three days to live. Contains swearing, sex scenes and nudity. ▦

Leslie Hope *Lucy Quick* • Peter Outerbridge *Randall Sloan* • Victor Ertmanis *Michael Quick* • Dan Lett *William* • Raoul Trujillo *Minter* ■ *Dir* Gerard Ciccoritti [Gérard Ciccoritti] • *Scr* Tom Walmsley, from his novel

Paris Holiday ★★ U
Comedy 1958 · US · Colour · 109mins

American comedian Bob Hope, while in Paris, buys a French script, unaware that it carries clues to a gang of counterfeiters. They send sexy blonde Anita Ekberg to lure Hope into their clutches, but she falls for him and shoves him into a lunatic asylum from where he is rescued by Fernandel. Wisecracker Hope and France's comic idol, Fernandel, prove an ill-matched pair in this frenetic nonsense, which surrounds them with an international ragbag of supporting players. Strictly for committed fans of the two stars, neither of whom is particularly funny.

Bob Hope *Robert Leslie Hunter* • Fernandel *Fernydel* • Anita Ekberg *Zara* • Martha Hyer *Ann McCall* • Preston Sturges *Serge Vitry* • André Morell *American Ambassador* • Maurice Teynac *Dr Bernais* • Yves Brainville *Inspector*

Dupont ■ *Dir* Gerd Oswald • *Scr* Edmund Beloin, Dean Riesner, from a story by Bob Hope

Paris Honeymoon ★★
Comedy 1939 · US · BW · 83mins

Texas millionaire Bing Crosby, complete with ten-gallon hat, falls for countess Shirley Ross, pursues her to Europe, and rents himself a castle. Once installed, he falls in love with a local peasant girl (Franciska Gaal). As insubstantial as gossamer, but nowhere near as pleasing, this nonsense, directed by Frank Tuttle with minimum style, includes a handful of forgotten songs and is definitely of interest only to Crosby fans. Miss Gaal returned to her native Budapest shortly after this film.

Bing Crosby *"Lucky" Lawton* • Franciska Gaal *Manya* • Akim Tamiroff *Peter Karloca* • Shirley Ross *Barbara Wayne* • Edward Everett Horton *Ernest Figg* • Ben Blue *Sitska* • Albert Dekker *Drunken peasant* ■ *Dir* Frank Tuttle • *Scr* Frank Butler, Don Hartman, from a story by Angela Sherwood • *Cinematographer* Karl Struss

Paris Is Burning ★★★★
Documentary 1990 · US · Colour · 76mins

A brilliantly entertaining documentary peek into the New York subculture of drag queens and transsexuals centred around "The Ball", a regular event that's part competition, part performance art and part ritual. Director Jennie Livingston's acerbic look at gay society's fringe-dwellers is a rapturous mixture of high spirits (the vogueing dance craze started in its hallowed Harlem venue), camp (the legendary Pepper Labeija living out an outlandish parody of a Hollywood star's life) and pathos (long-time pro Dorian Corey ashamed that the upcoming she-males don't even know who Marlene Dietrich is).

Dir Jennie Livingston

Paris Nous Appartient ★★★★
Mystery drama 1960 · Fr · BW · 158mins

Like many French New Wave film-makers, Jacques Rivette began his career as a critic. Indeed, he was still working for the famous journal *Cahiers du Cinéma* while making this intense conspiracy picture, for which he had to borrow film stock from François Truffaut and a camera from Claude Chabrol. The fact that the action was shot over a two-year period is clearly evident in the inconsistent quality of the performances, but Rivette still crafts a complex and intriguing story. Some critics labelled the film pretentious, but his fellow directors considered it one of the crowning achievements of the early New Wave. In French with English subtitles.

Betty Schneider *Anne Goupil* • Gianni Esposito *Gérard Lenz* • Françoise Prévost *Terry Yok* • Daniel Crohem *Philip Kaufman* • François Maistre *Pierre Goupil* • Jean-Claude Brialy *Jean-Marc* ■ *Dir* Jacques Rivette • *Scr* Jacques Rivette, Jean Gruault

Paris or Somewhere ★★

Drama 1995 · Can · Colour · 84mins

Based on J M Synge's masterpiece *The Playboy of the Western World*, this tale of claim and counterclaim has ideas quite some way above its station. Callum Keith Rennie stars as a stranger who divides a small Canadian community by confessing that he's a killer. While others debate whether he's a hero or a heel, one woman becomes his devoted admirer, much to the disgust of her beau, who is determined to expose the newcomer. Director Brad Turner urges his cast on to ever greater feats of overacting, and this overwrought barnstormer won't find many takers.

Callum Keith Rennie *Christy Mahon* • Molly Parker *Peg Kennedy* • John Vernon *Old Mahon* ■ *Dir* Brad Turner • *Scr* Lee Gowan, from the play by JM Synge

Paris Qui Dort ★★

Silent fantasy 1923 · Fr · BW · 61mins

René Clair's first feature, completed in three weeks, reflected some of the anarchic preoccupations of the surrealist and Dadaist artists with whom Clair associated at the time. The story, which he wrote in one night, tells of a crazed inventor who creates a "sleep ray" that suspends animation throughout Paris. Although the film is full of comic invention and absurdity, it is sometimes too self-consciously in love with its own cleverness, and some of the cinematic tricks begin to pall.

Henri Rollan *Albert* • Madeleine Rodrigue *Woman passenger* • Marcel Vallée *Thief* • Albert Préjean *Pilot* ■ *Dir/Scr* René Clair

Paris, Texas ★★★★★ 15

Drama 1984 · W Ger/Fr · Colour · 138mins

Character actor Harry Dean Stanton enjoys a rare leading role in German director Wim Wenders's emotionally charged road movie. The odyssey begins as restless drifter Travis Anderson (Stanton) walks out of the desert after a four-year absence and is reunited with his small son (Hunter Carson), who's being cared for by Travis's brother (Dean Stockwell). Travis then sets out to reclaim his family life by seeking out his estranged wife and the boy's mother (Nastassja Kinski), now a peep-show stripper. There's an urgency to the film, as Wenders brings an outsider's fresh eye to create this massive metaphor about rootless America.

Harry Dean Stanton *Travis Anderson* • Nastassja Kinski *Jane* • Dean Stockwell *Walter R Anderson* • Aurore Clément *Anne Anderson* • Hunter Carson *Hunter Anderson* • Bernhard Wicki *Dr Ulmer* ■ *Dir* Wim Wenders • *Scr* Sam Shepard, from his story adapted by LM Kit Carson

Paris Trout ★★★★ 18

Drama 1991 · US · Colour · 95mins

Paris Trout is a person: played by Dennis Hopper, he's a bigoted Deep South storekeeper who murders the young sister of a black man who has reneged on a debt. Appalled, Trout's wife (Barbara Hershey) finds herself becoming the target of his violence and eventually retreats to the arms of his lawyer (Ed Harris). This pressure cooker of a plot, set in 1949 and adapted by Pete Dexter from his own novel, is tensely directed by Stephen Gyllenhaal. But it's Hopper's picture – crewcut, wild-eyed and utterly horrific, he delivers a mesmerising portrayal of a monster who believes he's behaving normally. Contains violence.

Dennis Hopper *Paris Trout* • Barbara Hershey *Hanna Trout* • Ed Harris *Harry Seagraves* • Ray McKinnon *Carl Bonner* • Tina Lifford *Mary Sayers* • Darnita Henry *Rosie Sayers* • Eric Ware *Henry Ray Sayers* • Ronreaco Lee *Chester Sayers* ■ *Dir* Stephen Gyllenhaal • *Scr* Pete Dexter, from his novel

Paris Vu Par... ★★★ 15

Portmanteau drama 1965 · Fr · Colour · 91mins

Shot in 16mm and capturing the spontaneity of the *Nouvelle Vague*, this portmanteau picture is patchy but entertaining. Jean-Daniel Pollet chronicles a nervous man's encounter with a prostitute; an angry wife is too preoccupied to help a potential suicide in Jean Rouch's *Gard du Nord*; an American in Paris swaps boyfriends in Jean Douchet's *Saint-Germain-des-Prés*; Eric Rohmer puts Jean-Michel Rouzière through the emotional wringer; Jean-Luc Godard's *Montparnasse-Levallois* has a woman mixing up her billets-doux; and in Claude Chabrol's *La Muette*, a boy is frustrated by his parents' constant arguing. A French language film.

Nadine Ballot *Odile* • Barbet Schroeder *Jean-Pierre* • Micheline Dax *Prostitute* • Claude Melki *Léon* • Jean-Michel Rouzière *Jean-Marc* • Marcel Gallon *Victim* • Joanna Shimkus *Monica* • Philippe Hiquilly *Roger* • Stéphane Audran *Wife* • Claude Chabrol *Husband* ■ *Dir* Jean Douchet, Jean Rouch, Jean-Daniel Pollet, Eric Rohmer, Jean-Luc Godard, Claude Chabrol • *Scr* Jean Douchet, Georges Keller, Jean Rouch, Jean-Daniel Pollet, Eric Rohmer, Jean-Luc Godard, Claude Chabrol

Paris When It Sizzles ★★

Romantic comedy 1964 · US · Colour · 110mins

Gowned in her trademark Givenchy, the irresistible Audrey Hepburn does her best in director Richard Quine's leaden remake of a soufflé-light French comedy in which screenwriter William Holden, facing a deadline, is devoid of inspiration. He enlists the help of his secretary (Hepburn) in acting out possible scenarios, sending the film off into an unsuccessful hodgepodge of genres, periods and fantasy sequences. Though seeming understandably bemused at times, Hepburn is charming and keeps the nonsense and a dull Holden afloat, Noël Coward is the irate producer waiting for his script, and the Paris locations look gorgeous.

William Holden (1) *Richard Benson* • Audrey Hepburn *Gabrielle Simpson* • Grégoire Aslan *Police inspector* • Raymond Bussières *Gangster* • Christian Duvallex *Maître d'hôtel* • Noël Coward *Alexander Meyerheimer* • Tony Curtis *2nd policeman* • Marlene Dietrich *Guest star* • Mel Ferrer • Fred Astaire • Frank Sinatra ■ *Dir* Richard Quine • *Scr* George Axelrod, from the film *La Fête à Henriette* by Julien Duvivier, Henriette by *Henri Jeanson*

Park Plaza 605 ★ U

Crime thriller 1953 · UK · BW · 79mins

Tom Conway's long experience of playing sleuths shows to advantage in this fair British B-feature which tees off with the accidental death of a carrier pigeon. As the grandiloquently named private eye Norman Conquest, Conway can't resist courting danger on his day off by keeping a mysterious appointment with Eva Bartok's blonde diamond smuggler. Joy Shelton has the thankless role of the detective's wary girlfriend while there's offbeat casting of Sid James as a police superintendent and Richard Wattis as a villain.

Tom Conway *Norman Conquest* • Eva Bartok *Nadina Rodin* • Joy Shelton *Pixie Everard* • Sidney James *Supt Williams* • Richard Wattis *Theodore Feather* • Carl Jaffe *Boris Roff* • Anton Diffring *Gregor* • Robert Adair *Baron Von Henschel* ■ *Dir* Bernard Knowles • *Scr* Bertram Ostrer, Albert Fennell, Bernard Knowles, Clifford Witting, from the novel *Daredevil Conquest* by Berkeley Gray

Park Row ★★★★ U

Drama 1952 · US · BW · 82mins

Hard-boiled director Samuel Fuller returns to the profession that launched him – American big-city journalism – with this belter of a story about rivalry between two ruthless newspaper owners in the last century, as they battle to feed sleaze-hungry readers with all the news that's fit to print or get away with. Fuller's tabloid style is passionately suited to his first love and there's a fight sequence that's worth buying tickets for.

Gene Evans *Phineas Mitchell* • Mary Welch *Charity Hackett* • Bela Kovacs *Ottmar Mergenthaler* • Herbert Heyes *Josiah Davenport* • Tina Rome *Jenny O'Rourke* • George O'Hanlon *Steve Brodie* ■ *Dir/Scr* Samuel Fuller

Parker ★★ 15

Thriller 1984 · UK · Colour · 97mins

A routine British suspense film, with Bryan Brown as a businessman who claims to have been kidnapped in Munich, but who finds police oddly reluctant to accept his allegation. The paranoia-fuelled plot has potential, but it's largely unrealised because of needless obscurity and ambivalence. A more simple tack might have paid better dividends.

Bryan Brown *Parker* • Cherie Lunghi *Jenny* • Kurt Raab *Inspector Haag* • Hannelore Elsner *Jillian Schelm* • Bob Peck *Rohl* • Ingrid Pitt *Widow* • Tom Wilkinson *Tom* ■ *Dir* Jim Goddard • *Scr* Trevor Preston

Parker Kane ★★

Action thriller 1990 · US · Colour · 96mins

The eclectic cast is the most appealing thing about this otherwise formulaic TV movie, intended to spin off into a TV series . Jeff Fahey is the private investigator who stumbles across a gang of crooks dumping lethal waste products. There are no surprises in the story, so sit back instead and pick out the familiar faces: Marisa Tomei, in the days before her Oscar-winning turn in *My Cousin Vinny*, British model-turned-actress Amanda Pays and soul diva Patti LaBelle. Contains violence, swearing and nudity.

Jeff Fahey *Parker Kane* • Marisa Tomei *April Haynes* • Drew Snyder *Dunbar Fisk* • Stellan Skarsgård *Nathan Van Adams* • Amanda Pays *Sarah Taylor* • Patti LaBelle *Cartier* ■ *Dir* Steve Perry • *Scr* Peter Lenkov

Parlor, Bedroom and Bath ★★

Comedy 1931 · US · BW · 72mins

Suffocated by the studio system and uncomfortable with sound, Buster Keaton's spell at MGM became one of the unhappiest and least inspired of his career. Originally a Broadway hit and a popular 1920 silent, this frantic farce was bought specially for Keaton by production chief Irving G Thalberg to make amends after they fell out over the Great Stone Face's talkie debut, *Free and Easy*. A topnotch supporting cast was assembled and Keaton was given a measure of creative freedom, but farce just wasn't his forte and the strain shows.

Buster Keaton *Reginald Irving* • Charlotte Greenwood *Polly Hathaway* • Reginald Denny *Jeffery Haywood* • Cliff Edwards *Bellhop* • Dorothy Christy *Angelica Embrey* • Joan Peers *Nita Leslie* • Sally Eilers *Virginia Embrey* ■ *Dir* Edward Sedgwick • *Scr* Richard Schayer, Robert E Hopkins, from the play by Charles W Bell, Mark Swan

Parnell ★

Biographical drama 1937 · US · BW · 117mins

This is a worthy, though deadly dull, Hollywood biopic, suffers irredeemably from the chronic miscasting of the then king and queen of Hollywood, Clark Gable and Myrna Loy, as top Irish statesman Charles Stewart Parnell and his mistress Kitty O'Shea. For years afterwards Gable would joke about *Parnell* ruefully and with good cause. There's some attempt to use the tale as a then-topical aside to the Edward and Mrs Simpson affair, but, frankly, the whole is unwatchable except for fans of serious miscasting.

Clark Gable *Charles Stewart Parnell* • Myrna Loy *Katie O'Shea* • Edna May Oliver *Aunt Ben* • Edmund Gwenn *Campbell* • Alan Marshal *Willie O'Shea* • Donald Crisp *Davitt* • Billie Burke *Clara* • Donald Meek *Murphy* • Montagu Love *Gladstone* • Randolph Churchill *MP* ■ *Dir* John M Stahl • *Scr* John Van Druten, SN Behrman, from the play *Parnell* by Elsie T Schauffler • *Cinematographer* Karl Freund • *Costume Designer* Adrian

Parrish ★★

Drama 1961 · US · Colour · 137mins

One of several lurid and lengthy Warner Bros melodramas from writer/director Delmer Daves showcasing young players and aimed principally at juvenile audiences, this is just as risible but nowhere near as entertaining as *A Summer Place*. Blond hunk Troy Donahue plays the humble worker on a tobacco plantation who becomes involved with Connie Stevens, Diane McBain and Sharon Hugueny. It's sniggering fun for about half its running time, with Connie Stevens helpfully pointing out the location of her bedroom and her penchant for sleeping in the raw to the young stud, though its celebration of tobacco cultivation is now in rather bad taste. Claudette Colbert makes her

U = SUITABLE FOR ALL   Uc = SUITABLE FOR ALL, ESPECIALLY FOR YOUNG CHILDREN (VIDEO ONLY)   PG = PARENTAL GUIDANCE

final big screen appearance as Troy's mother.

Troy Donahue *Parrish McLean* • Claudette Colbert *Ellen McLean* • Karl Malden *Judd Raike* • Dean Jagger *Sala Post* • Connie Stevens *Lucy* • Diane McBain *Alison Post* • Sharon Hugueny *Paige Raike* ■ *Dir* Delmer Daves • *Scr* Delmer Daves, from the novel by Mildred Savage

The Parson and the Outlaw
★ U

Western   1957 · US · Colour · 70mins

In this B-western, Pat Garrett doesn't shoot Billy the Kid. He lets him go free when Billy promises to throw away his guns. But poor Billy can't escape his legend, nor those people who want to pick a fight with him. This nickel-and-dime effort may please devotees of sagebrush sagas because of its cast of has-beens like Sonny Tufts, Jean Parker and Charles ''Buddy'' Rogers who also produced it.

Anthony Dexter *Billy the Kid* • Charles ''Buddy'' Rogers *Reverend Jericho Jones* • Jean Parker *Mrs Jones* • Sonny Tufts *Jack Slade* • Robert Lowery *Colonel Morgan* • Marie Windsor *Tonya* ■ *Dir* Oliver Drake • *Scr* Oliver Drake, John Mantley

Part 2, Sounder
★★★

Drama   1976 · US · Colour · 98mins

On the back of the low-budget success of the original, an American TV network (ABC) funded this sequel as a TV movie but was so impressed they gave it a theatrical release. It continues the heart-rending story of the Morgan family of black sharecroppers in Depression-hit Louisiana in 1933, who are still fighting poverty and prejudice with the help of activist teacher Annazette Chase (in the role Janet MacLachlan played in the original). Her educational establishment is closed down by the white landowners but the black community get together to build their own school to ensure a better future for the next generation.

Harold Sylvester *Nathan Lee Morgan* • Ebony Wright *Rebecca Lee Morgan* • Taj Mahal *Ike Phillips* • Annazette Chase *Camille Johnson* • Darryl Young *David Lee Morgan* • Erica Young *Josie Mae Morgan* • Ronald Bolden *Earl Morgan* ■ *Dir* William A Graham • *Scr* Lonne Elder III, from a novel by William H Armstrong • *Music* Taj Mahal

Part 2 Walking Tall
★★ 15

Crime   1975 · US · Colour · 104mins

Whether we needed it or not here are the further adventures of real-life Tennessee sheriff Buford Pusser and his one-man crusade against organised crime, impersonated this time by the lightweight Bo Svenson, replacing original star Joe Don Baker. Pusser did agree to play himself but 24 hours after signing the contract he died in a car crash, and there were some among his devoted followers who refused to accept the crash as an accident. Although less violent than its predecessor, with a noticeable easing up on the glorification of vigilante cops, too often this comes across as a lame made-for-TV movie. ▦

Bo Svenson *Buford Pusser* • Luke Askew *Pinky Dobson* • Noah Beery Jr *Carl Pusser* • John Chandler [John Davis Chandler] *Ray Henry* • Robert DoQui *Obra Eaker* • Bruce

Glover *Grady Coker* • Richard Jaeckel *Stud Pardee* • Leif Garrett *Mike Pusser* ■ *Dir* Earl Bellamy • *Scr* Howard B Kreitsek

Part-Time Wife
★

Comedy   1961 · UK · BW · 69mins

Unsuccessful insurance salesman Anton Rodgers is a well-intentioned but gullible sort who's married to the vivacious Nyree Dawn Porter. Rodgers's ex-army friend, Kenneth J Warren, has a rich uncle visiting from Canada, and he is anxious to get in his good books. To this end, he persuades his friend to lend him his wife. However, Warren has a more sinister motive... Competent performances fail to add sparkle to the tired plot.

Anton Rodgers *Tom* • Nyree Dawn Porter *Jenny* • Kenneth J Warren *Drew* • Henry McCarthy *Whitworth* • Mark Singleton *Detective* ■ *Dir* Max Varnel • *Scr* MM McCormack

Une Partie de Campagne
★★★★★

Romantic drama   1936 · Fr · BW · 38mins

Based on the Maupassant story, Jean Renoir's short feature is one of the most lyrical pieces of cinema ever produced. Set in 1880, it follows a Parisian family on a Sunday outing that results in a stolen moment of passion and a lifetime of regret. Slyly observing middle-class foibles, the film is exuberantly played by the Groupe Octobre acting troupe and majestically photographed by Claude Renoir and Jean Bourgoin. Abandoned because of incessant rain (with only two scenes left to shoot), the picture was not released until 1946, and even then incomplete, with captions explaining the missing action. In French with English subtitles.

Sylvia Bataille *Henriette* • Georges Saint Saens *Henri* • Jeanne Marken *Mme Dufour* • Gabriello [AndréGabriello] *Monsieur Dufour* • Jacques Borel [Jacques Brunius] *Rudolph* • Paul Temps *Anatole* • Gabrielle Fontan *The Grandmother* • Jean Renoir *Papa Poulin* • Marguerite Renoir *Servant* ■ *Dir* Jean Renoir • *Scr* Jean Renoir, from the story by Guy de Maupassant

Une Partie de Plaisir
★★★ 18

Melodrama   1974 · Fr/It · Colour · 96mins

When Paul Gégauff, the screenwriter on many of Claude Chabrol's films, wrote this autobiographical account of the break-up of his marriage, Chabrol persuaded him, his real ex-wife and his daughter to play versions of themselves. Gégauff comes across as a chic poseur, who treats his wife abominably. Chabrol is obviously fascinated and disgusted by his friend's behaviour, and the audience might feel the same, though the exhibitionism of the whole enterprise sometimes outweighs the interest. Judging from this, it is not surprising that Gégauff was stabbed to death in 1983 by his second wife. In French with English subtitles. Contains violence, swearing and sex scenes. ▦

Paul Gégauff *Philippe* • Danièle Gégauff *Esther* • Paula Moore *Sylvia Murdoch* • Michel Valette *Katkof* ■ *Dir* Claude Chabrol • *Scr* Paul Gégauff

Parting Glances
★★★ 15

Drama   1985 · US · Colour · 86mins

Set during 24 hours in the Aids-ravaged confines of New York's swanky gay scene, director Bill Sherwood's earnestly tender drama is an old-fashioned love story at heart about two men finishing their relationship because one gets a job transfer abroad. Basically a series of heartfelt farewells to friends and family, this bold and outspoken, character-driven ensemble piece tells its bittersweet tale with warmth, grace and droll humour. Steve Buscemi puts in an early appearance as a dying musician. Sherwood himself died of an Aids-related illness in 1990. Contains swearing. ▦

Richard Ganoung *Michael* • Steve Buscemi *Nick* • John Bolger *Robert* • Adam Nathan *Peter* • Kathy Kinney *Joan* • Patrick Tull *Cecil* ■ *Dir/Scr* Bill Sherwood

Parting Shots
★ 12

Black comedy   1998 · UK · Colour · 98mins

Michael Winner's serial killer comedy is excruciatingly, embarrassingly awful, with every member of its august cast guilty of a gross error of judgement by agreeing to participate. As a dying man punishing those who've slighted him, singer Chris Rea's totally inadequate performance is made to look even more inept by a script of the smuggest sitcom variety, woefully one-dimensional direction and supremely shoddy editing (by Winner's alter ego Arnold Crust). Contains violence. ▦

Chris Rea *Harry Sterndale* • Felicity Kendal *Jill Saunders* • Bob Hoskins *Gerd Layton* • Ben Kingsley *Renzo Locatelli* • Joanna Lumley *Freda* • Oliver Reed *Jamie Campbell-Stewart* • Diana Rigg *Lisa* • John Cleese *Maurice Walpole* • Gareth Hunt *Inspector Bass* • Peter Davison *John* ■ *Dir* Michael Winner • *Scr* Michael Winner, Nick Mead, from a story by Michael Winner

Partner
★★★

Drama   1968 · It · Colour · 105mins

The fact that Pierre Clémenti speaks French while everyone else in this loose adaptation of Dostoevsky's novella converses in Italian, rather betrays the fact that Bernardo Bertolucci was totally enthralled with Jean-Luc Godard at this stage of his career. Yet the influence of the worldwide civil unrest that characterised 1968 and the experimental strategies of Julien Beck's Living Theatre can also be detected, as the repressed, middle-class Clémenti adopts a cockily anarchic alter ego in a bid to impress Stefania Sandrelli. Brimming over with political and cinematic ideas, this has an exhuberance that compensates for its naiveté. A French/Italian language film.

Pierre Clémenti *Jacob I/Jacob II* • Stefania Sandrelli *Clara* • Tina Aumont *Salesgirl* • Sergio Tofano *Petrushka* • Giulio Cesare Castello *Professor Mozzoni* ■ *Dir* Bernardo Bertolucci • *Scr* Bernardo Bertolucci, Gianni Amico, from the novel *The Double* by Fyodor Dostoyevsky

Partners
★★

Drama   1976 · Can · Colour · 96mins

Denholm Elliott was incapable of giving a bad performance, but he came very close to doing so in this lightweight Canadian film. He doesn't seem to care too much about his role as the owner of a large paper firm and the father of Hollis McLaren. She gets involved in a torrid love affair with dodgy character Michael Margotta, but when Dad's company is under threat from a rival corporation, both father and daughter discover their true capabilities. Mildly intriguing.

Denholm Elliott *John Grey* • Hollis McLaren *Heather Grey* • Michael Margotta *Paul Howard* • Lee Broker *Philip Rudd* • Judith Gault *Barbara* ■ *Dir* Don Owen • *Scr* Norman Snider, Don Owen

Partners
★★ 15

Comedy   1982 · US · Colour · 88mins

A twist is given to the stale conventions of the buddy-cop movie when two detectives, one straight (Ryan O'Neal) and one gay (John Hurt), step out on to the streets of Los Angeles. Hurt takes on the role of a gay cop with ease. O'Neal also pretends to be gay for the sake of the plot which involves a murder investigation in the homosexual community. ▦

Ryan O'Neal *Benson* • John Hurt *Kerwin* • Kenneth McMillan *Wilkins* • Robyn Douglass *Jill* • Jay Robinson *Halderstam* ■ *Dir* James Burrows • *Scr* Francis Veber

Partners in Love
★★

Romantic comedy   1992 · Can · Colour · 96mins

Eugene Levy has never really broken through to the mainstream after featuring on the fringe of the *Saturday Night Live*/*Second City* scene. Here he gets to flex his directorial muscles as well as starring in an amiable but hardly ground-breaking romantic comedy about an estranged couple who discover their divorce is invalid. Levy and Linda Kash spark off each other nicely, but there aren't enough funny lines to sustain the comedy.

Eugene Levy *David Grodin* • Linda Kash *Maxine Smith* • John James *Carey Mays* • Jayne Eastwood *Haddy Taylor* ■ *Dir* Eugene Levy • *Scr* Josh Goldstein, from a story by Josh Goldstein, Jonathon Prince

The Party
★★★ PG

Comedy   1968 · US · Colour · 94mins

Peter Sellers always had to be kept in check but director Blake Edwards was hardly the one to do it, especially in this straight-up farce which he'd promised Sellers as a diversion from Inspector Clouseau. The result is a one-joke idea in the two-reel style of a silent comedy as Sellers puts on his Indian accent – the one he used to woo Sophia Loren in *The Millionairess* – as the Bengali actor inadvertently wrecking a Hollywood producer's party. Some very funny moments but Sellers, like the character he plays, overstays his welcome. ▦

Peter Sellers *Hrundi V Bakshi* • Claudine Longet *Michèle Monet* • Marge Champion *Rosalind Dunphy* • J Edward Mckinley *Fred Clutterbuck* • Fay McKenzie *Alice Clutterbuck* •

Steve Franken *Levinson, the waiter* • Gavin MacLeod *CS Divot* ■ *Dir* Blake Edwards • *Scr* Blake Edwards, Tom Waldman, Frank Waldman, from a story by Blake Edwards

The Party and the Guests
★★★★ U

Political drama 1966 · Cz · BW · 70mins

A Kafkaesque portrait of modern Czechoslovakia, packed with resonating contemporary motifs, this sinister study of social conformity and political dissent was a collaboration between director Jan Nemec and his writer/designer wife, Ester Krumbachová. Set in Edenic woodlands, the film follows the pursuit, with savage dogs, of the sole self-determining individualist whose refusal to acquiesce in the system threatens the status quo. Ironically, the nonconformist was played by director Evald Schorm, whose *Return of the Prodigal Son* was then under government censure, a fate shared by Nemec's film, which was withheld for two years. In Czech with English subtitles.

Ivan Vyskocil *The Host* • Jan Klusák *Rudolf* • Jirí Nemec *Josef* • Zdenka Skvorecká *Eva* • Pavel Bosek *Frantisek* • Helena Pejsková *Marta* • Karel Mares *Karel* • Jana Pracharova *Wife* • Evald Schorm *Husband* ■ *Dir* Jan Nemec • *Scr* Ester Krumbachová, Jan Nemec, from a short story by Ester Krumbachová

Party Girl
★★★

Drama 1930 · US · BW · 67mins

A society drama about escort services and respectable businessmen. A rich young client (Douglas Fairbanks Jr) is blackmailed into marrying one of the girls (Marie Prevost). Even though this rather racy melodrama was made before the puritanical Hays Code came into being, it does try to suggest that the girls only ever dance and drink with their clients. Rather dated but enjoyable stuff, with lovely silent star Prevost, who starved herself to death aged 38, making her successful sound debut.

Douglas Fairbanks Jr *Jay Rountree* • Jeanette Loff *Ellen Powell* • Judith Barrie *Leeda Cather* • Marie Prevost *Diana Hoster* • John St Polis *John Rountree* • Lucien Prival *Paul Nucast* ■ *Dir* Victor Halperin • *Scr* Monte Katterjohn, George Draney, Victor Halperin, from their story, from the novel *Dangerous Business* by Edwin Balmer

Party Girl
★★

Crime drama 1958 · US · Colour · 98mins

On the surface, this has everything going for it: a tough and glossy MGM gangster melodrama starring a mature Robert Taylor and leggy Cyd Charisse, directed by Nicholas Ray. Trouble is, it doesn't quite come off, sabotaged by an over-the-top performance from chief villain Lee J Cobb and an uncertainty of tone, not helped by Charisse's relentlessly non-acting performance and an awkward, subdued Taylor. The main theme of corrupt lawyer Taylor assessing the morals of his equally corrupt gangster colleagues is not fully explored, and it's difficult to care about any of the characters.

Robert Taylor (1) *Thomas Farrell* • Cyd Charisse *Vicki Gaye* • Lee J Cobb *Rico Angelo* • John Ireland *Louis Canetto* • Kent Smith

Jeffery Stewart • Claire Kelly *Genevieve* • Corey Allen *Cookie* ■ *Dir* Nicholas Ray • *Scr* George Wells, from a story by Leo Katcher

Party Girl
★★

Comedy drama 1994 · US · Colour · 94mins

A comedy drama for the slacker generation of the eighties. Parker Posey is a flighty twentysomething who is puzzled by that pervasive Generation X question: "What should I do with my life?" Bored during the day and drawn to the bright Manhattan lights at night, she ends up getting nicked for hosting an illegal party. She asks her godmother Judy (played by director Daisy von Scherler Mayer's mother, Sasha von Scherler) for the bail money and has to work the debt off as a clerk in a library. Lightweight and skinny like its star but mildly fun.

Parker Posey *Mary* • Omar Townsend *Mustafa* • Sasha von Scherler *Judy Lindendorf* • Guillermo Diaz *Leo* • Anthony DeSando *Derrick* • Donna Mitchell *Rene* • Liev Schreiber *Nigel* • Nicole Bobbitt *Venus* ■ *Dir* Daisy von Scherler Mayer • *Scr* Daisy von Scherler Mayer, Harry Birckmayer, from a story by Daisy von Scherler Mayer, Harry Birckmayer, Sheila Gaffney

Party Line
★ 18

Thriller 1988 · US · Colour · 86mins

A sleazy schlocker about phone party-liners who, looking for love on the telephone lines, find they've dialled M for murder instead. A tough cop and the assistant DA join forces to track down the deadly brother and sister duo responsible for the slayings. Richard Roundtree and Richard Hatch star, along with short-lived seventies teen heart-throb Leif Garrett, who plays one of the killers. A film best described as "don't call us, we'll call you". ▣

Richard Hatch *Dan* • Leif Garrett *Seth* • Shawn Weatherly *Stacy* • Greta Blackburn *Angelina* • Richard Roundtree *Captain Barnes* ■ *Dir* William Webb • *Scr* Richard Brandes, from a story by Tom Byrnes

Party, Party
★ 18

Comedy 1983 · UK · Colour · 53mins

Pitched as a youthful British answer to *National Lampoon's Animal House*, this charmless comedy shambles is more like a geriatric *Carry On*. Set around a New Year's Eve celebration, only early glimpses of now-familiar TV faces such as Gary Olsen and Karl Howman (and, briefly, Nick Berry) make the hard slog worthwhile. Directed by film-school graduate Terry Winsor and co-scripted by *Comic Strip* regular Daniel Peacock (who also stars), this expanded student short will have everyone congregating in the kitchen in double-quick time. ▣

Daniel Peacock *Toby* • Karl Howman *Johnny* • Perry Fenwick *Larry* • Sean Chapman *Sam Diggins* • Phoebe Nicholls *Rebecca* • Gary Olsen *Terry* • Clive Mantle *Bobby* • Caroline Quentin *Shirley* ■ *Dir* Terry Winsor • *Scr* Terry Winsor, Daniel Peacock

The Party's Over
★

Drama 1965 · UK · BW · 93mins

This bizarre study in necrophilia was shot in 1963 and banned outright by the British film censor. When it was re-edited and then released in 1965, producer Anthony Perry and director

Guy Hamilton took their names off the credits. While one admires their integrity, the movie is a real stinker. Set in Chelsea in the Swinging Sixties, it's about the daughter of an American industrialist who falls in with a crowd of beatniks, led by a menacing Oliver Reed. The poor girl goes to the party, ends up dead and is then ravished. The intention was to show the decadence of the age, but no one need look beyond *The Servant* for that sort of thing.

Oliver Reed *Moise* • Clifford David *Carson* • Ann Lynn *Libby* • Catherine Woodville *Nina* • Louise Sorel *Melina* ■ *Dir* Guy Hamilton • *Scr* Marc Behm

Pascali's Island
★★★★ 15

Period drama 1988 · UK · Colour · 98mins

Helen Mirren is the prime suspect for acting honours in this adaptation of the Barry Unsworth novel about treachery and betrayal. Set in the year 1908, she's the painter torn between bogus archaeologist Charles Dance and spy Ben Kingsley, the Pascali of the title. Her love and loyalty are as divided as Nisi, the Turkish-occupied Greek island, part of the Ottoman empire which is crumbling around them. Pascali's sexual ambiguity is beautifully observed by Ben Kingsley, but it's the observed beauty of Helen Mirren which upstages languid atmospherics and lyrical vistas. ▣

Ben Kingsley *Basil Pascali* • Charles Dance *Anthony Bowles* • Helen Mirren *Lydia Neuman* • George Murcell *Herr Gesing* • Sheila Allen *Mrs Marchant* • Nadim Sawalha *Pasha* • TP McKenna *Dr Hogan* • Danielle Allan *Mrs Hogan* ■ *Dir* James Dearden • *Scr* James Dearden, from the novel by Barry Unsworth • *Cinematographer* Roger Deakins

Pass the Ammo
★★

Comedy satire 1988 · US · Colour · 97mins

This is a frantic, somewhat over-the-top comedy targetting TV evangelism. The Reverend Ray Potter (Tim Curry) and his wife (Annie Potts) have earned millions from their mission from donations made via the small screen but in actuality they are just con artists in it for the money. When Bill Paxton and *Crocodile Dundee's* Linda Kozlowski try and retrieve the $50,000 extorted from her grandmother they set in motion a train of events which culminate in a live-TV hostage taking.

Bill Paxton *Jesse* • Linda Kozlowski *Claire* • Annie Potts *Darla* • Glenn Withrow *Arnold Limpet* • Dennis Burkley *Big Joe Becker* • Tim Curry *Rev Ray Porter* ■ *Dir* David Beaird • *Scr* Neil Cohen, Joel Cohen

The Passage
★

Second World War drama 1978 · UK · Colour · 98mins

Ludicrous war movie with Anthony Quinn as a Basque shepherd who guides James Mason and his family to safety over the Pyrenees. Trotting out his usual Zorba act, Quinn's "life force" is exhausting while Malcolm McDowell camps it up as the SS sadist who wears a swastika on his jock strap and treats Michael Lonsdale's fingertips as a gourmet snack. It's laughable and repellent at the same time and a general embarrassment for all concerned.

Anthony Quinn *The Basque* • James Mason *Professor John Bergson* • Malcolm McDowell *Captain Von Berkow* • Patricia Neal *Ariel Bergson* • Kay Lenz *Leah Bergson* • Christopher Lee *Head Gypsy* • Michael Lonsdale [Michel Lonsdale] *Renoudot* ■ *Dir* J Lee Thompson • *Scr* Bruce Nicolaysen, from his novel *The Perilous Passage*

The Passage
★★

Supernatural drama 1986 · Fr · Colour · 100mins

Alain Delon stars as the pacifist animator who, following a car crash, is offered a deal by the physical personification of Death: unless Delon transforms his next film into a rallying cry for mass destruction, both he and his young son will die. Had there been greater concentration on the cinema's ability to manipulate the impressionable, this might have made for compelling viewing. But once Delon discovers the passage between existence and the afterlife, the emphasis shifts predictably on to abrasive action. French dialogue dubbed into English.

Alain Delon *Jean Diaz* • Christine Boisson *Catherine* • Alan Musey *David Diaz* • Jean-Luc Moreau *Patrick* • Alberto Lomeo *"The Surgeon"* ■ *Dir* René Manzor

Passage Home
★★

Drama 1955 · UK · BW · 102mins

Thirty men and one woman sail from South America to London in 1931. Tensions run high amongst the superstitious crew because of the presence of a woman passenger, played by sultry Diane Cilento. Captain Peter Finch turns to the bottle when she rebuffs him; first mate Anthony Steel saves her from the captain but fancies his chances and, below decks, Bryan Forbes, Gordon Jackson and others draw hard on their cigarettes. Never more than a B movie, this recycles old material with a modicum of style.

Anthony Steel *First Mate Vosper* • Peter Finch *Captain Lucky Ryland* • Diane Cilento *Ruth Elton* • Cyril Cusack *Bohannon* • Geoffrey Keen *Ike* • Hugh Griffith *Pettigrew* • Duncan Lamont *Llewellyn* • Gordon Jackson *Burne* • Bryan Forbes *Shorty* • Patrick McGoohan *McIsaacs* ■ *Dir* Roy Ward Baker • *Scr* William Fairchild, from the novel by Richard Armstrong

A Passage to India
★★★★★ PG

Drama 1984 · UK · Colour · 156mins

Nominated for 11 Academy Awards, David Lean's final feature trespasses on territory usually reserved for Merchant–Ivory, EM Forster and India. But Lean was the master of the stately epic and, in this lusciously photographed picture, the 75-year-old director showed that none of his powers had waned. Stripping away the sheen of Raj life, he exposes the tensions, prejudices and snobberies of imperialism with a satirical blade every bit as sharp as Forster's. Oscar-winning Peggy Ashcroft garnered the acting headlines, but she is surpassed by Judy Davis as the outsider who shatters the calm of this Indian Eden. ▣

Judy Davis *Adela Quested* • Victor Banerjee *Dr Aziz* • Peggy Ashcroft *Mrs Moore* • James Fox *Richard Fielding* • Nigel Havers *Ronny Heaslop*

• Alec Guinness *Professor Godbole* • Richard Wilson *Turton* • Antonia Pemberton *Mrs Turton* • Michael Culver *McBryde* • Art Malik *Mahmoud Ali* • Saeed Jaffrey *Hamidullah* ■ *Dir* David Lean • *Scr* David Lean, from he play by Santha Rama Rau, from the novel by EM Forster • *Cinematographer* Ernest Day

Passage to Marseille
★★★ PG

Second World War drama
1944 · US · BW · 104mins

You'd expect more from this Warner Bros reteaming of the director and most of the cast from *Casablanca*, but lightning seldom strikes twice. Despite the efforts of the eminently watchable Humphrey Bogart, Sydney Greenstreet, Peter Lorre and Claude Rains, the convoluted flashback plot is tiresome and hard to follow. As the girl in the flashbacks (the Ingrid Bergman role), Michèle Morgan doesn't really register and Bogart is strangely cast as French journalist Matrac, leading an escape from a penal colony to join the French Resistance. But director Michael Curtiz does what he can, and he's aided by great camerawork from James Wong Howe and a superb score (as ever) by Max Steiner.

Humphrey Bogart *Matrac* • Claude Rains *Captain Freycinet* • Michèle Morgan *Paula* • Philip Dorn *Renault* • Sydney Greenstreet *Major Duval* • Peter Lorre *Marius* • George Tobias *Petit* • Victor Francen *Captain Patain Malo* • Helmut Dantine *Garou* • John Loder *Manning* ■ *Dir* Michael Curtiz • *Scr* Casey Robinson, Jack Moffitt, from the novel *Men without a Country* by Charles Nordhoff, James Norman Hall

Passed Away
★★ 15

Black comedy 1992 · US · Colour · 92mins

This entertaining comedy grabs the attention thanks to some exceptional ensemble acting, but in the end settles for schmaltz and neatly tied loose ends. Gathering the members of his clan for their father's funeral, Bob Hoskins is nominally the star of the picture, but his mid-life crisis is never as interesting as brother William Petersen's problems, sister Pamela Reed's passion for embalmer Peter Riegert or liberated nun Frances McDormand's deadpan marxism. Sadly, director Charlie Peters's script runs out of steam too early, even though its quip count remains high throughout.

Bob Hoskins *Johnny Scanlan* • Blair Brown *Amy Scanlan* • Tim Curry *Boyd Pinter* • Frances McDormand *Nora Scanlan* • William Petersen *Frank Scanlan* • Pamela Reed *Terry Scanlan* • Peter Riegert *Peter Syracusa* • Maureen Stapleton *Mary Scanlan* • Nancy Travis *Cassie Slocombe* • Jack Warden *Jack Scanlan* ■ *Dir/Scr* Charlie Peters

Passenger
★★★★

Drama 1963 · Pol · BW · 60mins

Andrzej Munk was partway through his masterpiece when he was killed in a car crash. Yet, although Witold Lesiewicz used a voice-over and an adroit collage of stills to approximate its resolution, its very incompleteness reinforces the powerful message that while the Holocaust may belong to history, its legacy can never be forgotten. Aleksandra Slaska gives a chilling performance as the cruise liner

passenger who attempts to reinvent her career as an overseer at Auschwitz following a chance encounter with a survivor she thought long dead. Despite the horror of the camp sequences, there's no bitterness, just aching sadness. In Polish with English subtitles.

Aleksandra Slaska *Liza* • Jan Kreczmar *Walter* • Anna Ciepielewska *Marta* • Irena Malkiewicz *"Ober"* • John Rees *English narrator* ■ *Dir* Andrzej Munk, Witold Lesiewicz • *Scr* Zofia Posmysz-Piasecka, Andrzej Munk

The Passenger
★★★★ PG

Drama 1975 · Fr/It/Sp · Colour · 113mins

Michelangelo Antonioni's movie portrays what happens to a burnt-out TV reporter (Jack Nicholson) who adopts the identity of a dead man, a gun-runner, and loses himself in Africa's civil wars. There are two big themes here – the emptiness of existence and the exploitation of the Third World – and the film is a total blank on both counts. Similarly, Maria Schneider doesn't do much except look pretty, and the scenes in London with Jenny Runacre are terrible. However, the film has a wonderful hypnotic atmosphere, mainly due to Nicholson's excellent performance and to the location photography of the Sahara and the Gaudi buildings in Barcelona. And the long final sequence, shot without the aid of a Steadicam, is dazzling: the camera floats out of a hotel room, wanders around the town square for several minutes, and comes back again to gaze at what is either a very dramatic or a very disappointing climax.

Jack Nicholson *David Locke* • Maria Schneider *Girl* • Jenny Runacre *Rachel Locke* • Ian Hendry *Martin Knight* • Steven Berkoff *Stephen* • Ambrose Bia *Achebe* ■ *Dir* Michelangelo Antonioni • *Scr* Mark Peploe, Peter Wollen, Michelangelo Antonioni, from a story by Mark Peploe • *Cinematographer* Luciano Tovoli

Passenger 57
★★★ 15

Action adventure 1992 · US · Colour · 80mins

Die Hard provided such a perfectly structured action-movie template that Hollywood has been reluctant to leave the idea alone; cue this silly but hugely enjoyable airborne thriller. Wesley Snipes is the security expert who finds himself on the same aeroplane as British master criminal Bruce Payne, temporarily in police custody. Of course, Payne's henchmen have hitched a lift as well and when they duly free him, it's up to Snipes to save the day. Despite the hand-me-down plot and dialogue, director Kevin Hooks manages to wring the requisite suspense out of some expertly staged action set pieces. Contains violence and swearing. **DVD**

Wesley Snipes *John Cutter* • Bruce Payne *Charles Rane* • Tom Sizemore *Sly Delvecchio* • Alex Datcher *Marti Slayton* • Bruce Greenwood *Stuart Ramsey* • Robert Hooks *Dwight Henderson* • Elizabeth Hurley *Sabrina Ritchie* ■ *Dir* Kevin Hooks • *Scr* David Loughery, Dan Gordon, from a story by Stewart Raffill, David Gordon

The Passing of the Third Floor Back
★★★ U

Fantasy drama 1935 · UK · BW · 90mins

The German-born actor Conrad Veidt, so often cast in sinister roles, had one of the best parts of his career in this allegorical tale of a mysterious stranger who takes a back room in a boarding house run by a greedy landlord and populated by sad inhabitants. The newcomer profoundly affects their lives before disappearing as swiftly as he arrived. A British film, directed by Berthold Viertel, it was co-written by Alma Reville, better known as Mrs Alfred Hitchcock, from a play by Jerome K Jerome. Well observed and intriguing, with an excellent cast.

Conrad Veidt *The stranger* • René Ray *Stasia* • Frank Cellier *Wright* • Anna Lee *Vivian Tompkin* • John Turnbull *Major Tompkin* • Cathleen Nesbitt *Mrs Tompkin* • Barbara Everest *Cook* ■ *Dir* Berthold Viertel • *Scr* Michael Hogan, Alma Reville, from a play by Jerome K Jerome

Passion
★★ U

Western 1954 · US · Colour · 82mins

Passion is conspicuously missing from this dreary story of early California starring Cornel Wilde as the young hero seeking revenge on the band who have killed his wife and child. With glamorous Yvonne De Carlo as co-star and a great cameraman, John Alton, working with veteran director Allan Dwan, the film looks attractive enough but is slowed down by ponderous dialogue and predictable development. It was made on the cheap using standing Spanish sets around Hollywood but went for a visually strong climax in snow-covered mountains. Usually villainous at this period, Raymond Burr appears on the side of law and order.

Cornel Wilde *Juan Obreon* • Yvonne De Carlo *Tonya Melo/Rosa Melo* • Raymond Burr *Captain Rodriguez* • Lon Chaney Jr *Castro* • John Qualen *Gaspar Melo* • Rodolfo Acosta *Salvador Sandro* ■ *Dir* Allan Dwan • *Scr* Beatrice A Dresher, Joseph Leytes, Howard Estabrook, from a story by Beatrice A Dresher, Joseph Leytes, Miguel Padilla • *Cinematographer* John Alton

A Passion
★★★★

Drama 1969 · Swe · Colour · 100mins

The concluding instalment of Ingmar Bergman's "Faro" trilogy (following *Shame* and *Hour of the Wolf*) ranks among his most powerful, personal and pessimistic statements on the human condition. Utilising forbidding island landscape and the recurrence of dreams to emphasise the isolation of the protagonists, Bergman explores the impossibility of escaping from one's past and finding contentment in an irrational and violent society. Hell is definitely other people in this godless place, especially once Liv Ullmann drags Max von Sydow out of his reclusive self-sufficiency and into confrontation with both her neighbours and her ghosts. In Swedish with English subtitles.

Liv Ullmann *Anna Fromm* • Bibi Andersson *Eva Vergerus* • Max von Sydow *Andreas Winkelman* • Erland Josephson *Elis Vergerus* ■ *Dir/Scr* Ingmar Bergman • *Cinematographer* Sven Nykvist

Passion
★★ 15

Drama 1982 · Fr/Swi · Colour · 83mins

This marks Jean-Luc Godard's semi-return to a more commercial way of movie-making, reuniting him with Raoul Coutard, the man who photographed all the early, epoch-making films, and using big-name stars of the time such as Hanna Schygulla, Isabelle Huppert and Michel Piccoli. But despite the often gorgeous imagery, this movie is likely to mystify and bore most viewers. Its central story – about a Polish film director and his crew staying in a hotel – is almost lifted from François Truffaut's *Day for Night*, except in Godard's hands it is fragmented, vague and still experimental. In French with English subtitles.

Isabelle Huppert *Isabelle* • Hanna Schygulla *Hanna* • Jerzy Radziwilowicz *Jerzy* • Michel Piccoli *Michel* • Laszlo Szabo ■ *Dir/Scr* Jean-Luc Godard • *Cinematographer* Raoul Coutard

Passion
★★★

Musical drama 1996 · US · Colour · 114mins

This film version of Stephen Sondheim's 1994 Tony Award-winning Broadway musical – itself an adaptation of Iginio Ugo Tarchetti's classic novel *Fosca* – contains all the emotional intimacy and dramatic intensity that made the show such a success. In what is basically a *Beauty and the Beast* fable in reverse, Donna Murphy (re-creating her Tony Award-winning role) stars as the plain, mortally ill Fosca who falls for handsome officer Jere Shea and eventually melts his heart. The rich score is one of Sondheim's best, the performances are dazzling and anyone expecting the usual static and stilted approach to such stagebound material is in for a surprise.

Jere Shea *Giorgio* • Marin Mazzie *Clara* • Donna Murphy *Fosca* • Gregg Edelman *Colonel Ricci* • Tom Aldredge *Dr Tambourri* • Francis Ruivivar *Lt Torasso* ■ *Dir* James Lapine • *Scr* James Lapine, from the musical by Stephen Sondheim, from the novel *Fosca* by Iginio Ugo Tarchetti

Passion Fish
★★★★ 15

Drama 1992 · US · Colour · 129mins

Trust writer/director John Sayles to lift a theme that's often used in TV movies and transform it into something finer and richer. Mary McDonnell received an Oscar nomination for her performance as May-Alice, a daytime soap opera star who is paralysed after an accident and returns to her family home in Louisiana. Starting off as a "bitch on wheels" and taking to drink and self-pity, her disability and personality undergo a dramatic change with the help of her companion, played by Alfre Woodard. Sayles judges the tone expertly, deftly turning on the taps only to switch them off again with some sour wit, and creates a striking study of courageous individuals within a small community. Contains substance abuse and swearing.

Mary McDonnell *May-Alice* • Alfre Woodard *Chantelle* • David Strathairn *Rennie* • Vondie Curtis-Hall *Sugar LeDoux* • Angela Bassett *Dawn/Rhonda* • Lenore Banks *Nurse Quick* • William Mahoney *Max* ■ *Dir/Scr* John Sayles

Passion Flower ★★

Thriller 1986 · US · Colour · 78mins

Bruce Boxleitner gets involved in some strange goings-on in the Far East with the help of Barbara Hershey in this film which tries to be a romantic thriller but sadly lacks both romance and an involving plot. Joseph Sargent who won critical acclaim for *The Taking of Pelham 123* in 1974 seems to be on a downward career spiral.

Bruce Boxleitner *Larry Janson* • Barbara Hershey *Julia* • Nicol Williamson *Albert Coskin* • John Waters *Leslie* ■ *Dir* Joseph Sargent • *Scr* Richard A Guttman

A Passion for Murder ★★🔞

Thriller 1992 · US/Can · Colour · 87mins

Joanna Pacula is an undercover CIA agent who, following the death of her politician lover, ends up going on the run with cab driver Michael Nouri while being pursued by assassin Michael Ironside. Silly stuff indeed, but worth watching for bug-eyed Ironside, who seems to have made a career for himself playing mesmerising killers, bad guys and mercenaries. Contains swearing, violence, sex scenes and nudity. 📼 *DVD*

Joanna Pacula *Vanessa* • Michael Nouri *Ben Shorr* • Michael Ironside *Quinn* • Lee J Campbell *Sheriff* ■ *Dir* Neill Fearnley • *Scr* Arne Olsen, John Alan Schwartz

Passion in the Desert ★★★🔞

Historical drama 1998 · UK · Colour · 91mins

Based on a little-known novella by Balzac, Lavinia Currier's debut feature is clearly a labour of love. Set against the backdrop of Napoleon's Egyptian campaign, it opens as a treatise on man's disrespect for art, as painter Michel Piccoli and his officer escort Ben Daniels lament the wanton destruction of war. However, once circumstances force Daniels into the wilderness, the emphasis shifts to his primeval relationship with the leopardess that teaches him to survive his breathtaking but treacherous surroundings. Strikingly shot by Russian cinematographer Alexei Rodionov, this is a disconcerting and ultimately tragic tale. Contains some violence and nudity.

Ben Daniels *Augustin Robert* • Michel Piccoli *Jean-Michel Venture de Paradis* • Paul Meston *Grognard* • Kenneth Collard *Officer* • Nadi Odeh *Bedouin bride* ■ *Dir* Lavinia Currier • *Scr* Lavinia Currier, Martin Edmunds, from a novella by Honoré de Balzac

The Passion of Darkly Noon ★★★🔞

Drama 1995 · UK/Ger · Colour · 100mins

Beauty and the Beast meets *Twin Peaks* in an intellectual stalk-and-slasher picture about religion, redemption and repression. Brendan Fraser gives an eerie performance as the titular drifter Darkly Noon, sole survivor of a religious cult, who becomes obsessed with local beauty Callie, played by Ashley Judd. Written and directed by Philip Ridley (of *The Reflecting Skin* fame), this intriguingly warped fairy tale is a challenging, inventive and deeply stylish exploration of forbidden desire. Its gloom, doom,

and sexual foreboding, rendered in surrealistic American Gothic imagery, will delight arty horror aficionados. 📼

Brendan Fraser *Darkly Noon* • Ashley Judd *Callie* • Viggo Mortensen *Clay* • Loren Dean *Jude* ■ *Dir/Scr* Philip Ridley

The Passion of Joan of Arc ★★★★★

Classic silent drama 1928 · Fr · BW · 110mins

Based on authentic trial records and drawing on artistic styles from the Renaissance to the avant-garde, Danish director Carl Theodor Dreyer's film is one of the masterpieces of the silent era. Working with cinematographer Rudolph Maté, Dreyer used all manner of symbolic angles, zooms, tilts and pan shots to capture the dramatic intensity of the action, only for the flow to be interrupted too often by the descriptive captions. In her only screen appearance, Renée Maria Falconetti gives an astonishing performance, filmed almost exclusively in close-up both to convey her personal agony and to contrast her sincerity with the duplicity of her accusers.

Maria RenéFalconetti *Joan* • Eugène Silvain *Bishop Pierre Cauchon* • Maurice Schultz *Nicolas Loyseleur* • Michel Simon *Jean Lemaître* ■ *Dir* Carl Theodor Dreyer • *Scr* Carl Theodor Dreyer, Joseph Delteil, from a novel by Joseph Delteil

A Passion to Kill ★★

Erotic thriller 1994 · US · Colour · 93mins

Scott Bakula plays psychiatrist David, whose best friend John Getz comes back from a cruise with a new wife (Bakula's real-life wife, Chelsea Field). When she starts acting strangely, Getz asks Bakula to talk to her about her problems, but the doctor finds himself seduced by his patient's charms. Then Getz turns up dead. Only one tiny twist interrupts the pat progress of this predictable thriller. Bakula gives his earnest best to the role, but the flick is pure B-movie schlock.

Scott Bakula *Dr David Lawson* • Chelsea Field *Diana Chamberlain* • Sheila Kelley *Beth* • John Getz *Jerry Chamberlain* ■ *Dir* Rick King • *Scr* William Delligan

The Passionate Friends ★★🅿🅶

Romantic drama 1948 · UK · BW · 86mins

One of three films made by David Lean with Ann Todd, whom he married in 1949, this glossy, passionless movie ranks somewhere between the solid drama of *The Sound Barrier* and the wooden romance of *Madeleine*. In a stuffy drawing-room melodrama, Todd is forced to choose between luxury and love. Her cause is not helped by the script, which successfully buries one of HG Wells's more forgettable novels in a welter of confused flashbacks and clipped platitudes. Todd's haughty manner renders her eminently resistible and she is further disadvantaged by comparison with those astute screen actors Trevor Howard and Claude Rains. 📼

Ann Todd *Mary Justin* • Trevor Howard *Steven Stratton* • Claude Rains *Howard Justin* • Isabel Dean *Pat* • Betty Ann Davies *Miss*

Layton ■ *Dir* David Lean • *Scr* Eric Ambler, David Lean, Stanley Haynes, from the novel by HG Wells

The Passionate Plumber ★

Comedy 1932 · US · BW · 73mins

One of the last, and worst, comedies of the great Buster Keaton, due to MGM's poor choice of script and the studio's decision to combine him with the coarser comedy of Jimmy Durante. Directed with all the subtlety of an overflow by Edward Sedgwick, it's a remake of *Her Cardboard Lover*, with Keaton hired by Parisienne Irene Purcell to pose as her *amour* to make Gilbert Roland jealous. Keaton's own personal problems overwhelmed this underwhelming rubbish.

Buster Keaton *Elmer E Tuttle* • Jimmy Durante *Julius J McCracken* • Irene Purcell *Patricia Jardine* • Polly Moran *Albine* • Gilbert Roland *Tony Lagorce* ■ *Dir* Edward Sedgwick • *Scr* Laurence E Johnson, Ralph Spence, from the play *Her Cardboard Lover* by Valerie Wyngate, PG Wodehouse, from the play *Dans Sa Candeur Naïve* by Jacques Deval

The Passionate Stranger ★★

Comedy 1957 · UK · BW and Colour · 97mins

This feeble romantic comedy wastes the considerable talent of Margaret Leighton as a novelist who bases one of her characters on her chauffeur. Marital complications follow when he misunderstands her motives. Part of the film shows the central characters in real life and the rest dramatises sections of her book, but unfortunately the conceit does not work. Why the incomparable Ralph Richardson took the husband's role defeats questioning.

Ralph Richardson *Roger Wynter/Sir Clement Hathaway* • Margaret Leighton *Judith Wynter/Leonie* • Patricia Dainton *Emily/Betty* • Carlo Giustini *Carlo/Mario* ■ *Dir* Muriel Box • *Scr* Muriel Box, Sydney Box

Passionate Summer ★★★

Drama 1955 · Fr/It · BW · 97mins

A meticulous craftsman, who considered text as significant as visual signature, Charles Brabant was one of many French film-makers whose prospects were dimmed by the scathing proponents of auteur theory. This adaptation of Ugo Betti's play, *The Island of Goats*, was lambasted as a typical example of "cinéma du papa", the polished escapism that relied on literate dialogue and star performance. Yet, such was the animal magnetism of Raf Vallone, as the ugly man who exercises a fatal charm over Madeleine Robinson's household, that it scandalised contemporary audiences with its freakish eroticism. Yet, within seven years, Brabant's career was over. In French with English subtitles.

Madeleine Robinson *Agatha* • Raf Vallone *Angelo* • Magali Nöel *Pia* • Dany Carrel *Sylvia* ■ *Dir* Charles Brabant • *Scr* Charles Brabant, Maurice Clavel, from the play *The Island of Goats* by Ugo Betti

Passionate Summer ★★🅤

Romantic drama 1958 · UK · Colour · 103mins

Noted television producer Rudolph Cartier – best known for the *Quatermass* serials – made a rare foray into features with this hothouse Rank melodrama, set in a sweltering Jamaica. Virginia McKenna is the air hostess who lusts after Carl Mohner, while Bill Travers is in love with McKenna but being seduced by wicked Yvonne Mitchell. Travers and McKenna may have been a real-life couple, but they really are the most unconvincing of screen lovers here.

Virginia McKenna *Judy* • Bill Travers *Douglas Lockwood* • Yvonne Mitchell *Mrs Pawley* • Alexander Knox *Mr Pawley* • Carl Mohner *Louis* • Ellen Barrie *Silvia* • Guy Middleton *Duffield* ■ *Dir* Rudolph Cartier • *Scr* Joan Henry, from the novel *The Shadow and the Peak* by Richard Mason

La Passione ★🔞

Musical fantasy 1996 · UK · Colour · 89mins

A young boy's obsession with Ferraris and his hero worship of a German racing driver form the basis of rock star Chris Rea's script for this misfiring drama, set in Yorkshire in the early sixties. When his idol is killed at Monza, the boy becomes withdrawn and the film resorts to fantasies involving Shirley Bassey, even though when you think of her and cars you think of an Aston Martin DB5. You really want to like this movie, but, like many sixties sports cars, it looks good and goes wrong a lot. 📼

Shirley Bassey • Paul Shane *Papa* • Jan Ravens *Mama* • Carmen Silvera *Grandmother* • Gordon Kaye *PC Keecy* • Sean Gallagher *Jo* • Thomas Orange *Young Jo* • Keith Barron *Roy* ■ *Dir* John B Hobbs • *Scr* Chris Rea

Passions ★★

Drama 1984 · US · Colour · 83mins

Joanne Woodward puts in another good performance in this drama as a widow who discovers that her late husband had another life and a mistress. Lindsay Wagner is the quivering-lipped other woman, but her presence and Woodward's, still cannot save what is in fact a very predictable "women's" drama.

Joanne Woodward *Catherine Kennerly* • Lindsay Wagner *Nina Simon* • Richard Crenna *Richard Kennerly* • Mason Adams *Ron Sandler* • Heather Langenkamp *Beth Kennerly* • John Considine *Jack Blaine* • Viveca Lindfors *Lila* ■ *Dir* Sandor Stern • *Scr* Janet Green, Robin Maxwell, Sandor Stern

The Passover Plot ★★

Religious drama 1976 · Is · Colour · 108mins

Derived from the Hugh J Schonfield book, this is a controversial account of the life of Jesus Christ, depicting him as a zealot leader who brings about his own crucifixion in order to make a political point against the Roman authorities. Donald Pleasence and Biblical stalwarts Harry Andrews and Hugh Griffith feature in the cast, while Christ is played by Zalman King. The whole production is somewhat pedestrian, making the film's contentious issues rather bland.

🅤 = SUITABLE FOR ALL 🅤ᴄ = SUITABLE FOR ALL, ESPECIALLY FOR YOUNG CHILDREN (VIDEO ONLY) 🅿🅶 = PARENTAL GUIDANCE

Harry Andrews *Yohanan the Baptist* • Hugh Griffith *Caiaphas* • Zalman King *Yeshua* • Donald Pleasence *Pontius Pilate* • Scott Wilson *Judah* ■ *Dir* Michael Campus • *Scr* Millard Cohan, Patricia Knop, from the book by Hugh J Schonfield

Passport to Murder ★★★

Romantic thriller   1993 · US · Colour

This fast-moving TV thriller sweeps us across Europe as various spies and assassins pursue divorced socialite Connie Sellecca in the hope that she will lead them to the brains behind a nuclear arms smuggling ring. In addition, a private eye has been hired by her ex-husband's mistress to see whether she generates a very different kind of power and with whom. David Hemmings, one of the icons of sixties British cinema, directs without undue fuss, making the most of the fabulous locations around Paris and Budapest. There's also a change of pace for comedy actor Peter Bowles as a dogged police inspector. Contains violence, swearing and sex scenes.

Connie Sellecca *Helen Hollander* • Ed Marinaro *Hank McCabe* • Pavel Douglas *Charles Devon* • Peter Bowles *Inspector Bullion* • Laszlo Borbely *Zilka* ■ *Dir* David Hemmings • *Scr* Alfred Monacella

Passport to Pimlico ★★★★ 🅄

Comedy   1949 · UK · BW · 80mins

The cosiest of the Ealing comedies, this is essentially a one-joke affair that is spun out with masterly skill by that most gifted teller of shaggy dog stories, TEB Clarke, who received an Oscar nomination for his story and screenplay. Once local historian Margaret Rutherford discovers that Pimlico belongs to the Duchy of Burgundy, the scene could have been set for a sniping satire on the state of postwar England. Clarke and director Henry Cornelius's decision to cock only the gentlest of snooks at such bugbears as rationing and the breakdown of wartime camaraderie is slightly disappointing, but the majority of the situations are ingenious, and the cast is top quality. 📼

Stanley Holloway *Arthur Pemberton* • Margaret Rutherford *Professor Hatton-Jones* • Basil Radford *Gregg* • Naunton Wayne *Straker* • Hermione Baddeley *Edie Randall* • John Slater *Frank Huggins* • Betty Warren *Connie Pemberton* ■ *Dir* Henry Cornelius • *Scr* TEB Clarke

Passport to Shame ★★★

Drama   1958 · UK · BW · 92mins

In the late fifties, the BBFC reluctantly allowed producers to tackle prostitution as long as the films masqueraded as "Awful Warnings". This typical example is introduced by none other than Inspector Fabian, he of the Yard. Poor French waif Odile Versois comes to England and is tricked into working for a brothel run by evil Herbert Lom. A cheap, tawdry and utterly fascinating piece of vintage sexploitation. Somewhat incredibly, it is the work of Alvin Rakoff, responsible for many distinguished TV plays. Way down the cast list, Michael Caine plays a bridegroom.

Eddie Constantine *Johnny* • Diana Dors *Vicki* • Odile Versois *Malou* • Herbert Lom *Nick* • Brenda de Banzie *Madame* • Robert Brown *Mike* • Elwyn Brook-Jones *Heath* • Cyril Shaps *Willie* • Dennis Shaw [Denis Shaw] *Mac* • Joan Sims *Miriam* • Michael Caine *Bridegroom* ■ *Dir* Alvin Rakoff • *Scr* Patrick Alexander

Passport to Suez ★★

Spy detective drama   1943 · US · BW · 71mins

The last of nine Lone Wolf thrillers starring Warren William, this adequate outing presses the suave playboy sleuth into service on behalf of the British government, smashing a German spy ring in Egypt. As his butler and sidekick, Eric Blore figures prominently in the twist and turns of the plot while Ann Savage stands out as a shady war correspondent. This was Hungarian director Andre De Toth's first American assignment and he livens it up with considerable camera movement.

Warren William *Michael Lanyard aka The Lone Wolf* • Ann Savage *Valerie King* • Eric Blore *Llewellyn Jameson* • Robert Stanford *Donald Jameson* • Sheldon Leonard *Johnny Booth* • Lloyd Bridges *Fritz* ■ *Dir* Andre De Toth • *Scr* John Stone, from a story by Alden Nash, from characters created by Louis Joseph Vance

Passport to Treason ★ 🅄

Mystery   1956 · UK · BW · 83mins

Western star Rod Cameron should never have packed his passport to play the private eye in this dire British B-feature with its sub-Hitchcockian plot about neo-fascists in London concealing their activities within an organisation for world peace. A better actor than granite-jawed Cameron might have breathed some life into the line-up of hackneyed situations, from the vital clue in the book grasped by a dead man to the unsurprising revelation of the top man's identity and the climactic shoot-out.

Rod Cameron *Mike O'Kelly* • Lois Maxwell *Diane Boyd* • Clifford Evans *Orlando Sims* • Peter Illing *Giorgio Sacchi* • Marianne Stone *Miss Jones* ■ *Dir* Robert S Baker • *Scr* Norman Hudis, Kenneth R Hayles, from a novel by Manning O'Brine

The Password Is Courage ★★★ 🅄

Second World War drama   1962 · UK · BW · 115mins

Rather a forgotten film in Dirk Bogarde's canon, this is a fitfully amusing war offering, based on the true-life exploits of one Charles Coward, a cocky PoW who spent his time humiliating his guards and preparing his colleagues for escape. Writer/director Andrew L Stone occasionally pushes too hard for comic effect and Bogarde is hardly perfect casting, but the story of Coward's attempts to reach the Polish Resistance is fascinating and would have benefited from a more dramatic retelling. Alfred Lynch and Reginald Beckwith provide sterling support and, on the evidence of this performance, Maria Perschy should have become much better known.

Dirk Bogarde *Charles Coward* • Maria Perschy *Irena* • Alfred Lynch *Billy Pope* • Nigel Stock *Cole* • Reginald Beckwith *Unteroffizier* • Richard Marner *Schmidt* • Ed Devereaux

Aussie ■ *Dir* Andrew L Stone • *Scr* Andrew L Stone, from the biography of Charles Coward by John Castle

Past Midnight ★★

Romantic thriller
1992 · US · Colour · 100mins

Rutger Hauer is released from jail after 15 years for the murder of his wife, still proclaiming his innocence. His social worker Natasha Richardson starts to believe him after investigating on her own, and a romance blossoms. But is he really innocent? Viewers will figure it out long before Richardson does, and will predict the climax when they see that one of the main settings is an isolated cabin in the woods. It's professionally made, with good performances by the leads, but there are simply no surprises. 📼

Rutger Hauer *Ben Jordan* • Natasha Richardson *Laura Mathews* • Clancy Brown *Steve Lundy* • Kibibi Monie *Dorothy Coleman* • Tom Wright *Lee Samuels* • Dana Eskelson *Kathy Tudor* • Ted D'Arms *Bill Tudor* ■ *Dir* Jan Eliasberg • *Scr* Frank Norwood

Past Tense ★★ 🄸🄵

Thriller   1994 · US · Colour · 87mins

A would-be heady mix of sex, sleuthing and the supernatural, this TV movie concentrates more on style than substance, as detective Scott Glenn gets caught up in flashbacks involving neighbour Lara Flynn Boyle, who may or may not be involved in a murder case with his partner, Anthony LaPaglia. The result is a haphazard hotchpotch with little tension, although the cast tries its best. Contains violence, swearing, sex scenes and nudity. 📼

Scott Glenn *Gene Ralston* • Anthony LaPaglia *Larry* • Lara Flynn Boyle *Tory Bass* • David Ogden Stiers *Frank* ■ *Dir* Graeme Clifford • *Scr* Scott Frost, Miguel Tejada-Flores

Pastime ★★★

Sports drama   1991 · US · Colour · 94mins

Set in the fifties, this appealing low-key film chronicles the friendship of an ageing but chipper minor-league baseball player, Roy Dean Bream (William Russ) and a promising young black pitcher (Glenn Plummer) who has just joined Roy Dean's floundering team. Both men are used as scapegoats by the other players, who are frustrated at the team's overall performance. Naturally, the two form a bond in the face of this adversity. A real treat for baseball fans, but some may find Roy Dean's impossibly upbeat personality and the worship of this American sport difficult to tolerate.

William Russ *Roy Dean Bream* • Scott Plank *Randy Keever* • Reed Rudy *Spicer* • Ricky Paull Goldin *Hahn* • Peter Murnik *Simmons* • John Jones *Colbeck* • Glenn Plummer *Tyrone Debray* • Pat O'Bryan [Patrick O'Bryan] *Walsh* ■ *Dir* Robin B Armstrong • *Scr* David M Eyre Jr

Pastor Hall ★★★★

Second World War drama
1940 · UK · BW · 97mins

This highly impressive third feature from the Boulting brothers has been dismissed as a routine wartime flagwaver on the theme of Nazi intolerance. Rather, it is a bold and

often stirring tribute to the universal power of faith, courage and personal conviction. The picture is based on the life of the Protestant minister Martin Niemoller who was interned in a concentration camp for failing to preach against either socialism or Judaism. Wilfrid Lawson plays Pastor Hall with great dignity and he is admirably supported by Nova Pilbeam, Seymour Hicks, Marius Goring and the ever-excellent Hay Petrie.

Wilfrid Lawson *Pastor Hall* • Nova Pilbeam *Christine Hall* • Seymour Hicks *General von Grotjahn* • Marius Goring *Fritz Gerte* • Brian Worth *Werner von Grotjahn* • Percy Walsh *Herr Veit* • Lina Barrie *Lina Veit* • Hay Petrie *Nazi Pastor* ■ *Dir* Roy Boulting • *Scr* Leslie Arliss, Anna Reiner, Haworth Bromley, John Boulting, Roy Boulting, Miles Malcolm, from a play by Ernest Toller

Pat and Mike ★★★ 🅄

Sports comedy   1952 · US · BW · 91mins

A rollicking vehicle for the wonder team of Katharine Hepburn and Spencer Tracy: she's a sportswoman, he's a rugged, cynical sports promoter. The Ruth Gordon/Garson Kanin Oscar-nominated story and screenplay is, frankly, weakish compared with the divine sophistication of other Tracy/Hepburn films, and for non-sports fans there are only the stars to watch. Hepburn is born to play the all-round athlete, but Tracy has, despite his top billing, distinctly the secondary role, and seems uncomfortable at times. There's nice support, though, from gravel-voiced Aldo Ray, Charles Buchinski (later Bronson) and, in a tiny role as a policeman, Chuck Connors, making his film debut. 📼

Spencer Tracy *Mike Conovan* • Katharine Hepburn *Pat Pemberton* • Aldo Ray *Davie Hucko* • William Ching *Collier Weld* • Charles Buchinski [Charles Bronson] *Hank Tasling* • Sammy White *Barney Grau* • George Mathews *Spec Cauley* • Chuck Connors *Policeman* ■ *Dir* George Cukor • *Scr* Ruth Gordon, Garson Kanin

Pat Garrett and Billy the Kid ★★★★ 🄸🄸

Western   1973 · US · Colour · 116mins

Despite studio tinkering, this near-masterpiece from director Sam Peckinpah is almost on a par with *The Wild Bunch*. It's a brooding meditation on violence, honour and loyalty in the last days of the Old West, as gunman-turned-sheriff Garrett (James Coburn) relives the past before taking on his one-time partner Billy (Kris Kristofferson). It becomes an elegy for the father/son relationship that figures in so much American literature, as both men try to live up to the legend their lives have imposed upon them. Contains violence, swearing and nudity. 📼

James Coburn *Pat Garrett* • Kris Kristofferson *Billy the Kid* • Bob Dylan *Alias* • Jason Robards [Jason Robards Jr] *Governor Lew Wallace* • Richard Jaeckel *Sheriff Kip McKinney* • Katy Jurado *Mrs Baker* • Slim Pickens *Sheriff Baker* • Chill Wills *Lemuel* • John Beck *Poe* • Rita Coolidge *Maria* • Jack Elam *Alamosa Bill* • Harry Dean Stanton *Luke* ■ *Dir* Sam Peckinpah • *Scr* Rudolph Wurlitzer

Patch Adams ★★★ 12

Medical comedy drama
1998 · US · Colour · 115mins

Robin Williams is ideally cast in this hospital comedy drama, based on a true story, as an irrepressible spirit whose dream of becoming a doctor is threatened by his inability to conform to medical school dictates. Williams's penchant for playing the clowning do-gooder is indulged by director Tom Shadyac, however, and the pat manipulation of the emotions comes with a dangerously high level of saccharin. But anyone who's ever felt aggrieved by impersonal treatment from the medical establishment will enjoy the system-bucking antics and the sincerity of Patch's mission to treat the people as well as the disease. Contains some swearing and sexual references. ▢ **DVD**

Robin Williams *Hunter "Patch" Adams* • Daniel London *Truman* • Monica Potter *Carin* • Philip Seymour Hoffman *Mitch* • Bob Gunton *Dean Walcott* • Josef Sommer *Dr Eaton* • Irma P Hall *Joletta* • Frances Lee McCain *Judy* ▪ *Dir* Tom Shadyac • *Scr* Steve Oedekerk, from the book *Gesundheit, Good Health Is a Laughing Matter* by Hunter Doherty Adams, Maureen Mylander

A Patch of Blue ★★★

Drama
1965 · US · BW · 105mins

A bit of a weepie, with Elizabeth Hartman as a young blind woman and Sidney Poitier as the man she meets in the park who becomes her closest friend. Hartman is remarkably stable despite her tragic history, while Poitier is as solid as Mount Rushmore. Written and directed by Guy Green, the Oscar-winning cameraman, and photographed by Hitchcock regular Robert Burks, the picture lacks any semblance of subtlety: Shelley Winters as Hartman's monstrous mother goes straight for the jugular, and won an Oscar as best supporting actress.

Sidney Poitier *Gordon Ralfe* • Shelley Winters *Rose-Ann D'Arcy* • Elizabeth Hartman *Selina D'Arcy* • Wallace Ford *Ole Pa* • Ivan Dixon *Mark Ralfe* • Elisabeth Fraser *Sadie* ▪ *Dir* Guy Green • *Scr* Guy Green, from the novel *Be Ready with Bells and Drums* by Elizabeth Kata

Paternity ★★ 15

Romantic comedy
1981 · US · Colour · 88mins

Can you see Burt Reynolds as a broody dad? Well, in this featherweight romantic comedy he plays the middle-aged manager of Madison Square Gardens who decides he wants an heir to carry on his name. Of course, he doesn't want the wife to go with it. Beverley D'Angelo is a struggling musician waiting tables to save enough money to study in Paris, so she is more than happy to play surrogate mother to his progeny. Unfortunately love is bound to raise its head and complicate matters. An unlovely subject, with a script that fails to provide Reynolds with the arch charm he revels in. ▢

Burt Reynolds *Buddy Evans* • Beverly D'Angelo *Maggie Harden* • Norman Fell *Larry* • Paul Dooley *Kurt* • Elizabeth Ashley *Sophia Thatcher* • Lauren Hutton *Jenny Lofton* • Juanita Moore *Celia* • Peter Billingsley *Tad* ▪ *Dir* David Steinberg • *Scr* Charlie Peters

Father Panchali ★★★★★ U

Drama
1955 · Ind · BW · 119mins

Translating as *The Song of the Road*, Satyajit Ray's debut as director is one of the unqualified masterpieces of world cinema. The first in the acclaimed Apu trilogy, it astounded everyone when it won the Special Jury Prize at Cannes, particularly as it was filmed on weekends and holidays over a four year period, with Ray having to pawn his wife's jewellery to complete the shoot. Influenced by such Italian neorealist features as *Bicycle Thieves*, the story of a young Bengali boy's introduction to the ways of the world is remarkable for its simplicity, humanity and the restraint of its non-professional cast. In Bengali with English subtitles. ▢

Kanu Bannerjee *Harihar, the father* • Karuna Bannerjee *Sarbojaya, the mother* • Subir Bannerjee *Apu* • Runki Bannerjee *Durga, as a child* ▪ *Dir* Satyajit Ray • *Scr* Satyajit Ray, from a novel by Bibhuti Bhushan Bannerji

Pathfinder ★★★★ 15

Adventure drama 1987 · Fin · Colour · 82mins

Described as the very first film to be made in the Lapp language, *Pathfinder* is far more than a curiosity, being a splendid excursion into myth and legend above the Arctic Circle. The first scenes suggest a variant of *Conan*, with a young boy witnessing the massacre of his parents; but instead of growing into a strapping warrior, he remains a boy whose plan for vengeance takes us into a morass of betrayal and cunning in which the leading figure is a mythological reindeer. Set against this bleak and grand landscape, Nils Gaup's picture – a rites of passage saga – has an intense authenticity and exoticism. In Lappish with English subtitles. ▢

Mikkel Gaup *Aigin* • Ingvald Guttorm *Father* • Ellen Anne Buljo *Mother* • Inger Utsi *Sister* ▪ *Dir/Scr* Nils Gaup • *Cinematographer* Erling Thurmann-Andersen

Paths of Glory ★★★★★ PG

First World War drama
1957 · US · BW · 83mins

Winston Churchill claimed this film came closest to capturing the atmosphere of the First World War and exposing the workings of the military mind. Director Stanley Kubrick is said to be a great admirer of Napoleon, and this fearsome indictment of the futility of war can also be read as a lament for the decline of the once glorious French army. As the general who orders a hopeless attack on a German position, Adolphe Menjou is a villain not because he is an officer slavishly adhering to the letter of army law, but because he is an arrogant aristocrat, motivated more by fear of the lower classes than by hatred of the enemy. Kirk Douglas and Timothy Carey are outstanding among the troops on the front line, while Kubrick's relentlessly probing camera offers constant evidence of a film-maker at the height of his powers. ▢

Kirk Douglas *Colonel Dax* • Ralph Meeker *Corporal Paris* • Adolphe Menjou *General Broulard* • George Macready *General Mireau* • Wayne Morris *Lieutenant Roget* • Richard Anderson *Major Saint-Auban* • Joseph Turkel

Private Pierre Arnaud • Timothy Carey *Private Ferol* ▪ *Dir* Stanley Kubrick • *Scr* Stanley Kubrick, Calder Willingham, Jim Thompson from the novel by Humphrey Cobb • *Cinematographer* Georg Krause

Patlabor: the Mobile Police ★★★ PG

Animated adventure
1989 · Jap · Colour · 98mins

With *manga* movies, the emphasis is usually on ultra violence and stunning design, but this is a more cerebral affair. The plot revolves around an attempt by the Tokyo police, assisted by advanced robots to track down a gang of criminals intent on bringing down the city, and in many ways this works as a pure detective story. There are still the trademark scenes of explosive action, but director Mamoru Oshii takes a more measured approach to the tale, which may upset die-hard fans but is more digestible to those new to the genre. In Japanese with English subtitles. ▢

Dir Mamoru Oshii • *Scr* Kazunori Ito, from a story by Masami Yuuki

The Patricia Neal Story: an Act of Love ★★★

Drama based on a true story
1981 · US · Colour

A well-cast TV movie about the Oscar-winning actress Patricia Neal's recovery from a series of debilitating strokes, benefiting immensely from the sensitive playing of Glenda Jackson as Neal and an intelligent script from Robert Anderson. Although lacking Neal's American ranginess (and accent), Jackson almost uniquely possesses the resolute wilfulness the part needs, and she performs beautifully. Dirk Bogarde plays celebrated children's novelist Roald Dahl, who was married to Neal at the time of the story.

Glenda Jackson *Patricia Neal* • Dirk Bogarde *Roald Dahl* • Ken Kercheval *Dr Charles Carton* • Jane Merrow *Val Eaton* • John Reilly *Barry Farrell* • James Hayden *Martin Sheen* ▪ *Dir* Anthony Harvey, Anthony Page • *Scr* Robert Anderson, from the book *Pat and Roald* by Barry Farrell

Patrick ★★★ 18

Horror
1978 · Ausl · Colour · 107mins

Australian director Richard Franklin obviously has a thing about matricide. After this deeply disturbing picture, which opens with a son electrocuting his mother and her lover in the bath, he went on to make *Psycho II*. Although it rather loses its way, this Gothic grotesque benefits from the creepy atmosphere Franklin generates in the hospital ward, where the comatose Patrick develops a passion for nurse Susan Penhaligon that acts as a catalyst for a series of increasingly malevolent telekinetic happenings. Amid the mayhem, there is a delicious performance from ballet maestro Robert Helpmann as a sadistic doctor. ▢

Susan Penhaligon *Kathy Jacquard* • Robert Helpmann *Dr Roget* • Rod Mullinar *Ed Jacquard* • Bruce Barry *Dr Brian Wright* • Julia Blake *Matron Cassidy* • Helen Hemingway *Sister Williams* • Robert Thompson *Patrick* ▪ *Dir* Richard Franklin • *Scr* Everett de Roche

Patrick the Great ★★ U

Musical comedy
1944 · US · BW · 89mins

This breezy musical has the usual corny showbiz setting, but it allows Donald O'Connor and Peggy Ryan to shine in a few pleasant numbers and gives O'Connor the chance to perform some pleasant tap-dancing. The paper-thin plot has Donald and his father (a colourless Donald Cook) as rivals for the same part in a Broadway show. Eve Arden, usually relied on to perk up the dullest screenplay, only has a few wisecracks here.

Donald O'Connor *Pat Donahue Jr* • Peggy Ryan *Judy Watkins* • Frances Dee *Lynn Andrews* • Donald Cook *Pat Donahue, Sr* • Eve Arden *Jean Mathews* ▪ *Dir* Frank Ryan • *Scr* Dorothy Bennett, Bertram Millhauser, from a story by Jane Hall, Frederick Kohner, Ralph Block

The Patriot

Silent historical drama
1928 · US · BW · 113mins

Sadly, no prints exist of this now lost film, in which Emil Jannings is the tyrannical Tsar Paul I, in the grip of dangerous insanity, so his trusted confidante Lewis Stone puts aside loyalty to his ruler in an attempt to save his country. This full-blooded historical drama was the last silent to be directed by Ernst Lubitsch, here departing from his customary romantic comedies; it was also the first film made during his long and sparklingly successful tenure at Paramount. Jannings, a frequent Lubitsch star in Germany, was nearing the end of his Hollywood sojourn, his thick German accent unsuited to the talkies. Stone, Lubitsch and the picture were all nominated for Oscars, but the only winner was Hans Kräly's screenplay.

Emil Jannings *Tsar Paul the First* • Lewis Stone *Count Pahlen* • Florence Vidor *Countess Ostermann* • Neil Hamilton *Crown Prince Alexander* • Harry Cording *Stefan* • Vera Voronina *Mlle Lapoukhine* ▪ *Dir* Ernst Lubitsch • *Scr* Hans Kräly, Julian Johnson, from the novel *Der Patriot: Drama in 5 Akten* by Alfred Neumann, from its stage adaptation by Ashley Dukes, from the story *Paul I* by Dimitri Merejkowski

The Patriot ★ 15

Action drama   1986 · US · Colour · 88mins

This apology for a movie is unmitigated rubbish, and, because of, or in spite of, its dire production levels, its non-plot and its knowing but perhaps unintentionally camp air, there's an audience that may lap it up. However, more discerning viewers will switch off this would-be action adventure, in which Gregg Henry stars as a burned-out Vietnam vet redeeming his dignity by attempting to save the western world from nuclear annihilation. Don't blink or you'll miss a tongue-in-cheek Leslie Nielsen and Michael J Pollard. Contains violence and nudity. ▢

Gregg Henry *Lieutenant Matt Ryder* • Simone Griffeth *Sean* • Michael J Pollard *Howard* • Jeff Conaway *Mitchell* • Stack Pierce *Atkins* • Leslie Nielsen *Admiral Frazer* ▪ *Dir* Frank Harris • *Scr* Andy Ruben, Katt Shea Ruben

The Patriot ★★

Action adventure 1998 · US · Colour · 90mins

This epic from martial arts specialist Steven Seagal features the hunk ia a rancher and doctor in Montana whose neighbour is a militant extremist with a biological weapon that threatens human existence on earth. Seagal's peaceful, eco-friendly message sits beside a further message about native Americans and is sorted out with lashings of violence. The best thing about the picture is its magnificent landscapes, beautifully caught under the direction of Dean Semler, the Oscar-winning cameraman of *Dances with Wolves*. **DVD**

Steven Seagal *Wesley McClaren* • Gailard Sartain *Floyd Chisholm* • LQ Jones *Frank* • Silas Weir Mitchell *Pogue* • Dan Beene *Dr Richard Bach* • Damon Collazo *Lieutenant Johnson* • Brad Leland *Big Bob* • Molly McClure *Molly* ■ *Dir* Dean Semler • *Scr* Paul Mones, David Ayer, M Sussman, from the novel *The Last Canadian* by William Heine

The Patriot ★★★

Historical war drama
2000 · US · Colour · 164mins

What has Mel Gibson got against the English? Following his Scottish bagpipe-skirl of defiance in *Braveheart* (1995) here he repeats his against-the-Brits stance in this action drama set during the American War of Independence. He's Benjamin Martin, living peacefully in South Carolina, who along with his gung ho son, Gabriel (Heath Ledger), comes out fighting against the English. The battle scenes, with thousands of extras flailing all over the place, are well-staged while the English are not quite as Nazi-nasty as they have been before.

Mel Gibson *Benjamin Martin* • Heath Ledger *Gabriel Martin* • Joely Richardson *Charlotte Selton* • Tcheky Karyo *Major Jean Villeneuve* • Jason Isaacs *Colonel William Tavington* • Tom Wilkinson *General Cornwallis* • Chris Cooper *Colonel Harry Burwell* ■ *Dir* Roland Emmerich • *Scr* Robert Rodat

Patriot Games ★★★ 15

Thriller 1992 · US · Colour · 111mins

Not one to help the Irish peace process, even though it covers itself by saying its villains are "some ultra-violent faction of the IRA". Phillip Noyce's film, from the Tom Clancy novel, has ex-CIA man Harrison Ford rescuing politician James Fox and being hounded for his trouble by fanatic Sean Bean. But apart from one brilliant sequence showing a remote-controlled desert massacre it never gets its act together to provide the direct appeal all good action movies should have. Richard Harris's brief apologia for what's going on is lamely unconvincing. Contains swearing. ▭

Harrison Ford *Jack Ryan* • Anne Archer *Dr Cathy Ryan* • Patrick Bergin *Kevin O'Donnell* • Sean Bean *Sean Miller* • Thora Birch *Sally Ryan* • James Fox *Lord Holmes* • Samuel L Jackson *Robby Jackson* • Polly Walker *Annette* • James Earl Jones *Admiral James Greer* • Richard Harris *Paddy O'Neil* ■ *Dir* Phillip Noyce • *Scr* W Peter Iliff, Donald Stewart, Steve Zaillian, from the novel by Tom Clancy

Patriots ★★ 18

Thriller 1994 · Fr · Colour · 80mins

Eric Rochant's in-depth investigation into the methodology of modern espionage has been painstakingly researched and authentically staged. Its theme of personal morality versus national security echoes Le Carré. Yvan Attal plays the young Parisian Ariel, who joins the Mossad and is dispatched to obtain the blueprints of a French nuclear power plant. But for all the character's idealism and eventual disillusionment, he simply gets lost in the works. And Sandrine Kimberlain is underused as the prostitute he befriends, while Richard Masur's unreliable American agent is a woeful miscalculation. Interminably long and only fitfully interesting. In French with English subtitles. ▭

Yvan Attal *Ariel* • Yossi Banai *Yossi* • Sandrine Kiberlain *Marie-Claude* • Richard Masur *Jeremy Pelman* • Nancy Allen *Catherine Pelman* • Allen Garfield *Eagleman* • Christine Pascal *Laurence* ■ *Dir/Scr* Eric Rochant

The Patsy ★★★

Silent comedy drama 1928 · US · BW

Adapted from a play, King Vidor's silent retains some of the dialogue in the intertitles and showcases the not inconsiderable comedic talents of Marion Davies. The unimportant plot concerns the efforts of Davies to overcome her position as the family "patsy" and captivate her sister's boyfriend. The high point has Davies, for no particular reason, doing very funny impersonations of silent stars Mae Murray, Lillian Gish and the exotic Pola Negri.

Marion Davies *Patricia Harrington* • Orville Caldwell *Tony Anderson* • Marie Dressler *Ma Harrington* • Dell Henderson *Pa Harrington* • Lawrence Gray *Billy* • Jane Winton *Grace Harrington* ■ *Dir* King Vidor • *Scr* Agnes Christine Johnston, Ralph Spence (titles), from the play by Barry Connors

The Patsy ★★★ U

Comedy 1964 · US · Colour · 101mins

A very black premise indeed from Jerry Lewis, whose adulation by French cineastes is sometimes regarded with puzzlement here. Judge for yourself, as co-writer/director Lewis casts star Jerry as the bellboy who stumbles upon a group of desperate showbiz types who have lost their meal ticket and who groom Lewis to replace the noted comedian killed in a plane crash. Tasteless, but also clever and very funny, with a marvellous cast of movie veterans. Peter Lorre makes his last film appearance as the self-serving director, and watch out for unbilled guest slots from the likes of Hedda Hopper, George Raft and Rhonda Fleming. It may be a one-gag sketch stretched to feature length, but it works fine as a vehicle for the brilliant Lewis. ▭

Jerry Lewis *Stanley Belt* • Ina Balin *Ellen Betz* • Everett Sloane *Caryl Fergusson* • Keenan Wynn *Harry Silver* • Peter Lorre *Morgan Heywood* • John Carradine *Bruce Alden* • Phil Harris *Chic Wymore* • Hans Conried *Dr Mule-rrr* ■ *Dir* Jerry Lewis • *Scr* Jerry Lewis, Bill Richmond

Patterns ★★★

Drama 1956 · US · BW · 83mins

This exposé of unethical American big business lacked the star power of the similarly themed *Executive Suite* and went unnoticed.. *Patterns* is a remake of a live television play and in Rod Serling's strong script Van Heflin portrays the new business executive who is being groomed by the Machiavellian company head, Everett Sloane, to replace the ageing and likeable Ed Begley. Shooting in New York, director Fielder Cook extracts fine performances from the cast and the ending is not quite what you'd expect.

Van Heflin *Fred Staples* • Everett Sloane *Walter Ramsey* • Ed Begley *William Briggs* • Beatrice Straight *Nancy Staples* • Elizabeth Wilson *Marge Fleming* • Joanna Roos *Miss Lanier* ■ *Dir* Fielder Cook • *Scr* Rod Serling, from his TV play

Patti Rocks ★★★ 18

Comedy 1987 · US · Colour · 83mins

The characters from *Loose Ends* (1975) return in a tough-talking and provocative adult comedy. Patti Rocks (Karen Landry) is a man-wary Minnesotan who tells her chauvinist boyfriend Billy (Chris Mulkey) she's pregnant. Unfortunately, Mulkey is married with children and doesn't know how he's going to break it to her. An incisive look at masculine double-standards and hypocrisy, David Burton Morris's fiercely independent feature digs down deep and isn't afraid to get dirty doing it. A movie that is something of an acquired taste. ▭

Chris Mulkey *Billy Regis* • John Jenkins *Eddie Hassit* • Karen Landry *Patti Rocks* • David L Turk *Barge worker* • Stephen Yoakam *Bartender* ■ *Dir* David Burton Morris • *Scr* David Burton Morris, Chris Mulkey, John Jenkins, Karen Landry, from characters created by Victoria Wozniak in the film *Loose Ends*

Patton: Lust for Glory ★★★★★ PG

Biography 1970 · US · Colour · 163mins

Released while US forces were still deeply embroiled in Vietnam, this can be viewed as both a tribute to the indomitability of the fighting man and a satire on the myth of the American hero. The screenplay, by Francis Ford Coppola and Edmund H North, received one of the picture's seven Oscars, while director Franklin J Schaffner took another, thanks to the horrific majesty of the battle sequences. But the bedrock of this mammoth biopic is the performance in the title role of George C Scott, who became the first winner in Oscar history to refuse his award. Combining blimpish bluster with moments of monstrous ego and unexpected humanity, Scott makes this magnificent film unforgettable. ▭

George C Scott *General Patton* • Karl Malden *General Bradley* • Michael Bates *Field Marshal Montgomery* • Stephen Young *Captain Hansen* • Michael Strong *Brigadier General Carver* • Cary Loftin *General Bradley's driver* • Albert Dumortier *Moroccan minister* • Frank Latimore *Lt Col Davenport* ■ *Dir* Franklin J Schaffner • *Scr* Francis Ford Coppola, Edmund H North, from the books *Patton: Ordeal and Triumph* by Ladislas Farago and *A Soldier's Story* by General Omar N Bradley

Patty Hearst ★★ 18

Biography 1988 · US/UK · Colour · 103mins

The career low of writer/director Paul Schrader. Inspired by Patricia Hearst's autobiography, this was obviously meant to be a bold cinematic experiment to re-create the deprivations and sensations that transformed her from want-for-nothing press heiress into committed terrorist. Yet Schrader's use of darkness, dazzling light and off-screen voices fails to convey the fearful disorientation, and the Symbionese Liberation Army propaganda soon has the attention wandering. Natasha Richardson tries hard in the lead, but matters scarcely improve once she goes on active duty. Contains violence, swearing and nudity. ▭

Natasha Richardson *Patricia Campbell Hearst* • William Forsythe *Teko* • Ving Rhames *Cinque* • Frances Fisher *Yolanda* • Jodi Long *Wendy Yoshimura* • Olivia Barash *Fahizah* • Dana Delany *Gelina* ■ *Dir* Paul Schrader • *Scr* Nicholas Kazan, from the autobiography *Every Secret Thing* by Patricia Campbell Hearst, Alvin Moscow

Paul and Michelle ★

Romantic drama
1974 · Fr/UK · Colour · 102mins

Lewis Gilbert is one of British cinema's longest-serving and least-lauded film-makers. He had already been directing for 30 years when he signed up for this sequel to his own tale of teenage romance, *Friends* (1971). Yet, in all that time, he never missed his step as badly as this. Every emotion and every romantic interlude rings false, as Sorbonne student Sean Bury seeks to lure Anicée Alvina away from pilot Keir Dullea. The performances are insufferably inept and Claude Renoir's cloying soft-focus photography only makes things worse.

Anicée Alvina *Michelle Latour* • Sean Bury *Paul Harrison* • Keir Dullea *Garry* • Ronald Lewis *Sir Robert Harrison* • Catherine Allégret *Joanna* ■ *Dir* Lewis Gilbert • *Scr* Angela Huth, Vernon Harris, from a story by Lewis Gilbert

Paulie ★★★ U

Comedy adventure
1998 · US · Colour · 87mins

Refreshingly free of gratuitous pyrotechnics and sentimental moralising, this fine-feathered film should prove a playground talking point. Such is the technical ingenuity that, for much of the time, it's impossible to tell whether we're looking at one of the 14 blue-crown conures specially trained for the film or an animatronic replica, created by Michael "Tony" Meagher and his special-effects team. Voiced by Jay Mohr, Paulie lives in the basement of an animal study institute and how he got there and why he's so desperate to find the little girl he helped cure of a stammer forms the basis of the story, as told to the building's Russian janitor, Tony Shalhoub. There are longueurs, but this mostly flies by. ▭

Gena Rowlands *Ivy* • Tony Shalhoub *Misha* • Cheech Marin *Ignacio ["Cheech" Marin]* • Bruce Davison *Dr Reingold* • Jay Mohr *Paulie/Benny* • Trini Alvarado *Adult Marie* • Buddy Hackett *Artie* • Hallie Kate Eisenberg *Marie* ■ *Dir* John Roberts • *Scr* Laurie Craig

Pauline at the Beach
★★★★ 15

Comedy drama 1983 · Fr · Colour · 94mins

Earning Eric Rohmer the Best Director prize at Berlin, the third in his "Comedies and Proverbs" series was originally conceived in the fifties, with Brigitte Bardot in the role of the flirtatious divorcée that was eventually taken by Arielle Dombasle.
Considerably racier than Rohmer's earlier outings, but just as witty and eloquent, the film is light enough to be blown away on the same sea breeze which fans the flames of holiday lust felt by Dombasle and her inexperienced cousin, Amanda Langlet, as they dally between a trio of willing men. Sparklingly played, sunnily photographed and staged with a master's touch. In French with English subtitles.

Amanda Langlet *Pauline* • Arielle Dombasle *Marion* • Pascal Greggory *Pierre* • Feodor Atkine *Henry* • Simon de la Brosse *Sylvain* ■ *Dir/Scr* Eric Rohmer

Paw
★★★

Drama 1959 · Den · Colour · 93mins

Denmark received its first Oscar nomination for this perennially popular picture. Working from her own script, director Astrid Henning-Jensen draws on the documentary experience gained in partnership with her husband, Bjarne. There's a pleasing authenticity to this tale of a West Indian orphan billeted on his Danish aunt, and Jimmy Sterman's disillusion with his racist schoolmates is as convincing as his delight in the local wildlife. However, clumsy symbolism blights his relationship with poacher Edvin Adolphson, while the resolution is overly neat. The drama may be naive in both message and staging, but the intentions are admirable.

Jimmy Sterman *Paw* • Edvin Adolphson *Anders Nilsson* • Ninja Tholstrup *Aunt Frieda* • Asbjørn Andersen *Yvonne* ■ *Dir* Astrid Henning-Jensen • *Scr* Astrid Henning-Jensen, Bjarne Henning-Jensen, from the story *Paw, der Indianerjunge* by Torry Gredsted

The Pawnbroker
★★★★★ 18

Drama 1965 · US · BW · 58mins

Rod Steiger moved up from an imposing heavy to a protagonist of international standing with this complex psychological portrait of Holocaust survivor Sol Nazerman. He's a Jewish refugee in New York who has tried to withdraw from life in the small fortress of his Harlem pawn shop, but is inescapably haunted by his memories of the concentration camp. Director Sidney Lumet serves his material – adapted from Edward Lewis Wallant's searing novel – with solemnity and compassion, and the tone is sensitively enhanced by an evocative jazz score from first-time film composer Quincy Jones. ▦

Rod Steiger *Sol Nazerman* • Geraldine Fitzgerald *Marilyn Birchfield* • Brock Peters *Rodriguez* • Jaime Sanchez *Jesus Ortiz* • Thelma Oliver *Ortiz's Girl* • Marketa Kimbrell *Tessie* • Baruch Lumet *Mendel* ■ *Dir* Sidney Lumet • *Scr* David Friedkin, Morton Fine, from the novel by Edward Lewis Wallant • *Music* Quincy Jones

The Pawnshop
★★★★

Silent comedy 1916 · US · BW · 20mins

One of the first of the dozen short films that Charlie Chaplin made for Mutual, this is a slight, but extremely effective comedy with Chaplin as an assistant in a pawnbroker's shop "where the depressed poor come to try to redeem their pledges". There is some remarkable knockabout as Chaplin battles with his colleague John Rand and abuses his customers, but also more subtle moments such as the sequence in which the star tries to wash dishes by pushing them through a clothes wringer, repeats the process to dry them and then cleans his hands in the same way. For lovers of happy endings, the ever-loving Edna Purviance is in there along with the jokes.

Charles Chaplin *Pawnshop assistant* • Edna Purviance *Daughter* • John Rand *Clerk* • Henry Bergman *Pawnbroker* • Albert Austin *Customer* • Eric Campbell *Thief* ■ *Dir/Scr* Charles Chaplin

Paws
★★★ U

Comedy adventure 1997 · UK/Ausl · Colour · 80mins

A bright, breezy and good-natured family comedy about a computer literate Jack Russell terrier called PC who speaks with the aid of a microchip voice implant. Though the main story is made up of standard-issue elements – a missing fortune, a recently bereaved teenager – director Karl Zwicky whisks the slapstick humour, technical gimmickry, outrageous action and appealing animal whimsy into a subtle soufflé packed with emotional warmth. Billy Connolly is brilliant as PC's Scottish voice in another fine effort in the *Babe* mould. ▦

Billy Connolly *PC* • Nathan Cavaleri *Zac Feldman* • Emilie Francois *Samantha Arkwright* • Joe Petruzzi *Stephen Feldman* • Caroline Gillmer *Susie Arkwright* • Rachael Blake *Amy Feldman* ■ *Dir* Karl Zwicky • *Scr* Harry Cripps, from a story by Harry Cripps, from a story by Karl Zwicky, Stephen Dando-Collins

Pax
★★

Comedy 1994 · Por · Colour · 73mins

Amanda Plummer (who featured in *Pulp Fiction* opposite Tim Roth) can never be accused of opting for easy assignments. This one takes her to Portugal for a comedy that forms part of Eduardo Guedes's Lisbon trilogy. Plummer is in scatterbrain mode as an American tourist who teams up with ageing prostitute Isabel Ruth to discover the whereabouts of a mystery man to whom she's supposed to deliver a package. Unfortunately, the storyline is little more than an excuse for a nocturnal shuttle around the city, with its best-known landmarks playing second string to a series of seedy bars. The leads hit it off, but there's little else to report. A Portuguese language film.

Amanda Plummer *Franny* • Isabel Ruth *Esmeralda* • Joao Lagarto *Rui* ■ *Dir* Eduardo Guedes • *Scr* Bruno Heller

Pay Day
★★★★ U

Silent comedy 1922 · US · BW · 22mins

This was the last of Charlie Chaplin's short films, coming just after *The Kid*

(1921) and before his non-starring drama, *A Woman of Paris* (1923). It's about what happens when a pay check finally arrives in a working-class home and stars Chaplin as a construction worker struggling to avoid the wrath of his nagging wife. There are some inventive sight gags, but also some sour social significance – the lengths the needy will go to for money. A great two-reeler, but sometimes more Charles Dickens than Charles Chaplin. ▦

Charles Chaplin *Worker* • Phyllis Allen *His wife* • Mack Swain *The foreman* • Edna Purviance *Foreman's daughter* • Sydney Chaplin [Syd Chaplin] *Friend* ■ *Dir/Scr* Charles Chaplin

Pay or Die
★★★★

Drama based on a true story 1960 · US · BW · 111mins

From the opening religious ceremony in New York's Little Italy in which the evil force of the "Black Hand" cuts down a girl dressed as an angel, this is a powerful study, based on fact, of a community living in fear. Obviously relishing the opportunity to play a heroic role, Ernest Borgnine gives a vivid and rounded performance as the tough and incorruptible cop who heads a special force to fight the Mafia's secret terror organisation. As in his earlier *Al Capone*, director Richard Wilson brings a fresh look to familiar situations helped by a supporting cast of little-known players.

Ernest Borgnine *Lt Joseph Petrosino* • Zohra Lampert *Adelina Saulino* • Alan Austin *Johnny Viscardi* • Robert F Simon [Robert Simon] *Commissioner* • Renata Vanni *Mama Saulino* • Bruno Della Santina *Papa Saulino* ■ *Dir* Richard Wilson • *Scr* Richard Collins, Bertram Millhauser, from the short story *Pay-Off in Sicily* by Burnett Hershey

Payback
★★ 15

Drama 1997 · US · Colour · 83mins

A reunion of sorts for Edward Asner and Mary Tyler Moore, from the seventies TV sitcom *The Mary Tyler Moore Show*. This is altogether more serious fare, a fact-based drama that views police corruption from the outsider's point of view. Moore plays a shop owner who one night witnesses a gang of policemen beat a robbery suspect half to death. Reluctantly, she agrees to testify against them, only to find a campaign of harassment being launched against her entire family. The two leads deliver capable performances but are let down by the plodding direction of Ken Cameron. Contains violence and some swearing. ▦

Mary Tyler Moore *Kathryn Stanfill* • Edward Asner [Ed Asner] *Lieutenant Jack Patkanis* ■ *Dir* Ken Cameron • *Scr* Dennis Nemec

Payback
★★★★ 18

Action crime thriller 1999 · US · Colour · 96mins

The source material that provided Lee Marvin with an unforgettable role in *Point Blank* (Donald E Westlake's *The Hunter*, written under the pseudonym Richard Stark) is here expertly recycled for the solid directing debut of *LA Confidential* writer Brian Helgeland. Mel Gibson stars as violent antihero Porter, a professional thief who seeks

revenge when his wife and crime partner double-cross him during a successful hold-up of some Chinese gangsters and leave him for dead. Helgeland handles this cool-as-ice thriller with flair, intelligence and lethal doses of sardonic wit. Contains violence, some swearing and sex scenes. ▦ **DVD**

Mel Gibson *Porter* • Gregg Henry *Val* • Maria Bello *Rosie* • David Paymer *Stegman* • Bill Duke *Detective Hicks* • Deborah Kara Unger *Lynn* • John Glover *Phil* • William Devane *Carter* • Kris Kristofferson *Bronson* • James Coburn *Fairfax* ■ *Dir* Brian Helgeland • *Scr* Brian Helgeland, Terry Hayes, from the novel *The Hunter* by Richard Stark [Donald E Westlake]

Payday
★★★★

Road movie drama 1972 · US · Colour · 103mins

Rip Torn gives the definitive performance of a fading country-and-western star in this magnificently grim but sadly overlooked film that uncompromisingly captures the music business gone sour. Torn as Maury Dann is cruel, self-centred and as empty as the bottle he is always holding. The film follows his last 36 hours as he ping-pongs from one low-life honky-tonk bar to another, portraying the booze, the groupies, the hangers-on and the payoffs in a manner as far away from rhinestones and fringes as it is possible to get. There are no good guys and no bad ones, just the results of the endless grind of life on the road. Torn has never been better.

Rip Torn *Maury Dann* • Ahna Capri *Mayleen* • Elayne Heilveil *Rosamond* • Michael C Gwynne *Clarence* ■ *Dir* Daryl Duke • *Scr* Don Carpenter

Paydirt
★★ 15

Crime comedy 1992 · US · Colour · 84mins

Jeff Daniels, a prison psychiatrist, is beset by a run of bad luck which sees him lose his house and his girlfriend. Salvation comes in the dying statement of one of the prisoners, who tells him of a huge amount of loot stashed away in the basement of a house in Cherry Hill, New Jersey. This exchange is overheard by two other prisoners, who break out of jail with the intention of beating Willis to the loot. This thin but amiable comedy is held together by the likeable Daniels and a solid supporting cast. ▦

Jeff Daniels *Willis Embry* • Rhea Perlman *Lydia* • Dabney Coleman *Jeffrey* • Catherine O'Hara *Jessie* • Hector Elizondo *Norman* ■ *Dir/Scr* Bill Phillips

Payment Deferred
★★★

Murder drama 1932 · US · BW · 80mins

Short, but hardly sweet, adaptation of a stage play as a vehicle for Charles Laughton. He is brilliant, despite some pretty hokey dialogue, as a poverty-stricken bank teller, with a wife (Dorothy Peterson) and daughter (Maureen O'Sullivan) to support, who resorts to poisoning his wealthy nephew (a young, almost unrecognisable, Ray Milland). Directed by Lothar Mendes, who perfectly captures the grimly claustrophobic atmosphere of an ugly, constantly rain-

U = SUITABLE FOR ALL   Uc = SUITABLE FOR ALL, ESPECIALLY FOR YOUNG CHILDREN (VIDEO ONLY)   PG = PARENTAL GUIDANCE

drenched suburban house and the bleak lives of its inhabitants, this is a curiously intriguing little piece with a very neat twist.

Charles Laughton *William Marble* • Neil Hamilton *Gordon Holmes* • Maureen O'Sullivan *Winnie Marble* • Dorothy Peterson *Annie Marble* • Verree Teasdale *Mme Collins* • Ray Milland *James Medland* • Billy Bevan *Hammond* ■ *Dir* Lothar Mendes • *Scr* Ernest Vajda, Claudine West, from the play by Jeffrey Dell

Payment on Demand ★★★

Melodrama   1951 · US · BW · 90mins

Bette Davis is stunned when husband Barry Sullivan announces he loves Frances Dee and wants a divorce. At first she turns vindictive, until she realises her own contribution to the breakdown of her marriage. Curtis Bernhardt's movie eschews the more obvious clichés of the genre (no tug-of-war over children, for example) and charts the course of the central relationship in flashback. The first of Davis's films as a freelance following her rupture with Warner Bros after 18 years under contract, it was made before the hugely successful *All About Eve*, but released after. A good vehicle for the star's talents.

Bette Davis *Joyce Ramsey* • Barry Sullivan *David Ramsey* • Jane Cowl *Mrs Hedges* • Kent Taylor *Robert Townsend* • Betty Lynn *Martha Ramsey* • Frances Dee *Eileen Benson* • Peggie Castle *Diana Ramsey* ■ *Dir* Curtis Bernhardt • *Scr* Bruce Manning, Curtis Bernhardt

Payoff ★★

Thriller   1991 · US · Colour · 111mins

A made-for-cable thriller, starring the gaunt Keith Carradine as an ex-cop seeking revenge on the Mafia mobster who bombed his parents. If the script had been shorn of some of its cartwheeling subplots, a much tighter movie would have resulted. But there are some decent set pieces, the tackiness of Lake Tahoe's casino business is well evoked, and there are fine performances from heavies Harry Dean Stanton, John Saxon, Lawrence Monoson and love interest Kim Greist.

Keith Carradine *Peter "Mac" MacAllister* • Kim Greist *Justine Bates* • Harry Dean Stanton *Harvey Hook* • John Saxon *Rafael Concion* • Robert Harper *Benny Cowan* • Lawrence Monoson *Victor Concion* ■ *Dir* Stuart Cooper • *Scr* Douglas S Cook, David Weisberg, from the novel by Ronald T Owen

Payroll ★★PG

Crime drama   1961 · UK · BW · 102mins

Sidney Hayers is one of the forgotten journeymen of sixties British cinema. Coming between his accomplished chillers *Circus of Horrors* and *Night of the Eagle*, this is a solidly crafted crime story in which the perfect blag begins to unravel as the gang lies low. Michael Craig is on surprisingly good form as the gang leader, but it's Billie Whitelaw, as the widow of a murdered security van guard, who commands centre stage as she risks her own life to snare the culprits. While it could stand some tightening up, the action is robust and brisk. 🎬

Michael Craig *Johnny Mellors* • Françoise Prévost *Katie Pearson* • Billie Whitelaw *Jackie*

Parker • William Lucas *Dennis Pearson* • Kenneth Griffith *Monty* • Tom Bell *Blackie* ■ *Dir* Sidney Hayers • *Scr* George Baxt, from the novel by Derek Bickerton

The Peacekeeper ★★★15

Action thriller   1997 · Can · Colour · 94mins

Any resemblance to the George Clooney/Nicole Kidman vehicle *The Peacemaker* is, of course, completely intentional! Actually, this suspense thriller gives Clooney's post-Cold War adventure a good run for its money, as maverick air force major Dolph Lundgren gets in the way of a sinister plot to nuke Washington. An exciting roof-top car chase and an explosive attack on Mount Rushmore make up for the two-dimensional acting from Lundgren in this better-than-average flag-waver. Roy Scheider gives the action an extra touch of class. Contains swearing and violence. 🎬 **DVD**

Dolph Lundgren *Major Frank Cross* • Montel Williams *Lieutenant Colonel Northrop* • Michael Sarrazin *Lieutenant Colonel Douglas Murphy* • Roy Scheider *President Robert Baker* • Christopher Heyerdahl *Hettinger* ■ *Dir* Frederic Forestier • *Scr* Robert Geoffrion, James H Stewart

Peacemaker ★★★18

Science-fiction action thriller
1990 · US · Colour · 87mins

Despite an at times quite noticeable low budget this exhilarating sci-fi thriller really delivers the goods for action fans. A well-worn theme for sure – alien cop tracking down alien villain – but the twist comes when they crash-land on Earth and both claim to be the good guy. Cue a virtual non-stop montage of chases, explosions and shoot-outs. Kevin S Tenney keeps you engrossed, while Robert Forster and Lance Edwards as the humanoid and virtually indestructible aliens make it fun guessing who's who. 🎬

Robert Forster *Yates* • Lance Edwards *Townsend* • Hilary Shepard *Dori Caisson* • Robert Davi *Sergeant Frank Ramos* • Bert Remsen *Doc* • John Denos *Reeger* • Wally Taylor *Moses* ■ *Dir/Scr* Kevin S Tenney

The Peacemaker ★★★15

Action thriller   1997 · US · Colour · 118mins

This was the first film to be released by DreamWorks SKG, the studio founded by Steven Spielberg, Jeffrey Katzenberg and David Geffen. Critics were underwhelmed and it under-performed at the box office. However, action fans will be happy as all the formulaic set pieces are present and correct – ticking bomb, car chases etc. Although George Clooney's lead performance helped him continue the transition from small screen idol to international movie star, Nicole Kidman is not convincing as a nuclear scientist. Contains some violence and swearing. 🎬

George Clooney *Thomas Devoe* • Nicole Kidman *Julia Kelly* • Armin Mueller-Stahl *Dimitri Vertikoff* • Marcel Iures *Dusan Gavrich* • Alexander Baluev *Aleksander Kodoroff* • Rene Medvesek *Vlado Mirich* • Randall Batinkoff *Ken* ■ *Dir* Mimi Leder • *Scr* Michael Schiffer, from an article by Leslie Cockburn, Andrew Cockburn

The Peanut Butter Solution ★★★PG

Fantasy drama   1985 · Can · Colour · 90mins

A Roald Dahl-style children's fantasy from Canada, also known as *Michael's Fright*. After losing all his hair, young Michael (Mathew Mackay) is given a special type of peanut butter which is supposed to help his hair grow back. Unfortunately, he uses too much and is soon rivalling Samson in the long tresses department. A fun tale that will delight most children. 🎬

Mathew Mackay *Michael Baskin* • Michael Hogan *Father* • Alison Podbrey *Suzie* • Michael Maillot *Signor* ■ *Dir/Scr* Michael Rubbo

The Pearl of Death ★★★

Crime mystery   1944 · US · BW · 68mins

Basil Rathbone and Nigel Bruce did pick 'em! This is the one in which the Creeper (Rondo Hatton) creeps out of the crypt of bad dreams as homicidal sidekick to jewel thief Miles Mander. Not only is he encumbered with a zombie-lumbering walk and a nasty ability to break backs, but also an unhealthy obsession with Evelyn Ankers that results in the villain's comeuppance – a nightmare for us, but an elementary deduction for Holmes, if not Watson. The story's ostensibly about Napoleon statues, but it's the Creeper you'll be watching.

Basil Rathbone *Sherlock Holmes* • Nigel Bruce *Dr Watson* • Evelyn Ankers *Naomi Drake* • Dennis Hoey *Inspector Lestrade* • Miles Mander *Giles Conover* • Rondo Hatton *"Creeper"* ■ *Dir* Roy William Neill • *Scr* Bertram Millhauser, from the story *The Adventure of the Six Napoleons* by Sir Arthur Conan Doyle

Pearl of the South Pacific ★★U

Adventure   1955 · US · Colour · 84mins

This piece of tosh is immensely enjoyable if you're unsophisticated, aged under ten, or both. There's a great deal of period charm in the Technicolored tale for fans of both the exotic and of cheesy interior set dressing trying to look like authentic locations, but, although Virginia Mayo is just about adequate in the lead, her two male co-stars, Dennis Morgan and David Farrar, are well past their primes. Veteran director Allan Dwan knocked out some very good melodramas in the fifties, but sadly this isn't one of them.

Virginia Mayo *Rita Delaine* • Dennis Morgan *Dan Merrill* • David Farrar *Bully Hayes* • Lance Fuller *George* • Murvyn Vye *Halemano* ■ *Dir* Allan Dwan • *Scr* Talbot Jennings, Jesse Lasky Jr, from a story by Anna Hunger

La Peau Douce ★★★★PG

Comedy   1964 · Fr · BW · 112mins

The influence of Alfred Hitchcock is readily apparent in this darkly comic and wonderfully observed tale of *femmes fatales* and *crimes passionels*. François Truffaut depicts air hostess Françoise Dorléac (Catherine Deneuve's sister) as a blonde ice maiden whose passing fancy for hapless intellectual Jean Desailly has a life-shattering effect. There are also touches of Jean

Renoir's humanism and echoes of Jacques Tati's despair at the mechanised world in what was wrongly considered to be a coolly cynical melodrama. With Nelly Benedetti's passionate wife completing the brilliant central triangle, this is an overlooked gem. In French with English subtitles.

Jean Desailly *Pierre Lachenay* • Françoise Dorléac *Nicole Chomette* • Nelly Benedetti *Franca Lachenay* ■ *Dir* François Truffaut • *Scr* François Truffaut, Jean-Louis Richard

The Pebble and the Penguin ★★U

Animation   1995 · US · Colour · 70mins

This undistinguished offering from the Don Bluth studio owes little to nature and too much to the kind of clawing sentimentality that spoils so many animated features. The story of Hubie, the shy bird whose hopes of romance are dashed by the dastardly Drake, is further disadvantaged by the poor voice-overs of Martin Short, James Belushi and Tim Curry and the dreadful songs of Barry Manilow. But the most disappointing aspect about what is supposed to be kids entertainment is the implicit racism of the characterisations. 🎬

Shani Wallis *Narrator* • Martin Short *Hubie* • James Belushi *Rocko* • Tim Curry *Drake* • Annie Golden *Marina* • Scott Bullock *Chubby/Gentoo* ■ *Dir* Don Bluth • *Scr* Rachel Korestsky, Steve Whitestone • *Music* Barry Manilow • *Lyrics* Bruce Sussman

Pecker ★★15

Comedy drama   1998 · US · Colour · 86mins

Sweet, funny and inoffensive are not the usual adjectives attached to the work of cult director John *Pink Flamingos* Waters. But his sideways look at the pretentious art world is just that – and a crashing disappointment as a result. Baltimore teenager Edward Furlong is given an old camera by his thrift-shop-owning mum and becomes the toast of New York's photography galleries under the guidance of art dealer Lili Taylor. Yet fame comes with a price he ultimately decides not to pay in Waters's "No Place Like Home" fable. Contains nudity, sexual references and swearing. 🎬

Edward Furlong *Pecker* • Christina Ricci *Shelley* • Bess Armstrong *Dr Klompus* • Mark Joy *Jimmy* • Mary Kay Place *Joyce* • Martha Plimpton *Tina* • Brendan Sexton III *Matt* • Mink Stole *Precinct captain* • Lili Taylor *Rorey* • Patricia Hearst *Lynn Wentworth* ■ *Dir/Scr* John Waters

The Pedestrian ★★★

Drama   1974 · W Ger · Colour · 97mins

The career of Austrian actor/director Maximilian Schell seemed assured after he won the best actor Oscar for *Judgment at Nuremberg*, aged 30. But dross followed and he turned to direction, including this drama about war crimes during the Nazi era. He wrote, directed and starred in the film, influenced by his own experience of fleeing with his family to Switzerland in 1938. Through the story of a wealthy German industrialist – a former Nazi officer, who is exposed in the press – Schell examines the nature of collective guilt

and was subsequently coolly received in Germany. A German language film.

Gustav Rudolf Sellner *Heinz Alfred Giese* • Ruth Hausmeister *Inge Maria Giese* • Peter Hall *Rudolf Hartmann* • Maximilian Schell *Andreas Giese* • Gila Von Weitershausen *Karin* • Alexander May *Alexander Markowitz* • Peggy Ashcroft *Lady Gray* • Elisabeth Bergner *Frau Lilienthal* • Lil Dagover *Frau Eschenlohr* • Françoise Rosay *Frau Dechamps* ■ *Dir/Scr* Maximilian Schell

Pee-wee's Big Adventure
★★★ U

Comedy   1985 · US · Colour · 87mins

A film built around a cult children's TV character may seem a strange place for Tim Burton to start his feature career, but, actually, it's not that big a leap from Pee-Wee Herman to Edward Scissorhands, Batman or Ed Wood. At the centre of this cartoonish comedy, Paul Reubens is wonderful as the curious little chap whose world falls apart when his precious bicycle is stolen. But some of the gags are spectacularly unfunny and Pee-Wee's nervous prattling can become irritating. It's a bold attempt to do something dazzlingly original, but for a truly subversive road movie see *Beavis and Butt-head Do America*. ▣

Paul Reubens *Pee-wee Herman* • Elizabeth Daily *Dottie* • Mark Holton *Francis* • Diane Salinger *Simone* • Judd Omen *Mickey* • Monte Landis *Mario* • Damon Martin *Chip* • Daryl Roach *Chuck* ■ *Dir* Tim Burton • *Scr* Phil Hartman, Paul Reubens, Michael Varhol

Peeper
★★ PG

Detective comedy
1975 · US · Colour · 83mins

The lovely Natalie Wood and the equally lovely Michael Caine are cast together in this private-eye spoof and lift what is otherwise a fairly lame movie. (It was shot under the title *Fat Chance* and lay dormant for a year before 20th Century-Fox allowed it to creep out on release in a heavily edited version.) There is a prologue from a Bogart lookalike, then detective Caine starts sniffing around a mysterious family, searching for a missing daughter and finding Miss Wood, whose real parentage is the crux of the matter. It's clear that most of the effort went into the splendid forties settings. ▣

Michael Caine *Leslie Tucker* • Natalie Wood *Ellen Prendergast* • Kitty Winn *Mianne Prendergast* • Thayer David *Frank Prendergast* • Liam Dunn *Billy Pate* • Dorothy Adams *Mrs Prendergast* ■ *Dir* Peter Hyams • *Scr* WD Richter, from the novel *Deadfall* by Keith Laumer

Peeping Tom
★★★★★ 18

Thriller   1960 · UK · Colour · 101mins

This is probably Britain's most notorious movie of its time. Director Michael Powell's first film for 20 years away from his partner, Emeric Pressburger, still lives up to its enormous reputation as a Freudian nightmare about a film technician (Karlheinz Böhm) who photographs the look of terror in the eyes of the women he kills. Anna Massey, Maxine Audley and Moira Shearer are among those who encounter his lethal voyeurism, while Powell himself plays the father

who created a monster. Outrage against the film destroyed Powell in this country – he had to go to Australia to find work – and only in recent years has it been recognised, by directors such as Martin Scorsese, as a risk-all masterpiece from one of our greatest film-makers. Contains violence, swearing and nudity. ▣

Carl Boehm [Karlheinz Böhm] *Mark Lewis* • Moira Shearer *Vivian* • Anna Massey *Helen Stephens* • Maxine Audley *Mrs Stephens* • Esmond Knight *Arthur Baden* • Bartlett Mullins *Mr Peters* • Shirley Anne Field *Diane Ashley* • Michael Goodliffe *Don Jarvis* • Brenda Bruce *Dora* ■ *Dir* Michael Powell • *Scr* Leo Marks • *Cinematographer* Otto Heller

Peg o' My Heart
★★★

Comedy drama   1933 · US · BW · 86mins

The travails of the unspoilt, uneducated daughter of a widowed Irish fisherman after she inherits two million pounds. She is wrenched away from her beloved father to lodge with a gruesomely awful family in England, upper class but broke, who are being paid to turn her into a lady. Awash in sentimentality, this combines the poignant, the coyly comical and the melodramatic on the way to its fairy-tale climax. Marion Davies, replete with cod-Irish accent, does her hoydenish but limited best, directed by Robert Z Leonard.

Marion Davies *Peg O'Connell* • Onslow Stevens *Sir Jerry Markham* • J Farrell MacDonald *Pat O'Connell* • Juliette Compton *Ethel Chichester* • Irene Browne *Mrs. Chichester* • Tyrrell Davis *Alaric Chichester* • Alan Mowbray *Capt Christopher Brent* ■ *Dir* Robert Z Leonard • *Scr* Francis Marion, Frank R Adams, from the play *Peg O' My Heart* by J Hartley Manners

Peggy Su!
★★

Romantic comedy   1997 · UK · Colour

Despite good intentions and a limited amount of charm, this *My Beautiful Laundrette* clone (same setting, same paternal relationship, same ethnic banter) fails to jell. Instead of letting the slight tale speak for itself, the director, Frances-Anne Solomon, has mistakenly trussed up the film with would-be ''style'', from over-elaborate camera movements to superimposed love hearts. It's sad when the nicest thing you can say about a film is that the best jokes are in the subtitles. In English and Cantonese with subtitles.

Pamela Oei *Peggy* • Adrian Pang *Gilbert* • Sukie Smith *Rita* • Burt Kwouk *Dad* • Daniel York *Jack* • Daphne Cheung *Jackie* ■ *Dir* Frances-Anne Solomon • *Scr* Kevin Wong

Peggy Sue Got Married
★★★ 15

Comedy fantasy   1986 · US · Colour · 98mins

In production around the same time as Robert Zemeckis's time-travel blockbuster *Back to the Future*, this bittersweet comedy was originally to star Debra Winger before Kathleen Turner got the nod and turned in an Oscar-nominated performance. It's no surprise that Francis Coppola wasn't the first choice director, as this is hardly his sort of territory. He overplays the Capra card and spends too much time analysing Peggy Sue's responses to revisiting her youth, rather than

letting us make up our own minds. Turner is sublime, beautifully re-creating the traits of teenagehood, while Nicolas Cage is amazing as the boy she knows will grow up into a slob. Contains swearing. ▣

Kathleen Turner *Peggy Sue Bodell* • Nicolas Cage *Charlie Bodell* • Barry Miller *Richard Norvik* • Catherine Hicks *Carol Heath* • Joan Allen *Maddy Nagle* • Kevin J O'Connor *Michael Fitzsimmons* • Barbara Harris *Evelyn Kelcher* • Don Murray *Jack Kelcher* • Maureen O'Sullivan *Elizabeth Alvorg* • Leon Ames *Barney Alvorg* • Helen Hunt *Beth Bodell* • John Carradine *Leo* • Sofia Coppola *Nancy Kelcher* • Jim Carrey *Walter Getz* ■ *Dir* Francis Coppola [Francis Ford Coppola] • *Scr* Jerry Leichtling, Arlene Sarner

Peking Express
★★

Drama   1951 · US · BW · 84mins

A typical ''Red Menace'' yarn, with Chinese villains instead of Russian ones. The idea may originally have come from the old von Sternberg–Dietrich exotica, *Shanghai Express*, since it's set on the same train but going in the opposite direction. Aboard is UN doctor Joseph Cotten, who is going to perform an operation on a anti-communist leader; there's also Cotten's love interest, a priest and a communist apparatchik. The hefty doses of ideological dialogue make for a rather slow journey, but things liven up when bandits raid the train and take everyone hostage.

Joseph Cotten *Michael Bachlin* • Corinne Calvet *Danielle Grenier* • Edmund Gwenn *Father Joseph Murray* • Marvin Miller *Kwon* • Benson Fong *Wong* ■ *Dir* William Dieterle • *Scr* John Meredyth Lucas, Jules Furthman, from a story by Harry Hervey

Peking Opera Blues
★★★★ 18

Action comedy 1986 · HK · Colour · 104mins

Among the best films made in Hong Kong in the eighties, this dazzling period adventure will leave you breathless and begging for more. Director Tsui Hark packs so much into the movie that it's hard to know what to praise first – the spectacle, the athleticism, the sprawling storyline, the slapstick or the exhilarating action. Yet there isn't a martial arts hero in sight, as Cherie Chung, Lin Ching Hsia and Sally Yeh take centre stage to challenge the sexist prejudices that survived the republican uprising of 1911. Both brutally balletic and intricately frantic, this colourful picture will have you cheering out loud. In Cantonese with English subtitles. Contains violence.

Lin Ching Hsia *Tsao Wan* • Mark Cheng *Ling Pak Ho* ■ *Dir* Tsui Hark • *Scr* To Kwok Wai

The Pelican Brief
★★★★ 12

Thriller   1993 · US · Colour · 135mins

In the second of the big screen John Grisham adaptations, Julia Roberts is the aspiring young legal eagle who stumbles upon a massive conspiracy reaching right to the Oval Office. Her only ally turns out to be Denzel Washington, a sceptical reporter who finds himself investigating the scoop of a lifetime. The two leads are fine, but the real coup is the depth of talent in the supporting cast: Sam Shepard and

John Heard are among those delivering killer cameos, although all are eclipsed by Robert Culp's witty portrayal of a shifty president. The plot combines legal thriller with conspiracy movie, so it's no surprise that director Alan J Pakula (*Presumed Innocent* and *The Parallax View*) is able to weave his way adeptly through the myriad characters and subplots. Contains violence and swearing. ▣ DVD

Julia Roberts *Darby Shaw* • Denzel Washington *Gray Grantham* • Sam Shepard *Thomas Callahan* • John Heard *Gavin Verheek* • Tony Goldwyn *Fletcher Coal* • James B Sikking *Denton Voyles* • William Atherton *Bob Gminski* • Robert Culp *President* • Stanley Tucci *Khamel* • Hume Cronyn *Justice Rosenberg* • John Lithgow *Smith Keen* ■ *Dir* Alan J Pakula • *Scr* Alan J Pakula, from the novel by John Grisham

La Pelle
★★★

Second World War drama
1981 · It /Fr · Colour · 131mins

Set during the Allied liberation of Naples in 1943, this adaptation of Curzio Malaparte's episodic memoir uncompromisingly captures the moral collapse and social chaos of a decimated nation. Relating stories both shocking and dolorous, Liliana Cavani refuses to shy away from the city's grinding poverty and the desperate measures to which many resorted to survive, including the selling of children and the prostitution of young girls. Marcello Mastroianni holds the piece together as liaison officer Malaparte, while Burt Lancaster turns in a brusque cameo as the head of the US forces. In English, Italian and French with subtitles.

Marcello Mastroianni *Curzio Malaparte* • Burt Lancaster *General Mark Cork* • Claudia Cardinale *Princess Consuelo Caracciolo* • Ken Marshall *Jimmy Wren* • Alexandra King *Deborah Wyatt* • Carlo Giuffre *Eduardo Mazzullo* ■ *Dir* Liliana Cavani • *Scr* Robert Katz, Liliana Cavani, from the novel by Curzio Malaparte

Pelle the Conqueror
★★★★ 15

Drama   1987 · Den/Swe · Colour · 150mins

Although it deals with turn-of-the-century despair in Denmark, director Bille August's adaptation of the first part of Nobel Prize-winner Martin Andersen Nexø's four-volume novel is life-affirming stuff, thanks to Max von Sydow's towering performance as a slave-driven cowherd and Pelle Hvenegaard's cowering contribution as the young son who learns to stand up to adversity. So many strands of conflict are unravelled it's hard to keep track, but the sincerity of purpose and the rigour of narrative bind us to it hard and fast. This 19th-century drama went on to win the best foreign film Oscar and also found favour at Cannes where it received the Palme d'Or. In Danish with English subtitles. ▣

Max von Sydow *Lasse Karlsson* • Pelle Hvenegaard *Pelle Karlsson* • Erik Paaske *Farm manager* • Kristina Tornqvist *Anna* ■ *Dir* Bille August • *Scr* Bille August, from a novel by Martin Andersen Nexø

U = SUITABLE FOR ALL   Uc = SUITABLE FOR ALL, ESPECIALLY FOR YOUNG CHILDREN (VIDEO ONLY)   PG = PARENTAL GUIDANCE

The Penalty ★

Crime drama 1941 · US · BW · 80mins

A feeble attempt to resurrect the violent gangster film of the thirties, this stars burly character actor Edward Arnold as the ruthless and egotistical bank robber whose only soft spot is for his young son, played by Gene Reynolds, whom he grooms for a life of crime. But after the son is exposed to traditional family values on a farm, he turns against his father. The second half is predictable and Lionel Barrymore grates as the invalid grandfather.

Edward Arnold *Martin "Stuff" Nelson* • Lionel Barrymore *"Grandpop" Logan* • Marsha Hunt *Katherine Logan* • Robert Sterling *Edward McCormick* • Gene Reynolds *"Roosty"* • Emma Dunn *"Ma" McCormick* • Veda Ann Borg *Julie* • Phil Silvers ■ *Dir* Harold S Bucquet • *Scr* Harry Ruskin, John Q Higgins, from the play by Martin Berkeley

Pendulum ★★★ 15

Detective crime drama 1969 · US · Colour · 97mins

George Peppard turns in a tough performance in this above-par thriller as a police captain who becomes a murder suspect when his wife (Jean Seberg) and her lover are murdered. Ostracised by his former police colleagues and thrown in prison, he escapes to hunt down the real culprit. There's good support from Robert F Lyons, playing the murderer and rapist Peppard puts away at the outset, but who is then released on a technicality, and from Madeleine Sherwood as the bad guy's mother. ▭

George Peppard *Captain Frank Matthews* • Jean Seberg *Adele Matthews* • Richard Kiley *Woodrow Wilson King* • Charles McGraw *Deputy Chief Hildebrand* • Madeleine Sherwood *Mrs Eileen Sanderson* • Robert F Lyons *Paul Martin Sanderson* ■ *Dir* George Schaefer • *Scr* Stanley Niss

Penelope ★★ U

Comedy 1966 · US · Colour · 97mins

A glossy comedy with Natalie Wood as the compulsive thief who robs a bank and is then persuaded by her shrink to break into the bank again and put the money back. Then the plot obliges her to break into the bank yet again. Heist movies were very big in the mid-sixties and this one certainly has the most gorgeous-looking thief. If only it also had a wittier script, pacier direction and a real leading man – George Segal, say – to play opposite the vivacious Natalie Wood.

Natalie Wood *Penelope Elcott* • Ian Bannen *James B Elcott* • Dick Shawn *Dr Gregory Mannix* • Peter Falk *Lt Bixbee* • Jonathan Winters *Professor Klobb* ■ *Dir* Arthur Hiller • *Scr* George Wells, from the novel by EV Cunningham [Howard Fast]

The Penguin Pool Murder ★★★

Comedy mystery 1932 · US · BW · 65mins

A marvellous RKO B movie in which sleuthing teacher Hildegarde Withers (played by Edna May Oliver) and cigar-chewing cop Oscar Piper (James Gleason) team up to investigate a bizarre death in an aquarium. The experience is obviously mesmerising as the two characters end up contemplating marriage. Stuart Palmer's original stories were spun out into six films from 1932 to 1937, but Oliver only graced the first three – a pity, as it's the sparring stars that make this film so watchable.

Edna May Oliver *Hildegarde Martha Withers* • James Gleason *Inspector Oscar Piper* • Mae Clarke *Gwen Parker* • Robert Armstrong *Barry Costello* • Donald Cook *Philip Seymour* • Clarence Wilson *Bertrand B Hemingway* ■ *Dir* George Archainbaud • *Scr* Willis Goldbeck, from the novel by Stuart Palmer

The Penitent ★★★ 15

Drama 1988 · US · Colour · 90mins

Actor Cliff Osmond – best known as the hulking sap in Billy Wilder's *Kiss Me, Stupid* – turned writer/director with this weird, heavily symbolic tale about an isolated Hispanic village which has an annual religious festival which climaxes with a re-enactment of the Crucifixion. Few survive the ordeal, even though ropes are used instead of nails. The penitent this year is Raul Julia, trapped in a sexless marriage and watching his wife being easily seduced by Armande Assante. ▭

Raul Julia *Ramon Guerola* • Armand Assante *Juan Mateo* • Rona Freed *Celia Guerola* • Julie Carmen *Corina* • Lucy Reina *Margarita* ■ *Dir/Scr* Cliff Osmond

Penitentiary ★★★ 18

Blaxploitation prison drama 1979 · US · Colour · 99mins

This late entry in the blaxploitation cycle cleverly mixes gritty prison drama with the boxing movie, then enjoying huge popularity after the success of *Rocky*. Leon Isaac Kennedy is the clichéd innocent inmate who puts his fighting skills to good use competing in a prison boxing tournament where victory offers early parole. As written, directed and produced by Jamaa Fanaka, this is a relatively uncompromising look at daily prison life which dumps the usual blaxploitation stereotypes in a bid for more realistic and deeper characterisations, yet at the same time enforces the perception that prisons, particularly in America, are chock-full of black people. Successful enough to spawn two sequels. ▭

Leon Isaac Kennedy *Too Sweet* • Thommy Pollard *Eugene* • Hazel Spears *Linda* • Wilbur "Hi-Fi" White *Sweet Pea* • Gloria Delaney *Inmate* ■ *Dir/Scr* Jamaa Fanaka

Penn & Teller Get Killed ★

Black comedy 1989 · US · Colour · 89mins

It's hard to figure out why Arthur Penn (*Bonnie and Clyde*, *Little Big Man*) would suddenly direct a goofball comedy starring two magician comedians who are an acquired taste. There is a plot buried somewhere here – a psychopath sets his sights on assassinating one of the duo during their nationwide tour – but the movie constantly makes excuses to show the pair involved with unrelated material better suited for one of their talk-show appearances.

Penn Jillette *Penn* • Teller *Teller* • Caitlin Clarke *Carlotta* • Jon Cryer *3rd Frat Boy* • David Patrick Kelly *Fan* • Christopher Durang *Jesus Freak* • Leonardo Cimino *Ernesto* ■ *Dir* Arthur Penn • *Scr* Penn Jillette, Teller

Pennies from Heaven ★★★ U

Musical comedy drama 1936 · US · BW · 80mins

One of a stream of Depression-era movies that consolidated the starpower of crooner Bing Crosby, giving him the chance to warble the title song into posterity and an Oscar nomination. The slight plot and even slighter production values don't really matter, though these days it's hard to take Bing seriously as he befriends an orphaned little girl and wanders through life's incidents with her and her near-dotty grandad, played by the wonderful Donald Meek, the whiskey salesman from *Stagecoach*. Fans need no persuading, but those growing up in the post-Crosby era.

Bing Crosby *Larry Poole* • Madge Evans *Susan Sprague* • Edith Fellows *Patsy Smith* • Donald Meek *Gramp Smith* • John Gallaudet *Hart* • Louis Armstrong *Henry* • Tom Dugan *Crowbar* • Nana Bryant *Miss Howard* ■ *Dir* Norman Z McLeod • *Scr* Jo Swerling, from the novel *The Peacock's Feather* by Katherine Leslie Moore

Pennies from Heaven ★★★ 15

Musical romantic drama 1981 · US · Colour · 103mins

Dennis Potter's TV serial is given the Hollywood treatment here with Steve Martin in the driving seat as music salesman Arthur Parker. Set in Chicago during the Depression, Martin's frustrated marriage spurs him into a dangerous dalliance with feisty schoolteacher Bernadette Peters. The drama is offset and enriched by their happy-go-lucky musical numbers – by far the most enjoyable feature of the film. The cinematography is rich and slick, the leads engaging and the film is worth seeing for Christopher Walken doing his version of *The Full Monty* alone. ▭

Steve Martin *Arthur Parker* • Bernadette Peters *Eileen* • Christopher Walken *Tom* • Jessica Harper *Joan* • Vernel Bagneris *Accordion man* • John McMartin *Mr Warner* • John Karlen *Detective* • Jay Garner *Banker* ■ *Dir* Herbert Ross • *Scr* Dennis Potter, from his TV serial • *Cinematographer* Gordon Willis

Penny Gold ★★

Thriller 1973 · UK · Colour · 90mins

Never trust a twin sister if she looks like Francesca Annis and behaves with such suspicion-inviting self consciousness, especially as her sibling's been found dead. Director Jack Cardiff, taking time off from being one of British cinema's great cameramen, just couldn't come to terms with this thriller about up-market stamp dealing. The film lacks credibility, and the flashback structure employed to examine the jet-set lifestyle of the dead girl would have looked dated even back in the seventies.

Francesca Annis *Delphi Emerson* • James Booth *Matthews* • Nicky Henson *Roger* • Una Stubbs *Anna* • Joseph O'Conor *Charles Blachford* • Joss Ackland *Jones* • Richard Heffer *Claude Grancourt* • Sue Lloyd *Model* ■ *Dir* Jack Cardiff • *Scr* David Osborne, Liz Charles-Williams

Penny Paradise ★★ U

Comedy 1938 · UK · BW · 71mins

A Merseyside tugboat captain wins the football pools, celebrates with an uproarious party, and must cope with a grasping aunt and his daughter's unscrupulous suitor who both hope to profit from his good fortune. A simple and oft-told tale makes for a short and straightforward British film, given an authentic background by director Carol Reed, and beautifully played by Welsh character actor Edmund Gwenn, soon to find Hollywood stardom (notably in *Miracle on 34th Street*).

Edmund Gwenn *Joe Higgins* • Jimmy O'Dea *Pat* • Betty Driver *Betty Higgins* • Maire O'Neill *Widow Clegg* • Jack Livesey *Bert* ■ *Dir* Carol Reed • *Scr* Thomas Thompson, Thomas Browne, WL Meade, from a story by Basil Dean

The Penny Pool ★ U

Comedy 1937 · UK · BW · 89mins

Duggie Wakefield was a music-hall comedian who made his living playing dolts who, against all the odds, eventually came good. Released by Mancunian Films, which specialised in broad comedies with a distinctly regional feel, this hopelessly dated picture has our gormless hero getting mixed up with factory worker Luanne Shaw just as her winning pools coupon goes missing. For aficionados and the very bored only.

Duggie Wakefield *Duggie* • Billy Nelson *Billy* • Tommy Fields *Tommy Bancroft* • Luanne Shaw *Renee Harland* • Charles Sewell *Henry Bancroft* ■ *Dir* George Black • *Scr* Arthur Mertz

Penny Princess ★★★ U

Comedy 1952 · UK · Colour · 93mins

As a British spoof on the free market – New York girl inherits European principality and invigorates flagging economy – this is so gentle that the satire is scarcely as noticeable as the appearance of a young Dirk Bogarde as star Yolande Donlan's suitor. But Donlan, the wife of writer/director Val Guest, still puts in an effervescent performance despite the rather lacklustre plot.

Yolande Donlan *Lindy Smith* • Dirk Bogarde *Tony Craig* • Edwin Styles *Chancellor/Cobbler* • Reginald Beckwith *Finance minister/Blacksmith* • Kynaston Reeves *Burgomeister/Policeman* ■ *Dir/Scr* Val Guest

Penny Serenade ★★★★ U

Romantic melodrama 1941 · US · BW · 119mins

For this unforgettable weepie, one box of Kleenex simply won't be enough. Cary Grant (a superb performance) and Irene Dunne have a life story that will clutch at your hearts, expertly controlled by master director George Stevens, but don't watch if deaths of young children (albeit dramatised) are upsetting to you. Grant was rightly Oscar-nominated, and his subtly-shaded portrayal as he keeps sentimentality at bay is a lesson in screen acting. ▭

Cary Grant *Roger Adams* • Irene Dunne *Julie Gardiner Adams* • Beulah Bondi *Miss Oliver* • Edgar Buchanan *Applejack* • Ann Doran *Dotty* ■ *Dir* George Stevens • *Scr* Morrie Ryskind, from a story by Martha Cheavens

The Pentagon Wars
★★★★ 🔞

Comedy drama 1998 · US · Colour · 103mins

A wonderfully biting comedy based on a true story, the target is the American defence industry, in particular the gravy train responsible for developing new technology. Cary Elwes is the idealistic officer determined to crack down on dodgy practices, such as the use of cranes and electric hot elements in the testing of heatseeking missiles; *Frasier*'s Kelsey Grammer is his determined adversary. Director Richard Benjamin (who also makes a brief cameo) wisely allows the very funny script to take centre stage. Contains some swearing. 📼

Kelsey Grammer *General Partridge* • Cary Elwes *Colonel Burton* • Viola Davis *Fanning* • John C McGinley *Colonel Bock* • Clifton Powell *Sergeant Benjamin Dalton* • Richard Schiff *Smith* • Tom Wright *Major William Sayers* • Richard Benjamin *Casper Weinberger* ■ *Dir* Richard Benjamin • *Scr* Martyn Burke, Jamie Malanowski, from a non-fiction book by James G Burton

Pentathlon
★★ 🔞

Action thriller 1994 · US · Colour · 101mins

Dolph Lundgren returns to the sporting arena (he made his name in *Rocky IV*) for this strange action thriller. He plays a top East German athlete who defects to the West only to find himself pursued by his former trainer, David Soul. Made at the time when Lundgren was at the height of his video-star fame, this marked a departure from his usual crash, bang, wallop fare, although the mix of sporting and action heroics is deeply unconvincing. Contains scenes of violence, swearing and drug abuse. 📼

Dolph Lundgren *Eric Brogar* • Evan James Offerman • Barry Lynch *Horst* ■ *Dir* Bruce Malmuth • *Scr* William Stadiem. Gary MacDonald, Gary Devore, from a story by William Stadiem, Bruce Malmuth

Penthouse
★★★

Crime mystery 1933 · US · BW · 88mins

When a lawyer (Phillips Holmes) with seedy connections is framed for murder by a criminal heavy (C Henry Gordon), the crime is solved by respectable lawyer/sleuth Warner Baxter, with Myrna Loy co-starring as his helpmate. This Hunt Stromberg production was written by Albert Hackett and Frances Goodrich, who livened the formula up with a good seasoning of wit, directed with excellent judgement for the nuances of comedy-drama by WS Van Dyke. The following year, the same team, again with Loy but with William Powell in place of Baxter, perfected the formula with *The Thin Man* and launched one of MGM's most popular series.

Warner Baxter *Jackson Durant* • Myrna Loy *Gertie Waxted* • Charles Butterworth *Layton* • Mae Clarke *Mimi Montagne* • Phillips Holmes *Tom Siddall* • C Henry Gordon *Jim Crelliman* • Martha Sleeper *Sue Leonard* • Nat Pendleton

Tony Grazotti ■ *Dir* WS Van Dyke • *Scr* Frances Goodrich, Albert Hackett, from the novel by Arthur Somers Roche

The Penthouse
★

Thriller 1967 · UK · Colour · 96mins

Married estate agent Terence Morgan and his mistress Suzy Kendall are terrorised in their love nest by Tom and Dick (Tony Beckley and Norman Rodway), a knife-wielding pair of villains – Harry turns up later. After tying up the estate agent, they force him to watch them abuse the girlfriend as well as listen to self-justifying monologues and musings on the sad state of the world. The original stage play was probably more effective; the film version, however, comes across as grim, tasteless and pretentious.

Suzy Kendall *Barbara Willason* • Terence Morgan *Bruce Victor* • Tony Beckley *Tom* • Norman Rodway *Dick* • Martine Beswick *Harry* ■ *Dir* Peter Collinson • *Scr* Peter Collinson, from the play *The Meter Man* by C Scott Forbes

The Penthouse
★

Thriller 1989 · US · Colour · 95mins

Well-worn clichés provide the ingredients for this woman-in-jeopardy drama. Homicidal insane-asylum fugitive David Hewlett holds record-company executive's daughter Robin Givens hostage in her apartment. Wired with explosives, he keeps the increasingly frustrated cops at bay. Not even the solid support of Robert Guillaume as the girl's father can make up for the otherwise unappealing cast, poorly thought-out plot and stock situations.

Robin Givens *Dinah St Clair* • David Hewlett *Joe Dobson* • Robert Guillaume *Eugene St Clair* • Donnelly Rhodes *Lieutenant Valeri* • Alex Bruhanski *Captain Mundy* ■ *Dir* David Greene • *Scr* William Wood, Frank De Felitta, from the novel by Elleston Trevor

The People across the Lake
★★ 🔞

Thriller 1988 · US · Colour · 94mins

Valerie Harper and Gerald McRaney are the city slickers turned country mice who open up a surfboard business, only to find rural pollution can be worse than urban blight – there are bodies in the placid lake and skeletons in the community cupboard. Director Arthur Allan Seidelman's ramshackle made-for-TV thriller may be a slow starter, but it delivers a fair quota of chills.

Valerie Harper *Rachel Yoman* • Gerald McRaney *Chuck Yoman* • Barry Corbin *Malcolm Bryce* • Tammy Lauren *Lisa Yoman* • Daryl Anderson *Henry Link* ■ *Dir* Arthur Allan Seidelman • *Scr* Dalene Young, from a story by Bill McCutchen, Dalene Young

The People against O'Hara
★★★

Crime drama 1951 · US · BW · 102mins

James Arness may have the title role, but the main interest in this legal potboiler lies in watching longtime buddies Spencer Tracy and Pat O'Brien share the screen for the first time. Unfortunately, their time together is limited, as lawyer Tracy is mostly confined to a courtroom, attempting to

disprove DA John Hodiak's murder charge. Had director John Sturges taken a more direct route, this might have been a nifty little police procedures picture. But the pacing is often over-deliberate and the jibes made against the judicial system are far from original. Solid, but far from Tracy's best.

Spencer Tracy *James Curtayne* • Pat O'Brien *Vincent Ricks* • Diana Lynn *Ginny Curtayne* • John Hodiak *Louis Barra* • Eduardo Ciannelli *Knuckles Lanzetta* • James Arness *Johnny O'Hara* • Yvette Duguay *Mrs Lanzetta* • Jay C Flippen *Sven Norson* • Charles Bronson [Charles Bronson] *Angelo Korvac* ■ *Dir* John Sturges • *Scr* John Monks Jr, from the novel by Eleazar Lipsky

The People Next Door
★★

Drama 1970 · US · Colour · 93mins

A fifties-style drama about teenage angst and parental despair, starring Eli Wallach and Julie Harris as the married couple and Deborah Winters and Stephen McHattie as their teenage children. It's Winters who's the problem, indulging in drugs, getting close to overdosing and ending up in rehab. Wallach and Harris blame themselves, each other and society in general. The people next door, though, are Hal Holbrook and Cloris Leachman who offer neighbourly coffee and assurance, though their son turns out to be a drug dealer.

Eli Wallach *Arthur Mason* • Julie Harris *Gerrie Mason* • Deborah Winters *Maxie Mason* • Stephen McHattie *Artie Mason* • Hal Holbrook *David Hoffman* • Cloris Leachman *Tina Hoffman* • Don Scardino *Sandy Hoffman* • Rue McClanahan *Della* ■ *Dir* David Greene • *Scr* JP Miller, from his TV play

The People Next Door
★★ 🔞

Drama 1996 · US · Colour · 89mins

Nicollette Sheridan ditches her habitual glamour for this occasionally gripping slice of suburban paranoia. She plays a single mum with three young children who strikes up an instant rapport with new neighbours Michael O'Keefe and Tracy Ellis. However, she soon learns that the nice young couple have a very different and dangerous agenda. It's ably played – the supporting cast also includes Faye Dunaway – and slickly directed by Tim Hunter of *River's Edge* fame, although there are no real shocks or surprises.

Nicollette Sheridan *Anna Morse* • Faye Dunaway *Ellen Morse* • Michael O'Keefe *Garrett James* • Tracey Ellis *Donna James* • Ernie Lively *Lt Jack Driscoll* ■ *Dir* Tim Hunter • *Scr* Fred Mills

People on Sunday
★★★★★

Documentary drama 1929 · Ger · BW · 89mins

The semi-documentary that launched the careers of a number of film-makers who would subsequently make it in Hollywood: the Siodmak brothers (Robert and Curt), Edgar G Ulmer, Billy Wilder and Fred Zinnemann. Predating neo-realism by some years, being shot in a free-wheeling style on location with non-professional actors, the film follows 24 hours in the lives of a group of Berliners on a day's outing, among them a bachelor, his married friend, a model and a shopgirl. Still as fresh,

romantic and humorous as ever, it allows one to notice the details of everyday life in Berlin in the late twenties.

Dir Robert Siodmark [Robert Siodmak], Edgar G Ulmer • *Scr* Robert Siodmark, Kurt Siodmark [Curt Siodmak], Billy Wilder, from an idea by Kurt Siodmak [Curt Siodmak] • *Production assistant* Fred Zinnemann • *Cinematographer* Eugen Schüfftan

The People That Time Forgot
★★ 🔠

Adventure 1977 · UK · Colour · 86mins

An okay sequel to *The Land That Time Forgot* in which missing explorer Doug McClure is traced to an exotic prison on the lost island of Caprona. Not as trashy as the original Edgar Rice Burroughs adventure, but director Kevin Connor's constipated confection still features silly dinosaurs (ludicrous mechanised mock-ups) and hopeless acting from an interesting cast (John Wayne's son Patrick, David Bowie protégée Dana Gillespie and David Prowse). A few shots, composed around celebrated fantasy illustrations, compensate for all the film's shortcomings. 📼

Patrick Wayne *Major Ben McBride* • Doug McClure *Bowen Tyler* • Sarah Douglas *Lady Charlotte "Charly"* • Dana Gillespie *Ajor* • Thorley Walters *Dr Edward Norfolk* • Shane Rimmer *Hogan* • Tony Britton *Captain Lawton* • David Prowse [Dave Prowse] *Executioner* ■ *Dir* Kevin Connor • *Scr* Patrick Tilley, from the novel by Edgar Rice Burroughs

The People under the Stairs
★★★ 🔞

Horror 1991 · US · Colour · 97mins

Wes Craven was back to nearly his very best with this sly, satirical shocker, a modern-day fable in which the rich are literally feeding off the poor. Young Brandon Adams is the lad from the ghetto who gets trapped in the house owned by mad slum landlords Everett McGill and Wendy Robie, and discovers that he is not the only person to fall victim to the couple. The plot stretches credibility to the limit, but McGill – complete with leather bondage gear – and Robie have a ball as the monstrous duo, while Craven keeps the adrenalin pumping as well as delivering some sharp digs about injustices in American society. Contains violence and swearing. 📼

Brandon Adams *"Fool"* • Everett McGill *Man* • Wendy Robie *Woman* • AJ Langer *Alice* • Ving Rhames *LeRoy* • Sean Whalen *Roach* • Bill Cobbs *Grandpa Booker* ■ *Dir/Scr* Wes Craven

The People vs Dr Kildare
★

Medical drama 1941 · US · BW · 77mins

Moving out of the operating theatre into the courtroom, MGM's *Dr Kildare* series was showing signs of exhaustion by this seventh instalment (out of nine). Lew Ayres's James Kildare is sued for gross negligence by Bonita Granville's skating star after an emergency operation leaves her with a paralysed leg. Lionel Barrymore's wise old Dr Gillespie saves the day. On his way to bigger things, Red Skelton makes the first of two appearances in the series, providing some painful comedy relief as an orderly.

🇺 = SUITABLE FOR ALL   🇺c = SUITABLE FOR ALL, ESPECIALLY FOR YOUNG CHILDREN (VIDEO ONLY)   PG = PARENTAL GUIDANCE

Lew Ayres *Dr James Kildare* • Lionel Barrymore *Dr Leonard Gillespie* • Laraine Day *Mary Lamont* • Bonita Granville *Frances Marlowe* • Alma Kruger *Molly Byrd* • Red Skelton *Vernon Briggs, janitor* • Diana Lewis *Fay Lennox* • Paul Stanton *Mr Reynolds* ■ *Dir* Harold S Bucquet • *Scr* Willis Goldbeck, from a story by Lawrence P Bachmann, Max Brand, from characters created by Max Brand

The People vs Larry Flynt
★★★★ 18

Biographical drama
1996 · US · Colour · 124mins

An airbrushed version of the real-life story of America's most notorious and successful pornographer played with red-blooded bawdiness by Woody Harrelson, who runs a series of strip clubs and then publishes explicitly nude magazines such as *Hustler*. A long way from *Amadeus*, director Milos Forman would have you believe that obscenity is therapy, but he's made a film entertaining enough to gain him and Harrelson Oscar nominations. Contains swearing, sexual references, nudity and some violence. ▣ **DVD**

Woody Harrelson *Larry Flynt* • Courtney Love *Althea Leasure* • Edward Norton *Isaacman* • Brett Harrelson *Jimmy Flynt* • Donna Hanover *Ruth Carter Stapleton* • James Cromwell *Charles Keating* • Crispin Glover *Arlo* • Vincent Schiavelli *Chester* ■ *Dir* Milos Forman • *Scr* Scott Alexander, Larry Karaszewski

People Will Talk
★★★★

Comedy drama   1951 · US · BW · 109mins

The title is apt indeed: this is one of the talkiest movies Joseph L Mankiewicz ever wrote and directed. On paper, it's a romantic comedy about a doctor (Cary Grant) who treats, then marries already pregnant Jeanne Crain, much to the chagrin of both the academic fraternity and the moral majority. Along the way, however, Mankiewicz takes pot shots at American sexual morality, tax evasion, the Korean war, the McCarthy witch-hunts and a lot more besides. Though the film is bombastic and visually static, Grant is on top form, while you have to hand it to Mankiewicz for walking on eggshells.

Cary Grant *Dr Noah Praetorius* • Jeanne Crain *Annabel Higgins* • Finlay Currie *Shunderson* • Hume Cronyn *Professor Elwell* • Walter Slezak *Professor Barker* • Sidney Blackmer *Arthur Higgins* • Margaret Hamilton *Miss Pickett* ■ *Dir* Joseph L Mankiewicz • *Scr* Joseph L Mankiewicz, from the play *Dr Praetorius* by Curt Goetz

Pepe
★

Musical comedy 1960 · US · Colour · 157mins

An atrocious all-star mess, led by the singularly unappealing Mexican actor Cantinflas and evidently "inspired" by his 1956 hit, *Around the World in 80 Days*. It starts in Mexico, where Cantinflas plays a stupido ranch foreman whose beloved white stallion is sold to an American film director. The story then moves to Hollywood, where a mind-boggling array of stars drop in for a look, a line, a song or a scene with the befuddled Cantinflas. The joke might have just passed muster at 80 minutes, but the film originally lasted over three hours, stretching the plot and the audience's patience beyond endurance.

Cantinflas *Pepe* • Dan Dailey *Ted Holt* • Shirley Jones *Suzie Murphy* • Carlos Montalban *Auctioneer* • Vicki Trickett *Lupita* • Matt Mattox *Dancer* • Hank Henry *Manager* • Ernie Kovacs *Immigration inspector* • William Demarest *Studio gateman* • Joey Bishop • Maurice Chevalier • Charles Coburn • Bing Crosby • Tony Curtis • Bobby Darin • Sammy Davis Jr • Jimmy Durante • Zsa Zsa Gabor • Judy Garland • Greer Garson • Peter Lawford • Janet Leigh • Jack Lemmon • Dean Martin • Kim Novak • AndréPrevin • Debbie Reynolds • Edward G Robinson • Cesar Romero • Frank Sinatra ■ *Dir* George Sidney • *Scr* Dorothy Kingsley, Claude Binyon, from a story by Leonard Spigelgass, Sonya Levien

Pépé le Moko
★★★★★

Romantic melodrama 1937 · Fr · BW · 90mins

An unmissable French classic, a little bit frayed at the edges but still possessing irresistible Gallic glamour as Jean Gabin's fugitive from justice hangs out in the Algiers Casbah and is only tempted out of his hideaway by romantic love. Photographed like a thriller, with lots of shadows, the film is dominated by Gabin's superb portrayal of the self-sufficient loner – just one look at his sad face, and you know he's haunted by his past and doomed to life as an exile (or worse). A huge hit in France, *Pépé le Moko* was influenced by Howard Hawks's gangster classic *Scarface* (1932) and itself influenced a whole range of Hollywood movies, notably *Algiers* (1938) which was a remake of sorts, and, most famous of all, *Casablanca* (1942). In French with English subtitles. ▣

Jean Gabin *Pépé le Moko* • Mireille Balin *Gaby Gould* • Line Noro *Inès* • Lucas Gridoux *Inspector Slimane* • Gabriel Gabrio *Carlos* • Fernand Charpin *Régis* ■ *Dir* Julien Duvivier • *Scr* Julien Duvivier, Henri Jeanson, Detective Ashelbe [d'Henri La Barthe], Jacques Constant, from a novel by Detective Ashelbe [d'Henri La Barthe] • *Cinematographer* Jules Kruger, Marc Fossard

Pepi, Luci, Bom...
★★★ 18

Comedy   1980 · Sp · Colour · 77mins

The first full-length movie from Spanish director Pedro Almodóvar set the camp/trash/kitsch seal on his future output. Informed by the Andy Warhol pop art, photo romances and John Waters cult movies of his youth, Almodóvar's zany dissection of what constitutes happiness for people living on the edge is a flawed home-movie in which the flaws dictate a surreal style all their own. Featuring a cast of actual investors in the picture, including friends (and future leading ladies) Carmen Maura and Cecilia Roth, it tells the story of how three Madrid girls bond and set up house after rape, revenge, disco kidnapping, underwear commercials, erection competitions and sadistic lesbian fantasies throw them all together. In Spanish with English subtitles. ▣

Carmen Maura *Pepi* • Felix Rotaeta *Policeman* • Olvido "Alaska" Gara *Bom* • Eva Siva *Luci* • Cecilia Roth • Pedro Almodóvar ■ *Dir/Scr* Pedro Almodóvar

Peppermint Frappé
★★★

Drama   1967 · Sp · Colour · 94mins

Although dedicated to Luis Buñuel, the shadows of Alfred Hitchcock and

Michelangelo Antonioni fall just as heavily across this tale of repressed sexuality and physical transformation. The second in Carlos Saura's "Frustrations, Anxieties and Fantasies of Franco's Bourgeoisie" series, the film couches its political message in terms of a *Vertigo*-like plot, in which a rural physician transforms his comely nurse into the double of his stunning sister-in-law. That Saura won the best director prize at Berlin is due in no small measure to his future companion, Geraldine Chaplin, who handles the dual role with a panache that has since eluded her. In Spanish with English subtitles.

Geraldine Chaplin *Elena/Ana* • José Luis Lopez Vazquez *Julian* • Alfredo Mayo *Pablo* ■ *Dir* Carlos Saura • *Scr* Rafael Azcona, Angelino Fons, Carlos Saura

Perceval le Gallois
★★★★ PG

Period adventure
1978 · Fr/W Ger/It/Swi · Colour · 113mins

This adaptation of the 12th-century Arthurian poem by Chrétien de Troyes is an unexpected film from Eric Rohmer, the anatomist of French modern-day sexual relationships. Yet the episodic story about the naive young Welsh knight's quest for the Holy Grail is observed with much of the ironic wit of the director of "Six Moral Tales". Shot completely in the studio against stylised painted sets, it combines the means of cinema and theatre, with medieval music, mime and verse. It takes a while to adjust to the style and language and, at over two hours, the film needs quite a bit of concentration, but many sensual as well as intellectual pleasures can be gained. A French language film. ▣

Fabrice Luchini *Perceval* • André Dussollier *Gauvain* • Marie-Christine Barrault *Queen Guinevere* • Marc Eyraud *King Arthur* ■ *Dir* Eric Rohmer • *Scr* Eric Rohmer, from the poem by Chrétien de Troyes • *Cinematographer* Nestor Almendros

Percy
★

Comedy   1971 · UK · Colour · 103mins

Ralph Thomas made his name with the *Doctor* series of comedies, but you can bet your scalpel that Sir Lancelot Spratt wouldn't have touched *this* operation. However, Denholm Elliott clearly revels in the opportunity to perform the world's first penis transplant. Sadly, his wonderfully manic turn is the only reason to catch a film whose awfulness has earned it a certain cult kudos. Phallic gags abound as Hywel Bennett seeks the identity of the donor and becomes wrapped up in his complicated love life. No wonder he refused the equally dreadful sequel, *Percy's Progress*. Contains some swearing, a sex scene and nudity. ▣

Hywel Bennett *Edwin Anthony* • Denholm Elliott *Emmanuel Whitbread* • Elke Sommer *Helga* • Britt Ekland *Dorothy Chiltern-Barlow* • Cyd Hayman *Moira Warrington* • Janet Key *Hazel* • Julia Foster *Marilyn* ■ *Dir* Ralph Thomas • *Scr* Hugh Leonard, Terence Feel, from the novel by Raymond Hitchcock

Percy and Thunder
★★★

Drama   1993 · US · Colour · 90mins

Produced as part of Steven Spielberg's *Screenworks* experiment, this boxing drama marked a return to the ring for James Earl Jones, who had earned an Oscar nomination for *The Great White Hope* back in 1970. This time he's a washed-up champ, who scrapes along by coaching rookies, until he encounters contender Courtney B Vance. Billy Dee Williams wins several scenes on points, as an unscrupulous fight promoter. But it's the imposing Jones who stamps his authority on this unflinching look at the seedier side of the sport. Director Ivan Dixon also merits mention for his credibly choreographed fight sequences.

Courtney B Vance *Wayne "Thunder" Carter* • Zakes Mokae *Pee Wee* • James Earl Jones *Percy Banks* • Billy Dee Williams *Ralph Tate* • Robert Wuhl *Jim Keisling* • Gloria Foster *Sugar Brown* • Gloria Reuben *Suzanne* • Antonio Fargas *Spider* ■ *Dir* Ivan Dixon • *Scr* Art Washington

Percy's Progress
★ 15

Comedy   1974 · UK · Colour · 96mins

This sorry sequel to the dire sex comedy, *Percy*, was surely the career low of all who participated. It's hard to fathom why Vincent Price agreed to appear or why Denholm Elliott signed up again after his role in the original, but, following Hywel Bennett's refusal, it's clear that Leigh Lawson assumed the lead role in order to achieve greater exposure. Contains swearing and sex scenes.

Leigh Lawson *Percy Edward Anthony* • Elke Sommer *Clarissa* • Denholm Elliott *Sir Emmanuel Whitbread* • Judy Geeson *Dr Fairweather* • Harry H Corbett *Prime minister* • Vincent Price *Mammonian* • Adrienne Posta *Iris* • Julie Ege *Miss Hanson* • Barry Humphries *Dr Anderson/Australian TV lady* ■ *Dir* Ralph Thomas • *Scr* Sid Colin, from the novel *Percy* by Raymond Hitchcock

Perdita Durango
★★★ 18

Black comedy road movie
1997 · Sp/Mex/US · Colour · 118mins

An insanely violent, amoral black comedy thriller, inspired by the books of Barry Gifford, who also provided the source material for David Lynch's *Wild at Heart* (trivia nuts will know that Perdita Durango was the name of the Isabella Rossellini character in Lynch's version). Here she is flamboyantly played by Rosie Perez in a bonkers tale which finds her teaming up with black magic cult leader Javier Bardem to kidnap a couple of young lovers for human sacrifice, then moving on to smuggle a cargo of human fetuses to Las Vegas. Director Alex de la Iglesia sets out to offend just about everybody and pretty much succeeds, but the mix of Latin craziness and mind-blowing ultra-violence is utterly compulsive. ▣

Rosie Perez *Perdita Durango* • Javier Bardem *Romeo Dolorosa* • Harley Cross *Duane* • Aimee Graham *Estelle* • James Gandolfini *Dumas* • Screamin' Jay Hawkins *Adolfo* • Carlos Bardem *Reggie* • Santiago Segura *Shorty Dee* • Alex Cox *Agent Doyle* ■ *Dir* Alex de la Iglesia • *Scr* Álex de la Iglesia, David Trueba, Jorge Guerricaechevarría, Barry Gifford, from the novel *59 Degrees and Raining: the Story of Perdita Durango* by Barry Gifford

The Perez Family ★★★ 15
Romantic comedy drama
1995 · US · Colour · 108mins

A disappointing romantic comedy from director Mira Nair, with Marisa Tomei and Alfred Molina as Cubans, mistaken for husband and wife when they arrive in Miami because they have the same surname, who decide to take advantage of the coincidence. Set against the backdrop of a real-life drama (the 1980 Mariel Boatlift of Cuban refugees), this picks up considerably whenever Anjelica Huston (as Molina's wife, who's been waiting for him in Miami for 20 years) is on screen, but it never quite decides whether it's going to be a realistic portrayal of events or a slushy fable of love lost and found. Criticised on its release for having non-Cubans in its leading roles, this misfire has its moments. ▣

Marisa Tomei *Dottie Perez* • Anjelica Huston *Carmela Perez* • Alfred Molina *Juan Raul Perez* • Chazz Palminteri *Lieutenant John Pirelli* • Trini Alvarado *Teresa Perez* • Celia Cruz *Luz Paz* • Diego Wallraff *Angel Perez* • Angela Lanza *Flavia* ■ *Dir* Mira Nair • *Scr* Robin Swicord, from a novel by Christine Bell

Perfect ★★ 15
Drama 1985 · US · Colour · 115mins

Writing an exposé of the Californian fitness industry to keep busy while chasing a drug story, *Rolling Stone* reporter John Travolta falls in love with Jamie Lee Curtis, the aerobics guru whose club he intends to destroy in his feature. Director James Bridges's air-head film is one of the prime reasons Travolta fell out of favour before his *Pulp Fiction* rediscovery. Yet both he and Curtis look fabulous in their work-out sequences – of which there are far too many – and their appealing chemistry does get the now very dated premise over the rough patches and into shape. Contains swearing and brief nudity. ▣

John Travolta *Adam Lawrence* • Jamie Lee Curtis *Jessica Wilson* • Jann Wenner *Mark Roth* • Ann De Salvo *Frankie* • Stefan Gierasch *Charlie* • John Napierala *City news editor* • Laraine Newman *Linda* • Marilu Henner *Sally* • Carly Simon ■ *Dir* James Bridges • *Scr* Aaron Latham, James Bridges, from articles in *Rolling Stone* by Aaron Latham

Perfect Alibi ★★ 15
Thriller 1995 · US · Colour · 95mins

How perfect can an alibi be if Teri Garr can unravel it with one phone call? Garr plays the nosy friend of Kathleen Quinlan whose doctor husband (Alex McArthur) is having sex with their French au pair (Lydie Denier). Soon people begin to die, and it looks as if the wife is next. The doctor's plan for a perfect crime is so prosaic that the movie seems pointless, but Garr has some fun interaction with Hector Elizondo, who plays the cop assigned to the case. ▣

Teri Garr *Tolbert Laney* • Hector Elizondo *Detective Ryker* • Alex McArthur • Lydie Denier • Kathleen Quinlan *Melanie Bauers* ■ *Dir* Kevin Meyer • *Scr* Kevin Meyer, from the novel *Where's My Mommy Now?* by Rochelle Majer Krich

Perfect Blue ★★★ 18
Animated adventure
1998 · Jap · Colour · 81mins

Having previously concentrated on futuristic themes, Japanimation finally tackled a contemporary topic with this breakthrough study of psychological decline and the transience of fame. Clearly influenced by Katsuhiro Otomo, who directed that *anime* classic *Akira*, Satoshi Kon's atmospheric visuals disconcertingly mirror the growing paranoia of Mima, the clean-cut pop star whose drastic image change not only alienates her fans, but also puts her life in danger. Superbly drawn and packed with ambitious visuals, this impressive picture only stumbles in the later stages with a surfeit of dream sequences muddling an already unconvincing ending. Japanese dialogue dubbed into English. Contains violence, swearing and nudity.

Ruby Marlowe • Wendee Lee • Gil Starberry • Lia Sargent • Steve Bulen • James Lyon • Frank Buck • David Lucas ■ *Dir* Satoshi Kon • *Scr* Sadayuki Murai, from the novel *Perfect Blue* by Yoshikazu Takeuchi, from characters created by Hisashi Eguchi

A Perfect Couple ★★★
Romantic comedy
1979 · US · Colour · 111mins

Director Robert Altman abandons the scattershot technique that made *Nashville* so memorable to concentrate delightfully on an intimate, offbeat love story brought about by computer dating. Paul Dooley plays Alex, a strait-laced prude intimidated by his oppressive Greek-American family, who is drawn to Sheila (Marta Heflin), a member of the rock group Keepin' 'em Off the Streets. Gently awkward dilemmas and a well-earned happy ending result in a magic that only a fine director can create.

Paul Dooley *Alex Theodopoulos* • Marta Heflin *Sheila Shea* • Titos Vandis *Panos Theodopoulos* • Belita Moreno *Eleousa* • Henry Gibson *Fred Bott* • Dimitra Arliss *Athena* ■ *Dir* Robert Altman • *Scr* Robert Altman, Allan Nicholls

Perfect Day ★★★★★ U
Comedy 1929 · US · BW · 19mins

One of the very best of Laurel and Hardy's short comedies, with an alarming soundtrack – a bell is sounded when Stanley is struck on the head. Edgar Kennedy is the sublimely exasperated uncle with a gouty foot which is being continually attacked by the family dog. Our heroes are off on a picnic with wives Isabelle Keith and Kaye Deslys, but a series of incidents (a flat tyre, trouble with the neighbours) keep the car immovable until the end. Lovingly inventive and as cherishable as Stan and Ollie themselves. ▣

Stan Laurel *Stan* • Oliver Hardy *Ollie* • Edgar Kennedy *Uncle Edgar* • Kay Deslys *Mrs Hardy* • Isabelle Keith *Mrs Laurel* ■ *Dir* James Parrott • *Scr* HM Walker, from a story by Leo McCarey, Hal Roach

Perfect Friday ★★★
Crime comedy 1970 · UK · Colour · 94mins

This sprightly crime caper – a sort of *Lavender Hill Mob* with sex appeal – is hardly the kind of material normally associated with its director, Peter Hall. Stanley Baker stars as the timid banker who teams up with aristocratic wastrel David Warner and his bored wife Ursula Andress for a meticulously planned raid on his own bank. The raid never completely enthrals us, which is as much down to the script as Hall's discomfort with the genre, for, while the scam is smoothly staged, the moments of suspense seem contrived and the finale smacks slightly of desperation. Contains some swearing, sex scenes and brief nudity.

Ursula Andress *Britt* • Stanley Baker *Mr Graham* • David Warner *Nicholas* • Patience Collier *Nanny* • TP McKenna *Smith* • David Waller *Williams* ■ *Dir* Peter Hall • *Scr* Anthony Greville-Bell, C Scott Forbes, from a story by C Scott Forbes

The Perfect Furlough ★★
Comedy 1958 · US · Colour · 92mins

Tony Curtis and Janet Leigh star in their third film together, and the second Curtis made for director Blake Edwards. It's a sex comedy, with Curtis plucked by lottery from a secret military base in the Arctic and sent to Paris for a little R&R with dream girl Linda Cristal and army shrink Leigh, the idea being that Curtis's tales will raise morale when he gets back to base. Despite an inconvenient pregnancy and some "grown-up" dialogue about libido and suchlike, this is very much a fifties movie – glossily made and very coy, like the Doris Day–Rock Hudson picture *Pillow Talk* that Stanley Shapiro wrote after this effort.

Tony Curtis *Corporal Paul Hodges* • Janet Leigh *Lieutenant Vicki Loren* • Linda Cristal *Sandra Roca* • Keenan Wynn *Harvey Franklin* • Elaine Stritch *Liz Baker* • Marcel Dalio *Henri* • Les Tremayne *Colonel Leland* • Jay Novello *René* ■ *Dir* Blake Edwards • *Scr* Stanley Shapiro

Perfect Gentlemen ★★★ PG
Comedy thriller 1978 · US · Colour · 91mins

A heist movie with an ingenious twist: Lauren Bacall, Sandy Dennis and Lisa Pelikan plan a bank robbery because their husbands are all serving time in jail. They are joined by a cantankerous old biddy (Ruth Gordon) who happens to be a professional safe-cracker. This comedy thriller was directed for TV by former child star Jackie Cooper and was the first produced script by Nora Ephron. She later wrote *When Harry Met Sally* and went on to become a major director with such films as *Sleepless in Seattle*. ▣

Lauren Bacall *Lizzie Martin* • Ruth Gordon *Mama Cavagnaro* • Sandy Dennis *Sophie Rosenman* • Lisa Pelikan *Annie Cavagnaro* • Robert Alda *Ed Martin* • Stephen Pearlman *Murray Rosenman* ■ *Dir* Jackie Cooper • *Scr* Nora Ephron

A Perfect Little Murder ★★
Comedy mystery 1990 · US · Colour · 94mins

...but, sadly, not a perfect little film. Teri Garr stars as a suburban housewife who overhears a murder plot on her baby monitor in this light-hearted mystery from director Anson Williams (better known as Potsie from the *Happy Days* TV series). A cast that includes Robert Urich, Susan Ruttan and Jeffrey Tambor tries, but fails, to inject some life into the rapidly expiring script of this mediocre movie.

Teri Garr *Marsha Pegler* • Robert Urich *Ross Pegler* • Susan Ruttan *Judy Hecker* • Tom Poston *Don Corman* • Jeffrey Tambor *Don Hecker* ■ *Dir* Anson Williams • *Scr* Mark Stein

Perfect Match ★★ 15
Romantic comedy
1987 · US · Colour · 92mins

Marc McClure and Jennifer Edwards play a couple who meet through the personal ads. But their relationship gets extremely complicated after both of them lie about their real identities to make themselves more interesting, and the various twists and turns of the plot keep things moving nicely in this lightweight but always fun comedy. ▣

Marc McClure *Tim Wainwright* • Jennifer Edwards *Nancy Bryant* • Diane Stilwell *Vicki* ■ *Dir* Mark Deimel • *Scr* Nick Duretta, David Burr, Mark Deimel

The Perfect Murder ★ PG
Murder mystery
1988 · UK/Ind · Colour · 92mins

A simply dreadful adaptation of one of HRF Keating's Inspector Ghote yarns. Ghote is played by Naseeruddin Shah, a big star in Bombay talkies, who looks into diamond smuggling, teams up with a lumbering Swede and investigates the murder of a man named Perfect (that's the only clever thing in the picture). Madhur Jaffrey and her real-life daughter Sakeena also appear. Produced by the Merchant–Ivory stable, taking a rest from EM Forster, it's badly photographed by Walter Lassally and comes across like an amateur dramatics production.

Naseeruddin Shah *Inspector Ghote* • Madhur Jaffrey *Mrs Lal* • Stellan Skarsgård *Axel Svensson* • Dalip Tahil *Dilip Lal* • Dinshaw Daji *Mr Perfect* ■ *Dir* Zafar Hai • *Scr* Zafar Hai, HRF Keating, from a novel by HRF Keating

A Perfect Murder ★★ 15
Mystery thriller 1998 · US · Colour · 102mins

Dial M for Murder was not one of Hitchcock's best movies, but this remake isn't even in the same league, despite the appeal of its two stars, Michael Douglas and Gwyneth Paltrow. Douglas plots the demise of his beautiful, wealthy wife, Paltrow, by getting her lover, Viggo Mortensen, to murder her for a $500,000 fee. So far so good, but things quickly come unglued. So, too, does Andrew Davis's direction, which sometimes fails to maintain the tension of the first hour, while the script seems more interested in making obvious points about life and art in the late nineties. Contains swearing, violence and sex scenes. ▣ *DVD*

Michael Douglas *Steven Taylor* • Gwyneth Paltrow *Emily Bradford Taylor* • Viggo Mortensen *David Shaw* • David Suchet *Detective Mohamed Karaman* • Sarita Choudhury *Raquel Martinez* ■ *Dir* Andrew Davis • *Scr* Patrick Smith Kelly, from the play *Dial M For Murder* by Frederick Knott

U = SUITABLE FOR ALL Uc = SUITABLE FOR ALL, ESPECIALLY FOR YOUNG CHILDREN (VIDEO ONLY) PG = PARENTAL GUIDANCE

Perfect People ★★★ PG

Comedy drama 1988 · US · Colour · 93mins

A silly but enjoyable laugh at the expense of "beautiful people". Lauren Hutton and Perry King are the couple who decide to go in for a bit of physical self improvement, but find conventional methods like diet and exercise aren't enough. Soon they are undergoing plastic surgery, despite the fact that neither needed to go out with a paper bag over their head in the first place. Director Bruce Seth Green has a light enough touch, but allows the pace to flag towards the end. ▭

Lauren Hutton *Barbara Caldwell* • Perry King *Kenneth Caldwell* • Priscilla Barnes *Amy* • Cheryl Pollak *Irene Caldwell* • David Leisure *Derek* • Robert Estes [Rob Estes] *Monty* • June Lockhart *Esther* • Karen Valentine *Margo* ■ *Dir* Bruce Seth Green • *Scr* Gregory Goodell

Perfect Prey ★★ 18

Thriller 1998 · US · Colour · 99mins

The original (*When the Bough Breaks*) was a *Silence of the Lambs* cash-in and a genuinely chilling affair. This sequel (also known as *When the Bough Breaks 2*) is not in the same league – none of the original cast is on hand, either – but it is still a creepy affair, with Kelly McGillis stepping into Ally Walker's shoes as the Texas Ranger tracking a serial killer who's preying on successful female career women, torturing them and then dumping their suffocated bodies in a series of bizarre poses around the state. David Keith and Bruce Dern offer solid support. ▭

Kelly McGillis *Audrey MacLeah* • Bruce Dern *Captain Swaggert* • David Keith *Dwayne Alan Clay* • DW Moffett *Jimmy Cerullo* • Joely Fisher *Elizabeth Crane* ■ *Dir* Howard McCain • *Scr* Robert McDonnell

The Perfect Specimen ★★★ U

Comedy 1937 · US · BW · 99mins

Warner Bros gave their resident swashbuckler Errol Flynn a crack at contemporary comedy in this tale of a rich, upper-class young man who has been raised as an over-protected hothouse specimen and kept from any contact with the dangers of reality. Things change when attractive young Joan Blondell crashes her car through his fence and brings love into his life. Flynn, not quite in control of comedy technique, nonetheless is a perfect model of looks and charm and the film, directed by Flynn regular Michael Curtiz and featuring stalwarts Hugh Herbert, May Robson, and Edward Everett Horton, is a pleasing, if not too believable, romantic comedy romp.

Errol Flynn *Gerald Beresford Wicks* • Joan Blondell *Mona Carter* • Hugh Herbert *Killigrew Shaw* • Edward Everett Horton *Mr Grattan* • Dick Foran *Jinks Carter* • May Robson *Mrs Leona Wicks* • Beverly Roberts *Alicia* • Allen Jenkins *Pinky* ■ *Dir* Michael Curtiz • *Scr* Norman Reilly Raine, Lawrence Riley, Brewster Morse, Fritz Falkenstein, from a story by Samuel Hopkins Adams

The Perfect Storm ★★★ 12

Action drama based on a true story
2000 · US · Colour · 129mins

This truly tempestuous drama has to be the most waterlogged film since *Titanic*: those prone to *mal de mer* should take their sick bags along with them. A true story, it concerns the fishing vessel the *Andrea Gail* which was caught up in the century's worst storm, in 1991, in the North Atlantic. A stubbled George Clooney and a smooth-talking Mark Wahlberg come together again, even if at a stand-off, after being in *Three Kings*, while director Wolfgang Petersen, who made the submarine epic *Das Boot*, takes a deep breath and plunges audiences in and out of skyscraper-tall waves.

George Clooney *Captain Billy Tyne* • Mark Wahlberg *Bobby Shatford* • Diane Lane *Christina Cotter* • John C Reilly *Dale "Murph" Murphy* • William Fichtner *David "Sully" Sullivan* • Mary Elizabeth Mastrantonio *Linda Greenlaw* • Karen Allen *Melissa Brown* ■ *Dir* Wolfgang Petersen • *Scr* Bill Wittliff [William D Wittliff], from the non-fiction book *The Perfect Storm* by Sebastian Junger • *Music* James Horner

Perfect Strangers ★★★

Drama 1945 · UK · BW · 102mins

With the outbreak of the Second World War, a nondescript clerk (Robert Donat) and his dowdy wife (Deborah Kerr), locked in a staid and indifferent marriage, join the navy and the Wrens respectively. Their separate wartime experiences transform them and their postwar relationship. Adapted from a story by Clemence Dane, and produced and directed by Alexander Korda, this is an interesting, engaging and sympathetic film, guaranteed to please thanks to the presence of its attractive co-stars. The Americans loved it, and gave Miss Dane (who co-scripted with Anthony Pelissier) an Oscar for her story. Ann Todd, Glynis Johns and Roland Culver are excellent in the secondary roles.

Robert Donat *Robert Wilson* • Deborah Kerr *Catherine Wilson* • Glynis Johns *Dizzy Clayton* • Ann Todd *Elena* • Roland Culver *Richard* ■ *Dir* Alexander Korda • *Scr* Clemence Dane, Anthony Pelissier, from a story by Clemence Dane

Perfect Strangers ★★

Comedy 1950 · US · BW · 88mins

Married Dennis Morgan and divorced Ginger Rogers meet and fall in love while doing jury duty on a love-nest murder case. Sadly, these perfect strangers make for a less than perfect film, which suffers from a woolly script. Adapted from an American version of a Hungarian play, it aims for romantic comedy in a dramatic setting, but only gets real laughs from Thelma Ritter's splendid performance as a dumb housewife. Indeed, under Bretaigne Windust's direction, the stars are consistently outflanked by the supporting players, notably Harry Bellaver's bailiff, Margalo Gillmore's Park Avenue type and Alan Reed's barber.

Ginger Rogers *Terry Scott* • Dennis Morgan *David Campbell* • Thelma Ritter *Lena Fassler* • Margalo Gillmore *Isobel Bradford* • Anthony Ross *Robert Fisher* • Howard Freeman *Timkin* • Alan Reed *Harry Patullo* • Paul Ford *Judge Byron* • Harry Bellaver *Bailiff* ■ *Dir* Bretaigne Windust • *Scr* Edith Sommer, George Oppenheimer, from the play *Ladies and Gentlemen* by Ben Hecht, Charles Macarthur, from the play *Twelve in the Box* by Ladislaus Bus-Fekete

The Perfect Weapon ★★ 18

Martial arts thriller
1991 · US · Colour · 81mins

The latest crop of martial arts action stars have learnt a lesson from the likes of Chuck Norris and Jean-Claude Van Damme, and have realised that a smidgen of acting ability does come in handy in even the most rudimentary of biffers. Jeff Speakman falls into that category, and, while he doesn't possess the charisma of the late Brandon Lee, he gives every indication that he has mastered more than the basics and lifts this film out of the rut of B-movie martial arts thrillers. The plot holds few surprises, except that the Koreans rather than the Triads or Yakuza are the baddies, but there are some sharply choreographed fight sequences and familiar faces in the shape of Mako, and James Hong as the villain. Contains swearing. ▭

Jeff Speakman *Jeff Sanders* • John Dye *Adam* • Mako *Kim* • James Hong *Yung* • Dante Basco *Jimmy Ho* ■ *Dir* Mark DiSalle • *Scr* David Campbell Wilson

Perfect Witness ★★★ 15

Crime drama 1989 · US · Colour · 96mins

Films about witnesses who get cold feet are pretty formulaic affairs and this TV movie hasn't managed to rustle up any new tricks. However, it does have the virtue of an unusual background, the meat markets of New York, and a better than average cast. Brian Dennehy stars as a lawyer whose crusade against organised crime is given a boost when restaurant owner Aidan Quinn witnesses a gangland killing. Dennehy is typically imposing, but Quinn seems more than a little uncomfortable having to play scared. It's done with aplomb, but casting for dramatic impact rather than star rating might have paid dividends. Contains some violence and swearing. ▭

Brian Dennehy *James Falcon* • Aidan Quinn *Sam Paxton* • Stockard Channing *Liz Sapperstein* • David Cumming *Kevin O'Rourke* • Delroy Lindo *Assistant District Attorney Berger* ■ *Dir* Robert Mandel • *Scr* Terry Curtis Fox, Ron Hutchinson

The Perfect Woman ★★★ U

Comedy 1949 · UK · BW · 83mins

Patricia Roc, one of the most capable British second leads of the forties, was rarely given the chance to show what she could do in starring roles. When she did get her name above the title, she was invariably given a raw deal when it came to dialogue. This frantic comedy of errors is a case in point, for while she handles the dual role of a scientist's social-climbing niece and a beautiful robot with considerable ease, the choicest lines land in the laps of co-stars Stanley Holloway and Nigel Patrick. ▭

Patricia Roc *Penelope* • Stanley Holloway *Ramshead* • Nigel Patrick *Roger Cavendish* • Miles Malleson *Professor Belmond* • Irene Handl *Mrs Butter* • Pamela Devis *Olga, the robot* ■ *Dir* Bernard Knowles • *Scr* Bernard Knowles, JB Boothroyd, George Black, from the play by Wallace Geoffrey, Basil John Mitchell

A Perfect World ★★★★ 15

Drama 1993 · US · Colour · 132mins

It should have been perfect: Clint Eastwood was fresh from Oscar-winning success with *Unforgiven*, while Kevin Costner was challenging his heroic status forged in such hits as *The Bodyguard* by playing a bad guy. As it is, the chemistry isn't quite there and the film has to settle for being just very good indeed. Costner is perhaps a little too introspective as the escaped convict who kidnaps a young boy and heads for freedom in Alaska, developing a curious bond with the child en route. Eastwood is the veteran Texas Ranger on his trail, growling his way through some trademark throwaway lines and proving yet again that nobody directs Clint better than himself. Contains violence, swearing and a sex scene. ▭

Kevin Costner *Butch Haynes* • Clint Eastwood *Red Garnett* • Laura Dern *Sally Gerber* • TJ Lowther *Phillip Perry* • Keith Szarabajka *Terry Pugh* • Leo Burmester *Tom Adler* • Paul Hewitt *Dick Suttle* • Bradley Whitford *Bobby Lee* ■ *Dir* Clint Eastwood • *Scr* John Lee Hancock

Perfectly Normal ★★★ 15

Comedy 1990 · Can · Colour · 101mins

This Canadian comedy is so eager to please that it nearly sits up and begs, as a hockey-playing brewery worker (Michael Riley) teams up with an aspiring chef (Robbie Coltrane) to open a restaurant that serves up opera as a special addition to the menu. It means well, but it comes across as rather bizarre, though Coltrane's good nature here is in delightful contrast to all that forensic nastiness in *Cracker*. Contains swearing. ▭

Robbie Coltrane *Alonzo Turner* • Michael Riley *Renzo Parachii* • Deborah Duchene *Denise* • Eugene Lipinski *"Hopeless"* • Kenneth Welsh *Charlie Glesby* • Patricia Gage *Mrs Hathaway* • Jack Nichols *Duane Bickle* ■ *Dir* Yves Simoneau • *Scr* Eugene Lipinski, Paul Quarrington, from a story by Eugene Lipinski

Performance ★★★★★ 18

Drama 1970 · UK · Colour · 101mins

Warner Bros executives reeled in shock when they first saw it, and the censor reached for the aspirin. This seminal cult classic still has the power to disturb as it examines the lifestyles of a masochistic gangster (James Fox) and a bisexual pop star (played by Mick Jagger) within the same drugged-out parallel universe to extraordinary effect. With its fragmented narrative, hallucinatory images and arcane literary references, ranging from Jorge Luis Borges to Harold Pinter, this profound study of sexual identity is a sensibility-shattering masterpiece. Contains violence, swearing, sex scenes and nudity. ▭

James Fox *Chas Devlin* • Mick Jagger *Turner* • Anita Pallenberg *Pherber* • Michèle Breton *Lucy* • Ann Sidney *Dana* • Johnny Shannon *Harry Flowers* • John Bindon *Moody* • Anthony Valentine *Joey Maddocks* ■ *Dir* Nicolas Roeg, Donald Cammell • *Scr* Donald Cammell • *Cinematographer* Nicolas Roeg

Perfume of the Cyclone

★★ **18**

Thriller   1989 · US/SAfr · Colour · 85mins

The only surprising thing about this decidedly underwhelming thriller is that it managed to attract performers of the calibre of Kris Kristofferson and Marisa Berenson. This is one of the lower spots in Kristofferson's patchy career. Growling his lines with little enthusiasm, he plays a Chicago cop who uncovers a white slavery racket while searching an exotic island for his missing daughter. Contains swearing and nudity. ▣

Kris Kristofferson *Stan* • Marisa Berenson *Françoise* • Jeff Meek [Jeffrey Meek] *Adam* • Alla Kurot *Angélique* • Bud T Chud [Gerrit Graham] *Lt France* ■ *Dir* David Irving • *Scr* Patrick Lee

The Perils of Pauline

★★★ **U**

Musical comedy
1947 · US · Colour and BW · 88mins

Borrowing in title only from the twenty-chapter cliffhanger serial of 1914, this frisky period pic is in fact a biographical musical based very loosely on the life of Pearl White, the original peril-encountering Pauline and star of over 100 films before her death in 1938. An amateur performer who serenades her sweatshop co-workers, Betty Hutton hits the national bigtime when film director William Demarest, so impressed by her intrepid kicking of a lion on set, casts her as the star of a serial about a death-defying woman named Pauline. Hot air balloons and a not-so-true-to-life love interest also figure in the film, which rounds up a core of silent film stars, among them Paul Panzer (the villain in the 1914 original), Snub Pollard, James Finlayson and Chester Conklin, to add to the amusing distractions.

Betty Hutton *Pearl White* • John Lund *Michael Farrington* • Billy De Wolfe *Timmy* • William Demarest *George "Mac" McGuire* • Constance Collier *Julia Gibbs* • Frank Faylen *Joe Gurt* • William Farnum *Western saloon set hero* • Chester Conklin *Chef comic* • Paul Panzer *Drawing room agent* • Snub Pollard *Western set propman* • James Finlayson *Chef comic* • Creighton Hale *Marcelled leading man* ■ *Dir* George Marshall • *Scr* PJ Wolfson, Frank Butler, from a story by PJ Wolfson

The Perils of Pauline

★★★ **U**

Comedy adventure
1967 · US · Colour · 98mins

The famous 1914 silent cliffhanger serial *The Perils of Pauline* thrilled cinema audiences and made a star out of action heroine Pearl White. In 1947, a feature film of the same title told White's story, but this 1967 version returns to the original serial for inspiration. Pamela Austin plays Pauline, an orphan who enjoys adventures and escapades on her international travels. Pat Boone is a fellow orphan who romantically pursues her. Terry-Thomas brings an extra dash of class to proceedings, and the whole thing is an enjoyable romp played out to manic piano music from Vic Mizzy, who famously created the catchy theme for TV's *The Addams Family*.

Pat Boone *George* • Terry-Thomas *Sten Martin* • Pamela Austin *Pauline* • Edward Everett Horton *Mr Coleman* • Hamilton Camp *Thorpe* • Doris Packer *Mrs Carruthers* • Kurt Kasznar *Consul General* ■ *Dir* Herbert B Leonard, Joshua Shelley • *Scr* Albert Beich, from a story by Charles W Goddard

Period of Adjustment ★★★

Comedy drama   1962 · US · BW · 111mins

Based on one of Tennessee Williams's most light-hearted and accessible plays, this adult comedy drama receives a delightful screen treatment blessed with a superb cast provided by MGM. Everyone looks like the epitome of sixties' glamour, including sexy Jane Fonda and talented Jim Hutton as a pair of newlyweds concerned over the marriage troubles of friends Tony Franciosa and the sublime Lois Nettleton, who has the film's best moments. The black-and-white photography enhances the sense of period, and many viewers will find this neglected gem equally satisfying.

Tony Franciosa [Anthony Franciosa] *Ralph Baitz* • Jane Fonda *Isabel Haverstick* • Jim Hutton *George Haverstick* • Lois Nettleton *Dorothea Baitz* • John McGiver *Stewart P Mcgill* • Mabel Albertson *Mrs Alice McGill* • Jack Albertson *Desk sergeant* ■ *Dir* George Roy Hill • *Scr* Isobel Lennart, from the play by Tennessee Williams

Permanent Midnight ★★★

Biographical drama
1998 · US · Colour · 85mins

Ben Stiller, who has never been afraid to show a darker side (see *Your Friends and Neighbours*), makes the most of a meaty role in this gripping drugs drama, set in the Hollywood fast lane. It's based on the autobiography of Jerry Stahl, a writer working in television whose career self-destructed when his heroin addiction overtook his life. Stiller plays him warts and all and at times it's actually hard to work up any sympathy for his descent into drugs hell. There are good supporting turns from Maria Bello and Janeane Garofalo, while even Elizabeth Hurley acquits herself quite well as the naive producer who ends up in a marriage of convenience with Stiller.

Ben Stiller *Jerry Stahl* • Elizabeth Hurley *Sandra* • Janeane Garofalo *Jana* • Maria Bello *Kitty* • Owen Wilson *Nicky* • Lourdes Benedicto *Vola* • Jay Paulson *Phoenix Punk* • Jerry Stahl *Dr Murphy* ■ *Dir* David Veloz • *Scr* David Veloz, from the autobiography by Jerry Stahl

Permanent Record ★★ **15**

Drama   1988 · US · Colour · 88mins

An early, and affecting, performance from Keanu Reeves is the sole reason for bothering with this "social issue" movie about what drives teens to suicide. Reeves is the under-achieving best friend of the seemingly perfect pupil (Alan Boyce) who throws himself off a cliff. For what reason is endlessly discussed, although the self-obsessed, angst-ridden traumas of the classmates left behind provide more than enough motive. Only in Reeves's case does such vapid posturing ring heart-breakingly true and appealingly sincere. Contains swearing. ▣

Alan Boyce *David Sinclair* • Keanu Reeves *Chris Townsend* • Michelle Meyrink *MG* •

Jennifer Rubin *Lauren* • Pamela Gidley *Kim* • Michael Elgart *Jake* • Richard Bradford *Leo Verdell* ■ *Dir* Marisa Silver • *Scr* Jarre Fees, Alice Liddle, Larry Ketron

Permanent Vacation ★★★

Drama   1982 · US · Colour · 75mins

Jim Jarmusch signed up to the film programme at New York University, where he was tutored by the great film-maker Nicholas Ray. The dying Ray encouraged Jarmusch in the production of his graduation project, *Permanent Vacation*. The spare, quirky Jarmusch style is already in evidence in this slight story about a disillusioned New Yorker who decides his future lies in Europe. Jarmusch regular John Lurie provides both a typically deadpan performance and a slick score.

Chris Parker *Aloysious Parker* • Leila Gastil *Leila* • Maria Duval *Latin girl* • Ruth Bolton *Mother* • Richard Boes *War veteran* • John Lurie *Sax player* • Suzanne Fletcher *Girl in car* ■ • *Scr* Jim Jarmusch

Persecution ★★★ **15**

Psychological thriller
1974 · UK · Colour · 91mins

Lana Turner heaves her bosom and flutters her eyelashes and who's to blame her? She's a rich American widow in Britain with an oppressed son (Ralph Bates), and a past that's catching up with her. Director Don Chaffey's camera-lurking atmospherics try to make it more sinister than its plot deserves and, as a psychological thriller it's not a couch-case of neuroses but a basket-case of predictability. ▣

Lana Turner *Carrie Masters* • Ralph Bates *David Masters* • Trevor Howard *Paul Bellamy* • Olga Georges-Picot *Monique Kalfon* ■ *Dir* Don Chaffey • *Scr* Robert B Hutton, Rosemary Wootten, Frederick Warner

Persona ★★★★★

Drama   1966 · Swe · BW · 82mins

Ingmar Bergman devised this ambitious drama while recovering in hospital from debilitating dizziness. Inspired by the physical similarity between Liv Ullmann and Bibi Andersson – playing an actress struck mute and the nurse who treats her – it explores the very nature of art and reality. Everything about this most modern of films is designed to disorientate the viewer – the inclusion of off-screen voices and the paraphernalia of film-making, the sudden melting of the frame, the disjointed structure of the narrative and, finally, the famous melding of Ullmann and Andersson's faces into a single identity. Proclaiming the artist to be both communicator and charlatan, this is an audacious, complex and unforgettable piece of work.

Bibi Andersson *Alma, the nurse* • Liv Ullmann *Elisabeth Vogler* • Gunnar Björnstrand *Herr Vogler* ■ *Dir/Scr* Ingmar Bergman • *Cinematographer* Sven Nykvist

Personal Best ★★★ **18**

Sports drama   1982 · US · Colour · 122mins

Robert Towne was accused of voyeurism for his depiction of Mariel Hemingway and Patrice Donnelly in this lesbian love story played against the

backdrop of the Moscow Olympic Games. Although already one of Hollywood's top screenwriters, Towne here in his directorial debut demonstrates a sure visual sense, as he not only chronicles the athletes' romance, but also their physical progress under martinet coach Scott Glenn. The camerawork is occasionally fussy and over-reliant on sporting clichés, but this is still subtle, sensual stuff. ▣

Mariel Hemingway *Chris Cahill* • Scott Glenn *Terry Tingloff* • Patrice Donnelly *Tory Skinner* • Kenny Moore *Denny Stites* • Jim Moody *Roscoe Travis* • Kari Gosswiller *Penny Brill* • Jodi Anderson *Nadia "Pooch" Anderson* ■ *Dir/Scr* Robert Towne

Personal Foul ★★ **PG**

Romantic drama   1987 · US · Colour · 95mins

An intimate, character-driven independent film that reaches higher than it can touch. Adam Arkin (son of Alan and known primarily for TV's *Chicago Hope* and *Northern Exposure*) plays a committed teacher whose disillusionment with the system leads him to hit the road. He meets up with an introverted drifter, David Morse, who lives in a van making and selling paper flowers. Into this equation comes Susan Wheeler Duff, who merely serves to underscore the men's limited emotional capabilities. ▣

Adam Arkin *Jeremy* • David Morse *Ben* • Susan Wheeler Duff *Lisa* • F William Parker *Principal* ■ *Dir/Scr* Ted Lichtenheld

Personal Property ★★

Comedy   1937 · US · BW · 88mins

Starry but feeble comedy, with Robert Taylor as a London playboy given the job of overseeing a house belonging to a penniless American widow (Jean Harlow). Gone were the days when Hollywood movies could be fairly upfront about sexual matters; gone, too, were the days when Harlow could wear scarcely nothing on screen. A victim of censorship codes, this inoffensive picture dawdles from one non-event to the next, though the female audiences of the time appreciated the lingering shots of Taylor in the bathtub.

Robert Taylor (1) *Raymond Dabney* • Jean Harlow *Crystal Wetherby* • Reginald Owen *Claude Dabney* • Una O'Connor *Clara* • EE Clive *Mr Dabney* • Henrietta Crosman *Mrs Dabney* • Cora Witherspoon *Mrs Burns* ■ *Dir* WS Van Dyke II [WS Van Dyke] • *Scr* Hugh Mills, Ernest Vajda, from the play *The Man in Possession* by HM Harwood

Personal Services ★★★ **18**

Comedy   1987 · UK · Colour · 104mins

A gently witty, if curiously coy, attempt by director Terry Jones to re-create the odd career of "luncheon voucher madam" Cynthia Payne. Julie Walters is a good choice to portray her droll matter-of-factness about the sexual proclivities of a succession of middle-aged men, but in its jolly, almost seaside postcard approach, the movie loses edge and bite. Jones and Co basically bolster up the one-dimensional image of Walters's character as a cheery old duck whose early life was hard, but rich in experience, while its truly sad aspects

U = SUITABLE FOR ALL   **Uc** = SUITABLE FOR ALL, ESPECIALLY FOR YOUNG CHILDREN (VIDEO ONLY)   **PG** = PARENTAL GUIDANCE

are blithely glossed over. Contains swearing and nudity.

Julie Walters *Christine Painter* • Alec McCowen *Wing Commander Morton* • Shirley Stelfox *Shirley* • Danny Schiller *Dolly* • Victoria Hardcastle *Rose* • Tim Woodward *Timms* ■ *Dir* Terry Jones • *Scr* David Leland

The Personals ★★
Romantic comedy
1982 · US · Colour · 90mins

This weak romantic comedy features a middle-aged loser from Minnesota (Bill Schopperty) trying to deal with the loss of both his hair and his wife (she leaves him for another man) and finding life on the dating circuit something of a learning experience. This slight study was the first outing for director Peter Markle, who has spent most of his subsequent career in television.

Bill Schoppert *Bill* • Karen Landry *Adrienne* • Paul Eiding *Paul* • Michael Laskin *David* • Vicki Daki *Shelly* • Chris Forth *Jennifer* • Patrick O'Brien *Jay* ■ *Dir/Scr* Peter Markle

Persons Unknown ★★ 18
Thriller 1996 · US · Colour · 94mins

Before it turns into a soppy love story, this cynical thriller is a stylish and innovative take on the usual cops-and-robbers scenario. Joe Mantegna plays an ex-cop turned security systems rep whose new girlfriend (Kelly Lynch) steals files detailing the defences of the local drug dealers. It's when Mantegna gets involved at a distance, and Lynch's handicapped sister (Naomi Watts) arrives to take part in the robbery, that this suspenseful caper loses its way. Contains swearing, violence and sex scenes. ▭

Joe Mantegna *Holland* • Kelly Lynch *Amanda* • JT Walsh *Cake* • Naomi Watts *Molly* • Xander Berkeley *Tosh* • Jon Favreau *Terry* ■ *Dir* George Hickenlooper • *Scr* Craig Smith

Persuasion ★★★★ U
Period romance 1995 · UK · Colour · 102mins

Amanda Root glows as gentle Anne Elliot, past her bloom and thoughtlessly put-upon by her horrid, snobbish family when the once-poor suitor she was persuaded to reject returns in the shape of dashing Captain Wentworth (Ciaran Hinds). Now he's rich, socially desirable and eager to find a wife – just as long as she's not Anne. However, the attentions of a caddish admirer revive the resentful hero's interest. This artful BBC adaptation of Jane Austen's most mature love story is beautifully realised by *Notting Hill* director Roger Michell and a class ensemble who never let the superb period detail intrude on the emotional realism or romantic suspense. ▭ *DVD*

Amanda Root *Anne Elliot* • Ciaran Hinds *Captain Wentworth* • Susan Fleetwood *Lady Russell* • Corin Redgrave *Sir Walter Elliot* • Fiona Shaw *Mrs Croft* • John Woodvine *Admiral Croft* • Phoebe Nicholls *Elizabeth Elliot* • Samuel Morton *Mr Elliot* • Sophie Thompson *Mary Musgrove* • Judy Cornwell *Mrs Musgrove* • Simon Russell Beale *Charles Musgrove* ■ *Dir* Roger Michell • *Scr* Nick Dear, from the novel by Jane Austen

The Pest ★★ 12
Comedy 1997 · US · Colour · 80mins

Aptly-named comedy about a small-time con artist who owes the "Scottish Mob" $50,000. Offered a "cash scholarship" by Jeffrey Jones (expanding his repetoire of bad stereotypes to Germans this time), Pestario "Pest" Vargas (John Leguizamo) finds himself the prey in a remake of *The Most Dangerous Game*. The hunt ranges from Jones's private island to the streets of Miami, with Leguizamo cracking wise and spouting pop culture references all the way. As dumb as it sounds. Contains some swearing and sexual references. ▭

John Leguizamo *Pestario "Pest" Vargas* • Jeffrey Jones *Gustav* • Edoardo Ballerini *Himmel* • Freddy Rodriguez *Ninja* • Tammy Townsend *Xantha Kent* • Aries Spears *Chubby* • Joe Morton *Mr Kent* ■ *Dir* Paul Miller • *Scr* David Bar Katz, from a story by John Leguizamo, David Bar Katz

Pet Sematary ★★★ 18
Horror 1989 · US · Colour · 98mins

Morbid but compulsive horror, adapted by Stephen King from his own novel, about a young couple (Dale Midkiff and Denise Crosby), who discover that corpses, buried in the pet cemetery near their home, come back to life. For much of its length, the story, which seems to be yet another re-working of the classic short story *The Monkey's Paw*, provides only the occasional shudder and is interrupted by awkward flashbacks. But those who stick with it are rewarded with a really ghastly climax, cleverly engineered to tweak very raw nerves. ▭

Fred Gwynne *Jud Crandall* • Dale Midkiff *Louis Creed* • Denise Crosby *Rachel Creed* • Brad Greenquist *Victor Pascow* • Michael Lombard *Irwin Goldman* • Miko Hughes *Gage Creed* ■ *Dir* Mary Lambert • *Scr* Stephen King, from his novel

Pet Sematary II ★★ 18
Horror 1992 · US · Colour · 100mins

Although it begins unpromisingly with plodding, TV movie-style exposition, this sequel picks up speed when two boys discover the Indian burial ground that brings the dead back to life. The resurrected dog is a spine-chilling creature; later, wicked stepfather Clancy Brown returns from the grave to make love to his widow. The grossness culminates in carnage that almost rivals that of the original film, while a living corpse's shriek of "Dead is better!" could have become a catch phrase. The tone throughout is much more tongue-in-cheek than before. ▭

Anthony Edwards *Chase Matthews* • Edward Furlong *Jeff Matthews* • Clancy Brown *Gus Gilbert* • Jason McGuire *Drew Gilbert* • Jared Rushton *Clyde Parker* ■ *Dir* Mary Lambert • *Scr* Richard Outten

Pet Shop ★★ U
Comedy fantasy 1995 · US · Colour · 84mins

In the suburb of Cactus Flats, Arizona, a magical pet shop sells pets that are actually fantastic animals in disguise. A mob family in the witness protection programme end up with some of the magic animals, with supposedly hilarious consequences ensuing. The

characters (especially the mobsters) are so stereotypical, and the humour is so broad, that this low-budget kids' movie from the factory of Charles Band will probably appeal most to unsophisticated youngsters. ▭

Terry Kiser *Joe Yeagher* • Leigh Ann Orsi *Dena Yeagher* • Spencer Vrooman *Mike* • Joanne Baron *Marilyn Yeagher* • David Wagner *Charlie Yeagher* ■ *Dir* Hope Perello • *Scr* Mark Goldstein, Greg Suddeth, Brent Friedman, from an idea by Peter Von Sholly

Pétain ★★★★ 15
Historical war drama
1992 · Fr · Colour · 129mins

With the scars of the Occupation still running deep, it took director Jean Marboeuf six years to find willing collaborators for this meticulously researched history of the Vichy government. Much of the action takes place inside the infamous Hôtel du Parc, which tends to isolate the population at large from the enormity of the deeds carried out in its name by Pétain and his chief minister, Laval. As the Great War hero-cum-figurehead for the puppet regime, Jacques Dufilho turns in a momentous display of shabby pride and gullible opportunism, although Jean Yanne's performance is less subtly shaded. In French with English subtitles. ▭

Jacques Dufilho *Philippe Pétain* • Jean Yanne *Laval* • Jean-Pierre Cassel *Hans Roberto* • Jean-Claude Dreyfus *Dumoulin* • Antoinette Moya *Eugénie Pétain* ■ *Dir* Jean Marboeuf • *Scr* Jean-Pierre Marchand, Marc Ferro, Alain Riou, Jean Marboeuf, from a non-fiction book by Marc Ferro

Pete Kelly's Blues ★★★★ PG
Drama 1955 · US · Colour · 91mins

A marvellous one-off, directed by, produced by and starring *Dragnet*'s Jack Webb, a tale of a Kansas City cornet player that is one of the most sympathetic and understanding movies about jazz – not that there's exactly a plethora. Additionally, the film is superbly designed and photographed in early CinemaScope, deploying that letterbox frame to its best advantage, and perfectly cast. Not just moll Janet Leigh and bootlegger Edmond O'Brien, but also Ella Fitzgerald and Peggy Lee, the latter touching and Oscar-nominated for a performance that includes the affecting *Sing a Rainbow*. The melancholy tone is brilliantly sustained, the attitudes and language resolutely adult. ▭

Jack Webb *Pete Kelly* • Janet Leigh *Ivy Conrad* • Edmond O'Brien *Fran McCarg* • Peggy Lee *Rose Hopkins* • Andy Devine *George Tenell* • Lee Marvin *Al Gannaway* • Ella Fitzgerald *Maggie Jackson* ■ *Dir* Jack Webb • *Scr* Richard L Breen

Pete 'n' Tillie ★★★
Romantic comedy
1972 · US · Colour · 100mins

"When you're my age, blind dates are a way of life," says Carol Burnett to Walter Matthau at the start of this romantic comedy. Later, they get married and have a son with a terminal disease. Yes, *Pete 'n' Tillie* is unashamedly manipulative, but its saving grace is the acting: Burnett was making a big screen comeback after a decade's absence, and Matthau is a

sheer delight as a character who speaks in puns and riddles and lives for practical jokes. As Burnett's matchmaking friend, Geraldine Page is a classic busybody and won an Oscar nomination, as did the sudsy script.

Walter Matthau *Pete* • Carol Burnett *Tillie* • Geraldine Page *Gertrude* • Barry Nelson *Burt* • René Auberjonois *Jimmy* • Lee H Montgomery [Lee Montgomery] *Robbie* ■ *Dir* Martin Ritt • *Scr* Julius J Epstein, from the novella *Witch's Milk* by Peter De Vries

Peter and Pavla ★★★★
Crime 1964 · Cz · BW · 85mins

Having impressed with his short, *Konkurs* (*The Audition*), Milos Forman made his feature directorial debut with this story about a store detective pressurised by his parents to succeed in life and love. Although it's often been compared to François Truffaut's early work, the loudest echo comes from *Il Posto* (1961), Ermanno Olmi's gentle comedy about the shock of work and the everyday. Making atmospheric use of the Bohemian town of Kolin and coaxing wondrously naturalistic, improvised performances from Ladislav Jakim and Pavla Martinková, Forman began his perpetual fascination with the outsider with a sympathetic wit that would never desert him. In Czech with English subtitles.

Ladislav Jakim *Peter* • Pavla Martinková *Pavla* ■ *Dir* Milos Forman • *Scr* Milos Forman, Jaroslav Papousek • *Cinematographer* Jan Nemecek

Peter Gunn ★★ PG
Crime drama 1989 · US · Colour · 90mins

A second movie version of Blake Edwards's successful fifties television series that starred Craig Stevens. As ever, the real star here is Henry Mancini's theme tune, a hit for the Art of Noise, but there's also a welcome role for Broadway star Pearl Bailey, and Blake's own daughter Jennifer Edwards appears as Gunn's airhead secretary. Peter Strauss is notably uncharismatic as the titular private eye. After this rare foray into TV movies, Edwards returned to directing features.

Peter Strauss *Peter Gunn* • Pearl Bailey *"Mother"* • Barbara Williams *Edie* • Charles Cioffi *Tony Amatti* • Peter Jurasik *Lieutenant Jacoby* • Jennifer Edwards *Maggie* • David Rappaport *Speck* ■ *Dir/Scr* Blake Edwards

Peter Ibbetson ★★★★
Romantic fantasy drama
1935 · US · BW · 82mins

A Hollywood oddity that became a landmark for members of the European surrealist movement in the thirties, with Gary Cooper and Ann Harding as lovers who communicate their passion in dreams. Off-the-wall casting (Cooper is not very effective) adds to the sense of alienation in this adaptation of George du Maurier's novel and John Nathaniel Raphael's play, while the finale's fulfilment of *l'amour fou* received a rapturous reception from the surrealists.

Gary Cooper *Peter Ibbetson* • Ann Harding *Mary, Duchess of Towers* • John Halliday *Duke of Towers* • Ida Lupino *Agnes* • Douglass Dumbrille *Colonel Forsythe* • Virginia Weidler *Mimsey* • Dickie Moore *Gogo* • Elsa Prescott *Katherine* • Marcelle Corday *Maid* ■

Dir Henry Hathaway • *Scr* Vincent Lawrence, Waldemar Young, Constance Collier, John Meehan, Edwin Justus Mayer, from the play by John Nathaniel Raphael, from the novel by George du Maurier • *Cinematographer* Charles Lang

Peter Pan ★★★★ U
Animated fantasy adventure
1953 · US · Colour · 76mins
Although Peter Pan purists disliked the use of Bobby Driscoll's twangy American voice as the leader of JM Barrie's Lost Boys, this is still a well-crafted animated feature from Disney with such great songs by Sammy Cahn and Sammy Fain as *You Can Fly* and *What Makes the Red Man Red?*. The artists based Tinker Bell on a pout-lipped Marilyn Monroe, while the ongoing battle between Captain Hook and the crocodile is a delight. ▨

Bobby Driscoll *Peter Pan* • Kathryn Beaumont *Wendy* • Hans Conried *Capt Hook/Mr Darling* • Bill Thompson *Mr Smee* • Heather Angel *Mrs Darling* • Paul Collins *Michael Darling* • Tommy Luske *John* • Tom Conway *Narrator* ■ *Dir* Hamilton Luske, Clyde Geronimi, Wilfred Jackson • *Scr* Ted Sears, Bill Peet, Joe Rinaldi, Erdman Penner, Winston Hibler, Milt Banta, Ralph Wright, from the play by JM Barrie

Peter's Friends ★★★★ 15
Comedy 1992 · UK · Colour · 97mins
Seeming rather small, smug and insignificant when it first played in the cinema, Kenneth Branagh's engaging ensemble comedy is far more at home (and considerably more enjoyable) on the small screen. The air of ''luvviness'' still hangs heavy, but Rita Rudner's script (co-written with Martin Bergman) succeeds in being sharp and cosy without ever over-straining for effect, and Branagh's handling of his players is impeccable (if only he could get the hang of camera movement!). Tony Slattery looks woefully out of place in such accomplished company, but Emma Thompson's performance as the lonely, winsomely twee bachelor girl is a delight. Contains swearing and nudity. ▨

Hugh Laurie *Roger* • Imelda Staunton *Mary* • Stephen Fry *Peter* • Emma Thompson *Maggie* • Kenneth Branagh *Andrew* • Alphonsia Emmanuel *Sarah* • Rita Rudner *Carol* • Phyllida Law *Vera* • Alex Lowe *Paul* • Tony Slattery *Brian* ■ *Dir* Kenneth Branagh • *Scr* Rita Rudner, Martin Bergman

Petersen ★★
Drama 1974 · Ausl · Colour · 107mins
Infidelity in academia, with a blue-collar worker Down Under securing a university place and seeking solace from his fish-out-of-water feelings in a romance with his stuffy English professor's attractive wife. The romance looks doomed, however, when she lands a teaching post at Oxford. This offbeat love story benefits from a novel setting and nice playing by a cast headed by Aussie film veteran Jack Thompson.

Jack Thompson *Tony Petersen* • Jacki Weaver *Suzie Petersen* • Joey Hohenfels *Debbie* • Amanda Hunt *Carol* • George Mallaby *Executive* • Arthur Dignam *Charles Kent* •

David Phillips *Heinz* • Helen Morse *Jane* • Wendy Hughes *Patricia Kent* ■ *Dir* Tim Burstall • *Scr* David Williamson

Pete's Dragon ★★ U
Musical fantasy 1977 · US · Colour · 123mins
The magic largely left the Disney kingdom in the seventies and this mix of animation and live action is a long way from the likes of *Toy Story*. Sean Marshall is the lonely youngster who finds an unlikely friend in the shape of a dragon called Elliott (voiced by Charlie Callas). Despite a stellar cast, which includes Mickey Rooney, Jim Dale and singer Helen Reddy, the special effects pale alongside the sharper technologies of today, and, sadly, the tunes fail to provide much in the way of compensation. ▨ **DVD**

Helen Reddy *Nora* • Jim Dale *Dr Terminus* • Sean Marshall *Pete* • Mickey Rooney *Lampie* • Red Buttons *Hoagy* • Shelley Winters *Lena Gogan* • Jean Kean *Miss Taylor* • Jim Backus *Mayor* ■ *Dir* Don Chaffey • *Scr* Malcolm Marmorstein, from a story by Seton I Miller

Petit Con ★★★
Comedy 1984 · Fr · Colour · 90mins
Having already seen his comic strips filmed as *The Rat Race* (1980) and *Psy* (1981), Gérard Lauzier took on the megaphone duties for this adaptation of his book, *Souvenirs d'un Jeune Homme*. Like all rites of passage pictures, there are hard lessons to be learned about the big bad world. But few teenagers make as many cataclysmic errors of judgement as the thoroughly resistible Bernard Brieux, as he treats his undeserving father, Guy Marchand, to relentless socialist diatribes and allies with diverse bohemians, hobos and rebels in his rage against bourgeois conformity. An astute portrait of universal eighties attitudes. In French with English subtitles.

Bernard Brieux *Michel Choupon* • Guy Marchand *Bob Choupon* • Caroline Cellier *Annie Choupon* • Eric Carlos *Alain Choupon* ■ *Dir* Gérard Lauzier • *Scr* Gérard Lauzier, from his cartoon album *Souvenirs d'un Jeune Homme*

Le Petit Prince A Dit ★★★★ PG
Drama 1992 · Fr/Swi · Colour · 104mins
Although its main protagonist has been diagnosed with an inoperable brain tumour, rather than being a mawkish melodrama, Christine Pascal's unconventional road movie is a joyous celebration of life. While her divorced parents, scientist Richard Berry and actress Anémone, wallow in recrimination and self-pity, ten-year-old Marie Kleiber simply gets on with the business of getting the most out of each day, as Berry whisks her away on an Alpine tour that he desperately hopes will forestall the onset of the disease. Demonstrating wondrous maturity, Kleiber is a revelation, and her rapport with Berry is both persuasive and poignant. In French with English subtitles.

Richard Berry *Adam Leibovich* • Anémone *Melanie* • Marie Kleiber *Violette* • Lucie Phan *Lucie* • Mista Préchac *Minerve* ■ *Dir* Christine Pascal • *Scr* Christine Pascal, Robert Boner

Le Petit Soldat ★★★★
Spy drama 1960 · Fr · BW · 86mins
Jean-Luc Godard's second feature was a controversial dramatisation of the Algerian civil war that was then tearing France apart. Initially banned by the French government for its violence, the film concerns a secret agent sent to Geneva to assassinate a leading member of the Algerian resistance. Godard shoots it like a gangster thriller, with some disturbing sequences of bathroom torture, and achieves a chilling portrait of colonialism's last gasp. As the film's heroine, Godard cast Danish actress Anna Karina, who became his wife and the star of many of his subsequent films. In French with English subtitles.

Michel Subor *Bruno Forestier* • Anna Karina *Veronica Dreyer* • Henri-Jacques Huet *Jacques* • Paul Beauvais *Paul* • Laszlo Szabo *Laszlo* • Georges de Beauregard *Activist leader* • Jean-Luc Godard *Bystander at railway station* ■ *Dir/Scr* Jean-Luc Godard

La Petite Voleuse ★★★
Drama 1988 · Fr · Colour · 105mins
A teenage girl (Charlotte Gainsbourg, daughter of Serge), abandoned by her mother and living with her aunt and uncle in a small French town, longs for adulthood, freedom and excitement. She looks for it by stealing, working as a maid, losing her virginity to a married man and decamping with a young thief (Simon de la Brosse). Adapted and directed by François Truffaut's one-time assistant Claude Miller, working from a synopsis left by Truffaut who planned to make it before his premature death, the film is well-cast, well-made, accurately observed and hard to fault. However, those who fail to respond to the deeply irritating and fundamentally uninteresting heroine will find the whole thing utterly tedious. In French with English subtitles.

Charlotte Gainsbourg *Janine Castang* • Didier Bezace *Michel Davenne* • Simon de la Brosse *Raoul* • Raoul Billerey *André Rouleau* • Chantal Banlier *Aunt Léa* ■ *Dir* Claude Miller • *Scr* François Truffaut, Claude de Givray

The Petrified Forest ★★★★ PG
Drama 1936 · US · BW · 78mins
This studio-bound adaptation of playwright Robert Sherwood's Broadway success afforded character actor Humphrey Bogart the star-making role of his life as snarling Duke Mantee, the escaped thug who holds a motley group of travellers at bay as hostages. Star Leslie Howard insisted Bogie play the role, and in gratitude Bogart named his daughter ''Leslie''. Some of Sherwood's moralising may have dated, but there's no denying the power and conviction of the performances as Howard, Bogie and Bette Davis fire up the screen, setting the style and pace for future Warner Bros melodramas. ▨

Leslie Howard *Alan Squier* • Bette Davis *Gabrielle Maple* • Genevieve Tobin *Mrs Chisholm* • Dick Foran *Boze Hertzlinger* • Humphrey Bogart *Duke Mantee* • Joseph Sawyer *[Joe] Jackie* • Porter Hall *Jason Maple* • Charley Grapewin *Gramp Maple* ■ *Dir* Archie Mayo • *Scr* Charles Kenyon, Delmer Daves, from the play by Robert E Sherwood

Petticoat Pirates ★ U
Comedy 1961 · UK · Colour · 82mins
In his third tilt at movie stardom, TV comic Charlie Drake again finds himself up a well-known creek without a script. This time, however, he's only got himself to blame, as he co-wrote this woeful comedy, in which he plays a timid stoker ordered to disguise himself as a Wren in order to recover a battleship hijacked by a mutinous all-woman crew. Director David MacDonald had made some pretty ropey pictures since his debut in 193, but this was rock bottom. ▨

Charlie Drake *Charlie* • Anne Heywood *Anne Stephens* • Cecil Parker *Commander in chief* • John Turner *Captain Michael Patterson* • Maxine Audley *Superintendent* • Thorley Walters *Lieutenant Jerome Robertson* • Eleanor Summerfield *Mabel* • Victor Maddern *COC Nixon* ■ *Dir* David MacDonald • *Scr* Lew Schwartz, Charlie Drake, from a story by TJ Morrison

The Petty Girl ★★★
Musical 1950 · US · Colour · 87mins
No, the title's not a misprint for ''pretty'', though it amounts to the same thing. George Petty was a real-life popular mid-century illustrator akin to Vargas and this is a light-hearted Technicolored depiction of Petty's daily rounds, as portrayed here by affable Robert Cummings. The humour's very dated: he's a pin-up artist, whereas co-star Joan Caulfield is a bit of a prude, but it makes for agreeable viewing. The film is stolen by comedians Elsa Lanchester and the inimitable Mary Wickes, and watch closely for a glimpse of Hitchcock's ''discovery'' Tippi Hedren, a decade before *Marnie*.

Robert Cummings *George Petty* • Joan Caulfield *Victoria Braymore* • Elsa Lanchester *Dr Crutcher* • Melville Cooper *Beardsley* • Audrey Long *Connie* • Mary Wickes *Prof Whitman* • Tippi Hedren *Ice Box Petty Girl* ■ *Dir* Henry Levin • *Scr* Nat Perrin, from a story by Mary McCarthy

Petulia ★★★★ 15
Drama 1968 · US/UK · Colour · 100mins
Few directors embraced the technical trickery of the French New Wave with as much enthusiasm as Richard Lester. But the kind of narrative leap-frogging and camera eccentricity that worked a treat on *A Hard Day's Night* is something of a distraction in this Swinging Sixties story in which freewheeling Julie Christie cheats on dullard husband Richard Chamberlain with divorced surgeon George C Scott. Shot in San Francisco at the height of flower power, the film has dated just a tad, but Christie and Scott make a surprisingly potent couple and Joseph Cotten shows well as Chamberlain's blustering father. ▨

Julie Christie *Petulia Danner* • George C Scott *Archie Bollen* • Richard Chamberlain *David Danner* • Arthur Hill *Barney* • Shirley Knight *Polo* • Pippa Scott *May* • Kathleen Widdoes *Wilma* • Joseph Cotten *Mr Danner* ■ *Dir* Richard Lester • *Scr* Lawrence B Marcus, from the novel *Me and the Arch-Kook Petulia* by John Haase, adapted by Barbara Turner • *Cinematographer* Nicolas Roeg

U = SUITABLE FOR ALL • Uc = SUITABLE FOR ALL, ESPECIALLY FOR YOUNG CHILDREN (VIDEO ONLY) • PG = PARENTAL GUIDANCE

Peyton Place ★★★★ 15
Drama   1957 · US · Colour · 150mins

An excellent rendering of that steamy, sexy small-town novel that was a runaway bestseller for author Grace Metalious. Lana Turner is perfectly cast in this tight, taut film, and she shows what a riveting screen presence she could be, given a passable script. What distinguishes this *Peyton Place* from other versions is that nothing is crassly overt, but you can feel the tension of people wound-up like coiled springs. To this end, passion tugs at the skirts of hick morality throughout. A real fifties' treat. ▣

Lana Turner *Constance MacKenzie* • Hope Lange *Selena Cross* • Lee Philips *Michael Rossi* • Lloyd Nolan *Dr Matthew Swain* • Diane Varsi *Allison MacKenzie* • Arthur Kennedy *Lucas Cross* • Russ Tamblyn *Norman Page* ■ *Dir* Mark Robson • *Scr* John Michael Hayes, from the novel by Grace Metalious

Phaedra ★
Drama   1962 · US/Gr/Fr · BW · 115mins

Phaedra (Melina Mercouri), the second wife of Greek shipping tycoon Thanos (Raf Vallone), falls for her husband's son Alexis (Anthony Perkins). They embark on a steamy affair in Paris, before continuing to the island of Hydra where all is revealed to Thanos. This overheated updating of a classical Greek tragedy by Mercouri's producer/writer/director husband Jules Dassin, doubtless seriously intended, is risibly awful. The cast is unattractive, with Mercouri emoting all over the place, and Perkins a twitching wreck whose guilty passion for his stepmother is equalled only by his passion for his car. The embarrassing sight of Perkins caressing the vehicle with near sexual fervour is something to behold.

Melina Mercouri *Phaedra* • Anthony Perkins *Alexis* • Raf Vallone *Thanos* • Elizabeth Ercy *Ercy* • Olympia Papadouka *Anna* ■ *Dir* Jules Dassin • *Scr* Jules Dassin, Margarita Liberaki, from a story by Margarita Liberaki, from the play *Hippolytus* by Euripides

Phantasm ★★★ 18
Horror   1978 · US · Colour · 84mins

A fantasy horror with a science-fiction twist, director Don Coscarelli's lurid chiller is as wildly imaginative as it is totally illogical. Angus Scrimm impresses as the memorable celluloid demon who sends human victims into another dimension where they become slave dwarves. Don't even ask! Coscarelli's main concern is to shock you senseless while weaving a powerful primal spell. With the unforgettable flying sphere that drills out brains, a macabre fun-house mortuary, severed fingers and cemetery romance, he easily fulfils that lofty aim. ▣

A Michael Baldwin *Mike* • Bill Thornbury *Jody* • Angus Scrimm *Tall man* • Reggie Bannister *Reggie* • Kathy Lester *Lady in lavender* • Lynn Eastman *Sally* ■ *Dir/Scr* Don Coscarelli

Phantasm II ★★ 18
Horror   1988 · US · Colour · 92mins

Director Don Coscarelli waited ten years before making a follow-up to his weirdly different cult classic because he didn't want to be pigeonholed as a horror director. But he ended up merely rehashing the original with an equally gory but far less effective entry that barely carries the story forward. All the same ingredients are intact: the justly celebrated flying ball, and the return of Angus Scrimm's mysterious "Tall Man". Slickly made, but with all the attention-grabbing appeal of an empty crisp packet. ▣

James LeGros *Mike Pearson* • Reggie Bannister *Reggie* • Angus Scrimm *Tall Man* • Paula Irvine *Liz* • Samantha Phillips *Alchemy* ■ *Dir/Scr* Don Coscarelli

Phantasm III – Lord Of The Dead ★ 18
Horror   1994 · US · Colour · 85mins

Starting just after where the last entry ended, this third instalment in the series continues the adventures of Reggie (Reggie Bannister) and Mike (A Michael Baldwin) as they battle the "Tall Man" (Angus Scrimm) and his flying silver balls. Director Don Coscarelli tries to make things a little different with the addition of more humour and the addition of Gloria Henry as sexy female fighter Rocky. Yet another sequel followed in 1998. ▣

Angus Scrimm *The Tall Man* • Reggie Bannister *Reggie* • A Michael Baldwin *Mike Pearson* • Gloria Henry *Rocky* ■ *Dir/Scr* Don Coscarelli

The Phantom ★★★★ 12
Action adventure
1996 · US/Aus · Colour · 96mins

The equivalent of watching ten episodes of a Saturday matinée serial rolled into one *Die Hard* package, director Simon Wincer's pleasure cruise through the comic-book pages of Phantom creator Lee Falk's masked avenger story is retro fantasy adventure of the best kind. Billy Zane is the orphaned jungle "ghost" trying to stop master criminal Treat Williams unlocking the magical powers of three legendary skulls. A glamorous cocktail of lost kingdoms, supernatural excitement and flashy special effects, Wincer's gently self-mocking tone makes this pulp-fiction treasure a fabulous slice of exotic escapism. ▣

Billy Zane *The Phantom/Kit Walker* • Kristy Swanson *Diana Palmer* • Treat Williams *Xander Drax* • Catherine Zeta-Jones *Sala* • James Remar *Quill* • Cary-Hiroyuki Tagawa *Kabai Sengh* • Bill Smitrovich *Uncle Dave* ■ *Dir* Simon Wincer • *Scr* Jeffrey Boam, from a character created by Lee Falk

The Phantom Horsemen ★★
Adventure   1990 · Ausl · Colour

This has nothing to do with phantoms, ghosts and ghouls, but is an Australian adventure about a 19th-century sheep farming family battling against corruption as they try to make a new start in colonial Australia. That's pretty much it, and, although the barren scenery is impressive, it can't draw attention away from the uninspired script and mediocre performances.

Beth Buchanan *Charlotte Tremayne* • Brian Rooney *Toby Quinn* • Bryan Marshall *James Tremayne* • James Coates *Sir Peter Longworth* • Bill Conn *Reverend Samuel Marsden* ■ *Dir* Howard Rubie • *Scr* David Phillips

Phantom India ★★★★
Documentary   1968 · Fr · Colour · 378mins

In tune with the student rebellion in Paris in 1968, Louis Malle decided to give up fictional films for a while (it was three years, in fact) and embark on a six-month voyage to India to find both himself and the country. It resulted in this TV documentary series in seven 54-minute parts, later shown in theatres. Malle, who narrates, makes it a personal journey, and reveals quite a number of fascinating things about the people and society. The Indian government protested at what they saw as a negative view of their country, complaining that the director had put too much emphasis on the poverty and overcrowding.

Louis Malle *Narrator* ■ *Dir/Scr* Louis Malle • *Cinematographer* Etienne Becker

Phantom Lady ★★★★
Film noir mystery   1944 · US · BW · 86mins

This is one of the high points of *film noir*. Based on a Cornell Woolrich novel (written under the pseudonym William Irish), it's about businessman Alan Curtis, accused of strangling his wife, and the search for the woman – the phantom lady – who can give him an alibi and save him from the electric chair. Leading the search is Curtis's secretary Ella Raines, a policeman who believes in his innocence and his best friend Franchot Tone. The plot spins into spirals of cross and double-cross, all deliriously decked out by director Robert Siodmak with a dizzying array of camera angles, light and shadows.

Franchot Tone *Jack Marlow* • Ella Raines *Carol "Kansas" Richman* • Alan Curtis *Scott Henderson* • Aurora Miranda *Estela Monteiro* • Thomas Gomez *Inspector Burgess* • Fay Helm *Ann Terry* • Elisha Cook Jr *Cliff* ■ *Dir* Robert Siodmak • *Scr* Bernard C Schoenfeld, from the novel by William Irish [Cornell Woolrich] • *Cinematographer* Woody Bredell

The Phantom Light ★ U
Thriller   1934 · UK · BW · 76mins

This has gained a high reputation among Michael Powell's early films because of its good cast, lurid subject matter, continued availability, and tenuous links to later major works. But Powell is really sunk by the atrocious story, more suited to a Will Hay send-up, as new lighthouse keeper Gordon Harker uncovers a shipwreckers' plot. The director tried hard to create atmosphere with his limited location work at Portmadoc and by some dramatic lighting effects but he achieved far more in some of his other B-pictures of the period.

Binnie Hale *Alice Bright* • Gordon Harker *Sam Higgins* • Ian Hunter *Jim Pearce* • Donald Calthrop *David Owen* • Milton Rosmer *Dr Carey* • Reginald Tate *Tom Evans* • Mickey Brantford *Bob Peters* • Herbert Lomas *Claff Owen* ■ *Dir* Michael Powell • *Scr* J Jefferson Farjeon, Austin Melford, Ralph Smart, from the play *The Haunted Light* by Evadne Price, Joan Roy Byford

Phantom of Death ★★ 18
Horror   1988 · It · Colour · 87mins

A welcome return to the Italian horror thriller by director Ruggero Deodato, sidetracked by the success of his infamous and controversial *Cannibal Holocaust*. Famous classical pianist Michael York is diagnosed with a rare disease that prematurely ages him and twists his mind to such an extent he doesn't recall committing horrendous murders. An unexpectedly thoughtful production, mainly because York conveys his physical and mental disintegration extremely credibly. Horror staple Donald Pleasence and former Italian scream queen Edwige Fenech also add their lustre to the effective charnel-house chills. Some dialogue dubbed into English. ▣

Michael York *Robert Domenici* • Donald Pleasence *Inspector Downey* • Edwige Fenech • Mapi Galan • Fabio Sartor ■ *Dir* Ruggero Deodato • *Scr* Gigliola Battagnini, Vincenzo Mannino, Gianfranco Clerici

The Phantom of Hollywood ★★
Horror   1974 · US · Colour · 78mins

A passable TV movie update of Gaston Leroux's classic *The Phantom of the Opera* has Jack Cassidy taking revenge on the low-budget studio bigwigs who sell the backlot real estate where he lives to pay off debts. A formidable cast of Hollywood has-beens including Broderick Crawford, Jackie Coogan and Peter Lawford adds extra nostalgic zest to the pleasant proceedings, which often resemble an episode of *Murder, She Wrote*. Incidentally, it's the real MGM backlot being used to good effect.

Jack Cassidy *Otto Vonner/Karl Vonner* • Jackie Coogan *Jonathan* • Skye Aubrey *Randy Cross* • Broderick Crawford *Captain O'Neal* • Peter Haskell *Ray Burns* • John Ireland *Lieutenant Gifford* • Peter Lawford *Roger Cross* ■ *Dir* Gene Levitt • *Scr* Robert Thom, George Schenck, from a story by George Schenck

The Phantom of Liberty ★★★★ 15
Surreal drama   1974 · Fr · Colour · 99mins

Luis Buñuel's penultimate film shows him as mordantly comic and subversive as ever, but this series of loosely linked surreal sketches betrays a certain fatigue and laziness. The title refers to Karl Marx's phrase, and Buñuel's theme seems to be that most people are really afraid of freedom. The best-remembered sequence has elegant guests seated on individual lavatories around a table from which they excuse themselves to go and have a meal in a little room behind a locked door. Audacious, certainly, but it lacks the discreet charm of the other episodic French movies of his late period. In French with English subtitles. ▣

Michel Lonsdale *Hatter* • Jean-Claude Brialy *M Foucauld* • Michel Piccoli *Second Prefect of Police* • Adriana Asti *Prefect's sister* • Julien Bertheau *First Prefect of Police* • Adolfo Celi *Docteur Legendre* • Monica Vitti *Mme Foucauld* ■ *Dir* Luis Buñuel • *Scr* Luis Buñuel, Jean-Claude Carrière

The Phantom of the Opera ★★★★ PG
Classic silent horror
1925 · US · BW Tinted and Colour · 90mins

Now you can see where Andrew Lloyd Webber got most of his visual inspiration for his smash-hit musical. This is the influential classic silent first version of Gaston Leroux's novel about a deformed composer living in the Paris Opera House tunnels, who is obsessed by a young soprano (Mary Philbin). Despite outdated acting techniques and staging, this is a must-see for all cinema buffs, as make-up genius Lon Chaney's Phantom is a landmark. New prints restore the famous experimental two-colour section, including the awesome ''Masque of the Red Death'' sequence. 🎬

Lon Chaney *Erik/The Phantom* • Mary Philbin *Christine Daae* • Norman Kerry *Raoul de Chagny* • Snitz Edwards *Florine Papillon* • Gibson Gowland *Simon* • George B Williams *Monsieur Ricard* • Bruce Covington *Monsieur Moncharmin* • Edward Martindel *Philippe de Chagny* ■ *Dir* Rupert Julian, Edward Sedgwick • *Scr* Raymond Schrock, Elliott J Clawson, Tom Reed, Frank M McCormack, from the novel *Le Fantôme de l'Opéra* by Gaston Leroux

Phantom of the Opera ★★ PG

Melodrama 1943 · US · Colour · 88mins

Claude Rains plays the Phantom in this remake of the lavish silent film of 1925 that starred Lon Chaney. However, those expecting a horror movie will be disappointed from the outset when Nelson Eddy's name appears in the opening credits. Rains wears the mask and suffers as Eddy and his co-star Susanna Foster sing *Lullaby of the Bells*. Music director Edward Ward ''remixes'' Tchaikovsky and Chopin, while Fritz Leiber plays Franz Liszt and loses. Nevertheless, director Arthur Lubin's film won Oscars for its cinematography and art direction, with nominations for its score and sound. 🎬

Nelson Eddy *Anatole Garron* • Susanna Foster *Christine Dubois* • Claude Rains *Enrique Claudin* • Edgar Barrier *Inspector Raoul de Chagny* • Leo Carrillo *Signor Feretti* • Jane Farrar *Biancarolli* ■ *Dir* Arthur Lubin • *Scr* Eric Taylor, Samuel Hoffenstein, from the novel *Le Fantôme de l'Opéra* by Gaston Leroux, adapted by John Jacoby • *Cinematographer* Hal Mohr, W Howard Greene • *Art Director* Alexander Golitzen, John B Goodman

The Phantom of the Opera ★★★ PG

Horror 1962 · UK · Colour · 80mins

Hammer's film of Gaston Leroux's perennially popular story was treated with polite disdain in 1962, when it was released as one half of a double bill. It still appears a minor contribution to the *Phantom* cycle, and a pale shadow of the 1925 Lon Chaney version. The main problem is the casting, with perfectly competent actors such as Herbert Lom, Heather Sears and Edward De Souza playing at too low a key for the operatic passions. Hammer relocated the action from Paris to London and went to town on the art direction, particularly for the Phantom's subterranean lair – still the film's most impressive aspect. 🎬

Herbert Lom *The Phantom* • Heather Sears *Christine Charles* • Thorley Walters *Lattimer* • Michael Gough *Lord Ambrose D'Arcy* • Edward De Souza *Harry Hunter* • Martin Miller *Rossi*

■ *Dir* Terence Fisher • *Scr* Anthony Hinds, from the novel *Le Fantôme de l'Opéra* by Gaston Leroux

The Phantom of the Opera ★ 18

Horror 1989 · US · Colour · 88mins

This version of Gaston Leroux's timeless classic finds Robert Englund doing his Freddy Krueger routine and the story reduced to ''composer by day, serial killer by night'' basics. Coming on strong like a bad British sex farce crossed with junk Hammer horror, the look is heavily Gothic, the acting is hilariously mannered (songstress Stephanie Lawrence gives the worst diva performance in history), and the gore is shakily pizzicato (with the emphasis on the pits). 🎬

Robert Englund *Erik Destler, the Phantom* • Jill Schoelen *Christine* • Alex Hyde-White *Richard* • Bill Nighy *Barton* • Stephanie Lawrence *Carlotta* • Peter Clapham *Harrison* • Terence Harvey *Hawking* ■ *Dir* Dwight H Little • *Scr* Duke Sandefur, Gerry O'Hara, from the novel *Le Fantôme de l'Opéra* by Gaston Leroux

Phantom of the Paradise ★★★★

Satirical rock opera 1974 · US · Colour · 91mins

Arguably the best musical comedy fantasy on film after *The Rocky Horror Picture Show*, Brian De Palma's funky retelling of the Faust legend via *The Phantom of the Opera* is a savvy satire on the rock industry, delivering plenty of diabolical chills in the process. Paul Williams may be hard to take as the eternally youthful impresario who lusts after Jessica Harper, but Gerrit Graham is superb as the effeminate glam-rocker Beef. This being a De Palma film, the Hitchcock references are in abundance, including the wittiest *Psycho* shower scene send-up ever. Contains violence and swearing.

William Finley *Winslow the phantom* • Paul Williams *Swan* • Jessica Harper *Phoenix* • George Memmoli *Philbin* • Gerrit Graham *Beef* ■ *Dir* Brian De Palma • *Scr* Brian De Palma

Phantom of the Ritz ★ 15

Horror comedy 1988 · US · Colour · 88mins

A dire horror comedy that finds Peter Bergman buying an old disused cinema in order to put on a fifties rock show. As surviving members of the Coasters and an Elvis Presley impersonator are subjected to weird ''accidents'' in the supposedly haunted theatre, the management ask the audience to remain calm as they unmask the perpetrator. A strange mixture of rock revue and ersatz Gaston Leroux, with neither strand being well-served. 🎬

Peter Bergman *Ed Blake* • Deborah Van Valkenburgh *Nancy* • Cindy Vincino *Sally* • Joshua Sussman *The Phantom* • Russell Curry *Marcus* • Steve Geng *Detective Lassarde* • Frank Tranchina *Dutch* ■ *Dir* Allen Plone • *Scr* Allen Plone, Tom Dempsey, from the novel *Le Fantôme de l'Opéra* by Gaston Leroux

Phantom of the Rue Morgue ★

Horror 1954 · US · Colour · 83mins

A fairly naff adaptation of the Edgar Allan Poe yarn about a Paris psychiatrist who hypnotises a gorilla to

perform his murders of beautiful women. Whenever the gorilla hears the sound of bells, he goes absolutely ape and embraces whichever pretty girl happens to be close by. Karl Malden is much too nice a guy to play the shrink-on-the-blink, while Claude Dauphin seems far too elegant to play the French detective. The man in the monkey suit isn't very convincing, either. What seems to concern the producers most is the 3-D process; without that, the film will undoubtedly seem as flat as a pancake.

Karl Malden *Dr Marais* • Patricia Medina *Jeannette Revere* • Claude Dauphin *Inspector Bonnard* • Steve Forrest *Professor Paul Dupin* • Allyn McLerie [Allyn Ann McLerie] *Yvonne* • Veola Vonn *Arlette* • Dolores Dorn *Camille* • Anthony Caruso *Jacques* • Merv Griffin *Georges Brevert* ■ *Dir* Roy Del Ruth • *Scr* Harold Medford, James R Webb, from the story *Murders in the Rue Morgue* by Edgar Allan Poe

The Phantom President ★★ U

Musical comedy 1932 · US · BW · 77mins

George M Cohan is one of the great legends of American show business. A playwright, screenwriter, stage actor, songwriter, singer and dancer who was worshipped by Broadway and radio audiences, and famously portrayed by James Cagney in *Yankee Doodle Dandy*. Here Cohan plays a singing medicine quack commandeered to impersonate and undermine a presidential candidate. The result was a box office disaster, though it does offer a rare and valuable opportunity to see the legend in action.

George M Cohan *Theodore K Blair/Peter ''Doc'' Varney* • Claudette Colbert *Felicia Hammond* • Jimmy Durante *Curly Cooney* • George Barbier *Jim Ronkton* • Sidney Toler *Prof Aikenhead* • Louise Mackintosh *Sen Sarah Scranton* ■ *Dir* Norman Taurog • *Scr* Walter De Leon, Harlan Thompson, from the novel by George F Worts • *Music/Lyrics* Richard Rodgers, Lorenz Hart, George M Cohan

Phantom Raiders ★★★

Detective drama 1940 · US · BW · 70mins

The second of three films made by MGM featuring private detective Nick Carter, created on the page in 1886. All three were up-dated, given the studio polish that disguised their B-status, and fast-paced enough to overcome fanciful storylines. In this adventure, Carter (Walter Pidgeon) investigates sabotage in the Panama Canal, helped (or hindered) by series regular Bartholomew, a quizzical eccentric played by Donald Meek. Jacques Tourneur, getting started as a director, efficiently controls the action – two years later he would attract major attention with his outstanding thriller *Cat People*.

Walter Pidgeon *Nick Carter* • Donald Meek *Bartholomew* • Joseph Schildkraut *Al Taurez* • Florence Rice *Cora Barnes* • Nat Pendleton *''Gunboat'' Jacklin* • John Carroll *John Ramsell Jr* • Steffi Duna *Dolores* • Cecil Kellaway *Franklin Morris* ■ *Dir* Jacques Tourneur • *Scr* William R Lipman, from a story by Jonathan Latimer

The Phantom Tollbooth ★★★ U

Fantasy 1970 · US · Colour · 85mins

This is what happens when Bugs Bunny and Daffy Duck let Chuck Jones, their favourite artist, out on his own: he becomes a bit solemn and preachy. By and large an animated story, this has a live start and finish, but in between animates the adventures of a bored boy who passes through a magic tollbooth into a wondrous land where he has to rescue Rhyme and Reason from Ignorance Demons. Jones, teamed with Abe Levitow and David Monehan, has some wonderful ideas – especially a professor conducting a sunrise – but it's likely to be a bit above the heads of very young children. The rest should enjoy it, especially listening to the great Mel Blanc, Toonville's greatest ever voice. 🎬

Butch Patrick *Milo* • Mel Blanc ■ *Dir* Chuck Jones, Abe Levitow, David Monahan • *Scr* Chuck Jones, Sam Rosen, from the book by Norton Juster

Phantoms ★★ 15

Horror 1998 · US · Colour · 92mins

In a curiously clunky mix of sci-fi and horror Rose McGowan and Joanna Going play sisters who return to their isolated hometown and discover that virtually everyone has vanished. Ben Affleck is the puzzled local cop, while Peter O'Toole hams it up as a dotty scientist who holds the key to the mystery. However, despite the presence of *Scream* alumni McGowan and Liev Schreiber and a script from horror maestro Dean R Koontz (adapting his own novel), this fails in the fright department, with too much talk and not enough gore. Contains violence and swearing. 🎬

Peter O'Toole *Timothy Flyte* • Joanna Going *Dr Jennifer Pailey* • Rose McGowan *Lisa Pailey* • Ben Affleck *Sheriff Bryce Hammond* • Liev Schreiber *Deputy Stu Wargle* • Clifton Powell *General Leland Copperfield* • Nicky Katt *Deputy Steve Shanning* • Michael DeLorenzo *Soldier Velazquez* • Rick Otto *Scientist Lockland* ■ *Dir* Joe Chappelle • *Scr* Dean R Koontz, from his novel

Phar Lap ★★★★ PG

Drama 1983 · Ausl · Colour · 102mins

Thoroughbred drama about the Aussie superhorse that dominated world racing during the twenties and early thirties. The film follows the horse's career, up to and including its mysterious death in 1932. En route, it also takes a behind-the-scenes look at the cruel practices then prevalent in racehorse training. Impeccably staged and nicely acted, it survives the sort of turn-off title that could have brought it down within the first furlong to demonstrate genuine staying power.

Tom Burlinson *Tommy Woodcock* • Martin Vaughan *Harry Telford* • Judy Morris *Bea Davis* • Celia De Burgh *VI Telford* • Ron Leibman *Dave Davis* • Vincent Ball *Lachlan McKinnon* ■ *Dir* Simon Wincer • *Scr* David Williamson

Pharaoh ★★★
Historical epic   1966 · Pol · Colour · 180mins

Jerzy Kawalerowicz, who was one of the first post-war Polish directors to be internationally recognised, was also one of the first to make films set outside his native land. This historical epic, based on a classic Polish novel, tells of how the young prince Ramses incurs the wrath of the powerful high priest when he takes a Jewish girl as his mistress. When he becomes Ramses XIII, his battle with the priest continues unabated. More restrained, intelligent and veracious than its Hollywood counterparts, the film is rather pompous and plodding, and George Zelnik, though handsome, is not up to the lead role. In Polish with English subtitles.

George Zelnik *Ramses XIII* • Barbara Brylska *Kama* • Krystyna Mikolajewska *Sarah* • Piotr Pawlowski *Herbor* • Leszek Herdegen *Pentuer* ■ *Dir* Jerzy Kawalerowicz • *Scr* Jerzy Kawalerowicz, Tadeusz Konwicki, from a novel by Boleslaw Prus

Phase IV ★★ PG
Science-fiction thriller
1973 · UK/US · Colour · 79mins

This messy eco-upheaval picture was the first feature directed by title sequence maestro Saul Bass, whose work is notable for its animation and stylised use of colour and caption. Yet here, when he has a fuller range of visual techniques to experiment with, he fails to conjure up any sense of suspense. The special effects don't improve matters much, nor do the lacklustre performances of Nigel Davenport and Michael Murphy as scientists who discover that a desert ant colony is preparing to take over the planet before humans destroy it. 📺

Nigel Davenport *Ernest Hubbs* • Michael Murphy *James Lesko* • Lynne Frederick *Kendra* • Alan Gifford *Eldridge* • Robert Henderson *Clete* • Helen Horton *Mrs Eldridge* ■ *Dir* Saul Bass • *Scr* Mayo Simon

The Phenix City Story ★★★
Crime drama   1955 · US · BW · 86mins

Sensational in its day, this exposé of vice and corruption in an Alabama town was filmed in the wake of the infamous Senator Estes Kefauver investigations into crime across the United States, and expertly directed by Phil Karlson. Co-star Richard Kiley embodies moral uprightness as the returning lawyer, who finds his life dramatically changed by encroaching hometown vice. The movie is brutally unsparing in its depiction of corruption, and the sense of realism is heightened by a non-stellar cast, though both John McIntire and Edward Andrews may seem more familiar to today's movie watchers at the time.

John McIntire *Albert Patterson* • Richard Kiley *John Patterson* • Kathryn Grant *Ellie Rhodes* • Edward Andrews *Rhett Tanner* • Lenka Peterson *Mary Jo Patterson* • Biff McGuire *Fred Gage* • Truman Smith *Ed Gage* ■ *Dir* Phil Karlson • *Scr* Crane Wilbur, Daniel Mainwaring

Phenomenon ★★★ PG
Science-fiction fantasy drama
1996 · US · Colour · 118mins

A strange light in the sky gives small-town mechanic John Travolta paranormal powers in director John Turteltaub's feel-good sci-fi fable. As scientists attempt to evaluate his sudden escalation to genius, Travolta battles against an obvious script to focus all his energies on wooing divorced single mother Kyra Sedgwick. Hidden among the waves of sentiment are some genuinely funny moments, but, for all its well-meaning tear-jerking, this tribute to human potential is less than phenomenal. 📺 **DVD**

John Travolta *George Malley* • Kyra Sedgwick *Lace Pennemin* • Forest Whitaker *Nate Pope* • Robert Duvall *Doc* • David Gallagher *Al* • Ashley Buccille *Glory* • Tony Genaro *Tito* ■ *Dir* Jon Turteltaub • *Scr* Gerald DiPego

Phffft! ★★★
Comedy   1954 · US · BW · 88mins

The title derives, it is said, from the sound a marriage makes when it dies. This started as an unproduced play by George Axelrod, rewritten for the movies and specifically for Judy Holliday, who was so good as the dumb blonde in *Born Yesterday*. Like *The Seven Year Itch*, it's a comedy of sexual angst, with Holliday divorcing Jack Lemmon and relishing her freedom. He moves in with grouchy bachelor Jack Carson thereby inspiring *The Odd Couple* and starts to canoodle with Kim Novak. It's all very fifties, stagey and not particularly funny now, though Holliday was one of a kind and is always a pleasure to watch.

Judy Holliday *Nina Tracy* • Jack Lemmon *Robert Tracy* • Jack Carson *Charlie Nelson* • Kim Novak *Janis* • Luella Gear *Mrs Chapman* • Donald Randolph *Dr Van Kessel* • Donald Curtis *Rick Vidal* ■ *Dir* Mark Robson • *Scr* George Axelrod

Philadelphia ★★★★★ 12
Drama   1993 · US · Colour · 120mins

Tom Hanks is a star who isn't afraid of a challenge. Witness this, the first major Hollywood movie about Aids, in which Hanks won his first Academy Award. Hanks plays a homosexual lawyer who takes his powerful employers to court for sacking him. The company bigwigs claim he was dismissed for incompetence, but Hanks's character (Andrew Beckett) suspects the real reason is his Aids-related illness. Beckett's counsel is wheeler-dealer Joe Miller (Denzel Washington), who despises homosexuals but worships fair play, while Beckett's boss, Charles Wheeler (Jason Robards), is a bigot whose intolerance is hidden by bluff camaraderie. Hanks, meanwhile, portrays the ravaged, dying Beckett as a disabled Everyman whose life has lessons for all of us. His passionate crescendo of praise for opera is a tour de force of close-up acting not to be missed. 📺 **DVD**

Tom Hanks *Andrew Beckett* • Denzel Washington *Joe Miller* • Jason Robards [Jason Robards Jr] *Charles Wheeler* • Mary Steenburgen *Belinda Conine* • Antonio Banderas *Miguel Alvarez* • Ron Vawter *Bob Seidman* • Robert Ridgely *Walter Kenton* • Charles Napier *Judge Garnett* • Lisa Summerour *Lisa Miller* • Joanne Woodward *Sarah Beckett* ■ *Dir* Jonathan Demme • *Scr* Ron Nyswaner

The Philadelphia Experiment ★★★ PG
Science-fiction   1984 · US · Colour · 101mins

Michael Paré and Bobby DiCicco play a couple of American sailors from 1943 who are yanked into 1984 when an experiment to render ships invisible to radar backfires. They team up with gung ho Nancy Allen (whose character is named after the actress in *Attack of the 50 Foot Woman*) in a bid to get home. Enjoyably intriguing slice of sci-fi hokum, with the cast delivering their lines with deadpan élan. The project had been kicking around Hollywood since the late seventies; by the time it got going, Stewart Raffill had replaced original director John Carpenter, who installed himself as executive producer. 📺

Michael Paré *David Herdeg* • Nancy Allen *Allison Hayes* • Eric Christmas *Dr James Longstreet* • Bobby DiCicco *Jim Parker* • Kene Holliday *Major Clark* • Joe Dorsey *Sheriff Bates* ■ *Dir* Stewart Raffill • *Scr* William Gray, Michael Janover, from a story by Don Jakoby, from a story by Wallace Bennett, from the book by William I Moore, Charles Berlitz

The Philadelphia Experiment 2 ★★ 18
Science-fiction   1993 · US · Colour · 94mins

Brad Johnson steps into the time-travelling shoes vacated by Michael Paré and gets propelled onto an alternate 1993 where America has become a military state thanks to Hitler winning the Second World War. Then it's back to Germany, 1943, to set history straight. If you can follow the sometimes bewildering plot, this is a reasonably taut action fantasy, relying perhaps a little too heavily on slow-motion battles, black-and-white newsreel footage and wacky hallucination scenes. Contains some violence and mild swearing. 📺

Brad Johnson *David Herdeg* • Marjean Holden *Jess* • Gerrit Graham *Mailer/Mahler* • John Christian Graas *Benjamin* • Cyril O'Reilly *Decker* • Geoffrey Blake *Logan* ■ *Dir* Stephen Cornwell • *Scr* Kevin Rock, Nick Paine

Philadelphia, Here I Come ★★
Drama   1975 · US/Ire · Colour · 95mins

The old problem of expanding the themes of a stage play away from their theatrical origins rears its ugly head in this production of Brian Friel's first play. Disappointingly, director John Quested takes the easy way out here and places the emphasis firmly on text and performance rather than imagery. However, he's been well served by Des Cave and Donal McCann, who complement each other admirably playing the public and private sides of Gar, an Irishman preparing to leave his bullying father and provincial life for a fresh start in America. Contains swearing.

Donal McCann *Gareth (public)* • Des Cave *Gareth (private)* • Siobhan McKenna *Madge* • Eamon Kelly *SA O'Donnell* • Fidelma Murphy *Kate Doogan* • Liam Redmond *Senator Doogan* • Mavis Villiers *Liz Sweeney* ■ *Dir* John Quested • *Scr* Brian Friel, from his play

The Philadelphia Story ★★★★★ U
Classic comedy   1940 · US · BW · 107mins

With her unerring instinct for quality, Katharine Hepburn purchased the rights to the Philip Barry play as a vehicle for herself, and effectively controlled this wonderful MGM movie version, memorably directed by her old friend George Cukor. Cary Grant and James Stewart simply could not be bettered and weren't, in the popular musical remake *High Society*, as the men who both love Hepburn, and Stewart rightly won an Oscar for his magical portrayal of a frustrated reporter. The opening is hilarious and the wit never stops. If you've yet to see this, lucky you. If you know it and love it, you'll be viewing again. 📺

Cary Grant *CK Dexter Haven* • Katharine Hepburn *Tracy Lord* • James Stewart *Macauley Connor* • Ruth Hussey *Elizabeth Imbrie* • Virginia Weidler *Dinah Lord* • John Howard (1) *George Kittredge* ■ *Dir* George Cukor • *Scr* Donald Ogden Stewart, from the play by Philip Barry

Phobia ★ 15
Murder mystery   1980 · Can · Colour · 86mins

It's hard to believe when watching this shoddy Canadian tax-shelter movie, that five years earlier director John Huston had made *The Man Who Would Be King*. Paul Michael Glaser plays an unorthodox doctor who treats patients suffering from various phobias in eccentric ways. Soon, his patients start getting killed one by one in manners related to their individual phobias. The story is so poor, most viewers will be able to figure out who the killer is even before the first murder occurs. 📺

Paul Michael Glaser *Dr Peter Ross* • Susan Hogan *Jenny St Clair* • John Colicos *Inspector Barnes* • Alexandra Stewart *Barbara Grey* • Robert O'Ree *Bubba King* • David Bolt *Henry Owen* • David Eisner *Johnny Venuti* • Lisa Langlois *Laura Adams* ■ *Dir* John Huston • *Scr* Lew Lehman, Jimmy Sangster, Peter Bellwood, from a story by Gary Sherman, Ronald Shusett

Phoenix ★★★
Crime thriller   1998 · US · Colour · 103mins

Though it's obviously influenced by *Pulp Fiction*, this absorbing crime drama manages to do quite a lot on its own. Ray Liotta gives a commendable performance as a cop hopelessly addicted to gambling who gets involved in a "foolproof" plan with some fellow officers to rob a local loan shark. His protagonist's self-destructive behaviour is repulsive yet riveting, especially when interacting with a number of other well-developed characters. Having too many endings weakens the conclusion, while attempts at dialogue akin to *Pulp Fiction*'s "Royale with cheese"' conversation seem artificial. But there are some nice moments, the best of which feature Liotta courting tired barmaid Anjelica Huston.

Ray Liotta *Harry Collins* • Anjelica Huston *Leila* • Anthony LaPaglia *Mike Henshaw* • Daniel Baldwin *James Nutter* • Jeremy Piven *Fred Shuster* • Tom Noonan *Chicago* ■ *Dir* Danny Cannon • *Scr* Eddie Richey

Phone Call from a Stranger
★★★ U

Portmanteau drama 1952 · US · BW · 95mins

Portmanteau movies were a fashion in the late forties and early fifties, and this is an excellent example of such multi-chaptered works. A survivor from a plane crash calls the families of the three people with whom he became close on the flight. It's television fodder today, perhaps, but, in the hands of a grade-A 20th Century-Fox team, this is a fine, gripping drama, well acted by Gary Merrill and, especially, Keenan Wynn as the husband of a bedridden Bette Davis, on screen all too briefly.

Shelley Winters *Binky Gay* • Gary Merrill *David Trask* • Michael Rennie *Dr Fortness* • Keenan Wynn *Eddie Hoke* • Evelyn Varden *Sally Carr* • Warren Stevens *Marty Nelson* • Bette Davis *Marie Hoke* ■ *Dir* Jean Negulesco • *Scr* Nunnally Johnson, from the story by IAR Wylie

Photographing Fairies
★★★ 15

Fantasy drama 1997 · UK · Colour · 101mins

Made at the same time as *FairyTale a True Story* and inspired by the same report of two little girls who took photos of fairies at the bottom of their garden, Nick Willing's film stars Toby Stephens as a professional debunker of photographic forgeries who stumbles upon a genuine supernatural phenomenon. Convinced that the pixies caught on camera by two young sisters will allow him to contact his dead wife, Stephens's investigation becomes an obsession which brings him into conflict with local pastor Ben Kingsley. Imaginatively shot and featuring some nifty special effects, Willing's fantasy drama is also rather dour and carries a depressingly downbeat climax. Hardly surprising, then, that audiences favoured the other, more sanguine version of events. ▦

Toby Stephens *Charles Castle* • Emily Woof *Linda* • Ben Kingsley *Reverend Templeton* • Frances Barber *Beatrice Templeton* • Philip Davis *Roy* • Edward Hardwicke *Sir Arthur Conan Doyle* ■ *Dir* Nick Willing • *Scr* Chris Harrald, Nick Willing, from the book by Steve Szilagyi

Physical Evidence
★★ 18

Thriller 1989 · US · Colour · 95mins

A judicial lark from *Jurassic Park*'s Michael Crichton, directing, in dinosaur-lumbering fashion, this tough courtroom drama in which ex-cop Burt Reynolds is defended by Theresa Russell for a murder he says he didn't commit. Russell's ability to suggest obsession never matches up to her fatal attractiveness, but Reynolds manages a depressive attitude with real effectiveness. It never works up much tension, but it has its moments. Contains swearing. ▦

Burt Reynolds *Joe Paris* • Theresa Russell *Jenny Hudson* • Ned Beatty *James Nicks* • Kay Lenz *Deborah Quinn* • Ted McGinley *Kyle* • Tom O'Brien *Matt Farley* • Kenneth Welsh *Harry Norton* ■ *Dir* Michael Crichton • *Scr* Bill Phillips, from a story by Steve Ransohoff, Bill Phillips

Pi
★★★ 15

Psychological science-fiction thriller 1997 · US · BW · 80mins

An original, fascinating thriller about reclusive maths genius Sean Gullette, who becomes obsessed with the notion that everything in the universe can be broken down into mathematics and therefore follows a predictable pattern. This acclaimed black-and-white feature debut from Darren Aronofsky is filled with complex issues and makes arresting use of disorientating camerawork to depict Max's distorted view of the world. But, despite its many virtues, *Pi* becomes increasingly hard to follow because of an overload of intricate ideas that could have Stephen Hawking scratching his head. Contains swearing and some violence. ▦ **DVD**

Sean Gullette *Maximillian Cohen* • Mark Margolis *Sol Robeson* • Ben Shenkman *Lenny Meyer* • Pamela Hart *Marcy Dawson* • Stephen Pearlman *Rabbi Cohen* • Samia Shoaib *Devi* ■ *Dir* Darren Aronofsky • *Scr* Darren Aronofsky, from a story by Sean Gullette, Eric Watson, Darren Aronofsky • *Cinematographer* Matthew Libatique

Piaf: the Early Years
★★★

Biographical drama 1974 · Fr · Colour · 104mins

Based on the book by Edith Piaf's half-sister, Simone Berteaut, this biopic traces the Little Sparrow's life from her troubled childhood to her first hit song. Born in the gutter and raised in a brothel, Piaf recovered from infant blindness to join her father in performing on the pavements of Paris. However, there was also the tragedy of losing her child to tuberculosis to bear before she finally found fame. Brigitte Ariel is well cast in the title role, but it's a shame that impersonator Betty Mars was used to provide the vocals and not Piaf's original recordings. In French with English subtitles.

Brigitte Ariel *Edith Piaf* • Pascale Christophe *Simone Berteaut* • Guy Tréjan *Lucien Leplée* • Pierre Vernier *Raymond Asso* • Jacques Duby *Julien* • Anouk Ferjac *Madeleine* ■ *Dir* Guy Casaril • *Scr* Guy Casaril, Françoise Ferley, Marc Behm, from the biography *Piaf* by Simone Berteaut

The Piano
★★★★★ 15

Period drama 1993 · Ausl · Colour · 120mins

director Jane Campion's superbly staged tale of passion and obsession won her an Oscar for best screenplay. Like her earlier films, *The Piano* focuses on a woman whom society has dismissed as disabled. Holly Hunter, who chose to stop speaking at the age of six, communicates through her daughter Anna Paquin and her piano, which she brings with her to New Zealand when she is sent from Scotland to marry local landowner Sam Neill. The ability to make contact is one of the film's key themes; Ada's new husband can read her hurriedly written notes, but he does not appreciate her music and won't take the trouble to learn either her sign language or the local Maori dialect. The illiterate Harvey Keitel, on the other hand, has fully embraced the customs of his adopted home and, belying his uncouth outward appearance, proves to be much more tender and passionate than his social superiors. There's a masterly score by Michael Nyman and splendid photography from Stuart Dryburgh, and Campion coaxes stupendous performances from Hunter and Paquin, who both won Oscars Neill and Keitel were shamefully overlooked. In English and Maori with subtitles. Contains some violence and nudity. ▦ **DVD**

Holly Hunter *Ada* • Harvey Keitel *Baines* • Sam Neill *Stewart* • Anna Paquin *Flora* • Kerry Walker *Aunt Morag* • Genevieve Lemon *Nessie* • Tungia Baker *Hira* • Ian Mune *Reverend* ■ *Dir/Scr* Jane Campion

The Picasso Summer
★★

Drama 1969 · US · Colour · 94mins

Astonishingly based on a short story by the great science-fiction Ray Bradbury, this is an account of a young couple (Albert Finney and Yvette Mimieux) so addicted to Picasso's works that they wander through France in the hope of meeting him. Sadly for us, it's more of a dutiful trudge than a pleasurable ramble, though the animated sequence is worth staying awake for.

Albert Finney *George Smith* • Yvette Mimieux *Alice Smith* • Luis Miguel Dominguin • Theo Marcuse *The Host* • Jim Connell *The Artist* ■ *Dir* Serge Bourguignon, Robert Sallin • *Scr* Douglas Spaulding [Ray Bradbury], Edwin Boyd, from the short story *The Picasso Summer* by Ray Bradbury

Piccadilly
★★

Crime melodrama 1929 · UK · BW · 92mins

Directed by EA Dupont as a British silent, with sound added the following year, this crime melodrama, atmospherically designed by Alfred Junge, was much admired in its day as a stylish piece of work. Now, though, its old-fashioned acting is more likely to cause giggles. The plot has a nightclub owner (Jameson Thomas) fomenting rivalry between his fiancée (Gilda Gray) and his Chinese mistress (Anna May Wong). When the mistress is murdered, the fiancée is accused. Charles Laughton appears in the supporting cast, as does one Raymond (later Ray) Milland.

Gilda Gray *Mabel Greenfield* • Jameson Thomas *Valentine Wilmot* • Anna May Wong *Shosho* • King Ho Chang *Jim* • Cyril Ritchard *Victor Smiles* • Hannah Jones *Bessie* • Charles Laughton *Greedy nightclub diner* • Raymond Milland [Ray Milland] ■ *Dir* EA Dupont • *Scr* Arnold Bennett • *Art Director* Alfred Junge

Piccadilly Jim
★★★ U

Comedy 1936 · US · BW · 95mins

PG Wodehouse's story, previously filmed in 1920, glides through London's clubland and has an American cartoonist, Robert Montgomery, as its hero. The main plot has Montgomery converting the life of his sweetheart's family into a cartoon strip but it's the gallery of secondary characters and MGM's idea of what London Town is like that makes this creaky picture still watchable. Eric Blore plays an English butler to perfection and there are also turns from Robert Benchley and Billie Burke. The screenplay is co-written by Charles Brackett, later the partner of Billy Wilder on such classics as *The Lost Weekend* and *Sunset Boulevard*.

Robert Montgomery *Jim Crocker* • Frank Morgan *Mr Crocker* • Madge Evans *Ann Chester* • Eric Blore *Bayliss* • Billie Burke *Eugenia* • Robert Benchley *Macon* • Ralph Forbes *Lord Charles* • Cora Witherspoon *Nesta Pett* ■ *Dir* Robert Z Leonard • *Scr* Charles Brackett, Edwin Knopf, from the novel by PG Wodehouse

Piccadilly Third Stop
★

Crime thriller 1960 · UK · BW · 90mins

This is a plodding low-budget thriller, with Terence Morgan playing a London low-lifer who dates ambassador's daughter Yoko Tani in order to gain access to the embassy safe. Dennis Price, William Hartnell and Mai Zetterling are among those who obviously needed the work.

Terence Morgan *Dominic Colpoys-Owen* • Yoko Tani *Seraphina Yokami* • John Crawford *Joe Pready* • Mai Zetterling *Christine Pready* • William Hartnell *Colonel* • Dennis Price *Edward* ■ *Dir* Wolf Rilla • *Scr* Leigh Vance

The Pick-Up Artist
★ 15

Comedy drama 1987 · US · Colour · 77mins

A great cast is stymied by half-baked dialogue and a barely-there plot in cult director James Toback's dating disaster. Serial womaniser Robert Downey Jr puts the make on feisty Molly Ringwald and is amazed when she doesn't respond to his chat-up lines. Wise girl! Downey Jr emits none of his future star charisma in a thankless role that wears out its welcome way before the mercifully short running time is over. Contains swearing. ▦

Molly Ringwald *Randy Jensen* • Robert Downey Jr *Jack Jericho* • Dennis Hopper *Flash Jensen* • Danny Aiello *Phil* • Mildred Dunnock *Nellie, Jack's grandmother* • Harvey Keitel *Alonzo* • Brian Hamill *Mike* • Tamara Bruno *Karen* • Vanessa L Williams *Rae* ■ *Dir/Scr* James Toback

The Pickle
★

Comedy 1993 · US · Colour

Danny Aiello plays a film director (whose most recent movie is a sci-fi tale about a giant pickle hence the title) desperately in need of a career boost. Unfortunately, despite an interesting supporting cast that includes Shelley Winters, Isabella Rossellini, Dudley Moore and Little Richard, this is virtually unwatchable. It fails to find the appropriate tone and generally misfires on all cylinders, unlike the very successful *The Player* and *The Big Picture*. Don't blink or you'll miss Donald Trump.

Danny Aiello *Harry Stone* • Dyan Cannon *Ellen Stone* • Clotilde Courau *Francoise* • Shelley Winters *Yetta* • Barry Miller *Ronnie Liebowitz* • Jerry Stiller *Phil Hirsch* • Christopher Penn *Gregory Stone* • Little Richard *President* • Griffin Dunne *President's man* • Dudley Moore *Planet Cleveland Man* • Donald Trump ■ *Dir/Scr* Paul Mazursky

Pickpocket
★★★★

Crime drama 1959 · Fr · BW · 75mins

A mesmeric sequence in which a young thief learns the tricks of the trade from a master pickpocket is the highlight of this exceptional study by

U = SUITABLE FOR ALL   Uc = SUITABLE FOR ALL, ESPECIALLY FOR YOUNG CHILDREN (VIDEO ONLY)   PG = PARENTAL GUIDANCE

Robert Bresson of obsession, desperation and guilt. Inspired by Dostoyevsky's *Crime and Punishment*, the film follows a theme used several times by Bresson as lonely individuals lay bare their souls in the midst of personal torment. Martin Lassalle gives a performance of chilling restraint as the possessed "dip", but it is Bresson's control over his cast, the Parisian locations and the austere black-and-white imagery that makes this extraordinary film so compelling. In French with English subtitles..

Martin Lassalle *Michel* • Marika Green *Jeanne* • Pierre Leymarie *Jacques* • Jean Pelagri *Police Inspector* • Kassagi *Master Pickpocket* • Pierre Etaix *Accomplice* ■ *Dir/Scr* Robert Bresson • *Cinematographer* Henri Raichi

Pickup on South Street ★★

Film noir   1953 · US · BW · 76mins

A pick-up that's a hiccup for petty thief Richard Widmark, pocketing more than he bargained for by stealing Jean Peters's purse, only to find it loaded with espionage plans. Not one of director Sam Fuller's most successful outings – the anti-Communist spiel seems tacked on to cash in on contemporary hysteria – though it's worth a look for Thelma Ritter's acid-drop old lady betraying all and sundry to save up for "a plot and a stone". She carries conviction; the other characters deserve one.

Richard Widmark *Skip McCoy* • Jean Peters *Candy* • Thelma Ritter *Moe* • Murvyn Vye *Captain Dan Tiger* • Richard Kiley *Joey* ■ *Dir* Samuel Fuller • *Scr* Samuel Fuller, from a story by Dwight Taylor

The Pickwick Papers

                                        ★★★ U

Comedy   1952 · UK · BW · 104mins

Dickens's sprawling, episodic novel has been reined in by writer/director Noel Langley without sacrificing too much of its jaunty good nature. Brimming over with memorable characters, the film is well served by some solid performances. James Hayter is the embodiment of Pickwick, really hitting his stride during the breach of promise trial. Not all the vignettes come off, as the Pickwick Club crosses the country in its attempt to understand human nature, with the amorous misadventures of James Donald's Mr Winkle a touch too broad. But Nigel Patrick is bang on form as the disreputable Mr Jingle, and Kathleen Harrison is ever-excellent. ▭

James Hayter *Samuel Pickwick* • James Donald *Mr Winkle* • Alexander Gauge *Mr Tupman* • Lionel Murton *Mr Snodgrass* • Nigel Patrick *Mr Jingle* • Kathleen Harrison *Rachael Wardle* • Joyce Grenfell *Mrs Leo Hunter* • Hermione Gingold *Miss Tomkins* • Donald Wolfit *Sergeant Buzfuz* • Hermione Baddeley *Mrs Bardell* • Hattie Jacques *Mrs Nupkins* ■ *Dir* Noel Langley • *Scr* Noel Langley, from the novel by Charles Dickens

The Pickwick Papers ★★ U

Animated period drama
1985 · Ausl · Colour · 74mins

The Pickwick Papers is perhaps the least filmable Dickens novel, but this animated version makes a respectable stab at describing the picaresque adventures of Messrs Pickwick,

Tupman, Snodgrass and Winkle. The most fondly remembered episodes are covered: the hiring of Sam Weller as Pickwick's valet; the feud with the rascally Jingle and the breach of promise action taken by Mrs Bardell. Yet, while the film comes close to capturing the spirit of the original, the drawings are simply too cartoon-like to successfully conjure up the true magic of the characters and their pre-Victorian world. ▭

• *Scr* Steven Fosbery, from the novel by Charles Dickens

Picnic   ★★★ U

Drama   1955 · US · Colour · 108mins

Adapted by Daniel Taradash from William Inge's Pulitzer Prize-winning play, and directed for maximum cinematic effect by Joshua Logan, *Picnic* earned six Oscar nominations for its daringly frank depiction (by fifties standards) of the emotional havoc wrought on the women of a rustic Kansas town when a sexy itinerant wanders in to their Labor Day picnic. William Holden (not ideal for the role, but nonetheless giving a polished performance) is the attractive cat among the pigeons: tomboy Susan Strasberg, frustrated spinster Rosalind Russell and town beauty Kim Novak. Enjoyable drama with an edge. ▭

William Holden (1) *Hal Carter* • Rosalind Russell *Rosemary Sydney* • Betty Field *Flo Owens* • Kim Novak *Madge Owens* • Susan Strasberg *Millie Owens* • Cliff Robertson *Alan* ■ *Dir* Joshua Logan • *Scr* Daniel Taradash, from the play by William Inge

Picnic at Hanging Rock

                            ★★★★ PG

Psychological mystery
1975 · Ausl · Colour · 110mins

On St Valentine's Day in 1900 a party of schoolgirls enjoys a day at Hanging Rock, a local beauty spot. But something odd is at work: clocks stop at midday and three girls vanish. Dingo dogs, extraterrestrials, kidnappers or what? The director, Peter Weir, hasn't the foggiest, but he adores ambiguity, mysticism and metaphor. He leaves clues hanging in the air like a glistening spider's web, hears celestial choirs and thrumming insects. This is a very sexy picture, which stares an enigma straight in the eye and, in the process, proved to the world that the new Australian cinema was capable of making films other than those that featured gnarled and drunken sheep-shearers. There are fine performances from Rachel Roberts, Helen Morse and Dominic Guard, which, with the outstanding location work, add up to a decidedly class act. ▭

Rachel Roberts *Mrs Appleyard* • Dominic Guard *Michael Fitzhubert* • Helen Morse *Dianne de Potiers* • Jacki Weaver *Minnie* • Vivean Gray *Miss McCraw* • Kirsty Child *Dora Lumley* • Anne Lambert [Anne Louise Lambert] *Miranda* ■ *Dir* Peter Weir • *Scr* Cliff Green, from the novel by Joan Lindsay • *Cinematographer* Russell Boyd

Picture Bride   ★★ 12

Period drama   1994 · US · Colour · 94mins

Set in 1918, Kayo Hatta's debut feature recalls the old custom of using photographs to arrange marriages

between Japanese workers in Hawaii and girls back home. The action manages to capture a sense of period and place in spite of financial restraint. But there are few fresh insights into loveless marriage or the trials facing women in a patriarchal society, as 16-year-old Youki Kudoh attempts to escape the elderly husband who tricked her into emigrating. Boasting a cameo from Toshiro Mifune as an itinerant projectionist, this is heartfelt, but hard work. In English and Japanese with subtitles.

Youki Kudoh *Riyo* • Akira Takayama *Matsuji* • Tamlyn Tomita *Kana* • Cary-Hiroyuki Tagawa *Kanzaki* • Toshiro Mifune *The Benshi* • Yoko Sugi *Aunt Sode* ■ *Dir* Kayo Hatta • *Scr* Kayo Hatta, Mari Hatta, Kayo Hatta, Mari Hatta, Diane Mei Lin Mark

Picture Mommy Dead   ★★

Horror   1966 · US · Colour · 82mins

Typical sixties "shocker" with Susan Gordon (daughter of the film's director, Bert I Gordon) haunted by dim memories of her mother's mysterious death. Pure melodrama (wicked stepmother, scarred caretaker, an absurd chain of events) is punctuated by shock effects to enjoyably silly result. A bonus is the cast of old-timers (Don Ameche, Zsa Zsa Gabor, Maxwell Reed, Wendell Corey and Signe Hasso) trying to retain their dignity.

Don Ameche *Edward Shelley* • Martha Hyer *Francene Shelley* • Zsa Zsa Gabor *Jessica* • Susan Gordon *Susan Shelley* • Maxwell Reed *Anthony* • Wendell Corey *Clayborn* • Signe Hasso *Sister Rene* ■ *Dir* Bert I Gordon • *Scr* Robert Sherman

The Picture of Dorian Gray

                                ★★★★

Fantasy drama
1945 · US · BW and Colour · 109mins

Although MGM had enjoyed success with lavish literary adaptations such as *David Copperfield* and *Pride and Prejudice*, this big-budget version of Oscar Wilde's only novel was rather a curious venture for a studio that prided itself on its family entertainment. But flamboyant screenwriter/director Albert Lewin turned in a compelling picture that teeters between sophistication and vulgarity. Hurd Hatfield gives a muted performance as Dorian and is thus easily surpassed by Angela Lansbury, who plays the chirpy music-hall singer with whom he falls in lust, and by George Sanders as the languidly witty Lord Henry Wotton. The picture earned supervising art director Cedric Gibbons one of his record 40 Oscar nominations.

Hurd Hatfield *Dorian Gray* • George Sanders *Lord Henry Wotton* • Donna Reed *Gladys Hallward* • Angela Lansbury *Sibyl Vane* • Peter Lawford *David Stone* • Lowell Gilmore *Basil Hallward* • Richard Fraser *James Vane* ■ *Dir* Albert Lewin • *Scr* Albert Lewin, from the novel *The Picture of Dorian Gray* by Oscar Wilde • *Cinematographer* Harry Stradling

Picture Perfect   ★★★ PG

Romantic comedy
1997 · US · Colour · 97mins

Glenn Gordon Caron directs *Friends* star Jennifer Aniston in this good-natured romantic comedy. Aniston is

the single girl who discovers she needs a partner of the male kind to succeed at work. So she invents a fiancé using a photo of her with a complete stranger taken at a wedding. Of course, it's not long before her bosses want to meet the man (Jay Mohr), so she has to track him down, complicating the secret affair she's having with a corporate sleaze (a fun performance from Kevin Bacon). Preposterous perhaps, but sweetly done, with a suitably ditsy turn from Aniston. Contains some mild swearing and sexual references. ▭

Jennifer Aniston *Kate* • Jay Mohr *Nick* • Kevin Bacon *Sam* • Olympia Dukakis *Rita* • Illeana Douglas *Darcy* • Kevin Dunn *Mr Mercer* • Anne Twomey *Sela* • Faith Prince *Mrs Mercer* ■ *Dir* Glenn Gordon Caron • *Scr* Glenn Gordon Caron, Arleen Sorkin, Paul Slansky, from a story by May Quigley, Arleen Sorkin, Paul Slansky

The Picture Show Man   ★★

Comedy drama   1977 · Ausl · Colour · 99mins

Rod Taylor returned to his native Australia for a good-natured but rambling account of the early years of cinema, playing a villainous entrepreneur dogging the steps of the film's real hero, played by John Meillon. The two rivals slog their way around the outback drumming up enthusiasm for the picture show among the bemused citizens, and there's enough humour en route to keep the attention from flagging.

Rod Taylor *Palmer* • John Meillon *Mr Pym*, "*Pop*" • John Ewart *Freddie* • Harold Hopkins *Larry* • Sally Conabere *Lucy* • Patrick Cargill *Fitzwilliam* ■ *Dir* John Power • *Scr* Joan Long

Picture Snatcher   ★★★

Drama   1933 · US · BW · 74mins

Great title for a terrific James Cagney vehicle from that marvellous period at Warner Bros when pace was everything and dialogue just snapped and crackled its way across the screen. Cagney was making five or six movies a year at this time, creating and sustaining an image that chimed perfectly with Depression audiences, his cocky optimism at odds with the downbeat reality of everyday living. He is seldom more dynamic than here, under the frantically fresh direction of Lloyd Bacon. Cagney plays a whirlwind photographer, based on a true character, a cameraman who succeeded in getting published a gruesome photo of a murderess being electrocuted.

James Cagney *Danny Kean* • Ralph Bellamy *McLean* • Patricia Ellis *Patricia Nolan* • Alice White *Allison* • Ralf Harolde *Jerry* ■ *Dir* Lloyd Bacon • *Scr* Allen Rivkin, PJ Wolfson, Ben Markson, from a story by Danny Ahearn

Pictures of the Old World

                                    ★★★

Documentary   1972 · Cz · Colour · 74mins

The Slovakian director Dusan Hanak had the dubious distinction of having his first three films banned by the Czech authorities. Coming between his debut *322* and the comedy *I Love, You Love*, this rural documentary offended the Communist regime for daring to suggest that isolated shepherds and hill farmers had managed to resist

Party propaganda and retain their old ways and ideas. As with the aforementioned, it was banned until the late eighties when the democratically elected government opened up the film vaults. A Czech language film.

Dir/Scr Dusan Hanak

Pie in the Sky ★★★ 18

Drama   1995 · US · Colour · 90mins

A quirky romantic comedy that neatly avoids the usual slushy clichés. Josh Charles plays an offbeat teen, who was conceived during a traffic jam, and now remains obsessed with gridlock. That is, until the girl next door grows up into beautiful dancer Anne Heche. The two leads are charming, although the film is stolen by a typically larger-than-life performance from John Goodman as a wacky eye in the sky traffic reporter. Bryan Gordon's direction is unobtrusive and, even if it fades a little towards the end, there are plenty of funny moments. 🔲

Josh Charles *Charlie* • Anne Heche *Amy* • John Goodman *Alan Davenport* • Christine Lahti *Ruby* • Peter Riegert *Dad Dunlap* • Bob Balaban *Mr Entamen* • Christine Ebersole *Mom Dunlap* • Wil Wheaton *Jack* ■ *Dir/Scr* Bryan Gordon

A Piece of the Action ★★ 15

Comedy   1977 · US · Colour · 129mins

The third teaming of Sidney Poitier and Bill Cosby (after *Uptown Saturday Night* and *Let's Do It Again*) continues their comic misadventures as two con artists up to their ears in complications. This time they avoid a jail sentence by volunteering to work with under-privileged kids. Although a well-intentioned, occasionally funny farce, exploiting the easy charm and chemistry between the two able leads, Poitier's direction tends to overemphasise the more preachy and saccharine elements. 🔲

Sidney Poitier *Manny Durrell* • Bill Cosby *Dave Anderson* • James Earl Jones *Joshua Burke* • Denise Nicholas *Lila French* • Hope Clarke *Sarah Thomas* • Tracy Reed *Nikki McLean* • Titos Vandis *Bruno* ■ *Dir* Sidney Poitier • *Scr* Charles Blackwell, from a story by Timothy March

Pieces ★ 18

Horror   1982 · It/Sp · Colour · 84mins

Real-life husband-and-wife team Christopher and Lynda Day George must have rued the day they agreed to star in this twisted stalk-and-slash flick. George is a cop hunting down a psycho who chops up college girls for body parts in a grotesque human jigsaw. ("You don't have to go to Texas for a chain saw massacre!" bragged the poster.) Is one really to take Spanish director Juan Piquer Simón's effort seriously, riddled as it is with goofs and inane dialogue?

Christopher George *Lieutenant Bracken* • Edmund Purdom *Dean* • Lynda Day George *Mary Riggs* • Paul Smith *Willard* ■ *Dir* Juan Piquer Simón • *Scr* Dick Randall, John Shadow [Joe D'Amato]

The Pied Piper ★★★ U

Second World War drama
1942 · US · BW · 86mins

The Pied Piper theme is transferred to the Second World War, with Monty Woolley emotionally allergic to children but forced to lead two of them out of Nazi-occupied France. Woolley gives a fine performance, successfully overturning our belief in his pathological state, and helping what could have been a squeakily saccharine offering become an often intensely moving film, sadly spoilt overall by some very dull patches.

Monty Woolley *Howard* • Roddy McDowall *Ronnie Cavanaugh* • Anne Baxter *Nicole Rougeron* • Otto Preminger *Major Diessen* • J Carrol Naish *Aristide Rougeron* • Lester Matthews *Mr Cavanaugh* • Jill Esmond *Mrs Cavanaugh* • Ferike Boros *Madame* ■ *Dir* Irving Pichel • *Scr* Nunnally Johnson, from the novel by Nevil Shute.

The Pied Piper ★★ PG

Fantasy drama   1971 · UK · Colour · 86mins

From French director Jacques Demy, the master of enchantment, this is a lumpen disappointment. Based on the Grimm brothers' fairy tale and the Robert Browning poem about the medieval minstrel whose music rids the town of Hamelin of its plague of rats, the lead is played by British pop-singer Donovan – in one of his few films, and one can see why. But though prettily olde worlde to look at, it lacks the necessary ingredients of fantasy and appeal. 🔲

Donald Pleasence *Baron* • Donovan *The Pied Piper* • Jack Wild *Gavin* • John Hurt *Franz* • Michael Hordern *Melius* • Roy Kinnear *Burgermeister* • Diana Dors *Frau Poppendick* ■ *Dir* Jacques Demy • *Scr* Andrew Birkin, Jacques Demy, Mark Peploe, from the poem by Robert Browning, from the fairy tale by Jakob Grimm, Wilhelm Grimm,

Pièges ★★★★

Thriller   1939 · Fr · BW · 115mins

This was Robert Siodmak's last French-made film before his departure for Hollywood, and it is interesting to see how much this thriller, with its police investigation and seedy characters, prefigures the "night city" movies of his American period. The excellent cast includes Maurice Chevalier as a night club owner, Pierre Renoir (Jean's elder brother) and Erich von Stroheim as prime suspects connected with the disappearance of a number of young women. The film was remade in 1947 by Douglas Sirk as *Lured*, with Lucille Ball as the decoy played more convincingly here by Marie Déa. A French language film.

Maurice Chevalier *Robert Fleury* • Erich von Stroheim *Pears* • Pierre Renoir *Bremontière* • Marie Déa *Adrienne* • André Brunot *Ténier* ■ *Dir* Robert Siodmak • *Scr* Jacques Companeez, Ernest Neuville, Simon Gantillon

Pierrot le Fou ★★★★★ 15

Drama   1965 · Fr · Colour · 105mins

"*Pierrot le Fou* isn't really a film," said director Jean-Luc Godard on its release, "It's an attempt at cinema." Although it was based on Lionel White's novel *Obsession*, the action was nearly all improvised as Godard was inspired by the locations en route

from Paris to the south of France. Shot in razor sharp colour by Raoul Coutard, it is a bewildering blend of genres and visual styles, but the over-riding atmosphere is one of despair for both runaways Jean-Paul Belmondo and Anna Karina and the violent world of the mid-sixties. Godard's most political work thus far and certainly his most assured cinematically. In French with English subtitles. 🔲

Jean-Paul Belmondo *Ferdinand Griffon, "Pierrot"* • Anna Karina *Marianne Renoir* • Dirk Sanders *Fred, Marianne's brother* • Raymond Devos *Man on pier* • Graziella Galvani *Ferdinand's wife* • Sam Fuller [Samuel Fuller] ■ *Dir* Jean-Luc Godard • *Scr* Jean-Luc Godard, from the novel *Obsession* by Lionel White

Pigalle ★★

Crime drama   1994 · Fr/Swi · Colour · 93mins

Karim Dridi clearly set out to produce a throbbing portrait of Paris's notorious red-light district for his directorial debut. What he actually delivers in the doomed relationship between pickpocket François Renaud and stripper Vera Briole is a naive melodrama, in which clumsy caricatures veer from one clichéd situation to another, all to the incessant beat of bad pop music. In French with English subtitles.. Contains violence, swearing, sex scenes, drug abuse and nudity.

Vera Briole *Vera* • François Renaud *Fifi* • Raymond Gil *Fernande* • Philippe Ambrosini *Le Malfait* • Blanca Li *Divine* • Jean-Claude Grenier *L'Empereur* • Bobby Pacha *La Pacha* ■ *Dir/Scr* Karim Dridi

The Pigeon That Took Rome ★★

Second World War comedy
1962 · US · BW · 101mins

Charlton Heston is in Rome again: not driving a chariot this time, but playing an American army captain smuggled into the city under the nose of its German occupiers. He makes contact with the partisans – especially Elsa Martinelli – and falls in with a daft spy scheme involving a carrier pigeon. The plan actually calls for more than one pigeon; the rest get eaten by mistake. It's all a bit silly, and the American studio interiors make for some ugly joins with the exterior locations. Heston is miscast – his role should have been played by Cary Grant – though his discomfort proves to be the source of the film's biggest chuckles.

Charlton Heston *Capt Paul MacDougall* • Elsa Martinelli *Antonella Massimo* • Harry Guardino *Sgt Joseph Contini* • Salvatore Baccaloni *Ciccio Massimo* • Marietto *Livio Massimo* ■ *Dir* Melville Shavelson • *Scr* Melville Shavelson, from the novel *The Easter Dinner* by Donald Downes

A Pig's Tale ★★ U

Comedy   1994 · US · Colour · 89mins

When oddball youngster Milt (Joe Flaherty) is sent to summer camp, he finds himself sharing a cabin with three other losers. Together they manage to triumph against the odds stacked against them. Juvenile high jinks with the simple message that even misfits can make good – a sentiment echoed in such similar

pieces as *National Lampoon's Animal House* and *Meatballs*. 🔲

Joe Flaherty *Milt* • Graham Sack *Andy* • Mike Damus *Frank* • Andrew Harrison Leeds *Beckerwood* • Lisa Jakub *Tiffany* • Jake Beecham *Swackback* • Jimmy Zepeda *Cruz* ■ *Dir* Paul Tassie • *Scr* Charles Ransom, Scott Sandorf, Todd Richardson

Pigskin Parade ★★★ U

Musical comedy   1936 · US · BW · 92mins

A rather silly, if charming, 20th Century-Fox football musical, worth watching today for its cast, including a young Judy Garland in her first feature, loaned to Fox by her own studio MGM while they prepared projects for her, and appearing here with her future Tin Man, Jack Haley. Stuart Erwin and Patsy Kelly are the nominal leads in this likeable romp, but keep an eye out, too, for a gauche Tony Martin, Betty Grable a decade before she became Queen of the Lot, and don't blink or you'll miss Alan Ladd, singing with the Yacht Club Boys.

Stuart Erwin *Amos Dodd* • Patsy Kelly *Bessie Winters* • Jack Haley *"Slug" Winston Winters* • Johnny Downs *Chip Carson* • Betty Grable *Laura Watson* • Arline Judge *Sally Saxon* • Dixie Dunbar *Ginger Jones* • Judy Garland *Sairy Dodd* • Alan Ladd *Student* • Anthony Martin [Tony Martin] *Tommy Barker* ■ *Dir* David Butler • *Scr* Harry Tugend, Jack Yellen, William Conselman, from a story by Arthur Sheekman, Nat Perrin, Mark Kelly

The Pilgrim ★★★★★ U

Silent comedy   1923 · US · BW · 41mins

Charles Chaplin's genius at creating comedy out of desperate situations is well illustrated in as this film. He's in hot water in as an escaped convict who steals the clothes of a gospel minister and gets roped in to preaching to the congregation of Hell's Hinges, falling for Edna Purviance while bringing a former fellow inmate to justice. Inevitably, the film drew protests from both redneck religionists and the Ku-Klux-Klan.

Charlie Chaplin [Charles Chaplin] *The pilgrim* • Edna Purviance *The girl* • Kitty Bradbury *Her mother* • Mack Swain *The deacon* • Loyal Underwood *The elder* • Dinky Dean *The boy* • Mai Wells *his mother* • Sydney Chaplin [Syd Chaplin] *Her husband* • Chuck Reisner [Charles Reisner] *The crook* • Tom Murray *The sheriff* ■ *Dir* Charles Chaplin • *Scr* Charles Chaplin

Pilgrimage ★★★

Drama   1933 · US · BW · 96mins

A tough drama about a cruelly possessive mother (Henrietta Crosman) who, to keep her son from the girl he loves (Marian Nixon), enlists him in the army, resulting in his death on the Western Front. Nixon bears his son, who is also harshly treated by an even more hardened Crosman – until the woman goes on a pilgrimage to the war graves in France. This is uncharacteristic material for John Ford, but it's beautifully shot and a great showcase for the formidable stage actress Crosman. Its themes and incidents seem over-familiar now after many films about destructive mother love, but it offers depth, sweep and honest conviction, despite its slightly unrealistic "happy" ending.

Henrietta Crosman *Hannah Jessop* • Heather Angel *Suzanne* • Norman Foster *Jim Jessop* • Marian Nixon *Mary Saunders* • Maurice Murphy *Gary Worth* • Lucille La Verne *Mrs Hatfield* • Charley Grapewin *Dad Saunders* • Hedda Hopper *Mrs Worth* ■ *Dir* John Ford • *Scr* Philip Klein, Barry Connors, Dudley Nichols, from the story *Gold Star Mother* by IAR Wylie

Pillars of Society ★★

Drama   1935 · Ger · BW · 82mins

After an absence of 20 years in America, a man (Albrecht Schoenhals) returns to his native Norway and a reunion with his former business partner (Heinrich George). His presence causes upheaval, as he threatens to reveal dark secrets hiding behind the veneer of respectable society. This German adaptation of Ibsen's play never transcends its stage origins and plays out as a rather static and ponderous melodrama. Director Detlef Sierck, however, does display the touch which would bring him fame as Hollywood's Douglas Sirk. A German language film.

Heinrich George *Consul Bernick* • Maria Krahn *Betty, his wife* • Horst Teetzmann *Olaf, his son* • Albrecht Schoenhals *Johann Tonnessen* ■ *Dir* Detlef Sierck [Douglas Sirk] • *Scr* Dr Georg C Klaren, Karl Peter Gillman, from the play by Henrik Ibsen

Pillars of the Sky ★★

Western   1956 · US · Colour · 95mins

A handsome-looking CinemaScope western starring two of Universal's smouldering contract icons, silver-haired beefcake Jeff Chandler and bit-player-turned-star Dorothy Malone, in a tale with a decidedly sanctimonious tone (the none-too-subtle British title, *The Tomahawk and the Cross*, says it all). Veteran director George Marshall does what he can with a weak script, but there's a feeling that no one's heart is in tune with the sentiments expressed. A strong supporting cast headed by Ward Bond and Lee Marvin lends some much-needed western grit.

Jeff Chandler *First Sergeant Emmett Bell* • Dorothy Malone *Calla Gaxton* • Ward Bond *Doctor Joseph Holden* • Keith Andes *Captain Tom Gaxton* • Lee Marvin *Sergeant Lloyd Carracart* ■ *Dir* George Marshall • *Scr* Sam Rolfe, from the novel *Frontier Fury* by Will Henry

The Pillow Book ★★★★ 18

Erotic drama
1995 · Neth/Fr/UK · Colour and BW · 121mins

Extraordinary. Ravishing. Preposterous. The usual descriptions of director Peter Greenaway's work can all be applied here in spades. Even more overwrought and over-decorated than his previous films, Greenaway's Hong Kong-set tale of sex and power centres on the fetish of a woman (Vivian Wu) who enjoys having her flesh written upon, and who takes a dreadful revenge on the homosexual publisher who degraded her father. The split-screen motifs are a wonder to behold but, although it deals with white-hot emotions, the film (which co-stars Ewan McGregor) is as ice-cold as winter. Films with backing from the UK and France. In English and Japanese with subtitles. Contains violence, sex

scenes, drug abuse and nudity. 🖵
DVD

Vivian Wu *Nagiko* • Ewan McGregor *Jerome* • Yoshi Oida *Publisher* • Ken Ogata *Father* • Hideko Yoshida *Aunt/Maid* • Judy Ongg *Mother* • Ken Mitsuishi *Husband* ■ *Dir/Scr* Peter Greenaway

Pillow Talk ★★★★ PG

Romantic comedy
1959 · US · Colour · 98mins

The first and most entertaining of the series of comedies Doris Day made for Universal that gave the singing star a career lift and successfully teamed her with the likes of Cary Grant, James Garner and her most popular partner, Rock Hudson. This is ultra-glossy froth, and its smart plot about Day and Hudson sharing a telephone party line won an Oscar for best story and screenplay. Hudson displays a fine flair for adroit humour, but the funniest material goes to Tony Randall (never better) and the acerbic Thelma Ritter, and both shine through the heavily piled-on glamour (the hallmark of co-producer Ross Hunter). Director Michael Gordon's use of CinemaScope is exemplary. 🖵

Doris Day *Jan Morrow* • Rock Hudson *Brad Allen* • Tony Randall *Jonathan Forbes* • Thelma Ritter *Alma* • Nick Adams *Tony Walters* ■ *Dir* Michael Gordon • *Scr* Stanley Shapiro, Maurice Richlin, from a story by Russell Rouse, Clarence Greene

The Pilot ★★ PG

Drama   1979 · US · Colour · 93mins

Cliff Robertson directs, co-scripts and stars in this worthy drama about a once-lauded pilot's battle with alcoholism. It's a bit dull and, despite a quality supporting cast that includes Dana Andrews and Gordon MacRae, Robertson is clearly overstretched. Nevertheless, the fantastic aerial photography and stirring score help to stave off the ennui. 🖵

Cliff Robertson *Mike Hagan* • Diane Baker *Pat Simpson* • Frank Converse *Jim Cochran* • Dana Andrews *Randolph Evers* • Milo O'Shea *Dr O'Brian* • Gordon MacRae ■ *Dir* Cliff Robertson • *Scr* Cliff Robertson, Robert P Davis, from the novel by Robert P Davis • *Cinematographer* Walter Lassally • *Music* John Addison

Pilot #5 ★★

Second World War drama
1943 · US · BW · 70mins

A war effort melodrama about a lawyer, Franchot Tone, who's in league with a fascist politician. But then Tone atones for his misjudgment of character by becoming a fighter pilot. Told in a series of flashbacks, it's heavily contrived and rather dully directed by George Sidney, later famous for his musicals. Also famous for musicals was third-billed Gene Kelly, making his second film appearance as Tone's wartime buddy.

Franchot Tone *George Braynor Collins* • Marsha Hunt *Freddie* • Gene Kelly *Vito S Allesandro* • Van Johnson *Everett Arnold* • Alan Baxter *Winston Davis* • Dick Simmons *Henry Willoughby Clavens* • Steven Geray *Major Eichel* • Peter Lawford *Englishman* • Ava Gardner *Girl* ■ *Dir* George Sidney • *Scr* David Hertz

Pimpernel Smith ★★★★ U

Second World War spy drama
1941 · UK · BW · 115mins

A smashing piece of wartime propaganda with the screen's greatest Scarlet Pimpernel Leslie Howard updating the character to Nazi-occupied Europe. Howard also directs with style, and if the plot is preposterous – archaeologist Howard smuggles refugees out from under the very nose of the Gestapo and then goes back to Berlin to rescue a girl – it awakened the world, and particularly America, to Europe's plight. With this film, and both *The First of the Few* and *The Gentle Sex*, it became clear that Howard was a potent propaganda weapon.

Leslie Howard *Prof Horatio Smith* • Francis L Sullivan *Gen von Graum* • Mary Morris *Ludmilla Koslowski* • Hugh McDermott *David Maxwell* • Raymond Huntley *Marx* • Manning Whiley *Bertie Gregson* • Peter Gawthorne *Sidimir Kioslowski* • Allan Jeayes *Dr Beckendorf* • Michael Rennie *Officer at concentration camp* ■ *Dir* Leslie Howard • *Scr* Anatole De Grunwald, Roland Pertwee, Ian Dalrymple, from a story by AG MacDonell, Wolfgang Wilhelm

Pin ★★★★ 18

Psychological thriller
1988 · Can · Colour · 98mins

A first-rate psychological chiller, with David Hewlett giving the performance of his career as a schizophrenic who develops a symbiotic relationship with a medical mannequin called Pin. Broadly in the *Magic* vein, the film was written and directed by Sandor Stern, who also penned *The Amityville Horror*, and provides a truly spooky portrayal of a kid teetering on the tightrope between fantasy and reality. 🖵

David Hewlett *Leon* • Cyndy Preston *Ursula* • John Ferguson *Stan Fraker* • Terry O'Quinn *Dr Linden* • Bronwen Mantel *Mrs Linden* ■ *Dir* Sandor Stern • *Scr* Sandor Stern, from the novel by Andrew Neiderman

A Pin for the Butterfly ★★

Political drama
1994 · UK/Cz Rep · Colour · 113mins

Despite the excellent use of Prague locations and superb photography from Ivan Slapeta, this film lets itself down by its confused structure and an ill-chosen, but hard-working, British cast. Joan Plowright seems to have cornered the market in European matriarchs, and here her passively benign character is severely underwritten, while Ian Bannen merely reprises *Hope and Glory*'s Grandpa in a Slavonic setting. Most ill-at-ease,though, is Hugh Laurie's subversive uncle, while Imogen Stubbs as Zina at least enters into the spirit of the thing.

Florence Hoath *Marushka* • Imogen Stubbs *Mother* • Hugh Laurie *Uncle* • Ian Bannen *Grandpa* • Ian Hogg *Great Uncle* • Joan Plowright *Grandma* ■ *Dir/Scr* Hannah Kodicek

Pin Up Girl ★★ U

Musical comedy   1944 · US · Colour · 79mins

In her balmy days at 20th Century-Fox, pin-up queen Betty Grable was usually cushioned with glamorous leading men, zippy tunes and Technicolor to disguise the fact that, in her own words, she was "the original triple

threat – couldn't act, couldn't sing, couldn't dance". She might have also added "didn't matter", for her incandescent sheer good-naturedness won over the public's heart. In this opus, Betty's all there is, and bespectacled much of the time. There's a leading man (John Harvey) few people have heard of, little wit, few jokes, no decent songs and hardly any plot. Joe E Brown and Martha Raye add slight watchability, and the catchpennny title will attract die-hard fans, but, quite frankly, this one isn't terribly good.

Betty Grable *Lorry Jones* • John Harvey *Tommy Dooley* • Martha Raye *Marian* • Joe E Brown *Eddie* • Eugene Pallette *Barney Briggs* ■ *Dir H* Bruce Humberstone • *Scr* Robert Ellis, Helen Logan, Earl Baldwin, from a story by Libbie Block

Pink Cadillac ★★ 15

Comedy drama   1989 · US · Colour · 115mins

One of Clint Eastwood's rare mistakes. Lazily directed by his long-serving crony Buddy Van Horn, it's an overlong, straining-for-laughs comedy about a bounty hunter (Eastwood) and a runaway wife (Bernadette Peters) and various mentally challenged white supremacists. Instead of an orang-utan, Eastwood has to contend with Peters's baby. The car, though, looks great, even if it does hide a stash of drugs and another endless subplot, and if you blink you may miss the then unknown Jim Carrey. Contains violence and swearing.

Clint Eastwood *Tommy Nowak* • Bernadette Peters *Lou Ann McGuinn* • Timothy Carhart *Roy McGuinn* • John Dennis Johnston *Waycross* • Michael Des Barres *Alex* • Geoffrey Lewis *Ricky Z* • William Hickey *Barton* • Frances Fisher *Dinah* • Jim Carrey *Lounge entertainer* ■ *Dir* Buddy Van Horn • *Scr* John Eskow

Pink Flamingos ★★★★★ 18

Underground satire
1972 · US · Colour · 100mins

The film that not only defined bad taste, but also unashamedly celebrated it. Cult director John Waters's notorious gross-out has upstart perverts David Lochary and Mink Stole trying to wrest the honour of "Filthiest Person Alive" from the tenacious grip of sleaze superstar Divine. Chicken sex, a singing rectum, artificial insemination, lesbian motherhood and the incomparable Edith Massey are paraded before our increasingly appalled eyes in this screamingly funny shocker. Featuring the infamous coda where Divine eats a dog turd (for real), Waters's unique obscenity is the grandfather of midnight movies. Contains swearing, sex scenes and violence. 🖵

Divine *Babs Johnson/Divine* • David Lochary *Raymond Marble* • Mary Vivian Pearce *Cotton* • Mink Stole *Connie Marble* • Danny Mills *Crackers* • Edith Massey *Mama Edie* • Channing Wilroy *Channing* • Cookie Mueller *Cookie* ■ *Dir/Scr* John Waters

Pink Floyd – The Wall ★ 15

Musical drama   1982 · UK · Colour · 91mins

This indulgent monstrosity was dismissed at the time as a one and a half hour pop promo; hardly fair, as few of the music videos of the period were as banal as this adaptation of Pink Floyd's concept album. The subject is the disintegration of a rock star played by Bob Geldof, the style is derivative of *Tommy*, and, although exquisitely photographed, many of the images are unbelievably naive (the school system is represented by a line of faceless children falling into a mincing machine). What a waste of director Alan Parker's talent. 🖵 *DVD*

Bob Geldof *Pink* • Christine Hargreaves *Pink's mother* • James Laurenson *Pink's father* • Eleanor David *Pink's wife* • Kevin McKeon *Young Pink* • Bob Hoskins *Band manager* • David Bingham *Little Pink* • Jenny Wright *American groupie* ■ *Dir* Alan Parker • *Scr* Roger Waters, from the album by Pink Floyd • *Animator* Gerald Scarfe • *Cinematographer* Peter Biziou

The Pink Jungle ★★★ U

Crime caper   1968 · US · Colour · 103mins

James Garner plays a fashion photographer who is stranded in the South American jungle with model Eva Renzi when George Kennedy steals their helicopter in his quest to locate a hidden diamond mine. Blending elements from *North by Northwest*, *The Maltese Falcon* and *King Solomon's Mines*, this is a jolly caper that manages to be tense and spoofish at the same time. Garner is his usual charming self, while Kennedy, who plays everything for laughs, is very amusing.

James Garner *Ben Morris* • Eva Renzi *Alison Duquesne* • George Kennedy *Sammy Ryderbeit* • Nigel Green *Crowley* • Michael Ansara *Raul Ortega* ■ *Dir* Delbert Mann • *Scr* Charles Williams, from the novel *Snake Water* by Alan Williams

The Pink Panther ★★★★ PG

Comedy   1964 · US · Colour · 110mins

Peter Sellers went into this film as character support and came out an international star. David Niven is the ostensible lead in a rather dull setting-up of the plot, in which the bumbling Inspector Clouseau is called in to prevent the theft of a precious diamond – the Pink Panther. But Sellers's dud officer was so scene-stealingly comic that director Blake Edwards inserted new scenes. The rest is hysterical history. See it from the beginning: the cartoon title sequence with its Henry Mancini theme is an in-the-pink joy. 🖵

David Niven *Sir Charles* • Peter Sellers *Inspector Jacques Clouseau* • Robert Wagner *George* • Capucine *Simone Clouseau* • Claudia Cardinale *Princess Dala* • Brenda de Banzie *Angela Dunning* • John Le Mesurier *Defence attorney* ■ *Dir* Blake Edwards • *Scr* Maurice Richlin, Blake Edwards • *Title animator* DePatie-Freleng

The Pink Panther Strikes Again ★★★ PG

Comedy   1976 · UK · Colour · 98mins

The critics were divided on the fourth entry in Blake Edwards's *Pink Panther* series. Some thought that Chief Inspector Dreyfus's increasingly desperate attempts to bump off the incompetent Clouseau were a riot of bawdy humour and inspired slapstick, while others considered the film to be a repetitive rehash in which the same

gag was worked to death without ever really being funny. The box-office evidence seems to suggest that the public voted with the ''pro'' lobby, but there is a shortage of inspiration here, even though Herbert Lom gives his best performance of the series, while Peter Sellers ingeniously makes his blissful ignorance of events seem hilarious. 🖵

Peter Sellers *Jacques Clouseau* • Herbert Lom *Dreyfus* • Colin Blakely *Alec Drummond* • Leonard Rossiter *Superintendent Quinlan* • Lesley-Anne Down *Olga* • Bert Kwouk *Cato* • André Maranne *François* ■ *Dir* Blake Edwards • *Scr* Frank Waldman, Blake Edwards

Pink String and Sealing Wax ★★★

Crime drama   1945 · UK · BW · 95mins

Set in Victorian Brighton, this roaring melodrama is adapted from Roland Pertwee's stage success, which takes its title from the way in which pharmacists used to wrap parcels containing poison. There's not an ounce of subtlety in either the acting or in Robert Hamer's direction, but the film is none the worse for that, as restraint would have rendered the whole production ridiculous. The villains have all the fun, with Mervyn Johns unexpectedly severe as the tyrannical father, Garry Marsh on career best form as the brutal husband and Googie Withers gloriously wicked as the landlady leading timid Gordon Jackson astray.

Mervyn Johns *Mr Edward Sutton* • Googie Withers *Pearl Bond* • Gordon Jackson *David Sutton* • Sally Ann Howes *Peggy Sutton* • Mary Merrall *Mrs Ellen Sutton* • Catherine Lacey *Miss Porter* • Garry Marsh *Joe Bond* ■ *Dir* Robert Hamer • *Scr* Diana Morgan, Robert Hamer, from the play by Roland Pertwee

The Pink Telephone ★★

Drama   1975 · Fr · Colour · 93mins

Pierre Mondy is a naive, middle-aged provincial industrialist whose business problems lead him to consider selling his factory to an American company. The would-be buyers put him up in a luxury hotel and introduce him to Mareille Darc, with whom he falls in love. The film offers some impeccable acting, an attractive female lead in Darc, and the suggestion of insight into ruthless business methods; unfortunately, neither writer nor director seems certain whether this is comedy or drama. Eduoard Molinaro's crude direction only helps to wreck the enterprise. A French language film.

Mireille Darc *Christine* • Pierre Mondy *Benoît Castejac* • Michel Lonsdale *Morrison* • Daniel Ceccaldi *Levêque* • Françoise Prévost *Benoît's wife* ■ *Dir* Edouard Molinaro • *Scr* Francis Veber

Pinky ★★★

Drama   1949 · US · BW · 101mins

One of a group of important Hollywood movies – *Lost Boundaries*, *Gentlemen's Agreement*, *Home of the Brave* – that dealt with serious racial issues in the wake of the Second World War. Although these films may seem naive and dated to today's audiences, getting them made at all was in itself an achievement, and discussed by

the general public of the time little short of miraculous. Here, the white Jeanne Crain gives an affecting performance in the lead, though cast in a role patently requiring a black actress, but the film probably would not have been made otherwise, and Ethel Waters is marvellous as the southern grandmother she visits. Elia Kazan took over the directorial reins from John Ford and the result is extremely moving, despite the resolutely unconvincing studio interior sets.

Jeanne Crain *Pinky, Patricia Johnson* • Ethel Barrymore *Miss Em* • Ethel Waters *Granny Dysey Johnson* • William Lundigan *Dr Thomas Adams* • Basil Ruysdael *Judge Walker* • Kenny Washington *Dr Canady* ■ *Dir* Elia Kazan • *Scr* Philip Dunne, Dudley Nichols, from the novel *Quality* by Cid Ricketts Sumner

Pinocchio ★★★★★ U

Animated classic   1940 · US · Colour · 83mins

Some films you think you know well, until you revisit them, and are struck all over again by that sense of wonder that moved you in the first place. This is the case with all of Disney's early feature-length cartoons: they have enthralled us for so long that we take them for granted. There is just such a magic in this tale of the little wooden boy, and we have Walt Disney – not original author Carlo Collodi – to thank for the knowledge that telling lies makes your nose grow, and that your conscience should always be your guide. Meanwhile, Jiminy Cricket, Figaro, Geppetto and Monstro the Whale, and even those arch-felons who lead wayward boys to Pleasure Island, have all become a part of 20th-century mythology. The score, which includes the song that became Disney's anthem, *When You Wish upon a Star*, is magnificent, as is the artistic technique and use of early Technicolor. Oh, and children will enjoy it, too. 🖵

Dickie Jones *Pinocchio* • Cliff Edwards *Jiminy Cricket* • Christian Rub *Geppetto* • Evelyn Venable *The Blue Fairy* ■ *Dir* Ben Sharpsteen, Hamilton Luske • *Scr* Ted Sears, Otto Englander, Webb Smith, William Cottrell, Joseph Sabo, Erdman Penner, Aurelius Battaglia, from the story by Carlo Collodi

Pinocchio's Revenge ★★

Horror   1996 · US · Colour · 96mins

Despite centering on a wooden doll named Pinocchio, this film has no connection to the classic children's tale. The doll in question, previously owned by a father who murdered his son, comes into the possession of a troubled little girl. But is she or Pinocchio responsible for the ''accidents'' that befall her enemies soon after? The movie never says for sure, finishing instead with a weak and inconclusive ending. Its ample merits don't prevent it from being a fancily wrapped but fundamentally empty package.

Rosalind Allen *Jennifer Garrick* • Lewis Van Bergen *Vincent Gotto* • Brittany Alyse Smith *Zoe Garrick* • Todd Allen *David Kaminsky* • Aaron Lustig *Dr Edwards* ■ *Dir* Kevin Tenney [Kevin S Tenney] • *Scr* Kevin Tenney

Pipe Dreams ★★★ U

Drama   1976 · US · Colour · 89mins

Having launched a number of acting careers (including Sylvester Stallone's) in his own co-directing debut *The Lords of Flatbush*, director Stephen Verona focused on a first-time thespian of a different kind for his initial solo venture. Disco diva Gladys Knight acquits herself admirably as a woman who journeys to Alaska to find her husband (Barry Hankerson, to whom she was married in real life) who is working on the pipeline there. The scarcity of women in the frontier town means the only roommate she can find is prostitute Shirley Bain. Slight but sensitively handled, followers of the singer will welcome the chance to appreciate her talents in this mildly successful new context.

Gladys Knight *Maria Wilson* • Wayne Tippit *Mike Thompson* • Barry Hankerson *Rob Wilson* • Altovise Davis *Lydia* • Bruce French *Duke* • Sylvia Hayes *Sally* ■ *Dir/Scr* Stephen Verona

The Piper's Tune ★★ U

Historical adventure   1962 · UK · BW · 62mins

Muriel Box, the most prolific woman director in British screen history, made her first foray into costume adventure with this, her penultimate picture. Clearly aimed at a younger audience, it focuses on a gang of children whose attempts to flee the chaos of the Napoleonic Wars are jeopardised by a seemingly kindly doctor. Box and screenwriter Michael Barnes valiantly seek to convey the uncertainties of the period, and Frederick Piper shows well as the treacherous spy. But the inexperience of the juveniles, and a lack of finance, fatally undermines their efforts to bring weight and scale to the action.

Mavis Ranson *Anna* • Roberta Tovey *Suzy* • Angela White *Maria* • Malcolm Ranson *Thomas* • Brian Wills *Paul* • Graham Wills *Peter* ■ *Dir* Muriel Box • *Scr* Michael Barnes, from a story by Frank Wells

Pippi Longstocking ★★

Adventure   1968 · Swe · Colour · 99mins

This adventure for Astrid Lindgren's popular character was successful enough to warrant two sequels by the same team. Pippi is a super-strong, red-haired nine-year-old who leads a wild, independent life with her pet monkey and horse while her sea captain father is apparently lost at sea. The primitive dubbing may irritate grown-ups, but children will find it cheerful and enjoyable. Swedish dialogue dubbed into English.

Inger Nilsson *Pippi Longstocking* • Maria Persson *Annika* • Paer Sundberg *Tommy* • Oellegard Welton *Mother* • Fredrik Ohlsson *Father* • Hans Alfredson *Konrad* • Margot Trooger *Miss Prusselius* • Beppe Wolgers *Captain Longstocking* ■ *Dir* Olle Hellbom • *Scr* Astrid Lindgren

Pippi Longstocking ★★★ U

Animated adventure   1997 · Swe/Ger/Can · Colour · 75 mins.

Astrid Lindgren's perky heroine comes to the big screen in this lively animated adventure, packed with the uplifting values that characterise her

U = SUITABLE FOR ALL   Uc = SUITABLE FOR ALL, ESPECIALLY FOR YOUNG CHILDREN (VIDEO ONLY)   PG = PARENTAL GUIDANCE

original stories. Fans of *Home Alone* would be forgiven for thinking that Pippi and Kevin share an affinity for booby traps as the strongest girl in the world (appropriately voiced at full belt by Melissa Altro) battles a nosey, interfering neighbour and a couple of bungling burglars. Though not up to Disney standards, there's still enough here to keep little girls amused: animation that's full of colour and vitality, a couple of rousing musical numbers and some appealing animals in tow.

Melissa Altro *Pippi Longstocking* • Dave Thomas (2) *Thunder-Karlsson* • Catherine O'Hara *Mrs Prysselius* • Gordon Pinsent *Captain Longstocking* • Carole Pope *The Teacher* • Wayne Robson *Bloom* • Richard Binsley *Mr Nilsson/Dog* • Rick Jones *O'Malley* ■ *Dir* Clive Smith • *Scr* Catharina Stackelberg, from the books by Astrid Lindgren

Piranha ★★★ 18
Horror 1978 · US · Colour · 90mins

A sly, witty cash-in on *Jaws*, with director Joe Dante and writer John Sayles dreaming up a deliriously silly tale about a shoal of killer fish, bred by the army for use in Vietnam, which escapes and munches its way through the waterways of America. Bradford Dillman keeps an admirably straight face as the hero and there are neat supporting turns from Kevin McCarthy, Keenan Wynn, Dick Miller and Barbara Steele. Even at this early stage of his career, Dante embellishes the film with an array of references to other movies, and the laughs and blood flow in equal measure. Contains violence, swearing and brief nudity.

Bradford Dillman *Paul Grogan* • Heather Menzies *Maggie McKeown* • Kevin McCarthy *Dr Robert Hoak* • Keenan Wynn *Jack* • Dick Miller *Buck Gardner* • Barbara Steele *Dr Mengers* ■ *Dir* Joe Dante • *Scr* John Sayles, from a story by Richard Robinson, John Sayles

Piranha ★★
Horror 1996 · US · Colour · 90 mins

Not the Joe Dante *Jaws* parody, but a TV movie based on the same John Sayles script. Flesh and ferocity are the order of the day as scientists William Katt and Alexandra Paul accidentally let loose some genetically modified snappers into the tributary running through the holiday resort of Lost River. But Scott Levy's horror movie remake is devoid of the knowing references that always make Dante's films so much fun. It takes the premise far too seriously and is overly preoccupied with blood-letting special effects at the expense of character development and suspense. Contains swearing, violence and nudity.

William Katt *Paul Grogan* • Alexandra Paul *Maggie MacNamara* • Monte Markham *JR Randolph* • Darleen Carr *Dr Leticia Baines* • Mila Kunis *Susie Grogan* ■ *Dir* Scott Levy • *Scr* Alex Simon, from the film 1978 film

Piranha II: The Spawning ★ 18
Horror 1983 · Neth · Colour · 90mins

An appalling follow-up to Joe Dante's entertaining original. The performances are amateurish (even a young Lance Henriksen lacks conviction), the direction is leaden and the deadly fish are laughably bargain-basement. So it comes as a bit of a shock to find that this was the feature debut of James Cameron. There have been some really awful *Jaws* imitations, but you won't find a worse one than this.

Tricia O'Neil *Anne Kimbrough* • Steve Marachuk *Tyler* • Lance Henriksen *Steve Kimbrough* • Ricky G Paull *Chris Kimbrough* • Ted Richert *Raoul* • Leslie Graves *Allison* ■ *Dir* James Cameron • *Scr* HA Milton

The Pirate ★★★★ U
Musical 1948 · US · Colour · 97mins

A picturesque and largely enjoyable MGM musical swashbuckler that was a commercial flop in its day but has since picked up a considerable following. Its latter-day popularity stems more from the Cole Porter songs, opulent sets and lavish choreography than from the story about a sheltered young woman who dreams of escape and adventure with a glamorous pirate. Vincente Minnelli directs his wife Judy Garland and Gene Kelly with gusto and panache.

Judy Garland *Manuela* • Gene Kelly *Serafin* • Walter Slezak *Don Pedro Vargas* • Gladys Cooper *Aunt Inez* • Reginald Owen *Advocate* • George Zucco *Viceroy* ■ *Dir* Vincente Minnelli • *Scr* Albert Hackett, Frances Goodrich, from the play by SN Behrman

The Pirate Movie ★★ PG
Adventure 1982 · Ausl · Colour · 94mins

A peculiar Australian adaptation of Gilbert and Sullivan's operetta, *The Pirates Of Penzance*, released around the same time as a star-studded American version. Kristy McNichol plays a young girl who dreams she's involved in the *Penzance* plot – a leaden rewrite that's hardly helped by Ken Annakin's plodding direction. Aussie stalwart Bill Kerr also turns up; there are some who believe you can't make a movie Down Under without him.

Kristy McNichol *Mabel* • Christopher Atkins *Frederic* • Ted Hamilton *Pirate King* • Bill Kerr *Major General* • Maggie Kirkpatrick *Ruth* • Garry McDonald *Sergeant Inspector* • Chuck McKinney *Samuel* • Marc Colombani *Dwarf pirate* ■ *Dir* Ken Annakin • *Scr* Trevor Farrant, from the operetta *The Pirates of Penzance* by WS Gilbert, by Arthur Sullivan

Pirates ★ 15
Adventure 1986 · Fr/Tun · Colour · 107mins

One of the biggest flops in cinema history, Roman Polanski's *Pirates* began taking shape in 1974, immediately after *Chinatown*. Polanski wanted Jack Nicholson to play the lead in what would be a lark, a send-up of Errol Flynn movies and their ilk – a lark, however, that Hollywood wouldn't underwrite. But a dozen years later Polanski found Tunisian backers and shot the picture in the Seychelles with Walter Matthau hiding behind a forest of face-fur, walking on a wooden leg and talking Hollywood-cockney. The waste of money and talent, together with the sub-Python japes, make this a uniquely depressing experience. The spectacular million-dollar galleon built for the film was later moored at Cannes to serve as a warning to producers with grandiose ideas and no script.

Walter Matthau *Captain Red* • Cris Campion *Jean-Baptiste, "the Frog"* • Damien Thomas *Don Alfonso* • Olu Jacobs *Boumako* • Ferdy Mayne *Captain Linares* • David Kelly *Surgeon* • Charlotte Lewis *Dolores* • Anthony Peck *Spanish officer* • Anthony Dawson *Spanish officer* • Roy Kinnear *Dutch* ■ *Dir* Roman Polanski • *Scr* Gerard Brach, Roman Polanski, John Brownjohn

Pirates' Island ★★
Adventure 1990 · Ausl · Colour

A breezy Australian adventure straight out of childhood dreams, featuring youngsters marooned on a mysterious island, evil pirates and a rescue bid. There's plenty of enthusiasm from the cast, both young and old, and director Viktor Ritelis approaches his task with equal relish.

Les Hill *Tony* • Beth Buchanan *Sarah* • Matthew Doran *Grommet* • Dan Chesterman *Brad* • Daniel Funnell *Ahab* ■ *Dir* Viktor Ritelis

The Pirates of Blood River ★★ U
Swashbuckling adventure 1961 · UK · Colour · 94mins

In its present version, this Hammer swashbuckler is a colourful, action-packed adventure for undemanding kids. Kerwin Mathews, all-American hero in several other British films in the sixties, is a Huguenot who falls into the clutches of pirate king Christopher Lee, a buccaneer complete with eye-patch and hook. Lee attempts to use Mathews in a dastardly plan to steal Huguenot riches. There are wenches and scurvy knaves galore, but only tantalising vestiges of the X-rated bloodbath intended, as the film was reduced to U certificate derring-do for the school holidays after long sessions at the censor's office.

Christopher Lee *LaRoche* • Kerwin Mathews *Jonathan Standing* • Glenn Corbett *Henry* • Marla Landi *Bess* • Oliver Reed *Brocaire* • Andrew Keir *Jason Standing* • Dennis Waterman *Timothy* ■ *Dir* John Gilling • *Scr* John Gilling, John Hunter, from a story by Jimmy Sangster

The Pirates of Malaysia ★★
Swashbuckling action adventure 1964 · It/W Ger · Colour

Former Mr Universe Steve Reeves was coming to the end of his reign as the "sword and sandal" king of Italian movies when he took the lead in *Sandokan the Great* in 1963. He reprises the role in this brash spaghetti swashbuckler, in which he once more does battle with the forces of the British Empire. Director Umberto Lenzi keeps the action fast and furious as kidnappings, sea skirmishes, rescues and revolutions appear with alarming speed. Although beginning to look his age, Reeves plays the Tiger of Malaya with suitable vim. Italian dialogue dubbed into English.

Steve Reeves *Sandokan* • Jacqueline Sassard *Princess of Sarawak* • Andrea Bosic *Yanez* • Ananda Kumar *Tuang Olon* ■ *Dir* Umberto Lenzi • *Scr* Fulvio Gicca, Umberto Lenzi

The Pirates of Penzance ★★★ U
Musical 1983 · US · Colour · 107mins

Director Wilford Leach adapted Joseph Papp's famously successful stage production of Gilbert and Sullivan's popular operetta, retaining the original cast plus Angela Lansbury as Ruth. Kevin Kline repeated his rich performance as the Pirate King, with Linda Ronstadt as Mabel and George Rose as "the very model of a model major-general", while the familiar and much-loved score was pepped up with a contemporary treatment by William Elliott. The film nonetheless retains the essential spirit of the D'Oyly Carte original and provides an approximate record of Papp's 1980 smash hit. But the high-spirited energy of the experienced cast can't disguise the show's theatrical origins, and the whole enterprise is somewhat dwarfed by the Panavision screen.

Kevin Kline *Pirate King* • Angela Lansbury *Ruth* • Linda Ronstadt *Mabel* • George Rose *Major-General* • Tony Azito *Sergeant* ■ *Dir* Wilford Leach • *Scr* Wilford Leach, from the operetta by WS Gilbert and Arthur Sullivan

The Pit and the Pendulum ★★★★ 15
Horror 1961 · US · Colour · 76mins

Roger Corman's seminal series of Edgar Allan Poe adaptations ensures that he can never be dismissed as just a purveyor of schlock. This followed the first in the cycle, *The Fall of the House of Usher*, and boasts an intelligent script from Richard Matheson and another fine performance from Vincent Price. He plays the sinister Nicholas Medina, haunted by his father's tortuous past in the days of the Inquisition. Corman creates a suitably gothic air and works wonders with a limited budget.

Vincent Price *Nicholas Medina* • Barbara Steele *Elizabeth Barnard Medina* • John Kerr *Francis Barnard* • Luana Anders *Catherine Medina* • Antony Carbone *Dr Charles Leon* ■ *Dir* Roger Corman • *Scr* Richard Matheson, from the story by Edgar Allan Poe

The Pit and the Pendulum ★★★ 18
Horror 1991 · US · Colour · 92mins

Like the 1961 version, this film pretty much ignores Edgar Allan Poe's original story. The action takes place during the Spanish Inquisition and focuses on Inquisitor-General Torquemada (Lance Henriksen) who, attracted to a baker's wife (Rona De Ricci) accused of witchcraft, makes plans to do away with her husband (Jonathan Fuller). Henriksen hams it up in this slick period piece, while *Re-Animator* director Stuart Gordon gives the torture scenes a gleefully ghoulish edge. The screenplay also has an interesting serious side to it, illustrating how absolute power corrupts absolutely.

Lance Henriksen *Torquemada* • Rona De Ricci *Maria* • Jonathan Fuller *Antonio* • Frances Bay *Esmeralda* • Jeffrey Combs *Francisco* • Oliver Reed *Cardinal* ■ *Dir* Stuart Gordon • *Scr* Dennis Paoli, from the story by Edgar Allan Poe

Pit of Darkness ★ U
Crime drama 1961 · UK · BW · 76mins

William Franklyn had the misfortune to land the lead in this desperate B-feature, as a safe-maker who loses his memory and finds himself implicated in a jewel robbery. With assassination attempts coming thicker than clues, the plot plods along to its predictable conclusion at Leonard Sachs's nightclub. In spite of the best efforts of writer/director Lance Comfort and a talented cast, this is, sadly, awful.

William Franklyn *Richard Logan* • Moira Redmond *Julie Logan* • Bruno Barnabe *Maxie* • Leonard Sachs *Conrad* • Nigel Green *Jonathan* • Anthony Booth *Ted Mellis* • Nanette Newman *Mary* ■ *Dir* Lance Comfort • *Scr* Lance Comfort, from the novel *To Dusty Death* by Hugh McCutcheon

Pitch Black ★★★★ 15
Science-fiction thriller 2000 · Ausl/US · Colour · 110mins

It might start out resembling another assembly-line sci-fi saga. But once the eclectic crew of a doomed rocketship crash-land on an arid planet with three suns, David N Twohy's visually stunning, supremely scary and fast-paced adventure turns as thrilling as it is imaginatively striking. For a tri-solar eclipse occurs on this sun-bleached world, prompting screeching, flesh-hungry native creatures to emerge from its cavernous depths. Our heroes' one chance of survival is to find a disused spacecraft in the dark, and only hardened prisoner Vin Diesel can lead them there. So begins a dazzling matrix of breathtaking shock twists, with Diesel giving a charismatic performance.

Radha Mitchell *Fry* • Vin Diesel *Riddick* • Cole Hauser *Johns* • Keith David *Imam* • Lewis Fitz-Gerald *Paris* • Claudia Black *Shazza* ■ *Dir* David N Twohy • *Scr* Jim Wheat, Ken Wheat, David N Twohy, from a story by Jim Wheat, Ken Wheat • *Cinematographer* David Eggby • *Production Designer* Graham Walker

Pitfall ★★★★
Film noir 1948 · US · BW · 85mins

Bored with his perfect wife and son, an insurance agent falls for a charmer with tragic results in this excellent adult drama, which takes *film noir* into the world of middle-class domesticity. Unlike Fred MacMurray's character in *Double Indemnity*, this agent (Dick Powell) is basically honest, but that doesn't stop his momentary philandering leading to deceit and murder. Lizabeth Scott excelled in such roles as the seductive adventuress, and Raymond Burr is superbly sleazy as the villain of the piece. Andre De Toth maintains a tense pace in a film with a surprisingly modern view of the American Dream turned sour.

Dick Powell *John Forbes* • Lizabeth Scott *Mona Stevens* • Jane Wyatt *Sue Forbes* • Raymond Burr *Mack MacDonald* • John Litel *District Attorney* • Byron Barr *Bill Smiley* • Jimmy Hunt *Tommy Forbes* • Ann Doran *Maggie* ■ *Dir* Andre De Toth • *Scr* Karl Kamb, from the novel by Jay Dratler

Pittsburgh ★★
Melodrama 1942 · US · BW · 91mins

John Wayne, Marlene Dietrich and Randolph Scott star in this drama about coal mining in Pittsburgh. Wayne and Scott own the mine but operate it differently: Wayne is the ruthless capitalist, while Scott is more concerned with the health and safety of the workforce. Dietrich is sort of in the middle, though the movie isn't much interested in romance: it's 1942 and there's a war on. Dietrich, the exile from Hitler, weighs in with a stirring speech: "This is no time to think of personal feelings and personal grievances. The only question that should guide each of you is... devotion to your country. That's the one thing you should think about. Your country needs you."

Marlene Dietrich *Josie Winters* • Randolph Scott *Cash Evans* • John Wayne *Pittsburgh "Pitt" Markham* • Frank Craven *Doc Powers* • Louise Allbritton *Shannon Prentiss* ■ *Dir* Lewis Seiler • *Scr* Kenneth Gamet, Tom Reed, John Twist, from a story by George Owen, from Tom Reed

Pixote ★★★★★ 18
Drama 1981 · Bra · Colour · 119mins

The knowledge that Fernando Ramos Da Silva was killed in a shoot-out with the cops just six years after playing a 10-year-old orphan inexorably drawn into a living hell of prostitution, drugs and murder makes Hector Babenco's ultra-realistic picture of São Paulo streetlife all the more chilling. Da Silva genuinely lives a role that stands as an indictment of us all. Adapted from José Louzeiro's novel *Infancia dos Mortos*, the film has justifiably been compared to Luis Buñuel's *Los Olvidados* and François Truffaut's *The 400 Blows*, as it focuses on the facts of an appalling situation, without offering glib socio-political solutions. In Portuguese with English subtitles. ▣

Fernando Ramos Da Silva *Pixote* • Marilia Pêra *Sueli* • Jorge Juliao *Lilica* • Gilberto Moura *Dito* • José Nilson Dos Santos *Diego* • Jardel Filho *Sapatos Brancos* ■ *Dir* Hector Babenco • *Scr* Hector Babenco, Jorge Duran, from the novel *Infancia dos Mortos* by José Louzeiro

Pizza Man ★★
Comedy 1991 · US · Colour · 90mins

Comedian Bill Maher flexed his satirical muscles in this wacky political comedy about a pizza delivery man who stumbles upon a huge scandal featuring many of the top political figures of the day. A broad sideswipe at policies and personalities from all parties, the film casts its net wide but ends up like a pizza with too many toppings: it might look good on the menu, but it's a bit too much to swallow.

Bill Maher *Elmo Bunn* • Annabelle Gurwitch *The Dame* • David McKnight *Vince* • Andy Romano *The Hood* • Bob Delegall *Mayor Bradley* • Bryan Clark *Ronald Reagan* • Cathy Shambley *Geraldine Ferraro* • Ron Darian *Michael Dukakis* ■ *Dir/Scr* JF Lawton

A Place for Annie ★★★★ PG
Drama 1994 · US · Colour · 95mins

The year before she gave such an impressive performance as the HIV-positive Robin in *Boys on the Side*, Mary-Louise Parker produced another powerful portrayal of a young woman with Aids in this deeply affecting TV movie. She is admirably supported by Sissy Spacek as the nurse who wants to adopt the HIV-infected baby Parker has abandoned, and by Joan Plowright and S Epatha Merkerson as, respectively, a nanny and a social worker caught up in the case. This goes to show just what can be done with a true-life drama if it's handled with intelligence rather than sensationalism. ▣

Sissy Spacek *Susan Lansing* • Mary-Louise Parker *Linda Morsten* • Joan Plowright *Dorothy Kilgore* • S Epatha Merkerson *Alice Blakely* • Jack Noseworthy *David Lansing* • David Spielberg *Dr Palmer* ■ *Dir* John Gray • *Scr* Lee Guthrie, Cathleen Young, Nancy Barr

A Place for Lovers ★
Romantic drama 1969 · It/Fr · Colour · 88mins

Italy is the setting for this sudsy film in which American divorcee and fashion designer Faye Dunaway falls in love with engineer Marcello Mastroianni. Well, she would, wouldn't she? She did in reality as well, leading to a well-publicised affair with the archetypal Latin lover. The movie is trash of a fairly low order and might have been made in the thirties, possibly with Joan Crawford. The twist in the tale is that Dunaway is suffering from a terminal disease. Director Vittorio De Sica had clearly come a long way from such neorealist classics as *Bicycle Thieves* and *Umberto D*.

Faye Dunaway *Julia* • Marcello Mastroianni *Valerio* • Caroline Mortimer *Maggie* • Karin Engh *Griselda* ■ *Dir* Vittorio De Sica • *Scr* Vittorio De Sica, Julian Halevy [Julian Zimet], Peter Baldwin, Ennio de Concini, Tonino Guerra, Cesare Zavattini, from a story by Brunello Rondi

A Place in the Sun ★★★★
Drama 1951 · US · BW · 133mins

Elizabeth Taylor never looked lovelier, or the young Montgomery Clift more tortured than in this glossy adaptation of Theodore Dreiser's dour novel *An American Tragedy*, previously filmed by Josef von Sternberg. This film won six Oscars, including best director for George Stevens, whose trademark dissolves are most tellingly displayed as Clift and Taylor meet for the first time. Trouble is, this tale of love across the tracks has dated badly, and today seems rather drawn out. But Clift and, especially, Shelley Winters are brilliant, so forget the plot and just revel in what was once Hollywood's idea of classy movie-making.

Montgomery Clift *George Eastman* • Elizabeth Taylor *Angela Vickers* • Shelley Winters *Alice Tripp* • Anne Revere *Hannah Eastman* • Raymond Burr *Marlowe* • Herbert Heyes *Charles Eastman* • Keefe Brasselle *Earl Eastman* ■ *Dir* George Stevens • *Scr* Michael Wilson, Harry Brown, from the play *An American Tragedy* by Patrick Kearney, from the novel *An American Tragedy* by Theodore Dreiser • *Cinematographer* William C Mellor • *Costume Designer* Edith Head

A Place in the World ★★
Drama 1992 · Arg/Urug · Colour · 120mins

An enormous hit with Argentinian audiences, this story about the inhabitants of a small farming village uniting to oppose the forces of grasping capitalism is both naive and long-winded. Director Adolfo Aristarain is clearly determined to say something momentous but, as earnestly as his characters talk, they never come up with anything other than empty aphorisms. The gritty shepherd, the cursing nun and the poetic geologist all border on caricature, but in other places Aristarain's genuine sympathy for and understanding of the peasant population is both touching and astute. In Spanish with English subtitles.

Jose Sacristan *Hans* • Federico Luppi *Mario* • Cecilia Roth *Ana* • Leonor Benedetto *Nelda* ■ *Dir* Adolfo Aristarain • *Scr* Adolfo Aristarain, Alberto Lecchi

A Place of One's Own ★★★ U
Supernatural drama 1944 · UK · BW · 88mins

A genuinely eerie adaptation of Osbert Sitwell's novel of strange happenings in an English country house. Former cameraman turned director Bernard Knowles knows just how to achieve the right spine-chilling touch, keeping the supernatural themes cleverly light in tone. The cast is delightful, with James Mason and Barbara Mullen as the retired homeowners, and lovely Margaret Lockwood as their companion who is the catalyst for the ghostly goings-on. *Bride of Frankenstein* veteran Ernest Thesiger steals the show as old Dr Marsham, who isn't exactly what he appears, and there's nice support from Dennis Price and Dulcie Gray, too. Time has lent this Gainsborough picture a veneer of charm – well worth watching. ▣

Margaret Lockwood *Annette* • James Mason *Mr Smedhurst* • Barbara Mullen *Mrs Smedhurst* • Dennis Price *Dr Selbie* • Helen Haye *Mrs Manning-Tuthorn* • Michael Shepley *Major Manning-Tuthorn* • Dulcie Gray *Sarah* ■ *Dir* Bernard Knowles • *Scr* Brock Williams, from the novel by Osbert Sitwell

A Place to Go ★★
Crime drama 1963 · UK · BW · 88mins

Sometimes not even a gifted director can save a film from disintegrating. Basil Dearden had worked so often with Michael Relph (here the producer and co-scriptwriter) that it's tempting to suggest Dearden did this lacklustre crime movie so as not to hurt Relph's feelings. Michael Sarne goes all mean and moody to unfortunately comic effect as he bids to beat the Bethnal Green blues with an ill-conceived factory heist. Rita Tushingham and Bernard Lee do what they can with a dodgy script, while Dearden captures something of the flavour of the East End. But a simmering, realist classic this is not.

Bernard Lee *Matt Flint* • Rita Tushingham *Catherine* • Michael Same *Ricky Flint* • Doris Hare *Lil Flint* • Barbara Ferris *Betsy* • John Slater *Jack Ellerman* • David Andrews *Jim* • Roy Kinnear *Bunting* ■ *Dir* Basil Dearden • *Scr* Michael Relph, Clive Exton, from the novel *Bethnal Green* by Michael Fisher

Place Vendôme ★★★ 15
Romantic thriller 1998 · Fr · Colour · 118mins

Catherine Deneuve won the best actress prize at Venice for her performance as an alcoholic widow recovering her sense of worth in this mannered thriller from actress-turned-

U = SUITABLE FOR ALL   Uc = SUITABLE FOR ALL, ESPECIALLY FOR YOUNG CHILDREN (VIDEO ONLY)   PG = PARENTAL GUIDANCE

director Nicole Garcia. While her icy detachment and vulnerability are impressive, there's no real sense of danger underlying this tale of duplicitous diamond dealing. Evading industry regulators, Russian mafiosi and the lover who once betrayed her (Jacques Dutronc), Deneuve's attempts to sell the stolen gems left by her husband are not without intrigue. Yet, even with the dogged loyalty of disbarred lawyer Jean-Pierre Bacri and some neat circularity involving Dutronc's mistress, Emmanuelle Seigneur, the plot sparkles all too rarely. In French with English subtitles. Contains swearing.

Catherine Deneuve *Marianne* • Jean-Pierre Bacri *Jean-Pierre* • Emmanuelle Seigner *Nathalie* • Jacques Dutronc *Battistelli* • Bernard Fresson *Vincent Malivert* • François Berléand *Eric Malivert* • Philippe Clévenot *Kleiser* ■ *Dir* Nicole Garcia, Jacques Fieschi

Places in the Heart
★★★★ PG

Drama   1984 · US · Colour · 111mins

A beautifully paced and sumptuously shot heart-twanger that won Sally Field a richly deserved best actress Oscar, even if her acceptance speech will go down in the annals of excessive luvviedom. Field is wonderfully moving as the feisty, sorely tried small-town farmer battling the Depression and her emotions, and there's a fine supporting cast including John Malkovich, Danny Glover and Amy Madigan. Written and directed by Robert Benton, who won an Oscar for his screenplay, this is a lovingly crafted homage to the community values of his Texas home town. At the time, some cynics sneered at the sucrose level, but it's a hard heart that doesn't melt. [cc]

Sally Field *Edna Spalding* • Danny Glover *Moze* • John Malkovich *Mr Will* • Lindsay Crouse *Margaret Lomax* • Ed Harris *Wayne Lomax* • Amy Madigan *Viola Kelsey* • Yankton Hatten *Frank Spalding* • Gennie James *Possum Spalding* ■ *Dir/Scr* Robert Benton

The Plague
★★★ 15

Drama
1992 · Fr/UK/Arg/US · Colour · 116mins

The reunion of *Kiss of the Spider Woman* stars William Hurt and Raul Julia is something of a disappointment. Adapted from the Albert Camus novel by director Luis Puenzo, it involves a dedicated doctor (Hurt), a French reporter (Sandrine Bonnaire) and a TV cameraman (Jean-Marc Barr) whose lives become entangled during an outbreak of a lethal pestilence in a South American city. The existentialism of the original is lost in this version, which doesn't make up for it with action or tension. Contains swearing, sex scenes and some violence. [cc] **DVD**

William Hurt *Dr Bernard Rieux* • Sandrine Bonnaire *Martine Rambert* • Jean-Marc Barr *Jean Tarrou* • Robert Duvall *Joseph Grand* • Raul Julia *Cottard* • Lautaro Murua *Father Paneloux* • Victoria Tennant *Alice Rieux* ■ *Dir* Luis Puenzo • *Scr* Luis Puenzo, from the novel *La Peste* by Albert Camus

The Plague Dogs
★★★ PG

Animated adventure
1982 · US/UK · Colour · 98mins

After *Watership Down*, Martin Rosen went on to adapt another Richard Adams novel, though the film's troubling and downbeat nature possibly explains its comparative lack of success. Two laboratory dogs (voiced by John Hurt and Christopher Benjamin) escape from a British laboratory and seek a canine paradise while trying to avoid recapture. The animation does not reach modern standards, but it's pretty good for the period it was produced and still manages to convey the gritty emotion dictated by the bleak yet absorbing story. Even those not concerned with animal rights will feel something by the time the movie gets to its haunting finale, although the violence and general grimness make it inappropriate for younger viewers. [cc]

John Hurt *Snitter* • Christopher Benjamin *Rowf* • James Bolam *The Tod* • Nigel Hawthorne *Dr Robert Boycott* • Warren Mitchell *Tyson/Wag* • Bernard Hepton *Stephen Powell* ■ *Dir* Martin Rosen • *Scr* Martin Rosen, from the novel by Richard Adams

The Plague of the Zombies
★★★★ 15

Horror   1965 · UK · Colour · 86mins

Voodoo rituals in 18th-century Cornwall disguise a savage indictment of the British class system in a superior Hammer horror with a strong plotline. It's John Gilling's best work, and his tight direction and stylish visuals build the tension most effectively. Especially memorable moments include the green-tinted dream sequence, where churchyard corpses are resurrected, and a quite stunning decapitation scene. A vintage bloodcurdler from Hammer's golden era. [cc]

André Morell *Sir James Forbes* • Diane Clare *Sylvia Forbes* • John Carson *Clive Hamilton* • Alex Davion *Denver* • Jacqueline Pearce *Alice Thompson* • Roy Royston *Vicar* ■ *Dir* John Gilling • *Scr* Peter Bryan, John Elder [Anthony Hinds]

Plain Clothes
★★★ PG

Comedy thriller   1988 · US · Colour · 93mins

Some strong, gritty performances, particularly from George Wendt and Robert Stack, lift this workaday thriller above a script that lumbers along like an old car, accompanied by a man with a flag signalling "twist in the plot ahead". We've been undercover before with a disgruntled cop – in this case, he's posing as a student to clear his brother's name – so there is a strong whiff of familiarity about his quest. But this is still professional movie-making. Contains swearing. [cc]

Arliss Howard *Nick Dunbar/Nick Springsteen* • Suzy Amis *Robin Torrence* • George Wendt *Chet Butler* • Diane Ladd *Jane Melway* • Seymour Cassel *Ed Malmburg* • Larry Pine *Dave Hechtor* • Jackie Gayle *Coach Zeffer* • Abe Vigoda *Mr Wiseman* • Robert Stack *Mr Gardner* ■ *Dir* Martha Coolidge • *Scr* A Scott Frank, from a story by A Scott Frank, Dan Vining

The Plainsman
★★★★ U

Western   1936 · US · BW · 111mins

A no-holds-barred spectacle from Cecil B DeMille, impressively capturing the landscape of the Wild West, teeming with hordes of Sioux and Cheyenne Indians, and merrily ignoring historical truths. This western also presents us with a totally fictitious romance between Wild Bill Hickok and Calamity Jane, gloriously glamorised by Gary Cooper and Jean Arthur. A highly enjoyable action epic in true DeMille style, the film features James Ellison as Wild Bill's friend Buffalo Bill, John Miljan as General Custer and Frank McGlynn Sr as Abraham Lincoln. For what it's worth, the then unknown Anthony Quinn can be spotted, done up as a redskin.

Gary Cooper *Wild Bill Hickok* • Jean Arthur *Calamity Jane* • James Ellison *Buffalo Bill Cody* • Charles Bickford *John Latimer* • Porter Hall *Jack McCall* • Helen Burgess *Louisa Cody* • John Miljan *Gen George Armstrong Custer* • Victor Varconi *Painted Horse* • Anthony Quinn *Cheyenne warrior* • Frank McGlynn Sr *Abraham Lincoln* ■ *Dir* Cecil B DeMille • *Scr* Waldemar Young, Harold Lamb, Lynn Riggs, Grover Jones, from the novel *Wild Bill Hickok, the Prince of the Pioneers* by Frank J Wilstach and from stories by Courtney Ryley Cooper

Le Plaisir
★★★★★ PG

Drama   1951 · Fr · BW · 93mins

In the second of his four last masterpieces made in France, Max Ophüls approaches these three tales based on stories by Guy de Maupassant in a virtuoso manner. The first one tells of an old man who finds his youth again by wearing a magic mask; the second accompanies a group of prostitutes on a trip to the country; and the third relates how an artist marries his model after she tries to commit suicide. Each episode has memorable sequences, there is splendid period detail, and the wonderful cast includes Jean Gabin, Simone Simon, Danielle Darrieux and Madeleine Renaud as the madame of the brothel. [cc]

Claude Dauphin *The doctor* • Jean Galland *Ambroise, "The Mask"* • Daniel Gélin *Jean* • Simone Simon *Josephine* • Madeleine Renaud *Mme Tellier* • Jean Gabin *Joseph Rivet* • Danielle Darrieux *Rosa* • Peter Ustinov *Guy de Maupassant* ■ *Dir* Max Ophüls • *Scr* Max Ophüls, Jacques Natanson, from the stories *The Mask/The House of Madame Tellier/The Model* by Guy de Maupassant

Plan 9 from Outer Space
★ PG

Science-fiction thriller
1959 · US · BW · 75mins

Camp aliens attempt to take over the world by reviving the dead in Ed Wood Jr's science-fiction opus, built around a few minutes of footage Bela Lugosi shot days before he died and often cited as the worst movie ever made. While there is some unintentional humour to be had from the way Wood desperately incorporates his shots of Lugosi (and a fake body double) into a mess of stock footage, amateur acting, crude special effects (hub-caps as flying saucers) and wobbly sets, it's a tediously depressing experience. Tim Burton re-created many of its scenes in his entertaining biopic, *Ed Wood*. [cc]

Gregory Walcott *Jeff Trent* • Bela Lugosi *Ghoul man* • Mona McKinnon *Paula Trent* • Duke Moore *Lieutenant Harper* • Richard Powers *Colonel Tom Edwards* ■ *Dir/Scr* Edward D Wood Jr

Plan of Attack
★

Thriller   1992 · US · Colour · 95mins

One must assume Loni Anderson needed the money around the time of her separation from Burt Reynolds, as there can be no other logical explanation as to why she would appear in this drivel. She plays a woman who has started a new life in a new town after her attacker (Anthony John Denison) has been jailed for raping her, but, of course, as always happens in these movies, he is soon out and on her trail. Contains violence.

Loni Anderson *Lacey Stewart* • Anthony John Denison *Keith Welles* • Candy Clark *Marlene Thomas* • Stephen Meadows *Dan* • Coleby Lombardo *RT Stewart* ■ *Dir* Fred Walton • *Scr* Robert Foster, Phil Penningroth, from a play by Curtis Wilmot

Plan 10 from Outer Space
★★

Science-fiction spoof
1995 · US · Colour · 82mins

Why Salt Lake City film-maker Trent Harris would purposely want to invoke the memory of the worst movie ever made (Ed Wood's *Plan 9 from Outer Space*) is not the only cause of wonderment in this science-fiction spoof. While researching a book about local Mormon history, Stefene Russell finds a plaque which reveals faith founder Brigham Young married an alien queen from the planet Kolob (Karen Black) who's currently plotting a revenge attack on Utah. The chuckles may be few and far between, but good special effects and Black's over-the-top performance add to the eye-rolling bemusement.

Stefene Russell *Lucinda Hall* • Karen Black *Nehor* • Karen Nielson ■ *Dir/Scr* Trent Harris

Planes, Trains and Automobiles
★★★

Comedy   1987 · US · Colour · 88mins

Steve Martin and John Candy give excellent performances as the not-so-good companions desperately trying to get home for Thanksgiving in this amiable comedy, written and directed by John Hughes, which sends up the vagaries of the whole American transport system. Veering uneasily between slapstick and sentiment, the cheerfully astute playing by the disaster-prone "little-and-large" leads ensures the farcical proceedings are always fun to watch, even when the brain takes the strain. Contains swearing. [cc]

Steve Martin *Neal Page* • John Candy *Del Griffith* • Laila Robbins *Susan Page* • Michael McKean *State trooper* • Kevin Bacon *Taxi racer* • Dylan Baker *Owen* • Carol Bruce *Joy* • Olivia Burnette *Marti* ■ *Dir/Scr* John Hughes

Planet Earth
★★ PG

Futuristic adventure
1974 · US · Colour · 70mins

Gene Roddenberry may have struck gold with *Star Trek*, but his subsequent sci-fi creations have aged less well.

Working from a similar blueprint to Roddenberry's *Genesis II* (filmed the previous year), this is once again set in a post-apocalyptic future, with scientist John Saxon waking up after a deep sleep to find that women rule the roost. However, it's all a little po-faced compared to the racy fun of Kirk and co, and the cast (which includes Janet Margolin, Ted Cassidy and Diana Muldaur) struggles to breathe life into the concept. The sets, too, look suspiciously creaky today. ▭

John Saxon *Dylan Hunt* • Janet Margolin *Harper-Smythe* • Ted Cassidy *Isiah* • Diana Muldaur *Marg* • Majel Barrett *Yuloff* • Christopher Cary *Baylok* ■ *Dir* Marc Daniels • *Scr* Gene Roddenberry, Juanita Bartlett, from a story by Gene Roddenberry

Planet of Blood ★★
Science-fiction horror
1966 · US · Colour · 81mins

This largely unmemorable space opera from the Roger Corman stable is distinguished by an eclectic cast and may be viewed today as a precursor to *Alien* with its tale of a US manned space probe rescuing an alien craft that has ditched on the surface of Mars. Unfortunately, the green-skinned female occupant (Florence Marly) turns out to be a galactic vampire. Filmed in a week for just $65,000, the crude plot was concocted by writer/director Curtis Harrington to fit around cannibalised footage from a big-budget Russian sci-fi movie. To his credit, Harrington creates a potent feeling of eeriness and delivers a truly off-the-wall ending.

Basil Rathbone *Dr Farraday* • John Saxon *Allan* • Dennis Hopper *Paul* • Judi Meredith *Laura* • Florence Marly *Alien queen* ■ *Dir/Scr* Curtis Harrington

The Planet of Junior Brown
★
Drama   1999 · Can · Colour · 92mins
An underwritten script, typical of Canadian drama, makes this effort particularly incoherent. Centring around a homeless teen and his friendship with a child prodigy who is slowly losing his grip on reality, it frequently includes scenes and supporting characters without an obvious purpose. Key explanations are either avoided or were clearly butchered by slapdash editing, resulting in a film that feels greatly unfinished. With the language and sexual situations inappropriate for children, and a viewpoint on some serious subject material that is downright childish at times, it is unclear what audience was intended for this movie.

Martin Villafana *Junior Brown* • Lynn Whitfield *Mrs Brown* • Rainbow Sun Francks *Buddy Clark* • Clark Johnson *Mr Pool* • Sarah Polley *Butter* • Richard Chevolleau *Duckie* • Margot Kidder *Miss Peebs* ■ *Dir* Clément Virgo ■ *Scr* Clément Virgo, Cameron Bailey, from the novel by Virginia Hamilton

Planet of the Apes
★★★★ PG
Science-fiction adventure
1968 · US · Colour · 107mins
Charlton Heston is the leader of a team of astronauts who crash on a desolate planet that remains suspiciously reminiscent of Earth, but where apes rule and the humans are the dumb animals. Heston is appropriately square-jawed as the rebellious human and Roddy McDowall and Kim Hunter shine through the marvellous ape make-up from John Chambers, who received an honorary Oscar for his work. Rod Serling and Michael Wilson provide a sly, clever script and the twist at the end still delights. A smash hit that was followed by a number of increasingly inferior sequels, plus a rather mundane TV series. Contains violence. ▭

Charlton Heston *George Taylor* • Roddy McDowall *Cornelius* • Kim Hunter *Dr Zira* • Maurice Evans *Dr Zaius* • James Whitmore *President of the assembly* • James Daly *Honorius* • Linda Harrison *Nova* • Robert Gunner *Landon* • Lou Wagner *Lucius* ■ *Dir* Franklin J Schaffner • *Scr* Michael Wilson, Rod Serling, from the novel *Monkey Planet* by Pierre Boulle

The Plank ★★★ U
Silent comedy   1967 · UK · Colour · 54mins
A joyously inventive British "silent" comedy from writer/director Eric Sykes about the misadventures of two builders delivering wood to a house. Sykes himself is "Smaller workman" to Tommy Cooper's "Larger workman", and, although not all the jokes are completely fresh, the fun is in the effective sound effects, and the spotting of comedy icons such as Jimmy Edwards, Jimmy Tarbuck and Roy Castle in unfamiliar poses and surroundings. Music hall on the hoof. ▭

Tommy Cooper *Larger workman* • Eric Sykes *Smaller workman* • Jimmy Edwards *Policeman* • Roy Castle *Man covered in garbage* • Graham Stark *Amorous van driver* • Stratford Johns *Station sergeant* • Jim Dale *House painter* • Jimmy Tarbuck *Barman* • Hattie Jacques *Woman with rose* • Johnny Speight *Chauffeur* ■ *Dir/Scr* Eric Sykes

The Planter's Wife ★★
Drama   1952 · UK · BW · 91mins
She's Claudette Colbert, towards the end of her career, in the middle of a then-topical tale about the "troubles" in Malaya, drifting apart from hubby Jack Hawkins into the arms of Anthony Steel until the rebels attack their plantation and the threat to their lives reunites husband and wife. Interestingly, this picture, intended as a tribute to the courage of the rubber planters and their families, inadvertently ends up as a damning indictment of imperialism. Colbert seems uncomfortable, both in the location work and the ill-matched studio interiors, but, though uneven, the film is fascinating to watch as a period piece.

Claudette Colbert *Liz Frazer* • Jack Hawkins *Jim Frazer* • Anthony Steel *Inspector Hugh Dobson* • Ram Gopal *Nair* • Jeremy Spenser *Mat* • Tom Macauley *Jack Bushell* • Helen Goss *Eleanor Bushell* ■ *Dir* Ken Annakin • *Scr* Peter Proud, Guy Elmes, from the novel by SC George

Plastic Jesus ★★★★
Documentary drama
1971 · Yug · Sepia BW and Colour · 76mins
After a decade of unprecedented "novi film" innovation, Yugoslav cinema entered its so-called "black film" phase, in which the anti-socialist rhetoric became increasingly strident and nihilistic. Taking his title from a popular American song, student director Lazar Stojanovic found himself in the vanguard of this movement when he was sentenced to three years imprisonment for making anti-Tito statements in his debut feature, which was immediately banned. Combining newsreel footage challenging the official line on the Second World War and sepia-tinted scenes of a symbolically sexual nature, it's a technically audacious protest, that affects with its visual energy even without in-depth background knowledge. In Serbo-Croatian with English subtitles.

Dir/Scr Lazar Stojanovic

Platinum Blonde ★★★ U
Comedy   1931 · US · BW · 90mins
Jean Harlow is all aglow (and very revealing) in this fast-moving comedy satire. But the real star of the show is leading man Robert Williams (as the reporter who marries debutante Harlow), an inventive, screen-dominating light comedian who tragically died prematurely in the year of this, his greatest hit. The jokes at the expense of high society aren't as funny now, and much of the movie's shooting style has dated badly, but director Frank Capra keeps this zipping along, and the central trio of Harlow, Williams and lovely Loretta Young is a joy to behold.

Loretta Young *Gallagher* • Robert Williams *Stew Smith* • Jean Harlow *Anne Schuyler* • Louise Closser Hale *Mrs Schuyler* • Donald Dillaway *Michael Schuyler* • Reginald Owen *Dexter Grayson* ■ *Dir* Frank Capra • *Scr* Jo Swerling, Dorothy Howell, Robert Riskin, from a story by Harry E Chandlee, Douglas W Churchill

Platinum High School ★★
Drama   1960 · US · BW · 93mins
Mickey Rooney stars in this partly interesting, partly nonsensically sensationalist drama, directed by Charles Haas, whose supporting cast includes other old-timers Dan Duryea and Elisha Cook Jr. Rooney is the father, estranged from his son by divorce, who arrives at the military academy where his boy has been killed. There, he realises that the establishment is home to delinquent misfits from wealthy families, suspects foul play in his son's death and is himself endangered by his probing for the truth.

Mickey Rooney *Steven Conway* • Terry Moore *Jennifer Evans* • Dan Duryea *Major Redfern Kelly* • Yvette Mimieux *Lorinda Nibley* • Conway Twitty *Billy Jack Barnes* • Jimmy Boyd *Bud Starkweather* • Harold Lloyd Jr *Charley Boy Cable* • Richard Jaeckel *Hack Marlow* • Elisha Cook Jr *Harry Nesbitt* ■ *Dir* Charles Haas • *Scr* Robert Smith, from a story by Howard Breslin

Platoon ★★★★★ 15
War drama   1986 · US · Colour · 114mins
It took ten years for Oliver Stone to get his script made, but when it finally reached the screen it became a box-office smash and won four Oscars.

Unlike other directors who made major Vietnam movies, Stone has the edge in that he was actually there, as a volunteer who fought for patriotic reasons and got wounded before becoming disillusioned. From the scary opening when the new arrivals are greeted by the sight of body bags bound for home the movie is an authentically messy tour of duty through the paddy fields where two Americans (Willem Dafoe and Tom Berenger) are at war with each other and fight for the soul of rookie Charlie Sheen. A modern classic and a personal exorcism for its director, who went on to complete a trilogy of Vietnam movies with *Born on the Fourth of July* and *Heaven and Earth*. Contains violence and swearing. ▭

Tom Berenger *Sergeant Barnes* • Willem Dafoe *Sergeant Elias* • Charlie Sheen *Chris* • Forest Whitaker *Big Harold* • Francesco Quinn *Rhah* • John C McGinley *Sergeant O'Neill* • Richard Edson *Sal* • Kevin Dillon *Bunny* • Reggie Johnson *Junior* • Keith David *King* • Johnny Depp *Lerner* ■ *Dir/Scr* Oliver Stone • *Cinematographer* Robert Richardson

Platoon Leader ★★ 18
War drama   1988 · US · Colour · 91mins
This routine bit of wham bam, thank you Nam is one of the many Vietnam movies made in the wake of *Platoon*. (The similarity of the title is, of course, no coincidence.) The director is Aaron Norris, brother of martial arts movie star Chuck; one can only assume he passed on this one. The lead role is instead taken by Michael Dudikoff, a charisma-free prettyboy who was briefly "hunk of the month". ▭

Michael Dudikoff *Jeff Knight* • Robert F Lyons *Michael McNamara* • Michael DeLorenzo *Raymond Bacera* • Rick Fitts *Robert Hayes* ■ *Dir* Aaron Norris • *Scr* Rick Marx, Andrew Deutsch, David Walker, Harry Alan Towers, from a story by James R McDonough

Plato's Run ★★ 18
Action thriller   1996 · US · Colour · 92mins
First, we're supposed to believe that Gary Busey could have been a US Navy SEAL, one of the top agents during the Gulf War. Then we're meant to believe he's still able to carry out freelance covert missions, like "extracting" the son of a Miami crimelord from Cuba. Unfortunately, it's a double-cross courtesy of another crimelord, this one played by an extremely tanned Roy Scheider. The implausibilities pile up as Busey huffs and puffs his way through each action scene. Boredom abounds, punctuated by Scheider's chewing of the scenery. Contains violence and some swearing. ▭

Gary Busey *Plato* • Steven Bauer *Sam* • Roy Scheider *Senarkian* • Jeff Speakman *Dominick* • Tiani Warden *Marta* • Maggie Myatt *Kathy* ■ *Dir/Scr* James Becket

Play Dead ★ 18
Horror   1981 · US · Colour · 81mins
In her post-*Addams Family* years, Yvonne De Carlo lent dignity to a seemingly unending series of completely worthless scripts. This devilish drivel is yet another waste of her inestimable talents. As rich Aunt Hester, De Carlo makes a Satanic pact with a Rottweiler to kill off her

relatives, all because her late sister married her only true love. Electrocution, strangulation and poisoning are all in the canny canine's canon of carnage, as if anyone cares. Good dog – bad film! ▦

Yvonne De Carlo *Hester* • Stephanie Dunnam *Audrey* • David Cullinane *Jeff* • Glenn Kezer *Otis* • Ron Jackson *Richard* ■ *Dir* Peter Wittman • *Scr* Lothrop W Jordan

Play Dirty ★★★ 🅸🆅

Second World War drama
1969 · UK · Colour · 113mins

Co-written by Melvyn Bragg at his least cultured, and directed by Andre De Toth at his most action-led, this predictable wartime story of inexperienced officer Michael Caine leading a unit to blow up an enemy fuel dump has its moments – especially when roguish Nigel Davenport is around – but not many. If this seems familiar, it's another take on *The Dirty Dozen* and, though some of the skirmishes do have an impact, this is not in the same class as Robert Aldrich's film. Contains some violence and swearing. ▦

Michael Caine *Captain Douglas* • Nigel Davenport *Cyril Leech* • Nigel Green *Colonel Masters* • Harry Andrews *Brigadier Blore* • Bernard Archard *Colonel Homerton* • Daniel Pilon *Captain Attwood* ■ *Dir* Andre De Toth • *Scr* Lotte Colin, Melvyn Bragg, from a story by George Marton

Play It Again, Sam ★★★★ 🅸🆅

Comedy 1972 · US · Colour · 81mins

Adapted by Woody Allen from his own 1969 stage play, this is one of the very few entries on his CV that America's leading film auteur has not directed himself. That task fell to Herbert Ross, who adopts an overcautious approach to the story of film buff Allen's tentative relationship with Diane Keaton, the wife of best pal Tony Roberts. But such is the calibre of the playing and the assurance of the writing that it's almost impossible to resist. The more politically correct may feel their hackles rise from time to time, but the one-liners are among Allen's best and the Bogart allusions are priceless. ▦

Woody Allen *Allan Felix* • Diane Keaton *Linda Christie* • Tony Roberts *Dick Christie* • Jerry Lacy *Humphrey Bogart* • Susan Anspach *Nancy Felix* • Jennifer Salt *Sharon* • Joy Bang *Julie* ■ *Dir* Herbert Ross • *Scr* Woody Allen, from his play

Play It Cool ★★ 🆄

Drama 1963 · UK · BW · 78mins

A wonderfully nostalgic pre-Beatles teen fest, starring Britain's answer to Elvis, Billy Fury, in a genuine pop musical, as the Liverpool rocker who stops Anna Palk from straying off the straight and narrow – as if the plot matters! It's a real period artefact, with guest appearances from the likes of Bobby Vee, and a batch of splendid English veterans like Dennis Price and Richard Wattis along for the ride. It isn't any good, really, but at least it's fun and moves along briskly enough. The film's director, Michael Winner, was considered quite promising then, but today this could be regarded as one of his better pictures. ▦

Billy Fury *Billy Universe* • Michael Anderson Jr *Alvin* • Dennis Price *Sir Charles Bryant* • Richard Wattis *Nervous Man* • Anna Palk *Ann Bryant* ■ *Dir* Michael Winner • *Scr* Jack Henry

Play It to the Bone ★★★ 🅸🆅

Sports comedy drama
2000 · US · Colour · 123mins

Writer/director Ron Shelton specialises in movies about men in sport (*Bull Durham*, *Tin Cup*), so it was only a matter of time before he turned his wry gaze on the fight game. Antonio Banderas and Woody Harrelson play second-rate pugilists who get a shot at the big time when they are asked to box each other on the same bill as a Mike Tyson bout. The catch is they have less than 12 hours to get to Vegas, so the two friends hit the road with feisty Lolita Davidovich at the wheel. Too much chat and the aggravating presence of *Ally McBeal's* Lucy Liu as a hitchhiking nymphomaniac make the road trip a long haul. But things pick up during the climactic fisticuffs, with a host of star cameos (James Woods, Kevin Costner, Tony Curtis) suggesting Shelton's name still opens doors in Tinseltown.

Antonio Banderas *Cesar Dominguez* • Woody Harrelson *Vince Boudreau* • Lolita Davidovich *Grace Pasic* • Tom Sizemore *Joe Domino* • Lucy Liu *Lia* • Robert Wagner *Hank Goody* • Richard Masur *Artie* • George Foreman *HBO commentator* • Rod Stewart • Kevin Costner • James Woods • Drew Carey • Tony Curtis • Wesley Snipes • Natasha Gregson Wagner • Jennifer Tilly ■ *Dir/Scr* Ron Shelton

Play Me Something ★★ 🅸🅾

Drama 1989 · UK · Colour and BW · 71mins

Highly esoteric "film poem" based on the work of writer/critic John Berger, who appears as himself, telling a slight tale about romance in Venice to a group of passengers (one of whom is Tilda Swinton) waiting for a flight from Barra, in the Outer Hebrides, to Glasgow. Singer Hamish Henderson, about whom the director subsequently made a documentary, interjects. Fans of folk art may well be enchanted by the experimental blend of words and pictures. Others will avoid the kind of egghead chat that only a marriage of the British Film Institute and Channel 4 could produce.

Lucia Lanzarini *Marietta* • Charlie Barron *Bruno* • John Berger *Storyteller* • Hamish Henderson *Electrician* • Tilda Swinton *Hairdresser* • Stewart Ennis *Motorcyclist* • Robert Carr *Salesman* • Liz Lochhead *Pregnant woman* ■ *Dir* Timothy Neat • *Scr* Timothy Neat, John Berger, from a story by John Berger

Play Misty for Me ★★★★ 🅸🆅

Thriller 1971 · US · Colour · 97mins

Clint Eastwood's fine directorial debut, in which he also stars as DJ Dave Garland, rejecting a fan (Jessica Walter) after a one-night stand only to discover that she's determined to keep him whatever the cost – and all this 16 years before *Fatal Attraction*. Jealousy is one of the hardest emotions to delineate with any kind of subtlety in cinema, yet Walter is superb as the deranged woman. Eastwood's sideburns and flares lend the movie a period charm today, but

its power to grip and chill remains undiminished. Look out for *Dirty Harry* director Don Siegel as Murphy the bartender, and don't watch this one on your own. ▦

Clint Eastwood *Dave Garland* • Jessica Walter *Evelyn Draper* • Donna Mills *Tobie Williams* • John Larch *Sergeant McCallum* • James McEachin *Al Monte* • Don Siegel *Murphy the bartender* ■ *Dir* Clint Eastwood • *Scr* Jo Heims, Dean Riesner, from a story by Jo Heims • *Cinematographer* Bruce Surtees

Playback ★ 🅸🅾

Erotic thriller 1995 · US · Colour · 90mins

This erotic thriller is a calamitous comedown for someone of Harry Dean Stanton's ability. But, mercifully, he's spared the worst excesses of this tawdry tale, in which high-flying executive Charles Grant and wife Tawny Kitaen's penchant for shooting sexy home movies hands a potentially embarrassing initiative to his unscrupulous boss George Hamilton and voluptuous colleague Shannon Whirry. Director Oley Sassone is clearly more comfortable with soft-core than the more hard-edged aspects of what, laughingly, must be called the plot. Contains sex scenes and swearing. ▦

Charles Grant *David Burgess* • Tawny Kitaen *Sara Burgess* • Shannon Whirry *Karen Stone* • George Hamilton *Gil Braman* • Harry Dean Stanton *Ernie Fontonot* ■ *Dir* Oley Sassone • *Scr* Oley Sassone, David DuBos

The Playboys ★★ 🅿🅶

Drama 1992 · UK · Colour · 104mins

You wait ages for a film about a single Irish mother who refuses to name the father of her child to turn up, and then, typically, two come along at once. Roddy Doyle's *The Snapper* has the edge over *The Playboys*, although Shane Connaughton co-writer of *My Left Foot* cannot be faulted for his part in a script brimming with incident and credible characters. However, director Gillies MacKinnon is unable to prevent a bombastic Albert Finney from over-balancing the picture in the role of the village policeman, whose jealousy at Robin Wright's romance with travelling player Aidan Quinn spills over into violence. Contains violence and swearing. ▦

Albert Finney *Hegarty* • Aidan Quinn *Tom Casey* • Robin Wright [Robin Wright Penn] *Tara Maguire* • Milo O'Shea *Freddie* • Alan Devlin *Malone* • Niamh Cusack *Brigid* ■ *Dir* Gillies MacKinnon • *Scr* Shane Connaughton, Kerry Crabbe

The Player ★★★★★ 🅸🆅

Satire 1992 · US · Colour · 119mins

A satire on Hollywood at its worst told by Hollywood at its best. Director Robert Altman turns the spotlight on the industry hands that feed him and bites them with sardonic wit. The temptation is to play spot the star, but don't let the galaxy of cameos from such celebrities as Bruce Willis, Julia Roberts and Cher distract from the gloriously cynical plot and a towering turn from a marvellously oily Tim Robbins. He is a high-flying studio executive who is troubled by poison-pen postcards from a discarded scriptwriter, the ambitions of

wunderkind Peter Gallagher and the snooping of cop Whoopi Goldberg, who suspects him of murder. Altman had already employed his trademark roving technique on his country-and-western masterpiece *Nashville*. Here, everything he tries comes off to magnificent effect. Contains violence, swearing, and brief nudity. ▦

Tim Robbins *Griffin Mill* • Greta Scacchi *June Gudmundsdottir* • Fred Ward *Walter Stuckel* • Whoopi Goldberg *Detective Susan Avery* • Peter Gallagher *Larry Levy* • Brion James *Joel Levison* • Cynthia Stevenson *Bonnie Sherow* • Vincent D'Onofrio *David Kahane* • Dean Stockwell *Andy Civella* • Richard E Grant *Tom Oakley* • Sydney Pollack *Dick Mellen* ■ *Dir* Robert Altman • *Scr* Michael Tolkin, from his novel

Players ★★ 🅿🅶

Romantic drama
1979 · US · Colour · 115mins

This charts the rise of a young tennis player who makes it to the Wimbledon final, despite the distractions of a romance with a millionaire's mistress. Dean Paul Martin (Dean's son) stars, with Ali MacGraw as the love interest in a curate's egg that's very good as a tennis action movie but risibly poor away from the court. However, with Pancho Gonzalez playing the coach for director Anthony Harvey, a gripping final staged on Centre Court between the fictional hero and real champ Guillermo Vilas, and appearances by John McEnroe, Ilie Nastase and John Lloyd among others, this is sure to appeal to aficionados of the game. ▦

Ali MacGraw *Nicole* • Dean Paul Martin *Chris* • Maximilian Schell *Marco* • Pancho Gonzalez *Pancho* • Steve Guttenberg *Rusty* • Melissa Prophet *Ann* • Guillermo Vilas ■ *Dir* Anthony Harvey • *Scr* Arnold Schulman

The Players Club ★★

Comedy crime drama
1998 · US · Colour · 104mins

Showgirls meets *Boyz N the Hood* in this flawed curiosity, written and directed by rap star/actor Ice Cube (who also pops up in a brief cameo). Newcomer LisaRaye plays an aspiring journalist who takes up stripping to pay her way through college and soon finds herself drawn into the murkier aspects of the business. She delivers a feisty performance, although Bernie Mac steals the show as the motormouth owner of the club where she works. Ice Cube's heart is in the right place, but there's an exploitative nature to the whole affair, and both the writing and direction are erratic.

LisaRaye *Diana Armstrong/Diamond* • Monica Calhoun *Ebony* • Bernie Mac *Dollar Bill* • Jamie Foxx *Blue* • Chrystale Wilson *Ronnie* • Adele Givens *Tricks* • AJ Johnson [Anthony Johnson] *Li'l Man* • Ice Cube *Reggie* ■ *Dir* Ice Cube • *Scr* Ice Cube

Playgirl ★★

Drama 1954 · US · BW · 85mins

Old-fashioned melodrama given a fifties flavour as a simple Nebraska lass (Colleen Miller) arrives in New York to seek fame and fortune. She rapidly finds herself gracing the cover of *Glitter* magazine, incurring the jealousy of her roommate (Shelley Winters); other undesirable consequences include her descent into the sleazy party scene and her implication in a gangster's murder. Acceptable couch-potato fodder.

Shelley Winters *Fran Davis* • Barry Sullivan *Mike Marsh* • Colleen Miller *Phyllis Matthews* • Gregg Palmer *Tom Bradley* • Richard Long *Barron Courtney* • Kent Taylor *Ted Andrews* • Dave Barry *Jonathan* • Philip Van Zandt *Lew Martel* ■ *Dir* Joseph Pevney • *Scr* Robert Blees, from a story by Ray Buffum

Playing Away ★★★ 15
Satire   1986 · UK · Colour · 101mins

In Horace Ove's immensely likeable film, Britain's race relations and its imperial hangover are boiled down to a game of cricket, played on a village green between the local side and a team from Brixton. The country lads are confident of victory and are staging the match to raise money for the Third World. The cosy, quaint English movie of the pre-war years has been fondly updated and spiked with razor-sharp social observation.

Norman Beaton *Willy Boy* • Robert Urquhart *Godfrey* • Helen Lindsay *Marjorie* • Nicholas Farrell *Derek* • Brian Bovell *Stuart* • Suzette Llewellyn *Yvette* ■ *Dir* Horace Ove • *Scr* Caryl Phillips

Playing by Heart ★★★★ 15
Comedy drama 1998 · US · Colour · 121mins

A beautifully wrought multi-character love story, which not only provides great roles for legendary old-timers Sean Connery, Ellen Burstyn and Gena Rowlands, but also puts newer Hollywood hopefuls Ryan Phillippe, Gillian Anderson and Angelina Jolie in the spotlight. Director Willard Carroll's glossy ensemble brings to mind *Short Cuts* in both structure and format, as three couples grapple with the problems in their lives and relationships. Yet this is far more engaging and emotionally resonant as it cuts between a multitude of stormy confrontations, intriguing trysts and startling dates, and then neatly ties them all off with a bravura conclusion that's both extremely clever and deeply satisfying. Contains swearing.

Gillian Anderson *Meredith* • Angelina Jolie *Joan* • Madeleine Stowe *Gracie* • Anthony Edwards *Roger* • Ryan Phillippe *Keenan* • Gena Rowlands *Hannah* • Sean Connery *Paul* • Dennis Quaid *Hugh* • Ellen Burstyn *Mildred* • Nastassja Kinski *Melanie* ■ *Dir/Scr* Willard Carroll

Playing for Keeps ★ 15
Comedy   1986 · US · Colour · 102mins

An embarrassing attempt to make a youth movie. Having just finished high school, three friends inherit a run-down hotel in the Catskills and decide to turn it into the perfect place for rock-obsessed teenagers. They work hard on the hotel but there are local residents waiting to stop the lads from their dream, including a nefarious industrialist, hand in glove with the equally nasty president of the local council, who wants to use the site as a toxic waste dump. A film as awful as it sounds. ▭

Daniel Jordano *Danny D'Angelo* • Matthew Penn *Spikes* • Leon W Grant *Silk* • Mary B Ward *Chloe* • Marisa Tomei *Tracy* • Jimmy Baio *Steinberg* • Harold Gould *Rockerfeller* ■

Kim Hauser *Marie* ■ *Dir* Bob Weinstein, Harvey Weinstein • *Scr* Bob Weinstein, Harvey Weinstein, Jeremy Leven

Playing for Time ★★★
Drama based on a true story
1980 · US · Colour · 149mins

A highly acclaimed and well-acted tale, based on the experiences of a Jewish Holocaust survivor who managed to avoid death by forming an orchestra with fellow captives. Vanessa Redgrave, who caused controversy when she accepted the role owing to her Palestinian sympathies, is as impressive and heartfelt as ever, and she is given memorable support by Jane Alexander and Melanie Mayron. Perhaps too heart-rending for some tastes, this is nonetheless a thought-provoking and moving drama.

Vanessa Redgrave *Fania Fenelon* • Jane Alexander *Alma Rose* • Maud Adams *Mala* • Christine Baranski *Olga* • Robin Bartlett *Etalina* • Marisa Berenson *Elzvieta* • Verna Bloom *Paulette* ■ *Dir* Daniel Mann • *Scr* Arthur Miller, from the book by Fania Fenelon

Playing God ★★ 18
Crime thriller   1997 · US · Colour · 93mins

David Duchovny didn't go for the easy option when accepting his first post-*X Files* big-screen role, and despite his OK performance the movie itself is only a qualified success. Playing against type, Duchovny stars as a disgraced surgeon with a drug habit who becomes unofficial physician to slimy mobster Timothy Hutton and his gang. As he tries to wriggle out of the job, he finds himself caught between the FBI and the increasingly paranoid gangster. Both Hutton and Peter Stormare as an underworld rival are flamboyantly over the top, while Angelina Jolie supplies the glamour. The plot is ridiculously far-fetched while the direction from British TV's Andy Wilson is slick but a touch erratic. Contains violence and swearing. ▭

David Duchovny *Dr Eugene Sands* • Timothy Hutton *Raymond Blossom* • Angelina Jolie *Claire* • Michael Massee *Gage* • Peter Stormare *Vladimir* • Andrew Tiernan *Cyril* ■ *Dir* Andy Wilson • *Scr* Mark Haskell Smith

Playmaker ★
Mystery thriller 1994 · US · Colour · 88mins

Casting couch codswallop, with Jennifer Rubin as a wannabe actress willing to do almost anything in her bid for celluloid stardom. Colin Firth co-stars as a manipulative acting coach in a routine sexploitation movie that's far less erotic than it thinks it is. It's also marred by a first hour of appalling pop psychology and irritatingly vague plot development.

Colin Firth *Ross* • Jennifer Rubin *Jamie Harris* • John Getz *Eddie* ■ *Dir* Yuri Zeltser • *Scr* Yuri Zeltser, from a story by Darren Block, Kathryn Nemesh, from a screenplay (unproduced) by Michael Schroeder

Playmates ★ U
Musical comedy   1941 · US · BW · 95mins

The last film made by John Barrymore is a bizarrely awful comedy musical starring Kay Kyser and his band, with the usual Kyser appendages such as comedian Ish Kabibble. The ludicrous

plot presents the humiliating spectacle of a self-parodying Barrymore as a washed-up actor trying for a comeback on radio by teaching Shakespeare to Kyser. Adding to the comic chaos (which some might find amusing), is Lupe Velez, once known as the "Mexican Spitfire", exhibiting her particular brand of crude slapstick.

John Barrymore *John Barrymore* • Kay Kyser *Kay Kyser* • Lupe Velez *Carmen Del Toro* • Ginny Simms *Ginny* • May Robson *Grandma* • Patsy Kelly *Lulu Monahan* • Peter Lind Hayes *Peter Lindsey* • Ish Kabibble ■ *Dir* David Butler • *Scr* James V Kern, Arthur Phillips, from a story by James V Kern, MM Musselman

Playtime ★★★★★ U
Comedy   1967 · Fr · Colour · 114mins

It took Jacques Tati close to ten years to realise his greatest achievement, but it left him virtually broke. No wonder. He and his designer Eugène Roman built an ultramodern Paris of steel and glass skyscrapers through which Monsieur Hulot, Tati's marvellous comic creation, continues his battle with mechanical objects. The amiable, bumbling Hulot gets caught up with a group of American tourists, and finds himself at the opening of a nightclub that is far from ready. Ironically, given Tati's technophobe philosophy, his use of stereophonic sound and the 70mm screen has seldom been equalled. Unfortunately, the film, originally 152 minutes long, has mainly been shown since its first release in versions reduced in time and space. ▭

Jacques Tati *Monsieur Hulot* • Barbara Dennek *Young tourist* • Georges Montant *Giffard* • John Abbey *Lacs* • Billy Bourbon *Pilier* • Billy Kearns *Monsieur Schulz* ■ *Dir* Jacques Tati • *Scr* Jacques Tati, Jacques Lagrange, Art Buchwald • *Production Designer* Eugène Roman

Plaza Suite ★★★ PG
Comedy   1971 · US · Colour · 109mins

Three Walter Matthaus for the price of one, as he cynically bulldozes his way through three acts of Neil Simon's play about the goings-on in a swank hotel suite. As nervous comedy, it's best when it's most serious (Maureen Stapleton trying to keep husband Matthau from his mistress). Yet the more slapstick episodes (Hollywood producer trying to bed old flame; bemused father trying to coax bride-to-be daughter out of a locked loo) have their moments, even if the top-of-the-voice humour sometimes becomes so strident, it's inaudible. ▭

Walter Matthau *Sam Nash/Jesse Kiplinger/Roy Hubley* • Maureen Stapleton *Karen Nash* • Louise Sorel *Miss McCormack* • Barbara Harris *Muriel Tate* • Lee Grant *Norma Hubley* • Jenny Sullivan *Mimsey Hubley* • Tom Carey *Borden Eisler* ■ *Dir* Arthur Hiller • *Scr* Neil Simon, from his play

Pleasantville ★★★★ 12
Fantasy comedy drama
1998 · US · Colour · 124mins

Though *Pleasantville* boasts more special effects than *Jurassic Park*, many are so subtle you barely notice them. Tobey Maguire and Reese Witherspoon play sparring siblings who, while fighting over the TV remote control, get zapped inside Maguire's

favourite soap, a fifties re-run called *Pleasantville*. They find themselves in what is literally a black-and-white world – a time-warped tellyplace where the toilet stalls have no fittings because they couldn't be shown; where the library books have no words because they wouldn't be shown; where the men do all the work; and where a woman's place isn't just in the home, it's in the kitchen. How the youngsters' progressive attitudes to sex and marriage begin to induce unfamiliar feelings in the show's two-dimensional caricatures forms the basis of this witty and affectionate comedy. And how these new-found emotions are depicted by the gradual encroachment of colour into their monochrome lives is wherein lies its brilliance. It's a clever concept, beautifully acted by a crack cast. Contains some swearing and sexual situations. *DVD*

William H Macy *George Parker* • Joan Allen *Betty Parker* • Jeff Daniels *Mr Johnson* • Tobey Maguire *David* • Reese Witherspoon *Jennifer* • JT Walsh *Big Bob* • Don Knotts *TV repairman* ■ *Dir/Scr* Gary Ross

Please Don't Eat the Daisies ★★★★ U
Comedy   1960 · US · Colour · 110mins

A brash, colourful and fast-moving MGM comedy based on Jean Kerr's episodic reminiscences about life with hubby, Broadway's ace drama critic Walter Kerr. The couple are delightfully played here by Doris Day, whose company produced this movie for Metro, and the ever-urbane David Niven, who is hilarious in the scenes where he's pursued by panned Broadway actress Janis Paige. Director Charles Walters maintains a fast pace, as Day and Niven decamp from Manhattan to a country abode. This was one of a series of generally under-rated MGM comedies directed by Walters, that included such gems as *The Tender Trap, Ask Any Girl* and *Don't Go Near the Water*, all of which come up as fresh as, well, a daisy today.

Doris Day *Kate Mackay* • David Niven *Larry Mackay* • Janis Paige *Deborah Vaughn* • Spring Byington *Suzie Robinson* • Richard Haydn *Alfred North* • Patsy Kelly *Maggie* • Jack Weston *Joe Positamo* ■ *Dir* Charles Walters • *Scr* Isobel Lennart, from the book by Jean Kerr

Please Let the Flowers Live ★★
Drama   1986 · W Ger · Colour · 90mins

Duccio Tessari's weighty, symbolic "second chance" film about a lawyer who vows to reform after he is spared in a plane crash takes itself desperately seriously and is, thus, unintentionally hilarious. German dialogue dubbed into English.

Klaus-Jürgen Wussow *Charles Duhamel* • Birgit Doll • Hannelore Elsner • Gerd Böckmann • Kurt Meisel • Hans Christian Blech • Radost Bokel • Rainer Basedow ■ *Dir* Duccio Tessari • *Scr* Joachim Hammann, from a novel by Johannes Mario Simmel

Please Sir! ★★ U
Comedy   1971 · UK · Colour · 101mins

Inspired by the Sidney Poitier feature *To Sir with Love*, ITV's often hilarious sitcom ran for four years from 1968. The original class of 5C were all ready to depart for their own series, *The Fenn Street Gang*, when this shambolic film version was made, and you can tell that the minds of the ageing teens are elsewhere. The producers felt the need to shift the scene from Fenn Street school to a dingy holiday camp devoid of amenities and comic possibilities. John Alderton is typically good as put-upon form teacher Bernard Hedges, but the few funny moments belong to Joan Sanderson as the headmaster's formidable assistant. 🎞

John Alderton *Bernard Hedges* • Deryck Guyler *Norman Potter* • Noel Howlett *Mr Cromwell* • Joan Sanderson *Doris Ewell* • Richard Davies *Mr Price* • Erik Chitty *Mr Smith* • Patsy Rowlands *Angela Cutforth* ■ *Dir* Mark Stuart • *Scr* John Esmonde, Bob Larbey, from their TV series

Please Teacher ★★ 🅄

Comedy 1937 · UK · BW · 80mins

Believing the will bequeathing him a legacy is hidden in a bust that resides in a country-house girls' school, a young man inveigles himself into the premises by masquerading as the visiting explorer-brother of one of the pupils. Meanwhile, Oriental villains arrive in pursuit of a valuable jewelled fish. Bashful Bobby Howes and waif-like René Ray, both popular stars of stage and screen in thirties Britain, star in this *Boys' Own* farce with songs that's good-natured, inoffensive and belongs firmly to a bygone era.

Bobby Howes *Tommy Deacon* • René Ray *Ann Trent* • Wylie Watson *Oswald Clutterbuck* • Bertha Belmore *Agatha Pink* • Vera Pearce *Petunia Trundle* • Lyn Harding *Wing Foo* • Aubrey Dexter *Reeves* • Arthur Chesney *Round* ■ *Dir* Stafford Dickens • *Scr* Stafford Dickens, from the play by KRG Browne, RP Weston, Bert Lee

Please Turn Over ★★★

Comedy 1960 · UK · BW · 85mins

Notwithstanding its *Carry On* credentials, this gentle comedy of embarrassment could not be further from the bawdy humour of the celebrated series. Adapted by Norman Hudis from Basil Thomas's stage hit *Book of the Month*, it boasts Leslie Phillips, Joan Sims and Charles Hawtrey among those aghast at the revelations contained in a potboiling novel populated by local luminaries. It's a one-joke affair, but *Carry On* director Gerald Thomas ensures the cast of practised comics keeps it light and frothy. Parents Ted Ray and Jean Kent are overly priggish, but Julia Lockwood (daughter of Margaret) has a ball as the teenage novelist.

Ted Ray *Edward Halliday* • Jean Kent *Janet Halliday* • Leslie Phillips *Dr Henry Manners* • Joan Sims *Beryl* • Julia Lockwood *Jo Halliday* • Tim Seely *Robert Hughes* • Charles Hawtrey *Jeweller* • Dilys Laye *Millicent Jones* • Lionel Jeffries *Ian Howard* • Joan Hickson *Saleswoman* ■ *Dir* Gerald Thomas • *Scr* Norman Hudis, from the play *Book of the Month* by Basil Thomas

Pleasure at Her Majesty's ★★★★

Concert comedy documentary 1976 · UK · Colour · 100mins

The first in a long line of celebrity galas featuring major comedy and music stars performing in aid of Amnesty International. Originally screened on TV, then given a theatrical release, this elegantly filmed piece captures the magic of a special night. The Monty Python team dominate the proceedings, but there are wonderful contributions from all the artists involved (including Peter Cook, Dudley Moore, Alan Bennett, John Bird and John Fortune, among many others). This documentary, and the others that followed, provides an invaluable historical (and hysterical) record of many artists at the peak of their powers.

Eleanor Bron • Tim Brooke-Taylor • Carol Cleveland • Graeme Garden • Barry Humphries ■ *Dir* Roger Graef

The Pleasure Garden ★★★

Silent drama 1925 · UK/Ger · BW · 75mins

The trials and tribulations of a chorus girl (Virginia Valli) whose husband (Miles Mander), after their honeymoon on Lake Como, goes off to that ill-defined place known as the Tropics. Valli eventually follows him, only to discover he's really a psychotic alcoholic who's living with a native woman. All kinds of mayhem ensues. Made at the UFA studios in Germany as a co-production between Michael Balcon and Erich Pommer, this is a creaky, unconvincing and sometimes tedious silent melodrama. However, it does mark the solo feature directing debut of Alfred Hitchcock and, for all its shortcomings, reveals in embryo several of the master's stylistic devices (winding staircases, the theatre world, foreign locations, sly touches of humour). A must for students of his work.

Virginia Valli *Patsy Brand* • Carmelita Geraghty *Jill Cheyne* • Miles Mander *Levet* • John Stuart *Hugh Fielding* • Nita Naldi *Native girl* ■ *Dir* Alfred J Hitchcock [Alfred Hitchcock] • *Scr* Eliot Stannard, from the novel by Oliver Sandys • *Cinematographer* Baron Ventimiglia [Baron Gaetano Ventimiglia]

The Pleasure Girls ★★

Drama 1965 · UK · BW · 86mins

How did Klaus Kinski become mixed up with this? An attempt to show the problems facing a young model in the Swinging Sixties, it's an exasperating effort from writer/director Gerry O'Hara, who seems to think that incessant references to sexual freedom are enough to sustain a paper-thin story about the ever-changing relationships of Francesca Annis and her flatmates. It's difficult to see how the script, which strains every sinew to be gear and fab, was ever considered audacious, as the sting is drawn from almost every situation and the moralistic tone towards the end is unbearably Establishment.

Ian McShane *Keith Dexter* • Francesca Annis *Sally Feathers* • Klaus Kinski *Nikko* • Mark Eden *Prinny* • Tony Tanner *Paddy* • Rosemary Nicols *Marion* ■ *Dir/Scr* Gerry O'Hara

The Pleasure of His Company ★★ 🅄

Comedy 1961 · US · Colour · 113mins

Fred Astaire brings all his easy, debonair charm but not, alas, his twinkling feet to this, only the second non-musical of his long career. Adapted from a mildly diverting Broadway play in the vein of what used to be called drawing room comedy, the film shows what happens when ageing playboy Astaire, long-separated from his family, turns up for his daughter's wedding. Debbie Reynolds is delighted to see her father again; husband-to-be Tab Hunter is bemused; while Astaire's ex-wife Lilli Palmer, now remarried to Gary Merrill, is none too pleased. Renowned costume designer Edith Head (who did the gowns for this) makes a cameo appearance. Elegant and well-played, but also dull and dated.

Fred Astaire *Biddeford "Pogo" Poole* • Debbie Reynolds *Jessica Poole* • Lilli Palmer *Katharine Dougherty* • Tab Hunter *Roger Henderson* • Gary Merrill *James Dougherty* • Charles Ruggles *Mackenzie Savage* • Edith Head *Dress designer* ■ *Dir* George Seaton • *Scr* Samuel Taylor, from the play by Samuel Taylor, Cornelia Otis Skinner

The Pleasure Principle ★★ 🔞

Sex comedy 1991 · UK · Colour · 96mins

Peter Firth plays a philandering journalist who beds a succession of women before getting his comeuppance in this curious British sex comedy, very much in the tradition of the saucy romps of the seventies. It was unpopular with critics, who found its style outmoded in the Aids era. However, the surprisingly literate script does take into account the morals of the early nineties. The performances are also much more polished than in the rubbish of yore. Director David Cohen famously financed the shoot with a loan from the Nat West. 🎞

Peter Firth *Dick* • Lynsey Baxter *Sammy* • Haydn Gwynne *Judith* • Lysette Anthony *Charlotte* • Sara Mair-Thomas *Anne* • Ian Hogg *Malcolm* • Gordon Warnecke *Policeman* ■ *Dir/Scr* David Cohen

The Pleasure Seekers ★★★

Musical romance 1964 · US · Colour · 106mins

A rare example of a successful movie remade by the same director as the original, this is Jean Negulesco's reworking of his own *Three Coins in the Fountain*, this time set in Spain. The cast is exemplary, with sexy Ann-Margret, Pamela Tiffin and Carol Lynley more than a match for their glossy fifties predecessors, and there's Gene Tierney on hand to remind movie fans that this is a 20th Century-Fox romance. The novelty has worn a bit thin, and Fox's standard "three girls out on the town" plot looks stale, but this fun film is still worth a look.

Ann-Margret *Fran Hobson* • Tony Franciosa [Anthony Franciosa] *Emilio Lacaye* • Carol Lynley *Maggie Williams* • Gardner McKay *Pete Stenello* • Pamela Tiffin *Susie Higgins* • Andre Lawrence *Dr Andres Briones* • Gene Tierney *Jane Barton* • Brian Keith *Paul Barton* ■ *Dir*

Jean Negulesco • *Scr* Edith Sommer, from the novel *Coins in the Fountain* by John H Secondari

Pledge Night ★

Horror 1990 · US · Colour · 90 mins

Obnoxious horror quickie with a plot so risible and sleazy one must wonder at the sanity of its perpetrators. It's set at an American fraternity house, where an initiation prank ends with luckless new boy Sid being thrown into a vat of acid. Years later, a suitably peeved "Acid Sid" returns to wreak havoc on a new generation of freshmen. The young Sid is played by Joey Belladonna, better known as the lead singer of cult metal band Anthrax, who provide the film's music soundtrack.

Todd Eastland *Bonner* • Shannon McMahon *Wendy* • Will Kempe *Acid Sid* • Joey Belladonna *Young Sidney Snyder* • Dennis Sullivan *Bodine* • Craig Derrick *Cagle* • David Neal Evans *Goodman* • Robert Lentini *Silvera* ■ *Dir* Paul Ziller • *Scr* Joyce Snyder

Plein Soleil ★★★★ 🄿🄶

Crime drama 1960 · Fr/It · Colour · 113mins

Also known as *Purple Noon*, this shimmering and suspenseful *film noir* was based on the Patricia Highsmith novel, *The Talented Mr Ripley*. Rarely has such a sinister tale been told against such a gloriously sunny backdrop, yet Henri Decaë's picture-postcard views are every bit as atmospheric as the gloomiest monochrome cityscape. With more than a nod in the direction of Alfred Hitchcock, René Clément makes extensive use of a moving camera to pick up every nuance and detail as the murderous Alain Delon seeks to assume the identity of his well-to-do pal, Maurice Ronet. Stylish, impeccably played and utterly engrossing. In French with English subtitles. 🎞

Alain Delon *Tom Ripley* • Marie Laforêt *Marge* • Maurice Ronet *Philippe Greenleaf* • Bill Kearns [Billy Kearns] *Freddy Miles* • Erno Crisa *Inspector Riccordi* • Frank Latimore *O'Brien* ■ *Dir* René Clément • *Scr* René Clément, Paul Gégauff, from the novel *The Talented Mr Ripley* by Patricia Highsmith

Plenty ★★ 🄵

Drama 1985 · US · Colour · 119mins

A David Hare "special" on the postwar moral and political nosedive of our once great nation, complete with Hare's usual hectoring tone. His trenchant, deeply layered stage plays transfer badly to film and *Plenty* is a prime example of how the requisite small nervy performances, here from Meryl Streep, Charles Dance and Sam Neill, appear affected and over-stylised on screen. As always, Hare does have some interesting points to make through the contrast between Streep's memories of the Resistance and her current life of apathy, but everything is spelt out laboriously with a glum and squeakily pretentious air. Contains violence and swearing. 🎞

Meryl Streep *Susan Traherne* • Charles Dance *Raymond Brock* • Tracey Ullman *Alice Park* • John Gielgud *Sir Leonard Darwin* • Sting *Mick* • Ian McKellen *Sir Andrew Charleson* • Sam Neill *Lazar* • Bert Kwouk *Mr Aung* • Lim Pik Sen *Madame Aung* • André Maranne *Villon* ■ *Dir* Fred Schepisi • *Scr* David Hare, from his play

The Plot against Harry
★★★ PG

Comedy   1969 · US · BW · 80mins

Finally released 20 years after it was filmed, Michael Roemer's pseudo-*cinéma vérité* comedy was clearly ahead of its time. But, by 1989, its determinedly deadpan style had become such a familiar part of the comic landscape in the films of directors such as Jim Jarmusch that its impact was somewhat reduced. Newly sprung from jail, petty mobster Martin Priest is convinced that life has got it in for him. And a series of incidents, including a car accident that leads him to discover that he is the father of a family he never knew he had, seem to uphold his suspicions.

Martin Priest *Harry Plotnick* • Ben Lang *Leo Perlmutter* • Maxine Woods *Kay Skolnik* • Henry Nemo *Max* • Jacques Taylor *Jack* • Jean Leslie *Irene* • Ellen Herbert *Mae* • Sandra Kazan *Margie* • Ronald Coralian *Mel Skolnik* • Ruth Roemer *Linda Skolnik* ■ *Dir/Scr* Michael Roemer

The Plot Thickens
★★ U

Mystery   1936 · US · BW · 64mins

ZaSu Pitts took over the role of RKO's schoolmarm sleuth Hildegarde Withers from Helen Broderick, who herself succeeded Edna May Oliver, and was responsible for this more comedic entry in a most likeable series. Her flustery mode of performance isn't ideal for acutely rational detective Withers, but she's nevertheless fun to watch paired opposite series regular irascible James Gleason as the cigar-chomping cop Oscar Piper. As the title indicates, this is a particularly complex mystery, full of humour; Pitts and Gleason were to team again for one more title which was to be the last of the series.

James Gleason *Oscar Piper* • ZaSu Pitts *Hildegarde Withers* • Owen Davis Jr *Robert Wilkins* • Louise Latimer *Alice Stevens* • Arthur Aylesworth *Kendall* • Richard Tucker *John Carter* • Paul Fix *Joe* • Barbara Barondess *Marie* ■ *Dir* Ben Holmes • *Scr* Clarence Upson Young, Jack Townley, from a story by Stuart Palmer

The Plot to Kill Hitler
★★★ PG

Second World War drama
1990 · US · Colour · 89mins

Although this TV movie glamorises the facts and is weak on the hatching of the plot, it's still a fascinating if overfamiliar story, as members of the German high command led by Colonel von Stauffenberg (Brad Davis) try to dispose of the man who had led them to victory but was now in charge of a retreating army. The assassination attempt comes across as muddled both in organisation and execution, even though the film portrays the collaborators as heroic. Contains violence.

Brad Davis *Colonel Claus Von Stauffenberg* • Madolyn Smith *Countess Nina Von Stauffenberg* • Ian Richardson *General Ludwig Beck* • Michael Byrne *Friedrich Olbright* • Michael Gwilym [Mike Gwilym] *Adolf Hitler* • Helmut Grunn *Field Marshal Rommel* ■ *Dir* Lawrence Schiller • *Scr* Steven Elkins

The Plough and the Stars
★★

Drama   1936 · US · BW · 66mins

Barbara Stanwyck is magnificently miscast as the loyal wife fearing for the life of her IRA husband, played by the incredibly dreary Preston Foster, and the supporting cast is so authentically Irish that the two leads seem even more at sea. That said, the appearances of performers such as Barry Fitzgerald, his real-life brother Arthur Shields and FJ McCormick go a long way. It's truly dispiriting to watch a major Irish play sink into the Hollywood mire, particularly since John Ford should have known better, and the cheap production values and ill-chosen intercut newsreel clips don't help.

Barbara Stanwyck *Nora Clitheroe* • Preston Foster *Jack Clitheroe* • Barry Fitzgerald *Fluther Good* • Denis O'Dea *The Young Covey* • Eileen Crowe *Bessie Burgess* • FJ McCormick *Captain Brennon* • Arthur Shields *Padraic Pearse* ■ *Dir* John Ford • *Scr* Dudley Nichols, from the play by Sean O'Casey

The Ploughman's Lunch
★★★★ 15

Drama   1983 · UK · Colour · 102mins

Well-observed and thought-provoking drama about the way in which the private life of a BBC radio news producer affects his work. The background detail looks absolutely authentic, and the performances, particularly from Jonathan Pryce as the producer and Charlie Dore as the TV researcher he beds, are excellent. The film is a collaboration between novelist Ian McEwan and director Richard Eyre, who went on to head the National Theatre. It's remarkable how a film so critical of the media could wangle location facilities out of the BBC, LWT and even the 1982 Conservative Party conference in Brighton. Slow-starting, but stay with it.

Jonathan Pryce *James Penfield* • Tim Curry *Jeremy Hancock* • Rosemary Harris *Ann Barrington* • Frank Finlay *Matthew Fox* • Charlie Dore *Susan Barrington* • David De Keyser *Tom Gold* ■ *Dir* Richard Eyre • *Scr* Ian McEwan

The Plow that Broke the Plains
★★★★

Documentary   1934 · US · BW · 49mins

Sponsored by the United States Resettlement Administration, this piece of New Deal propaganda is usually considered the cornerstone of American documentary film-making. Made on a shoestring, yet filmed with evocative expertise by socialist cinematographers Ralph Steiner, Paul Strand and Leo Hurwitz, ex-critic Pare Lorentz's debut explored the history of the Great Plains and the ecological causes of the Dust Bowl that had made the Depression even more disastrous for the Mid-West's valiant farmers. With a superb score by Virgil Thompson and a rhythmic commentary delivered by baritone Thomas Chalmers, it is emotive, persuasive and powerful, both in its message and its imagery.

Thomas Chalmers *Narrator* ■ *Dir/Scr* Pare Lorentz

Plughead Rewired: Circuitry Man II
★

Science-fiction thriller
1994 · US · Colour · 97mins

It's distressing to see Dennis Christopher, so good in *Breaking Away*, wasted in a witless sequel that makes his character look even more foolish and aimless than he was in the original. The film feels like a collection of out-takes from the first *Circuitry Man*, even recycling some of its effects. The incomprehensible plot has something to do with Plughead (Vernon Wells) again setting his sights on capturing Danner (Jim Metzler).

Vernon Wells *Plughead* • Deborah Shelton *Kyle* • Jim Metzler *Danner* • Dennis Christopher *Leech* • Nicholas Worth *Rock* • Traci Lords *Norma* ■ *Dir/Scr* Steven Lovy, Robert Lovy

The Plumber
★★★

Black comedy   1979 · Ausl · Colour · 76mins

Peter Weir is revered as the director of *Witness*, *Dead Poets Society* and *The Truman Show* but even at the start of his career he established his serious credentials with *Picnic at Hanging Rock* and the mystical *The Last Wave*. This black comedy, made on 16mm in three weeks for Australian TV, is about a coarse plumber who arrives at a middle-class household, fixes the pipes, but refuses to budge, acting as a catalyst and provoking some very funny but also some scary responses. Behind it all is the evocation of otherness that Weir explores in all his films.

Judy Morris *Jill Cowper* • Robert Coleby *Brian Cowper* • Ivar Kants *Max, The Plumber* • Candy Raymond *Meg* ■ *Dir/Scr* Peter Weir

Plunder Road
★★★ U

Crime thriller   1957 · US · BW · 71mins

Veteran players Gene Raymond and Wayne Morris clearly relished the opportunity to star in this cleverly written story of a train hold-up and the robbers' doomed attempts to shift their massive haul of gold ingots. Elisha Cook Jr already knew his loser's part by heart but plays it, as usual, to perfection. Writer Steven Ritch also appears as Frankie, the former racing driver who teams up with Raymond to drive a tanker loaded with part of the booty. Aided by veteran cameraman Ernest Haller, new director Hubert Cornfield makes a visually exciting picture that squeezes every ounce of suspense from the story.

Gene Raymond *Eddie* • Jeanne Cooper *Fran* • Wayne Morris *Commando* • Elisha Cook Jr *Skeets* • Stafford Repp *Roly Adams* • Steven Ritch *Frankie* • Nora Hayden *Hazel* ■ *Dir* Hubert Cornfield • *Scr* Steven Ritch, from a story by Jack Charney, Steven Ritch

Plunkett & Macleane
★★ 15

Period action adventure
1999 · UK · Colour · 97mins

Despite having *Trainspotting* co-stars Robert Carlyle and Jonny Lee Miller reunite to play the infamous highwaymen who terrorised toffs in 18th-century London, Jake (son of Ridley) Scott's debut feature is a chaotic jumble of style over substance and sense. Contemporary dance music and startling production design deliberately flaunt period in a misguided attempt to make the larcenous odd couple a hip English version of Butch Cassidy and the Sundance Kid. Pouting Liv Tyler adds romantic window-dressing as Miller's aristocratic groupie, but it's a deucedly ragged romp. 📺 DVD

Robert Carlyle *Will Plunkett* • Jonny Lee Miller *James Macleane* • Liv Tyler *Lady Rebecca* • Ken Stott *Chance* • Michael Gambon *Lord Gibson* • Alan Cumming *Lord Rochester* ■ *Dir* Jake Scott • *Scr* Robert Wade, Neal Purvis, Charles McKeown, from a screenplay (unproduced) by Selwyn Roberts

Plymouth
★★

Science-fiction drama
1991 · US/It · Colour · 96mins

Plymouth (named after the rock that the Pilgrim Fathers allegedly landed on in 1620) is the first city on the Moon in this ho-hum TV movie that doesn't have the budget to properly do justice to its eventual disaster theme. Doctor Cindy Pickett tries keeping her pregnancy a secret from space hubby Dale Midkiff as a solar flare threatens to wipe out the lunar population. Aside from the few plot points raised – the most interesting being that a baby born on the Moon can't survive on Earth – it's a basic low-rent rescue mission adventure.

Cindy Pickett *Addy Mathewson* • Dale Midkiff *Gil Eaton* • Richard Hamilton *Wendell Mackenzies* • Jerry Hardin *Lowell* ■ *Dir/Scr* Lee David Zlotoff

Plymouth Adventure
★★ U

Historical drama
1952 · US · Colour · 104mins

Spencer Tracy is the stern skipper of the *Mayflower* as it sets sail for America in 1620. His heavyweight presence is sorely needed in a ponderous rendering of an unwieldy script that is overloaded with history. The special effects, which won an Oscar, and Miklos Rozsa's rousing score are among the few highlights in director Clarence Brown's rather dull depiction of the pilgrim fathers' epic journey.

Spencer Tracy *Captain Christopher Jones* • Gene Tierney *Dorothy Bradford* • Van Johnson *John Alden* • Leo Genn *William Bradford* • Dawn Addams *Priscilla Mullins* • Lloyd Bridges *Coppin* • Barry Jones *William Brewster* ■ *Dir* Clarence Brown • *Scr* Helen Deutsch, from a novel by Ernest Gebler

Pocahontas
★★★ U

Animated adventure
1995 · US · Colour · 77mins

Visually stunning but historically botched re-creation of the legendary romance between Indian maid Pocahontas (Irene Bedard) and captain John Smith (Mel Gibson) in the 17th-century New World. The first Disney animation to deal with a factual subject skilfully communicates both its "love conquers all" and ecological messages, although the greedy governor (David Ogden Stiers) is so over-the-top he's practically out of sight. 📺

Irene Bedard *Pocahontas* • Mel Gibson *John Smith* • Joe Baker *Lon* • Christian Bale *Thomas* • Billy Connolly *Ben* • Linda Hunt *Grandmother Willow* • David Ogden Stiers

U = SUITABLE FOR ALL   Uc = SUITABLE FOR ALL, ESPECIALLY FOR YOUNG CHILDREN (VIDEO ONLY)   PG = PARENTAL GUIDANCE

Governor Ratcliffe/Wiggins ■ Dir Mike Gabriel, Eric Goldberg • Scr Carl Binder, Susannah Grant, Philip LaZebnik

Pocahontas II: Journey to a New World ★★ **U**

Animated adventure
1998 · US · Colour · 70mins

An adequate sequel to one of Disney's less memorable recent cartoons, with the Indian princess sailing to England and finding herself torn between two cultures, and lovers. Predictably, her cute pet hummingbird and raccoon go along for the ride. The script takes the usual liberties with history (though the real-life Pocahontas *did* visit England, and in fact died there), though children will derive a fair amount of fun from the film. Like most Disney sequels, it bypassed cinemas and went straight to video. ▣

Irene Bedard *Pocahontas* • Billy Zane *John Rolfe* • David Ogden Stiers *Governor Ratcliffe* • Jean Stapleton *Mrs Jenkins* • Russell Means *Powhatan* • Linda Hunt *Grandmother Willow* • Donald Gibson *John Smith* ■ Dir Bradley Raymond, Tom Ellery • Scr Allen Estrin, Cindy Marcus, Flip Kobler

Pocahontas: the Legend ★★

Romantic drama
1995 · Can · Colour

Released the same year as Disney's animated blockbuster, this live-action version sticks pretty much to the core story line, as Pocahontas intercedes with her father, Powhatan, for the life of the English explorer, John Smith. Treading the tightrope of political correctness with considerable care, director Danièle J Suissa and her co-writer Donald Martin take pains to stress the rights of the Native Americans to their homelands and the sanctity of their customs and beliefs. But, such an educative approach leaves little room for drama and Sandrine Holt and Miles O'Keeffe (who was, of course, Bo Derek's Tarzan) struggle to make an impact.

Sandrine Holt *Pocahontas* • Miles O'Keefe [Miles O'Keeffe] *John Smith* • Tony Goldwyn *Sir Wingfield* • Billy Merasty *Kocoum* • Gordon Tootoosis *Chief Powhatan* ■ Dir Danièle J Suissa • Scr Danièle J Suissa, Donald Martin

Pocket Money ★★ **PG**

Western
1972 · US · Colour · 95mins

A tepid latter-day western. After Martin Ritt pulled out, Paul Newman installed his friend Stuart Rosenberg in the director's chair, but he never came to grips with Terrence Malick's rambling screenplay and the result is a directionless, if fitfully amusing, tale in which Newman and Lee Marvin try to round up some cattle for shady beef baron Strother Martin. Laszlo Kovacs's photography is so authentic it leaves you with dust in your eyes, but Newman and Marvin look like they're acting in different movies.

Paul Newman *Jim Kane* • Lee Marvin *Leonard* • Strother Martin *Garrett* • Christine Belford *Adelita* • Kelly Jean Peters *Wife* • Fred Graham *Herb* • Wayne Rogers *Stretch Russell* • Hector Elizondo *Juan* ■ Dir Stuart Rosenberg • Scr Terry Malick [Terrence Malick], John Gay, from the novel *Jim Kane* by JPS Brown

Pocketful of Miracles ★ **U**

Comedy
1961 · US · Colour · 136mins

Frank Capra's remake of his 1933 comedy *Lady for a Day* is a disaster from start to finish. Damon Runyon's yarn worked during the Depression, but here this tale of class envy and economic inequality seems lost in a time warp. It also drags on far too long, while Bette Davis is badly miscast as the apple-seller transformed into a wealthy socialite by a superstitious gangster (Glenn Ford) and his gang of hoodlums. A sad end to Capra's career, though some might say he never made a decent movie after *It's a Wonderful Life*.

Glenn Ford *Dave the Dude* • Bette Davis *Apple Annie* • Hope Lange *Queenie Martin* • Arthur O'Connell *Count Romero* • Peter Falk *Joy Boy* • Thomas Mitchell *Judge Henry G Blake* • Edward Everett Horton *Butler* • Mickey Shaughnessy *Junior* • David Brian *Governor* • Ann-Margret *Louise* • Mike Mazurki *Big Mike* ■ Dir Frank Capra • Scr Hal Kanter, Harry Tugend, Jimmy Cannon, from the film *Lady for a Day* by Robert Riskin, from the story *Madame La Gimp* by Damon Runyon

Poetic Justice ★★ **15**

Drama
1993 · US · Colour · 104mins

After making a big splash with his first film, *Boyz N the Hood*, John Singleton lost his control somewhat with this twee, right-on drama that charts the burgeoning romance between hairdresser and poetess Janet Jackson and postal worker Tupac Shakur as they get to know each other on the road to Oakland. Mawkish and well-intentioned instead of gritty and real, the movie is saved by the acting of the two leads – Shakur especially had a natural presence in front of the camera and his murder in 1996 brought a promising film career to an end. Maya Angelou wrote the poetry for Jackson's character. Contains violence, swearing and sex scenes. ▣

Janet Jackson *Justice* • Tupac Shakur *Lucky* • Tyra Ferrell *Jessie* • Regina King *Iesha* • Joe Torry *Chicago* • Roger Guenveur Smith *Heywood* • Lori Petty *Penelope* • Billy Zane *Brad* • Khandi Alexander *Simone* • Maya Angelou *Aunt June* ■ Dir/Scr John Singleton

Point Blank ★★★★ **18**

Thriller
1967 · US · Colour · 87mins

British director John Boorman's US directing debut (he'd previously made a Dave Clark Five musical in Britain) was this grim, violent, virtually metaphysical thriller, which is marred only by a flashback narrative that occasionally (deliberately?) confuses. Nevertheless, it's a gripping and sexy action movie, with a magnificent performance from Lee Marvin as the revenge-seeking Walker, the ultimate lethal weapon, whose insane quest to retrieve mob money assumes mythical proportions. Philip H Lathrop's brilliant cinematography and the Los Angeles night locations will inevitably suffer on TV, but repeated viewings actually make this film revealing the subtle complexity of the storytelling and clarifying the characterisations. MGM, by the way, was so worried by the rushes that it took an intervention from David Lean to ensure Boorman remained on the picture. Contains violence and some swearing. ▣

Lee Marvin *Walker* • Angie Dickinson *Chris* • Keenan Wynn *Yost* • Carroll O'Connor *Brewster* • Lloyd Bochner *Frederick Carter* • Michael Strong *Stegman* • John Vernon *Mal Reese* • Sharon Acker *Lynne* • James Sikking [James B Sikking] *Hired gun* ■ Dir John Boorman • Scr Alexander Jacobs, David Newhouse, Rafe Newhouse, from the novel *The Hunter* by Richard Stark [Donald E Westlake]

Point Blank ★ **18**

Action thriller
1997 · US · Colour · 85mins

Mickey Rourke's detractors will have a field day when they see the actor hilariously humiliated in this *Die Hard* rip-off. Rourke stars as an ex-Texas Ranger who sneaks into a shopping mall that's been taken over by a gang of escaped convicts. The star is only given about 25 lines of dialogue in the entire movie; to make matters worse, he doesn't even get the girl at the end. The rest of the movie mixes utter sleaze and graphic violence, greatly assisted by the shotgun-blasting Danny Trejo as one of the hostage-takers. ▣

Mickey Rourke *Rudy Ray* • Kevin Gage *Joe Ray* • Michael Wright *Sonny* • Danny Trejo *Wallace* • Frederic Forrest *Mac Bradford* ■ Dir Matt Earl Beesley • Scr James Bannon, Cary Solomon, Chuck Konzelman, Daniel Raskov, from a story by Daniel Raskov, Cary Solomon, Chuck Konzelman

Point Break ★★★★ **18**

Thriller
1991 · US · Colour · 122mins

Kathryn Bigelow shows the "boy's-own" adventure is not just the preserve of the lads in this silly but hugely enjoyable thriller. Keanu Reeves is the young FBI agent who unsurprisingly makes a very convincing surfing dude when he goes undercover to infiltrate a gang, headed by Patrick Swayze, suspected of carrying out a string of audacious bank robberies. Try to ignore the mystical claptrap and concentrate instead on Bigelow's stunningly conceived action set pieces, as well as some exhilarating sky-diving and surfing scenes. For Reeves, this proved to be a dry, or more accurately wet, run for *Speed*, and he acquits himself reasonably well, while Swayze makes a convincing enough villain. The reliable supporting players include Gary Busey, John McGinley and James LeGros. Contains violence, swearing and nudity. ▣ **DVD**

Patrick Swayze *Bodhi* • Keanu Reeves *Johnny Utah* • Gary Busey *Angelo Pappas* • Lori Petty *Tyler* • John C McGinley *Ben Harp* • James LeGros *Roach* ■ Dir Kathryn Bigelow • Scr W Peter Iliff, from a story by Rick King, W Peter Iliff

Point of No Return ★

Thriller
1986 · W Ger · Colour · 95mins

As with so many Euro crime movies, this below average heist thriller has not travelled well and once again the execrable dubbing makes following the cliché-ridden action even more of a chore. As the taxi driver, the blonde and the mechanic who carry out a daring raid on a security van, Winfried Glatzeder, Grazyna Dylong and Achim Reichel are eminently resistible and as writer/director Diethard Kuster has gambled everything on us sympathising with them as societal victims driven to crime by poverty, the picture is onto a loser from the start. German dialogue dubbed into English.

Winfried Glatzeder *Stefan* • Achim Reichel *Paul* • Grazyna Dylong *Helen* • Claus-Dieter Reents *Alfred S* ■ Dir/Scr Diethard Kuster

Point of No Return ★★

Thriller
1993 · US · Colour · 109mins

This serviceable American remake of Luc Besson's *Nikita* is a near scene-for-scene re-tread of the slick, sexy original. Bridget Fonda makes a far less convincing lead than Anne Parillaud, and her metamorphosis from psycho junkie to elegant assassin is much harder to swallow. The strong supporting cast (including Gabriel Byrne and Anne Bancroft) boost credibility, but there's an oddly cold, detached feeling about director John Badham's re-creation of the original's dynamic action scenes. Though well-shot and competently performed, it's one of the laziest and most unnecessary Hollywood remakes.

Bridget Fonda *Maggie* • Gabriel Byrne *Bob* • Dermot Mulroney *JP* • Miguel Ferrer *Kaufman* • Anne Bancroft *Amanda* • Olivia D'Abo *Angela* • Richard Romanus *Fahd Bahktiar* • Harvey Keitel *Victor the cleaner* ■ Dir John Badham • Scr Robert Getchell, Alexandra Seros, from the film *Nikita* by Luc Besson

Poison Ivy ★★ **PG**

Comedy
1985 · US · Colour · 92mins

A hopelessly tame comedy which would have remained long forgotten had it not provided a role for Michael J Fox. The setting is the obligatory summer camp, which provides the excuse for the usual teenage high jinks – except that it's a TV movie, so there are precious few gross-out laughs. Fox offers a few glimpses of his comic talents, but the rest of the cast is largely forgettable. ▣

Michael J Fox *Dennis Baxter* • Nancy McKeon *Rhonda Malone* • Adam Baldwin *Ike Dimick* • Caren Kaye *Margo Klopper* • Robert Klein *Big Irv Klopper* ■ Dir Larry Elikann • Scr Bennett Tramer

Poison Ivy ★★★ **18**

Thriller
1992 · US · Colour · 89mins

ET's Drew Barrymore came of age in this alluring tale about a poor girl from the wrong side of the tracks who befriends fellow loner Sara Gilbert and inveigles her way into her wealthy family, with deadly results. There's a touch of music-video style about director Katt Shea Ruben's over-glossy visuals, but she is well-served by the leads, particularly Barrymore, who's a sexy but vulnerable junior *femme fatale*. Look out, too, for *Charlie's Angels* star Cheryl Ladd as Gilbert's sickly mother and Leonardo DiCaprio in one of his earliest roles. Contains violence, swearing and nudity. ▣

Sara Gilbert *Sylvie Cooper* • Drew Barrymore *Ivy* • Tom Skerritt *Darryl Cooper* • Cheryl Ladd *Georgie Cooper* • Alan Stock *Bob* • Jeanne Sakata *Isabelle* • Leonardo DiCaprio *Guy* ■ Dir Katt Shea Ruben • Scr Katt Shea Ruben, Andy Ruben, from the story by Melissa Goddard , Peter Morgan

Poison Ivy II: Lily ★ 🔞

Erotic thriller 1995 · US · Colour · 101mins

The connection to the 1992 *Poison Ivy* comes with repressed college student Lily (Alyssa Milano) finding Drew Barrymore's old diary. After reading it, she is inspired to transform herself into a sexually liberated woman, confusing her boyfriend and generating lust in her professor (Xander Berkeley). After Lily's transformation, the movie doesn't know what to do, with Berkeley's sudden change in character only occurring to facilitate some kind of climax. The stereotypical supporting characters (quiet Asian, feminist lesbian) could easily have been eliminated. Another sequel, *Poison Ivy: The New Seduction*, followed in 1997. Contains swearing, sex scenes and some violence. 🖵

Alyssa Milano *Lily* • Xander Berkeley *Donald Falk* • Johnathon Schaech *Gredin* • Belinda Bauer *Angela Falk* ■ *Dir* Anne Goursaud • *Scr* Chloe King

Poison Pen ★★★

Psychological drama 1939 · UK · BW · 79mins

Here's an early and powerful working of an intrinsically downbeat subject, as a rash of anonymous letters cause major misery and distress among the inhabitants of an English hamlet. Catherine Lacey's seamstress is wrongly hounded as the likely perpetrator because she's an outsider, Robert Newton's volatile young labourer is persuaded his innocent wife is having an affair, and vicar's daughter Ann Todd nearly loses her Australian boyfriend. Could it possibly be that the saintly sinister sister of the vicar is not all she seems? When she's played by Flora Robson, you have to wonder.

Flora Robson *Mary Rider* • Robert Newton *Sam Hurrin* • Ann Todd *Ann Rider* • Geoffrey Toone *David* • Reginald Tate *Rev Rider* • Belle Chrystal *Sucal Hurrin* • Edward Chapman *Len Griffin* • Edward Rigby *Badham* • Catherine Lacey *Connie Fateley* • Wilfrid Hyde White *Postman* ■ *Dir* Paul L Stein • *Scr* Doreen Montgomery, William Freshman, NC Hunter, Esther McCracken, from the play by Richard Llewellyn

Pokémon the First Movie: Mewtwo Strikes Back ★ 🅿🇬

Animated fantasy adventure 1998 · Jap · Colour · 74mins

Parents may grit their teeth at the prospect of a full-length film with the cuddly Japanese monsters of trading card, video game and TV fame; their big-screen debut could hardly have been worse. The movie actually comprises two films, the first being a virtually plotless short (*Pikachu's Vacation*) whose eponymous hero, a cute yellow rodent, becomes irritating very quickly. In the main feature, genetically modified monster Mewtwo escapes from the lab and goes on the rampage. The climactic battle is repetitious and boring, while the film's anti-violence message is crassly expressed. Japanese dialogue dubbed into English.

Dir Kunihiko Yuyama, Michael Haigney • *Scr* English adaptation by Norman J Grossfeld,

Michael Haigney, John Touhey, from characters created by Satoshi Tajiri • *Chief Animator* Sayuri Ichiishi

Poker Alice ★★ 🅿🇬

Comedy western 1987 · US · Colour · 91mins

It's easy to see why Elizabeth Taylor was attracted to this rather paltry TV movie: if the leading role wasn't written for her, it was certainly (forgive the pun) tailored to her bawdy talents by distinguished veteran western writer James Lee Barrett. Yet the film overall is so poorly shot and directed that there's little of real interest, save watching the obvious on-screen chemistry between Taylor and her tanned co-star George Hamilton. 🖵

Elizabeth Taylor *"Poker Alice" Moffat* • George Hamilton *Cousin John* • Tom Skerritt *Jeremy Collins* • David Wayne *Old Man* • Richard Mulligan *Jake Sears* • Ed Adams *Harris* ■ *Dir* Arthur Allan Seidelman • *Scr* James Lee Barrett

Pola X ★★ 🔞

Drama 1999 · Fr/Ger/Swi · Colour · 134mins

Léos Carax's first movie since *Les Amants du Pont-Neuf* (1990) takes its acronymic name from the French title of Herman Melville's novel *Pierre, or the Ambiguities*; the "X" refers to the fact that there were ten drafts of the screenplay. Guillaume Depardieu plays Pierre, the carefree son of a wealthy widow (Catherine Deneuve) whose world is changed irrevocably when he meets a young woman who claims to be his illegitimate half-sister. Leaving his home, mother and fiancée, Pierre joins Isabelle (Katerina Golubeva) in Paris and adopts the life of a tortured, starving writer. Carax's grim fable recalls Mike Leigh's *Naked* with its nihilistic antihero and unfeeling urban landscape. Yet for all the gritty detail and hints of incest, this relentlessly bleak film is too dull to engage and almost too long to endure. In French with English subtitles.

Catherine Deneuve *Marie* • Guillaume Depardieu *Pierre Valombreuse* • Katerina Golubeva *Isabelle* • Delphine Chuillot *Lucie de Boisieux* • Laurent Lucas *Thibault* • Mathias Mlekuz *TV presenter* • Dine Oukili *Taxi driver* • Miguel Yeco *Augusto* ■ *Dir* Léos Carax • *Scr* LéosCarax, Jean-Pol Fargeau, Lauren Sedofsky, from the novel *Pierre, or the Ambiguities (Pierre, ou les Ambiguités)* by Herman Melville

Polar ★★★

Thriller 1984 · Fr · Colour · 97mins

This adaptation of Jean-Patrick Manchette's pulp novel, *Morgue Pleine* owes both its atmosphere and its complexity to *The Big Sleep*. However, Jacques Bral's direction lacks the incisiveness of Howard Hawks and Jean-François Balmer is certainly no Bogart, despite delivering his voiceover narrative in a suitably laconic drawl. But, the case is sufficiently twisting and sinister, with Balmer entering the seedy world of skin flicks after being lured by Sandra Montaigu into investigating the death of her roommate. Moreover, there's a chance to see thriller specialist Claude Chabrol in a rare acting role. French dialogue dubbed into English.

Jean-François Balmer *Eugène Tarpon* • Sandra Montaigu *Charlotte le Dantec* • Roland

Dubillard *Jean-Baptiste Haymann* • Pierre Santini *Insp Coccioli* • Claude Chabrol *Theodore Lyssenko* ■ *Dir* Jacques Bral • *Scr* Jacques Bral, Jean-Paul Leca, Julien Lévi, from the novel *Morgue Pleine* by Jean-Patrick Manchette

Police ★★★★ 🄸🄵

Crime thriller 1985 · Fr · Colour · 113mins

Sophie Marceau was the wunderkind of French cinema and Maurice Pialat her director, so the off-screen clashes were inevitable, but the tensions are also evident on the screen and they help give this superior crime drama an added charge. The opening sequences, in which bruising cop Gérard Depardieu muscles in on a Tunisian drugs-ring, make for compelling viewing thanks to Pialat's attention to authentic detail, but the erotic duel between Depardieu and the drug-dealing Marceau is less effective, even though sparks certainly fly from this oddly matched pair. Not your average thriller, but a cracking one, nevertheless. Contains violence, swearing and nudity.

Gérard Depardieu *Mangin* • Sophie Marceau *Noria* • Richard Anconina *Lambert* • Pascale Rocard *Marie Vedret* • Sandrine Bonnaire *Lydie* ■ *Dir* Maurice Pialat • *Scr* Maurice Pialat, Catherine Breillat, Sylvie Danton, Jacques Fieschi, from a story by Catherine Breillat

Police Academy ★★★ 🄸🄵

Comedy 1984 · US · Colour · 92mins

Back in 1984, it's hard to imagine that anyone thought this would go on to spawn six sequels as well as a cartoon series. However, it managed to strike a chord with audiences around the world and made a star (well, briefly anyway) out of Steve Guttenberg. And, while the follow-ups became increasingly puerile as the series went on, the original film produces its fair share of belly laughs. Guttenberg leads a group of oddballs, who probably shouldn't even be allowed to watch cops on television, into police training, where they clash with authority but prove themselves in the end. It's crude and juvenile but fans will be in heaven. Contains swearing, violence and nudity. 🖵 ***DVD***

Steve Guttenberg *Carey Mahoney* • Kim Cattrall *Karen Thompson* • GW Bailey *Lieutenant Harris* • Bubba Smith *Moses Hightower* • Donovan Scott *Leslie Barbara* • George Gaynes *Commandant Lassard* • Andrew Rubin *George Martin* • David Graf *Tackleberry* • Leslie Easterbrook *Sergeant Callahan* ■ *Dir* Hugh Wilson • *Scr* Neal Israel, Pat Proft, Hugh Wilson, from a story by Neal Israel, Pat Proft

Police Academy 2: Their First Assignment ★ 🄸🄵

Comedy 1985 · US · Colour · 83mins

The international success of the first movie in the *Police Academy* series meant that new director Jerry Paris wasn't going to mess with a winning formula. This time the misfits get the opportunity to cause chaos on the streets, but, while it features many members of the original cast, this is a lazy replay of the original outing, with grossness substituting for any genuine humour. An embarrassed looking

Howard Hesseman is the only major new addition. 🖵

Steve Guttenberg *Carey Mahoney* • Bubba Smith *Hightower* • David Graf *Tackleberry* • Michael Winslow *Larvell Jones* • Bruce Mahler *Doug Fackler* • Marion Ramsey *Laverne Hooks* • Colleen Camp *Kirkland* • Howard Hesseman *Pete Lassard* • Art Metrano *Lieutenant Mauser* • Bob Goldthwait [Bobcat Goldthwait] *Zed* ■ *Dir* Jerry Paris • *Scr* Barry Blaustein, David Sheffield, from characters created by Neal Israel, Pat Proft

Police Academy 3: Back in Training ★★ 🅿🇬

Comedy 1986 · US · Colour · 80mins

The title sums up the plot, really, although predictably the loveable losers eventually save the day as rival police academies battle for survival in an era of cutbacks in public spending. It is an improvement of sorts on the first sequel, but by this stage you were either a fan or holding the series up as the prime example of Hollywood puerility. The last film of director Jerry Paris, a former character actor who first stepped behind the camera on TV's *The Dick Van Dyke Show*. 🖵

Steve Guttenberg *Sergeant Mahoney* • Bubba Smith *Sergeant Hightower* • David Graf *Sergeant Tackleberry* • Michael Winslow *Sergeant Jones* • Marion Ramsey *Sergeant Hooks* • Leslie Easterbrook *Lieutenant Callahan* • Art Metrano *Commandant Mauser* • Bobcat Goldthwait *Cadet Zed* ■ *Dir* Jerry Paris • *Scr* Gene Quintano, from characters created by Neal Israel, Pat Proft

Police Academy 4: Citizens on Patrol ★ 🅿🇬

Comedy 1987 · US · Colour · 83mins

This sequel is only worth watching because it gives us the opportunity to watch a pre-*Basic Instinct* Sharon Stone stranded down the cast list with the thankless role of star Steve Guttenberg's girlfriend. By now Guttenberg was in search of better things and does little more here than go through the motions. So the best gags go to George Gaynes as the feeble-minded commander who finds himself training an even crazier bunch of recruits when citizens are encouraged to become part-time policemen. Contains swearing. 🖵

Steve Guttenberg *Mahoney* • Bubba Smith *Hightower* • Michael Winslow *Jones* • David Graf *Tackleberry* • Sharon Stone *Claire Mattson* • George Gaynes *Commandant Lassard* • Bobcat Goldthwait *Zed* • Leslie Easterbrook *Callahan* ■ *Dir* Jim Drake • *Scr* Gene Quintano, from characters created by Neal Israel, Pat Proft

Police Academy 5: Assignment Miami Beach ★ 🅿🇬

Comedy 1988 · US · Colour · 86mins

What could audiences have possibly done to deserve such torture? As this inane series progresses, each episode becomes sillier and more slapdash than the last. There's no Steve Guttenberg in this one (he must have read the script), and all you need to know is that the bumbling cops, as the title suggests, visit Miami for a convention, which is the only thing that differentiates this extremely mediocre

🅄 = SUITABLE FOR ALL, 🅄𝐜 = SUITABLE FOR ALL, ESPECIALLY FOR YOUNG CHILDREN (VIDEO ONLY) 🅿🇬 = PARENTAL GUIDANCE

movie from the four that went before. Contains some swearing. ▭

Matt McCoy *Nick* • Janet Jones *Kate Stratton* • George Gaynes *Commandant Lassard* • GW Bailey *Captain Harris* • René Auberjonois *Tony Stark* • Bubba Smith *Moses Hightower* • David Graf *Eugene Tackleberry* • Michael Winslow *Larvelle Jones* • Leslie Easterbrook *Debbie Callahan* ■ *Dir* Alan Myerson • *Scr* Stephen J Curwick, from characters created by Neal Israel, Pat Proft

Police Academy 6: City under Siege ★ PG

Comedy   1989 · US · Colour · 79mins

Evening all. What's all this then? Having run out of inventive gags and originality by the final scene of the very first *Police Academy*, the series had overstayed its welcome long before this fifth sequel by stretching a thin premise to breaking point. Aside from the vocal gymnastics of Michael Winslow, this laughter-free zone couldn't even get itself arrested for indecency, unlike our own far superior *Carry Ons*. You have the right to remain silent and unfortunately you probably will! Contains swearing. ▭

Bubba Smith *Hightower* • David Graf *Tackleberry* • Michael Winslow *Jones* • Leslie Easterbrook *Callahan* • Marion Ramsey *Hooks* • Lance Kinsey *Proctor* • Matt McCoy *Nick* • Bruce Mahler *Fackler* ■ *Dir* Peter Bonerz • *Scr* Stephen J Curwick, from characters created by Neal Israel, Pat Proft

Police Academy: Mission to Moscow ★ PG

Comedy   1994 · US · Colour · 79mins

All seemed well. Five years had passed since the execrable *Police Academy 6*. But to mark the tenth anniversary of the series, back came George Gaynes and his crew of cockeyed cops to prove once more the law of diminishing sequels. Christopher Lee can never have been in a more terrifying movie – terrifyingly bad, that is. Surely he had better things to do than play the Russian police chief unable to cope with computer crook Ron Perlman? There isn't a single joke worthy of the name in this humiliating farrago. ▭

George Gaynes *Commandant Lassard* • Michael Winslow *Sergeant Jones* • David Graf *Sergeant Tackleberry* • Leslie Easterbrook *Captain Callahan* • GW Bailey *Captain Harris* • Christopher Lee *Commandant Alexander Rakov* • Ron Perlman *Constantine Konali* ■ *Dir* Alan Metter • *Scr* Randolph Davis, Michele S Chodos, from characters created by Neal Israel, Pat Proft

Police Dog ★★ U

Crime drama   1955 · UK · BW · 74mins

Although mercifully brief and nowhere near as doggedly eager to please as *Turner and Hooch* or *K-9*, this competent quota quickie from Derek Twist is, in all honesty, "mutt ado about nothing". In one of his few movie excursions, Tim Turner plays a bobby who adopts an Alsatian stray and has reason to break out the Bonio when it helps him on the trail of his friend's murderer. It's hardly a baffling mystery – even Scooby Doo would have sussed it! However, it's nice to see class acts such as John Le Mesurier and Christopher Lee, no matter how briefly.

Joan Rice *Pat Lewis* • Tim Turner *Frank Mason* • Sandra Dorne *Blonde* • Charles Victor *Sergeant* • Jimmy Gilbert *Ken Lade* • Nora Gordon *Mrs Lewis* • John Le Mesurier *Inspector* ■ *Dir/Scr* Derek Twist

Police Story ★★

Crime drama   1975 · Fr/It · Colour · 107mins

Based on a real-life case – which explains the forties setting – this efficient thriller stars Alain Delon as a French detective and Jean-Louis Trintignant as his quarry, a psychotic killer and robber. Director Jacques Deray is clearly influenced by the work of Jean-Pierre Melville, and there are also traces of a Gallic *Dirty Harry* in Delon's parallel fight against bureaucratic red tape and liberal policies. Otherwise, this is a routine policier that was a big hit at the French box office. A French language film.

Alain Delon *Borniche* • Jean-Louis Trintignant *Buisson* • Renato Salvatori *Le Rital* • Maurice Barrier *Bollec* • André Pousse *Le Nus* ■ *Dir* Jacques Deray • *Scr* Deray Alphonse Boudard, from an autobiography by Roger Borniche

Police Story ★★ 15

Martial arts comedy thriller   1985 · HK · Colour · 95mins

Jackie Chan, as both director and star, proves to be Spring-Heeled Jackie as he progresses literally by leaps and bounds to bring drug-dealing gangsters to justice. The story is as lightweight as his levitation, but the stunts are seriously spectacular. As a monarch of martial arts, Jackie Chan is the King Kong of Hong Kong. Cantonese dialogue dubbed into English. Contains violence. ▭

Jackie Chan *Ka Kui Chan* • Brigitte Lin *Selina Fong* • Maggie Cheung *May* • Yuen Chua *Chu Tao* • Bill Tung *Inspector Wong* ■ *Dir* Jackie Chan • *Scr* Edward Tang

Police Story 2 ★★ 15

Martial arts thriller   1986 · HK · Colour · 101mins

Jackie directs, co-writes and stars as the policeman in this chop-socky sequel. Like many Hong Kong action films, its breathless pace cannot prevent it from becoming a drag, and the soundtrack seems to have been recorded in a cardboard box. Cantonese dialogue dubbed into English. Contains brief nudity. ▭

Jackie Chan *Kevin Chan* • Maggie Cheung *May* • Bill Tung *Inspector Wong* • Lam Kwok Hung *Superintendent Lee* ■ *Dir* Jackie Chan • *Scr* Edward Tang, Jackie Chan

Police Story III: Supercop ★ 15

Martial arts thriller   1992 · HK · Colour · 91mins

The best part of this typically lively Jackie Chan outing is the final credit sequence featuring the reckless stunts that failed to make the picture. That said, this is still a cracking romp in which Hong Kong cop Chan and Chinese police director Michelle Yeoh team up to infiltrate the gang of a vicious drugs baron. Chan hanging from a helicopter by a rope ladder, Yeoh leaping from a bike onto a speeding train and the knockabout shoot-out in which Yeoh finds herself

wearing a bullet-proof vest loaded with explosives are the highlights. But this is riotous fun throughout. Cantonese dubbed into English. Contains violence and swearing. ▭

Jackie Chan *Chen Chia-Chu* • Maggie Cheung *May* • Michelle Yeoh *Inspector Yang* ■ *Dir* Stanley Tong • *Scr* Edward Tang, Filre Ma, Lee Wai Yee

The Police War ★★

Police drama   1979 · Fr · Colour · 102mins

The bent cop is a familiar figure in French commercial cinema, but while Robin Davis manages to draw decent performances from his leading trio, he offers few new insights on the subjects of duty and criminality. Claude Brasseur plays the humane commissioner who is convinced that the detested head of a rival brigade, Claude Rich, is in cahoots with gangster Gérard Desarthe after he bungles an arrest ambush. The action has political implications, but they are scarcely touched upon. French dialogue dubbed into English.

Claude Brasseur *Fush* • Marlène Jobert *Marie* • Claude Rich *Ballestrat* • François Périer *Millard* • Rufus *Le Garret* • Gérard Desarthe *Hector Sarlat* ■ *Dir* Robin Davis • *Scr* Jacques Labib, Jean-Marie Guillaume

The Polish Bride ★★★★ 15

Romance drama   1998 · Neth · Colour · 89mins

This warmly sympathetic chamber-work certainly puts Dutch-based director Karim Traïdia on the map. It's an acute analysis of an oddball relationship: Henk (Jaap Spijkers) is a near-bankrupt farmer who gives shelter to Anna (Monic Hendrickx), a Polish prostitute on the run from abusing city pimps. She becomes his housekeeper and they form a relationship that turns to love. For all its heartache – she's forced to be apart from her daughter, his land is about to be taken away from him – this is an engrossing affirmation that's a tonic for the spirit. In Dutch, German and Polish with English subtitles. Contains violence and a brief sex scene.

Jaap Spijkers *Henk Woldring* • Monic Hendrickx *Anna Krzyzanowska* • Rudi Falkenhagen *Father* • Roef Ragas *Son* • Hakim Traïdia *Postman* ■ *Dir* Karim Traïdia • *Scr* Kees van der Hulst

Polish Wedding ★★ 15

Romantic comedy   1998 · US · Colour · 101mins

This tale of a Polish-American family in Detroit works quite well, but fails to stir up much emotion in the audience. Claire Danes is the teenager whose actions send her family into a turmoil – though perhaps they should be more alarmed at the casting. Not only are the leads not Polish; they're not even American! (Gabriel Byrne is Irish, while Lena Olin is a Swede.) They handle the accents well enough, but this is one of those slight films that can best be described as "nice" – damning with faint praise, indeed. Contains some swearing. ▭

Lena Olin *Jadzia Pzoniak* • Gabriel Byrne *Bolek Pzoniak* • Claire Danes *Hala Pzoniak* • Adam

Trese *Russell Schuster* • Mili Avital *Sofie Pzoniak* • Daniel Lapaine *Ziggy Pzoniak* • Rade Serbedzija *Roman* ■ *Dir/Scr* Theresa Connelly

Politically Correct Party Animals ★★ 15

Comedy   1994 · US · Colour · 77mins

A commendable, if flawed, attempt to revive that eighties' staple, the fraternity house flick. This brings it bang up to date by making political correctness, rather than teachers, the main enemy, with the slobbish devotees of the old-style of campus education (drink, sex, pranks and parties) declaring war on the caring, liberal face of responsible studenthood. It's a nice idea, but the members of the largely unknown cast don't have the charisma to carry off the antics, while Hart Bochner's direction is too restrained for the gross-out humour required. Contains swearing. ▭

Jeremy Piven *Droz* • Chris Young *Tom Lawrence* • Megan Ward *Katy* • Jon Favreau *Gutter* • Sarah Trigger *Samantha* • David Spade *Rand McPherson* ■ *Dir* Hart Bochner • *Scr* Adam Leff, Zak Penn

Polly ★★★ U

Musical   1989 · US · Colour · 89mins

Debbie Allen (the dance teacher in *Fame* and choreographer of many an Oscar ceremony dance number) here directs a Disney remake of the *Pollyanna* tale, adding music and a predominantly black cast. It's a fun romp, given added kudos by the presence of Hollywood veteran Celeste Holm, who looks as wonderful now as she did back in 1956 in *High Society*. ▭

Keshia Knight Pulliam *Polly* • Phylicia Rashad *Aunt Polly* • Dorian Harewood *Dr Shannon* • Barbara Montgomery *Mrs Conley* • TK Carter *George* • Vanessa Bell Calloway *Nancy* ■ *Dir* Debbie Allen • *Scr* William Blinn, from the film *Pollyanna* by David Swift, from the novel *Pollyanna* by Eleanor H Porter

Polly of the Circus ★★ U

Romantic drama   1932 · US · BW · 69mins

It took MGM some time to get the measure of their rising star Clark Gable and cast him according to his personality. This romantic drama, a perfect example of studio misjudgment, has Gable playing a man of the cloth who rescues a trapeze artist (a colourless Marion Davies) from physical and moral degradation in the face of disapproval from his bishop (C Aubrey Smith). A thin little film, devoid of sparks, despite Gable's flaming good looks.

Marion Davies *Polly Fisher* • Clark Gable *Reverend John Hartley* • C Aubrey Smith *Reverend James Northcott* • Raymond Hatton *Downey* • David Landau *Beef* • Ruth Selwyn *Mitzi* • Maude Eburne *Mrs Jennings* • Little Billy *Half-Pint* • Ray Milland *Rich young man* ■ *Dir* Alfred Santell • *Scr* Carey Wilson, Laurence Johnson, from the play by Margaret Mayo

Pollyanna ★★★★

Silent drama   1920 · US · BW · 60mins

This adaptation of Eleanor H Porter's book is probably Mary Pickford's most sugary confection. "The world's sweetheart" plays an orphan girl whose irresistible good nature converts the hard hearts of Aunt Polly (Katherine Griffith) and her grumpy New England neighours. (Her final, near-fatal illness is schmaltz with a temperature.) Pickford is wonderful, while director Paul Powell catches the mood of the time, and the town, with casual expertise. The kind of story that Disney might have made – and did, in 1960.

Mary Pickford *Pollyanna* • Wharton James *Rev Whittier* • Katherine Griffith *Aunt Polly Harrington* • Herbert Prior *Dr Chilton* • William Courtleigh *John Pendleton* • Helen Jerome Eddy *Nancy* • George Berrell *Tom* ■ *Dir* Paul Powell • *Scr* Frances Marion, from the novel by Eleanor H Porter

Pollyanna ★★★★U
Drama   1960 · US · Colour · 134mins

Writer/director David Swift made a splendid job of adapting Eleanor H Porter's 1912 children's classic for the screen. Disney spared no expense in re-creating the look and feel of small-town Vermont, and splashed out in no uncertain terms to land such top-line performers as Agnes Moorehead, Karl Malden, Adolphe Menjou and Jane Wyman. They play the cheerless citizens whose lives are transformed by the effervescent orphan Pollyanna (Hayley Mills) and her bottomless supply of "gladness". Mills won a special Oscar for her spirited performance. If there is a fault, it is that it's a bit too long for most children to take at a single sitting. ▭

Hayley Mills *Pollyanna* • Jane Wyman *Aunt Polly Harrington* • Richard Egan *Dr Edmond Chilton* • Karl Malden *Reverend Paul Ford* • Nancy Olson *Nancy Furman* • Adolphe Menjou *Mr Pendergast* • Donald Crisp *Mayor Warren* • Agnes Moorehead *Mrs Snow* ■ *Dir* David Swift • *Scr* David Swift, from the novel by Eleanor H Porter

Poltergeist ★★★★⒖
Horror   1982 · US · Colour · 109mins

Evil spirits enter the home of a typical suburban American family through their possessed television set in this spooktacular, co-produced and co-written by Steven Spielberg. After a deceptively cute opening, Tobe Hooper gets down to some serious haunting and piles on the thrilling special effects and grisly moments for a fun ghost-train ride. Hooper's direction may lack its usual edgy personality apparently over-ruled by Spielberg's script suggestions but he puts on a dazzling show and the intuitive performances are uniformly on the panic button. Contains swearing. ▭

JoBeth Williams *Diane Freeling* • Craig T Nelson *Steve Freeling* • Beatrice Straight *Dr Lesh* • Dominique Dunne *Dana Freeling* • Oliver Robbins *Robbie Freeling* • Heather O'Rourke *Carol Anne Freeling* • Michael McManus *Ben Tuthill* • Virginia Kiser *Mrs Tuthill* • Zelda Rubinstein *Tangina Barrons* ■ *Dir* Tobe Hooper • *Scr* Steven Spielberg, Michael Grais, Mark Victor, from a story by Steven Spielberg

Poltergeist II: the Other Side ★★★⒖
Horror   1986 · US · Colour · 90mins

The haunted Freeling family has moved to Arizona to stay with grandma, but the evil spirits aren't giving up their

pursuit of the family's daughter Heather O'Rourke. This sequel does little more than recycle the original story, yet there are enough supernatural visitations and grisly surprises to prevent the ghostly goings-on from getting dull. The ghouls this time are from a religious sect presided over by the creepy Julian Beck, giving a marvellous fire-and-brimstone performance. While director Brian Gibson thinks throwing assorted monsters from the screen is enough, it's the more bizarre gimmicks that provide the fun cheap chills. Contains swearing and violence. ▭

JoBeth Williams *Diane Freeling* • Craig T Nelson *Steve Freeling* • Heather O'Rourke *Carol Anne Freeling* • Oliver Robins *Robbie Freeling* • Zelda Rubinstein *Tangina Barrons* • Will Sampson *Taylor* • Julian Beck *Reverend Henry Kane* • Geraldine Fitzgerald *Gramma Jess* ■ *Dir* Brian Gibson • *Scr* Mark Victor, Michael Grais

Poltergeist III ★⒖
Horror   1988 · US · Colour · 93mins

"Enough, stop this stupid sideshow!" says the obnoxious psychiatrist in this repetitious and completely unnecessary second sequel. You'll give voice to the same sentiment long before he does in this slack, lifeless sequel. The end result is a disaster movie all right, but not the spectre spectacular director Gary Sherman thought he was making when he had the idea to relocate little Carol Anne Freeling (Heather O'Rourke) to a high rise Chicago condominium. Contains swearing. ▭

Tom Skerritt *Bruce Gardner* • Nancy Allen *Patricia Gardner* • Heather O'Rourke *Carol Anne Freeling* • Zelda Rubinstein *Tangina Barrons* • Lara Flynn Boyle *Donna Gardner* • Kip Wentz *Scott* • Richard Fire *Dr Seaton* ■ *Dir* Gary Sherman • *Scr* Gary Sherman, Brian Taggert

Polyester ★★★⒙
Comedy   1981 · US · Colour · 79mins

"Sultan of sleaze" John Waters revived fifties "Smell-O-Vision" for his first vaguely mainstream picture. "Odorama" scratch-and-sniff cards were handed out to audiences witnessing harried housewife Divine seeking romantic relief from her porn-merchant husband in hunky Tab Hunter's arms. Abortion and moral majority fanatics are the prime concerns of Waters's polemic, which is too soft for *Pink Flamingos* cultists and too close to home for those into Reaganite family values.

Divine *Francine Fishpaw* • Tab Hunter *Todd Tomorrow* • Edith Massey *Cuddles* • Mink Stole *Sandra* • David Samson *Elmer Fishpaw* ■ *Dir/Scr* John Waters • *Costume Designer* Van Smith

Le Polygraphe ★★★
Thriller   1996 · Can/Fr/Ger · Colour · 99mins

Reduced to its essentials, this is a thriller about an unsolved murder. But, working from his 1987 play, Robert Lepage's main concerns are art and artifice, repression and redemption. Still disturbed by the death of her friend, actress Josée Deschênes decides to make a movie about the case. But film and fiction are soon

blurring and coincidence is playing an increasingly unnerving role in the proceedings. Visually and psychologically complex, this is both intriguing and inventive, with Patrick Goyette convincingly tortured as the victim's ex-boyfriend, whose recollections are as unreliable as the polygraph test he takes to establish his innocence.

Patrick Goyette *François Tremblay* • Marie Brassard *Lucie* • Peter Stormare *Christof Haussman* • Maria de Medeiros *Claude* • Josée Deschênes *Judith* • James Hyndman *Hans* ■ *Dir* Robert Lepage • *Scr* Marie Brassard, Robert Lepage, Michael Mackenzie, Patrick Goyette, from the play by Robert Lepage

The Pompatus of Love ★
Romantic comedy
1995 · US · Colour · 99mins

Four affluent New York males (including co-writers Jon Cryer and Adam Oliensis) are confused about love in the nineties, regularly meeting to have long-winded discussions about it. There's no plot; just a series of choppily edited, unrelated vignettes of their unsatisfying love lives. Not one of the four actors manages to differentiate himself from his co-stars, all of whom are shallowly written and scripted to utter flip statements and observations that no one in real life would ever say. Roscoe Lee Browne's cameo stands out, in that he almost manages to pass off his trite dialogue.

Jon Cryer *Mark* • Adrian Pasdar *Josh* • Tim Guinee *Runyon* • Adam Oliensis *Phil* • Mia Sara *Cynthia* • Kristin Scott Thomas *Caroline* • Jennifer Tilly *Tarzaan* • Roscoe Lee Browne *Leonard Folder* ■ *Dir* Richard Schenkman • *Scr* Richard Schenkman, Jon Cryer, Adam Oliensis

Ponette ★★★🅟🅖
Drama   1996 · Fr · Colour · 93mins

Four-year-old Victoire Thivisol won the best actress prize at Venice for her remarkable work in this exquisite study of loss and the indomitability of innocence. Bruised and confused after surviving the car crash that killed her mother, she has to cope not only with the shocked anger of her father, but also the conflicting advice of her teachers and playmates on the nature of death and the afterlife. However, while director Jacques Doillon merits praise for coaxing from Thivisol a performance that ranks alongside Brigitte Fossey's in *Les Jeux Interdits*, he undermines the authenticity of Ponette's pain and bewilderment by tacking on a cosy, contrived ending. In French with English subtitles. ▭

Victoire Thivisol *Ponette* • Matiaz Bureau Caton *Matiaz* • Delphine Schiltz *Delphine* • Léopoldine Serre *Ada* • Luckie Royer *Luce* • Carla Ibled *Carla* • Antoine du Merle *Antoine* • Marie Trintignant *Ponette's mother* ■ *Dir/Scr* Jacques Doillon

Pontiac Moon ★★⒓
Comedy drama 1994 · US · Colour · 102mins

No "Cheers" to be had in this cloying drama starring Ted Danson as a rural science teacher who decides to take his son (Ryan Todd) on the road to discover the meaning of life. Mary Steenburgen and Cathy Moriarty go along for the mawkish ride, which even

features Danson singing *Cheek to Cheek*. Not a pretty sight! Peter Medak's direction errs on the side of the sentimentally mundane and only the good-natured cast give this pointless journey any drive at all. ▭

Ted Danson *Washington Bellamy* • Mary Steenburgen *Katherine Bellamy* • Ryan Todd *Andy Bellamy* • Eric Schweig *Ernest Ironplume* • Cathy Moriarty *Lorraine* • Max Gail *Jerome Bellamy* • Lisa Jane Persky *Alicia Frook* • JC Quinn *Bartender* • Don Swayze *Local* ■ *Dir* Peter Medak • *Scr* Finn Taylor, Jeffrey Brown, from an idea by Finn Taylor

Pontius Pilate ★★
Biblical drama 1961 · It/Fr · Colour · 100mins

The crucifixion is replayed from the viewpoint of the Roman procurator whose hand-wringing has earned him a place in the Christian faith. French superstar Jean Marais – after so many movies for Jean Cocteau – here has to make do with Hollywood stalwart Irving Rapper, who went to Europe for this concatenation on Pilate's love affairs. The muddled dubbing makes some of the plot almost impenetrable. Italian dialogue dubbed into English.

Jean Marais *Pontius Pilate* • Jeanne Crain *Claudia Procula* • Basil Rathbone *Caiaphas* • Leticia Roman *Sarah* • Massimo Serato *Nicodemus* • Riccardo Garrone *Galba* • Livio Lorenzon *Barabbas* • Gianni Garko *Jonathan* • John Drew Barrymore *Jesus/Judas* ■ *Dir* Irving Rapper, Gian Paolo Callegari • *Scr* O Biancolo, Gino DeSantis, Gian Paolo Callegari, from a story by Gino DeSanotis

The Pony Express ★★★
Silent western 1925 · US · BW · 110mins

This major silent western, directed by James Cruze for Paramount to follow up his smash hit, *The Covered Wagon*, was again about an historical aspect of the Old West. Ricardo Cortez plays the gambler turned pony express rider who carries vital news of the election of President Lincoln to California, thereby linking both sides of the huge country. Although overburdened with plot and subsidiary characters, it does have a spectacular climactic attack by Indians and some vivid, largely unpunished villainy from George Bancroft while Betty Compson makes an attractive job of the heroine. Cortez, however, looks too much like Buster Keaton.

Ricardo Cortez *Jack Weston* • Betty Compson *Molly Jones* • Ernest Torrence *"Ascension" Jones* • Wallace Beery *"Rhode Island" Red* • George Bancroft *Jack Slade* ■ *Dir* James Cruze • *Scr* Walter Woods, from a novel by Henry James Forman, Walter Woods

Pony Express ★★★U
Western   1953 · US · Colour · 101mins

Charlton Heston, always cast in roles where he can lead with his chin, is fuelled by purposeful action, decency and high moral fibre in a western which has all the expected shorthand of the genre. The lightweight plot revolves around the adventures of Heston, as Buffalo Bill Cody, and Forrest Tucker, as Wild Bill Hickok, and the opening of mail routes to California. This is a lumpy stew of lean crackerjack action and rather earnest, talky stretches.

Charlton Heston *Buffalo Bill Cody* • Rhonda Fleming *Evelyn* • Jan Sterling *Denny* • Forrest

🅤 = SUITABLE FOR ALL, 🅤🅢 = SUITABLE FOR ALL, ESPECIALLY FOR YOUNG CHILDREN (VIDEO ONLY) 🅟🅖 = PARENTAL GUIDANCE

Tucker *Wild Bill Hickok* • Michael Moore (3) *Rance Hastings* • Porter Hall *Bridger* • Richard Shannon *Barrett* ■ *Dir* Jerry Hopper • *Scr* Charles Marquis Warren, from a story by Frank Gruber

Pony Express Rider ★★

Western   1976 · US · Colour · 100mins

Stewart Peterson plays a cowboy who joins the Pony Express in the hope of finding the man who murdered his father. With such western stalwarts as Jack Elam, Dub Taylor and Slim Pickens on board, one might expect more from this western than it actually delivers. Sadly, the formulaic plot runs out of bullets long before the final showdown.

Stewart Petersen *Jimmy* • Henry Wilcoxon *Trevor* • Buck Taylor *Bovey* • Maureen McCormick *Rose* • Ken Curtis *Jed* • Joan Caulfield *Charlotte* • Slim Pickens *Bob* • Dub Taylor *Boomer* • Jack Elam *Crazy* ■ *Dir* Robert Totten, Hal Harrison Jr • *Scr* Lyman Dayton, Dan Greer, Hal Harrison Jr, Robert Totten

Pony Soldier ★★ U

Western   1952 · US · Colour · 82mins

The Mounties certainly had their day in the early fifties, what with Alan Ladd in *O'Rourke of the Royal Mounted* and Howard Keel and Ann Blyth in *Rose Marie*, and here's Tyrone Power sent to don the scarlet as MacDonald the Canadian Mounties (the film's British title). To be honest, Power looks thoroughly bored and ill-at-ease in this lame adventure. Why Fox didn't even give him a decent leading lady is anyone's guess, though Penny Edwards does her best.

Tyrone Power *Duncan MacDonald* • Cameron Mitchell *Konah* • Thomas Gomez *Natayo* • Penny Edwards *Emerald Neeley* • Robert Horton *Jess Calhoun* • Anthony Earl Numkena *Comes Running* • Adeline De Walt Reynolds *White Moon* • Howard Petrie *Inspector Frazer* ■ *Dir* Joseph M Newman • *Scr* John C Higgins, from a story by Garnett Weston in *The Saturday Evening Post*

Poodle Springs ★★ 15

Mystery   1998 · US · Colour · 95mins

Ageing private eye Philip Marlowe, laconically played by James Caan, gets mixed up with blackmail and murder among the elite sixties in-crowd in director Bob Rafelson's stilted take on Raymond Chandler. Despite a brave and literate attempt by scriptwriter Tom Stoppard to solve the contradictions of a story which existed only in sketch form at the time of the writer's death, this *faux film noir* is a thin stylistic oddity. Having Marlowe married to socialite Dina Meyer and give up his wild streak along with the moral grime of LA goes against every quintessential Chandleresque trademark, and the story never really convinces as a result. Contains swearing, nudity and violence. ▭ *DVD*

James Caan *Philip Marlowe* • Dina Meyer *Laura* • David Keith *Larry Victor* • Tom Bower *Arnie Burns* • Julia Campbell *Muffy Blackstone* • Brian Cox *Clayton Blackstone* • Nia Peeples *Angel* ■ *Dir* Bob Rafelson • *Scr* Tom Stoppard, from the novel by Robert B Parker, Raymond Chandler

Pool of London ★★

Crime drama   1950 · UK · BW · 85mins

An Ealing Studios thriller set in London's Docklands when there were ships and warehouses rather than wine bars and rooftop jacuzzis. Directed by Basil Dearden, it's a smuggling yarn involving a black stevedore, his white girlfriend and plenty of double-crosses before the cops close in. While the thriller elements of the picture are merely routine, it is the mixed-race romance that broke new ground for British cinema. The young Bermudan actor is Earl Cameron who appeared in later films about racial issues such as *Simba*, *Sapphire* and *Flame in the Streets*.

Bonar Colleano *Dan MacDonald* • Susan Shaw *Pat* • Renée Asherson *Sally* • Earl Cameron *Johnny* • Moira Lister *Maisie* • Max Adrian *Vernon* • Joan Dowling *Pamela* • James Robertson-Justice *Trotter* ■ *Dir* Basil Dearden • *Scr* Jack Whittingham, John Eldredge

Poor Cow ★★★ 15

Drama   1967 · UK · Colour · 97mins

Ken Loach made his feature debut with this adaptation of Nell Dunn's social realist (if unashamedly sensationalist) novel. The first of several films with working-class themes made by Loach, this isn't a patch on either his TV plays *Up the Junction* and *Cathy Come Home*, or his follow-up feature, *Kes*. This determinedly grim tale centres on the tangled love life of teenager Carol White, who turns to Terence Stamp after her thieving lover John Bindon is sent to prison. But only Queenie Watts impresses as White's prostitute aunt. Watch out for a debuting Malcolm McDowell. ▭

Carol White *Joy* • Terence Stamp *Dave* • John Bindon *Tom* • Kate Williams *Beryl* • Queenie Watts *Aunt Emm* • Geraldine Sherman *Trixie* • James Beckett *Tom's Friends* • Malcolm McDowell *Bill Murray* ■ *Dir* Kenneth Loach [Ken Loach] • *Scr* Kenneth Loach, Nell Dunn, the novel by Nell Dunn

Poor Little Rich Girl ★★★ U

Musical comedy   1936 · US · BW · 79mins

She's no-one but little Shirley Temple, and it's jolly difficult to care when such an obviously talented, bright-and-shiny youngster feels neglected and runs away from the home of her wealthy widower father. She's befriended by blonde Alice Faye and Tin Man-to-be Jack Haley and turned into a major radio star, which is as major as you could get back in the 1930s. Temple was the biggest movie star in the world at this time, and her studio, 20th Century-Fox, was hard-pressed to find suitable vehicles to showcase her talents. It did her proud with this one, and the militaristic finale is mesmerising. If you've never seen the curly haired moppet, check this out; if you can't stand her, stay well clear.

Shirley Temple *Barbara Barry* • Alice Faye *Jerry Dolan* • Gloria Stuart *Margaret Allen* • Jack Haley *Jimmy Dolan* • Michael Whalen *Richard Barry* • Sara Haden *Collins* • Jane Darwell *Woodward* • Billy Gilbert *Waiter* ■ *Dir* Irving Cummings • *Scr* Sam Hellman, Gladys Lehman, Harry Tugend, from stories by Eleanor Gates, Ralph Spence

Popcorn ★★ 15

Horror   1991 · US · Colour · 86mins

This quirky little movie puts too much on its plate, trying to mix a standard slasher tale with attempts to satirise campy old horror movies. The satire is more successful than the slash, with amusing and on-target homages to William Castle and failed cinematic innovations such as ''Smell-O-Vision''. The sporadic cuts to these segments are nice breaks in an otherwise predictable opus about a university film class sponsoring an all-night horror festival, not knowing that one of the audience members is out for blood. ▭

Jill Schoelen *Maggie* • Tom Villard *Toby* • Dee Wallace Stone *Suzanne* • Derek Rydall *Mark* • Malcolm Danare *Bud* • Elliott Hurst *Leon* ■ *Dir* Mark Herrier • *Scr* Alan Ormsby, from a story by Mitchell Smith

Pope Joan ★★

Period drama   1972 · UK · Colour · 140mins

Before he wrote his Oscar-winning script for *Gandhi*, John Briley penned this mythical tale of a woman who disguises herself as a monk and (to cut a long story short) ends up as pope. The main question is not what it all means, but why Liv Ullmann was such a riveting actress for Ingmar Bergman and such a prissy plum pudding for everyone else. The strong supporting cast pop in and out of the story, while the ninth-century settings are no more than perfunctory.

Liv Ullmann *Joan* • Keir Dullea *Dr Stevens* • Maximilian Schell *Adrian* • Olivia de Havilland *Mother Superior* • Lesley-Anne Down *Cecilia* • Trevor Howard *Pope Leo* ■ *Dir* Michael Anderson • *Scr* John Briley

The Pope Must Die ★★★ 15

Comedy   1991 · UK · Colour · 95mins

This *Comic Strip* team production remains a little ragged around the edges, but there are enough sharp gags to make this an entertaining time-passer. Robbie Coltrane is the simple, rock 'n' roll-loving priest who is mistakenly elected Pope, only to discover a hot-bed of corruption within the Vatican. Coltrane can do this sort of thing in his sleep, and the best performances come from canny scene-stealers not normally associated with the *Comic Strip*: Herbert Lom, Paul Bartel and, particularly, Alex Rocco. Contains violence, swearing and nudity. ▭

Robbie Coltrane *Dave Albinizi* • Beverly D'Angelo *Veronica Dante* • Herbert Lom *Vittorio Corelli* • Alex Rocco *Cardinal Rocco* • Paul Bartel *Monsignor Vitchie* • Balthazar Getty *Joe Don Dante* • William Hootkins *Cardinal Verucci* • Robert Stephens *Carmelengo* • Annette Crosbie *Mother Superior* • Steve O'Donnell *Rico* ■ *Dir* Peter Richardson • *Scr* Peter Richardson, Pete Richens

The Pope of Greenwich Village ★★★ 15

Crime drama   1984 · US · Colour · 115mins

This never once approaches the creatively crazed energy of Martin Scorsese's *Mean Streets*, on whose coat-tails it rather obviously hangs, even down to the wired/weird relationship between a small-potatoes hustler and his wired/weird cousin. But what the film lacks in imagination and drive it gains in rich character acting, particularly from those who look as if they've been pushed and pulled by New York life or just spent too long in its gutters. Contains swearing. ▭

Mickey Rourke *Charlie* • Eric Roberts *Paulie* • Daryl Hannah *Diane* • Geraldine Page *Mrs Ritter* • Kenneth McMillan *Barney* • Tony Musante *Pete* • M Emmet Walsh *Burns* ■ *Dir* Stuart Rosenberg • *Scr* Vincent Patrick, from his novel

Popeye ★★ U

Musical comedy   1980 · US · Colour · 92mins

When Robert Altman fails, he flops from a great height. And this is as high as it gets in terms of failed aspirations as the director tries to turn the comic strip *Popeye* into a live-action musical comedy. Robin Williams raps inarticulately as the heroic sailorman searching for his long-lost Pappy with the help of Shelley Duvall's witless though seductive Olive Oyl. There are compensations – the brilliantly designed town of Sweethaven and Harry Nilsson's songs, for example – but it's all too manic and jittery, and as overblown as a body-builder overdosed on spinach. ▭

Robin Williams *Popeye* • Shelley Duvall *Olive Oyl* • Ray Walston *Poopdeck Pappy* • Paul L Smith [Paul Smith] *Bluto* • Paul Dooley *Wimpy* • Richard Libertini *Geezil* • Roberta Maxwell *Nana Oyl* • Donald Moffat *Taxman* ■ *Dir* Robert Altman • *Scr* Jules Feiffer, from comic strip characters created by EC Segar

Popi ★★

Comedy   1969 · US · Colour · 113mins

A hard-working Puerto Rican tries to get his sons out of the New York ghetto by an elaborate hoax. Passing them off as Cuban refugees in Florida, he hopes to have them adopted by richer people. This pleasant and well-made comedy gives good parts to Alan Arkin and Rita Moreno while offering a believable, though ultimately rosy view of the rawer aspects of the American Dream.

Alan Arkin *Abraham, ''Popi''* • Rita Moreno *Lupe* • Miguel Alejandro *Junior* • Ruben Figueroa [Reuben Figueroa] *Luis* • John Harkins *Harmon* • Joan Tompkins *Miss Musto* • Anthony Holland *Pickett* • Amy Freeman *Diaz* ■ *Dir* Arthur Hiller • *Scr* Tina Pine, Les Pine

Poppy ★★★

Drama   1935 · Jap · BW · 72mins

Kenji Mizoguchi's adaptation of Soseki Natsume's novel has been somewhat overlooked. At its core lies the contrasting social attitudes of two women, dutiful daughter Yukichi Iwata, who reluctantly accedes to her betrothal to Daijiro Natsukawa, and his older, more liberated English student, Kuniko Miyake. The director abandoned his now customary long takes and adopted a traditional Hollywood narrative approach, with editing, not camera movement, creating the rhythm and significance of the action. In Japanese with English subtitles.

Kuniko Miyake *Fujio Kono* • Ichiro Tsukida *Seizo Ono* • Daijiro Natsukawa *Hajime Munechika* • Kazuyoshi Takeda *Kingo Kono* •

Yukichi Iwata *Tomotaka Inoue* • Chiyoko Okura *Sayoko Inoue* ■ *Dir* Kenji Mizoguchi • *Scr* Haruo Takayanagi, Daisuke Ito, from the novel *Gubijinso* by Soseki Natsume • *Cinematographer* Minoru Miki

Poppy ★★★★ U
Comedy   1936 · US · BW · 70mins

WC Fields made the role of travelling medicine seller Eustace McGargle his own when he first appeared in Dorothy Donnelly's play back in the early twenties. This film version finds him setting up his stall in a small town where his adopted daughter (Rochelle Hudson) falls in love with the mayor's son. There's more sentimentality than is usual for a Fields movie, but the sour delight of watching him never giving a sucker an even break (forging a marriage certificate, cheating a local yokel) is still a delight.

WC Fields *Prof Eustace McGargle* • Rochelle Hudson *Poppy* • Richard Cromwell *Billy Farnsworth* • Granville Bates *Mayor Farnsworth* • Catherine Doucet *Countess Maggie Tubbs DePuizzi* ■ *Dir* A Edward Sutherland • *Scr* Waldemar Young, Virginia Van Upp, from the play by Dorothy Donnelly

The Poppy Is Also a Flower ★★ PG
Crime thriller   1966 · US · Colour · 95mins

It's a testament to the United Nations that so many major stars appeared in this thriller about two UN agents who go up against the international heroin trade. For incurable star-spotters and collectors of 007 trivia, it's absolutely unmissable. James Bond author Ian Fleming had the original idea of opening with a shot of a pretty poppy growing in the fields of Iran and following its progress to the ugly streets of Harlem. Fleming took this idea to Terence Young, director of *Dr No* and *From Russia with Love*, who developed it after Fleming's death. Among the host of stars, Bond fans will immediately spot Harold Sakata, who played Oddjob in *Goldfinger*. It was first seen on American TV, then released in European cinemas as *Danger Grows Wild*. ▭

EG Marshall *Jones* • Trevor Howard *Lincoln* • Gilbert Roland *Marco* • Rita Hayworth *Monique* • Anthony Quayle *Captain* • Angie Dickinson *Linda Benson* • Yul Brynner *Col Salem* • Eli Wallach *Locarno* • Marcello Mastroianni *Inspector Mosca* • Omar Sharif *Dr Rad* • Grace Kelly *Introduction* • Harold Sakata *Dino* ■ *Dir* Terence Young • *Scr* Jo Eisinger, from an idea by Ian Fleming

Popsy-Pop ★
Crime drama   1970 · Fr · Colour · 88mins

Shot on location in the Caribbean, this dreary romantic thriller stars Stanley Baker as an incorruptible cop sent to arrest jewel smuggler Claudia Cardinale as she collects another consignment of stones from her double-crossing partner. Unsurprisingly, the couple fall in lust as their bad-tempered cat-and-mouse game grinds along to its predictable conclusion. There is absolutely no spark between the leads who look sulky throughout a picture that has no substance beneath the surface sheen. Cardinale's cabaret act and a midnight voodoo ceremony do little to relieve the gloom. French dialogue dubbed into English.

Stanley Baker *Silva* • Claudia Cardinale *Popsy* • Henri Charrière *Marco* • Georges Aminel *Priest* • Ginette Leclerc *Madame* ■ *Dir* Jean Herman • *Scr* Henri Charrière, Jean Herman

Porgy and Bess ★★★ PG
Opera   1959 · US · Colour · 183mins

Producer Samuel Goldwyn bowed out at the age of 75 with this film version of the George and Ira Gershwin–DuBose Heyward folk opera about crippled Porgy, his girl Bess and the inhabitants of Catfish Row. The familiar music, given Oscar-winning treatment by André Previn and Ken Darby, is gloriously intact. However, despite a starry cast of principals, the result disappoints. Otto Preminger's direction is heavy-handed, the singing not as good as it should be, and the whole production too lavish to convince as a poignant tale of slum life. ▭

Sidney Poitier *Porgy* • Dorothy Dandridge *Bess* • Sammy Davis Jr *Sportin' Life* • Pearl Bailey *Maria* • Brock Peters *Crown* • Leslie Scott *Jake* • Diahann Carroll *Clara* • Ruth Attaway *Serena* ■ *Dir* Otto Preminger • *Scr* N Richard Nash, from the opera by George Gershwin, Ira Gershwin, DuBose Heyward, from the stage play by DuBose Heyward, Dorothy Heyward

Pork Chop Hill ★★★★ PG
War drama   1959 · US · BW · 93mins

This is the definitive Korean War movie from director Lewis Milestone, who dealt with the Second World War impressively in *A Walk in the Sun* and the First World War unforgettably in the classic *All Quiet on the Western Front*. Bleak and grim, it boasts a superb all-male cast, headed by Gregory Peck at his glummest. Watch out for the young Martin Landau and Harry Dean Stanton (billed here as plain Dean Stanton) amid all the shrapnel. As with Milestone's other war films, the action sequences are terrific. ▭

Gregory Peck *Lieutenant Clemons* • Harry Guardino *Forstman* • Rip Torn *Lieutenant Russell* • George Peppard *Fedderson* • James Edwards *Corporal Jurgens* • Bob Steele *Kern* • Woody Strode *Franklin* • George Shibita *Lieutenant O'Hashi* • Norman Fell *Sergeant Coleman* • Robert Blake *Velie* • Biff Elliot *Bowen* • Barry Atwater *Davis* • Martin Landau *Marshall* • Dean Stanton [Harry Dean Stanton] *MacFarland* ■ *Dir* Lewis Milestone • *Scr* James R Webb, from a story by General SLA Marshall

Porky's ★★★ 18
Comedy   1981 · Can · Colour · 94mins

Set in the fifties, this crude, crass comedy centres around the elaborate revenge plotted by a group of students on the redneck owner of the local bar-cum-whorehouse, Porky's. Director Bob Clark makes a few misguided nods to serious issues such as anti-Semitism. For the most part, though, he sticks to a seamless mix of vulgar sexual gags and spectacular slapstick, which is most definitely not PC but is often hugely entertaining. The cast is largely forgettable, with only Kim Cattrall succeeding in fashioning a career in Hollywood. Contains swearing and nudity. ▭

Dan Monahan *Pee Wee* • Mark Herrier *Billy* • Wyatt Knight *Tommy* • Roger Wilson *Mickey* • Cyril O'Reilly *Tim* • Tony Ganios *Meat* • Kim

Cattrall *Honeywell* • Nancy Parsons *Ms Balbricker* • Susan Clark *Cherry Forever* • Chuck Mitchell *Porky* ■ *Dir/Scr* Bob Clark

Porky's II: The Next Day ★★ 18
Comedy   1983 · Can · Colour · 93mins

After the huge success of *Porky's*, all the leads reunited for this continuation of the story. This time the fifties Florida high school gang are trying to mount an evening of Shakespeare, but face opposition from the Righteous Flock, who deem the Bard obscene, and the KKK, who object to the casting of a Seminole Indian (Joseph Runningfox) as Romeo. A tighter plot than its predecessor, but with the same emphasis on sex – and, like the original, very funny in places. ▭

Dan Monahan *Pee Wee* • Wyatt Knight *Tommy* • Mark Herrier *Billy* • Roger Wilson *Mickey* • Cyril O'Reilly *Tim* • Tony Ganios *Meat* • Kaki Hunter *Wendy* • Scott Colomby *Brian* • Nancy Parsons *Ms Balbricker* • Joseph Runningfox *John Henry* ■ *Dir* Bob Clark • *Scr* Roger E Swaybill, Alan Ormsby, Bob Clark

Porky's Revenge ★ 18
Comedy   1985 · Can · Colour · 88mins

This third entry in the series is easily the worst. The energetic vulgarity of the first two films is replaced here by a leering coarseness – which is ironic, as the first two films were unfairly condemned by (those that hadn't seen them) for containing exactly this sort of crudity. The thin plot revolves around our heroes being forced to throw a basketball match by bar owner Porky (Chuck Mitchell). The world's oldest high school pupils finally graduate as the end credits roll – and not a moment too soon.

Dan Monahan *Pee Wee* • Wyatt Knight *Tommy* • Tony Ganios *Meat* • Mark Herrier *Billy* • Kaki Hunter *Wendy* • Scott Colomby *Brian* • Nancy Parsons *Ms Balbricker* • Chuck Mitchell *Porky Wallace* ■ *Dir* James Komack • *Scr* Ziggy Steinberg, from characters created by Bob Clark

Porridge ★★ PG
Comedy   1979 · UK · Colour · 89mins

The original TV series had been over for two years and Ronnie Barker had even been *Going Straight* before he was talked back into the role of Norman Fletcher for this movie spin-off. He's excellent and this is one of the best of its kind, but, sadly, that's not saying much. What worked in a tightly scripted half-hour falls apart over 90 minutes in a story about a Lags XI v Celebrity All-stars football match set up to cover an escape. ▭

Ronnie Barker *Norman Fletcher* • Richard Beckinsale *Lennie Godber* • Fulton Mackay *Mackay* • Brian Wilde *Barrowclough* • Peter Vaughan *"Grouty"* • Julian Holloway *Bainbridge* ■ *Dir* Dick Clement • *Scr* Dick Clement, Ian La Frenais, from their TV series

Port Djema ★★★
War thriller   1997 · Fr/It/Gr · Colour · 96mins

This is a fictionalised version of events that took place in the war-torn, famine-stricken East African country of Eritrea. Employing the stately style of Theo Angelopoulos (whose *Ulysses' Gate* he produced), director Eric Heumann

disconcertingly combines scenes of brutality with moments of pure pathos, as he follows emotionally and intellectually detached doctor Jean-Yves Dubois on a journey into his own heart of darkness, to keep his promise to a murdered friend to find a small boy trapped in spiralling civil unrest. As a thriller it's too deliberate to involve, but its views on post-colonial culpability and political indifference are powerfully expressed. In French with English subtitles.

Jean-Yves Dubois *Pierre Feldman* • Nathalie Boutefeu *Alice* • Christophe Odent *Jerome Delbos* • Edouard Montoute *Ousman* • Claire Wauthion *Sister Marie-Françoise* • Frédéric Pierrot *Antoine Barasse* ■ *Dir* Eric Heumann • *Scr* Eric Heumann, Jacques Lebas, Lam Le

Port of Call ★★★
Drama   1948 · Swe · BW · 100mins

An alienated girl (Nine-Christine Jönsson), recently released from a reformatory and tormented by her relationship with her destructive mother and the puritanical restraints placed on her by social workers, seeks solace in a love affair with a simple young sailor (Bengt Eklund), who is unable to comprehend her complexities. This interesting early entry from Ingmar Bergman, well-photographed in semi-documentary style on location in the Gothenburg docks, is, as one would expect, depressingly downbeat. It's marred by touches of melodrama that the more mature Bergman would avoid, but Jönsson's performance is compelling. In Swedish with English subtitles.

Nine-Christine Jönsson *Berit* • Bengt Eklund *Gösta* • Mimi Nelson *Gertrud* • Berta Hall *Berit's Mother* • Erik Hell *Berit's Father* ■ *Dir/Scr* Ingmar Bergman

Port of Hell ★★
Drama   1954 · US · BW · 79mins

The commies are up to their usual tricks in this minor melodrama, anchoring a freighter in Los Angeles harbour with an atomic bomb on board that will be detonated within hours. Fortunately, Dane Clark's stern harbourmaster is on hand to team up with an old adversary, Wayne Morris, and foil the dastardly plot. The film suggests that, as long as the atomic bomb is exploded out at sea, no real harm will occur. The under-rated Carole Mathews shines in the leading female role.

Dane Clark *Pardee* • Carole Mathews *Julie Povich* • Wayne Morris *Stanley Povich* • Marshall Thompson *Marsh Walker* • Harold Peary *Leo* ■ *Dir* Harold Schuster • *Scr* Tom Hubbard, Gil Doud, Fred Eggers, from a story by Gil Doud, DD Beauchamp

Port of New York ★★
Crime drama   1949 · US · BW · 81mins

The main interest in this minor thriller is the screen debut of Yul Brynner as a New York drug trafficker whose operation is infiltrated by narcotics agents Scott Brady and Richard Rober. Brynner had hair in those days and isn't easily recognisable as the mafioso who smuggles the drugs through the New York docks. Laslo Benedek directs in pseudo-documentary style, revelling in his

locations in a film clearly influenced by previous year's thriller, *The Naked City*.

Scott Brady *Michael "Mickey" Waters* • Richard Rober *Jim Flannery* • KT Stevens *Toni Cardell* • Yul Brynner *Paul Vicola* • Arthur Blake *Dolly Carney* ■ *Dir* Laslo Benedek • *Scr* Eugene Ling, Leo Townsend, from a story by Arthur A Ross, Bert Murray

Les Portes de la Nuit ★★★★

Drama	1946 · Fr · BW · 106mins

The film that marked the end of both the fruitful partnership between director Marcel Carné and screenwriter Jacques Prévert and the sombre, poetic-realist tradition of which they formed an important part. The action focuses on a quartet of doomed lovers and a tramp, who is the personification of Destiny. Pretty gloomy, portentous stuff, but it does have a heady, nocturnal forties atmosphere, impressive sets by Alexander Trauner and a haunting theme song, known in English as *Autumn Leaves*. The film, which misjudged the postwar mood, failed miserably at the box office. In French with English subtitles.

Nathalie Nattier *Malou* • Yves Montand *Diego* • Pierre Brasseur *Georges* • Saturnin Fabre *Monsieur Senechal* • Raymond Bussières *Raymond Lecuyer* • Serge Reggiani *Guy* ■ *Dir* Marcel Carné • *Scr* Jacques Prévert • *Production Designer* Alexander Trauner [Alexandre Trauner]

Portion d'Eternité ★★

Drama	1989 · Can · Colour

Told largely in flashback, Robert Favreau's film starts out as an engrossing human interest story but soon descends into a Michael Crichton-like medical thriller with decidedly *Frankenstein*-inspired overtones. The opening section is both provocative and moving, as French-Canadian couple Danielle Proulx and Marc Messier explore the artificial insemination options open to them at an expensive clinic when they try to start a family. The scene in which she learns of complications and has to decide which of her unborn children to abort is particularly well handled. But once we begin to discover their doctor's murky past and his involvement with corrupt pharmaceutical companies, the plot begins to unravel. In French with English subtitles.

Danielle Proulx *Marie* • Marc Messier *Pierre* ■ *Dir/Scr* Robert Favreau

Portnoy's Complaint ★ 18

Comedy drama	1972 · US · Colour · 96mins

For his directing debut, screenwriter Ernest Lehman (*Sabrina Fair, Sweet Smell of Success, North by Northwest* and many blockbusting musicals, including *The Sound of Music*, bear his imprimatur – chose Philip Roth's scandalous novel about the difficulties of being Jewish and the joys of masturbation. Portnoy (a smirking Richard Benjamin) has been a lonely, repressed child who has grown up playing obsessively with himself – as Woody Allen called it, "It's sex with someone you love." Various prostitutes and fashion models try and help Portnoy in this satire that should

really have been a hardcore porn movie but emerges as a limp, unfunny imitation of *The Graduate*. [VIDEO]

Richard Benjamin *Alexander Portnoy* • Karen Black *Mary Jane Reid/The Monkey* • Lee Grant *Sophie Portnoy* • Jack Somack *Jack Portnoy* • Renee Lippin *Hannah Portnoy* • Jeannie Berlin *Bubbles Girardi* ■ *Dir* Ernest Lehman • *Scr* Ernest Lehman, from the novel by Philip Roth

The Portrait ★★★

Drama	1993 · US · Colour · 89mins

Echoes of *On Golden Pond* reverberate throughout this stylish TV-movie. Following on from Henry and Jane Fonda, the real-life father and daughter feuding on the screen this time are Gregory and Cecilia Peck, with the former's longtime friend Lauren Bacall as the wife-mother with divided loyalties. Returning to television forty years after he got his start there, veteran director Arthur Penn coaxes admirable performances from his supporting cast, while wisely leaving his impeccable stars to their own devices. A little deliberate in places, but still eminently watchable.

Gregory Peck *Gardner Church* • Lauren Bacall *Fanny Church* • Cecilia Peck *Margaret Church* • Paul McCrane *Bartel* • Donna Mitchell *Marissa Pindar* • Joyce O'Connor *Samantha Button* ■ *Dir* Arthur Penn • *Scr* Lynn Roth, from the play *Painting Churches* by Tina Howe

Portrait from Life ★★

Drama	1948 · UK · BW · 90mins

Best known for its costume dramas, Gainsborough was also capable of turning out some pretty decent contemporary pictures. Terence Fisher's film tackles the then thorny topic of rehabilitating Nazi sympathisers within postwar German society. The cast is first rate, with Mai Zetterling particularly good as the amnesiac forced to explore her association with a high-ranking fascist. However, the dramatic demands of a reconciliation with her father and a romance with Robert Beatty soon swamp the infinitely more fascinating background story and a good opportunity for some serious social comment goes begging.

Mai Zetterling *Hildegarde* • Robert Beatty *Campbell Reid* • Guy Rolfe *Major Lawrence* • Herbert Lom *Hendlemann* • Patrick Holt *Ferguson* • Arnold Marle *Professor Menzel* • Thora Hird *Mrs Skinner* ■ *Dir* Terence Fisher • *Scr* Muriel Box, Sidney Box, Frank Harvey Jr, from a story by David Evans

Portrait in Black ★★

Mystery	1960 · US · Colour · 112mins

This is tosh, and don't think producer Ross Hunter didn't know it. Lana Turner stars in a film with a plot so full of holes that it's hard to stop the cast falling through them. But Hunter was shrewd enough to know that if it looked good and was cleverly cast you could get away with murder (almost). Trouble is, this drama really needed Joan Crawford to make it work; Turner is too genteel for the hysterics. Despite support from the likes of Lloyd Nolan, Sandra Dee and Anna May Wong, director Michael Gordon has a tough time pulling all the threads together.

Lana Turner *Sheila Cabot* • Anthony Quinn *Dr David Rivera* • Sandra Dee *Catherine Cabot* • John Saxon *Blake Richards* • Richard Basehart *Howard Mason* • Lloyd Nolan *Matthew Cabot* • Ray Walston *Cob O'Brien* • Virginia Grey *Miss Lee* • Anna May Wong *Tani* ■ *Dir* Michael Gordon • *Scr* Ivan Goff, Ben Roberts, from their play

Portrait of a Hitman ★★

Action adventure	1977 · US · Colour · 85mins

It's a shame that, in later years, Rod Steiger all but erased memories of his quality work with empty gestures and prime ham. Here Steiger is stranded between implausibility and emotional truth as a criminal who pays an assassin (Jack Palance) to bump off the killer's old chum (Bo Svenson), so that pursuer and pursued inhabit an awkward grey area. Furthermore, love arrives as an unlikely intrusion just to add to the fun. Palance looks both sinister and soulful, but the picture is generally a pretty shaky effort, appearing at times rather incomplete, as if the director had gone off to lunch and forgotten to come back. Contains violence and swearing.

Jack Palance *Jim Buck* • Rod Steiger *Max* • Ann Turkel *Kathy* • Bo Svenson *Dr Michaels* • Philip Ahn *Mr Wong* ■ *Dir* Allan A Buckhantz • *Scr* Harold "Yabo" Yablonsky

The Portrait of a Lady ★★★ 12

Period drama	1996 · NZ/UK/US · Colour · 138mins

Though not as successful for director Jane Campion as *The Piano*, this is nevertheless compelling viewing. Nicole Kidman is captivating as Henry James's heroine Isabel Archer, an independent, dynamic woman seduced into the machinations of Madame Merle (Barbara Hershey) and her lover, Gilbert Osmond (John Malkovich). Caught like a bright bird in their trap, her loss of spirit is the tragedy of the film, but it doesn't make for easy viewing. Where Stephen Frears's *Dangerous Liaisons* combined sexual games and social climbing with humour, there's nothing to laugh about here. It's beautifully shot and captures the spirit of the novel, but you walk away with a troubled brow. Contains brief nudity. [VIDEO]

Nicole Kidman *Isabel Archer* • John Malkovich *Gilbert Osmond* • Barbara Hershey *Madame Serena Merle* • Mary-Louise Parker *Henrietta Stackpole* • Martin Donovan *Ralph Touchett* • Shelley Winters *Mrs Touchett* • Richard E Grant *Lord Warburton* • Shelley Duvall *Countess Gemini* • Christian Bale *Edward Rosier* • Viggo Mortensen *Caspar Goodwood* • John Gielgud *Mr Touchett* ■ *Dir* Jane Campion • *Scr* Laura Jones, from the novel by Henry James • *Cinematographer* Stuart Dryburgh • *Costume Designer* Janet Patterson

Portrait of Clare ★★ U

Period drama	1950 · UK · BW · 99mins

British director Lance Comfort had a successful early career with films like *Hotel Reserve* and *Hatter's Castle*. Yet, by the time he came to make this flashback drama, he had rather lost the knack for this kind of "woman's picture", with its all-too-familiar blend of reminiscence, romance and regret. Australian-born actress Margaret Johnston fails to make much impact

as she recounts details of her three marriages to her curious granddaughter.

Margaret Johnston *Clare Hingston* • Richard Todd *Robert Hart* • Robin Bailey *Dudley Wilburn* • Ronald Howard *Ralph Hingston* • Jeremy Spenser *Steven Hingston* • Marjorie Fielding *Aunt Cathie* ■ *Dir* Lance Comfort • *Scr* Leslie Landau, Adrian Arlington, from the novel by Francis Brett Young

Portrait of Jennie ★★★★ U

Romance	1948 · US · BW and Colour · 86mins

Produced by David O Selznick as a monument to the beauty of his wife-to-be, Jennifer Jones, this is one of Hollywood's best romantic fantasies. A long opening title sequence ponders eternal questions of life, space and death, and then we meet Joseph Cotten as a struggling artist who falls in love with the mystical Jones. The movie has considerable passion and conviction and Jones is simply gorgeous, while Cotten's innate weakness and vulnerability are perfect for his role. With William Dieterle's stylish direction and composer Dimitri Tiomkin plagiarising Debussy, the movie melds into a surreally romantic world of its own. [VIDEO]

Jennifer Jones *Jennie Appleton* • Joseph Cotten *Eben Adams* • Ethel Barrymore *Miss Spinney* • Cecil Kellaway *Mr Matthews* • David Wayne *Gus O'Toole* • Albert Sharpe *Mr Moore* • Florence Bates *Mrs Jekes* • Lillian Gish *Mother Mary of Mercy* ■ *Dir* William Dieterle • *Scr* Paul Osborn, Peter Berneis, Leonardo Bercovici, from the novel by Robert Nathan

Portrait of Maria ★★★

Drama	1943 · Mex · BW · 101mins

Romanticising the spartan splendour of the Mexican countryside, director Emilio Fernandez and ace cinematographer Gabriel Figueroa came to international attention with this tragic tale of misunderstood motives and patriarchal prejudice. Returning to her native land after almost two decades gracing Hollywood, Dolores Del Rio gives a luminous performance as the woman who, like her mother, is stoned by the reactionary inhabitants of pre-revolutionary Xochimilco after they wrongly surmise she has posed nude for painter Alberto Galán. With Pedro Armendáriz also impressing as the heroine's impoverished suitor, this is simple but affecting. In Spanish with English subtitles.

Dolores Del Rio *Maria Candelaria* • Pedro Armendariz *Lorenzo Rafael* • Alberto Galán *Pintor* • Margarita Cortés *Lupe* ■ *Dir* Emilio Fernandez • *Scr* Emilio Fernandez, Mauricio Magdaleno

A Portrait of the Artist as a Young Man ★★★★

Drama	1977 · Ire · Colour · 91mins

American director Joseph Strick could never match talent to integrity, so his inability to compromise meant that attempts to film modern classics such as this one by James Joyce never lived up to his expectations. This is one of his most successful, with Bosco Hogan as the young Dubliner in an Ireland that is "the sow that eats her farrow", while John Gielgud preaches the famous hellfire sermon with an

eloquence and power Strick wanted for all his films, but which he seldom achieved.

Bosco Hogan *Stephen Dedalus* • TP McKenna *Simon Dedalus* • John Gielgud *Preacher* • Rosaleen Linehan *May Dedalus* • Maureen Potter *Dante* • Cecil Sheehan *Uncle Charles* ■ *Dir* Joseph Strick • *Scr* Judith Rascoe, from the novel by James Joyce

Portraits Chinois ★★★ 15

Drama 1996 · Fr/UK · Colour · 106mins

Set among the young Parisian smart set and echoing the work of both Eric Rohmer and Woody Allen, this is a slight, but easily enjoyable comedy from director Martine Dugowson. At the centre of a web of interweaving plot strands is fashion designer Helena Bonham Carter, whose personal and professional contentment is threatened by pushy newcomer Romane Bohringer. Everyone in the ensemble – which also includes Marie Trintignant and Jean-Philippe Ecoffey – gets their moment in the spotlight, although none can match shopaholic underachiever Elsa Zylberstein's gloriously awful cabaret routine. One totally unexpected outburst about racial intolerance aside, this is about as accessible a foreign film as you could wish for. In French and Vietnamese with English subtitles. Contains swearing. ▭

Helena Bonham Carter *Ada* • Romane Bohringer *Lise* • Marie Trintignant *Nina* • Elsa Zylberstein *Emma* • Yvan Attal *Yves* • Sergio Castellitto *Guido* • Jean-Claude Brialy *René Sandre* ■ *Dir* Martine Dugowson • *Scr* Martine Dugowson, Peter Chase

The Poseidon Adventure
★★★★ PG

Adventure 1972 · US · Colour · 112mins

A memorable calamity-at-sea epic, as an ocean liner turns turtle under a tidal wave and survivors fight their way to the ship's underside, hoping for an above-water exit. Novelist Paul Gallico meant it as a religious fable, though the film's more about tension than intention. But, in an upside-down world, it's minister Gene Hackman who's the only one upright enough to lead the passengers to safety. Ernest Borgnine, Stella Stevens and Red Buttons give some wonderfully poignant performances, but it's always Hackman's movie – not even the remarkable effects can upstage him. ▭

Gene Hackman *Reverend Frank Scott* • Ernest Borgnine *Mike Rogo* • Red Buttons *James Martin* • Carol Lynley *Nonnie Parry* • Roddy McDowall *Acres* • Stella Stevens *Linda Rogo* • Shelley Winters *Belle Rosen* • Jack Albertson *Manny Rosen* • Leslie Nielson *Ship's captain* • Pamela Sue Martin *Susan Shelby* ■ *Dir* Ronald Neame • *Scr* Stirling Silliphant, Wendell Mayes, from the novel by Paul Gallico

Positive ID ★★★

Thriller 1986 · US · Colour · 104mins

Stephanie Rascoe is a young housewife who discovers she cannot live her life as before following an assault. Instead, she takes on a new identity and proceeds to track down her attacker. This interesting thriller certainly has a different twist-in-the-tale from other movies on the same

subject, and Rascoe is a convincing victim-turned-avenger.

Stephanie Rascoe *Julie Kenner/Bobbie King* • John Davies *Don Kenner* • Steve Fromholz *Roy* • Laura Lane *Dana* • Gail Cronauer *Melissa* ■ *Dir/Scr* Andy Anderson

The Positively True Adventures of the Alleged Texas Cheerleader-Murdering Mom ★★★ 15

Comedy drama 1993 · US · Colour · 98mins

Director Michael Ritchie has had an erratic career, but here he has created a delightfully sardonic, stranger-than-fiction TV movie. Holly Hunter is the potty all-American mom, who decides the best way to get her daughter on to the cheerleading team is to resort to murder. In other hands, this could have been po-faced, but Ritchie exploits the comic potential of the story to the hilt and makes some neat satiric jibes at American family values. Hunter has a ball in the lead role and the talented supporting cast (Beau Bridges, Swoosie Kurtz, Matt Frewer) delivers broad comic performances. Contains swearing. ▭

Holly Hunter *Wanda Holloway* • Beau Bridges *Terry Harper* • Swoosie Kurtz *Marla Harper* • Matt Frewer *Troy McKinney* • Fred Koehler [Frederick Koehler] *Shane Holloway* ■ *Dir* Michael Ritchie • *Scr* Jane Anderson

Posse ★★★

Western 1975 · US · Colour · 93mins

A rare assignment behind the cameras for Kirk Douglas, who also stars in this likeably quirky western. Bruce Dern, cast against type, plays a Robin Hood-style bandit being hunted by a marshal (Douglas) who thinks Dern's capture will give his career a much-needed boost. Douglas the director takes a no-nonsense approach to the material and draws able performances from a winning support cast.

Kirk Douglas *Marshal Howard Nightingale* • Bruce Dern *Jack Strawhorn* • Bo Hopkins *Wesley* • James Stacy *Hellman* • Luke Askew *Krag* • David Canary *Pensteman* ■ *Dir* Kirk Douglas • *Scr* William Roberts, Christopher Knopf, from a story by Christopher Knopf

Posse ★★★ 15

Western 1993 · US · Colour · 105mins

Mario Van Peebles's ambitious attempt to fuse the spaghetti western with nineties black consciousness doesn't always work, but it remains a provocative and entertaining addition to the revitalised genre. Van Peebles himself plays the mean and moody leader of a disparate group of black soldiers, plus token white good guy Stephen Baldwin, who find themselves caught between a cruel, racist sheriff (Richard Jordan) and their psychopathic old colonel (Billy Zane). Van Peebles's flashy, hyperactive direction is sometimes at odds with the genre, as is some of the dialogue, but he succeeds with his astonishingly eclectic cast, which ranges from veteran black actor Woody Strode to seventies icons such as Pam Grier, Isaac Hayes and his own father, Melvin. Contains violence, swearing and nudity. ▭

Mario Van Peebles *Jessie Lee* • Stephen Baldwin *Little J* • Charles Lane (3) *Weezie* • Tiny Lister [Tom ''Tiny'' Lister Jr] *Obobo* • Big Daddy Kane *Father Time* • Billy Zane *Colonel Graham* • Blair Underwood *Sheriff Carver* • Melvin Van Peebles *Papa Joe* • Isaac Hayes *Cable* • Woody Strode *Storyteller* ■ *Dir* Mario Van Peebles • *Scr* Sy Richardson, Dario Scardapane

Posse from Hell ★★

Western 1961 · US · Colour · 85mins

Four convicts break out of jail and go on the rampage in a quiet orderly town called Paradise, killing the sheriff and taking a woman hostage. Local resident Audie Murphy, a former gunfighter, gathers a posse and heads off in pursuit. Not content with being a simple shoot-'em-up, *Posse from Hell* pitches itself as a deeply moral parable about the value of society and the nature of violence. This means that the action frequently grinds to a halt while Murphy squints his eyes, searches the horizon and disgorges nuggets of scripted wisdom.

Audie Murphy *Banner Cole* • John Saxon *Seymour Kern* • Zohra Lampert *Helen Caldwell* • Ward Ramsey *Marshal Webb* • Vic Morrow *Crip* • Robert Keith *Captain Brown* • Royal Dano *Uncle Billy Caldwell* • Rudolfo Acosta [Rodolfo Acosta] *Johnny Caddo* • Paul Carr *Jack Wiley* • Lee Van Cleef *Leo* ■ *Dir* Herbert Coleman • *Scr* Clair Huffaker, from his novel

Possessed ★★★

Melodrama 1931 · US · BW · 75mins

An MGM melodrama with some hard-edged dialogue and a positively glowing Joan Crawford playing the low-class mistress of aspiring politician Clark Gable. Crawford becomes the most famous courtesan in New York as Gable puts his career on the line in a genuinely witty movie.

Joan Crawford *Marian Martin* • Clark Gable *Mark Whitney* • Wallace Ford *Al Mannings* • Skeets Gallagher *Wally Stuart* • Frank Conroy *Travers* • Marjorie White *Vernice* ■ *Dir* Clarence Brown • *Scr* Lenore Coffee, from the play *The Mirage* by Edgar Selwyn

Possessed ★★ PG

Melodrama 1947 · US · BW · 103mins

Joan Crawford's second movie with the same title, this dotty study in dementia features a mature Joan deeply disturbed (and over-acting) as a guilt-ridden schizophrenic. The tale begins promisingly with a dazed and confused Crawford wandering the LA streets before being taken off to hospital. After that, it's pretentious psychological piffle, but nevertheless enjoyable for fans of Crawford's remarkable non-acting style. Van Heflin and Raymond Massey have little chance to strut their stuff in underwritten roles, but Geraldine Brooks (later Mrs Budd Schulberg) shines in her movie debut as Massey's daughter. ▭

Joan Crawford *Louise Howell Graham* • Van Heflin *David Sutton* • Raymond Massey *Dean Graham* • Geraldine Brooks *Carol Graham* • Stanley Ridges *Dr Harvey Willard* • John Ridgely *Lieutenant Harker* • Nana Bryant *Pauline Graham* • Moroni Olsen *Dr Ames* • Erskine Sanford *Dr Max Sherman* • Gerald Perreau *Wynn Graham* ■ *Dir* Curtis Bernhardt

• *Scr* Silvia Richards, Ranald MacDougall, from the story *One Man's Secret* by Rita Weiman

Possession ★★★ 18

Horror drama 1981 · Fr/W Ger · Colour · 118mins

The doppelgänger myth has long been a keystone of European horror, but rarely has it inspired such a downright weird movie. No précis can do justice to *Possession* 's dizzying visuals or the eccentricity of its story line, in which disgruntled wife, Isabelle Adjani, has an affair with a tentacled fungoid creature and produces a spitting image of her husband, Sam Neill. Any number of interpretations are valid. The setting of divided Berlin suggests split personalities, while Adjani's dangerous duality smacks of political allegory. Or was Andrzej Zulawski simply seeking to disturb with the explosive encounters, sickening blood-letting and the grandest of *Guignol* symbolism? Contains violence, swearing and sex scenes ▭

Isabelle Adjani *Anna/Helen* • Sam Neill *Marc* • Margit Carstensen *Margie* • Heinz Bennent *Heinrich* ■ *Dir* Andrzej Zulawski • *Scr* Andrzej Zulawski, Frédéric Tuten

The Possession of Joel Delaney ★★★

Supernatural horror 1972 · US · Colour · 107mins

For some, this occult thriller, based on the novel by Ramona Stewart, was superior to *The Exorcist*, but time has not been kind and it now feels ponderously slow while its modishly violent climax seems to belong to another film. Through the eyes of his rich bitch sister Shirley MacLaine, we see the gradual disintegration of Perry King, possessed by the spirit of a Puerto Rican psycho with a penchant for decapitation. The horror is dignified by social comment – antagonism between the haves and have-nots – although the message is garbled, possibly by what appear to be last-minute cuts. But the script and performances are strong enough for fans of the genre to make allowances.

Shirley MacLaine *Norah Benson* • Perry King *Joel Delaney* • Michael Hordern *Justin Lorenz* • Edmundo Rivera Alvarez *Don Pedro* • Robert Burr *Ted Benson* ■ *Dir* Waris Hussein • *Scr* Matt Robinson, Grimes Grice [Albert Maltz], from the novel by Ramona Stewart

Possums ★★★

Sports drama 1998 · US · Colour · 97mins

A charming slice of small-town life that had only a limited release in the States, despite enthusiastic receptions at a number of festivals. Country singer/songwriter Mac Davis stars as the ardent fan of a school football team (the Possums of the title) who are on the brink of being disbanded. Desperate to avert disaster, Davis starts broadcasting fictitious results on a local radio station, and soon the Possums are blazing an imaginary trail to the top of the league – until reality intervenes. It's a clever storyline, handled with a light touch by first-time director J Max Burnett.

Mac Davis *Will Clark* • Cynthia Sikes *Elizabeth Clark* • Gregory Coolidge *Jake Malloy* • Andrew

Prine *Charlie Lawton* • Dennis Burkley *Orville Moss* • Jerry Haynes *Bob* • Barry Switzer *Prattville Coach* ■ *Dir/Scr* J Max Burnett

Postcards from America ★★★ 18

Biographical drama
1994 · UK/US · Colour · 87mins

This moving and adroitly made feature is based on the life of New York multimedia artist and Aids activist David Wojnarowicz, who died in 1992. Divided into three segments (with the lead shifting between Olmo and Michael Tighe, and James Lyons), the film moves from his abused childhood, through a period of prostitution and petty crime, to an adulthood of audacious creativity, emotional instability and casual sex. Directed by Wojnarowicz's sometime British collaborator Steve McLean, this stylised drama reveals the influence of film-makers such as Gus Van Sant and Todd Haynes, as well as McLean's own background in pop videos and commercials. Contains violence and substance abuse. ▣

James Lyons *David Wojnarowicz* • Michael Tighe *Teenage David* • Olmo Tighe *Young David* • Michael Imperioli *The hustler* • Michael Ringer *Father* • Maggie Low *Mother* ■ *Dir* Steve McLean • *Scr* Steve McLean, from the books *Close to the Knives* and *Memories That Smell like Gasoline* by David Wojnarowicz

Postcards from the Edge ★★★★ 15

Comedy drama 1990 · US · Colour · 97mins

It bears little resemblance to Carrie Fisher's screamingly funny bestseller, yet director Mike Nichols's grand tour through ''Hollywood Babylon'' behaviour and Bel Air-head lifestyles still emerges as a reasonably savage showbiz satire. Meryl Streep is the selfish actress in celebrity detox who moves back home with her brittle-natured mother (Shirley MacLaine) in this thinly-veiled account of Fisher's own poignant love-hate relationship with real-life mother Debbie Reynolds. Both stars rise to the bitchy one-liner occasion and turn on the glitz, glamour and grit in an engaging ride on the hypocritical Hollywood highway. Contains swearing and drug abuse. ▣

Meryl Streep *Suzanne Vale* • Shirley MacLaine *Doris Mann* • Dennis Quaid *Jack Falkner* • Gene Hackman *Lowell* • Richard Dreyfuss *Dr Frankenthal* • Rob Reiner *Joe Pierce* • Mary Wickes *Grandma* • Conrad Bain *Grandpa* • Annette Bening *Evelyn Ames* • Simon Callow *Simon Asquith* ■ *Dir* Mike Nichols • *Scr* Carrie Fisher, from her novel

Il Postino ★★★★★ U

Romantic drama
1994 · It/Fr · Colour · 103mins

A delightfully different little international gem with an Italian/French cast and a British director (Michael Radford). Massimo Troisi stars as a shy postman on an Italian island whose only port of call is the residence of legendary exiled Chilean poet Pablo Neruda (Philippe Noiret). Too timid to talk to local beauty Maria Grazia Cucinotta, the postman turns to his new-found friend for poetic assistance to win her heart. Wonderful, contrasting performances from the two

stars, beautiful scenery and understated direction from Radford give this the radiance of a Mediterranean *Local Hero*. In a tragic footnote, Troisi died the day after completing this life-affirming movie. In Italian with English subtitles. ▣

Massimo Troisi *Mario* • Philippe Noiret *Pablo Neruda* • Maria Grazia Cucinotta *Beatrice Russo* • Linda Moretti *Donna Rosa* ■ *Dir* Michael Radford • *Scr* Anna Pavignano, Michael Radford, Furio Scarpelli, Giacomo Scarpelli, Massimo Troisi, from a story by Furio Scarpelli, Giacomo Scarpelli, from the novel *Il Postino di Neruda* by Antonio Skarmeta

The Postman ★ 15

Futuristic epic 1997 · US · Colour · 170mins

There's more than a touch of vanity about Kevin Costner's futuristic epic, which dawdles on for three hours and will surely test the patience of Costner's most ardent fans. Costing over $100 million, it has gone down as one of Hollywood's biggest flops. Kevin drifts across a post-apocalypse America, claiming to be a postman with 15-year-old mail. It's a metaphor about the need for communication, and it's fairly barmy. A complete dud. Contains violence and a sex scene. ▣ *DVD*

Kevin Costner *The Postman* • Will Patton *Bethlehem* • Larenz Tate *Ford* • Olivia Williams *Abby* • James Russo *Idaho* • Tom Petty *Bridge City mayor* • Daniel Von Bargen *Sheriff Briscoe* ■ *Dir* Kevin Costner • *Scr* Eric Roth, Brian Helgeland, from the novel by David Brin

The Postman Always Rings Twice ★★★★★ PG

Classic film noir 1946 · US · BW · 113mins

Sweaty and sensuous, this MGM *film noir* remains utterly electrifying today, thanks to the riveting sexual chemistry between its stars, Lana Turner and John Garfield, and Tay Garnett's tense directorial style. Garnett clearly understood the world of James M Cain's original novel, though he was forced to circumvent certain sections because of the censorship demands of the day. Despite competition from several other movies, notably Luchino Visconti's *Ossessione* and Bob Rafelson's 1981 film, this has proved to be the definitive interpretation of the novel, and the Turner/Garfield coupling undoubtedly the most incandescent – their first meeting remains a classic moment of screen desire. ▣

Lana Turner *Cora Smith* • John Garfield *Frank Chambers* • Cecil Kellaway *Nick Smith* • Hume Cronyn *Arthur Keats* • Leon Ames *Kyle Sackett* • Audrey Totter *Madge Gorland* ■ *Dir* Tay Garnett • *Scr* Harry Ruskin, Niven Busch, from the novel by James M Cain • *Costume Designer* Irene

The Postman Always Rings Twice ★★★ 18

Crime drama 1981 · US · Colour · 116mins

Following James M Cain's novel more closely than was allowed in the classic 1946 version, Bob Rafelson's take on the murderous morality fable opts for explicit action over extra adulterous tension. Despite luminous performances from Depression drifter Jack Nicholson and young wife Jessica

Lange as the plotters-in-lust, the loose ends and even looser ending point to a below par effort from Rafelson, and the final result is not up to the standard of his masterly work with Nicholson on *Five Easy Pieces* and *The King of Marvin Gardens*. Contains violence, swearing and sex scenes. ▣ *DVD*

Jack Nicholson *Frank Chambers* • Jessica Lange *Cora Papadakis* • John Colicos *Nick Papadakis* • Christopher Lloyd *Salesman* • Michael Lerner *Katz* • John P Ryan *Kennedy* • Anjelica Huston *Madge* • William Traylor *Sackett* ■ *Dir* Bob Rafelson • *Scr* David Mamet, from the novel by James M Cain

Postman's Knock ★ U

Comedy 1961 · UK · BW · 86mins

One of two comedies (the other is *Invasion Quartet*) created for Spike Milligan by John Briley and Jack Trevor Story, talented writers not noted for their eccentric humour. Consequently, the brilliant Goon flounders in the conventional, happy-go-lucky tale of a village postman who is transferred to London and comes up against mail robbers and streamlined sorting equipment. Disastrously, the supporting cast, especially sozzled old Wilfrid Lawson, are funnier than the star.

Spike Milligan *Harold Petts* • Barbara Shelley *Jean* • John Wood *PC Woods* • Archie Duncan *Inspector* • Wilfrid Lawson *Postman* • Miles Malleson *Psychiatrist* • Ronald Adam *Mr Fordyce* • Bob Todd *District Superintendent* • Warren Mitchell *Rupert* • Arthur Mullard *Sam* ■ *Dir* Robert Lynn • *Scr* John Briley, Jack Trevor Story, Spike Milligan, George Barclay, from a story by Jack Trevor Story

Postmark for Danger ★★

Murder mystery 1955 · UK · BW · 84mins

This B-movie, derived from a TV serial by Francis Durbridge called *Portrait of Alison*, was originally released under that title in cinemas. Robert Beatty investigates the mysterious death of his brother, a trail that leads to a smuggling ring and another brother, played by William Sylvester. Predictable and only moderately gripping, this was the third picture to be directed by Guy Green, who won an Oscar for his camerawork on David Lean's *Great Expectations* ten years earlier.

Terry Moore *Alison Ford* • Robert Beatty *Tim Forrester* • William Sylvester *Dave Forrester* • Josephine Griffin *Jill Stewart* • Geoffrey Keen *Inspector Colby* • Allan Cuthbertson *Henry Carmichael* ■ *Dir* Guy Green • *Scr* Guy Green, Ken Hughes, from the TV series *Portrait of Alison* by Francis Durbridge

Postmortem ★★ 18

Crime thriller
1999 · US/UK · Colour · 105mins

In terms of personnel, this has to go down as one of the oddest Scottish films in recent years. Director Albert Pyun, best known for his straight-to-video martial arts thrillers, here links up with Hollywood bad boy Charlie Sheen for a moody and surprisingly gritty thriller set in and around Glasgow. Sheen plays a boozy American ex-cop, now writing ''true crime'' books, who finds himself drawn into the hunt for a serial killer playing mind games with the police. ▣

Charlie Sheen [Charlie Sheen] *James McGregor* • Michael Halsey *Inspector*

Balantine • Stephen McCole *George Statler* • Gary Lewis *Wallace* ■ *Dir* Albert Pyun • *Scr* John Lowry Lamb, Robert McDonnell

Il Posto ★★★★ U

Comedy drama 1961 · It · BW · 99mins

True to his neorealist roots, former documentarist Ermanno Olmi employed a wholly non-professional cast for this vaguely autobiographical insight into the hostile world of work. As the provincial whose delight at finding a job in a Milanese office blinds him to the dehumanising effect of the daily urban grind, the impassive Sandro Panzeri proves himself to be a clown in the Buster Keaton mould as he performs mundane tasks with eager pride in the hope of impressing sympathetic colleague Loredano Detto. Yet it's Olmi's attention to satirical detail and his gentle pacing that make this episodic comedy so engaging. In Italian with English subtitles.

Sandro Panzeri *Domenico* • Loredano Detto *Antonietta* ■ *Dir/Scr* Ermanno Olmi

The Pot Carriers ★★★

Comedy drama 1962 · UK · BW · 84mins

Part social drama, part knockabout comedy, this is an odd but entertaining account of British prison life in the fifties. It's based on a 1960 TV play by Mike Watts, who used real-life experience for his story of an old lag (Ronald Fraser, the only member of the TV cast to reprise his role) who befriends new inmate Paul Massie and shows him the ropes. The depiction of repetitive prison routine (the title refers to the detested practice of ''slopping out'') still has an impact.

Ronald Fraser *Redband* • Paul Massie *James Rainbow* • Carole Lesley *Wendy* • Dennis Price *Smooth Tongue* • Paul Rogers *Governor* ■ *Dir* Peter Graham Scott • *Scr* Mike Watts, TJ Morrison, from the play by Mike Watts

Pound Puppies and the Legend of Big Paw ★★ U

Animated adventure
1988 · US · Colour · 73mins

Following in the pawprints of the *Care Bears Movie* and *My Little Pony*, this cartoon feature was made simply to sell more pups. Clearly not enough time or money was put into the project, with the animation way below the standard you'd expect from a children's TV show. The storyline is quite fun, however, as the cute canines take on a power-crazed villain who's searching for the two halves of a magical bone that will enable him to rule the world. The grown-ups watching might appreciate the doo-wop soundtrack, too. ▣

George Rose *McNasty* • BJ Ward *Whopper* • Ruth Buzzi *Nose Marie* ■ *Dir* Pierre DeCelles • *Scr* Jim Carlson, Terrence McDonnell

Pour Rire! ★★★

Comedy 1996 · Fr · Colour · 100mins

Although few would deny he has talent, Jean-Pierre Léaud has not always chosen his roles with care. However, as the cuckolded husband in Lucas Belvaux's assured comedy of manners, he's given free rein to demonstrate the offbeat amiability that illuminated the *Nouvelle Vague*. In a time of

impermanent relationships, Léaud's marriage appears rock solid, until wife, Ornella Muti, confesses her affair with sports photographer, Antoine Chappey. With the emphasis firmly on text and performance, this isn't a visually innovative film. But the humour is sophisticated and Léaud and Muti (whose filmography is also littered with unworthy projects) make splendid adversaries. A French language film.
Jean-Pierre Léaud *Nicolas* • Ornella Muti *Alice* • Tonie Marshall *Juliette* • Antoine Chappey *Gaspard* ■ *Dir/Scr* Lucas Belvaux

Pourquoi Pas! ★★★
Drama 1977 · Fr · Colour · 93mins
Coline Serreau's background in *café théâtre* is clearly evident in this gently subversive utopian tale. She inverts the traditional ménage à trois by having having homemaker Sami Frey, breadwinner Christine Murillo and musician Mario Gonzales take on a fourth member in Nicole Jamet. However, their idiosyncratic idyll is disturbed by the intrusion of police inspector Michel Aumont, whose investigation into an accident results in his having an affair himself. Dipping into genres at will, Serreau makes a convincing case for both social re-alignment and the importance of dreams. In French with English subtitles.
Sami Frey *Fernand* • Mario Gonzalez *Louis* • Christine Murillo *Alexa* • Nicole Jamet *Sylvie* • Michel Aumont *Inspector* • Alain Salomon *Roger* ■ *Dir/Scr* Coline Serreau

Powaqqatsi ★★★ U
Documentary 1988 · US · Colour · 98mins
Having censured the old world order for allowing itself to be enslaved by modern technology in *Koyaanisqatsi*, director Godfrey Reggio condemns it for the merciless manner in which it exploits the Third World in this heartfelt eco-documentary, whose title comes from the Hopi language word for "parasite". As in the original, it is an ambitious collage of images (some stunning, some shocking and some straining to make their point), combined with the futuristic music of Philip Glass. Ultimately it's an unsatisfactory exercise, as Reggio too often states the obvious and settles for gloss when grit might have been more effective. ▱
Dir Godfrey Reggio • *Scr* Godfrey Reggio, Ken Richards • *Music* Philip Glass

Powder ★★★★ 12
Science-fiction 1995 · US · Colour · 107mins
Extremely moving tale of a teenager whose mother was struck by lightning during labour, giving him a ghostly white appearance, an extraordinary intellect and strange powers. Completely shorn of body hair, Sean Patrick Flanery delivers a wonderfully sympathetic central performance as the "freak", and there's fine support from Jeff Goldblum, Mary Steenburgen and an unusually expressive Lance Henriksen. Victor Salva's intelligent script and assured direction take many familiar themes to some really unexpected places. ▱

Mary Steenburgen *Jessie Caldwell* • Sean Patrick Flanery *Powder* • Lance Henriksen *Sheriff Barnum* • Jeff Goldblum *Donald Ripley* • Brandon Smith *Duncan* • Bradford Tatum *John Box* • Susan Tyrrell *Maxine* ■ *Dir/Scr* Victor Salva

Powder River ★★ U
Western 1953 · US · Colour · 77mins
A taut little western, made with some style at 20th Century-Fox and featuring a topnotch, albeit second-string, cast. Rory Calhoun is on the right side of the law for once, looking for a killer, and Cameron Mitchell is excellent as the doctor who becomes his pal. Corinne Calvet makes a fetching heroine and Penny Edwards also scores as the other woman in the picture. Director Louis King (brother of Fox veteran Henry) knows how to handle this kind of film, and doesn't get in the way.
Rory Calhoun *Chino Bullock* • Corinne Calvet *Frenchie* • Cameron Mitchell *Mitch Hardin* • Penny Edwards *Debbie* • Carl Betz *Loney Hogan* • John Dehner *Harvey Logan* ■ *Dir* Louis King • *Scr* Geoffrey Homes [Daniel Mainwaring], from an idea by Sam Hellman, from a novel by Stuart N Lake

The Power ★★
Science-fiction 1968 · US · Colour · 109mins
A number of B-league players (George Hamilton, Suzanne Pleshette, Michael Rennie) can't invest much conviction or authority in this science-fiction tale about a group of scientists who discover that one of them can kill by willpower alone. Director Byron Haskin adds some clever touches of menace, but authenticity is sorely lacking.
George Hamilton *Jim Tanner* • Suzanne Pleshette *Margery Lansing* • Richard Carlson *NE Van Zandt* • Yvonne De Carlo *Sally Hallson* • Michael Rennie *Arthur Nordlund* ■ *Dir* Byron Haskin • *Scr* John Gay, from the novel by Frank M Robinson • *Music* Miklos Rozsa

Power ★★★ 15
Drama 1986 · US · Colour · 105mins
Not quite as sophisticated or as clever as it thinks it is, this political drama nevertheless has much to recommend it, despite cursory reviews at the time from critics who were snobby about its glamorous media-based theme. Newly-greying Richard Gere plays a public relations manipulator, heading all too clearly for a welcome comeuppance, undeterred by warnings from his alcoholic mentor (another of those seemingly effortless performances from the redoubtable Gene Hackman). This is eminently watchable nonsense, smoothly controlled by director Sidney Lumet, with a cast to whet any movie-goer's appetite, though it sank without trace on its theatrical release. ▱
Richard Gere *Pete St John* • Julie Christie *Ellen Freeman* • Gene Hackman *Wilfred Buckley* • Kate Capshaw *Sydney Betterman* • Denzel Washington *Arnold Billings* • Michael Learned *Governor Andrea Stannard* • JT Walsh *Jerome Cade* ■ *Dir* Sidney Lumet • *Scr* David Himmelstein

The Power and the Glory ★★
Drama 1933 · US · BW · 76mins
This is the movie that made a massive impact on the young Orson Welles, telling the story of a railway magnate's life in a series of non-chronological flashbacks, with different characters revealing different aspects of the great man himself. Sound familiar? Well, *Citizen Kane* this isn't. William K Howard's direction is turgid in the extreme and Preston Sturges's script is underdeveloped. Today, of course, *The Power and the Glory* can't help but seem historically interesting, but, despite its relatively short running time, it's actually something of an endurance test.
Spencer Tracy *Tom Garner* • Colleen Moore *Sally* • Ralph Morgan *Henry* • Helen Vinson *Eve* • Clifford Jones *Tom Garner Jr* • Henry Kolker *Mr Borden* ■ *Dir* William K Howard • *Scr* Preston Sturges

The Power and the Prize ★★
Drama 1956 · US · BW · 98mins
This drama about the ruthless nature of American big business is weak stuff compared to the earlier *Executive Suite* and *Patterns*. Robert Taylor is rather too old to convince as the ambitious executive being groomed by Burl Ives's tycoon to be his successor. Ives was branching out from his career as a folk singer and had scored as a dramatic actor on Broadway. Elisabeth Mueller is unexciting, but there is sterling supporting work from Mary Astor, Charles Coburn and Sir Cedric Hardwicke.
Robert Taylor (1) *Cliff Barton* • Elisabeth Mueller *Miriam Linka* • Burl Ives *George Salt* • Charles Coburn *Guy Eliot* • Cedric Hardwicke *Mr Carew* • Mary Astor *Mrs George Salt* ■ *Dir* Henry Koster • *Scr* Robert Ardrey, from the novel by Howard Swiggett

Power 98 ★ 18
Thriller 1996 · US · Colour · 85mins
This waste of celluloid features Eric Roberts as a radio "shock jock" who'll do anything to get good ratings, even if it means murder. Jason Gedrick is the eager youngster hired to partner him on air who really takes to the job, much to the dismay of his bland girlfriend (Jennie Garth). A stunningly bad pseudo-thriller that starts promisingly but goes downhill fast. ▱
Eric Roberts *Karlin Pickett* • Lisa Thornhill *Vivian Porter* • Jason Gedrick *John Price* • Stephen Tobolowsky *Rick Harris* • Jennie Garth *Sharon Penn* • Larry Drake *Detective DiMotto* ■ *Dir/Scr* Jaime Hellman

Power of Attorney ★★ 18
Crime drama 1994 · US · Colour · 92mins
A preposterous script leaves a talented cast floundering in this botched gangster drama. Elias Koteas plays a lawyer who improbably sells his soul to public enemy number one, the larger-than-life mobster Danny Aiello. It's hard to work up much enthusiasm about whether he will rediscover his conscience in time, while the finale itself beggars belief. It's a shame because both Koteas and Aiello deserve a lot better. ▱

Danny Aiello *Joseph Scassi* • Elias Koteas *Paul Diehl* • Rae Dawn Chong *Joan Armstrong* ■ *Dir* Howard Himelstein, George Erschbamer • *Scr* Jeff Barmash,

The Power of One ★★★ 15
Historical drama 1991 · US · Colour · 121mins
A solid and gritty adaptation of Bryce Courtenay's rites-of-passage novel set in South Africa in the thirties and forties. Stephen Dorff stars as an outsider whose friendship, as a young boy, with tutor Armin Mueller-Stahl and prisoner Morgan Freeman inspires him to fight against racial injustice. Dorff gives a mature performance, but he struggles to carry the action, while his experienced co-stars never put a foot wrong. As you would expect from the director of *Rocky*, John G Avildsen handles the boxing scenes with some skill, but his grasp of political discourse and teenage romance is less assured. Contains some violence and swearing. ▱
Stephen Dorff *PK, aged 18* • Morgan Freeman *Geel Piet* • Armin Mueller-Stahl *Doc* • John Gielgud *Headmaster St John* • Fay Masterson *Maria Marais* ■ *Dir* John G Avildsen • *Scr* Robert Mark Kamen, from the novel by Bryce Courtenay

Power Play ★ 18
Thriller 1978 · Can/UK · Colour · 97mins
Confused thriller in which an international cast struggles to get to grips with an uninspired script about a power struggle in an unnamed country. It's a Canadian/British production and Peter O'Toole, Donald Pleasence and David Hemmings bring a bit of class to the proceedings, but for the most part it is entirely forgettable. ▱
Peter O'Toole *Colonel Zeller* • David Hemmings *Colonel Anthony Narriman* • Donald Pleasence *Blair* • Barry Morse *Dr Jean Rousseau* ■ *Dir* Martyn Burke • *Scr* Martyn Burke, from a novel by Edward N Luttwak

Power Rangers 2 ★
Science-fiction adventure 1997 · US · Colour · 99mins
Viewers who have never seen the *Mighty Morphin Power Rangers* TV show will be absolutely lost in this second big-screen adaptation. Painfully bad dialogue and technical incompetence rule here as the Power Rangers face a new alien menace, Divatox. She is so powerful, the Rangers must get new weapons (read: more toys to make and sell to kids) and recruit a new and younger ranger (read: greater appeal to the younger viewers.) At least the previous movie had some ambition to entertain beyond being a toy commercial.
Nakia Burrise *Tanya* • Jason David Frank *Tommy* • Catherine Sutherland *Kat* • Johnny Yong Bosch *Adam* • Blake Foster *Justin* • Paul Schrier *Bulk* • Jason Narvy *Skull* • Richard Genelle *Ernie* • Hilary Shepard Turner [Hilary Shepard] *Divatox* ■ *Dir* David Winning, Shuki Levy • *Scr* Shuki Levy, Shell Danielson

Powwow Highway ★★★ 15
Drama 1988 · UK/US · Colour · 87mins
A film of great warmth and easy-going morality, which follows two men as they travel to New Mexico in an old

U = SUITABLE FOR ALL   Uc = SUITABLE FOR ALL, ESPECIALLY FOR YOUNG CHILDREN (VIDEO ONLY)   PG = PARENTAL GUIDANCE

Buick – one is a philosophical Cheyenne, the other a fiery activist and in the lead roles unknowns Gary Farmer and A Martinez deliver performances of charm and understanding. A courageous film that deserves to be better known, as does its director, Jonathan Wacks. Contains some violence and swearing. ▭

A Martinez *Buddy Red Bow* • Gary Farmer *Philbert Bono* • Amanda Wyss *Rabbit Layton* • Joanelle Nadine Romero *Bonnie Red Bow* • Sam Vlahos *Chief Joseph* ■ *Dir* Jonathan Wacks • *Scr* Janet Heaney, Jean Stawarz, from the novel by David Seals

Practical Magic ★★★⑫
Romantic comedy
1998 · US · Colour · 99mins

Nicole Kidman and Sandra Bullock star as two sisters who are descended from witches in this uneven romance. Kidman is the wilder sibling, while Bullock is the home-loving store owner who falls for hunky detective Aidan Quinn who investigates when Kidman's abusive boyfriend disappears. There are nice supporting performances from Stockard Channing and Dianne Wiest as the sisters' equally witchy aunts, but director Griffin Dunne ultimately fails to make either a moving comedy romance or a funny romantic comedy. This is *The Witches of Eastwick* with much of the humour and sizzle removed. Contains some horror scenes. ▭ *DVD*

Sandra Bullock *Sally Owens* • Nicole Kidman *Gillian Owens* • Stockard Channing *Aunt Frances* • Dianne Wiest *Aunt Jet* • Aidan Quinn *Gary Hallet* ■ *Dir* Griffin Dunne • *Scr* Robin Swicord, Akiva Goldsman, Adam Brooks, from the novel by Alice Hoffman

Praise Marx and Pass the Ammunition ★★★
Political comedy 1968 · UK · Colour · 89mins

Do not be deterred by this formidable-looking piece of political propaganda, made for virtually nothing and originally seen by virtually no one. Although it is part agitprop, with lots of facts and figures on social deprivation, it is, as the title suggests, mostly satire and takes amusing swipes at a Swinging Sixties stereotype, the Marxist-Leninist revolutionary with noble ideals and feet of clay. Partly shot during the Paris student riots, it is a fascinating testament to long-lost hopes. There is also considerable appeal in the fact that the activist dedicated to the overthrow of capitalism, but not averse to bedding a few dolly birds along the way, is played by a young John Thaw.

John Thaw *Dom* • Edina Ronay *Lucy* • Louis Mahoney *Julius* • Anthony Villaroel *Arthur* • Helen Fleming *Clara* ■ *Dir* Maurice Hatton • *Scr* Maurice Hatton, from an idea by Michael Wood, Maurice Hatton

The Pram ★★★
Drama 1963 · Swe · Colour · 93mins

Bo Widerberg's feature debut, which drew favourable comparisons with Ingmar Bergman, François Truffaut and Jean-Luc Godard. Inger Taube gives a truly Bergmanesque performance as an aimless young girl unable to decide between a dull, dependable friend and a wannabe pop singer. Using many of the tricks associated with the French

New Wave, Widerberg draws us into the heart of his tale, while also passing some astute asides on Swedish society. In Swedish with English subtitles.

Inger Taube *Britt* • Thommy Berggren *Bjorn* • Lars Passgard *Robban* ■ *Dir/Scr* Bo Widerberg

Prancer ★★★⑰
Christmas drama 1989 · US · Colour · 98mins

A charming and disarming family film. Rebecca Harrell plays a nine-year-old girl, recovering from the death of her mother, who finds an injured reindeer and thinks it belongs to Santa Claus. Unfortunately, her grief-stricken father (Sam Elliott) is struggling to save their farm from the bailiffs, and has little patience with his daughter's attempt to nurse the beast. Sentimental without being mawkish, with the grown-ups given as much character as the children, this is lump-in-the-throat stuff from start to finish. ▭

Sam Elliott *John Riggs* • Rebecca Harrell *Jessica Riggs* • Cloris Leachman *Mrs McFarland* • Rutanya Alda *Aunt Sarah* ■ *Dir* John Hancock • *Scr* Greg Taylor, from his story • *Music* Maurice Jarre

A Prayer for the Dying ★★★⑮
Crime thriller 1988 · UK · Colour · 103mins

Sadly, those involved in this political thriller could never decide what they wanted to make of Jack Higgins's novel about the moral dilemma of a priest unable to shop an IRA terrorist because he has identified himself in the confessional. The end result works relatively well as a fast-paced action adventure, but it is certainly shallow and melodramatic, and Bob Hoskins is hard to take as the priest. As the terrorist, Mickey Rourke was also unpopular, though his Belfast accent isn't at all bad. ▭

Mickey Rourke *Martin Fallon* • Bob Hoskins *Father Da Costa* • Alan Bates *Jack Meehan* • Liam Neeson *Liam Docherty* • Sammi Davis *Anna* ■ *Dir* Mike Hodges • *Scr* Edmund Ward, Martin Lynch, from the novel by Jack Higgins

Prayer of the Rollerboys ★★⑮
Futuristic adventure
1990 · US/Jap · Colour · 90mins

In a future where the American economy has failed, Los Angeles is run by a group of rollerblading junior fascists known as the Rollerboys. Standing against them is Griffin (Corey Haim), a pizza delivery boy who used to be a friend of the Rollerboys' leader, Gary Lee (Christopher Collet). Patricia Arquette plays Haim's love interest, and the action scenes are sometimes exciting. As dark futures go, though, it's rather silly. ▭

Corey Haim *Griffin* • Patricia Arquette *Casey* • Christopher Collet *Gary Lee* • JC Quinn *Jaworski* • Julius Harris *Speedbagger* • Devin Clark *Miltie* • Mark Pellegrino *Bingo* ■ *Dir* Rick King • *Scr* W Peter Iliff

Praying Mantis ★★⑮
Thriller 1993 · US · Colour · 85mins

When Theresa Russell in *Black Widow* preys on unsuspecting husbands and

artfully disposes of them to keep living in the style to which she has become accustomed, we can swallow it whole because of the evil glint behind the beauty. Yet when Jane Seymour attempts the same thing, playing a serial killer who marries and murders her victims, the effect is rather ridiculous, as you can't get away from the sweetness and light that make her ideal for her TV role as Dr Quinn. Frances Fisher does better as a suspicious potential sister-in-law. ▭

Jane Seymour *Linda Crandall* • Barry Bostwick *Don McAndrews* • Frances Fisher *Betty* • Chad Allen *Bob McAndrews* ■ *Dir* James Keach • *Scr* William Delligan, Duane Pool, from a story by William Delligan

The Preacher's Wife ★★★Ⓤ
Romantic fantasy
1996 · US · Colour · 118mins

This nineties version of *The Bishop's Wife* has Denzel Washington as the angel sent down to save the marriage of pastor Courtney B Vance and his gospel-singing wife (Whitney Houston), as well as restoring Vance's wavering faith. Unsurprisingly with diva Houston in the cast, there's lots of singing and close-ups of the singer, leaving Oscar-winner Washington and Vance on the sidelines to act as scenery for her musical moments. It tries to be one of those films you watch every holiday season, but ends up a pale imitation of the Cary Grant–David Niven original. ▭ *DVD*

Denzel Washington *Dudley* • Whitney Houston *Julia Biggs* • Courtney B Vance *Henry Biggs* • Gregory Hines *Joe Hamilton* • Jenifer Lewis *Marguerite Coleman* • Loretta Devine *Beverly* ■ *Dir* Penny Marshall • *Scr* Nat Mauldin, Allan Scott, from the film *The Bishop's Wife* by Robert E Sherwood, by Leonardo Bercovici, from the novel *The Bishop's Wife* by Robert Nathan

Preaching to the Perverted ★★⑱
Sex comedy 1997 · UK · Colour · 99mins

The first film to focus on the London fetish scene is an odd mix of traditional British sex comedy and serious message. It starts well with atmospheric, if glamorised scenes in a fetish club run by sexy Guinevere Turner. Thereafter, it doesn't seem to know where to go, and its story of a government man seduced by the depravity he's investigating is very weak. The result will probably shock the easily shocked and disappoint sensation-seekers hoping for something stronger. ▭

Guinevere Turner *Tanya Cheex* • Christien Anholt *Peter Emery* • Tom Bell *Henry Harding* • Julie Graham *Eugenie* • Julian Wadham *Prosecuting lawyer* • Georgina Hale *Miss Wilderspin* • Ricky Tomlinson *Fibbin' Gibbins* ■ *Dir/Scr* Stuart Urban

Precinct 45: Los Angeles Police ★★★★
Police drama 1972 · US · Colour · 103mins

Virtually dismissed on release, this cracking crime drama is violent and humorous by turns and superbly directed by the estimable Richard Fleischer from a top-notch screenplay by Stirling Silliphant. The real star of the movie, despite competition from a

high-calibre cast, is cop-turned-author Joseph Wambaugh, whose own police experiences form the basis of the movie. Fleischer clearly understands these characters, and many of the cast went on to play similar roles in TV series. This one, though, is the real thing, with star George C Scott particularly outstanding.

George C Scott *Sergeant Kilvinsky* • Stacy Keach *Roy Fehler* • Jane Alexander *Dorothy Fehler* • Scott Wilson *Gus* • Rosalind Cash *Lorrie* • Erik Estrada *Sergio* • Clifton James *Whitey* • Richard Kalk *Milton* • James Sikking *[James B Sikking] Sergeant Anders* ■ *Dir* Richard Fleischer • *Scr* Stirling Silliphant, from the novel *Precinct 45: Los Angeles Police* by Joseph Wambaugh

Precious Victims ★★★⑫
Drama based on a true story
1993 · US · Colour · 92mins

This true-life story generates a thought-provoking conflict between private rights and the government's duty to protect the helpless. When two babies from the same family disappear, one after the other, obsessed detective Frederic Forrest and tough prosecutor Richard Thomas pursue bizarre parents Park Overall and Robby Benson, who steadfastly maintain their innocence. An excellent cast, Deborah Dalton's inventive script and Peter Levin's sharp direction resulted in a solid drama whose unusual, dreamlike quality and ambiguous resolution should appeal to those who don't demand a tidy conclusion. ▭

Park Overall *Paula Sims* • Robby Benson *Robert Sims* • Richard Thomas *Don Weber* • Frederic Forrest *Frank Yocom* • Brion James *Jimmy Bivens* • Tim Grimm *Captain Kocis* ■ *Dir* Peter Levin • *Scr* Deborah Dalton, from a non-fiction book by Don W Weber, Charles Bosworth Jr

Predator ★★★★⑱
Science-fiction thriller
1987 · US · Colour · 106mins

It may not seem much of a compliment, but this is one of Arnold Schwarzenegger's most efficient movies: a stripped-down thriller that cheerfully sacrifices characterisation on the altar of exhilarating action and special effects. Schwarzenegger is the leader of an elite special forces team whose jungle mission is thrown into chaos when they are tracked by a lethal alien game-hunter. As with *Aliens*, much of the fun derives from watching a bunch of macho soldiers crack under pressure. Director John McTiernan ensures the tension is kept at snapping point, helped no end by the sci-fi gimmick of a "cloaking" device that keeps the predator hidden from view. Contains violence and swearing. ▭

Arnold Schwarzenegger *Major Alan "Dutch" Schaeffer* • Carl Weathers *Dillon* • Elpidia Carrillo *Anna* • Bill Duke *Mac* • Jesse Ventura *Sergeant Blain* • Kevin Peter Hall *Predator* ■ *Dir* John McTiernan • *Scr* Jim Thomas, John Thomas

Predator 2 ★★★⑱
Science-fiction thriller
1990 · US · Colour · 107mins

After playing straight man to Mel Gibson in *Lethal Weapon*, Danny Glover seized this opportunity to play a loose cannon, an unorthodox cop who is always turning his nose up at authority. The setting is Los Angeles in 1997, and Glover can't work out who or what is murdering the city's gangsters, or why sinister government official Gary Busey is so interested. However, it's not long before he realises that the culprit is far from human. The action sequences are ably staged but it lacks the sweaty, claustrophobic tension of the Arnold Schwarzenegger original. Contains swearing and violence. ▭

Danny Glover *Detective Mike Harrigan* • Gary Busey *Peter Keyes* • Rubén Blades *Danny Archuletta* • Maria Conchita Alonso *Leona Cantrell* • Kevin Peter Hall *Predator* • Bill Paxton *Jerry Lambert* ■ *Dir* Stephen Hopkins • *Scr* Jim Thomas, John Thomas

Prefontaine ★★
Sports biography
1997 · US · Colour · 106mins

For his follow-up to his acclaimed documentary, *Hoop Dreams*, writer/director Steve James made this biography of the Olympic runner who died in a car crash at the tragically young age of 24. Jared Leto does an excellent job impersonating Prefontaine and keeps a straight face while wearing some of the worst hairstyles the seventies had to offer. R Lee Ermey, best known as the drill sergeant in *Full Metal Jacket*, plays Steve's running coach. Fairly engrossing, even if, inevitably, there is no real third act.

Jared Leto *Steve Prefontaine* • R Lee Ermey *Bill Bowerman* • Ed O'Neill *Bill Dellinger* • Breckin Meyer *Pat Tyson* • Lindsay Crouse *Elfriede Prefontaine* ■ *Dir* Steve James • *Scr* Steve James, Eugene Corr

Prehysteria! ★★★ PG
Fantasy 1993 · US · Colour · 80mins

A junior-league *Jurassic Park*, with kids hatching a clutch of pygmy-dino eggs and a comic-book bad guy trying to force the family into handing them over. The dialogue is surprisingly good for a low-budget movie such as this and the diddly dinos, if not exactly state-of-the-art special effects, are cute and cuddly enough to keep younger kids enthralled. The film stars Austin O'Brien, the kid from that other dinosaur of a film, *The Last Action Hero*. ▭

Brett Cullen *Frank Taylor* • Colleen Morris *Vicki* • Austin O'Brien *Jerry Taylor* • Tony Longo *Louis* • Stuart Fratkin *Richie* • Stephen Lee *Rico Sarno* ■ *Dir* Charles Band, Albert Band • *Scr* Greg Suddeth, Mark Goldstein, from an idea by Peter Von Sholly

Prejudice ★★ U
Documentary drama
1988 · Ausl · Colour · 59mins

This Australian docudrama bites off rather more than it can chew. Writer Pamela Williams wastes director Ian Munro's realistic atmosphere by insisting on using melodramatic situations to prove that, if it is difficult for talented white women to succeed in their chosen professions, then it's next to impossible for those of a different race. It's inevitable that movies tackling such emotive subjects will lack detachment, because the makers care passionately about their

material, but they must involve before they can influence, and it's here that this film falls down.

Grace Parr *Leticia* • Patsy Stephen *Jessica* ■ *Dir* Ian Munro • *Scr* Pamela Williams

Prelude to a Kiss ★★★ PG
Romantic comedy fantasy
1992 · US · Colour · 98mins

An offbeat, gentle romantic fantasy. Alec Baldwin is the groom who begins to suspect something is up with new wife Meg Ryan, whose personality change may or may not be connected to the appearance of an elderly stranger at their wedding. This certainly isn't the usual romantic fare from Hollywood, but Norman René directs the proceedings with subtlety and summons up a charming, if slightly melancholic, air. The performances from Ryan and Baldwin are first rate, and there's excellent support from Sydney Walker, Kathy Bates, Patty Duke and Stanley Tucci. Contains swearing. ▭

Alec Baldwin *Peter Hoskins* • Meg Ryan *Rita Boyle* • Kathy Bates *Leah Blier* • Ned Beatty *Dr Boyle* • Patty Duke *Mrs Boyle* • Sydney Walker *Julius, the old man* ■ *Dir* Norman René • *Scr* Craig Lucas, from his play

Prelude to Fame ★★ U
Drama 1950 · UK · BW · 88mins

Dashing the highbrow aspirations of their producers, films about classical music have nearly always been box-office poison. This uninspired tale about a child prodigy whose tutor is his only refuge from expectation and exploitation was no exception. Adapted from a minor Aldous Huxley story, the film was directed with little flair by Fergus McDonell, who had obviously been instructed to keep the focus firmly on the sickly soloist, played rather well by Jeremy Spenser. The film was the last made using the ill-fated Independent Frame method, which aimed to cut costs by using back-projected interior scenery.

Guy Rolfe *John Morell* • Kathleen Byron *Signora Bondini* • Kathleen Ryan *Catherine Morell* • Jeremy Spenser *Guido* • Rosalie Crutchley *Carlotta* ■ *Dir* Fergus McDonell • *Scr* Robert Westerby, from the story *Young Archimedes* by Aldous Huxley

Prelude to War ★★
Second World War documentary
1943 · US · BW · 53mins

This was the first of director Frank Capra's *Why We Fight* series, which was originally intended for military use only. Theatrical release was the subject of prolonged debate, and only came after President Roosevelt's personal approval. It was one of four documentaries to win an Oscar in 1943. As the title suggests, it attempts to put the Second World War in some sort of context, but there is little historical or social analysis. This film simply demonises Hitler and it does so quite efficiently through footage, maps and graphics, with an uncredited voice-over by Walter Huston.

Walter Huston *Narrator* ■ *Dir* Ernst Lubitsch, Maj Anatole Litvak [Anatole Litvak], Robert Flaherty • *Scr* Eric Knight, Anthony Veiller, Robert Heller • *Music* Alfred Newman

The Premature Burial ★★★
Horror 1962 · US · Colour · 80mins

Originally not intended as one of Roger Corman's unofficial Edgar Allan Poe series – the reason Ray Milland starred instead of Vincent Price – this moody chiller jettisoned any pretence of a plot for an eerie essay on the terrors of being buried alive. Although somewhat starchily written and slightly static in approach, the B-movie master of the macabre still manages to raise the odd claustrophobic spine-tingle or two thanks to graveyard-loads of gloomy atmosphere.

Ray Milland *Guy Carrell* • Hazel Court *Emily Gault* • Richard Ney *Miles Archer* • Heather Angel *Kate Carrell* • Alan Napier *Dr Gideon Gault* ■ *Dir* Roger Corman • *Scr* Charles Beaumont, Ray Russell, from the story by Edgar Allan Poe

The Premonition ★★★ 15
Supernatural thriller
1975 · US · Colour · 88mins

A young girl is torn between her foster mother and her real mom, who's nutty as a fruitcake yet determined to regain custody. Shot in Mississipi, Robert Allen Schnitzer's eerie thriller evokes a murky swampland atmosphere and has some nicely spooky moments, while the cast deliver convincing performances. *The Blair Witch Project* did it better, though. ▭

Sharon Farrell *Sheri Bennett* • Richard Lynch *Jude* • Jeff Corey *Detective Mark Denver* • Ellen Barber *Andrea Fletcher* • Edward Bell *Miles Bennett* ■ *Dir* Robert Allen Schnitzer • *Scr* Anthony Mahon, Robert Allen Schnitzer

The Premonition ★★ 18
Thriller 1992 · Swe · Colour · 109mins

If disembowelled cats, teenage sexual fantasies, Peeping Toms, sadomasochistic murder and violent accidents are your idea of a good time, then this overwrought chiller is for you. Director Rumle Hammerich falls over himself to pack his picture with eerie images as schoolgirl Tova Magnusson experiences the premonitions with which she fills her distinctly weird diary. But too much of the symbolism (most of it borrowed from Hitchcock) is contrived and a good deal of it is totally irrelevant to a plot that pulls the viewer in all sorts of directions without really leading anywhere. In Swedish with English subtitles. ▭

Tova Magnusson *Mikaela* • Figge Norling *Joakim* • Björn Kjellman *Max* • Niklas Hjulström *Johan* ■ *Dir* Rumle Hammerich • *Scr* Carina Rydberg

Preppies ★ 18
Comedy 1984 · US · Colour · 79mins

Soft-core sex comedy. Three rich college kids are threatened with expulsion should they fail upcoming exams. One of them, Dennis Drake's Robert "Chip" Thurston, invites the others to his country home for some intensive study. Chip's cousin, however, realises Chip will be disinherited if he's sent down, so hires some call girls to distract the boys. A limp farce that offers late-night titillation of the lamest kind. ▭

Dennis Drake *Robert "Chip" Thurston* • Steven Holt *Bayard* • Peter Brady Reardon

Marc • Nitchie Barrett *Roxanne* • Cindy Manion *Jo* ■ *Dir* Chuck Vincent • *Scr* Rick Marx, Chuck Vincent, from a story by Todd Kessler

Presenting Lily Mars ★★ U
Musical comedy 1943 · US · BW · 103mins

Stage-struck singer Lily Mars (Judy Garland) leaves her small Indiana town to follow young Broadway producer John Thornway (Van Heflin) to Manhattan. There, despite falling foul of his temperamental star (Marta Eggerth), she eventually finds stardom and romance. A formula musical in the *Cinderella* vein, is enlivened by Garland's usual high-calibre performance and a climactic appearance from Tommy Dorsey and his Orchestra.

Judy Garland *Lily Mars* • Van Heflin *John Thornway* • Fay Bainter *Mrs Thornway* • Richard Carlson *Owen Vail* • Spring Byington *Mrs Mars* • Marta Eggerth *Isobel Rekay* • Tommy Dorsey ■ *Dir* Norman Taurog • *Scr* Richard Connell, Gladys Lehman, from the novel by Booth Tarkington

The President ★★★
Silent melodrama
1919 · Den · Tinted · 90mins

The tale of three women who are abused, impregnated and abandoned by shiftless, socially superior males, Carl Theodor Dreyer's directorial debut established several traits that would persist throughout his career. The influence of little-known Danish painter Vilhelm Hammershoi is evident in his austere interiors, while his choice of source material (Karl Emil Franzos's 1883 potboiler) began a lifetime of basing his films on works of little literary merit. But, most significantly, this narratively sophisticated and compositionally precise melodrama (which can now be seen in a lustrous, tinted print) introduced his perennial themes of life's cruelty, patriarchal bigotry and female suffering.

Halvard Hoff *Karl Victor von Sendlingen, president* • Elith Pio *The president's father* • Carl Meyer *The president's grandfather* • Olga Raphael-Linden *Victorine Lippert, president's daughter* • Betty Kirkebye *Hermine Lippert* • Richard Christensen *Georg Berger, the lawyer* ■ *Dir* Carl Th Dreyer [Carl Theodor Dreyer] • *Scr* Carl Th Dreyer [Carl Theodor Dreyer], from the novel by Karl Emil Franzos

The President's Analyst ★★★★
Political satire 1967 · US · Colour · 102mins

It may seem dated today, but this clever satire was the ultimate hip trip back in the Swinging Sixties, and it is still very, very funny. Talented iconoclast Theodore J Flicker wrote and directed, and profited from the presence of James Coburn in the lead as the suave psychiatrist earmarked for secret service assassination, only to be saved by other agencies interested in the information they assume has passed between the president and his shrink. Coburn leads them all a merry chase, notably causing international havoc during a hilarious sex romp with hippy Jill Banner. Contains some violence.

James Coburn *Dr Sidney Schaefer* • Godfrey Cambridge *Don Masters* • Severn Darden *Kropotkin* • Joan Delaney *Nan Butler* • Pat

U = SUITABLE FOR ALL   Uc = SUITABLE FOR ALL, ESPECIALLY FOR YOUNG CHILDREN (VIDEO ONLY)   PG = PARENTAL GUIDANCE

Harrington *Arlington Hewes* • Barry Maguire *Old Wrangler* • Jill Banner *Snow White* ■ *Dir/Scr* Theodore Flicker

The President's Child ★★ PG

Political thriller 1992 · US · Colour · 92mins

A political thriller with its own distinctive spin, this concerns a president-in-the-making whose ex-lover and secret child are threatened by a political thug. William Devane, whose demeanour is reminiscent of James Coburn in his prime, is particularly skilled at silent menace and generally looks as if he might bite his adversaries. Donna Mills – who, once she visited the world of the TV movie, never left – manages to look both spunky and terrified as the beleaguered mum. ▭

Donna Mills *Elizabeth Hemming* • William Devane *Eliot McSwain* • James Read *James Guthrie* ■ *Dir* Sam Pillsbury • *Scr* Edmond Stevens, from the novel by Fay Weldon

The President's Lady ★★★

Biographical drama 1953 · US · BW · 97mins

Charlton Heston takes on one of his iconic roles with this neat portrayal of American president Andrew Jackson and the two loves of his life. One, his country, naturally, in all its early 19th-century tumult and the other, luscious Susan Hayward as the woman with a dodgy past he is determined to marry. Based soundly on Irving Stone's novel rather than historical fact, it allows Heston once again to convey the heavy burden of office, be it chosen by God or the American people, with an endearing helping of agonising self-doubt. Like Hayward's concrete stays, however, the whole exercise does creak a bit.

Susan Hayward *Rachel Donelson Robards* • Charlton Heston *Andrew Jackson* • John McIntire *Jack Overton* • Fay Bainter *Mrs Donelson* ■ *Dir* Henry Levin • *Scr* John Patrick, from the novel by Irving Stone

The Presidio ★★★ 15

Mystery thriller 1988 · US · Colour · 94mins

Director Peter Hyams is an under-rated master of the high concept action thriller and this effort boasts his usual strengths and weaknesses. On the downside, the plotting – in which San Francisco cop Mark Harmon is paired with an old enemy, military policeman Sean Connery, to solve a murder mystery – is perfunctory to say the least. However, Hyams distracts attention from that with some humdinging action sequences. Meg Ryan is a feisty love interest and there are solid supporting turns from Jack Warden and Mark Blum. Contains swearing. ▭

Sean Connery *Lt Col Alan Caldwell* • Mark Harmon *Jay Austin* • Meg Ryan *Donna Caldwell* • Jack Warden *Sergeant Major Ross Maclure* • Mark Blum *Arthur Peale* ■ *Dir* Peter Hyams • *Scr* Larry Ferguson

Press for Time ★ U

Comedy 1966 · UK · Colour · 98mins

After headlining in 14 consecutive films, this was Norman Wisdom's last starring role, and a sorry swansong it makes. He is woefully out of form in this feeble comedy, which he co-adapted from a novel by journalist Angus McGill. There is nothing new in his performance as a bungling reporter on a local rag, but what makes matters worse is that he also crops up in a couple of unfunny cameos, one in drag and another in old-age make-up. The attempt to spice up his act with some Swinging Sixties sauce is also a non-starter. Even die-hard fans will look away with embarrassment.

Norman Wisdom *Norman Shields/Sir Wilfred Shields/Emily Shields* • Derek Bond *Major Bartlett* • Angela Browne *Eleanor* • Peter Jones *Willoughby* ■ *Dir* Robert Asher • *Scr* Norman Wisdom, Eddie Leslie, from the novel *Yea Yea Yea* by Angus McGill

Pressure Point ★★★★

Drama 1962 · US · BW · 86mins

Based on a real-life story, this case history about a black prison psychiatrist and his ongoing confrontations with a fascist, racist inmate was considered very controversial in its day. Sidney Poitier, as the doctor, gives a brilliantly controlled performance while singer Bobby Darin – in one of his rare dramatic appearances – is bellowingly obnoxious as the bigoted prisoner. Director Hubert Cornfield stresses the caged claustrophobia of life inside with casual expertise.

Sidney Poitier *Doctor* • Bobby Darin *Patient* • Peter Falk *Young psychiatrist* • Carl Benton Reid *Chief medical officer* ■ *Dir* Hubert Cornfield • *Scr* Hubert Cornfield, S Lee Pogostin, from a story by Robert Lindner

Presumed Guilty ★★

Crime drama based on a true story 1991 · US · Colour · 93mins

Ever-dependable Martin Sheen stars in this crime drama based on a true story about a father's struggle to get his son released from prison after he is wrongfully convicted of murder. Brendan Fraser is suitably tormented as Sheen's son, trying to stay alive in prison while dad campaigns on the outside. Yet in the end, despite the story's origins, this comes across as a formulaic drama in which every plot twist and turn is easy to predict.

Martin Sheen *Harold Hohne* • Carolyn Kava *Mary Hohne* • Brendan Fraser *Bobby McLaughlin* • Mark Metcalf *Police officer* ■ *Dir* Paul Wendkos • *Scr* Cynthia Whitcomb

Presumed Innocent ★★★★ 18

Thriller 1990 · US · Colour · 121mins

A glossy, highly polished blockbuster starring Harrison Ford at the peak of his popularity as a lawyer assigned to untangle the murder of his former mistress. Based on the multi-million-selling novel by Scott Turow, this could have been a great movie, but, despite being a darn good yarn well told, the essential magic is somehow missing. Quite what turns a competent movie into a classic remains the great Hollywood conundrum – the elements are here, but they're too tightly threaded for this to attain true classic status. Contains swearing, violence, sex scenes and nudity. ▭ DVD

Harrison Ford *Rozat "Rusty" Sabich* • Brian Dennehy *Raymond Horgan* • Raul Julia *Alejandro "Sandy" Stern* • Bonnie Bedelia *Barbara Sabich* • Paul Winfield *Judge Larren Lyttle* • Greta Scacchi *Carolyn Polhemus* ■ *Dir* Alan J Pakula • *Scr* Frank Pierson, Alan J Pakula, from the novel by Scott Turow

Prêt-à-Porter ★★★ 15

Satirical comedy 1994 · US · Colour · 127mins

Director Robert Altman was always going to struggle to surpass the sprawling perfection of his episodic drama *Short Cuts*, and when this satirical look at the fashion industry opened the backlash really kicked in. Yes, it does lack the bite and subtlety of Altman's best work, but it's not half as bad as some have made it out to be. Setting the action against the backdrop of the French spring fashion shows, Altman characteristically weaves a bewildering number of subplots through the piece, some of which you care about, some of which you don't. There's also a cast to die for – a fascinating failure, but a star-gazer's delight. Contains swearing, drug abuse and nudity. ▭ DVD

Julia Roberts *Anne Eisenhower* • Tim Robbins *Joe Flynn* • Stephen Rea *Milo O'Brannagan* • Lauren Bacall *Slim Chrysler* • Marcello Mastroianni *Sergei/Sergio* • Sophia Loren *Isabella de la Fontaine* • Anouk Aimée *Simone Lowenthal* • Kim Basinger *Kitty Potter* • Tracey Ullman *Nina Scant* • Rupert Everett *Jack Lowenthal* • Forest Whitaker *Cy Bianco* • Richard E Grant *Cort Romney, fashion designer* ■ *Dir* Robert Altman • *Scr* Robert Altman, Barbara Shulgasser

Pretty Baby ★★★ U

Comedy 1950 · US · BW · 91mins

An innocuous Warner Bros crowd-pleaser about, quite simply, what a working girl has to resort to in order to get a seat on the subway. Betsy Drake (Mrs Cary Grant at the time) is perky in the lead, and for once Dennis Morgan's bland performance matches his bland role, so no harm done there. Morgan is no match for sophisticated Zachary Scott, who yet again demonstrates why he was nicknamed "The Eyebrow". *Miracle on 34th Street's* Edmund Gwenn also makes a welcome appearance.

Dennis Morgan *Sam Morley* • Betsy Drake *Patsy Douglas* • Zachary Scott *Barry Holmes* • Edmund Gwenn *Cyrus Baxter* ■ *Dir* Bretaigne Windust • *Scr* Everett Freeman, from the book *Gay Deception* by Jules Furthman, John Klorer

Pretty Baby ★★★★ 18

Period drama 1978 · US · Colour · 104mins

"Scandal!" yelled the moralists of the time about the under-age sex theme of director Louis Malle's depiction of brothel life in the New Orleans of 1917. It's a cosier treatment than might have been expected, though, with Brooke Shields as the bordello girl awaiting her twelfth birthday – and the official loss of her virginity – while Keith Carradine is the photographer whose candid camera strips the romance from her naive view of life with the women who are the only family she's got. A difficult subject but treated sensitively in ways that might offend some, but intrigue others. ▭

Keith Carradine *EJ Bellocq* • Susan Sarandon *Hattie* • Brooke Shields *Violet* • Frances Faye *Madame Nell Livingston* • Antonio Fargas *Professor, piano player* • Barbara Steele *Josephine* ■ *Dir* Louis Malle • *Scr* Polly Platt, from a story by Polly Platt, Louis Malle, from the book *Storyville, New Orleans: Being an Authentic Account of the Notorious Redlight District* by Al Rose

Pretty Boy Floyd ★★

Crime biography 1960 · US · BW · 101mins

Pretty Boy Floyd was a thirties gangster who hung out with John Dillinger and Baby Face Nelson and created a vivid legend about himself. His great moment came in 1933 when he took part in the Kansas City Massacre, in which he reputedly machine-gunned to death an FBI agent, three cops and a prisoner they were escorting to jail. The story was first told in *"G" Men* (1935) and touched on in *The FBI Story* (1959), but here Floyd gets his own biography with John Ericson as the flamboyant killer.

John Ericson *Pretty Boy Floyd* • Barry Newman *Al Riccardo* • Joan Harvey *Lil Courtney* • Jason Evers *Blackie Faulkner* • Peter Falk *Shorty Walters* ■ *Dir/Scr* Herbert J Leder

Pretty in Pink ★★★ 15

Comedy drama 1986 · US · Colour · 92mins

Remember Molly Ringwald – the girl who never quite made it? This is one of her attempts to reverse the slide, but Molly could act and here she makes a game fist of rebellious teenie gal meets upmarket designer boy. Ringwald, all flaming red hair and grungy attire, gives a touch of charisma to this well-worn theme, with sterling support from Harry Dean Stanton as her feckless, deadbeat dad. The frenetic, hard-edged flick belts along pleasingly enough, carefully avoiding the beckoning jaws of the sucrose trap but, unfortunately for Ringwald, it's all a wee bit too hackneyed to effectively hit the mark. Contains swearing. ▭

Molly Ringwald *Andie Walsh* • Andrew McCarthy *Blane McDonough* • James Spader *Steff McKee* • Jon Cryer *Phil "Duckie" Dale* • Harry Dean Stanton *Jack Walsh* • Annie Potts *Iona* • Jim Haynie *Donnelly* ■ *Dir* Howard Deutch • *Scr* John Hughes

Pretty Maids All in a Row ★

Black comedy thriller 1971 · US · Colour · 91mins

After having made some chic 'n' sexy pics in Europe with Brigitte Bardot, Catherine Deneuve and Jane Fonda, Roger Vadim made his Hollywood debut with this dire sex satire. It also poses itself as a thriller, starting with a girl found murdered in a high school and suspicion initially falling on a shy, introverted boy. But then Rock Hudson takes the film over, laughingly playing the school counsellor who advises students on their sex lives. Mainly, though, Vadim just wants his cast of starlets to get their clothes off. Tacky and hopelessly dated.

Rock Hudson *Michael "Tiger" McDrew* • Angie Dickinson *Miss Smith* • Telly Savalas *Capt Sam Surcher* • John David Carson *Ponce de Leon Harper* • Roddy McDowall *Mr Proffer* • Keenan Wynn *Chief John Poldaski* • James Doohan *Follo* • William Campbell *Grady* ■ *Dir* Roger Vadim • *Scr* Gene Roddenberry, from a novel by Francis Pollini • *Music* Lalo Schifrin

Pretty Poison ★★★★ 15
Psychological crime thriller
1968 · US · Colour · 84mins

In of his more subtle variations on his Norman Bates character in *Psycho*, Anthony Perkins plays a young man, just released on parole from reform school, who hooks up with high school cheerleader Tuesday Weld to destroy a polluting factory. But she's rather more than he expected and he ends up shooting her mother. Shot on a low budget, and influenced by the French New Wave, Noel Black's first feature remained pretty poisonous at the box office, though it later gained cult status. Strangely, Black's subsequent films are of little interest. ▭

Anthony Perkins *Dennis Pitt* • Tuesday Weld *Sue Ann Stepanek* • Beverly Garland *Mrs Stepanek* • Ken Kercheval *Harry Jackson* ■ *Dir* Noel Black • *Scr* Lorenzo Semple Jr, from the novel *She Let Him Continue* by Stephen Geller

Pretty Polly ★★
Comedy drama 1967 · UK · Colour · 99mins

A soft-centred adaptation (by Keith Waterhouse and Willis Hall) of Noël Coward's harder-edged short story about the transformation from ugly duckling to swan of diffident young Polly (Hayley Mills), thanks to the accidental death of her wealthy aunt (Brenda de Banzie) in the swimming pool of a Singapore hotel. Mills is agreeably fresh, although hardly plain enough at the beginning, and Guy Green's direction of this pleasantly escapist but unmemorable film is helped by some attractive locations, Trevor Howard as Polly's unconventional uncle, and the attractive Indian actor Shashi Kapoor who provides the romantic interest.

Hayley Mills *Polly Barlow* • Trevor Howard *Robert Hook* • Shashi Kapoor *Amaz* • Brenda de Banzie *Mrs Innes-Hook* • Dick Patterson *Rick Preston* • Patricia Routledge *Miss Gudgeon* ■ *Dir* Guy Green • *Scr* Keith Waterhouse, Willis Hall, from the story *Pretty Polly Barlow* by Noël Coward

Pretty Village Pretty Flame ★★★★ 18
War drama 1996 · Ser · Colour · 123mins

Set at the height of the Bosnian conflict, yet continuously flashing back through the 15 years in which Yugoslavia fell apart, this is the sobering story of how the lifelong friendship between a Serb and a Muslim was shattered by civil war. Srdan Dragojević's film, like Emir Kusturica's *Underground*, was attacked for appearing pro-Serbian. Yet, as the Serb's unit is trapped inside the Tito-inspired tunnel that stood for unity and progress, it's clear that no one is immune from blame. Crisply acted and tautly directed, the action is strewn with striking scenes, but nothing can prepare you for the horror of the final image. In Serbo-Croatian with English subtitles. Contains violence.

Dragan Bjelogrlić *Milan* • Nikola Kojo *Velja Kozić* • Dragan Maksimović *Petar aka "Professor"* • Velimir Bata Zivojinović[Bata Zivojinović] *Gvozden Maksimović* • Zoran Cvijanović *"Speedy"* ■ *Dir* Srdjan Dragojević • *Scr* Vanja Bulić, Srdjan Dragojević, Nikola Pejaković, from a war report by Vanja Bulić as published in *Duga*

Pretty Woman ★★★★ 15
Romantic comedy
1990 · US · Colour · 114mins

Originally meant to be a serious drama (called *$3,000*) about a man buying a prostitute for the night, this turned into a delightful romantic comedy in the hands of Garry Marshall and helped send the career of star Julia Roberts into the stratosphere. Co-star Richard Gere didn't do badly either – his career had been on a downward spiral before the role of tycoon Edward Lewis came along. On screen, they make the "hooker falls for a millionaire in Beverly Hills" Cinderella tale completely plausible, aided by Marshall's glossy direction, the hit-filled soundtrack, a perky script from JF Lawton and hilarious support from Marshall stalwart Hector Elizondo. Abandon your preconceptions, grab a box of chocolates, sit back and enjoy. Contains swearing, nudity and a sex scene. *DVD*

Richard Gere *Edward Lewis* • Julia Roberts *Vivian Ward* • Ralph Bellamy *James Morse* • Laura San Giacomo *Kit De Luca* • Hector Elizondo *Hotel manager* • Jason Alexander *Philip Stuckey* • Alex Hyde-White *David Morse* ■ *Dir* Garry Marshall • *Scr* JF Lawton

PrettyKill ★★ 18
Crime thriller
1987 · US/Can · Colour · 97mins

Pretty awful exploitation thriller about a sleazy cop and his hooker girlfriend trying to track down a serial killer. Director George Kaczender seems to lose interest once the central idea has been set up, while the acting – especially one girl with a dual personality – is as convincing as a sex chatline. ▭

David Birney *Larry Turner* • Season Hubley *Heather Todd* • Susannah York *Toni* • Yaphet Kotto *Harris* • Suzanne Snyder *Francie* ■ *Dir* George Kaczender • *Scr* Sandra K Bailey

Prey of the Chameleon ★★ 18
Thriller 1991 · US · Colour · 90mins

Daphne Zuniga stars in a tough thriller as a deadly woman hitching a lift with James Wilder, who is unaware she is not what she seems – a murderous temptress who takes on the identity of her victims. Zuniga went on to play a key role in the American soap *Melrose Place*, but never quite made it on the big screen. Fun stuff, though not as edge-of-the-seat scary as *The Hitcher*. Contains violence.

Daphne Zuniga *Patricia* • Alexandra Paul *Carrie* • James Wilder *JD* • Don Harvey *Resnick* • Red West *Pritchard* ■ *Dir* Tex Fuller • *Scr* April Campbell Jones

Prey of the Jaguar ★★ 18
Action adventure 1996 · US · Colour · 89mins

The script for this duff superhero tale is about as ill-fitting as the lycra suit worn by its all-round good guy, Maxwell Caulfield. The cartoonish plotting seems tailor-made for younger audiences; the violence and huge body count aren't. Caulfield plays a former government agent who transforms himself into masked hero the Jaguar to get revenge on the drugs baron

responsible for the death of his wife and child. ▭

Maxwell Caulfield *Derek Leigh* • Linda Blair *Lt Cody Johnson* • Stacy Keach *The Commander* • Trevor Goddard *Damien Bandera* ■ *Dir* David DeCoteau • *Scr* Rory Johnston, Bud Robertson, Nick Spagnoli

A Price above Rubies ★★★ 15
Drama 1997 · US/Fr/UK · Colour · 111mins

A fierce assault on today's orthodox Jewish community in Brooklyn, featuring a wrenchingly sympathetic performance by Renee Zellweger as Sonia, a young Hasidic woman locked into a world where rules are laid down by men. Mendel (Glenn Fitzgerald) is her scholar husband whose devotion to prayer and aversion to sex drive her away, while Sender (Christopher Eccleston) is the brother-in-law who rapes her as the price of her independence. As feminist propaganda, the film overdoes the hypocrisy and bigotry; as a portrait of a religious community, it is unconvincing and provides little insight; but, as a fictional tale of repression and liberation, it presents a final spirited breakthrough for Sonia that makes you want to cheer. Contains swearing and sex scenes. ▭

Renee Zellweger *Sonia Horowitz* • Christopher Eccleston *Sender* • Allen Payne *Ramon* • Glenn Fitzgerald *Mendel* • Julianna Margulies *Rachel* • Kim Hunter *Rebbitzn* • John Randolph *Rebbe* ■ *Dir/Scr* Boaz Yakin

The Price of Heaven ★★
Drama 1997 · US · Colour · 96mins

It's a little hard to comprehend quite how *The Last Picture Show* director Peter Bogdanovich ended up working on such modest TV-movie fare. This quirky comedy drama is a low-key affair, but it's expertly played by a top-notch cast that includes Lori Loughlin, George Wendt and Cicely Tyson. The lead role goes to Grant Show, who plays a serviceman returning to small-town America in the fifties and struggling to cope with life.

Grant Show *Jerry Shand* • Cicely Tyson *Vesta Battle* • Lori Loughlin *Leslie* • George Wendt *Sam* • Cari Shayne *Claire* ■ *Dir* Peter Bogdanovich • *Scr* Joyce Eliason, from the novella *Blessed Assurance: a Moral Tale* by Allan Gurganus

The Price of Survival ★★
Drama 1980 · W Ger/Fr · Colour · 107mins

Shot in America by a German director with a British cinematographer and a French star, this conspiracy thriller gets off to an intriguing start, but loses its way as the action becomes too crowded and elaborate. When Martin West guns down the quintet responsible for his dismissal from a Missouri electronics company, he's bundled off to an asylum. But his daughter and a snooping journalist suspect there's more to the situation than the fury of an desperate man. Strictly run-of-the-mill. German and French dialogue dubbed into English.

Michel Piccoli *Rene Winterhalter* • Martin West *Joseph C Randolph* • Marilyn Clark *Betty Randolph* • Suzie Galler *Kathleen* • Daniel Rosen *Thomas* • Ben Dova *Old Jim* ■ *Dir/Scr* Hans Noever

Prick Up Your Ears ★★★★ 18
Biographical drama
1987 · UK · Colour · 105mins

The life of doomed gay British playwright Joe Orton gets a tart, no-holds-barred, sure-handed telling by director Stephen Frears, with Gary Oldman giving a marvellous performance as the promiscuous cheeky chappie. Wonderfully scripted by Alan Bennett, and full of hilarious one-liners, the compelling biography is more interesting when focusing on what it meant to be homosexual in the sixties than on Orton's lauded theatrical achievements. Yet, with Alfred Molina also a joy as his jealous lover, this is still British film-making at its finest. Contains violence, swearing and sex scenes. *DVD*

Gary Oldman *Joe Orton* • Alfred Molina *Kenneth Halliwell* • Vanessa Redgrave *Peggy Ramsay* • Wallace Shawn *John Lahr* • Lindsay Duncan *Anthea Lahr* • Julie Walters *Elsie Orton* • Frances Barber *Leonie Orton* ■ *Dir* Stephen Frears • *Scr* Alan Bennett, from the biography by John Lahr

Pride and Prejudice ★★★★ U
Drama 1940 · US · BW · 112mins

This Jane Austen adaptation, co-scripted by novelist Aldous Huxley, is set half a century in advance of the book's period, to take advantage of more glamorous costumes – a very MGM trick. Greer Garson is a spritely, lively Elizabeth Bennet, but Laurence Olivier, though dashing and handsome, seems slightly uncomfortable as Darcy: a Heathcliff in sheep's clothing. The supporting cast, notably Mary Boland's very funny Mrs Bennet and Maureen O'Sullivan as a very sweet-natured Jane, is utterly superb, and the interior set decoration won an Oscar. ▭

Greer Garson *Elizabeth Bennet* • Laurence Olivier *Mr Darcy* • Mary Boland *Mrs Bennet* • Edna May Oliver *Lady Catherine De Bourgh* • Maureen O'Sullivan *Jane Bennet* • Ann Rutherford *Lydia Bennet* • Frieda Inescort *Miss Caroline Bingley* ■ *Dir* Robert Z Leonard • *Scr* Aldous Huxley, Jane Murfin, from the play by Helen Jerome, from the novel by Jane Austen

The Pride and the Passion ★★★★ U
Epic adventure 1957 · US · Colour · 132mins

Much abused in its day, this is a splendidly calculated spectacle, with a priceless, eye-catching cast, though criticism at the time centred on Frank Sinatra's Spanish accent (excellent) and Cary Grant's British prissiness (unavoidable). Flamenco queen Sophia Loren is gorgeous, and the Franz Planer photography remarkable. No expense was spared by producer/director Stanley Kramer to tell the tale, based on CS Forester's novel *The Gun*, about a guerrilla band dragging a massive cannon across the Iberian Peninsula in 1810 to blow up a French stronghold. It's sincere, brutal and, above all else, satisfying.

Cary Grant *Capt Anthony Trumbull* • Frank Sinatra *Miguel* • Sophia Loren *Juana* • Theodore Bikel *General Jouvet* • John Wengraf *Sermaine* • Jay Novello *Ballinger* • Jose Nieto

Carlos ■ *Dir* Stanley Kramer • *Scr* Edna Anhalt, Edward Anhalt, from the novel *The Gun* by CS Forester

The Pride of St Louis ★★★▯

Sports biography   1952 · US · BW · 92mins

One of the most likeable baseball biopics, this is the tale of pitcher Dizzy Dean, a witty and talented player elevated to his sport's Hall of Fame. He is expertly played by the versatile Dan Dailey, an often under-rated, clever and skilful screen actor who is better remembered for his work in musicals, but who began and ended his screen career in dramas.

Dan Dailey *Dizzy Dean* • Joanne Dru *Patricia Nash Dean* • Richard Hylton *Johnny Kendall* • Richard Crenna *Paul Dean* • Hugh Sanders *Horst* • James Brown (2) *Moose* • *Dir* Harmon Jones • *Scr* Herman J Mankiewicz, from a story by Guy Trosper

Pride of the Blue Grass ★★▯

Drama   1954 · US · Colour · 70mins

Director William Beaudine's career spanned Mary Pickford silents through the television series *Lassie* to such bizarre projects as *Billy the Kid vs Dracula*, and his reputation for efficiency and lack of artistic pretention gained him plenty of work, albeit variable in quality as well as content. This enjoyable, sentimental tale features Lloyd Bridges as a stableman who spots racing potential in a plucky horse owned by Vera Miles.

Lloyd Bridges *Jim* • Vera Miles *Linda* • Margaret Sheridan *Helen* • Arthur Shields *Wilson* ■ *Dir* William Beaudine • *Scr* Harold Shumate, from his story

Pride of the Bowery ★★▯

Comedy   1941 · US · BW · 60mins

Also known as *Here We Go Again*, the fourth in the East Side Kids series is a sprightly comedy drama that reunites several of the gang that had first appeared on screen as the Dead End Kids, and would later be known as the Bowery Boys. It's pretty standard B-movie fare, with the kids befriending a boxer while staying at a training camp run by a welfare charity. Wise-cracking series regular Leo Gorcey is as rough and ready as ever, and he's well served by a cast that includes his brother David. While the boxing scenes aren't exactly up to *Raging Bull* standards, they'll do.

Leo Gorcey *Muggs Maloney* • Bobby Jordan *Danny* • Donald Haines *Skinny* • Carleton Young *Norton* • Kenneth Howell *Al* • David Gorcey *Peewee* • "Sunshine Sammy" Morrison *Scruno* ■ *Dir* Joseph H Lewis • *Scr* George Plympton, William Lively, from the story by Steven Clensos

The Pride of the Clan ★★★

Silent drama   1917 · US · BW · 84mins

Mary Pickford later admitted her Scottish accent was dreadful, so it's just as well this was a silent. Pickford plays a fisherman's daughter who becomes head of her clan after her father drowns at sea. She and Matt Moore are sweethearts, but their romance is threatened when it turns out he is the son of the Countess of Dunstable (Kathryn Browne Decker). Maurice Tourneur directs with the kind of conviction that pleased Pickford's legion of fans.

Mary Pickford *Marget MacTavish* • Matt Moore *Jamie Campbell* • Warren Cook *Robert, Earl of Dunstable* • Kathryn Browne Decker *Countess of Dunstable* ■ *Dir* Maurice Tourneur • *Scr* Elaine Sterne, Charles E Whittaker

Pride of the Marines ★★

Biographical drama   1945 · US · BW · 119mins

John Garfield gives a convincing performance as real-life marine and war hero Al Schmid who is blinded in the battle against Japanese forces at Guadalcanal in 1942 and dreads going home because he "don't want nobody to be a seeing-eye dog for me". Eleanor Parker is the girlfriend he married on the eve of war and Rosemary DeCamp is the nurse who gets him through the crisis. Designed to give comfort and even inspiration to returning war veterans, it's well meaning and upbeat, but often grossly oversentimental, and it's not a patch on William Wyler's similar *The Best Years of Our Lives*.

John Garfield *Al Schmid* • Eleanor Parker *Ruth Hartley* • Dane Clark *Lee Diamond* • John Ridgely *Jim Merchant* • Rosemary DeCamp *Virginia Pfeiffer* • Ann Doran *Ella Merchant* • Warren Douglas *Kebabian* ■ *Dir* Delmer Daves • *Scr* Albert Maltz, Marvin Borowsky, from a story by Roger Butterfield

The Pride of the Yankees ★★★★▯

Sports biography   1942 · US · BW · 122mins

Lou Gehrig played 2,130 consecutive games for the New York Yankees, becoming one of baseball's immortals. Not bad for a tenement kid who only began playing professionally because his mother needed an operation. There's not a lot of sporting action in Sam Wood's movingly inspirational biopic, as the tale concentrates on the romance between Gary Cooper and Teresa Wright, but there's drama aplenty as "Iron Horse" battles the neurological condition (amytropic lateral sclerosis) that has since become known as Lou Gehrig's disease. The Coop mannerisms aren't really suited to Gehrig, but he gives a typically sympathetic performance alongside Wright and real-life stars such as Babe Ruth. ▭

Gary Cooper *Lou Gehrig* • Teresa Wright *Eleanor Gehrig* • Walter Brennan *Sam Blake* • Babe Ruth ■ *Dir* Sam Wood • *Scr* Jo Swerling, Herman J Mankiewicz, from a story by Paul Gallico

Priest ★★★★▮

Drama   1994 · UK · Colour · 104mins

Antonia Bird's timely and compassionate portrait of a gay priest, struggling to live up to his vows is wryly written by *Cracker* creator Jimmy McGovern, and is a biting indictment of a religion that preaches love and forgiveness yet shuns another human for not conforming. A sensitive, if harrowing, tale of lives needlessly destroyed by hypocrisy, it pulls no punches dealing with the subjects of incest and homosexuality, and contains an unforgettably moving finale. Linus Roache gives an amazing performance as the torn cleric. Contains sex scenes and nudity. ▭

Linus Roache *Father Greg Pilkington* • Tom Wilkinson *Father Matthew Thomas* • Robert Carlyle *Graham* • Cathy Tyson *Maria Kerrigan* • James Ellis *Father Ellerton* • Lesley Sharp *Mrs Unsworth* • Robert Pugh *Mr Unsworth* ■ *Dir* Antonia Bird • *Scr* Jimmy McGovern

Priest of Love ★★▮

Biographical drama   1981 · UK · Colour · 94mins

Christopher Miles adapted DH Lawrence's *The Virgin and the Gypsy* and tried for years to make a film of Lawrence's risky Mexican novel *The Plumed Serpent*. Instead, as if in a mood of compromise, Miles made this biopic of the novelist, dealing with Lawrence's early life (in flashback) and the controversy his novels caused in England, bringing about his various exiles – to New Mexico and Provence where he coughs himself to death. The movie feels pacy, mainly due to Ian McKellen's pedantic, archly theatrical performance. Janet Suzman plays his German wife and there's a clutch of distracting cameos, from Ava Gardner to John Gielgud to Miles's sister, Sarah.

Ian McKellen *DH Lawrence* • Janet Suzman *Frieda Lawrence* • Ava Gardner *Mabel Dodge Luhan* • Penelope Keith *Honorable Dorothy Brett* • Jorge Rivero *Tony Luhan* • Maurizio Merli *Angelo Ravagli* • John Gielgud *Herbert G Muskett* • Sarah Miles *Actress* ■ *Dir* Christopher Miles • *Scr* Alan Plater, from the book by Harry T Moore

The Priest's Wife ★★

Comedy   1970 · It/Fr · Colour · 106mins

It's hard to convey to an Anglo-Saxon audience how controversial this title – *La Moglie del Prete* – would be to Italians. Singer Sophia Loren, therefore, should know better than to try to persuade priest Marcello Mastroianni out of his vows in order to wed and bed her. What sounds like a promising sex comedy turns out to be a wordy bore, and quite an unworthy vehicle for the two stars. Here, in the hands of prolific, though generally uninspired, Italian film-maker Dino Risi, the couple have little to do but bicker and argue, and what passes for humour falls very flat indeed. For some perverse artistic reason, Risi filmed this in deliberately muted colours. Italian dialogue dubbed into English.

Sophia Loren *Valeria Billi* • Marcello Mastroianni *Don Mario* • Venantino Venantini *Maurizio* • Jacques Stany *Jimmy Guitar* • Pippo Starnazza *Valeria's father* ■ *Dir* Dino Risi • *Scr* Ruggero Maccari, Bernardino Zapponi, from a story by Ruggero Maccari, Dino Risi, Bernardino Zapponi

Primal Fear ★★★★▮

Courtroom thriller   1996 · US · Colour · 125mins

Hotshot lawyer Richard Gere chases fame as much as justice in director Gregory Hoblit's enjoyably involving courtroom drama based on William Diehl's best-selling novel. But when Gere takes on the high-profile case of a bewildered altar boy (Edward Norton) accused of murdering an archbishop, his cut-and-dried life begins to unravel. Having squared up to a state prosecutor (Laura Linney) who just happens to be his ex-girlfriend, Gere begins to suspect that still waters run deep in his seemingly angelic client. The movie brims with humour and excitement – plus a twist guaranteed to drop jaws – while the performances of Gere and, particularly, the quite electric – and Oscar-nominated – Norton crackle with energy until the very last frame. Contains swearing, violence and a sex scene. ▭

Richard Gere *Martin Vail* • Laura Linney *Janet Venable* • Frances McDormand *Dr Molly Arrington* • John Mahoney *DA John Shaughnessy* • Edward Norton *Aaron Stampler* • AndréBraugher *Tommy Goodman* • Alfre Woodard *Judge Miriam Shoat* ■ *Dir* Gregory Hoblit • *Scr* Steve Shagan, Ann Biderman, from the novel by William Diehl

Primal Secrets ★★

Mystery   1994 · US · Colour · 93mins

An unremarkable thriller, this fails to make the most of either its intriguing idea or an admirable cast, as *trompe l'oeil* artist Meg Tilly discovers that she's been hired by wealthy Ellen Burstyn more for her looks than her flair with murals. From then on, it's downhill all the way towards some predictable revelations.

Ellen Burstyn *Frances Griffin* • Meg Tilly *Faith Crowell* • Barnard Hughes *Harry Pitt* • H Paxton Whitehead *Deane* ■ *Dir* Ed Kaplan • *Scr* John Gay, Jim Wheat, from the novel *Trick of the Eye* by Jane Stanton Hitchcock

Primary Colors ★★★★▮

Political comedy drama
1998 · US · Colour · 137mins

The rise and rise of a womanising Southern States governor, very like Bill Clinton, bought to persuasive life by John Travolta, on his first Presidential campaign, with a spot-on script by Elaine May and direction by her frequent partner, Mike Nichols. Adapted from a novel by Joe Klein, there are some great, cynical set-pieces while, as the combative wife, Emma Thompson gives as good as she gets. Great acting, but they're almost outshone by Kathy Bates as the future President's lesbian hatchet woman. Politics with an all too human face. Contains swearing. ▭

John Travolta *Governor Jack Stanton* • Emma Thompson *Susan Stanton* • Billy Bob Thornton *Richard Jemmons* • Adrian Lester *Henry Burton* • Maura Tierney *Daisy* • Paul Guilfoyle *Howard Ferguson* • Larry Hagman *Governor Fred Picker* • Kathy Bates *Libby Holden* • Diane Ladd *Mamma Stanton* • Rob Reiner *Izzy Rosenblatt* ■ *Dir* Mike Nichols • *Scr* Elaine May, from the novel *Primary Colors: a Novel of Politics* by Joe Klein

Primary Motive ★★★

Political thriller   1992 · US · Colour · 93mins

A political drama about duplicity and double-dealing in the corridors of power. Now, there's a novelty! However, while it breaks no new ground, it is a well-made film, with a strong central performance from the under-rated Judd Nelson. He plays an inexperienced press secretary who digs up some dirt on his candidate's opponent, and is morally torn as to what to do about it. The strong cast includes John Savage, Sally Kirkland and Justine Bateman.

Judd Nelson *Andrew Blumenthal* • John Savage *Wallace Roberts* • Sally Kirkland *Helen Poulas* • Justine Bateman *Darcy Link* • Frank Converse *John Eastham* • Joe Grifasi *Paul Melton* ■ *Dir* Daniel Adams • *Scr* Daniel Adams, William Snowden

Prime Cut ★★★ 18

Crime thriller   1972 · US · Colour · 82mins

In director Michael Ritchie's sleazy and irreverent crime thriller, Lee Marvin plays a Chicago mob enforcer sent to Kansas to teach renegade slaughterhouse owner Gene Hackman a lesson. While the engaging quirkiness initially comes thick and fast, Ritchie is unable to sustain the offbeat tenor for the whole duration. However, bloody bursts of violent action and great performances help this skewed movie through its rough patches. Look out for Sissy Spacek in her film debut. ▱

Lee Marvin *Nick Devlin* • Gene Hackman *"Mary Ann"* • Angel Tompkins *Clarabelle* • Gregory Walcott *Weenie* • Sissy Spacek *Poppy* • Bob Wilson *Reaper driver* ■ *Dir* Michael Ritchie • *Scr* Robert Dillon

Prime Evil ★ 18

Horror   1988 · US · Colour · 86mins

Notorious horror/porno director Roberta Findlay has had a hand in some of the most controversial and reprehensible exploitation movies in film history. Sadly, this dire Satanist drama isn't one of them. A 14th-century devil cult grants the Parkman family eternal life, which explains why they're now scouring contemporary New York for victims to sacrifice in the name of Lucifer. Although as tedious and amateurish as usual, this doesn't have the offensive shock value of Findlay's "best" work. ▱

William Beckwith *Thomas Seaton* • Christine Moore *Alexandra Parkman* • Tim Gail *Bill King* • Max Jacobs *George Parkman* ■ *Dir* Roberta Findlay • *Scr* Ed Kelleher, Harriette Vidal

The Prime Minister ★★ U

Biography   1940 · UK · BW · 109mins

The Victorian novelist and prime minister Benjamin Disraeli once said, "Never complain and never explain" but one wonders if he would have kept quiet after seeing this dull-as-ditchwater biopic. John Gielgud is plummy of tone, supercilious of manner and always convincing as the writer persuaded to run for parliament who ends up running the nation and the Empire. But it's a stodgy history lesson and soapy domestic drama (Mrs D is played by Diana Wynyard), made primarily to remind audiences embroiled in the second year of war of what they were fighting for and how "great" Great Britain was.

John Gielgud *Benjamin Disraeli* • Diana Wynyard *Mary Anne Wyndham-Lewis* • Will Fyffe *Agitator* • Stephen Murray *William E Gladstone* • Owen Nares *Lord Derby* • Fay Compton *Queen Victoria* ■ *Dir* Thorold Dickinson • *Scr* Brock Williams, Michael Hogan

The Prime of Miss Jean Brodie ★★★★★ 15

Drama   1969 · UK · Colour · 110mins

Although Vanessa Redgrave was a hit in the West End version of Jay Presson Allen's adaptation of Muriel Spark's novel, few would argue that the part of prim Edinburgh schoolmarm Jean Brodie now belongs solely to Maggie Smith. Never have such politically incorrect opinions been expressed with such disarming charm or been received with such trusting innocence. While Smith thoroughly deserved her Oscar, it is somewhat surprising that Celia Johnson was overlooked for her superb performance as the disapproving headmistress. Robert Stephens and Gordon Jackson are also on form as the men in Smith's life, and Pamela Franklin impresses as the pupil who turns Judas. *Crème de la crème*, indeed. Contains brief nudity. ▱

Maggie Smith *Jean Brodie* • Robert Stephens *Teddy Lloyd* • Pamela Franklin *Sandy* • Gordon Jackson *Gordon Lowther* • Celia Johnson *Miss MacKay* • Diane Grayson *Jenny* • Jane Carr (2) *Mary McGregor* • Shirley Steedman *Monica* ■ *Dir* Ronald Neame • *Scr* Jay Presson Allen, from her play, from the novel by Muriel Spark

Prime Risk ★★ PG

Action adventure   1985 · US · Colour · 94mins

Two bored kids concoct a scheme to rip off hole-in-the-wall cash machines, but find themselves out of their league when the scam brings them into contact with international baddies engaged in a similar but far more subversive activity. Lee Montgomery and Sam Bottoms are attractive leads, and there's a good baddie from veteran Keenan Wynn. Worth making a withdrawal. ▱

Toni Hudson *Julie Collins* • Lee Montgomery *Michael Fox* • Sam Bottoms *Bill Yeoman* • Clu Gulager *Paul Minsky* • Keenan Wynn *Dr Lasser* ■ *Dir/Scr* Michael Farkas

Prime Target ★★★ PG

Crime drama   1989 · US · Colour · 91mins

New York's policewomen are being targeted by a serial killer who may be a colleague. This is a standard-issue TV cop drama, often gritty and suspenseful and lifted by a good cast: Angie Dickinson, from the *Police Woman* series of the seventies, and David Soul of *Starsky and Hutch* fame. Joseph Bologna, Charles Durning and Yaphet Kotto complete the impressive line-up. Contains violence and swearing. ▱

Angie Dickinson *Kelly Mulcahaney* • David Soul *Peter Armetage* • Charles Durning *Earl Mulcahaney* • Joe Regalbuto *Tom Janssen* • Yaphet Kotto *Gilmore Brown* ■ *Dir* Robert Collins • *Scr* Robert Collins, from the novel *No Business Being a Cop* by Lillian O'Donnell

Prime Target ★★ 15

Action drama   1991 · US · Colour · 84mins

This routine action movie was written, produced and directed by one David Heavener, who positions himself in front of the camera as John Bloodstone, a tough, small town sheriff in the Chuck Norris mould, who's given the job of escorting Mob boss Tony Curtis to a different prison, unaware that it's a set-up. The mess that

follows is nothing you haven't seen before, though Curtis – in a new toupee – is watchable as ever. ▱

David Heavener *John Bloodstone* • Tony Curtis *Marrietta Copella* • Isaac Hayes *Captain Thompkins* • Andrew Robinson *Commissioner Garth* • Robert Reed *Agent Harrington* ■ *Dir/Scr* David Heavener

The Primitives ★★ U

Crime drama   1962 · UK · BW · 69mins

The Primitives are four jewel thieves – three men led by one woman – posing as entertainers, who draw upon their skill with disguises in their nefarious schemes. Jan Holden is Cheta, well named as the female cat burglar of the team, who becomes an inconvenient love interest. When they rob a London jewellers, the British police spot the unusual thespian quality of the crime and get on their tails. All pretty incredible yet watchable in a *Mission: Impossible* kind of way.

Jan Holden *Cheta* • Bill Edwards *Peter* • Rio Fanning *John* • George Mikell *Claude* • Terence Fallon *Sgt Henry* ■ *Dir* Alfred Travers • *Scr* Alfred Travers, Moris Farhi

Primrose Path ★★★

Melodrama   1940 · US · BW · 92mins

Determined to escape from the wrong side of the tracks, where her mother is a woman of easy virtue and her father a drunk, Ginger Rogers finds love and respectability with decent Joel McCrea – until he meets her family, that is. Director Gregory La Cava's film was quite daring within the censorious climate of the time, although it compromises its attempt at dramatic realism with a predictably sentimental, romantic outcome. Interesting, though, thanks to the standard of direction and the convincing cast. Marjorie Rambeau earned an Oscar nomination for her supporting actress as Ginger's mother.

Ginger Rogers *Ellie May Adams* • Joel McCrea *Ed Wallace* • Marjorie Rambeau *Mamie Adams* • Henry Travers *Gramp* • Miles Mander *Homer Adams* • Queenie Vassar *Grandma* ■ *Dir* Gregory La Cava • *Scr* Allan Scott, Gregory La Cava, from the play by Robert Buckner, Walter Hart, from the novel *February Hill* by Victoria Lincoln

The Prince and the Pauper ★★★ U

Historical swashbuckling adventure
1937 · US · BW · 113mins

A historical romp from the classic period at Warner Bros, this famous version of the much-filmed Mark Twain tale about a street urchin who swaps roles with the young Prince Edward was billed as an Errol Flynn feature, but Flynn doesn't even appear as swashbuckler Miles Hendon until nearly halfway through. The title youngsters are played by the Mauch twins, Billy and Bobby, and it's hard to summon up any interest in their adventures. The things that actually give this movie its verve and style are a fabulous score by Erich Wolfgang Korngold and a wonderful supporting cast headed by the urbane Claude Rains and featuring Eric Portman in a rare Hollywood role. ▱

Errol Flynn *Miles Hendon* • Claude Rains *Earl of Hertford* • Henry Stephenson *Duke of Norfolk* • Barton MacLane *John Canty* • Billy

Mauch *Tom Canty* • Bobby Mauch *Prince Edward* • Eric Portman *First Lord* ■ *Dir* William Keighley • *Scr* Laird Doyle, from the play by Catherine Chishold Cushing, from the novel by Mark Twain

The Prince and the Pauper ★★ U

Historical adventure
1962 · US · Colour · 93mins

This is an entertaining American TV-movie version of Mark Twain's classic story about the humble street urchin who trades places with a lookalike prince. The tale had already been told to more lavish effect on the big screen with Errol Flynn and Claude Rains in 1937, and would be made as an extravagant romp with Oliver Reed and Mark Lester in 1977. Here, Donald Houston and co do well enough, while Disney's stamp provides a minimum quality guarantee, at least for a young audience.

Sean Scully *Edward, Prince of Wales/Tom Canty* • Donald Houston *John Canty* • Niall MacGinnis *Father Andrew* • Jane Asher *Lady Jane Grey* • Laurence Naismith *Lord Hertford* ■ *Dir* Don Chaffey • *Scr* Jack Whittingham, from the novel by Mark Twain

The Prince and the Pauper ★★ PG

Historical adventure
1977 · Pan/US · Colour · 115mins

Oliver Reed, Charlton Heston and Raquel Welch, following on from the success of Richard Lester's two Musketeers films, don the costumes once again for another historical romp, this one based on Mark Twain's classic story. No expense was spared on production values and the distinguished cast (which also includes Rex Harrison and George C Scott) has a fine time hamming things up. Despite the extravagance, it remains a lifeless affair that isn't helped by an unconvincing lead performance from Mark Lester as the prince who swaps places with a beggar. ▱

Mark Lester (1) *Tom Canty/Prince Edward* • Oliver Reed *Miles Hendon* • Raquel Welch *Lady Edith* • Ernest Borgnine *John Canty* • George C Scott *Ruffler* • Rex Harrison *Duke of Norfolk* • David Hemmings *Hugh Hendon* • Charlton Heston *Henry VIII* • Harry Andrews *Hertford* ■ *Dir* Richard Fleischer • *Scr* George MacDonald Fraser, Berta Dominguez, Pierre Spengler, from the novel by Mark Twain

The Prince and the Showgirl ★★★ PG

Romantic comedy
1957 · UK · Colour · 111mins

What should have been an explosive pairing of Hollywood's golden girl, Marilyn Monroe, and England's greatest theatre actor, Laurence Olivier, doesn't quite come off, largely owing to the vapidity of the vehicle chosen: a tired Terence Rattigan play, written for the Coronation and already dated before it hit the West End boards. Yet there's much to be thankful for – as you would expect, Monroe sparkles, showing a terrific sense of comic timing in a performance of great skill and beauty, certainly helped by the white evening dress she wears throughout. Olivier, who also directed, seems overawed,

U = SUITABLE FOR ALL   Uc = SUITABLE FOR ALL, ESPECIALLY FOR YOUNG CHILDREN (VIDEO ONLY)   PG = PARENTAL GUIDANCE

and hampers himself with a Balkan accent that's a cross between Garbo and Bela Lugosi. Richard Wattis is splendid, however. ▱

Marilyn Monroe *Elsie Marina* • Laurence Olivier *Charles, Prince Regent* • Sybil Thorndike *Queen Dowager* • Richard Wattis *Northbrooke* • Jeremy Spenser *King Nicholas* ■ *Dir* Laurence Olivier • *Scr* Terence Rattigan, from his play *The Sleeping Prince* • *Costume Designer* Beatrice Dawson

Prince Jack ★★

Political drama 1984 · US · Colour · 100mins

The prince in question is JFK whose life and presidency are portrayed in "mockumentary" style. Starting off with Frank Sinatra singing *High Hopes* – which became JFK's campaign anthem – the movie takes in the major issues of the day, including the Bay of Pigs, the Cuban missile crisis, the civil rights movement and JFK's relationships with brother Bobby and Vice-President Lyndon Johnson. Conspicuous by her absence is Jackie, who was alive when the film was made, though a platinum blonde called Marilyn Monroe is mentioned in dispatches. As always, the main problem is that the actors don't look like the people they claim to be.

Robert Hogan *Jack Kennedy* • James F Kelly *Bobby Kennedy* • Kenneth Mars *Lyndon B Johnson* • Lloyd Nolan *Joseph Kennedy* • Cameron Mitchell *General Walker* • Robert Guillaume *Martin Luther King* • Theodore Bikel *Russian Ambassador* ■ *Dir/Scr* Bert Lovitt

Prince of Bel Air ★★▣

Comedy drama 1986 · US · Colour · 91mins

This is a mediocre TV movie with Mark Harmon as a swinging swimming pool repair man who begins to have doubts about his playboy lifestyle when he starts seeing his sponsor's niece. *Cheers* star Kirstie Alley and *The Man from UNCLE's* Robert Vaughn are left with very little to do, as this was obviously designed as a star vehicle for Harmon, but at least it has the novelty value of a brief supporting role for Patrick Swayze's brother Don. ▱

Mark Harmon *Robin Prince* • Kirstie Alley *Jamie Harris* • Robert Vaughn *Stanley Auerbach* • Patrick Labyorteaux *Justin Auerbach* ■ *Dir* Charles Braverman • *Scr* Dori Pierson, Marc Rubel

Prince of Darkness ★★▣

Horror 1987 · US · Colour · 101mins

In virtually a supernatural remake of his own *Assault on Precinct 13*, director John Carpenter takes one of his sporadic delves into Nigel Kneale sci-fi/horror territory (he even wrote the script as Martin Quatermass!) with tedious results. It's old superstitions versus the computer age in an awkward yarn about a weird container full of green liquid in an LA church that contains pure evil. Zombies, gore galore and metaphysical ramblings are overused to keep a mechanical plot moving relentlessly. Contains violence and swearing. ▱

Donald Pleasence *Priest* • Jameson Parker *Brian* • Victor Wong *Professor Birack* • Lisa Blount *Catherine* • Dennis Dun *Walter* • Susan Blanchard *Kelly* • Alice Cooper *Street people leader* ■ *Dir* John Carpenter • *Scr* Martin Quatermass [John Carpenter]

The Prince of Egypt ★★★★★ U

Animation 1998 · US · Colour · 98mins

DreamWorks's stunning animated interpretation of the story of Moses has a visual grandeur and emotional depth to match the best of Disney. Opening with a magical sequence of baby Moses's journey down the river and filled with extraordinary renderings of the parting of the Red Sea and the biblical plagues – the curse on the first born is particularly disturbing – this makes for epic, captivating cinema. A host of Hollywood heavyweights provide emotive vocal contributions, enhanced by Stephen Schwartz's stirring, Broadway-style songs (the moving *When You Believe* earned an Oscar). Admittedly, there are more than a few examples of dramatic licence taken along the way, but this is still an astonishing animated achievement, particularly for a studio still in its infancy. ▱

Val Kilmer *Moses* • Ralph Fiennes *Rameses* • Michelle Pfeiffer *Tzipporah* • Sandra Bullock *Miriam* • Jeff Goldblum *Aaron* • Danny Glover *Jethro* • Patrick Stewart *Pharaoh Seti* • Helen Mirren *The Queen* • Steve Martin *Hotep* • Martin Short *Huy* ■ *Dir* Brenda Chapman, Stephen Hickner, Simon Wells • *Scr* Philip LaZebnik • *Music/Lyrics* Stephen Schwartz

Prince of Foxes ★★★

Historical drama 1949 · US · BW · 106mins

This is a lavish historical pageant about the wicked Borgias, with Orson Welles giving a magnificently over-ripe performance as the Machiavellian Cesare Borgia, and Tyrone Power as his loyal aide. Filmed in Florence, Siena, Venice and San Gimignano by Oscar-nominated cameraman Leon Shamroy, the picture looks handsome, and Welles is clearly having a whale of a time. There was an intriguing postscript: because Welles wrote an article about Fascism in post-war Germany the picture was a big flop there and caused Fox to cancel the German release of Welles's follow-up, *The Black Rose*.

Tyrone Power *Andrea Corsini* • Orson Welles *Cesare Borgia* • Wanda Hendrix *Camilla Verano* • Everett Sloane *Mario Belli* • Marina Berti *Angela Borgia* ■ *Dir* Henry King • *Scr* Milton Krims, from the novel by Samuel Shellabarger

The Prince of Homburg ★★

Historical drama 1997 · It · Colour · 85 mins

Although Italian director Marco Bellocchio had built his reputation on uncompromising realism in movies such as 1967's *China Is Near*, he resorted to conservative pictorialism for this reworking of Heinrich von Kleist's 19th-century play about loyalty and patriotism. Andrea Di Stefano is suitably stiff as the aristocratic cavalry officer charged with recklessness after he leads a victorious charge against orders. It's a painstakingly crafted film, but the observations on the nature of honour and heroism are as old-fashioned as the imagery. In Italian with English subtitles..

Andrea Di Stefano *Prince of Homburg* • Barbara Bobulova *Natalia* • Toni Bertorelli

Elector • Anita Laurenzi *Electoress* ■ *Dir* Marco Bellocchio • *Scr* Marco Bellocchio, from the play by Heinrich von Kleist

Prince of Jutland ★

Historical drama 1994 · Den · Colour · 106mins

A basic great cast of British thespians – Helen Mirren, Kate Beckinsale, Gabriel Byrne and Ewen Bremner – are fronted by Christian Bale in this retelling of Shakespeare's Hamlet. More medieval Viking than Danish Royal Court this is a risible and mucky affair, sticking to the nutshell plot (man murders king, marries queen and father's ghost calls on son to avenge) it flails around mixing poor dialogue, laughable fight sequences and worse cinematography. The poor cast have all their considerable talent destroyed and doubtless feel this little effort is one best forgotten.

Christian Bale *Amled* • Helen Mirren *Queen Geruth* • Gabriel Byrne *Fenge* • Kate Beckinsale *Ethel* • Steven Waddington *Ribold* • Brian Cox *Aethelwine, Duke of Lindsey* • Brian Glover *Caedman* ■ *Dir* Gabriel Axel • *Scr* Gabriel Axel, Erik Kjersgaard, from the book *The Denmark Chronicle* by Saxo Grammaticus

The Prince of Pennsylvania ★▣

Comedy drama 1988 · US · Colour · 89mins

This dreadfully unbelievable small-town movie stars Keanu Reeves as Rupert, a misunderstood loner, whose father (Fred Ward) harbours dreams of being the King of Pennsylvania. Reeves's problems increase when he discovers his mother (Bonnie Bedelia) in bed with his father's best friend. He seeks solace in Amy Madigan, on feisty form as the hippy owner of a down-town drive-in. Together they concoct a ridiculous plan to kidnap his father while he's at work down the local mine shaft, at which the entire movie goes pear-shaped. A good cast can't rise above the absurdities of the plot. For Keanu completists only. ▱

Keanu Reeves *Rupert Marshetta* • Amy Madigan *Carla Headlee* • Bonnie Bedelia *Pam Marshetta* • Fred Ward *Gary Marshetta* • Jeff Hayenga *Jack Sike* • Jay O Sanders *Trooper Joe* ■ *Dir/Scr* Ron Nyswaner

Prince of Pirates ★★ U

Swashbuckling adventure 1953 · US · Colour · 80mins

A second-rate swashbuckler that used up existing studio costumes and sets (one of the last of its kind) and was tailored for then heart-throb John Derek, later to achieve a sort of notoriety as the photographer/director husband of Ursula Andress and the discoverer (and uncoverer) of Bo. Derek wears the period FrancoSpanish costume well but it's not really much good, and viewers will have to be very indulgent, or very young, to stay with it.

John Derek *Prince Roland of Haagen* • Barbara Rush *Nita Orde* • Carla Balenda *Princess Maria* • Whitfield Connor *Stephan* • Edgar Barrier *Count Blanco* ■ *Dir* Sidney Salkow • *Scr* John O'Dea, Samuel Newman, from the story by William Copeland, Herbert Kline

Prince of Players ★★★

Biographical drama 1955 · US · Colour · 102mins

A biopic of the American actor Edwin Booth who achieved another sort of notoriety by being the brother of Abraham Lincoln's assassin, John Wilkes Booth. Richard Burton plays Booth the actor and is at his best in the Bardian clips, starting with the time he played Richard III when his father was too drunk to go on. Marriage and extracts from *Hamlet*, *Othello* and *Romeo and Juliet* follow, building up to the Lincoln assassination and the public demonstrations against all actors that apparently followed.

Richard Burton *Edwin Booth* • Maggie McNamara *Mary Devlin* • John Derek *John Wilkes Booth* • Raymond Massey *Junius Brutus Booth* • Charles Bickford *Dave Prescott* • Elizabeth Sellars *Asia* ■ *Dir* Philip Dunne • *Scr* Moss Hart, from the biography by Eleanor Ruggles • *Music* Bernard Herrmann

Prince of Shadows ★★▣

Political thriller 1991 · Sp · Colour · 86mins

This moodily shot political thriller has Terence Stamp as Spanish exile Darman, sent back to Madrid in the early sixties to assassinate a traitor to the anti-fascist cause. Flashbacks reveal Darman's involvement in a similar assignment 16 years earlier. Nightclub performer Patsy Kensit demonstrates how not to imitate Rita Hayworth, with an ill-advised rendition of *Put the Blame on Mame*. Director Pilar Miró makes it looks splendid but the acting – apart from John McEnery – should face a firing squad. ▱

Terence Stamp *Darman* • Patsy Kensit *Rebeca* • José Luis Gómez *Valdivia/Ugarte* • Geraldine James *Rebeca Osorio* • Simon Andreu *Andrade* • [Aleksander Bardini] *Bernal* • John McEnery *Walter* ■ *Dir* Pilar Miró • *Scr* Pilar Miró, Mario Camus, Juan Antonio Porto

Prince of the City ★★★▣

Crime drama based on a true story 1981 · US · Colour · 160mins

New York-based director Sidney Lumet was responsible for delivering some of the most cinematically dynamic re-creations of urban police work, notably *Serpico* (1973) and *Dog Day Afternoon* (1975), both starring Al Pacino. This movie has a marvellously complex (and true) plot about a cop who reveals interdepartmental corruption, yet, sadly, it lacks both Pacino and an audience-friendly running time. With around three hours of screen time, Treat Williams, excellent though he is, doesn't have the star power to hold the attention and, despite sterling support from Jerry Orbach and sinister prosecutor James Tolkan, the film's length diminishes its impact. Contains violence and swearing. ▱

Treat Williams *Daniel Ciello* • Jerry Orbach *Gus Levy* • Richard Foronjy *Joe Marinaro* • Don Billett *Bill Mayo* • Kenny Marino *Dom Bando* • Carmine Caridi *Gino Mascone* ■ *Dir* Sidney Lumet • *Scr* Jay Presson Allen, Sidney Lumet, from a book by Robert Daley

The Prince of Tides
★★★★ 🔞

Drama   1991 · US · Colour · 126mins

Pat Conroy's epic novel about a dysfunctional Southern family is deftly translated to the screen under the subtle direction of Barbra Streisand, who also stars as the New York psychiatrist helping Nick Nolte to come to terms with his twin sister's attempted suicide. Nolte is superb as he wrestles with his family's demons, and Streisand sensibly stays on the sidelines (although the camera lingering occasionally on her talon-like fingernails provides some unwelcome distraction). Jason Gould (Streisand's son from her marriage to Elliott Gould) also features as, of course, Streisand's on-screen son. Contains violence and swearing. 📺

Nick Nolte *Tom Wingo* • Barbra Streisand *Susan Lowenstein* • Blythe Danner *Sallie Wingo* • Kate Nelligan *Lila Wingo Newbury* • Jeroen Krabbé *Herbert Woodruff* • Melinda Dillon *Savannah Wingo* • George Carlin *Eddie Detreville* • Jason Gould *Bernard Woodruff* • Brad Sullivan *Henry Wingo* ■ *Dir* Barbra Streisand • *Scr* Pat Conroy, Becky Johnston, from the novel by Pat Conroy

Prince Valiant
★★ 🔞

Historical adventure
1954 · US · Colour · 99mins

This jovial Arthurian spectacle, based on the comic strip by Harold Foster, is in that strange dialect called Hollywood Archaic, a tongue known to no one except Hollywood executives. James Mason plays Sir Brack, a Knight of the Round Table, and Robert Wagner in his first leading role is Valiant, the son of a beleaguered Swedish king who arrives in Camelot seeking assistance in the clanking armour and sword department. Janet Leigh swoons whenever Wagner's around, but goodness knows why considering the terrible wig he had to wear.

Robert Wagner *Prince Valiant* • Janet Leigh *Princess Aleta* • James Mason *Sir Brack* • Debra Paget *Ilene* • Sterling Hayden *Sir Gawain* • Victor McLaglen *Boltar* • Donald Crisp *King Aguar* • Brian Aherne *King Arthur* ■ *Dir* Henry Hathaway • *Scr* Dudley Nichols, from the comic strip by Harold R Foster

Prince Valiant
★★ 🔞

Fantasy action adventure
1997 · Ger/UK · Colour · 87mins

Cod-historical hokum derived from the popular US comic strip, in which King Arthur's sword, Excalibur, is stolen by marauding Vikings. Things go from bad to Norse when the legendary British symbol falls into the hands of an evil Euro king with designs on Arthur's seat. Fortunately, the heroic Prince Valiant rides to the sword's rescue. This could have been okay, but obvious cash restraints plus hamfisted hacking relegate the film to definite B-movie status. Familiar names among the film's cast include Edward Fox, Ron Perlman and Joanna Lumley, all of whom look uncomfortable. 📺

Stephen Moyer *Prince Valiant* • Katherine Heigl *Princess Ilene* • Thomas Kretschmann *Thagnar* • Edward Fox *King Arthur* • Udo Kier *Sligon* • Warwick Davis *Pechet* • Ron Perlman *Boltar* • Joanna Lumley *Morgan Le Fey* ■ *Dir* Anthony Hickox • *Scr* Michael Frost Beckner,

from a story by Anthony Hickox, Carsten Lorenz, from the comic strip by Harold R Foster

The Prince Who Was a Thief
★★

Adventure   1951 · US · Colour · 88mins

From the days when Tony Curtis was a tousle-haired idol for teenagers, this *Arabian Nights* nonsense showed him at his athletic, if not dramatic, best. He's a royal baby brought up by kindly thieves who then duels his way to his rightful throne. Perhaps most surprising, this non-magical fantasy was adapted from a story by Theodore Dreiser. Director Rudolph Maté was the cinematographer on films such as *Gilda* and *The Lady from Shanghai*.

Tony Curtis *Julna* • Piper Laurie *Tina* • Everett Sloane *Yussef* • Betty Garde *Mirna* • Jeff Corey *Mokar* • Peggie Castle *Princess Yasmin* ■ *Dir* Rudolph Maté • *Scr* Gerald Drayson Adams, Aeneas MacKenzie, from a story in the book *Chains* by Theodore Dreiser

Les Princes
★★★ 🔞

Drama   1982 · Fr · Colour · 99mins

This is the first instalment of Tony Gatlif's Romany trilogy, which was completed by *Latcho Drom* (1993) and *Gadjo Dilo* (1997). The villains of the piece are clearly the gendarmes who harass the despised *gitanes*. But Gatlif isn't blind to the problems caused by the patriarchal conservatism that prompts French Romany Gérard Darmon to disown his wife after discovering she's followed a social worker's advice on birth control. Living in squalor with his octogenarian mother and young daughter, and resorting to stealing food, he's bitter and unstable. Yet he's every bit as authentic as Jacques Loiseleux's gloomy photography. In French with English subtitles.

Gérard Darmon *Nara* • Muse Dalbray *Nara's grandmother* • Dominique Maurin *Petiton* • Hagop Arslanian *Chico* • Tony Gatlif *Leo* ■ *Dir/Scr* Tony Gatlif

Princes in Exile
★★★

Drama   1990 · Can · Colour · 104mins

A sensitive and skilled handling of a tough subject, that of teenagers with potentially terminal diseases. In other hands, it could have been just another "trauma of the week" film, but director Giles Walker handles the unknown cast with humour and intelligence. Firmly in the teen movie genre, but superior to most.

Zachary Ansley *Ryan Rafferty* • Nicholas Shields *Robert* • Stacie Mistysyn *Holly* • Andrea Roth *Marlene Lancaster* ■ *Dir* Giles Walker • *Scr* Joe Wiesenfeld, from the novel by Mark Schreiber

The Princess Academy
★★

Comedy   1987 · US/Yug/Fr · Colour · 90mins

Some questionable life values inform this light sex comedy about a girls finishing school which is dedicated to teaching its charges how to find rich husbands. Eva Gabor doesn't need to stretch herself as the girls' elegant lecturer, the Countess.

Eva Gabor *Countess* • Richard Paul *Drago* • Carole Davis *Sonia* • Lar Park-Lincoln *Cindy* •

Lu Leonard *Fraulein Stickenschmidt* • Britt Helfer *Lulu* ■ *Dir* Bruce A Block • *Scr* Sandra Weintraub, from a idea by Fred Weintraub

The Princess and the Goblin
★★★ 🇺

Animated fantasy adventure
1992 · UK/Hun · Colour · 81mins

Based on George MacDonald's Victorian fairy tale, this animated feature film will keep most children happy, although even they won't fail to notice that the drawings are way below the standard of Disney features. The story is easy enough to follow, with Princess Irene enlisting the help of her magical great-great-grandmother and of a miner's son called Curdi to try and prevent a tribe of goblins from capturing the royal palace. With their ugly faces, hatred of poetry and jealousy of humans (because people have toes and they don't), the goblins easily steal the show.

Joss Ackland *King* • Claire Bloom *Irene's great great grandmother* • Roy Kinnear *Mump* • Sally Ann Marsh *Princess Irene* • Rik Mayall *Froglip* • Peggy Mount *Goblin Queen* • Peter Murray *Curdi* • Victor Spinetti *Glump* ■ *Dir* József Gémes • *Scr* Robin Lyons, from a novel by George MacDonald

The Princess and the Pirate
★★★ 🇺

Swashbuckling comedy
1944 · US · Colour · 90mins

One of comedian Bob Hope's better vehicles. He plays the cowardly "Sylvester the Great Man of Seven Faces", an 18th-century variety artist with an aversion to – you guessed it – pirates. Hope is surrounded by superb character actors like buccaneer Victor McLaglen and governor Walter Slezak. There's also a hilarious turn from Walter Brennan, who seems to have based his part on Disney's cartoon dwarf Dopey. Virginia Mayo partners Hope ably, especially when they do their vaudeville number in the splendidly art-directed Bucket of Blood inn. Oh, and don't miss the gag at the very end – it's one of Hope's best. 📺

Bob Hope *Sylvester Crosby/"Sylvester The Great"* • Virginia Mayo *Princess Margaret/ "Margaret Warbrook"* • Walter Brennan *Featherhead* • Walter Slezak *Governor La Roche* • Victor McLaglen *The Hook* • Bing Crosby *Commoner* ■ *Dir* David Butler • *Scr* Don Hartman, Melville Shavelson, Everett Freeman, Allen Boretz, Curtis Kenyon, from the story by Sy Bartlett

The Princess Bride
★★★★ 🔞

Fantasy adventure
1987 · US · Colour · 94mins

Rob Reiner has always been careful to avoid typecasting as a director, so following the warm nostalgia of *Stand by Me* he opted for this curious, but ultimately charming, children's fable. The film opens with Peter Falk reading the story to the young Fred Savage, and this ironic distancing continues throughout the movie. Although the requisite monsters, giants and swordfights are present and correct for the children, Reiner also ensures there are plenty of quiet chuckles for adults, largely thanks to the eclectic cast. A delight for all the family. 📺

Cary Elwes *Westley* • Mandy Patinkin *Inigo Montoya* • Chris Sarandon *Prince Humperdinck* • Christopher Guest *Count Rugen* • Wallace Shawn *Vizzini* • Andréthe Giant *Fezzik* • Fred Savage *Grandson* • Robin Wright [Robin Wright Penn] *Buttercup, the Princess Bride* • Peter Falk *Grandfather* • Peter Cook *Impressive clergyman* • Billy Crystal *Miracle Max, the wizard* • Mel Smith *Albino* ■ *Dir* Rob Reiner • *Scr* William Goldman, from his novel • *Music* Mark Knopfler • *Production Designer* Norman Garwood

Princess Caraboo
★★★ 🔞

Historical romance
1994 · US · Colour · 92mins

Is exotic Phoebe Cates a Javanese princess, washed up on the Devon coastline after escaping from pirates? Or is she really a clever, if harmless, con artist using her suspect credentials to infiltrate the parlours and palaces of 19th-century England? Based on a true slice of history, co-writer/director Michael Austin's satirical fairy tale is disarming fluff with little more substance than a gooey marshmallow. Cates exudes the necessary glamour, but it's Jim Broadbent's boorish banker who nets the biggest laughs, while Kevin Kline (Cates's real-life husband) steals every scene he's in as a crazy butler. A romantic comedy for those with a very sweet tooth. Contains swearing. 📺

Phoebe Cates *Princess Caraboo* • Jim Broadbent *Mr Worrall* • Wendy Hughes *Mrs Worrall* • Kevin Kline *Frixos* • John Lithgow *Professor Wilkinson* • Stephen Rea *Gutch* • John Sessions *Prince Regent* • Peter Eyre *Lord Apthorpe* ■ *Dir* Michael Austin • *Scr* Michael Austin, John Wells

The Princess Comes Across
★★★

Comedy mystery   1936 · US · BW · 75mins

Carole Lombard is perfectly cast in this combination of romantic comedy and comedy detective thriller, set on board a transatlantic passenger ship, and directed with appropriate zip by William K Howard. Lombard stars as a Brooklyn showgirl with aspirations to be another Garbo. To this end, she poses as a Swedish princess during a sea voyage, but falls in love with ship's musician Fred MacMurray. Together they get caught up in trying to solve the murder of a blackmailing fellow passenger. Delightfully screwy nonsense, harmoniously played by the winning star combination.

Carole Lombard *Princess Olga* • Fred MacMurray *King Mantell* • Douglass Dumbrille *Lorel* • Alison Skipworth *Lady Gertrude Allwyn* • William Frawley *Benton* ■ *Dir* William K Howard • *Scr* Walter DeLeon, Francis Martin, Frank Butler, Don Hartman, from a story by Philip MacDonald, from a novel by Louis Lucien Rogger

Princess in Love
★★ 🔞

Drama   1996 · US · Colour · 89mins

Those who simply can't get enough of the Princess Diana story will no doubt tune to this made-for-TV dramatisation of her doomed affair with James Hewitt. Based on Anna Pasternak's book, it tells the story of the friendship between the Princess and her riding instructor, Hewitt, that later blossomed into romance. It all ends badly when

Hewitt betrays her by selling the story of their clandestine relationship to the press. Julie Cox and Christopher Villiers as the ill-starred couple and Christopher Bowen as Prince Charles. But this is a poorly-written and unnecessary footnote to a sad episode of royal history. ▫

Julie Cox *Princess Diana* • Christopher Bowen *Prince Charles* • Christopher Villiers *Captain James Hewitt* • Julia St John *Camilla Parker-Bowles* • Guy Witcher *Prince William* ■ *Dir* David Greene • *Scr* Cynthia A Cherbak, from the non-fiction book by Anna Pasternak

Princess Mononoke ★★★★
Animated action fantasy
1997 · Jap · Colour · 133mins
A luxuriously animated legend of ancient gods going head to head with mankind and industry over the balance of nature. This boldly surrealistic and starkly experimental cartoon is beautifully drawn, using the inspiration of classic Japanese artwork, and drums home a modern ecological message with a feminist bias. Set in the 14th century, it's a complicated tale of cursed Prince Ashitaka condemned to roam the land looking for a way to lift the malediction that has given him various supernatural gifts. After encountering bloodthirsty samurai, corrupt priests, friendly sprites and the evil Lady Eboshi who owns a giant iron foundry, he joins forces with San, the Wolf Princess, to ensure capitalistic progress will not be won at the expense of the woodland creatures.

Claire Danes *San* • Minnie Driver *Eboshi* • Gillian Anderson *Moro* • Billy Crudup *Ashitaka* ■ *Dir* Hayao Miyazaki • *Scr* Neil Gaiman, Hayao Miyazaki, from a story by Hayao Miyazaki

Princess of the Nile ★★ U
Adventure   1954 · US · Colour · 70mins
One of those costume pantomimes that 20th Century-Fox used to churn out as insurance against box-office failure elsewhere. Debra Paget is the medieval Egyptian princess who moonlights as an exotic dancer, a move that doesn't endear her to nasty Bedouin invader Michael Rennie. Fortunately Jeffrey Hunter comes to her rescue and – of course – they fall in love. Colourful nonsense that looks good but doesn't bear too much close analysis.

Debra Paget *Princess Shalimar/Taura the Dancer* • Jeffrey Hunter *Prince Haidi* • Michael Rennie *Rama Khan* • Dona Drake *Mirva* • Wally Cassell *Goghi* • Edgar Barrier *Shaman* • Michael Ansara *Captain Kral* • Jack Elam *Basra* ■ *Dir* Harmon Jones • *Scr* Gerald Drayson Adams

Princess O'Rourke ★★ U
Comedy   1943 · US · BW · 94mins
When ace flyer Robert Cummings and royal princess Olivia de Havilland fall in love with one another, they cause consternation at diplomatic levels which requires the intervention of President Franklin D Roosevelt. Writer/director Norman Krasna's screenplay for this frothy wartime romantic comedy won an Academy Award, and it offers a few good laughs and attractive star performances (with solid support

from Charles Coburn, Jack Carson, Jane Wyman and Gladys Cooper), but is ultimately no more than a pleasant time-waster.

Olivia de Havilland *Princess Maria* • Robert Cummings *Eddie O'Rourke* • Charles Coburn *Uncle* • Jack Carson *Dave* • Jane Wyman *Jean* • Harry Davenport *Supreme court judge* ■ *Dir/Scr* Norman Krasna

The Princess Yang Kwei Fei ★★★
Period romantic drama
1955 · Jap/HK · Colour · 91mins
Produced by the Shaw Brothers (who would go on to sponsor Hong Kong's kung fu boom), this colourful period drama was only undertaken with the greatest reluctance by director Kenji Mizoguchi. However, such was his consummate professionalism, that he overcame artistic misgivings and chronic health problems to fashion a dramatically involving and visually beguiling tale of court intrigue and familial feuding. Machiko Kyo gives a touching display of naivety and self-sacrificing nobility as the servant who marries one of the last T'ang emperors of 8th-century China and remains true to his love from beyond the grave. A Japanese language film.

Machiko Kyo *Yang Kwei Fei* • Masayuki Mori *Emperor Hsuan-tsung* • So Yamamura *An Lu-shan* • Sakae Ozawa [Eitaro Ozawa] *Yang Kuo-chung* ■ *Dir* Kenji Mizoguchi • *Scr* Yoshikata Yoda, T'ao Chin, Matsutaro Kawaguchi, Masashige Narusawa, from the poem *Ch'ang Hen Ko* by T'ien Pai Lo

The Principal ★★ 18
Drama   1987 · US · Colour · 105mins
This adequate reworking of an over-familiar tale stars James Belushi as a "problem" teacher whose career seems to have reached rock bottom when he is made principal of the worst school in the neighbourhood. His new charges are an unwholesome mixture of delinquents and drug addicts. Belushi is lightweight but likeable. But it's Louis Gossett Jr, as the school's tough-nut security chief, who takes the acting honours. The mix of comedy and drama is perhaps hard to take, but Belushi's showdown with the school's top tough – shades of *High Noon* – is exciting enough. ▫

James Belushi *Rick Latimer* • Louis Gossett Jr *Jake Phillips* • Rae Dawn Chong *Hilary Orozco* • Michael Wright *Victor Duncan* • JJ Cohen *"White Zac"* • Esai Morales *Raymi Rojas* ■ *Dir* Christopher Cain • *Scr* Frank Deese

Prison ★★★ 18
Prison horror   1987 · US · Colour · 98mins
A striking, low-budget horror film enlivened by classy direction from Renny Harlin, some startling make-up effects and atmospheric use of jail locations. This tale of the ghost of a wrongly executed prisoner on a vengeance spree pays unusual attention to its characters – you wouldn't know it was a scary movie for the first half hour – and when the gruesome fireworks begin, they certainly light up the screen. Decent performances from Viggo Mortensen and Lane Smith compensate for the film's unnecessary abundance of

prison clichés in between the creepy carnage ▫

Lane Smith *Ethan Sharpe* • Viggo Mortensen *Connie Burke* • Chelsea Field *Katherine Walker* • Lincoln Kilpatrick *Cresus* • Andrée De Shields *Sandor* • Steven Little *Rhino* ■ *Dir* Renny Harlin • *Scr* C Courtney Joyner, from a story by Irwin Yablans

Prison of Secrets ★★
Drama   1997 · US · Colour · 92mins
A tasteful "chicks in chains" movie may seem somewhat anomalous, but this is it. Yes, it involves a young woman (Stephanie Zimbalist) who discovers the brutality of life behind bars, but it hasn't got the obligatory titillating shower scenes or riots in the prison yard. Instead, this is a formulaic yet honest account of the often harrowing conditions in American prisons. There are good performances from Zimbalist and Dan Lauria, and the direction from Fred Gerber is resolutely non-exploitative. Contains violence.

Stephanie Zimbalist *Lynn* • Dan Lauria *Ed* • Gary Frank *Larry* • Finola Hughes *Angie* ■ *Dir* Fred Gerber • *Scr* Layce Gardner

Prison Stories: Women on the Inside ★★★ 15
Portmanteau prison drama
1991 · US · Colour · 79mins
A downbeat examination of the realities of life behind bars. The film is a compendium of three tales, directed by three of Hollywood's most successful women directors: Penelope Spheeris offers an affectionate portrait of two career criminals; Donna Deitch's segment looks at a woman trying to prevent her family making the same mistakes as her; while Joan Micklin Silver explores the insecurities of long-term prisoners about to be released back to the real world. Rae Dawn Chong, Rachel Ticotin, Annabella Sciorra, Lolita Davidovich and Grace Zabriskie deliver moving, believable portraits, and all three tales provide gritty yet sympathetic views of prison life. ▫

Rachel Ticotin *Iris Martinez* • Talisa Soto *Rosina* • Lolita Davidovich *Loretta* • Silvana Gallardo *Mercedes* • Rae Dawn Chong *Rhonda* • Annabella Sciorra *Nicole* ■ *Dir* Donna Deitch, Joan Micklin Silver, Penelope Spheeris • *Scr* Martin Jones, Marlane Meyer, Jule Selbo, Martin Jones, Dick Beebe

The Prisoner ★★★ U
Psychological drama 1955 · UK · BW · 89mins
Alec Guinness reprises his stage role in this adaptation of Bridget Boland's play about a Catholic cardinal's encounter with an official from the totalitarian government that has arrested him. Frequently shown in close-up, Guinness superbly conveys the humility, isolation and commitment of a man who is fighting as much for his flock as for his own survival. Yet, Peter Glenville's theatrical direction won't do much to persuade those without religious or political convictions to become involved. ▫

Alec Guinness *Cardinal* • Jack Hawkins *Interrogator* • Wilfrid Lawson *Cell warder* • Kenneth Griffith *Secretary* • Jeannette Sterke *Girl* • Ronald Lewis *Warder* ■ *Dir* Peter Glenville • *Scr* Bridget Boland, from her play

Prisoner of Honor ★★★★
Historical drama
1991 · US/UK · Colour · 88mins
A dramatisation of the famous Dreyfus case that obsessed France for more than a decade, and already the basis of several films. This one stars Richard Dreyfuss as a French officer, Lieutenant Colonel Picquart, who comes to believe that Dreyfus, a Jewish officer languishing on Devil's Island, was wrongly convicted for treason. Picquart's campaign and his own subsequent arrest implicate the religious and political establishment, uncovering a morass of corruption, treachery and anti-Semitism, and galvanising the Left, led by Emile Zola. The only complaint is that an hour and a half is far too short to tell such a complex story satisfactorily.

Richard Dreyfuss *Lieutenant Colonel Picquart* • Oliver Reed *General Boisdeffre* • Peter Firth *Major Henry* • Jeremy Kemp *General Depellieux* • Brian Blessed *General Gonse* • Peter Vaughan *General Mercier* • Kenneth Colley *Captain Alfred Dreyfus* ■ *Dir* Ken Russell • *Scr* Ron Hutchinson

Prisoner of Rio ★★ 15
Biographical drama
1988 · Bra · Colour · 100mins
The story of the efforts of a British copper (Steven Berkoff) to bring back notorious Great Train Robber Ronnie Biggs (Paul Freeman) from Brazil, has a cheap and cheerful look about it. The multi-talented Mr Biggs had a hand in the screenplay, ensuring that the fugitive is portrayed in a not entirely unsympathetic light. Meanwhile Berkoff, as his would-be captor, comes across as a bungling incompetent as his schemes to trap the wily Biggs meet with disaster. Desmond Llewelyn – better known as "Q" in the Bond movies – plays a policeman.

Steven Berkoff *Jack McFarland* • Paul Freeman *Ronald Biggs* • Peter Firth *Clive Ingram* • Florinda Bolkan *Stella* • Desmond Llewelyn *Police commissioner* • José Wilker *Salo* ■ *Dir* Lech Majewski • *Scr* Lech Majewski, Ronald Biggs, Julia Frankel

The Prisoner of Second Avenue ★★★ PG
Comedy   1974 · US · Colour · 93mins
Working from his own play, Neil Simon unusually fails to strike the right balance between wit and pathos in this strained study of mid-life crisis. Jack Lemmon pulls out all the stops as the executive who not only has to cope with being sacked after 22 years, but also with the evident delight with which wife Anne Bancroft embraces her new career at the local TV station. Gene Saks (who directed Lemmon in Simon's *The Odd Couple*) provides stiff support as his brother, while Sylvester Stallone pops up as an innocent bystander suspected of theft. ▫

Jack Lemmon *Mel* • Anne Bancroft *Edna* • Gene Saks *Harry* • Elizabeth Wilson *Pauline* • Florence Stanley *Pearl* • Maxine Stuart *Belle* • Sylvester Stallone *Youth in park* • F Murray Abraham *Cab driver* • M Emmet Walsh *Doorman* ■ *Dir* Melvin Frank • *Scr* Neil Simon, from his play

The Prisoner of Shark Island ★★★

Historical prison drama
1936 · US · BW · 95mins

Dr Samuel Mudd, a Maryland physician, was sentenced to life imprisonment on Shark Island for complicity in the assassination of Abraham Lincoln. John Ford's film about this unfortunate man is part adventure and part penal drama, beginning with John Wilkes Booth's visit to the theatre, where he shoots Lincoln and is injured escaping. Mudd treats Booth's leg and gets thrown into jail, where he helps fight an outbreak of yellow fever. The film, scripted by Nunnally Johnson, has a well-measured anger at the injustice and Warner Baxter's performance as the ordinary doctor penalised for his dedication to saving life is remarkably persuasive.

Warner Baxter *Dr Samuel A Mudd* • Gloria Stuart *Mrs Peggy Mudd* • Joyce Kay *Martha Mudd* • Claude Gillingwater *Colonel Dyer* • Douglas Wood *General Ewing* • John Carradine *Sergeant Rankin* ■ *Dir* John Ford • *Scr* Nunnally Johnson

Prisoner of the Mountains ★★★★ 15

War drama   1996 · Rus/Kaz · Colour · 94mins

Inspired by a Tolstoy short story, this was the first fictional film to tackle the Chechen conflict. Having been ambushed on patrol, along with battle-scarred sergeant Oleg Menshikov, rookie private Sergei Bodrov Jr, falls for Susanna Mekhralieva, the Muslim warlord's daughter, who is nearly tempted by passion to betray her own people. Exhausting combat stereotypes, director Sergei Bodrov reinforces his pacifist plea by unearthing wit and warmth amidst the war's brutal ethnic and political realities. But, even more impressive, are Pavel Lebeshev's photographed mountainscapes. In Russian with English subtitles. Contains swearing, sexual references and violence.

Oleg Menshikov *Sacha Kostylin* • Sergei Bodrov Jr *Ivan "Vania" Zhilin* • Susanna Mekhralieva *Dina* • Dzhemal Sikharulidze *Abdul-Murat* ■ *Dir* Sergei Bodrov • *Scr* Arif Aliev, Sergei Bodrov, Boris Giller, from an idea by Boris Giller, from the short story *Kavkazsky Plennik (Prisoner of the Caucasus)* by Leo Tolstoy • *Cinematographer* Pavel Lebeshev

Prisoner of War ★

War   1954 · US · BW · 80mins

Ronald Reagan parachutes behind enemy lines in North Korea and – unbelievably – allows himself to be taken prisoner. His mission is dangerous yet silly: he is there to verify reports that the Communists have been treating their prisoners harshly. Very harshly. For the most part the movie is as cretinous as Hollywood's "Red Scare" movies ever got. An important subject that deserved much better treatment.

Ronald Reagan *Web Sloane* • Steve Forrest *Corporal Joseph Robert Stanton* • Dewey Martin *Jesse Treadman* • Oscar Homolka *Colonel Nikita Biroshilov* ■ *Dir* Andrew Marton • *Scr* Allen Rivkin

Prisoner of War ★★★ 15

Drama based on a true story
1990 · US · Colour · 96mins

An overlong but intriguing TV movie about Bobby Garwood, the last prisoner of war to return to America from Vietnam, who, after 13 years of detention, found himself charged with collaborating with the enemy. Despite looking far too fresh-faced to play the part of a war-ravaged veteran, Ralph Macchio (best known as the Karate Kid) gives a decent performance in the leading role, while Martin Sheen is his usual imposing self as the captain of marines at the centre of his trial. It's hardly *Paths of Glory* or *Breaker Morant*, but it's well above the TV-movie average.

Ralph Macchio *PFC Robert Garwood* • Martin Sheen *Captain Ike Eisenbraun* • Russ Grisset • Tuan Le *Mr Ho* • Steve Park *Hom* • Joseph Hieu *Scarface* ■ *Dir* Georg Stanford Brown • *Scr* John Pielmeier, from a story by John Pielmeier, Edward Gold

The Prisoner of Zenda ★★★

Silent swashbuckling adventure
1922 · US · BW · 125mins

A year after his acclaimed *The Four Horsemen of the Apocalypse*, director Rex Ingram made this silent version of the Anthony Hope swashbuckler about the English commoner Rudolf Rassendyll (Lewis Stone), forced to impersonate his lookalike, the kidnapped king of the small kingdom of Ruritania. Not as stalwart or convincing as the later 1937 version, but Alice Terry makes an adorable princess and Stone excels in his dual role – he later became Judge Hardy in the *Andy Hardy* series.

Lewis Stone *Rudolf Rassendyll/King Rudolf* • Alice Terry *Princess Flavia* • Robert Edeson *Col Sapt* • Stuart Holmes *Duke "Black" Michael* • Ramon Samaniegos [Ramon Novarro] *Rupert of Hentzau* ■ *Dir* Rex Ingram • *Scr* Mary O'Hara, from the play by Edward E Rose, from the novel by Anthony Hope • *Cinematographer* John F Seitz

The Prisoner of Zenda ★★★★★

Swashbuckling adventure
1937 · US · BW · 101mins

After three silent adaptations, this was the first sound version of Anthony Hope's famous novel of derring-do in the mythical kingdom of Ruritania. Producer David O Selznick was determined to make a splash and raised a budget of $1.25 million, a more than generous sum at the time. The cast is top drawer, but director John Cromwell was less than happy with his stars, convinced that Ronald Colman didn't know his lines and that Douglas Fairbanks Jr and David Niven were indulging in too many wild nights. Selznick came down in favour of his stars and, with production nearly complete, he removed Cromwell and hired George Cukor to shoot some of the final scenes as well as using WS Van Dyke to do the action sequences, both without credit. There's no evidence of the behind the scenes crises, however, as the picture is seamlessly enjoyable, with Colman typically assured in the dual role of king and commoner. But it's Fairbanks Jr's swaggering Rupert of Hentzau that gives this swashbuckler its five-star status.

Ronald Colman *Rudolf Rassendyll/King Rudolf V* • Madeleine Carroll *Princess Flavia* • Douglas Fairbanks Jr *Rupert of Hentzau* • Mary Astor *Antoinette De Mauban* • C Aubrey Smith *Colonel Zapt* • Raymond Massey *Black Michael* • David Niven *Captain Fritz von Tarlenheim* ■ *Dir* John Cromwell, WS Van Dyke, George Cukor • *Scr* John Balderston, Wells Root, Donald Ogden Stewart, from the play by Edward Rose, from the novel by Anthony Hope • *Cinematographer* James Wong Howe • *Editor* James E Newcom • *Art Director* Lyle Wheeler • *Music* Alfred Newman

The Prisoner of Zenda ★★★★ U

Swashbuckling adventure
1952 · US · Colour · 96mins

There are those who prefer the popular 1937 Ronald Colman movie, but the Ruritanian romance cried out for this MGM Technicolor treatment, plus the dashing splendour of an experienced cast. Stewart Granger is simply marvellous as both Rudolf Rassendyll and King Rudolf, born to fence and carouse, and equally at ease romancing his Flavia (Deborah Kerr). Look out, too, for Lewis Stone as the Cardinal – he played the dual lead in the 1922 silent version. The special effects are brilliant – watch Granger shake hands with himself, and also walk around himself in a heavy wooden chair. The 1937 score by Alfred Newman is retained, and apparently a Moviola on set ensured that the camera set-ups were also copied. But in the year of Elizabeth II's accession, this re-filming had great resonance, and a great deal more panache than those which came before or since.

Stewart Granger *Rudolf Rassendyll/King Rudolf V* • Deborah Kerr *Princess Flavia* • James Mason *Rupert of Hentzau* • Louis Calhern *Colonel Zapt* • Lewis Stone *Cardinal* ■ *Dir* Richard Thorpe • *Scr* John L Balderston, Noel Langley, Wells Root, Donald Ogden Stewart, from the play by Edward Rose, from the novel by Anthony Hope • *Cinematographer* Joseph Ruttenberg • *Music* Alfred Newman

The Prisoner of Zenda ★★

Comedy adventure
1979 · US · Colour · 108mins

Spoof remake of the oft-filmed classic story featuring Peter Sellers as London cabbie Sydney Frewin who bears an uncanny likeness to Prince Rudolph of Ruritania. Sellers is conned into acting as a decoy for the Prince, whose throne is under threat. Sellers's real-life wife Lynne Frederick co-stars. The film was plagued by on-set troubles, most reputedly emanating from Sellers's increasingly bizarre behaviour and superstitious nature. On screen these troubles were all too evident, and the whole thing seems strained and unfunny, despite a script from Dick Clement and Ian La Frenais.

Peter Sellers *Prince Rudolph/Sydney Frewin/Old King* • Lynne Frederick *Princess Flavia* • Lionel Jeffries *General Sapt* • Elke Sommer *Countess* • Simon Williams *Fritz* ■ *Dir* Richard Quine • *Scr* Dick Clement, Ian La Frenais, from the novel by Anthony Hope

Prisoners of the Casbah ★

Romance adventure
1953 · US · Colour · 78mins

A threadbare and thoroughly dismal attempt at exotic adventure romance. Gloria Grahame, suitably veiled and gowned in gossamer robes, is a princess who, with her sheik-like suitor, Turhan Bey, hides out in the teeming Casbah to escape the clutches of Cesar Romero's villainous Grand Vizier. A sad comedown for Grahame, coming right after her stunning dramatic success in *The Big Heat*, it would be good for a laugh if it weren't so wooden and dreary.

Gloria Grahame *Princess Nadja* • Cesar Romero *Firouz* • Turhan Bey *Ahmed* • Nestor Paiva *Marouf* ■ *Dir* Richard Bare [Richard L Bare] • *Scr* DeVallon Scott, from a story by William Raynor

A Private Affair ★★

Second World War drama
1992 · It · Colour · 85mins

An obscure Second World War drama, made for Italian television, that's notable mainly for British star Rupert Graves's performance in the leading role. He plays a young Resistance fighter who returns from the guerrilla war against the Germans to discover his oldest friend has become involved with his former lover (Céline Beauvallet). Graves looks a tad uncomfortable as the young partisan, but the film is rescued by the assured direction of Alberto Negrin. In Italian with English subtitles.

Rupert Graves *Milton* • Céline Beauvallet *Fulvia* • Pina Cei *La Custode* • Alessandro Stefanelli *Hombre* • Rodolfo Corsato *Ferdi* • Luca Zingaretti *Sceriffo* ■ *Dir* Alberto Negrin • *Scr* Raffaele La Capria, Alberto Negrin, from the novel *Una Questione Privata* by Beppe Fenoglio

The Private Affairs of Bel Ami ★★★

Period drama
1947 · US · BW and Colour · 112mins

This is based on a novel by Guy de Maupassant and, in return for cutting out the more sordid aspects of the original story, director Albert Lewin gives it an extraordinary visual exoticism – he's Powell and Pressburger combined! George Sanders is marvellous as the lecherous rake and Angela Lansbury is the young widow he loves all along. It's weird, melodramatic, delirious, in black and white and suddenly colour, and how Lewin sneaked it around the studio's financial bosses is anyone's guess.

George Sanders *Georges Duroy* • Angela Lansbury *Clotilde de Marelle* • Ann Dvorak *Madeleine Forestier* • Frances Dee *Marie de Varenne* • John Carradine *Charles Forestier* ■ *Dir* Albert Lewin • *Scr* Albert Lewin, from the story by Guy de Maupassant

Private Benjamin ★★★ 15

Comedy   1980 · US · Colour · 105mins

A high octane tale about a Jewish princess who joins the US Army. It is basically a one-joke effort, but that joke has Goldie Hawn throwing herself with great gusto into the role of a bewildered spoilt brat who comes good, and her Oscar-nominated

U = SUITABLE FOR ALL   Uc = SUITABLE FOR ALL, ESPECIALLY FOR YOUNG CHILDREN (VIDEO ONLY)   PG = PARENTAL GUIDANCE

performance has huge charm. If only director Howard Zieff had allowed someone else to get a look in – the members of the supporting cast are mere satellites around a perky sun – and the screenplay had been broadened to contain more than just gags about broken fingernails. Even so, Eileen Brennan (as best supporting actress) and the writers also received Oscar nominations. Contains swearing, sex scenes and brief nudity. ▣ **DVD**

Goldie Hawn *Judy Benjamin* • Eileen Brennan *Captain Doreen Lewis* • Armand Assante *Henri Tremont* • Robert Webber *Colonel Clay Thornbush* • Sam Wanamaker *Teddy Benjamin* • Harry Dean Stanton *Sergeant Jim Ballard* • Albert Brooks *Yale Goodman* ■ *Dir* Howard Zieff • *Scr* Nancy Myers, Charles Shyer, Harvey Miller

Private Confessions ★★★

Period drama 1996 · Swe · Colour · 127mins

Ingmar Bergman reunited the key members of his creative family – Liv Ullmann, Sven Nykvist and Max von Sydow – for this concluding episode in the trilogy about his parents that began with *Fanny and Alexander* and *Best Intentions*. Samuel Froler and Pernilla August reprise their roles as the strict pastor and his unhappy wife, whose confession of an affair brings forth several shocking revelations and some long-suppressed emotions. Ullmann directs as inobtrusively as possible to foreground Bergman's screenplay. It's an excruciatingly personal film that dissects human nature with rare skill and almost flagellatory honesty. In Swedish with English subtitles.

Pernilla August *Anna* • Max von Sydow *Jacob* • Samuel Froler *Henrik Bergman* • Kristina Adolphson *Maria* • Anita Björk *Karin Åkerblom* ■ *Dir* Liv Ullmann • *Scr* Ingmar Bergman • *Cinematographer* Sven Nykvist

A Private Conversation ★★★ PG

Drama 1983 · USSR · Colour · 93mins

Also known as *Without Witnesses*, this is a two-hander about a divorced man who pays a surprise visit on his ex-wife at her apartment. Gradually they discuss their life together and the reasons for their separation, though his attempts to seduce her are not entirely successful. Strong performances, the constricted setting and the ''real time'' structure are major virtues, while the twist at the end is likely to surprise everyone. In Russian with English subtitles.

Irina Kupchenko *Woman* • Mikhail Ulyanov *Man* ■ *Dir* Nikita Mikhalkov • *Scr* Nikita Mikhalkov, Sofia Prokofyeva, Ramiz Fataliyev, from the play *A Talk without Witnesses* by Sofia Prokofyeva

The Private Eyes ★★★

Mystery spoof 1980 · US · Colour · 92mins

Another outing for comedy duo Tim Conway and Don Knotts who seemed destined to become the Abbott and Costello of the seventies and eighties. This time they're lampooning every private eye flick ever made, in a tall story of a murder investigation set in a 250-room English mansion. Huge amounts of slapstick is as usual with the pairing, but there are plenty of

good comic sequences to entertain the young.

Tim Conway *Dr Tart* • Don Knotts *Inspector Winship* • Trisha Noble *Mistress Phyllis Morley* • Bernard Fox *Justin* • Grace Zabriskie *Nanny* • Irwin Keyes *Jock* • Suzy Mandel *Hilda* ■ *Dir* Lang Elliott • *Scr* Tim Conway, John Myhers

The Private Files of J Edgar Hoover ★★★

Crime drama 1977 · US · Colour · 110mins

A lurid if immensely enjoyable exploitation flick from horror maestro Larry Cohen, purporting to reveal the truth about America's legendary head of the FBI. As Hoover, a closet homosexual cross-dresser, jowly Broderick Crawford is hard to beat, but Dan Dailey is actually even better as Hoover's long-time partner Clyde Tolson. If it all seems a mite unbelievable, only Hoover himself knew the whole truth, and he took it with him to the grave. Scored, surprisingly, by Miklos Rozsa, composer of *Ben-Hur* and *El Cid*. Contains swearing and violence.

Broderick Crawford *J Edgar Hoover* • José Ferrer *Lionel McCoy* • Michael Parks *Robert F Kennedy* • Ronee Blakley *Carrie Dewitt* • Rip Torn *Dwight Webb* • Celeste Holm *Florence Hollister* • Michael Sacks *Melvin Purvis* • Dan Dailey *Clyde Tolson* ■ *Dir/Scr* Larry Cohen

A Private Function ★★★★ 15

Comedy 1984 · UK · Colour · 92mins

With its gentle, witty portrait of postwar Britain and its sly digs at bourgeois aspirations, this could be described as a Handmade-Ealing comedy. Scripted by Alan Bennett, it is an often hilarious mixture of well-observed social comedy and sometimes laborious earthy humour, much of the latter being inspired by the bodily functions of a pig being fattened for a feast to celebrate the 1947 royal wedding. Michael Palin does a nice line in mortified meekness, but he is upstaged by Maggie Smith, as his scheming wife, and Liz Smith, whose eccentric antics and ramblings provide some of the highlights. ▣

Michael Palin *Gilbert Chilvers* • Maggie Smith *Joyce Chilvers* • Denholm Elliott *Dr Charles Swaby* • Richard Griffiths *Henry Allardyce* • Tony Haygarth *Bernard Sutcliff* • John Normington *Frank Lockwood* • Pete Postlethwaite *Douglas Nuttal* • Bill Paterson *Maurice Wormold* • Liz Smith *Mother* • Alison Steadman *Mrs Allardyce* • Jim Carter *Inspector Howard Noble* • Reece Dinsdale *PC Penny* ■ *Dir* Malcolm Mowbray • *Scr* Alan Bennett, from a story by Alan Bennett, Malcolm Mowbray

Private Hell 36 ★★★

Crime drama 1954 · US · BW · 81mins

Ida Lupino co-wrote and produced this tense thriller with ex-husband Collier Young, co-starred with then husband Howard Duff, and played her love scenes with Steve Cochran. He's the hard-up cop who pockets some loot so that she will marry him, and Howard Duff is the partner who reluctantly goes along with the lapse. Add Dorothy Malone as Duff's wife and Dean Jagger as the men's suspicious superior officer and this has a strong cast who perform well under director Don Siegel.

Ida Lupino *Lilli Marlowe* • Steve Cochran *Cal Bruner* • Howard Duff *Jack Farnham* • Dean

Jagger *Captain Michaels* • Dorothy Malone *Francey Farnham* • Bridget Duff *Farnham child* ■ *Dir* Don Siegel • *Scr* Collier Young, Ida Lupino • *Cinematographer* Burnett Guffey

Private Investigations ★★★ 18

Adventure drama 1987 · US · Colour · 75mins

The film that was meant to make actor Clayton Rohner a star back in 1987 manages to be a watchable if overly-complicated thriller, vaguely in the mould of *The Man Who Knew Too Much*. Rohner plays Los Angeles architecht Joey Bradley, who is falsely set up as being privy to a mob secret and finds himself hunted by hired guns as a consequence. Slickly made, it offers some decent performances, especially by the ever reliable Ray Sharkey as a hapless hitman. You'll watch worse. ▣

Clayton Rohner *Joey Bradley* • Ray Sharkey *Ryan* • Paul LeMat *Detective Wexler* • Talia Balsam *Jenny Fox* • Phil Morris *Eddie Gordon* • Martin Balsam *Cliff Dowling* ■ *Dir* Nigel Dick • *Scr* John Dahl, David Warfield, from a story by Nigel Dick

Private Lessons ★★ 18

Erotic drama 1981 · US · Colour · 79mins

Sylvia Kristel takes her notoriety as princess of soft-porn in European erotica such as *Emmanuelle* for an American makeover. But this suggestive fantasy – teenager Eric Brown being sexually initiated by maid Kristel – is the wish-fulfiller much as before, even though it's set in Arizona. A blackmail scheme is the feeble excuse for a plot, backed by a rather good rock soundtrack, but production problems didn't help the dislocated way it's put together, and even Kristel's passion is a fake – Judy Heldon is the stand-in for the nude scenes. ▣

Sylvia Kristel *Nicole* • Howard Hesseman *Lester* • Eric Brown *Philly* • Patrick Piccinnini *Sherman* • Ed Begley Jr *Jack Travis* • Pamela Bryant *Joyce* ■ *Dir* Alan Myerson • *Scr* Dan Greenburg, from his novel

Private Life ★★★

Drama 1982 · USSR · Colour · 104mins

Fifty-five years after he made his directorial debut with *Krug* (1927), Yuli Raizman earned himself an Oscar nomination for best foreign film for this wry parable on the growing detachment between the Communist Party and the People. Overlooked for promotion, Mikhail Ulyanov decides to focus on his family, only to discover that his careerism has alienated him from them, too. Laboured in its symbolism and languorous in its pacing, this is, nevertheless, a sincere, if occasionally sentimental, study in disillusion and redemption. The mournful Ulyanov is well supported by Iya Savvina as his wife and Irina Gubanova as his initially sympathetic former secretary. Russian dialogue dubbed into English.

Mikhail Ulyanov *Sergei Abrikosov* • Iya Savvina *Natalya Ilyinichna* • Irina Gubanova *Nelly Petrovna* ■ *Dir* Yuli Raizman • *Scr* Anatoly Grebnyev, Yuli Raizman

The Private Life of Don Juan ★★ U

Romantic adventure 1934 · UK · BW · 83mins

A rather sad end to the soaring, dynamic career of the original swashbuckler, Douglas Fairbanks Sr. The gang's all here – Merle Oberon, Benita Hume, Joan Gardner – and it's directed by the inimitable Alexander Korda. Sadly, Fairbanks is well past his swashbuckling prime – it's one of Hollywood's less engaging truisms that male sex symbols are rarely allowed to retire gracefully from the red-blooded fray. But there are still a few stylish moments to savour. ▣

Douglas Fairbanks *Don Juan* • Merle Oberon *Antonia* • Binnie Barnes *Rosita* • Joan Gardner *Carmen* • Benita Hume *Dolores* ■ *Dir* Alexander Korda • *Scr* Frederick Lonsdale, Lajos Biró, Arthur Wimperis, from the play *L'Homme à la Rose* by Henri Bataille

The Private Life of Helen of Troy ★★

Silent satire 1927 · US · BW

No more a serious slice of history than Alexander Korda's later and immeasurably more famous *Private Life of Henry VIII*, this irreverent dip into Ancient Greece was made during the Hungarian emigré's Hollywood period. Korda's wife, Maria Corda, stars as Helen, whisked off by Paris (Ricardo Cortez), away from her husband Menelaus (Lewis Stone). It's really a Flapper Era sex comedy in togas.

Maria Corda *Helen* • Lewis Stone *Menelaus* • Ricardo Cortez *Paris* • George Fawcett *Eteoneus* ■ *Dir* Alexander Korda • *Scr* Carey Wilson, from the novel by John Erskine and from the play *The Road to Rome, a Play* by Robert Emmet Sherwood

The Private Life of Henry VIII ★★★★ U

Biographical drama 1933 · UK · BW · 89mins

This was the British movie that finally cracked the American market: a superb, sexy, roistering biographical drama based on history's most flamboyant monarch. It caused a sensation and started a widespread trend for belching in public and tossing used meat bones over one's shoulder in imitation of the great Charles Laughton, whose subtle and clever portrayal rightly won him the best actor Oscar at the age of 33, the first time a British film had been honoured by the Academy. Director and co-producer Alexander Korda pulls out all the stops, and, although the style looks creaky today, the performances are simply splendid, especially Mrs Laughton, Elsa Lanchester, who is very funny as Anne of Cleves. ▣

Charles Laughton *Henry VIII* • Robert Donat *Thomas Culpepper* • Elsa Lanchester *Anne of Cleves* • Merle Oberon *Anne Boleyn* • Binnie Barnes *Katherine Howard* • Wendy Barrie *Jane Seymour* • Everley Gregg *Catherine Parr* • Franklyn Dyall *Thomas Cromwell* ■ *Dir* Alexander Korda • *Scr* Lajos Biro, Arthur Wimperis

The Private Life of Sherlock Holmes ★★★★★ PG

Mystery   1970 · UK · Colour · 120mins

Here we are on the Wilder shores of satire – Billy Wilder, that is! Casting a wondrously theatrical Robert Stephens as Holmes and a bemusedly stolid Colin Blakely as Dr Watson, director Wilder and his co-writer IAL Diamond give an affectionate comic spin to the great detective partnership, even hinting that others might think they had a gay relationship. Always one of Wilder's favourite films, the director was enraged when studio executives insisted on whittling the proposed four stories in the screenplay down to two. *Holmes in Love* (with Genevieve Page), though, is a sight to behold and *The Adventure of the Mini-Submarine*, featuring Queen Victoria, is bizarre and even wistful fun. The Baker Street set by the great Alexander Trauner is a joy of enormous craftsmanship an architectural metaphor for the film itself. 🎬

Robert Stephens *Sherlock Holmes* • Colin Blakely *Dr John H Watson* • Irene Handl *Mrs Hudson* • Christopher Lee *Mycroft Holmes* • Tamara Toumanova *Petrova* • Genevieve Page *Gabrielle Valladon* • Clive Revill *Rogozhin* • Catherine Lacey *Old lady* • Stanley Holloway *First gravedigger* • Mollie Maureen *Queen Victoria* ■ Dir Billy Wilder • Scr Billy Wilder, IAL Diamond, from characters created by Sir Arthur Conan Doyle • *Music* Miklos Rozsa

Private Lives ★★★

Romantic comedy   1931 · US · BW · 82mins

Norma Shearer and Robert Montgomery star in Noël Coward's most famous and enduring high comedy about divorced couple Amanda and Elyot, who were once "so ridiculously over-in love". They meet again unexpectedly while on their respective honeymoons and run away to start their fiery relationship all over again. Given how deeply English the play is and, with its tight three acts and confined sets, how uncinematic, MGM acquitted itself quite well by it, opening it up while retaining most of Coward's famous exchanges, albeit cut, fragmented, transposed and with new lines added. It lacks the brilliance of the original, but Shearer is perfect.

Norma Shearer *Amanda Chase Prynne* • Robert Montgomery *Elyot Chase* • Reginald Denny *Victor Prynne* • Una Merkel *Sibyl Chase* • Jean Hersholt *Oscar* ■ Dir Sidney Franklin • Scr Hans Kräly, Richard Schayer, Claudine West, from the play by Noël Coward

The Private Lives of Elizabeth and Essex ★★ U

Historical drama
1939 · US · Colour · 102mins

A ridiculous piece of pomp and circumstantial evidence, with Bette Davis as Elizabeth I, who's infatuated with the Earl of Essex, played by Errol Flynn. Unfortunately, without a buckle to swash, Flynn seems stranded in the reams of ripe Hollywood dialogue. Yet the stirring Erich Wolfgang Korngold music and lavish sets (seemingly modelled more on Beverly Hills than Hampton Court) almost compensate for the film's travesty of history. Davis herself hated doing the picture – she

wanted Laurence Olivier as Essex and didn't enjoy being cast against Flynn, though studio head Jack Warner knew they were a marriage made in box-office heaven. 🎬

Bette Davis *Queen Elizabeth I* • Errol Flynn *Robert Devereaux, Earl of Essex* • Olivia de Havilland *Lady Penelope Gray* • Donald Crisp *Francis Bacon* • Alan Hale *Earl of Tyrone* • Vincent Price *Sir Walter Raleigh* ■ Dir Michael Curtiz • Scr Norman Reilly Raine, Aeneas MacKenzie, from the play *Elizabeth the Queen* by Maxwell Anderson

The Private Navy of Sgt O'Farrell ★★ U

Second World War comedy
1968 · US · Colour · 92mins

Bob Hope was an unabashed Republican whose support for the war in Vietnam and Richard Nixon post-Watergate gave him the reputation of a stolid right-winger. Strange then to find him in this shipshape satire with antiwar undertones, co-produced by his own company, about lost beer and a wild and crazy nurse (Phyllis Diller). This final film of director Frank Tashlin, who made Hope's *Son of Paleface*, is no *M*A*S*H*, and Hope is no Phil Silvers, but the film worth a look.

Bob Hope *Dan O'Farrell* • Phyllis Diller *Nurse Nellie Krause* • Jeffrey Hunter *Lt Lyman Jones* • Gina Lollobrigida *Maria* • Mylene Demongeot *Gaby* • John Myhers *Lt Cdr Snavely* • Mako *Calvin Coolidge Ishimura* • Dick Sargent *Capt Prohaska* ■ Dir Frank Tashlin • Scr Frank Tashlin, from a story by John L Greene, Robert M Fresco

Private Parts ★★★★ 18

Biographical comedy
1997 · US · Colour · 104mins

Enthralling biopic of USA "shock jock" Howard Stern, notorious for his sexually explicit media broadcasts and for his bust-ups with just about everybody. Charting his rise from hopeless deejay to America's most outspoken radio celebrity, *Private Parts* presents Stern (here playing himself) as a deeply offensive human being, but it also reveals a softer off-air side, particularly in his relationship with Alison (Catherine McCormack). Although obviously toned down, this rude, crude and highly entertaining adaptation of Stern's own book doesn't flinch from re-creating many of his raunchier moments. Despite the sometimes extreme obnoxiousness, you find yourself rooting for the man. Contains swearing and sexual references. 🎬 **DVD**

Howard Stern • Robin Quivers • Mary McCormack *Alison Stern* • Fred Norris • Paul Giamatti *Kenny* • Gary Dell'Abate *Gary Dell'Abate* • Jackie Martling • Carol Alt *Gloria* • Ozzy Osbourne • Mia Farrow ■ Dir Betty Thomas • Scr Len Blum, Michael Kalesniko, from an autobiography by Howard Stern

Private Potter ★★ U

War drama   1963 · UK · BW · 88mins

Tom Courtenay is the eponymous soldier whose inexperience causes him to cry out while on a mission, leading to the death of a colleague. In his defence, Courtenay claims that at the critical moment he had a vision of God. This leads to a debate over whether he should be court martialled, his apparent pottiness, the existence

of God and a lot of other weighty issues. As with his next and far better movie, *King and Country*, Courtenay is utterly convincing as the delicate creature who wilts under pressure but Ronald Harwood's script, based on his TV play, is a sermon few actors could survive. Flashy direction doesn't help matters, either.

Tom Courtenay *Pvt Potter* • Mogens Wieth *Yannis* • Ronald Fraser *Doctor* • James Maxwell *Lt Col Gunyon* • Ralph Michael *Padre* • Brewster Mason *Brigadier* • Eric Thompson *Capt Knowles* • John Graham *Maj Sims* • Frank Finlay *Capt Patterson* ■ Dir Casper Wrede • Scr Casper Wrede, Ronald Harwood, from the TV play by Ronald Harwood

Private Resort ★★ 18

Comedy   1985 · US · Colour · 78mins

A typical eighties sun, sea, sand and sex movie about the exploits of two friends on the hunt for girls at a Miami resort. The main point of interest in what would otherwise be a forgettable movie is a first starring role for Johnny Depp. This followed his appearance in *A Nightmare on Elm Street* and predates his role in the TV series *21 Jump Street*, which made his name. Here he plays Jack, who with pal Ben (Rob Morrow from TV's *Northern Exposure*) seeks simple hedonistic pleasure – with the opposite sex. Even this early in his career Depp shows promise, demonstrating that most important screen attribute: presence. 🎬

Rob Morrow *Ben* • Johnny Depp *Jack Marshall* • Emily Longstreth *Patti* • Karyn O'Bryan *Dana* • Hector Elizondo *The Maestro* • Dody Goodman *Amanda Rawlings* ■ Dir George Bowers • Scr Gordon Mitchell, from a story by Ken Segall, Alan Wenkus, Gordon Mitchell

Private School ★ 18

Comedy   1983 · US · Colour · 84mins

Even fans of *Porky's* will loathe this witless teen sex comedy in which a bunch of voyeurs from an all-boy academy try to spy on the girls in the school next door. Sylvia Kristel (*Emmanuelle*) plays sex-education teacher Ms Regina Copuletta, which is about the level of humour to be expected here. Phoebe Cates and Matthew Modine are unlikely to have kept this on their CVs. 🎬

Phoebe Cates *Christine Ramsay* • Betsy Russell *Jordan Leigh-Jensen* • Kathleen Wilhoite *Betsy Newhouse* • Matthew Modine *Jim Green* • Ray Walston *Chauncey* • Sylvia Kristel *Ms Regina Copuletta* ■ Dir Noel Black • Scr Dan Greenburg, Suzanne O'Malley

The Private Secretary ★★ U

Comedy   1935 · UK · BW · 70mins

Fussy, ever-anxious and with an unrivalled gift for mismanagement, Edward Everett Horton was one of the great comic sidekicks of the studio era. However, he had to come to Twickenham Studios for this rare leading role. He plays an amiably muddled vicar who has to fend off the irate creditors on the trail of spendthrift playboy Barry Mackay. Based on Van Moser's popular German farce, the picture is pretty stagebound, but it trots along smoothly and Horton comes alive as he slips deeper into the mire.

Edward Everett Horton *Reverend Robert Spalding* • Barry MacKay *Douglas Cattermole* • Judy Gunn *Edith Marsland* • Oscar Asche *Robert Cattermole* • Sydney Fairbrother *Miss Ashford* • Henry Edwards • Scr George Broadhurst, Arthur Macrae, H Fowler Mear, from the play *Der Bibliotheker* by Van Moser

Private Sessions ★★★ 15

Drama   1985 · US · Colour · 89mins

Mike Farrell is a psychologist who gets a bit too involved in the lives of his patients, in this case a woman suffering from nymphomania. Although this TV pilot for a series that was never made is strictly run-of-the-mill stuff, it's worth tuning in for the talented and very recognisable cast which includes Maureen Stapleton, Tom Bosley, Robert Vaughn, and Kelly McGillis in her TV movie debut. 🎬

Mike Farrell *Dr Joe Braden* • Maureen Stapleton *Dr Liz Bolger* • Tom Bosley *Harry O'Reilly* • Kelly McGillis *Jennifer Coles* • Robert Vaughn *Oliver Coles* ■ Dir Michael Pressman • Scr Thom Thomas, David Seltzer

The Private War of Major Benson ★★★ U

Comedy   1955 · US · Colour · 104mins

Charlton Heston knocked off this dated but likeable comedy while on a month-long lay-off during the shooting of DeMille's gargantuan *The Ten Commandments*. Heston plays a hard-nosed army major, who displeases his superiors and winds up drilling the students at a military school run by nuns. Heston's intense physicality is often the source of the comedy and the Oscar-nominated story sometimes seems like a fusion of *From Here to Eternity* and *Rebel without a Cause*, delivering the message that in the post-war era the US military needn't be for tough nuts only.

Charlton Heston *Major Bernard Benson* • Julie Adams *Dr Kay Lambert* • William Demarest *John* • Tim Considine *Cadet Sergeant Hibler* • Sal Mineo *Cadet Colonel Dusik* ■ Dir Jerry Hopper • Scr William Roberts, Richard Alan Simmons, from a story by Joe Connelly, Bob Mosher

Private Worlds ★★★

Medical drama   1935 · US · BW · 80mins

Producer Walter Wanger bought Phyllis Bottome's novel because its setting – a mental hospital – had not been featured in an American film before, but both Fredric March and Warner Baxter turned down the male lead. Wanger then hired Charles Boyer, about to return to his native France after finding little success in Hollywood. The film brought him a huge female following and a reputation as "the great lover", and Claudette Colbert, as the fellow-doctor who initially encounters prejudice from Boyer, received an Oscar nomination.

Claudette Colbert *Dr Jane Everest* • Charles Boyer *Dr Charles Monet* • Joan Bennett *Sally MacGregor* • Helen Vinson *Claire Monet* • Joel McCrea *Dr Alex MacGregor* • Esther Dale *The matron* • Sam Hinds [Samuel S Hinds] *Dr Arnold* ■ Dir Gregory La Cava • Scr Lynn Starling, Gregory La Cava, Gladys Unger, from the novel by Phyllis Bottome • *Cinematographer* Leon Shamroy

U = SUITABLE FOR ALL   Uc = SUITABLE FOR ALL, ESPECIALLY FOR YOUNG CHILDREN (VIDEO ONLY)   PG = PARENTAL GUIDANCE

A Private's Affair ★★ U
Comedy   1959 · US · Colour · 92mins

Sal Mineo – the teenager who seemed far more troubled than James Dean in *Rebel without a Cause* – was neither comedian nor leading man, but he makes a stab at both in this service comedy. Mineo is one of three military cadets who form a vocal trio as part of their basic training. The three kids aren't convincing as cadets at all, the idea being that even rock 'n' roll beatnik types can wear a uniform – which is what Elvis Presley did, of course. And yes, that is Bing Crosby's boy Gary.

Sal Mineo *Luigi Maresi* • Christine Carere *Marie* • Barry Coe *Jerry Morgan* • Barbara Eden *Katey* • Gary Crosby *Mike* • Terry Moore *Louise Wright* • Jim Backus *Jim Gordon* • Jessie Royce Landis *Elizabeth T Chapman* ■ *Dir* Raoul Walsh • *Scr* Winston Miller, from a story by Ray Livingston Murphy

Privates on Parade ★★ 15
Comedy drama 1982 · UK · Colour · 107mins

A sort of *Virgin Soldiers* with pretentious knobs on, based on Peter Nichols's play in which a troupe of soldiers put on musical revues in Singapore. The Malay emergency, when communists threatened to topple the British colony, provides the background. In the foreground are John Cleese, Denis Quilley and lots of dodgy racial innuendo. The palm trees are all plastic as the picture was filmed in England, the jokes are a notch above the *Carry On* level and Cleese is an inch away from a nervous breakdown. But, as a whole, it's not nearly as funny as it should have been. Contains some violence and swearing. ▭

John Cleese *Major Giles Flack* • Denis Quilley *Captain Terri Dennis* • Nicola Pagett *Sylvia Morgan* • Patrick Pearson *Private Steven Flowers* ■ *Dir* Michael Blakemore • *Scr* Peter Nichols, from his play

Private's Progress ★★★★ U
Comedy   1956 · UK · BW · 95mins

This pleasing mix of satire and nostalgia was unusual at the time for suggesting that not every tommy who went to fight in the Second World War was a hero. Ian Carmichael is superbly cast as the hapless Stanley Windrush, whose natural ineptitude is seen as a God-given gift by the roguish Richard Attenborough and Dennis Price. Although the Boulting brothers rather lose track of the plot once Carmichael goes after Nazi art treasures, this is still richly entertaining, not least because of the smashing performance of Terry-Thomas. Several of the cast members would reunite with the Boultings for the classic *I'm All Right Jack* three years later. ▭

Richard Attenborough *Private Cox* • Dennis Price *Brigadier Bertram Tracepurcel* • Terry-Thomas *Major Hitchcock* • Ian Carmichael *Stanley Windrush* • Peter Jones *Egan* • William Hartnell *Sergeant Sutton* ■ *Dir* John Boulting • *Scr* John Boulting, Frank Harvey, from the novel by Alan Hackney

Privilege ★★
Satirical drama 1967 · UK · Colour · 102mins

Peter Watkins, who made the chilling atomic warning *The War Game*, directed this uneven satire in which real-life pop star Paul Jones is the rock idol who finds himself manipulated by the Church and the State, who seek to contain the violent instincts of his fans. This entails a change of image that transforms him into a religious leader. It's filled with confidence, but little conviction. Jean Shrimpton, one of the fashion icons of the time, is the singer's girlfriend – unfortunately her acting talent doesn't match her looks. Johnny Speight, creator of TV's Alf Garnett, wrote the story and Derek Ware directed the action sequences.

Paul Jones *Steve Shorter* • Jean Shrimpton *Vanessa Ritchie* • Mark London *Alvin Kirsch* • Max Bacon *Julie Jordan* • Jeremy Child *Martin Crossley* ■ *Dir* Peter Watkins, Derek Ware • *Scr* Norman Bogner, Peter Watkins, from a story by Johnny Speight

Prix de Beauté ★★★
Silent drama   1930 · Fr · BW · 109mins

One for Louise Brooks fans, and a perfect showcase for her specialist gifts as a tragic heroine, this was made as a silent in Paris by Italian director Augusto Genina. Disastrously badly dubbed as sound came into fashion, its American release, as *Miss Europe*, was an understandable failure. In its pure silent version, however, a print of which was rediscovered in Italy and restored, this tale of an ordinary girl of extraordinary beauty, who wins a beauty contest with tragic consequences, is replete with many exquisite images.

Louise Brooks *Lucienne Garnier* • Georges Charlia *André* • H Bandini *Antonin* ■ *Dir* Augusto Genina • *Scr* René Clair, Georg Wilhelm Pabst [GW Pabst], Bernard Zimmer, from a story by Augusto Genina, René Clair, Bernard Zimmer, Alessandro de Stefani • *Cinematographer* Rudolf Maté, Louis Née • *Editor* Edmond T Gréville

The Prize ★★★
Spy adventure 1963 · US · Colour · 134mins

The Nobel prizes are handed out in Stockholm, with Paul Newman winning his for literature and Edward G Robinson getting his for physics. But this is the Cold War, Russia is almost next door, and Newman smells a big fat communist conspiracy. Screenwriter Ernest Lehman wrote Hitchcock's classic chase picture *North by Northwest*; here he recycles some of those ideas and cares not a jot about plausibility. A bit long perhaps, but this is still an enjoyable romp that displays a healthy cynicism towards international politics and culture.

Paul Newman *Andrew Craig* • Edward G Robinson *Dr Max Stratman* • Elke Sommer *Inger Lisa Andersen* • Diane Baker *Emily Stratman* • Micheline Presle *Dr Denise Marceau* • Gérard Oury *Dr Claude Marceau* ■ *Dir* Mark Robson • *Scr* Ernest Lehman, from the novel by Irving Wallace

The Prize Fighter ★★
Comedy   1979 · US · Colour · 99mins

The regular collaborations between Don Knotts and Tim Conway proved popular to fans of the veteran comedy actors. In this one, Conway plays Bags, a dim-witted boxer and Knotts is Shake, his dispirited manager. The unsuccessful pair are down on their luck when they get involved with a gangster who promises them some big bucks. But as is the way with such shady deals, there is more to the scheme than meets the eye. Some farcical slapstick and passable comedy sequences, but it's hardly a knockout.

Tim Conway *Bags* • Don Knotts *Shake* • David Wayne *Pop Morgan* • Robin Clarke *Mike* • Cisse Cameron *Polly* • Mary Ellen O'Neill *Mama* ■ *Dir* Michael Preece • *Scr* Tim Conway, John Myhers

A Prize of Arms ★★★
Crime thriller 1961 · UK · BW · 104mins

A clever and exciting caper about the heist of army loot, starring Stanley Baker, who was never quite as effective in leading roles as he was playing the supporting villain. Master cameraman and later cult director Nicolas Roeg co-wrote the original story while under-rated Cliff Owen took on the directorial duties. The nail-biting climax is very well handled and there's a terrific co-starring performance from Tom Bell. Good reviews at the time didn't help this film's box office takings, and it became known as just another average British thriller; shame.

Stanley Baker *Turpin* • Helmut Schmid *Swavek* • Tom Bell *Fenner* • Tom Adams *Corporal Glenn* • Anthony Bate *Sergeant Reeves* • Rodney Bewes *Private Maynard* • Richard Bidlake *Lieutenant Waddington* ■ *Dir* Cliff Owen • *Scr* Paul Ryder, from a story by Nicolas Roeg, Kevin Kavanagh

A Prize of Gold ★★
Crime adventure
1955 · UK · Colour · 101mins

For reasons never satisfactorily explained, Mai Zetterling wants to take a number of orphaned children from their home in Germany to a new life in South America. Her lover, an American soldier played by Richard Widmark, agrees to help her and decides to steal a load of gold bullion which is being flown from Berlin to London. A gang of dubious types is assembled and, predictably, the thieves fall out – one of them quite literally out of the airplane. It's part routine thriller, part soggy melodrama with a lot of winsome kiddies, and Richard Widmark plays a softie! In a word, unconvincing.

Richard Widmark *Sergeant Joe Lawrence* • Mai Zetterling *Maria* • Nigel Patrick *Brian Hammell* • George Cole *Sergeant Roger Morris* • Donald Wolfit *Alfie Stratton* ■ *Dir* Mark Robson • *Scr* Robert Buckner, John Paxton, from the novel by Max Catto

The Prizefighter and the Lady ★★★
Sports romance 1933 · US · BW · 101mins

Heavyweight boxing champion Max Baer (displaying enough acting talent to go on to several more films) stars as fictional fighter Steve Morgan who falls for Myrna Loy. He marries her – with the permission of her former lover, gangster Otto Kruger – only to lose her through his own arrogance and womanising. The romantic plot, however, is incidental to the action in the ring, climaxing in a bloody battle with Primo Carnera. WS Van Dyke directed for MGM with his usual pace, enlisting the services of several fighters playing themselves, including Carnera, Jack Dempsey, Jess Willard

and Jim Jeffries. Definitely one for fight fans.

Myrna Loy *Belle Morgan* • Max Baer *Steve Morgan* • Primo Carnera • Jack Dempsey • Walter Huston *"Professor" Edwin J Bennett* • Otto Kruger *Willie Ryan* • Vince Barnett *Bugsie* • Jess Willard • Jim Jeffries ■ *Dir* WS Van Dyke • *Scr* John Lee Mahin, John Meehan, from a story by Frances Marion

Prizzi's Honor ★★★★★ 15
Black comedy 1985 · US · Colour · 123mins

A gloriously played and plotted joke at the Mafia's expense with Jack Nicholson hugely enjoying himself as a bumbling, mumbling, cerebrally challenged hit man falling madly in lust with Kathleen Turner's throaty, elegant, Machiavellian spider. The best scenes are between Nicholson and, at the time, real-life love Anjelica Huston, trading well-aimed insults and Cosa Nostra *bons mots* out of the corners of their mouths as if they've just been decanted off the Brooklyn A Train. Director John Huston takes a successful gamble by foregoing obvious knockabout farce and opting for a claustrophobic use of talking heads. But it works, wonderfully. Contains swearing, nudity, sex and violence. ▭

Jack Nicholson *Charley Partanna* • Kathleen Turner *Irene Walker* • Anjelica Huston *Maerose Prizzi* • Robert Loggia *Eduardo Prizzi* • William Hickey *Don Corrado Prizzi* • John Randolph *Angelo "Pop" Partanna* • Lee Richardson *Dominic Prizzi* ■ *Dir* John Huston • *Scr* Richard Condon, Janet Roach, from the novel by Richard Condon

Problem Child ★ PG
Comedy   1990 · US · Colour · 81mins

A dreadful mishmash of a comedy, starring John Ritter in hyperbolic mode as a man who adopts a child so dysfunctional it is a wonder any part of him works at all. Not only is this movie crude and deeply unfunny, but it fails to work on the simplest level as an object lesson in giving love and eventually receiving it. There is something offensive about using an unloved and rebellious child as the butt of bad jokes in this way. But, unfortunately, it has to be said that the American public flocked to it in their droves, spawning some even more obnoxious sequels. ▭

John Ritter *Ben Healy* • Jack Warden *"Big" Ben Healy Sr* • Michael Oliver *Junior* • Gilbert Gottfried *Mr Peabody* • Amy Yasbeck *Flo Healy* ■ *Dir* Dennis Dugan • *Scr* Scott Alexander, Larry Karaszewski

Problem Child 2 ★ PG
Comedy   1991 · US · Colour · 85mins

There are those who like nothing better than a full celluloid cacophony of life's more basic bodily functions and, if you find lavatorial humour a must, you will be well served by this execrable film. Continuing where the only marginally better original film left off, *Problem Child 2* was universally and justifiably slated on its release. A cinematic disaster zone – and another sequel appeared in 1995! Contains swearing and violence. ▭

John Ritter *Ben Healy* • Michael Oliver *Junior Healy* • Jack Warden *"Big" Ben Healy* • Laraine Newman *Lawanda Dumore* • Amy

Yasbeck *Annie Young* • Ivyann Schwan *Trixie Young* • Gilbert Gottfried *Mr Peabody* • Charlene Tilton *Debbie Claukinski* ■ *Dir* Brian Levant • *Scr* Scott Alexander, Larry Karaszewski

Problem Child 3 ★ PG

Comedy 1995 · US · Colour · 83mins

Continuing the truly dire tradition of the 1990 and 1991 feature films, this juvenile comedy follows obnoxious youngster Justin Chapman, son of divorced father William Katt, as he develops his first crush on a pretty schoolmate. He goes all out to win her affections, while fending off other suitors. The real problem is that inane situations and cardboard characters can't be salvaged, even by old pro Jack Warden, and wacky Gilbert Gottfried, who seem lost in this sea of pointlessness and bad taste. ▭

William Katt *Ben Healy* • Justin Chapman *Junior Healy* • Carolyn Lowery *Dr Gray* • Jack Warden *"Big" Ben Healy* • Gilbert Gottfried *Dr Peabody* ■ *Dir* Greg Beeman • *Scr* Michael Hitchcock, from characters created by Scott Alexander, Larry Karaszewski

Le Procès de Jeanne d'Arc ★★★★

Drama 1962 · Fr · BW · 65mins

With its stark, simple imagery, Carl Dreyer's *La Passion de Jeanne d'Arc* is one of the glories of French silent cinema. Like Dreyer, Robert Bresson, himself a master of minimalist technique, returned to the original trial transcripts to give an authentic feel to this remarkable featurette that deservedly won the Special Jury Prize at Cannes. Rather trapped between the astonishing silent performance of Renée Falconetti and Ingrid Bergman's gushing Hollywood saint in 1948's *Joan of Arc*, Florence Carrez seems overawed by the part, but this only helps make Joan's torment all the more credible. The deeply moving final shot will live long in the memory. In French with English subtitles.

Florence Carrez *Jeanne d'Arc* • Jean-Claude Fourneau *Bishop Cauchon* • Marc Jacquier *Jean Lemaître, Inquisitor* • Roger Honorat *Jean Beaupère* • Jean Gillibert *Jean de Châtillon* • André Régnier *d'Estivet* ■ *Dir/Scr* Robert Bresson

The Prodigal ★★

Biblical drama 1955 · US · Colour · 112mins

"Two years in the making!" shrieked the gaudily coloured posters for this very studio-bound MGM epic based on the New Testament tale of the prodigal son, but clearly less than two minutes were spent on the script. Director Richard Thorpe was obviously smitten by having hordes of extras, and, regrettably, lets himself linger, tableau-style. For the second time (the first was in *The Egyptian*), British matinée idol Edmund Purdom replaced Marlon Brando in a role rejected by the King of Method, but who today would argue with Brando? Top-billed Lana Turner, though perfectly typecast, is a shade too old for her predatory role, but is mesmerisingly watchable. They just don't make 'em like this any more, and with good reason.

Lana Turner *Samarra, High Priestess of Astarte* • Edmund Purdom *Micah* • Louis

Calhern *Nahreeb, High Priest of Baal* • Audrey Dalton *Ruth* • James Mitchell *Asham* • Neville Brand *Rhakim* • Walter Hampden *Eli, Micah's father* ■ *Dir* Richard Thorpe • *Scr* Maurice Zimm, Joe Breen Jr, Samuel James Larsen

The Prodigal ★ PG

Religious drama 1983 · US · Colour · 101mins

John Travolta's brother Joey, Scottish actor Ian Bannen and evangelist Billy Graham make for an eclectic mix in the cast of this ultra-conservative spiritual drama. The story follows a family who, pressured by the trials and tribulations of modern existence, are losing their faith and coming close to disintegration. As written and directed by James F Collier, it's squeaky clean and dreadfully dull. ▭

John Hammond *Greg Stuart* • Hope Lange *Anne Stuart* • John Cullum *Elton Stuart* • Morgan Brittany *Sheila Holt-Browning* • Ian Bannen *Riley Wyndham* • Joey Travolta *Tony* • Arliss Howard *Scott Stuart* • Sarah Rush *Laura* • Billy Graham ■ *Dir/Scr* James F Collier

The Prodigal Son ★★★ 18

Martial arts drama
1983 · HK · Colour · 100mins

One-time colleagues of Jackie Chan in the famous Seven Little Fortunes troupe, Yuen Biao and Samo Hung co-star in this action-packed but stylish tale of deception and revenge. With his cheeky grin and flying fists, the irrepressible Yuen is on top form as a disappointed streetfighter who joins a Chinese opera company to study under a martial arts master after he discovers that his over-protective father has been rigging all his bouts. Arch villain Frankie Chan provides a worthy opponent in a gut-wrenching massacre and stops-out finale, while the stocky Samo brings a typical touch of good humour. A Cantonese language film. Contains violence. ▭

Sammo Hung *Wong Wah Bo* • Yuen Biao *Leung Jan* • Frankie Chan *Lord Ngai* • Lam Ching Ying *Leung Yee Tai* ■ *Dir* Sammo Hung • *Scr* Samo Hung, Wong Bing Yiu

The Producers ★★★★ PG

Comedy 1968 · US · Colour · 84mins

The first, and still the very best, of Mel Brooks's films, a triumphantly tasteless affair that fully deserves its status as a comic classic. Zero Mostel is the sweaty, down-on-his-luck Broadway impresario who links up with shy accountant Gene Wilder in a scam to fleece theatrical investors with the worst play of all time: a musical biopic of Adolf Hitler. The two leads are wonderful, as is Dick Shawn as the hippy star who takes the lead role in their production, and, while the gags flow freely throughout, it's the jaw-dropping numbers from *Springtime for Hitler* that cement the film's place in cinema history. ▭

Zero Mostel *Max Bialystock* • Gene Wilder *Leo Bloom* • Kenneth Mars *Franz Liebkind* • Estelle Winwood *"Hold Me, Touch Me" Old Lady* • Renee Taylor *Eva Braun* • Christopher Hewett *Roger De Bris* • Lee Meredith *Ulla* • Andreas Voutsinas *Carmen Giya* • Dick Shawn *Lorenzo St Du Bois* • Josip Elic *Violinist* • Madlyn Cates *Concierge* • John Zoller *Drama critic* • William Hickey *Drunk in theatre bar* ■ *Dir/Scr* Mel Brooks

The Professional ★★★

Thriller 1981 · Fr · Colour · 105mins

This is an absorbing enough thriller, with Jean-Paul Belmondo in the title role as a French secret service agent sent to rub out the ruler of a minor African republic. However, a change in his political circumstances prompts the dictator to sue for an alliance and the contract is cancelled. But Belmondo is determined to fulfil his mission and now finds himself at the top of the French government hit list. Belmondo can play victimised heroes with his eyes shut, but his vigour here elevates the picture above the norm. French dialogue dubbed into English.

Jean-Paul Belmondo *Joss Beaumont* • Robert Hossein *Rosen* • Michel Baune *Valera* ■ *Dir* Georges Lautner • *Scr* Georges Lautner, Michel Audiard, from the novel *La Mort d'une Bête à la Peau Fragile* by Patrick Alexander

A Professional Gun ★★★

Spaghetti western
1968 · It/Sp · Colour · 105mins

Spiced up with much revolutionary relish, this spaghetti western with Franco Nero as the professional gun, Tony Musante as a workers' liberator and Jack Palance as a sadistic homosexual also lays on the gallows humour with bloodshot zest. That's because director Sergio Corbucci (who also worked with Nero in a couple of the *Django* movies) used to be a gag writer, so it's jokier than most of its kind, even if its jokes are as simple-minded as Nero striking a match on a villain's stubble. The body count is no laughing matter, though, but it's one of the better examples of the "giggles-through-the-gore" genre. Some dialogue dubbed into English.

Franco Nero *Sergei Cowalski* • Tony Musante *Eufemio* • Jack Palance *Ricciolo* • Giovanna Ralli *Columba* • Eduardo Fajardo *Alfonso Garcia* ■ *Dir* Sergio Corbucci • *Scr* Luciano Vincenzoni, Sergio Spina, Sergio Corbucci, from a story by Franco Solinas, Giorgio Arlorio

The Professionals ★★★★ PG

Western 1966 · US · Colour · 112mins

With more than a passing nod to *The Magnificent Seven*, made six years earlier, Richard Brooks's action western was a box-office smash, repairing the damage that the flop *Lord Jim* had done to his reputation two years before. Burt Lancaster, Lee Marvin, Robert Ryan and Woody Strode are the magnificent four, flawed and fearsome, hired to rescue Claudia Cardinale from the clutches of manic Mexican bandit Jack Palance. Grittily shot in canyon country, bursting with violence and with pit stops for pithy philosophising, this is one of the last westerns one can call a "classic". ▭

Burt Lancaster *Bill Dolworth* • Lee Marvin *Henry Rico Farden* • Robert Ryan *Hans Ehrengard* • Jack Palance *Captain Jesus Raza* • Claudia Cardinale *Maria Grant* • Ralph Bellamy *JW Grant* • Woody Strode *Jacob Sharp* • Joe De Santis *Ortega* ■ *Dir* Richard Brooks • *Scr* Richard Brooks, from the novel *A Mule for the Marquesa* by Frank O'Rourke

Profile ★★

Crime drama 1954 · UK · BW · 65mins

Steel-jawed magazine editor John Bentley is accused of forging a cheque

in the name of his publisher, who inconveniently keels over with a heart attack. Meanwhile, the publisher's wife (a totally wasted Kathleen Byron) lusts after Bentley (who's in love with her daughter), but is soon murdered herself. Rubbish? You bet, from Monarch, one of the lowest on the British B-movie totem pole: don't look for style here. Nevertheless, it was cheap movies such as this that got Bentley (all-too-briefly) to Hollywood.

John Bentley *Peter Armstrong* • Kathleen Byron *Margot Holland* • Thea Gregory *Susan Holland* • Stuart Lindsell *Aubrey Holland* • Garard Green *Charlie Pearson* ■ *Dir* Francis Searle • *Scr* John Gilling, from a story by John Temple-Smith, Maurice Temple-Smith

Profile for Murder ★★ 18

Erotic thriller 1996 · US · Colour · 94mins

The ever-reliable Lance Henriksen perks up this utterly routine straight-to-video serial killer thriller. He plays a wealthy businessman who is the prime suspect in the deaths of a string of young women. Detective Jeff Wincott only has circumstantial evidence to go on so he calls in criminal psychologist Joan Severance in a bid to wheedle a confession out of Henriksen, but things don't go to plan. Even on autopilot, Henriksen brings some much needed menace to the affair, but Severance lacks credibility as the shrink and director David Winning needs little prompting to slump into soft-core clichés. Contains violence, swearing and nudity. ▭

Joan Severance *Hanna Carras* • Lance Henriksen *Adrian Cross* • Jeff Wincott *Michael Weinberg* • Dwight McFee *Detective Williams* • Ryan Michael *Andy Sachs* • Jason Nash *Valet* • Fawnia Mondey *Diane Curtis* • Benjamin Ratner *Tony the coroner* ■ *Dir* David Winning • *Scr* Steve Fisher

Progeny ★★★ 18

Science-fiction horror
1998 · US · Colour · 91mins

A interesting change of pace for splatter specialist Brian Yuzna (*Society*, *Bride of Re-Animator*) in this *Outer Limits*-style tale of a pregnancy that might not be of this world. Although the alien abduction angle has been tackled more convincingly in films like *Communion*, Yuzna creates some unsettling imagery. Arnold Vosloo (*The Mummy*) isn't exactly leading man material, but he does convey an escalating sense of paranoia with some gusto, while Lindsay Crouse and Brad Dourif provide solid support. Although Yuzna does occasionally betray his roots with dollops of gore and nudity, this is a far more restrained and atmospheric tale than you might expect. Contains violence, nudity and some swearing. ▭ **DVD**

Arnold Vosloo *Dr Craig Burton* • Jillian McWhirter *Sherry Burton* • Brad Dourif *Dr Bert Clavell* • Lindsay Crouse *Dr Susan Lamarche* ■ *Dir* Brian Yuzna • *Scr* Aubrey Solomon, from a story by Stuart Gordon, Aubrey Solomon

The Program ★★ 15

Sports drama 1993 · US · Colour · 112mins

American sporting movies rarely translate well for British audiences and this is no exception despite its fine cast, this American football drama

U = SUITABLE FOR ALL, **Uc** = SUITABLE FOR ALL, ESPECIALLY FOR YOUNG CHILDREN (VIDEO ONLY), **PG** = PARENTAL GUIDANCE

went belatedly straight to video over here. James Caan is the hard-bitten coach (with the obligatory soft heart) who is told to transform the fortunes of his struggling college football team, whose players are suffering from myriad personal crises. The playing – both the football and the acting– is the best thing about the movie, with the dependable Caan receiving nice support from the likes of Craig Sheffer, Kristy Swanson and Halle Berry. Director David S Ward can't resist turning out all the usual clichés, but at least it is a step up from his inane *Major League* follow-up. Contains swearing, drug abuse and violence.

James Caan *Coach Sam Winters* • Halle Berry *Autumn* • Omar Epps *Darnell Jefferson* • Craig Sheffer *Joe Kane* • Kristy Swanson *Camille* • Abraham Benrubi *Bud-Lite* ■ *Dir* David S Ward • *Scr* Aaron Latham, David S Ward

Project A ★★★ 12

Action adventure
1983 · HK · Colour · 100mins

For those who think kung fu is kung-phooey, a chance to be converted by one of the masters. With an overworked soundtrack – thwack! kapow! crunch! – and fight choreography ballet companies would die for, Jackie Chan is a turn-of-the-century coastguard battling pirates. Credibility walks the buccaneers' plank, but the humour-leavened action takes some beating and dishes out plenty, as well. In Cantonese with English subtitles. Contains violence.

Jackie Chan *Dragon Ma* • Sammo Hung *Fei* • Yuen Biao *Hung Tin Tze* • Lau Hak Suen *Admiral* ■ *Dir* Jackie Chan • *Scr* Jackie Chan, Edward Tang

Project A: Part II ★★★ 15

Martial arts adventure
1987 · HK · Colour · 100mins

Starting and finishing with the sequences of previous picture highlights and hair-raising set piece out-takes that have become a familiar feature of a Jackie Chan sequel, this rattling if rambling chop-socky adventure has all the action and slapstick we've come to expect from this unique star. Corrupt cops, spies, revolutionaries and pirates hurtle across the screen as Chan teams with the rebellious Maggie Cheung to confound bent bobby David Lam. The handcuffed fight scene is a gem and the final chase proves again that Chan is the true heir of the great silent clowns. For good old-fashioned escapism, Chan's your man. In Cantonese with English subtitles. 🎞

Jackie Chan *Dragon Ma* • Maggie Cheung ■ *Dir* Jackie Chan • *Scr* Edward Tang

Project Alf ★★

Science-fiction comedy
1996 · US/Ger · Colour · 95mins

Spun off from an eighties American television series, director Dick Lowry's unassuming sci-fi comedy about an orange, furry and funny extraterrestrial – ALF stands for Alien Life Form – is amiable family fare. Here the wisecracking ET has close encounters with the military, who have taken him to a top secret base for analysis; but

others at the establishment wish to see him destroyed. Miguel Ferrer, Ed Begley Jr and Martin Sheen are the well known faces in an otherwise unfamiliar cast.

Miguel Ferrer *Moyers* • William O'Leary *Captain Rick Mulligan* • Jensen Daggett *Major Melissa Hill* • Scott Michael Campbell *Lieutenant Reese* • Ed Begley Jr *Dr Warner* • Martin Sheen *Colonel MIlfoil* ■ *Dir* Dick Lowry • *Scr* Tom Patchett, Paul Fusco

Project: Alien ★ 15

Science-fiction thriller
1990 · US/Ausl/Yug · Colour · 88mins

Michael Nouri plays journalist Milker, who investigates a plane crash and other mysterious events including a meteor shower and unexplained illness among a group of geologists. He enlists the help of renowned bush pilot Bird McNamara (actually a woman) but the authorities, including Colonel Clancy (Charles Durning) want everything to be hushed up. The convoluted plot will probably have lost your attention long before our hero gets to the bottom of the mystery. Even the flight sequences manage to be boring. 🎞

Michael Nouri *Jeff Milker* • Charles Durning *Colonel Clancy* • Maxwell Caulfield *George Abbott* • Darlanne Fluegel *Bird McNamara* ■ *Dir* Frank Shields • *Scr* David Peoples

Project: Kill ★★

Spy mystery   1976 · US · Colour · 90mins

In a movie made before *Airplane!* and the *Naked Gun* series reinvented him as a film funny man, Leslie Nielsen plays a kung fu-fighting secret agent who wants out of his way of work, but discovers the only exit door is the one marked "Death". When he goes on the run, friend and fellow agent Gary Lockwood is assigned to track him down. An adequate action film, but expect a few unintentional laughs from seeing comedy icon Nielsen playing it straight.

Leslie Nielsen • Gary Lockwood • Nancy Kwan ■ *Dir* William Girdler • *Scr* Donald G Thompson, from a story by David Sheldon, Donald G Thompson

Project Moonbase ★

Science-fiction   1953 · US · BW · 63mins

Science-fiction icon Robert Heinlein co-wrote the script for this talky space odyssey about man conquering the moon (in 1970, nearly right!). The highlights are communists sabotaging all chances of a return to Earth and the first lunar marriage, which is given a female president's blessing. A pseudo-scientific bore cobbled together from an unsold TV series with mind-boggling space outfit designs.

Donna Martell *Col Britels* • Hayden Rorke *Gen Greene* • Ross Ford *Maj Moore* • Larry Johns *Dr Wernher* • Ernestine Barrier *Mme President* ■ *Dir* Richard Talmadge • *Scr* Robert A Heinlein, Jack Seaman

Project S ★★ 18

Martial arts thriller
1993 · HK · Colour · 99mins

This below-par Hong Kong thriller (a sequel of sorts to *Police Story III: Supercop*) is distinguished only by the graceful high-kicking of Michelle Yeoh.

She plays a police inspector on the trail of bank robbers, who discovers that her ex-boyfriend is involved, leading to a bunch of flatly directed, by-the-numbers martial arts encounters. The siege opening and climactic heist push some of the right buttons, but there's a disappointing lack of style or substance on display. Bizarrely, Hong Kong superstar Jackie Chan has a one-scene cameo, as a cop foiling a jewellery store robbery – in drag. In Cantonese with English subtitles. 🎞 **DVD**

Michelle Yeoh • Jackie Chan • *Dir* Stanley Tong

Project: Shadowchaser ★ 15

Science-fiction action
1992 · UK/Can · Colour · 94mins

Mercenaries led by robot Romulus (Frank Zagarino) take over a hospital, holding the President's daughter (Meg Foster) to ransom. A convicted murderer (Martin Kove) is mistakenly brought in as the only person in the building who can save the hostages. Yes, it's *The Terminator* meets *Die Hard*, but even by cheap rip-off standards this movie is slavishly devoted to its models. Even the music bears a close resemblance to Danny Elfman's score to *Batman*. The only new wrinkle is that the daughter clashes romantically with our hero, like something out of *Moonlighting*. Save yourself the time and watch the originals. 🎞

Martin Kove *DaSilva* • Meg Foster *Sarah* • Frank Zagarino *Romulus* • Paul Koslo *Trevanian* • Joss Ackland *"Kinderman"* ■ *Dir* John Eyres • *Scr* Steven Lister

Project X ★★★

Science-fiction thriller
1968 · US · Colour · 96mins

As Hollywood's foremost hustler of horror, William Castle is a legend in his own spook-time. He directed this science fiction after producing *Rosemary's Baby*, but its story of Christopher George, from the next century, time-trapped in the present to discover a humankind destructor, is unlike Castle's usual scary stuff. A low-budget, low-key affair, it's imaginatively thought through, with enough data to convince. What's sadly missing, though, is the kind of gusto he brought to his other work. Ironically, he was a better salesman of trash than he was of quality – a more persuasive dealer in fool's gold than the real thing.

Christopher George *Hagen Arnold* • Greta Baldwin *Karen Summers* • Henry Jones *Dr Crowther* • Monte Markham *Gregory Gallea* • Harold Gould *Colonel Holt* • Phillip E Pine [Phillip Pine] *Lee Craig* ■ *Dir* William Castle • *Scr* Edmund Morris, from two novels by Leslie P Davies

Project X ★★★

Comedy thriller   1987 · US · Colour

There is plenty going on in this pleasing piece of monkey business. Matthew Broderick stars as a cocky USAF pilot who is sent to a strategic weapons unit to care for the chimpanzees being used to test flight simulators. However, when he learns that they are being subjected to radiation, he decides to stop the

programme before Virgil, an orphan chimp trained in sign language, is strapped into the hot seat. Helen Hunt proves an able accomplice, but Jonathan Kaplan fails either to sustain the suspense or sidestep the slushy ending. 🎞

Matthew Broderick *Jimmy Garrett* • Helen Hunt *Teresa "Teri" McDonald* • Bill Sadler [William Sadler] *Dr Lynnard Carroll* • Johnny Ray McGhee *Isaac Robertson* • Jonathan Stark *Sergeant "Kreig" Kreiger* • Robin Gammell *Colonel Niles* • Stephen Lang *Watts* ■ *Dir* Jonathan Kaplan • *Scr* Stanley Weiser, from a story by Stanley Weiser, Lawrence Lasker

The Projected Man ★★ PG

Science-fiction horror
1966 · UK · Colour · 86mins

A mid-sixties programmer, with special effects that have the distinct look of wobbly cardboard about them, especially when viewed from a post-*Star Wars* vantage point. The story is hardly original either, with a dotty scientist getting his sums wrong in a teleportation experiment and ending up hideously disfigured. However, for all its shortcomings, this still manages to pack a minor punch, largely due to the sense of menace engendered by Ian Curteis's direction and some passable acting by the likes of Ronald Allen and Derek Farr. The kids will snort with derision, though.

Bryant Halliday *Professor Paul Steiner* • Mary Peach *Dr Pat Hill* • Ronald Allen *Dr Mitchell* • Norman Wooland *Dr Blanchard* • Derek Farr *Inspector Davis* ■ *Dir* Ian Curteis • *Scr* John C Cooper, Peter Bryan, from a story by Frank Quattrocchi

The Projectionist ★★★★

Comedy fantasy   1970 · US · Colour · 84mins

An independent, low-budget pearl from writer/director Harry Hurwitz. Burly Chuck McCann is the lonely projectionist whose job leads him into flights of fantasy in which he is transformed into superhero Captain Flash, clashing with arch-enemy The Bat (Rodney Dangerfield). Film clips from other movies are well used, as McCann's daydreams lead him into adventures with fictional characters from Hollywood classics as well as historical characters. Steve Martin and Woody Allen later blurred the line between movies and reality in films like *Dead Men Don't Wear Plaid* and *The Purple Rose of Cairo*, but it's worth finding out why this early effort now enjoys a cult following.

Chuck McCann *Projectionist/Captain Flash* • Ina Balin *Girl* • Rodney Dangerfield *Renaldi/The Bat* • Jara Kohout *Candy Man/Scientist* • Harry Hurwitz *Friendly usher* • Robert Staats *TV pitchman* ■ *Dir/Scr* Harry Hurwitz

Prom Night ★★ 18

Horror   1980 · US · Colour · 88mins

Jamie Lee Curtis cemented her Scream Queen title with this inventively plotted, (relatively) light on gore, entry in the teenagers-in-jeopardy/stalk-and-slash cycle inaugurated by *Halloween* and appropriating the *Carrie* high school setting. Four youngsters cause the death of a fifth in the modishly formula opening prologue, and several years later an axe-wielding killer turns up at the school prom seeking belated revenge. An elongated and

suspenseful chase sequence through the campus and the surprise identity of the masked maniac lift it above average. Three sequels followed. Contains violence, swearing and some nudity. ▣

Leslie Nielsen *Mr Hammond* • Jamie Lee Curtis *Kim* • Casey Stevens *Nick* • Antoinette Bower *Mrs Hammond* • Eddie Benton *Wendy* • Michael Tough *Alex* • Robert Silverman *Sykes* • Pita Oliver *Vicki* ■ *Dir* Paul Lynch • *Scr* William Gray, from a story by Robert Guza Jr

La Promesse ★★★★
Drama
1996 · Bel/Fr/Tun/Lux · Colour · 93mins

Borrowing its uncompromising style from the British school of realism, this harrowing rites-of-passage story was partly inspired by Dostoevsky's *The Brothers Karamazov*. Depicting Europe as a soulless capitalist subjecting the underdeveloped world to a new form of slavery, the film focuses on the feud that develops between an apprentice mechanic and his immigrant-trafficking father over how to help the widow of an African worker who falls to his death. Consistently echoing Ken Loach, co-directors Luc and Jean-Pierre Dardenne pull no punches in this grimy study of human misery, saving their fiercest body blow for the very last scene. In French with English subtitles.

Jérémie Renier *Igor* • Olivier Gourmet *Roger* • Assita Ouedraogo *Assita* • Rasmane Ouedraogo *Amidou* ■ *Dir/Scr* Jean-Pierre Dardenne, Luc Dardenne

Prometheus ★★15
Drama 1998 · UK · Colour · 130mins

Somehow or other, British poet Tony Harrison raised the cash for this modern interpretation of the Greek myth, filmed all over Europe, with dialogue entirely in rhyming couplets. For those who persevere for more than two hours, there are some dazzling visuals, for example the collapsing cooling towers, but many will find Harrison's ideas either baffling or unoriginal. (The business with redundant Yorkshire miners plays like a throwback to the worthy political theatre of the seventies). Bit-player Walter Sparrow has a lead as a disgruntled ex-collier, while Steve Huison, a star of *The Full Monty*, appears in only a couple of scenes. Contains swearing.

Michael Feast *Hermes* • Fern Smith *Mam* • Steve Huison *Dad* • Walter Sparrow *Old Man* ■ *Dir/Scr* Tony Harrison

The Promise ★
Romantic drama 1979 · US · Colour · 97mins

Lovers Kathleen Quinlan and Stephen Collins are involved in an accident that leaves Quinlan disfigured and Collins in a coma. Collins's domineering mother (Beatrice Straight), persuades Quinlan to have plastic surgery and remove herself from the relationship. Quinlan acquiesces, acquires a new face, and finds a new life as an architect's assistant in California. Then – surprise, surprise – she is offered a new job by none other than Collins who, of course, doesn't recognise her. This dated bilge is the kind of film that gives soap opera a bad name.

Kathleen Quinlan *Nancy/Marie* • Stephen Collins *Michael* • Beatrice Straight *Marion* • Laurence Luckinbill *Dr Gregson* • William Prince *George Calloway* ■ *Dir* Gilbert Cates • *Scr* Garry Michael White, from a story by Fred Weintraub, Paul Heller

Promise ★★★★
Drama 1986 · US · Colour · 96mins

Party animal James Garner promises his dying mother that he will take care of his schizophrenic brother (James Woods) in this award-winning, critically acclaimed and heartfelt drama. Remarkably similar to *Rain Man*, made two years later, this emotional roller coaster ride is no less memorable in all artistic departments. A TV movie gem, beautifully written by Richard Friedenberg and shot entirely on location in Oregon.

James Garner *Bob* • James Woods *DJ* • Piper Laurie *Annie* • Peter Michael Goetz *Stuart* • Michael Alldredge *Gibb* • Alan Rosenberg *Dr Pressman* ■ *Dir* Glenn Jordan • *Scr* Richard Friedenberg, from a story by Richard Friedenberg, Tennyson Flowers, Kenneth Blackwell

The Promise ★★15
Romantic drama
1994 · Ger/Fr/Swi · BW and Colour · 115mins

Once one of the most vital forces in New German Cinema, Margarethe von Trotta has been forced into something of a festival backwater of late. The reasons are not hard to identify in this laboured romantic allegory about Germany in the era of the Wall. Initially, there's a certain sweetness about the doomed relationship between young easterners Anian Zollner and Meret Becker. But once she escapes to the West and the couple mature into August Zirner and Corinna Harfouch, the political ironies and cruel coincidences begin to mount up, among them a corny interlude during the Prague Spring. Heartfelt and plausibly played, but over-deliberate. In German with English subtitles.

Corinna Harfouch *Sophie* • Meret Becker *Sophie, as a young woman* • August Zirner *Konrad* • Anian Zollner *Konrad, as a young man* • Jean-Yves Gautier *Gerard* • Eva Mattes *Barbara* ■ *Dir* Margarethe von Trotta • *Scr* Peter Schneider, Margarethe von Trotta, Felice Laudadio, from a idea by Francesco Laudadio

Promise Her Anything ★
Comedy 1966 · UK · Colour · 96mins

The worst movie of Warren Beatty's career cast him as a porno film-maker redeemed by his relationship with next-door neighbour Leslie Caron and her baby son. Tacky and flashily directed, it is set in New York but was entirely shot in London since Beatty was living there with Caron who was unable to leave because of a court order regarding her children. Beatty only made the movie to fill in the time and to co-star with the woman he announced he was to marry. After this flop, Beatty and Caron toyed with another joint venture – *Bonnie and Clyde* – before their own separation.

Warren Beatty *Harley Rummel* • Leslie Caron *Michele O'Brien* • Bob Cummings [Robert Cummings] *Dr Peter Brock* • Hermione Gingold *Mrs Luce* • Lionel Stander *Sam* • Keenan Wynn *Angelo Carelli* • Asa Maynor *Rusty* • Michael Bradley *John Thomas* • Donald

Sutherland *Baby's father* ■ *Dir* Arthur Hiller • *Scr* William Peter Blatty, from a story by Arne Sultan, Marvin Worth

A Promise to Carolyn ★★
Drama based on a true story
1996 · US · Colour · 90mins

Based on a story so disturbingly unreal it could only be true, this TV movie traces the efforts of two sisters to prove their stepmother is guilty of the murder of their baby sister back in the mid-fifties. Child abuse needs to be handled with great sensitivity by film-makers, and thankfully director Jerry London stages the flashback sequences so well that the mere implication of violence is sufficiently chilling. Unfortunately, his account of Delta Burke and Swoozie Kurtz's attempt to bring cold-hearted Shirley Knight to justice is more laboured, with every significant event being milked for all its melodramatic worth. Contains violence.

Delta Burke *Debra Harper* • Swoosie Kurtz *Kay Wilbanks* • Shirley Knight *Jolene Maggart* • Grace Zabriskie *Francie Harper* ■ *Dir* Jerry London • *Scr* Scott Swanton

Promised a Miracle ★★★★
Drama based on a true story
1988 · US · Colour · 94mins

A classy and highly intelligent TV movie which takes a great moral conundrum and for once gives it the breadth and vision it deserves. Based on the true story of the Parkers, a deeply religious couple who were accused of manslaughter after refusing medical treatment for their diabetic son, it addresses a subject on which most people will have strong views. But, far from portraying the Parkers as negligent nutters, director Stephen Gyllenhaal extracts two wonderfully complex, compassionate performances from Rosanna Arquette and Judge Reinhold. All concerned acquit themselves exceptionally well.

Rosanna Arquette *Alice "Lucky" Parker* • Judge Reinhold *Larry Parker* • Tom Bower *Michael Elliott* • Vonni Ribisi [Giovanni Ribisi] *Wesley Parker* • Robin Pearson Rose *Beth* • John Vickery *Pastor Evans* ■ *Dir* Stephen Gyllenhaal • *Scr* David Hill, from the book *We Let Our Son Die* by Larry Parker, Donald Tanner

Promised Land ★★★15
Drama 1988 · US · Colour · 101mins

Michael Hoffman marked himself out as a promising young director on the strength of this under-rated coming of age drama. His subsequent career has been a series of hits and misses, but there is still much to enjoy in this accomplished tale of high school friends discovering that adulthood is not quite what they expected. Kiefer Sutherland gives one of his best performances as the drop-out of the group, on his way back to his old home town, who hooks up with misunderstood bad girl Meg Ryan (she, too, has rarely been better). Meanwhile, back home his old chum Jason Gedrick is now a cop with romantic problems of his own. The interweaving stories don't quite gel, but the cinematography is superb and Hoffman succeeds in summoning up

an air of quiet melancholy. Contains swearing and nudity. ▣

Jason Gedrick *Davey Hancock* • Tracy Pollan *Mary Daley* • Kiefer Sutherland *Danny Rivers* • Meg Ryan *Bev* • Googy Gress *Baines* • Deborah Richter *Pammie* • Oscar Rowland *Mr Rivers* • Sandra Seacat *Mrs Rivers* • Jay Underwood *Circle K Clerk* ■ *Dir/Scr* Michael Hoffman

Promises in the Dark ★★
Drama 1979 · US · Colour · 115mins

Occasionally, Hollywood's portrayal of terminal illness can be moving. This earlier, bleak drama focuses unblinkingly on the ravaging effects of cancer and the debilitating results of chemotherapy, and consequently was less successful at the box office. Kathleen Beller plays an ailing teenager, Ned Beatty and Susan Clark are her parents, and Marsha Mason is her doctor, a divorcee who is having an affair with radiologist Michael Brandon. A first-time directing effort from Jerome Hellman, the Oscar-winning producer of *Midnight Cowboy* and *Coming Home*. Contains swearing and nudity.

Marsha Mason *Dr Alexandra Kenda* • Ned Beatty *Bud Koenig* • Susan Clark *Fran Koenig* • Michael Brandon *Dr Jim Sandman* • Kathleen Beller *Buffy Koenig* • Paul Clemens *Gerry Hulin* • Donald Moffat *Dr Walter McInerny* ■ *Dir* Jerome Hellman • *Scr* Loring Mandel

Proof ★★★★15
Psychological drama
1991 · Ausl · Colour · 86mins

An astonishing Australian oddity that should have established the reputation of writer/director Jocelyn Moorhouse, but didn't, this is about a blind photographer (that's right) who relies on others to describe his work and who is lusted after by his cleaner. Rejected, she discovers that her employer has become friends with another young man and from this point the triangular eroticism strikes an even more bizarre note. Hugo Weaving, Genevieve Picot and Russell Crowe as the romantically inclined threesome pursue their outlandish course with skill and humour. Contains swearing and nudity. ▣

Hugo Weaving *Martin* • Genevieve Picot *Celia* • Russell Crowe *Andy* • Heather Mitchell *Martin's mother* • Jeffrey Walker *Young Martin* • Belinda Davey *Doctor* ■ *Dir/Scr* Jocelyn Moorhouse

Prophecy ★★15
Horror 1979 · US · Colour · 97mins

One of the earliest of the eco-shockers, this demonstrates the decline of director John Frankenheimer. Doctor Robert Foxworth and his pregnant classical musician wife, Talia Shire, go to investigate a report of mercury poisoning in the Maine backwoods and find themselves battling giant biological mutants. If only the direction had been as fluid as the mercury. ▣

Talia Shire *Maggie* • Robert Foxworth *Rob Vern* • Armand Assante *John Hawks* • Richard Dysart *Isley* • Victoria Racimo *Ramona* • George Clutesi *M'Rai* ■ *Dir* John Frankenheimer • *Scr* David Seltzer

U = SUITABLE FOR ALL   Uc = SUITABLE FOR ALL, ESPECIALLY FOR YOUNG CHILDREN (VIDEO ONLY)   PG = PARENTAL GUIDANCE

The Prophecy ★★★ 18
Supernatural horror
1994 · US · Colour · 93mins

Priest-turned-cop Elias Koteas gets caught up in an Earthly battle between renegade angels Christopher Walken and Eric Stoltz in a strangely ambiguous and slightly pretentious horror fantasy. The wildly imaginative premise and poetic development, along with a solid cast that includes Virginia Madsen and Amanda Plummer, make this often compelling, sometimes corny, chiller a bizarre cult item. Highly ambitious on the cerebral front but, except for one scene in Hell, lacking the sort of special effects you would expect from such an apocalyptic notion. Successful enough to spawn two sequels, though. ⌨

Christopher Walken *Angel Gabriel* • Elias Koteas *Thomas Dagget* • Eric Stoltz *Angel Simon* • Virginia Madsen *Katherine* • Moriah Shining Dove Snyder *Mary* • Adam Goldberg *Jerry* • Amanda Plummer *Rachael* • Viggo Mortensen *Lucifer* ■ *Dir/Scr* Gregory Widen

The Prophecy II ★★
Horror   1997 · US · Colour · 83mins

Carrying on from the first movie, Christopher Walken's archangel Gabriel, angered that God has favoured humans over his kind, returns to hunt down Jennifer Beals, who is pregnant with the saviour of mankind. But where the original boasted some good, offbeat ideas, this quickly degenerates into just another dumb chase movie, and even the sterling efforts of Walken can't save it.

Christopher Walken *Gabriel* • Jennifer Beals *Valerie Rosales* • Brittany Murphy *Izzy* • Russell Wong *Danyael* • William Prael *Rafayel* • Danny Strong *Julian* • Glenn Danzig *Samayel* • Eric Roberts *Michael* ■ *Dir* Greg Spence • *Scr* Matt Greenberg, Greg Spence

Prophet of Evil ★★ 15
Biographical drama
1993 · US · Colour · 88mins

Single-minded investigator Brian Dennehy obsessively pursues a charismatic cult leader for whom killing is part of his creed in director Jud Taylor's cliché-ridden drama. Dennehy offers his usual winning mix of decency and menace, lending a certain amount of credibility to an otherwise wayward outing that also features William Devane and Dee Wallace Stone, who played the mother in *ET*. ⌨

Brian Dennehy *Ervil LeBaron* • William Devane *Dan Fields* • Tracey Needham *Rena Chynoweth* • Philip Abbott *Dr Rulon Allred* • Lucy Butler *Naomi Kane* • Danny Cooksey *Isaac* • Dee Wallace Stone *Jackie Fields* ■ *Dir* Jud Taylor • *Scr* Fred Mills

The Proposition ★★★ 18
Period romantic drama
1996 · UK/US · Colour · 92mins

This period drama has a plot that sounds like a classic western, but it's actually set in 19th-century Napoleonic Wales around the time of the Napoleonic Wars. Theresa Russell plays a feisty widow who refuses to be forced into a marriage of convenience to local sheriff Richard Lynch, despite her dire financial situation. Instead she opts to save the estate by driving her herd of cattle to market herself — with a little help from Patrick Bergin. It's a strong story, well told, with good use of landscape, and memorable performances from Russell and co-stars Bergin and Lynch.

Theresa Russell *Catherine Morgan* • Patrick Bergin *Rhys Williams* • Richard Lynch *Sheriff Williams* ■ *Dir* Strathford Hamilton • *Scr* Paul Matthews

The Proposition ★★★ 12
Romantic crime drama
1998 · US · Colour · 107mins

The plot for this crime film set in Boston in the thirties is more suited to a lurid soap opera than a major movie, but it's saved by the quality of the acting on show. Director Lesli Linka Glatter's overwrought drama centres on impotent lawyer William Hurt, who "hires" Neil Patrick Harris to impregnate his wife Madeleine Stowe. The trouble starts when Harris falls in love with Stowe, and clergyman Kenneth Branagh arrives on the scene to further confuse matters. If it wasn't for Branagh and Co, this so easily could have descended into unintentional farce. Contains some swearing and sexual references. ⌨

Kenneth Branagh *Father Michael McKinnon* • Madeleine Stowe *Eleanor Barret* • William Hurt *Arthur Barret* • Neil Patrick Harris *Roger Martin* • Robert Loggia *Hannibal Thurman* • Blythe Danner *Syril Danning* • Josef Sommer *Father Dryer* ■ *Dir* Lesli Linka Glatter • *Scr* Rick Ramage

The Proprietor ★★ 12
Drama
1996 · UK/Fr/Tur/US · Colour · 108mins

Ismail Merchant's second solo directorial outing is a middlebrow misfire, especially when compared with his James Ivory collaborations. Pitted with clumsy flashbacks, the story turns around author Jeanne Moreau's memories of her mother, who was murdered by the Nazis, and her hopes for a screen version of her most famous novel. Romances and reunions provide engaging diversions, but the action too often lapses into kitsch and cultural snobbery, as Merchant gently mocks Indian musicals and over-earnest critics. Much of the meaning and emotion is registered on Moreau's exquisite face, but overall this is a disappointment. In French and English with subtitles. ⌨

Nell Carter *Milly* • Jeanne Moreau *Adrienne Mark* • Marc Tissot *Patrice Legendre* • Sean Young *Virginia Kelly/Sally* • Christopher Cazenove *Elliott Spencer* • Jean-Pierre Aumont *Franz Legendre* • Josh Hamilton *William O'Hara* • Austin Pendleton *Willy Kunst* • Sam Waterston *Harry Bancroft* ■ *Dir* Ismail Merchant • *Scr* Jean-Marie Besset, George Trow

Prospero's Books ★★★★ 15
Drama 1991 · Hol/Fr/It/UK · Colour · 120mins

Historically important both as a record of John Gielgud's celebrated stage rendition of Prospero, and as the first film to be shot entirely in High Definition Video, this visually stunning fantasy is more than just a straightforward adaptation of *The Tempest*. Focusing on the exiled Duke of Milan's beloved 24-volume library, Peter Greenaway overlays multiple images and textual information in what amounts to a meditation on the processes of thought and artistic creation, with Gielgud's voicing of all Shakespeare's characters underlining the omnipresence of the author. Casual viewers may find Greenaway's experiments with non-linear narrative challenging, but those with plenty of patience and a knowledge of the source material should find it rewarding. ⌨

John Gielgud *Prospero* • Michael Clark *Caliban* • Michel Blanc *Alonso* • Erland Josephson *Gonzalo* • Isabelle Pasco *Miranda* • Tom Bell *Antonio* • Kenneth Cranham *Sebastian* • Mark Rylance *Ferdinand* • Gérard Thoolen *Adrian* • Pierre Bokma *Francisco* ■ *Dir* Peter Greenaway • *Scr* Peter Greenaway, from the play *The Tempest* by William Shakespeare • *Music* Michael Nyman

The Protector ★★★ 18
Martial arts action
1985 · US · Colour · 90mins

This was one of Jackie Chan's early American productions, an efficient action movie tinged with 007-style hardware. He plays a tough cop battling bad guys in New York before being sent on assignment with Danny Aiello to Hong Kong to track down a drug kingpin. As usual with Chan movies, the plot and dialogue are forgettable but the all-out action scenes, including an impressive boat and helicopter pursuit around New York, dazzle the eye. While Aiello walks off with the acting honours this is Chan's movie, although director James Glickenhaus mistakenly tries to turn him into Asia's answer to Dirty Harry. Chan added extra footage of car chases and kung fu fights for the Chinese version. ⌨

Jackie Chan *Billy Wong* • Danny Aiello *Danny Garoni* • Sandy Alexander *Gang leader* • Roy Chiao *Mr Ko* • Victor Arnold *Police Captain* ■ *Dir/Scr* James Glickenhaus

Proteus ★★★ 18
Science-fiction horror
1995 · UK · Colour · 92mins

This typical monsters-on-the-loose movie is creepy all the way, floundering only slightly in its pacing and acting. A group of inept yuppies-turned-amateur drug-runners stumble upon a seemingly abandoned research rig in mid-ocean. The few people left seem terrified of something, but they never stick around long enough to say what. Have no fear, our heroes will discover what's plaguing the rig and fight it off – they hope. The dark industrial setting makes for good atmosphere, but it's still just a monster movie with much owed to earlier flicks like *Alien*. Director Bob Keen is probably better known for his make-up and special effects work on the *Hellraiser* films. Contains swearing and violence. ⌨

Craig Fairbrass *Alex* • Toni Barry *Linda* • William Marsh *Mark* • Jennifer Calvert *Rachel* • Robert Firth *Paul* • Margot Steinberg *Christine* ■ *Dir* Bob Keen • *Scr* John Brosnan, from the novel *Slimer* by Harry Adam Knight [John Brosnan]

Protocol ★★★ PG
Comedy   1984 · US · Colour · 90mins

Hardly A-grade Goldie Hawn, but a charming enough comedy all the same. She plays, unsurprisingly, a dizzy blonde, thrown into the world of intrigue in Washington when she saves the life of a Middle Eastern politician. The engaging cast (including Chris Sarandon, Richard Romanus and Ed Begley Jr) struggles valiantly with an uneven script from writer Buck Henry, but director Herbert Ross puts sufficient energy into his task to paper over the creative cracks. Contains violence and swearing. ⌨

Goldie Hawn *Sunny Davis* • Chris Sarandon *Michael Ransome* • Richard Romanus *Emir of Ohtar* • Andre Gregory *Nawaf Al Kabeer* • Gail Strickland *Mrs St John* • Cliff De Young *Hilley* • Keith Szarabajka *Crowe* • Ed Begley Jr *Hassler* ■ *Dir* Herbert Ross • *Scr* Buck Henry, from a story by Charles Shyer, Nancy Meyers, Harvey Miller

The Proud and Profane ★★
Second World War romance
1956 · US · BW · 111mins

You have to hand it to William Holden – a great actor who made a lot of bad films because he liked travelling the world, he liked drinking all over the world, and he liked women to share it all with him. So this movie finds him in New Caledonia in the south Pacific – well, they didn't actually go there, they went to the Virgin Islands which is almost as good. It's a war melodrama, with Holden as an officer who romances war widow Deborah Kerr, who becomes pregnant and then finds out Holden's married – a sort of "From Here to Maternity". Drivel, but Holden probably had a great time when he wasn't working.

William Holden (1) *Lieutenant Colonel Colin Black* • Deborah Kerr *Lee Ashley* • Thelma Ritter *Kate Connors* • Dewey Martin *Eddie Wodcik* • William Redfield *Chaplain Holmes* • Ross Bagdasarian *Louie* • Adam Williams *Eustace Press* • Marion Ross *Joan* ■ *Dir* George Seaton • *Scr* George Seaton, from the novel *The Magnificent Bastards* by Lucy Herndon Crockett

The Proud and the Damned ★★
Western action adventure
1972 · US · Colour · 94mins

A routine western, differentiated from a thousand others only by its use of slightly more exotic locales than usual. The plot centres on a wild bunch of mercenaries and ex-Civil War soldiers who get caught up in a revolution while way south of the border, down Latin America way. Familiar faces include Chuck Connors and Cesar Romero, the Joker in the *Batman* TV show. The action sequences are OK, but dire dialogue and dead direction speedily consign the film to the celluloid equivalent of Boot Hill.

Chuck Connors *Will* • Aron Kincaid *Ike* • Cesar Romero *Alcalde* • José Greco *Ramon* • Henry Capps *Hank* • Peter Ford *Billy* ■ *Dir/Scr* Ferde Grofe Jr

The Proud Ones ★★★
Drama   1953 · Fr/Mex · BW · mins

It's difficult to accept that this simmering Mexican melodrama was adapted from the Jean-Paul Sartre novel, *L'Amour Redempteur*. But, while it's deficient in the psychological department, Yves Allégret's tale of damaged souls and redemption through love and sacrifice has many

other things going for it, not least the atmospheric photography of Alex Phillips, who captures the stifling desperation of a small coastal town at the height of a meningitis epidemic. Michèle Morgan has rarely combined vulnerability and eroticism to better effect, as the stranded widow who rouses doctor Gérard Philipe from an alcoholic haze to recover his self-esteem and win her heart. French dialogue dubbed into English.

Michèle Morgan *Nellie* • Gérard Philipe *Georges* • Carlos Moctezuma *Doctor* • Victor Manuel Mendoza *Don Rodrigo* • Michèle Cordoue *Anna* • Andri Toffil *Tom* ■ *Dir* Yves Allégret • *Scr* Jean Aurenche, Yves Allégret, from the novel *L'Amour Redempteur* by Jean-Paul Sartre • *Cinematographer* Alex Phillips

The Proud Ones ★★★ U

Western 1956 · US · Colour · 94mins

Robert Ryan, so good at being bad, was in heroic mould for this minor-league western with some high-impact moments. As a sheriff, hampered by disability but psyching himself up for a showdown with a mixed bag of outlaws, his vulnerability is as credible as his courage. It's his performance that makes this modest tale better than average in the suspense stakes. Director Robert D Webb worked with most of the big names of the fifties without achieving premiere league status.

Robert Ryan *Marshal Cass Silver* • Virginia Mayo *Sally Kane* • Jeffrey Hunter *Thad Anderson* • Robert Middleton *Honest John Barrett* • Walter Brennan *Jake* • Arthur O'Connell *Jim Dexter* ■ *Dir* Robert D Webb • *Scr* Edmund H North, Joseph Petracca, from the novel *The Proud Ones* by Verne Athanas

The Proud Rebel ★★★★ U

Western 1958 · US · Colour · 99mins

Alan Ladd's finest achievement from the years following *Shane* carries echoes of that film, particularly in the prominence of a small boy. Ladd plays father to his own son, David, who's mute since witnessing his mother's death in the Civil War. It's about the search for a cure, the boy's beloved dog, Olivia de Havilland's kindly spinster farmer, and an evil brood of sheepherders that includes a young Harry Dean Stanton. Exquisitely photographed in burnished Technicolor, beautifully acted (with no-nonsense performances by Cecil Kellaway and Henry Hull) and directed with quiet mastery by Michael Curtiz, it's that rare breed of family film which should entrance kids and adults alike. [video]

Alan Ladd *John Chandler* • Olivia de Havilland *Linnett Moore* • Dean Jagger *Harry Burleigh* • David Ladd *David Chandler* • Cecil Kellaway *Dr Enos Davis* • James Westerfield *Birm Bates* • Henry Hull *Judge Morley* • Dean Stanton [Harry Dean Stanton] *Jeb Burleigh* • Thomas Pittman [Tom Pittman] *Tom Burleigh* • Eli Mintz *Gorman* ■ *Dir* Michael Curtiz • *Scr* Joe Petracca, Lillie Hayward, from the story *Journal of Linnett Moore* by James Edward Grant • *Cinematographer* Ted McCord

The Proud Valley ★★

Drama 1940 · UK · BW · 76mins

This rather dated parable on the need for community unity in the face of wartime tragedy was one of six films Paul Robeson made in Britain, and it gave him the rare opportunity to escape from typecasting as a tribal African. However, his majestic presence is the only thing not to ring true in this well-crafted tale about a mining disaster in a small Welsh village, as he is more prone to melodrama than the solid supporting cast. Director Pen Tennyson achieves the realistic atmosphere that would characterise many later British postwar films, although, sadly, he was killed in action the following year.

Paul Robeson *David Goliath* • Edward Chapman *Dick Parry* • Simon Lack *Emlyn Parry* • Rachel Thomas *Mrs Parry* • Dilys Thomas *Dilys* • Edward Rigby *Bert Rigby* ■ *Dir* Penrose Tennyson [Pen Tennyson] • *Scr* Roland Pertwee, Louis Goulding, Jack Jones, Penrose Tennyson, from a story by Herbert Marshall, Alfredda Brilliant

Providence ★★★★★ 15

Drama 1977 · Fr/Swi · Colour · 102mins

Alain Resnais' s English-language debut was voted the film of the seventies by an international panel of film-makers and critics. As ever playing intricate games with time and memory, the director has constructed a typically complex film that leaves you unsure whether the action is a flashback to a real event or a figment of the imagination of dying novelist John Gielgud. Intensifying the illusion, David Mercer's script is a perfect pastiche of the kind of florid dialogue found in purple fiction. Gielgud is outstanding, but Dirk Bogarde and Ellen Burstyn also give fine performances. Wonderful cinema from a true master of the art. Contains swearing. [video]

John Gielgud *Clive Langham* • Dirk Bogarde *Claude Langham* • Ellen Burstyn *Sonia Langham* • David Warner *Kevin Woodford* • Elaine Stritch *Helen Weiner/Molly Langham* • Denis Lawson *Dave Woodford* • Cyril Luckham *Dr Mark Eddington* ■ *Dir* Alain Resnais • *Scr* David Mercer • *Music* Miklos Rozsa

The Prowler ★★★ U

Film noir 1951 · US · BW · 92mins

While investigating a prowler in the neighbourhood, embittered policeman Van Heflin meets Evelyn Keyes whose sterile husband Emerson Treacy is a night-duty disc jockey. Cop and wife then embark on an affair that leads to murder. A taut, bleak *film noir*, well-handled by director Joseph Losey, and by the cast, notably Van Heflin. The film owes much to earlier, rather more memorable pieces such as *The Postman Always Rings Twice* and *Double Indemnity*, and doesn't draw much sympathy for its protagonists, but it's still a good watch. [video]

Van Heflin *Webb Garwood* • Evelyn Keyes *Susan Gilvray* • John Maxwell *Bud Crocker* • Katherine Warren *Mrs Crocker* • Emerson Treacy *William Gilvray* • Madge Blake *Martha Gilvray* ■ *Dir* Joseph Losey • *Scr* Dalton Trumbo, Hugo Butler, from a story by Robert Thoren, from a story by Hans Wilhelm

Prudence and the Pill ★★ 15

Comedy 1968 · UK · Colour · 88mins

David Niven and Deborah Kerr's marriage has degenerated into separate bedrooms and lovers. When their niece Judy Geeson steals her mother Joyce Redman's contraceptive pills, substituting aspirin, and Redman gets pregnant, Niven tries the same trick on Kerr, hoping she'll get pregnant by lover Keith Michell and give him grounds for divorce. Topical at the time with the coming of the pill, this British-made farce in which everybody winds up pregnant after a frenzy of pill-switching, was directed by Ronald Neame (taking over from Fielder Cook). The polished expertise of Niven and Kerr more or less holds this witless farrago together, providing a few laughs and a hint of a moral message about promiscuity. [video]

Deborah Kerr *Prudence Hardcastle* • David Niven *Gerald Hardcastle* • Robert Coote *Henry Hardcastle* • Irina Demick *Elizabeth* • Joyce Redman *Grace Hardcastle* • Judy Geeson *Geraldine Hardcastle* • Keith Michell *Dr Alan Hewitt* • Edith Evans *Lady Roberta Bates* ■ *Dir* Fielder Cook, Ronald Neame • *Scr* Hugh Mills, from his novel

Psych-Out ★★ 18

Drama 1968 · US · Colour · 85mins

After Jack Nicholson wrote the pro-LSD movie *The Trip*, he appeared in this other druggie epic, set in San Francisco's Haight-Ashbury district where deaf girl Susan Strasberg searches for her freaked-out brother, Bruce Dern, who think's he's Jesus Christ. As a relic of the flower power era, this takes some beating – and some watching, too – but Nicholson completists should get a buzz from seeing him as a rock musician and as the film's romantic lead. Also included are music from the Strawberry Alarm Clock, if that turns you on, and a *2001*-style acid trip to nowhere. [video]

Susan Strasberg *Jennie* • Dean Stockwell *Dave* • Jack Nicholson *Stoney* • Bruce Dern *Steve* • Adam Roarke *Ben* • Max Julien *Elwood* • Henry Jaglom *Warren* • IJ Jefferson *Pandora* ■ *Dir* Richard Rush • *Scr* E Hunter Willett [Betty Tusher], Betty Ulius, from a story by E Hunter Willett [Betty Tusher]

Psyche '59 ★★

Drama 1964 · UK · BW · 94mins

An intriguing though slightly over-the-top melodrama about the blind wife (Patricia Neal) of a businessman, who is forced to see (yes, her illness is psychosomatic) when her sister (Samantha Eggar), fresh from a divorce, comes to stay. You've seen it all before, and the cod psychology may be a bit irritating, but the cast is strong and the movie is glossily photographed.

Curt Jurgens *Eric Crawford* • Patricia Neal *Allison Crawford* • Samantha Eggar *Robin* • Ian Bannen *Paul* • Beatrix Lehmann *Mrs Crawford* • Elspeth March *Mme Valadier* • Sandra Lee *Susan* ■ *Dir* Alexander Singer • *Scr* Julian Halevy [Julian Zimet], from the novel _*Psyché 58,by Francoise des Ligneris*

Psychic Killer ★★ 18

Horror thriller 1975 · US · Colour · 85mins

This sensationalist low-budget thriller rips off *Psycho* so blatantly it's surprising that Hitchcock never sued. We have the gothic house, the mummy's boy, even a murder in a shower. Its story tells of a psychiatrist who unwittingly secures the release of a mental patient, who then uses psychic powers to revenge himself against those who wronged him in the past. Director Ray Danton, perhaps best known for his acting career, crudely mixes comedy with scenes of brutal murder, including a butcher put through his own meat grinder. Jim Hutton makes for a chilling killer, displaying both unsettling charm and plausible insanity. [video]

Paul Burke *Detective Morgan* • Jim Hutton *Arnold* • Julie Adams *Laura* • Nehemiah Persoff *Dr Gubner* • Neville Brand *Lemonowski* • Aldo Ray *Anderson* • Stack Pierce *Emilio* • Whit Bissell *Dr Taylor* • Della Reese *Mrs Gibson* ■ *Dir* Ray Danton • *Scr* Ray Danton, Greydon Clark, Mike Angel

Psycho ★★★★★ 15

Classic black comedy horror
1960 · US · BW · 108mins

The most talked about and shocked about horror thriller of all time. Who could ever get tired of checking into the Bates motel to witness Janet Leigh under the shower in the most appallingly brilliant movie murder in cinema history? The model for practically every terror vision made in the last 30 years, *Psycho* is the best-remembered movie of one of the world's best-known directors and Alfred Hitchcock made it as a joke! It typecast Anthony Perkins for ever as the shy Norman Bates and will always remain the ultimate study in scary schizophrenia. [video] DVD

Anthony Perkins *Norman Bates* • Janet Leigh *Marion Crane* • Vera Miles *Lila Crane* • John Gavin *Sam Loomis* • Martin Balsam *Milton Arbogast* • John McIntire *Sheriff Chambers* • Simon Oakland *Dr Richmond* ■ *Dir* Alfred Hitchcock • *Scr* Joseph Stefano, from the novel by Robert Bloch • *Cinematographer* John L Russell • *Music* Bernard Herrmann • *Editor* George Tomasini

Psycho ★ 15

Horror thriller 1998 · US · Colour · 99mins

Gus Van Sant must have been a little mad when he agreed to direct this near word-for-word, shot-for-shot impersonation of Hitchcock's most celebrated movie. It simply doesn't work, because every major character is horribly miscast – Anne Heche plays Marion Crane as a kooky cutie and Vince Vaughn's Norman is an effeminate hunk. Despite the hilarious modern references (Julianne Moore's dangling earphones are a hoot), the pointlessness of watching a stagey, badly-acted replica of one of cinema's true masterpieces cannot be ignored, and you have a film whose sole merit is being the strangest remake in cinema history. Contains violence and sex scenes. [video] DVD

Vince Vaughn *Norman Bates* • Anne Heche *Marion Crane* • Julianne Moore *Lila Crane* • Viggo Mortensen *Sam Loomis* • William H Macy *Milton Arbogast* • Robert Forster *Dr Simon* • Philip Baker Hall *Sheriff Chambers* • Anne Haney *Mrs Chambers* • Chad Everett *Tom Cassidy* ■ *Dir* Gus Van Sant • *Scr* Joseph Stefano, from the 1960 film

Psycho II ★★★ 18

Horror thriller 1983 · US · Colour · 107mins

Two decades after the motel murders, Norman Bates is released from the asylum and returns to the scene of his crimes but has "Mother" come too? Of course, this isn't Hitchcock, but it's a highly credible, nicely creepy and well-paced sequel, and Anthony Perkins

reprises his most famous role with no visible signs of ennui. There are several other enjoyable and gritty performances, most notably from original cast member Vera Miles, still seeking vengeance for her sister's demise in the first film, and Dennis Franz as the motel manager whose entrepreneurial skills are not appreciated by Mr Bates. Contains violence, swearing and nudity. ▣

Anthony Perkins *Norman Bates* • Vera Miles *Lila Loomis* • Meg Tilly *Mary* • Robert Loggia *Dr Raymond* • Dennis Franz *Toomey* • Hugh Gillin *Sheriff Hunt* • Claudia Bryar *Mrs Spool* ■ *Dir* Richard Franklin • *Scr* Tom Holland, from characters created by Robert Bloch

Psycho III ★★ 🔞
Horror 1986 · US · Colour · 88mins

Anthony Perkins stars in and directs a rather mean-spirited second sequel to the Hitchcock classic in which Norman falls in love with a suicidal nun, poignantly played by Diana Scarwid. Filled with overwrought in-jokes (the *Vertigo*-influenced opening), flashbacks to the original film (Janet Leigh's face turning into Scarwid's) and copious blood-letting (the studio added extra gore), Perkins goes for the jugular in a melodramatic, somewhat vulgar, way with the accent on sleazy humour and viciousness. Sadly, Perkins never matches the cleverer *Psycho II* for whodunit skilfulness, as he gamely stumbles on without a Hitch. Contains swearing and violence. ▣

Anthony Perkins *Norman Bates* • Diana Scarwid *Maureen Coyle* • Jeff Fahey *Duane Duke* • Roberta Maxwell *Tracy Venable* • Hugh Gillin *Sheriff Hunt* • Lee Garlington *Myrna* • Robert Alan Browne *Statler* ■ *Dir* Anthony Perkins • *Scr* Charles Edward Pogue, from characters created by Robert Bloch

Psycho IV: the Beginning ★★ 🔞
Horror 1990 · US · Colour · 92mins

The Norman Bates saga came to an end in this sorry made-for-TV finale. It's a shame because the plot at least offers up an intriguing twist: as the now rehabilitated Norman (Anthony Perkins, again excellent) discusses his fears over a radio phone-in, we flash back to the young Norman (played here by *ET's* Henry Thomas) and his troubled relationship with his mother. However, this is sloppily executed and the climax is just plain silly. Contains violence and nudity. ▣

Anthony Perkins *Norman Bates* • Henry Thomas *Young Norman* • Olivia Hussey *Norma Bates* • CCH Pounder *Fran Ambrose* • Warren Frost *Dr Leo Richmond* • Donna Mitchell *Connie Bates* • Thomas Schuster [Tom Schuster] *Chet Rudolph* ■ *Dir* Mick Garris • *Scr* Joseph Stefano, from characters created by Robert Bloch

Psychomania ★★
Murder mystery 1964 · US · BW · 93mins

Not, unfortunately, the delirious zombie biker flick of 1972 starring George Sanders and Beryl Reid, but an altogether more conventional affair. Lee Philips is an ex-serviceman and painter of nude women who becomes prime suspect in a serial murder case involving college girls. With the help of lawyer James Farentino, he attempts to clear his name.

Lee Philips *Elliot Freeman* • Shepperd Strudwick *Adrian Benedict* • Jean Hale *Carol Bishop* • Lorraine Rogers *Alice St Clair* • Margot Hartman *Lynn Freeman* • Kaye Elhardt *Dolores Martello* • James Farentino *Charlie Perone* • Richard Van Patten [Dick Van Patten] *Palmer* • Sylvia Miles *Silvia* ■ *Dir* Richard Hilliard [Richard L Hilliard] • *Scr* Robin MIller

Psychomania ★★★
Horror 1972 · UK · Colour · 90mins

A British horror cheapie that is so ridiculous it works. For much of the time this psychedelic zombie biker frightener is utter drivel, but director Don Sharp throws in some cracking scenes, notably the one in which leader of the gang Nicky Henson rises from the grave, bike and all. Henson has a hoot of a time as an Angel from Hell, and he is superbly supported by Beryl Reid as his devil-worshipping mum and George Sanders (alternately fighting off yawns, knowing winks and blushes) as her ghoulish butler. Sanders committed suicide shortly after this film was made.

Nicky Henson *Tom Latham* • Beryl Reid *Mrs Latham* • George Sanders *Shadwell* • Mary Larkin *Abby* • Roy Holder *Bertram* • Robert Hardy *Chief Inspector Hesseltine* • Patrick Holt *Sergeant* • Denis Gilmore *Hatchet* ■ *Dir* Don Sharp • *Scr* Arnaud D'Usseau

The Psychopath ★ 🔞
Horror thriller 1966 · UK · Colour · 90mins

Hammer's main rival, Amicus, produced some highly original shockers but, despite a screenplay by Robert Bloch, author of *Psycho*, this isn't one of them. Once again, a psychopath murders his enemies one by one, leaving a model of the victim next to each body, and it doesn't take much imagination to work out who the culprit is. Talented horror director Freddie Francis rather uncharacteristically creates little atmosphere and also allows Margaret Johnston to overplay almost to the point of burlesque. ▣

Patrick Wymark *Inspector Holloway* • Margaret Johnston *Mrs Von Sturm* • John Standing *Mark Von Sturm* • Alexander Knox *Frank Saville* • Judy Huxtable *Louise Saville* ■ *Dir* Freddie Francis • *Scr* Robert Bloch

P'Tang, Yang, Kipperbang ★★★★ 🅿🅶
Comedy 1982 · UK · Colour · 76mins

This surreal phrase chanted by 14-year-old schoolboys illustrates the gentle, oddball comedy of this story by TV playwright Jack Rosenthal. Alan (John Albasiny) has a crush on the prettiest girl in class (Abigail Cruttenden) but a host of obstacles are put in the way of his declaration of passion. Directed by Michael Apted, it's a wry and highly comic look at teenage lust with some splendid performances – especially Alison Steadman as a randy teacher – to round out a warm entertainment.

John Albasiny *Alan Duckworth* • Abigail Cruttenden *Ann* • Maurice Dee *Geoffrey* • Alison Steadman *Estelle Loup* • Mark Brailsford *Abbo* • Chris Karallis *Shaz* • Frances Ruffelle *Eunice* • Robert Urquhart *Headmaster* ■ *Dir* Michael Apted • *Scr* Jack Rosenthal

Pterodactyl Woman from Beverly Hills ★
Comedy 1996 · US · Colour · 99mins

''A perfect Beverly Hills housewife by day – a prehistoric flying reptile by night'', ran the ad line, which just about sums up the plot of this miserably unfunny comedy. Hovering somewhere between a satire of affluent American suburbia and a plain old monster movie spoof, it fails at both. Beverly D'Angelo plugs away gamely in the lead role but to little effect, hampered as she is by pricelessly naff dialogue and cheesy effects. For some unexplained reason Barry Humphries, in his Dame Edna Everage persona, crops up during a scene in a supermarket.

Beverly D'Angelo *Pixie Chandler* • Brad Wilson *Dick Chandler* • Brion James *Salvador Dali/Sam* • Barry Humphries *Bert/Lady shopper/manager* • Moon Zappa *Susie* • Aron Eisenberg *Tommy Chandler* • Sharon Martin *Jenny Chandler* ■ *Dir/Scr* Philippe Mora

Puberty Blues ★★ 🔞
Drama 1981 · Ausl · Colour · 82mins

Director Bruce Beresford's chequered career has included wonderful pieces such as *Driving Miss Daisy* and *Breaker Morant*, but also the less widely admired *King David*. Here two young Aussie women (Nell Schofield and Jad Capelja) try to break into the male bastion of the surfing set, experiencing all the frustrations and rejections that you'd expect. It's sensitively handled, if ultimately a little weak. Not one of Beresford's finest moments by any means. ▣

Nell Schofield *Debbie Vickers* • Jad Capelja *Sue Knight* • Geoff Rhoe *Garry* • Tony Hughes *Danny* • Sandy Paul *Tracy* ■ *Dir* Bruce Beresford • *Scr* Margaret Kelly, from the novel by Kathy Lette, Gabrielle Carey

Public Access ★★★★ 🔞
Thriller 1993 · US · Colour · 85mins

An intriguing thriller from Bryan Singer, who went on to make *The Usual Suspects*. Clean-cut Ron Marquette starts a show on public access cable TV in the small town of Brewster. Marquette encourages his viewers to call in and sound off about the problems in their town, stirring up antipathy. But what is his motive for getting people to reveal their grievances? This was Singer's first feature film as writer/director, and you can already see his propensity for camera tricks and intelligent, psychologically rich scripts. Ron Marquette is arresting as the mild-mannered Whiley and probably had an interesting career in front of him, but he committed suicide in 1995. ▣

Ron Marquette *Whiley Pritcher* • Dina Brooks *Rachel* • Burt Williams *Bob Hodges* • Larry Maxwell *Jeff Abernathy* • Charles Kavanaugh *Mayor Breyer* • Brandon Boyce *Kevin Havey* ■ *Dir* Bryan Singer • *Scr* Christopher McQuarrie, Michael Feit Dugan, Bryan Singer

The Public Enemy ★★★★★ 🅿🅶
Classic crime drama 1931 · US · BW · 84mins

The film that made James Cagney the world's favourite bootlegger. But it was not his brutal bootlegging methods, his machine-gun delivery of threats and wisecracks or his ruthless rubbing out of his enemies that secured his tough-guy image, but the shoving of a grapefruit into moll Mae Clarke's face. Cagney had originally been slated for the best-friend role (retiringly played by Edward Woods) and makes the most of his chance, giving a performance of raw power. Action expert William A Wellman keeps the story racing along at the speed of a getaway car, setting a style for Warner Bros (fast pace, crackling dialogue, unsentimental scripting and playing) and also glamorising the gangster and inadvertently helping to pave the way to the Hays Code and film censorship. ▣

James Cagney *Tom Powers* • Jean Harlow *Gwen Allen* • Edward Woods *Matt Doyle* • Joan Blondell *Mamie* • Beryl Mercer *Ma Powers* • Donald Cook *Mike Powers* • Mae Clarke *Kitty* • Mia Marvin *Jane* • Leslie Fenton *"Nails" Nathan* • Robert Emmett O'Connor *Paddy Ryan* ■ *Dir* William A Wellman • *Scr* Kubec Glasmon, John Bright, Harvey Thew, from the story *Beer and Blood* by John Bright, Kubec Glasmon

The Public Enemy #1 ★★★ 🔞
Action crime drama 1995 · US · Colour · 87mins

Theresa Russell is the real star in this retelling of the story of the Barker clan, including the infamous Ma Barker, who led her four sons on one of the bloodiest bank robbery campaigns in history. Several heartfelt performances make for an above average gangster-versus-FBI epic, replete with gun battles and epithets growled through gritted teeth. It's hard not to root for Ma and her boys, but don't expect a happy ending. ▣

Theresa Russell *Kate "Ma" Barker* • Alyssa Milano *Amaryllis* • Joseph Lindsey *Herman Barker* • James Marsden *Doc Barker* • Joseph Dain *Lloyd Barker* • Gavin Harrison *Freddie Barker* • Eric Roberts *Arthur Dunlop* ■ *Dir* Mark L Lester • *Scr* C Courtney Joyner

The Public Eye ★★★ 🔞
Crime drama 1992 · US · Colour and BW · 94mins

A rather downbeat tale of a forties' tabloid crime photographer (Joe Pesci) who secretly dreams of being recognised as an artist. When wealthy widow Barbara Hershey offers to help him create a book of his photographs in return for some information, he is pulled into her world which involves a war between opposing Mob families. Although this looks great – dark shadows and moody lighting aplenty – the *film noir* style needs a stronger script, and the final product, clearly inspired by real-life photographer Weegee, is rather tedious. It's still worth watching, though, for its breathtakingly beautiful visual impact alone. Contains swearing. ▣

Joe Pesci *Leon Bernstein* • Barbara Hershey *Kay Levitz* • Stanley Tucci *Sal Minetto* • Jerry Adler *Arthur Nabler* • Jared Harris *Danny the doorman* • Gerry Becker *Conklin* • Richard Riehle *Officer O'Brien* ■ *Dir/Scr* Howard Franklin • *Cinematographer* Peter Suschitzky

Public Hero No 1 ★★

Crime drama   1935 · US · BW · 88mins

Rapped over the knuckles for glorifying the American gangster, Hollywood obligingly promoted the forces of law and order – public heroes rather than public enemies. They're represented here by G-man Chester Morris who is planted in a cell with gangster Joseph Calleia and escapes with him to help bring his gang to justice. The final shooting in a variety theatre recalls the real-life end of the notorious John Dillinger. This minor film has a major plot contrivance introducing the always delightful Jean Arthur as the gangster's sister. It gives lead billing to Lionel Barrymore, heavy going as ever in the role of an alcoholic doctor.

Lionel Barrymore *Dr Josiah Glass* • Chester Morris *Jeff Crane* • Jean Arthur *Theresa O'Reilly* • Paul Kelly *Duff* • Lewis Stone *Warden Alcott* • Joseph Calleia *Sonny Black* • Walter Brennan *Farmer* ■ *Dir* J Walter Ruben • *Scr* Wells Root, from a story by J Walter Ruben, fWells Root

Pucker Up and Bark Like a Dog ★

Romantic comedy
1989 · US · Colour · 94mins

Robert Culp and Paul Bartel make appearances in this romantic comedy about a crushingly shy and isolated artist living in LA who finds love and with it the confidence to exhibit his work. It tries to be offbeat but ends up being only slightly less daft than its name.

Jonathan Gries *Max* • Lisa Zane *Taylor* • Robert Culp *Gregor* • Sal Lopez *Carlos* • Phyllis Diller *Mrs Frasco* • Wendy O Williams *Butch* • Paul Bartel *Director* ■ *Dir* Paul S Parco • *Scr* Mel Green, Gary Larimore, Jude Jansen, Walter Josten, Patricia Bando Josten

Puerto Escondido ★★★ 15

Comedy   1992 · It · Colour · 106mins

Gabriele Salvatores's follow-up to the Oscar-winning *Mediterraneo* was coolly received by the critics, who couldn't believe that the director capable of such quiet observation could now produce a work of such broad comedy and cack-handedness.However, Diego Abatantuono turns in a splendid performance as the Milan bankteller who is shot during a robbery by deranged police commissioner Renato Carpentieri and hides out in a Mexican backwater to avoid the corrupt copper's wrath. However, things are no better there, as he finds himself caught up in the hopeless schemes of fellow exiles Claudio Bisio and Valeria Golino. Slow in places, manic in others, but mostly entertaining. In Italian with English subtitles. ▭

Diego Abatantuono *Mario* • Valeria Golino *Anita* • Claudio Bisio *Alex* • Renato Carpentieri *Commissario Viola* • Antonio Catania *Di Gennaro* ■ *Dir* Gabriele Salvatores • *Scr* Enzo Monteleone, Diego Abatantuono, Gabriele Salvatores, from a novel by Pino Cacucci

Pufnstuf ★★ U

Fantasy   1970 · US · Colour · 94mins

An unoriginal, uninspired children's musical about the adventures of a young boy, led by his talking flute to a land where he encounters creatures, including a dragon and several witches. Based on an US TV series, it stars Jack Wild, a bunch of life-size puppets and Martha Raye as the leader of a witches' convention. Highlight of a forgettable score is Mama Cass, another witch, belting out a number called *Different*. OK entertainment for the youngest children.

Jack Wild *Jimmy* • Billie Hayes *Witchiepoo* • Martha Raye *Boss Witch* • "Mama" Cass Elliot *Witch Hazel* • Billy Barty *Googy Gopher* ■ *Dir* Hollingsworth Morse • *Scr* John Fenton Murray, Si Rose

Pull My Daisy ★★★★

Experimental drama 1959 · US · BW · 27mins

Directed by Alfred Leslie and by Robert Frank, the influential Swiss photographer who caught mid-century Americana when it wasn't yet looking, this delightful 27-minute short is the only film that the Beat writers of the 1950's actually created themselves. Largely a spontaneous experiment, it hovers around a slim storyline that's based on an incident in the life of Neal Cassady and his wife, when they invited a respectable neighbourhood bishop over for dinner with their unrespectable Beat friends, among them poets Allen Ginsberg, Gregory Corso and artist Larry Rivers. With the daddy of them all, Jack Kerouac, providing voice-over, it offers a fascinating glimpse into the lives of the major Beat writers, when they were still capable of just having fun.

Allen Ginsberg *Allen* • Gregory Corso *Gregory* • Peter Orlovsky *Peter* • Larry Rivers *Milo* • Delphine Seyrig *Milo's wife* • David Amram *Mez McGillicuddy* • Jack Kerouac *Narrator* ■ *Dir* Alfred Leslie, Robert Frank • *Scr* Jack Kerouac

Pulp ★★★

Comedy thriller 1972 · UK · Colour · 97mins

One of the more interesting teams in the British post-New Wave period was that of the three Michaels – star Caine, writer/director Hodges, producer Klinger – who failed to hit their former *Get Carter* pay dirt with this, their second outing. Nevertheless, the sheer knowing coolness of this bizarre original bears watching. The central theme involving the hiring of a ghostwriter is explored with wit and style, as Hodges deploys his camera cleverly through Maltese locations, and the uncompromising plot makes excellent use of Hollywood icons Mickey Rooney and Lizabeth Scott. Contains violence and swearing.

Michael Caine *Mickey King* • Mickey Rooney *Preston Gilbert* • Lionel Stander *Ben Dinuccio* • Lizabeth Scott *Princess Betty Cippola* • Nadia Cassini *Liz Adams* • Al Lettieri *Miller* • Dennis Price *Mysterious Englishman* ■ *Dir* Michael Hodges [Mike Hodges] • *Scr* Michael Hodges [Mike Hodges]

Pulp Fiction ★★★★★ 18

Crime drama   1994 · US · Colour · 147mins

While not as abrasive or compelling as *Reservoir Dogs*, Quentin Tarantino's follow-up not only confirmed his genius for writing hard-boiled comic dialogue, but also demonstrated a control over a wealth of characters and crossplots that was simply astonishing for a film-maker still, essentially, in the process of learning his trade. The picture went on to scoop the Palme d'Or at the Cannes film festival and win Oscars for Tarantino and his co-writer Roger Avary. Scorching though the writing is, it needed a high-calibre cast to carry it off. Uma Thurman, Bruce Willis, Maria de Medeiros and Christopher Walken are excellent, but the revitalised John Travolta and the then largely unknown Samuel L Jackson are unforgettable. As much pop as pulp, this is exhilarating stuff and clearly one of the best films of the nineties. Contains violence, swearing, sex scenes, drug abuse and nudity. ▭ *DVD*

John Travolta *Vincent Vega* • Samuel L Jackson *Jules Winnfield* • Uma Thurman *Mia Wallace* • Harvey Keitel *The Wolf* • Tim Roth *Pumpkin* • Amanda Plummer *Honey Bunny* • Maria de Medeiros *Fabienne* • Ving Rhames *Marsellus Wallace* • Eric Stoltz *Lance* • Rosanna Arquette *Jody* • Christopher Walken *Captain Koons* • Bruce Willis *Butch Coolidge* • Quentin Tarantino *Jimmie* • Steve Buscemi *Surly Buddy Holly Waiter* • Stephen Hibbert *The Gimp* • Peter Greene *Zed* ■ *Dir* Quentin Tarantino • *Scr* Quentin Tarantino, Roger Avary, from their stories • *Cinematographer* Andrzej Sekula

Pulse ★★★ 18

Science-fiction horror
1988 · US · Colour · 86mins

A quirky little horror tale that makes up for what it lacks in blood and gore with a neat line in suspense. Cliff De Young is the puzzled suburbanite who can't work out why all the appliances in the house are beginning to turn on their owners. Writer/director Paul Golding pokes some fun at life in the 'burbs, and makes ingenious use of the rogue electrical machines. ▭

Cliff De Young *Bill* • Roxanne Hart *Ellen* • Joey Lawrence *David* • Matthew Lawrence *Stevie* • Charles Tyner *Old Man* ■ *Dir/Scr* Paul Golding

Pummaro ★★★

Drama   1990 · It · Colour · 102mins

Actor Michele Placido made his directorial debut with this heartfelt drama in which a young Ghanaian comes to Naples in search of his brother. In the course of his travels, he witnesses racial prejudice, the exploitation of immigrant labour, the threat of organised crime and the contrasts between the two Italys – the impoverished south and the affluent north. In painting this picture of a nation coming to terms with its disparate ethnic make-up, Placido offers no easy answers and is careful to avoid sensationalism, sticking to everyday occurrences that would pass unnoticed by anyone other than an outsider. In Italian with English subtitles..

Thywill Ak Amenya *Kua Ku* • Pamela Villoresi *Eleonora* • Jacqueline Williams *Nanou* • Gerardo Scala *Professor* ■ *Dir* Michele Placido • *Scr* Sandro Petraglia, Stefano Rulli, Michele Placido, Vilko Filac

Pump Up the Volume ★★★ 15

Drama   1990 · US · Colour · 97mins

Christian Slater has been involved in some of the more thought-provoking teen movies to venture out of Hollywood – most notably the deliciously black *Heathers* – and he hardly puts a foot wrong here. He plays a quiet high-school student who metamorphoses into an anarchic radio shock jock, who enrages the authorities but becomes a cult hero to his fellow students. Director Allan Moyle shows a sensitive feel for adolescent angst, Samantha Mathis is impressive in an early role and the music is a cut above the FM pap that normally inhabits American teen movies. Contains swearing, drug abuse and nudity.

Christian Slater *Mark Hunter* • Samantha Mathis *Nora Diniro* • Ellen Greene *Jan Emerson* • Scott Paulin *Brian Hunter* • Cheryl Pollak *Paige* • Andy Romano *Murdock* • Mimi Kennedy *Marta Hunter* ■ *Dir/Scr* Allan Moyle

Pumping Iron ★★★★ PG

Documentary   1976 · US · Colour · 81mins

The real centre of attention in this entertaining tour of the body building world is an Austrian man-mountain by the name of Arnold Schwarzenegger, who is aiming to retain his Mr Olympia title. Big Arnie's personality is as overdeveloped as any of the pecs, biceps and triceps on display here, and whether he's explaining the enormous sexual pleasure he gets from lifting weights or psyching-out an opponent over breakfast, it's clear that you're witnessing a star in the making. And you'll never guess who wins! ▭

Charles Gaines *Narrator* ■ *Dir* George Butler, Robert Fiore • *Scr* George Butler, from the non-fiction book by Charles Gaines, George Butler

Pumping Iron II: the Women ★★★★ PG

Documentary   1984 · US · Colour · 102mins

The sequel to the film that made Arnold Schwarzenegger a star, this may be a little more contrived than some fly-on-the-wall documentaries, but it's still hugely entertaining and highly revealing of how so many men view the female form. Concentrating on the 1983 Caesar's Cup contest, director George Butler not only sets out to justify the sport of women's bodybuilding, but also proves that most of the competitors can intellectually knock spots off he-men and beauty queens alike. The Australian Bev Francis is the star of the show, even though the great sensation is caused by the better-known ex-champion Rachel McLish. ▭

Dir George Butler • *Scr* Charles Gaines, George Butler, from their book *Pumping Iron II: the Unprecedented Woman*

The Pumpkin Eater ★★★★

Drama   1964 · UK · BW · 119mins

A study of a marriage, based on Penelope Mortimer's novel, with Anne Bancroft as the mother of several screaming brats and the wife of adulterous screenwriter husband Peter Finch. She suffers a nervous collapse in Harrods, undergoes psychoanalysis, then a hysterectomy. Bancroft and Finch deliver blockbuster performances and the supporting cast is equally impressive – from James Mason as a boorish party guest and Maggie Smith

as one of Finch's lovers. There's also beautifully modulated direction from Jack Clayton but scriptwriter Harold Pinter's acidulated signature is all over it – not to mention the influence of Michelangelo Antonioni – for this British movie is so arty and so alienating it almost needs subtitles.

Anne Bancroft *Jo Armitage* • Peter Finch *Jake Armitage* • James Mason *Bob Conway* • Cedric Hardwicke *Mr James, Jo's father* • Richard Johnson *Giles* • Maggie Smith *Philpot* • Eric Porter *Psychiatrist* • Rosalind Atkinson *Mrs James, Jo's mother* ■ *Dir* Jack Clayton • *Scr* Harold Pinter, from the novel by Penelope Mortimer

The Punch and Judy Man ★★ U

Comedy   1962 · UK · BW · 88mins

Cast adrift from his regular scriptwriters Ray Galton and Alan Simpson for the first time in a decade studded with radio and TV triumphs, Tony Hancock comes unstuck in this glum comedy. While his earlier feature, *The Rebel*, had several scenes that showcased his genius for swaggering vainglory, this tale about a seaside showman driven to distraction by the petty dictates of the local authorities and the social ambitions of his grasping wife (Sylvia Syms) is overwhelmed by moments of unrelieved melancholy. Hancock's lack of finesse allows the despondency to descend into bathos, thus shrouding the whole picture with an out-of-season atmosphere.

Tony Hancock *Wally Pinner* • Sylvia Syms *Delia Pinner* • Ronald Fraser *Mayor Palmer* • Barbara Murray *Lady Jane Caterham* • John Le Mesurier *Charles the sandman* • Hugh Lloyd *Edward Cox* • Mario Fabrizi *Nevil Shanks* ■ *Dir* Jeremy Summers • *Scr* Tony Hancock, Phillip Oakes, from a story by Tony Hancock

Punchline ★★★ 15

Comedy drama   1988 · US · Colour · 117mins

Comedians sometimes have to be funny-peculiar in order to be funny ha-ha: well, who'd want to stand up and be laughed at for a living? David Seltzer's look at the laughter-makers has cracking wise-cracking performances by Tom Hanks, as a disorientated entertainer, and Sally Field, as a housewife with comic ambitions. But, in trying to escape the humdrum, they just create new restraints on their personalities. Slow in places, but both stars are good enough to help make this a thoughtful study as to why professional humour is no joke. Contains swearing.

Sally Field *Lilah Krytsick* • Tom Hanks *Steven Gold* • John Goodman *John Krytsick* • Mark Rydell *Romeo* • Kim Greist *Madeline Urie* • Paul Mazursky *Arnold* ■ *Dir/Scr* David Seltzer

The Punisher ★★ 18

Action crime
1989 · US/Ausl · Colour · 84mins

The Marvel Comics vigilante is brought to the screen in the guise of square-jawed giant Dolph Lundgren. He's no superhero though, merely a leather-clad man on a motorbike avenging the murder of his family by the New York mob, in this unremarkable thriller. Lundgren certainly looks every inch the comic book hero, plus there's better-

than-average support from Louis Gossett Jr and Jeroen Krabbé (the bad guy, naturally). The film also has one interesting genre twist up its sleeve – when Lundgren assists his adversary – but the lack of visual style, repetitive action scenes and a lifeless script place this in the second division of comic book adaptations.

Dolph Lundgren *Frank Castle/The Punisher* • Louis Gossett Jr *Jake Berkowitz* • Jeroen Krabbé *Gianni Franco* • Barry Otto *Shake* • Bryan Marshall *Dino Moretti* • Kim Miyori *Lady Tanaka* ■ *Dir* Mark Goldblatt • *Scr* Robert Mark Kamen, Boaz Yakin, from a story by Boaz Yakin

Punishment Park ★★★★

Documentary drama
1971 · US · Colour · 88mins

The best of the socio-political fantasies made by documentary film-maker Peter Watkins whose *Privilege* and *The War Game* also interpreted present ills through reconstructions of the future. Draft dodgers who oppose America's Indo-China war are put in detention camps where they must chose between a three-day ordeal in ''Punishment Park'' to win their freedom or a long jail sentence. Watkins plays the leader of a British documentary film unit observing one group of dissenters as they take the former option and run for their lives across a desert and face fascist terror tactics. Powerful and depressing, this virtual restaging of the Vietnam War in America's heartland is an outstanding indictment of repression and insidious state bullyboy tactics.

Jim Bohan *Captain, Dheriff's Department* • Van Daniels *County Sheriff* • Frederick Franklyn *Professor Daly* • Carmen Argenziano *Jay Kaufman* • Stan Armsted *Charles Robbins* • Gladys Golden *Mrs Jergens* • Sanford Golden *Sen Harris* • Patrick Boland *Defendant* • Peter Watkins *Documentarist* ■ *Dir/Scr* Peter Watkins

The Punk ★★ 15

Contemporary romantic drama
1993 · UK · Colour · 92mins

A romantic drama directed by Michael Sarne, the same cockney who serenaded the early sixties with ''Come Outside'' before directing films, most notoriously *Myra Breckinridge*. This punk-induced ode to Romeo and Juliet, set on the streets of Notting Hill, features another sixties star, Jess Conrad, as the father of a rich girl who falls for a local punk, much to the disgust of parents and the like. The director turns out something approaching a modern fairy tale. Contains swearing, some violence and sex scenes.

Charlie Creed-Miles *David* • Vanessa Hadaway *Rachel* • David Shawyer *David's father* • Jess Conrad *Rachel's father* • Jacqueline Skarvellis *David's mother* • Yolanda Mason *Rachel's stepmother* • Alex Mollo *Stray Cat* ■ *Dir* Mike Sarne [Michael Sarne] • *Scr* Michael Sarne, from the novel *The Punk* by Gideon Sams

The Punk Rock Movie ★★★ 15

Music documentary
1978 · UK · Colour · 79mins

An 8mm-blown-up-to-35mm record of the London punk scene just as it was exploding globally to irrevocably shake

up the moribund music world. Filmed by Don Letts, the road manager for various Brit-punk bands, this technically haphazard chronicle covers all the bases – tiny hothouse venues, cramped recording studios, road tours, pogo rituals (featuring a young Shane McGowan), razor blade fashions and drug-taking. The Sex Pistols sing *God Save the Queen*, The Clash *White Riot*, Wayne County *Cream in my Jeans*, and Siouxsie and the Banshees, Slaughter and the Dogs, X-Ray Spex, The Slits and The Heartbreakers also make appearances. Filmed mostly at London's Roxy Club, this is a simply presented but valuable history lesson.

Dir Don Letts

Puppet Master ★★ 18

Horror   1989 · US · Colour · 86mins

The first of seven horror films, all seen almost exclusively on the small screen, about the puppets given life by their creator, Toulon. A group of highly unlikely psychic researchers, including Paul LeMat, are terrorised in a hotel by the murderous marionettes. Director David Schmoeller, veteran of much low-grade horror, does little with the formulaic script, which is slow to get going, but finally delivers the gory goods. The puppets are cleverly animated by special effects expert David Allen.

Paul LeMat *Alex* • Irene Miracle *Dana Hadley* • Matt Roe *Frank* • Kathryn O'Reilly *Clarissa* • Robin Frates *Megan Gallagher* • Merrya Small [Marya Small] *Theresa* • Jimmie F Scaggs *Neil* • William Hickey *Toulon* ■ *Dir* David Schmoeller • *Scr* Joseph G Collodi, from a story by Charles Band, Kenneth J Hall

Puppet Master II ★★ 18

Horror   1990 · US · Colour · 84mins

The second in a remarkably durable series about killer puppets is pretty much a retread of episode one. A new batch of psychic researchers are at the mercy of the marionettes, who now need new brains to survive. David Allen, special effects man on the first film (and many other Charles Band productions), turned director here. He does a passable job, and clearly enjoys the sly references to other horror films, a practice later indulged by Wes Craven. Four more sequels followed.

Elizabeth MacClellan *Carolyn/Elsa* • Collin Bernsen *Michael* • Nita Talbot *Camille* • Gregory Webb *Patrick* • Charlie Spradling *Wanda* • Steve Welles *Toulon/Chanee* • Jeff Weston *Lance* • Sage Allen *Martha* ■ *Dir* David Allen • *Scr* David Pabian, from an idea by Charles Band

The Puppet Masters ★★ 15

Science-fiction   1994 · US · Colour · 104mins

A dumb incarnation of Robert Heinlein's excellent short science-fiction novel. Far from remaining faithful to the book, the film takes liberties with the story in such a way that Heinlein might have objected. If you've seen Donald Sutherland's other alien invasion flick, 1978's *Invasion of the Body Snatchers*, you've already got a pretty good idea of what's in store here. While technically competent, it offers little in the way of a story,

unless of course, you count the badly misplaced love scene dropped in the middle of the action, which only slows things down.

Donald Sutherland *Andrew Nivens* • Eric Thal *Sam Nivens* • Julie Warner *Mary* • Yaphet Kotto *Ressler* • Keith David *Holland* • Will Patton *Graves* • Richard Belzer *Jarvis* • Tom Mason *President Douglas* ■ *Dir* Stuart Orme • *Scr* David S Goyer, Ted Elliot, Terry Rossio, from the novel by Robert A Heinlein

Puppet on a Chain ★★ 15

Thriller   1970 · UK · Colour · 93mins

Along with the Bond movies, those based on the novels of Alistair MacLean are, in many ways, the precursors of the all-action blockbusters that have kept Hollywood's musclemen in work since the mid-eighties. Unfortunately, director Geoffrey Reeve is saddled with Swedish actor Sven-Bertil Taube, whose charmless playing makes involvement in the plot almost impossible. However, his performance serves to make the final speedboat chase along the canals of Amsterdam (a sequence directed by Don Sharp) even more thrilling. Contains violence and some swearing.

Sven-Bertil Taube *Paul Sherman* • Barbara Parkins *Maggie* • Alexander Knox *Colonel De Graaf* • Patrick Allen *Inspector Van Gelder* • Vladek Sheybal *Meegeren* • Ania Marson *Astrid Leman* ■ *Dir* Geoffrey Reeve • *Scr* Alistair MacLean, Paul Wheeler, Don Sharp, from the novel by Alistair MacLean

The Puppetmaster ★★★ 15

Biographical drama
1993 · Tai · Colour · 136mins

Steeped in the folklore of his beloved Taiwan, this hypnotic account of puppetmaster Li Tianlu's first 36 years features fleeting appearances from Li himself. Taking us from Li's troubled childhood in what was still essentially a feudal society to the liberation of the island from the Japanese at the end of the Second World War, the film is enlivened throughout by some compelling dramatic sequences and several wonderful displays of puppetry. Yet director Hou Hsiao-Hsien's sometimes heavy-handed symbolism and his decision to adopt such a funereal pace occasionally counts against the intricacy and the intrigue of the story. In Mandarin, Taiwanese and Japanese with English subtitles.

Li Tianlu *Li Tianlu* • Lim Giong [Lin Qiang] *Li Tianlu, young adult* • Chen Kuizhong *Li Tianlu, teenager* • Zuo Juwei *Li Tianlu, child* ■ *Dir* Hou Xiaoxian [Hou Hsiao-Hsien] • *Scr* Wu Nianzhen, Zhu Tianwen, from the book *Ximeng Rensheng* by Li Tianlu Li, Hou Xiaoxian [Hou Hsiao-Hsien], Zheng Yumen

The Purchase Price ★★★

Melodrama   1932 · US · BW · 66mins

Manhattan torch singer Barbara Stanwyck, eager to escape the clutches of her gangster lover, Lyle Talbot, becomes a mail order bride to North Dakota farmer George Brent. How the couple, especially Stanwyck, cope with adjusting to their unlikely alliance, and the series of dramatic incidents that attends them, is the stuff of this full-blooded melodrama. Director William A Wellman extracts as much humour as possible from clichéd secondary characters, while squeezing some credibility from the bizarre dramatic incidents. The sublime Stanwyck rises, as always, above the material. Her famous commitment to her work led her to insist on replacing her double in a dramatic fire scene, which left her burnt, blistered but undaunted.

Barbara Stanwyck *Joan Gordon* • George Brent *Jim Gilson* • Lyle Talbot *Ed Fields* • Hardie Albright *Don* • David Landau *Bull McDowell* • Murray Kinnell *Spike Forgan* ■ *Dir* William A Wellman • *Scr* Robert Lord, from the story *The Mud Lark* by Arthur Stringer

Pure Country ★★ PG

Drama 1992 · US · Colour · 107mins

''Pure Corn'' might have been a better title for this slice of country-and-western hokum. Your opinion of this tale of a troubled superstar will depend on your reaction to George Strait. There's no denying he's handy with a tune, but dialogue proves more difficult for him. It's a shame we couldn't spend more time with his tacky manager, played by Lesley Ann Warren, but, as she stands for everything Strait now detests, we have to make do with him, singing away on Isabel Glasser's cash-strapped ranch. Veteran Rory Calhoun is also wasted in an undemanding supporting role. ▭

George Strait *Dusty Wyatt Chandler* • Lesley Ann Warren *Lula Rogers* • Isabel Glasser *Harley Tucker* • Kyle Chandler *Buddy Jackson* • John Doe *Earl Blackstock* • Rory Calhoun *Ernest Tucker* • Molly McClure *Grandma Ivy Chandler* ■ *Dir* Christopher Cain • *Scr* Rex McGee

A Pure Formality ★★

Psychological mystery drama
1994 · It/Fr · Colour · 108mins

Director Giuseppe Tornatore had a hit with *Cinema Paradiso*, a near hit with *The Legend of 1900* and a big miss here. Gérard Depardieu takes the reins as a famous French writer fleeing from a mysterious gunshot. The movie centres round his interrogation by the Inspector (Roman Polanski) in a wet, seedy shed in the middle of a dank forest. Despite their pedigree, these two film giants cannot pull together a ponderous plot and meandering monologues. Polanski himself worked much better with a similar narrative in his adaptation of *Death and the Maiden*. In French with English subtitles.

Gérard Depardieu *Onoff* • Roman Polanski *Inspector* • Sergio Rubini *Andre, the young policeman* • Nicola DiPinto *The captain* • Paolo Lombardi *The warrant officer* • Tano Cimarosa *The old attendant* ■ *Dir* Giuseppe Tornatore • *Scr* Giuseppe Tornatore, Pascal Quignard, from a story by Giuseppe Tornatore

The Pure Hell of St Trinian's ★★ U

Comedy 1960 · US · BW · 99mins

Bereft of Alastair Sim, the third film in the St Trinian's series has its moments, but sadly all too few of them. With the school reduced to smouldering ashes, mysterious child psychologist Cecil Parker takes charge of the tearaways, in league with white-slaving sea captain Sid James. Woefully short on mayhem, the film

spends too much time in the company of eventual castaways Parker and Joyce Grenfell. What's worse, Frank Launder and Sidney Gilliat waste the opportunities presented by casting Irene Handl as the new headmistress and Eric Barker and Dennis Price as the men from the ministry.

Cecil Parker *Professor Canford* • Joyce Grenfell *Sergeant Ruby Gates* • George Cole *Flash Harry* • Thorley Walters *Butters* • Eric Barker *Culpepper-Brown* • Irene Handl *Miss Harker-Parker* • Sidney James *Alphonse O'Reilly* • Dennis Price *Gore-Blackwood* ■ *Dir* Frank Launder • *Scr* Frank Launder, Val Valentine, Sidney Gilliat, from the drawings by Ronald Searle

Pure Luck ★★ PG

Comedy 1991 · US · Colour · 91mins

A limp attempt to find life in the corpse of the buddy-buddy movie, this stars Danny Glover as a gumshoe and Martin Short as his idiotic sidekick who go shooting off to Mexico in search of a missing heiress. This lazy wheeze, which abandons any pretence at a decent script at an early stage, relies for the odd outbreak of energy on Short, who is required to shore up his film with a volley of pratfalls (only some work). Glover survives the proceedings without blushing once. Amazing. Contains swearing. ▭

Martin Short *Eugene Proctor* • Danny Glover *Raymond Campanella* • Sheila Kelley *Valerie Highsmith* • Sam Wanamaker *Mr Highsmith* • Scott Wilson *Grimes* • Harry Shearer *Monosoff* • Jorge Russek *Inspector Segura* ■ *Dir* Nadia Tass • *Scr* Herschel Weingrod, Timothy Harris

Purgatory ★

Prison drama 1988 · US · Colour · 93mins

This boring ''women in prison'' saga contains all the usual clichés, but not many of the needed lip-smacking exploitation elements to make it endearing to fans of the genre. Peace Corps worker Tanya Roberts (and that's only the first wild stretch of the imagination!) gets locked up on a phoney drugs charge while pounding her South African beat and discovers her fellow inmates are being used as prostitutes by the wardens. When her best friend commits suicide after being gang-raped, Roberts organises a break-out rebellion. Clearly mounted as a distaff *Midnight Express*, and with the former Charlie's Angel barely able to keep her head above the tough waters, this is utterly routine tosh.

Tanya Roberts *Carly Arnold* • Julie Pop *Melanie* • Hal Orlandini *Bledsoe* • Rufus Swart *Paul Cricks* ■ *Dir* Ami Artzi • *Scr* Felix Kroll, Paul Aratow

Purgatory ★★★ 15

Western 1999 · US · Colour · 90mins

A barmy but richly enjoyable western fable which stars Eric Roberts as a bank robber who holes up with his gang in a sleepy, weapons-free village south of the border. One of the young gang members (Brad Rowe) realises that this is Purgatory for legends of the West – Billy the Kid (Donnie Wahlberg), Doc Holliday (Randy Quaid), Jesse James (seventies soft rocker JD Souther) and Wild Bill Hickock (Sam Shepard). But if they take up arms against the newcomers, will they be

refused their place in heaven? Director Uli Edel plays it refreshingly straight, while the talented cast relish the chance to play their western heroes. Contains some violence, sexual references and swearing. ▭

Sam Shepard *Sheriff Forest* • Eric Roberts *Blackjack* • Randy Quaid *Director* • Peter Stormare *Cavin* • Brad Rowe *Sonny* • Donnie Wahlberg *Deputy Glen* • JD Souther *Brooks* ■ *Dir* Uli Edel • *Scr* Gordon Dawson

Purple Haze ★★ 18

Drama 1982 · US · Colour · 96mins

Another *American Graffiti*-inspired clone focusing on the summer of 1968 and the hippy antics of college drop-out Peter Nelson and his drugged-out best friend Chuck McQuary. Parental conflicts, the threat of the draft and the usual round of chemically fuelled parties are the familiar signposts in this not very insightful look at the turbulent late sixties. A great Golden Oldie soundtrack eases the bumps along director David Burton Morris's familiar nostalgia ride, and Jimi Hendrix provides the title track.

Peter Nelson *Matt Caulfield* • Chuck McQuary *Jeff Maley* • Bernard Baldan *Derek Savage* • Susanna Lack *Kitty Armstrong* • Bob Breuler *Walter Caulfield* • Joanne Bauman *Margaret Caulfield* ■ *Dir* David Burton Morris • *Scr* Victoria Wozniak, from a story by Tom Kelsey, David Burton Morris, Victoria Wozniak

The Purple Heart ★★★

Second World War drama
1944 · US · BW · 100mins

An unashamed wartime propaganda movie directed by Lewis Milestone, the man responsible for some of the greatest war films ever. Here, a group of US air force personnel are falsely accused of war atrocities after being captured by the Japanese. When they refuse to admit to the charges, they face a terrible ordeal. This isn't one of Milestone's best, mainly because every character seems such an obvious stereotype, despite the fact that the tragic events depicted are based on fact. Nevertheless, the film was potent enough for its day.

Dana Andrews *Captain Harvey Ross* • Richard Conte *Lieutenant Angelo Canelli* • Farley Granger *Sergeant Howard Clinton* • Kevin O'Shea *Sergeant Jan Skvoznik* • Donald Barry *Lieutenant Peter Vincent* • Trudy Marshall *Mrs Ross* ■ *Dir* Lewis Milestone • *Scr* Jerome Cady, from a story by Melville Crossman [Darryl F Zanuck]

Purple Hearts ★★ 15

War drama 1984 · US · Colour · 110mins

In this Vietnam romance, former *Charlie's Angel* Cheryl Ladd is the nurse who falls for doctor Ken Wahl during the war, intending to spend the rest of her medical career by his side. It's tosh, of course, but not unenjoyable, with a *Romeo and Juliet*-style series of endings, as you wonder who's been killed, or not, or whatever. Watch out for former military drill instructor Lee Ermey, appearing in a Vietnam feature three full years before *Full Metal Jacket*. Contains swearing. ▭

Ken Wahl *Don Jardian* • Cheryl Ladd *Deborah Solomon* • Stephen Lee *Wizard* • David Harris *Hanes* • Cyril O'Reilly *Zuma* • Lane Smith

Commander Market • Lee Ermey [R Lee Ermey] *Gunny* • Annie McEnroe *Hallaway* • Paul McCrane *Brenner* ■ *Dir* Sidney J Furie • *Scr* Rick Natkin, Sidney J Furie

The Purple Mask ★★ U

Period adventure 1955 · US · Colour · 81mins

A Napoleonic frolic with Tony Curtis in historical mode – that is to say, adding adenoidal timbre and generally camping it up. The plot is some nonsense about Napoleon and those irritating Royalists who keep losing their heads on the guillotine. Curtis sports a mask – just like Zorro or Percy Blakeney – and waves his rapier at arch rival, Dan O'Herlihy. Angela Lansbury is a milliner whose shop is also a cover for the Resistance, while the love interest is Colleen Miller.

Tony Curtis *Rene* • Colleen Miller *Laurette* • Gene Barry *Capt Laverne* • Dan O'Herlihy *Brisquet* • Angela Lansbury *Madame Valentine* • George Dolenz *Marcel Cadonal* • John Hoyt *Rochet* • Myrna Hansen *Constance* ■ *Dir* H Bruce Humberstone • *Scr* Oscar Brodney, from the play *Le Chevalier aux Masques* by Paul Armont, Jean Manoussi, adapted by Charles Latour

The Purple People Eater ★★★

Musical fantasy 1988 · US · Colour · 91mins

Thirty years after Sheb Wooley had a hit with the song of the title in 1958, this daft little movie attempted to rekindle the spirit of a time when aliens were synonymous with communists and rock 'n' roll was considered the Devil's music. Parts of the plot bear more than a passing resemblance to *Batteries Not Included*, but there's something irresistible about seeing Ned Beatty and Shelley Winters playing helpless pensioners. Neil Patrick Harris co-stars as the lad who brings the eponymous alien to Earth by playing Wooley's hit, and there are fascinating cameos from Little Richard and Chubby Checker.

Ned Beatty *Grandpa* • Neil Patrick Harris *Billy Johnson* • Shelley Winters *Rita* • Peggy Lipton *Mom* • James Houghton *Dad* • Thora Birch *Molly Johnson* • John Brumfield *Mr Noodle* • Little Richard *Mayor* • Chubby Checker *Singer* ■ *Dir* Linda Shayne • *Scr* Linda Shayne, from the song by Sheb Wooley

The Purple Plain ★★★

Second World War drama
1954 · UK · Colour · 101mins

A romantic adventure with Gregory Peck as the Canadian Second World War pilot, haunted by the death of his wife, who regains his confidence via a love affair and a bungled combat mission in Burma. Adapted by Eric Ambler from the novel by HE Bates, this is quite a classy production, directed by Robert Parrish, shot by Geoffrey Unsworth in the jungles of Ceylon and produced by John Bryan, who was David Lean's art director on *Oliver Twist* and *Great Expectations*. At times the picture anticipates Lean's *Bridge on the River Kwai*, shot in Ceylon a few years later.

Gregory Peck *Squadron Leader Forrester* • Than Min Win *Anna* • Bernard Lee *Dr Harris* • Maurice Denham *Blore* • Brenda de Banzie *Miss McNab* • Ram Gopal *Mr Phang* • Lyndon Brook *Carrington* • Anthony Bushell *Commander Aldridge* • Jack McNaughton

U = SUITABLE FOR ALL Uc = SUITABLE FOR ALL, ESPECIALLY FOR YOUNG CHILDREN (VIDEO ONLY) PG = PARENTAL GUIDANCE

Sergeant Brown • Harold Siddons *Navigator Williams* ■ *Dir* Robert Parrish • *Scr* Eric Ambler, from the novel by HE Bates

Purple Rain ★★★ 15

Musical drama 1984 · US · Colour · 106mins

The first and easily the best of pint-sized rock star Prince's forays into film. Breathtakingly egotistical, it follows the adventures of struggling rock singer "The Kid" as he battles to the top of the pop tree, despite the underhand tactics of his rivals. The less said about the lead performances the better although Morris Day eclipses the star with a charismatic turn but Prince and the Revolution were at the height of their powers and the hits *Purple Rain, Let's Go Crazy, When Doves Fly* are memorably captured by director Albert Magnoli. Contains swearing and sex scenes. ▣ **DVD**

Prince *The Kid* • Apollonia Kotero *Apollonia* • Morris Day *Morris* • Olga Karlatos *Mother* • Clarence Williams III *Father* • Jerome Benton *Jerome* • Billy Sparks *Billy* • Jill Jones *Jill* ■ *Dir* Albert Magnoli • *Scr* Albert Magnoli, William Blinn

The Purple Rose of Cairo ★★★★ PG

Fantasy comedy
1985 · US · Colour and BW · 78mins

In Woody Allen's short story *The Kugelmass Episode*, an academic is transported into the bedroom of the literary character Madame Bovary. *The Purple Rose of Cairo* is a film inversion of this idea, with Mia Farrow as a brutalised waitress who wins the heart of a character in her favourite movie (played by Jeff Daniels) who steps out of the screen to court her. Farrow and Daniels are charming and writer/director Allen poignantly recalls the importance of Hollywood dreams to people weighed down by the cares of the thirties. Technically polished and ingenious, the material is perhaps more suited to a shorter format. ▣

Mia Farrow *Cecilia* • Jeff Daniels *Tom Baxter/Gil Shepherd* • Danny Aiello *Monk* • Dianne Wiest *Emma* • Van Johnson *Larry* • Zoe Caldwell *Countess* • John Wood *Jason* • Milo O'Shea *Father Donnelly* ■ *Dir/Scr* Woody Allen • *Cinematographer* Gordon Willis

The Purple Taxi ★★★

Drama 1977 · Fr/US/Ire · Colour · 107mins

The multinational producers and cast give this curio a strange cross-cultural edge. Adapted by Michel Déon from his own novel, the drama centers on several moneyed expats of widely varying backgrounds who cross paths in the west of Ireland after escaping their previous lives. The doctor (Fred Astaire) drives the purple taxi, a millionaire (Edward Albert) searches for traces of his Irish ancestry, while the sexy wife of a German prince (Charlotte Rampling) tries to seduce a terminally ill patient. Offbeat and watchable.

Charlotte Rampling *Sharon* • Philippe Noiret *Philippe* • Agostina Belli *Anne Taubelman* • Peter Ustinov *Taubelman* • Fred Astaire *Dr Scully* • Edward Albert *Jerry* • Mairin O'Sullivan *Colleen* • Jack Watson *Sean* ■ *Dir* Yves Boisset • *Scr* Yves Boisset, Michel Déon, from a novel by Michel Déon

Pursued ★★★★ PG

Western 1947 · US · BW · 101mins

Not as well-known as *High Noon, The Searchers* or *Red River*, this was one of the first "psychological westerns" and has the same sort of story, theme and flashback structure usually found in the urban *film noir*. Robert Mitchum plays a tortured soul who was adopted as a child, murders his half-brother and then marries his brother's wife. Set against the stark buttes of the south-west, it has the feel of a classical tragedy, with Mitchum superb as the brooding hero who journeys back into his past. Critics have laid all the praise at the door of the director, Raoul Walsh, but it's largely the creation of screenwriter Niven Busch. He was married to Mitchum's co-star, the delightful Teresa Wright, and also wrote the novel *Duel in the Sun*, another Freud-on-horseback saga. ▣

Robert Mitchum *Jeb Rand* • Teresa Wright *Thorley Callum* • Judith Anderson *Mrs Medora Callum* • Dean Jagger *Grant Callum* • Alan Hale *Jake Dingle* • John Rodney *Adam Callum* • Harry Carey Jr *Prentice McComber* ■ *Dir* Raoul Walsh • *Scr* Niven Busch • *Cinematographer* James Wong Howe • *Music* Max Steiner

The Pursuers ★★

Crime 1961 · UK · BW · 63mins

The arrest and trial of Adolph Eichmann made the pursuit of Nazi war criminals a fitting topic for thrillers, such as this one released in early 1962, when Eichmann was executed in Israel. The plot resembles any fugitive on-the-run yarn, with the Nazi – a respected businessman – hiding out in a nightclub singer's flat in London, hunted by a German organisation and unable to flee the country because he's damaged his passport. Never more than a B-movie, it's worth seeing for its treatment of its subject and for the performance of Cyril Shaps, a B-movie regular who specialised in playing foreigners.

Cyril Shaps *Karl Luther* • Francis Matthews *David Nelson* • Susan Denny *Jenny Walmer* • Sheldon Lawrence *Rico* • George Murcell *Freddy* ■ *Dir* Godfrey Grayson • *Scr* Brian Clemens, David Nicholl

The Pursuit of DB Cooper ★★ 15

Comedy crime drama
1981 · US · Colour · 96mins

A thriller that begins with Treat Williams jumping out of a plane with a bag containing $200,000. Amazingly, this airborne robbery, with its James Bond-style stunt, really happened and DB Cooper vanished into myth. This is where fiction takes over, conjuring up Cooper's subsequent life and the attempts of a former Green Beret (Robert Duvall) to track him down. Sadly, the picture bungles a nifty idea and it's rarely more than routine. Buzz Kulik replaced John Frankenheimer as director before Roger Spottiswoode was brought in to finish the job. Contains violence. ▣

Robert Duvall *Gruen* • Treat Williams *Meade* • Kathryn Harrold *Hannah* • Ed Flanders *Brigadier* • Paul Gleason *Remson* • RG

Armstrong *Dempsey* ■ *Dir* Roger Spottiswoode • *Scr* Jeffrey Alan Fiskin, from the book *Free Fall* by JD Reed

The Pursuit of Happiness ★

Drama 1971 · US · Colour · 93mins

After directing minor classics such as *To Kill a Mockingbird* and *Love with the Proper Stranger*, Robert Mulligan's career began its sharp decline with this clichéd, hopelessly dated story of a disenchanted hippy who rejects the life style of his affluent Manhattan family. Michael Sarrazin's life goes wrong – he kills someone in an auto accident, goes to jail, gets embroiled in a knifing and then thinks he should escape and hop over the Canadian border, like any self-respecting draft dodger. Barbara Hershey is his girlfriend and there's a song, repeated often, by Randy Newman.

Michael Sarrazin *William Popper* • Barbara Hershey *Jane Kauffman* • Arthur Hill *John Popper* • Ruth White *Mrs Popper* • EG Marshall *Daniel Lawrence* • Robert Klein *Melvin Lasher* • William Devane *Pilot* ■ *Dir* Robert Mulligan • *Scr* Jon Boothe, George L Sherman, from a novel by Thomas Rogers • *Music/Lyrics* Randy Newman

Pursuit to Algiers ★★ U

Crime mystery 1945 · US · BW · 65mins

Basil Rathbone and Nigel Bruce just cruise through this, one of the worst of the Sherlock Holmes series from Universal Studios. They're aboard an ocean liner, escorting an imperilled prince to safety. Despite being a royalist loyalist, Holmes looks decidedly sniffy about the whole affair, probably lamenting the poor production values and sets which look like *Crossroads* on a bad day. Bruce's Dr Watson, though, makes the best of a mediocre job – at one point he even sings *Loch Lomond*. But, then, he always did look on the bright side which is more than the viewer can.

Basil Rathbone *Sherlock Holmes* • Nigel Bruce *Dr John H Watson* • Marjorie Riordan *Sheila Woodbury, Singer* • Rosalind Ivan *Agatha Dunham* • Martin Kosleck *Mirko* • John Abbott *Jodri* • Frederick Worlock *Prime Minister* • Morton Lowry *Sanford, ship's steward* ■ *Dir* Roy William Neill • *Scr* Leonard Lee, from characters created by Sir Arthur Conan Doyle

Pusher ★★★ 18

Crime drama 1996 · Den · Colour · 105mins

Although debuting Danish director Nicolas Winding Refn gives as his references such US indie icons as Quentin Tarantino and Abel Ferrara, the grungy handheld visuals, improvised dialogue and dark sense of humour mean this feels more like a European arthouse movie. Always a picture on the move, in keeping with drug dealer Kim Bodnia's occupational ducking and diving, the action becomes increasingly claustrophobic as his options run out. Capturing the predatory nature and paranoia of a hideous existence, this is a sobering and often violent drama, but even though Bodnia's problems are all of his own making, it's impossible not to empathise with him. In Danish with English subtitles. ▣

Kim Bodnia *Frank* • Zlatko Buric *Milo* • Laura Drasbaek *Vic* • Slavko Labovic *Radovan* ■ *Dir* Nicolas Winding Refn • *Scr* Nicolas Winding Refn, Jens Dahl

Pushing Hands ★★★

Comedy drama
1991 · Tai/US · Colour · 100mins

An early gem from director Ang Lee, *Pushing Hands* refers to the Oriental t'ai chi exercise where you keep your balance while unbalancing your opponent. This is an apt metaphor for the narrative about retired martial arts expert Lung Sihung, whose life is turned upside down when he moves in with his son and his American wife in a New York suburb. As in Lee's later film *The Wedding Banquet*, the cultural and generational gap between the elderly parent and the Americanised son is all too clear. While not as assured as his later works, Lee's subtle observations are worth watching as the older man struggles to fit in with his hostile daughter-in-law (Deb Snyder). An English/Mandarin language film.

Lung Sihung *Mr Chu* • Wang Lai *Mrs Chen* • Bo Z Wang *Alex Chu* • Deb Snyder *Martha Chu* • Lee Haan *Jeremy Chu* • Emily Liu *Yi Cui* ■ *Dir* Ang Lee • *Scr* Ang Lee, James Schamus

Pushing Tin ★★★ 15

Comedy drama 1999 · US · Colour · 123mins

This uneven but fascinating comedy-drama looks at the air traffic controllers who guide planes in and out of New York's airspace. Mike Newell's film focuses on two in particular: super-cool John Cusack and Zen-like Billy Bob Thornton, who challenges Cusack's claim to be the best controller in town. It's not only Cusack's ego which is bruised by his rivalry with Thornton; their wives (Cate Blanchett and Angelina Jolie) also get caught in the crossfire. Overly dramatic in places, *Pushing Tin* boasts superb performances from Thornton and the under-rated Cusack. Contains swearing. ▣

John Cusack *Nick Falzone* • Billy Bob Thornton *Russell Bell* • Cate Blanchett *Connie Falzone* • Angelina Jolie *Mary Bell* • Jake Weber *Barry Plotkin* • Kurt Fuller *Ed Clabes* • Vicki Lewis *Tina Leary* • Matt Ross *Ron Hewitt* ■ *Dir* Mike Newell • *Scr* Glen Charles, Les Charles, from the article *Something's Got to Give* by Darcy Frey

Pushover ★★★

Crime drama 1954 · US · BW · 87mins

A smart and unpredictable thriller with Fred MacMurray as the cop who puts a bank robber's girlfriend (Kim Novak) under surveillance, only to fall in love with her himself. Novak's glamorous and glacial presence, not to mention the easy-going charm of MacMurray, makes this movie a sort of forerunner to Hitchcock's *Vertigo*. The basic idea was reprised three decades later in the comedy *Stakeout*.

Fred MacMurray *Paul Sheridan* • Kim Novak *Lona McLane* • Phil Carey [Philip Carey] *Rick McAllister* • Dorothy Malone *Ann* • EG Marshall *Lt Carl Eckstrom* • Allen Nourse *Paddy Dolan* ■ *Dir* Richard Quine • *Scr* Roy Huggins, from a story and novel by Thomas Walsh, from the novel *Rafferty* by William S Ballinger

Putney Swope ★★

Satire 1969 · US · BW and Colour · 85mins

American independent film-maker Robert Downey had a modest hit with this satirical swipe at corporate and materialist America. Arnold Johnson plays the token black man on the board of directors of a Madison Avenue advertising agency. When the chairman keels over, Johnson surprisingly takes over and overturns the racial pecking order, hiring whites as janitors and elevator operators and banning accounts for booze, fags and toy guns. Unfortunately, Johnson's regime makes enemies of some of his staff, while its politically correct business policies arouse the suspicions of the pot-smoking US President. Among the cast of New York actors can be glimpsed a certain Mel Brooks.

Arnold Johnson *Putney Swope* • Antonio Fargas *Arab* • Laura Greene *Mrs Swope* • Eric Krupnik *Mark Focus* • Pepi Hermine *United States President* • Ruth Hermine *First Lady* • Lawrence Wolf *Mr Borman Six* • Stan Gottlieb *Nathan* • Mel Brooks *Mr Forget It* ■ *Dir/Scr* Robert Downey

Puzzle ★★

Thriller　1978 · Ausl · Colour · 90mins

It's not a hard-and-fast rule, but when a film's main character is a jaded tennis pro, you know you've got trouble. Even that excellent actress Wendy Hughes sleepwalks her way through this predictable thriller about a widow who seeks out her first husband when she discovers that her recently deceased spouse was up to his neck in shady deals. James Franciscus is at his least animated and not even a cameo by Robert Helpmann can enliven the proceedings. Although an accomplished horror director, Gordon Hessler struggles to sustain either the pace or the suspense.

James Franciscus *Harry Scott* • Wendy Hughes *Claudine Cunningham* • Robert Helpmann *Buckminster Shepherd* • Kerry McGuire *Diana* • Peter Gwynne *Det Sgt Knox* ■ *Dir* Gordon Hessler • *Scr* Herbert J Wright

Puzzle of a Downfall Child ★★

Drama　1970 · US · Colour · 104mins

A once-famous fashion model (Faye Dunaway), now in a state of disintegration as a result of her less than savoury lifestyle, retires to a beach house to pick up the shattered pieces of herself. There, she recounts her sordid past (in flashback) to photographer Barry Primus. Former fashion photographer Jerry Schatzberg made his directing debut with this visually excellent movie in which Dunaway, looking stunning, gives a good account of herself. However, the fundamentally sensationalist material would have done better to exploit itself as just that rather than adopting a tedious overlay of "arty" pretension.

Faye Dunaway *Lou Andreas Sand* • Barry Primus *Aaron Reinhardt* • Viveca Lindfors *Pauline Galba* • Barry Morse *Dr Galba* • Roy Scheider *Mark* • Ruth Jackson *Barbara Casey* • John Heffernan *Dr Sherman* ■ *Dir* Jerry Schatzberg • *Scr* Adrien Joyce [Carole Eastman], from a story by Jerry Schatzberg, Adrien Joyce [Carole Eastman] • *Cinematographer* Adam Holender

Pygmalion ★★★★★ Ⓤ

Comedy　1938 · UK · BW · 94mins

A superb rendering of George Bernard Shaw's most popular play, for which Shaw himself was awarded a special Academy Award for his contribution (the embassy ball scene) to the screenplay. The film actually won Oscars for the adaptors of the screenplay. Leslie Howard was never better as Henry Higgins (a role Shaw wanted to go to Charles Laughton) and both he and Wendy Hiller (quite brilliant as Eliza Doolittle) were unlucky not to win Oscars themselves. Although Howard took a co-directing credit, Anthony Asquith handled most of the action, acquiring himself an unrivalled reputation for stage adaptation in the process. ▣

Leslie Howard *Professor Henry Higgins* • Wendy Hiller *Eliza Doolittle* • Wilfrid Lawson *Alfred Doolittle* • Marie Lohr *Mrs Higgins* • Scott Sunderland *Colonel Pickering* • Jean Cadell *Mrs Pearce* • David Tree *Freddy Eynsford-Hill* • Everley Gregg *Mrs Eynsford-Hill* ■ *Dir* Anthony Asquith, Leslie Howard • *Scr* George Bernard Shaw, from his play, adapted by WP Lipscomb, Cecil Lewis, Ian Dalrymple

Pyrates ★★ 18

Comedy　1991 · US · Colour · 91mins

In this oddity, real-life husband-and-wife leads Kevin Bacon and Kyra Sedgwick play a young couple with a fiery love life, literally – when the pair get together, buildings tend to go up in smoke. It's an unusual concept, with the two stars giving it their best shot, but director Noah Stern doesn't take the original idea anywhere interesting and, in the end, it's far too self-consciously wacky for its own good. Englishman abroad Bruce Martyn Payne offers solid support as Bacon's best chum. Contains swearing, sex scenes and nudity. ▣

Kevin Bacon *Ari* • Kyra Sedgwick *Sam* • Bruce Martyn Payne [Bruce Payne] *Liam* • Kristin Dattilo *Pia* • Buckley Norris *Dr Weiss* • Deborah Falconer *Rivkah* • David Pressman *Carlton* • Raymond O'Conner *Fireman* ■ *Dir/Scr* Noah Stern

A Pyromaniac's Love Story ★★ PG

Romantic comedy
1995 · US · Colour · 90mins

Love-starved workers at Armin Mueller-Stahl's bakery try to find romance while dealing with a mystery arsonist in this witless comedy directed by Joshua Brand, the creator of *Northern Exposure*. Each of the game cast, including William Baldwin, John Leguizamo, Sadie Frost and Erika Eleniak, wants to be known as the pyromaniac responsible for the fire so they can say their motive was love. Despite some cute turns, this incomprehensible farce raises little heat and is too quirky for its own good. ▣

William Baldwin *Garet* • John Leguizamo *Sergio* • Sadie Frost *Hattie* • Erika Eleniak *Stephanie* • Michael Lerner *Perry* • Joan Plowright *Mrs Linzer* • Armin Mueller-Stahl *Mr Linzer* • Mike Starr *Sergeant Zikowski* • Julio Oscar Mechoso *Jerry* • Richard Crenna *Businessman* ■ *Dir* Joshua Brand • *Scr* Morgan Ward

Q & A ★★★ 18

Crime drama　1990 · US · Colour · 127mins

Sidney Lumet, who was once described as New York's Charles Dickens, chronicles yet another case of civic corruption and bigotry. He uses Nick Nolte as a hulking, dedicated if brutal cop suspected of killing a drug pusher. Seeking the truth behind the murder is Timothy Hutton, a squeaky-clean kid from upstairs. It's possible to view this tough movie as a liberal, East Coast version of a Clint Eastwood *Dirty Harry* yarn, and it is best appreciated now as a showcase for Nolte's explosive talent (which the public at the time clearly ignored, as the picture bombed). Contains violence, swearing and brief nudity. ▣

Nick Nolte *Lieutenant Mike Brennan* • Timothy Hutton *Al Reilly* • Armand Assante *Bobby Texador* • Patrick O'Neal *Kevin Quinn* • Lee Richardson *Leo Bloomenfeld* • Luis Guzman *Luis Valentin* • Charles S Dutton *Sam Chapman* • Jenny Lumet *Nancy Bosch* ■ *Dir* Sidney Lumet • *Scr* Sidney Lumet, from the novel by Edwin Torres

Q Planes ★★★ Ⓤ

Second World War spy drama
1939 · UK · BW · 78mins

A terrific Irving Asher/Alexander Korda production (originally planned as a Columbia British quickie) starring Laurence Olivier (as a test pilot) and Ralph Richardson (as a Scotland Yard officer), who all-too-obviously enjoy their casting together in this immediately pre-war espionage romp. Richardson is especially good value, as he tries to discover just how planes are disappearing off the coast of Cornwall. Rare to find intended lightheartedness working so well in a British film of the period, and much credit should go to the imported American director Tim Whelan, who keeps up the pace impressively. ▣

Laurence Olivier *Tony McVane* • Valerie Hobson *Kay Hammond* • Ralph Richardson *Charles Hammond* • George Curzon *Jenkins* • George Merritt *Barrett* ■ *Dir* Tim Whelan • *Scr* Ian Dalrymple, from a story by Jack Whittingham, Brock Williams, Arthur Wimperis

Q – the Winged Serpent ★★★★

Fantasy horror　1982 · US · Colour · 92mins

Another ace pulp horror classic from director Larry Cohen. The ancient Aztec god Quetzacoatl, a giant flying serpent-bird, is reincarnated by a Manhattan cult and decapitates New Yorkers from its nest atop the Chrysler Building. As detectives David Carradine and Richard Roundtree try to make sense of the myth, petty crook (and Cohen regular) Michael Moriarty holds the Big Apple to ransom in exchange for Q's hiding place. Part wonderfully entertaining cop thriller, part old-fashioned monster movie, Cohen's classic B picture sports great all-round performances and nifty stop-motion animation effects by David Allen. Contains violence, swearing and nudity.

Michael Moriarty *Jimmy Quinn* • David Carradine *Detective Shepard* • Candy Clark *Joan* • Richard Roundtree *Sergeant Powell* • James Dixon *Lt Murray* • Malachy McCourt *Police commissioner* ■ *Dir/Scr* Larry Cohen • *Special Effects* David Allen

Quackser Fortune Has a Cousin in the Bronx ★★★

Comedy drama　1970 · US · Colour · 90mins

The dreadful title apart, this is a charming Irish fable with Gene Wilder cast as Quackser Fortune – his duck imitations earn him the nickname – who shovels horse manure for a living, selling it to housewives all over Dublin. A know-all American student, Margot Kidder, distracts him romantically and patronises him intellectually, until the cousin in the Bronx brings about an ironic conclusion. The story is as soft as the constant drizzle that falls on Dublin and cameraman Gilbert Taylor turns the city's glistening Georgian buildings and cobbled streets into a tourist agent's dream.

Gene Wilder *Quackser Fortune* • Margot Kidder *Zazel Pierce* • Eileen Colgan *Betsy Bourke* • Seamus Ford *Mr Fortune* • May Ollis *Mrs Fortune* • Liz Davis *Kathleen Fortune* ■ *Dir* Waris Hussein • *Scr* Gabriel Walsh • *Cinematographer* Gilbert Taylor

Quadrophenia ★★★★ 18

Musical drama　1979 · UK · Colour · 114mins

The Who's "My Generation" musical tribute to Mods and Rockers in pre-Beatles England is a near-perfect integration of cinematic story and rousing pop. Specifically focusing on the parka-clad Phil Daniels (whose alienation, fuelled by pill-popping, scooter rave-ups and seaside battles in Brighton, ends in self-destruction), director Franc Roddam precisely evokes the budding Swinging Sixties and the teenage sense of frustration and disillusionment. Sting makes his acting debut in a musical milestone crackling with energy and great performances. Contains swearing, violence and sex scenes. ▣ *DVD*

Phil Daniels *Jimmy Michael Cooper* • Leslie Ash *Steph* • Philip Davis *Chalky* • Mark Wingett *Dave* • Sting *Ace Face* • Raymond Winstone [Ray Winstone] *Kevin* • Garry Cooper *Peter* • Toyah Willcox *Monkey* ■ *Dir* Franc Roddam • *Scr* Dave Humphries, Martin Stellman, Franc Roddam

Le Quai des Brumes ★★★★★ PG

Romantic melodrama　1938 · Fr · BW · 86mins

As war clouds gathered, French poetic realism grew increasingly pessimistic. None expressed this despondency more poignantly than Marcel Carné and screenwriter, Jacques Prévert, who collaborated on this mist-shrouded waterfront tale of doomed romance. Confining the action entirely to the sublime studio sets designed by Alexandre Trauner and evocatively shot by Eugen Schüfftan, Carné was able to

Ⓤ = SUITABLE FOR ALL　Ⓤⓒ = SUITABLE FOR ALL, ESPECIALLY FOR YOUNG CHILDREN (VIDEO ONLY)　PG = PARENTAL GUIDANCE

control every detail of his meticulous compositions and, thus, make the plight of army deserter Jean Gabin and waif Michèle Morgan all the more allegorically tragic. With seedy support from guardian Michel Simon and gangster, Pierre Brasseur, this is pure melancholic magic. In French with English subtitles.

Jean Gabin *Jean* • Michèle Morgan *Nelly* • Michel Simon *Zabel* • Pierre Brasseur *Lucien* • Robert Le Vigan *Michel Krauss* ■ *Dir* Marcel Carné • *Scr* Jacques Prévert, from the novel by Pierre MacOrlan [Pierre Dumarchais] • *Cinematographer* Eugen Schüfftan • *Production Designer* Alexandre Trauner

Quai des Orfèvres ★★★★
Thriller 1947 · Fr · BW · 102mins

The title of this wonderfully atmospheric thriller refers to the French equivalent of Scotland Yard. The story revolves around a seedy music hall, where singer Suzy Delair thinks she has committed a murder for which her husband becomes a suspect. The director Henri-Georges Clouzot portrays a Paris teeming with life and mystery in which he observes human frailty with wit and compassion. Outstanding is Louis Jouvet as a police inspector, part cynic, part sentimentalist, who wants to wrap up his last case in order to take care of his motherless son. It was Clouzot's first film for four years because his previous picture, *The Raven* (*Le Corbeau*), had been accused of being anti-French propaganda. In French with English subtitles.

Simone Renant *Dora* • Suzy Delair *Jenny Lamour* • Bernard Blier *Maurice Martineau* • Charles Dullin *Brignon the industrialist* • Louis Jouvet *Inspector Antoine* • RenéBlancard *Police commissioner* ■ *Dir* Henri-Georges Clouzot • *Scr* Henri-Georges Clouzot, Jean Ferry

Quake! ★
Disaster movie 1992 · US · Colour · 83mins

An earthquake hits San Francisco, but this film is too cheap to show us more than a few flimsy models and a lot of falling plaster. Rather than the usual disaster movie clichés, *Quake!* follows a beautiful attorney (Erika Anderson) who is kidnapped by obsessed Steve Railsback when he is supposed to be rescuing her from an unstable building. Railsback manages a performance that is slightly less restrained than the one he gave as Charles Manson in the TV mini-series *Helter Skelter.*

Steve Railsback *Kyle* • Erika Anderson *Jenny* • Eb Lottimer *David* • Burton Gilliam *Willie* • Richard Dean [Rick Dean] *Young tough* ■ *Dir* Louis Morneau • *Scr* Mark Evan Schwartz

Quality Street ★★ U
Comedy drama 1937 · US · BW · 82mins

JM Barrie's now hopelessly dated whimsey came to the screen as a vehicle for Katharine Hepburn in a last-ditch – and unsuccessful – attempt by RKO to arrest her box-office decline. Hepburn is the only girl in a gaggle of ageing spinsters who is likely to marry. She's in love with the dashing Franchot Tone, who goes off to the Napoleonic Wars for several years without declaring his intentions. Amid studio-bound Toytown sets, George

Stevens directs at a deadly pace for the first half (it livens up later along with the plot), and the star's stagey and hysterical performance is more deranged Southern belle than genteel Englishwoman. A handsome Franchot Tone, however, convinces despite the absurdity of his suitor's role.

Katharine Hepburn *Phoebe Throssel* • Franchot Tone *Dr Valentine Brown* • Fay Bainter *Susan Throssel* • Eric Blore *Recruiting Sergeant* • Cora Witherspoon *Patty the Maid* • Joan Fontaine *Charlotte Parratt* ■ *Dir* George Stevens • *Scr* Mortimer Offner, Allan Scott, from the play by JM Barrie

Quantez ★★
Western 1957 · US · Colour · 80mins

This is distinguished by its location photography and the tough performance of Dorothy Malone. Unfortunately, Malone is paired with an ageing – though still top-billed – Fred MacMurray and callow John Gavin to little advantage in this slow-paced tale about a group journeying to Mexico through Apache territory. It's worth watching to see James Barton, the Broadway star of *Paint Your Wagon*, as a travelling salesman and for *Dirty Harry's* John Larch as an outlaw.

Fred MacMurray *Gentry/John Coventry* • Dorothy Malone *Chaney* • James Barton *Minstrel* • Sydney Chaplin *Gato* • John Gavin *Teach* • John Larch *Heller* ■ *Dir* Harry Keller • *Scr* R Wright Campbell, from a story by R Wright Campbell, Anne Edwards

Quantrill's Raiders ★★ U
Wartime western 1958 · US · Colour · 70mins

This CinemaScope western programme filler is made interesting not by the presence of star Steve Cochran, but by Leo Gordon as the legendary William Quantrill himself, whom this movie kills off during the raid on an ammunitions dump at Lawrence, Kansas, and not, as actually happened, two years later in Kentucky. The thickset Gordon carved a sterling career in westerns, and also wrote several, including the interesting psychological outing *Black Patch* for George Montgomery. As an actor he specialised in psychotic villains, and eventually found a natural haven in Europe. Here, as Quantrill, his psychoses are given full rein.

Steve Cochran *Westcott* • Diane Brewster *Sue* • Leo Gordon *Quantrill* • Gale Robbins *Kate* • Will Wright *Judge* • Kim Charney *Joel* ■ *Dir* Edward Bernds • *Scr* Polly James

Quarantine ★ 15
Science-fiction thriller 1989 · Can · Colour · 91mins

Schlock Canadian horror, made in the creative mould of David Cronenberg's *Shivers* and *Rabid*, in which a deadly disease leads to the overthrow of democracy and the installation of a dictatorship that confines everyone to death camps. Cheap and shoddy, with subplots glued on, the film fires off metaphors and allegories and makes no sense at all. Charles Wilkinson directed, using a cast of unknowns. Contains swearing and violence.

Beatrice Boepple *Ivan Joad Honest!* • Garwin Sanford *Spencer Crown* • Jerry Wasserman *Senator Ford* • Michelle Goodger *Berlin Ford* ■ *Dir/Scr* Charles Wilkinson

The Quare Fellow ★★★ 15
Drama 1962 · Ire · Colour · 86mins

With his cult series *The Prisoner* still in the future when he starred in this anti-capital punishment treatise, Patrick McGoohan got a research headstart in this gloomily sincere adaptation of Brendan Behan's renowned play. He's the novice prison warder who has his hanging convictions severely shaken after meeting the wife of one ''Quare Fellow'', Irish slang for a criminal on death row. And they're rattled again when another reprieved murderer takes his own life. The claustrophobic prison atmosphere is expertly conjured up in a well-intentioned, if downbeat, protest movie.

Patrick McGoohan *Thomas Crimmin* • Sylvia Syms *Kathleen* • Walter Macken *Regan* • Dermot Kelly *Donnelly* • Jack Cunningham *Chief warder* • Hilton Edwards *Holy Healy* ■ *Dir* Arthur Dreifuss • *Scr* Arthur Dreifuss, Jacqueline Sundstrom, from the play by Brendan Behan

Quartet ★★★ PG
Portmanteau drama 1948 · UK · BW · 114mins

With W Somerset Maugham introducing the four vignettes based on his celebrated short stories, an air of literary portentousness hangs over this portmanteau picture. But, each tale is told with refreshing lightness. In *The Facts of Life*, Jack Watling enjoys the attentions of Monte Carlo gold-digger Mai Zetterling; *The Alien Corn* sees Dirk Bogarde driven to despair by his ambition to become a concert pianist; nerdy inventor George Cole is caught between wife Susan Shaw and hectoring mother, Hermione Baddeley in *The Kite*; while in *The Colonel's Lady*, Cecil Parker frets about the contents of a slim volume of love poems published by his wife, Nora Swinburne.

Basil Radford *Henry Garnet* • Jack Watling *Nicky* • Mai Zetterling *Jeanne* • Dirk Bogarde *George Bland* • Honor Blackman *Paula* • George Cole *Herbert Sunbury* • Hermione Baddeley *Beatrice Sunbury* • Susan Shaw *Betty* • Cecil Parker *Colonel Peregrine* • Nora Swinburne *Mrs Peregrine* ■ *Dir* Ralph Smart, Harold French, Arthur Crabtree, Ken Annakin • *Scr* RC Sherriff, from stories by W Somerset Maugham

Quartet ★★★ 18
Drama 1981 · UK/Fr · Colour · 96mins

Based on the novel by Jean Rhys, this is a typically classy piece of film-making from director James Ivory. In twenties Paris, Isabelle Adjani takes refuge with married couple Alan Bates and Maggie Smith after her husband (Anthony Higgins) is jailed. She eventually submits to the advances of Bates at the expense of his rather sad bullied wife, as the film explores with subtlety an upper-class lifestyle beset with moral corruption. It was sadly not as successful or lauded as Ivory's later EM Forster adaptations, but it's worth a look nevertheless.

Isabelle Adjani *Marya Zelli* • Anthony Higgins *Stephan Zelli* • Maggie Smith *Lois Heidler* • Alan Bates *HJ Heidler* • Pierre Clémenti *Theo the pornographer* • Daniel Mesguich *Pierre Schlamovitz* ■ *Dir* James Ivory • *Scr* Ruth Prawer Jhabvala, from the novel *Quartet* by Jean Rhys

Quartier Mozart ★★★
Drama 1992 · Cam · Colour · 80mins

Set in modern day Cameroon, this is a scathing insight into the ways that poverty and cultural conservatism are coupled with violence to maintain macho hegemony in a patriarchal society. Determined to beat the system, a young girl is turned into a swaggering man by a sorceress; she/he then discovers the harsh realities of sexual and economic exploitation. Made for just $30,000, Jean-Pierre Bekolo's film is as visually ambitious as it is politically daring, flouting the conventions of western cinema to make a strong statement of independence. In French with English subtitles.

Serge Amougou *Montype* • Sandrine Ola'a *Samedi* • Jimmy Biyong *Chien Mechant* • Essindi Mindja *Atango* • Atebass *Capo* ■ *Dir/Scr* Jean-Pierre Bekolo

Quatermass II ★★★
Science-fiction thriller 1957 · UK · BW · 84mins

The second in Hammer's *Quatermass* trilogy is a potent, low-budget roller coaster ride through government conspiracies and alien invasions, set against the chilling backdrop of postwar new town paranoia. Great writing by Nigel Kneale (based on his original BBC TV serial), superb direction by Val Guest and Gerald Gibbs's stark black-and-white photography make this British classic one of the best science-fiction allegories of the fifties.

Brian Donlevy *Quatermass* • John Longden *Inspector Lomax* • Sidney James *Jimmy Hall* • Bryan Forbes *Marsh* • William Franklyn *Brand* • Vera Day *Sheila* • Charles Lloyd Pack *Dawson* • Michael Ripper *Ernie* ■ *Dir* Val Guest • *Scr* Val Guest, Nigel Kneale, from the TV serial by Nigel Kneale • *Cinematographer* Gerald Gibbs

Quatermass and the Pit ★★★ PG
Science-fiction thriller 1967 · UK · Colour · 178mins

This remains the most popular of the movies taken from Nigel Kneale's acclaimed BBC TV serial. Although the Deluxe Color dissipates some of the atmosphere and mystery, the story of the Martian spaceship uncovered in a London tube station retains much of its intrigue and sense of disquiet thanks to Roy Ward Baker's careful direction and special effects that never attempt to exceed their technical or budgetary limitations. As well as providing a generous helping of shocks, Kneale's script gives his complex themes and theories plenty of space, and both action and argument are neatly judged by Andrew Keir, James Donald and Hammer favourite Barbara Shelley.

James Donald *Dr Matthew Roney* • Andrew Keir *Professor Bernard Quatermass* • Barbara Shelley *Barbara Judd* • Julian Glover *Colonel Breen* • Duncan Lamont *Sladden* ■ *Dir* Roy Ward Baker • *Scr* Nigel Kneale, from his TV serial

The Quatermass Conclusion ★★★ 15

Science-fiction thriller
1979 · UK · Colour · 101mins

After *Quatermass and the Pit*, the Professor returned to television in a four-part serial that was generally regarded as a failure. This cut-down feature film was released to cinemas abroad and on video in the UK. As author Nigel Kneale correctly observed, the serial was too long and the film too short. Nevertheless, the story, which uses a favourite Kneale theme, the re-emergence of old fears and religions, begins and ends well. Quatermass (a creditable stab at the role by John Mills) gradually realises that aliens are harvesting humans from places of congregation. The plot sags in the middle with the arrival of dippy flower children following ley lines – a dated concept even in the late seventies. 🖭

John Mills *Professor Bernard Quatermass* • Simon MacCorkindale *Joe Kapp* • Barbara Kellerman *Clare Kapp* • Margaret Tyzack *Annie Morgan* • Brewster Mason *Gurov* ■ *Dir* Piers Haggard • *Scr* Nigel Kneale, from his TV serial.

The Quatermass Experiment ★★★

Science-fiction thriller
1955 · UK · BW · 81mins

Hammer's film of Nigel Kneale's groundbreaking television serial was a huge success, encouraging the studio to concentrate on the production of horror films; in that regard, it can truly be said to have changed the course of British film history. The story, of an astronaut who returns to earth only to mutate gradually into a vegetable, was subsequently much emulated. Veteran director Val Guest detested the casting of American actor Brian Donlevy, though his portrayal of Quatermass was generally well-received at the time; while Jack Warner, PC George Dixon in *The Blue Lamp* and the long-running TV series *Dixon of Dock Green*, plays the inspector who helps the professor destroy the terror from outer space.

Brian Donlevy *Professor Bernard Quatermass* • Jack Warner *Inspector Lomax* • Margia Dean *Judith Carroon* • Richard Wordsworth *Victor Carroon* • Thora Hird *Rosie* • Gordon Jackson *TV producer* • Lionel Jeffries *Blake* ■ *Dir* Val Guest • *Scr* Val Guest, Richard Landau, from the TV serial by Nigel Kneale

Queen Bee ★★★ PG

Melodrama
1955 · US · BW · 90mins

Joan Crawford virtually breathes fire as the power-crazed woman who marries into an unhappy Southern family and then ruins their lives. Crawford is perfectly cast in her Tennessee Williams-style role and acts up a storm in one fabulous hostess gown after another, while expertly cutting the rest of the cast down to size. An overblown camp-bitch extravaganza much beloved by Crawford fans and lovers of glossy Hollywood melodramas in the grand tradition. 🖭

Joan Crawford *Eva Phillips* • Barry Sullivan *John Avery Phillips* • Betsy Palmer *Carol Lee Phillips* • John Ireland *Judson Prentiss* • Fay

Wray *Sue McKinnon* ■ *Dir* Ranald MacDougall • *Scr* Ranald MacDougall, from the novel by Edna Lee

Queen Christina ★★★★

Historical romantic drama
1933 · US · BW · 99mins

A treat for Greta Garbo fans, a historical romance in which she stars as a 17th-century queen of Sweden who falls in inappropriate love with the Spanish ambassador sent to deliver a marriage proposal from his king. Garbo is quintessentially Garboesque in one of her most famous roles, while John Gilbert, her crony from silent days, is the ambassador, a role he played only at her insistence, after she had failed to warm to Laurence Olivier. The action is better when Garbo is travelling the kingdom dressed as a man than when she is weighed down by the worries of her throne.

Greta Garbo *Queen Christina* • John Gilbert *Don Antonio de la Prada* • Ian Keith *Magnus* • Lewis Stone *Chancellor Oxenstierna* ■ *Dir* Rouben Mamoulian • *Scr* HM Harwood, Salka Viertel, SN Behrman, from a story by Salka Viertel, Margaret Levin • *Cinematographer* William Daniels

Queen Kelly ★★★ PG

Silent romantic melodrama
1928 · US · BW · 99mins

Despite Erich von Stroheim's legendary profligacy, Gloria Swanson hired him to direct this silent tale of the waif who is mistreated by both a Teutonic aristocrat and a mad Ruritanian monarch, in the hope he could turn a simmering melodrama into a sophisticated masterpiece. However, on learning her character would inherit a chain of brothels in German East Africa, Swanson pulled the plug and cobbled together a save-face version that included a musical number to cash in on the talkie boom. Von Stroheim evidently forgave her, as together they watch clips from this visual feast in *Sunset Boulevard*.

Gloria Swanson *Patricia Kelly, an orphan* • Walter Byron *Prince "Wild" Wolfram Von Hohenberg Falsenstein* • Seena Owen *Queen Regina V, his cousin and fiancée* • Sidney Bracey *Prince Wolfram's valet* • William von Brincken *Adjutant to Wolfram* ■ *Dir/Scr* Erich von Stroheim • *Cinematographer* Paul Ivano

Queen of Hearts ★★★★ PG

Drama
1989 · UK · Colour · 107mins

In Italy, sometime after the Second World War, Anita Zagaria breaks off her engagement to fierce Vittorio Amandola, and runs off to London with her lover, Joseph Long. But has she seen the last of her ex-fiancé? No chance. In later life, her ten-year-old son tells the whole magical tale. Jon Amiel debuts as director with a smashing mixture of vivid reality and dream-like surrealism. He introduces us to a world where people fly out of towers, where pigs dispense wisdom like Greek oracles, and where espresso machines puff out steam like mechanical dragons. Add terrific period atmosphere, and engaging performances from a largely unknown cast, and you've a terrific piece of offbeat entertainment that can be thoroughly recommended. 🖭

Vittorio Duse *Nonno* • Joseph Long *Danilo* • Anita Zagaria *Rosa* • Eileen Way *Mama Sibilla* • Vittorio Amandola *Barbariccia* • Jimmy Lambert *Bruno* • Anna Pernicci *Angelica* ■ *Dir* Jon Amiel • *Scr* Tony Grisoni

The Queen of Mean ★★★

Biographical drama
1990 · US · Colour · 94mins

Leona Helmsley, ruthless property magnate, gets the scandal-sheet treatment in a TV movie based on Ransdell Pierson's tabloid biography (although you'd swear Jackie Collins must have had something to do with it). Suzanne Pleshette's all-stops-out portrayal of the philanthropically challenged executive is pitched somewhere between Joan Crawford and *Valley of the Dolls*, yet it's perfectly in tune with what this trashy movie purports to be the whole unvarnished truth. And even if it isn't entirely true, you'll want it to be!

Suzanne Pleshette *Leona Helmsley* • Lloyd Bridges *Harry Helmsley* • Joe Regalbuto *Paul Summerton* • Raymond Singer *Jay* ■ *Dir* Richard Michaels • *Scr* Dennis Turner, from the non-fiction book by Ransdell Pierson

Queen of Outer Space ★ U

Science-fiction thriller
1958 · US · Colour · 79mins

A serious contender for the worst film ever made list, this idiotic would-be sexy sci-fi movie was actually based on an original story by Ben Hecht. The titular monarch is Laurie Mitchell (who?), but top-billed is Zsa Zsa Gabor, who succeeds in rescuing our astronaut heroes in trouble, headed by *Rawhide's* Eric Fleming, who should have known better than to land on Venus, anyway. The skimpy costumes are interesting – Anne Francis's complete *Forbidden Planet* wardrobe is recycled here. The colour gives the film an illusion of expense, but most British prints have faded to pink. Pink or restored, this one's for deadheads.

Zsa Zsa Gabor *Talleah* • Eric Fleming *Patterson* • Laurie Mitchell *Queen Yllana* • Paul Birch *Professor Konrad* • Barbara Darrow *Kaeel* ■ *Dir* Edward Bernds • *Scr* Charles Beaumont, from a story by Ben Hecht

The Queen of Spades ★★★★

Supernatural drama 1948 · UK · BW · 95mins

Set in Imperial Russia, this is the definitive film version of Pushkin's short story about an army captain who takes on more than he bargained for when he tries to discover the secret of an old countess's success at cards. Director Thorold Dickinson creates what is generally regarded as his best film: a handsomely mounted and highly atmospheric ghost story which still chills the blood. In her first major film, Edith Evans was heavily made up to add decades to her true age of 60. Surprisingly, Dickinson directed only two more films before retirement.

Anton Walbrook *Herman Savorin* • Edith Evans *Countess Ranevskaya* • Yvonne Mitchell *Lizavetta Ivanova* • Ronald Harwood *Andrei* • Mary Jerrold *Old Varvarushka* • Anthony Dawson *Fyodor* ■ *Dir* Thorold Dickinson • *Scr* Rodney Ackland, Arthur Boys, from a short story by Alexander Pushkin • *Cinematographer* Otto Heller • *Music* Georges Auric

Queen of the Pirates ★★ U

Action adventure
1960 · It/W Ger · Colour · 79mins

A good-looking adventure which is blighted by an overloaded script. There's tyranny, piracy, romance and tales of capture and recapture. The dull acting doesn't help, and the already inadequate package is further let down by a weak ending. Amazingly, there was more in store with a sequel called *Tiger of the Seven Seas*. Italian dialogue dubbed into English..

Gianna Maria Canale *Sandra* • Massimo Serato *Count Cesare* • Scilla Gabel *Isabella* • Paul Muller *Duke Zulian* ■ *Dir* Mario Costa • *Scr* Nino Stresa, from a story by Kurt Nachmann, Rolf Olsen

The Queen's Guards ★

Drama 1960 · UK · Colour · 110mins

''The most inept piece of film-making that I have ever produced or directed'', said Michael Powell of this wearisome slice of pomp and circumstance. It's a family drama about two brothers, one of whom dies at Tobruk leaving the other to maintain the family tradition by joining the Guards and fighting for the Empire in some fly-blown Arab state. Raymond Massey plays the father, Daniel Massey the son and it's all jolly well British, a sort of belated reaction to the humiliation of Suez.

Daniel Massey *John Fellowes* • Raymond Massey *Captain Fellowes* • Robert Stephens *Henry Wynne-Walton* • Jack Watson *Sergeant Johnson* ■ *Dir* Michael Powell • *Scr* Roger Milner, from his story, from an idea by Simon Harcourt-Smith

Queens Logic ★★★ 15

Comedy drama 1991 · US · Colour · 108mins

As in *The Big Chill*, a group of old friends are brought together by a life-changing event – in this case the impending marriage of Ray (Ken Olin) and Patricia (Chloe Webb). Gathering for Ray's bachelor party (in Queens, of course) are Al (Joe Mantegna), a fishmonger married to Linda Fiorentino, a gay but celibate John Malkovich as Eliot and Dennis (Kevin Bacon) now living in Hollywood. The film provides a gritty and thoroughly watchable group, but is essentially a series of well-written sketches. 🖭

Kevin Bacon *Dennis* • Linda Fiorentino *Carla* • John Malkovich *Eliot* • Joe Mantegna *Al* • Ken Olin *Ray* • Tony Spiridakis *Vinny* • Chloe Webb *Patricia* • Tom Waits *Monte* • Jamie Lee Curtis • Helen Hunt ■ *Dir* Steve Rash • *Scr* Tony Spiridakis, from a story by Joseph W Savino, Tony Spiridakis

Querelle ★★★ 18

Drama 1982 · W Ger/Fr · Colour · 104mins

Rainer Werner Fassbinder didn't live to see the release of this long-cherished adaptation of Jean Genet's once-banned novel, *Querelle de Brest*. By consistently deflecting away from the drama and by having the cast recite lines rather than give performances, Fassbinder was able to explore the cinematic quality of non-action. Moreover, his use of blatantly theatrical sets emphasises the unreality of the events that follow sailor Brad Davis's arrival at Jeanne Moreau's waterfront brothel. It's a despondent wallow in a world full of

U = SUITABLE FOR ALL   Uc = SUITABLE FOR ALL, ESPECIALLY FOR YOUNG CHILDREN (VIDEO ONLY)   PG = PARENTAL GUIDANCE

drugs, murder, alienation and suppressed emotion and is, therefore, more valuable as a final self-portrait than as a work of art. In German with English subtitles. 🔳

Brad Davis *Querelle* • Franco Nero *Lieutenant Seblon* • Jeanne Moreau *Lysiane* • Günther Kaufmann *Nono* • Laurent Malet *Roger Bataille* ■ *Dir* Rainer Werner Fassbinder • *Scr* Rainer Werner Fassbinder, Burkhard Driest, from the novel *Querelle de Brest* by Jean Genet • *Editor* Franz Walsch [Rainer Werner Fassbinder], Juliane Lorenz

The Quest ★★★ 18
Martial arts action
1996 · US · Colour · 90mins

In twenties New York City, Jean-Claude Van Damme is a small-time street criminal who finds himself a stowaway on a ship headed for the South China Seas. Following an attack by pirates, Van Damme meets Lord Edgar Dobbs (Roger Moore), and ends up in the charge of a martials arts master. Soon the two are scheming to enter Van Damme in the ''ultimate fighting match'' with its winning prize of a solid gold dragon statue. As Van Damme's debut directing effort, it's remarkably better than his usual films. Contains violence and some swearing. 🔳

Jean-Claude Van Damme *Chris Dubois* • Roger Moore *Lord Edgar Dobbs* • James Remar *Maxie Devine* • Janet Gunn *Carrie Newton* ■ *Dir* Jean-Claude Van Damme • *Scr* Steven Klein, Paul Mones, from a story by Frank Dux, Jean-Claude Van Damme

Quest for Fire ★★ 15
Prehistoric drama
1981 · Fr/Can · Colour · 95mins

The opening of Stanley Kubrick's *2001: a Space Odyssey* aside, the accepted wisdom is that cavemen movies don't work. Even if you dress them up with anthropological significance and call upon experts like Desmond Morris and Anthony Burgess to design the diverse gestures and grunts, the action will still be limited by the spartan simplicity of the prehistoric lifestyle. To his credit, Jean-Jacques Annaud succeeds in locating the characters within their hostile environment (variously Canada, Scotland, Iceland and Kenya) and explores the primitive intelligence of the questing Ulams without patronising them or the less civilised Ivakas. But it's still a trying experience. 🔳

Everett McGill *Naoh* • Ron Perlman *Amoukar* • Nameer El-Kadi *Gaw* • Rae Dawn Chong *Ika* • Gary Schwartz *Rouka* ■ *Dir* Jean-Jacques Annaud • *Scr* Gerard Brach, from the novel *La Guerre du Feu* by JH Rosny Sr

Quest for Justice ★★ 12
Drama based on a true story
1993 · US · Colour · 91mins

Jane Seymour, bless her, seems to have the uncanny ability to turn anything she works on into soap, and this racial TV drama, based on a true story, is no different. She plays a journalist in the Deep South in the fifties who discovers a political conscience and takes up the civil rights banner, much to the suspicion and dislike of the white community. It's a fascinating story, but director James Keach (brother of Stacy Keach and Seymour's husband) lays on the clichés with a trowel and the political

message is drowned out by soppy sentiment. Contains violence.

Jane Seymour *Hazel Brannon Smith* • Richard Kiley *Earl Clayburn* • DW Moffett *Smitty* • Lou Walker *Riley* ■ *Dir* James Keach • *Scr* Rama Laurie Stagner

Quest for Love ★★★ PG
Science-fiction drama
1971 · UK · Colour · 87mins

Before *Dynasty* became her destiny, Joan Collins made many attempts at acting, including this beguiling British science-fiction piece from *Carry On* producer Peter Rogers and *Doctor in the House* director Ralph Thomas. Tom Bell co-stars as a physicist who, after an explosion, finds himself in an alternative universe where his girlfriend Collins is dying. A supporting cast of the usual British stalwarts puts in a decent effort, while Bell is believably bemused. And Collins? A touchingly moving performance minus the power-shoulders. 🔳

Joan Collins *Ottilie* • Tom Bell *Colin Trafford* • Denholm Elliott *Tom Lewis* • Laurence Naismith *Sir Henry Lanstein* • Lyn Ashley *Jennifer* • Juliet Harmer *Geraldine Lambert* • Ray McAnally *Jack Kahn* ■ *Dir* Ralph Thomas • *Scr* Terence Feely, from the short story *Random Quest* by John Wyndham

Quest for Love ★★★ 15
Drama
1988 · SAfr · Colour · 90mins

Turning to Gertrude Stein's novel *Q.E.D.* for inspiration, Helen Nogueira became the first South African woman to direct a feature with this confident combination of political thriller and lesbian love story. Set in the fictional state of Mozania, shortly after black independence, the yacht-board action focuses on a romantic triangle comprising journalist Jana Cilliers, her passionate friend, Sandra Prinsloo, and her flighty lover, Joanna Weinberg. The film is primarily concerned with breaking with the stereotypical depiction of lesbian sensuality, but Cilliers's relationship with terrorist Wayne Bowman (and graphic scenes of torture and repressive violence) reinforce the political dimension. 🔳

Jana Cilliers *Alex* • Sandra Prinsloo • Joanna Weinberg *Mabel* • Wayne Bowman *Michael* • Lynn Gaines *Isabella* ■ *Dir* Helen Nogueira • *Scr* Helen Nogueira, from the novel *Q.E.D.* by Gertrude Stein

Quest of the Delta Knights ★
Action fantasy adventure
1993 · US · Colour · 97mins

This lame addition to the sword-and-sorcery genre is notable for its threadbare production values. In the Dark Ages, young Tee is sold into slavery, bought by mysterious beggar (David Warner), and trained to become one of the Delta Knights, a secret order whose mission is to help humanity. Together with painter Leonardo (of Vinci!), and lowly tavern girl Thena, he sets off to fulfil a prophecy and find the lost treasures of Archimedes before the villainous Lord Vultare (David Warner, again) does. Badly acted, the direction by James Dodson is almost as shaky as the sets.

David Warner *Lord Vultare/Raydoor* • Corbin Allred *Tee* • David Kriegel *Leonardo* • Brigid Conley Walsh *Thena* • Richard Kind *Wamthool* • Olivia Hussey *Mannerjay* ■ *Dir* James Dodson • *Scr* Redge Mahaffey

A Question of Silence ★★★★ 15
Crime drama
1982 · Neth · Colour · 95mins

Without any prior film-making experience, Marleen Gorris received state funding for this highly controversial debut, which unequivocally posits that patriarchal capitalism exists solely to exploit, repress and abuse women. One of the angriest (yet most lucid and undogmatic) feminist statements ever committed to celluloid, it uses cleverly contrasting flashbacks to chart court psychiatrist Cox Habbema's gradual appreciation of the motives that drove harassed housewife Edda Barends, divorced waitress Nelly Frijda and efficient secretary Henriette Tol to savagely beat to death the smug male boutique owner who caught Barends shoplifting. Compelling and provocative, from the shocking assault to the galvanising courtroom finale. In Dutch with English subtitles.

Edda Barends *Christine M* • Nelly Frijda *Waitress* • Henriette Tol *Secretary* • Cox Habbema *Dr Janine Van Den Bos* • Eddy Brugman *Rudd* ■ *Dir/Scr* Marleen Gorris

Quick ★★ 18
Action crime drama
1993 · US · Colour · 94mins

Unremarkable shoot-em up action filler notable for the performance of Teri Polo. She outshines the material as a hit woman in Los Angeles who does favours for her corrupt cop boyfriend (Jeff Fahey). Things really hot up when she's asked to kidnap a government witness (Martin Donovan) and allows a relationship to develop between them. It's a plot thinner than a negligee but there is adequate action and snappy dialogue. Among a credible support cast ex-Bond villain (*Licence to Kill*) Robert Davi is suitably slimy as a mobster, while *Wayne's World*'s Tia Carrere adds exotica to her role as a federal agent. 🔳

Jeff Fahey *Muncie* • Teri Polo *Quick* • Robert Davi *Davenport* • Tia Carrere *Janet* • Martin Donovan *Herschel Brewer* ■ *Dir* Rick King • *Scr* Frederick Bailey

The Quick and the Dead ★★★ PG
Western
1987 · US · Colour · 86mins

With a spaghetti-style plot and its overtones of *Shane* and *Friendly Persuasion*, this is a superior TV-movie western, that only lets itself down with its uncertain re-creation of the frontier of the 1870s. The story is involving and well told by director Robert Day, but it is the performances that elevate this above the pack. Tom Conti is admirable as the Indian war veteran whose pacifism is put to the test, and Sam Elliott obviously enjoys picking off baddies and smouldering around Conti's wife, played with some vigour, considering the shallowness of the part, by Kate Capshaw. 🔳

Sam Elliott *Con Vallian* • Tom Conti *Duncan McKaskel* • Kate Capshaw *Susanna McKaskel*

• Kenny Morrison *Tom McKaskel* ■ *Dir* Robert Day • *Scr* James Lee Barrett, from a story by Louis L'Amour

The Quick and the Dead ★★★ 15
Western
1995 · US · Colour · 103mins

Sharon Stone stars as a mysterious stranger, riding Clint Eastwood-style into a town called Redemption to take part in a gunfighting competition presided over by the evil Gene Hackman. This homage to the spaghetti-western style of Sergio Leone is as daft as they come, a sort of Roman epic with six-guns replacing tridents, and the point is rammed home by the cameo casting of Woody Strode, who almost killed Spartacus in 1960. *Evil Dead* director Sam Raimi smacks his lips in every OTT scene, but today this wacky movie will draw an entirely new audience because it also stars Leonardo DiCaprio as the freshest-faced, prettiest gunslinger in town. Contains violence, swearing and sex scenes. 🔳 *DVD*

Sharon Stone *Ellen* • Gene Hackman *John Herod* • Russell Crowe *Cort* • Leonardo DiCaprio *Kid* • Tobin Bell *Dog Kelly* • Lance Henriksen *Ace Hanlon* • Gary Sinise *Marshall* ■ *Dir* Sam Raimi • *Scr* Simon Moore

Quick Change ★★★ 15
Crime comedy
1990 · US · Colour · 84mins

Bill Murray chose an offbeat, small-scale project for his directorial debut, but the result was a warm, slightly melancholic comedy. Murray also stars, playing a reluctant robber who pulls off the perfect bank raid dressed as a clown but who is driven to despair trying to leave the city with partners in crime Geena Davis and Randy Quaid. The three leads are great and there is fine support, too, from Jason Robards Jr as the cop on their trail. You should find yourself chuckling away sympathetically throughout. Contains swearing. •

Bill Murray *Grimm* • Geena Davis *Phyllis* • Randy Quaid *Loomis* • Jason Robards Jr *Chief Rotzinger* • Dale Grand *Street Barker* • Bob Elliott *Bank guard* ■ *Dir* Howard Franklin, Bill Murray • *Scr* Howard Franklin, from the novel by Jay Cronley

Quick, Let's Get Married ★
Comedy
1964 · US · Colour · 100mins

The great Ginger Rogers bowed out of films in the fifties but returned briefly in the sixties to make two new movies, this one and later a biopic *Harlow*. This features Rogers as the madam of a brothel and was supposed to be the first of a new string of Rogers comedies produced by her ex-husband William Marshall. No further titles were made and this film itself wasn't released until 1971. Once it was unleashed it was easy to understand why it had been shelved for so long. Notable only for an early appearance by a young Elliott Gould.

Ginger Rogers *Mme Rinaldi* • Ray Milland *Mario Forni* • Barbara Eden *Pia* • Walter Abel *The thief* • Elliott Gould *The mute* • Michael Ansara *Mayor* ■ *Dir* William Dieterle • *Scr* Allan Scott

Quick Millions ★★ U

Crime drama　　1931 · US · BW · 61mins

A gangster movie with Spencer Tracy – in an early role – playing a truck driver who organises a protection racket and becomes a mobster, almost against his will since he really craves respectability. His bodyguard is played by George Raft. Boasting much less action than others of the genre, it was directed by the combative left-winger, Rowland Brown, who had written the source material for the 1930 film *Doorway to Hell*, a picture sometimes regarded by film historians as the first gangster movie to portray the mobster as the product of sexual, social and economic problems.

Spencer Tracy *Daniel J "Bugs" Raymond* • Marguerite Churchill *Dorothy Stone* • John Wray *Kenneth Stone* • George Raft *Jimmy Kirk* ■ *Dir* Rowland Brown • *Scr* Courtney Terrett, Rowland Brown

Quicker than the Eye ★★ PG

Action drama
1989 · Swi/Fr/W Ger · Colour · 88mins

The big question here is what on earth is Jean Yanne, one of French cinema's most bitingly satirical directors and veteran actor of such classy French features as *Weekend* and *Le Boucher*, doing in a cornball cheapie like this? That's not to say this ambitious story of a magician who uses his powers to confound a gang of killers is not without its merits. Ben Gazzara, also somewhat slumming it, obviously enjoys the sleights of hand, but Mary Crosby wanders through the action as if someone has put her in a trance. Some dialogue dubbed into English. Contains violence and swearing. 🖾

Ben Gazzara *Ben Norrell* • Mary Crosby *Mary Preston* • Catherine Jarrett *Catherine Lombard* • Jean Yanne *Inspector Sutter* • Wolfram Berger *Kurt* ■ *Dir* Nicolas Gessner • *Scr* Joseph Murhaim, Nicolas Gessner, from the novel by Claude Cueni

Quicksand ★★★

Crime drama　　1959 · US · BW · 79mins

This excellent but forgotten little programme-filler features a well-cast Mickey Rooney as a car mechanic who's got the hots for no-good *femme fatale* Jeanne Cagney (James's real-life sister). Rooney is superb, and his demented persona is admirably suited to this underlit half-world. Even better, however, is sleazy Peter Lorre in one of his finer depictions of screen menace as a penny arcade owner. Director Irving Pichel cleverly puts all the elements together to produce an undervalued *film noir*.

Mickey Rooney *Dan Brady, auto mechanic* • Jeanne Cagney *Vera Novak, cafe cashier* • Barbara Bates *Helen* • Peter Lorre *Nick Dramoshag, penny arcade owner* • Art Smith *Mackey, garage owner* ■ *Dir* Irving Pichel • *Scr* Robert Smith

Quicksand: No Escape

★★★ PG

Thriller　　1992 · US · Colour · 88mins

An excellent thriller starring Donald Sutherland as a detective hired by an architect's wife who suspects her husband of having an affair. From this conventional opening, the plot spins some clever webs of intrigue, but this TV movie's main attraction is Sutherland, whose character has some of the weird, repressed spookiness of his earlier creation, John Klute. 🖾

Donald Sutherland *Doc* • Tim Matheson *Scott Reinhardt* • Jay Avocone *Ted Herman* • Timothy Carhart *Charlie* • John Joseph Finn [John Finn] *Ken Griffith* ■ *Dir* Michael Pressman • *Scr* Peter Baloff, Dave Wollert

Quicksilver ★★ 15

Drama　　1986 · US · Colour · 101mins

The mind boggles at how films like this ever get the money to be made. Imagine the pitch to the studio: "Ok, there's this hot-shot financial whizzkid who drops out of the Wall Street rat race to become – wait for it – a bicycle messenger. But heh, I see bicycle messengers as America's new cowboys, wheels instead of hoofs, get it? And don't worry we'll paper over the fact the film's about absolutely nothing, with a hit-and-run murder, drug dealers, racial tension, even break-dancing on the bikes. Still not sold? How about roping in your usual eighties music soundtrack suspects – Giorgio Moroder and Ray Parker Jr. It could be another *Flashdance* or *Footloose*. Heh, that gives me a great idea, let's cast Kevin Bacon!'' ''Sounds great kid, here's $7 million, go make it!!!'' 🖾

Kevin Bacon *Jack Casey* • Jami Gertz *Terri* • Paul Rodriguez *Hector Rodriguez* • Rudy Ramos *Gypsy* • Andrew Smith *Gabe Kaplan* • Larry Fishburne [Laurence Fishburne] *Voodoo* ■ *Dir/Scr* Tom Donnelly [Thomas Michael Donnelly]

Quicksilver Highway ★★ 15

Supernatural horror
1997 · US · Colour · 86mins

Two masters of horror, Stephen King and Clive Barker, join forces in these unusual twin tales of the occult, their short stories *Chattering Teeth* and *The Body Politic*. A mysterious loner travels the highways in a trailer, recounting to strangers an eerie story of a hitchhiker whose life is saved by a set of novelty chattering teeth possessed by demons, and a second bizarre story of a doctor whose hands take on a life of their own. An attempt to recapture the classic supernatural feel of *The Twilight Zone* anthology, this is given a first-class pedigree with the slick direction of horror-meister director Mick Garris. Contains some violence and swearing. 🖾

Christopher Lloyd *Quicksilver* • Matt Frewer *Dr George* • Raphael Sbarge *Hector Hogan* • Silas Weir Mitchell *Hitchhiker* • Bill Nunn *Dr Jeudwine* ■ *Dir* Mick Garris • *Scr* Mick Garris, from the short stories *Chattering Teeth* by Stephen King and *The Body Politic* by Clive Barker

The Quiet American ★★★ PG

Drama　　1958 · US · BW · 116mins

America's most-decorated Second World War soldier was baby-faced Audie Murphy, who carved out a screen career with a gun in his hand, notably in a stream of support westerns, until his tragic death in 1971. Following the filming of his own autobiography *To Hell and Back*, Murphy became a major star for a short while, and was ideally cast as the naive American in this worthy but, unfortunately, rather dull adaptation of Graham Greene's novel about Saigon politics in the pre-Vietnam era. He is well cast, and actually very good, but at the time the critics over-praised co-star Michael Redgrave and, as ever, under-rated Murphy. Writer/director Joseph L Mankiewicz makes heavy weather of the subject. Nevertheless, it's an interesting failure. 🖾

Audie Murphy *The American* • Michael Redgrave *Fowler* • Giorgia Moll *Phuong* • Claude Dauphin *Inspector Vigot* • Kerima *Miss Hei* • Bruce Cabot *Bill Granger* ■ *Dir* Joseph L Mankiewicz • *Scr* Joseph LMankiewicz

Quiet Cool ★ 18

Action thriller　　1986 · US · Colour · 77mins

The only thing this movie has that differentiates it from other dreary action films (apart from characters actually running out of ammo in the shoot-outs) is the Pacific Northwest setting, though even that manages to look as grungy as the cast members. James Remar is the New York cop who travels there to help a former girlfriend living in a community under the thumb of violent marijuana growers, led by Nick Cassavetes. The meaning of the title is a long time coming, though it does manage to provide an unintentional laugh. 🖾

James Remar *Joe Dillon* • Nick Cassavetes *Valence* • Jared Martin *Mike Prior* • Adam Coleman Howard *Joshua Greer* • Daphne Ashbrook *Katy Greer* ■ *Dir* Clay Borris • *Scr* Clay Borris, Susan Vercellino

Quiet Days in Clichy ★★ 18

Biographical comedy
1969 · Den · BW · 99mins

The French New Wave meets the Danish skin flick in this wild adaptation of Henry Miller's novel. Badly showing its age, it now stands as a fascinating tribute both to the freewheeling spirit of Miller's sexual odyssey and to the technical excess that was hailed as progressive film-making in the sixties. Played out to the eccentric folk music of Country Joe McDonald, the amorous adventures of a lusty American in Paris are regularly punctuated by jump cuts, captions, speech bubbles and moments of rampaging soft-core sex and actorly incompetence. A Danish language film. Contains sex scenes. 🖾

Paul Valjean *Joey* • Louise White *Surrealist* • Wayne John Rodda *Carl* • Ulla Lemvigh-Mueller *Nys* ■ *Dir* Jens Jørgen Thorsen • *Scr* Jens Jørgen Thorsen, from the novel by Henry Miller • *Music* Country Joe McDonald

The Quiet Earth ★★★ 15

Science-fiction thriller
1985 · NZ · Colour · 87mins

A scientist awakes one morning only to realise he may be the only person left alive on earth after an experiment goes wrong. It's an intriguing if not altogether original concept. *The World, the Flesh and the Devil* and Charlton Heston's cult *The Omega Man* were there first. Bruno Lawrence gives a beguiling central performance as someone who is suddenly able to live out his fantasies, to enjoy the empty city without guilt or interference. Shot against stunning Auckland backdrops, the early section develops a strong sense of mystery, but after Lawrence discovers two other survivors, one male, one female, the script follows an all too predictable path.

Bruno Lawrence *Zac Hobson* • Alison Routledge *Joanne* • Peter Smith *Api* • Anzac Wallace *Api's mate* • Norman Fletcher *Perrin* • Tom Hyde *Scientist* ■ *Dir* Geoff Murphy • *Scr* Bill Baer, Bruno Lawrence, Sam Pillsbury

The Quiet Family ★★★

Black comedy thriller
1998 · S Kor · Colour · 98mins

Shades of *Arsenic and Old Lace* colour this dark South Korean romp. No sooner has the "Misty Lodge" opened its doors than the bodies start to pile up and the garden begins to resemble a cemetery. But there's worse to come when a murderous businessman lures his detested stepmother to the isolated hilltop cottage and the government announces plans for a new road – right past the front gate. This is a wickedly anarchic comedy of errors. A Korean language film.

Choi Min-sik • Mun-hee Na • Park In-hwan • Song Kang-ho ■ *Dir* Kim Ji-un • *Scr* Kim Ji-un

The Quiet Man ★★★★ U

Romantic adventure
1952 · US · Colour · 129mins

John Ford won his fifth best director Oscar for this immensely popular chunk of old blarney (why did he never win for his westerns?); today, however, this dated movie needs a very sympathetic audience. John Wayne is, of course, splendid as the boxer returning to his roots, with feisty Maureen O'Hara more than a match for him. Victor Young's lilting score is also very enjoyable, while Winton Hoch and Archie Stunt's Techincolor photography deservedly won the film a second Oscar. If you're in the right mood, *The Quiet Man* will make you laugh and cry but only if you're receptive to blarney. 🖾

John Wayne *Sean Thornton* • Maureen O'Hara *Mary Kate Danaher* • Barry Fitzgerald *Michaeleen Flynn* • Ward Bond *Father Peter Lonergan* • Victor McLaglen *"Red" Will Danaher* ■ *Dir* John Ford • *Scr* Frank S Nugent (uncredited), Richard Llewellyn, from the story by Maurice Walsh • *Cinematographer* Winton C Hoch • *Music* Victor Young

Quiet Please, Murder ★★

Crime drama　　1942 · US · BW · 70mins

An interesting little programme-filler starring the suave George Sanders, just after his acclaimed performance as a dissolute painter in *The Moon and Sixpence*. This time he plays a master forger, passing off his imitations as First Folio Shakespeare, in a clever and relatively sophisticated blend of romance and murder. His female co-star is Gail Patrick, who later went on to produce the *Perry Mason* TV series. Virtually unknown director John Larkin doesn't get in the way of some cleverish writing, though budgetary limitations don't help.

George Sanders *Fleg* • Gail Patrick *Myra Blandy* • Richard Denning *Hal Mcbyrne* • Lynne Roberts *Kay Ryan* • Sidney Blackmer *Martin Cleaver* ■ *Dir* John Larkin • *Scr* John Larkin, from a story by Lawrence G Blochman

Quiet Victory: the Charlie Wedemeyer Story ★★ PG

Drama based on a true story
1988 · US · Colour · 93mins

An often moving fact-based drama about an American football star – *Flashdance's* Michael Nouri – who developed Lou Gehrig's disease in the seventies, but refused to let it beat him, going on to become a high school football coach even when confined to a wheelchair. *Mork and Mindy* star Pam Dawber is his supportive wife in this tale that never gets too schmaltzy. ▭

Michael Nouri *Charlie Wedemeyer* • Pam Dawber *Lucy Wedemeyer* • Bess Meyer *Carri Wedemeyer* • Peter Berg *Bobby Manker* • Stephen Dorff *Kale Wedemeyer* ■ *Dir* Roy Campanella II • *Scr* Barry Morrow

Quiet Weekend ★★ U

Comedy
1946 · UK · BW · 90mins

As anyone familiar with Anthony Asquith's classic comedy of manners *Quiet Wedding* will know, the title of this disappointing sequel is ironic in the extreme. Although also based on an Esther McCracken play, the screenplay lacks the crisp chaos of the original co-written by Terence Rattigan. Consequently, the romantic tangles of Derek Farr and the poaching misadventures of George Thorpe and magistrate Frank Cellier fail to deliver the laughs deserving of such whole-hearted playing.

Derek Farr *Denys Royd* • Frank Cellier *Adrian Barrasford* • Marjorie Fielding *Mildred Royd* • George Thorpe *Arthur Royd* • Barbara White *Miranda Bute* • Helen Shingler *Rowena Hyde* ■ *Dir* Harold French • *Scr* Warwick Ward, Victor Skutezky, Stephen Black , TJ Morrison, from the play by Esther McCracken

The Quiet Woman ★ U

Crime thriller
1950 · UK · BW · 70mins

John Gilling was a vital cog in the conveyor belt that churned out quota quickie-style films in the fifties. He wrote and directed this feeble thriller. Jane Hylton stars as the woman whose fresh start is threatened when her jailbird ex-husband arrives on her doorstep demanding shelter. Romantic entanglements and a smuggling subplot can't save the picture from sinking deservedly into the mire.

Derek Bond *Duncan Mcleod* • Jane Hylton *Jane Foster* • Dora Bryan *Elsie* • Michael Balfour *Lefty* • Dianne Foster *Helen* ■ *Dir* John Gilling • *Scr* John Gilling

Quigley Down Under ★★★ 15

Western
1990 · US · Colour · 114mins

Entertaining attempt to transplant the western genre Down Under with a grizzled Tom Selleck as the laid-back sharpshooter who rebels against Australian land baron Alan Rickman, who wants him for a little Aborigine genocide. Director Simon Wincer makes full use of the grand Australian locations. Selleck is likeable enough in the title role, but unwittingly joins the list of Hollywood stars who have been effortlessly upstaged by Rickman, who delivers another wonderfully villainous performance.

Tom Selleck *Matthew Quigley* • Laura San Giacomo *Crazy Cora* • Alan Rickman *Elliott*

Marston • Chris Haywood *Major Ashley Pitt* • Ron Haddrick *Grimmelman* • Tony Bonner *Dobkin* ■ *Dir* Simon Wincer • *Scr* John Hill

The Quiller Memorandum ★★★★ PG

Spy drama
1966 · UK · Colour · 100mins

The menace of Harold Pinter's script is marvellously sustained by director Michael Anderson in this under-rated thriller, with George Segal giving one of his finest performances as the secret agent investigating a neo-Nazi movement in sixties' Berlin. Alec Guinness and Max von Sydow excel as, respectively, the British spy chief and his evil Nazi counterpart, and, for once, a woman plays a formidable part – Senta Berger in an ambiguous role, the true nature of which is only revealed in the final shots. ▭

George Segal *Quiller* • Alec Guinness *Pol* • Max von Sydow *Oktober* • Senta Berger *Inge* • George Sanders *Gibbs* • Robert Helpmann *Weng* ■ *Dir* Michael Anderson • *Scr* Harold Pinter, from the novel *The Berlin Memorandum* by Adam Hall [Elleston Trevor]

Quilombo ★★★

Historical drama
1984 · Bra · Colour · 114mins

Returning to the subject of his debut feature, *Ganga Zumba* (1963), Carlos Diegues seeks here to compare conditions in the 17th-century utopian settlement of Quilombo de Palmares with those in modern-day Brazil. The narrative, divided into three acts, involves a rebellion of plantation slaves and the establishing of a tolerant and prosperous community with an elected leader, Zumba (Toni Tornado). Also embracing the persecuted indigenous people and Jews fleeing the Inquisition, the community ultimately collapses through colonial brutality and internal division. This is an overly stylised, but engagingly powerful tract. In Portuguese with English subtitles.

Antonio Pompeo *Zumbi* • Zeze Motta *Dandara* • Toni Tornado *Ganga Zumba* • Vera Fischer *Ana de Ferro* ■ *Dir/Scr* Carlos Diegues

The Quince Tree Sun ★★★★ U

Documentary drama
1991 · Sp · Colour · 132mins

You'll get a whole new angle on the phrase ''as interesting as watching paint dry'' after seeing this wonderful documentary by the Spanish director Victor Erice. The film focuses on Antonio Lopez's meticulous execution of a painting of the quince tree in his garden. While this provides fascinating insights into the creative process, what is even more compelling is the artist's interaction both with the camera and the numerous visitors who drop in to see him. Best known for the haunting *Spirit of the Beehive*, Erice allows events to dictate the pace and what emerges is a mesmerising portrait. In Spanish with English subtitles. ▭

Dir Victor Erice • *Scr* Victor Erice, Antonio López, from an idea by Victor Erice, Antonio López García

Quintet ★★ 15

Science-fiction drama
1979 · US · Colour · 113mins

One of Robert Altman's more forgettable films, made during a spell when he was out of favour with critics and audiences alike (see also *Popeye*). An uncomfortable looking Paul Newman heads a largely European cast in a slow-moving and pretentious piece of post-apocalyptic sci-fi, about a deadly survival game played out in a deep-frozen future city. Everyone looks cold and watching it has a similar effect on the viewer. ▭

Paul Newman *Essex* • Vittorio Gassman *St Christopher* • Fernando Rey *Grigor* • Bibi Andersson *Ambrosia* • Brigitte Fossey *Vivia* • Nina Van Pallandt *Deuca* ■ *Dir* Robert Altman • *Scr* Robert Altman, Frank Barhydt, Patricia Resnick, from a story by Lionel Chetwynd, Robert Altman, Patricia Resnick

Quiz Show ★★★★ 15

Drama
1994 · US · Colour · 127mins

The riveting account of a true-life scandal of fifties' America, in which the winning contestant of the popular *Twenty-One* television game show was exposed as a fraud. Week after week, millions of viewers tuned in to watch a handsome and debonair professor (another memorable performance from Ralph Fiennes) flex his intellectual prowess, but it was later revealed he was given the answers in advance by a corrupt network seeking sponsorship dollars. John Turturro matches Fiennes as the show's unfairly deposed former champion, while Rob Morrow is the lawyer investigating the scam. Intelligently crafted by director Robert Redford, this absorbing drama says everything and more about American ethics, manners and morals, revealing the true price of fame during the days of TV's innocence. Contains some swearing. ▭ *DVD*

John Turturro *Herbie Stempel* • Rob Morrow *Dick Goodwin* • Ralph Fiennes *Charles Van Doren* • Paul Scofield *Mark Van Doren* • David Paymer *Dan Enright* • Hank Azaria *Albert Freedman* ■ *Dir* Robert Redford • *Scr* Paul Attanasio, from the book *Remembering America: a Voice from the Sixties* by Richard N Goodwin

Quo Vadis ★★★ PG

Historical epic
1951 · US · Colour · 161mins

Long and bloated, Mervyn LeRoy's *Quo Vadis* shows both the best and worst of depicting religious fervour in the Hollywood epic style. Alongside too-lengthy scenes of po-faced piety with pallid hero Robert Taylor and a wan Deborah Kerr, there is Peter Ustinov revelling in his role as the Emperor Nero. He pouts, simpers and fiddles while Rome burns, ad-libs to perfection and sends Christians to the lions in some spectacular arena scenes. Superbly cast against him is Leo Genn as Petronius, arbiter of fashion, whose speech before he opens his veins ''Do not mutilate the arts'' is a veiled attack on the then current McCarthy witch-hunts. ▭

Deborah Kerr *Lygia* • Robert Taylor (1) *Marcus Vinicius* • Peter Ustinov *Nero* • Leo Genn *Petronius* • Patricia Laffan *Poppaea* • Elizabeth Taylor ■ *Dir* Mervyn LeRoy • *Scr* John Lee Mahin, Sonya Levien, SN Behrman, from the novel by Henryk Sienkiewicz

Quo Vadis? ★★

Historical drama
1985 · It · Colour · 122mins

Franco Rossi's TV movie, based on the saga by Henryk Sienkiewicz, is an adaptation as ponderous as it is pretentious, with Francesco Quinn (Anthony Quinn's son) as the Roman soldier seduced into Christianity by a slave girl. The film is about as unviewable as the book is unreadable, though a vivid portrayal of regal megalomania by Klaus Maria Brandauer, as Emperor Nero, is worthy of attention.

Frederic Forrest *Petronius* • Francesco Quinn *Marcus Vinicius* • Klaus Maria Brandauer *Nero* • Marie-Theres Relin *Lygia* • Barbara De Rossi *Eunice* • Max von Sydow *Apostle Peter* ■ *Dir* Franco Rossi • *Scr* Franco Rossi, Ennio De Concini, Francesco Scardamaglia, from the novel by Henryk Sienkiewicz

RKO 281   ★★★★

Drama based on a true story
1999 · US · Colour · 90mins

When Orson Welles embarked upon his directorial debut, he described RKO as the biggest train set a boy could ever have. However, there was nothing juvenile about project 281, as *Citizen Kane* was to become the most critically lauded film of all time. Its production was anything but untroubled, though, as this stylish TV movie demonstrates. The feuds with co-scenarist Herman J Mankiewicz and media tycoon William Randolph Hearst are fully explored in this splendidly cast drama. Contains some swearing.

Liev Schreiber *Orson Welles* • James Cromwell *William Randolph Hearst* • Melanie Griffith *Marion Davies* • John Malkovich *Herman Mankiewicz* • Brenda Blethyn *Louella Parsons* • Roy Scheider *George Schaefer* • David Suchet *Louis B Mayer* • Fiona Shaw *Hedda Hopper* ■ *Dir* Benjamin Ross • *Scr* John Logan, from the original documentary script for *The Battle over Citizen Kane* by Richard Ben Cramer, Thomas Lennon

RPM – Revolutions per Minute   ★

Political drama   1970 · US · Colour · 91mins

A woeful, cheerless Stanley Kramer effort that tries to evoke the era of student protest and counterculture – hence the silly title. Written by Erich Segal, who also wrote *Love Story*, it stars Anthony Quinn as a campus professor, Ann-Margret as his mistress and Gary Lockwood (an astronaut from *2001: a Space Odyssey*) as the revolting student who organises a takeover of the university's computer and admin offices. Quinn decides to call the cops, which is when Kramer, never the subtlest of directors, gets heavy himself with obvious but empty parallels to the student riots in Chicago and at Kent State University.

Anthony Quinn *Perez* • Ann-Margret *Rhoda* • Gary Lockwood *Rossiter* • Paul Winfield *Dempsey* • Graham Jarvis *Thatcher* ■ *Dir* Stanley Kramer • *Scr* Erich Segal

Rabid   ★★★ 18

Horror   1976 · Can · Colour · 90mins

Another formative exercise in fear and loathing of the human body from director David Cronenberg, which takes up the themes of *Shivers*. This time a plague is let loose after accident victim Marilyn Chambers becomes the unwitting carrier of a rabid disease which turns people into bloodsuckers. This disturbing film lacks the claustrophobia of *Shivers*, but is an altogether slicker affair, and the spiralling violence still shocks. ▭

Marilyn Chambers *Rose* • Frank Moore *Hart Read* • Joe Silver *Murray Cypher* • Howard Ryshpan *Dr Dan Keloid* • Patricia Gage *Dr Roxanne Keloid* • Susan Roman *Mindy Kent* ■ *Dir/Scr* David Cronenberg

Rabid Grannies   ★★ 18

Comedy horror   1989 · Bel · Colour · 88mins

A badly-made Belgian splatter movie dubbed with inane British accents, that manages to be boring one minute and extremely offensive the next. A waft of smoke from a satanist turns two wealthy old aunts into slobbering, blood-crazed zombies during their birthday party in an old country mansion. The guests are all greedy relatives and obvious stereotypes (priest, lesbian, arms dealer, fat condom-maker) who want to worm themselves into the will but end up being savagely slaughtered instead. The gore may be unconvincing but it's relentlessly disgusting when it finally begins, as limbs are cut off, buttocks shredded, brains hit the walls and intestines ooze. French dialogue dubbed into English. ▭

Catherine Aymerie *Helen* • Caroline Braekman *Suzie* • Danielle Daven *Elisabeth Remington* • Richard Cotica *Gilbert* • Raymond Lescot *Reverend Father* ■ *Dir/Scr* Emmanuel Kervyn

Race against Fear   ★

Drama   1998 · US · Colour

In this instalment in the *Moment of Truth* original series of TV "teen in jeopardy" movies, the important subject matter of sexual harassment and abuse of power is given shallow treatment. A young runner has her dreams shattered when her coach and mentor rapes her. Despite a lack of support from her fellow teammates and a now-famous runner who was also abused by the coach, she decides to press charges. The cardboard characters lack depth and originality.

Ariana Richards *Mickey Carlyle* • Susan Blakely *Margaret Carlyle* • William Bumiller *Kurt Ansom* • Tracee Ellis Ross *Kaycee King* ■ *Dir* Joseph L Scanlan • *Scr* Jean Gennis, Phyllis Murphy, Sara Charno

Race against Time: the Search for Sarah   ★★ 12

Drama based on a true story
1996 · US · Colour · 85mins

Another well-meaning true-story TV movie, starring one of the genre's stalwarts, Patty Duke, as the mother of a kidnapped child. While the cast gives its all, this never rises above a cliché-ridden attempt to milk our emotions, despite taut direction from Fred Gerber (best known for episodes of TV series such as *ER* and *The X Files*). The main culprit is the predictable script from William Wood, Mimi Rothman Schapiro and Bill Wells.

Patty Duke *Natalie Porter* • Richard Crenna *John Porter* • Ele Keats *Sarah* • Caitlin Wachs *Amy* ■ *Dir* Fred Gerber • *Scr* William Wood, Bill Wells, Mimi Rothman Schapiro

Race for Glory   ★★ 15

Sports drama   1989 · US · Colour · 102mins

Peter Berg and Alex McArthur play friends from a small town who find their relationship under strain when one of them decides he wants to become an international motorcycling champion. Despite a well-known cast that includes Ray Wise and Burt Kwouk, this never rises above the average. But at least it's not as bad as the similarly plotted David Essex vehicle, *Silver Dream Racer*. Contains swearing. ▭

Alex McArthur *Cody Gifford* • Peter Berg *Chris Washburn* • Pamela Ludwig *Jenny Eastman* • Ray Wise *Jack Davis* • Oliver Stritzel *Klaus Kroeter* • Burt Kwouk *Yoshiro Tanaka* ■ *Dir* Rocky Lang • *Scr* Scott Swanton

Race for Your Life, Charlie Brown   ★★ U

Animation   1977 · US · Colour · 73mins

The *Peanuts* people leave the familiar neighbourhood for a summer camp in the third of Bill Melendez's animated tales featuring Charles M Schulz's enduring creations. As usual, Charlie Brown is the goat all the other kids mock as he fails hopelessly at each activity, with the feisty Peppermint Patty adding the kind of scathing encouragement only she can. However, the little round-headed kid finally proves his worth during a white-water raft race. There are plenty of the customarily witty observations on life, but the pace is slack and Snoopy seems to be involved in a different movie altogether. ▭

Dir Bill Melendez, Phil Roman • *Scr* Charles M Schulz, from his comic strip

Race the Sun   ★★★ PG

Comedy   1996 · US · Colour · 95mins

Disadvantaged Hawaiian high school students, inspired by their teacher (Halle Berry), build a solar-powered vehicle in the shape of a cockroach and enter it into the World Solar Challenge, a race across Australia. Along the way they get to prove they aren't quitters, and show up evil corporations and arrogant foreigners. Moderately entertaining, but noteworthy for featuring a number of young actors who would go on to greater success, including Casey Affleck (brother of Ben), Steve Zahn (*Happy, Texas, Out of Sight*) and Eliza Dushku from TV's *Buffy the Vampire Slayer*. ▭

Halle Berry *Sandra Beecher* • James Belushi *Frank Machi* • Bill Hunter *Commissioner Hawkes* • Casey Affleck *Daniel Webster* • Eliza Dushku *Cindy Johnson* • Kevin Tighe *Jack Fryman* • Steve Zahn *Hans Kooiman* ■ *Dir* Charles T Kanganis • *Scr* Barry Morrow

Race to Freedom: the Underground Railroad   ★★★

Historical drama   1994 · Can · Colour · 91mins

A superb cast brings to life one of the most shameful, and inspiring, chapters in American history. In 1850 four black plantation slaves flee from North Carolina to Canada, with the help of abolitionists. They are pursued by bounty hunters through a deadly, unknown wilderness. Though realistically brutal at times, this TV movie will reward those who want to understand more about the African-American experience.

Janet Bailey *Sarah* • Dawnn Lewis *Minnie* • Glynn Turman *Solomon* • Courtney B Vance *Thomas* • Tim Reid • Alfre Woodard • Michael Riley *Alexander Ross* ■ *Dir* Don McBrearty • *Scr* Diana Braithwaite, Nancy Trites Botkin

Race with the Devil   ★★ 15

Thriller   1975 · US · Colour · 84mins

Easy Rider was both a triumph and a millstone for its star and producer, Peter Fonda. Attempting to move on from that emblem of counterculture, Fonda lurched from one *Easy Rider* rip-off to the next. *Dirty Mary, Crazy Larry*, with Susan George and a lot of wrecked cars, was a momentary hit; *Race with the Devil* was a sort of sequel, with more high-speed chases. This time, the influence of *The Exorcist* and *Rosemary's Baby* was also present: the bad guys are satanists from the back of Texas beyond. It's a studio concoction and the characters are taken straight off the shelf, but director Jack Starrett keeps things moving and Fonda's co-star, Warren Oates, is always worth watching. Contains some swearing. ▭

Peter Fonda *Roger* • Warren Oates *Frank* • Loretta Swit *Alice* • Lara Parker *Kelly* • RG Armstrong *Sheriff Taylor* ■ *Dir* Jack Starrett • *Scr* Wes Bishop, Lee Frost

The Racers   ★

Sports drama   1955 · US · Colour · 91mins

Also known as *Such Men Are Dangerous*, this motor-racing saga barely gets into first gear. Set around Europe but shot on the backlot at 20th Century-Fox, with an overworked back projection machine, it stars Kirk Douglas as the reckless driver who trashes his car and kills a dog whose owner, Bella Darvi, falls in love with him and finances his new car. Polish-born Darvi was a compulsive gambler and then the mistress of studio boss Darryl F Zanuck. Mrs Zanuck had her banished from Hollywood, and she later committed suicide.

Kirk Douglas *Gino* • Bella Darvi *Nicole* • Gilbert Roland *Dell 'Oro* • Lee J Cobb *Maglio* ■ *Dir* Henry Hathaway • *Scr* Charles Kaufman, from a novel by Hans Ruesch

Rachel and the Stranger   ★★★

Romantic western   1948 · US · BW · 92mins

An utterly charming quasi-western, distinguished by one of Robert Mitchum's most likeable, deceptively throwaway roles, as the itinerant tracker who momentarily comes between husband and wife William Holden and Loretta Young. Mitchum's vocal talents are given full rein here; indeed, he had a hit record of sorts in the duet he performs with youngster Gary Gray, *Just Like Me*, which became a regular on *Children's Choice* in the fifties and sixties.

Loretta Young *Rachel* • William Holden (1) *Big Davey Harvey* • Robert Mitchum *Jim Fairways* • Gary Gray *Little Davey* • Tom Tully *Parson Jackson* ■ *Dir* Norman Foster • *Scr* Waldo Salt, from the stories *Rachel and Neighbor Sam* by Howard Fast.

The Rachel Papers   ★★ 18

Comedy drama   1989 · UK · Colour · 90mins

Why must film-makers always be such slaves to the lowest common denominator? Convinced that modern teenagers would be put off by the old-fashioned idea of paper, writer/director Damian Harris turns teenager Charles Highway's written catalogue into a computer database for future use, this misfiring adaptation of Martin Amis's novel. Dexter Fletcher does well enough as the lovesick youngster who keeps a record of former girlfriends to aid future seductions, but the fact that he spends so much time talking directly to camera (in a clumsy bid to reproduce the book's first-person perspective) says a good deal about Harris's uninspired direction. Contains swearing and nudity.

Dexter Fletcher *Charles Highway* • Ione Skye *Rachel Seth-Smith* • Jonathan Pryce *Norman* • James Spader *DeForest* • Bill Paterson *Gordon Highway* • Shirley Anne Field *Mrs Seth-Smith* • Michael Gambon *Dr Knowd* • Amanda De Cadenet *Yvonne* • Aubrey Morris *Sir Herbert* ■ *Dir* Damian Harris • *Scr* Damian Harris, from the novel by Martin Amis

Rachel, Rachel ★★★★
Drama   1968 · US · Colour · 101mins
This may have been Paul Newman's directorial debut, but it's the performance by his wife Joanne Woodward that makes it such a moving and memorable drama. As the bashful teacher for whom returning childhood friend James Olson presents the last chance of romance, she brilliantly conveys the timidity born of a frustrated life spent in the service of others. Woodward's quiet power also comes to Newman's rescue when his inexperience allows the tone and tempo to slip. Newman and Woodward's daughter Nell Potts plays the young Rachel.

Joanne Woodward *Rachel Cameron* • James Olson *Nick Kazlik* • Kate Harrington *Mrs Cameron* • Estelle Parsons *Calla Mackie* • Donald Moffatt *Niall Cameron* • Terry Kiser *Preacher* • Nell Potts *Rachel as a child* ■ *Dir* Paul Newman • *Scr* Stewart Stern, from the novel *A Jest of God* by Margaret Laurence

Rachel River ★★
Comedy drama   1987 · US · Colour · 88mins
A worthy, if occasionally silly reworking of a very successful PBS American Playhouse production about a Minnesota journalist and her dealings with the various characters in her small home town. Pamela Reed does a sterling job as the journalist giving just enough wit and bite to what could have been a totally unbelievable personality. But, overall, the movie misses by a mile, largely owing to its lack of courage in dealing with the issues raised.

Zeljko Ivanek *Momo* • Pamela Reed *Mary Graving* • Craig T Nelson *Marlyn* • Viveca Lindfors *Harriet* • James Olson *Jack* • Alan North *Beske* • Jo Henderson *Estona* • Jon De Vries [Jon DeVries] *Baker* ■ *Dir* Sandy Smolan • *Scr* Judith Guest, from stories by Carol Bly

Rachel's Man ★★
Religious drama 1975 · Is · Colour · 111mins
A reverent, hushed version of the Biblical love story between Jacob (Leonard Whiting) and Rachel (Michal Bat-Adam). Filmed in Israel by Moshe Mizari, it also features Rita Tushingham as Rachel's older sister, Lea, and Mickey Rooney as the father of the two girls. But the film is let

down by a script which brooks no conflict in its characterisation.

Mickey Rooney *Laban* • Rita Tushingham *Lea* • Leonard Whiting *Jacob* • Michal Bat-Adam *Rachel* • Avner Hiskiyahu *Isaac* • Dalia Cohen *Zilpah* • Robert Stevens *Narrator* ■ *Dir* Moshe Mizrahi • *Scr* Moshe Mizrahi, Rachel Fabien

Racing with the Moon ★★★15
Wartime romance
1984 · US · Colour · 103mins
Considering it was written by Steve Kloves when in his twenties and toplines such stars in the making as Sean Penn, Elizabeth McGovern and Nicolas Cage, this is a curiously old-fashioned rites-of-passage romance. The atmosphere of a wartime Christmas has been deftly achieved without undue nostalgia by director Richard Benjamin, who artfully masks the story's comparative lack of incident by allowing his cast to fully explore their characters. Penn particularly rises to the challenge as the teenager who falls in love above his station while waiting to join the Marines. Slight, but charmingly authentic.

Sean Penn *Henry "Hopper" Nash* • Elizabeth McGovern *Caddie Winger* • Nicolas Cage *Nicky* • John Karlen *Mr Nash* • Rutanya Alda *Mrs Nash* • Max Showalter *Mr Arthur* ■ *Dir* Richard Benjamin • *Scr* Steven Kloves

The Rack ★★
Drama   1956 · US · BW · 100mins
In this early starring role, Paul Newman plays the previously heroic army captain on trial for having collaborated with the enemy while a captive in Korea. This big-screen version of a TV drama by Rod Serling is an intelligent but overlong examination of the Newman character's psychological make-up and what brought him to the breaking point. Unfortunately, Newman's performance is mostly boorish and monotonous – in contrast to the forthright work of Wendell Corey as prosecutor, Edmond O'Brien as defence counsel and Walter Pidgeon as Newman's cold father.

Paul Newman *Capt Edward W Hall Jr* • Wendell Corey *Maj Sam Moulton* • Walter Pidgeon *Col Edward W Hall Sr* • Edmond O'Brien *Lt Col Frank Wasnick* • Lee Marvin *Capt John R Miller* • Cloris Leachman *Caroline* ■ *Dir* Arnold Laven • *Scr* Stewart Stern, from the TV play by Rod Serling

The Racket ★★★
Silent crime drama 1928 · US · BW · 60mins
Long unseen, *The Racket* was a notable entry in the silent gangster cycle of the late twenties, directed with considerable flair by Lewis Milestone for Howard Hughes's production company. The film's exposé of crooked cops and politicians was daring for its time and it was widely banned in the United States. There would be more pressure to revive it (if it still exists) had the star of the original Broadway play, Edward G Robinson, repeated his role as the big bootlegger, Nick Scarsi. Instead the film cast Louis Wolheim, now only remembered for *All Quiet on the Western Front*, opposite another forgotten name, Thomas Meighan, as the dogged police chief who brings about Scarsi's downfall. The 1951

remake with Robert Mitchum was updated and conventionalised.

Thomas Meighan *Capt McQuigg* • Marie Prevost *Helen Hayes, an entertainer* • Louis Wolheim *Nick Scarsi, bootleg king* • John Darrow *Ames, a cub reporter* ■ *Dir* George Stone, Lewis Milestone • *Scr* Harry Behn, Del Andrews, Eddie Adams, Bartlett Cormack, from the play by Bartlett Cormack

The Racket ★★★
Crime drama   1951 · US · BW · 88mins
A tough crime drama, made by RKO for peanuts, with Robert Mitchum as an honest cop who goes up against a gangster (Robert Ryan) who has leading politicians in his pocket. The movie would have worked just as well if the actors had switched roles, and the directorial team of John Cromwell and Nicholas Ray laces the rather hackneyed story with some decent action scenes, car chases and a welcome dash of political cynicism.

Robert Mitchum *Captain McQuigg* • Lizabeth Scott *Irene* • Robert Ryan *Nick Scanlon* • William Talman *Johnson* • Ray Collins *Welch* • Joyce Mackenzie *Mary McQuigg* ■ *Dir* John Cromwell, Nicholas Ray • *Scr* William Wister Haines, WR Burnett, from the play by Bartlett Cormack

Radiant City ★★★
Period drama   1996 · US · Colour · 97mins
A slight but expertly performed slice of nostalgia, which looks back affectionately at fifties' New York. Kirstie Alley relishes the opportunity for a meatier role and is excellent as the Brooklyn mother who dreams of a better life for her family. There are also fine supporting turns from a cast that includes *Ally McBeal's* Gil Bellows, while director Robert Allan Ackerman displays a quirky eye for detail. Contains violence.

Kirstie Alley *Gloria Goodman* • Clancy Brown *Al Goodman* • Gil Bellows *Bert Kramer* • Laraine Newman *Flo* ■ *Dir* Robert Allan Ackerman • *Scr* Lewis Colick

Radio City Revels ★★U
Musical comedy 1938 · US · BW · 89mins
This can be recommended only to die-hard musical fans, since the plot, about a composer who only functions when he is asleep, is not only skimpy but becomes tiresome as Milton Berle and Jack Oakie desperately try to get Bob Burns to nap in their presence so that they can steal his creations. Amid the dross, however, are some sparkling musical moments.

Bob Burns *Lester Robin* • Jack Oakie *Harry Miller* • Kenny Baker [2] *Kenny* • Ann Miller *Billie Shaw* • Victor Moore *Paul Plummer* • Milton Berle *Teddy Jordan* • Helen Broderick *Gertie Shaw* • Jane Froman *Jane* ■ *Dir* Ben Stoloff [Benjamin Stoloff] • *Scr* Eddie Davis, Matt Brooks, Anthony Veiller, Mortimer Offner, from a story by Matt Brooks

Radio Days ★★★★PG
Comedy   1987 · US · Colour · 84mins
An under-rated entry in the Woody Allen canon, this is an intelligent and endlessly delightful examination of childhood and the process of memory. Although it is subtly directed and played to a nicety by a splendid ensemble cast, the film stands and

falls on the wit and insight of the script and the minute period detail of the production design, and both Allen and production designer Santo Loquasto deserved more than just Oscar nominations. Cutting effortlessly from the crowded family home in Brooklyn to the empty glamour of Radioland, this celluloid scrapbook is evocative and irresistible. Contains some swearing and brief nudity.

Mia Farrow *Sally White* • Julie Kavner *Mother* • Michael Tucker *Father* • Seth Green *Little Joe* • Dianne Wiest *Aunt Bea* • Josh Mostel *Uncle Abe* • Danny Aiello *Rocco* • Diane Keaton *New Year's singer* • Woody Allen *Narrator* ■ *Dir/Scr* Woody Allen

Radio Flyer ★★★PG
Fantasy drama   1992 · US · Colour · 109mins
The importance of belief in the impossible is the central theme of director Richard Donner's difficult yet delicate fantasy about two boys who escape the physical abuse of their stepfather via their toy red wagon, the *Radio Flyer*. Reconciling the children's battered background with their desperate need for release, Donner punctuates his affecting fable with surreal and mystical twists that weave a powerful spell. Well acted by an excellent cast (Tom Hanks is the uncredited narrator), the *ET*-style ending will leave a lasting impression that's both painful and wonderful.

Lorraine Bracco *Mary* • John Heard *Daugherty* • Adam Baldwin *The King* • Elijah Wood *Mike* • Joseph Mazzello *Bobby* • Ben Johnson *Geronimo Bill* • Sean Baca *Fisher* • Tom Hanks *Narrator* ■ *Dir* Richard Donner • *Scr* David Mickey Evans

Radio Inside ★★★
Drama   1994 · US · Colour · 95mins
A romantic triangle is supposedly at the centre of this quirky, Miami-set melodrama, but debuting director Jeffrey Bell seems much happier exploring William McNamara's religious convictions than he does following the developing relationship between McNamara and the neglected girlfriend (*Leaving Las Vegas's* Elisabeth Shue) of his workaholic brother (Dylan Walsh). McNamara's conversations with Christ (Ara Madzounian) have none of the sentimentality that clouds the flashbacks or the confusion that mars the subplot featuring Pee Wee Love. Yet, while Bell's structuring is shaky, his grasp of character is impressive and he's rewarded with some deft performances. Contains swearing and brief nudity.

William McNamara *Matthew* • Elisabeth Shue *Nathalie* • Dylan Walsh *Michael* • Ilse Earl *Mrs Piccalo* • Pee Wee Love *TJ* • Steve Zurk *Father* • Ara Madzounian *Jesus* ■ *Dir/Scr* Jeffrey Bell

Radio On ★★★18
Road movie   1979 · UK/W Ger · BW · 99mins
A British road movie that reaches the dead end of existential despair, as a disc jockey (David Beames) drives haphazardly from London to Bristol to find out why his brother died. Much influenced by German director Wim Wenders (an associate producer) and made by former *Time Out* critic Christopher Petit, its attempt at a

multi-layered narrative is undercut by wooden acting. Yet its use of pop music and landscape make it a captivating, if cryptic experience. ▭

David Beames *Robert* • Lisa Kreuzer *Ingrid* • Sandy Ratcliff *Kathy* • Andrew Byatt *Deserter* • Sue Jones-Davies *Girl* • Sting *Just Like Eddie* • Sabina Michael *Aunt* ■ *Dir* Christopher Petit • *Scr* Christopher Petit, Heidi Adolph

Radioactive Dreams ★★ 18
Science-fiction fantasy comedy
1986 · US/Mex · Colour · 94mins

The warning sign of this movie – Albert Pyun was the writer and director – won't stop a number of viewers, because of the nutty but very promising premise. Two little boys are taken into a bomb shelter just as World War III breaks out and grow up reading the works of Raymond Chandler. As adults (Michael Dudikoff and John Stockwell), they rename themselves after Phillip Marlowe, take on the personality of the hero of Chandler's novels and set out on a journey across the wastelands. However, Pyun quickly forgets the private eye angle, and settles for a routine story concerning the heroes trying to stop some goofy *Mad Max*-type villains from getting their hands on a remaining nuclear bomb. ▭

John Stockwell *Phillip* • Michael Dudikoff *Marlowe* • Lisa Blount *Miles* • George Kennedy *Spade Chandler* • Don Murray *Dash Hammer* • Michele Little *Rusty Mars* • Norbert Weisser *Sternwood* ■ *Dir/Scr* Albert Pyun

Radioland Murders ★★ PG
Comedy thriller 1994 · US · Colour · 103mins

After his success with *The Tall Guy*, comic-turned-director Mel Smith was courted by Hollywood (apparently he was in line for the *Wayne's World* job). However, he ended up with this comedy misfire, a flop executive produced by George Lucas. Intended as a salute to the golden age of radio, this finds Brian Benben and Mary Stuart Masterson overacting frantically as they attempt to find out who is dispatching the employees of a radio station in 1939 Chicago. This is, frankly, a shapeless mess, an unsuccessful mix of lame gags and stodgy slapstick. ▭

Brian Benben *Roger* • Mary Stuart Masterson *Penny Henderson* • Ned Beatty *General Whalen* • George Burns *Milt Lackey* • Scott Michael Campbell *Billy* • Michael McKean *Rick Rochester* • Christopher Lloyd *Zoltan* ■ *Dir* Mel Smith • *Scr* Willard Huyck, Gloria Katz, Jeff Reno, Ron Osborne, from a story by George Lucas

Rafferty and the Gold Dust Twins ★★ 15
Comedy road movie
1974 · US · Colour · 87mins

A slow and meandering road movie that takes the same route as *Easy Rider* – from LA to New Orleans – but tries to mirror the working class ambience of *Alice Doesn't Live Here Anymore*. Rafferty (Alan Arkin) is an army veteran and drifter who is implausibly kidnapped by two vagrant women – a wannabe singer (wacky Sally Kellerman) and an orphaned, teenage runaway (Mackenzie Phillips from *American Graffiti*). The plot twists

and is easily seduced down secondary roads, but compensations include the southwest scenery and Rafferty's amazingly funky conveyance. ▭

Alan Arkin *Rafferty* • Sally Kellerman *Mac Beachwood* • Mackenzie Phillips *Frisbee* • Alex Rocco *Vinnie* • Charles Martin Smith *Alan* • Harry Dean Stanton *Billy Winston* ■ *Dir* Dick Richards • *Scr* John Kaye

The Raffle ★★
Romantic comedy adventure
1994 · Can · Colour · 100mins

An obvious shoestring budget continually undercuts the initially intriguing premise of this light Canadian affair about two down-on-their-luck men devising a money-making scheme to find the world's most beautiful woman and then setting up a raffle where the first prize is a date with her. But when they involve their sceptical friends in the deal, things go pear-shaped. A good cast, headlined by Nicholas Lea, works wonders with the schematic plot.

Nicholas Lea *David Lake* • Bobby Dawson *Frank Palmer* • Jennifer Clement *Margo Miller* • Teri-Lynn Rutherford *Anya Monroe* • Mark Hamill *Bernard Wallace* ■ *Dir* Gavin Wilding • *Scr* John Fairley

Raffles ★★★
Romantic crime adventure
1930 · US · BW · 70mins

Villainy is all very well if you can carry it off with a smile, smooth out misunderstandings with a mellifluous voice and look as handsome as Ronald Colman does here playing the elusive AJ Raffles. This urbane adaptation of EW Hornung's *The Amateur Cracksman* makes the toff thief amusingly likeable, a rogue with charm – unless you're his victim, of course. The result is a fascinating curio from a gentler age.

Ronald Colman *AJ Raffles* • Kay Francis *Lady Gwen Manders* • Bramwell Fletcher *Bunny Manders* • Frances Dade *Ethel Crowley* • David Torrence *McKenzie* • Alison Skipworth *Lady Kitty Melrose* • Frederick Kerr *Lord Harry Melrose* ■ *Dir* Harry d'Abbadie D'Arrast • *Scr* George Fitzmaurice, Sidney Howard, from the play *Raffles, the Amateur Cracksman* by Ernest William Hornung, Eugene Wiley Presbrey, from the novel *The Amateur Cracksman* by Ernest William Hornung

Raffles ★★★ U
Romantic crime adventure
1939 · US · BW · 68mins

A pleasant but mindless remake by producer Samuel Goldwyn of his 1930 Ronald Colman romantic adventure, with debonair David Niven lacking the suave charm of Colman's famed gentleman thief incarnation. Olivia de Havilland is lovely, however, and more than makes up for Niven's over-casual approach, a style that saw him through virtually five decades of cinema stardom, including an Academy Award. What is truly amazing is that this film is particularly strong on English mores and atmosphere, yet not a frame was shot outside Hollywood – all credit to under-rated co-director Sam Wood. ▭

David Niven *AJ Raffles* • Olivia de Havilland *Gwen Manders* • Douglas Walton *Bunny Manders* • Dudley Digges *Inspector McKenzie* • Dame May Whitty *Lady Kitty Melrose* • Lionel Pape *Lord Harry Melrose* ■ *Dir* Sam

Wood, William Wyler • *Scr* John Van Druten, Sidney Howard, F Scott Fitzgerald, from the novel *The Amateur Cracksman* by Ernest William Hornung

Rag Doll ★★
Drama 1960 · UK · BW · 66mins

A starring vehicle for would-be British heart-throb and teen idol Jess Conrad, perhaps best remembered for making some of the worst pop records ever, notably *This Pullover*. He's a singing burglar, really, who gets involved with teenage runaway Christina Gregg in this cheapie, directed without much flair by Lance Comfort, who regularly dished out these tepid programme fillers, often featuring pop acts. Conrad can't keep up with the likes of Hermione Baddeley, Patrick Magee and Kenneth Griffith in the acting stakes, but his bravado is part of the pleasure of watching the film.

Jess Conrad *Joe Shane* • Christina Gregg *Carol Flynn* • Hermione Baddeley *Princess Sophia* • Kenneth Griffith *Mort Wilson* • Patrick Magee *Flynn* • Patrick Jordan *Wills* ■ *Dir* Lance Comfort • *Scr* Brock Williams, Derry Quinn, from a story by Brock Williams

Ragan ★★ 15
Action adventure
1967 · Sp/It · Colour · 84mins

A Spanish-Italian co-production that is missing from most film biographies of star Ty Hardin and director Sidney Pink. Set in an unnamed South American republic, it goes some way to explaining why Pink was entrusted with only five bad B-movies in his brief career and why they handsome Hardin eventually also became a preacher. Hired to spring an anti-junta general from an inaccessible prison, Hardin and accomplice Jack Stewart play second fiddle to the stunning mountain scenery. The action looks stagey and the dubbed dialogue is embarrassing. A touch more tongue-in-cheek might have helped matters. Some dialogue dubbed into English. ▭

Ty Hardin *Ragan* • Antonella Lualdi *Janine* • Jack Stewart *Kohler* • Dick Palace *Flower* ■ *Dir* Sidney Pink • *Scr* Howard Berk, Sidney Pink, from a story by Howard Berk

Rage ★★★ 15
Melodrama 1966 · US/Mex · Colour · 99mins

Glenn Ford is the resident medico at a construction site in the wilds of Mexico. One day he's bitten by his pet dog which turns out to have rabies, so Ford has two days in which to get to a proper hospital and have the serum pumped into him before he starts foaming at the mouth. Instead of rushing, he tends to a pregnant woman who goes into labour; then his jeep breaks down; then Stella Stevens, as a tart with a heart, takes a shower, delaying things still further. You're always look closely at Ford's fraught face to see if he's growing any fangs in this race against the schlock. ▭

Glenn Ford *Reuben* • Stella Stevens *Perla* • David Reynoso *Pancho* • Armando Silvestre *Antonio* • Ariadna Welter *Blanca* ■ *Dir* Gilberto Gazcon • *Scr* Teddi Sherman, Gilberto Gazcon, Fernando Mendez, from a story by Jesus Velazquez, Guillermo Hernandez, Gilberto Gazcon

Rage ★★ 15
Drama 1972 · US · Colour · 95mins

A rancher (George C Scott) and his son (Nicolas Beauvy), are accidentally caught in the spray of what turns out to be a deadly nerve gas. When the boy dies, Scott learns the truth about the chemical and takes revenge by destroying the company where the gas was made. What might have been developed as a provocative social conscience drama emerges as thin and uninteresting melodrama. Actor Scott made his feature directing debut with the film, and might have been better advised to concentrate on one job or the other. ▭

George C Scott *Dan Logan* • Richard Basehart *Dr Caldwell* • Martin Sheen *Major Holliford* • Barnard Hughes *Dr Spencer* • Nicolas Beauvy *Chris Logan* ■ *Dir* George C Scott • *Scr* Philip Friedman, Dan Kleinman

Rage ★★ 18
Action thriller 1995 · US · Colour · 94mins

Gary Daniels is a typical martial arts-knowing LA schoolteacher with an English accent who's nabbed by corrupt government agents and drugged to become a super-fighting machine. When he kills his way to freedom, the same agents then frame him as an insane killer, and a statewide search and media frenzy erupts as he attempts to clear his name while on the run. Like other efforts from the PM Entertainment group, this not only has enough broken glass for ten movies, but some social commentary as well. ▭

Gary Daniels *Alex Gainer* • Kenneth Tigar *Harry* • Jillian McWhirter *Bobby T* • Fiona Hutchison *Mary* • Tom Colceri *Parrish* • Peter Jason *Griggs* ■ *Dir* Joseph Merhi • *Scr* Joseph John Barmettler, Jacobsen Hart

Rage and Honor ★ 18
Martial arts action thriller
1992 · US · Colour · 88mins

Martial arts action star Cynthia Rothrock plays schoolteacher Kris Fairchild who gets tangled up with a cop (Richard Norton) from Australia who was framed for the murder of a student. Inevitably they find themselves working together, beating everyone up in their path. Though this particular Rothrock effort has superior production values, the ho-hum fights and lengthy padding between them haven't changed a bit. Neither has her poor acting. ▭

Cynthia Rothrock *Kris Fairchild* • Richard Norton *Preston Michaels* • Terri Treas *Rita Carrion* • Brian Thompson *Conrad Drago* • Catherine Bach *Capt Murdock* ■ *Dir/Scr* Terence H Winkless

Rage at Dawn ★★ U
Western 1955 · US · Colour · 82mins

Handsome-looking but lethargic western in which special agent Randolph Scott goes undercover to trap one of the earliest bands of outlaws, that of the Reno brothers who committed the first train hold-up in 1866. Here played by Forrest Tucker, J Carrol Naish and Myron Healey, the Renos also have an attractive sister Laura (Mala Powers), which naturally complicates matters for Scott. The rage at dawn refers to the historically

U = SUITABLE FOR ALL, Uc = SUITABLE FOR ALL, ESPECIALLY FOR YOUNG CHILDREN (VIDEO ONLY) PG = PARENTAL GUIDANCE

accurate conclusion in which a lynch mob plucks the Renos from jail. 📺

Randolph Scott *James Barlow* • Forrest Tucker *Frank Reno* • Mala Powers *Laura Reno* • J Carrol Naish *Sim Reno* • Edgar Buchanan *Judge Hawkins* • Myron Healey *John Reno* ■ *Dir* Tim Whelan • *Scr* Horace McCoy, from a story by Frank Gruber

The Rage: Carrie 2 ★ 18

Horror   1999 · US · Colour · 107mins

A belated sequel to Brian De Palma's terrifying masterpiece *Carrie*, this abysmal travesty goes through the same narrative motions as the 1976 classic, even using clips as redundant flashbacks. Yet it repeatedly stomps on the memory of that class Stephen King act with utterly routine direction, tired gore and a complete lack of pathos. Emily Bergl takes a stab at filling Sissy Spacek's shoes as another vulnerable outsider with fatal telekinetic abilities who takes revenge on her taunting schoolmates at a party. However, she's fighting a losing battle in this colourless, crass and crude supernatural freak-out. 📺

Emily Bergl *Rachel Lang* • Jason London *Jesse Ryan* • Dylan Bruno *Mark* • Amy Irving *Sue Snell* ■ *Dir* Katt Shea [Katt Shea Ruben] • *Scr* Rafael Moreu, Howard A Rodman, from characters created by Stephen King

A Rage in Harlem ★★★★ 18

Crime thriller
1991 · UK/US · Colour · 103mins

Based on Chester Himes's novel, this is a stylish, fast-moving and often humorous thriller from *Deep Cover* director Bill Duke. Robin Givens, looking every inch the sex siren, is Imabelle, who arrives in fifties' Harlem with a bag full of stolen gold. As she tries to exchange the booty for cash, various seedy characters – including Danny Glover and Gregory Hines – get involved in her scheming, as does an innocent undertaker's assistant (played with charm and naivety by the ever-dependable Forest Whitaker). The cast is enjoyable to watch as the twisting tale unfolds, but the squeamish should beware: there is quite a lot of violence for a film that has such a strong vein of humour. Contains swearing and nudity. 📺

Forest Whitaker *Jackson* • Gregory Hines *Goldy* • Robin Givens *Imabelle* • Zakes Mokae *Big Kathy* • Danny Glover *Easy Money* • Badja Djola *Slim* • John Toles-Bey *Jodie* ■ *Dir* Bill Duke • *Scr* John Toles-Bey, Bobby Crawford, from the novel by Chester Himes

Rage in Heaven ★★

Drama   1941 · US · BW · 84mins

The English heir to a fortune (Robert Montgomery) returns home to his mother Lucile Watson after an absence in France where, unbeknown to her, he has been in a mental hospital. He marries his mother's social secretary (Ingrid Bergman), but his psychosis soon surfaces in unfounded jealousy of his wife and his friend (George Sanders), leading to violent and melodramatic events designed to have Sanders executed for murder. WS Van Dyke directed this overheated nonsense and was unable to rescue Montgomery from an unconvincing parody of a mad Englishman.

Robert Montgomery *Philip Monrell* • Ingrid Bergman *Stella Bergen* • George Sanders *Ward Andrews* • Lucile Watson *Mrs Monrell* ■ *Dir* WS Van Dyke • *Scr* Christopher Isherwood, Robert Thoeren, from the novel by James Hilton

The Rage of Paris ★★★

Romantic comedy 1938 · US · BW · 78mins

This is the kind of amoral, sophisticated romantic comedy commonly associated with Paramount, but it was made at Universal as a vehicle for French star Danielle Darrieux, making her Hollywood debut. Directed with a light touch by Henry Koster, the movie has Darrieux as a casino girl who, finding herself unemployed, turns model, and then, with the collusion and encouragement of two friends, gold-digger. These are the bare bones of an intricate plot that involves suspicions of blackmail and an unexpected love affair. The wildly glamorous Darrieux, in the kind of role usually reserved for Claudette Colbert, sparkles in this outrageous flim-flam.

Danielle Darrieux *Nicole de Cortillon* • Douglas Fairbanks Jr *Jim Trevor* • Mischa Auer *Mike* • Louis Hayward *Bill Jerome Duncan* • Helen Broderick *Gloria Patterson* • Charles Coleman *Rigley* ■ *Dir* Henry Koster • *Scr* Bruce Manning, Felix Jackson, from their story

Rage to Kill ★★ 18

Action drama 1988 · US · Colour · 88mins

Despite all the questions that have been asked about the rights and wrongs of American involvement in Grenada, this jingoistic exercise in exploiting the conflict now seems more than a little dated. James Ryan is the beefcake hero who's caught up in a military takeover while visiting his student brother. Pretty poor timing, particularly as the bad guy is Oliver Reed playing a hostage-taking Marxist general. Cameron Mitchell (*High Chaparral*) is the helpful CIA man. Pity he couldn't help this tedious exercise out of the straight-to-video abyss. 📺

James Ryan *Blaine Striker* • Oliver Reed *General Turner* • Cameron Mitchell *Miller* • Maxine John *Trishia Baker* ■ *Dir* David Winters • *Scr* David Winters, Ian Yule

A Rage to Live ★★

Melodrama 1965 · US · Colour · 101mins

Rich young nymphomaniac Suzanne Pleshette goes through a succession of men, beginning with her brother's best friend, and progressing through a hotel employee to a desperate marriage until infidelity (with Ben Gazzara) takes over and her husband Bradford Dillman leaves her. This superficial, watered-down account of John O'Hara's bestselling novel is rendered even more uninteresting by the casting of the inadequate Pleshette, when the movie screams out for a Stanwyck, a Hayward or a Joanne Woodward. Walter Grauman's dreary direction doesn't help either.

Suzanne Pleshette *Grace Caldwell* • Bradford Dillman *Sidney Tate* • Ben Gazzara *Roger Bannon* • Peter Graves (1) *Jack Hollister* • Bethel Leslie *Amy Hollister* ■ *Dir* Walter Grauman • *Scr* John T Kelley, from the novel by John O'Hara

Raggedy Ann and Andy ★★ U

Animation   1977 · US · Colour · 85mins

Somnolent cartoon musical since put to sleep by the two *Toy Story* films, about toys coming to life when their owners are away. Hailed as the adventures of ''America's favourite dolls'' and directed by Richard Williams, it succumbs to some songs – written by Joe Raposo – which stultify the action even more. The characters have appeal but no story that will interest children above the age of five.

Didi Conn *Raggedy Ann* • Mark Baker *Raggedy Andy* • Fred Stuthman *Camel with the wrinkled knees* • Niki Flacks *Babette* • George S Irving *Captain Contagious* ■ *Dir* Richard Williams • *Scr* Patricia Thackray, Max Wilk, from characters created by Johnny Gruelle

Raggedy Man ★★★ 15

Drama   1981 · US · Colour · 89mins

Sissy Spacek is a wartime divorcee who falls in love with a sailor played by Eric Roberts. This causes problems with her two children – one of whom is played by Henry Thomas, soon to become a star in *ET* – as well as the local predatory men, including Sam Shepard. Spacek had just won an Oscar for *Coal Miner's Daughter* and produces another trademark backwoods performance, heavy on the Texan accent and the wistful look. Her real-life husband, former art director Jack Fisk, directs the show with sensitivity, though the violent ending seems misjudged. 📺

Sissy Spacek *Nita Longley* • Eric Roberts *Teddy* • Sam Shepard *Bailey* • William Sanderson *Calvin* • Tracey Walter *Arnold* • RG Armstrong *Rigby* • Henry Thomas *Harry* ■ *Dir* Jack Fisk • *Scr* William D Wittliff

The Raggedy Rawney ★★★ 15

Drama   1987 · UK · Colour · 98mins

Much maligned on its original release, Bob Hoskins's directorial debut is undeniably ragged in places, but there is still much to admire in this plea for toleration and peace set in an unidentified war-torn European country at the turn of the century. Once you've accepted the premise that Dexter Fletcher (a deserter who has disguised himself as a woman) could be mistaken for a ''rawney'', a gypsy with magical powers, then this intriguing venture into the mysterious Romany world has many rewards. The different rituals and customs are handled with great reverence by Hoskins, whose efforts behind the camera are more impressive than his disappointing performance. Contains violence, swearing and nudity. 📺

Bob Hoskins *Darky* • Dexter Fletcher *Tom* • Zöe Nathenson *Jessie* • Zöe Wanamaker *Elle* • Dave Hill *Lamb* • Ian Dury *Weazel* • Ian McNeice *Stanley, the farmer* ■ *Dir* Bob Hoskins • *Scr* Bob Hoskins, Nicole de Wilde

Raging Bull ★★★★★ 18

Biographical drama
1980 · US · BW and Colour · 123mins

Film critics and film-makers are always being asked to reel off their desert-island movies. *Raging Bull*, without question, is one such great. Director

Martin Scorsese makes no concession to character likeability as he portrays Jake La Motta's downward slide from arrogant prizefighter to frustrated, hateful drop-out. Robert De Niro, who piled on the pounds to play the latter-day La Motta, proves he is the Method actor bar none, equally at home in the ring (the fight sequences are brutal, if spectacularly staged) and as the empty barrel abusing everyone (including his wife, Cathy Moriarty, and brother, Joe Pesci) at home. De Niro rightly won an Oscar for his efforts. Scorsese effortlessly fuses top-drawer acting, pumping narrative drive and a blitzkrieg camera technique to deliver this giddy, claustrophobic classic. 📺 *DVD*

Robert De Niro *Jake La Motta* • Cathy Moriarty *Vickie La Motta* • Joe Pesci *Joey La Motta* • Frank Vincent *Salvy* • Nicholas Colasanto *Tommy Como* • Theresa Saldana *Lenore* • Johnny Barnes *"Sugar" Ray Robinson* ■ *Dir* Martin Scorsese • *Scr* Paul Schrader, Mardik Martin, from the non-fiction book by Jake La Motta, Joseph Carter, Peter Savage • *Editor* Thelma Schoonmaker • *Cinematographer* Michael Chapman

The Raging Moon ★★ PG

Romantic drama
1970 · UK · Colour · 106mins

The suggestion that disabled people might enjoy a sexual relationship was still shocking when this romance in wheelchairs appeared, offering invaluable insight into a previously closed world. Malcolm McDowell is the young buck embittered by his crippling illness until he meets a woman (Nanette Newman) better adjusted to her fate. Director Bryan Forbes (Newman's husband in real life) tends to overdo everything, particularly the sentimentality, but the leads are sympathetic and there are many good cameos in the supporting cast. 📺

Malcolm McDowell *Bruce Pritchard* • Nanette Newman *Jill* • Georgia Brown *Sarah Charles* • Bernard Lee *Uncle Bob* • Gerald Sim *Reverend Corbett* • Michael Flanders *Clarence Marlow* ■ *Dir* Bryan Forbes • *Scr* Bryan Forbes, from the novel by Peter Marshall

The Ragman's Daughter ★★★

Romantic drama 1972 · UK · Colour · 94mins

Written by Alan Sillitoe from his own story, this is an intelligent, romantic drama that has unfortunately been tagged with the ''kitchen sink'' label. It features an ingenious thief (Simon Rouse) who falls for the astonishingly beautiful daughter (Victoria Tennant) of a rich rag-and-bone man. Beautifully acted and stylishly executed, this British independent feature marked the directorial debut of Harold Becker (*Sea of Love*). A little gem.

Simon Rouse *Tony Bradmore* • Victoria Tennant *Doris Randall* • Patrick O'Connell *Tony, aged 35* • Leslie Sands *Doris's father* • Rita Howard *Doris's mother* • Brenda Peters *Tony's mother* • Brian Murphy *Tony's father* • Sydney Livingstone *Prison officer* ■ *Dir* Harold Becker • *Scr* Alan Sillitoe, from his story

Ragtime ★★★ 15

Drama   1981 · US · Colour · 148mins

For some reason, EL Doctorow's novel was a publishing sensation and the rights to it were snapped up by producer Dino De Laurentiis for a

reported $5 million. Another $27 million was spent on re-creating (at Shepperton Studios) New York in 1906. But the novel is unfilmable, a chaotic bundle of characters and situations that relies solely on Doctorow's flashy wordplay. It's a total shambles, but it does have James Cagney (back on the screen after a 20-year retirement) and Norman Mailer as Stanford White, the real-life architect murdered by millionaire Harry K Thaw (played here by Robert Joy). Contains swearing and nudity. 🎬

James Cagney *Police commissioner Waldo* • Brad Dourif *Younger brother* • Moses Gunn *Booker T Washington* • Elizabeth McGovern *Evelyn Nesbit* • Kenneth McMillan *Willie Conklin* • Pat O'Brien *Delmas* • Mandy Patinkin *Tateh* • Norman Mailer *Stanford White* • Robert Joy *Thaw, Harry K* ■ *Dir* Milos Forman • *Scr* Michael Weller, from the novel by EL Doctorow

The Raid ★★★ U

Historical war drama
1954 · US · Colour · 82mins

This little-known Civil War drama, about a group of escaped Confederate soldiers who lay vengeful siege to a town near the Canadian border, has much to commend it: a tight construction, bursts of action, strong characters and a great cast. The script by *The Big Heat's* Sydney Boehm plays like an allegory of a wider conflict, while Hugo Fregonese (an Argentinian director who deserved greater public recognition) keeps the tension bubbling in the manner of *High Noon*.

Van Heflin *Major Neal Benton* • Anne Bancroft *Katy Bishop* • Richard Boone *Captain Foster* • Lee Marvin *Lieutenant Keating* • Tommy Rettig *Larry Bishop* • Peter Graves (1) *Captain Dwyer* ■ *Dir* Hugo Fregonese • *Scr* Sydney Boehm, from the story by Francis Cockrell, from the article *Affair at St Albans* by Herbert Ravenal Sass

Raid on Rommel ★★ 15

Second World War drama
1971 · US · Colour · 93mins

It says a lot for Richard Burton that he was able to plumb the depths in dreary Second World War action movies such as this one, about a British officer releasing prisoners to attack Tobruk, without doing any apparent damage to his career. Even the usually dependable director Henry Hathaway falters in this flawed effort that was originally meant for TV. 🎬

Richard Burton *Captain Foster* • John Colicos *MacKenzie* • Clinton Greyn *Major Tarkington* • Danielle de Metz *Vivi* • Wolfgang Preiss *General Rommel* • Karl Otto Alberty *Captain Schroeder* ■ *Dir* Henry Hathaway • *Scr* Richard Bluel

Raiders of the Lost Ark
★★★★★ PG

Action adventure fantasy
1981 · US · Colour · 110mins

Executive producer George Lucas and director Steven Spielberg minted fresh excitement from the cliffhanger serials of their youth in this breathless fantasy extravaganza. Archaeologist Indiana Jones (a part that fits Harrison Ford like a glove) searches the Holy Land for the fabled Ark of the Covenant, and finds himself up to his neck in booby-trapped caves, snake chambers, Nazi

spies, religious demons, damsels in distress and even a spot of romance. The climactic unleashing of the artefact's awesome holy fire remains a spine-tingling masterwork of visual effects ingenuity and ambitious dramatic force. No surprise then that one of the four Oscars this fabulous production picked up was for visual effects. Contains violence. 🎬

Harrison Ford *Indiana Jones* • Karen Allen *Marion Ravenwood* • Paul Freeman *Belloq* • Ronald Lacey *Toht* • John Rhys-Davies *Sallah* • Denholm Elliott *Brody* • Wolf Kahler *Dietrich* • Anthony Higgins *Gobler* • Alfred Molina *Satipo* • Vic Tablian *Barranca* ■ *Dir* Steven Spielberg • *Scr* Lawrence Kasdan, from a story by George Lucas, Philip Kaufman • *Cinematographer* Douglas Slocombe • *Editor* Michael Kahn • *Music* John Williams • *Production Designer* Norman Reynold • *Special Effects* Richard Edlund, Kit West, Joe Johnston, Bruce Nicholson • *Production Designer* Leslie Dilley

Raiders of the Seven Seas
★★ U

Swashbuckling adventure
1953 · US · Colour · 88mins

Red-bearded pirate John Payne commandeers a prison ship and takes on all-comers in this lively swashbuckler filmed in lush Technicolor. The love interest is supplied by Donna Reed (an Oscar winner for *From Here to Eternity* that same year) who, as is often the way in these by-the-book high-seas adventures, is won over, eventually, by our dashing hero's charms.

John Payne *Barbarossa* • Donna Reed *Alida* • Gerald Mohr *Salcedo* • Lon Chaney Jr *Peg Leg* ■ *Dir* Sidney Salkow • *Scr* John O'Dea, from a story by John O'Dea, Sidney Salkow

Railroaded ★★★

Crime melodrama 1947 · US · BW · 72mins

Anthony Mann, his glory days to come three years later with westerns like *Winchester '73*, brings a sure touch to this low-budget crime B-movie. Innocent youngster Ed Kelly is framed for murder by psychopathic professional John Ireland, whose penchant is spraying bullets with perfume before discharging them into his victims. Although formula stuff, it's taut, coolly violent and very tough, particularly in its treatment of female characters. Jane Randolph is excellent as Ireland's ill-fated confederate, who fronts scams with a beauty salon, and Hugh Beaumont is the cop who cleans up the escalating mess and is in love with the suspect's sister (Sheila Ryan).

John Ireland *Duke Martin* • Sheila Ryan *Rosa Ryan* • Hugh Beaumont *Mickey Ferguson* • Jane Randolph *Clara Calhoun* • Ed Kelly *Steve Ryan* ■ *Dir* Anthony Mann • *Scr* John C Higgins, from a story by Gertrude Walker

The Railrodder ★★★★ U

Comedy 1965 · Can · Colour · 24mins

A whimsical, poetic farewell to an elderly Buster Keaton in director Gerald Potterton's short film, a diminutive view of Keaton's *The General*, in which Keaton makes his way across Canada on a railway trolley. The solo slapstick is sweet-natured, the adoration of the director for his star is obvious and Buster Keaton recalls his silent days –

by not saying a word. Which makes it all the more poignant.

Buster Keaton *The Railrodder* ■ *Dir/Scr* Gerald Potterton

Rails into Laramie ★★ U

Western 1954 · US · Colour · 81mins

A routine western given distinction by a snarling study in black-hearted villainy by the ever-reliable Dan Duryea, who is trying to stop the railroad from reaching Laramie for his own devious purpose. Meanwhile, sexy Mari Blanchard aims to rustle up an all-female jury to put Duryea away. All this would be interesting were it not for the presence of John Payne, past his prime and looking ill-at-ease as the dull hero. Never mind, there's a throbbing theme song and a sullen Lee Van Cleef to remind us of *High Noon*.

John Payne *Jefferson Harder* • Mari Blanchard *Lou Carter* • Dan Duryea *Jim Shanessy* • Joyce MacKenzie *Helen Shanessy* • Barton MacLane *Lee Graham* • Lee Van Cleef *Ace Winton* ■ *Dir* Jesse Hibbs • *Scr* DD Beauchamp, Joseph Hoffman

The Railway Children
★★★★★ U

Drama 1971 · UK · Colour · 104mins

Directed by Lionel Jeffries, this adaptation of E Nesbit's much-loved novel is simply the finest children's film ever made in this country. Packed with memorable episodes, the story is not particularly involving, but it's far more intelligent than some of the fodder dished up for kids today. Sally Thomsett and Gary Warren are spirited as Phyllis and Peter, but it's Jenny Agutter's magnificent performance as Bobbie that stands out, balancing a child's passion for adventure with a growing sense of responsibility as she comes to understand her family's predicament. Of the grown-ups, Bernard Cribbins steals the show as the kindly stationmaster, Perks. 🎬

Jenny Agutter *Bobbie* • Sally Thomsett *Phyllis* • Gary Warren *Peter* • Dinah Sheridan *Mother* • Bernard Cribbins *Perks* • William Mervyn *Old gentleman* • Iain Cuthbertson *Father* • Peter Bromilow *Doctor* ■ *Dir* Lionel Jeffries • *Scr* Lionel Jeffries, from the novel by E Nesbit

Rain ★★★

Drama 1932 · US · BW · 95mins

Somerset Maugham's tale of a hellfire-and-damnation church missionary's lust for a prostitute who fetches up at a trading post on a rain-drenched South Sea island was a steamy shocker in its day, and has attracted three film versions and three major actresses. Gloria Swanson starred in the silent *Sadie Thompson* (1928), earning a best actress nomination in the first ever Oscars; Rita Hayworth was a Technicolored (and terrific) Miss Sadie Thompson, softened by censorship from whore to barroom singer in 1953. Here Joan Crawford, dressed and made-up to kill, gives her considerable all in a much under-rated performance that failed to please the customers in 1932. The faults lie more with co-star Walter Huston's hammy and unconvincing portrayal of the missionary, and screenplay and direction that fail to hit the right note.

Joan Crawford *Sadie Thompson* • Walter Huston *Rev Alfred Davidson* • William Gargan *Sgt "Handsome" O'Hara* • Guy Kibbee *Joe Horn* • Walter Catlett *Quartermaster Hal Bates* ■ *Dir* Lewis Milestone • *Scr* Maxwell Anderson, from the play by John Colton, Clemence Randolph, from the short story *Miss Thompson* by W Somerset Maugham

Rain Man ★★★★★ 15

Drama 1988 · US · Colour · 127mins

When Dustin Hoffman accepted his Oscar as best actor for *Rain Man*, he thanked his mom and dad, and his agent. Nothing unusual in that, except that this time Hoffman's agent, Michael Ovitz, can be considered the true creator of this film. The script had been doing the rounds for years – dozens of people tinkered with the tale about a used car hustler who must gain the confidence of his brother, an autistic savant, in order to divert a $3 million inheritance. Directors came and went, but Ovitz stuck with it, and when he saw how another of his clients, Tom Cruise, had partnered the older Paul Newman in *The Color of Money*, he realised how Cruise could work with another ageing client, Hoffman. It was a masterstroke designed to give Hoffman a juicy role and further Cruise's own career in serious movies. 🎬 *DVD*

Dustin Hoffman *Raymond Babbitt* • Tom Cruise *Charlie Babbitt* • Valeria Golino *Susanna* • Jerry Molen *Dr Bruner* • Jack Murdock *John Mooney* • Michael D Roberts *Vern* ■ *Dir* Barry Levinson • *Scr* Ronald Bass, Barry Morrow, from a story by Barry Morrow

Rain or Shine ★★

Comedy drama 1930 · US · BW · 90mins

A very early, too early, Frank Capra-directed peek beneath the big top, with a trio of clowns (Joe Cook, Dave Chasen and Tom Howard) attempting a lacklustre stab at the hackneyed "tears behind the greasepaint" scenario. The movie's problems stem from an overindulgence in leering acrobats and acres of sawdust at the expense of a plot and characterisation – the men are mere knockabout ciphers most of the time. A depressing experience for Capra fans.

Joe Cook *Smiley* • Louise Fazenda *Frankie* • Joan Peers *Mary* • William Collier Jr *Bud* • Tom Howard *Amos* • David Chasen *Dave* ■ *Dir* Frank Capra • *Scr* Jo Swerling, Dorothy Howell, from the play by James Gleason

The Rain People ★★

Drama 1969 · US · Colour · 101mins

This early outing from director Francis Ford Coppola is certainly not without interest today, but its sixties' attitudes have dated badly. Nevertheless, it is fascinating to see James Caan and Robert Duvall at a stage of their careers prior to *The Godfather*, and there's a superb performance from Shirley Knight in the neurotic leading role as the pregnant housewife who takes life on the lam. Uneven and slackly paced, this remains an adult drama of moderate curiosity. Contains swearing.

James Caan *Jimmie "Killer" Kilgannon* • Shirley Knight *Natalie Ravenna* • Robert Duvall *Gordon* • Marya Zimmet *Rosalie* • Tom

U = SUITABLE FOR ALL   Uc = SUITABLE FOR ALL, ESPECIALLY FOR YOUNG CHILDREN (VIDEO ONLY)   PG = PARENTAL GUIDANCE

Aldredge *Mr Alfred* • Laurie Crewes *Ellen* ■ *Dir* Francis Ford Coppola • *Scr* Francis Ford Coppola, from his story *Stir of Echoes*

The Rainbow ★★ **15**
Drama   1988 · UK · Colour · 106mins

Ken Russell and DH Lawrence – always a frightening combination. And the result here? A rather stilted, restrained and dated adaptation of the classic novel. Sammi Davis is plain irritating in the lead as a schoolteacher whose sexual awakening progresses from an affair with her mentor Amanda Donohoe to love and disappointment with soldier Paul McGann. Glenda Jackson is on fine form, playing the mother of the character she played in Russell's acclaimed 1969 version of *Women in Love*. But despite strong performances and shots of the English countryside, this doesn't quite work. Contains swearing and nudity. ▭

Sammi Davis *Ursula Brangwen* • Paul McGann *Anton Skrebensky* • Amanda Donohoe *Winifred Inger* • Christopher Gable *Will Brangwen* • David Hemmings *Uncle Henry* • Glenda Jackson *Anna Brangwen* • Dudley Sutton *MacAllister* • Jim Carter *Mr Harby* ■ *Dir* Ken Russell • *Scr* Ken Russell, Vivian Russell, from the novel by DH Lawrence

Rainbow ★ **PG**
Fantasy comedy
1995 · UK/Can · Colour · 94mins

Four kids go searching for the end of the rainbow in the second feature directed by Bob Hoskins. Unfortunately, when they find it in New Jersey, one of them takes pieces of gold from the spectrum causing all colour to drain from the real world and a crime wave to break out. One of the first features to be shot on Digital High Definition, the results – including the crucial rainbow special effects – are not entirely successful. Hoskins clearly doesn't have the feather-light touch such hokum demands as the whimsy he aims for never comes into focus. A charmless, clod-hopping fantasy. ▭

Bob Hoskins *Frank Bailey* • Dan Aykroyd *Sheriff Wyatt Hampton* • Willy Lavendal *Mike* • Saul Rubinek *Sam Cohen* ■ *Dir* Bob Hoskins • *Scr* Ashley Sidaway, Robert Sidaway

Rainbow Bridge ★★ **18**
Documentary drama
1971 · US · Colour · 73mins

Although it captures the mood of the late sixties, director Chuck Wein's mixture of hippy fact and impenetrable fiction is a rambling and tedious artefact from the era. Centred around model Pat Hartley making a pilgrimage to the Rainbow Bridge Occult Research Meditation Centre on the Hawaiian island of Maui, this disjointed mess is only worth watching to see Jimi Hendrix play a short concert by the side of the Haleakala volcano three months before his death. *Foxy Lady*, *Voodoo Chile*, *Purple Haze*, *Star Spangled Banner* and many more of his legendary songs are played either on screen or off as the commune of space children concern themselves with such riveting social issues as whether making love is a waste of cosmic energy. ▭

Dir/Scr Chuck Wein

Rainbow Drive ★ **18**
Murder mystery   1990 · US · Colour · 91mins

Peter Weller (*RoboCop*), Sela Ward (*The Fugitive*) and Bruce Weitz (*Hill Street Blues*) star in this tale of the sordid side of the glamour capital of the world. When a chief of homicide detectives uncovers a multiple murder in Hollywood, his efforts to crack the case are thwarted by a bizarre cover-up orchestrated by one of his superiors. A good cast is wasted in this poorly written and derivative mystery – a victim of its own loose ends. ▭

Peter Weller *Mike Gallagher* • David Caruso *Larry Hammond* • Sela Ward *Laura Demming* • Bruce Weitz *Dan Crawford* • Chris Mulkey *Ira Rosenberg* ■ *Dir* Bobby Roth • *Scr* Bill Phillips, Bennett Cohen, from the novel by Roderick Thorp

The Rainbow Jacket ★★ **PG**
Crime drama   1958 · UK · Colour · 96mins

Screenwriter TEB Clarke was the brains behind many of the Ealing comedies. Yet he also had a well-developed social conscience, as he proves in this unconvincing racing drama that reunited him with *Blue Lamp* director Basil Dearden. As the disgraced jockey who saves his protégé from a bribes scandal, Bill Owen has one of his meatiest screen roles. However, this is a workmanlike film, with some suitably downbeat photography from Otto Heller and neat cameos from Sid James and Wilfrid Hyde White. ▭

Robert Morley *Lord Logan* • Kay Walsh *Barbara Crain* • Edward Underdown *Geoffrey Tyler* • Bill Owen *Sam Lilley* • Honor Blackman *Monica Tyler* • Wilfrid Hyde White *Lord Stoneleigh* • Sidney James *Harry* ■ *Dir* Basil Dearden • *Scr* TEB Clarke

Rainbow on the River ★★ **U**
Period melodrama   1936 · US · BW · 88mins

The second, biggest and best known vehicle for Bobby Breen, a boy soprano. Always smiling in the face of on-screen adversity, this male answer to Shirley Temple, with a voice and repertoire to rival Deanna Durbin, was a relatively short-lived but popular and profitable phenomenon, whose fans were willing to overlook the dire sentimentality of scripts which made Shirley's material look like Shakespeare. This one has little orphan Bobby, poor but happy, ensconced down South in the care of his beloved "mammy" (Louise Beavers), only to be whipped away to his rich, hostile and unbending grandmother (May Robson) and a bunch of vile cousins in New York.

Bobby Breen *Philip* • May Robson *Mrs Ainsworth* • Charles Butterworth *Barrett, butler* • Louise Beavers *Toinette* • Alan Mowbray *Ralph Layton* • Benita Hume *Julia Layton* ■ *Dir* Kurt Neumann • *Scr* Earle Snell, Harry Chandlee, William Hurlbut, Clarence Marks, from the story *Toinnette's Philip* by Mrs CV Jamison

The Rainbow Thief ★★★
Fantasy   1990 · UK · Colour · 91mins

Alexandro Jodorowsky caused a real stir with *El Topo* but after making *The Holy Mountain* in the mid-seventies there was a long gap before his comeback film *Santa Sangre*. Jodorowsky's most ardent fans will

enjoy this obscure, whimsical fable about a man and his servant, played by Peter O'Toole and Omar Sharif. O'Toole is the eccentric who lives in the city sewers with Sharif, his servant who scavenges for food. Christopher Lee plays O'Toole's uncle who leaves his fortune to his dogs and his whores.

Peter O'Toole *Prince Meleagre* • Omar Sharif *Dima* • Christopher Lee *Uncle Rudolf* • Berta Dominguez D *Tiger Lily* ■ *Dir* Alexandro Jodorowsky • *Scr* Berta Dominguez D

Rainbow Warrior ★★★
Historical drama
1992 · US/NZ · Colour · 90mins

The true story of the bombing of the Greenpeace vessel, *Rainbow Warrior*, whose passive resistance to nuclear testing should have meant peaceful isolation – but didn't. Jon Voight and Sam Neill are the two men who embody the political complexities of the situation as the ship's skipper and the investigating cop respectively. Michael Tuchner directs vividly, but the script should have examined the complicated issues in greater depth.

Jon Voight *Peter Willcox* • Sam Neill *Alan Galbraith* • Kerry Fox *Andrea Joyce* • Greg Johnson *Bert White* ■ *Dir* Michael Tuchner • *Scr* Martin Copeland, Scott Busby

Raining Stones ★★★★★ **15**
Comedy drama   1993 · UK · Colour · 86mins

The genius of director Ken Loach lies in his ability to point out the comic ironies and absurdities of existence while exposing the prejudices and injustices of working-class life. While a touch uneven, this is one of his most effective films, showing the increasingly desperate measures an unemployed man is willing to take in order to raise the cash for his daughter's Communion dress. Bruce Jones occasionally loses his way, but mostly he conveys the stubborn pride and determination of his character with considerable skill. Julie Brown shows up well as his wife, while Ricky Tomlinson steals scenes as his scallywag mate. Contains violence and swearing. ▭ **DVD**

Bruce Jones *Bob Williams* • Julie Brown *Anne Williams* • Gemma Phoenix *Coleen Williams* • Ricky Tomlinson *Tommy* • Tom Hickey *Father Barry* • Mike Fallon *Jimmy* • Ronnie Ravey *Butcher* ■ *Dir* Ken Loach • *Scr* Jim Allen

The Rainmaker ★★★
Comedy drama   1956 · US · Colour · 121mins

Few remember this drama nowadays, but Burt Lancaster only made *Gunfight at the OK Corral* on condition that he star in it. Based on a Broadway flop, the story is set in Kansas, 1913, with Lancaster as the con man who promises he will bring an end to a serious drought, while also finding time to charm local spinster Katharine Hepburn. Director Joseph Anthony staged the original play and clearly has a reverential ear for dialogue; unfortunately, he has a blind eye when it comes to locations.

Burt Lancaster *Starbuck* • Katharine Hepburn *Lizzie Curry* • Wendell Corey *File* • Lloyd Bridges *Noah Curry* • Earl Holliman *Jim Curry* ■ *Dir* Joseph Anthony • *Scr* N Richard Nash, from his play

The Rainmaker ★★★★ **15**
Courtroom drama
1997 · US · Colour · 129mins

Francis Ford Coppola's riveting courtroom drama is an exceptionally well-crafted film that's a class above every other John Grisham adaptation. Matt Damon is excellent as the inexperienced lawyer thrown into the lion's den when he takes on the case of a young man dying of leukaemia, whose insurance company refuses to honour his claim. There's also a marvellous supporting cast including Jon Voight as the slimiest lawyer imaginable and Claire Danes as a battered wife sheltered by Damon. Grisham's scenarios often feel contrived, but this is courtroom cinema at its very best. Contains some swearing and violence. ▭

Matt Damon *Rudy Baylor* • Claire Danes *Kelly Riker* • Jon Voight *Leo F Drummond* • Mary Kay Place *Dot Black* • Mickey Rourke *Bruiser Stone* • Danny DeVito *Deck Shifflet* • Dean Stockwell *Judge Harvey Hale* • Teresa Wright *Miss Birdie* • Roy Scheider *Wilfred Keeley* • Danny Glover *Judge Tyrone Kippler* ■ *Dir* Francis Ford Coppola • *Scr* Francis Ford Coppola, Michael Herr, from the novel by John Grisham

The Rains Came ★★★
Romantic melodrama
1939 · US · BW · 104mins

Torrid stuff from 1939, Hollywood's *annus mirabilis*, and generally overlooked among the welter of great films on display. This is major tosh, set in a very 20th Century-Fox India with classy Myrna Loy chasing a turbaned Tyrone Power, face-darkened by make-up as Hindu doctor Major Rama Safti. The flood effects, tame by the standard of *The Abyss*, won an Oscar. George Brent as a ne'er-do-well and Brenda Joyce as a missionary's daughter attempt a semblance of reality – not that it matters, since author Louis Bromfield's novel was ruthlessly pared by the censorship of the time.

Myrna Loy *Lady Edwina Esketh* • Tyrone Power *Major Rama Safti* • George Brent *Tom Ransome* • Brenda Joyce *Fern Simon* • Nigel Bruce *Albert, Lord Esketh* ■ *Dir* Clarence Brown • *Scr* Philip Dunne, Julien Josephson, from the novel by Louis Bromfield

The Rains of Ranchipur ★★
Romantic drama
1955 · US · Colour · 103mins

A widescreen remake of the 1939 movie hit *The Rains Came*, this time with Richard Burton in ludicrous brown make-up as the Indian doctor Lana Turner decides to seduce. Does she get him? Who cares? The Oscar-nominated special effects are pathetic by today's standards, while co-stars Fred MacMurray, Joan Caulfield and Michael Rennie look particularly lost, as well they might, for director Jean Negulesco struggles to overcome the underdeveloped subplots.

Lana Turner *Edwina Esketh* • Richard Burton *Dr Safti* • Fred MacMurray *Tom Ransome* • Joan Caulfield *Fern Simon* • Michael Rennie *Lord Esketh* • Eugenie Leontovich *Maharani* ■ *Dir* Jean Negulesco • *Scr* Merle Miller, from the novel *The Rains Came* by Louis Bromfield

Raintree County ★★★★
Historical drama
1957 · US · Colour · 166mins

MGM's Civil War follow-up to its masterpiece *Gone with the Wind* failed to meet with much critical or public approval in its day. Such lack of enthusiasm now seems unfair and unwarranted, as this is a stunning, complex epic, dealing with issues and themes way ahead of its time. It's superbly cast and benefits from a particularly emotive and evocative vocal from Nat "King" Cole. This is the movie that Elizabeth Taylor should have got her Oscar for, as it contains some of the finest screen work she has ever done. But off screen the drama was even more absorbing, as Taylor saved co-star Montgomery Clift's life after a horrific car accident that resulted in Clift suffering both physical and mental scars.

Montgomery Clift *John Wickliff Shawnessy* • Elizabeth Taylor *Susanna Drake* • Eva Marie Saint *Nell Gaither* • Nigel Patrick *Professor Jerusalem Webster Stiles* • Lee Marvin *Orville "Flash" Perkins* • Agnes Moorehead *Ellen Shawnessy* • Rod Taylor *Garwood B Jones* ■ Dir Edward Dmytryk • Scr Millard Kaufman, from the novel by Ross Lockridge Jr

Raise the Red Lantern
★★★★★ PG

Drama
1991 · Chi · Colour · 119mins

Although a lesser film than the stunning *Ju Dou*, this is still one of the jewels of recent Chinese cinema. Once again making exceptional use of bright colour, symbolic compositions, stylised sets and the breathtaking rural landscape, director Zhang Yimou has fashioned a compelling and at times erotic story about the repression of women in twenties' China. Gong Li excels as the teenager who is forced to abandon her studies to become the fourth wife of a nobleman, but He Caifei, as the usurped third wife, matches her throughout their struggle for the right to the red lantern that signifies the master's favour. In Mandarin with English subtitles. Contains violence.

Gong Li *Songlian* • Ma Jingwu *Chen Zuoqian* • He Caifei *Meishan* • Cao Cuifeng *Zhuoyun* • Jin Shuyuan *Yuru* • Kong Lin *Yan'er* • Ding Weimin *Mother Song* • Cui Zhigang *Doctor Gao* ■ Dir Zhang Yimou • Scr Ni Zhen, from the short story by Su Tong

Raise the Titanic ★ PG
Adventure
1980 · US · Colour · 108mins

One of Lew Grade's most memorable flops, this deep sea exploration adventure cost a fortune, was touted as a major blockbuster and then proceeded to sink faster than the world famous liner on that fateful voyage in 1912. Jason Robards and Richard Jordan are among the unfortunate actors trying to raise the ship, believed to have a store of precious cargo in its hold, while Alec Guinness pops up as a crusty member of the *Titanic*'s original crew. All the usual disaster movie ingredients are here, but even a love triangle, a communist threat and lots of underwater photography cannot save this clunker from drowning. Contains some swearing.

Jason Robards [Jason Robards Jr] *Admiral James Sandecker* • Richard Jordan *Dirk Pitt* • David Selby *Dr Gene Seagram* • Anne Archer *Dana Archibald* • Alec Guinness *John Bigalow* • M Emmet Walsh *Vinnie Giordino* ■ Dir Jerry Jameson • Scr Adam Kennedy, from the novel by Clive Cussler

A Raisin in the Sun ★★ PG
Drama
1961 · US · BW · 122mins

Lorraine Hansberry's play opened on Broadway in 1959 and became a smash hit, showing white audiences what it was like to be black, working-class and living in a Chicago tenement. Within that social framework lies a melodrama of family life, built around a son's struggle to achieve some sort of status and independence away from his dominant mother and sister. For the film version, Daniel Petrie slavishly follows every last syllable of dialogue and stage direction. Though inherently and unavoidably theatrical, it should be viewed in the context of the developing civil rights movement.

Sidney Poitier *Walter Lee Younger* • Claudia McNeil *Lena Younger* • Ruby Dee *Ruth Younger* • Diana Sands *Beneatha Younger* • Ivan Dixon *Asagai* • John Fiedler *Mark Lindner* • Louis Gossett [Louis Gossett Jr] *George Murchison* ■ Dir Daniel Petrie • Scr Lorraine Hansberry, from her play

Raising a Riot ★★ U
Comedy
1955 · UK · Colour · 94mins

Left to cope with three unruly children during his wife's absence in Canada, naval officer Kenneth More takes his offspring to his father's converted windmill and institutes a strictly ordered regime. Inevitably, of course, chaos ensues. An inconsequential comedy, kept moving by the polished More, but old-fashioned and rather flat.

Kenneth More *Tony* • Shelagh Fraser *Mary* • Mandy Miller *Anne* • Gary Billings *Peter* • Fusty Bentine *Fusty* • Ronald Squire *Grampy* • Michael Bentine *Museum official* ■ Dir Wendy Toye • Scr Ian Dalrymple, Hugh Perceval, James Matthews, from the novel by Alfred Toombs

Raising Arizona ★★★★ 15
Comedy
1987 · US · Colour · 90mins

A delirious mix of slapstick, surrealism and sentimentality, this film by Joel and Ethan Coen – of *Fargo* fame – remains their warmest, most complete work next to that Oscar-winning triumph. Nicolas Cage and Holly Hunter are the couple who decide to kidnap one of a set of famous Arizona quintuplets when they discover they can't have children, only to find themselves pursued by the lone biker of the apocalypse. Cage and Hunter (in her breakthrough role) are superb, and there are winning supporting performances from John Goodman and William Forsythe as two cons on the run. However, in the end it is the dazzling invention of the Coen brothers that shines through. Contains some violence and swearing.

Nicolas Cage *Hi McDonnough* • Holly Hunter *Edwina* • Trey Wilson *Nathan Arizona Sr* • John Goodman *Gale* • William Forsythe *Evelle* • Frances McDormand *Dot* ■ Dir Joel Coen • Scr Ethan Coen, Joel Coen

Raising Cain ★★★★ 15
Thriller
1992 · US · Colour · 87mins

After the mauling he received for his disastrous adaptation of *The Bonfire of the Vanities*, director Brian De Palma went back to the disturbing Hitchcockian territory he knows so well. The result was his best movie in years: a sly, witty thriller in which the tortuous plot takes a back seat to a virtuoso display of cinematic technique as De Palma proceeds to pay tribute to Hitch and a host of his other favourite directors. John Lithgow, getting into the grisly, over-the-top spirit of the piece, plays a suspect in a series of kidnappings, Lolita Davidovich is his unfaithful wife, and there's solid support from Frances Sternhagen and Gregg Henry. Contains swearing.

John Lithgow *Carter/Cain/Dr Nix/Josh/Margo* • Lolita Davidovich *Jenny* • Steven Bauer *Jack* • Frances Sternhagen *Dr Waldheim* • Gregg Henry *Lieutenant Terri* • Tom Bower *Sergeant Cally* ■ Dir/Scr Brian De Palma

Raising Heroes ★★ 18
Crime drama
1995 · US · Colour · 85mins

A refreshing, if not entirely successful attempt to subvert the formula action/buddy/thriller genre by giving it a gay twist. An all-male couple, in the process of adopting a child, have their lives turned upside down when one of them witnesses a mob hit. Although painfully amateur in execution, this isn't just a limp-wristed *Lethal Weapon*, as director Douglas Langway's straight-to-video exercise delivers all the punch and predictability of the Hollywood mainstream but with its own fresh voice. It's just a shame the production values don't equal its often side-splitting hilarity. Contains swearing and violence.

Troy Sostillio *Josh* • Henry White *Paul* • Greg Bodkin ■ Dir Douglas Langway • Scr Douglas Langway, Edmond Sorel, Henry White

Raising the Wind ★★★ U
Comedy
1961 · UK · Colour · 87mins

Leslie Phillips stars in this laboured but likeable Gerald Thomas comedy as a penniless music student whose talent for writing pop songs while drunk jeopardises his scholarship at a top classical academy until gruff tutor James Robertson-Justice unexpectedly comes to his rescue. These accomplished funnymen go through their usual paces with aplomb, but the film belongs to the delightful Esma Cannon as a deaf landlady, Kenneth Williams as a toffee-nosed swot and Sid James as the publisher behind Phillips's predicament.

James Robertson-Justice *Sir Benjamin* • Leslie Phillips *Mervyn* • Sidney James *Sid* • Paul Massie *Malcolm* • Kenneth Williams *Harold* • Eric Barker *Morgan Rutherford* • Liz Fraser *Miranda* • Esma Cannon *Mrs Deevens* • Jim Dale *Bass trombone player* ■ Dir Gerald Thomas • Scr Bruce Montgomery

The Rake's Progress ★★★ U
Drama
1945 · UK · BW · 115mins

The first film produced by Frank Launder and Sidney Gilliat for their Individual Pictures company is a brisk comedy drama that, if not as elegant and sophisticated as it would have us believe, perfectly suits the debonair style of Rex Harrison. His exploits, first as a student at Oxford and then among the upper reaches of polite society, have a jaunty air and provide a nostalgic glimpse of Britain between the wars. Although some of its feel-good aura has diminished, the film still entertains over 50 years on.

Rex Harrison *Vivian Kenway* • Lilli Palmer *Rikki Krausner* • Godfrey Tearle *Colonel Kenway* • Griffith Jones *Sandy Duncan* ■ Dir Sidney Gilliat • Scr Frank Launder, Sidney Gilliat, from a story by Val Valentine

Rally 'round the Flag, Boys! ★★ PG
Comedy
1958 · US · Colour · 102mins

When the citizens of a nice, leafy commuter town learn they are to have a nuclear missile silo built nearby, local busybody Joanne Woodward sends her husband, Paul Newman, off to lobby Washington. This forgotten satire of the Cold War era strains for importance but fails to generate much humour, apart from Joan Collins's bubbly performance as the town flirt. It was the penultimate movie from veteran writer/director Leo McCarey, who made the Marx Brothers' classic *Duck Soup*.

Paul Newman *Harry Bannerman* • Joanne Woodward *Grace Bannerman* • Joan Collins *Angela Hoffa* • Jack Carson *Capt Hoxie* • Tuesday Weld *Comfort Goodpasture* ■ Dir Leo McCarey • Scr Leo McCarey, Claude Binyon, from the novel by Max Shulman

Rambling Rose ★★★ 15
Romantic comedy drama
1991 · US · Colour · 106mins

A neat, rather eccentric movie that shines for a while but ends up being rather aptly named. Laura Dern is very good as the sexually precocious girl with a big heart who arrives to work for a rich Southern family surrounded by thirties' poverty. Director Martha Coolidge does play the "whale I do deeclare" card a mite too often, but the movie is saved from parody by Robert Duvall's consummate performance as the clan's kindly patriarch. Dern and her real-life mother Diane Ladd were both rewarded with Oscar nominations.

Laura Dern *Rose* • Robert Duvall *Daddy Hillyer* • Diane Ladd *Mother Hillyer* • Lukas Haas *Buddy Hillyer* • John Heard *Willcox "Buddy" Hillyer* • Kevin Conway *Doctor Martinson* ■ Dir Martha Coolidge • Scr Calder Willingham, from his novel

Rambo: First Blood, Part II
★★★ 15
War drama
1985 · US · Colour · 91mins

Titanic director James Cameron shares the scriptwriting duties with star Sylvester Stallone in this explosive action sequel, directed by George Pan Cosmatos. The result is entertaining if implausible as Stallone flexes his muscles for some cartoon-like heroics, rescuing American prisoners in Vietnam but discovering that he's considered as expendable as the men he's trying to save. All this might be thought laughable, but it comes across as deadly serious and, therefore, rather scary. A bit of a come-down for

U = SUITABLE FOR ALL   Uc = SUITABLE FOR ALL, ESPECIALLY FOR YOUNG CHILDREN (VIDEO ONLY)   PG = PARENTAL GUIDANCE

Cameron after directing the previous year's massive sleeper hit, *The Terminator*. Contains violence and swearing. 📼 **DVD**

Sylvester Stallone *John Rambo* • Richard Crenna *Colonel Trautman* • Charles Napier *Marshall Murdock* • Steven Berkoff *Lieutenant Podovsky* • Julia Nickson [Julia Nickson-Soul] *Co Bao* ■ *Dir* George Pan Cosmatos • *Scr* Sylvester Stallone, James Cameron, from a story by Kevin Jarre, from characters created by David Morrell

Rambo III ★★ 18

Action drama 1988 · US · Colour · 94mins

Probably the most irredeemable of the *Rambo* series, in which Sylvester Stallone goes from slightly confused loner to the free world's white knight. In this one he reluctantly gives up his blissfully mystic life in Thailand, hilariously parodied in *Hot Shots! Part Deux*, to go on one more mission, seemingly taking on the entire Soviet army in Afghanistan when his old boss (Richard Crenna) is taken prisoner. If cartoon action is your bag, then this has it by the bucketful, but the mindless celebration of carnage leaves a nasty taste in the mouth. 📼 **DVD**

Sylvester Stallone *John Rambo* • Richard Crenna *Colonel Trautman* • Marc de Jonge *Colonel Zaysen* • Kurtwood Smith *Griggs* • Spiros Focas *Masoud* ■ *Dir* Peter MacDonald • *Scr* Sylvester Stallone, Sheldon Lettich, from characters created by David Morrell

Rampage ★★

Adventure 1963 · US · Colour · 94mins

Robert Mitchum in one of his lesser movies, a hunting saga involving the search for an elusive big cat, with Elsa Martinelli, who appeared in Howard Hawks's safari picture *Hatari!* the previous year, providing the human quarry. Mitchum virtually sleepwalks through the picture, as does his co-star Jack Hawkins, who has to sweat a lot and be mad when his mistress Martinelli switches her affections. Claiming to be set in Malaya, it was actually shot in Hawaii and at the San Diego zoo. Sabu makes his penultimate screen appearance.

Robert Mitchum *Harry Stanton* • Elsa Martinelli *Anna* • Jack Hawkins *Otto Abbot* • Sabu *Talib* • Cely Carrillo *Chep* • Emile Genest *Schelling* • Stefan Schnabel *Sakai chief* ■ *Dir* Phil Karlson • *Scr* Robert I Holt, Marguerite Roberts, from the novel by Alan Caillou

Rampage ★★ 18

Crime drama 1987 · US · Colour · 96mins

Unlike more recent movies like *Last Dance* and *Dead Man Walking* this is a story that actually seems to advocate the application of the death penalty – in some cases. Michael Biehn is a prosecutor who desperately wants to get an obviously psychotic killer (Alex McArthur) into the electric chair. McArthur seems to combine the attributes of every serial killer rolled into one easy-to-hate package as he goes about the business of slaughtering people. Despite his flair for controversy, director William Friedkin doesn't address the complexities of the issue of legal insanity, which forms the basis of the killer's defence. 📼

Michael Biehn *Anthony Fraser* • Alex McArthur *Charles Reece* • Nicholas Campbell *Albert Morse* • Deborah Van Valkenburgh *Kate Fraser* ■ *Dir* William Friedkin • *Scr* William Friedkin, from the novel by William P Wood

Ramparts of Clay ★★★

Documentary drama
1969 · Fr/Alg · Colour · 83mins

Jean-Louis Bertucelli made his feature debut with this adaptation of Jean Duvignaud's book, *Chebika*. Its themes resonate throughout African cinema – the clash between tradition and progress, the damaging legacy of colonial rule and the problems inherent in a patriarchal society. But, by filming in almost documentary fashion, Bertucelli is able to achieve a rare immediacy that is underscored by the personal liberation of Leila Schenna, the young Tunisian girl who comes to appreciate the harsh realities of so-called civilisation when the owner of a stone quarry calls in the troops to confront his striking workers. In French and Arabic with English subtitles.

Dir Jean-Louis Bertucelli • *Scr* Jean Duvignaud, from his book *Chebika (Change at Shebika)*

Ramrod ★★★ U

Western 1947 · US · BW · 94mins

War on the range, as sultry ranch owner Veronica Lake stakes her personal claim to land owned by her weak-willed father Charlie Ruggles, who's selling out to baddie Preston Foster. Joel McCrea is the titular ramrod (or ranch foreman) in this tense and violent western directed by Lake's then husband, the talented Andre De Toth. The stark black-and-white photography, the presence of dislocated, disenfranchised characters and Lake's *femme fatale*-like portrayal lend this the look of a western *film noir* in the same mould as *Pursued* and *Blood on the Moon*, both of which starred Robert Mitchum.

Veronica Lake *Connie Dickason* • Joel McCrea *Dave Nash* • Ian MacDonald *Walt Shipley* • Charles Ruggles *Ben Dickason* • Preston Foster *Frank Ivey* • Lloyd Bridges *Red Cates* ■ *Dir* Andre De Toth • *Scr* Jack Moffitt, Graham Baker, Cecile Kramer, from a story by Luke Short

Ran ★★★★★ 15

Epic drama 1985 · Jap/Fr · Colour · 153mins

Having reworked *Macbeth* in *Throne of Blood*, Akira Kurosawa tackled another Shakespearean tragedy, *King Lear*, in this majestic epic, in which a ruler's decision to partition his land between his sons plunges his realm into civil war. There is so much to admire here, but special mention must be made of Kurosawa's genius as a storyteller and his masterly movement of the camera (particularly in the stunning battle sequences), the remarkable performances of Tatsuya Nakadai as the repentant monarch and Mieko Harada as his Machiavellian daughter-in-law, and the sumptuous use of colour and period detail by production designers Yoshiro and Shinobu Muraki. A true classic. In Japanese with English subtitles.

Tatsuya Nakadai *Lord Hidetora* • Satoshi Terao *Taro* • Jinpachi Nezu *Jiro* • Daisuke Ryu *Saburo* • Mieko Harada *Lady Kaede* • Peter

The Fool • Hisashi Igawa *Kurogane* • Masayuke Yui *Tango* • Yoshiko Miyazaki *Lady Sué* ■ *Dir* Akira Kurosawa • *Scr* Akira Kurosawa, Hideo Oguni, Masato Ide, from the play *King Lear* by William Shakespeare

Rancho Deluxe ★★★ 15

Comedy western 1975 · US · Colour · 89mins

Not so much a modern buddy-buddy western as a younger generation nose-thumbing at the traditions of the range, with Jeff Bridges and Sam Waterston as disdainful young cattle rustlers who rightly end up behind bars but for the wrong reasons. Director Frank Perry's overwrought style, which unintentionally incited laughter in *Mommie Dearest*, is tightly reined in this time to make the most of the humour and the heroes, while cowboy specialist Thomas McGuane's screenplay is a joy. Contains swearing and nudity. 📼

Jeff Bridges *Jack McKee* • Sam Waterston *Cecil Colson* • Elizabeth Ashley *Cora Brown* • Charlene Dallas *Laura Beige* • Clifton James *John Brown* • Slim Pickens *Henry Beige* • Harry Dean Stanton *Curt* ■ *Dir* Frank Perry • *Scr* Thomas McGuane

Rancho Notorious ★★★ PG

Western 1952 · US · Colour · 85mins

A ridiculously over-the-top western that has developed quite a cult following. There is pleasure to be had from watching Marlene Dietrich past her prime, running a hole in the wall called "Chuck-a-Luck" and being romanced by louche Mel Ferrer. But director Fritz Lang's hand falls heavy on the proceedings, and the cheap studio settings don't help. The dialogue occasionally sparkles and writer Daniel Taradash certainly knows how to create and embellish a legend, complete with theme song and gambling wheel motif. 📼

Marlene Dietrich *Altar Keane* • Arthur Kennedy *Vern Haskell* • Mel Ferrer *Frenchy Fairmont* • Gloria Henry *Beth* • William Frawley *Baldy Gunder* • Jack Elam *Geary* ■ *Dir* Fritz Lang • *Scr* Daniel Taradash, from the story *Gunsight Whitman* by Sylvia Richards

Rancid Aluminium ★ 18

Comedy thriller 1999 · UK · Colour · 91mins

James Hawes brings his own cult novel to the screen with unengaging characters and incoherent plotting to match the unappetising title. Rhys Ifans is so preoccupied with his low sperm count and broody girlfriend (Sadie Frost), he's unsuspicious when scheming buddy Joseph Fiennes embroils them in a deadly partnership with a pair of cartoonish Russian gangsters (Steven Berkoff and Tara FitzGerald). Uncertain whether it wants to be a sex comedy or a thriller, this coarse, cluttered caper has lots of nudity and sex but little wit. 📼 **DVD**

Joseph Fiennes *Sean Deeny* • Rhys Ifans *Pete Thompson* • Tara FitzGerald *Masha* • Sadie Frost *Sarah* • Steven Berkoff *Mr Kant* • Keith Allen *Dr Jones* • Dani Behr *Charlie* • Andrew Howard *Trevor* ■ *Dir* Ed Thomas • *Scr* James Hawes, from his novel

Random Encounter ★★

Crime thriller 1998 · US · Colour · 89mins

Elizabeth Berkley, who will be forever enshrined in movie history thanks to the turkey that was *Showgirls*, tries unsuccessfully to ditch the airhead image in this middling, would-be erotic thriller. She plays an ambitious PR girl who gets enmeshed in a conspiracy involving murder and blackmail. Berkley isn't particularly convincing and the rest of the cast are hardly any more memorable.

Elizabeth Berkley *Alicia Brayman* • JH Wyman [Joel Wyner] *Kyle Jones* • Barry Flatman *Blake Preston* • Frank Schorpion *Detective Ed Royko* ■ *Dir* Doug Jackson • *Scr* Matt Dorff

Random Harvest ★★★★ U

Romance 1942 · US · BW · 126mins

Rightly, one of the best-loved and best-remembered movies of all time, teaming two of MGM's most romantic stars, Ronald Colman and Greer Garson, in a superb James Hilton story. Genuinely moving, under Mervyn LeRoy's masterly direction, and produced with all the wartime gloss MGM could muster, this film regularly seduces generation after cynical generation. Start watching, and if you're not totally hooked when Colman doesn't return to Garson after he's been hit by a car in Liverpool, you've no soul. This is clever, gracious and superbly satisfying.

Ronald Colman *Charles Rainier* • Greer Garson *Paula* • Philip Dorn *Dr Jonathan Benet* • Susan Peters *Kitty* • Reginald Owen *Biffer* • Henry Travers *Dr Sims* ■ *Dir* Mervyn LeRoy • *Scr* Claudine West, George Froeschel, Arthur Wimperis, from the novel by James Hilton

Random Hearts ★★★ 15

Romantic drama
1999 · US · Colour · 128mins

With a title that harks back to *Random Harvest*, one of cinema's greatest tear-jerkers, this is an affair of the heart intended for a mature box office. Harrison Ford is Dutch, a detective investigating another, crooked cop; Kristin Scott Thomas is a Republican congresswoman. They find out that their spouses have been killed together in an plane crash while conducting an extra-marital affair. To make up for the betrayal, the two marital leftovers fall in love. Sydney Pollack directs with real skill when it comes to sizing up the emotional weight that middle-age passion lays on a life, though the cop-pursuit gets in the way of the real problem – how to make a woman's picture that's an adult one as well. In that respect it succeeds, while the stars are marvellously attuned. 📼 **DVD**

Harrison Ford *Dutch Van Den Broeck* • Kristin Scott Thomas *Kay Chandler* • Charles S Dutton *Alcee* • Bonnie Hunt *Wendy Judd* • Dennis Haysbert *Detective George Beaufort* • Sydney Pollack *Carl Broman* • Peter Coyote *Cullen Chandler* • M Emmet Walsh *Bartender at Billy's* ■ *Dir* Sydney Pollack • *Scr* Kurt Luedtke, from the novel by Warren Adler

Randy Rides Alone ★★ U

Western 1934 · US · BW · 52mins

One of the more entertaining of John Wayne's Monogram Studio westerns, featuring not only the Duke singing (well, pretending to: he's dubbed by cowboy crooner Smith Ballew) but also starting on a chilling note – Wayne rides into a deserted town and finds a saloon full of dead men. The mystery is quite well sustained for what is no more or less than a routine B-western, but the production values let the cast down badly. ▭

John Wayne *Randy Bowers* • Alberta Vaughn *Sally Rogers* • George "Gabby" Hayes *Matt the Mute/Marvin Black* • Yakima Canutt *Spike* • Earl Dwire *Sheriff* • Tex Phelps *Deputy* ■ *Dir* Harry Fraser • *Scr* Lindsley Parsons, from his story

Rangeela ★★★ U
Drama 1995 · Ind · Colour · 149mins

A former tennis pro who followed his producer father and director uncle to Bollywood, Aamir Khan has made dozens of movies since hitting the big time in the 1988 film *Until Judgement Day*. Capable of a greater psychological depth than many of his contemporaries, he demonstrates his famed sense of comic timing in this romantic triangle, in which he plays a ticket tout who competes for the affections of a wannabe actress who the star who can grant her wishes. A typical mix of music and melodrama. In Hindi with English subtitles.

Jackie Shroff *Rajkamal* • Aamir Khan *Muna* • Urmila Matondkar *Mili* • Gulshan Grover *Steven Grover* ■ *Dir* Ram Gopal Varma

The Ranger, the Cook and a Hole in the Sky ★★★
Drama 1995 · US · Colour · 89mins

Like *A River Runs through It*, this homely TV movie comes from the autobiographical writings of Norman Maclean. Set in Montana in 1919, it's a rites-of-passage tale in which Jerry O'Connell learns all about girls, grub and gambling from the roughnecked crew of forest rangers led by avuncular Sam Elliott. Managing to evoke an attractive sense of period from his forest locations, director John Kent Harrison brings a feel of the old-time western to these amiable proceedings.

Sam Elliott *Bill Bell* • Jerry O'Connell *Mac* • Ricky Jay *Hawkes* • Molly Parker *Sue* • Don S Davis *Mr Smith* • Robert Wisden *Canada* ■ *Dir* John Kent Harrison • *Scr* Robert Wayne, from a short story by Norman Maclean

Ransom! ★★★
Crime drama 1956 · US · BW · 109mins

During the fifties Glenn Ford averaged three films a year. Mainly westerns and thrillers, they gave the stern-faced star angst-ridden roles on both sides of the law. Here he is in trouble as the wealthy father of a boy who has been kidnapped. In a novel idea for the period, he contacts the abductors on television, offering the ransom for their capture and threatening to kill them if they harm his son. The earliest version was made for television, although it will seem more familiar as the inspiration for Mel Gibson's 1996 film.

Glenn Ford *David G Stannard* • Donna Reed *Edith Stannard* • Leslie Nielsen *Charlie Telfer* • Juano Hernandez *Jesse Chapman* • Robert Keith *Chief Jim Backett* • Mabel Albertson *Mrs Partridge* ■ *Dir* Alex Segal • *Scr* Cyril Hume, Richard Maibaum

Ransom ★ PG
Drama 1975 · UK · Colour · 89mins

One of Sean Connery's very few total duds: a lamely directed, lousily written drama about international terrorism. Connery plays a security wiz tackling a ransom demand for a kidnapped British ambassador and also dealing with a hijacked plane. Apparently the British government has already caved in to the terrorists' demands, so Connery is left mired in a mass of red tape as actors' foreign accents wilt under the stress of it all. ▭

Sean Connery *Nils Tahlvik* • Ian McShane *Petrie* • Norman Bristow *Captain Denver* • John Cording *Bert* • Isabel Dean *Mrs Palmer* ■ *Dir* Casper Wrede • *Scr* Paul Wheeler

Ransom ★★★ 18
Action thriller 1996 · US · Colour · 116mins

In this entertaining remake of a 1956 Glenn Ford thriller, Mel Gibson stars as a maverick tycoon who must decide whether to pay a $2 million ransom for his kidnapped son or take the law into his own hands. There are no prizes for guessing the *Die Hard*-style avenue Gibson takes, but his method of action is an interesting one. The film suffers overall under Ron Howard's unusually starchy direction and Rene Russo is wasted as Gibson's concerned wife, but Gary Sinise gives his villainous role a few wry twists. ▭ DVD

Mel Gibson *Tom Mullen* • Rene Russo *Kate Mullen* • Brawley Nolte *Sean Mullen* • Gary Sinise *Jimmy Shaker* • Delroy Lindo *Agent Lonnie Hawkins* ■ *Dir* Ron Howard • *Scr* Richard Price, Alexander Ignon, from the 1956 film

Rapa Nui ★ 12
Drama 1994 · US · Colour · 102mins

The moai, the huge stone faces that dominate the landscape of Easter Island, make a hugely tempting topic for a film-maker. How did they get there? Who made them? What purpose did they serve? Kevin Reynolds succumbed to the temptation of the tale and persuaded Kevin Costner to co-produce. Sadly, the result is an insulting concoction, with anthropological speculation being replaced by leering travelogue, patronising tribalism and melodramatic ritual. The performers playing the Long Ear rulers and their Short Ear subjects struggle valiantly with the crass dialogue, but the idiocy of the plot and the flashiness of Reynolds's direction too often render their efforts ridiculous. Contains violence and nudity. ▭

Jason Scott Lee *Noro* • Esai Morales *Make* • Sandrine Holt *Ramana* • Emilio Tuki Hito *Messenger* • Gordon Hatfield *Riro* • Faenza Reuben *Heke* ■ *Dir* Kevin Reynolds • *Scr* Tim Rose Price, Kevin Reynolds

The Rape of Aphrodite ★★★
Drama 1985 · Cyp · Colour · 150mins

Cypriot cinema only released its first feature – Michael Papas's *Tomorrow's Warrior* – in 1981. It was followed by this sweeping study of 30 years of the country's turbulent history, one of the first Cypriot films to attract international attention. Costas Timvios stars as a former member of the Greek Cypriot terrorist group EOKA, who

dedicates his life to searching for his wife and child who vanished during the 1974 Turkish invasion that resulted in the island being partitioned. It's obviously an emotive story and the film is full of dramatic incident and provocative insight, but director Andreas Pantzis doesn't always keep far enough back from his subject. In Greek with English subtitles.

Costas Timvios *Evagoras* • Thalia Argiriou *Aphrodite* • Ilias Aletras *Taxi driver* ■ *Dir/Scr* Andreas Pantzis

The Rape of Dr Willis ★★ 15
Drama 1991 · US · Colour · 91mins

TV movie queen Jaclyn Smith stars as a distraught surgeon in this unfortunate soap opera-style tale: first her husband dies, then she is raped in the hospital car park on her first day at work. Both these events should be tragic, but director Lou Antonio succeeds in making them almost laughable, while Smith simply lets her lower lip quiver in relation to the seriousness of the moment. ▭

Jaclyn Smith *Dr Kate Willis* • Holland Taylor *Dr Carol Greenway* • Robin Thomas *Dr Wally Shaw* • Lisa Jakub *Carrie Willis* • Lonny Chapman *Dr McMahon* ■ *Dir* Lou Antonio • *Scr* Steven Gethers, Anne Gerard

The Rape of Richard Beck ★★★★ 18
Drama 1985 · US · Colour · 91mins

Director Karen Arthur has built a reputation for producing powerful films about women who draw on hidden resources to overcome all manner of ailments and abuses. That's why she was the ideal choice for this compelling TV movie in which macho cop Richard Crenna comes to appreciate the hell female sexual assault victims go through when he himself is raped. Crenna won an Emmy for his wonderfully aware performance. Contains violence. ▭

Richard Crenna *Richard Beck* • Meredith Baxter Birney [Meredith Baxter] *Barbara McKay* • Pat Hingle *Chappy Beck* • Frances Lee McCain *Caroline Beck* • Cotter Smith *Lieutenant Hugo* • George Dzundza *Blastig* ■ *Dir* Karen Arthur • *Scr* James G Hirsch

Rapid Fire ★★★ 18
Martial arts thriller 1992 · US · Colour · 91mins

Brandon Lee may have lacked the martial-arts grace of his father, but there was no denying his charisma, and this serviceable action thriller offered him the opportunity to make the transition from straight-to-video star to a man with genuine box-office appeal. There's not much subtlety involved in this story of a college student who finds himself on the run from villainous Powers Boothe, but the production values are a notch above the usual B-movie action adventures. Lee doesn't take things too seriously and shows that he was cut out to become one of the more interesting action stars. Contains swearing, sex scenes and nudity. ▭

Brandon Lee *Jake Lo* • Powers Boothe *Mace Ryan* • Nick Mancuso *Antonio Serrano* • Raymond J Barry *Agent Stuart* • Kate Hodge

Karla Withers • Ma Tzi *Kinman Tau* ■ *Dir* Dwight H Little • *Scr* Alan McElroy, from the story by Cindy Cirile, Alan McElroy

Rappin' ★ PG
Drama 1985 · US · Colour · 88mins

One of the many exploitation films released in the aftermath of the rap, break-dancing and hip-hop explosion, in which ex-con Mario Van Peebles takes on a crooked property baron who has recruited a gang to bully and evict the tenants from a run-down Pittsburgh ghetto. Van Peebles puts his rhyming skills to good use and manages to conquer the violence dominating the neighbourhood in this absurdly unrealistic social thriller teeming with offensive action and ludicrous stereotypes.

Mario Van Peebles *John Hood* • Tasia Valenza *Dixie* • Charles Flohe *Duane* • Leo O'Brien *Allan* • Eriq La Salle *Ice* • Richie Abanes *Richie* ■ *Dir* Joel Silberg • *Scr* Robert Litz, Adam Friedman

The Rapture ★★★ 18
Drama 1991 · US · Colour · 96mins

Mimi Rogers reminds us what a fine actress she can be with a bravura performance as a bored LA telephone operator and part-time swinger who joins a fundamentalist religious movement that believes the end of the world is nigh. Michael Tolkin, probably best known for his screenplay for *The Player*, makes a striking directorial debut with this admittedly imperfect but also ambitious, challenging and intelligent offering that perfectly captures the conspiratorial creepiness of such overly zealous religious sects. Fans of *The X Files* will want to catch a pre-Fox Mulder David Duchovny playing Rogers's husband. ▭

Mimi Rogers *Sharon* • David Duchovny *Randy* • Patrick Bauchau *Vic* • Kimberly Cullum *Mary* • Will Patton *Sheriff Foster* • Terri Hanauer *Paula* ■ *Dir/Scr* Michael Tolkin

The Rare Breed ★★★ U
Western 1966 · US · Colour · 96mins

A warm-hearted, sprawling western in which feisty widow Maureen O'Hara imports a prize Hereford bull to the Old West for breeding purposes. The pleasure's really in watching the languid by-play between O'Hara, loveable drifter James Stewart and rugged cattle baron Brian Keith. Novelty is provided by Juliet Mills, Hayley's sister, in cinematographer William H Clothier's landscapes. Director Andrew V McLaglen brings out the best in his actors, and if it is all a bit jovial and sub-John Ford, well, that's no bad thing.

James Stewart *Sam Burnett* • Maureen O'Hara *Martha Price* • Brian Keith *Alexander Bowen* • Juliet Mills *Hilary Price* • Don Galloway *Jamie Bowen* • Jack Elam *Deke Simons* ■ *Dir* Andrew V McLaglen • *Scr* Ric Hardman

A Rare Breed ★
Drama 1981 · US · Colour · 94mins

A horse-racing story, filmed in 1981 but left in the stables until 1984. The story is really *National Velvet* in different silks, about a teenage girl who falls in love with the horse which

U = SUITABLE FOR ALL   Uc = SUITABLE FOR ALL, ESPECIALLY FOR YOUNG CHILDREN (VIDEO ONLY)   PG = PARENTAL GUIDANCE

becomes a champion racer and is then kidnapped for ransom, much like Shergar. Set in Italy but shot in North Carolina, it can be safely recommended to horse fanciers.

George Kennedy Nathan Hill • Forrest Tucker Jess Cutler • Tracy Vaccaro Anne Cutler • Tom Hallick Luigi Nelson ■ Dir David Nelson • Scr Garner Simmons, from a story by Stanley S Canter

Rashomon ★★★★★ 12
Drama 1950 · Jap · BW · 86mins

Showered with prizes at festivals worldwide, this was the film that introduced western audiences to Japanese cinema. Exploring the relativity of truth, Akira Kurosawa presents four equally credible accounts of the woodland encounter between a wealthy married couple and a bandit that results in the husband's death. The endlessly moving camera, the stylised composition of the shots and the subtly shifting performances enable Kurosawa to challenge the notion that the camera never lies. Machiko Kyo as the wife and Toshiro Mifune as the bandit are superb, but it's Kurosawa's control that makes this exercise in emphasis and atmosphere so mesmerising. In Japanese with English subtitles.

Toshiro Mifune Tajomaru • Machiko Kyo Masago • Masayuki Mori Takehiro • Takashi Shimura Firewood dealer • Minoru Chiaki Priest ■ Dir Akira Kurosawa • Scr Shinobu Hashimoto, Akira Kurosawa, from the short story Yabu no Naka and the novel Rasho-Mon by Ryunosuke Akutagawa

Rasputin ★★★★ 15
Biographical drama
1996 · US · Colour · 100mins

An Emmy and Golden Globe-winning biopic made for cable by HBO. As far from staid costume television drama as you can get, Alan Rickman is dangerously dynamic as the Mad Monk and spiritual adviser to Russia's royals on the brink of dissolution. He's well matched by Greta Scacchi as Tsarina Alexandra and Ian McKellen as Tsar Nicholas II. This was a huge hit Stateside and while there are historical innacuracies, it captures the flavour of this often told tale of the enigmatic royals confronting the onset of revolution.

Alan Rickman Rasputin • Greta Scacchi Tsarina Alexandra • Ian McKellen Tsar Nicholas • David Warner Dr Botkin • John Wood Stolypin ■ Dir Uli Edel • Scr Peter Pruce

Rasputin and the Empress ★★
Historical drama 1932 · US · BW · 93mins

A trio of Barrymores is on display: Lionel as the demonic monk, Ethel as the tsarina and John as the nobleman who puts an end to Rasputin's sinister influence. Ethel had not made a picture for 13 years, and, in an effort to please her, Louis B Mayer hired Charles Brabin, who immediately became embroiled in sibling rivalry and John's excessive drinking. After a month of delays, Brabin was replaced by Richard Boleslawski. The resulting overlong stodge caused fireworks at MGM's legal department when

surviving members of Russia's aristocracy claimed they were misrepresented in the film.

John Barrymore Prince Paul Chegodieff • Ethel Barrymore Empress Alexandra • Lionel Barrymore Rasputin • Ralph Morgan Emperor Nikolai • Diana Wynyard Natasha • Tad Alexander Alexis • C Henry Gordon Grand Duke Igor ■ Dir Richard Boleslawski • Scr Charles MacArthur

Rasputin, the Mad Monk ★★★ 15
Historical drama 1965 · UK · Colour · 87mins

Christopher Lee's commanding presence is splendidly suited to his role here as the lecherous mystic who dominated the Romanov court of pre-revolutionary Russia and carved a debauched path through its ladies-in-waiting. But, although it was an intriguing change of pace for Hammer, with stylish studio regular Barbara Shelley present and correct as a different sort of scream queen, the tale eventually degenerates into wild-eyed hysteria.

Christopher Lee Rasputin • Barbara Shelley Sonia • Richard Pasco Dr Zargo • Francis Matthews Ivan • Suzan Farmer Vanessa • Joss Ackland Bishop ■ Dir Don Sharp • Scr John Elder [Anthony Hinds]

The Rat Pack ★★★
Biographical drama 1998 · US · Colour

Ray Liotta as Frank Sinatra, Joe Mantegna as Dean Martin, Don Cheadle as Sammy Davis Jr and Angus MacFadyen as Peter Lawford. You don't really believe it's them until they go on stage at one of JFK's fundraisers and sing High Hopes, JFK gives a speech, Marilyn coos and the movie snaps into gear. This TV film explores Sinatra's twin links to the mob and to Jack and Robert Kennedy, compromised when JFK enters the White House and when RFK declares war on organised crime. The pulse of the era is beautifully evoked.

Ray Liotta Frank Sinatra • Joe Mantegna Dean Martin • Don Cheadle Sammy Davis Jr • Angus MacFadyen Peter Lawford • William Petersen John F Kennedy • Zeljko Ivanek Bobby Kennedy • Bobby Slayton Joey Bishop ■ Dir Rob Cohen • Scr Kario Salem

The Rat Race ★★
Comedy 1960 · US · Colour · 105mins

Tony Curtis, still a saxophone player after Some Like it Hot, arrives from the sticks in New York, moves into a run-down tenement boarding house, and tries to make a career in the sleazy nightclub run by Don Rickles. He's just an inch away from crime and, in due course, a bit closer to Debbie Reynolds, a dance-hall "hostess". The Rat Race is Hollywood's idea of what a Beat movie should be like; the settings are picturesquely drab and Elmer Bernstein contributes a racy score but Curtis and Reynolds, charming as they are, are much too pretty and clean-looking to be convincing.

Tony Curtis Peter Hammond Jr • Debbie Reynolds Peggy Brown • Jack Oakie Mac • Kay Medford Soda • Don Rickles Nellie • Joe Bushkin Frankie ■ Dir Robert Mulligan • Scr Garson Kanin, from his play

Rat-Trap ★★★
Drama 1981 · Ind · Colour · 121mins

Considered by some critics to be the legitimate heir to Satyajit Ray, Adoor Gopalakrishnan concedes there is an autobiographical element to this weighty political drama, focusing on the slow emergence of the Kerala region of south-western India. With every action and gesture of his performance laced with symbolism, Karamana is compelling as the increasingly paranoid head of a redundant family of rent collectors, caught between the inevitable collapse of the traditional order and the caprices of his three sisters. In Malayalam with English subtitles.

Karamana Unni • Sarada Rajamma • Jalaja Sridevi • Rajam K Nair Janamma ■ Dir Adoor Gopalakrishnan • Scr Adoor Gopalakrishnan

Ratboy ★★ PG
Drama 1986 · US · Colour · 99mins

Sondra Locke directs and stars in yet another tale of an exploited misfit. This time it's a half boy, half rat creature (SL Baird) and again we have the archetypal outsider being exposed and promoted as a weird commercial fairground attraction. Plucked from the comfort of his Hollywood rubbish dump into a media circus, Ratboy is "rescued" by Locke, who is posing as a journalist. Her motives aren't altruistic though, as she has her own plans to exploit her media-friendly protégé.

Sondra Locke Nikki Morrison • Robert Townsend Manny • Christopher Hewett Acting coach • Larry Hankin Jewell • Sydney Lassick "Dial-a-Prayer" • SL Baird Ratboy ■ Dir Sondra Locke • Scr Rob Thompson

Ratcatcher ★★★★ 15
Drama 1999 · UK · Colour · 90mins

Lynne Ramsay makes her feature debut with this unsentimental portrait of growing up in Glasgow in the seventies. Achieving a lyrical realism that often recalls Jean Vigo's classic L'Atalante (1934), Ramsay manages to turn a rundown housing estate at the height of a refuse strike into fertile ground for the imagination of 12-year-old William Eadie, a neglected scallywag forced to bear the burden of accidentally drowning his friend in the canal. Alternately seeking solace in the shell of a green-belt dream house and the company of flirty teenager Leanne Mullen, Eadie gives a remarkably natural performance. Amiable, assured and affecting. Contains swearing

William Eadie James • Tommy Flanagan Da • Mandy Matthews Ma • Michelle Stewart Ellen • Lynne Ramsay Jr Anne Marie • Leanne Mullen Margaret Anne • John Miller Kenny ■ Dir/Scr Lynne Ramsay

Ratchet ★★ 18
Crime drama 1996 · US · Colour · 107mins

This contemporary film noir, overplotted and wilfully obscure, focuses on a writer/director suffering from writer's block who relocates to Nantucket Island hoping to rediscover his muse. There, he stumbles on a local writer with a great script, and deviously appropriates it for his own uses. Plagiarism comes to no good,

and the film descends into typically noir nastiness. Contains swearing, violence and sex scenes.

Tom Gilroy Elliot Callahan • Margaret Welsh Catherine Ripley • Mitchell Lichtenstein Tim Greenleaf • Nurit Koppel Julia Webb ■ Dir/Scr John S Johnson

The Ratings Game ★★★
Satire 1984 · US · Colour · 102mins

Hollywood powerhouse Danny DeVito here directs and stars as a cheesy TV producer who comes up with a really bad idea that becomes the hottest thing on the box. Sharper than that other satirical look at the world of TV, Broadcast News, this is a superior TV movie that also stars DeVito's real-life wife Rhea Perlman (Carla from Cheers), George Wendt (Norm from the same series), Kevin McCarthy and Steve Allen.

Danny DeVito Vic Desalvo • Rhea Perlman Francine Kester • Gerrit Graham Parker Braithwaite • Bernadette Birkett Mrs Sweeney • Barry Corbin Colonel • Kevin McCarthy Wes Vandergelder • George Wendt Mr Sweeney • Steve Allen ■ Dir Danny DeVito • Scr Jim Mulholland, Michael Barrie

The Rats ★★★
Drama 1955 · W Ger · BW · 97mins

Hollywood exile and film noir expert Robert Siodmak returned to his native Germany to make this drama about a refugee from the East who gives her newborn baby to a childless woman from the West. As an allegory it may now seem exceptionally crude but in 1955, when the still bombed-out Berlin was divided into four militarised zones, it carried enormous weight – indeed, the film won the main prize at the Berlin Film Festival. The refugee is played by Germany's then foremost actress Maria Schell, the older sister of actor/director Maximilian. A German language film.

Curt Jurgens Bruno Mechelke • Maria Schell Pauline Karka • Heidemarie Hatheyer Anna John • Gustav Knuth Karl John ■ Dir Robert Siodmak • Scr Jochen Huth, from a play by Gerhart Hauptmann

Rattle of a Simple Man ★★ 15
Comedy drama 1964 · UK · BW · 91mins

Harry H Corbett strays into Norman Wisdom territory in this disappointing comedy from the husband-and-wife team of Sydney and Muriel Box. In adapting his play for the big screen, Charles Dyer so overdoes the pathos that what few laughs there are seem rather cruel and out of place. As the innocent following his football team to Wembley, Corbett is unconvincingly wide-eyed, although his scenes with prostitute Diane Cilento have a certain sweetness about them.

Harry H Corbett Percy Winthram • Diane Cilento Cyrenne • Thora Hird Mrs Winthram • Michael Medwin Ginger • Charles Dyer Chalky • Hugh Futcher Ozzie • Brian Wilde Fred ■ Dir Muriel Box • Scr Charles Dyer, from his play

Rattled ★★ PG
Horror thriller 1996 · US · Colour · 85mins

Venomous snakes in the grass sink their fangs into suburbia in this nature-run-amok TV movie. Architect William

Katt (*Big Wednesday*), physician wife Shanna Reed and the kids find themselves the target of an immense den of rattlesnakes, blasted from hibernation during construction of dad's housing development. Not for the squeamish, this routine family-in-jeopardy tale coils to strike, then fails to deliver. 🎬

William Katt *Paul* • Shanna Reed *Krista* • Ed Lauter *Murray Hendershot* • Bibi Besch *Gail Hendershot* • Monica Creel *Michelle* ■ *Dir* Tony Randel • *Scr* Ken Wheat, Jim Wheat, from the book *Rattlers* by Joseph Gilmore

Ravager ★★★ 15

Science-fiction thriller
1997 · US · Colour · 88mins

Outbreak meets *Alien* in a competently made and acted science-fiction thriller. In the near future, a space cruiser commanded by Cooper (straight-to-video action hero Bruce Payne) crash-lands in an uncharted area – actually a dumping ground for biological weapons. While exploring the seemingly uninhabited site, one of the crew is infected by something nasty, known as "ravager" – a highly contagious disease which drives people insane after endowing them with super-human strength. Can Cooper and crew escape from the insidious terror? Contains violence and some swearing. 🎬

Bruce Payne *Cooper* • Yancy Butler *Avedon* • Salvator Xuereb *Lazarus* • Juliet Landau *Sarra* • Robin Sachs *Shepard* ■ *Dir* James D Deck • *Scr* Donald J Loperfido, James D Deck

The Raven ★★★★ 15

Horror
1935 · US · BW · 58mins

The second of Universal's horror vehicles to co-star Bela Lugosi and Boris Karloff is an unusually sadistic slice of shock from the Golden Age of *Grand Guignol*. Lugosi plays Dr Vollin, a crazed surgeon obsessed with the works of Edgar Allan Poe, who builds a dungeon with torture devices inspired by the writer. Karloff is the scarred criminal he promises to fix surgically if he carries out a few murderous tasks. Remarkably scripted, this vintage horror show, combining both the striking imagery and mournfully beautiful poetry of Poe, is brought to startling life by performances of twisted ferocity from the two kings of the genre. 🎬

Karloff [Boris Karloff] *Edmond Bateman* • Bela Lugosi *Dr Richard Vollin* • Lester Matthews *Dr Jerry Halden* • Irene Ware *Jean Thatcher* • Samuel S Hinds *Judge Thatcher* ■ *Dir* Louis Friedlander [Lew Landers] • *Scr* David Boehm, from the poem by Edgar Allan Poe

The Raven ★★★★

Mystery thriller
1943 · Fr · BW · 93mins

Such was the hostility levelled at this excoriating study of French provincial life that, on the Liberation, Henri-Georges Clouzot was accused of peddling collaborationist propaganda and banned from directing until 1947. Subsequently, this atmospheric thriller, about a poison-pen campaign that exposes the malicious hypocrisy simmering beneath the respectable surface of a tightly knit community, was reclaimed as an indictment of the paranoia that existed under the Nazi

occupation. In fact, Louis Chavance wrote his initial screenplay in 1937 and intended it to be, primarily, a riveting whodunit, which it most certainly is, thanks to exceptional ensemble playing and Clouzot's claustrophobic staging. In French with English subtitles.

Pierre Fresnay *Dr Germain* • Ginette Leclerc *Denise Saillens* • Micheline Francey *Laura Vorzet* ■ *Dir* Henri-Georges Clouzot • *Scr* Louis Chavance, Henri-Georges Clouzot

The Raven ★★★★

Comedy horror   1963 · US · Colour · 86mins

The most flippant of Roger Corman's Edgar Allan Poe cycle, this is, nevertheless, a minor B-movie classic, and a cast containing Vincent Price, Boris Karloff, Peter Lorre and a young Jack Nicholson alone makes it a must-see. But there is also a script littered with throwaway one-liners and some unashamedly home-made special effects that add considerably to the charm of this beautifully pitched gothic romp. As the duelling masters of the black arts, Price and Karloff selflessly send up their screen images, but it's Lorre's performance of tipsy comic incompetence that endures.

Vincent Price *Dr Erasmus Craven* • Peter Lorre *Dr Adolphus Bedlo* • Boris Karloff *Dr Scarabus* • Jack Nicholson *Rexford Bedlo* • Hazel Court *Lenore Craven* • Olive Sturgess *Estelle Craven* ■ *Dir* Roger Corman • *Scr* Richard Matheson, from the poem by Edgar Allan Poe

Raven Hawk ★

Action drama   1996 · US · Colour · 88mins

Rhyia Shadowfeather (Rachel McLish) is framed for the slaughter of her parents by evil businessman William Atherton who wants to put a factory on Native American land. Her efforts to wipe out all the bad guys are helped by the complicity of an agent investigating her case. The mixed messages in this decidedly low-budget, lowbrow revenge flick are almost lost in the orgy of killings. Even in Native American, environmental-friendly clothing, it's still senseless violence.

Rachel McLish *Rhyia Shadowfeather* • John Enos *Marshall Del Wilkes* • William Atherton *Philip Thorne* • Ed Lauter *Sheriff Daggert* ■ *Dir* Albert Pyun • *Scr* Kevin Elders

Ravenous ★★★★ 18

Period black comedy horror
1999 · US/UK · Colour · 100mins

Priest director Antonia Bird's stunning mix of gut-spilling gore and *Carry On*-style banter is a shocker that you'll either love for its edgy tone, or absolutely hate because it's so in-your-face. Inspired by the tragic Donner Pass disaster of 1846-7, the film stars Robert Carlyle as a devious maneater, decimating the inhabitants of a mountain outpost to keep human flesh on his winter menu. Bird's highly disturbing and thought-provoking film features a couple of impeccable performances. Carlyle etches the strongest portrait of pure evil since Anthony Hopkins in *The Silence of the Lambs*, while Guy Pearce is equally brilliant as the army captain who tries to stop his bloodthirsty exploits. The insane climax is yet another off-kilter

delight in this intensely hilarious chiller. Contains violence. 🎬

Robert Carlyle *Colqhoun/Ives* • Guy Pearce *Captain John Boyd* • David Arquette *Cleaves* • Jeremy Davies *Private Toffler* • Jeffrey Jones *Colonel Hart* ■ *Dir* Antonia Bird • *Scr* Ted Griffin

Raven's End ★★★

Drama   1963 · Swe · BW · 100mins

Lauded at the time for its uncompromising realism, Bo Widerberg's Oscar-nominated second feature is actually more notable for the economy of its storytelling. Constantly underplaying or not depicting key events, Widerberg forces us to concentrate on the characters enduring the harsh conditions that existed in Malmö during the thirties Depression. Thommy Berggren is ingratiatingly feckless as the budding novelist deliberating whether to break for freedom or accept the responsibility to his pregnant girlfriend, thus risking being trapped in the spirit-crushing ennui that has destroyed his parents. But the star turn is Keve Hjelm's drunken, work-shy father. In Swedish with English subtitles.

Thommy Berggren *Anders* • Keve Hjelm *Father* • Emy Storm *Mother* • Ingvar Hirdwall *Sixten* • Christina Frambäck *Elsie* ■ *Dir/Scr* Bo Widerberg

Raw Courage ★

Thriller   1984 · US · Colour · 90mins

Raw courage is what it takes to sit through this dreadful thriller. Three marathon runners (Ronny Cox, Lois Chiles and Art Hindle) are taken prisoner by a citizens' army in the New Mexico desert. The army is commanded by M Emmet Walsh which gives them a distinct edge in terms of acting, but Robert L Rosen directs with such a leaden-footed lack of momentum you wonder why you're watching.

Ronny Cox *Pete Canfield* • Lois Chiles *Ruth* • Art Hindle *Roger Bower* • M Emmet Walsh *Colonel Crouse* ■ *Dir* Robert L Rosen • *Scr* Ronny Cox, Mary Cox

Raw Deal ★★★★

Film noir   1948 · US · BW · 78mins

A smashing, low-budget thriller, photographed by John Alton so as to disguise the lack of money for sets by plunging whole areas of the screen into mysterious, menacing blackness. In and out of these voids stalk and flee some desperate characters – including gangster Dennis O'Keefe on the run from jail and aiming to kill the man who framed him, Raymond Burr. Marsha Hunt is his hostage and Claire Trevor is O'Keefe's girlfriend who helped him escape and who narrates the movie like an ode to the dead. A masterly exercise in atmospherics and tension from Anthony Mann.

Dennis O'Keefe *Joe Sullivan* • Claire Trevor *Pat Regan* • Marsha Hunt *Ann Martin* • John Ireland *Fantail* • Raymond Burr *Rick Coyle* ■ *Dir* Anthony Mann • *Scr* Leopold Atlas, John C Higgins, from a story by Arnold B Armstrong, Audrey Ashley

Raw Deal ★★★ 18

Action thriller   1986 · US · Colour · 101mins

Sadly, not the 1948 Anthony Mann *film noir*, but a superficially entertaining exercise in crash-bang policing from John Irvin, whose only previous action assignment was the dismal *Dogs of War*. Fresh from the equally disastrous *Red Sonja*, Arnold Schwarzenegger was probably so keen to get back to the old routine that he could only have given the script a cursory glance. Although he gets to blow away a generous quota of bad guys, the film is largely populated with stereotypes and riddled with situations that place more of a strain on the credibility that Arnie does on that vest as he loads up for action. If you can suspend your disbelief, you'll have a ball. Contains violence and swearing. 🎬 **DVD**

Arnold Schwarzenegger *Mark Kaminksi* • Kathryn Harrold *Monique* • Sam Wanamaker *Luigi Patrovita* • Paul Shenar *Rocca* • Robert Davi *Max* ■ *Dir* John Irvin • *Scr* Gary M DeVore, Norman Wexler, from a story by Luciano Vincenzoni, Sergio Donati

Raw Edge ★★★

Western   1956 · US · Colour · 76mins

One of those splendid Universal programme fillers produced by *Touch of Evil's* Albert Zugsmith, this time in lurid colour and boasting an equally lurid plot about a gang of ranch hands trying to kill Herbert Rudley so they can lay claim to his wife, Yvonne De Carlo. There's no direction to speak of from John Sherwood, but who cares?

Rory Calhoun *Tex Kirby* • Yvonne De Carlo *Hannah Montgomery* • Mara Corday *Paca* • Rex Reason *John Randolph* • Herbert Rudley *Gerald Montgomery* ■ *Dir* John Sherwood • *Scr* Harry Essex, Robert Hill, from a story by William Kozlenka, James Benson Nablo

Raw Force ★

Martial arts horror
1982 · US · Colour · 86mins

On Warriors Island, monks trade jade for regular shipments of bare-breasted women, whom they subsequently barbeque (not boil or bake, it's stressed) and eat. Nearby at the same time, the Burbank Karate Club is on a cruise, with Cameron Mitchell as their captain. They and several other passengers soon find themselves stranded on the island, and must fight the slave dealers, as well as ancient martial arts warriors rising from their graves. Obviously, not one minute of this movie is to be taken the least bit seriously, though it is played straight.

Cameron Mitchell *Captain* • Geoffrey Binney *Mike* • Jillian Kessner *Cookie* • John Dresden *John* ■ *Dir/Scr* Edward Murphy

Raw Justice ★★ 18

Crime thriller   1993 · US · Colour · 92mins

Notable mainly for giving Pamela Anderson an early opportunity to show her ability to wear very few clothes, this is an entertaining if extremely erratic comedy thriller. Robert Hays is the hapless executive who is forced to go on the run when he gets implicated in the murder of a powerful man's daughter. Anderson plays a prostitute who may or may not be an ally. The tone veers all over the place, but an

U = SUITABLE FOR ALL   **Uc** = SUITABLE FOR ALL, ESPECIALLY FOR YOUNG CHILDREN (VIDEO ONLY)   **PG** = PARENTAL GUIDANCE

eclectic cast means it's always watchable. Contains swearing, violence and sex scenes.

David Keith *Mace* • Robert Hays *Mitch* • Pamela Anderson *Sarah* • Charles Napier *Mayor Stiles* • Stacy Keach *Bob Jenkins* • Leo Rossi *Detective Atkins* ■ *Dir/Scr* David A Prior

Raw Nerve ★★★ 18

Thriller 1991 · US · Colour · 91mins

Hollywood legends often made late career appearances in movies they'd have been well advised to steer clear of. Who can forget Joan Crawford in *Trog*, or Bette Davis in *Return from Witch Mountain*? Glenn Ford, though, star of *The Blackboard Jungle* and *Gilda* fares rather better in this thriller about a racing driver who's having nightmares about a local killer in action. Schlock it may be, but it's superior schlock. 📼

Glenn Ford *Captain Gavin* • Jan-Michael Vincent *Lieutenant Ellis* • Sandahl Bergman *Gloria Freeman* • Randall "Tex" Cobb *Blake Garrett* • Traci Lords *Gina Clayton* ■ *Dir* David A Prior • *Scr* David A Prior, Lawrence L Simeone

Rawhead Rex ★★ 18

Horror 1986 · UK · Colour · 85mins

This was only the second Clive Barker script to be filmed and could have dealt a fatal blow to his career. No wonder the horror master practically disowned George Pavlou's movie. Beautifully shot in southern Ireland, the slender tale concerns a village farmer smashing an ancient Celtic monument, thus unleashing an age-old demon who terrorises the country, taking chunks out of people. This low-budget horror is derivative of every bad monster movie you've ever seen, complete with requisite unconvincing rubber-suited creature. Niall Toibin, as the local parish priest enslaved by the demon, contributes a suitably eccentric performance. 📼

David Dukes *Howard Hallenbeck* • Kelly Piper *Elaine Hallenbeck* • Ronan Wilmot *Declan O'Brien* • Niall Toibin *Reverend Coot* • Niall O'Brien *Detective Inspector Gissing* • Heinrich von Schellendorf *Rawhead Rex* ■ *Dir* George Pavlou • *Scr* Clive Barker, from his short story

Rawhide ★★★

Western 1951 · US · BW · 86mins

Initially evoking the romance of running a stagecoach line, this quickly turns into a superior suspense drama that happens to be set in the Old West, with the outlaws behaving rather like gangsters. Tyrone Power is too mature to play the young stageline trainee who becomes the captive of a hold-up gang, while Susan Hayward, as a passenger mistaken for his wife and imprisoned with him, has more to do at the climax. The villains are well characterised, with Hugh Marlowe as their businesslike leader and Jack Elam as a lecherous henchman.

Tyrone Power *Tom Owens* • Susan Hayward *Vinnie Holt* • Hugh Marlowe *Zimmerman* • Dean Jagger *Yancy* • Edgar Buchanan *Sam Todd* • Jack Elam *Tevis* • George Tobias *Gratz* ■ *Dir* Henry Hathaway • *Scr* Dudley Nichols

The Rawhide Years ★★

Western 1956 · US · Colour · 84mins

Universal used up sets and props from *The Mississippi Gambler* to decorate this vehicle for its young star Tony Curtis. Unfortunately, the plot's a bit of a hand-me-down as well. The supporting cast is good value, however, particularly Arthur Kennedy, fresh from menacing turns in *Where the River Bends* and *The Man from Laramie*, and *The Wages of Fear's* Peter Van Eyck as the chief baddie. Not very good, but watchable in parts.

Tony Curtis *Ben Mathews* • Colleen Miller *Zoe* • Arthur Kennedy *Rick Harper* • William Demarest *Brand Comfort* • William Gargan *Marshal Sommers* • Peter Van Eyck *Andre Boucher* ■ *Dir* Rudolph Maté • *Scr* Earl Felton, Robert Presnell Jr, DD Beauchamp, from the novel by Norman A Fox

Razor Blade Smile ★ 18

Erotic action horror 1998 · UK · Colour and BW · 97mins

A terminally trendy take on a tired theme, director Jake West's erotic popcorn vampire movie gives trash a bad name. *Femme fatale* Eileen Daly is made immortal in 1850 after a visit from aristocratic vampire Christopher Adamson. In modern London, she becomes a leather cat-suit clad assassin with a coffin full of weapons in her bedroom. Derivative, not even unintentionally funny, and technically inept – some scenes look like they were filmed on a camcorder – West serves up a mass of reheated clichés with little rhyme or reason. Contains violence and sex scenes, with some swearing. 📼

Eileen Daly *Lilith Silver* • Christopher Adamson *Sir Sethane Blake* • Jonathan Coote *Detective Inspector Ray Price* • Kevin Howarth *Platinum* ■ *Dir/Scr* Jake West

Razorback ★★ 18

Horror 1984 · Ausl · Colour · 90mins

Partly inspired by the dingo baby case that became the basis of the Meryl Streep drama *A Cry in the Dark*, this black horror tale about a giant wild pig terrorising the Australian outback borrows too from *The Texas Chain Saw Massacre* in its depiction of sick and depraved backwoods yokels. Making his directorial debut, Russell Mulcahy (*Highlander*) dishes up too rich a visual feast for what is a meandering man-against-nature storyline that plays like *Jaws* meets *Babe* on acid. The creature when it finally appears is also a big let-down, looking like something Jim Henson knocked up on a bad day. 📼

Gregory Harrison *Carl Winters* • Arkie Whiteley *Sarah Cameron* • Bill Kerr *Jake Cullen* • Chris Haywood *Benny Baker* ■ *Dir* Russell Mulcahy • *Scr* Everett DeRoche, from the novel by Peter Brennan

The Razor's Edge ★★★ PG

Drama 1946 · US · BW · 144mins

Tyrone Power plays a First World War veteran who, after a tragic love affair in Paris, goes to India for spiritual renewal. Based on W Somerset Maugham's novel (the author himself is played by Herbert Marshall), this big-budget melodrama bursts with incident

and was pitched by 20th Century-Fox as Power's return to the screen after distinguished war service. To mark the auspicious occasion, Fox cast two of its most glamorous stars – Gene Tierney and Anne Baxter – to tug on Power's sleeve and heartstrings. A big hit in its day, though rather laughable today for its cornball psychology. Contains swearing. 📼

Tyrone Power *Larry Darrell* • Gene Tierney *Isabel Bradley* • John Payne *Gray Maturin* • Anne Baxter *Sophie MacDonald* • Clifton Webb *Elliott Templeton* • Herbert Marshall *W Somerset Maugham* • Elsa Lanchester *Miss Keith* ■ *Dir* Edmund Goulding • *Scr* Lamar Trotti, from the novel by W Somerset Maugham

The Razor's Edge ★★ 15

Drama 1984 · US · Colour · 123mins

A limp remake of the 1946 Oscar-winning movie based on W Somerset Maugham's novel, relating how an American First World War survivor takes stock of his life as those close to him go through historically based personal crises. Comedian Bill Murray thought the *Gump*-like soap opera would smash his deadpan image and open up a whole new dramatic career. However, the overall success of John Byrum's routine potboiler is clearly evident, and we have yet to see Murray's Hamlet. Theresa Russell livens things up as a drunken hooker in Paris, but there's little else to enjoy. Contains swearing. 📼

Bill Murray *Larry Darrell* • Theresa Russell *Sophie* • Catherine Hicks *Isabel* • Denholm Elliott *Elliot Templeton* • James Keach *Gray Maturin* • Peter Vaughan *MacKenzie* • Saeed Jaffrey *Raaz* ■ *Dir* John Byrum • *Scr* Bill Murray, John Byrum, from the novel by W Somerset Maugham

Razzia sur la Chnouf ★★★★

Crime drama 1955 · Fr · BW · 105mins

Owing much to *Touchez Pas au Grisbi*, this is a gripping exposé of the criminal underworld in mid-fifties France. As in Jacques Becker's film, the inimitable Jean Gabin takes centre stage, as the hard-nosed narcotics expert hired by insidious dealer Marcel Dalio to run his Paris operation, only for vital information to begin falling into the hands of the police. Making the most of Pierre Montazel's thrilling nightscapes, Henri Decoin reveals his hand early, but expertly keeps the audience sweating on the outcome. Gabin is outstanding, but Lila Kedrova's junkie and Lino Ventura and Albert Rémy's heavies are also superb. A French language film.

Jean Gabin *Henri Ferré* • Magali Nöel *Lisette* • Marcel Dalio *Liski* • Lino Ventura *Le Catalan* • Albert Rémy *Bibi* • Pierre Louis *Leroux* • Lila Kedrova *Lea* • Alain Nobis *Decharme* ■ *Dir* Henri Decoin • *Scr* Henri Decoin, Maurice Griffe, from a novel by Auguste Le Breton

Reach for Glory ★★★

Drama 1962 · UK · BW · 86mins

A strange, haunting study of a family of Second World War evacuees and the young son who feels shamed by his conscientious objector brother and his shanghaied father. Joining up with a local gang of kids, he turns into a fervent nationalist who persecutes the local Jewish immigrant boy, then

befriends him, before the ritualistic tragedy that lies ahead. This drama poses some disturbing questions and is well worth seeking out.

Harry Andrews *Capt Curlew* • Kay Walsh *Mrs Curlew* • Michael Anderson Jr *Lewis Craig* • Oliver Grimm *Mark Stein* • Martin Tomlinson *John Curlew* ■ *Dir* Philip Leacock • *Scr* John Kohn, Jud Kinberg, John Rae, from the novel *The Custard Boys* by John Rae

Reach for the Sky ★★★★ U

Second World War biographical drama 1956 · UK · BW · 130mins

So many of Hollywood's war heroism biopics were tainted by smug patriotism and unwelcome sentiment. Thanks to its documentary heritage, postwar British cinema handled the events of the Second World War with greater fidelity and dignity, and this inspiring tale of unassuming courage is one of the finest. Lewis Gilbert masterfully makes the drama as compelling as the action sequences, and Kenneth More gives the performance of his career as Douglas Bader, the cocky pilot who overcame the loss of his legs in a pre-war flying accident to become one of the RAF's most decorated heroes. 📼 **DVD**

Kenneth More *Douglas Bader* • Muriel Pavlow *Thelma Bader* • Lyndon Brook *Johnny Sanderson* • Lee Patterson *Stan Turner* • Alexander Knox *Mr Joyce* • Dorothy Alison *Nurse Brace* • Michael Warre *Harry Day* ■ *Dir* Lewis Gilbert • *Scr* Lewis Gilbert, Vernon Harris, from the biography *Story of Douglas Bader* by Paul Brickhill

A Real American Hero ★★★

Crime drama 1978 · US · Colour · 94mins

Step forward the hero of countless TV movies, Brian Dennehy, cast this time as a sheriff bringing a moonshiner to book. A run-of-the-mill TV script is anchored by the reliable Dennehy, who has occasionally managed to step off the TV treadmill to lend his not-inconsiderable talents to acclaimed movies such as *Presumed Innocent*, *Cocoon* and *Gorky Park*.

Brian Dennehy *Sheriff Buford Pusser* • Forrest Tucker *Carl Pusser* • Brian Kerwin *Til Johnson* • Ken Howard *Danny Boy Mitchell* ■ *Dir* Lou Antonio • *Scr* Samuel A Peeples, from an idea by Mort Briskin

The Real Blonde ★★★ 15

Romantic comedy 1997 · US · Colour · 101mins

The pursuit of perfection in the shallow world of film, fashion and advertising lies at the core of writer/director Tom DiCillo's bright and breezy showbiz exposé, which ultimately resembles a soft-centred version of Robert Altman's *Short Cuts*. Matthew Modine is an idealistic aspiring actor in his mid-thirties, who draws everyone he meets into interlocking morality tales about sexism and image obsession that overlap in increasingly comic and complex ways. A wonderful cast – including Maxwell Caulfield (neatly sending up his *Colbys* persona) and Elizabeth Berkley (proving *Showgirls* was an aberration) – makes the most of the shrewd observations, even though the satire does meander at times. Contains swearing and sex scenes. 📼

Matthew Modine *Joe* • Catherine Keener *Mary* • Daryl Hannah *Kelly* • Maxwell Caulfield *Bob* • Elizabeth Berkley *Tina* • Christopher Lloyd *Ernst* • Kathleen Turner *Dee Dee Taylor* • Denis Leary *Doug* • Steve Buscemi *Nick* ■ *Dir/Scr* Tom DiCillo

Real Genius ★★★ 15

Comedy 1985 · US · Colour · 101mins

Enjoyable, if at times slightly silly, screwball comedy, moulded by some of the same minds that brought *Police Academy* and *Bachelor Party* to the screen. Val Kilmer plays one of a gang of scientific prodigies holed up in an institute for young boffins. But, while the youngsters are supposed to be expanding technology, and might be exploring the moral responsibilities of the post-nuclear arms race, they are far keener on getting up to fiendish japes in the corridor. No real genius here, but intermittent fun, nonetheless.

Val Kilmer *Chris Knight* • Gabe Jarret *Mitch Taylor* • Michelle Meyrink *Jordan Cochran* • William Atherton *Professor Jerome Hathaway* • Patti D'Arbanville [Patti D'Arbanville-Quinn] *Sherry Nugil* ■ *Dir* Martha Coolidge • *Scr* Neal Israel, Pat Proft, Peter Torokvei, from a story by Neal Israel, Pat Proft

The Real Glory ★★★ PG

War adventure 1939 · US · BW · 92mins

One of producer Samuel Goldwyn's expensively impressive pre-war movies, made the same year as his *Wuthering Heights*, and generally overlooked in that cinematic *annus mirabilis* of 1939. Intended to be a Spanish-American War rerun of the previously successful Gary Cooper/Henry Hathaway collaboration *The Lives of a Bengal Lancer*, this Philippines-based saga stints on nothing: the action sequences are particularly well staged and suitably bloody. Only an actor of Cooper's integrity could bring off a character (Dr Bill Canavan) so utterly brilliant at problem-solving, and he does so with aplomb, whether combating cholera or baddies, or riding down an overflowing river astride a log, hurling dynamite at rebels.

Gary Cooper *Dr Bill Canavan* • Andrea Leeds *Linda Hartley* • David Niven *Lieutenant Mccool* • Reginald Owen *Captain Steve Hartley* • Broderick Crawford *Lieutenant Swede Larson* • Kay Johnson *Mabel Manning* ■ *Dir* Henry Hathaway • *Scr* Jo Swerling, Robert R Presnell, from the novel by Charles L Clifford

The Real Howard Spitz ★★★★ PG

Comedy 1998 · UK/Can · Colour · 97mins

Barely released comic winner about a reclusive writer struggling to get his Raymond Chandler-esque pulp novels published. He finds success with his new Crafty Cow children's detective books, but goes to insane lengths to avoid public engagements. Kelsey Grammer (*Frasier*) is perfectly cast as the curmudgeon with a well-hidden heart, and the droll script is bursting with amusing dialogue, laugh-out-loud situations and cynical charm. Director Vadim Jean's skewed, cartoony direction is spot-on, as is the tongue-in-cheek score, plus there's delightful support from Amanda Donohoe and little Genevieve Tessier. Contains some strong language.

Kelsey Grammer *Howard Spitz* • Genevieve Tessier *Samantha* • Joseph Rutten *Lou* • Amanda Donohoe *Laura* • Kay Tremblay *Theodora Winkle* • Cathy Lee Crosby *Librarian* • Gary Levert *Allen* ■ *Dir* Vadim Jean • *Scr* Jurgen Wolff

Real Life ★★★ PG

Satirical comedy 1979 · US · Colour · 88mins

In 1973 on US TV, docusoap *An American Family* shocked audiences with its voyeuristic chronicling of the everyday life of an average US family – including on-screen divorce and the revelation that one of the kids was gay. For his directorial debut, Albert Brooks effectively spoofed the series and film documentaries in general, with this exposé of the destructive influence of TV on the family. Brooks (as a darker version of himself) is the director filming the lives of an average family just at the point when the family is going into meltdown. Brooks (real name Albert Einstein!) even involved his own relatives in the film to make sure it had an authentic look. A fine debut from a strangely under-appreciated comic talent.

Dick Haynes *Councilman Harris* • Albert Brooks • Matthew Tobin *Dr Howard Hill* • JA Preston *Dr Ted Cleary* • Mort Lindsey • Joseph Schaffler *Paul Lowell* • Phyllis Quinn *Donna Stanley* • James Ritz *Jack from Cincinnati* ■ *Dir* Albert Brooks • *Scr* Albert Brooks, Monica Johnson, Harry Shearer

The Real McCoy ★★ PG

Crime thriller 1993 · US · Colour · 90mins

World-class thief Kim Basinger is saddled with klutzy amateur partner Val Kilmer when she's forced by a crime boss into a heist she really doesn't want to pull in director Russell Mulcahy's fair comic thriller. While Mulcahy's cinematic eye for detail is on vivid show once more – the *Highlander* director really is one of cinemas most underrated visual stylists – the handsome stars have little to do except pose in front of his eye-popping backdrops. And, frankly, there doesn't seem to be much chemistry between the two leads either. As for Terence Stamp's daft southern accent, what was everyone thinking? Contains some swearing.

Kim Basinger *Karen McCoy* • Val Kilmer *JT Barker* • Terence Stamp *Jack Schmidt* • Gailard Sartain *Gary Buckner* • Zach English *Patrick* • Raynor Scheine *Baker* • Deborah Hobart *Cheryl Sweeney* • Pamela Stubbart *Kelly* ■ *Dir* Russell Mulcahy • *Scr* William Davies, William Osborne

Real Men ★★ 15

Spy comedy 1987 · US · Colour · 82mins

A prequel to *Dumb and Dumber*, perhaps? James Belushi is the hot-shot CIA agent, John Ritter is the shy insurance clerk he's forced to recruit as a courier. It's that mismatched-buddy/fish-out-of-water concept again, which can work so well (*Lethal Weapon*, for example), but all too often falls decidedly flat. Despite some moments of inventive farce, this spy comedy belongs in the latter category as it fails to gel under Dennis Feldman's overactive direction.

James Belushi *Nick Pirandello* • John Ritter *Bob Wilson* • Barbara Barrie *Mom* • Bill Morey *Cunard* • Iva Andersen *Dolly* • Gail Berle *Sherry* ■ *Dir/Scr* Dennis Feldman

Reality Bites ★★ 12

Comedy drama 1994 · US · Colour · 94mins

Ben Stiller made his directorial debut with this Generation X comedy, which wouldn't know reality if it jogged its arm during a showy but superficial hand-held camera movement. Strip away the attitude and all you'll find is an old-fashioned romantic comedy, in which Winona Ryder can't make up her mind between geek Stiller and tuned-in drop-out Ethan Hawke. This wouldn't be so bad if the characters were interesting, but, with the exception of Janeane Garofalo, they're self-obsessed twentysomethings with little grasp of the big, bad world. Yet, for all its faults, this still has moments of hip charm. Contains some swearing and drug abuse.

Winona Ryder *Lelaina Pierce* • Ethan Hawke *Troy Dyer* • Janeane Garofalo *Vickie Miner* • Steve Zahn *Sammy Gray* • Ben Stiller *Michael Grates* • Swoosie Kurtz *Charlane McGregor* • Harry O'Reilly *Wes McGregor* • Susan Norfleet *Helen Anne Pierce* • Joe Don Baker *Tom Pierce* • Renee Zellweger *Tami* ■ *Dir* Ben Stiller • *Scr* Helen Childress

Re-Animator ★★★★ 18

Black comedy horror
1985 · US · Colour · 83mins

A groundbreaking horror/black comedy that reintroduced HP Lovecraft to a new generation, and set a new level as to how far on-screen outrageousness can go. It also introduced cult star Jeffrey Combs, excellent as the funny and scary borderline-mad medical student working on a formula that brings the dead back to life. However, the dead don't come back in either tip-top or co-operative shape, leading to a number of wildly escalating problems. First-time director Stuart Gordon never lets up from the start, constantly pushing the limits with the gory antics, but also showing an absurd side to such sequences. Supporting players Barbara Crampton and David Gale (involved in a now-legendary scene near the end) give performances with a wink, as it should be. Contains violence and sex scenes.

Jeffrey Combs *Herbert West* • Bruce Abbott *Dan Cain* • Barbara Crampton *Megan Halsey* • Robert Sampson *Dean Halsey* • David Gale *Dr Carl Hill* • Gerry Black *Mace* • Peter Kent *Melvin, the Re-animated* ■ *Dir* Stuart Gordon • *Scr* Dennis Paoli, William J Norris, Stuart Gordon, from the story *Herbert West – the Re-Animator* by HP Lovecraft

Reap the Wild Wind ★★★

Drama 1942 · US · Colour · 123mins

This lurid melodrama seems to take an interminable amount of time to reach its famous Oscar-winning climax with a giant squid unless, of course, you happen to care whether it's John Wayne or a miscast Ray Milland that ends up with southern belle Paulette Goddard. If that little bit of romance isn't enough for Mills and Boon fans, there's another involving Susan Hayward and Robert Preston. The beginning and end are spectacular Cecil B DeMille proving yet again that, even as a director, he was a great producer, but this maritime vessel does get very watery amidships.

John Wayne *Captain Jack Stuart* • Ray Milland *Stephen Tolliver* • Paulette Goddard *Loxi Claiborne* • Raymond Massey *King Cutler* • Robert Preston *Dan Cutler* • Lynne Overman *Captain Phillip Philpott* • Susan Hayward *Drusilla Alston* ■ *Dir* Cecil B DeMille • *Scr* Alan LeMay, Charles Bennett, Jesse Lasky Jr, Jeanie Macpherson (uncredited), from a story by Thelma Strabel • *Special Effects* Gordon Jennings, Faricot Edouart, William L Pereira, Louis Mesenkop

Rear Window ★★★★★ PG

Classic thriller 1954 · US · Colour · 107mins

Like his earlier *Rope*, this masterpiece from director Alfred Hitchcock began as a technical stunt: "Hitch" wondered if he could make a film on just one set, from one single vantage point. James Stewart is a photojournalist with a broken leg and a high society girlfriend (Grace Kelly). Confined to his apartment, he whiles away the time gazing out of the window through his telephoto lens, becoming convinced that a neighbour who lives opposite (Raymond Burr) has murdered his wife and chopped her into disposable pieces. Hitchcock's "stunt" became a classic study of voyeurism – all those windows, shaped like movie screens, each containing a mini-drama of their own – and the tension builds brilliantly, complemented by the sexy repartee between Stewart and Kelly, plus the cynical humour provided by nurse Thelma Ritter. Often imitated, this extraordinary achievement has never been equalled.

James Stewart *LB "Jeff" Jeffries* • Grace Kelly *Lisa Carol Fremont* • Wendell Corey *Detective Thomas J Doyle* • Thelma Ritter *Stella* • Raymond Burr *Lars Thorwald* • Judith Evelyn *Miss Lonely Hearts* • David Seville [Ross Bagdasarian] *Songwriter* • Georgine Darcy *Miss Torso* • Sara Berner *Woman on fire escape* ■ *Dir* Alfred Hitchcock • *Scr* John Michael Hayes, from a story by Cornell Woolrich • *Cinematographer* Robert Burks

Rear Window ★★★

Thriller 1998 · US · Colour · 89mins

It takes a brave man to remake one of Alfred Hitchcock's finest ever films, and director Jeff Bleckner – who has divided his career between TV movies and series such as *Dynasty* – was always going to be on a hiding to nothing with this made-for-TV update of the classic original. Unsurprisingly, Bleckner isn't in the same league as the master, but where this scores is in the presence of Christopher Reeve in the lead role of the wheelchair-bound photographer. Reeve's own condition adds an extra dimension to the role, as does the range of high-tech equipment at his disposal. Contains violence and swearing.

Christopher Reeve *Jason Kemp* • Daryl Hannah *Claudia Henderson* • Robert Forster *Detective Charlie Moore* • Ruben Santiago-Hudson *Antonio* ■ *Dir* Jeff Bleckner • *Scr* Larry Gross, Eric Overmyer, from a story by Cornell Woolrich

Reason for Living: the Jill Ireland Story ★★★

Biographical drama
1991 · US · Colour · 96mins

Jill Clayburgh, who once played Carole Lombard (*Gable and Lombard*) here takes on the role of actress Jill Ireland in this TV movie. Along with her tough-guy actor-husband Charles Bronson (Lance Henriksen), Ireland struggles to help her adopted son, Jason, overcome addiction to heroin while dealing with her own battle with breast cancer. Though one might assume this is a routine disease-of-the-week tale, this complex movie concentrates on the strains illness and addiction place on a family, even a famous one. A fine script by Audrey Davis Levin, direction by Michael Ray Rhodes and supporting performance by veteran Elizabeth Ashley serve to round out this affecting TV film, which is much more than the typical celebrity tell-all.

Jill Clayburgh *Jill Ireland* • Lance Henriksen *Charles Bronson* • Neill Barry *Jason McCallum* • Elizabeth Ashley *Vicky* • Lila Kaye *Dorothy* • Jack Gwillim *Jack Ireland* ■ *Dir* Michael Ray Rhodes • *Scr* Audrey Davis Levin, from the autobiography *Life Lines* by Jill Ireland

Reasons of the Heart ★★★

Drama
1996 · US · Colour · 97mins

Written by Ron McGee and directed by Rick Jacobson, this TV-movie drama keeps threatening to become intriguing only to scurry back into the realms of predictability. There are two issues in the balance: will Terry Farrell persuade reclusive author Jim Davidson to resume his career and will she uncover the truth about her parents' cliff-top "suicide"? As he holds the key to both conundrums, Davidson keeps his character suitably mysterious, while Farrell allows herself to be shocked by the blatant and the unexpected alike. With more imaginative plotting, this would have been very entertaining.

Terry Farrell *Maggie Livingstone* • Jim Davidson *Berkeley Russell* • Mimi Kennedy *Celia* • Leon Russom *Mayor Drew Hadley* • Gloria Dorson *Lilly Barton* ■ *Dir* Rick Jacobson • *Scr* Ron McGee

Rebecca ★★★★★ PG

Classic romantic thriller
1940 · US · BW · 130mins

Director Alfred Hitchcock's first Hollywood film is a sumptuous and suspenseful adaptation of author Daphne du Maurier's romantic novel, produced by David O Selznick, immaculately played and rightly awarded the Oscar for best picture. Laurence Olivier as Maxim de Winter is superb, but it's mousey Joan Fontaine who is a revelation as the second Mrs de Winter. Lovers of lesbian subtexts will have a field day with Judith Anderson's sinister housekeeper, Mrs Danvers, as Hitchcock circumvents the censors who forced plot changes to the original story to accommodate the Hays Code. Fortunately no damage was done unless you think too hard, but, since the style and pace never let up, there's no danger of that happening! ▭

Laurence Olivier *Maxim de Winter* • Joan Fontaine *Mrs de Winter* • George Sanders *Jack Favell* • Judith Anderson *Mrs Danvers* •

Nigel Bruce *Major Giles Lacy* • C Aubrey Smith *Colonel Julyan* • Gladys Cooper *Beatrice Lacy* • Reginald Denny *Frank Crawley* • Florence Bates *Mrs Van Hopper* • Leo G Carroll *Dr Baker* ■ *Dir* Alfred Hitchcock • *Scr* Robert E Sherwood, Joan Harrison, from the novel by Daphne du Maurier, adapted by Philip MacDonald, Michael Hogan • *Cinematographer* George Barnes • *Editor* Hal C Kern • *Art Director* Lyle Wheeler • *Music* Franz Waxman

Rebecca of Sunnybrook Farm ★★★

Silent drama
1917 · US · BW

The first screen adaptation of the novel and play by Kate Douglas Wiggin stars "America's Sweetheart" Mary Pickford in one of the most famous of her perennial little girl roles. The tale of Rebecca, who is sent away to live with stern aunts, was recycled in sound in 1932, and lent its title and the vaguest strand of its plot to a well-known Shirley Temple musical in 1938. This silent version displays Pickford at her sympathetic, amusing best, as she matures from childish rebellion to young adulthood and romance under Marshall Neilan's direction. But only silent movie fans are likely to stay with it.

Mary Pickford *Rebecca Randall* • Eugene O'Brien *Adam Ladd* • Helen Jerome Eddy *Hannah Randall* • Charles Ogle *Mr Cobb* • Marjorie Daw *Emma Jane Perkins* • ZaSu Pitts ■ *Dir* Marshall Neilan • *Scr* Frances Marion, from the play by Kate Douglas Wiggin, Charlotte Thompson, from the novel by Kate Douglas Wiggin

Rebecca of Sunnybrook Farm ★★ U

Musical comedy
1938 · US · BW · 77mins

Unable to get Rebecca (Shirley Temple) a break in radio, her stepfather deposits her down on the farm to live with her rigid, puritanical, anti-show biz aunt, Helen Westley. Fate intervenes when new neighbour Randolph Scott who, entranced by the child, also turns out to be a radio executive. The classic tale was totally remodelled as a vehicle for the all-singing, all-dancing moppet, by then a ten-year-old veteran. Characteristic Temple drivel, directed by Allan Dwan, with Bill Robinson on the sidelines, Gloria Stuart as the romantic interest, and Shirley singing, among other numbers, a medley of her earlier hits including *Animal Crackers in My Soup* and *On the Good Ship Lollipop.* ▭

Shirley Temple *Rebecca Winstead* • Randolph Scott *Anthony Kent* • Jack Haley *Orville Smithers* • Gloria Stuart *Gwen Warren* • Phyllis Brooks *Lola Lee* • Helen Westley *Aunt Miranda Wilkins* • Slim Summerville *Homer Busby* • Bill Robinson *Aloysius* ■ *Dir* Allan Dwan • *Scr* Karl Tunberg, Don Ettlinger, from the novel by Kate Douglas Wiggin

Rebecca's Daughters ★★★ 15

Period comedy
1991 · UK/Ger · Colour · 92mins

Based on a screenplay by Dylan Thomas, this is inspired by the somewhat surreal events of the 1840s Rebecca Riots in which the Welsh poor, fed up with toll charges and taxes, and starving while the English landowners were getting fat, began

rioting, disguised as women. Each leader was known as Rebecca and followers were "her daughters", a reference from Genesis. Peter O'Toole hams it up as the drunken Lord Sarn and Paul Rhys is Anthony Raine, a liberal from the landowning class, who incites the rioters. Screenwriter Guy Jenkin (well-known to TV viewers for *Drop the Dead Donkey*) does Thomas's work proud. ▭

Paul Rhys *Anthony Raine* • Joely Richardson *Rhiannon* • Peter O'Toole *Lord Sarn* • Dafydd Hywel *Rhodri* • Sue Roderick *Sarah Hughes* • Simon Dormandy *Captain Marsden* • Clive Merrison *Sir Henry* • Keith Allen *Davy* ■ *Dir* Karl Francis • *Scr* Guy Jenkin, from a screenplay (unproduced) by Dylan Thomas

The Rebel ★★★ U

Comedy
1960 · UK · Colour · 100mins

Easily better than *The Punch and Judy Man*, Tony Hancock's first star vehicle is no masterpiece, but it is a fascinating misfire. Written by regular collaborators Ray Galton and Alan Simpson, the film has all the touches that made *Hancock's Half-Hour* so popular, although they seem a little strained over the course of a feature-length film. Happier in suburbia using landlady Irene Handl as a model for "Aphrodite by the Waterhole" than he is fooling the pretentious Parisians of the Left Bank, Hancock is his usual deluded, pompous self, while George Sanders's suave shiftiness is as watchable as ever. ▭

Tony Hancock *Anthony Hancock* • George Sanders *Sir Charles Brouard* • Paul Massie *Paul* • Margit Saad *Margot Carreras* • Grégoire Aslan *Aristotle Carreras* • Dennis Price *Jim Smith* • Irene Handl *Mrs Crevatte* • John Le Mesurier *Office manager* • Liz Fraser *Waitress* ■ *Dir* Robert Day • *Scr* Ray Galton, Alan Simpson, from the story by Ray Galton, Alan Simpson, Tony Hancock

Rebel ★★

Thriller drama
1973 · US · Colour · 84mins

Nothing to do with Tony Hancock, more's the pity. Sylvester E Stallone, as he is credited here, takes his first leading screen role in this conspiracy thriller about a group of antiwar hippies who are infiltrated by an FBI *agent provocateur* and encouraged to blow up a New York skyscraper. A straightforward paranoia drama which in the style of the time gives little kudos to America's political institutions. Contains violence and poor haircuts.

Anthony Page *Tommy* • Sylvester E Stallone [Sylvester Stallone] *Jerry* • Vickey Lancaster *Estelle* • Dennis Tate *Ray* • Barbara Lee Govan *Marlena* ■ *Dir* Robert Allen Schnitzer • *Scr* Robert Allen Schnitzer, Larry Beinhart

Rebel ★★ 15

Musical drama
1985 · Ausl · Colour · 89mins

This wildly ill-conceived curiosity from Australia – apparently intended as a *Cabaret* meets *From Here to Eternity* romance – is an obscure must for Matt Dillon fans, although he seems understandably ill at ease in a musical drama set in the Second World War. Dillon's troubled American GI who goes AWOL in Sydney and hides out with nightclub singer Debbie Byrne, who has a dance routine for every melodramatic development. Lots of

flashy production numbers fail utterly to evoke the right era or further the scanty plot, but Australian stalwarts like Bryan Brown and Bill Hunter bolster the bizarre proceedings. ▭

Matt Dillon *Rebel* • Debbie Byrne *Kathy* • Bryan Brown *Tiger* • Bill Hunter *Browning* • Ray Barrett *Bubbles* • Julie Nihill *Joycie* • John O'May *Bernie* • Kim Deacon *Hazel* ■ *Dir* Michael Jenkins • *Scr* Michael Jenkins, Bob Herbert, from the play *No Names ... No Packdrill* by Bob Herbert

Rebel in Town ★★★

Western
1956 · US · BW · 78mins

This post-Civil War drama takes as its starting point the accidental shooting of the small son of a former Union officer by a member of a Confederate family passing through a small town. Going on to explore the divisions that emerge within the killer's family, as well as the response of the parents, played by John Payne and Ruth Roman, it is more sober and thoughtful than most westerns, with veteran character actor J Carrol Naish scoring as the bearded Confederate patriarch.

John Payne *John Willoughby* • Ruth Roman *Nora Willoughby* • J Carrol Naish *Bedloe Mason* • Ben Cooper *Gray Mason* • John Smith *Wesley Mason* ■ *Dir* Alfred Werker • *Scr* Danny Arnold

Rebel Rousers ★★ 15

Drama
1967 · US · Colour · 73mins

When the most exciting part of this exploitation feature is the stripes on Jack Nicholson's trousers, you know you're in low-budget valley, though most of the young hopefuls have become today's stars. Here's Bruce Dern and Diane Ladd the year after they had daughter Laura Dern, and here's Dean Stanton before he added the Harry. The nominal lead is Cameron Mitchell, and the truly tasteless plot involves a drag race organised to offer Mitchell's pregnant girlfriend to the champion dragster. The release of this movie was delayed until after Nicholson had scored in *Easy Rider*. Contains some violence and swearing. ▭

Cameron Mitchell *Mr Collier* • Jack Nicholson *"Bunny"* • Bruce Dern *"JJ"* • Diane Ladd *Karen* • Dean Stanton [Harry Dean Stanton] ■ *Dir* Martin B Cohen • *Scr* Abe Polsky, Michael Kars, Martin B Cohen

The Rebel Set ★★

Crime drama
1959 · US · BW · 72mins

Three malcontents who hang out in a beat generation Hollywood coffee house – an unemployed actor, an unpublished novelist and a film star's delinquent son – are recruited to carry out an ingenious hold-up. Once shed of its beatnik trappings, *The Rebel Set* turns into an engrossing crime drama with character player Edward Platt given a rare chance to stand out as its rather unusual and devilish criminal mastermind. As his dupes, Gregg Palmer, John Lupton and Don Sullivan give capable performances under the direction of Gene Fowler Jr.

Gregg Palmer *John Mapes* • Kathleen Crowley *Jeanne Mapes* • Edward Platt *Mr Tucker* • John Lupton *Ray Miller* • Ned Glass *Sidney*

Horner • Don Sullivan *George Leland* ■ *Dir* Gene Fowler Jr • *Scr* Louis Vittes, Bernard Girard

Rebel without a Cause
★★★★★ PG

Classic drama   1955 · US · Colour · 106mins

The theme of the teenager as an alienated victim of family and society has never been done better. James Dean gives a superb, career-moulding performance as a frustrated youth from a well-to-do family, who rebels against his weak father and shrewish mother with such delinquent behaviour as boozing, knife-fighting and hazardous games of "chicken" driving hot rods. Natalie Wood and Sal Mineo also stand out in a superb, youthful cast that's wonderfully controlled by director Nicholas Ray, but it's Dean who remains most memorable, and his heartfelt portrayal epitomised his tragically short career. ■ *DVD*

James Dean *Jim* • Natalie Wood *Judy* • Jim Backus *Jim's father* • Ann Doran *Jim's mother* • William Hopper *Judy's father* • Rochelle Hudson *Judy's mother* • Corey Allen *Buzz* • Sal Mineo *Plato* • Dennis Hopper *Goon* ■ *Dir* Nicholas Ray • *Scr* Stewart Stem

Rebellion
★★★★

Period action drama
1967 · Jap · BW · 120mins

Rivalling any of Akira Kurosawa's famous samurai dramas, *Rebellion* stars the great Toshiro Mifune as a dishonoured samurai searching for revenge. In fact, it's the usual samurai stuff, given hardly any new twists, and seemingly influenced by Sergio Leone's *Dollars* films. But what is remarkable is Masaki Kobayashi's magnificent evocation of a vanished era in Japanese history and his stunning images, shot in the traditional black-and-white scope format. And Mifune's intensity is something to marvel at. In Japanese with English subtitles.

Toshiro Mifune *Isaburo Sasahara* • Go Kato *Yogoro Sasahara* • Tatsuyoshi Ehara *Bunzo Sasahara* • Michiko Otsuka *Suga Sasahara* • Yoko Tsukasa *Ichi Sasahara* ■ *Dir* Masaki Kobayashi • *Scr* Shinobu Hashimoto, from the story *Hairyo Zuma Shimatsu Yori* by Yasuhiko Takiguchi • *Cinematographer* Kazuo Yamada

Rebound
★★★ 18

Drama based on a true story
1996 · US · Colour · 111mins

Hardcourt action serves as a background to this true story of one man's quest to discover what is really important in life. In 1959, talented young Harlem playground basketball player Earl Manigault (Don Cheadle, of *Bulworth*) ruins his chances of sporting success by becoming addicted to heroin. Returning home after a prison sentence, he becomes determined to free his old Harlem park from the tyranny of drug dealers. An excellent script, sensitive direction by Eriq LaSalle (*ER*) and the presence of such sturdy pros as James Earl Jones and Ronny Cox (*Total Recall*), plus real-life hoop legend Kareem Abdul-Jabbar lend credibility to a cautionary tale. This moving TV movie, with its energetic Motown tunes, should prove a slam-dunk with audiences young and old. Contains swearing, drug abuse and some violence. ▣

Don Cheadle *Earl Manigault* • James Earl Jones *Dr McDuffie* • Forest Whitaker *Holcolm Rucker* • Michael Beach *Legrand* • Loretta Devine *Miss Mary* • Clarence Williams III *Coach Pratt* • Eriq La Salle *Diego* • Ronny Cox *Coach Scarpelli* • Kareem Abdul-Jabbar ■ *Dir* Eriq La Salle • *Scr* Alan Swyer, Larry Golin

Reckless
★★★

Romantic musical   1935 · US · BW · 96mins

Here's a preposterous bit of watchable tosh, a wildly unbelievable MGM vehicle for blonde bombshell Jean Harlow, which was reportedly based on the notorious shooting scandal involving real-life torch singer Libby Holman. Harlow plays a Broadway actress and she's ably backed up by on-screen husband Franchot Tone (their third film together) and suave, debonair William Powell, who actually fell for Harlow off-screen and left flowers on her grave for many years after her death in 1937. Glossy and contrived, but very watchable.

Jean Harlow *Mona Leslie* • William Powell *Ned Riley* • Franchot Tone *Bob Harrison* • May Robson *Granny* • Ted Healy *Smiley* • Nat Pendleton *Blossom* • Robert Light *Paul Mercer* • Rosalind Russell *Josephine* • Henry Stephenson *Harrison* • Louise Henry *Louise* ■ *Dir* Victor Fleming • *Scr* PJ Wolfson, from the story *A Woman Called Cheap* by Oliver Jeffries [David O Selznick], Victor Fleming

Reckless
★★

Black comedy   1995 · US · Colour · 91mins

A strange, nightmarish comedy thriller with Mia Farrow, suitably gauche and naive as a woman who discovers her husband has hired a hit man to knock her off on Christmas Eve. Escaping into the snow, Farrow begins a bizarre journey and has a series of encounters in which no one is what they seem. A collaboration between director Norman René and writer Craig Lucas, it is not as strong as their 1990 drama *Longtime Companion* but provides an interesting contrast to their previous film, the romantic comedy *Prelude to a Kiss*. Nevertheless, it's all a bit too *Twilight Zone* in the final analysis.

Mia Farrow *Rachel* • Scott Glenn *Lloyd* • Mary-Louise Parker *Pooty* • Tony Goldwyn *Tom* • Eileen Brennan *Sister Margaret* • Giancarlo Esposito *Game show host* • Stephen Dorff *Tom Jr* ■ *Dir* Norman René • *Scr* Craig Lucas, from his play

Reckless Kelly
★★ PG

Comedy   1993 · Ausl · Colour · 76mins

The spirit of Aussie outlaw Ned Kelly is alive and well and dwelling in director/star Yahoo Serious in this frantic and not particularly funny crime comedy. It begins well, as Yahoo's island idyll is threatened by evil banker Hugo Weaving and his explosive sidekick, Alexei Sayle. But, from the moment he arrives in the US intent on robbing banks to save his home, the gags begin to fall flat. Sloppily directed, this is, at least, superior to similar offerings from the likes of Carrot Top. Contains violence and swearing. ▣

Yahoo Serious *Reckless Kelly* • Melora Hardin *Robin Banks* • Alexei Sayle *Major Wimp* • Hugo Weaving *Sir John* • Kathleen Freeman *Mrs Delance* • John Pinette *Sam Delance* • Bob Maza *Dan Kelly* ■ *Dir* Yahoo Serious • *Scr* Yahoo Serious, Warwick Ross, Lulu Serious, David Roach

The Reckless Moment
★★★

Thriller melodrama   1949 · US · BW · 81mins

Adapted from Elisabeth Sanxay Holding's story *The Blank Wall*, this concluded a trio of brooding melodramas made in Hollywood by the ultra-sophisticated German director Max Ophüls. Short, sharp and to the point, it pitches anxious mother Joan Bennett against James Mason after her gauche daughter Geraldine Brooks has an affair with older married man Shepperd Strudwick. Paying less attention than usual to set detail and ornate camera movement, Ophüls directs with a cool detachment. But, while this allows Bennett to suffer and scheme without the histrionics of a Joan Crawford, it prevents Mason from trying out any new tricks as a blackmailing cad.

James Mason *Martin Donnelly* • Joan Bennett *Lucia Harper* • Geraldine Brooks *Beatrice Harper* • Henry O'Neill *Mr Harper* • Shepperd Strudwick *Ted Darby* ■ *Dir* Max Ophüls • *Scr* Henry Garson, Robert W Soderberg, Mel Dinelli, Robert E Kent, from the story *The Blank Wall* by Elisabeth Sanxay Holding

The Reckoning
★★★

Drama   1969 · UK · Colour · 111mins

A tough but troubled businessman is forced to deal with the chip on his shoulder when he learns his father is dying. Returning to Liverpool and his roots, he decides to take revenge on the teenager who attacked his father. An adult drama about class in Britain, held together with a muscular performance from Williamson as the dislikeable hero, it's by the same team that made *The Bofors Gun* the year before. This is no *Room at the Top*, but it's well handled nonetheless.

Nicol Williamson *Michael Marler* • Ann Bell *Rosemary Marler* • Lilita De Barros *Maria* • Tom Kempinski *Brunzy* ■ *Dir* Jack Gold • *Scr* John McGrath, from the play *The Harp That Once* by Patrick Hall

Recollections of the Yellow House
★★★ 18

Drama   1989 · Por · Colour · 122mins

Strewn with references to silent classics like *Greed*, *The Cabinet of Dr Caligari* and *Nosferatu*, this is a frustrating, yet persistently fascinating study on self-obsession and misery. Exercising rigid control over both the *mise-en-scène* and his elliptical storyline, writer/director João César Monteiro turns in a seedily anti-heroic performance, as the academic whose growing sense of dissatisfaction with life in general and his desolate Lisbon boarding house in particular results in an assault that sees him consigned to an asylum. No hope is even cursorily entertained, yet this is often as funny as it is despondent. In Portuguese with English subtitles.

João César Monteiro *Joao De Deus* • Manuela De Freitas *Dona Violeta* • Sabina Sacchi *Mimi* • Teresa Calado *Menina Julieta* • Ruy Furtado *Señor Armando* • Henrique Viana *Police Captain* ■ *Dir/Scr* João César Monteiro

Record of a Tenement Gentleman
★★★★

Drama   1947 · Jap · BW · 72mins

Recalling the visual style and emotional tone of pre-War Japanese social cinema, Yasujiro Ozu's delicate character drama combines unsentimental nostalgia and contemporary comment to poignant effect. Those familiar with the Brazilian charmer *Central Station*, will recognise the scenario, as self-contained widow Choko Iida slowly becomes fond of abandoned, bed-wetting urchin Hohi Aoki, whose tenacious desire to belong awakens Iida's suppressed maternal instincts. Cleverly using camera angles to create a sense of place and parallel motifs to unify the action, Ozu unobtrusively reveals his directorial genius. In Japanese with English subtitles.

Chishu Ryu *Tashiro, the fortune teller* • Choko Iida *Otane* • Takeshi Sakamoto *Kihachi* • Eitaro Ozawa *Kohei's father* ■ *Dir* Yasujiro Ozu • *Scr* Yasujiro Ozu, Tadao Ikeda

The Red and the White
★★★

Historical war drama
1967 · Hun/USSR · BW · 90mins

Made to celebrate the 50th anniversary of the Bolshevik Revolution, this is ostensibly a tribute to the Hungarian volunteers who fought with the Red Army against the pro-Tsarist Whites. But Miklós Jancsó clearly has an ironic contemporary agenda. Employing lateral tracking shots and meticulously composed widescreen images of the sweeping plains, he suggests the changing fortunes of the two armies and the enormity of the stakes for which they were fighting. Yet he is also implying that neither side had the monopoly on rectitude and that the governing strategy was simply a series of futile reactions to self-created chaos. A Hungarian language film.

József Madarás *Hungarian commander* • Tibor Molnár *András* • András Kozák *László* • Jácint Juhász *István* ■ *Dir* Miklós Jancsó • *Scr* Georgiy Mdivani, Gyula Hernádi, Miklós Jancsó

The Red Badge of Courage
★★★★ U

War drama   1951 · US · BW · 66mins

Apart from the brilliance of individual scenes, John Huston's American Civil War epic is also famous for having been butchered by the studio, a travesty well documented in Lillian Ross's book *Picture*, which charts the progress of the beleaguered production and remains one of the best accounts of events in Hollywood. Audie Murphy, America's most decorated soldier in the Second World War, plays the young recruit who is given a baptism of fire and emerges a hero, his experiences on the battlefield captured in some remarkable documentary-style, black-and-white photography. Although a shadow of the film Huston intended (James Whitmore's narration fills in the gaps created by MGM's scissor-happy editors), this is still a powerful study of the waste of war. ▣

Audie Murphy *Henry Fleming* • Bill Mauldin *Tom Wilson* • Douglas Dick *Lieutenant* • Royal

U = SUITABLE FOR ALL   Uc = SUITABLE FOR ALL, ESPECIALLY FOR YOUNG CHILDREN (VIDEO ONLY)   PG = PARENTAL GUIDANCE

Dano *Tattered man* • John Dierkes *Jim Conlin* • Arthur Hunnicutt *Bill Porter* ■ *Dir* John Huston • *Scr* John Huston, from the novel by Stephen Crane, adapted by Albert Band

Red Ball Express ★★★ U
Second World War drama
1952 · US · BW · 83mins

The king of the ''woman's picture'' and Alfred Hitchcock's favourite screenwriter of the fifties, John Michael Hayes was perhaps an odd choice to pen a war picture. But he managed to inject enough tension into this routine story about the problems facing a transportation unit as it accompanies General Patton on his push to Paris. By giving sergeant Alex Nicol a chip on his shoulder and corporal Sidney Poitier a sense of racial injustice, he makes unit leader Jeff Chandler seem a very human hero, which is exactly the kind of flawed action man that fascinated director Budd Boetticher. Intriguing and under-rated.

Jeff Chandler *Lieutenant Chick Campbell* • Alex Nicol *Sergeant Ernest Kalleck* • Charles Drake *Private Ronald Partridge* • Judith Braun *Joyce Mcclellan* • Hugh O'Brian *Private Wilson* • Jacqueline Duval *Antoinette Dubois* • Sidney Poitier *Corporal Andrew Robertson* ■ *Dir* Budd Boetticher • *Scr* John Michael Hayes, from the story by Marcel Klauber, Billy Grady Jr

Red Balloon ★★★★ U
Fantasy 1956 · Fr · Colour · 33mins

The first dialogue-less film to receive an Oscar nomination for its screenplay since the silent era (it went on to win), Albert Lamorisse's simple fable about the unique friendship between a lonely boy and a vibrant red balloon remains one of the most enchanting children's films ever made. Responding with adorable naturalism to his father's direction, Pascal Lamorisse seems lost in awe at the mischievous balloon's ingenuity as it follows him across Paris and into his classroom. The triumph of loyalty and love over envy and cruelty is a weighty message for such a slight tale. But Lamorisse carries it off magnificently with a joyous balloon-filled finale. ▭

Pascal Lamorisse *Little boy* • Sabine Lamorisse *Little girl* • *Dir/Scr* Albert Lamorisse

Red Beard ★★★★
Medical drama 1965 · Jap · BW · 185mins

The plot is simple: an ageing doctor (Toshiro Mifune) persuades his younger, rather feckless assistant to dedicate himself to work among the disadvantaged in 19th-century Japan. But what (almost) justifies the film's three-hour running time is Akira Kurosawa's wider interest in Japan's transition from its feudal past to its future as a modern industrialised society. Perhaps too slow for modern tastes, and too obscure for western audiences, it's a major work from a major director, whose use of architecture and the elements like wind and snow creates an indelible impression. In Japanese with English subtitles.

Toshiro Mifune *Doctor Kyojo ''Akahige''Niide* • Yuzo Kayama *Doctor Noboru Yasumoto* • Yoshio Tsuchiya *Doctor Handayu Mori* • Tatsuyoshi Ehara *Genzo Tsugawa* ■ *Dir* Akira Kurosawa • *Scr* Akira Kurosawa, Ryuzo

Kikushima, Hideo Oguni, Masato Ide, from the novel *Akahige Shinryo Tan* by Shugoro Yamamoto

The Red Beret ★★★ U
Second World War drama
1953 · UK · Colour · 88mins

A post-*Shane* Alan Ladd takes advantage of the tax breaks available to 18-month exiles from Hollywood in this rip-roaring Second World War drama, made in Britain. Wags recall that a trench was dug at Shepperton for the action sequences, but the diminutive Ladd was too small to use it. However, the star does look cool in Technicolor, blue eyes blazing, and puts in an excellent performance as a guilt-racked American, and he's well supported by British actors such as Leo Genn, Harry Andrews and Stanley Baker. An interesting note for film historians: this Warwick film was co-produced by ''Cubby'' Broccoli, co-written by Richard Maibaum and directed by Terence Young, the same team responsible for the first Bond movie, *Dr No*, nine years later.

Alan Ladd *Canada MacKendrick* • Leo Genn *Major Snow* • Susan Stephen *Penny Gardner* • Harry Andrews *Rsm* • Donald Houston *Taffy* • Anthony Bushell *General Whiting* • Stanley Baker *Breton* ■ *Dir* Terence Young • *Scr* Richard Maibaum, Frank S Nugent

Red Canyon ★★★ U
Western 1949 · US · Colour · 82mins

A charming western based on Zane Grey's novel *Wildfire*, with former radio actor Howard Duff playing a drifter trying to tame a wild stallion and falling for Ann Blyth, daughter of horse breeder George Brent. Blyth is particularly good, and there's an interesting supporting cast of western veterans such as Edgar Buchanan and Chill Wills, plus a youthful Lloyd Bridges. The Utah locations are beautifully shot by cinematographer Irving Glassberg.

Ann Blyth *Lucy Bostell* • Howard Duff *Lin Slone/Cordt* • George Brent *Mathew Boatel* • Edgar Buchanan *Jonah Johnson* • John McIntire *Floyd Cordt* • Chill Wills *Brackton* • Jane Darwell *Aunt Jane* • Lloyd Bridges *Virgil Cordt* ■ *Dir* George Sherman • *Scr* Maurice Geraghty, from the novel *Wildfire* by Zane Grey

The Red Circle ★★
Crime drama 1960 · W Ger · BW · 84mins

The crime movie is one of the staples of German cinema and this Scotland Yard mystery is one of three films featuring Fritz Rasp, a veteran from the golden age of German silents, who spent much of his later years in thrillers based on the novels of Edgar Wallace. How does he fit into the case of a serial killer who leaves his victims with a curious circular mark on their necks? You'll have to join inspector Karl Saebisch to find out. German dialogue dubbed into English.

Karl Saebisch *Inspector Parr* • Renate Ewert *Thalia Drummond* • Klaus-Jürgen Wussow *Derrik Yale* • Thomas Alder *Jack* • Fritz Rasp *Ulrich Berger* ■ *Dir* Jürgen Roland • *Scr* Trygve Larsen, Wolfgang Menge, from a novel by Edgar Wallace

The Red Circle ★★★★
Thriller 1970 · Fr/It · Colour · 136mins

Before he began writing *The Red Circle*, Jean-Pierre Melville made a list of his favourite thriller situations and came up with 19, noting that the only film to use them all was *The Asphalt Jungle*. Thus *The Red Circle* is a sort of condensation of all thrillers, with the sort of fully developed characters, ambiguities, betrayals, tense scenes and intricate plotting one expects from the best of them. It's about a robbery, of course, near the Ritz in Paris, immaculately performed by some of France's top male stars. Avoid seeing the English-dubbed version, which is cut by some 45 minutes; the four stars are for the original. French dialogue dubbed into English.

Alain Delon *Corey* • Yves Montand *Jansen* • Bourvil *Inspector Mattei* • Gian Maria Volonté *Vogel* • André Eykan *Rico* • François Périer *Santi* ■ *Dir/Scr* Jean-Pierre Melville

Red Corner ★★ 15
Courtroom thriller
1997 · US · Colour · 117mins

As this is a courtroom thriller set in Beijing, one might presume that the presence of Richard Gere – one of Hollywood's most prominent Buddhists and outspoken supporters of the Tibetan freedom movement – would make this a savage indictment of the Chinese occupiers of Tibet. But, instead, director Jon Avnet presents us with another variation on the lone wolf theme that has become a staple of modern action cinema. Something of the terror of being trapped in the machinery of a foreign legal system comes across, as Gere's smarmy American TV executive finds himself relying on a Chinese female lawyer, Bai Ling, to defend him on a fraudulent murder charge. Yet, for all its Zen idealism, the film lacks tension and focus. In English and Mandarin with subtitles. Contains some violence, swearing and a sex scene. ▭ **DVD**

Richard Gere *Jack Moore* • Bai Ling *Shen Yuelin* • Bradley Whitford *Bob Ghery* • Byron Mann *Lin Dan* • Peter Donat *David McAndrews* • Robert Stanton *Ed Pratt* ■ *Dir* Jon Avnet • *Scr* Robert King

The Red Dance ★★★★
Romantic drama 1928 · US · BW · 103mins

The influence of European art films affected even no-nonsense action directors such as Raoul Walsh, whose control of this novelettish excursion into the Russian Revolution – starring Charles Farrell and Dolores Del Rio – makes it a joy to look at. Camerawork is by Charles Clark and John Marta, and overall art direction by Ben Carrie. The story and action are incidental to the visuals, which makes it remarkable entertainment for its time – and for Raoul Walsh.

Charles Farrell *The Grand Duke Eugen* • Dolores Del Rio *Tasia* • Ivan Linow *Ivan Petroff* • Boris Charsky *Agitator* • Dorothy Revier *Princess Varvara* • Andrés De Segurola *General Tanaroff* • Demetrius Alexis *Rasputin* ■ *Dir* Raoul Walsh • *Scr* James Ashmore Creelman, Pierre Collings (adaptation), Philip Klein (adaptation), from a story by Eleanor Browne, from the novel *The Red Dancer of Moscow* by Henry Leyford Gates

The Red Danube ★★
War drama 1949 · US · BW · 118mins

American army officers Walter Pidgeon and Peter Lawford, stationed in Allied-occupied Vienna after the Second World War, are involved in the repatriation of Russians as a result of which, it is implied, they will suffer the cruel retribution of the Communist state. Janet Leigh is a ballerina loved by Lawford, which doesn't save her, and Ethel Barrymore a nun. Directed by George Sidney, this is heavy-handed drama, cashing in on the anti-Red climate of the times. Despite a large cast of authentic Europeans, it's ineffectual and unpersuasive.

Walter Pidgeon *Colonel Michael ''Jokey ''Nicobar* • Ethel Barrymore *Producer* • Peter Lawford *Major John ''Twingo'' McPhimister* • Angela Lansbury *Audrey Quail* • Janet Leigh *Maria Buhlen* • Louis Calhern *Colonel Piniev* • Francis L Sullivan *Colonel Humphrey ''Blinker'' Omicron* ■ *Dir* George Sidney • *Scr* Gina Kaus, Arthur Wimperis, from the novel *Vespers in Vienna* by Bruce Marshall

Red Dawn ★★ 15
Action drama 1984 · US · Colour · 109mins

A small band of American teenagers wages guerrilla warfare against Russian and Cuban troops staging an invasion of their small town in a ludicrously gung-ho fantasy from director John Milius, who co-wrote the script with regular Kevin Costner collaborator Kevin Reynolds. Some of Hollywood's finest including Patrick Swayze, Powers Boothe and Ben Johnson struggle with some highly unconvincing dialogue to justify the bombastic militarism, and the result is a scrambled action adventure smothered by political insensitivity. Contains violence and swearing. ▭

Patrick Swayze *Jed* • C Thomas Howell *Robert* • Lea Thompson *Erica* • Charlie Sheen *Matt* • Darren Dalton *Daryl* • Jennifer Grey *Toni* • Brad Savage *Danny* • Doug Toby *Aardvark* • Ben Johnson *Mason* • Harry Dean Stanton *Mr Eckert* • Powers Boothe *Andy* ■ *Dir* John Milius • *Scr* John Milius, Kevin Reynolds, from the novel by Kevin Reynolds

The Red Desert ★★ 15
Drama 1964 · Fr/It · Colour · 116mins

Michelangelo Antonioni's ''trilogy of urban alienation'' (*L'Avventura*, *La Notte* and *Eclipse*) made him an art-house darling. But by the time of *The Red Desert*, Antonioni had almost exhausted his theme and simply rehashed it in colour, taking his symbolism to artistic extremes as streets are repainted and a room changes hue. The story, though, is opaque – Monica Vitti plays a manic depressive who sleeps with her husband's friend (Richard Harris). Vitti is, as ever, convincingly neurotic, but Harris is totally miscast, dubbed and barely a presence. While Antonioni deserves praise for being prescient in his warning of the danger of industrial pollution, most viewers will regard this as pretentious twaddle, no matter how beautiful the photography is. In Italian with English subtitles. ▭ **DVD**

Monica Vitti *Giuliana* • Richard Harris *Corrado Zeller* • Carlo Chionetti *Ugo* • Xenia Valderi *Linda* • Rita Renoir *Emilia* • Aldo Grotti *Max* ■ *Dir* Michelangelo Antonioni • *Scr* Michelangelo

Antonioni, Tonino Guerra, from a story by Michelangelo Antonioni, Tonino Guerra • *Cinematographer* Carlo Di Palma

The Red Dragon ★★
Mystery 1945 · US · BW · 64mins

Sidney Toler's 18th Charlie Chan series outing was also the seventh to be released by Poverty Row studio Monogram, after it took over the franchise from 20th Century-Fox. By now the cases were becoming mundane affairs and, although Toler is suitably inscrutable as Earl Derr Biggers's sleuth, Benson Fong's Tommy Chan is nowhere near as effective as Keye Luke's "Number One Son". Moreover, Fortunio Bonanova (so superb as the singing teacher in *Citizen Kane*) is given too little to do as the police inspector left in Chan's wake as he searches for stolen plans.

Sidney Toler *Charlie Chan* • Fortunio Bonanova *Inspector Luis Carvero* • Benson Fong *Tommy Chan* • Robert E Keane *Alfred Wyans* • Willie Best *Chattanooga Brown* • Carol Hughes *Marguerite Fontan* ■ *Dir* Phil Rosen • *Scr and story* George Callahan, from characters created by Earl Derr Biggers

Red Dust ★★★★ PG
Romantic drama 1932 · US · BW · 79mins

Love in a hot climate is the theme of this melodrama, directed by Victor Fleming, better known for such films as *The Wizard of Oz* and *Gone with the Wind*, which risks looking clichéd, if not over-the-top, to our eyes half a century later. The film was a hit in its time, thanks not just to Fleming's direction, but also to sultry stylish performances by Clark Gable, as the macho boss of a rubber plantation in the tropics, and Jean Harlow and Mary Astor as the two very different women after whom he lusts. ▭

Clark Gable *Dennis Carson* • Jean Harlow *Vantine* • Mary Astor *Barbara Willis* • Gene Raymond *Gary Willis* • Donald Crisp *Guidon* • Tully Marshall *McQuarg* • Forrester Harvey *Limey* ■ *Dir* Victor Fleming • *Scr* John Mahin, from the play by Wilson Collison

Red Firecracker, Green Firecracker ★★★ 15
Romantic drama
1993 · HK/Chi · Colour · 111mins

There's a familiar feel to this intriguing drama from acclaimed Chinese director He Ping. But its story of an artist's forbidden love for the female head of a firework manufacturing family is right out of the ordinary. In a country where women are permitted to have only one child, this study of repressed sexuality takes on a whole new meaning. However, Da Ying's cumbersome screenplay and Ning Jing's unsubtle portrayal of the cross-dressing heiress undermine the beauty of He's direction and the irrepressible performance of Wu Gang, as the suitor who undertakes an explosive test to win his true love's hand. In Cantonese with English subtitles. Contains brief nudity. ▭

Ning Jing *Chun Zhi* • Wu Gang *Niu Bao, painter* • Zhao Xiaorui *Mr Mann* • Gai Yang *Mr Zhao* • Xu Zhengyun *Mr Xu* ■ *Dir* He Ping • *Scr* Da Ying, Feng Jicai

Red Garters ★★★ U
Western musical comedy
1954 · US · Colour · 90mins

In the year that *Seven Brides for Seven Brothers* broke box-office records, this musical spoof on the western passed unnoticed. Set in the fictional town of Paradise Lost, the action revolves around sharp-shooting cowboy Guy Mitchell out to avenge his brother's death, sassy saloon singer Rosemary Clooney and lawyer Jack Carson on whom her sights are set. The neither-here-nor-there plot, unremarkable script and hit-free score undermine an adventurously stylised production (the art direction was Oscar-nominated), lively performances and some genuinely funny upending of every heroic western cliché in the book.

Rosemary Clooney *Calaveras Kate* • Jack Carson *Jason Carberry* • Guy Mitchell *Reb Randall* • Pat Crowley *Susana Martinez De La Cruz* • Joanne Gilbert *Sheila Winthrop* • Gene Barry *Rafael Moreno* ■ *Dir* George Marshall • *Scr* Michael Fessier

Red-Headed Woman ★★★
Romantic drama 1932 · US · BW · 79mins

Infamously banned by the British censors at the time of its release, audiences here didn't have sight of this raunchy little opus until its TV bow some decades ago, and only then realised what all the fuss was about. This is a torrid tale that positively glorifies husband-stealing, and the electric Jean Harlow leaves no doubt where her sympathies lie. There's a sexual candour in the telling that provoked the pro-censorship lobby, which cited Harlow as a pervasive influence, but it's that startling erotic charge that makes this movie so electrifyingly watchable today. Look out for a young Charles Boyer, impressive as Harlow's uniformed chauffeur, Albert.

Jean Harlow *Lil Andrews* • Chester Morris *Bill Legendre Jr* • Lewis Stone *William Legendre Sr* • Leila Hyams *Irene Legendre* • Una Merkel *Sally* • Henry Stephenson *Gaersate* • May Robson *Aunt Jane* • Charles Boyer *Albert* • Harvey Clark *Uncle Fred* ■ *Dir* Jack Conway • *Scr* Anita Loos, from the novel by Katherine Brush

Red Heat ★★ 18
Prison drama
1985 · W Ger/US · Colour · 101mins

Most definitely not to be confused with the Arnie action film of the same name, this is routine "bras behind bars" stuff, about an American woman in West Germany who is mistakenly arrested as a spy and tossed into a prison packed with sadistic guards and even more unmentionable inmates. The film is most notable for co-starring *The Exorcist*'s Linda Blair and Emmanuelle herself, Sylvia Kristel, both of whom were, after their first big breaks, quickly reduced to making quickie tosh like this. ▭

Linda Blair *Christine Carlson* • Sylvia Kristel *Sofia* • Sue Kiel *Dr Hedda Kliemann* • William Ostrander *Michael Grainger* • Albert Fortell *Ernst* • Elisabeth Volkmann *Warden Einbech* ■ *Dir* Robert Collector • *Scr* Robert Collector, Gary Drucker

Red Heat ★★★ 18
Action thriller 1988 · US · Colour · 99mins

Routine as far as director Walter Hill is concerned, but this at least offered Arnold Schwarzenegger one of his more interesting action roles before he became a superstar. Playing a stony, monosyllabic Soviet cop posed no real acting problems for the big man, and in James Belushi he found an agreeably foul-mouthed foil, as the pair team up to hunt for an escaped Russian drug dealer. Hill stages a series of entertainingly violent, increasingly silly set pieces, and there's an eclectic support cast that includes Peter Boyle, Gina Gershon and Laurence Fishburne, when he was still calling himself Larry. Contains violence and swearing.

Arnold Schwarzenegger *Captain Ivan Danko* • James Belushi *Det Sgt Art Ridzik* • Peter Boyle *Lou Donnelly* • Ed O'Ross *Viktor Rostavili* • Larry Fishburne [Laurence Fishburne] *Lieutenant Stobbs* • Gina Gershon *Catherine Manzetti* ■ *Dir* Walter Hill • *Scr* Harry Kleiner, Walter Hill, from a story by Troy Kennedy Martin, Walter Hill

The Red House ★★★
Chiller 1947 · US · BW · 100mins

A splendid thriller with grand passions and Freudian undertones, which has grown in reputation. Now often described as *noir*, it is closer in style to the psychological horror of the sixties. Edward G Robinson has a meaty role as the tormented, crippled farmer, who warns juveniles Allene Roberts and Lon McCallister (their careers went nowhere) to keep away from the Red House, and hires hunky Rory Calhoun (in one of his first major roles) to make sure they do. There are longueurs during the build-up to the awful truth, but compensation is provided by the beautiful Sierra Nevada locations and Miklos Rozsa's score.

Edward G Robinson *Pete Morgan* • Lon McCallister *Nath Storm* • Judith Anderson *Ellen Morgan* • Allene Roberts *Meg Morgan* • Julie London *Tibby* • Rory Calhoun *Teller* ■ *Dir* Delmer Daves • *Scr* Delmer Daves, from the novel by George Agnew Chamberlain

Red King, White Knight ★★
Spy drama
1989 · US/UK/Can · Colour · 104mins

The Cold War heats up in this tale of international intrigue. Ex-CIA agent Tom Skerritt reluctantly comes out of retirement to try to foil an assassination attempt against the new liberal Soviet president. He's reunited with former lover Helen Mirren, a KGB agent who's part of the conspiracy. Wasting an appearance by great actor Max von Sydow, at his most sinister, this is a rather dated attempt to recapture the essence of John Le Carré espionage fiction. A TV movie, it fails to work as serious drama and, despite its graphic language and violence, also fails to satisfy on a James Bond-style action level. This is one spy movie that should have stayed out in the cold.

Tom Skerritt *Bill Stoner* • Helen Mirren *Anna* • Tom Bell *Tulayev* • Max von Sydow *Szasz* • Neil Dudgeon *Vlasek* • Gavan O'Herlihy *Clancy* ■ *Dir* Geoff Murphy • *Scr* Ron Hutchinson

Red Light ★★
Crime drama 1949 · US · BW · 83mins

This turgid crime drama from director Roy Del Ruth is not helped by the low-key performance of its star, the past-his-prime George Raft, here playing a businessman searching (seemingly interminably) for the killer of his army chaplain brother. What sexy Virginia Mayo sees in the gloomy Raft is a mystery known only to the casting department. It's redeemed only by its diamond-hard black-and-white photography and the sterling support work of gravel-voiced Barton MacLane and pre-*Perry Mason* Raymond Burr.

George Raft *John Torno* • Virginia Mayo *Carla North* • Raymond Burr *Nick Cherney* • Gene Lockhart *Warni Hazard* • Barton MacLane *Strecker* • Bill Phillips *Ryan* ■ *Dir* Roy Del Ruth • *Scr* George Callahan

The Red-Light Sting ★★ 15
Drama 1984 · US · Colour · 91mins

A by-the-numbers thriller, which, inevitably, is nowhere near as racy as it sounds. Farrah Fawcett is the high-class prostitute who is roped in to run a dodgy undercover operation to nail a nasty mobster with a taste for brothels. Fawcett acts her socks off and is helped by a strong supporting cast, which includes Beau Bridges and Harold Gould. However, the direction from TV-movie veteran Rod Holcomb is distinctly pedestrian and suspense is pretty thin on the ground. ▭

Farrah Fawcett *Kathy Dunne* • Beau Bridges *Frank Powell* • Harold Gould *Oliver Sully* • Paul Burke *John Brockelhurst* • Katherine Cannon *Diane Marks* • Conrad Janis *Bowman* • Sunny Johnson *Sonia* • Alex Henteloff *Jesse Lorner* ■ *Dir* Rod Holcomb • *Scr* Howard Berk, from the book *The Whorehouse Sting* by Henry Post

Red Line 7000 ★★★
Action drama 1965 · US · Colour · 110mins

Director Howard Hawks returns to territory that he'd first tackled in 1932's *The Crowd Roars*, but somehow this contemporary racetrack movie doesn't quite measure up. The Technicolor (photography by Milton Krasner and Haskell Boggs) is particularly fine, with that Paramount gloss much in evidence, but then new boy James Caan is a woeful lead, and the process shots are poor, making the whole look rather like an Elvis Presley movie with fewer songs. Still, for ardent Hawks fans, all of the director's themes are in place, and *Star Trek* enthusiasts will cherish an early film role for George Takei.

James Caan *Mike Marsh* • Gail Hire *Holly MacGregor* • Marianna Hill *Gabrielle Queneau* • Laura Devon *Julie Kazarian* • Charlene Holt *Lindy Bonaparte* • John Robert Crawford *Ned Arp* • James Ward *Dan McCall* • Norman Alden *Pat Kazarian* • George Takei *Kato* ■ *Dir* Howard Hawks • *Scr* George Kirgo, from a story by Howard Hawks

Red Mountain ★★
Western 1951 · US · Colour · 84mins

One of those Civil War dramas transposed to the Wild West, where the scenery is more dramatic and the Indians turn the dilemma of the Confederates and the Unionists into a "trilemma". Alan Ladd, a Confederate captain, kills a man, and

U = SUITABLE FOR ALL Uc = SUITABLE FOR ALL, ESPECIALLY FOR YOUNG CHILDREN (VIDEO ONLY) PG = PARENTAL GUIDANCE

another Southerner, Arthur Kennedy, gets blamed, but is saved from a lynch mob. Meanwhile, John Ireland has abandoned "The Cause" and is organising Indians and mercenaries for a war of his own. There's a decent moral, a dewy-eyed Lizabeth Scott, bright-as-a-button Technicolor and a rousing finale.

Alan Ladd *Captain Brett Sherwood* ● Lizabeth Scott *Chris* ● Arthur Kennedy *Lane Waldron* ● John Ireland *Quantrell* ● Jeff Corey *Skee* ● James Bell *Dr Terry* ● Bert Freed *Randall* ■ *Dir* William Dieterle ● *Scr* John Meredyth Lucas, George Slavin, George W George, from a story by George Slavin

Red Planet Mars ★★ U

Science-fiction drama
1952 · US · BW · 87mins

One of the oddest science-fiction movies ever made and worth sitting through every unwatchable preachy moment and ludicrous plot twist just to feel your jaw drop at various junctures. Could utopian Mars really be ruled by God? That's what TV contact via "hydrogen valve" reveals. But it's only a Nazi plot, controlled by Soviet agents, to destroy the world's economy. What can Earth do? Easy. Draft religious revolutionaries into Russia to overthrow the Communist government and replace them with a priestly monarchy. Possibly Billy Graham's favourite movie? Based on a play, hence the talky crusading, this simple-minded slice of po-faced seriousness is sci-fi's most explicit anti-Communist tract in disguise.

Peter Graves (1) *Chris Cronyn* ● Andrea King *Linda Cronyn* ● Orley Lindgren *Steward Cronyn* ● Bayard Vellier *Roger Cronyn* ● Walter Sande *Admiral Carey* ● Marvin Miller *Arjenian* ● Herbert Berghof *Franz Calder* ● Willis Bouchey *President* ■ *Dir* Harry Horner ● *Scr* Anthony Veiller, John L Balderson, from the play *Red Planet* by John L Balderson, John Hoare

The Red Pony ★★ PG

Drama
1949 · US · Colour · 84mins

John Steinbeck's tale of a boy and his horse is an awkward blend of children's picture and social realist drama, and it isn't really good enough in either department. However, while Myrna Loy seems miscast as the boy's mum, Robert Mitchum is impressive as the ranch hand. The boy is played by Peter Miles who, as Richard Miles, went on to write the novel *That Cold Day in the Park*, which in turn was filmed by Robert Altman. The most impressive thing here is the fine "outdoor" score by Aaron Copland, who had scored Milestone's earlier picture, *Of Mice and Men*. 🖵

Robert Mitchum *Billy Buck* ● Myrna Loy *Alice Tiflin* ● Louis Calhern *Grandpa* ● Shepperd Strudwick *Fred Tiflin* ● Peter Miles *Tom Tiflin* ● Beau Bridges *Beau* ● Margaret Hamilton *Teacher* ■ *Dir* Lewis Milestone ● *Scr* John Steinbeck, from his story

Red Riding Hood ★★

Fantasy
1987 · US · Colour · 80mins

Another in the erratic series of *Cannon Movie Tales* that also includes Christopher Walken's *Puss in Boots* and a marvellously wicked Diana Rigg as the evil queen in *Snow White*. Here the rather stolid Craig T Nelson gets to play twin brothers, one good, one bad,

in a somewhat drawn-out "full" version of the Brothers Grimm original. It's all a bit uneven, and the musical numbers in particular are uninspired, but Isabella Rossellini is as graceful as ever playing the good twin's wife-in-jeopardy. 🖵

Craig T Nelson *Godfrey/Percival* ● Isabella Rossellini *Lady Jeanne* ● Amelia Shankley *Linet aka Red Riding Hood* ● Rocco Sisto *Dagger the Wolf* ● Linda Kaye *Badger Kate* ● Helen Glazary *Nanny Bess* ■ *Dir* Adam Brooks ● *Scr* Carole Lucia Satrina, from the fairy tale by the Brothers Grimm

Red River ★★★★★ U

Classic western
1948 · US · BW · 127mins

This magnificent cattle-driving western is one of the greatest achievements of American cinema. Basing his film on co-screenwriter Borden Chase's novel, producer/director Howard Hawks created a rich masterpiece. Hawks is aided by arguably John Wayne's finest performance (as cattle boss Tom Dunson), and Wayne's matched by young Montgomery Clift (as Matthew Garth, his ward). This is Hollywood film-making at its highest level, with music by Dimitri Tiomkin and photography by Russell Harlan that enhances and embellishes the text. Not to be missed, and ideally watched on the biggest screen available. 🖵 **DVD**

John Wayne *Thomas Dunson* ● Montgomery Clift *Matthew Garth* ● Joanne Dru *Tess Millay* ● Walter Brennan *Groot Nadine* ● Coleen Gray *Fen* ● John Ireland *Cherry Valance* ● Noah Beery Jr *Buster McGee* ● Harry Carey Sr [Harry Carey] *Mr Melville* ● Harry Carey Jr *Dan Latimer* ● Shelley Winters *Dancehall girl* ■ *Dir* Howard Hawks ● *Scr* Borden Chase, Charles Schnee, from the novel *The Chisholm Trail* by Borden Chase

Red River ★★ PG

Western
1988 · US · Colour · 91mins

Some movies shouldn't be remade, but TV has an insatiable appetite, so it might have seemed a good idea at the time to rework Howard Hawks's majestic western for the small screen. The trouble is, without Hawks, his marvellous cast headed by John Wayne and Montgomery Clift and that Dimitri Tiomkin score, there's not much substance to this westernisation of *Mutiny on the Bounty*. Still, here's the same saddle-sore tale in colour and, to keep you watching, the cast is peppered with veteran cowboys. James Arness, himself once John Wayne's protégé, takes the Wayne role and does well by it, but Bruce Boxleitner is inadequate as Matthew Garth. It's the veteran supporting cast that really bears watching – there's not much else to enjoy. 🖵

Bruce Boxleitner *Matthew Garth* ● James Arness *Tom Dunson* ● Gregory Harrison *Cherry Valance* ● Ray Walston *Horace Groot* ● Stan Shaw *Jack Bird* ● Ty Hardin *Grogan* ● Robert Horton *Melville* ● John Lupton *Eli Pruitt* ● Guy Madison *Meeker* ■ *Dir* Richard Michaels ● *Scr* Richard Fielder, from the 1948 film

Red River Range ★★ U

Western
1938 · US · BW · 55mins

This "Three Mesquiteers" B-western, starring John Wayne just before John Ford borrowed him for *Stagecoach*, takes less than an hour to trot out its modern-day story of the trio (Wayne,

Ray Corrigan, Max Terhune) catching highly organised cattle rustlers. Veteran comedian Polly Moran takes a supporting role, while two of the younger members of the cast went on to better things – Kirby Grant as a B-western star and Adrian Booth (here billed as Lorna Gray) as one of Republic's leading ladies.

John Wayne *Stony Brooke* ● Ray Corrigan *Tucson Smith* ● Max Terhune *Lullaby Joslin* ● Polly Moran *Mrs Maxwell* ● Lorna Gray [Adrian Booth] *Jane Mason* ● Kirby Grant *Tex Reilly* ■ *Dir* George Sherman ● *Scr* Luci Ward, Stanley Roberts, Betty Burbridge, from a story by Luci Ward, from characters created by William Colt MacDonald

Red Rock West ★★★★ 15

Black comedy thriller
1992 · US · Colour · 94mins

The Last Seduction was the film that finally made people stand up and take notice of director John Dahl, but this *film noir* thriller is almost its equal. Nicolas Cage, this time in a non-comic variation on his innocent dupe persona, is the hapless drifter who is mistaken for a hit man by J T Walsh and is sent to murder Walsh's wife (Lara Flynn Boyle). Things go from bad to worse when the real assassin (the demonic Dennis Hopper) turns up. The plot twists and turns deliciously, and Dahl's direction strikes a deft balance between knowing humour and genuine suspense. The performances are good, with only Boyle's unconvincing *femme fatale* letting the side down. Contains violence and swearing. 🖵

Nicolas Cage *Michael Williams* ● Lara Flynn Boyle *Suzanne Brown* ● Dennis Hopper *Lyle* ● JT Walsh *Wayne Brown* ● Craig Reay *Jim* ● Vance Johnson *Mr Johnson* ● Robert Apel *Howard* ■ *Dir* John Dahl ● *Scr* John Dahl, Rick Dahl

Red Salute ★★ U

Romantic comedy road movie
1935 · US · BW · 79mins

General's daughter Barbara Stanwyck falls for a Communist and her father sends her to Mexico, where she meets a young soldier. Ensuing complications have them both on the run. Made when the radical movement in American universities was strong, this is basically a road comedy, with the spoiled daughter having to see the error of her leftist enthusiasms. At its premiere, students picketed and critics either condemned it as propaganda or felt it burlesqued the "American Way". Discounting the politics, it's diverting enough, with a particularly good-natured and disarming performance by Stanwyck.

Barbara Stanwyck *Drue Van Allen* ● Robert Young *Jeff* ● Hardie Albright *Leonard Arner* ● Ruth Donnelly *Mrs Edith Rooney* ● Cliff Edwards *PJ Rooney* ● Gordon Jones *Lefty* ● Paul Stanton *Louis Martin* ■ *Dir* Sidney Lanfield ● *Scr* Humphrey Pearson, Manuel Seff, from a story by Humphrey Pearson

Red Scorpion ★ 15

Action adventure
1989 · US · Colour · 100mins

The English language – and dialogue in particular – is a tricky blighter for action stars such as Jean-Claude Van Damme and Arnold Schwarzenegger, and it also proves a problem for the

heavily accented Dolph Lundgren in this awful action adventure. The makers played safe and cast the non-syllabic one as a Soviet agent, who is sent to a warring African state to take out a resistance leader. However, because Lundgren is the good guy, he has a change of heart and converts to the forces of freedom. Inexplicably, this was a big hit on video, perhaps because there's loads of mindless mass destruction, but the script and the performances make Rambo look positively Wildean. 🖵

Dolph Lundgren *Lt Nikolai* ● M Emmet Walsh *Dewey Ferguson* ● Al White *Kallunda* ● TP McKenna *General Vortek* ● Carmen Argenziano *Zayas* ● Alex Colon *Mendez* ● Brion James *Krasnov* ● Ruben Nthodi *Sundata* ■ *Dir* Joseph Zito ● *Scr* Arne Olsen, from a story by Robert Abramoff, Jack Abramoff

The Red Shoe Diaries ★★ 18

Erotic drama
1992 · US · Colour · 104mins

Before becoming a star in *The X Files*, David Duchovny toiled in the first of a series of sexually exploitative TV movies. Desperate to understand his fiancée's suicide, a distraught lover (Duchovny) discovers details of her obsessive passion for another man. Zalman King (*Wild Orchid*) has concocted a stylish but hollow drama bordering on soft-core porn. If you demand nothing more than comely, naked young women mouthing banal dialogue, then this may be enough. 🖵

David Duchovny *Jake* ● Brigitte Bako *Alex* ● Billy Wirth *Tom Workman* ● Bridget Ryan *Marlene* ● Karin Heidi *Martha* ■ *Dir* Zalman King ● *Scr* Patricia Louisiana Knop, Zalman King

The Red Shoes ★★★★★ U

Romantic dance drama
1948 · UK · Colour · 127mins

Moira Shearer stars as the ballerina whose life is torn between a career with a manipulative impresario (Anton Walbrook) and marriage to a young composer (Marius Goring). Based vaguely on the story of Sergei Diaghilev and Waslaw Nijinsky, *The Red Shoes* is arguably the best-loved dance film of all time, enabling the team of Michael Powell and Emeric Pressburger to ponder the power and nature of art and fantasy with some extravagant, exuberant dance sequences and a riot of Oscar-winning Technicolor designs. The performances from debutant Shearer and Walbrook, as the man filled with self-hate, are impeccable icons of innocence and tragedy at the service of art. Martin Scorsese often cites this as his all-time favourite movie. 🖵 **DVD**

Anton Walbrook *Boris Lermontov* ● Moira Shearer *Victoria Page* ● Marius Goring *Julian Craster* ● Leonide Massine *Grischa Ljubov* ● Robert Helpmann *Ivan Boleslawsky* ● Albert Basserman *Sergei Ratov* ● Esmond Knight *Livy* ● Ludmilla Tcherina *Irina Boronskaja* ■ *Dir* Michael Powell, Emeric Pressburger ● *Scr* Michael Powell, Emeric Pressburger, Keith Winter ● *Cinematographer* Jack Cardiff ● *Editor* Reginald Mills ● *Music* Brian Easdale ● *Art Director* Hein Heckroth, Arthur Lawson ● *Choreographer* Robert Helpmann

Red Skies of Montana ★★

Adventure drama 1952 · US · Colour · 89mins

Richard Widmark and Richard Boone just about make this old-time action adventure worth watching. Both charismatic tough guys, they play firefighters in the Rockies who parachute into forest fires and either hose them down or create corridors over which the flames can't jump. Of course, you can't do this for an entire movie so various subplots are trumped up, with Widmark haunted by the death of one of his colleagues while his wife (Constance Smith) gazes lovingly at him. Jeffrey Hunter is a troublesome trainee and there's an appearance by Charles Bronson, billed here as Charles Buchinsky.

Richard Widmark *Cliff Mason* • Constance Smith *Peg* • Jeffrey Hunter *Ed Miller* • Richard Boone *Dryer* • Warren Stevens *Steve* • James Griffith *Boise* • Joe Sawyer *Pop Miller* • Charles Buchinsky [Charles Bronson] *Neff* ■ *Dir* Joseph M Newman • *Scr* Harry Kleiner, from a story by Art Cohn

Red Sonja ★★ 15

Fantasy adventure
1985 · US · Colour · 84mins

Brigitte Nielsen (the ex-Mrs Sylvester Stallone) stars in the biggest role of her career as Red Sonja, a leather bikini-clad warrior who aims to avenge the death of her family by confronting wicked queen Sandahl Bergman. But it's Arnold Schwarzenegger who is the real star here, showing off his bulging biceps while trying to retain his dignity in a loincloth as the grunting hero who helps her. Based on a story by Robert E Howard (who also wrote the Conan tales), this is a sword-and-sorcery adventure for those who like their action fast and furious, their dialogue ropey and their acting filled with more ham than a butcher's shop. ▭

Brigitte Nielsen *Red Sonja* • Arnold Schwarzenegger *Kalidor* • Sandahl Bergman *Queen Gedren* • Paul Smith *Falkon* • Ernie Reyes Jr *Prince Tarn* • Ronald Lacey *Ikol* ■ *Dir* Richard Fleischer • *Scr* Clive Exton, George MacDonald Fraser, from the character created by Robert E Howard

Red Sorghum ★★★★★ 15

Drama 1987 · Chi · Colour · 87mins

Having made his name as a cinematographer on such pictures as Chen Kaige's *Yellow Earth*, Zhang Yimou established himself as one of the most important Chinese film-makers with this, his directorial debut. The start of his collaboration with then-partner Gong Li and the winner of the Golden Bear at Berlin, *Red Sorghum* has a visual bravura that has since become Zhang's trademark, making majestic use of colour and setting the scene with stunning long-shots of buildings or breathtaking landscapes. He is also a natural storyteller, switching with great skill from the cosiness of a simple family drama to the brutality of a heroic resistance struggle. A true modern classic. In Mandarin with English subtitles. Contains violence. ▭

Gong Li *Nine, "my grandma"* • Wen Jiang *Yu, "my grandpa"* • Teng Rujun *Liu Luohan* • Liu Ji *Douguan "my Dad"* • Qian Ming *Nine's father* • Ji Chunhua *Bandit Sanpao* • Zhai

Chunhua *Hu Er* ■ *Dir* Zhang Yimou • *Scr* Chen Jianyu, Zhu Wei and Mo Yan, from the short stories by Mo Yan

The Red Spider ★★ 18

Crime thriller 1988 · US · Colour · 89mins

A serial killer on the loose, a determined cop chasing him, the glamorous district attorney getting in the way, it all sounds far too familiar. James Farentino takes the central role in a follow-up to another TV movie, *One Police Plaza*, made two years earlier, which Jerry Jameson also directed. Farentino and co-star Jennifer O'Neill make this watchable, but it's a plotline which has been done to death, and significantly better. ▭

James Farentino *Lieutenant Daniel Malone* • Jennifer O'Neill *District Attorney Stephanie Hartford* • Amy Steel *Kate* • Philip Casnoff *Detective Shaunessy* • Soon-Teck Oh *Sonny Wu* ■ *Dir* Jerry Jameson • *Scr* Paul King

The Red Squirrel ★★★★ 18

Comedy drama 1993 · Sp · Colour · 109mins

Faintly recalling *Vertigo* and exploring such sundry themes as identity and memory, female intuition, male boorishness and Basque nationalism, this is a typically inventive and beguiling outing from director Julio Medem. The frantic pace and dazzling technique perfectly complement the endlessly diverging train of events that follows suicidal musician Nancho Novo's chance encounter with runaway amnesiac Emma Suarez. Unconventionally comic, yet deftly passionate in its themes, this virtuoso picture not only benefits from storming lead performances, but also from inspired character turns, notably from Maria Barranco as a housewife staying with the couple at the tacky camp site of the title. In Spanish with English subtitles. Contains violence, sex scenes and swearing. ▭

Nancho Novo *Jota* • Emma Suarez *Lisa* • Maria Barranco *Carmen* • Carmelo Gomez *Felix* ■ *Dir/Scr* Julio Medem

Red Sun ★★★ 15

Western 1971 · Fr/It/Sp · Colour · 108mins

Toshiro Mifune teams up with gunslinger Charles Bronson to recover a golden, ceremonial sword, stolen by black-clad Alain Delon from the Japanese Ambassador to the US. Ursula Andress and Capucine add glamour to the European-made yarn that's always entertaining and full of heavily stylised violence. Because the spaghetti western – specifically Sergio Leone's *Dollars* trilogy – owed its origins to the samurai movie, this is a clever example of fusion cinema, even though the script lacks the cultural insights and the wit one might have hoped for. ▭

Charles Bronson *Link* • Toshiro Mifune *Kuroda – samurai bodyguard* • Alain Delon *Gauche* • Ursula Andress *Cristina* • Capucine *Pepita* • Satoshi Nakamoura *Ambassador* ■ *Dir* Terence Young • *Scr* Laird Koenig, Denne Bart Petitclerc, William Roberts, Lawrence Roman, from a story by Laird Koenig

Red Sun Rising ★★★ 18

Martial arts action
1994 · US · Colour · 99mins

There were high hopes at one stage in the nineties that Don "The Dragon" Wilson could cross over into the mainstream. Even though he was consigned mainly to straight-to-video fodder, his charismatic skills marked him out as a name to watch. Sadly he faded from sight but this remains one of his stronger efforts, boasting a better than average script that still finds room for plenty of astonishing fight sequences. Here, Wilson plays a cop who comes up against his most lethal enemy in the shape of a black-hearted Japanese master (James Lew) with a "death touch". ▭

Don "The Dragon" Wilson *Thomas Hoshino* • Terry Farrell *Karen Ryder* • Michael Ironside *Captain Meisler* • Mako *Buntoro Iga* ■ *Dir* Francis Megahy • *Scr* David S Green, from a story by David S Green, Neva Friedden, Paul Maslak

Red Sundown ★★★ U

Western 1956 · US · Colour · 81mins

A terrific Universal co-feature, this western stars the excellent Rory Calhoun as a former gunslinger strapping on his guns one more time to thwart an evil cattle baron. Not terribly original but given zest by understanding director Jack Arnold (better known today for a series of horror flicks and Peter Sellers's opus *The Mouse That Roared*) and produced by exploitation king Albert Zugsmith of *Touch of Evil* fame. Martha Hyer gives a fine performance as a frontiers woman, and veterans Dean Jagger and Robert Middleton lend supporting class. There's a super linking ballad, too. Well worth catching.

Rory Calhoun *Alec Longmire* • Martha Hyer *Caroline Murphy* • Dean Jagger *Sheriff Jade Murphy* • Robert Middleton *Rufus Henshaw* • Grant Williams *Chet Swann* • Lita Baron *Maria* • James Millican *Purvis* ■ *Dir* Jack Arnold • *Scr* Martin Berkeley, from the novel *Black Trail* by Lewis B Patten

Red Surf ★ 18

Crime drama 1990 · US · Colour · 98mins

A relentlessly predictable, dumber-than-average thriller that has some interest value because it stars Hollywood heart-throb George Clooney in an early role. He plays a surfer dude, who together with best friend Doug Savant, deals drugs to make ends meet. Deciding to make one last big score, they involve their friend Doug McKeon in the plan. But when he gets arrested, he quickly names the local drug kingpin, who seeks revenge for the betrayal. A hokey, derivative exercise featuring Gene Simmons from the band Kiss as the surfers' mentor. ▭

George Clooney *Remar* • Doug Savant *Attila* • Gene Simmons *Doc* • Dedee Pfeiffer *Rebecca* • Rick Najera *Calavera* • Philip McKeon *True Blue* ■ *Dir* H Gordon Boos • *Scr* Vincent Robert, from a story by Brian Gamble, Jason Hoffs, Vincent Robert

The Red Tent ★★ U

Historical adventure
1969 · It/USSR · Colour · 120mins

An Italian-Soviet co-production, this ran at over four hours in Russia but was

half that length in Europe and the United States. The movie deals with the dramatic rescue in 1928 of an Italian expedition to the Arctic. Playing the leader of the expedition, Peter Finch had to endure the entire 16-month shoot – a near record – while Sean Connery's role, as Roald Amundsen, was added later in the hope of boosting the film's box-office appeal. As a survivalist epic, it has its moments and the authentic locations are often spectacular. Finch, too, is always excellent and there's an Ennio Morricone score as a bonus. But one must endure some clumsy Cold War politicking and a lot of dull stretches. The Oscar-winning British screenwriter, Robert Bolt, worked on the film without a screen credit. Some dialogue dubbed into English.

Sean Connery *Roald Amundsen* • Claudia Cardinale *Nurse Valeria* • Hardy Krüger *Aviator Lundborg* • Peter Finch *General Umberto Nobile* • Massimo Girotti *Romagna, rescue coordinator* • Luigi Vannucchi *Captain Zappi* • Mario Adorf *Biagi, radio operator* • Edward Marzevic *Finn Malmgren, meteorologist* ■ *Dir* Mikhail K Kalatozov [Mikhail Kalatozov] • *Scr* Ennio De Concini, Richard Adams

The Red Violin ★★★ 15

Drama 1998 · Can/It/UK · Colour · 130mins

Spanning 300 years, three continents and five languages, François Girard's musical chain letter looks and sounds superb. But, with locale and narrative carrying more weight than character, it's difficult to identify with any of the temporary owners of the violin, dyed red with the blood of his dead family by Italian craftsman, Carlo Cecchi. Cursed by its maker's obsessive pursuit of perfection, the instrument passes on down the centuries, bringing ill-fortune to Austrian child prodigy Christoph Koncz, English virtuoso Jason Flemyng and Chinese student Sylvia Chang, although, intriguingly, we're left unsure whether crooked antiquarian Samuel L Jackson will suffer the same fate. Contains some sex scenes.

Samuel L Jackson *Charles Morritz* • Greta Scacchi *Victoria Byrd* • Eva Marie Bryer *Sara* • Jason Flemyng *Frederick Pope* • Sylvia Chang *Xiang Pei* • Colm Feore *Auctioneer* ■ *Dir* François Girard • *Scr* François Girard, Don McKellar

The Redhead from Wyoming ★★★ U

Western adventure
1953 · US · Colour · 80mins

If ever anybody deserved to be filmed in colour, it was green-eyed, red-headed Irish beauty Maureen O'Hara, whose Hollywood career was as historic as it was colourful. Besides doing terrific work for John Ford, she invariably starred in swashbucklers and westerns that perfectly showcased her talents. In this movie, she falls for a sheriff while supposedly taking care of a rancher. The story is pure fluff, of course, but when O'Hara's on the screen the weaknesses in the plot aren't important. Watch out for a young Dennis Weaver (star of the *McCloud* TV series) in a minor role.

Maureen O'Hara *Kate Maxwell* • Alex Nicol *Stan Blaine* • William Bishop *Jim Averell* • Robert Strauss *"Knuckles" Hogan* • Alexander

Scourby *Reece Duncan* • Jack Kelly *Sandy* • Jeanne Cooper *Myra* ■ *Dir* Lee Sholem • *Scr* Polly James, Herb Meadow, from the story by Polly James

Redheads ★★ 15

Thriller   1992 · Ausl · Colour · 102mins

When she discovers she's videotaped the murder of her lover, a corrupt lawyer in the Justice Commission, Claudia Karvan goes on the run, only to be arrested for damaging a police car. Will she manage to convince her sceptical counsel, Catherine McClements, that she's in danger before the killer strikes again? Unfortunately, it's not too difficult to work out that one, or the identity of the culprit. Consequently, this conspiracy thriller, loosely based on Rosie Scott's play, *Say Thank You to the Lady*, went straight to video in its native Australia, despite creditable performances from its chalk and cheese leads. 📼

Claudia Karvan *Lucy Darling* • Catherine McClements *Diana Ferraro* • Alexander Petersons *Simon* • Sally McKenzie *Warden Zeida* • Anthony Phelan *Inspector Quigley* • Mark Hembrow *Brewster* • Jennifer Flowers *Carolyn* ■ *Dir* Danny Vendramini • *Scr* Danny Vendramini, from the play *Say Thank You to the Lady* by Rosie Scott

Redline ★★★ 18

Science-fiction thriller
1997 · Can/Neth · Colour · 94mins

Despite its alternative title of *Armageddon*, this is not the 1998 Bruce Willis blockbuster, but a rather routine revenge romp starring Mr Straight-to-Video himself, Rutger Hauer. He plays a virtual reality dealer murdered by a vicious syndicate who is then brought back to life as part of a sinister Russian experiment. Escaping from his futuristic laboratory prison, he goes after his gangster killer, Mr Straight-to-Video 2, Mark Dacascos. Although this low-grade *Strange Days* starts off well, it soon degenerates into a hopeless mess of unconvincing action, bad acting and s-l-o-w pacing. 📼

Rutger Hauer *John Anderson Wade* • Mark Dacascos *Merrick* • Yvonne Scio *Marina K/ Katya* • Patrick Dreikauss *Mishka* • Randall William Cook *Vanya the Special Prosecutor* • Michael Mehlmann *Serge* ■ *Dir* Tibor Takacs • *Scr* Tibor Takacs, Brian Irving

Redneck Zombies ★★

Horror   1988 · US · Colour · 83mins

Troma didn't actually make this *Night of the Living Dead* spoof (though they did distribute it), but it could easily be mistaken for one of their in-house productions. Shot on videotape, it concerns a drum of radioactive waste lost during a military transport through redneck country. Some locals find the drum and use it to repair their broken still, contaminating the moonshine they make and distribute. As a result, the area's residents become flesh-eating zombies. Aside from the plentiful (and extremely graphic) gore sequences, this is characterised by production values that hit a new low and a script that grabs every opportunity to use stereotypes and sophomoric humor. Viewers who admit they can find amusement in such material will find it

offers some laughs thanks to the enthusiasm of the movie's cast and crew. Contains violence.

Lisa DeHaven *Lisa Dubois* • WE Benson *Jed (Pa) Clemson* • William W Decker • James Housely *Wilbur* ■ *Dir/Scr* Pericles Lewnes

Reds ★★★★★ 15

Biographical historical drama
1981 · US · Colour · 186mins

It took Warren Beatty's ferocious energy to even attempt this chronicle of the Russian Revolution, focused through a radical love affair, and come up with a final product that is close to the project's original intentions. In telling the story of American journalist John Reed who wrote *Ten Days That Shook the World*, regarded by many as the definitive account of the revolution and his on-off romance with left-wing activist Diane Keaton, Beatty surrounded himself with massive talent: British writer Trevor Griffiths, cinematographer Vittorio Storaro, composer Stephen Sondheim, the great editor Dede Allen and a scene-stealing Jack Nicholson as playwright Eugene O'Neill. Beatty won a well-deserved Oscar for best direction, perhaps proving that it's not so much what you know as who you know. Contains swearing. 📼

Warren Beatty *John Reed* • Diane Keaton *Louise Bryant* • Jack Nicholson *Eugene O'Neill* • Edward Herrmann *Max Eastman* • Jerzy Kosinski *Grigory Zinoviev* • Maureen Stapleton *Emma Goldman* • Gene Hackman *Pete Van Wherry* • Paul Sorvino *Louis Fraina* • Nicolas Coster *Paul Trullinger* • M Emmet Walsh *Speaker at Liberal club* • Ian Wolfe *Mr Partlow* • Bessie Love *Mrs Partlow* ■ *Dir* Warren Beatty • *Scr* Warren Beatty, Trevor Griffiths

Redwood Curtain ★★

Drama   1995 · US · Colour · 99mins

An eclectic cast distinguishes this Hallmark Hall of Fame adaptation of Lanford Wilson's play. After the death of her adoptive father (John Lithgow, from TV's *Third Rock from the Sun*), Asian-American teen Lea Salonga (best known for the musical *Miss Saigon*) decides to look for her biological father. Her search takes her to the disenfranchised Vietnam veterans who've taken refuge in the California Redwood forest and she befriends disturbed vet Jeff Daniels, from whom she eventually learns the story of her birth. Though director John Korty elicits good performances from his cast, this TV movie wears its good intentions too obviously on its sleeve and never manages to really connect with the viewer. And although the ending wraps up the story nicely, the film takes far too long to get there.

Jeff Daniels *Lyman Fellers* • John Lithgow *Laird Riordan* • Lea Salonga *Geri Riordan* • Debra Monk *Geneva Simonson* • Catherine Hicks *Julia Riordan* • Vilma Silva *Zenaida* ■ *Dir* John Korty • *Scr* Ed Namzug, from the play by Lanford Wilson

Reed: Insurgent Mexico ★★★★

Historical drama
1971 · Mex · Sepia · 106mins

Long before he reported on the ten days that shook the world in 1917, American journalist John Reed

witnessed the Mexican Revolution of 1910. Paul Leduc may not have enjoyed the vast resources utilised by Warren Beatty's Reed opus *Reds*, but his modest film is a fine example of how depicting the past need not be as dry as a history lesson. The Mexican director's use of a sepia tint to convey both the time of the events and their authenticity is extremely shrewd, while his ability to put across factual information without swamping the human drama is most impressive. In Spanish with English subtitles.

Claudio Obregon • Eduardo Lopez Rojas • Ernesto Gomez Cruz • Juan Angel Martinez ■ *Dir* Paul Leduc • *Scr* from the book *Insurgent Mexico* by John Reed, Paul Leduc, Juan Tovar

The Reef ★★ U

Romantic drama   1996 · US · Colour

An old-fashioned weepie, based on a novel by Edith Wharton, that just about manages to rise above the glossy limitations of the TV-movie format. Timothy Dalton out in the cold a bit these days since handing in his licence to kill and Sela Ward play the tragic couple who find that the path of true love doesn't run smoothly. The two leads are fine and Robert Allan Ackerman's direction is respectful enough, but the film isn't in the same league as previous Wharton adaptations such as *Ethan Frome* and Martin Scorsese's marvellous *The Age of Innocence*. Contains sex scenes.

Timothy Dalton *Charles Darrow* • Sela Ward *Anna Leath* • Alicia Witt *Sophy Viner* • Jamie Glover *Owen Leath* • Leslie Caron *Regine De Chantelle* • Cynthia Harris *Adelaide* ■ *Dir* Robert Allan Ackerman • *Scr* William Hanley, from a novel by Edith Wharton

Reefer and the Model ★★★ 15

Comedy thriller   1988 · UK · Colour · 89mins

This spiky, acerbic tale of a small-time criminal and his involvement with a junkie "model", veers alarmingly at times between winsome charm and outré violence. It wins out in the end through sheer bravura of characterisation as director Joe Comerford cuts to the core of his cast's motivations. London's underbelly is exposed in all its visceral glory, the narrative occasionally roves all over the shop, but it's worth sticking with this unusually energetic thriller that contains just enough cutting wit and dark humour. 📼

Ian McElhinney *Reefer* • Carol Scanlan *Teresa, the model* • Eve Watkinson *Reefer's mother* • Sean Lawlor *Spider* • Ray McBride *Badger* • Birdy Sweeney "*Instant Photo*" ■ *Dir/Scr* Joe Comerford

Reefer Madness ★★ 15

Cult drama   1936 · US · Colour · 59mins

Initially released as *The Burning Question* and later retitled *Tell Your Children*, this exploitation classic emerged from decades of obscurity to become a campus classic in the early seventies. French-born Louis Gasnier had found Hollywood fame with the legendary serial, *The Perils of Pauline* (1914), but hard times forced him into directing this hilariously misinformed exposé of the perils of smoking dope. Exhortation comes a poor second to

sensationalism, as Dave O'Brien tempts his classmates into toking on the weed, resulting in Kenneth Craig accidentally shooting girlfriend Dorothy Short and Lillian Miles flinging herself from the courtroom window in drug-addled despair. Irresistibly risible. 📼

Dorothy Short *Mary* • Kenneth Craig *Bill* • Lillian Miles *Blanche* • Dave O'Brien *Ralph* • Thelma White *Mae* • Carleton Young *Jimmy* • Pat Royale *Agnes* • Josef Forte *Dr Carroll* ■ *Dir* Louis Gasnier • *Scr* Arthur Hoerl and Paul Franklin, from an original story by Lawrence Meade

The Reflecting Skin ★★ 15

Drama   1990 · UK · Colour · 91mins

The directorial debut of Philip Ridley, who wrote *The Krays*, is a wilfully perverse affair centred on a child (Jeremy Cooper) whose confused perceptions of the adults and events in his 1950s American farming community make for a disturbing vision of childhood. Ridley has a bad case of David Lynchitis, populating a striking rural landscape with weirdos, paedophiles and murderous kids. Coopers cruellest fantasies are fixed on reclusive widow Lindsay Duncan, whose liaison with the boy's hero-brother (Viggo Mortensen) inspires the child to connive at her ruin. Heavy portents and deep symbolism abound to absurd effect in a film of sumptuously overblown visuals and empty emotions. 📼

Viggo Mortensen *Cameron* • Lindsay Duncan *Dolphin Blue* • Jeremy Cooper *Seth* • Sheila Moore *Ruth* • Duncan Fraser *Luke* ■ *Dir/Scr* Philip Ridley • *Cinematographer* Dick Pope

A Reflection of Fear ★★★★ 18

Horror   1973 · US · Colour · 85mins

This weird thriller was very unpopular in its day – not least with its distributor, who shelved it, then released it on the bottom half of a double bill – but its unnervingly sinister atmosphere will repay another look. Strange teenager Sondra Locke lives with her mother Mary Ure, her grandmother Signe Hasso and her dolls. Then, when her absentee father (Robert Shaw, Ure's husband in real life) appears out of the blue, she goes completely off the rails, and the film leads to a truly mind-boggling ending. Director William A Fraker creates chills, à la *Cat People*, by never quite revealing the menace; primarily a cinematographer, everything looks great. Performances are also strong, especially from the ethereal-looking Locke. 📼

Robert Shaw *Michael* • Sally Kellerman *Anne* • Mary Ure *Katherine* • Sondra Locke *Marguerite* • Signe Hasso *Julia* • Mitchell Ryan *Inspector McKenna* ■ *Dir* William A Fraker • *Scr* Edward Hume, Lewis John Carlino, from the novel *Go to Thy Deathbed* by Stanton Forbes

Reflections in a Golden Eye ★★★ 15

Drama   1967 · US · Colour · 104mins

A weird John Huston effort, with Marlon Brando as the US Army officer and latent homosexual married to Elizabeth Taylor. Brian Keith is having an affair with Taylor because his wife, Julie Harris, performed a partial mastectomy on herself after the birth of her child. All this emanates from a novel by Carson McCullers, and very steamy it is, too. British cameraman Ossie Morris strikes some interesting angles and colour combinations, but it's hideously overblown and unintentionally funny. Buffs will note that shots of Brando in uniform were used later in *Apocalypse Now* to show the young Colonel Kurtz. Contains swearing. ▣

Elizabeth Taylor *Leonora Penderton* • Marlon Brando *Major Weldon Penderton* • Brian Keith *Lieutenant Colonel Morris Langdon* • Julie Harris *Alison Langdon* • Zorro David *Anacleto* • Gordon Mitchell *Stables Sergeant* • Irvin Dugan *Captain Weincheck* • Fay Sparks *Susie* • Robert Forster *Private Williams* • Douglas Stark *Dr Burgess* ■ *Dir* John Huston • *Scr* Chapman Mortimer, Gladys Hill, from the novel by Carson McCullers

Reflections on a Crime ★★

Psychological drama
1994 · US · Colour · 94mins

Although he will always be remembered for cult low-budget B movies, Roger Corman sometimes takes a chance on artier fare. The Jamie Lee Curtis drama *Love Letters* was one such example and this intriguing movie is another. The prison setting is what probably attracted Corman to the project (he's one of the executive producers), but writer/director Jon Purdy is more interested in exploring the disintegration of a marriage. Mimi Rogers puts in a mesmerising performance as a woman on death row for the murder of her husband, who reluctantly reveals her story in flashback to prison guard Billy Zane. It's too talky for its own good, but Purdy still delivers some chilling insights into domestic hell. Contains violence, swearing and nudity.

Mimi Rogers *Regina* • Billy Zane *Colin* • John Terry *James* • Kurt Fuller *Howard* • Lee Garlington *Tina* • Nancy Fish *Ellen* ■ *Dir/Scr* Jon Purdy

Reform School Girl ★

Prison crime drama 1957 · US · BW · 70mins

In this trashy exploitation picture aimed at the youth market, Gloria Castillo is the kind of well-developed teenager who has only to iron a dress in her underwear to be propositioned by her uncle. Sent to reform school after refusing to squeal on her car-thief boyfriend, she is victimised and almost murdered before settling down to a more wholesome future. A pre-*77 Sunset Strip* Edd Byrnes plays the vicious young criminal and among the bad girls later to become better known are Luana Anders and, if you look hard, Sally Kellerman.

Gloria Castillo *Donna Price* • Edward Byrnes [Edd Byrnes] *Vince* • Ross Ford *David Lindsay* • Ralph Reed *Jackie* • Yvette Vickers *Roxy* • Helen Wallace *Mrs Trimble* • Donna Jo Gribble *Cathy* • Luana Anders *Josie* • Sally Kellerman *Girl* ■ *Dir/Scr* Edward Bernds

Reform School Girl ★★ 18

Drama 1994 · US · Colour · 79mins

Given its title, one expects more than this rather bland teen drama delivers. Based loosely on a 50s flick of the same name, it features Aimee Graham as a sulky teen rebel who finds herself

way out of her depth when she is sent to reform school after being implicated in a case of manslaughter. The young cast which includes a pre-*Friends* Matt Le Blanc gives its all, but director Jonathan Kaplan, best known for worthy productions including *The Accused*, treats the premise too seriously, and exploitation fans are likely to be disappointed. Contains swearing and nudity. ▣

Aimee Graham *Donna* • Teresa Dispina *Maria* • Carolyn Seymour *Mrs Turnbull* • Eleanor O'Brien *Dink* • Matt LeBlanc *Vince* • Ashley Lister *Kathy Graham* • Harry Northrop *Uncle Charlie* ■ *Dir* Jonathan Kaplan • *Scr* Bruce Meade

Reform School Girls ★★ 18

Prison spoof 1986 · US · Colour · 90mins

Director Tom DeSimone had a string of enjoyably trashy pictures including porn to his credit, before making this "women behind bars" spoof and was already familiar with the genre, having made *The Concrete Jungle* a few years before. Youngster Linda Carol is sent to a harsh reform school where she has to deal with the usual unsympathetic female warden and a lesbian gang leader, played by one-time rock singer Wendy O Williams. Amusing and campy in spots, with plenty of nudity and gratuitous underwear. ▣

Sybil Danning *Sutter* • Wendy O Williams *Charlie* • Linda Carol *Jenny* • Pat Ast *Edna* • Charlotte McGinnis *Dr Norton* • Sherri Stoner *Lisa* • Denise Gordy *Claudie* • Laurie Schwartz *Nicky* ■ *Dir/Scr* Tom DeSimone

Regarding Henry ★★★ 15

Drama 1991 · US · Colour · 102mins

What looked like a sure-fire winner on paper – ruthless high-flying lawyer Harrison Ford fights back from brain injury and becomes a better person in the process – in fact emerged as a rather cold, lacklustre affair. Ford, who can be unnervingly emotionless on screen, was simply the wrong choice for the role, and director Mike Nichols invests the action with so much gloss and polish you feel as if your brain is swimming in an oil slick. Annette Bening looks lovely and gives one of the film's better performances, but from the start it's hard to sympathise with the family and their plight. A cynical, manipulative exercise that remains compulsively watchable despite its flaws thanks to the star power on board. Contains some swearing. ▣

Harrison Ford *Henry Turner* • Annette Bening *Sarah Turner* • Bill Nunn *Bradley* • Mikki Allen *Rachel Turner* • Donald Moffat *Charlie* • Aida Linares *Rosella* • Elizabeth Wilson *Jessica* • Robin Bartlett *Phyllis* • Bruce Altman *Bruce* • Rebecca Miller *Linda Palmer* ■ *Dir* Mike Nichols • *Scr* Jeffrey Abrams

Regeneration ★★★★ 15

First World War drama
1997 · UK/Can · Colour · 108mins

Four shell-shocked men help each other come to terms with their shared horrific First World War experiences in director Gillies MacKinnon's compelling, if sometimes highly romanticised, adaptation of the first book in Pat Barker's trilogy – the third,

The Ghost Road, won the Booker Prize. How they cope in a military psychiatric hospital – Siegfried Sassoon and Wilfred Owen (James Wilby and Stuart Bunce) wrote their most famous poetry in such institutions to exorcise their feelings – makes for a grim, intelligent drama suffused with haunting and harrowing images, none more so than the opening aerial shot of no man's land strewn with the casualties of war. Contains swearing and nudity. ▣

Jonathan Pryce *Dr William Rivers* • James Wilby *Siegfried Sassoon* • Jonny Lee Miller *Billy Prior* • Stuart Bunce *Wilfred Owen* • Tanya Allen *Sarah* • David Hayman *Dr Bryce* • Dougray Scott *Robert Graves* • John Neville *Dr Yealland* ■ *Dir* Gillies MacKinnon • *Scr* Allan Scott, from the novel by Pat Barker

Regina ★★★

Psychological drama
1982 · Fr/It · Colour · 95mins

Was ever a control freak so glamorous? Ava Gardner is the mother who dominates her husband (Anthony Quinn) and son (Ray Sharkey) to such an extent that, when the boy wants to marry, mum refuses, then takes to her bed with a psychosomatic illness. This rarely seen performance by Ava Gardner is one of her very best and director Jean-Yves Prate has contrived an atmosphere as morbid as the central character herself.

Ava Gardner *Mother* • Anthony Quinn *Father* • Anna Karina *Daughter* • Ray Sharkey *Son* ■ *Dir* Jean-Yves Prate • *Scr* from the play by Pierre Rey

La Règle du Jeu ★★★★★ PG

Comedy drama 1939 · Fr · Colour · 101mins

Jean Renoir's complex comedy of manners was such an all-time box office turkey on its first release in 1939, that it was not allowed out again at its original length until the late 50s, whereupon it was promptly acclaimed a masterpiece, going on a few years later to selection by an international poll of critics as the third greatest film of all time. Focusing on an up-market country house party, the film is a sophisticated, poignant and often funny study of social mores and the games people play. Renoir himself not only directs but co-writes and stars. The film may not suit all tastes, but who am I not to give five stars? ▣

Marcel Dalio *Robert la Chesnaye* • Nora Gregor *Christine* • Jean Renoir *Octave* • Roland Toutain *Jurieu* • Mila Parely *Geneviève de Marras* • Paulette Dubost *Lisette* • Carette [Julien Carette] *Marceau* • Gaston Modot *Schumacher* ■ *Dir* Jean Renoir • *Scr* Jean Renoir, in collaboration with Carl Koch, Camille Francois

Rehearsal for Murder
★★★ U

Mystery 1982 · US · Colour · 96mins

Richard Levinson and William Link, those prolific purveyors of TV movies and creators of that old favourite *Columbo*, are back on the murder trail with this hugely enjoyable drama. The pair put all their knowledge of stage and screen into this whodunit, in which movie star Lynn Redgrave is bumped off on the night of her Broadway bow. Robert Preston revels in the

opportunity to camp it up, although every member of the splendid supporting cast is in "dahling" mode. Taken at a fair lick by David Greene, this is good old-fashioned entertainment and, for once, the culprit isn't that easy to identify. ▣

Robert Preston *Alex Dennison* • Lynn Redgrave *Monica Welles* • Patrick Macnee *David Matthews* • Lawrence Pressman *Lloyd Andrews* • William Russ *Frank Heller* • Madolyn Smith *Karen Daniels* • Jeff Goldblum *Leo Gibbs* ■ *Dir* David Greene • *Scr* Richard Levinson, William Link

Reign of Terror ★★★★

Historical drama 1949 · US · BW · 89mins

A visually exhilarating, ingeniously-plotted political thriller about Robespierre's plot to become dictator after the French Revolution, this even extracts passable performances from usually limp Robert Cummings and insipid but beautiful Arlene Dahl in the starring roles. Richard Basehart makes a superbly malevolent Robespierre and supporting actor Arnold Moss has his finest moment as a sly opportunist. The Machiavellian intrigue unfolds in vivid *film noir* style as the powerful team of director Anthony Mann and cameraman John Alton is joined by the great art director William Cameron Menzies (taking credit only as the producer). The imagery conveys the terror and uncertainty of the period, while the pace overrides the script's contrivances. Heady stuff indeed.

Robert Cummings *Charles D'Aubigny* • Richard Basehart *Maximilien Robespierre* • Richard Hart *François Barras* • Arlene Dahl *Madelon* • Arnold Moss *Police chief Fouché* • Norman Lloyd *Tallien* • Charles McGraw *Sergeant* • Beulah Bondi *Grandma* ■ *Dir* Anthony Mann • *Scr* Philip Yordan, Aeneas MacKenzie, from a story by Philip Yordan, Aeneas MacKenzie • *Cinematographer* John Alton

The Reincarnation of Peter Proud ★★★ 18

Chiller 1975 · US · Colour · 101mins

Critically slated in its time, this has become almost a cult movie since. British director J Lee Thompson treated Max Ehrlich's adaptation of his own novel with a seriousness it didn't deserve – but his approach worked, nevertheless. Michael Sarrazin is the history professor who dreams his way back to the past and makes some discoveries about previous lives and loves. The plot never gets it together, but the mood and atmosphere are spot on. ▣

Michael Sarrazin *Peter Proud* • Jennifer O'Neill *Ann Curtis* • Margot Kidder *Marcia Curtis* • Cornelia Sharpe *Nora Hayes* • Paul Hecht *Dr Samuel Goodman* • Norman Burton *Dr Frederick Spear* ■ *Dir* J Lee Thompson • *Scr* Max Ehrlich, from his novel

La Reine Margot ★★

Historical drama
1954 · Fr/It · Colour · 93mins

Catherine de Medici (Françoise Rosay) rules France through her son, Charles IX, and hopes to avoid civil war between the Protestants and the Catholics by arranging a marriage between her daughter Margot (Jeanne Moreau) and a handsome count. Dumas's novel was originally adapted

by Abel Gance, the director of the legendary silent epic *Napoléon*, but the film that finally emerged was much more of a bodice-ripper and it suffered cuts for the American and British markets. It was lavishly remade in 1994 with Isabelle Adjani. A French language film. ▭

Jeanne Moreau *Marguerite de Valois –The Queen Margot* • Françoise Rosay *Catherine de Medici* • Armando Francioli *Joseph Peyrac de la Mole* • Robert Porte *Charles IX* • Henri Gènès *Annibal de Coconas* • AndréVersini *Henri de Navarre* ■ *Dir* Jean Dréville • *Scr* Abel Gance, from the novel by Alexandre Dumas

La Reine Margot ★★★ 🔞

Historical drama
1994 · Fr/Ger/It · Colour · 155mins

One of the dangers of historical film-making is that there is so much information available that the pace becomes fatally slow. Patrice Chéreau avoids this by taking the events described in the novel by Alexandre Dumas at such a furious lick, that the action becomes incomprehensible unless you pay keen attention. Isabelle Adjani won her fourth César as the Catholic Marguerite de Valois, who was married by her scheming mother Catherine de Medici (a César-winning Virna Lisi) to the Protestant leader Henri de Navarre (Daniel Auteuil). The illicit romance with Vincent Perez is deadly dull, but Jean-Hugues Anglade is outstanding as the deranged Charles IX. In French with English subtitles. Contains violence, sex scenes and nudity. ▭

Isabelle Adjani *Marguerite de Valois (Margot)* • Daniel Auteuil *Henri de Navarre* • Jean-Hugues Anglade *Charles IX* • Vincent Perez *La Mole* • Virna Lisi *Catherine de Médici* • Dominique Blanc *Henriette de Nevers* ■ *Dir* Patrice Chéreau • *Scr* Danièle Thompson, Patrice Chéreau, from the novel by Alexandre Dumas

The Reivers ★★★★

Drama 1969 · US · Colour · 110mins

Steve McQueen is well cast here as the ne'er-do-well guiding youngster Mitch Vogel through the minefield of adolescence in turn-of-the-century Mississippi. McQueen plays a hired hand working for Vogel's grandfather, Will Geer, who makes use of his employer's new car to take the lad on an adventure that includes a brothel and a racetrack. Former actor Mark Rydell directs with a gentle pace that suits the William Faulkner novel on which the film is based, and Burgess Meredith tightens it all up as narrator. There's also a scene-stealing, Oscar-nominated performance by Rupert Crosse.

Steve McQueen *Boon Hoggenbeck* • Sharon Farrell *Corrie* • Mitch Vogel *Lucius McCaslin* • Will Geer *Boss McCaslin* • Rupert Crosse *Ned McCaslin* • Michael Constantine *Mr Binford* • Lonny Chapman *Maury McCaslin* • Juano Hernandez *Uncle Possum* • Clifton James *Butch McCaslin* • Ruth White *Miss Reba* • Dub Taylor *Dr Peabody* • Burgess Meredith *Narrator* ■ *Dir* Mark Rydell • *Scr* Irving Ravetch, Harriet Jr Frank, from the novel by William Faulkner

The Rejuvenator ★★★ 🔞

Horror 1988 · US · Colour · 84mins

An offbeat and serious perversity pervades this oddly affecting gore fantasy version of *Sunset Boulevard*. Ageing actress Jessica Dublin is financing demented doctor John Mackay's experiments in eternal youth. When he finally creates a serum from human brains to make her young again, she pretends to be her actress niece in order to revive her film career. But sex makes her mutate into a giant-headed monster with huge claws, which she uses to decapitate victims before eating their brains. Well made by co-writer/director Brian Thomas Jones, this is oppressively creepy until it degenerates into over-done gooey silliness towards the end. ▭

Vivian Lanko *Elizabeth Warren/Monster* • John MacKay *Dr Gregory Ashton* • James Hogue *Wilhelm* • Katell Pleven *Dr Stella Stone* • Marcus Powell *Dr Germaine* • Jessica Dublin *Ruth Warren* • Roy MacArthur *Hunter* • Louis F Homyak *Tony* ■ *Dir* Brian Thomas Jones • *Scr* Simon Nuchtern, Brian Thomas Jones, from a story by Simon Nuchtern

Relative Fear ★★ 🔞

Thriller 1995 · Can · Colour · 93mins

Watchably daft thriller that plumps for nature not nurture as being the root of all evil. The tale tells of two kids who get switched at birth. One's the offspring of raving psychos, the other of normal parents. No prizes for guessing that the psychos' kid soon starts displaying all the characteristics of a natural born killer. The hokey subject matter is flattered by a strong cast which includes Darlanne Fluegel, James Brolin, Denise Crosby and M Emmet Walsh.

Darlanne Fluegel *Linda Pratman* • Martin Neufeld *Peter Pratman* • M Emmet Walsh *Earl* • James Brolin *Detective Atwater* • Denise Crosby *Connie Madison* ■ *Dir* George Mihalka • *Scr* Kurt Wimmer

Relative Values ★★★ 🅿🅶

Satire 2000 · UK · Colour · 89mins

Julie Andrews makes a big-screen comeback in Eric Styles's brittle adaptation of Noël Coward's comedy, shot on the Isle of Man with a sturdy British cast playing second fiddle to a pair of brash American interlopers. The narrative follows identical lines, with the unflappable Countess of Marshwood (Andrews) using all her feminine wiles to prevent her son (Edward Atterton) from marrying glamorous Hollywood starlet Miranda Frayle (Jeanne Tripplehorn). Miranda is, in fact, the sister of Andrews's personal maid, Moxie (Sophie Thompson), and arrives with her hell-raising boyfriend (William Baldwin) in hot pursuit. Snobbery and xenophobia are hardly the stuff of feel-good comedy, and Styles can't make Coward's creaky characters breathe on film. But Colin Firth and Stephen Fry play supporting roles with élan, while Andrews never puts a foot wrong.

Julie Andrews *Felicity* • Sophie Thompson *Moxie* • Edward Atterton *Nigel* • Jeanne Tripplehorn *Miranda* • William Baldwin *Don Lucas* • Colin Firth *Peter* • Stephen Fry *Crestwell* ■ *Dir* Eric Styles • *Scr* Paul Rattigan, Michael Walker, from the play *Relative Values* by Noël Coward

Relatives ★★ 🔞

Drama 1985 · Ausl · Colour · 83mins

Languishing on the shelves for five years before it was finally released on video, Anthony Bowman's tale of deep-seated resentments and emotional outbursts follows along all-too-familiar dysfunctional family lines. As Bill Kerr's kinfolk gather for his 80th birthday party, at his rundown Sydney estate, there's only one thing on the minds of all and sundry as they jockey for largess. Every tired feud imaginable is dusted down and pushed into service. But with Ray Barrett on blustering form as Kerr's oldest son and Norman Kaye providing some insouciant insinuation, it makes for brisk and abrasive entertainment. ▭

Bill Kerr *Grandfather* • Rowena Wallace *Nancy* • Alyson Best *Clare* • Ray Barrett *Geoffrey* • Brett Climo *Ross* • Michael Aitken *Peter* • Norman Kaye *Ed* ■ *Dir* Anthony Bowman [Antony J Bowman] • *Scr* Anthony Bowman

Relentless ★★ 🔞

Thriller 1989 · US · Colour · 88mins

One of those movies which spawned two sequels and no one can quite understand why. Judd Nelson undoubtedly turns in the greatest performance of his career so far – stay awake at the back there – as a serial killer who makes Jack the Ripper seem a dilettante. Apart from Mr Nelson acting his socks off, this is a very ho hum effort which is only passable fare if you're in an undemanding mood. There is some interesting support from Robert Loggia and Meg Foster. ▭

Judd Nelson *Buck Taylor* • Robert Loggia *Bill Malloy* • Leo Rossi *Sam Dietz* • Meg Foster *Carol Dietz* • Patrick O'Bryan *Todd Arthur* • Ken Lerner *Arthur* • Mindy Seger *Francine* • Angel Tompkins *Carmen* • Beau Starr *Ike Taylor* • Harriet Hall *Angela Taylor* ■ *Dir* William Lustig • *Scr* Jack TD Robinson [Phil Alden Robinson]

Relentless 2: Dead On ★★★ 🔞

Thriller 1991 · US · Colour · 89mins

This is a rarity in sequels, being an improvement over the original, and also the best entry in the four-part series. Leo Rossi returns as LA detective Sam Dietz, estranged from his wife (Meg Foster), and tracking down another serial killer, a surprisingly effective Miles O'Keeffe. When FBI agent Ray Sharkey starts to interfere, it becomes clear the killer isn't just another random slasher like Judd Nelson in the original. This extra plotting, plus excellent direction by Michael Schroeder are what gives the movie its edge, though Rossi's likeability and everyman quality also play an important part in its success.

▭ Miles O'Keeffe *Gregor* • Sven-Ole Thorsen *Mechanic* • Leo Rossi *Sam Dietz* • Meg Foster *Carol Dietz* • Dawn Mangrum *Reporter* • Ray Sharkey *Kyle Valsone* • Leilani Jones *Belinda Belos* ■ • *Scr* Mark Sevi

The Relic ★★★★ 🔞

Horror 1997 · US · Colour · 109mins

Director Peter Hyams pulls out all the stops in this unpretentious, super-slick gothic horror which rings few changes on the *Alien* blueprint, but still delivers the gory goods. An ancient Amazonian beast is creeping around Chicago's natural history museum on the night of a gala opening party. Can feisty scientist Penelope Ann Miller or detective Tom Sizemore overcome their fears to battle the blood-lusting demon of superstition? Throw some *Poseidon Adventure*-style panic into the monster mix and the result is a spectacular creature feature which gives a glossy veneer to the time-worn clichés. Harum-scarum jolts keep the seasoned suspense simmering and Hyams's full-tilt approach to the grisly mayhem is spot on. ▭

Penelope Ann Miller *Dr Margo Green* • Tom Sizemore *Lt Vince D'Agosta* • Linda Hunt *Dr Ann Cuthbert* • James Whitmore *Dr Albert Frock* • Clayton Rohner *Detective Hollingsworth* ■ *Dir* Peter Hyams • *Scr* Amy Holden Jones, John Raffo, Rick Jaffa, Amanda Silver, from the novel by Douglas Preston, Lincoln Child

La Religieuse ★★★★

Religious drama 1965 · Fr · Colour · 139mins

Adapted from the key Enlightenment text by encyclopedist Denis Diderot, Jacques Rivette's austere allegory was, initially, banned in France for its anti-clerical content. Rejected by her family, Anna Karina is forced to take the veil, only to be subjected to deprivations and beatings by mother superior, Micheline Presle, and then sexually harassed by the lesbian head of her new convent, Liselotte Pulver. Not even the priest who rescues her, Francisco Rabal, acts out of pure motives. However, this visually rigorous film is more about freedom of conscience than the severity or hypocrisy of religious celibacy and proves as provocative as it's tragic. In French with English subtitles.

Anna Karina *Suzanne Simonin* • Liselotte Pulver *Mme de Chelles* • Micheline Presle *Mme de Moni* • Christine Lenier *Mme Simonin* • Francine Bergé *Sister St Christine* • Francisco Rabal *Dom Morel* ■ *Dir* Jacques Rivette • *Scr* Jacques Rivette, Jean Gruault, from the novel *Memoirs of a Nun* by Denis Diderot

The Reluctant Agent ★

Comedy adventure
1989 · US · Colour · 94mins

This is a haphazard, unfunny action comedy, with an uneven performance by Jackée (yes, one of those actresses who thinks it will help her career if she forgets her surname). She plays the dual role of an FBI agent and her waitress twin sister, who team up for some contrived reason or other to catch a devious businessman. Most of the humour derives from that old (and worn out) chestnut which twin is which. You may even find yourself siding with the bad guys.

Jackée *Linda/Sharlene* • Richard Lawson *C* • Gabriel Dash • Dan Hedaya *John Fraser* • Harold Sylvester *Sam* ■ *Dir* Paul Lynch • *Scr* Jeff Cohn, Kristi Kane

The Reluctant Astronaut
★★ U

Science-fiction comedy
1967 · US · Colour · 101mins

Don Knotts gets shot into space in this one – a happy thought for the comedian's many detractors. Knotts's gormless comic style always polarised audiences, with some lapping it up and others unable to bear him. Here he plays Roy Fleming, a chap afraid of heights who is bullied by his father into going for a job at the NASA space centre. He ends up working as a trainee janitor. But as the Russians prepare to launch a man into space, US scientists bring forward their plans and urgently need a volunteer. Enter Roy. Simplistic comedy for serious Knotts fans only.

Don Knotts *Roy Fleming* • Arthur O'Connell *Buck Fleming* • Jeanette Nolan *Mrs Fleming* • Leslie Nielsen *Major Fred Gifford* • Joan Freeman *Ellie Jackson* • Jesse White *Donelli* ■ *Dir* Edward J Montagne • *Scr* Jim Fritzell, Everett Greenbaum, from a story by Don Knotts

The Reluctant Debutante
★★★ U

Comedy   1958 · US · Colour · 95mins

MGM, perhaps in the hope of recapturing the spirit of *Father of the Bride* (1950), hired that film's director, Vincente Minnelli, for this comedy adapted by William Douglas Home from his stage hit. However, the soft-centred dig at the London "season" was outmoded the moment it was made. A not very convincing change was the casting of two American teen idols, Sandra Dee, in the title role, and John Saxon, as her drum-playing sweetheart. Thankfully, Dee's father and stepmother were played delightfully by (recently married) Rex Harrison and Kay Kendall. (Kendall died of leukaemia the following year aged 33.) The nicely designed film was shot in Paris, because Harrison couldn't enter England for tax reasons.

Rex Harrison *Jimmy Broadbent* • Kay Kendall *Sheila Broadbent* • John Saxon *David Parkson* • Sandra Dee *Jane Broadbent* • Angela Lansbury *Mabel Claremont* • Peter Myers *David Fenner* • Diane Clare *Clarissa Claremont* ■ *Dir* Vincente Minnelli • *Scr* William Douglas Home, from his play

The Reluctant Dragon ★★ U

Documentary
1941 · US · BW and Colour · 73mins

American humorist Robert Benchley fronts this documentary about the Walt Disney studios, which takes its name from the 25-minute short that concludes the picture. Never more than a blatant plug for the studio, it encouraged the trade paper *Variety* to opine: "Dr Goebbels couldn't do a better propaganda job to show the workers in Disney's pen-and-ink factory as a happy and contented lot." In fact, the workers were on strike when the film was released in 1941. The demonstrations of the then up-to-date techniques, though, should interest fans and historians of animation. ▭

Dir Alfred Werker, Hamilton Luske, Jim Handley, Ford Beebe, Erwin Verity, Jasper Blystone • *Scr* Ted Sears, Al Perkins, Larry Clemmons, Bill Cottrell

The Remains of the Day
★★★★★ U

Period drama
1993 · UK/US · Colour · 128mins

An impeccable adaptation of Kazuo Ishiguro's Booker Prize-winning novel, with Anthony Hopkins as the emotionally repressed butler and Emma Thompson as the housekeeper he possibly loves. Framed in flashbacks, the story is an English twist on Jean Renoir's classic *La Règle du Jeu*, a broad view of a narrow class of aristocrats on the verge of self-destruction. Co-starring James Fox as a fascistic English lord and Christopher Reeve as an American diplomat (the past and present owners of Darlington Hall), it is as much a study in power and politics as it is Hopkins's blinkered view of the world from behind the gleaming silver salvers. The thirties' and forties' settings are immaculate, and, unlike James Ivory's earlier adaptations of EM Forster, this picture has real backbone: Ivory's direction is alive to every nuance and chink of the sherry glasses. ▭

Anthony Hopkins *Stevens* • Emma Thompson *Miss Kenton* • James Fox *Lord Darlington* • Christopher Reeve *Lewis* • Peter Vaughan *Father* • Hugh Grant *Cardinal* • Michael Lonsdale [Michel Lonsdale] *Dupont D'Ivry* • Tim Pigott-Smith *Benn* • John Haycraft *Auctioneer* • Caroline Hunt *Landlady* • Paula Jacobs *Mrs Mortimer* • Ben Chaplin *Charlie* • Steve Dibben *George* ■ *Dir* James Ivory • *Scr* Ruth Prawer Jhabvala, from the novel by Kazuo Ishiguro

The Remarkable Mr Pennypacker
★★★ U

Period comedy   1959 · US · Colour · 87mins

Clifton Webb is Pennypacker, son of sausage manufacturer Charles Coburn, for whom he works, and married to Dorothy McGuire in 1890s Harrisburg, Pennsylvania. Forced to spend much time at his father's Philadelphia plant, lonely Pennypacker takes a second wife, happily runs two families and fathers a total of 17 children before the truth is revealed. Scripted by Walter Reisch from a successful play and directed by Henry Levin, this is a good-natured, nicely observed period comedy, to which the polished and very "correct" Webb is ideally suited though he extracts rather too few laughs from the situation. ▭

Clifton Webb *Pa Pennypacker* • Dorothy McGuire *Ma Pennypacker* • Charles Coburn *Grampa* • Jill St John *Kate Pennypacker* • Ron Ely *Wilbur Fielding* • Ray Stricklyn *Horace Pennypacker III* • David Nelson *Henry Pennypacker* ■ *Dir* Henry Levin • *Scr* Walter Reisch, from the play by Liam O'Brien

Rembrandt
★★★ U

Biography   1936 · UK · BW · 80mins

One of the prestige productions that brought dignity to the British film industry, this distinguished film stars Charles Laughton in a remarkably affecting performance. His tendency to ham is brought under control by producer/director Alexander Korda, whose brother Vincent provides some particularly well-designed studio sets, quaintly converting Denham's sound stages to Rembrandt van Rijn's Amsterdam. No "Rembrandt" lighting, but excellent re-creations of the paintings, in particular a self-portrait that actually convinces you that Laughton and the Dutch master are one and the same. A rare screen performance from co-star Gertrude Lawrence reveals why this great lady of the stage wasn't loved by the movie camera. ▭

Charles Laughton *Rembrandt Van Rijn* • Gertrude Lawrence *Geertje Dirx* • Elsa Lanchester *Hendrickje Stoffels* • Edward Chapman *Fabrizius* • Walter Hudd *Banning Cocq* • Roger Livesey *Beggar Saul* • John Bryning *Titus Van Rijn* • Allan Jeayes *Dr Tulp* ■ *Dir* Alexander Korda • *Scr* Carl Zuckmayer, Lajos Biro, June Head, Arthur Wimperis • *Cinematographer* Georges Périnal • *Art Director* Vincent Korda

Remember?
★

Romantic comedy   1939 · US · BW · 83mins

Lew Ayres introduces his fiancée Greer Garson to his best friend Robert Taylor over lunch, whereupon friend sweeps her away and marries her, setting in train a series of events encompassing everything from divorce to amnesia-inducing potions. This must surely be one of the most witless romantic comedies ever dreamed up, despite a dozen or so amusing lines of dialogue. Ayres, looking and acting like a cut-price Jack Lemmon, emerges as a prize schnook and Taylor as a juvenile idiot, while Garson (with hints of her gracious performance in *Mrs Miniver*) rises above it all. Norman Z McLeod directed and co-wrote it, MGM produced it. Both should have known better.

Robert Taylor (1) *Jeff Holland* • Greer Garson *Linda Bronson* • Lew Ayres *Sky Ames* • Billie Burke *Mrs Bronson* • Reginald Owen *Mr Bronson* • George Barbier *Mr McIntyre* • Henry Travers *Judge Milliken* • Richard Carle *Mr Piper* ■ *Dir* Norman Z McLeod • *Scr* Corey Ford, Norman Z McLeod

Remember Last Night?
★★★

Comedy mystery   1935 · US · BW · 76mins

Universal assigned their star horror movie director James Whale and a first-rate cast, headed by Robert Young, Constance Cummings and Edward Arnold, to this offbeat comedy thriller, in which a group of socialites wake up with hangovers after a party, to find that one of their number was murdered during their carousals. A witty, sophisticated and suspenseful puzzler, the film combines, and cleverly parodies, a number of styles and genres to fascinating (if occasionally confusing) effect. Modern audiences might well appreciate the joke rather more than those of 1935 did. ▭

Edward Arnold *Danny Harrison* • Robert Young *Tony Milburn* • Constance Cummings *Carlotta, his wife* • George Meeker *Vic Huling* • Sally Eilers *Bette, his wife* • Reginald Denny *Jack Whitridge* • Louise Henry *Penny, his wife* • Gregory Ratoff *Faronea* • Robert Armstrong *Fred Flannagan* • Monroe Owsley *Billy Arliss* ■ *Dir* James Whale • *Scr* Harry Clork, Doris Malloy, Dan Totheroh, Murray Roth, from the novel *Hangover Murders* by Adam Hobhouse

Remember Me
★★★

Thriller   1985 · Ausl · Colour · 95mins

The same year that they collaborated on the Second World War medical drama *An Indecent Obsession*, Wendy Hughes, Richard Moir and director Lex Marinos reunited for this tense thriller. One of Australia's finest actresses, Hughes is given the chance to indulge in a little hysterical excess, as the return of her mentally disturbed ex-husband jeopardises both her new career and her second marriage. Torn between lingering passion and growing terror, Hughes brings some credibility to a potboiler that is otherwise played at fever pitch by Moir and Richard Grubb. Unsubtle, perhaps, but there's undeniable tension and tragedy in the finale.

Wendy Hughes *Jenny* • Richard Moir *Howard* • Robert Grubb *Geoff* • Carol Raye *Jenny's mother* • Peter Gwynne *Jenny's father* • Celia de Burgh *Barbara* • Sandy Gore *Adele* • Kris McQuade *Sue* ■ *Dir* Lex Marinos • *Scr* Anne Brooksbank

Remember Me
★★★

Psychological thriller   1995 · US · Colour

There's daft but entertaining gothic goings-on in this glossy made-for-TV chiller, based on the American bestseller by Mary Higgins Clark. Kelly McGillis is the grieving mother trying to get over the death of her young son, who decides to move to a summer home with her husband and new daughter. However, not only does the family find itself mixed up with a local murder, but also begins to suspect that the house may be haunted. McGillis deserves better material, but she still delivers a classy performance, and Michael Switzer succeeds in pushing the right directorial buttons. Contains violence and some swearing.

Kelly McGillis *Menley Nichols* • Shanna Reed *Elaine* • Cotter Smith *Adam Nichols* ■ *Dir* Michael Switzer • *Scr* Robert W Lenski, Michael Norell, from the novel by Mary Higgins Clark

Remember Me This Way
★★★ U

Drama   1988 · USSR · Colour · 58mins

Based on the play by Roman Solntsev, this intense family drama won the Special Jury Prize at the 1989 Tokyo TV Festival. Offering some provocative insights into life and expectations in Gorbachov's Soviet Union, it was directed by Pavel Chukhrai. Breaking with the traditions of socialist realism that dominated Communist film-making, Chukhrai uses the occasion of a family reunion to explore the political, social and moral issues widening the generation gap during the last days of Party rule. Iya Savvina, one of Soviet cinema's greatest actresses, gives an impressive performance as the woman at the centre of the feuding.

Iya Savvina • Oleg Borisov • Yelena Proklova • Yelena Finogeyeva ■ *Dir* Pavel Chukhrai • *Scr* M Zvereva, from the play *Mother and Son* by Roman Solntsev

Remember Me?
★★ PG

Comedy   1996 · UK · Colour · 77mins

Although the producers claimed this as a latter-day Ealing comedy, it's actually a single-pace, single-joke farce that leaves an expert cast floundering amid a myriad of clumsy plot contrivances. Yet Michael Frayn's tired script is only part of the problem, as Nick Hurran's

U = SUITABLE FOR ALL, **Uc** = SUITABLE FOR ALL, ESPECIALLY FOR YOUNG CHILDREN (VIDEO ONLY) **PG** = PARENTAL GUIDANCE

direction is rendered even more leaden by the painfully slow editing, which at times delays the reactions of the cast so long, it makes them look like amateur theatricals. There's a flicker of comic empathy between Imelda Staunton and Robert Lindsay, but Rik Mayall is unforgivably wasted and only Brenda Blethyn and James Fleet's cameos make it all bearable. 🎞️

Robert Lindsay *Jamie* • Rik Mayall *Ian* • Imelda Staunton *Lorna* • Brenda Blethyn *Shirley* • James Fleet *Donald* • Haydn Gwynne *Jamie's wife* ■ *Dir* Nick Hurran • *Scr* Michael Frayn

Remember My Name ★★★
Drama　　　1978 · US · Colour · 93mins
Written and directed by Alan Rudolph and produced by his mentor Robert Altman, this is a film full of fine moments, but, because of Rudolph's tendency to over-complicate, those moments ultimately add up to an unsatisfying whole. Returning from prison to make life hell for ex-husband Anthony Perkins, Geraldine Chaplin gives a scorching performance reminiscent of Joan Crawford and Barbara Stanwyck in their heyday. But even she gets bogged down in the subplots involving shopkeeper Jeff Goldblum and landlord Moses Gunn. You'll need to keep your wits about you because, once you lose the thread, it's virtually impossible to catch up. Contains swearing.

Geraldine Chaplin *Emily* • Anthony Perkins *Neil Curry* • Berry Berenson *Barbara Curry* • Moses Gunn *Pike* • Jeff Goldblum *Mr Nudd* • Timothy Thomerson [Tim Thomerson] *Jeff* • Alfre Woodard *Rita* • Marilyn Coleman *Teresa* ■ *Dir/Scr* Alan Rudolph

Remember the Day ★★★ U
Drama　　　1941 · US · BW · 86mins
One of those emotional chunks of Americana done so well by *In Old Chicago* director Henry King at 20th Century-Fox. What usually brought a tear to the eye of tough studio boss Darryl F Zanuck invariably worked with audiences worldwide, and this small-town soap opera is no exception. Claudette Colbert is cast against type as a schoolteacher who, in flashback, tells of her influence on a particular pupil, who – guess what? – grows up to be a presidential candidate. Meanwhile, Colbert falls for dull-but-worthy sports master John Payne. It's all professionally done and, if you like this sort of thing and can enjoy Colbert in a rare straight role, a fair slice of entertainment.

Claudette Colbert *Nora Trinell* • John Payne *Dan Hopkins* • John Shepperd [Shepperd Strudwick] *Dewey Roberts* • Ann E Todd *Kate Hill* • Douglas Croft *Dewey as a boy* • Jane Seymour (2) *Mrs Roberts* ■ *Dir* Henry King • *Scr* Tess Slesinger, Frank Davis, Allan Scott, from the play by Philo Higley, Philip Dunning

Remember the Night ★★★★
Romantic comedy drama
1940 · US · BW · 94mins
Barbara Stanwyck and Fred MacMurray, both at the top of their form and perfect foils for one another, co-star in this romantic comedy, written by Preston Sturges and directed by Mitchell Leisen. The action concerns a

shoplifter (Stanwyck) whose trial is delayed by the Christmas holiday, leaving her somewhat adrift. Sympathetic, assistant district attorney MacMurray takes pity on her and brings her home to his family's snowbound country home for Christmas. An absolute delight, combining warmth and charm with a little sentimentality and humour, woven together with stylish ease by all concerned.

Barbara Stanwyck *Lee Leander* • Fred MacMurray *John Sargent* • Beulah Bondi *Mrs Sargent* • Elizabeth Patterson *Aunt Emma* • Willard Roberton *Francis X O'Leary* • Sterling Holloway *Willie* • Charles Waldron *Judge –New York* • Paul Guilfoyle *District attorney* ■ *Dir* Mitchell Leisen • *Scr* Preston Sturges

Remembrance of Love ★★★
Drama　　　1982 · US · Colour · 100mins
Kirk Douglas is on form, as usual, as the ageing man who reunites with a woman he loved when he was young, in Poland during the Second World War. This is one of those movies that should come with free tissues, as tear-jerking moment follows tear-jerking moment. Well played, but tearfully sentimental grab some Kleenex and a box of chocolates and let yourself go.

Kirk Douglas *Joe Rabin* • Pam Dawber *Marcy Rabin* • Chana Eden *Leah Koenig* • Yoram Gal *David Berkman* • Robert Clary *Robert Clary* • Michael Goodwin *Ken Woodruff* • Eric Douglas *Young Joe Rabin* ■ *Dir* Jack Smight • *Scr* Harold Jack Bloom, from an article by Rena Dictor LeBlanc

Remo – Unarmed and Dangerous ★★★ 15
Action adventure
1985 · US · Colour · 110mins
A solid, unpretentious little action thriller, which is notable mainly for the presence of Joel Grey the Oscar-winning MC of *Cabaret*, making a rare return to the big screen. The Remo of the title is Fred Ward, a no-nonsense policeman who is transformed into a super agent by a wise old Oriental (Grey). Director Guy Hamilton probably would have preferred to have the same sort of budgets that were afforded him for his Bond movies, but he still keeps the action roaring along, and there are some neat supporting turns from Charles Cioffi and William Hickey. 🎞️

Fred Ward *Remo Williams* • Joel Grey *Chiun* • Wilford Brimley *Harold Smith* • JA Preston *Conn MacCleary* • George Coe *General Scott Watson* • Charles Cioffi *George S Grove* • Kate Mulgrew *Major Rayner Fleming* ■ *Dir* Guy Hamilton • *Scr* Christopher Wood, from *The Destroyer,series* by Richard Sapir, Warren Murphy

Remote Control ★★ 15
Science-fiction comedy
1988 · US · Colour and BW · 84mins
Kevin Dillon is good as a video-store clerk who stumbles into an alien conspiracy involving a video release of a cheesy fifties movie called *Remote Control*. Viewers of the tape are hypnotised into committing violent psychotic acts, leading Dillon and girlfriend Deborah Goodrich not just to gather and destroy the tapes, but also to try and take on the aliens. The black-and-white movie-within-a-movie is amusing, but although this is

ostensibly a sci-fi comedy, the entire enterprise is frequently stuck awkwardly between being funny and being serious. 🎞️

Kevin Dillon *Cosmo* • Deborah Goodrich *Belinda* • Jennifer Tilly *Allegra* • Christopher Wynne *Georgie* • Frank Beddor *Victor* • Kaaren Lee *Patricia* • Bert Remsen *Bill Denver* ■ *Dir/ Scr* Jeff Lieberman

Renaissance Man ★★ 12
Comedy　　　1994 · US · Colour · 122mins
Director Penny Marshall crosses *Stripes* with *Dead Poets Society* in this misconceived high-concept movie, which nevertheless just about manages to get by on the quality of its cast. Danny DeVito, as the unemployed advertising executive called up to teach English to stroppy army recruits, does his best to counteract the sentimentality that keeps rising to the surface, and he is ably supported by such top-line players as Gregory Hines, Cliff Robertson, Ed Begley Jr and Mark Wahlberg (billed here as Marky Mark). Ultimately, however, the film is just too nice for its own good. Contains some swearing. 🎞️

Danny DeVito *Bill Rago* • Gregory Hines *Sergeant Cass* • Cliff Robertson *Colonel James* • James Remar *Captain Murdoch* • Lillo Brancato Jr *Donnie Benitez* • Stacey Dash *Miranda Myers* • Kadeem Hardison *Jamaal Montgomery* • Richard T Jones *Jackson Leroy* • Khalil Kain *Roosevelt Hobbs* • Mark Wahlberg *Tommy Lee Haywood* • Ed Begley Jr *Jack Markin* ■ *Dir* Penny Marshall • *Scr* Jim Burnstein

Les Rendez-vous d'Anna ★★★
Drama
1978 · Fr/Bel/W Ger · Colour · 127mins
Made by Chantal Akerman, a young Belgian film director, the picture follows the meanderings of Anna, a young Belgian film director as she travels to several European cities to publicise her latest film. The overtly autobiographical element makes it a rather uncomfortable film to watch, especially in the long scene when she admits to her mother that she is in love with a woman. Previously, in medium long shots, mournful monologues and solemn silences, we have seen her on trains, in an impersonal hotel room with a man, and alone in her apartment. Some may find Akerman's minimalist cinema coolly captures the modern malaise, while others might suffer from a sense of malaise while watching it. In French with English subtitles.

Aurore Clément *Anna Silver* • Helmut Griem *Heinrich* • Magali Noël *Ida* • Lea Massari *Anna's mother* ■ *Dir/Scr* Chantal Akerman

Les Rendez-vous de Paris ★★★★ PG
Romance drama　　1995 · Fr · Colour · 98mins
Alighting on his favourite themes of pursuit and evasion, Eric Rohmer fashions three bittersweet vignettes in this fond tribute to capricious youth and the hidden beauties of Paris. As narcissistic as they are garrulous, each protagonist is a choice Rohmer archetype – whether it's the girl trying to catch her boyfriend in his infidelity in "The Seven O'Clock Rendezvous", the

student toying with an affair, while summoning the courage to break her engagement, in "The Benches of Paris", or the artist in "Mother and Child, 1907", who is gently rebuffed by a recently married woman. Minor perhaps, but still irresistible. In French with English subtitles.

Clara Bellar *Esther* • Antoine Basler *Horace* • Aurore Rauscher *Her* • Serge Renko *Him* • Michaël Kraft *Painter* • Bénédicte Loyen *Young woman* ■ *Dir/Scr* Eric Rohmer

Rendezvous ★★★ U
Spy comedy　　　1935 · US · BW · 94mins
A puzzle expert (William Powell), aching to see frontline action in France during the First World War, is reluctantly seconded to the American war ministry as a code-breaker to rescue a critical situation. He finds himself involved with a spy-ring and the assistant secretary of war's glamorous but dizzy niece (Rosalind Russell). An unusual, even daring, mixture of light – almost screwball – romantic comedy and espionage thriller, it features polished performances from Powell, Russell, Binnie Barnes, Lionel Atwill and Cesar Romero, and atmospheric, well-judged direction from William K Howard.

William Powell *Lt Bill Gordon/Anson Meridan* • Rosalind Russell *Joel Carter* • Binnie Barnes *Olivia Karloff* • Lionel Atwill *Maj Charles Brennan* • Cesar Romero *Capt Nikki Nikolajeff* • Samuel S Hlnds *John Carter, Assistant Secretary of War* ■ *Dir* William K Howard • *Scr* Bella Spewack, Samuel Spewack, PJ Wolfson, George Oppenheimer, from the novel *American Black Chamber* by Herbert O Yardley

Rendez-vous ★★★
Erotic drama　　　1985 · Fr · Colour · 83mins
Former critic and film teacher André Téchiné has certainly practiced what he formerly preached, having emerged as one of the more highly regarded French directors of the past three decades and winning for this chic film, the best director award at the Cannes Film Festival. It's an atmospheric, backstage drama in which Juliette Binoche plays Nina, a girl from the provinces who wants to become a star. She goes to Paris and decides that one way to success and home comfort is to sleep with the young men she meets. But when she gets a part in a production of *Romeo and Juliet*, it is the director, (Jean-Louis Trintignant), an older man, who becomes her salvation. Far from profound, but seldom, if ever, boring. In French with English subtitles.

Juliette Binoche *Nina Larrieu* • Lambert Wilson *Quentin* • Wadeck Stanczak *Paulot* • Jean-Louis Trintignant *Scrutzler* • Dominique Lavanant *Gertrude* ■ *Dir* André Téchiné • *Scr* André Téchiné, Olivier Assayas

Rendezvous with Annie ★★★
Wartime romantic comedy
1946 · US · BW · 89mins
American director Allan Dwan actually (and uniquely) notched up over 400 feature credits in a career that spanned from Douglas Fairbanks's silent epics to RKO co-features in the fifties. He hit a surprising run of box-office luck just as the Second World War ended, with a streak of comedies

such as *Getting Gertie's Garter*, *Up in Mabel's Room*, and the umpteenth remake of *Brewster's Millions*. This long-forgotten gem was next in that series – frantic, fast, and extremely entertaining especially for its glimpses of a very Hollywood England – as likeable GI Eddie Albert goes AWOL to check up on his stateside wife. Albert is immensely genial in the lead, making one regret his relegation to character roles (*Oklahoma!*, *Roman Holiday*) and Sir C Aubrey Smith brings a spurious dignity to the whole daft proceeding. Jolly good fun.

Faye Marlowe *Annie Dolan* • Gail Patrick *Dolores Starr* • Philip Reed *Lt Avery* • C Aubrey Smith *Sir Archibald Clyde* • Raymond Walburn *Everett Thorndyke* ■ *Dir* Allan Dwan • *Scr* Richard Sale, Mary Loos

Renegade ★★★ 18
Spaghetti western 1987 · It · Colour · 95mins

Directed by Enzo Barboni under the name of EB Clucher, this amiable latter day western gets off to an amusing start as Terence Hill (a drifter who gets by, repeatedly selling a horse with a homing instinct) hits the road with Ross Hill, the young son of a jailed buddy. Their encounters with truckers, bikers, flirts and a crooked knife thrower are all good value, but the picture falls away when villainous Robert Vaughn comes on the scene to steal the boy's farm in order to build a base for his drug business. Far more sedate than most spaghettis, but it has its moments. Some dialogue dubbed into English. ⌨

Terence Hill *''Renegade''* • Robert Vaughn *Tycoon* • Ross Hill • Norman Bowler • Beatrice Palme • Donald Hodson • Cyros Elias • Sandy • Valeria Sabel • Luisa Maneri • igi Bonos ■ *Dir* Enzo Barboni [EB Clucher] • *Scr* Marco Tullio Barboni, Mario Girotti [Terence HIll], Sergio Donati

Renegades ★★★
Adventure 1930 · US · BW · 90mins

Warner Baxter stars as an officer who leads a small group of Foreign Legionnaires against a band of warlike heathens in the desert and becomes a hero. Lots of blood and thunder, famous horror-star-to-be Bela Lugosi as The Marabout and the distracting, and disruptive, presence of female spy Myrna Loy contribute to a respectable early sound entry in the ''exotic heroic adventure melodrama'' genre. The movie, directed by Victor Fleming, does, however, suffer from a narrative confusion that hampers a solid cast.

Warner Baxter *Deucalion* • Myrna Loy *Eleanore* • Noah Berry Sr *Machwurth* • Gregory Gaye *Vologuine* • George Cooper *Bilox* • C Henry Gordon *Capt Mordiconi* • Colin Chase *Sgt Maj Olson* • Bela Lugosi *The Marabout* • Victor Jory *Young officer* ■ *Dir* Victor Fleming • *Scr* Jules Furthman, from the novel *Le Renégat* by André Armandy

Renegades ★★ 18
Action thriller 1989 · US · Colour · 101mins

As Kiefer Sutherland and Lou Diamond Phillips doubtless appreciate, this mindless, if energetic, thriller would have benefited considerably from a decent script. As it is, the endless action only serves to highlight that a single, scrawny idea is being stretched

to breaking point, and the attempts at ''serious'' dialogue between the set pieces are just embarrassing. Both actors were better employed in *Young Guns*. Contains swearing and violence. ⌨

Kiefer Sutherland *Buster* • Lou Diamond Phillips *Hank* • Jami Gertz *Barbara* • Rob Knepper [Robert Knepper] *Marino* • Bill Smitrovich *Finch* • Floyd Westerman [Floyd Red Crow Westerman] *Red Crow* • Joe Griffin *Matt* ■ *Dir* Jack Sholder • *Scr* David Rich

Rent-a-Cop ★★ 15
Action comedy 1988 · US · Colour · 92mins

The second teaming of stars Burt Reynolds and Liza Minnelli (remember *Lucky Lady*?) was one of five consecutive Reynolds features that never played in British cinemas. Seldom has a current favourite fallen from popularity so quickly, but this lacklustre thriller gives some indication why, despite its amazing A-list accomplished technicians, including editor Robert Lawrence (*El Cid*, *Spartacus*), art director Tony Masters (*2001: a Space Odyssey*) and Federico Fellini's cameraman Giuseppe Rotunno. Reynolds is an ex-cop with a seriously visible rotten toupee, and Minnelli's a flashy call girl working for ace madam Dionne Warwick. Say goodbye to credibility right there. The promotional T-shirt was more fun. Contains swearing and some violence. ⌨

Burt Reynolds *Tony Church* • Liza Minnelli *Della Roberts* • James Remar *Dancer* • Richard Masur *Roger* • Dionne Warwick *Beth* • Bernie Casey *Lemar* • Robby Benson *Pitts* • John Stanton *Alexander* ■ *Dir* Jerry London • *Scr* Dennis Shryack, Michael Blodgett

Rent-a-Kid ★★★ U
Comedy 1992 · Can · Colour · 85mins

Barely seen outside its native Canada, this is a children's film that doesn't patronise its audience by resorting to slapstick for its comedy or sentimentality for its message. Leslie Neilsen crops up in a showy cameo as the father of an orphanage owner, who rents out three children unwilling to have their family broken up, to a couple who can't decide whether parenting is for them. Although the antiques shop subplot and the final resolution are a tad corny, the scenes in which the couple try to please the threesome are good fun. It's patchy fun, but discriminating kids should warm to it. ⌨

Leslie Nielsen *Harry* • Christopher Lloyd *Lawrence Kady* • Matt McCoy *Russ Syracuse* • Sherry Miller *Val Syracuse* • Tabitha Lupien *Molly Ward* • Amos Crawley *Brandon Ward* • Cody Jones *Kyle Ward* • Tony Rosato *Cliff Haber* ■ *Dir* Fred Gerber • *Scr* Paul Bernbaum

Rentadick ★★ PG
Comedy 1972 · UK · Colour · 89mins

This woeful private-eye spoof started out as a project for *Monty Python* team members John Cleese and Graham Chapman, who wrote the original screenplay, but then disowned the film and had their names removed from the credits. John Wells and John Fortune were drafted in as replacements, but couldn't avert a disaster. Co-produced by Ned Sherrin, it should at least have

made up in wackiness what it lacked in wit. However, nearly everyone concerned seems to have been affected by the failure of vision at the core of the project, and not even brief appearances by Spike Milligan and Michael Bentine can enliven the proceedings. ⌨

James Booth *Hamilton* • Richard Briers *Gannet* • Julie Ege *Utta* • Ronald Fraser *Upton* • Donald Sinden *Armitage* • Kenneth Cope *West* • John Wells *Owltruss* • Richard Beckinsale *Hobbs* • Michael Bentine *Hussein* • Derek Griffiths *Henson* • Spike Milligan *Customs Officer* • Penelope Keith *Madge* ■ *Dir* Jim Clark • *Scr* John Wells, John Fortune

Repentance ★★★★
Political drama 1984 · USSR · Colour · 151mins

Not filmed for three years after it was written and then not released for another three after its completion, this was the first Soviet feature to be openly critical of Stalin and is one of the most daring films ever made in the former USSR. Ostensibly a black comedy about the repeated exhumation of the mayor of a small Georgian town, it is a defiant assault on revisionist history, that shows, through a series of harrowing flashbacks, that the crimes of the past cannot simply be buried and forgotten. Exceptionally played and unflinchingly directed by Tengiz Abuladze, it won a Special Jury Prize at Cannes. In Georgian with English subtitles. Contains some violence, swearing and brief nudity.

Avtandil Makharadze *Varlam Aravidze/Abel Aravidze* • Iya Ninidze *Guliko* • Merab Ninidze *Tornike* • Zeynab Botsvadze *Ketevan Barateli* ■ *Dir* Tengiz Abuladze • *Scr* Nana Janelidze, Tengiz Abuladze, Rezo Kveselava

The Replacement Killers ★★★ 18
Action thriller 1998 · US · Colour · 83mins

Forget the fact there's no plot whatsoever and focus on the high-energy action (who knew there were so many glass walls to smash?) and you'll enjoy this dumb, noisy and enjoyable thriller with Hong Kong superstar Chow Yun-Fat making his American debut. When he refuses to take out an assigned target Stateside, conscientious hit man Yun-Fat puts his family in danger back in China. Feisty Mira Sorvino is the expert passport forger who helps him out. Don't think, just thrill to the wild gunplay and slick stunts. Contains violence and some swearing. ⌨ 🄳🄳

Mira Sorvino *Meg Coburn* • Chow Yun-Fat *John Lee* • Michael Rooker *Stan ''Zeedo'' Zedkov* • Kenneth Tsang *Terence Wei* • Jürgen Prochnow *Michael Kogan* • Til Schweiger *Ryker* • Danny Trejo *Collins* ■ *Dir* Antoine Fuqua • *Scr* Ken Sanzel

Replacing Dad ★★
Drama 1999 · US · Colour · 120mins

Oscar-nominee Mary McDonnell (*Dances with Wolves*) portrays a small-town Florida woman who must pick up the pieces after husband William Russ (from TV's *Boy Meets World*) dumps her for their daughter's fifth-grade teacher. Initially angry and depressed, she slowly begins to pick up the

pieces of her life, much to the chagrin of her faithless spouse. What starts out as an interesting portrait of a wife struggling to find happiness deteriorates into a standard ''woman done wrong, then gets strong'' string of clichés. At its best when depicting the downward spiral of the jilted heroine, this TV movie stumbles with the tacked-on melodramatic ending. For viewers depressed about their life, the crises faced by McDonnell will make their problems seem positively trivial by comparison.

Mary McDonnell *Linda Marsh* • William Russ *George Marsh* • Jack Coleman *Dr Mark Chandler* • Tippi Hedren *Dixie* • Erik Von Detten *Drew Marsh* • Camilla Belle *Mandy Marsh* ■ *Dir* Joyce Chopra • *Scr* David J Hill, from the novel by Shelley Fraser Mickle

Replikator ★★ 18
Science-fiction action 1994 · Can · Colour · 96mins

A cyberpunk technological thriller about the race to create a machine that can reproduce human tissue, this is, unfortunately, low on thrills, focussing mainly on dark sets punctuated with neon lights and lots of talking heads. The future presented here has all the flashy toys you might expect, but shouldn't the television reception be better? Eventually a human is replicated and the results are unpleasant, of course. It could have been worse – they could have replicated Ned Beatty, who puts in a token appearance. ⌨

Michael St Gerard *Ludo/Ludovic* • Brigitte Bako *Kathy Moskow* • Ned Beatty *Inspector Valiant* • Cicciolina *Stripper* ■ *Dir* G Philip Jackson • *Scr* Michelle Bellerose, Tony Johnston, John Dawson

Repo Man ★★★★ 18
Science-fiction thriller 1984 · US · Colour · 88mins

Despite poor reviews on its initial release, Alex Cox's darkly satirical swipe at American urban low life mutated into one of the eighties' greatest cult movies. Emilio Estevez, who's never been in a better movie since, plays a novice car repossession man in Los Angeles, learning the tricks of the trade from veteran Harry Dean Stanton, while coming into contact with aliens and drug pushers. The film is a winning blend of sci-fi, social commentary and *film noir*, with lots of quotable dialogue. Estevez's new-wave punk and his friends are portrayed as characters existing on the fringes of society (note the names taken from beers – Bud, Miller and Lite) and it's a world that's beautifully captured by Wim Wenders's regular cinematographer Robby Müller. This film marked out Cox as a director to watch in the future, but alas nothing he's made since has ever been equally worth watching. This deserves multiple viewings. ⌨

Emilio Estevez *Otto* • Harry Dean Stanton *Bud* • Tracey Walter *Miller* • Olivia Barash *Leila* • Sy Richardson *Lite* • Susan Barnes *Agent Rogersz* • Fox Harris *J Frank Parnell* • Tom Finnegan *Oly* • Del Zamora *Lagarto* • Eddie Velez *Napo* ■ *Dir/Scr* Alex Cox

Report to the Commissioner ★★★ PG

Crime drama 1975 · US · Colour · 112mins

Also known as *Operation Undercover*, this cop drama resembles *Serpico* in its depiction of police corruption. Michael Moriarty stars as the idealistic rookie detective involved in the killing of an undercover cop, then embroiled in a vast cover-up. A solid script by Abby Mann and Ernest Tidyman (who wrote *The French Connection*) and some crisp action sequences, including a shoot-out in the Saks department store, make this eminently watchable, though most eyes now will be on Richard Gere, making his screen debut as a pimp. Hector Elizondo (Gere's stooge in *Pretty Woman*) and the excellent Bob Balaban also have early featured roles.

Michael Moriarty *Beauregard "Bo"Lockley* • Yaphet Kotto *Richard "Crunch"Blackstone* • Susan Blakely *Patty Butler* • Hector Elizondo *Captain d'Angelo* • Tony King *Thomas "Stick"Henderson* • Michael McGuire *Lt Hanson* • Edward Grover *Captain Strichter* • Dana Elcar *Chief Perna* • Robert Balaban [Bob Balaban] *Joey Egan* • William Devane *Asst district attorney Jackson* • Stephen Elliott *Police commissioner* • Richard Gere *Billy* ■ *Dir* Milton Katselas • *Scr* Abby Mann, Ernest Tidyman, from the novel by James Mills

Repossessed ★ 15

Horror spoof 1990 · US · Colour · 80mins

It must have seemed a good idea at the time. Give *The Exorcist* the *Airplane!* treatment, get Linda Blair to reprise her infamous head-turning/pea soup vomit role, cast *The Naked Gun's* Leslie Nielsen as Max von Sydow and wait for the laughs to come thick and fast. Sadly, they come thin and slow instead. Everything from Rambo films, Michael Jackson, TV evangelism to aerobics is spoofed in a lame-brained, mistimed fiasco. If there's an obvious target for humour, you can be sure it's missed in this dated *Porky's*-style satire. Contains swearing. 🖥

Linda Blair *Nancy Aglet* • Leslie Nielsen *Father Jedidiah Mayii* • Ned Beatty *Ernest Weller* • Anthony Starke *Father Luke Brophy* • Thom J Sharp *Braydon Aglet* • Lana Schwab *Fanny Weller* ■ *Dir/Scr* Bob Logan

The Reptile ★★★ 15

Horror 1966 · UK · Colour · 86mins

Snakes alive! Hysteria hits a 19th-century Cornish village when murder victims turn up with fang marks on their necks. Could sultry Jacqueline Pearce be the victim of a Malayan curse doomed to writhe the night away? A splendidly spooky vintage Hammer horror featuring an endearingly fifties-style monster, remarkably atmospheric art direction (the set at Hammer's Bray Studios was re-used for *The Plague of the Zombies*) and taut, stylish direction by John Gilling. One of the best examples of the economical approach Hammer took to horror while never sacrificing originality. 🖥

Noel Willman *Dr Franklyn* • Jennifer Daniel *Valerie* • Ray Barrett *Harry* • Jacqueline Pearce *Anna* • Michael Ripper *Tom Bailey* • John Laurie *Mad Peter* • Marne Maitland *Malay* • David Baron *Charles Spalding* • Charles Lloyd Pack *Vicar* • Harold Goldblatt *Solicitor* ■ *Dir* John Gilling • *Scr* John Elder [Anthony Hinds]

Repulsion ★★★★ 18

Psychological thriller 1965 · UK · BW · 100mins

Director Roman Polanski takes us on a deeply disturbing, hallucinatory trip into Catherine Deneuve's mental breakdown in this British psychological thriller, his first film in English. As Swinging London parties in the background, repressed Belgian manicurist Deneuve unsheathes her claws with deadly results. There are shades of Bunuel and Cocteau, but Polanski puts his personal stamp on the violent visuals (the killing of a boyfriend and landlord) and the terrifying soundtrack (the buzzing of flies, a slashing knife). The final panning shot revealing a photograph of Deneuve as a young girl, even then withdrawn and apart, is a truly cathartic moment. Contains violence. 🖥

Catherine Deneuve *Carol Ledoux* • Ian Hendry *Michael* • John Fraser *Colin* • Patrick Wymark *Landlord* • Yvonne Furneaux *Helen Ledoux* • Renee Houston *Miss Balch* • Helen Fraser *Bridget* • Roman Polanski *Spoons player* ■ *Dir* Roman Polanski • *Scr* Roman Polanski, Gerard Brach, David Stone • *Cinematographer* Gilbert Taylor

Requiem ★★

Fantasy drama 1998 · Swi/Fr/Por · Colour · 100mins

Returning to the scene of *In the White City*, Alain Tanner uses Lisbon as a stifling backdrop to this slow-moving treatise on memory and regret. Adapted from a novel by Antonio Tabucchi, the film is intended as a tribute to the Portuguese author, Fernando Pessoa, who puts in a guest appearance as one of the mysterious characters Francis Frappat encounters while awaiting a meeting with a ghost from his past. A pall of impossible sophistication hangs over the piece, which wears its intellectual credentials on its sleeve and makes little effort to invite the viewer into its rarified atmosphere. A French language film.

Francis Frappat *Paul* • AndréMarcon *Pierre* ■ *Dir* Alain Tanner • *Scr* Bernard Comment, Alain Tanner, from a novel by Antonio Tabucchi

Requiem for a Heavyweight ★★★

Sports drama 1962 · US · BW · 86mins

A boxing picture, based on an American live TV production written by Rod Serling, this stars Anthony Quinn as Mountain Rivera, an over-the-hill boxer. He has to continue fighting, risking permanent blindness, in order to pay off debts to the Mafia run up by his manager (Jackie Gleason). His devoted trainer is Mickey Rooney. In the ring (and on the moral message front) this is a bloody, brutal big-hitter of a movie – albeit with a rather soft centre – and Quinn's committed performance makes a welcome change from his usual Greek/Inuit/Mongolian offerings. He made the movie quickly, during a shutdown in the production of *Lawrence of Arabia*.

Anthony Quinn *Mountain Rivera* • Jackie Gleason *Maish Rennick* • Mickey Rooney *Army* • Julie Harris *Grace Miller* • Stan Adams *Perelli* • Herbie Faye *Bartender* • Jack

Dempsey • Cassius Clay [Muhammad Ali] *Ring opponent* ■ *Dir* Ralph Nelson • *Scr* Rod Serling, from his TV play

Requiem for Dominic ★★★

Historical political thriller 1990 · Aus · Colour · 88mins

Set in Ceausescu's Romania on the eve of the 1989 revolution, this intelligent film from Austria follows exile Felix Mitterer, in his quest to prove that his childhood friend August Schmölzer was not responsible for the murder of 80 factory workers in the town of Timisoara. Director Robert Dornhelm based his film on the experiences of his own friend, Dominic Paraschiv, a member of the notorious Securitate who was branded "the Butcher of Timisoara". Making studied use of news footage and fictional material, he has fashioned an engrossing, violent, political thriller that lays bare the soul of a troubled land. In German with English subtitles.

Felix Mitterer *Paul Weiss* • August Schmölzer *Dominic Paraschiv* • Viktoria Schubert *Clara* • Angelica Schutz *Codrata Paraschiv* • Antonia Rados *Antonia* ■ *Dir* Robert Dornhelm • *Scr* Michael Kohlmeier, Felix Mitterer

The Rescue ★★ PG

Action adventure 1988 · US · Colour · 92mins

A daft drama with Kevin Dillon (younger brother of the more successful Matt), as one of a group of teenagers who mount a rescue mission when they discover the US government isn't going to help their dads, a group of Navy SEALS who have been captured behind enemy lines. Director Ferdinand Fairfax was also responsible for the silly and rather plodding adventure *Spymaker: the Secret Life of Ian Fleming*, which has Jason Connery running around looking just as confused as these boys do. Contains swearing and violence.

Kevin Dillon *JJ Merrill* • Christina Harnos [Christine Harnos] *Adrian Phillips* • Marc Price *Max Rothman* • Ned Vaughn *Shawn Howard* • Ian Giatti *Bobby Howard* • Charles Haid *Commander Howard* • Edward Albert *Commander Merrill* ■ *Dir* Ferdinand Fairfax • *Scr* Jim Thomas, John Thomas

Rescue Me ★★ 15

Action comedy 1991 · US · Colour · 94mins

Everyone had a lot of fun making this silly spoof of the action adventure genre. Stephen Dorff (whose finest moment was as Stuart Sutcliffe in *BackBeat*) is Fraser, a high-school nerd who suffers from unrequited love for teen-queen Ami Dolenz (daughter of Monkee Micky Dolenz). Obsessed with cameras (Dorff is a collector of vintage cameras in real life), he takes pictures of Dolenz just as she is being kidnapped instead of rescuing her. He teams up with hard man Mac (Michael Dudikoff, taking the mickey out of his screen persona) to rescue his fair maiden. The film features nice support from Peter DeLuise (son of Dom DeLuise) and Dee Wallace Stone. 🖥

Michael Dudikoff *Daniel "Mac"MacDonald* • Stephen Dorff *Fraser Sweeney* • Ami Dolenz *Ginny Grafton* • Peter DeLuise *Rowdy* • William Lucking *Kurt* • Dee Wallace Stone *Sarah Sweeney* • Liz Torres *Carney* • Danny Nucci *Todd* ■ *Dir* Arthur Allan Seidelman • *Scr* Mike Snyder

The Rescuers ★★★★ U

Animation 1977 · US · Colour · 75mins

A thoroughly delightful Disney cartoon, this is about the all-mouse Rescue Aid Society and bids by its leading lights, Bernard and Miss Bianca, to free a little girl held hostage by hiss-boo baddie Madam Medusa. Bob Newhart, Eva Gabor and George C Scott are among the voice artists in a well-told tale with memorable characters. This was one of the animated features that indicated a return to form by Disney after a lengthy spell of cartoon mediocrity. The same characters appeared in a less successful sequel, *The Rescuers Down Under*. 🖥

Bob Newhart *Bernard* • Eva Gabor *Miss Bianca* • Michelle Stacy *Penny* • Geraldine Page *Madame Medusa* • Joe Flynn *Mr Snoops* ■ *Dir* Wolfgang Reitherman, John Lounsbery, Milt Kahl, Art Stevens • *Scr* Larry Clemmons, Ken Anderson, Vance Gerry, David Michener, Burny Mattinson, Frank Thomas, Fred Lucky, Ted Berman, Dick Sebast, from the books *The Rescuers* and *Miss Bianca* by Margery Sharp

The Rescuers Down Under ★★★ U

Animation 1990 · US · Colour · 80mins

This acceptable enough Disney animation is a sequel that came such a long time after *The Rescuers* (1977) that it could be forgiven for having lost the plot, because introductions to the "rescue mice" Miss Bianca and Bernard had to be made all over again. This time they're called to Australia to help a boy and golden eagle in danger from a fearsome trapper. It's likeable enough and the crocodile-snapping climax is exciting stuff. Bob Newhart and Eva Gabor are great as the voices of Bernard and Bianca, though it's a shame that fine actor George C Scott is only a disembodied presence. 🖥

Bob Newhart *Bernard* • Eva Gabor *Miss Bianca* • John Candy *Wilbur* • George C Scott *Percival McLeach* ■ *Dir* Hendel Butoy, Mike Gabriel • *Scr* Jim Cox, Karey Kirkpatrick, Byron Simpson, Joe Ranft, from the characters created by Margery Sharp

Rescuers: Stories of Courage – Two Women ★★ 12

Second-World War drama (based on a true story) 1997 · US · Colour · 102mins

Executive produced by Barbara Streisand, these are two fact-based dramas about heroic gentile women who shielded Jews from Nazi persecution. In *Mamusha*, Elizabeth Perkins (*Big*) stars as Polish-Catholic housekeeper Gertruda Babilinska, who devotes her life to raising a young Jewish boy after his mother dies during a terrifying Nazi raid. In *Woman on a Bicycle*, Sela Ward stars as Marie-Rose Gineste, who assists the French Resistance by bicycling underground pamphlets from town to town and, later, by hiding Jews from the Nazis. Setting these very personal stories against the terror of the holocaust makes for very affecting drama and the performances, under veteran director Peter Bogdanovich (*The Last Picture Show*), are uniformly above average. Contains some swearing and violence. 🖥

Elizabeth Perkins *Gertruda Babilinska ("Mamusha")* • Al Waxman *Dr Jacob Weinstock ("Mamusha")* • Nicky Guadagni *Lydia Stolowitzky ("Mamusha")* • George Morfogen *Adult Michael –narration* • Michael Cameron *Young Mickey* • Sela Ward *Marie-Rose Gineste* • Anne Jackson *Maman* • Fritz Weaver *Bishop Theas* ■ *Dir* Peter Bogdanovich • *Scr* Susan Nanus, Ernest Kinoy, from the book *Rescuers: Portraits of Moral Courage in the Holocaust* by Malka Drucker, Gay Block

Rescuers: Stories of Courage – Two Couples
★★ PG

Second-World War drama (based on a true story)
1998 · US · Colour · 104mins

This is one of a series of films about the rescue of Jews from the Holocaust by courageous gentiles, executive produced by Barbra Streisand. In the first of two stories, *Aart and Johtje Vos*, Dana Delaney and Martin Donovan star as a simple Dutch farming couple, who experience terrible strains on their family when they harbor Jews escaped from a concentration camp. In *Marie Taquet*, former Belgian army officer Emile (Alfred Molina) and pragmatic wife Marie (Linda Hamilton, *Terminator*), rekindle their loveless marriage when they hide Jewish children at the boarding school they run. The period settings are captured nicely and the worthwhile subject matter is eminently watchable. ▭

Dana Delany *Johtje Vos* • Martin Donovan *Aart Vos* • Jan Rubes *Hendrick DeVries* • Hugo Haenen *SS Lieutenant* • Tom Jansen *Ginkel* • Linda Hamilton *Marie Taquet* • Alfred Molina *Emile Taquet* ■ *Dir* Tim Hunter, Lynne Littman • *Scr* Paul Monash, Cy Chermak, Francine Carroll

Reservoir Dogs
★★★★★ 18

Crime drama   1991 · US · Colour · 94mins

As one of the slogans used to promote the video put it: "Robbery, blood, violence, torture all in the comfort of your own home." Yes, the film that many consider the most influential of the decade finally reaches our screens uncut and with its reputation intact, in spite of the revelation that it bears more than a passing resemblance to Hong Kong action director Ringo Lam's *City on Fire*. Shot in just five weeks on a minuscule $1.5 million budget, the film's runaway success came as something of a surprise even to its debuting writer/director Quentin Tarantino, who was hoping for a cult hit rather than a phenomenon that would inspire countless wannabes to churn out bungled blag flicks of their own. *Dogs* also ran into trouble with the British Board of Film Classification, which was rumoured to be considering digital realignment to lessen the impact of certain scenes – before passing the picture unscathed in the summer of 1995. Working wonders with Tarantino's pacey, attitude-laced dialogue (packed with references to pop music, TV shows and hip movies), the ensemble cast is uniformly excellent, with Michael Madsen's sadistic, ear-slashing Mr Blonde and Steve Buscemi's exasperated Mr Pink particularly outstanding. Brash, abrasive and unrelenting, this is a

must-see. Contains violence and swearing. ▭

Harvey Keitel *Mr White (Larry)* • Tim Roth *Mr Orange (Freddy)* • Michael Madsen *Mr Blonde (Vic Vega)* • Chris Penn [Christopher Penn] *Nice Guy Eddie* • Steve Buscemi *Mr Pink* • Lawrence Tierney *Joe Cabot* • Randy Brooks *Holdaway* • Kirk Baltz *Marvin Nash* • Eddie Bunker *Mr Blue* • Quentin Tarantino *Mr Brown* ■ *Dir/Scr* Quentin Tarantino • *Cinematographer* Andrzej Sekula

Resident Alien
★★★

Documentary   1990 · US · Colour · 85mins

Having become a celebrity because of John Hurt's portrayal in *The Naked Civil Servant*, Quentin Crisp moved to New York where he quickly became the darling of the cultural poseurs and a TV talk-show standby. In this thorough profile, directed by Jonathan Nossiter, Crisp exercises his wit and wisdom – "John Hurt played me and then played Caligula which is me in a sheet" – and is joined by Hurt, Sting and others who ruminate on the man who wears his camp credentials on his ruffled sleeves. We learn many nuggets of trivia (such as Crisp's deleted cameo in *Fatal Attraction*) and gain some deeper insights into this perpetual exile. A fascinating voyage on a Queen.

Dir/Scr Jonathan Nossiter

Resting Place
★★★★ PG

Drama   1986 · US · Colour · 98mins

Tautly scripted by Walter Halsey Davis and impeccably paced by director John Korty, this is one of the best TV movies ever made in America. Combining the themes of racial prejudice and military cover-up, this engrossing drama shuttles back and forth between Georgia and Vietnam as army officer John Lithgow seeks to discover why a black war hero has been denied burial in his hometown cemetery. Morgan Freeman and C C H Pounder also excel as the boy's proud parents, but it's the way in which Lithgow peels away the conspiratorial layers to reveal a shameful act of cowardice that provides the film's fascinating focus.

John Lithgow *Major Kendall Laird* • Morgan Freeman *Luther Johnson* • Richard Bradford *General Willard P Hauer* • CCH Pounder *Ada Johnson* • GD Spradlin *Sam Jennings* • Frances Sternhagen *Mrs Eudora McAlister* • M Emmet Walsh *Sarge* • John Philbin *Bradford Erskine* ■ *Dir* John Korty • *Scr* Walter Halsey Davis

The Restless Breed
★★ U

Western   1957 · US · Colour · 83mins

Director Allan Dwan is one of the great unsung Hollywood heroes, cutting his teeth at the birth of American cinema, directing such silent masterworks as Douglas Fairbanks's *Robin Hood* and *The Iron Mask*, and continuing through sound (*Sands of Iwo Jima*) to notch up over 400 directing credits, his last movie being planned at the age of 82. This is his last western, a cripplingly low-budgeted colour B movie starring deadpan Scott Brady in a routine tale, as a lawyer trying to unmask his father's killer, helped by a cast which includes a pre-*The Miracle Worker* Anne Bancroft and a pre-*Dallas* Jim Davis. Dwan manages some nice

directorial touches: watch how all the characters interact by appearing to eavesdrop on each other as the plot develops.

Scott Brady *Mitch Baker* • Anne Bancroft *Angelita* • Jay C Flippen *Marshal Steve Evans* • Rhys Williams *Ed Newton* • Jim Davis *Rev Simmons* • Leo Gordon *Cherokee* • Scott Marlowe *Allan* ■ *Dir* Allan Dwan • *Scr* Steven Fisher

Restless Natives
★★ PG

Comedy   1985 · UK · Colour · 85mins

A good comedy idea gone astray. Two Scottish lads become modern-day Robin Hoods, robbing tourists and giving the proceeds to the poor. Soon they are local, then international, heroes. The trouble is that much of the comedy is a parody of the work of the then-popular Scottish director Bill Forsyth, and jokes that were considered feeble in their day, now seem even more obscure. A treat, however, for lovers of the Scottish countryside, and an effective career spur for director Michael Hoffman, who went on to make more sophisticated comedies in Hollywood. The score is by Stuart Adamson of rock band *Big Country*. ▭

Joe Mullaney *Ronnie* • Vincent Friell *Will* • Ned Beatty *Bender* • Robert Urquhart *Det Insp Baird* • Teri Lally *Margot* • Bernard Hill *Will's Father* • Mel Smith *Pyle* • Bryan Forbes *Man in Car* • Nanette Newman *Woman in Car* ■ *Dir* Michael Hoffman • *Scr* Ninian Dunnett

The Restless Years
★★

Drama   1958 · US · Colour · 85mins

Family traumas abound in a conservative suburban community where Teresa Wright's major goal in life is to protect her teenage daughter Sandra Dee from the knowledge and stigma of illegitimacy, while John Saxon's young life is complicated by the reappearance of his long-absent failure of a father, James Whitmore. As a vehicle for teen-stars when teen culture was on the way up, this outmoded drama of small-town life was a curious choice, and it's difficult to know what audience it was aimed at. This remains true although, as directed by Helmut Kautner, it's OK as lower-case soap opera for lazy viewing. (Released as *The Wonderful Years* in the UK.)

John Saxon *Will Henderson* • Sandra Dee *Melinda Grant* • Teresa Wright *Elizabeth Grant* • James Whitmore *Ed Henderson* • Luana Patten *Polly Fisher* • Margaret Lindsay *Dorothy Henderson* • Virginia Grey *Miss Robson* • Alan Baxter *Alex Fisher* ■ *Dir* Helmut Kautner • *Scr* Edward Anhalt, from the play *Teach Me How to Cry* by Patricia Joudry

Restoration
★★★★ 15

Period romantic comedy
1995 · US · Colour · 112mins

Michael Hoffman's adaptation of Rose Tremain's novel is a period movie that, like Fellini's *Satyricon*, treats the past as something very, very strange. Filmed at Forde Abbey and other historic sites, the Oscar-winning design is astonishing. The court of Charles II resembles Nero's and the picture subversively suggests that the foppish king, surrounded by spaniels, sycophants and willing women, lit the Great Fire of London to purge the

plague and build a new capital, Rome. The casting is as weird as the settings: Sam Neill as the cholic King; Robert Downey Jr as a womanising medic; Hugh Grant splendidly pompous as artist in residence; but what on Earth is Meg Ryan doing as a traumatised hospital patient? This is a flawed picture with flashes of crazy brilliance. ▭

Robert Downey Jr *Robert Merivel* • Sam Neill *King Charles II* • David Thewlis *John Pearce* • Polly Walker *Celia* • Meg Ryan *Katherine* • Ian McKellen *Will Gates* • Hugh Grant *Finn* • Ian McDiarmid *Ambrose* ■ *Dir* Michael Hoffman • *Scr* Rupert Walters, from the novel by Rose Tremaine

Resurrected
★★★★ 15

Drama   1989 · UK · Colour · 88mins

A sombre, unsettling account of a soldier who goes AWOL in the Falklands War and returns to his North Country village, with cruelly ironic consequences. Directed by former documentarist Paul Greengrass – who also co-wrote the proscribed book *Spycatcher* – it depicts the combat in First World War terms, rather like Joseph Losey's *King and Country*, but with the political complexity of a Vietnam. "The main character is a blank sheet of paper on which everyone writes their own ideas about the Falklands," said Greengrass. He imbues the story with a wealth of religious imagery – walking on water, cruciform poses, resurrection – while examining a flagging nation's regeneration and the attendant jingoism. ▭

David Thewlis *Kevin Deakin* • Tom Bell *Mr Deakin* • Rita Tushingham *Mrs Deakin* • Rudi Davies *Julie* • Michael Pollitt *Gregory Deakin* • William Hoyland *Capt Sinclair* • Ewan Stewart *Cpl Byker* • Christopher Fulford *Slaven* • David Lonsdale *Hibbert* • Peter Gunn *Bonner* ■ *Dir* Paul Greengrass • *Scr* Martin Allen

The Resurrected
★★★

Horror mystery   1992 · US · Colour · 106mins

Director Dan O'Bannon is to be commended for this successful adaptation of the classic story *The Case of Charles Dexter Ward*, since most attempts to film the works of HP Lovecraft have proved to be directorial failures. The focus here is on mystery and atmosphere instead of gore, which makes the occasional necessary forays into blood and guts more repulsive and shocking. The story's progression is cleverly constructed, always tantalising the viewer with more questions as each answer is given. John Terry is adequate as the private detective investigating Ward, but the real star is Chris Sarandon, whose acting range gets an ideal showcase.

John Terry *John March* • Jane Sibbett *Claire Ward* • Chris Sarandon *Charles Dexter Ward/ Joseph Curwin* • Richard Romanus *Lonnie Peck* • Laurie Briscoe *Holly Tender* • Ken Cameroux *Captain Ben Szandor* ■ *Dir* Dan O'Bannon • *Scr* Brent V Friedman, from the novel by HP Lovecraft

Resurrection
★★★ 15

Fantasy drama   1980 · US · Colour · 98mins

After nearly dying in a car crash, Ellen Burstyn glimpses the "Gates of Heaven" and becomes endowed with healing powers. Is she Christ reborn?

U = SUITABLE FOR ALL   Uc = SUITABLE FOR ALL, ESPECIALLY FOR YOUNG CHILDREN (VIDEO ONLY)   PG = PARENTAL GUIDANCE

That's what neurotic preacher's son Sam Shepard thinks, leading to a provocative and tear-jerking climax. Superb scripting, a terrific cast and Daniel Petrie's heartfelt direction make this rural tale of faith and spirituality a rewarding experience. Burstyn is a revelation as the modest woman who soon realises how much of a burden her ''gift'' truly is. The moment she secretly cures a little boy of cancer with a loving hug is the emotional highlight of an underrated moral fantasy. ▭

Ellen Burstyn *Edna McCauley* • Sam Shepard *Cal Carpenter* • Richard Farnsworth *Esco* • Roberts Blossom *John Harper* • Clifford David *George* • Pamela Payton-Wright *Margaret* ■ *Dir* Daniel Petrie • *Scr* Lewis John Carlino

Resurrection Man ★★★ 18

Political crime drama
1997 · UK · Colour · 97mins

With the troubles in Northern Ireland providing a background, this thriller effectively creates an atmosphere of warfare and shows how the situation can affect – and even apparently excuse – the actions of psychopathic killer Stuart Townsend, who leads a gang of Loyalists on a killing spree. Director Marc Evans tends to favour the bloody and the obvious, over defining events and motives, but this is, nonetheless, certainly an engrossing, convincing account of humankind's inhumanity. Contains violence, swearing and sex scenes. ▭

Stuart Townsend *Victor Kelly* • Geraldine O'Rawe *Heather Graham* • James Nesbitt *Ryan* • John Hannah *Darkie Larche* • Brenda Fricker *Dorcas Kelly* • James Ellis *Ivor Coppinger* • Sean McGinley *Sammy McLure* • Derek Thompson *Herbie Ferguson* ■ *Dir* Marc Evans • *Scr* Eoin McNamee, from his novel

The Resurrection of Zachary Wheeler ★★

Science-fiction thriller
1971 · US · Colour · 100mins

Blending elements from John Frankenheimer's *Seconds* and Michael Crichton's *Coma*, this is an efficiently mounted thriller, shot on videotape. A playboy presidential hopeful (Bradford Dillman) is brought back from the dead thanks to organ transplants from synthetic zombies (called ''somas''), which have been bred for the purpose by mad doctor James Daly. Reporter Leslie Nielsen uncovers the grisly manufacturing plant in Almogordo, New Mexico and is about to suppress the story – thinking it's in America's best interests – when he learns Daly's next patient is a prominent Asian leader whose change in politics is to be the price of his rebirth. This suffers from too much Cold War philosophy and stodgy chase footage of Nielsen, which ultimately get in the way of the intriguing plot.

Leslie Nielsen *Harry Walsh* • Bradford Dillman *Senator Zachary Wheeler* • James Daly *Dr Redding* • Angie Dickinson *Dr Layle Johnson* • Robert J Wilke *Hugh Fielding* • Jack Carter *Dwight Childs* • Don Haggerty *Jake* ■ *Dir* Robert Wynn • *Scr* Jay Simms, Tom Rolf

Retreat, Hell! ★★

War drama
1952 · US · BW · 94mins

Cult B-movie director Joseph H Lewis – best known for *Gun Crazy* – turns in a conventional combat movie, set during the Korean War. All the clichés are firmly in place: the training routines, the heroic commanding officer; the platoon leader worried about the wife and kids he has left behind; the frayed nerves; and the camaraderie of the men as they are picked off by communist snipers. Made while the Korean War was actually being fought, this was shot on a low budget and isn't a patch on later films with the same theme, such as *Men in War* and *Pork Chop Hill*.

Frank Lovejoy *Steve Corbett* • Richard Carlson *Paul Hansen* • Rusty Tamblyn *Jimmy McDermid* • Anita Louise *Ruth Hansen* ■ *Dir* Joseph H Lewis • *Scr* Milton Sperling, Ted Sherdeman

Retroactive ★★ 18

Science-fiction action drama
1997 · US · Colour · 87mins

Although this major studio production was sent direct to video, it does have satisfying moments for more patient viewers who are in the mood for quirkiness. James Belushi is miscast as a lowlife involved in dirty deals in the desert, but Shannon Whirry compensates with an excellent, subtle performance as Belushi's abused wife. When they are unknowingly caught in a time loop caused by a nearby experiment, passer-by Kylie Travis repeatedly tries to ''do the right thing'' to prevent various disasters, though she never succeeds. It's fun and energetic until the end, but the plot is full of holes and afterwards viewers will probably come up with a long list of unanswered questions. Contains violence and some swearing. ▭

James Belushi *Frank Lloyd* • Kylie Travis *Karen* • Shannon Whirry *Rayanne* • Frank Whaley *Brian* • M Emmet Walsh *Sam* ■ *Dir* Louis Morneau • *Scr* Michael Hamilton-Wright, Robert Strauss

Return ★

Mystery
1985 · W Ger/US · Colour · 82mins

A ponderous and talky chiller revolving around hypnotic regression and dark family secrets. Karlene Crockett wants to know how her grandfather died 20-years ago and discovers that gardener John Walcutt could be his reincarnation and the key to unravelling the bizarre mystery. A disappointing adaptation of the Donald Harrington novel that squanders its few decent ideas through weak direction and over-earnest performances. Fifties *femme fatale* Anne (Lloyd) Francis, star of *Forbidden Planet* and TV's *Honey West*, puts in a rare appearance.

Karlene Crockett *Diana Stoving* • John Walcutt *Day Whittaker* • Lisa Richards *Ann Stoving* • Frederic Forrest *Brian Stoving* • Anne Lloyd Francis [Anne Francis] *Eileen Sedgely* • Lenore Zann *Susan* • Thomas Rolapp *Lucky* ■ *Dir* Andrew Silver • *Scr* Andrew Silver, from the novel *Some Other Place, the Right Place* by Donald Harrington

The Return ★★★ U

Drama
1994 · Viet · Colour · 40mins

Made when all Vietnamese films had to present a positive image of the ruling communists, *When the Tenth Month Comes* (1984) established Nhat Minh Dang among his country's most important film-makers. A decade later, with the prevailing political situation considerably more relaxed, he sampled more festival success with this astute study of how Vietnam's past impinges on its present. At the centre of events is Nguyen Thu Hien, an unhappily married schoolteacher, who is forced to reassess her life on the unexpected return of her first love, who fled three-years earlier as one of the infamous ''boat people''. In Vietnamese with English subtitles.

Nguyen Thu Hien • Tran Luc ■ *Dir* Nhat Minh Dang • *Scr* Nhat Minh Dang

Return from the Ashes ★★★

Crime thriller
1965 · UK/US · BW · 103mins

An extraordinary picture from British director J Lee Thompson in which a Jewish woman, Ingrid Thulin, returns to Paris from the Dachau concentration camp with her face and mind deeply scarred, so she has plastic surgery. Her husband Maxmilian Schell, a chess master, is now in love with his stepdaughter and at first believes Thulin is a ''double'' whom he can exploit for compensation money, but when she reveals her true identity, it leads to murder. Elements of *Vertigo*, *Les Diaboliques* and *Hiroshima, Mon Amour* combine in this bizarre tale that at times plumbs depths of awfulness yet rises to the giddiest heights of melodrama.

Maximilian Schell *Stanislaus Pilgrin* • Samantha Eggar *Fabienne* • Ingrid Thulin *Dr Michele Wolf* • Herbert Lom *Dr Charles Bovard* • Talitha Pol *Claudine* ■ *Dir* J Lee Thompson • *Scr* Julius J Epstein, Charles Blair, from the novel *Le Retour des Cendres* by Hubert Monteilhet

Return from the River Kwai ★★ 15

Second World War action adventure
1988 · UK · Colour · 97mins

A bid to recount with a certain level of realism, PoW life in the Far East during the closing months of the Second World War. Although there is no direct link with David Lean's 1957 classic film (it's even set two years later), comparisons are inevitable. Needless to say, this doesn't come close in terms of acting or direction, but still manages to be a tough, grim action movie. ▭

Edward Fox *Benford* • Denholm Elliott *Grayson* • Christopher Penn *Crawford* • George Takei *Tanaka* • Timothy Bottoms *Miller* • Richard Graham *Perry* ■ *Dir* Andrew V McLaglen • *Scr* Sargon Tamimi, Paul Mayersberg

Return from Witch Mountain ★★★★ U

Adventure
1978 · US · Colour · 89mins

Of course, it had to be Bette Davis who could disprove the old warning about scene-sharing with children few others would have the nerve or the

talent. She, however, is in her element, giving a scene-stealing performance as henchwoman to Christopher Lee's mad scientist. Lee is seeking world domination by gaining control of two extraterrestrial kids, who possess all kinds of strange powers (telekinesis, anti-gravity, cute expressions). A sequel to *Escape to Witch Mountain*, it's a Disney fantasy in which the usual milk-shake blandness has been spiked with an interesting touch of colour, courtesy of the film's legendary star. ▭

Bette Davis *Letha Wedge* • Christopher Lee *Dr Victor Gannon* • Kim Richards *Tia Malone* • Ike Eisenmann *Tony Malone* • Jack Soo *Mr Yokomoto* • Anthony James *Sickle* • Dick Bakalyan [Richard Bakalyan] *Eddie* • Ward Costello *Mr Clearcole* • Christian Juttner *Dazzler* • Poindexter *Crusher* • Brad Savage *Muscles* • Jeffrey Jacquet *Rocky* • Stu Gilliam *Dolan* ■ *Dir* John Hough • *Scr* Malcolm Marmorstein, from characters created by Alexander Key

Return Home ★★★★

Drama
1989 · Ausl · Colour · 87mins

Carefully directed by former cinematographer Ray Argall, this is a thoughtful treatise on family loyalty and the passing of traditional values. Dennis Coard turns in an impressive performance as a Melbourne stockbroker who reluctantly returns to his Adelaide roots to renew the ties he has allowed to lapse with his brother (Frankie J Holden), a small-time garage owner caught in the swell of consumerism. Also impressive is Ben Mendelsohn as the young mechanic with whom Coard strikes up a curious friendship. Unusual in its positive portrait of suburban life, this is a most pleasant surprise.

Dennis Coard *Noel McKenzie* • Frankie J Holden *Steve McKenzie* • Micki Camilleri *Judy McKenzie* • Ben Mendelsohn *Gary Wilson* • Rachel Rains *Wendy* • Alan Fletcher *Barry Marshall* ■ *Dir/Scr* Ray Argall

The Return of a Man Called Horse ★★★★ 15

Western
1976 · US · Colour · 118mins

And it's as if he'd never been away in this ''flay-it-again-m'lud'' sequel that's just as good as the original. Richard Harris is still the peer-turned-native, this time travelling from England to right the wrongs done to his adopted Sioux tribe. Sadomasochistic rituals such as the Sun Vow ceremony usually result in near-skinning alive, but director Irvin Kershner keeps it relevant to the story, while Gale Sondergaard, everyone's favourite female villain, breathes vengeful fire. Contains violence. ▭

Richard Harris *John Morgan* • Gale Sondergaard *Elk Woman* • Geoffrey Lewis *Zenas Morro* • Bill Lucking [William Lucking] *Tom Gryce* • Jorge Luke *Running Bull* • Claudio Brook *Chemin D'fer* • Enrique Lucero *Raven* • Jorge Russek *Blacksmith* • Ana De Sade *Moonstar* • Pedro Damien *Standing bear* ■ *Dir* Irvin Kershner • *Scr* Jack DeWitt, from characters created by Dorothy M Johnson

Return of a Stranger ★★

Crime drama
1937 · UK · BW · 63mins

In this creaky melodrama, a scientist disfigured in an explosion returns to London to clear his name, identify a killer and reclaim his girl. The plot is now a cliché, of course, but this remains mesmerisingly watchable because of its period production values and the sheer gall of the finale. Griffith Jones and Rosalyn Boulter are the lacklustre, but remarkably well-spoken, leads, and it's all ably directed by Victor Hanbury. Shown in the US as *Face behind the Scar* and copied in hundreds of B-movies.

Griffith Jones *James Martin* • Rosalyn Boulter *Carol* • Ellis Jeffreys *Lady Wall* • Athole Stewart *Sir Patrick Wall* • Cecil Ramage *John Forbes* • Constance Godridge *Esme* • Sylvia Marriott *Mary* • James Harcourt *Johnson* ■ *Dir* Victor Hanbury • *Scr* Akos Tolnay, Reginald Long, from a play by Rudolph Lothar

The Return of Bulldog Drummond ★

Mystery 1934 · UK · BW · 71mins

Based on a real Guards officer (Gerald Fairlie), the character of Bulldog Drummond was conceived by Fairlie's friend "Sapper" or, more correctly, H C McNeile and subsequently developed in novels and films. Drummond is a precursor to many sleuths and gentlemanly detectives. He enjoyed various incarnations including the urbane Jack Buchanan, but here Ralph Richardson takes the part. Based on *The Black Gang*, neither the role, nor the film, involving the kidnapping of Drummond's wife (Ann Todd) by a secret society of what are considered foreign undesirables, proved worthy of the great actor.

Ralph Richardson *Hugh Drummond* • Ann Todd *Phyllis Drummond* • Francis L Sullivan *Carl Peterson* • Claud Allister *Algy Longworth* • H Saxon-Snell *Zadowa* • Spencer Trevor *Sir Bryan Johnstone* • Charles Mortimer *Inspector McIver* ■ *Dir* Walter Summers • *Scr* Walter Summers, from the novel *The Black Gang* by Sapper [HC McNeile]

The Return of Captain Invincible ★★ PG

Spoof adventure 1983 · Ausl · Colour · 87mins

Intermittently enjoyable comic book spoof starring Alan Arkin as a down-and-out, alcoholic superhero dragged from his dazed retirement to save the world one last time. Christopher Lee rises to the occasion as the evil megalomaniac Mr Midnight in a cheaply-made Australian comedy fantasy, peppered with songs by *Rocky Horror Show* creator Richard O'Brien. Director Philippe (*Howling II*) Mora tries hard to combine all genres, but the film doesn't quite have the courage of his convictions. ▦

Alan Arkin *Captain Invincible* • Christopher Lee *Mr Midnight* • Michael Pate *US President* • Graham Kennedy *Australian PM* • Kate Fitzpatrick *Patty Patria* ■ *Dir* Philippe Mora • *Scr* Steven de Souza, Andrew Gaty

The Return of Count Yorga ★★★

Horror 1971 · US · Colour · 96mins

Robert Quarry dons the black cape once more in this polished picture that is superior in every way to the original *Count Yorga, Vampire*, the sexploitation movie that became a cult horror flick. This time he's developed a passion for Mariette Hartley, the daughter of the principal of the

orphanage close to his Los Angeles home. But before he can have his wicked way with her he has to overcome her dogged boyfriend Roger Perry. Everything's been done a dozen times before, but Bob Kelljan conjures up a few chills and Quarry turns on the menacing charm with some skill.

Robert Quarry *Count Yorga* • Mariette Hartley *Cynthia Nelson* • Roger Perry *Dr David Baldwin* • Yvonne Wilder *Jennifer* • Tom Toner *Reverend Thomas* ■ *Dir* Bob Kelljan • *Scr* Bob Kelljan, Yvonne Wilder

The Return of Dr Fu Manchu ★★

Mystery thriller 1930 · US · BW · 73mins

The second *Fu Manchu* movie to star Swedish character actor Warner Oland as Sax Rohmer's insidious Chinese villain, continues the evil mastermind's elaborate struggle with Scotland Yard's Nayland Smith for world domination. In this slow, but atmospheric entry, the Oriental madman, having used a secret drug that induces catalepsy to fake his death, comes back to get revenge on those responsible for killing his wife and son in the Boxer Rebellion. Oland shines in the star role, one he made his own before switching to the other side of the law and becoming the screen's most popular Charlie Chan.

Warner Oland *Dr Fu Manchu* • Neil Hamilton *Dr Jack Petrie* • Jean Arthur *Lila Eltham* ■ *Dir* Rowland V Lee • *Scr* Florence Ryerson, Lloyd Corrigan, from the novel by Sax Rohmer

The Return of Dr X ★★

Horror mystery 1939 · US · BW · 62mins

With Humphrey Bogart in a clichéd role as a murderous monster, this is a conventional account of a vampire terrorising a city. An attempt by Warner Bros to appeal to horror fans, it's notable for the inclusion of many members of the studio's acting B-league, including Dennis Morgan and Rosemary Lane. Only two years later, Bogart became a major star – and wisely steered clear of horror films for the rest of his career.

Humphrey Bogart *Marshall Quesne/Dr Maurice J Xavier* • Rosemary Lane *Joan Vance* • Wayne Morris *Walter Barnett* • Dennis Morgan *Michael Rhodes* • John Litel *Dr Francis Flegg* • Lya Lys *Angela Merrova* • Huntz Hall *Pinky* ■ *Dir* Vincent Sherman • *Scr* Lee Katz, from the story *The Doctor's Secret* by William J Makin

The Return of Dracula ★★

Horror 1958 · US · BW and Colour · 77mins

Dracula turns up in California masquerading as a refugee Transylvanian artist and starts his nasty nocturnal habits amongst the homely community. Released in the same year as Hammer's *Dracula*, this modern gothic thriller lost out in the vampire sweepstakes for being drearily highbrow in comparison. But undead Francis Lederer turning into a wolf, a bat and a curl of mist (hence the loony British retitling *The Fantastic Disappearing Man*) plus other nifty camera tricks, lift it above the average B-movie rut. Mainly for devotees who will find the more intelligent use of horror clichés a surprising bonus.

Francis Lederer *Bellac* • Norma Eberhardt *Rachel* • Ray Stricklyn *Tim* • Jimmy Baird

Mickey • Greta Granstedt *Cora* • Virginia Vincent *Jennie* • John Wengraf *Merriman* • Gage Clark [Gage Clarke] *Reverend* • John McNamara *Sheriff Bicknell* ■ *Dir* Paul Landres • *Scr* Pat Fielder

The Return of Eliot Ness ★★★ 15

Crime thriller 1991 · US · Colour · 90mins

Restoring Robert Stack to the role of Eliot Ness that he had made his own in the sixties' television series *The Untouchables*, this doughty TV movie was made in the wake of the phenomenally successful Kevin Costner/Sean Connery blockbuster of the same name. Set in 1947, 16 years after everybody's favourite T-man had put Al Capone behind bars, the film lacks both the raw edge of the original series and the style of De Palma's glossy remake. But, even though the years are showing, Stack still cuts an imposing figure as he roots out a murderer during a gang war. ▦

Robert Stack *Eliot Ness* • Charles Durning *Roger Finn* • Lisa Hartman *Madeline Whitfield* • Jack Coleman *Gil Labine* • Philip Bosco *Art Malto* • Anthony Desando *Bobby Malto* • Ron Lea *Pete Sheppard* ■ *Dir* James Contner [James A Contner] • *Scr* Michael Petryni

The Return of Frank Cannon ★★★ PG

Mystery 1980 · US · Colour · 96mins

Having starred in over a hundred episodes of the popular detective series on TV in the seventies, William Conrad was brought out of retirement for this comeback case, in which the portly private eye discovers that the suicide of an old secret service buddy might not be as clear cut as the authorities would have him believe. Directed by Corey Allen (who made his name as James Dean's "chicken-run" rival in *Rebel without a Cause*), this is a typically involving mystery, with Conrad as laconic as ever, and he's admirably supported by such small-screen stalwarts as Diana Muldaur, Joanna Pettet and Arthur Hill. ▦

William Conrad *Frank Cannon* • Allison Argo *Jessica Bingham* • Burr Debenning *Charles Kirkland* • Taylor Lacher *Sheriff Lew Garland* • Diana Muldaur *Sally Bingham* • Ed Nelson *Mike Danvers* • Joanna Pettet *Alana Richardson* ■ *Dir* Corey Allen • *Scr* James D Buchanan, Ronald L Austin

The Return of Frank James ★★★ U

Western 1940 · US · Colour · 92mins

Henry Fonda had played Frank to Tyrone Power's Jesse in the superb *Jesse James*, and in this disappointing follow-up he spends all his time searching for brothers Charles and, in particular, Bob Ford (John Carradine), the "dirty little coward" who shot his own brother. But, unfortunately, Hank has neither benefit of a decent script nor a sympathetic director, as Austrian émigré Fritz Lang makes heavy going of this lightweight material, dragging the pace to the point of boredom. The tedium of the tale is alleviated only slightly by the movie debut of God's gift to 20th Century-Fox, the beautiful Gene Tierney, who regrettably doesn't fulfil her acting potential. The

Technicolor helps, but the tempo is sluggish. ▦

Henry Fonda *Frank James/Ben Woodson* • Gene Tierney *Eleanor Stone* • Jackie Cooper *Clem/Tom Grayson* • Henry Hull *Major Rufus Cobb* • John Carradine *Bob Ford* • Charles Tannen *Charles Ford* • J Edward Bromberg *Runyon* • Donald Meek *McCoy* ■ *Dir* Fritz Lang • *Scr* Sam Hellman

The Return of Hunter: Everyone Walks in LA ★★

Drama 1995 · US · Colour · 85mins

In this murder mystery, Fred Dryer returns to the role of world-weary cop Rick Hunter, the TV detective of the eighties who owed more than a little to his feature-film inspiration, "Dirty" Harry Callahan. Here, Hunter's fiancée is murdered and her violent ex-husband becomes the prime suspect – until a complete stranger comes forward who's willing to confess to the crime. Even this intriguing twist can't lift director Bradford May's TV movie out of the ordinary, although such experienced character players as Barry Bostwick, Lisa Eilbacher and John C McGinley give it their best shot.

Fred Dryer *Rick Hunter* • Barry Bostwick *Matt Sherry* • Lisa Elibacher *Sally Vogel* • John C McGinley *Harry Mcbride* • *Dir* Bradford May

The Return of Jafar ★★ U

Animated musical 1994 · US · Colour · 73mins

An adequate, but unexceptional follow-up to Disney's *Aladdin* that, as now seems to be usual company policy, bypassed cinemas and went straight to video. Most of the original film's voice artists return as the lamp boy's good-guy genie battles an evil counterpart, but notably absent is genie-us Robin Williams, whose anarchic vocals are sorely missed. Fine for kids, though grown-ups will find less to chuckle at than they did first time round. ▦

Dan Castellaneta *Genie* • Scott Weinger *Aladdin* • Brad Kane *Aladdin (singing voice)* • Jason Alexander *Abis Mal* • Jonathan Freeman *Jafar* • Gilbert Gottfried *Iago* • Linda Larkin *Jasmine* • Liz Callaway *Jasmine (singing voice)* ■ *Dir* Toby Shelton, Tad Stones, Alan Zaslove, Ginny McSwain • *Scr* Kevin Campbell, Mirth Colao, Bill Motz, Steve Roberts, Dev Ross, Bob Roth, Jan Strand, Brian Swenlin, from a story by Douglas Langdale, Mark McCorkle, Robert Schooley, Tad Stones

The Return of Josey Wales ★ 15

Western 1986 · US · Colour · 87mins

Josey's back! But this time he ain't Clint Eastwood – so who cares? Josey is now played by Michael Parks who, in 1966, was plucked from B-movie obscurity to play Adam in John Huston's *The Bible... in the Beginning*. Tastefully lit or hiding behind the fig leaf of legend in that film, Parks did not go on to glory but sank back into B-movies. This sequel to the Eastwood classic is mainly just a series of shoot-outs. Parks also directs and he shot it in Mexico with an eye to the Latino market – much of the dialogue is in Spanish and the styling is reminiscent of those paella westerns of the seventies. An English/Spanish language film. ▦

U = SUITABLE FOR ALL Uc = SUITABLE FOR ALL, ESPECIALLY FOR YOUNG CHILDREN (VIDEO ONLY) PG = PARENTAL GUIDANCE

Michael Parks *Josey Wales* • Rafael Campos *Chato* • Bob Magruder *Ten Spot* • Paco Vela *Paco* • Everett Sifuentes *Escobedo* • Charlie McCoy *Charlie* ■ *Dir* Michael Parks • *Scr* Forrest Carter, Ro Taylor, from the novel *Vengeance Trail of Josey Wales* by Forrest Carter

The Return of Martin Guerre ★★★★ 15

Historical drama 1982 · Fr · Colour · 106mins

Infinitely superior to its Hollywood remake, *Sommersby*, Daniel Vigne's suspenseful riddle of identity is a fascinating study of the blind faith, superstition and prejudice that governed most rural communities in the mid-16th century. Gérard Depardieu typically imposes himself on proceedings as the farmer who returns a changed man after nine years at war. But just how changed is he? The winner of a César for its screenplay, this highly literate film benefits from some meticulous historical research and a sensitive performance from Nathalie Baye as the unquestioning wife. While the courtroom climax is compelling, however, several pertinent themes are left unexplored. In French with English subtitles. ▭

Gérard Depardieu *Martin Guerre* • Bernard Pierre Donnadieu *Martin Guerre* • Nathalie Baye *Bertrande de Rols* • Roger Planchon *Jean de Caros* • Maurice Jacquemont *Judge Rieux* • Isabelle Sadoyan *Catherine Boere* ■ *Dir* Daniel Vigne • *Scr* Daniel Vigne, Jean-Claude Carrière

The Return of October ★★

Comedy drama 1948 · US · Colour · 89mins

October's a racehorse, but he's also the reincarnation of Terry Moore's Uncle Willie – or so she believes in this whimsical comedy bolstered by Technicolor and an ingratiating performance by Glenn Ford, as the professor of psychology who writes a book about the girl's strange belief. James Gleason appears at the start as Willie and Dame May Whitty plays Moore's wealthy aunt. Director Joseph H Lewis shows some talent for comedy, but seems happiest shooting the racetrack sequences – although the races themselves are made up of stock shots from 1938's *Kentucky*, obtained in a deal with 20th Century-Fox. The dull title was changed for the film's original British release to the equally unexciting *A Date with Destiny*.

Glenn Ford *Prof Bentley Bassett, Jr* • Terry Moore *Terry Ramsey* • Albert Sharpe *Vince, the Tout* • James Gleason *Uncle Willie* • Dame May Whitty *Aunt Martha* • Henry O'Neill *President Hotchkiss* ■ *Dir* Joseph H Lewis • *Scr* Melvin Frank, Norman Panama, from a story by Connie Lee, Karen DeWolf

The Return of Peter Grimm ★★★

Fantasy 1935 · US · BW · 81mins

The theme of returning from the dead to see how the living are coping has always fascinated dramatists, and this adaptation of a David Belasco play has Lionel Barrymore as a crusty millionaire allowed after his death to see what a mess he made of things. Though the film suffers from an uncertain tone, with director George Nichols Jr not sure how seriously to treat the story,

the play's sound structure survives, performances are strong and the tale's premise remains intriguing and involving.

Lionel Barrymore *Peter Grimm* • Helen Mack *Catherine* • Edward Ellis *Dr Andrew MacPherson* • Donald Meek *Mr Batholomew* • George Breakston *William Van Dam* • Allen Vincent *Frederik* • James Bush *James* ■ *Dir* George Nichols Jr • *Scr* Francis Edwards Faragoh, from the play by David Belasco

The Return of Sam McCloud ★★ PG

Detective thriller 1989 · US · Colour · 89mins

The homespun homilies of the anachronistic lawman marked Sam McCloud out as a natural for politics, and in this belated sequel Dennis Weaver returns in the lead, now a senator with a greenie bent. However, when his niece is murdered in London, he goes back to his roots to solve the mystery. The English Tourist Board gets a free plug from the stock shots so beloved of American TV networks, while Brits such as Patrick Macnee, David McCallum and Roger Rees take the money and run. For fans only. ▭

Dennis Weaver *Senator Sam McCloud* • Terry Carter *Chief Joe Broadhurst* • Diana Muldaur *Chris Coughlin* • JD Cannon *Peter B Clifford* • Patrick Macnee *Tom Jamison* • David McCallum *Inspector Craig* • Roger Rees *Jason Cross* ■ *Dir* Alan J Levi • *Scr* Michael Sloan, from the character created by Herman Miller

The Return of Sherlock Holmes ★★ PG

Comedy mystery 1987 · US · Colour · 89mins

In this refreshingly original updating of a Sherlock Holmes mystery, the great detective himself is brought back to life after he's been cryogenically frozen. His rescuer is none other than the great granddaughter of his friend Dr Watson, a private eye whose visit to England turns up a lot more than she bargained for. Margaret Colin (*Independence Day*) has great fun with her part as the struggling detective who gets involved with Holmes in solving a murder case. An entertaining and clever TV movie, this will appeal not only to fans of Holmes but also to those simply looking for a good light mystery adventure. ▭

Margaret Colin *Jane Watson* • Michael Pennington *Sherlock Holmes* • Lila Kaye *Ms Houston* • Connie Booth *Violet* • Nicholas Guest *Toby* • Barry Morse *Carter Morstan* • William Hootkins *Spellman* • Tony Steedman *Doctor* • Paul Maxwell *Hopkins* • Shane Rimmer *Stark* ■ *Dir* Kevin Connor • *Scr* Bob Shayne

The Return of Swamp Thing ★★ 15

Spoof science-fiction thriller 1989 · US · Colour · 83mins

"Where do you come from?" asks a hillbilly saved from a mutant leech attack by the original (D C Comics) Swampy. "The bog", replies our leaf-in-cheek Jolly Green Giant. No comment! Louis Jourdan also returns as evil genius Dr Arcane, back in melodramatic Dr Moreau mode, and still gene-splitting to halt the ageing process. Soap queen Heather Locklear is his stepdaughter searching for the truth behind her mother's death, but

how and why she falls for Swampy in this bayou Garden of Eden fable has to be seen to be believed. It's a moss-eaten slice of splat-stick packed with laboured in-jokes, Jourdan's pet parrot is called "Gigi", and daffy heroics. ▭

Louis Jourdan *Dr Anton Arcane* • Heather Locklear *Abby Arcane* • Sarah Douglas *Dr Lana Zurrell* • Dick Durock *Swamp Thing* • Ace Mask *Dr Rochelle* • Joey Sagal *Gunn* ■ *Dir* Jim Wynorski • *Scr* Derek Spencer, Grant Morris, from the DC Comics character

Return of the Bad Men ★

Western 1948 · US · BW · 0mins

Stuff enough famous western desperadoes into one film to keep the action crowd happy and you don't have to worry too much about plot or characterisation. RKO Radio proved it with one Randolph Scott western, *Badman's Territory*, and again with this follow-up. There's the Youngers, the Daltons, Wild Bill Doolin and Billy the Kid all spoiling for a fight, but the real villainy comes from Robert Ryan's vicious Sundance Kid and the only man to stop him is Randolph Scott's marshal. Anne Jeffreys shows spirit as the reformed outlaw gal who tries to take Scott away from Jacqueline White, his decent but dull fiancée. George "Gabby" Hayes, providing comic relief as the banker, is just tiresome.

Randolph Scott *Vance* • Robert Ryan *Sundance Kid* • Anne Jeffreys *Cheyenne* • George "Gabby" Hayes *John Pettit* • Jacqueline White *Madge Allen* • Steve Brodie *Cole Younger* • Richard Powers *Jim Younger* • Robert Bray *John Younger* • Lex Barker *Emmett Dalton* • Walter Reed *Bob Dalton* • Michael Harvey *Grat Dalton* • Dean White *Billy the Kid* • Robert Armstrong *Wild Bill Doolin* ■ *Dir* Ray Enright • *Scr* Charles O'Neal, Jack Natteford, Luci Ward, from a story by Jack Natteford, Luci Ward

The Return of the Cisco Kid ★★★ U

Western 1939 · US · BW · 70mins

Third time out for matinée idol Warner Baxter as author O Henry's dashing Mexican hero, and, frankly, why not? After all, he received the first talkie best actor Oscar for the role in the 1929 film *In Old Arizona*, and did well commercially in the absurdly heroic 1931 sequel *The Cisco Kid*. But this time, eight long years later, Baxter's drinking, a decidedly substandard director (Herbert I Leeds) and a seemingly makeshift plot make for a disappointing outing, which proved to be Baxter's last as the Kid. But the poor quality didn't seem to matter to contemporary audiences, and this rollicking adventure led to a Cisco Kid movie series, starring Cesar Romero, who actually plays a supporting role here. Many viewers will recall the popular TV series with Duncan Renaldo as Cisco and Leo Carrillo as his trusty sidekick Pancho, but this is a rare chance to see the great originals.

Warner Baxter *Cisco Kid* • Lynn Bari *Ann Carver* • Cesar Romero *Lopez* • Henry Hull *Colonel Jonathan Bixby* • Kane Richmond *Alan Davis* • C Henry Gordon *Mexican Captain* • Robert Barrat *Sheriff McNally* ■ *Dir* Herbert I Leeds • *Scr* Milton Sperling, from the characters created by O Henry

Return of the Dragon ★★★

Martial arts action drama 1973 · HK · Colour · 93mins

Despite his icon status this was the only film Bruce Lee had complete control over, being director, writer and fight choreographer. It's a desperately thin tale of a country bumpkin (Lee), the antithesis of the Bond-like kung fu spy, that fans loved seeing him play in *Enter the Dragon*, who arrives in Rome to help out at a Chinese restaurant that's at the mercy of local gangsters. Typical of its genre, the dubbing is lousy, the characters are mere ciphers, dodgy seventies shirts plague the screen and there are too many clumsy comedy routines that play well in Hong Kong (it's why Jackie Chan movies are so broad humoured) but look merely amateurish to us. However, the action more than compensates: Lee's face-off with Chuck Norris inside Rome's Colosseum is one of the best two-man scraps in movie history. Norris had previously worked with Lee on the Matt Helm movie *The Wrecking Crew*, where Lee was karate advisor. Cantonese dialogue dubbed into English. ▭

Bruce Lee *Tang Lung* • Nora Miao *Chen Ching Hua* • Chuck Norris *Colt* • Wei Ping Au *Ho* • Wang Chung Hsin *Uncle Wang* • Tong Liu *Tony* • Ti Chin *Ah K'ung* ■ *Dir/Scr* Bruce Lee

Return of the Fly ★★ 15

Horror 1959 · US · BW · 76mins

The sequel to the original 1958 horror hit is a more standard black-and-white B-movie retelling of the same story, with Brett Halsey playing Al Hedison's son, repeating his father's teleportation tinkering with similarly disastrous results. Thankfully Vincent Price is back, again playing the concerned uncle, and goes a long way towards keeping things buzzing along. But, aside from a few horrific moments in a mortuary and the sick guinea pig experiment, director Edward Bernds (best known for his *Three Stooges* work) sadly stresses plot gimmicks, at the expense of an involving story. Price himself always joked that he wanted this inevitable follow-up to be called "The Zipper".

Vincent Price *François Delambre* • Brett Halsey *Phillipe Delambre* • David Frankham *Alan Hinds* • John Sutton *Inspector Charas* • Dan Seymour *Max Berthold* • Danielle de Metz *Cecile Bonnard* • Janine Graudel *Madame Bonnard* ■ *Dir* Edward Bernds • *Scr* Edward Bernds, from a story by George Langelaan

Return of the Idiot ★★★★

Drama 1999 · Cz Rep/Ger · Colour · 99mins

Based on Dostoyevsky's *The Idiot*, and clearly inspired by Milos Forman's deliciously droll sixties satires, *Peter and Pavla* and *A Blonde in Love*, this is the deceptively intricate tale of a seemingly simple man. Visiting distant relatives after a lengthy spell in an asylum, Pavel Liska is the epitome of innocence abroad as he artlessly dismantles the web of romantic deceit spun by a couple of small-town brothers and their adversarial sister lovers. The humour is as precise as it is gentle, although there are also some priceless moments of slapstick and some unexpectedly surreal imagery in Liska's recurrent nightmares. In Czech with English subtitles.

Pavel Liska *The Idiot/Frantisek* • Anna Geislerova *Anna* • Tatiana Vilhelmova *Olga* • Jiri Langmajer *Emil* • Jiri Machacek *Robert* ■ *Dir* Sasa Gedeon • *Scr* Sasa Gedeon, from the novel by Fyodor Dostoyevsky

Return of the Jedi ★★★★ U
Science-fiction fantasy
1983 · US · Colour · 131mins

Sequels are usually a case of diminishing returns, but this third instalment of the *Star Wars* saga is still essential viewing. Director Richard Marquand jumps straight in where the *The Empire Strikes Back* finished off with a stunning sequence involving the monstrous Jabba the Hutt and the pace rarely falters from then on, even if the plot is a dash stop-start at times. Mark Hamill still looks more like an enthusiastic schoolboy than an intergalactic hero, but his climactic scenes with Darth Vader work a treat, and, while adults will probably cringe at the cutesy Ewoks, their presence makes this a particular favourite with younger viewers. The massive success of the series' relaunch on video last year demonstrated that its popularity has not waned and fans are now eagerly waiting to see what George Lucas has come up with for his trilogy of prequels in updating the effects on the original film. 🖵

Mark Hamill *Luke Skywalker* • Harrison Ford *Han Solo* • Carrie Fisher *Princess Leia* • Billy Dee Williams *Lando Calrissian* • Anthony Daniels *C-3PO* • Peter Mayhew *Chewbacca* • Sebastian Shaw *Anakin Skywalker* • Ian McDiarmid *Emperor Palpatine* • Frank Oz *Yoda* • David Prowse [Dave Prowse] *Darth Vader* • James Earl Jones *Voice of Darth Vader* • Alec Guinness *Obi-Wan ''Ben''Kenobi* • Kenny Baker (1) *R2-D2* ■ *Dir* Richard Marquand • *Scr* Lawrence Kasdan, George Lucas, from a story by George Lucas

Return of the Killer Tomatoes ★ 15
Horror comedy   1988 · US · Colour · 94mins

As *Attack of the Killer Tomatoes* was a big video rental (solely because of its catchy title), a belated sequel was commissioned and it is even worse than the original. Professor Gangrene (John Astin) turns a tomato into a sexy babe by playing music at it and plans to take over the world with a bevy of similarly exposed red fruits. Stupid send-ups of popular TV commercials and movies (two Spielbergs get satirised – *1941* and *ET*) mix uneasily with broad science-fiction farce in director John DeBello's charmless wonder, which is only notable for an early appearance by future heart-throb George Clooney. 🖵

Anthony Starke *Chad* • Karen Mistal *Tara* • George Clooney *Matt* • Steve Lundquist *Igor* • John Astin *Professor Gangrene* ■ *Dir* John DeBello • *Scr* Constantine Dillon, John DeBello, John Stephen Peace [Steve Peace]

Return of the Living Dead ★★★ 18
Comedy horror   1985 · US · Colour · 86mins

This enjoyable horror comedy marked the directorial debut of long-time sci-fi scribe Dan O'Bannon, of *Dark Star* and *Alien* fame. This semi-sequel to George

A Romero's 1968 cult classic *Night of the Living Dead* is like an D C comic come alive, in that it'll make you laugh and squirm – often at the same time. ''They're back. They're hungry. And they're not vegetarian,'' blared the poster. O'Bannon cleverly makes the zombies – rather than the actors – the real stars of this movie and, unlike the Romero variety, these can speak, though they're mostly limited to spouting, ''Brains, more brains!'' The brain-eaters are the result of two bumbling workers who spill a missing army shipment of top-secret gas, which then contaminates the local cemetery where a gang of punks are holding a party. Later, after munching on some policemen, a zombie calls the local precinct and orders them to, ''Send more cops!''. A must for horror fans, this was followed by two sequels of varying quality. 🖵

Clu Gulager *Burt* • James Karen *Frank* • Don Calfa *Ernie* • Thom Mathews *Freddy* • Beverly Randolph *Tina* • John Philbin *Chuck* • Jewel Shepard *Casey* • Miguel A Nunez Jr *Spider* ■ *Dir* Dan O'Bannon • *Scr* Dan O'Bannon, from a story by Judy Ricci, John Russo, Russell Streiner

Return of the Living Dead Part II ★★ 18
Comedy horror   1988 · US · Colour · 85mins

Be warned: writer/director Ken Wiederhorn, who also made *Meatballs 2*, likened this movie to the *Police Academy* series. It's certainly true the emphasis is on humour at the expense of horror – most of it, it must be said, unintentional. Once again small-town America is overrun with brain-eating zombies, the by-products of toxic waste from bacteriological warfare, which has seeped into a local graveyard with familiar results. And it's up to the usual motley crew of teens to sort it out. This predictable sequel is dull and repetitive. Even the gore bores after a while and the zombies look like rejects from Michael Jackson's *Thriller* video. ''Just when you thought it was safe to be dead,'' said the poster. In fact, the scariest thing about this movie is the dawning realisation that a part three was bound to follow. 🖵

James Karen *Ed* • Thom Mathews *Joey* • Dana Ashbrook *Tom Essex* • Marsha Dietlein *Lucy Wilson* • Philip Bruns *Doc Mandel* • Michael Kenworthy *Jesse Wilson* • Suzanne Snyder *Brenda* • Thor Van Lingen *Billy* • Jason Hogan *Johnny* ■ *Dir/Scr* Ken Wiederhorn

Return of the Living Dead III ★★★ 18
Horror   1993 · US · Colour · 92mins

After the risible *Return of the Living Dead Part II* , the series got back on track with this splatter fest from Brian Yuzna, producer of the *Re-Animator* movies. Dispensing with the spoof elements of its predecessors, this is a darker and surprisingly intelligent mix of gore, special effects and tragic romance, which can only be described as *Romeo and Juliet* on acid. J Trevor Edmond is the lovelorn teen who uses the zombie gas that caused such chaos in the earlier movies to resurrect his girlfriend, after she is killed in a motorcycle accident, with predictable results. The subplot of a Pentagon general working on turning the dead

into soldiers, is an idea worthy of a movie on its own. Yuzna directs with his usual bursts of imaginative sensationalism, not least having a S M pierced zombie in the lead role – a movie first. 🖵

Mindy Clarke *Julie* • J Trevor Edmond *Curt Reynolds* • Kent McCord *Colonel John Reynolds* • Basil Wallace *Riverman* ■ *Dir* Brian Yuzna • *Scr* Jon Penney

The Return of the Man from UNCLE ★★ PG
Spy adventure   1983 · US · Colour · 92mins

Nostalgia rules in this periodically average resurrection of one of the sixties most famous TV shows. Back as the improbably named Napoleon Solo and Ilya Kuryakin, Robert Vaughn and David McCallum are lured out of retirement by new UNCLE boss Patrick Macnee (taking a siesta from *The Avengers*) to stop evil THRUSH agent Anthony Zerbe from holding the world to nuclear ransom. The plot is James Bond on the cheap and Ray Austin's direction is definitively lacklustre, but Vaughn and McCallum are one of those natural double acts and the chemistry between them hasn't faded with time. The Bond connection is underlined by a cheeky cameo from George Lazenby as the Aston Martin driving spy. This was intended as the pilot for a new television series that never materialised; ever since the huge success of *Mission Impossible*'s big-screen conversion, there have been rumours of a possible big-budget UNCLE movie. 🖵

Robert Vaughn *Napoleon Solo* • David McCallum *Illya Kuryakin* • Patrick Macnee *Sir John Raleigh* • Tom Mason *Benjamin Kowalski* • Gayle Hunnicutt *Andrea Markovitch* • Geoffrey Lewis *Janus* • Anthony Zerbe *Justin Sepheran* • Keenan Wynn *Piers Castillian* • George Lazenby *JB* ■ *Dir* Ray Austin • *Scr* Michael Sloan, from the TV series by Norman Felton, Sam H Rolfe

The Return of the Musketeers ★★ PG
Swashbuckling comedy adventure
1989 · UK/Fr/Sp · Colour · 101mins

Fifteen years after the success of his sparkling version of Alexandre Dumas's swashbuckling favourite, Richard Lester reunited the musketeers in this bid to save Charles I of England from the executioner's axe. Roy Kinnear's tragic death following a riding accident obviously sapped everyone's enthusiasm for the project and, while there are some witty jokes about the ravages of time, this might have been one occasion when the old adage ''the show must go on'' could have been ignored. The Dumas book, on which the story is based, *Twenty Years After*, inspired the marginally more successful Bertrand Tavernier 1994 film *D'Artagnan's Daughter*. Contains swearing and violence. 🖵

Michael York *D'Artagnan* • Oliver Reed *Athos* • Frank Finlay *Porthos* • C Thomas Howell *Raoul* • Kim Cattrall *Justine* • Geraldine Chaplin *Queen Anne* • Roy Kinnear *Planchet* • Christopher Lee *Rochefort* • Philippe Noiret *Cardinal Mazarin* • Richard Chamberlain *Aramis* ■ *Dir* Richard Lester • *Scr* George MacDonald Fraser, from the novel *Vingt Ans Après* by Alexandre Dumas

The Return of the Native ★★★
Period drama   1994 · US · Colour · 99mins

Catherine Zeta Jones is in ''perfick'' bloom as the entrancing Eustacia Vye, the ill-fated heroine of one of Thomas Hardy's greatest novels, buffeted by 19th-century superstition and gossip when she returns to the village of Egdon Heath. Orginally shown here in the BBC's *Screen Two* strand, it made its mark on US television in the *Hallmark Hall of Fame* series. Jack Gold, still remembered for his TV dramatisation of Quentin Crisp's autobiography *The Naked Civil Servant*, directs with a keen eye for period detail.

Catherine Zeta-Jones *Eustacia Vye* • Clive Owen *Damon Wildeve* • Joan Plowright *Mrs Yeobright* • Ray Stevenson *Clym Yeobright* • Steven Mackintosh *Diggory Venn* • Claire Skinner *Thomasin Yeobright* • Paul Rogers *Captain Vye* • Celia Imrie *Susan Nunsuch* ■ *Dir* Jack Gold • *Scr* Robert W Lenski, from the novel by Thomas Hardy

The Return of the Pink Panther ★★★ PG
Comedy   1974 · UK · Colour · 107mins

With his career flagging, Peter Sellers repeatedly returned to his Inspector Clouseau role, and everyone should be thankful. This is Blake Edwards and Sellers working together at their best, producing memorable moments of film comedy. Clouseau's attempts to woo Catherine Schell with his Bogart-style chat-up lines had even his co-star in fits of laughter, which they thankfully kept on screen. Not as good as the first in the series, but still great fun. 🖵

Peter Sellers *Inspector Clouseau* • Christopher Plummer *Sir Charles Litton* • Catherine Schell *Claudine* • Herbert Lom *Chief Inspector Dreyfus* • Peter Arne *Colonel Sharki* • Peter Jeffrey *General Wadafi* • Grégoire Aslan *Chief of Lugash Police* • David Lodge *Mac* • Graham Stark *Pepi* • Eric Pohlmann *Fat man* • André Maranne *François* • Burt Kwouk *Cato* ■ *Dir* Blake Edwards • *Scr* Frank Waldman, Blake Edwards, from a character created by Blake Edwards, Maurice Richlin

The Return of the Scarlet Pimpernel ★★ U
Historical drama   1937 · UK · BW · 74mins

Leslie Howard had such a hit with *The Scarlet Pimpernel* in 1934 that Alexander Korda immediately ordered a sequel – for far less than the budget of the original. The script was hashed by many hands and was intended to carry parallels with Hitler's Germany. A second-rung German director, Hanns Schwarz, was brought in and barely survived the production. After Howard turned the part down to play in a little something called *Gone with the Wind*, the role of Sir Percy Blakeney went to Barry K Barnes, a stage actor who made his screen debut. Being a Korda production, it looks handsome enough, but that's the best one can say. A second sequel (*The Elusive Pimpernel*), by Powell and Pressburger, also bombed in 1950. 🖵

Barry K Barnes *Sir Percy Blakeney/The Scarlet Pimpernel* • Sophie Stewart *Marguerite Blakeney* • Margaretta Scott *Theresa Cabarrus* • James Mason *Jean Tallien* • Francis Lister

Chauvelin • Anthony Bushell *Sir Andrew Ffoulkes* • Patrick Barr *Lord Hastings* • David Tree *Lord Harry Denning* • Henry Oscar *Maximilien de Robespierre* ■ *Dir* Hans Schwartz [Hanns Schwarz] • *Scr* Lajos Biro, Arthur Wimperis, Adrian Brunel, from the novel by Baroness Orczy

Return of the Secaucus Seven ★★★★

Drama   1980 · US · Colour · 109mins

John Sayles's directing debut was shot for a mere $60,000 and deals with the reunion of seven friends, all of whom were part of the student protest movement of the sixties and are now definitely older, richer and perhaps wiser. There's a teacher, a singer, a doctor and so on and they talk, attend a play, talk some more, have sex, get arrested and go their separate ways. It has the density of a novel and the non-starry cast is simply marvellous, each creating a real character, yet none making too big a show of it. This is a real ensemble piece that is often regarded as superior to the very similar, big-budgeted, starry Lawrence Kasdan film *The Big Chill*.

Bruce MacDonald *Mike* • Adam LeFevre *JT* • Gordon Clapp *Chip* • Karen Trott *Maura* • David Strathairn *Ron* • Marisa Smith *Carol* • Carolyn Brooks *Meg* • John Sayles *Howie* ■ *Dir/Scr* John Sayles

Return of the Seven ★★★

Western   1966 · US · Colour · 95mins

The title of this sequel to *The Magnificent Seven*, is more enticing than truthful, for only Yul Brynner actually returns from John Sturges's blistering translation of Akira Kurosawa's *Seven Samurai*. Of the newcomers, trusty tough guys Warren Oates and Claude Akins alone cut the mustard as Brynner and his band attempt to liberate a Mexican village from the slavery imposed by a megalomaniac father, grieving for his dead son. Director Burt Kennedy could always be depended upon to grind out robust westerns, but Larry Cohen's derivative script gives him too little to get his teeth into.

Yul Brynner *Chris* • Robert Fuller *Vin* • Warren Oates *Colbee* • Claude Akins *Frank* • Virgilio Texeira *Luis* • Julian Mateos *Chico* • Jordan Christopher *Manuel* • Emilio Fernandez *Lorca* • Rudy Acosta [Rodolfo Acosta] *Lopez* • Elisa Montes *Petra* • Fernando Rey *Priest* ■ *Dir* Burt Kennedy • *Scr* Larry Cohen

The Return of the Soldier ★★★PG

Period drama   1982 · UK · Colour · 98mins

Alan Bates is in the trenches, leaving wife, Julie Christie emotionally frozen in limbo and cousin, Ann-Margret worried sick and heaving with desire for him. Then Bates returns – shellshocked and an amnesiac, he may as well be dead. Instead he runs off with an old flame – dour Glenda Jackson, nursing a big social chip on her shoulder. Based on the novel by Rebecca West, this is an impeccably mounted costume drama in which every class division, every unsaid emotion and every napkin knows its place. But it also offers the spectacle of three fine actresses delicately jousting with each other over Bates,

the prettiest frock and the best lines. There are glimpses, too, of future TV stars Kevin Whately and Pauline Quirke in minor roles. ▭

Alan Bates *Captain Chris Baldry* • Ann-Margret *Jenny* • Glenda Jackson *Margaret Grey* • Julie Christie *Kitty Baldry* • Jeremy Kemp *Frank* • Edward De Souza *Edward* • Frank Finlay *William Grey* • Ian Holm *Dr Anderson* • Pauline Quirke *Girl searching in hospital* • Kevin Whately *Hostile soldier's mate* ■ *Dir* Alan Bridges • *Scr* Hugh Whitemore, from a novel by Rebecca West

The Return of the Texas Chainsaw Massacre ★★★18

Horror   1995 · US · Colour · 86mins

Written and directed by Kim Henkel – the co-scripter of Tobe Hooper's original – the fourth journey back to the Ed Gein well of gory inspiration still appalls, shocks and horrifies. An unofficial remake of the first film, which rings weird changes on the whole demented, ultra-sadistic atmosphere, this has four senior Prom revellers taking a wrong turning down a dark Texas road and coming into contact with the cannibal clan who humiliate, torture and, finally, kill them for fun. Early appearances by Renee Zellweger and Matthew McConaughey robustly rev Henkel's *Chainsaw* up to full power. Zellweger takes over the Marilyn Burns role to sympathetic perfection, while McConaughey's maniacal mood swings, dwarf the rest of the barking brood for sheer viciousness. A pulse-pounding chiller-diller making completely explicit what the original only hinted at.

Renee Zellweger *Jenny* • Matthew McConaughey *Vilmer* • Robert Jacks *Leatherface* • Tonie Perenski *Darla* • Joe Stevens *W E* • Lisa Newmyer *Heather* • John Harrison *Sean* • Tyler Cone *Barry* ■ *Dir/Scr* Kim Henkel

The Return of the Vampire ★

Horror   1943 · US · BW · 68mins

Playing a vampire for the first time since *Dracula* in 1931, Bela Lugosi is Armand Tesla (because Universal wouldn't let Columbia use its copyright name), a blood-sucker revived when a German bomb hits a cemetery during the Blitz. Our ill-humoured hero is then doomed to wander around foggy wartime London with a werewolf minion in tow to execute an aimless revenge plot. Crude and cornball, this graveyard and drawing-room exercise in plagiarist pastiche features a reasonable face-melting fade-out – if you last that long.

Bela Lugosi *Armand Tesla* • Frieda Inescort *Lady Jane Ainsley* • Nina Foch *Nicki Saunders* • Roland Varno *John Ainsley* • Miles Mander *Sir Frederick Fleet* • Matt Willis *Andreas Obry* • Ottola Nesmith *Elsa* • Gilbert Emery *Professor Saunders* ■ *Dir* Lew Landers • *Scr* Griffin Jay, Randall Faye, from an idea by Kurt Neumann

Return to Glennascaul ★★★U

Supernatural drama
1951 · US · Colour and BW · 23mins

Orson Welles was in the middle of his interminable *Othello* shoot when he cameoed in this diverting Irish ghost story, as a favour to writer/director

Hilton Edwards, whom he'd known since their days at Dublin's Gate Theatre. However, the brunt of the action is carried by Michael Lawrence, who relates the LeFanu-style tale of his midnight encounter with a long-deceased mother and daughter. Views of the isolated house, both in its baroque cosiness and its eerie desolation, are stylishly achieved. But the ending is more suited to a shaggy dog story than a genuinely Gothic chiller.

Orson Welles *Orson Welles* • Michael Lawrence *Sean Merriman* • Sheila Richards *Mrs Campbell* • Helena Hughes *Lucy Campbell* ■ *Dir/Scr* Hilton Edwards

Return to Green Acres ★

Comedy   1990 · US · Colour · 92mins

It has to be said that the original American sitcom *Green Acres* was hardly in the same league as other sixties' series such as *Get Smart* and *Bewitched*. So, unsurprisingly, a switch in decades has done little to improve its content. Eddie Albert and Eva Gabor reprise their roles, but, given that these city folk have now been living in the country for over 20 years, the original "fish out of water" concept doesn't really make much sense. The fact that it looks as cheap as the original TV series is no help either.

Eddie Albert *Oliver Douglas* • Eva Gabor *Lisa Douglas* • Pat Buttram *Mr Haney* • Tom Lester *Eb* • Mary Tanner *Daisy Ziffel* ■ *Dir* William Asher • *Scr* Craig Heller, Guy Shulman, from characters created by Jay Sommers

Return to Macon County ★★15

Drama   1975 · US · Colour · 85mins

This disappointing follow-up to the cult hit *Macon County Line*, is distinguished only by the casting of Nick Nolte and Don Johnson in early roles. This is really a sequel in name and setting only, since most of the characters in the first movie were killed off. And where the original focused on the horrors and violence of backwoods America, this goes down the *American Graffiti* route of a jukebox-friendly soundtrack for a tale of teen sex and hot-rod racing. Nolte and Johnson play two youngsters who spend most of the movie picking up girls, driving fast and being chased by a vengeful cop. Richard Compton is back in the director's chair but seems to have nothing of interest left to say to pad out a very thin potboiler. ▭

Nick Nolte *Bo Hollinger* • Don Johnson *Harley McKay* • Robin Mattson *Junell* • Eugene Daniels *Tom* • Matt Greene *Pete* • Devon Ericson *Betty* • Ron Prather *Steve* • Robert Viharo *Sergeant Whittaker* ■ *Dir/Scr* Richard Compton

Return to Me ★★PG

Romantic comedy drama
2000 · US · Colour · 116mins

A recently widowed architect, David Duchovny falls in love with beautiful young waitress Minnie Driver. The catch is – she's got his late wife's heart! You'll think twice about donating your organs after watching this mawkish romantic drama, which marks the directorial debut of actress Bonnie Hunt (*Jumanji*, *Beethoven*). The

Chicago locations are well used, and a colourful cast (Robert Loggia, Carroll O'Connor, James Belushi) deftly hint at the city's broad ethnic mix. Duchovny, however, is a dour leading man, while Driver is strangely subdued as his impossibly perfect love interest. Joely Richardson appears briefly as David's doomed spouse, while Hunt, who co-wrote the screenplay with Don Lake, takes a supporting role.

David Duchovny *Bob Rueland* • Minnie Driver *Grace Briggs* • Carroll O'Connor *Marty O'Reilly* • Robert Loggia *Angelo Pardipillo* • Bonnie Hunt *Megan Dayton* • David Alan Grier *Charlie Johnson* • Joely Richardson *Elizabeth Rueland* • Eddie Jones *Emmett McFadden* • James Belushi *Joe Dayton* ■ *Dir* Bonnie Hunt • *Scr* Bonnie Hunt, Don Lake, from a story by Bonnie Hunt, Don Lake, Andrew Stern, Samantha Goodman

Return to Oz ★★★PG

Fantasy   1985 · US · Colour · 105mins

Disney recaptures the dark side of L Frank Baum's *Oz* stories in this exciting sequel to the 1939 classic. Fairuza Balk is wonderful as Dorothy, who ends up back in a ruined Oz facing the evil Nome King and Princess Mombi with her friends Pumpkinhead, Tik Tok the clockwork man and a talking chicken. Sombre in tone it may be, but director Walter Murch's non-musical is imaginative and hugely appealing. Will Vinton's Claymation process animates the rock faces as part of the colourful special-effects extravaganza. ▭

Fairuza Balk *Dorothy Gale* • Nicol Williamson *Dr Worley/Nome King* • Jean Marsh *Nurse Wilson/Princess Mombi* • Piper Laurie *Aunt Em* • Matt Clark *Uncle Henry* • Michael Sundin *Tik Tok* • Sean Barrett *Tik Tok's voice* • Stewart Larange *Jack Pumpkinhead* • Brian Henson *Jack Pumpkinhead's Voice* • Steve Norrington *Gump* • Justin Case *Scarecrow* ■ *Dir* Walter Murch • *Scr* Walter Murch, Gill Dennis, from the books by L Frank Baum • *Cinematographer* David Watkin • *Art Director* Norman Reynolds

Return to Paradise ★★

Romance   1953 · US · Colour · 100mins

Gary Cooper, pursuing a peaceable devil-may-care beachcombing existence on a South Seas paradise, has a love affair with island girl Roberta Haynes and clashes with puritanical missionary Barry Jones. Haynes dies in childbirth and Cooper leaves, only to return during the Second World War when he meets his now grown-up daughter. Directed on location in the islands of Western Samoa by Mark Robson, utilising Technicolor and the islanders themselves in small parts and as extras, the film beguiles with its authentic atmosphere and flavour, but is too leisurely and erratic to be fully satisfying.

Gary Cooper *Mr Morgan* • Roberta Haynes *Maeva* • Barry Jones *Pastor Corbett* • Moira MacDonald *Turia* • John Hudson *Harry Faber* ■ *Dir* Mark Robson • *Scr* Charles Kaufman, from the short story *Mr Morgan* by James A Michener • *Cinematographer* Winton C Hoch

Return to Paradise ★★★★15

Drama   1998 · US · Colour · 107mins

Would you let a friend die in a Malaysian prison for an offence you committed? That's the dilemma facing Vince Vaughn and David Conrad when lawyer Anne Heche tells them Joaquin Phoenix will hang unless they go back to Asia and serve their part of his prison sentence. Based on the 1989 French success *Force Majeure*, director Joseph Ruben weaves a wrenching tragedy out of the awesome predicament, mining every ounce of indignation and empathy. Acted with anguished conviction, Ruben's crisis-of-conscience thriller doesn't take any easy options and the result casts a singularly provocative spell. With an eye on superior production values and its ear on truthful dialogue, this thematically complex *Midnight Express* revisited, is a great testament to the human spirit and its unerring strength in desperate times. Contains swearing, drug abuse and violence. ⬜

Vince Vaughn *Sheriff* • Anne Heche *Beth* • Joaquin Phoenix *Lewis* • David Conrad *Tony* • Vera Farmiga *Kerrie* • Nick Sandow *Ravitch* • Jada Pinkett Smith *MJ Major* • Ming Lee *Mr Chandran* • Joel De La Fuente *Mr Doramin* ▪ *Dir* Joseph Ruben • *Scr* Wesley Strick, Bruce Robinson

Return to Peyton Place ★★★

| Drama | 1961 · US · Colour · 121mins |

A sequel to the hit 1957 feature film *Peyton Place*, this offers the same sensational mix as before and needs little comment for devotees of its predecessor, Grace Metalious's original bestselling novel, or the long-running TV soap. Carol Lynley as Allison Mackenzie, who provokes outrage in her home town when she publishes her first novel, a thinly veiled exposé of the town's inhabitants. Utterly predictable glossy tosh, involving adultery, rape, bigotry and home truths, it showcases the then relative newcomer Tuesday Weld and offers a standout performance from Mary Astor, whose elegant presence had graced many a more refined melodrama in the past. Actor José Ferrer directed.

Carol Lynley *Allison MacKenzie* • Jeff Chandler *Lewis Jackman* • Eleanor Parker *Connie Rossi* • Mary Astor *Roberta Carter* • Robert Sterling *Mike Rossi* • Luciana Paluzzi *Raffaella Carter* • Tuesday Weld *Selena Cross* • Brett Halsey *Ted Carter* ▪ *Dir* José Ferrer • *Scr* Ronald Alexander, from the novel by Grace Metalious

A Return to Salem's Lot ★★★ 18

| Horror | 1987 · US · Colour · 96mins |

Larry Cohen can always be relied upon for quirky reinterpretations of horror myths. In this genuine treat for undead cultists, he pitches his tone a long way from the original Stephen King book for a loose semi-sequel. Cohen regular Michael Moriarty, plays an anthropologist arriving, with son Ricky Addison Reed, in the infamous title locale to take over an inherited farmhouse, only to find the vampire population want him to set down their venerable history for posterity. This is unique in the annals of fang-in-cheek fright for actually delving into the practicalities of being a vampire – how to touch up lipgloss after blood-sucking, breed daylight-tolerant offspring and buy real estate that will accrue in value. Cohen happily whittles

away at the American Dream, offering plenty of satire and allegory, as well as examining moral dilemmas, plus fine performances by old-timers June Havoc, Evelyn Keyes and director Samuel Fuller, who steals the show as a single-minded vampire hunter. ⬜

Michael Moriarty *Joe Weber –Dad* • Richard Addison Reed *Jeremy Weber* • Andrew Duggan *Judge Axel* • Samuel Fuller *Dr Van Meer* • June Havoc *Aunt Clara* • Ronee Blakley *Sally* • Evelyn Keyes *Mrs Axel* ▪ *Scr* Larry Cohen, James Dixon, from a story by Larry Cohen, from the novel *Salem's Lot* by Stephen King

Return to Snowy River ★★

Western adventure
1988 · Ausl · Colour · 110mins

Brian Dennehy steals the limelight in a role first played in 1982 by Kirk Douglas in this below-par sequel to *The Man from Snowy River*, the tale of feuding Australian ranchers. Tom Burlinson plays a strong and silent type, who left Snowy River to make his fortune, but now wants to come back to his former girlfriend. Burlinson and Sigrid Thornton reprise the roles they played better in George Miller's original film. But the spectacular scenery and the wonderful horses are some compensation for a story with insufficient focus and underdeveloped characters.

Tom Burlinson *Jim Craig* • Sigrid Thornton *Jessica Harrison* • Brian Dennehy *Harrison* • Nicholas Eadie *Alistair Patton* • Mark Hembrow *Seb* • Bryan Marshall *Hawker* ▪ *Dir* Geoff Burrowes • *Scr* John Dixon, Geoff Burrowes

Return to the Blue Lagoon
★ 15

Romantic adventure
1991 · US · Colour · 97mins

While 1980's *The Blue Lagoon* itself a remake of a 1949 film had a certain grimly humorous value, this sequel lacks even that, as Brian Krause playing the son of Brooke Shields's character from the original and *The Fifth Element*'s Milla Jovovich experience puberty and nudity on a deserted island. A textbook example of a disaster that amazingly manages not only to contain bad acting and an appalling script, but also some of the most unconvincing love scenes ever committed to film. Contains nudity. ⬜

Milla Jovovich *Lilli* • Brian Krause *Richard* • Lisa Pelikan *Sarah Hargrave* • Courtney Phillips *Young Lilli* • Garette Patrick Ratliff *Young Richard* ▪ *Dir* William A Graham • *Scr* Leslie Stevens, from the novel *The Garden of God* by Henry de Vere Stacpoole

Return to Treasure Island
★★ U

Adventure
1954 · US · Colour · 75mins

What kind of a name is Jamesina Hawkins? Still, it gives you an idea of how desperate the producers of this updating of Robert Louis Stevenson's classic adventure really were. Pirate descendant, Dawn Addams, is joined in her bid to find Captain Flint's treasure by archaeology student, Tab Hunter (a feeble forerunner of Indiana Jones), who relies on a little brawn to outwit bogus professor, Porter Hall and blind villain, James Seay. It's meagre fare, but what's most depressing is

that it was directed by E A Dupont, the maestro responsible for the silent classic *Variety*.

Tab Hunter *Clive Stone* • Dawn Addams *Jamesina Hawkins* • Porter Hall *Maximillian Harris* • James Seay *Felix Newman* • Harry Lauter *Parker* • William Cottrell *Cookie* • Henry Rowland *Williams* • Lane Chandler *Cardigan* ▪ *Dir* EA Dupont • *Scr* Aubrey Wisberg, Jack Pollexfen, from their story

Return to Two Moon Junction ★★ 18

| Erotic drama | 1994 · US · Colour · 92mins |

A passable revisiting of the torrid territory of Zalman King's original, this steamy slice of soft-core porn is about the bodice-ripping relationship between a well-to-do southern woman and a well-muscled sculptor. There's no King this time. And the original stars of *Two Moon Junction*, Sherilyn Fenn and Richard Tyson, are nowhere to be seen either. Otherwise, this mildly erotic "boy bonks girl" drama delivers exactly what genre fans demand. That means nice-looking leads, photogenic locations and oodles of softish sex scenes. ⬜

Louise Fletcher *Grandma Belle* • Mindy Clarke *Savannah* • John Clayton Schafer *Jake* • Montrose Hagins *Ruth* ▪ *Dir* Farhad Mann • *Scr* Dyanne Asimow

Return to Yesterday ★★ U

| Drama | 1940 · UK · BW · 69mins |

English actor Clive Brook, who enjoyed some success in Hollywood, stars in this British film about an English actor who has found success in Hollywood. Yearning for the simplicity of his past, however, he buys his way into a season with a humble British rep company. Leading lady, Anna Lee, complicates things by falling in love with him. Directed by Robert Stevenson, a pacifist who publicised his resentment of British film-makers escaping the war by fleeing to Hollywood, despite being a nice guy, this is a mediocre and technically inadequate film.

Clive Brook *Robert Maine* • Anna Lee *Carol Sands* • Dame May Whitty *Mrs Truscott* • Hartley Power *Regan* • Milton Rosmer *Sambourne* • David Tree *Peter Thropp, playwright* • Olga Lindo *Grace Sambourne* • Garry Marsh *Charlie Miller* ▪ *Dir* Robert Stevenson • *Scr* Robert Stevenson, Margaret Kennedy, Roland Pertwee, Angus MacPhail, from the play *Goodness How Sad!* by Robert Morley

Reuben, Reuben ★★★ 15

| Comedy | 1983 · US · Colour · 95mins |

Tom Conti was Oscar nominated for his tour de force as an impossible, alcoholic, womanising, flamboyantly verbose Scottish poet – a character shamelessly but affectionately inspired by Welsh icon Dylan Thomas and Ireland's Brendan Behan – who trades on his fading literary celebrity to scrounge off the generous hospitality of thrilled female admirers in a sleepy American university town. Inspiration to pull himself together comes in the shape of winsome young student Kelly McGillis (in her screen debut). The old-fashioned, but witty script by the venerable Julius J Epstein, co-writer of *Casablanca*, and charming

performances give this lightweight throwback appeal. ⬜

Tom Conti *Gowan McGland* • Kelly McGillis *Geneva Spofford* • Roberts Blossom *Frank Spofford* • Cynthia Harris *Bobby Springer* • E Katherine Kerr *Lucille Haxby* • Joel Fabiani *Dr Haxby* • Lois Smith *Mare Spofford* ▪ *Dir* Robert Ellis Miller • *Scr* Julius J Epstein, from a novel by Peter DeVries, from the play *Spofford* by Herman Shumlin

Reunion ★★ 15

Historical drama
1989 · Fr/W Ger/UK · Colour · 105mins

Samuel West and Christien Anholt give mature performances and Jason Robards turns in a dignified cameo in this thought-provoking drama, about the interracial implications of Hitler's rise to power and the pain of coming to terms with the past. But it's the behind the camera credits that make this co-production so fascinating. Jerry Schatzberg directs steadily from a Harold Pinter script, while the stylish sets were created by the veteran Alexandre Trauner, who had designed some of the most famous French films of all time during his 60-year career. The prolific Philippe Sarde provides a typically appropriate score.

Jason Robards [Jason Robards Jr] *Henry Strauss* • Christien Anholt *Hans Strauss* • Samuel West *Konradin Von Lohenburg* • Françoise Fabian *Countess Grafin Von Lohenburg* • Maureen Kerwin *Lisa, Henry's daughter* • Barbara Jefford *Madame Strauss* ▪ *Dir* Jerry Schatzberg • *Scr* Harold Pinter, from a novel by Fred Uhlman

Reunion ★★

| Drama | 1994 · US · Colour · 97mins |

The most surprising thing about this far-fetched drama which owes more than a little to *Ghost*, is that it was co-written by Ronald Bass, whose other credits include *Rain Man*, *Dangerous Minds* and the Julia Roberts comedy *My Best Friend's Wedding*. Marlo Thomas stars as a mother who is so grief-stricken at the death of one of her young twins that she finds consolation only in the periodic visits of his spirit. That excellent actress Lee Grant, directs without undue reliance on tear-jerking melodrama, but the rift that develops between Thomas and her neglected husband Peter Strauss, and their eventual making-up, follows entirely predictable lines.

Marlo Thomas *Jessie Yates* • Peter Strauss *Sam Yates* • Frances Sternhagen *Tobie Yates* • Courtney Chase *Meggie Yates* • Matthew Kelly *Jamie Yates* • LeeLee Sobieski *Anna* ▪ *Dir* Lee Grant • *Scr* Ronald Bass, John Pielmeier, from the novel *Points of Light* by Linda Gray Sexton

Reunion in France ★★★★ U

Second World War romantic drama
1942 · US · BW · 99mins

Joan Crawford a vain, thoughtless, wealthy French woman, interested only in her lover Philip Dorn and her wardrobe, undergoes a transformation after the Nazi occupation of France. Believing that wealthy industrialist Dorn is a high-level collaborator, she develops a new awareness and a sense of patriotism, which is further fuelled by her accidental involvement with an American airman (John Wayne) who is fleeing the Gestapo. Directed

with a European sensibility and a hard edge by Jules Dassin – despite some mawkish war drama is – despite some mawkish moments, mainly involving Wayne, and the odd lapse into melodrama – interesting, taut and compelling. It features what must surely be one of Crawford's best performances. ▱

Joan Crawford *Michele de la Becque* • John Wayne *Pat Talbot* • Philip Dorn *Robert Cortot* • Reginald Owen *Schultz* • Albert Basserman *Gen Hugo Schroeder* • John Carradine *Ulrich Windler* ▪ *Dir* Jules Dassin • *Scr* Jan Lustig, Marvin Borowsky, Marc Connelly, Charles Hoffman, from a story by Ladislaus Bus-Fekete [Leslie Bush-Fekete]

Reunion in Vienna ★★
Romantic comedy   1933 · US · BW · 97mins

Former lovers Elena (Diana Wynyard) and Rudolf (John Barrymore) meet after 10 years, at a monarchists' party in Vienna. Wynard is now married to a famous psychoanalyst (Frank Morgan), while Barrymore, the dethroned Hapsburg archduke, is now a taxi driver. He is determined to rekindle the flame: she is equally determined to resist. Set in the twenties, this adaptation of a play by Robert E Sherwood, is a largely tedious conversation piece, with Barrymore charmless and hammy for two-thirds of the action. The composed and classy Wynyard, however, is wonderful, as are the sets and clothes. Morgan convinces as the husband fighting for his wife, and Sidney Franklin directs the theatrical and outmoded proceedings with panache.

John Barrymore *Rudolf* • Diana Wynyard *Elena* • Frank Morgan *Anton* • Henry Travers *Father Krug* • May Robson *Frau Lucher* • Eduardo Ciannelli *Poffy* • Una Merkel *Isle* ▪ *Dir* Sidney Franklin • *Scr* Ernest Vajda, Claudine Westt, from the play by Robert E Sherwood

Revealing Evidence ★ 15
Crime thriller   1990 · US · Colour · 88mins

The pilot for a TV series that never happened, this has *Big Night* star Stanley Tucci and Mary Page Keller as a detective and a lawyer respectively trying to catch a serial killer in Hawaii. Yes, it's another cop show that's not much different to most of the others even the setting has been utilised better in series like *Magnum, PI* and *Hawaii Five-O*. Not worth watching and, to be honest, not worth the film it was processed on. ▱

Stanley Tucci *Detective Patrick Mcguire* • Mary Page Keller *Sydney Westin* • Finn Carter *Detective Maggie Luna* • Lori Tan Chinn *Pualani Keanu* • Jay O Sanders *Tom Marshall* • Wendy Kilbourne *Alyce Hewitt* • Stephen Meadows *Scott Parkes* ▪ *Dir* Michael Switzer • *Scr* Chris Abbott, from a story by Tom Selleck, Chris Abbott, Chas Floyd Johnson

Reveille with Beverly ★★★ U
Musical   1943 · US · BW · 77mins

One of many B movies churned out by super-hoofer Ann Miller, during her career with Columbia, this light-hearted and act-packed musical was actually based on the life and career of a real-life female disc jockey. Not that it matters, because Miller is simply fabulous, bringing her customary warm-heartedness and tap-dancing skills to

this insubstantial film. Watch for a young and skinny pre-film fame Frank Sinatra, before the Brooklyn Paramount concerts (the movie was reissued after that gig). Here's Duke Ellington and Count Basie, and the Mills Brothers, too, all appearing in a servicemen's show organised by Columbia juvenile Larry Parks, three years before he became famous for *The Jolson Story*. All Ann Miller's programme fillers were short, bright and sassy, and this stands out only slightly from the rest as a collector's item.

Ann Miller *Beverly Ross* • William Wright *Barry Lang* • Dick Purcell *Andy Adams* • Franklin Pangborn *Vernon Lewis* • Tim Ryan *Mr Kennedy* • Larry Parks *Eddie Ross* • Adele Mara *Evelyn Ross* • Frank Sinatra ▪ *Dir* Charles Barton • *Scr* Howard J Green, Jack Henley, Albert Duffy

Revenge ★★
Thriller   1971 · UK · Colour · 92mins

It was British films like this, that encouraged Joan Collins and James Booth to flee to Hollywood. The glamorous pair play a suburban couple who turn vigilantes and become involved in the kidnap and imprisonment of the man (Kenneth Griffith, made up to look like Richard Attenborough as Christie in *10 Rillington Place*) who they believe raped and murdered their daughter. What begins as a serious examination of a growing social problem becomes increasingly melodramatic, ending in a blaze of hysterical shrieking and stabbing. Quite unconvincing, enjoyable for all the wrong reasons.

Joan Collins *Carol Radford* • James Booth *Jim Radford* • Ray Barrett *Harry* • Kenneth Griffith *Seely* • Sinead Cusack *Rose* • Tom Marshall *Lee Radford* • Zuleika Robson *Jill Radford* ▪ *Dir* Sidney Hayers • *Scr* John Kruse

Revenge ★★ 18
Thriller   1990 · US · Colour · 118mins

Even die-hard fans of Kevin Costner will be disappointed by this daft drama which has retired navy pilot Costner going down to Mexico to visit old friend Anthony Quinn, only to incur the latter's wrath when he goes off with his wife, Madeleine Stowe (*Twelve Monkeys*). It all gets exceedingly silly, and overacting abounds as Costner and Stowe flee the understandably irate Quinn, who decides the murder of at least one of them is the best revenge. A boring blot in Costner's career, laboriously directed by the normally fluent action aficionado Tony Scott, (*Top Gun/Crimson Tide*). Contains swearing, violence and sex scenes. ▱

Kevin Costner *Cochran* • Anthony Quinn *Tiburon Mendez* • Madeleine Stowe *Miryea* • Tomas Milian *Cesar* • Joaquin Martinez *Mauro* • James Gammon *Texan* • Jesse Corti *Medero* • Sally Kirkland *Rock star* ▪ *Scr* Jim Harrison. Jeffrey Fiskin, from the novella by Jim Harrison

The Revenge of Al Capone ★★★
Crime drama   1989 · US · Colour · 92mins

This above-average TV-movie stars Ray Sharkey as probably the most filmed bad man ever, now conducting his crimes from inside prison, while

federal agent Keith Carradine gnashes his teeth on the outside. Directed by Michael Pressman, it's written, with real understanding of the ferocity of the robbin' hood, by Tracy Keenan Wynn. Sharkey's explosive performance comes at us fresh and fearsome. ▱

Ray Sharkey *Al Capone/Scarface* • Keith Carradine *Agent Michael Rourke* • Jayne Atkinson *Elizabeth Rourke* • Debrah Farentino *Jennie* • Charles Haid *Alex Connors* • Jordan Charney *J Edgar Hoover* ▪ *Dir* Michael Pressman • *Scr* Tracy Keenan Wynn

Revenge of Billy the Kid
★ 18
Horror   1991 · UK · Colour · 86mins

This tasteless, low-budget, British offering has a distinctly dubious antecedent in Thierry Zéno's Belgian bestiality shocker, *Vase de Noces* (1974), in which pig farmer Dominique Germy sires a litter of malevolent pork people. Jim Groom (who also directed *Beyond Bedlam*) plays this more for laughs than chills, but succeeds in raising neither. Old MacDonald is the perverted yeoman, whose nocturnal couplings result in the birth of a goat-headed dwarf, which embarks on a murderous rampage, only to be terminated by a chain saw. The location (an island off the Cornish coast) is the only thing to recommend this to the non-intoxicated. ▱

Michael Balfour *Gyles MacDonald* • Samantha Perkins *Ronnie MacDonald* • Jackie D Broad *Gretta MacDonald* • Trevor Peake *Ronald MacDonald* • Bryan Heeley *Ronald MacDonald* • Julian Shaw *Billy T Kid* • Norman Mitchell *Mr Allott* ▪ *Dir* Jim Groom • *Scr* Richard Mathews, James Groom, Tim Dennison

The Revenge of Frankenstein ★★★ 15
Horror   1958 · UK · Colour · 86mins

Hammer's first sequel to *The Curse of Frankenstein*, has the baron rescued from execution, changing his name to Dr Stein and continuing his body-part experiments in a charity hospital. The usual first-rate performances, excellent production values and gothic atmosphere are permeated by a macabre sense of humour in this superior spine-chiller, crisply directed as ever by studio regular Terence Fisher. The unexpectedly light-hearted moments counterpoint the more horrific elements, including cannibalism. ▱

Peter Cushing *Dr Victor Stein* • Francis Matthews *Dr Hans Kleve* • Eunice Gayson *Margaret* • Michael Gwynn *Karl* • John Welsh *Bergman* • Lionel Jeffries *Fritz* • Oscar Quitak *Karl* • Richard Wordsworth *Patient* • Charles Lloyd Pack *President* ▪ *Dir* Terence Fisher • *Scr* Jimmy Sangster, H Hurford Janes, from characters created by Mary Shelley

The Revenge of Pumpkinhead – Blood Wings ★★★ 18
Horror   1994 · US · Colour · 83mins

The slightly more engaging return of the monster from *Pumpkinhead*, dispenses with the previous story elements to create a mystery. This time, a small-town sheriff (Andrew Robinson) must deduce the monster's

reasons for picking particular victims. Pumpkinhead is used to better effect this time, although no explanation is given as to why a thunderstorm follows the monster wherever he goes. Look out for amusing bit-part turns by American presidential sibling Roger Clinton and Soleil Moon Frye (*Punky Brewster*). The principal actors mull the mystery while the teens scream, which is as it should be in a horror movie. ▱

Andrew Robinson *Sean Braddock* • Ami Dolenz *Jenny Braddock* • J Trevor Edmond *Danny Dixon* • Mark McCracken *Creature* • Gloria Hendry *Delilah Pettibone* • Alexander Polinsky *Paul* • Hill Harper *Peter* • Soleil Moon Frye *Marcie* • Roger Clinton *Mister Bubba* ▪ *Dir* Jeff Burr • *Scr* Steve Mitchell, Craig W Van Sickle

Revenge of the Creature ★★★
Horror   1955 · US · BW · 81mins

Almost as enjoyable as the original, director Jack Arnold's follow-up to *Creature from the Black Lagoon* has the ''Gill-Man'' (Ricou Browning) recaptured and taken to a sea-world park in Florida. There, ichthyologists John Agar and Lori Nelson try to teach him to speak, before the doggedly primeval monster goes on the inevitable rampage and drags Nelson back to his Everglades hideaway. Although the Gill-Man is dwelt on for too long, greatly dissipating his overall impact, Arnold accents the sexual nature of the beast to sinister and interesting effect. Look out for Clint Eastwood, in his first screen role, playing a laboratory technician. Though this was made in 3-D like the original, very few saw it projected that way after its initial release. A disappointing second sequel, *The Creature Walks Among Us*, followed in 1956, with a different director.

John Agar *Clete Ferguson* • Lori Nelson *Helen Dobson* • John Bromfield *Joe Hayes* • Robert B Williams *George Johnson* • Nestor Paiva *Lucas* • Grandon Rhodes *Foster* • Dave Willock *Gibson* • Charles Cane *Captain of Police* • Clint Eastwood *Lab technician* • Ricou Browning *Gill-Man* ▪ *Dir* Jack Arnold • *Scr* Martin Berkeley, from a story by William Alland

Revenge of the Nerds ★ 18
Comedy   1984 · US · Colour · 86mins

There is a theory that every Hollywood star has a turkey or two in their closet, so today, step forward Anthony Edwards, star of the hit TV series *ER*. In this puerile campus comedy, Edwards is one of the nerds of the title who decide to fight back in spectacular style against the bullying jocks at school. Among the other familiar faces in the cast are Robert Carradine, *Thirtysomething's* Timothy Busfield and *Moonlighting's* Curtis Armstrong, and all would undoubtedly wince now at the dire mix of lavatorial humour and tasteless slapstick. Even more amazing is the fact that this went on to spawn two sequels. Contains swearing and nudity. ▱

Robert Carradine *Lewis* • Anthony Edwards *Gilbert* • Timothy Busfield *Poindexter* • Andrew Cassese *Wormser* • Curtis Armstrong ''*Booger*'' • Larry B Scott *Lamar* • Brian Tochi Takashi • Julie Montgomery *Betty Childs* • Michelle Meyrink *Judy* • Ted McGinley *Stan Gable* ▪ *Dir* Jeff Kanew • *Scr* Steve

Zacharias, Jeff Buhai, from a story by Tim Metcalfe, Miguel Tejada-Flores, Steve Zacharias, Jeff Buhai

Revenge of the Ninja ★★ 18
Martial arts action
1983 · US · Colour · 80mins

There was an unpleasant rash of ninja movies in the early eighties and this sequel to *Enter the Ninja* probably ranks as one of the better ones, though admittedly that's not much of an endorsement. Japanese martial arts star, Sho Kosugi, is the ex-ninja seeking a life of serenity after moving to America from Japan following the murder of his family, only to discover that his new business partner is, in fact, a heroin smuggler and he must don his ninja clobber one last time – until the inevitable next sequel, that is. The by-the-numbers plot and trite dialogue – at one point someone says, "Only a ninja can stop a ninja!" "Oh yeah, well only a milkman can deliver milk!" – is redeemed by director Sam Firstenberg's staging of some impressive fight sequences. ▭

Sho Kosugi *Cho Osaki* • Keith Vitali *Dave Hatcher* • Virgil Frye *Lieutenant Dime* • Arthur Roberts *Braden* • Mario Gallo *Caifano* • Grace Oshita *Grandmother* • Ashley Ferrare *Cathy* ■ *Dir* Sam Firstenberg • *Scr* James R Silke

Revenge of the Pink Panther ★★★ PG
Comedy   1978 · US · Colour · 94mins

An immoderate helping of Inspector Clouseau from Peter Sellers, with so many comedy turns hanging from a slender plotline, that it tends to sag in places. Clouseau, on the trail of drug smugglers (takes his boss Herbert Lom beyond the end of his tether), is bemused when Dyan Cannon makes a play for him, and is constantly jumped by valet Bert Kwouk. Its comic parts are better than its incoherent whole. ▭

Peter Sellers *Chief Inspector Clouseau* • Herbert Lom *Chief Inspector Dreyfus* • Dyan Cannon *Simone Legree* • Robert Webber *Philippe Douvier* • Bert Kwouk *Cato* • Paul Stewart *Scallini* • Robert Loggia *Marchione* • Graham Stark *Dr Auguste Balls* • André Maranne *François* • Sue Lloyd *Claude Russo* ■ *Dir* Blake Edwards • *Scr* Frank Waldman, Ron Clark, Blake Edwards, from a story by Blake Edwards

Revenge of the Radioactive Reporter ★ 18
Comedy horror   1990 · Can · Colour · 80mins

This Canadian attempt to emulate the kind of movies the Troma studio is famous for, specifically the *Toxic Avenger* films, has none of the mayhem, outrageousness and cynicism for which Troma movies are famous. In fact, it frequently takes itself quite seriously, completely missing the point of its premise. Also, it somehow manages to look cheaper and cruder than Troma's ultra low-budget efforts, with little merit except for a few amusing one-liners and some comic rock songs. Like *The Toxic Avenger*, the plot concerns an unlucky hero forced into toxic waste by his enemies, then later coming back in a hideously mutated form for revenge. ▭

David Scammell *Mike R Wave* • Kathryn Boese *Richelle Darlington* • Derrick Strange *Richard Swell* • Randy Pearlstein *Joe Wave Junior* ■ *Dir* Craig Pryce • *Scr* Craig Pryce, David Wiechorek

Revenge of the Stepford Wives ★★
Science-fiction thriller
1980 · US · Colour · 95mins

Unwarranted and ill-judged, this sort-of-sequel is an insult to the Ira Levin source novel and the original movie, which was one of the most ambitious sci-fi thrillers of the mid-seventies. Arriving in Stepford to do a story on the town's remarkably low crime and divorce rates, a TV reporter discovers the womenfolk are being "programmed" to act as perfect domestic automatons for their husbands. A total dud and yet, incredibly, this was followed by two more inferior made-for-TV affairs, *The Stepford Children* and *The Stepford Husbands*. (What next? *The Stepford Gerbils*?) Among the cast are television superstars-in-waiting Don Johnson and Sharon Gless. Director Robert Fuest is perhaps best known for the superb Vincent Price *Dr Phibes* films.

Sharon Gless *Kay Foster* • Julie Kavner *Megan Brady* • Audra Lindley *Barbara Parkinson* • Don Johnson *Andy Brady* • Mason Adams *Wally* • Arthur Hill *Dale "Diz" Corbett* • Ellen Weston *Kitten* • Thomas Hill *Dr Edgar Trent* ■ *Dir* Robert Fuest • *Scr* David Wiltse, from the characters created by Ira Levin

The Revengers ★★
Western   1972 · US · Colour · 108mins

William Holden sets out to find and destroy the band of Comanches who killed his wife and children. Obviously he can't do this alone, so he springs six condemned men from prison. There are echoes of Holden's *The Wild Bunch* here, as well as *The Dirty Dozen* and *The Professionals*, and the movie provides the requisite number of bloody gunfights. However, Daniel Mann's direction is slack and easily diverted by flimsy subplots, including a longish dalliance with a frontier nurse played by Susan Hayward. It would prove to be her final feature film.

William Holden (1) *John Benedict* • Susan Hayward *Elizabeth* • Ernest Borgnine *Hoop* • Woody Strode *Job* • Roger Hanin *Quiberon* • René Koldehoff *Zweig* • Jorge Luke *Chamaco* • Scott Holden *Lieutenant* ■ *Dir* Daniel Mann • *Scr* Wendell Mayes, from a story by Steven W Carabatsos

The Revengers' Comedies ★★★
Black comedy   1997 · UK/Fr · Colour

Alfred Hitchcock's *Strangers on a Train* receives another reworking in this adept amalgamation of two Alan Ayckbourn plays. Meeting on Tower Bridge, Sam Neill and Helena Bonham Carter agree to abandon thoughts of suicide and do away with the other's chief tormentor instead. However, he soon discovers his co-conspirator's true nature after he becomes besotted with his intended victim, Kristin Scott Thomas. The main asset of this unfairly overlooked Britpic is its stellar cast, which includes such familiar TV faces as Martin Clunes and Steve

Coogan. But, unfortunately, Malcolm Mowbray's direction lacks the subtlety to exploit the story's dark farce. Contain violence, swearing.

Sam Neill *Henry Bell* • Helena Bonham Carter *Karen Knightly* • Kristin Scott Thomas *Imogen Staxton-Billing* • Rupert Graves *Oliver Knightly* • Martin Clunes *Anthony Staxton-Billing* • Steve Coogan *Bruce Tick* • John Wood *Colonel Marcus* • Liz Smith *Winnie* ■ *Dir* Malcolm Mowbray • *Scr* Malcolm Mowbray, from two plays by Alan Ayckbourn

Reversal of Fortune ★★★★ 15
Biographical drama
1990 · US · Colour · 106mins

Jeremy Irons won an Oscar for his portrayal of millionaire Claus von Bulow, who was found guilty of the attempted murder of his wife Sunny (Glenn Close), but acquitted on appeal. Even though there's no surprise about the outcome of this real-life story, this is a thoroughly absorbing and beautifully scripted drama, with events leading to the trial told in flashback and Close's comatose character bringing us up to date by a clever narration. Director Barbet Schroeder shoots *The Great Gatsby*-style setting with a documentary eye and gives the picture a deep sense of irony a quality enhanced by Irons's superb performance as the haughty, European aristocrat defended by a Jewish lawyer. This real-life tale marked the start of TV trials as soap opera: von Bulow's case obsessed America for months and made a star of his attorney, Alan Dershowitz, played here with scene-stealing bravura by Ron Silver. Contains violence, swearing. ▭

Jeremy Irons *Claus Von Bulow* • Glenn Close *Martha "Sunny" Von Bulow* • Ron Silver *Alan Dershowitz* • Annabella Sciorra *Sarah* • Uta Hagen *Maria* • Fisher Stevens *David Marriott* • Jack Gilpin *Peter Macintosh* • Christine Baranski *Andrea Reynolds* • Stephen Mailer *Elon Dershowitz* • Christine Dunford *Ellen* ■ *Dir* Barbet Schroeder • *Scr* Nicholas Kazan, from the book by Alan Dershowitz

The Revolt of Mamie Stover ★★★
Drama   1956 · US · Colour · 86mins

Great title for a strictly B-grade melodrama, dressed up with A-movie trappings by 20th Century-Fox, including filming on location in exotic Hawaii. But there's no disguising the fact that this movie really belongs to an earlier decade, with the same cast and director, but over at Warners or RKO. Jane Russell is, to be kind, a little past her prime. Warner's juvenile lead of the forties, Joan Leslie, while welcome, looks slightly weary, and Richard Egan, a leading man once touted as the new Clark Gable (the old one had just co-starred with Russell in director Raoul Walsh's previous film *The Tall Men*) proves to be all brawn and little else. Still, there's much fun to be had by guessing the real professions of these characters, hidebound as they were by fifties censorship.

Jane Russell *Mamie Stover* • Richard Egan *Jim* • Joan Leslie *Annalea* • Agnes Moorehead *Bertha Parchman* • Jorja Curtright *Jackie* • Michael Pate *Harry Adkins* • Richard Coogan

Eldon Sumac ■ *Dir* Raoul Walsh • *Scr* Sydney Boehm, from the novel by William Bradford Huie

Revolt of the Preatorians ★★
Historical adventure   1965 · It · Colour

In the style of the Caped Crusader himself, a masked man keeps turning up to dash the plans of a tyrannical emperor in this silly Italian costume escapade. Plenty of dramatic intent from director Brescia, but it soon becomes hard to take this film seriously. Italian dialogue dubbed into English.

Richard Harrison *Valerius Rufus* • Giuliano Gemma *Soterus* • Moira Orfei *Lucilla* • Piero Lulli *Domitian* • Paola Pitti *Artamne* • Ivy Holzer *Zusa* • Aldo Cecconi *Lucius Fabius* ■ *Dir* Alfonso Brescia • *Scr* Giampaolo Callegari

Revolution ★★★ PG
Historical war drama
1985 · UK/Nor · Colour · 120mins

Hugh Hudson's look at the American War of Independence was a famous mega-flop, sealing the fate of the already over-extended Goldcrest production house. It is the story of a father and son, and the way history intrudes on their relationship. On the plus side are: the battle scenes, brilliantly filmed with a handheld camera; a remarkable portrayal of a sadistic English officer by a deeply in period Donald Sutherland; and clever art direction which turns King's Lynn into New York. On the debit side is Al Pacino's ludicrous performance and laughable Scots/Irish/Brooklyn accent – an all-too evident case of Method madness and a star's egomania unbalancing an entire production. Another embarrassment is Nastassja Kinski's part – as a revolutionary heroine, she just gets in the way. ▭

Al Pacino *Tom Dobb* • Nastassja Kinski *Daisy McConnahay* • Donald Sutherland *Sergeant Major Peasy* • Joan Plowright *Mrs McConnahay* • Dave King *Mr McConnahay* • Steven Berkoff *Sergeant Jones* • Annie Lennox *Liberty Woman* • Dexter Fletcher *Ned Dobb* • Sid Owen *Young Ned* • John Wells *Corty* • Richard O'Brien *Lord Hampton* ■ *Dir* Hugh Hudson • *Scr* Robert Dillon

The Revolutionary ★★★★
Political drama
1970 · UK/US · Colour · 101mins

A compelling portrayal by Jon Voight of a political subversive, makes this worth the effort of watching. As "A", he moves from handing out revolutionary leaflets at college to an attempted assassination, in a moral tale that's too one-track for its own good but, which, nevertheless, poses hard questions for would-be revolutionaries who could become terrorists – for the best possible reasons. Writer Hans Koningsberger and director Paul Williams highlight the way that anything can be excused by strongly held belief. And Voight makes the idea stick.

Jon Voight *A* • Jennifer Salt *Helen Peret* • Seymour Cassel *Leonard* • Robert Duvall *Despard* • Collin Wilcox-Horne *Anne* • Lionel Murton *Professor* ■ *Dir* Paul Williams • *Scr* Hans Koningsberger, from the novel by Hans Koningsberger

U = SUITABLE FOR ALL   Uc = SUITABLE FOR ALL, ESPECIALLY FOR YOUNG CHILDREN (VIDEO ONLY)   PG = PARENTAL GUIDANCE

Revolver ★★ 🔞
Spy thriller 1992 · US/Sp · Colour · 96mins

TV-movie regular Robert Urich, stars as a paralysed spy who sets out to find the assassin responsible for his injuries, only to uncover a conspiracy. This old-fashioned espionage caper is a Spanish/US co-production and consequently shares many of the characteristics of the Euro-pudding: beautiful scenery, confused plotting and patchy performances. Director Gary Nelson, who is better known for sci-fi epic *The Black Hole*, does his best with the clichéd material.

Robert Urich *Nick Clayton* • Assumpta Serna *Countess Mariona Duran* • Steven Williams *Ken* • Dakin Matthews *Jim McCall* • David Ryall *Alfredo Testi* • Jordi Mollà *Jordi* • Garrick Hagon *Adam Vincent* • Ariadna Gil *Nuria* • Neil Dudgeon *Eric Volkner* • Gwen Humble *Claire* ◼ *Dir* Gary Nelson • *Scr* Mark Waxman, from a story by Rift Fournier and Mark Waxman

The Revolving Doors ★★★ 🆄
Drama 1988 · Can/Fr · Colour · 101mins

Cinema had recently celebrated the 70th anniversary of the switch to all-talking pictures. But this absorbing French/Canadian drama shows that the coming of sound meant the end of a unique form of entertainment, the silent movie, complete with its atmospheric piano accompaniment. As the pianist who leaves the dream palaces to find fame in the jazz joints of New York, Monique Spaziani gives an engaging performance, piling on the years for the bookend segments, in the latter of which she meets the grandson who has come to know her through her diary. Francis Mankiewicz directs neatly and there's a solid performance from French actress Miou-Miou.

Monique Spaziani *Céleste Beaumont* • Gabriel Arcand *Blaudelle* • Miou-Miou *Lauda* • Jacques Penot *Pierre Blaudelle* • François Méthé *Antoine* • Françoise Faucher *Simone Blaudelle* ◼ *Dir* Francis Mankiewicz • *Scr* Jacques Savoie

The Reward ★★★
Drama 1965 · US · Colour · 90mins

In the sixties, 20th Century-Fox hijacked a number of directors from Europe with admirable intent, but with little success. Along with Bernhard Wicki's *Morituri* and John Guillermin's *Rapture*, this slow, elegiac, contemporary western is one of the most interesting failures. A motley cast, headed by glum import Max von Sydow, spends a lot of time sitting around in the desert, very slowly motivated by greed to seek a bigger share of the title pay-out. It's not uninteresting, and is intelligently cast, with faces like Gilbert Roland, Henry Silva and Emilio Fernandez perfectly suited to the setting. But French director Serge Bourguignon, whose *Sundays and Cybèle* had achieved art-house kudos and won the best foreign language film Oscar, is well out of his *métier*, and the result, though fascinating, is not enjoyable.

Max von Sydow *Scott Swanson* • Yvette Mimieux *Sylvia* • Efrem Zimbalist Jr *Frank Bryant* • Gilbert Roland *Captain Carbajal* • Emilio Fernandez *Sergento Lopez* • Henry Silva *Joaquin* • Rafael Lopez *Indian Boy* ◼ *Dir*

Serge Bourguignon • *Scr* Serge Bourguignon, Oscar Milland, from the novel by Michael Barrett

Rhapsody ★★★ 🆄
Romantic drama
1954 · US · Colour · 115mins

Beautiful heiress Elizabeth Taylor is in love with classical violinist Vittorio Gassman, but leaves him – via a broken-hearted suicide attempt when he puts ambition first – for concert pianist John Ericson, who makes her his priority. There's much flitting back and forth between the two men and across Europe, before the final fade. An essentially hollow and old-fashioned romantic soap opera, this is given a cultural gloss by the outpouring of music, notably Ericson's rendition of the Rachmaninov's *Second Piano Concerto* (played by Claudio Arrau) and Gassman performing Tchaikowsky's *Violin Concerto in D major* (played by Michael Rabin). Taylor is good and at her loveliest, and the location photography in Technicolor and CinemaScope is eye-catching. Charles Vidor directs.

Elizabeth Taylor *Louise Durant* • Vittorio Gassman *Paul Bronte* • John Ericson *James Guest* • Louis Calhern *Nicholas Durant* • Michael Chekhov *Professor Schuman* • Barbara Bates *Effie Cahill* • Richard Hageman *Bruno Furst* • Richard Lupino *Otto Krafft* • Stuart Whitman *Dove* ◼ *Dir* Charles Vidor • *Scr* Fay Kanin, Michael Kanin, Ruth Goetz, Augustus Goetz, from the novel *Maurice Guest* by Henry Handel Richardson

Rhapsody in August ★★ 🆄
Drama 1990 · Jap · Colour · 97mins

This is comfortably the worst film made by the late Akira Kurosawa during his 50-year career. Rather than compelling his audience to re-examine their views on the nature of warfare and the impact of American cultural imperialism, the then 80-year-old film-maker merely trots out a series of platitudes that neither challenge nor enlighten. There is a certain charm in the interaction between Sachiko Murase and the four grandchildren, who spend the summer with her on the outskirts of Nagasaki, but the storyline is weak and Richard Gere looks distinctly out of place as a distant nephew. In Japanese with English subtitles.

Sachiko Murase *Kane* • Hisashi Igawa *Tadao* • Narumi Kayashima *Machiko* • Tomoko Ohtakara *Tami* • Mitsunori Isaki *Shinjiro* • Toshie Negishi *Yoshie* • Richard Gere *Clark* ◼ *Dir* Akira Kurosawa • *Scr* Akira Kurosawa, from the novel *Nabe-no-Naka* by Kiyoko Murata

Rhapsody in Blue ★★★ 🆄
Biographical drama 1945 · US · BW · 139mins

Splendid Warner Bros tosh, purporting to be the life story of genius composer George Gershwin, but actually a wonderfully enjoyable epic which manages to embrace every single cliché of the Lower East Side, Jewish-kid-makes-good, rags-to-riches saga, and almost brings it off. Unfortunately, Robert Alda (Alan's dad) lacks star power as Gershwin, and Herbert Rudley is seriously undercast as his brother Ira, but there's a wealth of fabulous support, including Al Jolson as himself

and the great Oscar Levant, who performs both *Concerto in F* and *Rhapsody in Blue* in their respective entireties, utterly justifying this movie. Technical credits, too, are extraordinarily accomplished, with beautiful editing from Folmer Blangsted, who later worked on the 1954 version of *A Star Is Born* with George Cukor, and classic art direction from Warners veteran Anton Grot and John Hughes. To the sophisticated and critical, this may seem overlong, dishonest and sentimental. But for most audiences, in the right mood, it's perfectly entertaining fare.

Robert Alda *George Gershwin* • Joan Leslie *Julie Adams* • Alexis Smith *Christine Gilbert* • Charles Coburn *Max Dreyfus* • Julie Bishop *Lee Gershwin* • Albert Basserman *Professor Frank* • Morris Carnovsky *Poppa Gershwin* • Rosemary DeCamp *Momma Gershwin* • Anne Brown *Bess* • Herbert Rudley *Ira Gershwin* ◼ *Dir* Irving Rapper • *Scr* Howard Koch, Elliott Paul, from a story by Sonya Levien

Rhinestone ★★ 🅿🅶
Comedy 1984 · US · Colour · 106mins

Contrary to popular belief, Sylvester Stallone does have the knack for comedy, albeit in a light form. However, he frequently lacks the ability to judge if a script is good, especially if he's involved in its writing, as he was with this modern take on *Pygmalion*. Country star, Dolly Parton takes a bet on whether she can turn cab driver Stallone into a country singer and the results, as far as both the wager and their interest in each other are concerned, are as expected. The two stars are up to it but, except for a hilarious scene in a funeral home, the movie simply isn't funny. Criticism of the movie always includes jabs at Stallone's singing – but it's actually passable. 📼

Sylvester Stallone *Nick* • Dolly Parton *Jake* • Richard Farnsworth *Noah* • Ron Leibman *Freddie* • Tim Thomerson *Barnett* • Steven Apostlee Peck *Father* ◼ *Dir* Bob Clark • *Scr* Phil Alden Robinson, Sylvester Stallone, from the story by Phil Alden Robinson, from the song *Rhinestone Cowboy* by Larry Weiss

Rhino! ★★
Adventure 1964 · US · Colour · 91mins

Best known as the producer who gave the world *Flipper*, Ivan Tors proved that his talents lay in writing and producing with this directorial debut. However, unlike other big game adventures, this one at least has the benefit of a conservationist message, as Hunter Harry Guardino and scientist Robert Culp go in search of a pair of white rhino that are threatened with extinction. Tors makes the most of his South African locations and the majestic wildlife, but his handling of the dramatic sequences is uncertain, with Shirley Eaton asked to do nothing more than look scared and regularly require rescuing.

Harry Guardino *Alec Burnett* • Shirley Eaton *Edith Arleigh* • Robert Culp *Dr Jim Hanlon* • Harry Mekela *Jopo* • George Lane *Haragay* ◼ *Dir* Ivan Tors • *Scr* Art Arthur, Arthur Weiss, from a story by Art Arthur

Rhinoceros ★★★ 🆄
Surreal comedy 1974 · US · Colour · 10mins

Producer Ely Landau's American Film Theater series of filmed plays has thrown up some interesting movies, including a superbly cast *The Iceman Cometh* and a magnificent *A Delicate Balance*. However, the allegorical material of Eugène Ionesco's absurdist play *Rhinoceros* has always been seen as self-defeating, and actors as distinguished as Laurence Olivier and Orson Welles, among others, have fallen foul of it. Here, the leads from *The Producers*, Zero Mostel and Gene Wilder, are reunited under the iconoclastic direction of Tom O'Horgan, *Futz*, and the result, though fascinating, is very much an acquired taste.

Zero Mostel *John* • Gene Wilder *Stanley* • Karen Black *Daisy* • Robert Weil *Carl* • Joe Silver *Norman* • Marilyn Chris *Mrs Bingham* ◼ *Dir* Tom O'Horgan • *Scr* Julian Barry, from the play by Eugène Ionesco

Rhubarb ★★★ 🅿🅶
Comedy 1951 · US · BW · 94mins

The second-best cat movie ever and it's only a whisker behind the greatest, *Harry and Tonto*. Rhubarb is a fiery alley cat who inherits a baseball team. Although he brings the team luck, he poses a triple headache for Ray Milland, the marketing man charged with caring for the new manager/mascot, for not only does Rhubarb insist on living on his own terms, but Milland's girlfriend Jan Sterling is allergic to him and a jilted benefactor is out to prove in the courts that he is an imposter. It's slight and silly, but there are plenty of laughs and Rhubarb is just perfect. 📼

Ray Milland *Eric Yeager* • Jan Sterling *Polly Sickles* • Gene Lockhart *Thaddeus J Banner* • William Frawley *Len Sickles* • Elsie Holmes *Myra Banner* • Taylor Holmes *P Duncan Munk* ◼ *Dir* Arthur Lubin • *Scr* Dorothy Reid, Francis Cockrell, David Stern, from the novel by H Allen Smith

Rhythm on the Range ★★ 🆄
Western musical comedy
1936 · US · BW · 85mins

Stepping into singing cowboy mode for the only time in his screen career, Bing Crosby is the star of this musical western romance in which he sings a song to a mightily large Hereford bull, as well as winning the hand of a rebellious heiress, played by the doomed Frances Farmer (subject of the biopic *Frances* with Jessica Lange). Bing had a huge hit with *I'm an Old Cowhand*, but the movie's main interest now, and extraordinary box-office success then, is down to motor-mouthed comedian and songstress Martha Raye, who makes her screen debut and delivers an all-stops-out rendition of *Mr Paganini*. Otherwise, a pleasantly nondescript movie, directed by Norman Taurog from the merest smidgen of a plot.

Bing Crosby *Jeff Larrabee* • Frances Farmer *Doris Halliday* • Bob Burns *Buck Burns* • Martha Raye *Emma* • Samuel S Hinds *Robert Halliday* • Lucille Webster Gleason *Penelope Ryland* • Warren Hymer *Big Brain* ◼ *Dir* Norman Taurog • *Scr* John C Moffitt, Sidney Salkow, Walter DeLeon, Francis Martin, from a story by Mervin J Houser

Rhythm on the River ★★★
Musical drama   1940 · US · BW · 92mins

With Bing Crosby and Mary Martin as the leads, a screenplay co-written by Billy Wilder and *Road to Singapore* (1940) director Victor Schertzinger in charge, it's no surprise that this amiable musical was a great hit on release. The third star is Basil Rathbone, taking time off from being Sherlock Holmes to play a composer who finds inspiration lacking and employs Bing and Mary to ghost write his work. They realise that they would be better off writing for themselves, only to discover that without the composer's name their talent is unacknowledged. Luckily the three join forces for a hit show. Good songs include Johnny Burke and James V Monaco's Oscar-nominated *Only Forever* and the director's own *I Don't Want to Cry Anymore*, plus as a bonus there's sad-faced pianist Oscar Levant in a supporting role.

Bing Crosby *Bob Summers* • Mary Martin *Cherry Lane* • Basil Rathbone *Oliver Courtney* • Oscar Levant *Charlie Starbuck* • Oscar Shaw *Charlie Goodrich* • Charley Grapewin *Uncle Caleb* • Lillian Cornell *Millie Starling* • William Frawley *Westlake* ■ *Dir* Victor Schertzinger • *Scr* Dwight Taylor, from a story by Billy Wilder, Jacques Thery • *Music Director* Victor Young

Rhythm Serenade ★★ U
Romantic musical   1943 · UK · BW · 0mins

During the Second World War, a schoolteacher does her bit for the war effort by opening a nursery school next door to a munitions factory so that the children's mothers can work. The enterprise only gets going after some problems regarding the premises she wants to rent, which belong to the mysterious chap who lives in the garden cottage. Directed by Gordon Wellesley for the British arm of Columbia, this sentimental and unremarkable film combines patriotic flag-waving with romance, some humour and a few songs, as a vehicle for ''Forces' Sweetheart'' Vera Lynn, who does her best. Peter Murray Hill co-stars and comics Jimmy Jewel, Irene Handl and Jimmy Clitheroe are in the large supporting cast.

Vera Lynn *Ann Martin* • Peter Murray Hill *John Drover* • Julien Mitchell *Mr Jimson* • Charles Victor *Mr Martin* • Jimmy Jewel *Jimmy Martin* • Ben Warriss *Ben Martin* • Irene Handl *Mrs Crumbling* • Jimmy Clitheroe *Joey* ■ *Dir* Gordon Wellesley • *Scr* Marjorie Deans, Basil Woon, Margaret Kennedy, Edward Dryhurst, from a story by Marjorie Deans

Rhythm Thief ★★★ 18
Drama   1994 · US · BW · 83mins

An extremely impressive no-budget film from the grubbier side of New York, revealing the sure hand of new director Matthew Harrison at the tiller. Much applauded at the 1994 World Film Festival in Montreal, it tells the story of a small-time hustler whose inner emptiness is filtered through his unfocused life of peanut butter scoffing and noisy neighbours, and whose hidden feelings are ignited by the arrival of an odd young girl. Harrison makes good use of his admirable cast, balancing the film's vital spark with a high degree of thoughtfulness. All this

in a movie that took 11 days to shoot. Contains violence, swearing. ▣

Jason Andrews *Simon* • Eddie Daniels *Marty* • Kimberly Flynn *Cyd* • Kevin Corrigan *Fuller* • Sean Hagerty *Shayme* ■ *Dir* Matthew Harrison • *Scr* Matthew Harrison, Christopher Grimm

Rice People ★★★ PG
Drama   1994 · Camb/Fr/Swi/Ger · Colour · 129mins

Cambodian director Rithy Panh – an exile in France since the genocidal regime of Pol Pot came to power in 1975 – returns to his roots and builds an entire film around a rice harvest. It's a harvest beset by nature's adversity and human nightmare – the father has visions of the Khmer Rouge and then a thorn infects his foot while the mother is menaced by a cobra. These calamities and others occur, but life goes on as it has for centuries. It's a bit of a slog at two hours, but connoisseurs of movies from the developing world should still find plenty to admire here. In Kymer with English subtitles.

Peng Phan *Yim Om, Mother* • Mom Soth *Vong Poeuv, Father* • Chhim Naline *Sakha, Oldest Daughter* ■ *Dir* Rithy Panh • *Scr* Rithy Panh, Eve Deboise, from a novel by Shahnon Ahmad

Rich and Famous ★★ 18
Comedy drama   1981 · US · Colour · 111mins

The last film from the great womens' director George Cukor is a disappointingly ho-hum remake of 1943's *Old Acquaintance*. Jacqueline Bisset and Candice Bergen step into roles Bette Davis and Miriam Hopkins made their own, as childhood friends who become rivals in their writing careers and in love. Playing spot the celeb is more entertaining than their tiresome jealous, bitchy confrontations or Bisset's crisis with a younger lover. Teenaged Meg Ryan, cute as a button, makes her film debut as Bergen's daughter; guests glimpsed in two party scenes include playboy film-maker Roger Vadim, and writers Christopher Isherwood and Ray Bradbury. ▣

Jacqueline Bisset *Liz Hamilton* • Candice Bergen *Merry Noel Blake* • David Selby *Doug Blake* • Hart Bochner *Chris Adams* • Steven Hill *Jules Levi* • Meg Ryan *Debby, aged 18* • Matt Lattanzi *Jim* ■ *Dir* George Cukor • *Scr* Gerald Ayres, from the play *Old Acquaintance* by John Van Druten

Rich and Respectable ★★
Comedy thriller   1975 · Fr/It · Colour · 105

Austrian director Franz Antel – a cinematic schizophrenic, who whenever he undertook a weighty topic, appended his own name. If he fancied doing something historical, erotic or parodic, however, he adopted the pseudonym François Legrand. Curiously, considering the emphasis is more on laughs than thrills, he owned up to this crime caper, in which a wannabe stuntman teams up with a bogus film-maker to rob a bank. Borrowing its central premise from Woody Allen's *Take the Money and Run*, this lightweight affair is notable only for the cameos of gangster Arthur Kennedy, mistress Carroll Baker and ambassador Curt Jurgens.

Arthur Kennedy *Jannacone* • Carroll Baker *Polly Moon* • Curt Jurgens *Senator Shelton* •

Angelo Infanti *Dino* • Vittorio Caprioli *Baron* • Christine Kaufmann *Biggi* • Silvia Dionisio *Moira* • Werner Pochath *Cotto* ■ *Dir/Scr* Franz Antel

Rich and Strange ★★
Comedy drama   1932 · UK · BW · 92mins

Alfred Hitchcock made this curious, often rather cruel and tiresome comedy when his career was in the doldrums. Henry Kendall and Joan Barry star as the young married couple who spend an inheritance on a world cruise during which their relationship comes under strain, particularly when they become shipwrecked in the Far East. The extensive location footage makes the film seem disconcertingly real at times. The stars are too sophisticated for their roles (although Joan Barry deserved to be seen after dubbing Anny Ondra's voice in *Blackmail*). Hitchcock's stylistic touches provide the main interest of the film today but even they are rather exaggerated for such slight subject matter.

Henry Kendall *Fred Hill* • Joan Barry *Emily Hill* • Percy Marmont *Commander Gordon* • Betty Amann *Princess* ■ *Dir* Alfred Hitchcock • *Scr* Val Valentine, Alma Reville, Alfred Hitchcock, from a novel by Dale Collins

The Rich Are Always with Us ★★★★
Romance   1932 · US · BW · 71mins

The brilliant Broadway actress Ruth Chatterton, is at the centre of this tale about an unusual and inordinately wealthy society hostess who resists the overtures of handsome young novelist George Brent – until she discovers her husband's infidelity, that is. Meanwhile, a very young Bette Davis sets her sights on Brent; the actor would later become her future and frequent co-star. Polished acting, surprise twists and a dialogue studded with archly witty gems make this period piece (directed by Alfred E Green) entertaining from start to finish. A sophisticated reflection of a bygone era, the film is high comedy with a satirical thrust and a bittersweet edge, populated by the Park Avenue *haut monde* and combining romance and poignancy to marvellous effect.

Ruth Chatterton *Caroline Grannard* • George Brent *Julian Tierney* • Adrienne Dore *Allison Adair* • Bette Davis *Malbro* • John Miljan *Greg Grannard* ■ *Dir* Alfred E Green • *Scr* Austin Parker, from the novel by Mrs Arthur Somers Roche [E Petit]

Rich in Love ★★★ PG
Drama   1992 · US · Colour · 100mins

Director Bruce Beresford, producers Richard and Lili Fini Zanuck and screenwriter Alfred Uhry, the team behind the Oscar-winning *Driving Miss Daisy*, reassembled in luscious South Carolina to make this marital drama. Jill Clayburgh walks out on Albert Finney, leaving him with their daughter, Kathryn Erbe, and a lot of excess emotional baggage. Among the supporting cast, Kyle MacLachlan is the ''other man'' who causes even more angst, and Piper Laurie plays a traditional Southern crackpot. Slow to start, slower to finish, it's nevertheless worth watching for Finney's heavily accented display of pique. ▣

Albert Finney *Warren Odom* • Jill Clayburgh *Helen Odom* • Kathryn Erbe *Lucille Odom* • Kyle MacLachlan *Billy McQueen* • Piper Laurie *Vera Delmage* • Ethan Hawke *Wayne Frobiness* • Suzy Amis *Rae Odom* • Alfre Woodard *Rhody Poole* ■ *Dir* Bruce Beresford • *Scr* Alfred Uhry, from the novel by Josephine Humphreys

Rich Kids ★★
Comedy drama   1979 · US · Colour · 96mins

The presence of Robert Altman on the credits (here as executive producer) is usually an indication of a classy piece of work – and while it's no masterpiece, *Rich Kids* does have a fair bit going for it. At the centre of the picture is 12-year-old Franny, who gradually comes to realise that her parents are about to get divorced; her friend Jamie, who has already gone through the process, and has an endless stream of advice for her on how to deal with the impending split. A rather heavy-handed message movie, demonstrating that the joyful innocence of childhood soon gives way to the murkier adult world, this features good performances all round but it's never quite the film it could have been.

Trini Alvarado *Franny Philips* • Jeremy Levy *Jamie Harris* • Kathryn Walker *Madeline Philips* • John Lithgow *Paul Philips* • Terry Kiser *Ralph Harris* • David Selby *Steve Sloan* • Roberta Maxwell *Barbara Peterfreund* • Paul Dooley *Simon Peterfreund* ■ *Dir* Robert M Young • *Scr* Judith Ross

The Rich Man's Wife ★★ 18
Mystery thriller   1996 · US · Colour · 90mins

What could have been a convincing thriller is sadly let down by an unfathomable twist in its tale. Before the unsuccessful ending, it's all rather good. Halle Berry is convincing as an unhappily married woman, whose flippant asides to a man she meets in a bar (Peter Greene) result in said man murdering her husband. Berry becomes a key suspect – she's been having an affair with another man (played by British actor Clive Owen) and she is after all, controversially, the black widow of a white man. But, all is not as it seems and, despite strong acting and a tight script, the balloon bursts all over the place at the end. Contains swearing, sexual references, violence. ▣

Halle Berry *Jane Potenza* • Christopher McDonald *Tony Potenza* • Clive Owen *Jake Golden* • Peter Greene *Cole Wilson* • Charles Hallahan *Dan Fredricks* • Frankie Faison *Ron Lewis* ■ *Dir/Scr* Amy Holden Jones

Rich Men, Single Women ★★
Romantic comedy   1990 · US · Colour · 96mins

Three single women Suzanne Somers, Deborah Adair and Heather Locklear team up to find millionaires to marry. Of course, they soon find out that money can't buy happiness in this often unintentionally funny, romantic comedy. This is the sort of movie that should have been made in the greedy eighties when *Dynasty* was on television. In the nineties, it looks dated and daft. Larry Wilcox, better known as one of the two stars of the

U = SUITABLE FOR ALL   Uc = SUITABLE FOR ALL, ESPECIALLY FOR YOUNG CHILDREN (VIDEO ONLY)   PG = PARENTAL GUIDANCE

cop show *Chips*, provides more than reliable support.

Heather Locklear *Tori Mitchell* • Suzanne Somers *Paige Williams* • Joel Higgins *Nicky Loomis* • Douglas Barr *Richard Hancock* • Larry Wilcox *Mark Wells* • John Allen Nelson *Travis Walton* ■ *Dir* Elliot Silverstein • *Scr* James Harmon Brown, Barbara Esensten, Rita Mae Brown, from the novel by Pamela Beck, Patti Massman

Richard Pryor: Live on the Sunset Strip ★★★ 18

Comedy concert 1982 · US · Colour · 77mins

Richard Pryor can be an acquired taste, and his concert films are variable, but on form there are few more astute comedians. In this, culled from two one-man shows at the Hollywood Palladium, he is in subdued mood. The Mafia, his drug abuse and his trip to Africa are among the diverse subjects covered, and he even picks up on some of the sick humour directed at his own accident, when he set himself alight while on a cocaine binge. Honest and funny.

Richard Pryor ■ *Dir* Joe Layton • *Scr* Richard Pryor

Richard III ★★★★ U

Historical drama
1955 · UK · Colour · 150mins

After turning *Henry V* into wartime propaganda and *Hamlet* into *film noir* on the battlements, Laurence Olivier made *Richard III* as outright melodrama, an historical pageant that looks like MGM's *Ivanhoe*. Olivier's stage portrayal of Richard is legendary and the film serves principally as a record of that triumph – thus, it is perhaps less of a movie than its two predecessors. The play's the thing, then, with Olivier's hunchback scowling and lurching around the sets like Charles Laughton's Quasimodo. While Ralph Richardson, John Gielgud and the gorgeous Claire Bloom give performances of great distinction and emotion, Olivier's is more a display of cold technique. Peter Sellers later devised a brilliant send-up of the "Now is the winter of our discontent" soliloquy to the lyrics of *A Hard Day's Night*.

Laurence Olivier *Richard III* • Ralph Richardson *Buckingham* • Claire Bloom *Lady Anne* • John Gielgud *Clarence* • Cedric Hardwicke *King Edward IV* • Mary Kerridge *Queen Elizabeth* • Pamela Brown *Jane Shore* • Alec Clunes *Hastings* • Stanley Baker *Henry Tudor* • Michael Gough *Dighton* ■ *Dir* Laurence Olivier • *Scr* Alan Dent, Laurence Olivier, Colley Cibber, David Garrick, from the play by William Shakespeare • *Production Designer* Roger Furse [Roger K Furse] • *Art Director* Carmen Dillon • *Cinematographer* Otto Heller

Richard III ★★★★ 15

Drama 1995 · UK/US · Colour · 99mins

Sir Ian McKellan authoritatively revisits one of the greatest roles in the English language in Richard Loncraine's daring, flashy reworking of the acclaimed National Theatre production, in which Richard was styled as a 1930s fascist dictator. The uniformly excellent cast includes Maggie Smith, Kristin Scott Thomas's drug-addicted Lady Anne, Annette Bening and a scene-stealing

Robert Downey Jr, as an American arriviste queen and her brother Earl. Although the artifice is dispassionately cold, the splashy nods to modern cinemagoers' frame of reference – sex, violence, explosions – do pep up the popular appeal without condescension or gutting the text, in a notable cinematic tackling of the Bard. Contains violence and sex scenes.

Ian McKellen *Richard III* • Annette Bening *Queen Elizabeth* • Robert Downey Jr *Earl Rivers* • Nigel Hawthorne *Clarence* • Maggie Smith *Duchess of York* • Jim Broadbent *Duke of Buckingham* • Kristin Scott Thomas *Lady Anne* ■ *Dir* Richard Loncraine • *Scr* Ian McKellen, Richard Loncraine, from the stage production by Richard Eyre of the play by William Shakespeare

The Richest Cat in the World ★★ U

Comedy 1986 · US · Colour · 83mins

This is a rather routine TV movie from Disney, about a talking cat who inherits a multi-million-dollar fortune and is then catnapped by his dead owner's cash-crazed kin. The twist in the tale is that the cat can talk. Though it's played for laughs, they're few and far between. It won't give grown-ups paws for thought, but younger kids might find it the cat's whiskers.

Steve Vinovich *Gus Barrett* • Jesse Welles *Louise* • Brandon Call *Bart* • Kellie Martin *Veronica* • George Wyner *Victor* ■ *Dir* Gregg Beeman [Greg Beeman] • *Scr* Alfa-Betty Olsen, Marshall Efron, from a story by Les Alexander, Steve Ditlea

The Richest Girl in the World ★★★

Romantic comedy 1934 · US · BW · 74mins

Desperate to find true romance and be loved for herself rather than for her money, heiress Miriam Hopkins, whom nobody can recognise since there are no pictures of her and few are privileged to meet her, swaps identities with her best-friend-cum-secretary Fay Wray to test the worth of a new man (Joel McCrea). Dorothy's protector (Henry Stephenson) and Sylvia's husband (Reginald Denny) join the conspiracy under William A Seiter's direction of Norman Krasna and Leona D'Ambry's Oscar-nominated screenplay. A sweetly sparkling romantic comedy with Hopkins on delightful form.

Miriam Hopkins *Dorothy Hunter* • Joel McCrea *Tony Travers* • Fay Wray *Sylvia Lockwood* • Henry Stephenson *John Connors* • Reginald Denny *Phillip Lockwood* • Beryl Mercer *Marie* • George Meeker *Donald* ■ *Dir* William A Seiter • *Scr* Norman Krasna, Leona D'Ambry, from a story by Norman Krasna

Richie Rich ★★ PG

Comedy 1994 · US · Colour · 90mins

Almost a last-gasp kiddie outing for Macaulay Culkin, who even here is entering that difficult period between childhood and adolescence. Based on the US comic strip, this features Culkin as a boy who has unlimited wealth but longs for a normal life. His wish is granted when he takes up with a ragbag gang of kids to foil nasty John Larroquette, who is trying to cheat Richie out of his fortune. All the usual clichés are present and correct,

Jonathan Hyde is the obligatory British butler and, although the kids will lap up the juvenile slapstick, it's not a patch on *Home Alone*.

Macaulay Culkin *Richie Rich* • John Larroquette *Van Dough* • Edward Herrmann *Mr Rich* • Christine Ebersole *Mrs Rich* • Jonathan Hyde *Cadbury* • Micheal McShane *Professor Keenbean* ■ *Dir* Donald Petrie • *Scr* Tom S Parker, Jim Jennewein, from a story by Neil Tolkin, from the Harvey Comics characters

Ricochet ★★★ 18

Action crime drama
1991 · US · Colour · 97mins

This enjoyable, totally over-the-top action thriller, has Denzel Washington's cop being systematically persecuted by John Lithgow's deranged killer, whom he had arrested years earlier in front of enraptured TV viewers. Writer Steven E De Souza, who co-scripted the first two *Die Hard* films, comes up with some fiendish acts of revenge. Director Russell Mulcahy (*Highlander*, *The Shadow*) keeps the energy levels high and the camera just about active enough to disguise the increasing ridiculousness of the story. Lithgow shows why he is one of modern cinema's premier psycho performers, but Washington's acting skills are somewhat wasted.

Denzel Washington *Nick Styles* • John Lithgow *Earl Talbot Blake* • Ice-T *Odessa* • Kevin Pollak *Larry Doyle* • Lindsay Wagner *Priscilla Brimleigh* • Victoria Dillard *Alice* ■ *Dir* Russell Mulcahy • *Scr* Steven E De Souza, from the story by Fred Dekker, Menno Meyjes

The Riddle of the Sands ★★★ U

Action adventure 1978 · UK · Colour · 98mins

Despite the riotous action contained in the original Erskine Childers turn-of-the-century adventure classic, this brave attempt to pin down the novel's narrative never quite succeeds, because it's too reverent for its own good. Michael York and Simon MacCorkindale, the best they've ever been, are the yachtsmen discovering a fiendish pre-emptive strike against England by the Germans, way ahead of the First World War. Tony Maylam's direction strives to make the most of authentic locations and the bleakest of headlands, but there's a glorious flaw in the production that itself launches a pre-emptive strike at our suspension of disbelief. In English and German with subtitles.

Michael York *Charles Carruthers* • Jenny Agutter *Clara* • Simon MacCorkindale *Arthur Davies* • Alan Badel *Dollmann* • Jurgen Andersen *Commander Von Brüning* • Michael Sheard *Böhme* ■ *Dir* Tony Maylam • *Scr* Tony Maylam, John Bailey, from the novel by Erskine Childers

Ride ★★ 15

Comedy road movie
1998 · US · Colour · 80mins

This cheap and cheerful hip-hop comedy thriller was made by the team behind *House Party*. Melissa DeSouza plays an aspiring film-maker who gets a job with a top music promo director and is given the task of chaperoning a rap group on their way from New York to Miami. Unbeknown to her, one of the number has stolen money from a

local gangster, prompting a frantic cross-country chase. Loud and brash, with a pumping hip-hop soundtrack, this also boasts cameos from rap luminaries such as Snoopy Doggy Dogg and Dr Dre.

Malik Yoba *Poppa* • Julia Garrison *Blacke* • Guy Torry *Indigo* • Melissa DeSouza *Leta* • John Witherspoon *Roscoe* • Cedric the Entertainer *Bo* • Fredro Starr *Geronimo* • Snoop Doggy Dogg *Mente* • Dr Dre *Eight* ■ *Dir* Millicent Shelton, Millicent Shelton • *Scr* Millicent Shelton

Ride a Crooked Trail ★★★ U

Western 1958 · US · Colour · 87mins

The series of westerns made by Universal starring baby-faced war hero Audie Murphy was extremely variable in quality, but it nevertheless made Murphy (who was actually very good in them) a household name. This is one of the better examples, using a basic mistaken identity plot from the great western screenwriter Borden Chase (who wrote the novel *The Chisholm Trail* on which *Red River* was based). Director Jesse Hibbs keeps things moving along and there's also a marvellous supporting cast: fiery beauty Gia Scala provides the romantic interest, hollow-cheeked Henry Silva is a baddie, and best of all a pre-stardom Walter Matthau is a drunken judge. Don't expect too much and you'll be pleasantly surprised.

Audie Murphy *Joe Maybe* • Gia Scala *Tessa Milotte* • Walter Matthau *Judge Kyle* • Henry Silva *Sam Teeler* • Joanna Moore *Little Brandy* • Eddie Little *Jimmy* • Mary Field *Mrs Curtis* • Leo Gordon *Sam Mason* • Mort Mills *Pecos* ■ *Dir* Jesse Hibbs • *Scr* Borden Chase, from a story by George Bruce

Ride a Wild Pony ★★★

Drama 1976 · US · Colour · 90mins

A highly moralistic and sentimental tale of love and jealousy adapted from the James Aldridge novel *A Sporting Proposition*. Set in 18th-century Australia, Robert Bettles plays a poor, farm schoolboy battling over the ownership of a prize horse with the rich, but polio-stricken, Eva Griffith. Typical Disney fare directed with compassion by Don Chaffey.

Robert Bettles *Scott Pirie* • Eva Griffith *Josie Ellison* • Alfred Bell *Angus* • Melissa Jaffer *Angus' Wife* • Michael Craig *James Ellison* • Lorraine Bayly *Mrs Ellison* • Graham Rouse *Bluey Waters* ■ *Dir* Don Chaffey • *Scr* Rosemary Anne Sisson, from the novel *A Sporting Proposition* by James Aldridge

Ride beyond Vengeance ★★★

Western 1966 · US · Colour · 100mins

A bartender tells a census taker a local story from the 1880s: as he returns to a wife he hasn't seen for 11 years, hunter Chuck Connors is mistaken for a rustler, sadistically branded and robbed. When he's rescued by the real rustler, he plans his revenge. Appropriately, given his affliction here, Connors had recently starred in the television series *Branded* (1965), and this tough, brutal western features several other TV stalwarts, such as Jamie Farr, James McArthur and, most pleasingly, Bill Bixby.

James MacArthur *Delahay, the census taker* • Arthur O'Connell *Narrator* • Ruth Warrick *Aunt Gussie* • Chuck Connors *Jonas Trapp* • Michael Rennie *Brooks Durham* • Kathryn Hays *Jessie* • Joan Blondell *Mrs Lavender* • Gloria Grahame *Bonnie Shelley* • Gary Merrill *Dub Stokes* • Bill Bixby *Johnsy Boy Hood* ■ *Dir* Bernard McEveety • *Scr* Andrew J Fenady, from the novel *The Night of the Tiger* by Al Dewlen

Ride Clear of Diablo ★★ U

Western   1954 · US · Colour · 80mins

Audie Murphy's up against a crooked sheriff and a corrupt lawyer, responsible for the murder of his rancher father and kid brother. With the help of Dan Duryea's likeable badman, he gains his revenge in this well-written but essentially by-the-numbers western. Susan Cabot plays the nice girl, while Abbe Lane is the far more interesting saloon singer. Duryea's rich performance steals the film from the ever stolid Murphy and Jack Elam registers as one of the bad guys.

Audie Murphy *Clay O'Mara* • Dan Duryea *Whitey Kincade* • Susan Cabot *Laurie* • Abbe Lane *Kate* • Russell Johnson *Ringer* • Paul Birch *Sheriff Kenyon* • Jack Elam *Tim* ■ *Dir* Jesse Hibbs • *Scr* George Zuckerman, DD Beauchamp, from a story by Ellis Marcus

Ride 'em Cowboy ★★★★ U

Musical comedy   1942 · US · BW · 85mins

Among the very best Abbott and Costello vehicles, made when the team's routines were still fresh and funny, this is given top-flight treatment by their studio, with some great music providing strong support in between the team's antics. Ella Fitzgerald sings her hit version of *A Tisket, a Tasket*, the superb close-harmony group *The Merry Macs* perform several numbers, and there is some spirited dancing by *The Congoroos* (including a young Dorothy Dandridge). The Don Raye and Gene DePaul songs include the classic *I'll Remember April*, given class-A treatment with a moonlit setting and a lovely choral arrangement backing the singer Dick Foran.

Bud Abbott *Duke* • Lou Costello *Willoughby* • Anne Gwynne *Anne Shaw* • Samuel S Hinds *Sam Shaw* • Dick Foran *Bronco Bob Mitchell* • Richard Lane *Peter Conway* • Ella Fitzgerald *Ruby* • Dorothy Dandridge ■ *Dir* Arthur Lubin • *Scr* True Boardman, John Grant, Harold Shumate, from a story by Edmund L Hartmann

Ride Him, Cowboy ★★ U

Western   1932 · US · BW · 85mins

The first of six B-westerns, largely based on old Ken Maynard silents – *The Unknown Cavalier* (1926) in this case – which a young John Wayne made for Warner Brothers in the early thirties. This cost the same as a mere two-reeler, but doesn't look it. The plot gives prominence to the white horse, Duke, with whom Wayne shares top billing. The steed is framed by the villains and sentenced to death for violent behaviour until Wayne comes to his rescue. Thereafter, the horse saves Wayne from death in the desert and corners the principal villain at the climax, last glimpsed apparently pounding him to death. ▣

John Wayne *John Drury* • Ruth Hall *Ruth Gaunt* • Henry B Walthall *John Gaunt* • Otis

Harlan *Judge Jones* ■ *Dir* Fred Allen • *Scr* Scott Mason, from a story by Kenneth Perkins, from the novel by Kenneth Perkins

Ride in the Whirlwind ★★ PG

Western   1966 · US · Colour · 77mins

Made back-to-back with *The Shooting*, this Jack Nicholson–Monte Hellman western is a loose remake of an Italian film they both admired called *Bandits of Orgosolo*. Three cowpokes, including Nicholson, stumble upon a gang of outlaws hiding out in a mountain shack. Invited to wet their whistles, the cowpokes stay the night and then find themselves surrounded by a gang of vigilantes. A pitched battle follows when Nicholson is obliged to act as an outlaw and a fugitive. It's not as good as the existentialist *Shooting* and is let down by scrappy photography and wooden acting, but the plot has a symbolic and moral power all its own. ▣

Cameron Mitchell *Vern* • Jack Nicholson *Wes* • Tom Filer *Otis* • Millie Perkins *Abby* • Katherine Squire *Catherine* • George Mitchell *Evan* • Brandon Carroll *Sheriff* • Rupert Crosse *Indian Joe* • Harry Dean Stanton *Blind Dick* ■ *Dir* Monte Hellman • *Scr* Jack Nicholson

Ride Lonesome ★★★★ U

Western   1959 · US · Colour · 72mins

Director Budd Boetticher and executive producer and star Randolph Scott, made a short cycle of fine westerns, unequalled in their classic simplicity and under-appreciated on their first release. This is one of the best. The finely tuned Burt Kennedy screenplay wastes not a moment as craggy-featured bounty hunter Scott goes after a young killer (the giggling James Best), ostensibly for the cash reward, but really to flush out his brother, the snarling Lee Van Cleef. Fine western stuff, with chases upon chases and brilliantly taut, terse dialogue. The use of CinemaScope is exemplary, and watch out for James Coburn's movie debut as a feckless outlaw.

Randolph Scott *Ben Brigade* • Karen Steele *Carrie Lane* • Pernell Roberts *Sam Boone* • James Best *Billy John* • Lee Van Cleef *Frank* • James Coburn *Wid* • Dyke Johnson *Charlie* • Boyd Stockman *Indian chief* ■ *Dir* Budd Boetticher • *Scr* Burt Kennedy

Ride the High Country ★★★★ PG

Western   1962 · US · Colour · 90mins

Director Sam Peckinpah proved his magisterial talent with this, his second movie (and many think his finest), a gentle requiem to the Old West, co-starring two icons of the genre, sturdy Joel McCrea and craggy Randolph Scott (in his last role). The casting provides constant delights as the two veterans bicker and cuss their way through a plot about a gold shipment, and should it be stolen or not. The action is superbly photographed by the great Lucien Ballard in eye-filling CinemaScope and Metrocolor, and there are marvellous supporting performances from Peckinpah regulars Warren Oates, LQ Jones and RG Armstrong. There's also a knockout vignette from Edgar Buchanan as a drunken judge. This is a deeply

satisfying, mature movie: don't miss it. ▣

Randolph Scott *Gil Westrum* • Joel McCrea *Steve Judd* • Mariette Hartley *Elsa Knudsen* • Ronald Starr *Heck Longtree* • RG Armstrong *Joshua Knudsen* • Edgar Buchanan *Judge Tolliver* • John Anderson *Elder Hammond* • LQ Jones *Sylvus Hammond* • Warren Oates *Henry Hammond* • James Drury *Billy Hammond* • John Davis Chandler *Jimmy Hammond* ■ *Dir* Sam Peckinpah • *Scr* NB Stone Jr

Ride the Man Down ★ U

Western   1952 · US · Colour · 89mins

Republic put more than enough stalwarts of the genre into this Trucolor western to keep undemanding fans happy. Rod Cameron is the heroic foreman who holds a cattle empire together when, after the death of its owner, Forrest Tucker and Brian Donlevy try to move in. Jim Davis, Paul Fix and Roy Barcroft are three villainous henchmen; Ella Raines and Barbara Britton take the female leads. It should add up to more, but a congested screenplay and indifferent direction by Joseph Kane rob it of dramatic impact.

Brian Donlevy *Bide Marriner* • Rod Cameron *Will Ballard* • Ella Raines *Celia Evarts* • Forrest Tucker *Sam Danfelser* • Barbara Britton *Lottie Priest* • Chill Wills *Ike Adams* • J Carrol Naish *Joe Kneen* • Jim Davis *Red Courteen* • Paul Fix *Ray Cavanaugh* • Roy Barcroft *Russ Schultz* ■ *Dir* Joseph Kane • *Scr* Mary McCall Jr, from a story by Luke Short first published in *The Saturday Evening Post*

Ride the Wild Surf ★★ U

Comedy drama   1964 · US · Colour · 101mins

A colourful and exuberant teen movie about three beach-bum pals who head for Hawaii for the surfing. However, though all three find romance, their new girlfriends (including Barbara Eden of *I Dream of Jeannie* fame) try to persuade them to change their ways. The characters are as flat as their surfboards, but the film is fun and well-made, and the surfing sequences eminently watchable.

Fabian *Jody Wallis* • Shelley Fabares *Brie Matthews* • Tab Hunter *Steamer Lane* • Barbara Eden *Augie Poole* • Peter Brown *Chase Colton* ■ *Dir* Don Taylor • *Scr* Jo Napoleon, Art Napoleon

The Ride to Hangman's Tree ★★★ U

Western   1967 · US · Colour · 89mins

An evocative title for a minor Universal western, utilising the studio's contract players and existing sets. It isn't bad, with Jack Lord (a year before he hit the TV big time with *Hawaii Five-O*) and the ever-excellent James Farentino and Don Galloway playing a trio of outlaws vaguely reminiscent of those cowboy stars whose adventures enthralled young audiences at the Saturday morning pictures. This begins with a cleverly directed and remarkably well-staged robbery: stick with it, it's fun.

Jack Lord *Guy Russell* • James Farentino *Matt Stone* • Don Galloway *Nevada Jones* • Melodie Johnson *Lillie Malone* • Richard Anderson *Steve Carlson* • Robert Yuro *Jeff Scott* • Ed Peck *Sheriff Stewart* • Paul Reed *Corbett* ■ *Dir* Alan Rafkin • *Scr* Luci Ward, Jack Natteford, William Bowers, from a story by Luci Ward, Jack Natteford

Ride, Vaquero! ★★ U

Western   1953 · US · Colour · 90mins

This poorly written western arouses interest from MGM's offbeat casting of the three stars: Robert Taylor, as the quiet but deadly right-hand man of a Mexican bandit; Howard Keel, in a non-singing role as a foolhardy rancher; and Ava Gardner, as the rancher's virtuous wife. Only Anthony Quinn, playing the flamboyant, egotistical Mexican bandit chief who attacks the American ranchers invading his domain, seems cast to type – and he walks away with the picture. John Farrow's direction, Robert Surtees's photography and Bronislau Kaper's music are superior to the script, with its feeble echoes of better westerns.

Robert Taylor (1) *Rio* • Ava Gardner *Cordelia Cameron* • Howard Keel *King Cameron* • Anthony Quinn *Jose Esqueda* • Kurt Kasznar *Father Antonio* • Ted De Corsia *Sheriff Parker* • Charlita *Singer* • Jack Elam *Barton* ■ *Dir* John Farrow • *Scr* Frank Fenton, John Farrow

Ride with the Devil ★★★★★ 15

Historical war drama   1999 · US · Colour · 138mins

Director Ang Lee (*The Ice Storm*, *Sense and Sensibility*) turns in another handsome and moving piece of cinema, this time set against the backdrop of the American Civil War. Jack Bull (Skeet Ulrich) and Jake (Tobey Maguire) are two members of the "Bushwhackers" – Southern guerrillas who secretly ambush Yankee platoons along the Missouri backroads. When they have to hide out for the winter, the pair and two fellow irregulars – one an ex-slave – hole up in a cave cut out of a hill, where they are sent food and water by a beautiful young widow (singer *Jewel*). It's an epic yet intimate portrayal of relationships and war, boasting superb performances from the almost completely male cast and a compelling script by writer/producer James Schamus. Unmissable.

Skeet Ulrich *Jack Bull Chiles* • Tobey Maguire *Jacob Friedel Roedel, "Dutchman"* • Jewel *Sue Lee Shelley* • Jeffrey Wright *Daniel Holt* • Simon Baker *George Clyde* • Jonathan Rhys-Meyers *Pitt Mackeson* • James Caviezel *Black John* • Thomas Guiry *Riley Crawford* • Tom Wilkinson *Orton Brown* ■ *Dir* Ang Lee • *Scr* James Schamus, from the novel *Woe to Live On* by Daniel Woodrell

Ride with the Wind ★★ U

Drama   1994 · US · Colour · 95mins

The name of Craig T Nelson crops up throughout the credits for this overlong and often unashamedly sentimental TV movie. In addition to starring, he also produced and co-wrote this story about a gritty motorcycle rider who willingly blows his chances of the championship, when he vows to improve the lot of a little boy in hospital battling against leukaemia. Nelson is still best known as the dad in the first two *Poltergeist* movies and, try as he might, he fails to convince here either as tough biker or big softie. Hankies may be needed, but only by the very soppy.

Craig T Nelson *Frank Shelby* • Helen Shaver *Katherine Barnes* • Bradley Pierce *Danny*

Barnes • Max Gail *Jack Hayes* • Tracey Walter *Francis Bartley* • Henry G Sanders *Dr Dailey* • Travis McKenna *Travis* ■ *Dir* Bobby Roth • *Scr* Craig T Nelson, Harry Grant, from a story by Grant

Rider from Tucson ★ U

Western   1950 · US · BW · 60mins

One of seven Tim Holt B-westerns released in 1950, this has a competent cast but is sunk by the usual idiotic script and plot in which, as a stagecoach driver notes, the villains steal his passenger but ignore the strongbox. Amid its mechanical storytelling, a chance glimpse of a cat fleeing the hooves of a heavy's mount is refreshingly natural. The only character of interest is Veda Ann Borg's hard-boiled Gypsy, a villainess who cold-bloodedly shoots a lesser heavy and generally acts tough when not sneering at her weak-kneed husband, played by Robert Shayne.

Tim Holt *Dave* • Richard Martin *Chito Rafferty* • Elaine Riley *Jane* • Douglas Fowley *Rankin* • Veda Ann Borg *Gypsy* • Robert Shayne *Avery* ■ *Dir* Lesley Selander • *Scr* Ed Earl

Rider on the Rain ★★★ 18

Thriller   1970 · Fr/It · Colour · 109mins

Marlène Jobert kills the man who rapes her and then tries to cover it up, but she's thwarted by Charles Bronson, who starts sniffing around while keeping his identity a mystery. A solid piece of work from veteran director René Clément, who orchestrates subplots galore, this is a sharp portrait of life in a French seaside town, with echoes of Hitchcock in its concern with the burden of guilt. Bronson, who had just made *Once upon a Time in the West*, had still to become a major star in America. His wife, Jill Ireland, has a supporting role. French dialogue dubbed into English. ▭

Marlène Jobert *Mellie* • Charles Bronson *Colonel Harry Dobbs* • Jean Gaven *Inspector Toussaint* • Corinne Marchand *Tania* • Jill Ireland *Nicole* • Annie Cordy *Juliette* ■ *Dir* René Clément • *Scr* Sébastien Japrisot, Lorenzo Ventavoli

Riders in the Sky ★★ U

Western   1949 · US · BW · 69mins

One of an interminable series of Gene Autry programme fillers, this film allows the singing cowboy to break into the hit song *Ghost Riders in the Sky*. The plot, grafted on to the song, is the usual one about freeing someone framed for murder, but the structure is interesting for this type of production-line fare: a flashback within a flashback that's certainly original and quite amusing. Also, for reasons best known to Autry, his sartorial outfits are far less gaudy and grandiose this time out. Otherwise, strictly for fans only.

Gene Autry *Gene Autry* • Gloria Henry *Ann Lawson* • Pat Buttram *Chuckwalla Jones* • Mary Beth Hughes *Julie Steward* • Robert Livingston *Rock McCleary* • Steve Darrell *Ralph Lawson* • Alan Hale Jr *Marshal Riggs* ■ *Dir* John English • *Scr* Gerald Geraghty, from a story by Herbert A Woodbury

Riders of Destiny ★★ U

Western   1933 · US · BW · 49mins

Historically important, and prophetically titled, this is the first of a dozen or so B-westerns made by John Wayne for Monogram Pictures under producer Paul Malvern's Lone Star trademark, before Wayne was rescued and steered towards stardom by John Ford and *Stagecoach*. Here Wayne plays "Singin' Sandy", a government agent sent a-hunting villains, who (are you ready for this?) sings as he guns them down. The villain of the piece is played by stuntman Yakima Canutt, and this is a movie where, to establish the character's black heart, he actually kicks a dog on his entrance. This style of baddie was therefore known as a "dog heavy", and was a popular cliché in westerns for many years – watch the dog slink away from Jack Palance in *Shane*. The fights between Canutt and Wayne are particularly well staged, but elsewhere the paucity of the $10,000 budget is much in evidence. Fascinating to view today but, unfortunately, not terribly good. ▭

John Wayne *Singin' Sandy Saunders* • Cecilia Parker *Fay Denton* • George Hayes [George "Gabby" Hayes] *Sheriff Denton* • Forrest Taylor *Kincaid* • Lafe McKee *Sheriff* • Fern Emmett *Farm woman* • Yakima Canutt ■ *Dir* Robert North Bradbury [Robert N Bradbury] • *Scr* Robert NorthBradbury

Riders of the Purple Sage ★★★★

Silent western   1925 · US · BW · 56mins

Tom Mix, the most famous cowboy-star of his time, rides tall in the saddle for this engrossing yarn, from the novel by western writer Zane Grey. Its story vaguely echoes John Wayne's *The Searchers* (1956), with Texas Ranger Mix in pursuit of his sister (Beatrice Burnham) and niece, who have been kidnapped by the evil Warner Oland. Lots of fine "head 'em off at the pass" stuff.

Tom Mix *Jim Lassiter* • Beatrice Burnham *Millie Erne* • Arthur Morrison *Frank Erne* • Seesel Ann Johnson *Bess Erne as a child* • Warner Oland *Lew Walters/Judge Dyer* • Fred Kohler *Metzger* ■ *Dir* Lynn Reynolds • *Scr* Edfrid Bingham, from the novel by Zane Grey

Riders of the Purple Sage ★★

Western   1931 · US · BW · 58mins

Zane Grey's huge popularity as a western novelist made his name the principal selling point of Fox's third filming of his first bestseller, dating from 1912. Early in his career as a series cowboy star, George O'Brien follows Tom Mix as the laconic westerner, seeking the man who killed his sister. Superbly photographed by George Schneiderman and – outside of stilted dialogue sequences – briskly directed by Hamilton MacFadden, the film has a strong plot with a decidedly offbeat ending. O'Brien later married leading lady Marguerite Churchill.

George O'Brien *Lassiter* • Marguerite Churchill *Jane Withersteen* • Noah Beery *Judge Dyer* • Yvonne Pelletier *Bess* • James Todd *Venters* • Stanley Fields *Oldring* • Lester Dorr *Judkins* • Shirley Nails *Fay* • Frank McGlynn Sr *Jeff Tull*

■ *Dir* Hamilton MacFadden • *Scr* John F Goodrich, Philip Klein, Barry Connors, from the novel by Zane Grey

Riders of the Purple Sage ★★ U

Western   1941 · US · BW · 65mins

The fourth movie based on the great Zane Grey western novel, and not a patch on the definitive 1925 Tom Mix version. Here it's poker-faced George Montgomery who's wrestling with the multiple twists and turns of the complex plot, though the story has been simplified this time around. The bleak, nihilistic ending still works, proving quite a startling climax to what is basically an ordinary 20th Century-Fox B-western. Fox was grooming Montgomery at the time, and he shows a distinct romantic ability that would soon allow him to move up to main features, co-starring with the likes of Ginger Rogers and Dorothy Lamour.

George Montgomery *Jim Lassiter* • Mary Howard *Jane Withersteen* • Robert Barrat *Judge Dyer* • Lynne Roberts *Bess* • Kane Richmond *Adam Dyer* • Patsy Patterson *Fay Larkin* • Richard Lane *Oldring* • Oscar O'Shea *Judkins* • James Gillette *Venters* • Frank McGrath *Pete* • LeRoy Mason *Jerry Card* ■ *Dir* James Tinling • *Scr* William Bruckner, Robert Metzler, from the novel by Zane Grey

Riders of the Purple Sage ★★★ 12

Western   1996 · US · Colour · 93mins

This made-for-cable feature from husband-and-wife team Ed Harris and Amy Madigan is the fifth screen version of novelist Zane Grey's great trail tale. As producers, it took them ten years to get the project off the ground, but this labour of love was worth the effort. Madigan stars as the rancher who enlists the help of gunslinger Harris, when she's threatened by members of her church after turning down Norbert Weisser's marriage proposal. Director Charles Haid keeps the tone mysterious throughout and, tactfully, Dyer's evil Mormons from the book are not identified as such. In a far cry from the more famous 1925 Tom Mix version, Madigan and Harris prove a formidable twosome. Contains some violence. ▭

Ed Harris *Jim Lassiter* • Amy Madigan *Jane Withersteen* • Henry Thomas *Bern Venters* • Robin Tunney *Bess* • Norbert Weisser *Deacon Tull* • GD Spradlin *Pastor Dyer* • Lynn Wanlass *Hester Brandt* • Bob L Harris *Collier Brandt* ■ *Dir* Charles Haid • *Scr* Gill Dennis, from the novel by Zane Grey

Riders of the Storm ★★ 15

Satirical comedy 1986 · UK · Colour · 100mins

A group of Vietnam veterans start up a pirate radio station to hound right-wing senators in this limp satire on American politics. All the offbeat elements are present and correct – weirdo duo Dennis Hopper and Michael J Pollard doing their "wacky" thing, the presidential candidate etched as a full-blown drag queen, the station situated inside an old B-52 bomber – but the whole strange enterprise simply refuses to gel or elicit much laughter. Boredom soon sets in, and it's not hard to see why this oddball curio was

shelved for three years before getting a release. ▭

Dennis Hopper *Captain* • Michael J Pollard *Doc* • Eugene Lipinski *Ace* • James Aubrey *Claude* • Al Matthews *Ben* • William Armstrong *Jerry* • Nigel Pegram *Sen Willa Westinghouse* • Michael Ho *Minh* • Josie Lawrence *Guerillette* • Ozzy Osbourne ■ *Dir* Maurice Phillips • *Scr* Scott Roberts

Ridicule ★★★★ 15

Historical drama 1996 · Fr · Colour · 97mins

Winner of four Césars and the Bafta for best foreign language film, Patrice Leconte's insight into life at Louis XVI's Versailles, sends an icy chill through the cosy corridors of the costume picture. The rapiers in Remi Waterhouse's script may not be tipped with venom, but there's enough sophistication in the repartee to produce a slyly credible vision of a world founded solely on ambition and indolence. Entering this mausoleum of mordant wit, Charles Berling's country Jekyll turns courtly Hyde, as he seeks to outwit influential black widow Fanny Ardant and her provocative priest, Bernard Giraudeau. An acute, acerbic delight. In French with English subtitles. Contains violence, sex scenes and nudity. ▭

Charles Berling *Ponceludon de Malavoy* • Jean Rochefort *Marquis de Bellegarde* • Fanny Ardant *Madame de Blayac* • Judith Godrèche *Mathilde de Bellegarde* • Bernard Giraudeau *L'Abbée Vilecourt* • Bernard Dhéran *Monsieur de Montalieri* ■ *Dir* Patrice Leconte • *Scr* Remi Waterhouse, Michel Fessler, Eric Vicaut

Riding High ★★ U

Musical western 1943 · US · Colour · 88mins

Not to be confused with Frank Capra's 1950 film of the same name, starring Bing Crosby, this more minor entry features another crooner, Dick Powell, out west. He's the owner of a silver mine that's not paying. Enter burlesque queen, Dorothy Lamour, who does her act at a dude ranch, run by shrieking singer, Cass Daley, to help Powell and his partner, the irritatingly whiny Victor Moore, pay off the mortgage on the mine. Pretty forgettable material, with unmemorable songs, the film does at least have the benefit of the glorious Technicolor and of the period. Released as *Melody Inn* in the UK.

Dorothy Lamour *Ann Castle* • Dick Powell *Steve Baird* • Victor Moore *Mortimer J Slocum* • Gil Lamb *Bob "Foggy" Day* • Cass Daley *Tess Connors* • Bill Goodwin *Chuck Stuart* • Rod Cameron *Sam Welch* ■ *Dir* George Marshall • *Scr* Walter DeLeon, Arthur Phillips, Art Arthur, from the play *Ready Money* by James Montgomery

Riding High ★★★

Musical comedy 1950 · US · BW · 112mins

Director Frank Capra remade his 1934 hit *Broadway Bill* as a Bing Crosby vehicle, yet still managed to incorporate stock footage from the original – watch closely! – and even recast some of the same actors. The result is not entirely without charm and the slight plot changes are an improvement (the hero is now engaged to the heroine, not married to her), but it lacks the feeling of sheer goodwill of the Warner Baxter/Myrna Loy original. The added songs though, don't hurt the narrative and Crosby's real-life affection for horse racing is evident. There's also a rare late appearance from the great Oliver Hardy, but *Red River's* Coleen Gray is a rather bland co-star among all those swell character actors.

Bing Crosby *Dan Brooks* • Coleen Gray *Alice Higgins* • Charles Bickford *JL Higgins* • William Demarest *Happy McGuire* • Frances Gifford *Margaret Higgins* • Raymond Walburn *Professor Pettigrew* • James Gleason *Racing Secretary* • Ward Bond *Lee* • Clarence Muse *Whitey* • Percy Kilbride *Pop Jones* ■ *Dir* Frank Capra • *Scr* Robert Riskin, Nelville Shavelson, Jack Rose, from the story *Broadway Bill* by Mark Hellinger

Riding Shotgun ★★ U

Western 1954 · US · Colour · 74mins

Throughout the fifties, western fans were well-served by colour programme fillers, invariably featuring either baby-faced Audie Murphy or craggy Randolph Scott. Eventually Scott managed to fashion his co-features into a remarkable series of westerns, the Ranown cycle. Prior to that, however, Randy rode a tall saddle, invariably directed by Warners hack-of-all-trades, the one-eyed Andre De Toth, of whose work this is a prime example. The plot is the usual one of Scott attempting to clear his name, and down the cast list as a baddie is one Charles Buchinsky, who changed his name to Bronson a year later. Nothing spectacular, then, but still reasonably undemanding entertainment.

Randolph Scott *Larry Delong* • Wayne Morris *Tub Murphy* • Joan Weldon *Orissa Flynn* • Joe Sawyer *Tom Biggert* • James Millican *Dan Maraday* • Charles Buchinski [Charles Bronson] *Pinto* ■ *Dir* Andre De Toth • *Scr* Tom Blackburn, from the story *Riding Solo* by Kenneth Perkins

Rien Ne Va Plus ★★★★ 15

Comedy thriller
1997 · Fr/Swi · Colour · 101mins

Claude Chabrol's 50th movie is a smashing comedy thriller about a pair of con artists, played by Isabelle Huppert and Michel Serrault, best known for his camp performance in *La Cage aux Folles*. Criss-crossing France in search of victims, Huppert and Serrault are exuberant partners in crime, who nearly come unstuck when Huppert sets her sights on a business executive with a suitcase bursting with mob money. The mood swings wonderfully from comedy to romance, to occasionally shocking violence. In French with English subtitles.

Isabelle Huppert *Elisabeth/"Betty"* • Michel Serrault *Victor* • François Cluzet *Maurice Biagini* • Jean-François Balmer *Monsieur K* • Jackie Berroyer *Robert Châtillon* • Thomas Chabrol *Hotel Waldhaus bellboy* ■ *Dir/Scr* Claude Chabrol

Rien sur Robert ★★★ 18

Comedy drama 1998 · Fr · Colour · 106mins

Hamstrung by highbrow pomposity and crippling self-doubt, trapped within a circle of friends vying to become his severest critic, Fabrice Luchini gives a wonderful performance of bourgeois neuroticism in this assured satire from writer/director Pascal Bonitzer. Lacing Rohmer-esque discourses with wisecracks Woody Allen would be proud of, the literate screenplay is seized upon by an excellent cast, with Michel Piccoli particularly relishing his bombastic rants. However, there are also some inspired set pieces involving Piccoli's eccentric daughter (Valentina Cervi) and Luchini's permanently dissatisfied ex (Sandrine Kiberlain). It's just a shame the picture loses momentum as it approaches its disappointingly flat finale. In French with English subtitles.

Fabrice Luchini *Didier Temple* • Sandrine Kiberlain *Juliette Sauvage* • Valentina Cervi *Aurélie Coquille* • Michel Piccoli *Lord Ariel Chatwick-West* • Bernadette Lafont *Madame Sauvage* • Laurent Lucas *Jérôme Sauveur* ■ *Dir/Scr* Pascal Bonitzer

Riff-Raff ★★★★ 15

Drama 1991 · UK · Colour · 95mins

Ken Loach's film about life on a London building site gave Robert Carlyle his first shot at stardom, which he seized with both hands. Working from a script by Bill Jesse, who died before the film was finished, this exploration of a gang of ethnically diverse labourers as they work on a closed-down hospital, is lighter in mood than many Loach movies, though Carlyle's romantic dalliance with Emer McCourt never quite convinces. It also features one of Ricky Tomlinson's first screen performances. DVD

Robert Carlyle *Stevie* • Emer McCourt *Susan* • Jimmy Coleman *Shem* • George Moss *Mo* • Ricky Tomlinson *Larry* • David Finch *Kevin* • Richard Belgrave *Kojo* ■ *Dir* Ken Loach • *Scr* Bill Jesse

Riffraff ★★★

Drama 1936 · US · BW · 94mins

No, not Ken Loach's 1991 construction worker drama, but the genuine starry article, an MGM major feature about a pair of fisherfolk who end up on the wrong side of the law. At any other studio this would be a potboiler, but here it earns its place in posterity thanks to luminous star performances from blonde bombshell Jean Harlow (disguised in a brown wig) and her likeable co-star, dependable Spencer Tracy. Their scenes together reveal an easy camaraderie that's very pleasant to watch, a sort of "hey we know the plot's not up to much but we're having a good time anyway" quality which gives the movie a distinction that rises above J Walter Ruben's pallid direction and an uneasiness of tone. Frankly, with real movie stars like Harlow and Tracy in the leads, does anything else really matter? Switch off before the tacked-on, glutinous ending.

Jean Harlow *Hattie* • Spencer Tracy *Dutch Miller* • Joseph Calleia *Nick Appopolis* • Una Merkel *Lil* • Mickey Rooney *Jimmy* • Victor Kilian *Flytrap* • J Farrell MacDonald *Brains* • Roger Imhof *Pops* • Baby Jane "Juanita" Quigley *Rosie* ■ *Dir* J Walter Ruben • *Scr* Frances Marion, HW Hanemann, Anita Loos, from a story by Frances Marion

Rififi ★★★★

Crime caper 1955 · Fr · BW · 118mins

Little did Jules Dassin know, as he sent Jean Servais and his gang into a Rue de Rivoli jewellery store, that he was giving birth to that ever-popular sub-genre, the caper movie. However, no one since has matched the tension and cinematic mastery of the near 30-minute robbery sequence, which is executed in the minutest detail and without resort to dialogue or ambient score. The change of pace, as rival mobster Marcel Lupovici moves in for an undeserved cut, is also neatly accomplished. But there's precious little happening beneath the dazzling surface. Incidentally, that's Dassin playing César, under the pseudonym, Perlo Vita. In French with English subtitles.

Jean Servais *Tony le Stephanois* • Carl Mohner *Jo le Suedois* • Robert Manuel *Mario* • Perlo Vita [Jules Dassin] *César* • Marie Sabouret *Mado* • Janine Darcey *Louise* • Claude Sylvain *Ida* • Marcel Lupovici *Pierre Grutter* ■ *Dir* Jules Dassin • *Scr* Jules Dassin, Rene Wheeler, Auguste Le Breton, from a novel by Auguste Le Breton • *Production Designer* Trauner [Alexandre Trauner]

Right Bank, Left Bank ★★

Thriller 1984 · Fr · Colour · 105mins

A much-amended, yet still muddled script and inexact casting, undermine this lightweight melodrama from Philippe Labro. Bringing together the stars of *The Return of Martin Guerre*, the film has a similar feel, despite its contemporary setting, as divorced publicist Nathalie Baye (who has just quit her job because of sexual harassment) slowly comes to trust smooth media lawyer, Gérard Depardieu, as he regains his principles through her influence and exposes corrupt client, Bernard Fresson. There are also hints of a future Depardieu vehicle, *Trop Belle pour Toi*, as he abandons his perfect wife, Carole Bouquet, for this risky romance. French dialogue dubbed into English.

Gérard Depardieu *Paul Senanques* • Nathalie Baye *Sacha Vernakis* • Bernard Fresson *President* • Charlotte De Turckheim *Catherine* • Robert Bruce *Bobby* • Marcel Bozonnet *Michel Monblanc* ■ *Dir* Philippe Labro • *Scr* Philippe Labro, Françoise Labro

Right Cross ★★★ U

Sports drama 1950 · US · BW · 89mins

A boxing drama, directed by John Sturges, in which Mexican, Ricardo Montalban, has a chip on his shoulder about his racial origins, but faces a real problem when injury to his hand prevents him from fighting. There's a love triangle involving Montalban, June Allyson and sports writer Dick Powell and Lionel Barrymore features as the fight manager. The movie does capture the flavour of the boxing world, but the introduction of a racial theme seems to be an attempt to provide depth to an otherwise unremarkable plot. Look out for the brief, unbilled appearance of soon-to-be-a star Marilyn Monroe.

June Allyson *Pat O'Malley* • Dick Powell *Rick Gavery* • Ricardo Montalban *Johnny Monterez* • Lionel Barrymore *Sean O'Malley* • Teresa Celli *Marian Monterez* • Barry Kelley *Allan Goff* • Tom Powers *Robert Balford* • Marilyn Monroe *Blonde* ■ *Dir* John Sturges • *Scr* Charles Schnee

The Right Hand Man ★

Period drama 1986 · Ausl · Colour · 100mins

The single saving grace here is decent cinematography – that aside this is a Bernard Matthews of a movie. Rupert Everett stars as a foppish heir, whose mama wishes to mate in a similar manner to the stud horses in her stables. Meanwhile, Everett manages to faint, kill his papa and lose an arm in an accident. It's here, during amputation, that the doctor's daughter falls in love with him and their ridiculous romance starts. Appalling in every sense, this is one that Everett must wish would stay in its country of origin – down under.

Rupert Everett *Harry Ironminster* • Hugo Weaving *Ned Rowlands* • Catherine McClements *Sarah Redbridge* • Arthur Dignam *Dr Redbridge* • Jennifer Claire *Lady Ironminster* ■ *Dir* Di Drew • *Scr* Helen Hodgman, Kit Denton, from the novel by Kathleen Peyton • *Cinematographer* Peter James

Right of Way ★★

Drama 1983 · US · Colour · 106mins

With a combined total of over 100 years in pictures, Bette Davis and James Stewart co-starred for the first time in this cloying made-for-TV study of voluntary euthanasia, that was not only unworthy of their talents, but was also badly botched by the producers, who tinkered with the ending, late in post-production, to avoid undue controversy. Initially it's hard to accept these highly distinctive performers as a devoted couple. But once Stewart begins defending to daughter Melinda Dillon his decision to join his terminally ill wife in death, the union begins to gel – making the front-office cowardice all the more disappointing.

Bette Davis *Mini Dwyer* • James Stewart *Teddy Dwyer* • Melinda Dillon *Ruda Dwyer* • Priscilla Morrill *Louise Finter* • John Harkins *G Clayburn* • Louis Schaefer *Kahn* ■ *Dir* George Schaefer • *Scr* Richard Lee, from his play

The Right Stuff ★★★★ 15

Historical drama
1983 · US · Colour · 184mins

An exhilarating, if sprawling, adaptation of Tom Wolfe's bestseller, *The Right Stuff* is a striking Oscar-winning chronicle about the training of the first American astronauts. The point of director Philip Kaufman's visually dazzling epic, is to ally the early test pilots, such as Chuck Yeager (stoically played by Sam Shepard) who clearly have the "right stuff" for the job, with the pioneering heroes of the Old West. Borrowing a great deal from the work of maverick director John Ford in terms of mythological scope and story structuring, Kaufman's drama documentary is a great tribute to the space race packed with terrific performances – Ed Harris, Fred Ward, Dennis Quaid – thought-provoking satire, nail-biting aerial scenes and emotional resonance. DVD

Sam Shepard *Chuck Yeager* • Scott Glenn *Alan Shepard* • Ed Harris *John Glenn* • Dennis Quaid *Gordon Cooper* • Fred Ward *Gus Grissom* • Barbara Hershey *Glennis Yeager* • Veronica Cartwright *Betty Grissom* • Pamela Reed *Trudy Cooper* • Lance Henricksen *Walter Schirra* • Donald Moffat *Lyndon B Johnson* • Levon Helm *Jack Ridley* ■ *Dir* Philip Kaufman • *Scr* Kim Stanley, Philip Kaufman • *Cinematographer* Caleb Deschanel • *Music* Bill Conti

1190 U = SUITABLE FOR ALL Uc = SUITABLE FOR ALL, ESPECIALLY FOR YOUNG CHILDREN (VIDEO ONLY) PG = PARENTAL GUIDANCE

Right to Die ★★ 15

Drama based on a true story
1987 · US · Colour · 92mins

Sex goddess Raquel Welch, typically known for much less dramatic fare, tries her hand at a serious role and does a surprisingly affecting job. In this fact-based story, a young psychologist stricken by the incurable degenerative disease ALS, better known as Lou Gehrig's Disease, asks her husband Michael Gross (Michael J Fox's father in TV's *Family Ties*) to help her commit suicide so that she can die with dignity. This well-worn formula is given a fresh feel, thanks to sharp direction by TV-movie specialist Paul Wendkos and solid performances by both Welch and Gross. However you might feel about the controversial subject of euthanasia, this TV drama deserves a look. ▭

Raquel Welch *Emily Bauer* • Michael Gross *Bob Bauer* • Bonnie Bartlett *Lilian* • Ed O'Neill *Bob's partner* • Mark Shera *Emily's brother* • Joanna Miles *Psychiatrist* ■ *Dir* Paul Wendkos • *Scr* Phil Penningroth

Right to Kill? ★★★ 15

Drama based on a true story
1985 · US · Colour · 90mins

Frederic Forrest turns in a high-class performance as the brutal, if not deranged, man who tyrannises his wife and teenage children with a regime of relentless physical and mental abuse. Forrest gives a gritty performance in a difficult role, and Christopher Collet does well as the son who realises that he must take action. This American film was shot in Texas, but the real-life character portrayed by Forrest lived in South Dakota. A superior TV drama. ▭

Frederic Forrest *Richard Jahnke Sr* • Christopher Collet *Richard Jahnke Jr* • Justine Bateman *Deborah Jahnke* • Ann Wedgeworth *Eve Whitcomb* • JT Walsh *Major Vegvary* ■ *Dir* John Erman • *Scr* Joyce Eliason

Rigoletto ★★★ U

Opera
1946 · It · BW · 104mins

Inspired by Victor Hugo's play, *Le Roi s'amuse*, Verdi's opera is adapted with reverence by veteran director, Carmine Gallone. The celebrated baritone, Tito Gobbi, stars as Rigoletto, the acerbic crookbacked jester of the dilettante Duke of Mantua, who, labouring under the curse of an abused count, unknowingly participates in the kidnapping of his own daughter, Gilda. Determined to avenge himself on the Duke, he hires Sparafucile, the assassin, to waylay him at a country inn, but his scheme tragically backfires. The decor is undeniably theatrical, but the music and the performances (with Lina Pagliughi voicing Marcella Govoni's Gilda) are admirable. An Italian language film.

Tito Gobbi *Rigoletto* • Mario Filippeschi *Duke of Mantua* • Marcella Govoni *Gilda* • Lina Pagliughi *Gilda (singing voice)* • Anna Maria Canali *Maddalena* • Giulio Neri *Sparafucile* • Marcello Giorda *Monterone* ■ *Dir* Carmine Gallone • *Scr* from the opera by Giuseppe Verdi

Rigoletto ★★

Drama
1995 · US · Colour · 98mins

Before any opera buffs get excited, this isn't the Pavarotti version of Verdi's classic work, but a tacky melodrama that should never have been allowed to use the revered title. The full-throated Joseph Paur stars as the mean-spirited mystery man whose heart is melted by a young girl so moved by the story of Rigoletto, that she will do anything to become a diva. Utterly lacking in finesse, the film is a sanitised version of the *Phantom of the Opera* story. A well-meaning attempt to interest kids in opera, but it's unlikely to succeed.

Joseph Paur *Ribaldi* • Ivey Lloyd *Bonnie* • Tracey Williams *Gabriella* • Frank Gerrish *Papanickolas* ■ *Dir/Scr* Leo Paur

Rikky and Pete ★★

Comedy drama 1988 · Ausl · Colour · 103mins

Less innocent or effective than its predecessor, *Malcolm* (1986), Nadia Tass and husband David Parker's second feature is a considerable disappointment. Many of the same elements are in place, notably the fascination with eccentric gadgets. But, there's nothing intriguing about the sister-and-brother act of geologist, Nina Landis and inventor, Stephen Kearney. Whether they're taunting blustering Melbourne cop, Bill Hunter, or putting their offbeat talents to more constructive use in the backwater mining town of Mount Isa. Dorothy Alison and Bruno Lawrence provide some serviceable support, but there's a rehashed feel to the storyline, the characters and the comedy.

Stephen Kearney *Pete* • Nina Landis *Rikky* • Tetchie Agbayani *Flossie* • Bill Hunter *Sergeant Whitstead* • Bruno Lawrence *Sonny* • Bruce Spence *Ben* • Dorothy Alison *Mrs Menzies* ■ *Dir* Nadia Tass • *Scr* David Parker, from his story

Rikyu ★★★★

Biographical drama
1989 · Jap · Colour · 135mins

Fascinated by the life of Rikyu, Hiroshi Teshigahara emerged from a 12-year feature film-making hiatus to discover Kei Kumai tackling the identical topic in the Toshiro Mifune vehicle, *Death of a Tea Master*. But, notwithstanding its greater star wattage, it lacked the stylised realism and structural rigour of this stately, allegorical study of 16th-century ritual and intrigue. Befitting Teshigahara's status as a master flower arranger, every image is laden with precise symbolism and the clash between coarse warrior-turned-ruler, Tsutomu Yamazaki, and culturally refined Buddhist monk, Rentaro Mikuni, is as much about a proposed invasion of China, as the niceties of the tea ceremony. A Japanese language film.

Rentaro Mikuni *Sen-no Rikyu* • Tsutomu Yamazaki *Hideyoshi Toyotomi* • Yoshiko Mita *Riki, Rikyu's wife* ■ *Dir* Hiroshi Teshigahara • *Scr* Hiroshi Teshigahara, Genpei Akasegawa, from a novel by Yaeko Nogami

The Ring ★★★ U

Silent drama 1927 · UK · BW · 109mins

Alfred Hitchcock's silent, sixth, credited feature concerns a champion fairground boxer (Carl Brisson), the girl he loves and eventually marries (Lillian Hall-Davies), and the Australian fighter (Ian Hunter) who almost tempts her away. On the surface, a routine drama, but watch it closely and it reveals the psychological undertow, signalled in carefully chosen images, that are the hallmarks of the Master's better known, later films. The very word "ring", for example, alludes not only to the men's occupation, but the circular artefacts of the fairground (the tents, the carousel), the bracelet Hunter gives the girl, the wedding ring Brisson places on her finger, and the circular emotional journey of the protagonists. ▭

Carl Brisson *Jack Sander* • Lillian Hall-Davies *Nelly* • Ian Hunter *Bob Corby* ■ *Dir* Alfred Hitchcock • *Scr* Alfred Hitchcock, Alma Reville, from a story by Alfred Hitchcock

The Ring ★★ U

Drama 1952 · US · BW · 79mins

A little-known but interesting drama about racial discrimination, it concerns a young Mexican-American who tries to earn the respect of whites by succeeding as a prizefighter. The star, Lalo Rios, takes third billing to minor Hollywood lead Gerald Mohr, playing his manager, and to then little-known Rita Moreno as the youngster's girlfriend. The film is refreshingly small scale, the story sensibly rather than sensationally resolved with an excellent script by Irving Shulman and careful direction by Kurt Neumann, which develops a documentary-like atmosphere.

Gerald Mohr *Pete* • Rita Moreno *Lucy* • Lalo Rios *Tommy* • Robert Arthur *Billy Smith* • Robert Osterloh *Freddy* • Martin Garralaga *Vidal* • Jack Elam *Harry Jackson* ■ *Dir* Kurt Neumann • *Scr* Irving Shulman, from the novel *Cry Tough* by Irving Shulman

Ring of Bright Water ★★★ U

Drama 1969 · UK · Colour · 106mins

Born Free stars, Bill Travers and Virginia McKenna, yet again allow themselves to be upstaged by an adorable creature in this delightful adaptation of Gavin Maxwell's bestseller. While Mij the otter hasn't the majestic presence of Elsa the lioness or the voice of Babe the sheep-pig, he'll still win the hearts of children with his mischievous escapades, whether careering around a cramped city-flat, splashing in his private swimming tank or romping in the snow. There's even room for a few tears in one tragic scene, but the lasting impression will be one of a wonderful little animal with a larger-than-life personality. ▭

Bill Travers *Graham Merrill* • Virginia McKenna *Mary MacKenzie* • Peter Jeffrey *Colin Clifford* • Roddy McMillan *Bus driver* • Jameson Clark *Storekeeper* • Jean Taylor-Smith *Sarah Chambers* • Helena Gloag *Flora Elrich* ■ *Dir* Jack Couffer • *Scr* Jack Couffer, Bill Travers, from the book by Gavin Maxwell

Ring of Fire ★★★

Action adventure 1961 · US · Colour · 90mins

TV's *The Fugitive*, David Janssen, is an Oregon deputy sheriff who arrests and is then kidnapped by three juvenile delinquents. While the plot's twists and turns take some believing, the pace is fast enough and the action spectacular enough – notably a climactic forest fire that engulfs a township – to make such considerations redundant. Directed, produced, written and edited by the "rolling" Stones – that is, Andrew and Virginia, husband-and-wife, whose work still awaits critical "rediscovery" – the picture has the old-fashioned virtues of an outdoor adventure that's gutsy in all the right places.

David Janssen *Sergeant Steve Walsh* • Joyce Taylor *Bobbie Adams* • Frank Gorshin *Frank Henderson* • Joel Marston *Deputy Pringle* • James Johnson *Roy Anderson* • Ron Myron *Sheriff Niles* ■ *Dir/Scr* Andrew L Stone

Ring of Fire ★★ 18

Martial arts drama
1991 · US · Colour · 92mins

Don "The Dragon" Wilson plays Johnny Wu, a young medical intern with great martial arts skills who falls in love with a Caucasian woman (Maria Ford), to the disapproval of his friends. After all the fights are done, will these star-crossed lovers be together? Just because it's based on the *Romeo and Juliet* story, don't expect Shakespearean acting, especially from kick-boxing champ Wilson. However, *Ring of Fire* is much more good natured and endearing than most films of this type. ▭

Don "The Dragon"Wilson *Johnny Wu* • Eric Lee *Kwong* • Dale Edmund Jacoby *Brad* • Steven Vincent Leigh *Terry* • Marie Ford *Julie* • Vince Murdocco *Chuck* ■ *Dir* Richard W Munchkin • *Scr* Richard W Munchkin, Jake Jacobs

Ring of Spies ★★★

Spy drama based on a true story
1963 · UK · BW · 90mins

Throughout his career, Frank Launder proved himself to be just as capable of turning out a nail-biting thriller, as he was of crafting a chortle-worthy comedy. For once, separated from his usual partner, Sidney Gilliatt (although the latter's brother Leslie acted as producer), Launder and co-writer Peter Barnes capably retell the story of the Portland spy ring, whose activities prompted "Reds under the bed" scare stories in the popular press. The docudramatic style rather undermines director Robert Tronson's attempts to build suspense, but there's a nice irony in the casting of Bernard Lee ("M" from the Bond movies) as a blackmail target.

Bernard Lee *Henry Houghton* • William Sylvester *Gordon Lonsdale* • Margaret Tyzack *Elizabeth Gee* • David Kossoff *Peter Kroger* • Nancy Nevinson *Helen Kroger* • Thorley Walters *Commander Winters* • Gillian Lewis *Marjorie Shaw* • Brian Nissen *Lieutenant Downes* ■ *Dir* Robert Tronson • *Scr* Frank Launder, Peter Barnes

Ring of Steel ★★ 🔞

Martial arts action
1994 · US · Colour · 89mins

A disgraced fencing champion joins an illegal sword-fighting club – the Ring of Steel. Lots of fights follow and the champion finds out that the Ring exacts a price from its combatants that's too high to pay. The plot is simple and fairly compelling, even if much of the acting is sub-par. A touch of surrealism is added to the proceedings by the casting of beefy Joe Don Baker as the Man in Black, who runs the whole show. In a couple of early scenes, Baker seems to be putting on a European accent, but happily he drops it later on. ▢

Joe Don Baker *Man in Black* • Carol Alt *Tanya* • Robert Chapin *Alex Freyer* • Darlene Vogel *Elena* • Gary Kasper *Jack* • Jim Pirri *Brian* ∎ *Dir* David Frost • *Scr* Robert Chapin

Ring of the Musketeers ★★ 🔞

Action adventure 1994 · US · Colour · 82mins

This is the sort of crackpot concept that you can imagine a bunch of Hollywood film developers dreaming up during a "brainstorming" sessions. "How about doing *The Musketeers*?" "Nah, its been done. And, besides, we can't afford the costumes." "How about updating it? Then they can all wear their street clothes." "Brilliant!" And update it is just what they've done. Umpteen generations on, the descendents of the old swashbucklers get together for an "all for one, and one for all" bid to rescue a boy from a mob boss. Either the makers couldn't afford, or couldn't interest, any A-list stars. So, instead, there's David Hasselhoff, Alison Doody, Richard "Cheech" Marin and John Rhys-Davies, all obviously having fun in a mildly entertaining piece of hokum. ▢

David Hasselhoff *John Smith D'Artagnan* • Thomas Gottschalk *Peter Porthos* • Corbin Bernsen *Harry* • Alison Doody *Anne-Marie* • John Rhys-Davies *Maurice Treville* • Richard "Cheech" Marin *Burt Aramis* • Catherine E Coulson *Lina* • Andy Romano *Vince Pellito* ∎ *Dir* John Paragon • *Scr* John Paragon, Joel Surnow

Ringo and His Golden Pistol ★★★ 🆄

Spaghetti western 1966 · It · Colour · 87mins

Sergio Corbucci spent much of his career in the shadow of spaghetti western master, Sergio Leone. Lacking Leone's storytelling gifts, Corbucci was prone to fall back on violence and camera trickery when short on plot inspiration. Here, he is content to enliven this unremarkable, but occasionally explosive, tale of banditry and bounty-hunting with ideas borrowed from such contemporary (and far superior) offerings as Leone's *The Good, the Bad and the Ugly*, Duccio Tessari's *A Pistol for Ringo* and Corbucci's own cult classic, *Django*. The success of Tessari's film prompted the changing of the original title, *Johnny Oro*, for this English language version. Star, Mark Damon is now a successful independent producer in Hollywood, with *Rudyard Kipling's The Jungle Book*, *High Spirits* and *Flight of the Navigator* among his

credits. Italian dialogue dubbed into English.

Mark Damon *Ringo* • Valeria Fabrizi *Margie* • Ettore Manni *Sheriff Norton* • Giulia Rubini *Norton's wife* • *Dir* Sergio Corbucci • *Scr* Adriano Bolzoni, Franco Rossetti

Rings on Her Fingers ★★★ 🆄

Comedy 1942 · US · BW · 86mins

After the popular and critical success of *The Lady Eve*, Henry Fonda's portrayal of naivety was used again as the springboard for a wily female's confidence trick, only this time beautiful Gene Tierney is the fleecer who falls for her victim. Alas, she's no Barbara Stanwyck, any more than director Rouben Mamoulian is a match for the great Preston Sturges. There's a regrettable coldness about the Fonda/Tierney partnership, but Laird Cregar and Spring Byington are very watchable as Tierney's crooked partners, and the movie is genuinely funny and absorbing throughout its first half. Unfortunately, it runs out of steam as Tierney reforms her ways.

Henry Fonda *John Wheeler* • Gene Tierney *Susan Miller* • Laird Cregar *Warren* • John Shepperd [Shepperd Strudwick] *Tod Fenwick* • Spring Byington *Mrs Maybelle Worthington* • Frank Orth *Kellogg* • Henry Stephenson *Colonel Prentice* • Marjorie Gateson *Mrs Fenwick* ∎ *Dir* Rouben Mamoulian • *Scr* Ken Englund, from a story by Robert Pirosh, Joseph Schrank

Ringside Maisie ★★★

Comedy 1941 · US · BW · 96mins

Out in the cold in the Adirondacks, where she had hoped for a job as a dancer in a hotel, Maisie (Ann Sothern) is rescued by an up-and-coming boxer (Robert Sterling). She becomes the companion of his crippled mother (Margaret Moffat) and falls for his initially hostile manager (George Murphy). Edwin L Marin was again at the helm, there is a nifty piece of eccentric characterisation in Sterling's compulsive-eater girlfriend (Natalie Thompson) and the *Maisie* formula is enlivened with some fight scenes.

Ann Sothern *Maisie Ravier* • George Murphy *Skeets Maguire* • Robert Sterling *Terry Dolan* • Natalie Thompson *Cecelia Reardon* • Maxie Rosenbloom *Chotsie* • Margaret Moffat *Mrs Dolan* • John Indrisano *Peaches* • Virginia O'Brien *Virginia O'Brien* ∎ *Dir* Edwin L Marin • *Scr* Mary C McCall Jr

The Rink ★★★★ 🆄

Silent action comedy
1916 · US · BW · 20mins

In his eighth short for Mutual, Charles Chaplin plays both waiter and skater in this celebration of the roller-skating craze that swept Europe and America during the late 19th/early 20th centuries. At once victim and dominant force, he evades heavy Eric Campbell to win the hand of Edna Purviance with a ferocious cascade of pratfalls and near-miss pirouettes. This typically hilarious piece of sophisticated slapstick was based on a routine dating back to his vaudeville days with Fred Karno. ▢

Charles Chaplin *A waiter, posing as Sir Cecil Seltzer* • Edna Purviance *The girl* • James T

Kelley *Her father* • Eric Campbell *Mr Stout* • Henry Bergman *Mrs Stout* ∎ *Dir/Scr* Charles Chaplin

Rio Bravo ★★★★★ 🅿🅶

Western 1959 · US · Colour · 135mins

Under-rated at the time of its release, this majestically paced western is one of the finest achievements of the genre, and stands as a career-best for many of its participants, its above-average length and simplistic plot mask a work of depth and artistry. Originally intended by director Howard Hawks as a riposte to the liberal *High Noon*, the quality and class of this movie owe little to what had gone before, save some dialogue lifted from Hawks's earlier *To Have and Have Not*. This is a definitive study of male camaraderie, particularly in the wordless opening sequence as John Wayne attempts to preserve the drunken Dean Martin's dignity. The casting is perfect (if you believe Ricky Nelson as a gunslinger) and the sense of fun contagious. Superb Technicolor photography and a Dimitri Tiomkin score provide the icing on a very impressive cake. ▢

John Wayne *John T Chance* • Dean Martin *Dude* • Ricky Nelson *Colorado Ryan* • Angie Dickinson *Feathers* • Walter Brennan *Stumpy* • Ward Bond *Pat Wheeler* • John Russell *Nathan Burdette* ∎ *Dir* Howard Hawks • *Scr* Jules Furthman, Leigh Brackett, from a story by Barbara Hawks McCampbell • *Cinematographer* Russell Harlan

Rio Conchos ★★

Western 1964 · US · Colour · 106mins

This is a violent near remake (uncredited) of *The Comancheros*, a reasonable hit for 20th Century Fox in 1961, sadly this time without Big John Wayne, though Richard Boone is a sturdy, if stolid, substitute. Stuart Whitman makes a return from the earlier movie and Edmond O'Brien puts in a reliable performance. It is competently handled by veteran director Gordon Douglas, who evokes *The Charge at Feather River* in the climactic attack, but the whole just isn't involving enough. Still, today, any such gritty western in CinemaScope is welcome, and this is interesting for the feature film debut of American football star Jim Brown, who would later walk away with *100 Rifles*, a film with a very similar story.

Richard Boone *Lassiter* • Stuart Whitman *Captain Haven* • Tony Franciosa [Anthony Franciosa] *Rodriguez* • Wende Wagner *Sally* • Edmond O'Brien *Colonel Theron Pardee* • Warner Anderson *Colonel Wagner* • Jim Brown *Sgt Ben Franklyn* ∎ *Dir* Gordon Douglas • *Scr* Joseph Landon, Clair Huffaker, from the novel *Guns of the Rio Conchos* by Clair Huffaker

Rio Diablo ★★★

Western 1993 · US · Colour · 120mins

Not content with robbing a bank and shooting up a town, bandits kidnap a bride on her wedding day, in this TV-movie western that's co-produced by country singer Kenny Rogers's own company. And the country connections don't stop there, as bounty hunter Rogers rides in to help bewildered groom Travis Tritt (who's not bad), while Naomi Judd crops up as the owner of a bar. Veteran Stacy Keach

makes sure that the singers don't grab all the limelight, giving good value as a heavy. Contains violence.

Kenny Rogers *Quinton Leech* • Travis Tritt *Benjamin Tabor* • Naomi Judd *Flora Mae Pepper* • Stacy Keach *Kansas* • Brion James *Jake Walker* • Bruce Greenwood *Jarvis Walker* • Laura Harring *Maria Gutierrez* • Michael G Hagerty *Dyke Holland* • Luis Contreras *Almenzar* • Kelly Junkermann *Carson* ∎ *Dir* Rod Hardy • *Scr* Frank Q Dobbs, David Cass, Stephen Lodge

Rio Grande ★★★★★ 🆄

Western 1950 · US · BW · 104mins

The third, great, John Ford cavalry western – following *Fort Apache* and *She Wore a Yellow Ribbon* – tells the story of a daring off-the-record solution to Indian raids from across the border. It also features a powerful romantic relationship between John Wayne and Maureen O'Hara as the fort commander and his long-separated wife. O'Hara was the strongest leading lady Wayne ever had and almost his match in stubborn pride (they co-starred in four more films). Here, she re-enters Wayne's life seeking to protect their son (Claude Jarman Jr), a private sent out west to serve under him. Once again, Ford creates a stirring picture of the Old West – if this wasn't the way it was, it's the way it should have been. ▢

John Wayne *Lt Colonel Yorke* • Maureen O'Hara *Mrs Yorke* • Ben Johnson *Trooper Tyree* • Claude Jarman Jr *Trooper Jeff Yorke* • Harry Carey Jr *Trooper Boone* • Chill Wills *Dr Wilkins* • J Carrol Naish *General Sheridan* • Victor McLaglen *Quincannon* ∎ *Dir* John Ford • *Scr* James Kevin McGuinness

Rio Lobo ★★★ 🅿🅶

Western 1970 · US · Colour · 109mins

A mite saddle-weary, maybe, but John Wayne's last film with director Howard Hawks, the third, after *Rio Bravo* and *El Dorado*, with scripts from novelist Leigh Brackett, has a wonderful sense of western occasion. The sardonic humour lights up a listless story of Union gold being snatched by Confederate bad guys, Jorge Rivero and Bob's son, Chris Mitchum. Wayne is the colonel trying to find the traitor who's feeding information to the robbers, while wild-eyed Jack Elam looks askance at the whole business. Leisurely, sure, but the characters and circumstance make a real impression. ▢

John Wayne *Colonel Cord Mcnally* • Jennifer O'Neill *Shasta Delaney* • Jack Elam *Phillips* • Chris Mitchum *[Christopher Mitchum] Sergeant Tuscarora* • Jorge Rivero *Captain Pierre Cordona* • Victor French *Ketcham* ∎ *Dir* Howard Hawks • *Scr* Leigh Brackett, Burton Wohl, from a story by Burton Wohl

Rio Rita ★★★

Musical revue
1929 · US · BW and Colour · 140mins

Little more than canned theatre, with a static camera filming the spectacular Ziegfeld show of the twenties, this early film musical, which took 24 days to shoot, is, nevertheless, of historical interest. The slim plot has dashing John Boles as a Texas ranger on the trail of a notorious bandit. He loves Bebe Daniels, in the title role, but boy loses girl (temporarily), when he

🆄 = SUITABLE FOR ALL 🆄🅴 = SUITABLE FOR ALL, ESPECIALLY FOR YOUNG CHILDREN (VIDEO ONLY) 🅿🅶 = PARENTAL GUIDANCE

suspects her brother of being the outlaw. Tiresome Bert Wheeler and Robert Woolsey provide what is called "comic relief". The numbers are good and the finale is in pleasing two-strip Technicolor. In 1942, there was an updated remake starring Kathryn Grayson and Abbott and Costello.

Georges Renavent *Gen Ravinoff* • Eva Rosita *Carmen* • Bebe Daniels *Rita Ferguson* • John Boles *Capt Jim Stewart* • Don Alvarado *Roberto Ferguson* • Dorothy Lee *Dolly* • Bert Wheeler *Chick* • Robert Woolsey *Lovett* ■ *Dir* Luther Reed • *Scr* Luther Reed, Russell Mack, from the musical by Guy Bolton, Fred Thompson

Rio Rita ★★ U
Wartime musical comedy
1942 · US · BW · 90mins

MGM borrowed Abbott and Costello from Universal and placed them in this remake of 1929's *Rio Rita* (which had starred comedy double-act Wheeler and Woolsey). The updated version, featuring Nazis and saboteurs, was a bit of an odd fish and didn't serve Abbott and Costello too well – the pair find themselves squeezing their comedy routines in between the love story of John Carroll and Kathryn Grayson. Predictably the film's best moments come when the boys take centre stage and do their stuff.

Bud Abbott *Doc* • Lou Costello *Wishy* • Kathryn Grayson *Rita Winslow* • John Carroll *Ricardo Montera* • Patricia Dane *Lucille Brunswick* • Tom Conway *Maurice Craindall* ■ *Dir* S Sylvan Simon • *Scr* Richard Connell, Gladys Lehman, John Grant

Rio Shannon ★★★
Drama
1993 · US · Colour · 96mins

Mimi Leder hit the headlines in 1997 as the director of the first feature released by Steven Spielberg's DreamWorks company, the George Clooney/Nicole Kidman film *The Peacemaker*. This TV movie could hardly be more different, as newly widowed Blair Brown sells up and relocates to New Mexico, where she plans to transform a neglected ranch into a cosy tourist hotel. Naturally, the locals ain't got no time for the new-fangled ideas of city folk and a feud ensues. Apart from a few neat touches, Leder largely lets her experienced cast get on with it and what emerges is an amiable if unremarkable movie.

Blair Brown *Liz Cleary* • Patrick Van Horn *Jack Cleary* • Michael DeLuise *Patrick Cleary* • Shay Astar *Bridget Cleary* • Robert Beltran *Tito Carson* • Penny Fuller *Beatrice* ■ *Dir* Mimi Leder • *Scr* Linda Bergman, from a story by John Egan

Riot ★★
Prison drama
1969 · US · Colour · 96mins

Produced by master of schlock William Castle, this jailhouse drama was filmed inside Arizona State Prison, with the real warden and real prisoners appearing as extras. While the warden's away, Gene Hackman leads a revolt and takes over the prison's isolation wing, holding several guards hostage. Jim Brown is a prisoner who thinks Hackman has made a big mistake, a view confirmed when the 35 convicts start to dig a tunnel, knife each other and form a society of

drunken bigots, complete with a party with men in drag that's strongly reminiscent of *Stalag 17*. Strong performances from the leads and a half-decent script based on a real-life incident, place this film a notch above similar exploitation fare.

Jim Brown *Cully Briston* • Gene Hackman *Red Fletcher* • Ben Carruthers *Surefoot* • Mike Kellin *Bugsy* • Gerald S O'Loughlin *Grossman* ■ *Dir* Buzz Kulik • *Scr* James Poe, from the novel *The Riot* by Frank Elli

Riot in Cell Block 11 ★★★★ 15
Prison drama
1954 · US · BW · 80mins

Don Siegel emerged as more than just a Hollywood journeyman director with this hard-hitting, realistic prison picture, which presents a credible account of the riot and the conditions that caused it. Warden, Emile Meyer, could be accused of being overly sympathetic to the inmates' demands and Frank Faylen is far too dogmatic as the uncompromising senator. But, otherwise, the characters ring true, with Neville Brand's ringleader-turned-scapegoat particularly well realised. Russell Harlan's brooding photography heightens both the tension and the realism, and this remains a powerful indictment of the dehumanising effects of the penal system. ▭

Neville Brand *Dunn* • Emile Meyer *Warden* • Frank Faylen *Haskell* • Leo Gordon *Carnie* • Robert Osterloh *Colonel* • Paul Frees *Monroe* • Don Keefer *Reporter* • Alvy Moore *Gator* • Dabbs Greer *Schuyler* • Whit Bissell *Snader* ■ *Dir* Don Siegel • *Scr* Richard Collins

Ripe ★
Drama
1996 · US · Colour · 93mins

Monica Keena and Daisy Eagan are adolescent twin sisters who go on the run after their parents get killed in a car crash. Somehow, they end up living with a handyman on an army base, where they learn about sex and violence. This coming-of-age story is often distasteful and is hardly realistic – the US Army would hardly let a 14-year-old girl carry a handgun. The girls' performances are heartfelt – but heartfelt doesn't mean talented.

Monica Keena *Violet* • Daisy Eagan *Rosie* • Gordon Currie *Pete* • Ron Brice *Ken* • Karen Lynn Gorney *Janet Wyman* • Vincent Laresca *Jimmy* • Scott Sowers *Colonel Wyman* • Eric Jensen *Dave* ■ *Dir/Scr* Mo Ogrodnik

The Ripening Seed ★★★★
Romantic drama
1953 · Fr · BW · 110mins

Condemned by the Catholic Church and banned in various parts of the world, this adaptation of Colette's erotic novel may have seemed daring back in 1953. But today, it stands simply as a delicate – and often touching – account of a young man's initiation into the delights of physical love. Under Claude Autant-Lara's watchful eye, Pierre-Michel Beck is suitably bashful as the 16-year-old, who exploits a seaside holiday to spare his childhood sweetheart (Nicole Berger) the humiliation of untutored lovemaking. However, it's Edwige Feuillère's exquisite performance, as the ethereal woman in white, that gives the film its soul. In French with English subtitles.

Nicole Berger *Vinca* • Pierre-Michel Beck *Phil* • Edwige Feuillère *Madame Dalleray* ■ *Dir* Claude Autant-Lara • *Scr* Pierre Bost, Jean Aurenche, Claude Autant-Lara, from the novel by Colette

The Ripper ★★ 15
Crime mystery
1997 · US/Ausl · Colour · 95mins

Astonishing isn't it, how the intervening years have done nothing to dull the sensationalism of the Jack the Ripper case? Writers still churn out countless books, plays and films all offering their own conclusions. This pale made-for-TV affair follows the most controversial line of inquiry, already touched upon in 1978's *Murder by Decree*, which connects the Prince Regent to the murders. Patrick Bergin stars as the inspector leading the hunt for the Whitechapel butcher, who amid slayings, has time to romance Gabrielle Anwar (*Scent of a Woman*). Combining fact with fiction, this slow-moving tale is packed with diversionary social commentary, but the screenplay takes such huge liberties with the story, that Ripper fans will feel like slashing the film-maker's collective throats. British support players include Samuel West and the ever reliable Michael York. Contains some swearing and violence. ▭

Patrick Bergin *Inspector Jim Hansen* • Gabrielle Anwar *Florry Lewis* • Samuel West *Prince Eddy* • Michael York *Sir Charles Warren* • Adam Couper *Sergeant Tommy Bell* ■ *Dir* Janet Meyers • *Scr* Robert Rodat

Riptide ★★★
Romantic drama
1934 · US · BW · 92mins

The unusual meeting of British aristocrat Herbert Marshall and Park Avenue party girl with a past Norma Shearer leads to an idyllic love affair, then marriage and a child. However, when the wife is caught up in a scandal in Cannes, through the drunken antics of an old flame (Robert Montgomery), the husband is consumed with jealousy and wants a divorce. Written and directed by Edmund Goulding, the film is an intriguing, but sometimes uneasy, mix of romance, farce, arch comedy of manners and moral dilemma. Shearer carries it off superbly, Montgomery (as so often) irritates, Marshall is polished and the cast includes the legendary Mrs Patrick Campbell. Very 1930s.

Norma Shearer *Lady Mary Rexford* • Robert Montgomery *Tommy Trent* • Herbert Marshall *Lord Philip Rexford* • Mrs Patrick Campbell *Lady Hetty Riversleigh* • Richard "Skeets" Gallagher *Erskine* • Ralph Forbes *David Fenwick* • Lilyan Tashman *Sylvia* • Arthur Jarrett *Percy* ■ *Dir/Scr* Edmund Goulding

The Rise and Fall of Legs Diamond ★★★★ PG
Biographical crime drama
1960 · US · BW · 97mins

A sharply observed and crisply photographed attempt by Warner Bros to revive its gangster cycle. Budd Boetticher, better known for his Randolph Scott westerns, does a terrific job of directing the ice-cold Ray Danton in the leading role, and of sustaining a thoroughly amoral atmosphere on a tight schedule and a

very low budget. The black-and-white cinematography by Lucien Ballard is also a major plus. Watch out for an early appearance by Warren Oates and a glimpse of Dyan Cannon. ▭

Ray Danton *Jack "Legs" Diamond* • Karen Steele *Alice Shiffer* • Elaine Stewart *Monica Drake* • Jesse White *Leo Bremer* • Simon Oakland *Lieutenant Moody* • Robert Lowery *Arnold Rothstein* • Judson Pratt *Fats Walsh* • Warren Oates *Eddie Diamond* ■ *Dir* Budd Boetticher • *Scr* Joseph Landon

The Rise and Rise of Michael Rimmer ★★
Satirical political comedy
1970 · UK · Colour · 102mins

Having played a minor role in Kevin Billington's debut feature, *Interlude*, John Cleese reteamed with the director for this patchy political satire. In addition to co-starring, Cleese and fellow Python, Graham Chapman contributed to the script, which charts the meteoric rise of efficiency expert Michael Rimmer (played by Peter Cook), who bluffs his way into high office. Although the gags gradually fall flat, there are several scathing swipes at the British character and the nature of power. But, by the end, only the expertise of such familiar faces as Arthur Lowe, Denholm Elliott and Dennis Price will prevent you from voting with your remote.

Peter Cook *Michael Rimmer* • Denholm Elliott *Peter Niss* • Ronald Fraser *Tom Hutchinson* • Arthur Lowe *Ferret* • Vanessa Howard *Patricia Cartwright* • George A Cooper *Blackett* • Graham Crowden *Bishop of Cowley* • Harold Pinter *Steven Hench* • James Cossins *Crodder* • Richard Pearson *Wilting* • Ronnie Corbett *Interviewer* • Dennis Price *Fairburn* • John Cleese *Pumer* • Julian Glover *Col Moffat* ■ *Dir* Kevin Billington • *Scr* Peter Cook, John Cleese, Graham Chapman, Kevin Billington

Rise and Walk: the Dennis Byrd Story ★★ PG
Drama based on a true story
1994 · US · Colour · 85mins

Peter Berg, the much under-rated actor who played Linda Fiorentino's small-town target in *The Last Seduction*, is in moving form in this true story for which the phrase "heart-rending" could have been created. He stars as an American football player who is left paralysed after an accident during a game and then has to face up to his responsibilities as a husband, a parent and an individual. There are some classy supporting players in the cast, including Carrie Snodgress and Zakes Mokae, but it's really one for dedicated TV melodrama fans only. ▭

Peter Berg *Dennis Byrd* • Kathy Morris *Angela Byrd* • Johann Carlo *Joanne Giametti* • Wolfgang Bodison *Marvin Washington* • Carrie Snodgress *Nancy Byrd* • R Lee Ermey *Dan Byrd* ■ *Dir* Michael Dinner • *Scr* Sally Nemeth, John Miglis, Mark Levin

The Rise to Power of Louis XIV ★★★★
Historical drama
1966 · Fr · BW · 100mins

Achieving the ingenious illusion of historical contemporaneity, Roberto Rossellini authoritatively explores the routines and intrigues of Louis XIV's court, without once threatening to turn this docu-drama into a stylised history lesson. Employing tracks and zooms to animate the elaborate tableaux, he reveals how the Sun King tamed his treacherous nobility and turned the uncertainties of his regency into a regal dictatorship based at Versailles. With the cast of unknowns adding to the aura of authenticity, this engrossing film (which was originally made for TV) is the perfect riposte to those who denounce costume dramas for their empty spectacle. In French with English subtitles.

Jean-Marie Patte *Louis XIV* • Raymond Jourdan *Colbert* • Silvagni *Cardinal Mazarin* • Katharina Renn *Anne of Austria* • Dominique Vincent *Mme du Plessis* • Pierre Barrat *Fouquet* ■ *Dir* Roberto Rossellini • *Scr* Jean Gruault, Philippe Erlanger

Rising Damp   ★★★ PG

Comedy   1980 · UK · Colour · 94mins

The absence of Richard Beckinsale does much to sap the enjoyment of this acceptable movie version of the enduring Yorkshire TV sitcom. Eric Chappell, who wrote the series and the original stage play about Rigsby the scheming landlord, overwrites to compensate and the film suffers from too many padded scenes and too few hilarious situations. Newcomer, Denholm Elliott, looks a tad out of place alongside regulars Frances de la Tour and Don Warrington, but he makes a solid foil for the magnificent Leonard Rossiter, who pursues his romantic quest with a seedy chivalry that both disgusts and amuses. Contains swearing. ▭

Leonard Rossiter *Rigsby* • Frances de la Tour *Miss Jones* • Don Warrington *Philip* • Christopher Strauli *John* • Denholm Elliott *Seymour* • Carrie Jones *Sandra* • Glynn Edwards *Cooper* • John Cater *Bert* • Derek Griffiths *Alec* ■ *Dir* Joe McGrath [Joseph McGrath] • *Scr* Eric Chappell, from his TV series

The Rising of the Moon   ★★

Comedy drama   1957 · Ire · BW · 81mins

A cloying, sentimental slice of Oirish whimsy from John Ford, comprising three stories: the first is about a potty aristocrat jailed for assaulting a poteen brewer; the second is about a consignment of lobsters; the last one is a comedy about an IRA killer who escapes the gallows with the help of an actress who disguises herself as a nun, and a policeman who takes pity on him. All the cast overact shamelessly in this mix of booze, poetry and religion. When he was in Monument Valley, with horses and John Wayne, Ford was a master filmmaker, a poet, but when he was in Ireland he could be a dreadful bore.

Tyrone Power *Introduction* • Cyril Cusack *Inspector Michael Dillon* • Noel Purcell *Dan O'Flaherty the old man* • Jack MacGowran *Mickey J, the poteen maker* • Jimmy O'Dea *Porter* • Tony Quinn *Station master* • Paul Farrell *Engine driver* • Denis O'Dea *The police sergeant* • Eileen Crowe *His wife* ■ *Scr* Frank S Nugent, from the following three sources: the short story *The Majesty of the Law* by Frank O'Connor, the play *A Minute's Wait* by Martin J McHugh, the play by Lady Augusta Gregory

Rising Son   ★★★

Drama   1990 · US · Colour · 92mins

The recession hits the home of Brian Dennehy, a supervisor at a car factory faced with closure. Always seen as the bedrock of the family, Dennehy's self-esteem crumbles as his two sons lose face with their friends and learn that their school fees can't be paid. Dennehy, a mountain of a man, here plays a sort of Samson sapped of strength and it's a touching performance even if the script contains the kind of oversentimentality that mars many made-for-TV movies. It's also good to see that fine actress Piper Laurie, best remembered as Paul Newman's girlfriend in *The Hustler*, as the suffering wife and mother.

Brian Dennehy *Gus Robinson* • Piper Laurie *Martha Robinson* • Matt Damon *Charlie Robinson* • Emily Longstreth *Carol* • Jane Adams *Meg Bradley* • Graham Beckel *Billy* • Ving Rhames *Ed* • Richard Jenkins *Tommy* • Earl Hindman *Victor* ■ *Dir* John David Coles • *Scr* Bill Phillips, from a story by Bill Phillips, Rafael Yglesias, Lewis Cole

Rising Sun   ★★★ 18

Thriller   1993 · US · Colour · 124mins

Michael Crichton's novel caused a stir for its portrait of Japan as a tentacular monster, devouring every American corporation in its path. Since Hollywood studios were being gobbled up along with computer companies and most of Hawaii, any movie version had to tread carefully, and this one was finally bankrolled by Rupert Murdoch-owned 20th Century Fox. The picture is still a wimp, though, stopping well short of Crichton's xenophobic chauvinism, and seems more of a rehash of Ridley Scott's *Black Rain*, with dazzling surface textures plus Sean Connery's inimitable presence as a cop investigating a murder. Connery's sidekick is played by Wesley Snipes, and there's quirky character support from Harvey Keitel. It's often exciting, occasionally brutal and kinky, but a bit of a letdown from Philip Kaufman, director of the masterly *The Right Stuff*. Contains violence, swearing, sex scenes, nudity. ▭
DVD

Sean Connery *John Connor* • Wesley Snipes *Web Smith* • Harvey Keitel *Tom Graham* • Cary-Hiroyuki Tagawa *Eddie Sakamura* • Kevin Anderson *Bob Richmond* • Mako *Yoshida-San* • Ray Wise *Senator John Morton* • Stan Egi *Ishihara* • Stan Shaw *Phillips* • Tia Carrere *Jingo Asakuma* • Steve Buscemi *Willy "The Weasel" Wilhelm* ■ *Dir* Philip Kaufman • *Scr* Philip Kaufman, Michael Crichton, Michael Backes, from the novel by Michael Crichton

Risk   ★★

Romantic drama   1993 · US · Colour · 85mins

The "lovers on the run" genre is a popular one for independent films, but this effort, by first-time film-maker Deirdre Fishel, fails to do anything special with it. Karen Sillas is a painter's model who falls for petty criminal and big-time loser David Ilku, after meeting him on a New York bus. Later, on the spur of the moment, the pair steal a car and drive out to see Ilku's sister in Connecticut, where they encounter a heap of trouble related to his past. A film full of good intentions, but ultimately a bit disappointing.

Karen Sillas *Maya* • David Ilku *Joe* • Molly Price *Nikki* • Jack Gwaltney *Karl* • Christie MacFadyen *Alice* • Barry Snider *Phil* • David Lansing *Todd* • Gloria Maddox *Mrs Thompson* ■ *Dir/Scr* Deirdre Fishel

Risky Business   ★★★★ 18

Comedy   1983 · US · Colour · 94mins

Teenager Tom Cruise starts making money from sin and making tracks from respectability, when his family home becomes the "Best Little Whorehouse in Suburbia". Writer/director Paul Brickman has honed a sharp satire on American go-getting as Cruise – parents away – picks up hooker Rebecca De Mornay and turns the house into an overnight brothel for his buddies. The danger, though, comes when a killer-pimp arrives on the scene ("never muck with a man's business"); that's when a comedy of embarrassment becomes a near-tragedy of class collisions. There's no such thing as a totally free enterprise. Contains swearing, sex scenes. ▭
DVD

Tom Cruise *Joel Goodson* • Rebecca De Mornay *Lana* • Joe Pantoliano *Guido* • Richard Masur *Rutherford* • Bronson Pinchot *Barry* • Curtis Armstrong *Miles* • Nicholas Pryor *Joel's father* • Janet Carroll *Joel's mother* • Shera Danese *Vicki* • Raphael Sbarge *Glenn* ■ *Dir/Scr* Paul Brickman

Rita, Sue and Bob Too   ★★★★ 18

Comedy   1987 · UK · Colour · 89mins

Adapted by Andrea Dunbar from two of her controversial plays, this caused a right old rumpus on its release. Although much of the shock value has been distilled by seeing so much of the same on weekly soaps nowadays, this still makes you squirm as you find yourself unable to decide who is exploiting who, where the blame lies and how to respond to jokes that are uproariously funny despite their political incorrectness. A decade on, the three characters still exist in abundance, and it is to the credit of Michelle Holmes, Siobhan Finneran and George Costigan that they pitch their performances so perfectly. Contains swearing, sex scenes. ▭

Siobhan Finneran *Rita* • Michelle Holmes *Sue* • George Costigan *Bob* • Lesley Sharp *Michelle* • Willie Ross *Sue's father* • Patti Nicholls *Sue's mother* ■ *Dir* Alan Clarke • *Scr* Andrea Dunbar, from her plays *The Arbour* and *Rita, Sue and Bob Too*

The Rite   ★★★★

Drama   1969 · Swe · BW · 74mins

Initially made for television, but awarded a cinema release, this intense drama takes its cue from Ingmar Bergman's own Fårö films, by subjecting a self-contained community (in this case an acting troupe) to the pressures of the real world. When their show is banned because of an allegedly obscene sketch, Gunnar Björnstrand, Ingrid Thulin and Anders Ek are given a humiliating grilling by the aptly named judge, Erik Hell, whose inquisition not only exposes their own artistic and personal insecurities, but also his own hypocrisy. Stiflingly photographed by Sven Nykvist and

unconditionally played, this is Bergman at his most self-denigratingly pessimistic. In Swedish with English subtitles.

Ingrid Thulin *Thea Winkelmann* • Anders Ek *Albert Emanuel Sebastian Fischer* • Gunnar Björnstrand *Hans Winkelmann* • Erik Hell *Judge Abramson* • Ingmar Bergman *Clergyman* ■ *Dir/Scr* Ingmar Bergman

The Ritz   ★★ 15

Comedy   1976 · US · Colour · 86mins

Director Richard Lester made his name with the Beatles films *A Hard Day's Night* and *Help!*, but almost lost it with this tasteless camp comedy in which straight Jack Weston, takes refuge in a New York gay bathhouse. Hiding from his gangster father-in-law (George Coulouris) and brother-in-law (Jerry Stiller), Weston encounters Rita Moreno, who is superb as a talentless singer entertaining the patrons. Terrence McNally's script (adapted from his Broadway play) keeps the clichés flowing. Contains violence and swearing. ▭

Jack Weston *Gaetano Proclo* • Rita Moreno *Googie Gomez* • Jerry Stiller *Carmine Vespucci* • Kaye Ballard *Vivian Proclo* • F Murray Abraham *Chris* • Paul B Price *Claude* • Treat Williams *Michael Brick* • John Everson *Tiger* ■ *Dir* Richard Lester • *Scr* Terrence McNally, from the play by Terrence McNally

The River   ★★★★★ U

Documentary   1937 · US · BW · 31mins

Much more cinematically accomplished than its rough-and-ready predecessor, *The Plow That Broke the Plains* (1934), Pare Lorentz's second keystone documentary was sponsored by the Tennessee Valley Authority to expound the significance of its conservation policies. Following a prologue recalling Walt Whitman's poetry, Lorentz charts the history and ecological importance of the Mississippi and its tributaries, with an audiovisual harmony that compensates for its sentimental New Deal liberalism. With clips from *Come and Get It* (1936) and *Show Boat* (1936) juxtaposed with Einsteinian montage sequences, it was widely admired, although Walt Disney vetoed its Oscar nomination. However, it won the Best Documentary at Venice instead.

Thomas Chalmers *Narrator* ■ *Dir/Scr* Pare Lorentz • *Music* Virgil Thomson

The River   ★★★ U

Romantic drama
1951 · US/Ind · Colour · 98mins

After its creatively stifling years in Hollywood, the celebrated French director Jean Renoir, venturing into Technicolor for the first time, filmed Rumer Godden's semi-autobiographical novel in India. The focus is on the adolescent longings of Patricia Walters, the eldest daughter of an English family, and her friends, sophisticated Adrienne Corri and Eurasian Radha, all hankering after a handsome, embittered American pilot Thomas E Breen, who has lost a leg in the war. Exquisitely photographed by Claude Renoir, capturing the local colour and culture, it's more travelogue than narrative entertainment, but as the first film made in India to eschew

gung-ho heroics or exotic adventure, its influence was profound, opening the way for Roberto Rossellini, Louis Malle, James Ivory and others.

Nora Swinburne *Mother* • Esmond Knight *Father* • Arthur Shields *Mr John* • Thomas E Breen *Captain John* • Suprova Mukerjee *Nan* • Patricia Walters *Harriet* • Radha *Melanie* • Adrienne Corri *Valerie* ■ *Dir* Jean Renoir • *Scr* Rumer Godden, Jean Renoir

The River ★★ 15

Drama 1984 · US · Colour · 118mins

Rural couple, Mel Gibson and Sissy Spacek, battle against nature and the machinations of a local landowner (Scott Glenn) in Mark Rydell's well-shot, but fairly inconsequential drama. Besides the pretty scenery, the film is chiefly of interest for a pre-stardom Gibson, taking the kind of unsympathetic role that would give studios heartburn nowadays. He offers a strong performance, but is hampered by a superficial script that gives the protagonists an unlikely "love rivals" back story. If you like water, however, you won't be disappointed. ▭

Mel Gibson *Tom Garvey* • Sissy Spacek *Mae Garvey* • Scott Glenn *Joe Wade* • Billy Green Bush *Harve Stanley* • Shane Bailey *Lewis Garvey* • Becky Jo Lynch *Beth Garvey* • James Tolkan *Simpson* • Jack Starrett *Swick* • Barry Primus *Roy* • Amy Rydell *Betty Gaumer* ■ *Dir* Mark Rydell • *Scr* Robert Dillon, Julian Barry, from a story by Robert Dillon

The River ★★★★ 18

Drama 1997 · Tai · Colour · 113mins

This is an alarming study of familial dysfunction in Taiwan. When Li Kangsheng contracts a mysterious neck ailment, after working as a floating extra for a visiting film-maker (Ann Hui), neither of his parents can break their routine to tend to him – father, Miao Tien, frequents gay saunas, while mother, Lu Xialin, panders to a lover who pirates porn videos. Presenting water as a corrupting force, Tsai Ming-Liang shoots the almost wordless action in lingering long takes, which make the final incidence of incest all the more shocking. A Mandarin language film. Contains sex scenes. ▭

Miao Tien *Father* • Li Kangsheng *The boy* • Lu Xiaolin *Mother* • Ann Hui *Film director* • Chen Xiangqi *The boy's girlfriend* • Chen Zhaorong *Young man at sauna* • Lu Shiao-Lin *Mother's lover* ■ *Dir* Tsai Ming-Liang • *Scr* Tsai Ming-Liang, Yang Pi-Ying, Tsai Yi-Chun

The River and Death ★★★

Drama 1954 · Mex · BW · 90mins

Considering the author of the source novel this soap-operatic, plains western was Luis Buñuel's longtime friend, career diplomat Miguel Alvarez Acosta, this was a surprisingly disharmonious project. The main bone of contention was Buñuel's open contempt for the key idea that higher education was the panacea to the ills of this intemperate, macho society. Denied the chance to alter the ending, to show the graduate heirs intellectually justifying their age-old family feud, Buñuel had to content himself with sly digs at the duplicity of the Catholic Church and the ignorance

of the peasant nobility. In Spanish with English subtitles.

Columba Dominguez *Mercedes* • Miguel Torruco *Felipe Anguiano* • Joaquin Cordero *Gerardo Anguiano* • Jaime Fernandez *Romulo Menchaca* • Victor Alcocer *Polo Menchaca* ■ *Dir* Luis Buñuel • *Scr* Luis Buñuel, Luis Alcoriza, from the novel *Muro Blanco en Roca Negra* by Miguel Alvarez Acosta

River Beat ★ U

Crime drama 1954 · UK · BW · 70mins

Hollywood's Phyllis Kirk, gives a dash of much needed class to this minor British crime thriller. She plays the radio operator on an American freighter docked in the Thames, who's caught with diamonds hidden in her cigarettes. It helps in such circumstances to have an inspector in the river police for a boyfriend and John Bentley proves she was an innocent carrier. Leading cinematographer Guy Green switched over to direction for the first time and proved he could do an efficient job, especially in the climactic chase along the Thames. However, the dull script sinks the picture.

Phyllis Kirk *Judy Roberts* • John Bentley *Inspector Dan Barker* • Robert Ayres *Captain Watford* • Glyn Houston *Charlie Williamson* • Leonard White *Sergeant Mcleod* • Ewan Roberts *Customs Officer Blake* • Harold Ayer *Al Gordon* • Charles Lloyd Pack *Hendrick* ■ *Dir* Guy Green • *Scr* Rex Rienits

The River Niger ★★★

Drama 1976 · US · Colour · 105mins

An overflow of compassion and self-understanding makes this story of life in a black ghetto an intelligent and moving movie. Based on a 1972 Tony Award-winning play about a family trying to get it together in a world which seems geared against them, it's directed by Krishna Shah and features remarkable portrayals by James Earl Jones and Cicely Tyson.

Cicely Tyson *Mattie Williams* • James Earl Jones *Johnny Williams* • Louis Gossett Jr *Dr Dudley Stanton* • Glynn Turman *Jeff Williams* • Roger E Mosley *Big Moe Hayes* • Jonelle Allen *Ann Vanderguild* • Hilda Haynes *Wilhemina* • Geneva Brown ■ *Dir* Krishna Shah • *Scr* Joseph A Walker, from a play by Joseph A Walker

River of Death ★ 15

Action adventure 1989 · US · Colour · 97mins

Adventurer Michael Dudikoff travels up the "river of death" in search of a woman and a Nazi scientist. Accompanying him on his quest is (a toupee-wearing) Donald Pleasence and a bunch of other people who all have their own agendas. This extremely violent and unpleasant action film, includes too many of the modern jungle movie clichés and the ending turns out to be particularly pointless. Just about the only fun to be had is the accent Robert Vaughn puts on in his role as the Nazi scientist. ▭

Michael Dudikoff *John Hamilton* • Robert Vaughn *Wolfgang Manteuffel* • Donald Pleasence *Heinrich Spaatz* • Herbert Lom *Colonel Ricardo Diaz* • LQ Jones *Hiller* • Sarah Maur-Thorp *Anna Blakesley* ■ *Dir* Steve Carver • *Scr* Andrew Deutsch, Edward Simpson, from the novel by Alistair MacLean

River of No Return ★★★ PG

Western 1954 · US · Colour · 87mins

Here's a chance to see Robert Mitchum mumble away to Marilyn Monroe and show what a great job two stars can do with a creaking script and poor dialogue. This is an "event" movie, in that we do not really believe in Mitchum and Monroe cast adrift in the glorious scenery of the Canadian Rockies, but we enjoy seeing them do it. In his only western, Otto Preminger directs with enough sense to let the actors shine within the confines of a far-fetched adventure tale. It's good entertainment as long as you suspend your critical faculties and the sight of starry charisma suffice. ▭

Robert Mitchum *Matt Calder* • Marilyn Monroe *Kay Weston* • Rory Calhoun *Harry Weston* • Tommy Rettig *Mark Calder* • Murvyn Vye *Dave Colby* • Douglas Spencer *Sam Benson* • Ed Hinton *Gambler* ■ *Dir* Otto Preminger • *Scr* Frank Fenton, from a story by Louis Lantz

The River Rat ★★★ 15

Drama 1984 · US · Colour · 88mins

Tommy Lee Jones is well cast as the ex-con, released after serving a long prison sentence for accidental murder, meeting his teenage daughter (Martha Plimpton) for the first time. Determined to go straight and be the perfect dad, Jones's plans unravel when his parole officer, Brian Dennehy, turns nasty. Set in the eerie Mississippi swamps, the picture is written and directed by Tom Rickman, who wrote *Coal Miner's Daughter* which co-starred Jones. Michael Apted, who directed *Coal Miner's Daughter*, here serves as executive producer. Contains some violence, swearing. ▭

Tommy Lee Jones *Billy* • Martha Plimpton *Jonsy* • Brian Dennehy *Doc* • Shawn Smith *Wexel* • Nancy Lea Owen *Vadie* • Norman Bennett *Sheriff Cal* • Frank Tony *Poley* • Angie Bolling *Joyce* ■ *Dir/Scr* Tom Rickman

A River Runs through It ★★★★ PG

Drama 1992 · US · Colour · 118mins

When Tom Skerritt, Brad Pitt and Craig Sheffer go down to the water's edge and cast their lines, they are not fishing for fish: they are fishing for metaphors. This movie may not star Robert Redford (he merely directs and narrates) but Pitt resembles the young Redford to a quite startling degree – golden highlights and faded denim costumes – and is full of his brand of outdoors mythology. Based on Norman Maclean's bestselling 1976 novella, it shows us how to fly-fish and live in a state of grace, harmoniously with the land and water. Set in Montana in the early part of the century, the story focuses on the relationships between stern Presbyterian clergyman, Skerritt and his two sons, Sheffer and Pitt, who grow increasingly apart aside from their common love of fly-fishing. Philippe Rousselot's exquisite photography deservedly won an Oscar – Montana looks simply gorgeous. Contains swearing, nudity. ▭

Craig Sheffer *Norman Maclean* • Brad Pitt *Paul Maclean* • Tom Skerritt *Reverend Maclean* • Brenda Blethyn *Mrs Maclean* • Emily Lloyd *Jessie Burns* • Edie McClurg *Mrs*

Burns • Stephen Shellen *Neal Burns* ■ *Dir* Robert Redford • *Scr* Richard Friedenberg, from a story by Norman Maclean

River Street ★★★

Comedy drama 1996 · Ausl · Colour · 88mins

The good-looking, Canadian-born actor, Aden Young, has appeared in a number of Australian movies, including this romantic comedy, in which he takes the lead. Young is Ben Egan, a ruthless, unfeeling estate agent who is sentenced to community service after he hits a policeman. He is assigned to work at a centre for the homeless and, realising immediately that the building has enormous potential, cons the owner into selling it to him cheaply. However, encounters with a homeless teenager and Essie Davis, the caring woman who runs the centre, lead to a change of heart. Predictable but endearing entertainment.

Aden Young *Ben Egan* • Bill Hunter *Vincent Pierce* • Essie Davis *Wendy Davis* • Tammy McIntosh *Sharon Pierce* • Sullivan Stapleton *Chris* • Joy Smithers *Marcia* ■ *Dir* Tony Mahood • *Scr* Philip Ryall

The River Wild ★★★★ 12

Adventure thriller
1994 · US · Colour · 106mins

A distaff *Deliverance* with a bit of *Dead Calm* thrown in, this excellent thriller has Streep and family white-water rafting. What promises to be an enjoyable break soon turns into a nightmare when armed robbers, Kevin Bacon and John C Reilly, hitch a ride on the raft with $250,000 of stolen loot. Directed by Curtis Hanson, who made *The Hand That Rocks the Cradle* and the brilliant *LA Confidential*, this is a real roller-coaster ride, filled with hair-raising action scenes (shot in Montana and Oregon) and some equally tense moments on the river bank. Bullets fly and no one stays dead for long as the family's vacation takes a dark turn. In a dramatic break from her usual roles of urban angst and foreign accents, Streep is utterly convincing as the strong-willed wife and mother, taking charge as husband David Strathairn wimps out. She performs many of her own stunts (indeed, at one point she was thrown overboard to resurface 500 yards downstream where she was rescued by a kayak crew) and put in a lot of training for the role. Her muscles are as pumped-up as the plot, which is little more than a thrill machine, plus juicy nuggets of political correctness about the family unit and sexual equality. But the incredible action and Streep's performance more than compensate for any shortcomings. Contains swearing, violence. ▭ **DVD**

Meryl Streep *Gail Hartman* • Joseph Mazzello *Roarke Hartman* • David Strathairn *Tom Hartman* • Kevin Bacon *Wade* • John C Reilly *Terry* • William Lucking *Frank* • Benjamin Bratt *Ranger Johnny* ■ *Dir* Curtis Hanson • *Scr* Denis O'Neill

The River's Edge ★★★

Comedy adventure
1957 · US · Colour · 87mins

What looks at first glance like a routine action film, actually has some surprisingly ironic twists up its sleeve and delivers a rather bleak moral message. Ray Milland is a bank robber on the run who forces Anthony Quinn and his wife, Debra Paget, to guide him and his stolen dollars across the mountainous border to Mexico. An avalanche, the pouting Paget and sundry other inconveniences hinder their progress. Although Milland is slightly miscast, Quinn delivers his usual ethnic exuberance and veteran director Allan Dwan, clearly enjoying his Mexican locations, doesn't dawdle.

Ray Milland *Nardo Denning* • Anthony Quinn *Ben Cameron* • Debra Paget *Meg Cameron* • Harry Carey Jr *Chet* • Chubby Johnson *Whiskers* • Byron Foulger *Barry* ■ *Dir* Allan Dwan • *Scr* Harold Jacob Smith, James Leicester, from the story *The Highest Mountain* by Harold Jacob Smith

River's Edge ★★★★ 18

Drama 1987 · US · Colour · 95mins

A chilling chronicle of the differing reactions given by a group of disaffected high school teenagers over the course of a few days, when a friend shows them the body of the girl he murdered. A vivid study of alienation and moral vacuity, Tim Hunter's confident direction underlines the bleakness of the sorry tale, based on a true incident. Keanu Reeves scores as the decent guy who doesn't think the killing should go unpunished, but the stand-out performance comes from Crispin Glover as the speed-freak friend of the killer whose own sorry life is given pathetic meaning by the slaying.

Crispin Glover *Layne* • Keanu Reeves *Matt* • Ione Skye *Clarissa* • Daniel Roebuck *Samson "John" Tollette* • Dennis Hopper *Feck* • Joshua Miller *Tim* • Josh Richman *Tony* ■ *Dir* Tim Hunter • *Scr* Neal Jimenez

Riviera ★★

Spy thriller 1987 · US · Colour · 100mins

A TV movie in need of some energy, this boring thriller was originally credited to director Alan Smithee (the name directors use when they want to be unidentified), until John Frankenheimer later owned up. It's hardly surprising that he wanted to remain incognito, as this tepid offering pales in comparison to his better known works such as *Birdman of Alcatraz* or *The Manchurian Candidate* (although why he didn't adapt the same anonymous approach to the turkeys *Year of the Gun* or *Dead-Bang* is a total mystery). Ben Masters is unimaginative as the ex-agent who comes out of hiding to save his father's house in the South of France, and in the process reveals himself to all the enemies still out to get him.

Ben Masters *Jonathan Patrick Kelly* • Elyssa Davalos *Ashley Stevens* • Patrick Bauchau *Rykker* • Richard Hamilton *Kennedy* • Michael Lonsdale [Michel Lonsdale] *Detective Dubois* • Jon Finch *Jeffers* • Shane Rimmer *Doc Donovan* • Lalla Ward *Laura* • Geoffrey Chater *Grayson* • Patrick Monckton *Spiros* ■ *Dir* Alan Smithee [John Frankenheimer] • *Scr* Michael Sloan

Road Agent ★★ U

Western 1941 · US · BW · 59mins

Crooning cowboy star, Dick Foran, went to Universal for this western, having made his name at Warner Bros. Although Foran and co-stars Leo Carrillo and, particularly, heavyweight Andy Devine look good together and do their own hard ridin', they can't change the plot, which is fast-moving nonsense about the wrongly accused threesome being let out of jail to prove their own innocence. It's enjoyable enough for fans of B westerns, but non-fans should avoid. (Occasionally referred to as *Texas Road Agent* to differentiate it from the Tim Holt series western of the early fifties.)

Dick Foran *Duke Masters* • Leo Carrillo *Pancho* • Andy Devine *Andy* • Anne Gwynne *Patricia Leavitt* • Samuel S Hinds *Sam Leavitt* • Anne Nagel *Lola* ■ *Dir* Charles Lamont • *Scr* Morgan Cox, Arthur Strawn, Maurice Tombragel, from a story by Sherman Loew, Arthur St Claire

Road Ends ★

Crime drama 1999 · US · Colour · 98mins

With no point and no purpose, there's no particular reason to watch this boring drama. Chris Sarandon is a shady character who escapes from the mob and hangs around in sheriff, Dennis Hopper's small town, waiting for something or someone. By the time viewers find out what he's waiting for, they will have long stopped caring, due to the meandering plotline and the fact that it's never clear just who are the villains and who are the heroes. The only merit is the PM Entertainment trademark, superior photography.

Chris Sarandon *Estaban Maceda* • Dennis Hopper *Gilchrist* • Peter Coyote *Gene Gere* • Mariel Hemingway *Kat* • Joanna Gleason *Armacost* ■ *Dir* Rick King • *Scr* Bill Mesce Jr

Road Games ★★ 15

Thriller 1981 · Aus · Colour · 96mins

The cars driving on the left-hand side of the road of the road is as close as this Australian Hitchcock imitation gets to local colour – especially since Americans play the leads. Stacy Keach plays a truck driver hauling pork across the Outback, who picks up hitchhiker Jamie Lee Curtis during one journey. When she later disappears, Keach suspects one of the other drivers on the road took her. But the police start to suspect him. The classic themes of Hitchcock are here: an innocent man on the run; people placed in inescapable danger; and an emphasis on suspense over actual violence. However, since little actually happens along the journey, it's hard for the movie to maintain suspense as it progresses. Contains violence, swearing, sexual references.

Stacy Keach *Patrick Quid* • Jamie Lee Curtis *Pamela Rushworth/"Hitch"* • Marion Edward *Madeleine "Sunny" Day/Frita Frugal* • Grant Page *"Smith or Jones"* • Thaddeus Smith *Abbott* • Stephen Millichamp *Costello* ■ *Dir* Richard Franklin • *Scr* Everett DeRoche

The Road Home ★ 15

Drama 1989 · US · Colour · 111mins

Anxious to make a break from historical epics such as *Chariots of Fire* and *Revolution*, director Hugh Hudson unwisely chose this story of teenage angst, starring *Beastie Boy*, Adam Horovitz, as an institutionalised youth and Donald Sutherland as his shrink. Set in Los Angeles, the film was originally punningly titled *Lost Angels* , it tries hard to mirror *Rebel without a Cause*, but fails dismally in all departments. The clichéd script, wooden performances and contrived ending are dispiriting to watch, and the resulting shambles put Hudson's career into reverse. Contains swearing, nudity, violence.

Donald Sutherland *Dr Charles Loftis* • Adam Horovitz *Tim Doolan* • Amy Locane *Cheryl Anderson* • Don Bloomfield *Andy Doolan* • Celia Weston *Felicia Marks* • Graham Beckel *Richard Doolan* • Patricia Richardson *Mrs Anderson* • Ron Frazier *Barton Marks* ■ *Dir* Hugh Hudson • *Scr* Michael Weller

The Road Home ★★★

Adventure 1995 · US · Colour · 90mins

Two sons of Irish immigrants are orphaned and then separated when the younger brother is adopted. The older brother then absconds with his sibling and together they make for the one place they imagine they can be together – Boys Town. *The Road Home* never strays far from the established stereotypes you usually find in this kind of movie – a kind-hearted king of the hobos (Danny Aiello), the uncaring nun who heads the orphanage – but it's touching nonetheless. In an ironic bit of casting, Mickey Rooney, who as a teenager appeared in the most famous film version of *Boys Town*, plays Father Flanagan in this TV movie.

Danny Aiello *Duke* • Will Estes *Michael* • Kris Kristofferson *Davis* • Keegan Macintosh *John* • Sheila Patterson *Sister Elizabeth* • Mickey Rooney *Father Flanagan* • Charles Martin Smith *Merriman* • Dee Wallace Stone *Mrs Bastian* ■ *Dir* Dean Hamilton • *Scr* Keith O'Leary

The Road Home ★★★★

Drama 2000 · Chi · Colour and BW · 89m

Adapted from Bao Shi's novel, *Remembrance*, and prompted by a son returning for his father's funeral, this is, ostensibly, a touching love story shot through with painstaking attention to the detail of everyday life in a fifties rural community. But Zhang Yimou is also keen to extol virtues forgotten in modern consumerist China, such as loyalty, faith and permanence, which is why he shoots the present-day book ends in sombre monochrome and the romance between the teenage Zhang Ziyi and the village's new teacher, Zheng Hao, in vibrantly warm colour. Lyrical, but shrewd, nostalgic, but unsentimental, moving and just a touch despondent. In Mandarin with English subtitles.

Zhang Ziyi *Zhao Di as a young woman* • Sun Honglei *Luo Yusheng* • Zheng Hao *Luo Changyu* ■ *Dir* Zhang Yimou • *Scr* Bao Shi, from the novel *Remembrance* by Bao Shi

Road House ★★★★

Crime melodrama 1948 · US · BW · 94mins

Blues singer, Ida Lupino, gets a job at Richard Widmark's joint, but ill-advisedly falls for his general manager, Cornel Wilde. Lupino plays the floozy to perfection, her unsmoked cigarettes burning lines in the piano, as she plays and sings her tragic ballads. As the rejected lover, Widmark gives one of his trademark psychotics, framing his employee and then going ballistic at the end, when Lupino and Wilde hide out in a hunting cabin on the Canadian border. Not one of the great *film noirs*, but still a very gripping movie. Contains strong language.

Ida Lupino *Lily Stevens* • Cornel Wilde *Pete Morgan* • Celeste Holm *Susie Smith* • Richard Widmark *Jefty Robbins* • OZ Whitehead *Arthur* • Robert Karnes *Mike* • George Beranger *Lefty* ■ *Dir* Jean Negulesco • *Scr* Edward Chodorov, from a story by Margaret Gruen, Oscar Saul

Road House ★★★ 18

Action drama 1989 · US · Colour · 109mins

This gloriously brainless, modern-day western, is a treat from start to finish and possibly the one and only time that a bouncer will ever get the full Hollywood hero treatment. Patrick Swayze, with a stoical straight face, plays the softly spoken doorman who brings order and just a little karma to the unruly Double Deuce bar, which is under threat from unsavoury characters and local hoodlums. Kelly Lynch plays the token love interest, but the best roles go to Sam Elliott, as Swayze's old buddy, and Ben Gazzara, as the villain of the piece. It's directed by the aptly named Rowdy Herrington. Contains swearing, violence, sex scenes, drug abuse, nudity.

Patrick Swayze *Dalton* • Kelly Lynch *Dr Elizabeth "doc" Clay* • Sam Elliott *Wade Garrett* • Ben Gazzara *Brad Wesley* • Marshall Teague *Jimmy* • Julie Michaels *Denise* • Red West *Red Webster* • Sunshine Parker *Emmet* • Jeff Healey *Cody* • Kevin Tighe *Tilghman* ■ *Dir* Rowdy Herrington • *Scr* David Lee Henry, Hilary Henkin, from a story by David Lee Henry

The Road Raiders ★★ PG

Action adventure 1989 · US · Colour · 91mins

A rather belated entry in the *Dirty Dozen* stakes, this looks suspiciously like a pilot for a TV series that never got off the ground. TV veteran, Bruce Boxleitner, is the loveable rogue in the war-torn Philippines who assumes the identity of a dead officer, only to discover he has been put in charge of a team of convicts and eccentrics. The ever-reliable Noble Willingham is the best-known face among the supporting players, although the eagle-eyed will spot a young Tia Carrere of *Wayne's World* fame in a small role. Director, Richard Lang does his best, but it ends up looking like an extended episode of *The A-Team* in period trappings. Produced by Glen A Larson, whose TV successes include *McCloud*, *The Six Million Dollar Man* and *Battlestar Galactica*.

Bruce Boxleitner *Captain Rhodes* • Susan Diol *Lieutenant Johanson* • Noble Willingham *Crankcase* • Reed McCants *Harlem* • Mark Blankfield *Schizoid* • David Paul *Bruise Brother* • Peter Paul *Bruise Brother* ■ *Dir* Richard Lang • *Scr* Glen A Larson, Mark Jones, from a story by Glen A Larson

Road Show ★★★ U

Comedy 1941 · US · BW · 87mins

Millionaire John Hubbard, committed to a lunatic asylum by a vengeful woman, becomes friendly with fellow inmate Colonel Caraway "of caraway seeds" (Adolphe Menjou), who is the inventor of a camera that takes no pictures. Together, they escape and join a carnival owned by Carole Landis, where Hubbard becomes a lion tamer and the carnival runs into riotous (in both senses of the word) trouble. Zany, manic, broad farce from the Hal Roach stable, this was written by a trio of writers, one of whom was Harry Langdon, and directed by Gordon Douglas with Roach and Roach Jr (both uncredited).

Adolphe Menjou *Col Carleton Carraway* • Carole Landis *Penguin Moore* • John Hubbard *Drogo Gaines* • Charles Butterworth *Harry Whitman* • Patsy Kelly *Jinx* • George E Stone *Indian* • Margaret Roach *Priscilla* ■ *Dir* Gordon Douglas • *Scr* Arnold Belgard, Harry Langdon, Mickell Novak, from the novel by Eric Hatch

Road to Bali ★★★ U

Musical comedy 1952 · US · Colour · 91mins

A wonderfully wacky and surreal entry in Paramount's "Road" series. This was the penultimate of the seven made and the only one in colour. Alongside Bing Crosby, Bob Hope and Dorothy Lamour (whose camaraderie was by now honed to perfection), there are a variety of star cameos (don't blink!) and a number of enjoyable special effects, from materialisation by a snake charmer's flute to volcanic eruption, all done with a warmth generally missing from today's digital wizardry. Five songs enhance the narrative, including the lovely *Moonflowers*.

Bob Hope *Harold Gridley* • Bing Crosby *George Cochran* • Dorothy Lamour *Lalah* • Murvyn Vye *Ken Arok* • Peter Coe *Gung* • Ralph Moody *Bhoma Da* • Leon Askin *Ramayana* ■ *Dir* Hal Walker • *Scr* Frank Butler, Hal Kanter, William Morrow, from a story by Frank Butler, Harry Tugend

The Road to Denver ★ U

Western 1955 · US · Colour · 90mins

No wonder John Payne looks more morose than ever – he's reduced to playing in a Republic western and his part requires him to be upstaged by his younger brother's wild behaviour, when he's not stationed at a sink washing dishes. Skip Homeier is convincingly hot-headed as the youngster, but veteran Joseph Kane's direction is tepid and the script is as dull as dishwater. True, some action sequences liven up the second half of the film, but its ending is a cop-out – in sorry contrast to the more rigorous and dynamic handling of fraternal conflict between Robert Taylor and John Cassavetes in the later *Saddle the Wind*.

John Payne *Bill Mayhew* • Skip Homeier *Sam Mayhew* • Mona Freeman *Elizabeth Sutton* • Lee J Cobb *Jim Donovan* • Ray Middleton *John Sutton* • Andy Clyde *Whipsaw* • Lee Van Cleef *Pecos Larry* • Karl Davis *Hunsaker* ■ *Dir* Joseph Kane • *Scr* Horace McCoy, Allen Rivkin, from the novel *Man From Texas* by Bill Gulick

The Road to El Dorado ★★★ PG

Animated adventure 2000 · US · Colour · 89mins

The third animated feature from DreamWorks – following *Antz* and *The Prince Of Egypt* – features Kevin Kline and Kenneth Branagh, voicing a duo of rascally 16th-century Spaniards who stumble on the fabled South American city of gold. Mistaken for gods, the two must fake divinity long enough to run

off with the loot, but evil High Priest Amand Assante has other ideas. The film starts and finishes strongly, and boasts at least two terrific action set pieces, while the talky in-between sequences noticeably drag on. The mix of conventional animation and computer graphics is good, but the voices carry the day. Not quite up to the best of Disney, but along with *The Iron Giant* and *The Magic Sword*, it's proof that the Mouse's monopoly on quality cartooning can no longer be taken for granted.

Elton John *Narrator* • Kevin Kline *Tulio* • Kenneth Branagh *Miguel* • Rosie Perez *Chel* • Armand Assante *Tzekel-Kan* • Edward James Olmos *Chief* • Jim Cummings *Cortes* • Frank Welker *Altivo* • Tobin Bell *Zaragoza* ■ *Dir* Eric "Bibo" Bergeron, Don Paul, Will Finn, David Silverman • *Scr* Ted Elliott, Terry Rossio • *Music* Elton John • *Lyrics* Tim Rice

The Road to Galveston ★★ PG

Drama based on a true story 1996 · US · Colour · 89mins

Cicely Tyson stars as a Texas widow who, suffering from the loss of her husband's income, saves her farm by turning it into a nursing home for three women with Alzheimer's disease. Deciding to fulfil a lifelong dream, she takes the women on a drive to Galveston to see the ocean. There she finally deals with her suppressed grief. With a strong ensemble cast of actresses, including Piper Laurie, this TV drama provides the perfect showcase for Cicely Tyson's considerable talents. Although the road is a bit winding, the trip to Galveston is worth taking. ▭

Cicely Tyson *Jordan Roosevelt* • Piper Laurie *Wanda Kirkman* • Tess Harper *Julia Archer* • James McDaniel *Marcus Roosevelt* • Starletta DuPois *Sally McGowan* • Penny Johnson *Laney Roosevelt* ■ *Dir* Michael Toshiyuki Uno • *Scr* Tony Lee

The Road to Glory ★★

First World War drama 1936 · US · BW · 102mins

This has no connection with Howard Hawks's directorial debut, a 1926 silent movie of the same name. Instead, Hawks recycled ideas from another film of his, *The Dawn Patrol*, changing the focus from the war in the air, to the war in the trenches. And that wasn't the only instance of recycling. Fox studio boss Darryl F Zanuck had bought a 1932 French movie, *Les Croix des Bois*, a French *All Quiet on the Western Front*, but Zanuck decided not to release it in the US. Instead he took all the battle footage from the French movie and got Hawks to graft a plot onto it and glue Hollywood actors around in.

Fredric March *Lt Michel Denet* • Warner Baxter *Capt Paul Laroche* • Lionel Barrymore *Papa Laroche* • June Lang *Monique* • Gregory Ratoff *Bouffiou* • Victor Kilian *Regnier* • Paul Stanton *Relief Captain* • John Qualen *Duflous* ■ *Dir* Howard Hawks • *Scr* Joel Sayre and William Faulkner, from the film *Les Croix des Bois* by Raymond Bernard, André Lang, from the novel by Roland Dorgèles

The Road to Hong Kong ★★ U

Musical comedy 1962 · US/UK · BW · 102mins

Bing Crosby and Bob Hope reteamed ten years after *Road to Bali*, for the seventh and last in a once fabulously funny series. Sadly, by now the spark had gone from the relationship and the English locations and parsimonious filming in black and white make the movie look shabby. Worse is the graceless demoting of Dorothy Lamour to "guest star", with the co-starring role being taken by an ill-suited Joan Collins. The film's not without interest, of course, and there's super work from some distinguished supporting players – especially Peter Sellers – but on the whole this is neither funny nor attractive. Children unfamiliar with the classics in the series might enjoy it.

Bing Crosby *Harry Turner* • Bob Hope *Chester Babcock* • Joan Collins *Diane* • Dorothy Lamour • Robert Morley *The Leader* • Walter Gotell *Dr Zorbb* • Roger Delgado *Jhinnah* • Felix Aylmer *Grand Lama* • Peter Madden *Lama* • Peter Sellers • Frank Sinatra • Dean Martin • David Niven • Zsa Zsa Gabor ■ *Dir* Norman Panama • *Scr* Norman Panama, Melvin Frank

The Road to Mandalay ★★★

Silent melodrama 1926 · US · BW

Lon Chaney, the master of disguise, created a grotesque white cataract in his eye with the skin of an eggshell to play the villainous Chinese owner of a Singapore dive. The evil character who has sent his daughter Lois Moran to a convent in Mandalay, kidnaps her sweetheart Owen Moore – he's a former partner-in-crime and Chaney wants the best for his little girl. As eerily atmospheric as the other collaborations between Chaney and director Tod Browning, who shared the star's taste for the macabre, it is by today's standards, an overripe melodrama and strictly non-PC.

Lon Chaney *Singapore Joe* • Lois Moran *Joe's daughter* • Owen Moore *The Admiral* • Henry B Walthall *Father James* ■ *Dir* Tod Browning • *Scr* Elliott Clawson, Joe Farnham [Joseph Farnham], from a story by Tod Browning, Herman Mankiewicz [Herman J Mankiewicz]

Road to Morocco ★★★★ U

Musical comedy 1942 · US · BW · 78mins

"Like Webster's Dictionary, we're Morocco-bound," sing Bob Hope and Bing Crosby in arguably the funniest and best – of their zany *Road* series for Paramount. There's much to cherish here: Dorothy Lamour and *Moonlight Becomes You*; Anthony Quinn as a villainous Arab; the utterly delectable Dona Drake as a slave girl and, especially the talking camels. These comedies may seem to have dated – and certainly they remain sadly and stubbornly unfashionable – but for sheer inventiveness and innate good humour they're hard to beat. In these post-modern times, they're simply full of surreal cinematic in-jokes. Not just for forties nostalgics. ▭

Bing Crosby *Jeff Peters* • Bob Hope *Orville "Turkey" Jackson* • Dorothy Lamour *Princess Shalmar* • Anthony Quinn *Mullay Kasim* •

Dona Drake *Mihirmah* • Mikhail Rasumny *Ahmed Fey* • Vladimir Sokoloff *Hyder Khan* ■ *Dir* David Butler • *Scr* Frank Butler, Don Hartman

Road to Nhill ★★★

Comedy 1997 · Ausl · Colour · 95mins

This award-winning art house movie takes a whimsical look at the effect of a road accident on the inhabitants of an Australian country town. When a car containing four lady bowlers from Pyramid Hill overturns on the Nhill road, an escalating comedy of errors is put into motion. The local emergency services spring into action, but set off in the wrong destination, while the townsfolk contemplate what the accident may mean to their lives. An absorbing, warm and gentle comedy on the theme of fate and destiny, it features wonderful performances from the cast. However, the intrusive presence of the "Voice of God" grates.

Patricia Kennedy *Jean* • Monica Maughan *Nell* • Lois Ramsey *Carmel* • Lynette Curran *Margot* • Phillip Adams *Voice of God* ■ *Dir* Sue Brooks • *Scr* Alison Tilson

Road to Rio ★★★★ U

Musical comedy 1947 · US · BW · 102mins

The fifth of the seven *Road* movies was also one of the best, even though the formula remained much as before – entertainers Bing Crosby and Bob Hope, on the run, fall for Dorothy Lamour, become rivals for her love and land in hot water. This time, Dorothy is being hypnotised by her guardian (the delightfully wicked Gale Sondergaard) so that she'll marry the guardian's brother, who is after Dorothy's estate. "I find myself saying things and I don't know why I say them," says Dot. "Why don't you just run for Congress," Hope quips. Added attractions are the Andrew Sisters singing *You Don't Have to Know the Language* with Bing, and the zany Weire Brothers doing their famous hat routine.

Bing Crosby *"Scat" Sweeney* • Bob Hope *"Hot Lips" Barton* • Dorothy Lamour *Lucia Maria De Andrade* • Gale Sondergaard *Catherine Vail* • Frank Faylen *Trigger* • Joseph Vitale *Tony* • Frank Puglia *Rodrigues* • Nestor Paiva *Cardoso* ■ *Dir* Norman Z McLeod • *Scr* Edmund Beloin, Jack Rose

Road to Ruin ★★ 15

Romantic comedy 1992 · US/Fr · Colour · 90mins

The original Robocop, Peter Weller, isn't the first person you'd bring up in a discussion on romantic comedy, but that's what is attempted in this Parisian frippery. The city looks glorious, thanks to cinematographer Jean-Yves LeMener, but Erick Anjou's script is right out of the bottom drawer, taking increasingly ludicrous turns to prove to Weller's wealthy exile that model, Carey Lowell, loves him for more than his money. There's little spark between them and, as the elaborate scams come thick and fast, you're left wondering how anyone so harebrained came to be so rich. However, Duchaussoy supplies a neat turn as Weller's duplicitous partner. Contains swearing and sex scenes. ▭

Peter Weller *Jack Sloan* • Carey Lowell *Jessie Taylor* • Michel Duchaussoy *Julien Boulet* • Rebecca Pauly *Arabella* • Sylvie Laguna *Sarah* • Takashi Kawahara *Toshi* • Pierre Belot *Jason* ■ *Dir* Charlotte Brandstrom • *Scr* Erick Anjou, from the story by Richard Gitelson, Eric Freiser

Road to Salina ★

Drama   1969 · Fr/It · Colour · 97mins

The last years of Rita Hayworth's life were saddened by illness and films made towards the end of her career, including this co-production, were of little or no merit. Nevertheless the film achieves what interest it has from Hayworth's portrayal of Mara, the mother to Mimsy Farmer who gets very involved with the young and wayward Robert Walker Jr. Not much problem there you might think, except that Walker could possibly be Hayward's son. There's more incident than plot in this rather trashy movie, with a couple of killings, some fairly explicit sex and a variety of nationalities clashing badly on the soundtrack. We'd all soon remember her in her prime as Gilda.

Mimsy Farmer *Billie* • Robert Walker [Robert Walker Jr] *Jonas* • Rita Hayworth *Mara* • Ed Begley *Warren* • Bruce Pecheur *Charlie* ■ *Dir* Georges Lautner • *Scr* Georges Lautner, Pascal Jardin, Jack Miller, from the novel *Sur la Route de Salina* by Maurice Cury

Road to Singapore ★★★ Ⓤ

Musical comedy   1940 · US · BW · 81mins

Not the best of the *Road* series, but the first, originally intended as a vehicle for a sarong-clad Dorothy Lamour. Several other stars were mooted, notably Jack Oakie with a number of partners, but eventually crooner Bing Crosby and comedian Bob Hope were recruited to team with Lamour in a script which, by then, was nearly ten years old. The public loved the resultant comedy and seeming ad-libs, although the tone of the series (Bing and Bob moon over Lamour, or money, or both) wasn't really established until the second, *Road to Zanzibar*. However, what was once intended for adult entertainment, may now be more suited to youngsters, but they may be bored by Lamour's musical interludes.

Bing Crosby *Josh Mallon* • Bob Hope *Ace Lannigan* • Dorothy Lamour *Mima* • Charles Coburn *Joshua Mallon IV* • Judith Barrett *Gloria Wycott* • Anthony Quinn *Caesar* • Jerry Colonna *Achilles Bombanassa* • Johnny Arthur *Timothy Willow* • Pierre Watkin *Morgan Wycott* ■ *Dir* Victor Schertzinger • *Scr* Don Hartman, Frank Butler, from a story by Harry Hervey

Road to Utopia ★★★★ Ⓟⓖ

Musical comedy   1945 · US · BW · 85mins

Sadly, they really don't make them like this anymore. Released 20-months after it was completed, this is among the best of a much-loved series, with Bing and Bob as down-at-heel entertainers posing as hardened prospectors in order to get their hands on a Klondike gold map. Told as an elongated flashback and blessed with a mocking commentary by Robert Benchley, the film contains a wealth of insider gags that were a trademark of these freewheeling comedies. Complete with obligatory squabble over Dorothy Lamour, talking animals and

the familiar "pat-a-cake" fight sequence, the time simply flies by.

Bing Crosby *Duke Johnson* • Bob Hope *Chester Hooton* • Dorothy Lamour *Sal Van Hoyden* • Hillary Brooke *Kate* • Douglass Dumbrille *Ace Larson* • Jack LaRue *Lebec* • Robert Barrat *Sperry* • Robert Benchley *Narrator* ■ *Dir* Hal Walker • *Scr* Norman Panama, Melvin Frank

The Road to Wellville ★★ 18

Black comedy   1994 · US · Colour · 114mins

Evita director, Alan Parker, comes unstuck with this tasteless farce about turn-of-the-century health habits. Anthony Hopkins is all-wavering accent and buckteeth as Dr John Harvey Kellogg (yes, he of cornflakes fame), who ran a notorious sanatorium in Battle Creek, Michigan, where idle rich Americans flocked to have enemas, salt scrubs, yogurt therapy and bowel inspections. Matthew Broderick turns up with chronic constipation, his sexually frustrated wife Bridget Fonda in tow, to indulge in numerous high-class *Carry On*-style shenanigans among the handsome period detailing and gorgeous spa sets. About as funny as it sounds. Contains swearing, sex scenes, nudity.

Anthony Hopkins *Dr John Harvey Kellogg* • Bridget Fonda *Eleanor Lightbody* • Matthew Broderick *Will Lightbody* • John Cusack *Charles Ossining* • Dana Carvey *George Kellogg* • Michael Lerner *Goodloe Bender* • Colm Meaney *Dr Lionel Badger* • John Neville *Endymion Hart-jones* • Lara Flynn Boyle *Ida Muntz* • Traci Lind *Nurse Irene Graves* ■ *Dir* Alan Parker • *Scr* Alan Parker, from the novel by T Coraghessan Boyle

The Road to Yesterday ★★★★

Silent romantic drama
1925 · US · BW · 136mins

Lively reincarnation fantasy in which a spectacle-specialist, Cecil B DeMille, transports two unhappily-married modern-day couples into the past to teach them a lesson for the future. Unconscious following a train crash, the crotchety quartet find themselves back in 16th century England, where their bigotry and unkindness is given its head only to backfire horribly. Joseph Schildkraut, Jetta Goudal, William Boyd (before he was Hopalong Cassidy) and Vera Reynolds each make their presences felt in this agreeable slice of hokum, while DeMille proves once again what a crowd-pleaser he is.

Joseph Schildkraut *Kenneth Paulton* • Jetta Goudal *Malena Paulton* • Vera Reynolds *Beth Tyrell* • William Boyd *Jack Moreland* ■ *Dir* Cecil B De Mille [Cecil B DeMille] • *Scr* Beulah Marie Dix, Jeanie Macpherson, from a story by Beulah Marie Dix, from the play by Evelyn Greenleaf Sutherland

Road to Zanzibar ★★★ Ⓟⓖ

Musical road movie comedy
1941 · US · BW · 87mins

The first two "Road" pictures (this is the second) seem somewhat disappointing now in light of the wonderful three that followed (Morocco, Utopia and Rio), but this still has Bob Hope, Bing Crosby and Dorothy Lamour, some zany gags and some catchy tunes, so it more than gets by. Bing and Bob are carnival

performers this time, on the run from a gangster to whom they sold a phoney diamond mine, and their ensuing trek through the jungle with Lamour and Una Merkel cues some great satire on jungle pictures in general.

Bob Hope *"Fearless" Frazier* • Bing Crosby *Chuck Reardon* • Dorothy Lamour *Donna Latour* • Una Merkel *Julia Quimby* • Eric Blore *Charles Kimble* ■ *Dir* Victor Schertzinger • *Scr* Frank Butler, Don Hartman, from the story *Find Colonel Fawcett* by Don Hartman, Sy Bartlett

Road Trip ★★ 15

Comedy   2000 · US · Colour · mins

Executive producer, Ivan Reitman, updates the humour of his earlier production *National Lampoon's Animal House* (1978) here, with middling results. There are some raunchy and hilarious moments as student Breckin Meyer, races from New York to Texas with his friends to avert a disaster that could ruin his relationship with his girlfriend, but the movie is a jumbled mess. Several lengthy and redundant subplots keep diverting attention from the central story, and the central characters come across as stereotypes, sharing the same "wild" college guy persona. The exception is Tom Green, whose insane character is as unforgettable and hilarious as John Belushi's Bluto in *Animal House*, yet he's put in a supporting role that doesn't give him a chance to stretch himself.

Breckin Meyer *Josh* • Seann William Scott *E L* • Amy Smart *Beth* • Paulo Costanzo *Rubin* • DJ Qualls *Kyle* • Rachel Blanchard *Tiffany* ■ *Dir* Todd Phillips • *Scr* Todd Phillips, Scot Armstrong

Roadblock ★★★

Crime thriller   1951 · US · BW · 73mins

Playing against type, square-jawed Charles McGraw gives a surprisingly layered performance in this claustrophobic *film noir*. With Nicholas Musuraca's camerawork making Los Angeles and its environs look like a series of forbidding dead ends, Harold Daniels is able to give the impression of a world closing in on MacGraw's hard-working insurance investigator, who becomes involved in a million-dollar mail robbery in order to finance new wife, Joan Dixon's expensive tastes. The shootout in a dried-up river bed is arresting, but it's the dank cityscapes that give the film both its atmosphere and its sense of middle-class malaise.

Charles McGraw *Joe Peters* • Joan Dixon *Diane* • Lowell Gilmore *Kendall Webb* • Louis Jean Heydt *Harry Miller* • Milburn Stone *Egan* • Joseph Crehan *Thompson* • Joe Forte *Brissard* ■ *Dir* Harold Daniels • *Scr* Steve Fisher, George Bricker, from a story by Richard Landau, Geoffrey Holmes

Roadflower ★★★ 18

Crime action drama
1994 · US · Colour · 85mins

There are shades of *The Hills Have Eyes* in this intriguing action thriller, which boasts a high quality, if eclectic, cast. Christopher Lambert is the head of a family driving across the Nevada desert who find themselves locked in combat with a gang of psychos led by Craig Scheffer. Lambert is a tad

unconvincing as the humble businessman, but there are unlikely, but solid, supporting performances from former Hal Hartley favourite Adrienne Shelly, David (*Scream*) Arquette, Christopher (*The Faculty*) McDonald and Joseph Gordon-Levitt, best known for his role in *Third Rock from the Sun*.

Christopher Lambert *Jack* • Craig Sheffer *Cliff* • David Arquette *Bobby* • Joseph Gordon-Levitt *Richie* • Adrienne Shelly *Red* • Michelle Forbes *Helen* • Josh Brolin *Tom* • Christopher McDonald *Glen* ■ *Dir* Deran Sarafian • *Scr* Tedi Sarafian

Roadhouse 66 ★★ 18

Comedy drama   1984 · US · Colour · 89mins

A youth movie, set over Labor Day weekend on the mythical Route 66. Willem Dafoe – still trying to get his career into top gear – plays a cool dude who hitches a ride with University dropout Judge Reinhold. When their car collapses in the one-horse town of Bowman, Arizona, they hang out with the locals, cause some trouble, play pool and finally enter a drag race, winning it despite the presence of a scorpion in the cabin. Almost every cliché of the youth movie – from *The Wild One* to *Rebel without a Cause* to *American Graffiti* – is tossed into the blender, together with a non-stop soundtrack of jukebox faves.

Willem Dafoe *Johnny Harte* • Judge Reinhold *Beckman Hallsgood Jr* • Kaaren Lee *Jesse Duran* • Kate Vernon *Melissa Duran* • Stephen Elliott *Sam* • Alan Autry *Hoot* ■ *Dir* John Mark Robinson • *Scr* Galen Lee, George Simpson, from a story by Galen Lee

The Roadhouse Murder ★★★

Crime drama   1932 · US · BW · 71mins

This terrific idea for a movie has journalist, Eric Linden, deciding to incriminate himself as a killer for a series of newspaper articles, only to find that it's not that easy to extricate himself from the morass of his own making. B-feature stuff, of course, but part-written by real-life journalist Gene Fowler (although also partly based on both a novel and a Hungarian play) who brings plenty of life and colour to the proceedings. Linden is an acceptably harassed hero and Dorothy Jordan a fine hapless heroine, while Bruce Cabot and Roscoe Ates provide redoubtable support. Suspenseful stuff.

Eric Linden *Chick Brian* • Dorothy Jordan *Mary Agnew* • Bruce Cabot *Fred Dykes* • Phyllis Clare *Louise Rand* ■ *Dir* J Walter Ruben • *Scr* J Walter Ruben, Gene Fowler, from the play *Lame Dog Inn* by Ladislaus Bus-Fekete, from a novel by Maurice Level

Roadie ★★

Music comedy   1980 · US · Colour · 89mins

The biggest novelty in this movie is the inspired casting of pop melodramatist Meat Loaf as a wide-eyed innocent lost in the corruptible world of rock 'n' roll. Proving in films like "Fight Club" what an affecting actor he can be, Meat Loaf brings an engaging credibility to the role of a Texas mechanic-turned-roadie, who strikes up an unlikely friendship with a groupie who's been saving herself for *Alice Cooper*. But

Robert Altman protégé, Alan Rudolph punctuates this straightforward tale with tiresome bar room brawls and noisy knockabout comic moments made bearable only by the occasional celebrity cameo from the likes of Blondie, Roy Orbison and, years before his joke appearance in Wayne's World, Alice Cooper.

Meat Loaf Travis W Redfish • Kaki Hunter Lola Bouilliabase • Art Carney Corpus C Redfish • Gailard Sartain BB Muldoon • Don Cornelius Mohammed Johnson • Rhonda Bates Alice Poo • Richard Marion George • Sonny Davis Bird • Joe Spano Ace ■ Dir Alan Rudolph • Scr Big Boy Medlin, Michael Ventura, from a story by Big Boy Medlin, Michael Ventura, Zalman King, Alan Rudolph

Roadkill ★★★

Surreal road movie 1989 · Can · BW · 85mins
A distinct curio from Canadian director Bruce McDonald, a road movie with a difference. Slowly gaining confidence behind the wheel, Valerie Buhagiar does remarkably well in the role of a naive assistant sent by an unscrupulous promoter to find a rock band that's gone missing on tour. En route, she encounters a taxi driver who bores everyone with tales of his days as a roadie, an eccentric documentary-maker and a maniac who wants to put Canadian serial killing on the map. The episodic structure hinders character development, but it also prevents any situation from outstaying its welcome.

Valerie Buhagiar Ramona • Gerry Quigley Roy Seth • Larry Hudson Buddie • Bruce McDonald Bruce Shack • Shaun Bowring Matthew • Don McKellar Russel • Mark Tarantino Luke ■ Dir Bruce McDonald • Scr Don McKellar

Roadracers ★★ 15

Drama 1994 · US · Colour · 89mins
A chance to see the early work of one of Hollywood's hippest young directors, Robert Rodriguez, chum of Quentin Tarantino and responsible for the likes of Desperado and From Dusk till Dawn. Made as part of a series of TV remakes of teen B movies from the fifties (John Milius is another luminary who has contributed a film), Rodriguez keeps his tongue firmly in his cheek as he recounts the story of cool singer David Arquette, who finds himself caught between a tough gang leader and a cruel detective (William Sadler). It's a tad indulgent and the film's kitsch appeal gradually begins to fade, but it's enthusiastically played and Rodriguez never lets the pace slacken for a moment. Female lead Salma Hayek teamed up again with Rodriguez for Desperado. Contains swearing. ▣

David Arquette Dude • Salma Hayek Donna • John Hawkes Nixer • Jason Wiles Teddy • William Sadler Sarge • O'Neal Compton J T ■ Dir Robert Rodriguez • Scr Robert Rodriguez, Tommy Nix

Roads to the South ★★

Political drama
1978 · Fr/Sp · Colour · 100mins
Conceived by Jorge Semprun and Yves Montand as a companion piece to The War Is Over (1966) on which they'd worked with Alain Resnais, this downbeat drama about the growing disillusionment of an old-style socialist has none of the intellectual intensity of

its predecessor and comes across as an old man's lament for past times and missed opportunities. Originally intended for the small screen, Joseph Losey's film has touching moments, particularly when Montand and his young lover, Miou-Miou, head back to Spain on the death of Franco. But, mostly, it's an interminably polemical picture, which offers few historical or contemporary insights. In French with English subtitles.

Yves Montand Larrea • Miou-Miou Julia • France Lambiotte Eve • Laurent Malet Laurent • JoséLuis Gómez Miguel ■ Scr Joseph Losey • Scr Joseph Losey, Patricia Losey, Jorge Semprun

Roadside Prophets ★★★ 15

Road movie comedy drama
1992 · US · Colour · 92mins
Ultra-hip road movie, with many of the leading roles acted out by cutting-edge rock, rap and folk musicians. John Doe, of LA punk band X, and Beastie Boy rapper Adam Horovitz, play bikers who hit the highway to deliver a dead friend's ashes for scattering in a remote Nevada town. En route, they encounter deadbeats, philosophers, fighters and loose women. Pitched as an Easy Rider for the 90s, Roadside Prophets eclectic cast also includes psychedelia guru Timothy Leary, folk singer Arlo Guthrie, and actors John Cusack and David Carradine. Highly rated by US critics, this manic ride of a movie maybe doesn't push quite the same buttons on this side of the Atlantic. But certain viewers might well turn on, tune in and drop out to it. ▣

John Doe Joe Mosely • Adam Horovitz Sam • Arlo Guthrie Harvey • David Carradine Othello Jones • John Cusack Caspar • David Anthony Marshall Dave Coleman • Don Cheadle Happy Days manager • Timothy Leary Salvadore ■ Dir Abbe Wool • Scr Abbe Wool, from an idea by David Swinson

Roar ★★★ PG

Adventure 1981 · US · Colour · 96mins
The title refers to the lions who star in this sadly self-conscious travelogue featuring wild animals and film-maker Noel Marshall. He's a biological researcher who sends for his family– including his real-life then-wife Tippi Hedren – to come stay at his ranch in the African Bush. That's about all, apart from the yelps of delight from the young humans as they communicate with the oh-so-friendly beasts. Floods and fire held up filming of this profit-losing comedy adventure, but it managed to reach the screen – and kids' hearts – without a roar of approval from critics. Cameraman Jan de Bont went on to direct both Speed and Twister ▣

Noel Marshall Hank • Tippi Hedren Madeleine • John Marshall John • Jerry Marshall Jerry • Melanie Griffith Melanie • Kyalo Mativo Mativo • Frank Tom Frank ■ Dir/Scr Noel Marshall

The Roaring Twenties ★★★★ PG

Crime drama 1939 · US · BW · 101mins
Despite its plentiful shoot-outs, this is not so much a gangster movie in the mould of Scarface or Little Caesar, but a morality story about a First World War veteran who tries to go straight,

then yields to the lure of bootlegging and other crimes. James Cagney is on terrific form as the good-guy turned bad and Humphrey Bogart is a vicious hoodlum whose motto might be "don't blame me, blame society". Raoul Walsh skilfully creates a convincing Prohibition world of smoky speakeasys and gleaming black cars parked in dark alleys, a world of endless opportunity and rampant corruption, though the script is a typical Warner Bros blend of slang and sermon. ▣

James Cagney Eddie Bartlett • Humphrey Bogart George Hally • Jeffrey Lynn Lloyd Hart • Priscilla Lane Jean Sherman • Gladys George Panama Smith • Frank McHugh Danny Green ■ Dir Raoul Walsh • Scr Jerry Wald, Richard Macaulay, Robert Rossen, from a story by Mark Hellinger

Rob Roy ★★★★ 15

Historical adventure
1995 · US · Colour · 132mins
Mel Gibson may have grabbed the Oscar glory for Braveheart, but this rip-snorting early 18th-century tartan romp is a lot more fun. Liam Neeson plays the principled Robert MacGregor, who becomes reluctant rebel, Rob Roy, when his money is stolen and his wife, Jessica Lange, is raped by evil English aristocrat Tim Roth. Neeson is suitably heroic, but Roth is a diabolical delight, stealing every scene in which he appears, and he's matched by fellow villains, John Hurt and Brian Cox. Scottish-born director, Michael Caton-Jones, makes striking use of the rugged locations and stages the action sequences with robust glee – the flashing duel between Neeson and Roth is a highlight. Terrific stuff. Contains violence and swearing. ▣
DVD

Liam Neeson Robert MacGregor • Jessica Lange Mary Of Comar • John Hurt Marquis of Montrose • Tim Roth Archie Cunningham • Eric Stoltz McDonald • Andrew Keir Argyll • Brian Cox Killearn • Brian McCarde Alasdair • Gilbert Martin Guthrie • Vicki Masson Betty ■ Dir Michael Caton-Jones • Scr Alan Sharp

Rob Roy, the Highland Rogue ★★ U

Historical adventure
1953 · UK/US · Colour · 81mins
Heavy on starch and lacing the prerequisite thigh-slapping, this stiff biographical account of the 18th-century Scots clansman, is a reminder of the days when Disney would travel to these shores, re-write a bit of history, and provide work for half the British film industry in the process. Richard Todd and Glynis Johns head a cast which also includes anyone who was anyone in 50s British cinema (James Robertson-Justice, Michael Gough, Finlay Currie), but the principals can't quite compare with Liam Neeson and Jessica Lange in the recent remake. Todd would be seen to fair better soon after as Wing Commander, Guy Gibson, in The Dam Busters.

Richard Todd Rob Roy MacGregor • Glynis Johns Helen Mary MacGregor • James Robertson-Justice Duke of Argyll • Michael Gough Duke of Montrose • Jean Taylor-Smith Lady Glengyll • Geoffrey Keen Killearn • Finlay Currie Hamish MacPherson • Archie Duncan Dougal MacGregor ■ Dir Harold French • Scr Lawrence E Watkin

Robbers of the Sacred Mountain ★★ 15

Adventure fantasy
1983 · Can/US · Colour · 92mins
A Raiders Of The Lost Ark clone – one of many made in the early 80s, in a bid to keep up with the (Indiana) Joneses. Most from this timely genre went straight or nearly straight to video, a medium which at the time was new, voracious and indiscriminate in its appetite. And this archaeological dig was no exception. The title tells all plotwise, while any attempts at matching the quality of Raiders were sabotaged by both dodgy acting and ragged editing (its 90-minute running time suggests some hacking back from something rather longer). ▣

John Marley Christopher Falcon • Simon MacCorkindale Hank Richards • Louis Vallance Tracey Falcon • Bianca Guerra BG Alvarez • George Touliatos Murdoch • Jorge Reynoso Marquez ■ Dir Robert Schulz • Scr Olaf Pooley, Walter Bell, from a story by Sir Arthur Conan Doyle

Robbery ★★★ PG

Crime drama 1967 · UK · Colour · 109mins
Following the Glasgow-London, mail train robbery of 1963, several film projects were announced, but this is the only British production to have got off the ground. It never fulfils the promise of its opening car chase, during which one vehicle mows down a policeman and a procession of schoolchildren. Thereafter, the plotting and execution of the Great Train Robbery seems rather trite, cops-and-robbers stuff, and the fictitious characters are not half as colourful as the real-life Ronnie Biggs and company. But there is more action towards the end, enough to impress Hollywood, who summoned Peter Yates to direct Bullitt. Incidentally, the West German film, The Great British Train Robbery (1966), is truer to life. ▣

Stanley Baker Paul Clifton • Joanna Pettet Kate Clifton • James Booth Inspector Langdon • Frank Finlay Robinson • Barry Foster Frank ■ Dir Peter Yates • Scr Edward Boyd, Peter Yates, George Markstein, from a story by Gerald Wilson

Robbery under Arms ★★ U

Crime adventure 1957 · US · Colour · 99mins
The fourth, screen-telling of Rolf Boldrewood's popular tale about bushranger, Captain Starlight, is saved only by Peter Finch in the lead and the panoramic photography of Harry Waxman. Away from the savage beauty of the Australian wilderness, former documentary film-maker, Jack Lee, drains all the drama from the round of robberies, escapes and betrayals that engulf brothers, David McCallum and Ronald Lewis, when they join the bandits. Finch is not seen enough, leaving us stuck with the tensions within the gang and the stormy relationship between Lewis and the duplicitous Maureen Swanson. The 1985 version (starring Sam Neill) was scarcely better.

Peter Finch Captain Starlight • Ronald Lewis Dick Marston • David McCallum Jim Marston • Maureen Swanson Kate Morrison • Laurence Naismith Ben Marston • Jill Ireland Jean •

Jean Anderson *Ma* ■ *Dir* Jack Lee • *Scr* WP Lipscomb, Alexander Baron, from the novel by Rolf Boldrewood

Robbery under Arms ★★PG

Crime adventure
1985 · Ausl · Colour · 105mins

Hacked-back version of a TV mini-series about two farming brothers who become sidekicks to the notorious Aussie bushranger, Captain Starlight. Donald Crombie's film has some exciting action moments, but its main interest lies in Sam Neill's swashbuckling performance as Starlight. The story, combining elements of *Dick Turpin* and *Robin Hood*, had been filmed several times before, most notably in 1957, with Peter Finch as the Captain. ▣

Sam Neill *Capt Starlight* • Christopher Cummins *Jim Marston* • Steven Vidler *Dick Marston* • Tommy Lewis *Warrigal* • Ed Devereaux *Ben Marston* • Liz Newman *Gracey* ■ *Dir* Ken Hannam, Donald Crombie • *Scr* Graeme Koestveld, Tony Morphett, from a novel by Rolf Boldrewood

The Robe ★★★U

Religious drama 1953 · US · Colour · 133mins

Best known as the first film to be released in CinemaScope, *The Robe* is a plodding, pious epic, with Richard Burton as the Roman officer who wins Christ's robe in a game of dice during the Crucifixion. The torn and bloody piece works its magic and, before long, Burton and Jean Simmons are hauled before the crazed Roman emperor Caligula. Based on a doorstop bestseller by Lloyd C Douglas, it's awkwardly directed by Henry Koster and scripted as if by a committee anxious not to offend any race or creed. But there are compensations: Jean Simmons is always on the verge of giggles, Burton is incredibly handsome in a mini-skirt and Jay Robinson makes an unforgettably melodramatic Caligula. Victor Mature took it seriously enough to be called on for the sequel, *Demetrius and the Gladiators*. ▣

Richard Burton *Marcellus Gallio* • Jean Simmons *Diana* • Victor Mature *Demetrius* • Michael Rennie *Peter* • Jay Robinson *Caligula* • Dean Jagger *Justus* • Torin Thatcher *Senator Gallio* • Richard Boone *Pilate* • Betta St John *Miriam* • Ernest Thesiger *Emperor Tiberius* ■ *Dir* Henry Koster • *Scr* Albert Maltz (uncredited), Philip Dunne, from the novel by Lloyd C Douglas, adapted by Gina Kaus • *Costume Designer* Charles LeMaire, Emile Santiago • *Cinematographer* Leon Shamroy

Robert Altman's Jazz '34: Remembrances of Kansas City Swing ★★★★

Music documentary
1996 · US · Colour · 72mins

Director Robert Altman's 1996 film, *Kansas City* – a jazz-tinged melodrama about a corrupt politician and a determined gangster – was notable if only for some remarkable thirties music as arranged by the innovative John Cale. This documentary is the offspring of that movie, featuring sessions recorded on the set of the earlier film. With *Jazz '34*'s pumping, grinding blues all set to elevate the spirits, it's a shame that Altman hadn't done a better job on the original move.

Harry Belafonte *Narrator* ■ *Dir* Robert Altman • *Production Designer* Stephen Altman

Robert et Robert ★★★

Comedy drama 1978 · Fr · Colour · 105mins

Often dismissed for promoting style over content, Claude Lelouch is still capable of producing hugely entertaining films. While this odd couple comedy may not have anything resounding to say about the modern French male, it's still full of good-natured humour and spirited performances. The pairing of Charles Denner and Jacques Villeret, as the eponymous bachelors who embark on a series of comic misadventures, is inspired, with the former's outgoing cabby contrasting splendidly with the latter's timid everyman. The Waterloo day trip is very funny, but the music-hall subplot is a touch contrived. In French with English subtitles.

Charles Denner *Robert Goldman* • Jacques Villeret *Robert Villiers* • Jean-Claude Brialy *Manager* • Germaine Montero *Madame Goldman* • Regine *Madame Villiers* • Macha Meril *Agathe* ■ *Dir/Scr* Claude Lelouch

Roberta ★★★U

Musical romantic comedy
1935 · US · BW · 102mins

Fred Astaire and Gingers Rogers (billed below nominal star Irene Dunne) and Jerome Kern's ravishing eighteen-carat score, are the attractions of this otherwise quite silly musical, adapted from Kern and Otto Harbach's Broadway show. The plot, such as it is, has he-man footballer, Randolph Scott inheriting a chic, Paris fashion house and designer, Dunne (who renders *Smoke Gets in Your Eyes* most touchingly) falling for him. But it's the musical numbers (especially *I'll be Hard to Handle*) performed by Fred and Ginger (displaying her comedic gifts as a phony Polish countess) on the verge of mega-stardom, that has kept the film alive. Lucille Ball can be spotted briefly in the interminable fashion-show finale. The rich cornucopia of ballads also includes the Oscar-nominated and enduring *Lovely to Look At* from which the 1952 remake took its name.

Irene Dunne *Princess Stephanie* • Fred Astaire *Huck Haines* • Ginger Rogers *Comtesse "Tanka" Scharwenka aka Lizzie Gatz* • Randolph Scott *John Kent* • Helen Westley *Roberta aka Minnie* • Victor Varconi *Prince Ladislaw* • Claire Dodd *Sophie Teale* • Luis Alberni *Alexander Petrovich Moskovitch Voyda* • Lucille Ball *Model* ■ *Dir* William A Seiter • *Scr* Jane Murfin, Sam Mintz, Allan Scott, Glenn Tryon (additional dialogue), Dorothy Yost (contributed to treatment), from the musical by Jerome Kern, Otto Harbach, from the novel *Gowns by Roberta* by Alice Duer Miller

Robin and Marian ★★★★

Adventure 1976 · UK · Colour · 106mins

An older and disillusioned Robin Hood returns from the Crusades to find Sherwood empty of outlaws, Marian in a nunnery and the Sheriff of Nottingham still fiddling the books. James Goldman's script has a wonderful way with satire and myth-mongering, while Richard Lester has the sharpest eye for historical detail – watch how Robin and his band awake to the forest dawn, all damp and shivery as they scratch their bums and

brush their teeth with twigs. Audrey Hepburn was lured out of retirement to play Marian and she is exquisite, but it's Sean Connery's gruff, greybeard performance that ennobles, rather than dominates the picture. Great support, too, from Robert Shaw's Sheriff and Ronnie Barker's perfectly judged "heavy relief" as Friar Tuck. The ending is devastating – Robin and the Sheriff hack at each other like two bull elephants, there's a suicide pact and one last arrow. What a pity this gorgeous, masterly elegy for a vanished age of chivalry flopped at the box-office.

Sean Connery *Robin Hood* • Audrey Hepburn *Maid Marian* • Robert Shaw *Sheriff of Nottingham* • Richard Harris *King Richard* • Nicol Williamson *Little John* • Denholm Elliott *Will Scarlett* • Kenneth Haigh *Sir Ranulf* • Ronnie Barker *Friar Tuck* • Ian Holm *King John* • Bill Maynard *Mercadier* • Esmond Knight *Old defender* • Veronica Quilligan *Sister Mary* • Peter Butterworth *Surgeon* ■ *Dir* Richard Lester • *Scr* James Goldman • *Cinematographer* David Watkin

Robin and the 7 Hoods ★★★★U

Comedy 1964 · US · Colour · 117mins

This musical, crime comedy by Warner veteran director, Gordon Douglas, was the final fling of Frank Sinatra's Rat Pack. It's Robin Hood in Prohibition-era Chicago, with gangsters battling for control of the city. Sinatra introduces *My Kind of Town (Chicago Is...)*, Bing Crosby and Dean Martin join him in *Style*, and Peter Falk, Barbara Rush (Marian) and Edward G Robinson, no less, decorate the fringes. Funny, irreverent and very enjoyable, this movie really has the look and feel of a warm-hearted treat. ▣

Frank Sinatra *Robbo* • Dean Martin *John* • Sammy Davis Jr *Will* • Peter Falk *Guy Gisborne* • Barbara Rush *Marian* • Victor Buono *Sheriff Potts* • Bing Crosby *Allen A Dale* • Hank Henry *Six Seconds* • Allen Jenkins *Vermin* • Jack LaRue *Tomatoes* • Edward G Robinson *Big Jim* ■ *Dir* Gordon Douglas • *Scr* David R Schwartz

Robin Cook's Formula for Death ★★★15

Thriller 1995 · US · Colour · 89mins

If we tell you that this TV movie is also known as *Virus* and was taken from a Robin Cook novel entitled *Outbreak*, you'll have a pretty shrewd idea what it's all about. And, although not on a par with the film of Cook's best-known book, *Coma*, this is still quite a decent little thriller, even though the audience has twigged who was responsible for the spread of a supposedly extinct plague, long before ace medical researcher, Nicollette Sheridan manages to do so. But, as Alfred Hitchcock knew so well, feeling superior to the characters accounts for a good deal of the viewer's pleasure. No nailbiter, then, but a well-told tale nonetheless. Contains some violence and sexual references. ▣

Nicollette Sheridan *Dr Marissa Blumenthal* • William Devane *Dr Ralph Harbuck* • William Atherton *Dr Reginald Holloway* • Stephen Caffrey *Tad Shockley* • Dakin Matthews *Cyrill Dubcheck* • Barry Corbin *Dr Jack Clayman* • Jim Minjares *Dr Newman* ■ *Dir* Armand Mastroianni • *Scr* Roger Young, from the novel *Outbreak* by Robin Cook

Robin Cook's Terminal ★★

Medical thriller 1996 · US · Colour · 87mins

Whenever a writer's name is appended to a title, it usually means that the film isn't much cop and the producers are desperately hoping that the name-check will reel in devoted fans. This isn't that bad an adaptation, but anyone familiar with Cook's work will know that he's hot on medical cover-ups and so, from the moment a rich teen dies in an institution with a 100 per cent cure rate, you know that the nasty smell isn't formaldehyde. *Melrose Place* star Doug Savant risks all, taking on the bigwigs, with only an innate sense of justice and nurse, Nia Peeples, to rely on. Contains violence, swearing.

Doug Savant *Sean O'Grady* • Nia Peeples *Janet Reardon* • Michael Ironside *Rombauer* • Roy Thinnes ■ *Dir* Larry Elikann • *Scr* Nancy Isaak, from the novel by Robin Cook

Robin Hood ★★★★PG

Silent romantic adventure
1922 · US · BW · 117mins

One of the showiest (and slowest) of all the epics starring the actionman of the silents, Douglas Fairbanks. The crowds are imaginatively handled by director Allan Dwan, with Fairbanks, as the eponymous, ever-grinning Robin, swashbuckling his way around Sherwood Forest at the behest of Enid Bennett's, Maid Marian. And while Wallace Beery weighs in heavily as Richard the Lion-Hearted, it's Sam De Grasse, as Prince John, who gives the film's best performance. ▣

Douglas Fairbanks *The Earl of Huntington/Robin Hood* • Wallace Beery *Richard the Lion-Hearted* • Sam De Grasse *Prince John* • Enid Bennett *Lady Marian Fitzwalter* • Paul Dickey *Sir Guy of Gisbourne* • William Lowery *The High Sheriff of Nottingham* • Roy Coulson *The King's Jester* • Willard Louis *Friar Tuck* • Alan Hale *Little John* ■ *Dir* Allan Dwan • *Scr* Lotta Woods, from a story by Elton Thomas [Douglas Fairbanks] • *Costume Designer* Mitchell Leisen

Robin Hood ★★★U

Animated adventure
1973 · US · Colour · 79mins

A lesser Disney cartoon, that may not have the heart or the memorable songs of the studio's classics, but is still pleasant and entertaining diversion for the children. Here, it's Robin Hood and his Merry Men-agerie, as all the legendary Nottingham characters have been drawn as animals in an unexceptional retelling of the "rob from the rich, give to the poor" Sherwood Forest fable. Villainous Prince John (voiced by Peter Ustinov) and the slimy Sir Hiss (Terry-Thomas) provide the funniest moments, while the archery contest-turned-American football match lends the tale an upbeat, all-action climax. ▣

Brian Bedford *Robin Hood* • Phil Harris *Little John* • Monica Evans *Maid Marian* • Peter Ustinov *Prince John* • Terry-Thomas *Sir Hiss* • Andy Devine *Friar Tuck* ■ *Dir* Wolfgang Reitherman • *Scr* Larry Clemmons, from a story and the characters created by Ken Anderson

Robin Hood ★★★★ PG
Adventure   1990 · UK/US · Colour · 99mins

This version of the classic tale had the misfortune to come out around the same time as Kevin Costner's epic and unsurprisingly was overshadowed by that Hollywood blockbuster. It's a shame because this, in many ways, is an infinitely better film. Patrick Bergin sparkles in the title role, doing battle with an enjoyable trio of baddies (Jeroen Krabbé, Jurgen Prochnow and Edward Fox), while Uma Thurman makes for a rather sympathetic Maid Marian. Director John Irvin authentically re-creates the murky medieval settings, while staging some grand action sequences and rousing sword fights. But, best of all, there's no sign of that dreadful Bryan Adams. Contains some violence.

Patrick Bergin *Robert Hode/"Robin Hood"* • Uma Thurman *Maid Marian* • Jürgen Prochnow *Sir Miles Folcanet* • Edward Fox *Prince John* • Jeroen Krabbé *Baron Daguerre* • Owen Teale *Will Redding "Will Scarlett"* • David Morrissey *Little John* • Alex Norton *Harry* • Gabrielle Reidy *Lily* • Jeff Nuttall *Friar Tuck* ■ *Dir* John Irvin • *Scr* Mark Allen Smith, John McGrath

Robin Hood: Men in Tights ★★ PG
Comedy   1993 · US · Colour · 99mins

While it's sad that Mel Brooks has hung up his megaphone, there's a certain sense of merciful release, as his last few pictures have veered from poor, to downright awful. This Sherwood spoof sits towards the top of this scale of underachievement, thanks to the occasional flash of vintage Brooks and the wonderfully po-faced performances of Cary Elwes, as Robin and Amy Yasbeck, as Marian. On the down side are Roger Rees's ghastly Sheriff of Rottingham, the untidy structure and the fact that the bawdy gags are more notable for their antiquity than their quality. Watch your *Blackadder* videos instead. Contains swearing.

Cary Elwes *Robin Hood* • Richard Lewis *Prince John* • Roger Rees *Sheriff of Rottingham* • Amy Yasbeck *Marian* • Mark Blankfield *Blinkin* • Dave Chappelle *Ahchoo* • Isaac Hayes *Asneeze* • Megan Cavanagh *Broomhilde* • Eric Allan Kramer *Little John* • Matthew Poretta *Will Scarlet O'Hara* • Tracey Ullman *Latrine* • Patrick Stewart *King Richard* • Dom DeLuise *Don Giovanni* • Mel Brooks ■ *Dir* Mel Brooks • *Scr* Mel Brooks, Evan Chandler, J David Shapiro, from a story by J David Shapiro, Evan Chandler

The Robin Hood of El Dorado ★★★
Biographical drama   1936 · US · BW · 85mins

Spurred by the success of *Viva Villa!*, its biopic of Pancho Villa, MGM turned out this vigorous account of the life and death in early California of another legendary figure, Joaquin Murrieta. He is depicted as the peaceful farmer who is branded a bandit, after avenging the death of his wife at the hands of four gringos. Former Cisco Kid, Warner Baxter, takes the role and William A Wellman's typically uneven direction veers from hard-hitting action, to poetic lyricism and sheer sentimentality. At least 11 writers toiled on the script (only three were credited), including Wellman and actor Joseph Calleia (originally slated to play the rival Mexican bandit played by J Carrol Naish).

Warner Baxter *Joaquin Murrieta* • Ann Loring *Juanita De La Cuesta* • Bruce Cabot *Bill Warren* • Margo *Rosita* • J Carrol Naish *Three Fingered Jack* • Soledad Jimenez [Soledad Jiminez] *Madre Murrieta* • Eric Linden *Jose Murrieta* • carlos De Valdez *johnnie Warren* • Edgar Kennedy *Sheriff Judd* • Charles Trowbridge *Ramon De La Cuesta* ■ *Dir* William A Wellman • *Scr* William A Wellman, Joseph Calleia, Melvin Levy, from a novel by Walter Noble

Robin Hood: Prince of Thieves ★★★★ PG
Action adventure   1991 · US · Colour · 136mins

Buckles are truly swashed and derring-do effectively done in Kevin Reynolds's 12th-century road movie, which simply sets out to entertain handsomely and does so with a great deal of dash, flash and panache. Alan Rickman is a joy to behold as the panto-styled Sheriff of Nottingham, while Morgan Freeman's cultured Moor Robin's early saviour is a commanding, if unlikely, medieval presence. Kevin Costner is more "Indiana Hood" than the Locksley lad of yore in this popcorn epic of romp and circumstance. But it's director Reynolds, who deserves the most praise for disguising such overfamiliar events with imaginative staging and a constantly roving camera. Contains swearing, violence. DVD

Kevin Costner *Robin of Locksley/Robin Hood* • Mary Elizabeth Mastrantonio *Maid Marian* • Alan Rickman *Sheriff of Nottingham* • Morgan Freeman *Azeem* • Christian Slater *Will Scarlett* • Geraldine McEwan *Mortianna* • Micheal McShane *Friar Tuck* • Brian Blessed *Lord Locksley* • Michael Wincott *Guy of Gisborne* • Nick Brimble *Little John* • Soo Drouet *Fanny* • Sean Connery *King Richard* ■ *Dir* Kevin Reynolds • *Scr* Pen Densham, John Watson, from a story by Pen Densham

Robin of Locksley ★★
Romantic comedy adventure   1996 · US · Colour · 97mins

It's one thing to turn *Dangerous Liaisons* into *Cruel Intentions*, but to transpose the legend of Robin Hood to a swanky private school, is pushing postmodernism a bit too far. Director Michael Kennedy takes events at a clip in this made-for-cable film, not allowing you to dwell on the worst anachronisms for too long. He also has a good eye for young talent, with heartthrob-in-waiting Devon Sawa making an athletic Robin, as he uses his prowess on the archery team to protect his beloved Marion (Sarah Chalke) from Agent Walter Nottingham, the sidekick of *Dawson's Creek* star Joshua Jackson, as the villainous John Prince Jr. Geddit?

Devon Sawa *Robin McAllister* • Sarah Chalke *Marion Fitzwater* • Josh Jackson [Joshua Jackson] *John Prince Jr* • Billy O'Sullivan *Will Scarlett* • Tyler Labine *Little John* • Colin Cunningham *Agent Walter Nottingham* ■ *Dir* Michael Kennedy • *Scr* Larry Sugar

Robinson in Space ★★★★ PG
Documentary drama   1997 · UK · Colour · 78mins

Patrick Keiller was inspired to make this follow-up to 1994's *London* by the closure of the old Morris Motors works in Oxford. Visiting factories and ports the length and breadth of the country, he seeks to gauge the impact of 18-years of Tory rule on Britain's traditional manufacturing industries and assess how far we have become a service economy. Complete with a voice-over from Paul Scofield that blends socio-economic data, literary references and the quirky opinions of his fictional companion, Robinson, the film has more of a political agenda than its predecessor, but it's every bit as compelling.

Paul Scofield *Narrator* ■ *Dir/Scr* Patrick Keiller

Robo Warriors ★★ 15
Science-fiction action   1996 · US/Phil · Colour · 89mins

Glum, joyless sci-fi tale of a legendary resistance leader (a thoroughly miserable James Remar), who emerges from hiding to pilot a robot-fighting machine against the Teridaxx aliens, who have declared martial law on Earth. *Predator*, *Jurassic Park* and *Terminator 2* are among the influences evident in this slow-moving and thoroughly unlikely tale – the fascistic villains agree to leave Earth peaceably if they lose the climactic robot fracas. Even the occasional action sequences are sunk by static, unexciting direction and mundane effects. A sense of humour might have helped. Contains violence, swearing.

Kyle Howard • James Lew • James Remar ■ *Dir* Ian Barry • *Scr* Michael Berlin, from a character created by Stuart Gordon

RoboCop ★★★★★ 12
Satirical science-fiction thriller   1987 · US · Colour · 85mins

High-tech meets *High Noon* in Dutch director Paul Verhoeven's deft science-fiction masterpiece, amply delivering on both violent action and satirical fronts. Peter Weller gives a great mime performance as the Detroit cop of the near future resurrected as a cyborg, who goes head-hunting the sadistic gang responsible for his plight as his human memory begins to return. But it's Verhoeven's scabrous dissection of American social issues, trashy sitcom culture and corporate greed that makes this comic-book poem a subversive and thought-provoking edge-of-the-seat epic. Contains violence, swearing, drug abuse, brief nudity.

Peter Weller *Murphy/RoboCop* • Nancy Allen *Officer Anne Lewis* • Daniel O'Herlihy [Dan O'Herlihy] *Old man* • Ronny Cox *Dick Jones* • Kurtwood Smith *Clarence Boddicker* • Miguel Ferrer *Robert Morton* • Robert DoQui *Sergeant Reed* • Ray Wise *Leon* ■ *Dir* Paul Verhoeven • *Scr* Edward Neumeier, Michael Miner

RoboCop 2 ★★★ 18
Science-fiction thriller   1990 · US · Colour · 111mins

An efficient, but rather empty retread of the original, with Peter Weller returning as the cyborg policeman patrolling the mean streets of Detroit. Daniel O'Herlihy, ostensibly the good tycoon from the first film, becomes the bad guy this time around, teaming up with psycho Tom Noonan to destroy his company's creation. It's once again a spectacularly violent affair and the satirical news items still provide a chuckle or two, but, sadly, it lacks the gloriously black excess of Paul Verhoeven's original. Nevertheless, it has proved to be a very serviceable franchise; a second sequel, a children's animated series and a live action TV spin-off followed. Contains swearing, strong violence.

Peter Weller *Robocop* • Nancy Allen *Officer Anne Lewis* • Belinda Bauer *Dr Juliette Faxx* • Daniel O'Herlihy [Dan O'Herlihy] *Old man* • Tom Noonan *Cain* • Gabriel Damon *Hob* • Willard Pugh *Mayor Kuzak* • Stephen Lee *Duffy* • Felton Perry *Donald Johnson* • Patricia Charbonneau *Dr Garcia* ■ *Dir* Irvin Kershner • *Scr* Frank Miller, Walon Green, from a story by Frank Miller, from characters created by Edward Neumeier, Michael Miner

RoboCop 3 ★★★ 15
Science-fiction thriller   1993 · US · Colour · 100mins

Robert Burke, who made a big impression in the title role of British horror thriller, *Dust Devil*, replaces Peter Weller as the unstoppable cyborg cop in director, Fred Dekker's more comedy driven, and far less violent, futuristic fantasy, which returns the series to the central themes of Verhoeven's original "Christian fairy tale". The mechanised flatfoot this time defends the downtrodden homeless when an amoral Japanese magnate decides to clean up downtown Detroit, to build a luxury apartment complex. Complete with "splatterpunk" villains, cyborg samurai and Burke flying to trouble spots using a jet pack, Dekker's fun sequel is well directed and written with a firm eye on the family TV series the concept eventually became. Contains violence. DVD

Robert John Burke [Robert Burke] *Robocop/Alex J Murphy* • Nancy Allen *Officer Anne Lewis* • Rip Torn *Merrit W Morton, CEO* • John Castle *Paul McDaggett* • Jill Hennessy *Dr Marie Lazarus* • CCH Pounder *Bertha* • Mako Kanemitsu ■ *Dir* Fred Dekker • *Scr* Frank Miller, Fred Dekker, from a story by Frank Miller, from the characters created by Edward Neumeier, Michael Miner

A Robot Called Golddigger ★★ PG
Comedy   1993 · US · Colour · 85mins

Even the canniest character actors seem occasionally to like the idea of taking star billing. And that can be the only explanation for the appearance of Joe Pantolino in this dire *Short Circuit* rip-off. As the kindly inventor who builds a robot to save his family from financial ruin, Pantoliano can do nothing with the juvenile script and unimaginative direction. Talented performers Amy Wright and John Rhys-Davies are also left stranded by the wafer-thin material.

Joe Pantoliano *Jack Shamir* • Amy Wright *Kristina Shamir* • John Rhys-Davies *Eli Taki* ■ *Dir* Mark Richardson, Jack Shaoul • *Scr* Jack Shaoul

Robot Jox ★★ 15

Science-fiction action
1989 · US · Colour · 80mins

In a post-nuclear world of banished warfare, nations settle scores with one another via televised games, in which representative heroes battle it out while inside hulking, transformer-like robots. A fascinating premise sadly let down by a scrawny budget and script to match. Gary Graham, from TV's *Alien Nation*, stars as one of the fighters who, having quit the game following a fatal accident involving spectators, returns to battle when his girlfriend enlists. This plagued production was actually shut down for a year once the money ran out. And while the robot miniature work is highly effective, the rest of the film has a shoddy, cheap look about it. A sort of pulp, hi-tech *Rollerball*, this was something of a departure for horror director Stuart Gordon, known for the notorious *Re-Animator*. ▣

Gary Graham *Achilles* • Anne-Marie Johnson *Athena* • Paul Koslo *Alexander* • Robert Sampson *Commissioner Jameson* • Danny Kamekona *Doctor Matsumoto* • Hilary Mason *Professor Laplace* • Michael Alldredge *Tex Conway* ■ *Dir* Stuart Gordon • *Scr* Joe Haldeman, from a story by Stuart Gordon

Robot Monster ★ U

Science-fiction
1953 · US · BW · 62mins

After *Plan 9 from Outer Space*, this is the best known bad movie in the science-fiction genre. The last six human survivors in existence struggle against the dreaded Ro-Man (a man dressed in a gorilla suit and a plastic diving helmet), whose race has destroyed the planet with their "calcinator ray" to stop Earthlings going into space and causing intergalactic friction. Made for next-to-nothing in four days, and padded out with bizarre stock footage montages (from *Man and His Mate* and *Flight to Mars*), this legendary trash masterpiece is hilariously banal, naive and threadbare. And it was all originally presented in 3-D!

George Nader *Roy* • Claudia Barrett *Alice* • Selena Royle *Mother* • Gregory Moffett *Johnny* • John Mylong *Professor* • Pamela Paulson *Carla* • George Barrows *Ro-Man* ■ *Dir* Phil Tucker • *Scr* Wyott Ordung

Robot Wars ★ PG

Science-fiction western
1993 · US · Colour · 69mins

This dire, futuristic tale from cheapo father and son director/producer team, Albert and Charles Band, may be set in 2041, but it's got the production values of 1970. The stop-frame animation of the giant robot vehicles is passable, but the acting and dialogue ("You're way too negative. You're a walking minus sign.") is beyond bad. Although *Re-Animator*'s (1985) Barbara Crampton adds a little feistiness to the heroine, Don Michael Paul's, Han Solo-esque robot pilot, barely has a pulse. Chuck in a co-pilot called Stumpy and some of the shoddiest back projection work ever seen and you have a film of considerable awfulness. ▣

Don Michael Paul *Captain Drake* • Barbara Crampton *Dr Leda Fannon* • James Staley

Stumpy • Lisa Rinna *Annie* ■ *Dir* Albert Band • *Scr* Jackson Barr, from an idea by Charles Band

Rocco and His Brothers ★★★★ 15

Drama
1960 · It · BW · 170mins

Neo-realism meets soap-style melodrama in this episodic family saga. A grimly naturalistic subject – peasant family from southern Italy moves to the corrupting urban jungle of Milan – gets the grand operatic treatment from Luchino Visconti whose initial restraint should have been maintained throughout. Instead, he goes for empty flourishes of over-the-top despair with which Alain Delon, as the self-sacrificing Rocco, seems somewhat uncomfortable. A long haul at nearly three hours, but worth seeing for Renato Salvatori as the brutish elder brother and the accomplished black-and-white photography of Giuseppe Rotunno. In Italian with English subtitles. ▣

Alain Delon *Rocco Pafundi* • Renato Salvatori *Simone* • Annie Girardot *Nadia* • Katina Paxinou *Rosaria Pafundi* • Claudia Cardinale *Ginetta* • Roger Hanin *Morini* ■ *Dir* Luchino Visconti • *Scr* Luchino Visconti, Vasco Pratolini, Suso Cecchi D'Amico

Rocinante ★★ PG

Political drama
1986 · UK · Colour · 92mins

After a meaningful conversation about film narrative with an ex-projectionist, recluse, John Hurt , leaves the derelict cinema where he has been hiding out and hitches a ride to Dartmoor in a truck named Rocinante (a reference to Don Quixote's horse). On his aimless quest he meets political activist Maureen Douglass who, inspired by the 1984 miners' strike, is intent on industrial sabotage. The resulting blend of road movie, British folklore and the Don Quixote myth is a mind-boggling, often inaccessible slice of pretentious art that's rich in ironic symbolism, yet occasionally haunting. You'll find it wonderfully thought-provoking or hopelessly obscure. Late pop star *Ian Dury* pops up occasionally as a jester to quote poetry and make incisive/prosaic – asides to the camera.

John Hurt *Bill* • Maureen Douglass *Jess* • Ian Dury *Jester* • Carol Gillies *Molly* • Jimmy Jewel *Projectionist* ■ *Dir/Scr* Ann Guedes, Eduardo Guedes

The Rock ★★★★ 15

Action thriller   1996 · US · Colour · 140mins

Undeterred by the premature death of his business partner Don Simpson in 1996, producer Jerry Bruckheimer has still dominated the late-nineties action movie scene with a steady stream of blockbusters. *The Rock* is perhaps the most satisfying of these movies, for it's neither as cartoonish as *Con Air*, nor as sentimental as *Armageddon*, but certainly easier to follow than *Enemy of the State*. And it deserves further kudos for establishing Nicolas Cage as one of Hollywood's unlikeliest action heroes. The setting is Alcatraz, which has been taken over by disenchanted general, Ed Harris and his crack team of marines, who are threatening to launch deadly poison-

gas rockets to contaminate San Francisco. In desperation, the FBI pair chemical warfare expert, Cage with jailed former SAS man, Sean Connery, who as the only man to ever escape from the notorious island prison is seen as their best option to break in. Director Michael Bay's boyish enthusiasm for outlandish stunts and carefree destruction is extremely contagious and even the most cynical of viewers will find it difficult not to feel rushes of adrenalin during the numerous slick set pieces. Extra slickness is added in the shape of subtle touches such as Dick Clement and Ian La Frenais's gags, while Harris supplies an unexpectedly human villain of the piece. Contains swearing and violence. ▣ *DVD*

Sean Connery *John Patrick Mason* • Nicolas Cage *Stanley Goodspeed* • Ed Harris *General Francis X Hummel* • John Spencer *FBI Director Womack* • David Morse *Major Tom Baxter* • William Forsythe *Ernest Paxton* • Michael Biehn *Commander Anderson* • Vanessa Marcil *Carla Pestalozzi* • John C McGinley *Marine Captain Hendrix* ■ *Dir* Michael Bay • *Scr* David Weisberg, Mark Rosner, Douglas S Cook, from a story by David Weisberg, Douglas S Cook

Rock-a-Bye Baby ★★ U

Comedy   1958 · US · Colour · 106mins

A famous movie star (Marilyn Maxwell), whose marriage has been kept secret in order to preserve her glamorous image, gives birth to triplets, another event that needs hushing up, and turns to a lifelong besotted fan, a bachelor, to take care of the infant trio. He is Jerry Lewis, pursuing his post-Dean Martin, solo career and calling on his full repertoire of frenzied lunacy. The effect, without Martin as foil, is akin to being hit on the head with a sandbag, but Lewis addicts should be happy with that.

Jerry Lewis *Clayton Poole* • Marilyn Maxwell *Carla Naples* • Connie Stevens *Sandy Naples* • Reginald Gardiner *Harold Herman* • Baccaloni [Salvatore Baccaloni] *Salvatore Naples* • Hans Conried *Mr Wright* • Isobel Elsom *Mrs Van Cleve* • James Gleason *Dr Simkins* • Ida Moore *Bessie Polk* • Gary Lewis *Young Clayton* ■ *Dir* Frank Tashlin • *Scr* Frank Tashlin, from the play *The Miracle of Morgan's Creek* by Preston Sturges.

Rock-a-Doodle ★★ U

Animated musical
1990 · US · Colour · 71mins

So-so animation from Don Bluth which isn't really a patch on Disney fare or even Bluth's own, *Land Before Time* series. It's the tale of Chanticleer, a rooster who accidentally neglects his duty of heralding the arrival of the dawn and so, humiliated, decides to leave his farmyard home. Bizarrely, he ends up in a city, much like Las Vegas and embarks on a career as an Elvis impersonator – events which are unlikely to impress younger viewers a great deal. They're also unlikely to be moved by the news that Chanticleer's singing and speaking voice is provided by singer Glen Campbell. Misjudged kids fare. ▣

Glen Campbell *Chanticleer* • Eddie Deezen *Snipes* • Sandy Duncan *Peepers* • Charles Nelson Reilly *Hunch* • Ellen Greene *Goldie* • Phil Harris *Patou* • Christopher Plummer *The Duke* • Toby Scott Ganger *Edmond* ■ *Dir* Don

Bluth • *Scr* David N Weiss, David Steinberg, from a story by Don Bluth, John Pomeroy, TJ Kuenster, Gary Goldman

Rock All Night ★★

Crime drama   1957 · US · BW · 73mins

If Roger Corman is the king of B-movies, then Dick Miller is one of its most loyal subjects. Fresh from a supporting role in Corman's *Not of This Earth*, he landed the lead in this trashy teen crime drama, about a couple of killers who besiege the Cloud Nine rock 'n' roll club. Shot in under a week, this is the kind of quickie that Tarantino tarts up with a little street talk and a lot of gunfire. For once playing the good guy, Miller is great value as the nerdy barman who saves the day. *The Platters*, in their original line-up with Tony Williams and Zola Taylor and at the height of their fame, make the screen sizzle, despite the economy of footage used to film them. A real curio, and mercifully short.

Dick Miller *Shorty* • Abby Dalton *Julie* • Robin Morse *Al* • Richard Cutting *Steve* • Bruno Vesota *Charley* • Chris Alcaide *Angie* ■ *Dir* Roger Corman • *Scr* Charles B Griffith, from the story by David P Harmon

Rock around the Clock ★★★ U

Musical   1956 · US · BW · 74mins

A low-budget, 77-minute movie, directed by Fred F Sears (hardly a name to conjure with!) in which disc jockey, Alan Freed, discovers a rock band in a village in the faraway hills, and promotes them in New York. And that would be that, except for the fact that the band is Bill Haley and the Comets, and this little film now history for the effect they had on teen audiences worldwide and on the music business. Boasting an abundance of hits, including Haley's *See You Later, Alligator*, this rock-pop fest features numerous other artists, including The Platters.

Bill Haley and the Comets *Bill Haley and the Comets* • Alan Freed • Johnny Johnston *Steve Hollis* • Alix Talton *Corinne* • Lisa Gaye *Lisa Johns* • John Archer *Mike Dennis* ■ *Dir* Fred F Sears • *Scr* Robert E Kent, James B Gordon

Rock Hudson ★★★

Biographical drama
1990 · US · Colour · 97mins

Amazingly, it's 12-years since Hudson's Aids-related death stunned fans. This TV movie traces his rise to fame, relives some of his smash-hit movies and reveals the secret life that would ultimately contribute to his demise. The action is loosely based on a memoir written by Phyllis Gates, the woman Hudson married on the advice of the studio publicity machine to reinforce his screen image. Thomas Ian Griffith battles bravely in the title role, but he always seems more like the truck driver that Hudson once was, than the star manufactured with such care by Universal.

Thomas Ian Griffith *Rock Hudson* • Daphne Ashbrook *Phyllis Gates* • William R Moses *Marc Christian* • Andrew Robinson *Henry Willson* • Thom Mathews *Tim Murphy* • Michael Ensign *Mark Miller* • Diane Ladd *Kay,*

U = SUITABLE FOR ALL   Uc = SUITABLE FOR ALL, ESPECIALLY FOR YOUNG CHILDREN (VIDEO ONLY)   PG = PARENTAL GUIDANCE

Rock Hudson's mother ■ *Dir* John Nicolella • *Scr* Dennis Turner, from the book *My Husband, Rock Hudson* by Phyllis Gates

Rock Hudson's Home Movies ★★★
Documentary 1992 · US · Colour · 63mins

A hip, smart and sassy probe into the uneasy synthesis of homosexuality and the Hollywood star system. Director, Mark Rappaport's camp delight features a Rock Hudson look-alike who takes the viewer on a *That's Entertainment*-style journey of cleverly edited film clips from the heart-throb's life, hilariously underlining their gay connotations. Although tinged with a melancholic sadness over the matinée idol's subsequent Aids-related death in 1985, Rappaport's take on Rock is a far more militant version of the ageing closeted star who, in this post-Queerdom incarnation, never fails to slyly point out an ultra-modern way of assessing his *Pillow Talk* persona.

Eric Farr *Rock Hudson* ■ *Dir/Scr* Mark Rappaport

Rock'n'Roll Cop ★★★
Police thriller 1994 · HK · Colour

With 1997 very much in mind, Kirk Wong's acclaimed cop film is a touch more thought-provoking than the average "chop socky" movie. When a triad gang decimates a Kowloon gambling joint, unconventional Hong Kong islander, Anthony Wong, crosses to the mainland in pursuit of mobster Wing-Kwong Yu. The film makes little advance on the usual crime drama themes, and there is nothing new about a cop and a villain harbouring a passion for the same girl (Carrie Ng). But there are plenty of insights into Sino-colonial relations and some spirited action sequences. In Cantonese with English subtitles.

Anthony Wong *Inspector Hung* • Wu Hsing-Kuo *Wang Jun* • Carrie Ng *Hou-yee* • Yu Wing-Kwong *Shum Chi-hung* • Chan Ming-Yuan *Singer* ■ *Dir* Che Kirk Wong [Kirk Wong] • *Scr* Winky Wong

Rock 'n' Roll High School ★★★ 15
Musical comedy 1979 · US · Colour · 87mins

A punk homage to the high-school rock 'n' roll films of the fifties and sixties, trailing cult credits like a pair of ripped bondage pants. Roger Corman is the executive producer, Joe Dante co-wrote the story, with director, Allan Arkush and *The Ramones* appear live and contribute to the score. There is an excuse for a teenage romance plot but the meat has P J Soles, a Ramones fan at war with rock-hating high-school principal Mary Woronov. A scorchingly brilliant soundtrack, a great deal of ludicrous fun, comic-book humour and an explosive ending make this head and shoulders above all other teenage music films, including the miserable follow-up *Rock 'n' Roll High School Forever* (1991). Apparently Soles was terrified throughout the gig scene because real Ramones fans were used as the extras. ▭

PJ Soles *Riff Randell* • Vincent Van Patten *Tom Roberts* • Clint Howard *Eaglebauer* • Dey Young *Kate Rambeau* • Mary Woronov *Evelyn*

Togar • Dick Miller *Police Chief Klein* • Paul Bartel *Mr McGree* ■ *Dir* Allan Arkush • *Scr* Richard Whitley, Russ Dvonch, Joseph McBride, from a story by Allan Arkush, Joe Dante

Rock 'n' Roll Mom ★
Comedy 1988 · US · Colour · 96mins

In an utterly daft Disney comedy, Dyan Cannon stars as a female rock singer, who's trying to be both a musician and a mother. However, in a film concerning rock 'n' roll, it isn't helpful that the music is made up of horrible eighties drivel. The only area of interest is the cast, which includes *Melrose Place*'s Heather Locklear, *Dempsey and Makepeace* star Michael Brandon, and Joe Pantoliano (*The Matrix*). Maybe they should have known better, though.

Dyan Cannon *Annie Hackett* • Michael Brandon *Jeff Robbins* • Telma Hopkins *Etta* • Nancy Lenehan *Connie* • Josh Blake *Nicky Hackett* • Amy Lynne *Emma Hackett* • Alex Rocco *Jerry Weiss* • John Snyder *Jake* • Joe Pantoliano *Ronnie Dewlap* ■ *Dir* Michael Schultz

Rock, Pretty Baby ★★
Musical 1956 · US · BW · 89mins

This was made strictly for a teenage audience at the time, and is still likely to appeal mostly to those who were growing up in the fifties, though fans of the era's music (shockingly radical at the time but amazingly tame-sounding now) will appreciate seeing the stars of the day performing their hits. The slight plot has John Saxon as the leader of a high-school band, intent on winning a major contest against the wishes of his father, who feels he should have loftier ambitions. Sal Mineo as a fellow student and King Kong star, Fay Wray (as Saxon's mother) are also in the cast, struggling to make some impression amid the countless rock'n'roll numbers.

Sal Mineo *Angelo Barrato* • John Saxon *Jimmy Daley* • Luana Patten *Joan Wright* • Edward C Platt [Edward Platt] *Thomas Daley Sr* • Fay Wray *Beth Daley* • Rod McKuen *"Ox" Bentley* • John Wilder *"Fingers" Porter* • Alan Reed Jr *"Sax" Lewis* ■ *Dir* Richard Bartlett • *Scr* Herbert Margolis, William Raynor • *Music* Henry Mancini

Rock, Rock, Rock! ★★ U
Musical 1956 · US · BW · 85mins

This is very much a period piece for aficionados, a cheap quickie made by producer Milton Subotsky, who went on to a stream of British horror flicks under the Amicus banner. Featuring the man who actually coined the phrase "rock 'n' roll", Alan Freed, the wafer-thin plot hinges on whether teenager, Tuesday Weld (songs dubbed by Connie Francis), will get the prom dress of her dreams. Still, miming to their records, there's Chuck Berry performing *You Can't Catch Me*, the fabulous LaVern Baker's version of *Tra La La*, and, best of all, Frankie Lymon and the Teenagers' hit *I'm Not a Juvenile Delinquent*. Production values? Plot? Acting? It didn't matter then, Daddy-O, and it still doesn't. ▭

Tuesday Weld *Dori* • Jacqueline Kerr *Gloria* • Ivy Schulman *Baby* • Fran Manfred *Arabella* • Jack Collins *Father* • Carol Moss *Mother* • Eleanore Swayne *Miss Silky* • Lester Mack *Mr*

Bimble • Bert Conway *Mr Barker* ■ *Dir* Will Price • *Scr* Milton Subotsky, from a story by Milton Subotsky, Phyllis Coe

Rockabye ★
Drama 1932 · US · BW · 66mins

Fraught with problems throughout its making, this David O Selznick production of a tearjerking melodrama, is recorded in the annals of RKO's troubled history as a major critical catastrophe. The overwrought tale of an actress who has clawed her way to the top, only to torment herself over her children and sacrifice her lover, it stars the stylish and restrained Constance Bennett in a role to which she is totally unsuited. George Fitzmaurice, a veteran of several silents including Valentino's *Son of the Sheik*, was wheeled in on loan from MGM to direct, and Phillips Holmes was cast as Bennett's leading man. The resulting film was so awful that Joel McCrea was bundled in to replace Holmes and George Cukor called in to direct a slew of retakes.

Constance Bennett *Judy Carroll* • Joel McCrea *Jacobs "Jake" Van Riker Pell* • Paul Lukas *Antoine "Tony" de Sola* • Jobyna Howland *"Snooks" Carroll* • Walter Pidgeon *Commissioner Al Howard* • Clara Blandick *Brida* • Walter Catlett *Jimmy Dunn* ■ *Dir* George Cukor, George Fitzmaurice • *Scr* Jane Murfin, Kubec Glasmon, from the play by Lucia Bonder, from the short story *Our Judy* by Lucia Bonder

Rockabye ★★
Drama 1986 · US · Colour · 100mins

A silly drama with *I'll Take Manhattan's* Valerie Bertinelli, as a naive young woman who has to track down her child when he's snatched soon after she arrives on the mean streets of New York. Yes, the Big Apple is portrayed as the real criminal in this daft tale, which becomes even more so when Rachel Ticotin (*Total Recall*) appears as one of those characters you only get in movies – the wise-talking reporter who steps in to help because she's after a good story.

Valerie Bertinelli *Susannah Bartok* • Rachel Ticotin *Victoria Garcia* • Jason Alexander *Lieutenant Ernest Foy* • Ray Baker *Donald F Donald* • Roderick Cook *Christopher Zellner* • David Carroll *Joey* ■ *Dir* Richard Michaels • *Scr* Laird Koenig, from his novel

Rockers ★★★
Action comedy 1978 · Jam · Colour · 99mins

This story of a young Rastafarian trying to drum his way into the music business may well have a see-through story, but it's also high on fruitcake whimsy and meandering charm. Even though the film invites the audience into a world of Rasta ritual and peer-group activity, it always does so with plenty of nimbleness, wit and grace. A relevant and classy soundtrack is provided by the *Mighty Diamonds*, *Peter Tosh* et al.

Leroy Wallace *Horsemouth* • Richard Hall *Dirty Harry* • Monica Craig *Madgie* • Marjorie Norman *Sunshine* • Jacob Miller *Jakes* • Gregory Isaacs *Jah Tooth* • Winston Rodney *Burning Spear* ■ *Dir/Scr* Theodoros Bafaloukos

---

Rocket Gibraltar ★★★ PG
Drama 1988 · US · Colour · 94mins

A family gathers on Long Island to celebrate the 77th birthday of its patriarch, Burt Lancaster. And, in the manner of such cinematic gatherings, there are the customary resentments and jealousies to exercise and/or exorcise. In this case, the only daughter is a sex addict, while the sons are a faded baseball pitcher and a dried-up, stand-up comedian. Grandpa Lancaster is a former blacklisted writer and general egghead. As usual with such dramas, the benefits are solely in the casting and here the future-star spotting is exceptional: Bill Pullman and Kevin Spacey in early roles and even little Macaulay Culkin in his screen debut. The movie was made during David Puttnam's brief stewardship of Columbia and was barely released anywhere. ▭

Burt Lancaster *Levi Rockwell* • Suzy Amis *Aggie Rockwell* • Patricia Clarkson *Rose Black* • Frances Conroy *Ruby Hanson* • Sinead Cusack *Amanda "Billi" Rockwell* • John Glover *Rolo Rockwell* • Bill Pullman *Crow Black* • Kevin Spacey *Dwayne Hanson* • Macaulay Culkin *Cy Blue Black* ■ *Dir* Daniel Petrie • *Scr* Amos Poe

The Rocketeer ★★★★ PG
Fantasy adventure 1991 · US · Colour · 104mins

Based on a cult graphic novel blending Second World War adventure and superhero thrills, *Honey, I Shrunk the Kids* director, Joe Johnston's vastly entertaining swashbuckler will jet-propel you back to your most cherished childhood fantasies. A brilliant ode to those corny thirties movie serials, with an added Art Deco sheen, this pleasure cruise through sophisticated nostalgia also benefits from Timothy Dalton's hissably slimy Nazi agent, masquerading as a devil-may-care, Errol Flynn-inspired matinée idol. A treat. ▭ **DVD**

Bill Campbell *Cliff Secord* • Jennifer Connelly *Jenny* • Alan Arkin *Peevy* • Timothy Dalton *Neville Sinclair* • Paul Sorvino *Eddie Valentine* • Terry O'Quinn *Howard Hughes* • Ed Lauter *Fitch* • James Handy *Wooly* • Tiny Ron *Lothar* • Robert Guy Miranda *Spanish Johnny* ■ *Dir* Joe Johnston • *Scr* Danny Bilson, Paul DeMeo, from a story by Danny Bilson, Paul DeMeo, William Dear, from the graphic novel by Dave Stevens

Rocketman ★★★ PG
Science-fiction comedy 1997 · US · Colour · 89mins

Computer genius Fred Z Randall finally gets his chance to be an astronaut. Unfortunately, he's a bit too eccentric for his NASA colleagues, who are treated to a touch more slapstick chaos than they'd bargained for. This goofy comedy, aimed primarily at kids, will succeed mostly with those younger viewers predisposed to humour of the flatulent variety. *Rocketman* is really a vehicle for the antics of Harland Williams as Randall, but credit must be given to William Sadler as Mission Commander "Wild Bill" Overbeck, who does a slow burn while Randall inadvertently spoils his dreams. Contains strong language. ▭

Harland Williams *Fred Z Randall* • Jessica Lundy *Mission Specialist Julie Ford* • William Sadler *Comdr ''Wild Bill''Overbeck* • Jeffrey DeMunn *Chief Flight Director Paul Wick* • James Pickens Jr *Ben Stevens* • Beau Bridges *Bud Nesbitt* • Peter Onorati *Gary Hackman* • Shelley Duvall *Mrs Randall* ■ *Dir* Stuart Gillard • *Scr* Craig Mazin, Greg Erb, from a story by Oren Aviv

Rockets Galore ★★ U

Comedy　　　1958 · UK · Colour · 91mins

Made a decade after Ealing's classic comedy *Whisky Galore!*, this sequel (albeit adapted from another novel by Compton Mackenzie) was on a hiding to nothing, for no matter how good it might be, it would never be favourably compared with its predecessor. In the event, it is an undeniably feeble follow-up, with only a handful of the original Todday islanders remaining, and the story of their battle to prevent the construction of a missile base lacking both charm and satirical bite. Scriptwriter Monja Danischewsky tries to bring the ''little folk against the system'' formula to life, but laughs galore there are not.

Jeannie Carson *Janet MacLeod* • Donald Sinden *Hugh Mander* • Roland Culver *Captain Waggett* • Noel Purcell *Father James McAllister* • Ian Hunter *Air Commodore Watchorn* • Duncan Macrae *Duncan Ban* • Gordon Jackson *George Campbell* • Ronnie Corbett *Drooby* ■ *Dir* Michael Relph • *Scr* Monja Danischewsky, from the novel by Compton Mackenzie

The Rocking Horse Winner ★★★★ PG

Drama　　　1949 · UK · BW · 87mins

A largely unsung, but truly terrific British feature based on a story from D H Lawrence about a young boy with the gift of picking racetrack winners. The imaginative story leaves plenty of space for director Anthony Pelissier's aptitude for surprise and emotional complexity. He elicits measured, insightful performances from the likes of John Mills and Valerie Hobson, and wrings the last ounce of pathos from an intriguing, thought-provoking tale. A film that has always been a favourite among critics and deserves wider recognition from the public at large. ▣

Valerie Hobson *Hester Grahame* • John Howard Davies *Paul Grahame* • Ronald Squire *Oscar Cresswell* • John Mills *Bassett* • Hugh Sinclair *Richard Grahame* • Charles Goldner *Mr Tsaldouris* • Susan Richards *Nannie* • Cyril Smith *Bailiff* ■ *Dir* Anthony Pelissier • *Scr* Anthony Pelissier, from the story by DH Lawrence

Rockshow ★★★

Concert movie　1979 · US · Colour · 103min

Paul McCartney spreading his Wings with a filmed concert tour featuring his first post-Beatles band. The line-up includes wife Linda, ex-*Moody Blues* man Denny Laine and former *Thunderclap Newman* sidekick Jimmy McCullough. The filming is simple and straightforward (no director is credited). Originally recorded in Dolby stereo, it's best seen in cinemas or on a decent home system. A rarity of late, but surely worth a reissue in light of renewed interest in all things Beatle.

• *Cinematographer* Jack Priestly • *Editor* Robin Clarke, Paul Stein

Rocky ★★★★ PG

Sports drama　1976 · US · Colour · 114mins

Though dusting down the classic Hollywood story of the little man winning big, this triple Oscar-winner is shot through with genuine impassioned commitment, born of the fact that Sylvester Stallone realised this was his best shot at stardom. The notion, then, of success hanging by a thread unites both the character of boxer Rocky Balboa and of Stallone himself. Sly, in fact, is highly convincing as a mumbling Philadelphia no-hoper who is finally galvanised by his own aspirations and ends up having a crack at the loquacious Heavyweight Champion of the World, Apollo Creed (Carl Weathers, by way of Muhammed Ali). Sly also wrote the script and was rewarded with an Oscar nomination. Contains some violence, sexual references. ▣ **DVD**

Sylvester Stallone *Rocky Balboa* • Talia Shire *Adrian* • Burt Young *Paulie* • Carl Weathers *Apollo Creed* • Burgess Meredith *Mickey* • Thayer David *Jergens* • Joe Spinell *Gazzo* • Joe Frazier ■ *Dir* John G Avildsen • *Scr* Sylvester Stallone • *Editor* Richard Halsey • *Music* Bill Conti

Rocky II ★★★ PG

Sports drama　1979 · US · Colour · 114mins

Sly Stallone, as writer, director and star, took his cue from those B pictures set in the inner city where decency and success were able to triumph in the midst of adversity. Taking a clutch of simple ideas and comic-strip characters, he creates a giddy whirlwind of sentiment and fisticuffs. Having gone the distance with the heavyweight champ in the first bout, and now married to the love of his life (Talia Shire), Rocky Balboa is contemplating a return to the ring. The big-fight finale is executed with skill, passion and glee, and it's good to see the rasping Burgess Meredith back in the trainer's chair. ▣

Sylvester Stallone *Rocky Balboa* • Talia Shire *Adrian* • Burt Young *Paulie* • Carl Weathers *Apollo Creed* • Burgess Meredith *Mickey* • Tony Burton *Apollo's trainer* • Joe Spinell *Gazzo* • Sylvia Meals *Mary Anne Creed* ■ *Dir/Scr* Sylvester Stallone

Rocky III ★★ PG

Sports drama　1982 · US · Colour · 95mins

By now the formula was already starting to look a little stale, although two further sequels were still to follow. The opponent this time around is subsequent *The A-Team* star, Mr T, who takes Sylvester Stallone's championship crown; Rocky then battles to reclaim it. Writer/director Stallone, once again finds roles for Talia Shire as his long-suffering wife, Carl Weathers, Burt Young and Burgess Meredith, but the story is predictable and it all goes a little flat outside the ring. Contains violence and swearing. ▣

Sylvester Stallone *Rocky Balboa* • Carl Weathers *Apollo Creed* • Mr T *Clubber Lang* • Talia Shire *Adrian Balboa* • Burt Young *Paulie*

• Burgess Meredith *Mickey* • Ian Fried *Rocky Jr* • Hulk Hogan *Thunderlips* ■ *Dir/Scr* Sylvester Stallone

Rocky IV ★★ PG

Sports drama　1985 · US · Colour · 87mins

Sylvester Stallone goes back on the *Rocky* road to success with decidedly mixed results. Nobody boxes clever in this lazy sequel, also directed by the Sly guy, which introduced both Dolph Lundgren and Brigitte Nielsen to the movie world. It's still impossible not to get caught up in Rocky's Russian training programme, or to root for his climactic victory, but mawkish montages accompanied by blaring music ineptly pass for plot shading. Stallone's silly post-fight speech echoes *Rambo* more than this Italian Stallion. Contains swearing. ▣

Sylvester Stallone *Rocky Balboa* • Talia Shire *Adrian Balboa* • Burt Young *Paulie* • Carl Weathers *Apollo Creed* • Brigitte Nielsen *Ludmilla* • Tony Burton *Duke* • Michael Pataki *Nicoli Koloff* • Dolph Lundgren *Drago* • RJ Adams *Sports announcer* • James Brown (1) *Godfather of Soul* ■ *Dir/Scr* Sylvester Stallone

Rocky V ★★ PG

Drama　　　1990 · US · Colour · 99mins

Despite John G Avildsen being back as director (he did the first *Rocky*, with Stallone himself directing the intervening rounds), the emotional clout of the original has now given way to simple gestures and acting-by-numbers. Given that it would be impossible to surprise with such a prescriptive format, it's a shame that the only real spark comes courtesy of Sly's own offspring (Sage Stallone) as his screen son. Contains violence, swearing. ▣

Sylvester Stallone *Rocky Balboa* • Talia Shire *Adrian Balboa* • Burt Young *Paulie* • Sage Stallone *Rocky Jr* • Burgess Meredith *Mickey* • Tommy Morrison *Tommy Gunn* • Richard Gant *George Washington Duke* • Tony Burton *Tony* ■ *Dir* John G Avildsen • *Scr* Sylvester Stallone

The Rocky Horror Picture Show ★★★★ 15

Cult comedy musical
1975 · UK · Colour · 95mins

The Queen Mother of cult movies is a campy, vampy, kinky musical send-up of old horror flicks that's surprisingly witty and wickedly naughty. Telling what happens when strait-laced Brad and Janet get stranded at the weird castle of Frank N Furter, Tim Curry wrings every ounce of deranged humour from his glam-rock role in a landmark performance that cleverly satirises *Frankenstein*, haunted house mysteries, science-fiction clichés and *Carry On* sexual identity confusion. The score is justifiably famous; stand-out songs are *Touch-a Touch-a Touch Me*, and *Sweet Transvestite*. If you've never seen it give yourself a treat. If you have, then let's do *The Time Warp* again! Contains swearing, brief nudity. ▣

Tim Curry *Frank N Furter* • Susan Sarandon *Janet Weiss* • Barry Bostwick *Brad Majors* • Richard O'Brien *Riff Raff* • Jonathan Adams *Dr Everett Scott* • Nell Campbell *Columbia* • Peter Hinwood *Rocky Horror* • Patricia Quinn *Magenta* • Meat Loaf *Eddie* • Charles Gray *Criminologist* ■ *Dir* Jim Sharman • *Scr* Jim

Sharman, Richard O'Brien, from the musical by Richard O'Brien • *Music Director* Richard Hartley • *Costume Designer* Richard Pointing, Gillian Dods

Rocky Marciano ★★

Sports biography
1999 · US · Colour · 100mins

This biography traces the rise of the legendary boxer who never lost a professional fight. Jon Favreau (*Swingers*) in the title role does a decent job as the son determined to escape the fate suffered by his immigrant labourer father. With perseverance and raw power he soon becomes a contender. Director, Charles Winkler, continues in the sports tradition of his father, Irwin, who produced the classic *Rocky*. The strong cast includes Judd Hirsch and Penelope Ann Miller, whose performances enliven this TV movie, which, if it must be said, is less than a knockout.

Jon Favreau *Rocky Marciano* • Judd Hirsch *Al Weill* • Penelope Ann Miller *Barbara* • Tony LoBianco *Frankie Carbo* • Duane Davis *Joe Louis* ■ *Dir* Charles Winkler • *Scr* Larry Golin, Charles Winkler, Dick Beebe

Rocky Mountain ★★ U

Western　　　1950 · US · BW · 82mins

This was really the last of Errol Flynn's mainstream Hollywood movies, and it received a lot of publicity at the time as Flynn married his leading lady, Patrice Wymore, just after shooting ended. It's a western, with Flynn as a Confederate leader trying to forge an alliance with outlaws in California. Alas, Indians soon scupper that plan. The script is co-written by Alan LeMay, best known as the author of the novel which John Ford made into *The Searchers*.

Errol Flynn *Lafe Barstow* • Patrice Wymore *Johanna Carter* • Scott Forbes *Lt Rickey* • Guinn ''Big Boy'' Williams [Guinn Williams] *Pap Dennison* • Dick Jones [Dickie Jones] *Jim Wheat* • Howard Petrie *Cole Smith* • Slim Pickens *Plank* ■ *Dir* William Keighley • *Scr* Alan LeMay, Winston Miller, from the story by Alan LeMay

Rodan ★★★

Science-fiction thriller
1956 · Jap · Colour · 70mins

Two years after Inoshirô Honda launched the ''creature feature'' with *Godzilla*, he moved into colour production with this all-action tale of the Cretaceous pterodactyl, which was hatched in a coal mine and gained its powers from consuming giant dragonflies called Meganuron. The atomic theme is once more to the fore, with the seismic shocks created by Rodan's supersonic speeds capable of reducing cities to rubble. But there's also a tragic element, as Rodan seeks to protect its brooding mate from prying scientists. The monster may be a man may be a suit, but the urban decimation and volcanic explosion are effectively staged. Japanese dialogue dubbed into English.

Kenji Sahara *Shigeru* • Yumi Shirakawa *Kiyo* • David Duncan *Narrator* ■ *Dir* Ishiro Honda [Inoshiro Honda] • *Scr* Takeshi Kimura, Takeo Murata, from a story by Takashi Kuronuma • *Special Effects* Eiji Tsuburaya

U = SUITABLE FOR ALL　Uc = SUITABLE FOR ALL, ESPECIALLY FOR YOUNG CHILDREN (VIDEO ONLY)　PG = PARENTAL GUIDANCE

Rodgers & Hammerstein's Cinderella ★★★

Musical fantasy   1997 · US · Colour · 88mins

A fanciful, multiracial TV remake of the 1965 telemusical (which featured Lesley Ann Warren as Cinderella and Celeste Holm as the Fairy Godmother), with a lovely score from Broadway's incomparable songwriting team. Superstar warbler, Whitney Houston plays the Fairy Godmother, with singer/ actress Brandy, donning a glass slipper for the title role in this timeless fairy story about a poor lass, her evil stepmother, odious stepsisters, a Fairy Godmother and a dashing prince. Director Rob Iscove (*She's All That*), skillfully handles a talented cast, who sing and dance with more than a little bit of gusto. A delightful film for most of the family.

Brandy Norwood [Brandy] *Cinderella* • Whitney Houston *The Fairy Godmother* • Jason Alexander *Lionel* • Victor Garber *King* • Whoopi Goldberg *Queen Constantina* • Bernadette Peters *Wicked Stepmother* • Veanne Cox *Stepsister* • Natalie Desselle *Stepsister* • Paolo Montalban *Prince* ■ *Dir* Robert Iscove • *Scr* Robert L Freedman, Oscar Hammerstein II, Richard Rodgers, from a story by by Charles Perrault

Roe vs Wade ★★★★

Drama   1989 · US · Colour · 92mins

This Emmy-winning TV film from 1989 tackles the heated subject of abortion rights in the United States. Academy Award winner Holly Hunter (*The Piano*) stars as Ellen ''Jane Roe'' Russell, the destitute unwed mother at the centre of the historic Supreme Court case, with Amy Madigan (*Field of Dreams*) as her novice attorney. Complex layered performances highlight this ground-breaking film, which deservedly provided Hunter with an Emmy. The script manages to promote a balanced point of view, while the sensitive direction by Gregory Hoblit (*Primal Fear*, *Frequency*) further enhances this excellent TV drama.

Holly Hunter *Ellen Russell aka Jane Roe* • Amy Madigan *Sarah Weddington* • James Gammon *Jimmy Russell* • Terry O'Quinn *Jay Floyd* • Dion Anderson *Bob Flowers* • Kathy Bates *Jessie* • Micole Mercurio *Ida Russell* • Chris Mulkey *Ron Weddington* • Annabella Price *Linda Coffey* • Stephen Tobolowsky *Daryl Horwood* ■ *Dir* Gregory Hoblit • *Scr* Alison Cross

Roger and Me ★★★★★

Documentary   1989 · US · Colour · 87mins

This is a glorious ''one off'', refusing to fit neatly into any celluloid category, which considerably irked some nit-picking critics at the time. A wonderfully intrusive Michael Moore spent three years roaming his Michigan home town after General Motors chairman, Roger Smith, announced his cold-hearted plan to close down operations, thus decimating its working population. Moore's keen eye for truthful quirky detail shines through via the vividly incandescent cast of characters with whom we become instantly involved. Roger deserves everything he gets – with interest – and Moore supplies it with a compelling mixture of impish

nerve and investigative flair. Essential viewing.

Dir/Scr Michael Moore (2)

RoGoPaG ★★★ PG

Portmanteau drama

1962 · It/Fr · Colour · 117mins

With its bizarre shorthand title and introductory biblical references, this contemporary critique is the least satisfying of the sixties portmanteau pictures. Roberto Rossellini's *Virginity* is the dull tale of a passenger's obsession with an air hostess. Anticipating the futuristic *Alphaville*, Jean-Luc Godard's *The New World* chronicles a doomed post-apocalyptic romance, while Pier Paolo Pasolini received a four-month suspended sentence for defamation for *Cream Cheese*, in which an actor in Orson Welles's religious epic dies on the cross during an orgiastic shoot. The weakest segment, however, is *The Range-Grown Chicken*, Ugo Gregoretti's take on aggressive marketing, which lacks satirical bite. In Italian with English subtitles. ⬚

Rosanna Schiaffino *Anna Maria* • Bruce Balaban *Joe* • Alexandra Stewart *Alexandra* • Jean-Marc Bory *Narrator* • Jean-Luc Godard *Pill-popping pedestrian* • Orson Welles *The Director* • Mario Cipriani *Stracci* • Laura Betti *The Star* • Ugo Tognazzi *Togni* • Lisa Gastoni *His wife* ■ *Dir/Scr* Roberto Rossellini, Jean-Luc Godard, Pier Paolo Pasolini, Ugo Gregoretti

Rogue Cop ★★★

Crime drama   1954 · US · BW · 92mins

Robert Taylor plays a cop on the take from the mob, led by George Raft. But as this is an MGM film, Taylor can't really be the bad guy and so, following the murder of his brother and fellow cop, Taylor sees the error of his ways and goes after Raft and his murderous henchmen. The script, by author of *The Big Heat* Sydney Boehm, is surprisingly keen to bump off major characters and is at its sharpest when dealing with Taylor's moral quagmire: is he avenging his brother, redeeming himself or on a suicide mission? Director, Roy Rowland, maintains a sprint throughout and offers the usual barrage of *film noir* shadows and doomy ambience.

Robert Taylor (1) *Christopher Kelvaney* • Janet Leigh *Karen Stephanson* • George Raft *Dan Beaumonte* • Steve Forrest *Eddie Kelvaney* • Anne Francis *Nancy Corlane* ■ *Dir* Roy Rowland • *Scr* Sydney Boehm, from a novel by William P McGivern

The Rogue Song

Musical romance

1930 · US · Colour · 115mins

One of the things the Hollywood studios did in the early years of sound, was sign as many Broadway actors or singers as they could. One of MGM's catches was Lawrence Tibbett, star of the New York Met and described as one of the world's greatest baritones. *The Rogue Song* (sadly, no prints exist of this lost film) was his Oscar-nominated debut, an operatic showcase about a Russian bandit who kidnaps a princess. Apparently the public flocked to see this all-talking, all-singing, all-Technicolor concoction,

lured by the voice of Tibbett and by Laurel and Hardy who provided some laughs between arias and plotting.

Lawrence Tibbett *Yegor* • Catherine Dale Owen *Princess Vera* • Judith Vosselli *Countess Tatiana* • Nance O'Neil *Princess Alexandra* • Stan Laurel *Ali-Bek* • Oliver Hardy *Murza-Bek* • Florence Lake *Nadja* • Lionel Belmore *Ossman* ■ *Dir* Lionel Barrymore • *Scr* Frances Marion, John Colton, from the operetta *Gypsy Love* by Franz Lehár, AM Willner, Robert Bodansky

The Rogue Stallion ★★

Adventure drama   1990 · NZ · Colour · 93mins

A young girl named Anna (Beth Buchanan), befriends a wild stallion that a local landowner has been trying to kill in a sweet *Black Beauty*-style drama set in New Zealand. Alas, nice photography of the horse galloping like the wind cannot hold a thinly plotted movie together, but the equine frolics and the performance of Buchanan should keep young horse lovers glued to their seats.

Beth Buchanan *Anna Peterson* • Michelle Fawdon *Rose Peterson* • Peter McCallum *Garrett* • Brian Rooney *Wayne Garrett* • Dean O'Gorman *Tony Garrett* • Jodie Rimmer *Ginny Garrett* • Andrew Shepherd *Mike Peterson* • Rawiri Paratene *Brian* ■ *Dir* Henri Safran

Rogue Trader ★★ 15

Biographical drama

1998 · UK/US · Colour · 101

You'd think the true story of how Watford wide boy, Nick Leeson brought about the collapse of Barings Merchant Bank, one of the oldest financial institutions in the City, would make a cracking movie brimming with personal intrigues and trader insights. Sadly, under James Dearden's lacklustre direction, the tabloid tale is reduced to the level of a bland TV movie with its futures-market setting and bewildering jargon making it wilfully obscure to the point of abject disinterest. Leeson will doubtless be thrilled by Ewan McGregor's performance, painting him as a gambling cheeky chappie with a heart of gold. Everyone else will see it as spin-doctoring on heavy rotation. Nor is this long-on-the-shelf film helped by Anna Friel's awful performance as Mrs Leeson. But then even Meryl Streep would have had a hard time with the join-the-dots script, which patently doesn't ring true in any area it purports to explore.

Ewan McGregor *Nick Leeson* • Anna Friel *Lisa Leeson* • Yves Beneyton *Pierre Beaumarchais* • Betsy Brantley *Brenda Granger* • Caroline Langrishe *Ash Lewis* • Nigel Lindsay *Ron Baker* • Tim McInnerny *Tony Hawes* • Irene Ng *Bonnie Lee* ■ *Dir* James Dearden • *Scr* James Dearden, from the non-fiction book by Nick Leeson, Edward Whitley

Rogues of Sherwood Forest ★★ U

Swashbuckling adventure

1950 · US · Colour · 79mins

Those men in Lincoln-green tights are at it again, this time with John Derek as Robin Hood's son, battling to get anti-democratic villain, George Macready, to sign the Magna Carta. Another example of how Hollywood rewrites history, though this meagre

script couldn't plump out its entertainment with much value.

John Derek *Robin, Earl of Huntington* • Diana Lynn *Lady Marianne* • George Macready *King John* • Alan Hale *Little John* • Paul Cavanagh *Sir Giles* • Lowell Gilmore *Count of Flanders* • Billy House *Friar Tuck* • Lester Matthews *Alan-a-Dale* ■ *Dir* Gordon Douglas • *Scr* George Bruce, from a story by Ralph Bettinson

Rogue's Yarn ★

Crime drama   1956 · UK · BW · 83mins

When Derek Bond is persuaded by his mistress, Nicole Maurey, to murder his rich invalid wife, he concocts a seemingly waterproof alibi by appearing to be in charge of his yacht on a Channel crossing at the time of her demise. But the scheme proves full of holes under the close inspection of Elwyn Brook-Jones's Scotland Yard inspector. Co-written and directed by Vernon Sewell, a keen sailor in his spare time, it was a watchable enough thriller in its day, but even then it had a long delay obtaining a release. The film was partly shot on location at Shoreham and Le Havre.

Nicole Maurey *Michele Carter* • Derek Bond *John Marsden* • Elwyn Brook-Jones *Insp Walker* • Hugh Latimer *Sgt Adams* • John Serret *Insp Lefarge* ■ *Dir* Vernon Sewell • *Scr* Vernon Sewell, Ernie Bradford

Roja ★★★ PG

Political drama   1992 · US · Colour · 132mins

Even with a solid understanding of the complexities of Indian politics, this is a labyrinth of sensibilities. A colossal and controversial hit on its release, the film recounts the true story of a wife who battles almost single-handedly for the release of her husband, after he is kidnapped by Kashmiri rebels demanding the liberation of their leader. Director Mani Rathnam, is so vehement in his support for the Tamil couple that the film provoked a wave of anti-Muslim feeling in parts of the subcontinent, while Hindus resented his stance in the wake of Rajiv Gandhi's assassination by Tamil terrorists. In Hindi with English subtitles. ⬚

Arvind Swamy *Rishi Kumar* • Madhubala *Roja* • Pankaj Kapur *Liaqat* ■ *Dir/Scr* Mani Rathnam

Roller Boogie ★

Musical drama   1979 · US · Colour · 103mins

Beware the movie made swiftly to cash in on a fad. Sometimes, like the Sam Katzman rock'n'roll quickies, they retain a period charm. Sometimes, like this quasi-amateurish mishmash about roller disco fans ganging together to stop the closure of the local boogie centre, they're virtually unwatchable. Fans of *The Exorcist*'s Regan may well wonder what happened to her, but the sad truth is that Linda Blair lurched from one cheapo exploiter to another, and she's usually much better than the movies in which she found herself. Director, Mark L Lester (no, not the kid from *Oliver!*), is probably better known for helming the early Schwarzenegger vehicle *Commando*.

Linda Blair *Terry Barkley* • Jim Bray *Bobby James* • Beverly Garland *Lillian Barkley* • Roger Perry *Roger Barkley* • Jimmy Van Patten [James Van Patten] *Hoppy* • Kimberly Beck

Lana • Rick Sciacca *Complete Control Conway* ■ *Dir* Mark L Lester • *Scr* Barry Schneider, from a story by Irwin Yablans

Rollerball ★★★ 15
Futuristic drama
1975 · US · Colour · 119mins

It's the early 21st-century, street violence has been outlawed and the world is divided into huge conglomerates that govern the world sport of rollerball, through which violent passions are controlled and vented. Sound familiar? It wasn't back in pre-*Mad Max* 1975 when this splendidly presented, futuristic drama hit the screens. James Caan and John Beck make a pair of convincing athletes, while John Houseman and Ralph Richardson provide the thespian muscle. However the film is as soulless as the world it depicts, and resolutely unenjoyable, with the sport itself no more exciting than the average roller derby. Or have we become blasé in the last 20 years, and was this movie unusually prescient? 🎬

James Caan *Jonathan E* • John Houseman *Bartholomew* • Maud Adams *Ella* • John Beck *Moonpie* • Moses Gunn *Cletus* • Pamela Hensley *Mackie* • Barbara Trentham *Daphne* • Ralph Richardson *Librarian* ■ *Dir* Norman Jewison • *Scr* William Harrison, from his story *Rollerball Murders* • *Cinematographer* Douglas Slocombe

Rollercoaster ★★★
Disaster 1977 · US · Colour · 116mins

Universal Studios, cleverly promoting it's studio tour while knocking rival attractions, came up with this disaster movie in which a terrorist (Timothy Bottoms), targets popular theme parks, planting bombs on the giant rides of the title. The strain of tracking him down prevents Segal's safety inspector from quitting smoking and makes Richard Widmark twitch uncontrollably. One of the best disaster movies of the mid-seventies, and originally released in Sensurround, a short-lived process that made cinema seats shake at appropriate moments, it was difficult to simulate in the home. Contains swearing.

George Segal *Harry Calder* • Richard Widmark *Hoyt* • Timothy Bottoms *Young Man* • Henry Fonda *Simon Davenport* • Harry Guardino *Keefer* • Susan Strasberg *Fran* • Helen Hunt *Tracy Calder* • Dorothy Tristan *Helen* • Harry Davis *Benny* • Stephen Pearlman *Lyons* ■ *Dir* James Goldstone • *Scr* Richard Levinson, William Link, from a story by Sanford Sheldon, Richard Levinson, William Link

Rollercoaster ★★★
Drama 1999 · Can · Colour · 90mins

A Canadian teenage gang break into a dilapidated fairground in order to get high on drugs and alcohol and fool around on the rides. But when the security guard catches them, his outwardly friendly demeanour hides a twisted sexual agenda of his own. A thought-provoking, compelling and disturbing look at hot sexual issues and the protection of the innocent, director Scott Smith's moral fable is made all the more potent by his cool approach to the controversial subject matter, his disarming visuals and an expert cast of unknowns. Many will find

this ultimate teen nightmare an upsetting viewing experience.

Brendan Fletcher *Stick* • Kett Turton *Darrin* • Crystal Buble *Chloe* • Brent Glenen *Justin* • Sean Amsing *Sanj* • David Lovgren *Ben* ■ *Dir/Scr* Scott Smith

The Rolling Stones Rock and Roll Circus ★★
Concert movie 1995 · UK · Colour · 65 mins.

Intended for American television, but vetoed by Mick Jagger, this legendary 1968 concert, set in a circus tent, surfaced on bootleg video in 1995. Ringmaster Jagger cracks the whip under the big-top set, as the Rolling Stones perform several songs in costume and *John Lennon* and *Yoko Ono*, Jethro Tull, *The Who*, Marianne Faithfull, Eric Clapton and Taj Mahal also do turns. Accompanied by a full orchestra and assorted animal and juggling acts, the psychedelic melange also features Lennon leading an all-star jam of *Yer Blues*. The Who's segment turned up in *The Kids Are Alright* and other footage was cannibalised for the documentary *25 X 5: the Continuing Adventures of the Rolling Stones*.

Dir Michael Lindsay-Hogg

Rolling Thunder ★★★ 18
Drama 1977 · US · Colour · 95mins

Paul Schrader who wrote *Taxi Driver* and *Raging Bull* is usually a disciplined screenwriter, but (working with Heywood Gould) runs amok with this story of an embittered Vietnam vet (William Devane), who returns home to an ungrateful society and a thankless wife (Lisa Richards) who's fallen for another man. The antagonists after the murder of his family lead to a bloody conclusion that, if director John Flynn had been more in control, might have made us care. As it is, despite fine acting from Devane and Tommy Lee Jones as his Vietnam buddy, we don't. Contains swearing, violence. 🎬

William Devane *Major Charles Rane* • Tommy Lee Jones *Johnny Vohden* • Linda Haynes *Linda Forchet* • Lisa Richards *Janet* • Dabney Coleman *Maxwell* • James Best *Texan* • Cassie Yates *Candy* ■ *Dir* John Flynn • *Scr* Paul Schrader, Heywood Gould

Rollover ★★★ 15
Thriller 1981 · US · Colour · 110mins

Before the National Lottery made "rollover" a buzz word for millions, it was out of reach for most audiences set as it was in the rarefied world of international high finance, and this was an attempt to explain it in dramatic terms. Jane Fonda is the film star widow of a murdered financier, confronted with the news that the Arab world is threatening to withhold monetary reserves, thus putting the global economy at risk. Alan J Pakula's political thriller lays on too much romance; Kris Kristofferson in widow-wooing mode trys to convince that mercantile mayhem could ensue, yet its moments of financial panic are topical in the light of the recent dive in the Asian markets. Contains violence, swearing. 🎬

Jane Fonda *Lee Winters* • Kris Kristofferson *Hub Smith* • Hume Cronyn *Maxwell Emery* •

Josef Sommer *Roy Lefcourt* • Bob Gunton *Sal Naftari* • Macon McCalman *Mr Fewster* • Ron Frazier *Gil Hovey* ■ *Dir* Alan J Pakula • *Scr* David Shaber, from a story by David Shaber, Howard Kohn, David Weir

Roman Holiday ★★★★★ U
Romantic comedy 1953 · US · BW · 113mins

A sublime and utterly charming fable which rightly secured a best actress Oscar for the divine Audrey Hepburn (in a role originally intended for Jean Simmons) and resulted in both Audrey and Rome (not to mention motor scooters!) becoming the very epitome of post-war chic. The film could be viewed merely as a love story: princess falls for a reporter, but, not intending to detract from the charm of the story, the background is perhaps more interesting: the script was written by the uncredited, blacklisted Dalton Trumbo, a fact not revealed for almost 40 years, and actually deals in some depth with personal freedom and responsibilities, the setting and characters distancing the tale far from the witch-hunts of McCarthyite America. Immaculately directed by William Wyler, written and played with style and grace, this is a film to treasure, with both sequences and performances that will live for ever. 🎬

Audrey Hepburn *Princess Anne* • Gregory Peck *Joe Bradley* • Eddie Albert *Irving Radovich* • Hartley Power *Mr Hennessy* • Margaret Rawlings *Countess Vereberg* • Harcourt Williams *Ambassador* • Laura Solari *Mr Hennessy's Secretary* • Tullio Carminati *General Provno* • Paolo Carlini *Mario Delani* • Claudio Ermelli *Giovanni* ■ *Dir* William Wyler • *Scr* Ian McLellan Hunter, John Dighton, from a story by Ian McLellan Hunter (front for Dalton Trumbo) • *Costume Designer* Edith Head • *Cinematographer* Henri Alekan, Franz Planer • *Music* Georges Auric

Roman Scandals ★★★ PG
Musical comedy 1933 · US · BW · 87mins 🎬

Producer, Samuel Goldwyn's six Eddie Cantor vehicles were great fun, and four of them gave choreographer Busby Berkeley his grounding before he decamped to Warner Bros and *42nd Street*. Here, Cantor falls asleep and finds himself back in pre-censorship ancient Rome, where naked Goldwyn Girls in long blond wigs besport themselves in a wonderfully lewd Berkeley production number. Watch closely and you'll spot youngster Lucille Ball among those chorus girls trying to *Keep Young and Beautiful*. Cantor is an acquired taste, but he's very amusing as food-taster to emperor Edward Arnold, and the climactic chariot race is an amusing shot at the silent 1925 version of *Ben Hur*. Vocalist Ruth Etting, played by Doris Day in *Love Me or Leave Me*, is the female lead. 🎬

Eddie Cantor *Eddie* • Ruth Etting *Olga* • Gloria Stuart *Princess Sylvia* • David Manners *Josephus* • Verree Teasdale *Empress Agrippa* • Edward Arnold *Emperor Valerius* • Alan Mowbray *Major-Domo* ■ *Dir* Frank Tuttle • *Scr* William Anthony McGuire, George Oppenheimer, Arthur Sheekman, Nat Perrin, from a story by George S Kaufman, Robert E Sherwood

The Roman Spring of Mrs Stone ★★★
Drama 1961 · US · Colour · 104mins

Making her penultimate screen appearance, Vivien Leigh is superbly cast as a fading beauty who uses her wealth to lure the young lover who will make her life worthwhile. Warren Beatty, in only his second film, is equally impressive as her conquest, while Lotte Lenya thoroughly merited her Oscar nomination as a calculating matchmaker. But this adaptation of Tennessee Williams's one and only novel, is somewhat bungled by Gavin Lambert's precious dialogue and the plodding direction of the inexperienced Jose Quintero. Curiously, this overly euphemistic misfire was produced by screen realism pioneer and *March of Time* creator, Louis de Rochemont.

Vivien Leigh *Karen Stone* • Warren Beatty *Pablo di Leo* • Coral Browne *Meg* • Jill St John *Bingham* • Lotte Lenya *Contessa Magda Terribili-Gonzales* • Jeremy Spenser *Young man* • Stella Bonheur *Mrs Jamison-Walker* • Josephine Brown *Lucia* • Cleo Laine *Singer* ■ *Dir* Jose Quintero • *Scr* Gavin Lambert, Jan Read, from the novel by Tennessee Williams

Romance ★★
Romantic drama 1930 · US · BW · 62mins

A bishop (Gavin Gordon) relives in flashback his ill-fated love affair with an opera star (Greta Garbo) who is the mistress of a rich businessman (Lewis Stone). The amazing idea of making Garbo, in her second talking picture after *Anna Christie*, an operatic soprano – Italian to boot – boggles the imagination; added to which the film's plot is flimsy and uninteresting. But who cares? The usual rules of judgement don't apply to Garbo movies, beyond recognising that some are better than others. This is worse than several, but the star (Oscar-nominated) transcends the material and her dreary leading man with her usual mesmerising beauty and conviction. Her A-team is in place: cinematographer William H Daniels and director Clarence Brown (Oscar-nominated).

Greta Garbo *Rita Cavallini* • Lewis Stone *Cornelius Van Tuyl* • Gavin Gordon *Tom Armstrong* • Elliott Nugent *Harry* • Florence Lake *Susan Van Tuyl* • Clara Blandick *Miss Armstrong* ■ *Dir* Clarence Brown • *Scr* Bess Meredyth, Edwin Justus Mayer, from the play *Signora Cavallini* by Edward Sheldon

Romance ★★ 18
Psychological drama
1998 · Fr · Colour · 98mins

A woman's sexuality is explored in gynaecological detail in Catherine Breillat's boundary-pushing drama. It's a dull, emotionless movie whose heroine, Caroline Ducey, isn't getting "the full monty" from her man. So she wanders aimlessly from one bed to another, having pretentious, penetrative thoughts. Supposedly a feminist tale, Breillat's frank film reveals little (apart from Ducey's flesh) and seems to be saying that sex between men and women is passionless and mechanical. Why, then, does her camera linger so lustily on the male and female genitalia? Undeniably bold, but as lifeless an experience as you'll ever have,

Romance is dead from the waist up. In French with English subtitles. Contains nudity, sex scenes.

Caroline Ducey *Marie* • Sagamore Stevenin *Paul* • François Berleand *Robert* • Rocco Siffredi *Paolo* • Reza Habouhossein *Man in the stairs* • Ashley Wanninger *Ashley* • Emma Colberti *Charlotte* • Fabien de Jomaron *Claude* ■ *Dir* Catherine Breillat • *Scr* Catherine Breillat, Severine Siaut

Romance in Manhattan ★★★ U

Drama   1934 · US · BW · 76mins

Ginger Rogers was desperately anxious to prove that she wasn't just Fred Astaire's screen dance partner, and in 1934 made seven features, only one of which co-starred the great Fred. This little gem slotted in neatly between *The Gay Divorce* and the following year's *Roberta*, as Ginger took second billing to debonair foreign import Francis Lederer, handsome star of G W Pabst's *Pandora's Box*, amongst others. Ironically, he's an illegal alien who's helped by our Ginger, playing as she so often did, a soubrette from the chorus line. Naturally they fall for each other and, underrated and now forgotten, director Stephen Roberts treats this lightweight nonsense with respect, ensuring a polished and charming romantic movie, a little sub-Capra, maybe, but none the worse for that. Deft and droll, and well worth spending time with.

Ginger Rogers *Sylvia Dennis* • Francis Lederer *Karel Novak* • Arthur Hohl *Attorney* • Jimmy Butler *Frank Dennis* ■ *Dir* Stephen Roberts • *Scr* Jane Murfin, Edward Kaufman, from a story by Norman Krasna, Don Hartman

Romance of a Horse Thief ★★

Comedy drama
1971 · US/Yug · Colour · 78mins

The French-based, English actress Jane Birkin is probably best known here for the heavy-breathing sixties' record *Je T'Aime*. Yet in France she is known as the star of over 30 films. This movie gave her one of her first starring roles, as a Jewish woman who returns from education in France to urge her Polish peasant community to fight back against their Cossack oppressors, led by Yul Brynner. The film is also notable for reuniting Brynner and Eli Wallach, two of the stars of *The Magnificent Seven*. A well-meaning but at times plodding drama.

Yul Brynner *Stoloff* • Eli Wallach *Kifke* • Jane Birkin *Naomi* • Oliver Tobias *Zanvill Kradnik* • Lainie Kazan *Estusha* • David Opatoshu *Schloime Kradnik* • Serge Gainsbourg *Sigmund* ■ *Dir* Abraham Polonsky • *Scr* David Opatoshu, from a story by Joseph Opatoshu

A Romance of the Redwoods ★★

Silent western   1917 · US · BW

In the same year that she played the title child in *Rebecca of Sunnybrook Farm*, Mary Pickford scored a success in this early Cecil B DeMille western, filmed on location in California's redwood country and set against a background of the 1849 gold rush. Pickford is a young woman who, having lost her father in an Indian attack, falls in love with outlaw, Elliott Dexter and

saves him from the full force of the law by pretending to be pregnant by him. Good enough in its day, but of purely historical interest now.

Mary Pickford *Jenny Lawrence* • Elliott Dexter *"Black" Brown* • Charles Ogle *Jim Lyn* • Tully Marshall *Sam Sparks* • Raymond Hatton *Dick Roland* • Walter Long *Sheriff* • Winter Hall *John Lawrence* ■ *Dir* Cecil B DeMille • *Scr* Jeanie Macpherson, Cecil B DeMille

Romance on the High Seas ★★★

Musical comedy   1948 · US · Colour · 98mins

A young Doris Day croons classics, like *It's Magic*, aboard an ocean-going liner alongside regular co-star Jack Carson and Janis Paige. Day throws herself into her movie debut like a woman aiming for a passing lifeboat from the deck of the *Titanic*. But this was a fledgling performance from an actress determined to succeed – even if it took a few years of belting 'em out in froth like this. One of those movies to watch with a box of chocolates on a rainy afternoon, it requires nothing more than an open mind and a light heart.

Doris Day *Georgia Garrett* • Jack Carson *Peter Virgil* • Janis Paige *Elvira Kent* • Oscar Levant *Oscar Farrar* • SZ Sakall *Uncle Lazlo* • Fortunio Bonanova *Plinio* • Eric Blore *Ship's doctor* ■ *Dir* Michael Curtiz • *Scr* Julius J Epstein, Philip G Epstein, Ial Diamond, from the story *Romance in High C* by S Pondal Rios, Carlos A Olivari

Romance on the Orient Express ★★

Romance   1985 · UK/US · Colour · 96mins

You know you're in trouble when the scenery is better than the story. In this British/American made-for-TV co-production, the lovely Cheryl Ladd (*Charlie's Angels*) plays an American magazine editor who jumps aboard the Orient Express and meets up with Englishman Stuart Wilson, with whom she had an ill-fated love affair ten years earlier. Will they rekindle their love while sipping champagne in the dining car? Only ardent romantics or zealous train buffs will want to buy a ticket on this locomotive of love.

Cheryl Ladd *Lily Parker* • Stuart Wilson *Alex Woodward* • Renée Asherson *Beatrice* • Ralph Michael *Harry* • Ruby Wax *Susan Lawson* • Julian Sands *Sandy* • John Gielgud *Theodore Woodward* ■ *Dir* Lawrence Gordon Clark • *Scr* Jan Worthington

Romancing the Stone ★★★★★ PG

Adventure comedy
1984 · US · Colour · 100mins

Director, Robert Zemeckis, superbly soups up a deliberately old-fashioned matinée adventure with tongue-in-cheek gags, unpredictably clever touches and top-of-the-range action. Novelist, Kathleen Turner, swaps the Manhattan urban jungle, where she's an easy touch, for the real Colombian McCoy, where she becomes as hards as nails. Turner dazzles in a spot-on performance that proved a career turning point, and there's a wonderful hate-each-other chemistry between Turner and her world-weary co-star Michael Douglas. A cracker of a roller-coaster ride. Contains swearing, violence.

Michael Douglas *Jack Colton* • Kathleen Turner *Joan Wilder* • Danny DeVito *Ralph* • Zack Norman *Ira* • Alfonso Arau *Juan* • Manuel Ojeda *Zolo* • Holland Taylor *Gloria* • Mary Ellen Trainor *Elaine* ■ *Dir* Robert Zemeckis • *Scr* Diane Thomas

Romanoff and Juliet ★★★ U

Comedy   1961 · US · Colour · 102mins

Written and directed by Peter Ustinov from his stage play, this is one of those wish-fulfilling fables – like *The Mouse That Roared* – which blunts its Cold War satire with queasy romanticism. The Americans and Russians are being held to atomic ransom by the tiny nation of Concordia ruled over by Ustinov. But, while vocal warfare goes on, the kids of the US and Soviet ambassadors (Sandra Dee and John Gavin) fall in love, which should be the answer to everything – but isn't. Charming, but far too simplistic.

Peter Ustinov *The General* • Sandra Dee *Juliet Moulsworth* • John Gavin *Igor Romanoff* • Akim Tamiroff *Vadim Romanoff* • Alix Talton *Beulah Moulsworth* • John Phillips *Hooper Moulsworth* • Tamara Shayne *Evdokia Romanoff* ■ *Dir* Peter Ustinov • *Scr* Peter Ustinov, from the play by Peter Ustinov

The Romantic Age ★

Romantic comedy   1949 · UK · BW · 93mins

A schoolgirl (Mai Zetterling), feeling put down by her friend's father (Hugh Williams), takes revenge by seducing him, but he eventually manages to extricate himself and hold on to his wife and family. The stars of this British film, directed by Edmond T Greville, must really have been desperate for work in 1949. This combination of prurience and coyness, with Zetterling a mite mature to pass as a schoolgirl, is an embarrassment. A large, and largely unknown, supporting cast includes such stalwarts of the British acting profession as Adrienne Corri and Jean Anderson, as well as a young Petula Clark.

Mai Zetterling *Arlette* • Hugh Williams *Arnold Dickson* • Margot Grahame *Helen Dickson* • Petula Clark *Julie Dickson* • Carol Marsh *Patricia* • Raymond Lovell *Hedges* • Paul Dupuis *Henri Sinclair* • Margaret Barton *Bessie* • Adrienne Corri *Nora* • Jean Anderson ■ *Dir* Edmond T Gréville • *Scr* Edward Dryhurst, Peggy Barwell, from the novel *Lycee des Jeunes Filles* by Serge Weber

Romantic Comedy ★ 15

Comedy   1983 · US · Colour · 97mins

Two Broadway playwrights, Dudley Moore and Mary Steenburgen, enjoy a fruitful professional partnership. Their working relationship keeps threatening to teeter over the edge into romance, except that it's never the right time. Each marries someone else, but that doesn't stop them wondering what might have been. A weak script and storyline contributed to Moore's rapid post-*Arthur* (1981) decline.

Dudley Moore *Jason Carmichael* • Mary Steenburgen *Phoebe Craddock* • Frances Sternhagen *Blanche* • Janet Eilber *allison St James* • Robyn Douglass *Kate Mallory* • Ron Leibman *Leo* ■ *Dir* Arthur Hiller • *Scr* Bernard Slade, from his play

The Romantic Englishwoman ★★ 15

Comedy drama
1975 · UK/Fr · Colour · 111mins

Show-business hack, Thomas Wiseman, wrote the preposterous novel on which this is based, and here he tries to make sense of it with the help of co-scriptwriter Tom Stoppard, director Joseph Losey, and actors Glenda Jackson, Michael Caine and Helmut Berger. They don't succeed. Jackson goes on an emotional bender with drug-dealer Berger at Baden-Baden, and husband Caine amazingly invites him to their English country home. The result is high-falutin', puddle-shallow soap opera giving itself airs. Contains swearing, sex scenes, nudity. 🖬

Glenda Jackson *Elizabeth Fielding* • Michael Caine *Lewis Fielding* • Helmut Berger *Thomas* • Marcus Richardson *David Fielding* • Kate Nelligan *Isabel* • Rene Kolldehof *Herman* • Michael Lonsdale *[Michel Lonsdale] Swan* • Béatrice Romand *Catherine* • Anna Steele *Annie* • Nathalie Delon *Miranda* ■ *Dir* Joseph Losey • *Scr* Tom Stoppard, Thomas Wiseman, from the novel by Thomas Wiseman

Romantic Undertaking ★★

Comedy   1995 · Can · Colour · 95mins

A Canadian comedy which, sadly, is not quite as quirky as it would like to believe. Valerie Buhagiar plays a young woman who takes over her dead father's funeral business. Forced by debts to rent out part of her home, she finds her life becoming complicated when she falls for mysterious new lodger, William Katt. The two leads turn in warm enough performances but, despite its unusual setting, this is formulaic stuff.

William Katt *Richard Tennant* • Valerie Buhagiar *Jenny Tanner* • Ishwar Mooljee *Oscar* • Paul Berry *Squirrelly* • Greg Blanchard *Harry* ■ *Dir* Peter McCubbin • *Scr* Melissa R Byer, Treena Hancock, from a story by Chuck Micallef

Rome Express ★★★★ U

Crime drama   1932 · UK · BW · 86mins

A wonderfully entertaining Gaumont-British melodrama featuring a rich variety of passengers (including an art thief, double-crossed accomplices, an American film star, a philanthropist, adulterous lovers and a French police inspector) on a train journey between Paris and Rome. This set the pattern for dozens of later pictures using the same confined setting, including *The Lady Vanishes* and *Night Train to Munich*. A splendid cast includes; Conrad Veidt (in his first British film), Cedric Hardwicke, Gordon Harker, Esther Ralston and Frank Vosper. Walter Forde directed it on the cramped sound stages of Shepherd's Bush, cleverly maintaining a sense of continual movement and foreign atmosphere.

Esther Ralston *Asta Marvelle* • Conrad Veidt *Zurta* • Hugh Williams *Tony* • Donald Calthrop *Poole* • Joan Barry *Mrs Maxted* • Harold Huth *Grant* • Gordon Harker *Tom Bishop* • Eliot Makeham *Mills* • Cedric Hardwicke *Alistair McBane* ■ *Dir* Walter Forde • *Scr* Clifford Grey, Sidney Gilliat, Frank Vosper, Ralph Stock, from the story by Clifford Grey

Rome, Open City ★★★★★
Second World War drama
1945 · It · BW · 101mins

Roberto Rossellini came to international prominence with this emotive Cannes Grand Prize-winning resistance drama, which formed part of a wartime trilogy that was completed by *Paisà* (1946) and *Germany, Year Zero*. (1946) Based on actual events and shot on location, during the last days of the Nazi occupation of Rome, using fragments of painstakingly-spliced film stills, it is one of the landmarks of neorealist cinema, even though its melodramatic storyline, montage structure and star performances (Aldo Fabrizi and Anna Magnani head a primarily non-professional cast) somewhat undermine the social commitment, visual authenticity and technical rigour demanded by the movement's intellectual founder, Cesare Zavattini. In Italian with English subtitles.

Anna Magnani *Pina* • Aldo Fabrizi *Don Pietro Pellegrini* • Marcello Pagliero *Giorgio Manfredi, AKA Luigi Ferraris* • Maria Michi *Marina Mari* • Harry Feist *Maj Bergmann* ■ *Dir* Roberto Rossellini • *Scr* Sergio Amidei, Federico Fellini, Roberto Rossellini, from a story by Sergio Amidei, Alberto Consiglio

Romeo and Juliet ★★★★ U
Romantic tragedy 1936 · US · BW · 124mins

Shakespeare as a star vehicle, with Norma Shearer and a too-mature Leslie Howard as the doomed lovers. Made at the instigation of MGM boss Irving Thalberg, the film contains hugely enjoyable performances from studio regulars Basil Rathbone and Edna May Oliver, plus a breathtaking turn from John Barrymore as Mercutio. George Cukor directs with a reverent eye for the text and period detail, and it's all worth seeing as a superb example of Hollywood studio kitsch.

Norma Shearer *Juliet* • Leslie Howard *Romeo* • John Barrymore *Mercutio* • Basil Rathbone *Tybalt* • Edna May Oliver *Nurse* • C Aubrey Smith *Lord Capulet* ■ *Dir* George Cukor • *Scr* Talbot Jennings, from the play by William Shakespeare

Romeo and Juliet ★★★★ U
Romance drama
1954 · UK/It · Colour · 141mins

This adaptation of Shakespeare's tragedy of star-crossed lovers tends to be forgotten in the shuffle between George Cukor's all-star thirties version, Franco Zeffirelli's exquisite 1968 film and Baz Luhrmann's exciting modern take. But, Renato Castellani's classically elegant production, beautifully shot on location in Italy with jewel-bright design inspired by Renaissance paintings, did win the Golden Lion at the Venice Film Festival and can boast attractive, textbook performances. Most memorable is Laurence Harvey's soulful, poetic Romeo, unknown Susan Shentall is a gentle, dreamy Juliet and *grande dame* Flora Robson is delicious as her loquacious nurse, while John Gielgud provides the narration.

Laurence Harvey *Romeo* • Susan Shentall *Juliet* • Flora Robson *Nurse* • Mervyn Johns *Friar Laurence* • Bill Travers *Benvolio* • Enzo Fiermonte *Tybalt* • Aldo Zollo *Mercutio* • Giovanni Rota *Prince of Verona* • John Gielgud

Chorus ■ *Dir* Renato Castellani • *Scr* Renato Castellani, from the play by William Shakespeare

Romeo and Juliet ★★★ U
Ballet 1966 · UK · Colour · 127mins

Filmed performance of the Kenneth MacMillan-choreographed ballet that, if nothing else, acts as archive footage of the greatest dance partnership of the last century. Although Margot Fonteyn was 46 at the time, hardly appropriate for the 14-year-old Juliet, her astonishing technicality and musical sense soon overcomes any credibility gap. Rudolf Nureyev was always at his best with Fonteyn and their chemistry is almost captured in this stage-bound production. With the stately and beautiful score by Prokofiev, the ballet is enjoyable even for non-balletomanes, telling the story of the star-cross'd lovers with a spoken prologue before each of the three acts.

Rudolf Nureyev *Romeo* • Margot Fonteyn *Juliet* • David Blair *Mercutio* • Desmond Doyle *Tybalt* • Anthony Dowell *Benvolio* • Derek Rencher *Paris* • Michael Somes *Lord Capulet* • Julia Farron *Lady Capulet* ■ *Dir* Paul Czinner • *Scr* Kenneth MacMillan, from the ballet by Sergei Prokofiev, from the play by William Shakespeare

Romeo and Juliet ★★★★ PG
Drama 1968 · UK/It · Colour · 132mins

Franco Zeffirelli's bold adaptation was notorious for its jettisoning of almost half of the text and its chaste use of nudity. But it's tame indeed beside Baz Luhrmann's scintillating update in *William Shakespeare's Romeo + Juliet*. Olivia Hussey and Leonard Whiting might have met the age criteria required to play Verona's star-crossed lovers, but neither can hold a candle to their latter-day counterparts Leonardo DiCaprio and Clare Danes. They're bailed out, to some extent, by the support playing of Peter McEnery, Michael York and Milo O'Shea, as well as Pasqualino De Santis's Oscar-winning photography. 📺

Laurence Olivier *Narrator* • Leonard Whiting *Romeo* • Olivia Hussey *Juliet* • Milo O'Shea *Friar Laurence* • Michael York *Tybalt* • John McEnery *Mercutio* • Pat Heywood *Nurse* • Natasha Parry *Lady Capulet* ■ *Dir* Franco Zeffirelli • *Scr* Franco Zeffirelli, from the play by William Shakespeare, adapted by Franco Brusati, Masolino D'Amico • *Cinematographer* Pasqualino De Santis

Romeo Is Bleeding
★★★★ 18
Thriller 1992 · US · Colour · 104mins

Deliriously bonkers, black comedy thriller, that makes little sense but is powered along by a sheer disregard for anything approaching good taste and some wonderfully over-the-top performances. Gary Oldman is the corrupt cop whose life falls apart completely when he encounters psychotic Lena Olin. Don't worry too much about the niceties of the plot, just sit back and enjoy Olin's whirlwind performance as the *femme fatale* from hell who is near indestructible. Oldman is equally good and there are fine turns from an exceptional supporting cast that includes Annabella Sciorra, Juliette Lewis, Will Patton, Michael

Wincott and Roy Scheider. The *film noir* and comic elements don't always jell, but director Peter Medak ensures that it's always an exhilarating ride. Contains violence, swearing, sex scenes, nudity. 📺

Gary Oldman *Jack Grimaldi* • Lena Olin *Mona Demarkov* • Annabella Sciorra *Natalie Grimaldi* • Juliette Lewis *Sheri* • Roy Scheider *Don Falcone* • Michael Wincott *Sal* • Ron Perlman *Jack's attorney* • Dennis Farina *Nick Gazzara* • David Proval *Scully* • Will Patton *Martie Cuchinski* ■ *Dir* Peter Medak • *Scr* Hilary Henkin

Romeo Must Die ★★
Romantic action drama
2000 · US · Colour · 115mins

Jet Li takes his first starring role in a US movie, as an ex-cop convict who flees to America to avenge the death of his brother and gets entangled in a mob war. During his investigation, he continually mixes with Aaliyah Houghton, daughter of the rival gang's head thug, but the film-makers are too cowardly to take the inter-racial relationship beyond mere friendliness. Even for an American movie, the martial arts sequences are very badly choreographed, and there is far more hip-hop music and lingo than either plot or action. Anthony Anderson provides some welcomed comic relief as a dim-witted henchman.

Jet Li *Han Sing* • Aaliyah Houghton [Aaliyah] *Trish O'Day* • Isaiah Washington *Mac* • Russell Wong *Kai* • DM X *Silk* • Delroy Lindo *Isaak O'Day* • Henry O *Ch'u Sing* • DB Woodside *Colin* • Anthony Anderson *Maurice* ■ *Dir* Andrzej Bartkowiak • *Scr* Eric Bernt, John Jarrell, Jerrold E Brown, from a story by Mitchell Kapner

Romero ★★★ 15
Political biographical drama
1989 · US · Colour · 100mins

Powerful biopic of Oscar Romero, the El Salvadoran archbishop who, during the late seventies, voiced the Roman Catholic Church's opposition to his country's ruling repressive regime, and was subsequently assassinated for his outspokenness. The first film ever funded by officials of the US Roman Catholic Church, *Romero* is very much a message movie, but its tendency towards heavy-handedness is offset by an understated and dignified performance by Raul Julia as the martyred liberal. Anglo-Australian director John Duigan, also made *Flirting* and *Sirens*. 📺

Raul Julia *Archbishop Oscar Romero* • Richard Jordan *Father Rutilio Grande* • Ana Alicia Arista *Zalada* • Eddie Velez *Lieutenant Columa* • Alejandro Bracho *Father Alfonzo Osuna* • Tony Plana *Father Manuel Morantes* • Harold Gould *Francisco Galedo* • Lucy Reina *Lucia* ■ *Dir* John Duigan • *Scr* John Sacret Young

Romper Stomper ★★★ 18
Drama 1992 · Ausl · Colour · 88mins

Russell Crowe stars as the leader of a racist gang that preys on Australia's immigrant population in writer/director Geoffrey Wright's unsettling portrait of neo-Nazi thugs. Unflinching in its depiction of the lifestyle of the protagonists, the film caused A Clockwork Orange-style controversy Down Under when it was released. Much of the film's power comes from

the bruising, raw performances of Crowe (later to become a major Hollywood star with *LA Confidential* and *The Insider*), best friend Daniel Pollock and lover Jacqueline McKenzie, who has even deeper psychological problems than the guys. Although some may find the violent subject matter a major turn-off, Wright's stylised camerawork and pacey editing make this more than just an exercise in screen brutality. 📺

Russell Crowe *Hando* • Daniel Pollock *Davey* • Jacqueline McKenzie *Gabe* • Alex Scott *Martin* • Leigh Russell *Sonny Jim* • Daniel Wyllie [Dan Wyllie] *Cackles* • James McKenna *Bubs* ■ *Dir/Scr* Geoffrey Wright

Romuald et Juliette ★★★ PG
Romantic comedy
1989 · Fr · Colour · 111mins

This cultured, romantic comedy, features Daniel Auteuil as a yoghurt-company boss who's framed for a food-poisoning scandal, and finds that the only person who can help him, commercially and emotionally, is his company's black cleaning lady (Firmine Richard). Directed with skill and style by Coline Serreau, maker of the original French version of *Three Men and a Baby*, and played with aplomb by the two leads, this is lightweight French film-making at its most likeable best. In French with English subtitles.

Daniel Auteuil *Romuald* • Firmine Richard *Juliette Bonaventure* • Pierre Vernier *Blache* • Maxime Leroux *Cloquet* • Gilles Privat *Paulin* • Muriel Combeau *Nicole* • Catherine Salviat *Françoise* ■ *Dir/Scr* Coline Serreau

Romy and Michele's High School Reunion ★★★ 15
Comedy 1997 · US · Colour · 88mins

A fun comedy with Mira Sorvino (*Mighty Aphrodite, Mimic*) and *Friends* star Lisa Kudrow as the two dim-witted, down-on-their-luck blondes of the title, who pretend they are high-powered businesswomen at their high school reunion to impress those ex-school mates who once made fun of them. It's a simple enough premise (a sort of *Clueless* for twentysomethings) that is enlivened by two infectious performances from the leads as well as slick support from Janeane Garofalo and Alan Cumming. Contains swearing, sexual references. 📀 *DVD*

Mira Sorvino *Romy* • Lisa Kudrow *Michele* • Janeane Garofalo *Heather* • Alan Cumming *Sandy Frink* • Julia Campbell *Christie* • Mia Cottet *Cheryl* • Kristin Bauer *Kelly* • Elaine Hendrix *Lisa* • Vincent Ventresca *Billy* ■ *Dir* David Mirkin • *Scr* Robin Schiff

La Ronde ★★★★★ PG
Drama 1950 · Fr · Colour · 88mins

The Arthur Schnitzler play on which *La Ronde* is based was a metaphor for the spread of venereal disease. However, director Max Ophüls buried this message beneath a surface elegance and sophistication that characterised his 1950s style. From the dazzling opening sequence, in which master of ceremonies Anton Walbrook flits between studio sets to start this carousel of careless caresses, Ophüls keeps his prying camera on the move in time to the

waltz music of Oscar Straus. Each tryst is played to perfection by the remarkable cast, in which Simone Signoret, Simone Simon and Danielle Darrieux are exceptional. In French with English subtitles.

Anton Walbrook *Storyteller* • Simone Signoret *Leocadie, the prostitute* • Serge Reggiani *Franz, the soldier* • Simone Simon *Marie, the maid* • Daniel Gélin *Alfred, the young man* • Danielle Darrieux *Emma Breitkopf, the wife* • Fernand Gravey [Fernand Gravet] *Charles, Emma's husband* ■ *Dir* Max Ophüls • *Scr* Jacques Natanson, Max Ophüls, from a play by Arthur Schnitzler

La Ronde ★★

Drama 1964 · Fr/It · Colour · 110mins

The first of the four films Jane Fonda made with one-time husband, Roger Vadim, this reworking of Arthur Schnitzler's elegantly subversive play suffers in every aspect on comparison with Max Ophüls's 1950 version. Switching the action to Paris on the eve of the Great War, Vadim makes stylish use of Henri Decaë's widescreen imagery. But, the screenplay is surprisingly coarse considering it was written by acclaimed playwright, Jean Anouilh, while too many of the all-star cast, with the exception of Catherine Spaak and Francine Bergé, but including New Wave icons Jean-Claude Brialy and Anna Karina, seem to misread their characters. A French language film.

Marie Dubois *Prostitute* • Claude Giraud *Soldier* • Anna Karina *Maid* • Valérie Lagrange *Maid's friend* • Jean-Claude Brialy *Young man* • Jane Fonda *Married woman* • Maurice Ronet *Husband* • Catherine Spaak *Midinette* • Francine Bergé *Maximilienne de Poussy* ■ *Dir* Roger Vadim • *Scr* Jean Anoilh, from the play *Reigen* by Arthur Schnitzler

Ronin ★★★★ U

Action thriller
1998 · US · Colour · 118 mins. (V)

Resembling a seventies European espionage caper in atmosphere and style, director John Frankenheimer's deliberate retro thriller bounds along at a cracking pace. In an engrossing action adventure with a sobering political slant, De Niro travels to Paris to join an international gang of criminals (including the always watchable Jean Reno) who have been hired by an Irish revolutionary, Natascha McElhone, to steal an important briefcase. No excuse is missed for a frenzied car chase in the *Bullitt* tradition, or the chance to add a menacing hard edge to the deliciously convoluted plot. The word "ronin" is taken from a Japanese legend about 47 samurai who avenge the killing of their master then commit mass suicide. DVD

Robert De Niro *Sam* • Jean Reno *Vincent* • Natascha McElhone *Deirdre* • Stellan Skarsgård *Director* • Sean Bean *Spence* • Skipp Sudduth *Larry* • Michael Lonsdale [Michel Lonsdale] *Jean-Pierre* • Jan Tríska *Dapper gent* • Jonathan Pryce *Seamus* ■ *Dir* John Frankenheimer • *Scr* JD Zeik, Richard Weisz [David Mamet], from a story by JD Zeik

Rooftops ★★ 15

Romantic drama 1989 · US · Colour · 90mins

Twenty-eight years after winning an Oscar for *West Side Story*, director Robert Wise returns to broadly similar turf. This time around, though, the results are decidedly less spectacular. *Rooftops* is a routine, urban musical about the forbidden love between a white boy and a Hispanic girl. With his eye obviously on the blockbuster takings of the similarly flavoured *Dirty Dancing* two years earlier, Wise structured his film around its footwork – a form of combat dancing that's like kung fu but without the contact. The dance form quickly got the chop, and the film died a death at the box office. Certainly not worth shouting from the rooftops about.

Jason Gedrick *T* • Troy Beyer *Elana* • Eddie Velez *Lobo* • Tisha Campbell *Amber* • Alexis Cruz *Squeak* • Allen Payne *Kadim* • Steve Love *Jackie-Sky* • Rafael Baez *Raphael* • Jaime Tirelli *Rivera* ■ *Dir* Robert Wise • *Scr* Terence Brennan, from a story by Allan Goldstein, Tony Mark

The Rookie ★★ 18

Action thriller 1990 · US · Colour · 115mins

As both a talented director and actor, Clint Eastwood has a distinctive creative style, which he keeps for the likes of *Unforgiven* and *Bird*, but he still manages to maintain a spirit of lethargic cynicism when working on formula fare such as this all-action buddy movie. For fans, there's plenty of Clint as a firecracker cop, here part of a double act with Charlie Sheen, but Clint the director makes little effort to freshen up plot, character or car chase. Still, by wrestling manfully with a bad script, Sheen does provide a few laughs along the tired way. Contains swearing, violence, sex scene.

Clint Eastwood *Nick Pulovski* • Charlie Sheen *David Ackerman* • Raul Julia *Strom* • Sonia Braga *Liesl* • Tom Skerritt *Eugene Ackerman* • Lara Flynn Boyle *Sarah* • Pepe Serna *Lieutenant Ray Garcia* ■ *Dir* Clint Eastwood • *Scr* Boaz Yakin, Scott Spiegel

Rookie of the Year ★★★ PG

Sports comedy 1993 · US · Colour · 99mins

With a few honourable exceptions (*Bull Durham* and *Major League* among them), the British have never really warmed to baseball movies and this one slipped by virtually unnoticed in the UK. It's a slight but affectionate family comedy that follows the adventures of a youngster (Thomas Ian Nicholas) who, after breaking his arm, becomes a wonder pitcher. Actor-turned-director Daniel Stern – familiar from supporting roles in *Home Alone* and *City Slickers* – plays down the cute aspects of the story, while Nicholas is helped along by some sterling support work from Gary Busey, Dan Hedaya and Stern himself.

Thomas Ian Nicholas *Henry Rowengartner* • Gary Busey *Chet Steadman* • Albert Hall *Martinella* • Amy Morton *Mary Rowengartner* • Dan Hedaya *Larry "Fish" Fisher* • Bruce Altman *Jack Bradfield* • Eddie Bracken *Bob Carson* ■ *Dir* Daniel Stern • *Scr* Sam Harper

Room at the Top ★★★★★ 15

Drama 1958 · UK · BW · 112mins

A gritty, trenchant film which burst upon the late fifties and stirred a hornet's nest of controversy for its treatment of sex as passionate rather than a merely procreative exercise. Laurence Harvey is at his slit-eyed, manipulative, lizard-like best as the ambitious antihero of John Braine's novel, with Simone Signoret, glorious and sexy as his ill-fated mistress. For once, the North is portrayed as a shade more complicated than previous "flat cap and whippet" outings had shown, in a movie which perfectly captures the gradual demise of Victorian morality and traditional class culture. You can almost smell the coming sixties in the air.

Laurence Harvey *Joe Lampton* • Simone Signoret *Alice Aisgill* • Heather Sears *Susan Brown* • Donald Wolfit *Mr Brown* • Ambrosine Philpotts *Mrs Brown* • Donald Houston *Charles Soames* • Raymond Huntley *Mr Hoylake* • John Westbrook *Jack Wales* • Allan Cuthbertson *George Aisgill* • Mary Peach *June Samson* ■ *Dir* Jack Clayton • *Scr* Neil Paterson, from the novel by John Braine

Room for One More ★★★ U

Comedy drama 1952 · US · BW · 94mins

Cary Grant brings much-needed charm to this peculiar comedy drama, in which his then real-life wife Betsy Drake plays his spouse, a woman with a compulsive need to adopt. It's somewhat surprisingly based on a true story and is quite watchable, especially when Grant is pitted against that formidable child actor, the deadpan George "Foghorn" Winslow, perhaps best remembered now for *Gentlemen Prefer Blondes*. Director Norman Taurog, became renowned for his ability to get performances out of youngsters and non-actors, achieving notable success wth Mickey Rooney, Judy Garland and Elvis Presley.

Cary Grant *"Poppy" Rose* • Betsy Drake *Anna Rose* • Lurene Tuttle *Miss Kenyon* • Randy Stuart *Mrs Foreman* • John Ridgely *Harry Foreman* • Irving Bacon *Mayor* • Mary Lou Treen [Mary Treen] *Mrs Roberts* • Hayden Rorke *Doctor* • Iris Mann *Jane* • George "Foghorn" Winslow [George Winslow] *Teensie* • Clifford Tatum Jr *Jimmy-John* • Gay Gordon *Trot* • Malcolm Cassell *Tim* ■ *Dir* Norman Taurog • *Scr* Jack Rose, Melville Shavelson, from the autobiography by Anna Perrott Rose

A Room for Romeo Brass ★★★★ 15

Romantic comedy drama
1999 · UK/Can · Colour · 90mins

Having developed a nice little fan base for their excellent feature debut *TwentyFourSeven*, director Shane Meadows and his writing partner Paul Fraser haven't taken the easy option. *Romeo Brass* is a risky, difficult and very impressive little movie about two 12-year-old mates – the spirited Andrew Shim and the sickly Ben Marshall – who are befriended by likeable, albeit peculiar loner Paddy Considine. Beginning as an earthy but light-hearted study of adolescent friendship, the film takes a sharp turn into quite shocking drama once Considine reveals his darker side. Although the sudden shift in tone won't please everyone, this honest, unsentimental movie offers more insights into the weirdness of human relationships than many, while newcomer Considine is definitely a name to watch.

Andrew Shim *Romeo Brass* • Ben Marshall *Gavin "Knock Knock" Woolley* • Paddy Considine *Morell* • Frank Harper *Joseph Brass* • Julia Ford *Sandra Woolley* • James Higgins *Bill Woolley* • Vicky McClure *Ladine Brass* • Ladene Hall *Carol Brass* • Bob Hoskins *Steven Laws* • Shane Meadows *Fish and chip shop man* ■ *Dir* Shane Meadows • *Scr* Paul Fraser, Shane Meadows

Room Service ★★ U

Comedy 1938 · US · BW · 74mins

An oddity in the careers of the Marx Brothers in which a little of their well-established humour is applied to a hit Broadway farce. The anarchic personalities of Groucho, Harpo and Chico are fatally weakened by being tied to a situation comedy plot and Groucho is the only brother with a real part, as a penniless Broadway producer trying to put on a new play. There are odd inspired moments from all three, but far too few of them. The film looks cheap and a young Lucille Ball and Ann Miller make no impression in small roles. RKO later turned the play into a musical, *Step Lively*, with Frank Sinatra.

Groucho Marx *Gordon Miller* • Chico Marx *Binelli* • Harpo Marx *Faker Englund* • Lucille Ball *Christine Marlowe* • Ann Miller *Hilda Manny* ■ *Dir* William A Seiter • *Scr* Morrie Ryskind, Glenn Tryon, Philip Loeb, from a play by Allan Boretz, John Murray

Room to Let ★★

Crime thriller 1949 · UK · Colour · 65mins

Hammer Films took a step towards its future specialty with this early B-feature from a radio play by mystery writer Margery Allingham. Is Valentine Dyall's creepy Victorian lodger a missing mental patient or possibly even Jack the Ripper? How was murder committed behind a locked and bolted door? Jimmy Hanley headlines the cast playing the reporter Curley Minter, while Constance Smith, as his girlfriend and landlady's daughter, gains useful practice for her later role in Hollywood's *The Man in the Attic*, an official screen version of Marie Belloc Lowndes' famous novel, *The Lodger*, which seems to have inspired some of this modest tale.

Jimmy Hanley *Curley Minter* • Valentine Dyall *Dr Fell* • Christine Silver *Mrs Musgrave* • Merle Tottenham *Alice* • Charles Hawtrey *Mike Atkinson* • Constance Smith *Molly Musgrave* ■ *Dir* Godfrey Grayson • *Scr* John Gilling, Godfrey Grayson, from the radio play by Margery Allingham

The Room Upstairs ★★★ PG

Romantic comedy drama
1987 · US · Colour · 97mins

The ever-dependable Stockard Channing, is presented with a rare romantic lead in this pleasing, if predictable TV movie. As a lonely teacher who discovers there is more to life than the disabled youngsters in her care, she manages a combination of dedication and regret that is totally true to life. There's fine support from Linda Hunt, Sarah Jessica Parker and Sam Waterston, as the cellist who becomes both her lodger and her lover. Directed by Stuart Margolin, this is hardly profound, but such is the quality of the acting that the gentle blend of comedy and drama slowly begins to draw you in.

Stockard Channing *Leah Lazenby* • Sam Waterston *Travis Coles* • Linda Hunt *Mrs*

Sanders • Joan Allen *Ellie* • Clancy Brown *Kevin* • Sarah Jessica Parker *Mandy* ■ *Dir* Stuart Margolin • *Scr* Steve Lawson, from the novel by Norma Levinson

A Room with a View
★★★★ PG

Period drama   1985 · UK · Colour · 111mins

This is the first of the Merchant-Ivory adaptations of E M Forster. While *Howards End* was the one that scooped the major international awards, this is, in many ways, a more vibrant and infinitely more influential picture, as it confirmed the marketability of the "heritage" film that was, until recently, this country's most profitable movie export. Everything about the production proclaims its class: Ruth Prawer Jhabvala's script is witty and erudite, Tony Pierce-Roberts's images of Florence and the English countryside are breathtaking and the performances of Helena Bonham Carter, Julian Sands and, in particular, Daniel Day-Lewis and Maggie Smith, are of masterclass quality. There are longueurs, but the air of Edwardian charm is irresistible. Contains nudity. 🎬

Maggie Smith *Charlotte Bartlett* • Helena Bonham Carter *Lucy Honeychurch* • Denholm Elliott *Mr Emerson* • Julian Sands *George Emerson* • Daniel Day-Lewis *Cecil Vyse* • Simon Callow *Reverend Arthur Beebe* • Judi Dench *Miss Eleanor Lavish* • Rosemary Leach *Mrs Honeychurch* • Rupert Graves *Freddy Honeychurch* ■ *Dir* James Ivory • *Scr* Ruth Prawer Jhabvala, from the novel by EM Forster

The Roommate
★★★★ PG

Comedy   1984 · US · Colour · 92mins

This is a superior TV adaptation of John Updike's story, *The Christian Roommates*, about university students in the 1950s. Lance Guest is Orson Ziegler, an unworldly undergrad who finds himself sharing a room with disruptive Bohemian Barry Miller, an early exponent of the sort of alternative lifestyle that would be embraced wholesale throughout the second half of the next decade. The film, from PBS's *American Playhouse* series, plays out like a low-key but enjoyable, juvenile version of *The Odd Couple*. Miller is especially effective, while the production on the whole has a classy feel. 🎬

Lance Guest *Orson Ziegler* • Barry Miller *Henry "Hub" Palamountain* • Elmer Two Crow *Lester* • Melissa Ford *Emily* ■ *Dir* Nell Cox • *Scr* Neal Miller, from the story *The Christian Roommates* by John Updike

Roommates
★★★

Drama   1994 · US · Colour · 100mins

Not to be confused with Peter Yates's 1995 slush-fest, this TV movie comes closer than most to discussing Aids without being mawkish. Films about people dying slowly from this terrible condition, inevitably tread similar plot paths and only the remarkable documentary *Silverlake Life: the View from Here* has successfully demonstrated the shattering effect it has on the lives of sufferers and their friends. However, thanks to the restrained performances of Eric Stoltz and Randy Quaid, *Roommates* is an affecting and believable film, having

much in common with the pioneering Aids movie, *Longtime Companion* and being mercifully free of the manipulative set pieces and extended sermons that rendered *Philadelphia* at times almost unwatchable.

Randy Quaid *Jim Riley* • Eric Stoltz *Bill Thomas* • Charles Durning *Barney Riley* • Elizabeth Pena *Lisa Elliott* • Frank Buxton *Mr Thomas* • Jill Teed *Barbara Thomas* ■ *Dir* Alan Metzger • *Scr* Robert W Lenski

Roommates
★★ 12

Comedy drama   1995 · US · Colour · 104mins

Peter Falk stars as an elderly baker who adopts his grandson to prevent him from being sent to an orphanage. With the help of Oscar-nominated make-up, the film chronicles their relationship over the next three decades. They come to blows when little Michael, played by D B Sweeney, is a full-blown adult and studying medicine. Grandad, now over a hundred, is at odds with Sweeney's Chinese roommates and girlfriend Julianne Moore. Daft and overlong, this twaddle is bearable if only for the conviction of Falk's performance. 🎬

Peter Falk *Rocky* • DB Sweeney *Michael Holczek* • Julianne Moore *Beth* • Ellen Burstyn *Judith* • Jan Rubes *Bolek Krupa* ■ *Dir* Peter Yates • *Scr* Max Apple, Stephen Metcalfe, from the autobiography *Roommates: My Grandfather's Story* by Max Apple

Rooney
★★★ U

Comedy   1958 · UK · BW · 87mins

Ah, the blarney overflows in this very Pinewood version of Catherine Cookson's novel of an Irish dustman in love. Liverpool-born John Gregson makes a likeable stab at the title role, but sadly lacks grit alongside the more authentic Marie Kean, Jack MacGowran, Noel Purcell, Liam Redmond and bedridden Barry Fitzgerald. And if they're all a little too much for you, then so be it, but the result is really quite charming. As un-Irish as they come are sweet Muriel Pavlow as Rooney's girlfriend and popular British crooner Michael Holliday off screen warbling, Bing-like, the title song. Produced by Tina Brown's dad, George H.

John Gregson *James Ignatius Rooney* • Muriel Pavlow *Maire Hogan* • Barry Fitzgerald *Grandfather* • June Thorburn *Doreen O'Flynn* • Noel Purcell *Tim Hennessy* • Marie Kean *Mrs O'Flynn* • Liam Redmond *Mr Doolan* • Jack MacGowran *Joe O'Connor* ■ *Dir* George Pollock • *Scr* Patrick Kirwan, from the novel *Rooney* by Catherine Cookson

Rooster Cogburn
★★★ U

Western   1975 · US · Colour · 102mins

A memorable collaboration between John Wayne and Katharine Hepburn, with Wayne reprising his Oscar-winning role in *True Grit* and Hepburn playing the same kind of Bible-punching spinster she portrayed in *The African Queen*. Here, Hepburn is the missionary who tames the truculence of one-eyed Wayne as they search for her father's killers. The performances are wonderful, but the film relies too much on its elderly stars and is fatally flawed by Stuart Millar's sluggish direction. However, it remains

eminently watchable, as great stars go through their paces. 🎬

John Wayne *Rooster Cogburn* • Katharine Hepburn *Eula Goodnight* • Anthony Zerbe *Breed* • Richard Jordan *Hawk* • John McIntire *Judge Parker* • Richard Romancito *Wolf* • Strother Martin *McCoy* ■ *Dir* Stuart Millar • *Scr* Martin Julien, from the character created by Charles Portis in his novel *True Grit*

Roosters
★★

Drama   1993 · US · Colour · 93mins

A who's who of Hispanic acting talent, with the likes of Edward James Olmos, Sonia Braga and Maria Conchita Alonso teaming up for a heavy-handed poetic tale of poultry and patriarchy. Olmos plays an ex-con who returns home to reclaim his place as head of a poverty-line household. The film's title refers to Olmos's job of raising fighting cocks. The quality of the cast ensures some passionate acting, but the direction is dour in a film that weighs in too lightly on subtlety and too heavily on pretentious dialogue and symbolism. Nothing to crow about.

Edward James Olmos *Gallo Morales* • Sonia Braga *Juana* • Maria Conchita Alonso *Chata* • Danny Nucci *Hector* • Sarah Lassez *Angela* • Valente Rodriguez *Adan* ■ *Dir* Robert M Young • *Scr* Milcha Sanchez-Scott, from her play

The Root of All Evil
★★

Drama   1946 · UK · BW · 110mins

Attempting to break from her wholesome image, Phyllis Calvert here found herself in a role much more suited to her *Man in Grey* co-star, Margaret Lockwood. Her transformation from fresh-faced farm girl to scheming oil tycoon, by way of a breach of promise suit against fiancé Hubert Gregg, is totally implausible, and the harder she tries to be wicked, the more ludicrous the action becomes. Scripting from JS Fletcher's potboiler, director Brock Williams has slightly more joy with Michael Rennie and an accomplished supporting cast. Without the costumes to provide a distraction, however, this is one of Gainsborough's lesser outings.

Phyllis Calvert *Jeckie Farnish* • Michael Rennie *Charles Mortimer* • John McCallum *Joe Bartle* • Brefni O'Rourke *Mr Farnish* • Arthur Young *George Grice* • Hubert Gregg *Albert Grice* • Pat Hicks *Lucy Grice* ■ *Dir* Brock Williams • *Scr* Brock Williams, from the novel by JS Fletcher

The Roots of Heaven
★★

Drama   1958 · US · Colour · 0mins

Seven years after *The African Queen*, John Huston had another gruelling location adventure shooting in French Equatorial Africa for this ecological drama. With Errol Flynn and Trevor Howard in the cast, it was a boozy set, to say the least, and the movie rather staggers and lurches along. Howard is in Africa to save the elephant from ivory poachers and extinction – something of a relief as Huston spent much of his time on *The African Queen* trying to shoot one. Flynn supports Howard's campaign and as does TV reporter Orson Welles. As a narrative it's sadly muddled and the raddled Flynn looks more endangered than any elephant.

Errol Flynn *Major Forsythe* • Juliette Greco *Minna* • Trevor Howard *Morel* • Eddie Albert

Abe Fields • Orson Welles *Cy Sedgewick* • Paul Lukas *Saint Denis* • Herbert Lom *Orsini* • Grégoire Aslan *Habib* ■ *Dir* John Huston • *Scr* Romain Gary, Patrick Leigh-Fermor, from the novel by Romain Gary

Rope
★★★★ PG

Thriller   1948 · US · Colour · 76mins

This thriller is one of Alfred Hitchcock's strangest films. It's weirdly macabre rather than especially tense, as it relates the story of the Leopold and Loeb murder case that also formed the basis of Richard Fleischer's 1959 film *Compulsion* and a later, low-budget movie called *Swoon*. Essentially, it's the corpse and will-they-find-it plot. The body is that of a college boy, his murderers are two fellow students (John Dall, Farley Granger) and James Stewart is one of the donnish guests at the party hosted by the killers. The fact that the characters played by Dall and Granger are homosexuals is hinted at rather than stated, though for Hitchcock the main attraction was a technical stunt: he wanted to make a film that appeared as a single shot, with daylight turning to night outside the studio set window. 🎬

James Stewart *Rupert Cadell* • John Dall *Shaw Brandon* • Farley Granger *Philip Morgan* • Cedric Hardwicke *Mr Kentley* • Joan Chandler *Janet Walker* • Constance Collier *Mrs Atwater* • Edith Evanson *Mrs Wilson* ■ *Dir* Alfred Hitchcock • *Scr* Arthur Laurents, Hume Cronyn, Ben Hecht (uncredited), from the play *Rope's End* by Patrick Hamilton

Rope of Sand
★★

Adventure drama   1949 · US · BW · 104mins

In an improbable Hollywood version of South Africa, heroic big-game hunter Burt Lancaster foils the nefarious activities of gem seekers and rescues the lady caught in the complicated plot. Directed by William Dieterle with Claude Rains as a suave schemer, Paul Henreid a chilling sadist, and Peter Lorre a whining opportunist on the edge of things, this gathering of half the cast of *Casablanca*, plus French actress Corinne Calvet making a less than persuasive Hollywood debut, is a nonsensical adventure of no merit whatsoever. However, seen now, and with Lancaster in tough, action-adventure mode, it makes for fairly hilarious enjoyment.

Burt Lancaster *Mike Davis* • Paul Henreid *Commandant Paul Vogel* • Claude Rains *Arthur Fred Martingale* • Peter Lorre *Toady* • Corinne Calvet *Suzanne Renaud* • Sam Jaffe *Dr Francis "Doc" Hunter* • John Bromfield *Thompson, guard* ■ *Dir* William Dieterle • *Scr* Walter Doniger, John Paxton, from a story by Walter Doniger

Rosa Luxemburg
★★★★ PG

Biographical drama
1986 · W Ger · Colour · 123mins

Despite her surname, Rosa Luxemburg was actually born in Poland, resident in Germany and widely considered one of the most dangerous women of her age: a revolutionary, internationalist, pacifist, Jew and troublemaker and probably vegetarian to boot. Award-winning actress Barbara Sukowa was rightly rewarded for for portraying her in this praised German film. An intelligent biopic, of historical, personal and

dramatic interest. In German with English subtitles.

Barbara Sukowa *Rosa Luxemburg* • Daniel Olbrychski *Leo Jogiches* • Otto Sander *Karl Liebknecht* • Adelheid Arndt *Luise Kautsky* • Jürgen Holtz *Karl Kautsky* ■ *Dir/Scr* Margarethe von Trotta

Rosalie ★★ U
Musical comedy 1937 · US · BW · 124mins

Nelson Eddy teams with tap-dancer Eleanor Powell in this crass and kitschy cross between operetta and college musical. Nelson is a West Point cadet in love with Powell, playing Princess Rosalie of Romanza, who is studying at Vassar The best song in the so-so Cole Porter score is *In the Still of the Night*, while the gigantic title number (hated by its composer) had Powell in a frothy tutu and pom-poms and a cast of thousands including dancers in scanty slave-girl outfits.

Nelson Eddy *Dick Thorpe* • Eleanor Powell *Rosalie* • Ray Bolger *Bill Delroy* • Frank Morgan *King* • Ilona Massey *Brenda* • Edna May Oliver *Queen* • Billy Gilbert *Oloff* • Reginald Owen *Chancellor* • William Demarest *Army's coach* ■ *Dir* WS Van Dyke • *Scr* William Anthony McGuire, from the musical by William Anthony McGuire, by Guy Bolton

Rosalie Goes Shopping ★★★ 15
Comedy 1989 · W Ger · Colour · 89mins

Critics at the time considered German director Percy Adlon's follow-up to the cult favourite *Bagdad Café* to have been something of a disappointment. Yet, in many ways, this is a more assured piece of film-making, largely because Adlon's grasp of modern American mores was much firmer. This is a stinging satire on the consumerist boom that occurred during the Reagan presidency, when acquisition made life worthwhile and payment was an inconvenience. Adlon regular Marianne Sägebrecht gives a beguiling performance as the shopaholic of the title, while Brad Davis provides solid support as her crop-dusting husband. Contains swearing. 🖭

Marianne Sägebrecht *Rosalie Greenspace* • Brad Davis *Ray Greenspace, "Liebling"* • Judge Reinhold *Priest* • Erika Blumberger *Rosalie's mum* • Willy Harlander *Rosalie's dad* • John Hawkes *Schnuki* ■ *Dir* Percy Adlon • *Scr* Percy Adlon, Eleonore Adlon, Christopher Doherty

The Rosary Murders ★★★ 18
Murder mystery 1987 · US · Colour · 100mins

The sometimes mildly threatening Donald Sutherland makes an unlikely Detroit priest, but his fine, controlled performance in this dark, unsettling film lifts its rather plodding pace. Sutherland is the recipient of every priest's occupational nightmare, the serial killer who picks his church to confess in. We witness a neat tussle of conscience, as victims are felled like ninepins for most of the film. One of those promising efforts which starts out at a decent lick but ends up running out of steam and ideas. Contains violence and swearing. 🖭

Donald Sutherland *Father Bob Koesler* • Charles Durning *Father Ted Nabors* • Josef Sommer *Lieutenant Walt Koznicki* • Belinda

Bauer *Pat Lennon* • James Murtaugh *Javison* ■ *Dir* Fred Walton • *Scr* Elmore Leonard, Fred Walton, from the novel by William X Kienzle

The Rose ★★ 15
Musical drama 1979 · US · Colour · 128mins

Trapped by the usual conventions of rock-star biopics – drugs, booze and blues – Bette Midler, playing a singer loosely based on Janis Joplin, is only really effective during her raunchy concert numbers. For the rest of the film she's at the mercy of a script as ridiculous as the hairstyles. Alan Bates gives a skilful performance that makes his ruthless manager a plausible man you love to hate, but Midler just muddles through. Contains swearing and nudity. 🖭

Bette Midler *Rose* • Alan Bates *Rudge* • Frederic Forrest *Dyer* • Harry Dean Stanton *Billy Ray* • Barry Primus *Dennis* • David Keith *Mal* • Sandra McCabe *Sarah* ■ *Dir* Mark Rydell • *Scr* Bo Goldman, William Kerby, Michael Cimino, from the story by William Kerby

The Rose and the Jackal ★★
Historical drama 1990 · US · Colour · 94mins

A lightweight but passably enjoyable romp based on the true story of the founder of the famous Pinkerton detective agency. Christopher Reeve is the Scottish-born Allan Pinkerton who, during the American Civil War, finds himself wooing Southern belles and foiling dastardly Confederate plots. British director Jack Gold marshals the action competently enough and there is a pleasing support cast which includes Madolyn Smith Osborne, Carrie Snodgress and Kevin McCarthy.

Christopher Reeve *Allan Pinkerton* • Madolyn Smith Osborne [Madolyn Smith] *Rose O'Neal Greenhow* • Granville Van Dusen *Thomas Scott* • Carrie Snodgress *Joan Pinkerton* • Kevin McCarthy *Senator Wilson* ■ *Dir* Jack Gold • *Scr* Eric Edson, from the book *Revelry in Washington* by Margaret Leech

The Rose Garden ★★ 15
Historical courtroom drama 1989 · W Ger/US · Colour · 108mins

Winner of the best foreign film Oscar for his 1986 movie *The Assault*, Dutch director Fons Rademakers returned to the subject of the Second World War with this study of anguished memory and unpunished guilt. Set in modern-day Germany, the story of Maximilian Schell's prosecution for attacking the former commandant of the concentration camp where his sister died eschews the cheap sentimentality that blights so many films about the Holocaust and its aftermath. However, it also mistakes slowness for sincerity and spends too much time exploring lawyer Liv Ullmann's relationship with her estranged husband, Peter Fonda. 🖭

Liv Ullmann *Gabriele Schlueter-Freund* • Maximilian Schell *Aaron Reichenbach* • Peter Fonda *Herbert Schlueter* • Jan Niklas *George Paessler* • Katarina Lena Muller *Tina* ■ *Dir* Fons Rademakers • *Scr* Paul Hengge

Rose Marie ★★★★ U
Musical romantic comedy 1936 · US · Colour · 111mins

Admittedly, the phenomenally successful thirties musicals of "America's Sweethearts", Jeanette MacDonald and Nelson Eddy, creak mightily now, but there is still abundant fun in this loose adaptation of the popular operetta combined here with a manhunt melodrama. Opera singer MacDonald falls in love with Canadian Mountie Nelson while trying to shield her ne'er-do-well fugitive kid brother Jimmy Stewart from the lawman's dogged pursuit. A highlight is the fabled twosome's duet of *Indian Love Call*. Watch, too, for a brief appearance by newcomer David Niven as Rose Marie's would-be suitor.

Jeanette MacDonald *Marie de Flor* • Nelson Eddy *Sgt Bruce* • James Stewart *John Flower* • Reginald Owen *Myerson* • George Regas *Boniface* • Robert Greig *Cafe manager* • Una O'Connor *Anna* • James Conlin [Jimmy Conlin] *Joe, the piano player* • Lucien Littlefield *Storekeeper* • Mary Anita Loos *Corn Queen* • David Niven *Teddy* ■ *Dir* WS Van Dyke II [WS Van Dyke] • *Scr* Frances Goodrich, Albert Hackett, Alice Duer Miller, from the operetta by Otto A Harbach, Oscar Hammerstein II, Rudolf Friml, Herbert Stothart

Rose Marie ★★★ U
Musical romantic comedy 1954 · US · Colour · 99mins

MGM's remake of its phenomenally successful 1936 vehicle for Jeanette MacDonald and Nelson Eddy is the first colour CinemaScope musical and takes advantage of locations in the Canadian Rockies, but is nowhere near as beguiling as its predecessor. It stars Ann Blyth, Howard Keel as the Mountie, "Latin Lover" Fernando Lamas as an unlikely fur trapper, and Joan Taylor as Wanda, the daughter of a tribal chief and a new character in the much reworked plot of the original operetta. The highspot in the film, directed by Mervyn LeRoy, has Taylor and a hundred Indian braves performing a ceremonial war dance to *Totem Tom Tom*. 🖭

Ann Blyth *Rose Marie Lemaitre* • Howard Keel *Mike Malone* • Fernando Lamas *James Severn Duval* • Bert Lahr *Barney McCorkle* • Marjorie Main *Lady Jane Dunstock* • Joan Taylor *Wanda* • Ray Collins *Inspector Appleby* • Chief Yowlachie *Black Eagle* ■ *Dir* Mervyn LeRoy • *Scr* Ronald Millar, George Froeschel, from the operetta by Otto A Harbach, Oscar Hammerstein II, Rudolf Friml, Herbert Stothart • *Choreographer* Busby Berkeley

Rose of Cimarron ★★ U
Western 1952 · US · Colour · 72mins

Mala Powers is best remembered as Roxanne to José Ferrer's Oscar-winning Cyrano de Bergerac. Here, as Rose, she's an orphan brought up by native Americans who is seeking revenge for the death of her parents. Powers's co-star is Jack Buetel, once Howard Hughes's Billy the Kid in the infamous *The Outlaw*, but it's up to western veterans such as Jim Davis, Bill Williams and old hand Bob Steele to keep this production on its feet. Incidentally, this was published as a one-off comic book in the fifties with a knockout cover: mint copies are now much prized by collectors.

Jack Buetel *Marshal Hollister* • Mala Powers *Rose of Cimarron* • Bill Williams *George Newcomb* • Jim Davis *Willie Whitewater* • Dick Curtis *Clem Dawley* • Tom Monroe *Mike Finch* • William Phipps *Jeb Dawley* • Bob Steele *Rio* ■ *Dir* Harry Keller • *Scr* Maurice Geraghty

Rose of Washington Square ★★
Musical 1939 · US · BW · 86mins

Twentieth Century-Fox's leading blonde Alice Faye plays Rose in a very thinly disguised biopic of Ziegfeld headliner Fanny Brice, later more memorably incarnated by Barbra Streisand in the show and movie *Funny Girl* (and its sequel). Here, Faye falls for handsome but no-good, and severely underwritten, gambler Tyrone Power, and is inspired by him to sing Brice's theme song *My Man*. But the real treat of the movie (unless you're a Faye fanatic) is the appearance of the great Al Jolson, who sings a batch of his own top hits. There's no direction to speak of, but *Intermezzo*'s Gregory Ratoff is credited.

Tyrone Power *Bart Clinton* • Alice Faye *Rose Sargent* • Al Jolson *Ted Cotter* • William Frawley *Harry Long* • Joyce Compton *Peggy* • Hobart Cavanaugh *Whitey Boone* • Moroni Olsen *Buck Russell* ■ *Dir* Gregory Ratoff • *Scr* Nunnally Johnson, from a story by John Larkin, Jerry Horwin

The Rose Tattoo ★★★
Drama 1955 · US · BW · 116mins

Anna Magnani goes wild with desire for Burt Lancaster who has a tattoo on his chest like that of her virile dead husband. Magnani's daughter, who sets a sailor's pulse racing, adds another layer of smouldering compost to this already earthy tale which could only have come from the pen of Tennessee Williams. Audiences gasped in 1955 but they will be more likely to giggle today as the serio-comic malarkey unfolds. Williams wrote the play for Magnani but she chickened out of doing it on stage; however on film, she carted off an Oscar, a Bafta and a New York Film Critics Circle award, though a more OTT performance would be hard to find.

Anna Magnani *Serafina Delle Rose* • Burt Lancaster *Alvaro Mangiacavallo* • Marisa Pavan *Rosa Delle Rose* • Ben Cooper *Jack Hunter* • Virginia Grey *Estelle Hohengarten* • Jo Van Fleet *Bessie* ■ *Dir* Daniel Mann • *Scr* Tennessee Williams, Hal Kanter, from the play by Tennessee Williams

Roseanna McCoy ★★
Romantic drama 1949 · US · BW · 89mins

The bucolic Ozark mountain feuds between rival family factions have barely been touched on in cinema, and neither this movie nor the later *Lolly Madonna War* really conveyed what internecine warfare over moonshine and sex must've really been like. Producer Samuel Goldwyn used the famous Hatfield–McCoy feud to feature his young contract glamour stars Farley Granger and Joan Evans in a story that owes much to *Romeo and Juliet*, but unfortunately the two leads look far too urbane. Granger became a star of sorts, but Joan Evans sunk via B-movies without trace, eventually turning up as a Los Angeles educationalist in real life. 🖭

Farley Granger *Johnse Hatfield* • Joan Evans *Roseanna McCoy* • Charles Bickford *Devil Anse Hatfield* • Raymond Massey *Old Randall McCoy* • Richard Basehart *Mounts Hatfield* ■ *Dir* Irving Reis • *Scr* John Collier, from the novel by Alberta Hannum

Roseanna's Grave ★★★ 🔞
Romantic comedy
1996 · US/UK · Colour · 93mins

Jean Reno is Marcello, whose beloved, dying wife Roseanna (Mercedes Ruehl) has her weak heart set on being buried in the village churchyard. The problem is there are few plots left, so the bistro proprietor embarks on a frantic mission as local protector, rescuing the death-threatened and concealing inconvenient corpses to save Roseanna's cemetery space. This lightweight, genial lark captures the vivacity and mini-dramas of rural Italian life around Reno and Ruehl's heart-warming performances, and while it sometimes skitters uncertainly between gentle whimsy and laboured farce, it has undeniable charm. Contains swearing and some sex scenes. ▭

Jean Reno *Marcello Beatto* • Mercedes Ruehl *Roseanna Beatto* • Polly Walker *Cecilia* • Mark Frankel *Antonio* • Trevor Peacock *Iacoponi* • Fay Ripley *Francesca* ■ *Dir* Paul Weiland • *Scr* Saul Turteltaub

Roseanne ★★
Biographical drama
1994 · US · Colour · 90mins

Sensationalistic, trailer-trash account of Roseanne Barr, the mother of all sitcom divas. Denny Dillon (*Dream On*) stars in this unauthorised TV biography that charts the brazen comedian's beginnings in a "dysfunctional" family through early years as a waitress and subsequent breakthroughs as a stand-up, before resurrecting well-documented battles on the set of her groundbreaking TV comedy and her tempestuous marriage to Tom Arnold (played by David Graf of the *Police Academy* series). Slapped together, this unfortunate venture lacks depth and empathy for its subject. If you're a true fan of the tabloid press, you'll feel right at home.

Denny Dillon *Roseanne* • David Graf *Tom Arnold* • Dawn Zeek *Young Roseanne* • John Walcutt *Bill Pentland* • Judith Scarpone *Helen* • John Karlen *Jerry Barr* ■ *Dir* Paul Schneider • *Scr* Karen Harris

Roseanne and Tom: Behind the Scenes ★★
Biographical drama
1994 · US · Colour

The troubled marriage of Roseanne Barr and Tom Arnold accounted for more newsprint than just about any other showbiz liaison of recent times. This TV movie traces their relationship from romance to recriminations and will make compelling viewing for any fans of the long-running sitcom *Roseanne*. Patrika Darbo (one of those familiar faces to whom it's next to impossible to put a name) is well cast as Barr, but Stephen Lee is less convincing as her husband as hardly surprising in a film that obviously has little sympathy for Arnold or his well-publicised problems.

Patrika Darbo *Roseanne Barr* • Stephen Lee *Tom Arnold* • Tom Ormeny *Bud Roker* • Heather Paige Kent *Kim Silva* ■ *Dir* Richard A Colla • *Scr* Eugenie Ross-Leming, Brad Buckner

Les Roseaux Sauvages ★★★★ 🔞
Drama 1994 · Fr · Colour · 109mins

For all its shimmering images of the beautiful French countryside and its painstaking attention to period detail, this magnificent rites-of-passage drama tackles such complex themes as war, class, sexuality, the age gap and civic responsibility with an intelligence and a naturalism that one has come to expect of director André Téchiné. Rather than delivering a rose-tinted lament for the lost innocence of youth, he takes the emotions, opinions and confusions of teenagers seriously and is rewarded with exceptional performances from the members of his young cast who can clearly identify with the concerns of their characters. In French with English subtitles. ▭

Frédéric Gorny *Henri* • Gaël Morel *François* • Elodie Bouchez *Maïté* • Stéphane Rideau *Serge* • Michèle Moretti *Madame Alvarez* ■ *Dir* André Téchiné • *Scr* André Téchiné, Gilles Taurand, Olivier Massart

Rosebud ★★ 🔞
Political action thriller
1975 · US · Colour · 121mins

A depressing bloom, indeed, from director Otto Preminger in which PLO terrorists kidnap five women who are holidaying aboard a yacht. Intercutting between the women's plight and what's being done to help them slows the idea down to stasis, despite the efforts of CIA agent Peter O'Toole, Richard Attenborough and Adrienne Corri to salvage it. Adapted by Preminger's son – but why did he bother? Contains violence and swearing. ▭

Peter O'Toole *Larry Martin* • Richard Attenborough *Sloat* • Cliff Gorman *Hamlekh* • Claude Dauphin *Fargeau* • John V Lindsay *United States Senator Donovan* • Peter Lawford *Lord Carter* • Raf Vallone *George Nikolaos* • Adrienne Corri *Lady Carter* ■ *Dir* Otto Preminger • *Scr* Erik Lee Preminger, from a novel by Joan Hemingway, Paul Bonnecarrere

Roseland ★★★★
Dance drama 1977 · US · Colour · 103mins

Merchant–Ivory's American films are less celebrated than their famously lovely English and Indian literary adaptations, but the American James Ivory is also at his least cosy exploring his homeland. This bittersweet collection of tales set in New York's Roseland ballroom sees a marvellous ensemble of lonely hearts trip the light fantastic reminiscing about life and love. Making one of her rare screen appearances after a premature 1959 retirement, Teresa Wright is particularly moving as the widow with a new lease of life after striking up a dance partnership with Lou Jacobi. Lilia Skala and Geraldine Chaplin also score, and Christopher Walken (a trained dancer early in his career) makes an oily impression as a dancehall predator.

Teresa Wright *May* • Lou Jacobi *Stan* • Don DeNatale *Master of Ceremonies* • Louise Kirtland *Ruby* • Hetty Galen *Red-haired lady* • Geraldine Chaplin *Marilyn* • Christopher Walken *Russel* • Lilia Skala *Rosa* ■ *Dir* James Ivory • *Scr* Ruth Prawer Jhabvala • *Executive Producer* Ismail Merchant

Roselyne and the Lions ★★★ 🔞
Drama 1989 · Fr · Colour · 136mins

Apart from showcasing the Bardot-esque beauty of Isabelle Pasco, it's hard to fathom exactly what director Jean-Jacques Beineix was up to with this too-leisurely parable on the theme of creation and the ever-present spectre of death. As the couple whose desire to tame lions leads to passion, Pasco and Gérard Sandoz look good enough, and the hours of off-screen training they put in with the big cats fully pays off. But the tensions that arise once Pasco is encouraged by a lustful German circus owner are nowhere near as interesting as the tentative manoeuvres of the opening scenes in the Marseille zoo. In French with English subtitles. ▭

Isabelle Pasco *Roselyne* • Gérard Sandoz *Thierry* • Philippe Clevenot *Bracquard* • Gunter Meisner *Klint* • Wolf Harnisch *Koenig* • Gabriel Monnet *Frazier* • Jacques Le Carpentier *Markovitch* ■ *Dir* Jean-Jacques Beineix • *Scr* Jean-Jacques Beineix, Jacques Forgeas

Rosemary's Baby ★★★★★ 🔞
Horror 1968 · US · Colour · 131mins

Ira Levin's bestseller about Antichrist cultism in Manhattan is impeccably and faithfully brought to the screen by director Roman Polanski in a genuinely horrifying chiller that quietly builds unbearable tension. Mia Farrow is the perfect Satanic foil in a supernatural classic of conspiratorial evil meshed with apocalyptic revelations, and Ruth Gordon won a deserved Oscar for her busy-body portrayal of eccentric menace. The rest of the cast is equally excellent, including director John Cassavetes as Farrow's husband. It's one of the most powerful films ever made about Devil worship because Polanski expertly winds up the paranoia with spooky atmospherics and morbid humour. Contains nudity. ▭

Mia Farrow *Rosemary Woodhouse* • John Cassavetes *Guy Woodhouse* • Ruth Gordon *Minnie Castevet* • Sidney Blackmer *Roman Castevet* • Maurice Evans *Hutch* • Ralph Bellamy *Dr Sapirstein* • Tony Curtis *Voice of Donald Baumgart* ■ *Dir* Roman Polanski • *Scr* Roman Polanski, from the novel by Ira Levin

Rosencrantz and Guildenstern Are Dead ★★★★ 🔞
Comedy 1990 · US · Colour · 117mins

Tom Stoppard's screen version of his own hit play, beginning with a splendid long shot of Rosencrantz and Guildenstern making their way to Elsinore, has largely been dismissed by the critics, who disapproved both of his opening out what had been a delightful theatrical experience and his audacity in penning new material. They were also pretty scathing of the performances by Gary Oldman and Tim Roth. Yet, combining verbal dexterity

with precise slapstick timing, they capture the boredom and bewilderment of these two *Hamlet* also-rans with disarming charm. Richard Dreyfuss as the Player and Ian Richardson as Polonius also score palpable hits. Undeservedly much-maligned.

Gary Oldman *Rosencrantz* • Tim Roth *Guildenstern* • Richard Dreyfuss *Player* • Joanna Roth *Ophelia* • Iain Glen *Prince Hamlet* • Donald Sumpter *King Claudius* • Joanna Miles *Queen Gertrude* • Ian Richardson *Polonius* ■ *Dir/Scr* Tom Stoppard

Rosetta ★★★ 🔞
Drama 1999 · Bel/Fr · Colour · 95mins

Inspired by Kafka and booed on winning the Palme d'Or at Cannes, Luc and Jean-Pierre Dardenne's starkly realistic insight into life on the lowest rung undoubtedly makes for difficult viewing. However, as the debuting Emilie Dequenne clings to the soul-destroying routine she hopes will land the job she needs for self-esteem as much as pay, the film begins to grip in much the same way as Chantal Akerman's *Jeanne Dielman*. Spurning both the optimism of American "trailer trash" pictures and the politicking of British social realism, this gruelling film makes no commercial concessions and is all the better for it. In French with English subtitles.

Emilie Dequenne *Rosetta* • Fabrizio Rongione *Riquet* • Anne Yernaux *Rosetta's mother* • Olivier Gourmet *Boss* ■ *Dir/Scr* Luc Dardenne, Jean-Pierre Dardenne

Rosewood ★★★ 🔞
Historical drama
1997 · US · Colour · 136mins

A powerful historical drama from *Boyz N the Hood* director John Singleton that re-creates with shocking intensity a twenties atrocity that was hushed up until a journalist came across the story by chance in the early eighties. Sparked by a false charge of rape, the annihilation of a black settlement by a mob of Florida rednecks in 1923 was motivated purely out of racial hatred. Singleton reconstructs the incident with care, but the intervention of Ving Rhames's fictional American Civil War hero and the unconvincing repentance of adulterous shopkeeper Jon Voight undermine this otherwise noble attempt at depicting the attitudes and actions of an unenlightened age. ▭

Jon Voight *John Wright* • Ving Rhames *Mann* • Don Cheadle *Sylvester Carrier* • Bruce McGill *Duke Purdy* • Loren Dean *James Taylor* • Esther Rolle *Aunt Sarah* • Elise Neal *Scrappie* ■ *Dir* John Singleton • *Scr* Gregory Poirier

Rosie! ★ 🅤
Comedy drama 1967 · US · Colour · 97mins

The grasping daughters of a wealthy, off-the-wall widow with an overdeveloped penchant for spending her money, have her committed to a spartan "rest home" in order to curb her extravagance. Naturally, mother emerges as the heroine after a court case. Rosalind Russell, giving her considerable all as a cut-price version of Auntie Mame, is unable to rescue this unspeakable rubbish adapted, for no good reason, from a failed Broadway play by Ruth Gordon. David Lowell Rich directed, with an excellent

🅤 = SUITABLE FOR ALL 🆄🅲 = SUITABLE FOR ALL, ESPECIALLY FOR YOUNG CHILDREN (VIDEO ONLY) 🅿🅶 = PARENTAL GUIDANCE

cast, their good work wasted on this witless drama – or is it a comedy? Who cares!

Rosalind Russell *Rosie Lord* • Sandra Dee *Daphne* • Brian Aherne *Oliver Stevenson* • Audrey Meadows *Mildred* • James Farentino *David* • Vanessa Brown *Edith* • Leslie Nielsen *Cabot* • Margaret Hamilton *Mae* ■ *Dir* David Lowell Rich • *Scr* Samuel Taylor, from the play *A Very Rich Woman* by Ruth Gordon, from the play *Les Joies de la Famille* by Philippe Heriat

Rosie the Riveter ★★ U

Wartime comedy 1944 · US · BW · 74mins

A wartime tribute to the women working in the factories (retitled *In Rosie's Room* in the UK, where few knew what a riveter was), this B-movie is best remembered for its popular title tune. Appealing Jane Frazee plays Rosie, who has to share an apartment with three other factory workers (two of them men) due to the housing shortage. Many years later Frazee recalled, "The picture people always mention to me is Rosie the Riveter, which surprises me. It was just a six-day wonder thrown together overnight to capitalise on the wartime novelty song."

Jane Frazee *Rosalind "Rosie" Warren* • Frank Albertson *Charlie Doran* • Vera Vague [Barbara Jo Allen] *Vera Watson* • Frank Jenks *Kelly Kennedy* • Maude Eburne *Grandma Quill* • Lloyd Corrigan *Clem Prouty* ■ *Dir* Joseph Santley • *Scr* Jack Townley, Aleen Leslie, from the story *Room for Two* by Dorothy Curnow Handley

Rosie: the Rosemary Clooney Story ★★ PG

Biographical drama
1982 · US · Colour · 91mins

This tale of the breakdown (and recovery, it is a TV movie!) of fifties' pop and movie star Rosemary Clooney is as interesting as made-for-TV movies get. Today Clooney's probably better known as George's aunt rather than for her undoubted vocal talents. The tale is well told, but directed by former child star Jackie Cooper as though using the zoom lens is the only way he knows how to start a scene. Sondra Locke struggles hard in the lead, but her lip-synching (to the real Rosie on the soundtrack) is often awry, and she resembles the voluptuous Clooney not a whit. [video]

Sondra Locke *Rosemary Clooney* • Tony Orlando *José Ferrer* • Penelope Milford *Betty Clooney* • John Karlen *Uncle George* • Cheryl Anderson *Aunt Jean* • Robert Ridgely *Mort Weiner* • Joey Travolta *Dante* • Katherine Helmond *Frances Clooney* • Kevin McCarthy *Dr Jones* ■ *Dir* Jackie Cooper • *Scr* Katherine E Coker, from the autobiography *This for Remembrance* by Rosemary Clooney, Raymond Strait

Rosita ★★

Silent period romance 1923 · US · BW

The King of Spain (Holbrook Blinn) wants guitar-strumming dancing girl Rosita (Mary Pickford) for his mistress, but she loves dashing nobleman Don Diego (George Walsh, director Raoul Walsh's brother) who is under sentence of death for treason. This romantic period melodrama, set in 18th-century Toledo, marked Pickford's failed bid to transform herself from America's "Little Mary" into a tempestuous romantic star. More importantly, it marked the Hollywood debut of director Ernst Lubitsch, whom Pickford imported from Germany for the occasion. The European sophisticate and the co-founding queen of United Artists didn't hit it off and the film was completed amid a multitude of disagreements.

Mary Pickford *Rosita* • Holbrook Blinn *The King* • Irene Rich *The Queen* • George Walsh *Don Diego* • Charles Belcher *The Prime Minister* ■ *Dir* Ernst Lubitsch • *Scr* Edward Knoblock, from a story by Norbert Falk, from Hans Kräly, from the play *Don César de Bazan* by Adolphe Philippe Dennery, Philippe François Pinel

The Rossiter Case ★

Crime mystery 1950 · UK · BW · 75mins

This obscure melodrama from Hammer's early B-movie days never escapes its stage origins. Helen Shingler stars as the wife who's paralysed after a car accident, only to discover that her sister (Sheila Burrell) is having an affair with her husband (Clement McCallin). A quarrel leads to the accidental shooting of one sister and the husband's arrest on a murder charge. Silent star Henry Edwards plays a small role as a doctor.

Helen Shingler *Liz Rossiter* • Clement McCallin *Peter Rossiter* • Shelia Burrell *Honor* • Frederick Leister *Sir James Ferguson* • Henry Edwards *Dr Bendix* ■ *Dir* Francis Searle • *Scr* Kenneth Hyde, John Gilling, Francis Searle, from the play by Kenneth Hyde

Roswell ★★★★ 12

Drama 1994 · US · Colour and BW · 87mins

A fascinating drama about an event that would have made a perfect case for the *X Files* team if only they had been born at the time. The year is 1947, and Kyle MacLachlan is the military intelligence officer who begins investigating what appears to be the crash-landing of a flying saucer and starts to suspect a cover-up. MacLachlan is convincing as the questioning officer, there are neat supporting turns from Martin Sheen and country singer Dwight Yoakam, and director Jeremy Kagan summons up an air of paranoia that Mulder and Scully would have felt quite at home with. The film is based on a true story that has long intrigued those investigating extraterrestrial phenomena. Contains swearing. [video]

Kyle MacLachlan *Major Jesse Marcel* • Martin Sheen *Townsend* • Dwight Yoakam *Mac Brazel* • Xander Berkeley *Sherman Carson* • Bob Gunton *Frank Joyce* • Kim Greist *Vy Marcel* • Peter MacNicol *Lewis Rickett* ■ *Dir* Jeremy Kagan [Jeremy Paul Kagan] • *Scr* Arthur Kopit, from a story by Paul Davids, Jeremy Kagan, from the book *UFO Crash at Roswell* by Donald R Schmitt, Steven Poster

Rothschild's Violin ★★★ U

Biographical drama
1996 · Fr/Swi/Fin/Hun · Colour · 101mins

Following the acclaimed *Citizen Langlois*, Argentinian-born director Edgardo Cozarinsky continued the theme of state intervention in the arts in this astute re-creation of a little-known episode in Stalinist history. Constrained by the dictates of socialist realism, the composer Shostakovich sought to make a stand by performing the unfinished opera of his disciple Benjamin Fleischmann, a Jew who had died in the siege of Leningrad. Cozarinsky first combines archive footage and re-enacted material to explore Soviet classical music in the 1930s, before presenting a full performance of *Le Violon de Rothschild* and a scathing assessment of Stalin's rule. Difficult, but rewarding. In Russian with English subtitles.

Sergei Makovetsky *Dmitri Shostakovich* • Dainius Kazlauskus *Benjamin Fleischmann* • Miklos B Szekely *Bronze* • Mari Torocsik *Marfa* • Sándor Zsótér *Rothschild* • Ferenc Jávori *Chakhkes* ■ *Dir/Scr* Edgardo Cozarinsky

Rotten to the Core ★★

Crime comedy 1965 · UK · BW · 89mins

Everywhere you looked during the early sixties, there was a comic criminal mastermind planning an audacious raid that was doomed to failure because his gang were paid-up members of Dolts Anonymous. Anton Rodgers is the great brain here, posing as a top-ranking general in order to rob an army camp. Charlotte Rampling is slinkily amusing as the moll who seduces pompous army officer Ian Bannen to secure some inside information, but what few laughs there are come from Eric Sykes as the private eye hired by wealthy Peter Vaughan to spy on daughter Rampling. Fitfully funny, but hardly the Boulting brothers at their best.

Eric Sykes *Hunt* • Ian Bannen *Vine* • Dudley Sutton *Jelly* • Kenneth Griffith *Lenny* • James Beckett *Scapa* • Avis Bunnage *Countess* • Anton Rodgers *Duke* • Charlotte Rampling *Sara* • Victor Maddern *Anxious* ■ *Dir* John Boulting • *Scr* John Warren, Len Heath, Jeffrey Dell, Roy Boulting, from their story, from an idea by John Warren, Len Heath

La Roue ★★★★★

Silent tragedy 1923 · Fr · BW · 303mins

Even before he made *Napoleon* (1927), Abel Gance was considered the Griffith of France; on seeing this masterpiece, Jean Cocteau opined: "There is cinema before and after *La Roue* as there is painting before and after Picasso." The story concerns the suffering of railway engineer Séverin-Mars and his violin-making son Gabriel de Gravone over the marriage of adopted family member Ivy Close to ageing inspector Pierre Magnier. Shot on location over 16 months and originally running some nine hours, it was eventually released by Pathé at just 144 minutes. Yet, even in truncated form the audacious blend of realism and romanticism achieved by superbly-controlled accelerated and associative montage is clearly evident. A restored 303-minute version was completed by Marie Epstein in 1980. With French titles and simultaneous English translation.

Séverin-Mars *Sisif* • Gabriel de Gravone *Elie* • Pierre Magnier *Jacques de Hersan, the engineer* • Ivy Close *Norma* • Georges Terof *Mâchefer* ■ *Dir/Scr* Abel Gance

Rouge ★★★★ 15

Fantasy romance 1987 · HK · Colour · 92mins

Directed by Stanley Kwan, this ghost story-cum-satire oozes quality, from the sublime photography of Bill Wong to the outstanding performance of Anita Mui as the troubled spirit of a thirties courtesan, condemned to wander the streets of Hong Kong until she meets the lover with whom she entered into a suicide pact. Perfectly re-creating the decadent elegance of the thirties and gently mocking the consumerism of the eighties, Kwan tells his story (co-adapted by Li Bihua from her own novel) with a lightness of touch few modern directors can rival. If you think subtitled films aren't for you, give this delightful love story a try. In Cantonese with English subtitles. Contains drug abuse. [video]

Anita Mui *Fleur* • Leslie Cheung *Chan Chen-Pang* • Alex Man *Yuen* • Emily Chu *Ah Chor* • Irene Wan *Suk-Yin* ■ *Dir* Stanley Kwan • *Scr* Li Bihua, Qiu-Dai Anping, from the novel by Li Bihua

Rouge Baiser ★★★ 15

Drama based on a true story
1985 · Fr · Colour · 108mins

With its faithful re-creation of the atmosphere of Parisian jazz clubs in the early fifties, its perceptive insights into the emotional and intellectual naivety of teenagers, and its inch-perfect performances, this neatly observed, semi-autobiographical film should have been a joy. Charlotte Valandrey plays her heart out as the 15-year-old Communist whose world comes tumbling down with the onset of romance and disturbing news from inside Stalin's empire. But what spoils all the good work is an overindulgence in flashy camerawork by director Véra Belmont that too often distracts from the action without adding anything of dramatic or symbolic significance. In French with English subtitles.

Charlotte Valandrey *Nadia* • Lambert Wilson *Stéphane* • Marthe Keller *Bronka* • Günter Lamprecht *Herschel* • Laurent Terzieff *Moische* ■ *Dir* Véra Belmont • *Scr* Véra Belmont, Guy Konopnicki, David Milhaud

Le Rouge et le Noir ★★★

Period romantic drama
1954 · Fr · Colour · 153mins

Having already headlined Christian-Jaque's *The Charterhouse of Parma* (1948), Gérard Philipe returned to play another Stendahl anti-hero in this pictorialist adaptation of his 1830 novel. Claude Autant-Lara was frequently accused by such critics as François Truffaut for producing "cinéma du papa" or traditionalist narratives that were more literary than filmic. Certainly, for all the surface sheen, a paucity of visual imagination was expended on this tale of the young man who seduces his way up the socio-political ladder. But, then, there's little of the book's biting irony, either, even though the bowdlerising screenplay was penned by adaptation specialists, Jean Aurenche and Pierre Bost. In French with English subtitles.

Gérard Philipe *Julien Sorel* • Danielle Darrieux *Mme Louise de Renal* • Antonella Lualdi *Mathilde de la Mole* • Jean Martinelli *Mons de Renal* • Antoine Balpêtré *Abbé Pirard* • Anna-Maria Sandri *Elisa* • Jean Mercure *Marquis de la Mole* • André Brunot *Abbé Chelan* ■ *Dir* Claude Autant-Lara • *Scr* Jean Aurenche, Pierre Bost, from the novel by Stendhal

The Rough and the Smooth ★★

Erotic thriller 1959 · UK · BW · 99mins

Hollywood director Robert Siodmak, a *film noir* specialist, brought his talents to Britain for this thriller that trades on its steamy sex scenes. Tony Britton stars as an archeologist who has a fling with a shady lady – the alluring Austrian import Nadja Tiller – who plays secretary to rich and ugly William Bendix. A trademark hammy Donald Wolfit represents the gutter press, to which the sordid story is leaked. It's based on a novel by Robin Maugham, and like his better-known novel, *The Servant*, it's intended to show the decadence and corruption that lies at the heart of the British establishment.

Nadja Tiller *Ila Hansen* • Tony Britton *Mike* • William Bendix *Reg Barker* • Norman Wooland *David* • Natasha Parry *Margaret Goreham* • Donald Wolfit *Lord Drewell* • Tony Wright *Jack* • Adrienne Corri *Jane* • Joyce Carey *Mrs Thompson* ■ *Dir* Robert Siodmak • *Scr* Dudley Leslie, Audrey Erskine-Lindop, from the novel by Robin Maugham

Rough Cut ★★★ PG

Crime comedy 1980 · US · Colour · 106mins

Burt Reynolds does his Cary Grant impersonation in a stylish caper comedy where even the criminals have a touch of class. It's a mellow throwback to those elegant light entertainments of the fifties (David Niven adding further nostalgia), and director Don Siegel injects irony and droll humour into a bright and breezy script that gives charming gentleman burglar Reynolds every opportunity to shine. Rather an atypical movie from action man Siegel who was, in fact, fired and rehired during filming. It has an attractively blasé gloss that suits the light-hearted approach perfectly. Contains swearing.

Burt Reynolds *Jack Rhodes* • Lesley-Anne Down *Gillian Bromley* • David Niven *Chief Inspector Cyril Willis* • Timothy West *Nigel Lawton* • Patrick Magee *Ernst Mueller* • Al Matthews *Ferguson* • Susan Littler *Sheila* • Joss Ackland *Inspector Vanderveld* • Isabel Dean *Mrs Willis* ■ *Dir* Don Siegel • *Scr* Francis Burns [Larry Gelbart], from the novel *Touch the Lion's Paw* by Derek Lambert

Rough Diamonds ★★ PG

Romantic comedy
1994 · Ausl · Colour · 84mins

Angie Milliken leaves her successful lawyer husband and takes to the Australian outback road with her daughter to find herself. What she finds instead is cattleman Jason Donovan struggling to make ends meet on the ranch he inherited from his parents. Will his prize bull win the cash jackpot in the Brisbane championship and solve his financial problems? Will Milliken revive her country-and-western singing career? Prize bull indeed, but harmless enough even though the script is depressingly devoid of convincing character development or genuine humour. Soaper-turned-pop star Donovan doesn't have what it takes to avoid all the one-dimensional pitfalls either. Contains some strong language and brief violence.

Jason Donovan *Mike Tyrrell* • Angie Milliken *Chrissie Bright* • Peter Phelps *Dozer Brennan* • Max Cullen *Magistrate Roy* • Haley Toomey *Sam Tyrrell* • Jocelyn Gabriel *Lisa Bright* • Kit Taylor *Les Finnigan* ■ *Dir* Donald Crombie • *Scr* Donald Crombie, Christopher Lee

Rough Magic ★★ 12

Fantasy road movie romance
1995 · Fr/UK · Colour · 100mins

Director Clare Peploe (Mrs Bernardo Bertolucci) wrestles with a mix of genres in the quirky tale of magician's assistant and runaway bride Bridget Fonda, who flees fifties LA for Mexico, pursued by various men including a cynical detective (Russell Crowe) hired by her peeved millionaire fiancé. En route she discovers her genuine magical powers, after getting caught up in the discovery of a miracle elixir and Mayan shamanism. It's an oddball road movie, gumshoe romance and fantasy of magic realism whose clumsy peculiarity doesn't best serve its engaging stars. Contains swearing, sexual references and some violence.

Bridget Fonda *Myra Shumway* • Russell Crowe *Alex Ross* • Kenneth Mars *Magician* • DW Moffett *Cliff Wyatt* • Jim Broadbent *Doc Ansell* • Paul Rodriguez *Diego* ■ *Dir* Clare Peploe • *Scr* Clare Peploe, William Brookfield, Robert Mundy, from the novel *Miss Shumway Waves a Wand* by James Hadley Chase

Rough Night in Jericho ★★

Western 1967 · US · Colour · 103mins

Surprisingly violent (for its day), this Universal western stars an unlikely Dean Martin as the baddie who owns the town of the title and is bent on owning Jean Simmons's stagecoach line and tying up the territory. Ex-marshal George Peppard ain't gonna let him, though, and all hell breaks loose. Although expertly directed by Arnold Laven, both Martin and Peppard look far too urbane for this kind of savage western, and there's really little to recommend here, save for the lovely Simmons, wasted in a thankless role. Contains violence.

Dean Martin *Alex Flood* • George Peppard *Dolan* • Jean Simmons *Molly Lang* • John McIntire *Ben Hickman* • Slim Pickens *Yarbrough* • Don Galloway *Jace* • Brad Weston *Torrey* ■ *Dir* Arnold Laven • *Scr* Sidney Boehm, Marvin H Albert, from the novel *The Man in Black* by Marvin H Albert

Rough Riders' Roundup ★★

Musical western 1939 · US · BW · 58mins

One of eight starring vehicles for Roy Rogers released by Republic in 1939, his second year as a western lead, this features the singing cowboy as a former rough rider in the Spanish-American war who joins the border patrol in the south-west. Between musical interludes, he and sidekicks Raymond Hatton and Eddie Acuff put an end to a spate of gold bullion robberies. Dorothy Sebastian stands out in a small part as a mine foreman's disgruntled girlfriend while Glenn Strange and Duncan Renaldo are among the familiar western faces way down the cast.

Roy Rogers *Roy* • Mary Hart [Lynne Roberts] *Dorothy* • Raymond Hatton *Rusty* • Eddie Acuff *Tommy* • William Pawley *Arizona Jack* • Dorothy Sebastian *Rose* • George Meeker *Lanning* • Jack Rockwell *Harrison* • Glenn Strange *Henchman* ■ *Dir* Joe Kane [Joseph Kane] • *Scr* Jack Natteford, Duncan Renaldo

Rough Shoot ★★★ U

Spy thriller 1952 · UK · BW · 86mins

A postwar lull in Joel McCrea's career found him relegated as happened to most ageing male stars to co-feature westerns, but he still found time to make this interesting thriller in England, a Geoffrey Household spy story scripted by Eric Ambler, which actually has one of the oldest western plots: the hero believes that he has killed someone accidentally. The English period setting affords much pleasure today, with a cast of West End veterans offering sterling support, notably Marius Goring and Roland Culver. Under-rated former editor Robert Parrish does a fine directing job, and became an Anglophile in the process. In America, the movie was retitled *Shoot First*, and did little business.

Joel McCrea *Lt Col Robert Taine* • Evelyn Keyes *Cecily Taine* • Herbert Lom *Peter Sandorski* • Marius Goring *Hiart* • Roland Culver *Randall* • Frank Lawton *Richard Hassingham* • Patricia Laffan *Magda Hassingham* ■ *Dir* Robert Parrish • *Scr* Eric Ambler, from the novel by Geoffrey Household

Roughly Speaking ★★★

Biography 1945 · US · BW · 117mins

This likeable, sprawling account of the life of the engagingly eccentric Louise Randall Pierson, an early exponent of women's lib, covers 40 years of her life in episodic fashion. There are many fine moments here, but Warner Bros possibly erred in allowing Pierson to adapt her own autobiography, for she was by all accounts reluctant to leave anything out. Giving great performances are Rosalind Russell, loaded with grit as the determined wife and mother, and Jack Carson, as her quixotic husband obsessed with get-rich-quick schemes, who buoy the proceedings, as do the ever dependable directon of Michael Curtiz (*Casablanca, Mildred Pierce*) and a charming score by Max Steiner.

Rosalind Russell *Louise Randall* • Jack Carson *Harold Pierson* • Robert Hutton *John, aged 20-28* • Jean Sullivan *Louise Jr, aged 18-26* • Donald Woods *Rodney Crane* • Alan Hale *Mr Morton* • Andrea King *Barbara, aged 21-29* • Ann Doran *Alice Abbott* ■ *Dir* Michael Curtiz • *Scr* Louise Randall Pierson, from her autobiography

Roughshod ★★★

Western 1949 · US · BW · 88mins

A likeable western made with unusual care and intelligence, *Roughshod* is also a curiously modest, small-scale undertaking which failed to make a star out of its leading man, Robert Sterling. With the help of kid brother Claude Jarman Jr, Sterling directs a herd of thoroughbred horses, rescues a troupe of saloon girls, and has a run-in with three vicious outlaws. Gloria Grahame plays the leading floozie with her customary panache while John Ireland makes for a mean killer. Mark Robson's direction is assured but the material would have benefitted from the poetic touch of a John Ford.

Robert Sterling *Clay Phillips* • Gloria Grahame *Mary Wells* • John Ireland *Lednov* • Claude Jarman Jr *Steve Phillips* • Jeff Donnell *Elaine Wyatt* • Myrna Dell *Helen Carter* • Martha Hyer *Marcia* • George Cooper *Jim Clayton* • Jeff Corey *Jed Graham* ■ *Dir* Mark Robson • *Scr* Geoffrey Homes [Daniel Mainwaring], Hugo Butler, from a story by Peter Viertel

Roujin Z ★★★★ 15

Animated thriller 1991 · Jap · Colour · 80mins

Written by Katsuhiro Otomo, who made perhaps the best-known *manga* movie, *Akira*, this animated feature concentrates more on character than on the futuristic concepts and designer violence that tends to dominate the genre. Translating roughly as "Old Man Z", this is primarily a "people versus the powers that be" picture, with a student nurse siding with the elderly when they discover that a luxury bed experiment is the front for more sinister activities. However, it's also a mischievously romantic ghost story and an ironic study of male-female hegemony, while for action fans there's a storming robot battle finale. In Japanese with English subtitles.

Dir Hiroyuki Kitakubo • *Scr* Katsuhiro Otomo, from his story

'Round Midnight ★★★★ 15

Musical drama
1986 · US/Fr · Colour · 125mins

According to cinematic formula, when they're not living in poverty until the world finally tunes in to their unique style, jazz musicians are on the skids, playing great music through a drug or booze-induced haze. Bertrand Tavernier's superb film is of this school, but has none of the glib clichés of the Hollywood jazz movie. This is a harrowing and truthful study of talent suffocating under the pressures of creativity. Film debutant and jazz veteran Dexter Gordon earned an Oscar nomination for his remarkable performance, while Herbie Hancock's Oscar-winning soundtrack will send shivers down your spine. Contains swearing.

Dexter Gordon *Dale Turner* • François Cluzet *Francis Borier* • Gabrielle Haker *Bérangère* • Sandra Reaves-Phillips *Buttercup* • Lonette McKee *Darcey Leigh* • Christine Pascal *Sylvie* • Herbie Hancock *Eddie Wayne* • Bobby Hutcherson *Ace* ■ *Dir* Bertrand Tavernier • *Scr* Bertrand Tavernier, David Rayfiel, from the lives of Francis Paudras, Bud Powell

Round Trip to Heaven ★★ 15

Comedy adventure
1992 · US · Colour · 92mins

Co-scripted by Shuki Levy, who had a hand in the *Power Rangers* franchise, this is a slightly more grown-up but equally brainless teen comedy. Corey Feldman and Zach Galligan play two lazy chums who get into all sorts of trouble when they borrow a Rolls-Royce belonging to villain Ray Sharkey for a weekend break. There's a lot of mindless slapstick and the usual obsession with beer and babes, none of which raises more than the occasional chuckle.

Corey Feldman *Larry* • Ray Sharkey *Stoneface* • Zach Galligan *Steve* • Julie McCullough *Lucille* • Rowanne Brewer *April* • Lloyd Battista *Mike* • Joey Travolta *Ed* • Shuki Levy *2nd Man* ■ *Dir* Alan Roberts • *Scr* Shuki Levy, Winston Richards

The Round-Up ★★★★★★

Historical drama   1966 · Hun · BW · 84mins

Set during the 1848 revolution against Hapsburg imperialism, Miklós Jancsó's dispassionate depiction of the mechanics of power and the vulnerability underlying even the most heroic resistance has powerful contemporary resonance. Just as no concession is made by the sadistic police to the peasants trapped inside an isolated stockade, so none is made to the viewer, who is presented with geometrical arrangements of oppressors and victims instead of tangible heroes and villains. The refusal to surrender the rebels testifies to the indomitability of the human spirit, but the film's chilling conclusion, as the Austrians triumph, is that totalitarianism can be ruthlessly effective. In Hungarian with English subtitles.

János Görbe *János Gajdor* • Tibor Molnár *Kabai* • István Avar *1st interrogator* • Lajos Oze *2nd interrogator* ■ *Dir* Miklós Jancsó • *Scr* Gyula Hernádi

The Rounders ★★★ U

Comedy drama   1965 · US · Colour · 84mins

An amiable comedy western, pairing two of the screen's most watchable veterans, Glenn Ford and Henry Fonda, with a determined horse. The film is basically a series of incidents, affectionately directed by cowboy specialist Burt Kennedy and featuring a nice line in very sixties risqué humour. In the UK this went out as a co-feature, but, although MGM did little to promote it, the movie proved to be a nice little earner for the studio. No great surprises, but very pleasant viewing. Contains some swearing. ▭

Glenn Ford *Ben Jones* • Henry Fonda *Howdy Lewis* • Sue Anne Langdon [Sue Ane Langdon] *Mary* • Hope Holiday *Sister* • Chill Wills *Jim Ed Love* • Edgar Buchanan *Vince Moore* • Kathleen Freeman *Agatha Moore* • Joan Freeman *Meg Moore* • Denver Pyle *Bull* • Barton MacLane *Tanner* ■ *Dir* Burt Kennedy • *Scr* Burt Kennedy, from the novel by Max Evans

Rounders ★★★ 15

Drama   1998 · US · Colour · 115mins

A stroll – not even a fast walk – on the wild side of gambling, with Matt Damon as the legal student-turned-poker player who keeps his cards – and his emotions – close to his chest, which means that there's very little on view that hits the dramatic jackpot. The theme of the gambler trying to defeat his addiction is old hat and this never really overcomes its hackneyed origins. A major disappointment from director John Dahl, whose superb *The Last Seduction* established the vogue for "nouveau" film noir. Contains swearing, some violence and a sex scene. ▭

Matt Damon *Mike McDermott* • Edward Norton *Worm* • John Turturro *Joey Kinish* • Gretchen Mol *Jo* • Famke Janssen *Petra* • John Malkovich *Teddy KGB* • Martin Landau *Abe Petrovsky* • Josh Mostel *Zagosh* ■ *Dir* John Dahl • *Scr* David Levien, Brian Koppelman

The Roundup ★★★

Western   1941 · US · BW · 90mins

A fascinating western from one of the great unsung directors of the genre, Lesley Selander, whose credits number over a hundred and who finished his career making segments of *Laramie* for TV. However, this is primarily a melodrama about an interrupted wedding, which could have done with a little more blood and thunder in the styling. It's interesting from the off, though, with Patricia Morison's former fiancé Preston Foster turning up when she is about to marry Richard Dix. Not bad, but more forceful direction would have helped.

Richard Dix *Steve* • Patricia Morison *Janet* • Preston Foster *Greg* • Don Wilson *Slim* • Ruth Donnelly *Polly* • Betty Brewer *Mary* • Douglass Dumbrille *Captain Lane* ■ *Dir* Lesley Selander • *Scr* Harold Shumate, from a story by Edmund Day

Roustabout ★★★ U

Musical   1964 · US · Colour · 95mins

Elvis films are basically unashamed reconstituted fluff, plus songs and girls with curiously pointed breasts. Chirpy but very silly, *Roustabout* sticks firmly to tradition with Elvis playing the role of a mean, moody general handyman, embittered orphan and karate expert with a very large motorcycle. Barbara Stanwyck plays the fairground owner as if on autopilot, and this time the girl is Joan Freeman as her deeply smitten daughter. Very daft, very immature and great fun. ▭

Elvis Presley *Charlie Rogers* • Barbara Stanwyck *Maggie Morgan* • Joan Freeman *Cathy Lean* • Leif Erickson *Joe Lean* • Sue Ann Langdon [Sue Ane Langdon] *Madame Mijanou* • Pat Buttram *Harry Carver* • Joan Staley *Marge* • Raquel Welch ■ *Dir* John Rich • *Scr* Paul Nathan, Anthony Lawrence, Allan Weiss, from a story by Allan Weiss

Route 9 ★★

Crime drama   1998 · US · Colour · 105mins

Two backwoods cops discover several corpses and a bag containing $1.5 million. When one of the corpses proves to be somewhat lively, they finish him off and bury the loot, planning to start spending when the heat dies down. But things gets spectacularly unglued: the authorities arrive and our lads discover that the man they finished off was in fact a federal undercover agent. While the relentless twistiness of the script is admirable, this thriller really needs gutsier direction and a better cast: Kyle MacLachlan's glacial personality may have worked well in *Blue Velvet* but it's a drawback here.

Kyle MacLachlan *Booth Parker* • Peter Coyote *Dwayne Hogan* • Amy Locane *Sally Hogan* • Roma Maffia *Ellen Marks* ■ *Dir* David Mackay • *Scr* Brendan Broderick, Rob Kerchner

The Rover ★★

Historical war drama
1967 · It · Colour · 103mins

This slow adventure, based on Joseph Conrad's minor novel, finds Anthony Quinn as a piratical rebel in the Napoleonic Wars. He is drawn to a mentally ill young woman, but she is fond of an officer in the French navy. Not lively enough in the action sequences and not intelligent enough in the dialogue, but it's unusual enough to be watchable. Directed by Shanghai-born British director Terence Young between his hits *Thunderball* and *Wait Until Dark*.

Anthony Quinn *Peyrol* • Rosanna Schiaffino *Arlette* • Rita Hayworth *Aunt Caterina* • Richard Johnson *Real* • Ivo Garrani *Scevola* ■ *Dir* Terence Young • *Scr* Luciano Vincenzoni, Jo Eisinger, from the novel by Joseph Conrad

Rover Dangerfield ★★ U

Animated comedy
1991 · US · Colour · 70mins

Did somebody really think the world needed a movie that featured a cartoon dog with the voice and likeness of Rodney Dangerfield? And if such a movie had to be made, whose idea was it to let Dangerfield sing? Somebody threw a fair amount of money at this animated story of a wise-cracking Las Vegas dog named Rover who is separated from his showgirl owner and forced to live on a farm. But the animation is nothing special and Dangerfield's schtick doesn't get any funnier just because it's coming from a canine. ▭

Rodney Dangerfield *Rover* • Susan Boyd *Daisy* • Dana Hill *Danny* • Sal Landi *Rocky* • Ned Luke *Raffles* ■ *Dir* James George, Robert Seeley • *Scr* Rodney Dangerfield, from a story by Rodney Dangerfield, Harold Ramis

A Row of Crows ★★ 15

Thriller   1991 · US · Colour · 98mins

It's mismatched policemen again in this tough mystery thriller, as big city cop Steven Bauer gets sent to Arizona to team up with local sheriff John Beck. As they squabble about various police matters, they have to try to solve the murder of a young woman who is found decapitated in the desert. Fairly standard crime fare, boasting a decidedly ropey script and an unusual role for Katharine Ross as a hard-drinking coroner. Contains swearing, violence, sex scenes and nudity. ▭

John Beck *Kyle Shipp* • Katharine Ross *Grace Hines* • Mia Sara *Elise Shipp* • Steven Bauer *Paul McGraw* • Dedee Pfeiffer *Donna* • John Diehl *Wayne Paris* ■ *Dir/Scr* JS Cardone

Rowing with the Wind ★★

Romantic melodrama
1987 · Sp/Nor · Colour · 126mins

The double-act of Hugh Grant and Elizabeth Hurley has shared many a tabloid headline since this somewhat dazed account of how *Frankenstein* came to be written – not that Hurley has much of a role. Grant, though, is at his least flustered and thus most convincing in this peculiar production, as Mary Shelley recalls events from a ship sailing around the Arctic. Director Gonzalo Suarez takes a sometimes surreal advantage of a situation that was more gruesomely exploited by Ken Russell's *Gothic*.

Hugh Grant *Lord Byron* • Lizzy McInnerny *Mary Shelley* • Elizabeth Hurley *Claire Clairmont* • Valentine Pelka *Percy Bysshe Shelley* • Jose Luis Gomez *Polidori* • Virginia Mataix *Elisa* • Ronan Vibert *Fletcher* • Jose Carlos Rivas *Creature* ■ *Dir/Scr* Gonzalo Suarez

Roxanne ★★★★ PG

Romantic comedy
1987 · US · Colour · 102mins

This is surely the pinnacle of Steve Martin's career so far. Nimbly adapted by Martin himself (for which he won the American Writers' Guild prize) from the celebrated Edmond Rostand play *Cyrano de Bergerac*, this is romantic comedy as it is used to be, with Martin playing CD Bales, the nasally gifted fire chief who falls for heavenly stargazer Daryl Hannah. Directed by Fred Schepisi, *Roxanne* is remarkably faithful to Rostand's original work, cleverly transplanting the action from 17th-century Paris to present-day small-town America, and imbuing the sensitive CD Bales with considerable duelling skills. From the moment he swashbuckles with a tennis racket, it's clear Martin is on peak form, acquitting himself during the hilarious nose-jokes sequence. Schepisi keeps the action as buoyant as Martin's performance, while also coaxing a deliciously doltish turn from Rick Rossovich, who woos Hannah using Martin's eloquence. ▭ *DVD*

Steve Martin *CD Bales* • Daryl Hannah *Roxanne Kowalski* • Rick Rossovich *Chris* • Shelley Duvall *Dixie* • John Kapelos *Chuck* • Fred Willard *Mayor Deebs* • Max Alexander *Dean* • Michael J Pollard *Andy* ■ *Dir* Fred Schepisi • *Scr* Steve Martin, from the play *Cyrano de Bergerac* by Edmond Rostand

Roxanne: the Prize Pulitzer ★★

Drama based on a true story
1989 · US · Colour · 97mins

It's nowhere near as trashy as it should be, but this true story still provides some tabloid-style fun. Richard Colla's film tracks the romance between the young Roxanne Ulrich and Herbert Pulitzer, heir to a publishing fortune, and their subsequent scandalous separation hearings. Chynna Phillips and Perry King are the bland leads; *Friends* star Courteney Cox pops up in a supporting role. Contains swearing.

Chynna Phillips *Roxanne Pulitzer* • Perry King *Herbert Pulitzer* • Courteney Cox *Jacquie Kimberly* • Caitlin Brown *Lorraine Odasso* • Betsy Russell *Liza Pulitzer* ■ *Dir* Richard Colla [Richard A Colla] • *Scr* Elizabeth Gill, Roxanne Pulitzer, from the autobiography by Roxanne Pulitzer

Roxie Hart ★★★★

Crime comedy   1942 · US · BW · 74mins

Terrifically hard-boiled and funny Ginger Rogers vehicle, based on Maurine Watkins's famous play *Chicago*, first filmed in 1928 with Phyllis Haver, and recently reworked by Bob Fosse as a stunning Broadway musical under the original title. There's a crackling script, a magnificent picture-stealing performance from Adolphe Menjou and some super by-play from the supporting cast. Rogers simply scintillates as the on-trial heroine of the title, and, if William A Wellman's direction isn't quite spot-on (if ever a movie needed Howard Hawks, it was this one), or if George Montgomery is a colourless leading man, it doesn't really matter. By now *Roxie Hart* should have achieved minor classic status, and is always a treat to watch.

Ginger Rogers *Roxie Hart* • Adolphe Menjou *Billy Flynn* • George Montgomery *Homer Howard* • Lynne Overman *Jake Callahan* • Nigel Bruce *E Clay Benham* • Phil Silvers *Babe* • Sara Allgood *Mrs Morton* • William Frawley *O'Malley* • Spring Byington *Mary Sunshine* ■ *Dir* William Wellman [William A Wellman] • *Scr* Nunnally Johnson, from the play *Chicago* by Maurine Watkins

Royal Affairs in Versailles ★★★

Historical drama 1953 · Fr · Colour · 165mins

In its day, this was one of the most lavish and expensive French films ever made, a three-hour, all-star evocation of the reigns of three men named Louis – XIV, XV and XVI – and their little cottage outside Paris called Versailles. The director, Sacha Guitry – an alleged Nazi collaborator – himself plays Louis XIV and gets the lion's share of scenes, supported by a gallery of French stars who perform with a lot of pomp and pompadour. Hollywood queen Claudette Colbert (born in Paris in 1905) makes an appearance as do Orson Welles as American President Benjamin Franklin and, briefly, songbird Edith Piaf. In French with English subtitles.

Claudette Colbert *Madame de Montespan* • Sacha Guitry *Louis XIV* • Orson Welles *Benjamin Franklin* • Jean-Pierre Aumont *Cardinal de Rohan* • Edith Piaf *Woman of the People* • Gérard Philipe *D'Artagnan* • Micheline Presle *Madame du Pompadour* • Jean Marais *Louis XV* • Gilbert Boka *Louis XVI* • Brigitte Bardot *Mademoiselle de Rosille* ■ *Dir/Scr* Sacha Guitry

The Royal Family of Broadway ★★ [U]

Comedy 1930 · US · BW · 106mins

Said to be loosely modelled on the Barrymore dynasty, this once relevant attempt at some kind of satirical comedy is now largely a monumental bore. Fredric March was Oscar-nominated for his performance as the wayward matinée idol son of dowager trouper Henrietta Crosman, but that honour should have gone to Ina Claire as his actress sister who, like her own daughter, is briefly torn between career and personal happiness. Although intermittently amusing, and certainly a confirmation that an acting obsession is an incurable illness, it's painfully stagey. The snail's-pace direction is by George Cukor and Cyril Gardner.

Ina Claire *Julia Cavendish* • Fredric March *Tony Cavendish* • Mary Brian *Gwen Cavendish* • Henrietta Crosman *Fanny Cavendish* • Charles Starrett *Perry Stewart* • Arnold Korff *Oscar Wolff* ■ *Dir* George Cukor, Cyril Gardner • *Scr* Herman Mankiewicz, Gertrude Purcell, from the play by George S Kaufman, Edna Ferber

Royal Flash ★★ [15]

Comedy adventure
1975 · UK · Colour · 97mins

Author George MacDonald Fraser's series of novels featuring a grown-up Harry Flashman, the bully from *Tom Brown's Schooldays*, were fun, but the character doesn't survive the transition to film. Fraser had worked on the screenplay of director Richard Lester's *Three Musketeers*, but that film has a far stronger cast than this one. As Flashman, Malcolm McDowell lacks the necessary public school veneer and, despite effective support from the likes of Alan Bates (who would have been better cast in the lead role) and Oliver Reed (ditto), it's really hard to care what happens to him. [video]

Malcolm McDowell *Captain Harry Flashman* • Alan Bates *Rudi von Starnberg* • Florinda Bolkan *Lola Montez* • Oliver Reed *Otto von Bismarck* • Britt Ekland *Duchess Irma of Strakenz* • Lionel Jeffries *Kraftstein* • Tom Bell *de Gautet* • Joss Ackland *Sapten* • Christopher Cazenove *Eric Hansen* • Roy Kinnear *Old roué* • Alastair Sim *Mr Greig* • Michael Hordern *Headmaster* ■ *Dir* Richard Lester • *Scr* George MacDonald Fraser, from his novel

The Royal Hunt of the Sun ★★★ [U]

Historical drama
1969 · UK/US · Colour · 121mins

Peter Shaffer's play is made over, in rather skeletal fashion, into a duet for two egoes as Spanish conquistador Pizarro (Robert Shaw) embarks on his South American trek to conquer the Inca god-king, Atahualpa (Christopher Plummer) for the gold he thinks the Incas have. Directed by Irving Lerner, this is surprisingly stagey and static although the acting is extraordinarily powerful.

Robert Shaw *Francisco Pizarro* • Christopher Plummer *Atahualpa* • Nigel Davenport *Hernando De Soto* • Leonard Whiting *Young Martin* • Michael Craig *Estete* • Andrew Keir *Valverde* • James Donald *King Carlos V* ■ *Dir* Irving Lerner • *Scr* Philip Yordan, from the play by Peter Shaffer

A Royal Scandal ★★

Period biographical comedy
1945 · US · Colour · 93mins

Alexei (William Eythe), a young soldier passionately loyal to Catherine the Great (Tallulah Bankhead), arrives at court as her self-appointed protector, but finds himself dangerously out of his depth when the empress falls for his charms. A sporadically entertaining but silly and antediluvian period comedy, produced by Ernst Lubitsch but directed by Otto Preminger without any of the sophisticated Lubitsch touches it badly needs. Bankhead is good; so are Charles Coburn as her chancellor and Anne Baxter as the lady-in-waiting, who is also Eythe's fiancé. Released as *Czarina* in the UK.

Tallulah Bankhead *Czarina Catherine the Great* • Charles Coburn *Chancellor Nicolai Ilyitch* • Anne Baxter *Countess Anna Jaschikoff* • William Eythe *Lt Alexei Chernoff* • Vincent Price *Marquis de Fleury* • Mischa Auer *Captain Sukov* • Sig Ruman *General Ronsky* ■ *Dir* Otto Preminger • *Scr* Edwin Justis Mayer, Bruno Frank, from the play *The Czarina* by Lajos Biró, Melchior Lengyel

Royal Wedding ★★★ [U]

Musical comedy 1951 · US · Colour · 89mins

Here's a totally delightful oddity: a topical MGM musical, timed to chime in with the wedding of then Princess Elizabeth and Prince Philip, and actually incorporating library footage. Choreographer-turned-director Stanley Donen makes the most of his solo directing debut, despite an over-dependence on English stereotypes and fake fog. Donen has the inestimable benefit of the great Fred Astaire in the leading role, who furnishes his director with the movie's highlight, an incredible routine in which he dances effortlessly up the walls and on the ceiling of his room. A charming musical from a Hollywood studio at its height. [video]

Fred Astaire *Tom Bowen* • Jane Powell *Ellen Bowen* • Peter Lawford *Lord John Brindale* • Sarah Churchill *Anne Ashmond* • Keenan Wynn *Irving Klinger/Edgar Klinger* • Albert Sharpe *James Ashmond* ■ *Dir* Stanley Donen • *Scr* Alan Jay Lerner

Royce ★★ [15]

Spoof spy thriller 1994 · US · Colour · 93mins

James Belushi is at his best portraying slightly seedy characters – in *K9*, for instance – so he's less than convincing here playing a spy in the James Bond mould. He does well enough in this romp, however, making a decent fist of his role as a laid-back secret agent. Director Rod Holcomb ensures there are plenty of set pieces to take one's mind off the silly plot involving renegade agents and stolen nuclear weapons and he makes good use of an experienced support cast that includes Miguel Ferrer, Peter Boyle and Anthony Head. Contains swearing, violence and some nudity. [video]

James Belushi *Shayne Royce* • Miguel Ferrer *Gribbon* • Peter Boyle *Huggins* • Chelsea Field *Marnie* • Michael J Shannon *Senator Scanlon* ■ *Dir* Rod Holcomb • *Scr* Paul Bernbaum

Rubdown ★★★ [15]

Thriller 1993 · US · Colour · 87mins

This is an enjoyably convoluted, semi-erotic TV thriller, which served as a reunion of sorts for some familiar faces from the *Dynasty/Dallas/Knots Landing* era, including Catherine Oxenberg and Michelle Phillips. Jack Coleman (who starred as Steven in *Dynasty* after the plastic surgery) plays a down-on-his-luck masseur who is offered $50,000 by millionaire William Devane (who numbers *Knots Landing* among his credits) to sleep with his wife so Devane can get away with a cheap divorce. However, when Devane turns up dead, Coleman becomes the chief suspect. There are enough sharp twists in the plot to keep you hooked and Stuart Cooper keeps the story bustling along. [video]

Jack Coleman *Marion Pooley* • Michelle Phillips *Jordonna* • William Devane *Harry Orwitz* • Catherine Oxenberg *Jordy/Natalie Browning* • Alan Thicke *Raymond Holliman* • Kent Williams *Detective Armstrong* ■ *Dir* Stuart Cooper • *Scr* Clyde Allen Hayes

Rubin & Ed ★★★

Road movie comedy drama
1991 · UK · Colour · 82mins

This unconventional road movie features one of cinema's oddest characters, Rubin Farr (Crispin Glover), a recluse who spends most of his life in a motel room mourning the loss of his cat, whose body lies frozen in the icebox. Prompted by his mother to get out of the house more, Glover meets up with salesman Howard Hesseman, who is trying to bring in clients for an upcoming sales seminar. He agrees to accompany Hesseman to the seminar, but only if the two journey via the desert, where Rubin can bury his beloved cat. Of course things start to go haywire once they hit the road. Decidedly odd but with a certain twisted appeal, it's worth checking out.

Crispin Glover *Rubin Farr* • Howard Hesseman *Ed Tuttle* • Karen Black *Rula* • Michael Greene *Mr Busta* • Brittney Lewis *Poster girl* ■ *Dir/Scr* Trent Harris

Ruby ★★ [15]

Horror 1977 · US · Colour · 163mins

Star Piper Laurie isn't the only reason you'll think of *Carrie* while watching this tall terror tale. She plays an ex-torch singer, now owner of a drive-in movie theatre, whose deaf-mute daughter seems to be linked to a series of mystifying and chilling deaths. It's mainly a mindless muddle, partly owing to a story cobbled together from numerous chiller clichés and also to director Curtis Harrington's replacement during production by Stephanie Rothman. However, Laurie still manages to hold the fifties-set bijou blood bath together by the sheer force of her overpowering acting ability. Contains violence. [video]

Piper Laurie *Ruby Claire* • Stuart Whitman *Vince Kemper* • Roger Davis *Doc Keller* • Janit Baldwin *Leslie Claire* • Crystin Sinclaire *Lila June* • Paul Kent *Louie* • Len Lesser *Barney* ■ *Dir* Curtis Harrington • *Scr* George Edwards, Barry Schneider, from a story by Steve Krantz

Ruby ★★★ [15]

Crime drama 1992 · US · Colour · 105mins

Danny Aiello, one of America's best big-screen brooders, leaps at the complexity of Jack Ruby, the man who shot alleged Kennedy assassin Lee Harvey Oswald, and so creates maximum energy from Ruby's insecurity, arrogance and morose, haunted nature. John MacKenzie, who directed *The Long Good Friday*, returns with something of the same raw power, and sensibly skews his film in the direction of a character piece, which helps it transcend the largely fictionalised and sometimes fuzzy plot. Released too close to Oliver Stone's fascinating *JFK* to avoid comparison, *Ruby* is still an interesting take on events, made as it was just before the 30th anniversary of Kennedy's death. Contains violence and swearing. [video]

Danny Aiello *Jack Ruby* • Sherilyn Fenn *Sheryl Ann Dujean/"Candy Cane"* • Frank Orsatti *Action Jackson* • Jeffrey Nordling *Hank* • Jane Hamilton *Telephone Trixie* • Maurice Bernard *Diego* • Joe Cortese *Louie Vitali* • Marc Lawrence *Santos Alicante* • Arliss Howard *Maxwell* • David Duchovny *Officer Tippit* ■ *Dir* John Mackenzie • *Scr* Stephen Davis, from his play *Love Field*

Ruby and Rata ★★★

Comedy drama 1990 · NZ · Colour · 111mins

Yvonne Lawley and Vanessa Rare turn in spirited performances as, respectively, the elderly Auckland suburbanite and the Maori dole scrounger whose feud takes an unexpected turn thanks to Rare's tearaway son, Lee Mete-Kingi. Originally conceived by director Gaylene Preston as a TV series, the film suffers slightly from some underdrawn secondary characters. However, it doesn't hold back in its consideration

1216

[U] = SUITABLE FOR ALL [Uc] = SUITABLE FOR ALL, ESPECIALLY FOR YOUNG CHILDREN (VIDEO ONLY) [PG] = PARENTAL GUIDANCE

of such topics as middle-class snobbery, the iniquities of the social security system and anti-Maori prejudice. Contains swearing.

Yvonne Lawley *Ruby* • Vanessa Rare *Rata* • Lee Mete-kingi *Willie* • Simon Barnett *Buckle* ■ *Dir* Gaylene Preston • *Scr* Graeme Tetley

Ruby Cairo ★★ 15

Mystery 1992 · US/Jap · Colour · 105mins

Gone are the days when a little globetrotting could transport audiences away from their daily routine and into a world of adventure and romance. Sadly, director Graeme Clifford seems convinced that all he has to do to keep us on the edge of our seats is to whisk Andie MacDowell across three continents in search of the clues that will explain the disappearance of errant husband Viggo Mortensen. This is never a dull film, with MacDowell conveying vulnerability and tenacity in just the right measures, but you can't quite believe in her love either for naughty Morty or for hunky charity worker Liam Neeson. Released in America as *Deception*. Contains swearing and nudity. 🖭

Andie MacDowell *Bessie Faro* • Liam Neeson *Fergus Lamb* • Jack Thompson *Ed* • Viggo Mortensen *Johnny* • Paul Spencer *Young Johnny* • Chad Power *Niles Faro* • Monica Mikala *Alexandria Faro* ■ *Dir* Graeme Clifford • *Scr* Robert Dillon, Michael Thomas, from a story by Robert Dillon

Ruby Gentry ★★★ PG

Melodrama 1952 · US · BW · 82mins

Hot 'n' steamy southern melodrama reuniting the star and director of that torrid classic *Duel in the Sun*, Jennifer Jones and King Vidor. Ruby Gentry is quite the seductive equal of the former film's Pearl Chavez, setting her cap at Charlton Heston and marrying Karl Malden to spite him. This is a classic of melodrama, unintentionally hilarious or totally turgid depending on your point of view. Jones is amazingly sexy, clad in the clingiest of jeans, but Heston looks more perplexed than enamoured, and perhaps Clark Gable or Robert Mitchum might have propelled the movie on to those wilder shores of lust that it obviously seeks to embrace. For lovers of Hollywood at its most baroque, this is a real one-off. 🖭

Jennifer Jones *Ruby Gentry* • Charlton Heston *Boake Tackman* • Karl Malden *Jim Gentry* • Tom Tully *Jud Corey* • Bernard Phillips *Dr Saul Manfred* • James Anderson *Jewel Corey* • Josephine Hutchinson *Letitia Gentry* ■ *Dir* King Vidor • *Scr* Sylvia Richards, from a story by Arthyr Fitz-Richard

Ruby in Paradise ★★★★ 15

Drama 1993 · US · Colour · 114mins

A gentle, if at times bordering on the comatose, little elegy to finding oneself, starring Ashley Judd in a debut performance of engaging clarity. Writer/director Victor Nunez does a sterling job with a budget that wouldn't keep the likes of Sharon Stone in mineral water for a week, neatly blending Judd's home territory of Tennessee with the laid-back freedoms of her chosen Florida beach community without resorting to either redneck or post-hippie clichés. As usual with such

small American independent movies, this suffered from lack of marketing when it was released and undeservedly disappeared without trace. Contains swearing, sex scenes and nudity. 🖭

Ashley Judd *Ruby Lee Gissing* • Todd Field *Mike McCaslin* • Bentley Mitchum *Ricky Chambers* • Allison Dean *Rochelle Bridges* • Dorothy Lyman *Mildred Chambers* • Betsy Douds *Debrah Ann* • Felicia Hernandez *Persefina* ■ *Dir/Scr* Victor Nunez

Ruby Jean and Joe ★★★

Drama 1996 · US · Colour · 99mins

This amiable but unremarkable road movie was produced by Tom Selleck, who also stars as a world-weary rodeo rider whose friendship with a black hitcher ruffles a few feathers as they cross the American south-west. Selleck doesn't quite have the depth to convince in a role demanding this level of soul-searching, so he simply pours on the macho charm and makes the most of the wry humour. Rebekah Johnson gives a good account of herself as the strong-willed Ruby Jean and there's typically solid support from JoBeth Williams and Ben Johnson.

Tom Selleck *Joe* • Rebekah Johnson *Ruby Jean* • JoBeth Williams *Rose* • Ben Johnson *Big Man* • Eileen Seeley *Margaret Johnson* • John Diehl *Harris Johnson* ■ *Dir* Geoffrey Sax • *Scr* James Lee Barrett

Rude ★★★ 18

Drama 1995 · Can · Colour · 85mins

Like *Short Cuts*, *Magnolia* and countless other examples, the enigmatically titled *Rude* follows the indy-spirited route of intertwined tales of urban angst. Writer/director Clément Virgo's Toronto-set drama finds a woman trying to come to terms with a break-up, a decidely straight-acting athlete with doubts about his sexuality, and an ex-con resisting temptations to get back in the drug dealing business. A low-profile cast do justice to this nicely directed, predominantly black Canadian effort. 🖭

Maurice Dean Wint *The General* • Rachael Crawford *Maxine* • Clark Johnson *Reece* • Richard Chevolleau *Jordan* • Sharon M Lewis *Rude* • Melanie Nicholls-King *Jessica* ■ *Dir/Scr* Clément Virgo

Rude Awakening ★★ 15

Comedy 1989 · US · Colour · 96mins

One of a series of Rip Van Winkle comedies made in recent years. Here, Eric Roberts and Cheech Marin haven't exactly been sleeping between the sixties and the eighties – they've been living in a South American commune. When they return to America, they discover life has moved on and – shock, horror– their former pals are yuppies. Nice idea, but this is silly rather than comical, and the jokes are hammered home far too hard by heavy-handed directors Aaron Russo and David Greenwalt. Contains some swearing. 🖭

Eric Roberts *Fred* • Richard "Cheech" Marin *Hesus* • Petra Hagerty *Julie* • Robert Carradine *Sammy* • Buck Henry *Lloyd* • Louise Lasser *Ronnie* • Cindy Williams *June* • Andrea Martin *April* • Cliff De Young *Brubaker* ■ *Dir* Aaron Russo, David Greenwalt • *Scr* Neil Levy, Richard LaGravenese, from a story by Neil Levy

Rude Boy ★★ 18

Music documentary drama 1980 · UK · Colour · 127mins

A muddled blend of documentary footage and part-improvised, part-scripted scenes, this concert drama revolves around the trials and tribulations of sex shop salesman Ray Gange (the Rude Boy of the title) employed by the Clash as their roadie in Scotland around the time of their second album *Give 'Em Enough Rope*. Teeming with unconvincing political sermonising and paying lip service to the social and racist issues of the day, the well-staged performances of *London's Burning*, *I Fought the Law* and *All the Young Punks* (shown being recorded by nervous singer Joe Strummer) make this anti-establishment comic book more memorable than it deserves to be. 🖭

Ray Gange *Ray* • John Green *Road manager* ■ *Dir* Jack Hazan, David Mingay • *Scr* Jack Hazan, David Mingay, Ray Gange

Rudy ★★ PG

Sports biography 1993 · US · Colour · 109mins

Director David Anspaugh made his name with the gritty if over-rated basketball drama *Hoosiers*, and he's back battling for the underdog in this less than convincing American football feature that's based on a true story. Sean Austin plays the pint-sized gridiron fanatic who is determined to play for a college team, despite the lack of encouragement from the sporting establishment and his parents. Austin is adequate and he has effective support from the likes of Ned Beatty, and youngsters Jon Favreau (*Swingers*) and Lili Taylor (*The Haunting*). However, at times it is both overly sentimental and unintentionally funny. Contains swearing. 🖭

Sean Astin *Rudy* • Jon Favreau *D-Bob* • Ned Beatty *Daniel* • Greta Lind *Mary* • Scott Benjaminson *Frank* • Mary Ann Thebus *Betty* • Charles S Dutton *Fortune* • Lili Taylor *Sherry* ■ *Dir* David Anspaugh • *Scr* Angelo Pizzo

Rudyard Kipling's The Jungle Book ★★★ PG

Drama 1994 · US · Colour · 119mins

This live-action rumble-in-the-jungle version of the story of Mowgli, the boy brought up to adulthood by wolves, may lack the songs and the magic, but it is closer to Kipling's original tale than was the classic feature-length cartoon. Jason Scott Lee is very effective as the wolf-man battling villain Cary Elwes for the treasure buried beneath the lost city. The animal training is extraordinary, and John Cleese's regular appearances add a much-needed lightness to the tale: he even gets to mention "the bare necessities" without a glimmer of Pythonesque irony. 🖭 **DVD**

Jason Scott Lee *Mowgli* • Cary Elwes *Captain Boone* • Lena Headey *Kitty Brydon* • Sam Neill *Major Brydon* • John Cleese *Doctor Plumford* • Jason Flemyng *Wilkins* • Stefan Kalipha *Buldeo* ■ *Dir* Stephen Sommers • *Scr* Stephen Sommers, Ronald Yanover, Mark D Geldman, from a story by Ronald Yanover, Mark D Geldman, from the novel by Rudyard Kipling

Rue Cases Nègres ★★★★ PG

Drama 1983 · Fr · Colour · 105mins

Inspired by Joseph Zobel's novel and based on a script she'd been refining since student days, Euzhan Palcy's feature debut is remarkable for her total immersion in its environment and her complete understanding of its characters. Set in a thirties Martinique shantytown abutting a French-run sugar cane plantation, this is no mere rites of passage picture, but an affirmation of the vital part love plays in childhood, even in the midst of oppression and poverty. Winner of the best actress prize at Venice, Darling Legitimus is superb as the proud woman who sacrifices everything for her grandson's education. In French with English subtitles.

Garry Cadenat *Jose* • Darling Legitimus *M'Man Tine* • Douta Seck *Medouze* • Joby Bernabe *Monsieur Saint-Louis* • Francisco Charles *Le Gereur* ■ *Dir* Euzhan Palcy • *Scr* Euzhan Palcy, from the novel by Joseph Zobel

Ruggles of Red Gap ★★★

Silent comedy 1923 · US · BW · 89mins

This earlier version of the classic comedy known best for its 1935 outing with Charles Laughton features Edward Everett Horton as the quintessential British valet whose services are won in a game of poker but who is then whisked away from Europe to the Wild Western town of Red Gap, where he's introduced to the locals as a colonel. Horton, before his trademark of dither took hold and elevated him to a kind of character-actor stardom, is wonderfully funny here, with James Cruze directing the story adapted from Henry Leon Wilson's novel. Bob Hope was to star in yet another version, *Fancy Pants* (1950), but neither he nor Horton are a match for Laughton in the role of the charming Ruggles.

Edward Horton [Edward Everett Horton] "Colonel" Ruggles • Ernest Torrence *Cousin Egbert Floud* • Lois Wilson *Kate Kenner* • Fritzi Ridgeway *Emily Judson* • Charles Ogle *Jeff Tuttle* • Louise Dresser *Mrs Effie Floud* • Anna Lehr *Mrs Belknap-Jackson* • Thomas Holding *Earl of Brinstead* ■ *Dir* James Cruze • *Scr* Walter Woods, Anthony Coldeway, from the novel by Harry Leon Wilson

Ruggles of Red Gap ★★★★★ U

Comedy 1935 · US · BW · 89mins

Charles Laughton is Ruggles, an English butler of impeccable credentials and phlegmatic rectitude, is sold by his titled employer Roland Young to a visiting American couple at the insistence of the pretentious wife Mary Boland. He is taken out west charged with, among other things, making a gentleman out of his employer's husband (Charlie Ruggles). Once there, events take a surprising turn. A brilliant, hilarious and fondly satirical look at Anglo-American relations and culture gaps, faultlessly directed by Leo McCarey with Laughton in masterly form – funny and touching, magnificently suffering the vulgarities that offend his dignity while slowly learning to profit from another way of life and even falling in love (with ZaSu Pitts). Nobody else could have played it, and the Oscar-nominated film itself

could never have emerged with such nuanced perfection in any other era (though its ideas were plundered for Bob Hope and *Fancy Pants* in 1950). The supporting performances are every inch as good as film and star deserve.

Charles Laughton Colonel Marmaduke "Bill" Ruggles • Mary Boland Effie Floud • Charlie Ruggles [Charles Ruggles] Egbert "Sourdough" Floud • ZaSu Pitts Mrs Prunella Judson • Roland Young Earl of Burnstead • Leila Hyams Nell Kenner • Maude Eburne "Ma" Pettingill • Lucien Littlefield Charles Belknap-Jackson ■ Dir Leo McCarey • Scr Walter DeLeon, Harlan Thompson, Humphrey Pearson, from the novel by Harry Leon Wilson

The Rugrats Movie ★★★ 🅤
Animated comedy adventure
1998 · US · Colour · 76mins

Nickelodeon TV favourites the Rugrats get their own movie in this fun feature-length animated adventure featuring, among many, the voices of Tim Curry, Iggy Pop and Whoopi Goldberg. Cute one-year-old Tommy persuades his pals to help him return his newborn brother Dil to the hospital so he can have his parents back all to himself. Of course, their journey doesn't go as planned, and the group end up in a scary forest. There are messages about bravery and friendship here, but they're woven into the fun in a way that won't spoil the enjoyment for the kiddies, while adults will get more than a few laughs out of the Rugrats' adventures, not to mention the scattering of movie homages. ▭

EG Daily [Elizabeth Daily] Tommy Pickles • Christine Cavanaugh Chuckie Finster • Kath Soucie Philip Deville/Lillian Deville/Betty Deville • Melanie Chartoff Didi Pickles/Minka • Phil Proctor Howard Deville/Igor • Cree Summer Susie Carmichael • Busta Rhymes Reptar Wagon • Iggy Pop Newborn baby • Tim Curry Rex Pester • Whoopi Goldberg Ranger Margaret • David Spade Ranger Frank ■ Dir Norton Virgien, Igor Kovalyov • Scr J David Stem, David N Weiss, from characters created by Arlene Klasky, Gabor Csupo, Paul Germain

Rulers of the Sea ★★★ 🅤
Historical drama   1939 · US · BW · 96mins

Glasgow-born Frank Lloyd, a master craftsman who directed the Academy Award-winning *Mutiny on the Bounty* in 1935, returned to the world of ships to make this excellent, reasonably exciting adventure about the building and maiden voyage of the first steamship. Genuine Scotsman Will Fyffe made a rare excursion into Hollywood, while another import – England's Margaret Lockwood, not yet the nation's favourite wicked lady – was paired with Douglas Fairbanks Jr to supply the romantic subplot that leavens the action. A young, unknown Alan Ladd is in the cast.

Douglas Fairbanks Jr Gillespie • Margaret Lockwood Mary Shaw • Will Fyffe John Shaw • George Bancroft James Oliver • Montagu Love Malcolm Grant • Vaughan Glaser Junius Smith • David Torrence Donald Fenton • Lester Matthews Lieutenant Commander Roberts • Alan Ladd Colin Farrell ■ Dir Frank Lloyd • Scr Talbot Jennings, Frank Cavett, Richard Collins

Rules of Engagement ★★ 🄸🄵
Courtroom melodrama
2000 · US · Colour · 127mins

William Friedkin's courtroom melodrama revolves around colonel Samuel L Jackson's decision to fire on a crowd of Arabs storming the US embassy in Yemen. Old comrade-in-arms Tommy Lee Jones reluctantly defends him at his court martial, knowing only too well that Jackson has a tendency to go potty under pressure. A terrific cast is wasted as the two leads duke it out with tough prosecution attorney Guy Pearce. Alas, the film is scuppered by a Vietnam flashback which suggests the stars have not aged a day in 30 years, while the sequences in Yemen show Hollywood has lost none of its appetite for unsavoury stereotypes.

Tommy Lee Jones Col Hays Hodges • Samuel L Jackson Col Terry Childers • Guy Pearce Maj Mark Biggs • Bruce Greenwood National Security Adviser William Sokal • Blair Underwood Captain Lee • Philip Baker Hall Gen H Lawrence Hodges • Anne Archer Mrs Mourain • Ben Kingsley Ambassador Mourain ■ Dir William Friedkin • Scr Stephen Gaghan, from a story by James Webb

The Ruling Class ★★★
Black comedy   1972 · UK · Colour · 154mins

A black-hearted assault on British social institutions and the class system, this boasts moments of cruel comedy and real anger thanks to Peter Medak's inspired direction of Peter Barnes's play. Peter O'Toole stars as the madman who inherits the title of the Earl of Gurney. His relatives – played by a flurry of great character actors from Alastair Sim to Arthur Lowe – then bury their snouts in the trough of expected riches, but O'Toole fools them all: he switches from being Jesus Christ to Jack the Ripper. The film is dated in its approach, though it still has the power to shock, while cynics may claim that the satirical targets are very much alive and well. Contains swearing and nudity.

Peter O'Toole Jack • Alastair Sim Bishop Lampton • Arthur Lowe Tucker • Harry Andrews 13th Earl of Gurney • Coral Browne Lady Claire Gurney • Michael Bryant Dr Herder • Nigel Green McKyle • William Mervyn Sir Charles Gurney • Carolyn Seymour Grace Shelley • James Villiers Dinsdale Gurney • Hugh Burden Matthew Peake • Graham Crowden Truscott • Kay Walsh Mrs Piggot-Jones • Patsy Byrne Mrs Treadwell ■ Dir Peter Medak • Scr Peter Barnes, from his play

Rumba ★★
Romance   1935 · US · BW · 70mins

A moneyed New York society girl meets a Broadway dancer as a result of a duplicated lottery ticket, falls for him and, predictably, steps in to the big number of his new show when his regular partner (Margo) lets him down. Paramount's shamelessly recycled version of the previous year's hugely successful *Bolero*, once again starring George Raft and Carole Lombard but directed by Marion Gering in place of Wesley Ruggles, lacks both the novelty and the enjoyable melodramatics of its predecessor. Not to mention the hypnotic, erotic effect of Ravel's music that lent so much to the first movie.

George Raft Joe Martin • Carole Lombard Diane Harrison • Lynne Overman Flash • Margo Carmelita • Gail Patrick Patsy • Iris Adrian Goldie Allen • Clara Lou Sheridan [Ann Sheridan] Dance girl ■ Dir Marion Gering • Scr Howard J Green, Harry Ruskin, Frank Partos, from an idea by Guy Endore, Seena Owen

Rumble Fish ★★★★ 🄸🄸
Drama   1983 · US · BW and Colour · 90mins

The second of Francis Ford Coppola's youth problem pictures adapted from S E Hinton's popular novels and Matt Dillon's third (*Tex*). Unlike his more conventional *The Outsiders*, this alienated teen allegory finds Coppola pulling out all the stylistic stops. The drama is extremely mannered, and the symbolism a mite overdone, but it's a visually startling knockout, brilliantly filmed in moody black-and-white, with some dashes of colour. Stewart Copeland composed the brooding score. Contains swearing. ▭

Matt Dillon Rusty-James • Mickey Rourke Motorcycle Boy • Diane Lane Patty • Dennis Hopper Father • Diana Scarwid Cassandra • Vincent Spano Steve • Nicolas Cage Smokey • Christopher Penn BJ Jackson • Larry Fishburne [Laurence Fishburne] Midget • Tom Waits Benny ■ Dir Francis Ford Coppola • Scr SE Hinton, Francis Ford Coppola, from the novel by SE Hinton • Cinematographer Stephen H Burum

Rumble in the Bronx ★★★ 🄸🄵
Martial arts crime drama
1996 · HK/US · Colour · 85mins

Clumsily dubbed and with Vancouver standing in for New York, this is a typical Jackie Chan outing, as he joins his uncle and the new owner of his market stall in seeing off a gang of doltish villains. Anita Mui and Françoise Yip are big stars back in Hong Kong, but they are given little room for manoeuvre in this lightweight adventure. As ever, there's plenty of thrilling action, but Chan always manages to invest his set-pieces with an element of balletic humour, so that you feel you are watching violent slapstick rather than an expertly executed martial art. Cantonese dialogue dubbed into English. ▭

Jackie Chan Keung • Anita Mui Elaine • Bill Tung Uncle Bill • Françoise Yip Nancy ■ Dir Stanley Tong • Scr Edward Tang, from a story by Stanley Tong

Rumpelstiltskin ★ 🄸🄸
Fantasy   1986 · US · Colour · 83mins

The bad news is that this dire film based on the Brothers Grimm story was intended as the first of a series of such adaptations aimed at children. The good news is that others in the dozen or so mooted failed to materialise. The adaptation and direction by David Irving is undernourished and he has tried to compensate for over-the-top performances from an international cast (it was filmed in Israel) who flail around in search of a style. ▭

Amy Irving Katie • Clive Revill King Mezzer • Billy Barty Rumpelstiltskin • Priscilla Pointer Queen Grizelda • Robert Symonds Victor, Katie's father • John Moulder-Brown Prince ■ Dir David Irving • Scr David Irving, from the fairy tale by Wilhelm Grimm, Jacob Grimm

Run ★★ 🄸🄵
Action thriller   1991 · US · Colour · 87mins

Patrick Dempsey is one of those actors (like Michael J Fox) who is cursed with looking like the eternal teenager, so this attempt to stretch himself into more adult, serious material was almost doomed to fail before it began. Dempsey is a young college student who inadvertently incurs the wrath of a small-town crime lord and then spends the rest of the film running from assorted hit men and bent policemen. Director Geoff Burrowes appears to be aiming for some sort of cross between a crime thriller and a yuppie-in-peril drama but the end result is convincing as neither, even though he does engineer some slick action sequences. Contains violence. ▭

Patrick Dempsey Charlie Farrow • Kelly Preston Karen Landers • Ken Pogue Matt Halloran • Alan C Peterson Denny Halloran • James Kidnie Sammy • Sean McCann Marv ■ Dir Geoff Burrowes • Scr Dennis Shryack, Michael Blodgett

Run, Angel, Run ★
Drama   1969 · US · Colour · 94mins

This William Smith motorcycle movie would have been better had it been made under the eye of New World or American International Pictures; they would have known that the audience would be expecting action in the middle of the movie. It actually gets to a good start, with turncoat biker Smith fleeing into hiding with his girlfriend after he rats out the gang to a magazine. Once they settle down on a sheep farm, the movie then focuses on their new and tedious ordinary lives, occasionally cutting back to Smith's ex-gang searching for him. The multi-image sequences and some of the camerawork date this more than other motorcycle movies of the period.

William Smith Angel • Valerie Starrett Lauri • Gene Shane Ron • Lee DeBroux Pappy • Eugene Cornelius Space • Paul Harper Chic • Earl Finn Turk • William Bonner Duke ■ Dir Jack Starrett • Scr Jerome Wish, VA Furlong, from a story by Richard Compton

Run for Cover ★★★ 🅤
Western   1955 · US · Colour · 92mins

A wistful, almost elegiac western from director Nicholas Ray which pits an ageing Jimmy Cagney against youthful John Derek. The themes are those of a thousand traditional cowboy films: old man teaches young pup new tricks, young pup goes to the bad, but it's handled so sensitively that one forgets its hackneyed origins. Cagney is understated and effective, Derek holds his own and a fine supporting cast provides sound ballast.

James Cagney Mat Dow • Viveca Lindfors Helga Swenson • John Derek Davey Bishop • Jean Hersholt Mr Swenson • Grant Withers Gentry • Jack Lambert Larsen • Ernest Borgnine Morgan • Ray Teal Sheriff ■ Dir Nicholas Ray • Scr Winston Miller, from a story by Harriet Frank Jr, Irving Ravetch

Run for the Dream: the Gail Devers Story ★★★

Biographical sports drama
1996 · US · Colour · 99mins

A standout debut performance by Charlayne Woodard highlights this inspiring, true sports story of American track star Gail Devers, who overcomes tremendous physical and spiritual hurdles after contracting a thyroid disease. With the support of her coach, Bob Kersee (Louis Gossett Jr), family and friends, she crawls back to win a gold medal in the 1992 Olympic Games. A fine script, insightful direction by Neema Barnette and a cast that includes Robert *Benson* Guillaume, give wings to this televisual account of Devers's plight.

Louis Gossett Jr *Bob Kersee* • Charlayne Woodard *Gail Devers* • Jeffrey D Sams *RJ Hampton* • Tina Lifford *Jackie Joyner-Kersee* • Robert Guillaume *Reverend Devers* • Paula Kelly *Mrs Devers* ■ *Dir* Neema Barnette • *Scr* Scott Abbott, Dianne Houston

Run for the Roses ★★ PG

Drama
1978 · US · Colour · 89mins

This is a shamelessly sentimental story about a boy and his horse. Veteran performers Vera Miles and Stuart Whitman were somehow lured into it – she's a horse fancier whose nephew is a 12-year-old Puerto Rican boy with a lame horse, while Whitman is the boy's stepfather, who beams with pride when the horse is nursed back to health and entered for the Kentucky Derby. Henry Levin, an old-time studio hack, hung up his megaphone after this effort. 🖭

Vera Miles *Clarissa* • Stuart Whitman *Charlie* • Sam Groom *Jim* • Panchito Gomez *Juanito* • Theodore Wilson *[Teddy Wilson] Flash* • Lisa Eilbacher *Carol* ■ *Dir* Henry Levin • *Scr* Joseph G Prieto, Mimi Avins

Run for the Sun ★★

Adventure thriller 1956 · US · Colour · 99mins

Yet another remake of *The Hounds of Zaroff*, sometimes known as *The Most Dangerous Game*. This time disillusioned author Richard Widmark and woman journalist Jane Greer are the human prey hunted down in the jungle by Nazis Trevor Howard and Peter Van Eyck. British director Roy Boulting – making one of his few Hollywood films – piles on the tension with a skilful hand, but this is fairly negligible compensation for what the film could have said about postwar relations.

Richard Widmark *Mike Latimer* • Trevor Howard *Browne* • Jane Greer *Katy Connors* • Peter Van Eyck *Van Anders* • Carlos Henning *Jan* ■ *Dir* Roy Boulting • *Scr* Dudley Nichols, Roy Boulting, from the story *The Most Dangerous Game* by Richard Connell

A Run for Your Money ★★ U

Comedy
1949 · UK · BW · 83mins

Directed by Charles Frend, this is one of the weakest comedies produced by Ealing Studios. Chronicling the misadventures of Welsh miners Donald Houston and Meredith Edwards after they win a day out in London, it is nothing more than a string of cheap jokes at the expense of the naive boys from the Valleys lost in the urban

jungle. It's hard to summon up any interest in Edwards's encounter with harpist Hugh Griffith, while Houston's involvement with con artist Moira Lister similarly tests the patience. More galling than the patronising humour is the waste of Alec Guinness as their journalist guide.

Donald Houston *Dai Jones* • Moira Lister *Jo* • Alec Guinness *Whimple* • Meredith Edwards *Twm Jones* • Hugh Griffith *Huw Price* • Clive Morton *Editor* • Leslie Perrins *Barney* • Joyce Grenfell *Mrs Pargiter* ■ *Dir* Charles Frend • *Scr* Charles Frend, Leslie Norman, Richard Hughes, Diana Morgan, from a story by Clifford Evans

Run Lola Run ★★★★ 15

Crime drama
1998 · Ger · Colour · 80mins

This breathtakingly enjoyable German film is faster than a speeding bullet, with a mind-boggling pace that seizes audiences by the scruff of the neck and forces them along with ruthless momentum. Franka Potente receives a phone call from boyfriend Moritz Bleibtreu, who's left the money he owes the mob on the subway. If it's not delivered, he'll be killed. Can she either find the loot or scrounge it in the short time her boyfriend has left? Director Tom Tykwer pushes cinema to superhuman limits – jump cuts and replays, colour turning to monochrome, action sped to a blur. Like Lola, you end up winded and breathless. Not so much a movie as an obstacle course. In German with English subtitles. Contains swearing and violence. 🖭
DVD

Franka Potente *Lola* • Moritz Bleibtreu *Manni* • Herbert Knaup *Lola's father* • Armin Rohde *Mr Schuster* • Ludger Pistor *Herr Meier* • Suzanne von Borsody *Frau Jäger* • Sebastian Schipper *Mike* • Heino Ferch *Ronnie* ■ *Dir/Scr* Tom Tykwer

Run of the Arrow ★★★★ U

Western
1957 · US · Colour · 85mins

Rod Steiger's least favourite film (he and director Samuel Fuller didn't get on) but the personality clash sparked one of his greatest performances. He's the bigoted southerner who, after the American Civil War, joins the Sioux tribe as a way of getting back at the Yankees. Surviving the torturous initiation rite, he manages to reveal the macho ethic at its most dangerous, while at the same time investing an unlikeable character with a certain naive dignity. Some brutish action is made necessary because of what the tale has to say.

Rod Steiger *O'Meara* • Sarita Montiel *Yellow Moccasin* • Brian Keith *Captain Clark* • Ralph Meeker *Lieutenant Driscoll* • Jay C Flippen *Walking Coyote* • Charles Bronson *Blue Buffalo* • Olive Carey *Mrs O'Meara* ■ *Dir/Scr* Samuel Fuller

The Run of the Country ★★★ 15

Drama
1995 · Ire · Colour · 104mins

Albert Finney gives a towering performance as an Irish policeman trying to cope with his wayward son Matt Keeslar in director Peter Yates's moving drama. Unfortunately, the film's glowing portrayal of the Irish countryside rather softens the rites-of-passage roots of the drama, in which

Keeslar is taught a few hard lessons in life when he falls for Victoria Smurfit, a girl from north of the border. Politics rarely intrude, with Yates more content to explore how a mundane existence in rural Ireland effects the young. It's beautiful to look at, but ultimately too nice for its own good, though Finney's commanding presence makes this well worth watching. 🖭

Albert Finney *Father* • Matt Keeslar *Danny* • Victoria Smurfit *Annagh* • Anthony Brophy *Prunty* • David Kelly *Father Gaynor* • Dearbhla Molloy *Mother* ■ *Dir* Peter Yates • *Scr* Shane Connaughton, from his novel

Run, Rebecca, Run ★★★

Adventure 1981 · Ausl · Colour · 80mins

Short, sharp action adventure, about a young girl who falls into the hands of an illegal immigrant hiding out on a remote Australian island. Captive becomes captivated, and she winds up working with him to persuade the Aussie authorities to let him legally enter the country. Director Peter Maxwell shows early signs of the skills that he'd later bring to the acclaimed Aussie war film *The Highest Honour*.

Simone Buchanan *Rebecca Ann Porter* • Henri Szeps *Manuel Cortes* • Adam Garnett *Rod* • John Stanton *Bob Porter* • Mary Anne Severne *Jean Porter* ■ *Dir* Peter Maxwell • *Scr* Charles Stamp

Run Silent, Run Deep ★★★★ U

Second World War drama
1958 · US · BW · 88mins

One of the best submarine movies – Quentin Tarantino even referred to it as such in his additions to the screenplay of *Crimson Tide* – this is a terse, brilliantly directed study in revenge, as commander Clark Gable returns to the dreaded Bongo Stits where he had previously lost a sub and his men. Of course, second-in-command Burt Lancaster isn't happy, feeling that he should be in charge, and his reticence and the resentfulness of the crew make for fine drama in a confined space. The opening, pre-title sequence of this film is a classic example of movie storytelling. Even if you don't like this particular sub-genre (excuse the pun), this film merits watching for its star power alone. 🖭

Clark Gable *Commander Richardson* • Burt Lancaster *Lieutenant Jim Bledsoe* • Jack Warden *Mueller* • Brad Dexter *Cartwright* • Don Rickles *Ruby* • Nick Cravat *Russo* ■ *Dir* Robert Wise • *Scr* John Gay, from a novel by Commander Edward L Beach

Run, Simon, Run ★★

Drama
1970 · US · Colour · 74mins

Before movie stardom beckoned, Burt Reynolds paid his small screen dues with a number of made-for-TV movies. As in *Navajo Joe* and a couple of other films, Reynolds goes native playing an American Indian. Here, he's just released from prison for murdering his brother and swears to kill the man who really did it. After playing this role Reynolds apparently told his agent, "The only Indian I haven't played is Pocahontas." Unfortunately, Reynolds's co-star, Swedish-born Inger Stevens, was found dead of a drugs

overdose shortly after shooting was completed.

Burt Reynolds *Simon Zuniga* • Inger Stevens *Carroll Rennard* • Royal Dano *Sheriff Tackaberry* • James Best *Henry Burroughs* • Rodolfo Acosta *Manuel* • Don Dubbins *Freddy* • Ken Lynch *Warden Loomis* ■ *Dir* George McCowan • *Scr* Lionel E Siegel

Run Wild, Run Free ★★★ U

Drama
1969 · UK · Colour · 94mins

Adapted by David Rook from his novel, *The White Colt*, this rural fable owes much to the earthy evocation of the wild beauty of Dartmoor. Complete with a tense finale and directed with old-fashioned care by Richard C Sarafian, the story of the timid boy whose love of a free-spirited horse brings him out of his shell should appeal to more discriminating youngsters. Fresh from his success in *Oliver!*, Mark Lester has few problems looking vulnerable, while John Mills provides seasoned support as the retired colonel who provides the affection denied by parents Sylvia Syms and Gordon Jackson.

John Mills *The Moorman* • Gordon Jackson *Mr Ransome* • Sylvia Syms *Mrs Ransome* • Mark Lester (1) *Philip Ransome* • Bernard Miles *Reg* • Fiona Fullerton *Diana* ■ *Dir* Richard C Sarafian • *Scr* David Rook, from the novel *The White Colt* by David Rook • *Cinematographer* Wilkie Cooper

Runaway! ★★

Action drama 1973 · US · Colour · 73mins

Made for American TV but released to cinemas in Britain as *The Runaway Train*, this hokey disaster movie stars Ben Johnson as the driver whose train runs out of control down a mountain and across a field of the corniest clichés. Aboard the train are 200 skiers wishing they'd gone by car; they're all carrying lots of emotional baggage, of course, which fills the gap between brake failure and climactic buffers. Contains swearing and violence.

Ben Johnson *Holly Gibson* • Ben Murphy *Les Reaver* • Ed Nelson *Nick Staffo* • Darleen Carr *Carol Lerner* • Lee H Montgomery *[Lee Montgomery] Mark Shedd* • Martin Milner *John Shedd* • Vera Miles *Ellen Staffo* ■ *Dir* David Lowell Rich • *Scr* Gerald DiPego

Runaway ★★ 15

Futuristic action thriller
1984 · US · Colour · 95mins

Although Tom Selleck was unable to break free of his *Magnum, PI* contract to make *Raiders of the Lost Ark*, he did abscond for this silly futuristic thriller, written and directed by *Jurassic Park* creator Michael Crichton. Selleck is a cop who suffers from vertigo (sound familiar?) and the villain is Gene Simmons, leader of the rock group Kiss, who has an army of deadly spider-like robots at his command. Apart from some amusing romantic banter between Selleck and his police partner Cynthia Rhodes and a fairly exciting climax, it's routinely made. Contains swearing and violence. 🖭

Tom Selleck *Jack Ramsay* • Cynthia Rhodes *Karen Thompson* • Gene Simmons *Dr Charles Luther* • Kirstie Alley *Jackie Rogers* • Stan Shaw *Marvin* • GW Bailey *Chief* • Joey Cramer *Bobby Ramsay* • Chris Mulkey *Johnson* ■ *Dir/Scr* Michael Crichton

Runaway Bride ★★★ PG

Romantic comedy
1999 · US · Colour · 116mins

Pretty Woman co-stars Julia Roberts and Richard Gere reunite with that film's director, Garry Marshall, for this predictable but well-played romantic comedy. Roberts is the small-town girl who has left a trio of heartbroken men at the altar, while Gere is the cynical columnist keen to see if she will actually go through with it on her fourth attempt. Of course, you'll have worked out the ending before you reach the last line of this review. However, thanks to Roberts's deft comedic touch, a zippy script and some nice support from Hector Elizondo and the always reliable Joan Cusack, this is a sweet romance that will warm the cockles of wedding fanatics everywhere. Marriage phobics, however, should steer clear – they may well be converted. Contains some strong language and sexual references.
▣ *DVD*

Julia Roberts *Maggie* • Richard Gere *Ike* • Joan Cusack *Peggy* • Hector Elizondo *Fisher* • Rita Wilson *Ellie* • Paul Dooley *Walter* • Christopher Meloni *Coach Bob* • Reg Rogers *George* • Laurie Metcalf *Mrs Trout* ■ *Dir* Garry Marshall • *Scr* Josann McGibbon, Sara Parriott

The Runaway Bus ★★ U

Comedy thriller   1954 · UK · BW · 76mins

Written and directed by Val Guest and owing much to Arnold Ridley's twice-filmed play, *The Ghost Train*, this comedy thriller proved the ideal debut vehicle for Frankie Howerd. Never totally at home on film, he wisely follows Bob Hope's lead in combining cowardice and wisecracks as he substitutes for the driver of an airport shuttle bus, blissfully unaware that on this foggy night he has a stash of stolen gold onboard. However, he is roundly upstaged by both that expert scene-stealer Margaret Rutherford and the under-rated Belinda Lee, whose pulp-addicted blonde has a touch of Judy Holliday about her.

Frankie Howerd *Percy Lamb* • Margaret Rutherford *Cynthia Beeston* • Petula Clark *Lee Nichols* • George Coulouris *Edward Schroeder* • Belinda Lee *Janie Grey* • Reginald Beckwith *Collector* ■ *Dir/Scr* Val Guest

Runaway Car ★★ PG

Action comedy based on a true story
1997 · US · Colour · 90mins

Judge Reinhold has never managed to capitalise on the leading-man potential he showed in such early hits as *Ruthless People* and *Vice Versa*. Here he delivers another in a long line of pleasant but undistinguished performances, playing a computer programmer trapped in the passenger seat – along with Leon and a young baby – when goofy nurse Nina Siemaszko's brakes decide to pack in. Although the tale is supposedly inspired by a true incident, it doesn't really add up, and Reinhold himself has been quoted as wondering why the driver "didn't just turn the car off".
▣

Nina Siemaszko *Jenny Todd* • Judge Reinhold *Ed Lauter* • Brian Hooks *Dex* • Leon *Isaiah Beaufort* • Alec Murdock *Dr Mason* ■ *Dir* Jack Sholder • *Scr* Paul F Edwards

Runaway Daughters ★★★ 12

Drama   1994 · US · Colour · 78mins

Having cut his teeth in Roger Corman's B-movie empire, Joe Dante was an obvious choice for this remake of Edward L Cahn's 1957 drive-in classic, and he doesn't disappoint. This follows the adventures of a trio of mildly rebellious teenage girls newcomers Julie Brown, Jenny Lewis and Holly Field who hit the road when Field gets pregnant and her boyfriend attempts to avoid his responsibilities by enlisting. Although the film lacks the joyous anarchy of Dante's best works such as *Gremlins* and *Matinee*, there's still space for some knowing digs at fifties' America and Dante is well served by an excellent supporting cast. Watch out for cameos from his mentor Corman, old regular Dick Miller, Dee Wallace Stone and former teen idol Fabian. Contains some swearing and sexual references. ▣

Holly Fields *Mary* • Julie Bowen *Angie* • Jenny Lewis *Laura* • Paul Rudd *Jimmy* • Chris Young *Bob* • Dick Miller *Farrell* • Dee Wallace Stone *Mrs Gordon* • Christopher Stone *Mr Gordon* • Roger Corman *Mr Randolph* • Fabian *Mr Rusoff* ■ *Dir* Joe Dante • *Scr* Charlie Haas, from characters created by Lou Rusoff

Runaway Heart ★★

Romantic comedy
1990 · US · Colour · 97mins

Michael Tucker and Jill Eikenberry the real-life husband-and-wife stars of TV's *LA Law* play an inept bank robber and the woman he kidnaps in this romantic comedy from *The Muppet Movie* director James Frawley. Although both leads and co-stars Elaine Stritch and Ray Wise give pleasant enough performances, there is nothing special here to raise this out of the ordinary.

Jill Eikenberry *Bunny Brown* • Michael Tucker *Walter Sharphorn* • Elaine Stritch *Rowena Sharphorn* • Ray Wise *Archie Brown* • Noah Blake *Joe* • Alison Tucker *Tanya* ■ *Dir* James Frawley • *Scr* Walter Lockwood

Runaway Train ★★★★ 18

Action adventure
1985 · US · Colour · 105mins

This is a fast-paced thriller based on a screenplay co-written by celebrated Japanese director Akira Kurosawa, which takes it a notch above the average Hollywood action film. Escaping convicts Jon Voight and Eric Roberts have far more depth than your typical gung-ho hero – both landed Oscar nominations, as did Henry Richardson, whose dynamic editing gives Andrei Konchalovsky's superior direction the breakneck pace that will keep you on the edge of your seat. John P Ryan as a sadistic warden and Rebecca De Mornay as a trapped passenger also rise to the occasion. Contains swearing and violence. ▣

Jon Voight *Manny* • Eric Roberts *Buck* • Rebecca De Mornay *Sara* • Kyle T Heffner *Frank Barstow* • John P Ryan *Ranken* • TK Carter *Dave Prince* • Kenneth McMillan *Eddie MacDonald* ■ *Dir* Andrei Konchalovsky • *Scr* Djordje Milicevic, Paul Zindel, Edward Bunker, from a screenplay (unproduced) by Akira Kurosawa, Ryuzo Kikushima, Hideo Oguni

The Runestone ★★ 15

Horror   1991 · US · Colour · 98mins

An archaeologist uncovers a Norse artefact which turns him into a murderous hairy beast in this old-fashioned monster movie with a few good scares. Highly regarded in some genre quarters for its eerie atmosphere, graphic blood-letting and neat acting turns by Peter Riegert and Lawrence Tierney as hard-nosed NYPD cops, writer/director Willard Carroll unfortunately drags the excitement down with elongated passages of pretentious mumbo-jumbo. ▣

Alexander Godunov *Clockmaker* • Peter Riegert *Fanducol* • Joan Severance *Marla Stewart* • William Hickey *Lars Hagstron* • Tim Ryan *Sam Stewart* • Mitchell Laurance *Martin Almquist* • Lawrence Tierney *Chief Richardson* ■ *Dir* Willard Carroll • *Scr* Willard Carroll, from a novella by Mark E Rogers

The Runner ★★★★ PG

Drama   1984 · Iran · Colour · 86mins

Amir Naderi's film furthers the Iranian cinematic tradition of viewing the world through the eyes of disadvantaged children. Living alone in an abandoned boat in the port of Abadan, Majid Nirumand struggles to compete with the bigger lads in the scramble for redeemable bottles carried on the tide, but he's spurred on by his determination to forge a better life for himself. While this neorealist study of post-revolutionary conditions could have been hopelessly pessimistic, Naderi invests it with startling exhilaration through the simple, joyful thrill this uncomplaining waif derives from running. In Farsi with English subtitles. ▣

Majid Nirumand *Amiro* • A Gholamzadeh *Uncle Gholam* • Musa Torkizadeh *Musa* • Reza Ramezani *Ramezan* ■ *Dir* Amir Naderi • *Scr* Amir Naderi, Behruz Gharibpur

The Runner ★★★

Crime drama   1999 · US · Colour · 95mins

Ron Eldard is the Las Vegas loser who becomes a runner for gangster John Goodman. It's the plot of *Wall Street* relocated to Vegas, with Eldard placing bets all over the neon city, falling in love with cocktail waitress Courteney Cox and buying her an engagement ring with Goodman's money. There are some fairly macabre twists in store and Goodman is superbly menacing as the man who has reduced everything in life to a matter of chance. *Friends* star Cox is also alluring in a low-rent Julia Roberts sort of way, but the weakness is Eldard who hasn't quite got the required charisma to play the butt of one of Goodman's cosmic wagers.

Ron Eldard *Edward Harrington* • Courteney Cox *Karina* • Bokeem Woodbine *477* • John Goodman *Deep Throat* • Joe Mantegna *Rocco* • David Arquette *Bartender* ■ *Dir* Ron Moler • *Scr* Anthony E Zuiker

The Runner Stumbles ★

Drama   1979 · US · Colour · 88mins

Stanley Kramer is Hollywood's big game hunter. He tracks down the weightiest issues of the day – Darwinian theory, nuclear war, racism, student unrest – and turns them into corny melodramas. This one stars Dick Van Dyke, of all people, as a priest accused in the 1920s of killing a nun he lusted after. There is hardly a line, let alone a scene, that rings true as Kramer bludgeons us with a new moral dilemma every minute. After this snail-paced, insanely cast and generally execrable effort, Kramer threw in the towel and hasn't made a movie since.

Dick Van Dyke *Father Rivard* • Kathleen Quinlan *Sister Rita* • Maureen Stapleton *Mrs Shandig* • Ray Bolger *Monsignor Nicholson* • Tammy Grimes *Erna* • Beau Bridges *Toby* ■ *Dir* Stanley Kramer • *Scr* Milan Stitt, from a play by Milan Stitt

Runners ★★★ 15

Drama   1983 · UK · Colour · 102mins

With his teenage daughter on the disappearance list for two years, James Fox refuses to accept that she's dead and sets out on a journey to London to find her. He meets Jane Asher, the member of a support group who has lost her son, and his search turns from a contemporary social issue drama into a fully blown cryptic thriller. Idiosyncratically written by Stephen Poliakoff, directed with an accent on documentary realism by Charles Sturridge and well performed by the sympathetic Fox, this drama succeeds in engaging the attention and holding it until the anticlimactic ending. ▣

Kate Hardie *Rachel* • James Fox *Tom* • Jane Asher *Helen* • Eileen O'Brien *Gillian* • Ruti Simon *Lucy* ■ *Dir* Charles Sturridge • *Scr* Stephen Poliakoff

Running ★★ PG

Drama   1979 · Can · Colour · 96mins

In a typical tale of "The American Dream", Michael Douglas is an unemployed father of two who tries to sort out all of his domestic problems by bidding to join the Olympic marathon team. Not really illustrative of Douglas's subsequent career, this is an obvious attempt to cash in on the running craze of the late seventies, but fails to get off the starting blocks. ▣

Michael Douglas *Michael Andropolis* • Susan Anspach *Janet Andropolis* • Lawrence Dane *Coach Walker* • Eugene Levy *Richard Rosenberg* • Charles Shamata [Chuck Shamata] *Howard Grant* ■ *Dir/Scr* Steven Hilliard Stern

Running against Time ★★★ U

Fantasy drama   1990 · US · Colour · 88mins

Yet another time-travelling movie, but this time a surprisingly good one. *Airplane!*'s Robert Hays discovers a time machine and uses it to go back to that fateful day in American history, 22 November 1963, to try to prevent John F Kennedy's assassination in Dallas. Of course, things don't go quite as planned, but that's part of the fun in this often highly entertaining tale, which also stars Catherine Hicks and Sam Wanamaker.

Robert Hays *David Rhodes* • Catherine Hicks *Laura Whittaker* • Sam Wanamaker *Dr Koopman* • James Distefano *Lee Harvey Oswald* • Brian Smiar *President Lyndon Johnson* • Tracy Fraim *Teddy* ■ *Dir* Bruce Seth Green • *Scr* Robert Glass, Stanley Shapiro, from the book *A Time to Remember* by Stanley Shapiro

Running Brave ★★ PG

Biographical drama
1983 · Can · Colour · 97mins

With its liberal credentials pinned proudly to its sleeve, this is a worthy but predictable true story of triumph over adversity. Robby Benson plays a native American determined to find glory as an athlete, who eventually forces his way into the Olympic team. Benson puts in an impassioned performance and there are canny supporting turns from the likes of Pat Hingle and a young Graham Greene. However, DS Everett's direction is heavy-handed and he too readily resorts to sentimentality. ▣

Robby Benson *Billy Mills* • Pat Hingle *Coach Easton* • Claudia Cron *Pat Mills* • Jeff McCracken *Dennis* • August Schellenberg *Billy's father* • Denis Lacroix *Frank* • Graham Greene *Eddie* ■ Dir DS Everett • Scr Henry Bean, Shirl Hendryx

Running Cool ★★ 18

Action drama   1993 · US · Colour · 101mins

An uninspired low-budget movie that tells the predictable story of a pair of bikers who get caught up in a battle against an evil property magnate. Andrew Divoff is the nominal star, although Paul Gleason (as the tycoon) is probably the best known name in the cast, while Dedee Pfeiffer pops up in a supporting role. It's written and directed by exploitation specialists Ferd and Beverly Sebastian. Contains violence, swearing and brief nudity. ▣

Andrew Divoff *Bone* • Tracy Sebastian *Blue Hogg* • Dedee Pfeiffer *Michele* • Paul Gleason *Calvin Hogg* • Arlen Dean Snyder *Sheriff* ■ Dir/Scr Beverly Sebastian, Ferd Sebastian

Running Delilah ★

Science-fiction thriller
1992 · US · Colour · 92mins

Only serving to remind the audience of her less-than-grand contribution to *Porky's* and *Police Academy*, Kim Cattrall is here saddled with unintentionally hilarious dialogue. Clearly unaware that the James Bond genre has already reached self-parody, director Richard Franklin (whose mentor was, gasp, Alfred Hitchcock) bungles the action plot, featuring a dead Cattrall who becomes a vengeance-seeking cyborg. Ludicrous hardly begins to describe later events.

Kim Cattrall *Delilah* • François Guetary *Kercharian* • Billy Zane *Paul* ■ Dir Richard Franklin

Running Hot ★★★ 18

Crime   1983 · US · Colour · 88mins

Eric Stoltz plays a young man, wrongfully convicted of murdering his father, who is then sentenced to death. After a hasty escape from a squad car, Stoltz hooks up with Monica Carrico, a prostitute, who is drawn to him by a sense of déjà vu. Stoltz then blunders across the country with Carrico in tow, killing several people who get in his way. A bit long and bleak, but well acted, especially by the two leads. For a good laugh, don't miss the early scene involving a Nixon Halloween mask.

Monica Carrico *Charlene Andrews* • Eric Stoltz *Danny Hicks* • Stuart Margolin *Officer Trent* • Virgil Frye *Ross, the pimp* • Richard Bradford *Tom Bond* ■ Dir/Scr Mark Griffiths

The Running, Jumping and Standing Still Film ★★★ U

Silent comedy   1959 · UK · Sepia · 11mins

Having directed several episodes of *The Goon Show*, Richard Lester was able to call on the services of Peter Sellers and Spike Milligan for this anarchic short, which marked his cinematic debut. Shot in two days for just £700, using Sellers's new 16mm camera, it boasts such bizarre images as a couple of women washing a field, a man playing a record on a tree stump and Graham Stark getting carried away by his kite before being punched on the nose by Leo McKern in boxing gloves. Nominated for an Oscar, it lost out to Jacques-Yves Cousteau's *The Golden Fish*.

Peter Sellers • Spike Milligan • Leo McKern • Graham Stark • Mario Fabrizi • David Lodge • Bruce Lacey ■ Dir Dick Lester [Richard Lester] • Scr Peter Sellers, Spike Milligan, Mario Fabrizi, Dick Lester [Richard Lester]

The Running Man ★★★

Crime drama   1963 · UK · Colour · 108mins

This is one of those cinematic sleights of hand that only exceptional film-makers can hope to pull off. Armed with a clever script by John Mortimer (of Rumpole fame), director Carol Reed turns a thoroughly run-of-the-mill potboiler into a hugely entertaining three-handed thriller, thanks to his unerring ability to conjure up atmosphere, the striking photography of Robert Krasker and the canny performances of his splendid cast. Laurence Harvey is gleefully extravagant as a cocky con man, Alan Bates doggedly decent as the insurance assessor on his trail, and Lee Remick beguiling as the "widow" caught between them.

Laurence Harvey *Rex Black* • Lee Remick *Stella Black* • Alan Bates *Stephen Maddox* • Felix Aylmer *Parson* • Eleanor Summerfield *Hilda Tanner* • Allan Cuthbertson *Jenkins* • Harold Goldblatt *Tom Webster* ■ Dir Carol Reed • Scr John Mortimer, from the novel *The Ballad of the Running Man* by Shelley Smith

The Running Man ★★★ 18

Science-fiction action thriller
1987 · US · Colour · 96mins

Given TV's increasingly desperate search for new programme formats, this futuristic blockbuster about a game show where a pumped-up audience bays for the blood of convicts on a lethal combat course isn't so far-fetched. Arnold Schwarzenegger is the former police helicopter pilot who is forced into the game of death when he rebels against his totalitarian superiors. While it's a long way from the original Stephen King (writing as Richard Bachman) novel, Schwarzenegger gets to do what he does best – destroying baddies with a quip and director Paul Michael Glaser handles the action sequences with some panache. Maria Conchita Alonso is Arnie's reluctant partner, while Richard Dawson steals the acting honours as the game show host. Contains swearing and violence. ▣

Arnold Schwarzenegger *Ben Richards* • Maria Conchita Alonso *Amber Mendez* • Yaphet Kotto *Laughlin* • Jim Brown *Fireball* • Jesse Ventura *Captain Freedom* • Erland Van Lidth *Dynamo* • Marvin J McIntyre *Weiss* • Gus Rethwisch *Buzzsaw* • Richard Dawson *Damon Killian* ■ Dir Paul Michael Glaser • Scr Steven E DeSouza, from the novel *The Running Man* by Richard Bachman [Stephen King]

Running Mates ★★★

Political romance 1992 · US · Colour · 88mins

There's clearly a hidden agenda behind a film that has a leading lady who's the spitting image of Hillary Clinton and was shown for the first time on the last day of the 1992 presidential election campaign. Speculation aside, this is a pleasingly sniping satire of the American political system, with Diane Keaton (making her TV-movie debut) in superb form as the widowed children's novelist whose involvement with ambitious senator Ed Harris results in a media frenzy. British director Michael Lindsay-Hogg takes the action at a fair clip and gets neat support performances from Ed Begley Jr and Russ Tamblyn.

Diane Keaton *Aggie Snow* • Ed Harris *Hugh Hathaway* • Ed Begley Jr *Chapman Snow* • Ben Masters *Mel Fletcher* • Robert Harper *Gordy Faust* • Russ Tamblyn *Frank Usher* • Edgar Small *Senator Seaton* • Brandon Maggart *Jack Delaney* ■ Dir Michael Lindsay-Hogg • Scr AL Appling

Running on Empty ★★★★ 15

Drama   1988 · US · Colour · 111mins

An interesting twist on the effect the sixties really had on America, this is also a sad reminder of the late River Phoenix's talents as an actor. He plays Danny, a teenager who leads an unusual life – he and his parents (Judd Hirsch and Christine Lahti) have been on the run from the FBI for 17 years since the couple bombed a university research centre, blinding a janitor in the blast. But now Phoenix wants a more settled existence, and the film focuses on the family's attempts to keep together. Director Sidney Lumet manages to keep the drama subtle instead of dissolving into mush. A moving treat. Contains swearing. ▣

Christine Lahti *Annie Pope* • River Phoenix *Danny Pope* • Judd Hirsch *Arthur Pope* • Martha Plimpton *Lorna Phillips* • Jonas Abry *Harry Pope* • Ed Crowley *Mr Phillips* • LM Kit Carson *Gus Winant* ■ Dir Sidney Lumet • Scr Naomi Foner

Running Out of Luck ★ 18

Music drama   1985 · UK · Colour · 86mins

An obscure musical drama, directed by Julien Temple and made to accompany a Mick Jagger album, it's basically a feature-length music video with an incredibly bizarre plot filling in the gaps between songs. Its self-reflexive start has Jagger, partner Jerry Hall and Dennis Hopper filming a music video in Rio, but the shoot breaks up and somehow Jagger finds himself being beaten up by transvestites and, with the world thinking him dead, forced into sex slavery on a faraway banana plantation with Rae Dawn Chong. Though it may sound intriguing, it's really not worth the bother of trying to find a copy. ▣

Mick Jagger • Jerry Hall • Dennis Hopper *Video director* • Rae Dawn Chong *Slave girl* • Jim Broadbent ■ Dir Julien Temple • Scr Julien Temple, Mick Jagger

Running Scared ★★★ 15

Comedy action thriller
1986 · US · Colour · 102mins

An enjoyable buddy-buddy cop thriller that was comic Billy Crystal's breakthrough movie. Both he and Gregory Hines play streetwise Chicago cops, firing wisecracks like bullets, who've decided to retire to Florida. The only problem is they have to work out a month's notice and underworld boss Jimmy Smits is determined to rub them out. Hines and Crystal make an endearing screen partnership that deserved resurrection in another movie, although their stream of funny one-liners and Peter Hyams's set-piece spectacles sit uneasily with the gritty look of the production. ▣

Billy Crystal *Danny Costanzo* • Gregory Hines *Ray Hughes* • Steve Bauer [Steven Bauer] *Frank* • Darlanne Fluegel *Anna Costanzo* • Joe Pantoliano *Snake* • Dan Hedaya *Capt Logan* • Jimmy Smits *Julio Gonzales* ■ Dir Peter Hyams • Scr Gary DeVore, Jimmy Huston, from a story by Gary DeVore

Running Wild ★★

Silent comedy   1927 · US · BW · 68mins

Fresh from *So's Your Old Man*, WC Fields and director Gregory La Cava re-teamed on this unofficial reworking of the Will Rogers comedy, *One Glorious Day*. As the henpecked milquetoast, whose only friend is at the toy shop where he works is a nodding donkey, Fields is given little room for manoeuvre by a substandard script. However, the vaudeville sequence, in which he's hypnotised into becoming a world-beater, provides a perfect showcase for his pantomimic skills.

WC Fields *Elmer Finch* • Mary Brian *Elizabeth* • Claud Buchanan *Jerry Harvey* • Marie Shotwell *Mrs Finch* • Barney Raskle *Junior* ■ Dir Gregory La Cava • Scr Roy Briant, from a story by Gregory La Cava

Running Wild ★★

Crime drama   1955 · US · BW · 81mins

Like Fagin before him, Keenan Wynn runs a gang of young criminals – car thieves rather than pickpockets. William Campbell is a cop who disguises himself as a teenager and infiltrates the gang. Mamie Van Doren acts with her chest and plays the gang's swoon centre. Aimed exclusively at the teen market, it features several rock 'n' roll numbers which belt out of the nearest jukebox. The major flaw is that none of the cast look remotely young or thuggish enough – but then James Dean wore a tie in *Rebel without a Cause*. Director Abner Biberman was a one-time acting coach to Marilyn Monroe and Tony Curtis, who remembered him as "vain and pompous".

William Campbell *Ralph Barclay* • Mamie Van Doren *Irma Bean* • Keenan Wynn *Ken Osanger* • Kathleen Case *Leta Novak* • Jan Merlin *Scotty Cluett* • John Saxon *Vince Pomeroy* ■ Dir Abner Biberman • Scr Leo Townsend, from a novel by Ben Benson

Running Wild ★★★ U

Drama   1973 · US · Colour · 96mins

Set in charming and beautiful scenery, this pleasant family drama concerns a news photographer whose horror at the treatment of wild mustangs inspires an exposé. Classy Dina Merrill makes a welcome big-screen return in the pivotal leading role, while gritty veterans Lloyd Bridges, Gilbert Roland, and RG Armstrong give her staunch company. This is a strong and intelligently written piece with its heart in the right place. ▢

Lloyd Bridges *Jeff Methune* • Dina Merrill *Whit Colby* • Pat Hingle *Quentin Hogue* • Morgan Woodward *Crug Crider* • Gilbert Roland *Chief Tomacito* • Fred Betts *Cap Methune* • RG Armstrong *Bull* ■ *Dir/Scr* Robert McCahon

La Rupture ★★★★

Thriller   1970 · Fr/It/Bel · Colour · 120mins

Part of Claude Chabrol's absorbing "Hélène cycle" of films, featuring his wife, the seductive Stéphane Audran, this is another of the director's attacks on the bourgeois family. Here, Audran is less scheming than usual as a woman fighting to gain custody of her child from her drug addict husband and nasty father-in-law. Chabrol's terse and suspenseful style works to great advantage in this neat thriller based on Charlotte Armstrong's novel, *The Balloon Man*. The excellent cast includes Jean-Pierre Cassel as a seedy detective and, as the father-in-law, Chabrol favourite Michel Bouquet. In French with English subtitles.

Jean-Pierre Cassel *Paul* • Stéphane Audran *Hélène* • Annie Cordy *Mme Pinelli* • Michel Bouquet *Ludovic Regnier* ■ *Dir* Claude Chabrol • *Scr* Claude Chabrol, from the novel *The Balloon Man* by Charlotte Armstrong

Rush ★★★ 18

Thriller   1991 · US · Colour · 115mins

It's rare these days to hear Eric Clapton music that smacks of commitment. And yet it's his sensitive soundtrack which contributes to the intensity of a movie that successfully captures the unnerving world of the drug addict. Debut director Lili Fini Zanuck sustains the right air of stifling claustrophobia, while Jennifer Jason Leigh and Jason Patric, as two narcotics cops who get hooked, go on their downward spiral with a great deal of force. Contains violence, swearing and substance abuse. ▢

Jason Patric *Jim Raynor* • Jennifer Jason Leigh *Kristen Cates* • Sam Elliott *Larry Dodd* • Max Perlich *Walker* • Gregg Allman *William Gaines* • Tony Frank *Police Chief Nettle* • William Sadler *Monroe* ■ *Dir* Lili Fini Zanuck • *Scr* Pete Dexter, from the book by Kim Wozencraft

Rush Hour ★★★★ 12

Action comedy thriller
1998 · US · Colour · 93mins

Hong Kong action superstar Jackie Chan teams up with loudmouth American comedian Chris Tucker for this blockbuster thriller. It's essentially an east-meets-west buddy movie about two cops trying to solve an international kidnapping, but director Brett Ratner allows plenty of time for character development between the spectacular set pieces, and Chan and Tucker's inspired double act elevates it above the norm. Equally adept at comic martial arts, Chaplin-esque gymnastic displays and near-superhuman stunts, Chan has never been more engaging, with Tucker as his likeably cocky foil, complete with machine-gun patter. Memorable moments include the pair singing Edwin Starr's *War* and rolling over each other's backs to biff the villains. ▢

DVD

Jackie Chan *Detective Inspector Lee* • Chris Tucker *Detective James Carter* • Tom Wilkinson *Griffin/Juntao* • Chris Penn [Christopher Penn] *Clive* • Elizabeth Pena *Tania Johnson* • Rex Linn *Agent Whitney* • Philip Baker Hall *Captain Diel* ■ *Dir* Brett Ratner • *Scr* Ross LaManna, Jim Kouf, from a story by Ross LaManna

Rush to Judgment ★★★

Documentary   1967 · US · BW

A more thought-provoking than polemical documentary about the assassination of John F Kennedy and its aftermath, not only of interest to conspiracy buffs. Using witness interviews and footage, the Warren Commission's lone assassin conclusions are challenged and the conspiracy theory of Mark Lane's landmark article is presented. Director Emile de Antonio made several interesting documentaries on aspects of American politics, including his highly admired film about the Vietnam War, *In the Year of the Pig* (1969).

Mark Lane *Narrator* ■ *Dir* Emile de Antonio • *Scr* Mark Lane, from his article *Rush to Judgement: a Critique of the Warren Commission Inquiry into the Murder of President John F Kennedy, Officer JD Tippit and Lee Harvey Oswald*

Rushmore ★★★★ 15

Black comedy drama
1998 · US · Colour · 92mins

Director Wes Anderson and his co-writer Owen Wilson – who first caught the eye with their low-budget debut *Bottle Rocket* – score again with this unusual black comedy, which centres around an extremely unconventional teen hero. The boy in question is 15-year-old Max Fischer (Jason Schwartzman), one of the least popular pupils at Rushmore Academy, who nonetheless runs just about every club and school activity in a megalomaniacal effort to further himself. Schwartzman gives a superbly nerdy performance, but Bill Murray – playing a depressed millionaire – steals every scene in this quirky, edgy and very funny tale of an outsider who just might end up leading all those who laugh at him. Contains swearing. ▢ **DVD**

Jason Schwartzman *Max Fischer* • Bill Murray *Herman Blume* • Olivia Williams *Rosemary Cross* • Brian Cox *Dr Guggenheim* • Seymour Cassel *Bert Fischer* • Mason Gamble *Dirk Calloway* ■ *Dir* Wes Anderson, Wes Anderson • *Scr* Wes Anderson, Owen Wilson

The Russia House ★★★★ 15

Spy drama   1990 · US · Colour · 117mins

Adapted by Tom Stoppard from John le Carré's novel, this espionage thriller is a class act in every respect, not least in its clever use of authentic Russian locations. Sean Connery is a tweedy, irascible British publisher and reluctant spy who goes to Russia to check out the truth behind a potentially explosive manuscript. Michelle Pfeiffer is his contact and her moving performance is simply astonishing, with a wholly convincing accent that never comes across as studied. It's a tense, often puzzling picture, subtly directed by Fred Schepisi and with a great supporting cast. Contains swearing. ▢

Sean Connery *Barley Blair* • Michelle Pfeiffer *Katya* • Roy Scheider *Russell* • James Fox *Ned* • John Mahoney *Brady* • Klaus Maria Brandauer *Savelev/"Dante"* • Ken Russell *Walter* • JT Walsh *Quinn* • Michael Kitchen *Clive* • David Threlfall *Wicklow* • Mac McDonald *Bob* • Nicholas Woodeson *Niki Landau* • Martin Clunes *Brock* • Ian McNeice *Merrydew* ■ *Dir* Fred Schepisi • *Scr* Tom Stoppard, from the novel by John le Carré

The Russians Are Coming, the Russians Are Coming ★★★★ U

Comedy   1966 · US · Colour · 120mins

Norman Jewison's comedy – an Oscar nominee for best picture – now seems funnier than ever and survives, along with Stanley Kubrick's *Dr Strangelove*, as a key artefact of the Cold War era. The story is simple: Russian Alan Arkin grounds his submarine on the American coast, he goes ashore for help and panic ensues. It's just like that other William Rose script, *It's a Mad, Mad, Mad, Mad World*, with nuclear bombs instead of stolen loot. It's a little long and there's some rather sticky moralising as well, but these are minor flaws when set beside the general level of comic invention. ▢

Carl Reiner *Walt Whittaker* • Eva Marie Saint *Elspeth Whittaker* • Alan Arkin *Rozanov* • Brian Keith *Link Mattocks* • Jonathan Winters *Norman Jonas* • Theodore Bikel *Russian captain* • Paul Ford *Fendall Hawkins* ■ *Dir* Norman Jewison • *Scr* William Rose, from the novel *The Off-Islanders* by Nathaniel Benchley

Rustler's Rhapsody ★★★ PG

Western spoof   1985 · US · Colour · 84mins

A fun spoof of the popular "singing cowboy" films of the thirties, forties and fifties. They're the ones where someone like Roy Rogers or Gene Autry would beat off the baddies, while still finding time to sing to his horse and ride Dale Evans. Or was it the other way round? Whatever, Tom Berenger plays the cowboy crooner here, and has the hunky good looks to carry it off. The parody suffers, though, from the fact that the singing cowboy genre never took itself so seriously in the first place, and that anyone under 50 will have probably never seen one.

Tom Berenger *Rex O'Herlihan* • Marilu Henner *Miss Tracy* • GW Bailey *Peter* • Fernando Rey *Railroad colonel* • Andy Griffith *Colonel Ticonderoga* ■ *Dir/Scr* Hugh Wilson

Ruthless ★★★ PG

Drama   1948 · US · BW · 100mins

This splendid chunk of Hollywood B-movie tosh stars Zachary Scott as the man who ruins everyone in his path. Dames he two-times, men he just destroys. Better enjoyed as cheap junk than taken seriously, it was directed by cult maestro Edgar G Ulmer, a man who knew how to stretch a budget and a schedule. The screenplay is somewhat clumsy, but the cast here is better than expected, particularly the women: *The Big Sleep's* Martha Vickers, winsome Diana Lynn in a dual role, and MGM's fading musical star Lucille Bremer. Sydney Greenstreet overacts as a Southern tycoon, but mesmerises as ever.

Zachary Scott *Horace Vendig* • Louis Hayward *Vic Lambdin* • Diana Lynn *Martha Burnside/Mallory Flagg* • Martha Vickers *Susan Dunne* • Sydney Greenstreet *Buck Mansfield* • Lucille Bremer *Christa Mansfield* • Raymond Burr *Peter Vendig* ■ *Dir* Edgar G Ulmer • *Scr* Alvah Bessie (uncredited), SK Lauren, Gordon Kahn, from the novel *Prelude to Night* by Dayton Stoddart

Ruthless People ★★★★ 18

Comedy   1986 · US · Colour · 90mins

Airplane! partners Jim Abrahams, Jerry Zucker and David Zucker teamed up again for this fun comedy about a pair of bumbling kidnappers – Helen Slater and Judge Reinhold – who snatch wealthy Bette Midler, unaware that her husband Danny DeVito doesn't want her back. The movie twists and turns as a whole host of other people get involved (including Anita Morris as DeVito's mistress and a young Bill Pullman as her mentally challenged lover). DeVito and Midler are superb in their roles as the greedy philanderer and his screaming, overbearing other half. Contains swearing and nudity. ▢

Danny DeVito *Sam Stone* • Bette Midler *Barbara Stone* • Judge Reinhold *Ken Kessler* • Helen Slater *Sandy Kessler* • Anita Morris *Carol* • Bill Pullman *Earl* • William G Schilling *Police commissioner* • Art Evans *Lieutenant Bender* • Clarence Felder *Lieutenant Walters* ■ *Dir* Jim Abrahams, David Zucker, Jerry Zucker • *Scr* Dale Launer

The Ryan White Story ★★★ 15

Drama based on a true story
1989 · US · Colour · 92mins

Witness star Lukas Haas heads the cast in the moving and sad true story of a young haemophiliac boy who contracts the Aids virus and is then banned from attending school. Judith Light plays his mom, who campaigns for him to return. Unlike other TV movies of its kind, there's a minimum of melodrama, and the strong supporting cast includes George C Scott. ▢

Lukas Haas *Ryan White* • George C Scott *Charles Vaughan* • Judith Light *Jeanne White* • Nikki Cox *Andrea White* • George Dzundza • Sarah Jessica Parker ■ *Dir* John Herzfeld • *Scr* Phil Penningroth

Ryan's Daughter ★★★★ 15

Romantic epic   1970 · UK · Colour · 186mins

David Lean's follow-up to *Doctor Zhivago*, *Ryan's Daughter* was not so much roasted by the critics as incinerated. The story of a dreamy girl who marries a stolid village teacher and then has an affair with a shell-shocked British officer, it began as a script of Flaubert's *Madame Bovary* that Robert Bolt had written for his wife, Sarah Miles. Set in a bleak Irish village in 1916, it co-stars a

U = SUITABLE FOR ALL   Uc = SUITABLE FOR ALL, ESPECIALLY FOR YOUNG CHILDREN (VIDEO ONLY)   PG = PARENTAL GUIDANCE

courageously cast Robert Mitchum as the teacher. Stories about the year-long making of the picture have duly entered movie legend; as an overblown romance it has no equal and now looks like a masterpiece. Freddie Young's Oscar-winning images of the wild Dingle Peninsula need to be seen on the big screen. Contains a sex scene and brief nudity. 🖵

Robert Mitchum *Charles Shaughnessy* • Sarah Miles *Rosy* • Trevor Howard *Father Collins* • John Mills *Michael* • Christopher Jones *Major Doryan* • Leo McKern *Thomas Ryan* • Barry Foster *Tim O'Leary* • Arthur O'Sullivan *Mr McCardle* • Marie Kean *Mrs McCardle* ■ *Dir* David Lean • *Scr* Robert Bolt • *Music* Maurice Jarre

SFW ★★★ 18

Satirical drama 1994 · US · Colour · 91mins

It's beginning to show its age, but this satirical drama remains a topical dissection of the American fascination with the cult of the non-celebrity. Stephen Dorff is the angry young man who is among a group taken hostage by camcorder-wielding anarchists. They force the networks to broadcast their tapes, but it's the rebellious Dorff who soon becomes the star attraction, making him, unwillingly, the hottest thing on TV. Dorff is suitably surly as the man fighting against his 15 minutes of fame and there's good support from a pre-fame Reese Witherspoon and Jake Busey. Director Jefery Levy, demonstrates an understanding of nineties teenage alienation, but the grunge soundtrack now sounds dated. Contains violence, swearing, nudity. 🖵

Stephen Dorff *Cliff Spab* • Reese Witherspoon *Wendy Pfister* • Jake Busey *Morrow Streeter* • Joey Lauren Adams *Monica Dice* • Pamela Gidley *Janet Streeter* ■ *Dir* Jefery Levy • *Scr* Jefery Levy, Danny Rubin, from the novel by Andrew Wellman

SIS Extreme Justice ★★ 18

Action 1993 · US · Colour · 95mins

As with *The First Power*, Lou Diamond Phillips is grossly miscast as a tough-as-nails cop, this time recruited into a secret LA police squad. With Scott Glenn, Yaphet Kotto, and Andrew Divoff (all three giving good performances), the squad trails ex-cons until they commit a felony, using the crimes as a legal excuse to subsequently shoot and kill them. There are some interesting ideas and topics brought up, but they are quickly put aside to allow scenes of unbelievably graphic gunplay. It's capped with an ending that's both unsatisfying and unfinished. 🖵

Lou Diamond Phillips *Jeff Powers* • Scott Glenn *Dan Vaughn* • Ed Lauter *Captain Shafer* • Chelsea Field *Kelly Daniels* • Yaphet Kotto *Larsen* • Andrew Divoff *Angel* ■ *Dir* Mark L Lester • *Scr* Frank Sacks, Robert Boris

SLC Punk! ★★★

Comedy drama 1999 · US · Colour · 97mins

They may be geographically and musically miles apart, but this is the Mohawk-sporting cousin of *Detroit Rock City*. As Salt Lake's only hardcore punks, Matthew Lillard and Michael Goorjian have a take on rednecks, posing cultists and the all-pervading influence of Mormonism, that's as sharply witty as it's jaundiced. How can you be an anarchist, though, when you have good grades, ambitious parents and a social conscience?

Writer/director James Merendino's decision to let Lillard address the audience directly personalises the overly familiar teen-pic tropes, but the stomping soundtrack and some archly designed threads can't forestall the inevitable triumph of conventionality.

Matthew Lillard *Stevo* • Michael Goorjian *Bob* • Annabeth Gish *Trish* • Jennifer Lien *Sandy* • Christopher McDonald *Father* • Devon Sawa *Sean* • Jason Segel *Mike* • Summer Phoenix *Brandy* ■ *Dir/Scr* James Merendino

SOB ★★★

Comedy 1981 · US · Colour · 121mins

You don't expect this sort of vitriol from Blake Edwards, creator of the amiable, if idiotic, Inspector Clouseau, especially when Edwards's wife Julie Andrews is the star. Yet this attack on Hollywood values is one of the crudest satires ever made at the expense of Tinseltown, as Richard Mulligan, playing a director, decides to turn his art-movie stinker into a soft-porn success, with screen-wife Andrews in the leading role. As the showbiz in-fighting gets worse, it's obvious that Edwards is paying off old, rancorous scores, but such personal venom slows down the pace and the point. Contains swearing and nudity.

Julie Andrews *Sally Miles* • William Holden (1) *Tim Culley* • Marisa Berenson *Mavis* • Larry Hagman *Dick Benson* • Robert Loggia *Herb Maskowitz* • Stuart Margolin *Gary Murdock* • Richard Mulligan *Felix Farmer* • Robert Preston *Dr Irving Finegarten* • Craig Stevens *Willard Gaylin* • Loretta Swit *Polly Reed* • Robert Vaughn *David Blackman* • Shelley Winters *Eva Brown* • Jennifer Edwards *Lila* • Rosanna Arquette *Babs* ■ *Dir/Scr* Blake Edwards

SOS Iceberg ★★

Adventure drama 1933 · Ger · BW · 77mins

A German crew under Dr Arnold Fanck, shot 58 hours of Arctic footage; Hollywood director Tay Garnett then went to Berlin to help devise a dual-language drama using some of this material, which included a glacier exploding into thousands of icebergs. On a frozen Swiss lake they shot a formula story of a scientific expedition in trouble, the few survivors sheltering on an ice floe to await rescue. The natural spectacle dwarfs the cast, which in the English-speaking version includes Rod La Rocque and Gibson Gowland (star of the silent, *Greed*).

Rod La Rocque *Dr Carl Lawrence* • Leni Riefenstahl *Ellen Lawrence* • Sepp Rist *Dr Johannes Brand* • Gibson Gowland *John Dragan* • Dr Max Holzboer [Max Holzboer] *Dr Jan Matushek* ■ *Dir* Tay Garnett • *Scr* Tom Reed, Edwin H Knopf, from a story by Dr Arnold Fanck

SOS Pacific ★★★

Action drama 1959 · UK · BW · 90mins

The secret of a good disaster movie is to ensure that the victims hardly have chance to draw breath after one crisis, before another follows hot on its heels. In this Rank adventure, a plane crash-lands on an island, only for the survivors to discover that it is the site for an imminent atomic test. Considering there is only one outcome, director Guy Green sustains the suspense remarkably well, helped in no small measure by a sound cast led

by Richard Attenborough, Pier Angeli and Eddie Constantine.

Eddie Constantine *Mark Reisener* • Pier Angeli *Teresa* • Richard Attenborough *Whitey* • John Gregson *Jack Bennett* • Eva Bartok *Maria* • Jean Anderson *Miss Shaw* • Harold Kasket *Monk* ■ *Dir* Guy Green • *Scr* Robert Westerby, from a story by Gilbert Travers

SOS Titanic ★★ PG

Drama 1979 · US · Colour · 97mins

Originally made for American TV, but released in cinemas over here, this detailed account of the famous shipping disaster, mixes fact and fiction as uneasily as it mixes its Anglo-American cast. Director William Hale's grip on the drama is rather tenuous, and the result is regrettably rather low key and cheap looking. Still, Helen Mirren, Ian Holm, Harry Andrews, David Warner, David Janssen and Susan Saint James suffer nobly, and the game to play while watching is, who gets to go down with the ship and who doesn't. 🖵

David Janssen *John Jacob Astor* • Cloris Leachman *Molly Brown* • Susan Saint James *Leigh Goodwin* • David Warner *Laurence Beesley* • Ian Holm *J Bruce Ismay* • Helen Mirren *May Sloan* • Harry Andrews *Captain Edward J Smith* • Beverly Ross *Madeline Astor* • Ed Bishop *Henry Harris* ■ *Dir* William Hale • *Scr* James Costigan

Saadia ★★ U

Drama 1953 · US · Colour · 87mins

Albert Lewin was assistant to Irving Thalberg during the great days of MGM, credited on classics like *Mutiny on the Bounty* and *The Good Earth*. A former critic for the *Jewish Tribune*, he was an intelligent, literate man, who latterly directed six interesting features, including *The Picture of Dorian Gray*, which grew increasingly mediocre as he chased his special muse – *Saadia* was the penultimate, and by far the most preposterous. Mysticism and religiosity obscure a simple Moroccan love story, as Cornel Wilde and Mel Ferrer slug it out for love of dancer Rita Gam.

Cornel Wilde *Si Lahssen* • Mel Ferrer *Henrik* • Rita Gam *Saadia* • Michel Simon *Bou Rezza* • Cyril Cusack *Khadir* • Wanda Rotha *Fatima* • Marcel Poncin *Moha* • Anthony Marlowe *Captain Sabert* ■ *Dir* Albert Lewin • *Scr* Albert Lewin, from the novel *Echeck au Destin* by Francis D'Autheville

Saagar ★★ 15

Romantic drama
1985 · Ind · Colour · 186mins

Director Ramesh Sippy's bittersweet love story focuses on a poor fisherman's affection for a tavern owner's daughter, but she only has eyes for the grandson of a millionairess. The youngsters' romance gets in the way of his grandmother's plot to put the poor fishing folk out of business. A charming mix of fantasy and social comment. In Hindi with English subtitles. 🖵

Madhur Jaffrey • Rishi Kapoor ■ *Dir* Ramesh Sippy

Saajan ★★★ 🅄
Romantic drama
1991 · Ind · Colour · 173mins

Salman Khan, the hunky pin-up of both India's gay community and the nation's teenage girls, stars here as a playboy on one side of a love triangle in Lawrence D'Souza's amiable Bollywood romance. But, unusually for a masala ménage à trois, he and impoverished poet Sanjay Dutt appear more than willing to see each other's merits and leave poor old Madhuri Dixit feeling rather neglected. In Punjabi with English subtitles.. 🖳

Salman Khan *Akash* • Sanjay Dutt *Aman/ Sagar* • Madhuri Dixit *Pooja* ■ *Dir* Lawrence D'Souza • *Scr* Reema Rakeshnath

Saajan Chale Sasural ★★ 🅿🄶
Drama
1997 · Ind · Colour · 133mins

A farmer who remarries after losing his wife in a flood, finds himself in a dramatic predicament when she miraculously returns. This love triangle is played out for all it is worth by an enthusiastic cast, but director David Dhawan can't decide whether he should aim for tears or laughter. In Hindi with English subtitles.. 🖳

Govinda *Shamu* • Satish Kaushik *Mutthu Swamy* • Tabu *Divya* • Kader Khan *Khurana* • Karishma Kapoor *Pooja* ■ *Dir* David Dhawan • *Scr* Rumi Jaffery

Sabotage ★★★★ 🅿🄶
Mystery thriller 1936 · UK · BW · 73mins

There was no such thing as accepted behaviour for suspense master Alfred Hitchcock, and his non-conformity was never more apparent than in the unnerving scene from this movie in which a small boy (Desmond Tester) carries a time-bomb aboard a bus. Movie-goers suddenly had to confront the unexpected (a Hitchcock trademark) in this adaptation of Joseph Conrad's novel *The Secret Agent*, in which terrorist Oscar Homolka uses his marriage to submissive Sylvia Sidney and his business as a cinema owner as front for his subversive activities. Hitchcock later described the film as "playful" but, as usual for him, it is, in fact, a deadly game with cruel conclusions. 🖳

Sylvia Sidney *Sylvia Verloc* • Oscar Homolka *Carl Verloc* • John Loder *Sergeant Ted Spencer* • Desmond Tester *Steve* • Joyce Barbour *Renee* • Matthew Boulton *Superintendent Talbot* ■ *Dir* Alfred Hitchcock • *Scr* Charles Bennett, Ian Hay, Alma Reville, Helen Simpson and EVH Emmett, from the novel *The Secret Agent* by Joseph Conrad

Sabotage ★★ 🔞
Action adventure 1996 · US · Colour · 98mins

Mark Dacascos has an ounce more charisma and acting talent than his fellow martial arts stars, although it hasn't helped him escape from straight-to-video fare such as this. But at least this action thriller boasts a stronger than usual storyline, with moody Dacascos playing an ex-navy commando-turned bodyguard, who gets mixed up in a sinister CIA conspiracy. The supporting cast is fine, but Tibor Takacs's ultra-stylised direction quickly becomes wearying. Contains swearing and violence. 🖳

Mark Dacascos *Michael Bishop* • Carrie-Anne Moss *Lou Castle* • Tony Todd *Sherwood* • Graham Greene *Nicholas Tolliver* • John Neville *Follenfont* • James Neville Purcel *Putley* • Richard Coulter *Jeffrey Trent* • Heidi Von Palleske *Susan Trent* ■ *Dir* Tibor Takacs • *Scr* Michael Stokes, Rick Filon

Saboteur ★★★★ 🅿🄶
Spy thriller 1942 · US · BW · 104mins

Dorothy Parker contributed to the screenplay of this cracking Hitchcock thriller, which cleverly served the dual purpose of warning Americans against Fifth Columnists and providing much needed escapism. Although Hitch was unhappy with the stars chosen for him by Universal (Robert Cummings and Priscilla Lane), he clearly enjoyed hurtling them around deserts, ghost towns and luxury mansions in a manner that both recalled *The 39 Steps* and anticipated *North by Northwest*. The Statue of Liberty finale is the film's best known set piece, but the encounter with a circus troupe and the Radio City Music Hall shoot-out are bang on the money. 🖳

Priscilla Lane *Patricia Martin* • Robert Cummings *Barry Kane* • Otto Kruger *Charles Tobin* • Alan Baxter *Freeman* • Clem Bevans *Neilson* • Norman Lloyd *Frank Fry* • Alma Kruger *Mrs Henrietta Sutton* ■ *Dir* Alfred Hitchcock • *Scr* Peter Viertel, Joan Harrison, Dorothy Parker

The Saboteur, Code Name Morituri ★★★★
Spy drama 1965 · US · BW · 123mins

Despite the clashing egos on the set of *Mutiny on the Bounty*, Marlon Brando and Trevor Howard signed on for another shipboard drama. For Brando it was a legal obligation to 20th Century-Fox: he had walked off *The Egyptian* in 1954 and still owed the studio a movie. A Second World War spy drama, Brando plays a German pacifist recruited by British agent Howard to destroy a German supply vessel, skippered by Yul Brynner. While Brynner is far from being a card-carrying Nazi, Brando impersonates an SS officer, setting up a complex relationship based on moral deception. Taking place almost entirely aboard the ship, this is a claustrophobic, often very tense movie that deserves to be better known.

Marlon Brando *Robert Crain* • Yul Brynner *Captain Mueller* • Janet Margolin *Esther* • Trevor Howard *Colonel Statter* • Martin Benrath *Kruse* • Hans Christian Blech *Donkeyman* • Wally Cox *Dr Ambach* ■ *Dir* Bernhard Wicki • *Scr* Daniel Taradash, from a novel by Werner Jorg Luddecke

Sabrina ★★★ 🅿🄶
Romantic comedy 1995 · US · Colour · 121mins

Sydney Pollack must have known before he embarked on this remake of Billy Wilder's 1954 comedy classic, that the ghosts of Humphrey Bogart, Audrey Hepburn and William Holden would be hovering over his production. Yet, with canny casting and some subtle updating, he succeeded in coming up with a charming variation on this Cinderella story, in which the chauffeur's daughter romances the billionaire boss. Julia Ormond and Harrison Ford take a while to settle into their roles, unlike Greg Kinnear, who gives a vibrant special performance as Ford's brattish brother. Fans of the original won't be satisfied, but, by the end, there's no doubt Pollack achieves a sparkle to match the picture's undoubted polish. 🖳

Harrison Ford *Linus Larrabee* • Julia Ormond *Sabrina Fairchild* • Greg Kinnear *David Larrabee* • Nancy Marchand *Maude Larrabee* • John Wood *Fairchild* • Richard Crenna *Patrick Tyson* • Angie Dickinson *Ingrid Tyson* • Lauren Holly *Elizabeth Tyson* ■ *Dir* Sydney Pollack • *Scr* Barbara Benedek, David Rayfiel, from the 1954 film *Sabrina Fair* , from the play by Samuel Taylor

Sabrina Fair ★★★★★ 🅄
Romantic comedy 1954 · US · BW · 108mins

Ignore the critics who say this is one of Billy Wilder's minor works. It is a major movie, a masterpiece of romantic comedy. *Sabrina Fair* is a Cinderella story about a chauffeur's daughter (Audrey Hepburn) and two brothers, Humphrey Bogart as the workaholic zillionaire and William Holden as the playboy. Because Hepburn's infatuation with Holden is unwittingly wrecking a business deal, Bogart decides to divert her – with predictable results. For a film that is so funny, so sophisticated and so technically polished, it comes as a surprise to learn that the production was a difficult one. The performances are impeccable, with Hepburn radiant, Holden showing real star quality and Bogart perfectly cast against his tough-guy image so that his entry into a new age of innocence is all the more funny and all the more moving. 🖳

Humphrey Bogart *Linus Larrabee* • Audrey Hepburn *Sabrina Fairchild* • William Holden (1) *David Larrabee* • Walter Hampden *Oliver Larrabee* • John Williams *Thomas Fairchild* • Martha Hyer *Elizabeth Tyson* • Joan Vohs *Gretchen Van Horn* • Marcel Dalio *Baron* • Marcel Hillaire *The Professor* • Nella Walker *Maude Larrabee* ■ *Dir* Billy Wilder • *Scr* Billy Wilder, Samuel Taylor, Ernest Lehman, from the play by Samuel Taylor • *Costume Designer* Edith Head

Sacco and Vanzetti ★★★★
Historical drama
1971 · It/Fr · Colour · 123mins

Based on the real lives and true deaths of two American political martyrs, this drama pulls out all the stops of sympathy to support the two Italian immigrants – and acknowledged anarchists – who were caught between a Communist witch hunt and legal negligence in the twenties; they were wrongfully arrested and then executed. Directed by Giuliano Montaldo, and featuring Gian Maria Volonté and Riccardo Cucciolla, it won the best film at Cannes in 1971.

Gian Maria Volonté *Bartolomeo Vanzetti* • Riccardo Cucciolla *Nicola Sacco* • Cyril Cusack *Frederick Katzmann* • Rosanna Fratello *Rosa Sacco* • Geoffrey Keen *Judge Webster Thayer* ■ *Dir* Giuliano Montaldo • *Scr* Fabrizio Onofri, Giuliano Montaldo, Ottavio Jemma

Sacred Flesh ★ 🔞
Erotic drama 2000 · UK · Colour · 72mins

Three years after he finally lost his long struggle to reverse the BBFC's decision to withhold video certification from his film, *Visions of Ecstasy*, on the grounds of blasphemy, Nigel Wingrove returns with another assault on the taboos surrounding the depiction of Christianity on screen. Many will proclaim this as a courageous affirmation of free speech, but it's nothing more than porn in wimples, posing as a high-minded treatise on the mental, physical and spiritual dangers of enforced chastity.

Sally Tremaine *Sister Elizabeth, the Mother Superior* • Moyna Cope *The Abbess* • Simon Hill *Father Henry, The Abbott* • Kristina Bill *Mary Magdalene* • Rachel Taggart *Catechism* • Eileen Daly *Repression* • Daisy Weston *Sister Brigitte* ■ *Dir/Scr* Nigel Wingrove

Sacred Ground ★★
Drama 1983 · US · Colour · 100mins

Charles B Pierce is a genuine maverick director and invariably makes independently financed, would-be-commercial, low- to medium-budgeters with unusual casts or themes. This native American drama concerns a frontiersman with an Apache wife and mixed-race baby, homesteading on sacred Paiute burial grounds, and it generates more issues than it can comfortably cope with. Tim McIntyre, late son of western character actor John McIntyre, is good as the troubled mountain man, and walleyed Jack Elam offers strong support, as does western veteran L Q Jones. The film's good intentions are let down by weaker performances from the female members of the cast, however.

Tim McIntire *Matt* • Jack Elam *Witcher* • LQ Jones *Tolbert* • Ty Randolph *Wannetta* • Eloy Casados *Prairie Fox* • Serene Hedin *Little Doe* • Vernon Foster *Wounded Leg* ■ *Dir/Scr* Charles B Pierce

The Sacrifice ★★★★ 🅿🄶
Drama
1986 · Fr/Swe · Colour and BW · 142mins

With its location (Faro), themes (alienation, faith and death), cinematographer (Sven Nykvist) and star (Erland Josephson) all primarily associated with Ingmar Bergman, his influence is all-pervasive throughout Andrei Tarkovsky's final film. But the Soviet visionary's tormented lyricism is also very much in evidence, both as he suggests the horror of nuclear war through retired intellectual Josephson's desperate, Faustian reaction to the terrible news broadcast, and as he presents the possibility of redemption, through the intercession of mystical mailman, Allan Edwall. In Swedish with English subtitles. 🖳

Erland Josephson *Alexander* • Susan Fleetwood *Adelaide* • Allan Edwall *Otto* • Sven Wollter *Victor* ■ *Dir/Scr* Andrei Tarkovsky • *Cinematographer* Sven Nykvist

Sacrificed Youth ★★★★ 🅿🄶
Drama 1985 · Chi · Colour · 95mins

Having waited 20 years from film school graduation to directing her first feature, Zhang Nuanxin emerged as a key member of the Fourth Generation directors. Although Chinese cinema was changing rapidly, this partly autobiographical tale of a city girl's rural re-education owes much to the post-revolutionary humanist tradition, as Li Fengxu learns more about life from the people around her, than from political dictates. Sent to a collective farm in Yunnan during the Cultural Revolution, Li's medical student also matures as a woman, giving the film a subtle eroticism to place alongside its contrast between Han (city) and Dai (country) attitudes. In Mandarin with English subtitles..

Li Fengxu • Yu Da • Fen Yuanzheng ■ *Dir* Zhang Nuanxin • *Scr* Zhang Nuanxin, from the novel *You Yige Meilide Difang (There Was a Beautiful Place)* by Zhang Manling

The Sad Horse ★★★ U

Adventure drama 1959 · US · Colour · 77mins

A late entry in the seemingly unending series of 20th Century-Fox family films about a boy/girl and his/her horse/dog which included *Kentucky* and *My Friend Flicka*, this story (filmed on location) benefits from sympathetic direction of former Fox film editor James B Clark. Alan Ladd's son David plays the leading role here, and firm support comes from the ever-reliable Chill Wills, sturdy Rex Reason, and the former Mrs Errol Flynn, Patrice Wymore. Young viewers might need hankies at the ready.

David Ladd *Jackie Connors* • Chill Wills *Captain Connors* • Rex Reason *Bill MacDonald* • Patrice Wymore *Leslie MacDonald* • Gregg Palmer *Bart Connors* • Leslie Bradley *Jonas* ■ *Dir* James B Clark • *Scr* Charles Hoffman, from a story by Zoe Akins

The Sad Sack ★★ U

Comedy 1957 · US · BW · 98mins

After making 17 films with Dean Martin, Jerry Lewis took his unique brand of comedy shtick with him and went solo in 1957. In this effort, surrounded by a notable supporting cast that includes Peter Lorre, Jerry inflicts his screwy antics on the armed forces. He plays an unwilling army recruit with a photographic memory who, in addition to the predictable disasters that befall a misfit, gets himself caught up with spies and an Arab conspiracy. Only fitfully funny, but under veteran George Marshall's direction, there's enough here to keep Lewis addicts happy.

Jerry Lewis *Bixby* • David Wayne *Dolan* • Phyllis Kirk *Major Shelton* • Peter Lorre *Abdul* • Joe Mantell *Private Stan Wenaslawsky* • Gene Evans *Sergeant Pulley* • George Dolenz *Ali Mustapha* ■ *Dir* George Marshall • *Scr* Edmund Beloin, Nate Monaster

Saddle the Wind ★★★

Western 1958 · US · Colour · 84mins

Robert Taylor (Hollywood professional) and John Cassavetes (New York king of improvisation) star as a rancher and no-good brother, heading for their last showdown. The clash of acting styles makes for some decently intriguing drama, directed with flair by Robert Parrish, but this is a film with added rarity value because it's the only western ever been written by *The Twilight Zone*'s Rod Serling, early television's greatest fantasist.

Robert Taylor (1) *Steve Sinclair* • Julie London *Joan Blake* • John Cassavetes *Tony Sinclair* • Donald Crisp *Mr Deneen* • Charles McGraw *Larry Venables* • Royal Dano *Clay Ellison* ■ *Dir* Robert Parrish • *Scr* Rod Serling, from a story by Thomas Thompson

Saddle Tramp ★★★ U

Western 1950 · US · Colour · 76mins

An engaging western starring the laconic Joel McCrea, as a loner who secures food for a handful of lost prairie youths. Made as a family film, but note how talented director Hugo Fregonese manages to keep sentimentality in check while embracing the sentimental: no mean feat. The Technicolor location photography by Charles Boyle is particularly attractive, and Wanda Hendrix (Mrs Audie Murphy at the time) makes a perky heroine. Very appealing, very charming.

Joel McCrea *Chuck Conner* • Wanda Hendrix *Della* • John Russell *Rocky* • John McIntire *Hess Higgins* • Jeanette Nolan *Ma Higgins* • Russell Simpson *Pop* ■ *Dir* Hugo Fregonese • *Scr* Harold Shumate

Sadgati ★★★

Drama 1981 · Ind · Colour · 50mins

The second of a pair of short rural dramas (after *Pikoo*) from India's most respected director, Satyajit Ray, that tells the simple, but cruel story of a high-caste bully who forces a low-caste labourer to work to his death. It is one of Ray's most politically militant films, not only attacking the prejudices of the caste system, but also protesting about the socio-economic hardships faced by the sub-continent's poorest people. Om Puri (the star of Ismail Merchant's *In Custody*) gives a performance of great strength and dignity as the repressed bonded labourer, and the final scene is heart-rending. In Hindi with English subtitles.

Om Puri *Dukhi* • Smita Patil *Dukhi's wife* • Mohan Agashe *Brahmin* ■ *Dir/Scr* Satyajit Ray

Sadhna ★★★ U

Drama 1958 · Ind · BW · 136mins

Sunil Dutt made his name playing clean-cut heroes in the late fifties and here, he is perfectly cast as a college lecturer who pretends that he is going to be married to please his ailing mother, Leia Chitnis. His ruse backfires when he discovers that his "intended" is really a prostitute, but when his proud family throws her into the street in disgust he finds his vehement opposition to marriage beginning to crumble. Although typical of director BR Chopra's influential blend of social comment and stylish entertainment, this *masala* melodrama is not regarded as one of his more significant pictures. In Hindi with English subtitles. 📼

Vyjayanthimala • Sunil Dutt • Radia Krishna • Nandini ■ *Dir* BR Chopra • *Scr* Mukhram Sharma, from a story by Mukhram Sharma

Sadie McKee ★★

Melodrama 1934 · US · BW · 90mins

A typical rags-to-riches melodrama, with maid Joan Crawford, embarking on another romantic roller-coaster ride as she tries to climb the social ladder. Crawford virtually carries this entertaining Cinderella saga single-handedly through star charisma alone – only Edward Arnold's performance as her drunken husband survives

Crawford's bid to obliterate her co-stars from the spotlight.

Joan Crawford *Sadie McKee* • Gene Raymond *Tommy Wallace* • Franchot Tone *Michael Alderson* • Esther Ralston *Dolly* • Edward Arnold *Jack Brennon* ■ *Dir* Clarence Brown • *Scr* John Meehan, from the story *Pretty Sadie McKee* by Vina Delmar

Sadie Thompson ★★★

Silent drama 1928 · US · BW · 90mins

This silent version of Somerset Maugham's *Rain*, about a prostitute marooned on a South Seas island where she is almost destroyed by a reforming religious zealot, whose attraction to her undoes him in the end, is the most interesting of three attempts to film it. Directed by Raoul Walsh, it stars Gloria Swanson (who produced it) and Lionel Barrymore, and it's worth sitting through the now tedious, somewhat heavy-handed first half-hour for the powerful melodrama that follows. Claustrophobic and atmospheric, with Barrymore frightening and Swanson mesmerising in her beauty and commitment.

Gloria Swanson *Sadie Thompson* • Lionel Barrymore *Alfred Atkinson* • Raoul Walsh *Sgt Tim O'Hara* • Blanche Frederici *Mrs Atkinson* • Charles Lane (2) *Dr McPhail* • Florence Midgely *Mrs McPhail* • Will Stanton *Quartermaster Bates* ■ *Dir* Raoul Walsh • *Scr* Raoul Walsh, C Gardner Sullivan (titles), the play *Rain; a Play in Three Acts* by John Colton, Clemence Randolph, from the short story *Rain* by Somerset Maugham

Safari ★★★ U

Action adventure 1956 · US · Colour · 41mins

A marvellously batty African adventure romp from Warwick Films, photographed, to its credit, on genuine locations and in CinemaScope. There's a real sense of the terror of the Mau Maus – *Simba* and *Something of Value* were the only other mainstream features to deal with this subject. Victor Mature plays the hero and Janet Leigh is at her most beguiling, whether terrorised by snakes or taking a bath in the jungle. *Dr No* director Terence Young was very good at this sort of thing, and it shows. 📼

Victor Mature *Ken Duffield* • Janet Leigh *Linda Latham* • John Justin *Brian Sinden* • Roland Culver *Sir Vincent Brampton* • Orlando Martins *Jerusalem* ■ *Dir* Terence Young • *Scr* Anthony Veiller, from a story by Robert Buckner

Safe ★★★★ 15

Drama 1995 · US · Colour · 118mins

This claustrophobic study of a dysfunctional Californian housewife who becomes allergic to the chemical by-products of the 20th century casts an eerie spell with its hypnotic camerawork and unusual soundtrack. It's a modern-day psychological horror story, that's made even more harrowing by the intense and impressive performance by Julianne Moore as a woman personally and medically devastated by her surroundings. Contains swearing, nudity 📼

Julianne Moore *Carol White* • Xander Berkeley *Greg White* • Peter Friedman *Peter Dunning* • Kate McGregor-Stewart *Claire* • Mary Carver *Nell* • Susan Norman *Linda* • Steven Gilborn *Dr Hubbard* • Ronnie Farer *Barbara* • James LeGros *Chris* ■ *Dir/Scr* Todd Haynes

Safe at Home ★★ U

Sports musical 1962 · US · BW · 84mins

The subject of baseball has always been considered anathema to British audiences, with even such fine films as *The Stratton Story* (1949) getting limited release, so it is not surprising that this movie was barely shown in the UK. The sentimental tale of a "Little League" youngster who brags that he and his dad are close friends of New York Yankees heroes Mickey Mantle and Roger Maris, then has to make good his boast, is wish-fulfilment stuff and makes no claims to subtlety. William Frawley adds a touch of grit as a grouchy coach. 📼

Mickey Mantle • Roger Maris • William Frawley *Bill Turner* • Patricia Barry *Johanna Price* • Don Collier *Ken Lawton* • Bryan Russell *Hutch Lawton* • Eugene Iglesias *Mr Torres* • Flip Mark *Henry* ■ *Dir* Walter Doniger • *Scr* Robert Dillon, from a story by Tom Naud, Steve Ritch

Safe House ★★★ 15

Thriller 1997 · US · Colour · 94mins

This quirky mix of black comedy and conspiracy thriller stars Patrick Stewart plays a retired civil servant diagnosed with the early stages of Alzheimer's disease, who becomes convinced that the president is trying to kill him. But can he persuade his disbelieving daughter that his life is under threat? Director Eric Steven Stahl, doesn't quite manage to hold it together, but it's a good deal better than most TV-movie fare, and Stewart is always good value. Contains swearing and violence. 📼

Patrick Stewart *Mace Sowell* • Kimberly Williams *Andi Travers* • Hector Elizondo *Dr Simon* ■ *Dir* Eric Steven Stahl • *Scr* Eric Steven Stahl, John Schalter, Sean McLain

Safe Men ★★ 15

Crime comedy 1998 · US · Colour · 84mins

Yet another comedy based around the cobweb-covered "incompetent guys mistaken for experienced criminals" premise. This one is given a lift by two very watchable leads in Steve Zahn (*Out of Sight*) and Sam Rockwell (*Galaxy Quest*) and an enjoyably caricatured supporting cast which includes Michael Lerner and Harvey Fierstein as OTT Jewish gangsters. It's a shame then that the material is so run-of-the-mill as this pair of dumb, fifth-rate musicians find themselves forced into cracking a safe (hence the title). Zahn and Rockwell's likeability factor stretches so far, but the plot is paper thin, as is the humour. Contains swearing. 📼

Sam Rockwell *Samuel* • Steve Zahn *Eddie* • Mark Ruffalo *Frank* • Josh Pais *Mitchell* • Paul Giamatti *Veal Chop* • Michael Schmidt *Bernie Jr* • Christina Kirk *Hannah* • Raymond Serra *Barber* ■ *Dir/Scr* John Hamburg

Safe Passage ★★ 15

Drama 1994 · US · Colour · 93mins

Susan Sarandon is stunning yet again as a frustrated mother of seven boys, who struggles to cope with husband Sam Shepard's bouts of periodic and seemingly psychosomatic blindness. When one of their boys, a US marine, is blown to bits during a clash in the Sinai desert, the entire family gathers

– an opportunity to resolve age-old conflicts and tensions. Despite Sarandon and a good performance from Shepard, the formula is stale – a safe passage through predictable waters. ▣

Susan Sarandon *Mag Singer* • Sam Shepard *Patrick Singer* • Robert Sean Leonard *Alfred Singer* • Nick Stahl *Simon Singer* • Jason London *Gideon Singer* • Marcia Gay Harden *Cynthia* • Matt Keeslar *Percival Singer* • Sean Astin *Izzy Singer* ■ *Dir* Robert Allan Ackerman • *Scr* Deena Goldstone, from the novel by Ellyn Bache

A Safe Place ★★ PG

Experimental fantasy drama
1971 · US · Colour · 94mins

A fantasy which is wildly incoherent or poetically experimental, depending on your tastes. Tuesday Weld plays a vulnerable woman who escapes the pressures of New York life into a dream world, courtesy of a magician (Orson Welles). There's a low-budget feel to this, director Henry Jaglom's first release, and indeed it was filmed at his parent's flat, with the cast largely made up of his pals. However, it gives the impression of having been a labour of love. Jack Nicholson is good value as Weld's old lover.

Tuesday Weld *Susan/Noah* • Orson Welles *Magician* • Jack Nicholson *Mitch* • Philip Proctor [Phil Proctor] *Fred* • Gwen Welles *Bari* • Dov Lawrence *Dov* • Fanny Birkenmaier *Maid* ■ *Dir/Scr* Henry Jaglom

The Safecracker ★★ U

Second World War crime thriller
1958 · UK · BW · 96mins

Ray Milland directs himself in this lightly entertaining Second World War drama, playing the criminal whose digital dexterity comes in useful to the Allies as he's persuaded to join a Commando unit and prise open a Nazi safe in a Belgian castle. At times, it's rather too apt to recall better movies – re-working a gag from the Marx Brothers' *Duck Soup* and a fatal weakness of character from *The Asphalt Jungle* – but it does in its own modest way foreshadow *The Dirty Dozen* .

Ray Milland *Colley Dawson* • Barry Jones *Bennett Carfield* • Jeannette Sterke *Irene* • Ernest Clark *Major Adbury* • Melissa Stribling *Angela* • Victor Maddern *Morris* • Cyril Raymond *Inspector Frankham* • Barbara Everest *Mrs Dawson* ■ *Dir* Ray Milland • *Scr* Paul Monash, from the book *The Willie Gordon Story* by Rhys Davies, Bruce Thomas

Safety Last ★★★★★ U

Classic silent comedy
1923 · US · BW · 73mins

The film that best illustrates the thrill-comedy of Harold Lloyd with his climactic clock-hanging bravado. Lloyd is the country boy who suggests a high-rise climber as a publicity stunt for the big city store that employs him, and then finds he has to substitute for the original daredevil. No wonder Mildred Davis loves him. As a feature-length expansion of his remarkable acrobatic skills displayed in earlier shorts, it's a movie chock full of incidents to make audiences laugh – and gasp. ▣

Harold Lloyd *Boy* • Mildred Davis *Girl* • Bill Strother *Pal* • Noah Young *Law* • Westcott B

Clarke *Floorwalker* ■ *Dir* Fred C Newmeyer, Sam Taylor • *Scr* Hal Roach, Tim Whelan, Sam Taylor

The Saga of Anatahan ★★★★

Drama based on a true story
1953 · Jap · BW · 91mins

In Josef von Sternberg's curious final film, the director shows what can be done with a simple studio set and lighting. Narrated by Sternberg himself, it tells the true story of a group of Japanese merchant seamen shipwrecked on the island of Anahatan in 1944 who believed, seven years after the war had ended, that Japan was still fighting. Von Sternberg, who was the cinematographer as well, shot the film on a sound stage in a Japanese studio, using synthetic sets made of cellophane and papier maché, sprayed with aluminium paint, making it look as artificial as possible. The acting of the cast, consisting of members of the Kabuki theatre, add to the stylisation of the whole picture. A Japanese/English language film.

Akemi Negishi *Keiko, the "Queen Bee"* • Tadashi Suganuma *Kusakabe, the "King"* • Josef von Sternberg *Narrator* ■ *Dir* Josef von Sternberg • *Scr* Josef von Sternberg, from the story *Anatahan* and an article in *Life,magazine*

The Saga of Hemp Brown ★★★ U

Western 1958 · US · Colour · 77mins

In this under-rated Universal western, Rory Calhoun stars as a disgraced cavalry officer seeking to clear his name with the help of medicine man, Fortunio Bonanova. Behind the camera is actor-turned-director Richard Carlson, best known for battling with 3-D monsters in movies such as *Creature from the Black Lagoon*. Calhoun's co-star is cult favourite, Beverly Garland and if this is nothing special, it is competently done and mercifully unpretentious. Contains violence.

Rory Calhoun *Hemp Brown* • Beverly Garland *Mona Langley* • John Larch *Jed Givens* • Russell Johnson *Hook* • Fortunio Bonanova *Serge Bolanos, medicine man* • Allan Lane *Sheriff* • Morris Ankrum *Bo Slauter* ■ *Dir* Richard Carlson • *Scr* Bob Williams, from a story by Bernard Girard

Sagebrush Trail ★★ U

Western 1934 · US · BW · 53mins

This is John Wayne's second Monogram Studios western, and is really only of interest to B-western fans: the plot's average, the direction plods and the cast is unremarkable. What really brings it to life are the stunts, planned and carried out by the incredible Yakima Canutt. Watch out for Canutt doubling for Wayne and hiding underwater – the stunt must have been exceptionally dangerous. ▣

John Wayne *John Brant* • Nancy Shubert *Sally Blake* • Lane Chandler *Bob Jones* • Yakima Canutt *Ed Walsh* ■ *Dir* Armand Schaefer • *Scr* Lindsley Parsons

Sahara ★★★ PG

Second World War action adventure
1943 · US · BW · 93mins

Humphrey Bogart spent most of the war years playing loners in civilian clothes, who stuck their necks out for no one until Lauren Bacall or Ingrid Bergman forced him to take sides. It is something of a surprise, then, to find him here as a resourceful army sergeant, leading a bunch of no-hopers across the desert in a dilapidated tank, dodging Nazis as they search for water. Directed by Zoltan Korda, co-written by John Howard Lawson (later blacklisted in the communist witch-hunt), shot by Rudolph Maté and scored by Miklos Rozsa, there's solid talent behind the camera and a lot of derring-do in front of it. ▣

Humphrey Bogart *Sergeant Joe Gunn* • Bruce Bennett *Waco Hoyt* • Lloyd Bridges *Fred Clarkson* • Rex Ingram *Sergeant Tambul* • J Carrol Naish *Giuseppe* • Dan Duryea *Jimmy Doyle* • Richard Nugent *Captain Jason Halliday* ■ *Dir* Zoltan Korda • *Scr* John Howard Lawson, Zoltan Korda, James O'Hanlon, from a story by Philip MacDonald

Sahara ★ PG

Adventure 1983 · US · Colour · 106mins

After her father dies, flapper Brooke Shields disguises herself as a man and takes his place in the 1920s trans-Sahara automobile race, somehow ending up as the wife of dashing desert sheik Lambert Wilson. A pathetic bodice-ripper that tries to emulate the atmosphere and heated eroticism of Rudolph Valentino silent epics, but ends up as a badly plotted and shoddily produced *Mills & Boon*. This isn't even remotely entertaining on a camp level and sets a new low standard for period romances. ▣

Brooke Shields *Dale Gordon* • Lambert Wilson *Jaffar* • John Rhys-Davies *Rasoul* • Horst Buchholz *Von Glessing* • Perry Lang *Andy* • Cliff Potts *String* • John Mills *Cambridge* ■ *Dir* Andrew V McLaglen • *Scr* James R Silke, from a story by Menahem Golan

Sahara ★★ 15

Second World War drama
1995 · Ausl/US · Colour · 106mins

James Belushi as Humphrey Bogart? Even Belushi's most devoted fans will be raising their eyebrows in disbelief. However, if you can get over the eccentric casting, this is a proficient remake of the 1943 Bogart war movie, which finds Belushi making a last stand against the Germans when his group of survivors is stranded in the desert. Director Brian Trenchard-Smith makes hard work of characterisation and the interplay between the motley crew of Allied soldiers, but is more at home with the action sequences. The result is a moderately entertaining adventure that passes the time harmlessly enough. ▣

James Belushi *Sergeant Joe Gunn* • Alan David Lee *Bates* • Simon Westaway *Williams* • Mark Lee *Jimmy Doyle* • Michael Massee *Leroux* • Jerome Ehlers *Captain Halliday* ■ *Dir* Brian Trenchard-Smith • *Scr* David Phillips

Saigon ★★

Drama 1948 · US · BW · 94mins

Ex-army pilot Alan Ladd washes up in Saigon with one healthy buddy and

another, terminally ill, but not knowing he's got a month left to live. The three guys go out on the town – but without that song – and rope Veronica Lake into joining them on a caper that goes more than slightly wrong. This sort of malarkey lives or dies on the charm of its stars and Ladd and Lake were never in the Bogart–Bacall league. It also could have done with a better supporting cast. Saigon appears on the back projection screen while the foreground is pure studio backlot.

Alan Ladd *Maj Larry Briggs* • Veronica Lake *Susan Cleaver* • Douglas Dick *Capt Mike Perry* • Wally Cassell *Sgt Pete Rocco* • Luther Adler *Lt Keon* ■ *Dir* Leslie Fenton • *Scr* PJ Wolfson, Arthur Sheekman, from a story by Julian Zimet

Saigon ★★★ 18

Action thriller 1988 · US · Colour · 97mins

Despite its pretensions, this is no more than a variant of *Lethal Weapon*'s "white cop, black cop" formula transposed to *Apocalypse Now* territory. Willem Dafoe and Gregory Hines are gripping as army cops tracking down a serial killer – who may or may not be military top brass – among the sleazy back alleys of Saigon circa 1968. It's undeniably well crafted, with much macho posturing, and debut director Crowe offers plenty of twists and turns amid the well-staged action scenes – including an old fashioned non-consummated affair between Dafoe and a streetwise nun (Amanda Pays). ▣

Willem Dafoe *Buck McGriff* • Gregory Hines *Albaby Perkins* • Fred Ward *Dix* • Amanda Pays *Nicole* • Scott Glenn *Colonel Armstrong* • Lim Kay Tong *Lime Green* • Keith David *Maurice* ■ *Dir* Christopher Crowe • *Scr* Christopher Crowe, Jack Thibeau

Sail a Crooked Ship ★★ U

Comedy 1961 · US · BW · 87mins

A wacky heist comedy with ex-Navy man Robert Wagner re-fitting a ship for leisure purposes, but tricked into sailing it to Boston with a dubious skipper (Ernie Kovacs) and a crew of criminals intent on robbing a bank. Perpetually caught somewhere in the charm and macho league between Cary Grant and Paul Newman (with a dash of Rock Hudson), Wagner sails through effortlessly, trading sexy banter with Carolyn Jones and coping well with the almost slapstick antics of the stormy sea crossing. It's likable, but probably seemed dated in 1961.

Robert Wagner *Gilbert Barrows* • Dolores Hart *Elinor Harrison* • Carolyn Jones *Virginia* • Frankie Avalon *Rodney* • Ernie Kovacs *The Captain* • Frank Gorshin *George Wilson* ■ *Dir* Irving Brecher • *Scr* Ruth Brooks Flippen, Bruce Geller, from a novel by Nathaniel Benchley

Sailing Along ★ U

Musical 1938 · UK · BW · 90mins

One of the many substandard – not to say dire – films in which the adored British musical comedy star Jessie Matthews found herself during the thirties. Directed (and co-written) by her then husband, actor Sonnie Hale, it finds Matthews as a female bargee with aspirations to become a stage star, while her co-worker Barry Mackay dreams of being a financier. With the

help of eccentric millionaire Roland Young, they achieve their ambitions before falling into each other's arms and sailing off into the sunset. 🎞️

Jessie Matthews *Kay Martin* • Barry MacKay *Steve Barnes* • Jack Whiting *Dicky Randall* • Roland Young *Anthony Gulliver* • Noel Madison *Windy* • Frank Pettingell *Skipper Barnes* • Alastair Sim *Sylvester* ■ *Dir* Sonnie Hale • *Scr* Lesser Samuels, Sonnie Hale, from a story by Selwyn Jepson

Sailor Beware ★★ U

Comedy　　　　　1951 · US · BW · 103mins

The fifth film pairing of Dean Martin and Jerry Lewis is easily one of their worst. You are either a fan or you can't bear to be in the same room as the duo who took American showbiz by storm in the late 1940s. Putting the comic style to one side, what really makes this hard to take are the smug references to their fame, as the boys do a stint in the navy. Minor consolations are an uncredited guest appearance by Betty Hutton and a blink-and-miss bit for James Dean.

Jerry Lewis *Melvin Jones* • Dean Martin *Al Crowthers* • Corinne Calvet *Guest Star* • Marion Marshall *Hilda Jones* • Robert Strauss *Lardoski* • Vincent Edwards [Vince Edwards] *Blayden* • Leif Erickson *Commander Lane* • James Dean *Sailor* • Dan Willis *Sailor* • Betty Hutton ■ *Dir* Hal Walker • *Scr* James Allardice, Martin Rackin, from a play by Kenyon Nicholson

Sailor Beware! ★★ U

Comedy　　　　　1956 · UK · BW · 80mins

Based on a long-running stage success, this politically incorrect comedy established Peggy Mount in the booming shrew persona that was to make her such a hit in TV series like *George and the Dragon*. Here she terrorises hubby Cyril Smith and prospective son-in-law Ronald Lewis, on the eve of daughter Shirley Eaton's wedding. However, while she dominates the proceedings, she has every scene stolen from under her nose by the peerless Esma Cannon.

Peggy Mount *Emma Hornett* • Cyril Smith *Henry Hornett* • Shirley Eaton *Shirley Hornett* • Ronald Lewis *Albert Tufnell* • Esma Cannon *Edie Hornett* • Joy Webster *Daphne* • Gordon Jackson *Carnoustie Bligh* • Thora Hird *Mrs Lack* • Geoffrey Keen *Reverend Purefoy* • Jack MacGowran *Toddy* • Michael Caine ■ *Dir* Gordon Parry • *Scr* Philip King, Falkland L Cary

The Sailor from Gibraltar ★

Romantic drama　　1967 · UK · BW · 90mins

One of the two grandiose flops Tony Richardson made with Jeanne Moreau, of whom he was much enamoured at the time. Based on a Marguerite Duras novel, adapted by Christopher Isherwood, it's an insufferably arty exercise in alienation with Ian Bannen as the bored office clerk, who has an affair with the La Moreau who sails around exotic Arabian ports, consorting and philosophising with the likes of Orson Welles. An amazing cast, including Richardson's jilted real-life wife Vanessa Redgrave. But movies come no more pretentious than this.

Jeanne Moreau *Anna* • Ian Bannen *Alan* • Vanessa Redgrave *Sheila* • Orson Welles *Louis of Mozambique* • Zia Mohyeddin *Noori* • Hugh Griffith *Llewellyn* • Umberto Orsini *Postcard vendor* ■ *Dir* Tony Richardson • *Scr*

Christopher Isherwood, Don Magner, Tony Richardson, from the novel *Le Marin de Gibraltar* by Marguerite Duras

A Sailor-Made Man ★★★★ U

Silent comedy　1921 · US · BW · 36mins

Yet another Harold Lloyd movie, in which he's the bespectacled wimp who redeems himself by an unexpected show of guts and bravery. Here, he's a wealthy playboy who's told to get a job by the father of the girl he loves (Mildred Davis) – so he joins the Navy. Initially the enemy of tough crew mate Noah Young, they soon become best friends and team-up to save Davis from the lecherous intentions of a maharajah. An entertaining swimming pool dip and a marriage proposal via semaphore contribute towards a very enjoyable Lloyd outing.

Harold Lloyd *The Boy* • Mildred Davis *The Girl* • Noah Young *Rough-House O'Rafferty* • Dick Sutherland *Maharajah* ■ *Dir* Fred C Newmeyer • *Scr* Hal Roach, Sam Taylor, HM Walker (titles), Jean Havez

Sailor of the King ★★★ U

Second World War drama
1953 · UK · BW · 84mins

Originally released in the UK as *Single-Handed*, this is a rather good second screen version of author CS Forester's novel *Brown on Resolution* (the earlier one being the weakish 1935 film *Forever England* starring John Mills), made by 20th Century-Fox in England, with Roy Boulting at the helm. Hollywood heart-throb Jeffrey Hunter is impressive as the courageous Brown, descended from a long line of seafarers, his unlikely parents being Michael Rennie and Wendy Hiller.

Jeffrey Hunter *Seaman Andrew Brown* • Michael Rennie *Captain Richard Saville* • Wendy Hiller *Lucinda Bentley* • Bernard Lee *Petty Officer Wheatley* • Peter Van Eyck *Kapitan von Falk* • Victor Maddern *Signalman Earnshaw* ■ *Dir* Roy Boulting • *Scr* Valentine Davies, from the novel *Brown on Resolution* by CS Forester

The Sailor Takes a Wife ★★

Comedy　　　　　1945 · US · BW · 90mins

Following their pairing in *Her Highness and the Bellboy*, June Allyson and Robert Walker were reunited for this lightweight version of Chester Erskine's play. Director Richard Whorf makes the most of the limited laughs that follow the whirlwind courtship, leaving our newlyweds with nothing but illusions to be shattered. Discharged from the navy, Walker struggles to make an impact on anyone other than Audrey Totter, whose ditzy vamping enlivens the proceedings.

Robert Walker *John* • June Allyson *Mary* • Hume Cronyn *Freddie* • Audrey Totter *Lisa* • Eddie "Rochester" Anderson *Harry* • Reginald Owen *Mr Amboy* • Gerald Oliver Smith *Butler* ■ *Dir* Richard Whorf • *Scr* Chester Erskine, Anne Morrison Chapin, Whitfield Cook, from a play by Chester Erskine

The Sailor Who Fell from Grace with the Sea ★★★ 18

Drama　　　　　1976 · UK · Colour · 100mins

A weird, sometimes disturbing, sometimes downright laughable adaptation of a novel by the Japanese

writer Yukio Mishima – who formed his own right-wing army, committed ritual suicide and became the subject of a brilliant Paul Schrader biopic. This story is about a sensual widow whose teenage son is a member of a strange secret society. Experts felt that the core elements of Mishima's novel went AWOL in the transition from Japan to England (the film was shot at seaside locations), but there's no denying the strangeness of the story, the sexually charged atmosphere or the commitment of Sarah Miles's emotionally naked performance. 🎞️

Sarah Miles *Anne Osborne* • Kris Kristofferson *Jim Cameron* • Jonathan Kahn *Jonathan Osborne* • Margo Cunningham *Mrs Palmer* ■ *Dir* Lewis John Carlino • *Scr* Lewis John Carlino, from the novel by Yukio Mishima

The Sailor's Return ★

Drama　　　　　1978 · UK · Colour · 112mins

A Victorian tragedy, based on the novel by Bloomsbury writer David Garnett, about an English sailor (Tom Bell), whose return from the sea in the company of a black bride (Shope Shodeinde, in her only film to date) scandalises the local community. The period settings are pretty , but nothing much goes on and bigger issues are left unexplored. After his success with *The Naked Civil Servant* (1975), this was one of several disappointments from director Jack Gold.

Tom Bell *William Targett* • Shope Shodeinde *Tulip* • Mick Ford *Tom* • Paola Dionisotti *Lucy* • George Costigan *Harry* • Clive Swift *Reverend Pottock* • Ray Smith *Fred Leake* • Ivor Roberts *Molten* • Bernard Hill *Carter* ■ *Dir* Jack Gold • *Scr* James Saunders, from the novel by David Garnett

Sailors Three ★★ U

Comedy　　　　　1940 · UK · BW · 86mins

Talk about a clash of styles! Who on earth thought that wisecracking Tommy Trinder, silly ass Claude Hulbert and smoothie Michael Wilding would make a winning comedy team? Frankly, even the Ritz Brothers were funnier. Yet, as with most flag-waving pictures made during the Second World War, the aim was to raise morale and not make masterpieces. In that light, this is an effective-enough piece of nonsense from Ealing, with our trio of tars taking on the Nazi navy after a boozy shore leave in Buenos Aires, though it would appear that jokes were subject to war rationing, too.

Tommy Trinder *Tommy Taylor* • Claude Hulbert *Admiral* • Michael Wilding *Johnny* • Carla Lehmann *Jane* • Jeanne de Casalis *Mrs Pilkington* • James Hayter *Hans* • Henry Hewitt *Professor Pilkington* ■ *Dir* Walter Forde • *Scr* Angus Macphail, John Dighton, Austin Melford

The Saint ★★ 12

Crime action thriller
1997 · US · Colour · 111mins

An empty, lumbering spectacular that turns author Leslie Charteris's gallant law-breaker into a cat-burgling James Bond clone. Both Val Kilmer, in the title role, and scientist Elisabeth Shue, are miscast in a mundane tale about a Russian billionaire who's trying to discover a way to glean energy from tap water. Shue has the "cold fusion" formula stuffed into her bra and

practically the whole of director Phillip Noyce's misjudged fiasco has her and Kilmer being chased by the Russian Mafia. Sloppily plotted, unexciting and laughable. Contains some violence, swearing. 🎞️

Val Kilmer *Simon Templar* • Elisabeth Shue *Dr Emma Russell* • Rade Serbedzija *Ivan Tretiak* • Valery Nikolaev *Ilya Tretiak* • Henry Goodman *Dr Lev Botvin* • Alun Armstrong *Chief Inspector Teal* ■ *Dir* Phillip Noyce • *Scr* Jonathan Hensleigh, Wesley Strick, from a story by Jonathan Hensleigh, from the character created by Leslie Charteris

St Elmo's Fire ★★★ 15

Drama　　　　　1985 · US · Colour · 103mins

A Brat Pack movie that most of the cast would probably like to forget, this is now a great example of the excesses of the eighties. Ally Sheedy, Emilio Estevez, Rob Lowe, Andrew McCarthy and Judd Nelson – all of whose careers have never been the same again – are the college pals trying to make their way in the world while wrestling with problems like drug abuse, a teenage marriage, unrequited love and hidden sexuality. This is glossy and glib like so much else from the decade it represents, but it's also a fascinating record of what that generation was watching, wearing and listening to. Contains swearing and drug abuse. 🎞️ **DVD**

Emilio Estevez *Kirby* • Rob Lowe *Billy* • Demi Moore *Jules* • Andrew McCarthy *Kevin* • Judd Nelson *Alec* • Ally Sheedy *Leslie* • Mare Winningham *Wendy* • Martin Balsam *Mr Beamish* • Andie MacDowell *Dale Biberman* ■ *Dir* Joel Schumacher • *Scr* Joel Schumacher, Carl Kurlander

The Saint in London ★★★ PG

Detective adventure
1939 · UK/US · BW · 72mins

Mention the name Simon Templar nowadays and many will think of Roger Moore, some Ian Ogilvy, and a few Val Kilmer. But the finest Saint of them all was undoubtedly George Sanders, who inherited the role from Louis Hayward in 1939. Based on Leslie Charteris's novel *The Million Pound Day*, this tale has our hero pitted against a ruthless counterfeit gang with only dizzy deb Sally Gray in his corner. This was Sanders's second outing as the debonair detective and a rattlingly good yarn it is, too. 🎞️

George Sanders *Simon Templar "The Saint"* • Sally Gray *Penelope Parker* • David Burns *Dugan* • Gordon McLeod *Inspector Teal* • Henry Oscar *Bruno Lang* • Ralph Truman *Kussella* ■ *Dir* John Paddy Carstairs • *Scr* Lynn Root, Frank Fenton, from the novel *The Million Pound Day* by Leslie Charteris

The Saint in New York ★★ PG

Crime adventure　1938 · US · BW · 72mins

The first film in RKO's resolutely low-budget nine-film series has Louis Hayward perfectly cast as the haloed hero. This was rumoured to be one of the movies that Alfred Hitchcock was offered for his US directing debut. Subsequent Saints were George Sanders and Hugh Sinclair, but Hayward returned for the last film *The Saint's Girl Friday* made in 1954; the next time the Saint appeared on

screen was in the guise of smoothie Roger Moore in the sixties TV series. However, no other adaptation followed Charteris's source material as closely as this one. 🖭

Louis Hayward *Simon Templar "The Saint"* • Sig Rumann [Sig Ruman] *Hutch Rellin* • Kay Sutton *Fay Edwards* • Jonathan Hale *Inspector Fernack* • Jack Carson *Red Jenks* • Paul Guilfoyle *Hymie Fanro* ■ *Dir* Ben Holmes • *Scr* Charles Kaufman, Mortimer Offner, from the novel by Leslie Charteris

The Saint in Palm Springs
★★★

Crime adventure   1941 · US · BW · 65mins

George Sanders bade farewell to the role of Simon Templar after this, his fifth outing as Leslie Charteris's suave troubleshooter. There's a pronounced end-of-term feel to the story, in which Sanders crosses swords with a gang intent on preventing him from delivering some rare stamps to their rightful owner. It's not as dull as Sanders's weary expression would have you believe, with director Jack Hively (handling his third Templar adventure) keeping the action brisk, and there is a surprisingly high body count for what was supposed to be a pretty light-hearted series.

George Sanders *Simon Templar "The Saint"* • Wendy Barrie *Elna* • Paul Guilfoyle *Pearly Gates* • Jonathan Hale *Fernack* • Linda Hayes *Margaret Forbes* ■ *Dir* Jack Hively • *Scr* Jerry Cady, from a story by Leslie Charteris

St Ives
★★ 15

Thriller   1976 · US · Colour · 90mins

A rather silly, if glossy, thriller starring an improbable Charles Bronson as a writer embroiled in a murder plot. Veteran director J Lee Thompson ensures that it all moves along at a reasonable pace and looks technically proficient, but there's really little here to get excited about. Jacqueline Bisset has nothing to do but look lovely, and John Houseman and Maximilian Schell are sadly wasted. Keep a sharp eye out for Jeff Goldblum and Robert Englund at the start of their careers. 🖭

Charles Bronson *Raymond St Ives* • John Houseman *Abner Procane* • Jacqueline Bisset *Janet Whistler* • Maximilian Schell *Doctor John Constable* • Harry Guardino *Detective Deal* • Elisha Cook [Elisha Cook Jr] *Eddie the bell boy* • Daniel J Travanti *Johnny Parisi* • Robert Englund *Hood* • Mark Thomas *Hood* • Jeff Goldblum *Hood* ■ *Dir* J Lee Thompson • *Scr* Barry Beckerman, from the novel *The Procane Chronicle* by Oliver Bleeck

Saint Jack
★★★

Drama   1979 · US · Colour · 115mins

One of director Peter Bogdanovich's least known movies, based on Paul Theroux's novel, this black comedy is an effective character study of American Jack Flowers (Ben Gazzara in fine form), a well-educated Korean War hero who pimps and wheeler-deals throughout Singapore in the early seventies. Needing a big cash injection, he accepts an offer to secretly photograph a visiting senator (one-time James Bond actor, George Lazenby) with a male prostitute. But will his sense of moral decency actually allow him to carry out the

scheme? An evocative and whimsical portrait of sleazy Singapore during the Vietnam era.

Ben Gazzara *Jack Flowers* • Denholm Elliott *William Leigh* • James Villiers *Frogget* • Joss Ackland *Yardley* • Rodney Bewes *Smale* • Mark Kingston *Yates* • Peter Bogdanovich *Eddie Schuman* • George Lazenby *Senator* ■ *Scr* Howard Sackler, Paul Theroux, Peter Bogdanovich, from the novel by Paul Theroux

Saint Joan
★★★ U

Drama   1957 · US · BW · 110mins

This is one of Hollywood's celebrated disasters, panned by the critics at the time and seen by almost no one. Loosely based on George Bernard Shaw's play, the script is by none other than Graham Greene and, instead of hiring a major star, director Otto Preminger took a huge gamble with a then unknown young actress called Jean Seberg, who was the right age to play France's great heroine. "Poor Jean Seberg wasn't up to it," said Greene later. "Anyway, I got a few laughs that were not in Bernard Shaw; at least I can claim that." Flops are rarely as fascinating as this one.

Jean Seberg *Joan* • Richard Widmark *Charles the dauphin* • Richard Todd *Dunois* • Anton Walbrook *Cauchon, Bishop of Beauvais* • John Gielgud *Earl of Warwick* • Felix Aylmer *Inquisitor* • Harry Andrews *John de Stognumber* • Barry Jones *De Courcelles* • Finlay Currie *Archbishop of Rheims* • Bernard Miles *Master executioner* ■ *Dir* Otto Preminger • *Scr* Graham Greene, from the play by George Bernard Shaw

St Louis Blues
★★ U

Musical biography   1958 · US · BW · 95mins

Nat King Cole stars as the legendary and influential blues composer WC Handy in this disappointing biopic, which deals with Handy's pursuit of his calling in the face of his Bible-punching father's disapproval, and his complicated relationships with the two women in his life (Eartha Kitt, Ruby Dee). The movie is a sadly wasted opportunity, unimaginatively directed and dramatically dull, with Cole woodenly unconvincing, as is the script. There is compensation, however, in watching (and listening to) a cast that includes Pearl Bailey, Mahalia Jackson, Cab Calloway and, as herself, Ella Fitzgerald.

Nat King Cole *WC Handy* • Eartha Kitt *Gogo Germaine* • Pearl Bailey *Aunt Hagar* • Cab Calloway *Blade* • Ella Fitzgerald • Mahalia Jackson *Bessie May* • Ruby Dee *Elizabeth* ■ *Dir* Allen Reisner • *Scr* Robert Smith, Ted Sherdeman

St Martin's Lane
★★★

Melodrama   1938 · UK · BW · 86mins

This prestigious British melodrama was meticulously designed – to the extent that the extras who formed the theatre queues were cast in descending order of height. Yet, for all this preparation, the film was mauled by the critics and flopped at the box office. There's no denying it's a sentimental tale, but it presents a fascinating portrait of theatre land and, while Vivien Leigh overdoes it as the waif yearning for stardom, Charles Laughton is superb as the busker who supports her.

Charles Laughton *Charles Saggers* • Vivien Leigh *Libby* • Rex Harrison *Harley Prentiss* • Larry Adler *Constantine* • Tyrone Guthrie *Gentry* • Gus McNaughton *Arthur Smith* • Bart Cormack *Strang* ■ *Dir* Tim Whelan • *Scr* Clemence Dane, from her story

The Saint Meets the Tiger
★★

Detective adventure
1943 · US/UK · BW · 78mins

After a two-year gap, RKO continued its wildly inconsistent Saint series with this feeble story of smuggled ingots and worthless gold-mine shares. Hugh Sinclair is simply dreadful as Simon Templar in this cheapskate mystery.

Hugh Sinclair *Simon Templar "The Saint"* • Jean Gillie *Pat Holmes* • Gordon McLeod *Inspector Teal/Professor Kahn* • Clifford Evans *Tidmarsh* • Wylie Watson *Horace* ■ *Dir* Paul Stein [Paul L Stein] • *Scr* Leslie Arliss, Wolfgang Wilhelm, James Seymour, from the novel *Meet the Tiger* by Leslie Charteris

The Saint of Fort Washington
★★ 15

Drama   1993 · US · Colour · 99mins

A well-meaning, but self-conscious social drama, which tackles the rather unfashionable (well, for Hollywood at least) subject of homelessness. Matt Dillon is the mentally disabled young man who finds himself on the streets; salvation comes in the shape of Vietnam veteran Danny Glover. The two leads deliver moving performances, and the good support cast includes Ving Rhames and Nina Siemaszko. Contains violence. 🖭

Danny Glover *Jerry* • Matt Dillon *Matthew* • Rick Aviles *Rosario* • Nina Siemaszko *Tamsen* • Ving Rhames *Little Leroy* • Joe Seneca *Spits* • Robert Beatty Jr *Ex-pharmacist* ■ *Dir* Tim Hunter • *Scr* Lyle Kessler

The Saint Strikes Back
★★★

Crime adventure   1939 · US · BW · 64mins

Super-suave George Sanders stepped into the shoes of Simon Templar for this sprightly mystery, based on Charteris's novel *Angels of Doom*. Here, Sanders takes on the San Francisco underworld in order to prove the innocence of Wendy Barrie's cop father. Jonathan Hale also joins the series in the recurring role of Inspector Fernack, who starts every case by putting Templar at the top of the list of suspects. Briskly directed by John Farrow, the film boasts atmospheric sets by Van Nest Polglase, who designed the Astaire/Rogers musicals as well as *Citizen Kane*.

George Sanders *Simon Templar "The Saint"* • Wendy Barrie *Valerie Travers* • Jonathan Hale *Henry Fernack* • Jerome Cowan *Cullis* • Neil Hamilton *Allan Breck* • Barry Fitzgerald *Zipper Dyson* • Robert Elliott *Webster* ■ *Dir* John Farrow • *Scr* John Twist, from the novel *Angels of Doom* by Leslie Charteris

The Saint Takes Over
★★★

Crime adventure   1940 · US · BW · 69mins

RKO had to borrow George Sanders back from 20th Century-Fox for this entry in the ever-popular *Saint* series. Scripted by Frank Fenton and Lynn Root, it was the first not to be based on a Leslie Charteris story, but the tale

of racetrack hoods who implicate Inspector Fernack (Jonathan Hale) in their race-rigging scam is packed with incident and taken at a fair gallop by director Jack Hively. Wendy Barrie makes the second of her three appearances in the series (all as different characters), while Paul Guilfoyle makes his debut as Simon Templar's light-fingered assistant Clarence "Pearly" Gates.

George Sanders *Simon Templar "The Saint"* • Wendy Barrie *Ruth* • Jonathan Hale *Inspector Henry Fernack* • Paul Guilfoyle *Clarence "Pearly" Gates* • Morgan Conway *Sam Reese* • Robert Emmett Keane *Leo Sloan* • Cyrus W Kendall [Cy Kendall] *Max Bremer* • James Burke *Mike* ■ *Dir* Jack Hively • *Scr* Lynn Root, Frank Fenton, from characters created by Leslie Charteris

The St Valentine's Day Massacre
★★★

Crime drama   1967 · US · Colour · 99mins

The most authentic documentary-style account – complete with narration giving precise time and location details – of the Chicago gang wars between crime lords Al Capone (Jason Robards) and Bugs Moran (Ralph Meeker), that led to the infamous 1929 massacre. Offbeat casting, lots of bloody action and cult director Roger Corman working for a major studio – and with a decent budget for the first time – make for a compelling and always fascinating throwback to the quick-fire gangster movies of the thirties. Contains violence, swearing.

Jason Robards [Jason Robards Jr] *Al Capone* • George Segal *Peter Gusenberg* • Ralph Meeker *George "Bugsy" Moran* • Jean Hale *Myrtle Nelson* • Clint Ritchie *"Machinegun Jack" McGurn* • Frank Silvera *Nicholas Sorello* • Joseph Campanella *Al Weinshank* • Bruce Dern *John May* • Jack Nicholson *Gino* ■ *Dir* Roger Corman • *Scr* Howard Browne

The Sainted Sisters
★★

Period comedy
1948 · US · BW · 89mins

In 1895 Maine, sexy con-women Veronica Lake and Joan Caulfield have the misfortune to come up against broth of a boy Barry Fitzgerald, who has a sneaky method of showing them the error of their ways. An appealing idea is ploddingly developed by William D Russell, a no-count director who moved swiftly to television (*Gunsmoke, Bewitched*). The contrivances and folksy comedy make the going tough.

Veronica Lake *Letty Stanton* • Joan Caulfield *Jane Stanton* • Barry Fitzgerald *Robbie McCleary* • William Demarest *Vern Tewilliger* • George Reeves *Sam Stoaks* • Beulah Bondi *Hester Rivercomb* • Chill Wills *Will Twitchell* ■ *Dir* William D Russell • *Scr* Harry Clork, Richard Nash [N Richard Nash], Mindret Lord, from the play by Elisa Bialk, Alden Nash, from the story *Sainted Sisters of Sandy Creek* by Elisa Bialk

A Saintly Switch
★★

Comedy fantasy   1999 · US · Colour · 96mins

A typical American family is turned upside-down in this light-hearted comedy from director Peter Bogdanovich. Kids, afraid that their bickering parents might split, cast a spell and feminine Mom finds herself trapped inside Dad's pro quarterback body, while macho Dad struts around

U = SUITABLE FOR ALL   Uc = SUITABLE FOR ALL, ESPECIALLY FOR YOUNG CHILDREN (VIDEO ONLY)   PG = PARENTAL GUIDANCE

in Mom's body, spouting football statistics. Although the roles are stereotyped, there is much fun to be had in this gender-bending Disney telefilm.

David Alan Grier *Dan Anderson* • Vivica A Fox *Sara Anderson* • Rue McClanahan *Fanny Moye* • Al Waxman *Coach Beasily* ■ *Dir* Peter Bogdanovich • *Scr* Harris Orkin

Saints and Sinners ★★ 18

Erotic crime drama
1995 · US · Colour · 94mins

Damian Chapa returns to his old neighbourhood and is reunited with childhood friend Scott Plank. Although on the surface their friendship is as strong as ever, there is more to the relationship than meets the eye: Plank is now a successful gangster and Chapa is an undercover cop on assignment to arrest him. Into the mix add Jennifer Rubin, a vivacious, but off-centre young woman. With guns, gansters and nudity, it should be loads of fun. Unfortunately, it isn't. ▭

Damian Chapa *Pooch* • Jennifer Rubin *Eva* • Scott Plank *Big Boy* • William Atherton *McCone* • Damon Whitaker *Rockitt* ■ *Dir/Scr* Paul Mones

The Saint's Double Trouble
★★

Crime adventure   1940 · US · BW · 67mins

Perhaps the least accomplished film in RKO's popular B series, this entry, nevertheless, has the added bonus of George Sanders pursuing himself, as he plays both Simon Templar and a criminal mastermind called "The Boss". The scene in which Templar, posing as his criminal double, meets "The Boss" impersonating Templar, is a classic example of back-projected trickery. The film also has the distinction of being one of Bela Lugosi's final bids to prove he was capable of more than just horror, but here, his Egyptian smuggler made so little impact that he was condemned to spend his twilight years in ghouldom.

George Sanders *Simon Templar ''The Saint ''/ ''The Boss''* • Helene Whitney *Anne* • Jonathan Hale *Fernack* • Bela Lugosi *Partner* ■ *Dir* Jack Hively • *Scr* Ben Holmes, from a story by Leslie Charteris

The Saint's Vacation   ★★

Detective adventure
1941 · US/UK · BW · 78mins

Hugh Sinclair assumed the role of Simon Templar for this tame thriller, made in Britain by RKO. Although co-scripted by Leslie Charteris from his own story, it's hardly mystery, with Sinclair racing ruthless Nazi agents to a musical box that contains a vital code. Switzerland has never looked quite so much like a series of hurriedly built studio sets, but then Sinclair is nothing like the genuine article either. The chief interest lies in the solid supporting cast, which includes Cecil Parker, Felix Aylmer and Sally Gray.

Hugh Sinclair *Simon Templar ''The Saint''* • Sally Gray *Mary Langdon* • Arthur Macrae *Monty Hayward* • Cecil Parker *Rudolph Hauser* • Leueen MacGrath *Valerie* • Gordon McLeod *Inspector Teal* • John Warwick *Gregory* • Ivor Barnard *Emil* • Manning Whiley *Marko* • Felix

Aylmer *Charles Leighton* ■ *Dir* Leslie Fenton • *Scr* Jeffry Dell, Leslie Charteris, from the novel *Getaway* by Leslie Charteris

Salaam Bombay! ★★★★ 15

Drama   1988 · Ind/Fr/UK · Colour · 109mins

Dickensian in its empathy with the poor, uncompromising in its realism and ambitious in both scope and technique, Mira Nair's debut feature is one of the most arresting studies of street life ever made. Shot on location after numerous workshops had drawn together a cast made up mostly of homeless kids, the tale of a runaway's assimilation into the dangerous world of petty crime, drugs and prostitution draws on Nair's documentary experience. But it also demonstrates her skill in coaxing a performance of disarming naturalism from Shafiq Syed as the 11-year-old whose indomitability prevents the film from becoming too painful or sentimental. In Hindi with English subtitles. ▭

Shafiq Syed *Krishna/Chaipau* • Raghubir Yadav [Raghuvir Yadav] *Chillum* • Aneeta Kanwar *Rekha* • Nana Patekar *Baba* • Hansa Vithal *Manju* ■ *Dir* Mira Nair • *Scr* Sooni Taraporevala, from a story by Mira Nair, Sooni Taraporevala

The Salamander   ★ 15

Thriller   1981 · US/It /UK · Colour · 97mins

Morris West's novel becomes a heavy-handed drama about a failed right-wing coup in Italy, with Franco Nero as a spy and Anthony Quinn as a millionaire businessman, who also hunts down war criminals. First time director Peter Zinner (whose editing of *The Deer Hunter* won him an Oscar) gets bogged down in plot and then wastes time on travelogue material, reducing the impressive cast to bystanders. ▭

Anthony Quinn *Bruno Manzini* • Franco Nero *Dante Matucci* • Martin Balsam *Stefanelli* • Sybil Danning *Lili Anders* • Christopher Lee *Director Baldassare* • Claudia Cardinale *Elena* • Cleavon Little *Major Malinowski* • Eli Wallach *Leporello* ■ *Dir* Peter Zinner • *Scr* Robert Katz, from a novel by Morris West

Salem's Lot   ★★★ 18

Horror   1979 · US · Colour · 105mins

More blood and stronger horror was added to the spooky theatrical version of the truncated television miniseries based on Stephen King's bestseller. Novelist David Soul moves to the New England town to accumulate research for a new book and finds the place troubled by vampirism after mysterious antiques man James Mason moves into the sinister house on the hill. *The Texas Chain Saw Massacre* director Tobe Hooper, plunders *Psycho* and *Nosferatu* to good effect in a brisk bloodsucker saga featuring the very creepy looking Reggie Nalder as the undead nemesis. ▭

David Soul *Ben Mears* • James Mason *Richard K Straker* • Bonnie Bedelia *Susan Norton* • Lance Kerwin *Mark Petrie* • Lew Ayres *Jason Burke* • Ed Flanders *Dr Bill Norton* • Geoffrey Lewis *Mike Ryerson* • Kenneth McMillan *Parkins Gillespie* ■ *Dir* Tobe Hooper • *Scr* Paul Monash, from the novel by Stephen King

Sallah   ★★★ U

Comedy   1964 · Is · BW · 104mins

In 1948, Topol, his wife and seven children arrive in Israel – only to be housed in a transit camp rather than the roomy flat they were expecting. Needing £1,000 to jump the queue and secure the flat, he throws himself into a number of dodgy schemes to raise the money. Warm-hearted satire with Topol (then known under his full name Haym – or Chaim – Topol) playing Sallah like an early, Jewish version of *Minder's* ''Arfur'' Daley. Perhaps a bit overburdened with local colour and characters, but still a pleasant enough time-passer.

Chaim Topol [Topol] *Sallah Shabati* • Geula Noni *Habbubah Shabati* • Gila Almagor *Bathsheva Sosialit* • Arik Einstein *Ziggi* • Shraga Friedman *Neuman* ■ *Dir* Ephraim Kishon • *Scr* Ephraim Kishon, from a story by Ephraim Kishon

Sally in Our Alley   ★

Romantic musical drama
1931 · UK · BW · 75mins

Of interest only to historians or those addicted to ''Our Gracie'', this worse-than-mediocre film made Gracie Fields a star and gave her her lifelong signature song, *Sally*. Directed by Maurice Elvey and co-starring Ian Hunter, the plot has Gracie as a teashop entertainer who believes her boyfriend has been killed in the war. Of course he hasn't, and they are happily reunited after Florence Desmond loses the competition for his affections.

Gracie Fields *Sally Winch* • Ian Hunter *George Miles* • Florence Desmond *Florrie Small* • Ivor Barnard *Tod Small* • Fred Groves *Alf Cope* ■ *Dir* Maurice Elvey • *Scr* Miles Malleson, Alma Reville, Archie Pitt, from the play *The Likes of 'Er* by Charles McEvoy

Sally, Irene and Mary   ★★

Silent comedy drama
1925 · US · BW · 58mins

The salutary experiences of three chorus girls on the make. Edmund Goulding directs Constance Bennett as Sally, the most worldly of the trio; Sally O'Neil as Mary, sprightly and cheerful, who wisely relinquishes the bright lights in favour of her faithful beau; and Joan Crawford as Irene, who comes to a horrible end. The kind of tale that has been done to death over the decades, this film version of a stage musical inevitably lost much in its transfer to the silent screen and offers little interest now, apart from its leading ladies.

Constance Bennett *Sally* • Joan Crawford *Irene* • Sally O'Neil *Mary* • William Haines *Jimmy Dugan* ■ *Dir* Edmund Goulding • *Scr* Edmund Goulding, from a play by Edward Dowling, Cyrus Wood

Sally, Irene and Mary
★★★ U

Musical comedy   1938 · US · BW · 85mins

Borrowing the title, but nothing else of an early stage musical, this romantic musical comedy from Fox stars Alice Faye and her then husband Tony Martin. It's movie jam-packed with plot, action, songs, and a cast that includes Jimmy Durante, Fred Allen, Gregory Ratoff and, as a middle-aged

moneybags widow with her sights set on Martin, Louise Hovick – better known as stripper, Gypsy Rose Lee. This genial nonsense begin with three girls (Faye, Joan Davis, Marjorie Weaver), working as manicurists while looking for the big break into showbiz .

Alice Faye *Sally Day* • Tony Martin *Tommy Reynolds* • Fred Allen *Gabriel ''Gabby'' Green* • Jimmy Durante *Jefferson Twitchell* • Gregory Ratoff *Baron Zorka* • Joan Davis *Irene Keene* • Marjorie Weaver *Mary Stevens* • Louise Hovick [Gypsy Rose Lee] *Joyce Taylor* ■ *Dir* William A Seiter • *Scr* Harry Tugend, Jack Yellen, from a story by Karl Tunberg, Don Ettinger, from a play by Edward Dowling, Cyril Wood

Sally of the Sawdust   ★★ U

Silent comedy   1925 · US · BW · 86mins

After the death of her mother, who was disowned for marrying a circus performer, Carol Dempster is raised by juggler and conman WC Fields. Having reached womanhood, McGargle decides to find her grandparents, and sets a multiplicity of complications into motion. Adapted from the play *Poppy*, under which title it was remade in 1936 with Fields again starring, this silent version was the only feature-length comedy made by D W Griffith.

Carol Dempster *Sally* • WC Fields *Prof Eustace P McGargle* • Alfred Lunt *Peyton Lennox* ■ *Dir* DW Griffith • *Scr* Forrest Halsey, from the play *Poppy* by Dorothy Donnelly

Salmonberries   ★★★ 15

Drama   1991 · Ger · Colour · 90mins

Deprived of star Marianne Sägebrecht after a trio of angular films, Percy Adlon seemed to lose his way with this story set in the frozen wastes of Alaska and the newly unified Berlin. Ultimately, it's an optimistic film about the true nature of love and coming to terms with the past, but from its confused opening *Salmonberries* is hard to engage with, for all the efforts of kd lang as an Eskimo trying to conceal her sexual identity and Rosel Zech as the shy German unsure how best to love her. There are some moving moments, but the pace is sadly lacking. Contains swearing and nudity ▭

kd lang *Kotzebue* • Rosel Zech *Roswitha* • Chuck Connors *Bingo Chuck* • Jane Lind *Noayak* • Oscar Kawagley *Butch* • Wolfgang Steinberg *Albert* ■ *Dir* Percy Adlon • *Scr* Percy Adlon, Felix O Adlon

Salo, or the 120 Days of Sodom   ★★★★★

Political drama
1975 · It/Fr · Colour · 117mins

Relocating the Marquis de Sade's infamous novel to wartime Italy, this film has become synonymous with sexual deviance and bestial violence. Yet, the soon-to-be-murdered Pier Paolo Pasolini had loftier ambitions than simply shocking the complacent who thought his work obscene. Each of the libertines committing the unspeakably heinous acts represents a social pillar that had delivered the nation into the hands of the Fascists – the law, the merchants, the aristocracy and the church. By depicting their crimes from a distance and by cutting away at the most distasteful moments, he reveals the culpability of the viewer for their passive reponse to the barbarism. So devastating, it's almost unwatchable. In Italian with English subtitles. Contains graphic violence, sex scenes.

Paolo Bonacelli *The Duke* • Giorgio Cataldi *The Bishop* • Uberto Paulo Quintavalle *Chief Magistrate* • Caterina Boratto *Signora Castelli* • Hélène Surgère *Signora Vaccari* ■ *Dir* Pier Paolo Pasolini • *Scr* Pier Paolo Pasolini, Sergio Citti, from the novel *Les 120 Journées de Sodome* by Marquis de Sade

Salome ★★
Silent drama   1922 · US · BW · 38mins

Hailed as America's first art film, silent movie star Alla Nazimova lost a personal fortune producing this extravagant version of Oscar Wilde's controversial play, which re-created Aubrey Beardsley's sumptuous text illustrations for the screen. The infamous, Russian-born phenomenon plays the lead in this ornate, if stagey, reading of the biblical story of King Herod and his unbridled passion for his adolescent stepdaughter Salome, who demands the head of her own lust object Jokanaan (John the Baptist), in return for the Dance of the Seven Veils. All the sets and costumes were designed by the future Mrs Rudolph Valentino, Natacha Rambova, and the entire cast and crew were allegedly homosexual in homage to Wilde. A camp curiosity, it features men in drag and outrageous make-up, arch posing and hilariously unsubtle titles.

Nazimova [Alla Nazimova] *Salome* • Rose Dione *Herodias* • Mitchell Lewis *Herod* • Nigel De Brulier *Jokaanan* ■ *Dir* Charles Bryant • *Scr* Peter M Winters [Natacha Rambova], from the play by Oscar Wilde

Salome ★★★ PG
Drama   1953 · US · Colour · 98mins

Superbly cast tosh from Columbia, directed at a deathly pace by veteran William Dieterle, and given credence only by Alan Badel's sincere portrayal of John the Baptist. But credence isn't what this film's about. You watch it for the stars; the dashing Stewart Granger, flexing his armoured torso for the benefit of ravishing Rita Hayworth, while Charles Laughton chews the scenery as Herod. And wait until you see what they've done to the *Dance of the Seven Veils*! Stage luminaries Cedric Hardwicke, Judith Anderson, Basil Sydney and Maurice Schwartz are in there, too – for the money, no doubt. ▭

Rita Hayworth *Princess Salome* • Stewart Granger *Commander Claudius* • Charles Laughton *King Herod* • Judith Anderson *Queen Herodias* • Cedric Hardwicke *Caesar Tiberius* • Alan Badel *John the Baptist* • Basil Sydney *Pontius Pilate* ■ *Dir* William Dieterle • *Scr* Harry Kleiner, from a story by Harry Kleiner, Jesse Lasky Jr

Salome's Last Dance ★★ 18
Drama   1988 · UK · Colour · 85mins

Ken Russell's career continued to slide downwards with this execrable re-working of Oscar Wilde's banned play, as an end of the pier show acted by some of his pals. The whole grossly over-the-top farrago shrieks excess and truly abominable acting, particularly from Russell himself, who bounces

around the small enclosed set as a leering, ruddy-faced photographer. Glenda Jackson, who turns in a bizarre Herodias, must be greatly regretting her involvement in this one. Worth watching only for Stratford Johns's ability to invest a tiresome Herod with a wry, mischievous air. Contains swearing, nudity. ▭

Glenda Jackson *Herodias/Lady Alice* • Stratford Johns *Herod/Alfred Taylor* • Nickolas Grace *Oscar Wilde* • Douglas Hodge *Lord Alfred Douglas/John the Baptist* • Imogen Millais-Scott *Salome/Rose* • Denis Ull *Tigellenus/Chilvers* • Ken Russell *Kenneth* ■ *Dir* Ken Russell • *Scr* Ken Russell, from the play *Salomé* by Oscar Wilde

Salon Kitty ★★ 18
Erotic drama
1976 · It/W Ger · Colour · 112mins

In independent director Giovanni Tinto Brass's trashy tale of fascist decadence in Berlin in 1939, young women are trained to entertain Nazi officers with degrading perversions in the famous high-class brothel of the title. A wild and arty mix of graphic sex, fetishistic art direction, heavy-handed political statements and gore, this trendsetter spawned a rash of nasty Nazi exploitation flicks. In Italian with English subtitles. Contains nudity. ▭

Helmut Berger *Captain Helmut Wallenberg* • Ingrid Thulin *Kitty Kellermann* • Teresa Ann Savoy *Margherita* • Bekim Fehmiu *Captain Hans Reiter* • John Steiner *Biondo* ■ *Dir* Giovanni Tinto Brass • *Scr* Ennio De Concini, Maria Pia Fusco, Giovanni Tinto Brass

Saloon Bar ★★★
Crime mystery   1940 · UK · BW · 75mins

Gordon Harker was a familiar face in British thrillers during the thirties, his mournful expression and throaty cockney accent enabled him to play characters on either side of the law. In this engaging Ealing whodunit, he has a fine old time as a bookie playing detective in his local. Director Walter Forde makes effective use of the claustrophobic set to build tension, and he is well served by an efficient cast of suspects.

Gordon Harker *Joe Harris* • Elizabeth Allan *Queenie* • Mervyn Johns *Wickers* • Joyce Barbour *Sally* • Anna Konstam *Ivy* • Cyril Raymond *Harry Small* • Judy Campbell *Doris* • Al Millen *Fred* • Norman Pierce *Bill Hoskins* • Alec Clunes *Eddie Graves* ■ *Dir* Walter Forde • *Scr* Angus MacPhail, John Dighton, from a play by Frank Harvey Jr

Salsa ★ PG
Musical romantic drama
1988 · US · Colour · 93mins

Miserable effort to give a Latin spin to the successful dance flicks like *Saturday Night Fever* and *Dirty Dancing*. Unfortunately, Boaz Davidson forgot to make the plot, about a grease monkey going for the King of Salsa crown, remotely involving. But since this was made before the explosion of interest in salsa, and *Strictly Ballroom* made dancing hip again, it might just be worth a second look. Yet, given that and the pluses of Kenny Ortega's choreography and Tito Puente's soundtrack, it's still low-rent and pedestrian. ▭

Bobby Rosa *Rico* • Rodney Harvey *Ken* • Magali Alvarado *Rita* • Miranda Garrison *Luna* • Moon Orona *Lola* • Loyda Ramos *Mother* ■ *Dir* Boaz Davidson • *Scr* Boaz Davidson, Tomas Benitez, Shepard Goldman, by Eli Tabor, by Boaz Davidson

Salt and Pepper ★★★
Comedy   1968 · UK · Colour · 102mins

Sinatra clan members, Sammy Davis Jr and Peter Lawford came to Britain to make this amiable, though strictly routine, comedy crime caper. They play Soho club-owners involved in a series of murders that turn out to be part of an international conspiracy. The attempt to jump on the "Swinging London" bandwagon, pathetic at the time, now has high camp value and some of the lines are still funny. A number of experienced British character actors raise the amusement level by playing stock figures of authority. Although loathed by the press and eventually released as a second-feature, it produced a sequel (*One More Time*) in 1970.

Sammy Davis Jr *Charles Salt* • Peter Lawford *Christopher Pepper* • Michael Bates *Inspector Crabbe* • Ilona Rodgers *Marianne Renaud* • John Le Mesurier *Colonel Woodstock* • Graham Stark *Sergeant Walters* • Ernest Clark *Colonel Balsom* • Jeanne Roland *Mai Ling* ■ *Dir* Richard Donner • *Scr* Michael Pertwee

Salt of the Earth ★★★★★
Drama   1954 · US · BW · 94mins

Probably the most left-wing movie ever made in America, *Salt of the Earth* represents an extraordinary act of defiance against McCarthyism and the Hollywood blacklist. Its subject is a miners' strike, but the picture opens a pandora's box of themes, ranging from immigrant workers, racism, the rights of women and the way that America's post-war economic boom passes these people by. Director Herbert J Biberman, producer Paul Jarrico, Oscar-winning writer Michael Wilson, composer Sol Kaplan and actor Will Geer were all blacklisted at the time and the film, financed by the Miners Union, was subject to constant FBI harassment and barely shown in cinemas. Not only a milestone in the political history of the cinema, it's a riveting piece of work.

Rosaura Revueltas *Esperanza Quintero* • Juan Chacon *Ramon Quintero* • Will Geer *Sheriff* • David Wolfe *Barton* • Melvin Williams *Hartwell* • David Sarvis *Alexander* • Henrietta Williams *Teresa Vidal* ■ *Dir* Herbert J Biberman • *Scr* Michael Wilson

Salt on Our Skin ★★ 18
Romantic drama
1992 · Ger/Can/Fr · Colour · 106mins

Also known as *Desire*, this tale of attracting opposites provides Greta Scacchi with another opportunity to indulge in a little steamy romance. As the globetrotting feminist whose principles founder on the rippling torso of Scottish fisherman Vincent D'Onofrio, she is a touch too glamorous to convince. But then nothing about Andrew Birkin's drama is particularly credible, especially the manner in which the star-crossed lovers keep running into each other. Much more interesting is the striking scenery (shot by Rainer Werner

Fassbinder's regular cinematographer, Dietrich Lohmann) and the guest turns from popular French stars Claudine Auger and Charles Berling. ▭

Greta Scacchi *George* • Vincent D'Onofrio *Gavin* • Anaïs Jeanneret *Frederique* • Claudine Auger *George's mother* • Rolf Illig *George's father* • Shirley Henderson *Mary* • Charles Berling *Roger* ■ *Dir* Andrew Birkin • *Scr* Bee Gilbert, from the novel *Les Vaisseaux du Coeur* by Benoîte Groult

Salt Water Moose ★★★
Adventure   1996 · Can · Colour · 90mins

The symbolism couldn't be much more blatant, but there's an old-fashioned charm about this family feature from actor-turned-director Stuart Margolin. Set in the Canadian countryside, it focuses on the efforts of Katharine Isobel and newcomer Johnny Morina to build a raft in order to pair a lonely bull moose with a mate. Predictably, their river adventure proves more perilous than they imagined and it takes her boat-builder father and his determined mother to save the day. Timothy Dalton and Lolita Davidovich play along as the single parents, but the real star is the Nova Scotia scenery. Contains some swearing.

Timothy Dalton *Lester Parnell* • Lolita Davidovich *Eva Scofield* • Johnny Morina *Bobby Scofield* • Katherine Isobel *Josephine "Jo" Parnell* • Corinne Conley *Grandma* • Maurice Godin *Richard* ■ *Dir* Stuart Margolin • *Scr* Bruce McKenna

Salty O'Rourke ★★★★
Sports comedy drama
1945 · US · BW · 97mins

Alan Ladd is on top form as a likeable heel in this brightly written racetrack story. A gambler in debt to gangsters, Ladd recruits an obnoxious but talented young jockey, convincingly played by Stanley Clements, to ride a vital race for him. Ladd then has to charm Gail Russell's schoolteacher into tolerating the youth's classroom insolence, as expulsion would bar him from racing. With strong support from William Demarest it's a delight from start to finish, thanks to Walsh's polished direction, excellent casting and – most particularly – the original screenplay by Milton Holmes, which gained an Academy Award nomination.

Alan Ladd *Salty O'Rourke* • Gail Russell *Barbara Brooks* • William Demarest *Smitty* • Stanley "Stash" Clements [Stanley Clements] *Johnny Cates* • Bruce Cabot *Doc Baxter* • Spring Byington *Mrs Brooks* • Rex Williams *The Babe* • Darryl Hickman *Sneezer* ■ *Dir* Raoul Walsh • *Scr* Milton Holmes

Saludos Amigos ★★★ U
Animation   1943 · US · Colour · 40mins

Produced to support the United States' "Good Neighbour" policy towards Latin America and to prevent its nations from allying with the Axis powers during the Second World War, *Saludos Amigos* and its 1944 companion *The Three Caballeros* are among the least seen Disney films. While perhaps better propaganda than entertainment, this short feature still has plenty to enjoy. Donald Duck's tour of Peru includes a hilarious meeting with a pesky llama, while gaucho Goofy comes a cropper on the pampas. ▭

   U = SUITABLE FOR ALL,   Uc = SUITABLE FOR ALL, ESPECIALLY FOR YOUNG CHILDREN (VIDEO ONLY)   PG = PARENTAL GUIDANCE

Dir Bill Roberts, Jack Kinney, Hamilton Luske, Wilfred Jackson

Salut Cousin! ★★★ 15
Comedy drama
1996 · Fr/Bel/Alg/Lux · Colour · 102mins
Returning to France after a sojourn in his native Algeria, Merzak Allouache opted for a droll approach in relating this sly variation on the town-and-country-mouse theme. In Paris to pick up some clothing, rag-trade gofer Gad Elmaleh accepts the hospitality of his cousin Mess Hattou, who has adapted to the Parisian lifestyle in a way that both shocks and intrigues Elmaleh. This accessible character comedy stands in contrast to the director's earlier *Bab el-Oued City*, which sacrificed narrative cogency for political statement. In French with English subtitles. Contains swearing and nudity.
Gad Elmaleh *Alilo* • Mess Hattou *Mokrane "Mok" Bensalem* • Magaly Berdy *Fatoumata* • Ann-Gisel Glass *Laurence* • Jean Benguigui *Maurice* ■ *Dir* Merzak Allouache • *Scr* Merzak Allouache, Caroline Thivel

The Salute of the Jugger ★★
Science-fiction action adventure
1989 · US/Ausl · Colour · 102mins
Mad Max meets *Rollerball* in this lame post-apocalyptic action adventure that resembles TV's *Gladiators* on the cheap. Rutger Hauer stars as a veteran player of a savage future sport that combines rugby, basketball and gratuitous violence, who's reduced to leading a ragbag outfit of semi-pros from village to village to take on all comers. That is, until ambitious apprentice Joan Chen spurs him towards a return to the big city. Both trite and dull, even the sport action lacks the required knockout element. Contains violence, swearing and nudity.
Rutger Hauer *Sallow* • Joan Chen *Kidda* • Vincent Phillip D'Onofrio [Vincent D'Onofrio] *Young Gar* • Delroy Lindo *Mbulu* • Anna Katarina *Big Cimber* • Gandhi MacIntyre *Gandhi* • Justin Monju *Dog Boy* • Max Fairchild *Gonzo* • Hugh Keays-Byrne *Lord Vile* ■ *Dir* David Peoples [David Webb Peoples] • *Scr* David Peoples [David Webb Peoples]

Salute to the Marines ★★
Second World War comedy drama
1943 · US · Colour · 101mins
MGM pays tribute to the US Marine Corps by casting plug-ugly star Wallace Beery as the marine who has spent 30-odd years without seeing active duty. Hitting the bottle – and then some merchant seamen – he ends up in the brig, much to the dismay of his pacifist wife. A physical and emotional wreck, Beery is thrown out of the service. Then the Japanese invade the Philippines and, naturally, Beery is on hand to help with the evacuation. To watch the script's contortions is an amusement in itself, but most audiences today will find Beery's self-pity easy to resist.
Wallace Beery *Sgt Major Bailey* • Fay Bainter *Jennie Bailey* • Reginald Owen *Mr Caspar* • Ray Collins *Col Mason* • Keye Luke *"Flashy"*

Logaz • Marilyn Maxwell *Helen Bailey* ■ *Dir* Sylvan Simon • *Scr* George Bruce, Wells Root, from a story by Robert D Andrews

Salvador ★★★★★ 18
Drama   1986 · US · Colour · 117mins
Oliver Stone's first major film also made a star out of James Woods who gives a stunning, Oscar-nominated performance as a zapped-out journalist who heads down to Latin America in search of sex, drugs and rock 'n' roll. What he finds is a nation in chaos with death squads, CIA spooks and the media circus in full cry. He also finds redemption. Stone's message here is "No more Vietnams," delivered in a ferocious, pseudo-documentary style that plunges us pell-mell into the middle of street fighting where tracheotomies are performed with ballpoint pens and photographers get high on carnage. ▭
James Woods *Richard Boyle* • James Belushi *Dr Rock* • Michael Murphy *Ambassador Thomas Kelly* • John Savage *John Cassady* • Elpidia Carrillo *Maria* • Tony Plana *Major Max* • Colby Chester *Jack Morgan* • Cynthia Gibb *Cathy Moore* ■ *Dir* Oliver Stone • *Scr* Oliver Stone, Richard Boyle

Salvage ★★
Science-fiction comedy   1979 · US · Colour
Steptoe and Son in space! Junkman Andy Griffith and his young friends fly to the moon to salvage all the scientific equipment, rusty rockets and disused satellites littering the lunar surface and have an assortment of amiable adventures. A good-natured TV movie pilot, which became a short-lived series that failed to capitalise on its interesting premise.
Andy Griffith *Harry Broderick* • Joel Higgins *Skip Carmichael* • Trish Stewart *Melanie Slozer* • Richard Jaeckel *Jack Klinger* • J Jay Saunders *Mack* ■ *Dir* Lee Philips • *Scr* Mike Lloyd Ross

The Salvation Hunters ★★★★
Silent drama   1925 · US · BW
Though often ponderous and pretentious – "Our aim has been to photograph thought" – this dockyard drama was a remarkable first film by Josef von Sternberg, who produced, directed, wrote and edited. Shot rapidly in actual locations, with a cast and crew of semi-amateurs, it dealt with the world of waterfront derelicts in a detached and stylised way. Sternberg got Charles Chaplin, Mary Pickford and Douglas Fairbanks to watch it, they bought it for more than it cost to make (a paltry $6000) and released it through United Artists, although it was more prestigious than profitable.
George K Arthur *The boy* • Georgia Hale *The girl* • Bruce Guerin *The child* ■ *Dir/Scr* Josef von Sternberg

Salvation! Have You Said Your Prayers Today? ★★ 18
Comedy   1987 · US · Colour · 76mins
Beth B and her husband Scott B were at the vanguard of the New York Super 8 movement of the 1980s, crossing B-movie sensibility with *film noir* and punk rock attitude. Beth B's first solo feature is a raucous satire on

television evangalism, at the same time as the real-life Bakker scandal was hitting the broadcasters of religious television. It's a wild, undisciplined production utilising contrasting techniques and acting styles with the result an intriguing, but chaotic mix that doesn't quite gel. Bonus points however for a cutting edge soundtrack. ▭
Stephen McHattie *Reverend Edward Randall* • Dominique Davalos *Lenore Finley* • Exene Cervenka *Rhonda Stample* • Viggo Mortensen *Jerome Stample* ■ *Dir* Beth B • *Scr* Beth B, Tom Robinson

Salvatore Giuliano ★★★★
Historical crime drama
1961 · It · BW · 123mins
Francesco Rosi won the best director prize at Berlin for this documentary-style account of the rise and fall of the eponymous mobster, who was gunned down by disillusioned members of his own gang in Sicily in 1950. Just as the cast comprises a mixture of full-time and non-professional performers, so the elliptical narrative style is a combination of flashbacks, reconstructions and interviews seeking to explore the influence of a corrupt, violent and deeply divided homeland on this self-styled Robin Hood. This controversial epic prompted a far-reaching government inquiry into Mafia activity. An Italian language film.
Frank Wolff *Gaspare Pisciotta* • Salvo Randone *President of Viterbo Assize Court* • Federico Zardi *Pisciotta's Defense Counsel* • Pietro Cammarata *Salvatore Giuliano* ■ *Dir* Francesco Rosi • *Scr* Francesco Rosi, Suso Cecchi D'Amico, Enzo Provenzale, Franco Solinas

The Salzburg Connection ★★ PG
Spy drama   1972 · US · Colour · 89mins
A convoluted, if scenic spy yarn set in Austria. The plot turns on a chest found by Anna Karina's husband, who is bumped off early on. Seems that the chest contains the names of Nazi collaborators and this sends everyone into a spin, resulting in the kidnapping of Karina and the torture of her brother (Klaus Maria Brandauer in his screen debut). There was, it seems, a major problem with the music, with both Jerry Goldsmith and Bronislau Kaper being credited on press releases, but Lionel Newman – listed as music supervisor – is the only name on the screen. ▭
Barry Newman *William Mathison* • Anna Karina *Anna Bryant* • Klaus Maria Brandauer *Johann Kronsteiner* • Karen Jensen *Elissa Lang* • Joe Maross *Chuck* • Wolfgang Preiss *Felix* • Helmut Schmid *Grell* • Udo Kier *Anton* ■ *Dir* Lee H Katzin • *Scr* Oscar Millard, from the novel by Helen MacInnes

Sam and Me ★★
Drama   1991 · Can · Colour · 94mins
This gentle study of cultural displacement, from Indian director Deepa Mehta, might have worked better if it had stuck to the point and not wandered off into some sitcom-style cul-de-sacs. The relationship between ageing Israeli Peter Borestski and reluctant exile Ranjit Choudhry is neatly developed from its frosty beginnings. But it settles for too many

cheap gags and fails to explore the status of two ancient cultures within the context of modern Canada.
Ranjit Chowdhry *Nikhil* • Peter Boretski *Sam Cohen* • Om Puri *Chetan Parikh* • Heath Lamberts *Morris Cohen* • Javid Jafri *Xavier* ■ *Dir* Deepa Mehta • *Scr* Ranjit Chowdhry

Sam Whiskey ★★
Comedy western   1969 · US · Colour · 96mins
Amiability covers a multitude of sins, as Burt Reynolds narrows his eyes and widens his smile in his familiar way, to try to distract us from a broken-down nag of a story about a gambler hired to recover loot from a Colorado river. The movie surrounds him with a trio of western icons; Clint Walker, Ossie Davis and Angie Dickinson, in an effort to beef up an anorexic story, but all it succeeds in being is, well, amiable.
Burt Reynolds *Sam Whiskey* • Angie Dickinson *Laura Breckenridge* • Clint Walker *OW Bandy* • Ossie Davis *Jed Hooker* • Rick Davis *Fat Henry Hobson* ■ *Dir* Arnold Laven • *Scr* William W Norton, from his story

Samar ★★
Prison adventure   1962 · US · Colour · 89mins
A capable second-rank star for 20 years, George Montgomery showed enterprise by producing, directing and writing (as well as starring in) some passably entertaining, low-budget pictures, shot in colour in the Philippines with the help of local film-maker Ferde Grofe Jr. The Second World War film *The Steel Claw*, was followed by this story of Spanish oppression in the 1870s. Gilbert Roland is the humane administrator of a colony for political prisoners, who responds to criticism of his methods by leading the inmates to a new life in a remote valley. Montgomery is the doctor who joins the trek, which encounters typhoons and headhunters.
George Montgomery *Dr John Saunders* • Gilbert Roland *Colonel Salazar* • Ziva Rodann *Ana* • Joan O'Brien *Cecile Salazar* • Nico Minardos *De Guzman* ■ *Dir* George Montgomery • *Scr* Ferde Grofe Jr, George Montgomery

Samba Traore ★★★ U
Drama   1992 · Burkina Faso · Colour · 85mins
Tracing the misfortunes that befall a decent man when he is prompted by poverty to steal money to open a bar in his home village, this is a remarkable merger of the African social drama and the Hollywood genre film by the Burkinabe director Idrissa Ouedraogo. Anxious to create a picture with an indigenous setting and a universal theme, Ouedraogo has produced what amounts to the first sub-Saharan *film noir*, even though it retains the brilliant outdoor lighting typical of most of the region's films. In Bambara with English subtitles.
Bakary Sangare *Samba* • Mariam Kaba *Saratou* • Abdoulaye Komboudri *Salif* • Irene Tassembedo *Binta* ■ *Dir* Idrissa Ouedraogo • *Scr* Idrissa Ouedraogo, Jacques Arhex, Santiago Amigorena

Same Time, Next Year
★★★★ 15

Romantic comedy drama
1978 · US · Colour · 113mins

This cosy apologia for adultery has all you'd expect from a smash Broadway play (by Bernard Slade) brought faithfully to the screen, about a married (not to each other) couple who meet every year until the silver anniversary of their coupling, to revive their first fine, careless rapture. There are superb performances from Alan Alda and Ellen Burstyn, sensitive direction by Robert Mulligan, and a total lack of realism. Affection and sentimentality are in glorious abundance, but there are few insights into the emotional trauma involved in such a relationship. Contains swearing.

Ellen Burstyn *Doris* • Alan Alda *George* • Ivan Bonar *Chalmers* • Bernie Kuby *Waiter* • Cosmo Sardo *Second Waiter* • David Northcutt *First Pilot* ■ *Dir* Robert Mulligan • *Scr* Bernard Slade, from his play

Sammy and Rosie Get Laid
★★ 18

Drama   1987 · UK · Colour · 96mins

This follow-up to *My Beautiful Laundrette* sees director Stephen Frears and writer Hanif Kureishi washing some political dirty linen. A retired Pakistani government torturer (Shashi Kapoor) comes to England to stay with his son (Ayub Khan Din) and daughter-in-law (Frances Barber), and anti-Thatcher messages get spelled out in riots and sexual promiscuity – a case of over-copulation. Well-acted, but the characters are totally unsympathetic, except for Claire Bloom as the old man's former mistress. As a blast of yuppie culture, it now looks like a dated whimper.

Frances Barber *Rosie Hobbs* • Ayub Khan Din *Sammy* • Shashi Kapoor *Rafi Rahman* • Claire Bloom *Alice* • Roland Gift *Danny/Victoria* • Wendy Gazelle *Anna* • Suzette Llewellyn *Vivia* • Meera Syal *Rani* ■ *Dir* Stephen Frears • *Scr* Hanif Kureishi

Sammy Going South ★★★ U

Adventure   1963 · UK · Colour · 128mins

Coming between *Mandy* and *A High Wind in Jamaica*, this is the weakest of Alexander Mackendrick's bittersweet trio of films in which the foibles of the adult world are exposed to the gaze of an artless child. The format is essentially that of a road movie, as ten-year-old Fergus McClelland heads for South Africa after he is orphaned during the Suez crisis. But its episodic structure prevents the picture from picking up pace and, because it is populated by caricatures, the insights into human nature are pretty trite. However, McClelland is a likeable lad and his scenes with wizened diamond smuggler Edward G Robinson are of a very high order.

Edward G Robinson *Cocky Wainwright* • Fergus McClelland *Sammy Hartland* • Constance Cummings *Gloria Von Imhoff* • Harry H Corbett *Lem* • Paul Stassino *Spyros Dracondopolous* • Zia Mohyeddin *Syrian* • Zena Walker *Aunt Jane* ■ *Dir* Alexander Mackendrick • *Scr* Denis Cannan, from the novel by WH Canaway

Sammy Stops the World ★

Musical   1978 · US · Colour · 105mins

A stage production crudely put on film, this version of the Anthony Newley–Leslie Bricusse musical *Stop the World – I Want to Get Off*, starring Sammy Davis Jr and "updated", is dire stuff and an unworthy record of the great performer. Quickly made, with cameras placed rigidly at the front of the stage (and two focused on the audience), it highlights all the deficiencies of the show and its production – the libretto's heavy-handed attempts at allegory, the off-key, klutzy chorus, and the self-consciously "hip" performances.

Sammy Davis Jr *Littlechap* • Dennis Daniels *Baton Twirler* • Donna Lowe *Schoolgirl* • Marian Mercer *Evie* ■ *Dir* Melvin Shapiro • *Scr* Leslie Bricusse, Anthony Newley

Sammy, the Way Out Seal
★★★ U

Comedy   1962 · US · Colour · 85mins

A Disney animal feature that was originally made for TV in the sixties, this has found a new lease of life on video in the States. It's very much of its time (check out the title, man), but still is entertaining thanks to the talent of its watery-eyed star. Two young brothers (Michael McGreevey and Bill Mumy) find the injured seal and hide him from parents Robert Culp and Patricia Barry, only for the slippery one to escape from the beach-house and wreck cute havoc around town. As written and directed by Norman Tokar, this is deep Disney, but there's actually much to enjoy.

Robert Culp *Father* • Patricia Barry *Mother* • Michael McGreevey *Arthur Loomis* • Billy Mumy [Bill Mumy] *Petey Loomis* • Jack Carson *Harold Sylvester* • Elisabeth Fraser *Lovey* • Ann Jillian *Rocky* ■ *Dir/Scr* Norman Tokar

Le Samouraï
★★★★★ PG

Thriller   1967 · Fr/It · Colour · 100mins

Alain Delon excels in this ultra-stylish study of the ultimate professional. The way in which director Jean-Pierre Melville sets up hit man Delon's next job is mesmerising. Yet, as in every good *film noir*, there is a *femme fatale* waiting in the shadows to tempt the hero away from his purpose, and Cathy Rosier is about as chic as an angel of doom could be. Almost devoid of dialogue, the film owes everything to the subtlety of the acting, the sinister beauty of Henri Decaë's photography and the intricacy of Melville's direction. In French with English subtitles..

Alain Delon *Jef Costello* • François Périer *Inspector* • Nathalie Delon *Jane Lagrange* • Cathy Rosier *Valerie* ■ *Dir* Jean-Pierre Melville • *Scr* Jean-Pierre Melville, from the novel *The Ronin* by Joan McLeod

Sam's Son
★★★ 15

Drama   1984 · US · Colour · 107mins

Anyone familiar with *Little House on the Prairie* and *Highway to Heaven* will know that Michael Landon is no stranger to sentiment. But he reins in the schmaltz in this neglected drama that is as much a tribute to his stern father, as an account of his own transformation from high school athlete to Hollywood hopeful. In

addition to writing and directing, Landon also appears in a cameo as the returning prodigal, leaving Timothy Patrick Murphy to impress as the young Gene Orowitz (Landon's real surname) and real-life couple Eli Wallach and Anne Jackson to steal the picture as his parents. Contains swearing, sex.

Eli Wallach *Sam Orowitz* • Anne Jackson *Harriet* • Timothy Patrick Murphy *Gene* • Hallie Todd *Cathy Stanton* • Alan Hayes *Robert Woods* • Jonna Lee *Bonnie Barnes* • Michael Landon *Gene Orman* • Howard Witt *Cy Martin* ■ *Dir/Scr* Michael Landon

Sam's Song ★

Drama   1969 · US · Colour · 92mins

In 1980, Cannon Films tried to cash in on Robert De Niro's burgeoning fame by re-releasing an obscure 1969 independent movie, in which he stars as a film editor spending the weekend on Long Island. Although it was a total flop, Cannon still thought it had commercial value and reworked the De Niro footage into a newly shot film. In the re-edited version, flashbacks show De Niro getting killed while editing a porno movie. Ten years later his ex-con brother Anthony Charnota searches for his murderer. No matter which incarnation is seen, it's all a dull disaster.

Robert De Niro *Sam* • Jennifer Warren *Erica* • Jered Mickey *Andrew* • Terrayne Crawford *Carol* • Martin Kelley *Mitch* • Phyllis Black *Marge* • Viva *Girl with the hourglass* • Anthony Charnota *Vito* ■ *Dir* John Shade [Jordan Leondopoulos], John C Broderick

Samson and Delilah ★★★ U

Biblical epic   1949 · US · Colour · 122mins

Scooping Oscars for its sets and costumes, this thumping epic prompted veteran American critic Pauline Kael to suggest that Cecil B DeMille considered God to be his co-director. Victor Mature stars as the biblical hero whose strength lies in the length of his hair, while Hedy Lamarr brings a gorgeous woodenness to the role of the Philistine, whose jealousy over Samson's fondness for Angela Lansbury leads to treachery. The fight with the lion is so lousy it's brilliant, while the oily villainy of George Sanders provides the only acting highlight.

Victor Mature *Samson* • Hedy Lamarr *Delilah* • George Sanders *Saran of Gaza* • Angela Lansbury *Semadar* • Henry Wilcoxon *Ahtur* • Olive Deering *Miriam* • Fay Holden *Hazelelponit* • Julia Faye *Hisham* • Rusty Tamblyn *Saul* ■ *Dir* Cecil B DeMille • *Scr* Vladimir Jabotinsky, Harold Lamb, Jesse L Lasky Jr, Frederic M Frank, from the book *Judge and Fool* by Vladimir Jabotinsky • *Costume Designer* Edith Head, Dorothy Jeakins, Elois Jenssen, Gile Steele, Gwen Wakeling

Samson and Delilah ★★ PG

Biblical drama   1984 · US · Colour · 91mins

A larger-than-life story of lust and vengeance fills the small screen in this stylish TV movie. Biblical strongman Samson (Antony Hamilton) is seduced and betrayed by the beauteous Delilah (Belinda Bauer), who cuts his hair to rob him of his strength. Blinded and imprisoned, he rekindles his faith in God and strikes back at his

oppressors. Campy, with a dash of the old Cecil B DeMille hokum, this tale is enlivened by spectacular Mexican locations and an all-star cast, including Victor Mature (Samson in the 1949 version) as Samson's father. There's enough action and spectacle here to satisfy the sword-and-sandal set.

Antony Hamilton *Samson* • Belinda Bauer *Delilah* • Max von Sydow *Sidka* • Stephen Macht *Malchuk* • Clive Revill *Raul* • Daniel Stern *Micah* • JoséFerrer *High Priest* • Maria Schell *Deborah* • Victor Mature *Manoah* ■ *Dir* Lee Philips • *Scr* John Gay, from the book *Husband of Delilah* by Eric Linkletter

Samson and the Mighty Challenge ★★

Action adventure   1965 · It · Colour

This colourful, fantasy-tinged saga brings you not one, but four muscle-bound superheroes – Hercules, Samson, Maciste and Ursus – all in one preposterously macho adventure that's a must for Mr Universe completists only. By the way, this is the cheap and cheerful movie that was redubbed/revamped into David Parker's Australian cult hit, *Hercules Returns*. To be perfectly honest, though, it's funnier in this original. Italian dialogue dubbed into English.

Alan Steel • Red Ross ■ *Dir* Giorgio Capitani

Samurai ★★★

Period action adventure
1954 · Jap · Colour · 92mins

With over 100 features to his credit, Hiroshi Inagaki was no stranger to the Meiji-mono, or historical drama. Based on an epic tome by Eiji Yoshikawa, it opens by exploring the humble origins and reckless, womanising youth of Musashi Miyamoto, the 17th-century peasant who rose to become the finest swordsman of his generation. Depicting the samurai's rigorous training and explaining the significance of the Bushido Code, the film was initially released in the US with narration from William Holden. A Japanese language film.

Toshiro Mifune *Takesho/Miyamoto Musashi* • Kaoru Yachigusa *Otsu* • Rentaro Mikuni *Matahachi* • William Holden (1) *Narrator* ■ *Dir* Hiroshi Inagaki • *Scr* Tokuhei Wakao, Hiroshi Inagaki, Hideji Hojo, from the novel *Miyamoto Musashi* by Eiji Yoshikawa

Samurai Cowboy ★★★ PG

Western comedy drama
1993 · US/Can · Colour · 96mins

After a friend dies from "overwork", Japanese businessman Hiromi Gô decides to live out his dream and buys a cattle ranch in Montana. Unfortunately, the previous owner left the place a bit untidy, and Gô barely has time to overcome local xenophobia before another problem presents itself: the big boss in town wants to sell the entire valley in a real estate deal. A fish-out-of-water story that actually works, despite resorting to the usual "save the ranch" routine.

Hiromi Gô *Yutaka Sato* • Catherine Mary Stewart • Matt McCoy • Conchata Ferrell • Robert Conrad *Gabe* ■ *Dir* Michael Keusch • *Scr* Michael Keusch, Deborah Tilton

U = SUITABLE FOR ALL   Uc = SUITABLE FOR ALL, ESPECIALLY FOR YOUNG CHILDREN (VIDEO ONLY)   PG = PARENTAL GUIDANCE

San Antonio ★★ PG
Western 1945 · US · Colour · 104mins

A bloated Errol Flynn western, boasting lovely Technicolor and the high production values of a big-budget Warner Bros feature, but lacking a decent script (despite being the work of two notable writers, Alan LeMay and WR Burnett). Alexis Smith co-stars as the dance hall singer working for villain Paul Kelly, while Flynn sports some fancy outfits including holsters specially designed to give him a lightning-fast draw. The climactic shoot-out that extends from the saloon to the ruins of the Alamo is well worth catching. ▭

Errol Flynn *Clay Hardin* • Alexis Smith *Jeanne Starr* • SZ Sakall *Sacha Bozic* • Victor Francen *Legare* • Florence Bates *Henrietta* ■ *Dir* David Butler • *Scr* Alan LeMay, WR Burnett

San Demetrio London
★★★ PG

Second World War drama
1943 · UK · BW · 93mins

Thanks to a fine ensemble cast and the authenticity of the action, this Second World War drama about an oil tanker struggling to cross the Atlantic after being attacked by German planes not only did its bit in boosting Britain's morale, but also played a key role in the evolution of Ealing studios. Based on a true story, it served as an allegory for the nation's fortunes since 1939. The ship may have been damaged, but its gallant crew successfully salvage it and bring it into port ready to fight another day. Although Charles Frend is credited as sole director, he was indisposed for much of the production and co-writer/producer Robert Hamer actually called the shots. ▭

Walter Fitzgerald *Chief Engineer Charles Pollard* • Ralph Michael *Second Officer Hawkins* • Frederick Piper *Bosun WE Fletcher* • Gordon Jackson *John Jamieson* • Mervyn Johns *Greaser John Boyle* • Robert Beatty *"Yank" Preston* ■ *Dir* Charles Frend • *Scr* Robert Hamer, Charles Frend, from a story by F Tennyson Jesse

San Francisco ★★★★ U
Disaster movie 1936 · US · BW · 110mins

MGM's classic disaster epic is driven by sheer star power. Clark Gable's cynical saloon keeper, Jeanette MacDonald's showgirl and Spencer Tracy's priest, battle for one another's souls until San Francisco gets clobbered by the earthquake of 1906. The quake, itself a magnificent testimony to the studio's special effects department, remains one of the most elaborate and exciting action sequences ever filmed, and it's well worth enduring the 90-minute wait while the three heroes squabble over love and life. Epic master DW Griffith reportedly directed one of the scenes. ▭

Clark Gable *Blackie Norton* • Jeanette MacDonald *Mary Blake* • Spencer Tracy *Father Tim Mullin* • Jack Holt *Jack Burley* • Jessie Ralph *Maisie Burley* • Ted Healy *Mat* • Shirley Ross *Trixie* ■ *Dir* WS Van Dyke II [WS Van Dyke] • *Scr* Anita Loos, Erich von Stroheim (uncredited), from a story by Robert Hopkins • *Special Effects* A Arnold Gillespie, James Basevi

The San Francisco Story
★★

Drama 1952 · US · BW · 79mins

Hunky Joel McCrea, plays a miner who opposes corrupt politician Sidney Blackmer's plans to take over the city and the state of California. It all ends with a preposterous duel on horseback, by which the point of dispute isn't political morality, but the fairly blatant charms of Yvonne De Carlo, who starts off in Blackmer's camp but switches sides when McCrea swaggers in like a bargain-basement Clark Gable. There's a lot of rough-house stuff – and every interior set is so overdressed it makes San Francisco in the 1850s look like a bordello – and one waits in vain for an earthquake to liven things up.

Joel McCrea *Rick Nelson* • Yvonne De Carlo *Adelaide McCall* • Sidney Blackmer *Andrew Cain* • Richard Erdman *Shorty* • Florence Bates *Sadie* • Onslow Stevens *Jim Martin* • John Raven *Lessing* ■ *Dir* Robert Parrish • *Scr* DD Beauchamp, from the novel *Vigilante* by Richard Summers

San Quentin ★★★
Prison drama 1937 · US · BW · 71mins

A highly enjoyable Warner Bros prison melodrama – with absolutely no redeeming social significance – that revolves around Humphrey Bogart as a hardened young hoodlum who goes inside. His precious sister (Ann Sheridan) is dating the fair-minded new captain of the prison yard, while he's powerless to do anything about it. O'Brien is the nominal star of the picture, but broody Bogart and perky young Sheridan are the centre of interest. Anyone could have directed it; Lloyd Bacon did.

Pat O'Brien *Capt Stephen Jameson* • Humphrey Bogart *Joe "Red" Kennedy* • Ann Sheridan *May Kennedy* • Barton MacLane *Lt Druggin* • Joseph Sawyer *[Joe Sawyer] "Sailor Boy" Hansen* • Veda Ann Borg *Helen* • James Robbins *Mickey Callahan* • Joseph King *Warden Taylor* ■ *Dir* Lloyd Bacon • *Scr* Peter Milne, Humphrey Cobb, from a story by Robert Tasker, John Bright

San Quentin ★★
Crime drama 1946 · US · BW · 66mins

Claiming social significance with a filmed introduction by Lewis E Lawes, the reform-minded ex-warden of Sing Sing prison, this is an energetic RKO crime thriller with ideas above its station. Barton MacLaine is the prisoner who has completed a San Quentin reform programme, does a bunk on the way to address a press club. A fully rehabilitated ex-con, Lawrence Tierney, steps in to save the reputation of the governor and his scheme – cue for a well handled, documentary-style manhunt that helped director Gordon Douglas to move up the ladder to bigger things.

Lawrence Tierney *Jim Rolands* • Barton MacLane *Nick Taylor* • Marian Carr *Betty* • Harry Shannon *Warden Kelly* • Carol Forman *Ruthie* • Richard Powers *Schaeffer* • Joe Devlin *Broadway* ■ *Dir* Gordon M Douglas [Gordon Douglas] • *Scr* Lawrence Kimble, Arthur A Ross, Howard J Green

Sanctuary ★★
Melodrama 1961 · US · BW · 89mins

High drama in the Greek tradition reduced to swamp melodrama in the Tennessee Williams tradition, though the source is William Faulkner's novel of the same title with elements from his *Requiem for a Nun*. Directed by Tony Richardson and starring Lee Remick, it concerns a Mississippi governor's daughter who is raped by a bootlegger. She goes to live in a New Orleans brothel with him and her black maid Odetta which, of course, leads to several tragedies. An opaque, turgid and unsuccessful attempt to bring Faulkner to the screen.

Lee Remick *Temple Drake* • Yves Montand *Candy Man* • Bradford Dillman *Gowan Stevens* • Harry Townes *Ira Bobbitt* • Odetta *Nancy Mannigoe* • Howard St John *Governor* ■ *Dir* Tony Richardson • *Scr* James Poe, from the play *Requiem for a Nun* by Ruth Ford, from the novels *Sanctuary* and *Requiem for a Nun* by William Faulkner

Sanctuary ★★ 18
Action thriller 1998 · US · Colour · 99mins

This is what happens when you take the retired assassin premise of The Long Kiss Goodnight and replace the amnesiac housewife with a hunky clergyman. It may sound ludicrously far-fetched, but Tibor Takacs is no mug when it comes to action, so there are plenty of shootouts and explosions to occupy Mark Dacasco and Jaimz Woolvett. Basic, but crudely effective. ▭ **DVD**

Mark Dacascos *Luke Kovak* • Kylie Travis *Rachel Malcolm* • Jaimz Woolvett *Dominic Grace* • Alan Scarfe *William Dyson* • Monika Schnarre *Colette Fortier* • Nigel Bennett *Senator Stephen Macguire* ■ *Dir* Tibor Takacs • *Scr* Michael Stokes

The Sand Castle ★★★ U
Fantasy drama
1961 · US · BW and Colour · 65mins

A curious and charming feature from writer/director Jerome Hill, this children's fantasy follows a young boy whose elaborate sand castle attracts a diverse range of admirers during the course of a day on the beach. The action is shot in black and white (originally on 16mm), shifting to colour for an animated sequence in which the boy imagines his castle inhabited by the people he has met. This effect is created with the use of 19th-century-style paper cut-outs, a technique familiar to fans of TV's *Paddington*. The end result is surprisingly beguiling – even if it was just a dream.

Barry Cardwell *Boy* • Laurie Cardwell *Girl* • George Dunham *Artist* • Alec Wilder *Fisherman* • Maybelle Nash *Shade lady* • Erica Speyer *Sun lady* ■ *Dir/Scr* Jerome Hill

The Sand Pebbles ★★★ 15
War drama 1966 · US · Colour · 174mins

Set on a US gunboat patrolling the Yangtze River in 1926, this blend of action and melodrama was something of a surprise hit in its day, earning itself no fewer than eight Oscar nominations (although it won none). Part of the reason for its success can be found in its thinly veiled apology for American intervention in Vietnam, but there are some more enduring plus

points, too. Steve McQueen and Richard Attenborough both turn in pleasing performances and Joseph MacDonald's cinematography is outstanding. The romances are rather contrived, but, to director Robert Wise's credit, this long film never feels like a slog. ▭

Steve McQueen *Jake Holman* • Richard Attenborough *Frenchy Burgoyne* • Richard Crenna *Captain Collins* • Candice Bergen *Shirley Eckert* • Marayat Andriane *Emmanuelle Arsan Maily* • Mako *Po-Han* • Larry Gates *Jameson* • Charles Robinson *Ensign Bordelles* ■ *Dir* Robert Wise • *Scr* Robert W Anderson, from the novel by Richard McKenna

Sanders of the River
★★★ U

Adventure 1935 · UK · BW · 84mins

A famous title of its day, this Alexander Korda production looks patronising and imperialistic to modern eyes. The titular Sanders (Leslie Banks), is a police commissioner in colonial Nigeria, but the real interest here is the performance of the great African-American bass Paul Robeson, as the escaped convict Bosambo (the film's American title), and the "native" chants which greatly enhanced the film's popularity and lead to an infinite number of Robeson impressions in the music halls. The movie still impresses, but it's really best viewed as a production of its time and as a fascinating historic document. ▭

Leslie Banks *RG Sanders* • Paul Robeson *Bosambo* • Nina Mae McKinney *Lilongo* • Robert Cochran *Tibbets* • Martin Walker *Ferguson* • Richard Grey *Hamilton* • Tony Wane *King Mofolaba* ■ *Dir* Zoltan Korda • *Scr* Lajos Biro, Jeffrey Dell, from the stories by Edgar Wallace

The Sandlot ★★★ PG
Comedy adventure
1993 · US · Colour · 96mins

An adult does occasionally intrude upon the world of baseball, lifeguards and savage dogs described in this pleasing rites-of-passage picture. However, this enchanted summer really belongs to the kids, in particular Tom Guiry, the pre-teen who makes Charlie Brown look like Babe Ruth. Although the games on the sand lot provide the focus, this isn't just another sports movie. It's about self-discovery and learning how to deal with the scuffed knees of life. Mike Vitar shines alongside Guiry, but the entire pre-teen cast is so good you almost overlook the likes of Denis Leary, Karen Allen and James Earl Jones. ▭

Tom Guiry *Scotty Smalls* • Mike Vitar *Benjamin Franklin Rodriguez* • Patrick Renna *Hamilton "Ham" Porter* • Chauncey Leopardi *Michael "Squints" Palledorous* • Marty York *Alan "Yeah-Yeah" McClennan* • Brandon Adams *Kenny DeNunez* • Victor DiMattia *Timmy Timmons* • Denis Leary *Bill* • Karen Allen *Mom* • James Earl Jones *Mr Mertle* ■ *Dir* David Mickey Evans • *Scr* David Mickey Evans, Robert Gunter

Sandokan against the Leopard of Sarawak ★ U
Adventure 1964 · It · Colour · 88mins

Ray Danton had a variable career with plenty of duff patches. Here, in one of the duffest, he plays the "Tiger", the famous Malaysian warrior, played by Steve Reeves in the earlier *Sandokan the Great*. A somewhat unengaging action adventure, but with some virile skirmishes. Contains some violence. Italian dialogue dubbed into English.

Ray Danton *Sandokan* • Guy Madison • Franca Bettoja • Mario Petri ■ *Dir* Luigi Capuano

Sandokan Fights Back
★★ PG

Action adventure   1964 · It · Colour · 86mins

Italian director Luigi Capuano was churning them out back in 1964, so he could be forgiven for running out of steam by the time he shot this, one of two sequels to Umberto Lenzi's swashbuckling adventure, *Sandokan the Great*. Ray Danton returns in the title role, while Guy Madison again provides the villainy, as he steals the throne of Sarawak. The sets look as if they could fall down at any second but, for a spot of mindless escapism, you could do a lot worse. Italian dialogue dubbed into English. 🎞

Ray Danton *Sandokan* • Guy Madison *Yanez* • Franca Bettoja • Mino Doro ■ *Dir* Luigi Capuano

Sandokan the Great ★★ U

Adventure   1963 · Fr/It/Sp · Colour · 109mins

A sturdy adventure set in Victorian Borneo. When British forces begin wiping out East Indian villagers, a band of rebels led by warrior Sandokan take on the colonists, kidnapping the commander's niece. Steve Reeves doesn't get to flash as much musculature as in his "sword and sandal" epics, such as *Hercules Unchained*, but he makes an athletic lead and there are enough colourful action sequences to hold the interest. Italian dialogue dubbed into English.

Steve Reeves *Sandokan* • Geneviève Grad *Mary Ann* • Andrea Bosic *Yanez* • Maurice Poli *Giro Batol* • Rik Battaglia *Sambigliong* ■ *Dir* Umberto Lenzi • *Scr* Umberto Lenzi, Fulvio Gicca, Victor A Catena, from the novel *Le Tigri di Mompracem* by Emilio Salgari

The Sandpiper ★ 15

Romantic drama
1965 · US · Colour · 112mins

In every major director's career, it's inevitable that you'll find the odd turkey. This truly terrible movie was made by the great Vincente Minnelli. It's a full-blown example of the Elizabeth Taylor/Richard Burton vehicle, and as mindless and inept as it comes. Of course, its sheer awfulness and desperate pretension create a numbing watchability: you have been warned. The California coastline at Big Sur and Charles Bronson emerge with some credit, but Eva Marie Saint is totally wasted, and these days the only thing worth remembering from this utter no-no is the schmaltzy theme song, *The Shadow of Your Smile*. 🎞

Richard Burton *Dr Edward Hewitt* • Elizabeth Taylor *Laura Reynolds* • Eva Marie Saint *Claire Hewitt* • Charles Bronson *Cos Erickson* • Peter O'Toole ■ *Dir* Vincente Minnelli • *Scr* Dalton Trumbo, Michael Wilson, Irene Kamp, Louis Kamp, from a story by Martin Ransohoff

Sands of Iwo Jima ★★★ PG

Second World War drama
1949 · US · Colour · 109mins

John Wayne leads his marines to hell and back and they love him for it, every bloodsoaked, heroic foot of the way. Apparently, Kirk Douglas was in line for the role of Sergeant Stryker, but, according to the film's producer, Wayne wanted the role so badly "he could taste it." If you believe Wayne's son, though, the Duke worried about the script and only relented when war veterans lobbied him to play the part. The result was a gung-ho classic, made on the cheap, often risible, and nowadays offensive to Japanese sensibilities. But it's still eminently watchable and the Duke nabbed his first Oscar nomination to boot. 🎞

John Wayne *Sgt Stryker* • John Agar *Pte Conway* • Forrest Tucker *Cpl Thomas* • Adele Mara *Allison Bromley* • Wally Cassell *Pte Ragazzi* • James Brown (2) *Pte Bass* • Richard Webb *Pte Shipley* ■ *Dir* Allan Dwan • *Scr* Harry Brown, Edward James Grant, from a story by Harry Brown

Sands of the Desert ★ U

Comedy   1960 · UK · Colour · 88mins

Poor old Charlie Drake. To call his flirtation with film fame an unmitigated disaster, would be understating the extent to which he failed to translate his stage, radio and TV success to the big screen. Director John Paddy Carstairs, who guided Norman Wisdom through many a comedy, also co-wrote this silly story in which travel agent Drake sets out to uncover the saboteur at a holiday camp. With a cheapness that makes a *Carry On* look like a lavish blockbuster, this is better than Drake's other efforts, but, sadly, that's not saying much. 🎞

Charlie Drake *Charlie Sands* • Peter Arne *Sheikh El Jabez* • Sarah Branch *Janet Brown* • Raymond Huntley *Bossom* • Peter Illing *Sheikh Ibrahim* • Harold Kasket *Abdullah* • Marne Maitland *Sheikh's advisor* • Neil McCarthy *Hassan* ■ *Dir* John Paddy Carstairs • *Scr* John Paddy Carstairs, Charlie Drake, from a story by Robert Hall, Anne Burnaby, Stafford Byrne

Sands of the Kalahari ★★★

Action drama   1965 · UK · Colour · 119mins

The team behind *Zulu* converge upon South Africa for another gritty adventure. It's a well-cast survival picture, in which a charter plane is grounded by a plague of locusts, leaving the United Nations of passengers to bicker, rape, kill and generally abuse each other in the desert. That is, until a tribe of baboons makes a monkey out of everyone. In case no one notices, it's an allegory showing how, given half a chance, humans will regress to ape-like behaviour, with Stuart Whitman taking on the role of the prime primate. It's not in the class of Endfield's previous epic, but it has a raw intensity all of its own thanks to some excellent performances and imposing locations .

Stuart Whitman *O'Brien* • Stanley Baker *Bain* • Susannah York *Grace Monckton* • Harry Andrews *Grimmelman* • Theodore Bikel *Dr Bondarahkai* • Nigel Davenport *Sturdevant* • Barry Lowe *Detjens* ■ *Dir* Cy Endfield • *Scr* Cy Endfield, from the novel by William Mulvihill

The Sandwich Man ★★ U

Comedy   1966 · UK · Colour · 91mins

Known as the Goon that got away, and as the genius behind *Potty Time*, Michael Bentine was yet another British comedian who failed to repeat his TV and/or radio success on the big screen. This virtually silent comedy was politely considered "ahead of its time" on its release, but, over 30 years later, this euphemism for "not very good" still applies. The cast is all-star, but the film's few pleasures come from Bentine's often inspired mime as he wanders the streets of London with his sandwich board. 🎞

Michael Bentine *Horace Quilby* • Dora Bryan *Mrs de Vere* • Harry H Corbett *Stage doorkeeper* • Bernard Cribbins *Photographer* • Diana Dors *Billingsgate woman* • Ian Hendry *Motorcycle cop* • Stanley Holloway *Gardener* • Wilfrid Hyde White *Lord Uffingham* • Michael Medwin *Sewer man* • Ron Moody *Coach* • Anna Quayle *Billingsgate woman* • Terry-Thomas *Scoutmaster* • Norman Wisdom *Father O'Malley* • Suzy Kendall *Sue* • Alfie Bass *Yachtsman* • John Le Mesurier *Sandwich man* • Peter Jones *Escapologist* • Warren Mitchell *Gypsy Syd* ■ *Dir* Robert Hartford-Davis • *Scr* Robert Hartford-Davis, Michael Bentine

Sango Malo ★★★

Drama   1991 · Cam · Colour

Novelist Bassek Ba Kobhio made his directorial debut with this fervent appeal to prioritise education in order to give the Cameroons a chance finally to lay both the ghosts of colonial rule and the mistakes made in the name of independence. However, as his scathing portrayal of village life suggests, it's not going to be an easy task, with patriarchal tradition, corruption and indolence all in the way of progress. As the teacher trying to give his students some practical schooling, Jerome Bolo is suitably zealous, while Marcel Mvondo II is amusing as the lazily bookish headmaster. In English, French and various African dialects with subtitles.

Jerome Bolo • Marcel Mvondo II • Edwige Ntongon a Zock ■ *Dir/Scr* Bassek Ba Kobhio

Sanjuro ★★★ 12

Period action drama 1962 · Jap · BW · 91mins

Following the success of *Yojimbo*, Akira Kurosawa was persuaded (somewhat against his better judgement) to make a further adventure featuring the self-seeking samurai who uses his own guile and the efforts of others to achieve his ends. Toshiro Mifune returns as Sanjuro, who joins forces with a band of eager warriors to rescue a kidnapped landowner. Until the final eruption of violence, Kurosawa plays the film for laughs, sending up the conventions of the *jidai-geki* (or period costume drama) with an unerring eye, while Mifune bestrides the action with gleeful gravitas. In Japanese with English subtitles .. 🎞

Toshiro Mifune *Sanjuro* • Tatsuya Nakadai *Muroto* • Masao Shimizu *Kikui* • Yunosuke Ito *Mutsuta, the Chamberlain* • Takako Irie *Chamberlain's wife* ■ *Dir* Akira Kurosawa • *Scr* Ryuzo Kikushima, Akira Kurosawa, Hideo Oguni, from the short story *Hibi Heian* by Shugoro Yamamoto

Sans Soleil ★★★★ 15

Documentary   1983 · Fr · Colour · 99mins

Still most widely known for his sci-fi short *La Jetée*, Chris Marker emerged in the sixties as a key practitioner of the *cinéma vérité* documentary style. This is tantamount to a postcard from "a life", as Marker tries to convey his impressions and recollections of cultures as far afield as Africa, Iceland and Japan. Exploiting what was then the latest in video and imaging technology, the film is an exhilarating collage of sights and sounds, faces and places. Unlike many documentarists, Marker doesn't force his views upon you, but, like a good guide, draws your attention to what you might otherwise have missed. 🎞

Alexandra Stewart *English narration* ■ *Dir/Scr* Chris Marker

Sanshiro Sugata ★★★

Adventure drama   1943 · Jap · BW · 80mins

An intriguing work, as the first film directed by the legendary Japanese director Akira Kurosawa, who went on to international fame with *The Seven Samurai*. Made in the latter part of the war, when he was in his early thirties, it was inevitably influenced by the authorities, which may have accounted for its economical and straightforward storytelling. This concerns Sugata, who in the late 1800s develops the art of Judo, showing its superiority over the martial art of Ju-Jitsu. There was a second part to the story made a couple of years later. In Japanese with English subtitles.

Susumu Fujita *Sanshiro Sugata* • Denjiro Okochi *Shogoro Yano* • Takashi Shimura *Hansuke Murai* • Yukiko Todoroki *Sayo, his daughter* ■ *Dir* Akira Kurosawa • *Scr* Akira Kurosawa, from the novel *Sugata Sanshiro* by Tsuneo Tomita

Sansho the Bailiff ★★★★★

Epic drama   1954 · Jap · BW · 116mins

One of the masterworks of Japanese cinema, this powerful, poignant period drama not only discusses tyranny and liberalism, but also the psychological differences between the sexes. Reworking a traditional folktale, Kenji Mizoguchi considers how someone can be driven to barbarism simply to survive, with kidnap victim Yoshiaki Hanayagi's collusion with the barbarous bailiff, Eitaro Shindo, contrasting sharply with the idealism that condemned his father to exile, his mother to prostitution and his sister to death, while contriving his escape. Shooting primarily in long takes from a withdrawn, fluid camera, Mizoguchi conveys a sense of intimacy through flashbacks and the intense performances of his superlative cast. In Japanese with English subtitles..

Yoshiaki Hanayagi *Zushio* • Kyoko Kagawa *Anju* • Kinuyo Tanaka *Tamaki* • Eitaro Shindo *Sansho* ■ *Dir* Kenji Mizoguchi • *Scr* Yahiro Fuji, Yoshikata Yoda, from the story by Ogai Mori • *Cinematographer* Kazuo Miyagawa

Santa Claus ★★ U

Seasonal comedy
1985 · UK/US · Colour · 103mins

Cuddly Dudley Moore is the elf who loses his job with Santa and decides

to sell his former employer's secrets to evil toy manufacturer John Lithgow, in this rather daft family comedy. It boasts a great opening (which explains who Santa really is), but gets bogged down with infantile humour, a silly script and plot twists that a five-year-old would find insulting. One wonders whether Szwarc had presents delivered down his chimney the year this was made.

Dudley Moore *Patch* • John Lithgow *B Z* • David Huddleston *Claus* • Burgess Meredith *Ancient Elf* • Judy Cornwell *Anya* • Jeffrey Kramer *Towzer* • Christian Fitzpatrick *Joe* ■ *Dir* Jeannot Szwarc • *Scr* David Newman, from a story by David Newman, Leslie Newman

The Santa Clause ★★★ U
Seasonal fantasy
1994 · US · Colour · 105mins

Bearing in mind Phoebe Cates's account of her father's rooftop misadventures in *Gremlins*, Tim Allen gets off rather lightly in this engaging Yuletide comedy. Allen's feature debut brims over with good ideas; the only trouble is, they are all stocking-fillers when what the action really needs is a couple of huge gift-wrapped set pieces. However, as the sceptic bound by the Claus clause, the *Home Improvement* star slips from Scrooge into Santa with some skill and is far more amiable than Arnold Schwarzenegger was as a similarly workaholic father in *Jingle All the Way*. 🎞 **DVD**

Tim Allen *Scott Calvin* • Judge Reinhold *Neal* • Wendy Crewson *Laura* • Eric Lloyd *Charlie* • David Krumholtz *Bernard* • Larry Brandenburg *Detective Nunzio* ■ *Dir* John Pasquin • *Scr* Leo Benvenuti, Steve Rudnick

Santa Fe ★★
Western
1951 · US · Colour · 89mins

Made virtually back-to-back with *Man in the Saddle* (same year, star, producer and writer) this is a much more routine western. This time granite-faced Confederate soldier Randolph Scott is involved in unseemly sibling rivalry at the end of the Civil War, as his brothers turn against him when he decides to work for the railroad of the title. Neither Irving Pichel's colourless direction, nor Janis Carter's uninspiring leading lady help this over-familiar tale, and Scott just goes through the motions.

Randolph Scott *Britt Canfield* • Janis Carter *Judith Chandler* • Jerome Courtland *Terry Canfield* • Peter Thompson *Tom Canfield* • John Archer *Clint Canfield* • Warner Anderson *Dave Baxter* ■ *Dir* Irving Pichel • *Scr* Kenneth Gamet, from a story by Louis Stevens, from the novel by James Marshall

Santa Fe Passage ★★ U
Western
1955 · US · Colour · 90mins

An average second-division western, given moderate interest by its trio of stars, well past their primes but still able to hold the attention. John Payne plays an ostracised wagon-train scout battling former B hero Rod Cameron (here cast against type) for the hand of part-Indian maiden Faith Domergue.

John Payne *Kirby Randolph* • Faith Domergue *Aurelie St Clair* • Rod Cameron *Jess Griswold* • Slim Pickens *Sam Beekman* • Irene Tedrow

Ptewaquin • George Keymas *Satank* ■ *Dir* William Witney • *Scr* Lillie Hayward, from a short story by Clay Fisher

Santa Fe Stampede ★★ U
Western
1938 · US · BW · 55mins

The Three Mesquiteers grubstake an old miner, who strikes it rich and summons them to share in his good fortune. A pre-*Stagecoach* John Wayne is the star of this routine B-western, along with Ray Corrigan and Max Terhune. Silent star William Farnum plays the old-timer, who is killed off by the bad guys who then try to pin the blame on Wayne.

John Wayne *Stony Brooke* • Ray Corrigan *Tucson Smith* • Max Terhune *Lullaby Joslin* • William Farnum *Dave Carson* • June Martel *Nancy Carson* • LeRoy Mason *Gil Byron* ■ *Dir* George Sherman • *Scr* Luci Ward, Betty Burbridge, from a story by Luci Ward, from characters created by William Colt MacDonald

Santa Fe Trail ★★ U
Action adventure
1940 · US · BW · 109mins

One of the weakest of the Errol Flynn/Olivia de Havilland series at Warners, this rambling saga concerns the attempts of future Civil War cavalryman Jeb Stuart (played by Flynn) to nail the great abolitionist John Brown (a ranting Raymond Massey). As history, this is wild fiction, even for Hollywood, and, despite a watchable supporting cast including Ronald Reagan as Stuart's West Point pal George Armstrong Custer, there's precious little actually going on here. 🎞

Errol Flynn *Jeb Stuart* • Olivia de Havilland *Kit Carson Halliday* • Raymond Massey *John Brown* • Ronald Reagan *George Armstrong Custer* • Alan Hale *Tex Bell* • Guinn Williams *Windy Brody* • Van Heflin *Rader* ■ *Dir* Michael Curtiz • *Scr* Robert Buckner

Santa Sangre ★★★ 18
Surreal horror drama
1989 · It/Mex · Colour · 118mins

More extravagant, but less controlled than his infamous allegorical western, *El Topo*, Alexandro Jodorowsky's cross-cultural collage of ideas and images borrows freely from Freud, Fellini and Ferrara, de Milo, Marceau and *Psycho*. Using the circus as a microcosm, Jodorowsky combines the sacred and the psychedelic, the psychological and the symbolic, as a magician (played variously by the director's sons, Adan and Axel) goes on a murderous rampage to avenge the aerialist mother whose arms were severed by the knife-throwing husband she caught *in flagrante delicto* with the tattooed lady. Unsurprisingly, salvation comes in the form of deaf-mute, Sabrina Dennison. Some subtitling. 🎞

Axel Jodorowsky *Fenix* • Blanca Guerra *Concha* • Guy Stockwell *Orgo* • Thelma Tixou *Tattooed woman* • Sabrina Dennison *Alma* • Adan Jodorowsky *Young Fenix* ■ *Dir* Alexandro Jodorowsky • *Scr* Alexandro Jodorowsky, Roberto Leoni, Claudio Argento, from a story by Roberto Leoni, Alexandro Jodorowsky

Santa with Muscles ★★
Comedy action adventure
1996 · US · Colour · 97mins

The main gag here is that arrogant health-food millionaire Hulk Hogan loses his memory and adopts the role

of Santa to protect a local church orphanage. We're supposed to laugh as he submits himself to various indignities along the way in the name of doing good. The problem with this joke is that a guy named "Hulk" doesn't have any dignity to begin with. Ed Begley Jr paints his role with broad strokes as the villain who wants the orphanage property.

Hulk Hogan *Blake Thorne* • Ed Begley Jr *Ebner Frost* • Don Stark *Lenny* • Robin Curtis *Leslie* • Garrett Morris *Clayton* • Clint Howard *Hinkley* ■ *Dir* John Murlowski • *Scr* Jonathan Bond, Fred Mata, Dorrie Krum Raymond

Santee ★★★ 15
Western
1973 · US · Colour · 86mins

Glenn Ford is a bounty hunter, long embittered by the memory of his son who was gunned down by a gang he hunts still. In a twist of fate he becomes the surrogate father to another boy – whose father he has killed – and still the ironies pile upon Ford, turning him into a figure from Greek tragedy. While this does not even approach the westerns that Anthony Mann made with James Stewart, its similar classical allegiances and convincingly tormented hero make for an immensely satisfying drama.

Glenn Ford *Santee* • Michael Burns *Jody* • Dana Wynter *Valerie* • Jay Silverheels *John Crow* • Harry Townes *Sheriff Carter* • John Larch *Banner* • Robert Wilke [Robert J Wilke] *Deake* ■ *Dir* Gary Nelson • *Scr* Tom Blackburn, from a story by Brand Bell

Santiago ★★
Adventure drama
1956 · US · Colour · 91mins

A cracking script by Martin Rackin and John Twist goes some way to redeeming this period bunkum about gunrunners Alan Ladd and Lloyd Nolan paddle-boating rifles to Cuban revolutionaries fighting Spanish oppression. Gordon Douglas's dull direction backs it all into Cliché Corner, but the writing quite often forces a way out.

Alan Ladd *Cash Adams* • Rossana Podesta *Isabella* • Lloyd Nolan *Clay Pike* • Chill Wills *Sidewheel* • Paul Fix *Trasker* • LQ Jones *Digger* ■ *Dir* Gordon Douglas • *Scr* Martin Rackin, John Twist, from the novel *The Great Courage* by Martin Rackin

The Saphead ★★★
Silent comedy
1921 · US · BW · 77mins

Buster Keaton's first feature was for Metro who, having lost Fatty Arbuckle, didn't quite know what to do with Buster, so installed him in a Fatty-prepared vehicle. Buster is Bertie Van Alstyne, naive son of a rich father, devoted to his father's ward (Carol Holloway). Determined to be "bad", in fact his goodness ensures that he takes the blame for another stockbroker's error. A bit of a letdown for Keaton fans, but the character was the basis for many of his later creations.

William H Crane *Nicholas Van Alstyne* • Buster Keaton *Bertie Van Alstyne* • Carol Holloway *Rose Turner* • Edward Connelly *Musgrave* ■ *Dir* Herbert Blaché • *Scr* June Mathis, from the play *The New Henrietta* by Winchell Smith, Victor Mapes, Bronson Howard

Sapnay ★★★ U
Drama
1997 · Ind · Colour · 147mins

Director Rajiv Menon's deft camerawork and sense of dramatic tension are well to the fore in this engaging love triangle drama. The well-travelled and dashing Arvind Swamy falls for gorgeous teenager Kajol, who has unfortunately decided to enter a convent. Matters are not helped when Swamy employs Prabhu Deva, the local honey-tongued barber, to plead his cause, little suspecting that he too will succumb to Priya's abundant charms. In Hindi with English subtitles. 🎞

Kajol *Priya* • Arvind Swamy *Thomas/Mr Dancing Shoes* • Prabhu Deva *Deva* ■ *Dir* Rajiv Menon • *Scr* VC Guhanathan, Rajiv Menon

Sapphire ★★★
Crime mystery
1959 · UK · Colour · 92mins

A young woman's murder leaves many questions unanswered in this intriguing detective tale. The relatively innovative racial element – the victim is a young black woman who has been passing as white – adds to the historic interest, and gives the search for the murderer a wider resonance. Yvonne Mitchell was nominated for best actress at that year's British Academy Awards, while the film itself scooped the Best British Film award.

Nigel Patrick *Detective Superintendent Hazard* • Michael Craig *Detective Inspector Learoyd* • Yvonne Mitchell *Mildred* • Paul Massie *David Harris* • Bernard Miles *Mr Harris* • Olga Lindo *Mrs Harris* • Earl Cameron *Dr Robbins* • Gordon Heath *Paul Slade* • Harry Baird *Johnnie Fiddle* • Orlando Martins *Barman* • Jocelyn Britton *Patsy* • Rupert Davies *Ferris* • Robert Adams *Horace Big Cigar* ■ *Dir* Basil Dearden • *Scr* Janet Green, Lukas Heller

Saps at Sea ★★ U
Comedy
1940 · US · BW · 57mins

This inconsistent comedy was Laurel and Hardy's last film for Hal Roach, and the first of the highly derivative features with which they saw out their distinguished careers. Driven bonkers by honking horns at work, Ollie is prescribed a tranquil sea voyage, during which he and Stan are shanghaied by a fugitive killer. The opening sections are fast and furious – with Ben Turpin joining in the horn factory hijinks and James Finlayson cracking value as a quack psychiatrist. But the action becomes becalmed the moment the boys are afloat. 🎞

Stan Laurel *Stan* • Oliver Hardy *Ollie* • James Finlayson *Dr JH Finlayson* • Ben Turpin *Mixed-up plumber* • Rychard Cramer [Richard Cramer] *Nick Grainger* ■ *Dir* Gordon Douglas • *Scr* Charles Rogers, Felix Adler, Gil Pratt [Gilbert W Pratt], Harry Langdon, from their story

Saraband for Dead Lovers ★★★ U
Romantic historical drama
1948 · UK · Colour · 91mins

A sumptuous British movie – audiences wanted colour, upholstery and royalty in the postwar era – about a claim to the Hanoverian throne of England. Joan Greenwood is married to the king but fancies Stewart Granger, a Swedish count of indifferent pedigree and accent, previously involved with Flora Robson, who goes into a fit of jealous rage. Basil Dearden and Michael Relph direct with straight faces, but no one could suppress Greenwood in full flounce and, later on, mourning glory. ▣

Stewart Granger *Count Philip Konigsmark* • Joan Greenwood *Sophie Dorothea* • Françoise Rosay *Electress Sophie* • Flora Robson *Countess Platen* • Frederick Valk *Elector Ernest Augustus* • Peter Bull *Prince George-Louis* • Anthony Quayle *Durer* • Megs Jenkins *Frau Busche* • Michael Gough *Prince Charles* ■ *Dir* Basil Dearden, Michael Relph • *Scr* John Dighton, Alexander Mackendrick, from the novel by Helen Simpson

Sarafina! ★★★ 🔞
Musical drama
1992 · S Africa/US/UK/Fr · Colour · 111mins

Based on the anti-apartheid Broadway musical, this traces the transformation of a schoolgirl in the South African townships of the 1970s from innocent teenage dreamer to political activist. In her school there is only one teacher (Whoopi Goldberg) who refuses to toe the white-endorsed party line and pays a terrible price for her courage. The upbeat musical numbers are invigorating but seem sometimes at odds with the theme. Miriam Makeba, the singer/actress and *grande dame* of the anti-apartheid movement is in a supporting role. ▣

Whoopi Goldberg *Mary Masombuka* • Leleti Khumalo *Sarafina* • Miriam Makeba *Angelina* • John Kani *School principal* • Dumisani Diamini *Crocodile* ■ *Dir* Darrell James Roodt • *Scr* William Nicholson, Mbongeni Ngema, from the musical by Mbongeni Ngema • *Music* Stanley Meyers

Sarah and Son ★★★
Drama
1930 · US · BW · 86mins

Following her success in *Madame X* as a mother deprived of her child as punishment for her infidelity, Ruth Chatterton returned in this tear-sodden variation on the theme. Here, she is a woman wronged by her cad of a husband who sells their baby to a wealthy couple. The rest of the film is spent with Chatterton as she searches for her lost son while managing to become an opera star. Directed with requisite feeling by Dorothy Arzner, and well-played by the polished Chatterton (Oscar-nominated) and Fredric March, it adds up to a predictable but effective entry in the canon of melodramas about suffering women.

Ruth Chatterton *Sarah Storm* • Fredric March *Howard Vanning* • Fuller Mellish Jr *Jim Gray* • Gilbert Emery *John Ashmore* • Doris Lloyd *Mrs Ashmore* • William Stack *Cyril Belloc* • Philippe De Lacy *Bobby* ■ *Dir* Dorothy Arzner • *Scr* Zoe Akins, from a novel by Timothy Shea

Sarah, Plain and Tall
     ★★★ 🅿️
Drama
1991 · US · Colour · 98mins

A strong performance from Glenn Close, who doesn't often do TV movies, brings to life the schoolteacher heroine of Patricia MacLachlan's treasured children's book. Close is deeply affecting as a lonely but determined woman in turn-of-the-century Kansas forming a relationship with the family of a widowed farmer. An apt supporting

cast, including Christopher Walken, moves effortlessly around the movie's star. ▣

Glenn Close *Sarah Wheaton* • Christopher Walken *Jacob Witting* • Christopher Bell *Caleb Witting* • Lexi Randall *Anna Witting* • Jon De Vries [Jon DeVries] *Matthew Grant* ■ *Dir* Glenn Jordan • *Scr* Patricia MacLachlan, Carol Sobieski, from a novel by Patricia MacLachlan

Sarah T: Portrait of a Teenage Alcoholic ★★
Drama
1975 · US · Colour · 97mins

Two years after she shot to fame in *The Exorcist*, Linda Blair was possessed by the demon drink in this unremarkable TV movie. Clearly a well-meaning attempt to alert parents to the problem of teenage drinking, the film falls back on melodrama when a dash of realism might have been more effective. Blair is credible, but Larry Hagman and the remainder of what is quite a starry cast for a TV production are less committed.

Linda Blair *Sarah Travis* • Larry Hagman *Jerry Travis* • Verna Bloom *Jean Hodges* • William Daniels *Matt Hodges* • Michael Lerner *Dr Martin Kittredge* • Mark Hamill *Ken Newkirk* • M Emmet Walsh *Mr Peterson* ■ *Dir* Richard Donner • *Scr* Richard Shapiro, Esther Shapiro

Saratoga ★★★
Comedy
1937 · US · BW · 92mins

This robust racetrack romance had its back broken by the tragic and untimely death (during filming) of its star, blond bombshell Jean Harlow. Her demise cast a pall over the production and resulted in the movie being finished by the necessary use of a none-too-clever double (stand-in Mary Dees) in certain scenes, voice-matched and photographed back-to-camera. The morbidly curious will be able to spot the non-Harlow sections easily. For the rest, it's one of those intelligently crafted, glossy movies from MGM's golden era, with Clark Gable at his most dashing and Lionel Barrymore at his most crusty. Harlow sparkles, sadly for the last time.

Jean Harlow *Carol Clayton* • Clark Gable *Duke Bradley* • Lionel Barrymore *Grandpa Clayton* • Walter Pidgeon *Hartley Madison* • Frank Morgan *Jesse Kiffmeyer* • Una Merkel *Fritzi O'Malley* • Cliff Edwards *Tip O'Brien* ■ *Dir* Jack Conway • *Scr* Anita Loos, Robert Hopkins

Saratoga Trunk ★★
Melodrama
1945 · US · BW · 135mins

A lavish film of Edna Ferber's novel which reunited Ingrid Bergman, Gary Cooper, and Sam Wood, the stars and director of *For Whom the Bell Tolls*. Bergman plays a half-Creole beauty, resentful of her illegitimacy, and Cooper is a gambler who fancies her while she sets her sights on a tycoon. Set in New Orleans and Saratoga Springs, it's an obvious attempt to haul in the audience for *Gone with the Wind*. Among the embarrassments is Oscar nominee Flora Robson as a maid, blacked up like Hattie McDaniel.

Gary Cooper *Colonel Clint Maroon* • Ingrid Bergman *Clio Dulaine* • Flora Robson *Angelique Buiton* • Jerry Austin *Cupidon* • John Warburton *Bartholomew Van Steed* • Florence Bates *Mrs Coventry Bellop* • Curt Bois

Augustin Haussy ■ *Dir* Sam Wood • *Scr* Casey Robinson, from the novel by Edna Ferber

Sardar ★★★ 🔞
Biographical drama
1993 · Ind · Colour · 134mins

An eclectic director associated with the "middle cinema" tradition between the staple masala musicals and the social realism of "parallel cinema", Ketan Mehta is best known as the first Indian director to show naked breasts in his 1992 version of *Madame Bovary*. This controversial biopic focuses on the career of the man who was prime minister Nehru's deputy, and also the minister responsible for domestic affairs in India in the days after Partition. Paresh Rawl does sterling work in the title role, but it's Mehta's frank exploration of the policies and prejudices that still divide the peoples of the subcontinent that makes this so engrossing. In Hindi with English subtitles.

Paresh Rawl *Sardar* • Annu Kapoor ■ *Dir* Ketan Mehta • *Scr* Vijay Tendulkar

Sarraouina ★★★★
Drama
1986 · Fr/Burkina Faso · Colour · 120mins

Both a celebration of African culture and a warning against perpetuating the divisions that delivered much of the continent into European rule, Med Hondo's epic account of the battles waged by Sarraounia (Aï Këta), the 19th-century warrior queen of the Aznas, is both inspiring and impressively cinematic. While Guy Famechon's photography conveys the enormity of the Lugu region, Hondo concentrates on the personal problems besetting Këta's resistance to a local tribe and the marauding French. A landmark in Third World Cinema. In French with English subtitles.

Aï Këta *Sarraounia* • Jean-Roger Milo *Captain Voulet* • Feodor Atkine *Captain Chanoine* • Didier Sauvegrain *Doctor Henric* ■ *Dir* Med Hondo • *Scr* Med Hondo, Abdul War

Sartana ★★★ 🔞
Spaghetti western 1968 · It · Colour · 91mins

A no-nonsense spaghetti western from Gianfranco Parolini, directing under the name of Frank Kramer. John Garko is the eponymous gunfighter who is forced to draw on all his experience and cunning to clear his name after he is accused of masterminding a bank robbery. Parolini has a firm grasp of the conventions of the genre, switching between passages of terse dialogue and outbursts of stylised violence with some aplomb. Garko looks the part, but he is easily outshone by co-stars Klaus Kinski and William Berger. Italian dialogue dubbed into English. ▣

John Garko [Gianni Garko] *Sartana* • Klaus Kinski • William Berger ■ *Dir* Frank Kramer [Gianfranco Parolini]

Sartana, Angel of Death ★★
Spaghetti western 1969 · It · Colour · 92mins

After the success of *Sartana*, Gianni Garko and Klaus Kinski were reteamed the following year for this unremarkable sequel. Sticking pretty closely to the trusted spaghetti

western recipe, it follows the unflinching gunfighter as he tries to discover who's behind a series of vicious bank robberies. Whereas Gianfranco Parolini kept the action swift and simple in the original picture, director Giuliano Carnimeo (hiding behind the pseudonym Anthony Ascott) is prepared to allow it to meander and rarely rouses his stars from their lethargy. An Italian language film.

Gianni Garko *Sartana* • Frank Wolff • Klaus Kinski ■ *Dir* Anthony Ascott [Giuliano Carnimeo] • *Scr* Tito Carpi, Enzo Dell'Aquila

Saskatchewan ★★ 🅄
Western 1954 · US · Colour · 87mins

An under-rated actor, Alan Ladd seemed content to make formula pictures rather than stretch himself. His first western after the memorable *Shane* was this routine story of cavalry versus Indians – only this time the troops are Mounties and the location is Canada. Ladd's the Indian-raised officer who defies his superior officer to deal with hostile Sioux crossing the border. Shelley Winters is thrown in as the woman prisoner of Hugh O'Brian's marshal. The uninvolved direction of veteran Raoul Walsh doesn't help.

Alan Ladd *Sergeant O'Rourke* • Shelley Winters *Grace Markey* • J Carrol Naish *Batoche* • Hugh O'Brian *Marshal Smith* • Robert Douglas *Inspector Benton* • George Lewis [George J Lewis] *Lawson* • Jay Silverheels *Cajou* ■ *Dir* Raoul Walsh • *Scr* Gil Doud

Sasquatch ★ 🅄
Adventure 1978 · US · Colour · 101mins

Of all the monsters that cinema has unleashed, Bigfoot, supposed inhabitant of the North American forests, seems to be one of the most benign – perhaps because we know so little about him (or her). He's even more harmless in this semi-documentary about an expedition – featuring a lot of B-movie actors – that goes in search of the creature. Some blurred photos are supposed to strike a chill, but they are faintly risible – as is the film.

George Lauris *Chuck Evans* • Steve Boergadine *Hank Parshall* • Jim Bradford *Barney Snipe* • Ken Kenzle *Josh Bigsby* • William Emmons *Dr Paul Markham* • Joe Morello *Techka Blackhawk* ■ *Dir* Ed Ragozzini • *Scr* Edward H Hawkins, from a story by Ronald B Olson

The Satan Bug ★★★ 🅿️
Science-fiction thriller
1965 · US · Colour · 109mins

Compared to the more straightforward heroics of other Alistair MacLean hits such as *The Guns of Navarone* and *Where Eagles Dare*, this is an altogether more subtle affair, with George Maharis searching for the madman who is threatening to unleash a deadly virus. There's a solid supporting cast in the shape of Richard Basehart, Anne Francis, Ed Asner, and Dana Andrews, and director John Sturges never lets the suspense slip for a minute. Contains some violence and strong language. ▣

George Maharis *Lee Barrett* • Richard Basehart *Dr Hoffman/Ainsley* • Anne Francis *Ann* • Dana Andrews *The General* • Edward

Asner [Ed Asner] *Veretti* • Frank Sutton *Donald* • John Larkin *Michaelson* ■ *Dir* John Sturges • *Scr* James Clavell, Edward Anhalt, from the novel by Ian Stuart [Alistair MacLean]

Satan in High Heels ★★

Thriller 1962 · US · BW · 89mins

Great title, shame about the movie! Burlesque dancer Meg Myles robs her junkie boyfriend, heads for New York and quickly becomes a cabaret club owner's mistress, in a typical exploitation item from the early sixties featuring very little strip but lots of tease. Aside from a stand-out sequence where Myles (a future American soap-opera star) sings *More Deadly Than the Male* wearing full leather and brandishing a riding crop, this is strictly routine trash.

Meg Myles *Stacey Kane* • Grayson Hall *Pepe* • Earl Hammond *Rudy* • Mike Keene *Arnold Kenyon* • John Nicholas *Peter* ■ *Dir* Jerald Intrator • *Scr* John Chapman

Satan Met a Lady ★

Crime comedy drama
1936 · US · BW · 75mins

A reworked version of Dashiell Hammett's *The Maltese Falcon*, this was clearly intended as a sophisticated spoof but emerged as a clumsy, unfunny bore. There is some interest to be had in identifying the worked-over characters – for Madame Barabbas read Sidney Greenstreet, for example – and plot points – several questionable characters are after an ancient ivory horn filled with jewels – but that's about it. Warren William stars as Ted Shayne, scriptwriter Brown Holmes's version of Sam Spade, Bette Davis is the girl in the case. Davis regarded the movie as one of the low points in her career.

Bette Davis *Valerie Purvis* • Warren William *Ted Shayne* • Alison Skipworth *Mme Barabbas* • Arthur Treacher *Anthony Travers* • Winifred Shaw *Astrid Ames* • Marie Wilson *Murgatroyd* • Porter Hall *Mr Ames* • Maynard Holmes *Kenneth* ■ *Dir* William Dieterle • *Scr* Brown Holmes, from the novel *The Maltese Falcon* by Dashiell Hammett

Satan Never Sleeps ★

Drama 1962 · US · Colour · 126mins

Director Leo McCarey made that cringe-making tale of Hollywood religiosity, *Going My Way*. This – his last movie – was a similar yarn, about two priests, Clifton Webb and William Holden, whose enemy is not juvenile delinquency but godless communism. Set in China in its revolutionary year of 1949, this tells of Holden arriving at a Chinese mission to relieve the old priest (Webb). The pair are attacked by communist soldiers, who also rape and impregnate a native girl. A self-important piece of anti-communist propaganda from a once-great director, with lazy performances from two woefully miscast stars.

William Holden (1) *Father O'Banion* • Clifton Webb *Father Bovard* • France Nuyen *Sin Lan* • Athene Seyler *Sister Agnes* • Martin Benson *Kuznietsky* • Edith Sharpe *Sister Theresa* ■ *Dir* Leo McCarey • *Scr* Claude Binyon, Leo McCarey, from the novel *The China Story* by Pearl Buck

The Satanic Rites of Dracula ★ 🔞

Horror 1973 · UK · Colour · 83mins

Christopher Lee masquerades as a mysterious Howard Hughes-style business mogul, plotting to control the world with a vampire virus, in his disappointing final appearance as the count. Lacking in Hammer's usual Gothic flavour and detail, this proved to be the final nail in the Dracula coffin, despite the indefatigable Peter Cushing performing his usual miracle as a descendant of the original Van Helsing, with Joanna Lumley as his daughter. The contrived final showdown features an undead first death by hawthorn bush but it's a shoddy memorial to the Lee/Cushing Hammer golden years. Contains nudity. 📼

Christopher Lee *Count Dracula* • Peter Cushing *Van Helsing* • Michael Coles *Inspector Murray* • William Franklyn *Torrence* • Freddie Jones *Professor Keeley* • Joanna Lumley *Jessica* • Richard Vernon *Mathews* • Patrick Barr *Lord Carradine* ■ *Dir* Alan Gibson • *Scr* Don Houghton, from the character created by Bram Stoker

Satan's Brew ★★★

Black comedy
1976 · W Ger · Colour · 112mins

Rainer Werner Fassbinder is at his most scathingly anti-bourgeois in this portrayal of a worthless world. His pessimistic conclusion is that all relationships are based on power and that sado-masochism, blind fealty and financial gain have replaced emotion. Playing the burned-out poet capable only of expressing himself in acts of cruelty or self-loathing, Kurt Raab exhibits no redeeming features as a character Fassbinder clearly invests with autobiographical disgust. Contemptuously blurring the line between illusion and reality, Fassbinder makes no concessions towards the viewer, who is left to experience either anger or guilt. In German with English subtitles.

Kurt Raab *Walter Kranz* • Margit Carstensen *Andrée* • Helen Vita *Luise Kranz* • Volker Spengler *Ernst* • Ingrid Caven *Lilly* • Marquard Bohm *Rolf* • Ulli Lommel *Lauf* ■ *Dir/Scr* Rainer Werner Fassbinder

Satan's Cheerleaders ★★

Horror 1977 · US · Colour · 92mins

A bunch of cheerleaders on their way to a football game are kidnapped by backwood Satanists eager for a virgin sacrifice, in this bottom-of-the-barrel horror movie. So why choose cheerleaders? Luckily one of the girls happens to be descended from a witch and her tormentors get more than they bargained for. Despite the inspired title this is in no way funny or horrific enough to be truly effective. Veterans John Ireland, Yvonne De Carlo and John Carradine are all totally wasted by director Greydon Clark.

John Ireland *Sheriff Bub/High Priest* • Yvonne De Carlo *Emm Bub, Sheriff's wife/High Priestess* • Jack Kruschen *Billy the janitor* • John Carradine *Bum* • Sydney Chaplin *Mond* • Jacqueline Cole *Ms Johnson* ■ *Dir* Greydon Clark • *Scr* Greydon Clark, Alvin L Fast

Satan's Harvest ★

Detective thriller
1965 · SAfr · Colour · 104mins

American detective George Montgomery inherits a ranch in South Africa, only to discover it's being used as the centre for an international drug-smuggling operation. A slow and banal thriller, set against a spectacular backdrop and featuring a rare screen turn by crooner Matt Monro. Conservationist actress Tippi Hedren made this potboiler not long after *The Birds*, but it was kept on the shelf until 1970. Easy to see why.

George Montgomery *Cutter Murdock* • Tippi Hedren *Marla Oaks* • Matt Monro *Bates* • Davy Kaye • Brian O'Shaughnessy *Andrew* ■ *Dir/Scr* George Montgomery

Satisfaction ★ 15

Drama 1988 · US · Colour · 89mins

Justine Bateman, Julia Roberts, Trini Alvarado and Britta Phillips are the four girls in a rock band who spend the summer playing music at a resort and trying to find eligible men. Club owner Liam Neeson is the older man Bateman falls for in this mediocre teenage tale, notable mainly for a cameo from Blondie singer Debbie Harry, and a chance to see a pre-stardom Roberts and Neeson. You know it's time these girls had their instruments confiscated when you hear Bateman's rendition of *(I Can't Get No) Satisfaction* and the soul classic *Knock on Wood*. 📼

Justine Bateman *Jennie Lee* • Liam Neeson *Martin Falcon* • Julia Roberts *Daryle Shane* • Trini Alvarado *May "Mooch" Stark* • Britta Phillips *Billy Swan* • Scott Coffey *Nickie Longo* • Deborah Harry *Tina* ■ *Dir* Joan Freeman • *Scr* Charles Purpura

Saturday Night and Sunday Morning ★★★★★ PG

Drama 1960 · UK · BW · 85mins

Arthur Seaton was the only "kitchen sink" hero to accept that, while life was nasty, brutish and short, you had to make the best of it. And there was no one better to convey that complex mix of cynicism, laddishness and resignation than Albert Finney, in only his second film. Both he and Rachel Roberts won British Film Academy awards, while the film itself took the best British picture honour. Author Alan Sillitoe draws on his own experiences of factory life which are given a truly authentic ring by director Karel Reisz. For the first time, the working classes were treated with respect, not condescension. Finney's belligerence towards authority is as convincing as his touching tenderness towards the married woman (Roberts) he seduces, and, while he may not always live by his words – "What I want is a good time. The rest is all propaganda" – as he conforms to marriage with Shirley Anne Field, the film's affirmation that he can never really be beaten survives. 📼

Albert Finney *Arthur Seaton* • Shirley Anne Field *Doreen Gretton* • Rachel Roberts *Brenda* • Hylda Baker *Aunt Ada* • Norman Rossington *Bert* • Bryan Pringle *Jack* • Robert Cawdron *Robboe* ■ *Dir* Karel Reisz • *Scr* Alan Sillitoe, from his novel

Saturday Night at the Palace ★★★

Drama 1987 · SAfr · Colour · 88mins

Precious little South African cinema reaches this country, so Paul Slabolepszy's adaptation of his own much-praised play is all the more welcome. Unfortunately, the story of a broken-down footballer, whose drunken antics result in tragedy at an out-of-town burger bar, is a thoroughly predictable affair that rarely breaks out of its stage confines. Yet, there's undoubted power in the anti-apartheid rhetoric, and Slabolepszy himself gives a chilling performance revealing the ignorance and intolerance of the racist. Contains violence and swearing.

Bill Flynn *Forcie* • John Kani *September* • Paul Slabolepszy *Vince* ■ *Dir* Robert Davies • *Scr* Paul Slabolepszy, Bill Flynn, from a play by Paul Slabolepszy

Saturday Night Fever ★★★★ 18

Musical drama 1977 · US · Colour · 118mins

It was John Travolta's role in *Saturday Night Fever* as Tony Manero, the bum from Brooklyn who becomes king of the New York disco scene, that first turned him from a B-list TV actor into, for a time, the hottest movie star in the world. Some may find the whole thing a cringeworthy period piece and a reminder that the seventies really were the naffest decade. But most will sit back and enjoy the snazzy dancing (much of it with co-star Karen Lynn Gorney), the memorable soundtrack featuring classic hits from the Bee Gees, as well as Tavares and KC and the Sunshine Band and the all-round, high energy entertainment. Contains swearing and sex scenes. 📼

John Travolta *Tony Manero* • Karen Lynn Gorney *Stephanie* • Barry Miller *Bobby C* • Joseph Cali *Joey* • Paul Pape *Double J* • Donna Pescow *Annette* • Bruce Ornstein *Gus* • Julie Bovasso *Flo* ■ *Dir* John Badham • *Scr* Norman Wexler, from the article *Tribal Rites of the New Saturday Night* by Nik Cohn • *Choreographer* Lester Wilson

The Saturday Night Kid ★★

Romantic comedy 1929 · US · BW · 62mins

With her scandalous off-screen antics escalating, Paramount's megastar Clara Bow would soon receive her exit visa from the studio. But she survived the transition to sound and here – as in *It* – she is a department store assistant. Jean Arthur, playing Clara's sister, is surprisingly the bigger vamp of the two and both girls have their sights set on James Hall. The script offers some snappy one-liners as well as the attraction of the leading ladies. Future sex symbol Jean Harlow has a bit part.

Clara Bow *Mayme* • James Hall *Bill* • Jean Arthur *Janie* • Charles Sellon *Lem Woodruff* • Ethel Wales *Ma Woodruff* • Frank Ross *Ken* • Edna May Oliver *Miss Streeter* • Jean Harlow *Hazel* ■ *Dir* A Edward Sutherland • *Scr* Lloyd Corrigan, Ethel Doherty, Edward E Paramore Jr, from the play *Love 'em and Leave 'em* by George Abbott, John VA Weaver

Saturday Night Out ★★★

Drama   1963 · UK · BW · 96mins

This gritty, low-budget, black-and-white exploitation film was very daring in its day but wouldn't cause a stir now. The plot is negligible: five merchant seamen and their passenger spend a long day's leave in London, but it's the location charm and period cast that keep the movie watchable today. On board are such British stalwarts as Vera Day, David Lodge, Nigel Green, and ex-boxer Freddie Mills. The nominal stars are the lovely sweet-faced Heather Sears, and that venerable old grouch Bernard Lee (James Bond's "M"). Francesca Annis and Colin (*The Leather Boys*) Campbell also impress.

Heather Sears *Penny* • Bernard Lee *George Hudson* • Erika Remberg *Wanda* • Francesca Annis *Jean* • John Bonney *Lee* • Colin Campbell *Jamie* • Nigel Green *Paddy* • Vera Day *Arlene* • Freddie Mills *Joe* • David Lodge *Arthur* ■ *Dir* Robert Hartford-Davis • *Scr* Donald Ford, Derek Ford

Saturday the 14th ★ 15

Spoof horror   1981 · US · Colour · 72mins

Despite its title, this childish parody is more a monster-movie spoof than a send-up of slasher movies such as *Friday the 13th*. Real-life couple Richard Benjamin and Paula Prentiss move into a haunted house where their son Kevin Brando opens an ancient *Book of Evil* and a horde of monsters, aliens and vampires pop out eager to take up residence. There are some flashes of humour – a *Creature from the Black Lagoon* in the bubble bath and nothing but *Twilight Zone* episodes on the TV set – but for the most part this juvenile affair is a crudely produced rag-bag of sketches. ▭

Richard Benjamin *John* • Paula Prentiss *Mary* • Severn Darden *Van Helsing* • Jeffrey Tambor *Waldemar* • Kari Michaelsen *Debbie* • Kevin Brando *Billy* • Rosemary De Camp *Aunt Lucille* ■ *Dir* Howard R Cohen • *Scr* Howard R Cohen, from a story by Jeff Begun

Saturday the 14th Strikes Back ★ PG

Spoof horror   1988 · US · Colour · 75mins

Director Howard R Cohen clearly didn't learn from the mistakes of his original sub-standard spoof as this sequel is an even more pitiful parody. This time husband and wife Avery Schreiber and Patty McCormack move into a haunted house built over the entrance to Hell which cracks open and unleashes yet another surfeit of monsters, vampires and werewolves. Footage lifted from bad Roger Corman B-movies replaces the arch-satire of the first movie but with the same poor result on the entertainment front. ▭

Jason Presson *Eddie Baxter* • Ray Walston *Gramps* • Avery Schreiber *Frank* • Patty McCormack *Kate* • Julianne McNamara *Linda* • Rhonda Aldrich *Alice* • Daniel Will-Harris *Bert* ■ *Dir/Scr* Howard R Cohen

Saturday's Children ★★★

Drama   1940 · US · BW · 101mins

A young inventor (John Garfield) meets obstacles to his plans and dreams: marriage to an ambitious girl (Anne Shirley) and the devastating effects of the Depression. Directed by Vincent Sherman with an excellent cast that includes Claude Rains, this was Garfield's successful bid to break out of the slum boy/crime movie mould. Its social concerns are clear but, like the era it explores, the movie is downbeat and depressing.

John Garfield *Rimes Rosson* • Anne Shirley *Bobby Halevy* • Claude Rains *Mr Halevy* • Lee Patrick *Florrie Sands* • George Tobias *Herbie Smith* • Roscoe Karns *Willie Sands* • Dennie Moore *Gertrude Mills* ■ *Dir* Vincent Sherman • *Scr* Julius J Epstein, Philip G Epstein, from the play by Maxwell Anderson

Saturn 3 ★★ 15

Science-fiction adventure
1980 · UK · Colour · 83mins

Kirk Douglas and Farrah Fawcett live an idyllic Adam and Eve existence in a synthetic food-making factory on Titan, the third moon of Saturn. Then along comes snake Harvey Keitel, a psychopath on the run from Earth, with his equally disturbed robot Hector. Great sets and futuristic hardware paper over the black holes in a ridiculous space shocker directed by Stanley Donen, who is unable to overcome the mass of contrivance and plot confusion. Note Keitel's dubbed English accent. ▭ **DVD**

Farrah Fawcett *Alex* • Kirk Douglas *Adam* • Harvey Keitel *Benson* • Douglas Lambert *Captain James* • Ed Bishop *Harding* ■ *Dir* Stanley Donen • *Scr* Martin Amis, from a story by John Barry

Satyamev Jayate ★★★ 15

Crime thriller   1987 · Ind · Colour · 148mins

Director Raj Sippy's epic crime thriller follows the trials and tribulations of a dedicated police officer, who's desperately trying to pick up the pieces of his life following the accidental killing of a young boy. Vinay Shukla's screenplay remains faithful to the genre and, as a result, contains few surprises. In Hindi with English subtitles. ▭

Vinod Khanna • Meenakshi Seshadri • Madhavi ■ *Dir* Raj Sippy • *Scr* Vinay Shukla

Satyricon ★★★★

Historical fantasy drama
1969 · Fr/It · Colour · 129mins

Federico Fellini received an Oscar nomination for best director for this deliriously surreal moving fresco of ancient Rome. This is *La Dolce Vita* out of Petronius by way of Pasolini and DeMille, with the antics of Nero's empire being used to comment on contemporary godlessness. The adventures of squabbling hedonists Martin Potter and Hiram Keller don't matter a fig beside the debauchery and depravity, which for all their seeming excess are not that divorced from historical reality. Over-indulgence, indiscipline and sexual immaturity are the usual accusations hurled at this hellish vision, but few film-makers would have had the courage to make it. In Italian with English subtitles.

Martin Potter *Encolpius* • Hiram Keller *Ascyltus* • Salvo Randone *Eumolpus* • Max Born *Giton* • Fanfulla *Vernacchio* • Mario Romagnoli *Trimalchio* • Capucine *Tryphaena* • Alain Cuny *Lichas* ■ *Dir* Federico Fellini • *Scr* Federico Fellini, Bernardino Zapponi, Brunello Rondi, from the novel by Gaius Petronius

The Savage ★★ U

Western   1953 · US · Colour · 94mins

Charlton Heston was the sole star of his fourth Hollywood film. He makes a sturdy job of portraying the white man raised by the Sioux who becomes an army scout, trusted by neither side. As conflict threatens, he has to decide where his loyalties lie. Blandly directed by George Marshall, the western is far too long and the way the Heston character is handled at the end smacks of box-office compromise.

Charlton Heston *Warbonnet/Jim Ahern* • Susan Morrow *Tally Hathersall* • Peter Hanson *Lt Weston Hathersall* • Joan Taylor *Luta* • Richard Rober *Capt Arnold Vaugant* ■ *Dir* George Marshall • *Scr* Sydney Boehm, from the novel *The Renegade* by LL Foreman

Savage ★ 18

Science-fiction action thriller
1995 · US · Colour · 98mins

Most of the blame for this underwhelming movie goes to Patrick Highsmith and Peter Sagal's script, which does not properly explain the mysterious alien force that awakens shooting victim Olivier Gruner from his stupor, and subsequently drives him to destroy an evil corporation headed by Kario Salem. While director Avi Nesher usually brings a sharp look and high impact action, Gruner's martial arts sequences are cramped and generic. Contains swearing, violence and a sex scene. ▭

Olivier Gruner *Alex Verne/Savage* • Jennifer Grant *Nicky Carter* • Kario Salem *Reese Burroughs* • Sam McMurray *Edgar Wallace* • Kristin Minter *Marie* ■ *Dir* Avi Nesher • *Scr* Patrick Highsmith, Peter Sagal, from a story by Patrick Highsmith

Savage Dawn ★ 18

Action drama   1985 · US · Colour · 98mins

It's an unwritten rule among film critics that movies with titles that start with the word "savage" are invariably awful. *Savage Dawn* confirms it beyond any reasonable doubt. Ploughing the same furrow as a thousand other B-movies, it's the violent, foul-mouthed tale of a biker gang that takes over a small desert town. You can guess exactly what happens, and you'd be right. The major mystery is how such tosh managed to attract such a recognisable and half-decent cast. ▭

George Kennedy *Tick Rand* • Richard Lynch *Reverend Romano* • Karen Black *Rachel* • Lance Henriksen *Ben Stryker* • Claudia Udy *Kate Rand* • Bill Forsythe [William Forsythe] *Pigiron* • Leo Gordon *Sheriff* ■ *Dir* Simon Nuchtern • *Scr* William P Milling

The Savage Eye ★★

Drama   1959 · US · BW · 66mins

This part-documentary offers a sour and biased view of urban American life, built around Barbara Baxley as a new arrival in a big city, alone and unhappy in a hostile environment. Individual sequences provide a depressing picture of people on their worst behaviour – watching wrestlers and strippers – or at their most gullible and ridiculous, flocking to faith healers and undergoing cosmetic surgery and beauty treatments. Overlaid on the visuals is a pretentious dialogue between the woman and a poet (voiced by Gary Merrill). Made over four years – often with hidden cameras – this gained a wide arthouse release.

Barbara Baxley *Judith McGuire* • Gary Merrill *The poet* • Herschel Bernardi *Kirtz* ■ *Dir/Scr* Ben Maddow, Sidney Myers, Joseph Strick

Savage Harvest ★★★ 15

Adventure drama 1981 · US · Colour · 82mins

This Kenyan-set adventure has an intriguing premise: Michelle Phillips and children are cornered on a plantation by a group of starving lions, but these are no ordinary lions, they exhibit seemingly preternatural intelligence in their tactics. Safari guide (and Phillips ex-husband) Tom Skerritt comes to the rescue. Phillips does a nice line in frayed nerves as the tension mounts, while Skerritt has plenty of opportunities to squint into the sun and look wiry. The film never manages fully capitalise on the potential offered by both the setting and story, but it still has its moments. ▭

Tom Skerritt *Casey* • Michelle Phillips *Maggie* • Shawn Stevens *Jon* • Anne-Marie Martin *Wendy* • Derek Partridge *Derek* • Arthur Malet *Dr MacGruder* • Tana Helfer *Kristie* ■ *Dir* Robert Collins • *Scr* Robert Collins, Robert Blees, from a story by Ralph Helfer, Ken Noyle

Savage Hearts ★★ 18

Comedy thriller 1995 · UK · Colour · 106mins

The collision between British caper film and Tarantino-esque "crooks on the run" scenario produces predictably confused, if occasionally entertaining results. Con-man turned Jamie Harris teams up with terminally ill drug courier Maryam d'Abo, who has decided to rob her paymasters blind before she dies. Along the way the pair tangle with an assortment of creaky stereotypes – including an amusing turn from Harris's dad, Richard, as a dodgy aristocrat – but the smattering of B-list celebrities serves only to make the whole feel like TV out-takes rather than a feature film. Watch out for Angus Deayton, looking rather uncomfortable as a hit man. Contains some swearing, violence and sexual references. ▭

Jamie Harris *Johnny* • Maryam D'Abo *Beatrice* • Myriam Cyr *Jennifer* • Richard Harris *Sir Roger Foxley* • Stephen Marcus *Hector* • Angus Deayton *Leonard* • Julian Fellowes *Bishop* • Jerry Hall *Lady* ■ *Dir/Scr* Mark Ezra

The Savage Innocents ★★

Adventure drama
1960 · It /Fr/UK · Colour · 107mins

What started out as a sort of *Nanook of the North*-style look at Inuit culture, with Anthony Quinn in fur and full ethnic mode, was apparently plagued by production problems. These included Peter O'Toole's Mountie sporting his original nose but not his original voice, which was dubbed against the actor's wishes. Quinn makes a creditable attempt at portraying the harsh Inuit lifestyle – hunting, fishing, watching polar bears – but even he can't save this oddity from

director Nicholas Ray. A shambles, but with noble intentions.

Anthony Quinn *Inuk* • Yoko Tani *Asiak* • Marie Yang *Powtee* • Peter O'Toole *First Trooper* • Carlo Giustini *Second Trooper* • Kaida Horiuchi *Imina* ▪ *Dir* Nicholas Ray • *Scr* Nicholas Ray, Hans Ruesch, Franco Solinas, from the novel *Top of the World* by Hans Ruesch

The Savage Is Loose ★

Adventure drama
1974 · US · Colour · 115mins

Directed, produced and starring George C Scott, this is a tale of incest between mother and son after they've been stranded on a desert island with father for some years. Trish Van Devere (Scott's real wife) and John David Carson feature in a story that plumbs the shallows rather ineptly and does Scott's reputation no good.

George C Scott *John* • Trish Van Devere *Maida* • John David Carson *David* • Lee H Montgomery [Lee Montgomery] *Young David* ▪ *Dir* George C Scott • *Scr* Max Ehrlich, Frank De Felitta

Savage Islands ★★ PG

Adventure 1983 · US/NZ · Colour · 95mins

This has to be a low point in the rollercoaster career of Tommy Lee Jones, who didn't get real recognition until his award-winning turn as the US marshal hunting Harrison Ford in *The Fugitive*. Belonging to the bygone age of Saturday morning pictures, this bloodless romp has Jones as a crusty rogue helping missionary Michael O'Keefe to rescue fiancée Jenny Seagrove from the pirates who've kidnapped her. It's a case of all buckle and no swash. 📺 •

Tommy Lee Jones *Captain "Bully" Hayes* • Michael O'Keefe *Nathaniel Williamson* • Jenny Seagrove *Sophie* • Max Phipps *Ben Pease* • Grant Tilly *Count Von Rittenberg* • Peter Rowley *Louis Beck* • Bill Johnson *Reverend Williamson* ▪ *Dir* Ferdinand Fairfax • *Scr* John Hughes, David Odell, from a screenplay (unproduced) by David Odell and a story by Lloyd Phillips

Savage Messiah ★★★

Romantic drama 1972 · UK · Colour · 96mins

After the excesses of *The Music Lovers* and *The Devils*, director Ken Russell handled the platonic love affair between sculptor Henri Gaudier and his muse Sophie Brzeska, with pleasing restraint (apart from a couple of unnecessary song and dance numbers). Set in Paris and London prior to the First World War, Dorothy Tutin and newcomer Scott Antony give superb, impassioned performances as the seemingly ill-matched couple. For Russell, it was a labour of love (he put his own money into the project); he asked Derek Jarman to design the film because of Jarman's fondness for the period, and this shows as well.

Dorothy Tutin *Sophie Brzeska* • Scott Antony *Henri Gaudier-Brzeska* • Helen Mirren *Gosh Smith-Boyle* • Lindsay Kemp *Angus Corky* • Peter Vaughan *Louvre attendant* • Michael Gough *Mons Gaudier* ▪ *Dir* Ken Russell • *Scr* Christopher Logue, from a book by HS Ede

Savage Sam ★★ PG

Western 1963 · US · Colour · 103mins

This is a hugely disappointing sequel to the popular doggy tale, *Old Yeller*. The story focuses on Yeller's son, Savage Sam, who leads Brian Keith to the Indian camp where brothers Tommy Kirk and Kevin Corcoran and their neighbour Marta Kristen, are being held hostage. The brutal battle at the end of the film might be a little strong for younger children, but most parents will be slightly concerned at the stereotypical depiction of the native Americans. 📺

Brian Keith *Uncle Beck Coates* • Tommy Kirk *Travis Coates* • Kevin Corcoran *Arliss Coates* • Dewey Martin *Lester White* • Jeff York *Bud Searcy* • Marta Kristen *Lisbeth Searcy* ▪ *Dir* Norman Tokar • *Scr* Fred Gipson, William Tunberg, from a book by Fred Gipson

Savage Streets ★★ 18

Action drama 1984 · US · Colour · 80mins

Following her appearance in *The Exorcist* and its less than popular sequel, Linda Blair made a career out of trashy exploitation flicks. She stars as a typical LA girl who turns into "Charles Bronson in a dress" when her deaf mute sister is raped by a gang of lowlife punks. Linda leads her all-girl gang against those responsible, armed with such niceties as bear traps and a crossbow. Blair's performance is actually quite strong, but is swamped by the vulgar dialogue and gratuitous bouts of violence. 📺

Linda Blair *Brenda* • John Vernon *Principal Underwood* • Robert Dryer *Jake* • Johnny Venocur *Vince* • Sal Landi *Fargo* • Scott Mayer *Red* ▪ *Dir* Danny Steinmann • *Scr* Norman Yonemoto, Danny Steinmann

Savannah Smiles ★★ PG

Comedy drama 1982 · US · Colour · 99mins

Bridgette Andersen runs away from her uncaring politician father and makes the mistake of hiding in the car of two not-so-bright crooks. The duo decide to hold her to ransom, but gradually become more like surrogate parents than opportunistic kidnappers as the police close in. Written by co-star Mark Miller, this winsome comedy thriller throws some fresh comic twists into the plot to stop it becoming too mechanical and manipulative. 📺

Mark Miller *Alvie* • Donovan Scott *Boots* • Bridgette Andersen *Savannah Driscoll* • Peter Graves (1) *Harland Dobbs* • Chris Robinson *Richard Driscoll* • Michael Parks *Lt Savage* • Barbara Stanger *Joan Driscoll* ▪ *Dir* Pierre De Moro • *Scr* Mark Miller

Save Me ★★ 18

Erotic thriller 1994 · US · Colour · 89mins

This movie must be one of the low points of Harry Hamlin's career. His character is suffering a crisis of faith: his wife is leaving him, his performance as a stockbroker is suffering, and the office jerk just got the big promotion. Then he meets Ellie (Lysette Anthony), a beautiful but troubled young woman who surreptitiously leaves him a note reading "Save me". This silly story is basically an excuse to get the two stars naked as often as possible.

Contains swearing, nudity, sex scenes and violence. 📺

Harry Hamlin *Jim Stevens* • Lysette Anthony *Ellie* • Michael Ironside *Oliver Moran* • Olivia Hussey *Gail* • Bill Nunn *Detective Vincent* ▪ *Dir* Alan Roberts • *Scr* Neil Ronco

Save the Dog! ★★★

Comedy 1988 · US · Colour · 95mins

Cindy Williams (one half of *Laverne and Shirley*) and Tony Randall (one half of TV's *The Odd Couple*) star in this silly canine caper about a woman trying to save her dog, although the only threat to its life seems to be from overeating. It's daft in the extreme, but very entertaining, nonetheless (and the dog's cute), and there are certainly worse ways to spend your time.

Cindy Williams *Becky Dale* • Tony Randall *Director* • Katherine Helmond *Agent* • Tom Poston *Veterinarian* ▪ *Dir* Paul Aaron • *Scr* Haris Orkin, John McNamara

Save the Tiger ★★★

Drama 1973 · US · Colour · 100mins

Jack Lemmon stars as a struggling Los Angeles garment manufacturer who contemplates burning down his factory in order to claim the insurance and pay off his debts. This drama about the consumer rat race is bludgeoning rather than hard-hitting, and Lemmon's role seems very much in the tradition of Arthur Miller's Willy Loman in *Death of a Salesman*. Though it won Lemmon a best actor Oscar, he has given far better performances in films such as *The Apartment*. The Academy loves a comedian being serious, however, and the movie was said to have caught the Watergate mood of sleaze and disenchantment. Contains swearing.

Jack Lemmon *Harry Stoner* • Jack Gilford *Phil Greene* • Laurie Heineman *Myra* • Norman Burton *Fred Mirrell* • Patricia Smith *Janet Stoner* • Thayer David *Charlie Robbins* • William Hansen *Meyer* ▪ *Dir* John G Avildsen • *Scr* Steve Shagan

Saved By the Light ★

Supernatural drama based on a true story
1995 · US · Colour · 95mins

A true story plucked from the tabloid headlines forms the basis of this plodding TV movie. In 1975, violent and nasty Dannion Brinkley (Eric Roberts) is struck dead by lightning, but comes back to life in the morgue. His near-death experience brings purpose to his life and he becomes an inspirational public speaker. Cheap production values and an uninspired performance by Roberts relegate this film to the don't-waste-your-time list.

Eric Roberts *Dannion Brinkley* • Lynette Walden *Casey* • Don McManus *Dr Raymond Moody* • Don Harvey *TM* ▪ *Dir* Lewis Teague • *Scr* John Mandel, from the non-fiction book by Dannion Brinkley, Paul Perry

Saving Grace ★★ PG

Comedy drama 1985 · US · Colour · 106mins

The essential decency of Tom Conti just about holds this fragile fable together. As a Pope who slips out of the Vatican to minister to people who truly need him, he wrinkles his brow and smiles sadly with a concern that convinces in a situation that doesn't.

Director Robert M Young shoots the southern Italian countryside with the glossy eye of a postcard photographer, while Joaquin Montana's script is overly dependent on easy solutions and glib platitudes. For all its good intentions, this is more of a penance than a pleasure. 📺

Tom Conti *Pope Leo XIV* • Fernando Rey *Cardinal Stefano Biondi* • Erland Josephson *Monsignor Francesco Ghezzi* • Giancarlo Giannini *Abalardi* • Donald Hewlett *Monsignor Colin McGee* • Edward James Olmos *Ciolino* ▪ *Dir* Robert M Young • *Scr* Joaquin Montana, from the novel by Celia Gittelson

Saving Grace ★★ PG

Comedy 2000 · UK · Colour · 111mins

An updated, Ealing-style comedy, with marijuana instead of whisky galore and Brenda Blethyn in the role that, 50 years ago, would have gone to Margaret Rutherford. Blethyn is the eponymous Grace, a recently widowed housewife whose late husband has left her with a mountain of debts to pay. The only way to keep her beautiful Cornish mansion is to grow ganja with the aid of her Scottish handyman, Craig Ferguson. A host of familiar TV faces jockey for position, but the screenplay is more juvenile than risqué and makes tittering pot-shots at the expense of credible characterisation and plot development.

Brenda Blethyn *Grace* • Craig Ferguson *Matthew* • Martin Clunes *Dr Bamford* • Tcheky Karyo *Jacques* • Jamie Foreman *China* • Bill Bailey *Vince* • Valerie Edmond *Nicky* • Diana Quick *Honey* • Leslie Phillips *Vicar* ▪ *Dir* Nigel Cole • *Scr* Craig Ferguson, Mark Crowdy, from a story by Mark Crowdy

Saving Private Ryan ★★★ 15

Second World War drama
1998 · US · Colour · 162mins

Steven Spielberg can't resist rewriting history. He did it with both *Schindler's List* and *Amistad*, but with this Oscar-winning attempt to reshape the past through fiction, he comes closer than ever before to depicting historical truth. The action opens brutally with a wrenching re-creation of the Second World War D-Day landing on Omaha beach. Spielberg and cinematographer Janusz Kaminski succeed in capturing the terrifying and bewildering chaos of the encounter. Yet, away from the fighting, *Saving Private Ryan* occasionally lapses into combat picture cliché, with too many members of Tom Hanks's unit recalling stereotypical troopers from morale-boosting movies made during the war itself. But (apart from its corny bookend sequences) this is still well-meaning, strongly acted and slickly mounted, and ranks among the director's better films. Contains violence, language and horror. 📺

Tom Hanks *Captain Miller* • Tom Sizemore *Sergeant Horvath* • Edward Burns *Private Reiben* • Barry Pepper *Private Jackson* • Adam Goldberg *Private Mellish* • Vin Diesel *Private Caparzo* • Giovanni Ribisi *T/4 Medic Wade* • Jeremy Davies *Corporal Upham* • Matt Damon *Private Ryan* • Ted Danson *Captain Hamill* • Kathleen Byron *Old Mrs Ryan* ▪ *Dir* Steven Spielberg • *Scr* Robert Rodat • *Editor* Michael Kahn

Savior ★★★★ 18
War drama 1997 · US · Colour · 99mins

Although at times an odd marriage between numbingly brutal fact and commercial Hollywood packaging, this Oliver Stone-produced, Yugoslavian-set tale of human cruelty still carries a haunting and shocking impact. Mercenary Dennis Quaid joins the Foreign Legion after his wife and child are killed by Islamic terrorists. While fighting on the Serbian side against the Muslims, circumstances throw him together with a pregnant rape victim caught in the crossfire and he begins to regain his humanity in the face of Bosnian atrocities. Grim, unrelenting and necessarily very violent, Serbian director Peter Antonijevic draws on his personal experiences to devastating effect and comes up with a poignant end product of rare emotional depth. Contains swearing and violence. 🖵
DVD

Dennis Quaid *Joshua Rose/Guy* • Nastassja Kinski *Maria Rose* • Stellan Skarsgård *Peter* • Natasa Ninkovic *Vera* • Pascal Rollin *Paris Priest* ■ *Dir* Peter Antonijevic • *Scr* Robert Orr

Saviors of the Forest ★★★
Documentary 1992 · US · Colour · 75mins

Taking their cue from Michael Moore, those self-styled "video warriors", director Bill Day and writer Terry Schwartz cast a satirical eye over the world of eco-politics in this mischievous, yet still highly perceptive investigation into the battle to save the Ecuadorian rainforest. Wryly exploring the paradoxes inherent in environmental crusading, the "camera Guys" unashamedly throw in their lot with the local "colonos", whose agricultural needs often bring them into conflict with both big business and the green lobby. They also highlight the culpability of Hollywood, which shoots impassioned eco-dramas on sets built from rainforest timber.

Dir Bill Day • *Scr* Terry Schwartz

Sawdust and Tinsel ★★★★
Drama 1953 · Swe · BW · 94mins

This symbolic circus drama is now recognised as a landmark in Ingmar Bergman's film career. Two cinematographers reproduced the oppressive compositions reminiscent of EA Dupont's expressionist classic, *Variety* (1925). Yet, while the narrative seems similarly fractured (with its bleached out flashback to clown Anders Ek's humiliation before a platoon of mocking soldiers and a Freudian dream sequence), there is an artistic unity about this tale of ageing ringmaster, Ake Gronberg, whose encounter with the wife he deserted, almost costs him the love of his mistress, Harriet Andersson. In Swedish with English subtitles.

Harriet Andersson *Anne* • Ake Gronberg *Albert Johansson* • Hakke Ekman *Frans* • Anders Ek *Frost* • Annika Tretow *Agda, Albert's wife* ■ *Dir/Scr* Ingmar Bergman • *Cinematographer* Sven Nykvist, Bladh Hilding

The Saxon Charm ★★★
Drama 1948 · US · BW · 88mins

Stage producer Robert Montgomery, an arrogant, amoral egomaniac and bully, causes misery to all who come into his orbit – particularly writer John Payne, whose play he is preparing to stage, Payne's wife Susan Hayward, his own girlfriend Audrey Totter and wealthy backer Harry Von Zell. Reputedly based on Broadway's notoriously unpleasant Jed Harris, this is interesting niche-market stuff for backstage aficionados; it carries an alarming ring of truth, but it's relentlessly unpleasant and lacking in edge.

Robert Montgomery *Matt Saxon* • Susan Hayward *Janet Busch* • John Payne *Eric Busch* • Audrey Totter *Alma Wragg* • Henry Morgan [Harry Morgan] *Hermy* • Harry Von Zell *Zack Humber* • Cara Williams *Dolly Humber* • Chill Wills *Captain Chatham* • Heather Angel *Vivian Saxon* ■ *Dir* Claude Binyon • *Scr* Claude Binyon, from the novel by Frederic Wakeman

Say Anything ★★★ 15
Comedy drama 1989 · US · Colour · 96mins

Not deemed worthy of a UK theatrical release, this little gem from Cameron Crowe, author of *Fast Times at Ridgemont High*, is a cleverly formatted teenage romance in which nothing is quite as it seems. John Cusack stars (and his sister Joan guests, playing his character's sister) as an underachieving student who falls for Ione Skye, "Miss Priss", the brain of the class, but meets opposition from her divorced dad (the excellent John Mahoney). Director Crowe continued his studies of Seattle courtship in 1992 with the beguiling *Singles*. Contains swearing 🖵

John Cusack *Lloyd Dobler* • Ione Skye *Diane Court* • John Mahoney *James Court* • Lili Taylor *Corey Flood* • Amy Brooks *D C* • Pamela Segall *Rebecca* • Jason Gould *Mike Cameron* • Loren Dean *Joe* • Glenn Walker Harris Jr *Jason* • Bebe Neuwirth *Mrs Evans* • Eric Stoltz *Vahlere* ■ *Dir/Scr* Cameron Crowe

Say Hello to Yesterday ★
Comedy 1971 · UK · Colour · 91mins

The beautiful and witty Jean Simmons is the only reason to watch this dreadful, Swinging Sixties relic. Simmons plays a bored housewife from the stockbroker belt who takes the train to London and is hounded by a young dropout, played by Zeffirelli's Romeo, Leonard Whiting. He wants to seduce her and pursues her across London to her mother's house. This is *Brief Encounter* in the style of *Blow-Up*, taking a tourist's-eye view of London before settling down to its chaste sex scene and Antonioni-esque finale of cold alienation.

Jean Simmons *Woman* • Leonard Whiting *Boy* • Evelyn Laye *Woman's mother* • John Lee *Woman's husband* • Jack Woolgar *Boy's father* • Constance Chapman *Boy's mother* • Gwen Nelson *Char* ■ *Dir* Alvin Rakoff • *Scr* Alvin Rakoff, Peter King, from a story by Ray Mathew, Alvin Rakoff

Say It With Songs ★★
Musical drama 1929 · US · BW · 95mins

Soon after the sound-breaking *The Jazz Singer*, Al Jolson embarked on this miscalculated musical drama, co-written by Darryl F Zanuck. Jolson plays a radio singer imprisoned for manslaughter and yearning for his wife and small boy. It's obvious lump-in-the-throat stuff but almost ends up as a joke with the song *Little Pal* trying to be another *Sonny Boy*.

Al Jolson *Joe Lane* • Davey Lee *Little Pal* • Marian Nixon *Katherine Lane* • Fred Kohler *Joe's cellmate* • Holmes Herbert *Dr Robert Merrill* • John Bowers *Surgeon* ■ *Dir* Lloyd Bacon • *Scr* Joseph Jackson, from a story by Darryl F Zanuck, Harvey Gates

Say One for Me ★★ U
Musical comedy 1959 · US · BW · 119mins

Bing Crosby had two enormous hits playing a priest back in the forties with *Going My Way* (which won him an Oscar) and *The Bells of St Mary's*, so he probably thought that doing it again might revive a fading film career. Here, the ageing crooner plays a cleric in charge of a Broadway church for showbiz folk. Alas, this overlong and thinly-scripted affair bears no comparison with the earlier hits, and Frank Tashlin was the wrong man to direct. Debbie Reynolds, like Crosby, has to struggle with both the script and weak musical material (James Van Heusen and Sammy Cahn working well below par) as well as a colourless romantic partner in Robert Wagner.

Bing Crosby *Father Conroy* • Debbie Reynolds *Holly LaMaise* • Robert Wagner *Tony Vincent* • Ray Walston *Phil Stanley* • Les Tremayne *Harry LaMaise* • Connie Gilchrist *Mary Manning* • Frank McHugh *Jim Dugan* ■ *Dir* Frank Tashlin • *Scr* Robert O'Brien

Sayonara ★★★ PG
Drama 1957 · US · Colour · 141mins

Marlon Brando's electric acting, not to mention sturdy contributions from Miyoshi Umeki and Red Buttons (both of whom scooped Oscars), forms an almost other-worldly contrast to the travelogue blandness of Joshua Logan's direction. With Brando capably holding centre screen as the Korean War soldier in Japan, and in love, Logan's scenic tendencies are occasionally interrupted by some proper art direction, the quality of which also merited an Oscar. The lovely theme song by Irving Berlin will haunt you. 🖵

Marlon Brando *Major Lloyd "Ace" Gruver* • Ricardo Montalban *Nakamura* • Red Buttons *Joe Kelly* • Patricia Owens *Eileen Webster* • Martha Scott *Mrs Webster* • James Garner *Captain Mike Bailey* • Miyoshi Umeki *Katsumi* ■ *Dir* Joshua Logan • *Scr* Paul Osborn, from the novel by James A Michener • *Art Director* Ted Haworth • *Set Designer* Robert Priestley

Scalawag ★
Adventure 1973 · US/It · Colour · 92mins

For his first film as a director, Kirk Douglas chose to remodel *Treasure Island* as a landlocked yarn. Set in Mexico, Douglas is the one-legged pirate Peg, trying to get his hands on some treasure hidden by his former colleagues. Mark Lester is the cute kid who brings out Peg's paternal qualities, and Danny DeVito has a small part. A catastrophe from start to finish.

Kirk Douglas *Peg* • Mark Lester (1) *Jamie* • Neville Brand *Brimstone/Mudhook* • Lesley-Anne Down *Lucy-Ann* • Don Stroud *Velvet* • Danny DeVito *Flyspeck* • Mel Blanc *Barfly the parrot* ■ *Dir* Kirk Douglas • *Scr* Albert Maltz, Sid Fleischman, from the story by Robert Louis Stevenson

The Scalphunters ★★★ PG
Comedy western 1968 · US · Colour · 99mins

Released at the height of civil rights awareness in America, this intelligent and highly enjoyable western might be described as *The Defiant Ones* in reverse, for here the uneasy black/white partnership is doing the pursuing rather than the escaping. If director Sydney Pollack presses home his points about racial tolerance with a heavy hand, he nevertheless coaxes spirited performances from his big-name cast. Trapper Burt Lancaster and runaway slave Ossie Davis play off each other to good effect, but the real sparks fly when scalphunter Telly Savalas and his mistress Shelley Winters are on the screen. 🖵

Burt Lancaster *Joe Bass* • Shelley Winters *Kate* • Telly Savalas *Jim Howie* • Ossie Davis *Joseph Winfield Lee* • Armando Silvestre *Two Crows* • Dan Vadis *Yuma* • Dabney Coleman *Jed* ■ *Dir* Sydney Pollack • *Scr* William Norton, from his story

Scam ★★★ 15
Thriller 1993 · US · Colour · 97mins

This crime thriller has ex-FBI agent Christopher Walken and crafty con woman Lorraine Bracco joining forces to lay an elaborate sting on Mafia money-launderer Martin Donovan, whose bodyguard "Headache" likes to chop people's heads off. The story shifts from Miami to Jamaica where our two unlikely heroes hide out and hopefully hang on to their heads when the scam doesn't go quite as planned. Gripping if a little too clever at the end (like *The Sting*), and altogether gutsier than the usual made-for-TV fodder, with Walken as excellent as ever. Contains violence and swearing. 🖵

Christopher Walken *Jack Shanks* • Lorraine Bracco *Maggie Rohrer* • Miguel Ferrer *Barry Landers* • Martin Donovan *Gordon Wexler* • James McDaniel *Daniel Poole* • Daniel Von Bargen *Albert Magliocco* • Erick Avari *Mr Ayub* ■ *Dir* John Flynn • *Scr* Craig Smith, from the novel *Ladystinger*

The Scamp ★★★
Drama 1957 · UK · BW · 88mins

Having made his name in the Australian-set drama *Smiley*, contemporary critics had high hopes for ten-year-old Colin Petersen. He tries hard in this well intentioned story of a delinquent given a second chance, but he never convinces either as the urchin son of alcoholic music-hall actor Terence Morgan or as the confused kid cajoled by teacher Richard Attenborough and his wife Dorothy Alison. It must have been a relief to Attenborough not to have been given the juvenile lead himself, but that doesn't excuse his overdoing the bourgeois benevolence.

Richard Attenborough *Stephen Leigh* • Colin Petersen *Tod Dawson* • Dorothy Alison *Barbara Leigh* • Terence Morgan *Mike Dawson* • Jill Adams *Julie Dawson* • Maureen Delaney *Mrs Perryman* • Margaretta Scott *Mrs Blundell* • David Franks *Eddie* ■ *Dir* Wolf Rilla • *Scr* Wolf Rilla, from the play *Uncertain Joy* by Charlotte Hastings

U = SUITABLE FOR ALL   **Uc** = SUITABLE FOR ALL, ESPECIALLY FOR YOUNG CHILDREN (VIDEO ONLY)   **PG** = PARENTAL GUIDANCE

Scandal ★★★ 18

Historical drama
1988 · UK · Colour · 108mins

A capable cast struggles to inject life into a by-the-numbers reconstruction of the Profumo affair, a scandal that contributed to the downfall of the Conservative government in 1964. Rather tame in the sleaze department, despite all the hype over the ''orgy'' scenes, Joanne Whalley-Kilmer makes a fine Christine Keeler and John Hurt a suitably shallow Stephen Ward. But it's Bridget Fonda who steals the show with her spot-on impersonation of Mandy Rice-Davies. Contains violence, swearing, sex scenes and nudity. 🎞

John Hurt *Stephen Ward* • Joanne Whalley-Kilmer [Joanne Whalley] *Christine Keeler* • Bridget Fonda *Mandy Rice-Davies* • Ian McKellen *John Profumo* • Leslie Phillips *Lord Astor* • Britt Ekland *Mariella Novotny* • Daniel Massey *Mervyn Griffith-Jones* • Roland Gift *Johnnie Edgecombe* • Jean Alexander *Mrs Keeler* • Jeroen Krabbé *Eugene Ivanov* ■ • *Scr* Michael Thomas, from the book *Nothing But* by Christine Keeler, Sandy Fawkes; the book *Mandy* by Mandy Rice-Davies, Shirley Flack; the book *Stephen Ward Speaks* by Warwick Charlton; the book *The Profumo Affair: a Summing Up* by Judge Sparrow; and the book *Scandal '63* by Clive Irving, Ron Hall, Jeremy Wallington

Scandal at Scourie ★★ U

Drama
1953 · US · Colour · 89mins

Walter Pidgeon, leading political, business and religious light of the Protestant community at Scourie – a small town in Canada – reluctantly allows his childless wife Greer Garson to adopt a little girl from a Catholic orphanage that has burnt down. The nuns extract a promise that the child (Donna Corcoran) will be raised a Catholic, and the situation is used as ammunition by Pidgeon's political rivals to discredit him. Directed by Jean Negulesco, this over-plotted, simplistic, anti-bigotry morality tale was the last outing for the once potent Pidgeon–Garson partnership.

Greer Garson *Mrs Patrick McChesney* • Walter Pidgeon *Patrick J McChesney* • Agnes Moorehead *Sister Josephine* • Donna Corcoran *Patsy* • Arthur Shields *Father Reilly* • Philip Ober *BG Belney* • Rhys Williams *Bill Swazey* • Margalo Gillmore *Alice Hanover* ■ *Dir* Jean Negulesco • *Scr* Norman Corwin, Leonard Spigelgass, Karl Tunberg, from a story by Mary McSherry

Scandal in a Small Town ★★ 15

Drama
1988 · US · Colour · 91mins

A waitress discovers that her daughter's history teacher is encouraging anti-Semitism and ends up waging a one-woman fight against the community. This TV movie has a potentially interesting plot, but since the woman in question is none other than Raquel Welch, it ends up as more exploitative than thought-provoking. Raquel is still beautiful but she lacks the emotional acting strength to carry off the role. 🎞

Raquel Welch *Leda Beth Vincent* • Christa Denton *Julie Vincent* • Ronny Cox *George Baker* • Frances Lee McCain *Gwendolyn McLeod* • Katherine McGrath *Verna* • Robin Gammell *Professor Paul Martin* ■ *Dir* Anthony Page • *Scr* Robert Avrech

Scandal Sheet ★★ PG

Drama
1985 · US · Colour · 94mins

In this exploitative TV potboiler, Burt Lancaster plays the sleazy editor of a gossip tabloid who goes after a famous Hollywood couple whose secret, if exposed, could ruin them. Robert Urich and Lauren Hutton star as the beleaguered pair, but none of the performers can do much with this material. All of the characters are defined by stereotypes instead of nuance, and an a vapid plot weighs down its impressive cast. 🎞

Burt Lancaster *Harold Fallen* • Lauren Hutton *Meg North* • Pamela Reed *Helen Grant* • Robert Urich *Ben Rowan* ■ *Dir* David Lowell Rich • *Scr* Howard Rodman

Scandalous ★ 15

Comedy thriller 1983 · US · Colour · 88mins

Rob Cohen got off to a distinctly shaky start as a director with the dismal *A Small Circle of Friends* and this unfunny comedy. As a TV reporter up to his neck in murder, Robert Hays shows flashes of the talent that made him such a hit in the *Airplane!* spoofs, but he doesn't stand a chance with a script so utterly bereft of ideas. John Gielgud does little for his reputation as a master of disguise, but what's most scandalous is that the whole sorry mess was shot by legendary cinematographer Jack Cardiff. Contains nudity and swearing. 🎞

Robert Hays *Frank Swedlin* • John Gielgud *Uncle Willie* • Pamela Stephenson *Fiona Maxwell Sayle* • M Emmet Walsh *Simon Reynolds* • Nancy Wood *Lindsay Manning* • Conover Kennard *Francine Swedlin* ■ *Dir* Rob Cohen • *Scr* Rob Cohen, John Byrum, from a story by Larry Cohen, Rob Cohen, John Byrum

Scandalous John ★★★ U

Comedy western
1971 · US · Colour · 109mins

Nice nostalgia piece, with grizzled Brian Keith excellent as an eccentric rancher who is wild about the west. He is touchingly trying to keep to cowboy ways in a world that's long since consigned them to history, and even cattle-drives a single steer. Predictably, though, engaging pottiness brings him into conflict with the authorities. Elegiac and moving, with more than a few laughs, the film also benefits from familiar cowboy-film faces among the supporting cast. 🎞

Brian Keith *John McCanless* • Alfonso Arau *Paco Martinez* • Michele Carey *Amanda McCanless* • Rick Lenz *Jimmy Whittaker* • Harry Morgan *Sheriff Pippin* • Simon Oakland *Barton Whittaker* • Bill Williams *Sheriff Hart* • Christopher Dark *Card dealer* • John Ritter *Wendell* ■ *Dir* Robert Butler • *Scr* Bill Walsh, Don DaGradi, from a book by Richard Gardner

Scanner Cop ★★★ 18

Science-fiction action
1994 · US · Colour · 90mins

The fourth entry in the *Scanners* series gets a boost with its change in locale (moving from Canada to LA) and introducing a new psychic hero, who happens to be a police officer. The irresistible setup has scanner cop Daniel Quinn after B-movie bad guy Richard Lynch, a scientist with a grudge against policemen. Lynch is fun as usual, hypnotising innocent people into killing cops in his usual hammy fashion, and the whole movie is executed with zip. 🎞

Daniel Quinn *Samuel Staziak* • Darlanne Fluegel *Dr Joan Alden* • Richard Lynch *Glock* • Hilary Shepard *Zena* • Richard Grove *Commander Peter Harrigan* ■ *Dir* Pierre David • *Scr* George Saunders, John Bryant

Scanners ★★★★ 18

Science-fiction horror
1981 · Can · Colour · 102mins

Evil Michael Ironside and derelict Stephen Lack go head to head as telepathists or ''scanners'' in David Cronenberg's modern horror classic. The Canadian director seamlessly blends science fiction, horror and conspiracy thriller into an exhilarating ride. While the stunning (and occasionally stomach-churning) set pieces, the exploding heads and the final apocalyptic battle will delight horror fans, Cronenberg is more interested in exploring the horrors lurking within the human body and our inability to control them. 📀

Patrick McGoohan *Dr Paul Ruth* • Jennifer O'Neill *Kim* • Stephen Lack *Cameron Vale* • Lawrence Dane *Keller* • Charles Shamata [Chuck Shamata] *Gaudi* • Michael Ironside *Darryl Revok* ■ *Dir/Scr* David Cronenberg

Scanners II: The New Order ★★ 18

Science-fiction thriller
1991 · Can · Colour · 99mins

This lacks the thought-provoking script of Cronenberg's original *Scanners*, opting for a more conventional and exploitable story. David Hewlett is the naive ''scanner'' recruited by police chief Yvan Ponton on the pretext of helping out the city. In fact Ponton plans to use Hewlett's telepathic powers to pursue his own political agenda. Director Christian Duguay (in his movie debut) brings more style and a much slicker look to the movie, and never allows the pacing to falter for long. Splatter fans will particularly enjoy both the quality and the quantity of the exploding head sequences. 🎞

David Hewlett *David Kellum* • Deborah Raffin *Julie Vale* • Yvan Ponton *Commander John Forrester* • Isabelle Mejias *Alice Leonardo* • Tom Butler *Doctor Morse* • Raoul Trujillo *Drak* • Vlasta Vrana *Lieutenant Gelson* ■ *Dir* Christian Duguay • *Scr* BJ Nelson, from characters created by David Cronenberg

The Scapegoat ★★

Crime mystery 1959 · UK · BW · 119mins

Robert Hamer and Alec Guinness made one of the blackest, greatest comedies of all time – *Kind Hearts and Coronets* – but they can't quite repeat that magic here. Guinness restricts his talents to just two roles – the French count who wants to murder his wife and his double, the meek English teacher who might be tricked into doing it. A hammy Bette Davis plays his mother and Irene Worth is the inconvenient spouse. Based on the Daphne du Maurier novel and co-scripted by Gore Vidal, it's fitfully amusing.

Alec Guinness *Jacques De Gue/John Barrett* • Bette Davis *Countess* • Nicole Maurey *Bella* • Irene Worth *Françoise De Gue* • Pamela Brown *Blanche* • Annabel Bartlett *Marie-Noël* • Geoffrey Keen *Gaston* ■ *Dir* Robert Hamer • *Scr* Gore Vidal, Robert Hamer, from the novel by Daphne du Maurier

Scapegoat ★

Thriller 1982 · Sp · Colour

This Spanish thriller proves conclusively that even industries in the arthouse heartland are capable of producing substandard action dross. Written and directed without imagination by Carlos Benpar and played with lumpen efficiency by a third-string cast, this road movie has that unmistakable direct-to-video feel. The plot, for those still interested, has model Sean Catherine Derek (who has accidentally killed her corrupt judge lover) and terrorist Craig Hill (who's just detonated a lorryload of nuclear waste) getting caught up in the same desperate getaway. Spanish dialogue dubbed into English.

Sean Catherine Derek • Francisco Rabal • Robert Gras • Craig Hill ■ *Dir/Scr* Carlos Benpar

Scaramouche ★★★★ U

Swashbuckling adventure
1952 · US · Colour · 114mins

Rafael Sabatini's rousing adventure was first filmed in 1923 by the master of the silent swashbuckler, Rex Ingram. This colourful version has been pared down to the bone by its writers, so that only the feuding, flirting and fencing remain of the classic novel's vivacious and complex portrait of Revolutionary France. Stewart Granger exudes charm in his scenes with Janet Leigh and cuts a dash as the mysterious swordsman out on the trail of arrogant aristocrat Mel Ferrer. The final duel has the distinction of being the longest in movie history.

Stewart Granger *Andre Moreau/Scaramouche* • Eleanor Parker *Lenore* • Janet Leigh *Aline de Gavrillac* • Mel Ferrer *Noel, Marquis de Maynes* • Henry Wilcoxon *Chevalier de Chambrillaine* • Nina Foch *Marie Antoinette* • Richard Anderson *Philippe de Valmorin* • Robert Coote *Gaston Binet* ■ *Dir* George Sidney • *Scr* Ronald Millar, George Froeschel, from the novel by Rafael Sabatini

Scarecrow ★★★★

Silent comedy 1920 · US · BW · 17mins

After comedian Fatty Arbuckle's scandal, Buster Keaton took on many of his projects and this was one of the first silent movies for Buster Keaton Productions. The film is filled with sight gags, concentrating on the domestic set-up enjoyed by him and Joe Roberts: a gramophone converts into a stove, all table items are lowered on strings and the table itself – with plates attached – is hung up for washing. As the caption proclaims: ''What is home without a mother?!''

Buster Keaton • Joe Roberts ■ *Dir* Buster Keaton • *Scr* Edward F Cline, Buster Keaton

Scarecrow ★★ 18

Road movie drama
1973 · US · Colour · 107mins

Ex-con Gene Hackman and drifter Al Pacino hook up in California and travel east together, with the latter hoping to reconcile with the wife and child he abandoned in Detroit. On the journey they meet numerous other social misfits who regale them with various life lessons. An arty road movie that can't quite harmonise its bleak realism with its glossy Hollywood approach to suffering. Pacino is no match for Hackman in an underwritten role, but the film did win the Palme d'Or at the 1973 Cannes festival.

Gene Hackman *Max* • Al Pacino *Lion* • Dorothy Tristan *Coley* • Ann Wedgeworth *Frenchy* • Richard Lynch *Riley* • Eileen Brennan *Darlene* • Penny Allen [Penelope Allen] *Annie* • Richard Hackman *Mickey* ■ *Dir* Jerry Schatzberg • *Scr* Garry Michael White

The Scarecrow ★★ 15

Comedy thriller 1982 · NZ · Colour · 84mins

Hollywood horror veteran John Carradine stars in a fifties-set thriller that mixes the mystical and the mundane in its tale of a New Zealand teen battling both his local bully and a crazed killer. The film's opening, with the mystery disappearance of some chickens setting in motion a spooky chain of events, grabs the attention. Ultimately, though, it never quite sustains this momentum.

John Carradine *Hubert Salter* • Tracy Mann *Prudence Poindexter* • Jonathan Smith *Ned Poindexter* • Daniel McLaren *Les Wilson* • Denise O'Connell *Angela Potroz* • Anne Flannery *Mrs Poindexter* ■ *Dir* Sam Pillsbury • *Scr* Michael Heath, Sam Pillsbury, from a novel by Ronald Hugh Morrieson

Scared Stiff ★★★ U

Musical comedy 1953 · US · BW · 107mins

Comic teams always get around to a haunted house vehicle and this is the one from Dean Martin and Jerry Lewis – then at their peak. It's a remake of *The Ghost Breakers*, one of Bob Hope's funniest films, and though not as good as the earlier version, it is passable fare from the dynamic duo with veteran director George Marshall neatly combining genuine chills with the laughter. Lizabeth Scott is the heiress in distress and Brazilian bombshell Carmen Miranda makes her final film appearance, cueing an impersonation by Jerry Lewis which is, to put it kindly, not very good.

Dean Martin *Larry Todd* • Jerry Lewis *Myron Mertz* • Lizabeth Scott *Mary Carroll* • Carmen Miranda *Carmelita Castina* • George Dolenz *Mr Cortega* • Dorothy Malone *Rosie* • William Ching *Tony Warren* • Paul Marion *Carriso Twins* • Jack Lambert *Zombi* • Bob Hope • Bing Crosby ■ *Dir* George Marshall • *Scr* Herbert Baker, Walter De Leon, Ed Simmons, Norman Lear, from the play *Ghost Breakers* by Paul Dickey, Charles W Goddard

Scarface ★★★★★

Crime drama 1932 · US · BW · 170mins

The greatest gangster movie of the thirties – and that means the greatest ever. Producer Howard Hughes told director Howard Hawks to make it "as realistic, as exciting, as grisly as possible". Hawks happily obliged, though Hollywood's moral watchdog, the Hays Office later insisted the ending was softened and a subtitle was added – *Shame of the Nation*. The story is a thinly-disguised biography of Al Capone, with Paul Muni as Tony Camonte, a monster who lusts after his own sister, Ann Dvorak, yet whose business acumen embodies the American Dream. It's filled with moments that define the gangster genre – terrific shoot-outs, psychotic characters and George Raft spinning a coin. *Scarface* remains a bracingly violent and subversive tragicomedy that says crime pays and that mowing people down is fun.

Paul Muni *Tony Camonte* • Ann Dvorak *Cesca Camonte* • Karen Morley *Poppy* • Osgood Perkins *Johnny Lovo* • Boris Karloff *Gaffney* • George Raft *Guino Rinaldo* • Vince Barnett *Angelo* • C Henry Gordon *Inspector Guarino* • Howard Hawks *Man on bed* ■ *Dir* Howard Hawks • *Scr* Ben Hecht, Seton I Miller, John Lee Mahin, WR Burnett, Fred Pasley, from the novel by Armitage Trail

Scarface ★★★★ 18

Crime thriller 1983 · US · Colour · 162mins

Director Brian De Palma's scorching update of Howard Hawks's 1932 classic relocates events to Miami and follows the rapid rise and violent fall of a Cuban refugee turned cocaine-smuggling kingpin. Al Pacino is the ruthless criminal pursuing the American dream, and he gets top support from Michelle Pfeiffer as his wife, Steven Bauer as his partner in crime and Mary Elizabeth Mastrantonio as his sister. The accurate, if four-letter-word heavy, dialogue and sharp wit contained in Oliver Stone's script and the vivid cinematography of John A Alonzo help make De Palma's urban shocker a modern-day classic and one of the best movies ever made about the subject. Contains violence, swearing, sex scenes and nudity.

Al Pacino *Tony Montana* • Steven Bauer *Manny Ray* • Michelle Pfeiffer *Elvira* • Mary Elizabeth Mastrantonio *Gina* • Robert Loggia *Frank Lopez* • Miriam Colon *Mama Montana* • F Murray Abraham *Omar* ■ *Dir* Brian De Palma • *Scr* Oliver Stone, from the 1932 film

The Scarlet and the Black ★★★ PG

Second World War drama
1983 · US/It · Colour · 137mins

Gregory Peck made his TV-movie debut in this true story of wartime hide-and-seek. Although it's far too long, it is certainly one of the more impressive efforts made for the small screen. In addition to a cameo from John Gielgud as Pope Pius XII, the film boasts photography by Giuseppe Rotunno and a score by the great Ennio Morricone. Peck's character is a sort of Oskar Schindler in vestments, who gives sanctuary to Jews and other persecuted peoples prior to smuggling them to safety. Christopher Plummer is suitably villainous as the Nazi who can't pin down the elusive priest.

Gregory Peck *Monsignor Hugh O'Flaherty* • Christopher Plummer *Colonel Herbert Kappler* • John Gielgud *Pope Pius XII* • Raf Vallone *Father Vittorio* • Kenneth Colley *Captain Hirsch* ■ *Dir* Jerry London • *Scr* David Butler, from the non-fiction book *The Scarlet Pimpernel of the Vatican* by JP Gallagher

The Scarlet Blade ★★ U

Period adventure drama
1963 · UK · Colour · 84mins

Oliver Reed is on form here as a renegade swordsman with an eye for the ladies in a period drama from Hammer set during the English Civil War. Swordfights abound as sadistic Cromwellian colonel Lionel Jeffries discovers his daughter has Royalist sympathies. There's capable support from Jack Hedley and June Thorburn, but writer/director John Gilling was on surer ground with later horror films such as *The Plague of the Zombies*.

Lionel Jeffries *Colonel Judd* • Oliver Reed *Sylvester* • Jack Hedley *Edward* • June Thorburn *Clare* • Michael Ripper *Pablo* • Harold Goldblatt *Jacob* ■ *Dir/Scr* John Gilling

The Scarlet Claw ★★★★ PG

Crime mystery 1944 · US · BW · 73mins

Here's the greatest of all Sherlocks (Basil Rathbone) and the most bumbling of all Watsons (Nigel Bruce) in possibly the best of the Universal Studios series, with the pair in Canada investigating ghostly and ghastly murders. The under-rated Roy William Neill causes consternation with some memorably uneasy visuals: a dead woman's hand clutching a bell-rope, a luminous "monster" stalking Holmes across a marsh and, best of all, the fog which just avalanches down.

Basil Rathbone *Sherlock Holmes* • Nigel Bruce *Dr John H Watson* • Gerald Hamer *Potts* • Paul Cavanagh *Lord William Penrose* • Arthur Hohl *Emile Journet* • Kay Harding *Marie Journet* ■ *Dir* Roy William Neill • *Scr* Roy William Neill, Edmund L Hartmann, from a story by Paul Gangelin, Brenda Weisberg, from characters created by Sir Arthur Conan Doyle

The Scarlet Coat ★★ U

Historical spy drama
1955 · US · Colour · 100mins

An espionage drama set during the American War of Independence, dealing with the famous traitor Benedict Arnold. Playing the hero is Cornel Wilde, an American who becomes a double agent and joins the British in order to expose Arnold's treachery. This being a Hollywood movie, there is some romantic intrigue as well as a fairly cavalier treatment of historical fact. A very camp George Sanders steals every scene he's in.

Cornel Wilde *Major John Bolton* • Michael Wilding *Major John Andre* • George Sanders *Dr Jonathan Odell* • Anne Francis *Sally Cameron* • Robert Douglas *Benedict Arnold* • John McIntire *General Robert Howe* • Rhys Williams *Peter* • John Dehner *Nathanael Greene* ■ *Dir* John Sturges • *Scr* Karl Tunberg

Scarlet Dawn ★

Period drama 1932 · US · BW · 58mins

The dawn here is the colour of the Russian Revolution. In the thick of it is Douglas Fairbanks Jr, an aristocrat from St Petersburg who has no truck with Lenin and instead runs off to Constantinople with Nancy Carroll. He marries her, leaves her for one of his own class and then returns. Is Fairbanks a bourgeois cad or a closet Bolshevik? Made when Hollywood was just discovering that movies could talk and that Fairbanks Jr had charm aplenty but somewhat less talent.

Douglas Fairbanks Jr *Baron Nikiti Krasnoff* • Nancy Carroll *Tanyusha* • Lilyan Tashman *Vera Zimina* • Guy Kibbee *Murphy* • Sheila Terry *Marjorie Murphy* • Earle Fox *Boris* • Ivan Linow *Ivan* ■ *Dir* William Dieterle • *Scr* Niven Busch, Edwin Gelsey, Douglas Fairbanks Jr, from the novel *Revolt* by Mary McCall Jr

The Scarlet Empress ★★★★★

Historical drama 1934 · US · BW · 98mins

This is more fun than you could ever imagine, more suggestive than you'd thought possible, even in those days prior to the imposition of the Hays Production Code. Director Josef von Sternberg fills the screen with typically lustrous images and staggeringly rich art direction. This movie, which does have its detractors, was influential on Russian director Sergei Eisenstein and his acclaimed epic *Ivan the Terrible*. More than just a vehicle for the marvellous Marlene Dietrich, the film conveys a real sense of the lusts and intrigues of the court of Catherine the Great.

Gerald Fielding *Lieutenant Dmitri* • Marlene Dietrich *Sophia Frederica, Catherine II* • John Lodge *Count Alexei* • Sam Jaffe *Grand Duke Peter* • Louise Dresser *Empress Elizabeth* • C Aubrey Smith *Prince August* • Gavin Gordon *Gregory Orloff* • Ruthelma Stevens *Countess Elisabeth* • Hans von Twardowski *Ivan Shuvolov* ■ *Dir* Josef von Sternberg • *Scr* Manuel Komroff, from the diaries of Catherine II • *Cinematographer* Bert Glennon • *Costume Designer* Travis Banton • *Set Designer* Hans Dreier, Peter Ballbusch, Richard Kollorsz

The Scarlet Letter ★★★★

Silent drama 1926 · US · BW · 80mins

Lillian Gish gives here what many regard as her finest performance. The fifth screen version of Nathaniel Hawthorne's novel, this is by far the finest adaptation of any era. With Hendrik Sartov's photography bringing a painterly austerity to the already puritanical setting, Hester Prynne's adultery with Pastor Dimmesdale assumes a social enormity that is often disregarded by those concentrating on the story's human aspects. Yet director Victor Sjöström is not blind to the lyrical tragedy of the couple's disgrace, as he locates beauty and sensitivity amid the bigotry.

Lillian Gish *Hester Prynne* • Lars Hanson *The Reverend Arthur Dimmesdale* • Henry B Walthall *Roger Prynne* • Karl Dane *Giles* • William H Tooker *The governor* • Marcelle Corday *Mistress Hibbins* ■ *Dir* Victor Seastrom [Victor Sjöström] • *Scr* Frances Marion, from the novel by Nathaniel Hawthorne

The Scarlet Letter ★★ 15

Period drama 1995 · US · Colour · 129mins

Give Demi Moore a role that requires any kind of subtlety and she just looks confused. In this absurd version of Nathaniel Hawthorne's classic novel, Moore stars as the 17th-century wife who has an affair and is ostracised by the community, which forces her to wear a scarlet "A" (for adultery). Gary Oldman is ludicrously over the top as the preacher with whom Moore has a passionate fling, while Robert Duvall, as her cuckolded husband, gives a performance that is totally out of place with the period. Contains some violence, sex scenes and nudity

Demi Moore *Hester Prynne* • Gary Oldman *Arthur Dimmesdale* • Robert Duvall *Roger Prynne* • Lisa Joliff-Andoh *Mituba* • Edward Hardwick *John Bellingham* • Robert Prosky *Horace Stonehall* • Roy Dotrice *Thomas Cheever* • Joan Plowright *Harriet Hibbons* •

Jodhi May *Pearl* ■ *Dir* Roland Joffé • *Scr* Douglas Day Stewart, from the novel by Nathaniel Hawthorne

The Scarlet Pimpernel
★★★ U

Swashbuckling adventure
1934 · UK · BW · 93mins

Leslie Howard stars as Sir Percy Blakeney, master of disguise, outwitting Raymond Massey's evil Chauvelin during the French Revolution and fooling his wife, Merle Oberon, who thinks he's just a boorish fop. Produced by Alexander Korda and aimed firmly in mid-Atlantic, its chief virtues are Howard's portrait of strength masquerading as superciliousness and some lavish production design. But it seems rather creaky nowadays, mainly because of the stagey direction from Harold Young (with uncredited assistance from Rowland Brown and Korda) and the servants who speak with Mayfair accents. A big success in its day, though.

Leslie Howard *Sir Percy Blakeney/the Scarlet Pimpernel* • Merle Oberon *Lady Marguerite Blakeney formerly Marguerite St Just* • Raymond Massey *Chauvelin* • Nigel Bruce *The Prince of Wales (HRH the Prince Regent)* • Bramwell Fletcher *Priest* • Anthony Bushell *Sir Andrew Ffoulkes* • Joan Gardner *Suzanne de Tournay* • Walter Rilla *Armand St Just* ■ *Dir* Harold Young • *Scr* SN Behrman, Robert Sherwood, Arthur Wimperis, Lajos Biró, from the novel by Baroness Orczy • *Production Designer* Vincent Korda

The Scarlet Pimpernel
★★★ PG

Swashbuckling adventure
1982 · UK/US · Colour · 135mins

This is distinctly superior small screen fare, with director Clive Donner making the most of the period plushness to fashion a lively swashbuckler true to the spirit of the novels of Baroness Orczy. As dashing as predecessors Leslie Howard and David Niven, Anthony Andrews is on *Brideshead* form as Sir Percy Blakeney, the foppish English noble who risks all to rescue French aristocrats from the guillotine during the Reign of Terror. Jane Seymour also surpasses herself as the neglected Lady Marguerite, while Ian McKellen has a ripe old time as the villainous Chauvelin.

Anthony Andrews *Sir Percy Blakeney* • Jane Seymour *Marguerite St Just* • Ian McKellen *Paul Chauvelin* • James Villiers *Baron de Batz* • Eleanor David *Louise Lenjean* • Malcolm Jamieson *Armand St Just* • Julian Fellowes *Prince Regent* ■ *Dir* Clive Donner • *Scr* William Bast, from the novel by Baroness Orczy

Scarlet Street
★★★ PG

Film noir
1945 · US · BW · 101mins

Edward G Robinson stars (brilliantly) as a diffident cashier with a termagant wife (Rosalind Ivan) and limited means, whose only pleasure is painting in his spare time. He falls in love with Joan Bennett who, under the sway of her sadistic boyfriend Dan Duryea, leads him into a tangle of deceptions, embezzlement and murder. An effective *noir* drama, directed by Fritz Lang, a master of the genre, the movie is grim, downbeat and well-played, with some

imaginative and unusual plot developments and an audacious ending. The script, though, does strain credibility at times.

Edward G Robinson *Christopher Cross* • Joan Bennett *Kitty March* • Dan Duryea *Johnny Prince* • Margaret Lindsay *Millie* • Rosalind Ivan *Adele Cross* • Jess Barker *Janeway* • Arthur Loft *Dellarowe* ■ *Dir* Fritz Lang • *Scr* Dudley Nichols, from the novel *La Chienne* by Georges de la Fouchardiere, from the play *La Chienne* by Georges de la Fouchardière, André Mouëzy-Eon

The Scarlet Tunic
★★★ 12

Period drama
1997 · UK · Colour · 92mins

Minimally budgeted, this British period drama really belongs on television. Concerning the ill-starred romance between a rich man's daughter and a foreign mercenary who's about to set off to fight Napoleon, the melodramatic crunch comes when the soldier has to do a *High Noon* and choose between love and duty. Emma Fielding and *The Big Blue*'s Jean-Marc Barr play the lovers while Simon Callow chews the scenery as Barr's brutal military commander. Contains some violence and sexual situations.

Jean-Marc Barr *Sergeant Matthaus Singer* • Emma Fielding *Frances Elizabeth Groves* • Simon Callow *Captain John Fairfax* • Jack Shepherd *Dr Edward Groves* • John Sessions *Humphrey Gould* ■ *Dir* Stuart St Paul • *Scr* Stuart St Paul, Mark Jenkins, Colin Clements, from the story *The Melancholy Hussar* by Thomas Hardy

Scarred City
★★

Thriller
1998 · US · Colour · 96mins

Unexceptional action thriller which, to its credit, boasts a cast that doesn't deserve the film's video-dustbin status. Stephen Baldwin is a cop facing investigation after killing some criminal suspects in rather dubious circumstances. Police lieutenant Chazz Palminteri offers him a way out with his very secret squad, although it soon transpires that this force takes neither prisoners nor witnesses.

Stephen Baldwin *John Trace* • Chazz Palminteri *Lieutenant Laine Devon* • Tia Carrere *Candy* • Michael Rispoli *Sam Bandusky* • Gary Dourdan *Sergeant Creedy* • Bray Poor *Zero* ■ *Dir/Scr* Ken Sanzel

The Scars of Dracula
★★★ 18

Horror
1970 · UK · Colour · 91mins

Christopher Lee thinks this is his weakest *Dracula* sequel, but Hammer horror fans like it because the Count has more screen time than in any other episode. There's also a palpable dark fairy-tale atmosphere achieved by director Roy Ward Baker as Dracula tries sinking his fangs into naive Transylvanian travellers Dennis Waterman and Jenny Hanley. Propping up the formula vampire tale are a memorable death by lightning climax, and more blood, sadism and silly rubber bats than ever before.

Christopher Lee *Count Dracula* • Dennis Waterman *Simon Carlson* • Christopher Matthews *Paul Carlson* • Jenny Hanley *Sarah Framsen* • Patrick Troughton *Klove* • Michael Gwynn *Priest* • Wendy Hamilton *Julie* •

Anouska Hempel *Tania* ■ *Dir* Roy Ward Baker • *Scr* John Elder [Anthony Hinds], from characters created by Bram Stoker

Scattered Dreams
★★★ 15

Drama based on a true story
1993 · US · Colour · 89mins

A well made TV drama that provides a meaty role for Tyne Daly of *Cagney and Lacey* fame. Set in fifties Florida, it follows a couple's bid to regain custody of their children after the pair are wrongly sent to prison. Daly and Gerald McRaney, as her husband, give stoical performances, and there's an early screen appearance for *Clueless* star Alicia Silverstone. Director Neema Barnette gives sentimentality the full orchestral treatment, but it remains an affecting slice of drama. Contains some violence.

Tyne Daly *Kathryn Messenger* • Gerald McRaney *George Messenger* • Alicia Silverstone *Phyllis Messenger* • Sonny Shroyer *Sheriff Ashford* • Blair Struble *June Messenger* • Andrew Prine *Sandstrom* ■ *Dir* Neema Barnette • *Scr* Karen Croner

Scavenger Hunt
★★

Comedy
1979 · US · Colour · 116mins

It's a Mad, Mad, Mad, Mad World was an honourable but failed attempt to make the "comedy to end all comedies". *Scavenger Hunt* treads a similar path with its star-studded cast involved in a frantic hunt for a hidden fortune. Mad games inventor Vincent Price leaves a will which stipulates that his relatives have to participate in a grand scavenger hunt, with the winner inheriting his millions. Even wider of the mark than its illustrious predecessor, this is, at least, a lot shorter. Megastar-to-be Arnold Schwarzenegger makes a (miniscule) appearance.

Richard Benjamin *Stuart Selsome* • James Coco *Henri* • Scatman Crothers *Sam* • Cloris Leachman *Mildred Carruthers* • Cleavon Little *Jackson* • Roddy McDowall *Jenkins* • Robert Morley *Bernstein* • Richard Mulligan *Marvin Dummitz* • Tony Randall *Henry Motley* • Dirk Benedict *Jeff Stevens* • Vincent Price *Milton Parker* • Arnold Schwarzenegger *Lars* ■ *Dir* Michael Schultz • *Scr* Steven A Vail, Henry Harper, John Thompson, Gerry Woolery, from a story by Steven A Vail

A Scene at the Sea
★★★★

Surfing drama
1991 · Jap · Colour · 102mins

A drastic change of pace for Takeshi Kitano, this surfing odyssey came between those explosive Yakuza pictures, *Boiling Point* and *Sonatine*. A deaf garbage collector, Kurodo Maki, finds a discarded surfboard and after reconditioning it, battles to conquer the waves. The Kitano proclivity for slapstick is very much in evidence: Maki repeatedly comes a cropper as he masters the basic skills of surfing and then competes in local championships before the unflinchingly supportive gaze of his deaf girlfriend, Hiroko Oshima. A slight delight. In Japanese with English subtitles.

Kurodo Maki *Shigeru* • Hiroko Oshima *Takako* • Sabu Kawahara *Tamukai, garbage truck driver* • Toshizo Fujiwara *Nakajima, owner of surfing goods shops* ■ *Dir/Scr* Takeshi Kitano

Scene of the Crime
★★

Crime drama
1949 · US · BW · 94mins

Van Johnson is Los Angeles detective, Mike Conovan, investigating the murder of one of his colleagues. Part of the late forties fad for documentary realism and police procedure, the movie spends much time depicting our hero's dogged, dedicated work as well as his blissfully ordinary home life with Arlene Dahl. But a movie about routine inevitably becomes routine.

Van Johnson *Mike Conovan* • Gloria De Haven [Gloria DeHaven] *Lili* • Tom Drake *CC Gordon* • Arlene Dahl *Gloria Conovan* • Leon Ames *Captain AC Forster* • John McIntire *Fred Piper* • Norman Lloyd *Sleeper* • Donald Woods *Herkimer* ■ *Dir* Roy Rowland • *Scr* Charles Schnee, from the story *Smashing the Bookie Gang Marauders* by John Bartlow Martin

The Scene of the Crime
★★★

Thriller
1986 · Fr · Colour · 90mins

Catherine Deneuve heads a quality cast in this fine French thriller from director André Téchiné (*Les Voleurs*, *Ma Saison Preferée*). The action takes place over an eventful four-day period, in which a run-in between a 13-year-old boy and two escaped convicts leads to murder, and to the forging of an unlikely alliance between the killer and the boy's mother. In French with English subtitles.

Catherine Deneuve *Lili* • Danielle Darrieux *Grandmother* • Nicolas Giraudi *Thomas* • Wadeck Stanczak *Martin* • Victor Lanoux *Maurice* • Jean Bousquet *Grandfather* ■ *Dir* André Téchiné • *Scr* André Téchiné, Pascal Bonitzer, Olivier Assayas

Scene of the Crime
★★

Crime thriller
1996 · US · Colour

This serial killer thriller went straight to video in the States, and it's easy to see why. As disgraced cop Ben Gazzara looks for links between the Ladykiller and the Piggybank Murderer, he is joined by Alex McArthur, an actor researching a slasher role, who just happens to fall for Gazzara's daughter, Renee Ammann. The plethora of false leads may provide some interest, but there's no chemistry between the stars, Gazzara merely slouches through the action and there's simply no excuse for the sloppy finale.

Ben Gazzara *Jack Lasky* • Alex McArthur *Richard Darling* • Renee Ammann *Jennifer* • Terri Treas *Capt Hanover* ■ *Dir* Terence H Winkless • *Scr* Craig J Nevius

Scenes from a Mall ★★★ 15

Comedy
1991 · US · Colour · 83mins

The notion of Woody Allen and Bette Midler playing a smugly successful couple whose marriage begins to crumble as they go shopping must have brought a big smile to the faces of the producers. Unfortunately, director Paul Mazursky reduces the satirical potential to a torrent of words. Woody's lines, unsurprisingly the best, are not matched by the dialogue or performance of the too-loud Midler, and the added irony of a marriage teetering at Christmas is too corny. Despite the leaden weight of the script, there are some fine moments,

thanks to the die-hard personalities of the two leads. Contains swearing. ▭

Bette Midler *Deborah Fifer* • Woody Allen *Nick Fifer* • Bill Irwin *Mime* • Daren Firestone *Sam* • Rebecca Nickels *Jennifer* • Paul Mazursky *Dr Hans Clava* ■ *Dir* Paul Mazursky • *Scr* Paul Mazursky, Roger L Simon

Scenes from a Marriage
★★★★🔞

Drama 1973 · Swe · Colour · 162mins

Originally a six-part TV series, this was edited for feature release by writer/director Ingmar Bergman. Mostly shot in tight close-ups to enhance the tensions between the main protagonists, this is not easy viewing: some of the insights seem too blatant for a film-maker of Bergman's intellect to be bothered with. However, when the rambling gives way to fierce infighting and wounding insults, the film exerts a much firmer grip. Liv Ullmann as the betrayed wife, Erland Josephson as the philandering husband and Bibi Andersson as the other woman are all quite superb. In Swedish with English subtitles. ▭

Liv Ullmann *Marianne* • Erland Josephson *Johan* • Bibi Andersson *Katarina* • Jan Malmsjo *Peter* • Anita Wall *Interviewer* ■ *Dir/Scr* Ingmar Bergman

Scenes from the Class Struggle In Beverly Hills
★★★★🔞

Comedy 1989 · UK · Colour · 99mins

Jacqueline Bisset gets a juicy role as a recently widowed soap star who invites her neighbour and her son to stay while their house is being defumigated. Joining them are a hilarious mixture of the rich and famous that reach across the sexual and racial divides, along the leafy, private boulevards, down shopping nirvana, Rodeo Drive, and into areas like body fascism, freak diets and weird sex. A guest spot is reserved for Paul Mazursky, director of both *Bob & Carol & Ted & Alice* and *Down and Out in Beverly Hills*, both touchstones for Paul Bartel's subversive brand of humour that sets out to offend almost everyone.

Jacqueline Bisset *Clare Lipkin* • Ray Sharkey *Frank* • Robert Beltran *Juan* • Mary Woronov *Lisabeth Hepburn-Saravian* • Ed Begley Jr *Peter* • Wallace Shawn *Howard Saravian* • Arnetia Walker *To-bel* • Paul Mazursky *Sidney Lipkin* ■ *Dir* Paul Bartel • *Scr* Bruce Wagner, from a story by Paul Bartel, Bruce Wagner

Scent of a Woman
★★★

Comedy drama 1974 · It · Colour · 103mins

Somewhat overlooked since Al Pacino's Oscar-winning remake, Dino Risi's twice-nominated adaptation of Giovanni Arpino's novel boasts a similarly show-stopping performance from Vittorio Gassman. He won the best actor prize at Cannes for his portrayal of the blind army captain with a stubborn streak to match his simmering sense of resentment. However, that's where the similarities end, as Gassman journeys from Turin to Naples to enter into a suicide pact with a soldier disfigured in the accident that disabled him. There's sly humour in his relationship with rookie escort Alessandro Momo, but the romantic

reunion with Agostina Belli is cringingly sentimental. An Italian language film.

Vittorio Gassman *Fausto* • Alessandro Momo *Ciccio* • Agostina Belli *Sara* • Moira Orfei *Mirka* • Franco Ricci *Raffaele* • Elena Veronese *Michelina* ■ *Dir* Dino Risi • *Scr* Ruggero Maccari, Dino Risi, from the novel *Il Buio e il Miele* by Giovanni Arpino

Scent of a Woman
★★★★🔞

Drama 1992 · US · Colour · 149mins

This lengthy melodrama is kept vibrantly alive and out of the clutches of sickly sentimentality by a towering Oscar-winning performance from Al Pacino. He plays the blind ex-soldier who heads for New York to sample once more life's little luxuries over the Thanksgiving weekend. As his unworldly teenage escort, Chris O'Donnell gives a quietly impressive portrayal, but it's Pacino's picture, whether waltzing with Gabrielle Anwar, berating O'Donnell's cowardly schoolmates or barking out his famous "hoo-ha" cough. Loosely based on Dino Risi's 1974 film of the same name. Contains swearing. ▭ **DVD**

Al Pacino *Lieutenant Colonel Frank Slade* • Chris O'Donnell *Charlie Simms* • James Rebhorn *Mr Trask* • Gabrielle Anwar *Donna* • Philip S Hoffman [Philip Seymour Hoffman] *George Willis Jr* • Richard Venture *WR Slade* • Bradley Whitford *Randy* ■ *Dir* Martin Brest • *Scr* Bo Goldman, from a character in the 1974 film

The Scent of Green Papaya
★★★★★🅄

Drama 1993 · Fr · Colour · 99mins

Set in pre-Vietnam War Saigon, this is the leisurely, minutely observed and thoroughly involving story of a servant girl and the relationships she develops with her employers and a handsome family friend. The opening segment is quite captivating, thanks to the guileless performance of Man San Lu as the ten-year-old maid, but the intensity of the drama as it moves into the sixties compensates for the mannered innocence of Tran Nu Yen-Khe as the older Mui. A delightful study of duty, devotion and the quiet power of female dignity, it won director Tran Anh Hung the Camera d'Or at Cannes for best debut feature. In Vietnamese with English subtitles. ▭

Tran Nu Yen-Khe *Mui, aged 20* • Man San Lu *Mui, aged 10* • Thi Loc Truong *Mother* • Anh Hoa Nguyen *Old Thi* • Hoa Hoi Vuong *Khuyen* • Ngoc Tran Trung *Father* ■ *Dir* Tran Anh Hung • *Scr* Tran Anh Hung

Scent of Mystery
★★🅄

Mystery 1960 · US · Colour · 132mins

The only film ever shot in "smell-o-vision" – a process which squirted appropriate odours at the audience. Denholm Elliott wanders through Spain and finds he has to protect Beverly Bentley who's being menaced by such classy heavies as Peter Lorre and Paul Lukas. The great cameraman Jack Cardiff directed the attenuated narrative, which was produced by the American showman Mike Todd who liked gimmicks but, the smellier the better. Not exactly a stinker, but nearly.

Denholm Elliott *Oliver Larker* • Beverly Bentley *The Decoy Sally* • Peter Lorre *Smiley, chauffeur* • Paul Lukas *Baron Saradin* • Diana

Dors *Winifred Jordan* • Liam Redmond *Johnny Gin, derelict* • Elizabeth Taylor *The Real Sally Kennedy* ■ *Dir* Jack Cardiff • *Scr* William Rose, from a story by Kelley Roos

Schemes
★★★

Thriller 1994 · US · Colour · 92mins

Bad guy John Glover has a ball in this enjoyably convoluted thriller. The story is pretty formulaic: architect James McCaffrey is awarded half a million dollars when his wife dies in an accident, a tidy sum that attracts the villainous intentions of *femme fatale* Leslie Hope and creepy private eye Glover. However, writer/director Derek Westervelt manages to keep the viewer in the dark right to the very end. Contains swearing and violence.

James McCaffrey *Paul Stewart* • Leslie Hope *Laura Pierce* • John Glover *Victor Kraft* • Polly Draper *Evelyn Hayes* ■ *Dir/Scr* Derek Westervelt

Schindler's List
★★★★★🔞

Drama 1993 · US · BW and Colour · 187mins

Steven Spielberg's outstanding Holocaust drama, based on Thomas Keneally's bestseller *Schindler's Ark* won seven Oscars, including best picture, director, adapted screenplay and score. Telling the story of Second World War entrepreneur Oskar Schindler (played by Liam Neeson), whose profiteering operations for the German army led him to be the unexpected saviour of more than 1,000 Jewish factory workers in Poland, Spielberg uses stark, brutal realism to put over his powerful points about racism and ethnic cleansing. The use of stunning black-and-white photography and gritty hand-held camera footage give it a potent documentary-style resonance. Ralph Fiennes draws an awesome mixture of revulsion and sympathy as the inhuman Nazi commandant, Amon Goeth, and Neeson matches him with a heartfelt performance as the enigmatic Schindler. Ben Kingsley is also superb as Schindler's Jewish accountant and conscience. Contains swearing. ▭

Liam Neeson *Oskar Schindler* • Ben Kingsley *Itzhak Stern* • Ralph Fiennes *Amon Goeth* • Caroline Goodall *Emilie Schindler* • Jonathan Sagalle *Poldek Pfefferberg* • Embeth Davidtz *Helen Hirsch* • Andrzej Seweryn *Julian Scherner* ■ *Dir* Steven Spielberg • *Scr* Steven Zaillian, from the novel *Schindler's Ark* by Thomas Keneally • *Cinematographer* Janusz Kaminski • *Music* John Williams • *Editor* Michael Kahn

Schizopolis
★★🔞

Experimental comedy drama 1996 · US · Colour · 96mins

An inspired surrealist swipe at the American mainstream or a vanity project gone off the rails? The answer lies somewhere in between these verdicts on Steven Soderbergh's ambitious satire on language, identity, fidelity, advertising, self-help and dentistry. Writer/director Soderbergh also stars as a speech writer, whose wife (Betsy Brantley) is having an affair with a dentist (also played by Soderbergh). Mixing the absurd with the autobiographical, this is a riot of ideas – characters speaking in gibberish or unsubtitled foreign

tongues; speeded-up footage; bookends from a cinema stage – but not enough of them come off. ▭

Steven Soderbergh *Fletcher Munson/Dr Jeffrey Korchek* • Betsy Brantley *Mrs Munson/ Attractive Woman No 2* • David Jensen *Elmo Oxygen* • Eddie Jemison *Nameless Numberheadman* • Scott Allen *Right Hand Man* • Mike Malone *T Azimuth Schwitters* ■ *Dir/Scr* Steven Soderbergh

Schlock
★

Science-fiction horror spoof
1971 · US · Colour · 77mins

Before *The Blues Brothers* and *National Lampoon's Animal House*, director John Landis donned an ape suit in his debut as a director. The monkey-suited title character – a thawed prehistoric missing link – runs amok in a small town, and leaves a trail of banana skins in his murderous wake. Nothing more than a poor excuse to lampoon Kubrick's *2001*, this is a game, but lame, student effort. Future Oscar winner Rick Baker designed the hairy costume.

John Landis *The Schlockthropus* • Saul Kahan *Detective/Sgt Wino* • Joseph Piantadosi *Prof Shlibovitz* • Eliza Garrett *Mindy Binerman* • Eric Allison *Joe Puzman* • Enrica Blankey *Mrs Binerman* ■ *Dir/Scr* John Landis

School Daze
★★🔞

Musical comedy 1988 · US · Colour · 120mins

In attempting to present campus life as a microcosm of African-American society, Spike Lee succeeds in raising many points without reaching any conclusions. He attacks the conventions of college life without exploring any alternatives and takes pot shots at sexism, racism and the age and class divides without steadying his aim. A couple of the songs are well staged and Laurence Fishburne gives a steady performance, but, overall, this is a disjointed and disappointing satire. Contains swearing and nudity. ▭

Larry Fishburne [Laurence Fishburne] *Vaughn "Dap" Dunlap* • Giancarlo Esposito *Julian "Big Brother Almighty" Eaves* • Tisha Campbell *Jane Toussaint* • Kyme *Rachel Meadows* • Joe Seneca *President McPherson* • Ellen Holly *Odrie McPherson* • Art Evans *Cedar Cloud* • Ossie Davis *Coach Odom* • Bill Nunn *Grady* • Branford Marsalis *Jordan* • Spike Lee *Half-Pint* • Samuel L Jackson ■ *Dir/Scr* Spike Lee

School for Postmen
★★★★

Comedy 1947 · Fr · BW · 18mins

Returning behind the camera for the first time since the mid-thirties, Jacques Tati here tried out the routines that would form the core of his feature debut, *Jour de Fête*. A winner on the festival circuit, this hilarious short introduces the character of François, the work-shy postman, as well as containing two scenes – a hilarious tutorial and an eccentric dance – which didn't make the feature. Bearing the influence of Max Linder, Buster Keaton and Charlie Chaplin, the film showcases the athletic slapstick style honed over many years in the French music hall, but it also demonstrates an innate understanding of the cinematic medium. A French language film.

🅄 = SUITABLE FOR ALL, 🆄c = SUITABLE FOR ALL, ESPECIALLY FOR YOUNG CHILDREN (VIDEO ONLY) 🅿🅶 = PARENTAL GUIDANCE

Jacques Tati *Postman* • Paul Demange *Head Postman* ■ *Dir/Scr* Jacques Tati

School for Scoundrels ★★★ U
Comedy   1960 · UK · BW · 90mins

Based on Stephen Potter's popular one-upmanship books, this hit-and-miss comedy just about passes muster thanks to the willing performances of Ian Carmichael and Terry-Thomas. There are some amusing moments as Carmichael learns how to "confound a bounder" under the tutelage of Alastair Sim, but director Robert Hamer handles the subtle humour with a heavy hand and fails to knit the various sketches into a convincing whole. Our sympathy is firmly with the loveable rogue, and, whether crowing with caddishness or beaten and bemused, Terry-Thomas is the star of the show. ▭

Ian Carmichael *Henry Palfrey* • Terry-Thomas *Raymond Delauney* • Alastair Sim *Stephen Potter* • Janette Scott *April Smith* • Dennis Price *Dunstan Dorchester* • Peter Jones *Dudley Dorchester* • Edward Chapman *Gloatbridge* • John Le Mesurier *Head waiter* • Irene Handl *Mrs Stringer* • Hattie Jacques *First instructress* ■ *Dir* Robert Hamer • *Scr* Hal E Chester, Patricia Moyes, Peter Ustinov, from the books by Stephen Potter

School for Secrets ★★★
Wartime drama   1946 · UK · BW · 107mins

After the war the RAF and the Ministry of Defence wanted to boast about their invention of radar and the job of producing, directing and writing the account went to the 25-year-old Peter Ustinov. Ralph Richardson plays the boffin and there are some half-hearted action scenes and mini-melodramas to flesh out the reams of technospeak. Fortunately, Ustinov's refusal to make a blatant back-slapper suffuses the film with both a distorted attitude to heroism and a cartoonish wit.

Ralph Richardson *Prof Heatherville* • Richard Attenborough *Jack Arnold* • Raymond Huntley *Prof Laxton-Jones* • John Laurie *Dr McVitie* • Ernest Jay *Dr Dainty* • David Tomlinson *Mr Watlington* • Finlay Currie *Sir Duncan Wilson Wills* • Norman Webb *Dr Wainwright* • Michael Hordern *Lt Cdr Lowther* • Alvar Liddell *BBC announcer* ■ *Dir/Scr* Peter Ustinov

The School of Flesh ★★
Romantic drama   1998 · Fr · Colour · 105mins

Divorced, middle-aged fashion executive Isabelle Huppert is aided in her pursuit of bisexual hustler Vincent Martinez by transvestite Vincent Lindon. Instead of tension, tantrums and tempestuous sex, it's chat and heartache, as her manipulative strategies misfire. Problems with class and cultural identity are director Benoît Jacquot's staples, but, for once his laconic, gynocentric approach fails, as in transferring Yukio Mishima's tale of sexual obsession to a chic Parisian setting, he and screenwriter Jacques Fieschi have dissipated the novel's reckless passion by coating it with a sheen of empty sophistication. A French language film.

Isabelle Huppert *Dominique* • Vincent Martinez *Quentin* • Vincent Lindon *Chris* • Marthe Keller *Madame Thorpe* • François Berleand *Soukaz* • Danièle Dubroux *Domonique's friend* •

Bernard Le Coq *Cordier* • Jean-Claude Dauphin *Louis-Guy* • Dir Benoît Jacquot • *Scr* Jacques Fieschi, from the novel *Nikutai no Gakko* by Yukio Mishima

School Spirit ★ 15
Comedy   1985 · US · Colour · 86mins

Tom Nolan is a dislikeably sex-mad high school kid who is killed in a car crash, but returns in spirit form for one last day of trying to get it on with the girls. Post-mortem powers give him a ghost of a chance. Far less haunting than Nolan is, the film mixes slapstick and sexism to unfunny and unpleasant effect. Audiences "exorcised" their right to stay away in droves. ▭

Tom Nolan *Billy Batson* • Elizabeth Foxx *Judy Hightower* • Roberta Collins *Mrs Grimshaw* • John Finnegan *Pinky Batson* • Larry Linville *President Grimshaw* ■ *Dir* Alan Holleb • *Scr* Geoffrey Baere

School Ties ★★★ PG
Drama   1992 · US · Colour · 102mins

Although responsible and challenging, *School Ties* isn't just a sermon sugared by the forceful presence of Chris O'Donnell and Brendan Fraser. The film is a mix of *Gentleman's Agreement* and the code-of-honour subplot of *Scent of a Woman*, as aspiring American footballer Fraser hides his Judaism to ensure that he succeeds at an exclusive school where racist remarks are part of polite conversation. Not all the pitfalls are avoided, but the performances are impressive. Contains some swearing and brief nudity.

Brendan Fraser *David Greene* • Matt Damon *Charlie Dillon* • Chris O'Donnell *Chris Reece* • Randall Batinkoff *Rip Van Kelt* • Andrew Lowery *McGivern* • Cole Hauser *Jack Connors* • Ben Affleck *Chesty Smith* • Anthony Rapp *McGoo* • Amy Locane *Sally Wheeler* • Kevin Tighe *Coach McDevitt* • Ed Lauter *Alan Greene* ■ *Dir* Robert Mandel • *Scr* Dick Wolf, Darryl Ponicsan, from the story by Dick Wolf

Schpaaa ★★★
Drama   1999 · Nor · Colour · 77mins

Divided into six daily instalments, Erik Poppe's uncompromising portrait of street life seeks to do for Oslo what Mathieu Kassovitz's *La Haine* did for Paris. There's a depressing familiarity about the wheeling and dealing and the sense of racial exclusion. But there's a refreshing naturalism about the performances, with Maikel Andressen impressive as the white teenager who tries to extricate his gang from the mess in which his Yugoslav buddy has landed them. Poppe's relentlessly downbeat film presents a side of Norway little seen on screen. The efficiency of the boys' violent crimes is chillingly detached, but the ending smacks of contrivance. A Norwegian language film.

Maikel Abou-Zelof Andressen *Jonas* • Jalal Zahedjekta *Emir* • Sharjil Arshed Vaseer *Jack* • Mickael Marman *Ali* ■ *Dir* Erik Poppe • *Scr* Erik Poppe, Hans Petter Blad

Schtonk! ★★ 15
Satire   1992 · Ger · Colour · 106mins

Named after a word spluttered by Charlie Chaplin during one of Adenoid Hynkel's speeches in *The Great*

Dictator, this German farce cashed in on the "Hitler Diaries" fiasco and was a huge domestic hit. However, it fared less well abroad, where the satirical digs at modern German ambivalence towards the Nazi past meant little to the average overseas viewer. Uwe Ochsenknecht, as the hoarder of Hitler memorabilia, and Götz George as the journalist who seizes on the diaries to make his reputation, give it everything they've got, but a little restraint would not have gone amiss. In German with English subtitles. ▭

Götz George *Hermann Willié* • Uwe Ochsenknecht *Fritz Knobel* • Christiane Hörbiger *Freya von Hepp* • Rolf Hoppe *Karl Lentz* • Dagmar Manzel *Biggi* ■ *Dir* Helmut Dietl • *Scr* Helmut Dietl, Ulrich Limmer

Sci-Fighters ★★ 18
Science-fiction   1996 · Can · Colour · 90mins

Roddy Piper stars in this rip-off of *Blade Runner*. But instead of an android, Piper is hunting a seemingly deceased rapist (Billy Drago) who has somehow developed the ability to infect people with a disgusting alien virus. The movie is drab, and the actors seem to have taken their cue from their surroundings. Do yourself a favour and rent the real thing. ▭

Roddy Piper *Cameron Grayson* • Jayne Heitmeyer *Dr Kirbie Younger* • Billy Drago *Adrian Dunn* • Tyrone Benskin *Gene Washington* • Richard Raybourne *Casper* ■ *Dir* Peter Svatek • *Scr* Mark Sevi

Scissors ★★ 18
Psychological thriller
1991 · US · Colour · 90mins

Sandwiched between her breakthrough role in *Total Recall* and her star making performance in *Basic Instinct*, Sharon Stone starred in this little known thriller as a sexually traumatised woman suffering from nightmares and illusions which are in fact a bold plot to drive her insane. Stone gives the part her all and there's creepy support from Steve Railsback in a dual role as her neighbour and his disabled brother. But Frank De Felitta's leaden direction ultimately stifles the life out of what could have been a decent little thriller. Contains violence, swearing and nudity. ▭

Sharon Stone *Angie* • Steve Railsback *Alex/Cole* • Ronny Cox *Dr Carter* • Michelle Phillips *Ann* • Vicki Frederick *Nancy* • Leonard Rogel *Red Beard* ■ *Dir* Frank De Felitta • *Scr* Frank De Felitta, from a story by Joyce Selznick

Scorchers ★ 18
Drama   1991 · US · Colour · 77mins

Talk about a misnomer! But, then, talk is all they ever do in this dismal stage to screen transfer. An unusually strong cast including Faye Dunaway and James Earl Jones rant and rave to little effect in a philosophical tale of sex and southern girl Emily Lloyd who would rather hide under the bed than be in it on her wedding night. She plays Splendid and her name is the only thing that is in a tepid Tennessee Williams inspired, high-decibel shouting match barely held together by globs of blue bayou mysticism. Contains swearing and sex scenes. ▭

Faye Dunaway *Thais* • Denholm Elliott *Howler* • Emily Lloyd *Splendid* • James Earl Jones

Bear • Jennifer Tilly *Talbot* • James Wilder *Dolan* • Anthony Geary *Preacher* • Leland Crooke *Jumper* • Luke Perry *Ray Ray* ■ *Dir* David Beaird • *Scr* David Beaird, from his play

Scorchy ★★
Action crime   1976 · US · Colour · 97mins

Forgettable action film, a mid-career low for Connie Stevens, better known for her earlier roles in a slew of dumb-but-fun sixties beach flicks. Here she's an undercover cop tackling a high-profile drugs ring in Seattle. Heavy on the violence, and light on anything else – such as plot and characters. Stevens and a solid supporting cast do their best: but they're required to do little other than carry the film from one shootout to the next.

Connie Stevens *Sergeant Jackie Parker* • Cesare Danova *Philip Bianco* • William Smith *Carl Henrich* • Norman Burton *Chief Frank O'Brien* • John Davis Chandler *Nicky* • Joyce Jameson *Mary Davis* ■ *Dir/Scr* Howard Avedis

Scorned and Swindled ★★★
Drama based on a true story
1984 · US · Colour · 97mins

In this fun TV drama Tuesday Weld acts suitably tough as a woman who discovers her hubby has not only left her, but taken everything she owns as well. As Weld goes after the serial swindler you realise the idea is a bit daft, but *Gidget* director Paul Wendkos manages to keep things moving along at a good pace.

Tuesday Weld *Sharon Clark* • Keith Carradine *John Boslett* • Peter Coyote *Anthony Ristelli* • Sheree North *Maxine Wagner* • Fionnula Flanagan *Margaret* ■ *Dir* Paul Wendkos • *Scr* Karol A Hoeffner, Jerome Kass, from an article by Cable Neuhaus

Scorpio ★★★ 15
Spy thriller   1973 · US · Colour · 109mins

All the ingredients are here for a presentable thriller – treachery, murder, intrigue and a handful of foreign locations – but a garbled script and Michael Winner's rather slipshod direction undoes much of the good work put in by his admirable cast. As the CIA agent suspected of having double standards, Burt Lancaster manages to combine the fear of the fugitive with the toughness and resourcefulness we have come to expect of him. Alain Delon's performance suffers from comparisons with his classic portrayal of a hitman in *Le Samouraï*, but he still does a solid job of blending duty and doubt. ▭

Burt Lancaster *Cross* • Alain Delon *Laurier* • Paul Scofield *Zharkov* • John Colicos *McLeod* • Gayle Hunnicutt *Susan* • JD Cannon *Filchock* ■ *Dir* Michael Winner • *Scr* David W Rintels, Gerald Wilson, from a story by David W Rintels

Scorpio Rising ★★★★
Underground erotic parody
1963 · US · Colour · 31mins

One of the most famous American underground films and a seminal force in gay cinema, Kenneth Anger's orgiastic study of leather bike boys, was banned as obscene in places as far apart as California and Belgium. Anger injects black humour into the homoeroticism, such as intercutting the action with sequences of Marlon Brando in *The Wild One*. There's also

Nazi symbolism, occultism and 13 rock songs on the soundtrack. Tasteless, self-indulgent and juvenile at times, the brilliantly-edited film has some fascination even for the uninitiated.

Bruce Byron *Scorpio* • Johnny Sapienza *Taurus* • Frank Carifi *Leo* • Bill Dorfman *The Back* • John Palone *Pin* • Ernie Allo *Joker* ■ *Dir/Scr* Kenneth Anger

Scorpion Spring ★★★ 18
Road movie thriller
1995 · US · Colour · 85mins

Quentin Tarantino has a lot to answer for. His slick genre pastiches have inspired a whole slew of imitations of his imitations. Here's one of the better ones: a sweaty Tex-Mex border yarn about a cross-country driver who's daft enough to give a ride to a couple of drug runners. Though ultimately it lacks a genuine sting in its tale, the plot is twisty and violent enough to hold the interest. The superior cast includes Britain's Alfred Molina, and Matthew McConaughey. Contains violence, drug abuse and swearing. 🖭

Alfred Molina *Denis Brabant* • Patrick McGaw *Zac Cross* • Esai Morales *Astor* • Angel Aviles *Nadia* • Rubén Blades *Sam Zaragosa* • Kevin Tighe *Rawley Gill* • Matthew McConaughey *El Rojo* ■ *Dir/Scr* Brian Cox

La Scorta ★★★ 15
Thriller
1993 · It · Colour · 91mins

This involving Mafia thriller centres on the story of a mainland judge sent to Sicily to smash mob control of the water supply. The film has a gritty semi-documentary look, which is reinforced by the episodic nature of the action and the naturalistic performances. The *carabinieri* detailed to escort the judge may be sketchily drawn macho types, but their petty problems soon come to matter as much as the success of the racket-busting mission. In Italian with English subtitles. Contains violence, swearing and nudity. 🖭

Claudio Amendola *Angelo Mandolesi* • Enrico Lo Verso *Andrea Corsale* • Carlo Cecchi *Judge Michele de Francesco* • Ricky Memphis *Fabio Muzzi* • Leo Gullotta *Policeman* • Tony Sperandeo *Raffaele Frasca* • Angelo Infanti *Judge Barresi* • Ugo Conti *Nicola* ■ *Dir* Ricky Tognazzi • *Scr* Graziano Diana, Simona Izzo, from an idea by Stefano Sudrie, Giovanni Romoli

Scott Joplin ★★
Musical biography
1977 · US · Colour · 96mins

Motown produced this biopic of another great black musical star, after the success of *Lady Sings the Blues* which also starred Billy Dee Williams. Shot quickly as a TV movie, it was given a limited theatrical release. It traces the career of the ragtime pianist who created a nationwide craze from his struggle for recognition to his death. Great performances and terrific music do not always a great movie make, but it's not a bad shot.

Billy Dee Williams *Scott Joplin* • Clifton Davis *Louis Chauvin* • Margaret Avery *Belle Joplin* • Eubie Blake *Will Williams* • Godfrey Cambridge *Tom Turpin* • Seymour Cassel *Dr Jaelki* ■ *Dir* Jeremy Paul Kagan • *Scr* Christopher Knopf

Scott of the Antarctic ★★★★ U
Drama
1948 · UK · Colour · 105mins

This is a documentary-like account of the ill-fated British expedition to the South Pole that ended in 1912. Although sticking closely to Scott's journal, it plays down his probable errors of judgement in order to concentrate on his reckless courage and the unswerving loyalty of his men. Using many of the team's actual possessions to increase the authenticity, the cast is only rarely allowed to demonstrate the humanity behind the stiff upper lips. John Mills is splendidly British in the title role, although he nearly came a cropper when he fell through the snow while filming in the Alps. 🖭

John Mills *Captain Scott* • Derek Bond *Captain Oates* • Harold Warrender *Dr Wilson* • Diana Churchill *Kathleen Scott* • Anne Firth *Oriana Wilson* • Reginald Beckwith *Lieutenant Bowers* • James Robertson-Justice *Taffy Evans* • Kenneth More *Teddy Evans* ■ *Dir* Charles Frend • *Scr* Ivor Montagu, Walter Meade, Mary Hayley Bell

The Scoundrel ★★★
Drama
1935 · US · BW · 73mins

Noël Coward considered this to be his screen debut, though he had appeared briefly in Griffith's *Hearts of the World* in 1918. Written and directed jointly by Ben Hecht and Charles MacArthur, *The Scoundrel* is a fantasy about a publisher who comes back from the dead bearing a bunch of seaweed which he claims will guarantee him true love. Coward liked the idea and was also lured by the promise that his co-star would be Helen Hayes (later Mrs Charles MacArthur), but she dropped out at the last minute and was replaced by Julie Haydon.

Noël Coward *Anthony Mallare* • Julie Haydon *Cora Moore* • Stanley Ridges *Paul Decker* • Rosita Moreno *Carlotta* • Martha Sleeper *Julia Vivian* • Hope Williams *Maggie* • Ernest Cossart *Jimmy Clay* • Ben Hecht *Flophouse bum* • Charles MacArthur *Flophouse bum* • Burgess Meredith ■ *Dir* Ben Hecht, Charles MacArthur • *Scr* Ben Hecht, Charles MacArthur, from their story

The Scout ★★★★ 12
Sports comedy drama
1994 · US · Colour · 97mins

Engaging human comedy, with Albert Brooks excellent as a struggling talent scout for big-league baseball teams, and Brendan Fraser likeable as ever as an unsigned super-pitcher whom Brooks discovers on a scouting trip down Mexico way. Trouble is, Fraser gets "moundfright", and can't pitch straight when crowds are watching. So Brooks turns for help to psychiatrist Dianne Wiest. A watchable film, that doesn't require an understanding of the rules of baseball. 🖭

Albert Brooks *Al Percolo* • Brendan Fraser *Steve Nebraska* • Dianne Wiest *Doctor Aaron* • Anne Twomey *Jennifer* • Lane Smith *Ron Wilson* • Michael Rapaport *Tommy Lacy* ■ *Dir* Michael Ritchie • *Scr* Andrew Bergman, Albert Brooks, Monica Johnson, from an article by Roger Angell

Scram! ★★★★ U
Comedy
1932 · US · BW · 20mins

A title that could only be appplied to Laurel and Hardy, whose disreputable appearance ensures they are ordered out of town because they might spoil the town's chances of winning a civic prize. However, several adventures later, they find a judge's wife on their side and it all ends in a lengthy laughfest. A short from producer Hal Roach, the small-town hypocrisy is never punctured as it should be, but the mythic laughmakers are at their most sweet-hearted and endearing. 🖭

Stan Laurel *Stanley* • Oliver Hardy *Oliver* • Arthur Housman *Drunk* • Vivien Oakland *Mrs Beaumont* • Richard Cramer *Judge Beaumont* ■ *Dir* Ray McCarey • *Scr* HM Walker

Scream ★★★★★ 18
Horror comedy 1996 · US · Colour · 106mins

The nineties horror revival started here, with director Wes Craven's intelligent reinvention of the slasher genre. Gleefully exploring the relationship between gore movies and their core audience, while paying clever homage to such key titles as *Halloween* and *Friday the 13th*, the elaborate script subversively keeps things scary even when sinister events are at their funniest. A sick maniac on the loose in a small suburban town murdering anyone who gets horror trivia questions wrong is all Craven needs to expose the genre's knee-jerk devices while deftly employing them at the same time. An instant classic, with gasps galore and a genuinely surprising denouement. Contains swearing and violence. 🖭 **DVD**

Drew Barrymore *Casey Becker* • David Arquette *Deputy Dwight "Dewey" Riley* • Neve Campbell *Sidney Prescott* • Skeet Ulrich *Billy Loomis* • Lawrence Hecht *Mr Prescott* • Linda Blair *Obnoxious reporter* • Courteney Cox *Gale Weathers* • Rose McGowan *Tatum Riley* • Henry Winkler *Principal Himbry* • Matthew Lillard *Stuart* • Jamie Kennedy *Randy* • Liev Schreiber *Cotton Weary* • Wes Craven *Fred, the janitor* ■ *Dir* Wes Craven • *Scr* Kevin Williamson

Scream 2 ★★★ 18
Horror comedy 1997 · US · Colour · 115mins

The body count increases in this easily digestible sequel from director Wes Craven. But the scare factor is considerably diluted in this reheated outing that picks up on events two years after the notorious Woodsboro murders, just as *Stab*, the movie based on them by news reporter Courteney Cox, hits town. When two members of the audience are killed during the screening, student target Neve Campbell finds herself flung back into the unwanted limelight. Although once more cleverly twisting the genre rules, this lacks the satirical originality of the first recursive nightmare and coasts, rather than builds, on the shrewd achievements of the far superior first film. Contains violence and swearing 🖭 **DVD**

David Arquette *Dwight "Dewey" Riley* • Neve Campbell *Sidney Prescott* • Courteney Cox *Gale Weathers* • Sarah Michelle Gellar *Casey "Cici" Cooper* • Jamie Kennedy *Randy Meeks* • Laurie Metcalf *Debbie Salt* • Elise Neal *Hallie* • Jerry O'Connell *Derek* • Jada Pinkett [Jada Pinkett Smith] *Maureen Evans* • Omar

Epps *Phil Stevens* • Liev Schreiber *Cotton Weary* • David Warner *Gus Gold* ■ *Dir* Wes Craven • *Scr* Kevin Williamson

Scream 3 ★★ 18
Horror comedy 1999 · US · Colour · 116mins

The *Scream* trilogy ends, not with a bang, but a whimper in director Wes Craven's unconvincing wrap-up to the franchise. With the surviving cast members of the previous episodes now merely going through the expected self-referential motions, the worst thing about *Scream 3* is that it makes you forget how original and inventive the first outing was in slicing and dicing slasher movie conventions. Despite the addition of feisty Parker Posey to the cast and a reasonably surprising ending, the film runs out of steam and becomes exactly what the first *Scream* so smartly sent up.

David Arquette *Dwight "Dewey" Riley* • Neve Campbell *Sidney Prescott* • Courteney Cox Arquette *[Courteney Cox] Gale Weathers* • Patrick Dempsey *Mark Kincaid* • Parker Posey *Jennifer Jolie* • Scott Foley *Roman Bridger* • Lance Henriksen *John Milton* • Matt Keeslar *Tom Prinze* • Jenny McCarthy *Sarah Darling* • Liev Schreiber *Cotton Weary* • Carrie Fisher *Bianca* • Kevin Smith *Silent Bob* • Roger L Jackson *"The Voice"* • Roger Corman *Studio executive* ■ *Dir* Wes Craven • *Scr* Ehren Kruger, from characters created by Kevin Williamson

Scream and Scream Again ★★★ 18
Horror chiller 1969 · UK · Colour · 90mins

A highly regarded, but confusing, sci-fi horror tale tinged with political allegory. Vincent Price is a scientist creating an artificial super-race via gruesome transplant surgery for a foreign fascist power. Peter Cushing is an ex-Nazi and Christopher Lee a British agent in veteran genre director Gordon Hessler's imaginative blood-curdler, but the three leads' highly publicised (at the time) teaming is a cheat, as they have virtually no scenes together. Price lends dignity and class to some credible chills. Contains violence, swearing and some nudity. 🖭

Vincent Price *Dr Browning* • Christopher Lee *Fremont* • Peter Cushing *Major Benedek Heinrich* • Judy Huxtable *Sylvia* • Alfred Marks *Superintendent Bellaver* • Anthony Newlands *Ludwig* • Peter Sallis *Schweitz* • David Lodge *Det Insp Strickland* ■ *Dir* Gordon Hessler • *Scr* Christopher Wicking, from the novel *The Disorientated Man* by Peter Saxon

Scream Blacula Scream ★★ 15
Blaxploitation horror
1973 · US · Colour · 91mins

Blacula was one of the more outrageous novelties of the blaxploitation era, further distinguished by its tongue-in-cheek approach. This flat sequel is merely a routine vampire yarn in which the characters happen to be black. William Marshall returns to his role of the African prince bitten in the 18th century by Dracula. He is resuscitated with an incantation and joins forces with voodoo priestess Pam Grier. There is some appeal in the film's depiction of the swinging Los Angeles scene – all parties, flares and big hair. 🖭

U = SUITABLE FOR ALL   Uc = SUITABLE FOR ALL, ESPECIALLY FOR YOUNG CHILDREN (VIDEO ONLY)   PG = PARENTAL GUIDANCE

William Marshall *Manuwalde* • Don Mitchell *Justin* • Pam Grier *Lisa* • Michael Conrad *Sheriff Dunlop* • Richard Lawson *Willis* • Lynne Moody *Denny* • Janee Michelle *Gloria* ■ *Dir* Bob Kelljan • *Scr* Joan Torres, Raymond Koenig, Maurice Jules, from a story by Raymond Koenig, Joan Torres

Scream of Fear ★★★★
Psychological thriller
1961 · UK · BW · 82mins

Hammer's first *Psycho*-inspired thriller, also known as *Taste of Fear*, is the best the House of Horror ever made. Squeezing maximum shocks from a clichéd story a plot to drive someone insane Seth Holt dazzles with his direction and gives Susan Strasberg her greatest role as the wheelchair-bound young woman haunted by her father's corpse at his French villa. Just when you think you know what's going on, the marvellous script takes another labyrinthine twist into the unknown. Shot in moody black and white, the creepy swimming pool scene is justifiably famous.

Susan Strasberg *Penny Appleby* • Ronald Lewis *Bob, the chauffeur* • Ann Todd *Jane Appleby* • Christopher Lee *Dr Gerrard* • John Serret *Inspector Legrand* • Leonard Sachs *Spratt* ■ *Dir* Seth Holt • *Scr* Jimmy Sangster

Scream of Stone ★★★
Drama 1991 · Can/Ger/Fr · Colour · 105mins

The "mountain film" has been a key German genre since the silent era, but Werner Herzog's film lacks the dramatic drive to match its stunning photography. It's as if he's dissipated his trademark intensity by dividing the obsession that motivates nearly all his protagonists between two characters, mountaineer Vittorio Mezzogiorno and indoor climbing champion, Stefan Glowacz, whose race to scale El Toro in Patagonia is intensified by a rivalry for the affections of Mathilda May.

Mathilda May *Katharina* • Vittorio Mezzogiorno *Roccia* • Stefan Glowacz *Martin* • Donald Sutherland *Ivan* • Brad Dourif *"Fingerless"* ■ *Dir* Werner Herzog • *Scr* Hans-Ulrich Klenner, Walter Saxer, Robert Geoffrion, from an idea by Reinhold Messner • *Cinematographer* Rainer Klausmann

Screamers ★★ 18
Science-fiction thriller
1995 · Can/US/Jap · Colour · 103mins

This dingy adaptation of a Philip K Dick short story is only a moderate success. Peter Weller (*Robocop*) plays the soldier brokering peace with his futuristic enemies, who comes up against the eponymous deadly defence units, which have evolved into increasingly sophisticated adversaries. Although there are decently mounted action sequences and the post-nuclear production design is nicely realised, there are far too many lulls in the story. ▭ *DVD*

Peter Weller *Colonel Hendricksson* • Andy Lauer [Andrew Lauer] *Ace* • Roy Dupuis *Becker* • Charles Powell *Ross* • Jennifer Rubin *Jessica* • Ron White *Elbarak* ■ *Dir* Christian Duguay • *Scr* Dan O'Bannon, Miguel Tejada-Flores, from the short story *Second Variety* by Philip K Dick

Screaming Mimi ★★
Thriller 1958 · US · BW · 77mins

This would-be lurid and sexy thriller, filmed in gritty black and white and directed by Gerd Oswald (*A Kiss before Dying*), falls far short of expectation. A tortuous and virtually incomprehensible plot, and an almost unwatchable hero played by an expressionless Phil Carey are the main culprits. Anita Ekberg is splendidly awful as an assault victim, and there's a palpable sexual tension whenever she's on screen. For fifties freaks, fans of the bizarre and anyone interested in that late *film noir* style when all the streets were wet ones. Sadly, it's just not very good.

Anita Ekberg *Virginia Wilson* • Phil Carey [Philip Carey] *Bill Sweeney* • Gypsy Rose Lee *Joann Mapes* • Harry Townes *Dr Greenwood* • Linda Cherney *Ketti* • Romney Brent *Charlie Wilson* • Alan Gifford *Captain Bline* ■ *Dir* Gerd Oswald • *Scr* Robert Blees, from the book by Frederic Brown

Screwballs ★ 18
Comedy 1983 · US/Can · Colour · 76mins

Five students on detention at Taft and Adams High School blame the school's last remaining virgin, Purity Busch, for their predicament, and plan revenge by contriving to see her ample breasts. But the various schemes they cook up, backfire badly. This is one of the very worst *American Graffiti*-inspired youth comedies. A leering, juvenile slice of limp titillation and corny sexual situations that spawned an equally naff sequel. ▭

Peter Keleghan *Rick McKay* • Lynda Speciale *Purity Busch* • Alan Deveau *Howie Bates* • Kent Deuters *Brent Van Dusen III* • Jason Warren *Melvin Jerkovski* • Linda Shayne *Bootsie Goodhead* ■ *Dir* Rafal Zielinski • *Scr* Linda Shayne, Jim Wynorski

Scrooge ★★ U
Fantasy drama 1935 · US · BW · 77mins

Seymour Hicks plays the old curmudgeon and Donald Calthrop is Bob Cratchit in the first talking version of Dickens's *A Christmas Carol*. Viewers who expect something deeply sentimental and technically creaky will not be disappointed but it should not really be compared to the classic Alastair Sim version of 1951.

Seymour Hicks *Ebenezer Scrooge* • Donald Calthrop *Bob Cratchit* • Robert Cochran *Fred* • Mary Glynne *Belle* • Garry Marsh *Belle's husband* • Oscar Asche *Spirit of Christmas Present* • Marie Ney *Spirit of Christmas Past* • CV France *Spirit of Christmas Future* ■ *Dir* Henry Edwards • *Scr* Seymour Hicks, H Fowler Mear, from the story *A Christmas Carol* by Charles Dickens

Scrooge ★★★★★ U
Christmas drama 1951 · UK · Colour · 86mins

Released in the US under Dickens's original title, *A Christmas Carol*, this is easily the best screen version of the much-loved yuletide tale. The ever-versatile Alastair Sim is impeccable as the miser who comes to see the error of his ways through the promptings of the spirits of Christmas Past, Present and Future. Michael Hordern makes a splendid Jacob Marley and Mervyn Johns a humble Bob Cratchit, while George Cole does well as the younger, carefree Scrooge. Beautifully designed by Ralph Brinton and directed with unexpected finesse by Brian Desmond Hurst, this is not to be missed. ▭

Alastair Sim *Scrooge* • Kathleen Harrison *Mrs Dilber* • Jack Warner *Mr Jorkins* • Michael Hordern *Jacob Marley* • Mervyn Johns *Bob Cratchit* • Hermione Baddeley *Mrs Cratchit* • John Charlesworth *Peter Cratchit* • Glyn Dearman *Tiny Tim* • George Cole *Scrooge as young man* • Rona Anderson *Alice* • Carol Marsh *Fan, Scrooge's sister* • Brian Worth *Fred, Scrooge's nephew* • Hattie Jacques *Mrs Fezziwig* • Patrick Macnee *Young Marley* ■ *Dir* Brian Desmond Hurst • *Scr* Noel Langley, from the story *A Christmas Carol* by Charles Dickens

Scrooge ★★ U
Musical 1970 · UK · Colour · 108mins

This feeble sub-Dickensian fable features an overly made-up grouch in Albert Finney, who gives the impression he'd be happier somewhere else. Director Ronald Neame oversees matters with the heaviest of hands, but there's some compensation in watching fine twilight-year performances from Dame Edith Evans and Kenneth More. Only Alec Guinness really registers. ▭

Albert Finney *Ebenezer Scrooge* • Alec Guinness *Jacob Marley's Ghost* • Edith Evans *Ghost of Christmas Past* • Kenneth More *Ghost of Christmas Present* • Michael Medwin *Scrooge's nephew* • Laurence Naismith *Fezziwig* • David Collings *Bob Cratchit* • Anton Rodgers *Tom Jenkins* • Suzanne Neve *Isabel* • Roy Kinnear *Portly gentleman* • Gordon Jackson *Nephew's friend* ■ *Dir* Ronald Neame • *Scr* Leslie Bricusse, from the story *A Christmas Carol* by Charles Dickens • *Music/Lyrics* Leslie Bricusse

Scrooged ★★★ PG
Seasonal comedy 1988 · US · Colour · 96mins

For the opening quarter, this is a joyously black Christmas treat with Bill Murray at his sour-faced best as a monstrous TV executive preparing for the festive break by sacking staff, planning a season of violence and ordering mini antlers to be stapled on the heads of mice. This being an update of *A Christmas Carol*, it is not long before sentimentality starts seeping in, as Murray is shown what a miserable heel he is by unconventional ghosts John Forsythe, Carol Kane and David Johansen. A missed opportunity, but some of the gags still hit the mark and there is a starry stream of cameos. Contains some swearing ▭

Bill Murray *Frank Cross* • Karen Allen *Claire Phillips* • John Forsythe *Lew Hayward* • Bobcat Goldthwait *Eliot Loudermilk* • Robert Mitchum *Preston Rhinelander* • Carol Kane *Ghost of Christmas Present* • John Glover *Brice Cummings* • David Johansen *Ghost of Christmas Past* • Alfre Woodard *Grace Cooley* ■ *Dir* Richard Donner • *Scr* Mitch Glazer, Michael O'Donoghue, from the story *A Christmas Carol* by Charles Dickens

Scrubbers ★★★ 15
Drama 1982 · UK · Colour · 88mins

Bursting at the seams with all manner of GBH and blaspheming, director Mai Zetterling's moderately successful attempt at showing the gritty and depressing underbelly of life in a girls' borstal and beyond was highly controversial. Utilising inventive moody camerawork and incisive editing, Zetterling does well in portraying the problems facing her two main protagonists, who emote like fury in realistic performances, but this is dreadfully depressing. Contains some violence and swearing. ▭

Amanda York *Carol* • Chrissie Cotterill *Annetta* • Elizabeth Edmonds *Kathleen* • Kate Ingram *Eddie* • Debbie Bishop *Doreen* • Dana Gillespie *Budd* • Camille Davis *Sharon* • Amanda Symonds *Mac* • Kathy Burke *Glennis* • Robbie Coltrane *Pam St Clement* ■ *Dir* Mai Zetterling • *Scr* Mai Zetterling, Roy Minton, Jeremy Watt • *Cinematographer* Ernest Vincze • *Editor* Rodney Holland

Scum ★★★ 18
Prison drama 1979 · UK · Colour · 92mins

Originally written for the BBC's *Play for Today* series, Roy Minton's stark, bruising drama about conditions inside a juvenile detention centre was banned by the BBC in 1978. Minton persuaded director Alan Clarke to make a cinema version on a shoestring budget the following year. Beefing up the incidents that had informed dozens of Hollywood prison pictures, Minton presents an uncompromising picture of borstal life, made all the more shocking by Clarke's docudramatic approach, with the scenes of sexual and physical violence still having the power to revolt and arouse anger. Contains violence and swearing. ▭ *DVD*

Ray Winstone *Carlin* • Mick Ford *Archer* • John Judd *Sands* • Phil Daniels *Richards* • John Blundell *Banks* • Ray Burdis *Eckersly* • Julian Firth *Davis* • Alrick Riley *Angel* ■ *Dir* Alan Clarke • *Scr* Roy Minton

The Sea Chase ★★★ U
Second World War adventure
1955 · US · Colour · 112mins

John Wayne stars as a German sea captain in this Second World War adventure. However, the real villain of the piece is first mate Lyle Bettger, whose murder of some defenceless fishermen prompts British naval officer David Farrar to pursue Wayne's freighter across the Pacific. Director John Farrow adopts a no-nonsense approach, but Wayne's dalliance with sultry passenger Lana Turner slows up the action. However, the shark attack and the final battle are briskly staged and the rivalry between the Duke and Farrar gives the picture extra edge. ▭

John Wayne *Captain Karl Ehrlich* • Lana Turner *Elsa Keller* • David Farrar *Commander Napier* • Lyle Bettger *Kirchner* • Tab Hunter *Cadet Wesser* • James Arness *Schlieter* • Richard Davalos *Cadet Walter Stemme* ■ *Dir* John Farrow • *Scr* James Warner Bellah, John Twist, from the novel by Andrew Geer

Sea Devils ★★
Action drama 1937 · US · BW · 87mins

A highly predictable modern sea drama and star vehicle for the expansive personality of Victor McLaglen. He's the petty officer in the US Coastguard who wants his precious daughter, played by Ida Lupino, to marry Donald Woods's decent but dull seaman while she prefers Preston Foster's man of the world. McLaglen has Foster under his command and tries to break him at sea. An accident while testing explosives on an iceberg and a sudden hurricane resolve matters.

Victor McLaglen *Medals Malone* • Preston Foster *Mike O'Shay* • Ida Lupino *Doris Malone* • Donald Woods *Steve Webb* • Helen Flint *Sadie* • Gordon Jones *Puggy* ■ *Dir* Ben Stoloff [Benjamin Stoloff] • *Scr* Frank Wead, John Twist, PJ Wolfson

Sea Devils ★★ U

Period adventure
1952 · UK/US · Colour · 86mins

A routine seafaring yarn directed by the one-eyed, macho action maestro Raoul Walsh. The svelte Yvonne De Carlo plays a spy for George III who slips into France to try to uncover Napoleon's invasion plans. Rock Hudson, sporting designer stubble, is a smuggler from Guernsey who, after being duped by her, becomes a patriotic hero. Filmed in the Channel Islands and Brittany, the picture often looks good, but it still falls well below Walsh's usually high standards. ▣

Yvonne De Carlo *Drouette* • Rock Hudson *Gilliatt* • Maxwell Reed *Rantaine* • Denis O'Dea *Lethierry* • Michael Goodliffe *Ragan* • Bryan Forbes *Willie* • Jacques Brunius *Fouche* • Gérard Oury *Napoleon* ■ *Dir* Raoul Walsh • *Scr* Borden Chase, from the novel *The Toilers of the Sea* by Victor Hugo

Sea Devils ★★

Period adventure 1982 · Sp · Colour · 84mins

Based on a Jules Verne novel, this frantic Spanish-made adventure does provide a few thrills amid the endless spills. Ships slip into Davy Jones's locker with monotonous regularity in the opening scenes, as six youngsters, heading for reunions with their parents in Australia, fall foul of pirates, storms and an unfriendly whale. But that's nothing compared to the African flesh-eating ants that await them when they encounter old sea dog Frank Brana, who is also a slave trader in his spare time. Spanish dialogue dubbed into English. Contains violence.

Ian Sera *Mark* • Patty Shepard *Mrs Waldom* • Frank Brana *Van Hassel* • Flavia Zarzo *Jenny* • Gaby Jiminez *Dick Sand* • Aldo Sambrell *Negoro* ■ *Dir* J Piquer Simon [Juan Piquer Simon] • *Scr* Joaquin Grau, J Piquer Simon, from the novel *A Fifteen Years Old Captain* by Jules Verne

Sea Fury ★★★

Adventure 1958 · UK · BW · 97mins

After the success of *Hell Drivers*, star Stanley Baker and writer/director Cy Endfield teamed up again for this modest but strangely effective action movie set in Spain. Baker plays a drifter who gets a job aboard Victor McLaglen's salvage vessel. The pair end up competing for local siren Luciana Paluzzi – culminating in a rescue bid in a storm for Baker and a drunken binge for McLaglen. A study in macho posturing, failing sexuality and the virility of the weather: a heady brew that also features an early role for Robert Shaw.

Stanley Baker *Abel Hewson* • Victor McLaglen *Captain Bellew* • Luciana Paluzzi *Josita* • Grégoire Aslan *Fernando* • David Oxley *Blanco* • Robert Shaw *Gorman* • Dermot Walsh *Kelso* • Barry Foster *Vincent* ■ *Dir* C Raker Endfield [Cy Endfield] • *Scr* C Raker Endfield [Cy Endfield], John Kruse

The Sea Gull ★★★

Drama 1968 · UK · Colour · 141mins

Solid if unsensational version of the Chekhov play about life, loves and hates on a 19th-century Russian estate. Director Sidney Lumet clearly likes filming plays: he'd done *Long Day's Journey into Night* six years earlier, and would later make *Equus*. But it's the cast that really catches the eye here. The veritable who's who of sixties British cinema includes James Mason, David Warner, Vanessa Redgrave, Harry Andrews and Denholm Elliott, as well as Simone Signoret.

James Mason *Trigorin* • Vanessa Redgrave *Nina* • Simone Signoret *Arkadina* • David Warner *Konstantin* • Harry Andrews *Sorin* • Ronald Radd *Shamraev* • Eileen Herlie *Polina* • Kathleen Widdoes *Masha* • Denholm Elliott *Dorn* ■ *Dir* Sidney Lumet • *Scr* Moura Budberg, from the play by Anton Chekhov

The Sea Gypsies ★★ U

Adventure 1978 · US · Colour · 97mins

Robert Logan enjoyed a brief period of fame at the end of the seventies in a string of family films, most of which found him battling against the elements. In this one, he and his family find themselves trapped on the Alaskan coast when their ship sinks during a storm. All the usual clichés are present and correct, but children will lap it up and the scenery looks great. It's competently directed by Stewart Raffill, who worked with Logan on similar projects *Across the Great Divide* and *The Adventures of the Wilderness Family*. ▣

Robert Logan *Travis Maclaine* • Mikki Jamison-Olsen *Kelly* • Heather Rattray *Courtney* • Cjon Damitri Patterson *Jesse* • Shannon Saylor *Samantha* ■ *Dir/Scr* Stewart Raffill

The Sea Hawk ★★★★

Silent swashbuckling adventure
1924 · US · BW · 129mins

Rivalling anything produced by Douglas Fairbanks, this thrilling adventure sweeps from Georgian England to the Algerian bazaar, in pursuit of baronet, Milton Sills, as he seeks revenge on his treacherous half-brother, Wallace MacDonald. Working from the swashbuckling classic by Rafael Sabatini, Frank Lloyd is most heavily indebted to art director Stephen Goosson, whose sets for everything from a country manor to a desert palace, a Spanish galleon to a Moorish pirate ship give the action a splendour to match its zest. The performances are also top notch, with Sills's clean-cut hero complemented by Enid Bennett's chaste beloved and Wallace Beery's scowling villain.

Milton Sills *Sir Oliver Tressilian, the Sea Hawk* • Enid Bennett *Rosamund Godolphin* • Lloyd Hughes *Master Lionel Tressilian* • Wallace MacDonald *Master Peter Godolphin* • Marc MacDermott *Sir John Killigrew* • Wallace Beery *Jasper Leigh, a freebooter* ■ *Dir* Frank Lloyd • *Scr* JG Hawks, Walter Anthony, from a novel by Rafael Sabatini

The Sea Hawk ★★★★ U

Classic swashbuckling adventure
1940 · US · BW · 121mins

A rip-roaring adventure yarn, made at lavish expense. Directed by Michael Curtiz, who was soon to make *Casablanca*, and starring Errol Flynn in his swashbuckling prime, it's stronger in its scenes of derring-do and Spanish galleons on the high seas than it is when detailing the political intrigue at the court of Elizabeth I. All in all, a film that even improves on the rousing 1924 silent movie of the same name – praise indeed. ▣

Errol Flynn *Captain Geoffrey Thorpe* • Claude Rains *Don Jose Alvarez de Cordoba* • Brenda Marshall *Doña Maria Alvarez de Cordoba* • Donald Crisp *Sir John Burleson* • Flora Robson *Queen Elizabeth I* • Alan Hale *Carl Pitt* • Henry Daniell *Lord Wolfingham* • Una O'Connor *Martha, Miss Latham* ■ *Dir* Michael Curtiz • *Scr* Seton I Miller, Howard Koch

The Sea of Grass ★★

Western 1947 · US · BW · 123mins

This New Mexico-set western wasn't one of the more interesting vehicles for the stellar partnership of Katharine Hepburn and Spencer Tracy. Tracy is the steely cattle rancher who becomes increasingly ruthless in his efforts to protect his livelihood from the influx of homesteaders. Hepburn is his wife, who finds herself driven into the arms of Melvyn Douglas. Her subsequent pregnancy creates further complications. Despite the high-powered cast, director Elia Kazan fails to engender interest in anyone's plight or in the story itself.

Spencer Tracy *Col Jim Brewton* • Katharine Hepburn *Lutie Cameron* • Melvyn Douglas *Brice Chamberlain* • Robert Walker *Brock Brewton* • Phyllis Thaxter *Sara Beth Brewton* • Edgar Buchanan *Jeff* • Harry Carey *Doc Reid* • Ruth Nelson *Selina Hall* ■ *Dir* Elia Kazan • *Scr* Marguerite Roberts, Vincent Lawrence, from the novel by Conrad Richter

Sea of Love ★★★★ 18

Erotic thriller 1989 · US · Colour · 108mins

There's a real sexual charge to this tough thriller, with New York cop Al Pacino and chief murder suspect Ellen Barkin conveying a highly plausible erotic tension. It's a rather lurid story about Manhattan men being killed after advertising in the lonely-hearts columns, with a screenplay by Richard Price that's as serrated as a dozen *Jagged Edges*. The film is effectively directed by Harold Becker, who gives it an air of realism that only adds to the suspense. The title record (playing at the scene of each murder) is a bit of an irrelevance, but is still a treat to listen to. Contains nudity and sex scenes. ▣ **DVD**

Al Pacino *Frank Keller* • Ellen Barkin *Helen* • John Goodman *Sherman Touhey* • Michael Rooker *Terry* • Lorraine Bracco *Denise* • William Hickey *Frank Keller Sr* • Richard Jenkins *Gruber* • Paul Calderon *Serafino* ■ *Dir* Harold Becker • *Scr* Richard Price

Sea of Sand ★★ U

Second World War action adventure
1958 · UK · BW · 94mins

Guy Green was a leading British cameraman (*Great Expectations*, *Oliver Twist*) who, when he became a director, lost his way nearly as badly as this desert patrol of British stalwarts (Richard Attenborough, John Gregson, Michael Craig) out to blow up an Axis fuel dump before the battle of El Alamein. Green handles the macho element with credibility, but the sentimentality that finally consigned him to directing weepie movies proves to be an irritating distraction. ▣

Richard Attenborough *Trooper Brody* • John Gregson *Captain Williams* • Michael Craig *Captain Cotton* • Vincent Ball *Sergeant Nesbitt* • Percy Herbert *Trooper White* • Barry Foster *Corporal Matheson* • Ray McAnally *Sergeant Hardy* ■ *Dir* Guy Green • *Scr* Robert Westerby, from a story by Sean Fielding

The Sea Shall Not Have Them ★★ U

Second World War adventure
1954 · UK · BW · 91mins

Lewis Gilbert fails to generate much excitement with this stiff wartime tale of pluck and endurance, about a plane-load of heroes pitching into the briny. The calamities are utterly predictable, and there is no palpable tension between the castaways (clichés to a man). Each member of the stellar cast, including Michael Redgrave and Dirk Bogarde, is seemingly more preoccupied with holding his own in such august company than contributing to the ensemble effort. ▣

Michael Redgrave *Air Commodore Waltby* • Dirk Bogarde *Flight Sergeant Mackay* • Anthony Steel *Flying Officer Treherne* • Nigel Patrick *Flight Sergeant Slingsby* • Bonar Colleano *Sergeant Kirby* • Jack Watling *Flying Officer Harding* ■ *Dir* Lewis Gilbert • *Scr* Lewis Gilbert, Vernon Harris, from the novel by John Harris

Sea Wife ★★

Second World War romantic adventure
1957 · UK · Colour · 81mins

An adventure romance that doesn't quite come off, mainly owing to a change of directors mid-production. Richard Burton, Joan Collins, Basil Sydney and Cy Grant play the only survivors of a ship wrecked off the coast of Singapore during the evacuation in 1942. As millionaire Sydney is a committed atheist, Collins hides the fact that she is a nun and wards off Burton's increasingly fervent attentions by suggesting she is already attached. Director Bob McNaught – he took over from Roberto Rossellini – makes a fair job of it, but the characters are predictable types and not even a shark attack can enliven the chatty lifeboat sequences. ▣

Joan Collins *Sea Wife* • Richard Burton *Biscuit* • Basil Sydney *Bulldog* • Cy Grant *Number four* • Ronald Squire *Teddy* • Harold Goodwin *Daily Telegraph clerk* • Joan Hickson *Scribe* ■ *Dir* Bob McNaught • *Scr* George K Burke, from the novel *Sea Wyf and Biscuit* by JM Scott

The Sea Wolf ★★★★ PG

Drama 1941 · US · BW · 84mins

Exciting nautical melodrama from director Michael Curtiz, based on the classic Jack London tale. Edward G Robinson is terrific as Wolf Larsen, the tormented skipper of the *Ghost*, trading intellectual barbs with rescued novelist Alexander Knox. John Garfield and Ida Lupino are both wasted in relatively minor roles, and their shipboard romance takes clear second place to the captain's fiendish desire to break the spirits of his crew members. ▣

Edward G Robinson *Wolf Larsen* • John Garfield *George Leach* • Ida Lupino *Ruth*

U = SUITABLE FOR ALL   Uc = SUITABLE FOR ALL, ESPECIALLY FOR YOUNG CHILDREN (VIDEO ONLY)   PG = PARENTAL GUIDANCE

Webster • Alexander Knox *Humphrey van Weyden* • Gene Lockhart *Dr Louie Prescott* • Barry Fitzgerald *Cooky* • Stanley Ridges *Johnson* ■ *Dir* Michael Curtiz • *Scr* Robert Rossen, from the novel by Jack London

The Sea Wolf ★ PG

Adventure drama 1993 · US · Colour · 89mins

An all-star cast sinks like a lead anchor in this torpid retelling of Jack London's classic novel. In 1890, San Francisco aristocrat Christopher Reeve is shipwrecked and rescued by a brutal and sadistic sea captain (Charles Bronson) who presses him into service aboard his schooner. Reeve and the wooden Bronson are without chemistry and, along with the uninspired direction of Michael Anderson (*Logan's Run*) drown in this leaky made-for-cable effort. ▭

Charles Bronson *Captain Wolf Larsen* • Catherine Mary Stewart *Flaxen Brewster* • Christopher Reeve *Humphrey Van Weyden* • Len Cariou *Doc Picard* • Marc Singer *Johnson* • Clive Revill *Cookie* ■ *Dir* Michael Anderson • *Scr* Andrew J Fenady, from the novel by Jack London

The Sea Wolves ★★

Second World War drama 1980 · UK/US/Swi · Colour · 121mins

Encouraged by his success with the action romp *The Wild Geese*, intrepid producer Euan Lloyd came up with this maritime Second World War version. Starring a trio of venerable old sea dogs, the exploits are headed up by Gregory Peck, attempting a most ill-advised British accent, which is especially disturbing when pitched, literally, alongside Roger Moore and David Niven, with whom he once stormed the cliffs at Navarone. This tosh was directed with some verve by Andrew McLaglen, but there's little point in pretending this has any real merit. It's not boring, though, for all sorts of strange reasons.

Gregory Peck *Lieutenant Colonel Lewis Pugh* • David Niven *Colonel Bill Grice* • Roger Moore *Captain Gavin Stewart* • Trevor Howard *Jack Cartwright* • Barbara Kellerman *Mrs Cromwell* • Patrick Macnee *Major "Yogi" Crossley* • Patrick Allen *Colin Mackenzie* ■ *Dir* Andrew V McLaglen • *Scr* Reginald Rose, from the novel *Boarding Party* by James Leasor

Seagulls over Sorrento ★★★ U

Second World War drama 1954 · UK · BW · 91mins

One of the stranger products of the Cold War, this stage hit was "opened out" considerably by the Boultings for this film version. In a weird bit of casting, Gene Kelly plays an American navy scientist working on torpedo research on a Scottish island. The British boffins have already blown themselves to bits when the Yanks arrive, thus sparking a lot of transatlantic rivalry and resentment. It's a pity Richaed Attenborough and/or John Mills aren't around but this is still an enjoyable and often quirky drama about the "Special Relationship".

Gene Kelly *Lieutenant Bradville, USN* • John Justin *Lieutenant Wharton* • Bernard Lee *Lofty Turner* • Jeff Richards *Butch Clelland, USN* • Sidney James *Charlie Badger* • Patric Doonan

PO Herbert ■ *Dir* John Boulting, Roy Boulting • *Scr* Frank Harvey, Roy Boulting, from the play by Hugh Hastings

Sealed Cargo ★★ U

Second World War drama 1951 · US · BW · 89mins

Newfoundland fisherman Dana Andrews comes across a sailing ship called *The Gaunt Woman* (the title of the original novel by Edmund Gilligan) with its hold full of guns, bombs and torpedoes, and manned by Nazis in disguise headed by an urbane but miscast Claude Rains. RKO gave Andrews sideburns and Carla Balenda as his leading lady, neither of which makes this film any more convincing. Despite some good action sequences, this is a long haul.

Dana Andrews *Pat Bannon* • Claude Rains *Skalder* • Carla Balenda *Margaret McLean* • Philip Dorn *Conrad* • Onslow Stevens *McLean* • Skip Homeier *Steve* • Eric Feldary *Holger* ■ *Dir* Alfred Werker • *Scr* Dale Van Every, Oliver HP Garrett, Roy Huggins, from the novel *The Gaunt Woman* by Edmund Gilligan

Seance on a Wet Afternoon ★★★

Drama 1964 · UK · BW · 115mins

Kim Stanley gives a compelling, Oscar-nominated performance as an unbalanced medium in this engrossing and imaginative drama. She orders her brow-beaten husband, Richard Attenborough, to kidnap a wealthy industrialist's daughter so she can enhance her reputation as a spiritualist by "finding" the youngster. The tension screws are chillingly turned when Attenborough realises his wife will go to any lengths to achieve celebrity status. Director Bryan Forbes skilfully conjures up suspenseful uncertainty as the ghastly implications of Stanley's plan unfold.

Kim Stanley *Myra Savage* • Richard Attenborough *Billy Savage* • Mark Eden *Charles Clayton* • Nanette Newman *Mrs Clayton* • Judith Donner *Amanda Clayton* • Patrick Magee *Supt Walsh* • Gerald Sim *Sergeant Beedle* ■ *Dir* Bryan Forbes • *Scr* Bryan Forbes, from the novel by Mark McShane

The Search ★★★★ U

Drama 1948 · US · BW · 103mins

Although Montgomery Clift had already made his first movie *Red River*, protracted delays kept that film off the screen until after *The Search* had premiered, giving movie-goers their first sight of the actor who was the forerunner of the Method style of acting. This semi-documentary won an Oscar for best motion picture story, but Clift largely improvised his own dialogue for his portrayal of a soldier in postwar Germany, who befriends a nine-year-old homeless boy. Clift gives a casual, unaffected performance, and Ivan Jandl, as the boy, was awarded a special juvenile Oscar.

Montgomery Clift *Ralph Stevenson* • Aline MacMahon *Mrs Murray* • Jarmila Novotna *Mrs Malik* • Wendell Corey *Jerry Fisher* • Ivan Jandl *Karel Malik* • Mary Patton *Mrs Fisher* • Ewart G Morrison *Mr Crookes* • William Rogers *Tom Fisher* ■ *Dir* Fred Zinnemann • *Scr* Richard Schweizer, David Wechsler, Paul Jarrico

Search and Destroy ★★ 15

Action drama 1978 · US · Colour · 89mins

This potboiler is indistinguishable from the hundreds of other movies that have been made for the lucrative and undemanding video market. The plot involves a Vietnamese officer who, after the war, seeks violent revenge against the American GIs who crossed him. You'd expect the likes of George Kennedy and Don Stroud to pop up in something like this: they do. ▭

Perry King *Kip Moore* • Don Stroud *Buddy Grant* • Tisa Farrow *Kate* • Park Jong Soo *Assassin* • George Kennedy *Anthony Fusqua* • Tony Sheer *Frank Malone* ■ *Dir* William Fruet • *Scr* Don Enright

Search and Destroy ★★ 18

Black comedy drama 1995 · US · Colour · 87mins

This hopelessly misconceived would-be black comedy was the disappointing debut feature from controversial New York visual artist David Salle. Griffin Dunne stars as a Florida film producer, his business and private life down the tubes, whose last throw of the dice is putting together a film deal with kooky TV guru Dennis Hopper. Salle has assembled a dream cast (Christopher Walken, John Turturro, Ethan Hawke, Martin Scorsese) that only partially redeems this poorly directed film, where almost every laugh seems forced and which relies too heavily on its weird assortment of characters and events to sustain the thin narrative. Contains swearing, nudity, sexual references and some violence. ▭

Griffin Dunne *Martin Mirkheim* • Illeana Douglas *Marie Davenport* • Christopher Walken *Kim Ulander* • Dennis Hopper *Dr Luther Waxling* • John Turturro *Ron* • Rosanna Arquette *Lauren Mirkheim* • Ethan Hawke *Roger* • Martin Scorsese *The accountant* ■ *Dir* David Salle • *Scr* Michael Almereyda, from the play by Howard Korder

Search and Rescue ★★

Action drama 1994 · US · Colour · 96mins

A decidedly cheesy slice of family entertainment focusing on a volunteer mountain rescue team led by Robert Conrad, which comes to the aid of a variety of injured or stranded people in and around the Sierra Mountains. Children and undemanding adults may lap up the *Boys' Own* heroics, but this relies too much on tired old formulae, while the performances and direction are studiously bland.

Robert Conrad • Dee Wallace Stone • Chad McQueen ■ *Dir* Paul Krasny • *Scr* George Schenk, Frank Cardea

Search for Grace ★★ 15

Drama 1994 · US · Colour · 89mins

Echoes of Kenneth Branagh's *Dead Again* can be heard throughout this TV movie in which a woman discovers that she's the reincarnated victim of an unsolved twenties' murder. If you took away the plot contrivances, the whole film would be over in a matter of minutes. Just sit back and admire the way Lisa Hartman Black and her co-stars ham to their hearts' content, as an idyllic romance turns into a murderous chase across time, culminating at Niagara Falls. ▭

Lisa Hartman Black *Ivy/Grace* • Ken Wahl *Jake/Johnny* • Don Michael Paul *Dave/Sam* • Richard Masur *Dr Randolph* • Suzzanne Douglas *Melody/Margaret* • Lori Lindberg *Dr Sanders* ■ *Dir* Sam Pillsbury • *Scr* Alex Ayres

Search for Justice ★★ PG

Crime thriller 1996 · US · Colour · 87mins

Peggy Lipton (*Twin Peaks*) takes a rare leading role in this passable drama that also stars *Hill Street Blues*'s Bruce Weitz. Suffering as only a TV-movie mother can, Lipton becomes convinced that it would take more than a broken marriage to drive her daughter to suicide. Yet the authorities seem reluctant to assist in her pursuit of the eccentric couple whom her daughter visited before her death. ▭

Peggy Lipton *Carol Mills* • Bruce Weitz *Detective McAdams* • Danica McKellar *Annie Mills Carman* • Terry David Mulligan *George Preston* • Gwynyth Walsh *Lydia Sawyer* • Teryl Rothery *Laura Kane* • Martin Cummins *Ken Carman* • Susan Ruttan *Helen Preston* ■ *Dir* Noel Nosseck • *Scr* Joyce Brotman

The Search for One-Eye Jimmy ★★

Comedy 1996 · US · Colour · 82mins

Holt McCallany is an aspiring film-maker who decides to shoot a movie documenting life in his own South Brooklyn neighbourhood. While conducting interviews with various colourful local characters he stumbles across a mystery – the disappearance of one of their number: "One-Eye" Jimmy. He's convinced his film will break him into the big time if he can follow (and solve) the mystery. A valiant low-budget attempt at character comedy with well-known faces in caricature roles – Steve Buscemi, Samuel L Jackson, John Turturro – it's too meandering for its own good.

Nick Turturro [Nicholas Turturro] *Junior* • Steve Buscemi *Ed Hoyt* • Michael Badalucco *Joe Head* • Ray "Boom Boom" Mancini [Ray Mancini] *Lefty* • Holt McCallany *Les* • Anne Meara *Holly Hoyt* • John Turturro *Disco Bean* • Samuel L Jackson *Colonel Ron* • Jennifer Beals *Ellen* • Tony Sirico *The Snake* ■ *Dir/Scr* Sam Henry Kass

The Search for Signs of Intelligent Life in the Universe ★★★

Comedy drama 1991 · US · Colour · 106 mins

The filmed version of comedian-turned-movie star Lily Tomlin's hit one-woman Broadway show. In the movie version, the bare stage is transformed with colourful sets to reflect the history of each individual, purposely breaking the seamless stand-up illusion. All of Tomlin's familiar characters do a turn: Trudy, the bag lady; Chrissy, the under-achiever; Kate, the socialite who values appearance and status; and Lyn, who's going through a mid-life crisis. It's a sustained monologue by Lyn – where all her sixties hippy and feminist revolutionary dreams are catalogued with despair – which ends this engrossing record of Tomlin's talent for accents and expert mimicry.

Lily Tomlin ■ *Dir* John Bailey • *Scr* Jane Wagner, from her play

The Searchers ★★★★★ U
Classic western 1956 · US · Colour · 113mins

Like Monument Valley, where it was filmed, John Ford's masterpiece western of revenge and reconciliation is massive and unmissable. It touches the heart of racist darkness and cleanses itself in the process. As John Wayne's Ethan sets out to kill both the "redskin" butcher of his brother's family and the abducted niece who, in his eyes, has turned native, his five-year quest becomes a search for his own soul. Jeffrey Hunter is the conscience along for the ride, but it's the complexity of Ethan – as the antihero being redeemed – that reveals him as a rootless pioneer, forever framed in the doorways of family homesteads of which he can never become part. Ford's great allegory is of a people lost and found. ▭ **DVD**

John Wayne *Ethan Edwards* • Jeffrey Hunter *Martin Pawley* • Natalie Wood *Debbie Edwards* • Vera Miles *Laurie Jorgensen* • Ward Bond *Sam Clayton* • John Qualen *Lars Jorgensen* • Olive Carey *Mrs Jorgensen* • Henry Brandon *Chief Scar* • Ken Curtis *Charlie McCorry* • Harry Carey Jr *Brad Jorgensen* ■ *Dir* John Ford • *Scr* Frank S Nugent, from the novel by Alan LeMay • *Cinematographer* Winton C Hoch

The Searching Wind ★★★
War drama 1946 · US · BW · 107mins

A high-toned – in both content and production – exploration of political and ideological issues as represented by an American career diplomat (Robert Young) of vacillating opinions. Set in the thirties, with the spectre of war hovering over it, the screenplay was written by Lillian Hellman from her own Broadway play, and is directed with suitable gravity by William Dieterle. It's well-played by Young, and an excellent cast that includes Sylvia Sidney as a hard-boiled but high-minded journalist and Young's sometime mistress. Interesting, literate material, but more suited to its stage origins than to the cinema.

Robert Young *Alex Hazen* • Sylvia Sidney *Cassie Bowman* • Ann Richards *Emily Hazen* • Douglas Dick *Sam* • Dudley Digges *Moses* • Albert Basserman *Count Von Stammer* • Dan Seymour *Torrone* ■ *Dir* William Dieterle • *Scr* Lillian Hellman, from her play

The Seashell and the Clergyman ★★★★
Silent experimental classic
1928 · Fr · BW · 29mins

Although dismissed by the Surrealist group at the time, this is generally accepted as the first Surrealist film. The cryptic scenario was written by Antonin Artaud, but the avant-garde theorist, writer and actor, who had intended to direct it and play the lead, later repudiated it – perhaps because it was directed by a woman. Germaine Dulac brought her technical skill to bear on the plotless film which shows, by automatic association, the dreams of a frustrated and celibate clergyman. An interesting, but fruitless attempt at "pure cinema", free from the influence of literature, the theatre and other visual arts. A French language film.

Alex Allin *The clergyman* • Génica Athanasiou *The woman* ■ *Dir* Germaine Dulac • *Scr* Antonin Artaud

Season of Dreams ★ PG
Drama 1987 · US · Colour · 90mins

A disappointing coming-of-age drama which milks the golden hues of rural America for all their worth but sinks under an uninvolving script. Megan Follows takes the lead as the troubled young teenager, but not even the presence of such charismatic performers as Christine Lahti, Frederic Forrest, Jason Gedrick and Peter Coyote can rescue this dud. Contains swearing. ▭

Christine Lahti *Kathleen Morgan* • Frederic Forrest *Buster McGuire* • Megan Follows *Anna Mae Morgan* • Jason Gedrick *Gary Connaloe* • Peter Coyote *Photographer* ■ *Dir* Martin Rosen • *Scr* Victoria Jenkins

Season of Fear ★
Thriller 1989 · US · Colour · 89mins

A young man visits his famous inventor father in the Midwestern heartland to rekindle their relationship after a 20-year estrangement and becomes romantically entangled with his sexy new stepmother. It all ends very badly with a shoot-out and much writhing in dirt. Completely fatuous and dragged out beyond belief, writer/director Doug Campbell's odd erotic thriller could almost pass as avant-garde because it's so confused and affected.

Michael Bowen *Mick Drummond* • Ray Wise *Fred Drummond* • Clancy Brown *Ward* • Clare Wren *Sarah Drummond* • Michael J Pollard *Bob* • Heather Jane MacDonald *Penny* • Dean Fortunato *David* ■ *Dir* Doug Campbell • *Scr* Doug Campbell, from a story by Scott J Mulvaney, Doug Campbell

Season of Passion ★★★
Romantic drama 1960 · Ausl · BW · 94mins

This willing Australian melodrama slowly creeps under the skin thanks to the fascinating contrasts in the acting styles of its star quartet. John Mills and Ernest Borgnine are cleverly cast as chalk and cheese sugar cane cutters in Sydney for their annual holiday, while Anne Baxter and Angela Lansbury are their feisty sheilas who refuse to tolerate their rough and ready notions of romance any longer. Director Leslie Norman wisely showcases the performances, but occasionally lets the authentic Aussie atmosphere slip.

Ernest Borgnine *Roo* • John Mills *Barney* • Anne Baxter *Olive* • Angela Lansbury *Pearl* • Vincent Ball *Dowd* • Ethel Gabriel *Emma* • Janette Craig *Bubba* ■ *Dir* Leslie Norman • *Scr* John Dighton, from the play *Summer of the Seventeenth Doll* by Ray Lawler

Sebastian ★★★
Comedy thriller 1968 · UK · Colour · 99mins

A semi-spoof of Swinging Sixties spy stories that ends up packing so much plot into the final third that its careful characterisation and smart satire go out of the window. The tensions within John Gielgud's eavesdropping unit are far more intriguing than spymaster Ronald Fraser's attempts to compromise codebuster Dirk Bogarde, and the cast seems more at ease with the knowing humour and hushed tones of this opening segment than it does with the blaring muzak and trippy dreams of the finale.

Dirk Bogarde *Sebastian* • Susannah York *Becky Howard* • Lilli Palmer *Elsa Shahn* • John Gielgud *Head of Intelligence* • Janet Munro *Carol* • Margaret Johnston *Miss Elliott* • Nigel Davenport *General Phillips* • Ronald Fraser *Toby* • Donald Sutherland *American* • Alan Freeman *TV disc jockey* ■ *Dir* David Greene • *Scr* Gerald Vaughan-Hughes, from a story by Leo Marks • *Music* Jerry Goldsmith

Sebastiane ★★ 18
Historical drama 1976 · UK · Colour · 81mins

Sebastian was a favourite at the court of Roman Emperor Diocletian and Derek Jarman's explicit biopic (co-directed by Paul Humfress) details his death at the hands of fellow soldiers while in naked exile. Shot on a semi-improvisational basis, with a largely non-professional cast, Jarman explores with frank honesty why Renaissance artists found this gay hero to be the perfect vehicle to depict homoeroticism in their paintings. Naturally, a must for gay viewers, but others may find it rather a hard slog. In Latin with English subtitles. ▭

Leonardo Treviglio *Sebastian* • Barney James *Severus* • Neil Kennedy *Max* • Richard Warwick *Justin* • Donald Dunham *Claudius* • Ken Hicks *Adrian* ■ *Dir* Derek Jarman, Paul Humfress • *Scr* Derek Jarman, James Waley, Jack Welch (Latin translation)

Second Best ★★★ 12
Drama 1994 · US · Colour · 100mins

This largely overlooked drama perfectly illustrates the genius for restraint that is the basis of William Hurt's acting talent. As the shy Welsh postmaster who decides to adopt a son, he brilliantly exposes the mixed emotions of a lonely, self-contained fortysomething trying to break with the habits of a lifetime and start anew. He's well supported by young Chris Cleary Miles and such familiar faces as John Hurt, Prunella Scales and Jane Horrocks. Director Chris Menges nearly loses control in the scenes featuring Miles's disturbed dad, Keith Allen, but mostly gets the tone right. Contains some violence and swearing ▭

William Hurt *Graham* • John Hurt *Uncle Turpin* • Chris Cleary Miles *James* • Nathan Yapp *Jimmy* • Keith Allen *John* • Jane Horrocks *Debbie* • Prunella Scales *Margery* ■ *Dir* Chris Menges • *Scr* David Cook, from his novel

Second Chance ★★★
Crime romance 1953 · US · Colour · 82mins

Originally shown in 3-D, this relies on the potency of its starpower, as laconic boxer Robert Mitchum falls for lovely gangster's moll Linda Darnell, who is on the run from killer Jack Palance. Director Rudolph Maté keeps this moving along, and the Mexican scenery is certainly striking. This is very much a product of RKO under its new boss Howard Hughes, featuring good-looking stars in exotic locations.

Robert Mitchum *Russ Lambert* • Linda Darnell *Clare Shepperd* • Jack Palance *Cappy Gordon* ■ *Dir* Rudolph Maté • *Scr* Oscar Millard, Sydney Boehm, DM Marshman Jr, from a story by DM Marshman Jr

Second Chance ★★★
Drama 1976 · Fr · Colour · 99mins

Charged as an accessory to murder, a young woman gives birth to a baby while in prison. Freed many years later, she is reunited with her teenage son, who falls in love with her friend from prison, while she herself finds happiness with the boy's teacher. This glossy, glamorised and superficial melodrama was written and directed by Claude Lelouch, stars Catherine Deneuve, with Anouk Aimée as her friend and features music by Francis Lai. Undemanding viewing for the romantically minded. In French with English subtitles.

Catherine Deneuve *Catherine Berger* • Anouk Aimée *Sarah Gordon* • Charles Denner *Lawyer* • Francis Huster *Patrick* • Niels Arestrup *Henri Lano* • Colette Baudot *Lucienne Lano* • Jean-Jacques Briot *Simon Berger* ■ *Dir/Scr* Claude Lelouch

Second Chance ★
Comedy 1995 · US · Colour

Cocoon meets *Big*, but without the budget, charm or expertise. Three scientists discover a drug that allows them to literally roll back the years; however, when they try it on themselves they go too far and turn into six-year-olds. The direction is ham-fisted and Arte Johnson, probably the best known name in the cast, really should have known better.

Richard Hatch • Cylk Cozart • George LePorte • Arte Johnson ■ *Dir/Scr* Lyman Dayton

Second Chorus ★★★ U
Musical comedy 1940 · US · BW · 84mins

Playing an undergraduate at the age of 41, Fred Astaire considered this the worst film he ever made. But an off-form Fred is still worth watching, even though his dancing style is undeniably cramped by Paulette Goddard, who is the subject of his romantic rivalry with Burgess Meredith. Goddard (then Mrs Charlie Chaplin) married Meredith in 1942. Artie Shaw earned an Oscar nomination for best score and shared another with Johnny Mercer for the song *Love of My Life*.

Fred Astaire *Danny O'Neill* • Paulette Goddard *Ellen Miller* • Burgess Meredith *Hank Taylor* • Charles Butterworth *Mr Chisholm* • Frank Melton *Stu* ■ *Dir* HC Potter • *Scr* Frank Cavett, Elaine Ryan, Johnny Mercer, Ian McLellan Hunter, from a story by Frank Cavett

The Second Civil War ★★★
Political satire 1997 · US · Colour · 97mins

America finds itself on the brink of another civil war when the US President (Phil Hartman) allows a group of refugee children to settle in Idaho. Governor Beau Bridges has other ideas and decides to close the state borders. Media frenzy escalates the conflict as the nation takes sides over the controversial issue. Bridges won an Emmy for his performance and he's well supported by James Coburn, Joanna Cassidy and James Earl Jones, in this wicked social satire.

Beau Bridges *Governor Jim Farley* • Joanna Cassidy *Helena Newman* • James Coburn *Jack Buchan* • Kevin Dunn *Jimmy Cannon* • Phil Hartman *The President* • Dan Hedaya *Mel Burgess* • James Earl Jones *Jim Calla* ■ *Dir* Joe Dante • *Scr* Martyn Burke

The Second Coming of Suzanne ★

Fantasy drama   1974 · US · Colour · 90mins

Pretentious blip in the early career of Richard Dreyfuss, made in between *American Graffiti* and *Jaws*. Dreyfuss plays a frustrated film-maker obsessed with the idea that Christ was a woman. He tries to film his vision, with Sondra Locke as the sex-swapped Messiah. Just about as bad as it sounds, the film was reportedly inspired by the lyrics of the Leonard Cohen song, *Suzanne*, which features on the soundtrack.

Sondra Locke *Suzanne* • Paul Sand *Artist* • Jared Martin *Film-maker* • Richard Dreyfuss *Clavius* • Gene Barry *TV commentator* ■ *Dir/Scr* Michael Barry

Second Fiddle ★★★ U

Musical comedy   1939 · US · BW · 86mins

You'd be forgiven if you couldn't tell one Sonja Henie vehicle from the next, but this is the one with the Irving Berlin score, where Tyrone Power plays the Hollywoodite who starts off promoting a romance for La Henie but, surprise, surprise, ends up falling for her himself. The 20th Century-Fox production values are all high gloss, and the ever-professional and under-rated director Sidney Lanfield keeps the fluffy proceedings running smoothly. Also on hand, for nostalgia buffs, are the delightful Rudy Vallee and Edna May Oliver.

Sonja Henie *Trudi Hovland* • Tyrone Power *Jimmy Sutton* • Rudy Vallee *Roger Maxwell* • Edna May Oliver *Aunt Phoebe Hovland* • Mary Healy *Jean Varick* • Lyle Talbot *Willie Hogger* • Alan Dinehart *George "Whit" Whitney* ■ *Dir* Sidney Lanfield • *Scr* Harry Tugend, from a story by George Bradshaw • *Music/Lyrics* Irving Berlin

The Second Jungle Book ★★ PG

Adventure   1997 · US · Colour · 85mins

Loosely based on the Rudyard Kipling original, and most definitely nothing to do with Disney, this live-action family film has jungle boy Mowgli and bear-friend Baloo driven deep into the interior by the unwanted attentions of a talent scout for PT Barnum's circus. There, they stumble on a lost city whose sole inhabitant is deranged British soldier Roddy McDowall. Inferior to other *Jungle Book* versions, this offers some fun for kids, but grown-ups will wonder why the animal sequences look like they've been spliced in from another film altogether. ▭

Jamie Williams *Mowgli* • William Campbell [Bill Campbell] *Harrison* • Roddy McDowall *King Murphy* • David Paul Francis *Chuchundra* • Dyrk Ashton *Karait* • Cornelia Hayes *O'Herlihy Emily Reece* ■ *Dir* Duncan McLachlan • *Scr* Matthew Horton, Bayard Johnson, from the books by Rudyard Kipling

Second Serve ★★★★ 15

Drama   1986 · US · Colour · 90mins

On paper it has all the signs of a tacky hagiography, but a towering performance from Vanessa Redgrave and a taut, insightful script make this a TV movie of unusual depth and sensitivity. The true story of transsexual surgeon-turned-tennis star

Renee Richards, based closely on her autobiography, is adapted by director Anthony Page into an intriguing, multi-layered look at the agonies and resourcefulness of a truly extraordinary personality. But this is ultimately Redgrave's film and she plays both Richards's male and female personae wonderfully.

Vanessa Redgrave *Richard Radley/Renee Richards* • Martin Balsam *Dr Stone* • William Russ *Josh* • Alice Krige *Gwen* • Kerrie Keane *Meriam* ■ *Dir* Anthony Page • *Scr* Stephanie Liss, Gavin Lambert, from the non-fiction book by Renee Richards, John Ames

Second Sight ★★ PG

Comedy   1989 · US · Colour · 80mins

Few would give this lame cop comedy a second glance. It's one of those "everything but the kitchen sink" movies that throws in any plot device it can think of, the most prominent of which is partnering ex-cop John Larroquette and psychic Bronson Pinchot as dumb detectives in search of laughs. Larroquette's finest movie hour to date is probably his uncredited narration of *The Texas Chain Saw Massacre*. Here he once again fails to set the big screen alight. ▭

John Larroquette *Willis* • Bronson Pinchot *Bobby* • Bess Armstrong *Sister Elizabeth* • Stuart Pankin *Dr Preston Pickett* • John Schuck *Manoogian* ■ *Dir* Joel Zwick • *Scr* Tom Schulman, Patricia Resnick

Second Thoughts ★ 15

Melodrama   1982 · US · Colour · 93mins

Second thoughts are what you should have before deciding to view this turkey. Lucie Arnaz (Lucille Ball for mum and Desi Arnaz for dad) is Amy, a bored attorney who swaps her stuffy hubby for a hippy misfit (Craig Wasson) in an attempt to spice up her life. The relationship founders but not before Amy gets pregnant. From there on the film descends into a right-to-life debate that is neither informative nor insightful. Unpleasant. ▭

Lucie Arnaz *Amy Ash* • Craig Wasson *Will Thorson* • Ken Howard *John Michael Tombs* • Anne Schedeen *Janis* • Arthur Rosenberg *Dr Eastman* • Peggy McCay *Dr Martha Carpenter* • Joe Mantegna *Orderly* ■ *Dir* Lawrence Turman • *Scr* Steve Brown, from a story by Terry Louise Fisher, Steve Brown

The Second Time Around ★★ U

Comedy western   1961 · US · Colour · 98mins

Debbie Reynolds stars as a young widow from the east who moves to an Arizona frontier town to start life afresh. Unfazed by the culture shock, she labours in the mud as a humble ranch-hand (for the always admirable Thelma Ritter) before becoming sheriff and ridding the town of its lawless elements. The spirited Reynolds is the attraction of this innocuous but pleasant movie, which can't decide whether it's a western, a comedy, a romance or a drama. Steve Forrest supplies romantic interest, and Juliet Prowse is a dance hall girl who performs a flamenco number.

Debbie Reynolds *Lucretia Rogers* • Steve Forrest *Dan Jones* • Andy Griffith *Pat Collins* • Juliet Prowse *Rena* • Thelma Ritter *Aggie* • Ken Scott *Sheriff John Yoss* • Isobel Elsom

Mrs Rogers ■ *Dir* Vincent Sherman • *Scr* Oscar Saul, Cecil Dan Hansen, from the novel *Star in the West* by Richard Emery Roberts

The Second Victory ★★ 15

Drama   1986 · UK · Colour · 98mins

Adapted from his own novel by Morris West, this is a drama set in Austria shortly after the Second World War. Anthony Andrews is the bold soldier in pursuit of the sniper who shot and killed his sergeant. From thereon in, it's strictly action fare, with Andrews looking ill-at-ease, having to tote a gun and look vengeful at the same time. Nice scenery, though. ▭

Anthony Andrews *Major Hanlon* • Max von Sydow *Dr Huber* • Helmut Griem *Karl Fischer* • Mario Adorf *Dr Sepp Kunzli* • Birgit Doll *Anna Kunzli* • Wolfgang Reichmann *Max Holzinger* • Renée Soutendijk *Traudi Holzinger* • Immy Schell *Liesl Holzinger* ■ *Dir* Gerald Thomas • *Scr* Morris West, from his novel

The Second Woman ★★

Thriller   1951 · US · BW · 91mins

This minor melodrama explains why Robert Young's architect suffers from blackouts and memory loss and is driven to attempt suicide. More usually it's a female who is being victimised in the psychological thrillers of this period, but here it's girlfriend Betsy Drake who exposes the villain who is out to deprive Young of his sanity. The best feature is the photography by Hal Mohr, which aims at a *film noir* moodiness. Morris Carnovksy makes one of his last appearances before being blacklisted.

Robert Young *Jeff Cohalan* • Betsy Drake *Ellen Foster* • John Sutton *Keith Ferris* • Henry O'Neill *Ben Sheppard* • Florence Bates *Amelia Foster* • Morris Carnovsky *Dr Hartley* ■ *Dir* James V Kern • *Scr* Robert Smith, Mort Briskin

Seconds ★★★★

Science-fiction thriller
1966 · US · BW · 105mins

An absolutely brilliant social science-fiction movie that's years ahead of its time in both theme and style, it deals with the uncomfortable subject of spiritual rebirth. As elderly businessman Mr Hamilton, John Randolph – a blacklisted actor – is transmuted into Tony Wilson, a deeply uncomfortable Rock Hudson, in one of this under-rated screen actor's finest performances. This was X-rated on original release, its deeply frightening premise intensified by the stark black-and-white photography and use of distorting fisheye lenses of ace cameraman James Wong Howe. One of John Frankenheimer's best movies, which established him as a seminal sixties American director.

Rock Hudson *Antiochus "Tony" Wilson* • Salome Jens *Nora Marcus* • John Randolph *Arthur Hamilton* • Will Geer *Old man* • Jeff Corey *Mr Ruby* • Richard Anderson *Dr Innes* ■ *Dir* John Frankenheimer • *Scr* Lewis John Carlino, from the novel by David Ely

The Secret ★★

Drama   1992 · US · Colour · 92mins

Screen legend Kirk Douglas gives a human face to a little-understood affliction in this generational family drama. After a lifetime of struggle to

keep his dyslexia a secret, an old man must now confront his problem in order to help his grandson (Jesse R Tendler), who has been diagnosed with the same learning disorder. Sentimentality teeters on the edge of bathos, but rough-hewn old-pro Douglas does manage to add some much-needed grit to what is otherwise just another predictable problem-of-the-week TV movie.

Kirk Douglas *Mike Dunmore* • Brock Peters *Thurgood Carver III* • Bruce Boxleitner *Patrick Dunmore* • Laura Harrington *Meredith Dunmore* • Jesse R Tendler *Danny Dunmore* • Anne Twomey *Dr Meyers* ■ *Dir* Karen Arthur • *Scr* Cynthia A Cherbak

Secret Admirer ★ 15

Comedy   1985 · US · Colour · 93mins

An unsigned love letter leads the unwary into a repulsive comedy of errors that verges on the insulting to both teenagers and adults alike. Fred Ward and Dee Wallace Stone do what they can as the parents and C Thomas Howell and Lori Loughlin try to elevate it above the level of farcical teen-sex comedy but ultimately fail. ▭

C Thomas Howell *Michael Ryan* • Lori Loughlin *Toni* • Kelly Preston *Deborah Anne Fimple* • Dee Wallace Stone *Connie Ryan* • Cliff De Young *George Ryan* • Fred Ward *Lou Fimple* • Leigh Taylor-Young *Elizabeth Fimple* • Casey Siemaszko *Roger Despard* ■ *Dir* David Greenwalt • *Scr* Jim Kouf, David Greenwalt

The Secret Adventures of Tom Thumb ★★ 12

Animated fantasy 1993 · UK · Colour · 57mins

An adult animated version of the Grimm tale that you won't be taking the kids to. Into a surreal landscape of mutants and insects is born poor Tom. His parents fail to protect him from kidnappers who conduct a series of bizarre medical experiments on our hero. Escaping, Tom befriends a giant who inadvertently kills him, releasing him into an afterlife that is not harps, clouds and angels. Director Dave Borthwick's ten-minute short has been expanded into a full length feature but not everyone will enjoy his nightmarish vision. ▭

Nick Upton *Pa Thumb* • Deborah Collard *Ma Thumb* • Frank Passingham *Man/Giant* • John Schofield *Man/Giant* ■ *Dir/Scr* Dave Borthwick

Secret Agent ★★★★ U

Spy thriller   1936 · UK · BW · 82mins

John Gielgud might not be everyone's ideal Hitchcock hero, and contemporary critics were quick to point out his lack of derring-do, but, in fact, he acquits himself admirably in this engaging thriller. The script has more than its fair share of loose ends, but such is the committed playing, particularly by Robert Young and the amazing Peter Lorre, and the director's genius for generating suspense out of ordinary situations and locations, that they scarcely seem to matter. ▭

John Gielgud *Edgar Brodie/Richard Ashenden* • Madeleine Carroll *Elsa Carrington* • Peter Lorre *The General* • Robert Young *Robert Marvin* • Percy Marmont *Caypor* • Florence Kahn *Mrs Caypor* • Lilli Palmer *Lilli* ■ *Dir* Alfred Hitchcock • *Scr* Charles Bennett, Ian

Hay, Jesse Lasky Jr, Alma Reville, from the play by Campbell Dixon, from the stories by W Somerset Maugham

The Secret Agent ★★12

Period spy thriller
1996 · US/UK · Colour · 90mins

A dull adaptation of Joseph Conrad's novel, despite the presence of Bob Hoskins and Patricia Arquette. He plays Adolph Verloc, an anarchist living in London at the end of the 19th century, who becomes involved in a terrorist attack on the Greenwich Observatory. Writer/director Christopher Hampton's film never really gets off the ground, despite a good performance from Arquette as Verloc's wife, and a supporting cast that includes Christian Bale (as her mentally-disabled brother), Gérard Depardieu, Jim Broadbent and an uncredited Robin Williams as an explosives expert. Contains some swearing and violence.

Bob Hoskins *Adolph Verloc* • Patricia Arquette *Winnie Verloc* • Gérard Depardieu *Tom "Alexander" Ossipon* • Jim Broadbent *Chief Inspector Heat* • Christian Bale *Stevie Verloc* • Eddie Izzard *Vladimir* • Elizabeth Spriggs *Winnie's mother* • Peter Vaughan *The driver* • Robin Williams *The professor* ■ *Dir* Christopher Hampton • *Scr* Christopher Hampton, from the novel by Joseph Conrad

The Secret Agent Club ★PG

Action comedy   1995 · US · Colour · 86mins

Hulk Hogan briefly becomes charming as his secret agent character returns to his civilian disguise as a nerdy single father. Then he's kidnapped by arms dealers, and spends most of the movie under sedation. His young son gets his friends to help track down and spring his father, dodging bullets and killers while having a jolly good time. Reprehensible in its attitude towards violence while children are present, this also contains blatant racist stereotypes. It's a pity the audience couldn't be as unconscious as Hogan was throughout this travesty. **DVD**

Hulk Hogan *Ray* • Lesley-Anne Down *Eve* • Barry Bostwick *Vincent Scarletti* • Mathew McCurley *Jeremy* • Edward Albert *Max* • Richard Moll *Wrecks* • Lyman Ward *SHADOW General* • Jack Nance *Doc* ■ *Dir* John Murlowski • *Scr* Rory Johnston

A Secret between Friends ★★

Drama   1996 · US · Colour

Lynda Carter (*Wonder Woman*) stars in this well-directed "disease of the week" TV movie as a recently divorced mother confronted by an all-too-common disorder in her family. Her teenage daughter befriends a popular but secretly bulimic girl at her new high school, resulting in a secret weight loss pact that costs the popular girl her life and involves the other in an almost fatal battle with the disease. Carter gives a solid turn as the concerned mother.

Lynda Carter *Kathryn Archer* • Katie Wright *Lexi Archer* • Marley Shelton *Jennifer* • Josh Taylor *Peter Archer* ■ *Dir* James A Contner • *Scr* Elizabeth Gill

Secret beyond the Door ★★PG

Thriller melodrama   1948 · US · BW · 93mins

A woman marries an architect whose house contains his painstaking re-creations of rooms in which brutal murders were committed. Furthermore, there's a first wife she never knew about and a jealous secretary. The echoes of Hitchcock's *Rebecca* attracted director Fritz Lang to the project, his third collaboration with Joan Bennett after *The Woman in the Window* and *Scarlet Street*. It is visually accomplished but, with Michael Redgrave lacking any romantic appeal as the architect, a complicated flashback structure and a climax that combines lurid melodrama with Freudian explanations, the result is heavy going and pretentious.

Joan Bennett *Celia Lamphere* • Michael Redgrave *Mark Lamphere* • Anne Revere *Caroline Lamphere* • Barbara O'Neil *Miss Robey* • Natalie Schafer *Edith Potter* • Paul Cavanagh *Rick Barrett* ■ *Dir* Fritz Lang • *Scr* Silvia Richards, from the story *Museum Piece No.13* by Rufus King

The Secret Bride ★

Political drama   1934 · US · BW · 76mins

Attorney general Warren William and governor's daughter Barbara Stanwyck marry in secret but, about to break the happy news to her father, they learn that he is to be impeached for taking a bribe. A nonsensical farrago involving political corruption, murder and a frame-up, typical of the kind of rubbish the peerless Stanwyck was so often forced to endure. Even she can't rise above the comically bad dialogue and unbelievable plot.

Barbara Stanwyck *Ruth Vincent* • Warren William *Robert Sheldon* • Glenda Farrell *Hazel Normandie* • Grant Mitchell *Willie Martin* • Arthur Byron *Gov Vincent* • Henry O'Neill *Jim Lansdale* • Douglass Dumbrille *Dave Breedeen* ■ *Dir* William Dieterle • *Scr* Tom Buckingham, F Hugh Herbert, Mary McCall Jr, from a play by Leonard Ide

Secret Ceremony ★★

Drama   1969 · US · Colour · 109mins

A typically bitter, twisted and pretentious morality tale from cerebral director Joseph Losey. This moody mistaken-identity melodrama quickly becomes a macabre muddle of daft sexual psychosis and suspect psychology when nympho Mia Farrow adopts prostitute Elizabeth Taylor as her surrogate mother after a meeting on a London bus. The return of Farrow's stepfather Robert Mitchum provides this meandering morsel of Swinging Sixties Gothic with a suitably off-the-wall climax.

Elizabeth Taylor *Leonora* • Mia Farrow *Cenci* • Robert Mitchum *Albert* • Peggy Ashcroft *Hannah* • Pamela Brown *Hilda* • Michael Strong *Dr Walter Stevens* • Robert Douglas *Sir Alex Gordon* ■ *Dir* Joseph Losey • *Scr* George Tabori, from the short story *Ceremonia Secreta* by Marco Denevi

Secret Command ★★

Second World War spy drama
1944 · US · BW · 81mins

Pat O'Brien is a naval intelligence agent who goes undercover to prevent a Nazi sabotage operation. Chester Morris runs the shipyard under threat, and since he happens to be O'Brien's brother, he's understandably bewildered by O'Brien's sudden arrival with a wife and two children in tow. In fact, the FBI have drafted in another agent, Carole Landis, to play O'Brien's imaginary wife. You can guess what happens to them in between all the fist fights and propaganda.

Pat O'Brien *Sam Gallagher* • Carole Landis *Jill McCann* • Chester Morris *Jeff Gallagher* • Ruth Warrick *Lea Damaron* • Barton MacLane *Red Kelly* • Tom Tully *Brownell* • Wallace Ford *Miller* • Howard Freeman *Max Lessing* ■ *Dir* A Edward Sutherland • *Scr* Roy Chanslor, from the story *The Saboteurs* by John Hawkins, Ward Hawkins

Secret Defense ★★★PG

Mystery drama
1997 · Fr/Swi/It · Colour · 173mins

Jacques Rivette continues his career-long preoccupation with the nature of real-screen time and the concept of plot as conspiracy in this leisurely, but still intriguing anti-thriller. Investigating the murder of her father, scientist Sandrine Bonnaire becomes embroiled in a cover-up of her own after an accidental shooting. With a subplot involving the mysterious death of Bonnaire's sister (Laure Marsac, who also plays the woman Bonnaire kills), this is more a study of motives, methods and responses than a tension-packed nailbiter, but it still exercises a slow-burning fascination. In French with English subtitles.

Sandrine Bonnaire *Sylvie Rousseau* • Jerzy Radziwilowicz *Walser* • Laure Marsac *Véronique Lukachevski/Ludivine Lukachevski* • Grégoire Colin *Paul Rousseau* ■ *Dir* Jacques Rivette • *Scr* Jacques Rivette, Pascal Bonitzer, Emmanuelle Cuau

The Secret Diary of Sigmund Freud ★

Comedy   1984 · US · Colour · 99mins

A game cult cast waste their collective energies in this painful comedy based on the early life and psychoanalytical theories of Doctor Sigmund Freud, performed by Bud Cort in his typical deadpan manner. *Baby Doll* Carroll Baker plays his mother, Klaus Kinski the doctor she has an affair with, and Carol Kane his lisping nurse. Each are primarily there to take turns at being the butt of pretty pathetic gags covering the expected Freudian spectrum. Comedian Dick Shawn puts in a marvellous turn, but the lethargic pace and annoying script are enough to put anyone in therapy.

Bud Cort *Sigmund Freud* • Carol Kane *Martha Bernays* • Klaus Kinski *Dr Max Bauer* • Marisa Berenson *Emma Herrmann* • Carroll Baker *Mama Freud* • Dick Shawn *Ultimate patient* • Ferdy Mayne *Herr Herrmann* ■ *Dir* Danford B Greene • *Scr* Roberto Mitrotti, Linda Howard

Secret Friends ★★★15

Fantasy drama
1991 · UK/US · Colour · 93mins

Dennis Potter was one of Britain's greatest TV playwrights, but this directorial debut – an adaptation of his novel, *Ticket to Ride* – is an embittered mess about sex ("a bloody hoot ") and the violent impulses that drive his hero John (Alan Bates) to amnesia and beyond, with Gina Bellman as the sexual catalyst. Compelling enough, but the love-making is sleazy and the intercutting flashbacks make an already muddled narrative even more murky.

Alan Bates *John* • Gina Bellman *Helen* • Frances Barber *Angela* • Tony Doyle *Martin* • Joanna David *Kate* • Colin Jeavons *Vicar* ■ *Dir* Dennis Potter • *Scr* Dennis Potter, from his novel *Ticket to Ride*

Secret Games ★★18

Erotic thriller   1992 · US · Colour · 92mins

Michelle Brin is haunted by her Catholic school upbringing, and she is unhappy with her married life to a successful real estate developer Billy Drago. So obviously, the best remedy for her problems is to become a high-priced call girl specialising in kinky sex with millionaires! So goes the male fantasy logic in this erotic thriller. Brin is a better actress than most of the people who star in this kind of film, and you have to give some credit for being ambitious enough to rip-off Buñuel's *Belle de Jour*. Contains nudity and sex scenes.

Martin Hewitt *Eric* • Michelle Brin *Julianne* • Billy Drago *Mark Langford* • Delia Sheppard *Celeste* ■ *Dir* Gregory Hippolyte • *Scr* Georges Des Esseintes

The Secret Garden ★★★U

Drama   1949 · US · BW and Colour · 88mins

Compared with Agnieszka Holland's magnificent 1993 adaptation, some may find this MGM version of Frances Hodgson Burnett's delightful children's classic deeply disappointing. Although mounted on an equally lavish scale, it simply cannot compete in terms of performance. But Margaret O'Brien makes a spirited Mary Lennox, the orphan whose mischievous optimism brightens up life at her morbid uncle's mansion, and Elsa Lanchester is typically splendid as the kindly maid. But Gladys Cooper overdoes the tyranny as the housekeeper and Herbert Marshall is a damp squib as the grieving uncle.

Margaret O'Brien *Mary Lennox* • Herbert Marshall *Archibald Craven* • Dean Stockwell *Colin Craven* • Gladys Cooper *Mrs Medlock* • Elsa Lanchester *Martha* • Brian Roper *Dickon* • Reginald Owen *Ben Weatherstaff* ■ *Dir* Fred M Wilcox • *Scr* Robert Ardrey, from the novel by Frances Hodgson Burnett

The Secret Garden ★★★

Drama   1987 · US · Colour · 100mins

Fine performances and an opulent production distinguish this TV film of Frances Hodgson Burnett's classic children's novel. In Victorian England, a spoiled little orphan girl (Gennie James), now living with her nasty uncle, stumbles upon an enchanted garden on their eerie estate, which transforms her life and those of the people around her. Alan Grint's perceptive direction and veteran British stage actors Derek Jacobi and Michael Hordern fill this timeless tale with warmth, humour and wonder.

Gennie James *Mary Lennox* • Michael Hordern *Ben* • Billie Whitelaw *Mrs Medlock* • Derek Jacobi *Archibald Craven* • Jadrien Steele *Colin Craven* • Barret Oliver *Dickon Sowerby* • Colin Firth *Adult Colin* • Julian Glover *Col McGraw* •

U = SUITABLE FOR ALL   Uc = SUITABLE FOR ALL, ESPECIALLY FOR YOUNG CHILDREN (VIDEO ONLY)   PG = PARENTAL GUIDANCE

Lucy Gutteridge *Mrs Lennox* ■ *Dir* Alan Grint • *Scr* Blanche Hanalis, from the novel by Frances Hodgson Burnett

The Secret Garden ★★★★ U

Drama   1993 · US · Colour · 97mins

Originally filmed in 1949, Frances Hodgson Burnett's enchanting children's classic is given a new lease of life in this imaginative adaptation by Polish film-maker Agnieszka Holland. Always a skilled director of children, she draws a spirited performance out of Kate Maberly as the orphan who sweeps away the cobwebs from Misselthwaite Manor. Scripted by Caroline Thompson – who wrote *Edward Scissorhands* – the film retains the gothic atmosphere of the book and looks amazing, thanks to Roger Deakins's photography. Stealing the show is Maggie Smith as the beastly housekeeper. ▭ **DVD**

Kate Maberly *Mary Lennox* • Heydon Prowse *Colin Craven* • Andrew Knott *Dickon* • Maggie Smith *Mrs Medlock* • Laura Crossley *Martha* • John Lynch *Lord Craven* • Walter Sparrow *Ben Weatherstaff* • Irène Jacob *Mary's mother/ Lilas Craven* ■ *Dir* Agnieszka Holland • *Scr* Caroline Thompson, from the novel by Frances Hodgson Burnett

The Secret Heart ★★

Drama   1946 · US · BW · 96mins

Widowed by the suicide of the alcoholic husband she married and in spite of loving another man (Walter Pidgeon), Claudette Colbert has devotedly cared for her stepchildren. Now she faces problems with her psychologically traumatised stepdaughter June Allyson. Robert Z Leonard directs this attempt to make a serious domestic drama out of a soap opera, but the material stubbornly refuses to budge. However, the inimitable Colbert and the polished Pidgeon ensure audience involvement in a plot whose outcome is obvious after 15 minutes.

Claudette Colbert *Lee Addams* • Walter Pidgeon *Chris Matthews* • June Allyson *Penny Addams* • Lionel Barrymore *Dr Rossiger* • Robert Sterling *Chase Addams Jr* • Marshall Thompson *Brandon Reynolds* • Elizabeth Patterson *Mrs Stover* • Richard Derr *Larry Addams Sr* ■ *Dir* Robert Z Leonard • *Scr* Whitfield Cook, Anne Morrison Chapin, Rose Franken, from a story by Rose Franken, William Brown Meloney

Secret Honor ★★★★ 15

Biographical political drama
1984 · US · Colour · 86mins

Maverick director Robert Altman's stunning portrayal of a drunken President Richard Milhous Nixon features Philip Baker Hall as Tricky Dicky. Set after his ignominious resignation, he rants and raves about his contemporaries in his White House study, comparing his "secret honour with his public shame". Altman's prowling camera keeps this one-character drama cinematic and on its toes, and ensures that the man's insane, bigoted mediocrity has a certain vivid poignancy. ▭

Philip Baker Hall *Richard M Nixon* ■ *Dir* Robert Altman • *Scr* Donald Freed, Arnold M Stone, from the play *Secret Honor, The Last Will and Testament of Richard M Nixon* by Donald Freed

The Secret Invasion ★★ PG

Second World War action drama
1964 · US · Colour · 93mins

Cult director Roger Corman's snappily-paced action/adventure bears a strikingly similarity to *The Dirty Dozen* – but lacks the powerhouse cast. British Intelligence officer Stewart Granger leads five hardened criminals into Dubrovnik during the Second World War to rescue an Italian general from the Nazis. Although cheaply produced, the veteran cast (including *77 Sunset Strip*'s Edd "Kookie" Byrnes) wring every ounce of conviction from a routine script. ▭

Stewart Granger *Maj Richard Mace* • Raf Vallone *Roberto Rocca* • Mickey Rooney *Terence Scanlon* • Edd Byrnes *Simon Fell* • Henry Silva *John Durrell* • Mia Massini *Mila* • William Campbell *Jean Saval* ■ *Dir* Roger Corman • *Scr* R Wright Campbell

The Secret Laughter of Women ★★ 15

Romantic comedy
1998 · UK/Can · Colour · 95mins

There's little love and even less humour in this stiffly staged Riviera story of a Nigerian single mother's encounter with an exiled English writer of comic books. Nia Long struggles to suppress her American accent as the former, while Colin Firth mistakes monotone for laconicism as the latter. Even less well-defined is the ex-pat community that tries to force Long into marrying pontificating preacher, Ariyon Bakare.

Colin Firth *Matthew Field* • Nia Long *Nimi Da Silva, "Big Eyes"* • Dan Lett *John* • Joke Silva *Nene* • Ariyon Bakare *Reverend Fola* ■ *Dir* Peter Schwabach • *Scr* OO Sagay

The Secret Life of an American Wife ★★

Comedy   1968 · US · Colour · 92mins

Now, here's a few interesting connections: George Axelrod wrote *The Seven Year Itch* which Billy Wilder directed and which almost starred Walter Matthau. Then Wilder made *Kiss Me, Stupid*, a rasping comedy in which a housewife and a hooker swap roles in order to charm a recording star. Here, Anne Jackson plays a housewife who, thinking she's lost her sexual charm, impersonates a hooker and sets out to seduce a big movie star, Matthau – whose agent happens to be Jackson's husband. While the playing is a constant delight, the sets are like amateur rep and the dialogue, thought to be very risqué in 1968, will seem very dated indeed.

Walter Matthau *The Movie Star* • Anne Jackson *Victoria Layton* • Patrick O'Neal *Tom Layton* • Edy Williams *Suzie Steinberg* • Richard Bull *Howard* • Paul Napier *Herb Steinberg* • Gary Brown *Jimmy* • Albert Carrier *Jean-Claude* ■ *Dir/Scr* George Axelrod

The Secret Life of Kathy McCormick ★★★

Romantic comedy
1988 · US · Colour · 96mins

Barbara Eden (*I Dream of Jeannie*) turns on the charm as a supermarket worker whose brief entry into high society results in a whirlwind romance with a well-heeled beau who has no idea of her true identity. Known as both *Happily Ever After* and *The Secret Life of Marlene MacFadden* in its earlier incarnations, this cheerful Cinderella story also provides a decent supporting role for Judy Geeson.

Barbara Eden *Kathy McCormick* • Josh Taylor *Grant Sherwood* • Robert Costanzo *Sid Thompson* • Judith-Marie Bergan *Janice* • Jenny O'Hara *Lisa Mason* • Judy Geeson *Babs* ■ *Dir* Robert Lewis • *Scr* Jim Brecher, from a story by Gloria Goldsmith

The Secret Life of Walter Mitty ★★★★ U

Comedy   1947 · US · Colour · 105mins

James Thurber's short story becomes a marvellous Technicolored cavalcade for Danny Kaye, who plays both the daydreaming Mitty and the amazingly heroic characters of his fantasies. Kaye's on top form here, as a surgeon performing a near-impossible operation, an ace gunslinger (the "Perth Amboy Kid") and a pernickety RAF pilot, among others. The energetic star is not so popular today, but this is generally acknowledged to be his finest screen performance and is certainly his most endearing. There's marvellous support from the great Boris Karloff as a homicidal psychiatrist, while future director Robert Altman is an extra in the *Symphony for Unstrung Tongues* number. ▭

Danny Kaye *Walter Mitty* • Virginia Mayo *Rosalind van Hoorn* • Boris Karloff *Dr Hugo Hollingshead* • Fay Bainter *Mrs Mitty* • Ann Rutherford *Gertrude Griswold* • Thurston Hall *Bruce Pierce* • Konstantin Shayne *Peter van Hoorn* • Florence Bates *Mrs Griswold* • Gordon Jones *Tubby Wadsworth* • Reginald Denny *RAF colonel* ■ *Dir* Norman Z McLeod • *Scr* Ken Englund, Everett Freeman, from the story by James Thurber

The Secret Mark of D'Artagnan ★★ U

Adventure   1962 · Fr/It · Colour · 92mins

Yet another from the Musketeers industry, this time from Italy with American actor George Nader sword-fighting against those would do do down Louis XIII and Richelieu. The plot is several blades short of a scabbard, but director Siro Marcellini moves it at enough of a pace to cover that inadequacy. French/Italian dialogue dubbed into English.

George Nader *D'Artagnan* • Magali Noel *Carlotta, maid* • Georges Marchal *Duke of Montserant* • Mario Petri *Porthos* • Alessandra Panaro *Diana* • Massimo Serato *Cardinal Richelieu* ■ *Dir* Siro Marcellini • *Scr* Ottario Poggi, Milton Krims, Siro Marcellini, from characters created by Alexandre Dumas

Secret Mission ★★ U

Second World War spy drama
1942 · UK · BW · 89mins

It's hard to see how this flag-waver could have raised anyone's spirits during the darkest days of the Second World War. There's a modicum of excitement in the attempt by Michael Wilding, Hugh Williams and Roland Culver, along with their French guide James Mason, to glean information about Nazi invasion plans. But the comic subplot involving Wilding and his French wife, and the romance that develops between Williams and Mason's sister (Carla Lehmann), are embarrassing. Credit to director Harold French for keeping the pace brisk, but this is unremarkable fare. ▭

Hugh Williams *Peter Garnett* • Carla Lehmann *Michele de Carnot* • James Mason *Raoul de Carnot* • Roland Culver *Red Gowan* • Michael Wilding *Nobby Clark* • Nancy Price *Violette* • Herbert Lom *Medical officer* • Stewart Granger *Sublieutenant Jackson* ■ *Dir* Harold French • *Scr* Anatole de Grunwald, Basil Bartlett, from a story by Shaun Terence Young

The Secret Nation ★★★★

Drama   1989 · Bol · Colour · 125mins

Although the theme of this remarkable study in existential angst is atonement, Jorge Sanjines is also keen to highlight the marginalisation of Bolivia's indigenous Aymara peoples, who have been consigned to shanties on the edge of the major cities by the European descendants, who continue to resist full national integration. Recalling Miklos Jancso with his use of lingering long takes, Sanjines employs a flashback structure to explain why Reynaldo Yujra, a man whose life has been one long act of betrayal, is returning to his village on the altiplano to perform a ritual cleansing dance that will end in his death. In Bolivian dialect with English subtitles.

Reynaldo Yujra *Sebastian* • Delfina Mamani *Basilia* • Orlando Huanca *Vicente* • Roque Salgado *Clarividente* ■ *Dir* Jorge Sanjines

The Secret of Blood Island ★★

Second World War drama
1964 · UK · Colour · 83mins

Secret agent Barbara Shelley has to go into hiding after her plane is shot down on a Japanese-occupied island during the Second World War. A lurid but fairly enjoyable jungle-bound war movie from Quentin Lawrence, director of *The Trollenberg Terror*.

Barbara Shelley *Elaine* • Jack Hedley *Sergeant Crewe* • Charles Tingwell *Major Dryden* • Bill Owen *Bludgin* • Peter Welch *Richardson* • Lee Montague *Levy* ■ *Dir* Quentin Lawrence • *Scr* John Gilling

The Secret of Convict Lake ★★

Western   1951 · US · BW · 83mins

In this routine melodrama set in 19th-century California, escaped prisoners take over a town populated just by women, while the menfolk are away prospecting. The studio boosted the hackneyed plot by putting in top-class players such as Glenn Ford, Gene Tierney, Ethel Barrymore and Zachary Scott, and their presence helps make the rather predictable scenario much more enjoyable.

Glenn Ford *Canfield* • Gene Tierney *Marcia Stoddard* • Ethel Barrymore *Granny* • Zachary Scott *Greer* • Ann Dvorak *Rachel* • Barbara Bates *Barbara Purcell* • Cyril Cusack *Limey* ■ *Dir* Michael Gordon • *Scr* Oscar Saul, Victor Trivas, from a story by Anna Hunger, Jack Pollexfen

---

The Secret of Dr Kildare
★★★

Medical drama   1939 · US · BW · 84mins

The relationship between Lew Ayres's idealistic young Dr Kildare and Lionel Barrymore's curmudgeonly old Dr Gillespie was beginning to mature in the third of MGM's popular series. Kildare, concerned for Gillespie's health, tries to get his superior to take a holiday. At the same time, he manages to cure a woman with psychosomatic blindness. All the regulars are on hand, including nurse Mary Lamont (Laraine Day), who provides Kildare with some romance.

Lew Ayres _Dr James Kildare_ • Lionel Barrymore _Dr Leonard Gillespie_ • Lionel Atwill _Paul Messenger_ • Laraine Day _Mary Lamont_ • Helen Gilbert _Nancy Messenger_ • Nat Pendleton _Joe Wayman_ • Sara Haden _Nora_ • Samuel S Hinds _Dr Stephen Kildare_ ■ _Dir_ Harold Bucquet [Harold S Bucquet] • _Scr_ Willis Goldbeck, Harry Ruskin, from the story by Max Brand

The Secret of Madame Blanche
★★★

Period melodrama   1933 · US · BW · 78mins

Respectable musical actress Irene Dunne is swept off her feet by Phillips Holmes, a charming but weak upper class idler. She marries him and falls pregnant, but when his cruel and rigid father Lionel Atwill refuses to acknowledge the union, Holmes kills himself. She is stranded in France with her newborn son, whose grandfather steals the baby away... An 18-carat weepie, this wonderful wallow is best described as _Madame X_ meets _The Sin of Madelon Claudet_ though Dunne – enchanting as the young woman, less successful as middle-aged "Madame Blanche" – plays a morally blameless character, and is rewarded with something of a happy ending.

Irene Dunne _Sally Sanders St John/Madame Blanche_ • Lionel Atwill _Aubrey St John_ • Phillips Holmes _Leonard St John_ • Una Merkel _Ella_ • Douglas Walton _Leonard St John Jr_ ■ _Dir_ Charles Brabin • _Scr_ Frances Goodrich, Albert Hackett, from the play _The Lady_ by Martin Brown

The Secret of My Success
★★

Comedy   1965 · UK · Colour · 107mins

Yet another in the seemingly endless parade of lacklustre British comedies, this features James Booth as a naive, Panglossian mother's boy who starts the film as a PC and ends up unwittingly helping to overthrow a foreign dictator, becoming a hero in the process. Not very funny, though Booth is generally worth watching, and Lionel Jeffries gets to play four roles in what are the _Kind Hearts and Coronets_ style then.

Shirley Jones _Marigold Marado_ • Stella Stevens _Violet Lawson_ • Honor Blackman _Baroness von Lukenberg_ • James Booth _Arthur Tate_ • Lionel Jeffries _Inspector Hobart/ Baron von Lukenberg/President Esteda/Earl of Aldershot_ • Amy Dolby _Mrs Tate_ ■ _Dir/Scr_ Andrew L Stone

The Secret of My Success
★★ PG

Comedy   1987 · US · Colour · 105mins

Another tailor-made Michael J Fox role – he didn't succeed in playing a grown-up until _The American President_ in 1995 – in which he plays a mailroom boy who tries to make his way to the top by spending half his day impersonating an executive. Lots of pratfalls ensue, and Fox is reasonably engaging as he runs around frantically trying to keep up the charade. Margaret Whitton, as the scheming boss's wife, steals the show, however, and makes this rather basic comedy worth watching. ▭

Michael J Fox _Brantley Foster_ • Helen Slater _Christy Wills_ • Richard Jordan _Howard Prescott_ • Margaret Whitton _Vera Prescott_ • John Pankow _Fred Melrose_ • Christopher Murney _Barney Rattigan_ • Gerry Bamman _Art Thomas_ • Mercedes Ruehl _Sheila_ ■ _Dir_ Herbert Ross • _Scr_ Jim Cash, Jack Epps, AJ Carothers, from a story by AJ Carothers

The Secret of NIMH ★★★ U
Animated fantasy 1982 · US · Colour · 78mins

Animator Don Bluth rebelled against the mighty Mouse and set out to remind a then-struggling Disney about the glory days of animation. He largely succeeded (the sentimentality which would cloud his _An American Tail_ and _The Land before Time_ is the only drawback) with this story of a proud mouse who strikes up an unlikely friendship with the rat branch of Mensa. The animation is lovingly rendered and there is a pedigree cast (Dom DeLuise, Derek Jacobi, John Carradine) providing voices. ▭

Derek Jacobi _Nicodemus_ • Elizabeth Hartman _Mrs Brisby_ • Arthur Malet _Mr Ages_ • Dom DeLuise _Jeremy_ • Hermione Baddeley _Auntie Shrew_ • John Carradine _Great Owl_ • Peter Strauss _Justin_ • Paul Shenar _Jenner_ • Shannen Doherty _Teresa_ ■ _Dir_ Don Bluth • _Scr_ John Pomeroy, Gary Goldman, Don Bluth, Will Finn, from the novel _Mrs Frisby and the Rats of N.I.M.H._ by Robert C O'Brien

The Secret of NIMH II: Timmy to the Rescue ★ U
Animated adventure 1998 · US · Colour · 65mins

This made-for-video sequel to animator Don Bluth's one good movie makes his other wretched efforts look like masterpieces. The screenplay here freely ignores or alters key characters and events from the previous movie in this tale of now grown-up mouse Timmy traveling to Thorn Valley to save his furry friends from the returning menace of NIMH. A frenzied pace and extremely choppy editing suggest that this short feature was originally longer before post-production. However, more coherence would not have saved the movie, which is blighted by poor animation and art design, and also by its surprisingly grim tone. ▭

Dom DeLuise _Jeremy_ • Andrew Ducote _Timmy, aged 10_ • Eric Idle _Martin_ • Harvey Korman _Floyd_ • Ralph Macchio _Timmy, aged 19_ • Peter MacNicol _Narrator_ ■ _Dir_ Dick Sebast • _Scr_ Sam Graham, Chris Hubbell, from characters created by Robert C O'Brien

The Secret of Roan Inish
★★★★ PG

Fantasy   1993 · US · Colour · 97mins

This is a gem of a film from talented writer/director John Sayles. Without sentiment and accompanied by stunning cinematography from veteran Haskell Wexler, Sayles spins a tale of ten-year-old Fiona living in 1940s Ireland who believes her family are descendants from selkies: half-seal, half-human creatures from the island of Roan Inish. While staying with her grandparents near the now-deserted island, the youngster starts to uncover her true heritage. The result is a mythical and magical film which will entrance children and adults alike. ▭

Jeni Courtney _Fiona Coneelly_ • Mick Lally _Hugh Coneelly, Fiona's Grandfather_ • Eileen Colgan _Tess Coneelly, Fiona's Grandmother_ • Richard Sheridan _Eamon_ • John Lynch _Tadhg Coneelly_ • Cillian Byrne _Jamie_ • Susan Lynch _Selkie_ ■ _Dir_ John Sayles • _Scr_ John Sayles, from the novel _The Secret of the Ron Mor Skerry_ by Rosalie K Fry

The Secret of Santa Vittoria
★★★★

Comedy   1969 · US · Colour · 139mins

This under-rated film is based on a supposedly true incident during the Second World War, when the population of a small village in the Italian hills secreted its stocks of wine to prevent them from falling into the hands of the Germans. Producer/director Stanley Kramer has crafted an irresistible game of cat and mouse as town drunk-cum-mayor Anthony Quinn and Nazi officer Hardy Kruger try to outsmart each other. Quinn and fiery Anna Magnani make a dynamic duo and you'll be hard pressed to choose between tears and cheers.

Anthony Quinn _Italo Bombolini_ • Anna Magnani _Rosa Bombolini_ • Virna Lisi _Caterina Malatesta_ • Hardy Kruger _Sepp Von Prum, German Commander_ • Sergio Franchi _Tufa_ ■ _Dir_ Stanley Kramer • _Scr_ William Rose, Ben Maddow, from the novel by Robert Crichton

Secret of the Incas ★★★ U
Adventure   1954 · US · Colour · 104mins

An adventure yarn about a fabled Inca icon, the "Sunburst", which is a sort of Treasure of the Sierra Maltese Falcon. Add some romance and Cold War intrigue, so fashionable in 1954, and you have the gist of it. What distinguishes the film are the location shots of the fabled Inca city of Machu Picchu, which sits swathed in Andean clouds. Machu was discovered in 1911 by an American adventurer-archaeologist named Hiram Bingham, on whom Charlton Heston's character is based. There has, of course, been another – rather better known – character inspired by Bingham... named Indiana Jones.

Charlton Heston _Harry Steele_ • Nicole Maurey _Elena Antonescu_ • Robert Young _Dr Stanley Moorehead_ • Thomas Mitchell _Ed Morgan_ • Glenda Farrell _Jane Winston_ • William Henry _Phillip Lang_ ■ _Dir_ Jerry Hopper • _Scr_ Ranald MacDougall, Sydney Boehm, from the story _Legend of the Incas_ by Sydney Boehm

The Secret of the Purple Reef
★ U

Murder mystery   1960 · US · Colour · 79mins

An early role for Peter Falk and the screen debut of Richard Chamberlain may be the sole reasons to watch this seaborne schlock. The plot has Jeff Richards and brother Chamberlain looking into the death of another brother who went down in his fishing sloop in the Caribbean. The weather is good, the acting less so, the script scrapes the bottom, and there are any number of suspects, notably local heavy Falk, whose girlfriend, Margia Dean, switches sides in mid-drama.

Jeff Richards _Mark Christopher_ • Margia Dean _Rue Amboy_ • Peter Falk _Tom Weber_ • Richard Chamberlain _Dean Christopher_ • Robert Earle _Tobias_ • Terence DeMarney _Ashby_ ■ _Dir_ William Witney • _Scr_ Harold Yablonsky, Gene Corman, from a serial in _The Saturday Evening Post_ by Dorothy Cottrell

Secret of Treasure Mountain
★★ U

Western adventure   1956 · US · BW · 67mins

The moral of this routine western must be that if you're going to bury some treasure, don't do it on Indian land. Snarling villain Raymond Burr and Valerie French lead the desultory crew looking for some gold buried by the Spanish and now protected by a particularly potent Apache curse. Third-billed William Prince also appeared in _Lust for Gold_, an almost identical yarn tossed out by Columbia in 1949.

Valerie French _Audrey Lancaster_ • Raymond Burr _Cash Larsen_ • William Prince _Robert Kendall_ • Lance Fuller _Juan Alvarado_ • Susan Cummings _Tawana_ • Pat Hogan _Vahoe_ ■ _Dir_ Seymour Friedman • _Scr_ David Lang

Secret of Treasure Mountain
★★

Adventure   1993 · US · Colour

The sequel to _The Butter Cream Gang_ finds the eager band of do-gooders on the horns of a dilemma. Do they pocket the proceeds of a treasure map or do they help a neighbour who's about to be made homeless? Of course, there are the small matters of locating the concealed crypt in a derelict monastery, escaping from a mountain cave and confounding a trio of desperadoes before thoughts turn to sharing out the loot all of which should keep the pre-teens entertained.

Brandon Blaser _Eldon_ • Jason Glenn _Lanny_ • Jason Johnson _Scott_ • Rick Macy _Almodovar_ • Frank Gerrish _Mugfat_ ■ _Dir_ Scott Swofford

The Secret Partner
★★

Crime drama   1961 · UK · BW · 91mins

In this implausible but ingenious British thriller, a hooded man forces a dentist to drug a shipping executive during an appointment so that he will reveal the combination of his company's strongroom. It remains watchable thanks to some skilful characterisation and the strong performances of Stewart Granger as the executive, Norman Bird as the dentist, and Bernard Lee as the dogged, chain-smoking policeman.

Stewart Granger _John Brent_ • Haya Harareet _Nicole Brent_ • Bernard Lee _Det Supt Hanbury_

• Hugh Burden *Charles Standish* • Lee Montague *Det Inspector Henderson* • Norman Bird *Ralph Beldon, dentist* ■ *Dir* Basil Dearden • *Scr* David Pursall, Jack Seddon

The Secret People ★

Crime drama 1951 · UK · BW · 95mins

Given carte blanche by Ealing Studios, director Thorold Dickinson set out to make a polemical film about the ethics of political assassination, and encouraged the young Lindsay Anderson to write a book documenting its production. Sadly, the result was a wordy, pretentious and boring picture, too coldly characterised, too unspecific in detail, too cerebral by far. Shunned by critics and audiences, its sole interest lies in the casting of Audrey Hepburn, in one of her earliest roles.

Valentina Cortesa [Valentina Cortese] *Maria Brentano* • Serge Reggiani *Louis* • Charles Goldner *Anselmo* • Audrey Hepburn *Nora Brentano* • Angela Fouldes *Nora as a child* • Megs Jenkins *Penny* • Irene Worth *Miss Jackson* • Reginald Tate *Inspector Eliot* • Bob Monkhouse *Barber* ■ *Dir* Thorold Dickinson • *Scr* Thorold Dickinson, Wolfgang Wilhelm, Christianna Brand, from a story by Thorold Dickinson, Joyce Carey

Secret Places ★★ 15

Drama 1984 · UK · Colour · 94mins

In the claustrophobic atmosphere of an all-girl's school at the beginning of the Second World War, two disparate pupils (Marie-Theres Relin and Tara MacGowran) strike up a friendship which is so close, the other schoolgirls and teachers (including Jenny Agutter) suspect "something is going on". Warm, low-key and somewhat lacking in drama. ▭

Marie-Theres Relin *Laura Meister* • Tara MacGowran *Patience* • Claudine Auger *Sophy Meister* • Jenny Agutter *Miss Lowrie* • Cassie Stuart *Nina* • Ann-Marie Gwatkin *Rose* • Pippa Hinchley *Barbara* ■ *Dir* Zelda Barron • *Scr* Zelda Barron, from the novel by Janice Elliott

The Secret Policeman's Ball ★★★★ 15

Comedy performance
1980 · UK · Colour · 91mins

This recording of the comedy fundraiser for Amnesty International enjoyed a theatrical release (in a much longer form) following its TV screening. A brilliant cast of comedians and performers (including John Cleese, Peter Cook, Clive James, Rowan Atkinson, Billy Connolly, Pete Townshend), and some wonderful sketches provide guaranteed entertainment. The same formula was repeated with *The Secret Policeman's Other Ball* which had a theatrical debut as well as the *Third Ball* in 1987. All feature wonderful moments from some of the most popular comedians of the last 35 years. ▭

Dir Roger Graef

The Secret Rapture

★★★★ 15

Drama 1993 · UK · Colour · 96mins

Writer David Hare can veer from nuance to crassness in one giddy swoop. Here, for once, he has merged the personal and the political without letting us see too much of the join.

Set on the cusp of the shark-toothed eighties and the more introspective nineties, this tale of sisterly rivalry is shot through with fine acting, particularly from Juliet Stevenson and Penelope Wilton as the sisters, Joanne Whalley-Kilmer as the stepmother and Neil Pearson as the boyfriend.

Juliet Stevenson *Isobel Coleridge* • Joanne Whalley-Kilmer [Joanne Whalley] *Katherine Coleridge* • Penelope Wilton *Marion French* • Neil Pearson *Patrick Steadman* • Alan Howard *Tom French* • Robert Stephens *Max Lopert* • Hilton McRae *Norman* • Robert Glenister *Jeremy* ■ *Dir* Howard Davies • *Scr* David Hare, from his play

Secret Sins of the Father

★★★ 15

Crime mystery 1994 · US · Colour · 88mins

Very much a family affair for the Bridges clan and it's their chemistry which lifts this TV drama out of the ordinary. Beau Bridges is the local cop who begins to think the unthinkable – that his father Lloyd may have murdered his mother (Dorothy Dean Bridges). There's even room for a small part for Beau's son Jordan and the family scenes carry a powerful sense of authenticity. It's just a shame that Beau the director didn't manage to bring more of a cutting edge to the mechanics of the murder mystery. ▭

Beau Bridges *Tom Thielman* • Lloyd Bridges *Louis Thielman* • Lee Purcell *Ann Thielman* • Frederick Coffin *LJ Thielman* • Victoria Rowell *Prosecutor Yolanda Seely* • Patrika Darbo *Leslie Holcomb* • Michael McManus *Rod Holcomb* • Ed Lauter *Arnold Carter* • Dorothy Dean Bridges • Jordan Bridges ■ *Dir* Beau Bridges • *Scr* Lillian Samuel

The Secret Six ★★

Crime 1931 · US · BW · 83mins

Bootlegger Wallace Beery rises to gangland supremo, only to be brought down by a six-man consortium of influential men, with a little help from newspaperman Clark Gable (in a supporting role). Slow to start, this is a serviceable, though superficially characterised, gangster movie. George Hill directed, with Lewis Stone excellent as a crooked attorney and, in small but key parts, John Mack Brown and Jean Harlow.

Wallace Beery *Louis Scorpio* • Lewis Stone *Richard Newton* • John Mack Brown [Johnny Mack Brown] *Hank Rogers* • Jean Harlow *Anne Courtland* • Marjorie Rambeau *Peaches* • Paul Hurst *Nick Mizoski the Gouger* • Clark Gable *Carl Luckner* • Ralph Bellamy *Johnny Franks* ■ *Dir* George W Hill [George Hill] • *Scr* Frances Marion, from her story

The Secret Steak ★★

Drama 1992 · Fr · Colour

A title as rare as the sirloin it celebrates, but this French TV movie is in effect one of those petit-bourgeois burnt offerings about a vegetarian bank manager (Daniel Ceccaldi) who, in succumbing to eating steak, also falls prey to other temptations of the flesh. Predictable enough, but the acting (especially from Danièle Lebrun as the manager's wife) successfully highlights the situation of a man who is lifted out of the frying pan into the fire, despite all his good resolutions. In French with English subtitles.

Daniel Ceccaldi *Mr Berthaud* • Danièle Lebrun *Mrs Berthaud* • Florence Darel *Claire* • Gérard Sergue *Lardut* • Jacques Seyres *Baron* • Jean Rougerie *Mr Dulatre* • Danièle Ajoret *Mrs Dulatre* • Stéphane Jobert *Richard* • Cecile Auclert *Lucy* ■ *Dir* Lazare Iglesis • *Scr* François-Olivier Rousseau, from a short story by Marcel Ayme

The Secret War of Harry Frigg ★★★ U

Second World War comedy
1967 · US · Colour · 109mins

Paul Newman was never fully convincing as a comedian, though he makes a fair stab at it here, as a deadbeat private whose one gift is the ability to escape from military prisons. Given the temporary rank of full general, he is sent to Italy to engineer the escape of five Allied generals, who are enjoying their imprisonment in a lavish villa owned by Countess Sylva Koscina. This is a jolly jape, lifted by some lovely turns from the supporting cast, notably John Williams as one of the two terribly English generals.

Paul Newman *Harry Frigg* • Sylva Koscina *Countess di Montefiore* • Andrew Duggan *General Armstrong* • Tom Bosley *General Pennypacker* • John Willams *General Mayhew* • Charles Gray *General Cox-Roberts* ■ *Dir* Jack Smight • *Scr* Peter Stone, Frank Tarloff, from a story by Frank Tarloff

The Secret War of Jackie's Girls ★★

Adventure 1980 · US · Colour · 98mins

Biggles meets Charlie's Angels in this daft and undistinguished made-for-TV film. A pilot for a television series that never got off the ground, it finds Ann Dusenberry, Dee Wallace and Lee Purcell among a team of plucky female fliers who are sent on secret missions during the Second World War. Despite some enthusiastic performances, this is sadly predictable stuff.

Lee Purcell *Casey McCann* • Ann Dusenberry *Donna* • Tracy Brooks Swope *Zimmy* • Dee Wallace [Dee Wallace Stone] *Maxine* • Caroline Smith *Patti* • John Reilly *Russ Hamilton* • Ben Murphy *Buck Wheeler* ■ *Dir* Gordon Hessler • *Scr* Theodore Jonas, D Guthrie, from a story by Theodore Jonas, from an idea by Jean Ross Kondek, Mary Ann Donahue

The Secret Ways ★★★

Spy thriller 1961 · US · BW · 111mins

A Cold War drama with the always watchable Richard Widmark as an American soldier-of-fortune helping a noted Hungarian intellectual and anti-communist escape from behind the Iron Curtain. The tone wavers between realism and satire, the result of a dispute between Widmark and director Phil Karlson. "I told Widmark I wanted to do it as a James Bond," said Karlson, "but he hadn't heard of Bond. I said, 'If we do this tongue-in-cheek we'll be the first ones.' He said, 'No, I don't want to do it that way.' We had a big fight and I never finished the picture."

Richard Widmark *Michael Reynolds* • Sonja Ziemann *Julia* • Charles Regnier *The Count* • Walter Rilla *Jansci* • Howard Vernon *Colonel Hidas* • Senta Berger *Elsa* • Heinz Moog *Minister Sakenov* ■ *Dir* Phil Karlson • *Scr* Jean Hazlewood, from a novel by Alistair MacLean

---

Secret Weapon ★★

Drama based on a true story
1990 · US/Ausl · Colour · 95mins

This fact-based TV movie dramatises the plight of an Israeli nuclear power plant technician (Griffin Dunne) who, after he exposes secret atomic weapon production, is hunted by a beautiful Mossad agent (Karen Allen). Intense performances highlight this drama, filmed on various locations, from London to Australia and Israel. However, it's let down by strained and somewhat predictable plotting.

Griffin Dunne *Mordechai Vanunu* • Karen Allen *Ruth* • Jeroen Krabbé *Asher* • Stuart Wilson *Peter Hounam* • Joe Petruzzi *Felix Romero* • John Rhys-Davies *Mossad chief* • Brian Cox *Andrew Neil* ■ *Dir* Ian Sharp • *Scr* Nick Evans

Secret Wedding ★★★★

Romantic political drama
1989 · Arg/Neth/Can · Colour · 95mins

Blending political allegory, black humour and touching romance, Argentinian director Alejandro Agresti provides a fascinating insight into the problems facing the "disappeared", imprisoned under the junta, and now released back into society with the restoration of democracy. From the moment we find him naked on the streets of Buenos Aires, Tito Haas dominates the action, whether coming to terms with the years he has lost, attempting to win back the love of Mirtha Busnelli, or coping with the suspicions of his new neighbours. Ricardo Rodriguez's photography is superb, complementing the unusual camera angles favoured by Agresti. In Spanish with English subtitles.

Tito Haas *Fermin Garcia* • Mirtha Busnelli *Tota* • Sergio Poves Campos *Pipi* • Nathan Pinzon *Priest* • Floria Bloise *Dona Patricia* • Elio Marchi *Leandro* ■ *Dir/Scr* Alejandro Agresti

Secrets ★

Period drama 1933 · US · BW · 84mins

This remake of their 1924 silent film, by writer Frances Marion and director Frank Borzage was a mistake. It was Mary Pickford's last film and made for an ignominious end to her long career as "America's Sweetheart". Pickford cast herself as a pioneering woman bravely enduring hardships and tragedy – and nobly standing by her philandering husband through 50 years of marriage. Leslie Howard, not surprisingly, is uncharacteristically ill at ease as the wayward spouse in a creaky melodrama that had already passed its sell-by date in the 1930s.

Mary Pickford *Mary Marlowe/Mary Carlton* • Leslie Howard *John Carlton* • C Aubrey Smith *Mr William Marlowe* • Blanche Frederici *Mrs Martha Marlowe* • Doris Lloyd *Susan Channing* • Herbert Evans *Lord Hurley* • Ned Sparks *"Sunshine"* ■ *Dir* Frank Borzage • *Scr* Frances Marion, Salisbury Field, Leonard Praskins, from the play by Rudolf Besier

Secrets ★★★ 15

Comedy drama
1992 · Ausl/NZ · Colour · 91mins

Set on the day the Beatles arrived in Melbourne at the start of their 1964 Australian tour, this potentially winning tale of teenage self-discovery is rather weighed down by heavy-handed symbolism and two-dimensional characterisation. Robert Zemeckis's first movie *I Wanna Hold Your Hand* provides the obvious inspiration, as four Beatles fans get trapped overnight in a hotel basement with an Elvis freak. Michael Pattinson directs a little self-consciously, but the young cast is fine, notably Noah Taylor (*Shine*). Contains swearing. ▭

Beth Champion *Emily* • Malcolm Kennard *Danny* • Dannii Minogue *Didi* • Willa O'Neill *Vicki* • Noah Taylor *Randolph* ■ *Dir* Michael Pattinson • *Scr* Jan Sardi

Secrets ★★
Period drama   1995 · US · Colour · 92mins

The subject of baby kidnapping is transposed to 1910 Iowa in this melodramatic TV movie. A teenager (Jessica Bowman) discovers she is adopted when her domineering mother (Veronica Hamel) and passive doctor father (Richard Kiley), who have hidden their inability to have children, buy the illegitimate baby of their housemaid and then banish the poor girl. Serviceable acting by Thomas Gibson (*Dharma and Greg*), and veterans Kiley and Hamel, can't redeem this corny, slow-moving soap opera.

Veronica Hamel *Etta Berter* • Richard Kiley *Will Berter* • Julie Harris *Mrs Phelan* • Jessica Bowman *Anna Berter* • Shae D'Lyn *Edwina Phelan* • Thomas Gibson *Hailus Tuckman* ■ *Dir* Jud Taylor • *Scr* Jerome Kass, from the novel *The Other Anna* by Barbara Esstman

Secrets & Lies ★★★★★ 15
Drama   1995 · UK · Colour · 136mins

Acclaimed director Mike Leigh finally scored a resounding box-office hit with this bittersweet snoop into the nooks and crannies of family life. The winner of the Palme d'Or at Cannes, this is a return to the familiar battleground of suburbia, but without the caricature that occasionally undermines Leigh's razor-sharp social observation. The teasing statements on the original poster best sum up the film's labyrinthine relationships: "Roxanne drives her mother crazy. Maurice never speaks to his niece. Monica can't talk to her husband. Hortense has never met her mother. Cynthia has a shock for her family." But even the secrets and lies themselves are of less significance than how the different characters respond to the revelations. Brenda Blethyn's café scene with fellow Oscar nominee Marianne Jean-Baptiste is a highlight. Timothy Spall and Claire Rushbrook are also impressive in the ensemble cast. Contains swearing. ▭ **DVD**

Timothy Spall *Maurice* • Brenda Blethyn *Cynthia* • Marianne Jean-Baptiste *Hortense* • Phyllis Logan *Monica* • Claire Rushbrook *Roxanne* • Elizabeth Berrington *Jane* • Michele Austin *Dionne* • Lee Ross *Paul* • Lesley Manville *Social worker* • Ron Cook *Stuart* ■ *Dir/Scr* Mike Leigh

Secrets d'Alcove ★★★
Portmanteau comedy
1954 · Fr/It · BW · 110mins

A bed links this amusing collection of short stories, told by a trio of diplomats and their chauffeur. In Henri Decoin's *Le Billet de Logement* Richard Todd parachutes into occupied France and helps Jeanne Moreau deliver a

baby; Vittorio De Sica has to spend a night with professional co-respondent, Dawn Addams, in Gianni Franciolini's *Le Divorce*; the mysteries of the night haunt trucker Marcel Mouloudji when he stops to help the stranded François Périer in Ralph Habib's *Riviera-Express*, while Martine Carol seeks verification of the bed's historical importance in Jean Delannoy's *Le Lit de la Pompadour*. In English and French with subtitles.

Jeanne Moreau *Mother* • Richard Todd *Soldier* • Martine Carol *Agnes* • Bernard Blier *President* • François Périer *Alfred* • Vittorio De Sica *Bob* • Dawn Addams *Janet* • Mouloudji *Ricky* ■ *Dir* Henri Decoin, Jean Delannoy, Ralph Habib, Gianni Franciolini • *Scr* Maurice Auberge, Jean Delannoy, Roland Laudenbach, Sergio Amidei, Antoine Blondin, Janet Wolf, Jacques Fano, Niccolo Theodoli, Paul Andreota, Richard Todd

Secrets of the Heart ★★★
Fantasy drama
1997 · Sp/Fr/Por · Colour · 108mins

Admirers of Victor Erice's *The Spirit of the Beehive* will be intrigued by this Oscar-nominated tale of childhood innocence and the lure of the unknown. Set in the Basque country around Pamplona in the sixties, the film doesn't overplay its allegorical hand, even though the symbolism of the abandoned house, with its locked rooms and buried secrets, is pretty blatant. Instead, Montxo Armendariz focuses on the curiosity and incomprehension of nine-year-old Andoni Erburu, who is more interested in rumours that whispering ghosts inhabit the basement than in the relationship between his widowed mother and his uncle. A Spanish language film.

Andoni Erburu *Javi-Javier Zabalza* • Carmelo Gomez *Uncle* • Maria Charo Lopez *Aunt* • Silvia Munt *Mother* • Vicky Peña *Aunt Rosa* ■ *Dir/Scr* Montxo Armendariz

Secrets of the Phantom Caverns ★★ 15
Action thriller   1984 · UK · Colour · 87mins

Robert Powell's presence is so negligible as to be negative in this lost-world fantasy, which should never have been found. Director Don Sharp, who could usually turn out high action from low budgets, never got to grips with this story of an albino tribe discovered in South American caves. With the quality of acting from Lisa Blount and Richard Johnson, besides the pathetic Powell, a stranglehold wouldn't have been enough.

Robert Powell *Wolfson* • Timothy Bottoms *Major Stevens* • Lisa Blount *Leslie Peterson* • Richard Johnson *Ben Gannon* • Anne Heywood *Frida Shelley* • Jackson Bostwick *Hunter* ■ *Dir* Don Sharp • *Scr* Christy Marx, Robert Vincent O'Neil, from a story by Ken Barnett

The Sect ★★★ 18
Horror   1991 · It · Colour · 111mins

Fans of spaghetti shockers will lap up this offering from Dario Argento acolyte Michele Soavi who, after Argento-influenced fare such as *The Church*, finally established himself as a horror stylist in his own right with this highly atmospheric fantasy about a coven of devil worshippers carrying out ritualistic

killings in modern-day Frankfurt. It's less a story than a succession of surreal and bravura set pieces; Soavi holds back on the gore (for the most part) emphasising suspense instead and succeeds in coming up with a good deal of genuine frights. He wrings good performances from Kelly Leigh Curtis as a schoolteacher caught up in the murders and, most notably, from Herbert Lom as the cult leader. Italian dialogue dubbed into English. ▭

Kelly Leigh Curtis [Kelly Curtis] *Miriam* • Herbert Lom *Gran Vecchio* • Maria Angela Giordano *Kathryn* • Tomas Arana *Damon* • Erica Sinisi *Sara* • Donald O'Brien *Jonathan* • Michel Hans Adatte *Franz* ■ *Dir* Michele Soavi • *Scr* Dario Argento, Giovanni Romoli, Michele Soavi, from a story by Dario Argento, Giovanni Romoli, Michele Soavi

Security Risk ★
Action spy drama   1954 · US · BW · 69mins

While FBI agent John Ireland is on holiday at a ski resort, an atomic scientist is murdered by his assistant – who plans to sell secret papers to the KGB. Ireland's girlfriend, Dolores Donlon, witnesses the crime and takes the papers, intending to sell them herself. The bodies pile up before Ireland saves the day. Cold War, Red Scare movies like this were a dime a dozen in Hollywood in the fifties, and this one probably cost a dime to make.

John Ireland *Ralph Payne* • Dorothy Malone *Donna Weeks* • Keith Larsen *Ted* • John Craven *Dr Lanson* • Joe Bassett *Malone* • Murray Alper *Mike* ■ *Dir* Harold Schuster • *Scr* Jo Pagano, Frank McDonald, John Rich, from a story by John Rich

Seduced ★★ 15
Crime drama   1985 · US · Colour · 90mins

A good cast, including Cybill Shepherd, Ray Wise and *The Fog*'s Adrienne Barbeau, makes the most of this average TV movie about a district attorney trying to track down the murderer of the wealthy businessman husband of his former mistress. José Ferrer and his namesake son also give some edge to the tale, but you'll have guessed whodunit well before the end credits. ▭

Gregory Harrison *Michael Riordan* • Cybill Shepherd *Vicki Orloff* • José Ferrer *James Killian* • Michael C Gwynne *Keith Fitzgibbons* • Ray Wise *Bartecki* • Karmin Murcelo *Lieutenant Alvarado* • Paul Stewart *Norman Weinglass* • Jordan Christopher *Howell* • Adrienne Barbeau *Barbara Orloff* • Mel Ferrer *Arthur Orloff* ■ *Dir* Jerrold Freedman • *Scr* Charles Robert Carner

Seduced and Abandoned ★★★
Comedy drama   1964 · Fr/It · BW · 117mins

Less subtle than its predecessor, *Divorce – Italian Style*, Pietro Germi's scatter-shot assault on the Sicilian code of honour is deflected in its satirical purpose by the broad ebullience of its situation comedy. Depicting island society as archaic, prejudicial, superstitious and sex-ridden, Germi relies on caricature to expose the patriarchal tyranny that still claims proprietorial right over its womenfolk. This is a bitterly realistic film, with Aldo Puglisi impregnating his fiancée's teenage sister, Stefania

Sandrelli, only to discard her because she's no longer a virgin. Yet, it's also scurrilously funny, with hypocritical father Saro Urzi thoroughly meriting his best actor prize at Cannes. In Italian with English subtitles.

Stefania Sandrelli *Agnese Ascalone* • Aldo Puglisi *Peppino Califano* • Saro Urzi *Vincenzo Ascalone* • Lando Buzzanca *Antonio Ascalone* • Leopoldo Trieste *Baron Rizieri* ■ *Dir* Pietro Germi • *Scr* Pietro Germi, Luciano Vincenzoni, Age, Furio Scarpelli, from an idea by Pietro Germi, Luciano Vincenzoni

Seduced and Betrayed ★★
Erotic thriller   1995 · US · Colour · 87mins

Former *Baywatch* star David Charvet swaps the sun and surf for the 'burbs, though he only manages to keep marginally more clothes on in this hokey erotic thriller. He plays a happily married carpenter who falls into the clutches of rich woman Susan Lucci, who wants him to nail more than just planks of wood. All the usual clichés are present but fans of the genre won't be disappointed. Contains violence and swearing.

Susan Lucci *Victoria Sanders* • David Charvet *Dan Hiller* • Gabrielle Carteris *Cheryl Hiller* • Peter Donat *Judge Van Owen* • Mary Ellen Trainor *Charlotte* ■ *Dir* Felix Enriquez Alcala • *Scr* Cameron Kent

Seduced by Evil ★★
Supernatural thriller
1994 · US · Colour · 90mins

Adapted from the novel *Brujo* by Jann Arrington Wolcott, this TV movie might have been a hair-raising chiller had it had a little more money spent on it and a lot more imagination invested in it by its creative team. Suzanne Somers occasionally looks genuinely scared as the journalist who is tormented by the nightmares and traumas visited upon her by small-town sorceror John Vargas in his bid to possess her. But her efforts can't overcome the blandness of the visual terrors dreamt up by director Tony Wharmby, which are as likely to induce giggles as cold sweats.

Suzanne Somers *Lee Lindsay* • James B Sikking *Nick Lindsay* • John Vargas *Ceiro* • Mindy Spence *Melissa Lindsay* • Nancy Moonves *Dr Mallory* • Julie Carmen *Rayna* ■ *Dir* Tony Wharmby • *Scr* Bill Svanoe, from the novel *Brujo* by Jann Arrington Wolcott

Seduction in a Small Town ★★
Drama based on a true story
1996 · US · Colour · 97mins

It never happened in *Little House on the Prairie*. This modern-day rural melodrama finds Melissa Gilbert battling to keep her family together when she is falsely accused of abusing her kids. The story is depressingly familiar and, in the hands of director Charles Wilkinson, a tad overwrought. However, Gilbert gives a plucky performance and there is solid support from the likes of Dennis Weaver, GW Bailey and Joely Fisher, familiar to TV viewers as Paige Clark in *Ellen*.

Melissa Gilbert *Sarah Jenks* • Dennis Weaver *Sam Jenks* • GW Bailey *Pat Carter* • Brian McNamara *Paul Jenks* • Joel Palmer *David*

Ⓤ = SUITABLE FOR ALL, Ⓤₛ = SUITABLE FOR ALL, ESPECIALLY FOR YOUNG CHILDREN (VIDEO ONLY), Ⓟ Ⓖ = PARENTAL GUIDANCE

Jenks • Joely Fisher *Sandy Barlow* ■ *Dir* Charles Wilkinson • *Scr* William Phillips, from a treatment by Ned Welsh

The Seduction of Joe Tynan ★★★ 15

Political drama 1979 · US · Colour · 102mins

You always get the feeling with this portrait of American political life that it has more than a ring of truth about it. Unfortunately, the echo has a hollowness that undermines the satire. Alan Alda's performance is superior to his script, capturing the glib, Kennedy-like charm that can still win votes, and Meryl Streep is convincing as a ruthless lawyer. There's also a clever cameo from Melvyn Douglas, but it's Barbara Harris's worrying wife that still impresses most. However, some of the Senate scenes seem far-fetched, while the melodramatic finale is a shoddy way to end an otherwise well-constructed drama. Contains swearing and brief nudity.

Alan Alda *Joe Tynan* • Barbara Harris *Ellie Tynan* • Meryl Streep *Karen Traynor* • Rip Torn *Senator Hugh Kittner* • Melvyn Douglas *Senator Birney* • Charles Kimbrough *Francis* • Carrie Nye *Althena Kittner* ■ *Dir* Jerry Schatzberg • *Scr* Alan Alda

The Seduction of Mimi ★★★

Satire 1972 · It · Colour · 92mins

Remade in 1977 as the Richard Pryor vehicle *Which Way Is Up?* (1977), Lina Wertmuller's third collaboration with actor Giancarlo Giannini earned her best director kudos at Cannes. A study in sexual hypocrisy and political expediency, it stars Giannini as Mimi, a Sicilian labourer who manages to alienate both the mob and the communists, lose his wife and his mistress, and impregnate the spouse of the man who cuckolded him. Despite exposing the immoderate importance placed on honour and the perils of macho boorishness, Wertmuller is scarcely more sympathetic in her depiction of the female characters, although Mariangela Melato's party activist is at least loyal to her word and principles. An Italian language film.

Giancarlo Giannini *Mimi* • Mariangela Melato *Fiore* • Agostina Belli *Rosalia* • Elena Fiore *Amelia* • Turi Ferro *Tricarico* • Luigi Diberti *Pippino* ■ *Dir/Scr* Lina Wertmuller

The Seduction of Miss Leona ★★★

Romantic drama 1980 · US · Colour · 100mins

Better than average, this is an intelligent made-for-TV drama, based on the novel *Bliss* by Elizabeth Gundy. Lynn Redgrave is a shy, middle-aged teacher who finds herself in an unlikely love triangle with old flame Anthony Zerbe and blue collar handyman Brian Dennehy. The direction from Joseph Hardy is formulaic, but there are topnotch performances from the cast, especially the charismatic Dennehy.

Lynn Redgrave *Leona DeVos* • Anthony Zerbe *Clem Steggman* • Conchata Ferrell *Hazel Dawson* • Brian Dennehy *Bliss Dawson* ■ *Dir* Joseph Hardy • *Scr* Dan Wakefield, from the novel *Bliss* by Elizabeth Gundy

Seduction: the Cruel Woman ★★★ 18

Drama 1985 · W Ger · Colour · 84mins

The influence of Rainer Werner Fassbinder can be felt throughout this dark exploration of the politics of desire. Recalling both the stylised visuals and intellectual melodramatics of films such as *The Bitter Tears of Petra Von Kant* (1972), this lesbian *ménage à trois* combines sadomasochism, fetishism and erotic fantasy to explore everything from Germany's relationship with the USA, to consumerism, bourgeois hypocrisy and the battle of the sexes. Udo Kier gives a Calibanesque performance as the slave of dominatrix Mechthild Grossmann, who divides her time between running a taboo-shattering cabaret and disciplining her lovers, shoe seller Carola Regnier and naive American Sheila McLaughlin. In German with English subtitles.

Mechthild Grossmann *Wanda* • Udo Kier *Gregor* • Sheila McLaughlin *Justine* • Carola Regnier *Caren* ■ *Dir* Elfi Mikesch, Monika Treut • *Scr* Elfi Mikesch, Monika Treut, from the novel *Venus in Furs* by Leopold von Sacher-Masoch

Seduction: Three Tales from the Inner Sanctum ★★

Erotic thriller 1992 · US · Colour · 100mins

The Inner Sanctum was an American radio show in the late thirties. The series spawned six B-movies, each of which starred Lon Chaney Jr and blended mystery with horror in a *Twilight Zone* sort of way. None of them was particularly good and this TV movie upholds that tradition of mediocrity. Victoria Principal takes three roles in this anthology, which focuses on obsessive love. The film affords her the chance to demonstrate her versatility but, saddled with such poor material, her task proves impossible.

John Terry • John O Hurley • W Morgan Sheppard [Morgan Sheppard] • Andreas Katsulas • Joseph Lambie [Joe Lambie] • Richard Heard • Victoria Principal ■ *Dir* Michael Ray Rhodes • *Scr* Robert Glass, Stephen Whitney, Barry Brown, from the radio show *The Inner Sanctum* by Himan Brown

See Here, Private Hargrove ★★★

Second World War comedy drama 1944 · US · BW · 101mins

This is a pleasant enough boot-camp tale, based on the memoirs of Marion Hargrove. Robert Walker does well as the hapless private, infuriating his senior officers in much the same way as he drove his editor up the wall during his civilian career as a reporter. There's echoes of Sergeant Bilko, as Walker schemes a way to visit his girlfriend in New York, but the picture lacks the commanding comic presence of a Phil Silvers here. However, it's well directed by Wesley Ruggles – plus an uncredited Tay Garnett, who handled the tacked-on upbeat ending – and there's a ring of observational truth behind the humour.

Robert Walker *Pvt Marion Hargrove* • Donna Reed *Carol Holliday* • Robert Benchley *Mr Holliday* • Keenan Wynn *Pvt Mulvehill* • Bob Crosby *Bob* • Ray Collins *Brody S Griffith* •

Chill Wills *First Sgt Cramp* ■ *Dir* Wesley Ruggles • *Scr* Harry Kurnitz, from the book by Marion Hargrove

See How They Fall ★★★★ 18

Drama 1993 · Fr · Colour · 95mins

Although it's taken from Teri White's novel, *Triangle*, the inspiration for this frankly homoerotic crime drama is hard-boiled French *film noir* as practised by director Jacques Audiard's screenwriter father, Michel, in the immediate postwar era. Stripping down motives to loyalty and survival, the story follows two distinct avenues, which, through the supremely controlled, convoluted structure, eventually coincide with explosive consequences. Ageing con man Jean-Louis Trintignant and reckless rookie Mathieu Kassovitz encounter Jean Yanne, a travelling salesman whose life has fallen apart through his obsessional crusade to avenge the death of the undercover cop to whom he'd become attached. In French with English subtitles. Contains swearing, violence and sex scenes.

Jean-Louis Trintignant *Marx* • Jean Yanne *Simon* • Mathieu Kassovitz *Johnny* • Bulle Ogier *Louise* • Christine Pascal *Sandrine* • Yvon Back *Mickey* ■ *Dir* Jacques Audiard • *Scr* Alain Le Henry, Jacques Audiard, from the novel *Triangle* by Teri White

See Jane Run ★★★

Thriller 1995 · US · Colour · 95mins

Joanna Kerns comes round to find $10,000 stashed in a pocket of her blood-soaked clothes. Adapted from Joy Fielding's bestseller, this TV movie's one major plus point is that the action provides as much of a surprise for us as it does for the bemused heroine, guaranteeing more than a little suspense along the way. While not perhaps as gripping as the page-turning original, it's still worth the odd nibble at the nails.

Joanna Kerns *Jane Ravenson* • John Shea *Michael Ravenson* • Katy Boyer *Paula* • Tiffany Taubman *Amy* • Lee Garlington *Carole Garson* ■ *Dir* John Patterson • *Scr* Ellen Weston, from the book by Joy Fielding

See No Evil, Hear No Evil ★ 15

Comedy 1989 · US · Colour · 97mins

As well as being an original comic talent, Richard Pryor has had the dubious distinction of appearing in a plethora of truly execrable movies. The man has a homing instinct for a dreadful script and this is certainly one of them. The two-handed comedy – Gene Wilder is Pryor's partner in puerile nonsense in their third movie together – manages to waste both men's ability, and to be simultaenously boring and deeply offensive. Contains violence and swearing.

Gene Wilder *Dave Lyons* • Richard Pryor *Wally Karew* • Joan Severance *Eve* • Kevin Spacey *Kirgo* • Alan North *Captain Braddock* • Anthony Zerbe *Sutherland* • Louis Giambalvo *Gatlin* • Kirsten Childs *Adele* ■ *Dir* Arthur Hiller • *Scr* Earl Barret, Arne Sultan, Eliot Wald, Andrew Kurtzman, Gene Wilder, from a story by Earl Barret, Arne Sultan, Marvin Worth

See You in the Morning ★★ 15

Romantic drama 1989 · US · Colour · 113mins

This is one of those intense relationship dramas in which everyone behaves like an adult – including the children. Jeff Bridges deserves a pat on the back for not howling with laughter during a bedtime story about a dolphin and he keeps the film on the rails, as a psychiatrist who spends so much time analysing his motives it's a wonder he's got any time left for living. Lukas Haas and Drew Barrymore are very subdued as Bridges's stepchildren, but they are certainly more interesting than their mother (Alice Krige). Heavygoing.

Jeff Bridges *Larry Livingston* • Alice Krige *Beth Goodwin* • Farrah Fawcett *Jo Livingston* • Drew Barrymore *Cathy Goodwin* • Lukas Haas *Petey Goodwin* • David Dukes *Peter Goodwin* • Frances Sternhagen *Neenie* • George Hearn *Martin* ■ *Dir/Scr* Alan J Pakula

Seeds of Deception ★★ 15

Drama based on a true story 1993 · US · Colour · 90mins

The American health service throws up some compulsive true stories and this doesn't disappoint. George Dzundza plays a doctor specialising in fertility who seems to have an uncanny knack of helping barren couples give birth. However, it's all a little too good to be true and, when one of the hopeful parents (Melissa Gilbert) digs a little deeper, she uncovers some shocking secrets. The direction is as lumpen as it is with most TV movies, but Dzundza has a ball as the shifty doc.

George Dzundza *Dr Cecil Jacobson* • Melissa Gilbert *Mary Bennett* • Tom Verica *Greg Bennett* • Shanna Reed *Sue Castellano* • RH Thomson *Bill Castellano* ■ *Dir* Arlene Sanford • *Scr* Phil Penningroth, Sharon Elizabeth Doyle

Seeds of Tragedy ★★★ 18

Crime crime 1991 · US · Colour · 87mins

Director Martin Donovan, who made his name with the chilling *Apartment Zero*, brings a similar cool objectivity to this thoughtful examination of the drugs trade. By focusing on just one consignment of cocaine, Donovan is able to touch on all aspects of the drugs chain. This begins with the cultivation of the coca plants in South America and ends up in the more familiar environment of the Los Angeles gangs. There are no star names in the cast but, if anything, that just adds to the film's power and strong sense of authenticity. Contains drug abuse.

Jeff Kaake *Coggins* • Norbert Weisser *Gunter* • Michael Fernandes *Saavedra* • Sarah Buxton *Amy* • Page Moseley *Marion* ■ *Dir* Martin Donovan • *Scr* Alex Lasker

Seeing Red ★★★

Political documentary 1983 · US · BW and Colour · 100mins

This Oscar-nominated documentary about American Marxists examines their beliefs, their efforts to transform American society, their victimisation at the hands of ambitious politicians and their responses to political developments in Soviet Russia. It makes for fascinating viewing – a little reminiscent of the witnesses in Warren Beatty's *Reds*. The film's only real weakness is that none of the politicians of the time – such as future presidents Nixon and Reagan – are interviewed. While we get plenty of retrospective thought from the persecuted, it would have been nice to have had some thoughts from their persecutors as well.

Dir James Klein, Julia Reichert

The Seekers ★★
Period adventure 1954 · UK · Colour · 90mins

Ealing blazed the trail for British film-makers Down Under with their Australian outback pictures of the mid-forties. In contrast, this costume adventure from director Ken Annakin is set in 19th-century New Zealand and, apart from Geoffrey Unsworth's striking cinematography, has none of the freshness of Ealing's pseudo-documentaries. The major influence on this story of colonial expansion at the expense of the Maoris is undoubtedly the Hollywood western and, consequently, it is hardly the most enlightened interpretation of the colonial spirit ever committed to film. Jack Hawkins cuts a dash as the leader of the expedition – and keep an eye out for Kenneth Williams.

Jack Hawkins *Philip Wayne* • Glynis Johns *Marion Southey* • Noel Purcell *Paddy Clarke* • Inia Te Wiata *Hongi Tepe* • Kenneth Williams *Peter Wishart* • Laya Raki *Moana* ■ *Dir* Ken Annakin • *Scr* William Fairchild, from the novel by John Gutherie

Seems like Old Times ★★ PG
Comedy 1980 · US · Colour · 97mins

Despite the presence of stars Goldie Hawn, Chevy Chase and Charles Grodin, plus a screenplay by Neil Simon, this tribute to the heyday of screwball comedy falls as flat as a pancake under the leaden hand of Jay Sandrich making his film-directing debut. Some sharp lines pass muster, but the plot is limp and witless, while the ending is spectacularly pointless. Contains swearing.

Goldie Hawn *Glenda* • Chevy Chase *Nick* • Charles Grodin *Ira* • Robert Guillaume *Fred* • Harold Gould *Judge* • George Grizzard *Governor* • Yvonne Wilder *Aurora* • TK Carter *Chester* ■ *Dir* Jay Sandrich • *Scr* Neil Simon

Seize the Day ★★★ PG
Drama 1986 · US · Colour · 93mins

This intriguing drama, based on a novel by Saul Bellow, gave Robin Williams the chance to prove that he was capable of much more than mere comic exuberance. However, heartfelt as his performance is as the perpetual loser who returns to his roots to rebuild his life, it's the supporting turns of unforgiving father Joseph Wiseman and shifty, stockbroking quack Jerry Stiller that give this well-acted piece its impetus. Director Fielder Cook admirably captures the dog-eat-dog atmosphere of mid-fifties New York, but doesn't always exploit the full dramatic potential of Williams's plight. Contains swearing.

Robin Williams *Tommy Wilhelm* • Joseph Wiseman *Dr Adler* • Jerry Stiller *Dr Tamkin* • Glenne Headly *Olive* • Richard B Shull *Rojax* •

William Hickey *Perls* • Tony Roberts *Bernie Pell* • Jo Van Fleet *Mrs Einhorn* • Jayne Heller *Mrs Adler* ■ *Dir* Fielder Cook • *Scr* Ronald Ribman, from the novel by Saul Bellow

Seizure ★★★
Horror 1974 · US · Colour · 94mins

For a long time after he hit the Hollywood big time, Oliver Stone refused to acknowledge this low-budget horror movie as his directorial debut. If it was bad, one could understand it. But it isn't. In fact, it's an unusually gripping gem starring ex-*Dark Shadows* vampire Jonathan Frid as a demented writer dreaming up three characters (Queen of Evil Martine Beswick, evil dwarf Herve Villechaize and towering Henry Baker) who spring to life to do his murderous bidding. Gory and scary, this is easily recognisable as a talented debut from someone who would clearly go the distance.

Jonathan Frid *Edmund Blackstone* • Martine Beswick *Queen of Evil* • Joseph Sirola *Charlie* • Christina Pickles *Nicole Blackstone* • Herve Villechaize *The Spider* • Anne Meacham *Eunice* • Roger De Koven *Serge* • Troy Donahue *Mark* • Henry Baker *Jackal* ■ *Dir* Oliver Stone • *Scr* Edward Mann, Oliver Stone

Sélect Hôtel ★★★ 18
Drama 1996 · Fr · Colour · 81mins

Starting as a vox-pop documentary before assuming a stylised form of *cinéma vérité*, Laurent Bouhnik's debut feature attempts to achieve a visual edginess to match the marginalisation of its characters. It's a rough-and-ready, nineties version of that poetic realist classic *Hôtel du Nord* (hence the dedication to Arletty), with prostitute Julie Gayet caught between her thieving, junkie brother (Jean-Michel Fête) and her scheming pimp (Marc Andréoni). The decision to use Serge Blumenthal's shopkeeper as a bourgeois everyma doesn't quite pay off, but Bouhnik's empathy with the disenfranchised otherwise seems authentic. In French with English subtitles. Contains swearing, sex scenes and some violence.

Julie Gayet *Nathalie* • Jean-Michel Fée *Tof* • Serge Blumenthal *Pierre* • Marc Andréoni *Denis* • Sabine Bail *Clémentine* ■ *Dir/Scr* Laurent Bouhnik

Selena ★★ PG
Biographical musical drama 1997 · US · Colour · 122mins

Virtually unknown outside the Latino community, Selena Quintanilla was a major figure in Tejano music until, on the very brink of her crossover into mainstream pop charts (à la Gloria Estefan) she was murdered by the president of her fan club. This glossy, slick and predictable biography centres on her relationship with her father Abraham (Edward James Olmos) and her determination to hit the big time. Unsurprisingly, as Abraham is the executive producer, the film does not linger on her tragic death, but it provides a perfect vehicle for singer/actress Jennifer Lopez, who was nominated for a Golden Globe in the best actress in a musical category.

Jennifer Lopez *Selena Quintanilla* • Edward James Olmos *Abraham Quintanilla* • Jon Seda

Chris Perez • Jackie Guerra *Suzette Quintanilla* • Constance Marie *Marcela Quintanilla* • Jacob Vargas *Abie* ■ *Dir/Scr* Gregory Nava

A Self-Made Hero ★★★★ 15
Wartime comedy drama 1995 · Fr · Colour · 101mins

Brilliantly exploiting the confusion precipitated by the Liberation, Jacques Audiard's fascinating film is doubly audacious. It not only ventures into the "forbidden" territory of resistance and collaboration, but also gently mocks its simmering sensibilities in the process. Mathieu Kassovitz, the son of a Nazi kept-woman, so credibly reinvents his Occupation past that he becomes part of a crack war-crimes unit. Forever on the verge of exposure, Kassovitz gives a nerve-end portrayal of an opportunist whose very survival depends on his addiction to deception, while Audiard's direction slyly captures the chilling postwar atmosphere of cameraderie tinged with suspicion. In French with English subtitles.

Mathieu Kassovitz *Young Albert Dehousse* • Anouk Grinberg *Servane* • Sandrine Kiberlain *Yvette* • Albert Dupontel *Dionnet* • Jean-Louis Trintignant *Old Albert Dehousse* ■ *Dir* Jacques Audiard • *Scr* Jacques Audiard, Alain Le Henry, from the novel *Un Héros Très Discret* by Jean-François Deniau

The Sellout ★★★
Crime drama 1951 · US · BW · 83mins

Using one of the most common themes in American films, this crime drama has small-town decency once more opposing corruption in high places. Even though the film is a touch predictable, it gains considerably from the performance of Walter Pidgeon as a crusading newspaper editor and from its short, sharp style, created by director Gerald Mayer.

Walter Pidgeon *Haven D Allridge* • John Hodiak *Chick Johnson* • Audrey Totter *Cleo Bethel* • Paula Raymond *Peggy Stauton* • Thomas Gomez *Sheriff Kellwin C Burke* • Cameron Mitchell *Randy Stauton* • Karl Malden *Buck Maxwell, policeman* • Everett Sloane *Nelson S Tarsson, attorney* ■ *Dir* Gerald Mayer • *Scr* Charles Palmer, from a story by Matthew Rapf

The Sellout ★★ 15
Spy drama 1975 · UK/It · Colour · 96mins

Before his premature death in 1980, British director Peter Collinson achieved a certain notoriety with a ragbag of action adventures like this one, set and filmed in Israel. It's not surprising to find Oliver Reed and Gayle Hunnicutt on hand, since they tended to prop up international co-productions on attractive locations, but sad to see the great Richard Widmark slumming it. This would-be thriller about spies brings credit to no one, and it's sad to recall that its director once made *The Italian Job*, so leaden is this film's pace.

Richard Widmark *Sam Lucas* • Oliver Reed *Gabriel Lee* • Gayle Hunnicutt *Deborah* • Sam Wanamaker *Sickles* • Vladek Sheybal *The Dutchman* • Ori Levy *Major Benjamin* • Assaf Dayan *Lieutenant Elan* • Shmuel Rodensky *Zafron* ■ *Dir* Peter Collinson • *Scr* Murray Smith, Judson Kinberg, from a story by Murray Smith • *Cinematographer* Arthur Ibbetson

Seminole ★★ U
Western 1953 · US · Colour · 86mins

This otherwise effective western from Universal Studios is hobbled by a combination of its own earnestness and a weak leading performance by Rock Hudson. Nevertheless, it's beautifully filmed (with Technicolor photography by Russell Metty) and has a striking turn from Hugh O'Brian. Anthony Quinn, however, is as unlikely as an Indian chief as Hudson is as a West Point veteran, and a stronger script would have helped. At least the climax works.

Rock Hudson *Lieutenant Lance Caldwell* • Barbara Hale *Revere Muldoon* • Anthony Quinn *Osceola/John Powell* • Richard Carlson *Major Harlan Degan* • Hugh O'Brian *Kajeck* • Russell Johnson *Lieutenant Hamilton* • Lee Marvin *Sergeant Magruder* ■ *Dir* Budd Boetticher • *Scr* Charles K Peck Jr

Semi-Tough ★★★ 15
Sports comedy 1977 · US · Colour · 103mins

A good-natured, often very funny, Burt Reynolds comedy vehicle, this is set around the world of American football. Reynolds is the star player who finds himself competing with team-mate and good pal Kris Kristofferson for the attentions of Jill Clayburgh, whose dad owns the team. Reynolds and Kristofferson exude an easy-going charm and there is some expert comic support from the likes of Richard Masur and Robert Preston, plus early outings for Brian Dennehy and Ron Silver. The humour is largely knockabout stuff, but director Michael Ritchie slips in some sly satiric jabs at the commercialisation of American sport. Contains swearing.

Burt Reynolds *Billy Clyde Puckett* • Kris Kristofferson *Marvin "Shake" Tiller* • Jill Clayburgh *Barbara Jane Bookman* • Robert Preston *Big Ed Bookman* • Bert Convy *Friedrich Bismark* • Roger E Mosley *Puddin* • Lotte Lenya *Clara Pelf* • Richard Masur *Phillip Hooper* • Carl Weathers *Dreamer Tatum* • Brian Dennehy *TJ Lambert* • Ron Silver *Vlada* ■ *Dir* Michael Ritchie • *Scr* Walter Bernstein, from the novel by Dan Jenkins

The Senator Was Indiscreet ★★★ U
Comedy 1947 · US · BW · 81mins

An interesting satire on Capitol Hill, starring a very tongue-in-cheek William Powell as the senator with an interest in more than just the latest crop sharers' bill. This Universal comedy is unusual for its time, in that it pokes very obvious fun at political institutions when other movies were considerably less direct. Inexplicably, this was the only directorial outing for playwright George S Kaufman, who acquits himself well. Perhaps his brand of no-holds-barred satire was a little too strong for forties Hollywood.

William Powell *Senator Melvin G Ashton* • Ella Raines *Poppy McNaughton* • Peter Lind Hayes *Lew Gibson* • Arleen Whelan *Valerie Shepherd* • Ray Collins *Houlihan* • Allen Jenkins *Farrell* • Charles D Brown *Dinty* • Hans Conried *Waiter* • Myrna Loy *Mrs Ashton* ■ *Dir* George S Kaufman • *Scr* Charles MacArthur, from a story by Edwin Lanham

U = SUITABLE FOR ALL · Uc = SUITABLE FOR ALL, ESPECIALLY FOR YOUNG CHILDREN (VIDEO ONLY) · PG = PARENTAL GUIDANCE

Send Me No Flowers ★★★★
Romantic comedy
1964 · US · Colour · 99mins

Riotously funny, or extraordinarily tasteless, depending on your point of view, this ''comedy'' stars Rock Hudson as a hyper-hypochondriac who's convinced he's dying. Doris Day is his put-upon wife and Tony Randall the friend and neighbour who takes the news of Hudson's impending demise badly. This is sophisticated stuff, the last of the Day/Hudson collaborations, and it's shot through with a mordant wit that may chime better with today's audience than it did with movie-goers back in the sixties. Paul Lynde is hysterical as a cemetery plot salesman, and there are telling performances from Edward Andrews and big Clint Walker. Hudson was invariably under-rated as a performer. Here he's excellent, lending grace to a difficult role and imbuing his character with sly, winning humour.

Rock Hudson *George Kimball* • Doris Day *Judy Kimball* • Tony Randall *Arnold Nash* • Paul Lynde *Mr Akins* • Hal March *Winston Burr* • Edward Andrews *Dr Ralph Morrissey* • Patricia Barry *Linda Bullard* • Clint Walker *Bert Power* ■ *Dir* Norman Jewison • *Scr* Julius J Epstein, from the play by Norman Barasch, Carroll Moore

The Sender ★★★ 18
Science-fiction thriller
1982 · UK · Colour · 87mins

Former art director Roger Christian's directorial debut was this piece of metaphysical sci-fi, in which psychiatrist Kathryn Harrold pieces together the bizarre circumstances of amnesiac Zeljko Ivanek's condition. At times extremely disturbing, and regularly punctuated by set pieces highlighting Nick Allder's special effects, this mystery keeps one constantly alert and on the edge of one's seat. The scene in which an entire hospital is convulsed by Ivanek's shock treatment is electrifying. Too bad about the many loose ends. ▭

Kathryn Harrold *Gail Farmer* • Zeljko Ivanek *Sender* • Shirley Knight *Jerolyn* • Paul Freeman *Dr Denman* • Sean Hewitt *Messiah* • Harry Ditson *Dr Hirsch* • Olivier Pierre *Dr Erskine* • Marsha A Hunt *Nurse Jo* ■ *Dir* Roger Christian • *Scr* Thomas Baum

The Sender ★
Science-fiction action drama
1997 · US · Colour · 98mins

A listless Michael Madsen is Dallas Grayson, a naval officer endowed with a mysterious power that makes him a target for the government. There are superior special effects and large-scale action sequences, but everything seems wrong, from the position of the camera to how the action moves on the screen. The closing credits list a number of assistant directors, suggesting that there were some problems during the production. Cult favorites R Lee Ermey and Robert Vaughn liven things up during their brief appearances.

Michael Madsen *Dallas Grayson* • Robert Vaughn *Fairfax* • Dyan Cannon *Gina Fairfax* • R Lee Ermey *Rosewater* • Shelli Lether *Angel* • Brian Bloom *Jack Greyson* ■ *Dir* Richard Pepin • *Scr* Richard Preston Jr, Nathan Long

Senior Prom ★★ U
Musical   1958 · US · BW · 81mins

Passing itself off as a campus musical, the college girl-meets-boy-then meets-another-boy wisp of a plotline serves only as an excuse for stringing together 20 unmemorable musical numbers. Five of the songs spotlight the girl at the centre (Jill Corey), with the other 15 supplied by a line-up that includes Louis Prima and Keely Smith, Bob Crosby, and Connee Boswell. The boys between whom Corey's affections travel – if anyone cares – are rich Tom Laughlin (who picked up some fame in the seventies for *Billy Jack*) and penniless Paul Hampton.

Jill Corey *Gay Sherridan* • Paul Hampton *Tom Harper* • Jimmie Komach *Dog* • Barbara Bostock *Flip* • Tom Laughlin *Carter Breed III* • Frieda Inescort *Mrs Sherridan* • Selene Walters *Caroline* • Marvin Miller *Narrator* • Louis Prima • Keely Smith • Ed Sullivan • Mitch Miller • Connee Boswell • Bob Crosby ■ *Dir* David Lowell Rich • *Scr* Hal Hackady

The Seniors ★★
Comedy   1978 · US · Colour · 87mins

Screenwriter Stanley Shapiro (a co-Oscar winner for *Pillow Talk*) turned his hand to the frat-pack genre here, with uneven results. A young Dennis Quaid is one of a group of students who set up a phony sex clinic, only for the prank to turn into a multi-million-dollar concern – while teaching them valuable lessons about life and love, of course. Released in the same year as the hugely successful (and far superior) *Animal House*, this is too tame to provoke and too lame to amuse. Quaid would prove himself a year later in *Breaking Away*, but he displays little charm in this movie.

Dennis Quaid *Alan* • Jeffrey Byron *Larry* • Gary Imhoff *Ben* • Lou Richards *Steve* • Priscilla Barnes *Sylvia* • Rockey Flinterman *Arnold* • Alan Reed *Professor Helgner* • Edward Andrews *Banker* • Ian Wolfe *Mr Bleiffer* ■ *Dir* Rod Amateau • *Scr* Stanley Shapiro

La Señora ★★ 18
Drama   1987 · Sp · Colour · 103mins

This is what happens when a director trespasses on Buñuel territory, without having the wit, insight or film-making skills to prevent a dark story and a couple of slick scenes from descending into a pretentious mess. Catalan director Jordi Cadena obviously fancies himself as a scathing satirist in this tale of greed and just deserts, but he is so fascinated by the cruel sexual games played by Silvia Tortosa (a gripping performance) and her paranoid husband that he never delves deeply enough into his socio-political themes. In Spanish with English subtitles.

Silvia Tortosa *Teresa* • Hermann Bonnin *Don Nicolau* • Luis Merlo *Rafael* • Fernando Guillen-Cuervo *Josep* • Jeannine Mestre *Aina* ■ *Dir* Jordi Cadena • *Scr* Jordi Cadena, Silvia Tortosa, from the novel by Antoni Mus

Sensations ★★★★ U
Musical   1944 · US · BW · 85mins

This is one of those of those musicals with a mouthwatering cast list that promises much more than it delivers. Director Andrew Stone also produced and co-wrote the script so must take most of the blame. Top-billed Eleanor Powell had been MGM's brightest dancing star, but was freelancing when she made this modest affair (originally called *Sensations of 1945*). She could still dance up a storm and her numbers are the best things in the movie, though the one where she's inside a pinball machine has strictly novelty value. The efforts of Powell's character to obtain publicity make up the wispy plot, welcome relief from which is provided by the guest spots of Sophie Tucker, WC Fields (in his last film appearance) and Cab Calloway.

Eleanor Powell *Ginny Walker* • Dennis O'Keefe *Junior Crane* • C Aubrey Smith *Dan Lindsay* • Eugene Pallette *Gus Crane* • Mimi Forsythe *Julia Westcott* • Lyle Talbot *Randall* • Hubert Castle *The Great Gustafson* • WC Fields ■ *Dir* Andrew L Stone • *Scr* Dorothy Bennett, Andrew L Stone, from a story by Frederick Jackson, Andrew L Stone

Sensations ★★ 18
Erotic comedy drama
1987 · US · Colour · 91mins

The advent of video allowed Chuck Vincent to shift from his trademark seventies straight porn to soft-core features such as this cheapo comedy from 1987. The slenderest of plots revolves around two bitter enemies — a stripper and a hooker – who are forced to learn to like each other when they have to share a big win on the lottery. The no-name cast shed their kit with enthusiasm but struggle somewhat when they are obliged to keep their clothes on. ▭

Rebecca Lynn *Jenny Hunter* • Blake Bahner *Brian Ingles* • Jennifer Delora *Della Randall* • Rick Savage *Dave Salt* • Frank Stewart *Harold Nichols* ■ *Dir* Chuck Vincent • *Scr* Craig Horrall, from a story by Chuck Vincent

Sense and Sensibility ★★★★ U
Period romantic comedy
1995 · US · Colour · 130mins

If the past is a foreign country, then the decision to bring over Taiwan's Ang Lee to direct this adaptation of Jane Austen's first published novel was totally inspired. Rejecting the chocolate-box visuals that cheapen so many British costume films, Ang brings a refreshing period realism to this tale of two sisters that allows Emma Thompson's respectful script to flourish. Kate Winslet's spirited Marianne stands out from a solid display of ensemble acting, but the mystery remains why Lee, who became the first director to win Berlin's Golden Bear twice, was not among the film's seven Oscar nominations. ▭ **DVD**

Emma Thompson *Elinor Dashwood* • Alan Rickman *Colonel Brandon* • Kate Winslet *Marianne Dashwood* • Hugh Grant *Edward Ferrars* • James Fleet *John Dashwood* • Tom Wilkinson *Mr Dashwood* • Harriet Walter *Fanny Dashwood* • Greg Wise *John Willoughby* ■ *Dir* Ang Lee • *Scr* Emma Thompson, from the novel by Jane Austen

A Sense of Loss ★★
Documentary
1972 · US/Swi · Colour · 132mins

Marcel Ophüls's follow-up to his acclaimed 1971 Holocaust epic, *The Sorrow and the Pity*, this fatally flawed investigation into the Troubles in Northern Ireland was considered sufficiently inflammatory by the BBC for them to ban it. However, such is the evident bias in his assessment of the situation that it has precious little value, either as reportage or propaganda. His presentation of key Protestant apologists such as Ian Paisley is so dismissive that, rather than exposing the prejudice in their polemic, he succeeds only in ridiculing them, thus making the pronouncements of the Republican cause seem wholly acceptable. Incalculably disappointing.

Dir Marcel Ophüls

Senseless ★ 15
Comedy   1998 · US · Colour · 89mins

A poor man's imitation of a Jim Carrey movie, *Senseless* is weak on all fronts. Marlon Wayans stars as a student so desperate to get a junior analyst's job that he agrees to take a sense-enhancing potion. Inevitably this lends him super senses that soon spiral out of control. Both Wayans and love interest Tamara Taylor are bearable, and Rip Torn is more than adequate in yet another corporate role, but Matthew Lillard is sorely misused in a subplot of zero consequence. Contains sexual references. ▭

Marlon Wayans *Darryl Witherspoon* • Matthew Lillard *Tim LaFlour* • Rip Torn *Randall Tyson* • David Spade *Scott Thorpe* • Brad Dourif *Dr Wheedon* ■ *Dir* Penelope Spheeris • *Scr* Greg Erb, Craig Mazin • *Music* Yello

Senso ★★★ PG
Period drama   1954 · It · Colour · 116mins

A full-blown melodrama from Luchino Visconti about an Italian countess, trapped in a sexless marriage, falling in love with a dashing Austrian cavalry officer who is invading Italy. As usual with Visconti, there is a welter of baroque effects and an acute sense of history, as the countess betrays her country and her social class for the sake of passion. Visconti wanted Ingrid Bergman for the countess but Roberto Rossellini put his foot down and said she only worked for him. So Visconti went with Alida Valli (*The Third Man*) and he cast Farley Granger (*Strangers on a Train*) as her lover. Italian dialogue dubbed into English. ▭

Alida Valli *Contessa Livia Serpieri* • Farley Granger *Lieut Franz Mahler* • Massimo Girotti *Marquis Roberto Ussoni* • Heinz Moog *Count Serpieri* • Rina Morelli *Laura* ■ *Dir* Luchino Visconti • *Scr* Luchino Visconti, Suso Cecchi D'Amico, Giorgio Prosperi, Carlo Alianello, Giorgio Bassani, from the *Senso: Nuove Storielle Vane* by Camillo Boito

Sentimental Journey ★★ U
Melodrama   1946 · US · BW · 94mins

A stage actress (Maureen O'Hara) with a heart condition adopts an orphan child so that, if she succumbs, her husband, John Payne, won't be left alone. Weepies don't come much weepier than this offering, which is crassly manipulative and the sort of emotional rollercoaster that American audiences responded to immediately after the Second World War, when husbands were returning to their wives to raise a family. There have been two remakes: with Lauren Bacall in 1958 as *The Gift of Love* and a 1984 TV-movie with Jaclyn Smith.

John Payne *Bill* • Maureen O'Hara *Julie* • William Bendix *Donnelly* • Cedric Hardwicke *Dr Miller* • Glenn Langan *Judson* • Mischa Auer *Lawrence Ayres* ■ *Dir* Walter Lang • *Scr* Samuel Hoffenstein, Elizabeth Reinhardt, from a story by Nelia Gardner White

Sentimental Journey ★★
Drama 1984 · US · Colour · 97mins

A glossy if largely pointless take on a story that had been filmed twice before, in 1946 and in 1958 as *The Gift of Love*. Jaclyn Smith and David Dukes are the married luvvies who find their lives up-ended by the arrival of an unbearably cute orphan. Despite the modern-day settings, this is an unashamedly old-fashioned weepie, but Smith and Dukes are no match for the previous pairings of Maureen O'Hara with John Payne and Lauren Bacall with Robert Stack.

Jaclyn Smith *Julie Ross-Gardner* • David Dukes *Bill Gardner* • Maureen Stapleton *Ruthie* • Jessica Rene Carroll *Libby* • Elia Enid Cadilla *Alicia* ■ *Dir* James Goldstone • *Scr* Darlene Craviotto, Frank J Cavestani, from a story by Nelia Gardner White

The Sentinel ★★ 18
Horror 1977 · US · Colour · 87mins

Michael Winner is one of our most frequently disparaged directors, and it isn't difficult to see why on the evidence of this risible attempt to jump on *The Exorcist's* demonic band wagon. Cristina Raines plays a fashion model who moves into a stately old Brooklyn mansion, is menaced by ghastly apparitions and finds the place is built over a gateway to hell. Even those disposed to find Winner's direction enjoyably trashy – as opposed to clumsy and sensationalist – will be shocked by his decision to use genuinely handicapped people in one scene. ▣

Chris Sarandon *Michael Lerman* • Cristina Raines *Alison Parker* • Martin Balsam *Professor* • John Carradine *Father Halliran* • JoséFerrer *Robed figure* • Ava Gardner *Miss Logan* • Arthur Kennedy *Franchino* • Burgess Meredith *Chazen* • Eli Wallach *Gatz* • Christopher Walken *Rizzo* • Jerry Orbach *Director* • Beverly D'Angelo *Sandra* • Tom Berenger *Man at end* • Jeff Goldblum *Jack* ■ *Dir* Michael Winner • *Scr* Michael Winner, Jeffrey Konvitz, from his novel

Separate Lives ★ 18
Thriller 1995 · US · Colour · 97mins

James Belushi and Linda Hamilton have both shown themselves as capable actors, but here they are consigned to B-movie hell in a limp psychological thriller from David Madden. Belushi plays a former detective who is persuaded by his college lecturer (Hamilton) to watch for her for signs of a murderous multiple personality. Tedious and predictable, despite the best efforts of the under-rated Belushi. Contains violence, sex scenes and swearing. ▣

James Belushi *Tom Beckwith* • Linda Hamilton *Lauren Porter/Lena* • Vera Miles *Dr Ruth Goldin* • Elisabeth Moss *Ronnie Beckwith* • Drew Snyder *Robert Porter* • Mark Lindsay

Chapman *Keno Sykes* • Marc Poppel *Detective Joe Gallo* ■ *Dir* David Madden • *Scr* Steven Pressfield

Separate Tables ★★★★★ PG
Drama 1958 · US · BW · 95mins

David Niven won an Oscar as the retired "major" whose libido gets the better of him in this wonderfully – and perhaps surprisingly – cast version of Terence Rattigan's play. Wendy Hiller is the proprietor of a Bournemouth boarding house, presiding over a small group of paying guests whose neuroses start to unravel. Deborah Kerr's mother-dominated mousiness is too insistent, but Burt Lancaster's Hemingwayesque turn is great fun and Rita Hayworth, as his ex-wife, is marvellously convincing as a woman who knows that time and her beauty are running out. Delbert Mann's film is both moving and entertaining. ▣

Rita Hayworth *Ann Shankland* • Deborah Kerr *Sibyl Railton-Bell* • David Niven *Major Pollock* • Burt Lancaster *John Malcolm* • Wendy Hiller *Miss Pat Cooper* • Gladys Cooper *Mrs Railton-Bell* • Cathleen Nesbitt *Lady Matheson* • Rod Taylor *Charles* ■ *Dir* Delbert Mann • *Scr* Terence Rattigan, John Gay, from the play by Terence Rattigan

Separate Tables ★★★ PG
Drama 1983 · US · Colour · 113mins

Julie Christie teamed with director John Schlesinger for the fourth time (to date) for this TV-movie version of the celebrated Terence Rattigan play. She's far too beautiful for the role of the mousey Sibyl, but her hesitant performance just about stands comparison with Deborah Kerr's. Alan Bates, her co-star in *Far from the Madding Crowd*, is a touch too ebullient in the role that earned David Niven an Oscar, but it's clear the couple enjoy working together. Interestingly, Schlesinger retains the "Table by the Window" and the "Table Number Seven" structure of the play. ▣

Julie Christie *Ann Shankland/Sibyl Railton-Bell* • Alan Bates *John Malcolm/Major Pollock* • Claire Bloom *Miss Cooper* • Irene Worth *Mrs Railton-Bell* • Sylvia Barter *Lady Matheson* • Bernard Archard *Mr Fowler* • Liz Smith *Miss Meachum* • Kathy Staff *Mabel* • Brian Deacon *Charles Stratton* ■ *Dir* John Schlesinger • *Scr* Terence Rattigan, from his play

Separate Vacations ★★ 18
Comedy 1986 · Can · Colour · 87mins

David Naughton of *American Werewolf in London* fame gets a rare starring role in this Canadian comedy. It's a shame the material isn't more deserving of his talents. He plays a child-harried husband who opts out of the family skiing holiday in favour of a business trip to Mexico, with hopes of a bit of sauce on the side. Predictably, his lust-fueled fantasies end in rejection, while wife Jennifer Dale finds ski instuctor Mark Keyloun keen to show her a few moves away from the slopes. Co-produced by the Playboy organisation, this is a mildly "swinging" comedy that attempts to hide its intrinsic tackiness behind a moralistic theme of marital strife. The end result is unengaging. ▣

David Naughton *Richard Moore* • Jennifer Dale *Sarah Moore* • Mark Keyloun *Jeff Ferguson* •

Laurie Holden *Karen* • Blanca Guerra *Alicia* • Suzie Almgren [Susan Almgren] *Helen Gilbert* • Lally Cadeau *Shelley* • Jackie Mahon *Annie Moore* ■ *Dir* Michael Anderson • *Scr* Robert Kaufman, from the novel by Eric Webber

Separate Ways ★
Romantic drama 1981 · US · Colour · 92mins

An uninspired romantic drama about an upper middle-class couple having to re-evaluate their relationship in the wake of non-blissful domesticity. Karen Black starts an affair with a student at her community college just as her relationship with her former racing-driver husband Tony LoBianco, who is also having it on the side, goes into the pits. Despite the presence of the singularly watchable Black, the film is a real non-starter.

Karen Black *Valentine Colby* • Tony LoBianco *Ken Colby* • Arlene Golonka *Annie* • David Naughton *Jerry* • Sharon Farrell *Karen* • Jack Carter *Barney* • William Windom *Huey* • Robert Fuller *Woody* ■ *Dir* Howard Avedis • *Scr* Leah Appet, from a story by Leah Appet, Howard Avedis, Marlene Schmidt

Separated by Murder ★★ 12
Crime drama based on a true story
1994 · US · Colour · 92mins

Also known as *Black Widows: the Alabama Twins*, this TV movie gives Sharon Gless the chance to play two roles – and go right over the top in both of them. Since *Cagney and Lacey* passed into TV legend, things haven't exactly gone smoothly career-wise for Gless. This undemanding fact-based shocker, in which the twins conspire to murder one of their husbands, is about par for the course. Steve Railsback hasn't exactly set the world alight, either, since his promising performance in *The Stunt Man*, and his amateur hit man isn't a character he will look back on with much pride. Contains some swearing. ▣

Sharon Gless *Holly Fay Walker/Lily Mae Stokely* • Steve Railsback *Jesse Dixon* • Steve Watson *Colin Walker* • Ed Bruce *Daryl Kelso* • Mark W Johnson *Bobby Joe Howell* • Jim Ostrander *Dwight Stokely* • Bob Penny *David Walker* ■ *Dir* Donald Wrye • *Scr* Jeff Andrus, Bobby Roth, from a story by Bobby Roth

La Séparation ★★★ PG
Drama 1994 · Fr · Colour · 84mins

Although a masterclass in actorly restraint, the agonisingly slow deterioration of Isabelle Huppert and Daniel Auteuil's relationship makes for painful viewing. It would have been much more effective with a more balanced presentation of emotions and events – by siding with Auteuil's character, director Christian Vincent makes Huppert's Anne seem unnecessarily callous and allows Auteuil to become increasingly pathetic. The political subtext, on how radicals conform with time, is much more engaging than the disappointingly detached melodrama. Impressive, but too impassive. In French with English subtitles. ▣

Isabelle Huppert *Anne* • Daniel Auteuil *Pierre* • Jerôme Deschamps *Victor* • Karin Viard *Claire* • Laurence Lerel *Laurence* • Louis Vincent *Loulou* • Nina Morato *Marie* ■ *Dir* Christian Vincent • *Scr* Christian Vincent, Dan Franck, from the novel by Dan Franck

September ★★★★ PG
Drama 1987 · US · Colour · 171mins

Woody Allen's autumnal film has a story straight out of Chekhov, as relationships fray between intellectuals in a Vermont mansion and Mia Farrow, Denholm Elliott, Dianne Wiest and Sam Waterston vent their frustrations on each other. One of Allen's "serious" pieces, without his angst-prone presence, this was originally filmed with Maureen O'Sullivan (Farrow's real-life mother), Sam Shepard and Charles Durning. Allen was so unsure about its balance that he largely re-shot it and was forced to find alternative actors because of the cast's other commitments. The result is wonderfully stylish and beautifully shot, but don't expect a barrel of laughs – except from Elaine Stritch, as a former film star who is visiting her daughter Farrow. ▣

Denholm Elliott *Howard* • Dianne Wiest *Stephanie* • Mia Farrow *Lane* • Elaine Stritch *Diane* • Sam Waterston *Peter* • Jack Warden *Lloyd* • Ira Wheeler *Mr Raines* • Jane Cecil *Mrs Raines* ■ *Dir/Scr* Woody Allen • *Cinematographer* Carlo Di Palma

September Affair ★★★
Romantic drama 1950 · US · BW · 105mins

Set in various Italian locations, this soapy romance might have been more appealing in colour. What it does have, however, are two likeable leads in Joseph Cotten and Joan Fontaine and Kurt Weill's *September Song*, sung by Walter Huston on the soundtrack. The contrived plot has Fontaine, a concert pianist (cue for some emotive Rachmaninoff), and wealthy married Cotton falling in love when they miss their plane back to the USA. The plane crashes and they are listed among the dead. Now they can start a new life together. Or can they? Thankfully William Dieterle's direction avoids oversentimentality.

Joan Fontaine *Manina Stuart* • Joseph Cotten *David Lawrence* • Françoise Rosay *Maria Salvatini* • Jessica Tandy *Catherine Lawrence* • Robert Arthur *David Lawrence Jr* • James Lydon *Johnny Wilson* ■ *Dir* William Dieterle • *Scr* Robert Thoeren, from a story by Fritz Rotter • *Music* Victor Young

September Gun ★★★
Comedy western 1983 · US · Colour · 94mins

The estimable Robert Preston clearly had a ball making this TV-movie western. As the gunslinger well past his draw-by date, he brings a grizzled edge to what might have been a sickly sweet story about a nun trying to reclaim her mission for Apache orphans from the outlaws who have occupied it. The by-play between Preston and Patty Duke is decidedly spicy as they trek across the plains and then cross swords with outlaw chief Christopher Lloyd.

Robert Preston *Ben Sunday* • Patty Duke Astin [Patty Duke] *Sister Dulcina* • Geoffrey Lewis *Sheriff Bill Johnson* • Sally Kellerman *Mama Queen* • David Knell *Jason Farragut* • Jacques Aubuchon *Father Jerome* • Christopher Lloyd *Jack Brian* ■ *Dir* Don Taylor • *Scr* William Norton, from characters created by Hal Goodman, Larry Klein

Serena ★★★ U

Crime drama 1962 · UK · BW · 62mins

Rising well above the usual quota-quickie standards, this entertaining little whodunit shoehorns about two hours of plot into its short running time. Directed at a fair lick by Peter Maxwell, it revolves around the complicated sex life of smoothie artist Emrys Jones, who wants to leave his wife for his model mistress. When the body of an unknown woman is found in an isolated country cottage, inspector Patrick Holt is called in to investigate. It marked a change of pace for Honor Blackman, then at the height of her fame as Cathy Gale in the TV series *The Avengers*.

Patrick Holt Inspector Gregory • Emrys Jones Howard Rogers • Honor Blackman Ann Rogers • Bruce Beeby Sergeant Conway • John Horsley Mr Fisher • Robert Perceval Bank Manager ■ Dir Peter Maxwell • Scr Edward Abraham, Reginald Hearne, from a story by Edward Abraham, Valerie Abraham

Serenade ★★★★ U

Musical drama 1956 · US · Colour · 121mins

This film version of James M Cain's steamy novel about a singer who has a homosexual relationship with his patron seems an unlikely vehicle for Hollywood's top tenor Mario Lanza. But, even with the book's plot substantially changed (the patron is now a woman), this is compulsive viewing thanks to director Anthony Mann's skill, the urbane villainy of Vincent Price and the sheer soap-opera pleasure of watching cool Joan Fontaine and sultry Sarita Montiel vie for Lanza. The Warner Bros production values are topnotch, and the tubby tenor belts out a couple of popular songs as well as the expected arias. It's a bit long, though.

Mario Lanza Damon Vincenti • Joan Fontaine Kendall Hale • Sarita Montiel Juana Montes • Vincent Price Charles Winthrop • Joseph Calleia Maestro Marcatello • Harry Bellaver Monte • Vince Edwards Marco Roselli ■ Dir Anthony Mann • Scr Ivan Goff, Ben Roberts, John Twist, from the novel by James M Cain

The Sergeant ★★★

Drama 1968 · US · Colour and BW · 108mins

Rod Steiger boldly goes where few actors have dared to go, even in the liberated Swinging Sixties, by portraying a homosexual character. As a US Army sergeant serving in postwar Paris he finds a love-object in young private John Phillip Law, though it takes a long time for him to realise why the hands-off relationship means so much to him. John Flynn directs with ponderous seriousness, but Steiger is believably vulnerable as the man caught up in a system that won't allow him to reveal his sexuality.

Rod Steiger Master Sergeant Albert Callan • John Phillip Law Private Tom Swanson • Ludmila Mikael Solange • Frank Latimore Captain Loring • Elliott Sullivan Pop Henneken • Ronald Rubin Corporal Cowley • Phillip Roye Aldous Brown ■ Dir John Flynn • Scr Dennis Murphy, from his novel

Sgt Bilko ★★ PG

Comedy 1996 · US · Colour · 90mins

Steve Martin must have known the comparisons with Phil Silvers were not

going to be favourable when he took on this tepid TV spin-off. But he dexterously combines elements of Silvers's character with his own comic personality. Andy Breckman's script is strongest in its double-talk, as Bilko seeks to bamboozle suckers and superiors alike. The plot – about a top-secret hover-tank – is less than involving, however, and the feud between Martin and his longtime adversary (Phil Hartman) is overcooked. Mediocre, but a total disaster. ▣

Steve Martin Master Sgt Ernest G Bilko • Dan Aykroyd Colonel Hall • Phil Hartman Major Thorn • Glenne Headly Rita Robbins • Daryl Mitchell Wally Holbrook • Max Casella Dino Paparelli • Eric Edwards Duane Doberman • Dan Ferro Tony Morales ■ Dir Jonathan Lynn • Scr Andy Breckman, from the TV series The Phil Silvers Show by Nat Hiken

Sergeant Deadhead ★★ U

Musical comedy 1965 · US · Colour · 88mins

One-time pop star Frankie Avalon plays a dual role in this watchable, if rowdy, musical comedy. Sergeant OK Deadhead is the kind of nervous, Jerry Lewis-style klutz the US Air Force doesn't need when it's about to launch a top-secret rocket. Deadhead is accidentally blasted off into space with a chimpanzee and, on his return, temporarily becomes a crazed rebel. So his commander substitutes Deadhead with his double. Buster Keaton, in one of his final movies, supplies some quieter visual humour as a mad electrician.

Frankie Avalon Sgt OK Deadhead/Sgt Donovan • Deborah Walley Col Lucy Turner • Fred Clark Gen Rufus Fogg • Cesar Romero Adm Stoneham • Gale Gordon Capt Weiskopf • Harvey Lembeck Pvt McEvoy • John Ashley Pvt Filroy • Buster Keaton Pvt Blinken ■ Dir Norman Taurog • Scr Louis M Heyward

Sgt Kabukiman NYPD ★★★ 18

Action comedy adventure 1991 · US/Jap · Colour · 100mins

Gleefully disregarding trifles such as quality and taste, Troma has produced some of the most delirious B-movies of recent times. However, none can rival the silliness of this comic-book caper. Doltish cop Rick Gianasi, is possessed by the spirit of a kabuki actor and masters the heat-seeking chopsticks and suffocating sushi rolls that will prevent The Evil One from taking over the world. Mercilessly – and with large dollops of political incorrectness – mocking the superhero tradition, directors Michael Herz and Lloyd Kaufman resort too readily to stereotypes and socko slapstick. But, somehow, the manic mixture gets laughs.

Rick Gianasi Harry Griswold/Sergeant Kabukiman • Susan Byun Lotus • Bill Weeden Reginald Stuart • Thomas Crnkovich Rembrandt • Larry Robinson Reverend Snipes • Noble Lee Lester Captain Bender • Brick Bronsky Jughead ■ Dir Lloyd Kaufman, Michael Herz • Scr Lloyd Kaufman, Andrew Osborne, Jeffrey W Sass

Sergeant Madden ★★

Drama 1939 · US · BW · 82mins

Josef von Sternberg, under contract to MGM to make two films, was forced to

take on this typical sentimental Wallace Beery vehicle after being removed from *I Take This Woman* with Hedy Lamarr. The director was not happy, either with the screenplay or his pug-ugly star, with whom he had many a row. The result was a mediocre crime melodrama about an Irish cop (Beery), whose son (Alan Curtis) goes wrong. Sternberg had previously made two much better gangster movies (*Underworld* and *The Dragnet*) in the silent days – but then he had had more freedom.

Wallace Beery Shaun Madden • Tom Brown Al Boylan Jr • Alan Curtis Dennis Madden • Laraine Day Eileen Daly • Fay Holden Mary Madden • Marc Lawrence "Piggy" Ceders • Marion Martin Charlotte • David Gorcey "Punchy" ■ Dir Josef von Sternberg • Scr Wells Root, from the story A Gun in His Hand by William A Ullman Jr

Sgt Pepper's Lonely Hearts Club Band ★★ U

Musical 1978 · US · Colour · 110mins

A daft attempt to further conceptualise the classic Beatles album by linking its songs via a contrived connective storyline. Some sequences are OK, but others are downright embarrassing. Some interest resides in its pick 'n' mix cast of musicians and actors. Musicians include The Bee Gees, soul band Earth Wind & Fire, and seventies pin-up Peter Frampton, a multi-million seller way back when with Show Me The Way. Actors in the cast include Steve Martin, George Burns, Donald Pleasence and Frankie Howerd.

Peter Frampton Billy Shears • Barry Gibb Mark Henderson • Robin Gibb Dave Henderson • Maurice Gibb Bob Henderson • Frankie Howerd Mr Mustard • Paul Nicholas Dougie Shears • Donald Pleasence BD Brockhurst • Steve Martin Dr Maxwell Edison • Alice Cooper Father Sun • Billy Preston Sgt Pepper • George Burns Mr Kite ■ Dir Michael Schultz • Scr Henry Edwards

Sergeant Rutledge ★★★ PG

Western drama 1960 · US · Colour · 106mins

This is director John Ford's racial apologia movie. Having been accused of depleting the native American population and of rarely featuring an uncaricatured Jew or African-American in his films, the grand master of the western delivered this uncharacteristic, rather static courtroom drama about a black cavalry officer accused of rape and murder. Daring in its time, it's still powerful today. Woody Strode (*Spartacus*) gets the part of his life in the title role and a sequence in which he sings *Captain Buffalo* (the film's original title) and crosses the River Pecos is one of the most significant in Hollywood's treatment of blacks in cinema up until the sixties. ▣

Jeffrey Hunter Lt Thomas Cantrell • Woody Strode Sgt Braxton Rutledge • Constance Towers Mary Beecher • Willis Bouchey Colonel Fosgate • Billie Burke Mrs Fosgate • Carleton Young Captain Shattuck • Judson Pratt Lieutenant Mulqueen • Juano Hernandez Sgt Skidmore ■ Dir John Ford • Scr Willis Goldbeck, James Warner Bellah, from the novel Captain Buffalo by James Warner Bellah

Sergeant Ryker ★★ U

Courtroom drama 1968 · US · Colour · 85mins

Military prosecutor Bradford Dillman is persuaded that a bitter, convicted traitor (Lee Marvin), who is awaiting execution, may not have received a fair hearing, and he agrees to a retrial. As it was originally an extended TV play and not intended as a film, the copurtroom drama jars occasionally, but the intelligent writing and reliable supporting cast – including Vera Miles, Peter Graves and Lloyd Nolan – make it worth watching.

Lee Marvin Sergeant Paul Ryker • Bradford Dillman Captain David Young • Vera Miles Ann Ryker • Peter Graves (1) Major Whitaker • Lloyd Nolan General Amos Bailey • Norman Fell Sergeant Max Winkler • Walter Brooke Colonel Arthur Merriam ■ Dir Buzz Kulik • Scr Seeleg Lester, William D Gordon, from a story by Seeleg Lester

Sergeant York ★★★★ U

Biographical war drama 1941 · US · BW · 128mins

Nominated for 11 Oscars and winning Gary Cooper his first best actor statuette, this is a model of biopic making. As decent and determined as ever, Cooper is Alvin C York, the Tennessee backwoodsman who swears off violence after lightning strikes his rifle during a land dispute, only to become a national hero after single-handedly killing 20 Germans and capturing 132 more during a First World War offensive in October 1918. Director Howard Hawks handles the action sequences with customary confidence, but he also creates several fully fledged supporting characters, who are convincingly played by Joan Leslie and Oscar nominees Walter Brennan and Margaret Wycherly. ▣

Gary Cooper Alvin C York • Walter Brennan Pastor Rosier Pile • Joan Leslie Gracie Williams • George Tobias "Pusher" Ross • Stanley Ridges Major Buxton • Margaret Wycherly Mother York • Ward Bond Ike Botkin ■ Dir Howard Hawks • Scr Abem Finkel, Harry Chandlee, Howard Koch, John Huston, from the War Diary of Sergeant York by Alvin C York and edited by Sam K Cowan, and the biographies Sergeant York and His People by Sam K Cowan and Sergeant York – Last of the Long Hunters by Tom Skeyhill • Cinematographer Sol Polito, Arthur Edeson • Music Max Steiner

Sergeants 3 ★★★ U

Western comedy 1962 · US · Colour · 112mins

Following on from *Ocean's Eleven*, this rambunctious on-screen get-together of the "Rat Pack" – Frank Sinatra, Dean Martin, Peter Lawford, Sammy Davis Jr, Joey Bishop – finds the first three on horseback, as brawling cavalry officers out to repulse marauding Indians, which they succeed in doing with the help of bugle-blowing ex-slave Davis. Directed by John Sturges from a WR Burnett script that transposes *Gunga Din* to the American west and spoofs that film's heroics, this long, loud and exhausting romp only entertains in parts. However, the passage of time and the reputation of its stars have invested in with some nostalgic value.

Frank Sinatra 1st Sergeant Mike Merry • Dean Martin Sgt Chip Deal • Sammy Davis Jr Jonah Williams • Peter Lawford Sgt Larry Barrett •

Joey Bishop *Sgt Major Roger Boswell* • Henry Silva *Mountain Hawk* • Ruta Lee *Amelia Parent* ■ *Dir* John Sturges • *Scr* WR Burnett

Sergei Eisenstein: Mexican Fantasy ★★★★
Documentary   1998 · Rus · BW · 98mins
Que Viva Mexico!, Sergei Eisenstein's first (and only) non-Soviet venture was dogged throughout by authorial disputes. Spurned by Paramount in 1930, he received sufficient sponsorship from left-wing novelist Upton Sinclair to shoot some 50 hours of footage, only for it to be delivered to Hollywood producer Sol Lesser, who used it for the bowdlerised feature *Thunder over Mexico* (1933). Eisenstein's biographer Marie Seton and former student Jay Leyda both reworked the material (the former as co-writer of 1939's *Time in the Sun*), as is related in this fascinating documentary on the travelogue that turned into a tract on the colonial abuses that instilled revolutionary fervour into a land of stark beauty and cultural complexity. A Russian language film.
Alexandra Scheff *Narrator* ■ *Dir/Scr* Oleg Kovalov • *Cinematographer* Yevgeny Shermergor, Edouard Tissé

Serial ★★★ 18
Satirical comedy 1980 · US · Colour · 88mins
Christopher Lee plays a gay Hell's Angel in an under-rated satire about the worst excesses in 1970s America. Bizarre religious cults, ludicrous fashions, absurd self-help groups, marital fidelity and love affairs with poodle-parlour workers all come under the social mores microscope, in a scatter-shot spoof centred around the Beautiful People of Marin County, California. Lee rises to the occasion, enjoying playing against type, and the rest of the eclectic cast make their oddball moments count. ▭
Martin Mull *Harvey* • Tuesday Weld *Kate* • Jennifer McAllister *Joan* • Sam Chew Jr *Bill* • Sally Kellerman *Martha* • Anthony Battaglia *Stokeley* • Nita Talbot *Angela* • Bill Macy *Sam* • Sally Kellerman *Martha* • Christopher Lee *Luckman/Skull* • Pamela Bellwood *Carol* ■ *Dir* Bill Persky • *Scr* Rich Eustis, Michael Elias, from the novel by Cyra McFadden

Serial Killer ★★★ 18
Thriller   1996 · Can · Colour · 90mins
Here's a film that states its intentions up front. Tobin Bell is the serial killer, recently escaped from captivity and out to exact revenge on Kim Delaney, the FBI psychological profiler who put him away. The film's only real attractions are the unusual method of revenge Bell has in mind for his former captor and the gleam of menace in his eye. Pam Grier is the police captain who keeps tabs on Delany's officious cop boyfriend. It's no *Silence of the Lambs*, but it does have a definite twist. ▭
Kim Delaney *Selby Younger* • Gary Hudson *Cole Grayson* • Tobin Bell *William Lucian Morrano* • Pam Grier *Capt Maggie Davis* • Marco Rodriguez *Manny Ramirez* • Joel Polis *Jack Blund* • Andrew Prine *Perry Jones* ■ *Dir* Pierre David • *Scr* Mark Sevi

Serial Mom ★★★ 18
Black comedy   1994 · US · Colour · 89mins
Kathleen Turner is the archetypal cheerful Baltimore mother – until someone disrupts her orderly life. Then she turns into the homicidal housewife from hell. Didn't rewind your videotape? Wearing white shoes after Labour Day? Watch out! Cult director John Waters's darkly funny look at the murderer-as-celebrity phenomenon trashes American family values and sends up splatter movies, mining each target for maximum screwball outrage. While not as perverse as some of Waters's previous bad-taste epics, this "Doris Day goes *Psycho*" comedy still retains his trademark shocking edge. A truly tacky delight. Contains violence, swearing and sex scenes. ▭
Kathleen Turner *Mom/Beverly Sutphin* • Sam Waterston *Dad/Eugene Sutphin* • Ricki Lake *Misty Sutphin* • Matthew Lillard *Chip Sutphin* • Scott Wesley Morgan *Detective Pike* • Walt MacPherson *Detective Gracey* • Justin Whalin *Scotty* • Patricia Dunnock *Birdie* • Lonnie Horsey *Carl* ■ *Dir/Scr* John Waters

Serious Charge ★★★ PG
Drama   1959 · UK · BW · 95mins
One of those unassuming British movies that suddenly veers off into very risky areas. Anthony Quayle plays a former army vicar who arrives in a new town (an early Milton Keynes) to run a youth club. Sarah Churchill throws herself at him but Quayle prefers football. Then a local teddy boy accuses Quayle of sexual assault. The movie is especially good at subverting British movie decorum – people exchanging mild gossip over cups of tea – by focusing on the sterility of life in the New Britain of purpose-built towns. All this plus Cliff Richard making his screen debut. ▭
Anthony Quayle *Howard Phillips* • Sarah Churchill *Hester Peters* • Andrew Ray *Larry Thompson* • Irene Browne *Mrs Phillips* • Percy Herbert *Mr Thompson* • Noel Howlett *Mr Peters* • Cliff Richard *Curley Thompson* ■ *Dir* Terence Young • *Scr* Mickey Delamar, Guy Elmes, from the play by Philip King

The Serpent ★★
Spy drama   1972 · Fr/It/W Ger · Colour · 121mins
As well as an outstanding cast – Yul Brynner, Henry Fonda, Dirk Bogarde – this boasts exemplary technical credits, with Claude Renoir behind the camera and Ennio Morricone composing the score. Alas, it turns out to be a distinctly muted cloak-and-dagger affair. Brynner is a top Russian diplomat whose defection to the west is complicated by a series of deaths. Interrogations, mysterious meetings at airports and other genre clichés ensure that spy fans are kept happy. The whole production is given a glossy look by director Henri Verneuil and his set pieces display a fine eye for detail, but the overly complicated story never grips the viewer.
Yul Brynner *Vlassov* • Henry Fonda *Allan Davies* • Dirk Bogarde *Philip Boyle* • Philippe Noiret *Lucien Berthon* • Michel Bouquet *Tavel* • Farley Granger *Computer programming chief* • Virna Lisi *Annabel Lee* ■ *Dir* Henri Verneuil • *Scr* Henri Verneuil, Gilles Perrault, Tom Rowe, from the novel *Le Suicide* by Pierre Nord

The Serpent and the Rainbow ★★★ 18
Horror   1987 · US · Colour · 93mins
Inspired by Wade Davis's non-fiction account of scouring Haiti for authentic "zombie powder" on behalf of a pharmaceutical company wanting to market a new anaesthetic, *A Nightmare on Elm Street* director Wes Craven turns his intriguing quest into nothing more than a high-tone fright flick. However, this literal Hollywood interpretation, while paying scant attention to the role political terror plays in some parts of the West Indies, is well appointed in the creepy atmosphere department, veering from chilling fact to hallucinatory horror via Craven's sure-handed shock tableaux of live burials, voodoo brainwashing and decomposing hands in the dinner party soup. Contains violence and swearing. ▭
Bill Pullman *Dennis Alan* • Cathy Tyson *Dr Marielle Duchamp* • Zakes Mokae *Dargent Peytraud* • Paul Winfield *Lucien Celine* • Brent Jennings *Mozart* • Conrad Roberts *Christophe* • Badja Djola *Gaston* • Theresa Merritt *Simone* • Michael Gough *Schoonbacher* ■ *Dir* Wes Craven • *Scr* Richard Maxwell, AR Simoun, from the book by Wade Davis

Serpent of the Nile ★ U
Historical drama   1953 · US · Colour · 81mins
If Perry Mason is your idea of Mark Antony, this risible historical drama is for you. For, verily, Raymond Burr plays the noble Roman, with red-headed Rhonda Fleming as Queen Cleopatra, seducing him and heading for a suicide pact. Made on a budget that would only have paid for a day's linguini lunches on the Burton/Taylor *Cleopatra*, this effort from director William Castle is lamentable in every respect.
Rhonda Fleming *Cleopatra* • William Lundigan *Lucilius* • Raymond Burr *Mark Antony* • Jean Byron *Charmion* • Michael Ansara *Florus* ■ *Dir* William Castle • *Scr* Robert E Kent

The Serpent's Egg ★★★ 18
Drama   1977 · W Ger/US · Colour · 119mins
The critics have been unkind to this film, attacking it for its noise, its depiction of pain and prejudice and its echoes of the portrait of Germany painted in *Cabaret*. Admittedly, this is one of Ingmar Bergman's lesser pictures – he wasn't used to working in English, his knowledge of the period was somewhat limited and he was still nursing the hurt caused by his brush with the Swedish inland revenue that had driven him into temporary exile. But, occasionally, this bold experiment in style throws up some striking images, which capture the mix of decadence and danger of life in the Weimar Republic. Contains some violence and swearing. ▭
Liv Ullmann *Manuela Rosenberg* • David Carradine *Abel Rosenberg* • Gert Frobe *Inspector Bauer* • Heinz Bennent *Doctor Hans Vergerus* • James Whitmore *Priest* • Toni Berger *Mr Rosenberg* • Christian Berkel *Student* ■ *Dir/Scr* Ingmar Bergman

The Serpent's Kiss ★
Period mystery
1997 · Fr/Ger/UK · Colour · 110mins
Given Ewan McGregor's popularity, it's a sure sign of a bad movie that this sank into obscurity. In a thinly-disguised rip-off of Peter Greenaway's *The Draughtsman's Contract*, McGregor plays a landscape architect hired by wealthy Pete Postlethwaite to design a garden for his wife (Greta Scacchi). Not surprisingly, McGregor becomes embroiled in a plot by scheming Richard E Grant to bankrupt Postlethwaite. Despite the attractive cast and cinematography (by Jean-François Robin), you'd be better off doing some weeding of your own.
Greta Scacchi *Juliana* • Ewan McGregor *Meneer Chrome* • Pete Postlethwaite *Thomas Smithers* • Richard E Grant *James Fitzmaurice* • Carmen Chaplin *Thea* ■ *Dir* Philippe Rousselot • *Scr* Tim Rose Price

Serpent's Lair ★★ 18
Erotic horror thriller
1995 · US · Colour · 88mins
This fairly steamy mix of sex and shocks features Jeff Fahey as a happily married man whose wife is hospitalised shortly after they move into a strange apartment block with a dubious history. Soon Fahey finds himself stalked by a slinky seductress, played by model and singer Lisa B, who turns out to be a man-eater in more ways than one. The cast does its best and director Jeffrey Reiner summons up the odd spooky moment. Contains violence, swearing and sex scenes. ▭
Jeff Fahey *Tom Bennett* • Lisa B [Lisa Barbuscia] *Lilith* • Heather Medway *Alex Bennett* • Patrick Bauchau *Sam* • Anthony Palermo *Mario* • Kathleen Noone *Betty* ■ *Dir* Jeffrey Reiner • *Scr* Marc Rosenburg

Serpent's Path ★★★
Psychological thriller
1998 · Jap · Colour · 85mins
Completed in just a fortnight, Kiyoshi Kurosawa's stark Yakuza drama presents a far more credible insight into the murky world of snuff movies than commercially minded offerings such as *Mute Witness* or *8mm*. However, while it eschews cheap sensationalism, the film doesn't shy away from the depiction of pitiless violence, as astrophysics expert Sho Aikawa subjects various underlings to savage beatings in order to discover who was responsible for the rape and murder of the eight-year-old daughter of unstable gangster Miyashita (Teruyuki Kagawa). With the motives behind Aikawa's actions only gradually becoming clear, this is considerably more downbeat than its companion piece, *Eyes of the Spider*. In Japanese with English subtitles.
Sho Aikawa *Niijima* • Teruyuki Kagawa *Miyashita* ■ *Dir* Kiyoshi Kurosawa • *Scr* Hiroshi Takahashi

Serpico ★★★★ 18
Biographical police thriller
1973 · US · Colour · 124mins
Al Pacino's outstanding, ground-breaking performance as real-life New York cop Frank Serpico makes this a vivid portrayal of a whistle-blower as

hero and victim. After 11 years of police service, Serpico helped expose corruption among colleagues for whom hush-money and bribes were a way of life and his idealism cost him dear in terms of love affairs and friendships. Director Sidney Lumet shows, in fascinating detail, how Serpico distances himself from his colleagues with his hippy clothes and his snappy attitude. Though he has revisited similar territory in later films, Lumet has never found a better purveyor of idealism than Pacino. ▭

Al Pacino *Frank Serpico* • John Randolph *Sidney Green* • Jack Kehoe *Tom Keough* • Biff McGuire *McClain* • Barbara Eda-Young *Laurie* • Cornelia Sharpe *Leslie* • Tony Roberts *Bob Blair* • John Medici *Pasquale* ■ *Dir* Sidney Lumet • *Scr* Waldo Salt, Norman Wexler, from the book by Peter Maas

The Servant ★★★★ 15

Drama   1963 · UK · BW · 110mins

This claustrophobic tale of envy and manipulation sees James Fox descend from a champagne lifestyle into a decadent dependence upon his servant, Dirk Bogarde. The snarling story is handled with great insight by director Joseph Losey, who had keenly studied the British class system since being exiled from Hollywood in 1951 during the Communist witch-hunt. Sarah Miles and Wendy Craig impress as the women caught in the powerplay, but this is essentially a two-hander, with Fox admirable as a latter-day Sebastian Flyte and Bogarde (finally nailing his matinée reputation) chilling as the mercenary valet. ▭

Dirk Bogarde *Hugo Barrett* • Sarah Miles *Vera* • Wendy Craig *Susan* • James Fox *Tony* • Catherine Lacey *Lady Mounset* • Richard Vernon *Lord Mounset* • Ann Firbank *Society woman* • Harold Pinter *Society man* ■ *Dir* Joseph Losey • *Scr* Harold Pinter, from the novel by Robin Maugham • *Cinematographer* Douglas Slocombe • *Music* John Dankworth

The Servants of Twilight ★★★ 15

Thriller   1991 · US · Colour · 91mins

Many sci-fi/fantasy aficionados speak of Dean R Koontz in the same revered terms as Stephen King. Invariably, even the best adaptations have an author's fans protesting, but this TV movie should not disappoint the converted – and might just persuade the uninitiated to check the shelves at their local bookshop. The strong point here is undoubtedly the storyline, which tells of a race against time to prevent a group of religious fanatics murdering a young boy they are convinced is the Antichrist. What makes this particularly disturbing is the fact that it's all so plausible. Contains violence and swearing. ▭

Bruce Greenwood *Charlie Harrison, Private Investigator* • Belinda Bauer *Christine Scavello* • Grace Zabriskie *Grace Spivey* • Richard Bradford *Henry Rankin* • Jarrett Lennon *Joey Scavello* • Carel Struycken *Kyle* ■ *Dir* Jeffrey Obrow • *Scr* Dean R Koontz, from his novel

Serving in Silence ★★★ PG

Drama based on a true story
1995 · US · Colour · 87mins

Boasting Barbra Streisand as one of its executive producers and the

heavyweight presence of Glenn Close and Judy Davis, this is a provocative TV movie. Close is typically impressive in the lead as a much-decorated US Army nurse, who is discharged after she reveals her homosexuality during a security screening. Davis has less chance to shine as her lover, whose reluctance to face the glare of publicity makes her seem skittish and selfish beside the dignified and determined Close. As drama it's pretty predictable, but as social comment it's committed and timely. ▭

Glenn Close *Col Margarethe Cammermeyer* • Judy Davis *Diane* • Jan Rubes *Far* • Wendy Makkena *Mary Newcombe* • Susan Barnes *Captain Kern* • Vic Polizos *Jim* ■ *Dir* Jeff Bleckner • *Scr* Alison Cross

Set It Off ★★★ 18

Action crime drama
1996 · US · Colour · 123mins

Four down-on-their-luck African-American women from Los Angeles – resentful of the "system" – band together to pull off a string of bank robberies. The subplots are numerous, resulting in romance, serious statements about ghetto life and thrilling bullet-strewn action scenes being crammed in together, yet they still manage to grab the attention. Jada Pinkett does well in the lead, but it's the commanding Queen Latifah who has the acting ability and personality to stand out, though Blair Underwood gives a nice supporting performance. ▭ **DVD**

Jada Pinkett [Jada Pinkett Smith] *Stony* • Queen Latifah *Cleo* • Vivica A Fox *Frankie* • Kimberly Elise *Tisean* • John C McGinley *Detective Strode* • Blair Underwood *Keith* • Dr Dre *Black Sam* ■ *Dir* F Gary Gray • *Scr* Kate Lanier, Takashi Bufford, from a story by Takashi Bufford

The Set-Up ★★★★ PG

Sports drama   1949 · US · BW · 68mins

Arguably one of the best boxing films ever made, this is a knockout from the great days of RKO. It was among the first to show the crippling confrontation between good and evil in the ring, when an over-the-hill, down-the-bill boxer is sold out by his manager, and then has to face the consequences of his gangster connections. The usually villainous Robert Ryan is wonderful and plausibly decent as the fighter, though Audrey Totter as his wife is miscast. Director Robert Wise, long before his success with *The Sound of Music*, controversially depicts the ringside audience as sadists lusting for blood. And there is plenty of it, as Milton Krasner's camera darts around in a flurry of action to create boxing scenes of brain-jarring ferocity. A savage morality tale, not to be missed. ▭

Robert Ryan *Bill "Stoker" Thompson* • Audrey Totter *Julie* • George Tobias *Tiny* • Alan Baxter *Little Boy* • Wallace Ford *Gus* • Percy Helton *Red* ■ *Dir* Robert Wise • *Scr* Art Cohn, from a poem by Joseph Moncure March

The Set Up ★★★ 18

Thriller   1995 · US · Colour · 89mins

This superior TV movie benefits from a tightly plotted story and a stellar cast led by Billy Zane and featuring thriller icon James Coburn. Zane gives a

dogged performance as a cat burglar whose plans to go straight are waylaid by ex-con James Russo, who threatens to kill Zane's girlfriend unless he dismantles the security system he has installed at Coburn's bank. The excellent Russo gives another rendition of his unhinged villain routine, while Mia Sara scores as Zane's lover. The boxing scene is strong meat, but stick with it because the finale is a belter. Contains violence and sex scenes. ▭

Billy Zane *Charlie Thorpe* • Mia Sara *Gina Sands* • James Russo *Kliff* • James Coburn *Jeremiah Cole* • Louis Mandylor *Pauly* • Tiny "Zeus" Lister [Tom "Tiny" Lister Jr] *Leon* • Mark Rolston *Ray Harris* • Margaret Avery *Olivia Dubois* ■ *Dir* Strathford Hamilton • *Scr* Michael Thoma, from the book *My Laugh Comes Last* by James Hadley Chase

Settle the Score ★★ 18

Thriller   1989 · US · Colour · 93mins

Jaclyn Smith stars in this average TV movie as a policewoman trying to turn the tables on a serial attacker who left her for dead 20 years before. Smith isn't a very effective stalker of the criminal fraternity and the pace of this potentially disturbing movie is inconsistent. What starts out as a worthy idea – the empowerment of female victims of violence– merely makes the women themselves look rather stupid. There are better ways of raising the profile of this issue than turning Smith into Charles Bronson. ▭

Jaclyn Smith *Kate Whately* • Jeffrey DeMunn *Josh* • Louise Latham *Mother* • Howard Duff *Father* • Amy Wright *Becky* • Richard Masur *Lincoln* • Frederick Coffin *Tucker* ■ *Dir* Ed Sherin [Edwin Sherin] • *Scr* Steve Sohmer

The Settlement ★★★

Drama   1982 · Ausl · Colour · 91mins

Reminiscent of George and Lennie in *Of Mice and Men*, Bill Kerr and John Jarratt arrive in an outback town looking to hustle a few quid. But, when they hook up with barmaid Lorna Lesley, they incur the wrath of the conservative locals. Without forcing the issue, director Howard Rubie succeeds in celebrating individuality rather than sniping at the muddled morality of the Australian majority. His only false step is in allowing Catholic cop's wife Katy Wild to be so shrill in whipping up animosity. The performances of May-December lovers Lesley and Kerr and the guileless Jarratt are spot-on.

Bill Kerr *Kearney* • John Jarratt *Tommy Martin* • Lorna Lesley *Joycie* • Tony Barry *Sgt Crowe* • Alan Cassell *Lohan* • Katy Wild *Mrs Crowe* ■ *Dir* Howard Rubie • *Scr* Ted Roberts

Seul contre Tous ★★★★ 18

Drama   1998 · Fr · Colour · 92mins

Setting out to rouse the lethargic cinema establishment, Gaspar Noé succeeded in turning a barrage of shocking images, abrasive captions and jarring sounds into a grotesquely credible portrait of furious misery that enervates and repels in equal measure. Whether spouting self-pitying, misanthropic bile or assaulting his pregnant mistress and handicapped daughter, butcher Philippe Nahon (in an alarmingly courageous performance) still commands our pity, as a victim of

poverty, injustice and his own twisted logic. From the frantic opening montage to the ambiguously upbeat ending, this is an assault on the senses that irresistibly recalls the early work of Jean-Luc Godard. In French with English subtitles. Contains violence, sex scenes and swearing. ▭

Philippe Nahon *The butcher* • Bladine Lenoir *His daughter, Cynthia* • Frankye Pain *His mistress* • Martine Audrain *Mother-in-law* ■ *Dir/Scr* Gaspar Noé

Seven ★★★ 18

Action comedy   1979 · US · Colour · 96mins

Director Andy Sidaris carved out a niche for himself making enjoyable low-budget action films destined for video, rather than big-screen exposure. *Seven* is such a film. Veteran hunk William Smith stars as Drew Savano, leader of a seven-strong team of experts assembled by a government agent to combat a syndicate of seven gangsters planning mayhem in Hawaii. Lots of fisticuffs, gunplay and female flesh comes as no surprise for fans of this genre – fine if you like that sort of thing. ▭

William Smith *Drew* • Barbara Leigh *Alexa* • Guich Koock *Cowboy* • Art Metrano *Kinsella* • Martin Kove *Skip* • Richard LePore *Professor* ■ *Dir* Andy Sidaris • *Scr* William Driskill, Robert Baird, from a story by Andy Sidaris

Se7en ★★★★★ 18

Thriller   1995 · US · Colour · 121mins

Director David Fincher's brilliant postmodern *film noir* is a grim and disturbing tale about a vicious serial killer on the loose in Los Angeles. Intelligently scripted by Andrew Kevin Walker, it is a work of extraordinary style, upsetting power and narrative daring. It also boasts fine performances from Morgan Freeman as a disillusioned detective on the brink of retirement and Brad Pitt as his enthusiastic replacement. With only seven days left on the job, Freeman finds himself drawn to a puzzling case of a psychopath who murders his victims in a gruesome manner to atone for the sins he deems them to have committed. Draining his landscapes of colour, and setting all the tense action against rain-washed streets and underlit interiors, Fincher evokes an atmosphere of nightmare proportions. Contains swearing and violence. ▭ **DVD**

Brad Pitt *Detective David Mills* • Morgan Freeman *Lieutenant William Somerset* • Gwyneth Paltrow *Tracy Mills* • Richard Roundtree *Talbot* • John C McGinley *California* • R Lee Ermey *Police captain* • Kevin Spacey *John Doe* • Daniel Zacapa *Detective Taylor* ■ *Dir* David Fincher • *Scr* Andrew Kevin Walker • *Cinematographer* Darius Khondji

Seven Alone ★ U

Western adventure based on a true story
1974 · US · Colour · 97mins

This is the tale of the Sager children who were orphaned in the American northwest of the 1840s during a wagon train journey to Oregon. The seven children, lead by oldest child Stewart Petersen, make the rest of the journey by themselves, encountering various low-budget dangers along the way. Based on his performance,

Petersen must have secured his role in this "family values" movie (and others in the seventies) only because he had the same Mormon background as the producers. In fact, the real trials of the Sager family were even less exciting than what happens here.

Dewey Martin *Henry Sager* • Aldo Ray *Dr Dutch* • Anne Collings *Naome Sager* • Dean Smith *Kit Carson* • James Griffith *Billy Shaw* • Stewart Petersen *John Sager* • Dehl Berti *White Elk* ■ *Dir* Earl Bellamy • *Scr* Douglas Stewart, Eleanor Lamb, from the book *On to Oregon* by Honore Morrow

Seven Angry Men ★★ U

Historical drama 1955 · US · BW · 91mins

Raymond Massey had powerfully portrayed the fanatical abolitionist John Brown in *Santa Fe Trail*, but what was good in moderation becomes tiresome here, as Massey takes centre stage. The verbose script by Daniel B Ullman and the heavy-handed direction by Charles Marquis Warren concentrate on Brown's increasingly savage campaign in Kansas to abolish slavery, culminating in his attack on Harper's Ferry.

Raymond Massey *John Brown* • Debra Paget *Elizabeth* • Jeffrey Hunter *Owen* • Larry Pennell *Oliver* • Leo Gordon *White* • John Smith *Frederick* • James Best *Jason* • Dennis Weaver *John Jr* • Guy Williams *Salmon* ■ *Dir* Charles Marquis Warren • *Scr* Daniel B Ullman

Seven Beauties ★★★★ 18

Satirical war drama
1976 · It · Colour · 111mins

This really is a film with something to offend everyone. A sizzling satire on the political naivety and military incompetence of the Italian male, it also passes scathing comment on such sensitive issues as obesity, female emancipation, the Mafia and concentration camps. Not all of the jokes come off. But Lina Wertmuller, who received Oscar nominations for both her writing and direction, takes events at a ferocious pace and gets a superb performance from her regular collaborator Giancarlo Giannini, who is the everyman struggling to survive the war and feed his indolent family. In Italian with English subtitles. Contains violence and sex scenes.

Giancarlo Giannini *Pasqualino Settebellezze* • Fernando Rey *Pedro* • Shirley Stoler *Hilde* • Elena Fiore *Concetta* • Piero Di Iorio *Francesco* ■ *Dir/Scr* Lina Wertmuller

Seven Brides for Seven Brothers ★★★★★ U

Musical 1954 · US · Colour · 97mins

Rightly a sensational commercial success in its day, especially in Britain, this joyous romp remains one of the freshest and most satisfying of movie musicals. A screen original, based on Stephen Vincent Benet's updating of *The Rape of the Sabine Women*, it was fashioned by director Stanley Donen and choreographer Michael Kidd into an exciting, heart-warming and technically accomplished (though perhaps a shade politically incorrect) musical. The central barn dance is magnificent, and the early use of CinemaScope is as exquisite as the beautifully stylised MGM interiors. Although generally cleverly cast, the movie gains strength from the two leading performances. Keel, in particular, brings variety to what could have been a boorish role. A treat.

Howard Keel *Adam Pontipee* • Jane Powell *Milly* • Russ Tamblyn *Gideon* • Jeff Richards *Benjamin* • Tommy Rall *Frank* • Marc Platt *Daniel* • Matt Mattox *Caleb* • Jacques d'Amboise *Ephraim* • Howard Petrie *Pete Perkins* ■ *Dir* Stanley Donen • *Scr* Albert Hackett, Frances Goodrich, Dorothy Kingsley, from the story *The Sobbin' Women* by Stephen Vincent Benet • *Music/Lyrics* Gene De Paul, Johnny Mercer • *Cinematographer* George Folsey • *Music Director* Adolph Deutsch, Saul Chaplin

Seven Chances ★★★

Silent farce
1925 · US · BW and Colour · 56mins

Made immediately after three Keaton masterpieces, culminating with *The Navigator*, this enjoyable comedy has been somewhat neglected, partly because the highlight is in the last reel. Buster plays his usual doleful character who discovers that he has been left seven million dollars, provided he marries within the day. There are soon plenty of hopefuls and the climax of the film finds him pursued first by would-be brides and then by an avalanche of rocks.

Buster Keaton *James Shannon* • T Roy Barnes *His partner* • Snitz Edwards *Lawyer* • Ruth Dwyer *Mary Jones* • Jean Arthur ■ *Dir* Buster Keaton • *Scr* Jean Havez, Clyde Bruckman, Joseph Mitchell, from the play *Seven Chances: a Comedy in Three Acts* by Roi Cooper Megrue

Seven Cities of Gold ★★ U

Historical adventure
1955 · US · Colour · 102mins

It's the late 18th century, and Richard Egan and Anthony Quinn ride out from Mexico in an attempt to load their saddlebags with gold. In their way stands pious and pompous Michael Rennie, bent on bringing Christianity to the land and converting the Indians, represented by Jeffrey Hunter and Rita Moreno. Although pitched as an action drama, the historical context of Spanish colonialism, in which the church and army are sidekicks, is not ignored. Shot in Mexico by Lucien Ballard, who later worked on *The Wild Bunch*, it was directed by Robert D Webb who specialised in westerns with Spanish accents.

Richard Egan *Jose* • Anthony Quinn *Captain Portola* • Michael Rennie *Father Junipero Serra* • Jeffrey Hunter *Matuwir* • Rita Moreno *Ula* • Eduardo Noriega *Sergeant* • Leslie Bradley *Galvez* ■ *Dir* Robert D Webb • *Scr* Richard L Breen, John C Higgins, Joseph Petracca, from the novel *The Nine Days of Father Serra* by Isabelle Gibson Ziegler

Seven Days in May ★★★★ U

Political thriller 1964 · US · BW · 117mins

An outstanding cast that includes Burt Lancaster, Fredric March, Kirk Douglas and Ava Gardner could make even the most outlandish of conspiracy theories credible. They do so magnificently with this story of a military group trying to topple the US President (March) because he has signed a nuclear disarmament treaty with the Soviet Union. Director John Frankenheimer uses all the mechanical tricks of the surveillance trade – TV monitors, hidden cameras and electronic devices – to suggest the omnipresent miltary machine. Not that all the hardware upstages the actors.

Burt Lancaster *General James M Scott* • Kirk Douglas *Colonel Martin "Jiggs" Casey* • Fredric March *President Jordan Lyman* • Ava Gardner *Eleanor Holbrook* • Edmond O'Brien *Senator Raymond Clark* • Martin Balsam *Paul Girard* • George Macready *Christopher Todd* • Whit Bissell *Senator Prentice* • Hugh Marlowe *Harold McPherson* ■ *Dir* John Frankenheimer • *Scr* Rod Serling, from the novel by Fletcher Knebel, Charles Waldo Bailey II

Seven Days' Leave ★★★ U

Wartime musical comedy
1942 · US · BW · 87mins

This endearing RKO romp effectively teams a pre-*I Love Lucy* Lucille Ball and handsome hunk Victor Mature, both of whom seem to be having a jolly good time and manage to convey that pleasure to the audience. The plot's a clunker, with army private Mature inheriting $100,000 if he can marry socialite Ball. There's fun and frolics along the way, plus some terrific music from top bands of the era.

Victor Mature *Johnny Grey* • Lucille Ball *Terry* • Harold Peary *Great Gildersleeve* • Mapy Cortes *Mapy* • Ginny Simms *Ginny* • Marcy McGuire *Mickey* • Peter Lind Hayes *Jackson* • Walter Reed *Ralph Bell* • Wallace Ford *Sergeant Mead* ■ *Dir* Tim Whelan • *Scr* William Bowers, Ralph Spence, Curtis Kenyon, Kenneth Earl

Seven Days to Noon ★★★★

Science-fiction drama
1950 · UK · BW · 96mins

Doomsday movies were everywhere in the early fifties, as the Cold War chill began to bite. This is the finest British contribution to that sub-genre, indeed, a pretty convincing case could be made for its nomination as one of this country's best ever sci-fi films. Although the threat of an atomic explosion in London makes for compelling viewing, the true power of the picture comes from a magnificent performance by Barry Jones as the professor driven to suicidal despair by the misappropriation of his work. Thanks to Jones and cinematographer Gilbert Taylor's eerie images of the capital, the Boulting brothers maintain an unbearable tension.

Barry Jones *Professor Willingdon* • Olive Sloane *Goldie* • André Morell *Superintendent Folland* • Sheila Manahan *Ann Willingdon* • Hugh Cross *Stephen Lane* • Joan Hickson *Mrs Peckett* ■ *Dir* John Boulting • *Scr* Roy Boulting, Frank Harvey, from a story by Paul Dehn, James Bernard

The Seven Deadly Sins ★★★

Portmanteau drama
1952 · Fr/It · BW · 155mins

Gerard Philipe introduces each of these tales with more charm than they really merit. The main interest in these modern parables – five of them in French and two in Italian – is how much they reveal about the attitude to sex in the early 1950s. Inevitably there are a few duds in the collection, with the best being Roberto Rossellini's *Envy*, based on a story by Colette, about a woman becoming more attached to her cat than her husband. Yves Allégret's *Lust* effectively reveals the difference between puppy and adult love, and Carlo Rim's *Gluttony* tells how a piece of cheese comes between a man and a woman. A French/Italian language film.

Eduardo De Filippo *Eduardo* • Jacqueline Plessis *Laziness* • Frank Villard *Ravila* • Francette Vernillat *Chantel* • Gérard Philipe *Master of Ceremonies* • Noël-Noël *The Director* • Michèle Morgan *Anne-Marie* ■ *Dir* Eduardo De Filippo, Jean Dréville, Yves Allégret, Roberto Rossellini, Carlo Rim, Claude Autant-Lara, Georges Lacombe • *Scr* Charles Spaak, Carlo Rim, Pierre Bost, Jean Aurenche, Roberto Rossellini, Carlo Rim, Pierre Bost, Jean Aurenche, Claude Autant-Lara, Pierre Bost, Jean Aurenche

The Seven Deadly Sins ★★★

Portmanteau drama
1961 · Fr/It · BW · 115mins

It must have seemed a good idea at the time to get several of the New Wave French directors to give their slant on the seven deadly sins. But the result is a hit-and-miss affair, as with so many portmanteau films, with a mixture of good, average and awful. Among the better episodes are Philipe de Broca's *Gluttony*, Roger Vadim's *Pride*, Jacques Demy's *Lust*, and Jean-Luc Godard's *Sloth* – about a film star (Eddie Constantine) who is too lazy to have sex even when offered to him on a plate. The other three sins were committed by Claude Chabrol (*Greed*), Edouard Molinaro (*Envy*) and Sylvain Dhomme (*Anger*). In French with English subtitles.

Danièle Barraud *Suzon* • Jacques Charrier *Antoine* • Nicole Mirel *Starlet* • Eddie Constantine *Eddie* • Micheline Presle *Mother* • Jean-Louis Trintignant *Paul* • Michèle Girardon *La maîtrese* • Marcelle Arnold *The wife* • Georges Wilson *Valentin* • Perrette Pradier *TV announcer* • Marie-José Nat *Young wife* ■ *Dir* Claude Chabrol, Edouard Molinaro, Jean-Luc Godard, Jacques Demy, Roger Vadim, Philippe de Broca, Sylvain Dhomme • *Scr* Félicien Marceau, Claude Chabrol, Claude Mauriac, Jean-Luc Godard, Roger Peyrefitte, Jacques Demy, Félicien Marceau, Daniel Boulanger, Eugène Ionesco

711 Ocean Drive ★★

Crime drama 1950 · US · BW · 101mins

Released at a time when bookmaking scandals were journalistic currency, this early fifties crime drama features Edmond O'Brien as a telephone engineer lured into organised crime by the mob. At first he just fixes the phone lines that link the racetracks, but then he gets a taste for power and starts cutting people off at the neck. It's a little moral tale, which says that crime doesn't pay – except that the mob are still all-powerful and in control after the spectacular climax on the Hoover Dam.

Edmond O'Brien *Mal Granger* • Joanne Dru *Gail Mason* • Donald Porter [Don Porter] *Larry Mason* • Sammy White *Chippie Evans* • Dorothy Patrick *Trudy Maxwell* • Barry Kelley *Vince Walters* • Otto Kruger *Carl Stephans* ■ *Dir* Joseph M Newman • *Scr* Richard English, Frances Swan

1264 U = SUITABLE FOR ALL Uc = SUITABLE FOR ALL, ESPECIALLY FOR YOUNG CHILDREN (VIDEO ONLY) PG = PARENTAL GUIDANCE

7 Faces of Dr Lao ★★★ Ⓤ
Fantasy western drama
1963 · US · Colour · 99mins

This odd, almost surrealistic, fantasy western hit a nerve at the time and became a major success largely, because of the mesmerising performance of Tony Randall, who plays the titular doctor and no less than six other roles. This is the classic tale of a strange travelling circus, which arrives in town puts the fear of God into the locals and teaches them a few of life's lessons along the way. What distinguishes this intriguing movie is the glorious make-up, which won William Tuttle a much-deserved Oscar. The townsfolk are a trifle stereotypical – staring eyes and toothless leers under frayed bonnets – but Randall engages from reel on reel.

Tony Randall *Dr Lao/Merlin the Magician/Medusa/Apollonius of Tyana/Pan/The Abominable Snowman/Giant Serpent* • Arthur O'Connell *Clint Stark* • John Ericson *Ed Cunningham* • Barbara Eden *Angela Benedict* • Kevin Tate *Mike Benedict* • Noah Beery Jr *Tim Mitchell* • Lee Patrick *Mrs Howard T Cassan* ■ *Dir* George Pal • *Scr* Charles Beaumont, from the novel *The Circus of Dr Lao* by Charles G Finney

Seven Hills of Rome ★★ Ⓤ
Musical
1957 · US · Colour · 103mins

Tenor Mario Lanza's last two movies were sorry affairs compared to what had gone before (*The Great Caruso*, *Because You're Mine*). But an insatiable appetite coupled with appalling manners made him hard both to cast and to like, and, although his robust voice was undeniably attractive, his screen persona became awkward and contrived. Here, under the expert directorial hand of Roy Rowland, his performance is a little more mellow – but when those lungs open, nothing seems able to contain him. This film is really for fans only.

Mario Lanza *Marc Revere* • Renato Rascel *Pepe Bonelli* • Marisa Allasio *Rafaella Marini* • Peggie Castle *Carol Ralston* • Clelia Matania *Beatrice* • Rossella Como *Anita* • Amos Davoli *Carlo* • Guido Celano *Luigi* ■ *Dir* Roy Rowland • *Scr* Art Cohn, Giorgio Prosperi, from a story by Giuseppi Amato

Seven Hours to Judgment ★★★ 15
Thriller
1988 · US · Colour · 89mins

Beau Bridges directs and stars in this revenge thriller, playing a judge who's forced to acquit a gang of killer thugs on a technicality. The victim's husband (Ron Leibman) blames Beau, kidnaps the judge's wife and forces him to run the gauntlet through the gang's tough home turf. The direction is a bit twitchy and Beau is far too baby-faced to be credible in a role that requires a lot more visual gravitas. Brother Jeff would have been better. This nevertheless remains a solid and watchable if preposterous action thriller. ▭

Beau Bridges *John Eden* • Ron Leibman *David Reardon* • Julianne Phillips *Lisa Eden* • Tiny Ron Taylor [Tiny Ron] *Ira* • Al Freeman Jr *Danny Larwin* • Reggie Johnson *Chino* ■ *Dir* Beau Bridges • *Scr* Walter Davis, Elliot Stephens, from a story by Walter Davis

Seven Keys to Baldpate ★★ Ⓤ
Comedy mystery 1935 · US · BW · 69mins

Across four decades, film-makers were drawn to this story from a novel by Earl Derr Biggers. A writer who needs peace and quiet to finish a book in 24 hours, takes himself off to the remote Baldpate Inn, only to find himself in the hub of activity involving a constant stream of mysterious strangers chasing $200,000 worth of illicit cash. The tale was adapted for the stage by George M Cohan who, in 1917, starred in the first of two silent versions. Here, Gene Raymond does his usual uninspired best, but the intriguing aspects of the movie take second place to the creaking tedium. William Hamilton and Edward Killy co-directed – providing atmosphere, but at snail's pace.

Gene Raymond *Magee* • Margaret Callahan *Mary* • Eric Blore *Bolton* • Erin O'Brien-Moore *Myra* • Moroni Olsen *Cargan* • Walter Brennan *Station agent* ■ *Dir* William Hamilton, Edward Killy • *Scr* Wallace Smith, Anthony Veiller, from the play by George M Cohan, from the novel by Earl Derr Biggers

Seven Keys to Baldpate ★★
Comedy mystery 1947 · US · BW · 68mins

Yet another remake of the cold, dark house mystery about a novelist who, forced to finish a book to a 24-hour deadline, seeks refuge in the isolated Baldpate Inn, but is disturbed by the arrival of thieves come to split the proceeds of a heist. It's directed by Lew Landers at programme-filler length, with Philip Terry as Magee and there are a couple of minor variations in the convoluted plot, but it's really hard to understand why RKO returned yet again to this dated material.

Phillip Terry *Magee* • Jacqueline White *Mary* • Eduardo Ciannelli *Cargan* • Margaret Lindsay *Connie Lane* • Arthur Shields *Bolton* • Jimmy Conlin *Hermit* ■ *Dir* Lew Landers • *Scr* Lee Loeb, from the play by George M Cohan, from the novel by Earl Derr Biggers

Seven Little Foys ★★★ Ⓤ
Musical biography
1955 · US · Colour · 92mins

In one of his straighter roles, Bob Hope plays real-life comedian Eddie Foy who, after the early death of his wife, trained his seven children to join him in his vaudeville act. The trouble is that Hope's character is hard to like, and the musical routines are lacklustre, apart from one memorable sequence featuring guest star James Cagney. Reprising his portrayal of George M Cohan from *Yankee Doodle Dandy*, Cagney joins Hope in a song-and-soft-shoe routine to two Cohan favourites, momentarily lifting the film into a classier category altogether.

Eddie Foy Jr *Narrator* • Bob Hope *Eddie Foy* • Milly Vitale *Madeleine Morando* • George Tobias *Barney Green* • Angela Clarke *Clara* • Herbert Heyes *Judge* • James Cagney *George M Cohan* ■ *Dir* Melville Shavelson • *Scr* Melville Shavelson, Jack Rose

Seven Men from Now ★★★★
Western 1956 · US · Colour · 77mins

John Wayne's production company made this modestly budgeted Randolph Scott western and it turned out so well that the Duke wished he'd starred in it himself. Burt Kennedy's lean script has Scott grimly tracking down the seven men who killed his wife during a hold-up, with Lee Marvin's gunman following close behind hoping to grab the loot they've hidden. Wayne gave his former co-star Gail Russell the female lead. Director Budd Boetticher makes terrific use of outdoor settings and he, Scott and Kennedy teamed up on three more outstanding westerns: *The Tall T*, *Ride Lonesome* and *Comanche Station*.

Randolph Scott *Ben Stride* • Gail Russell *Annie Greer* • Lee Marvin *Big Masters* • Walter Reed *John Greer* • John Larch *Pate Bodeen* ■ *Dir* Budd Boetticher • *Scr* Burt Kennedy, from his story • *Cinematographer* William H Clothier [William Clothier]

The Seven Minutes ★★
Courtroom drama 1971 · US · Colour · 93mins

This adaptation of Irving Wallace's pornography-on-trial tale – about a man accused of rape who claims reading a dirty book incited him to do it – is a real hoot. It's chiefly notable as the only "straight" film of director Russ Meyer, better known as the purveyor of mega-bosomed babes in such cult "classics" as *Faster Pussycat! Kill! Kill!* and *Beyond the Valley of the Ultra Vixens*. Although the cast is populated by such fine character actors as Philip Carey, Yvonne De Carlo and John Carradine, and there's an early appearance by Tom Selleck, there's no *Magnum* force here. Consequently Meyer decided nothing succeeds like excess and retreated back to big bosoms and camp outrageousness.

Wayne Maunder *Mike Barrett* • Yvonne De Carlo *Constance Cumberland* • Marianne McAndrew *Maggie Russell* • Philip Carey *Elmo Duncan* • Jay C Flippen *Luther Yerkes* • Edy Williams *Faye Osborn* • Lyle Bettger *Frank Griffith* • Charles Drake *Sgt Kellog* • John Carradine *Sean O'Flanagan* • Harold J Stone *Judge Upshaw* • Tom Selleck *Phil Sanford* ■ *Dir* Russ Meyer • *Scr* Richard Warren Lewis, from the novel by Irving Wallace

Seven Minutes ★★★★ 15
Second World War thriller
1989 · W Ger · Colour · 91mins

This is an intelligent, auspicious directorial debut from Klaus Maria Brandauer, who also stars as a determined, methodical would-be assassin of one Adolf Hitler. Brandauer's strong, impressive performance overlays a thriller that intrigues and grips in equal measure. The cast is excellent, with the always watchable Brian Dennehy chilling but understated as a Gestapo chief. Celebrated cinematographer Lajos Koltai gives the film a suitably dense, atmospheric air. ▭

Klaus Maria Brandauer *Elser* • Rebecca Miller *Anneliese* • Brian Dennehy *Wagner* • Nigel Le Vaillant *Mayer* • Maggie O'Neill *Berta* • Roger Ashton-Griffiths *Watchman* ■ *Dir* Klaus Maria Brandauer • *Scr* Stephen Sheppard, from his novel *The Artisan*

Seven Nights in Japan ★ PG
Romantic drama
1976 · UK/Fr · Colour · 99mins

Seven Nights seems a lot longer. Considering he's been saddled with screenwriter Christopher Wood's wincingly twee reworking of *Roman Holiday* and Lewis Gilbert's guileless direction, Michael York looks far less embarrassed than he should be, as the British prince who evades his bodyguards to indulge in a spot of romance with tour guide Hidemi Aoki. As toffs such as James Villiers and Charles Gray fret patriotically, we are treated to cinematographer Henri Decaë's postcard vistas and the delirious efforts of York and Aoki to look besotted. ▭

Michael York *Prince George* • Hidemi Aoki *Somi* • Charles Gray *Ambassador Hollander* • Ann Lonnberg *Jane Hollander* • Eléonore Hirt *Mrs Hollander* • James Villiers *Finn* ■ *Dir* Lewis Gilbert • *Scr* Christopher Wood

The Seven-Per-Cent Solution ★★
Mystery 1976 · US · Colour · 119mins

Sherlock Holmes's fans will immediately recognise that the title refers to the sleuth's preferred mixture of cocaine, but that's as clever as it gets. The spoof plot is a simple one involving a mystery kidnapping. Although the cast is impressive – Nicol Williamson and Robert Duvall as Holmes and Watson, Alan Arkin, Laurence Olivier and Vanessa Redgrave (as the damsel in distress) – the solution is rather less so.

Nicol Williamson *Sherlock Holmes* • Robert Duvall *Dr Watson* • Alan Arkin *Sigmund Freud* • Laurence Olivier *Professor Moriarty* • Vanessa Redgrave *Lola Deveraux* • Joel Grey *Lowenstein* • Samantha Eggar *Mary Watson* • Jeremy Kemp *Baron von Leinsdorf* ■ *Dir* Herbert Ross • *Scr* Nicholas Meyer, from his novel, from the characters created by Sir Arthur Conan Doyle

Seven Samurai ★★★★★ PG
Classic action drama
1954 · Jap · BW · 190mins

One of the undisputed masterpieces of world cinema, Akira Kurosawa's epic was inspired by the westerns of John Ford and had the compliment repaid with John Sturges's classic reworking, *The Magnificent Seven*. Showered with international awards, the film is a mesmerising combination of historical detail, spectacular action and poignant humanism. Over 18 months in production, it has been described as "a tapestry of motion", with the final battle standing out for its audacious use of moving camera, telephoto lenses, varied film speeds and precision editing. Takashi Shimura and Toshiro Mifune are the pick of an excellent cast, but it's the director's genius that leaves an impression. In Japanese with English subtitles. Contains violence. ▭ **DVD**

Takashi Shimura *Kambei* • Toshiro Mifune *Kikuchiyo* • Yoshio Inaba *Gorobei* • Seiji Miyaguchi *Kyuzo* • Minoru Chiaki *Heihachi* • Daisuke Kato *Shichiroji* • Isao Kimura *Katsushiro* • Kamatari Fujiwara *Manzo* ■ *Dir* Akira Kurosawa • *Scr* Akira Kurosawa, Shinobu Hashimoto, Hideo Oguni • *Cinematographer* Asakasu Nakai • *Editor* Akira Kurosawa

Seven Seas to Calais ★★★ U

Swashbuckling adventure
1962 · It/US · Colour · 101mins

Swashbucklers don't come more buckled than this one, which has Rod Taylor chasing Spanish treasure as Sir Francis Drake. Keith Michell and Irene Worth articulate the ''prithee-avast'' language with clarity, but director Rudolph Maté, who had made some great *films noirs* – *Union Station* among them – was in decline and this movie follows that downhill trend in lacking tension and credibility.

Rod Taylor *Sir Francis Drake* • Keith Michell *Malcolm Marsh* • Irene Worth *Queen Elizabeth I* • Anthony Dawson *Burleigh* • Basil Dignam *Walsingham* • Mario Girotti [Terence Hill] *Babington* ■ *Dir* Rudolph Maté, Primo Zeglio • *Scr* Filippo Sanjust, George St George, Lindsay Galloway

Seven Sinners ★★★

Drama　　　　1940 · US · BW · 86mins

Marlene Dietrich is sultry cabaret singer Bijou, who arrives on a South Sea island to perform at the Seven Sinners Café. There, her erotic presence inflames every man in sight and captures the heart of navy lieutenant John Wayne. He wants to marry her, but she's wise enough to know that's a bad idea. Dietrich, giving a knowing, self-mocking parody of the Shanghai Lil stereotype, sings (if that's the right word) three numbers and inflames a climactic bar-room brawl in this rumbustious nonsense. It's directed by Tay Garnett, who benefits from the services of some terrific character actors. ▦

Marlene Dietrich *Bijou Blanche* • John Wayne *Lieutenant Dan Brent* • Broderick Crawford *''Little Ned''*, *Edward Patrick Finnegan* • Mischa Auer *Sasha* • Albert Dekker *Dr Martin* • Billy Gilbert *Tony* • Oscar Homolka *Antro* • Anna Lee *Dorothy Henderson* • Reginald Denny *Captain Church* • Samuel S Hinds *Governor* ■ *Dir* Tay Garnett • *Scr* John Meehan, Harry Tugend, from a story by Ladislaus Fodor, Laslo Vadnay

Seven Thieves ★★★

Crime drama　　1960 · US · BW · 101mins

Three Hollywood veterans – star Edward G Robinson, producer/writer Sydney Boehm and director Henry Hathaway – try to breathe life into a caper plot that itself had seen better days. Edward G does manage to add a certain validity to the story of an ageing criminal planning a last assault on a Monte Carlo casino and his acting meshes surprisingly well with that of comparative newcomer and Method actor Rod Steiger.

Edward G Robinson *Theo Wilkins* • Rod Steiger *Paul Mason* • Joan Collins *Melanie* • Eli Wallach *Poncho* • Michael Dante *Louis* • Alexander Scourby *Raymond Le May* • Berry Kroeger *Hugo Baumer* ■ *Dir* Henry Hathaway • *Scr* Sydney Boehm, from the novel *Lions at the Kill* by Max Catto • *Cinematographer* Sam Leavitt • *Music* Dominic Frontiere

Seven Thunders ★★ PG

Wartime chiller　　1957 · UK · BW · 96mins

A British oddity set in wartime France. James Robertson-Justice plays a French physician, who is ostensibly helping escaped PoWs including

---

Stephen Boyd, but in reality is mass-poisoning refugees for their money and goods. Sadly, Robertson-Justice is like a whale out of water away from his much loved Sir Lancelot in the light-hearted *Doctor* movies. Based on a real-life killer, the character he plays here was more fully realised in the 1990 French film *Docteur Petiot*, which had Michel Serrault playing the title role to chillingly merciless effect. ▦

Stephen Boyd *Dave* • James Robertson-Justice *Dr Martout* • Kathleen Harrison *Madame Abou* • Tony Wright *Jim* • Anna Gaylor *Lise* • Eugene Deckers *Emile Blanchard* • Rosalie Crutchley *Therese Blanchard* • Katherine Kath *Madame Parfait* ■ *Dir* Hugo Fregonese • *Scr* John Baines, from the novel by Rupert Croft-Cooke

The Seven-Ups ★★★

Police drama　1973 · US · Colour · 103mins

The nerve-scraping car-chase in this fast-moving New York police thriller is quite the equal of those pacey pile-ups in *Bullitt* and *The French Connection*. It's not surprising, really, as the producer of those movies, Philip D'Antoni, directed this police drama. Roy Scheider stars as an undercover cop in an unorthodox unit, whose chief informant uses Scheider's criminal lists for his own purposes. It's one of those movies in which you can't tell the good guys from the bad guys, and character development is given the elbow in favour of violent action. Contains some violence and swearing.

Roy Scheider *Buddy Manucci* • Victor Arnold *Barilli* • Jerry Leon *Mingo* • Ken Kercheval *Ansel* • Tony LoBianco *Vito Lucia* • Larry Haines *Max Kalish* • Richard Lynch *Moon* • Bill Hickman *Bo* ■ *Dir* Philip D'Antoni • *Scr* Albert Ruben, Alexander Jacobs, from a story by Sonny Grosso

Seven Ways from Sundown ★★★ U

Western　　　1960 · US · Colour · 86mins

A satisfying Audie Murphy western, in which he plays a Texas Ranger bringing in a killer, played by the ever-excellent Barry Sullivan, who gives Murphy more than a run for his money in the acting stakes. There's a nice wryness running through this Universal feature, with a cast of western veterans (John McIntire, Kenneth Tobey) to lend credibility. Although Murphy would continue filming big-screen westerns, this was his last one of any real merit. The title comes from Murphy character's name: Seven-ways-from-sundown Jones!

Audie Murphy *Seven Jones* • Barry Sullivan *Jim Flood* • Venetia Stevenson *Joy Karrington* • John McIntire *Sergeant Hennessy* • Kenneth Tobey *Lieutenant Herly* • Mary Field *Ma Kerrington* • Ken Lynch *Graves* • Suzanne Lloyd *Lucinda* ■ *Dir* Harry Keller • *Scr* Clair Huffaker, from his novel

7 Women ★★★★

Period drama　1966 · US · Colour · 86mins

The last movie from great American director John Ford is, as one might expect, a transplanted western. It's set in Manchuria in 1935, where a group of remarkably resolute women missionaries are threatened by the local Mongolian warlord (a cleverly-cast Mike Mazurki). Ford has the benefit of

---

a superb cast, headed by Anne Bancroft as a cynical physician who ends up risking everything to protect the mission. This may seem unlikely Ford material on the surface, but the old maestro certainly makes it his own, treating such skilled performers as Flora Robson, Margaret Leighton and Sue Lyon as though they were members of the US cavalry.

Anne Bancroft *Dr Cartwright* • Sue Lyon *Emma Clark* • Margaret Leighton *Agatha Andrews* • Flora Robson *Miss Binns* • Mildred Dunnock *Jane Argent* • Betty Field *Florrie Pether* • Anna Lee *Mrs Russell* • Eddie Albert *Charles Pether* • Mike Mazurki *Tunga Khan* ■ *Dir* John Ford • *Scr* Janet Green, John McCormick, from the novel *Chinese Finale* by Norah Lofts

The Seven Year Itch ★★★★ PG

Comedy　　　1955 · US · Colour · 99mins

One of the great moments from this film, when Marilyn Monroe lets the updraft from a subway ventilation shaft lift her skirt, has passed into movie legend; true cineastes will delight in noting that the sequence is divided into two horizontal cuts, since the film was one of Fox's early CinemaScope productions, and director Billy Wilder made it all look so seamless. If you haven't seen it before, you could well wonder what all the fuss was about, but in the more prudish fifties this film – and the George Axelrod Broadway hit it was based on – were very risqué indeed, the title giving a catchphrase to the nation and a new insight into marriage. The film is still very funny, and beautifully played by Monroe and Tom Ewell (plus veteran Victor Moore, as a plumber!). Just make allowances for the period and enjoy yourself. ▦

Marilyn Monroe *The Girl* • Tom Ewell *Richard Sherman* • Evelyn Keyes *Helen Sherman* • Sonny Tufts *Tom McKenzie* • Robert Strauss *Mr Kruhulik* • Oskar Homolka [Oscar Homolka] *Dr Brubaker* • Marguerite Chapman *Miss Morris* • Victor Moore *Plumber* ■ *Dir* Billy Wilder • *Scr* Billy Wilder, George Axelrod, from the play by George Axelrod • *Cinematographer* Milton Krasner • *Music* Alfred Newman

Seven Years in Tibet ★★★ PG

Adventure drama
1997 · US/UK · Colour · 130mins

Jean-Jacques Annaud's magnificently photographed Dalai Lama drama is strong on visual appeal and spiritual ambience, but makes one fatal error – the miscasting of Brad Pitt as real-life German mountaineer Heinrich Harrer, whose eventful life was capped by a lengthy stay in Tibet. The camera loves him, but his catalogue model looks and ropey Teutonic accent undermine the whole movie. David Thewlis, however, is excellent as his climbing partner, as is Annaud's feeling for time and place. Contains some strong language. ▦ **DVD**

Brad Pitt *Heinrich Harrer* • David Thewlis *Peter Aufschnaiter* • BD Wong *Ngawang Jigme* • Mako *Kungo Tsarong* • Danny Denzongpa *Regent* • Victor Wong *Chinese ''Amban''* ■ *Dir* Jean-Jacques Annaud • *Scr* Becky Johnston, from the memoirs of Heinrich Harrer • *Music* John Williams • *Cinematographer* Robert Fraisse

---

Seventh Cavalry ★★★ U

Western　　　1956 · US · Colour · 76mins

Randolph Scott played a key role in the emergence of the psychological western in the late fifties in films such as *Ride Lonesome* and *The Tall T*, in which motives mattered more than action. This disjointed picture does manage to combine excitement and emotion, as Scott seeks to disprove a charge of cowardice by leading a cavalry detail to reclaim the dead after the Battle of the Little Bighorn. The skirmishes are solidly staged by B-movie specialist Joseph H Lewis, but the film's real interest lies in the way that Scott's character comes to believe General Custer was an incompetent rather than a glorious hero.

Randolph Scott *Captain Tom Benson* • Barbara Hale *Martha Kellogg* • Jay C Flippen *Sergeant Bates* • Jeanette Nolan *Mrs Reynolds* • Frank Faylen *Krugger* • Leo Gordon *Vogel* • Denver Pyle *Dixon* • Harry Carey Jr *Corporal Morrison* • Michael Pate *Captain Benteen* ■ *Dir* Joseph H Lewis • *Scr* Peter Packer, from a story by Glendon F Swarthout

The Seventh Coin ★★

Mystery thriller　1993 · US · Colour · 92mins

On holiday in old Jerusalem, American teenager Alexandra Powers hangs out with an Arab boy who steals a precious coin that once belonged to King Herod. Soon the duo are being pursued by dotty Peter O'Toole, who believes that he is the reincarnation of the ancient monarch and the coin is his. This is a mild-mannered family orientated thriller, high on lush visuals, but low on basic action and adventure trappings. O'Toole goes hilariously over the top.

Alexandra Powers *Ronnie Segal* • Navin Chowdhry *Salim Zouabi* • Peter O'Toole *Emil Saber* • John Rhys-Davies *Captain Galil* • Ally Walker *Lisa* ■ *Dir* Dror Soref • *Scr* Dror Soref, Michael Lewis

The Seventh Cross ★★★

Drama　　　1944 · US · BW · 111mins

Seven inmates escape from a German concentration camp in 1936, but only one (Spencer Tracy), against all the odds, evades capture and execution. This is a gripping story that evokes the poisonous atmosphere of threat and terror and the dangers and difficulties for the Resistance in Nazi Germany. Directed with full command by Austrian émigré Fred Zinnemann and played by Tracy as you would expect, there's also excellent support from Agnes Moorehead, Signe Hasso, Jessica Tandy and an Oscar-nominated Hume Cronyn. The cross refers to the one nailed to a tree upon which the camp authorities plan to execute Tracy.

Spencer Tracy *George Heisler* • Signe Hasso *Toni* • Hume Cronyn *Paul Roeder* • Jessica Tandy *Liesel Roeder* • Agnes Moorehead *Mme Marelli* • Herbert Rudley *Franz Marnet* ■ *Dir* Fred Zinnemann • *Scr* Helen Deutsch, from the novel *Das Siebte Kreuz* by Anna Seghers

The 7th Dawn ★

Drama　　　1964 · UK · Colour · 125mins

Set in Malaya in the period immediately after the Second World War, this dismal melodrama is directed at a funereal pace and with mini-series

---

U = SUITABLE FOR ALL　　Uc = SUITABLE FOR ALL, ESPECIALLY FOR YOUNG CHILDREN (VIDEO ONLY)　　PG = PARENTAL GUIDANCE

subtlety by Lewis Gilbert. This tale of wartime comrades divided by the cause of independence is packed with clichéd characters who pompously spout political platitudes and entangle themselves in shabby love affairs. Grumpy William Holden gives one of the worst performances of his career.

William Holden (1) *Ferris* • Susannah York *Candace* • Capucine *Dhana* • Tetsuro Tamba *Ng* • Michael Goodliffe *Trumphey* • Allan Cuthbertson *Cavendish* • Maurice Denham *Tarlton* • Beulah Quo *Ah Ming* ■ *Dir* Lewis Gilbert • *Scr* Karl Tunberg, from the novel *The Durian Tree* by Michael Koen

Seventh Floor ★★
Psychological thriller
1995 · Ausl/Jap/Uk · Colour · 99mins

A muddled thriller set in the Australian advertising world, this stars a cast-against-type Brooke Shields as a widow, first blackmailed by one of her husband's business partners, then terrorised in her high-tech Sydney apartment by the deranged Masaya Kato. The cast is let down by Tony Morphett's inept script and the ineffective direction of Ian Barry. Though it aspires to be in the same league, *Demon Seed* it ain't. Contains violence and swearing.

Brooke Shields *Kate Fletcher* • Masaya Kato *Mitsuru* • Craig Pearce *Ed* • Linda Cropper *Vivian* • Russell Newman *Detective Riley* ■ *Dir* Ian Barry • *Scr* Tony Morphett

7th Heaven ★★★★
Silent romantic drama
1927 · US · BW · 120mins

A poor, lonely, and religious Parisian sewer worker (Charles Farrell) takes in a girl (Janet Gaynor) off the streets. They fall in love and marry, he is sent to the First World War battlefront, and she, hearing that he has been killed, loses her faith in God. Although thickly coated in molasses, this classic tearjerker is an effective romantic drama about love triumphing over adversity and still has the power to draw tears. With its impressive battle scenes and atmospheric production, the film featured large in the first ever Academy Awards, winning Oscars for Frank Borzage, Gaynor, and Benjamin Glazer's script, and nominations for best picture and Harry Oliver's art direction.

Janet Gaynor *Diane* • Charles Farrell *Chico* • Ben Bard *Colonel Brissac* • David Butler *Gobin* • Marie Mosquini *Mme Gobin* • Albert Gran *Boul* ■ *Dir* Frank Borzage • *Scr* Benjamin Glazer, Katherine Hilliker (titles), HH Caldwell (titles), from the play by Austin Strong

Seventh Heaven ★★★
Romantic drama 1937 · US · BW · 102mins

Directed by Henry King and starring James Stewart and Simone Simon, this is a serviceable remake of the 1927 silent film. It tells of the love affair, tested by war and tragedy, between a Parisian sewer worker and a homeless girl. Gale Sondergaard plays the heartless sister who throws Simon out onto the streets, while Hollywood's resident screen medic Jean Hersholt exchanges his stethoscope for a priest's dog-collar. Reworked in certain areas (the hero starts out as an atheist, the heroine is a prostitute), it dilutes the sugar quotient of the

original, but fails to achieve its dream-like poignancy. The stars don't quite ring true as French slum-dwellers, but the story still convinces.

Simone Simon *Diane* • James Stewart *Chico* • Gale Sondergaard *Nana* • Gregory Ratoff *Boul* • Jean Hersholt *Father Chevillon* • J Edward Bromberg *Aristide* ■ *Scr* Melville Baker, from the play by Austin Strong

The Seventh Seal ★★★★★ PG
Period drama 1957 · Swe · BW · 92mins

Spoofed by Woody Allen, French and Saunders, Bill and Ted (on their *Bogus Journey*) and Arnold Schwarzenegger in *Last Action Hero*, *The Seventh Seal* is an undoubted masterpiece of world cinema. It tells of a crusader knight (Max von Sydow) who refuses to accompany Death (Bengt Ekerot) until he has found a flicker of hope in a world stricken by plague, corruption and fear. While this is a highly personal film, in which director Ingmar Bergman (the son of the chaplain of the Swedish royal family) resolves his own doubts about the existence of God, its conclusions will leave even the most cynical filled with optimism. In Swedish with English subtitles. ▭

Max von Sydow *Antonius Block, the knight* • Gunnar Björnstrand *Jons, Block's squire* • Bengt Ekerot *Death* • Nils Poppe *Jof* • Bibi Andersson *Mia* ■ *Dir* Ingmar Bergman • *Scr* Ingmar Bergman, from his play *Tramalning, (Sculpture in Wood)*

The Seventh Sign ★★ 15
Supernatural horror thriller
1988 · US · Colour · 92mins

Great! Demi Moore is given the opportunity to save the world. As blood rains from the sky and earthquakes shake cities, Demi is more worried about having a successful pregnancy. But with a weirdo reading Hebrew in her garage and CNN broadcasting apocalyptic bulletins on the hour, having the baby and saving humanity become synonymous. Moore is good but the rest of the movie is a marvellous mess: fans of the biblical horror genre will be in seventh heaven, but if that's not your bag, it's a bomb. ▭ **DVD**

Demi Moore *Abby Quinn* • Michael Biehn *Russell Quinn* • Jürgen Prochnow *David the Boarder* • Peter Friedman *Father Lucci* • Manny Jacobs *Avi* • John Taylor *Jimmy* • John Heard *Reverend* ■ *Dir* Carl Schultz • *Scr* WW Wicket, George Kaplan

The Seventh Veil ★★★ PG
Melodrama 1945 · US · BW · 89mins

The Oscar-winning screenplay for this all-stops-out melodrama was written by the husband-and-wife team of Sydney and Muriel Box. But, whichever way you slice it, there's no escaping the fact that, for all its aspirations to musical and psychological gravity, this is nothing more than home-cured ham. Ann Todd is at her drippiest as a persecuted pianist whose love-hate relationship with crippled guardian James Mason is founded on romantic clichés that first appeared in Victorian penny-dreadfuls. Nonetheless, it's still irresistible entertainment, done with considerable style, and Mason is tremendous as a brooding brute. ▭

The Seventh Victim ★★
Horror 1943 · US · BW · 70mins

This marks the directing debut of former editor Mark Robson, who later made *The Inn of the Sixth Happiness* and *Earthquake*. Like *Cat People* and other cultish Val Lewton productions, it's an underwritten but atmospheric and creepy tale about a sect of Satanists who live in deepest Greenwich Village. Tom Conway, best known for the title role in the *Falcon* series, is a pallid lead, out-performed by Kim Hunter, who screams on cue with considerable conviction. If the main set looks vaguely familiar, it's because it was originally built the previous year for Orson Welles's *The Magnificent Ambersons*, on which Robson had worked as co-editor.

Kim Hunter *Mary Gibson* • Tom Conway *Dr Louis Judd* • Jean Brooks *Jacqueline Gibson* • Isabel Jewell *Frances Fallon* • Evelyn Brent *Natalie Cortez* • Erford Gage *Jason Hoag* • Ben Bard *Brun* • Hugh Beaumont *Gregory Ward* ■ *Dir* Mark Robson • *Scr* DeWitt Bodeen, Charles O'Neal • *Cinematographer* Nicholas Musuraca

The 7th Voyage of Sinbad ★★★★ U
Fantasy adventure
1958 · US · Colour · 84mins

The first Sinbad adventure saga from stop-motion genius Ray Harryhausen is still the best. Sokurah the Magician (Torin Thatcher) demands that Sinbad (Kerwin Matthews) find a magic lamp that is being guarded by an ingenious gallery of monsters – brought to fabulous life by Harryhausen's expertise and Bernard Herrmann's rousing score. A 30-foot-tall cyclops, a two-headed bird, a fire-breathing dragon and a warrior skeleton effortlessly combine with swashbuckling spectacle and thrilling escapism under Nathan Juran's sure-handed direction. The result is a fantastic family favourite. ▭ **DVD**

Kerwin Mathews *Captain Sinbad* • Kathryn Grant *Princess Parisa* • Richard Eyer *Barroni the Genie* • Torin Thatcher *Sokurah the Magician* • Alec Mango *Caliph* • Danny Green *Karim* • Harold Kasket *Sultan* ■ *Dir* Nathan Juran • *Scr* Kenneth Kolb

A Severed Head ★★★
Black comedy 1970 · UK · Colour · 99mins

Though not a patch on Iris Murdoch's 1961 novel, nor its subsequent stage adaptation, this is still an amusing, sophisticated comedy which, in its highly polished way, recalls Ross Hunter's Hollywood films of the fifties and sixties. Screenwriter Frederic Raphael was obviously writing about people he knew – academics and posh folk indulging in a mad charade of partner-swapping. In his first screen lead, Ian Holm is the harassed wine merchant juggling a wife and mistresses. Dick Clement directs with confidence.

James Mason *Nicholas* • Ann Todd *Francesca Cunningham* • Hugh McDermott *Peter Gay* • Albert Lieven *Maxwell Leyden* • Yvonne Owen *Susan Brook* • David Horne *Dr Kendal* ■ *Dir* Compton Bennett • *Scr* Sydney Box, Muriel Box

Lee Remick *Antonia Lynch-Gibbon* • Richard Attenborough *Palmer Anderson, psychiatrist* • Ian Holm *Martin Lynch-Gibbon, wine merchant* • Claire Bloom *Honor Klein* • Jennie Linden *Georgie Hands* • Clive Revill *Alexander Lynch-Gibbon* • Ann Firbank *Rosemary Lynch-Gibbon* ■ *Dir* Dick Clement • *Scr* Frederic Raphael, from the play by Iris Murdoch, JB Priestley, from the novel by Iris Murdoch

Sex and the Married Woman ★★ 18
Drama 1977 · US · Colour · 57mins

The director who brought you *Creature from the Black Lagoon* and *The Incredible Shrinking Man* lays before you the "Nosey Neighbour with a Typewriter" in this hugely resistible TV movie. Jack Arnold was one of the kings of the fifties' exploitation movie and it's sad to see him straining every sinew to get laughs out of Michael Norell's sorry script. Barry Newman mugs adequately, as he sees his quiet life fly out of the window after wife Joanna Pettet writes a bestseller inspired by their friends' sex lives. Keenan Wynn and F Murray Abraham provide welcome distractions. ▭

Barry Newman *Alan Fitch* • Joanna Pettet *Leslie Fitch* • Keenan Wynn *Uncle June* • F Murray Abraham *Duke Skaggs* ■ *Dir* Jack Arnold • *Scr* Michael Norell

Sex and the Other Man ★★★
Comedy 1995 · US · Colour · 89mins

In this blackish comedy, Ron Eldard (*ER*), suffering from impotence, is shocked when he catches his girlfriend, Kari Wuhrer, in bed with her boss (Stanley Tucci). But this scene has a positive affect on Eldard's libido, and he and Wuhrer then hold Tucci captive while they work out their sexual frustrations. Based on Paul Weitz's stage play *Captive*, this off-centre farce is lifted by the brilliant performance of Tucci. At the time of the film's release, he was making a name for himself in Steven Bochco's landmark TV series *Murder One*. He's since gone on to show his skills as a writer/director (*Big Night*, *The Imposters*).

Ron Eldard *Billy* • Stanley Tucci *Arthur* • Kari Wuhrer *Jessica* ■ *Dir* Karl Slovin • *Scr* Karl Slovin, from the play *Captive* by Paul Weitz

Sex and the Single Girl ★★★
Satirical comedy
1964 · US · Colour · 119mins

Tony Curtis and Natalie Wood make an attractive couple in this comedy, which was regarded as very risqué in 1964. It's based on an enormous bestseller by Helen Gurley Brown, the legendary editor of *Cosmopolitan*. Warner's paid a reputed $200,000 for the rights, then realised it didn't have a story, so Joseph Heller, author of *Catch-22*, wrote the script as a satire on sex therapy in general and Brown's book in particular. Wood played Miss Brown as a virginal sexologist and Curtis is the journalist who interviews her, posing as a man with deep sexual problems.

Tony Curtis *Bob Weston* • Natalie Wood *Dr Helen Brown* • Henry Fonda *Frank Broderick* • Lauren Bacall *Sylvia Broderick* • Mel Ferrer *Rudy DeMeyer* • Fran Jeffries *Gretchen* • Leslie Parrish *Susan* • Edward Everett Horton

The Chief • Larry Storch *Motorcycle cop* ■ *Dir* Richard Quine • *Scr* Joseph Heller, David R Schwartz, from the story by Joseph Hoffman, from the book by Helen Gurley Brown

Sex and Zen ★★★ 18
Period sex comedy
1992 · HK · Colour · 86mins

Adapted from Li Yu's Ming Dynasty novel, *The Carnal Prayer Mat*, this is the best-known example of the soft-core genre known in Hong Kong as Category III. Although the scenes involving concubine-wife Amy Yip have a high erotic content, director Michael Mak largely plays the film for laughs. Envious scholar Lawrence Ng undergoes a transplant of equine proportions and, after many energetic misadventures, comes to repent at leisure at a Buddhist monastery. A frantic mixture of morality tale and bedroom farce, the film gained a cult following, not least because of its glorious costumes and authentic period details. A Cantonese language film. Contains sex scenes and violence. ▱

Kent Cheng *Doctor* • Lo Lieh *Choi Run Lun* • Amy Yip *Yuk Heung* • Isabella Chow *Kuen's wife* • Lawrence Ng *Mei Yang* • Elvis Kam-Kong Tsui *Kuen* ■ *Dir* Michael Mak • *Scr* Lee Ying Kit, from the book *Yu Ou Tuan (The Carnal Prayer Mat)* by Li Yu

Sex and Zen II ★ 18
Period sex comedy
1996 · HK · Colour · 82mins

Golden Harvest's inevitable sequel to the wildly successful *Sex and Zen* shares its predecessor's period gloss, but still ranks among the poorest Category III films ever made. With Elvis (Kam-Kong) Tsui chomping on the scenery and eroticism being replaced by cartoon-like coupling, Chin Man-Kei's film is neither amusing nor sensuous. In Cantonese with English subtitles. Contains sex scenes and violence. ▱

Loletta Lai-Chun Lee *Yau* • Qi Shu *Mirage Lady* • Elvis Kam-Kong Tsui *Squire, Yau's father* ■ *Dir* Chin Man-Kei • *Scr* Simon Kin Sai-Moon

Sex, Drugs, Rock & Roll ★★★
Satirical monologue
1991 · US · Colour · 96mins

Filmed at Boston's Wilbur Theatre, this record of comic performance artist Eric Bogosian's hit Broadway one-man show is directed to hilarious perfection by John (*Henry: Portrait of a Serial Killer*) McNaughton. Bogosian offers up an assortment of unpleasant characters to laugh at uncontrollably, including a drug-addled youth remembering a debauched stag night, an entertainment lawyer driven by success, and an ageing English rock star about to play a benefit concert for Amazon Indians. In between his blisteringly astute monologues, he also rants on about the excesses and delusions of pop-culture-obsessed baby boomers. Often surreal, always outrageous and very funny.

Eric Bogosian ■ *Dir* John McNaughton • *Scr* Eric Bogosian

Sex Kittens Go to College ★★ 15
Sex comedy
1960 · US · BW · 103mins

The pneumatic charms of Mamie Van Doren graced many a B-movie feature in the fifties and sixties, always adding an extra frisson to nostalgic viewings of such fare. Mamie plays a brilliant science teacher whose previous incarnation as a stripper catches up with her. Corny dialogue and inept slapstick abound. There are appearances from Vampira and Brigitte Bardot's sister, Mijanou. Tuesday Weld, Jackie Coogan and John Carradine are also present in this sexploitation flick, which – in its truncated form at least – cannot quite live up to its lurid title. ▱

Mamie Van Doren *Dr Mathilda West* • Tuesday Weld *Jody* • Mijanou Bardot *Suzanne* • Mickey Shaughnessy *Boomie* • Louis Nye *Dr Zorch* • Pamela Mason *Dr Myrtle Carter* • Marty Milner [Martin Milner] *George Barton* • Jackie Coogan *Wildcat MacPherson* • John Carradine *Professor Watts* • Vampira [Maila Nurmi] *Etta Toodie* • Conway Twitty ■ *Dir* Albert Zugsmith • *Scr* Robert F Hill [Robert Hill], from a story by Albert Zugsmith

sex, lies, and videotape ★★★★ 18
Drama
1989 · US · Colour · 95mins

The winner of the Palme d'Or at Cannes, Steven Soderbergh's debut feature was made for just $1.2 million. Although it took an uncompromisingly adult approach to sex, it wasn't explicit nudity (of which there is none) that made this intelligent film so controversial, but the intimacy of the drama and the frankness of the dialogue. A genuine slow-burner, it takes its time introducing us to the quartet of main characters. Peter Gallagher is a lawyer having an affair with his sister-in-law (Laura San Giacomo), who has always resented the prissiness of her perfect sibling (Andie MacDowell). However, we never really discover anything about Graham (James Spader), the long-lost friend who forces the other three to re-examine their motives and desires. Where does his money come from and why does he have tapes of women confiding their innermost sexual secrets? It's this ambiguity that makes Spader's character the most fascinating of the quartet and goes some way to explaining why he won best actor at Cannes. Contains swearing and sex scenes. ▱

James Spader *Graham Dalton* • Andie MacDowell *Ann Millaney* • Peter Gallagher *John Millaney* • Laura San Giacomo *Cynthia Bishop* • Ron Vawter *Therapist* • Steven Brill *Barfly* ■ *Dir/Scr* Steven Soderbergh

Sex, Love and Cold Hard Cash ★★★ 15
Crime adventure 1993 · US · Colour · 82mins

JoBeth Williams is in hot pursuit of ne'er-do-wells in this fast-moving caper. This time she's a high-class hooker who teams up with recently sprung armed robber Anthony John Denison to recover her purloined life savings – a mere matter of $20 million. Written and directed by Harry S Longstreet, the film rattles along, just about managing to stay on course, despite the endless twists and turns, right through to its luxury liner finale. ▱

JoBeth Williams *Sara Gallagher* • Anthony John Denison *Doug* • Robert Forster *Sid* • Eric Pierpoint *Andy* • Randle Mell *Jack* • Tobin Bell *Tom Mansfield* • Richard Sarafian [Richard C Sarafian] *Abe Lederman* ■ *Dir/Scr* Harry S Longstreet

The Sex Monster ★★
Sex comedy 1998 · US · Colour · 96mins

Writer/director Mike Binder as a wealthy Californian who wants to spice up his sex life and talks his wife, Mariel Hemmingway, into a threesome with another woman. Although initially reluctant to satisfy this clichéd male fantasy, Hemmingway finds herself increasingly intrigued by lesbianism, and before long Binder has unleashed a bisexual monster on the LA swingers scene. This is an amiable, if unsophisticated, farce that dabbles in political incorrectness and wonky gay sensibilities with glee. Hemmingway stands out as the experimental dyke on a pleasure mission.

Mariel Hemingway *Laura Barnes* • Mike Binder *Marty* • Renee Humphrey *Didi* • Missy Crider *Diva* ■ *Dir/Scr* Mike Binder

Sex, Shame and Tears ★★
Romantic comedy
1999 · Mex · Colour · 107mins

In reworking his own play for the screen, Mexican director Antonio Serrano has been unable to take the staginess out of either the acting or the narrative, and the entire cast seems to be projecting to the back of an auditorium. An impotent would-be intellectual is piqued by the arrival of his wife's flashy photographer ex, while across the street the long-suffering wife of a philandering executive finally reaches boiling point with the entry of his smouldering old flame. A Spanish language film.

Demian Bichir *Tomas* • Susana Zabaleta *Ana* • Monic Dionne *Maria* • Jorge Salinas *Miguel* • Cecilia Suarez *Andrea* • Victor Hugo Martin *Carlos* ■ *Dir/Scr* Antonio Serrano, Antonio Serrano

Sex: the Annabel Chong Story ★★★ 18
Sex documentary 1999 · US · Colour · 86mins

Grace Quek, the Singaporean student who re-created herself as porn queen Annabel Chong, may believe she set the world gang-bang record in the name of gynocentric emancipation. However, as Gough Lewis's documentary discloses, it was just another act of self-loathing by a fiercely intelligent but deeply confused innocent abroad in a world of frauds and exploiters. With on-screen acts of self-mutilation undermining the hardcore antics and aggressive psychobabble, this is a film that prompts one to question both the director's motives and those of his convent-educated star.

Annabel Chong [Grace Quek] *Student/Porn star* • John Bowen *Director, World's Biggest Gang Bang 1 & 2* • Ed Powers *Director/performer, Dirty Debutante series* • Dr Walter Williams *Professor of anthropology University of Southern California* • Dick James *President, Annabel Chong Fan Club* ■ *Dir* Gough Lewis

Sexpionage ★ 15
Spy adventure 1985 · US · Colour · 91mins

Directed by former actor Don Taylor, this is an attempt to tell the story of how the KGB allegedly trained beautiful Russian girls to work as spies in the USA. When you learn that *Terminator* star Linda Hamilton is cast as an innocent schoolgirl trained by top agent Sally Kellerman, you realise this isn't documentary-style material. A young Geena Davis pops up (bet she doesn't mention this one on her CV), but neither she nor the rest of the cast can hide the fact that this is utter rubbish. ▱

Sally Kellerman *Major Vera Malevich* • Linda Hamilton *Elena/Joanna* • James Franciscus *Colonel Victor Khudenko* • Hunt Block *Jack Spaulding* • Geena Davis *Tamara/Brenda* • Christopher Atkins *Allen Collier* • Viveca Lindfors *Aunt Roza* ■ *Dir* Don Taylor • *Scr* Thomas Baum, Sandor Stern

Sextette ★★ PG
Musical comedy 1978 · US · Colour · 84mins

They don't come any stranger than this too-late vehicle for the octogenarian (and virtually embalmed) Mae West. The musical exists in its own inspired limboland, where salaciousness and dated vulgarity ineptly combine to render it mesmerisingly, appallingly, watchable. Interspersed with what attempts to pass for a plot, the movie is padded with some bizarre London locations. The cast is truly astonishing: you'll shudder for their collective embarrassment if you last to the end. Ken Hughes's direction makes tack-meister Ed Wood look like Orson Welles, but at least he knows it. ▱

Mae West *Marlo Manners* • Timothy Dalton *Sir Michael Barrington* • Dom DeLuise *Dan Turner* • Tony Curtis *Alexei Karansky* • Ringo Starr *Laslo Karolny* • George Hamilton *Vance* • Alice Cooper *Waiter* • Rona Barrett • Keith Moon *Dress designer* • George Raft ■ *Dir* Ken Hughes • *Scr* Herbert Baker, from the play by Mae West

Sexton Blake and the Hooded Terror ★★
Crime drama 1938 · UK/US · BW · 68mins

Unlike so many other suave English sleuths, Sexton Blake has never really come to life on the big screen. Tod Slaughter is admittedly below par as the master crook, but the film's failure lies squarely at the door of George Curzon in the title role. He lacks the necessary looks and charm to match those that Ronald Colman brought to Bulldog Drummond or with which George Sanders imbued Simon Templar. While packed with ne'er-do-wells such as the Snake and the members of the Black Quorum, AR Rawlinson's script lacks the zip of Hal Meredith's original story.

George Curzon *Sexton Blake* • Tod Slaughter *Michael Larron* • Greta Gynt *Mademoiselle Julie* • Charles Oliver *Max Fleming* • Tony Sympson *Tinker* • Marie Wright *Mrs Bardell* ■ *Dir* George King • *Scr* AR Rawlinson, from the novel by Pierre Quiroule

Sexual Advances ★★
Drama 1992 · US · Colour · 96mins

When the loss of a major account threatens the position of executive

William Russ, he retaliates against Stephanie Zimbalist with a vengeful plan of sexual harassment. There's nothing new or shocking here, and it's hobbled by an awkward subplot involving Zimbalist's shaky marriage, but Michele Gallery's tight script, perceptive direction by Donna Deitch (*Desert Hearts*) and a committed cast make this women's issue piece surprisingly engaging.

Stephanie Zimbalist *Paula Pratt* • William Russ *Jack French* • Ken Pogue *Treadway* • Deborah May *Rita* • Peter Stebbings ■ *Dir* Donna Deitch • *Scr* Michele Gallery

The Sexual Life of the Belgians 1950-1978 ★★★ 18

Satirical comedy drama
1994 · Bel · Colour · 78mins

Prior to this semi-autobiographical satire, director Jan Bucquoy's greatest claim to fame was as the curator of Belgium's National Museum of Underpants. Whether his intention was to chart his own voyage of sexual discovery or expose every guilty secret in Belgian culture, Bucquoy only partially fulfils his ambitions. In spite of a bravura performance by Jean-Henri Compère as the director's alter ego, the personal side of the story too often finds itself suffocating under the bedclothes or wallowing in the bottom of a glass. The social observations, however, are much more successful and often very amusing. Unashamedly sexist, this won't be to everyone's taste. In Flemish with English subtitles. Contains swearing. ▭

Jean-Henri Compère *Jan Bucquoy* • Noé Francq *Jan as a child* • Isabelle Legros *Noella Bucquoy* • Sophie Schneider *Thérèse* • Pascale Binneri *Ariane Bucquoy* • Michele Shor *Aunt Martha* ■ *Dir/Scr* Jan Bucquoy

Sexual Malice ★ 18

Erotic thriller　1994 · US · Colour · 98mins

Even though the whole point of an erotic thriller is to pack in as much soft-core sex as possible, you would have thought at least someone involved in this tiresome trash would have the professional pride to devise an original storyline. But it's clichés all the way in this utterly predictable offering from Jag Mundhra, in which business executive Diana Barton ends up in deep water after embarking on a dangerous affair. However, sibling spotters should enjoy the atrocious performance of Patrick Swayze's brother, Don. Contains violence, swearing and sex scenes. ▭

Edward Albert *Richard Chandler* • Chad McQueen *David Chandler* • John Laughlin *Jack* • Diana Barton *Christine* • Don Swayze *Curran* • Douglas Jeffery *Quinn* ■ *Dir* Jag Mundhra • *Scr* Carl Austin, from a story by Jag Mundhra

Sexual Outlaws ★ 18

Erotic thriller　1994 · US · Colour · 97mins

A convoluted erotic thriller with little in the way of either eroticism or thrills. Mute Mitch Gaylord pays prostitutes to strip and sends the photographs to the sexually frustrated wife of the editor of the magazine *Sexual Outlaws*. As they strike up a flirtatious relationship by mail, one of Gaylord's hookers is murdered and he becomes the prime suspect. How his sexual pen pal helps

to prove him innocent after numerous coincidences is unbelievable and scarcely watchable. ▭

Mitch Gaylord *Francis Badham* • Erika West *Lisa Bauer* • Kim Dawson *Jeannie* • Nicole Grey *Rita* ■ *Dir* Edwin Brown • *Scr* Edwin Brown, Summer Brown

Sexual Response ★★ 18

Erotic thriller　1992 · US · Colour · 90mins

A routine "disrober" for hard-working Shannon Tweed, cast once again as a sex expert (the first of the *Indecent Behavior* films would follow a year later). Here she passes her expertise over the airwaves, even though her own marriage is in trouble and her lover has other things than adultery on his mind. Former *Dynasty* babe Catherine Oxenberg pops up in a supporting role, although she has more success than the star in keeping her clothes on. One for genre and Tweed fans only. ▭

Shannon Tweed *Eve* • Catherine Oxenberg *Kate* • Vernon Wells *Philip* • Emile Levisetti *Edge* • David Kriegel *Peter* ■ *Dir* Yaki Yosha • *Scr* Brent Morris, Eric Diamond

Shaan ★★★ PG

Action drama　1980 · Ind · Colour · 181mins

This exciting, action-packed Hindi film pitches an evil crime genius, with a bewildering array of electronic weapons, against brave young men and women out to avenge the death of a policeman. Traditional Hindi-film virtues are married to James Bond-style effects in this colourful extravaganza. In Hindi with English subtitles. ▭

Shashi Kapoor *Ravi* • Amitabh Bachchan *Vijay* ■ *Dir* Ramesh Sippy

Shack Out on 101 ★★★

Drama　1955 · US · BW · 80mins

Lee Marvin delivers the stand-out performance in this Cold War melodrama centred around a remote and ramshackle roadside café near a top-secret research station. Marvin relishes the part of the dimwitted cook, known as Slob, who's not all that he seems. Frank Lovejoy plays the nuclear scientist who romances Terry Moore's waitress and is apparently willing to sell secrets to the other side. Keenan Wynn is around as the easy-going proprietor. Directed on a low budget by Edward Dein, it's a distinctly unconventional picture that holds the interest, with an unusual weapon of death featured in the climax.

Terry Moore *Kotty, the waitress* • Frank Lovejoy *Professor* • Keenan Wynn *George* • Lee Marvin *Slob, the cook* • Whit Bissell *Eddie* • Jess Barker *Artie* • Donald Murphy *Pepe* • Frank De Kova *Dillon* ■ *Dir* Edward Dein • *Scr* Edward Dein, Mildred Dein

Shades of Fear ★★

Mystery comedy romance
1993 · UK/US · Colour · 92mins

Director Beeban Kidron and writer Jeanette Winterson failed to repeat the success of *Oranges Are Not the Only Fruit* with this disappointing TV movie set in the 1950s. Aspiring pilot Rakie Ayola finds herself on a cruise ship bound for England in the company of bizarre set of characters, including

(perhaps) a forger and a murderer. Unfortunately, the mixture of romance and mystery doesn't work and even the combined acting talents of Vanessa Redgrave, Jonathan Pryce, John Hurt and Dorothy Tutin can't save it.

Vanessa Redgrave *Dr Angela Bead* • John Hurt *Rex Goodyear* • Jonathan Pryce *Duncan Stewart* • Dorothy Tutin *Gwendolyn Quinn* • Rakie Ayola *Gabriel Angel* ■ *Dir* Beeban Kidron • *Scr* Jeanette Winterson

Shades of Gray ★★★

Crime drama　1992 · US · Colour · 96mins

George Dzundza is one of America's most charismatic character actors and his presence lifts this TV movie out of the routine. He plays the policeman father of ambitious young lawyer Valerie Bertinelli, who causes ructions at the district attorney's office and conflict at home when she starts probing organised crime. Director Kevin James Dobson never really reconciles the family drama with the more menacing elements of the plot, but the spirited performances of the two leads keep it watchable. Contains violence.

Valerie Bertinelli *Molly Kilcoin* • George Dzundza *Detective Jack Kilcoin* • Dobson Peter *Joey Martinelli* • David Marshall Grant *Brad* • Micole Mercurio *Lorraine Kilcoin* • Vondie Curtis-Hall *Vinnie* ■ *Dir* Kevin James Dobson • *Scr* Andy Tennant, Timothy Stack, from a story by Billy Goldenberg

Shades of Gray ★★

Erotic thriller　1995 · US · Colour · 95mins

Director Jag Mundhra specialises in cheap, steamy, erotic thrillers for the straight-to-video market and this is his usual efficient mix of skin and thrills. The story centres around Kelly Burns, playing a former police sketch artist who moves to a small town to take up a new career as a teacher, only to find herself dragged back into the world of crime when one of her students is murdered. The acting could be diplomatically termed enthusiastic, and you don't need to be a member of Mensa to spot the killer. But, as exploitation goes, it's competent enough. Contains violence, swearing and sex scenes.

Kelly Burns *Gray Goodman* • Doug Jeffrey *Jack Kincaid* • Tom Reilley *Frank Maxwell* • Kathy Shower *Joyce* • Michelle Helm *Amy* ■ *Dir* Jag Mundhra • *Scr* Carl Austin

Shadey ★ 15

Black comedy　1985 · UK · Colour · 102mins

The idea is a good one – a clairvoyant, who can transfer his precognitions to film, is exploited by big business and British Intelligence – and the production values are glossy. But the treatment is a mystifying mishmash of transexualism, incest, insanity and ESP. Described as black comedy, it is indulgent in the extreme. A distinguished cast of character actors, including Katherine Helmond (*Soap*) is headed by Antony Sher, who would not find his feet in film for another ten years. ▭

Antony Sher *Oliver Shadey* • Patrick Macnee *Sir Cyril Landau* • Leslie Ash *Carol Landau* • Bernard Hepton *Capt Amies* • Katherine Helmond *Lady Landau* • Larry Lamb *Dick Darnley* • Billie Whitelaw *Dr Cloud* ■ *Dir* Philip Saville • *Scr* Snoo Wilson

The Shadow ★

Murder mystery　1936 · UK · BW · 75mins

A hooded figure is murdering the inhabitants of a rambling mansion in this creaky chiller, which has nothing in common with the American radio serial of the same name made famous by Orson Welles. Director George A Cooper's musty "old dark house" yawn adds nothing to the fear formula you've all seen before. Others more cognisant of the rules of the genre have done it far better.

Henry Kendall *Reggie Ogden/The Shadow* • Elizabeth Allan *Sonya Stuart* • Jeanne Stuart *Moya Silverton* • Felix Aylmer *Sir Richard* • Cyril Raymond *Silverton* • Viola Compton *Mrs Bascomb* • John Turnbull *Inspector* • Sam Livesey *Sir Richard Bryant* ■ *Dir* George A Cooper • *Scr* H Fowler Mear, Terence Egan, from a play by Donald Stuart

The Shadow ★★★ 12

Action adventure
1994 · US · Colour · 102mins

"Who knows what evil lurks in the hearts of men?". Alec Baldwin does, here playing both wealthy socialite Lamont Cranston and his mysterious alter ego, the Shadow, who uses psychic powers to render himself invisible at will. The famous thirties' pulp crime-fighter takes on a descendant of Genghis Khan who's out to conquer the world in *Highlander* director Russell Mulcahy's comic-strip fantasy. It's stuffed with fun clichés of the genre, and the spectacle of the design easily matches the visual punch of the special effects. Unfortunately, the flashy production values rather overshadow the performances of Baldwin and the star-studded supporting cast, while the plot rarely grips. Contains swearing and violene. ▭

Alec Baldwin *Lamont Cranston/The Shadow* • John Lone *Shiwan Khan* • Penelope Ann Miller *Margo Lane* • Peter Boyle *Moe Shrevnitz* • Ian McKellen *Reinhardt Lane* • Tim Curry *Farley Claymore* • Jonathan Winters *Wainwright Barth* • Sab Shimono *Dr Tam* ■ *Dir* Russell Mulcahy • *Scr* David Koepp, from the characters created by Walter Gibson • *Cinematographer* Stephen H Burum • *Producer* Joseph Nemec III

The Shadow Box ★★★ 15

Drama　1980 · US · Colour · 103mins

Co-produced by his daughter Susan, and starring his wife, Joanne Woodward, this was Paul Newman's TV-movie debut as a director. Adapted from the play by Michael Cristofer and set in a clinic for the terminally sick, it takes an age to develop, and helped by Newman's insistence on long takes of talking heads. However, the drama intensifies as the relationship between Woodward, ex-husband Christopher Plummer and his gay lover (Ben Masters) draws to its tragic conclusion. The most impressive work comes from Melinda Dillon, as the dutiful daughter trying to make mother Sylvia Sydney's last days more bearable. ▭

Joanne Woodward *Beverly* • Christopher Plummer *Brian* • Valerie Harper *Maggie* • James Broderick *Joe* • Sylvia Sidney *Felicity Thomas* • Melinda Dillon *Agnes* • Ben Masters *Mark* ■ *Dir* Paul Newman • *Scr* Michael Cristofer, from his play

Shadow Conspiracy ★★★ 15

Political action thriller
1996 · US · Colour · 98mins

An A-minus cast makes a good fist of this conspiracy thriller that is never less than gripping. Charlie Sheen is a presidential spin merchant whose life is on the line when he stumbles upon a top level White House plot. Linda Hamilton is the political journalist in peril who teams up with Sheen, while Donald Sutherland is a high-ranking official whose motives may not be as pure as they seem. One set piece follows another at a cracking pace as Sheen finds he is being hunted by a merciless killer intent on silencing him before he can blow the whistle. Contains violence and some swearing. ▨

Charlie Sheen *Bobby Bishop* • Linda Hamilton *Amanda Givens* • Donald Sutherland *Conrad* • Stephen Lang *The Agent* • Sam Waterston *The President* • Ben Gazzara *Vice President Saxon* • Nicholas Turturro *Grasso* • Theodore Bikel *Professor Pochenko* • Gore Vidal *Congressman Page* ■ *Dir* George Pan Cosmatos • *Scr* Adi Hasak, Ric Gibbs

Shadow Makers ★★★ PG

Drama
1989 · US · Colour · 121mins

While it's hugely enjoyable to have Paul Newman as a nastily punctilious army officer, this account of the secret project that developed the first American atom bomb never detonates into real drama. There is conflict between the by-the-book soldiers and off-the-wall scientists, and also among the scientists themselves, but, despite a quality cast, the story comes to life only when there's the threat of illness on the base. Director Roland Joffé and his co-writer Bruce Robinson worked together to better effect on *The Killing Fields*. Contains strong language and some violence. ▨

Paul Newman *General Leslie R Groves* • Dwight Schultz *J Robert Oppenheimer* • Bonnie Bedelia *Kitty Oppenheimer* • John Cusack *Michael Merriman* • Laura Dern *Kathleen Robinson* • Ron Frazier *Peer de Silva* • John C McGinley *Richard Schoenfield* • Natasha Richardson *Jean Tatlock* ■ *Dir* Roland Joffé • *Scr* Roland Joffé, Bruce Robinson, from a story by Bruce Robinson

The Shadow Men ★★ 12

Science-fiction thriller
1997 · US · Colour · 90mins

These were the original Men in Black, but the dark-suited characters are a far cry from Will Smith and Tommy Lee Jones. The Shadow Men here are a sinister force out to silence Eric Roberts and Sherilyn Fenn, who have inadvertently witnessed extraterrestrial activity. It's *The X Files* on the cheap, but this TV-movie thriller is entertaining enough, and Dean Stockwell adds a touch of class in a supporting role. ▨

Eric Roberts *Bob Wilson* • Sherilyn Fenn *Dez Wilson* • Dean Stockwell *Stan Mills* • Brendon Ryan Barrett *Andy Wilson* • Andrew Prine *First man in black* • Chris McCarty *Second man in black* • Tom Poster *Third man in black* ■ *Dir* Timothy Bond • *Scr* Eric Miller, Justin Stanley

Shadow of a Doubt

★★★★★ PG

Classic thriller   1943 · US · BW · 103mins

Alfred Hitchcock's personal favourite of his own movies begins when a train, belching out a cloud of ominous black smoke, pulls into Santa Rosa, California. Joseph Cotten has arrived and is met by his adoring niece, Teresa Wright. Both are called "Charlie". She is pumpkin-pie innocence: he is a suave killer, wanted back east for relieving widows of their wealth and their lives. Although Hitchcock blurs the line between good and evil (endorsing Cotten's outbursts against the cosy complacency of the town), the two Charlies are inevitably pitched against each other, as suspicion increases and the police start nosing around. The movie may lack the show-off set pieces that Hitchcock turned into his trademark, yet its tension never falters. Contains some swearing. ▨

Joseph Cotten *Uncle Charlie* • Teresa Wright *Young Charlie* • Macdonald Carey *Jack Graham* • Henry Travers *Joseph Newton* • Patricia Collinge *Emma Newton* • Hume Cronyn *Herbie Hawkins* • Edna May Wonacott *Ann Newton* • Wallace Ford *Fred Saunders* ■ *Dir* Alfred Hitchcock • *Scr* Thornton Wilder, Sally Benson, Alma Reville, from a story by Gordon McDonell

Shadow of a Doubt ★★ PG

Thriller   1991 · US · Colour · 95mins

An unnecessary TV-movie remake of Alfred Hitchcock's classic 1943 thriller starring Joseph Cotten and Teresa Wright, this has Mark Harmon as the man who preys on older, rich women, and Margaret Welsh as his adoring niece, who begins to suspect him. It's nowhere near as gripping, atmospheric or tense as the original. Tippi Hedren and Diane Ladd do add some class to the proceedings. Harmon spoils their efforts, however, by overacting and displays none of the menace he showed in his finest hour as serial killer Ted Bundy in *The Deliberate Stranger*. ▨

Mark Harmon *Charles Spencer/Uncle Charlie* • Diane Ladd *Emma Newton* • Margaret Welsh *Charlie Newton* • William Lanteau *Henry Newton* • Norm Skaggs *Gary Graham* • Rick Lenz *Herb Hawkins* • Tippi Hedren *Mrs Mathewson* • Shirley Knight *Mrs Potter* ■ *Dir* Karen Arthur • *Scr* John Gay, from the film by Thorton Wilder, Sally Benson, Alma Reville, from the story by Gordon McDonell

Shadow of a Doubt ★★★

Courtroom drama
1995 · US · Colour · 107mins

Actor Brian Dennehy's debut as a director, this is a courtroom drama in which Dennehy plays a lawyer, battling against the bottle, who takes on a case brought to him by a former girlfriend, Bonnie Bedelia. Her stepdaughter, it seems, has murdered her father, though in stories like this you know that the truth will emerge either just before or just after the jury has delivered its verdict. Dennehy has the heavyweight presence of Raymond Burr's Perry Mason and he's nearly matched by Fairuza Balk's turn as the troubled teen.

Brian Dennehy *Charley Sloan* • Bonnie Bedelia *Robin Harwell* • Fairuza Balk *Angel Harwell* •

Mike Nussbaum *Nate Golden* • Kevin Dunn *Mark Evola* • Joe Grifasi *Sidney* • Ken Pogue *Judge Brown* • *Dir* Brian Dennehy • *Scr* Bill Phillips, William J Coughlin, from the novel by William J Coughlin

Shadow of a Stranger ★★ 15

Thriller   1992 · US · Colour · 87mins

Dynasty's Emma Samms and ex-*Baywatch* actor Parker Stevenson are an otherwise successful couple trying to save their marriage by getting away from it all on an exotic holiday. Unfortunately, their travel agent gives them a bit of a bad deal and they end up on the coast just as a severe storm breaks. Matters get worse when they save a couple whose boat sinks but who may not be all they seem. While Samms spends most of the movie in hysterics, the rest of the cast battles against the predictable script (*Dead Calm II*, anybody?) while trying to look surprised, as enough dead bodies to fill a morgue turn up. ▨

Emma Samms *Sarah Klein* • Parker Stevenson *Ted Klein* • Joan Chen *Vanessa* • Michael Easton *Shawn* • John Pyper-Ferguson *Robert* ■ *Dir/Scr* Richard Friedman

A Shadow of Doubt

★★★★ 15

Psychological thriller
1992 · Fr · Colour · 101mins

When 11-year-old Alexandrine (Sandrine Blancke) accuses her father of molestation, no one believes her except social worker, Josiane Balasko. It would have been easy to have turned this situation into a grimly effective melodrama. But, director Aline Issermann allows the doubt to linger, exploring both the torment of the suspected father and the loneliness of a child trapped in the misery and fear of incest. Staged without sensationalism or sermonising, this impeccably played picture has an emotional messiness that owes everything to life, not the movies. In French with English subtitles. ▨

Mireille Perrier *Marie* • Alain Bashung *Jean* • Sandrine Blancke *Alexandrine* • Emmanuelle Riva *Grandma* • Michel Aumont *Grandpa* • Josiane Balasko *Sophia* ■ *Dir/Scr* Aline Issermann

Shadow of Doubt ★

Courtroom thriller
1998 · US · Colour · 102mins

In this highly contrived courtroom drama, Melanie Griffith is the attorney defending a rap star against murder charges from prosecutor and ex-lover Tom Berenger. The proceedings, especially towards the end, are so jam-packed with wild plot twists, subplots, and unnecessary details that it comes close to being entertaining in its badness. However, director Randal Kleiser shows no sign of a sense of humour, and makes everything so overly slick that even the opening credits generate a headache.

Melanie Griffith *Kitt Devereux* • Tom Berenger *Jack Campioni* • Huey Lewis *Al Gordon* • Nina Foch *Sylvia Saxon* • Kimberley Kates *Bridget* • Wade Dominguez *Bobby Medina* ■ *Dir* Randal Kleiser • *Scr* Myra Byanka, Raymond DeFelitta

Shadow of Evil ★★ U

Spy thriller   1964 · Fr/It · Colour · 92mins

That James Bond wannabe, OSS 117 (Kerwin Mathews) dons the superspy's gunbelt to thwart Robert Hossein's insane scheme to wipe out what he considers "inferior races" in order to head a perfect world. Although the subject matter is decidedly unpleasant for such a tongue-in-cheek romp, director André Hunebelle knows enough about swashbucklers to keep the action moving along and the romance between Mathews and Pier Angeli spicy. French dialogue dubbed into English.

Kerwin Mathews *OSS 117* • Robert Hossein *Dr Sinn* • Pier Angeli *Lila* • Dominique Wilms *Eva Davidson* ■ *Dir* André Hunebelle • *Scr* André Hunebelle, Pierre Foucard, Raymond Borel, Michel Lebrun, Richard Caron, Patrice Rondard, from the novel *Lila de Calcutta* by Jean Bruce

Shadow of Fear ★ U

Spy drama   1963 · UK · BW · 60mins

Paul Maxwell has the misfortune to star in this risible tale of an oil mogul who agrees to have himself kidnapped so he can root out a mole operating within the British secret service. Ernest Morris directs with such little enthusiasm for the material that he can hardly expect his audience to bother sitting all the way through a story that is shrouded in about as much mystery as an oil well under a belly-dancer's veil.

Paul Maxwell *Bill Martin* • Clare Owen *Barbara* • Anita West *Ruth* • Alan Tilvern *Warner* • John Arnatt *Sharp* • Eric Pohlmann *Spiroulos* • Reginald Marsh *Oliver* ■ *Dir* Ernest Morris • *Scr* Ronald Liles, James O'Connolly, from the novel *Decoy Be Damned* by TF Fotherby

Shadow of Obsession ★★

Thriller   1994 · US · Colour

Watchable, if routine thriller, involving that popular TV-movie stand-by, the stalker. Former *Hill Street Blues* star Veronica Hamel plays a divorcee and dedicated college psychology professor whose life is thrown into turmoil when slimeball Jack Scalia develops an increasingly dangerous obsession with her. There's the odd suspenseful moment, but the performances are strictly average and the direction from Kevin Connor is equally forgettable.

Veronica Hamel *Rebecca Kendall* • Jack Scalia *Michael Carvella* • Kim Miyori *Angela Casaretti* • Page Moseley *Benjamin Nash* • Sam Behrens *Philip Parrish* ■ *Dir* Kevin Connor • *Scr* Ellen Weston, from the novel *Unwanted Attentions* by KK Beck

The Shadow of the Cat ★★

Horror   1961 · UK · BW · 78mins

Hammer removed their credit from director John Gilling's bizarre curiosity for legal quota reasons. But this tale of a manic moggy exacting a terrible revenge on those who conspired to kill its mistress was only serviceable melodrama at best despite the addition of House of Horror heroine Barbara Shelley. Notable for the way Gilling shows the deaths of the terrified murderers through the eyes of the avenging feline, but not much else.

U = SUITABLE FOR ALL   Uc = SUITABLE FOR ALL, ESPECIALLY FOR YOUNG CHILDREN (VIDEO ONLY)   PG = PARENTAL GUIDANCE

André Morell *Walter Venable* • Barbara Shelley *Beth Venable* • William Lucas *Jacob* • Freda Jackson *Clara* • Conrad Phillips *Michael Latimer* ■ *Dir* John Gilling • *Scr* George Baxt

Shadow of the Eagle ★★ U

Historical swashbuckling drama
1950 · UK · BW · 95mins

This is typical of the clutch of second-rate swashbucklers made by Sidney Salkow during a mid-career crisis that saw him switch from lively detective thrillers to B-westerns. It's certainly a shadow of the kind of picture he could have made on the same budget had he stayed in Hollywood. The grim monochrome doesn't help conjure up the grandeur of 18th-century Venice, but it is Salkow's pedestrian direction that prevents us becoming caught in the web of intrigue surrounding Russian diplomat Richard Greene and intended royal kidnap victim Valentina Cortese.

Richard Greene *Count Alexei Orloff* • Valentina Cortese [Valentina Cortese] *Princess Tarakanova* • Greta Gynt *Countess Camponiello* • Binnie Barnes *Empress Catherine* • Charles Goldner *General Korsakov* • Walter Rilla *Prince Radziwill* ■ *Dir* Sidney Salkow • *Scr* Doreen Montgomery, Hagar Wilde, from the story by Jacques Companeez

Shadow of the Past ★★

Drama 1995 · US · Colour · 105mins

This showcase role for country superstar Dwight Yoakam has him as a former top rodeo clown reluctant to re-enter the ring. Yoakam is laid back, but effective in this moving tale that follows Kidder as he attempts to tackle the hang-ups from his past before he can settle comfortably back in the saddle. An offbeat and likeable character study, with sturdy support by the likes of Bo Hopkins, Cindy Pickett and John Getz. Watch out for a cameo appearance from Peter Fonda.

Dwight Yoakam *Virgil Kidder* • Michelle Joyner *Katelin* • Kiersten Warren *Teresa* • Cindy Pickett *Sadie* • John Getz *Sheriff Acuff* • Bo Hopkins *Brownie* • Peter Fonda ■ *Dir* Terry Benedict • *Scr* Terry Benedict, Stan Bertheaud

Shadow of the Thin Man ★★

Detective comedy drama
1941 · US · BW · 96mins

While Nick and Nora Charles (William Powell and Myrna Loy), now the proud parents of a baby son, are at the races, a jockey is murdered. Nick refuses to investigate, but gets involved when a reporter is also bumped off. By this fourth entry in the popular series, quality was on the decline, with the original sharp wit lessened by injections of broader comedy and more convoluted plotting. But Powell and Loy's polish is undimmed.

William Powell *Nick* • Myrna Loy *Nora* • Barry Nelson *Paul* • Donna Reed *Molly* • Sam Levene *Lieutenant Abrams* • Alan Baxter *"Whitey" Barrow* ■ *Dir* Major WS Van Dyke II [WS Van Dyke] ■ *Scr* Irving Brecher, Harry Kurnitz, from a story by Harry Kurnitz, from characters created by Dashiell Hammett

Shadow of the Wolf ★★ 15

Historical drama
1992 · Can/Fr · Colour · 107mins

This costly wilderness epic about the conflict between the Inuit and encroaching whites in the Arctic of the thirties proves to be an insipid watch. Lou Diamond Phillips stars as a young Inuit hunter banished from his tribe only to be hunted down himself for murder by Donald Sutherland's cop. Director Jacques Dorfmann allows his narrative to become convoluted and cluttered with mystical mumbo jumbo, though there are some moments of pictorial beauty, courtesy of Oscar-winning cinematographer Billy Williams. If you ever wanted to learn how to build an igloo, this is the film for you. 🎬

Lou Diamond Phillips *Agaguk* • Toshiro Mifune *Ramook* • Jennifer Tilly *Iriook* • Donald Sutherland *Henderson* • Bernard-Pierre Donnadieu *Brown* • Qalingo Tookalak *Tulugak* • Harry Hill *McTavish* ■ *Dir* Jacques Dorfmann • *Scr* Rudy Wurlitzer, Evan Jones, from the novel *Agaguk* by Yves Theriault

Shadow Play ★★ 15

Supernatural thriller
1986 · US · Colour · 93mins

In this routine haunted house tale, a New York playwright becomes so obsessed by her dead lover that, on returning to the island where he died, she ends up playing host to his ghost. Unfortunately for the audience, the spirit helps her ghost-write some pretty awful poetry. And that's about it. 🎬

Dee Wallace Stone *Morgan Hanna* • Cloris Leachman *Millie Crown* • Ron Kuhlman *John Crown* • Barry Laws *Jeremy Crown* • Al Strobel *Byron* ■ *Dir/Scr* Susan Shadburne

Shadowlands ★★★★★ U

Romantic biographical drama
1993 · UK/US · Colour · 125mins

This intimate drama set far from the world stage remains one of director Richard Attenborough's best pictures to date. It charts the tragic love affair between the author CS Lewis and an American poet, Joy Gresham. Anthony Hopkins and Debra Winger give performances that you dream about but rarely see, and the tone is set by Winger's entrance into Oxford's Randolph Hotel: "Anyone here named Loowis?" she rasps, upsetting the decorum of academe and rattling Hopkins's tea cup. Thereafter, Hopkins's life as an emotionally frigid bachelor is transformed. With its immaculate fifties' setting, the film creates a totally convincing world and Attenborough gets beneath the skin of his characters as never before. 🎬

Anthony Hopkins *CS "Jack" Lewis* • Debra Winger *Joy Gresham* • John Wood *Christopher Riley* • Edward Hardwicke *Warnie Lewis* • Joseph Mazzello *Douglas Gresham* • Julian Fellowes *Desmond Arding* • Roddy Maude-Roxby *Arnold Dopliss* • Michael Denison *Harry Harrington* • Peter Firth *Doctor Craig* ■ *Dir* Richard Attenborough • *Scr* William Nicholson, from his play

Shadows ★★★★★ PG

Drama 1959 · US · BW · 77mins

Format-breaking social drama by actor-turned-director John Cassavetes who, in this his first film, created a mainly-improvised story of three black siblings – Lelia Goldoni, Ben Carruthers and Hugh Hurd – making their way in Manhattan. Goldoni, who passes for white, begins a love affair with a white man, which gives Cassavetes plenty of scope for inter-racial discussion (unusual in the sixties), while jazz trumpeter Hugh finds life full of sour notes. Cassavetes's style of ad-lib acting and situations became a benchmark for future independent film-making. 🎬

Hugh Hurd *Hugh* • Lelia Goldoni *Lelia* • Ben Carruthers *Ben* • Anthony Ray *Tony* • Dennis Sallas *Dennis* • Tom Allen *Tom* • David Pokitillow *David* ■ *Dir* John Cassavetes • *Music* Charlie Mingus

Shadows and Fog ★★★ 15

Comedy drama 1991 · US · BW · 81mins

Reworking his 1972 one-act play *Death*, Woody Allen originally intended this esoteric drama to be a homage to German Expressionism. However, he opted for a look owing more to Universal's pre-war horror movies and, thus, deprived an already slight premise of some visual power. As the nobody who is co-opted into the search for a strangler in an eastern European town, Allen is typically twitchy amid a galaxy of guest stars, including John Malkovich, Madonna and Jodie Foster. Short on humour, perhaps, but this curio is laced with ideas that took on a new relevance when news broke of his split with Mia Farrow. Contains some violence. 🎬

Woody Allen *Kleinman* • Mia Farrow *Irmy* • John Malkovich *Clown* • Madonna *Marie* • Donald Pleasence *Doctor* • Kathy Bates *Prostitute* • Jodie Foster *Prostitute* • Lily Tomlin *Prostitute* • John Cusack *Student Jack* • Julie Kavner *Alma* ■ *Dir/Scr* Woody Allen

Shadows in the Night ★★

Mystery 1944 · US · BW · 66mins

The third in Columbia's series based on a radio show called *Crime Doctor*, in which the hero, Robert Ordway, is a famous criminal psychiatrist and brilliant sleuth who's really a criminal mastermind suffering from amnesia. Warner Baxter, a silent star and Oscar winner for 1929's *In Old Arizona*, played Ordway throughout the series, despite a nervous breakdown. In this episode, Baxter assists haunted heiress Nina Foch, who keeps threatening suicide.

Warner Baxter *Dr Robert Ordway* • Nina Foch *Lois Garland* • George Zucco *Frank Swift* • Minor Watson *Frederick Gordon* • Lester Matthews *Stanley Carter* • Ben Welden *Nick Kallus* ■ *Dir* Eugene J Forde [Eugene Forde] • *Scr* Eric Taylor, from the radio programme *Crime Doctor* by Max Marcin

Shadows of Our Forgotten Ancestors ★★★★★ 12

Drama 1964 · USSR · Colour and BW · 91mins

A radical departure from his previous films, Sergei Paradjanov's masterpiece sought to challenge accepted notions of narrative and visual representation. Inspired by the stories of Mikhaylo Kotsyubinsky, this expressionist variation on the Tristan and Isolde theme is not just cinematically subversive, but also politically contentious, through its bold assertion of Ukrainian heritage. Nothing can be taken at face value in this psychologically dense exercise in deconstruction. The hallucinatory affects achieved through camera movement, lens manipulation and cutting, the daringly shifting diegetic perspectives, the brilliant "dramaturgy of colour" and the disorientating use of sound all ran counter to existing norms in Soviet art and made its director a marked man. In Russian with English subtitles. 🎬

Ivan Mikolaychuk *Ivan* • Larisa Kadochnikova *Marichka* • Tatyana Bestayeva *Palagna* • Spartak Bagashvili *Yurko the Sorcerer* ■ *Dir* Sergei Paradjanov • *Scr* Sergey Paradzhanov, Ivan Chendey, from the novelette *Tini Zabutykh Predkiv* by Mikhaylo Mikhaylovich Kotsyubinsky

Shadows of the Past ★ 15

Thriller 1991 · Can · Colour · 91mins

Anyone who sat through the rather implausible Tom Berenger movie *Shattered* will know that thrillers based around a lead character with memory loss are, often as not, ludicrous. This, alas, is no exception. Erika Anderson stars as a woman who survives a car accident only to wake up with amnesia. And if things weren't bad enough, she also realises someone may be trying to kill her, and there is an equally silly connection to illegal arms dealing. 🎬

Erika Anderson *Jackie Delaney* • Nicholas Campbell *Sean MacFern* • Daniel Martin • Heidi Von Palleske *Sara Davis* • Lorne Brass *Haaring* • Dennis O'Connor *Banner* • Jacques Herlin *Inspector Grenier* ■ *Dir* Gabriel Pelletier • *Scr* David Preston

Shadows of the Peacock ★★

Drama 1987 · Ausl · Colour · 92mins

Before decamping for Hollywood, Australian director Phillip Noyce signed off with this uneven drama. Wendy Hughes is the mother trying to rebuild her life after discovering that her husband has been cheating on her and finding romance in Thailand with the bewitching John Lone. It looks glorious and is superbly played by the talented cast, although the suspicion remains that there is less going on here than meets the eye.

Wendy Hughes *Maria* • John Lone *Raka* • Steven Jacobs [Steve Jacobs] *George* • Peta Toppano *Judy* • Rod Mullinar *Terry* ■ *Dir* Phillip Noyce • *Scr* Jan Sharp, Anne Brooksbank

Shadows on the Stairs ★

Mystery 1941 · US · BW · 63mins

One of those irritating thrillers that explain away an implausible plot through a cheat ending. Murder is committed in the Bloomsbury boarding house run by Frieda Inescort and Miles Mander and investigated by a resident, Bruce Lester's budding playwright. Turhan Bey plays a shady Asian businessman in one of his earliest screen appearances while Paul Cavanagh and Lumsden Hare are familiar faces in the cast list.

Paul Cavanagh *Mr Reynolds* • Heather Angel *Sylvia* • Turhan Bey *Ram Singh* • Frieda Inescort *Mrs Armitage* • Miles Mander *Mr Armitage* • Bruce Lester *Bromilow* • Phyllis

Barry *Lucy* • Lumsden Hare *Inspector* • Mary Field *Miss Snell* ◼ *Dir* D Ross Lederman • *Scr* Anthony Coldeway, from the play *Murder on the 2nd Floor* by Frank Vosper

Shadowzone ★★★ 18

Science-fiction horror
1990 · US · Colour · 84mins

In this intriguing and competent low-budget shocker, a team of scientists working in an isolated underground complex investigate the mysteries of dreams and long-term sleep but accidentally unleash a shape-shifting monster from another dimension. One of literally countless *Alien* rip-offs, but writer/director JS Cardone heightens the sense of foreboding inherent within the claustrophobic situation and pumps up the suspense. Although, like so many of these movies, the unveiling of the monster is a big let-down. 🎬

Louise Fletcher *Dr Erhardt* • Miguel A Nunez Jr *Wiley* • David Beecroft *Captain Hickock* • Lu Leonard *Mrs Cutter* • James Hong *Dr Van Fleet* • Shawn Weatherly *Dr Kidwell* • Frederick Flynn *Tommy Shivers* ◼ *Dir/Scr* JS Cardone

Shaft ★★★ 15

Blaxploitation crime thriller
1971 · US · Colour · 100mins

The film that firmly established the blaxploitation genre in the early seventies is nothing more than an urban ghetto James Bond thriller. But ex-male model Richard Roundtree brings a casual charm to the vicious proceedings as the private dick ("a sex machine to all the chicks") enlisted to find a Harlem racketeer's kidnapped daughter, and director Gordon Parks gives it a fast and furious style. Isaac Hayes won an Oscar for the landmark theme song that laid down the ground rules for all the funky satin-sheet sounds that followed in its ground-breaking wake. Contains violence, swearing and brief nudity. 🎬

Richard Roundtree *John Shaft* • Moses Gunn *Bumpy Jonas* • Charles Cioffi *Lieutenant Vic Androzzi* • Christopher St John *Ben Buford* • Gwenn Mitchell *Ellie Moore* • Lawrence Pressman *Sergeant Tom Hannon* • Victor Arnold *Charlie* • Sherri Brewer *Marcy* ◼ *Dir* Gordon Parks • *Scr* Ernest Tidyman, John DF Black, from the novel by Ernest Tidyman

Shaft in Africa ★★★ 18

Blaxploitation thriller
1973 · US · Colour · 107mins

Richard Roundtree's portrayal of the supercool black private eye is still, in this sequel, the film's most persuasive quality. With a screenplay by Stirling Silliphant, this tale has Shaft lured out of his ghetto domain to break Frank Finlay's slave-smuggling racket. The film gets across its message with some cracking dialogue and bursts of violent skulduggery, with British director John Guillermin showing an acute eye for sadistic detail. Contains nudity, violence and swearing. 🎬

Richard Roundtree *John Shaft* • Frank Finlay *Amafi* • Vonetta McGee *Aleme* • Neda Arneric *Jazar* • Debebe Eshetu *Wassa* • Cy Grant *Emir Ramila* • Spiros Focas *Sassari* ◼ *Dir* John Guillermin • *Scr* Stirling Silliphant, from the characters created by Ernest Tidyman

Shaft's Big Score! ★★★ 15

Blaxploitation thriller
1972 · US · Colour · 100mins

Richard Roundtree and Moses Gunn return in the sequel to the huge blockbuster *Shaft*, which kicked off the early seventies' blaxploitation craze. This time the private-eye hero acts more like a hip James Bond than a retro Sam Spade, in a routine social conscience tale that finds him avenging the murder of a friend while retrieving money stolen by warring gangsters. It's not as tightly directed by Gordon Parks as the first movie, but the New York harbour ending is memorably exciting. 🎬

Richard Roundtree *John Shaft* • Moses Gunn *Bumpy Jonas* • Drew Bundini Brown *Willy* • Joseph Mascolo *Gus Mascola* • Kathy Imrie *Rita* • Wally Taylor *Kelly* • Julius W Harris [Julius Harris] *Captain Bollin* • Rosalind Miles *Arna Asby* ◼ *Dir* Gordon Parks • *Scr* Ernest Tidyman, from his characters

Shag ★★★ 15

Comedy 1988 · UK/US · Colour · 95mins

An unfortunately titled (it's a dance) youth movie, directed by former continuity girl Zelda Barron. The film features an attractive American cast plus Britain's own Shirley Anne Field, but nobody has anything significant to do. Phoebe Cates is on the verge of matrimony, and her buddies Bridget Fonda, Annabeth Gish and Darryl Hannah's younger sister, Page, decide to throw her one last fling at Myrtle Beach. Since it's 1963 and the Yanks have yet to discover the Beatles and the Pill, not much happens. Slight and undemanding, but fun in places. Contains mild swearing. 🎬

Phoebe Cates *Carson McBride* • Scott Coffey *Chip Guillyard* • Bridget Fonda *Melaina Buller* • Annabeth Gish *Caroline "Pudge" Carmichael* • Page Hannah *Luanne Clatterbuck* • Robert Rusler *Buzz Ravenel* • Tyrone Power Jr *Harley Ralston* • Jeff Yagher *Jimmy Valentine* • Shirley Anne Field *Mrs Clatterbuck* ◼ *Dir* Zelda Barron • *Scr* Robin Swicord, Lanier Laney, Terry Sweeney, from a story by Lanier Laney, Terry Sweeney

The Shaggy DA ★★★ U

Comedy 1976 · US · Colour · 87mins

A belated follow-up to Disney's 1959 hit, *The Shaggy Dog*, finds lawyer Dean Jones turning into a pooch at the slightest provocation. Unfortunately, this peculiar canine condition occurs just as he's up for election as district attorney against the unscrupulous Keenan Wynn. Notable for a juicy scene involving some cherry pies and an ingenious breakout from the dog pound, this is one of those rare occasions when the sequel is superior to the original. 🎬

Dean Jones *Wilby Daniels* • Suzanne Pleshette *Betty Daniels* • Keenan Wynn *District Attorney John Slade* • Tim Conway *Tim* • Jo Anne Worley *Katrinka Muggelberg* • Dick Van Patten *Raymond* ◼ *Dir* Robert Stevenson • *Scr* Don Tait, from the novel *The Hound of Florence* by Felix Salten

The Shaggy Dog ★★ U

Fantasy comedy 1959 · US · BW · 100mins

This was the first of Disney's contemporary slapstick fantasies and typifies the generally reviled genre.

However, in its day it was a big success and led to a belated sequel. With his usual aplomb, Fred MacMurray plays the troubled *paterfamilias* whose son turns into a sheepdog (you'd be troubled, too), while Jean Hagen has a thankless role as mom. Disney regulars Annette Funicello and Tommy Kirk head the support cast, but today's audience might still be disappointed with this tale.

Fred MacMurray *Wilson Daniels* • Jean Hagen *Frieda Daniels* • Tommy Kirk *Wilby Daniels* • Annette Funicello *Allison D'Allessio* • Tim Considine *Buzz Miller* • Kevin Corcoran *Moochie Daniels* • Cecil Kellaway *Professor Plumcutt* • Alexander Scourby *Doctor Mikhail Andrassy* ◼ *Dir* Charles Barton • *Scr* Bill Walsh, Lillie Hayward, from the novel *The Hound of Florence* by Felix Salten

The Shaggy Dog ★★

Fantasy comedy 1994 · US · Colour · 96mins

This is Disney's TV-movie reworking of its 1959 smash-hit comedy. The ever-willing Ed Begley Jr valiantly tries to fill the shoes of Fred MacMurray, but Scott Weinger (as the boy who turns himself into a pooch while experimenting with an ancient spell) lacks Tommy Kirk's charm and Natasha Gregson Wagner is clearly no Annette Funicello.

Scott Weinger *Wilby Daniels* • Ed Begley Jr *Ron Daniels* • Sharon Lawrence *Beth Daniels* • Jordan Blake Warkol *Moochie Daniels* • James Cromwell *Charlie Mulvihill* • Sarah Lassez *Francesca* • Natasha Gregson Wagner *Allison* ◼ *Dir* Dennis Dugan • *Scr* Tim Doyle, from the 1959 film, from the novel *The Hound of Florence* by Felix Salten

Shaheed ★★★

Political melodrama 1948 · Ind · BW

Set in the final days of the Raj, this surprisingly outspoken drama focuses on the tensions placed on the already strained relationship between a mandarin in the imperial civil service and his freedom fighter son, when the latter is charged with a political killing. Director Ramesh Saigal tackles the thorny subject of divided loyalties with admirable restraint, considering that he had been forced to abandon his native Punjab the previous year after it became part of Pakistan. The intelligent performances of matinée idol Dilip Kumar and Chandra Mohan ensure the action never descends into melodrama. In Urdu and Hindi with English subtitles.

Dilip Kumar • Kamini Kaushal • Chandra Mohan ◼ *Dir* Ramesh Saigal • *Scr* Ramesh Saigal, Qamar Jalalabadi, from a story by Ramesh Saigal

Shai'r ★★★ U

Comedy 1949 · Ind · BW · 135mins

Fuelled by caprice, confusion and coincidence, the *masala* musical melodramas produced by the studios of Bombay (Bollywood) are something of an acquired taste. But if you can forgive the plot contrivances and cope with the highly individual musical style, there is much to enjoy in lively extravaganzas like this popular story about a poet who loves a singer, unaware of the effect he has on an innocent country girl. It may not be one of the best films made by future pin-up

Dev Anand or former child star Suraiya, but it's a fair starting point for the uninitiated. In Urdu and Hindi with English subtitles. 🎬

Dev Anand • Kamini Kashai • Suraiya ◼ *Dir* Chawla

Shake Hands with the Devil ★★★

Political drama 1959 · Ire/US · BW · 110mins

A distinguished cast of British and Irish actors, plus American Don Murray, bolster James Cagney in this somewhat grim and melodramatic but well-made mix of politics, romance, and violence. Cagney is a professor of medicine in 1921 Dublin, whose respectability is a cover for his IRA activities. When his student Murray, an Irish-American, is beaten up by British officers, a vengeful Cagney abducts the daughter (Dana Wynter) of a British functionary, paving the way for romance between her and his protégé. Meanwhile the political bloodshed continues to rage. A provocative, if undeveloped proposition.

James Cagney *Sean Lenihan* • Don Murray *Kerry O'Shea* • Dana Wynter *Jennifer Curtis* • Glynis Johns *Kitty Brady* • Michael Redgrave *The General* • Sybil Thorndike *Lady Fitzhugh* • Cyril Cusack *Chris Noonan* • Marianne Benet *Mary Madigan* ◼ *Dir* Michael Anderson • *Scr* Ben Roberts, Marian Thompson, Ivan Goff, from the novel by Rearden Conner

Shake, Rattle and Rock! ★★★ U

Drama 1957 · US · BW · 76mins

Quintessential viewing for rock 'n' roll fans and a key film of its era. Plotwise it's the usual stuff about a town's parents at odds with the new music craze. What makes it worth watching is the music. Highlights include the legendary Joe Turner performing *Lipstick, Powder and Paint* and the great Fats Domino belting out *I'm in Love Again* and the fabulous *Ain't That a Shame*. The cast is headed by Touch Connors, who as Mike Connors achieved stardom of sorts in the TV series *Mannix*, and it's good to see Margaret Dumont (the Marx Brothers' stooge) making an appearance.

Touch Connors [Mike Connors] *Garry Nelson* • Lisa Gaye *June* • Sterling Holloway *Axe* • Margaret Dumont *Georgianna* • Douglass Dumbrille *Eustace* ◼ *Dir* Edward L Cahn • *Scr* Lou Rusoff

Shake, Rattle and Rock ★★★ PG

Drama 1994 · US · Colour · 79mins

Part of a series of remakes of fifties B-movies, this is a slight but affectionate take on that old staple: the teen musical. Howie Mandel has a ball as a rebel with a cause allowing teenagers to get down to the rock 'n' roll music hated by their conservative elders. The eclectic cast includes Renee Zellweger, Roger Corman regular Dick Miller, singer Ruth Brown and cult icon Mary Woronov. Director Allan Arkush – another Corman protégé – keeps his tongue firmly in his cheek and conjures up the same atmosphere of cheerful irreverence he brought to the Ramones vehicle *Rock 'n' Roll High School*.

U = SUITABLE FOR ALL · Uc = SUITABLE FOR ALL, ESPECIALLY FOR YOUNG CHILDREN (VIDEO ONLY) · PG = PARENTAL GUIDANCE

Contains some sexual references and strong language. 🖵

Renee Zellweger *Susan Doyle* • Patricia Childress *Cookie* • Max Perlich *Tony* • Howie Mandel *Danny Klay* • Latanyia Baldwin *Sireena Cooper* • Mary Woronov *Joyce* • Stephen Furst *Frank* • Dick Miller *Officer Miller* • Ruth Brown *Ella* • PJ Soles *Evelyn* ■ *Dir* Allan Arkush • *Scr* Trish Soodik

The Shakedown ★★
Crime drama 1959 · UK · BW · 91mins

Terence Morgan plays a photographer with an eye for extortion in this film that sets out to shock with sleazy settings and sensationalist suggestions of nudity. However, few of the misdemeanours from this period piece would raise even a blush today. Director John Lemont forgets to concentrate on the storyline, which grinds to its inevitable conclusion.

Terence Morgan *Augie Cortona* • Hazel Court *Mildred* • Donald Pleasence *Jessel* • Bill Owen *Spettigue* • Robert Beatty *Inspector Jarvis* • Harry H Corbett *Gollar* • Gene Anderson *Zena* • Eddie Byrne *George* ■ *Dir* John Lemont • *Scr* John Lemont, Leigh Vance

Shakedown on the Sunset Strip ★ 15
Crime drama based on a true story
1988 · US · Colour · 89mins

Seasoned TV actors Perry King and Joan Van Ark star in this uneven film about an LA cop determined to arrest a rich madam, despite the fact she has friends in high places. Perhaps actor King should get friendly with some of these people in real life, then he wouldn't have to star in movies like this. 🖵

Perry King *Sergeant Charles Stoker* • Season Hubley *Officer Audre Davis* • Joan Van Ark *Brenda Allen* • Vincent Baggetta *Sergeant Fuller* • Alan Blumenfeld *Officer Parslow* • David Graf *Officer Ruggles* ■ *Dir* Walter Grauman • *Scr* Harold Gast

Shaker Run ★★ 15
Thriller 1985 · NZ · Colour · 86mins

Lush New Zealand landscape emphasises the clichéd inanity and inadequacy of this car-chase melodrama in whch Cliff Robertson and Leif Garrett are two American stunt drivers helping a naive girl (Lisa Harrow) transport a deadly virus cross-country. Crashes and pursuits are beautifully shot by director Bruce Morrison, but otherwise, it's totally predictable. 🖵

Cliff Robertson *Judd Pierson* • Leif Garrett *Casey Lee* • Lisa Harrow *Dr Christine Rubin* • Shane Briant *Paul Thoreau* • Peter Hayden *Michael Connolly* ■ *Dir* Bruce Morrison • *Scr* James Kouf Jr, Henry Fownes, Bruce Morrison

Shakes the Clown ★★ 18
Comedy 1991 · US · Colour · 82mins

Stand-up comedian Bobcat Goldthwait exploited the sinister side of the classic circus clown, writing, directing and starring in this bizarre, harsh fantasy. Set in the mythical town of Palukaville, Goldthwait is the eponymous Shakes, an alcoholic clown and regular barfly. When his boss, the clown dispatcher, is found murdered Shakes is the prime suspect and is forced to go on the run to clear

himself. The depiction of a hierarchical clown society is one of the film's strong points, but in the end it's more funny peculiar than funny ha-ha. Robin Williams appears in a cameo role and the film does have an almost masochistic cult status. Contains swearing and drug abuse. 🖵

Bobcat Goldthwait *Shakes the Clown* • Julie Brown *Judy* • Bruce Baum *Ty the Rodeo Clown* • Blake Clark *Stenchy the Clown* • Paul Dooley *Owen Cheese* • Marty Fromage [Robin Williams] *Mime Jerry* • Florence Henderson *The Unknown Woman* • Tom Kenny *Binky the Clown* • Sydney Lassick *Peppy the Clown* • Adam Sandler *Dink the Clown* ■ *Dir/Scr* Bobcat Goldthwait

Shakespeare in Love ★★★★★ 15
Period romantic comedy
1998 · US · Colour · 118mins

Taking the creation of Shakespeare's *Romeo and Juliet* as its inspiration, John Madden's follow-up to *Mrs Brown* combines contemporary humour with an authentic 16th-century setting. Young Will (Joseph Fiennes) falls for the soon-to-be-married Viola (Gwyneth Paltrow) and casts her, disguised as a boy, as his Romeo. As their love affair unfolds, so does the play in a film that is passionate, intelligent and hysterically funny in turns. Fiennes and Paltrow are supported by an outstanding cast that includes Geoffrey Rush, Tom Wilkinson and Colin Firth, while Judi Dench delivers an Oscar-winning portrayal of Elizabeth I. Contains sex scenes. 🖵 **DVD**

Gwyneth Paltrow *Viola De Lesseps* • Joseph Fiennes *Will Shakespeare* • Colin Firth *Lord Wessex* • Geoffrey Rush *Philip Henslowe* • Judi Dench *Queen Elizabeth* • Tom Wilkinson *Hugh Fennyman* • Ben Affleck *Ned Alleyn* • Simon Callow *Tilney, Master of the Revels* • Jim Carter *Ralph Bashford* • Martin Clunes *Richard Burbage* • Imelda Staunton *Nurse* • Rupert Everett *Christopher Marlowe* ■ *Dir* John Madden • *Scr* Marc Norman, Tom Stoppard • *Costume Designer* Sandy Powell • *Art Director* Martin Childs, Jill Quertier • *Music* Stephen Warbeck • *Cinematographer* Richard Greatrex

Shakespeare Wallah ★★★
Romantic drama 1965 · Ind · BW · 124mins

With its gentle pacing and keen eye for atmospheric detail, this might be mistaken for the work of director Satyajit Ray. But while he provided both the score and the cinematographer (Subrata Mitra), this tale of strolling players was, in fact, the second collaboration between Merchant–Ivory and screenwriter Ruth Prawer Jhabvala. Based on their own experiences performing the Bard around the subcontinent, Geoffrey and Felicity Kendall effortlessly avoid condescension, while Shashi Kapoor is suitably dashing as Felicity's culture-crossed lover. But no one stands a chance alongside Madhur Jaffrey's hilarious Bollywood bitch.

Shashi Kapoor *Sanju* • Felicity Kendal *Lizzie Buckingham* • Madhur Jaffrey *Manjula* • Geoffrey Kendal *Tony Buckingham* • Laura Liddell *Carla Buckingham* • Utpal Dutt *The Maharajah* ■ *Dir* James Ivory • *Scr* Ruth Prawer Jhabvala, James Ivory • *Producer* Ismail Merchant

The Shakiest Gun in the West ★★ U
Comedy western
1967 · US · Colour · 100mins

Don Knotts steps into the shoes first worn by Bob Hope in this feeble reworking of that classic comedy western *The Paleface*. Never one to underplay when some shameless mugging will do, the ever-nervous Knotts (*The Ghost and Mr Chicken*) overcooks every gag. However, this story of the dentist mistaken for a gunfighter isn't entirely as painful as root-canal surgery, thanks to the welcome appearance of western veteran Don Barry. T.

Don Knotts *Jesse W Haywood* • Barbara Rhoades *Penelope Cushings* • Jackie Coogan *Matthew Basch* • Don "Red" Barry [Donald Barry] *Reverend Zachary Grant* • Ruth McDevitt *Olive* • Frank McGrath *Mr Remington* ■ *Dir* Alan Rafkin • *Scr* Jim Fritzell, Everett Greenbaum, from the film *The Paleface* by Frank Tashlin, Edmund Hartmann

Shaking the Tree ★★ 15
Drama 1990 · US · Colour · 102mins

A retreat of over-familiar territory, as a bunch of Chicago pals, all from differing backgrounds and circumstances, come together to make the collective transition from wild youth to responsible adulthood. There are the usual trials and tribulations en route – getting married, paying off gambling debts, adultery – and it's well enough acted by a cast which includes Arye Gross and *Scream* star Courteney Cox. But a po-faced approach and an abiding sense of "haven't I seen it all before?" do the film no favours. Contains swearing.

Arye Gross *Barry* • Gale Hansen *John "Sully" Sullivan* • Doug Savant *Michael* • Steven Wilde *Terry "Duke" Keegan* • Courteney Cox *Kathleen* • Christina Haag *Michelle* ■ *Dir* Duane Clark • *Scr* Duane Clark, Steven Wilde

Shalako ★★ PG
Western 1968 · UK · Colour · 112mins

"Dinna walk alone in these hills, no' even for modestee's sake". Thus warns cowboy Sean Connery to aristocrat Brigitte Bardot, screen icons well adrift out west, though technically not so far from their respective manors since this would-be epic western was filmed entirely in Spain. Despite director Edward Dmytryk, this is a slow-moving, high-camp fiasco that is oddly cast – British actors Jack Hawkins and Eric Sykes are, not surprisingly, like fish out of water. Cherishable mainly for the sight of Honor Blackman choking to death on her own diamonds. 🖵

Sean Connery *Shalako* • Brigitte Bardot *Countess Irina Lazaar* • Stephen Boyd *Bosky Fulton* • Jack Hawkins *Sir Charles Daggett* • Peter Van Eyck *Frederick von Hallstatt* • Honor Blackman *Lady Julia Daggett* • Woody Strode *Chato* • Eric Sykes *Mako* • Alexander Knox *Henry Clarke* • Valerie French *Elena Clarke* ■ *Dir* Edward Dmytryk • *Scr* JJ Griffith, Hal Hopper, Scot Finch, from a story by Clarke Reynolds, from the novel by Louis L'Amour

Shall We Dance ★★★ U
Musical comedy 1937 · US · BW · 103mins

This is a particularly silly Fred Astaire/ Ginger Rogers movie, the one about

him chasing her across the Atlantic. He's a Russian ballet dancer called Petrov, and there's a chorus of cardboard Ginger cut-outs at the finale. Forget the daftness and enjoy the wonderful George and Ira Gershwin score, especially, that melancholy joy *They Can't Take That Away from Me*. 🖵

Fred Astaire *Petrov/Pete Peters* • Ginger Rogers *Linda Keene* • Edward Everett Horton *Jeffrey Baird* • Eric Blore *Cecil Flintridge* • Jerome Cowan *Arthur Miller* • Ketti Gallian *Lady Tarrington* ■ *Dir* Mark Sandrich • *Scr* Allan Scott, Ernest Pagano, PJ Wolfson, from the story *Watch Your Step* by Lee Loeb, Harold Buchman

Shall We Dance? ★★★★ PG
Romantic comedy drama
1995 · Jap · Colour · 114mins

Koji Yakusho exudes a salaryman dignity worthy of Chishu Ryu in this acute study of social embarrassment, Japanese style. Having established the tyranny of national reserve, Masayuki Suo presents Tamiyo Kusakari's ballroom dancing studio as a foreign sanctuary, in which inhibition succumbs to the illicit sensuality and liberating grace of the rhythm. Making a delicious contrast to the timid Yakusho (whose wife is too reserved to confront him with suspicions of adultery) and the melancholic Kusakari (who once lost a big competition in Blackpool) is Naoto Takenaka, the office nobody who is transformed into a rumba monster by his macho wig and tight duds. A delight. In Japanese with English subtitles. 🖵

Koji Yakusho *Shohei Sugiyama* • Tamiyo Kusakari *Mai Kishikawa* • Naoto Takenaka *Tomio Aoki* • Eriko Watanabe *Toyoko Takahashi* ■ *Dir/Scr* Masayuki Suo

Shallow Grave ★★★★★ 18
Black comedy thriller
1994 · UK · Colour · 93mins

An incredibly slick and inventive and, at times, gruesome thriller, owing a great deal to the Coen brothers' *Blood Simple*. It starts with a dead body and a stash of money lying in a huge flat. The deceased man's flatmates decide to dismember and dispose of the corpse. Things go slightly haywire after that. Director Danny Boyle's picture bursts with energy and springs some deliciously macabre surprises. Especially brilliant are the use of the cavernous flat and city locations and the performances from Kerry Fox, Christopher Eccleston and Ewan McGregor who are all outwardly ordinary, inwardly strange. Deservedly a box-office smash everywhere, it gave a much-needed shot in the arm to a British film industry preoccupied by Jane Austen. Contains violence, swearing and nudity. 🖵

Kerry Fox *Juliet Miller* • Christopher Eccleston *David Stephens* • Ewan McGregor *Alex Law* • Ken Stott *Detective Inspector McCall* • Keith Allen *Hugo* • Colin McCredie *Cameron* ■ *Dir* Danny Boyle • *Scr* John Hodge

Shame ★★★★
Drama 1968 · Swe · BW · 103mins

This is a relentlessly bleak study of communal and moral collapse. Apolitical concert violinists Max von Sydow and Liv Ullmann take refuge on a remote island but are dragged back into society when civil war soldiers arrive in huge numbers. As loyalties shift around a corrupt, quisling colonel, Gunnar Björnstrand, Ullmann's strength and tenderness come to the fore, while von Sydow turns into a selfish, immature, treacherous coward. Rigorously played and staged as a hideously realistic nightmare, this is a chilling vision of a world without beauty, trust or love. In Swedish with English subtitles.

Liv Ullmann *Eva Rosenberg* • Max von Sydow *Jan Rosenberg* • Gunnar Björnstrand *Colonel Jacobi* • Sigge Furst *Filip* • Birgitta Valberg *Mrs Jacobi* ■ *Dir/Scr* Ingmar Bergman

Shame ★★★★ 15
Drama 1987 · Ausl · Colour · 89mins

Released in the same year as the more sensationalised *The Accused*, *Shame* is a more down-to-earth, responsible and raw look at the subject of gang rape. Deborra-Lee Furness is the barrister whose bike breaks down in the Australian outback, where she meets rape victim Simone Buchanan. Standing up against the male-led community who believe the girl asked for it, the lawyer takes on her case, battling not only the criminal who must be brought to justice but the prejudices of the town. Excellent, restrained performances and a careful treatment of a difficult and emotive subject turn this into a powerful and moving piece of cinema. ▭

Deborra-Lee Furness *Asta Cadell* • Tony Barry *Tim Curtis* • Simone Buchanan *Lizzie Curtis* • Gillian Jones *Tina Farrel* • Peter Aanensen *Sergeant Wal Cuddy* • Margaret Ford *Norma Curtis* ■ *Dir* Steve Jodrell • *Scr* Beverly Blankenship, Michael Brindley

Shame ★★★
Crime drama 1992 · US · Colour · 96mins

No bad deed goes unpunished in this woman's revenge drama. After female lawyer Amanda Donohoe's motorcycle breaks down in a small out-of-the-way town, she befriends teenage rape victim Fairuza Balk. When the girl files charges against her attacker, the whole angry town comes after them both. Hampered only by the nearly invisible performance of Dean Stockwell as the girl's father, this frank and brutal TV movie boasts an excellent script by writer Rebecca Soladay – based on the 1987 Australian original.

Amanda Donohoe *Diana Cadell* • Fairuza Balk *Lizzie Curtis* • Dean Stockwell *Tim Curtis* • Shelley Owens *Lorna* • Dan Gauthier *Danny* ■ *Dir* Dan Lerner • *Scr* Rebecca Soladay, from the 1987 film by Michael Brindley, Beverly Blankenship

Shampoo ★★★ 18
Comedy 1975 · US · Colour · 105mins

This one-time *succès de scandale* grossed over $60 million at the box office in its day. While it is delightfully amoral, producer, co-writer and star Warren Beatty never quite pulled his themes together, and the movie remains relentlessly Beverly Hills navel-inward looking. Nevertheless, there are striking moments, not least of which is Julie Christie's now classic appearance at a memorable dinner table. The

model for Beatty's crimper was widely believed to be Jon Peters, but was actually Jay Sebring, killed in the Sharon Tate massacre. The action is set on 4 November 1968 – the day Richard Nixon became president. Contains swearing and nudity. ▭

Warren Beatty *George Roundy* • Julie Christie *Jackie Shawn* • Goldie Hawn *Jill* • Lee Grant *Felicia Carr* • Jack Warden *Lester Carr* • Tony Bill *Johnny Pope* • Carrie Fisher *Lorna Carr* • Jay Robinson *Norman* ■ *Dir* Hal Ashby • *Scr* Warren Beatty, Robert Towne

Shamus ★★★ 18
Comedy thriller 1973 · US · Colour · 94mins

A violent (by seventies' standards), fast-moving, but not very original, this Burt Reynolds vehicle was stylishly directed on New York locations by thriller specialist Buzz Kulik. Reynolds is well cast here as the tough-as-nails Brooklyn private eye who gets called in by a tycoon to find some stolen diamonds. There's some terrific character work along the way from the likes of Joe Santos and Giorgio Tozzi, and Dyan Cannon is particularly fine as the moll in the tale. Trouble is, Reynolds made one too many movies like this, and audiences swiftly tired of him and his toupee. Contains swearing. ▭

Burt Reynolds *Shamus McCoy* • Dyan Cannon *Alexis Montaigne* • John Ryan *Colonel Hardcore* • Joe Santos *Lieutenant Promuto* • Giorgio Tozzi *Il Dottore* • Ron Weyland *EJ Hume* • Larry Block *Springy* ■ *Dir* Buzz Kulik • *Scr* Barry Beckerman

Shane ★★★★★ PG
Classic western 1953 · US · Colour · 112mins

A marvellous distillation of all that is fine about Hollywood cinema. *Shane* is a revelation, sweeping you up via magnificent editing and Loyal Griggs's Technicolor photography into a tale of a man, a woman and, especially, a boy, whose lives are changed by the man dressed in buckskin who rides on to their farm. Alan Ladd gives the performance of a lifetime in the title role, and the rest of the cast is also impeccable, notably Jean Arthur as the married woman whose relationship with Shane is subtly understated. Victor Young's majestic main theme lingers long after the movie is over. This is one of the finest American motion pictures, brilliantly constructed and beautifully filmed, and a constant source of pleasure. ▭

Alan Ladd *Shane* • Jean Arthur *Marion Starrett* • Van Heflin *Joe Starrett* • Brandon de Wilde *Joey Starrett* • Jack Palance *Wilson* • Ben Johnson *Chris* • Edgar Buchanan *Lewis* • Emile Meyer *Ryker* • Elisha Cook Jr *Torrey* • Douglas Spencer *Mr Shipstead* • Dierkes John *Morgan* • Ellen Corby *Mrs Torrey* ■ *Dir* George Stevens • *Scr* AB Guthrie Jr, Jack Sher, from the novel by Jack Schaefer • *Editor* William Hornbeck, Tom McAdoo

Shanghai Express ★★★★ PG
Romance drama 1932 · US · BW · 88mins

The fourth collaboration between Marlene Dietrich and director Josef von Sternberg, this arch melodrama divides audiences. Fans love its exotic lighting (cinematographer Lee Garmes won an Oscar) and its clever, intimate use of confined space; detractors laugh at its high camp histrionics and its ludicrous

(but stylish) plot and dialogue ("It took more than one man to change my name to Shanghai Lily"). With a drink in your hand and a generous disposition, this dated hokum is immensely enjoyable, as notorious hooker Dietrich is amazingly reunited with her former true love Clive Brook (wooden, as ever, but well cast) aboard the titular train that's hijacked by brigand Warner Oland. Dietrich is, as ever, unforgettable. ▭

Marlene Dietrich *Shanghai Lily* • Clive Brook *Captain Donald "doc" Harvey* • Anna May Wong *Hui Fei* • Warner Oland *Henry Chang* • Eugene Pallette *Sam Salt* • Lawrence Grant *Reverend Carmichael* • Louise Closser Hale *Mrs Haggerty* ■ *Dir* Josef von Sternberg • *Scr* Jules Furthman, from a story by Harry Hervey

The Shanghai Gesture ★★★★★
Melodrama 1941 · US · BW · 98mins

Though the title recalls an earlier von Sternberg classic made at the height of his and Dietrich's collaborative fame, this melodrama conjures up a different universe altogether. A spoilt rich girl using the alias of Poppy Smith – Gene Tierney at her loveliest – enters a Shanghai casino and is seduced by its " incredible evil", unaware that her entrepreneur dad (Walter Huston) is intent on closing down the iniquitous establishment, domain of the glacial "Mother" Gin Sling (Ona Munson in a series of lacquered, Medusa-like wigs). Sternberg was forced to sanitise his adaptation of John Colton's stage play, but his vision suggestively offers more than the salacious detail he was forced to cut from the script. The film's masterful use of musical rhythms, stylised dialogue and close-ups makes it a high point among films from the studio age.

Gene Tierney *Poppy Smith* • Walter Huston *Sir Guy Charteris* • Victor Mature *Doctor Omar* • Ona Munson *"Mother" Gin Sling* • Phyllis Brooks *Dixie Pomeroy* • Albert Basserman *Commissioner* • Maria Ouspenskaya *Amah* • Eric Blore *Caesar Hawkins, the bookkeeper* ■ *Dir* Josef von Sternberg • *Scr* Josef von Sternberg, Geza Herczeg, Jules Furthman, Kurt Vollmoeller, from the play by John Colton • *Cinematographer* Paul Ivano

Shanghai Joe ★★
Spaghetti western 1974 · It · Colour · 91mins

With its stylised violence, dark humour and bold visuals, the spaghetti western breathed new life into the genre in the mid-sixties. But by the time *Shanghai Joe* was released, formula had stifled invention and sundry novelties were incorporated with little discrimination. Borrowing heavily from the 1972 TV movie *Kung Fu*, this undistinguished picture has Chen Lee as a wannabe cowboy who disproves charges of cowardice by helping a judge to thwart evil town boss Klaus Kinski and his band of outlaws. Italian dialogue dubbed into English.

Klaus Kinski • Chen Lee • Karen Field • Tommy Polgar • Claudio Giorgi ■ *Dir* Bitto Albertini [Adalberto Albertini] • *Scr* Bitto Albertini [Adalberto Albertini], Carlo Alberto Alfieri, from a story by Mario Caiano, Luigi Russo

Shanghai Noon ★★★ 12
Period action comedy 2000 · US · Colour · mins

Visually authentic and deliciously anachronistic in its gentle sending up of the genre, Jackie Chan's western is a hugely enjoyable combination of martial artistry, buddy comedy and adventure. Sent to the States to rescue kidnapped princess Lucy Liu, Chan's Imperial Palace guard hooks up with outlaw Owen Wilson, who proves to be his equal in the fish-out-of-water stakes. Using antlers, sheriff's badges and horseshoes to prise himself out of a tight corner, Chan is pure slapstick poetry in motion: falling off horses, getting riotously drunk and confusing slave-owning louse Roger Yuan and corrupt sheriff, Xander Berkeley.

Jackie Chan *Chon Wang* • Owen Wilson *Roy O'Bannon* • Lucy Liu *Princess Pei Pei* • Brandon Merrill *Indian wife* • Roger Yuan *Lo Fong* • Xander Berkeley *Van Cleef* • Walton Goggins *Wallace* • Jason Connery *Andrews* ■ *Dir* Tom Dey • *Scr* Miles Millar, Alfred Gough

The Shanghai Story ★
Spy drama 1954 · US · BW · 90mins

Director of the smash hits *Cavalcade* and *Mutiny on the Bounty*, Frank Lloyd ended his career at Republic making this plodding Cold War melodrama followed by his swansong, *The Last Command*. Here Edmond O'Brien is an American doctor imprisoned with other foreigners in a Shanghai hotel by Marvin Miller's police chief who's seeking to identify a western spy believed to be among them. As the mysterious woman who's friendly with both sides, Ruth Roman fails to add any spice to the drawn-out proceedings.

Ruth Roman *Rita King* • Edmond O'Brien *Dr Dan Maynard* • Richard Jaeckel *"Knuckles" Greer* • Barry Kelley *Ricki Dolmine* • Whit Bissell *Paul Grant* • Basil Ruysdael *Reverend Hollingsworth* • Marvin Miller *Colonel Zorek* ■ *Dir* Frank Lloyd • *Scr* Seton I Miller, Steve Fisher, from a story by Lester Yard

Shanghai Surprise ★ 15
Adventure 1986 · UK · Colour · 92mins

If you can buy the Material Girl as a nun then you may be slightly entertained by this infamous fiasco that was an uncharacteristic flop for George Harrison's HandMade Films. Madonna's then husband Sean Penn is OK as a rogue salesman, hired to look for stolen opium in pre-war China. Otherwise, director Jim Goddard's heavy-handed and over-inflated screwball adventure is desperately seeking laughs at every vulgar turn and is woefully short of the madcap antics that go to define the genre. A witless embarrassment. Contains swearing and brief nudity. ▭

Sean Penn *Glendon Wasey* • Madonna *Gloria Tatlock* • Paul Freeman *Walter Faraday* • Richard Griffiths *Willie Tuttle* • Philip Sayer *Justin Kronk* • Clyde Kusatsu *Joe Go* • Lim Kay Tong *Mei Gan* • Sonserai Lee *China Doll* • Michael Aldridge *Mr Burns* • George Harrison *Night club singer* ■ *Dir* Jim Goddard • *Scr* John Kohn, Robert Bentley, from the novel *Faraday's Flowers* by Tony Kenrick

U = SUITABLE FOR ALL   Uc = SUITABLE FOR ALL, ESPECIALLY FOR YOUNG CHILDREN (VIDEO ONLY)   PG = PARENTAL GUIDANCE

Shanghai Triad ★★★★ 🔞15

Crime drama 1995 · HK/Fr · Colour · 103mins

Longtime companions Gong Li and Zhang Yimou parted during the production of this, their seventh collaboration. As a result, perhaps, this is their least effective picture, with the plot allowed to ramble and the pacing sluggish when swift, *noir*ish strokes would have heightened the tension. But the stunning beauty of both Li and director Zhang's imagery give this an undeniable allure. In particular, the teasing sensuality of Li's musical numbers and the sudden realisation that her gangster lover has discovered her deceptions, together with the shimmering golden interiors and misty blue island vistas, are unforgettable. In Mandarin with English subtitles. Contains violence. 📼

Gong Li *Xiao Jinbao, "Jewel"* • Wang Xiaowing *Shuisheng* • Li Baotian *Gangster* • Li Xuejian *Uncle Liu* ■ *Dir* Zhang Yimou • *Scr* Bi Feiyu, from the novel *Men Gui [Gang Law]* by Li Xiao

Shanks ★★

Horror comedy 1974 · US · Colour · 93mins

An extremely offbeat horror-comedy, this is the last film directed by William Castle, a showman often attracted to horror, comedy and gimmicks, but never with such bizarre results as here. It marked virtually the beginning and end of Marcel Marceau's screen career. The world's most famous mime doesn't speak in his role as a puppeteer bequeathed a gadget that brings the dead back to life. The section where Marceau learns how to animate corpses (played by other mime artists) is very funny, but much of the rest looks contrived and confused.

Marcel Marceau *Malcolm Shanks/Old Walker* • Tsilla Chelton *Mrs Barton* • Philippe Clay *Mr Barton* • Cindy Eilbacher *Celia* • Larry Bishop *Napoleon* • William Castle *Grocer* ■ *Dir* William Castle • *Scr* Ranald Graham

Shannon's Deal ★★★★

Drama 1989 · US · Colour · 95mins

Writer/director John Sayles generally adds flavour to even his smallest characters and creates the power of suggestion through dialogue. Writing for director Lewis Teague, Sayles transforms what could so easily have been a trawl through inanity and cliché into a work of edgy, dramatic clout. He takes the gumshoe genre and puts his own spin on events, and lifts it considerably, with the forces of morality and idealism, and the grubby reality of the gutter, forming a strong presence throughout. The insinuating, unnerving score by Wynton Marsalis for this TV pilot perfectly matches the psychology of the key character.

Jamey Sheridan *Jack Shannon* • Elizabeth Pena *Lucy* • Jenny Lewis *Neala* • Miguel Ferrer *Todd Snyder* • Stefan Gierasch *Klaus* ■ *Dir* Lewis Teague • *Scr* John Sayles

Sharaz ★★

Adventure 1968 · Sp/It · Colour · 92mins

A spot of Eastern delight in a Spanish setting which is so teeth-grindingly awful that it becomes well worth watching for a laugh. Take one son of the Sultan of Granada, one dastardly interloper, one flashing eyed female genie, a loyal slave who badly needs to raise his political consciousness and stew well with a phalanx of bloodcurdling Spanish extras all dressed to the nines and bumping into each other. Spanish dialogue dubbed into English.

Jeff Cooper *Omar* • Luciana Paluzzi *Sharaz* • Raf Vallone *Hixem* • Perla Cristal *"Favourite"* ■ *Dir* Joe Lacy

Sharing Richard ★

Comedy 1988 · US · Colour · 93mins

An odd romantic comedy. Without his knowledge, three women (Eileen Davidson, Nancy Frangione and Hillary Bailey Smith) arrange to share freshly-divorced plastic surgeon Ed Marinaro, but rivalry and complications ensue. A distasteful and misguided attempt to reduce relationships to the level of a time-share condominium, quickly degenerates from light-hearted whim to back-biting competition between the distaff trio. A leaden script, Peter Bonerz's lifeless direction and a bland cast make this TV movie a poor viewing choice.

Ed Marinaro *Dr Richard Bronowski* • Eileen Davidson *Hillary Bailey Smith* • Nancy Frangione *Bonnie Griswold* • Janet Carroll *Amanda* • Lisa Jane Persky *Roberta* ■ *Dir* Peter Bonerz • *Scr* Ann Donahue, Marion Zola, Kristi Kane

Shark! ★ 🔞15

Action drama 1969 · US/Mex · Colour · 88mins

Before Spielberg's *Jaws* there was... this watery tale about underwater treasure that cast barely a ripple – except for a public row between the producers and director Sam Fuller who wanted his name removed from the credits, claiming the film had been re-edited against his will. Fuller's army of fans accepted this, overlooking the fact that in 1967 Fuller was reduced to making dime-budget stuff in Mexico to pay the rent. The movie spent three years on the shelf only seeing the light of day when Burt Reynolds became a major box-office draw.

Burt Reynolds *Caine* • Barry Sullivan *Mallare* • Arthur Kennedy *Doc* • Silvia Pinal *Anna* • Enrique Lucero *Barok* ■ *Dir* Samuel Fuller • *Scr* Samuel Fuller, John Kinsgbridge, from the novel *His Bones Are Coral* by Victor Canning

Shark's Treasure ★ 🔞PG

Adventure 1975 · US · Colour · 91mins

For all its trendy references to *Jaws* (released earlier that year), this feels like a relic of those deadly dull deep-sea diving movies of the fifties. Apart from the odd shark, the camera only has eyes for Cornel Wilde, which is hardly surprising, considering he also wrote and directed this hokum about an old man of the sea who sacrifices his beloved boat in the hope of finding buried treasure. Yaphet Kotto provides burly support and Al Giddings's underwater photography is fine. But this is a distinctly fishy enterprise. 📼

Cornel Wilde *Jim* • Yaphet Kotto *Ben* • John Neilson *Ron* • Cliff Osmond *Lobo* • David Canary *Larry* ■ *Dir/Scr* Cornel Wilde

Sharky's Machine ★★★ 🔞18

Crime thriller 1981 · US · Colour · 116mins

As both director and star, Burt Reynolds proves just a bit too ambitious. His vice cop on the tail of some nasties is not only packed with bull-necked aggression but also has a sensitive interest in woodcarving, while his direction similarly moves abruptly from the overbearing to the light'n'easy and back again. Neither character nor situation is built up enough to obscure the crude joins. However, Burt-the-director has picked a clutch of good locations to portray the world of sleaze and he has a nifty way with the boisterous action set pieces, in which Burt-the-star is at his best. Contains some violence and swearing. 📼

Burt Reynolds *Sharky* • Vittorio Gassman *Victor* • Brian Keith *Papa* • Charles Durning *Friscoe* • Earl Holliman *Hotchkins* • Bernie Casey *Arch* • Henry Silva *Billy Score* • Richard Libertini *Nosh* • Rachel Ward *Dominoe* ■ *Dir* Burt Reynolds • *Scr* Gerald Di Pego, from the novel by William Diehl

Sharon's Secret ★★ 🔞15

Psychological thriller 1995 · US · Colour · 86mins

Things go bump in the night in this psychological thriller. A traumatised teenage girl (Candace Cameron) slips into catatonia when she's accused of murdering her wealthy parents in their mansion. Dedicated psychiatrist Mel Harris tries to uncover the truth, but sinister forces begin stalking her – trying to get her off the case. Enlivened by its believable cast and old-dark-house locale, this complex, tightly-plotted whodunit only falters in its reliance on a too-easily-identified villain. 📼

Mel Harris *Dr Laurel O'Connor* • Alex McArthur *Frank Bodin* • Candace Cameron *Sharon* • Paul Regina *Dr Gordon Davies* • Gregg Henry *Detective Thomas McGregor* ■ *Dir* Michael Scott • *Scr* Mark Homer

Shatter ★

Martial arts action thriller 1974 · UK · Colour · 90mins

When Hammer's horror movies started to bomb at the box-office, the studio forged a short-lived partnership with Hong Kong studios and made kung fu action films, though they stopped short of calling the company Hammer and Tongs. What everyone failed to appreciate was that while Bruce Lee could invade the west, it was a one-way traffic. Stuart Whitman just isn't credible as the chop-socky hero, and Peter Cushing and Anton Diffring are simply Hammer's end of the contractual bargain.

Stuart Whitman *Shatter* • Peter Cushing *Rattwood* • Ti Lung *Tai Pah* • Anton Diffring *Hans Leber* • Yemi Ajibade *M'Goya* • Huang Pei-Chi *Bodyguard* ■ *Dir* Michael Carreras, Monte Hellman • *Scr* Don Houghton

Shattered ★★★ 🔞15

Thriller 1991 · US · Colour · 93mins

Modern directors show no sign of losing their desire to pay their respects to Alfred Hitchcock, and this intriguing thriller from Wolfgang Petersen succeeds better than most. Tom Berenger wakes up after a horrific car accident with amnesia and attempts to put his life back together again with the help of a private detective (Bob Hoskins); Greta Scacchi is the *femme fatale* who may or may not be trying to kill him. There's a very neat twist at the end, but there are so many bluffs and double bluffs it becomes quite exhausting to follow. Petersen directs with some panache and there's an excellent supporting cast, including Joanne Whalley-Kilmer and *LA Law's* Corbin Bernsen. Contains swearing, violence and nudity. 📼

Tom Berenger *Dan Merrick* • Bob Hoskins *Gus Klein* • Greta Scacchi *Judith Merrick* • Joanne Whalley-Kilmer [Joanne Whalley] *Jenny Scott* • Corbin Bernsen *Jeb Scott* • Debi A Monahan *Nancy Mercer* ■ *Dir* Wolfgang Petersen • *Scr* Wolfgang Petersen, from the novel *The Plastic Nightmare* by Richard Neely

Shattered Dreams ★★ 🔞15

Drama based on a true story 1990 · US · Colour · 89mins

Somehow you never think of wife-beating occurring within the higher echelons of society. But that's the arresting theme of this TV movie, which, like so many others, is based on a true story. That doyenne of the teleplay, Lindsay Wagner, stars as the wife of a top-flight government official who knows that no one will believe her charismatic husband (Michael Nouri) is a sadistic thug. Unfortunately, what could have been a disturbing drama is turned into a glitzy soap opera by director Robert Iscove. Contains violence. 📼

Lindsay Wagner *Charlotte Fedders* • Michael Nouri *John Fedders* • Georgann Johnson *Helen O'Donnell* • James Karen *Charles O'Donnell* • Marilyn Rockafellow *Ellen O'Hare* ■ *Dir* Robert Iscove • *Scr* David Hill, from the non-fiction book by Charlotte Fedders, Laura Elliot

Shattered Family ★★ 🔞PG

Drama based on a true story 1993 · US · Colour · 88mins

In the 1984 comedy *Irreconcilable Differences*, a young Drew Barrymore attempted to sue her parents for divorce. Now, in an odd case of life imitating art, this made-for-TV drama traces the true-life court battle in which 12-year-old Tom Guiry attempts to sever his ties with his uncaring biological family. Richard Crenna plays the caring family man who wants to adopt the young lad and helps him in his fight. The sensationalist storyline will keep viewers hooked, but the direction is strictly routine. 📼

Richard Crenna *George Russ* • Rhea Perlman *Jerri Blair* • Linda Kelsey *Liz Russ* • Tom Guiry *Gregory Kingsley/Shawn Russ* • Cyril O'Reilly *Ralph Kingsley* • Cotter Smith *Mike Caldwell* ■ *Dir* Sandy Smolan • *Scr* Blair Ferguson

Shattered Image ★★ 🔞18

Thriller mystery 1998 · US · Colour · 90mins

Schizophrenic after a brutal rape, hit woman Jessie (Anne Parillaud) finds herself drifting in and out of reality. The action flips between Seattle and Jamaica and as fantasy begins to take hold, Jessie must decide what's real: Is she a pitiless revenge-killer of men, or a happy wife on holiday with new husband William Baldwin? Then again, maybe she's a bit of both. A solidly made psychodrama that just about keeps you watching. 📼

William Baldwin *Brian* • Anne Parillaud *Jessie* • Lisanne Falk *Paula/Laura* • Graham Greene *Conrad/Mike* • Billy Wilmott *Lamond* • O'Neil Peart *Simon* • Bulle Ogier *Mrs Ford* ■ *Dir* Raúl Ruiz • *Scr* Duane Poole

Shattered Innocence ★★ 15

Drama based on a true story
1988 · US · Colour · 89mins

An intriguing American TV movie about a teenage girl being pulled into the world of pornography. But this drama, based on the tragic real-life story of American porn star Shauna Grant, is only ordinary as entertainment and enlightenment. The main problem is that the film lacks punch, depth and complexity. Still, it is well played by Jonna Lee as the teenage girl who discovers the reality behind Hollywood's glamour, and there is strong support from Melinda Dillon, Dennis Howard and John Pleshette. Inevitably, the controversial subject matter is toned down by the restraints of American television. 🎞

Jonna Lee *Pauline* • Melinda Dillon *Sharon* • John Pleshette *Mel Erman* • Dennis Howard *Del* • Nadine Van Der Velde *Nora* ■ *Dir* Sandor Stern • *Scr* Sandor Stern, Thanet Richard

Shattered Silence ★★★ 15

Drama based on a true story
1992 · US · Colour · 91mins

An impassioned performance by Bonnie Bedelia lifts this true-life TV movie well above the norm. She plays a doctor who sparks a bitter court battle when she refuses to disclose the whereabouts of her daughter to her estranged husband (Terence Knox), whom she believes has been abusing the child. Bedelia's playing is matched by the supporting cast, which includes seasoned scene stealers Pam Grier and Rip Torn, while Linda Otto's direction is equally committed. 🎞

Bonnie Bedelia *Dr Elizabeth Morgan* • Terence Knox *Eric Foretich* • Caroline Dollar *Hilary* • Pam Grier *Linda Holman* • Patricia Neal *Antonia Morgan* • Rip Torn *Bill Morgan* ■ *Dir* Linda Otto • *Scr* Lucretia Baxter, Alan Landsburg

Shattered Spirits ★★★ PG

Drama
1986 · US · Colour · 88mins

A chillingly believable performance from Martin Sheen marks this out as an unusually compelling TV drama. He plays a father whose painful descent into alcoholism threatens to destroy the fabric of his family's life. Sheen's intense acting is matched by co-stars Matthew Laborteaux, Melinda Dillon and a young Lukas Haas (still best known for his role in *Witness* opposite Harrison Ford), while Robert Greenwald's direction is pleasingly unsensational. 🎞

Martin Sheen *Lyle Mollencamp* • Melinda Dillon *Joyce Mollencamp* • Matthew Laborteaux *Kenny Mollencamp* • Roxana Zal *Lesley Mollencamp* • Lukas Haas *Brian Mollencamp* • Jill Schoelen *Allison* ■ *Dir* Robert Greenwald • *Scr* Gregory Goodell

Shattered Trust ★★ 15

Drama
1993 · US · Colour · 88mins

Melissa Gilbert has never really shaken off the image she gained during her lengthy stint on *Little House on the Prairie*. But here she proves that there might just be life after Laura Ingalls, playing a high-flying attorney whose world comes tumbling down when a courtroom incident releases long-suppressed memories of childhood abuse at the hands of her father. While director Bill Corcoran occasionally allows melodrama to get the better of restraint, he handles the family feuds and Gilbert's crusade with some care. Of course, it helps having actresses like Ellen Burstyn and Kate Nelligan in the cast. 🎞

Melissa Gilbert *Shari Karney* • Ellen Burstyn *Joan Delvecchio* • Kate Nelligan *Stephanie Crawford* ■ *Dir* Bill Corcoran • *Scr* Susan Nanus

Shattering the Silence ★★ 15

Drama
1992 · US · Colour · 87mins

A well-meaning but soporific TV examination of the tricky subject of child abuse. Joanna Kerns plays the seemingly content woman who starts behaving strangely following the birth of her first child. When it becomes apparent that her behaviour may be connected to her own upbringing, subsequent revelations start to tear the family apart. Kerns gets solid support from the likes of Michael Brandon, Tony Roberts and former Charlie's Angel Shelley Hack, but director Linda Otto lays on the melodrama with a shovel. 🎞

Joanna Kerns *Veronica Ricci* • Michael Brandon *Ted Ricci* • Tony Roberts • Dina Merrill *Clair Worth* • George Grizzard *Malcolm Worth* • Shelley Hack *Becky Worth* ■ *Dir* Linda Otto • *Scr* Joe Cacaci, Michael Love, Martin Salinas

The Shawshank Redemption ★★★★★ 15

Prison drama
1994 · US · Colour · 136mins

Frank Darabont's moving version of Stephen King's short story *Rita Hayworth and Shawshank Redemption* is one of the best adaptations of the novelist's work. Tim Robbins plays Andy Dufresne, a Maine banker sent to Shawshank State Prison for murdering his wife and her lover. Regularly brutalised by the inmates and the penal system in general, his existence improves when he befriends fellow lifer and prison fixer Red, played by Morgan Freeman. Under Darabont's inspired direction, Robbins and Freeman both rise to the challenge of portraying world-weary dignity against the odds, while the severity of the prison system is underlined in the poignant performance of James Whitmore as a veteran convict trying to make it on parole, but ill-equipped to do so. Contains violence, swearing and nudity. 🎞 **DVD**

Tim Robbins *Andy Dufresne* • Morgan Freeman *Ellis Boyd "Red" Redding* • Bob Gunton *Warden Norton* • William Sadler *Heywood* • Clancy Brown *Captain Hadley* • Gil Bellows *Tommy* • Mark Rolston *Bogs Diamond* • James Whitmore *Brooks Hatlen* ■ *Dir* Frank Darabont • *Scr* Frank Darabont, from the short story *Rita Hayworth and Shawshank Redemption* by Stephen King

She ★★★

Fantasy adventure   1935 · US · BW · 94mins

The first talkie verison of H Rider Haggard's romantic adventure about the explorer lured by the woman who – having bathed in the Flame of Life – becomes immortal, provides only short-lived interest. Randolph Scott is a grim-jawed explorer, Helen Gahagan a rather muted siren and the story is transferred from Africa to the Arctic Circle. The result is dialogue and acting that's as frozen stiff as the setting. Merian C Cooper (who helped King Kong shamble into legend) produces, while Irving Pichel directs.

Helen Gahagan *Hash-A-Mo-Tep, "She"* • Randolph Scott *Leo Vincey* • Helen Mack *Tanya Dugmore* • Nigel Bruce *Archibald Holly* • Gustav von Seyffertitz *Prime Minister Billali* • Samuel S Hinds *John Vincey* • Noble Johnson *Amahagger chief* • Lumsden Hare *Dugmore* ■ *Dir* Irving Pichel, Lansing C Holden • *Scr* Ruth Rose, Dudley Nichols, from the novel by H Rider Haggard

She ★★★ U

Fantasy adventure
1965 · UK · Colour · 101mins

Swiss sex goddess Ursula Andress is destined always to be remembered for her voluptuous performance in the first Bond movie, *Dr No*. However, she acquits herself better than you might expect in this adaptation of H Rider Haggard's much-filmed fantasy. Indeed, she looks in great shape for a 2,000-year-old queen of a lost kingdom, who is still yearning for the embrace of a lover she killed centuries ago. The exotic backdrops are easily matched by Andress's own brand of exotic beauty and, while there's plenty to criticise, there's also much to enjoy. 🎞

Ursula Andress *Ayesha* • John Richardson *Leo Vincey* • Peter Cushing *Major Horace Holly* • Bernard Cribbins *Job* • Rosenda Monteros *Ustane* • Christopher Lee *Billali* ■ *Dir* Robert Day • *Scr* David T Chantler, from the novel by H Rider Haggard

The She Beast ★★★

Horror   1965 · UK/It · Colour · 75mins

Cult director Michael Reeves made his feature debut with this painfully cheap shocker that nevertheless revealed the powerful use of horrific imagery he would harness to perfection in his masterpiece, *Witchfinder General*. Honeymooners Barbara Steele and Ian Ogilvy visit modern-day Transylvania, only to crash their car in the lake where vengeful witch Vardella was tortured to death in the 18th century. Steele transforms into the decrepit hag and goes on a murder spree in this amalgam of stark terror and facile humour (although the communist gag where a bloody scythe lands on a hammer is unique in the genre). Fans of Queen of Horror Steele be warned: she only makes a token appearance before being possessed. Some Italian dialogue dubbed into English.

Barbara Steele *Veronica/Vardella* • Ian Ogilvy *Philip* • John Karlsen *Count von Helsing* ■ *Dir* Michael Reeves • *Scr* Michael Byron

The She-Creature ★★

Horror   1956 · US · BW · 80mins

Chester Morris hypnotises sexy Marla English back to prehistoric times, and has her reptilian alter ego materialise in the present to help him and money-grabbing promoter Tom Conway con the police. He predicts a murder and the scaly, large-breasted amphibian carries it out. One of those bonkers fifties sci-fi quickies that are so awful they become irresistibly compelling. Incidentally, the monster is an impressive work of trash art.

Chester Morris *Carlo Lombardi* • Marla English *Andrea* • Tom Conway *Timothy Chappel* • Cathy Downs *Dorothy* • Lance Fuller *Ted Erickson* ■ *Dir* Edward L Cahn • *Scr* Lou Rusoff, from his play

She Dances Alone ★★★

Documentary drama
1981 · US/Aus · Colour · 87mins

This intriguing blend of fact and fiction has Bud Cort as a director trying to make an objective documentary about the legendary dancer Nijinsky. Unfortunately he's blocked at every turn by Nijinsky's daughter, Kyra. Well over 60 years old at the time, Kyra is a huge presence in the film in every sense, and it is as much about her strong-willed desire to make her own career with the burden/blessing of such a famous father as it is about the great man himself. To blur the edges even further, Max von Sydow plays himself and is the voice reading Nijinsky's diary.

Max von Sydow *Voice of Nijinsky* • Jon Bradshaw *Narrator* • Bud Cort *Director* • Patrick Dupond *Dancer* ■ *Dir* Robert Dornhelm • *Scr* Paul Davids, from an idea by Robert Dornhelm

She Demons ★

Horror   1958 · US · BW · 79mins

They don't come any more ludicrously inept than this Z-movie trash about a Nazi war criminal turning gorgeous shipwreck survivors into ugly monsters on his uncharted island, in an effort to restore beauty to his wife's scarred face. Connoisseurs will enjoy the wobbly sets, a ritual jungle dance and a volcanic eruption climax. This incredible schlock from *Missile to the Moon* director Richard E Cunha has to be seen to be believed – if you can actually bear sitting through it.

Irish McCalla *Jerrie Turner* • Tod Griffin *Fred Maklin* • Victor Sen Yung *Sammy Ching* • Rudolph Anders *Herr Osler* • Gene Roth *Egore* ■ *Dir* Richard E Cunha • *Scr* Richard E Cunha, HE Barrie, from their story

She-Devil ★★ 15

Comedy   1989 · US · Colour · 95mins

Fay Weldon's dark, acerbic tale of rejection and revenge receives the full Hollywood "wash and brush up" treatment, reducing its saturnine charm to frothy candyfloss. The whole farrago is hopelessly miscast with a wet and vapid Meryl Streep as the vamp novelist Mary Fisher, a cardboard cut-out Ed Begley Jr as the errant husband she snares, and, most disappointing of all, Roseanne Barr as a curiously weak and woolly She-Devil. Watching this makes you appreciate once more the celebrated BBC TV adaptation that starred Patricia Hodge, Dennis Waterman and Julie T Wallace. Contains some swearing, sex scenes and brief nudity. 🎞

Meryl Streep *Mary Fisher* • Roseanne Barr [Roseanne] *Ruth Patchett* • Ed Begley Jr *Bob Patchett* • Linda Hunt *Nurse Hooper* • Sylvia Miles *Francine Fisher* • Elisebeth Peters *Nicolette Patchett* • Bryan Larkin *Andy Patchett* • Robin Leach ■ *Dir* Susan Seidelman • *Scr* Barry Strugatz, Mark R Burns, from the novel *The Life and Loves of a She-Devil* by Fay Weldon

She Done Him Wrong ★★★★

Comedy   1933 · US · BW · 66mins

Probably *the* classic Mae West movie and a perfect opportunity to make the acquaintance of "the finest woman that ever walked the streets". The truly outrageous West is today mainly regarded as a camp icon, a sort of female drag artist. The predatory creature known as Lady Lou in this opus was once West's infamous "Diamond Lil" in her own play, but the requirements of both national and local censors caused the modification of nickname and dialogue for the movie. Young Cary Grant is the person she asks to "come up sometime and see me", a phrase that is now well established as part of cinema iconography. Well worth watching, especially if you're not yet acquainted with the redoubtable West.

Mae West *Lady Lou* • Cary Grant *Captain Cummings* • Owen Moore *Chick Clark* • Gilbert Roland *Serge Stanieff* • Noah Beery Sr [Noah Beery] *Gus Jordan* • David Landau *Dan Flynn* ■ *Dir* Lowell Sherman • *Scr* Mae West, Harvey Thew, John Bright, from the play *Diamond Lil* by Mae West

She Fought Alone ★★ 15

Drama based on a true story
1995 · US · Colour · 87mins

Beverly Hills 90210 stars Tiffani-Amber Thiessen and Brian Austin Green aim for a somewhat grittier look at school life in this story centring on the controversial issue of teenage rape. Unfortunately, this suffers from the same shallowness that afflicts the glossy TV series and ultimately fails to do justice to the subject matter. Christopher Leitch directs the proceedings at a deadening pace, robbing the tale of its emotional impact. Contains violence and swearing. ▣

Tiffani-Amber Thiessen *Caitlin Rose* • Brian Austin Green *Ethan* • Isabella Hoffman *Avon* ■ *Dir* Christopher Leitch

She Freak ★ 15

Cult horror   1967 · US · Colour · 79mins

Sleaze expert David F Friedman (the producer of the legendary *Blood Feast* and *2000 Maniacs*) takes elements from Tod Browning's 1932 classic *Freaks*, relocates it to redneck country and hopes for the best. Sadly, director Byron Mabe isn't up to the challenge and lets the tale slip from promising camp trash into complete ineptitude. While the story – an ambitious greasy spoon waitress marries the owner of a seedy side show with gruesome results – is not without its compelling moments, you can see the money drain away from the micro-budget as this grade Z flick staggers to its rip-off climax of Browning's masterpiece. ▣

Claire Brennen *Jade Cochran* • Lee Raymond *Blackie Fleming* • Lynn Courtney *Pat Mullins* • Bill McKinney *Steve St John* • Marsha Drake *Olga* • Bobby Matthews *Max* ■ *Dir* Byron Mabe • *Scr* David F Friedman

She Knows Too Much ★ 15

Comedy thriller 1989 · US · Colour · 89mins

Robert Urich and Meredith Baxter star in this torpid caper of a po-faced detective springing a feisty young con from the slammer in order to catch a bigger criminal fish. Lots of silly chases, bungled attempts to be amusing, ham-fisted political in-fighting (this is Washington DC) and all-round ineptitude follow. However, this is nothing compared to the incompetence of director Paul Lynch. ▣

Meredith Baxter Birney [Meredith Baxter] *Samantha White* • Robert Urich *Harry Schofield* • John Bennett Perry *Matthew Bream* • Dennis Lipscomb *Ivan Fletcher* • Erik Estrada *Jimmy Alvarez* ■ *Dir* Paul Lynch • *Scr* Michael Norell

She Loves Me Not ★★★

Musical comedy   1934 · US · BW · 80mins

Showgirl Miriam Hopkins, fleeing from mobsters, hides out in a boys' college in this enjoyable early musical starring Bing Crosby. Though Hopkins is basically miscast as a burlesque queen, the complications as she is forced to masquerade as a male are fun, and Crosby oozes affable charm. Kitty Carlisle has her best screen role, and gets to introduce with Crosby the Ralph Rainger–Leo Robin song *Love in Bloom*, which reached number one in the hit parade.

Bing Crosby *Paul Lawton* • Miriam Hopkins *Curly Flagg* • Kitty Carlisle *Midge Mercer* • Edward Nugent *Buzz Jones* • Henry Stephenson *Dean Mercer* • Warren Hymer *Mugg Schnitzel* • Lynne Overman *Gus McNeal* ■ *Dir* Elliott Nugent • *Scr* Benjamin Glazer, from the play by Lindsay Howard. from the novel by Edward Hope

She Married Her Boss ★★★ U

Comedy   1935 · US · BW · 88mins

This movie finds Claudette Colbert under the deft and witty direction of Gregory La Cava, with a screenplay by Columbia's arch-sophisticate Sidney Buchman cleverly balancing a couple of rather slight plotlines together: that of Melvyn Douglas, the titular "boss", and his own relationship with Claudette; and the concurrent theme of Claudette's treatment by Douglas's awful stepdaughter and his drama queen of a sister. The movie is genuinely funny but runs out of comedic steam towards the end. Nevertheless, there are some wonderful performances, most notably Raymond Walburn as a squiffy butler.

Claudette Colbert *Julia Scott* • Michael Bartlett *Lonnie Rogers* • Melvyn Douglas *Richard Barclay* • Raymond Walburn *Franklin* • Jean Dixon *Martha* • Katherine Alexander *Gertrude* • Edith Fellows *Annabel* ■ *Dir* Gregory La Cava • *Scr* Sidney Buchman, from the story by Thyra Samter Winslow

She Said No ★★★ 15

Drama   1990 · US · Colour · 91mins

A well written and well played variation on the courtroom drama, with Veronica Hamel as the successful businesswoman who sues a lawyer after he rapes her, only to find her counter-sues for slander. Judd Hirsch – still best known for his role as nice guy Alex in the TV series *Taxi* – is good, playing against type as the nasty lawyer: you can't wait for him to get his comeuppance. ▣

Veronica Hamel *Beth Early* • Judd Hirsch *Martin Knapek* • Becky Ann Baker *Gail Maguire* • Ray Baker *Sergeant Frank Igus* • Lee Grant *Doris Cantore* ■ *Dir* John Patterson • *Scr* Michael O'Hara

She Stood Alone: the Tailhook Scandal ★★★ 12

Drama based on a true story
1995 · US · Colour · 92mins

Former *NYPD Blue* star Gail O'Grady gives a brave, gutsy performance in this made-for-TV drama based on an incident that rocked the US military establishment. She plays a promising navy flier who is the victim of sexual harassment at the hands of her fellow officers while at a convention. However, when she tries to report the incident, her superiors not only attempt to cover it up, but also set out to wreck her career. Contains violence and nudity. ▣

Gail O'Grady *Paula Coughlin* • Hal Holbrook *Admiral Frank Kelso* • Rip Torn *Rear Admiral Jack Snyder* • Robert Urich *Rear Admiral Mac Williams* • Bess Armstrong *Asst Secretary of the Navy* ■ *Dir* Larry Shaw • *Scr* Suzette Couture

She Was Marked for Murder ★★ 15

Thriller   1988 · US · Colour · 90mins

Does this sound familiar? A well-off widow falls for a seemingly nice young man, marries him within a matter of weeks, then realises he's not quite the great chap she thought he was. The plot should ring a few bells as it has already been done on numerous occasions. Stefanie Powers, Lloyd Bridges and Hunt Block try to inject as much tension here as possible, but even their experienced presence can't prevent you from guessing the outcome of this TV movie. ▣

Stefanie Powers *Elena Forrester* • Hunt Block *Eric Chandler* • Debrah Farentino *Claire Potter* • Lloyd Bridges *Justin Matthews* • Polly Bergen *Laura Lee Webster* ■ *Dir* Chris Thomson • *Scr* David Stenn

She Woke Up ★★

Thriller   1992 · US · Colour · 100mins

Lindsay Wagner wakes from a coma nearly two years after a brutal attack. But viewers are going to be fighting drowsiness within minutes of the start of this ludicrously contrived and overblown melodrama, in which just about everyone heiress Wagner knows has a motive for killing her. You can't trust anyone these days! In fairness, Wagner shows what a good actress she is with another committed performance and British director Waris Hussein piles on the glitz, but it's a pretty tatty tale, not very well told.

Lindsay Wagner *Claudia Parr* • David Dukes *Sloane* • Maureen Mueller *Alix* • Frances Sternhagen *Noelle* • Ron Frazier *Dr Bigelow* ■ *Dir* Waris Hussein • *Scr* Claire Labine

She Wore a Yellow Ribbon ★★★★ PG

Western   1949 · US · Colour · 99mins

A first-class cavalry western from director John Ford containing one of John Wayne's finest screen performances, marvellously in character as retiring commander Nathan Brittles a performance that even those vehemently anti-Wayne, and all he stood for, feel forced to admire. This is one of the great Technicolor movies, justly winning an Oscar for its cinematography, which expertly captures Ford's favourite Monument Valley locations. The picture is marred by some ludicrous Irish whimsy involving Victor McLaglen, but the supporting cast is mighty fine, particularly Ben Johnson and Harry Carey Jr, and the lovely Joanne Dru as she of the yellow ribbon. ▣

John Wayne *Captain Brittles* • Joanne Dru *Olivia* • John Agar *Lieutenant Cohill* • Ben Johnson *Tyree* • Harry Carey Jr *Lieutenant Pennell* • Victor McLaglen *Sergeant Quincannon* • Mildred Natwick *Mrs Allshard* • Arthur Shields *Dr O'Laughlin* • Harry Woods *Toucey Rynders* ■ *Dir* John Ford • *Scr* Frank Nugent, Laurence Stallings, from the stories *War Party* and *The Big Hunt* by James Warner Bellah • *Cinematographer* Winton C Hoch

Sheena, Queen of the Jungle ★★ 15

Romantic adventure
1984 · US · Colour · 111mins

Raised by African natives when orphaned as a little girl, a hopelessly miscast Tanya Roberts learns how to talk to animals and use mystical powers to protect her people against political intrigue and an intrusive newsreel crew in a miserable adaptation of the thirties jungle woman comic strip. John Guillermin directs the colourful adventure yarn with a straight face and completely avoids the campy tone such exotica cries out for. The result is a deadly dull turkey full of unintentional laughs (the horse painted to look like a zebra) underscored by a truly great soundtrack. ▣

Tanya Roberts *Sheena* • Ted Wass *Vic Casey* • Donovan Scott *Fletcher* • Elizabeth of Toro *Shaman* • France Zobda *Countess Zanda* • Trevor Thomas *Prince Otwani* • Clifton Jones *King Jabalani* ■ *Dir* John Guillermin • *Scr* David Newman, Lorenzo Semple Jr • *Music* Richard Hartley

The Sheep Has Five Legs ★★★

Comedy   1954 · Fr · BW · 107mins

Seizing the opportunity to demonstrate his genius for comic characterisation, Fernandel takes on six roles in this engaging family album, compiled by Henri Verneuil. In addition to playing the disapproving vitner father, he also essays the five sons, who are reunited on their 40th birthday. The vignettes involving the prissy beautician and the Parisian agony aunt are unremarkable, but Fernandel excels as the hypochondriac window cleaner feuding with a grasping undertaker, the old salt

reduced to betting on flies landing on sugar lumps, and the priest weary of being reminded he resembles Don Camillo (a part the star made famous). In French with English subtitles.

Fernandel Papa Saint Forget • Delmont Dr Bollene • Louis De Funès Pilate, the undertaker ▪ Dir Henri Verneuil • Scr Albert Valentin

The Sheepman ★★★★ U

Western   1958 · US · Colour · 85mins

Directed with wit and style by veteran George Marshall (*Destry Rides Again*), this wonderful Glenn Ford comedy western co-stars a splendidly raucous and unusually sympathetic Shirley MacLaine. The opening is a real humdinger, and sets the style for the rest of the movie as Ford's milk-drinking sheep farmer (in cattle country!) picks a fight with local character Mickey Shaughnessy, proving that he's not a man to trifle with. A reminder that Ford was not only Hollywood's most popular star of this period, but one of America's finest.

Glenn Ford Jason Sweet • Shirley MacLaine Dell Payton • Leslie Nielsen Johnny Bledsoe • Mickey Shaughnessy Jumbo McCall • Edgar Buchanan Milt Masters • Willis Bouchey Mr Payton • Pernell Roberts Choctaw • Slim Pickens Marshal ▪ Dir George Marshall • Scr William Bowers, James Edward Grant, William Roberts, from a story by James Edward Grant

The Sheik ★★★★

Silent adventure melodrama
1921 · US · BW · 80mins

Having found fame in *The Four Horsemen of the Apocalypse*, Rudolph Valentino achieved iconic status with his performance as the dashing Ahmed Ben Hassan in this overheated desert melodrama. Female fans swooned as he delivered Agnes Ayres from the clutches of the lascivious Walter Long, while their dates looked on in disbelief at his effete heroics and impassioned wooing. There were even those who demanded the film should be banned for its dubious morality and acceptance of miscegenation. Yet, for all its surface glamour and romantic abandon, the story actually hurtles towards a rather traditional conclusion.

Agnes Ayres Diana Mayo • Rudolph Valentino Sheik Ahmed Ben Hassan • Adolphe Menjou Raoul de Saint Hubert • Walter Long Omair • Lucien Littlefield Gaston ▪ Dir George Melford • Scr Monte M Katterjohn, from the novel by Edith Maude Hull

Sheila Levine Is Dead and Living in New York ★★

Comedy   1975 · US · Colour · 113mins

Pathetic conversion of Gail Parent's bestselling comic novel about a spoilt girl trying to make it in New York, with Jeannie Berlin as the Jewish Princess fighting prejudice and her own nature. Director Sidney J Furie blots the copybook created by *The Ipcress File*, failing to grasp the comedy but squeezing too hard on the social significance.

Jeannie Berlin Sheila • Roy Scheider Sam • Rebecca Dianna Smith Kate • Janet Brandt Bernice • Sid Melton Manny • Charles Woolf Wally • Noble Willingham School Principal ▪ Dir Sidney J Furie • Scr Kenny Solms, from the novel by Gail Parent

Shelf Life ★★★

Comedy drama   1993 · US · Colour · 83mins

On the day President Kennedy is assassinated, a suburban sixties family retreat to their bomb shelter and stay there for 30 years. When their parents die of food poisoning, the three children resort to acting out scenes from their favourite TV shows to stay sane. Based on a play, the stars – Jim Turner, O-Lan Jones and Andrea Stein – wrote the film script which was filmed on one claustrophobic set by cult director Paul Bartel. Much surreal fun is had when the trio indulge in cultural rituals based upon the famous sitcoms of the era.

Andrea Stein Pam/Mrs St Cloud • O-Lan Jones Tina • Jim Turner Scotty/Mr St Cloud • Paul Bartel Various Apparitions ▪ Dir Paul Bartel • Scr Jim Turner, O-Lan Jones, Andrea Stein, from their play

She'll Be Wearing Pink Pyjamas ★★ 15

Comedy drama   1984 · UK · Colour · 86mins

All talk and no trousers, pyjama or otherwise, in this tiresome natter-fest about a bunch of women who go on a wilderness survival course as part of a company "bonding" scheme. Julie Walters stars and, as always, gives it her all. But neither she nor the supporting girls are particularly well served by the tedious dialogue and aimless plotting. The awful title doesn't help. ▭

Julie Walters Fran • Anthony Higgins Tom • Jane Evers Catherine • Janet Henfrey Lucy • Paula Jacobs Doreen • Penelope Nice Ann • Maureen O'Brien Joan • Alyson Spiro Anita ▪ Dir John Goldschmidt • Scr Eva Hardy

She'll Have to Go ★★ U

Comedy   1961 · UK · BW · 89mins

Known in the States as *Maid for Murder*, this mediocre comedy was something of a family affair. The Asher brothers co-produced the picture, with Robert also directing and his younger sibling, Jack, acting as cinematographer. They might have been better off having a crack at the script, too, as John Waterhouse's adaptation of Ian Stuart Black's play, *We Must Kill Toni*, is so slipshod that not even Hattie Jacques can bring it to life. But most sympathy goes to Jean-Luc Godard's then wife Anna Karina, who looks lost and embarrassed fighting off gold-digging brothers Bob Monkhouse and Alfred Marks.

Bob Monkhouse Francis Oberon • Alfred Marks Douglas Oberon • Hattie Jacques Miss Richards • Anna Karina Toni • Dennis Lotis Gilbert • Graham Stark Arnold • Clive Dunn Chemist ▪ Dir Robert Asher • Scr John Waterhouse, from the play We Must Kill Toni by Ian Stuart Black

She'll Take Romance ★★ PG

Comedy   1990 · US · Colour · 89mins

In *To Die For*, Nicole Kidman gave TV weathergirls a bad name, but the balance is somewhat restored by Linda Evans in this cosy TV movie. Saddled with judging a Mr Romance contest on her local Seattle station, she finds herself inundated with amorous invitations. Basking in the candlelight, Evans shows a surprisingly sure touch

with light comedy as all the male attention causes her to rethink her engagement to judge Tom Skerritt. The string of hot pursuits could have become a tad tedious, but director Piers Haggard keeps it bubbling. ▭

Linda Evans Jane McMillan • Tom Skerritt Judge Warren Danvers • Larry Poindexter Mike Heller • Delane Matthews April August • Heather Tom Caroline McMillan ▪ Dir Piers Haggard • Scr James Henerson, James G Hirsch

The Sheltering Sky ★★★ 18

Drama   1990 · UK/It · Colour · 132mins

Following the international success of *The Last Emperor*, Bernardo Bertolucci then produced this immensely ambitious film of Paul Bowles's strange, mystical, metaphysical novel. The tale concerns an American married couple (John Malkovich and Debra Winger) and a friend (Campbell Scott) touring North Africa in 1947 in search of the mystery that is the desert. Filmed in arduous conditions in Algeria and Niger, the movie tries to be bookish and introspective yet full of vast landscapes. Despite the obvious commitment of Winger, who gives an intensely physical performance, it remains a rather soulless and aloof experience. ▭

Debra Winger Kit Moresby • John Malkovich Port Moresby • Campbell Scott George Tunner • Jill Bennett Mrs Lyle • Timothy Spall Eric Lyle • Eric Vu-An Belqassim • Amina Annabi Mahrnia ▪ Dir Bernardo Bertolucci • Scr Mark Peploe, Bernardo Bertolucci, from the novel by Paul Bowles • Cinematographer Vittorio Storaro

Shenandoah ★★★★ PG

Western   1965 · US · Colour · 100mins

This marvellous and moving late western features a superb performance from James Stewart as a widower trying to ignore the Civil War until the tide of history washes over his whole family. Unusually, the deliberate sentimentality does work, and the scene where Stewart offers a moving soliloquy beside his wife's grave was so popular that it was released on record. Director Andrew V McLaglen (Victor's son) achieves a real sense of scale here, and the supporting cast, including many veterans from John Ford's repertory company, is particularly well chosen. ▭

James Stewart Charlie Anderson • Doug McClure Sam • Glenn Corbett Jacob Anderson • Patrick Wayne James Anderson • Rosemary Forsyth Jennie Anderson • Phillip Alford Boy Anderson • Katharine Ross Ann Anderson • Charles Robinson Nathan Anderson ▪ Dir Andrew V McLaglen • Scr James Lee Barrett

The Shepherd of the Hills ★★★

Adventure melodrama
1941 · US · Colour · 97mins

The heavyweight presence of John Wayne helps make this one of the best adaptations of Harold Bell Wright's Missouri-set novel. Wayne stars as the backwoods boy who blames his absent father for the death of his mother and spends his days plotting revenge. Betty Field plays the girl who won't marry Wayne while he's consumed with hate. Wayne makes the

most of his opportunity here, cementing his new-found stardom after *Stagecoach*, while director Henry Hathaway just stands back and lets the splendid cast get on with it.

John Wayne Young Matt Matthews • Betty Field Sammy Lane • Harry Carey Daniel Howitt • Beulah Bondi Aunt Mollie • James Barton Old Matt • Samuel S Hinds Andy Beeler • Marjorie Main Granny Becky • Ward Bond Wash Gibbs ▪ Dir Henry Hathaway • Scr Grover Jones, Stuart Anthony, from the novel by Harold Bell Wright

The Sheriff of Fractured Jaw ★★★★ U

Comedy western
1958 · UK · Colour · 103mins

This is the first western shot in Spain, its standing set later used for Sergio Leone's *Dollars* trilogy. The title role in this super spoof is played by British actor Kenneth More at his most diffident, and the director is the great Raoul Walsh, who films in the grand tradition of the genre. Fifties sex symbol Jayne Mansfield provides the love interest and there's a touching musical interlude in which she croons *In the Valley of Love*, dubbed by Connie Francis. The film's soundtrack is especially witty, and there's the added value of an entertaining Anglo-American supporting cast.

Kenneth More Jonathan Tibbs • Jayne Mansfield Kate • Henry Hull Mayor Masters • William Campbell Keno • Bruce Cabot Jack • Robert Morley Uncle Lucius • Ronald Squire Toynbee • David Horne James ▪ Dir Raoul Walsh • Scr Arthur Dales [Howard Dimsdale], from a short story by Jacob Hay • Music Robert Farnon

Sheriff of Sage Valley ★★ U

Western   1942 · US · BW · 55mins

Buster Crabbe was an Olympic swimmer who in swift succession played hero figures Tarzan, Flash Gordon and Buck Rogers in series and serials throughout the thirties that are still recalled with affectionate nostalgia today. But Crabbe was no actor, and he soon became a leading man in B-westerns, of which this is a typical example. The star was 48 in all, 31 in this series of rather skimpy-on-plot but action-packed programme fillers for poverty row producers PRC.

Buster Crabbe [Larry "Buster" Crabbe] Billy The Kid/Kansas Ed • Al St John Fuzzy Jones • Tex O'Brien Jeff • Maxine Leslie Janet • Charles King Sloane ▪ Dir Sherman Scott [Sam Newfield] • Scr George W Sayre, Milton Raison

Sherlock Holmes ★★★

Mystery   1932 · US · BW · 62mins

Call it "the Case of the Clueless Sleuth". Before Basil Rathbone put his definitive imprint on Conan Doyle's famous private detective, matinée idol Clive Brook was a refined and far too discreet Holmes, with Reginald Owen as a very ineffectual Dr Watson. The film loses a lot of gaslight appeal as Chicago gangsters, brought in by the monstrous Moriarty, invade a bewildered London. Holmes's nemesis is given such a wonderfully OTT presence by Ernest Torrence that, in the end, you almost hope he'll win.

U = SUITABLE FOR ALL   Uc = SUITABLE FOR ALL, ESPECIALLY FOR YOUNG CHILDREN (VIDEO ONLY)   PG = PARENTAL GUIDANCE

Clive Brook *Sherlock Holmes* • Ernest Torrence *Professor Moriarty* • Reginald Owen *Dr Watson* • Miriam Jordan *Alice Faulkner* • Howard Leeds *Little Billy* • Alan Mowbray *Gore-King* ■ *Dir* William K Howard • *Scr* Bertram Milhauser, from a play by William Gillette, from stories by Sir Arthur Conan Doyle

Sherlock Holmes and the Secret Weapon ★★★ PG
Mystery   1942 · US · BW · 68mins

The Nazis stood no chance once they knew they were up against the Allies' own secret weapon, Basil Rathbone as Holmes, ably assisted as always by Nigel Bruce as Dr Watson. This modernised, morale-boosting story drew only a fraction of its plot (the ''dancing men'' code) from Conan Doyle, as Holmes searches for a unique bombsight. As the baleful Moriarty, Lionel Atwill walks the corridors of glower with real malevolence, and the film was the first in the series to be directed by Roy William Neill. He must have been doing something right; he went on to make ten more. ▦

Basil Rathbone *Sherlock Holmes* • Nigel Bruce *Dr Watson* • Kaaren Verne *Charlotte Eberli* • Lionel Atwill *Professor Moriarty* • William Post Jr *Dr Franz Tobel* • Dennis Hoey *Inspector Lestrade* ■ *Dir* Roy William Neill • *Scr* Edward T Lowe, Scott Darling, Edmund L Hartmann, from the story *The Dancing Men* by Sir Arthur Conan Doyle

Sherlock Holmes and the Voice of Terror ★★ U
Mystery   1942 · US · BW · 62mins

The first of Universal's 11-film series featuring Basil Rathbone and Nigel Bruce as the slender sleuth and his rotund sidekick, though the two actors had already played the roles in two films for 20th Century-Fox. The wartime plot is simplistic, with Holmes searching for the traitor in the government supplying a Nazi broadcaster with news of sabotage and disaster. Not the best of the series, with the informer as obvious as the Union flag raised so laboriously in Holmes's patriotic speeches. ▦

Basil Rathbone *Sherlock Holmes* • Nigel Bruce *Dr Watson* • Evelyn Ankers *Kitty* • Reginald Denny *Sir Evan Barham* • Montagu Love *General Jerome Lawford* • Henry Daniell *Anthony Lloyd* • Thomas Gomez *RF Meade* ■ *Dir* John Rawlins • *Scr* Lynn Riggs, John Bright, Robert Andrews, from the story *His Last Bow* by Sir Arthur Conan Doyle

Sherlock Holmes and the Spider Woman ★★★ U
Mystery   1944 · US · BW · 59mins

Dr Watson shooting at Sherlock Holmes? The mind boggles. Have no fear: it's not deliberate, though it could be lethal. The serene elegance of Basil Rathbone as Holmes is just a tad ruffled when he's set up in a shooting gallery by the great Gale Sondergaard – as vicious a foe as Holmes has faced in a film as effective as any in the series. The only fly, or flaw, in the web is that Nigel Bruce's Dr Watson is at his most boringly bumbling. ▦

Basil Rathbone *Sherlock Holmes* • Nigel Bruce *Dr Watson* • Gale Sondergaard *Andrea Spedding* • Dennis Hoey *Inspector Lestrade* • Vernon Downing *Norman Locke* • Alec Craig

Radlik • Arthur Hohl *Adam Gilflower* ■ *Dir* Roy William Neill • *Scr* Bertram Millhauser, from the story *The Sign of the Four* by Sir Arthur Conan Doyle

Sherlock Holmes Faces Death ★★★ U
Mystery   1943 · US · BW · 65mins

.One of the best of the Basil Rathbone/Nigel Bruce movies, in which a clock strikes 13 and murder comes in triplicate. For once Dr Watson is the plot's prime mover, in charge of an army officers' convalescent home at Musgrave Manor where shell-shocked patients are the cover for misdeeds in a hidden cellar. With distinctive echoes from its Conan Doyle source story, *The Musgrave Ritual* – watch Holmes using suspects as giant chess pieces – it's one of the most old-fashioned of the series, which explains the craftsmanlike grip it exerts. ▦

Basil Rathbone *Sherlock Holmes* • Nigel Bruce *Dr Watson* • Dennis Hoey *Inspector Lestrade* • Arthur Margetson *Dr Sexton* • Hillary Brooke *Sally Musgrave* • Halliwell Hobbes *Brunton, the butler* • Minna Phillips *Mrs Howells* ■ *Dir* Roy William Neill • *Scr* Bertram Millhauser, from the story *The Musgrave Ritual* by Sir Arthur Conan Doyle

Sherlock Holmes in New York ★★★ U
Mystery   1976 · US · Colour · 98mins

Roger Moore as Sherlock Holmes, Patrick Macnee as Dr Watson and John Huston as Professor Moriarty enliven this TV movie outing for Conan Doyle's inimitable hero, which involves Huston messing with the world's gold supply. Asked why he decided to play the part, he said: ''Well, I have the time, I can use the money and Moriarty is a part I was born to play.'' Having already created one of the modern cinema's great villains – Noah Cross in *Chinatown* – Huston slips into Moriarty's wardrobe with ease and dominates this enjoyable movie.

Roger Moore *Sherlock Holmes* • John Huston *Professor James Moriarty* • Patrick Macnee *Dr John Watson* • David Huddleston *Inspector Lafferty* • Signe Hasso *Fraulein Reichenbach* • Gig Young *Mortimer McGraw* • Charlotte Rampling *Irene Adler* • Jackie Coogan *Hotel Haymarket Proprietor* ■ *Dir* Boris Sagal • *Scr* Alvin Sapinsley, from characters created by Sir Arthur Conan Doyle

Sherlock Holmes in Washington ★★ U
Mystery   1943 · US · BW · 68mins

Shock! Horror! Sherlock Holmes (Basil Rathbone) smokes a cigarette – what happened to his treatise on tobacco? – while Dr Watson (Nigel Bruce) puffs petulantly on his pipe in the first of the series not connected, however tenuously, to a story by Arthur Conan Doyle. A weakish update of the character, Holmes is after a microfilm passed to the wrong stranger on a train and a prime target for nasty Nazis. Holmes does get to quote Winston Churchill, however, and waxes paternal about democracy. ▦

Basil Rathbone *Sherlock Holmes* • Nigel Bruce *Dr Watson* • Marjorie Lord *Nancy Partridge* • Henry Daniell *William Easter* • George Zucco *Stanley* • John Archer *Lt Peter Merriam* • Gavin Muir *Bart Lang* ■ *Dir* Roy William Neill •

Scr Bertram Millhauser, Lynn Riggs, from a story by Bertram Millhauser, from characters created by Sir Arthur Conan Doyle

Sherlock Junior ★★★★★ U
Silent comedy   1924 · US · BW · 45mins

One of Buster Keaton's finest comedies, certainly his most inventive and technically audacious. He plays an amateur detective and cinema projectionist who dreams himself into the movie he is showing and, hopefully, into the arms of the girl he loves. As early as 1924 Keaton recognised the cinema's role in society as escapism, and constructed an entire film about it. The result is richly romantic and oddly educational: audiences were shown all the tricks of the trade, notably editing, back projection and other special effects. But mostly it works as a brilliant comedy, full of the clever bits of business and ambitious stunts one associates with Keaton.

Buster Keaton *Sherlock Jr* • Kathryn McGuire *Girl* • Ward Crane *Rival* • Joseph Keaton [Joe Keaton] *Father* ■ *Dir* Buster Keaton • *Scr* Clyde Bruckman, Jean Havez, Joseph Mitchell

Sherlock – Undercover Dog ★ PG
Comedy adventure
1994 · US · Colour · 75mins

You'd think that a children's movie with a title like this would be terrible. And you'd be right. On Catalina Island, a Scottish detective is kidnapped by drug smugglers, and it's up to his pal Sherlock – a talking police dog that speaks only to children – to convince two youngsters to help him save his master. Why a Scottish detective is dealing with a crime in California is just one of the many plot stupidities that will have adults grimacing. ▦

Benjamin Eroen *Billy* • Brynne Cameron *Emma* • Anthony Simmons *William* ■ *Dir/Scr* Richard Harding Gardner

She's All That ★★★ 12
Romantic comedy
1999 · US · Colour · 95mins

Preposterous but fun romantic comedy, with Rachael Leigh Cook as the gawky teen who gets a make-over from popular soccer star Freddie Prinze Jr because he's made a secret bet with his pals that he can turn even the most unlikely girl in their high school into a prom queen. Both the leads are enjoyable and the central story is fun, but equally worth catching are the supporting stars, especially Matthew Lillard as an egotistical oaf, Anna Paquin as Prinze's sister and Kieran Culkin as Cook's gutsy younger brother. Contains some swearing and sexual references. ▦ **DVD**

Freddie Prinze Jr *Zack Siler* • Rachael Leigh Cook *Laney Boggs* • Matthew Lillard *Brock Hudson* • Paul Walker *Dean Sampson* • Jodi Lyn O'Keefe *Taylor Vaughan* • Kevin Pollak *Wayne Boggs* • Kieran Culkin *Simon Boggs* • Anna Paquin *Mackenzie Siler* ■ *Dir* Robert Iscove • *Scr* R Lee Fleming Jr

She's Gotta Have It ★★★★ 18
Comedy drama   1986 · US · BW and Colour · 80mins

Spike Lee's directorial debut hasn't lost any of its vitality over the years and remains his most genuinely entertaining work, refreshingly free of much of the political rhetoric which occasionally overcomes his other projects. Tracy Camila Johns is the strong willed young woman who not only has to have it, but also refuses to be tied down to one of three suitors out to tame her. Lee has plenty of fun deflating the macho egos on parade, grabbing many of the best lines for himself as the irritatingly persistent Mars Blackmon. Vividly shot in black and white apart from one lovely colour sequence at the end. Contains swearing and nudity. ▦

Tracy Camila Johns *Nola Darling* • Tommy Redmond Hicks *Jamie Overstreet* • John Canada Terrell *Greer Childs* • Spike Lee *Mars Blackmon* • Raye Dowell *Opal Gilstrap* • Joie Lee *Clorinda Bradford* • Epatha Merkinson [S Epatha Merkerson] *Dr Jamison* • Bill Lee *Sonny Darling* ■ *Dir/Scr* Spike Lee • *Cinematographer* Ernest Dickerson

She's Having a Baby ★★ 15
Comedy   1988 · US · Colour · 101mins

A rather humdrum look at young love turning into disgruntled parenthood, starring a highly believable Kevin Bacon and a less rooted-in-reality Elizabeth McGovern. There are some neat jokes about bulges, nappies and loss of freedom, and Bacon's terror at the impending event is almost palpable. But the movie fails to break any new ground, and, after a while, there is a familiar jaded ring to every hackneyed scenario. This is a shame, as director John Hughes tries his best to give everything a sparky, pacey feel, but the end result is simply just not funny enough. Contains swearing. ▦

Kevin Bacon *Jefferson ''Jake'' Briggs* • Elizabeth McGovern *Kristy Briggs* • Alec Baldwin *Davis McDonald* • Isabel Lorca *Fantasy girl* • William Windom *Russ Bainbridge* ■ *Dir/Scr* John Hughes

She's Out of Control ★★ 15
Comedy   1989 · US · Colour · 90mins

Tony Danza here plays a single father worried about his daughter's burgeoning sexuality who becomes embroiled in a number of increasingly embarrassing situations as he tries to curb her romantic liaisons. This is all in vain, however, as daughter Ami Dolenz is a level-headed sort who can manage perfectly without dad's over-attentiveness. A fifties story in eighties clothes, and we know what a great decade the eighties was for sartorial elegance. ▦

Tony Danza *Doug Simpson* • Catherine Hicks *Janet Pearson* • Ami Dolenz *Katie Simpson* • Wallace Shawn *Dr Fishbinder* • Dick O'Neill *Mr Pearson* • Laura Mooney *Bonnie Simpson* ■ *Dir* Stan Dragoti • *Scr* Seth Winston, Michael J Nathanson

She's So Lovely ★★★ 15
Romantic drama   1997 · US · Colour · 92mins

At one time Nick Cassavetes looked as if he would be just another actor with a more famous relative. However, he has successfully reinvented himself as a director and, although the influences of his independent film-maker father John are clear to see, this affectingly offbeat drama stands up in its own right. Sean Penn is a mentally troubled young man who is locked away in a psychiatric hospital. Ten years later he is released and sets out to find his wife (Robin Wright Penn) who, unbeknown to him, has divorced him and married John Travolta. It's a slight tale, but the performances are finely judged. Contains swearing and some violence. ▣

Sean Penn *Eddie* • Robin Wright [Robin Wright Penn] *Maureen* • John Travolta *Joey* • Harry Dean Stanton *Shorty* • Debi Mazar *Georgie* • Gena Rowlands *Miss Green* • James Gandolfini *Kiefer* ■ *Dir* Nick Cassavetes • *Scr* John Cassavetes

She's the One ★★ 🔞15

Romantic comedy
1996 · US · Colour · 92mins

Edward Burns's follow-up to *The Brothers McMullen* is a lightly comic family affair. Two brothers, Burns and Mike McGlone, banter about love and marriage: one still smarts from an ex-fiancée's infidelity, the other happily plays away from his wife without conscience. John Mahoney stars as their father, with Cameron Diaz and Jennifer Aniston as the women in question. Witty and well observed by Burns, again both directing and starring, the problem is that though it's instantly watchable, it's also instantly forgettable. Contains swearing and sexual references. ▣

John Mahoney *Mr Fitzpatrick* • Edward Burns *Mickey Fitzpatrick* • Mike McGlone *Francis Fitzpatrick* • Maxine Bahns *Hope* • Jennifer Aniston *Renee* • Cameron Diaz *Heather* • Malachy McCourt *Tom* ■ *Dir/Scr* Edward Burns

She's Working Her Way through College ★★★ 🔞U

Musical comedy 1952 · US · Colour · 101mins

An attractive Warner Bros musical version of James Thurber and Elliott Nugent's stage play *The Male Animal*, filmed previously in 1942 with Henry Fonda. Here Ronald Reagan is the college professor who makes a stand for freedom of expression, and it's not often that you get to see a future US president watching voluptuous Virginia Mayo perform saucy dance routines! The generally under-rated Mayo is super as the showgirl determined to improve her mind, and there's nice back-up from hoofer Gene Nelson.

Virginia Mayo *Angela Gardner/"Hot Garters Gertie"* • Ronald Reagan *John Palmer* • Gene Nelson *Don Weston* • Don DeFore *Shep Slade* • Phyllis Thaxter *Helen Palmer* • Patrice Wymore *Ivy Williams* • Roland Winters *Fred Copeland* ■ *Dir* H Bruce Humberstone • *Scr* Peter Milne, from the play *The Male Animal* by James Thurber, Elliott Nugent

Shield for Murder ★★

Crime drama 1954 · US · BW · 82mins

Edmond O'Brien co-directed and starred in this meaty drama of a city cop "gone sour", a veteran of the force who hankers after the good life in suburbia. Killing a crook for the loot

he's carrying, the cop then tries to deal with the complications, including his betrayal of John Agar's young detective who has always looked up to him. O'Brien's sweaty performance is better than his uneven direction, but there are tense moments and the climax on the front lawn of the cop's dream home is typically forceful.

Edmond O'Brien *Barney Nolan* • Marla English *Patty Winters* • John Agar *Mark Brewster* • Emile Meyer *Captain Gunnarson* • Carolyn Jones *Girl at bar* • Claude Akins *Fat Michaels* ■ *Dir* Edmond O'Brien, Howard W Koch • *Scr* Richard Alan Simmons, John C Higgins, from the novel by William P McGivern

Shiloh ★★★★ 🔞U

Drama 1996 · US · Colour · 86mins

In a first-rate family entertainment, a boy befriends a hunting dog that's being cruelly treated by its owner, a neighbouring farmer. The boy's dad reckons it's the neighbour's business, and that he shouldn't get involved. But, convinced by a kindly shopkeeper that a boy's gotta do what a boy's gotta do, the kid takes the paw into his own hands and fights doggedly to become the beagle's new owner. Refreshingly unsentimental and impeccably acted, *Shiloh* is a minor treat for kids and grown-ups alike. A sequel followed in 1999. ▣

Michael Moriarty *Ray Preston* • Rod Steiger *Doc Wallace* • Blake Heron [Blake Heron] *Marty Preston* • Scott Wilson *Judd Travers* • Bonnie Bartlett *Mrs Wallace* • Ann Dowd *Louise Preston* ■ *Dir* Dale Rosenbloom • *Scr* Dale Rosenbloom, from a novel by Phyllis Reynolds Naylor

Shimmering Light ★★

Drama 1978 · Ausl · Colour · 92mins

A small and decidedly lacklustre Australian TV movie about surfing, the prospect of which managed to persuade two of the Bridges clan, Lloyd and Beau, to head down under. The tale of a dropout who disobeys his rich father in his search for the perfect wave is hardly an original one, and this has no new twists to impart. The Australian coast looks magnificent, Lloyd and Beau are as thoroughly professional as ever and the supporting cast jog competently through their paces. It is just all so horribly predictable.

Beau Bridges *Kevin* • Lloyd Bridges *Sean* • John Meillon *Eric Stuart* • Victoria Shaw *Moira* ■ *Dir* Don Chaffey • *Scr* George Kirgo, Paul Savage

Shinbone Alley ★★

Animated musical comedy 1971 · US · Colour · 83mins

This less-than-animated animation features the characters archy and mehitabel – a love-struck cockroach and the happy-go-lucky cat who's the object of his affection. Created by Don Marquis and originally adapted into a stage musical by Joe Darion and Mel Brooks, Eddie Bracken and Carol Channing take up the big-screen vocal roles and breathe some much needed life into this listless cartoon.

Carol Channing *mehitabel* • Eddie Bracken *archy* • Alan Reed *Big Bill Sr* • John Carradine *Tyrone T Tattersall* ■ *Dir* John David Wilson •

Scr Joe Darion, from the musical by Mel Brooks, Joe Darion, from characters created by Don Marquis

Shine ★★★★★ 🔞12

Biographical drama 1996 · Ausl/UK · Colour · 101mins

Although reservations have been expressed about the accuracy of the "facts" in this film based on the life of Australian pianist David Helfgott, the resulting drama is still an exhilarating and uplifting screen experience. While it was Geoffrey Rush who took many of the plaudits, including a best actor Oscar, it's the acumen of Scott Hicks that prevents this often harrowing story from turning into a melodramatic mush. The director proves himself to be a film-maker of rare perception and imagination, never more so than in the excruciating scene in which the young David (the overlooked Noah Taylor) collapses during his performance of the "Rach 3" at the Royal College of Music. Contains swearing and brief nudity. ▣ **DVD**

Geoffrey Rush *David as an adult* • Armin Mueller-Stahl *Peter* • Noah Taylor *David as an adolescent* • Lynn Redgrave *Gillian* • John Gielgud *Cecil Parkes* • Googie Withers *Katharine Susannah Prichard* • Sonia Todd *Sylvia* ■ *Dir* Scott Hicks • *Scr* Jan Sardi, from a story by Scott Hicks

Shine On, Harvest Moon ★★ 🔞U

Western 1938 · US · BW · 55mins

Not to be confused with the splendid Ann Sheridan musical of 1944, this is an early Roy Rogers western, made when Rogers was beginning a challenge to Gene Autry's popularity that would culminate in 1942 when Autry joined up and Rogers officially became "King of the Cowboys". Veteran western director Joseph Kane made dozens of these B-movies with both Autry and Rogers, and knew how to keep the action swift and the running time short.

Roy Rogers *Roy* • Mary Hart [Lynne Roberts] *Claire* • Stanley Andrews *Jackson* • William Farnum *Brower* ■ *Dir* Joseph Kane • *Scr* Jack Natteford

Shine On, Harvest Moon ★★★ 🔞U

Musical biography 1944 · US · BW and Colour · 112mins

Marvellous lively vehicle for sexy and talented "Oomph Girl" Ann Sheridan. She plays Broadway star Nora Bayes in one of those post-*Yankee Doodle Dandy* Warner Bros biopics that owes little to the truth but manages to include a load of period songs. Dennis Morgan is terrific as songwriter Jack Norworth – also Nora's husband – and there are telling contributions from Warners regulars SZ "Cuddles" Sakall and Jack Carson. If you want the sordid truth about the Bayes/Norworth vaudeville-to-Broadway affair, this isn't the place to look, but it's a jolly enjoyable movie nonetheless.

Ann Sheridan *Nora Bayes* • Dennis Morgan *Jack Norworth* • Jack Carson *The Great Georgetti* • Irene Manning *Blanche Mallory* • SZ Sakall *Poppa Karl* ■ *Dir* David Butler • *Scr* Sam Hellman, Richard Weil, Francis Swan, James Kern, from the story by Richard Weil

The Shining ★★★★★ 🔞18

Horror 1980 · US/UK · Colour · 114mins

Based on Stephen King's novel, Stanley Kubrick's horror show stars Jack Nicholson, Shelley Duvall and young Danny Lloyd as the family who are invited to look after a remote mountain hotel when it's closed for the winter. It's not long before Nicholson becomes unhinged as a series of apparitions, hallucinations and time-warps begin to affect his sanity. Trust Kubrick to be different: this horror film chills rather than shocks, works by stealth and provides nothing but eerie discomfort. Filmed on an amazing set built at Elstree (the opening aerial scenes were shot by Kubrick's daughter at the Timberline Lodge in Oregon) and using a gliding Steadicam throughout, the technique is as overpowering as Nicholson's performance, which is both hammy and deeply disturbing. Contains violence, swearing and nudity. ▣

Jack Nicholson *Jack Torrance* • Shelley Duvall *Wendy Torrance* • Danny Lloyd *Danny* • Scatman Crothers *Dick Halloran* • Barry Nelson *Ullman* • Philip Stone *Grady* • Joe Turkel [Joseph Turkel] *Lloyd* • Anne Jackson *Doctor* ■ *Dir* Stanley Kubrick • *Scr* Stanley Kubrick, Diane Johnson, from the novel by Stephen King • *Cinematographer* John Alcott

The Shining Hour ★★★

Drama 1938 · US · BW · 76mins

Ultra-wealthy landowner Melvyn Douglas, ignoring the disapproval of his brother Robert Young and his possessive, embittered sister Fay Bainter, marries nightclub dancer with a past Joan Crawford. Emotional havoc is unleashed as Young, adored by his wife Margaret Sullavan, falls for his sister-in-law. Director Frank Borzage's film is highly entertaining, marked by committed performances, lots of atmosphere and a luminous portrayal of bruised emotion and self-sacrifice from Sullavan.

Joan Crawford *Olivia Riley* • Margaret Sullavan *Judy Linden* • Robert Young *David Linden* • Melvyn Douglas *Henry Linden* • Fay Bainter *Hannah Linden* • Allyn Joslyn *Roger Franklin* • Hattie McDaniel *Belvedere* ■ *Dir* Frank Borzage • *Scr* Jane Murfin, Ogden Nash, from the play by Keith Winters

A Shining Season ★★★

Drama based on a true story 1979 · US · Colour · 100mins

Timothy Bottoms, still best remembered for his performance in the 1971 film *The Last Picture Show*, here brings a touch of class to the true story of athlete John Baker. Bottoms tugs at the heartstrings as he battles against terminal illness, but is nevertheless determined to coach a girl's track team in his last few months. It could have been syrupy, but, thanks to the central performance and director Stuart Margolin (*The Glitter Dome*), this is, in fact, an interesting and often affecting tale.

Timothy Bottoms *John Baker* • Allyn Ann McLerie *Polly Baker* • Constance Forslund *Mary Anne* • Ed Begley Jr *John Haaland* • Rip Torn *Jack Baker* ■ *Dir* Stuart Margolin • *Scr* William Harrison, from the non-fiction book by William Buchanan

🔞U = SUITABLE FOR ALL   🔞Uc = SUITABLE FOR ALL, ESPECIALLY FOR YOUNG CHILDREN (VIDEO ONLY)   🔞PG = PARENTAL GUIDANCE

Shining Through ★★ 15

Second World War spy drama
1992 · US · Colour · 127mins

Melanie Griffith is the half-Jewish, German-speaking American who goes to work for US spy Michael Douglas shortly before Pearl Harbor, and volunteers to risk her life by going to Berlin to spy on debonair Nazi Liam Neeson. Although there's some tension as Griffith runs the risk of being caught, what spoils the film is the firmly nineties dialogue in the forties setting, the often ludicrous plot twists and the fact that Griffith never seems quite at home in her period role. Add a pinch of salt and you might just enjoy it. Contains some violence, swearing and brief nudity. [video]

Michael Douglas *Ed Leland* • Melanie Griffith *Linda Voss* • Liam Neeson *Franze-Otto Dietrich* • Joely Richardson *Margrete Von Eberstien* • John Gielgud *Konrad Friedrichs, "Sunflower"* • Francis Guinan *Andrew Berringer* • Sylvia Syms *Linda's mother* ■ *Dir* David Seltzer • *Scr* David Seltzer, from the novel by Susan Isaacs • *Cinematographer* Jan De Bont

Shining Victory ★★

Drama 1941 · US · BW · 79mins

An adaptation of AJ Cronin's play, *Jupiter Laughs*, in which every character seems to be a doctor and every scene is a crisis of some sort. James Stephenson plays a research scientist who is forced out of Hungary and washes up in a Scottish sanatorium. There his theories of psycho-biology are swallowed whole, especially by Geraldine Fitzgerald.

James Stephenson *Dr Paul Venner* • Geraldine Fitzgerald *Dr Mary Murray* • Donald Crisp *Dr Drewett* • Barbara O'Neil *Miss Leeming* • Montagu Love *Dr Blake* • Sig Ruman *Professor Herman Von Reiter* ■ *Dir* Irving Rapper • *Scr* Howard Koch, Anne Froelick, from the play *Jupiter Laughs* by AJ Cronin

Ship Ahoy ★★★ U

Musical comedy 1942 · US · BW · 94mins

Forget the silly story of this spy spoof, which culminates with dancer Eleanor Powell sending a morse code message in taps, and enjoy her sensational dancing, including one of her greatest routines – a breathtaking ship-board tap dance climaxing in some dextrous by-play with drummer Buddy Rich. Several of the first-rate songs are by Burton Lane and EY Harburg, and include the plaintive *Poor You*, sung by a skinny vocalist with Tommy Dorsey's orchestra – Frank Sinatra. Comics Red Skelton and Bert Lahr are among others contributing to the above-average entertainment quotient.

Eleanor Powell *Tallulah Winters* • Red Skelton *Merton K Kibble* • Bert Lahr *Skip Owens* • Virginia O'Brien *Fran Evans* • William Post Jr *HU Bennett* • James Cross *Stump* • Eddie Hartman *Stumpy* • Frank Sinatra ■ *Dir* Edward N Buzzell [Edward Buzzell] • *Scr* Harry Clork, Harry Kurnitz, Irving Brecher, from a story by Matt Brooks, Bradford Ropes, Bert Kalmar

Ship of Fools ★★★

Drama 1965 · US · BW · 149mins

A big, bloated and often boring drama that marked the final screen appearance of Vivien Leigh. The story concerns a group of refugees – exiles, Jews, aristocrats, and oddballs – who leave Mexico for Germany in 1933, just as Hitler was lying in wait for them. It's a giant allegory that takes itself very seriously indeed. Leigh's performance as a lonely divorcee is absolutely riveting to watch, and there's an amazing supporting cast.

Vivien Leigh *Mary Treadwell* • Simone Signoret *La Condesa* • José Ferrer *Rieber* • Lee Marvin *Tenny* • Oskar Werner *Dr Schumann* • Elizabeth Ashley *Jenny* • George Segal *David* • José Greco *Pepe* • Werner Klemperer *Lieutenant Heebner* ■ *Dir* Stanley Kramer • *Scr* Abby Mann, from the novel by Katherine Anne Porter • *Cinematographer* Ernest Laszlo • *Art Director* Robert Clatworthy, Joseph Kish

The Ship of Lost Men ★★

Silent drama 1929 · Ger · BW · 121mins

The last silent movie made by Marlene Dietrich before *The Blue Angel* sent her star soaring. The future Hollywood legend plays Miss Ethel, an heiress who crash-lands during a transatlantic flight and is secretly picked up by a good doctor (British Robin Irvine) and a gentle cook (Vladimir Sokoloff). Taken on board a strange ship loaded with escaped convicts, murderers and smugglers, the pair try to keep Dietrich from the motley crew. Although contrived at times, the characters are convincing, the plot is skilfully developed and director Maurice Tourneur's striking visuals and moody atmosphere keep the high seas adventure on an even keel.

Fritz Kortner *Captain Fernando Vela* • Marlene Dietrich *Ethel Marley* • Gaston Modot *Morain* • Robin Irvine *William Cheyne* • Vladimir Sokoloff *Grischa* ■ *Dir* Maurice Tourneur • *Scr* Maurice Tourneur, from the novel by Franzos Keremen

The Ship That Died of Shame ★★ PG

Drama 1955 · UK · BW · 88mins

Adapted from the novel by Nicholas Monsarrat, this is one of the more peculiar civvy street pictures made in the decade after the war. With Basil Dearden and his regular co-director Michael Relph at the helm, it lurches uncomfortably between comedy, social drama and thriller as it follows the fortunes of the washed-up crew of a motor torpedo boat, who recondition the old tub and turn to smuggling because Britain no longer has anything to offer its one-time heroes. Ducking and weaving in characteristic style, Richard Attenborough is the star of the show, but the uncertainty of tone finally gets the better of him. [video]

Richard Attenborough *Hoskins* • George Baker *Bill* • Bill Owen *Birdie* • Virginia McKenna *Helen* • Roland Culver *Fordyce* • Bernard Lee *Customs officer* • Ralph Truman *Sir Richard* ■ *Dir* Michael Relph, Basil Dearden • *Scr* Michael Relph, Basil Dearden, John Whiting, from the novel by Nicholas Monsarrat

A Ship to India ★★★

Drama 1947 · Swe · BW · 98mins

The influence of Marcel Carné can be detected in Ingmar Bergman's third feature. Set on the Stockholm waterfront, it begins with a happy ending, from which the action flashes back to chronicle the rivalry between captain Holger Lowenadler (whose dreams of seeing the world have been dashed by incipient blindness) and his hunchbacked son, Birger Malmsten, for the affections of dance-hall waif, Gertrud Fridh. Piercing the poetic gloom are themes that would recur throughout the director's career – spiritual imprisonment, unrequited love, physical and emotional imperfection – but the structure allows the intensity to wane and the handling is decidedly melodramatic. In Swedish with English subtitles.

Holger Lowenadler *Captain Alexander Blom* • Anna Lindahl *His wife* • Birger Malmsten *Johannes* • Gertrud Fridh *Sally* • Naemi Briese *Selma* • Hjordis Petterson *Sofie* ■ *Dir* Ingmar Bergman • *Scr* Ingmar Bergman, from the play *Skepp till India land* by Martin Söderhjelm

Ships with Wings ★

Second World War action drama
1942 · UK · BW · 105mins

An hour could easily be cut from this endless flagwaver designed to glorify the aircraft carrier *Ark Royal* and the men of the Fleet Air Arm. No one doubts their bravery, but did they really deserve this awful mess of soap opera and derring-do? John Clements is the hero who almost turns himself into a kamikaze pilot, his suicidal tactics reportedly worrying Churchill who wanted the film shelved. The fine cast is at the mercy of wonky model shots, a dreadful script and Sergei Nolbandov's static direction.

John Clements *Lt Dick Stacey* • Leslie Banks *Admiral Wetherby* • Jane Baxter *Celia Wetherby* • Ann Todd *Kay Gordon* • Basil Sydney *Captain Fairfax* • Edward Chapman *Papadopulous* • Michael Wilding *Lt Grant* ■ *Dir* Sergei Nolbandov • *Scr* Patrick Kirwan, Austin Melford, Diana Morgan, Sergei Nolbandov

Shipwrecked ★★★ U

Period adventure 1990 · US · Colour · 89mins

Norwegian director Nils Gaup is best known for the 1987 feature *Pathfinder*, which had the distinction of being the first in the Lapp language. Scandinavian cinema has an international reputation for children's films, a renown recognised by the Disney studio, who hired Gaup to make this lively action tale. There are calm waters to wade through between the swashbuckling, but Gabriel Byrne shivers the odd timber as the pirate captain and Stian Smestad impresses as the cabin boy embarking on the adventure of a lifetime. [video]

Stian Smestad *Haakon Haakonsen* • Gabriel Byrne *Lieutenant Merrick* • Louisa Haigh *Mary* • Trond Peter Stamso Munch *Jens* • Bjorn Sundquist *Mr Haakonsen* • Eva Von Hanno *Mrs Haakonsen* • Kjell Stormoen *Captain Madsen* ■ *Dir* Nils Gaup • *Scr* Nils Gaup, Bob Foss, Greg Dinner, Nick Thiel, from the novel *Haakon Haakonsen* by OV Falck-Ytter

The Shiralee ★★★

Adventure drama 1957 · UK · BW · 99mins

One of several features Ealing Studios made in Australia, *The Shiralee* stars genuine Aussie Peter Finch as a poacher who finds his wife shacked up with another man. Consequently, he leaves for a life on the road with his daughter, who becomes his shiralee – an aboriginal word for "burden". The result is a captivating double-act between Finch and the bright-as-a-button Dana Wilson as each of them realises they have a lot to learn. The location photography is incredible, though attempts to inject some humour with cameos from Sid James and Tessie O'Shea backfire.

Peter Finch *Jim Macauley* • Elizabeth Sellars *Marge Macauley* • Dana Wilson *Buster Macauley* • Rosemary Harris *Lily Parker* • Tessie O'Shea *Bella* • Sidney James *Luke* • George Rose *Donny* ■ *Dir* Leslie Norman • *Scr* Leslie Norman, Neil Paterson, from the novel by D'Arcy Niland • *Cinematographer* Paul Beeson

The Shiralee ★★★

Drama 1986 · Ausl · Colour · 120mins

The edited feature film version of the top-rated Australian television mini-series loses a few subplots but still remains an emotionally moving look at father-daughter relationships. Bryan Brown is swagman Macauley, odd-jobbing his way through forties Australia looking for permanent work, who gets landed with his daughter Buster (Rebecca Smart) when he returns to Adelaide and finds his boozy, unfaithful wife romancing the town bookie. On the road the two bond through illness, separation and the final hurdle of his wife's threat to get Buster back. High-class comfort viewing, superbly acted by the leads.

Bryan Brown *Macauley* • Noni Hazlehurst *Lily* • Rebecca Smart *Buster* • Lewis Fitz-Gerald *Tony* • Lorna Lesley *Marge* • Ned Manning *Jim* ■ *Dir* George Ogilvie • *Scr* Tony Morphett, from the novel by D'Arcy Niland

Shirley Valentine ★★★★ 15

Comedy 1989 · US/UK · Colour · 104mins

The movie that gladdened a generation of women's hearts and brought cinema stardom to Pauline Collins at an age when actresses are often resigned to sitcom suburbia. Collins's performance as the long-suffering housewife who decamps to a Greek island and Tom Conti is quite sublime and carefully crafted. The movie manages to retain the best of Willy Russell's theatrical devices (Collins talking to the kitchen wall, for instance) while opening out the action to embrace a big-screen atmosphere. The supporting cast, particularly Bernard Hill as her Neanderthal husband, is equally convincing, with only the hammy Conti striking a momentary false note. Contains swearing and brief nudity. [video]

Pauline Collins *Shirley Valentine* • Tom Conti *Costas Caldes* • Julia McKenzie *Gillian* • Alison Steadman *Jane* • Joanna Lumley *Marjorie* • Sylvia Syms *Headmistress* • Bernard Hill *Joe Bradshaw* • George Costigan *Dougie* ■ *Dir* Lewis Gilbert • *Scr* Willy Russell, from his play

Shiver of the Vampires ★★

Horror 1970 · Fr · Colour · 71mins

French director Jean Rollin is the latest eccentric personality to be lionised by exploitation genre fans. His banal poverty row output from the early seventies is now considered chic thanks to its up-front sexual content and hallucinatory visuals streaked with eerie sadism. This honeymooners-meet-hippy vampires saga verges on boredom, but nonetheless ranks as one of his better efforts from the period, occasionally throwing up the odd surreal image and macabre moment of delirium. An acquired taste. In French with English subtitles. Contains violence and nudity.

Dominique *Isolde* • Sandra Julien • Jean-Marie Durand • Nicole Nancel • Michel Delahaye ■ *Dir/Scr* Jean Rollin

Shivers ★★★★ 18
Horror   1975 · Can · Colour · 84mins

David Cronenberg's first important horror film may now look a little crude, but the obsessions that would colour his later works are already apparent. The story is centred around a vaguely futuristic apartment complex where a parasite is gradually working its way through the occupants, transforming them into sex-obsessed zombies. It's not exactly subtle, but Cronenberg delights in some stomach-churning imagery and the stark, chilling design would later be revisited in films such as *Dead Ringers* and *The Fly*. There are no big names in the cast, although horror aficionados will be pleased to see Hammer stalwart Barbara Steele. Contains swearing and violence. ▭

Paul Hampton *Roger St Luc* • Joe Silver *Rollo Linsky* • Lynn Lowry *Forsythe* • Alan Migicovsky *Nicholas Tudor* • Susan Petrie *Janine Tudor* • Barbara Steele *Betts* ■ *Dir/Scr* David Cronenberg

Shoah ★★★★★ PG
Documentary   1985 · Fr · Colour · 565mins

Claude Lanzmann spent over a decade shooting the 350 hours of interviews and location footage – he purposely did not use archive material – that were distilled into this cinematic monument to those who perished in the death camps and ghettos of the Second World War. Several decades on, the ruins of Auschwitz, Chelmno and the rest still induce revulsion, as do the remorseless recollections of the Polish peasants who remain tainted with the hatred that made the Holocaust possible. Yet this is also a testament to the survivors who refused to let their spirit be broken by the daily horrors they witnessed. Putting a face on inhuman misery, this remarkable achievement demonstrates film's unique power and its underperformed duty. In French with English subtitles.

Dir Claude Lanzmann

Shock ★★★
Thriller   1982 · Fr · Colour · 100mins

The hardships of a professional killer when he decides to retire are well known, but none more so than those suffered by Alain Delon when he decides to rest his trigger finger. His boss wants him to keep working, while Catherine Deneuve offers sympathetic compensation. A touch of the French amoralities, directed with some style by Robin Davis from a bestselling novel, it's a romantic thriller of dubious ethics but great pace. French dialogue dubbed into English.

Alain Delon *Martin Terrier* • Catherine Deneuve *Claire* • Philippe Léotard *Felix* • Etienne Chicot *Michel* • Stéphane Audran *Mme Faulques* • François Perrot *Cox* ■ *Dir* Robin Davis • *Scr* Alain Delon, Robin Davis,

Claude Veillot, Dominique Robelet, from the novel *La Position du Tireur Couché* by Jean-Patrick Manchette

Shock Corridor ★★★★ 15
Melodrama
1963 · US · BW and Colour · 95mins

The characters talk in slogans, the idea verges on the outrageous, but Sam Fuller's direction barrels us through discrepancies in this film's plot with a gut-punching style that flattens objections. Journalist Peter Breck has himself committed to a mental hospital to find a killer and discovers more than he bargained for. Pitting himself against many ideas of good taste, Fuller's film still has the stifling grip of a straitjacket. ▭

Peter Breck *Johnny Barrett* • Constance Towers *Cathy* • Gene Evans *Boden* • James Best *Stuart* • Hari Rhodes [Harry Rhodes] *Trent* • Larry Tucker *Pagliacci* • William Zuckert *Swanee* • Philip Ahn *Dr Fong* ■ *Dir* Samuel Fuller • *Scr* Samuel Fuller, from his treatment

A Shock to the System ★★★ 15
Black comedy   1990 · US · Colour · 84mins

Dulwich College public school has made a major contribution to world cinema over the years. Director Michael Powell and oft-filmed writers such as Raymond Chandler, PG Wodehouse, AEW Mason and CS Forester are all old boys, as is *The English Patient* author Michael Ondaatje. So, too, is novelist Simon Brett, but this adaptation of one of his superb tales lacks the forceful direction that turned Ondaatje's story into a multi-Oscar-winning success. Nevertheless, Michael Caine gives a terrific performance as the cold-blooded advertising executive who realises that he can get away with anything, even murder, in his ruthless climb to the top, and there are a few fair swipes at some obvious targets. Contains swearing. ▭

Michael Caine *Graham Marshall* • Elizabeth McGovern *Stella Anderson* • Peter Riegert *Robert Benham* • Swoosie Kurtz *Leslie Marshall* • Will Patton *Lieutenant Laker* • Jenny Wright *Melanie O'Connor* • Samuel L Jackson *Ulysses* ■ *Dir* Jan Egleson • *Scr* Andrew Klavan, from the novel by Simon Brett

Shock Treatment ★★
Mystery drama   1964 · US · Colour · 94mins

This mystery melodrama should not be confused with Samuel Fuller's genuinely disturbing *Shock Corridor*, made a year earlier and also about a man feigning insanity to solve a mystery. This is the unpleasant story of an actor, played by Stuart Whitman, who has himself committed to a mental hospital and undergoes electro-therapy and other ordeals while seeking a fortune hidden by Roddy McDowall's apparently crazed murderer. True to cliché, Lauren Bacall's psychiatrist proves to be nuttier than any of her patients.

Stuart Whitman *Dale Nelson* • Carol Lynley *Cynthia* • Roddy McDowall *Martin Ashly, gardener* • Lauren Bacall *Dr Edwina Beighley* • Olive Deering *Mrs Mellon* • Ossie Davis *Capshaw* • Douglass Dumbrille *Judge* ■ *Dir* Denis Sanders • *Scr* Sidney Boehm, from the novel by Winfred Van Atta

Shock Treatment ★★★
Horror   1973 · Fr/It · Colour · 90mins

A short sequence of Alain Delon and Annie Girardot frolicking stark naked gained this film a notoriety that detracted from its value as a Frankensteinian chiller. Girardot has checked into a clifftop clinic to rebuild her self-esteem after a fractured love affair. However, following a friend's death, she deduces that Delon's miraculous rejuvenation treatment consists of cells removed from the institute's ever-changing roster of Portuguese servants. With its sinister antiseptic interiors, brutal Darwinian logic, satirical undercurrent, and twist ending, Alain Jessua's third feature is a much more than mere exploitation fodder. French dialogue dubbed into English. Contains nudity.

Alain Delon *Dr Devilers* • Annie Girardot *Hélène Masson* • Michel Duchaussoy *Dr Bernard* • Robert Hirsch *Jerome Savignat* • Jean-François Calvé *Rene Gassin* ■ *Dir/Scr* Alain Jessua

Shock Treatment ★★ PG
Musical satire   1981 · UK · Colour · 91mins

Typical teenagers Brad and Janet reappear in this calamitous and now largely forgotten sequel to *The Rocky Horror Picture Show*, in which life resembles not a B-movie but a TV game show. In the small American town of Denton, everyone participates in 24-hour television in some way. The idea has potential, but once again Brad and Janet are the victims of a megalomaniac, and this time a confusing and unfunny story goes nowhere. Wonderful visuals were not enough to provide another cult hit for author Richard O'Brien. ▭

Cliff De Young *Farley Flavors/Brad Majors* • Jessica Harper *Janet Majors* • Patricia Quinn *Nation McKinley* • Richard O'Brien *Cosmo McKinley* • Charles Gray *Judge Oliver Wright* • Nell Campbell *Nurse Ansalong* • Ruby Wax *Betty Hapschatt* • Barry Humphries *Bert Schnick* • Rik Mayall *''Rest Home'' Ricky* ■ *Dir* Jim Sharman • *Scr* Richard O'Brien, Jim Sharman, Brian Thomson • *Music/Lyrics* Richard O'Brien

Shock Waves ★★★ 15
Horror drama   1975 · US · Colour · 84mins

Survivors of a shipwreck are washed up on a tropical island where fugitive Gestapo officer Peter Cushing is busy re-animating drowned Nazi soldiers to form a zombie army. Relying more on atmosphere and tension than gore or jolts, Ken Wiederhorn's directorial debut is a genuinely eerie cult favourite featuring a fine performance from Cushing as evil personified. The sub-aqueous undead marching along the ocean floor in jackboots is one of the creepiest sequences in this Florida-shot independent, which also stars John Carradine, the king of B-movie horror, as the doomed sea captain. A surprisingly effective shocker that's well worth a look. ▭

Peter Cushing *Scar, SS Commander* • John Carradine *Captain Ben* • Brooke Adams *Rose* • Fred Buch *Chuck* • Jack Davidson *Norman* • Luke Halpin *Keith* • DJ Sidney *Beverly* • Don Stout *Dobbs* ■ *Dir* Ken Wiederhorn • *Scr* John Harrison, Ken Wiederhorn

Shocker ★ 18
Horror thriller 1989 · US · Colour · 104mins

This dud from Wes Craven charts the murderous exploits of an electrocuted maniac TV repair man who can appear wherever someone switches on a set. Sci-fi TV fans will recognise the television bogeyman Horace Pinker as Mitch Pileggi, who went on to play Director Skinner in *The X Files*. Confusing and tedious, it's a shame such a neat concept was wasted by Craven in his worst movie. ▭

Michael Murphy *Lt Don Parker* • Peter Berg *Jonathan Parker* • Mitch Pileggi *Horace Pinker* • Cami Cooper [Camille Cooper] *Alison* • Heather Langenkamp *Victim* • Richard Brooks *Rhino* • John Tesh *TV newscaster* ■ *Dir/Scr* Wes Craven

The Shocking Miss Pilgrim ★★★ U
Musical   1947 · US · Colour · 84mins

This was a rare box-office dud in Betty Grable's series of hit movies for 20th Century-Fox. Today, though, this looks like courageous casting on Fox's part, with Grable as a feisty suffragette in strait-laced 19th-century Boston, and there's a Gershwin brothers score to enjoy as well. Particularly pleasing is co-star Dick Haymes, whose mastery of the romantic ballad does not prevent him having fun with Grable during the up-tempo numbers. Despite all that, a horde of disgruntled fans wrote in pleading for Grable to get back to the garish flicks that made her name.

Betty Grable *Cynthia Pilgrim* • Dick Haymes *John Pritchard* • Anne Revere *Alice Pritchard* • Allyn Joslyn *Leander Woolsey* • Gene Lockhart *Saxon* • Elizabeth Patterson *Catherine Dennison* ■ *Dir* George Seaton • *Scr* George Seaton, from the story by Ernest Maas, Frederica Maas

Shockproof ★★★
Film noir   1949 · US · BW · 79mins

A deliciously tense *film noir* in which parole officer Cornel Wilde is drawn into the tangled past of ex-convict Patricia Knight. *Shockproof* comes from a period in the late forties when directors such as Douglas Sirk were honing and refining movies edited with exquisite timing and redolent of shadows and whispered asides. Unfortunately here, Sirk's initial pace and stylishness run out of steam, and the denouement can only be described as a cop-out. However, although the final destination is a disappointment, you can still luxuriate in the journey.

Cornel Wilde *Griff Marat* • Patricia Knight *Jenny Marsh* • John Baragrey *Harry Wesson* • Esther Minciotti *Mrs Marat* • Howard St John *Sam Brooks* • Russell Collins *Frederick Bauer* • Charles Bates *Tommy Marat* ■ *Dir* Douglas Sirk • *Scr* Helen Deutsch, Samuel Fuller

The Shoes of the Fisherman ★★★ U
Drama   1968 · US · Colour · 146mins

Anthony Quinn, in one of his best performances, plays a Russian priest, a political prisoner for many years, who is suddenly elected to be Pope at a time of superpower instability. Unfortunately, what was exciting stuff in Morris West's bestseller, takes itself far too seriously in the movie.

Michael Anderson's leaden direction seems more in awe of the Vatican bureaucracy when it should be inspecting it for story interest. A celebrity cast – Laurence Olivier, John Gielgud, Oskar Werner – lighten the gravitas, but to waste it in such a long slog is a cardinal sin.

Anthony Quinn *Kiril Lakota* • Laurence Olivier *Piotr Ilyich Kamenev* • Oskar Werner *Father David Telemond* • David Janssen *George Faber* • Barbara Jefford *Dr Ruth Faber* • Leo McKern *Cardinal Leone* • Vittorio De Sica *Cardinal Rinaldi* • John Gielgud *Elder Pope* ■ *Dir* Michael Anderson • *Scr* John Patrick, James Kennaway, from the novel by Morris L West

Shoeshine ★★★★★
Drama 1946 · It · BW · 91mins
The recipient of the first best foreign film Oscar (albeit honorary), Vittorio De Sica's unblinking (and, at the time, controversial) portrait of postwar Italian society has none of the sentimentality that would coat his other neorealist classics, *Bicycle Thieves* and *Umberto D*. Co-scripted by the movement's co-founder, Cesare Zavattini, the fall from innocence of street scamps Rinaldo Smordoni and Franco Interlenghi is clearly allegorical. But, even bearing in mind the prominence of their longed-for white horse, the symbolism is as unforced as the performances. In Italian with English subtitles.

Rinaldo Smordoni *Giuseppe* • Franco Interlenghi *Pasquale* • Aniello Mele *Raffaele* • Bruno Ortensi *Arcangeli* • Pacifico Astrologo *Vittorio* ■ *Dir* Vittorio De Sica • *Scr* Cesare Zavattini, Sergio Amidei, Adolfo Franci, Cesare Giulio Viola, Vittorio De Sica

Shogun ★★ 15
Period drama 1980 · US · Colour · 118mins
As you battle through this tedious adaptation of James Clavell's blockbuster novel, be thankful you have been spared the marathon that was the original miniseries. That enough material for another three features has gone AWOL should alert you to the fact that what remains is so packed with unexplained characters and implausible events that it is virtually impossible to decipher what's going on. Unaware that most of his performance was destined for the cutting-room floor, but only too aware that Toshiro Mifune is acting him off the screen, Richard Chamberlain is wildly OTT as the English sailor washed up in 17th-century Japan.

Richard Chamberlain *Pilot Major John Blackthorne* • Toshiro Mifune *Lord Toranaga* • Yoko Shimada *Lady Toda Buntaro Mariko* • Frankie Sakai *Kasigi Yabu* • Alan Badel *Father Dell'Aqua* • Michael Hordern *Friar Domingo* ■ *Dir* Jerry London • *Scr* Eric Bercovici, from the novel by James Clavell

Shogun Warrior ★★★
Historical action adventure
1991 · Jap · Colour · 90mins
Boasting a fine cast and some rousing action, it's hard to see why this period adventure went straight to video in America. Sho Kosugi (best known for the *Enter the Ninja* movies) stars as a 17th-century samurai who leaves behind the ravages of a Japanese civil war only to find himself plunged into a rebellion against the Spanish king

(Christopher Lee). With more traitors, rebels, pirates and princesses than Errol Flynn encountered in his entire career, this is swashbuckling entertainment, martial-arts style. Contains swearing and nudity.

Sho Kosugi *Mayeda* • David Essex *Don Pedro* • Kane Kosugi *Yorimune* • Christopher Lee *King Philip* • Polly Walker *Cecilia* • Norman Lloyd *Father Vasco* • Ronald Pickup *Captain Crawford* • John Rhys-Davies *El Zaidan* • Toshiro Mifune *Lord Akugawa Leyasu* ■ *Dir* Gordon Hessler • *Scr* Nelson Gidding, from the story by Nelson Gidding, Sho Kosugi

Sholay ★★★ 15
Adventure 1975 · Ind · Colour · 155mins
In making what is considered to be a classic of Indian cinema, director Ramesh Sippy combined elements of Bollywood music, comedy and romance with the spaghetti western genre, creating a technically lauded, as well as massively popular, adventure movie. Told as a couple of extended flashbacks which lead to an all-action finale, the story concerns the rivalry between Amjad Khan's fabled bandit and Sanjeev Kumar, a courageous former policeman, who hires adventurers Amitabh Bachchan and Dharmendra to avenge his murdered family. The performances are impressive, especially that of Khan. In Hindi with English subtitles.

Sanjeev Kumar *Thakur Baldev Singh* • Dharmendra *Veeru* • Amitabh Bachchan *Jaidev* • Amjad Khan *Gabbar Singh* ■ *Dir* Ramesh Sippy • *Scr* Salim-Javed, from his story

Shoot ★
Action drama 1976 · Can · Colour · 92mins
Cliff Robertson, Henry Silva and Ernest Borgnine find themselves deep in *Deliverance* territory in this little-known Canadian movie. It starts well as they go into the woods to hunt and find themselves in a shoot-out with a group of hostile hunters. The rest of the movie focuses on their complex, deadly and increasingly improbable plans to wreak revenge on the attackers. Things pick up towards the end, but it's too little and too late.

Cliff Robertson *Major Rex Jeanette* • Ernest Borgnine *Lou* • Henry Silva *Zeke Springer* • James Blendick *Pete* • Larry Reynolds *Bob* • Les Carlson *Jim* • Helen Shaver *Paula* ■ *Dir* Harvey Hart • *Scr* Dick Berg, from the novel by Douglas Fairbairn

Shoot First: a Cop's Vengeance ★★
Police drama 1991 · US · Colour · 97mins
The fine line between cop and criminal forms the basis of this story of a pair of partnered police rookies fighting growing crime in San Antonio, Texas. While one follows the straight-and-narrow path, the other goes off the deep end and becomes a vigilante. Though robbed of any real suspense due to the film's revelation as to which officer is honest and which is not, the well-defined characters and earnest intensity of actors Dale Midkiff and Alex McArthur make up for most of its deficiencies. Beyond that, this remains a rousing action-filled saga that, for the most part, hits its target.

Alex McArthur *Stephen Smith* • Dale Midkiff *Farrell Tucker* • Loryn Locklin *Lea Smith* •

Lucinda Jenney *Beth Tucker* • GD Spradlin *Chief Hogan* • Terry O'Quinn *Sergeant Nicholas* ■ *Dir* Mel Damski • *Scr* Garry Michael White, Joseph Gunn

Shoot Out ★★
Western 1971 · US · Colour · 94mins
Henry Hathaway, fresh from directing John Wayne's Oscar-winning performance in *True Grit*, returned to the Rocky Mountains with Gregory Peck for this disappointing revenge western. Peck plays the ''good'' bad guy, a bank robber who comes out of jail swearing vengeance on the members of the gang who betrayed him. Chief target is Robert F Lyons as an unhinged gunman, but there's also love interest in the shape of Pat Quinn. The violence is of the fashionable, post-*Wild Bunch* school, with all the blood but none of the resonance. As for Peck, this film sadly shows how far he'd fallen by the end of the sixties. Contains swearing.

Gregory Peck *Clay Lomax* • Pat Quinn *Juliana Farrell* • Robert F Lyons *Bobby Jay* • Susan Tyrrell *Alma* • Jeff Corey *Trooper* • James Gregory *Sam Foley* • Rita Gam *Emma* • Dawn Lyn *Decky* • Pepe Serna *Pepe* ■ *Dir* Henry Hathaway • *Scr* Marguerite Roberts, from the book *The Lone Cowboy* by Will James

Shoot-Out at Medicine Bend ★★★ U
Western 1957 · US · BW · 86mins
A standard Randolph Scott revenge western is given a fresh suit of clothes as three ex-soldiers dress up and talk like Quakers to bring about the downfall of James Craig's ruthless town boss. Scott leads the trio and James Garner, working his way toward stardom, plays one of Randy's two sidekicks in his usual ingratiating manner. On the other hand, Angie Dickinson can do little with the undemanding role of Scott's gal.

Randolph Scott *Cap Devlin* • James Craig *Clark* • Angie Dickinson *Priscilla* • Dani Crayne *Nell* • James Garner *Maitland* ■ *Dir* Richard L Bare • *Scr* John Tucker Battle, DD Beauchamp

Shoot the Moon ★★★★ 15
Drama 1982 · US · Colour · 118mins
In this alarming story of marital collapse, Albert Finney – demonstrating what accomplished screen acting credentials he has – plays a writer parting from housebound wife Diane Keaton and their four children. Creating a character more sympathetic than you'd expect, you can almost hear the ticking timebomb of his enraged personality and, although the photography does Keaton no favours, she subdues the quirkiness of her Woody Allen pictures. One of Alan Parker's most interesting essays in intimate drama, it has an an uneven, but literate, script by Bo Goldman.

Albert Finney *George Dunlap* • Diane Keaton *Faith Dunlap* • Peter Weller *Frank Henderson* • Karen Allen *Sandy* • Dana Hill *Sherry* • Viveka Davis *Jill* • Tracey Gold *Marianne* ■ *Dir* Alan Parker • *Scr* Bo Goldman

Shoot the Pianist ★★★★★ 15
Crime drama 1960 · Fr · BW · 77mins
Coming between *The 400 Blows* and *Jules et Jim*, this is François Truffaut's

forgotten masterpiece. Adapted from David Goodis's pulp novel *Down There*, its a knowing homage to Hollywood *films noirs*, with Charles Aznavour excelling as the pianist whose descent from the classical stage to a seedy Parisian bar culminates in his involvement with some unforgiving gangsters. A grab bag of fond memories, both cinematic and personal, this is Truffaut at his most exuberant, with the stylistic flourishes of the *nouvelle vague* enhancing the romantic melancholy of this tragi-comic tale. Endlessly inventive and bustling with life, it will restore your faith in film. In French with English subtitles. Contains violence, swearing and brief nudity.

Charles Aznavour *Charlie Kohler/Edouard Saroyan* • Marie Dubois *Léna* • Nicole Berger *Thérésa* • Michèle Mercier *Clarisse* • Albert Rémy *Chico Saroyan* • Jacques Aslanian *Richard Saroyan* • Richard Kanayan *Fido Saroyan* ■ *Dir* François Truffaut • *Scr* François Truffaut, Marcel Moussy, from the novel *Down There* by David Goodis • *Cinematographer* Raoul Coutard

Shootdown ★★★ PG
Drama based on a true story
1988 · US · Colour · 93mins
Very often, TV movies based on true stories have a lazy or hysterical grab at the facts and nosedive towards blandness in the process. Here the usual A to Z of what happened is saved by the majesty of Angela Lansbury, whose TV stardom in recent years has tended to obscure her versatility. As the mother of a victim in the Korean Air Lines disaster of 1983, she brings sensitivity, determination, anxiety and outrage to her role, and convincingly portrays the human tragedy behind the event.

Angela Lansbury *Nan Moore* • George Coe *David* • Kyle Secor *John* • Molly Hagan *Elizabeth* • Jennifer Savidge *Mary* • Diana Bellamy *Lillian* ■ *Dir* Michael Pressman • *Scr* Judy Merl, Paul Eric Myers

The Shooter ★★ 18
Thriller
1994 · US/UK/Sp/Cz Rep · Colour · 100mins
The unmistakeable whiff of a Euro-pudding hangs over this fairly dim addition to the Dolph Lundgren canon. Playing a US marshal – he wouldn't last two minutes with Tommy Lee Jones – Lundgren finds himself mixed up in all sorts of international intrigue when he hunts for a glamorous hit woman (Maruschka Detmers) at a major Cuban/American summit in Prague. Director Ted Kotcheff handles the set pieces with skill, but the film fails because of the needlessly complicated plotting. Contains swearing and violence.

Dolph Lundgren *Michael Dane* • Maruschka Detmers *Simone Rosset* • Assumpta Serna *Marta* • John Ashton *Alex Reed* • Gavan O'Herlihy *Dick Powell* ■ *Dir* Ted Kotcheff • *Scr* Billy Ray, Meg Thayer, from a story by Yves Andre Martin

The Shooting ★★★ PG
Western 1967 · US · Colour · 71mins
A weird, legendary western whose existentialism and minimalism is as much the result of having no budget as the philosophical inclinations of its

director, Monte Hellman, and its star, Jack Nicholson. Shot in the empty deserts of Utah, it has Nicholson as a grinning hired killer involved with bounty hunters and a mysterious woman in a journey into the real or imaginary past. It's like Dali made a western, or *Treasure of Sierra Madre* set in Marienbad, a puzzle picture that's either intentionally metaphorical or just ineptly made. Hellman and Nicholson made a second western, *Ride in the Whirlwind*, on the same location trip. ▭

Jack Nicholson *Billy Spear* • Millie Perkins *Woman* • Warren Oates *Willett Gashade* • Will Hutchins *Coley* • BJ Merholz *Leland Drum* ■ *Dir* Monte Hellman • *Scr* Adrien Joyce [Carole Eastman]

Shooting Fish ★★★ 12
Romantic comedy
1997 · UK · Colour · 107mins

Director Stefan Schwartz's daft, yet endearing romantic comedy sees two friends – American Dan Futterman and British Stuart Townsend – trying to pull off a series of money-making scams. From selling bogus voice-recognition computers to nonexistent loft insulation, the boys are doing well until mutual love interest Kate Beckinsale sets them at odds. This is an Ealing comedy style caper in a contemporary setting with both a high cute factor and some imaginative gags. But it overstays its welcome and succumbs to a schmaltzy conclusion. ▭

Dan Futterman *Dylan* • Stuart Townsend *Jez* • Kate Beckinsale *Georgie* • Nickolas Grace *Mr Stratton-Luce* • Claire Cox *Floss* • Ralph Ineson *Mr Ray* • Dominic Mafham *Roger* • Peter Capaldi *Mr Gilzean* • Annette Crosbie *Mrs Cummins* ■ *Dir* Stefan Schwartz • *Scr* Stefan Schwartz, Richard Holmes

The Shooting Party
★★★★ 15
Drama
1984 · UK · Colour · 92mins

On target with regard to upper-class attitudes just prior to the First World War, James Mason's penultimate feature film casts him as Sir Randolph Nettleby, the aristocratic organiser of a weekend shoot at his country mansion, where class exploitation and numerous infidelities are also on the menu. Similar to Renoir's *La Règle du Jeu* in its theme of a disintegrating social order, it has a cast to die for in Edward Fox, John Gielgud and Gordon Jackson, among others. Connoisseurs of British television drama may have seen it all before, but this still has acting class in abundance. ▭

James Mason *Sir Randolph Nettleby* • Edward Fox *Lord Gilbert Hartlip* • Dorothy Tutin *Lady Minnie Nettleby* • John Gielgud *Cornelius Cardew* • Gordon Jackson *Tom Harker* • Cheryl Campbell *Lady Aline Hartlip* • Robert Hardy *Lord Bob Lilburn* • Rupert Frazer *Lionel Stephens* • Judi Bowker *Lady Olivier Lilburn* ■ *Dir* Alan Bridges • *Scr* Julian Bond, from the novel by Isabel Colegate

Shooting the Moon ★★★★
Drama
1998 · It · Colour · 90mins

Rome emerges as a soulless city in Francesca Archibugi's unflinching yet warm-hearted study of brotherly love and innocent determination. Furthering a tradition of juvenile excellence dating

back to *Bicycle Thieves*, Niccolo Senni carries the film as the teenage son of heroin-addict Valeria Golina, who so distrusts the adults around him that when his half-sister accidentally pricks herself on one of their mother's needles, he assumes the responsibility of having her Aids-tested. Francesca di Giovanni is also impressively natural as his toddling co-star, which speaks volumes for Archibugi's unforced yet eminently sympathetic direction. An Italian language film.

Valeria Golino *Silvia* • Sergio Rubini *Massimo* • Stefano Dionisi *Roberto* • Niccolo Senni *Siddharta* • Francesca di Giovanni *Domitilla* ■ *Dir/Scr* Francesca Archibugi

The Shootist ★★★★ PG
Western
1976 · US · Colour · 94mins

John Wayne's last movie, with the Duke playing a retired gunfighter stricken with cancer, turned out to be a fitting tribute to a great talent. *Dirty Harry* director Don Siegel was not a man to dwell on the maudlin, however, and this fine western plays like a *Shane* for the seventies. Director Ron Howard appears as the wide-eyed innocent to Wayne's Alan Ladd, and the supporting cast (James Stewart, Lauren Bacall and, especially, the under-used Hugh O'Brian as the Duke's nemesis) is superb. The opening titles form a touching montage to an outstanding career; how often does a star of Wayne's magnitude leave the stage with such dignity? ▭

John Wayne *John Bernard Books* • Lauren Bacall *Bond Rogers* • James Stewart *Dr Hostetler* • Ron Howard *Gillom Rogers* • Richard Boone *Sweeney* • Hugh O'Brian *Pulford* • Bill McKinney *Cobb* • Harry Morgan *Marshall Thibido* ■ *Dir* Don Siegel • *Scr* Miles Hood Swarthout, Scott Hale, from the novel by Glendon Swarthout

The Shop around the Corner
★★★★ U
Romantic drama
1940 · US · BW · 98mins

Based on Nikolaus Laszlo's play *Parfumerie*, this is a truly wonderful film, deftly directed by the great Ernst Lubitsch and containing a delightful performance by Margaret Sullavan, full of grace and warmth. The plot, about pen pals who fall in love after realising they work together, is paper-thin, but charm is there in abundance, and the young James Stewart is a portrait in perfection.

James Stewart *Alfred Kralik* • Margaret Sullavan *Klara Novak* • Frank Morgan *Hugo Matuschek* • Joseph Schildkraut *Ferencz Vadas* • Sara Haden *Flora* • Felix Bressart *Pirovitch* • William Tracy *Pepi Katona* • Inez Courtney *Ilona* ■ *Dir* Ernst Lubitsch • *Scr* Samson Raphaelson, from the play *Parfumerie* by Nikolaus Laszlo

The Shop at Sly Corner ★★
Crime drama
1948 · UK · BW · 94mins

Retitled *Code of Scotland Yard* in the States, this reworking of Edward Percy's hit play is a splendid showcase for that master of malevolence Oscar Homolka. With an accent thicker than his eyebrows, he is suitably shifty as an antiques dealer who not only trades in stolen goods but is also a fugitive from Devil's Island. However, he is occasionally in serious danger of

having the picture filched from under his nose by Kenneth Griffith, who is revoltingly effective as a blackmailing assistant who threatens to ruin the musical career of Homolka's daughter.

Oscar Homolka *Descius Heiss* • Derek Farr *Robert Graham* • Muriel Pavlow *Margaret Heiss* • Kenneth Griffith *Archie Fellowes* • Manning Whiley *Corder Morris* • Kathleen Harrison *Mrs Catt* • Garry Marsh *Major Elliot* ■ *Dir* George King • *Scr* Katherine Strueby, from a play by Edward Percy

The Shop on the High Street ★★★★ 15
Second World War drama
1965 · Cz · BW · 119mins

Winner of the 1965 Oscar for best foreign film, Czech writer/director Jan Kadar's intimate portrait of two simple people destroyed by the Nazi occupation is exquisitely sensitive, brilliantly played and utterly heartbreaking. Ida Kaminska gives a miraculous performance as an old Jewish woman who owns a little button shop where a humble carpenter (a superb Jozef Kroner) is appointed "Aryan comptroller" by the occupiers. He discovers that Kaminska's stock of buttons is depleted almost to nothing, and that she's totally deaf and quite unaware of the war. His growing affection for her leads Kroner into muddled efforts to protect her, with tragic results for both of them. In Czech with English subtitles. ▭

Ida Kaminska *Rozalie Lautmannova* • Jozef Kroner *Tono Brtko* • Frantisek Zvarik *Markus Kolkocky* • Hana Slivkova *Evelyna Brtkova* ■ *Dir* Jan Kadar, Elmar Klos • *Scr* Jan Kadár, Elmar Klos

Shopping ★★★ 18
Drama
1993 · UK · Colour · 102mins

Paul Anderson's first feature is a slick, superficial exercise which doesn't quite reach the heights of the Hollywood blockbusters to which he aspires, but is a riveting ride nevertheless. Jude Law is the adrenalin freak who, along with Sadie Frost, gets his kicks by joyriding and ram raiding. However, his nihilistic lifestyle is threatened both by the forces of law and order and rival rider Sean Pertwee, who views Law's hobby as a profession. The two leads are unconvincing, but Pertwee excels as a villain and there is a solid turn from Jonathan Pryce as a sympathetic policeman. Contains violence and swearing. ▭

Sadie Frost *Jo* • Jude Law *Billy* • Sean Pertwee *Tommy* • Fraser James *Be Bop* • Sean Bean *Venning* • Marianne Faithfull *Bev* • Jonathan Pryce *Conway* • Danny Newman *Monkey* ■ *Dir/Scr* Paul Anderson

Shopworn ★★
Melodrama
1932 · US · BW · 68mins

The plot is as shopworn as Barbara Stanwyck's notorious showgirl in this perfunctory melodrama which the actress aptly described as "one of those terrible pictures they sandwiched in when you started". She starts out as a waitress loved by a college student. Framed on morals charges by his wealthy, disapproving mother, she is sent to reform school. Heavy censorship trimmed the details of her subsequent rise in show business via

rich "admirers", leaving some obvious gaps and loose ends. Stanwyck's terrific performance makes it enjoyable but she's ill-served by the miscasting of Regis Toomey as her great love.

Barbara Stanwyck *Kitty Lane* • Regis Toomey *Dave Livingston* • ZaSu Pitts *Dot* • Lucien Littlefield *Fred* ■ *Dir* Nicholas Grinde [Nick Grinde] • *Scr* Jo Swerling, Robert Riskin, from a story by Sarah Y Mason

The Shopworn Angel ★★★
Silent romantic drama
1928 · US · BW · 82mins

An innocent young Texan (Gary Cooper), about to be shipped off to France with the army, meets a showgirl (Nancy Carroll) when she knocks him down (not seriously) with her car. To the displeasure of her wealthy lover (Paul Lukas), she befriends the young man, who falls passionately in love with her, causing all sorts of problems with Lukas. A superior romantic drama, directed by Richard Wallace and attractively cast and played, this is still worth watching, though it's now understandably superceded by the better-known 1938 remake. The coming of sound allowed Carroll to burst effectively into song at the end of this silent version.

Nancy Carroll *Daisy Heath* • Gary Cooper *William Tyler* • Paul Lukas *Bailey* • Emmett King *The chaplain* • Mildred Washington *Daisy's maid* • Roscoe Karns *Dance director* ■ *Dir* Richard Wallace • *Scr* Howard Estabrook, Albert Shelby Le Vino, Tom Miranda (titles), from the story *Private Pettigrew's Girl* by Dana Burnet

The Shopworn Angel ★★★★★
Wartime romantic drama
1938 · US · BW · 85mins

Benefiting from sound, technical advance and dream casting, this triumphantly successful remake offers the always magical pairing of James Stewart and Margaret Sullavan. With his youthful, gawky attractiveness, Stewart is perfect as the naive and idealistic cowboy in love, while Sullavan is exemplary as the self-centred, kept showgirl whose hard-boiled exterior hides a soft heart buried by life's knocks. Other than one key plot adjustment, and a change of emphasis in making Sullavan's lover (Walter Pidgeon) sympathetic rather than threatening, the film stays close to the original. The stars are marvellous in their scenes together, resolutely unsentimental and extracting every shred of truth from the tale.

Margaret Sullavan *Daisy Heath* • James Stewart *Bill Pettigrew* • Walter Pidgeon *Sam Bailey* • Nat Pendleton *Dice* • Hattie McDaniel *Martha the maid* • Charley Grapewin *Wilson the caretaker* • Charles D Brown *Mr Gonigle the stage manager* ■ *Dir* HC Potter • *Scr* Waldo Salt, from the short story *Pettigrew's Girl* by Dana Burnet

Short Circuit ★★★ PG
Fantasy comedy
1986 · US · Colour · 94mins

A government robot gets struck by lightning, goes AWOL, takes on hilarious human characteristics and befriends vegetarian animal lover Ally Sheedy. Goofy inventor Steve Guttenberg must locate his missing Number Five model. Cue madcap misadventures, during which our cute

cyborg mimics John Wayne, the Three Stooges and John Travolta. Youngsters will especially love this hip spoof on hardware movies, neatly directed with the lightest of touches by John Badham. Others may find Number Five's incessant whine of ''Stephanie'' a little grating and start reaching for a handy screwdriver. Contains some swearing. 🖭

Ally Sheedy *Stephanie Speck* • Steve Guttenberg *Newton Crosby* • Fisher Stevens *Ben Jabituya* • Austin Pendleton *Howard Marner* • GW Bailey *Skroeder* • Brian McNamara *Frank* • Tim Blaney *Number Five* ■ *Dir* John Badham • *Scr* SS Wilson, Brent Maddock

Short Circuit 2 ★★ PG

Fantasy comedy 1988 · US · Colour · 105mins

Yet another attempt to humanise technology, this sequel about the former military robot Number Five, now Johnny Five, has several moments of humour (becoming involved with a bank robbery, for example), but too many minutes of tedium as it wonders whether to be social satire or pratfall parody. Fisher Stevens returns as the Indian co-inventor of the robot, and again his clichéd character is infuriating, representing the kind of prejudice Johnny Five is supposed to be against. Contains swearing. 🖭

Fisher Stevens *Ben Jahrvi* • Michael McKean *Fred Ritter* • Cynthia Gibb *Sandy Banatoni* • Jack Weston *Oscar Baldwin* • Dee McCafferty *Saunders* • David Hemblen *Jones* • Don Lake *Manic Mike* ■ *Dir* Kenneth Johnson • *Scr* SS Wilson, Brent Maddock

Short Cut to Hell ★

Crime drama 1957 · US · BW · 89mins

Look in vain for any sign of the vitality you'd expect from the directing debut of James Cagney. He himself appears only in a very brief prologue to introduce two newcomers, Robert Ivers and Georgann Johnson, as the stars of this updated remake of *This Gun for Hire*. In 1942 it did wonders for the careers of Alan Ladd and Veronica Lake, but not here.

Robert Ivers *Kyle* • William Bishop *Stan* • Georgann Johnson *Glory Hamilton* • Jacques Aubuchon *Bahrwell* • Peter Baldwin *Adams* • Yvette Vickers *Daisy* • Murvyn Vye *Nichols* ■ *Dir* James Cagney • *Scr* Ted Berkman, Raphael Blau, from the film *This Gun for Hire* by Albert Maltz, WR Burnett, from the novel *A Gun for Sale* by Graham Greene

Short Cuts ★★★★★ 18

Episodic drama 1993 · US · Colour · 187mins

Admirers of Raymond Carver, whose stories inspired *Short Cuts*, were less than impressed by Robert Altman's reworking and interweaving of his tales into this tapestry of southern Californian mores. But, for those less wedded to or ignorant of the originals, this is a superbly controlled piece of film-making that invites comparison with Altman's own *Nashville*. The only discordant note is provided by the sole non-Carver story, involving jazz singer Annie Ross and her daughter Lori Singer. The rest, however, are engaging in their own right and spellbinding when taken as a whole. Lily Tomlin, Tim Robbins, Jennifer Jason Leigh and Andie MacDowell stand out in a brilliant cast, but the real star is Altman. Contains violence, swearing, sex scenes and nudity. 🖭

Andie MacDowell *Ann Finnigan* • Bruce Davison *Howard Finnigan* • Jack Lemmon *Paul Finnigan* • Julianne Moore *Marian Wyman* • Matthew Modine *Dr Ralph Wyman* • Anne Archer *Claire Kane* • Fred Ward *Stuart Kane* • Jennifer Jason Leigh *Lois Kaiser* • Christopher Penn *Jerry Kaiser* • Robert Downey Jr *Bill Bush* • Madeleine Stowe *Sherri Shepard* • Tim Robbins *Gene Shepard* • Lily Tomlin *Doreen Piggot* • Tom Waits *Earl Piggot* • Peter Gallagher *Stormy Weathers* • Frances McDormand *Betty Weathers* • Annie Ross *Tess Trainer* • Lori Singer *Zoe Trainer* ■ *Dir* Robert Altman • *Scr* Robert Altman, Frank Barhydt, from stories by Raymond Carver

A Short Film about Killing ★★★★★ 18

Crime drama 1988 · Pol · Colour · 84mins

Krzysztof Kieslowski, who was arguably Poland's greatest contemporary director, made a series of television films about the Ten Commandments called *Dekalog*. This harrowing full-length entry in the series won the Special Jury Prize at Cannes. Powerful precisely because of its subdued, matter-of-fact approach, this judgement on murder (be it illegal or state-sanctioned) concerns a youth who kills a cab driver and must face the consequences. The late Kieslowski was a true master of narrative construction, and many of his thoughtful compositions linger long in the memory. In Polish with English subtitles.

Miroslaw Baka *Yatzek* • Krzysztof Globisz *Lawyer* • Jan Tesarz *Taxi driver* ■ *Dir* Krzysztof Kieslowski • *Scr* Krzysztof Kieslowski, Krzysztof Piesiewicz

A Short Film about Love ★★★ 15

Drama 1988 · Pol · Colour · 83mins

From its bitingly ironic title to its downbeat conclusion, this is one of the most damning pictures of modern city life ever made. Expanding on the seventh part of the *Dekalog* series he made for TV, director Krzysztof Kieslowski revisits the themes of obsession and voyeurism touched on by Alfred Hitchcock in *Rear Window* and Michael Powell in *Peeping Tom*. But his main preoccupation here is with the impossibility of love and the breakdown of community. It's impressive and provocative film-making, but ultimately the dispassion and the pessimism may render you little more than a detached observer. In Polish with English subtitles. Contains sex scenes and nudity. 🖭

Grazyna Szapolowska *Magda* • Olaf Lubaszenko *Tomek* • Stefania Iwinska *Gospodyni* • Piotr Machalica *Roman* • Artur Barcis *Mlody Mezczyzna* ■ *Dir* Krzysztof Kieslowski • *Scr* Krzysztof Kieslowski, Krzysztof Piesiewicz

Short Time ★★★ 15

Comedy drama 1990 · US · Colour · 93mins

A rare leading role for that accomplished comedy actor Dabney Coleman. He plays a cop on the verge of retirement who discovers that not only is he dying, but that the insurers will pay out only if he dies in the line of duty. To the astonishment of partner Matt Frewer, Coleman is then transformed into the craziest risk-taking policeman since Mel Gibson. It's an intriguing concept and Coleman milks it for all it is worth, but director Gregg Champion doesn't look entirely comfortable juggling the action and comedy. The talented supporting players include Teri Garr, Joe Pantoliano and Barry Corbin. Contains violence and swearing. 🖭 **DVD**

Dabney Coleman *Burt Simpson* • Matt Frewer *Ernie Dills* • Teri Garr *Carolyn Simpson* • Barry Corbin *Captain* • Joe Pantoliano *Scalese* • Xander Berkeley *Stark* ■ *Dir* Gregg Champion • *Scr* John Blumenthal, Michael Berry

The Shot ★★ 15

Satirical comedy 1996 · US · Colour · 84mins

A little seen but enthusiastic satire on Hollywood, notable mainly for a cameo appearance by Dana Carvey. Yet it is another actor from *Wayne's World*, Dan Bell, who stars here, as well as serving as writer/director. Bell plays a jobless actor who hits upon an insane scheme to hold a blockbuster film to ransom. Unfortunately, no one wants to play ball. Despite sterling support from the likes of Ted Raimi, a regular in the TV series *Xena, Warrior Princess*, it lacks the satirical precision of similarly themed major-league films such as *The Player* and *The Big Picture*. Contains violence and swearing. 🖭

Dan Bell *Dern Reel* • Michael Rivkin *Patrick St Patrick* • Ted Raimi *Detective Corelli* • Michael DeLuise *Bob Mann* • Jude Horowitz *Anna* • Vincent Ward *Smith* • Mo Gaffney *Sheila Ricks* • Dana Carvey ■ *Dir* Dan Bell • *Scr* Dan Bell, from his play

A Shot in the Dark ★

Mystery 1933 · UK · BW · 53mins

A typically mediocre British ''quota quickie'' thriller full of unlikely coincidences and false clues. A Bromley Davenport plays an aged recluse, always fearful of being murdered, who apparently commits suicide. OB Clarence, as the local clergyman, suspects foul play and uses the gathering of the family for the reading of the will to get at the truth. This mystery takes less than an hour to unspool, but is so sluggish it feels much longer.

Dorothy Boyd *Alaris Browne* • OB Clarence *Rev John Malcolm* • Jack Hawkins *Norman Paul* • Russell Thorndike *Dr Stuart* • Michael Shepley *Vivian Waugh* • Davy Burnaby *Colonel Browne* • A Bromley Davenport *Colonel Browne* ■ *Dir* George Pearson • *Scr* H Fowler Mear, from a novel by Gerard Fairlie

A Shot in the Dark ★★★★ PG

Mystery farce 1964 · US · Colour · 98mins

''Give me ten men like Clouseau and I could destroy the world!'' says the inept inspector's despairing commander (Herbert Lom) when the self-righteous buffoon takes on a murder case in a millionaire's Paris apartment that houses a saucy Elke Sommer and a suave George Sanders. This was the movie in which Peter Sellers first headed the cast as Clouseau (after stealing every scene from nominal stars David Niven and Capucine in *The Pink Panther* the year before), and he mingles accents and mangles motives with his usual skill, producing some of the most hilarious moments in the series. 🖭

Peter Sellers *Inspector Jacques Clouseau* • Elke Sommer *Maria Gambrelli* • George Sanders *Benjamin Ballon* • Herbert Lom *Chief Inspector Charles Dreyfus* • Tracy Reed *Dominique Ballon* • Graham Stark *Hercule Lajoy* • Bert Kwouk *Kato* ■ *Dir* Blake Edwards • *Scr* Blake Edwards, William Peter Blatty, from the plays *A Shot in the Dark* by Harry Kurnitz and *L'Idiote* by Marcel Achard

Shotgun ★★

Western 1955 · US · Colour · 80mins

A well-cast western that was, for its time, rather brutal and violent. Yvonne De Carlo is splendidly sultry as the half-breed staked out in a snake trap by Apaches and left to die. Rescued by Sterling Hayden's deputy marshal, she tags along with him as he pursues a killer. Zachary Scott joins them as a bounty hunter after the same man. The harsh landscape is striking in Technicolor and the characters are strongly etched in a screenplay co-written by actor Rory Calhoun.

Sterling Hayden *Clay* • Yvonne De Carlo *Abby* • Zachary Scott *Reb* • Guy Prescott *Thompson* • Robert Wilke [Robert J Wilke] *Bentley* • Angela Greene *Aletha* • Paul Marion *Delgadito* • Harry Harvey Jr *Davey* ■ *Dir* Lesley Selander • *Scr* Clark E Reynolds, Rory Calhoun, John C Champion

Shoulder Arms ★★★★★ U

Silent comedy drama
1918 · US · BW · 29mins

Charles Chaplin's genius at creating comedy out of desperate situations is well illustrated in this short film. But this film also drew howls of protests, as Chaplin dares make fun of conditions for men in the trenches of the First World War. He co-stars with vermin, a sniper, flooding rain, mud and fear, proving he could laugh in the face of the most horrifying extremes.

Charles Chaplin *Recruit* • Edna Purviance *French girl* • Sydney Chaplin [Syd Chaplin] *The American sergeant/The Kaiser* • Loyal Underwood *Short German officer* ■ *Dir/Scr* Charles Chaplin

The Shout ★★★ 15

Horror drama 1978 · UK · Colour · 82mins

Robert Graves's weird story becomes a weird movie, directed by Polish émigré Jerzy Skolimowski and starring Alan Bates as the mysterious interloper who claims to have murdered his family in Australia and is the custodian of various aboriginal curses. Chief of these is the ability to shout so loudly that it can kill. John Hurt and Susannah York are among those reaching for their earplugs. Obscurity is at the heart of the matter, but there is some tension in waiting for the moment when Bates lets his larynx rip. Contains some swearing. 🖭

Alan Bates *Crossley* • Susannah York *Rachel* • John Hurt *Anthony* • Robert Stephens *Medical officer* • Tim Curry *Robert* • Julian Hough *Vicar* • Carol Drinkwater *Cobbler's wife* • Nick Stringer *Cobbler* ■ *Dir* Jerzy Skolimowski • *Scr* Jerzy Skolimowski, Michael Austin, from a story by Robert Graves

Shout ★★ 15

Drama   1991 · US · Colour · 197mins

Until his rebirth as the master of cool in *Pulp Fiction*, which proved he could do more than swivel his hips and slick back his hair, John Travolta was sunk by embarrassments such as this. He plays a music teacher at a tough school who just loves rock 'n' roll (what a surprise) and, on the run himself, reaches out naturally to rebel pupil James Walters. Lumpy direction of the first order (by *Flashdance* choreographer Jeffrey Hornaday) is enlivened by occasional, unexpected charm. Contains some swearing. ▨

John Travolta *Jack Cabe* • James Walters [Jamie Walters] *Jesse Tucker* • Heather Graham *Sara Benedict* • Richard Jordan *Eugene Benedict* • Linda Fiorentino *Molly* • Scott Coffey *Bradley* • Glenn Quinn *Alan* ■ *Dir* Jeffrey Hornaday • *Scr* Joe Gayton, from his story

Shout at the Devil ★★ 15

Action adventure
1976 · UK · Colour · 114mins

Mixing the rough (Lee Marvin) with the smooth (Roger Moore) wasn't such a good idea, even if their oddball partnership was supposed to be for king and country in the First World War. Based on a Wilbur Smith novel, the tale follows the undynamic duo as they set out to sabotage a German cruiser berthed in an East African delta. More action than you'd expect, but, as neither hero is very likeable, you really don't care. Contains swearing. ▨

Lee Marvin *Flynn* • Roger Moore *Sebastian Oldsmith* • Barbara Parkins *Rosa* • Ian Holm *Mohammed* • Rene Kolldehoff *Commissioner Fleischer* • Maurice Denham *Mr Smythe* • Jean Kent *Mrs Smythe* ■ *Dir* Peter Hunt • *Scr* Wilbur Smith, Stanley Price, Alastair Reid, from the novel by Wilbur Smith

Shout Loud, Louder... I Don't Understand ★★

Comedy   1966 · It · Colour · 100mins

Alberto Saporito (Marcello Mastroianni) is a timid chap with a vivid imagination who suffers from flights of fantasy. When he sees his neighbours commit a murder, Alberto is unsure whether this is real or another fantasy. But when the bautiful Tania (Raquel Welch) supports his story, Alberto realises they are both in very real danger. A typically wacky sixties Italian comedy with Welch, fresh from fur-bikined breakthrough in *One Million Years BC* turning in another eye-catching performance. That said, this is a bit of an odd fish, of only real interest to fans of the leads or director Eduardo De Filippo. An Italian language film.

Marcello Mastroianni *Alberto Saporito* • Raquel Welch *Tania Mottini* • Guido Alberti *Pasquale Cimmaruta* • Leopoldo Tieste *Carlo Saporito* • Tecla Scarano *Aunt Rosa Cimmaruta* • Eduardo De Filippo *Uncle Nicola* ■ *Dir* Eduardo De Filippo • *Scr* Eduardo De Filppo, Suso Cecchi D'Amico, from the play *Le Voci di Dentro* by Eduardo De Filippo

The Show ★★ 15

Music documentary
1995 · US · Colour and BW · 89mins

This adequate hip-hop documentary features talk and squawk from all the leading exponents of the musical genre, including Dr Dre, Naughty by Nature, Run-DMC, Wu-Tang Clan and Snoop Doggy Dogg. Aren't any of them just called Bob or Jeff? Billed on release as the first "rapumentary", the film could frustrate hip-hop fans by being overlong on talk, and overshort on actual hip-hopping. ▨

Dir Brian Robbins

Show Boat ★★★★ U

Musical   1936 · US · BW · 114mins

Arguably the finest creation of the Broadway musical theatre, this Jerome Kern/Oscar Hammerstein II stage masterpiece has been blessed by two equally fine talkie versions. This one is aided by a screenplay from Hammerstein himself, and by the appearances of the great bass Paul Robeson as Joe, who gets to sing *Ol' Man River*, and torch singer Helen Morgan. Irene Dunne is a fine Magnolia, strutting and cakewalking as though to the manner born, but Allan Jones is nowhere near as dashing a Gaylord Ravenal as Howard Keel in the 1951 Technicolor remake. However, there's little to choose between the versions: both are splendid and well worthy of their superb source material.

Irene Dunne *Magnolia Hawks* • Allan Jones *Gaylord Ravenal* • Charles Winninger *Captain Andy Hawks* • Helen Westley *Parthy Hawks* • Paul Robeson *Joe* • Helen Morgan *Julie* • Donald Cook *Steve* • Sammy White *Frank Schultz* • Queenie Smith *Ellie* ■ *Dir* James Whale • *Scr* Oscar Hammerstein II, from the musical by Oscar Hammerstein II, Jerome Kern, from the novel by Edna Ferber • *Art Director* Charles D Hall

Show Boat ★★★★★ U

Musical   1951 · US · Colour · 103mins

A magnificent musical achievement, and unquestionably one of the finest MGM Technicolor features, this triumph from producer Arthur Freed and director George Sidney is supremely satisfying. The cast couldn't be bettered, with Ava Gardner hitting a career high as Julie LaVerne, never more moving than in the scene where she's left on the river bank to the strains of William Warfield singing *Ol' Man River*. The show was, and is, Broadway at its peak, and here the Kern–Hammerstein score receives a definitive rendering. The plot, with its themes of miscegenation and compulsive gambling, is shamelessly adult, while the opening sequence of the show boat's arrival is a superb marriage of music, style and colour. Don't miss it. ▨

Kathryn Grayson *Magnolia Hawks* • Ava Gardner *Julie LaVerne* • Howard Keel *Gaylord Ravenal* • Joe E Brown *Captain Andy Hawks* • Marge Champion *Ellie May Shipley* • Gower Champion *Frank Schultz* • Robert Sterling *Stephen Baker* • Agnes Moorehead *Parthy Hawks* • William Warfield *Joe* ■ *Dir* George Sidney • *Scr* John Lee Mahin, George Wells, Jack McGowan, from the musical by Oscar Hammerstein II, Jerome Kern, from the novel by Edna Ferber

Show Business ★★★ U

Musical   1944 · US · BW · 92mins

After 35 years in show business, saucer-eyed comedian Eddie Cantor decided to produce a film based on his early days in vaudeville. The result was a cliché-packed musical, beginning in 1914, about the ups and downs of two contrasting couples – hoofer George Murphy and singer Constance Moore (almost broken up by vamp Nancy Kelly), and Cantor and the tiresomely madcap Joan Davis. But there are a lot of good old tunes, including *It Had To Be You*, and Cantor favourites such as *Making Whoopee*. ▨

Eddie Cantor *Eddie Martin* • Joan Davis *Joan Mason* • George Murphy *George Doane* • Nancy Kelly *Nancy Gaye* • Constance Moore *Constance Ford* • Don Douglas *Charles Lucas* ■ *Dir* Edwin L Marin • *Scr* Joseph Quillan, Dorothy Bennett, Irving Elinson, from a story by Bert Granet

The Show Goes On ★★ U

Musical   1937 · UK · BW · 94mins

Gracie Fields has the dubious distinction here of starring in a *film à clef* about her own rise to showbiz fame. As the chorus girl who becomes the darling of the music halls, Gracie shows occasional flashes of her unique Lancastrian charm. But, curiously, her regular director Basil Dean stifles her exuberance by saddling her with some woefully unsuitable material, although he could always blame Owen Nares, who plays the impresario who tries to give her highbrow appeal. The backstage details ring false, while the film has a shoddiness that would have been unthinkable in Hollywood.

Gracie Fields *Sally Scowcroft* • Owen Nares *Martin Fraser* • John Stuart *Mack* • Horace Hodges *Sam Bishop* • Edward Rigby *Mr Scowcroft* • Amy Veness *Mrs Scowcroft* ■ *Dir* Basil Dean • *Scr* Austin Melford, Anthony Kimmins, EG Valentine, from a story by Basil Dean

Show Me Love ★★★ 15

Comedy drama   1998 · Swe · Colour · 89mins

A colossal hit in its native Sweden, this charming rite of passage picture marks the feature debut of acclaimed poet and short film-maker, Lukas Moodysson. However, its treatment of alienated adolescence, provincial ennui and sexual confusion is every bit as superficial as the numerous American indies that have tackled the subject of lesbian first love. Rebecca Liljeberg's performance as the 15-year-old outsider who falls for school stunner Alexandra Dahlström brims with anti-parental resentment and repressed longing. Alas, such perspicacity is absent from the depiction of more peripheral characters, particularly the roughly caricatured boys. In Swedish with English subtitles.

Alexandra Dahlström *Elin* • Rebecca Liljeberg *Agnes* • Erica Carlson *Jessica* • Mathias Rust *Johan Hult* ■ *Dir/Scr* Lukas Moodysson

A Show of Force ★★ 15

Political thriller   1990 · US · Colour · 88mins

This movie from Brazilian director Bruno Barreto is loosely based on a supposedly true event, when some Puerto Rican student activists were shot as terrorists during an action instigated by a renegade FBI agent. Unfortunately, Barreto's film takes a potentially interesting and controversial subject and turns it into a rather tedious and violent political thriller. However, it does feature a strong cast, including Andy Garcia, Robert Duvall, Kevin Spacey and Amy Irving. ▨

Amy Irving *Kate Melendez* • Andy Garcia *Luis Angel Mora* • Robert Duvall *Howard* • Lou Diamond Phillips *Jesus Fuentes* • Kevin Spacey *Frank Curtin* • Erik Estrada *Machado* • Juan Fernandez *Captain Correa* ■ *Dir* Bruno Barreto • *Scr* Evan Jones, John Strong, from the non-fiction book *Murder under Two Flags* by Anne Nelson

The Show of Shows ★★★

Musical revue   1929 · US · BW · 128mins

An early, technically primitive forerunner of the studio star-parade revues that would remain in the repertoire over the next 15 years, filmed entirely as a stage show and compered by languid, quirky, deadpan comedian Frank Fay. Basically an experimental PR exercise, directed by John G Adolfi, to showcase Warners contract artists, it demonstrates how rapidly and radically tastes in humour, music and performing styles change. On the one hand a lengthy exercise in indescribable tedium, which only the dedicated will endure; on the other hand, a unique and fascinating social-historical document, encompassing many names from a forgotten past.

Frank Fay *Master of ceremonies/Mexican general* • William Courtenay *The Minister* • HB Warner *The Victim* • Hobart Bosworth *The Executioner* • Myrna Loy *Floradora girl/Chinese fantasy girl* • Douglas Fairbanks Jr *Ambrose* • John Barrymore *Duke of Gloucester* ■ *Dir* John G Adolfi • *Scr* Frank Fay, J Keirn Brennan

Show People ★★★★★ U

Silent comedy   1928 · US · BW · 84mins

Here's a wonderful chance to see Marion Davies, the mistress of billionaire William Randolph Hearst as well as the model for Susan Alexander in *Citizen Kane*. How Orson Welles wronged her! In truth, she was a highly intelligent comedian, here playing a young hopeful in Hollywood who graduates from Keystone Kops custard pies to a Gloria Swanson-style *femme fatale*. Hearst didn't want to entrust any old director with Marion, so chose his old friend, King Vidor, who makes an appearance in the film-within-a-film at the end. A sparkling, gentle satire.

Marion Davies *Peggy Pepper* • William Haines *Billy Boone* • Dell Henderson *Colonel Pepper* • Paul Ralli *André* • Charles Chaplin • Douglas Fairbanks • John Gilbert ■ *Dir* King Vidor • *Scr* Wanda Tuchock, Agnes Christine Johnston, Laurence Stallings, Ralph Spence

Showdown ★★★

Western   1963 · US · BW · 78mins

Baby-faced Audie Murphy and bluff Charles Drake star as escaped convicts who become involved in a robbery. There's a marvellous supporting cast of western regulars, including *The Gunfighter*'s nemesis Skip Homeier, and Strother Martin and LQ Jones, six years before *The Wild Bunch*. Director RG Springsteen tells the tale tersely and tautly, and, unusually for a Murphy western, it's in grim black and white. Ten years later the title was hijacked for a dull Rock Hudson/Dean Martin western.

U = SUITABLE FOR ALL, **Uc** = SUITABLE FOR ALL, ESPECIALLY FOR YOUNG CHILDREN (VIDEO ONLY) **PG** = PARENTAL GUIDANCE

Audie Murphy *Chris Foster* • Kathleen Crowley *Estelle* • Charles Drake *Bert Pickett* • Harold J Stone *Lavalle* • Skip Homeier *Calson* • LQ Jones *Foray* • Strother Martin *Charlie Reeder* ■ *Dir* RG Springsteen • *Scr* Bronson Howitzer

Showdown ★★ PG

Western 1973 · US · Colour · 94mins

An unremarkable western with Rock Hudson as a sheriff and Dean Martin as a train robber. Both were the closest of childhood friends until Hudson went into crime and married Martin's sweetheart, Susan Clark, who has to stand referee while these two movie stars slug it out and reach a compromise. There are times when the script scratches around for a classical allusion, though mostly it's a matter of furrowed brows, running sweat and New Mexican vistas. This was the last piece of direction by George Seaton, whose previous film had been the blockbusting *Airport.*

Dean Martin *Billy* • Rock Hudson *Chuck* • Susan Clark *Kate* • Donald Moffat *Art Williams* • John McLiam *PJ Wilson* • Charles Baca *Martinez* • Jackson D Kane *Clem* • Ben Zeller *Perry Williams* • Ed Begley Jr *Pook* ■ *Dir* George Seaton • *Scr* Theodore Taylor, from a story by Hank Fine

Showdown at Boot Hill ★★★

Western 1958 · US · BW · 71mins

Charles Bronson plays a US marshal who rides into a strange town, kills the man he has been pursuing, and is then thwarted by the local residents who regarded the deceased as a respectable citizen. Denied his bounty money, Bronson turns all moody and reflective, pondering the ethics of his line of work. Within the conventions of the B-western, this develops into a fairly complex character study, using the townspeople – the brothel keeper, the undertaker and so on – with imagination. The director, Gene Fowler Jr, is perhaps best known for trash classics like *I Was a Teenage Werewolf* and for his more mainstream work as an Oscar-nominated editor.

Charles Bronson *Luke Welsh* • Robert Hutton *Sloane* • John Carradine *Doc Weber* • Carole Mathews *Jill* • Paul Maxey *Judge* • Thomas Browne Henry *Con Maynor* • Fintan Meyler *Sally* ■ *Dir* Gene Fowler Jr • *Scr* Louis Vittes

Showdown in Little Tokyo ★★ 18

Martial arts action adventure 1991 · US · Colour · 75mins

This brainless martial arts kickabout teams Dolph Lundgren with a pre-*Crow* Brandon Lee as cops hunting down a vicious Yakuza gang operating in Los Angeles. Mark L Lester packs in enough shootouts and fights to keep undemanding fans of the genre happy, while *Wayne's World*'s Tia Carrere crops up as a singer in the gangster's nightclub. However, the best thing about this movie is the mercifully short running time.

Dolph Lundgren *Detective Chris Kenner* • Brandon Lee *Johnny Murata* • Cary-Hiroyuki Tagawa *Yoshida* • Tia Carrere *Minako Okeya* • Toshishiro Obata *Sato* • Philip Tan *Tanaka* ■ *Dir* Mark L Lester • *Scr* Stephen Glantz, Caliope Brattlestreet

Showgirls ★★ 18

Erotic drama 1995 · US · Colour · 125mins

According to director Paul Verhoeven, his controversial and much-reviled showbiz exposé is an incisive look at sleazy Las Vegas life. To almost everyone else, it was an instant camp kitsch classic charting the rise of small-town girl Elizabeth Berkley from tawdry lap dancer to famed topless revue headliner. Practically nothing works in this tacky sashay through *Valley of the Dolls* cliché and unerotic burlesque. Apart from head showgirl Gina Gershon, everyone else is miscast and the end result is nothing more than a posh sexploitation flick with tarnished good intentions. Contains nudity, swearing and some violence. *DVD*

Elizabeth Berkley *Nomi Malone* • Kyle MacLachlan *Zack Carey* • Gina Gershon *Cristal Connors* • Glenn Plummer *James Smith* • Robert Davi *Al Torres* • Alan Rachins *Tony Moss* ■ *Dir* Paul Verhoeven • *Scr* Joe Eszterhas

The Shrike ★★

Drama 1955 · US · BW · 88mins

José Ferrer made his directing debut with this record of his stage performance in Joseph Kramm's play about a Broadway director who suffers a nervous breakdown and then starts to have flashbacks in a mental hospital. Ferrer acts his socks off, as does June Allyson as his wife, an unsuccessful actress who resents her husband's success and makes sure he never gets to read his good reviews. As a depiction of Broadway's egotism and bitchery, it may be quite accurate but as an entertainment it's gloomy.

José Ferrer *Jim Downs* • June Allyson *Ann Downs* • Joy Page *Charlotte Moore* • Kendall Clark *Dr Bellman* • Isabel Bonner *Dr Barrow* • Jay Barney *Dr Kramer* • Edward Platt *Harry Downs* ■ *Dir* José Ferrer • *Scr* Ketti Frings, from the play by Joseph Kramm

The Shrimp on the Barbie ★★

Comedy 1990 · NZ/US · Colour · 87mins

Crocodile Dundee made Down Under flavour of the month for a while and this co-production planned to cash in on the craze. The film mirrored the Paul Hogan smash hit by having a fish-out-of-water type thrown together with his perceived opposite. Rich heiress Alex (Samms) is going out with a chunky Aussie, much to the chagrin of her father who thinks she can do better. To make her dad try and see things her way she hires Mexican-American waiter Carlos (Marin) to pretend to be her new suitor. Although directed by Michael Gottlieb, the film is credited to Alan Smithee – usually an indication of unrest behind the scenes.

Richard "Cheech" Marin *Carlos* • Emma Samms *Alexandra Hobart* • Bruce Spence *Wayne* • Vernon Wells *Bruce Woodley* • Carole Davis *Dominique* • Terence Cooper *Sir Ian Hobart* • Jeanette Cronin *Maggie* ■ *Dir* Alan Smithee [Michael Gottlieb] • *Scr* Grant Morris, Ron House, Alan Shearman

Shrunken Heads ★ 18

Horror comedy 1994 · US · Colour · 82mins

Three New York teenagers are killed by hoodlums and brought back to life by voodoo-practising news vendor Julius Harris as severed, shrunken heads eager to wreak revenge and turn other street gangs into zombie monsters. Aside from a few flashes of inspired gore – the truly bizarre moment where one of the heads has a romantic liaison – and Meg Foster as a lesbian gangster, this interminable horror comedy has shrunken thrills and sense to match its cranial capacity. Contains violence and swearing

Aeryk Egan *Tommy* • Becky Herbst *Sally* • Meg Foster *Big Moe* • Julius Harris *Mr Sumatra* • AJ Damato *Vinnie* ■ *Dir* Richard Elfman • *Scr* Matthew Bright, from an idea by Charles Band • *Music* Danny Elfman

The Shuttered Room ★★★

Horror 1967 · UK · Colour · 99mins

This superior tale of the supernatural was based on a short story by August Derleth and HP Lovecraft. Twenty years after she was driven away from her childhood home by a series of sinister happenings, Carol Lynley returns with her new husband, Gig Young. But the old mill is as daunting as ever and deliriously malevolent cousin Oliver Reed and his gang of New England delinquents are far from the ideal welcoming committee. David Greene leaks the secret of the room at the top of the stairs early on, but he still conveys a genuine sense of evil.

Gig Young *Mike Kelton* • Carol Lynley *Susannah Kelton* • Oliver Reed *Ethan* • Flora Robson *Aunt Agatha* • William Devlin *Zebulon Whateley* • Bernard Kay *Tait* ■ *Dir* David Greene • *Scr* DB Ledrov, Nathaniel Tanchuk, from a story by HP Lovecraft, August Derleth

Shuttlecock ★★★

Drama 1991 · UK/Fr · Colour · 99mins

Director Andrew Piddington struggles to bring to life Graham Swift's complex tale of a son investigating his father's sudden nervous breakdown, the roots of which lie in the father's wartime activities under the code-name "Shuttlecock". Lambert Wilson is suitably intense as the son whose own sanity begins to shatter in his quest for the truth; Alan Bates simmers powerfully as the war hero repressing a grim secret. But as with *Waterland*, the other notable Graham Swift adaptation, the film – though absorbing – fails to match the source novel's intricate layering of past and present.

Alan Bates *Major James Prentis VC* • Lambert Wilson *John Prentis* • Kenneth Haigh *Dr Quinn* • Jill Meager *Marian* • Gregory Chisholm *Martin* • Beatrice Buccholz *Beatrice Carnot* ■ *Dir* Andrew Piddington • *Scr* Tim Rose Price, from the novel by Graham Swift

Shy People ★★★ 15

Drama 1987 · US · Colour · 114mins

There are no duelling banjos, as in *Deliverance*, but Russian director Andrei Konchalovsky succeeds in coming up with an intriguing, if flawed, variation on the swamp melodrama. Jill Clayburgh is the snooty New Yorker who sets out on a *Roots*-style journey to the bayous, sulky teenage daughter

Martha Plimpton in tow, to locate some long-lost relatives, headed up by Barbara Hershey. The ensuing culture clash is a tad predictable, but Konchalovsky does well in invoking a spooky gothic atmosphere.

Jill Clayburgh *Diana* • Barbara Hershey *Ruth* • Martha Plimpton *Grace* • Merritt Butrick *Mike* • John Philbin *Tommy* • Don Swayze *Mark* • Pruitt Taylor Vince *Paul* • Mare Winningham *Candy* ■ *Dir* Andrei Konchalovsky • *Scr* Gerard Brach, Andrei Konchalovsky, Marjorie David, from a story by Andrei Konchalovsky

Siam Sunset ★★★

Comedy adventure 1999 · Ausl · Colour · 92mins

A distraught widower's quest to create the perfect paint colour takes him on a wild adventure through the Australian outback in John Polson's quirky road movie. Perry (Linus Roache) is dogged by disaster – his wife was killed by a refrigerator unit that fell from a passing jumbo – and catastropes occur wherever he goes. Salvation comes in the shape of Grace (Danielle Cormack) a free-spirited young woman who's as accident-prone as he is. The laughs come from a hilarious battle of wills between a pair of rival coach tour operators and from Grace's drug-dealing ex-boyfriend (Ian Bliss). However, the movie's biggest achievement is to make us really care about these bizarre characters and their off-kilter universe.

Linus Roache *Perry* • Danielle Cormack *Grace* • Ian Bliss *Martin* • Roy Billing *Bill* • Alan Brough *Stuart* • Rebecca Hobbs *Jane* • Terry Kenwrick *Arthur* ■ *Dir* John Polson • *Scr* Max Dann, Andrew Knight

Siberia ★★★ 18

Black comedy 1998 · Neth · BW and Colour · 86mins

A bouncy Dutch black comedy set in Amsterdam, about two friends and flatmates who seduce female backpackers of all nationalities and keep a page from their passport as a memento. Driven by a soundtrack by techno band Junkie XL, this immoral low-budget game of sexual rivalry is full of free-spirited, bed-hopping zeal and has a couple of winning actors in Hugo Metsers and Roeland Fernhout. When Vlatca Simac shows up as the spunky, enigmatic Lara, a dark and dirty *ménage à trois* ensues, but the film retains its cynical anti-romantic stance to the very end. In Dutch and English with subtitles.

Hugo Metsers *Hugo* • Roeland Fernhout *Goof* • Nicole Eggert *Kristy* • Vlatca Simac *Lara* • Johnny Lion *Freddy* ■ *Dir* Robert Jan Westdijk • *Scr* Jos Driessen, Robert Jan Westdijk

Sibling Rivalry ★★★ 15

Black comedy 1990 · US · Colour · 83mins

This movie contains a highly ingenious plotline, with some subtle twists and turns that are negotiated skilfully by the likes of Kirstie Alley and Carrie Fisher. They are supported by several familiar American TV faces (including Scott Bakula and Ed O'Neill), who throw themselves wholesale into the frantic, vulgar action with varying degrees of success, and it's all pulled together by the stylish direction of Carl Reiner, but the result still disappoints.

Contains swearing and sex scenes.

Kirstie Alley *Marjorie Turner* • Bill Pullman *Nick Meany* • Jami Gertz *Jeanine* • Carrie Fisher *Iris Turner-Hunter* • Scott Bakula *Harry Turner* • Sam Elliott *Charles Turner Jr* • Ed O'Neill *Wilbur Meany* • Frances Sternhagen *Rose Turner* ■ *Dir* Carl Reiner • *Scr* Martha Goldhirsh

The Sicilian ★★ 18

Crime drama   1987 · US · Colour · 109mins

A plodding and sententious account of the postwar Sicilian rebel Salvatore Giuliano, whose mania for independence from Italy inspired him to a career of murder and pillage. Christopher Lambert stars as a remarkably uncharismatic Giuliano, who nonetheless charms his way into the hearts of the Sicilian people and even the Mafia (in the person of the sinister Joss Ackland). Director Michael Cimino lets the action swing between huge messy gunfights and tedious moralising from Lambert. It's not a total disaster, but botched editing and leaden acting win the day. Contains swearing, violence and nudity.

Christopher Lambert *Salvatore Giuliano* • John Turturro *Aspanu Pisciotta* • Terence Stamp *Prince Borsa* • Joss Ackland *Don Masino Croce* • Richard Bauer *Professor Hector Adonis* • Ray McAnally *Minister Trezza* ■ *Dir* Michael Cimino • *Scr* Steve Shagan, from the novel by Mario Puzo

The Sicilian Clan ★★★ 15

Crime drama   1969 · Fr · Colour · 113mins

Imagine if you can Clark Gable, Humphrey Bogart and Paul Newman starring in a movie together. Well, in French terms, *The Sicilian Clan* has just that sort of charismatic threesome – Alain Delon, Jean Gabin and Lino Ventura – and that alone guaranteed the film's success at the box office in France and abroad. Delon is a Mafia hitman, sprung from jail by godfather Gabin who's planning to heist some jewellery. Ventura is the dogged cop on the case. It's an old-fashioned thriller, expertly made by its veteran director and boasting a score by Ennio Morricone. A French language film.

Jean Gabin *Vittorio Manalese* • Alain Delon *Roger Sartet* • Lino Ventura *Inspector Le Goff* • Irina Demick *Jeanne Manalese* • Amedeo Nazzari *Tony Nicosia* ■ *Dir* Henri Verneuil • *Scr* Henri Verneuil, José Giovanni, Pierre Pelegri, from the novel *Le Clan des Siciliens* by Auguste Le Breton

The Sicilian Cross ★★

Thriller   1976 · It · Colour · 101mins

It's a double-cross obviously, considering the country of origin of this very conventional Mafia thriller. The only novelty is the pairing of Stacy Keach and Roger Moore as a racing driver and half-Sicilian lawyer who probe the disappearance of a consignment of heroin. Amazingly, it took six writers to come up with such a humdrum idea. Mind you, the shock of watching Moore play a Mafia mouthpiece is a stunning enough concept in itself. Italian dialogue dubbed into English.

Roger Moore *Ulysses* • Stacy Keach *Charlie* • Ivo Garrani *Salvatore Francesco* • Fausto Tozzi *Nicoletta* ■ *Dir* Maurizio Lucidi • *Scr* Maurizio

Lucidi, Ernest Tidyman, Gianfranco Bucceri, Randal Kleiser, Roberto Leoni, Nicola Badalucco, from a story by Gianfranco Bucceri, Roberto Leoni

The Sicilians ★★ U

Crime thriller   1964 · UK · BW · 69mins

Known for his brisk approach to shooting and his no-nonsense style, Ernest Morris was able to make even the flimsiest of crime thrillers watchable, including this one about a dancer and a diplomat who search for a mafioso's kidnapped son. Robert Hutton is the imported Hollywood has-been and, even though he was never more than a second division star, he is streets ahead of this material.

Robert Hutton *Calvin Adams* • Reginald Marsh *Inspector Webb* • Ursula Howells *Madame Perrault* • Alex Scott *Henri Perrault* • Susan Denny *Carole Linden* • Robert Ayres *Angelo Di Marco* • Eric Pohlmann *Inspector Bressin* • Patricia Hayes *Passenger* • Warren Mitchell *O'Leary* ■ *Dir* Ernest Morris • *Scr* Ronald Liles, Reginald Hearne

Sick: the Life and Death of Bob Flanagan, Supermasochist ★★★★

Sex documentary 1997 · US · Colour · 90mins

This is an excruciatingly painful documentary about the extraordinary life and dying days of Californian comedian and performance artist Bob Flanagan, who used his own sexual masochism as a means of articulating the suffering caused by cystic fibrosis. His partner, Sheree Rose, at first objected to the intrusion of director Kirby Dick's camera into their private practices, but came to terms with it as Flanagan approached death. The result, though not for the squeamish, is sad, shocking and very moving.

Dir Kirby Dick

Sid and Nancy ★★★★ 18

Biographical drama
1986 · UK · Colour · 108mins

This punk love story is an authentic, uncompromising insight into the obsession of Sid Vicious, who played bass guitar for the Sex Pistols, with drug addict groupie Nancy Spungen, and their inexorable descent into death. Co-scripted by Abbe Wool and Alex Cox, it brilliantly recaptures the rage, cynicism and self-destructiveness of the late seventies punk scene, while never setting up the rock 'n' roll lifestyle as a blissful idyll. Cox directs with an eye for the age and its absurdities, mixing gritty realism with moments of charming romance and black comedy. Gary Oldman and Chloe Webb are outstanding as the lovers whose tragic affair managed to shock even in those unshakable times. Contains violence, swearing, sex scenes, drug abuse and nudity.

Gary Oldman *Sid Vicious* • Chloe Webb *Nancy Spungen* • Andrew Schofield *Johnny Rotten* • David Hayman *Malcolm McLaren* • Debby Bishop *[Debbie Bishop] Phoebe* • Tony London *Steve* • Courtney Love *Gretchen* ■ *Dir* Alex Cox • *Scr* Alex Cox, Abbe Wool

Siddhartha ★★

Drama   1972 · US · Colour · 89mins

Herman Hesse's 1922 novel is brought to the screen with the reverence of a true devotee by American writer/director Conrad Rooks. However, such is the unquestioning dogmatism of the screenplay, the lushness of Sven Nykvist's Indian landscapes and the stylised earnestness of Bollywood icon Shashi Kapoor in the title role that instead of a moving journey to spiritual enlightenment, this comes across as a glossy promo for Buddhism, in which self-discovery is trampled under foot by clumsy symbolism. Bypassing life in its quest for significance, this is an airless adaptation of an obdurate text.

Shashi Kapoor *Siddhartha* • Simi Garewal *Kamala* • Romesh Sharma *Govinda* • Pinchoo Kapoor *Kamaswami* • Zul Vellani *Vasudeva* ■ *Dir* Conrad Rooks • *Scr* Conrad Rooks, from the novel by Hermann Hesse

Side by Side ★★

Comedy   1975 · UK · Colour · 83mins

Who'll win the only nightclub licence in town? Old-timer Terry-Thomas at the Golden Nugget, or those groovy new kids on the block at Sound City? Glam rockers Mud and the Rubettes are joined by seventies sensations Kenny, Fox and Stephanie De Sykes for this candyfloss movie directed by none other than Bruce Beresford, of *Driving Miss Daisy* fame. Barry Humphries also appears in what must rank as one of the strangest musical comedies. Lynsey de Paul and Barry Blue supplied the title song.

Barry Humphries *Rodney* • Terry-Thomas *Max Nugget* • Stephanie De Sykes *Julia* • Billy Boyle *Gary* • Dave Mount *Flip* • Frank Thornton *Inspector Crumb* ■ *Dir* Bruce Beresford • *Scr* Garry Chambers, Ron Inkpen, Peter James, Bruce Beresford

Side by Side ★★

Drama   1982 · US · Colour · 100mins

It's a quarter of a century since the Osmonds, the singing sensation from Salt Lake City, first hit the British charts. A few old teenyboppers out there and those caught up in the current wave of seventies nostalgia might have found something to amuse them in a film covering the Osmonds' years at the top, but a biopic of their parents? Please! Marie Osmond plays her mother Olive with daughterly devotion, while some of the band's own offspring play them as children.

Marie Osmond *Olive Osmond* • Joseph Bottoms *George Osmond* • Karen Alston *Belva* • Cheryl Hudock *Marianne* • Scott Wilkinson *Lieutenant Gonez* ■ *Dir* Russ Mayberry • *Scr* EF Wallengren, from a story by Tom Lazarus, EF Wallengren

Side by Side ★★ PG

Comedy   1988 · US · Colour · 90mins

Veteran comics Milton Berle, Sid Caesar and Danny Thomas have been well and truly stitched up in this distinctly average *Prêt-à-Porter* for pensioners, in which the themes are old hat and the smug humour is in the worst back-slapping tradition of American showbiz. They play a trio of rag traders whose decision to launch a

collection of sportswear for the elderly puts a strain on their resources and their friendship. Director Jack Bender's rather tacky TV movie is awash with sentimental subplots dealing with secret mistresses and ungrateful offspring, and culminates in a fashion show that can only be described as embarrassing. Yet, despite the film's many flaws, Berle, Caesar and Thomas still prove moderately watchable.

Milton Berle *Abe Mercer* • Sid Caesar *Louie Hammerstein* • Danny Thomas *Charlie Warren* • Morey Amsterdam *Moe* • Marjorie Lord *Lillian Hammerstein* • Georgann Johnson *Alice Grayson* • Richard Kline *Matt Reinhorn* ■ *Dir* Jack Bender • *Scr* Rosemary Edelman, Sheldon Keller, from a story by Anthony Velona, Rosemary Edelman

Side Out ★★ 15

Sports drama   1990 · US · Colour · 99mins

This poor attempt to cash in on the largely American craze for beach volleyball became yet another turkey for former bratpacker C Thomas Howell. He plays a naive young law student who comes to California to work for his uncle and gets mixed up with a dropout volleyball star (Peter Horton). It apparently features appearances from the real-life stars of the sport, but that won't mean much to audiences here, and it ends up largely resembling an extended trailer for *Baywatch*. Contains nudity.

C Thomas Howell *Monroe Clark* • Peter Horton *Zack Barnes* • Courtney Thorne-Smith *Samantha* • Harley Jane Kozak *Kate Jacobs* • Christopher Rydell *Wiley Hunter* ■ *Dir* Peter Israelson • *Scr* David Thoreau

Side Street ★★★

Thriller   1950 · US · BW · 82mins

An absolutely first-rate MGM co-feature, one of those super programme-fillers that's not quite a main feature, but far above the average B-movie. The studio's customary production gloss and intelligence is here provided by masterly director Anthony Mann, not long before he hit his stride as one of the finest ever western directors. The film is a virtual *film noir* about a postman (Farley Granger) whose solitary act of theft changes the shape of his life forever.

Farley Granger *Joe Norson* • Cathy O'Donnell *Ellen Norson* • James Craig *Georgie Garsell* • Paul Kelly *Captain Walter Anderson* • Edmon Ryan *Victor Backett* • Paul Harvey *Emil Lorrison* • Jean Hagen *Harriet Sinton* • Charles McGraw *Stanley Simon* ■ *Dir* Anthony Mann • *Scr* Sydney Boehm, from his story

Side Streets ★★ 15

Drama   1998 · US · Colour · 130mins

Executive produced by Ismail Merchant, director/co-writer Tony Gerber's debut depicts New York as a city of self-contained immigrant conclaves that only interact through necessity. While this makes an important sociological point, it doesn't help the structure of this meandering collection of short cuts. Of the five stories, the tragedy of faded Bollywood star Shashi Kapoor has the most heart, while fashion wannabe Valeria Golino's encounter with the pinball of fate offers both satire and slapstick. But the episodes involving a Puerto

Rican Iothario, a Romanian gambler and a squabbling Afro-Caribbean couple lack focus. Contains swearing and sex scenes. 📺
Valeria Golino *Sylvie Otti* • Shashi Kapoor *Vikram Raj* • Leon *Errol Boyce* • Art Malik *Bipin Raj* • Shabana Azmi *Chandra Raj* • Mirjana Jokovic *Elena Iscovescu* • Miho Nikaido *Yuki Shimamura* ■ *Dir* Tony Gerber • *Scr* Lynn Nottage, Tony Gerber

Sidekicks ★★ 🅿🅖
Martial arts comedy
1993 · US · Colour · 92mins
Viewers who are the same age or younger than protagonist Jonathan Brandis might enjoy this rehash of the superior *The Karate Kid*, especially if they haven't seen the original. As a bullied asthmatic teenager who constantly dreams of fighting beside Chuck Norris, Brandis is likeable and sympathetic. Joe Piscopo is outrageous as a lunk-headed karate instructor, though Mako counter-balances that with a nice little performance as another tutor. The main quibble with the movie is not really in its lack of originality, but that it frequently comes across as a commercial for Chuck Norris. 📺
Chuck Norris • Jonathan Brandis *Barry Gabrewski* • Beau Bridges *Jerry Gabrewski* • Joe Piscopo *Kelly Stone* • Danica McKellar *Lauren* • Mako *Mr Lee* • Julia Nickson-Soul *Noreen Chan* ■ *Dir* Aaron Norris • *Scr* Donald G Thompson

The Sidelong Glances of a Pigeon Kicker ★★
Drama   1970 · US · Colour · 86mins
A little late for the psychedelic sixties, this self-satisfied and barely screened little movie was a rare US feature outing for talented theatre and opera director John Dexter, whose main claim to cinematic fame was the dire but popular *The Virgin Soldiers*. Manhattan, as ever, looks good, and the cast of Broadway ladies (Jill O'Hara, Elaine Stritch, Lois Nettleton) is not without interest, but Jordan Christopher is wholly inadequate as a forerunner to Travis Bickle in *Taxi Driver*. Contains swearing. 📺
Jordan Christopher *Jonathan* • Jill O'Hara *Jennifer* • Robert Walden *Winslow Smith* • Kate Reid *Mother* • William Redfield *Father* • Lois Nettleton *Mildred* • Boni Enten *Naomi* • Elaine Stritch *Tough lady* ■ *Dir* John Dexter • *Scr* Ron Whyte, from the novel by David Boyer

Sidewalk Stories ★★★★ 🆕
Silent drama   1989 · US · BW · 100mins
Written, directed, produced by and starring Charles Lane, this remarkable tribute to the art of Charlie Chaplin is virtually without dialogue. As a struggling Greenwich Village artist, Lane pays his debt to the Little Tramp in a knockabout scene that recalls a dozen stand-offs between Chaplin and bushy-browed Eric Campbell. In keeping with the homage there's as much pathos as well as slapstick, as Lane takes in an abandoned child (played by his own daughter, Nicole Alysia). Rarely has the modern city looked less sinister than in Bill Dill's stylish black-and-white images, while Marc Marder's score is almost a character in itself. Contains nudity.

Charles Lane (3) *Artist* • Nicole Alysia *Child* • Sandye Wilson *Young woman* • Darnell Williams *Father* • Trula Hoosier *Mother* • George Riddick *Street partner* • Tom Hoover *Portrait artist* ■ *Dir/Scr* Charles Lane (3)

Sidewinder One ★
Sports action drama
1977 · US · Colour · 96mins
Fans of motocross (the fancy name for scrambling) won't find much to enjoy in this seventies action drama featuring Susan Howard as the wealthy owner of a company specialising in stripped-down racing bikes. When not wandering the tracks between the interminable, identical-seeming runs, she enjoys the attentions of biker Michael Parks. Parks's buddy is played by the oddly repellent Marjoe Gortner, the real-life evangelist turned actor.
Marjoe Gortner *Digger* • Michael Parks *JW Wyatt* • Susan Howard *Chris Gentry* • Alex Cord *Packard Gentry* • Charlotte Rae *Mrs Holt* ■ *Dir* Earl Bellamy • *Scr* Nancy Voyles Crawford, Thomas A McMahon

The Siege ★★ 🔞
Action thriller 1998 · US · Colour · 111mins
Denzel Washington and Annette Bening go head to head in a muddled thriller that can't decide if it's a serious issue raiser or a patriotic action adventure. Islamic terrorists are attacking New York and different Government agencies are competing to deal with the violent outbreak that's putting civilians at risk. Listlessly directed by Edward Zwick and curiously understated in key plot areas, this routine potboiler lacks both basic credibility and suspense. Contains swearing and violence. 📺 **DVD**
Denzel Washington *Anthony "Hub" Hubbard* • Annette Bening *Elise Kraft/Sharon Bridger* • Bruce Willis *General William Devereaux* • Tony Shalhoub *Frank Haddad* • Sami Bouajila *Samir Nazhde* • Ahmed Ben Larby *Sheik Ahmed Bin Talal* ■ *Dir* Edward Zwick • *Scr* Lawrence Wright, Menno Meyjes, Edward Zwick, from a story by Lawrence Wright

The Siege at Red River ★★★ 🆄
Western   1954 · US · Colour · 85mins
Routine programme filler from producer Leonard Goldstein, whose Panoramic production company had a deal with 20th Century-Fox, guaranteeing cinema distribution. The canny Goldstein cleverly hijacked the colour climax of an earlier Fox western 1944's *Buffalo Bill* and used it virtually intact in this movie, inserting new close-ups of his principal players. The cast is headed by the ever interesting, and once hugely popular, Van Johnson. Director Rudolph Maté keeps the film moving, and the fifties Technicolor, along with the appearance of Joanne Dru make it still worth watching today.
Van Johnson *Jim Farraday* • Joanne Dru *Nora Curtis* • Richard Boone *Brett Manning* • Milburn Stone *Benjy* • Jeff Morrow *Frank Kelso* • Craig Hill *Lieutenant Braden* ■ *Dir* Rudolph Maté • *Scr* Sydney Boehm, from a story by J Robert Bren, Gladys Atwater

The Siege of Pinchgut ★★ 🆄
Thriller   1959 · UK · BW · 106mins
Ealing Studios had already made several films in Australia, including *Bitter Springs* and *The Shiralee*. Among the company's last productions was this muddled crime drama about an escaped prisoner who wants a new trial, holding captives on the tiny island of Pinchgut in the middle of Sydney Harbour. Aldo Ray was uninspired casting for the central role, and the resolution is rather unsatisfactory. At least the picture gains a strong documentary look from director Harry Watt's use of the locations.
Aldo Ray *Matt Kirk* • Heather Sears *Ann Fulton* • Neil McCallum *Johnny Kirk* • Victor Maddern *Bert* • Carlo Justini *Luke* • Alan Tilvern *Supt Hanna* • Barbara Mullen *Mrs Fulton* • Gerry Duggan *Pat Fulton* ■ *Dir* Harry Watt • *Scr* Inman Hunter, Lee Robinson, Harry Watt, John Cleary, from a story by Inman Hunter, Lee Robinson

The Siege of Sidney Street ★★
Historical drama   1960 · UK · BW · 93mins
Alfred Hitchcock drew on this famous piece of Edwardian history for *The Man Who Knew Too Much*, but this reconstruction sticks a mite closer to the facts. The East End locale looks rather thrown together and the early scenes get bogged down in background information. But once the Russian anarchists have barricaded themselves in, the action begins to come to life. Donald Sinden plods along as the inspector on the trail of Peter Wyngarde and his compatriots, Kieron Moore and Leonard Sachs.
Donald Sinden *Inspector John Mannering* • Nicole Berger *Sara* • Kieron Moore *Yoska* • Peter Wyngarde *Peter the Painter* • Godfrey Quigley *Blakey* • Angela Newman *Nina* • TP McKenna *Lapidos* • Leonard Sachs *Svaars* ■ *Dir* Robert S Baker, Monty Berman • *Scr* Jimmy Sangster, Alexander Baron, from a story by Jimmy Sangster

The Siege of Syracuse ★★
Historical epic   1959 · It · Colour · 97mins
A mere four years after he became one of the heart-throbs of world cinema after wooing Katharine Hepburn in *Summertime*, Rossano Brazzi found himself in this rather ridiculous sword-and-sandal adventure. He manages to keep a straight face as Archimedes, the mathematician and engineer who is torn between duty and ambition during a war between Rome and Carthage. If all the intrigue and treachery weren't enough, there is also a romantic triangle involving a dancer, a Roman consul and a son Brazzi didn't know he had. The destruction of the Roman fleet with giant mirrors is a stroke of bargain basement brilliance. In Italian with English subtitles.
Rossano Brazzi *Archimedes* • Tina Louise *Diana* • Sylva Koscina *Clio* • Enrico Maria Salerno *Gorgia* • Gino Cervi *Gerone* ■ *Dir* Pietro Francisci • *Scr* Pietro Francisci, Giorgio Graziosi, Ennio De Concini

The Siege of the Saxons ★★ 🆄
Historical adventure
1963 · UK · Colour · 85mins
Second-rate British thespians clank around in chain mail while women blush demurely in this Arthurian tosh. The sword Excalibur is still the weapon of choice, sought after by outlaw hero Ronald Lewis, the wooden Mark Dignam as King Arthur himself, and Jerome Willis as a villain with a dodgy leg. Chief damsel is Janette Scott, the daughter of Thora Hird and a leading British starlet of the day. If a modern audience hadn't been spoilt by parodies such as *Monty Python and the Holy Grail*, this cheesy plod might have seemed rather amusing; instead, it's just several knights short of a round table.
Ronald Lewis *Robert Marshall* • Janette Scott *Katherine* • Ronald Howard *Edmund of Cornwall* • Mark Dignam *King Arthur* • John Laurie *Merlin* • Jerome Willis *Limping man* • Richard Clarke *Saxon Prince* • Charles Lloyd Pack *Doctor* ■ *Dir* Nathan Juran • *Scr* Jud Kinberg, John Kohn

Sierra ★★ 🆄
Western   1950 · US · Colour · 82mins
America's most decorated war hero, Audie Murphy, was just settling into his western stride when he starred in this Technicolor remake of a forgotten 1938 film called *Forbidden Valley*, in which Murphy accompanies his wrongly accused father Dean Jagger into hiding. He also had a decent director in Alfred E Green to help him, but the result was still routine. The cast helps: Murphy met and married co-star Wanda Hendrix, and there is an obvious on-screen chemistry between them. There's also strong back-up from Jagger and Burl Ives, plus James Arness in his pre-Marshal Dillon days.
Wanda Hendrix *Riley Martin* • Audie Murphy *Ring Hassard* • Burl Ives *Lonesome* • Dean Jagger *Jeff Hassard* • Richard Rober *Big Matt* • Anthony Curtis [Tony Curtis] *Brent Coulter* • James Arness *Little Sam* ■ *Dir* Alfred E Green • *Scr* Edna Anhalt, Milton Gunzberg, from the novel by Stuart Hardy

Sierra Baron ★★ 🆄
Western   1958 · US · Colour · 79mins
A standard western plot is moved to the early California of 1848 as Brian Keith's gunslinger is hired to kill Rick Jason's young Spanish rancher by Steve Brodie's Yankee landgrabber. Rita Gam, as the Spaniard's beautiful sister, is instrumental in making Keith change sides. Brian Keith does well in one of his first leading roles. Mexican locations stand in for California and are outstandingly well photographed by Alex Phillips under the direction of former editor James B Clark.
Brian Keith *Jack McCracken* • Rick Jason *Miguel Delmonte* • Rita Gam *Felicia Delmonte* • Mala Powers *Sue Russell* • Steve Brodie *Rufus Bynum* ■ *Dir* James B Clark • *Scr* Houston Branch, from a novel by Thomas Wakefield Blackburn

Siesta ★ 🔞
Psychological drama
1987 · US · Colour · 92mins
An interesting cast – Ellen Barkin, Gabriel Byrne, Jodie Foster, Martin

Sheen and Isabella Rossellini – flounder in a plotless scenario which lands (with skydiver Barkin!) in steamy Spain. There, Barkin's murder and rape fantasies entwine as ineffectually as a soft porn movie while the film explores her sexual history. One is left wondering why and feeling conned by an array of stars all purporting to be in something far more interesting than this actually is.

Ellen Barkin *Claire* • Gabriel Byrne *Augustine* • Julian Sands *Kit* • Isabella Rossellini *Marie* • Martin Sheen *Del* • Alexei Sayle *Cabbie* • Grace Jones *Conchita* • Jodie Foster *Nancy* • Anastassia Stakis *Desdra* ■ *Dir* Mary Lambert • *Scr* Patricia Louisianna Knop, from the novel by Patrice Chaplin • *Music* Miles Davis

Sign o' the Times ★★ 15

Music concert 1987 · US · Colour · 81mins

Prince's filmed treatment of his 1987 European concert tour, with short scenes filmed in his Paisley Park studios linking together the live tracks, which were shot in Rotterdam. His Royal Purpleness androgynously bumps and grinds his way through one limp MTV-inspired sexual fantasy after another, all of which run the gaudy gamut between laughable machismo and arch feminism. Sheena Easton and Sheila E puncture his posing with their nifty musical contributions, but this isn't in the same class as *Purple Rain*. Contains swearing.

Dir Prince

The Sign of Four ★★★ PG

Mystery 1983 · UK/US · Colour · 103mins

Ian Richardson gives a sly performance as Sherlock Holmes in director Desmond Davis's entertaining version of Conan Doyle's sensationalist novel. Davis invests the material with a keen sense of atmosphere and mystery as Holmes is called in to investigate events at Pondicherry Lodge, and soon finds himself embroiled in a case of murder and betrayal revolving around a note with the words "the sign of the four" written upon it and some stolen Indian treasure. The solution is ingenious and the midnight pursuit along the Thames superbly staged. By choosing to focus on Holmes's brusqueness and his insufferable vanity rather than his remarkable powers of deduction, Davis brings a fresh slant to the genre.

Ian Richardson *Sherlock Holmes* • David Healy *Dr Watson* • Thorley Walters *Major John Sholto* • Terence Rigby *Inspector Layton* • Joe Melia *Jonathan Small* • Cherie Lunghi *Mary Morstan* ■ *Dir* Desmond Davis • *Scr* Charles Pogue, from the novel by Sir Arthur Conan Doyle

The Sign of Leo ★★★★ PG

Drama 1959 · Fr · BW · 98mins

Eric Rohmer (born Jean-Marie Maurice Scherer) was the editor of the influential French film magazine *Cahiers du Cinéma* when he made his first feature in 1956, which was only released three years later. It told of a 40-year-old American in Paris, borrowing money on the expectation of an inheritance. However, when it is not forthcoming, he becomes a tramp begging outside cafés. The film, which gives little indication as to the

direction Rohmer was to take, is an insightful portrait of a good-natured but hopelessly irresponsible man slowly disintegrating in the face of reality. In French with English subtitles.

Jess Hahn *Pierre Wesselrin* • Van Doude *Jean-Francois Santeuil* • Michèle Girardon *Dominique* • Jean Le Poulain *The clochard* • Stéphane Audran *Concierge at Hotel de Seine* • Jean-Luc Godard *Man listening to gramophone at party* ■ *Dir/Scr* Eric Rohmer

The Sign of the Cross ★★★★

Historical epic 1932 · US · BW · 118mins

Anyone unsure why Cecil B DeMille's name is synonymous with epic showmanship must see this. The territory is familiar: ancient Rome under the rule of the deranged, debauched Nero (Charles Laughton) and his wife Poppaea, and the hunting down of Christians to throw to the lions. The narrative is pegged to a doomed love between Nero's chief prefect (Fredric March) and a young Christian convert (Elissa Landi), but this is secondary to the opulence, high camp, decadence, and graphic cruelty of the climactic sequences in the gladiatorial arena.

Fredric March *Marcus Superbus* • Elissa Landi *Mercia* • Claudette Colbert *Empress Poppaea* • Charles Laughton *Emperor Nero* • Ian Keith *Tigellinus* • Vivian Tobin *Dacia* • Harry Beresford *Flavius* • Ferdinand Gottschalk *Glabrio* ■ *Dir* Cecil B DeMille • *Scr* Waldemar Young, Sidney Buchman, from the play by Wilson Barrett • *Cinematographer* Karl Struss

The Sign of the Gladiator ★

Historical epic
1958 · Fr/ W Ger/It · Colour · 84mins

A trashy sword-and-sandal epic about Queen Zenobia, a wanton Syrian beauty whose desert stronghold, Palmyra, is a thorn in Rome's side until they send in the heavy mob to rape and pillage. Zenobia is taken as a slave and loves happily ever after. Released around the same time as *Ben-Hur*, this pathetic effort is crude in every department, with wobbly sets, wonky swords and wooden acting. Sergio Leone, no less, contributed to the script but, as *Variety* said at the time, "the deepest thing about it is Anita Ekberg's cleavage". In Italian with English subtitles.

Anita Ekberg *Zenobia, Queen Of Palmyra* • Georges Marchal *Marcus Valerius, Roman general* • Folco Lulli *Semanzio* • Chelo Alonso *Erica, slave dancer* • Jacques Sernas *Julian* • Lorella De Luca *Bathsheba* ■ *Dir* Guido Brignone • *Scr* Francesco De Feo, Antonio Thellung, Roberti Sergio Leone [Sergio Leone], Giuseppe Mangione

Sign of the Pagan ★★★ U

Historical epic 1954 · US · Colour · 92mins

Jack Palance has a whale of a time playing the ferocious Attila, king of the Huns. His bold attempt to sack Rome is only halted by a welter of plot contrivances, but Jeff Chandler's centurion seems no real match for the ruthless barbarian. Lustily staged by director Douglas Sirk and strikingly photographed in early CinemaScope by Russell Metty (who would later shoot *Spartacus*), this is that rarity, an epic

with a short running time that doesn't overstay its welcome.

Jeff Chandler *Marcian* • Jack Palance *Attila* • Ludmilla Tcherina *Princess Pulcheria* • Rita Gam *Kubra* • Jeff Morrow *Paulinus* • George Dolenz *Theodosius* • Eduard Franz *Astrologer* • Allison Hayes *Ildico* ■ *Dir* Douglas Sirk • *Scr* Oscar Brodney, Barre Lyndon, from a story by Oscar Brodney

Signal 7 ★★★

Comedy drama 1983 · US · Colour · 92mins

Rob Nilsson began his career directing documentaries about farmers, making his feature debut with *Northern Lights*. This movie is surely dedicated to the patron saint of experimental low-budget drama, John Cassavetes. He would doubtless have approved of the episodic structure, the use of improvisational acting techniques and the method of recording on videotape and transferring to film stock to cut costs. The casual viewer, however, might struggle to identify with Bill Ackridge and Dan Leegant, the taxi drivers whose opinions, concerns and aspirations are the focus of this talkative drama. Contains swearing.

Bill Ackridge *Speed* • Dan Leegant *Marty* • John Tidwell *Johnny* • Herb Mills *Steve* • Don Bajema *Roger* • Phil Polakoff *Phil* ■ *Dir/Scr* Rob Nilsson

La Signora di Tutti ★★★

Drama 1934 · It · BW · 89mins

Made during the nomadic phase of his career, Max Ophüls's sole Italian venture bears the slight influence of the glossy "white telephone" pictures then dominating the local industry. However, this is very much an Ophüls picture, giving early glimpses of the structural fragmentation and visual fluidity that would characterise his best work, notably *Lola Montès*. Told in a series of flashbacks, as actress Ise Miranda undergoes emergency surgery following a suicide attempt, this melodic melodrama reveals the price she has paid for her brush with fame, as her relationships inevitably culminate in misery or death. In Italian with English subtitles.

Isa Miranda *Gabriella Murge, "Gaby Doriot"* • Memo Benassi *Leonardo Nanni* • Tatiana Pavlova *Alma Nanni* • Federico Benfer *Roberto Nanni* • Nelly Corradi *Anna* ■ *Dir* Max Ophüls • *Scr* Max Ophüls, Hans Wilhelm, Curt Alexander, from a novel by Salvator Gotta

La Signora senza Camelie ★★★

Drama 1953 · It · BW · 105mins

Michelangelo Antonioni's third feature continues to explore the alienating effects of modern society in what was originally conceived as a vehicle for Gina Lollobrigida. Instead, Lucia Bosé shoulders the burden of a faintly improbable storyline, in which her naive shopgirl is transformed into a starlet, only for her to be destroyed through a combination of limited ability, media pressure and the self-seeking ambition of her producer husband, Andrea Checchi, who pushes her into a doomed Joan of Arc project. Although casting a dismissive eye over the Cinecittà ballyhoo, Antonioni is more concerned with the psychological

impact of Bosé's lonely predicament. An Italian language film.

Lucia Bosé *Clara Manni* • Andrea Checchi *Gianni Franchi* • Gino Cervi *Ercole "Ercolino"* • Ivan Desny *Nardo Rusconi* • Alain Cuny *Lodi* • Enrico Glori *Director* ■ *Dir* Michelangelo Antonioni • *Scr* Suso Cecchi D'Amico, Francesco Maselli, PM Pasinetti, from a story by Michelangelo Antonioni

Signpost to Murder ★★

Thriller 1964 · US · BW · 77mins

A well acted but relentlessly stagey opus, made by MGM in black-and-white when they still felt the need to produce co-features, and based on a one-set West End play of no particular distinction. Joanne Woodward makes it watchable, and Irish-born Edward Mulhare, Rex Harrison's New York replacement in *My Fair Lady*, surfaces in one of his few screen roles, prior to re-creating Harrison's part for the TV series of *The Ghost and Mrs Muir*.

Joanne Woodward *Molly Thomas* • Stuart Whitman *Alex Forrester* • Edward Mulhare *Dr Mark Fleming* • Joyce Worsley *Mrs Barnes* • Leslie Denison *Supt Bickley* ■ *Dir* George Englund • *Scr* Sally Benson, from the play by Monte Doyle

The Silence ★★★ 15

Drama 1963 · Swe · BW · 91mins

The early work of Swedish director Ingmar Bergman is very much an acquired taste, and this enigmatic contemplation on loneliness and obsessive desire is one of his most obscure passion plays. It symbolically explores the bleak lives of two sisters as they embark on individual odysseys to find emotional warmth and tenderness. The overt sexuality caused censorship problems at the time, but now it's hard to see what all the fuss was about. In Swedish with English subtitles.

Gunnel Lindblom *Anna* • Ingrid Thulin *Ester* • Jörgen Lindström *Johan* ■ *Dir/Scr* Ingmar Bergman

Le Silence de la Mer ★★★★★

Drama 1947 · Fr · BW · 86mins

Filmed using non-union labour and without the rights to Jean Vercours's clandestine tribute to the Resistance, Jean-Pierre Melville's debut feature is a master class in nuance and gesture. Employing camera angles derived from Carl Theodor Dreyer, Melville conveys the impact on a patriotically silent uncle and niece of the cultured nostalgia and political idealism espoused by a convalescing Nazi officer. Howard Vernon delivers the monologues to perfection, but the dramatic power comes from the heroic stoicism of Jean-Marie Robain and Nicole Stéphane. A French language film.

Howard Vernon *Werner von Ebrennac* • Nicole Stéphane *Niece* • Ami Aaroé *Werner's fiancée* • Jean-Marie Robain *Uncle* ■ *Dir* Jean-Pierre Melville • *Scr* Jean-Pierre Melville, from the novel by Jean Vercors

Silence like Glass ★★

Drama 1989 · W Ger · Colour · 105mins

Jami Gertz heads a cracking cast in a routine disease-of-the-month movie, a

U = SUITABLE FOR ALL Uc = SUITABLE FOR ALL, ESPECIALLY FOR YOUNG CHILDREN (VIDEO ONLY) PG = PARENTAL GUIDANCE

contrived three-hanky tear-jerker about a ballet dancer struck down by cancer. With a cast of the calibre of Martha Plimpton, George Peppard, Rip Torn and Gayle Hunnicutt, you'd expect better. But even their combined talents can't transcend a formula film and an especially clichéd screenplay.

Jami Gertz *Eva* • Martha Plimpton *Claudia* • George Peppard *Eva's father* • Bruce Payne *Dr Burton* • Rip Torn *Dr Markowitz* • Gayle Hunnicutt *Eva's mother* ■ *Dir* Carl Schenkel • *Scr* Carl Schenkel, Bea Hellmann

Silence of Adultery ★★

Drama 1995 · US · Colour · 97mins

A soppy TV movie that manages to combine disabled children, cute animals and adultery in one fluffy confection. Kate Jackson is the caring mum working with autistic children whose saintly credentials take a knock when she embarks on an affair. Art Hindle is the only other well-known face in the cast, but, while both he and Jackson manage to keep commendably straight faces throughout, most viewers will find it just a little too much.

Kate Jackson *Dr Rachel Lindsey* • Art Hindle *David* • Robert Desiderio *Michael* ■ *Dir* Steven Hilliard Stern • *Scr* Susan Rhinehart, from a book by Bonnie Eaker Weil, Ruth Winter

The Silence of the Hams
★ **15**

Spoof horror 1993 · It/US · Colour · 78mins

Possibly the worst film spoof ever made and it's not hard to identify the guilty party: step forward one Ezio Greggio, who not only gets top billing but also wrote, directed and produced this tripe. Character names such as Jo Dee Fostar and Dr Animal Cannibal Pizza illustrate the supposed target, but more tellingly demonstrate the crass level of the (alleged) humour. Let's hope the likes of Billy Zane, Dom DeLuise, Martin Balsam and Joanna Pacula have already erased this from their CVs. This film is so bad it makes *Spaceballs* look good. ▭

Ezio Greggio *Antonio Motel* • Dom DeLuise *Dr Animal Cannibal Pizza* • Billy Zane *Jo Dee Fostar* • Joanna Pacula *Lily* • Charlene Tilton *Jane* • Martin Balsam *Detective Balsam* • Shelley Winters *The mother* • Phyllis Diller *Old secretary* ■ *Dir/Scr* Ezio Greggio

The Silence of the Lambs
★★★★★ **18**

Psychological thriller 1991 · US · Colour · 113mins

Although mass murderers have long been a fixture in the movies, they were almost always mad, bad or pathetic. Then along came Hannibal Lecter, a witty, cultured psychiatrist. So what if he was an incarcerated cannibal? The masterful Anthony Hopkins won an Oscar for his performance; so did Jodie Foster for her role as fledgling FBI agent Clarice Starling, who is drawn into a disturbingly close relationship with Lecter as she hunts for serial killer "Buffalo Bill". With a track record for directing quirky comedies, director Jonathan Demme made a seemingly effortless switch to terror, summoning up a magnificent air of gothic gloom. Spare a thought, too,

for the talented supporting players: stoical Scott Glenn as Foster's boss, Ted Levine as the tormented killer and Anthony Heald as the ill-fated hospital head, the butt of the movie's flip end gag. A modern masterpiece. Contains violence, swearing and nudity. ▭

Jodie Foster *Clarice Starling* • Anthony Hopkins *Dr Hannibal Lecter* • Scott Glenn *Jack Crawford* • Ted Levine *Jame Gumb* • Anthony Heald *Dr Frederick Chilton* • Kasi Lemmons *Ardelia Mapp* • Chris Isaak *Swat Commander* ■ *Dir* Jonathan Demme • *Scr* Ted Tally, from the novel by Thomas Harris

Silence of the North ★★ **PG**

Historical adventure
1981 · Can · Colour · 89mins

Based on a true story, this woman-and-wilderness drama from documentary film-maker Allan King zeroes in on the trials and tribulations that befall a trapper, his soon-to-be-widowed wife and their family in the Canadian wilds in 1919. Ellen Burstyn stars as Olive Fredrickson, who raises her family alone and in harsh conditions before succumbing to a second marriage. The scenery is stunning. ▭

Ellen Burstyn *Olive Fredrickson* • Tom Skerritt *Walter Reamer* • Gordon Pinsent *John Fredrickson* • Jennifer McKinney *Little Olive* • Donna Dobrijevic *Vala Reamer* • Jeff Banks *Lewis Reamer* ■ *Dir* Allan King • *Scr* Patricia Knop, from a non-fiction book by Ben East, Olive Fredrickson

The Silencers ★★★ **PG**

Action comedy 1966 · US · Colour · 97mins

Quintessential sixties spy spoof, the first (and best) of four colourful Matt Helm features, with debonair Dean Martin cleverly cast as author Donald Hamilton's womanising smoothie. The attitudes may have dated, but the women continue to delight, especially Stella Stevens as a divine klutz. Also making an impact are former Miss Israel Daliah Lavi and one-time MGM siren Cyd Charisse, whose title song is a highlight. If you care, the plot's about Helm trying to divert a Chinese-aimed missile to avoid global warfare.
▭ **DVD**

Dean Martin *Matt Helm* • Stella Stevens *Gail* • Daliah Lavi *Tina Batori* • Victor Buono *Tungtze* • Arthur O'Connell *Wigman* • Robert Webber *Sam Gunther* • James Gregory *MacDonald* • Cyd Charisse *Sarita* ■ *Dir* Phil Karlson • *Scr* Oscar Saul, from the novels *The Silencers* and *Death of a Citizen* by Donald Hamilton • *Music* Elmer Bernstein

The Silencers ★★ **18**

Science-fiction thriller
1995 · US · Colour · 96mins

This isn't the spy spoof that launched Dean Martin's Matt Helm series, and don't be fooled by the fact that there are several close encounters with "Men in Black". This is sci-fi, but strictly of the third-rate kind. Director Richard Pepin clearly hoped to overcome his budgetary restrictions by recalling the alien invasion pictures of the fifties. But neither undercover agent Jack Scalia's discovery of a plot involving government officials and an army of shape-changing ETs nor his alliance with Dennis Christopher's intergalactic troubleshooter is going to hook anyone but genre fanatics. ▭

Jack Scalia *Chuck Rafferty* • Dennis Christopher *Comdor* ■ *Dir* Richard Pepin • *Scr* Joseph John Barmettler, from a story by Joseph John Barmettler, Richard Preston Jr, William Applegate Jr

The Silences of the Palace
★★★★ **12**

Drama 1994 · Fr/Tun · Colour · 123mins

Moufida Tlatli's directorial debut is a slow, multi-layered drama set during the reign of Tunisia's last king, Sidi Ali. Life within his palace is so cloistered that the mounting protests against royal collaboration with the French barely intrude upon the life of a young servant girl, whose talent for music sparks a bitter rivalry between her mother and the king's barren wife. Well served by a fine ensemble cast, Tlatli superbly contrasts the shabby grandeur of the palace and the rigid protocol of a decaying system with the young girl's innocent beauty and the subtle simplicity of the music. In Arabic with English subtitles. ▭

Ahmel Hedhili *Khedija* • Hend Sabri *Young Alia* • Najia Ouerghi *Khalti Hadda* • Ghalia Lacroix *Adult Alia* ■ *Dir/Scr* Moufida Tlatli

Silencing Mary ★★ **12**

Drama 1998 · US · Colour · 84mins

College journalist Melissa Joan Hart (*Sabrina the Teenage Witch*) is terrorised by her school's football squad after she uncovers a conspiracy of silence surrounding her roommate's rape by the team's star player. She fights back by exposing the university's preferential treatment of athletes' behavior. Steve Johnson's fine dramatic script touches on all the relevant aspects. Contains some swearing. ▭

Melissa Joan Hart *Mary Stuartson* • Corin Nemec *David MacPherson* • Josh Hopkins *Clay Roberts* • Lisa Dean Ryan *Holly Shavers* • Peter MacNicol *Lawrence Dixon* • James McDaniel *Professor Thiel* • Lochlyn Munro *Billy* ■ *Dir* Craig R Baxley • *Scr* Steve Johnson

Silent Assassins ★ **18**

Action 1988 · US · Colour · 86mins

A group of hired killers eccentric enough to be at home in a *Batman* comic book kidnap a scientist who has invented some sort of biological weapon. The only person who can rescue him is Sam Jones, a standard issue cop on the edge whose partners were, of course, victims of these same assassins. A further cop movie cliché has Jones teaming up with another grieving relative, Jun Chong. Even by action movie standards, this scrapes the bottom of the barrel. ▭

Sam J Jones [Sam Jones] *Sam Kettle* • Linda Blair *Sara* • Jun Chong *Jun Kim* • Phillip Rhee *Bernard* • Bill Erwin *Dr London* • Gustav Vintas *Kendrick* • Mako *Oyama* ■ *Dir* Doo-yong Lee, Scott Thomas • *Scr* Will Gates, Ada Lin, from a story by John Bruner

The Silent Bell ★★★

Historical drama 1944 · US · Colour · 69mins

In one of the least known of Val Lewton's low-budget productions for RKO, Simone Simon, the star of *Cat People*, plays a common laundress in an adaptation of two Guy de Maupassant stories (one of which had

inspired John Ford's *Stagecoach*). Set during the Prussian invasion of France in the 1870s (paralleling the Nazi occupation of France during the Second World War), the story enables Simon to display real patriotism that shames her aristocratic fellow passengers on a coach journey. Simon and Kurt Kreuger (as a sadistic Prussian) are both excellent.

Simone Simon *Elizabeth Rousset* • John Emery *Jean Cornudet* • Kurt Kreuger *Lt von Eyrick, "Mademoiselle Fifi"* • Alan Napier *Count de Breville* • Helen Freeman *Countess de Breville* • Jason Robards *Wine wholesaler* ■ *Dir* Robert Wise • *Scr* Josef Mischel, Peter Ruric, from the short stories *Mademoiselle Fifi* and *Boule de Suif* by Guy de Maupassant

Silent Conflict ★★ **U**

Western 1948 · US · BW · 61mins

The long-running Hopalong Cassidy series was on its last legs when William Boyd saddled up once more to help a chum who had been hypnotised into a life of crime. Despite the presence of regulars Andy Clyde and Rand Brooks, this entry is long on talk and low on action.

William Boyd *Hopalong Cassidy* • Andy Clyde *California Carlson* • Rand Brooks *Lucky Jenkins* • Virginia Belmont *Rene Richards* • Earle Hodgins *Doc Richards* • James Harrison *Speed Blaney* • Forbes Murray *Randall* ■ *Dir* George Archainbaud • *Scr* Charles Belden, from characters created by Clarence E Mulford

Silent Dust ★

Drama 1948 · UK · BW · 81mins

Georges Auric composed scores for almost 100 films in France, Britain and Hollywood, winning awards galore. In 1949 he wrote the music for the Ealing classic *Passport to Pimlico* and *Queen of Spades*, so what on earth was he doing working on this rather weak offering? Adapted by Michael Pertwee from the play he co-wrote with his father Roland, it is supposed to be a provocative treatise on the nature of heroism, but is nothing more than a mawkish drama with a shamelessly sentimental performance by Stephen Murray, whose rose-tinted image of his son is tarnished by the truth.

Sally Gray *Angela Rawley* • Stephen Murray *Robert Rawley* • Derek Farr *Maxwell Oliver* • Nigel Patrick *Simon Rawley* • Beatrice Campbell *Joan Rawley* ■ *Dir* Lance Comfort • *Scr* Michael Pertwee, from the play *The Paragon* by Michael Pertwee, Roland Pertwee

The Silent Enemy ★★★ **PG**

Second World War drama
1958 · UK · BW · 107mins

A distinguished British war film about the exploits of celebrated Royal Navy frogman Lieutenant Lionel "Buster" Crabb (no, not the movie star), played here by Laurence Harvey, whose explosive temperament is a perfect match for the volatile character he plays. The underwater shooting (by Egil Woxholt) is well done, and the plot has more excitement than many fictional tales. Reliable Michael Craig plays Crabb's partner, while stern John Clements represents the Admiralty. The saga is shot through with a rich vein of humour, a credit to the film's writer/director William Fairchild. ▭

Laurence Harvey *Lieutenant Lionel Crabb* • Dawn Addams *Third Officer Jill Masters* • Michael Craig *Leading Seaman Knowles* • John Clements *The Admiral* • Sidney James *Chief Petty Officer Thorpe* • Alec McCowen *Able Seaman Morgan* • Nigel Stock *Able Seaman Fraser* ■ *Dir* William Fairchild • *Scr* William Fairchild, from the non-fiction book *Commander Crabb* by Marshall Pugh

Silent Fall ★★★🅸🅵

Thriller 1994 · US · Colour · 96mins

Director Bruce Beresford is one of Hollywood's safer pairs of hands and he hardly misses a beat with this absorbing, if somewhat predictable thriller. Richard Dreyfuss is the retired child psychologist called in to help unlock the memory of an autistic child who holds the key to the murder of his parents. Ben Faulkner is movingly believable as the boy and Dreyfuss is as dependable as ever, even though John Lithgow and JT Walsh steal every scene they're in. Look out to for a charismatic debut from Liv Tyler. Contains violence and swearing. ▭

Richard Dreyfuss *Jake Rainer* • Linda Hamilton *Karen Rainer* • John Lithgow *Doctor Harlinger* • JT Walsh *Sheriff Mitch Rivers* • Ben Faulkner *Tim Warden* • Liv Tyler *Sylvie Warden* ■ *Dir* Bruce Beresford • *Scr* Akiva Goldsman

Silent Hunter ★★🅸🅱

Action thriller 1995 · US · Colour · 92mins

The writers of *Silent Hunter* included every cop movie cliché they could think of in the script, apparently on the theory that quantity trumps quality. Beefy Miles O'Keeffe plays Jim, a cop who discusses his future plans with his affable black partner at a birthday party. However, while driving home, violent masked bank robbers hijack Jim and his beautiful family, and Jim's wife and daughter are killed. Two years later, Jim has an opportunity to take revenge. Predictable and low-budget, it's directed by blaxploitation legend Fred Williamson, who also has a neat supporting role. Contains violence, swearing and nudity. ▭

Miles O'Keeffe *Jim Paradine* • Fred Williamson *Sheriff Mantee* • Peter Colvey *Bo* • Lynne Adams *Anna* • Jason Cavalier *Dewey* • Sabine Karsenti *Laura* ■ *Dir* Fred Williamson • *Scr* Errol Da Silva, Bud Fleisher, Richard Loncar

Silent Motive ★★★

Thriller 1991 · US · Colour · 90mins

Thirtysomething's Patricia Wettig stars in this thriller as a scriptwriter who discovers people are being murdered using the same methods contained in her scripts. Although the "I wrote it, so I can't be the killer" alibi is a familiar one, borrowed from murder mysteries of old and used a year later to greater effect by Sharon Stone in *Basic Instinct*, this is still an above-average TV movie distinguished by the performances of Wettig and the ever-reliable Ed Asner as her agent. Contains swearing.

Patricia Wettig *Laura Bardell* • Mike Farrell *Detective Paul Trella* • Ed Asner *Sam Van Drake* • Rick Springfield *Brad* ■ *Dir* Lee Philips • *Scr* William P Bekkala

Silent Movie ★★★🅿🅶

Comedy 1976 · US · Colour · 87mins

In a (virtually) dialogue-free movie, Brooks plays film director Mel Funn who plans to make a modern-day silent movie in an attempt to save ailing film corporation Big Picture Studios. Aided by his henchmen Marty Feldman and Dom DeLuise, Brooks sets out to shoot his masterpiece and on the way runs into a number of well-known movie faces (Liza Minnelli, Burt Reynolds, James Caan) in cameo roles. There's some well-honed slapstick and a number of fair gags, but the film is always more of a Brooks comedy than a homage to the silent era. Amiable enough, but certainly not something to shout about. ▭

Mel Brooks *Mel Funn* • Marty Feldman *Marty Eggs* • Dom DeLuise *Dom Bell* • Bernadette Peters *Vilma Kaplan* • Sid Caesar *Studio Chief* • Harold Gould *Engulf* • Ron Carey *Devour* ■ *Dir* Mel Brooks • *Scr* Mel Brooks, Ron Clark, Rudy DeLuca, Barry Levinson, by Ron Clark

Silent Night, Bloody Night ★★

Horror 1972 · US · Colour · 88mins

Seriously humdrum horror movie that's even lower in imagination as it is obviously low in budget. The much under-rated Patrick O'Neal plays a lawyer sent to a small provincial American town to sell off an old mansion which used to be an insane asylum. It transpires that the inmates were released and now form the bulk of the townsfolk, who are being bumped off by a mystery killer. Director Theodore Gershuny delivers a few atmospheric chills but not enough to lift this above the purely mundane.

Patrick O'Neal *Carter* • John Carradine *Towlman* • James Patterson *Jeffrey Butler* • Walter Abel *Mayor* • Mary Woronov *Diane Adams* • Candy Darling ■ *Dir* Theodore Gershuny • *Scr* Theodore Gershuny, Jeffrey Konvitz, Ami Artzi, Ira Teller

Silent Night, Deadly Night ★★

Horror 1984 · US · Colour · 79mins

This routine stalk-and-slasher movie gained notoriety when American parents protested about the effect that portraying Father Christmas as a mad murderer would have on children. Billy sees his parents slain at Christmas by someone dressed as Santa. He suffers a miserable childhood in an orphanage and, not surprisingly, grows up hating the festive season. Working in a department store, he's forced into a Santa outfit by his boss and goes on a homicidal rampage himself armed with an axe, a bow and arrows and fairy lights. The murders are perfunctorily dismissed by undistinguished direction and, aside from a few on-the-button lines about the greed and phoney sentiment of Christmas, it's a shallow and depressing affair.

Lilyan Chauvin *Mother Superior* • Gilmer McCormick *Sister Margaret* • Toni Nero *Pamela* • Robert Brian Wilson *Billy aged 18* • Britt Leach *Mr Sims* ■ *Dir* Charles E Sellier Jr • *Scr* Michael Hickey, from a story by Paul Caimi

Silent Night, Deadly Night Part 2 ★

Horror 1987 · US · Colour · 88mins

The Santa Claus killer's brother Ricky (Eric Freeman) from the original movie, locked up in a maximum security orphanage, tells the whole shocking family history to his psychiatrist in this dreadful sequel that reuses some 40 minutes of footage from the first episode as couch flashbacks. The second half of this sorry mess then has the afflicted brother going on a killing spree of his own. The worst kind of mean-spirited exploitation.

Eric Freeman *Ricky Caldwell* • James L Newman *Dr Henry Bloom* • Elizabeth Cayton *Jennifer* • Jean Miller *Mother Superior* ■ *Dir* Lee Harry • *Scr* Lee Harry, Joseph H Earle, from a story by Dennis Paterson, Lawrence Appelbaum, Lee Harry, Joseph H Earle, from characters created by Paul Caimi, Michael Hickey

Silent Night, Deadly Night 3: Better Watch Out! ★

Horror 1989 · US · Colour · 92 mins

Although a marginal improvement over the second in the once-controversial Santa Claus series, this tedious ramble lacks suspense, energy or even the inventive murder methods which usually provide some incentive to stay awake. The *Part 2* killer Ricky (now played by Bill Moseley) is restored to life by mad scientist Richard Beymer on Christmas Eve and goes on a murder spree. Only this time he's psychically linked to blind girl Samantha Scully and his brain is visible under a plexi-glass dome! Two more sequels followed.

Robert Culp *Lieutenant Connely* • Richard Beymer *Doctor Newbury* • Bill Moseley *Ricky* • Samantha Scully *Laura* • Eric DaRe *Chris* ■ *Dir* Monte Hellman • *Scr* Carlos Laszlo, from a story by Monte Hellman, Richard N Gladstein, Carlos Laszlo

Silent Night, Lonely Night ★★

Drama 1969 · US · Colour · 98mins

A nice, though not terribly original, made-for-television soap opera, in which middle-aged Lloyd Bridges and Shirley Jones find romance amid clichés galore in a New England setting. Based on Robert Anderson's play, this could have done with a more adult treatment from director Daniel Petrie, but, thanks to the skilled performances of Bridges and Jones, it remains watchable. Lloyd's son Jeff puts in an appearance and there's some excellent support from Carrie Snodgress and Cloris Leachman.

Lloyd Bridges *John Sparrow* • Shirley Jones *Katherine Johnson* • Lynn Carlin *Jennifer Sparrow* • Carrie Snodgress *Janet* • Robert Lipton *Philip* • Cloris Leachman *Ginny* • Jeff Bridges *Young John* ■ *Dir* Daniel Petrie • *Scr* John Vlahos, from the play by Robert Anderson

The Silent One ★★★

Spy thriller 1973 · Fr/It · Colour · 117mins

Nobody did the chase thriller better than Alfred Hitchcock and on the evidence of this stylish, suspenseful espionage story, Claude Pinoteau had clearly been taking notes. From the moment Soviet nuclear scientist Lino Ventura is revealed to be a kidnapped Frenchman, nothing can be taken for granted, apart from the excellence of the star whose mournful response to freedom is very much that of a spy coming in from the cold with the greatest reluctance. Fascinating in its insights into the nature of liberty and riveting in its sweeping pursuit of a mysterious orchestra conductor, this is both intelligent and entertaining. French dialogue dubbed into English.

Lino Ventura *Tibère* • Lea Massari *Maria* • Suzanne Flon *Jeanne* • Leo Genn *Man from MI5* • Robert Hardy *MI5 assistant* ■ *Dir* Claude Pinoteau • *Scr* Jean-Loup Dabadie, Claude Pinoteau, from the novel *Drôle de Pistolet* by Francis Ryck

The Silent One ★★★

Fantasy 1984 · NZ · Colour · 95mins

Charming children's film, about an abandoned boy who's washed up on a remote South Pacific island. He can't hear or speak, but the islanders discover he can communicate with the local sea turtles. Shot on location in the Cook Islands, with many of the locals taking supporting roles, this overturns conventional notions of family entertainment, being just about as exotic as you can get.

Telo Malese *Jonasi* • George Henare *Paui Te Po* • Pat Evison *Luisa* • Anzac Wallace *Tasiri* ■ *Dir* Yvonne Mackay • *Scr* Ian Mune, from the novel by Joy Cowley

The Silent Partner ★★★

Crime caper 1978 · Can · Colour · 105mins

This Canadian-made thriller boasts a sort of retro sixties cast and an ingenious script by Curtis Hanson, who later won an Oscar for his adaptation of *LA Confidential*. It's about a bank, which is robbed by Christopher Plummer dressed as Santa Claus, though part of his potential haul is stolen by devious bank clerk Elliott Gould. What develops then is a game of cat and mouse as the slightly deranged Plummer puts on the pressure to get the rest of his stash. Both the male leads are in fine fettle but Susannah York has too little to do.

Susannah York *Julie Carver* • Christopher Plummer *Harry Reikle* • Elliott Gould *Miles Cullen* • Celine Lomez *Elaine* • Michael Kirby *Charles Packard* • Ken Pogue *Detective Willard* • John Candy *Simonsen* ■ *Dir* Daryl Duke • *Scr* Curtis Hanson, from the novel *Think of a Number* by Anders Bodelsen

Silent Rage ★🅸🅱

Action drama 1982 · US · Colour · 95mins

Chuck Norris doesn't say much in his movies, which is just as well given scripts like this one. As a former karate champion turned actor he lets his feet do the talking. Here we discover him in one of those ubiquitous small Texas towns that seem to have, and need, sheriffs like Chuck, especially when an axe killer (Brian Libby) he's already dealt with is back in town. But now he's been genetically engineered by an insane scientist, so the psychopath is not just mad and bad but indestructible as well. Norris looks bemused in a preposterously silly film which is less fun than it should be. ▭

🅄 = SUITABLE FOR ALL 🅄🅲 = SUITABLE FOR ALL, ESPECIALLY FOR YOUNG CHILDREN (VIDEO ONLY) 🅿🅶 = PARENTAL GUIDANCE

Chuck Norris *Dan Stevens* • Ron Silver *Dr Tom Halman* • Steven Keats *Dr Philip Spires* • Toni Kalem *Alison Halman* • William Finley *Dr Paul Vaughn* • Brian Libby *John Kirby* • Stephen Furst *Charlie* ■ *Dir* Michael Miller • *Scr* Joseph Fraley

Silent Running ★★★★ U
Science-fiction adventure
1971 · US · Colour · 85mins

Special-effects ace Douglas Trumbull (of *2001* fame) turned director with this ecologically based science-fiction thriller about the last of Earth's plant-life preserved on the *Valley Forge* spaceship, lovingly cared for by space ranger Bruce Dern and his three cute "drone" robots. Dern mutinies when orders arrive to destroy the precious cargo. Although the film may seem rather hippy-influenced now (those syrupy Joan Baez ballads!), Trumbull's gentle direction highlights a sensitive performance by Dern, and there are some spectacular images of the spacecraft floating between planets, exploding suns and solar storms. Imaginative and much admired. ▭

Bruce Dern *Freeman Lowell* • Cliff Potts *Wolf* • Ron Rifkin *Barker* • Jesse Vint *Keenan* ■ *Dir* Douglas Trumbull • *Scr* Deric Washburn, Mike Cimino, Steve Bocho

Silent Scream ★★ 15
Biographical drama
1989 · UK · Colour · 81mins

Extremely powerful in parts, director David Hayman's heartfelt biographical drama, based on the life of convicted murderer Larry Winters, is very much a mixed blessing. Iain Glen gives a marvellous performance as the manic-depressive Winters, jailed for killing a barman, recalling his life while dying from a drugs overdose in prison. But Hayman drenches his potent polemic in an earnest and inappropriately fractured style, creating distance from the subject matter rather than empathy. It's a slog, with some rewards if you stick at it. Contains swearing and drug abuse. ▭

Iain Glen *Larry Winters* • Paul Samson *Jimmy* • Andrew Barr *Shuggie* • Kenneth Glenaan *Rab* • Steve Hotchkiss *Mo* • Jim Murtagh *Ken Murray* • Robert Carlyle *Big Woodsy* ■ *Dir* David Hayman • *Scr* Bill Beech, Jane Beech, from the life and writings of Larry Winters

Silent Thunder ★★ 15
Drama
1992 · US · Colour · 87mins

Stacy Keach turns in his usual solid work in this otherwise unremarkable revenge drama, supposedly based on a true story. He plays an ordinary dad who becomes a vigilante when his young son is killed by a hit-and-run truck driver. Aside from Keach, the acting is undistinguished, with icy blonde Sandahl Bergman looking a mite ridiculous as a trucker called Python, but director Craig R Baxley shows some neat touches in the action sequences and it passes the time harmlessly enough. Contains violence and swearing. ▭

Stacy Keach *Claude Sams* • Thomas Wilson Brown *Paul Sams* • Sandahl Bergman *Python* • Lisa Banes *Vi Sams* ■ *Dir* Craig R Baxley • *Scr* Dennis Sharyack

Silent Tongue ★★ 12
Supernatural western
1993 · US · Colour · 97mins

A western, written and directed by Sam Shepard for French television and with a bizarre cast headed by two survivors of sixties British cinema, Alan Bates and Richard Harris, and dysfunctional former child star River Phoenix in his final credited screen appearance. Bates plays the drunken proprietor of a mystical, crazy Wild West show in the wilderness. Years before, Bates sold Harris his half-American Indian daughter, who later married Harris's legitimate son, Phoenix. But the girl has died in childbirth and Phoenix has become insane. Most viewers will wonder what the heck it all means. ▭

Richard Harris *Prescott Roe* • Sheila Tousey *Awbonnie/Ghost* • Alan Bates *Eamon McCree* • River Phoenix *Talbot Roe* • Dermot Mulroney *Reeves McCree* • Jeri Arredondo *Velada McCree* • Tantoo Cardinal *Silent Tongue* ■ *Dir/Scr* Sam Shepard

The Silent Touch ★★★ 15
Romantic comedy
1992 · UK /Pol/Den · Colour · 91mins

A complex display of frustrated creativity, simmering fury and manipulative cunning from Max von Sydow dominates this intense study of the sacrifices art demands of life. Roused from his reclusive ennui by Polish musicologist Lothaire Bluteau, von Sydow's exiled composer battles the bottle, physical pain and his emotional demons to complete his masterpiece, a snatch of which had lingered elusively in the mind of his mystical visitor. This turbulent relationship is delineated with care by director Krzysztof Zanussi, although it leaves little room to explore von Sydow's troubled marriage to a resigned Sarah Miles. ▭

Max von Sydow *Henry Kesdi* • Lothaire Bluteau *Stefan Bugajski* • Sarah Miles *Helena Kesdi* • Sofie Grabol [Sofie Gråbøl] *Annette Berg* • Aleksander Bardini *Professor Jerzy Kern* ■ *Dir* Krzysztof Zanussi • *Scr* Peter Morgan, Mark Wadlow, from a story by Krzysztof Zanussi, Edward Zebrowski

Silent Trigger ★★ 18
Action thriller
1996 · UK/Can · Colour · 89mins

Dolph Lundgren and Gina Bellman play a pair of hired killers, waiting in an eerie building for their next target, in a sleep-inducing thriller. Among Dolph's fans, this is considered one of his better outings – though let's face it, the competition isn't that stiff. Here his role isn't mere beefcake but demands emotional depth as his character begins to have reservations about the morality of his "job", brought on by disturbing flashbacks of a bungled assassination attempt. But Dolph's still guilty of delivering dialogue like a foreign exchange student on his first day in class. Contains violence, swearing, drug abuse and nudity. ▭

Dolph Lundgren *Shooter* • Gina Bellman *Spotter* • Conrad Dunn *Supervisor* • Christopher Heyerdahl *O'Hara* • Emma Stevens *Target woman* ■ *Dir* Russell Mulcahy • *Scr* Sergio Altieri

Silent Witness ★ 18
Drama
1985 · US · Colour · 91mins

What do you do if you're a respectable married woman and witness your own brother-in-law raping a woman in a bar? Do you remain silent, tell the police, or sell your story to a TV company and have it turned into a 90-minute drama? Quite a poser this conscience business, and this movie makes as much as it can out of it. Valerie Bertinelli looks suitably troubled, the two men in her life are Chris Nash and John Savage, and the rest of the cast make the best of the weak material. Contains violence. ▭

Valerie Bertinelli *Anna Dunne* • John Savage *Kevin Dunne* • Chris Nash *Michael Dunne* • Melissa Leo *Patti Mullen* • Jacqueline Brookes *Ma Dunne* • Katie McCombs *Jean Dunne* ■ *Dir* Michael Miller • *Scr* Conrad Bromberg

The Silent Woman ★★
Thriller
1989 · Fr · Colour · xxmins

Marie-Christine Barrault emerged from the shadow of her celebrated uncle Jean-Louis when she was Oscar-nominated for her role in *Cousin, Cousine*. Joyce Buñuel, on the other hand, has found it next to impossible to match the achievements of her illustrious father-in-law, Luis, and this overwrought thriller, which she directed, does little to redress the balance. While Buñuel sets the scene neatly, having murder witness Barrault hide away at an isolated country cottage unaware that a terrorist is hot on her trail, she allows the action to lapse into high melodrama as the siege begins. It won't jangle any nerves, but it's diverting enough. In French with English subtitles. ▭

Marie-Christine Barrault • Veronique Genest • Pierre Clementi ■ *Dir* Joyce Buñuel • *Scr* Jean-Claude Carrière

Silhouette ★★★ 15
Thriller
1990 · US · Colour · 84mins

Faye Dunaway is such a formidable presence, it's hard to think of her in any kind of jeopardy. But that's her lot in this predictable but tension-building TV movie about terrors in a Texas town. She's the architect forced to stay in the area when her car breaks down, only to witness a waitress being stabbed to death. Bringing the architect's daughter into the drama is an obvious attempt to engage the youth market, but Dunaway will have none of it. In the tradition of Joan Crawford and Bette Davis, she's the supreme scene-stealer, the last of the queens of the silver screen. ▭

Faye Dunaway *Samantha Kimball* • David Rasche *Sheriff Kyle Lauder* • John Terry *Deputy Pete Schroeder* • Carlos Gomez *Eddie Herrera* • Talisa Soto *Marianna Herrera* • Ron Campbell *Ben Styles* ■ *Dir* Carl Schenkel • *Scr* Jay Wolf, Victor Buell

Silhouette ★★ 15
Thriller
1994 · US · Colour · 86mins

A thriller with a familiar plot about a stranger suddenly appearing and recognising a murder victim as his wife: a sort of *Laura* meets *The Three Faces of Eve*, but done for TV. The cast performs with conviction, but it would be nice to see the likes of Stephanie

Zimbalist (playing the victim) and JoBeth Williams (her musician sister) back on the big screen in decent roles. ▭

JoBeth Williams *Nancy Parkhurst* • Corbin Bernsen *Mark Reichard* • Stephanie Zimbalist *Ann Parkhurst* • Winston Rekert *Paul Gatlin* ■ *Dir* Eric Till • *Scr* Karol Ann Hoeffner

Silk Stockings ★★★ U
Musical comedy 1957 · US · Colour · 112mins

A musical remake of *Ninotchka* with a Cole Porter score might have seemed a good idea at the time, but this MGM CinemaScope special is more than a little heavy-handed under the arthritic direction of veteran Rouben Mamoulian. Nevertheless, the splendid cast and choreography keep it all eminently watchable, even if the anti-Russian jokes and the anti-rock 'n' roll number leave a sour taste in the mouth. Plus points abound: the above-the-line casting reteams those *Band Wagon* co-stars Fred Astaire and Cyd Charisse in numbers like *All of You* and *Paris Loves Lovers*, but the real highlight is a movie parody by Astaire and Janis Paige called *Stereophonic Sound*. The commissars, headed by Peter Lorre, are funny, but it lacks the sparkle of MGM's best. ▭

Fred Astaire *Steve Canfield* • Cyd Charisse *Ninotchka* • Janis Paige *Peggy Dainton* • Peter Lorre *Brankov* • Jules Munshin *Bibinski* • Joseph Buloff *Ivanov* • George Tobias *Commissar Vassili Markovich* ■ *Dir* Rouben Mamoulian • *Scr* Leonard Gershe, Leonard Spigelgass, Harry Kurnitz, from the musical by George S Kaufman, Leueen McGrath, Abe Burrows, from the film *Ninotchka* by Charles Brackett, Billy Wilder, Walter Reisch, from a story by Melchior Lengyel • *Choreographer* Hermes Pan

The Silken Affair ★★ U
Comedy 1957 · UK · BW · 95mins

David Niven is the accountant who goes off the rails when he decides to indulge in a spot of creative book-keeping in this frivolous romantic comedy. His ill-gotten gains are used to fund a romantic spree with French girl Genevieve Page (appearing in her first British film), but all good things must come to an end. There are lots of well-known faces in the supporting cast but the theme was exploited much more effectively 20 years later in *Something Wild*.

David Niven *Roger Tweakham/New accountant* • Genevieve Page *Genevieve Gerard* • Ronald Squire *Marberry* • Beatrice Straight *Theora* • Wilfrid Hyde White *Sir Horace Hogg* • Howard Marion-Crawford *Baggott* • Dorothy Alison *Mrs Tweakham* • Miles Malleson *Mr Blucher* ■ *Dir* Roy Kellino • *Scr* Robert Lewis Taylor, from an idea by John McCarten

Silkwood ★★★★ 15
Biographical drama
1983 · US · Colour · 125mins

A moving film based on a true story about a female nuclear power plant worker who died under mysterious circumstances on her way to a meeting with the press, at which she intended to show them proof of improprieties at her workplace. Meryl Streep is charismatic and convincing in the lead and there's strong support from Cher and Kurt Russell. Unfortunately, the interesting premise, particularly topical at the time of its Cold War release, is let down by a lack of tension and director Mike Nichols's tendency to digress into the romantic subplot. Nevertheless, it's a thought-provoking film that asks questions about the safety of the nuclear power industry that are still pertinent. 🖵

Meryl Streep *Karen Silkwood* • Kurt Russell *Drew Stephens* • Cher *Dolly Pelliker* • Craig T Nelson *Winston* • Diana Scarwid *Angela* • Fred Ward *Morgan* • Ron Silver *Paul Stone* ■ *Dir* Mike Nichols • *Scr* Nora Ephron, Alice Arlen

Silver Bears ★ PG

Comedy adventure
1978 · US · Colour · 107mins

Michael Caine has made some odd choices in his career, but none as peculiar as this high-finance drama in which he sets up a bank in Switzerland for gangster Martin Balsam and becomes involved in a scam involving an Iranian silver mine. There's an elegant cast (Louis Jourdan, Cybill Shepherd, Stéphane Audran), but hardly any sympathetic characters. 🖵

Michael Caine *Doc Fletcher* • Cybill Shepherd *Debbie Luckman* • Louis Jourdan *Prince Di Siracusa* • Stéphane Audran *Shireen Firdausi* • David Warner *Agha Firdausi* • Martin Balsam *Joe Fiore* • Jay Leno *Albert Fiore* • Tony Mascia *Marvin Skinner* • Joss Ackland *Henry Foreman* ■ *Dir* Ivan Passer • *Scr* Peter Stone, from the novel by Paul E Erdman

The Silver Brumby ★★★★ U

Adventure   1992 · Ausl · Colour · 91mins

Less sentimental than most American family films, this "outback western" will transfix those teenagers who are obsessed with all things equine. Shooting both the landscape and the fabulous horses with a genuine passion, director John Tatoulis foregoes the easy rites-of-passage clichés as Ami Daemion learns the lessons contained in her mother Caroline Goodall's book about a wild stallion, the "brumby" of the title. With Russell Crowe cutting a dash as the cattleman intent on possessing the beast, the film makes demands of its audience and offers no cosy conclusions, but it's all the better for that. 🖵

Caroline Goodall *Elyne* • Russell Crowe *The man* • Ami Daemion [Amiel Daemion] *Indy* ■ *Dir* John Tatoulis • *Scr* Elyne Mitchell, John Tatoulis, Jon Stephens, from the novel by Elyne Mitchell

Silver Bullet ★★ 18

Horror   1985 · US · Colour · 90mins

Scripted by Stephen King from his own story *Cycle of the Werewolf*, this half-hearted lycanthropic horror is a tired sheep in werewolf's clothing. Disabled Corey Haim (his wheelchair is the silver bullet of the title) knows there's a werewolf on the prowl in his small town and convinces his sister (Megan Fellows) and their alcoholic uncle (Gary Busey) to help him unmask its human identity. First-time director Daniel Attias draws credible performances from his able cast but the deliberately irony-rich murders draw more laughter than terror. *ET* creator Carlo Rambaldi's embarrassingly artificial werewolf doesn't help matters. 🖵

Gary Busey *Uncle Red* • Corey Haim *Marty Coslaw* • Megan Follows *Jane Coslaw* • Everett McGill *Reverend Lowe* • Terry O'Quinn *Sheriff Joe Haller* • Lawrence Tierney *Owen Knopfler* ■ *Dir* Daniel Attias • *Scr* Stephen King, from his story *Cycle of the Werewolf*

The Silver Chalice ★★ U

Religious drama 1954 · US · Colour · 143mins

A biblical epic focusing on a Greek slave, freed from bondage to design and make a chalice to hold the silver cup used at the Last Supper, this was the film that launched the career of Paul Newman. Unfortunately, the underdeveloped script gave him no chance to display his considerable acting gifts. Despite William V Skall's Oscar-nominated CinemaScope photography, which made the most of the visual spectacle (including the feminine pulchritude of Virginia Mayo and Pier Angeli as the women in Newman's life), and Franz Waxman's sweeping score (also nominated), the dreary writing and Victor Saville's lifeless direction make for a movie that's too long by half.

Virginia Mayo *Helena* • Pier Angeli *Deborra* • Jack Palance *Simon* • Paul Newman *Basil* • Walter Hampden *Joseph* • Joseph Wiseman *Mijamin* • Alexander Scourby *Luke* • Lorne Greene *Peter* • Natalie Wood *Helena as a child* ■ *Dir* Victor Saville • *Scr* Lesser Samuels, from the novel by Thomas B Costain

Silver City ★★ 15

Romantic drama
1984 · Ausl · Colour · 97mins

This is a disappointingly flat and unconvincing melodrama, considering that the screenplay boasted contributions from *Schindler's Ark* author, Thomas Keneally. Recalled in flashback, the romantic triangle involving aspiring teacher Gosia Dobrowolska, lawyer Ivar Kants and his put-upon wife, Anna Jemison, develops along all-too-predictable lines, wasting both the unusual backdrop (an immigrant camp nicknamed Silver City on account of its dehumanising corrugated huts) and the inevitable culture clashes between the refugee Poles and the local Australians. Earnestly acted, yet mediocre. 🖵

Gosia Dobrowolska *Nina* • Ivar Kants *Julian* • Anna Jemison *Anna* • Steve Bisley *Viktor* • Debra Lawrance *Helena* • Ewa Brok *Mrs Bronowska* ■ *Dir* Sophia Turkiewicz • *Scr* Sophia Turkiewicz, Thomas Keneally

The Silver Cord ★★★

Drama   1933 · US · BW · 75mins

Although this adaptation of a play by Sidney Howard retains the style, atmosphere, small cast of characters and theatrical speeches that betray its origins, it is nonetheless one of the most frightening and powerful studies of poisonously destructive mother-love you are likely to see. Laura Hope Crews delivers something of a tour de force as the selfish, manipulative and unhealthily possessive mother of two adult sons, bent on destroying the engagement of one (Eric Linden) and the marriage of the other (Joel McCrea). John Cromwell directs, drawing solid portrayals from the men and a shining performance from Irene Dunne as McCrea's wife.

Irene Dunne *Christina Phelps* • Joel McCrea *David Phelps* • Frances Dee *Hester Phelps* • Eric Linden *Robert Phelps* • Laura Hope Crews *Mrs Phelps* • Helen Cromwell *Delia* ■ *Dir* John Cromwell • *Scr* Jane Murfin, from the play by Sidney Howard

The Silver Darlings ★★ U

Drama   1947 · UK · BW · 93mins

The silver darlings are the herrings that provide a precarious living for the fishermen of the Hebrides in the mid-19th century. This Scottish enterprise was a work of love, made over a two-year span by writer/director Clarence Elder in collaboration with leading actor and associate director Clifford Evans. A pity, then, that the location footage not only overwhelms the commonplace narrative but is too often back-projected behind actors in the studio. Sorely lacking is the poetic vision of Robert Flaherty's *Man of Aran*, while Evans's Welsh accent and Helen Shingler's English one are a hindrance to cultivating an authentic tone.

Clifford Evans *Roddy* • Helen Shingler *Catrine* • Carl Bernard *Angus* • Norman Shelley *Hendry* • Jean Shepherd *Mrs Hendry* • Simon Lack *Don* • Norman Williams *Tormad* • Phyllis Morris *Tormad's mother* ■ *Dir* Clarence Elder, Clifford Evans • *Scr* Clarence Elder, from a novel by Neil M Gunn

Silver Dream Racer ★ 15

Action drama   1980 · UK · Colour · 106mins

Whatever happened to David Essex? Here he is, near the end of his heyday, racing motorbikes, dressing in leather, trying to be James Dean and keeping Brylcreem in business. He wrote the music, too. The plot kicks in when Essex is given the mean machine of the title, a space-age ride designed to leave American ace rider Beau Bridges on the starting grid. A vanity project from beginning to end, it tries hard to be a British *Electra Glide in Blue*, but rarely rises above the level of a clapped out Vespa. 🖵

David Essex *Nick Freeman* • Beau Bridges *Bruce McBride* • Cristina Raines *Julie Prince* • Clarke Peters *Cider Jones* • Harry H Corbett *Wiggins* • Diane Keen *Tina* • Lee Montague *Jack Freeman* ■ *Dir/Scr* David Wickes

The Silver Fleet ★★★ U

Second World War drama
1943 · UK · BW · 84mins

This British wartime flag-waver boasts the magic names of Michael Powell and Emeric Pressburger. But they were only producers of this film, which was actually written and directed by Vernon Sewell and Gordon Wellesley. Their influence may well account for the too-stately progress of its tale of shipping engineer Ralph Richardson, posing as a traitor in Nazi-occupied Holland in order to destroy the U-boat he's just had built. Richardson's performance is never less than convincing and neither is the story once it gets going. 🖵

Ralph Richardson *Jaap Van Leyden* • Googie Withers *Helene Van Leyden* • Esmond Knight *Von Schiller* • Beresford Egan *Krampf* • Frederick Burtwell *Captain Muller* • Willem Akkerman *Willem Van Leyden* • Dorothy Gordon *Janni Peters* • Charles Victor *Bastiaan Peters* ■ *Dir* Vernon Campbell Sewell [Vernon Sewell], Gordon Wellesley • *Scr* Vernon Campbell Sewell, Gordon Wellesley

Silver Lode ★★★

Western   1954 · US · Colour · 80mins

A B-western that's well worth catching. On his wedding day, John Payne is accused of murder and has to go on the run from a posse led by a bogus sheriff, played by Dan Duryea. As with the earlier and far better known *High Noon*, also set on a wedding day, many critics regard this tale as an allegory about the political witch-hunts of the time Duryea's character, after all, is called McCarthy! Tightly directed by veteran Allan Dwan and nicely photographed by maestro John Alton, this is one of many RKO productions that belies its dime budget.

John Payne *Dan Ballard* • Lizabeth Scott *Rose Evans* • Dan Duryea *McCarthy* • Dolores Moran *Dolly* • Emile Meyer *Sheriff Woolley* • Robert Warwick *Judge Cranston* • John Hudson *Mitch Evans* • Harry Carey Jr *Johnson* ■ *Dir* Allan Dwan • *Scr* Karen De Wolfe

Silver River ★★★ U

Western   1948 · US · BW · 104mins

After *Gentleman Jim* and *They Died with Their Boots On*, director Raoul Walsh and ageing stud Errol Flynn renewed their partnership in this run-of-the-mill Warner Bros western, not even considered worthy of shooting in colour. Still, movie fans today will find much to enjoy, since the film shows the Hollywood system in fine fettle. Flynn's the former soldier turned gambler who'll stop at nothing to win the affection of sexy – but married – Ann Sheridan. The pair strike erotic sparks off one another and there's novelty value in the fact that the plot is a western version of the Biblical tale of David and Bathsheba. 🖵

Errol Flynn *Capt Mike McComb* • Ann Sheridan *Georgia Moore* • Thomas Mitchell *John Plato Beck* • Bruce Bennett *Stanley Moore* • Tom D'Andrea *Pistol Porter* • Barton MacLane *Banjo Sweeney* • Monte Blue *Buck Chevigee* • Jonathan Hale *Maj Spencer* ■ *Dir* Raoul Walsh • *Scr* Stephen Longstreet, Harriet Frank Jr, from a novel by Stephen Longstreet

Silver Strand ★★ 18

Drama   1995 · US · Colour · 99mins

It won't take you very long to recognise that this naval base romance was penned by Douglas Day Stewart, the screenwriter of *An Officer and a Gentleman*. Fresh from working on a different kind of seal movie (the family hit *Andre*) George Miller directs this potboiler, in which showy SEAL Gil Bellows beds bored officer's wife Nicollette Sheridan, earning the approval of naughty Jennifer O'Neill and the fury of bullish instructor Tony Plana in the process. There's a little steamy love-making and a lot of yelling on the parade ground, but we've seen just about everything here somewhere else, and done much better too. 🖵

Nicollette Sheridan *Michelle Hughes* • Gil Bellows *Brian Del Piso* • Jennifer O'Neill *Louellen Peterson* • Jay O Sanders *Captain Lucas Hughes* • Tony Plana *Richie Guttierez* ■ *Dir* George Miller (1) • *Scr* Douglas Day Stewart

Silver Streak ★★★★ PG

Comedy   1976 · US · Colour · 108mins

Gene Wilder and Richard Pryor star in a spectacular comedy thriller set

aboard the Los Angeles-Chicago *Silver Streak* train. Publisher Wilder witnesses a murder and thief Pryor helps to hide him as Patrick McGoohan and his gang of villains close in. It harks back to those British thrillers of the thirties, *The 39 Steps* and *The Lady Vanishes*, with some screwball antics thrown in for good measure, plus the delectable Jill Clayburgh sorting out the men from the boys. With such an endearing trio of characters, it makes you wonder why there wasn't a sequel, though it paved the way for Wilder and Pryor's 1980 collaboration, *Stir Crazy*. 🖼

Gene Wilder *George Caldwell* • Jill Clayburgh *Hilly Burns* • Richard Pryor *Grover Muldoon* • Patrick McGoohan *Roger Devereau* • Ned Beatty *Sweet* • Clifton James *Sheriff Chauncey* • Ray Walston *Mr Whiney* • Richard Kiel *Reace* • Scatman Crothers *Ralston* ■ *Dir* Arthur Hiller • *Scr* Colin Higgins

Silverado ★★★★ 🅿🄶
Western 1985 · US · Colour · 127mins

Billed as the movie that was going to revive the ailing western, Lawrence Kasdan's film merely performed a little resuscitation before Clint Eastwood's *Unforgiven* proved there was life in the old genre yet. Just as Steven Spielberg plundered the Saturday serial for his *Raiders* trilogy, so this rousing tale rustles ideas from virtually every B-western ever made. While this makes for an invigorating adventure, it's also rather untidy. Nevertheless, Kevin Kline, Kevin Costner, Danny Glover and Scott Glenn make attractive heroes, Brian Dennehy is a hissable villain and John Cleese enjoys his cameo as an English lawman. Pity the thundering hooves didn't drown out Bruce Broughton's lousy score. Contains some swearing. 🖼 *DVD*

Kevin Kline *Paden* • Scott Glenn *Emmett* • Kevin Costner *Jake* • John Cleese *Sheriff Langston* • Brian Dennehy *Cobb* • Danny Glover *Mal* • Jeff Goldblum *Slick* • Linda Hunt *Stella* • Rosanna Arquette *Hannah* ■ *Dir* Lawrence Kasdan • *Scr* Lawrence Kasdan, Mark Kasdan

Silverlake Life: the View from Here ★★★★
Documentary
1992 · US · Colour and BW · 99mins

After *Longtime Companion*, this is the best movie made about the Aids experience. A profoundly moving and multi-award-winning documentary charting the lives of gay lovers Tom Joslin and Mark Massi as they enter the final stages of the disease. Using home-movie footage of their 20-odd years living together in the gay-friendly Silverlake area of Los Angeles, intercut with the harsh reality of their present situation, this is an incredibly thought-provoking tribute to the agony, pain and candid self-revelation of two fascinating and brave individuals. Often unbearably distressing to watch, it's their humanity and spirit in the face of adversity you will remember.

Dir Tom Joslin, Peter Friedman

Simba ★★
Drama
1955 · UK · Colour · 99mins

Simba is the Swahili word for lion, though this is no wildlife adventure

frolic. It's a drama about the Mau Mau troubles in Kenya, bit it reduces a complex political crisis to a feeble love story and colonial posturings on the verandah, while a back-projected Africa wobbles in the distance. Dirk Bogarde was then at the height of his matinée idol period, while Donald Sinden and Virginia McKenna are pretty lightweight in support. Nowadays, it comes over as an example of how British cinema still strove to make Imperial yarns even as the Empire was falling apart.

Dirk Bogarde *Alan Howard* • Donald Sinden *Inspector Tom Drummond* • Virginia McKenna *Mary Crawford* • Basil Sydney *Mr Crawford* • Marie Ney *Mrs Crawford* • Joseph Tomelty *Dr Hughes* ■ *Dir* Brian Desmond Hurst • *Scr* John Baines, Robin Estridge, from a novel by Anthony Perry

Simon ★★ 🅿🄶
Comedy 1980 · US · Colour · 93mins

This half-baked satirical comedy from Woody Allen associate Marshall Brickman (the pair shared *Annie Hall's* best screenplay Oscar) is too clever by half. In truth, it's not funny where it's meant to be, and tiresome long before it reaches its conclusion. But there's some compensation in Alan Arkin's strong central performance as a professor of psychology who's brainwashed into thinking he's an alien, and clever support from a cast clearly hand-picked for their eccentricity: bucktoothed Austin Pendleton, sexy Madeline Kahn, Fred Gwynne from *The Munsters* and the great, slack-jawed Adolph Green, co-author of *Singin' in the Rain* and *The Band Wagon*. Contains swearing.

Alan Arkin *Simon Mendelssohn* • Madeline Kahn *Cynthia* • Austin Pendleton *Becker* • Judy Graubart *Lisa* • Wallace Shawn *Van Dongen* • Max Wright *Hundertwasser* • Fred Gwynne *Korey* • Adolph Green *Commune leader* ■ *Dir/Scr* Marshall Brickman

Simon and Laura ★★
Comedy 1955 · UK · Colour · 90mins

Simon and Laura (Peter Finch and Kay Kendall) are a husband-and-wife acting team, publicly celebrated, privately bankrupt and one step from the divorce court. But the BBC, no less, comes to the rescue, offering them a series in which they play a happily married couple. Oh, the irony. Directed by Muriel Box (one of the few women directing in Britain at the time), this starts out as a brisk satire on celebrity, emancipation and cinema's enemy, TV. It goes soft by the end, of course, and now looks terribly dated.

Peter Finch *Simon Foster* • Kay Kendall *Laura Foster* • Muriel Pavlow *Janet Honeyman* • Hubert Gregg *Bertie Burton* • Maurice Denham *Wilson* • Ian Carmichael *David Prentice* • Richard Wattis *Controller* • Thora Hird *Jessie* ■ *Dir* Muriel Box • *Scr* Peter Blackmore, from the play by Alan Melville

Simon Birch ★★★ 🅿🄶
Drama 1998 · US · Colour · 113mins

American buddy-buddy movies start young. This, with faint echoes of Peter Chelsom's *The Mighty*, is set in the fifties and sixties, and tells of the friendship between the illegitimate pre-adolescent Joe (Joseph Mazzello) and Simon (Ian Michael Smith), a dwarf

with an answer for everything and a question for everyone. Narrated by Jim Carrey (its one concession to popularity at the box office) and set in a Norman Rockwell-type small town, it tells how the boys cope with the strictures of their enemies – the local clergyman and the Sunday-school teacher. Predictable enough, but the acting lifts it into the heart. 🖼

Ian Michael Smith *Simon Birch* • Joseph Mazzello *Joe Wenteworth* • Ashley Judd *Rebecca Wenteworth* • Oliver Platt *Ben Goodrich* • David Strathairn *Reverend Russell* • Dana Ivey *Grandmother Wenteworth* ■ *Dir* Mark Steven Johnson • *Scr* Mark Steven Johnson, from the novel *A Prayer for Owen Meany* by John Irving

Simon Magus ★★ 🅿🄶
Romantic fantasy
1998 · UK · Colour · 106mins

Opening with a pseudo-silent movie view of 19th-century Silesia, Ben Hopkins's feature debut quickly descends into costume melodramatics as he loses control of both his multinational cast and his folkloric tale of progress, prejudice and superstition. As the titular village outcast who's convinced he's in the thrall of Satan, Noah Taylor partially conveys the incomprehending resentment that prompts him to spy for anti-Semitic aristo, Sean McGinley, as the latter seeks to confound farmer Stuart Townsend's bid to link their circumcised settlement to the railroad. With widow Embeth Davidtz and poet Rutger Hauer left out on a limb, this bombastic muddle misfires on every conceivable level.

Noah Taylor *Simon* • Stuart Townsend *Dovid* • Embeth Davidtz *Leah* • Sean McGinley *Hase* • Rutger Hauer *Squire* ■ *Dir/Scr* Ben Hopkins

Simon of the Desert ★★★ 🄸🄸
Drama 1965 · Mex · BW · 43mins

Winner of the special jury prize at the Venice Film Festival in 1965, this is one of Luis Buñuel's least strident assaults on Roman Catholicism. How much this was influenced by a consciously playful mood or by having to make do when funds dried up after only 25 days (hence its short running time) is open to conjecture. Based loosely on the story of the fifth-century saint, Simeon Stylites, the film is packed with ribald comments on the improbability of miracles, the hypocrisy of the faithful and the impossibility of holiness. Stylishly photographed by Gabriel Figueroa, it's a minor film, but it's still evidently the work of a master. In Spanish with English subtitles. 🖼

Claudio Brook *Simon* • Silvia Pinal *The Devil* • Hortensia Santovena *Simon's mother* • Jesus Fernandez *Goatherd* • Enrique Alvarez Felix *Brother Matias* ■ *Dir/Scr* Luis Buñuel

Simon Sez ★ 🄸🄸
Action comedy adventure
1999 · Bel/Ger · Colour · 81mins

The producer of *Double Team* (1997) didn't learn his lesson with the casting of basketball pro Dennis Rodman in that movie, casting him again in this action comedy that actually seems to be an unofficial sequel. Actually, except for being in one of the most

unintentionally funny sex scenes ever filmed, Rodman actually looks good when compared to his sidekick Dane Cook, who comes across as Jim Carrey on cocaine. Only the attractive French Rivera backdrop prevents this from being a complete waste of time.

Dennis Rodman *Simon* • Dane Cook *Nick* • Natalia Cigliuti *Claire* • Filip Nicolic *Michael* • John Pinette *Macro* ■ *Dir* Kevin Elders • *Scr* Andrew Miller, Andrew Lowery, from a story by Moshe Diamant, Rudy Cohen

Simon, Simon ★★ 🅄
Comedy 1970 · UK · Colour · 31mins

Unsung character actor Graham Stark made his debut as the writer and director of this fond, if laboured tribute to the silent slapstick style of the Keystone Kops. Comedy stars like Peter Sellers, Morecambe and Wise, Bob Monkhouse and Bernie Winters, crop up in cameo roles, as does movie star Michael Caine. But the main focus falls on the rivalry between Stark's council workman and fireman Norman Rossington, as they use their elevator vehicles to woo typist Julia Foster. The mugging mime and the excessive crane shots soon become wearisome, but essentially this is harmless fun.

Graham Stark *First workman* • John Junkin *Second workman* • Julia Foster *Typist* • Norman Rossington *Fireman* • Peter Sellers • Michael Caine • Eric Morecambe • Ernie Wise • Bob Monkhouse *Photographer* • Bernie Winters ■ *Dir/Scr* Graham Stark

Simpatico ★★★ 🄸🄵
Drama 1999 · US/Fr · Colour · 106mins

A great cast (Jeff Bridges, Nick Nolte, Sharon Stone) and impeccable credentials (it's based on a Sam Shepard play) still make for an awkward drama. The first film from stage director Matthew Warchus, it tells of a millionaire racehorse owner, Lyle Carter (Bridges), who answers an SOS from former friend Vincent (Nolte). The alcoholic Vinnie has a precarious hold over Carter: they used to fix races together, a scam which ended in the ruin of course official Albert Finney. Both men are still in love with Stone, but her appearance, often in a fragile nightie, seems merely gratuitous. It all comes across as stilted and stagey.

Nick Nolte *Vincent "Vinnie" T Webb* • Jeff Bridges *Lyle Carter* • Sharon Stone *Rosie Carter* • Catherine Keener *Cecilia Ponz* • Albert Finney *Simms* ■ *Dir* Matthew Warchus • *Scr* Matthew Warchus, David Nicholls, from a play by Sam Shepard

The Simple Life of Noah Dearborn ★★★
Drama 1999 · US · Colour · 87mins

Screen icon Sidney Poitier makes a rare small-screen appearance in this tale of quiet determination and inner strength. An elderly small-town craftsman/farmer refuses to sell his land to a greedy developer, who then tries to get his psychiatrist girlfriend (Mary Louise Parker) to declare the man mentally incompetent. Sterling Anderson's observant screenplay, Gregg Champion's sensitive direction and compelling performances by stars Poitier and Parker paint a vivid picture of innocent dignity under siege.

Sidney Poitier *Noah Dearborn* • Dianne Wiest *Sarah McClellan* • Mary-Louise Parker *Valerie Crane* • George Newbern *Christian Nelson* • Bernie Casey *Silas* ■ *Dir* Gregg Champion • *Scr* Sterling Anderson

Simple Men ★★★★ 🖪
Comedy drama
1992 · US/UK · Colour · 100mins
One of the most accessible of writer/director Hal Hartley's oddball accounts of his slightly-skewed world. This begins mid-robbery and then follows a white-collar crook Bill (Robert Burke) and his younger brother Dennis (William Sage) as they search for their father, a former baseball star and suspected bomber who's been on the run for years. Along the way there's a fight between a nun and a cop, romantic interludes and musings on the meaning of life. The usual Hartley repertory company respond as to a puppeteer's twitch. 🖭

Robert Burke *Bill McCabe* • William Sage *Dennis McCabe* • Karen Sillas *Kate* • Elina Lowensohn *Elina* • Martin Donovan *Martin* • Chris Cooke *Vic* ■ *Dir/Scr* Hal Hartley

The Simple-Minded Murderer ★★★★
Drama   1982 · Swe · Colour · 107mins
Winning international awards for writer/director Hans Alfredson and star Stellan Skarsgård, this is a chilling period piece with a slow-burning fuse. Alfredson, who co-stars, gives a performance of terrifying brutality as the vicious landowner whose persecution of Skarsgård's village idiot ends in inevitable tragedy. With its persuasive evocation of rural life in the thirties and its perceptive insights into the prejudices of enclosed communities, this is a disturbing film that is all the more effective for its sedate pacing and restrained playing. In Swedish with English subtitles..

Stellan Skarsgård *The Idiot* • Hans Alfredson *Hoglund* • Maria Johansson *Anna* • Per Myrberg *Andersson* • Lena-Pia Bernhardsson *Mrs Andersson* ■ *Dir* Hans Alfredson • *Scr* Hans Alfredson, from his novel *En ond man*

A Simple Plan ★★★★ 🖪
Thriller
1998 · US/UK/Jap/Ger/Fr · Colour · 121mins
Shallow Grave meets *Fargo* in director Sam Raimi's change-of-pace thriller about the corrupting influence of greed. Three men find a crashed plane in thick snow containing over $4 million and hesitantly decide to split the loot once they are sure they won't be suspected. Of course, everything that could go wrong does in Raimi's grim fairy tale. Completely eschewing the frenetic approach of his *Evil Dead* work, Raimi comes up with a poetic suspense film that delves unassumingly into the cryptic regions of human nature, and the uneasy mood is underscored by two marvellous performances from Bill Paxton and Billy Bob Thornton as the two brothers in the pledge triangle. Contains violence and swearing. 🖭

Bill Paxton *Hank Mitchell* • Billy Bob Thornton *Jacob Mitchell* • Bridget Fonda *Sarah Mitchell* • Gary Cole *Baxter* • Brent Briscoe *Lou* •

Becky Ann Baker *Nancy* • Chelcie Ross *Carl* • Jack Walsh *Tom Butler* ■ *Dir* Sam Raimi • *Scr* Scott B Smith, from a novel by Scott B Smith

A Simple Twist of Fate ★★★ 🄿🄶
Drama   1994 · US · Colour · 101mins
Steve Martin likes to have an audience on his side, and nowhere is that more evident than in this personally-scripted drama, updated from George Eliot's *Silas Marner*. Martin plays a reclusive cabinet-maker who "adopts" the illegitimate toddler of local magnate Gabriel Byrne when the child's mother dies in the snow near his isolated home. The Victorian poignancy of the tale still grips, even in modern-day dress, but Martin unfortunately comes across as a bit of a wimp. The charm that seemed to flow effortlessly in Martin's earlier update *Roxanne* is not very evident here, though the end result is still very watchable. 🖭

Steve Martin *Michael McMann* • Gabriel Byrne *John Newland* • Laura Linney *Nancy Newland* • Catherine O'Hara *Mrs Simon* • Alana Austin *Mathilda McCann aged ten* • Alyssa Austin *Mathilda McCann aged five* • Stephen Baldwin *Tanny Newland* ■ *Dir* Gillies MacKinnon • *Scr* Steve Martin, from the novel *Silas Marner* by George Eliot

A Simple Wish ★★★ 🅄
Fantasy comedy   1997 · US · Colour · 85mins
Fun family romp with Martin Short as a fumbling fairy godmother who gets into all sorts of trouble when he tries to grant little Mara Wilson's wish that her actor dad (Robert Pastorelli) finally finds success. More interesting, though, is the conflict as the fairy godmothers (including Teri Garr and Ruby Dee) are facing against struck-off fairy turned witch Kathleen Turner, who chews up the scenery and spits it out with hilarious venom in a deliciously evil turn. It's gets a bit flabby towards the middle, but young viewers will no doubt enjoy the special effects. 🖭

Martin Short *Murray* • Kathleen Turner *Claudia* • Mara Wilson *Anabel* • Robert Pastorelli *Oliver* • Amanda Plummer *Boots* • Francis Capra *Charlie Greening* • Ruby Dee *Hortense* • Teri Garr *Rena* ■ *Dir* Michael Ritchie • *Scr* Jeff Rothberg

Simply Irresistible ★ 🄿🄶
Supernatural romantic comedy
1999 · US · Colour · 95mins
A very unfortunate title for a film which, quite frankly, is incredibly easy to resist. *Buffy the Vampire Slayer* star Sarah Michelle Gellar is the mediocre chef of a small New York bistro who suddenly discovers she can magically make wonderful food which affects people's emotions. Sean Patrick Flanery is the Manhattan businessman who offers her a culinary opportunity and possible romance. Unfortunately, the pair have no chemistry whatsoever, while first-time director Mark Tarlov can't decide whether he is making a romantic comedy or a quirky magical drama along the lines of *Like Water for Chocolate*. Contains sexual references and some strong language.

Sarah Michelle Gellar *Amanda Shelton* • Sean Patrick Flanery *Tom Bartlett* • Patricia Clarkson *Lois McNally* • Dylan Baker *Jonathan Bendel* •

Christopher Durang *Gene O'Reilly* • Larry Gilliard Jr *Nolan Traynor* • Betty Buckley *Aunt Stella* ■ *Dir* Mark Tarlov • *Scr* Judith Roberts

Sin ★★ 🖪
Romantic drama   1972 · US · Colour · 86mins
An incredibly daft seventies drama from director George Pan Cosmatos, who went on to make *Rambo: First Blood Part II* and the infinitely more impressive *Tombstone*. Raquel Welch, looking stunning (of course), gets involved in some serious passion, Mills and Boon style, in a case of forbidden love on a Mediterranean island, which you just know is going to end in tears. Never mind, because both the scenery and Miss Welch look beautiful, and that's all the excuse you need to watch this. 🖭

Raquel Welch *Elena* • Richard Johnson *Orestes* • Frank Wolff *Hector* • Flora Robson *Antigone* • Jack Hawkins *Father Nicholas* ■ *Dir/Scr* George Pan Cosmatos

The Sin of Madelon Claudet ★★★★
Melodrama   1931 · US · BW · 74mins
Broadway legend Helen Hayes, who walked off with an Oscar for her performance as the unfortunate heroine, plays an innocent French country girl who elopes to Paris with an American artist, is deserted and left pregnant. How she sacrifices herself for the child who thinks she's dead (shades of *Madame X*) is the stuff of an archetypal five-handkerchief weepie. Lewis Stone is splendid as Madelon's protector-lover, while Jean Hersholt is the mentor of her "orphan" son.

Helen Hayes *Madelon Claudet* • Lewis Stone *Carlo Boretti* • Neil Hamilton *Larry* • Robert Young *Dr Claudet* • Cliff Edwards *Victor* • Jean Hersholt *Dr Dulac* • Marie Prevost *Rosalie* ■ *Dir* Edgar Selwyn • *Scr* Charles Macarthur, Ben Hecht, from the play *The Lullaby* by Edward Knoblock

The Sin Ship ★
Crime drama   1931 · US · BW · 65mins
Riding high after co-starring as the tough veteran soldier of *All Quiet on the Western Front*, Louis Wolheim not only starred in this lurid drama but made his directing debut. Dead from stomach cancer before it opened, he was spared the bad reviews. His hard-boiled skipper of a cargo ship takes on board Ian Keith and Mary Astor, a fleeing bank robber and his moll posing as a church minister and wife. Wolheim falls heavily for Astor and becomes a reformed character while she, unbelievably, is attracted to him.

Louis Wolheim *Captain McVeigh* • Mary Astor *"Frisco" Kitty* • Ian Keith *Marsden* • Hugh Herbert *Charlie* ■ *Dir* Louis Wolheim • *Scr* Hugh Herbert, from a story by Keane Thompson, Agnes Brand Leahy

Sin Town ★★
Western   1942 · US · BW · 73mins
An average little western, kept moving at a rate of knots by one of those unsung heroes of the studio system, director Ray Enright. There's a certain gritty realism in the script, thanks to the presence of the young Richard Brooks, a former reporter, as one of the screenwriters. It's always good to

see Broderick Crawford, but it's the ever elegant Constance Bennett who sweeps up the acting honours. The film packs a surprising amount into its short running time, but sadly little that is above programme-filler standard.

Constance Bennett *Kye Allen* • Broderick Crawford *Dude McNair* • Anne Gwynne *Laura Kirby* • Patric Knowles *Wade Crowell* • Andy Devine *Judge Eustace Vale* • Leo Carrillo *Angelo Colina* • Ward Bond *Rock Delaney* ■ *Dir* Ray Enright • *Scr* W Scott Darling, Gerald Geraghty, Richard Brooks

Sinbad and the Eye of the Tiger ★★★ 🅄
Fantasy adventure
1977 · UK/US · Colour · 108mins
Not up to the previous two *Sinbad* adventures from the Ray Harryhausen fantasy factory – it's too long and Patrick Wayne is a distinctly charisma-free hero. As you'd expect, special effects wizard Harryhausen enhances this romantic exotica with his distinctive brand of visual thrills. Highlights include a chess-playing baboon, three axe-wielding ghouls, a sabre-toothed tiger and a one-horned troglodyte. It all helps to pass the time away agreeably between the frothy *Arabian Nights* nonsense standing in for the plot.

Patrick Wayne *Sinbad* • Taryn Power *Dione* • Jane Seymour *Princess Farah* • Margaret Whiting *Zenobia* • Patrick Troughton *Melanthius* • Kurt Christian *Rafi* • Nadim Sawalha *Hassan* ■ *Dir* Sam Wanamaker • *Scr* Beverley Cross, from a story by Beverley Cross, Ray Harryhausen

Sinbad the Sailor ★★★ 🅄
Adventure   1947 · US · Colour · 111mins
A splendid Technicolor romp with Douglas Fairbanks Jr ably following in the dashing footsteps of his late father and falling for green-eyed, red-headed Maureen O'Hara. The costumes lack flair (as does the plot), and the whole's very juvenile. But there's no denying the film's sense of *joie de vivre*, and that's a very cherishable commodity. The right tone is defined from the opening; this is great fun. 🖭

Douglas Fairbanks Jr *Sinbad* • Maureen O'Hara *Shireen* • Walter Slezak *Melik* • Anthony Quinn *Emir* • George Tobias *Abbu* • Jane Greer *Pirouze* • Mike Mazurki *Yusuf* ■ *Dir* Richard Wallace • *Scr* John Twist, from a story by John Twist, George Worthing

Since You Went Away ★★★ 🅄
Drama   1944 · US · BW · 163mins
Everything is absolutely certain in this vision of wartime middle-class America. Claudette Colbert waits faithfully, keeping the home fires burning, while husband Neil Hamilton (his only appearance in the film is in a photograph) and family friend Joseph Cotten are off saving everyone from Hitler. Marriage is wonderful, children are dreamboats and democracy rules OK. It's all syrupy nonsense, of course, which has weathered the years with little to recommend it apart from a wonderful cast, including an appearance from the brilliant Agnes Moorehead, always good value no matter how bad the material. 🖭

🅄 = SUITABLE FOR ALL   🅄🄲 = SUITABLE FOR ALL, ESPECIALLY FOR YOUNG CHILDREN (VIDEO ONLY)   🄿🄶 = PARENTAL GUIDANCE

Claudette Colbert *Anne Hilton* • Jennifer Jones *Jane Hilton* • Shirley Temple *Bridget Hilton* • Joseph Cotten *Lieutenant Anthony Willett* • Monty Woolley *Colonel Smollett* • Robert Walker *Corporal William G Smollett II* • Lionel Barrymore *Clergyman* • Hattie McDaniel *Fidelia* • Agnes Moorehead *Emily Hawkins* ■ *Dir* John Cromwell • *Scr* David O Selznick, Margaret Buell Wilder, from the novel *Together* by Margaret Buell Wilder

Since You've Been Gone ★★

Comedy 1998 · US · Colour · 94mins

Doctor David Schwimmer is persuaded to attend his high school reunion, despite the humiliation he suffered at the hands of the school bully on graduation day. Once there, Schwimmer begins to understand that the rest of his high school class is far more troubled than he is. A largely talented cast (Teri Hatcher, Rachel Griffiths) is overshadowed by a juvenile plot and silly innuendo, but there are some enjoyable moments and some might even call it a date movie.

David Schwimmer *Robert S Levin* • Philip Rayburn Smith *Kevin MacEldowney* • Joey Slotnick *Zane Levy* • Teri Hatcher *Maria Goldstein* • Lara Flynn Boyle *Grace Williams* • Rachel Griffiths *Sally Zalinsky* ■ *Dir* David Schwimmer • *Scr* Jeff Steinberg

Sincerely Yours ★ U

Drama 1955 · US · Colour · 120mins

"Insincerely yours" might have been a more honest title for this ill-judged, ineptly updated and ludicrous remake of *The Man Who Played God*, the unusual, fantastical and rather powerful 1932 melodrama starring George Arliss and Bette Davis. Liberace takes the Arliss role of a concert pianist who goes deaf, learns to lip-read and anonymously helps people in trouble on whose conversations he "eavesdrops" through binoculars. The film, in which Dorothy Malone co-stars, would be funny if it weren't so awful.

Liberace *Anthony Warrin* • Joanne Dru *Marion Moore* • Dorothy Malone *Linda Curtis* • Alex Nicol *Howard Ferguson* • William Demarest *Sam Dunne* • Lori Nelson *Sarah Cosgrove* • Lurene Tuttle *Mrs McGinley* • Richard Eyer *Alvie Hunt* ■ *Dir* Gordon Douglas • *Scr* Irving Wallace, from the play *The Man Who Played God* by Jules Eckert Goodman

Sinful Davey ★★

Period comedy adventure
1969 · UK · Colour · 94mins

John Hurt is Scot Davey Haggart, who deserts the British army and, like his father before him, becomes a highwayman, always just an inch away from the hangman's noose. John Huston included this extremely lightweight and modestly enjoyable romp amongst his failures – rightly so if you compare it to *The Maltese Falcon* or *The Man Who Would Be King*. Filmed in Ireland, where Huston owned an estate at St Clerans, County Galway for many years, it boasts some nice camerawork by Freddie Young, a cute performance by Pamela Franklin and the fleeting screen debut of the director's daughter, Anjelica.

John Hurt *Davey Haggart* • Pamela Franklin *Annie* • Nigel Davenport *Constable Richardson* • Ronald Fraser *MacNab* • Robert Morley

Duke of Argyll • Maxine Audley *Duchess of Argyll* • Fionnuala Flanagan [Fionnula Flanagan] *Penelope* • Anjelica Huston ■ *Dir* John Huston • *Scr* James R Webb, from the autobiography *The Life of David Haggart* by David Haggart

A Sinful Life ★★

Comedy 1989 · US · Colour · 90mins

Adapted by Melanie Graham from her play *Baby Bump and the Last of the Pom Pom Girls*, this low-budget comedy finds Anita Morris opting for single motherhood, having once danced for Sonny and Cher. When the authorities threaten to take away her unusual daughter Blair Tefkin, she enters the arena of domestic respectabilty, complete with dutiful husband. Actor/director William Schreiner's comedy is a nice, if extremely slight vehicle for Morris's talents.

Anita Morris *Claire* • Rick Overton *Janitor Joe* • Dennis Christopher *Nathan Flowers* • Blair Tefkin *Baby* • Mark Rolston *Teresa Tremaine* ■ *Dir* William Schreiner • *Scr* Melanie Graham, from her play *Baby Bump and the Last of the Pom Pom Girls*

Sing ★★★ 15

Musical drama 1989 · US · Colour · 94mins

A teen romance that's as corny as Kansas in August, September *and* October, but that's so sweet and disingenuous it's hard to dislike it, however clichéd. Richard Baskin's musical drama is set in a Brooklyn high school where the students take part in an annual "Sing" contest. Participating bad boy Peter Dobson and nice Jewish girl Jessica Steen share a certain talent for each other, while empathetic teacher Lorraine Bracco must shield the kids from the nasty education authorities, who want to shut the school down. ▭

Lorraine Bracco *Miss Lombardo* • Peter Dobson *Dominic* • Jessica Steen *Hannah* • Louise Lasser *Rosie* • George DiCenzo *Mr Marowitz* • Patti LaBelle *Mrs DeVere* • Susan Peretz *Mrs Tucci* • Laurnea Wilkerson *Zena* ■ *Dir* Richard Baskin • *Scr* Dean Pitchford

Sing, Baby, Sing ★★★★

Musical comedy 1936 · US · BW · 87mins

A fast-moving musical comedy which set Alice Faye on the road to becoming 20th Century-Fox's top singing star. Appearing with a softened, more alluring hairstyle, Faye is a nightclub singer who attracts the attentions of a drunken Shakespearean actor. Adolphe Menjou is hilarious in this role, which is obviously based on that great tippler John Barrymore. The film marked the debut of the Ritz Brothers, who have a few funny moments. The singer with the band is Tony Martin, recently married to Alice Faye, who sings the Oscar-nominated song *When Did You Leave Heaven*.

Alice Faye *Joan Warren* • Adolphe Menjou *Bruce Farraday* • Gregory Ratoff *Nicky* • Ted Healy *Al Craven* • Patsy Kelly *Fitz* • Montagu Love *Robert Wilson* ■ *Dir* Sidney Lanfield • *Scr* Milton Sperling, Jack Yellen, Harry Tugend

Sing, Boy, Sing ★★

Musical drama 1958 · US · BW · 90mins

Tommy Sands, singing idol of the rock 'n' roll era, had a chequered career,

but his screen debut in this adaptation of a television play was impressive and promised better things. The story has teen idol Sands being manipulated by a ruthless manager (Edmond O'Brien) while – shades of *The Jazz Singer* – being torn between his love of pop music and his obligation to succeed his grandfather as a preacher. The tale has too much angst and too little originality to be more than mildly entertaining, but Sands gets to sing a dozen songs and gives an agreeably believable performance.

Tommy Sands *Virgil Walker* • Lili Gentle *Leora Easton* • Edmond O'Brien *Joseph Sharkey* • John McIntire *Reverend Walker* • Nick Adams *CK Judd* • Diane Jergens *Pat* • Josephine Hutchinson *Caroline Walker* • Jerry Paris *Fisher* ■ *Dir* Henry Ephron • *Scr* Claude Binyon, from the TV play *The Singin' Idol* by Paul Monash

Singapore ★★

Adventure drama 1947 · US · BW · 79mins

Pearl-smuggling sailor Fred MacMurray returns to Singapore after the Second World War to retrieve a valuable bag of pearls he left hidden in his hotel room. In flashback, he relives his romance with Ava Gardner, apparently killed in the Japanese invasion which coincided with their wedding. Back in present time, he discovers her alive but suffering total amnesia and married to wealthy Roland Culver. A familiar formula farrago, directed by John Brahm and combining romance, melodrama and thriller elements in an exotic setting, this much-derided piece of nonsensical escapism is really quite entertaining and could be a lot worse.

Fred MacMurray *Matt Gordon* • Ava Gardner *Linda* • Roland Culver *Michael Van Leyden* • Richard Haydn *Chief Inspector Hewitt* • Thomas Gomez *Mr Mauribus* • Spring Byington *Mrs Bellows* • Porter Hall *Mr Bellows* • George Lloyd *Sascha Barda* ■ *Dir* John Brahm • *Scr* Seton I Miller, Robert Thoeren, from a story by Seton I Miller

The Singer Not the Song ★★ U

Western 1960 · UK · Colour · 132mins

With Dirk Bogarde strutting around a small Mexican town in the tightest black leather trousers the censors would allow and John Mills spouting Catholic dogma in an abominable Irish accent, this has all the makings of a cult classic. Sadly, the story, penned by Nigel Balchin from a long-forgotten novel by Audrey Erskine Lindop, is so dull that your mind is soon numbed to the actorly excesses of the stars. Director Roy Ward Baker doesn't help matters with his leaden pacing and over-deliberate staging. French actress Mylene Demongeot looks lost and far from home at the centre of this scene-stealing tug-of-war.

Dirk Bogarde *Anacleto* • John Mills *Father Keogh* • Mylene Demongeot *Locha* • Laurence Naismith *Old Uncle* • John Bentley *Chief Of Police* • Leslie French *Father Gomez* • Eric Pohlmann *Presidente* ■ *Dir* Roy Ward Baker • *Scr* Nigel Balchin, from the novel by Audrey Erskine Lindop

Singin' in the Rain ★★★★★ U

Classic musical 1952 · US · Colour · 98mins

Never, in the whole history of the American cinema, has such a collection of talents come together at the peak of their abilities to generate such an enjoyable and clever movie. Not only is this utterly irrepressible, but the story also beautifully evokes the excitement and pleasure of making motion pictures. Gene Kelly was responsible in his lifetime for providing enormous pleasure to movie audiences, and his joyous rendition of the title song in this film stands as a lasting tribute. For those who don't know, this film is an affectionate parody of the days when sound came to Hollywood in the wake of *The Jazz Singer*, and every incident wittily referred to in Betty Comden and Adolph Green's sparkling screenplay actually happened.

Gene Kelly *Don Lockwood* • Debbie Reynolds *Kathy Selden* • Donald O'Connor *Cosmo Brown* • Jean Hagen *Lina Lamont* • Millard Mitchell *RF Simpson* • Rita Moreno *Zelda Zanders* • Douglas Fowley *Roscoe Dexter* • Cyd Charisse *Dancer* ■ *Dir* Gene Kelly, Stanley Donen • *Scr* Adolph Green, Betty Comden • *Cinematographer* Harold Rosson • *Music/Lyrics* Nacio Herb Brown • *Music Director* Lennie Hayton

The Singing Fool ★★

Musical drama 1928 · US · BW · 105mins

Al Jolson's follow-up to *The Jazz Singer*, another part-talkie, was even more popular and was Hollywood's most financially successful sound film until *Gone with the Wind* in 1939. Its blatant assault on the tear ducts and Jolson's performance take a lot of swallowing now, and its appeal rests purely on its important place in Hollywood history. Jolson plays a singer/composer who suffers the loss of his wife and small son, the demise of the latter prompting the film's most famous sequence, as Jolson serenades the dying tot with *Sonny Boy*. The song's composers, BG DeSylva, Lew Brown and Ray Henderson, later insisted they wrote the song as a joke and were surprised not only that Jolson took it seriously but that it became the nation's number one hit and sold three million copies.

Al Jolson *Al Stone* • Betty Bronson *Grace* • Josephine Dunn *Molly Winton* • Reed Howes *John Perry* • Edward Martindel *Louis Marcus* • Arthur Housman *Blackie Joe* • Davey Lee *Sonny Boy* ■ *Dir* Lloyd Bacon • *Scr* Joseph Jackson, C Graham Baker, from a story by Leslie S Barrows

The Singing Kid ★★★ U

Musical comedy 1936 · US · BW · 85mins

If ever a musical was saved by its songs, this is it. Though Al Jolson had been the saviour of Warner Bros when he starred in *The Jazz Singer*, the studio was happy to terminate his contract by the time this film was released. Tastes had changed and Jolson's extrovert style was going out of fashion. Mundane scripts like this one did not help, with Jolson a stage star who loses his voice and goes to the country to convalesce. There he finds true love. Fortunately, the songs by Harold Arlen and EY Harburg crop up often enough to provide some much-needed adrenaline.

Al Jolson *Al Jackson* • Allen Jenkins *Joe Eddy* • Lyle Talbot *Bob Carey* • William Davidson *Barney Hammond* • Frank Mitchell *Dope* • Edward Keane *Potter* • Sybil Jason *Sybil Haines* • Edward Everett Horton *Davenport Rogers* ■ *Dir* William Keighley • *Scr* Warren Duff, Pat C Flick, from a story by Robert Lord

The Singing Nun ★★ U

Musical drama 1966 · US · Colour · 96mins

Audiences in the mid-sixties must have had sweet teeth for this mawkish musical biopic to be a box-office success. Piously pert Debbie Reynolds plays Soeur Sourire, the guitar-strumming Belgian nun who composed the song *Dominique*, written for a motherless boy, which ended up as an international hit. Greer Garson pours more syrup over it as the Mother Prioress. The schmaltzy direction was by Henry Koster, who steered Deanna Durbin through many of her less sentimental movies.

Debbie Reynolds *Sister Ann* • Ricardo Montalban *Father Clementi* • Greer Garson *Mother Prioress* • Agnes Moorehead *Sister Cluny* • Chad Everett *Robert Gerarde* • Katharine Ross *Nicole Arlien* • Ed Sullivan ■ *Dir* Henry Koster • *Scr* Sally Benson, John Furia Jr, from a story by John Furia Jr

The Singing Sheriff ★★ U

Comedy western 1944 · US · BW · 62mins

Intended as a satire on westerns, this works better today as a vehicle for bandleader Bob Crosby (brother of Bing) playing a Broadway cowboy finding himself out in the real Wild West. Much of the spoofing is heavy-handed, but some of it does work and it's all good-natured stuff with Crosby a likeable lead. Most fun is to be had, however, from veteran sidekick Fuzzy Knight making a joke of his own screen persona, and there are times you wonder if this was an influence on Mel Brooks's *Blazing Saddles*.

Bob Crosby *Bob Richards* • Fay McKenzie *Caroline* • Fuzzy Knight *Fuzzy* • Iris Adrian *Lefty* • Samuel S Hinds *Seth* • Edward Norris *Vance* ■ *Dir* Leslie Goodwins • *Scr* Henry Blankfort, Eugene Conrad, from a story by John Grey

Single Bars, Single Women ★★ 15

Comedy drama 1984 · US · Colour · 95mins

Smug comedy drama that's quite convinced it has something revolutionary to say about swinging singles and the dating game. It hasn't. Against the backdrop of a typical pick-up joint, assorted loners, both male and female, meet, mate and indulge their fantasies in the bits in between. The film was inspired by the Dolly Parton song of same name, which just about says it all really. Although basically a one star film, it earns a second solely for its flattering cast of television perennials, including Tony Danza from *Taxi* and Paul Michael Glaser from *Starsky and Hutch*. 🖵

Tony Danza *Dennis* • Paul Michael Glaser *Gabe* • Keith Gordon *Lionel* • Shelley Hack *Frankie* • Christine Lahti *Elsie* • Mare Winningham *Bootsie* ■ *Dir* Harry Winer • *Scr* Michael Bortman

The Single Standard ★★★

Romantic drama 1929 · US · BW · 73mins

Greta Garbo's last film with Nils Asther presents her in the familiar mix of convention-defying free spirit and penitent coming to her senses. She plays Arden Stuart, a San Francisco socialite who jaunts off on a yacht for an affair with Asther, a macho sailor-turned-artist. When he has second thoughts, she returns home to find herself a social outcast but is rescued by marriage to John Mack Brown, who has always loved her. Soft-edged stuff, directed with almost puritan discretion by John S Robertson.

Greta Garbo *Arden Stuart* • Nils Asther *Packy Cannon* • John Mack Brown [Johnny Mack Brown] *Tommy Hewlett* • Dorothy Sebastian *Mercedes* • Lane Chandler *Ding Stuart* • Robert Castle *Anthony Kendall* • Mahlon Hamilton *Mr Glendenning* • Kathlyn Williams *Mrs Glendenning* ■ *Dir* John S Robertson • *Scr* Josephine Lovett, from a story by Adela Rogers St Johns

Single White Female ★★★★ 18

Thriller 1992 · US · Colour · 103mins

Jennifer Jason Leigh is the lodger from hell who makes nice Bridget Fonda's life a misery in this ludicrous but hugely enjoyable thriller from *Reversal of Fortune* director Barbet Schroeder. Based on John Lutz's novel, this has Fonda as a chic Manhattanite looking for a roommate, and Leigh as the shy, frumpy "perfect" candidate. That is, until she starts dressing like Fonda and tries to steal her boyfriend. Yes, you may be able to guess the end from the first five minutes, but that doesn't make this any less enthralling, and it should certainly win a few plaudits for the most ingenious use of a stiletto heel in a movie. Contains violence, swearing, sex scenes and nudity. 🖵 **DVD**

Bridget Fonda *Allison Jones* • Jennifer Jason Leigh *Hedra Carlson* • Steven Weber *Sam Rawson* • Peter Friedman *Graham Knox* • Stephen Tobolowsky *Mitchell Myerson* • Frances Bay *Elderly neighbour* ■ *Dir* Barbet Schroeder • *Scr* Don Roos, from the novel *SWF Seeks Same* by John Lutz

Single Women, Married Men ★★ 15

Drama 1989 · US · Colour · 90mins

What would you do if your husband deserted you? Michele Lee decides against revenge and gets involved with a community support group instead. Far more sensible, but not so much fun for either Ms Lee or the audience, who are treated to an extremely po-faced lecture about the perils of having an affair. Lee does her best with a distinctly ropey script, but nothing can save this over-earnest, preachy film from boring us rigid. 🖵

Michele Lee *Susan Parmel* • Lee Horsley *Ross* • Mary Frann *Pat Michaels* • Carrie Hamilton *April* • Julie Harris *Lucille* ■ *Dir* Nick Havinga • *Scr* Hilma Wolitzer

Singles ★★★★ 15

Romantic comedy 1992 · US · Colour · 95mins

Director Cameron Crowe received much attention for the Oscar-winning *Jerry*

Maguire starring Tom Cruise. But the former rock journalist had already made an equally interesting romantic comedy with this wonderfully funny look at love among Seattle's twentysomethings. Matt Dillon is the self-centred grunge rocker in love with Bridget Fonda, while Campbell Scott and Kyra Sedgwick are the couple too scared of commitment because of past experiences. They head an exemplary cast involved in the sort of dating rituals that recall the acerbic wit of early Woody Allen, but appealingly countered with a touching sweetness. Contains swearing and sex scenes. 🖵

Bridget Fonda *Janet Livermore* • Campbell Scott *Steve Dunne* • Kyra Sedgwick *Linda Powell* • Sheila Kelley *Debbie Hunt* • Jim True *David Bailey* • Matt Dillon *Cliff Poncier* • Bill Pullman *Dr Jamison* • James LeGros *Andy* ■ *Dir/Scr* Cameron Crowe

Sink or Swim ★★★

Historical drama 1971 · Fr · Colour · 98mins

Jean-Paul Rappeneau likened this rousing costume adventure to a collaboration between Mozart and bullish Hollywood director, Raoul Walsh. Certainly, there's plenty of Walsh brio about the proceedings, which see anti-royalist Jean-Paul Belmondo return from New World exile to revolutionary France in order to secure the divorce he needs to marry an American heiress. However, he's soon entangled in the schemes of his duplicitous wife, Marlène Jobert, as she seeks to exploit both marquis Sami Frey and prince Michel Auclair. Smartly satirising period politics while keeping the action light and furious, this is a tailor-made vehicle for the ever-popular Belmondo. In French with English dialogue.

Jean-Paul Belmondo *Nicolas* • Marlène Jobert *Charlotte* • Laura Antonelli *Pauline* • Michel Auclair *Prince* • Sami Frey *Marquis* • Pierre Brasseur *Gosselin* ■ *Dir* Jean-Paul Rappeneau • *Scr* Daniel Boulanger, Jean-Paul Rappeneau, Claude Sautet, Maurice Clavel

Sink the Bismarck! ★★★★ U

Second World War drama 1960 · UK · BW · 97mins

The postwar British film industry relied heavily on "now the story can be told" accounts of engagements that helped turn the Second World War in favour of the Allies. Too many were smug action adventures that devalued the true heroism of the exploits they depicted, but this fine film fully captures the tensions, dangers and complexities of battle by concentrating on the unsung back-room planners as much as on the combatants themselves. There are necessarily caricatures on both sides, but at the same time there is a respect for the enemy that is missing in many previous flag-wavers. 🖵

Kenneth More *Captain Jonathan Shepard* • Dana Wynter *Anne Davis* • Carl Mohner *Captain Lindemann* • Laurence Naismith *First Sea Lord* • Geoffrey Keen *ACNS* • Karel Stepanek *Admiral Lutjens* • Michael Hordern *Commander on King George V* • Maurice Denham *Commander Richards* ■ *Dir* Lewis Gilbert • *Scr* Edmund H North, from the non-fiction book by CS Forester

Sinners in Paradise ★

Drama 1938 · US · BW · 64mins

Scraping the bottom of the barrel of stories about strangers thrown together by unusual and unfortunate circumstances, this is the plane crash version. Here the passengers are stranded on a remote tropical island, seemingly deserted until escaped convict John Boles shows himself. The characters, played by a middle-of-the-road cast, all happen to be in critical situations: Madge Evans, for example, is running from her husband and gunman Bruce Cabot from the Mafia, while Gene Lockhart is a crooked politician. Happily, it only takes 64 minutes for their dreary skeletons to come rattling out of the cupboard under the less than inspired direction of James Whale.

Madge Evans *Anne Wesson* • John Boles *Jim Taylor* • Bruce Cabot *Robert Malone/"The Torpedo"* • Marion Martin *Iris Compton* • Gene Lockhart *Senator Corey* • Charlotte Wynters *Thelma Chase/Doris Bailey* ■ *Dir* James Whale • *Scr* Lester Cole, Harold Buckley, Louis Stevens, from the story *Half Way to Shanghai* by Harold Buckley

Sinners in the Sun ★★

Romance 1932 · US · BW · 60mins

Dress-shop model Carole Lombard and mechanic Chester Morris, madly in love, part after a difference of opinion about their planned marriage. She becomes the kept mistress of wealthy Walter Byron; he graduates from chauffeur to husband of rich socialite Adrienne Ames. Both come to see the error of their ways. Paramount's sophisticated house style is only celluloid deep, a surface cover for a clichéd and simplistic demonstration that money doesn't buy happiness. The subsidiary plot involves Cary Grant as the lover of Lombard's friend.

Carole Lombard *Doris Blake* • Chester Morris *Jimmie Martin* • Adrienne Ames *Claire Kinkaid* • Alison Skipworth *Mrs Blake* • Cary Grant *Ridgeway* • Walter Byron *Eric Nelson* • Rita La Roy *Lil* ■ *Dir* Alexander Hall • *Scr* Waldemar Young, Samuel Hoffenstein, Vincent Lawrence, from the short story *The Beachcomber* by Mildred Cram

Sins of Desire ★★ 18

Erotic thriller 1993 · US · Colour · 86mins

Teaming up with private investigator Nick Cassavetes, former Bond girl Tanya Roberts dons a nurse's uniform in a bid to discover why her sister died following her stay at a fashionable sex therapy institute. Director Jim Wynorski would argue that the energetic fumblings are essential to the plot (in a *Don't Look Now* kind of way), but don't be fooled: this fetishistic thriller is nothing more than soft core with an even softer storyline. Contains violence, swearing and nudity. 🖵

Tanya Roberts *Kay* • Nick Cassavetes *Barry* • Jan-Michael Vincent *Warren Robillard* • Delia Sheppard *Jessica Callister* • Jay Richardson *Dr Scott Callister* ■ *Dir* Jim Wynorski • *Scr* Mark McGee, Peter Liapis, from a story by Jim Wynorski

The Sins of Rachel Cade ★★★

Melodrama   1960 · US · Colour · 122mins

Almost single-handedly, Warner Bros cut a melodramatic swathe through the late fifties and sixties with a series of star-studded colourful dramas, tackling "adult" themes and featuring their contract players. *A Summer Place* was by far the most successful, and one of the best, and *The Nun's Story* easily the most prestigious. Well, here's "The Nun's Summer Place", as missionary nurse Angie Dickinson sweats it out with Peter Finch in the Belgian Congo, while Roger Moore looks on in lust. Veteran director Gordon Douglas understands the quintessential trashiness of the material and does well by it.

Angie Dickinson *Rachel Cade* • Peter Finch *Colonel Henri Derode* • Roger Moore *Paul Wilton* • Errol John *Kulu, Rachel's assistant* • Woody Strode *Muwango* • Juano Hernandez *Kalanumu* • Scatman Crothers *Musinga* ■ *Dir* Gordon Douglas • *Scr* Edward Anhalt, from the novel *Rachel Cade* by Charles E Mercer

Sins of Silence ★★

Drama based on a true story
1995 · US · Colour · 86mins

The concept of a bionic nun raises all sorts of interesting possibilities. Sadly for this well-meaning TV movie, Lindsay Wagner is only human. The former bionic woman plays a former sister turned rape counsellor who comes to the aid of a teenager who has been brutally assaulted by the son of the local pillar of the community. She suffers under the law in order to keep secure her own moral code and the confidence of her young client. Wagner is her usual reliable self, but Sam Pillsbury's direction is routine.

Lindsay Wagner *Molly McKinley* • Holly Marie Combs *Sophie DiMatteo* • Jason Cadieux *Tommy Bickley* • Victor Argo *Nick DiMatteo* • Sean McCann *Lee Keating* ■ *Dir* Sam Pillsbury • *Scr* Shelley Evans, from a story by Shelley Evans, Kathryn Montgomery

Sins of the Mind ★ 15

Drama   1997 · US · Colour · 88mins

An examination of modern morality is at the heart of this trashy TV movie. A model family's strait-laced daughter (Missy Crider) emerges from a car-crash-induced coma with psychological problems, loss of all inhibitions and a ravenous sexual appetite, which threaten to destroy her family. Veteran actors Mike Farrell and Jill Clayburgh are wasted in this shallow and unbelievable variation of the classic Jekyll-and-Hyde formula, which stumbles in concept and plunges downhill from there. Contains sexual situations and some swearing and violence. 📹

Missy Crider *Michelle Widener* • Mike Farrell *William Widener* • Jill Clayburgh *Eve Widener* • Cyia Batten *Allegra Widener* • Louise Fletcher *Dr Anna Bingham* ■ *Dir* James Frawley • *Scr* Sharon Elizabeth Doyle

Sins of the Mother ★★★

Drama based on a true story
1991 · US · Colour · 96mins

An unsavoury but well-written and forceful psychodrama, based on the true story of the aberrant relationship between an overbearing mother and her son, a serial rapist. Elizabeth Montgomery will forever be remembered for the sixties sitcom *Bewitched*, but here delivers an impressive performance in a very different role as the domineering mum, while Dale Midkiff does equally well as the son. A superior, engrossing TV movie. Contains violence.

Elizabeth Montgomery *Ruth Coe* • Dale Midkiff *Kevin Coe* • Richard Roat *Gordon Coe* • Talia Balsam *Liz Trent* • Heather Fairfield *Gini Perham* • Jerry Bossard *Jay Williams* ■ *Dir* John K Patterson [John Patterson] • *Scr* Michael K Krohn, Christopher Lofton, Richard Fielder, from the book *Son* by Jack Olsen

Sins of the Night ★★ 18

Erotic thriller   1993 · US · Colour · 85mins

Gregory Hippolyte is one of the prime movers behind the erotic thriller genre and this typical example of his output is packed with the usual naked limbs. The story this time involves an investigator working for an insurance firm who gets too close to the stripper he is meant to be investigating, stirring up all sorts of trouble. Nick Cassavetes, Deborah Shelton, Miles O'Keeffe and Richard Roundtree are among the actors trying not to look embarrassed. Contains violence, swearing, sex scenes and nudity. 📹

Deborah Shelton *Roxanne Flowers* • Nick Cassavetes *Jack Nietzshe* • Miles O'Keefe [Miles O'Keeffe] *Tony Falcone* • Matt Roe *Ted Quinty* • Michelle Brin *Laura Winters* • Courtney Taylor *Danielle* • Richard Roundtree *Les* ■ *Dir* A Gregory Hippolyte [Gregory Hippolyte] • *Scr* Russell LaValle

Sir Henry at Rawlinson End ★★ 15

Surreal comedy   1980 · UK · Sepia · 67mins

A mercifully brief British oddity, with Trevor Howard as an eccentric, boozy aristocrat at odds with an army of characters seemingly left over from other comedies. *The Goon Show* it isn't, though it would like to be. The fault lies firmly at the door of former Bonzo Dog (Doo Dah) Band member Vivian Stanshall, who wrote the film and contributed the music. 📹

Trevor Howard *Sir Henry Rawlinson* • Patrick Magee *Reverend Slodden* • JG Devlin *Old Scrotum* • Sheila Reid *Florrie* • Denise Coffey *Mrs E* • Harry Fowler *Buller Bullethead* • Vivian Stanshall *Hubert Rawlinson* • Jeremy Child *Peregrine Maynard* ■ *Dir* Steve Roberts • *Scr* Vivian Stanshall, Steve Roberts, from the radio series by Vivian Stanshall

Sirens ★★ 15

Erotic comedy
1994 · Ausl/UK/Ger · Colour · 90mins

Following the success of *Four Weddings and a Funeral*, this prettified period piece came as something of a shock to Hugh Grant's new-found legion of fans. He plays a prudish clergyman whose first task in his new Australian parish is to prevent bohemian artist Norman Lindsay (Sam Neill) from exhibiting both his models and his portraits of them. Director John Duigan contents himself with a few gentle barbs and elegant *bons mots*, but rather loses his way once Grant's less inhibited wife, Tara FitzGerald, joins Elle MacPherson and her fellow poseurs. Visually pleasing, but films of this sort need to be more than just something to look at. Contains swearing, sex scenes and nudity. 📹

Hugh Grant *Anthony Campion* • Tara FitzGerald *Estella Campion* • Sam Neill *Norman Lindsay* • Elle MacPherson *Sheela* • Portia De Rossi *Giddy* • Kate Fischer *Pru* • Pamela Rabe *Rose Lindsay* ■ *Dir/Scr* John Duigan

Sirocco ★★★ PG

Spy drama   1951 · US · BW · 94mins

This pretty blatant imitation of *Casablanca* was made by Humphrey Bogart's own production company, Santana. Set in Syria in the twenties, this was by his own admission not one of Bogart's best pictures, but it's still a moodily gripping yarn about gunrunners, political commitment and various other intrigues. What it sadly lacks is a decent heroine – Swedish actress Marta Toren is not in the Ingrid Bergman league – though Lee J Cobb is excellent in what might be termed the Claude Rains part. 📹

Humphrey Bogart *Harry Smith* • Marta Toren *Violette* • Lee J Cobb *Colonel Feroud* • Everett Sloane *General LaSalle* • Gerald Mohr *Major Leon* • Zero Mostel *Balukjian* • Nick Dennis *Nasir Aboud* ■ *Dir* Curtis Bernhardt • *Scr* Al Bezzerides, Hans Jacoby, from the novel *Coup de Grace* by Joseph Kessel

Sister Act ★★★★ PG

Comedy   1992 · US · Colour · 96mins

Ghost may have won Whoopi Goldberg an Oscar, but it was *Sister Act* that turned her into a huge Hollywood star. Whoopi is the Reno lounge singer who witnesses lover Harvey Keitel killing a man, so she accepts a police offer of protection that entails hiding out in a convent. That's about it for plot in this comedy from the Disney stable, while the remainder of the movie follows our heroine as she tries to bring the nuns and Maggie Smith's strict Mother Superior into the 20th century. Relying on some great songs and a superb cast (including Kathy Najimy as sunny Sister Mary Patrick), this gets past the slight story to become a hugely enjoyable, very funny comedy. Contains some swearing. 📹

Whoopi Goldberg *Deloris Van Cartier* • Maggie Smith *Mother Superior* • Kathy Najimy *Sister Mary Patrick* • Wendy Makkena *Sister Mary Robert* • Mary Wickes *Sister Mary Lazarus* • Harvey Keitel *Vince LaRocca* • Bill Nunn *Eddie Souther* • Robert Miranda *Joey* ■ *Dir* Emile Ardolino • *Scr* Joseph Howard

Sister Act 2: Back in the Habit ★★★ PG

Musical comedy 1993 · US · Colour · 102mins

Las Vegas cabaret singer Whoopi Goldberg dons her Sister Mary Clarence habit again to teach music to a bad-attitude class at a run-down high school in this OK sequel. Goldberg delivers the good-education/family-values/follow-your-dream messages with likeable enough charm, even if the familiar "nuns just want to have fun" concept is treated in heavy-handed fashion by director Bill Duke and the nuns from the original are relegated to mere background. Still, the musical sequences are lively enough and Maggie Smith gives her usual sterling support. 📹 **DVD**

Whoopi Goldberg *Deloris Van Cartier/Sister Mary Clarence* • Kathy Najimy *Sister Mary Patrick* • Barnard Hughes *Father Maurice* • Mary Wickes *Sister Mary Lazarus* • James Coburn *Mr Crisp* • Michael Jeter *Father Ignatius* • Wendy Makkena *Sister Mary Robert* • Maggie Smith *Mother Superior* • Lauryn Hill *Rita Watson* • Jennifer Love Hewitt *Margaret* ■ *Dir* Bill Duke • *Scr* James Orr, Jim Cruickshank, Judi Ann Mason, from characters created by Joseph Howard

Sister Kenny ★★★★

Biographical drama 1946 · US · BW · 116mins

An engrossing and moving biographical drama that contains possibly Rosalind Russell's finest performance on screen as Australian nurse Elizabeth Kenny, who fought the medical establishment to gain acceptance for her pioneering work with polio sufferers. The Oscar-nominated Russell totally eschews the maudlin and banal in a sterling, deep portrayal of a woman compelled to battle a feared and potentially fatal disease, and aficionados of the star will probably be able to quote much of the dialogue. It's based on Kenny's autobiography *And They Shall Walk*.

Rosalind Russell *Elizabeth Kenny* • Alexander Knox *Dr McDonnell* • Dean Jagger *Kevin Connors* • Philip Merivale *Dr Brack* • Beulah Bondi *Mary Kenny* • Charles Dingle *Michael Kenny* ■ *Dir* Dudley Nichols • *Scr* Dudley Nichols, Alexander Knox, Mary McCarthy, Milton Gunzburg, from the autobiography *And They Shall Walk* by Elizabeth Kenny, Martha Ostenso

Sister My Sister ★★★ 15

Historical crime drama
1994 · UK · Colour · 85mins

In 1933, two French maids murdered their employer and her daughter. This brutal act gave rise to Jean Genet's classic play *The Maids* and, decades later, also inspired American playwright Wendy Kesselman to write *My Sister in This House* on which director Nancy Meckler based this strange but haunting little oddity. Joely Richardson and Jodhi May are the pair who allow their repressions to surface when in the service of Madame Danzard, played with gusto by Julie Walters. Tautly directed by Meckler, this sinister portrait of corrupted innocence and sisterly love beyond the norm is quite a chilling curiosity. Contains violence and sex scenes.

Julie Walters *Madame Danzard* • Joely Richardson *Christine* • Jodhi May *Lea* • Sophie Thursfield *Isabelle Danzard* • Amelda Brown *Visitor* • Lucita Pope *Visitor* • Kate Gartside *Sister Veronica* ■ *Dir* Nancy Meckler • *Scr* Wendy Kesselman, from her play *My Sister in This House*

Sisterly Love ★

Comedy   1988 · Ausl · Colour

Rivalry between sisters has been a popular topic in the movies, from the excellent *sex, lies, and videotape* to the dreadful *Sibling Rivalry*. This Australian TV movie is no great addition to the genre, with Joan Sydney deciding to visit her sister in Australia who she hasn't seen for 20 years. Soon after her arrival the pair are at loggerheads, and even their neighbour gets caught up in their battles. Yes, this is supposed to be a hilarious comedy, but instead it's a tedious, often bitchy tale that lacks originality.

Maggie King *Sylvia* • Joan Sydney *Jean* • Martin Vaughan *Bob* • Sandra Eldridge *Birdy* ■ *Dir* Mark DeFriest • *Scr* Ray Harding, from an idea by Jeremy Higgins

The Sisters ★★★
Drama 1938 · US · BW · 98mins

Sisters be damned! This costume drama is all about how far poor Bette Davis can fall after she's abandoned by drunken husband Errol Flynn. Admittedly, director Anatole Litvak drops in on Anita Louise and Jane Bryan from time to time to see how they're getting along, but Davis dominates the action, whether eloping with sports reporter Flynn, surviving the San Francisco earthquake or flitting around an Oakland bordello. Orry-Kelly's costumes are a delight and Max Steiner's soundtrack neatly captures the feel of the period and the melodramatics of the plot. It's typical penny dreadful fare, but with Davis on this sort of form, who cares? ⬚

Bette Davis *Louise Elliott* • Errol Flynn *Frank Medlin* • Anita Louise *Helen Elliott* • Jane Bryan *Grace Elliott* • Ian Hunter *William Benson* • Henry Travers *Ned Elliott* • Beulah Bondi *Rose Elliott* • Susan Hayward *Telephone operator* ■ *Dir* Anatole Litvak • *Scr* Milton Krims, from the novel by Myron Brinig

Sisters ★★★★18
Psychological thriller
1973 · US · Colour · 88mins

The first foray into fully-fledged fright by director Brian De Palma is a masterful Hitch-cocktail of the sinister and the satirical. De Palma established his flashy style in this well-choreographed shocker about a journalist (Jennifer Salt) who's compelled to investigate when she witnesses her neighbour (Margot Kidder) appear to commit murder. To some extent a modified version of *Psycho* dealing with duality and psychosis in an incredibly insightful way, this *Peeping Tom* nightmare is a well-tuned slice of cinematic frenzy complete with red herrings, a fantasy sequence and split-screen suspense. Along with *Carrie*, De Palma's most coherent work. ⬚

Margot Kidder *Danielle Breton* • Jennifer Salt *Grace Collier* • Charles Durning *Larch* • William Finley *Emil Breton* • Lisle Wilson *Phillip Woode* • Barnard Hughes *Mr McLennen* • Mary Davenport *Mrs Collier* ■ *Dir* Brian De Palma • *Scr* Louisa Rose, Brian De Palma, from a story by Brian De Palma

Sisters ★★15
Comedy 1988 · US · Colour · 89mins

Also known as *Some Girls*, this has Patrick Dempsey as the student who looks forward to spending Christmas with his girlfriend's family in Canada, only to fall prey to both of her sisters while trying to avoid the watchful eye of her eccentric parents. Directed by Michael Hoffman (who also made the hysterical comedy *Soapdish*), this has occasional moments of hilarity, but not enough to sustain interest in what is supposed to be a funny film. Contains swearing, sex scenes and nudity. ⬚

Patrick Dempsey *Michael* • Jennifer Connelly *Gabby* • Sheila Kelley *Irenka* • Andre Gregory

Father • Ashley Greenfield *Simone* • Florinda Bolkan *Mother* ■ *Dir* Michael Hoffman • *Scr* Rupert Walters

Sisters of the Gion ★★★★★
Drama 1936 · Jap · BW · 70mins

Two Japanese sisters, both Geisha girls, differ in their outlook: the elder (Yoko Umemura) subscribes to tradition, while the younger (Isuzu Yamada) embraces a more modern view of life. Both, however, come to grief at the hands of men, one physically abused by a jealous ex-lover, the other deserted by the man she has loved. An acknowledged masterpiece from Kenji Mizoguchi, one of the truly great directors in world cinema, this restrained, beautifully composed film, replete with gentle sadness and a touch of humour, well demonstrates the film-maker's empathy with women, and his implied critique of society's treatment of them, that is the focus of much of his work. Those already acquainted with Mizoguchi will need no urging to watch this. Others may find it a wonderful new experience. A Japanese language film.

Isuzu Yamada *Omocha* • Yoko Umemura *Umekichi* • Benkei Shiganoya *Shimbei Furusawa* • Fumio Okura *Jurakudo, the antiques dealer* ■ *Dir* Kenji Mizoguchi • *Scr* Yoshikata Yoda, from a story by Kenji Mizoguchi

Sisters, or the Balance of Happiness ★★★★15
Drama 1979 · W Ger · Colour · 95mins

Margarethe von Trotta considered this study of sibling misunderstanding to be a "soul painting", in which the personalities of the protagonists took priority over the political climate that created them. However, the fact that mollycoddling elder sister Jutta Lampe is a super-efficient executive secretary and Gudrun Gabriel is a depressive biology student suggests that a pronounced socio-feminist vein still runs through the piece. Similarly, the sisters play much more subtle power games than are insinuated by outward appearance and Lampe's attempt to turn typist Jessica Früh into a surrogate. With the *mise en scène* taking on symbolic significance, this is both cinematically accomplished and psychologically intriguing. In German with English subtitles.

Jutta Lampe *Maria* • Gudrun Gabriel *Anna* • Jessica Früh *Miriam* • Konstantin Wecker *Robert* • Rainer Delventhal *Maurice* ■ *Dir* Margarethe von Trotta • *Scr* Margarethe von Trotta, Luisa Francia, Martje Grohmann, from the story *Traumprotokolle* by Wolfgang Bachler

Sitcom ★★★★18
Comedy horror 1997 · Fr · Colour · 80mins

A rare stab by France at genre film-making, François Ozon's send-up of soap opera conventions is raunchy, kitsch and hilariously funny. In this John Waters-tilted farcical fantasy, a bourgeois family's existence is disrupted when the head of the household brings home a pet rat. How this outsider's evil influence causes them all to jettison their sexual inhibitions and embark on a round robin of escalating perversion is ultra camp and very cutting edge. In French

with English subtitles. Contains sex scenes and sexual references.

Evelyne Dandry *Hélène, the mother* • François Marthouret *Jean, the father* • Marina de Van *Sophie, the daughter* • Adrien de Van *Nicolas, the son* • Stéphane Rideau *David* ■ *Dir/Scr* François Ozon

Sitting Bull ★ U
Western 1954 · US · Colour · 105mins

Superficially spectacular, this independent production relied on early use of CinemaScope and on hordes of Mexican extras to fill its wide screen, playing both the Indians and the US Cavalry. Something went wrong with the colour, however, while the routine story takes forever to unfold. There's Douglas Kennedy as the usual glory-seeking Custer, Dale Robertson as the honest cavalry major trying to bring about lasting peace, and J Carrol Naish as the dignified, fair-minded Chief Sitting Bull. The only real native American around is Iron Eyes Cody as the warrior Crazy Horse.

Dale Robertson *Parrish* • Mary Murphy *Kathy* • J Carrol Naish *Sitting Bull* • Iron Eyes Cody *Crazy Horse* • John Litel *General Howell* • Bill Hopper *Wentworth* • Douglas Kennedy *Colonel Custer* ■ *Dir* Sidney Salkow • *Scr* Jack DeWitt, Sidney Salkow

Sitting Ducks ★★★★
Comedy caper 1979 · US · Colour · 87mins

Michael Emil and Zack Norman rip off a cool $724,000 from their mobster bosses and flee New York. Ostensibly they are bound for a flight to Central America, but Zack has other ideas and instead the pair find themselves hitting the road. En route they pick up genial gas-station attendant Richard Romanus and two girls, Patrice Townsend and Irene Forrest. An enjoyable mix of oddball comedy and romance follows. The sadly under-rated Jaglom, a great exponent of improvisation, hits pay dirt here with a thoughtful, constantly amusing road movie. It's also a family affair: Townsend was Mrs Jaglom at the time, and Emil is his brother.

Michael Emil *Simon* • Zack Norman *Sidney* • Patrice Townsend *Jenny* • Irene Forrest *Leona* • Richard Romanus *Moose* • Henry Jaglom *Jenny's friend* ■ *Dir/Scr* Henry Jaglom

Sitting in Limbo ★★★15
Drama 1986 · Can · Colour · 38mins

This well-intentioned drama about the limited opportunities available to African-American teenagers living in Montreal, has much in common with such American "in your face" films as *Just Another Girl on the IRT*. Aiming for a hard-hitting but freewheeling realism, director John N Smith casts engaging non-professionals Fabian Gibbs and Pat Dillon in the leading roles and uses rough-and-ready, documentary-style camera techniques to capture the transient joys and incessant despairs of their hand-to-mouth existence. The relentless round of sackings, debts, rows, pregnancies and partings takes a toll on one's sympathies, but it's worth sticking with. Contains swearing.

Pat Dillon *Pat* • Fabian Gibbs *Fabian* • Sylvie Clarke *Sylvie* • Debbie Grant *Debbie* • Compton McLean *John* ■ *Dir* John N Smith • *Scr* John N Smith, David Wilson

Sitting Pretty ★★★
Musical comedy 1933 · US · BW · 80mins

Jack Oakie and Jack Haley, an aspiring Tin Pan Alley songwriting team, are advised by their music publisher and their rehearsal pianist – Mack Gordon and Harry Revel respectively, who also composed the movie's song score – to try their luck in Hollywood. Which they do, finding fame, fortune and lunch-room waitress Ginger Rogers. "Cheerful" is the word for this musical, zippily played and directed by Harry Joe Brown from a script co-written by humorist SJ Perelman that offers some nice Hollywood-satirising-Hollywood comedy. Also featuring are flamboyant Gregory Ratoff as an agent and lovely Thelma Todd, who would soon be found dead in a never-solved suspected murder.

Jack Oakie *Chick Parker* • Jack Haley *Pete Pendleton* • Ginger Rogers *Dorothy* • Thelma Todd *Gloria Duval* • Gregory Ratoff *Tannenbaum* • Lew Cody *Jules Clark* • Harry Revel *Pianist* • Mack Gordon *Song publisher* ■ *Dir* Harry Joe Brown • *Scr* Jack McGowan, SJ Perelman, Lou Breslow, from a story by Harry Stoddard, Nina Wilcox Putnam

Sitting Pretty ★★★U
Comedy 1948 · US · BW · 84mins

Clifton Webb had been an actor in silent movies and a major Broadway star, but it wasn't until he played Waldo Lydecker in Otto Preminger's classic *Laura* that he achieved genuine public recognition. Lydecker was an effete, waspish newspaper columnist, and Webb wittily transforms that screen image in this popular comedy hit as the self-centred, pompous Mr Belvedere. Webb takes a job as a baby-sitter to Hummingbird Hill parents Robert Young and Maureen O'Hara, and the memorable scene where the toddler pours porridge over Webb's head was not only used as the film's poster motif, but also became part of the cultural imagery of post-war America. Two sequels followed.

Robert Young *Harry* • Clifton Webb *Lynn Belvedere* • Maureen O'Hara *Tacey* • Richard Haydn *Mr Appleton* • Louise Allbritton *Edna Philby* • Randy Stuart *Peggy* • Ed Begley *Hammond* ■ *Dir* Walter Lang • *Scr* F Hugh Herbert, from the novel *Belvedere* by Gwen Davenport

Sitting Target ★★★18
Crime thriller 1972 · US/UK · Colour · 90mins

British cinema in the early seventies seemed preoccupied with crime and violence, as evidenced by such films as *A Clockwork Orange*, *Villain* and *Get Carter*. *Sitting Target* also came out of that period and gave Oliver Reed the chance to brutalise and barnstorm as convicted murderer Harry Lomart who escapes from jail in order to bump off his wife, Jill St John – she's been putting herself about a bit and now has some other man's bun in the oven. A splendid supporting cast of TV familiars and peculiars make this a juicy and none too subtle excursion into the underworld.

Oliver Reed *Harry Lomart* • Jill St John *Pat Lomart* • Ian McShane *Birdy Williams* • Edward Woodward *Inspector Milton* • Frank Finlay *Marty Gold* • Freddie Jones *MacNeil* •

Jill Townsend *Maureen* ■ *Dir* Douglas Hickox • *Scr* Alexander Jacobs, from a novel by Laurence Henderson

Situation ★★

Thriller 1973 · Aus · Colour · 90mins

Peter Patzak is certainly the most prolific and probably the best-known Austrian director of recent years. Made for television at the outset of his career, this thriller starts off like a sixties heist caper, with criminal mastermind Michael Haussermann painstakingly planning a scam in which, *Yojimbo* style, he tricks the cops and three gangs of bank robbers into a turf war. However, he hadn't bargained on student Rita Tushingham breaking through his steely reserve, and the plan violently begins to unravel. It's efficient but unremarkable fare. A German language film.

Rita Tushingham • Michael Haussermann • Frederick Jaeger • William Berger • Gordon Mitchell • Klaus Dahlen ■ *Dir* Peter Patzak • *Scr* Peter Patzak, Ossi Bronner

Situation Hopeless – but Not Serious ★★★

Second World War comedy 1965 · US · BW · 97mins

A maverick, oddball film version of actor Robert Shaw's novel *The Hiding Place*, a wartime story about two Allied airmen who think they are taking refuge when they are actually imprisoned in a comfortable cellar for seven years by a meek little shop assistant. It's mildly allegorical, faintly satirical and almost funny. A nearly movie, then, but worth seeing for Alec Guinness's performance as Herr Frick, whose demure exterior conceals a card-carrying Nazi on the verge of emotional meltdown. At times, Guinness makes the movie seem like an Ealing comedy with an umlaut. Notable for an early appearance by Robert Redford as one of the unwitting kidnap victims.

Alec Guinness *Herr Wilhelm Frick* • Michael Connors [Mike Connors] *Lucky Finder* • Robert Redford *Hank Wilson* • Anita Hoefer *Edeltraud* • Mady Rahl *Lissie* • Paul Dahlke *Herr Neusel* • Frank Wolff *QM Master Sergeant* • John Briley *Sergeant* ■ *Dir* Gottfried Reinhardt • *Scr* Silvia Reinhardt, Jan Lustig, from the novel *The Hiding Place* by Robert Shaw

Six Black Horses ★★

Western 1962 · US · Colour · 80mins

This film originated as a screenplay written by Burt Kennedy and was intended for Randolph Scott in the series of westerns directed by Budd Boetticher at Columbia. It actually ended up at Universal as a vehicle for that studio's resident baby-faced cowboy star, Audie Murphy. It's good to see snarling Dan Duryea in his element, and the plot – determined Joan O'Brien hires Murphy and Duryea to apprehend her husband's killer – is unusually seasoned with humour.

Audie Murphy *Ben Lane* • Dan Duryea *Frank Jesse* • Joan O'Brien *Kelly* • George Wallace [George D Wallace] *Boone* • Phil Chambers *Undertaker* ■ *Dir* Harry Keller • *Scr* Burt Kennedy

Six Bridges to Cross ★★★

Crime drama 1955 · US · BW · 95mins

Sal Mineo made his screen debut here playing a juvenile delinquent and recidivist who grows into a criminal big shot, despite the best efforts of kindly cop George Nader, who shoots Mineo in the opening sequence. As the years pass by, Mineo metamorphoses into Tony Curtis (spot the join) who carries the movie across its various moral hurdles. Inspired by Boston's notorious Brinks Robbery of 1950, the film was scipted by noted crime scenarist Sidney Boehm, who went on to write *The Big Heat* (1953).

Tony Curtis *Jerry Florea* • Julie Adams *Ellen Gallagher* • George Nader *Edward Gallagher* • Jay C Flippen *Vincent Concannon* • Ken Clark *Sanborn* • Sal Mineo *Jerry as a boy* ■ *Dir* Joseph Pevney • *Scr* Sydney Boehm, from the story *They Stole $2,000,000 and Got Away With It* by Joseph Dineen

Six Days Seven Nights ★★★12

Romantic comedy adventure 1998 · US · Colour · 97mins

This sub-*Romancing the Stone* adventure comedy stars Anne Heche as a New York fashion magazine journalist who sets out on a romantic island trip with her fiancé (David Schwimmer from *Friends*) but ends up stranded on an even more remote island with drunken local pilot Harrison Ford. Unfortunately, director Ivan Reitman (*Ghostbusters*) decides that pirates and ludicrous plot twists are more intriguing than exploring the far more interesting chemistry between the two leads. Enjoyable, thanks to the attractive screen presence of Heche and Ford, but ultimately annoying: it could have been so much better. Contains swearing, sexual references and some violence. ▭ **DVD**

Harrison Ford *Quinn Harris* • Anne Heche *Robin Monroe* • David Schwimmer *Frank Martin* • Jacqueline Obradors *Angelica* • Temuera Morrison *Jager* • Allison Janney *Marjorie* ■ *Dir* Ivan Reitman • *Scr* Michael Browning

Six Days, Six Nights ★★

Drama 1994 · Fr/UK · Colour · 90mins

Diane Kurys has forged her reputation by focusing on modern women and their problems. However, the naturalistic style and keen, witty social insights for which she is renowned are notably absent from this disappointing outing. Indeed, there's a distinct shortage of tension and sexual ambiguity in this otherwise carefully constructed tale of female rivalry, as Béatrice Dalle abandons her family in a bid to destroy artist Anne Parillaud's romance with Patric Aurignac. An intriguing premise, undermined by the slack scripting and inconsistent acting. In French with English subtitles. Contains violence, sex scenes and nudity.

Anne Parillaud *Alice* • Béatrice Dalle *Elsa* • Patric Aurignac *Franck* • Bernard Verley *Sanders* • Alain Chabat *Thomas* ■ *Dir* Diane Kurys • *Scr* Diane Kurys, Antoine Lacomblez • *Music* Michael Nyman

Six Degrees of Separation ★★★★15

Drama 1993 · US · Colour · 107mins

As an alien-chaser in *Independence Day* and *Men in Black*, Will Smith served notice on Eddie Murphy that he was the new, smarter, cheekier black kid on the block. But, with this earlier bourgeois satire, he had already displayed the talents that were to elevate him to the superstar stratosphere. As the young man who talks his way into the rich New York household of liberal-minded art dealer Donald Sutherland and his wife Stockard Channing by purporting to be the friend of their student children, Smith is as busy as a gadfly. While John Guare has perhaps been too careful in transferring his play to the screen and Fred Schepisi's direction is too safe for a real sarcastic sting, Smith's performance shines above these limitations, transcending the too-glib spelling-out of the gulf between integrity and hypocrisy. Contains swearing and nudity. ▭

Stockard Channing *Ouisa Kittredge* • Will Smith *Paul* • Donald Sutherland *Flan Kittredge* • Ian McKellen *Geoffrey* • Mary Beth Hurt *Kitty* • Bruce Davison *Larkin* • Richard Masur *Doctor Fine* • Anthony Michael Hall *Trent* • Heather Graham *Elizabeth* ■ *Dir* Fred Schepisi • *Scr* John Guare, from his play

6.5 Special ★★U

Musical 1958 · UK · BW · 57mins

Here's the film version of one of BBC TV's much-loved nostalgic teenfests, a programme that grew out of the need to fill the Saturday slot between children's telly and early evening viewing. It was hosted by Josephine Douglas and Pete Murray, both on hand here, and became a key showcase for British pop music in the pre-Beatles era. Ignore the wisp of a plot about two girls taking the titular train to London to crash showbiz: this is a real period treat.

Josephine Douglas • Pete Murray ■ *Dir* Alfred Shaughnessy • *Scr* Norman Hudis

Six of a Kind ★★★★

Comedy 1934 · US · BW · 62mins

Director Leo McCarey was a wiz where comedy was concerned and triumphed whether the theme was slapstick, screwball or, as in this case, sheer anarchy. Here he has a dream comedy cast, and an unruly Great Dane, fizzing together on a crazy car trip. WC Fields and Alison Skipworth appear late in the film but still manage to steal it from the other two double acts, Charles Ruggles and Mary Boland, and George Burns and Gracie Allen. Fields gets to perform his famous "billiards" routine, a miniature masterpiece in itself.

Charles Ruggles *J Pinkham Whinney* • Mary Boland *Flora Whinney* • WC Fields *Sheriff "Honest" John Hoxley* • George Burns *George* • Gracie Allen *Gracie Devore* • Alison Skipworth *Mrs K Rumford* ■ *Dir* Leo McCarey • *Scr* Walter DeLeon, Harry Ruskin, from a story by Keene Thompson, Douglas MacLean

Six Pack ★★

Action comedy 1982 · US · Colour · 107mins

After proving his worth as an actor in a number of TV roles (most famously *The Gambler*), Kenny Rogers made his big-screen debut in this middle-of-the-road tale of an ex-stock car driver and six orphaned youngsters. The car-crazy kids help Rogers in his attempts to make a comeback in the sport. *Six Pack* also gives a big screen role to Erin Gray, well known at the time as the love interest in sci-fi TV show, *Buck Rogers in the 25th Century*.

Kenny Rogers *Brewster Baker* • Diane Lane *Breezy* • Erin Gray *Lilah* • Barry Corbin *Sheriff* • Terry Kiser *Terk* • Bob Hannah *Diddler* ■ *Dir* Daniel Petrie • *Scr* Mike Marvin, Alex Matter

633 Squadron ★★★PG

Second World War action drama 1964 · UK/US · Colour · 92mins

A film that inevitably suffers in comparison with that other tribute to the Royal Air Force, *The Dam Busters*. The mission is less audacious, the casting is less precise (Cliff Robertson as an American in the RAF and George Chakiris as a Norwegian Resistance fighter) and the theme tune is far harder to sing along to. The flying sequences are, undeniably, more thrilling (particularly the Scottish Highlands training exercises), but they cannot compensate for the dullness of the Norwegian-set scenes, which smack of Hollywood's wartime vision of occupied Europe in which the Nazis resemble the Keystone Kops. ▭

Cliff Robertson *Wing Commander Roy Grant* • George Chakiris *Lieutenant Erik Bergman* • Maria Perschy *Hilde Bergman* • Harry Andrews *Air Marshal Davis* • Donald Houston *Wing Commander Tom Barrett* • Michael Goodliffe *Squadron Leader Bill Adams* ■ *Dir* Walter E Grauman [Walter Grauman] • *Scr* James Clavell, Howard Koch, from the novel by Frederick E Smith

Six Ways to Sunday ★★★18

Drama 1997 · US · Colour · 93mins

A bleak, bitter and very brutal American drama which went straight to video in Britain. Norman Reedus plays a sociopathic teenager with an unhealthily close relationship with his mother (an almost unrecognisable Deborah Harry), who gets involved with mobsters impressed with his capacity for violence. Finely performed by the eclectic cast – Adrien Brody and Isaac Hayes have supporting roles – and directed with seedy style by Adam Bernstein. Contains swearing, nudity and violence. ▭ **DVD**

Norman Reedus *Harry Odum* • Deborah Harry *Kate Odum* • Elina Lowensohn *Iris* • Adrien Brody *Arnie Finklestein* • Isaac Hayes *Bill Bennet* • Jerry Adler *Louis Varga* • Peter Appel *Abie "The Bug" Pinkwise* ■ *Dir* Adam Bernstein • *Scr* Adam Bernstein, Marc Gerald, from the novel *Portrait of a Young Man Drowning* by Charles Perry

Six Weeks ★PG

Drama 1982 · US · Colour · 107mins

Distinctly yucky, TV movie-style fodder dressed up as tear-jerking drama. The cancer-stricken daughter of Mary Tyler Moore melts the heart of Congressional candidate Dudley Moore, who helps the girl win a role in a ballet. At this point, you'll be either blubbing helplessly or sneering at the crass contrivances of the plot. If you think that politicians are wonderful, this manipulative monstrosity will be right up your street.

Dudley Moore *Patrick Dalton* • Mary Tyler Moore *Charlotte Dreyfus* • Katherine Healy *Nicole Dreyfus* • Shannon Wilcox *Peg Dalton* • Bill Calvert *Jeff Dalton* • John Harkins *Arnold Stillman* • Joe Regalbuto *Bob Crowther* ■ *Dir* Tony Bill • *Scr* David Seltzer, from a novel by Fred Mustard Stewart • *Music* Dudley Moore

Sixteen Candles ★★★ 15

Comedy drama   1984 · US · Colour · 88mins

John Hughes made his directorial debut as the master of the teen pic with this sharp comedy, which not only has a keen ear for the idiom of teenspeak, but also a genuine sympathy with its various geeks, jocks, seniors and girls next door. Molly Ringwald is the personification of the sulky, sweet 16-year-old whose birthday goes from bad to worse as her parents forget the occasion and the school pest begins showing off her underwear to his classmates. Beaming through his braces, Anthony Michael Hall is nigh-on perfect as the nerd trying too hard to impress. Contains swearing and brief nudity. 🔲

Molly Ringwald *Samantha* • Justin Henry *Mike Baker* • Michael Schoeffling *Jake* • Haviland Morris *Caroline* • Gedde Watanabe *Long Duk Dong* • Anthony Michael Hall *Ted, the geek* • John Cusack *Bryce* • Joan Cusack *First geek girl* • *Dir/Scr* John Hughes

Sixth and Main ★★

Comedy drama   1977 · US · Colour · 103mins

Three years before Leslie Nielsen's career as a deadpan comic took off with *Airplane!*, he made this indie production about life on Skid Row – or Skid Drive as it's known in Beverly Hills. Playing John Doe, a once-famous writer, Nielsen lives in a trailer crammed with unpublished manuscripts, which are uncovered by Beverly Garland during her snoop researching a book on LA's derelicts. While Nielsen is celebrated as an author of genius, his friends on Skid Row carry on living on the rubbish heap. Among the cast of characters enlivening the procedures are Roddy McDowall as a disabled man and Leo Penn as a doctor.

Leslie Nielsen *John Doe* • Roddy McDowall *Skateboard* • Beverly Garland *Monica* • Leo Penn *Doc* • Joe Maross *Peanut* • Bard Stevens *Carlsburg* • Sharon Tomas *Tina* ■ *Dir/Scr* Christopher Cain

Sixth Happiness ★★★

Biographical drama
1997 · UK · Colour · 97mins

Firdaus Kanga not only wrote the screenplay for this moving drama from his autobiographical novel, *Trying to Grow*, but he also turns in a riveting performance in this extraordinary account of what it's like being gay, Parsee and disabled in seventies Bombay. With the endless round of suicides, betrayals and doomed relationships going on around him, it almost seems as though being born with osteoporosis is the least of Kanga's problems. Mocking Indian cinema as well as its social prejudices, the film suffers slightly from Waris Hussein's fussy direction, but it

remains a brave attempt to convey true courage. Contains nudity.

Firdaus Kanga *Brit Kotwal* • Souad Faress *Sera Kotwal* • Khodus Wadia *Sam Kotwal* • Nina Wadia *Dolly Kotwal* • Ahsen Bhatti *Cyrus* ■ *Dir* Waris Hussein • *Scr* Firdaus Kanga, from his autobiography *Trying to Grow*

The Sixth Man ★★ 12

Sports comedy   1997 · US · Colour · 103mins

Judging from its first half-hour, *The Sixth Man* could be a touching drama about two brothers with hoop dreams. When the older brother dies, the younger one is lost without him. Lost, that is, until older bro shows up as a ghost with a wacky sense of humour and a drive to win the college basketball championships! Unless you're a huge fan of poltergeist comedy or basketball, this Marlon Wayans vehicle probably won't score too many points. It certainly doesn't go much beyond the obvious gimmick. Contains some swearing and sexual references. 🔲

Marlon Wayans *Kenny Tyler* • Kadeem Hardison *Antoine Tyler* • David Paymer *Coach Pederson* • Michael Michele *RC St John* • Kevin Dunn *Mikulski* ■ *Dir* Randall Miller • *Scr* Christopher Reed, Cynthia Carle

The Sixth Sense ★★★★ 15

Supernatural drama
1999 · US · Colour · 103mins

Successful Bruce Willis movies are no rarity, but here he's not even the lead. Instead he plays second fiddle to Haley Joel Osment's compelling performance as a troubled young boy who receives visitations from the dead. Director M Night Shyamalan's film is no cheesy ghost story, though. The script is smart and believable, the emotional content is higher than average, and the scary moments are truly hair-prickling. Willis is on sensitive, subdued form as a sympathetic child psychologist, proving there's more to him than quips and gun clips. 🔲 **DVD**

Bruce Willis *Malcolm Crowe* • Toni Collette *Lynn Sear* • Olivia Williams *Anna Crowe* • Haley Joel Osment *Cole Sear* • Donnie Wahlberg *Vincent Gray* • Glenn Fitzgerald *Sean* • Mischa Barton *Kyra Collins* • Trevor Morgan *Tommy Tammisimo* • M Night Shyamalan *Doctor Hill* • *Dir/Scr* M Night Shyamalan

Sixty Glorious Years ★★★ U

Historical drama   1938 · UK · Colour · 91mins

Following the success of *Victoria the Great* starring his wife Anna Neagle, producer/director Herbert Wilcox continued the saga up to and including Victoria's death. Peopled with a cast of dignified upper-crust actors such as C Aubrey Smith and Felix Aylmer, the film has Neagle presiding regally, and sometimes touchingly, over events personal, political and public – among them her wedding to Albert (Anton Walbrook), the opening of the Great Exhibition, Albert's death and the Diamond Jubilee. 🔲

Anna Neagle *Queen Victoria* • Anton Walbrook *Prince Albert* • C Aubrey Smith *Duke of Wellington* • Walter Rilla *Prince Ernst* • Charles Carson *Sir Robert Peel* • Felix Aylmer *Lord Palmerston* ■ *Dir* Herbert Wilcox • *Scr* Charles de Grandcourt, Miles Malleson, Robert Vansittart

Sizzle Beach, USA ★★ 18

Sex comedy   1974 · US · Colour · 83mins

A creaky soft-core sexploitation movie whose own history is of far more interest than the story it tries to tell. The film details the sexual adventures of a trio of girls who share a Malibu beach house. One of their conquests is the young Kevin Costner (making his screen debut). Years later this appearance returned to haunt him when the schlock horror film company Troma acquired the rights in the late eighties and cheekily touted it round the Cannes Film Festival as Costner's latest flick. Rumours at the time suggested Costner was trying to buy the rights, but its subsequent video release did little to harm the superstar's career. 🔲

Terry Congie *Janice* • Leslie Brander *Sheryl* • Roselyn Royce *Dit* • Kevin Costner *John Logan, horse trainer* ■ *Dir* Richard Brander • *Scr* Craig Kusaba

Skateboard ★

Sports drama   1978 · US · Colour · 95mins

Owing money to everyone from his ex-wife to the mob, talent agent Allen Garfield organizes several neighborhood kids and teenagers into a touring skateboard team, promising them fame but with dreams of big bucks in his heart. Made during the height of the skateboard craze in the late seventies, there is surprisingly little skateboarding, and its presentation here makes the sport look boring. The incompetent direction extends to the shallow characters and story: with no one ever in focus, there is a bizarre, surreal feel to every scene.

Allen Garfield *Manny Bloom* • Kathleen Lloyd *Millicent Broderick* • Leif Garrett *Brad Harris* • Richard Van Der Wyk *Jason Maddox* • Tony Alva *Tony Bluetile* ■ *Dir* George Gage • *Scr* Richard A Wolf, George Gage, from a story by Richard A Wolf

The Skateboard Kid ★

Fantasy   1993 · US · Colour · 83mins

Foisted on an undeserving public by Roger Corman's Concorde-New Horizons company, this film featuring a talking skateboard marks a new low in teen movies. Trevor Lissauer is the charmless kid who brings a little life to the hick town of Mill Creek by taking on a gang of bullies, humiliating a crooked car dealer, matchmaking his widowed father and finding long-lost treasure. Not bad for a nerd, but where would he have been without his chatty four-wheeled buddy? Dom DeLuise voices Rip the secondhand skateboard, which should have been allowed to gather dust in peace.

Timothy Busfield *Frank Tyler* • Trevor Lissauer *Zack Tyler* • Bess Armstrong *Maggie* • Dom DeLuise *Rip* ■ *Dir* Larry Swerdlove • *Scr* Larry Swerdlove, Gary Stuart Kaplan

The Skateboard Kid II ★★ U

Fantasy   1995 · US · Colour · 88mins

Andrew Stevens, who is better known for directing Shannon Tweed's erotic dramas than family adventures, is behind this routine children's outing. From Roger Corman's production outfit Concorde, this stars Trenton Knight as

the lucky owner of a magic skateboard whose fantastic exploits attract the attention of jealous skate punks. There are steady performances from grown-ups such as Dee Wallace Stone, Bruce Davison and Stevens himself, but it's not very memorable stuff. 🔲

Dee Wallace Stone *Lois Curtis* • Bruce Davison *Burt Squires* • Andrew Stevens *Ken Fields* • Trenton Knight *Sammy Curtis* ■ *Dir* Andrew Stevens • *Scr* Karen Kelly

Skatetown, USA ★★

Comedy   1979 · US · Colour · 98mins

The first to hop on the minor roller-disco bandwagon that pulled up at the fag end of the seventies, this brainless little comedy has good guy Greg Bradford in a roller-skating dance duel with bullying nasty Patrick Swayze. A period curiosity at best, it features not only Patrick Swayze's movie debut but also a roll call of fading American TV stars, including Scott Baio (of *Happy Days*), stand-up comedian Flip Wilson and *Laugh-In*'s Ruth Buzzi. Further down the cast list is Playboy playmate Dorothy Stratten, who appeared in a tiny handful of films before her shocking murder in 1980.

Scott Baio *Richie* • Flip Wilson *Harvey Ross* • Ron Palillo *Frankey* • Ruth Buzzi *Elvira* • Greg Bradford *Stan* • Patrick Swayze *Ace* • Dorothy Stratten *Girl who orders pizza* ■ *Dir* William A Levey • *Scr* Nick Castle

Skeeter ★ 15

Science-fiction horror
1993 · US · Colour · 91mins

It's the old story about radiation mutating insects into bigger and deadlier versions of themselves, but a slower and sometimes even shoddier retelling. It all takes place in the desert, which conveniently doesn't require many sets or complicated shots to arrange. An evil industrialist dumps toxic waste into an abandoned mine, which gets into a water supply full of mosquito eggs, and very low-budget havoc erupts. 🔲

Jim Youngs *Boone* • Tracy Griffith *Sarah* • Michael J Pollard *Hopper* • Charles Napier *Sheriff Buckle* • Jay Robinson *Drake* • William Sanderson *Gordon Perry* ■ *Dir* Clark Brandon • *Scr* Clark Brandon, Lanny Horn, from an idea by Joe Rubin

Skeletons ★★★ 15

Thriller   1996 · US · Colour · 86mins

After a heart attack, journalist Ron Silver and his family move out to the country for a year of rest and relaxation, and are welcomed by the surprisingly friendly small town residents, including James Coburn and local reverend Christopher Plummer. When Silver starts investigating the case surrounding a local resident accused of murder, the town's mood quickly turns ugly. The big revelation at the end, while a little unlikely, is still reasonably believable, and the characters' actions before it are quite plausible. Much of the credit for the movie's success goes to the cast for their excellent performances. Contains violence and swearing. 🔲 **DVD**

Ron Silver *Peter Crane* • Christopher Plummer *Reverend Carlyle* • Dee Wallace Stone *Heather Crane* • Kyle Howard *Zach Crane* •

U = SUITABLE FOR ALL   **Uc** = SUITABLE FOR ALL, ESPECIALLY FOR YOUNG CHILDREN (VIDEO ONLY)   **PG** = PARENTAL GUIDANCE

James Coburn *Frank Jove* • Arlene Golonka *Melanie Jove* ■ *Dir* David DeCoteau • *Scr* Joshua Michael Stern

The Sketch Artist ★★ 18

Thriller 1992 · US · Colour · 85mins

Director Phedon Papamichail wastes a clever idea here as police sketch artist Jeff Fahey tries to cover up the fact that the face described by murder witness Drew Barrymore belongs to his own wife, Sean Young. The worlds of fashion and interior design provide a stylish backdrop to a story that should have been a nail-biting affair, especially with such solid character actors as Tcheky Karyo and James Tolkan among the cast. But it's hard to accept Fahey's methods of investigation, particularly after he becomes the killer's next target. 🎞

Jeff Fahey *Jack Whitfield* • Sean Young *Rayanne Whitfield* • Drew Barrymore *Daisy* • Frank McRae *Milon* • Tcheky Karyo *Paul Corbeil* • James Tolkan *Tonelli* ■ *Dir* Phedon Papamichail • *Scr* Michael Angeli

Ski Party ★★ U

Musical comedy 1965 · US · Colour · 79mins

An amiable, if vastly inferior take on *Some Like it Hot*, set in a ski resort where college chums Frankie Avalon and Dwayne Hickman do what any red-blooded American males would do on discovering their girlfriends fancy another man – dress up in drag. Predictably, the cross-dressed students then become the focus for male interest. James Brown gets to perform his classic *I Got You (I Feel Good)*, probably the best thing in the movie.

Frankie Avalon *Todd Armstrong/Jane* • Dwayne Hickman *Craig Gamble/Nora* • Deborah Walley *Linda Hughes* • Yvonne Craig *Barbara Norris* • Robert Q Lewis *Donald Pevney* • Bobbi Shaw *Nita* • Lesley Gore • Annette Funicello ■ *Dir* Alan Rafkin • *Scr* Robert Kaufman

Ski Patrol ★★ PG

Comedy 1989 · US · Colour · 87mins

Owner of the Snowy Peaks ski lodge, Ray Walston, has maintained a safely run operation in his 40 years in the business. But now he has a rival, Martin Mull, who schemes to sabotage the safety record in order to take over the resort himself. It's up to the motley Ski Patrol team to save the day. Like a sort of *Police Academy* on snow, *Ski Patrol* features a team of misfits having to overcome their differences and natural shortcomings for a greater cause. Fairly standard of its type, but enlivened by some spectacular ski stunts. 🎞

Roger Rose *Jerry* • Yvette Nipar *Ellen* • TK Carter *Iceman* • Leslie Jordan *Murray* • Paul Feig *Stanley* • Sean Gregory Sullivan *Suicide* • Ray Walston *Pops* • Martin Mull *Maris* ■ *Dir* Rich Correll [Richard Correll] • *Scr* Steven Long Mitchell, Craig W Van Sickle, from a story by Wink Roberts, Steven Long Mitchel, Craig W Van Sickle

Ski School ★★ 18

Comedy 1991 · Can · Colour · 84mins

Having discovered the public's appetite for teenage sex-themed comedies with such fare as *Porky's* and *Screwballs*, the Canadian film industry continued to mine this lucrative vein. *Ski School* provides a similar mix of sexy hi-jinks and laughs. Set around a ski school at Vancouver's Whistler Mountain, the film squeezes in the usual quota of wild parties, practical jokes and acres of female flesh. Although relentlessly par for the course, it delivers exactly what it promises (simple titillation) and was successful enough to spawn a sequel, *Ski School 2*, in 1995. Contains swearing and nudity. 🎞

Mark Thomas Miller *Reid* • Tom Breznahan *Johnny* • Dean Cameron *Dave* • John Pyper-Ferguson *Erich* • Spencer Rochfort *Derek* • Patrick Labyorteaux *Ed* • Stuart Fratkin *Fitz* ■ *Dir* Damian Lee • *Scr* David Mitchell

Skidoo ★

Comedy 1968 · US · Colour · 97mins

A rack of top-line comedy stars, not to mention a good score by Harry Nilsson, is wasted in this bizarre and unfunny satire. Reformed gangster Jackie Gleason is bullied out of retirement by gang boss "God" (Groucho Marx, in his final picture) for an unwanted job: to get sent to jail, murder Mickey Rooney, then escape. But within those walls he discovers the alleged joys of LSD. Meanwhile, his daughter brings home a hippy boyfriend who turns the house into a commune. In any poll of the most misguided movies ever made, this would surely be in the top ten, so it is probably worth watching just to see how director Otto Preminger could have got it so wrong.

Jackie Gleason *Tony Banks* • Carol Channing *Flo Banks* • Frankie Avalon *Angie* • Fred Clark *Tower Guard* • Michael Constantine *Leech* • Frank Gorshin *Man* • John Phillip Law *Stash* • Peter Lawford *Senator* • Burgess Meredith *Warden* • George Raft *Captain Garbaldo* • Mickey Rooney *"Blue Chips" Packard* • Groucho Marx *"God"* ■ *Dir* Otto Preminger • *Scr* Doran William Cannon, Elliott Baker (uncredited), Stanley Ralph Ross (uncredited), from a story by Erik Kirkland

Skin Deep ★★★

Melodrama 1985 · Ausl · Colour · 92mins

Luckily, this is not the disastrous Blake Edwards comedy, but a Jackie Collins-style tale set behind the scenes in the fashion industry. Barbara (Briony Behets) and Vanessa (Carmen Duncan) are just two of the ambitious women who will stop at nothing to get what they want, which of course leads to secrets, betrayal, conflict and lots of close-ups of their trembling, well-glossed red lips. It's as superficial as the business it portrays, but entertaining nonetheless.

Briony Behets *Barbara* • Carmen Duncan *Vanessa* • James Smillie *Cliff* • David Reyne *Grant* • Antoinette Byron *Christina* ■ *Dir* Chris Langman, Mark Joffe • *Scr* Anne Lucas

Skin Deep ★ 18

Comedy 1989 · US · Colour · 96mins

An ugly and deeply unappealing sex comedy from Blake Edwards. John Ritter is the womaniser attempting to win back his ex-wife but finding old habits die hard. The fact that its most memorable gag involves fluorescent condoms is an indication of the level of the humour and, while Edwards professes to be tackling adult themes, it's easily as infantile as his *Pink Panther* movies but not nearly as funny. Only Vincent Gardenia as a sympathetic barman emerges with any dignity. Contains swearing.

John Ritter *Zach Hutton* • Vincent Gardenia *Barney* • Alyson Reed *Alex Hutton* • Joel Brooks *Jake* • Julianne Phillips *Molly* • Chelsea Field *Amy* • Peter Donat *Sparky* • Don Gordon *Curt* ■ *Dir/Scr* Blake Edwards

The Skin Game ★★

Drama 1931 · UK · BW · 88mins

Alfred Hitchcock enjoyed the challenge of the seemingly theatrical confines of restricted space – *Lifeboat*, *Rear Window*, *Rope* – creating works of extraordinary fluidity. But the actual theatre pieces which dominated his early British career defeated even his genius and this adaptation of Galsworthy's London success is inevitably dated. It concerns a wealthy family, the Hillcrests, dominated by the aristocratic mother (Helen Haye in the film's best performance) which is at loggerheads with a neighbouring builder who wants to replace farms with factories. The situation raises themes of class and "progress" and rattles a few skeletons.

Phyllis Konstam *Chloe Hornblower* • Edmund Gwenn *Mr Hornblower* • John Longden *Charles Hornblower* • Frank Lawton *Rolf Hornblower* • CV France *Mr Hillcrest* • Jill Esmond *Jill Hillcrest* • Edward Chapman *Dawker* • Helen Haye *Mrs Hillcrest* ■ *Dir* Alfred Hitchcock • *Scr* Alfred Hitchcock, Alma Reville, from the play by John Galsworthy

Skin Game ★★★ PG

Comedy western 1971 · US · Colour · 97mins

An enjoyable comedy western which teams James Garner and Lou Gossett as con men in the years before the Civil War. Their scam is an ingenious and contentious one: Garner poses as a slave trader who sells Gossett for big bucks, only for Gossett to escape and rejoin Garner at the next town where someone else is cheated. Garner trades heavily on his *Maverick* persona, Gossett skilfully transforms himself from a free man to a "Stepin Fetchit" menial, and Ed Asner impresses as a slave dealer. 🎞

James Garner *Quincy* • Lou Gossett [Louis Gossett Jr] *Jason* • Susan Clark *Ginger* • Brenda Sykes *Naomi* • Edward Asner [Ed Asner] *Plunkett* • Andrew Duggan *Calloway* • Henry Jones *Sam* ■ *Dir* Paul Bogart • *Scr* Pierre Marton [Peter Stone]

Skip Tracer ★★★

Crime thriller 1977 · Can · Colour · 94mins

A smashing Canadian indie production, shot for around $150,000, *Skip Tracer* made quite an impact at international film festivals with its story of a debt collector who's determined to be the best in the business. But the repossession of a car goes slightly wrong when the owner, who has legitimately paid for it, turns bad-tempered and has murder on his mind. Directed by first-timer Zale Dalen and acted out by a cast of Vancouver stage performers, this is a tough, witty and gloriously quirky thriller.

David Peterson *John Collins* • John Lazarus *Brent Solverman* • Rudy Szabo *Leo Gabrowski* ■ *Dir/Scr* Zale Dalen

Skippy ★★★ U

Comedy drama 1931 · US · BW · 85mins

Drawing its idea from a comic strip, this wholesome, unbelievably successful entertainment for all the family recounts the tale of how two youngsters (Jackie Cooper, Robert Coogan) set about earning enough money to buy their mutt back from the neighbourhood dog-catcher. Nine-year-old Cooper, a recruit from the *Our Gang* shorts, and the nephew of director Norman Taurog, went on to MGM and became the biggest child star since Jackie Coogan (*The Kid*), young Robert's elder brother. Co-written by Joseph L Mankiewicz and Norman Z McLeod, this simple little movie garnered Oscar nominations for story, script and Cooper, and won Taurog the director's statuette.

Jackie Cooper *Skippy Skinner* • Robert Coogan *Sooky* • Mitzi Green *Eloise* • Jackie Searl [Jackie Searle] *Sidney* • Willard Robertson *Dr Herbert Skinner* • Enid Bennett *Mrs Ellen Skinner* • David Haines *Harley Nubbins* • Helen Jerome Eddy *Mrs Wayne* ■ *Dir* Norman Taurog • *Scr* Joseph L Mankiewicz, Norman McLeod [Norman Z McLeod], Don Marquis, Sam Mintz, from the comic strip and novel by Percy Crosby

Skirts Ahoy! ★★★ U

Musical 1952 · US · Colour · 109mins

It's three girls rather than boys in the navy for a change in this musical which puts Esther Williams, Vivian Blaine and Joan Evans into uniform . Evans is not really happy with song and dance (she replaced Sally Forrest, reputedly because Forrest's hair colour was too similar to Williams) and Blaine, fresh from her Broadway triumph in *Guys and Dolls*, is not given enough opportunity, but the film is pleasant escapist fare. Debbie Reynolds and Bobby Van liven things up, and one of the film's songs *What Good Is a Gal (Without a Guy)* became a modest hit.

Esther Williams *Whitney Young* • Joan Evans *Mary Kate Yarbrough* • Vivian Blaine *Una Yancy* • Barry Sullivan *Lt Cmdr Paul Elcott* • Keefe Brasselle *Dick Hallson* • Billy Eckstine • Dean Miller *Archie O'Conovan* • Debbie Reynolds • Bobby Van ■ *Dir* Sidney Lanfield • *Scr* Isobel Lennart

Skokie ★★★★ PG

Drama based on a true story
1981 · US · Colour · 120mins

Head and shoulders above the majority of fact-based television dramas, this award-winning reconstruction of the stand-off between the citizens of Skokie, Illinois, and a gang of militant neo-Nazis is a sobering reminder that anti-Semitism did not end with the defeat of Hitler. In his only TV movie, Danny Kaye gives a genuinely moving performance as the Holocaust survivor refusing to be intimidated by the bully boys. But then everyone in this stellar cast is totally credible, including acting guru Lee Strasberg in what proved to be his last role. Directed with admirable restraint by Herbert Wise, this is long but enthralling. 🎞

Danny Kaye *Max Feldman* • John Rubinstein *Herb Lewisohn* • Carl Reiner *Abbot Rosen* • Kim Hunter *Bertha Feldman* • Eli Wallach *Bert Silverman* • Lee Strasberg *Morton Weisman*

Brian Dennehy *Chief Arthur Buchanan* • George Dzundza *Frank Collin* ■ *Dir* Herbert Wise • *Scr* Ernest Kinoy

The Skull ★★

Horror   1965 · UK · Colour · 83mins

Horror stars Peter Cushing and Christopher Lee are strongly cast in Freddie Francis's disappointing adaptation of Robert Bloch's story about the strange properties of the Marquis de Sade's skull. There are some good moments and impressive special effects, though, while Francis's direction has panache. The film's original title *The Skull of the Marquis de Sade* had to be changed when the French descendants of the Marquis complained.

Peter Cushing *Professor Christopher Maitland* • Patrick Wymark *Marco* • Christopher Lee *Sir Matthew Phillips* • Jill Bennett *Jane Maitland* • Nigel Green *Inspector Wilson* • Michael Gough *Auctioneer* • George Coulouris *Dr Londe* • Patrick Magee *Police doctor* ■ *Dir* Freddie Francis • *Scr* Milton Subotsky, from the story *The Skull of the Marquis de Sade* by Robert Bloch

Skullduggery ★★

Adventure drama
1969 · US · Colour · 105mins

Burt Reynolds managed to rise above unworthy material with a good-natured charm and skill in the early days of his film career, and this weak adventure is a good example of that ability. Reynolds plays an adventurer who accompanies archaeologist Susan Clark to New Guinea. There they discover a tribe that could be a clue to human evolution, but evil scientist Paul Hubschmid forces them to take their find to the courts. Skullduggery behind the camera didn't help conference: director Gordon Douglas was fired after a week and replaced by Richard Wilson, while French author Vercours was so incensed by the outcome he demanded his name be taken off the credits. Nobody really noticed.

Burt Reynolds *Doug Temple* • Susan Clark *Dr Sybil Greame* • Roger C Carmel *Otto Kreps* • Paul Hubschmid *Vancruysen* • Chips Rafferty *Father "Pop" Dillingham* • Alexander Knox *Buffington* • Pat Suzuki *Topazia* • Edward Fox *Bruce Spofford* • Wilfrid Hyde White *Eaton* ■ *Dir* Gordon Douglas, Richard Wilson • *Scr* Nelson Gidding, from the novel *Les Animaux Denatures (You Shall Know Them)* by Vercours [Jean Marcel Brewer]

The Skulls ★★★ 15

Thriller   2000 · US · Colour · mins

Joshua Jackson (*Dawson's Creek*'s Pacey Witter) places his first foot firmly on the road to Hollywood stardom with a leading role in this preposterous but entertaining thriller about a college secret society called the Skulls, which counts politicians and rich businessmen among its alumni and offers them flash benefits. Jackson plays Luke, a non-wealthy student who is given the opportunity to join. Shortly after his initiation (which involves a lot of running to answer phones and climbing up college steeples) his best friend (who'd been investigating the group) suspiciously commits suicide, leaving Jackson to choose between his jet set pals or Doing The Right Thing. An initially tense set-up gets

increasingly daft as the Skulls go to bizarre lengths to harbour their secrets, but Jackson holds your interest until the end.

Joshua Jackson *Luke McNamara* • Paul Walker *Caleb Mandrake* • Hill Harper *Will Beckford* • Leslie Bibb *Chloe* • Christopher McDonald *Martin Lombard* • Steve Harris *Detective Sparrow* • William Petersen *Senator Ames Levitt* • Craig T Nelson *Litten Mandrake* ■ *Dir* Rob Cohen • *Scr* John Pogue

The Sky above, the Mud below ★★★

Documentary
1960 · Bel/Fr/Neth · Colour · 90mins

Considering it only had the official Rome Olympics film as competition, it was no surprise that Pierre-Dominique Gaisseau's ethnographical exercise won the feature documentary Oscar. Although it could now be accused of patronising its subjects, this study of life in Dutch New Guinea, as seen during a seven-month Franco-Dutch expedition, at least provides a valuable record of tribal customs – cannibalism, headhunting and so on – and the region's flora and fauna. A version with English-language narration also exists. A French language film.

William Peacock *Narrator* ■ *Dir/Scr* Pierre-Dominique Gaisseau • *Cinematographer* Gilbert Sarthre

Sky Heist ★★

Action thriller   1975 · US · Colour · 92mins

This TV movie boasts several well-staged aerial sequences, but it's on terra firma that things fall flat. Clearly delighting in his own ingenuity, director Lee Katzin needlessly strings out what might have been a passable 50-minute episode to feature length. Frank Gorshin (the Riddler in TV's *Batman*) and Stefanie Powers lay on the villainy with a trowel as they plan to hijack a police helicopter as a diversion from their real target – a $10 million bullion consignment. But they hadn't counted on the LAPD's finest, Don Meredith and Joseph Campanella.

Don Meredith *Sergeant Doug Trumbell* • Joseph Campanella *Captain Monty Ballard* • Larry Wilcox *Deputy Jim Schiller* • Ken Swofford *Deputy Pat Connelly* • Stefanie Powers *Terry Hardings* • Frank Gorshin *Ben Hardings* • Shelley Fabares *Lisa* ■ *Dir* Lee H Katzin • *Scr* William F Nolan, Rick Rosner

Sky Murder ★

Second World War detective drama
1940 · US · BW · 72mins

Nick Carter, one of the 20th century's earliest pulp fiction detectives and the focus of some early French silent movies, finally made it to the American screen in 1939 with *Nick Carter, Master Detective*. However, only two more movies followed before the series died and this last instalment explains why. The plot, such as it is, concerns killer spies and a millionaire, but the action quotient is almost nil, with the sleuth helping romantic interest Joyce Compton to wind knitting wool one of the high points.

Walter Pidgeon *Nick Carter* • Donald Meek *Bartholomew* • Karen Verne [Kaaren Verne] *Pat Evens* • Edward Ashley *Cortland Grand* • Joyce Compton *Christina Cross* • Tom Conway

Andrew Hendon • George Lessey *Senator Monrose* • Dorothy Tree *Kathe* ■ *Dir* George B Seitz • *Scr* William R Lipman

Sky Pirates ★★ PG

Science-fiction adventure
1986 · Ausl · Colour · 83mins

John Hargreaves does his best as the pilot flying into a time warp, in this Australian attempt to recapture the excitement and adventure of the old Saturday morning serials. But, whereas Spielberg and Lucas showed in their *Indiana Jones* escapades that the secret of remaking old B-movies for modern audiences is to apply A-movie polish and production values, this effort struggles to rise above C-movie standards of writing and effects.

John Hargreaves *Flight Lieutenant Harris* • Meredith Phillips *Melanie Mitchell* • Max Phipps *Squadron Leader Savage* • Bill Hunter *O'Reilly* • Simon Chilvers *Reverend Kenneth Mitchell* • Alex Scott *General Hackett* ■ *Dir* Colin Eggleston • *Scr* John Lamond

Sky Riders ★★ PG

Action adventure
1976 · US/Gr · Colour · 86mins

Action man violence that gives itself airs as the family of an American businessman (Robert Culp) in Greece is kidnapped by a terrorist group and taken to a monastery on top of a needle-shaped mountain. But never fear, to the rescue comes a group of hang-gliding freaks led by soldier-of-fortune James Coburn. Appearing to let us know it's on the side of democracy, instead it shows us that wife Susannah York isn't wearing a bra and that Coburn is as emotionless as a cold fish. Excellent hang-gliding stunts, though.

James Coburn *Jim McCabe* • Susannah York *Ellen Bracken* • Robert Culp *Jonas Bracken* • Charles Aznavour *Inspector Nikolidis* • Werner Pochath *No 1, terrorist leader* • Zouzou *No 6, female terrorist* • Kenneth Griffith *Wasserman* ■ *Dir* Douglas Hickox • *Scr* Jack DeWitt, Stanley Mann, Garry Michael White, from a story by Hall T Sprague, Bill McGaw

Sky West and Crooked ★★★

Drama   1965 · UK · Colour · 105mins

John Mills's sole assignment behind the camera is something of a family affair: it was co-scripted by his novelist wife, Mary Hayley Bell, and stars their daughter Hayley Mills. Intended to help Hayley distance herself from the kind of kiddie roles she had undertaken at Disney, the film is a variation on DH Lawrence's *The Virgin and the Gypsy*, with Hayley's slightly touched teen falling for romantic Romany Ian McShane. It's all somewhat melodramatic, with Hayley's problems compounded by mother Annette Crosbie's drinking and local hostility towards McShane. Mills Sr directs with a steady hand.

Hayley Mills *Brydie White* • Ian McShane *Roibin* • Laurence Naismith *Edwin Dacres* • Geoffrey Bayldon *Philip Moss* • Annette Crosbie *Mrs White* • Norman Bird *Cheeseman* ■ *Dir* John Mills • *Scr* Mary Hayley Bell, John Prebble, from a story by Mary Hayley Bell

Skyjacked ★★★ PG

Disaster movie   1972 · US · Colour · 96mins

Before he made the mother of all disaster movies, *The Towering Inferno*, John Guillermin worked out with this aerial jeopardy epic which cashed in on the rash of terrorist hijackings as well as the box-office success of *Airport*. Charlton Heston is the stoical pilot, Yvette Mimieux the plucky stewardess, and James Brolin the psychotic hijacker who orders Heston to head for Moscow. Passengers either stay calm or go bonkers, the Russians launch their jet fighters and Heston worries about running out of gas.

Charlton Heston *Captain O'Hara* • Yvette Mimieux *Angela Thacher* • James Brolin *Jerome K Weber* • Claude Akins *Sgt Ben Puzo* • Jeanne Crain *Mrs Shaw* • Susan Dey *Elly Brewster* • Roosevelt Grier [Rosey Grier] *Gary Brown* • Walter Pidgeon *Senator Arne Lindner* ■ *Dir* John Guillermin • *Scr* Stanley R Greenberg, from the novel *Hijacked* by David Harper

Skylark ★★

Comedy   1941 · US · BW · 94mins

After five years of marriage to Ray Milland, Claudette Colbert is fed up with her wifely role as second fiddle to her husband's career. When charming Brian Aherne appears on the scene, he offers just the diversion she's seeking. Adapted from a Broadway play that had starred Gertrude Lawrence, this is standard romantic comedy of the period, played with style and given the Paramount studio gloss. Profiting from the attractive personalities of the stars, it amuses but is nothing special.

Claudette Colbert *Lydia Kenyon* • Ray Milland *Tony Kenyon* • Brian Aherne *Jim Blake* • Binnie Barnes *Myrtle Vantine* • Walter Abel *George Gore* • Grant Mitchell *Frederick Vantine* ■ *Dir* Mark Sandrich • *Scr* Zion Myers, Allan Scott, from the play and novel by Samson Raphaelson

Skylark ★★

Period drama   1993 · US · Colour · 95mins

A perfect example of returning to a successful formula but leaving out the magic. On first sight, there is nothing missing from this effective sequel to the wonderfully moving *Sarah, Plain and Tall*, in which Glenn Close gave a stirring portrayal of a repressed but insightful Maine schoolteacher who uproots to Kansas to look after a widowed farmer and his young family. But, despite all the previous excellent ingredients being present and correct, prairie dust and all, there is a dullness which sadly blights this sequel.

Glenn Close *Sarah Wheaton* • Christopher Walken *Jacob Witting* • Lexi Randall *Anna Witting* • Christopher Bell *Caleb Witting* • Margaret Sophie Stein *Maggie Grant* • Jon De Vries [Jon DeVries] *Matthew Grant* ■ *Dir* Joseph Sargent • *Scr* Patricia MacLachlan

The Sky's the Limit ★★ U

Musical comedy   1943 · US · BW · 86mins

The most forgettable – and largely forgotten – of Fred Astaire's musicals pairs him with Joan Leslie in a wafer-thin romance about a flying hero (Astaire) on leave in New York where, to escape adulation, he pretends to be an idle civilian. Leslie is the news photographer more interested in the

war effort than his attempts to woo her. The movie yielded a couple of great songs, including *One For My Baby*, and the dance routines staged by the star aren't bad. However, in this instance, Fred without Ginger is like flat champagne. ▢

Fred Astaire *Fred Atwell* • Joan Leslie *Joan Manyon* • Robert Benchley *Phil Harriman* • Robert Ryan *Reginald Fenton* • Elizabeth Patterson *Mrs Fisher* • Eric Blore *Jasper* • Marjorie Gateson *Canteen lady* • Peter Lawford *Naval commander* ∎ *Dir* Edward H Griffith • *Scr* Frank Fenton, Lynn Root, from their story *A Handful of Heaven*

The Slab Boys ★★★ 🔟

Drama   1997 · UK · Colour · 97mins

John Byrne's love of fifties rock 'n' roll shone through his superb TV series *Tutti Frutti* and it also forms a musical background to this flawed but quirkily entertaining drama. Based on two of Byrne's plays, it's a coming-of-age tale about three young lads employed in a carpet factory who dream of escape from their bleak working-class surroundings. Byrne draws out fine performances from a largely unknown cast and lovingly evokes the era, shooting almost entirely on studio sets to give his movie a magical, stylised feel. The superb soundtrack mixes Little Richard and Chuck Berry with Scottish contemporary artists like Edwyn Collins and the Proclaimers.

Robin Laing *Phil McCann* • Russell Barr *George "Spanky" Farrell* • Bill Gardiner *Hector McKenzie* • Louise Berry *Lucille Bentley* • Julie Wilson Nimmo *Bernadette Rooney* • Duncan Ross *Alan Downie* • Tom Watson *Willie Curry* • Anna Massey *Miss Elsie Walkinshaw* ∎ *Dir* John Byrne • *Scr* John Byrne, from his plays *The Slab Boys* and *Cuttin' a Rug*

Slacker ★★★★ 🔟

Cult comedy   1989 · US · Colour · 96mins

Director Richard Linklater made his name with this offbeat, low-budget effort, whose title was taken up by the bored twentysomethings of nineties America. There's no plot to speak of, with Linklater instead taking a rather hazy ramble through the lives of a large number of eccentrics living in Austin, Texas. It's an occasionally over-indulgent affair, but the natural performances and dizzying number of barmy conspiracy theories and philosophies win you over in the end. Contains swearing. ▢

Richard Linklater *Should have stayed at the bus station* • Rudy Basquez *Taxi driver* • Jean Caffeine *Roadkill* • Jan Hockey *Jogger* • Stephan Hockey *Running late* • Mark James *Hit-and-run son* ∎ *Dir/Scr* Richard Linklater

Slam ★★★ 🔟

Prison drama   1998 · US · Colour · 103mins

Unusual film about the redemptive power of poetry, with a small-time drug dealer discovering his true calling courtesy of an arts course he signs up for while in prison. Back on the outside, he becomes a leading light of Washington's black rap-poetry scene. Preachy but powerful, the film makes extensive use of handheld cameras to give it a genuine feel of the real. Performances are in-your-face and convincing, but the subject matter won't appeal to all tastes. Contains swearing and a sex scene.

Saul Williams *Ray Joshua* • Bonz Malone *Hopha* • Sonja Sohn *Lauren Bell* • Beau Sia *Jimmy Huang* • Lawrence Wilson *Big Mike* • Andre Taylor *China* ∎ *Dir* Marc Levin, Marc Levin • *Scr* Marc Levin, Richard Stratton, Saul Williams, Sonja Sohn, Bonz Malone, from a story by Marc Levin, Richard Stratton

Slam Dance ★★★ 🔟

Thriller   1987 · US · Colour · 95mins

Director Wayne Wang (*Smoke*, *The Joy Luck Club*) shows his versatility with this intriguing excursion into the thriller genre. Tom Hulce is the harassed cartoonist who finds himself suspected of murder after a brief liaison with Yolanda (Virginia Madsen). Wang cleverly uses the device of Hulce being hounded by both cops and the violent Buddy (Don Opper) to invoke a disturbing atmosphere of individual paranoia and general psychosis. The film could have disintegrated into a muddle – there are many delicious surprises and red herrings are scattered around like confetti – but Wang keeps things moving at a brisk rate. Contains swearing. ▢

Tom Hulce *CC Drood* • Mary Elizabeth Mastrantonio *Helen Drood* • Adam Ant *Jim Campbell* • Don Opper *Buddy* • John Doe *Gilbert* • Harry Dean Stanton *Detective Smiley* • Robert Beltran *Frank* • Virginia Madsen *Yolanda Caldwell* • Millie Perkins *Bobby Nye* ∎ *Dir* Wayne Wang • *Scr* Don Opper

Slam Dunk Ernest ★ 🇺

Comedy   1995 · US · Colour · 92mins

The consistently unfunny Jim Varney returns as Ernest P Worrell in another edition in the film series about the madcap adventures of a trouble-prone simpleton. When the dumber than dumb Ernest comes into possession of a pair of magic basketball shoes, he and his work colleagues come up against the professionals of the game. Help comes in the form of real-life basketball star Kareem Abdul-Jabbar as Ernest's sporting fairy godfather. Puerile humour is interspersed with the usual lashings of childish slapstick and sentimentality. ▢

Jim Varney *Ernest P Worrell* • Kareem Abdul-Jabbar *Archangel* • Jay Brazeau *Mr Moloch* ∎ *Dir* John Cherry [John R Cherry III] • *Scr* John R Cherry III, Daniel Butler

The Slams ★★ 🔟

Prison drama   1973 · US · Colour · 86mins

No-brain prison drama, with athlete turned actor Jim Brown the star behind bars. He finds himself under pressure from fellow inmates to reveal where he's hidden a heroin-and-cash stash. The film starts off as a drama, but oddly transmutes into something resembling a comedy. Yet it's neither particularly exciting, nor particularly funny. Something of a teeth-cutter for director Jonathan Kaplan, who'd later make the likes of *The Accused*, *Love Field* and *Unlawful Entry*. ▢

Jim Brown *Curtis Hook* • Judy Pace *Iris Daniels* • Roland "Bob" Harris *Stambell* • Paul Harris *Jackson Barney* • Frank De Kova *Capiello* • Ted Cassidy *Glover* ∎ *Dir* Jonathan Kaplan • *Scr* Richard L Adams

Slap Shot ★★★

Comedy drama   1977 · US · Colour · 122mins

Paul Newman is reunited with his *Butch Cassidy* director George Roy Hill for this sharp, satirical look at unethical tactics in professional ice hockey. Fashioned as a series of deliberately crude epithets by scriptwriter Nancy Dowd, the film follows the fortunes of a minor-league team that is encouraged to play dirty to win by ambitious coach Newman. Unfortunately, the relentless violence and profanity that provide the film with its great strength are usually toned down in TV versions, with much of the locker-room language removed. ▢

Paul Newman *Reggie Dunlop* • Strother Martin *Joe McGrath* • Michael Ontkean *Ned Braden* • Jennifer Warren *Francine Dunlop* • Lindsay Crouse *Lily Braden* • Jerry Houser *"Killer" Carlson* • Andrew Duncan *Jim Carr* ∎ *Dir* George Roy Hill • *Scr* Nancy Dowd

Slapstick of Another Kind ★★

Science-fiction comedy   1982 · US · Colour · 87mins

The handful of attempts made to bring the work of cult novelist Kurt Vonnegut to the big screen have all met with less than resounding success. *Slapstick of Another Kind* is no exception. A would-be satirical comedy about the birth of huge, hideously ugly twins (Jerry Lewis and Madeline Kahn) who in reality are super-intelligent beings from another planet, the film widely misses the mark. A strong cast ensure that some good moments survive but all in all it demonstrates the difficulty certain idiosyncratic novelists have with their on-screen adaptations. The film was unseen in the US until 1984.

Jerry Lewis *Wilbur Swain/Caleb Swain* • Madeline Kahn *Eliza Swain/Letitia Swain* • Marty Feldman *Sylvester* • John Abbott *Dr Frankenstein* • Jim Backus *United States President* • Samuel Fuller *Colonel Sharp* • Merv Griffin *Anchorman* • Pat Morita *Ambassador Ah Fong* • Orson Welles *Alien Father* ∎ *Dir* Steven Paul • *Scr* Steven Paul, from the novel *Slapstick* by Kurt Vonnegut Jr

Slate, Wyn & Me ★★ 🔟

Crime drama   1987 · Ausl · Colour · 87mins

An intriguing title for this watchable, violent and foul-mouthed Australian drama which concerns two brothers who rob a bank, kill a cop, and take hostage the eponymous "Me", a girl witness. The ensuing triangle creates various roadblocks in the getaway process. Don McLennan's crime drama is strong for the first 30 minutes, but doesn't quite know how to fulfil its early potential. Yet there's a quirkiness to it that sustains viewer interest. ▢

Sigrid Thornton *Blanche McBride* • Simon Burke *Wyn Jackson* • Martin Sacks *Slate Jackson* • Tommy Lewis *Morgan* • Lesley Baker *Molly* • Harold Baigent *Sammy* • Michelle Torres *Daphne* • Murray Fahey *Martin* ∎ *Dir* Don McLennan • *Scr* Don McLennan, from a novel by Georgia Savage

Slattery's Hurricane ★★★

Disaster drama   1949 · US · BW · 83mins

Pilot Richard Widmark's post-Second World War career has included flying for a front company for the mob and

an affair with the boss's girlfriend, Veronica Lake. Learning that his former flying buddy John Russell is married to his old flame Linda Darnell, Widmark, now a weather bureau pilot, tries to wreck the marriage and get her back, but atones by taking Russell's place on a dangerous assignment into the eye of a hurricane. This forgettable drama, told in flashback, is not to be taken seriously. But it's entertaining enough, especially in the storm-tossed aerial sequences.

Richard Widmark *Willard Francis Slattery* • Linda Darnell *Aggie Hobson* • Veronica Lake *Dolores Greeves* • John Russell *Lt FJ "Hobby" Hobson* • Gary Merrill *Comdr ET Kramer* • Walter Kingsford *RJ Milne* • Raymond Greenleaf *Adm William F Ollenby* • Stanley Waxman *Frank* ∎ *Dir* Andre De Toth • *Scr* Herman Wouk, Richard Murphy, from a story by Herman Wouk

Slaughter ★★ 🔞

Blaxploitation crime   1972 · US · Colour · 88mins

With a title to die for, literally, this piece of blaxploitation tries to cash in on the supercool black avenger image institutionalised by *Shaft* (1971). But it's set at such a fast pace by director Jack Starrett that you scarcely feel the potholes of the plot. Jim Brown is the former Green Beret on a trigger-happy vendetta against the underworld mob responsible for killing his parents. It has the ruthless efficiency of a well-oiled automatic weapon – and about as much characterisation. ▢

Jim Brown *Slaughter* • Stella Stevens *Ann* • Rip Torn *Dominick* • Cameron Mitchell *Price* • Don Gordon *Harry* • Marlene Clark *Kim* • Norman Alfe *Mario* ∎ *Dir* Jack Starrett • *Scr* Mark Hanna, Don Williams

Slaughter of the Innocents ★ 🔞

Thriller   1993 · US · Colour · 99mins

This ugly serial-killer thriller cashes in on the fact that its star Scott Glenn was in the far superior multiple-murder movie, *The Silence of the Lambs*. Here Glenn plays an FBI special agent whose golden-haired son (played by the director's real-life son) is his unofficial helper. Together they solve the mystery of the atrocities committed by a Christian fundamentalist who's collecting carcasses for his personal Noah's Ark. Contains swearing, violence and nudity. ▢

Scott Glenn *Stephen Broderick* • Jesse Cameron-Glickenhaus *Jesse Broderick* • Sheila Tousey *Agent Roxanne Lemar* • Darlanne Fluegel *Susan Broderick* • Zitto Kazann *Mordechai Booth* • Armin Shimerman *Dr Mort Seger* • Kevin Sorbo *John Willison* ∎ *Dir/Scr* James Glickenhaus

Slaughter on Tenth Avenue ★★★

Crime drama   1957 · US · BW · 102mins

Three years after *On the Waterfront*, this formula movie discovered the waterfront racket all over again. Craftily directed by Arnold Laven, it has assistant DA Richard Egan at war with the crime around the docks, and finding true love with longshoreman's widow Jan Sterling. Dan Duryea is the heavy, but there's no Marlon Brando this time around.

Richard Egan *William Keating* • Jan Sterling *Madge Pitts* • Dan Duryea *John Jacob Masters* • Julie Adams *Dee* • Walter Matthau *Al Dahlke* • Charles McGraw *Lieutenant Anthony Vosnick* ■ *Dir* Arnold Laven • *Scr* Lawrence Roman, from the memoirs *The Man Who Rocked the Boat* by William J Keating, Richard Carter

Slaughter Trail ★★ U

Western　　　　1951 · US · Colour · 76mins

A small band of outlaws disturbs the peace between Navajos and whites in this Cinecolor western, which is enlivened by the pre-*Cat Ballou* novelty of a commentary which is sung at intervals by guitar-strumming cavalrymen. Gig Young also makes the principal villain colourful. The film's release was delayed by the blacklisting of actor Howard Da Silva, as RKO's owner, Howard Hughes, insisted that all Da Silva's scenes as the cavalry commander were re-shot with Brian Donlevy in the role.

Brian Donlevy *Captain Dempster* • Gig Young *Vaughn* • Virginia Grey *Lorabelle Larkin* • Andy Devine *Sgt McIntosh* • Robert Hutton *Lt Morgan* ■ *Dir* Irving Allen • *Scr* Sid Kuller

Slaughterhouse-Five ★★★★

Science-fiction satire
1972 · US · Colour · 102mins

Kurt Vonnegut's science-fiction masterpiece is done marvellous justice by director George Roy Hill's wildly complex, truly bizarre and poignant commentary on the absurdity of human existence. In this postmodern *Pilgrim's Progress*, Michael Sacks is Billy Pilgrim, a man "unstuck in time" who constantly leaves the present to either return to the past, when he was a prisoner of war in Dresden, or flit to the future, where his existence with half-naked actress Valerie Perrine is viewed under glass by aliens. A wry, intelligent and thought-provoking parable with a haunting surreal quality.

Michael Sacks *Billy Pilgrim* • Ron Leibman *Paul Lazzaro* • Eugene Roche *Derby* • Sharon Gans *Valencia* • Valerie Perrine *Montana Wildhack* • Roberts Blossom *Wild Bob Cody* • Sorrell Booke *Lionel Merble* • Kevin Conway *Weary* ■ *Dir* George Roy Hill • *Scr* Stephen Geller, from the novel by Kurt Vonnegut Jr

Slaughter's Big Rip-Off ★★★

Blaxploitation crime
1973 · US · Colour · 90mins

Black Vietnam vet/urban warrior Jim Brown returns to his avenge the murder of his mother and father by gangsters, led this time around by Ed McMahon. Jim Brown goes in for a lot of violent confrontations but is really too good for this blaxploitation fix – as is *Them!* and *In like Flint* director Gordon Douglas. A hint of humour would have helped.

Jim Brown *Slaughter* • Ed McMahon *Duncan* • Brock Peters *Reynolds* • Don Stroud *Kirk* • Gloria Hendry *Marcia* • Richard Williams *Joe Creole* • Judith Brown *Norji* ■ *Dir* Gordon Douglas • *Scr* Charles Johnson, from a character created by Don Williams

Slave Ship ★★★

Adventure　　　1937 · US · BW · 90mins

Warner Baxter should really have known better than to buy a "blood ship" called the *Albatross*, for no

sooner has he sworn to cease slave trading than he has a mutiny on his hands. Wallace Beery plays his trademark soft-centred sourpuss with typical gusto, and he's ably supported by George Sanders as the chief mutineer and Mickey Rooney as a cheeky cabin boy. But the soggy performance of Baxter as the Captain Bligh of the piece makes it almost impossible for director Tay Garnett to keep the wind in the sails of this otherwise boisterous picture, co-written by novelist William Faulkner.

Warner Baxter *Jim Lovett* • Wallace Beery *Jack Thompson* • Elizabeth Allan *Nancy Marlowe* • Mickey Rooney *Swifty* • George Sanders *Lefty* • Jane Darwell *Mrs Marlowe* • Joseph Schildkraut *Danelo* ■ *Dir* Tay Garnett • *Scr* Sam Hellman, Lamar Trotti, Gladys Lehman, William Faulkner, from the novel *The Last Slaver* by Dr George S King

Slavers ★ 18

Drama　　　1977 · W Ger · Colour · 94mins

In this bloody repellent mess, Trevor Howard and Ray Milland are slumming, playing Victorian-era slave traders. Howard owns the trading post, à la Mr Kurtz in *Heart of Darkness*, while Milland is browned-up as a shifty Arab, Hassan, who shoots his slaves as target practice (which doesn't make very sound economic sense). Britt Ekland introduces some love interest, while Zimbabwe (then Rhodesia) provides the scenery. A German language film.

Trevor Howard *Alec MacKenzie* • Ron Ely *Steven Hamilton* • Britt Ekland *Anna von Erken* • Jürgen Goslar *Max von Erken* • Ray Milland *Hassan* • Don Jack Rousseau *Mazu* • Helen Morgan *Malika* ■ *Dir* Jürgen Goslar • *Scr* Henry Morrisson, Nathaniel Kohn, Marcia MacDonald

Slaves ★★★

Drama　　　1969 · US · Colour · 105mins

Herbert J Biberman, the blacklisted director of *Salt of the Earth* (1954), had to wait 15 years before his next film, a study of slavery. Ossie Davis plays the hero who is sold to Stephen Boyd, a Mississippi landowner who keeps a black mistress, played by singer Dionne Warwick in her screen debut. While Davis and Warwick are fairly conventional archetypes, both desperate to escape, it's Boyd who has the best material, playing a satisfyingly complex character – brutal yet haunted by a religious upbringing which draws him to the Christian-motivated Davis. The director's wife Gale Sondergaard – herself both an Oscar winner and a blacklist victim – appears in the New Orleans sequence. It was her first film since 1949.

Stephen Boyd *Nathan MacKay* • Dionne Warwick *Cassy* • Ossie Davis *Luke* • Robert Kya-Hill *Jericho* • Barbara Ann Teer *Esther* • Marilyn Clark *Mrs Bennett* • Gale Sondergaard *New Orleans lady* ■ *Dir* Herbert J Biberman • *Scr* Herbert J Biberman, John O Killens, Alida Sherman

Slaves of New York ★★★ 15

Comedy drama　1989 · US · Colour · 119mins

The genteel style of the James Ivory–Ismail Merchant duo sits uneasily on a series of inter-related short stories about middle-class thirtysomethings in a district of New

York. The abiding relationship is that between kooky hat designer Bernadette Peters and self-centred artist Adam Coleman Howard, but that's as doomed to fail as the rest of the characters. Ivory and Merchant are more at home with period pieces and they seem out of touch with this inconsequential movie. Contains swearing, sex scenes and brief nudity. ▦

Bernadette Peters *Eleanor* • Chris Sarandon *Victor Okrent* • Mary Beth Hurt *Ginger Booth* • Madeleine Potter *Daria* • Adam Coleman Howard *Stash Stotz* • Nick Corri *Marley Mantello* • Mercedes Ruehl *Samantha* • Steve Buscemi *Wilfredo* ■ *Dir* James Ivory • *Scr* Tama Janowitz, from her stories • *Producer* Ismail Merchant

Slayground ★★ 18

Thriller　　　1983 · UK · Colour · 84mins

Not a horror film, despite the lurid title, but a tepid thriller based on a hard-boiled novel by Richard Stark (crime writer Donald E Westlake). The hero of the book was a tough-nut criminal, but for the film, he's been softened into a whiny petty thief. This sweetening of his character does the film no favours; neither does the dreary plot, which sees the crook on the run from a contract killer. Peter Coyote stars, while other familiar faces include Billie Whitelaw and Mel Smith. ▦

Peter Coyote *Stone* • Mel Smith *Abbatt* • Billie Whitelaw *Madge* • Philip Sayer *Costello* • Bill Luhrs *Sheer* • Marie Master *Joni* • Clarence Felder *Orzel* ■ *Dir* Terry Bedford • *Scr* Trevor Preston, from a novel by Richard Stark [Donald E Westlake]

Sleep, Baby, Sleep ★★★ PG

Thriller　　　1995 · US · Colour · 92mins

Armand Mastroianni made his name with low-budget horrors such as *Cameron's Closet* and *He Knows You're Alone*, but he is surprisingly at home here with this gripping made-for-TV thriller. Tracey Gold is the young mother who suffers from attention deficit disorder, and finds herself in hot water when her baby vanishes without trace. Gold delivers a gutsy performance and is well supported by the likes of Kyle Chandler and Joanna Cassidy, while Mastroianni puts his horror background to good use by evoking a creepy air of suspense. Contains some violence. ▦

Tracey Gold *Sylvie Walker* • Kyle Chandler *Peter Walker* • Joanna Cassidy *Hannah Pierson* • Thomas Calabro *Detective Martinson* • Missy Crider *Joanna Blessing* • Karla Tamburrelli *Tracy Corbett* ■ *Dir* Armand Mastroianni • *Scr* John Grey

Sleep, My Love ★★ PG

Murder mystery　1948 · US · BW · 92mins

Shades of that old favourite *Gaslight* haunt this psycho-melodrama, which pairs one-time romantic comedy team Claudette Colbert and Don Ameche. Colbert is the wealthy wife of Ameche, for once swapping his debonair persona to play the impassive, cold husband systematically sending Colbert mad so he can inherit her money and marry siren Hazel Brooks. Robert Cummings is the hero figure in a plot too familiar for surprises, but still somewhat suspenseful. The

expertise of director Douglas Sirk holds together what would otherwise have been a very minor work. ▦

Claudette Colbert *Alison Courtland* • Don Ameche *Richard Courtland* • Robert Cummings *Bruce Elcott* • Rita Johnson *Barby* • George Coulouris *Charles Vernay* • Hazel Brooks *Daphne* • Queenie Smith *Mrs Vernay* • Keye Luke *Jimmie* ■ *Dir* Douglas Sirk • *Scr* St Clair McKelway, Leo Rosten, Cyril Endfield [Cy Endfield], Decla Dunning, from a novel by Leo Rosten

Sleep with Me ★★★ 18

Romantic comedy
1994 · US · Colour · 82mins

Suggested by Eric Stoltz and director Rory Kelly, this is a fascinating experiment in film-making. Six writers each penned a different episode; if the end result is a little uneven, the shifts in tone give the picture vibrance and variety. Though the narrative focus is on the twists and trysts involving Stoltz, Meg Tilly and Craig Sheffer, it's the incidentals that stand out, notably Quentin Tarantino's wonderful party piece and Adrienne Shelly's unerring talent for social gaffs. Hilarious when it hits the mark, but never less than amiable. Contains swearing, sex scenes and nudity. ▦

Eric Stoltz *Joseph* • Meg Tilly *Sarah* • Craig Sheffer *Frank* • Todd Field *Duane* • Susan Traylor *Deborah* • Dean Cameron *Leo* • Quentin Tarantino *Sid* • Adrienne Shelly *Pamela* ■ *Dir* Rory Kelly • *Scr* Duane Dell'Amico, Roger Hedden, Neal Jimenez, Joe Keenan, Rory Kelly, Michael Steinberg

Sleeper ★★★ PG

Comedy　　　1973 · US · Colour · 83mins

With this energetic but over-eager tribute to such silent clowns as Charlie Chaplin, Buster Keaton, Harry Langdon and Harold Lloyd, Woody Allen proved once and for all that his talents did not lie in physical comedy. Fun though some of the slapstick is, it's Allen's satirical view of the future and his priceless one-liners that linger longest in the memory. Once more he strikes up an effortless rapport with Diane Keaton, but too many of the other characters fail to register, while the plot too often slows down the comic pace. The costumes were designed by director Joel Schumacher. Contains swearing. ▦

Woody Allen *Miles Monroe* • Diane Keaton *Luna Schlosser* • John Beck *Erno Windt* • Marya Small *Dr Nero* • Bartlett Robinson *Dr Orva* • Mary Gregory *Dr Melik* • Chris Forbes *Rainer Krebs* ■ *Dir* Woody Allen • *Scr* Woody Allen, Marshall Brickman

The Sleepers ★★★ 15

Spy thriller　　1988 · US · Colour · 92mins

Sleepers were spies planted in key locations with orders to live unremarkable lives so that, when activated, their operations would not arouse suspicion. The sleepers in this case are the parents of teenager River Phoenix, whose application to join the US Air Force arouses the suspicions of FBI agent Sidney Poitier. The intriguing premise behind this picture, also known as *Little Nikita*, is wasted by director Richard Benjamin, who settles for a game of cat and mouse as Poitier and Phoenix join forces to catch the real Soviet snakes. ▦

Sidney Poitier *Roy Parmenter* • River Phoenix *Jeff Grant* • Richard Jenkins *Richard Grant* • Caroline Kava *Elizabeth Grant* • Richard Bradford *Konstantin Karpov* • Richard Lynch *Scuba* ■ *Dir* Richard Benjamin • *Scr* John Hill, Bo Goldman, from a story by Tom Musca, Terry Schwartz

Sleepers ★★★ 18

Drama 1996 · US · Colour · 140mins

With its powerhouse cast and an A-list director, *Sleepers* is long and exudes importance and integrity. So why does it come across as bogus? Though based on a controversial autobiography, the plot mechanism and its moral stance – that violent revenge is fully justified – is not totally believable. The story concerns four teenagers who are brought up by a priest, accidentally commit a murder and are sent to jail where they are repeatedly raped by their guard. Years later, they plot revenge. The big themes pile up but director Barry Levinson keeps the story rolling and vividly evokes the hothouse atmosphere of New York's Hell's Kitchen. Contains violence and swearing. [video] DVD

Kevin Bacon *Sean Nokes* • Robert De Niro *Father Bobby* • Dustin Hoffman *Danny Snyder* • Jason Patric *Lorenzo "Shakes"* • Brad Pitt *Michael* • Billy Crudup *Tommy* • Ron Eldard *John* • Vittorio Gassman *King Benny* • Minnie Driver *Carol Martinez* ■ *Dir* Barry Levinson • *Scr* Barry Levinson, from the autobiography by Lorenzo Carcaterra

Sleeping Beauty ★★★ U

Animated fantasy 1959 · US · Colour · 71mins

Based on Charles Perrault's enduring fairy tale, this was Disney's most expensive cartoon to date and the first one to bomb at the box office. It was an ambitious project that made use of the latest technology and state-of-the-art rotoscoping (that is, creating the character by tracing the filmed actions of real people), but no one was impressed and, even though the score was based on Tchaikovsky's *Sleeping Beauty* ballet, few went away whistling the tunes. The fairies Flora, Fauna and Merryweather are fun and Maleficent is a great villainess, but Aurora is one of Disney's least endearing heroines and the whole thing is a mite slow. [video]

Eleanor Audley *Maleficent* • Verna Felton *Flora* • Vera Vague [Barbara Jo Allen] *Fauna* • Barbara Luddy *Merryweather* • Taylor Holmes *King Stefan* • Bill Thompson *King Hubert* • Candy Candido *Goons* • Mary Costa *Princess Aurora* • Bill Shirley *Prince Phillip* ■ *Dir* Clyde Geronimi, Eric Larson, Wolfgang Reitherman, Les Clark • *Scr* Erdman Penner, from the fairy tale by Charles Perrault

The Sleeping Car Murders ★★★

Crime thriller 1965 · Fr · BW · 91mins

After years assisting René Clair and Jacques Demy, the Greek-born film-maker Constantin Costa-Gavras finally made his feature debut with this teasing whodunit. The members of the all-star cast fall like flies as police inspector Yves Montand tries to discover who killed a woman on the Marseilles-Paris express. In addition to a grotesquely lecherous Michel Piccoli, the limelight is hogged by Simone Signoret, whose daughter Catherine Allégret also appears. Costa-Gavras takes the picture at a fast pace and keeps the clues well hidden, so you can forgive him the preposterous ending. French dialogue dubbed into English.

Yves Montand *Inspector Grazzi* • Simone Signoret *Eliane Darres* • Pierre Mondy *Commissioner* • Catherine Allégret *Bambi* • Pascale Roberts *Georgette Thomas* • Michel Piccoli *Cabourg* • Jean-Louis Trintignant *Eric* ■ *Dir* Costa-Gavras • *Scr* Costa-Gavras, Sebastien Japrisot, from the novel *Compartiment Tueurs* by Sebastien Japrisot

Sleeping Car to Trieste ★★ PG

Spy drama 1948 · UK · BW · 91mins

While 1932's *Rome Express* was a sleek, fast-moving turbo of a crime drama, this unnecessary remake is something of a branch-line diesel that director John Paddy Carstairs insists on stopping at every country halt. The story remains basically the same as before, with Albert Lieven and Jean Kent as thieves in pursuit of a diary packed with state secrets, which passes from one shifty passenger to another. Comparisons are inevitable, if slightly unfair, but none of the cast improves on the original characterisations. Lieven does a nice line in villainy, though. [video]

Jean Kent *Valya* • Albert Lieven *Zurta* • Derrick de Marney *George Grant* • Paul Dupuis *Jolif* • Rona Anderson *Joan Maxted* • David Tomlinson *Tom Bishop* • Finlay Currie *Alastair MacBain* ■ *Dir* John Paddy Carstairs • *Scr* Allan MacKinnon, from the story *Rome Express* by Clifford Grey

The Sleeping City ★★★

Crime drama 1950 · US · BW · 83mins

A documentary-style thriller which critics at the time thought was heavily derived from the 1948 drama *The Naked City*. Set in a New York's notorious Bellevue hospital – scene of Ray Milland's drying-out nightmares in *The Lost Weekend* – it weaves together several strands of narrative and the deaths of two interns who have been stealing drugs to pay off gambling debts. George Sherman's film was one of the earliest Hollywood movies to confront the drug problem and it doesn't stint on the grim details. Richard Conte is the cop on the case, Coleen Gray the nurse who is also involved in the drug trade.

Richard Conte *Fred Rowan* • Coleen Gray *Ann Sebastian* • Peggy Dow *Kathy Hall* • John Alexander *Inspector Gordon* • Alex Nicol *Dr Bob Anderson* • Richard Taber *Pop Ware* ■ *Dir* George Sherman • *Scr* Jo Eisinger

The Sleeping Tiger ★★★★ U

Crime drama 1954 · UK · BW · 85mins

A highly charged British melodrama, made in England by Hollywood blacklistees, director Joseph Losey (hiding behind the name of the film's actual producer, Victor Hanbury) and co-writer Carl Foreman (under the alias Derek Frye). An important film, it brought together for the first time one of British cinema's most accomplished pairings in director Losey and star Dirk Bogarde, who would create a stunning body of work including *The Servant* and *Accident*. Losey seemed able to tap Bogarde's smouldering sexual and social ambivalence, and his scenes here with Alexis Smith are electric. The plot, about a psychiatrist taking a known criminal into his home, is reminiscent of Hollywood at its battiest. [video]

Dirk Bogarde *Frank Clements* • Alexis Smith *Glenda Esmond* • Alexander Knox *Dr Clive Esmond* • Hugh Griffith *Inspector Simmons* • Patricia McCarron *Sally* • Maxine Audley *Carol* • Glyn Houston *Bailey* • Harry Towb *Harry* • Billie Whitelaw *Receptionist* ■ *Dir* Victor Hanbury [Joseph Losey] • *Scr* Derek Frye [Harold Buchman, Carl Foreman], from the novel by Maurice Moiseiwitsch

Sleeping with the Devil ★★

Drama based on a true story
1997 · US · Colour

Domestic violence forms the basis of this TV true-crime story. Young nurse Shannen Doherty weds bodybuilding Texas tycoon Tim Matheson, who's 24 years her senior. Two tempestuous years later, she learns that he is a wife-abusing bigamist and leaves, only for the psychotic spouse to put a hit man on her trail. What is an otherwise engrossing tale of deceit and betrayal is itself betrayed by Doherty's insipid, colourless and unsympathetic portrayal of a real-life victim.

Shannen Doherty *Rebecca Dubrovich/Janni Smith* • Tim Matheson *Dick Strang* • Bonnie Bartlett *Stasha Dubrovich* • Steve Eastin *Wes Dubrovich* ■ *Dir* William A Graham • *Scr* Ellen Weston, from the non-fiction book by Suzanne Finstad

Sleeping with the Enemy ★★★ 18

Thriller 1991 · US · Colour · 94mins

Fatal Attraction turned on its head, with the obsessive this time being a husband who just won't let his wife go. Julia Roberts is the abused spouse who stages her own death to escape her marriage from hell with Patrick Bergin. She begins her life anew and meets nice Kevin Anderson but her crazed husband is never far behind. This was Roberts's bid for grittier material and she acquits herself rather well, while Bergin relishes his role as the bad guy. Director Joseph Ruben established his reputation with this sort of thriller, and, although this never equals his earlier *The Stepfather*, he still manages some chilling sequences. Contains violence, sex scenes and swearing. [video]

Julia Roberts *Laura Burney/Sara Waters* • Patrick Bergin *Martin Burney* • Kevin Anderson *Ben Woodward* • Elizabeth Lawrence *Chloe* • Kyle Secor *Fleishman* • Claudette Nevins *Dr Rissner* • Tony Abatemarco *Locke* • Marita Geraghty *Julie* ■ *Dir* Joseph Ruben • *Scr* Ronald Bass, from the novel by Nancy Price

Sleepless in Seattle ★★★★ PG

Romantic comedy
1993 · US · Colour · 100mins

Nora Ephron, the writer of *When Harry Met Sally...*, comes up trumps again as co-writer and director of this gloriously old-fashioned and unashamedly manipulative romantic comedy. Tom Hanks, recently widowed, moves to a new home in Seattle where he just grieves and grieves. His young son, concerned over his dad's state of mind, calls a radio phone-in and when Hanks himself takes the phone, he pours his heart out. That's storyline one. Storyline two features Meg Ryan, a Baltimore journalist who hears the broadcast, recognises a kindred lonely heart and starts tracking Hanks down. For nearly two hours, Ephron keeps her marvellous stars apart, a potentially dangerous tactic that works superbly. *Sleepless in Seattle* proved to be a box-office smash; the team subsequently reunited for *You've Got Mail* in 1998. [video] DVD

Tom Hanks *Sam Baldwin* • Meg Ryan *Annie Reed* • Ross Malinger *Jonah Baldwin* • Rosie O'Donnell *Becky* • Rob Reiner *Jay* • Bill Pullman *Walter* • Rita Wilson *Suzy* • Victor Garber *Greg* • David Hyde Pierce *Dennis Reed* ■ *Dir* Nora Ephron • *Scr* Nora Ephron, David S Ward, Jeff Arch, from a story by Jeff Arch

Sleepwalkers ★ 18

Fantasy horror 1992 · US · Colour · 85mins

Hailed as the first Stephen King story expressly written for the screen, this minor horror entry revolves around the gory small-town exploits of shape-shifting, incestuous, psychic vampires with feline, reptilian and human traits. Director Mick Garris tries to inject life into the pathetic script by gyrating the camera, adding some neat computer-generated transformations and flashily accenting what little action there is, but this underdeveloped material is so poor he's constantly fighting a losing battle. Apart from playing spot-the-cameo, there's little to engage the attention in this idiotic potboiler. [video]

Brian Krause *Charles Brady* • Mädchen Amick *Tanya Robertson* • Alice Krige *Mary Brady* • Jim Haynie *Sheriff Ira* • Cindy Pickett *Mrs Robertson* • Ron Perlman *Captain Soames* • John Landis *Lab technician* • Joe Dante *Lab assistant* • Stephen King *Cemetery caretaker* • Clive Barker *Forensic technician* • Tobe Hooper *Forensic technician* ■ *Dir* Mick Garris • *Scr* Stephen King

Sleepy Hollow ★★★★ 15

Gothic horror fantasy
1999 · US · Colour · 105mins

An alchemic combination of visual splendour, dreamy bloodthirstiness and sly humour, this supernatural Gothic whodunit is another beautifully crafted offering from eccentric maestro Tim Burton. With a perfect cast milking every sinister nuance, his clever revision of Washington Irving's timeless tale of terror enlists the classic retro look of Hammer's golden horror era to stunning effect. Johnny Depp, sporting a clipped English accent, is brilliant as radical-thinking police constable Ichabod Crane, sent to the small Dutch community of Sleepy Hollow to investigate three mysterious beheadings the locals are blaming on the ghost of the legendary Headless Horseman. The ultimate Tim Burton movie. [video] DVD

Johnny Depp *Ichabod Crane* • Christina Ricci *Katrina Van Tassel* • Miranda Richardson *Lady Van Tassel/Crone* • Michael Gambon *Baltus Van Tassel* • Casper Van Dien *Brom Van Brunt* • Jeffrey Jones *Reverend Steenwyck* • Richard Griffiths *Magistrate Philipse* • Christopher Walken *Hessian Horseman* ■ *Dir* Tim Burton • *Scr* Andrew Kevin Walker, from a story by Kevin Yagher, Andrew Kevin Walker,

from the story *The Legend of Sleepy Hollow* by Washington Irving • *Cinematographer* Emmanuel Lubezki • *Production Designer* Rick Heinrichs • *Set Decorator* Peter Young

The Slender Thread ★★★

Drama   1965 · US · BW · 98mins

Two years before working on the Oscar-winning *In the Heat of the Night*, Sidney Poitier and writer Stirling Silliphant made this tense little thriller about a volunteer social worker (Poitier) trying to locate a woman (Anne Bancroft) who's taken a drugs overdose. Based upon an actual incident, what led this wife and mother to take such desperate steps is told in flashback. In his feature debut, director Sydney Pollack concentrates on the telephoned interchange between the two principals, and the suspense that the conversation generates is what keeps this particular race against time so engrossing.

Sidney Poitier *Alan Newell* • Anne Bancroft *Inga Dyson* • Telly Savalas *Doctor Coburn* • Steven Hill *Mark Dyson* • Greg Jarvis *Chris Dyson* • Edward Asner [Ed Asner] *Detective Judd Ridley* • Indus Arthur *Marion* • Dabney Coleman *Charlie* ■ *Dir* Sydney Pollack • *Scr* Stirling Silliphant, from the story *Decision To Die* by Shana Alexander

Sleuth ★★★★🄵

Mystery   1972 · UK · Colour · 138mins

Both leading players in this mystery were nominated for the best actor Oscar. Neither Michael Caine nor Laurence Olivier won, but they surely had their reward in the fun they evidently had in making this engrossing sleight of hand from playwright Anthony Shaffer. As theatrical duplicity inevitably packs more of a punch than its cinematic counterpart, the impact of the elaborate role-playing is undeniably weakened by its translation to the screen. However, the corkscrew plot and the delicious hamming of the leads ensure that it still remains a thundering good watch. Contains some swearing and sexual references. ▦

Laurence Olivier *Andrew Wyke* • Michael Caine *Milo Tindle* ■ *Dir* Joseph L Mankiewicz • *Scr* Anthony Shaffer, from his play

Sliding Doors ★★★🄵

Romantic fantasy comedy
1997 · UK/US · Colour · 95mins

If you could live your life again, would you do it differently? That's the thought behind this lightweight British comedy directed by ex-*Bread* actor Peter Howitt, in which Gwyneth Paltrow plays out two different scenarios after she misses/doesn't miss a tube train home. In one reality she finds out her boyfriend is a two-timing louse, so she leaves him and gets a cute new haircut. In her parallel world the hair is long and boring – very much like her life. Paltrow handles her English accent with ease, and she gets some nice support from John Hannah and John Lynch. But because her life is far more interesting in one half than the other the movie never quite gels. Contains swearing. ▦

Gwyneth Paltrow *Helen* • John Hannah *James* • John Lynch *Gerry* • Jeanne Tripplehorn *Lydia*

• Zara Turner *Anna* • Douglas McFerran *Russell* • Paul Brightwell *Clive* • Nina Young *Claudia* ■ *Dir/Scr* Peter Howitt

A Slight Case of Murder ★★★🄤

Crime comedy   1938 · US · BW · 86mins

A terrific fast-paced Warner Bros movie, which provides a knockout role for Edward G Robinson as the bootlegging hood left high and dry at the end of Prohibition. Robinson hogs the picture, though there's super support from the likes of Ruth Donnelly (as Robinson's wife) and a wry Allen Jenkins, and there's a very funny climax during which four corpses have all the best moments. This was based on a popular Broadway play by Damon Runyon and Howard Lindsay, and the theatrical structure does show through at times, but Robinson and his cohorts don't let you dwell on it for a second.

Edward G Robinson *Remy Marko* • Jane Bryan *Mary Marko* • Willard Parker *Dick Whitewood* • Ruth Donnelly *Nora Marko* • Allen Jenkins *Mike* • John Litel *Post* • Eric Stanley *Ritter* • Margaret Hamilton *Mrs Cagle* ■ *Dir* Lloyd Bacon • *Scr* Earl Baldwin, Joseph Schrank, from the play by Damon Runyon, Howard Lindsay

Slightly Dangerous ★★🄤

Comedy   1943 · US · BW · 94mins

At this point in her career, Lana Turner had already successfully co-starred with Clark Gable and Robert Taylor, and could afford to relax in this tosh about a waitress who lies about her origins. MGM was preparing the definitive waitress movie for Turner, but in the end it was Judy Garland who made *The Harvey Girls*, leaving Turner to find everlasting notoriety with *The Postman Always Rings Twice*.

Lana Turner *Peggy Evans/Carol Burden/Narrator* • Robert Young *Bob Stuart* • Walter Brennan *Cornelius Burden* • Dame May Whitty *Baba* • Eugene Pallette *Durstin* • Alan Mowbray *English gentleman* • Florence Bates *Mrs Roanoke-Brooke* • Howard Freeman *Mr Quill* ■ *Dir* Wesley Ruggles • *Scr* Charles Lederer, George Oppenheimer, from a story by Ian McLellan Hunter, Aileen Hamilton

Slightly French ★★

Musical comedy   1949 · US · BW · 81mins

In this take on *Pygmalion*, a Brooklyn hoochy-cooch dancer (Dorothy Lamour) is given a crash-course in conduct by film director Don Ameche, who digs himself out of a hole by passing her off as a quality French actress. Smoothly directed by Douglas Sirk and played with pleasing nonchalance by the stars, it's a slightly good idea, slightly amusing, and bears a slight resemblance to *Let's Fall in Love* (1934) – hardly surprising, since it's a makeover of that film's story.

Dorothy Lamour *Mary O'Leary/Rochelle Olivier* • Don Ameche *John Gayle* • Janis Carter *Louisa Gayle* • Willard Parker *Douglas Hyde* • Adele Jergens *Yvonne La Tour* • Jeanne Manet *Nicolette* ■ *Dir* Douglas Sirk • *Scr* Karen De Wolf, from a story by Herbert Fields

Slightly Honorable ★★

Mystery   1939 · US · BW · 85mins

Suspected of murder, lawyer Pat O'Brien determines to track down the

real killer. He eventually does so with the help of Broderick Crawford and uncovers the villainy of corrupt politician Edward Arnold. Heavily populated with corpses, suspects and jokes – several of them delivered by ace wisecracker Eve Arden – this comedy thriller veers uncertainly between laughter and suspense, with the former winning to the detriment of the latter. Tay Garnett directs, with a large cast of supporting players.

Pat O'Brien *John Webb* • Edward Arnold *Vincent Cushing* • Broderick Crawford *Russ Sampson* • Ruth Terry *Ann Seymour* • Claire Dodd *Alma Brehmer* ■ *Dir* Tay Garnett • *Scr* Ken Englund, John Hunter Lay, Robert Tallman, from the novel *Send Another Coffin* by Frank G Presnell

Slightly Scarlet ★★★

Crime drama   1956 · US · Colour · 92mins

In the dying days of RKO following Howard Hughes's ownership, producer Benedict Bogeaus mounted a series of westerns and melodramas using up leftover sets and contract artists, glossily directed by the talented and estimable veteran Allan Dwan. This is one of the better examples, a crime drama about a guy (John Payne) involved with a pair of redheaded sisters (Rhonda Fleming and Arlene Dahl). The theme is well handled, and Dahl is terrific as the slightly sozzled sister. These Dwan/Bogeaus/Payne movies deserve to be better known, and are certainly worth watching now for their fascinating range of themes and attitudes.

John Payne *Ben Grace* • Rhonda Fleming *June Lyons* • Arlene Dahl *Dorothy Lyons* • Kent Taylor *Frank Jansen* • Ted De Corsia *Sol Caspar* • Lance Fuller *Gauss* • Buddy Baer *Lenhardt* ■ *Dir* Allan Dwan • *Scr* Robert Blees, from the novel *Love's Lovely Counterfeit* by James M Cain

Slim ★★★

Drama   1937 · US · BW · 86mins

A young and handsome Henry Fonda is Slim, a farm boy who realises his dream of becoming an electric lineman when hardened expert Pat O'Brien makes him his protégé (later his partner) and exposes him to the addiction of a dangerous and wandering life on the pylons. Ray Enright directs, and Margaret Lindsay supplies the romantic complication in a tightly made movie that holds the attention, despite a beginning that plays like a propaganda film for the men who risk their lives, and an ending you can see coming a mile off.

Pat O'Brien *Red Blayd* • Henry Fonda *Slim* • Margaret Lindsay *Cally* • Stuart Erwin *Stumpy* • J Farrell MacDonald *Pop Traver* • Jane Wyman *Stumpy's girlfriend* ■ *Dir* Ray Enright • *Scr* William Wister Haines, from his novel

Sling Blade ★★★★🄵

Drama   1996 · US · Colour · 134mins

This shockingly moving drama brought debutant director Billy Bob Thornton to international attention. In addition to winning an Oscar for his screenplay, he also drew a best actor nomination for his mesmerising performance as Karl Childers, the hesitant, seemingly harmless handyman who befriends a lonely boy on being released from the

secure hospital where he'd been held for 25 years after murdering his mother and her beau. With unseen sparks flying around an emotional powder keg, it's a case of Norman Bates meeting Tennessee Williams in a sleepy Deep South hollow. Darkly comic, superbly acted and utterly compelling. Contains swearing and sexual references.

Billy Bob Thornton *Karl Childers* • Dwight Yoakam *Doyle Hargraves* • JT Walsh *Charles Bushman* • John Ritter *Vaughan Cunningham* • Lucas Black *Frank Wheatley* • Natalie Canerday *Linda Wheatley* • James Hampton *Jerry Woolridge* • Jim Jarmusch *Dairy Queen boy* ■ *Dir/Scr* Billy Bob Thornton

The Slingshot ★★★🄻🄶

Biographical drama
1993 · Swe · Colour · 98mins

Scandinavian cinema has a reputation for films about childhood and echoes of *My Life as a Dog* ring around this evocation of growing up in twenties Stockholm. Touching upon such topics as sex, sibling rivalry, poverty, royalty and anti-Semitism, this is an incredibly busy film. Stellan Skarsgård contributes some uncompromising support and Jesper Salen looks suitably put-upon as the incomprehending son of a lame socialist and the punchbag brother of an aspiring boxer. But Ake Sandgren's episodic approach to his fact-based material means that the action never really gains momentum. In Swedish with English subtitles. ▦

Jesper Salen *Roland Schutt* • Stellan Skarsgård *Fritiof Schutt* • Basia Frydman *Zipa Schutt* • Niclas Olund *Bertil Schutt* ■ *Dir* Ake Sandgren • *Scr* Ake Sandgren, from the novel by Roland Schütt

The Slipper and the Rose ★★🄤

Musical fantasy 1976 · UK · Colour · 136mins

This lavish British musical has neither the magic nor the songs to turn it into the shimmering extravaganza that director Bryan Forbes obviously had in mind. Gemma Craven has the voice but not the allure to give Cinders a fairy-tale sheen, and Richard Chamberlain looks a little long in the tooth to play the charming Prince Edward. But the veterans in the cast have a ball, and Annette Crosbie makes a wonderfully world-weary fairy godmother. ▦

Richard Chamberlain *Prince* • Gemma Craven *Cinderella* • Annette Crosbie *Fairy Godmother* • Edith Evans *Dowager Queen* • Christopher Gable *John* • Michael Hordern *King* • Margaret Lockwood *Stepmother* • Kenneth More *Lord Chamberlain* ■ *Dir* Bryan Forbes • *Scr* Bryan Forbes, Robert B Sherman, Richard M Sherman

Slipstream ★★🄿🄶

Science-fiction adventure
1989 · US/UK · Colour · 87mins

The forgotten man of *Star Wars*, Mark Hamill, attempted to get his career airborne again with a return to the sci-fi genre. However, this muddled, British-shot affair barely got off the ground itself. The concept – a post-apocalyptic world where the favoured form of transportation is the glider – has potential, but director Steven Lisberger

never makes up his mind whether this is an escapist fantasy or a more cerebral affair. Nevertheless, the flight sequences are pretty good and there is an eclectic cast that includes Bob Peck, Bill Paxton, Ben Kingsley and F Murray Abraham. 🖭

Mark Hamill *Tasker* • Bob Peck *Byron* • Bill Paxton *Matt Owen* • Kitty Aldridge *Belitski* • Tony Allen *Bartender* • Susan Leong *Abigail* • F Murray Abraham *Cornelius* • Ben Kingsley *Avatar* ■ *Dir* Steven Lisberger • *Scr* Tony Kayden, Charles Pogue, Steven Lisberger, from a story by Bill Bauer

Slither ★★★ 15

Comedy thriller 1973 · US · Colour · 92mins

Easy Rider, *Vanishing Point* and *Two-Lane Blacktop* started a vogue for counterculture road movies. *Slither* took it to extremes, a comedy thriller that has the frenetic absurdity of a *Roadrunner* cartoon and a stash of stolen loot as the reason for it all. MGM, wanting out of its cosy middle-American image, hired the combustible James Caan and surrounded him with oddball characters from the likes of Peter Boyle and Sally Kellerman. Played largely deadpan and set in mobile home parks and bingo parlours, it's a charming mess. 🖭

James Caan *Dick Kanipsia* • Peter Boyle *Barry Fenaka* • Sally Kellerman *Kitty Kopetzky* • Louise Lasser *Mary Fenaka* • Allen Garfield *Vincent J Palmer* • Richard B Shull *Harry Moss* ■ *Dir* Howard Zieff • *Scr* WD Richter

Sliver ★★★ 18

Erotic thriller 1993 · US · Colour · 103mins

Sharon Stone consolidated her reputation as Hollywood's hottest sex symbol in another steamy thriller from the pen of Joe Eszterhas (adapting Ira Levin's novel), who also scripted her breakthrough hit *Basic Instinct*. Stone is the rather unlikely book editor who moves into a highly desirable apartment block, where the tenants have a worrying habit of moving to the morgue rather than new residences. At the same time, she finds herself pursued by two of her neighbours, the oafish author Tom Berenger and the mysterious William Baldwin, either one of whom could be a murderer or a voyeur. Director Phillip Noyce cranks up the tension, and there are some pretty raunchy sex scenes. However, it lacks *Basic Instinct's* drive and Eszterhas's trademark final pay-off is a little weak. 🖭

Sharon Stone *Carly Norris* • William Baldwin *Zeke Hawkins* • Tom Berenger *Jack Lansford* • Polly Walker *Vida Jordan* • Colleen Camp *Judy* • Amanda Foreman *Samantha* • Martin Landau *Alex* • CCH Pounder *Lieutenant Victoria Hendrix* ■ *Dir* Phillip Noyce • *Scr* Joe Eszterhas, from the novel by Ira Levin

Slow Dancing in the Big City ★

Drama 1978 · US · Colour · 110mins

Rocky director John G Avildsen finds himself mired in cliché and sentimentality in this misconceived drama. Journalist Paul Sorvino falls in love with ballerina Anne Ditchburn while performing his Good Samaritan act on an eight-year-old street urchin. Connoisseurs of the soap-opera-as-social-tract won't be surprised to learn

that Ditchburn's dancing days are numbered and that the kid has a drug problem. The tear-jerking bathos gets piled on in ever increasing measures until the absolutely breathtaking ending. You have been warned.

Paul Sorvino *Lou Friedlander* • Anne Ditchburn *Sarah Gantz* • Nicolas Coster *David Fillmore* • Anita Dangler *Franny* • Thaao Penghlis *Christopher* • Linda Selman *Barbara Bass* ■ *Dir* John G Avildsen • *Scr* Barra Grant

Slow Motion ★★★ 18

Drama 1980 · Fr/Swi · Colour · 84mins

This was Godard's first bona fide movie for ten years, the previous decade having been dedicated to increasingly impoverished and experimental video, documentary and TV work. There is nod to the autobiographical – a character who's a washed-up film-maker called Godard – but it's also about the director's pet themes of prostitution, exploitation and cultural politics. No Godard movie is ever conventional, and this one isn't either, but the presence of major stars like Isabelle Huppert and Nathalie Baye is oddly reassuring and shows the respect Godard enjoys amongst the French film community. In French with English subtitles. 🖭

Isabelle Huppert *Isabelle Rivière* • Jacques Dutronc *Paul Godard* • Nathalie Baye *Denise Rimbaud* • Anna Baldaccini *Isabelle's sister* • Fred Personne *1st client* • Roland Amstutz *2nd client* • Nicole Jacquet *Woman* ■ *Dir* Jean-Luc Godard • *Scr* Jean-Luc Godard, Jean-Claude Carrière, Anne-Marie Miéville

The Slugger's Wife ★ 15

Romantic comedy 1985 · US · Colour · 99mins

Any cinematic expectations that might be raised by the combination of Neil Simon and baseball are quickly dispelled in this dismal comedy that fails to provide either laughs or romance. Rebecca De Mornay looks jaded in the role of a rock singer who (inexplicably) falls for the crude charms of baseball star Michael O'Keefe. They marry and are soon beset by career conflicts, not to mention ridiculous baseball double entendres in the bedroom department. A waste of a good cast and director.

Michael O'Keefe *Darryl Palmer* • Rebecca De Mornay *Debby Palmer* • Martin Ritt *Burly DeVito* • Randy Quaid *Moose Granger* • Cleavant Derricks *Manny Alvarado* • Lisa Langlois *Aline Cooper* • Loudon Wainwright III *Gary* ■ *Dir* Hal Ashby • *Scr* Neil Simon

Slumber Party '57 ★★

Comedy drama 1976 · US · Colour · 88mins

Six high school girls at a slumber party recount how they lost their virginity via some variable flashbacks – the best revolving around making a movie. Sloppy direction and continuity matches the Golden Oldie soundtrack which is mainly comprised of sixties hits; a drive-in movie episode also shows a trailer for *Cauldron of Blood* from 1967. Debra Winger makes an inauspicious film debut, appearing topless and suggestively eating a banana. A mess, but not devoid of entertainment value.

Noelle North *Angie* • Bridget Holloman *Bonnie May* • Debra Winger *Debbie* • Mary Ann

Appleseth *Jo Ann* • Cheryl Smith *Sherry* • Janet Wood *Smitty* ■ *Scr* Frank Farmer, from a story by William A Levey

The Slumber Party Massacre ★ 18

Horror 1982 · US · Colour · 76mins

Given the feminist credentials of author Rita Mae Brown and director Amy Jones, the most shocking thing about this late-in-the-day addition to the stalk-and-slash cycle is that it's just as crass and exploitative as most other low-budget entries. Student Michele Michaels is holding a slumber party at her house while her parents are away. Homicidal gate-crasher Michael Villela spoils the fun, decimating her friends and visiting guests with his power drill. Gory, stupid and sexist.

Michele Michaels *Trish Devereaux* • Robin Stille *Valerie* • Michael Villela *Russ Thorn* • Andree Honore *Jackie* • Debra Deliso *Kim* ■ *Dir* Amy Jones [Amy Holden Jones] • *Scr* Rita Mae Brown

Slums of Beverly Hills ★★★★ 15

Comedy drama 1998 · US · Colour · 87mins

Writer/director Tamara Jenkins made her feature debut with this quirky comedy drama about the bizarreness of growing up. The Abramowitz family live on the slum fringes of Beverly Hills, and we see their problematic existence through the eyes of daughter Vivian (Natasha Lyonne), who has to deal with her two brothers and a dad (Alan Arkin, superb as usual) trying hard to keep it all together. While all the family and their various acquaintances are both funny and well-realised, the film belongs to Lyonne, who gives a terrific turn as the girl finding pubescent life a very strange experience indeed. Contains swearing, sex scenes and nudity. 🖭

Alan Arkin *Murray Abramowitz* • Natasha Lyonne *Vivian Abramowitz* • Kevin Corrigan *Eliot* • Jessica Walter *Doris* • Rita Moreno *Belle* • David Krumholtz *Ben Abramowitz* • Eli Marienthal *Rickey Abramowitz* • Carl Reiner *Mickey Abramowitz* • Marisa Tomei *Rita* ■ *Dir/Scr* Tamara Jenkins

Smack and Thistle ★★★

Crime drama 1989 · UK · Colour · 90mins

Barely noticed on its release, this Channel 4-funded feature is an intelligent thriller that also provides a perceptive (and often depressing) analysis of Britain at the end of the eighties. In the light of recent revelations about sleaze in high places, this story about an ex-con who stumbles across a briefcase full of dodgy deals has an added pertinence, with the camera lens almost turning into a crystal ball. However, writer/director Tunde Ikoli might have resisted a sensationalist romantic subplot involving a smack-shooting blue blood that slows down the action without making any telling social point.

Charlie Caine *Abel* • Rosalind Bennett *Elizabeth* • Patrick Malahide *Dirk-Brown* • Geoffrey Palmer *Sir Horace Wimbol* • John Elmes *Edward Tulip* • James Saxon *Henry Wilks* • Connie Booth *Ms Kane* ■ *Dir/Scr* Tunde Ikoli

The Small Back Room ★★★ PG

Second World War drama 1949 · UK · BW · 102mins

After the sumptuous theatrics of *Black Narcissus* and *The Red Shoes*, Michael Powell and Emeric Pressburger returned to the muted naturalism of their earlier collaborations for this adaptation of Nigel Balchin's novel about scientists feeling the strain in wartime. The pair were obviously uninspired by the lengthy passages of chat in which the backroom boffins bicker about their latest inventions. But they hit true to form with the surreal sequence in which David Farrar's disillusioned hero loses himself in alcoholic oblivion and the bomb disposal finale, which is given an unbearable tension by their masterful use of camera angles and cutting. 🖭

David Farrar *Sammy Rice* • Kathleen Byron *Susan* • Jack Hawkins *RB Waring* • Leslie Banks *Colonel Holland* • Cyril Cusack *Corporal Taylor* • Robert Morley *Minister* • Emrys Jones *Joe* • Renée Asherson *ATS Corporal* ■ *Dir* Michael Powell, Emeric Pressburger • *Scr* Michael Powell, Emeric Pressburger, from the novel by Nigel Balchin

Small Change ★★

Drama 1976 · Fr · Colour · 105mins

François Truffaut's anecdotal return to the charmed world of childhood suffers from protracted bouts of mawkishness and inconsequence. Gone is the insight revealed in *The 400 Blows* or *L'Enfant Sauvage* as Truffaut strains to celebrate this "state of grace" which no adult has the right to corrupt. The linked episodes involving Geory Desmouceaux (a boy caring for his disabled father) and Philippe Goldman (a tearaway beaten by his parents) are the best developed, but even these are tainted by the moralising of their teacher, Jean-François Stévenin. A French language film.

Geory Desmouceaux *Patrick* • Philippe Goldman *Julien* • Claudio Deluca *Mathieu Deluca* • Franck Deluca *Richard Golfier* • Laurent Devlaeminck *Laurent Riffle* • Jean-François Stévenin *Jean-François Richet* ■ *Dir* François Truffaut • *Scr* François Truffaut, Suzanne Schiffman

A Small Circle of Friends ★★

Drama 1980 · US · Colour · 112mins

In an unremarkable period drama, three bosom buddies live and love their way through the campus unrest of an American college during the sixties. Karen Allen, Brad Davis and Shelley Long lead a strong cast, but there's little they can really do with patchy material that never quite gels. Director Rob Cohen is better known for such films as *DragonHeart* and *Dragon: the Bruce Lee Story*.

Brad Davis *Leonardo Da Vinci Rizzo* • Karen Allen *Jessica Bloom* • Jameson Parker *Nick Baxter* • Shelley Long *Alice* • John Friedrich *Alex Haddox* • Gary Springer *Greenblatt* • Harry Caesar *Jimmy* • Nan Martin *Mrs Baxter* ■ *Dir* Rob Cohen • *Scr* Ezra Sacks

Small Faces ★★★★ 🅸🅵

Drama   1995 · US · Colour · 108mins

Rather lost in the swell created by *Trainspotting*, Gillies MacKinnon's excellent memoir of late-sixties Glasgow was co-written with his producer brother, Billy. Iain Robertson is absolutely superb as the razor-sharp teenager unsure which of his brothers is the best role model – emotionally stunted hardcase JS Duffy or art student Joseph McFadden. Whether running with street gangs, suffering the agonies of a family get-together or driving mother Clare Higgins to distraction, Robertson never fails to convince, which can't always be said for some of the period details. Contains violence and swearing.

Iain Robertson *Lex Maclean* • Joseph McFadden *Alan Maclean* • JS Duffy *Bobby Maclean* • Laura Fraser *Joanne MacGowan* • Garry Sweeney *Charlie Sloan* • Clare Higgins *Lorna Maclean* • Kevin McKidd *Malky Johnson* ■ *Dir* Gillies MacKinnon • *Scr* Gillies MacKinnon, Billy MacKinnon

Small Hotel ★★ 🅄

Comedy   1957 · UK · BW · 59mins

Belligerent Cockney character Gordon Harker's last success was this adaptation of a stage farce in which he plays a waiter refusing to be dismissed from his job at the hotel of the title. In this, his penultimate film, japes with guests and other staff make do for the plot. This is a pared-down, low-budget film version, which is no great shakes as comedy, but interesting as a vehicle built around a much-loved British star at the end of his career.

Gordon Harker *Albert* • Marie Lohr *Mrs Samson-Fox* • John Loder *Mr Finch* • Irene Handl *Mrs Gammon* • Janet Munro *Effie* • Billie Whitelaw *Caroline Mallet* ■ *Dir* David MacDonald • *Scr* Wilfred Eades, from a play by Rex Frost

A Small Killing ★★★ 🅸🅵

Crime drama   1981 · US · Colour · 96mins

If you wrote a script about a cop and a female professor going undercover as tramps, both falling in love as a result, it's just possible it wouldn't be taken seriously. However, despite too many mechanical moves, this unlikely premise is given ballast by Edward Asner, who is as charismatically gruff-but-kindly as he is in any other role, and Jean Simmons, who lends her own special glow to the crime drama. Venerable screen veterans such as Sylvia Sidney add to the interest. ▭

Edward Asner [Ed Asner] *Simon Shaber* • Jean Simmons *Margaret Lawrence* • Andrew Prine *Lieutenant Ward Arlen* • J Pat O'Malley *Charley* • Mary Jackson *Rose* • Sylvia Sidney *Sadie Ross* ■ *Dir* Steven Hilliard Stern • *Scr* Burt Prelutsky, from the novel *The Rag Bag Clan* by Richard Barth

Small Soldiers ★★★ 🅿🅶

Fantasy action adventure
1998 · US · Colour · 105mins

Action Man-type dolls fitted with deadly microprocessors go on menacing manoeuvres in director Joe Dante's *Gremlins* meets *Toy Story* war fantasy. The slick professionalism and technical brilliance keep the awkward mixture of comedy and carnage from becoming a too uncomfortable experience. Crafty

nods to classic war films of the *Patton* ilk, the creepy deformed Gwendy Doll sequence and the GI Joes being voiced by the likes of Tommy Lee Jones, Ernest Borgnine and Bruce Dern also help maintain the interest for adults as well as youngsters. Contains violence and some swearing. ▭

Denis Leary *Gil Mars* • Kirsten Dunst *Christy Fimple* • Gregory Smith *Alan Abernathy* • Ann Magnuson *Irene Abernathy* • Phil Hartman *Phil Fimple* • Frank Langella *Archer* • Tommy Lee Jones *Major Chip Hazard* • Ernest Borgnine *Kip Killagin* • Bruce Dern *Link Static* • George Kennedy *Brick Bazooka* ■ *Dir* Joe Dante • *Scr* Gavin Scott, Adam Rifkin, Ted Elliott, Terry Rossio

Small Time ★★★ 🅸🅱

Crime drama   1990 · US · BW · 58mins

Structured as a five-act morality play, this is an uncompromising study of New York street life. There were so many movies about inner-city problems in the early nineties that the abrasive attitudes of the participants became as clichéd as having rap hits on the soundtrack. But here writer/director Norman Loftis plays fast and loose with a variety of styles to produce a compelling portrait of Vince (Richard Barboza), a kid driven to crime to survive and now suffering the consequences of his errant lifestyle. The dramatic segments are rough and ropey, but Loftis's documentary footage of Harlem and the talking-head sequences are pretty impressive. Contains violence and swearing. ▭

Richard Barboza *Vince Williams* • Carolyn Kinebrew *Vicki* ■ *Dir/Scr* Norman Loftis

Small Town Girl ★★

Drama   1936 · US · BW · 105mins

Robert Taylor had scored so well as a wastrel turned brain surgeon in *Magnificent Obsession* that he was obvious casting for the role in this romantic drama of a wealthy surgeon who marries Janet Gaynor's small-town girl while drunk. Jean Harlow, originally cast, would have given the proceedings more zest and it's a rising young actor called James Stewart who stands out in the thankless part of Gaynor's beau, destined to lose out to Taylor. Director William A Wellman, who fell out with Gaynor, brings no particular distinctiveness to the picture.

Janet Gaynor *Kay Brannan* • Robert Taylor (1) *Bob Dakin* • Binnie Barnes *Priscilla* • James Stewart *Elmer* • Lewis Stone *Dr Dakin* • Elizabeth Patterson *Ma Brannan* • Frank Craven *Pa Brannan* ■ *Dir* William A Wellman • *Scr* John Lee Mahin, Edith Fitzgerald, Frances Goodrich, Albert Hackett, from the novel by Ben Ames Williams

A Small Town in Texas ★★ 🅸🅵

Action drama   1976 · US · Colour · 92mins

The title and the star, Timothy Bottoms, may promise a drama in the vein of *The Last Picture Show* but this is a car chase flick, directed by Jack Starrett who the previous year crossed the chase movie with *The Exorcist* and came up with *Race with the Devil*. Bottoms plays an ex-con, returning home to his white trash girlfriend, Susan George, and their baby son. Bottoms also swears revenge on the

redneck cop who busted him, Bo Hopkins, which results in a lot of revving up and wasted gasoline. Aimed fair and square at what *Variety* used to call "yahoo audiences". ▭

Timothy Bottoms *Poke* • Susan George *Mary Lee* • Bo Hopkins *Duke* • Art Hindle *Boogie* • John Karlen *Lenny* • Morgan Woodward *CJ Crane* • Patrice Rohmer *Trudy* ■ *Dir* Jack Starrett • *Scr* William Norton

The Small World of Sammy Lee ★★

Comedy drama   1963 · UK · BW · 108mins

This fast-moving drama, expanded from a BBC TV play, finds Anthony Newley as a smart-aleck strip-show compère, spending a frantic night trying to raise cash to pay off his gambling debts. Newley was involved with several offbeat and nearly forgotten projects, such as the surreal *The Strange World of Gurney Slade*, but this is worth seeing for a string of appearances by familiar British TV faces including Wilfred Brambell, Warren Mitchell and Miriam Karlin. The black-and-white photography makes the suitably grim Soho locations even grimmer.

Anthony Newley *Sammy Lee* • Julia Foster *Patsy* • Robert Stephens *Gerry* • Wilfrid Brambell *Harry* • Warren Mitchell *Lou* • Miriam Karlin *Milly* • Roy Kinnear *Lucky Dave* ■ *Dir* Ken Hughes • *Scr* Ken Hughes, from his TV play *Sammy*

The Smallest Show on Earth ★★★★ 🅄

Comedy   1957 · UK · BW · 76mins

In praise of fleapits everywhere, this charming comedy will bring back happy memories for anyone who pines for the days when going to the pictures meant something more than being conveyor-belted in and out of a soulless multiplex. Fondly scripted by John Eldridge and William Rose and deftly directed by Basil Dearden, it stars Bill Travers and Virginia McKenna as a couple who inherit a crumbling cinema. The cast alone makes the movie a must-see, and the sequence in which projectionist Peter Sellers, pianist Margaret Rutherford and doorman Bernard Miles relive the glories of the silent era is adorable. ▭

Virginia McKenna *Jean Spenser* • Bill Travers *Matt Spenser* • Peter Sellers *Percy Quill* • Margaret Rutherford *Mrs Fazackalee* • Leslie Phillips *Robin Carter* • Bernard Miles *Old Tom* • Sidney James *Mr Hogg* ■ *Dir* Basil Dearden • *Scr* William Rose, John Eldridge, from a story by William Rose

Smalltime ★★★ 🅸🅱

Comedy drama
1996 · UK · Colour and BW · 61mins

It was *TwentyFourSeven* that propelled Nottingham director Shane Meadows into the mainstream, but this earlier work, made on half a shoestring, is a welcome introduction to his raw, gritty and amusing universe. By turns amateurish and professional, funny and depressing, it follows the lives of a bunch of small-time crooks (all wearing the most ridiculous cheap wigs) whose botched attempts at crime make an art form out of incompetence. A sweet-and-sour suburban satire that's touching in a grotesque way. Contains swearing.

Mat Hand *Malc* • Dena Smiles *Kate* • Shane Meadows *Jumbo* • Gena Kawecka *Ruby* • Jimmy Hynd *Willy* • Leon Lammond *Bets* • Tim Cunningham *Lenny the Fence* • Dominic Dillon *Mad Terrance* ■ *Dir/Scr* Shane Meadows

Smart Money ★★★

Crime drama   1931 · US · BW · 83mins

This is as tough as they come, and, incidentally, the only movie to co-star those two gangster heavyweights James Cagney and Edward G Robinson. Robinson plays a lucky small-time barber who hits it big, and Cagney is his mate. Both actors knew one another from the New York stage, and their naturalistic delivery owes much to their theatre background. Directed by Alfred E Green, this gambling-racket crime drama also features, in a small role, Boris Karloff in the sixth of more than a dozen movies he made in 1931, one of which was *Frankenstein*.

Edward G Robinson *Nick "The Barber" Venizelos* • James Cagney *Jack* • Evalyn Knapp *Irene Graham* • Ralf Harolde *Sleepy Sam* • Noel Francis *Marie* • Margaret Livingston *District attorney's girl* • Maurice Black *Greek barber* • Boris Karloff *Sport Williams* ■ *Dir* Alfred E Green • *Scr* Kubec Glasmon, John Bright, Lucien Hubbard, Joseph Jackson, from the story *The Idol* by Lucien Hubbard, Joseph Jackson

Smart Woman ★★

Drama   1948 · US · BW · 93mins

Constance Bennett's last fling as a star provided her with this last leading role in a film, named after the character she plays: a resourceful defence lawyer pitted against Brian Aherne's special prosecutor – her lover – in an election fraud trial. Bennett chose cameraman Stanley Cortez for the glamour lighting he had given Susan Hayward in *Smash-Up, the Story of a Woman* but most of the budget seems to have gone on her wardrobe by Adrian. A pity she didn't choose a more positive director than Edward A Blatt.

Brian Aherne *Robert Larrimore* • Constance Bennett *Paula Rogers* • Barry Sullivan *Frank McCoy* • Michael O'Shea *Johnny Simons, Reporter* • James Gleason *Sam Corkle* ■ *Dir* Edward A Blatt • *Scr* Alvah Bessie, Louis Morheim, Herbert Margolis, Adela Rogers St Johns, from the story by Leon Gutterman, Edwin V Westrate

Smash Palace ★★★★ 🅸🅱

Drama   1981 · NZ · Colour · 108mins

Among the films that put New Zealand cinema on the map, this is an engrossing study of one man's retreat into despair. Bruno Lawrence gives a painfully truthful performance as the one-time Grand Prix hero whose idyllic life as a mechanic in the middle of nowhere drives his French wife, Anna Jemison, to adultery. Equally impressive is 10-year-old Greer Robson, as the daughter who becomes a pawn in her parents' increasingly bitter wrangle. This deeply disturbing drama was directed by Roger Donaldson, who has yet to achieve anything of comparable power since his arrival in Hollywood. Contains violence, swearing and nudity. ▭

🅄 = SUITABLE FOR ALL   🆄c = SUITABLE FOR ALL, ESPECIALLY FOR YOUNG CHILDREN (VIDEO ONLY)   🅿🅶 = PARENTAL GUIDANCE

Bruno Lawrence *Al Shaw* • Anna Jemison *Jacqui Shaw* • Greer Robson *Georgie Shaw* • Keith Aberdein *Ray Foley* • Desmond Kelly *Tiny* ■ *Dir* Roger Donaldson • *Scr* Roger Donaldson, Peter Hansard, Bruno Lawrence

Smash-Up on Interstate 5
★★★ 15

Drama 1976 · US · Colour · 91mins

One of the better TV movies begins with a stunningly well-staged 39-car pile-up on the eponymous freeway. Since the tale is cleverly told in flashback, we don't know who lives or dies. Unfortunately, we don't care too much, since the characters comprise a collection of clichés. Yet the casting's astute, involving a compulsively watchable parade of names old and new, including former film stars Vera Miles and Sue Lyon. Robert Conrad is the rather vapid lead, but keep your eyes peeled for Tommy Lee Jones, who would later win a best supporting actor Oscar for *The Fugitive*. ▣

Robert Conrad *Sergeant Sam Marcum* • Sian-Barbara Allen *Barbara Hutton* • Buddy Ebsen *Al Pearson* • Herbert Edelman *Danny* • David Groh *Dale* • Sue Lyon *Burnsey* • Vera Miles *Erica* • Donna Mills *Laureen* • Tommy Lee Jones *Officer Hutton* ■ *Dir* John Llewellyn Moxey • *Scr* Eugene Price, Robert Presnell Jr, from the novel *Expressway* by Elleston Trevor

Smash-Up, the Story of a Woman
★★★

Drama 1947 · US · BW · 103mins

Adapted from a story co-written by the estimable Dorothy Parker, this overblown melodrama, released in the UK as *A Woman Destroyed*, seems to have been concocted by putting *A Star Is Born* and *The Lost Weekend* in a cocktail mixer and shaking well. Susan Hayward received an Oscar nomination for her performance as a singer who begins to view the world through the bottom of a glass at the same time as her shiftless husband's showbiz stock begins to rise. Lee Bowman is out of his depth as Hayward's husband, but it's still worth a watch.

Susan Hayward *Angie Evans* • Lee Bowman *Ken Conway* • Marsha Hunt *Martha Gray* • Eddie Albert *Steve* • Carl Esmond *Dr Lorenz* • Carleton Young *Mr Elliott* • Charles D Brown *Mike Dawson* ■ *Dir* Stuart Heisler • *Scr* John Howard Lawson, Lionel Wiggam, from a story by Dorothy Parker, Frank Cavett

The Smashing Bird I Used to Know
★★★

Drama 1969 · UK · Colour · 96mins

A British prison drama that provides an opportunity to see the youthful early careers of Dennis Waterman and Maureen Lipman. It's a rather bizarre tale concerning the murder of Madeline Hinde's mother's boyfriend and the attendant mayhem wreaked on several relationships and individual psyches. They used to crank them out in this mould for the cartload in the sixties, and this is not the worst example of the genre by any means. Additional interest may come from spotting today's middle-aged sitcom stars.

Madeline Hinde *Nicki Johnson* • Renée Asherson *Anne Johnson* • Dennis Waterman *Peter* • Patrick Mower *Harry Spenton* • Faith Brook *Dr Sands* • Maureen Lipman *Sarah* •

Derek Fowlds *Geoffrey* • Sheila Steafel *Gilda* • Megs Jenkins *Matron* ■ *Dir* Robert Hartford-Davis • *Scr* John Peacock

Smashing the Rackets
★★

Crime drama 1938 · US · BW · 68mins

This efficient, if undistinguished crime drama was the result of a conscious effort by RKO executives to produce the kind of topical, if sensationalist, fare known as ''exploitation''. Loosely based on the career of New York DA Thomas E Dewey, this fast-talking insight into underworld machinations and corruption in high places makes racket-busting look remarkably easy, as every illegal operation crumbles at the mere sight of Chester Morris and his team. However, director Lew Landers brings such a sense of urgency and importance to the proceedings that its sheer verve carries you along.

Chester Morris *Jim Conway* • Frances Mercer *Susan Lane* • Bruce Cabot *Steve Lawrence* • Rita Johnson *Letty Lane* • Donald Douglas [Don Douglas] *Spaulding* • Ben Welden *Whitey Clark* • Edward Pawley *Chin Martin* • Frank M Thomas *Judge Wend* ■ *Dir* Lew Landers • *Scr* Lionel Houser, from a story by Forrest Davis

Smashing Time
★★

Comedy 1967 · UK · Colour · 96mins

The fact that some of the character names come from the poems of Lewis Carroll provides the clue that this Swinging Sixties comedy is trying too hard to be both clever and cool. Scripted as satire by George Melly, with Lynn Redgrave and Rita Tushingham as the iconoclastic northern lasses trying to gate-crash the fame game. Desmond Davis (who directed the duo in *Girl with Green Eyes*) draws some knowing cameos from the likes of Ian Carmichael and Irene Handl, but otherwise seems ill at ease with the slapstick excesses.

Rita Tushingham *Brenda* • Lynn Redgrave *Yvonne* • Michael York *Tom Wabe* • Anna Quayle *Charlotte Brilling* • Irene Handl *Mrs Gimble* • Ian Carmichael *Bobby Mome-Rothlan* • Jeremy Lloyd *Jeremy Tove* • Toni Palmer *Toni* • Arthur Mullard *Caféboss* ■ *Dir* Desmond Davis • *Scr* George Melly

Smash-Up Alley
★★ U

Action sports drama 1972 · US · Colour · 77mins

With its fender-bending, full-throttled action, stock-car racing should make excellent movie material. But as everything from *Fireball 500* to *Days of Thunder* proves, it doesn't matter what happens on the track if the dramatic sequences stink. Richard Petty (playing himself) may be an ace behind the wheel, but in front of a camera he looks like a rabbit dazzled by headlights. Darren McGavin adds a touch of steel as his father, but the rest of the cast, including Noah Beery Jr, are clearly suffering from an advanced case of *dramatis mortis*.

Darren McGavin *Lee Petty* • Richard Petty • Kathy Brown *Elizabeth Petty* • Noah Beery Jr *Uncle Julie* • Pierre Jalbert *Curtis Cross* • Lynne Marta *Lynda Petty* • LQ Jones *Koler* ■ *Dir/Scr* Edward J Lakso

Smile
★★★★

Satire 1975 · US · Colour · 112mins

A minor masterpiece of wit and observation, Michael Ritchie's picture records the run-up to and the staging of the horrendous Young American Miss competition in Santa Rosa, California, in which 33 wide-eyed girls subject themselves to personality interviews, dance sessions, photo calls and every other cringe-making ritual known to man. Ritchie's camera is unblinking: it's like a documentary, but it isn't. Bruce Dern is the chief judge, a car salesman, and among the hopefuls are Melanie Griffith and Annette O'Toole. A total joy. Contains swearing.

Bruce Dern ''*Big Bob*'' *Freelander* • Barbara Feldon *Brenda DiCarlo* • Michael Kidd *Tommy French* • Geoffrey Lewis *Wilson Shears* • Nicholas Pryor *Andy DiCarlo* • Colleen Camp *Connie Thompson, ''Miss Imperial County''* • Annette O'Toole *Doria Houston, ''Miss Anaheim''* • Melanie Griffith *Karen Love, ''Miss Simi Valley''* ■ *Dir* Michael Ritchie • *Scr* Jerry Belson

Smile, Jenny, You're Dead
★★

Murder mystery 1974 · US · Colour · 92mins

Made as the pilot for the *Harry O* detective series, which ran for three years in the mid-seventies, this TV movie features David Janssen as a retired cop whose quiet life by the beach is disrupted when a former police colleague hires him to investigate the death of his son-in-law. Of interest to fans of the genre, but also for an early appearance by 12-year-old actress Jodie Foster.

David Janssen *Harry Orwell* • John Anderson *Col John Lockport* • Howard Da Silva *Lt Humphrey Kenney* • Andrea Marcovicci *Jennifer English* • Tim McIntire *Charley English* • Zalman King *Roy St John* • Martin Gabel *Meade De Ruyter* • Jodie Foster *Liberty* ■ *Dir* Jerry Thorpe • *Scr* Howard Rodman

A Smile like Yours
★★ 12

Romantic comedy
1997 · US · Colour · 93mins

Greg Kinnear and Lauren Holly are both miscast in this comedy (or is it a drama?) about infertility. The couple's happy marriage comes under fire when they realise they can't have children and instigate a series of visits to a fertility clinic. Their troubles are compounded when Holly suspects Kinnear of beginning an affair and they experience the inevitable bumpy ride back to togetherness. Cameos from Joan Cusack and Shirley MacLaine are entertaining and the script is strong, but the direction is unfocused and the end result is patchy. Contains swearing and sexual references. ▣

Greg Kinnear *Danny Robertson* • Lauren Holly *Jennifer Robertson* • Joan Cusack *Nancy Tellen* • Jay Thomas *Steve Harris* • Jill Hennessy *Lindsay Hamilton* • Christopher McDonald *Richard Halstrom* • Shirley MacLaine *Jennifer's mother* ■ *Dir* Keith Samples • *Scr* Kevin Meyers, Keith Samples

Smiles of a Summer Night
★★★★★ PG

Romantic comedy 1955 · Swe · BW · 104mins

Ingmar Bergman's sprightly comedy of sexual manners has a distinguished lineage, inspired as it is by William Shakespeare's *A Midsummer Night's Dream*, the operas of Mozart, the plays of Marivaux and Mauritz Stiller's film *Erotikon*. Its progeny includes Stephen Sondheim's musical *A Little Night Music* and Woody Allen's *A Midsummer Night's Sex Comedy*. Bergman's comedies can be laboured and precious, but here he strikes exactly the right note of levity. Led by Eva Dahlbeck as the mischievous actress who assembles a weekend party of past, present and prospective lovers, the cast is uniformly excellent. In Swedish with English subtitles. ▣

Gunnar Björnstrand *Fredrik Egerman* • Eva Dahlbeck *Desirée Armfeldt* • Ulla Jacobsson *Anne Egerman* • Margit Carlquist *Charlotte Malcolm* • Harriet Andersson *Petra the maid* • Birgitta Valberg *Actress* • Bibi Andersson *Actress* ■ *Dir/Scr* Ingmar Bergman

Smiley
★★ U

Adventure drama 1956 · UK · Colour · 96mins

A British movie made entirely in Australia that shows life in an outback town. Smiley is a small boy obliged to become independent because his mum is a washer woman and his dad is a drunken stockman who spends months in the bush. So Smiley rings the church bells for the local vicar (Ralph Richardson no less), innocently gets involved with drug smugglers and yearns to own a bicycle. It's a rather sickly affair that trades on stereotypes which modern Australian viewers may regard as the clincher in the debate about becoming a republic. A sequel followed three years later.

Ralph Richardson *Rev Lambeth* • John McCallum *Rankin* • Chips Rafferty *Sgt Flaxman* • Colin Petersen *Smiley Greevins* • Jocelyn Hernfield *Miss Workman* ■ *Dir* Anthony Kimmins • *Scr* Moore Raymond, Anthony Kimmins, from the novel by Moore Raymond

Smiley Gets a Gun
★★ U

Comedy drama 1959 · UK · Colour · 89mins

Smiley was a huge hit with British family audiences, many of whom were queuing up to emigrate Down Under to escape the grimness of the British economy and weather. This sequel retains writer/director Anthony Kimmins but exchanges one grand thespian (Ralph Richardson) for another, namely Dame Sybil Thorndike. The story has the local copper, Chips Rafferty, promising to give Smiley a gun if he can catch the man who stole Thorndike's horde of gold.

Sybil Thorndike *Granny McKinley* • Chips Rafferty *Sgt Flaxman* • Keith Calvert *Smiley Greevins* • Bruce Archer *Joey* • Margaret Christensen *Ma Greevins* • Reg Lye *Pa Greevins* ■ *Dir* Anthony Kimmins • *Scr* Anthony Kimmons, Rex Rienits, from the novel by Moore Raymond

Smilin' Through
★★★★

Melodrama 1932 · US · BW · 98mins

The famous and much-loved stage play *Smilin' Through* was filmed as a silent with Norma Talmadge in 1922. This first sound version, Oscar-nominated for best picture, showcases Norma Shearer – en route to mega-stardom – with Fredric March and Leslie Howard under the polished direction of Sidney Franklin. Set in England and spanning the years from 1868 to 1918, it's a sentimental romantic drama, with a crucial fantasy element and a message of love and forgiveness. The complicated plot involves Howard, reclusive and bitter after his adored bride (Shearer) was shot at the altar by a jealous suitor (March), his orphaned niece who is the spitting image of his dead beloved, and the anguish suffered by all when she falls in love with the killer's son.

Norma Shearer *Moonyean Clare/Kathleen* • Fredric March *Kenneth Wayne/Jeremy Wayne* • Leslie Howard *John Carteret* • OP Heggie *Dr Owen* • Ralph Forbes *Willie Ainley* • Beryl Mercer *Mrs Crouch* • Margaret Seddon *Ellen* ■ *Dir* Sidney Franklin • *Scr* Ernest Vajda, Claudine West, Donald Ogden Stewart, James Bernard Fagan, from the play by Jane Cowl, Jane Murfin, Langdon McCormick

Smilin' Through ★★

Musical drama   1941 · US · Colour · 100mins

The second sound version of this romantic drama stars Jeanette MacDonald in the dual role of the dead wife and niece of bereaved husband Brian Aherne, and accordingly works in several songs. Director Frank Borzage hits new heights in treacly, melodramatic sentimentality; MacDonald acts well, as does Aherne, but Gene Raymond (the star's real-life husband) is an unattractive disaster as a drunken jealous suitor and his son. If the classic original is hard to take, this is near impossible to sit through, yet it still manages to bring a tiny lump to the throat.

Jeanette MacDonald *Kathleen Clare/ Moonyean Clare* • Brian Aherne *Sir John Carteret* • Gene Raymond *Kenneth Wayne/ Jeremy Wayne* • Ian Hunter *Rev Owen Harding* • Frances Robinson *Ellen* • Patrick O'Moore *Willie* • Eric Lonsdale *Charles* ■ *Dir* Frank Borzage • *Scr* Donald Ogden Stewart, John Balderston, from the play by Jane Cowl, Jane Murfin, Langdon McCormick

The Smiling Lieutenant ★★★★★

Musical comedy   1931 · US · BW · 82mins

Nowhere is director Ernst Lubitsch's famous "touch" more frequently in evidence than in this delicious trifle adapted from the stage operetta *A Waltz Dream*, its charming score given witty lyrics by Clifford Grey. Maurice Chevalier plays a sexy Viennese guards officer enjoying a love affair with Claudette Colbert, the fiddle-playing leader of a ladies' café orchestra, who attracts the attention of the prim and dowdy daughter (Miriam Hopkins) of a visiting monarch. Assigned, at her request, as official aide to the visitors, he is then ordered to marry her. The plot serves as a foundation on which to build a breathless series of heavenly encounters, alternating between the risqué, the romantic, the hilarious and the poignant.

Maurice Chevalier *Niki* • Claudette Colbert *Franzi* • Miriam Hopkins *Princess Anna* • George Barbier *King Adolf* • Charles Ruggles *Max* • Hugh O'Connell *Orderly* ■ *Dir* Ernst Lubitsch • *Scr* Ernest Vajda, Samson

Raphaelson, Ernst Lubitsch, from the operetta *A Waltz Dream* by Leopold Jacobson, Felix Doermann, from the novel *Nux der Prinzgemahl* by Hans Müller

Smilla's Feeling for Snow ★★ 15

Mystery thriller
1996 · Ger/Den/Swe · Colour · 116mins

Fans of the bestselling book *Miss Smilla's Sense of Snow* will be disappointed by this plodding adaptation by Bille August (*The House of the Spirits*). Julia Ormond doesn't have the depth or experience to carry the film as the scientist investigating the death of a young boy who plunges from the roof of her Copenhagen apartment building. While occasionally moody in places, this thriller never quite pushes you to the edge – or even the middle – of your seat, and Ormond is overshadowed at every turn by her impressive co-stars, Gabriel Byrne and Richard Harris. Disappointing.

Julia Ormond *Smilla Jasperson* • Gabriel Byrne *Mechanic* • Richard Harris *Tork* • Vanessa Redgrave *Elsa Lubing* • Robert Loggia *Moritz Johnson* • Jim Broadbent *Lagermann* • Bob Peck *Ravn* ■ *Dir* Bille August • *Scr* Ann Biderman, from the novel *Miss Smilla's Sense of Snow* by Peter Høeg

Smith! ★★ U

Western comedy drama
1969 · US · Colour · 97mins

This is a Disney western, so don't expect Sam Peckinpah levels of violence or Sergio Leone levels of stylisation. But it's a solidly crafted account of a rancher who tries to prevent the execution of a young American Indian in the custody of a racist sheriff. Playing to the memory of his role in *The Sheepman* (1958), Glenn Ford is happily married to Nancy Olson and oozes decency and liberal values while Keenan Wynn pushes every button marked "hiss" or "villain". Shot on location in the Nez Pierce territory of Idaho, it marked the screen debut of Chief Dan George, whose next film, *Little Big Man*, would earn him an Oscar nomination. ⊞

Glenn Ford *Smith* • Nancy Olson *Norah Smith* • Dean Jagger *Judge* • Keenan Wynn *Vince Heber* • Warren Oates *Walter Charlie* • Chief Dan George *Ol' Antoine* • Frank Ramirez *Gabriel Jimmyboy* • John Randolph *Mr Edwards* ■ *Dir* Michael O'Herlihy • *Scr* Louis Pelletier, from the novel *Breaking Smith's Quarter Horse* by Paul St Pierre

Smithereens ★★★ 15

Drama   1982 · US · Colour · 93mins

A low-budget movie packing an adrenalin-charged punch. It features a raucously poignant portrayal by Susan Berman of a punkish, working-class girl trying to make it in the rock 'n' roll world of Manhattan's Lower East Side. The debut film of director Susan Seidelman, who gave Madonna an early start in movies with *Desperately Seeking Susan*, this has a terrific soundtrack, and what it lacks in production values it makes up for in verve and gaiety. ⊞

Susan Berman *Wren* • Brad Rinn *Paul* • Richard Hell *Eric* • Nada Despotovich *Cecile* • Roger Jett *Billy* ■ *Dir* Susan Seidelman • *Scr* Ron Nyswaner, Peter Askin, from a story by Ron Nyswaner, Susan Seidelman

Smoke ★★★★ 15

Drama   1995 · US · Colour and BW · 107mins

Novelist Paul Auster's first original screenplay is clearly the product of a literary mind, as the dialogue hangs on the air like the aroma of a good cigar. But without director Wayne Wang's insouciant control and nuanced performances from the likes of William Hurt, Stockard Channing and Forest Whitaker, this episodic roundelay about the inevitability of chance and coincidence would have seemed stiff and unconvincing. Instead, it's a vibrant portrait of the small community that congregates around Harvey Keitel's Brooklyn cigar shop, whose customers meet fortune and tragedy alike with enviable equanimity. ⊞

Harvey Keitel *Auggie Wren* • William Hurt *Paul Benjamin* • Harold Perrineau *Rashid* • Forest Whitaker *Cyrus* • Stockard Channing *Ruby* • Ashley Judd *Felicity* • Giancarlo Esposito *Tommy* • Jose Zuniga *Jerry* ■ *Dir* Wayne Wang • *Scr* Paul Auster, from his short story *Auggie Wren's Christmas Story*

Smoke Signal ★★ U

Western   1955 · US · Colour · 87mins

A buckskin-clad Dana Andrews leads the survivors of an Indian massacre to safety in a very routine western, distinguished only by its majestic Grand Canyon setting. Piper Laurie is the only woman in the cast, which includes Universal's handsome heart-throb Rex Reason and veteran Milburn Stone, "Doc" from TV's *Gunsmoke*. In London, this was released as a double bill with the first ever nudist flick, *Garden of Eden*.

Dana Andrews *Brett Halliday* • Piper Laurie *Laura Evans* • Rex Reason *Lieutenant Wayne Ford* • William Talman *Captain Harper* • Gordon Jones *Corporal Rogers* • Milburn Stone *Sergeant Miles* • Douglas Spencer *Garode* ■ *Dir* Jerry Hopper • *Scr* George Slavin, George W George

Smoke Signals ★★★

Road movie   1998 · US · Colour · 89mins

A double winner at the Sundance Festival, this is the first US feature to be written, directed and performed solely by native Americans. Adapted by Sherman Alexie from stories in his own collection, *The Lone Ranger and Tonto Fistfight in Heaven*, it follows Adam Beach and Evan Adams on their trek to Phoenix to collect the ashes of Gary Farmer, the abusive father Beach despises and the hero who pulled Adams out of the fire that killed his parents. Chris Eyre's debut may be a cinematic landmark, but with its sharp, self-deprecating humour, it's also a warm, vibrant and totally human story.

Adam Beach *Victor Joseph* • Evan Adams *Thomas Builds-the-Fire* • Irene Bedard *Suzy Song* • Gary Farmer *Arnold Joseph* • Tantoo Cardinal *Arlene Joseph* • Cody Lightning *Young Victor Joseph* • Simon Baker *Young Thomas Builds-the-Fire* ■ *Dir* Chris Eyre • *Scr* Sherman Alexie, from his stories *The Lone Ranger and Tonto Fistfight in Heaven*

Smokescreen ★★ U

Thriller   1964 · UK · BW · 65mins

An above-average programme filler that, for once, has a passable plot (involving a little bit of skulduggery in suburban Brighton) which is kept

moving swiftly by director Jim O'Connolly. Adultery, embezzlement and murder are all taken in his stride by Peter Vaughan as an insurance claims inspector who suspects that there is more to a blazing car wreck than meets the eye. While all around him give typically second-division performances, Vaughan plays with a dogged determination that is efficient, engaging and quite at odds with the more sinister characterisations he would essay later in his career.

Peter Vaughan *Ropey Roper* • John Carson *Trevor Baylis* • Yvonne Romain *Janet Dexter* • Gerald Flood *Graham Turner* • Glynn Edwards *Inspector Wright* ■ *Dir/Scr* Jim O'Connolly

Smokey and the Bandit ★★★★ PG

Comedy   1977 · US · Colour · 91mins

A smash hit in its day, this is a marvellously good-natured chase movie, as Burt Reynolds ("Bandit") carts a rather too obviously product-placed truckload of Coors beer across the state lines, outpacing Sheriff Jackie Gleason ("Smokey" in the local lingo) by way of a variety of spectacular stunts. Unsurprising, since the movie is the directorial debut of former stuntman Hal Needham. Several sequels were spawned, but none captured the freshness and charm of this terrific original, which greatly benefits from the real-life, as well as on-screen, sexual chemistry between co-stars Burt Reynolds and the vivacious Sally Field. ⊞

Burt Reynolds *Bandit* • Sally Field *Carrie* • Jackie Gleason *Sheriff Buford T Justice* • Jerry Reed *Cledus Snow* • Mike Henry *Junior Justice* • Paul Williams *Little Enos Burdette* • Pat McCormick *Big Enos Burdette* ■ *Dir* Hal Needham • *Scr* James Lee Barrett, Charles Shyer, Alan Mandel, from a story by Hal Needham, Robert L Levy

Smokey and the Bandit II ★★★ PG

Comedy   1980 · US · Colour · 96mins

Not so much of a chase comedy as the first film, this battle of wits between trucker Burt Reynolds and man-mountain cop Jackie Gleason is more a series of sight gags with cars and lorries piling up like a motorway collision. The tone is set from the beginning when Reynolds emerges from behind a huge heap of beer cans. He has always been capable of much more than this genial, show-off role, but it's what he obviously likes best. What you see is what you get. ⊞

Burt Reynolds *Bandit* • Jackie Gleason *Sheriff Buford T Justice/Reginald Van Justice/Gaylord Van Justice* • Jerry Reed *Cledus* • Dom DeLuise *Doc* • Sally Field *Carrie* • Paul Williams *Little Enos* • David Huddleston *John Conn* ■ *Dir* Hal Needham • *Scr* Jerry Belson, Brock Yates, from a story by Michael Kane, from characters created by Hal Needham, Robert L Levy

Smokey and the Bandit III ★ 18

Comedy   1983 · US · Colour · 81mins

A truly dire entry in what was always a crass comedy series. Jerry Reed (Burt Reynolds's sidekick from the first two movies) takes over as the number one bandit, once again setting off on a

U = SUITABLE FOR ALL   Uc = SUITABLE FOR ALL, ESPECIALLY FOR YOUNG CHILDREN (VIDEO ONLY)   PG = PARENTAL GUIDANCE

cross-country trek and being pursued by the moronic police force. Dick Lowry takes over the directorial reins, but he simply throws car crash after car crash at the screen in increasingly desperate fashion. Contains swearing and brief nudity.
Jackie Gleason *Buford T Justice* • Jerry Reed *Cletus/Bandit* • Paul Williams *Little Enos* • Pat McCormick *Big Enos* • Mike Henry *Junior* • Colleen Camp *Dusty Trails* • Faith Minton *Tina* • Burt Reynolds *The Real Bandit* ■ *Dir* Dick Lowry • *Scr* Stuart Birnbaum, David Dashev, from characters created by Hal Needham, Robert L Levy

Smokey and the Good Time Outlaws ★★ U
Comedy adventure
1978 · US · Colour · 89mins
When in doubt over the plot, have a car crash. That seems to be the attitude of the producers of this comedy adventure about two aspiring country and western singers who travel to Nashville to seek fame, fortune and fist fights. Despite a title that cashes in on the *Smokey and the Bandit* series, this rang no box-office bells, though it's always pleasant to hear Slim Pickens's drawl-in-the-saddle enunciation.
Jesse Turner *JD Todd* • Dennis Fimple *Salt Flat Kid* • Slim Pickens *Sheriff Leddy* • Dianne Sherrill *Sandy* • Marcie Barkin *Linda* • Hope Summers *Marcie* ■ *Dir* Alex Grasshoff • *Scr* Frank Dobbs, Robert Walsh, Jesse Turner, from a story by Jesse Turner

Smoking/No Smoking ★★★★ PG
Drama
1993 · Fr · Colour · 292mins
The eight plays in Alan Ayckbourn's *Intimate Exchanges* cycle are presented in an unashamedly theatrical manner by Alain Resnais in this mammoth two-part, 292-minute adaptation. It takes a while to get used to hearing the clichéd expressions of the English middle classes in colloquial French, but the exceptional performances of Sabine Azéma and Pierre Arditi will soon have you hooked. Although this was an exhausting cinematic experience when seen in its entirety, it is worth trying to watch in one sitting (with the judicious use of a video recorder) as the interweaving between the two films is ingenious. In French with English subtitles. Contains swearing.
Sabine Azéma *Celia Teasdale/Rowena Coombes/Sylvie Bell/Irene Pridworthy/ Josephine Hamilton* • Pierre Arditi *Toby Teasdale/Miles Coombes/Lionel Hepplewick/ Joe Hepplewick* ■ *Dir* Alain Resnais • *Scr* Alan Ayckbourn, Agnès Jaoui, Jean-Pierre Bacri, from the plays *Intimate Exchanges* by Alan Ayckbourn

Smoky ★★★ U
Western
1946 · US · Colour · 84mins
This heartbreaking tale of a horse will bring a lump to the hardiest of throats. Based on the once-popular Will James story, previously filmed in 1933, and again remade in 1966, the adventures of Smoky put *Black Beauty* to shame. This version is well photographed in glorious forties Technicolor and sympathetically directed by Louis King, lesser-known younger brother of

veteran Henry King. Fred MacMurray and Anne Baxter are eminently likeable, but the real scene-stealer, making his movie debut here, is "Big Daddy" Burl Ives, 12 years before *Cat on a Hot Tin Roof* and his Oscar-winning performance in *The Big Country*.
Fred MacMurray *Clint Barkley* • Anne Baxter *Julie Richards* • Burl Ives *Bill* • Bruce Cabot *Frank* • Esther Dale *Gram* • Roy Roberts *Jeff* ■ *Dir* Louis King • *Scr* Lillie Hayward, Dwight Cummins, Dorothy Yost, from the novel *Smoky, the Cowhorse* by Will James

Smooth Talk ★★★ 15
Drama
1985 · US · Colour · 87mins
This American coming-of-age movie features Laura Dern as a gauche teenager unable to relate to her mother (Mary Kay Place), who unfavourably compares the 15-year-old to her peaches and cream sister. Rebelling, Dern hangs out with her girlfriends and gets up to mischief, finally biting off more than she can chew when she encounters the charismatic but sexually aggressive Treat Williams. It's a well-judged piece by director Joyce Chopra, with Dern excelling in the lead role.
Treat Williams *Arnold Friend* • Laura Dern *Connie* • Mary Kay Place *Katherine* • Levon Helm *Harry* • Sara Inglis [Sarah Inglis] *Jill* • Margaret Welsh *Laura* ■ *Dir* Joyce Chopra • *Scr* Tom Cole, from the short story *Where Are You Going, Where Have You Been* by Joyce Carol Oates

Smorgasbord ★★ PG
Comedy
1983 · US · Colour · 85mins
"A variety of savoury dishes" says the dictionary, and that's just what this movie is trying to be. Consisting of a number of skits, it's linked by the story of failure related to a psychiatrist by a hapless loser (Lewis). The same year *Smorgasbord* finally saw the light of day, Lewis made a triumphant comeback in Scorsese's *King of Comedy*, and reputedly the director is also a fan of this film. However many people simply hate it, citing it as an unfunny, self-indulgent mess. The French had no doubts, though, and the influential magazine *Cahiers du Cinéma* named it as their joint tenth best film of 1983.
Jerry Lewis *Warren Nefron/Dr Perks* • Herbert Edelman *Dr Jonas Pletchick* • Zane Busby *Waitress* • Foster Brooks *Pilot* • Buddy Lester *Passenger* • Milton Berle *Female patient* • Sammy Davis Jr *Mr Billings* ■ *Dir* Jerry Lewis • *Scr* Jerry Lewis, Bill Richmond

The Smugglers ★★★
Mystery thriller
1968 · US · Colour · 97mins
No matter what you think of this TV movie, you will be in a better position to judge than the American audience watching its premiere on Christmas Eve in 1968. Just as the plot was hotting up, the action was interrupted by news of Apollo 8's arrival at the Moon. Shirley Booth, in her sole TV movie, is on lively form alongside stepdaughter Carol Lynley as a couple of Americans in Europe who find themselves mixed up with murderous smugglers. Director Norman Lloyd spices up the suspense with some jaunty humour, while Gayle Hunnicutt,

Emilio Fernandez and Kurt Kasznar round out a quality cast.
Shirley Booth *Mrs Hudson* • Carol Lynley *Jo Hudson* • Kurt Kasznar *Willi Raben* • David Opatoshu *Alfredo Faggio* • Emilio Fernandez *Inspector Cesare Brunelli* • Charles Drake *Harry Miller* • Michael J Pollard *Piero* • Gayle Hunnicutt *Adrianna* ■ *Dir* Norman Lloyd • *Scr* Alfred Hayes, from the novel by Elizabeth Hely

Snake Eyes ★★★ 15
Mystery thriller 1998 · US · Colour · 94mins
The US Secretary of Defence is assassinated in full view of a huge audience gathered in an Atlantic City casino for a boxing championship. Can supercharged detective Nicolas Cage use his own recollections and those of key witnesses to find out whodunit and unravel an ever-widening conspiracy? Although a stunning visual tour de force by director Brian De Palma (a virtuoso opening sequence, split screens, acrobatic cameras, the replaying of interconnected events from different angles and perspectives), this jigsaw murder mystery lacks suspense and disappoints as a thriller, with the expected slam-bang finale never materialising. Contains violence and some swearing.  **DVD**
Nicolas Cage *Rick Santoro* • Gary Sinise *Kevin Dunne* • John Heard *Gilbert Powell* • Carla Gugino *Julia Costello* • Stan Shaw *Lincoln Tyler* • Kevin Dunn *Lou Logan* ■ *Dir* Brian De Palma • *Scr* David Koepp, from a story by Brian De Palma, David Koepp • *Cinematographer* Stephen H Burum

The Snake Pit ★★★★
Psychological drama 1948 · US · BW · 99mins
In its day, this was a truly harrowing and extremely controversial adaptation of Mary Jane Ward's semi-autobiographical novel about life in a mental institution. In Britain, the film was perceived to be so disturbing that it suffered from over-zealous censor cuts. The film still retains its power to shock, and, although the medical department may seem slightly antiquated, the performances of the women inmates are still incredibly moving, particularly Olivia de Havilland in the lead, and Celeste Holm, Beulah Bondi and a young Betsy Blair in support. The sequence where they sing *Going Home* is still deeply touching. Anatole Litvak's direction may seem on the strident side, but there's no denying this film's power and impact.
Olivia de Havilland *Virginia Stuart Cunningham* • Mark Stevens *Robert Cunningham* • Leo Genn *Dr Mark Kirk* • Celeste Holm *Grace* • Glenn Langan *Dr Terry* • Helen Craig *Miss Davis* • Leif Erickson *Gordon* • Beulah Bondi *Mrs Greer* ■ *Dir* Anatole Litvak • *Scr* Frank Partos, Millen Brand, from the novel by Mary Jane Ward

Snake Treaty ★★★
Drama 1989 · US · Colour · 93mins
Shot in Quebec, this TV movie is a good old-fashioned melodrama, at the centre of which is a farming family torn asunder when son Timothy Daly sides with the local native Americans in a struggle over land rights. Familiar faces abound in an impressive cast, with Ralph Waite (who played John Walton for so many years) as Daly's pa and Richard Farnsworth fighting the "Indian" corner. Caught in the middle

is the ever-dependable Genevieve Bujold.
Timothy Daly *Guy Pehrsson* • Ralph Waite *Martin Pehrsson* • Geneviève Bujold *Madeline* • Billy Merasty *Tom Redfox* • Richard Farnsworth *Helmer Pehrsson* • Alberta Watson *Cassandra* ■ *Dir* David Greene • *Scr* Michael DeGuzman, from the novel *Red Earth, White Earth* by Will Weaver

Snapdragon ★ 18
Erotic thriller 1993 · US · Colour · 94mins
Pamela Anderson is Felicity, an amnesiac woman who has dreams about killing the men she has sex with. When she wakes up, she finds out that her dreams have come true. Steven Bauer plays the police psychologist who takes a long time to figure out that Anderson may be the victim of some bizarre oriental intrigue that turns women into concubine-assassins. Don't expect too many action scenes in this film, the baby-voiced Anderson knows that her talents lie in the sex scenes. Too bad those aren't very good either.
Steven Bauer *David* • Chelsea Field *Sergeant Peckham* • Pamela Anderson *Felicity* • Matt McCoy *Bernie* • Kenneth Tigar *Captain* • Irene Tsu *Hua* ■ *Dir* Worth Keeter • *Scr* Gene Church

The Snapper ★★ 15
Comedy drama 1993 · UK · Colour · 90mins
Adapted by Roddy Doyle from his own novel, this sassy comedy drama was something of a disappointment after his earlier slice of working-class Dublin life, *The Commitments*. Sometimes funny, sometimes touching, the film benefits from a few snorting one-liners and some solid ensemble playing, although the cast occasionally gets carried away during the very stagey shouting matches. The main problem, however, is that director Stephen Frears too often allows the comedy to slip into sitcom and the drama to come across as something from a social-conscience soap opera. *The Van*, the final part of the trilogy, was released in late 1996.
Tina KelleghER *Sharon Curley* • Colm Meaney *Dessie Curley* • Ruth McCabe *Kay Curley* • Eanna MacLiam *Craig Curley* • Peter Rowen *Sonny Curley* • Joanne Gerrard *Lisa Curley* • Colm O'Byrne *Darren Curley* • Brendan Gleeson *Lester* ■ *Dir* Stephen Frears • *Scr* Roddy Doyle, from his novel

Sneakers ★★★★ 15
Comedy thriller 1992 · US · Colour · 120mins
After the feel-good mythology of *Field of Dreams*, director Phil Alden Robinson changed tack completely and came up with a smart and snappy caper that is blessed with a sparkling script and an outstanding ensemble cast. Robert Redford, graciously sending himself up a little, is the former student radical, who now makes a living heading a team which is paid to break into high-tech buildings to show up lapses in security systems. However, his past returns to haunt him when he is blackmailed into stealing the ultimate codebreaker. Ignore the holes in plot logic and savour the relaxed and unselfish comic interplay from a cast that includes River Phoenix, Dan Aykroyd, Sidney Poitier,

David Strathairn and Mary McDonnell. Contains some swearing. 💻 📀 *DVD*

Robert Redford *Martin Bishop* • Dan Aykroyd *"Mother"* • Ben Kingsley *Cosmo* • Mary McDonnell *Liz* • River Phoenix *Carl* • Sidney Poitier *Crease* • David Strathairn *Whistler* • Timothy Busfield *Dick Gordon* • James Earl Jones *Bernard Abbott* ■ *Dir* Phil Alden Robinson • *Scr* Phil Alden Robinson, Lawrence Lasker, Walter F Parkes

The Sniper ★★★★
Crime drama   1952 · US · BW · 87mins

An excellent psychological exploration of what drives one man to shoot at random with no apparent thought or feeling. The man in question has a deep grudge against women and the camera follows his gun as if we, the audience, are his eyes, the effect of this visual trick being both eerie and strangely compelling. Arthur Franz gives a powerful performance as the madman and this is neither a eulogy to violence, nor a total condemnation of society, but an intelligent movie that poses many complex questions. However it is not to everyone's taste.

Adolphe Menjou *Lieutenant Kafka* • Arthur Franz *Eddie Miller* • Gerald Mohr *Sergeant Ferris* • Marie Windsor *Jean Darr* • Frank Faylen *Inspector Anderson* • Richard Kiley *Dr James C Kent* ■ *Dir* Edward Dmytryk • *Scr* Harry Brown, from a story by Edward Anhalt, Edna Anhalt

Sniper ★★★ 🔳
Action adventure 1992 · US · Colour · 94mins

Though it doesn't quite come off, this is a surprisingly intelligent spin on the action thriller. Tom Berenger is a seasoned marksman on a covert mission to terminate a Panamanian rebel leader. However, he soon discovers he has more than enough on his plate dealing with his twitchy new partner, Billy Zane. The pair's claustrophobic relationship generates plenty of jungle-bound tension and the action set pieces, notably the pair's long-range assassinations, are stylishly staged by director Luis Llosa. Contains swearing, violence. 💻

Tom Berenger *Tom Beckett* • Billy Zane *Richard Miller* • Aden Young *Doug Papich* • Ken Radley *El Cirujano* • JT Walsh *Beckett's senior officer* • Reinaldo Arenas [Reynaldo Arenas] *Cacique* ■ *Dir* Luis Llosa • *Scr* Michael Frost Beckner, Crash Leyland

The Snoop Sisters ★★★
Detective comedy thriller
1972 · US · Colour · 100mins

Paulette Goddard came out of retirement to play a faded film star who is bumped off in sinister circumstances in this sprightly TV movie, which is also known as *The Female Instinct*. A forerunner of *Murder, She Wrote*, the two sleuth sisters are played with sly prissiness by Mildred Natwick and Helen Hayes (who would go on to play the ultimate spinster sleuth, Miss Marple), and are kept out of trouble by their ex-cop-turned-chauffeur, Art Carney. While not the most impenetrable of mysteries, this is still an enjoyable diversion, played to perfection by real pros.

Helen Hayes *Ernesta Snoop* • Mildred Natwick *Gwendolyn "G" Snoop Ostrowski* • Art Carney *Barney* • Paulette Goddard *Norma Treat* • Craig Stevens *Charles Corman* • Lawrence

Pressman *Lieutenant Steven Ostrowski* • Fritz Weaver *Anton De Touralay* • Jill Clayburgh *Mary Nero* ■ *Dir* Leonard B Stern • *Scr* Leonard B Stern, Hugh Wheeler

Snoopy, Come Home ★★★ 🔳
Animation   1972 · US · Colour · 76mins

Second in the series of feature-length *Peanuts* adventures. Charles M Schulz's beagle takes centre stage, vowing that life *isn't* going to the dogs, and, with bird-brained buddy Woodstock in tow, heading off in search of something better. Cutely animated, and packed with all the gentle charm and humour of the *Peanuts* comic strip, this could still delight a whole new generation of kids. 💻

Chad Webber *Charlie Brown* • Robin Kohn *Robin Van Pelt* • Stephen Shea *Linus Van Pelt* • David Carey *Schroeder* ■ *Dir* Bill Melendez • *Scr* from the comic strip by Charles M Schulz

Snow Day ★★ 🔳
Comedy   2000 · US · Colour · 89mins

A "snow day" is that special day, traditionally recognised in America, when a freak blizzard causes an unexpected break from school. Mark Webber uses the opportunity to make a play for the glamorous Emmanuelle Chriqui, while his younger sister Zena Grey tries to keep the Snow-plowman (Chris Elliott) occupied so that her school remains closed. Director Chris Koch piles on the teen movie clichés with all the lumbering tenacity of a plough. Yet the picture is good-natured and energetic enough to make it watchable, if not memorable.

Chris Elliott *Snow-plowman* • Mark Webber *Hal Brandston* • Jean Smart *Laura Brandston* • Schuyler Fisk *Lane Leonard* • Iggy Pop *Mr Zellweger* • Pam Grier *Tina* • John Schneider *Chad Symmonz* • Chevy Chase *Tom Brandston* • Zena Grey *Natalie Brandston* • Emmanuelle Chriqui *Claire Bonner* ■ *Dir* Chris Koch • *Scr* Will McRobb, Chris Viscardi

Snow Falling on Cedars ★★★★ 🔳
Courtroom drama
1999 · US · Colour · 127mins

It's rare to experience an adaptation of a novel as true to the spirit of the original as director Scott Hicks's follow-up to the Oscar-winning *Shine*. David Guterson's book is vivid, poetic and sensual, qualities this film, about prejudice within a small fishing community in the years following the Second World War, shares in abundance. Ethan Hawke plays a local journalist fascinated by the trial of a Japanese-American war hero accused of murdering a fellow fisherman. The trial becomes the focus for fear and scapegoating in a mixed-race community torn apart by Pearl Harbor. Hicks sacrifices narrative thrust for atmosphere, resulting in a slow but very special and beautiful film.

Ethan Hawke *Ishmael Chambers* • Youki Kudoh *Hatsue Miyamoto* • Reeve Carney *Young Ishmael Chambers* • Anne Suzuki *Young Hatsue Imada* • Rick Yune *Kazuo Miyamoto* • Max von Sydow *Nels Gudmundsson* • James Rebhorn *Alvin Hooks* • James Cromwell *Judge Fielding* • Sam

Shepard *Arthur Chambers* ■ *Dir* Scott Hicks • *Scr* Ron Bass [Ronald Bass], Scott Hicks, from the novel by David Guterson

Snow Job ★
Crime drama   1972 · US · Colour · 90mins

Also known as *The Ski Raiders*, this was intended as a vehicle for former Olympic ski champion, Jean-Claude Killy. The beauty of the Alpine scenery and Killy's sporting prowess are plain for all to see, but so is the fact that this crime caper is just no good. As the ski instructor who robs the local bank, Killy falls flat on his face every time he comes off the piste. The sole bright spot is provided by legendary director Vittorio De Sica, whose slyly debunking cameo as an insurance investigator, shows why he was such a matinée idol in the thirties and forties.

Jean-Claude Killy *Christian Biton* • Daniele Gaubert *Monica Scotti* • Cliff Potts *Bob Skinner* • Vittorio De Sica *Enrico Dolphi* • Lelio Luttazzi *Bank manager* • Delia Boccardo *Lorraine Borman* ■ *Dir* George Englund • *Scr* Ken Kolb, Jeffrey Bloom, from the story *$125,000 Ski Bum Holdup* by Richard Gallagher

The Snow Queen ★★★
Part-animated fantasy
1959 · USSR · Colour · 54mins

Live-action, directed by Phil Patton and featuring Art Linkletter with Tammy Marihugh, bookends an animated feature from the Soviet Union, based on the Hans Christian Andersen story of the ice-bound queen, thawed by true love. Lev Atamanov directed the animation in 1955, though the voice-overs (including Sandra Dee and Tommy Kirk) are American.

Sandra Dee *Gerda* • Tommy Kirk *Kay* • Patty McCormack *Angel* • Louise Arthur *The Snow Queen* • Paul Frees *Ol' Dreamy/The Raven* ■ *Dir* Phil Patton • *Scr* Alan Lipscott, Bob Fisher, from a fairy tale by Hans Christian Andersen, Art Linkletter, Tammy Marihugh

Snow White ★★★
Fantasy   1989 · Cz/W Ger · Colour · 90mins

Such is the hold of Walt Disney's 1937 animated adaptation (*Snow White and the Seven Dwarfs*) on the imagination of generations of young viewers, that it is easy to forget other versions exist. Markedly less lavish, this Czech-German co-production is a solid reworking of the dark Brothers Grimm tale, which, like many other eastern European children's films, entertains without ever talking down to its audience. Natalie Minko is fine in the title role, while Gudrun Landgrebe makes a suitably sinister Queen. German dialogue dubbed into English.

Natalie Minko *Snow White* • Gudrun Landgrebe *Queen* • Alessandro Gassman *Court Jester* • Eberhard Feik *Priest* • Dietmar Schonherr *King* • Sandor Koleseri *Black Knight* ■ *Dir* Ludvik Raza • *Scr* Bernd Fiedler, from a fairy tale by Jacob Grimm, Wilhelm Grimm

Snow White: a Tale of Terror ★★★ 🔳
Gothic horror 1996 · UK/US · Colour · 96mins

Director Michael Cohn puts the grim back in to the Grimm Brothers dark fairy tale. All Disney expectation is turned on its head as the sexual

tensions and bloody obsessions are accentuated in this highly sinister fable with a richly textured Hammer Horror look. The dwarfs are barbaric outcasts in this intriguing revision (scarred, simple-minded, branded) that's too sombre for kids, but too light in the fright department for adults. However, Sigourney Weaver gives the performance of her career as Claudia the wicked stepmother. Contains swearing and violence. 💻

Sigourney Weaver *Claudia Hoffman* • Sam Neill *Frederick Hoffman* • Gil Bellows *Will* • Taryn Davis *Little Lilli* • Brian Glover *Lars* • David Conrad *Peter Gutenberg* • Monica Keena *Lilli Hoffman* • Anthony Brophy *Rolf* ■ *Dir* Michael Cohn • *Scr* Tom Szollosi, Deborah Serra, from the fairy tale by Jacob Grimm, Wilhelm Grimm

Snow White and the Seven Dwarfs ★★★★★ 🔳
Animated fantasy 1937 · US · Colour · 81mins

Disney's first animation feature is a joyous folk tale, from the Grimm Brothers, which comes fresh to each generation. As Snow White flees her wicked stepmother to find a forest refuge with the minute miners, some great, tuneful songs counterpoint their setting up home together and the dark tension of the stepmother's poisoned apple. Cute, maybe, but it's a landmark experience for all children – and grown-ups – infused with a haunting Gothic sub-text. 💻

Adriana Caselotti *Snow White* • Harry Stockwell *Prince Charming* • Lucille La Verne *The queen/The witch* • Moroni Olsen *Magic Mirror* • Billy Gilbert *Sneezy* • Pinto Colvig *Sleepy/Grumpy* • Otis Harlan *Happy* • Scotty Mattraw *Bashful* • Roy Atwell *Doc* ■ *Dir* David Hand • *Scr* Ted Sears, Otto Englander, Earl Hurd, Dorothy Ann Blank, Richard Creedon, Dick Richard, Merrill De Maris, Webb Smith, from the fairy tale by Jacob Grimm, Wilhelm Grimm • *Music* Leigh Harline

Snowball Express ★★ 🔳
Comedy   1972 · US · Colour · 93mins

Beating a retreat from the city is many a suburbanite's dream. This comedy shows that dream turning sour, when Manhattan family man Dean Jones inherits a ski-resort hotel in the Rockies and tries to make a go of it with wife, Nancy Olson. Being a Disney confection that aims to please, the bad succumbs to the beautiful, with lots of ski sequences and a snowmobile race, and the tales of financial hardship tend to get buried under a pile of slush.

Dean Jones *Johnny Baxter* • Nancy Olson *Sue Baxter* • Harry Morgan *Jesse McCord* • Keenan Wynn *Martin Ridgeway* • Johnny Whitaker *Richard Baxter* • Michael McGreevey *Wally Perkins* ■ *Dir* Norman Tokar • *Scr* Don Tait, Jim Parker, from the novel *Chateau Bon Vivant* by Frankie O'Rear, John O'Rear

Snowbeast ★★
Thriller   1977 · US · Colour · 96mins

This risible TV movie is, surprisingly, written by *Psycho*'s Joseph Stefano. It has pretensions of being *Jaws* on ice, but has more in common with a Scooby Doo mystery, as a crummy-looking monster terrorises a mountain resort. Bo Svenson and Clint Walker try to bring a semblance of credibility to the proceedings, but their efforts are

confounded by the predictable plot and Herb Wallerstein's fumbling direction. More interesting is the fact that Donna Mills and Gloria Swanson were originally cast, only to be replaced by Yvette Mimieux and Sylvia Sidney as shooting began.

Bo Svenson *Gar Seberg* • Yvette Mimieux *Ellen Seberg* • Robert Logan *Tony Rill* • Clint Walker *Sheriff Paraday* • Sylvia Sidney *Carrie Rill* • Michael J London *The Beast* ■ *Dir* Herb Wallerstein • *Scr* Joseph Stefano

Snowbound ★★ U
Adventure   1948 · UK · BW · 81mins

A ludicrous Alpine adventure, based on Hammond Innes's *The Lonely Skier*, which too often betrays its pulp novel roots among resolutely studio-bound snow. Nevertheless, the cast is splendid, with Dennis Price and Robert Newton positively outdoing each other for the (over-) acting honours: the former plays a film extra-cum-scriptwriter sent by the latter, a film director, to write a script in the Dolomites, knowing full well there's Nazi gold in them there Alps. It becomes slightly less ludicrous when the snow traps everybody, and director David MacDonald ploughs through the tosh with a certain conviction, achieving a fine sense of claustrophobia. 🎞

Robert Newton *Derek Engles* • Dennis Price *Neil Blair* • Herbert Lom *Keramikos* • Marcel Dalio *Stefan Valdini* • Stanley Holloway *Joe Wesson* • Guy Middleton *Gilbert Mayne* ■ *Dir* David MacDonald • *Scr* David Evans, Keith Campbell, from the novel *The Lonely Skier* by Hammond Innes

Snowbound ★★
Drama based on a true story
1993 · US · Colour

''Sugarbound'' would have made an equally appropriate title this TV movie, because snow isn't the only thing the cast is struggling to escape from in this otherwise quite gripping true story. Neil Patrick Harris, still sporting the baby-faced looks first seen in *Doogie Howser MD*, and Kelli Williams play the young couple who, with their baby, get stranded in a terrifying blizzard while on the way to a funeral. The two leads are niceness personified, and director Christian Duguay injects a bit of grittiness into the proceedings, but everyone's efforts are let down by the syrupy script.

Neil Patrick Harris *Jim Stolpa* • Kelli Williams *Jennifer Stolpa* • Susan Clark *Muriel* • Michael Gross *Kevin* • Richard Cox *Jason* • Alexander Ahnert *Clayton Stolpa* ■ *Dir* Christian Duguay • *Scr* Jonathan Rintels

The Snowman ★★
Crime thriller   1985 · W Ger · Colour

A tricky one this. Continental commercial pulp is never going to attract the art-house crowd, so there's little point in presenting such humdrum thrillers with subtitles. Yet, dubbing of this quality robs a movie of much-needed authenticity and renders it almost unwatchable for the casual viewer. Here, for example, director Peter F Bringmann makes atmospheric use of his Maltese locations and concocts a decent drama around drifter Marius Müller-Westermhagen's

bid to keep out of the clutches of cops who are convinced he's a killer and rival drug gangs who are concerned he's a threat. But any tension is frittered away by those dispassionate voiceovers. German dialogue dubbed into English.

Marius Müller-Westermhagen *Dorn* • Polly Eltes *Cora* • Heinz Wanitschek *Roda* • Riad Gholmie *Habib* ■ *Dir* Peter F Bringmann

The Snows of Kilimanjaro ★★★ PG
Romantic drama
1952 · US · Colour · 109mins

This prettified 20th Century-Fox film version of Ernest Hemingway's novella, is almost totally wrecked by the miscasting of Gregory Peck. He is much too nice to play the hard-drinking, macho-obsessed, animal-hunting hero suffering from flashback syndrome, as wrong here as he was in the later *Moby Dick*. But Ava Gardner, Hildegarde Neff and Susan Hayward are right, seductively rivalling the African and Riviera landscapes and making Peck's life a misery. Studio hack Henry King, keeps it rolling. 🎞

Gregory Peck *Harry* • Susan Hayward *Helen* • Ava Gardner *Cynthia* • Hildegarde Neff *Countess Liz* • Leo G Carroll *Uncle Bill* • Torin Thatcher *Johnson* • Ava Norring *Beatrice* • Helene Stanley *Connie* ■ *Dir* Henry King • *Scr* Casey Robinson, from the short story by Ernest Hemingway

So Big ★★★ U
Period drama   1953 · US · BW · 101mins

Author Edna Ferber achieved tremendous cinematic success with filmed versions of *Show Boat* , *Cimarron*, and *Giant*, and this Pulitzer Prize winner also spawned three film versions, this one being the last, and weakest. Jane Wyman, a huge star after her Oscar for *Johnny Belinda*, follows Colleen Moore and Barbara Stanwyck as the New Holland schoolmistress bringing up son, Steve Forrest against all odds. The Warner Bros gloss is not too intrusive, and there are nicely honed performances from big Sterling Hayden and lovely Nancy Olsen in support.

Jane Wyman *Selina Dejong* • Sterling Hayden *Pervus Dejong* • Nancy Olson *Dallas O'Mara* • Steve Forrest *Dirk Dejong* • Elisabeth Fraser *Julie Hempel* • Martha Hyer *Paula Hempel* ■ *Dir* Robert Wise • *Scr* John Twist, from the novel by Edna Ferber

So Close to Life ★★★
Drama   1957 · Swe · BW · 84mins

Ingrid Thulin, Eva Dahlbeck and Bibi Andersson shared the best actress prize at the 1958 Cannes Film Festival, but it's not just the performances that makes *So Close to Life* significant. This is the film that signalled Ingmar Bergman's shift towards what are usually called ''Chamber Dramas'', intense conversation pieces that take place in symbolically confined spaces (in this case, a maternity ward). Ultimately, Bergman hedges his bets about the wisdom of bringing a child into such a troubled world but, for all its purple passages and cosy conclusions, the film leaves you with plenty to think

about. In Swedish with English subtitles.

Eva Dahlbeck *Stina* • Ingrid Thulin *Cecilia* • Bibi Andersson *Hjordis* • Barbro Hiort Af Ornas *Brita* • Erland Josephson *Anders* • Max von Sydow *Harry* • Gunnar Sjoberg *Doctor* ■ *Dir* Ingmar Bergman • *Scr* Ingmar Bergman, from a story by Ulla Isaksson

So Dark the Night ★★★
Crime drama   1946 · US · BW · 70mins

It's not often that character actors have the chance to play leading roles and Steven Geray, an east European actor usually cast as bartender, foreign agent or small-time criminal, does a splendid job in this outstanding B-feature. Playing a famous French detective on holiday, he finds himself investigating murders in a small village. Although the rest of the cast is little known, the well-written story has a memorably original twist and the setting is skilfully evoked.

Steven Geray *Henri Cassin* • Micheline Cheirel *Nanette Michaud* • Eugene Borden *Pierre Michaud* • Ann Codee *Mama Michaud* • Egon Brecher *Dr Boncourt* ■ *Dir* Joseph H Lewis • *Scr* Martin Berkeley, Dwight Babcock, from a story by Audrey Wisberg

So Dear to My Heart ★★★ U
Part-animated musical
1949 · US · Colour · 78mins

The first actor to sign a long-term contract at Disney, Bobby Driscoll won a special Oscar for his work in 1949, although it clearly had more to do with *The Window*, than this slight blend of live-action and animation. Although the nominated song, *Lavender Blue*, was one of Uncle Walt's favourites, today's youngsters will get more enjoyment out of numbers like *Stick-with-it-ivity*, one of the many animated sequences in which farm boy Driscoll (who'd also starred in the studio's similarly folksy *Song of the South*) learns the lessons of life as he trains his black lamb, Danny, for a country fair.

Burl Ives *Uncle Hiram* • Beulah Bondi *Granny Kincaid* • Harry Carey *Judge* • Bobby Driscoll *Jeremiah Kincaid* ■ *Dir* Harold Schuster, Hamilton Luske • *Scr* John Tucker Battle, Maurice Rapf, Ted Sears, from the novel *Midnight and Jeremiah* by Sterling North

So Ends Our Night ★★★
Wartime drama   1941 · US · BW · 121mins

Released before the US entered the War, this strong drama relates the experiences of three Germans who flee the rise of Hitler in 1937, only to encounter persecution wherever they journey. Fredric March, an anti-Nazi German, risks danger to return to his dying wife (Frances Dee), while Jewish girl Margaret Sullavan and half-Jewish Glenn Ford make it to safety, falling in love en route. Adapted from Erich Maria Remarque's novel, the subject matter can hardly fail to be moving, especially with such a cast, and is frequently tense and gripping. No thanks, though, to director John Cromwell, who tends to use a sledgehammer to kill a gnat.

Fredric March *Joseph Steiner* • Margaret Sullavan *Ruth Holland* • Frances Dee *Marie Steiner* • Glenn Ford *Ludwig Kern* • Anna Sten

Lilo • Erich von Stroheim *Brenner* ■ *Dir* John Cromwell • *Scr* Talbot Jennings, from the novel *Flotsam* by Erich Maria Remarque

So Fine ★★★ 15
Comedy   1981 · US · Colour · 87mins

Clever comic writer Andrew Bergman's directorial debut is an absolutely hilarious wacky comedy about the inventor of see-through jeans – yes, really! Although fresh-faced Ryan O'Neal isn't ideal as the intellectual heir of a New York City clothing manufacturer, his bookish quality is well-used, and his reluctance to make a career in the garment jungle is wittily observed. The whole descends into a delirious farce, and one wonders when we'll see those sexy see-through trousers on the streets. 🎞

Ryan O'Neal *Bobby Fine* • Jack Warden *Jack Fine* • Mariangela Melato *Lire* • Richard Kiel *Mr Eddie* • Fred Gwynne *Chairman Lincoln* • Mike Kellin *Sam Schlotzman* • David Rounds *Prof Dick McCarthy* • Joel Steadman *Prof Yarnell* ■ *Dir/Scr* Andrew Bergman

So Goes My Love ★★★ U
Comedy   1946 · US · BW · 91mins

This light tale of eccentric family life in the 19th century, is based on the memoir *A Genius in the Family* by Hiram Percy Maxim, (Bobby Driscoll). Since Driscoll's parents are inventor Don Ameche and the fussing Myrna Loy, it's not without period charm, but it needed a more forceful director than Frank Ryan. However, one should be thankful that Hollywood could at one time produce movies whose charm alone outweighed their content.

Myrna Loy *Jane* • Don Ameche *Hiram Stephen Maxim* • Rhys Williams *Magel* • Bobby Driscoll *Percy Maxim* • Richard Gaines *Mr Josephus* • Molly Lamont *Anty Gannet* ■ *Dir* Frank Ryan • *Scr* Bruce Manning, James Clifden, from the book *A Genius in the Family* by Hiram Percy Maxim

So I Married an Axe Murderer ★★★ 15
Comedy   1993 · US · Colour · 89mins

Mike Myers's first stab at flying solo from his *Wayne's World* partner Dana Carvey is a mixed bag. He plays an aspiring poet who always manages to talk himself out of long-term relationships with women. All that seems to change when he falls madly in love with Nancy Travis, until evidence starts mounting that she may be a black widow who has left a trail of dead husbands in her wake. There are some nicely black comic moments, but Myers tries too hard and mugs shamelessly to the camera. The best performances come from supporting players Amanda Plummer, Brenda Fricker and, most notably, Anthony LaPaglia as his best friend. Sadly, it fails to live up to the promise of the title. Contains swearing, nudity. 🎞

Mike Myers *Charlie Mackenzie/Stuart Mackenzie* • Nancy Travis *Harriet Michaels* • Anthony LaPaglia *Tony Giardino* • Amanda Plummer *Rose Michaels* • Brenda Fricker *May Mackenzie* • Matt Doherty *Heed* • Charles Grodin *Comandeered car driver* • Phil Hartman *Park ranger ''Vickie''* • Debi Mazar *Tony's girlfriend ''Susan''* • Steven Wright *Pilot* ■ *Dir* Thomas Schlamme • *Scr* Robbie Fox, Mike Myers, Neil Mullarkey, from a story by Robbie Fox

So Long at the Fair ★★ U

Mystery 1950 · UK · BW · 85mins

Everything's set here for an attention-grabbing little mystery. In addition to David Tomlinson's unexplained disappearance, there's the unique backdrop of the 1889 Great Exhibition in Paris, a solid supporting cast and the exciting prospect of seeing Dirk Bogarde woo Jean Simmons. Yet, somehow, it fails to gell and, by the time the shocking solution is revealed, everyone's too numb to care. Definitely a wasted opportunity.

Jean Simmons *Victoria Barton* • Dirk Bogarde *George Hathaway* • David Tomlinson *Johnny Barton* • Marcel Poncin *Narcisse* • Cathleen Nesbitt *Madam Herve* • Honor Blackman *Rhoda O'Donovan* • Betty Warren *Mrs O'Donovan* ■ *Dir* Terence Fisher, Anthony Darnborough • *Scr* Hugh Mills, Anthony Thorne, from a novel by Anthony Thorne

So Proudly We Hail ★★★

Second World War drama
1943 · US · BW · 125mins

When major Hollywood stars such as John Wayne, Gary Cooper and James Stewart were winning the Second World War, major Hollywood actresses tended to lose out on heroism and were cast as *femme fatales* or dewy-eyed wives. But this lavish Paramount flag-waver puts Claudette Colbert, Paulette Goddard and Veronica Lake into army nurse uniform and packs them off to the Pacific where they get on in a no nonsense, "pass the plasma please" way. Each of them has a personal problem to overcome and each of them battles with Miklos Rozsa's music. Overlong, but watchable for the stars on parade.

Claudette Colbert *Lt Janet Davidson* • Paulette Goddard *Lt Joan O'Doul* • Veronica Lake *Lt Olivia D'Arcy* • George Reeves *Lt John Summers* • Barbara Britton *Lt Rosemary Larson* • Walter Abel *Chaplain* • Sonny Tufts *Kansas* ■ *Dir* Mark Sandrich • *Scr* Allan Scott

So Proudly We Hail ★★ 15

Drama 1990 · US · Colour · 90mins

Sadly, not the 1943 Claudette Colbert/ Veronica Lake drama of the same name, but a rather dull and uninvolving film from director Lionel Chetwynd (who made the equally tedious *The Hanoi Hilton*) about a university professor becoming involved with a white supremacist group, which uses his theories on racism for its own ends. David Soul and co-star Edward Herrmann (*The Lost Boys*) are both woefully miscast in what is essentially, a very superficial and heavy-handed look at a serious subject.

David Soul *Alden Ernst* • Chad Lowe *Billy Kincaid* • Edward Herrmann *James Wagner* • Raphael Sbarge *Henry Ernst* • Peter Dobson *Rocco Inucci* • Harley Jane Kozak *Susan McCarran* • Gloria Carlin *Angie* ■ *Dir/Scr* Lionel Chetwynd

So Red the Rose ★★★ U

Romantic drama 1935 · US · BW · 82mins

This is the period movie that convinced Hollywood producers that there was no money to be made in movies about the American Civil War, so they all rejected *Gone with the Wind*, letting it go to independent David O Selznick who turned it into screen history. This isn't at all bad, though, and Margaret Sullavan is particularly touching as she waits for Randolph Scott to return from the "war between the states". There's fine support from the likes of Walter Connolly and Janet Beecher, and keep an eye peeled for a very young and effective Robert Cummings. King Vidor's direction is restrained and masterly, making this a rewarding, if little known movie.

Margaret Sullavan *Vallette Bedford* • Walter Connolly *Malcolm Bedford* • Janet Beecher *Sally Bedford* • Harry Ellerbe *Edward Bedford* • Robert Cummings *George Pendleton* • Charles Starrett *George McGehee* • Johnny Downs *Yankee Boy* • Randolph Scott *Duncan Bedford* ■ *Dir* King Vidor • *Scr* Laurence Stallings, Edwin Justus Mayer, Maxwell Anderson, from a novel by Stark Young

So This Is Love ★★ U

Biographical musical drama
1953 · US · Colour · 100mins

Kathryn Grayson was undeniably talented, as her career-best work in *Show Boat* and *Kiss Me Kate* for MGM demonstrates. However, in this Warner Bros biopic she is seriously miscast, lacking the class to portray real-life tragic Metropolitan Opera star Grace Moore, whose screen career faded as her weight ballooned. The songs are worthy and the Technicolor is fine to watch, but leading man Merv Griffin (later a chat-show host) is dull, and in truth there's little of substance.

Kathryn Grayson *Grace Moore* • Merv Griffin *Buddy Nash* • Joan Weldon *Ruth Obre* • Walter Abel *Colonel Moore* • Rosemary De Camp *Aunt Laura Stokley* • Jeff Donnell *Henrietta Van Dyke* • Ann Doran *Mrs Moore* ■ *Dir* Gordon Douglas • *Scr* John Monk Jr, from the autobiography *You're Only Human Once* by Grace Moore • *Music* Max Steiner

So This Is New York ★★★

Comedy 1948 · US · BW · 77mins

This attractive vehicle for radio star Henry Morgan was an early effort from Richard Fleischer, whose career would embrace *The Vikings*, *Compulsion* and *10 Rillington Place*, among others. This is based on Ring Lardner's autobiographical novel *The Big Town*, but Lardner's recollections, once transferred to film, are so good-natured they ultimately become tiresome. Still, there's no denying young Fleischer's talent behind the camera, and film buffs should note that this was also Hollywood legend Stanley Kramer's first producer credit.

Henry Morgan *Ernie Finch* • Virginia Grey *Ella Finch* • Dona Drake *Kate Goff* • Rudy Vallee *Herbert Daley* • Bill Goodwin *Jimmy Ralston* • Hugh Herbert *Mr Trumball* • Leo Gorcey *Sid Mercer* • Jerome Cowan *Francis Griffin* ■ *Dir* Richard O Fleischer [Richard Fleischer] • *Scr* Carl Foreman, Herbert Baker, from the novel *The Big Town* by Ring Lardner

So This Is Paris ★★★

Silent comedy 1926 · US · BW · 74mins

German import Ernst Lubitsch's seventh American film is an elegant, sophisticated and satirical silent comedy, in which the unique Lubitsch touch, spoke as eloquently as any words could. It made a mint for Warner Bros and was voted one of the year's ten best by the *New York Times*. The plot revolves around the light-hearted complications that ensue when a husband-and-wife dance duo (Lilyan Tashman, André Beranger) decide to spice up their relationship by indulging in criss-cross flirtations with a doctor and his wife (Monte Blue, Patsy Ruth Miller). Very "French", very ooh-la-la, and a lot of fun. Look out for the maid – she's Myrna Loy.

Monte Blue *Dr Eisenstein* • Patsy Ruth Miller *Rosalind Eisenstein* • Lilyan Tashman *Adela, a dancer* • AndréBeranger *Alfred, her husband* • Myrna Loy *Maid* ■ *Dir* Ernst Lubitsch • *Scr* Hans Kräly, from the play *Le Réveillon* by Henri Meilhac, Ludovic Halévy

So This Is Paris ★★ U

Musical comedy 1954 · US · Colour · 96mins

This retread of every tired old musical cliché about sailors on the town or Americans in Paris, stars Tony Curtis, Gene Nelson and Paul Gilbert as three mariners on the make in the French capital, with Gloria De Haven, Mara Corday and Corinne Calvet as the girls. The musical numbers are reasonably pleasing, if totally forgettable, but the script hits a level of such mind-numbing imbecility that the sentimental element – De Haven masquerading as French and dancing in a nightclub to help support a bunch of cute orphans – is actually a welcome relief.

Tony Curtis *Joe Maxwell* • Gloria De Haven [Gloria DeHaven] *Colette D'Avril/Jane Mitchell* • Gene Nelson *Al Howard* • Corinne Calvet *Suzanne Sorel* • Paul Gilbert *Davey Jones* • Mara Corday *Yvonne* ■ *Dir* Richard Quine • *Scr* Charles Hoffman, from a story by Ray Buffum

So This Is Romance? ★★

Romantic comedy
1997 · UK · Colour · 92mins

A comedy tagged as "the date movie of the year" and by the few who saw it, as anything but. The story, stylised to be hip in the vein of *Swingers*, but set in a New York arts world, centers on a guy and his serial failures at finding a girlfriend. The good cast is led by Reece Dinsdale, with better suppport than the movie merits from the likes of Frank Finlay, Susannah York and Maryam D'Abo. The director of this unfortunte romantic comedy is Kevin W Smith, the "W" informing you that this isn't the Kevin Smith who made *Clerks* and *Chasing Amy*.

Reece Dinsdale *Mike* • John Hannah *Tony* • Victoria Smurfit *Helen* • Frank Finlay *Dad* • Clara Bellar *Sara* • Rowena King *Moira* • Maryam D'Abo *Sara 2* • Susannah York *Mum* ■ *Dir/Scr* Kevin W Smith

Soapdish ★★★★ 15

Comedy 1991 · US · Colour · 92mins

The inside dope on daytime soap, with Sally Field (she began her career in TV shows such as *Gidget* and its ilk), Carrie Fisher and Whoopi Goldberg among the stars and creators of a ghastly TV show called *The Sun Also Sets*. Actors are written out, has-beens stage comebacks, real life echoes fiction, emotional wreckage piles up, you know the rest. As for the always brilliant Kevin Kline, he's been off the show for years. But, executive producer Robert Downey Jr and Field's co-star and rival (Cathy Moriarty) want him back to induce Field to leave. Despite some longueurs, this farce has genuinely hysterical moments, and can be seen as a sly reworking of *All about Eve* for couch potatoes. Contains swearing.

Sally Field *Celeste Talbert* • Kevin Kline *Jeffrey Anderson* • Robert Downey Jr *David Barnes* • Whoopi Goldberg *Rose Schwartz* • Carrie Fisher *Betsy Faye Sharon* • Cathy Moriarty *Montana Moorehead* • Teri Hatcher *Ariel Maloney* • Paul Johansson *Bolt Brennan* • Elisabeth Shue *Lori Craven* • Kathy Najimy *Tawny Miller* ■ *Dir* Michael Hoffman • *Scr* Robert Harling, Andrew Bergman, from a story by Robert Harling

Society ★★★ 18

Horror 1989 · US · Colour · 94mins

A truly unique shocker, this mixture of social comment and splatter horror will definitely not be to everyone's taste. Is Bill Warlock just paranoid about his well-respected Beverly Hills family? Or do they really get up to unspeakable taboo-breaking orgies when he's not around? The answer involves a great deal of special make-up effects, including torso distortion, melting flesh, deviant gender blurring and surreal spectacle. Disturbing and silly in roughly equal amounts, this over-the-top exposé of what the rich are really doing to the poor, marked the directing debut of Brian Yuzna. Contains swearing, nudity. DVD

Bill Warlock [Bill Warlock] *Bill Whitney* • Devin Devasquez *Clarisa* • Evan Richards *Milo* • Ben Meyerson *Ted Ferguson* • Charles Lucia *Jim* • Connie Danese *Nan* ■ *Dir* Brian Yuzna • *Scr* Woody Keith, Rick Fry • *Makeup Special Effects* Screaming Mad George

Sodbusters ★★

Comedy western 1994 · Can · Colour · 98mins

Is there anything more embarrassing than a spoof that isn't funny? Kris Kristofferson isn't noted for sending audiences into paroxysms of laughter. But, to be fair to him here, as the battle-scarred gunslinger helping some Colorado farmers keep the railroad off their land, he's only been armed with blanks, thanks to the leaden script co-written by director Eugene Levy. The intention is clearly to parody pictures like *Shane*, but the sniggering way in which the clichés of the old homesteader westerns are trotted out is no way to set about it. The inclusion of a couple of gay cowboys doesn't help much, either. Contains violence, swearing.

Kris Kristofferson *Destiny* • John Vernon *Slade Cantrell* • Fred Willard *Clarence Gentry* • Wendel Meldrum *Lilac Gentry* • Steve Landesberg *Gunther Schteuppin* • Max Gail *Tom Partridge* ■ *Dir* Eugene Levy • *Scr* Eugene Levy, John Hemphill

Sodom and Gomorrah ★★★ PG

Biblical epic
1962 · US/Fr/It · Colour · 153mins

Lot (Stewart Granger) leads his people away from Sodom and Gomorrah, the twin cities of sin, just as God lays waste to them both. "Don't look back!" Lot tells his wife, but she does and is turned into a pillar of salt (one of the strangest special effects in movie history). Ridiculous in so many ways, Robert Aldrich's biblical epic has

1316

U = SUITABLE FOR ALL Uc = SUITABLE FOR ALL, ESPECIALLY FOR YOUNG CHILDREN (VIDEO ONLY) PG = PARENTAL GUIDANCE

an energy and a knowing hypocrisy that makes it very watchable. Sergio Leone directed the Italian version and some of the action sequences. ▭

Stewart Granger *Lot* • Anouk Aimée *Queen Bera* • Stanley Baker *Astaroth* • Rossana Podesta *Shuah* • Pier Angeli *Ildith* ▪ *Dir* Robert Aldrich, Sergio Leone • *Scr* Hugo Butler, Giorgio Prosperi

Sofie ★★★ PG

Drama
1992 · Den/Nor/Swe · Colour · 145mins

Based on Henri Nathansens's 1932 novel, *Mendel Philipsen and Sons*, Liv Ullmann's full-feature-length directorial debut, is a Bergmanesque examination of the pressures placed on women in late 19th-century Denmark. A study in dignified strength amidst the ruins of her romantic ideals, Karen-Lise Mynster gives a performance worthy of her director, as the mature Jewish woman, who abandons a passionate Gentile painter to marry her repressed shopkeeping cousin and bear him a rebellious son. With Ghita Norby and Erland Josephson similarly outstanding as her parents and Jorgen Persson's compositions suggesting the rigidity of the period, this is a deliberate, theatrical, but heartfelt film. In Swedish with English subtitles. ▭

Karen-Lise Mynster *Sofie* • Erland Josephson *Semmy* • Ghita Norby *Frederikke* • Jesper Christensen *Hojby* • Torben Zeller *Jonas* ▪ *Dir* Liv Ullmann • *Scr* Liv Ullmann, Peter Poulsen, from the novel *Mendel Philipsen and Son* by Henri Nathansen

Soft Beds, Hard Battles ★★

Comedy 1973 · UK · Colour · 106mins

This film reunited Peter Sellers with the Boulting Brothers who had been responsible for one of his greatest screen triumphs, *I'm All Right Jack*. Alas *Soft Beds, Hard Battles* – an X-rated Second World War romp – was not in the same class. Sellers plays multiple roles (including Adolf Hitler) in a story of murder and duplicity set around a Parisian brothel in 1940. The production was reportedly dogged with problems and the cracks are all too evident in the finished film. Still, there are some flashes of the Sellers talent, but oh, so few.

Peter Sellers *General Latour/Major Robinson/ Schroeder/Hitler/Prince Kyoto/President of France/Radio newsreader* • Lila Kedrova *Madame Grenier* • Curt Jurgens *General von Grotjahn* • Béatrice Romand *Marie-Claude* ▪ *Dir* Roy Boulting • *Scr* Leo Marks, Roy Boulting

Soft Deceit ★★★ 18

Erotic thriller 1994 · US · Colour · 91mins

Made in Canada by writer/director Jorge Montesi, this erotic thriller is packed to the rafters with clichés and contrivances. Yet, you can't quite pull yourself away from watching undercover cop Kate Vernon struggle with her feelings for slippery crook Patrick Bergin. Does she follow her heart, or turn him in along with the six-million dollars that he has stashed away? Every trick is thrown into the mix to keep the plot rattling along and Vernon gives a gutsy performance, but Bergin lacks the menace he brought to

Sleeping with the Enemy. Contains swearing, violence, sex. ▭

Patrick Bergin *Adam Trent* • Kate Vernon *Anne Fowler* • John Wesley Shipp *Detective John Hobart* ▪ *Dir/Scr* Jorge Montesi

Soft Fruit ★★★

Comedy drama
1999 · Ausl/US · Colour · 101mins

Jane Campion's former assistant, Christina Andreef, made her feature debut with this spikey, but unfocused comedy drama about a splintered family coming to terms with a mother's terminal cancer. Always a sympathetic matriarch, Jeanie Drynan provides a warm focus for the reunion of her larger-than-life siblings in the hellhole steel town of Port Kembla. But the episodic structure, while making for copious laughs, deprives the action of dramatic and emotional unity. Even though there's an autobiographical element to the picture, several incidents feel contrived, particularly those involving strict immigrant dad Linal Haft and his feckless son Russell Dykstra. Over-determinedly offbeat.

Jeanie Drynan *Patsy* • Linal Haft *Vic* • Russell Dykstra *Bo* • Genevieve Lemon *Josie* • Sacha Horler *Nadia* • Alicia Talbot *Vera* • Dion Bilios *Bud* ▪ *Dir/Scr* Christina Andreef • *Executive Producer* Jane Campion

Soft Top, Hard Shoulder ★★ 15

Road movie 1992 · UK · Colour · 90mins

As small British movies go, this is among the smallest. From its contrived title downwards, virtually everything about this odd couple comedy (apart from the playing of Peter Capaldi and Elaine Collins) is ill-judged. As in his Oscar-winning short *Franz Kafka's It's a Wonderful Life*, Capaldi bases his script on a Frank Capra classic, with several situations here reminiscent of scenes from *It Happened One Night*. However, Capaldi not only misfires with the screwball antics, but is also wide of the mark with the Bill Forsyth-style whimsy he is obviously striving for. Contains swearing.

Peter Capaldi *Gavin Bellini* • Elaine Collins *Yvonne* • Frances Barber *Miss Trimble* • Catherine Russell *Animal Rights activist* • Jeremy Northam *John* • Richard Wilson *Uncle Salvatore* • Sophie Hall *Nancy* • Scott Hall *Mr Young* • Simon Callow *Eddie Cherdowski* • Phyllis Logan *Karla* ▪ *Dir* Stefan Schwartz • *Scr* Peter Capaldi

Soigne Ta Droite ★★

Experimental fantasy
1986 · Fr/Swi · Colour · 82mins

Writer/director Jean-Luc Godard appears as the idiot and the prince in this impenetrable in-joke, complete with whispered mock-philosophical narration. There are several main stories, inseparable but unconnected, including one about an airline pilot apparently about to commit suicide in mid-air. The film has been described as a "metaphysical cartoon", but what it all means is anyone's guess, though casual viewers might just be impressed by the odd shot or two. A cinematic doodle plus a brief guest spot from Jane Birkin. A French language film.

Jean-Luc Godard *The idiot/The prince* • Jacques Villeret *The individual* • François Périer *The man* • Jane Birkin *The cricket* • Michel Galabru *The admiral* • Dominique Lavanant *The admiral's wife* ▪ *Dir/Scr* Jean-Luc Godard

Sol Madrid ★★

Action drama 1968 · US · Colour · 89mins

In a feeble thriller with a touch of James Bond about it, David McCallum, then the star of *The Man From UNCLE*, gets a chance to go solo and shine in a movie. McCallum plays a US narcotics agent on the trail of Rip Torn, whose mistress Stella Stevens has betrayed him. Telly Savalas plays a drug runner while Ricardo Montalban lounges about in some fancy shirts playing the Latin lover – some things never change. Director Brian G Hutton maintains a breathless pace and makes the most of the jet-set location of Acapulco.

David McCallum *Sol Madrid* • Stella Stevens *Stacey Woodward* • Telly Savalas *Dano Villanova* • Ricardo Montalban *Jalisco* • Rip Torn *Dano Villanova* • Pat Hingle *Harry Mitchell* • Paul Lukas *Capo Riccione* • Michael Ansara *Captain Ortega* ▪ *Dir* Brian G Hutton • *Scr* David Karp, from the novel *Fruit of the Poppy* by Robert Wilder

Solar Crisis ★★ 15

Science-fiction thriller
1990 · Jap/US · Colour · 107mins

This expensive US/Japan co-production was filled with production problems, including director Richard C Sarafian opting for a pseudonym when the producers dictated additional shooting after the movie bombed in Japan. Despite the new footage, it's easy to see why the movie went straight to video in North America. Though the story of a 21st-century space station crew working to save the broiling Earth by firing a special bomb into the Sun (while industrialist Peter Boyle attempts to sabotage the mission) has plenty of impressive special effects, the proceedings are bogged down by a lack of tension, awe, and excitement. This and a virtually unrelated subplot (wasting Jack Palance and Charlton Heston) about a runaway teenager. ▭

Charlton Heston *Skeet Kelso* • Peter Boyle *Teague* • Tetsuya Bessho *Ken Minami* • Jack Palance *Travis* • Tim Matheson *Steve Kelso* • Annabel Schofield *Alex* • Corin "Corky" Nemec [Corin Nemec] *Mike Kelso* • Brenda Bakke *Claire* ▪ *Dir* Alan Smithee [Richard C Sarafian] • *Scr* Joe Gannon, Crispan Bolt [Ted Sarafian], from a novel by Takeshi Kawata

Solaris ★★★ PG

Science-fiction
1972 · USSR · Colour · 159mins

For some, director Andrei Tarkovsky's philosophical cult movie is the Soviet equivalent of *2001*; for others, it's an obscure intellectual snore-fest. Based on Polish writer Stanislaw Lem's 1961 novel, the tale involves astronauts on an alien planet who are confronted by illusions from their subconscious memories (usually their morose girlfriends back on earth). Tarkovsky's highly influential and cerebral science-fiction epic is ponderous, very talky and contains minimal special effects, but its remote strangeness exerts a compelling hypnotic power that's often

extraordinarily potent. In Russian with English subtitles. ▭

Natalya Bondarchuk *Hari* • Donatas Banionis *Kris Kelvin* • Yuri Jarvet *Snow* • Anatoli Solonitsin [Anatoli Solonitsyn] *Sartorius* • Vladislav Dvorjetzki *Burton* ▪ *Dir* Andrei Tarkovsky • *Scr* Andrei Tarkovsky, Friedrich Gorenstein, from the novel by Stanislaw Lem

Solarwarriors ★ 15

Science-fiction adventure
1986 · US · Colour · 90mins

This feeble futuristic fantasy about roller-skating orphans, arrived too late to cash in on the teen market of the eighties. The orphans, imprisoned by tyrant Richard Jordan, try to bring moisture to a universe as parched as the Yorkshire Water Board. There's an age-old mystical force at work à la *Star Wars*, other science-fiction films are ripped off without mercy, and the kids aren't even all that likeable. Contains violence. ▭

Jami Gertz *Terra* • Jason Patric *Jason* • Lukas Haas *Daniel* • Richard Jordan *Grock* • James LeGros *Metron* • Claude Brooks *Rabbit* • Peter DeLuise *Tug* • Adrian Pasdar *Darstar* • Charles Durning *Warden* • Alexei Sayle *Malice* ▪ *Dir* Alan Johnson • *Scr* Walon Green, Douglas Anthony Metrov

Soldier ★ 18

Science-fiction action thriller
1998 · US · Colour · 94mins

Shane goes to outer space in director Paul (*Event Horizon*) Anderson's depressingly unoriginal slice of science fiction from David Webb Peoples, the writer of *Blade Runner*. Kurt Russell is the brainwashed army killing machine dumped on a garbage planet when a newer DNA manipulated model is developed. There he finds a forgotten outpost of stranded humans who adopt him as their warrior saviour, when Jason Scott Lee's genetically enhanced battalion arrive for practice manoeuvres. With hardly an original bone in its body, Anderson trots out familiar clichés against a tired post-apocalyptic backdrop with zero emotional engagement, lots of mindless slam-bang action and heaps of unintentional laughs. A by-the-numbers empty spectacle with Russell's performance consisting of barely a hundred words in total. Contains violence. ▭ **DVD**

Kurt Russell *Todd* • Jason Scott Lee *Caine 607* • Connie Nielsen *Sandra* • Gary Busey *Captain Church* • Jason Isaacs *Colonel Mekum* • Sean Pertwee *Mace* ▪ *Dir* Paul Anderson • *Scr* David Webb Peoples

Soldier Blue ★★★ 18

Western drama 1970 · US · Colour · 109mins

Very controversial on its release, this dramatisation of the Sand Creek Massacre of 1864, does not stint on the appalling carnage meted out to the Cheyenne by the US Cavalry. Scenes of women and children being raped and mutilated were cut by the British censor and the film was widely condemned for its extreme violence. It closely resembles *Little Big Man* in its tale of a white person – in this case Candice Bergen – who is kidnapped by Indians and becomes culturally enriched rather than bigoted. Like Arthur Penn's critically rated film, the vilified *Soldier Blue* owed a lot to the hugely influential book *Bury My Heart At Wounded Knee* and is an explicit allegory of the My Lai massacre in Vietnam. Contains violence and swearing. ▣

Candice Bergen *Cresta Marybelle Lee* • Peter Strauss *Private Honus Gant* • Donald Pleasence *Isaac Q Cumber* • Bob Carraway *Lieut John McNair* • Jorge Rivero *Spotted Wolf* • Dana Elcar *Captain Battles* • John Anderson *Colonel Iverson* ■ *Dir* Ralph Nelson • *Scr* John Gay, from the novel *Arrow in the Sun* by Theodore V Olsen

Soldier in the Rain ★★★★ U

Comedy drama   1963 · US · BW · 87mins

Made the same year Steve McQueen starred in *The Great Escape* and *Love with the Proper Stranger*, this unfashionable film is one of the most neglected in his filmography. The story of scamming and shirking at an army base is *Bilko* with bitterness and sentiment stirred in to give the comedy its unique flavour. McQueen engagingly blends naivety with nous, as he tries to persuade scheming sergeant Jackie Gleason to quit the service and cut a dash on civvy street. An odd couple, but they work well together and make the most of every nugget in the accomplished script.

Steve McQueen *Supply Sgt Eustice Clay* • Jackie Gleason *Master Sgt Maxwell Slaughter* • Tuesday Weld *Bobby Jo Pepperdine* • Tony Bill *Private Jerry Meltzner* • Tom Poston *Lieutenant Magee* • Paul Hartman *Chief of Police* • Adam West *Captain Blekeley* ■ *Dir* Ralph Nelson • *Scr* Maurice Richlin, Blake Edwards, from the novel by William Goldman

Soldier of Fortune   ★★★

Romantic adventure
1955 · US · Colour · 95mins

Clark Gable's first movie as an independent freelancer, away from the shackles of his 25-year stint as "King" of MGM. Twentieth Century-Fox was trying out its new CinemaScope process in a variety of locations, and here Gable finds himself in Hong Kong as a smuggler, hired to locate Susan Hayward's husband Gene Barry, who's either dead or over in Red China, or both. Skilled director Edward Dmytryk makes this melodramatic tosh seem extremely exciting, and Gable and Hayward strike suitably starry sparks from each other.

Clark Gable *Hank Lee* • Susan Hayward *Jane Hoyt* • Michael Rennie *Inspector Merryweather* • Gene Barry *Louis Hoyt* ■ *Dir* Edward Dmytryk • *Scr* Ernest K Gann, from his novel

Soldier of Orange   ★★★★

War drama   1977 · Neth · Colour · 165mins

Paul Verhoeven's lavish, personal war epic re-creates the Nazi invasion of his native Holland and shows the effects it has on six university students, all but one of whom become involved in the Resistance. Known for his graphic depiction of sex and violence, Verhoeven's approach here is more traditional and boasts two splendid leading performances from Rutger Hauer and Jeroen Krabbé. Edward Fox appears as the head of British military intelligence and Susan Penhaligon is on hand to give both Hauer and Krabbé a squeeze when they escape to Britain. In Dutch with English subtitles.

Rutger Hauer *Erik* • Jeroen Krabbé *Gus* • Peter Faber *Will* • Derek De Lint *Alex* • Edward Fox *Colonel Rafelli* • Susan Penhaligon *Susan* ■ *Dir* Paul Verhoeven • *Scr* Gerard Soeteman, Kees Holierhoek, Paul Verhoeven, from an autobiography by Erik Hazelhoff Roelfzema

A Soldier's Daughter Never Cries   ★★★ 15

Drama   1998 · US · Colour · 126mins

James Ivory may have freed himself from the Henry James/EM Forster orbit, but this remains a bookish story about a young girl and her relationship with her mum and novelist dad (loosely based on James Jones, author of *From Here to Eternity*). Divided into three sections, the daughter is seen as a girl in Paris coping with an adopted brother, as a troubled teenager and then, back in America, as a promiscuous twentysomething. There are good performances behind that terrible title, though Kris Kristofferson rather overdoes the Hemingway/James Jones routine. Contains swearing. ▣

Kris Kristofferson *Bill Willis* • Barbara Hershey *Marcella Willis* • LeeLee Sobieski *Channe, aged 14* • Jesse Bradford *Billy, aged 14* • Dominique Blanc *Candida* • Jane Birkin *Mrs Fortescue* ■ *Dir* James Ivory • *Scr* James Ivory, Ruth Prawer Jhabvala, from the novel by Kaylie Jones • *Producer* Ismail Merchant

A Soldier's Story   ★★★★ 15

Drama   1984 · US · Colour · 96mins

Never has a whodunit packed such a loaded punch. Adapted by Charles Fuller from his own Pulitzer Prize-winning play, this is not just a gripping mystery, but also a far-reaching investigation into the widely differing aspirations and expectations that divide, as much as unite, America's black population. Howard Rollins gives a showy performance as the army captain sent to a camp in the Deep South, to discover who murdered a black sergeant. Everyone seemingly has motive and opportunity and, under Norman Jewison's tight direction, the supporting cast, led by Denzel Washington and the Oscar-nominated Adolph Caesar, give nothing away. ▣

Howard E Rollins Jr *Captain Davenport* • Adolph Caesar *Master Sergeant Vernon C Waters* • Art Evans *Private Wilkie* • David Alan Grier *Corporal Cobb* • David Harris *Private Smalls* • Dennis Lipscomb *Captain Taylor* • Larry Riley *CJ Memphis* • Robert Townsend *Corporal Ellis* • Denzel Washington *Private Peterson* • Patti LaBelle *Big Mary* ■ *Dir* Norman Jewison • *Scr* Charles Fuller, from his play

A Soldier's Sweetheart   ★★ 15

War drama   1998 · US · Colour · 106mins

The mystical side of warfare is explored in this small-screen offering. Shy young woman Georgina Cates sneaks into Vietnam to join medic boyfriend Kiefer Sutherland during the height of jungle combat. She soon adjusts to her surroundings, but her growing fascination with, and eventual participation in the activities of a mysterious Green Beret unit threaten her romance. Her descent into the brotherhood of killers is more implied than explicit, though the film does contain its fair share of profanity,

violence and bloody hospital scenes. Contains swearing and some violence. ▣

Kiefer Sutherland *Rat Kiley* • Skeet Ulrich *Mark Fossie* • Georgina Cates *Marianne Bell* • Daniel London *Eddie Diamond* • Louis Vanaria *Bobbie D* ■ *Dir* Thomas Michael Donnelly • *Scr* Thomas Michael Donnelly, from the short story *Sweetheart of the Song Tra Bong* by Tim O'Brien

A Soldier's Tale   ★★★

Second World War drama
1988 · NZ · Colour · 99mins

Touching, offbeat wartime drama that did not even get a video release in the UK. Gabriel Byrne is the British soldier in France in the latter years of the Second World War, who falls for a French girl (Marianne Basler) who may or may not be a collaborator. Although it's a little too downbeat for its own good, the two leads deliver moving performances and it's directed with some sensitivity by New Zealander Larry Parr. Look out, too, for a brief appearance from Judge Reinhold. Contains violence, swearing and nudity.

Gabriel Byrne *Saul* • Marianne Basler *Belle* • Paul Wyett *Charlie* • Judge Reinhold *Yank* ■ *Dir* Larry Parr • *Scr* Grant Hinden Miller, Larry Parr, from the novel by MK Joseph

Soldiers Three   ★★★ U

Adventure   1951 · US · BW · 91mins

A rumbustious North-West Frontier tale, in which several Rudyard Kipling stories have been put through the MGM blender and reduced to pulp. The soldiers are a likeable bunch; Stewart Granger, Walter Pidgeon and David Niven among them, who cope with revolting natives, dusky maidens and other problems of that ilk. Whenever the plot stalls, which is often, a horde of Indians appears on the horizon. It's not as funny as *Carry On Up the Khyber*, but it is played for laughs.

Stewart Granger *Private Archibald Ackroyd* • Walter Pidgeon *Colonel Brunswick* • David Niven *Captain Pindenny* • Robert Newton *Private Jock Sykes* • Cyril Cusack *Private Dennis Malloy* • Greta Gynt *Crenshaw* • Frank Allenby *Colonel Groat* • Robert Coote *Major Mercer* • Dan O'Herlihy *Sergeant Murphy* • Michael Ansara *Manik Rao* ■ *Dir* Tay Garnett • *Scr* Marguerite Roberts, Tom Reed, Malcolm Stuart Boylan, from the short stories by Rudyard Kipling

The Solid Gold Cadillac   ★★★ U

Comedy   1956 · US · BW and Colour · 95mins

A clever idea and perfect casting make a delightful comedy. Judy Holliday is the small shareholder who embarrasses the crooked directors of a big company by innocently questioning their high salaries and is given a meaningless job to keep her quiet. In the tradition of Frank Capra, the little woman eventually triumphs over the pompous bosses. No one suggests Judy could run the company any better and Paul Douglas figures as the former chairman who becomes her ally and romantic interest. Richard Quine ably directed the comedy in black-and-white with a flash of colour at the end. ▣

Judy Holliday *Laura Partridge* • Paul Douglas *Edward L McKeever* • Fred Clark *Clifford Snell* • John Williams *John T Blessington* • Hiram Sherman *Harry Harkness* • Neva Patterson *Amelia Shotgraven* • Ralph Dumke *Warren Gillie* • Ray Collins *Alfred Metcalfe* • Arthur O'Connell *Jenkins* ■ *Dir* Richard Quine • *Scr* Abe Burrows, from the play by George S Kaufman, Howard Teichmann

Solitaire for 2   ★ 15

Romantic comedy
1994 · UK · Colour · 100mins

An unwatchable romantic comedy that sent punters away groaning in droves. Amanda Pays is implausible as a woman who reads minds, aware that all the men she dates are only interested in one thing. Academic philanderer Mark Frankel is determined to conquer Pays and their battle forms the bedrock of a bad film. Utterly ridiculous, despite support from Maryam D'Abo, Helen Lederer and Annette Crosbie, this comedy simply doesn't work. Contains swearing and sexual references. ▣

Mark Frankel *Daniel Becker* • Amanda Pays *Katie* • Roshan Seth *Sandip Tamar* • Jason Isaacs *Harry* • Maryam D'Abo *Caroline* • Helen Lederer *Cop* • Malcolm Cooper *Cop* • Annette Crosbie *Mrs Dwyer* • Neil Mullarkey *Parris* ■ *Dir/Scr* Gary Sinyor

Solo   ★★ 18

Science-fiction action thriller
1996 · US/Mex · Colour · 89mins

A pumped-up Mario Van Peebles plays a cyber-soldier who refuses to kill innocent Latin American villagers and becomes their friend, in this derivative, but amiable sci-fi action thriller. You'll recognise themes, scenes and characters from dozens of other movies –particularly *Terminator 2* – but Van Peebles isn't bad as a lower budget Arnie and it displays much less violence and more heart than you would expect. That said, there are a few too many moments of unintentional comedy, caused by the ropey macho dialogue and the hammy performances of bad guys William Sadler and Barry Corbin. ▣ DVD

Mario Van Peebles *Solo* • Barry Corbin *General Clyde Haynes* • William Sadler *Colonel Madden* • Jaime Gomez *Lorenzo* ■ *Dir* Norberto Barba • *Scr* David Corley, from the novel *Weapon* by Robert Mason

Solo for Sparrow   ★★

Crime drama   1962 · UK · BW · 56mins

What's it all about, Michael? Two years before his career-making performance in *Zulu*, the future double Oscar-winner was marking time taking small parts in humdrum crime dramas such as this. The nominal star is Donald Houston, playing a policeman who takes a leave of absence to set up his own detective agency. The film was not seen in America until 1966, when the producers took advantage of Caine's newfound success and released it with his name above the title.

Anthony Newlands *Mr Reynolds* • Glyn Houston *Inspector Sparrow* • Nadja Regin *Mrs Reynolds* • Michael Coles *Pin Norman* • Allan Cuthbertson *Chief Supt Symington* • Ken Wayne *Baker* • Jerry Stovin *Lewis* • Michael Caine *Mooney* ■ *Dir* Gordon Flemyng • *Scr* Roger Marshall, from the novel *The Gunner* by Edgar Wallace

U = SUITABLE FOR ALL   Uc = SUITABLE FOR ALL, ESPECIALLY FOR YOUNG CHILDREN (VIDEO ONLY)   PG = PARENTAL GUIDANCE

Solomon and Gaenor

★★★ **15**

Period romance 1998 · UK · Colour · 103mins

Filmed in both Welsh and English, director/writer Paul Morrison's debut feature is a tragic tale of forbidden love. Set in 1911 in the Welsh valleys, the Romeo and Juliet-esque narrative finds chapel-goer Gaenor (Nia Roberts) falling for door-to-door salesman Solomon (Ioan Gruffudd). Yet Solomon has concealed his Jewish identity and, in a heated atmosphere of anti-Semitism, the couple take desperate measures to preserve their love. Both Gruffudd and Roberts are outstanding as the lovers; their performances rising out of the bleak depression and sodden landscape of the Black Mountains. Ultimately, however, this is a grim and sorry tale, and definitely not for the faint at heart. In English, Welsh and Yiddish with subtitles. Contains sex scenes, violence.

Ioan Gruffudd *Solomon* • Nia Roberts *Gaenor* • Sue Jones Davies *Gwen* • William Thomas *Idris* • Mark Lewis Jones *Crad* • Maureen Lipman *Rezl* • David Horovitch *Isaac* • Bethan Ellis Owen *Bronwen* • Adam Jenkins *Thomas* ■ *Dir/Scr* Paul Morrison

Solomon and Sheba ★★ **PG**

Biblical epic 1959 · US · Colour · 135mins

Historically dodgy, generally stodgy epic with a black-wigged Yul Brynner courting scantily clad Gina Lollobrigida in days of Biblical yore. While *Ben-Hur*, *Barabbas* and *El Cid* show how good epics can be, *Solomon and Sheba* has all the weaknesses of the genre, notably a script brimming with non sequiturs and inane Americanisms. Despite some eye-catching designs and photography by Freddie Young, the picture was probably doomed when the original star, Tyrone Power, died on set. That disaster, together with a critical drubbing and poor audiences, caused the director, King Vidor, to abandon the movie business for good. 🖭

Yul Brynner *Solomon* • Gina Lollobrigida *Magda, Queen Of Sheba* • George Sanders *Adonijah* • Marisa Pavan *Abishag* • David Farrar *Pharaoh* • Jim Crawford *Joab* • Laurence Naismith *Hezrai* • Jose Nieto *Ahab* • Alejandro Rey *Sittar* ■ *Dir* King Vidor • *Scr* Anthony Veillier, Paul Dudley, George Bruce, from a story by Crane Wilbur • *Art Director* Richard Day, Alfred Sweeney

Solomon's Choice ★★★ **PG**

Drama 1992 · US · Colour · 92mins

Unlike Hollywood, where films often begin with the plausible and end with the hysterical, American television movies generally contain a great deal of sense. Writers and directors regularly anchor their films in an emotional reality and supply scenes with plenty of detail so that authenticity seeps into every scene. Congratulations, then, to Sandra Jennings, Maggie Kleinman (writers) and Andy Tennant (director) who combine a teenager with cheerleader looks and her leukaemia, a family rift and her younger brother as possible saviour, with conviction and fresh performances. Only occasionally does their temptation to load the dice cause the film to teeter. 🖭

Joanna Kerns *Mary Ellen Robbins* • Bruce Davison *Richard Robbins* • Joe Mazzello [Joseph Mazzello] *Willy Robbins* • Reese Witherspoon *Cassie Robbins* ■ *Dir* Andy Tennant • *Scr* Sandra Jennings, Maggie Kleinman, from a story by Sandra Jennings

Some Came Running

★★★ **PG**

Drama 1958 · US · Colour · 130mins

Dismissed in its day as hokum, this can now be fully appreciated for what it is: a highly stylised MGM melodrama from ace director Vincente Minnelli. The fireworks of the finale are exemplary and there is an extraordinarily watchable cast, headed by Frank Sinatra at his most convincing. Perhaps the real acting revelation is Dean Martin as Bama Dillert, the man who steadfastly refuses to remove his hat, but gals Shirley MacLaine and, particularly, Martha Hyer are also mighty fine. High-blown stuff, and a little long, but Elmer Bernstein's score keeps it all moving. 🖭

Frank Sinatra *Dave Hirsh* • Dean Martin *Bama Dillert* • Shirley MacLaine *Ginny Moorhead* • Arthur Kennedy *Frank Hirsh* • Martha Hyer *Gwen French* • Nancy Gates *Edith Barclay* ■ *Dir* Vincente Minnelli • *Scr* John Patrick, Arthur Sheekman, from the novel by James Jones

Some Girls ★★★ **18**

Romantic comedy drama 1998 · US · Colour · 81mins

Engagingly quirky and often filthily funny twentysomething ensemble piece,which sadly disappeared straight to video over here. The story focuses on a disparate group of friends all looking for love in nineties LA, but none with any particular luck. Marissa Ribisi, who also co-wrote it, heads a hot young cast which also encompasses brother Giovanni, Michael Rapaport, Juliette Lewis and Jeremy Sisto (*Suicide Kings*), all of whom deliver exemplary performances. The film earned director Rory Kelly (*Sleep With Me*) a best director gong at last years Los Angeles Independent Film Festival. 🖭

Marissa Ribisi *Claire* • Juliette Lewis *April* • Giovanni Ribisi *Jason* • Jeremy Sisto *Chad* • Pamela Segall Adlon [Pamela Segall] *Jenn* • Kristen Dattilo *Suzanne* • Michael Rapaport *Neal* ■ *Dir* Rory Kelly • *Scr* Marissa Ribisi, Brie Shaffer

Some Girls Do ★★

Spy comedy thriller 1969 · UK · Colour · 93mins

Having played Bulldog Drummond with some aplomb in *Deadlier than the Male* in 1966, Richard Johnson is left high and dry in this risible sequel about a missing supersonic jet. Desperately seeking to spoof James Bond and cash in on the swinging sauciness of the sixties, director Ralph Thomas is content to operate with a plot that manages to be even flimsier than the costumes worn by the bevy of bad beauties.

Richard Johnson *Hugh Drummond* • Daliah Lavi *Baroness Helga Hagen* • Beba Loncar *Pandora* • James Villiers *Carl Petersen* • Sydne Rome *Flicky* • Ronnie Stevens *Peregrine Carruthers* • Robert Morley *Miss Mary* • Maurice Denham *Mr Mortimer* ■ *Dir*

Ralph Thomas • *Scr* David Osborn, Liz Charles-Williams, from the character created by HC ''Sapper'' McNeile

Some Kind of Hero ★★ **15**

Comedy 1982 · US · Colour · 92mins

Brilliant stand-up comedian Richard Pryor enjoyed mixed fortunes when he swapped the stage for the silver screen. *Some Kind of Hero* tells the story of Vietnam vet Eddie Keller, who returns to the USA after six years imprisonment by the Viet Cong to find the life he left behind has disappeared. Jobs are scarce and Eddie is tempted to try crime to survive. It's an uneasy mix of comedy and drama with its worthy sentiments undermined by feeble attempts at humour. 🖭

Richard Pryor *Eddie Keller* • Margot Kidder *Toni* • Ray Sharkey *Vinnie* • Ronny Cox *Colonel Powers* • Lynne Moody *Lisa* • Olivia Cole *Jesse* • Paul Benjamin *Leon* ■ *Dir* Michael Pressman • *Scr* Robert Boris, James Kirkwood, from a novel by James Kirkwood

Some Kind of Wonderful

★★★★ **15**

Romantic drama 1987 · US · Colour · 90mins

Producer and writer John Hughes effectively remade *Pretty in Pink* here (even hiring the same director, Howard Deutch), only pausing to swap Molly Ringwald with Eric Stoltz in the role of the teen who can't choose between the neighbourhood beauty and the less glamorous (but infinitely nicer) best friend as his love interest. This is gentler and more subtle than *Pretty in Pink*, with *Back to the Future*'s Lea Thompson in one of her best roles as the spoilt girl that garage attendant Stoltz falls for, and Mary Stuart Masterson delightful as the tomboy who secretly harbours deeper feelings for her male friend. Stoltz makes an effective leading man, giving a touching performance in what is a genuinely charming film. 🖭

Eric Stoltz *Keith Nelson* • Mary Stuart Masterson *Watts* • Lea Thompson *Amanda Jones* • Craig Sheffer *Hardy Jenns* • John Ashton *Cliff Nelson* • Elias Koteas *Skinhead* • Molly Hagan *Shayne* • Chynna Phillips *Mia* ■ *Dir* Howard Deutch • *Scr* John Hughes

Some Like It Hot ★★★★★ **U**

Classic comedy 1959 · US · BW · 116mins

Everyone must be familiar with this cracking cross-dressing comedy by now, so how about a little trivia? Amazingly, director Billy Wilder originally wrote the film for Bob Hope and Danny Kaye, and considered Frank Sinatra as an alternative to Jack Lemmon in the Daphne role. Not content with imitating the voice of Cary Grant, Tony Curtis based his body language on Grace Kelly. He had little time for Marilyn Monroe and described kissing her as like kissing Hitler (ironically, the name she gave to Wilder for bullying her on the set). Yet the personality clashes sparked a true film classic, for, as Joe E Brown famously says at the end of the movie, ''Nobody's perfect!''. 🖭

Marilyn Monroe *Sugar Kane Kowa* • Tony Curtis *Joe/Josephine* • Jack Lemmon *Jerry/Daphne* • George Raft *Spats Columbo* • Pat O'Brien *Mulligan* • Joe E Brown *Osgood E*

Fielding III • Nehemiah Persoff *Little Bonaparte* • Joan Shawlee *Sweet Sue* • Billy Gray *Sig Poliakoff* ■ *Dir* Billy Wilder • *Scr* Billy Wilder, Ial Diamond, from the film *Fanfares of Love* by Robert Thoeren, M Logan • *Costume Designer* Orry-Kelly

Some Mother's Son

★★★★ **15**

Political drama 1996 · Ire/US · Colour · 106mins

This, while it touches the raw nerve of Northern Irish politics, shows Helen Mirren's formidable ability; as a widowed mother who discovers her son is involved with the IRA and fighting for him when he is on the prison hunger strike during which ten activists died in the early eighties. Director Terry George makes no secret of whose side he's on, but Helen Mirren extends propaganda into an unsentimental, but poignant, portrait of universal motherhood. Contains swearing, violence. 🖭

Helen Mirren *Kathleen Quigley* • Fionnula Flanagan *Annie Higgins* • Aidan Gillen *Gerard Quigley* • David O'Hara *Frank Higgins* • John Lynch *Bobby Sands* • Tom Hollander *Farnsworth* • Tim Woodward *Tim Harrington* • Ciaran Hinds *Damny Boyle* ■ *Dir* Terry George • *Scr* Jim Sheridan, Terry George

Some People ★★★

Melodrama 1962 · UK · Colour · 93mins

This coffee bar musical arrived two months before the Beatles, but its moral values are those of the early fifties: motorbikes and pop music equal juvenile delinquency, and what young tearaways need is spiritual guidance. (The film's profits went to the Duke of Edinburgh's relatively new Award Scheme, which is heavily plugged.) Ray Brooks and David Hemmings are among the ton-up boys who are taken under the wing of loveable church organist Kenneth More. Not only naive charm, but unusual Bristol locations and a bouncy title song.

Kenneth More *Mr Smith* • Ray Brooks *Johnnie* • Annika Wills *Anne Smith* • David Andrews *Bill* • Angela Douglas *Terry* • David Hemmings *Bert* • Timothy Nightingale *Tim* • Frankie Dymon Jr *Jimmy* ■ *Dir* Clive Donner • *Scr* John Eldridge

Some Will, Some Won't

★ **PG**

Comedy 1969 · UK · Colour · 86mins

Some people really will find this comic calamity funny, but they'll be in a very small minority. If this insipid remake of *Laughter in Paradise* is supposed to be a comedy, it's not only an insult to the memory of the original, but it also breaches the Trades Descriptions Act. What makes this an even more depressing experience is the utter waste of fine cast. 🖭

Ronnie Corbett *Herbert Russell* • Thora Hird *Agnes Russell* • Michael Hordern *Deniston Russell* • Leslie Phillips *Simon Russell* • Barbara Murray *Lucille* • Wilfrid Brambell *Henry Russell* • Dennis Price *Benson* • James Robertson-Justice *Sir Charles Robson* ■ *Dir* Duncan Wood • *Scr* Lew Schwarz, from the film *Laughter in Paradise* by Jack Davies, Michael Pertwee

Somebody Has to Shoot the Picture ★★★ 18

Drama 1990 · US · Colour · 99mins

Frank Pierson, the acclaimed scriptwriter of *Cat Ballou* and *Dog Day Afternoon* and the director of Barbra Streisand's *A Star Is Born*, is at the helm of this above-average TV movie. Roy Scheider gives a typically gritty performance as a photo-journalist hired by a drug dealer on Florida's death row to record his execution. Adapting from his own book, *Slow Coming Dark*, co-writer Doug Magee lays out the clues behind a possible miscarriage of justice with great skill, while Pierson's astute pacing will have you nibbling your nails as the fatal deadline approaches. ▭

Roy Scheider *Paul Marish* • Bonnie Bedelia *Hannah McGrath* • Robert Carradine *Jerry Brown* • Tom Nowicki *Steve March* • Arliss Howard *Raymond Eames* • AndréBraugher *Dan Weston* • Tom Schuster *Rusher* ■ *Dir* Frank Pierson • *Scr* Doug Magee, Daniel Pyne, from the book *Slow Coming Dark* by Doug Magee

Somebody Killed Her Husband ★★ PG

Comedy mystery 1978 · US · Colour · 92mins

Farrah Fawcett (in her first starring feature role) turns amateur detective with Jeff Bridges to find out who killed her husband in this lame comedy mystery. Director Lamont Johnson is clearly aiming for a sophisticated caper in the Hitchcock vein, and the engaging climax during the Macy's Thanksgiving Parade almost gets there. The ex-Charlie's Angel isn't bad but she's a little too lightweight to carry the melodramatic load in such inconsequential fluff. ▭

Farrah Fawcett-Majors [Farrah Fawcett] *Jenny Moore* • Jeff Bridges *Jerry Green* • John Wood *Ernest Van Santen* • Tammy Grimes *Audrey Van Santen* • John Glover *Hubert Little* • Patricia Elliott *Helene* • Mary McCarty *Flora* ■ *Dir* Lamont Johnson • *Scr* Reginald Rose

Somebody Loves Me ★★★ U

Musical biography
1952 · US · Colour · 90mins

This typical high fictionalised musical biopic was Betty Hutton's penultimate picture, and her last for Paramount. When studio executives refused to give in to her demand that her second husband, Charles O'Curran, who choreographed the film, be allowed to direct her subsequent pictures, she left, and her career was almost over. Hutton is as energetic as ever in this rags-to-riches story of vaudeville entertainer Blossom Seeley, and delivers several fine songs in her raucous and sentimental manner. Ralph Meeker, rarely seen outside dark melodramas, is good as her husband and stage partner Benny Fields.

Betty Hutton *Blossom Seeley* • Ralph Meeker *Benny Fields* • Robert Keith *Sam Doyle* • Adele Jergens *Nola Beach* • Billie Bird *Essie* • Henry Slate *Forrest* • Sid Tomack *Lake* • Ludwig Stossel *Mr Grauman* • Jack Benny ■ *Dir/Scr* Irving Brecher

Somebody to Love ★★★ 18

Romantic drama 1994 · US · Colour · 98mins

A meandering menagerie of characters merge here in this stream of consciousness, urban drama. Steve Buscemi, Stanley Tucci, Quentin Tarantino and Anthony Quinn all have bizarre cameos in this story of the unrequited love felt by aspiring actress Rosie Perez, for down on his luck TV cowboy Harvey Keitel. Perez is the energy and fun in the film and it needs her. However, though both an interesting and perceptive exercise by director Alexandre Rockwell, Perez just isn't dynamic enough to make this any more than a strange and slightly nihilistic trip. Ultimately it says very little and goes nowhere. ▭

Rosie Perez *Mercedes* • Harvey Keitel *Harry* • Michael DeLorenzo *Ernesto* • Stanley Tucci *George* • Steve Buscemi *Mickey* • Anthony Quinn *Emilio* • Samuel Fuller *Old man on highway* • Quentin Tarantino *Bartender* ■ *Dir* Alexandre Rockwell • *Scr* Alexandre Rockwell, Sergei Bodrov

Somebody Up There Likes Me ★★★★ PG

Biographical drama 1956 · US · BW · 108mins

The role of middleweight champ Rocky Graziano was intended for James Dean, who unfortunately had a date with destiny on the highway. Into the ring stepped Paul Newman in only his third film after *The Silver Chalice* and *The Rack* (released at the same time as this), and he became a star overnight. Newman brings to the role a lot of Marlon Brando's Method mannerisms and the script drags in rather too many social issues for comfort. It's very much a product, albeit an important one from the Actors Studio of New York in the fifties, directed by Robert Wise. If you watch closely, you might catch Steve McQueen making his screen debut. ▭

Paul Newman *Rocky Graziano* • Pier Angeli *Norma* • Everett Sloane *Irving Cohen* • Eileen Heckart *Ma Barbella* • Sal Mineo *Romolo* • Harold J Stone *Nick Barbella* • Steve McQueen *Fidel* • Robert Loggia *Frankie Peppo* ■ *Dir* Robert Wise • *Scr* Ernest Lehman, from the autobiography by Rocky Graziano, Rowland Barber • *Cinematographer* Joseph Ruttenberg • *Art Director* Cedric Gibbons, Malcolm Brown

Someone at the Door ★★

Comedy thriller 1936 · UK · BW · 74mins

This is one of those rare instances when the remake is superior to the original, although, in this case, that's not saying much, as the 1950 version of Campbell and Dorothy Christie's old theatrical chestnut wasn't very good either. Contrived only goes part way to describing this creaky thriller, in which a reporter desperate for a scoop stumbles across a real mystery while staging a fake murder. Noah Beery Sr and Edward Chapman add a touch of spice as jewel thieves, but it's Billy Milton and Aileen Marson who are highly resistible as the hack and his accomplice sister.

Billy Milton *Ronald Martin* • Aileen Marson *Sally Martin* • Noah Beery Sr [Noah Beery] *Harry Kapel* • Edward Chapman *Price* • John Irwin *Bill Reid* • Hermione Gingold *Mrs Appleby* • Charles Mortimer *Sergeant Spedding* ■ *Dir*

Herbert Brenon • *Scr* Jack Davies, Marjorie Deans, from the play by Dorothy Christie, Campbell Christie

Someone at the Door ★★ U

Crime comedy 1950 · UK · BW · 61mins

A remake of Herbert Brenon's 1936 version of the hit West End play, this is Hammer hokum of the hoariest kind. There isn't a semblance of suspense in the shenanigans that follow journalist Michael Medwin's bizarre decision to make headlines with the fake killing of his sister. Not even the arrival of jewel thieves at the haunted house they've inherited can revive one's fast-fading interest. However, there is one good wheeze, during the credit sequence, when director Francis Searle reveals that the front of the old house is merely a flat piece of scenery erected in a field.

Michael Medwin *Ronnie Martin* • Garry Marsh *Kapel* • Yvonne Owen *Sally Martin* • Hugh Latimer *Bill Reid* • Danny Green *Price* • Campbell Singer *Inspector Spedding* • John Kelly *PC O'Brien* ■ *Dir* Francis Searle • *Scr* AR Rawlinson, from a play by Dorothy Christie, Campbell Christie

Someone behind the Door ★

Crime drama 1971 · Fr /UK · Colour · 95mins

The strange pairing of Anthony Perkins and Charles Bronson (and Bronson's wife Jill Ireland) is the most interesting thing about this psychological suspense drama. It's also interesting to see Bronson cast in a different role for a change, playing a lost and befuddled amnesiac who doesn't know he's a fugitive psychotic. When doctor Perkins discovers who he is, he decides to use him as a tool in his plans for revenge against his adulterous wife. From the American cast to the European setting, the movie never seems to have its finger on exactly where everything is or what it's all about, and drifts along at a pretty slow pace.

Charles Bronson *Stranger* • Anthony Perkins *Laurence Jeffries* • Jill Ireland *Frances Jeffries* • Henri Garcin *Paul Damien* • Adriano Magestretti *Andrew* • Agathe Natanson *Lucy* ■ *Dir* Nicolas Gessner • *Scr* Marc Behm, Jacques Robert, Nicolas Gessner, Lorenzo Ventavoli, by Jacques Robert

Someone Else's America ★★★ 15

Comedy drama
1995 · Fr/UK/Ger · Colour · 95mins

Winner of the audience prize at Cannes, this well-meaning drama gave Tom Conti another chance to play a heavily accented Mediterranean type. As the Spanish bar owner living in Brooklyn with his blind mother, Conti gives a heartfelt performance that's matched by Miki Manojlovic as the illegal immigrant from Montenegro who becomes his lodger. Released at a time when the Balkan crisis was front-page news, this gentle, if unfocused, fable takes on a more serious tone when Manojlovic's grandmother decides to leave Montenegro and head for the promised land of America to reunite her grandchildren with their father. In English and Serbo-Croatian with subtitles. Contains swearing. ▭

Tom Conti *Alonso* • Miki Manojlovic *Bayo* • Maria Casarès *Alonso's mother* • Zorka Manojlovic *Bayo's mother* ■ *Dir* Goran Paskaljevic • *Scr* Gordon Mihic

Someone Else's Child ★★ PG

Drama based on a true story
1994 · US · Colour · 92mins

They leap out at you from the pages of your newspaper and induce gasps of surprise when they reach the TV bulletins, but, for all their drama and human interest, true-life stories only occasionally make for good cinema. America's TV-movie industry churns them out by the dozen, the less likely the better. Here, a mother discovers her baby was switched at birth and then crusades to regain her natural child from its abusive adoptive parents as well as fighting to keep custody of her ''son''. ▭

Lisa Hartman Black *Cory Maddox* • Bruce Davison *John Callahan* • Louise Fletcher *Faye* • Jonathan Hoog *Christopher Maddox* ■ *Dir* John Power • *Scr* Cindy Myers

Someone Is Bleeding ★★★

Thriller 1974 · Fr · Colour · 100mins

Making the eleventh of her thirteen appearances for Georges Lautner, Mireille Darc plays against type in this engrossing psychological thriller. As the sociopathic drug addict who spells trouble for all the men she encounters, Darc displays an icy detachment that ensnares television writer Claude Brasseur. Although he usually injected a note of levity into his thrillers, Lautner plays this adaptation of Richard Matheson's novel dead straight, casting a wintry pall over the Riviera coastline that not only reflects Darc's cold heart, but also the film's effectively downbeat ending. French dialogue dubbed into English..

Alain Delon *Marc* • Claude Brasseur *Francois* • Mireille Darc *Peggy* • Nicoletta Machiavelli *Jacqueline* • Fiora Altoviti *Denis* ■ *Dir* Georges Lautner • *Scr* Georges Lautner, from the novel by Richard Matheson

Someone She Knows ★★

Thriller 1994 · US · Colour

Another tragic, American crime story gets the airbrushed TV-movie treatment in this occasionally moving melodrama. Markie Post is the distraught mother whose five-year-old daughter is murdered, possibly by someone close to the family. When the FBI and the local cops fail to find the killer, she then decides to carry out her own investigation with the help of sympathetic neighbour Gerald McRaney. Director Eric Laneuville handles the material competently enough, although it's indistinguishable from many other similar movies.

Markie Post *Laurie Philips* • Gerald McRaney *Frank Mayfield* • Jeffrey Nordling *Greg Philips* • Sharon Lawrence *Sharon* • Shawn Modrell *Cheryl Mayfield* ■ *Dir* Eric Laneuville • *Scr* Carol Monpere

Someone to Die For ★★ 18

Thriller 1995 · US · Colour · 97mins

Director Clay Borris does his best to keep you involved in this convoluted thriller, coaxing a suitably angst-ridden performance from his star Corbin

U = SUITABLE FOR ALL Uc = SUITABLE FOR ALL, ESPECIALLY FOR YOUNG CHILDREN (VIDEO ONLY) PG = PARENTAL GUIDANCE

Bernsen, who plays a cop suspected of murdering the colleagues whose negligence led to his daughter's death. But not even the surfeit of plot can prevent you from picking out the culprit almost immediately. It's a pity that Shell Danielson, who co-stars with Ally Walker, couldn't put *Fatal Attraction* to the back of her mind when she concocted the story on which this TV movie is based. Contains swearing, violence, sex scenes. ▣

Corbin Bernsen *Detective Jack Davis* • Ally Walker *Alex Donaldson* • Robert Stewart [Rob Stewart] *Sergeant Holliman* • Shell Danielson *Lydia Kellerman* ■ *Dir* Clay Borris • *Scr* Douglas J Sloan, Shuki Levy, from a story by Shell Danielson

Someone to Love ★★★ 15

Comedy drama 1987 · US · Colour · 104mins
Initially to be titled *Is It You?*, this discussion of love and loneliness was written and directed by leading independent Henry Jaglom. He also stars, playing a film-maker who seeks to solve his romantic problems by getting his friends to reveal their deepest emotions during a Valentine's party. While there are a few profound insights and the odd smart remark, it's not an easy picture to get involved in, although it's hard to resist Sally Kellerman's kooky performance. The highlight is Orson Welles making his final film appearance. Contains swearing. ▣

Orson Welles *Danny's friend* • Henry Jaglom *Danny Sapir* • Andrea Marcovicci *Helen Eugene* • Michael Emil *Mickey Sapir* • Sally Kellerman *Edith Helm* ■ *Dir/Scr* Henry Jaglom

Someone to Love Me ★

Drama 1998 · US · Colour
Jessica Bowman stars as a lonely teenager whose promiscuous ways come back to haunt her when she is date-raped by a star student. Because of her reckless behaviour, she has trouble convincing the police and her mother (Lynda Carter of *Wonder Woman* fame) that this time, she said "No". Good intentions and a social conscience don't justify this sort of simple-minded manipulative drama, while the cheap production values make this just another by-the-numbers TV movie.

Lynda Carter *Diane Young* • Jessica Bowman *Cayley Young* • Scott Foley *Ian Hall* • Mary Ellen Trainor *Jocelyn Hart* ■ *Dir* Chuck Bowman • *Scr* Elizabeth Gill

Someone to Watch over Me ★★★★ 15

Thriller 1987 · US · Colour · 102mins
This intelligent thriller remains one of Ridley Scott's most quietly satisfying works. Tom Berenger plays a tough police detective who gets to sample the high life when he is assigned to protect beautiful, wealthy Mimi Rogers, the key witness in a murder trial. It may lack the power of the director's *Thelma and Louise* and *Blade Runner*, but this is still a beautifully shot, stylish affair. Howard Franklin's clever script touches upon issues of class and voyeurism, while still producing the goods in the suspense stakes and the performances are first rate: Berenger is grumpily charismatic, while Rogers

shines as the woman in distress. Contains swearing, and some violence and nudity. ▣

Tom Berenger *Mike Keegan* • Mimi Rogers *Claire Gregory* • Lorraine Bracco *Ellie Keegan* • Jerry Orbach *Lieutenant Garber* • John Rubinstein *Neil Steinhart* • Andreas Katsulas *Joey Venza* ■ *Dir* Ridley Scott • *Scr* Howard Franklin • *Cinematographer* Steven Poster

Someone's Watching ★★★ 18

Erotic thriller 1993 · US · Colour · 87mins
Also known as *Caroline at Midnight*, this erotic thriller has the dual advantage of a nail-biting script and a splendid cast to make the endless twists seem totally convincing. What with phone calls from dead girlfriends, drug-dealing cops and romances with terrified wives, director Scott McGinnis's film never lets up for a second, right down to its unexpected ending. It's certainly racy in places, but not all of the action takes place in the bedroom. Mia Sara stands out in a cast that also boasts Tim Daly, Judd Nelson and Virginia Madsen. Contains violence, swearing, nudity. ▣

Timothy Daly *Ray Dillon* • Mia Sara *Victoria Dillon* • Paul LeMat *Emmett Rourke* • Clayton Rohner *Jack Lynch* • Judd Nelson *Phil Gallo* • Virginia Madsen *Susan Prince* ■ *Dir* Scott McGinnis • *Scr* Travis Rink

Someone's Watching Me! ★★★

Thriller 1978 · US · Colour · 100mins
A rare excursion into TV movie thrillerdom for horror director John Carpenter. A peeping tom with a telescope bugs Lauren Hutton's apartment and terrorises her with scary phone calls. Only best friend Adrienne Barbeau believes her story and sets out to prove it. Taking all its cues from *Rear Window*, Carpenter's script and direction are full of tight, taut little touches that raise it above the TV norm and disguise its blatant Hitchcock homages. The atmosphere of unexpectancy and dread is well sustained even though Hutton leaves much to be desired as the central focus of the puzzle.

Lauren Hutton *Leigh Michaels* • David Birney *Paul Winkless* • Adrienne Barbeau *Sophie* • Charles Cyphers *Gary Hunt* • Michael Laurence *TV announcer* ■ *Dir/Scr* John Carpenter

Something about Love ★★★ 15

Drama 1987 · Can · Colour · 89mins
Resisting the temptation to wallow in nostalgia, this is an engaging variation on the theme of the returning exile. In addition to his starring role, Stefan Wodoslawsky wrote the semi-autobiographical script, in which a Los Angeles TV producer comes home to Nova Scotia to visit his dying father. The Ukrainian background adds to the interest, but there's nothing particularly new about the squabbles between father and son. However, both Wodoslawsky and Jan Rubes throw themselves into their roles, and there's a nice strain of humour to leaven the mix of regret and recrimination. ▣

Stefan Wodoslawsky *Wally Olynyk* • Jan Rubes *Stan Olynyk* • Jennifer Dale *Bobbie* • Diana Reis *Elaine* ■ *Dir* Tom Berry • *Scr* Tom Berry, Stefan Wodoslawsky

something big ★

Comedy western 1971 · US · Colour · 108mins
The only other movie title alongside *Tom Thumb*, to insist on lower case lettering in its original publicity – apt because this tasteless, would-be comedy western is very lower case indeed. Dean Martin enjoys his post-Matt Helm stardom by offering such a perilously lazy performance against veteran stalwarts Brian Keith and Ben Johnson, that you just want to shut your eyes and nod off. If you did, you'd miss British imports Carol White and Honor Blackman, but little else.

Dean Martin *Joe Baker* • Brian Keith *Colonel Morgan* • Honor Blackman *Mary Anna Morgan* • Carol White *Dover MacBride* • Ben Johnson *Jesse Bookbinder* • Albert Salmi *Johnny Cobb* • Don Knight *Tommy MacBride* • Joyce Van Patten *Polly Standall* • Denver Pyle *Junior Frisbee* ■ *Dir* Andrew V McLaglen • *Scr* James Lee Barrett

Something Borrowed, Something Blue ★★ 12

Romantic drama 1997 · US · Colour · 87mins
This is a disjointed hotch-potch of stories, loosely linked together by a contrived premise: an engaged magazine editor (Connie Sellecca), writing a story about three first-time brides, discovers each woman is concealing a secret from her fiancé that threatens to destroy the marriage plans. This TV movie also features ex-supermodel Twiggy who, along with Sellecca, manages to rise above this melodrama. ▣

Connie Sellecca *Monique D'Arcy* • Twiggy Lawson [Twiggy] *Eve Hamel* • Dina Merrill *Lydia D'Arcy* • Ken Howard *John Farrell* • Jameson Parker *Richard Ives* • Shawnee Smith *Teri* ■ *Dir* Gwen Arner • *Scr* Karol Ann Hoeffner, from the novel by Jillian Karr

Something for Joey ★★★★

Drama based on a true story 1977 · US · Colour · 96mins
A fine screenplay, superior acting and classy direction save this made-for-TV drama – based on the true-life relationship between a US college football star and his kid brother who is dying of leukaemia – from sentimentality. Geraldine Page and Steve Guttenberg both won praise for their performances and went on to greater fame and fortune. However, it is Jeff Lynas's sensitive portrayal of the afflicted brother, that provides the key to making this such a surprisingly effective, moving and uplifting film.

Geraldine Page *Anne Cappelletti* • Gerald S O'Loughlin *John Cappelletti Sr* • Marc Singer *John Cappelletti* • Jeff Lynas [Jeffrey Lynas] *Joey Cappelletti* • Linda Kelsey *Joyce Cappelletti/Narrator* • Brian Farrell *Marty Cappelletti* • Kathleen Beller *Jean Cappelletti* • Steve Guttenberg *Mike Cappelletti* ■ *Dir* Lou Antonio • *Scr* Jerry McNeely

Something for the Boys ★★★ U

Musical 1944 · US · Colour · 86mins
Cole Porter's 1943 stage production lost a lot on its transfer to the screen, including Ethel Merman and most of its score. What remains is a typically garish 20th Century-Fox musical, interesting today for the array of talent on display. The plot's about cousins Carmen Miranda, Vivian Blaine and Phil Silvers opening up their inherited southern plantation to army wives, and putting on a show to fund it. Silvers is terrific in a routine that owes much to his vaudeville background, while the gals (including Sheila Ryan and Cara Williams) and that new young crooner Perry Como, also put over numbers with style and verve.

Carmen Miranda *Chiquita Hart* • Michael O'Shea *Staff Sergeant Rocky Fulton* • Vivian Blaine *Blossom Hart* • Phil Silvers *Harry Hart* • Sheila Ryan *Melanie Walker* • Perry Como *Sergeant Laddie Green* • Glenn Langan *Lieutenant Ashley Crothers* ■ *Dir* Lewis Seiler • *Scr* Robert Ellis, Helen Logan, Frank Gabrielson, from a musical comedy by Herbert Fields, Dorothy Fields, Cole Porter

Something in Common ★★★ 15

Romantic comedy 1986 · US · Colour · 93mins
Ellen Burstyn, one of America's finest dramatic actresses, makes the most of a rare chance to demonstrate her comic prowess in this lively TV movie, in which she tries to come to terms with the fact that her 22-year-old son is having an affair with Tuesday Weld, a divorcee twice his age. The banter between the leads has a real zip to it, thanks to Susan Rice's sparkling script, while there's also some self-deprecating support from Eli Wallach. Contains swearing. ▣

Ellen Burstyn *Lynn Hollander* • Tuesday Weld *Shelly Grant* • Patrick Cassidy *Nick Hollander* • Don Murray *Theo Fontana* • Eli Wallach *Norman Voss* • Amanda Wyss *Laura Grant* ■ *Dir* Glenn Jordan • *Scr* Susan Rice

Something in the City ★★ U

Comedy 1950 · UK · BW · 76mins
After 40 years as a circus clown and music-hall comic, Richard Hearne finally found fame on TV as the fumbling old fool, Mr Pastry. But, as is often the case, the performer was less fond of the character to whom he owed his fortune than the public, and Hearne frequently sought to escape from the corny slapstick of his children's shows. Here, he plays a pavement artist who convinces his wife he is a high financier. The cheery street folk simply don't ring true and the pathos makes Chaplin look like a cynic.

Richard Hearne *William Ningle* • Garry Marsh *Mr Holley* • Ellen Pollock *Mrs Holley* • Betty Sinclair *Mrs Ningle* • Tom Gill *Richard* • Dora Bryan *Waitress* ■ *Dir* Maclean Rogers • *Scr* HF Maltby

Something Is Out There ★★★ 15

Science-fiction drama 1988 · US · Colour · 166mins
The pilot for an extremely short-lived series, this is a sci-fi thriller in the

same mould as *Alien Nation*, although this time the ET agent working alongside the LA cop is female and has a thing about her partner's hands. Hot on the trail of the shape-changing "xenomorph", Maryam D'Abo works well alongside the cynical Joe Cortese. But all eyes will be on the special effects created by John Dykstra and the make-up designs of Rick Baker, who worked together on *Star Wars*. Contains violence and swearing. ▣

Joseph Cortese [Joe Cortese] *Jack* • Maryam D'Abo *Ta'ra* • George Dzundza *Frank Dileo* • Gregory Sierra *Victor Maldonado* • Kim Delaney *Mandy Estabrook* • John Putch *Wendle* ■ *Dir* Richard A Colla • *Scr* Frank Lupo

Something of Value ★★★

Drama 1957 · US · BW · 113mins

Directed by Richard Brooks, who adapted it from Robert Ruark's novel based on the Mau Mau uprisings in Kenya, the film graphically conveys the horror of slaughter, but is dull. The more personal plot at the centre of the upheaval between white farmers and black tribesman, focuses on Rock Hudson and Sidney Poitier, close friends plunged into conflicting loyalties by the bloody divide with Poitier, excellent in the role, succumbing to tribal allegiance. Vivid East African locations add to the reality of this tale.

Rock Hudson *Peter McKenzie* • Dana Wynter *Holly Keith* • Wendy Hiller *Elizabeth* • Sidney Poitier *Kimani* • Juano Hernandez *Njogu* • William Marshall *Leader* • Robert Beatty *Jeff Newton* • Walter Fitzgerald *Henry McKenzie* ■ *Dir* Richard Brooks • *Scr* Richard Brooks, from a novel by Robert C Ruark

Something Short of Paradise ★★★ 15

Romantic comedy 1979 · US · Colour · 86mins

A late seventies romantic comedy with *Annie Hall* on the brain. David Steinberg and Susan Sarandon star as a moviehouse manager and a journalist who fall in love, despite obstacles thrown in their paths by conniving acquaintances. Performances from the two leads are good, though Steinberg's character is perhaps more unlikeable than he needs to be. Film buffs will go ga-ga over the title sequence, which cleverly strings together old movie ads. ▣

Susan Sarandon *Madeleine Ross* • David Steinberg *Harris Soane* • Jean-Pierre Aumont *Jean-Fidel Mileau* • Marilyn Sokol *Ruthie Miller* • Joe Grifasi *Barney Collins* ■ *Dir* David Helpern Jr • *Scr* Fred Barron

Something So Right ★★★ PG

Comedy drama 1982 · US · Colour · 100mins

This more than acceptable TV movie was made in the days when Rick Schroder was called Ricky and was still trying to live down *The Champ* and *Little Lord Fauntleroy*, and Patty Duke still appended Astin to her surname. With *Something for Joey* and *The Outside Woman* among his many credits, director Lou Antonio has shown that he can tell a good story without overdosing it with melodramatics. Here, he coaxes decent performances from his leading trio, including a barely recognisable

James Farentino as the man who transforms the lives of a mother and her troublesome son. ▣

Ricky Schroder [Rick Schroder] *Joey Bosnick* • Patty Duke Astin [Patty Duke] *Jeanne Bosnick* • James Farentino *Arnie Potts* • Fred Dryer *Mike Bosnick* • Annie Potts *Sunday* ■ *Dir* Lou Antonio • *Scr* Jonathan Estrin, Shelley List

Something to Believe In ★ PG

Romantic drama 1997 · UK/Ger · Colour · 108mins

Schmaltz, saccharine and sentimentality overwhelm this melodrama, despite a strong cast of recognisable faces (Roddy McDowall, Robert Wagner). William McNamara plays a concert pianist off to compete in Naples and en route he encounters terminally-ill Las Vegas croupier Maria Pitillo. She's in Italy seeking a miracle cure, but with love interest from McNamara do, we think she'll need it? Tom Conti, Maria Schneider and Ian Bannen flail equally with this all too "sweet" material, but to no avail. Contains strong language. ▣

William McNamara *Mike* • Maria Pitillo *Maggie* • Tom Conti *Monsignor Calogero* • Maria Schneider *Maria* • Ian Bannen *Don Pozzi* • Robert Wagner *Brad* • Jill St John *Dr Joann Anderson* • Roddy McDowall *Gambler* ■ *Dir* John Hough • *Scr* John Goldsmith, John Hough, from a idea by John Hough, David Purcell

Something to Hide ★

Thriller 1971 · UK · Colour · 106mins

For ten minutes, as Peter Finch and Shelley Winters hurl drunken abuse at each other, this melodrama looks as if it could be a scorcher. But then, disastrously, Winters departs the scene and Finch is left to wallow in what must be the worst movie hangover since Ray Milland had his lost weekend. Finch's encounter with pregnant waif Linda Hayden is utterly unbelievable, and the preposterous dialogue lacks insight, while the lingering images are packed with thick-ear symbolism.

Peter Finch *Harry Field* • Shelley Winters *Gabrielle Field* • Colin Blakely *Blagdon* • John Stride *Sergeant Tom Winnington* • Linda Hayden *Lorelei* • Harold Goldbatt *Dibbick* • Rosemarie Dunham *Elsie* • Helen Fraser *Miss Bunyan* • Graham Crowden *Lay preacher* ■ *Dir* Alastair Reid • *Scr* Alastair Reid, from the novel by Nicholas Monsarrat

Something to Live For ★★

Melodrama 1952 · US · BW · 89mins

Seven years after winning his Oscar for playing an alcoholic in *The Lost Weekend*, Ray Milland was involved with booze again in this less ambitious vehicle, produced and directed by George Stevens. As a member of Alcoholics Anonymous, Milland helps actress Joan Fontaine battle the demon drink and falls for her in the process. Teresa Wright plays Milland's wife, and all three stars, though past the peak of their film careers, give excellent performances. Director Stevens, must take the blame for the film's dull tone and turgid progress.

Joan Fontaine *Jenny Carey* • Ray Milland *Alan Miller* • Teresa Wright *Edna Miller* • Richard Derr *Tony Collins* • Douglas Dick *Baker* •

Herbert Heyes *Mr Crawley* • Harry Bellaver *Billy* • Paul Valentine *Albert* ■ *Dir* George Stevens • *Scr* Dwight Taylor

Something to Sing About ★★ U

Musical comedy 1937 · US · BW · 87mins

As this is one of James Cagney's all too few musicals, we should be grateful even for this mistitled low-budget affair in which he gets to sing and dance his way through a few numbers. (The film was released ten years later with the worse title: *The Battling Hoofer*. Cagney plays a Hollywood star, who discovers that the small print in his contract says that he must remain a bachelor while with the studio, so he can't marry his sweetheart Evelyn Daw. Victor Schertzinger, who wrote the tunes, directed the film in sequence. ▣

James Cagney *Terry Rooney* • Evelyn Daw *Rita Wyatt* • William Frawley *Hank Meyers* • Mona Barrie *Stephanie Hajos* • Gene Lockhart Bennett *O Regan* ■ *Dir* Victor Schertzinger • *Scr* Austin Parker, from a story by Victor Schertzinger

Something to Talk About ★★★ 15

Drama 1995 · US · Colour · 100mins

For all its pretensions, this tale of a modern woman giving as good as she gets, is little more than a sophisticated soap opera. Reversing the tactics she employed in *Thelma and Louise*, screenwriter Callie Khouri has disgruntled wife Julia Roberts stand and fight rather than take to the road. But it's not much of a contest, as who could possibly have any sympathy for either play-away husband Dennis Quaid or her overbearing father Robert Duvall? It's directed with care, but no flair by Lasse Hallström, while Roberts is outclassed by both sparky sister Kyra Sedgwick and snobby mom Gena Rowlands. ▣

Julia Roberts *Grace* • Dennis Quaid *Eddie* • Robert Duvall *Wyly King* • Gena Rowlands *Georgia King* • Kyra Sedgwick *Emma Rae* • Brett Cullen *Jamie Johnson* ■ *Dir* Lasse Hallström • *Scr* Callie Khouri

Something Wicked This Way Comes ★★★★ PG

Gothic fantasy drama 1983 · US · Colour · 91mins

Generally thought of as a disappointingly crude adaptation by Ray Bradbury of his own novel, this fantasy promises more than it delivers, but is still a good, spooky horror yarn for children with imagination. Jonathan Pryce is suitably evil as the owner of the Pandemonium Carnival, which appears to grant the wishes of the inhabitants of a small American town. Director Jack Clayton piles on the suspense and atmosphere, especially when Pryce goes in search of two young boys who have discovered too many of his secrets. He's aided by Pam Grier's alluring Dust Witch, but arachnophobes should beware. ▣

Jason Robards [Jason Robards Jr] *Charles Halloway* • Jonathan Pryce *Mr Dark* • Diane Ladd *Mrs Nightshade* • Pam Grier *Dust Witch* • Royal Dano *Tom Fury* • Vidal Peterson *Will*

Halloway • Shawn Carson *Jim Nightshade* • Arthur Hill *Narrator* ■ *Dir* Jack Clayton • *Scr* Ray Bradbury, from his novel

Something Wild ★★★★ 18

Comedy drama 1986 · US · Colour · 108mins

Jonathan Demme's oddball "yuppie nightmare" finds meek Jeff Daniels dragged into boozing and bondage after an accidental meeting with flaky *femme fatale* Melanie Griffith, who persuades him to attend her high-school reunion. The film moves up a violent gear when her crazed ex-con husband Ray Liotta, kidnaps them both for his own vengeful purposes. Constantly confounding expectations as to where it's going, Demme's jet black anarchic comedy features a marvellous rock soundtrack and a great performance by Griffith. Just watch out for those shocking shifts in style as the lethal paranoia builds. Contains swearing. ▣

Jeff Daniels *Charles Driggs* • Melanie Griffith *Audrey "Lulu" Hankel* • Ray Liotta *Ray Sinclair* • Margaret Colin *Irene* • Tracey Walter *Country squire* • Dana Preu *"Peaches"* • Jack Gilpin *Larry Dillman* • Su Tissue *Peggy Dillman* ■ *Dir* Jonathan Demme • *Scr* E Max Frye

Sometimes They Come Back ★★ 15

Supernatural thriller 1991 · US · Colour · 96mins

Teacher Tim Matheson returns to his home town where he's haunted by the ghosts of the boys responsible for killing his brother 27 years before, in this so-so shocker from the Stephen King horror conveyor belt. Matheson stumbles with suitable dread through the fights with the juvenile delinquents from hell, but while director Tom McLoughlin aims to engross and gross-out in equal measure, the numerous plot inconsistencies scupper everyone's good intentions. Successful enough, though, to spawn two sequels. ▣

Tim Matheson *Jim Norman* • Brooke Adams *Sally Norman* • Robert Rusler *Lawson* • Chris Demetral *Wayne* • Robert Hy Gorman *Scott Norman* • William Sanderson *Carl Mueller* ■ *Dir* Tom McLoughlin • *Scr* Lawrence Konner, Mark Rosenthal, from the short story by Stephen King

Sometimes They Come Back... Again ★★ 18

Horror 1996 · US · Colour · 94mins

Michael Gross returns to his hometown after his mother dies, to take care of her estate, only to find the town absolutely awash with the occult. Jerry Seinfeld lookalike Alexis Arquette is Tony Reno, the demonically powered teenager who has his eyes on Gross's daughter, played by Hilary (*Boys Don't Cry*) Swank. Despite being a needless sequel to a movie that was barely based on a Stephen King short story, it's slickly produced, but after a while you begin to wonder why all this supernatural stuff keeps happening in this particular town. ▣

Michael Gross *Jon Porter* • Hilary Swank *Michelle Porter* • Jennifer Elise Cox *Jules Martin* • Alexis Arquette *Tony Reno* ■ *Dir* Adam Grossman • *Scr* Guy Reidel, Adam Grossman, from characters created by Stephen King

Somewhere beyond Love ★★★★

Romantic drama   1974 · It · Colour · 106mins

Boasting performances as authentic as Dante Ferretti's sets and directed without frills or affectation, this unashamedly linear study of Italy's North-South divide and the gulf between men and women is social conscience cinema at its most poignant and persuasive. The basic premise is as unprepossessing as life itself, as Sicilian Catholic Stefania Sandrelli and Milanese Communist Giuliano Gemma refuse to allow pride, principle and prejudice to derail their unlikely romance. In confronting them with cruel fate, Luigi Comencini is able to explore the danger in which factory owners place their employees, while also forcing the couple to reassess their priorities. Italian dialogue dubbed into English.

Giuliano Gemma *Nullo* • Stefania Sandrelli *Carmela* ■ *Dir* Luigi Comencini • *Scr* Luigi Comencini, Ugo Pirro, from a story by Ugo Pirro

Somewhere I'll Find You ★★★

Romantic wartime drama
1942 · US · BW · 107mins

The relationship of two brothers (Clark Gable, Robert Sterling), both war correspondents, is upset by their involvement with a female journalist (Lana Turner), who is sent to report in Indochina where they all meet up again. She becomes a nurse, they all go to Bataan, and one of them doesn't return. It's a standard Second World War romance with a convenient resolution, efficiently directed by Wesley Ruggles, which allows Turner to go through the melodramatic mill. A huge box-office success in its day, the film is remembered because Gable's wife, Carole Lombard, was killed three days into shooting, becoming an early Hollywood war casualty. A grief-stricken Gable insisted on finishing the picture, but gives an understandably subdued and lacklustre performance.

Clark Gable *Jonathan "Johnny" Davis* • Lana Turner *Paula Lane* • Robert Sterling *Kirk Davis* • Reginald Owen *Willie Manning* • Lee Patrick *Eve Manning* • Charles Dingle *George L Stafford* • Van Johnson *Lt Wade Halls* • Keenan Wynn *Sgt Tom Purdy* ■ *Dir* Wesley Ruggles • *Scr* Marguerite Roberts, Walter Reisch, from a story by Charles Hoffman

Somewhere in Europe ★★★★

Drama   1947 · Hun · BW · 104mins

A landmark film in that it was Hungary's first international success for decades and led to the Hungarian cinema becoming a nationalised industry. Béla Balázs – the film theorist and author who had returned from exile in the USSR – co-wrote the screenplay which dealt with the bitter realities of post-war Hungary in a direct manner. It involved a band of thieving, begging orphans who take refuge in a castle, where they find a new and better way of life. Obviously influenced by the Italian neo-realists, the film is more lyrical and optimistic. A Hungarian language film.

Ladislas Horvath *Kuksi* • Arthur Somlay *Peter Simon* • Miklos Gabor *Ossup* • Zsuzsa Banky *The girl* ■ *Dir* Géza von Radványi • *Scr* Géza von Radványi, Béla Balázs, Judit Féjer, Félix Máriássy

Somewhere in Sonora ★★

Western   1933 · US · BW · 59mins

From early in the period when John Wayne was languishing in B-movies, comes this remake of an old Ken Maynard silent. Wayne is the hero foiling a plot to rob the silver mine owned by the father (Ralph Lewis) of the girl he loves (Ann Fay). Also in the cast are silent star Henry B Walthall and a young Paul Fix, frequently associated with Wayne later on.

John Wayne *John Bishop* • Henry B Walthall *Bob Leadly* • Shirley Palmer *Mary Burton* • JP McGowan *Monte Black* • Ann Fay *Patsy Ellis* • Ralph Lewis *Burton* • Paul Fix *Bart Leadly* ■ *Dir* Mack V Wright • *Scr* Joseph Anthony Roach, from a story by Will Levington Comfort, from the novel *Somewhere South in Sonora* by Will Levington Comfort

Somewhere in Time ★★★ PG

Romantic drama   1980 · US · Colour · 98mins

A now-poignant outing from Christopher Reeve as a disaffected playwright in this highly schmaltzy love story. Reeve is serviceable and moist-eyed enough, and Jane Seymour sleepwalks her way through a familiar role in a tale that resembles the plot of a Barbara Cartland novel with a supernatural twist. Made after the phenomenal success of *Superman*, but before the eponymous series began to fade, this is one of Reeve's not terribly successful attempts to show us there was more to his acting than a pair of underpants over his tights. His lack of flair in that department does not, however, detract from what is basically a rather charming, old-fashioned love story that will prove an entertaining tear-jerker for those in the mood. [VIDEO]

Christopher Reeve *Richard Collier* • Jane Seymour *Elise McKenna* • Christopher Plummer *William Fawcett Robinson* • Teresa Wright *Laura Roberts* • Bill Erwin *Arthur* • Victoria Michaels *Maude* • William P O'Hagan *Rollo* ■ *Dir* Jeannot Szwarc • *Scr* Richard Matheson, from his novel

Somewhere on Leave ★★ U

Musical comedy   1942 · UK · BW · 96mins

Of the music hall turns who made films, the Lancashire comedian Frank Randle was among the most successful. But his appeal inevitably exemplifies the North-South divide and his success was largely confined to home ground. Here, Randle and three of his regular army pals are invited by a fellow private to have some off-duty fun at his stately home. Their host is too busy courting an ATS girl to realise what chaos the quartet are causing. Unsophisticated perhaps, and more a series of incidents than a cohesive narrative, but great fun.

Frank Randle *Private Randle* • Harry Korris *Sgt Korris* • Robbie Vincent *Private Enoch* • Dan Young *Private Young* • Toni Lupino *Toni Beaumont* • Pat McGrath *Private Roy Desmond* ■ *Dir* John E Blakeley • *Scr* Roney Parsons, Anthony Toner, Frank Randle

Somewhere Tomorrow ★★

Romantic drama   1983 · US · Colour · 91mins

A likeable curiosity, notable mainly for the appearance of a young Sarah Jessica Parker, eight years before her scene-stealing performance in Steve Martin's *LA Story*. Here, she plays a teenager who strikes up an offbeat friendship with the ghost of youngster Tom Shea, who was killed in an airplane crash. Robert Wiemer's direction is a touch uneven, but Parker shows early promise and it's a good deal less cloying than other similarly themed American films.

Sarah Jessica Parker *Lori Anderson* • Nancy Addison *Betty Anderson* • Tom Shea *Terry Stockton* • Rick Weber *Alex Peiski* ■ *Dir/Scr* Robert Wiemer

Somewhere under the Broad Sky ★★★

Melodrama   1954 · Jap · Colour

Along with *Three Loves*, this low-key shomin-geki (or lower-middle-class movie) was virtually an act of atonement on behalf of Masaki Kobayashi to the head of the Shochiku studio, for the embarrassment caused by *The Thick-Walled Room* (1953), which drew on the diaries of war criminals to suggest that Japan's real warmongers had escaped punishment. Scripted by Kobayashi's sister, and set in the industrial city of Kawasaki, this unflinching melodrama typified the director's detailed style and commitment to the exposure of social injustice that would find its greatest expression in his *Human Condition* trilogy. A Japanese language film.

Keiji Sata • Yoshiko Kuga • Hideko Takamine • Akira Ishihama ■ *Dir* Masaki Kobayashi • *Scr* Yoshiko Kusuda

Sommersby ★★★ 12

Period romantic drama
1993 · US · Colour · 108mins

This is the American reworking of the Gérard Depardieu/Nathalie Baye modern classic *The Return of Martin Guerre*, and it isn't a patch on the original, either in terms of tension, intelligence or performance. Nevertheless, there is still much to enjoy and engross in the central mystery surrounding the true identity of returning Civil War veteran Richard Gere, in particular the sensitive playing of the excellent Jodie Foster as his confused "widow". Unfortunately, neither Gere nor Bill Pullman, as Foster's embittered suitor, can hold a candle to her, and the resolution will not satisfy everybody. Contains some swearing, a sex scene and brief nudity. [VIDEO]

Richard Gere *Jack Sommersby* • Jodie Foster *Laurel Sommersby* • Bill Pullman *Orin Meecham* • James Earl Jones *Judge Isaacs* • Lanny Flaherty *Buck* • William Windom *Reverend Powell* • Wendell Wellman *Travis* • Brett Kelley *Little Rob* • Clarice Taylor *Esther* • Frankie Faison *Joseph* • Ronald Lee Ermey [R Lee Ermey] *Dick Mead* ■ *Dir* Jon Amiel • *Scr* Nicholas Meyer, Sarah Kernochan, from a story by Nicholas Meyer, Anthony Schaffer, from the film *The Return of Martin Guerre* by Daniel Vigne, Jean-Claude Carrière

Son in Law ★★ 15

Comedy   1993 · US · Colour · 91mins

Pauly Shore could never be accused of subtlety. The humour in this rustic comedy is as broad as a barn door and twice as creaky. Yet he puts so much energy into his manic mugging that no matter how irritating he is, he still manages to coax at least one smile. But it is only a solitary moment of mirth in this hackneyed variation on the town-and-country mouse theme, in which Shore's campus nerd not only wins over Carla Gugino's folksy family, but also exposes her despicable boyfriend. [VIDEO]

Pauly Shore *Crawl* • Carla Gugino *Rebecca* • Lane Smith *Walter Warner* • Cindy Pickett *Connie Warner* • Mason Adams *Walter Sr* • Patrick Renna *Zack* • Dennis Burkley *Theo* • Tiffani-Amber Thiessen *Tracy* ■ *Dir* Steve Rash • *Scr* Shawn Schepps, Fax Bahr, Adam Small, from a story by Patrick J Clifton, Susan McMartin, Peter M Lenkov

Son of Ali Baba ★★ U

Satirical swashbuckling adventure
1952 · US · Colour · 74mins

When good looks mattered more than good acting for Tony Curtis, this is the sort of pantomime stuff he appeared in. As Kashma Baba, son of Ali, he must protect the Princess Kiki from an evil caliph, who also wants to get his greedy hands on Baba Sr's treasure. It's a satirical tale of kidnapping, sword crossing and falling in love, but without a genie or flying carpet, it's less than magical.

Tony Curtis *Kashma Baba* • Piper Laurie *Kiki* • Susan Cabot *Tala* • William Reynolds *Mustafa* • Hugh O'Brian *Hussein* • Victor Jory *Caliph* • Morris Ankrum *Ali Baba* ■ *Dir* Kurt Neumann • *Scr* Gerald Drayson Adams

Son of Dracula ★★★

Horror   1943 · US · BW · 79mins

Lon Chaney Jr plays the famous Count under the pseudonym Alucard (Dracula spelt backwards, a device destined to be used in numerous inferior horrors), and recruits vampires in the Deep South because Universal wouldn't pay for Transylvanian sets. It didn't matter. This has atmosphere to spare, super make-up and fun man-to-bat transformations, with Chaney clearly having a ball as the sinister bloodsucker. A neglected highlight from the golden age of vintage horror.

Lon Chaney Jr *Count Alucard* • Robert Paige *Frank Stanley* • Louise Allbritton *Katherine Caldwell* • Evelyn Ankers *Claire Caldwell* • Frank Craven *Dr Harry Brewster* • J Edward Bromberg *Professor Lazlo* • Samuel S Hinds *Judge Simmons* ■ *Dir* Robert Siodmak • *Scr* Eric Taylor, from a story by Curtis Siodmak

Son of Flubber ★★★ U

Comedy   1962 · US · BW · 98mins

You will remember that "flubber" was the flying rubber invented by Fred MacMurray in the fun family comedy *The Absent-Minded Professor*. Disney reassembled many of the same cast two years later, but usually reliable director Robert Stevenson could not repeat the winning formula. Keenan Wynn enjoys himself as the villain and veterans Leon Ames and Charlie Ruggles demonstrate the value of

experienced character support. MacMurray simply looks flubbergasted.

Fred MacMurray *Professor Ned Brainard* • Nancy Olson *Betsy Brainard* • Keenan Wynn *Alonzo Hawk* • Tommy Kirk *Biff Hawk* • Elliott Reid *Shelby Ashton* • Joanna Moore *Desiree de la Roche* • Leon Ames *President Rufus Daggett* • Ed Wynn *AJ Allen* • Ken Murray *Mr Hurley* • Charlie Ruggles [Charles Ruggles] *Judge Murdock* • William Demarest *Mr Hummel* • Paul Lynde *Sportscaster* ■ *Dir* Robert Stevenson • *Scr* Bill Walsh, Don DaGradi, from the story *A Situation of Gravity* by Samuel W Taylor, from novels by Jay Williams, Raymond Abrashkin

Son of Frankenstein ★★★★

Horror 1939 · US · BW · 95mins

The third instalment of Universal's classic series features Boris Karloff's last fling as the Monster and is a superior shocker all round. Basil Rathbone (the Baron), Bela Lugosi (Ygor) and Lionel Atwill (the police chief with a noisy artificial arm) all turn in unforgettably eccentric performances along with the ever-imposing Karloff. Add Rowland V Lee's eerie direction and the result is a majestically macabre chiller. After this, the Monster became a stumbling cliché.

Basil Rathbone *Baron Wolf von Frankenstein* • Boris Karloff *The Monster* • Bela Lugosi *Ygor* • Lionel Atwill *Inspector Krogh* • Josephine Hutchinson *Elsa von Frankenstein* • Donnie Dunagan *Peter von Frankenstein* ■ *Dir* Rowland V Lee • *Scr* Willis Cooper, from characters created by Mary Shelley

Son of Fury ★★★ U

Period adventure 1942 · US · BW · 98mins

Historical nonsense set during the reign of George III. Tyrone Power, cheated out of his inheritance by George Sanders, falls in love with Frances Farmer and ends up on a Polynesian island with a heavily made-up, but skimpily costumed native girl, played by Gene Tierney. Having cast its most alluring stars, 20th Century-Fox threw money (though not much-needed Technicolor) at the production and the result was big box office. The stars perform well, especially Sanders as a snarling villain, and the supporting cast is worth a look, too.

Tyrone Power *Benjamin Blake* • Gene Tierney *Eve* • George Sanders *Sir Arthur Blake* • Frances Farmer *Isabel Blake* • Roddy McDowall *Benjamin as a boy* • John Carradine *Caleb Green* • Elsa Lanchester *Bristol Isabel* ■ *Dir* John Cromwell • *Scr* Philip Dunne

Son of Godzilla ★★ U

Science-fiction 1967 · Jap · Colour · 81mins

Intense heat from Japanese weather experiments causes cute Godzilla offspring, Minya, to hatch. Then mother (and who knew Godzilla was female?) must protect her son from a giant hairy spider, and other insect life enlarged by the atmospheric conditions. The eighth in the Toho monster series is an inept juvenile adventure with comical episodes spliced into the miniature special effects mayhem. Japanese dialogue dubbed into English.

Tadao Takashima *Dr Kuzumi* • Akira Kubo *Goro* ■ *Dir* Jun Fukuda • *Scr* Shinichi Sekizawa, Kazue Shiba

Son of Kong ★★★

Fantasy adventure 1933 · US · BW · 69mins

Rushed out within a year of its predecessor *King Kong*'s release, the official sequel took a more light-hearted and whimsical approach and was dismissed by critics because of the accent on comedy. From a distance, it now plays as short, inoffensive and good fun. The ludicrous story has Carl Denham (Robert Armstrong) returning to Skull Island in a hunt for treasure in order to pay off Manhattan's rebuilding costs after Kong's destructive rampage, and finding the giant ape's cute, albino, 25-foot offspring stuck in quicksand. As always, Willis O'Brien's stop-motion animation is as endearing as it was ground-breaking. More *ET* than *KK*.

Robert Armstrong *Carl Denham* • Helen Mack *Hilda Peterson* • Frank Reicher *Captain Englehorn* • John Marston *Helstrom* • Victor Wong *Charlie* • Lee Kohlmar *Mickey* • Ed Brady *Red* • Clarence Wilson *Peterson* ■ *Dir* Ernest B Schoedsack • *Scr* Ruth Rose

Son of Lassie ★★★ U

Drama 1945 · US · Colour · 100mins

A sequel to the tremendously popular *Lassie Come Home*, that consolidated the stardom of the most successful canine performer since Rin Tin Tin. It benefits from a fine supporting cast of caring humans, including Peter Lawford and June Lockhart, but is very much of its time, as Lassie's son Laddie accompanies Lawford into Nazi-occupied Norway. Connoisseurs may care to note that the collie Pal plays both Lassie and her offspring.

Peter Lawford *Joe Carraclough* • Donald Crisp *Sam Carraclough* • June Lockhart *Priscilla* • Nigel Bruce *Duke of Rudling* • William Severn *Henrik* • Leon Ames *Anton* ■ *Dir* S Sylvan Simon • *Scr* Jeanne Bartlett, from characters created by Eric Knight

Son of Monte Cristo ★★★ U

Period swashbuckling adventure 1940 · US · BW · 95mins

This long-gestating sequel to the marvellous 1934 *Count of Monte Cristo* features Louis Hayward (replacing Robert Donat, who refused to return) as the swashbuckling son of the famous Edmond Dantes, and Joan Bennett as an imprisoned queen. The plot assumes a deliberate political relevance as it deals with an evil Balkan dictator, suavely played by George Sanders, attempting to conquer her country, a reminder to contemporary audiences of then-current events in Europe.

Louis Hayward *Count of Monte Cristo* • Joan Bennett *Grand Duchess Zona* • George Sanders *Gurko Lanen* • Florence Bates *Mathilde* • Lionel Royce *Colonel Zimmerman* • Montagu Love *Baron von Neuhoff* • Ian MacWolfe *Conrad Stadt* ■ *Dir* Rowland V Lee • *Scr* George Bruce

Son of Paleface ★★★★ U

Spoof western 1952 · US · Colour · 94mins

In this very funny follow-up to *The Paleface* (1948), Bob Hope plays his own son, a cowardly dude who gets entangled with Jane Russell, a bandit who sings in a saloon called "The Dirty Shame". Roy Rogers is delightfully self-mocking as himself, particularly when singing *A Four-Legged Friend* to Trigger. All the clichés of the western are here played for laughs by Frank Tashlin, a former animator who sets up many of the sequences like a cartoon, especially a scene in which Hope finds himself sharing a bed with Trigger.

Bob Hope *Junior Potter* • Jane Russell *Mike* • Roy Rogers *Roy Barton* • Bill Williams *Kirk* • Harry Von Zell *Stoner* • Douglass Dumbrille *Sheriff McIntyre* • Lyle Moraine *Waverly* • Lloyd Corrigan *Doc Lovejoy* • Cecil B DeMille ■ *Dir* Frank Tashlin • *Scr* Frank Tashlin, Robert L Welch, Joseph Quillan

Son of Robin Hood ★★ U

Adventure 1958 · UK · Colour · 80mins

The son of Sherwood's finest is in fact a girl, played by June Laverick, and she takes over the remnants of her father's outlaw band to fight against the Black Duke (David Farrar) who wants the British throne. All the most hilarious aspects of Hollywood-on-Trent are present in this jolly jape – the Middle Ages dialogue, the classy grovelling, as well as an undercurrent of cross-dressing – and Laverick makes a pleasing heroine. Resolutely Home Counties, but plucky with it.

Al Hedison [David Hedison] *Jamie* • June Laverick *Deering Hood* • David Farrar *Des Roches* • Marius Goring *Chester* • Philip Friend *Dorchester* • Delphi Lawrence *Sylvia* • George Coulouris *Alan A Dale* • George Woodbridge *Little John* ■ *Dir* George Sherman • *Scr* George W George, George Slavin

Son of Sinbad ★★ U

Fantasy adventure 1955 · US · Colour · 85mins

Howard Hughes allegedly produced this frothy fantasy nonsense, solely to placate the screen ambitions of all the starlets to whom he'd promised a career. There can be no other explanation for this "forty thieves" exotica. Even Vincent Price, as comical poet Omar Khayham, considered it the worst script ever written. As a result, Dale Robertson, playing Sinbad with a Texas accent, seems perfectly in synch with the rest of the colourfully camp confection, and if you look closely, you'll notice one of the lovelies is a young Kim Novak, in an early bit part.

Dale Robertson *Sinbad* • Sally Forrest *Ameer* • Vincent Price *Omar Khayham* • Lili St Cyr *Nerissa* • Mari Blanchard *Kristina* • Jay Novello *Jiddah* • Kim Novak ■ *Dir* Ted Tetzlaff • *Scr* Aubrey Wisberg, Jack Pollexfen

Son of the Pink Panther ★ PG

Action comedy 1993 · US · Colour · 88mins

One can understand Blake Edwards's frustration at seeing a successful series stopped in its tracks by the death of Peter Sellers. Yet surely the critical mauling meted out to those cut-and-paste jobs *Trail* and *Curse*, should have clued him in to the fact that the public were simply not interested in Clouseau clones. Here, he puts Italian comic Roberto Benigni through his paces as a gormless gendarme, whose only talent is to annoy poor old Herbert Lom. The kidnapping plot is inane, the slapstick inept and the cast ineffectual. All in all, mind-bogglingly bad.

Roberto Benigni *Jacques Gambrelli* • Herbert Lom *Inspector Dreyfus* • Shabana Azmi *the Queen* • Debrah Farentino *Princess Yasmin* • Jennifer Edwards *Yussa* • Robert Davi *Hans* • Burt Kwouk *Cato* • Mark Schneider *Arnon* • Graham Stark *Dr Balls* • Liz Smith *Madame Balls* • ■ *Dir* Blake Edwards • *Scr* Blake Edwards, Madeline Sunshine, Steve Sunshine, from a story by Blake Edwards, from characters created by Maurice Richlin, Blake Edwards

The Son of the Sheik ★★★★

Silent adventure 1926 · US · BW · 68mins

Abandon all resistance to the technique and conventions of blood-and-sand romance as filmed in the silent era. Remind yourself that there has been no greater male screen idol than Rudolph Valentino, and surrender to this, his last film before his premature death. The star plays two roles, Prince Ahmed, and his father, the all-powerful Sheik. Marvellously photographed by George Barnes, directed by George Fitzmaurice and drawing excellent work from Valentino, this tongue-in-cheek tale, combining passion, violence and swashbuckling action with humour, has lost none of its charm or entertainment value.

Rudolph Valentino *Ahmed/The Sheik* • Vilma Banky *Yasmin* • George Fawcett *André* • Montague Love [Montagu Love] *Ghabah* • Karl Dane *Ramadan* • Agnes Ayres *Diana* ■ *Dir* George Fitzmaurice • *Scr* Frances Marion, Fred De Gresac, George Marion Jr (titles), from the novel *The Sons of the Sheik* by Edith Maude Hull

Sonatine ★★★

Crime drama 1984 · Can · Colour · 91mins

Writer/director Micheline Lanctot stages this Antonioni-esque study of social alienation as a "small sonata" in three movements. In the first two movements, a series of glances and gestures prompts Pascale Bussières to become distantly enamoured of a married bus driver, while runaway Marcia Pilote shares a brief moment of tenderness on a cargo boat with a Bulgarian sailor, before she's handed over to the authorities. Yet there's little in the opening episodes to prepare you for the teenagers' tragic response to the world's neglect. Delicately directed, persuasively played and, ultimately, as inevitable as it is sad. In French with English subtitles. Contains violence, nudity.

Pascale Bussières *Chantal* • Marcia Pilote *Louisette* • Kliment Demtchev *Sailor* ■ *Dir/Scr* Micheline Lanctot

Sonatine ★★★★★ 18

Crime drama 1993 · Jap · Colour · 89mins

This violent gang war thriller is a stunning piece of film-making. Director Takeshi "Beat" Kitano shows a complete understanding of the Hollywood gangster movie and its Japanese counterpart, the Yakuza film. Moreover, he demonstrates a mastery of technique in the magnificent beach hideout segment in which he uses trick effects, imaginative camera angles and a range of comic styles to question the value of the Yakuza's existence and build tension towards the superb silhouette shoot-out. He also gives a towering performance as a

1324 U = SUITABLE FOR ALL Uc = SUITABLE FOR ALL, ESPECIALLY FOR YOUNG CHILDREN (VIDEO ONLY) PG = PARENTAL GUIDANCE

disillusioned hit man. In Japanese with English subtitles. Contains violence and nudity. 🖳

''Beat'' Takeshi [Takeshi Kitano] *Murakawa* • Aya Kokumai *Miyuki* • Tetsu Watanabe *Uechi* • Masanobu Katsumura *Ryoji* ■ *Dir/Scr* Takeshi Kitano • *Cinematographer* Katsumi Yanagishima

A Song for Beko ★★★★
Wartime drama
1992 · Ger/Arm · Colour · 86mins

A teacher not a fighter, Turkish Kurd Nizamettin Aric goes in search of his rebel brother with a diligence and dignity that characterises his relationship with orphan refugee Bezara Arsen. The first-ever Kurdish feature, Aric's directorial debut is remarkable not just for its courage, but also for the restraint with which it depicts everyday reality and passionately espouses its cause. The flashback-packed storyline contrasts the persistent prejudice of the Turks with Saddam Hussein's pitiless poison gas attack on a village slowly returning to normality after the Iran-Iraq War. In Kurdish with English subtitles.

Nizamettin Aric *Beko* • Bezara Arsen *Zine* ■ *Dir/Scr* Nizamettin Aric

A Song for Europe ★★★
Drama   1985 · UK/W Ger · Colour · 95mins

British stage and television actor David Suchet (*Poirot*) and *Last Tango in Paris* star Maria Schneider head the mostly German cast of this international co-production. It tells the story of how a drug company executive was imprisoned for industrial espionage after taking evidence of his company's malpractice to Common Market officials. Focusing on the injustices suffered by the executive at the hands of the authorities, director John Goldschmidt offers a disturbing indictment of corporate power that's at odds with the wishy-washy atmosphere of most of his other films.

David Suchet *Stephen Dyer* • Maria Schneider *Madeline* • Anne-Marie Blanc *Maman* • Reinhard Glemnitz *Weigel* ■ *Dir* John Goldschmidt • *Scr* Peter Prince

A Song Is Born ★★★🄿🄶
Musical comedy 1948 · US · Colour · 119mins

Director Howard Hawks's remake of his classic *Ball of Fire* with Danny Kaye in the original Gary Cooper role. Cooper played a gauche professor compiling a dictionary of slang; here the plot's updated to a study of jazz, and on hand are some of its greatest exponents, including Benny Goodman, Louis Armstrong, Charlie Barnet and Tommy Dorsey. That in itself should be recommendation enough. In Hawks's canon this is a trifle, though it has interest as the director's first film in colour. Unfortunately, it's all rather silly. 🖳

Danny Kaye *Professor Hobart Frisbee* • Virginia Mayo *Honey Swanson* • Benny Goodman *Professor Magenbruch* • Hugh Herbert *Professor Twingle* • Steve Cochran *Tony Crow* ■ *Dir* Howard Hawks • *Scr* Harry Tugend, from the story *From A to Z* by Thomas Monroe, Billy Wilder

Song O' My Heart ★★
Musical   1930 · US · BW · 85mins

Designed as a vehicle for the film debut of the internationally popular Irish tenor, John McCormack, this blarney was directed by that skilful engineer of sentimentality, Frank Borzage. McCormack plays a singer whose great love (Alice Joyce) is forced to marry another. Abandoned, several children later by her husband, her old flame steps in to save her from starvation. It allows McCormack to sing a clutch of songs, including *Rose of Tralee*. Ecstatically received in its day, it's all rather maudlin now, but McCormack fans are in for a treat.

John McCormack *Sean O'Carolan* • Maureen O'Sullivan *Eileen O'Brien* • John Garrick *Fergus O' Donnell* • JM Kerrigan *Peter Conlon* ■ *Dir* Frank Borzage • *Scr* Tom Barry

The Song of Bernadette ★★★★🅄
Biographical drama 1943 · US · BW · 155mins

A desperately sincere slice of now unfashionable Hollywood sermonising which still contrives to move audiences, largely because of the amazing story of young Bernadette Soubirous, who, in 1858, saw a vision of the Virgin Mary in a grotto at Lourdes. Jennifer Jones won the best actress Oscar for her openly affecting Bernadette, the Virgin is portrayed by Linda Darnell and an unusually restrained Vincent Price is impeccable. Cynics won't be converted, but sceptics may find the movie posits a sincere argument. Another Oscar went to Arthur Miller's luminous black-and-white photography. 🖳

Jennifer Jones *Bernadette Soubirous* • William Eythe *Antoine* • Charles Bickford *Peyremaie* • Vincent Price *Dutour* • Lee J Cobb *Dr Dozous* • Gladys Cooper *Sister Vauzous* • Anne Revere *Louise Soubirous* • Roman Bohnen *François Soubirous* • Linda Darnell *Blessed Virgin* ■ *Dir* Henry King • *Scr* George Seaton, from the novel by Franz Werfel

Song of Ceylon ★★★★★🅄
Documentary   1934 · UK · BW · 39mins

Although sponsored by the Ceylon Tea Propaganda Board, this extraordinarily beautiful film is far more concerned with the ancient customs and Buddhist heritage of what is now called Sri Lanka. Basil Wright divided his odyssey into four sections and used the 17th-century travelogue of Robert Knox to counterpoint his poetic and ethnographically invaluable images. Tea is only introduced in the third segment and, then, is clearly presented as a corrupting influence on an idyllic scene. Every bit as impressive as, but less celebrated than *Night Mail* (which Wright co-directed with Harry Watt), this is one of the glories of the British documentary.

Lionel Wendt *Narrator* ■ *Dir* Basil Wright • *Scr* John Grierson, Basil Wright, from a travel book by Robert Knox • *Producer* John Grierson • *Cinematographer* Basil Wright

Song of Freedom ★★★★🅄
Drama   1936 · UK · BW · 78mins

Paul Robeson unearthed the legend of the singing king while shooting *Sanders of the River*. Even though he

had just completed *Show Boat*, he considered this the first film to showcase his talent without demeaning his race. As the London stevedore who is discovered by an operatic impresario, only to cast off his fame to return to the island kingdom from which he was kidnapped years before, Robeson not only gets to sing several fine songs, but also explores such themes as interracial marriage, the evils of superstition and slavery, and the clash between tradition and progress. It's dated, but still powerful.

Paul Robeson *John Zinga* • Elisabeth Welch *Ruth Zinga* • Esme Percy *Gabriel Donezetti* • Robert Adams *Monty* • Ecce Homo Toto *Mandingo* ■ *Scr* Fenn Sherie, Ingram D'Abbes, Michael Barringer (uncredited), Philip Lindsay (uncredited), from a story by Claude Wallace, from a story by Dorothy Holloway

Song of Love ★★★🅄
Musical biography 1947 · US · BW · 118mins

It's the Clara Wieck Schumann story that's not as awful as you might expect, thanks to Katharine Hepburn's portrayal. Hubby is an austere Paul Henreid and close mate Brahms is a beardless Robert Walker. Fictional tosh, certainly, but expertly produced with just the requisite amount of MGM gloss. Director Clarence Brown, who gave us *The Yearling* and stacks of Garbos, seems overawed by his subject, and his usual sureness of touch lapses into a slow pace.

Katharine Hepburn *Clara Wieck Schumann* • Paul Henreid *Robert Schumann* • Robert Walker *Johannes Brahms* • Henry Daniell *Franz Liszt* • Leo G Carroll *Prof Wieck* ■ *Dir* Clarence Brown • *Scr* Ivan Tors, Irmgard Von Cube, Allen Vincent, Robert Ardrey, from the play by Bernard Schubert, Mario Silva

Song of Norway ★🅄
Musical biography
1970 · US · Colour · 138mins

Let's be honest: this horrendously overlong biopic of composer Edvard Grieg has precious little going for it, except for the magnificent Scandinavian locations. Otherwise, one-time talented director Andrew L Stone has assembled a motley cast, including Edward G Robinson and Harry Secombe, to surround the woefully ill-equipped Toralv Maurstad (who?) in this supremely uninteresting saga. Lyrics were added to Grieg's greatest hits by Robert Wright and George Forrest, a team that had achieved greater success in 1955 with the music of Borodin in *Kismet*. 🖳

Toralv Maurstad *Edvard Grieg* • Florence Henderson *Nina Grieg* • Christina Schollin *Therese Berg* • Frank Porretta *Rikard Nordraak* • Harry Secombe *Bjornsterne Bjornson* • Robert Morley *Berg* • Edward G Robinson *Krogstad* • Elizabeth Larner *Mrs Bjornson* • Oscar Homolka *Engstrand* ■ *Dir* Andrew L Stone • *Scr* Andrew L Stone, from the musical by Milton Lazarus, Robert Wright and George Forrest, from a play by Homer Curran

Song of Scheherazade ★★★
Musical biography
1947 · US · Colour · 105mins

Supposedly a biopic of Rimsky-Korsakov, this is one of the campest of all Universal's gaudy costume

pictures. Jean Pierre Aumont plays the young Russian composer, who meets and falls for sultry dancer Yvonne De Carlo on his way back to Russia. They fall in love, she inspires him to write *Scherherazade* and dances at the premiere in St Petersburg. Eve Arden, only ten years De Carlo's senior, plays her wisecracking mother in this enjoyable nonsense.

Yvonne De Carlo *Cara de Talavera/ Scheherazade* • Brian Donlevy *Captain Vladimir Gregovich* • Jean-Pierre Aumont *Nikolai Rimsky-Korsakov* • Eve Arden *Mme Conchita de Talavera* • Philip Reed *Prince Mischetsky* ■ *Dir/Scr* Walter Reisch • *Music Director* Miklos Rozsa

The Song of Songs ★★
Comedy drama   1933 · US · BW · 85mins

After disappointing box-office returns for *Blonde Venus*, Paramount engineered a trial separation between Marlene Dietrich and director Josef von Sternberg – with little reward. Rouben Mamoulian was entrusted with the task of making something of this tale about a German peasant girl who falls in love with a sculptor and becomes his model, but marries a baron, turns café singer, and has several lovers. The stylish and intelligent Mamoulian did what he could, helped by a reliable cast, notably Brian Aherne, but this tired old material – previously a novel, play and two silent films – obstinately refused to come to life.

Marlene Dietrich *Lily Czepanek* • Brian Aherne *Richard Waldow* • Lionel Atwill *Baron von Merzbach* • Alison Skipworth *Mrs Rasmussen* ■ *Dir* Rouben Mamoulian • *Scr* Leo Birinski, Samuel Hoffenstein, the play by Edward Brewster Sheldon, from the novel *Das Hohe Lied* by Hermann Sudermann, and

Song of Texas ★★🅄
Western   1943 · US · BW · 50mins

This comparatively lavish Roy Rogers western gives priority to the songs: there are ten delivered by Roy, Bob Nolan and the Sons of the Pioneers including the popular *Moonlight and Roses* and *Mexicali Rose*. There's also a speciality number from a Mexican dance troupe. A wagon race in the last reel provides the only big action sequence and the plot is an old one: Roy and friends try to help Harry Shannon's impoverished old-timer, fool his visiting daughter, Sheila Ryan, into thinking he's the ranch owner he's claimed to be. 🖳

Roy Rogers *Roy* • Sheila Ryan *Sue Bennett* • Barton MacLane *Jim Calvert* • Harry Shannon *Sam Bennett* • Arline Judge *Hildegarde* ■ *Dir* Joseph Kane • *Scr* Winston Miller

Song of the Exile ★★★
Drama   1990 · HK/Tai · Colour · 100mins

Surviving an indifferent start, Ann Hui's semi-autobiographical drama, gradually develops into a moving study of a strained mother-daughter relationship. Returning to Hong Kong in the early seventies after studying broadcasting in London, Maggie Cheung is resentful of Chang Shwu-Fen's dismissive attitude towards her newly-acquired western ways. Typically revealing the tempest beneath the surface, Hui directs a touch methodically, but the performances, especially Cheung's, are

deeply affecting. In Cantonese with English subtitles.

Chang Shwu-Fen • Maggie Cheung • Lu Shao-fen ■ *Dir* Ann Hui • *Scr* Wu Nien-Jen

Song of the Islands ★★★ U
Romantic musical
1942 · US · Colour · 75mins

Immensely entertaining 20th Century-Fox Technicolor romp, starring pin-up Betty Grable as a Hawaiian "hula" girl in a sunny musical wherein hunk Victor Mature claims her, despite interference from a pair of feudin' fathers. There's some robust comic playing from reliable Jack Oakie, who's involved in some super by-play with Hilo Hattie. Unsurprisingly, this movie was a massive wartime hit, and is still mightily pleasing today.

Betty Grable *Eileen O'Brien* • Victor Mature *Jefferson Harper* • Jack Oakie *Rusty Smith* • Thomas Mitchell *Dennis O'Brien* • George Barbier *Harper* • Hilo Hattie *Palola* ■ *Dir* Walter Lang • *Scr* Joseph Schrank, Robert Pirosh, Robert Ellis, Helen Logan

Song of the Open Road ★★
Musical comedy   1944 · US · BW · 93mins

The only notable thing about this "let's-put-on-a-show" musical, was the screen debut of 15-year-old radio singing star Jane Powell. Virtually a showcase for her vocal talent, it soon led to an MGM contract and blonde hair. Powell plays a juvenile movie star, who runs away from home to work on a youth farm where everyone seems to have a musical gift. The show they put on to save the farm includes turns by WC Fields and ventriloquist Edgar Bergen with Charlie McCarthy.

Edgar Bergen • Jane Powell • WC Fields • Bonita Granville *Bonnie* • Peggy O'Neill *Peggy* • Jackie Moran *Jack* • Bill Christy *Bill* ■ *Dir* S Sylvan Simon • *Scr* Albert Mannheimer, from a story by Irving Phillips, Edward Verdier

Song of the Road   ★★★ U
Drama   1937 · UK · BW · 73mins

John Baxter was one of the most original British film-makers. In addition to some rather clumsy (but surprisingly commercial) regional comedies, he also made a string of socially aware dramas in which the heroes were either everyday workers or outsiders unwilling to march in step with progress. A sobering, if sentimental view of Britain emerging from the Depression, this old-fashioned, but curiously compelling picture follows Bransby Williams and his horse Polly as they tour the country looking for work. Keep an eye out for that inveterate barnstormer Tod Slaughter in a cameo as a travelling showman.

Bransby Williams *Old Bill* • Ernest Butcher *Foreman* • Muriel George *Mrs Trelawney* • Davy Burnaby *Mr Keppel* • Tod Slaughter *Showman* • John Turnbull *Bristow* • Edgar Driver *Titch* ■ *Dir* John Baxter • *Scr* John Baxter, from a story by Michael Kent

Song of the South   ★★★ U
Part-animated fantasy
1946 · US · Colour · 90mins

This wonderful piece of Southern Disneyana is a technically clever and charming work, blending live action and animation together with wit and brilliance, most notably in the now-classic *Zip-a-Dee Doo-Dah* sequence where James Baskett's Oscar-winning Uncle Remus meets the woodland folk of his tales. But seen today, such quaint simplicity looks patronising, and makes many contemporary viewers squirm. It's best to remember the film's period and relaxed attitudes, and thereby enjoy to the full the sheer innocence of the film. 🖵

Bobby Driscoll *Johnny* • James Baskett *Uncle Remus/Brer Fox* • Ruth Warrick *Sally* • Luana Patten *Ginny* • Lucile Watson *Grandmother* • Hattie McDaniel *Aunt Tempy* ■ *Dir* Wilfred Jackson, Harve Foster • *Scr* Dalton Raymond, Morton Grant, Maurice Rapf, from a story by Dalton Raymond, William Peet, Ralph Wright, and George Stallings, from the story collection *Tales of Uncle Remus* by Joel Chandler Harris

The Song Remains the Same   ★★★ 15
Concert documentary
1976 · UK · Colour · 136mins

The thunderous rock riffs of Led Zeppelin were a favourite among seventies acid-droppers and it looks as if the makers of this odd documentary had more than their fair share. Footage of a 1973 New York concert (with the highlight being jukebox giant *Stairway to Heaven*) are interspersed with behind-the-scenes mishaps, trippy effects and ultra-weird fantasy sequences from the heads of Robert Plant, Jimmy Page *et al*, which makes *Tommy* look like social realism. The dated sound quality might bother those with a re-mastered Led Zep CD collection. 🖵 **DVD**

Dir Peter Clifton, Joe Massot

A Song to Remember   ★★★ U
Biographical drama
1945 · US · Colour · 107mins

Hollywood biographies of classical composers are usually fair game for jest, and this account of Chopin's life is no exception. It features some flowery dialogue, a wildly over-the-top performance by Paul Muni as the composer's tutor and Merle Oberon miscast as the trousered George Sand who tells her lover to "Discontinue that so-called *Polonaise* jumble you've been playing for days." But the melodies, gorgeous Technicolor photography, opulent production and the seductive piano playing of Jose Iturbi (who dubbed for Cornel Wilde in the title role) add up to a lush, irresistible experience.

Cornel Wilde *Chopin* • Paul Muni *Joseph Elsner* • Merle Oberon *George Sand* • Stephen Bekassy *Franz Liszt* • Nina Foch *Constantia* • George Coulouris *Louis Pleyel* • George Macready *Alfred de Musset* ■ *Dir* Charles Vidor • *Scr* Sidney Buchman, from a story by Ernst Marischka • *Cinematographer* Tony Gaudio, Allen M Davey

Song without End   ★★★ U
Musical biography
1960 · US · Colour · 142mins

Rank matinée idol Dirk Bogarde made his Hollywood debut playing Franz Liszt in this ultra-glamorous Columbia biopic, turning down the role of Gaston Lachaille in MGM's *Gigi* in the process.

Bogarde swiftly returned to European film-making, and no wonder, for excellent though he is, this is preposterous tosh, redeemed only by Jorge Bolet's off-screen piano and the panache of veteran cameraman James Wong Howe. Alas, the soul went out of the project when the original director, Charles Vidor, died and George Cukor took over. The international supporting cast is also impressive, if lifeless.

Dirk Bogarde *Franz Liszt* • Capucine *Princess Carolyne* • Genevieve Page *Countess Marie* • Patricia Morison *George Sand* • Ivan Desny *Prince Nicholas* • Martita Hunt *Grand Duchess* ■ *Dir* Charles Vidor, George Cukor • *Scr* Oscar Millard

Songwriter   ★★★ 15
Musical comedy drama
1984 · US · Colour · 90mins

Sheer heaven for country music fans, with Willie Nelson and Kris Kristofferson as former singer-songwriter partners, who reunite to take on unscrupulous elements of the country music biz. The former is a C&W superstar, while the latter has clung on to his wayward lifestyle. The usual cocktail of drugs, booze and sleazy industry professionals is enlivened by the requisite musical number. An amiable and entertaining work from Robert Altman protegé Alan Rudolph. 🖵

Willie Nelson *Doc Jenkins* • Kris Kristofferson *Blackie Buck* • Melinda Dillon *Honey Carder* • Rip Torn *Dino McLeish* • Lesley Ann Warren *Gilda* ■ *Dir* Alan Rudolph • *Scr* Bud Shrake

Sons   ★★★
Comedy drama   1989 · US · Colour

A modest, but intriguing comedy drama about an attempt by three men to take their elderly father back to France to see the woman he fell in love with during the Second World War. While not saying anything particularly new, it benefits from the neat performances by leads D B Sweeney, William Forsythe and Robert Miranda. Look out, too, for appearances by legendary American director Samuel Fuller, French actress Stéphane Audran and *Flashdance's* Jennifer Beals as a transvestite. Contains swearing.

William Forsythe *Mike* • DB Sweeney *Rich* • Robert Miranda *Fred* • Samuel Fuller *Father* • Stéphane Audran *Florence* • William Hickey *Roger* • Jennifer Beals *Transvestite* ■ *Dir* Alexandre Rockwell • *Scr* Alexandre Rockwell, Brandon Cole

Sons and Lovers   ★★★
Drama   1960 · UK · BW · 99mins

The great cameraman Jack Cardiff made a directorial outing with this forthright adaptation of DH Lawrence's semi-autobiographical novel, about a boy caught between the Nottinghamshire rock and the hard place of his possessive mother (Wendy Hiller) and miner father (Trevor Howard). The trouble is that Dean Stockwell, as the teenager, is unconvincing in such great acting company. Ironically, the film won an Oscar for Freddie Francis's cinematography, while Cardiff was nominated as director.

Trevor Howard *Walter Morel* • Dean Stockwell *Paul Morel* • Wendy Hiller *Mrs Morel* • Mary Ure *Clara Dawes* • Heather Sears *Miriam Lievers* • William Lucas *William* • Conrad Phillips *Baxter Dawes* • Donald Pleasence *Pappleworth* • Ernest Thesiger *Henry Hadlock* ■ *Dir* Jack Cardiff • *Scr* Gavin Lambert, T EB Clarke, from the novel by DH Lawrence

The Sons of Katie Elder   ★★★★ U
Western   1965 · US · Colour · 116mins

A terrific western containing a wonderful score from Elmer Bernstein, who worked on *The Magnificent Seven*. Brothers John Wayne and Dean Martin ride out to avenge the death of their father. Stirring stuff, beautifully photographed on Panavisioned exteriors, with a fine support cast headed by Martha Hyer, who dignifies the movie by making a heartfelt speech about matriarchal virtue. Director Henry Hathaway and the Duke would team again for the Oscar-winning *True Grit*. 🖵

John Wayne *John Elder* • Dean Martin *Tom Elder* • Michael Anderson Jr *Bud Elder* • Earl Holliman *Matt Elder* • Martha Hyer *Mary Gordon* • George Kennedy *Curley* • Dennis Hopper *Dave Hastings* ■ *Dir* Henry Hathaway • *Scr* Allan Weiss, William H Wright, Harry Essex, from a story by Talbot Jennings • *Cinematographer* Lucien Ballard • *Music* Elmer Bernstein

Sons of the Desert   ★★★★★ U
Comedy   1933 · US · BW · 64mins

Probably the finest, and fastest, of all Laurel and Hardy's feature films, it involves the boys going to the Chicago convention of their fraternity lodge, having fooled their intimidating wives (Mae Busch and Dorothy Christy), but there's the inventive devil to pay when their spouses find out. The ridiculous men-only antics of the lodge are wonderfully exploited, especially by a burpingly bumptious Charley Chase, and the international society devoted to Stan and Ollie bears the name of this comedy gem – an indication of how highly it is thought of. 🖵

Stan Laurel *Stan* • Oliver Hardy *Ollie* • Charley Chase • Mae Busch *Mrs Lottie Chase Hardy* • Dorothy Christy *Mrs Betty Laurel* ■ *Dir* William A Seiter • *Scr* Frank Craven, Byron Morgan

Sons of the Musketeers   ★★★ U
Adventure   1951 · US · Colour · 81mins

Gloriously Technicolored hokum, which imagines that the offspring of the Musketeers are just as nifty with swords as their fathers. One of them is female (Athos's daughter, in fact), and played by Maureen O'Hara, who tosses her red tresses to the wind and buckles a swash as if to the manor born. Co-star Cornel Wilde, a former member of the US Olympic fencing team, is no match for our Maureen. Splendid fun.

Maureen O'Hara *Claire* • Cornel Wilde *D'Artagnan* • Robert Douglas *Lavalle* • Gladys Cooper *Queen* • Dan O'Herlihy *Aramis* • Alan Hale Jr *Porthos* • June Clayworth *Claudine* • Blanche Yurka *Madame Michom* • Nancy Gates *Princess Henriette* ■ *Dir* Lewis Allen • *Scr* Walter Ferris, Joseph Hoffman, from a story by Aubrey Wisberg, Jack Pollexfen • *Cinematographer* Ray Rennahan

U = SUITABLE FOR ALL   Uc = SUITABLE FOR ALL, ESPECIALLY FOR YOUNG CHILDREN (VIDEO ONLY)   PG = PARENTAL GUIDANCE

A Son's Promise ★★ U

Drama based on a true story
1990 · US · Colour · 90mins

Get out the Kleenex and prepare for a seriously weepie TV movie. When his mother is diagnosed as having terminal cancer, teenage son Rick Schroder promises to keep the family of seven sons together, no matter what. Despite good performances from a cast that includes Stephen Dorff (*Backbeat*), this film flounders in a sea of sentimentality. Any message about family unity is lost behind clichés and "meaningful" moments. ▭

Rick Schroder *Terry O'Kelley* • Donald Moffat *Cecil O'Kelley* • Veronica Cartwright *Guardian* • Stephen Dorff *Charles* • Andrew Lowery *Tommy O'Kelley* • Boyd Gaines *Businessman* • Ryan Marshall *David O'Kelley* ■ *Dir* John Korty • *Scr* Bill Stratton, Robert Inman, from a story by Bill Stratton

Sophie's Choice ★★★★ 15

Drama 1982 · US · Colour · 144mins

Meryl Streep confirmed her status as the Queen of Accents, with her Oscar-winning performance in this moving adaptation of William Styron's bestselling novel. Yet, for all the significance of the revelations about Sophie's past, it is the interaction between the three central characters that gives the story its strength, and it is quite bewildering that, in spite of the quality of Kevin Kline's temperamental zest and Peter MacNicol's adoring timidity, neither merited even a nomination. Alan J Pakula's direction is much less constricted than his overly reverential script, thanks to the beautiful and evocative photography by Nestor Almendros. ▭ **DVD**

Meryl Streep *Sophie Zawistowska* • Kevin Kline *Nathan Landau* • Peter MacNicol *Stingo* • Rita Karin *Yetta Zimmerman* • Stephen D Newman *Larry Landau* • Greta Turken *Leslie Lapidus* • Josh Mostel *Morris Fink* • Marcel Rosenblatt *Astrid Weinstein* • Moishe Rosenfeld *Moishe Rosenblaum* ■ *Dir* Alan J Pakula • *Scr* Alan J Pakula, from the novel by William Styron • *Cinematographer* Nestor Almendros • *Music* Marvin Hamlisch

Sorcerer ★★

Thriller 1977 · US · Colour · 92mins

William Friedkin's follow-up to *The French Connection* and *The Exorcist* was a remake of Clouzot's 1953 classic *The Wages of Fear*, about two trucks and their desperate crews who take a load of high explosives through the South American jungle, knowing that the slightest jolt will blow them sky-high. Friedkin's insistence on absolute realism took the budget from $3m to $22m and resulted in some simply staggering footage as the trucks heave through the jungle, across rivers and over dilapidated rope bridges. As an allegory about Third World exploitation it works, often powerfully, but the vital ingredient – tension – is missing. One of Hollywood's most infamous critical and box-office flops, it's a fascinating failure and a monument to one director's ego. (Rarely shown and unavailable on video, due to a dispute between Paramount and Universal, both of whom financed it.)

Roy Scheider *Jackie Scanlon/"Dominguez"* • Bruno Cremer *Victor Manzon/"Serrano"* •

Francisco Rabal *Nilo* • Amidou *Kassem/"Martinez"* • Ramon Bieri *Corlette* • Peter Capell *Lartigue* ■ *Dir* William Friedkin • *Scr* Walon Green, from the novel *Le salaire de la Peur (The Wages of Fear)* by Georges Arnaud

The Sorcerers ★★★

Science-fiction horror
1967 · UK · Colour · 85mins

Prior to *Witchfinder General* and his death at the age of 24, Michael Reeves directed this intelligent shocker. Boris Karloff invents a mesmeric machine to control the mind of bored, swinging Londoner Ian Ogilvy, which can absorb and pass on the sensations he experiences. Unfortunately, Karloff's wife gets hooked on the voyeuristic thrills, and wills the mod zombie to steal and kill. Cult brilliance on a small budget, with Karloff adding his adroit touches.

Boris Karloff *Professor Monserrat* • Catherine Lacey *Estelle Monserrat* • Ian Ogilvy *Mike* • Elizabeth Ercy *Nicole* • Victor Henry *Alan* • Susan George *Audrey* ■ *Dir* Michael Reeves • *Scr* Michael Reeves, Tom Baker, from a idea by John Burke

Sorority Girl ★★

Drama 1957 · US · BW · 60mins

A torrid fifties teen-flick from schlock-meister Roger Corman, with Susan Cabot as a James Dean figure in a dress, rebelling without much cause, blackmailing and pulling the hair of her college colleagues until she's banished to the American equivalent of Coventry. This deeply moral tale, filmed in a fortnight, was aimed at an undemanding drive-in audience. The pretty Miss Cabot, by the way, retired in 1959 to raise a family and in 1986 she was tragically murdered by her son.

Susan Cabot *Sabra Tanner* • Dick Miller *Mort* • Barboura O'Neill *Rita Joyce* • June Kenney *Tina* • Barbara Crane *Ellie Marshall* • Fay Baker *Mrs Tanner* • Jeane Wood *Mrs Fessenden* ■ *Dir* Roger Corman • *Scr* Ed Waters, Lou Lieberman

The Sorrow and the Pity ★★★★★

Political documentary
1970 · Fr/Swi/W Ger · BW · 260mins

Divided into two parts – *The Collapse* and *The Choice* – Marcel Ophüls's monumental documentary is not just an investigation into what occurred in France during the Nazi Occupation, but how the nation has elected to remember it. Probing the selective memory of his occasionally evasive witnesses (who range from heroes and survivors to traitors and oppressors), he uncovers contradictions among the half-truths, as well as provoking outbursts of bitter fury and expressions of genuine remorse. Topics such as collaboration and co-operation, resistance and indifference are painfully explored. The archive material may be manipulative, but it retains the power to chill and cast doubt.

Dir Marcel Ophüls • *Scr* Marcel Ophüls, André Harris

Sorrowful Jones ★★★ U

Comedy 1949 · US · BW · 88mins

Damon Runyon's warm-hearted story, *Little Miss Marker* – about a tightwad Broadway bookie forced to look after a gambler's child – had been a huge success as a film with Shirley Temple. Paramount then ingeniously adapted it into a Bob Hope vehicle, taking attention away from the moppet played competently, but not memorably, by Mary Jane Saunders. Although well supplied with characteristic quips, Hope is more restrained and brings out the sentimentality inherent in the story. Lucille Ball was obvious casting as the Runyon doll, and the film proved such a hit, that director and star teamed up for another Runyon adaptation, *The Lemon Drop Kid*.

Bob Hope *Sorrowful Jones* • Lucille Ball *Gladys O'Neill* • William Demarest *Regret* • Bruce Cabot *Big Steve Holloway* • Thomas Gomez *Reardon* ■ *Dir* Sidney Lanfield • *Scr* Melville Shavelson, Edmund Hartmann, Jack Rose, from the film *Little Miss Marker* by Gladys Lehman, William R Lipman, Sam Hellman, and from the story by Damon Runyon

Sorry, Wrong Number ★★★★

Thriller 1948 · US · BW · 89mins

Originally a radio play by Lucille Fletcher, this taut drama centres on a bedridden heiress who, left alone in her apartment, tries to call her husband and overhears her own murder being planned. Fletcher opened out the screenplay just enough to allow beefy Burt Lancaster to share a crumb of the honours with Barbara Stanwyck, and to heighten the claustrophobia of the victim's bedroom by contrasting it with a murky outside world. Anatole Litvak directed this classic *film noir*, a real nail-biter, which earned Stanwyck an Oscar-nomination for her tour de force as the domineering, neurotically ill Leona, at the mercy of her self-induced helplessness.

Barbara Stanwyck *Leona Stevenson* • Burt Lancaster *Henry Stevenson* • Ann Richards *Sally Lord Dodge* • Wendell Corey *Dr Alexander* • Ed Begley *James Cotterell* • Leif Erickson *Fred Lord* • William Conrad *Morano* ■ *Dir* Anatole Litvak • *Scr* Lucille Fletcher, from her radio play

Sorry, Wrong Number ★★ 15

Thriller 1989 · US · Colour · 85mins

Loni Anderson gives a surprisingly credible performance in this TV suspense thriller, a remake of the 1948 film which starred Barbara Stanwyck. A bed-bound woman accidentally overhears a phone conversation involving her planned murder. Although not as strong as the original, the story still holds up, and Anderson portrays the lead role with convincing vulnerability. Hal Holbrook co-stars in this taut nail-biter which, under Tony Wharmby's well-paced direction, is well-worth ringing up. ▭

Loni Anderson *Angela Stevenson* • Hal Holbrook *Jim Coltrane* • Carl Weintraub *Charlie Stevenson* • Patrick Macnee *Nigel Evans* ■ *Dir* Tony Wharmby • *Scr* Ann Louise Bardach, from the1948 film

Le Souffle au Coeur ★★★★ 18

Drama 1971 · Fr/It/W Ger · Colour · 113mins

On hearing the word incest, the moral guardians who delight in blaming cinema for society's ills almost fell over themselves in the rush to condemn *Le Souffle au Coeur*. Even the critics got caught up in the fuss, and devoted more column space to a brief, tender scene at the end of the film than they did to the fond, very funny portrait of the French middle-classes in the mid-fifties. This is classic rites-of-passage stuff from Louis Malle, with non-actor Benôt Ferreux giving a wonderfully natural performance as the Dijon teenager curious about everything from sex to art forgery. Lea Massari is equally outstanding as his flirtatious mother. In French with English subtitles. Contains sex scenes, nudity. ▭

Lea Massari *Clara Chevalier* • Benôt Ferreux *Laurent Chevalier* • Daniel Gélin *Father* • Marc Winocourt *Marc* • Michel Lonsdale *Father Henri* ■ *Dir/Scr* Louis Malle

Soul Food ★★★★ 15

Drama 1997 · US · Colour · 110mins

This well-acted and well-made drama focuses, as the title suggests, on the Sunday dinner get-togethers of a large African-American family. Matriarch Irma P Hall's home cooking , just about keeps her three grown-up daughters and their partners from each other's throats, until a tragedy forces them to reconcile their differences. This is a terrific ensemble piece, boosted by the unfussy script and direction of George Tillman Jr. There are also solid performances from Vanessa Williams, Viveca A Fox, Nia Long and Mekhi Phifer. Contains swearing and sex scenes. ▭

Vanessa L Williams *Teri* • Vivica A Fox *Maxine* • Nia Long *Bird* • Michael Beach *Miles* • Mekhi Phifer *Lem* • Brandon Hammond *Ahmad* • Jeffrey D Sams *Kenny* ■ *Dir/Scr* George Tillman Jr

Soul in the Hole ★★★★ 15

Sports documentary
1995 · US · Colour · 98mins

From *Hoop Dreams* to *He Got Game*, basketball has appeared the homeboy's only conceivable route out of the ghetto. But never has the human drama and the simple beauty of the game been combined with such pace, passion and personality as in Danielle Gardner's documentary. Following the fortunes of "Bed-Stuy" team Kenny's Kings, and particularly its wayward star Ed "Booger" Smith, it may not break stylistic ground with its blend of talking heads and big game highlights. However, with its concentration on character and locale, this clipped, comic film takes a grip, but its real strength is that it never loses sight of life.

Dir Danielle Gardner

Soul Man ★★ 15

Comedy 1986 · US · Colour · 100mins

This charade was supposed to be a daring and right-on attempt to explore the prejudices on either side of the American racial divide, from the

perspective of a middle-class white boy who is being penalised for not being black! Even though the social comment is totally subservient to the endless round of cheap-shot gags, the critics were inexplicably charitable to the film on its release, pointing to the sly satire and the courageous performance of C Thomas Howell as the kid who gulps down suntan pills in order to win a law school scholarship. Surely someone else noticed that this is insidious and offensive? ▱

C Thomas Howell *Mark Watson* • Arye Gross *Gordon Bloomfield* • Rae Dawn Chong *Sarah Walker* • James Earl Jones *Professor Rutherford Banks* • Melora Hardin *Whitney Dunbar* • Leslie Nielsen *Mr Dunbar* • James B Sikking *Bill Watson* ■ *Dir* Steve Miner • *Scr* Carol Black

Soul of the Game ★★★

Sports drama 1996 · US · Colour · 105mins
A terrific cast toplines this historical docu-drama about the racial integration of American baseball, told from the point of view of three Negro League baseball greats and friends. Kevin Sullivan deftly directs Delroy Lindo, Mykelti Williamson and Blair Underwood in an excellent drama, which rises above the sports genre with its intense look at loyalty, racism and morality. Due to the subject matter there is strong language, but, with superb technical credits, especially the authentic period locations and atmosphere, you don't have to be a baseball fan to appreciate this winning tale.

Delroy Lindo *Satchel Paige* • Mykel T Williamson *Josh Gibson* • Blair Underwood *Jackie Robinson* • Edward Herrmann *Branch Rickey* • R Lee Ermey *Wilkie* ■ *Dir* Kevin Rodney Sullivan [Kevin Sullivan] • *Scr* David Himmelstein, by Gary Hoffman

Souls at Sea ★★★

Drama 1937 · US · BW · 90mins
Released in competition with 20th Century-Fox's *Slave Ship* (1937), this Paramount spectacular features Gary Cooper as the strong, silent opponent of slavery, on trial for shooting survivors of a sinking vessel who clung to the oars of his crowded lifeboat. Co-star George Raft revived his flagging career with a winning performance as Cooper's loyal, but slow-witted companion with a ring in his ear. The story is rather awkwardly presented (with too much reported rather than shown), but Henry Hathaway's direction is swift and incisive, and the period setting is superbly evoked.

Gary Cooper *Michael "Nuggin" Taylor* • George Raft *Powdah* • Frances Dee *Margaret Tarryton* • Henry Wilcoxon *Lt Stanley Tarryton* • Harry Carey *Captain* • Olympe Bradna *Babsie* • Robert Cummings *George Martin* • Virginia Weidler *Tina* ■ *Dir* Henry Hathaway • *Scr* Grover Jones, Dale Van Every, Richard Talmadge, from a story by Ted Lesser

Soultaker ★★ 15

Horror 1991 · US · Colour · 90mins
Two lovers are separated from their souls in a car crash and must get them back before time runs out, in this tedious suspense fantasy. Martin Sheen's brother Joe Estevez is the titular terror who takes a shine to the female victim and wants to spend

eternity with her. An awkward combination of cartoon action, comic horror and tame romance, director Michael Rissi's mystic mix-up comes too close to *Naked Gun* parody for comfort, especially with lines like: "Led Zeppelin was wrong, man! There is no stairway to heaven!" Contains violence. ▱

Joe Estevez *Soultaker* • Vivian Schilling *Natalie* • Gregg Thomsen *Zach Taylor* • Robert Z'Dar *Angel of Death* • David Shark *Brad* • Chuck Williams *Tommy* ■ *Dir* Michael Rissi • *Scr* Vivian Schilling, from a story by Vivian Schilling, Eric Parkinson

The Sound and the Fury ★★★

Drama 1959 · US · Colour · 115mins
Joanne Woodward is the young misfit in this less intense companion piece to the earlier William Faulkner adaptation, *The Long Hot Summer*, by the same director, screenwriters and leading lady. But there's no escaping Jason, played by Yul Brynner (with hair), the cruel-to-be-kind outsider, who bullies a decayed southern family into some semblance of self respect. It's a delightfully played battle of wills between Woodward and Brynner, with a fine supporting cast that includes Margaret Leighton as a Blanche DuBois wreck.

Yul Brynner *Jason* • Joanne Woodward *Quentin* • Margaret Leighton *Caddy* • Stuart Whitman *Charles Busch* • Ethel Waters *Dilsey* • Jack Warden *Ben* • Françoise Rosay *Mrs Compson* ■ *Dir* Martin Ritt • *Scr* Irving Ravetch, Harriet Frank Jr, from the novel by William Faulkner

The Sound Barrier ★★★★ U

Drama 1952 · UK · BW · 111mins
Terence Rattigan's script was Oscar-nominated, but the main honours in this David Lean film are shared between the stunning aerial sequences and the fine performance by Ralph Richardson as an aeroplane designer driven to produce the first craft to outstrip the speed of sound. The film is an illustration of Bernard Shaw's dictum, that history is made by unreasonable people or, by those single-minded enough to pursue their visions, regardless of the emotional cost to their families or themselves. Not one of Lean's masterpieces, but a solid enough effort.

Ralph Richardson *John Ridgefield* • Ann Todd *Susan Garthwaite* • Nigel Patrick *Tony Garthwaite* • John Justin *Phillip Peel* • Dinah Sheridan *Jess Peel* • Joseph Tomelty *Will Sparks* • Denholm Elliott *Christopher Ridgefield* • Jack Allen *Windy Williams* • Ralph Michael *Fletcher* • Vincent Holman *ATA officer* • Douglas Muir *Controller* • Leslie Phillips *Controller* ■ *Dir* David Lean • *Scr* Terence Rattigan • *Cinematographer* Jack Hildyard

The Sound of Fury ★★★★ PG

Crime drama 1950 · US · BW · 88mins
This extraordinarily stark and uncompromising low-budget drama features Lloyd Bridges as a hardened criminal of the Depression period who recruits an out-of-work family man, played by Frank Lovejoy, as his accomplice in a kidnapping. After their victim dies, a journalist whips up local feeling and in a terrifying climax, the

two men are seized by an hysterical lynch mob. Only the unnecessary moral comments of an Italian doctor lessen the film's impact. The critical view of American mores contributed to the blacklisting of its director, Cyril Endfield, who moved to Britain. ▱

Frank Lovejoy *Howard Tyler* • Lloyd Bridges *Jerry Slocum* • Kathleen Ryan *Judy Tyler* • Richard Carlson *Gil Stanton* • Katherine Locke *Hazel* • Adele Jergens *Velma* ■ *Dir* Cyril Endfield [Cy Endfield] • *Scr* Jo Pagano, from his novel *The Condemned*

Sound of Love ★★

Romantic drama 1977 · US · Colour · 74mins
Struggling at times between the authentic and overemphasised, this is a sometimes touching portrait of the love between two people with hearing difficulties. He's a mechanic rendered deaf through an accident, she's a drifter. John Power rightly opts for uncluttered direction and gives his characters a chance to breathe. John Jarratt and Celia De Burgh portray the hearing-impaired couple without a hint of self-consciousness.

John Jarratt *Dave* • Celia De Burgh *Eileen* ■ *Dir* John Power • *Scr* John Power, from a screenplay by Lew Hunter

The Sound of Music ★★★★★ U

Classic musical 1965 · US · Colour · 165mins
The hills are still alive for the, then, biggest money-maker in the history of cinema. It's an artful and professionally made crowd-pleaser that reaches out to every generation, thanks to expert and unsentimental handling from director Robert Wise (replacing William Wyler) and a magnificent performance from Julie Andrews. She is perfectly cast as Maria, the reluctant nun who discovers her true calling as governess to a houseful of youngsters. It still looks lovely, in particular the stunning opening panoramic sweep on to the mountain top and the *Do Re Mi* tour around Salzburg, and the Rodgers and Hammerstein score is as refreshing as ever. For those who have never seen it, do. For those who love it, no persuasion is needed – it's as fresh and as magical as Andrews's smile. ▱

Julie Andrews *Maria* • Christopher Plummer *Captain Von Trapp* • Eleanor Parker *Baroness* • Richard Haydn *Max Detweiler* • Peggy Wood *Mother Abbess* • Charmian Carr *Liesl* • Heather Menzies *Louisa* • Nicholas Hammond *Friedrich* • Duane Chase *Kurt* • Angela Cartwright *Brigitta* • Debbie Turner *Marta* • Kym Karath *Gretl* • Daniel Truhitte *Rolfe* ■ *Dir* Robert Wise • *Scr* Ernest Lehman, from the musical by Richard Rodgers, Oscar Hammerstein II, Howard Lindsay, Russel Crouse • *Cinematographer* Ted McCord • *Production Designer* Boris Leven • *Music Director* Irwin Kostal • *Editor* William Reynolds

Sounder ★★★★ U

Drama 1972 · US · Colour · 105mins
A sentimental, but still powerful movie about a family of black sharecroppers in thirties Depression-hit Louisiana that was heavily Oscar-nominated, but failed to win anything. Directed by Martin Ritt and beautifully photographed, it boasts fine

performances from Paul Winfield as the dad who is snatched from his family for stealing a ham and Cicely Tyson as the mother of three who struggles to carry on the farm without him. Kevin Hooks (who won a Golden Globe for best newcomer and went on to become a director) is the son who embarks on an odyssey to find Winfield. Accompanied by faithful dog Sounder, he meets schoolteacher Jane McLachlan, who irrevocably changes his life. A sequel followed in 1976.

Cicely Tyson *Rebecca Morgan* • Paul Winfield *Nathan Lee Morgan* • Kevin Hooks *David Lee Morgan* • Carmen Mathews *Mrs Boatwright* • Taj Mahal *Ike* • James Best *Sheriff Young* ■ *Dir* Martin Ritt • *Scr* Lonne Elder III, from the novel by William H Armstrong • *Cinematographer* John A Alonzo

Sour Grapes ★ 15

Comedy 1998 · US · Colour · 88mins
Two goombah cousins hit it rich playing slot machines in Atlantic City – or rather, one of them does, using the quarters he borrowed from his relative. His refusal to split the winnings means the end of their friendship and the start of an endless round of recriminations and snappy repartee. The brain behind this one was Larry David, co-creator of sitcom *Seinfeld*, but even fans of the TV series will have trouble laughing at any of this. Contains swearing and sexual references. ▱

Steven Weber *Evan* • Craig Bierko *Richie* • Karen Sillas *Joan* • Robyn Peterman *Roberta* • Jack Burns *Eulogist* • Viola Harris *Selma* ■ *Dir/Scr* Larry David

Soursweet ★★★ 15

Drama 1988 · UK · Colour · 105mins
Before he went on to bigger, if not necessarily better, things with *Four Weddings and a Funeral* and *Pushing Tin*, Mike Newell came up with this sweet and sour drama of immigrant life in London, about a Chinese couple who set up their own small restaurant. It could have been chop phooey, but, with the help of a fine screenplay by Ian McEwan, and thoughtful direction, it becomes a charming and moving character study of one of the many ethnic strands that make up multiracial Britain. ▱

Sylvia Chang *Lily* • Danny An-Ning Dun *Chen* • Jodi Long *Mui* • Soon-Teck Oh *Red Cudgel* • William Chow *White Paper Fan* • Jim Carter *Mr Constantinides* ■ *Dir* Mike Newell • *Scr* Ian McEwan, from the novel by Timothy Mo

Sous les Toits de Paris ★★★★

Drama 1930 · Fr · BW · 91mins
Deriving much neighbourhood charm from Lazare Meerson's sets and full of memorable songs and pleasing performances, René Clair's sound debut was a fluent delight at a time when everyone else's talkies were little more than animated radio. Indeed, he places so much emphasis on the narrative power of the image, that he mischievously stages conversations where the dialogue simply couldn't be heard. Keeping the camera on the move and the action light, he utterly enchants with the story of Parisian street singer, Albert Préjean, whose

U = SUITABLE FOR ALL   Uc = SUITABLE FOR ALL, ESPECIALLY FOR YOUNG CHILDREN (VIDEO ONLY)   PG = PARENTAL GUIDANCE

beloved, Pola Illery, is also pursued by his best friend, Edmond Gréville, and the lecherous Gaston Modot. In French with English subtitles.

Albert Préjean *Albert* • Pola Illery *Pola* • Gaston Modot *Fred* • Edmond T Gréville *Louis* • Bill Bocket *Bill* • *Dir/Scr* René Clair • *Cinematographer* Georges Périnal

South ★★★

Silent documentary
1919 · UK · Tinted · 81mins

A milestone in Britain's proud documentary history, Frank Hurley's silent account of Sir Ernest Shackleton's doomed Antarctic expedition (1914-16) is heavily reliant on captions that don't always provide adequate information or explanation. Nor does Hurley come clean about the fate of the 70 sled dogs on whom he lavishes so much attention, until they are abandoned when the mission becomes a desperate bid for survival. However, the tinted footage is compelling, with the hauntingly beautiful night shots of the *Endurance* run aground, standing out as symbols of our nation's love affair with flawed heroism.

Dir Frank Hurley

South American George ★★★ 🆄

Comedy   1941 · UK · BW · 95mins

The first film that ukulele-playing comic George Formby made after he left Ealing Studios and signed with Columbia, gives him a dual role as an opera singer and his double, a stagehand who agrees to take the singer's place then finds himself fleeing gangsters. Sometimes cited as the start of Formby's decline on the screen, this has more plot than usual for a Formby vehicle and although some of his fans missed the "old" George, they still turned out in their millions and maintained his position as Britain's top box-office draw.

George Formby *George Butters/Gilli Vanetti* • Linden Travers *Carole Dean* • Enid Stamp-Taylor *Frances Martinique* • Jacques Brown *Enrico Richardo* • Felix Aylmer *Mr Appleby* • Ronald Shiner *Swifty* ■ *Dir* Marcel Varnel • *Scr* Leslie Arliss, Norman Lee, Austin Melford

South Central ★★★ 15

Drama   1992 · US · Colour · 98mins

Based on the novel *Crips* by schoolteacher Donald Bakeer, this is another stark look at life on the streets of South Central Los Angeles. Although it begins in standard *Boyz N the Hood* territory, the action takes a dramatic turn when jailed murderer Glenn Plummer discovers Islam. There's something of the Malcolm X story about this transformation, but the struggle for control of his ten-year-old between Plummer and gang leader Byron Keith Minns, and his girlfriend's descent into addiction and prostitution, makes for powerful human drama. Featuring uncompromising direction by Steve Anderson, this is not for the faint-hearted.

Glenn Plummer *Bobby Johnson* • Carl Lumbly *Ali* • Byron Keith Minns [Byron Minns] *Ray Ray* • Lexie D Bigham [Lexie Bigham] *Bear* • Vincent Craig Dupree *Loco* • LaRita Shelby

Carole • Kevin Best *Genie Lamp* ■ *Dir* Steve Anderson • *Scr* Steve Anderson, from the novel *Crips* by Donald Bakeer

South of Algiers ★★★ PG

Drama   1952 · UK · Colour · 86mins

An exciting, richly Technicolored movie about a sun-scorched search in the Sahara for a fabled "golden mask" (the American title). Imaginatively shot by under-rated documentarist Jack Lee, it features sturdy Van Heflin as the archaeologist with a mission and Eric Portman as his rapacious adversary. Wanda Hendrix, once Mrs Audie Murphy in real life, is the female lead. Stirring stuff, and beautifully filmed by veteran British cameraman Oswald Morris, with some strikingly authentic sequences. 📼

Van Heflin *Nicholas Chapman* • Wanda Hendrix *Anne Burnet* • Eric Portman *Dr Burnet* • Charles Goldner *Petris* • Jacques François *Jacques Farnod* • Jacques Brunius *Kress* • Aubrey Mather *Professor Sir Arthur Young* ■ *Dir* Jack Lee • *Scr* Robert Westerby

South of Pago Pago ★★★ 🆄

Adventure   1940 · US · BW · 97mins

Pago Pago – pronounced Pango Pango – is the main town of American Samoa and infamous as the watery hang-out for Sadie Thompson, the heroine of Somerset Maugham's torrid South Seas story *Rain*. In this well-barnacled adventure, Victor McLaglen runs a pearl-diving operation while dodging hostile Polynesians and watching his divers fail to come up for air. Romance is supplied by the alluring, but doomed Frances Farmer who catches the eye of native hunk Jon Hall. Exciting action and fine photography keep it above the merely routine.

Victor McLaglen *Bucko Larson* • Jon Hall *Kehane* • Frances Farmer *Ruby Taylor* • Olympe Bradna *Malia* • Gene Lockhart *Lindsay* • Douglass Dumbrille *Williams* • Francis Ford *Foster* ■ *Dir* Alfred E Green • *Scr* George Bruce • *Cinematographer* John Mescall

South of St Louis ★★ 🆄

Western   1949 · US · Colour · 86mins

This routine western about three ranchers wasn't particularly memorable in its day, but today is well worth a look for nostalgic value alone. The three leads –Joel McCrea, Alexis Smith and Zachary Scott– are eminently watchable, their sheer professionalism a delight. In a post-war return to Warner Bros, director Ray Enright proves as competent as ever, this time helped by the great cameraman Karl Freund's outdoor Technicolor photography. But the basic material remains relentlessly routine, and the movie, while pleasant enough, has little real merit.

Joel McCrea *Kip Davis* • Alexis Smith *Rouge de Lisle* • Zachary Scott *Charlie Burns* • Dorothy Malone *Deborah Miller* • Douglas Kennedy *Lee Price* • Alan Hale *Jake Evarts* • Victor Jory *Luke Cottrell* ■ *Dir* Ray Enright • *Scr* Zachary Gold, James R Webb

South Pacific ★★★ 🆄

Musical   1958 · US · Colour · 143mins

This screen version of the fabulous Rodgers and Hammerstein Broadway show has always been better liked by

the public than the critics. Unfortunately, though, it has several flaws, not least of which is the bizarre use of colour filters that will turn your TV picture orange, mauve and green. Wonderful though Mitzi Gaynor is in the big numbers, her character's brashness grows tiresome, while Rossano Brazzi is wooden and the war sequences seem to belong to a different movie. But the score is wonderful, and no one could fail to be carried away by some of the finest songs ever written, including *Some Enchanted Evening*. 📼

Mitzi Gaynor *Nellie Forbush* • Rossano Brazzi *Emile de Becque* • John Kerr *Lieutenant Cable* • Ray Walston *Luther Billis* • Juanita Hall *Bloody Mary* • France Nuyen *Liat* • Russ Brown *Captain Brackett* • Joan Fontaine *Polynesian woman* ■ *Dir* Joshua Logan • *Scr* Paul Osborn, from the musical by Richard Rodgers, Oscar Hammerstein II, Joshua Logan, from the novel *Tales of the South Pacific* by James A Michener

South Park: Bigger, Longer & Uncut ★★★★ 15

Animated comedy
1999 · US · Colour · 81mins

Trey Parker and Matt Stone's tasteless animated series gets a big screen supercharge in this dark, demented, deliriously funny feature-length tale. Stan, Kyle, Cartman and Kenny go on an outing to see Terrence and Philip's profanity-laced movie and their resultant change in vocabulary is the catalyst for an escalating bout of moral guardian madness, culminating in the outbreak of World War Three (well, America versus Canada). A sharp, inventive TV spin-off, it doesn't pad its plot or waste widescreen opportunities. The crude, taboo-assaulting story is enjoyably ambitious and the surprisingly tuneful songs cleverly parody everything from Disney ditties to *Les Misérables*. Bad taste at its best. Contains swearing, sexual references. 📼 **DVD**

Trey Parker *Stan Marsh/Eric Cartman/Mr Garrison/Mr Hat/Officer Barbrady* • Matt Stone *Kyle Broflovski/Kenny McCormick/Pip/Jesus/Jimbo* • Mary Kay Bergman *Mrs Cartman/Sheila Broflovski/Sharon Manson/Mrs McCormick/Wendy Testaburger/Principal Victoria* • Isaac Hayes *Chef* • George Clooney *Doctor Gouache* • Brent Spiner *Conan O'Brien* • Minnie Driver *Brooke Shields* • Eric Idle *Doctor Vosknocker* ■ *Dir* Trey Parker • *Scr* Trey Parker, Matt Stone, Pam Brady

South Riding ★★★

Romantic drama   1938 · UK · BW · 68mins

Victor Saville makes an admirable job of bringing Winifred Holtby's bubbling cauldron of upper-class insanity, misguided philanthropy and council-chamber corruption to the screen. Deftly capturing the sights and sounds of this Yorkshire neverland, he only loses his grasp at the close as sentimentality is allowed to wash away the grit. Ralph Richardson reins in his customary screen excesses to give a sensitive reading of the misguided squire unable to come to terms with his wife's madness.

Ralph Richardson *Robert Carne* • Edna Best *Sarah Burton* • Ann Todd *Madge Carne* • Edmund Gwenn *Alfred Huggins* • John Clements *Joe Astell* • Marie Lohr *Mrs Beddows* • Milton Rosmer *Alderman Snaith* •

Glynis Johns *Midge Carne* ■ *Dir* Victor Saville • *Scr* Ian Dalrymple, Donald Bull, from the novel by Winifred Holtby

South Sea Woman ★★

Comedy adventure   1953 · US · BW · 98mins

Even stars as big as Burt Lancaster had to serve their Hollywood apprenticeship in tacky movies such as this, in which he's an eager-to-fight marine sparking with sultry Virginia Mayo on a tropical island. Director Arthur Lubin had made six movies about Francis the Talking Mule, so Burt's reported mulish behaviour off-set was forgivably in character. Sadly, not much character in the rest of the cast, though.

Burt Lancaster *Sergeant James O'hearn* • Virginia Mayo *Ginger Martin* • Chuck Connors *Davey White* • Barry Kelley *Colonel Hickman* • Hayden Rorke *Lieutenant Fears* • Leon Askin *Marchand* ■ *Dir* Arthur Lubin • *Scr* Edwin Blum, Earl Baldwin, Stanley Shapiro, from a play by William M Rankin

Southern Comfort ★★★★ 15

Action drama   1981 · US · Colour · 101mins

Nine National Guardsmen – including Keith Carradine and Powers Boothe – are sent on exercises through the Louisiana swamplands and find themselves drawn into a guerrilla war with the local Cajuns. Set in 1973, Walter Hill's movie is evidently an allegorical treatment of the Vietnam conflict, with the Cajuns cast as the shadowy, but lethal Vietcong. Few movies are as single-minded as this one: Hill establishes the bayou as a grey, formless labyrinth and ultimately creates a purely abstract action movie that's creepy, tense and never remotely comfortable. 📼

Keith Carradine *Spencer* • Powers Boothe *Hardin* • Fred Ward *Reece* • Franklyn Seales *Simms* • TK Carter *Cribbs* • Lewis Smith *Stuckey* • Les Lannom *Casper* • Peter Coyote *Poole* • Carlos Brown *Bowden* • Brion James *Trapper* ■ *Dir* Walter Hill • *Scr* Michael Kane, Walter Hill, David Glier

Southern Roses ★★ 🆄

Musical comedy   1936 · UK · BW · 80mins

Small-scale, long-forgotten, expendable, British, romantic comedy, in which a naval officer is smitten with a musical comedy actress, while his friend is required to pose as her husband, this is notable only for the presence of famous musical hall comedian George Robey, known as "the prime minister of mirth". With additional appearances from silent film star Chili Bouchier and character actress Sara Allgood.

George Robey *Mr Higgins* • Neil Hamilton *Reggie* • Gina Malo *Mary Rowland* • Chili Bouchier *Estrella Estrello* • Vera Pearce *Carrie* • Richard Dolman *Bill Higgins* • Athene Seyler *Mrs Rowland* • DA Clarke-Smith *Senor Estrello* • Sara Allgood *Miss Florence* ■ *Dir* Frederick Zelnik [Fred Zelnik] • *Scr* Ronald Gow, from a play by Rudolph Bernauer

The Southern Star ★★★ PG

Comedy adventure
1969 · Fr/UK · Colour · 101mins

Splendidly photographed African adventure filmed on authentic Senegalese locations, but alas bearing the curse of international co-

production. Under-rated editor-turned-director Sidney Hayers tries to pull together the Jules Verne-inspired plot and a cast that verges on the preposterous, headed by George Segal (far too urban for this type of trek), Ursula Andress and Orson Welles, who was obviously in need of the money. This romp isn't sure whether it's comedy or adventure or both, but it looks good nevertheless. ▣
George Segal *Dan* • Ursula Andress *Erica Kramer* • Orson Welles *Plankett* • Ian Hendry *Karl* • Harry Andrews *Kramer* ■ *Dir* Sidney Hayers • *Scr* David Pursall, Jack Seddon, Jean Giono, from the novel *L'Etoile du Sud, le Pays des Diamants* by Jules Verne • *Cinematographer* Raoul Coutard

A Southern Yankee ★★★
Comedy   1948 · US · BW · 90mins
Fans of Buster Keaton's *The General* may well recognise an occasional overlap here. That's because not only was Keaton happy for Red Skelton to borrow ideas from that silent classic, he was also in charge of many comic sequences, which unsurprisingly turn out to be those that make the film really sing. Otherwise proceedings oscillate from swirling exuberance to blandness, though Skelton's comic knack is never in doubt. As he depicts his foolish Civil War spy with precision, the silent era and its sense of slapstick are brought to mind.
Red Skelton *Aubrey Filmore* • Arlene Dahl *Sallyann Weatharby* • Brian Donlevy *Curt Devlyn* • George Coulouris *Major Jack Drumman* • Minor Watson *General Watkins* • Lloyd Gough *Captain Steve Lorford* • John Ireland *Captain Jed Calbern* ■ *Dir* Edward Sedgwick • *Scr* Harry Tugend, from a story by Melvin Frank

The Southerner ★★★★★
Drama   1945 · US · BW · 92mins
The only American film by the great French director Jean Renoir to receive critical praise and break even at the box office, the screenplay, on which Renoir was advised by William Faulkner, told of a year in the life of a cotton farmer who has to fight a malicious neighbour, the elements and malnutrition. In order to achieve pictorial splendour and realism, the film was shot almost entirely on location in the San Joaquin valley in California (standing in for Texas) and produced an effective slice of Americana. Zachary Scott, cast against type in a role refused by Joel McCrea, gives one of his finest performances.
Zachary Scott *Sam Tucker* • Betty Field *Nona Tucker* • J Carrol Naish *Devers* • Beulah Bondi *Granny* • Jean Vanderwilt *Daisy* • Jay Gilpin *Jot* • Percy Kilbride *Harmie* • Blanche Yurka *Ma* • Charles Kemper *Tim* • Norman Lloyd *Finley* • Jack Norworth *Doctor* • Nestor Paiva *Bartender* • Estelle Taylor *Lizzie* ■ *Dir* Jean Renoir • *Scr* Jean Renoir, Hugo Butler, William Faulkner (uncredited), Nunnally Johnson (uncredited), from the novel *Hold Autumn in Your Hands* by George Sessions Perry

Southpaw ★★★★▣
Sports documentary
1998 · Ire/UK · Colour · 79mins
A documentary about the rise to fame of Francis Barrett, an Irish boxer and one of a community of Galway travellers. A national hero, he qualied

for the Irish Olympic team, carrying his country's flag during the opening ceremony at Atlanta in 1996. Training in a ramshackle gym, under a boxing-addicted barber, he encounters bigotry, but settles into marriage easily – if not celebrity. He explains he's a southpaw – a boxer who leads with his right, and punches with his left – which is what director Liam McGrath does with this hard-hitting account of a real-life fighter who is naturally appealing. Contains swearing.
Dir Liam McGrath

Souvenir ★★▣
Drama   1987 · UK · Colour · 92mins
Heavy-handed, wordy exploration of guilt and individual responsibility, with Christopher Plummer as an elderly German, former Second World War soldier, now resident in New York. He returns to France to try to atone for a massacre he was involved in 40 years earlier. Plummer, an excellent actor, is wasted on such predictable and plodding material. Co-stars Catherine Hicks and Christopher Cazenove fare slightly better, perhaps because of one's low expectations of them.
Christopher Plummer *Ernst Kestner* • Catherine Hicks *Tina* • Michael Lonsdale [Michel Lonsdale] *Xavier Lorion* • Christopher Cazenove *William Root* • Lisa Daniely *Madame Lorion* • Jean Badin *Henri* ■ *Dir* Geoffrey Reeve • *Scr* Paul Wheeler, from the novel *The Pork Butcher* by David Hughes

Soylent Green ★★★▣
Science-fiction thriller
1973 · US · Colour · 92mins
Charlton Heston in serious jaw-jutting mode as the lone honest cop in a polluted and over-populated 21st century New York, investigating an industrial espionage murder at the company responsible for a new synthetic food product. A curious blend of the private eye genre with grim glimpses of a future consumer society run amok, Harry Harrison's sober novel has been rather ploddingly adapted by director Richard Fleischer, but the film still manages to retain the book's anti-Utopian sentiments. Edward G Robinson, in his final performance, gives a very poignant turn as a citizen past his sell-by date, who remembers the tastes and smells of real life. Contains violence. ▣
Charlton Heston *Detective Thorn* • Leigh Taylor-Young *Shirl* • Chuck Connors *Tab Fielding* • Joseph Cotten *William Simonson* • Brock Peters *Hatcher* • Edward G Robinson *Sol Roth* ■ *Dir* Richard Fleischer • *Scr* Stanley R Greenberg, from the novel *Make Room! Make Room!* by Harry Harrison

Space Jam ★★★▣
Part-animated fantasy comedy
1997 · US · Colour · 83mins
American basketball star Michael Jordan makes a charismatic big screen acting debut, as he teams up with the entire Warner Bros cartoon catalogue, in this part-animated, part live-action adventure with a sci-fi twist. Aliens from failing intergalactic theme park Moron Mountain want Bugs Bunny, Daffy Duck *et al* to be their new attraction. So the animated brigade challenge their would-be captors to a

basketball game and up their chances by kidnapping Jordan. The humour cleverly mixes typical Looney Tunes gags with references to *Reservoir Dogs*, comic jibes at the sports star's new choice of career (baseball) and some hilarious moments provided by Bill Murray. Children will love the energy of both the actors and animated characters, and there's plenty here to keep adults amused, too. ▣ **DVD**
Michael Jordan • Wayne Knight *Stan Podolak* • Danny DeVito *Swackhammer* • Theresa Randle *Juanita Jordan* • Eric Gordon *Marcus Jordan* • Penny Bae Bridges *Jasmine Jordan* • Bill Murray ■ *Dir* Joe Pytka • *Scr* Leo Benvenuti, Steve Rudnick, Timothy Harris, Herschel Weingrod

Space Master X 7 ★★
Science-fiction horror
1958 · US · BW · 70mins
Treat this *Blob/Quatermass* derivative as farce and you'll have a good time. Fungus from a space probe mixes with human blood and turns deadly, in this prime example of a fifties' copycat chiller. Told in routine, and extremely padded out, semi-documentary style, the presence of Three Stooges funnyman Moe Howard (playing a cab driver), suggests director Edward Bernds thought it was a comedy, too. Unfortunately, the other actors take it all very seriously which only adds to the hilarity.
Bill Williams *John Hand* • Lyn Thomas *Lora Greeling* • Robert Ellis *Radigan* • Paul Frees *Charles Palmer* • Joan Nixon *Barry Miss Meyers* • Thomas Browne Henry *Professor West* • Fred Sherman *Morse* • Rhoda Williams *Miss Archer* ■ *Dir* Edward Bernds • *Scr* George Worthing Yates, Daniel Mainwaring

Space Raiders ★★▣
Science-fiction adventure
1983 · US · Colour · 79mins
Writer/director Howard R Cohen seems to have concocted his tale of a boy who stows away on a ship belonging to a motley band of space mercenaries, merely to fit around special effects footage lifted from producer Roger Corman's own *Battle Beyond the Stars*. Even the score by the celebrated James Horner is the same. Still, undemanding kids may find some enjoyment in its strictly limited thrills and cheap gags, such as the pastiche of the famous *Star Wars* Cantina scene, where a seductively dressed lady turns to reveal herself to be a grotesque alien.
David Mendenhall *Peter Tracton* • Vince Edwards *Hawk* • George Dickerson *Arthur Tracton* • Thom Christopher *Flightplan* • Drew Snyder *Alderbarian* • Patsy Pease *Amanda* ■ *Dir/Scr* Howard R Cohen

Space Truckers ★★★▣
Science-fiction action comedy
1996 · US/Ire · Colour · 92mins
Off-the-wall, cheesy sci-fi romp, with a better than expected cast and a naughty sense of humour. Amongst the folk along for this intergalactic brush with killer robots, pirates and motorised body parts are Dennis Hopper, Stephen Dorff and Debi Mazar, while Charles Dance's bio-mechanical adversary even out-camps his pantomime *Last Action Hero* villain.

By director Stuart Gordon's standards, there are more than a few dollars on screen and at a time when sci-fi seems to have lost its sense of fun, this is a colourful, unpretentious slice of spoofy nonsense. ▣
Dennis Hopper *John Canyon* • Stephen Dorff *Mike Pucci* • Debi Mazar *Cindy* • George Wendt *Mr Keller* • Barbara Crampton *Carol* • Charles Dance *Nabel/Macanudo* • Shane Rimmer *EJ Saggs* ■ *Dir* Stuart Gordon • *Scr* Ted Mann, by Stuart Gordon, by Ted Mann

Spaceballs ★★▣
Science-fiction spoof
1987 · US · Colour · 92mins
Mel Brooks seems to think that just by appearing on screen, assembling assorted clowns (Rick Moranis and John Candy among them) and substituting noise for wit, hilarity will somehow ensue. Unfortunately, Brooks has descended to a pick 'n' mix approach to comedy. In this limp spoof of *Star Wars* (where the obvious is never avoided), visual and verbal gags leap across the screen with manic abandon. At least a handful of decent jokes and japes do brighten the mundane proceedings. Contains strong language. ▣
Mel Brooks *President Skroob/Yogurt* • John Candy *Barf the Mawg* • Rick Moranis *Lord Dark Helmet* • Bill Pullman *Lone Starr* • Daphne Zuniga *Princess Vespa* • Dick Van Patten *King Roland* • George Wyner *Colonel Sandurz* • Michael Winslow *Radar technician* • Joan Rivers *Dot Matrix* (voice only) • Lorene Yarnell *Dot Matrix* • John Hurt • Dom DeLuise *Pizza the Hutt* ■ *Dir* Mel Brooks • *Scr* Mel Brooks, Thomas Meehan, Ronny Graham

SpaceCamp ★▣
Adventure   1986 · US · Colour · 106mins
This space opera for youngsters brought Kate Capshaw (later to become Mrs Steven Spielberg) down to earth with something of a bump from the heady heights of *Indiana Jones and the Temple of Doom*. Younger teenagers might well relish the idea of a group of aspiring astronauts who accidentally blast off into orbit, but they will be less forgiving about the cut-price special effects. Several of the cast notably Kelly Preston and Tate Donovan went on to better things, altugh, bearing in mind their dim-witted performances here, it's not easy to see why. ▣
Lea Thompson *Kathryn* • Tate Donovan *Kevin* • Kelly Preston *Tish* • Larry B Scott *Rudy* • Leaf Phoenix [Joaquin Phoenix] *Max* • Kate Capshaw *Andie Bergstrom* • Tom Skerritt *Zach Bergstrom* • Barry Primus *Brennan* ■ *Dir* Harry Winer • *Scr* WW Wicket, Casey T Mitchell, from a story by Patrick Bailey, Larry B Williams

Spacehunter: Adventures in the Forbidden Zone ★★▣
Science-fiction adventure
1983 · US · Colour · 86mins
Galactic adventurer Peter Strauss aims to rescue cosmic travellers held prisoner by an evil man-machine on the plague-ridden planet of Terra Eleven, in this messy jump on the science-fiction bandwagon. Directed with a weary eye by Lamont Johnson, the feeble script gives Strauss's bratty sidekick Molly Ringwald nothing to do, and only the

▣ = SUITABLE FOR ALL   ▣ = SUITABLE FOR ALL, ESPECIALLY FOR YOUNG CHILDREN (VIDEO ONLY)   ▣ = PARENTAL GUIDANCE

sheer force of Michael Ironside's personality, proving he can be good in anything, turns the mutant cyborg Overdog into a decently hissable villain. Originally shown in strained 3-D, it's of even lesser interest without that added "comin' at ya" dimension. ▭

Peter Strauss *Wolff* • Molly Ringwald *Niki* • Ernie Hudson *Washington* • Andrea Marcovicci *Chalmers* • Michael Ironside *Overdog McNabb* • Beeson Carroll *Grandma Patterson* • Hrant Alianak *Chemist* • Deborah Pratt *Meagan* ■ *Dir* Lamont Johnson • *Scr* David Preston, Edith Rey, Dan Goldberg, Len Blum, from a story by Stewart Harding, Jean LaFleur

The Spaceman and King Arthur ★★★ U

Adventure 1979 · US/UK · Colour · 89mins

Also known, with delightful Disney whimsy, as *Unidentified Flying Oddball*, this reworking of Mark Twain's *A Connecticut Yankee in King Arthur's Court* has a frantic charm and provides a chance to see the desperately amiable Jim Dale as a baddie. The tale involves Nasa technician Dennis Dugan who, along with his lookalike robot, ends up in aristocratic Camelot with an engagingly elderly King Arthur (Kenneth More) and John Le Mesurier as a hesitant Sir Gawain. Lots of science "friction" and jolly japes make this a worthwhile tale, especially for younger viewers. ▭

Dennis Dugan *Tom Trimble* • Jim Dale *Sir Mordred* • Ron Moody *Merlin* • Kenneth More *King Arthur* • John Le Mesurier *Sir Gawain* • Rodney Bewes *Clarence* • Sheila White *Alisande* • Robert Beatty *Senator Milburn* ■ *Dir* Russ Mayberry • *Scr* Don Tait, from the novel *A Connecticut Yankee in King Arthur's Court* by Mark Twain

The Spacemen of St Tropez ★★

Comedy 1978 · Fr · Colour

The last entry in the comedy cop series to be completed by writer/director Jean Girault (who died while shooting *The Gendarme Wore Skirts*) borrows its premise from *Invasion of the Body Snatchers* in order to both exploit and satirise the vogue for all things interstellar in the wake of *Star Wars*. However, the action is utterly reliant on broad slapstick, as the bungling Louis De Funès assaults the cream of St Tropez in a bid to expose some oil-swilling aliens with a gift for impersonation who seem set to take over the Riviera. The script is weak, but the cast is willing. French and Italian dialogue dubbed into English.

Michel Galabru *Insp Gerber* • Maurice Risch *Beaupied* • Maria Mauban *Josepha* • Guy Grasso *Tricard* • Jean-Pierre Rambal *Taupin* • Louis De Funès *Ludovic Cruchot* ■ *Dir/Scr* Jean Girault

Spaceways ★ U

Science-fiction fantasy
1953 · UK · BW · 77mins

This big-screen version of Charles Eric Maine's space-age whodunit leaves the viewer with one burning question: why did anybody who read the radio play think it was worth doing anything with it other than hurl it across the room? The plot has leads Howard Duff and Eva Bartok blasting off in pursuit of a satellite to prove Duff's innocence

following an accusation of double murder. Sci-fi was never the strong suit of Hammer or horror specialist Terence Fisher, and his funereal pace kills this cheaply-made picture stone dead long before the denouement.

Howard Duff *Stephen Mitchell* • Eva Bartok *Lisa Frank* • Alan Wheatley *Smith* • Philip Leaver *Dr Keppler* • Michael Medwin *Toby Andrews* ■ *Dir* Terence Fisher • *Scr* Paul Tabori, Richard Landau, from a radio play by Charles Eric Maine

The Spaniard's Curse ★ U

Murder mystery 1958 · UK · BW · 79mins

When an innocent man is sentenced to be hanged for murder, he invokes an old Spanish curse on the judge, prosecuting counsel and jury. After deaths begin to take place, suspicion falls on the condemned man but his sudden death only enhances the mystery. Tony Wright has the most colourful part as the judge's wayward son, a crime reporter, but Michael Hordern as the judge gives the sharpest performance. It's the only film directed by top editor Ralph Kemplen, who wisely returned to his real talent.

Tony Wright *Charlie Manton* • Lee Patterson *Mark Brett* • Michael Hordern *Judge Manton* • Ralph Truman *Sir Robert Wyvern* • Henry Oscar *Mr Fredericks* • Susan Beaumont *Margaret Manton* • Brian Oulton *Frank Porter* ■ *Dir* Ralph Kemplen • *Scr* Kenneth Hyde, from the novel *The Assize of the Dying* by Edith Pargiter

The Spanish Gardener ★★★ U

Drama 1956 · UK · Colour · 91mins

Dirk Bogarde posted notice that he was much more than Rank's "Mr Charm" in this brooding drama. Although it was supposed to be buried safely beneath the surface, the film's homosexual subtext is clearly detectable as diplomat Michael Hordern comes to resent his son's burgeoning relationship with gardener Bogarde. Thanks to Christopher Challis's sultry cinematography, director Philip Leacock is able to convey the rising emotional temperature of the action, while also coaxing a creditable performance from young Jon Whiteley. ▭

Dirk Bogarde *Jose* • Jon Whiteley *Nicholas Brande* • Michael Hordern *Harrington Brande* • Cyril Cusack *Garcia* • Maureen Swanson *Maria* • Lyndon Brook *Robert Burton* • Josephine Griffin *Carol Burton* • Bernard Lee *Leighton Bailey* ■ *Dir* Philip Leacock • *Scr* Lesley Storm, John Bryan, from the novel by AJ Cronin

The Spanish Main ★★ U

Swashbuckling adventure
1945 · US · Colour · 95mins

This hopelessly inadequate swashbuckler is partially redeemed by its ravishing forties Technicolor, used to best effect when photographing red-headed Maureen O'Hara, who here proves more than a match for leading man Paul Henreid. Walter Slezak makes a splendidly corrupt villain, but director Frank Borzage hasn't a clue how to buckle a swash, and the result is very studio-bound and dull for long stretches. ▭

Maureen O'Hara *Francisca* • Paul Henreid *Laurent Van Horn, "The Barracuda"* • Walter Slezak *Don Alvarado* • Binnie Barnes *Anne Bonny* • John Emery *Maria Da Bilar* • Barton MacLane *Captain Benjamin Black* • JM Kerrigan *Pillory* • Fritz Leiber *Bishop* ■ *Dir* Frank Borzage • *Scr* George Worthing Yates, Herman J Mankiewicz, from a story by Aeneas MacKenzie

The Spanish Prisoner ★★★★ PG

Mystery thriller 1997 · US · Colour · 105mins

Writer/director David Mamet returns to the themes of his first film (*House of Games*) in this adroit fable about the simple-mindedness of complex-minded executives. Campbell Scott is the corporation inventor, creator of "the Process", who's concerned about his employer's integrity. Cue smoothly plausible Steve Martin and an elaborate and totally convincing con trick played on us as well as the hapless Scott. There's no Spanish, no prisoners, though everyone's in thrall to *femme fatale* Rebecca Pidgeon. A tale told with all the entertaining sleight of hand of a three-card trick: now you see it, now you don't. Contains some swearing. ▭

Ben Gazzara *Joe Klein* • Felicity Huffman *Pat McCune* • Ricky Jay *George Lang* • Steve Martin *Jimmy Dell* • Rebecca Pidgeon *Susan Ricci* • Campbell Scott *Joe Ross* ■ *Dir/Scr* David Mamet

Spanking the Monkey ★★★★ 18

Drama 1994 · US · Colour · 95mins

A low-budget cult hit that caused a big stir owing to its story of incest between mother and son. It was not so much the subject matter but the movie's sanguine, almost blasé attitude towards its theme that offended many, yet this view profoundly misunderstood an original and daring film. A largely unknown cast brings great assurance and subtlety to an often funny, sometimes moving and always intriguing look at the essential complexities between parent and child. One to make many men shift uneasily in their seats, but still an intelligent treat that rightly won great critical credit. Contains swearing, sex scenes, drug abuse and nudity. ▭

Jeremy Davies *Raymond Aibelli* • Alberta Watson *Susan Aibelli* • Benjamin Hendrickson *Tom Aibelli* • Carla Gallo *Toni Peck* • Matthew Puckett *Nicky* • Zak Orth *Curtis* • Josh Weinstein *Joel* ■ *Dir/Scr* David O Russell

Spare a Copper ★★ U

Second World War comedy
1940 · UK · BW · 78mins

The docks of Liverpool provide the setting for another of George Formby's films for Ealing Studios. Wartime audiences were grateful for any relief from the conflict and this did very tidy business at the box office, thanks largely to the jokes at the expense of the special constabulary. But the story, in which George confounds a gang of Nazi saboteurs, is too far-fetched and there were mutterings in high places that the depiction of the enemy as such easily defeated dolts could lull audiences into a false sense of

security. Nowadays, though, it will just lull them to sleep.

George Formby *George Carter* • Dorothy Hyson *Jane Grey* • Bernard Lee *Jake* • John Warwick Shaw • Warburton Gamble *Sir Robert Dyer* • John Turnbull *Inspector Richards* • George Merritt *Edward Brewster* ■ *Dir* John Paddy Carstairs • *Scr* Roger Macdougall, Basil Dearden, Austin Melford

Spare the Rod ★★★

Drama 1961 · UK · BW · 92mins

Although he didn't make many films, Max Bygraves is a surprisingly sympathetic screen presence in this docudramatic story about a benevolent teacher in a tough inner-city school. Of course, he's not in the same league as those old pros Donald Pleasence and Geoffrey Keen, who give completely credible performances as the wishy-washy headmaster and the staffroom tyrant respectively. A young Richard O'Sullivan is his trademark perky self as a cheeky pupil. Directed with care by Leslie Norman, the film's production values are too spartan to disguise the lack of a cutting edge.

Max Bygraves *John Saunders* • Donald Pleasence *Mr Jenkins* • Geoffrey Keen *Arthur Gregory* • Betty McDowall *Ann Collins* • Peter Reynolds *Alec Murray* • Jean Anderson *Mrs Pond* • Eleanor Summerfield *Mrs Harkness* • Richard O'Sullivan *Fred Harkness* ■ *Dir* Leslie Norman • *Scr* John Cresswell, from the novel by Michael Croft

Sparks: the Price of Passion ★★ 15

Thriller 1990 · US · Colour · 100mins

Victoria Principal plays a mayor who teams up with FBI agent Ted Wass to track a serial killer, while also trying to keep the historical parts of her city free from the clutches of a property developer. With all this on her plate, Principal doesn't seem to find much time to act, but at least her hair is always perfectly coiffed. Reasonably watchable. ▭

Victoria Principal *Patricia Sparks* • Ted Wass *Steve Warner* • Ralph Waite *Orville Lemon* • Hector Elizondo *Vic Ramos* • Gary Farmer *Pete Russell* • Elaine Stritch *Marti Sparks* • William Lucking *Cam Wilson* ■ *Dir* Richard Colla [Richard A Colla] • *Scr* John Robert Bensink

Sparrow ★ 12

Period drama 1993 · It/Ger · Colour · 102mins

Since his debut film, Franco Zeffirelli has directed only about ten more features (excluding operas). Of these, *Sparrow* has been the most vilified. Set in the mid-1850s, it tells the story of a young girl who enters a convent. A cholera outbreak results in her returning to her father's villa, where she falls in love with handsome young Johnathon Schaech. The plague over, she returns to the convent to battle with her religious calling and her love for Schaech. Zeffirelli lets rip with full-blown theatrics, but the story and the inexperienced leads are not enough to carry his ambitious film. ▭

Angela Bettis *Mana* • Johnathon Schaech *Nino* • Sinead Cusack *Matilde* • John Castle *Giuseppi* • Vanessa Redgrave *Sister Agata* • Sarah Jane Alexander *Annetta* • Frank Finlay *Father Nunzio* ■ *Dir* Franco Zeffirelli • *Scr* Franco Zeffirelli, Allan Baker, from the novel *A Sparrow's Tale* by Giovanni Verga

Sparrows ★★★
Silent chiller 1926 · US · BW · 81mins

A near classic of the silent era featuring twenties superstar Mary Pickford in her last juvenile role. She plays Molly, the leader of a rag-tag bunch of orphans treated as slaves by evil Mr Grimes on his farm in the Deep South swamplands. When a gang in league with Grimes kidnaps the daughter of a rich man and hides her on his farm, Molly leads her flock out through alligator-infested waters as the police close in. Although the film is poorly paced, Pickford is as touchingly poignant as ever in an American-style Grimm fairy tale.

Mary Pickford *Mama Mollie* • Gustav von Seyffertitz *Grimes* • Roy Stewart *Richard Wayne* • Mary Louise Miller *Doris Wayne* ■ *Dir* William Beaudine • *Scr* C Gardner Sullivan, George Marion Jr (titles), from a story by Winifred Dunn

Sparrows Can't Sing ★ PG
Comedy drama 1962 · UK · BW · 88mins

You can't capture the sights and sounds of East End life simply by packing the cast with cockneys and touting a camera round the streets of Stepney. Colourful phrases in Bow Bells accents might have convinced theatregoers, but on screen this supposed slice of everyday realism has sham written all over it. James Booth is eminently resistible as the sailor searching for wife Barbara Windsor and her bus-driving fancy man, George Sewell. Missing both social statement and fond characterisation, director Joan Littlewood has succeeded only in being patronising. ▭

James Booth *Charlie Gooding* • Barbara Windsor *Maggie Gooding* • Roy Kinnear *Fred Gooding* • Avis Bunnage *Bridgie Gooding* • Brian Murphy *Jack* • George Sewell *Bert* ■ *Dir* Joan Littlewood • *Scr* Stephen Lewis, Joan Littlewood, from the play by Stephen Lewis • *Music/Lyrics* Lionel Bart

Spartacus ★★★★★ PG
Historical epic 1960 · US · Colour · 186mins

The restored version of this Roman epic about the famous slave revolt has additional blood, more lingering death agonies of Kirk Douglas on the cross and a risible bath scene with Laurence Olivier and Tony Curtis, which was originally cut because of its alleged homosexual innuendo. Despite the film's length and overemphasis in the latter half on wordy speeches from Douglas, the action leading up to the revolt of the gladiators is brilliantly re-created, with Peter Ustinov, Charles Laughton and Olivier (as the Romans) addictively greedy scene-stealers. The early sequences, set in the Libyan desert, were directed by Anthony Mann, who was fired by Douglas and replaced by Stanley Kubrick. ▭

Kirk Douglas *Spartacus* • Laurence Olivier *Marcus Crassus* • Tony Curtis *Antoninus* • Jean Simmons *Varinia* • Charles Laughton *Gracchus* • Peter Ustinov *Batiatus* • John Gavin *Julius Caesar* • Nina Foch *Helena Glabrus* ■ *Dir* Stanley Kubrick • *Scr* Dalton Trumbo, from the novel by Howard Fast • *Cinematographer* Russell Metty • *Music* Alex North • *Costume Designer* Bill Thomas, Valles

Spartacus and the Ten Gladiators ★★ U
Adventure 1964 · It/ Fr/Sp · Colour · 98mins

An Italian co-produced rehash of the Kirk Douglas blockbuster, with the epic-sounding John Heston as the revolting Spartacus, and Dan Vadis as a gladiator hired by the Senate to destroy the slave army. As always with these European co-productions, the dubbing is appalling, but some money was obviously spent on several hundred extras and whatever chariots were left over from *Ben-Hur*. Italian dialogue dubbed into English.

Helga Liné *Daria* • John Heston *Spartacus* • Dan Vadis *Roccia* • Ursula Davis *Lydia* • Gianni Rizzo *Varro* ■ *Dir* Nick Nostro • *Scr* Nick Nostro, Simon Sterling

Spawn ★★ 12
Science-fiction horror adventure 1997 · US · Colour · 92mins

A live-action comic book spin-off that promised to duplicate the grim and extremely violent images that are the bestselling comic's hallmarks, but ended up being distributed in an edited "12" certificate version and then an 18-rated video "director's cut". Michael Jai White plays Al Simmons, a special forces assassin betrayed by boss Martin Sheen and left to fry in a burning chemical factory. Somehow passing beyond death, he is revived as Spawn, scarred costumed henchman to the demonic Malebolgia who is also bent on revenge against Sheen. Dark in tone and crammed with computer-generated effects, it found a cult popularity and spawned a follow-up animated series. ▭ *DVD*

Michael Jai White *Al Simmons/Spawn* • Martin Sheen *Jason Wynn* • John Leguizamo *Clown* • Theresa Randle *Wanda* • Nicol Williamson *Cogliostro* • Melinda Clarke *Jessica Priest* • DB Sweeney *Terry Fitzgerald* ■ *Dir* Mark AZ Dippé • *Scr* Alan McElroy, from a story by Mark AZ Dippé, Alan McElroy, from the comic book by Todd McFarlane

Spawn of the North ★★★
Drama 1938 · US · BW · 105mins

Henry Fonda stars as the skipper of an American fishing crew in Alaska, circa 1890, whose best buddy (George Raft) deserts him for some villainous Russian poachers, led by Akim Tamiroff. It's an entertaining action adventure, with some high drama, a little romance (supplied by Dorothy Lamour and Louise Platt), satisfying heroics, and a convincing John Barrymore as a heavy-drinking newspaper reporter. A big hit in its day, with the authentic exteriors specially filmed on location in Alaska, the film spawned a feeble remake, *Alaska Seas*, in 1954.

George Raft *Tyler Dawson* • Henry Fonda *Jim Kimmerlee* • Dorothy Lamour *Nicky Duval* • Akim Tamiroff *Red Skain* • John Barrymore *Windy Turlon* • Louise Platt *Dian Turlon* • Lynne Overman *Jackson* • Fuzzy Knight *Lefty Jones* ■ *Dir* Henry Hathaway • *Scr* Jules Furthman, Talbot Jennings, from the novel by Florence Barrett Willoughby

Spawn of the Slithis ★
Fantasy adventure 1978 · US · Colour · 86mins

The title should warn viewers in advance that this is a B-movie, but that alone cannot convey how silly the film is. A mutated form of sea life is squelching around the California coastline, understandably annoyed that it has evolved from a radiation spillage from a local power plant and prepared to ooze over everything in its path. Stephen Traxler, who wrote, produced and directed this daft tale, obviously saw far too many schlock movies while growing up, since he borrows the worst bits from all of them.

Alan Blanchard • Judy Motulsky • Dennis Lee Falt • Win Condict • Mello Alexandria • Hy Pyke ■ *Dir/Scr* Stephen Traxler

Speak Easily ★★★★ U
Comedy 1932 · US · BW · 81mins

When Buster Keaton gave up independent production and signed with MGM in 1928 it was a move he later considered the worst of his career. But of the eight sound films he made for the studio, this was his favourite. It features Keaton as a sheltered university professor who decides to see life and becomes involved with a run-down theatrical troupe. Keaton's co-star Jimmy Durante has some fine moments, including his song *Can Broadway Do without Me?*, and though Keaton disliked working with the brash comic, the two became good friends. The film is a hit-and-miss affair but Keaton is superb as the innocent at sea in a world of showbiz sharpies. ▭

Buster Keaton *Prof Post* • Jimmy Durante *James* • Ruth Selwyn *Pansy Peets* • Thelma Todd *Eleanor Espere* • Hedda Hopper *Mrs Peets* • William Pawley *Griffo* • Sidney Toler *Stage director* • Lawrence Grant *Dr Bolton* ■ *Dir* Edward Sedgwick • *Scr* Ralph Spence, Laurence E Johnson, from the novel by Clarence Budington Kelland

Speaking Parts ★★ 18
Drama 1989 · Can · Colour · 91mins

Gabrielle Rose watches videos of her dead brother while pursuing a movie project about his life. She gets involved with aspiring actor Michael McManus who, coincidentally, resembles her sibling, and is himself a lust object for lovelorn Arsinée Khanjian. Writer/director Atom Egoyan returns to our ambiguous relationship with technology, particularly video, and he successfully connects the characters in his strange story through the medium. But in focusing on intellectual dissection, and images which cloak familiar objects in a hyper-reality, the director sacrifices the emotional pay-off essential in this story of a three-way relationship. Contains nudity.

Michael McManus *Lance* • Arsinée Khanjian *Lisa* • Gabrielle Rose *Clara* • Tony Nardi *Eddy* • David Hemblen *Producer* • Patricia Collins *Housekeeper* ■ *Dir/Scr* Atom Egoyan

Special Agent ★★
Crime drama 1935 · US · BW · 77mins

"Miss Davis is too valuable a performer to be doing stories such as this one," said *Variety*, slamming this crime drama which Warners "encouraged" her to do. Davis plays the secretary to a mobster, Ricardo Cortez, whose operation is being investigated by plucky newspaper man George Brent. Davis takes a shine to Brent and gives him secrets.

Bette Davis *Julie Carston* • George Brent *Bill Bradford* • Ricardo Cortez *Nick Cartson* • Joseph Sawyer [Joe Sawyer] *Rich* • Joseph Crehan *Chief of Police* • Henry O'Neill *District Attorney* • Irving Pichel *US District Attorney* ■ *Dir* William Keighley • *Scr* Laird Doyle, Abem Finkel, from an idea by Martin Mooney

A Special Day ★★
Historical drama 1977 · It/Can · Colour · 105mins

Marcello Mastroianni earned an Oscar nomination for performing so subtly against type in this contrived romance dressed up as a sweeping statement about the human condition and Italy's Fascist past. It's beautifully set up, with Marcello's suicidal gay radio announcer and Sophia Loren's harassed mother of six meeting in a Roman tenement on the day in 1938 that Mussolini first played host to Hitler. But, for all the evident chemistry between the leads, the symbolism is heavy-handed and the dialogue drips with portentous pronouncements.

Sophia Loren *Antonietta* • Marcello Mastroianni *Gabriele* • John Vernon *Emanuele* • Francoise Berd *Concierge* ■ *Dir* Ettore Scola • *Scr* Ettore Scola, Ruggero Maccari, Maurizio Costanzo, from a story by Ettore Scola

Special Delivery ★★ U
Political satirical comedy 1955 · US/W Ger · BW · 86mins

Even when lumbered with a banal script and mediocre performances from everyone but Joseph Cotten, director John Brahm (who made the excellent *Hangover Square*) can't help but conjure atmosphere in this story of an American diplomat being assigned behind the Iron Curtain, where he has to cope with an abandoned baby. The romantic interest is supplied by Eva Bartok, who appeared in more gossip columns than movies.

Joseph Cotten *Jonathan Adams* • Eva Bartok *Sonia* • Rene Deltgen *Kovak* • Bruni Loebel *Lila* • Niall MacGinnis *Sidney* • Lexford Richards *Wayne* ■ *Dir* John Brahm • *Scr* Philip Reisman Jr, Dwight Taylor, from an idea by Geva Radvanyi

Special Delivery ★★★ 15
Crime comedy 1976 · US · Colour · 94mins

Surprisingly, this Bo Svenson vehicle is a neat little caper movie, with Svenson doing a respectable job as a bank robber who stashes his loot in the mail while fleeing the police. But the real star of the movie is Cybill Shepherd – excellent as the woman who witnesses Svenson at the mailbox, she boldly strikes a deal with him. Taking place over a span of several hours, the strength of the movie comes from the many interesting interactions the central characters have with other parties, all realistically done. ▭

Bo Svenson *Jack Murdock* • Cybill Shepherd *Mary Jane* • Tom Atkins *Zabelski* • Sorrell Booke *Bank Manager Hubert Zane* • Gerrit

Graham *Swivot* • Michael C Gwynne *Carl Graff* • Jeff Goldblum *Snake* ■ *Dir* Paul Wendkos • *Scr* Don Gazzaniga, Gil Ralston

A Special Kind of Love ★★★

Drama   1978 · US · Colour · 104mins

As an actor, Lee Philips was best known for playing Michael Rossi in the screen version of *Peyton Place*. He has since directed over 20 TV movies, including biopics of Mae West and Louis Armstrong, and he shows in this genuinely touching film that he can handle emotive subjects without descending into mawkishness. The action centres on a mentally disabled boy who finds fulfilment through his sporting skill. Charles Durning gives a solid performance as his widowed father, but of more interest are the early appearances of Mare Winningham and Debra Winger.

Charles Durning Carl Gallitzin • Irene Tedrow *Elmira Gallitzin* • Mare Winningham *Janice Gallitzin* • Phil Brown *Michael Gallitzin* • George Parry *Matthew Gallitzin* • Debra Winger *Sherrie Hensley* ■ *Dir* Lee Philips • *Scr* John Sacret Young

Special Report: Journey to Mars ★★ U

Science-fiction drama
1996 · US · Colour · 86mins

In the year 2015 an international TV audience watches the first manned space mission to Mars as it suffers a computer malfunction, possibly due to sabotage, endangering the crew and the entire mission. This formulaic TV movie is anything but special, which American audiences obviously knew ahead of time: the film has the dubious distinction of being the lowest-rated primetime network movie in TV history. A surprisingly capable group of actors collectively lowered their usual standards for this predictable "what-if" sci-fi scenario, including Keith Carradine and Alfre Woodard.

Keith Carradine Captain Eugene Slader • Judge Reinhold *Ryan West* • Alfre Woodard *Tamara O'Neil* • Philip Casnoff *Nick Van Pelt* • Rosalind Chao *Dr Lin Yo Yu* • Elizabeth Wilson *President Richardson* • Michael Murphy *Dean Rumplemeyer* • Dean Jones *Dr Scott Berlin* ■ *Dir* Robert Mandel • *Scr* Augustus Taylor

The Specialist ★★★ 18

Thriller   1994 · US · Colour · 105mins

James Woods has a knack for spotting mediocre movies with roles that give him the chance to shine when all around are floundering. This is a case in point, as he strides off with Luis Llosa's bomb thriller without even getting his hair mussed. Sylvester Stallone was clearly tempted by the prospect of sharing erotic phone calls with Sharon Stone, and, to be fair, they do create a surprising number of sparks. Even with Rod Steiger and Eric Roberts as Miami mobsters, however, this is essentially straight-to-video fare. Contains swearing, violence, sex scenes and nudity.

Sylvester Stallone Ray Quick • Sharon Stone *May Munro* • James Woods *Ned Trent* • Rod Steiger *Joel Leon* • Eric Roberts *Tomas Leon* • Mario Ernesto Sanchez *Charlie* • Sergio Dore Jr *Strongarm* ■ *Dir* Luis Llosa • *Scr* Alexandra Seros, from the novels by John Shirley

Species ★★★ 18

Science-fiction horror
1995 · US · Colour · 103mins

Natasha Henstridge is the dangerous spawn of combined alien and human DNA in director Roger Donaldson's sexy sci-fi shocker. Ben Kingsley, Michael Madsen and Alfred Molina are among the inept government scientists speaking daft dialogue as they attempt to track down the genetic engineering experiment gone awry, before she devours half the male population of LA. Nifty designs by surrealist HR Giger (who gave the extraterrestrial in *Alien* its incredible look) and some engaging, tongue-in-cheek thrills go part way to disguising the fact that this is essentially clichéd B-movie stuff, albeit delivered with a pleasingly glossy sheen. Contains violence, swearing, sex scenes and nudity. *DVD*

Ben Kingsley Fitch • Michael Madsen *Press* • Alfred Molina *Arden* • Forest Whitaker *Dan* • Marg Helgenberger *Laura* • Natasha Henstridge *Sil* ■ *Dir* Roger Donaldson • *Scr* Dennis Feldman

Species II ★★★ 18

Science-fiction horror
1998 · US · Colour · 89mins

Head explosions, torso-bursting and computer-generated aliens in heat: it's all here in Peter Medak's science-fiction howler which continues the half-human/half-alien DNA experiment as a sex rampage saga. Far gorier and camper than the original film, this lascivious popcorn treat is a spectacularly lunatic shocker revelling in soft-core sleaze and grisly death. Piling up the unintentional laughs alongside the bloodied victims, the actors coast through the mayhem as if they couldn't be bothered bringing an iota of credibility to this terminally daft scenario. Contains sex scenes, swearing and violence. *DVD*

Michael Madsen Press Lennox • Natasha Henstridge *Eve* • Marg Helgenberger *Doctor Laura Baker* • Mykel T Williamson *Dennis Gamble* • George Dzundza *Colonel Carter Burgess Jr* • James Cromwell *Senator Ross* • Myriam Cyr *Anne Sampas* ■ *Dir* Peter Medak • *Scr* Chris Brancato, from characters created by Dennis Feldman

Specter of the Rose ★★★

Comedy drama   1946 · US · BW · 90mins

An unusual and ambitious undertaking by Ben Hecht – one of the sharpest writers in Hollywood – this film purports to be based in part on the ballet *Spectre de la Rose*. One suspects, however, that Nijinsky couldn't have been far from Hecht's mind in this tale of a progressively deranged dancer (Ivan Kirov) driven to attempt murder and suicide by the eponymous ballet. Admittedly "arty", the film is also camp, inventive and eccentric; though it may provoke derisive mirth, it is still fascinating and unusual.

Judith Anderson Madame La Sylph • Michael Chekhov *Max "Poli" Polikoff* • Ivan Kirov *Andre Sanine* • Lionel Stander *Lionel Gans* • Ben Hecht *Waiter* ■ *Dir* Ben Hecht • *Scr* Ben Hecht, from his short story

The Spectre ★★

Horror   1963 · It · Colour · 95mins

Inferior sequel to *The Horrible Dr Hichcock* in which the doctor, apparently murdered by his wife, returns as a ghost. Like the earlier film, this was shot quickly in Rome and all but ignored when it was released in the UK as a second feature. Although the story is utterly conventional, with none of the outrageous elements of its predecessor, the film is liked by fans of stylish director Riccardo Freda (here credited as Robert Hampton) and vampish horror star Barbara Steele. Others should not expect anything too sophisticated; the "surprise" towards the end will surprise nobody. Italian dialogue dubbed into English.

Barbara Steele Margaret • Peter Baldwin *Dr Charles Livingstone* • Leonard Elliott *Dr Hichcock* • Harriet White *Catherine* • Raoul H Newman [Umberto Raho] *Canon* ■ *Dir* Robert Hampton [Riccardo Freda] • *Scr* Robert Hampton [Riccardo Freda], Robert Davidson, from a story by Robert Davidson

Speechless ★★★ 12

Romantic comedy
1994 · US · Colour · 94mins

Bewilderingly, this starry comedy bypassed cinemas and went straight to video in this country. It's a shame, because it's a smart and sassy affair from director Ron Underwood. Michael Keaton and Geena Davis spark off each other nicely, playing a pair of rival political speech writers who fall in and out of love with each other while on the campaign trail. There are excellent supporting turns from Bonnie Bedelia and Christopher Reeve, and Underwood has some gentle fun at the expense of the American political system. Contains swearing.

Michael Keaton Kevin Vallick • Geena Davis *Julia Mann* • Christopher Reeve *Bob Freed* • Bonnie Bedelia *Annette* • Ernie Hudson *Ventura* • Charles Martin Smith *Kratz* ■ *Dir* Ron Underwood • *Scr* Robert King

Speed ★★

Sports drama   1936 · US · BW · 65mins

Bearing no relation to the 1994 mega-hit, this minor B-movie about motor racing is notable only for the presence of James Stewart in the leading role – one of many parts he played in 1936 while on his way to major stardom. He plays a test-car driver who, when not romancing the boss's daughter (Wendy Barrie), finds time to develop a high-speed carburettor to use in the Indianapolis 500. The film's depiction of an ultra-modern auto-plant in 1936 makes interesting viewing, but there is also too much evidence of back projection and stock shots.

James Stewart Terry Martin • Wendy Barrie *Jane Mitchell* • Ted Healy *Gadget* • Una Merkel *Josephine Sanderson* • Weldon Heyburn *Frank Lawson* • Patricia Wilder *Fanny Lane* • Ralph Morgan *Mr Dean* • Robert Livingston *George Saunders* ■ *Dir* Edwin L Marin • *Scr* Michael Fessier, from a story by Milton Krims, Larry Bachman

Speed ★★★★★ 15

Action thriller 1994 · US · Colour · 111mins

Pure adrenalin-pumping entertainment of the highest order, as action man Keanu Reeves and Sandra Bullock are trapped on a crowded LA bus that crazed extortionist Dennis Hopper has primed to explode if its speed falls below 50mph. Slipping smoothly into top gear from the nail-biting scene-setting opening, director Jan De Bont's "Die Hard" on the Buses" moves into the fast lane with a nonstop barrage of nerve-jangling thrills and death-defying stunts. Outrageous, over-the-top and as exciting as can be, this wild ride will make you wish your sofa came equipped with seat belts. Contains swearing and violence. *DVD*

Keanu Reeves Jack Traven • Dennis Hopper *Howard Payne* • Sandra Bullock *Annie* • Joe Morton *Captain McMahon* • Jeff Daniels *Harry* • Alan Ruck *Stephens* • Glenn Plummer *Jaguar owner* • Richard Lineback *Norwood* ■ *Dir* Jan De Bont • *Scr* Graham Yost

Speed 2: Cruise Control ★★ PG

Action thriller 1997 · US · Colour · 119mins

Director Jan De Bont's listlessly routine sequel to his own powerhouse original is a massive disappointment. Sandra Bullock reprises her role as Annie Porter who, with cop boyfriend Jason Patric, boards a luxury liner for a holiday. Before you can say "Where's Keanu Reeves gone?", disgruntled computer genius Willem Dafoe puts his extortion plan into operation and turns their voyage into a titanic nightmare. Bloated set pieces and predictable suspense scupper De Bont's waterlogged effort to re-create on sea what worked so brilliantly on land. Contains swearing and some violence. *DVD*

Sandra Bullock Annie • Jason Patric *Alex* • Willem Dafoe *Geiger* • Temuera Morrison *Juliano* • Brian McCardie *Merced* • Christine Firkins *Drew* • Michael G Hagerty *Harvey* ■ *Dir* Jan De Bont • *Scr* Randall McCormick, Jeff Nathanson, from a story by Jan DeBont, Randall McCormick, from characters created by Graham Yost

Speedway ★ U

Musical drama   1968 · US · Colour · 90mins

A bland, cheap and hopelessly unhip musical made when both the recording and screen careers of Elvis Presley were at rock bottom. Recently wed to Priscilla Beaulieu, the pre-*Comeback* rock 'n' roll king seems to be going through the motions as a stock car driver pursued by income tax investigator Nancy Sinatra. The songs sound as though very old men had written them. There was certainly little here to interest youngsters in 1968 and the film was released on the second half of a double bill with a *Man from UNCLE* adventure.

Elvis Presley Steve Grayson • Nancy Sinatra *Susan Jacks* • Bill Bixby *Kenny Donford* • Gale Gordon *RW Hepworth* • William Schallert *Abel Esterlake* • Victoria Meyerink *Ellie Esterlake* • Ross Hagen *Paul Dado* ■ *Dir* Norman Taurog • *Scr* Phillip Shuken

Speedy ★★★ U

Silent comedy   1928 · US · BW · 86mins

Coming 15 years after his screen debut, Harold Lloyd's silent swansong is something of a disappointment considering the glorious high-risk clowning that had gone before. Still nurturing go-getting ambitions, his baseball-crazy soda jerk takes on some ruthless traffic tycoons after they try to drive the last horse-drawn trolley bus off the road. Naturally, love is at the heart of Harold's heroism, although the romantic outing to Coney Island lacks both the period charm of the New York street scenes and the comic zest of the concluding chase. It's a crowd-pleaser, but, sadly, the work of a waning talent.

Harold Lloyd *Harold "Speedy" Swift* • Ann Christy *Jane Dillon* • Bert Woodruff *Pop Dillon* • Brooks Benedict *Steven Carter* • George Herman *"Babe" Ruth [Babe Ruth]* ■ *Dir* Ted Wilde • *Scr* John Grey, Lex Neal, Howard Emmett Rogers, Jay Howe

The Spellbinder ★★

Crime drama   1939 · US · BW · 69mins

If you're not allergic to Lee Tracy's fast, attention-grabbing performances, there's an ingenious story told in this courtroom melodrama. Tracy is well cast as a defence lawyer whose tricks get murderers off. He doesn't like it one bit, however, when his precious daughter, played by Barbara Read, elopes with a killer, Patric Knowles, that she believes is innocent because papa's clever tactics persuaded the jury to acquit him. It's Tracy's show, with weak back-up in a film never intended to be anything but double-feature material.

Lee Tracy *Jed Marlow* • Barbara Read *Janet Marlow* • Patric Knowles *Tom Dixon* • Allan Lane *Steve Kendall* • Linda Hayes *Miss Simpson* • Morgan Conway *Carrington* • Robert Emmett Keane *Judge Butler* ■ *Dir* Jack Hively • *Scr* Thomas Lennon, Joseph A Fields, from a story by Joseph Anthony

Spellbinder ★ 18

Thriller   1988 · US · Colour · 94mins

American TV actor Timothy Daly (brother of *Cagney and Lacey's* Tyne) stars in this silly and completely unthrilling chiller about a lawyer who becomes obsessed with a woman (Kelly Preston) on the run from an evil coven. A disaster. ☐

Timothy Daly *Jeff Mills* • Kelly Preston *Miranda Reed* • Rick Rossovich *Derek Clayton* • Audra Lindley *Mrs White* • Anthony Crivello *Aldys* • Diana Bellamy *Grace Woods* • Cary-Hiroyuki Tagawa *Lieutenant Lee* ■ *Dir* Janet Greek • *Scr* Tracey Torme

Spellbound ★★★ PG

Psychological thriller
1945 · US · BW · 110mins

In his eagerness to make the first serious film about psychoanalysis, Alfred Hitchcock so diluted the fantastical elements in Francis Beeding's novel *The House of Dr Edwardes*, all that remained was a melodramatic plot and an awful lot of psychobabble. Not even dream sequences designed by Salvador Dali could enliven the turgid script, made all the less palatable by the robotic performance of Gregory Peck as the amnesiac trying to unravel his troubled past with the help of sympathetic shrink, Ingrid Bergman. Hitch himself was disappointed with the picture, but there are enough masterly touches to prevent the attention straying. ☐

Ingrid Bergman *Dr Constance Peterson* • Gregory Peck *John Ballantine/Dr Anthony*

Edwardes* • Michael Chekhov *Dr Alex Brulov* • Leo G Carroll *Dr Murchison* • Rhonda Fleming *Mary Carmichael* • John Emery *Dr Fleurot* ■ *Dir* Alfred Hitchcock • *Scr* Ben Hecht, Angus MacPhail, from the novel *The House of Dr Edwardes* by Francis Beeding

Spencer's Mountain ★★★

Drama   1963 · US · Colour · 119mins

Although it was a considerable commercial success, Henry Fonda absolutely loathed this cosy melodrama, claiming it "damned near set film-making back 25 years". With Fonda playing the church-hating head of a Wyoming hill family, it's not immediately apparent that Earl Hamner Jr's novel also provided the inspiration for that enduringly popular TV show, *The Waltons*. The connection becomes clearer as James MacArthur's character Clayboy (rather than John Boy) struggles to choose between his education and his inheritance. As mom and grandpa respectively, Maureen O'Hara and Donald Crisp provide expert support, and it all comes together under the watchful eye of director Delmer Daves.

Henry Fonda *Clay Spencer* • Maureen O'Hara *Olivia* • James MacArthur *Clayboy* • Donald Crisp *Grandpa* • Wally Cox *Preacher Goodson* • Mimsy Farmer *Claris* • Virginia Gregg *Miss Parker* ■ *Dir* Delmer Daves • *Scr* Delmer Daves, from the novel by Earl Hamner Jr

Spendthrift ★★★

Comedy   1936 · US · BW · 77mins

Millionaire playboy Henry Fonda is temporarily out of cash but can't bring himself to break the news to mercenary spouse Mary Brian. Eventually he gets to see how the other half lives when he takes a job as a sports announcer and falls for Pat Paterson. Action director Raoul Walsh has a light enough touch, and the streak of social conscience - very necessary at the time - is eased in almost painlessly. What's so delightfully manipulative about the movie is the way it shows us how the rich live, spiking those lush vistas with Depression era home truths.

Henry Fonda *Townsend Middleton* • Pat Paterson *Valerie "Boots" O'Connell* • Mary Brian *Sally Barnaby* • George Barbier *Uncle Morton Middleton* • Edward Brophy *Bill* • Richard Carle *Popsy* • JM Kerrigan *Pop O'Connell* • Spencer Charters *Col Barnaby* ■ *Dir* Raoul Walsh • *Scr* Raoul Walsh, Bert Hanlon, from the novella by Eric Hatch

Spetters ★★★★ 18

Drama   1980 · Neth · Colour · 102mins

Fans of Paul Verhoeven's Hollywood output will be amazed by this garish Dutch take on the teen pic. Punctuated with graphic scenes of straight and gay sex, played to the melodramatic hilt and deliriously over-stylised, it owes its greatest debt to Rainer Werner Fassbinder as a trio of dirt-bike dreamers strive to emulate their motocross hero, Rutger Hauer. Meanwhile, hot dog waitress Renée Soutendijk seeks to seduce one of them into delivering her from dead-end hell. You name it, Verhoeven nails it, whether it's religious fanaticism, homophobia, small-town ennui, media manipulation or just plain adolescent

lust. Rough and unrepentant. In Dutch with English subtitles. ☐

Hans Van Tongeren *Reen* • Renée Soutendijk *Fientje* • Toon Agterberg *Eve* • Maarten Spanjer *Hans* • Marianne Boyer *Maya* • Rutger Hauer *Gerrit Witkamp* • Jeroen Krabbé *Frans Henkhof* ■ *Dir* Paul Verhoeven • *Scr* Gerard Soeteman

Sphere ★★★ 12

Science-fiction thriller
1998 · US · Colour · 128mins

A submerged spacecraft from the future containing a golden sphere that has the ability to physically manifest the darkest fears of anyone who enters its enigmatic interior is at the centre of director Barry Levinson's cerebral adaptation of Michael Crichton's bestselling novel. Alternating between being genuinely creepy (the aquanauts' phobias are all unseen) and overly tame through the deliberate under-use of shock effects, this underwater *Solaris* relies on moody dread rather than cheap thrills to weave its spell. A wittily scripted science-fiction chamber piece that focuses on characters thrust into an extraordinary situation rather than the situation itself. ☐ *DVD*

Dustin Hoffman *Dr Norman Goodman* • Sharon Stone *Dr Beth Halperin* • Samuel L Jackson *Harry Adams* • Peter Coyote *Harold C Barnes* • Liev Schreiber *Dr Ted Fielding* • Queen Latifah *Fletcher* ■ *Dir* Barry Levinson • *Scr* Stephen Hauser, Paul Attanasio, from the novel by Michael Crichton

The Sphinx ★

Mystery   1933 · US · BW · 62mins

The old evil twin device is given another airing in an unremarkable programmer courtesy of Monogram, one of the cheapest exploitation studios in thirties Hollywood. Lionel Atwill has the perfect alibi for murder - he is deaf-mute, and a witness heard the killer speak. However, he has a deaf-mute twin hidden behind a panel. He substitutes his brother in court, but equally clever justice wins the day. A sorry mix of low-grade suspense and comic relief means *The Sphinx* stinks!

Lionel Atwill *Jerome Breen* • Sheila Terry *Jerry Crane, society editor* • Theodore Newton *Jack Burton, reporter* • Paul Hurst *Terrence Hogan* ■ *Dir* Phil Rosen • *Scr* Albert DeMond

Sphinx ★★ 15

Adventure   1980 · US · Colour · 112mins

Rarely since *The Perils of Pauline* has so much been endured by a heroine as by Lesley-Anne Down here, starring as an Egyptologist who comes up against a gang smuggling artefacts from the Valley of the Kings. After witnessing John Gielgud's demise, she's shot at, nearly raped, attacked by bats, thrown into a dungeon of rotting corpses and has a tomb cave in on her. She screams a lot, though co-star Frank Langella seems not to hear. Contains swearing and violence. ☐

Lesley-Anne Down *Erica Baron* • Frank Langella *Ahmed Khazzan* • Maurice Ronet *Yvon* • John Gielgud *Abdu Hamdi* • Vic Tablian *Khalifa* • Nadim Sawalha *Gamal* • Saeed Jaffrey *Selim* ■ *Dir* Franklin J Schaffner • *Scr* John Byrum, from the novel by Robin Cook

Spice World ★★ PG

Musical comedy   1997 · UK · Colour · 88mins

For fans of Baby, Scary, Sporty, Posh and Ginger and children under five only. Not only do the members of the band display zero acting talent, but their lack of ability appears to have rubbed off on everybody else in the movie. In a feeble attempt to capture the chaotic style of early Beatles films such as *Help!* and *A Hard Day's Night*, the girls go on tour, play gigs, meet their fans and change clothes in a vague semblance of a plot. But they don't have the cool of the Fab Four and, unless you're a devotee, this is a very painful experience. Contains some swearing. ☐ *DVD*

Victoria Adams *Posh Spice* • Melanie Brown *Scary Spice* • Emma Bunton *Baby Spice* • Melanie Chisholm *Sporty Spice* • Geraldine Halliwell *Ginger Spice* • Richard E Grant *Clifford* • Alan Cumming *Piers Cuthbertson-Smyth* • George Wendt *Martin Barnfield* ■ *Dir* Bob Spiers • *Scr* Kim Fuller, Jamie Curtis, from an idea by the Spice Girls, Kim Fuller

Spider and Rose ★★

Comedy   1994 · Ausl · Colour · 90mins

Coming between a series of impressive docudramas and the 1997 antipodean box-office smash *Kiss or Kill*, this is something of a disappointment from Australian writer/director Bill Bennett. There haven't been too many age-gap road movies and this goes some way to explaining why. Bennett's direction is steady enough, but his script is littered with predictable situations, as a 70-year-old is driven back to her family farm by an aimless young ambulance driver. The relationship between Ruth Cracknell and Simon Bossell occasionally flickers into life, but it's all too obvious how things will turn out once her loathsome son (Lewis Fitz-Gerald) enters the picture. Contains some swearing. ☐

Ruth Cracknell *Rose* • Simon Bossell *Spider* • Lewis Fitz-Gerald ■ *Dir/Scr* Bill Bennett

The Spider and the Fly ★★★★ U

Crime drama   1949 · UK · BW · 90mins

Predating *Father Brown* by five years, this was Robert Hamer's first attempt at depicting the grudging respect that exists between a master thief and a brilliant detective. Evoking the Paris of Louis Feuillade's *Fantomas* serials, Hamer superbly captures the conspiratorial pre-First World War atmosphere, while artfully keeping the tone as light as it is suspenseful, as Eric Portman initially attempts to capture Guy Rolfe and then enlists him to procure some top-secret German plans. With a mutual passion for Nadia Gray intensifying the rivalry, this is a cat-and-mouse thriller of the highest order and a film that deserves to be much better known. ☐

Eric Portman *Maubert* • Guy Rolfe *Philippe* • Nadia Gray *Madeleine* • George Cole *Marc* • Edward Chapman *Minister of War* • Maurice Denham *Col de la Roche* ■ *Dir* Robert Hamer • *Scr* Robert Westerby

   U = SUITABLE FOR ALL   Uc = SUITABLE FOR ALL, ESPECIALLY FOR YOUNG CHILDREN (VIDEO ONLY)   PG = PARENTAL GUIDANCE

Spider-Man ★★ U

Action crime   1977 · US · Colour · 88mins

Tinseltown's first attempt to bring Marvel Comics' greatest cartoon character to life was an unmitigated disaster, resulting in a charmless, by-the-numbers thriller made worse by shoddy effects. Nicholas Hammond does an adequate job of imitating our hero, alias Peter Parker – bitten by a radioactive spider which gives him superhuman strength – but is hampered by EW Swackhamer's failure to capture the style or character of the original comic book. What makes this even more of a disappointment is the fact that Marvel guru Stan Lee consulted on the production. Actually made as the pilot for a television show but released to theatres in Europe, it spawned two movie-length sequels, *Spider-Man Strikes Back* and *Spider-Man: the Dragon's Challenge*.

Nicholas Hammond *Peter Parker/Spider-Man* • Lisa Eilbacher *Judy Tyler* • David White *J Jonah Jameson* • Michael Pataki *Captain Barbera* • Hilly Hicks *Robbie Robinson* • Thayer David *Edward Byron* ■ *Dir* EW Swackhamer • *Scr* Alvin Boretz, from the comic book by Stan Lee

The Spiders ★★★★

Silent adventure melodrama
1919 · Ger · BW · 72mins

Fritz Lang's first commercial success is an adventure melodrama on a theme popular at the time: arch criminals hoping to take over the world. Inspired by the German pulp writer Karl May and the serials of Louis Feuillade, it was made in two parts, but broken up into episodes like a serial. It tells of a hero pitted against an Asian criminal and a gang called the Spiders, who are after a diamond shaped like the head of Buddha. The earliest of Lang's surviving works, it already has many Langian elements: the use of mirrors, hypnosis and underground chambers.

Carl de Vogt *Kay Hoog* • Lil Dagover *Naela, Priestess of the Sun* • Ressel Orla *Lio Sha* • Georg John *Dr Telphas* • Rudolph Lettinger [Rudolf Lettinger] *John Terry, the Diamond King* • Edgar Pauly *Four Finger John* ■ *Dir/Scr* Fritz Lang

The Spider's Stratagem ★★★★★ PG

Drama   1970 · It · Colour · 94mins

One of the all-time great movies of Italian cinema, this shows director Bernardo Bertolucci at the zenith of his consummate talent in the days when he excelled at illuminating the effect of cultural differences on the human spirit. His hero, brilliantly played by Giulio Brogi, returns home to find his sense of family shattered by unseen events from the past. As he struggles to attain greater knowledge of his heroic father's assassination, we are taken on a fascinating psychological journey with enormous verve and wit, while Italy's Po valley looks marvellous thanks to the luminous camerawork of Vittorio Storaro. In Italian with English subtitles.

Giulio Brogi *Athos Magnani/His father* • Alida Valli *Draifa* • Tino Scotti *Costa* • Pippo Campanini *Gaibazzi* ■ *Dir* Bernardo Bertolucci • *Scr* Bernardo Bertolucci, Eduardo De

Gregorio, Marilu Parolini, from the story *Theme of the Traitor and the Hero* by Jorge Luis Borges • *Cinematographer* Vittorio Storaro

Spies ★★★★

Silent spy thriller   1928 · Ger · BW · 86mins

Perhaps the most under-rated of Fritz Lang's silent spectacles, this tale of master criminality has all the visceral thrill and visual atmospherics of one of Louis Feuillade's *Fantomas* serials. Many of the *Metropolis* alumni were reunited for the picture, with Karl Vollbrecht and Otto Hunte creating Expressionist sets which added menace to the dastardly deeds laid at the door of the Mabuse-like Rudolf Klein-Rogge by Lang and Thea von Harbou's breathless script. However, once again, this is very much Lang's own vision, as he abandons political allegory to place the emphasis firmly on escapism and his genius for the awe-inspiring set piece.

Rudolf Klein-Rogge *Haghi* • Gerda Maurus *Sonia Barranikova* • Willy Fritsch *Number 326* ■ *Dir* Fritz Lang • *Scr* Fritz Lang, Thea von Harbou, from their story

Spies, Lies and Naked Thighs ★★ PG

Comedy thriller   1988 · US · Colour · 87mins

James Frawley has had a chequered career. One moment he's directing Jean Renoir in *The Christian Licorice Store*; the next he's guiding Kermit and Miss Piggy through *The Muppet Movie*. His career highlight was the disaster spoof *The Big Bus* and he's back on the pastiche path with this manic TV movie from the pen of Ed Self. Your enjoyment of this espionage comedy will largely depend on your ability to stomach improvisational comic Harry Anderson, who tears through the action like the Tasmanian Devil.

Harry Anderson *Freddie Fallon* • Ed Begley Jr *Alan Rossmore* • Linda Purl *Beverly Rossmore* • Wendy Crewson *Evelyn Fallon* • Brent Carver *Gunther* • Rachel Ticotin *Sonia* ■ *Dir* James Frawley • *Scr* Ed Self

Spies like Us ★★ PG

Spy comedy   1985 · US · Colour · 97mins

With films such as *The Blues Brothers* to his credit, John Landis had forged himself the reputation of being one of Hollywood's slickest comedy directors. But with this highly resistible spoof, he stepped on to a slippery slope on which he is still stranded. Paired for the first time in a film, former *Saturday Night Live* alumni Dan Aykroyd and Chevy Chase simply fail to gel, and there's little fun to be had once the boisterous training school gags are exhausted. Movie aficionados can while away the time playing spot the famous film-makers in a variety of cameo roles.

Chevy Chase *Emmett Fitz-Hume* • Dan Aykroyd *Austin Millbarge* • Steve Forrest *General Sline* • Donna Dixon *Karen Boyer* • Bruce Davison *Mr Ruby* • Bernie Casey *Colonel Rhombus* • William Prince *Mr Keyes* • Tom Hatten *General Miegs* • Bob Hope ■ *Dir* John Landis • *Scr* Dan Aykroyd, Lowell Ganz, Babaloo Mandel, from a story by Dan Aykroyd, Dave Thomas

Spike of Bensonhurst ★★

Sports comedy   1988 · US · Colour · 101mins

Andy Warhol alumnus Paul Morrissey is the unlikely director of this sub-*Rocky* crime and boxing comedy. Sasha Mitchell is a local wide-boy working for the mob and making a living by taking the odd dive in the boxing ring. Life is fine until he makes the mistake of falling for Maria Pitillo, the daughter of local Mafia don Ernest Borgnine. Some charm but certainly no knockout.

Sasha Mitchell *Spike Fumo* • Ernest Borgnine *Baldo Cacetti* • Anne DeSalvo *Sylvia Cacetti* • Sylvia Miles *Congresswoman* • Geraldine Smith *Helen Fumo* • Maria Pitillo *Angel* • Talisa Soto *India* ■ *Dir* Paul Morrissey • *Scr* Alan Bowne, Paul Morrissey

The Spikes Gang ★★ 15

Western   1974 · US · Colour · 92mins

It's a shame that this was filmed in Spain, for it's the European look and corny Almeria locations that undermine any grit that director Richard Fleischer and star Lee Marvin can bring to this intriguing screenplay from Irving Ravetch and Harriet Frank Jr, the team responsible for such estimable westerns as *Hud* and *Hombre*. Like *Bad Company* and *The Cowboys*, this is a story of awestruck youths out West, including *The Culpepper Cattle Co's* Gary Grimes and *Happy Days's* Ron Howard, now better known as director of such major features as *Apollo 13* and *Ransom*. The lads idolise Marvin's Harry Spikes (the film's original title) who teaches them to rob banks. The then-fashionable dashes of violence don't help.

Lee Marvin *Harry Spikes* • Gary Grimes *Will Young* • Ron Howard *Les Richter* • Charlie Martin Smith [Charles Martin Smith] *Tod Mayhew* • Arthur Hunnicutt *Kid White* • Noah Beery Jr *Jack Bassett* • Marc Smith *Abel Young* ■ *Dir* Richard Fleischer • *Scr* Irving Ravetch, Harriet Frank Jr

The Spiral Road ★

Melodrama   1962 · US · Colour · 135mins

American director Robert Mulligan followed this dire religious medical drama with *To Kill a Mockingbird*, thus making both his best and possibly worst films within the same 12 months. This jungle-set drama is disadvantaged from the start in its casting of the amiable Rock Hudson as an aggressively ambitious doctor who, in the mid-thirties, travels to Java to learn and then profit from the ideas of guru physician Dr Jansen. The matinée idol was never known for being ruthless in films, and he's equally implausible as a born-again reformer. Over two hours of witchcraft, leprosy, voodoo and alcoholism prove to be a long and winding road.

Rock Hudson *Dr Anton Drager* • Gena Rowlands *Els* • Burl Ives *Dr Brits Jansen* • Geoffrey Keen *Willem Wattereus* • Neva Patterson *Louise Kramer* • Will Kuluva *Dr Sordjano* • Philip Abbott *Frolick* ■ *Dir* Robert Mulligan • *Scr* John Lee Mahin, Neil Paterson, from the novel by Jan de Hartog

The Spiral Staircase ★★★★ PG

Thriller   1946 · US · BW · 83mins

Thought-provoking and disturbing, this masterly thriller is directed with touches of sheer genius by Robert Siodmak, who beckons us into a voyeuristic nightmare with taut, creeping camerawork that makes the hairs on your neck stand up. However, while this is undoubtedly a classic of forties' Hollywood Gothic, the movie treads a fine line between acceptable menace and uncomfortable sadism with its story of a serial killer murdering maimed and disabled women. That said, this remains a masterwork, with a fine performance from Dorothy McGuire.

Dorothy McGuire *Helen Capel* • George Brent *Professor Warren* • Ethel Barrymore *Mrs Warren* • Kent Smith *Dr Parry* • Rhonda Fleming *Blanche* • Gordon Oliver *Steve Warren* • Elsa Lanchester *Mrs Oates* • Sara Allgood *Nurse Barker* ■ *Dir* Robert Siodmak • *Scr* Mel Dinelli, from the novel *Some Must Watch* by Ethel Lina White • *Cinematographer* Nicholas Musuraca

The Spirit of St Louis ★★★★ U

Historical drama
1957 · US · Colour · 134mins

One of the greatest achievements of director Billy Wilder, best known for such mordant comedies as *Some Like It Hot* and *Sunset Boulevard*. It is a staggering conceit to film such a seemingly uncinematic tale as Charles A Lindbergh's solo flight across the Atlantic, confined as it is to one man in a small cockpit. Wilder makes it an emotional tour de force, utilising flashbacks and narration with wit and skill, aided by Franz Waxman's superb score and Robert Burks and J Peverell Marley's magnificent photography. James Stewart is a shade too old for Lindbergh, but no other actor could better his unique all-American combination of intensity, tenderness and wry concern.

James Stewart *Charles A Lindbergh* • Murray Hamilton *Bud Gurney* • Patricia Smith *Mirror Girl* • Bartlett Robinson *BF Mahoney* • Robert Cornthwaite *Knight* • Sheila Bond *Model/Dancer* • Marc Connelly *Father Hussman* ■ *Dir* Billy Wilder • *Scr* Billy Wilder, Wendell Mayes, Charles Lederer, from the autobiography by Charles A Lindbergh

The Spirit of the Beehive ★★★★★ PG

Drama   1973 · Sp · Colour · 93mins

Set in 1940, Victor Erice's remarkable debut is a controlled assault on the indolence into which Spain slipped under Franco, and a biting allegory on the evil of which the seemingly benevolent state could be capable. A vision of trust and gentleness, Ana Torrent is enchanting as the small girl who watches *Frankenstein* and becomes fascinated by the monster, mistakenly believing that its spirit is embodied in the fugitive soldier she has befriended. It is her way of trying to alleviate the misery of life in her post-Civil War village. Told with a disarming realism and simplicity, this charming film is one of the gems of

Spanish cinema. In Spanish with English subtitles. ▣

Ana Torrent *Ana* • Isabel Telleria *Isabel* • Fernando Fernan Gomez *Father* • Teresa Gimpera *Mother* • Jose Villasante *Frankenstein's monster* ■ *Dir* Victor Erice • *Scr* Francisco J Querejeta

Spirit of the Eagle ★★★ U
Adventure   1991 · US · Colour · 88mins

Those who have not had enough of Dan Haggerty in his "Grizzly" Adams incarnation will probably enjoy this good-natured, Great Outdoors adventure. Haggerty is Big Eli, a cartographer who makes the mistake of leaving son Little Eli home alone, only to find that he's been kidnapped. It's a great advertisement for the attractions of Oregon, even though the story itself could do with more hills and valleys, light and shade. Still, this peek into family harmony is affecting, and the sumptuous locations provide the eye with a rich, ready meal. ▣

Dan Haggerty *Big Eli McDonaugh* • Bill Smith [William Smith] *One-Eye* • Trever Yarrish *Little Eli* • Jeri Arredondo *Watawna* • Taylor Lacher *Weasel* • Ken Carpenter *Jake* • Don Shanks *Running Wolf* ■ *Dir/Scr* Boon Collins

Spiritual Love ★★★ 15
Comedy   1987 · HK · Colour · 88mins

Inspired by the writings of the 17th-century chronicler of the supernatural, Master Liaozhai, the female ghost story developed into a popular sub-genre of Hong Kong fantasy horror in the eighties. Made just before the emphasis shifted away from atmosphere and on to special effects, David Lai and Taylor Wong's film also slips in plenty of comedy, notably the bizarre manner in which Chow Yun-Fat's jealous lover, Pauline Wong, is transformed into his "girlfiend". Yet, for all Wong's vengeful antics and the grisliness of the final showdown, this is essentially a romance between Chow and Cherie Chung, who died centuries before they met. In Cantonese with English subtitles.

Chow Yun-Fat *Pok* • Cherie Chung *Butterfly* • Pauline Wong ■ *Dir* David Lai, Taylor Wong • *Scr* Stephen Shiu

Spite Marriage ★★★
Silent comedy   1929 · US · BW · 76mins

Despite a couple of uproarious scenes, it was clear – in only his second feature for the studio – that MGM was slowly eroding Buster Keaton's creative autonomy and corrupting his comic instincts. Never had Keaton's stone-faced bewilderment been so apposite, as he hurtles through increasingly shoddy plot contrivances that culminate in him confronting a rum-runner on his yacht. Much more sure-footed are the scenes between his daydreaming dry cleaner and Dorothy Sebastian, the actress who exploits him to get back at her feckless beau. The chaos Buster causes as a stage stand-in and the sequence when he tries to put a drunken woman to bed just about save the day.

Buster Keaton *Elmer* • Dorothy Sebastian *Trilby Drew* • Edward Earle *Lionel Denmore* ■ *Dir* Edward Sedgwick • *Scr* Richard Schayer, Ernest S Pagano, Robert Hopkins, from a story by Lew Lipton

Spitfire ★
Drama   1934 · US · BW · 85mins

This ludicrous melodrama was an early nail in the coffin of Katharine Hepburn's reputation, that would see her labelled as "box-office poison" by the end of the decade. Improbably cast as a badly educated, uncouth mountain girl, she alienates the backwoods community with her faith-healing ideas, and is caught in a dreary and unbelievable love triangle with Robert Young and Ralph Bellamy. The script is dreadful, and the patrician Hepburn is badly miscast. Her hysterically mannered and frenzied performance is at best highly irritating, at worst an intolerable embarrassment.

Katharine Hepburn *Trigger Hicks* • Robert Young *John Stafford* • Ralph Bellamy *George Fleetwood* • Martha Sleeper *Eleanor Stafford* ■ *Dir* John Cromwell • *Scr* Jane Murfin, Lula Vollmer, from the play *Trigger* by Lula Vollmer

The Spitfire Grill ★★★ 12
Drama   1996 · US · Colour · 111mins

A mesmerising performance from Alison Elliott (*The Wings of the Dove*) is the highlight of this moving if slightly unbelievable drama. Elliott plays Percy, the young ex-con paroled to a small (and small-minded) Maine town, where she goes to work at the local diner run by worldly-wise Ellen Burstyn. Well played by a cast that includes Marcia Gay Harden and the always watchable Will Patton, and featuring some luscious, rugged scenery, this is tear-jerking, female bonding stuff – perfect fare for a Sunday afternoon by the fire with a man-size box of tissues. ▣

Alison Elliott *Percy Talbott* • Ellen Burstyn *Hannah Ferguson* • Marcia Gay Harden *Shelby Goddard* • Will Patton *Nahum Goddard* • Kieran Mulroney *Joe Sperling* ■ *Dir/Scr* Lee David Zlotoff

Splash ★★★★ PG
Romantic comedy   1984 · US · Colour · 105mins

A charming romantic comedy that touched a chord with audiences around the world and propelled its stars Tom Hanks and Daryl Hannah, along with director Ron Howard, to Hollywood's front rank. Hannah is the innocent mermaid who docks on dry land to locate the boy (now the grown-up Hanks) she saved from drowning many years ago. Hanks and Hannah make a pair of charismatic leads, although John Candy (another player on the road to stardom) gets most of the best gags. Howard ensures the good-natured fun keeps flowing and manages to keep soppiness largely at bay. The film was followed four years later by a dismal TV-movie sequel. Contains swearing. ▣ **DVD**

Tom Hanks *Allen Bauer* • Daryl Hannah *Madison* • Eugene Levy *Walter Kornbluth* • John Candy *Freddie Bauer* • Dody Goodman *Mrs Stimler* • Shecky Greene *Mr Buyrite* • Richard B Shull *Dr Ross* ■ *Dir* Ron Howard • *Scr* Lowell Ganz, Babaloo Mandel, Bruce Jay Friedman, from a story by Brian Grazer, Bruce Jay Friedman

Splash, Too ★ U
Comedy   1988 · US · Colour · 87mins

What do you get when you cross a hit movie with a sitcom? The answer is

this soggy TV pilot, a sequel of sorts to the comedy hit that starred Tom Hanks and Daryl Hannah. You can't really blame Todd Waring and Amy Yasbeck, as their predecessors are an impossible act to follow. It's the script that is the principal culprit, with the opening scenes in New York cringingly unfunny and the finale embarrassingly twee. ▣

Todd Waring *Allen Bauer* • Amy Yasbeck *Madison* • Donovan Scott *Freddie* • Rita Taggart *Fern Hooten* • Noble Willingham *Karl Hooten* ■ *Dir* Greg Antonacci • *Scr* Bruce Franklin Singer, from characters created by Brian Grazer, Bruce Jay Friedman

Splendor ★★★ U
Melodrama   1935 · US · BW · 73mins

Producer Samuel Goldwyn commissioned playwright Rachel Crothers to write this (on a royalty basis) as a vehicle for Miriam Hopkins. Handsome Joel McCrea marries poor girl Hopkins, instead of the rich heiress his mother has set her sights on. Hopkins is a take-her-or-leave-her actress, and she can't quite bring off the early stages of the movie, clearly being anything but a naive newlywed. Yet her later scenes with Helen Westley as McCrea's thwarted mother have a ferocity all their own. ▣

Joel McCrea *Brighton Lorrimore* • Miriam Hopkins *Phyllis Manning Lorrimore* • Paul Cavanagh *Martin Deering* • Helen Westley *Mrs Lorrimore* • David Niven *Clancey Lorrimore* ■ *Dir* Elliott Nugent • *Scr* Rachel Crothers

Splendor in the Grass ★★★★ 15
Drama   1961 · US · Colour · 118mins

Warren Beatty couldn't have had a better start to his movie career than this, with collaborators such as co-star Natalie Wood and director Elia Kazan. Beatty and Wood play star-crossed lovers in playwright William Inge's tragi-romantic screenplay, set in twenties Kansas. The young couple who spend the film attempting to cross the sexual morality divide are too easily dominated by interfering parents (Audrey Christie, Pat Hingle), so that what should be splendid is seen to be squalid. The psychology may be simplistic, but the powerful portrayals make that weakness seem like an irrelevance. Contains sexual references. ▣

Natalie Wood *Wilma Dean Loomis* • Warren Beatty *Bud Stamper* • Pat Hingle *Ace Stamper* • Audrey Christie *Mrs Loomis* • Barbara Loden *Ginny Stamper* • Zohra Lampert *Angelina* • Fred Stewart *Del Loomis* • Sandy Dennis *Kay* ■ *Dir* Elia Kazan • *Scr* William Inge

The Split ★★★
Crime thriller   1968 · US · Colour · 89mins

A gutsy crime thriller that boasts a splendid supporting cast of tough guys and a script based on a novel by Richard Stark, who also wrote *Point Blank*. For that film producers Robert Chartoff and Irwin Winkler imported a British director, John Boorman, and they did the same for *The Split*, with only slightly less spectacular results. The movie spins around Jim Brown, who plans to rob a football stadium and recruits his team in the manner of *The Dirty Dozen*. It's a formula picture,

though director Gordon Flemyng relishes his Los Angeles locations just as much as Boorman did.

Jim Brown *McClain* • Diahann Carroll *Ellie* • Julie Harris *Gladys* • Ernest Borgnine *Bert Clinger* • Gene Hackman *Lt Walter Brill* • Jack Klugman *Harry Kifka* • Warren Oates *Marty Gough* • Donald Sutherland *Dave Negli* ■ *Dir* Gordon Flemyng • *Scr* Robert Sabaroff, from the novel *The Seventh* by Richard Stark [Donald E Westlake]

Split Image ★★★ 15
Drama   1982 · US · Colour · 106mins

The eighties were a quiet time for Peter Fonda, but here he delivers a powerful performance that shows a different side to the counterculture hero. He plays a cult leader who ensnares Michael O'Keefe, only to discover that the latter's father (the ever-reliable Brian Dennehy) is not giving up without a fight. The film additionally provides juicy roles for James Woods and Karen Allen, while director Ted Kotcheff lends a dark edge to the proceedings. Contains swearing and nudity.

Michael O'Keefe *Danny Stetson* • Karen Allen *Rebecca* • Peter Fonda *Neal Kirklander* • James Woods *Charles Pratt* • Elizabeth Ashley *Diana Stetson* • Brian Dennehy *Kevin Stetson* • Ronnie Scribner *Sean Stetson* ■ *Dir* Ted Kotcheff • *Scr* Scott Spencer, Robert Kaufman, Robert Mark Kamen, from a story by Scott Spencer

Split Infinity ★
Drama   1992 · US · Colour · 90mins

Teenagers simply aren't going to sit through a movie about a stroppy, money-mad girl learning the harsh facts of the Great Depression, and adults aren't going to be fooled by the accompanying sentimentality. So it's hard to see just who is going to enjoy this TV movie in which 14-year-old Melora Slover is transported back to 1929 to become her own great aunt and discovers just how hard her grandfather tried to save the family farm. Director Stan Ferguson thumps the tub far too hard, producing a story that both looks and feels like a rejected episode of *The Waltons*.

Melora Slover *Aj Knowlton* • Marcia Dangerfield *Mary Ellen* • Devin Healey *Joey* • Dave Jensen *George* • Heath Ezell *Dewey* ■ *Dir* Stan Ferguson • *Scr* Leo D Paur, from a story by Forrest S Baker III

Split Second ★★★
Drama   1953 · US · BW · 80mins

A cracking thriller from Dick Powell, here making his dirctorial debut and managing to crank up a fair amount of suspense. Slimy escaped convict Stephen McNally ends up in a Nevada ghost town with a clutch of hostages to keep the law at bay. The catch is that the town is actually part of a nuclear test site. This is clever stuff, particularly well cast, with fine work from Alexis Smith and Jan Sterling, and reliable veterans like Paul Kelly and Arthur Hunnicutt turning in their usual well-honed character studies.

Stephen McNally *Sam Hurley* • Alexis Smith *Kay Garven* • Jan Sterling *Dottie* • Keith Andes *Larry Fleming* • Arthur Hunnicutt *Asa* • Paul Kelly *Bart Moore* • Robert Paige *Arthur Ashton*

U = SUITABLE FOR ALL,   Uc = SUITABLE FOR ALL, ESPECIALLY FOR YOUNG CHILDREN (VIDEO ONLY)   PG = PARENTAL GUIDANCE

• Richard Egan *Dr Garven* ■ *Dir* Dick Powell • *Scr* William Bowers, Irving Wallace, from a story by Chester Erskine, Irving Wallace

Split Second ★★ 18

Science-fiction horror thriller
1991 · UK · Colour · 86mins

Rutger Hauer mugs shamelessly in a nonsensical science-fiction effort from Tony Maylam, the director of *The Burning*. Hauer's an on-edge cop in the flooded London of 2008, in search of a monstrous heart-ripping serial killer with Satanic origins with whom he shares a psychic link. Sidekick Neil Duncan and love interest Kim Cattrall take their places for the daft battle denouement in Cannon Street tube station. Cartoon gore, noisy violence, plot strands left hanging in the air and a few fleeting glimpses of a black rubber creature aren't enough to satisfy anyone but the most undiscriminating trash addict. ▭

Rutger Hauer *Harley Stone* • Kim Cattrall *Michelle* • Neil Duncan *Dick Durkin* • Michael J Pollard *The Rat Catcher* • Pete Postlethwaite *Paulsen* • Ian Dury *Jay Jay* • Roberta Eaton *Robin* • Alun Armstrong *Thrasher* ■ *Dir* Tony Maylam • *Scr* Gary Scott Thompson

Splitting Heirs ★★ 15

Comedy   1993 · UK · Colour · 83mins

Eric Idle is mistakenly allowed to roam free here as both star and scriptwriter by director Robert M Young, who should have boxed him in tight. Had the other participants (Rick Moranis, John Cleese and Barbara Hershey) been similarly reined in, Young might have been able to deliver a focused comedy. Odd moments do resurrect the barmy surrealism so familiar from Monty Python, but on the whole this is a rather disorganised comedy. Contains some violence, swearing, sex scenes and nudity. ▭

Eric Idle *Tommy* • Rick Moranis *Henry* • Barbara Hershey *Duchess Lucinda* • Catherine Zeta-Jones *Kitty* • John Cleese *Shadgrind* • Sadie Frost *Angela* • Stratford Johns *Butler* • Brenda Bruce *Mrs Bullock* • Eric Sykes *Jobson the doorman* ■ *Dir* Robert Young [Robert M Young] • *Scr* Eric Idle

Spoiler ★★ 18

Science-fiction thriller
1998 · US · Colour · 90mins

If one considers its low budget and 18-day shooting schedule, this movie can be considered more of an accomplishment that it otherwise is. Martial arts actor Gary Daniels is miscast as a prisoner in the future, whose frequent attempts to escape see him recaptured, frozen for several years and put through various hells. The underlying weakness of the story is that Daniels's stubborn and seemingly illogical behavior is never properly explained, making one wonder if he deserves his fate after all. The sets and most of the special effects are appallingly cheap; various B-movie stars make cameos throughout. Contains swearing and violence. ▭

Jeffrey Combs *Captain* • Gary Daniels *Roger Mason* • Jean Speegle Howard *Jennifer* ■ *Dir* Michael Kalesniko

The Spoilers ★★★

Western   1942 · US · BW · 87mins

A version Rex Beach's popular, Alaska-set western novel, this time with its plot slightly altered to accommodate Marlene Dietrich as the saloon keeper. What always distinguishes movie versions of this tale is the exciting, protracted fist-fight between the leading men that marks the story's climax. Here the macho cuffing is between John Wayne and Randolph Scott.

Marlene Dietrich *Cherry Malotte* • John Wayne *Roy Glennister* • Randolph Scott *McNamara* • Margaret Lindsay *Helen Chester* • Harry Carey Sr [Harry Carey] *Dextry* • Richard Barthelmess *Bronco Kid* ■ *Dir* Ray Enright • *Scr* Lawrence Hazard, Tom Reed, from the novel by Rex Beach

The Spoilers ★★ U

Western   1955 · US · Colour · 83mins

Another version of Rex Beach's novel about claim jumping during the Alaskan gold rush and the first to be filmed in colour with a new generation of stars – Anne Baxter, Jeff Chandler, Rory Calhoun – who later match up to Marlene Dietrich, Randolph Scott and John Wayne in the version 13 years earlier. The preceding films have become noted for the climactic fist-fights between hero and villain and this makes a determined effort to compete as Chandler and Calhoun (and their stunt doubles) slug it out from the floor above the saloon down the stairs and out into the muddy main street. But the story is tired and the picture is never more than mildly engrossing.

Anne Baxter *Cherry Malotte* • Jeff Chandler *Roy Glennister* • Rory Calhoun *Alex McNamara* • Ray Danton *"Bronco" Blackie* • Barbara Britton *Helen Chester* • John McIntire *Dextry* • Carl Benton Reid *Judge Stillman* • Wallace Ford *Flapjack Simms* ■ *Dir* Jesse Hibbs • *Scr* Oscar Brodney, Charles Hoffman, from the novel by Rex Beach

Spoils of War ★★★ PG

Romantic drama   1994 · US · Colour · 89mins

This flimsy romantic drama scarcely deserves a cast of this calibre but, thanks to the efforts of Kate Nelligan and John Heard, its story of regret and reconciliation is a surprisingly good watch. Nelligan is a divorcee whose determination to make a fresh start is coloured by the lingering hope that her marriage could be revived. You might shudder at the thought of her teenage son acting as matchmaker, but the performances have a lifelike ring about them and the action is never allowed to become mawkish. Contains swearing. ▭

Kate Nelligan *Elise* • John Heard *Andrew* • Tobey Maguire *Martin* ■ *Dir* David Greene • *Scr* Michael Weller

Spooks Run Wild ★★ U

Comedy   1941 · US · BW · 64mins

Having made the minor horror classics *The Black Cat* with Basil Rathbone and *The Wolf Man* with Lon Chaney Jr also in 1941, this seventh entry in the East Side Kids series must have seemed something of a comedown for Bela Lugosi. However, an even more surprising credit for this harum-scarum

old-dark-house adventure is that of co-scriptwriter Carl Foreman, who later received five Oscar nominations for pictures such as *High Noon*. Lugosi is mildly sinister and the Kids wisecrack like popcorn machines.

Bela Lugosi *Nardo, the monster* • Leo Gorcey *Muggsy* • Huntz Hall *Glimpy* • Bobby Jordan *Danny* • David Gorcey *Pee Wee* • "Sunshine Sammy" Morrison *Scruno* • Donald Haines *Skinny* ■ *Dir* Phil Rosen • *Scr* Carl Foreman, Charles Marion, Jack Henley

Sporting Blood ★★★ U

Comedy drama   1931 · US · BW · 82mins

Top-billed Clark Gable is the only big name in this "biography" of a horse named Tommy Boy, which follows him from a Kentucky stud farm, through the abuse he suffers at the hands of several racehorse owners, to his eventual rescue and triumph as the Derby winner. This unusual movie is part exposé of the ugly elements who indulge in the sport of kings, and part tribute to and plea on behalf of dumb animals. Featuring a charming Madge Evans as the female interest this is an absolute must for all horse lovers and Gable fans.

Clark Gable *Rid Riddell* • Ernest Torrence *Jim Rellence* • Madge Evans *Ruby* • Lew Cody *Tip Scanlon* • Marie Prevost *Angela* • Hallam Cooley *Ludeking* • J Farrell MacDonald *MacGuire* ■ *Dir* Charles Brabin • *Scr* Wanda Tuchock, from the novel *Horseflesh* by Frederick Hazlitt Brennan

Spotswood ★★★ PG

Comedy drama   1991 · Ausl · Colour · 94mins

Director Mark Joffe's appealing feature is similar to an Aussie Ealing comedy. At his most hesitant and human, Anthony Hopkins stars in a role that would have been ideal for Peter Sellers as a time-and-motion man whose dealings with the workers in a suburban moccasin factory cause him to re-evaluate a life dictated by emotional sterility and ruthless efficiency. The satire is gentle, the comedy often delightfully offbeat and the character traits neatly observed. There are promising performances from Toni Collette and Russell Crowe.

Anthony Hopkins *Wallace* • Ben Mendelsohn *Carey* • Toni Collette *Wendy* • Alwyn Kurts *Mr Ball* • Dan Wyllie *Fletcher* • Bruno Lawrence *Robert* • Rebecca Rigg *Cheryl* • Russell Crowe *Kim Barrett* ■ *Dir* Mark Joffe • *Scr* Max Dann, Andrew Knight

The Spring ★★ 15

Action adventure
1990 · US · Colour · 101mins

A tired rehash of *Cocoon* that finds archaeologists Dack Rambo and Gedde Watanabe setting out to uncover a fabled spring which keeps people eternally young. The action elements are routine and the playing of Rambo and Shari Shattuck as the mysterious beauty who holds the secret to the fountain is bland. Contains some nudity. ▭

Dack Rambo *Andy Peterson* • Shari Shattuck *Dianne Windsor* • Gedde Watanabe *Matty* • Steven Keats *Mark* • Virginia Watson *Palinya* ■ *Dir* John D Patterson [John Patterson] • *Scr* Hugh Parks

Spring and Port Wine ★★★

Comedy   1969 · UK · Colour · 100mins

Any film adaptation of a play in which the critical action takes place around a dining table is likely to be slightly stagebound. That Bill Naughton's screen version of his own generation-gap comedy works as a movie is partly down to its commonplace, but utterly compelling, content and director Peter Hammond's deft opening out of events. However, the key element is unquestionably the playing of James Mason, Susan George and a host of sitcom celebrities, with Mason alternately infuriating and endearing as the dour Lancastrian feuding with daughter George.

James Mason *Rafe Crompton* • Susan George *Hilda Crompton* • Diana Coupland *Daisy Crompton* • Rodney Bewes *Harold Crompton* • Hannah Gordon *Florence Crompton* • Len Jones *Wilfred Crompton* • Keith Buckley *Arthur Gasket* ■ *Dir* Peter Hammond • *Scr* Bill Naughton, from his play

Spring in Park Lane ★★★ U

Romantic comedy   1948 · UK · BW · 95mins

Another of those fatuous fantasies about lords pretending to be servants, as wealthy Anna Neagle falls for footman Michael Wilding. Even though Herbert Wilcox's direction tends to be heavy-handed, there are many deft touches, mainly supplied by Nicholas Phipps's light-as-air screenplay. The two leads carry off the plot with some aplomb, and Wilding plays his role of charming wimp surprisingly well. A big hit in postwar Britain.

Anna Neagle *Judy Howard* • Michael Wilding *Richard* • Tom Walls *Uncle Joshua Howard* • Peter Graves (2) *Basil Maitland* • Marjorie Fielding *Mildred Howard* • Nicholas Phipps *Marquis of Borechester* ■ *Dir* Herbert Wilcox • *Scr* Nicholas Phipps, from the play *Come Out of the Kitchen* by Alice Duer Miller

Spring River Flows East ★★★★

Drama   1947 · Chi · BW · 190mins

Arguably the finest director of the pre-communist era, Cai Chusheng and documentarist Zheng Junli teamed for this convoluted account of the chaos and corruption that afflicted Chinese society around the Sino-Japanese war. Parallel narratives chart the diverging fortunes of schoolteacher Tao Jin and Bai Yang, the wife he leaves behind when he volunteers to fight, with his postwar prosperity contrasting with the poverty and despair she endures in various refugee camps and menial jobs. The strongest performances all come from actresses, with Bai's selfless suffering being matched by the loyalty of mother-in-law Wu Yin. A Mandarin language film.

Bai Yang *Sufen* • Tao Jin *Zhang Zhongliang* • Shu Xiuwen *Wang Lizhen* • Yunzhu Shangguan *He Wenyan* ■ *Dir* Cai Chusheng, Zheng Junli • *Scr* Cai Chusheng, Zheng Junli

Springfield Rifle ★★★ U

Western   1952 · US · Colour · 92mins

The same year that Gary Cooper won an Oscar for *High Noon* he also starred in this perfunctory Warner Bros western. Directed with some style by *House of Wax*'s André De Toth, this

feature resembles a Randolph Scott programme filler, wherein Cooper instead of Scott rides with a batch of second-string actors to infiltrate a gang. Cooper is a little too old for this kind of lark, but there's a certain pleasure to be gained from watching a great star at work.

Gary Cooper *Major "Lex" Kearney* • Phyllis Thaxter *Erin Kearney* • David Brian *Austin McCool* • Paul Kelly *Lieutenant Colonel Hudson* • Philip Carey *Captain Tennick* • Lon Chaney Jr *Elm* • James Millican *Matthew Quint* • Martin Milner *Olie Larsen* ■ *Dir* Andre De Toth • *Scr* Charles Marquis Warren, Frank Davis, from a story by Sloan Nibley

Springtime in the Rockies ★★★ U

Musical comedy 1942 · US · Colour · 87mins
Soon-to-be-wed Betty Grable and Harry James appear together in one of the better musicals produced by 20th Century-Fox during the Second World War. Grable and John Payne play a sparring Broadway duo, and that's all you really need to know! The music includes the wonderful Helen Forrest performing Harry Warren and Mack Gordon's *I Had the Craziest Dream*, and the supporting cast includes such eccentrics as Carmen Miranda (attempting *Chattanooga Choo Choo*), Charlotte Greenwood, and the redoubtable Edward Everett Horton. Grable expertly showed off her slim talents to best effect, and confidently consolidated her stardom on her way to becoming the Forces' "pin-up".

Betty Grable *Vicky Lane* • John Payne *Dan Christy* • Carmen Miranda *Rosita Murphy* • Cesar Romero *Victor Prince* • Charlotte Greenwood *Phoebe Gray* • Edward Everett Horton *McTavish* • Jackie Gleason *The commissioner* • Harry James ■ *Dir* Irving Cummings • *Scr* Walter Bullock, Ken Englund, Jacques Thery, from the short story *Second Honeymoon* by Philip Wylie

Springtime in the Sierras ★★

Western 1947 · US · Colour · 75mins
One of the earliest Roy Rogers westerns to be filmed in colour, this has a plotline with an ecological slant. In support of the preservation of wildlife, the "King of the Cowboys" exposes a gang who are killing game out of season. There's a villainess behind it all, played by Stephanie Bachelor who ends up in a fierce tussle with heroine Jane Frazee while Roy is slugging it out with her beefy henchman, Roy Barcroft.

Roy Rogers • Jane Frazee *Taffy Baker* • Andy Devine *"Cookie" Bullfincher* • Stephanie Bachelor *Jean Loring* • Hal Landon *Bert Baker* • Roy Barcroft *Matt Wilkes* ■ *Dir* William Witney • *Scr* A Sloan Nibley

Sprung ★★ 15

Romantic comedy
1997 · US · Colour · 104mins
Best friends Rusty Cundieff (who also wrote and directed) and Joe Torry pick up inseparable friends Tisha Campbell and Paula Jai Parker at a party, but while Torry and Parker hit it off, the other two end up despising each other. Their friendship threatened by the hot-and-heavy liaison, Cundieff and Campbell call a truce and do

everything in their power to separate the new lovers. Brash and likeable in parts, ordinary and uneven in others, the engaging actors bring more sparkle to the overly familiar material than it deserves. Contains swearing and sex scenes.

Tisha Campbell *Brandy* • Rusty Cundieff *Montel* • Paula Jai Parker *Adina* • Joe Torry *Clyde* • John Witherspoon *Detective* • Jennifer Lee *Veronica* • Clarence Williams III *Grand Daddy* • Isabel Sanford *Sista* ■ *Dir* Rusty Cundieff • *Scr* Rusty Cundieff, Darin Scott

Spy Hard ★★ PG

Spy spoof 1996 · US · Colour · 77mins
The blockbuster action thriller genre is ripe for sending up, but this lazy effort has to go down as a miss despite the presence of spoofmeister Leslie Nielsen. The basic story is firmly rooted in James Bond – Nielsen is superagent Dick Steele battling supervillain Andy Griffith – but to ensure all the bases are covered director Rick Friedberg tosses in largely irrelevant send-ups of *Speed*, *Pulp Fiction* and *In the Line of Duty*. The cast gives its all, but is defeated by the determinedly juvenile script. Contains strong language. DVD

Leslie Nielsen *Dick Steele* • Nicollette Sheridan *Veronique Ukrinsky* • Charles Durning *The Director* • Marcia Gay Harden *Miss Cheevus* • Barry Bostwick *Norman Coleman* • John Ales *Kabul* • Andy Griffith *General Rancor* ■ *Dir* Rick Friedberg • *Scr* Rick Friedberg, Dick Chudnow, Aaron Seltzer, from a story by Jason Friedberg, Aaron Seltzer

The Spy in Black ★★★ U

First World War spy drama
1939 · UK · BW · 78mins
A bold and atmospheric espionage thriller-cum-melodrama-cum-romance, made on the eve of the Second World War, but set during the First World War, with Conrad Veidt turning in a convincing performance as a German submarine commander dispatched to the Orkney Islands on a mission to sink the British fleet. Strong writing combines with striking cinematography and talented direction to make this a satisfying entertainment, the first collaboration of celebrated film-makers Michael Powell and Emeric Pressburger.

Conrad Veidt *Captain Hardt* • Valerie Hobson *Joan, the schoolmistress* • Sebastian Shaw *Commander Davis Blacklock* • Marius Goring *Lieutenant Schuster* • June Duprez *Anne Burnett* • Athole Stewart *Reverend Hector Matthews* • Agnes Lauchlan *Mrs Matthews* • Helen Haye *Mrs Sedley* ■ *Dir* Michael Powell • *Scr* Emeric Pressburger, Roland Pertwee, from the novel by J Storer Clouston • *Cinematographer* Bernard Browne

The Spy in the Green Hat ★★★

Spy drama 1966 · US · Colour · 92mins
The Man from UNCLE TV show spawned a hit and miss series of spinoff movies of which this is arguably the most accomplished. It features the series' best villains in the guise of Jack Palance's pill-popping megalomaniac and his kinky female secretary/assassin played with delicious malice by Janet Leigh. The plot is even more tongue in cheek than usual with the ever unflappable

Napoleon Solo and Illya Kuryakin teaming up with with a pack of stereotypical Italian-American gangsters to thwart THRUSH's latest plan for world domination. It's directed with stylish aplomb by Joseph Sargent, and Jerry Goldsmith's familiar theme tune sounds as fresh as ever.

Robert Vaughn *Napoleon Solo* • David McCallum *Illya Kuryakin* • Jack Palance *Louis Strago* • Janet Leigh *Miss Diketon* • Letitia Roman *Pia Monteri* • Leo G Carroll *Alexander Waverly* • Eduardo Ciannelli *Arturo "Fingers" Stilletto* • Allen Jenkins *Enzo "Pretty" Stilletto* • Jack La Rue [Jack LaRue] *Frederico "Feet" Stilletto* • Joan Blondell *Mrs "Fingers" Stilletto* • Elisha Cook [Elisha Cook Jr] *Arnold* ■ *Dir* Joseph Sargent • *Scr* Peter Allan Fields

The Spy Who Came in from the Cold ★★★★ PG

Spy drama 1965 · UK · BW · 112mins
This gritty adaptation of John Le Carré's gruelling novel finally offered Richard Burton a role worthy of his wonderfully world-weary style. Bitterness seeps from every pore as he goes behind the Iron Curtain for a final showdown with his East German counterpart. With agents trapped behind state secrecy and false identities, this isn't the glitzy neverland of James Bond, but a dangerous reality in which suppressed emotion matters more than derring-do. Martin Ritt's icy direction and Oswald Morris's bleak black-and-white photography make this not just the most authentic Cold War film, but also one of the best.

Richard Burton *Alec Leamas* • Claire Bloom *Nan Perry* • Oskar Werner *Fiedler* • Peter Van Eyck *Hans-Dieter Mundt* • Sam Wanamaker *Peters* • Rupert Davies *George Smiley* • Cyril Cusack *Control* ■ *Dir* Martin Ritt • *Scr* Paul Dehn, Guy Trosper, from the novel by John Le Carré

The Spy Who Loved Me ★★★★ PG

Spy adventure 1977 · UK · Colour · 120mins
"Nobody Does It Better" than Roger Moore in the best post-Connery James Bond adventure. Well-acted (with less reliance on slapstick humour than normal), smartly cast (metal-toothed Jaws, played by Richard Kiel, makes his first appearance) and lavishly directed (by Lewis Gilbert), this exceptional spy escapade is far-fetched mayhem of the highest order, with a welcome accent on character realism rather than just spectacular sets. Barbara Bach is the alluring Russian agent Anya Amasova. Contains some violence.

Roger Moore *James Bond* • Barbara Bach *Major Anya Amasova* • Curt Jurgens *Karl Stromberg* • Richard Kiel *Jaws* • Caroline Munro *Naomi* • Walter Gotell *General Gogol* • Geoffrey Keen *Minister of Defence* • Bernard Lee *"M"* • Shane Rimmer *Captain Carter* • Bryan Marshall *Commander Talbot* • Desmond Llewelyn *"Q"* • Lois Maxwell *Miss Moneypenny* ■ *Dir* Lewis Gilbert • *Scr* Christopher Wood, Richard Maibaum, from the novel by Ian Fleming

The Spy with a Cold Nose ★★★ U

Comedy 1966 · UK · Colour · 98mins
Ace sitcom writers Galton and Simpson (*Hancock*, *Steptoe and Son*) here offer

their contribution to the spy boom that was dominating popular cinema in the sixties. Their sub-Bondian farce stars Laurence Harvey and fine comedy actor Lionel Jeffries in a story of Cold War espionage which features a bulldog with a listening bug grafted to its insides for spying on the Russians. The script was held up as a model of its type but the genius of the words lost a little something in translation.

Laurence Harvey *Dr Francis Trevellyan* • Lionel Jeffries *Stanley Farquhar* • Daliah Lavi *Princess Natasha Romanova* • Eric Sykes *Wrigley* • Eric Portman *British ambassador* • Colin Blakely *Russian prime minister* • Denholm Elliott *Pond-Jones* ■ *Dir* Daniel Petrie • *Scr* Ray Galton, Alan Simpson

The Spy with My Face ★★★

Spy drama 1966 · US · Colour · 86mins
The Man from UNCLE was such a cult hit in this country that the seven movie spin-offs were made almost exclusively with the British box office in mind. In this second film in the series, Robert Vaughn as Napoleon Solo is sent to deal with a devilish doppelgänger. As always David McCallum provides the dependable support as Illya Kuryakin, while Senta Berger is the naughty Napoleon's partner in crime.

Robert Vaughn *Napoleon Solo* • David McCallum *Illya Kuryakin* • Senta Berger *Serena* • Leo G Carroll *Alexander Waverly* • Michael Evens *Darius Two* • Sharon Farrell *Sandy Wister* • Fabrizio Mioni *Arsena Coria* ■ *Dir* John Newland • *Scr* Clyde Ware, Joseph Caivelli, from a story by Clyde Ware

Spymaker: the Secret Life of Ian Fleming ★★ 15

Biographical drama
1990 · US · Colour · 95mins
Fans of 007 will appreciate the Bond movie references (and the casting of Jason Connery, son of first Bond Sean, as Ian Fleming), but anyone who isn't a zealous Fleming fan may be left out in the cold by this semi-fictionalised account of the author's life. Following shortly after another movie made in 1989 on the same subject, *Goldeneye* starring Charles Dance, this certainly boasts more excitement as it details the years before he picked up a pen to write about everyone's favourite secret agent. Mildly entertaining, but wouldn't you rather be watching a real Bond movie? Contains sex scenes.

Jason Connery *Ian Fleming* • Kristin Scott Thomas *Leda St Gabriel* • Joss Ackland *General Helstein* • David Warner *Admiral Godfrey* • Patricia Hodge *Lady Evelyn* • Colin Welland *George Fowler* • Richard Johnson *General Hormsby* ■ *Dir* Ferdinand Fairfax • *Scr* Robert J Avrech

S*P*Y*S ★★ PG

Comedy 1974 · US · Colour · 99mins
Donald Sutherland and Elliott Gould, a great comedy partnership in *MASH* five years earlier, found the magic hard to repeat. This espionage spoof that attempts to cash in on their double act reputation is both clichéd and unfunny. They play CIA agents who mishandle the defection of a Russian ballet dancer and end up on the run from their own side and the KGB. Compared with their first movie this has neither the verve nor the nerve.

U = SUITABLE FOR ALL **Uc** = SUITABLE FOR ALL, ESPECIALLY FOR YOUNG CHILDREN (VIDEO ONLY) **PG** = PARENTAL GUIDANCE

Elliott Gould *Douglas "Griff" Griffin* • Donald Sutherland *Eric Brulard* • Zouzou *Sybil* • Joss Ackland *Martinson* • Kenneth Griffith *Lippet* • Vladek Sheybal *Borisenko* • Kenneth J Warren *Grubov* ■ *Dir* Irvin Kershner • *Scr* Mal Marmorstein, Laurence J Cohen, Fred Freeman

The Square Circle ★★ 🅸🅵

Drama   1996 · Ind · Colour · 107mins

Combining Bollywood-style melodrama with passages of stark realism, director Amol Palekar clearly intended this film to entertain as well as provoke. An intriguing study of gender politics set in rural India, it benefits from the splendidly mannered performances of Nirmal Pandey, as an itinerant female impersonator, and Sonali Kulkarni, as the young girl who adopts men's attire after escaping from the brothel thugs who abducted her on the eve of her wedding. However, Palekar overcooks the masala ingredients and thus reduces the impact of his socio-sexual insights. In Hindi with English subtitles. Contains violence.

Nirmal Pandey *The transvestite* • Sonali Kulkarni *The girl* • Faiyyaz *Madam* • Rekha Sahay *Bar owner* • Nina Kulkarni *Widow* ■ *Dir* Amol Palekar • *Scr* Timeri N Murari, Chitra Palekar, Shashank Shanker, Amol Palekar

Square Dance ★★★ 🅸🅵

Drama   1987 · US · Colour · 107mins

This was Winona Ryder's second film and her role as the scripture-spouting Gemma Dillard ultimately proves too much for her. But she is definitely one of the plus points in a film that deals solely with eccentrics. Jason Robards is lazily effective as Ryder's crotchety grandpa and Jane Alexander lets off plenty of steam as her city-corrupted mother. However, it's Rob Lowe's wildly unbelievable performance as the mentally disabled Rory (which seems to belong to another film altogether) that you'll be discussing once the movie's over. Contains swearing.

Jason Robards Jr *Dillard* • Jane Alexander *Juanelle* • Winona Ryder *Gemma Dillard* • Rob Lowe *Rory* • Deborah Richter *Gwen* • Guich Koock *Frank* • Elbert Lewis *Beecham* • Charlotte Stanton *Aggie* ■ *Dir* Daniel Petrie • *Scr* Alan Hines, from his novel

The Square Jungle ★★★

Sports drama   1955 · US · BW · 86mins

Tony Curtis stars as a grocery-store clerk who joins the beasts of the "square jungle", otherwise known as the boxing ring, to earn the money to bail out his drunken father (Jim Backus). However he finds the fight game fraught with dangers. With Ernest Borgnine as Curtis's trainer, Paul Kelly as the cop who sponsors him, some peripheral romantic interest, and an appearance by heavyweight champ Joe Louis as himself, this is unremarkable but entertaining fare.

Tony Curtis *Eddie Quaid/Packy Glennon* • Patricia Crowley *[Pat Crowley]* *Julie Walsh* • Ernest Borgnine *Bernie Browne* • Paul Kelly *Jim McBride* • Jim Backus *Pat Quaid* • Leigh Snowden *Lorraine Evans* • David Janssen *Jack Lindsay* • Joe Louis ■ *Dir* Jerry Hopper • *Scr* George Zuckerman, from his story

The Square Peg ★★ 🆄

Second World War comedy   1958 · UK · BW · 85mins

Norman Wisdom's comedy appealed because his "little man" character struggled valiantly in situations with which many in the audience could identify. Yet this loose reworking of the Will Hay classic *The Goose Steps Out*, in which Norman becomes a war hero by impersonating a top Nazi general, misfires because the commonplace is forsaken for the fantastic and it becomes hard to sympathise, let alone laugh, with him.

Norman Wisdom *Norman Pitkin/General Schreiber* • Honor Blackman *Lesley Cartland* • Edward Chapman *Mr Grimsdale* • Campbell Singer *Sergeant Loder* • Hattie Jacques *Gretchen Von Schmetterling* • Brian Worth *Henri Le Blanc* • Terence Alexander *Captain Wharton* • John Warwick *Colonel Layton* ■ *Dir* John Paddy Carstairs • *Scr* Jack Davies, Henry E Blyth, Norman Wisdom, Eddie Leslie

The Square Ring ★★ 🅿🅶

Portmanteau drama   1953 · UK · BW · 79mins

The portmanteau movie meets the boxing film in this clash of the genres. Covering one night at a seedy boxing ring allows this movie to veer off into separate mini-dramas, each dealing with one boxer – ranging from a wide-eyed beginner to a punch-drunk veteran. Inevitably it's uneven, wavering between comedy and tragedy, but given the dangerous nature of the game there's uncertainty about the future of the pugilists.

Jack Warner *Danny Felton* • Robert Beatty *Kid Curtis* • Bill Owen *Happy Burns* • Maxwell Reed *Rick Martell* • George Rose *Whitey Johnson* • Bill Travers *Rowdie Rawlings* • Alfie Bass *Frank Forbes* • Ronald Lewis *Eddie Lloyd* • Sidney James *Adams* • Joan Collins *Frankie* • Kay Kendall *Eve Lewis* • Joan Sims *Bunty* ■ *Dir* Michael Relph, Basil Dearden • *Scr* Robert Westerby, Peter Myers, Alec Grahame, from the play by Ralph W Peterson

The Squaw Man ★★

Western   1931 · US · BW · 106mins

His career floundering in the early years of the talkies, Cecil B DeMille made his third screen version of Edwin Milton Royle's smash hit play. It was horribly dated material by this time, resulting in a huge box-office failure, but its strong cast and lavish production values give it some interest. Warner Baxter is the honourable Englishman who makes a new life for himself in Arizona, marries Lupe Velez's American Indian woman, but is then located by his old love, Eleanor Boardman. Charles Bickford and Roland Young are also prominent.

Warner Baxter *Capt James Wynegate/Jim Carsten* • Lupe Velez *Naturich* • Eleanor Boardman *Lady Diana* • Charles Bickford *Cash Hawkins* • Roland Young *Sir John Applegate Kerhill* • Paul Cavanaugh *[Paul Cavanagh] Henry, Earl of Kerhill* • Raymond Hatton *Shorty* ■ *Dir* Cecil B DeMille • *Scr* Lucien Hubbard, Lenore Coffee, Elsie Janis, from the play by Edwin Milton Royle

The Squeaker ★★★ 🆄

Crime drama   1937 · UK · BW · 73mins

Edmund Lowe reprises his stage role as the methodical Scotland Yard inspector who doggedly pursues arch criminal Sebastian Shaw. Confined within starchy studio sets, William K Howard directs steadily, but the removal of that touch of mystery leaves him with precious little to play with, to the extent that he has to bolster the action with protracted love scenes between Lowe and Ann Todd. Robert Newton and Alastair Sim put in pleasing support appearances.

Edmund Lowe *Inspector Barrabal* • Sebastian Shaw *Frank Sutton* • Ann Todd *Carol Stedman* • Tamara Desni *Tamara* • Robert Newton *Larry Graeme* • Allan Jeayes *Inspector Elford* • Alastair Sim *Joshua Collie* ■ *Dir* William K Howard • *Scr* Bryan Wallace, Edward O Berkman, from the novel by Edgar Wallace

The Squeeze ★★★ 🔞

Crime drama   1977 · UK · Colour · 102mins

Comedian Freddie Starr shows that there's more to him than pratfalls and doubles entendres. He acquits himself surprisingly well as a small-time London crook, but the focus here falls firmly on Stacy Keach as the booze-sodden former cop who is forced to clean up his act when his ex-wife is kidnapped. With Edward Fox, David Hemmings and Stephen Boyd giving the action more class than it deserves, this is a violent and abrasive thriller – creaky perhaps, but still disturbingly plausible.

Stacy Keach *Naboth* • Freddie Starr *Teddy* • Edward Fox *Foreman* • Stephen Boyd *Vic* • David Hemmings *Keith* • Carol White *Jill* • Alan Ford *Taff* • Roy Marsden *Barry* ■ *Dir* Michael Apted • *Scr* Leon Griffiths, from the novel *Whose Little Girl Are You?* by David Craig

The Squeeze ★ 🅸🅵

Thriller   1987 · US · Colour · 97mins

Beetle Juice was arguably the only Michael Keaton film ever to make full use of its star's prodigious comic talents. This dreary comedy-thriller, about a con man who gets caught up in murder and mayhem, is a case in point. What few laughs there are derive from Keaton while the remainder of this time-filler is a mirth-free zone of titanic proportions.

Michael Keaton *Harry Berg* • Rae Dawn Chong *Rachel Dobs* • John Davidson *Honest Tom T Murray* • Ric Abernathy *Bouncer* • Danny Aiello III *Ralph Vigo* • Bobby Bass *Poker player* • Leslie Bevis *Gem Vigo* • Jophrey Brown *Poker player* ■ *Dir* Roger Young • *Scr* Daniel Taplitz

Squibs ★★ 🆄

Musical   1935 · UK · BW · 77mins

Betty Balfour had been hailed as the English Mary Pickford during the silent era, but by the mid-thirties she was reduced to taking chirpy supports. Here she reprised the role of Squibs, the tousle-haired cockney flower girl she had played several times at the height of her fame. The story of the waif who becomes wealthy overnight was an old theatrical warhorse in the twenties, and this version has little new to offer.

Betty Balfour *Squibs Hopkins* • Gordon Harker *Sam Hopkins* • Stanley Holloway *PC Charley Lee* • Margaret Yarde *Mrs Lee* • Morris Harvey *Inspector Lee* • Michael Shepley *Colin Barrett* ■ *Dir* Henry Edwards • *Scr* Michael Hogan, H Fowler Mear, from the play by Clifford Seyler, George Pearson

Squirm ★★★ 🔞

Horror   1976 · US · Colour · 92mins

The worm turns in this cheap but cheerfully repellent horror film. A pylon, struck by lightning, electrifies the earth in typical small town, USA, and the worms go on the offensive. Writer/ director Jeff Lieberman, making the most of a limited budget, builds the tension expertly, and limits the shock effects, giving full value to the scenes (created by master of the art Rick Baker) in which worms crawl through human flesh. This black comedy is seen by some as a satire of American small town values.

Don Scardino *Mick* • Patricia Pearcy *Geri* • RA Dow *Roger* • Jean Sullivan *Naomi* • Peter MacLean *Sheriff* • Fran Higgins *Alma* • William Newman *Quigley* ■ *Dir/Scr* Jeff Lieberman • *Special Effects* Rick Baker

Sssssss ★★★

Horror   1973 · US · Colour · 99mins

The marvellously villainous Strother Martin is a mad doctor who wants to turn men into snakes in this outrageous but often nightmarish horror. Playing cleverly on the audience's fear of snakes, it sustains a strange and suspenseful atmosphere virtually throughout, aided by the excellent make-up work of John Chambers, who had won an Oscar for *Planet of the Apes*. It is only towards the end that the temperature falls as the contrivances pile up and the special effects show their age. Nevertheless this is still a very effective shocker.

Strother Martin *Dr Carl Stoner* • Dirk Benedict *David Blake* • Heather Menzies *Kristine Stoner* • Richard B Shull *Dr Ken Daniels* • Jack Ging *Sheriff Dale Hardison* • Tim O' Connor *Kogen* ■ *Dir* Bernard L Kowalski • *Scr* Hal Dresner, from a story by Dan Striepeke

Stacy's Knights ★★

Drama   1983 · US · Colour · 95mins

Kevin Costner's star did not begin to shine until he played Eliot Ness in *The Untouchables*, but his creative potential and charisma are evident even in this latter-day B-movie. The film has occasional tense moments in between rather too many flat sequences, though it benefits from Costner's lively performance and screenwriter Michael Blake's realistic portrayal of gambling addiction. Contains swearing and violence.

Andra Millian *Stacy* • Kevin Costner *Will* • Eve Lilith *Jean* • Mike Reynolds *Shecky* • Ed Semenza *Kid* • Don Hackstaff *Lawyer* ■ *Dir* Jim Wilson • *Scr* Michael Blake

Stag ★★★ 🔞

Thriller   1996 · US · Colour · 90mins

A group of pals hold a stag party, but in a haze of booze and drugs one of the strippers they've hired for the night is accidentally killed. What do they do? Call the police or attempt to cover it up. The film chillingly explores what extremes will people go to save themselves. Andrew McCarthy is in fine form as the most unscrupulous of the bunch, though Mario Van Peebles almost pips him. Gavin Wilding's film adopts a dramatically dark narrative and ends up being an ambitious if flawed moral tale of conscience and loyalty. Contains swearing, violence, nudity and drug abuse. DVD

Mario Van Peebles *Michael* • Andrew McCarthy *Peter* • Kevin Dillon *Dan* • William McNamara *Jon* • John Stockwell *Victor* • Ben Gazzara *Frank* • John Henson *Timan* • Taylor Dayne *Serena* • Jerry Stiller *Ted* ■ *Dir* Gavin Wilding • *Scr* Evan Tylor, Pat Bermel, from a story by Jason Schombing

Stage Door ★★★★ U

Comedy drama 1937 · US · BW · 90mins

Marvellous adaptation of the witty Edna Ferber/George S Kaufman play, set mainly in a boarding house for theatrical hopefuls. Scintillating casting gives bravura roles to a batch of Hollywood greats, most notably the fabulous Katharine Hepburn and the sassy Ginger Rogers. Points, too, for acerbic Eve Arden, dippy Constance Collier and a teenaged Ann Miller. Only Andrea Leeds in the obligatory tragic role isn't up to the demands of the plot or her co-stars. A true joy, especially for stage-struck female hopefuls.

Katharine Hepburn *Terry Randall* • Ginger Rogers *Joan Maitland* • Adolphe Menjou *Anthony Powell* • Gail Patrick *Linda Shaw* • Constance Collier *Miss Catherine Luther* • Andrea Leeds *Kaye Hamilton* • Samuel S Hinds *Henry Sims* • Lucille Ball *Judy Canfield* • Eve Arden *Eve* • Ann Miller *Annie* ■ *Dir* Gregory La Cava • *Scr* Morrie Ryskind, Gregory La Cava, from the play by Edna Ferber, George S Kaufman

Stage Door Canteen ★★★ U

Musical 1943 · US · BW · 131mins

New York's Stage Door Canteen was the venue where servicemen on leave during the Second World War would meet, and be entertained by the stars of stage and screen. Producer Sol Lesser's film (directed by Frank Borzage) is a revue-style show, set in the Canteen and populated by countless entertainers giving their services free. A redundant wisp of romantic plot occasionally interrupts the parade of celebrities.

Cheryl Walker *Eileen* • William Terry *Ed "Dakota" Smith* • Marjorie Riordan *Jean Rule* • Lon McCallister *"California"* • Ralph Bellamy • William Demarest • Gracie Fields • Helen Hayes • Katharine Hepburn • Jean Hersholt • Sam Jaffe • Otto Kruger • Gertrude Lawrence • Gypsy Rose Lee • Harpo Marx • Yehudi Menuhin • Ethel Merman • Paul Muni • Merle Oberon • George Raft • Johnny Weissmuller ■ *Dir* Frank Borzage • *Scr* Delmer Daves

Stage Fright ★★★★

Mystery 1950 · UK · BW · 111mins

Hitchcock's overlooked and under-rated *Stage Fright* stars Jane Wyman as a stage-struck RADA student implausibly forced to play a real-life role in order to solve a murder. Marlene Dietrich is spot-on as the jaded international singing star, with Richard Todd on the run as Wyman's former boyfriend. The film offers frequent comic diversions from great supporting players like Alastair Sim, Joyce Grenfell and Sybill Thorndike. It's a comic charade, really – a whodunit about role-playing and duplicity; even the flashback lies.

Jane Wyman *Eve Gill/Doris Tinsdale* • Marlene Dietrich *Charlotte Inwood* • Michael Wilding *Detective Wilfrid "Ordinary" Smith* • Richard Todd *Jonathan Cooper* • Alastair Sim *Commodore Gill* • Kay Walsh *Nellie Goode* • Sybil Thorndike *Mrs Gill* • Miles Malleson *Mr Fortesque* • Joyce Grenfell *"Lovely Ducks"* ■ *Dir* Alfred Hitchcock • *Scr* Whitfield Cook, Alma Reville, James Bridie, from the stories *Man Running* and *Outrun the Constable* by Selwyn Jepson

Stage Fright – Aquarius ★★★ 18

Horror thriller 1987 · It · Colour · 86mins

Michele Soavi, a former assistant to horror icon Dario Argento, makes his big screen directorial debut with an impressive horror movie which is not only packed with gross-out gore, but also hasn't forgotten how to frighten its audience. Soavi tackles the conventional storyline of an asylum escapee locked in a theatre where a dance company is rehearsing a ballet based on the Jack the Ripper legend in much the same style as Argento would. In typical body count fashion, the killer dispatches the pretentious cast members with clinical explicitness using such handy implements as drills, chainsaws and axes. Horror fans and lovers of Italian exploitation cinema will not want to miss this one. An Italian language film.

David Brandon • Barbara Cupisti • Robert Gligorov • Martin Philips • Mary Sellers ■ *Dir* Michele Soavi • *Scr* Michele Soavi, George Eastman [Luigi Montefiori]

Stage Struck ★★★

Silent comedy 1925 · US · BW and Colour

Gloria Swanson threw off her famous *haute couture* clothes to star as a grease-stained waitress trying to become an actress via mail order lessons in order to hang on to her stage-struck boyfriend (Lawrence Gray). As directed by Allan Dwan, it's knockabout comedy, emphasised by the presence of one-time Keystone Kop Ford Sterling, and even has Gloria at one moment wearing trousers – and dropping them. It was her last major hit for Paramount.

Gloria Swanson *Jennie Hagen* • Lawrence Gray *Orme Wilson* • Gertrude Astor *Lillian Lyons* • Marguerite Evans *Hilda Wagner* • Ford Sterling *Waldo Buck* ■ *Dir* Allan Dwan • *Scr* Forrest Halsey, Sylvia La Varre, from a story by Frank R Adams

Stage Struck ★ U

Musical comedy 1936 · US · BW · 93mins

Empty-headed celebrity Joan Blondell, with Broadway aspirations but no talent, backs a show but has problems with dance director Dick Powell (her real-life husband at the time). This miserable apology for a backstage musical was directed by Busby Berkeley but suffers from an almost total absence of music or dance numbers. The script is atrocious, and the comedy relief from Frank McHugh pathetic. Blondell, of course, is incapable of a bad performance, and Warren William's producer manages to bring some life to the otherwise painful proceedings.

Dick Powell *George Randall* • Joan Blondell *Peggy Revere* • Warren William *Fred Harris* • Jeanne Madden *Ruth Williams* • Frank McHugh *Sid* • Carol Hughes *Grace* • Hobart Cavanaugh *Wayne* • Spring Byington *Mrs Randall* ■ *Dir* Busby Berkeley • *Scr* Tom Buckingham, Pat C Flick, from a story by Robert Lord, Warren Duff

Stage Struck ★★★ U

Drama 1958 · US · Colour · 94mins

Interesting, sophisticated and compulsively watchable remake of *Morning Glory* (the movie which won Katharine Hepburn her first Oscar), cleverly updated to the fifties Broadway circuit, and directed by Sidney Lumet. This time Susan Strasberg, daughter of Actors Studio great Lee Strasberg, takes the lead, and unfortunately isn't quite up to the demands of the role. Her distinguished co-stars include the brilliant Joan Greenwood, who has all the best dialogue as the temperamental actress Strasberg replaces. However, Henry Fonda and Christopher Plummer look as though they belong on Broadway, which indeed they do, and the authentic use of Manhattan locations helps immensely.

Henry Fonda *Lewis Easton* • Susan Strasberg *Eva Lovelace* • Joan Greenwood *Rita Vernon* • Herbert Marshall *Robert Hedges* • Christopher Plummer *Joe Sheridan* • Daniel Ocko *Constantine* • Pat Harrington *Benny* • Frank Campanella *Victor* ■ *Dir* Sidney Lumet • *Scr* Ruth Goetz, Augustus Goetz, from the play *Morning Glory* by Zoe Akins

Stagecoach ★★★★★ U

Classic western 1939 · US · BW · 91mins

Orson Welles prepared for *Citizen Kane* by watching John Ford's masterpiece some 40 times. And why not, because this is textbook film-making by the only cinematic poet Hollywood ever produced. Owing its origins to Guy de Maupassant's story *Boule de Suif*, the plot is simplicity itself, but with just a few deft touches screenwriter Dudley Nichols created a coachload of credible characters whose vices and virtues are not as apparent as they initially seem. Ford's first venture into Monument Valley was also his first picture starring John Wayne, the man with whom he would transform the very nature of the western. From Yakima Canutt's breathtaking stunts (although Wayne did most of his own) to the brilliant support playing, everything about this picture is perfection.

John Wayne *Ringo Kid* • Claire Trevor *Dallas* • Thomas Mitchell *Dr Josiah Boone* • Andy Devine *Buck Rickabaugh, stagecoach driver* • John Carradine *Hatfield* • George Bancroft *Sheriff Curly Wilcox* • Louise Platt *Lucy Mallory* • Tim Holt *Lt Blanchard* • Chris-Pin Martin *Chris* • Donald Meek *Mr Samuel Peacock* ■ *Dir* John Ford • *Scr* Dudley Nichols, from the short story *Stage to Lordsburg* by Ernest Haycox • *Cinematographer* Bert Glennon

Stagecoach ★★

Western 1966 · US · Colour · 113mins

This remake of John Ford's revered classic is no masterpiece, but it's not a total disaster, either. The producers shrewdly decided against filming in Monument Valley, electing for the plains and mountains of Colorado instead. Alex Cord is certainly no John Wayne, but Van Heflin and Ann-Margret contribute solid performances. It's also notable as being Bing Crosby's final screen appearance.

Ann-Margret *Dallas* • Bing Crosby *Doc Boone* • Red Buttons *Mr Peacock* • Alex Cord *Ringo* • Van Heflin *Curly* • Michael Connors [Mike Connors] *Hatfield* • Bob Cummings [Robert Cummings] *Mr Gatewood* • Slim Pickens *Buck* • Stefanie Powers *Lucy Mallory* • Keenan Wynn *Luke Plummer* ■ *Dir* Gordon Douglas • *Scr* Joseph Landon, from the 1939 film by Dudley Nichols

Stagecoach Kid ★★ U

Western 1949 · US · BW · 59mins

A routine western spiced up with a cross-dressing subplot, as a rail magnate's daughter dons stetson and chaps to sneak away from her overbearing father. Actress Jeff (born Jean Marie) Donnell is the young woman in question, falling for stagecoach owner Tim Holt as he tries to keep her from the clutches of two of her father's crooked employees. Holt is an uninspired lead, and journeyman director Lew Landers brings nothing of note to the proceedings.

Tim Holt *Dave Collins* • Richard Martin *Chito Rafferty* • Jeff Donnell *Jessie Arnold* • Joe Sawyer *Thatcher* • Thurston Hall *Arnold* • Carol Hughes *Birdie* • Robert Bray *Clint* • Robert B Williams *Parnell* ■ *Dir* Lew Landers • *Scr* Norman Houston, from his story

Stagecoach to Dancer's Rock ★★★

Western 1962 · US · BW · 72mins

An unprepossessing but interesting minor Universal western dealing with a tricky moral issue – the unceremonious dumping of six passengers from a stagecoach when it transpires that one of them has smallpox. Veteran western director Earl Bellamy makes the most of the film's short duration, and he's helped by the excellent performances of the under-rated Warren Stevens, "B" girl Jody Lawrence and the ineffable Martin Landau. A bigger budget might have helped, though.

Warren Stevens *Jess Dollard* • Martin Landau *Dade Coleman* • Jody Lawrence [Jody Lawrance] *Dr Ann Thompson* • Judy Dan *Loi Yan Wu* • Del Moore *Hiram Best* • Don Wilbanks *Major John Southern* • Bob Anderson *Carl Whip Mott* ■ *Dir* Earl Bellamy • *Scr* Kenneth Darling

Staggered ★★★ 15

Comedy 1993 · UK · Colour · 95mins

Martin Clunes's debut as actor/director is packed with neat cameos, tasty situations and well-timed gags. Yet it suffers from the cinematic equivalent of long stretches of motorway without a service station. Deposited on a Scottish island after his riotous stag night by a best man with designs on his bride, Clunes has to thumb his way across the country to make it to the church on time. There's a wonderful sequence involving Griff Rhys Jones, and Clunes is amiable, but the comedy is, occasionally, rather ridiculous. Contains swearing and brief nudity.

Martin Clunes *Neil Price* • Michael Praed *Gary* • John Forgeham *Inspector Lubbock* • Anna Chancellor *Carmen Sfennipeg* • Sylvia Syms *Mother* • Sarah Winman *Hilary* • Griff Rhys Jones *Graham* • Michele Winstanley *Tina* ■ *Dir* Martin Clunes • *Scr* Paul Alexander, Simon Braithwaite

The Stain ★★★

Drama 1987 · USSR · Colour · 90mins

This drama about a student whose gambling activities get him into trouble with local hoods is notable more for the fact that it was shown uncut on Soviet TV than for its cinematic quality. In fact, it's merely a moderate example of the "everyday life" films that were made in the USSR during the *perestroika* period. Given the freedom to shed some light into the dark corners of the Soviet underworld and to expose the grip it exerts on the lives of ordinary people, director Aleko Tsabadze rather disappoints by becoming too engrossed in the melodramatic events of his story. In Russian with English subtitles.

Kishwa Glunchadze • Rusudan Kvlividze • Z Begalishvit ■ *Dir/Scr* Aleko Tsabadze

Staircase ★

Comedy drama 1969 · UK · Colour · 97mins

The sight of Richard Burton and Rex Harrison – two of the most notorious serial husbands and womanisers in showbusiness – parading about as ageing homosexual hairdressers made for one of the silliest sights in sixties cinema. Both are desperately miscast and act accordingly, trying hard not to be camp and failing completely. Harrison later admitted that he shouldn't have made the film "even to pay for my villa and vineyards".

Richard Burton *Harry Leeds* • Rex Harrison *Charlie Dyer* • Cathleen Nesbitt *Harry's mother* • Beatrix Lehmann *Charlie's mother* • Stephen Lewis *Jack* ■ *Dir* Stanley Donen • *Scr* Charles Dyer, from his play

Stakeout ★★★ 15

Comedy thriller 1987 · US · Colour · 112mins

The always watchable Richard Dreyfuss elevates this thriller above the norm. For all its determined attempts to up the comedy content of the *Lethal Weapon* pictures without cutting down on their violence, it manages to be both too abrasive for family viewing and too soft for the six-pack brigade. Emilio Estevez struggles with the verbal ping-pong, but Dreyfuss's scenes with Madeleine Stowe more than atone. Contains swearing, violence, sex scenes and nudity.

Richard Dreyfuss *Chris Leece* • Emilio Estevez *Bill Reimers* • Madeleine Stowe *Maria McGuire* • Aidan Quinn *Richard "Stick" Montgomery* • Dan Lauria *Phil Coldshank* • Forest Whitaker *Jack Pismo* • Ian Tracey *Caylor Reese* • Earl Billings *Captain Giles* ■ *Dir* John Badham • *Scr* Jim Kouf

Stalag 17 ★★★★ PG

Second World War drama 1953 · US · BW · 115mins

William Holden won the best actor Oscar for his unsympathetic portrayal here of an imprisoned opportunist in a German PoW camp – an emotive subject just eight years after the end of the Second World War. Director Billy Wilder superbly balances elements of drama, satire and comedy, and captures the claustrophobia of camp life, aided by fine performances from inmates Robert Strauss and Harvey Lembeck, both of whom were veterans of the tale's original Broadway run.

Director Otto Preminger is mesmerising as a nasty Nazi. ▭

William Holden (1) *Sefton* • Don Taylor *Dunbar* • Otto Preminger *Oberst Von Scherbach* • Robert Strauss *Stosh* • Harvey Lembeck *Harry* • Neville Brand *Duke* • Richard Erdman *Hoffy* • Peter Graves (1) *Price* • Gil Stratton Jr [Gil Stratton] *Cookie* • Jay Lawrence *Bagradian* • Sig Rumann [Sig Ruman] *Schultz* ■ *Dir* Billy Wilder • *Scr* Billy Wilder, Edwin Blum, from the play by Donald Bevan, Edmund Trzcinski

Stalin ★★★ PG

Biographical drama 1992 · US · Colour · 166mins

Shot in authentic locations, this sprawling historical epic traces the career of the savage Soviet dictator from the 1917 Revolution to his death in 1953. The removal of Trotsky, the decimation of the kulaks and the political purges of the thirties are all graphically re-created. But director Ivan Passer is also at pains to show how Stalin dragged his backward nation into the 20th century through his ambitious economic strategies. Robert Duvall gives an imperious performance, but it's Julia Ormond, as his tyrannised wife, Nadya, who brings a human aspect to this exhaustively detailed portrait of a man demonised by power. Contains violence and swearing.

Robert Duvall *Stalin* • Julia Ormond *Nadya* • Jeroen Krabbé *Bukharin* • Joan Plowright *Olga* • Maximilian Schell *Lenin* • Frank Finlay *Sergei Alliluyeva* • Daniel Massey *Trotsky* ■ *Dir* Ivan Passer • *Scr* Paul Monash

Stalingrad ★★★ 15

War drama 1992 · Ger · Colour · 132mins

Produced to coincide with the 50th anniversary of the Soviet rearguard that cost the Nazis all but 6,000 of their besieging army, Joseph Vilsmaier's combat epic makes its points about the barbarity and futility of war through the sheer scale of the enterprise. However, the lack of a human focus for our horror and pity reduces the impact of the impeccably-reconstructed battle sequences. Mightily impressive, but insufficiently involving or cautionary. A German language film. ▭ **DVD**

Thomas Kretschmann *Hans* • Dominique Horwitz *Fritz* • Jochen Nickel *Rollo* • Karel Hermanek *Musk* • Dana Vavrova *Irina* • Sebastian Rudolph *GeGe* • Martin Benrath *General Hentz* • Sylvester Groth *Otto* ■ *Dir* Joseph Vilsmaier • *Scr* Johannes Heide, Jurgen Buscher, Joseph Vilsmaier

Stalk the Wild Child ★★

Drama 1976 · US · Colour · 78mins

This TV-movie combination of *The Jungle Book* and François Truffaut's moving drama *The Wild Child* can't decide whether it wants to be a serious anthropological study or a slice of tabloid sensationalism. There's also something rather patronising about the script, and David Janssen, as a behavioural psychologist, often seems more interested in his own reputation than in the welfare of the boy who was unceremoniously plucked from the pack of dogs that raised him. However, brothers Benjamin and Joseph Bottoms convey much of the child's bemusement as he grows up under the watchful eye of Janssen and speech therapist Trish Van Devere.

David Janssen *Dr James Hazard* • Trish Van Devere *Maggie* • Benjamin Bottoms *Cal as a youth* • Joseph Bottoms *Cal as a young man* • Jamie Smith Jackson *Andrea* • Allan Arbus *Gault* • Rhea Perlman *Jean* ■ *Dir* William Hale • *Scr* Peter Packer

Stalker ★★★★ PG

Science-fiction 1979 · USSR · Colour and BW · 154mins

Andrei Tarkovsky could always be relied upon for visual lyriciscm, but the terrain traversed during this gruelling trek is anything but picturesque. Chillingly shot in muted colour by Aleksandr Knyazhinsky, the Zone is an area of the post-meteoric wilderness, that can only be crossed by "stalkers" like Aleksandr Kaidanovsky He has been hired to guide writer Anatoli Solonitsyn and professor Nikolai Grinko to the Room, a place in which truth and innermost desire can be attained. The metaphysical discussion feels somewhat mundane after what has gone before, but it still leaves you questioning your own beliefs and values. In Russian with English subtitles. ▭

Alexander Kaidanovsky *Stalker* • Anatoly Solonitsin [Anatoli Solonitsyn] *Writer* • Nikolai Grinko *Professor* • Alisa Freindlikh *Stalker's wife* • Natasha Abramova *Stalker's daughter* ■ *Dir* Andrei Tarkovsky • *Scr* Arkady Strugatsky, Boris Strugatsky, from the book *Picnic by the Roadside* by Arkady Strugatsky

Stalking Back ★★ 15

Drama based on a true story 1993 · US · Colour · 88mins

A worthy if predictable true story that delves into that very nineties phenomenon stalking. Shanna Reed plays a mother who takes legal action when she discovers that her teenage daughter is being pestered by a disturbed man. Part of a loose series of made-for-TV films examining the pressures of modern life under the banner *Moment of Truth*, this does indeed have its moments, even if the direction and the acting are unexceptional. Contains some violence.

Shanna Reed *Linda Anello* • Luanne Ponce *Laurisa* • Tom Kurlander *Curt* • John Martin Nelson *Anello* • Cassie Yates *Sandy Boyer* ■ *Dir* Corey Allen • *Scr* Priscilla English

Stalking Laura ★★

Thriller based on a true story 1993 · US · Colour · 92mins

Despite her squeaky-clean off-screen image, *Blue Lagoon* star Brooke Shields appears here in the darkly ambiguous star role of Laura, where she becomes an obsession in the fixated mind of a colleague. In this disturbing, based-on-truth tale, he then hounds her for four years. Director Michael Switzer delivers efficient thrills but never really gets a handle on the psychological depths of his characters.

Richard Thomas *Richard Farley* • Brooke Shields *Laura Black* • Viveka Davis *Mary Ann* • William Allen Young *Chris* • Richard Yniguez *Lt Grijalva* • Scott Bryce *Sam Waters* ■ *Dir* Michael Switzer • *Scr* Frank Abatemarco

The Stalking Moon ★★

Western 1968 · US · Colour · 109mins

Charles Lang's Panavision landscape photography is the redeeming feature in this suspense western, but the pacing leaves much to be desired. Gregory Peck is sadly dull as the scout who agrees to lead Eva Marie Saint and her half-Apache son to safety. The boy's father has other ideas. The screenplay fails to convey the threat inherent in Theodore V Olsen's novel, where the unseen Indian is truly menacing.

Gregory Peck *Sam Varner* • Eva Marie Saint *Sarah Carver* • Robert Forster *Nick Tana* • Noland Clay *Boy* • Russell Thorson *Ned* • Frank Silvera *Major* • Lonny Chapman *Purdue* • Lou Frizzell *Stationmaster* ■ *Dir* Robert Mulligan • *Scr* Alvin Sargent, Wendell Mayes, from the novel by Theodore V Olsen

Stamboul Quest ★★★

First World War spy romance 1934 · US · BW · 86mins

An espionage drama conducted in shadows courtesy of some moody lighting by the ace cameraman James Wong Howe. Myrna Loy plays a German spy who claims to have ended Mata Hari's career, but in Istanbul she breaks her own rule by falling in love – with US medical student George Brent – right in the middle of the First World War. There's a preposterous ending, but fans of thirties Hollywood will find much to enjoy.

Myrna Loy *Annemarie/Fraülein Doktor/Helena Bohlen* • George Brent *Douglas Beall* • Lionel Atwill *Von Strum* • C Henry Gordon *Ali Bey* • Douglass Dumbrille *General* • Mischa Auer *Ameel* ■ *Dir* Sam Wood • *Scr* Herman Mankiewicz, from a story by Leo Birinski

Stan and George's New Life ★★

Romantic comedy 1990 · Ausl · Colour · 104mins

This well acted curio should have been a charming character comedy, but director Brian McKenzie's uncertain pacing and his insistence on focusing on a sinister conspiracy upset the film's delicate balance. The relationship between shy barber's son Paul Chubb and plain country girl Julie Forsyth is subtly established, as is the atmosphere of the regional weather station where they both work. Their contretemps over a series of misleading weather forecasts is less well handled, however, and unconvincing coincidences replace the mood of quietly satirical observation.

Julie Forsyth *George* • Paul Chubb *Stanley Harris* • Margaret Ford *Sheila Harris* • John Bluthal *Stan Senior* • Roy Baldwin *Boss – Thomas Stearns* • Bruce Alexander *Geoffrey* ■ *Dir* Brian McKenzie • *Scr* Brian McKenzie, Deborah Cox

Stand against Fear ★★

Drama based on a true story 1996 · US · Colour · 120 mins

This "woman against the system" tale features a gutsy high school student who takes on the entire football team for sexually harrassing her and her fellow cheerleaders. When nothing is done by the school board, angry parents and fearful students take their case to court. The first hour is compelling, with convincing characterisations from the swaggering boys, led by newcomer Lochlyn Munro. However, the second half becomes a standard courtroom drama.

Shanna Reed *Anne Wilson* • Sarah Chalke *Krista Munro* • Josh Taylor *Ted Wilson* • Brigitta Dau *Ruth Gayle* • Lochlyn Munro *Josh Kelly* • Gwynyth Walsh *Vicky Cooke* ■ *Dir* Joseph L Scanlan • *Scr* Natalie Chaidez

Stand Alone ★★ 18

Action drama 1985 · US · Colour · 89mins

In an effort to mount a vigilante thriller where the hero doesn't look as if he chews metal as a hobby, director Alan Beattie has made his righteous avenger (Charles Durning) so ordinary and so overweight that he looks incapable of anything other than watching TV. The film never recovers from this grave central flaw. Durning is a fine actor who deserves better material, as does his co-star Pam Grier. 🎞

Charles Durning *Louis Thibido* • Pam Grier *Catherine* • James Keach *Isgro* • Bert Remsen *Paddie* • Barbara Sammeth *Meg* ■ *Dir* Alan Beattie • *Scr* Roy Carlson

Stand and Deliver ★★★★ PG

Drama based on a true story
1988 · US · Colour · 98mins

A real heart-lifter from Edward James Olmos, who stars in this LA *barrio* tale that he also helped power into existence. Based on the true story of teacher Jaime Escalante (Olmos), who transformed a classroom full of disaffected young gang members into such a top-scoring exam team that the examination board refused to believe it and made them sit everything again. Olmos gives an infectious, driven performance that carries everyone else along. Contains swearing.

Edward James Olmos *Jaime Escalante* • Lou Diamond Phillips *Angel* • Rosana De Soto *Fabiola Escalante* • Andy Garcia *Dr Ramirez* • Virginia Paris *Chairwoman Raquel Ortega* • Carmen Argenziano *Principal Molina* • Mark Eliot *Tito* ■ *Dir* Ramon Menendez • *Scr* Ramon Menendez, Tom Musca

The Stand at Apache River ★★ U

Western 1953 · US · Colour · 76mins

A very ordinary Universal western using up stock sets and contract artists with little real distinction. There are colourful support turns from two newcomers who would soon flourish in TV's golden age of westerns, Hugh O'Brian and Jack Kelly, but the leads sheriff Stephen McNally and fiancée Julia (later Julie) Adams just go through the motions, unaided by Lee Sholem's pedestrian direction.

Stephen McNally *Sheriff Lane Dakota* • Julia Adams [Julie Adams] *Valerie Kendrick* • Hugh Marlowe *Colonel Morsby* • Jaclynne Greene *Ann Kenyon* • Hugh O'Brian *Tom Kenyon* • Russell Johnson *Greiner* • Jack Kelly *Hatcher* ■ *Dir* Lee Sholem • *Scr* Arthur Ross, from the novel *Apache Landing* by Robert J Hogan

Stand by for Action ★★

Second World War drama
1942 · US · BW · 100mins

Despite being co-written by Herman J Mankiewicz (of *Citizen Kane* fame) and

boasting the heavyweight lustre of Charles Laughton, the story of snooty Harvard graduate Robert Taylor coming to terms with the gritty reality of life on an ancient destroyer is as much junk as the ship itself. Sentimentality waterlogs the studio-harboured craft.

Robert Taylor (1) *Lt Gregg Mastermann* • Charles Laughton *Rear Adm Stephan "Iron Pants" Thomas* • Brian Donlevy *Lt Comdr Martin J Roberts* • Walter Brennan *Chief Yeoman Henry Johnson* ■ *Dir* Robert Z Leonard • *Scr* George Bruce, John L Balderston, Herman J Mankiewicz, from a story by Capt Harvey Haislip, RC Sherriff, from the story *A Cargo of Innocence* by Laurence Kirk

Stand by Me ★★★★★ 15

Drama 1986 · US · Colour · 84mins

Rob Reiner made his name as a director with his debut feature, the masterly spoof rockumentary *This Is Spinal Tap*. This coming-of-age drama marked a departure from the satire and comedy Reiner had become associated with, and he proved his versatility with a smart, sensitive, fifties-set tale taken from the unlikely source of Stephen King's story *The Body*. The rich dialogue and intelligent performances are a joy to behold as four school friends set out to find the corpse of a missing boy. 🎞

Wil Wheaton *Gordie Lachance* • River Phoenix *Chris Chambers* • Corey Feldman *Teddy Duchamp* • Jerry O'Connell *Vern Tessio* • Richard Dreyfuss *Ace Merrill* • Kiefer Sutherland *Ace Merrill* • Casey Siemaszko *Billy Tessio* • Gary Riley *Charlie Hogan* • Bradley Gregg *Eyeball Chambers* • John Cusack *Denny Lachance* ■ *Dir* Rob Reiner • *Scr* Raynold Gideon, Bruce A Evans, from the story *The Body* by Stephen King

Stand by Your Man ★★★

Biographical drama
1981 · US · Colour · 100mins

In this TV movie about country-and-western legend Tammy Wynette, events have occasionally been D-I-V-O-R-C-E-D from the truth in the interests of dramatic impact. What with five marriages and a headline-making kidnapping, her life was certainly colourful, but director Jerry Jameson spends too much time meandering around her early days and her stormy relationship with fellow singer George Jones. Annette O'Toole is hardly a dead ringer, but she gives a gutsy performance that should please fans.

Annette O'Toole *Tammy Wynette* • Tim McIntire *George Jones* • Cooper Huckabee *Euple Byrd* • James Hampton *Billy Sherrill* • Helen Page Camp *Mother Pugh* • John Horn *Charlie Carter* • Monica Parker *Jane* • Ivy Bethune *Clara Jones* ■ *Dir* Jerry Jameson • *Scr* John Gay, from the autobiography by Tammy Wynette, Joan Dew

Stand-In ★★★ U

Comedy 1937 · US · BW · 86mins

A funny and perceptive Hollywood-set tale about the dangers of non-film people involving themselves in making movies. Leslie Howard stars as an accountant sent west to audit the books of the fictional Colossal Studios, with the titular stand-in played by Joan Blondell, whose career is being guided by producer Humphrey Bogart. It's an

independent satire produced by Walter Wanger, whose views on labour relations in Los Angeles as depicted here are still relevant today. The second half doesn't really live up to the wacky initial premise, but *Postman Always Rings Twice* director Tay Garnett gets what he can out of it. 🎞

Leslie Howard *Atterbury Dodd* • Joan Blondell *Lester Plum* • Humphrey Bogart *Douglas Quintain* • Alan Mowbray *Koslofski* • Marla Shelton *Thelma Cheri* • C Henry Gordon *Ivor Nassau* • Jack Carson *Tom Potts* ■ *Dir* Tay Garnett • *Scr* Gene Towne, Graham Baker, from a story in *The Saturday Evening Post* by Clarence Budington Kelland

Stand up and Cheer! ★★ U

Musical 1934 · US · BW · 81mins

A Broadway theatrical producer (Warner Baxter) is summoned to Washington by the fictitious president of the USA and appointed "Secretary of Entertainment" with a brief to cheer up a Depression-weary nation. This is the excuse for a revue featuring various musical entertainers and comedians, including a performing penguin, but the film is remembered for the attention it brought a four-year-old moppet named Shirley Temple. Relentlessly cheerful and cheerily propagandistic, it is unlikely to make much of an impression now.

Warner Baxter *Lawrence Cromwell* • Madge Evans *Mary Adams* • Nigel Bruce *Eustace Dinwiddie* • Stepin Fetchit *Stepin Fetchit/George Bernard Shaw* • Frank Melton *Fosdick* • Lila Lee *Zelda* • Ralph Morgan *Secretary to the President* • Frank Mitchell *Senator Danforth* • Shirley Temple *Shirley Dugan* ■ *Dir* Hamilton MacFadden • *Scr* Lew Brown, Ralph Spence, Rian James, Edward T Lowe Jr, Malcolm Stuart Boylan, Hamilton MacFadden, from an idea by Will Rogers, Philip Klein

Stand Up Virgin Soldiers ★★ 15

Comedy 1977 · UK · Colour · 87mins

Writer Leslie Thomas revisits his Malayan war memoirs but this time the result is more akin to "Confessions of a National Serviceman". Nigel Davenport returns from the original *The Virgin Soldiers*, but Robin Askwith is a crude substitute for Hywel Bennett and the lavatorial humour sits uneasily alongside the stabs at drama. 🎞

Robin Askwith *Private Brigg* • George Layton *Private Jacobs* • Pamela Stephenson *Bernice* • Lynda Bellingham *Valerie* • Edward Woodward *Sergeant Wellbeloved* • Nigel Davenport *Sergent Driscoll* • John Le Mesurier *Colonel Bromley-Pickering* • Warren Mitchell *Morris Morris* • Irene Handl *Mrs Phillimore* ■ *Dir* Norman Cohen • *Scr* Leslie Thomas, from his novel

Standing Room Only ★★ U

Romantic comedy 1944 · US · BW · 82mins

The great comedy based on wartime overcrowding in Washington DC is *The More the Merrier* and this later variation is too poorly written and contrived to compete. Fred MacMurray is an executive arriving in town in the hope of landing a government contract for his factory. Paulette Goddard is his inept secretary who bungles their accommodation, forcing them to take up work as husband-and-wife servants for somewhere to sleep. The comic highlight is probably MacMurray's

efforts – while serving fruit salad – to retrieve a cherry that's dropped into a guest's lap without her noticing.

Paulette Goddard *Jane Rogers* • Fred MacMurray *Lee Stevens* • Edward Arnold *TJ Todd* • Roland Young *Ira Cromwell* • Hillary Brooke *Alice Todd* • Porter Hall *Hugo Farenhall* • Clarence Kolb *Glen Ritchie* ■ *Dir* Sidney Lanfield • *Scr* Darrell Ware, Karl Tunberg, from a story by Al Martin

Stanley & Iris ★★★ 15

Drama 1989 · US · Colour · 100mins

Although virtually unrecognisable from Pat Barker's source novel *Union Street*, this well meaning blue-collar drama is carried by striking performances from Robert De Niro and Jane Fonda. De Niro is the uneducated factory worker who is slowly drawn out of his shell by recently widowed Fonda. Martin Ritt's direction is curiously anonymous and if it wasn't for the cast, this would be little more than just another "issue of the week" TV movie. However, the two stars are on top form and the supporting players can't be faulted, either. Contains swearing. 🎞

Jane Fonda *Iris King* • Robert De Niro *Stanley Cox* • Swoosie Kurtz *Sharon* • Martha Plimpton *Kelly King* • Harley Cross *Richard* • Jamey Sheridan *Joe* • Feodor Chaliapin [Feodor Chaliapin Jr] *Leonides Cox* • Zohra Lampert *Elaine* ■ *Dir* Martin Ritt • *Scr* Harriet Frank Jr, Irving Ravetch, from the novel *Union Street* by Pat Barker

Stanley and Livingstone ★★★★ U

Historical adventure
1939 · US · BW · 100mins

This is one of the best 20th Century-Fox historical biopics, despite necessary tamperings with history to enable the inclusion of one of the most famous greetings in history. Avoiding any sense of parody whatsoever are the two fine main performances the redoubtable Spencer Tracy as an obsessed, fever-ridden Henry Morton Stanley, and Cedric Hardwicke, genuinely convincing as Dr Livingstone. Director Henry King is in his element, but he would have been surprised to see much footage from this film in *Monster from Green Hell* nearly 20 years after.

Spencer Tracy *Henry M Stanley* • Nancy Kelly *Eve Kingsley* • Richard Greene *Gareth Tyce* • Walter Brennan *Jeff Slocum* • Charles Coburn *Lord Tyce* • Cedric Hardwicke *Dr David Livingstone* • Henry Hull *James Gordon Bennett Jr* • Henry Travers *John Kingsley* ■ *Dir* Henry King • *Scr* Philip Dunne, Julien Josephson, from research and story outline by Hal Long, Sam Hellman

Stanley's Magic Garden ★★ U

Animated musical fantasy
1994 · US · Colour · 72mins

An instantly forgettable animated fantasy from Don Bluth (*An American Tail*, *Anastasia*) geared towards a young audience, it's a sickly-sweet tale about a benevolent troll who's banished to New York's Central Park. There's a good voice cast though, which includes Dom DeLuise, Cloris Leachman and Jonathan Pryce. 🎞

U = SUITABLE FOR ALL   Uc = SUITABLE FOR ALL, ESPECIALLY FOR YOUNG CHILDREN (VIDEO ONLY)   PG = PARENTAL GUIDANCE

Dom DeLuise *Stanley* • Cloris Leachman *Queen Gnorga* • Phillip Glasser *Gus* • Tawney Sunshine Glover *Rosie* • Hayley Mills *Hilary* • Jonathan Pryce *Alan* ■ *Dir* Gary Goldman, Don Bluth • *Scr* Stu Krieger

The Star ★★★

Drama 　　　　　1953 · US · BW · 90mins

The star is Bette Davis, three years after *All about Eve*, in a role with which she clearly identifies, as an over-the-hill movie star. This is a relatively low-budget independent feature, which gains great strength from the casting of Davis, as a former Oscar winner, and Sterling Hayden, a pillar of integrity as her admirer. There's nice work, too, from a young and precocious Natalie Wood. Well worth watching, despite a few over-the-top scenes this minor movie echoes with a ring of truth.

Bette Davis *Margaret Elliot* • Sterling Hayden *Jim Johannson* • Natalie Wood *Gretchen* • Warner Anderson *Harry Stone* • Minor Watson *Joe Morrison* • June Travis *Phyllis Stone* • Katherine Warren *Mrs Morrison* ■ *Dir* Stuart Heisler • *Scr* Katherine Albert, Dale Eunson

Star! ★★ U

Biographical musical
1968 · US · Colour · 218mins

Julie Andrews spends over three mind-boggling hours trying to convince us that she is the legendary stage star Gertrude Lawrence. Daniel Massey does a rather better job portraying Noël Coward (his godfather in real life). Some believe Andrews is a deeply under-rated actress while others think she can only portray herself. If you tend towards the latter view, then this is excruciatingly tedious fare, saved only by some spectacular production numbers.

Julie Andrews *Gertrude Lawrence* • Richard Crenna *Richard Aldrich* • Michael Craig *Sir Anthony Spencer* • Daniel Massey *Noël Coward* • Robert Reed *Charles Fraser* • Bruce Forsyth *Arthur Lawrence* • Beryl Reid *Rose* • Jenny Agutter *Pamela* ■ *Dir* Robert Wise • *Scr* William Fairchild

The Star Chamber ★★★ 15

Thriller 　　　　1983 · US · Colour · 104mins

The title is misleading, conveying as it does more of a futuristic feel than an urban exposé, for this gripping thriller revolves around the moral dilemma of a young judge having to free dangerous criminals because of legal technicalities. As a result, he discovers the existence of a sort of legal vigilante committee. The drawn-out storyline ultimately fails to convince, and Michael Douglas in the leading role is too callow and inexperienced (at that time) as an actor to bring it off. Contains swearing and violence. ▭

Michael Douglas *Steven R Hardin* • Hal Holbrook *Benjamin Caulfield* • Yaphet Kotto *Detective Harry Lowes* • Sharon Gless *Emily Hardin* • James B Sikking *Dr Harold Lewin* • Joe Regalbuto *Arthur Cooms* ■ *Dir* Peter Hyams • *Scr* Roderick Taylor, Peter Hyams, from a story by Roderick Taylor

Star Dust ★★★ U

Drama 　　　　1940 · US · BW · 85mins

Walter Lang directs Linda Darnell in this tale of the struggles and disappointments suffered by an attractive young woman spotted by a Hollywood talent scout, only to be turned down by the studio boss. About to go home, she meets and falls in love with former singing football star John Payne, who pushes her into persevering. A familiar tale to be sure, but well told here with an unromantic air of authenticity that convinces.

Linda Darnell *Carolyn Sayres* • John Payne *Bud Borden* • Roland Young *Thomas Brooke* • Charlotte Greenwood *Lola Langdon* • William Gargan *Dane Wharton* • Mary Beth Hughes *June Lawrence* • Mary Healy *Mary Andrews* • Donald Meek *Sam Wellman* ■ *Dir* Walter Lang • *Scr* Robert Ellis, Helen Logan, from a story by Jesse Malo, Kenneth Earl, Ivan Kahn

Star 80 ★★★★ 18

Biographical drama
1983 · US · Colour · 98mins

The true story of Canadian *Playboy* playmate-turned-Hollywood actress Dorothy Stratten who was on the verge of stardom when she was murdered by her small-time hustler husband Paul Snider. Director Bob Fosse's last movie is a disturbing look at the high cost of fame. Stratten is brilliantly portrayed by Mariel Hemingway (complete with breast enlargements), but it's Eric Roberts as her psychotically jealous mentor/spouse who registers the strongest impact. A downbeat and dark fairy tale of Tinseltown's tarnished ethics. ▭

Mariel Hemingway *Dorothy Stratten* • Eric Roberts *Paul Snider* • Cliff Robertson *Hugh Hefner* • Carroll Baker *Dorothy's mother* • Roger Rees *Aram Nicholas* • David Clennon *Geb* • Josh Mostel *Private detective* ■ *Dir* Bob Fosse • *Scr* Bob Fosse, from the story *Death of a Playmate* by Teresa Carpenter

Star in the Dust ★★★★ U

Western 　　　1956 · US · Colour · 80mins

A very fine but generally under-rated western. Produced by *Touch of Evil's* Albert Zugsmith and directed by Charles Haas, this taut film contains its action between twilight and dawn as sheriff John Agar gets ready to hang killer Richard Boone, while Boone's hired guns (at the behest of banker villain Leif Erickson) menace the town. Sultry fifties icon (and Zugsmith veteran) Mamie Van Doren is Agar's gal and – to add to the plot – Erickson's relation. Watch closely for a very young Clint Eastwood.

John Agar *Sheriff Bill Jorden* • Mamie Van Doren *Ellen Ballard* • Richard Boone *Sam Hall* • Coleen Gray *Nellie Mason* • Leif Erickson *George Ballard* • James Gleason *Orval Jones* • Randy Stuart *Nan Hogan* • Clint Eastwood ■ *Dir* Charles Haas • *Scr* Oscar Brodney, from the novel *Law Man* by Lee Leighton

A Star Is Born ★★★★ U

Drama 　　　1937 · US · Colour · 110mins

One of the most famous movie titles of all time in its second incarnation (the first was called *What Price Hollywood?*), with Janet Gaynor as the young star on the way up and Fredric March as the ageing star on the way out in Tinseltown. Gaynor and March are superb and Hollywood itself is well depicted in early three-strip Technicolor. The now classic screenplay by Dorothy Parker and husband Alan Campbell, among others, is still caustic and vibrant, and, of course, contains one of the greatest last lines in all cinema. Not up to the Judy Garland version, but streets ahead of Barbra Streisand's. ▭

Janet Gaynor *Esther Blodgett/Vicki Lester* • Fredric March *Norman Maine* • Adolphe Menjou *Oliver Niles* • May Robson *Lettie, Grandmother Blodgett* • Andy Devine *Danny McGuire* • Lionel Stander *Matt Libby* • Owen Moore *Casey Burke* • Peggy Wood *Miss Phillips, Central Casting Corp clerk* • Elizabeth Jenns *Anita Regis* ■ *Dir* William A Wellman • *Scr* Dorothy Parker, Alan Campbell, Robert Carson, William A Wellman, Ring Lardner Jr, Bud Schulberg, John Le Mahin, from a story by Robert Carson, William A Wellman

A Star Is Born ★★★★★ U

Musical drama 1954 · US · Colour · 167mins

One of the most superlative melodramas in Hollywood's history, this remake (of the 1937 Janet Gaynor movie) contains the greatest ever performance by the lustrous Judy Garland, paired with the brilliant James Mason at the very zenith of their talents. These portrayals, plus superb direction from George Cukor, ensure that this film enriches more lives each time it is screened. But on first release, the movie was overlong, and was trimmed. In the eighties some of this missing material was discovered, with other scenes re-created using stills. This "restoration", though of historical value, may alienate a first-time viewer. Anyhow, this movie's a stunner, and superbly portrays a side of Hollywood at its self-centred best: when Judy Garland lost that year's Oscar to Grace Kelly (for *The Country Girl*), Groucho Marx quipped, "it's the biggest robbery since Brink's!". ▭

Judy Garland *Esther Blodgett/Vicki Lester* • James Mason *Norman Maine* • Jack Carson *Matt Libby* • Charles Bickford *Oliver Niles* • Tommy Noonan *Danny McGuire* • Lucy Marlow *Lola Lavery* • Amanda Blake *Susan Ettinger* • Irving Bacon *Graves* • Hazel Shermet *Miss Wheeler* • James Brown (2) *Glenn Williams* ■ *Dir* George Cukor • *Scr* Moss Hart, from the 1937 film • *Cinematographer* Sam Leavitt

A Star Is Born ★★★ 15

Musical drama 1976 · US · Colour · 133mins

Sadly not the 1937 nor the 1954 version, but the 1976 remake that didn't quite work, starring Barbra Streisand and Kris Kristofferson as the star-crossed lovers on self-destruct. They tried to bring the action screechingly up to date with a contemporary rock soundtrack, but there's little finesse as everyone rushes around in seventies gear that already looked pretty dated on release. The movie's basic problem is that we simply cannot believe that Streisand and Kristofferson are in the throes of a passionate love affair. Babs can sure belt out a tune, though, particularly that Oscar-winning theme song *Evergreen*. Contains swearing and brief nudity. ▭

Barbra Streisand *Esther Hoffman* • Kris Kristofferson *John Norman Howard* • Gary Busey *Bobby Ritchie* • Oliver Clark *Gary Danziger* • Marta Heflin *Quentin* • MG Kelly *Bebe Jesus* • Sally Kirkland *Photographer* • Paul Mazursky *Brian* ■ *Dir* Frank Pierson • *Scr* John Gregory Dunne, Joan Didion, Frank Pierson, from the 1937 film

Star Kid ★★★ PG

Science-fiction adventure
1997 · US · Colour · 96mins

Joseph Mazzello gives an engaging performance as an ignored and bullied child who isn't having much luck with girls either. In a scrap yard he comes across a combat-enhancement suit (with its own intelligence) from an alien race. After using it to get revenge against the school bully, he is confronted by an alien determined to capture the suit. Cyborsuit's intelligence – taking everything Mazzello says literally – provides much amusement, and the rest of the movie serves up enough action to satisfy the kids and their parents. Contains some strong language. ▭

Joseph Mazzello *Spencer Griffith* • Richard Gilliland *Roland Griffith* • Corinne Bohrer *Janet Holloway* • Alex Daniels *Cyborsuit* • Joey Simmrin *Turbo Bruntley* • Ashlee Levitch *Stacey Griffith* • Jack McGee *Hank Bruntley* ■ *Dir/Scr* Manny Coto

The Star Maker ★★ U

Musical drama 1939 · US · BW · 93mins

This minor musical drama stars Bing Crosby as a showman and songwriter, inspired by the career of Gus Edwards (who discovered Eddie Cantor among others). Failed singer Edwards, forced to work as a store salesman, hits on the idea of setting up a vaudeville act with youngsters. Success is cut short when he falls foul of child labour laws, but he then turns to the new medium of radio. Crosby dispenses easy charm and croons a handful of numbers.

Bing Crosby *Larry Earl* • Linda Ware *Jane Gray* • Louise Campbell *Mary* • Ned Sparks *"Speed" King* • Walter Damrosch • Laura Hope Crews *Carlotta Salvina* • Thurston Hall *Mr Proctor* ■ *Dir* Roy Del Ruth • *Scr* Frank Butler, Don Hartman, Arthur Caesar, from a story by Arthur Caesar, William A Pierce

Star Maps ★★★★

Drama 　　　1997 · US · Colour · 90mins

Luis Buñuel's *Los Olvidados* haunts this sordid, surreal, yet curiously sympathetic study of immigrant exploitation, familial dysfunction and male prostitution. In revealing the flip side of Hollywood life, debut director Miguel Arteta recognises the parallels with the ruthless world of glamour by having Mexican pimp Efrain Figueroa order his boys to sell maps of the stars' houses as a front for their activities, while Figueroa's son, Douglas Spain, an aspiring actor, regards each trick as a Method opportunity. From deluded soap star Kandeyce Jorden to Spain's Cantinflas-obsessed mother, Martha Velez, everyone has his or her own motives here and that's why the film works.

Douglas Spain *Carlos* • Efrain Figueroa *Pepe* • Kandeyce Jorden *Jennifer* • Martha Velez *Teresa* • Lysa Flores *Maria* • Annette Murphy *Letti* • Robin Thomas *Martin* • Vincent Chandler *Juancito* ■ *Dir* Miguel Arteta • *Scr* Miguel Arteta, from a story by Matthew Greenfield

Star of India ★ U

Period swashbuckling adventure
1954 · UK · Colour · 92mins

Virtually unwatchable swashbuckler, with Cornel Wilde as the French

nobleman who, stripped of his estates, starts a search for a priceless jewel. Jean Wallace isn't stripped of anything but tags along anyway. Herbert Lom hisses like a panto villain and seems to have an unhealthy relationship with his Siamese cats.

Cornel Wilde *Pierre St Laurent* • Jean Wallace *Katrina* • Herbert Lom *Narbonne* • Yvonne Sanson *Madame De Montespan* • John Slater *Emile* • Walter Rilla *Van Horst* • Basil Sydney *King Louis XIV* ■ *Dir* Arthur Lubin • *Scr* Herbert Dalmas, Denis Freeman

Star of Midnight ★★★

Mystery comedy   1935 · US · BW · 89mins

Capitalising on William Powell's success in *The Thin Man*, RKO plagiarised the attributes of both the Nick Charles character and the actor himself, casting him as Clay Dalzell, a witty and debonair lawyer. Nicely directed by Stephen Roberts, this comedy suspenser sees Dalzell trying to prove himself innocent of the murder of a gossip columnist by turning sleuth, with the assistance of his girlfriend Ginger Rogers. A characteristic thirties mixture of cops, criminals, and cocktails – sophisticated and entertaining.

William Powell *Clay Dalzell* • Ginger Rogers *Donna Mantin* • Paul Kelly *Jimmy Kinland* • Gene Lockhart *Horace Swayne* • Ralph Morgan *Roger Classon* • Leslie Fenton *Tim Winthrop* • J Farrell MacDonald *Inspector Doremus* • Russell Hopton *Tommy Tennant* ■ *Dir* Stephen Roberts • *Scr* Howard J Green, Anthony Veiller, Edward Kaufman

The Star Packer ★★ Ⓤ

Western   1934 · US · BW · 53mins

Between *The Big Trail* of 1930 and his resurrection in *Stagecoach* in 1939, John Wayne laboured in a series of programme fillers for Monogram. The ludicrous plot about a mysterious "Shadow" who traverses the town via an underground tunnel is made palatable by sprightly casting: George Hayes, and the friendly Indian, played by ace stuntman Yakima Canutt, usually cast as the heavy in these B-movies. Meanwhile, Duke continues the long haul to stardom. 🖳

John Wayne *John Travers* • Verna Hillie *Anita Matlock* • George "Gabby" Hayes *Matt Matlock* • Yakima Canutt *Yak* • Earl Dwire *Mason* • Ed Parker *(Eddie Parker) Parker* • George Cleveland *Old Jake* • William Franey *Pete* ■ *Dir/Scr* Robert N Bradbury

Star Spangled Rhythm ★★★ Ⓤ

Musical comedy   1942 · US · BW · 100mins

One of the better wartime revue-format shows, for which Paramount corralled just about everybody on the payroll. The screwy premise for the musical and comedy extravaganza is the impending visit of a sailor on leave (Eddie Bracken), who believes that his Paramount gateman father (Victor Moore) is really the studio's executive vice-president. Encouraged by switchboard operator Betty Hutton, Moore pretends he is the studio head, whereupon the mighty organisation co-operates in the deception and stages a show for son Johnny and his navy pals.

Bing Crosby • Bob Hope *Master of Ceremonies* • Fred MacMurray *Man playing cards* • Ray Milland *Man playing cards* • Franchot Tone *Man playing cards* • Victor Moore *"Pop" Webster/"Bronco Billy"* • Dorothy Lamour • Paulette Goddard • Veronica Lake • Vera Zorina • Mary Martin • Dick Powell • Betty Hutton *Polly Judson* • Eddie Bracken *Johnny Webster* • Alan Ladd *Scarface* • William Bendix *Husband* • Macdonald Carey *Louie the Lug* • Walter Abel *BG De Soto* • Susan Hayward *Genevieve* • Cecil B DeMille • Preston Sturges • Anne Revere *Sarah* ■ *Dir* George Marshall • *Scr* Harry Tugend, Arthur Phillips, George Kaufman, Arthur Ross, Fred Saidy, Norman Panama, Melvin Frank • *Music/Lyrics* Harold Arlen, Johnny Mercer

Star Trek: the Motion Picture ★★★ Ⓤ

Science-fiction adventure   1979 · US · Colour · 138mins

Dubbed "The Motionless Picture" when it was first released, it is rather talky, yet the long-delayed big-screen debut of the cult TV series hits epic heights fans can't fail to be moved by. Director Robert Wise purposely went for *2001* grandeur rather than *Star Wars* mock heroics in an effort to give the beloved characters an enduring film career beyond TV repeats. And it worked, as time has shown, despite the plot merely combining The *Changeling* and The *Doomsday Machine* episodes in one glorious space glob. 🖳

William Shatner *Captain James T Kirk* • Leonard Nimoy *Mr Spock* • DeForest Kelley *Dr Leonard "Bones" McCoy* • Stephen Collins *Commander Willard Decker* • Persis Khambatta *Ilia* • James Doohan *Scotty* • George Takei *Sulu* • Nichelle Nichols *Uhura* • Walter Koenig *Chekov* • Majel Barrett *Dr Christine Chapel* ■ *Dir* Robert Wise • *Scr* Harold Livingston, Gene Roddenberry, from a story by Alan Dean Foster, from the TV series created by Gene Roddenberry

Star Trek II: the Wrath of Khan ★★★★ ⑮

Science-fiction adventure   1982 · US · Colour · 108mins

The big screen sequel to the 1967 TV episode *Space Seed* is truer in spirit to the beloved space opera than the first feature. Emphasising the narrative values that made the original series so great and vibrantly weaving the thematic motifs of life, loss and adventure together, this continues the saga of genetic superman Ricardo Montalban wreaking vengeance against the *Enterprise* crew for sending him to a prison colony. Leonard Nimoy has rarely been so moving. 🖳

William Shatner *Admiral James T Kirk* • Leonard Nimoy *Spock* • DeForest Kelley *Dr Leonard "Bones" McCoy* • James Doohan *Scotty* • Walter Koenig *Chekov* • George Takei *Sulu* • Nichelle Nichols *Commander Uhura* • Bibi Besch *Dr Carol Marcus* • Merritt Butrick *David* • Paul Winfield *Starship Reliant Captain Terrell* • Kirstie Alley *Saavik* • Ricardo Montalban *Khan* ■ *Dir* Nicholas Meyer • *Scr* Jack B Sowards, from a story by Harve Bennett, Jack B Sowards, from the TV series created by Gene Roddenberry

Star Trek III: the Search for Spock ★★★ ⑫

Science-fiction adventure   1984 · US · Colour · 100mins

There are no real surprises in this ponderous journey to the final frontier, in which Admiral Kirk hijacks the starship *Enterprise* to help in the rejuvenation of the deceased Spock on the planet Genesis. It's a good character-driven story, marred by Leonard Nimoy's workmanlike direction, a pseudo-mystical ending and an all-pervasive funereal tone. Amazing special effects supply the wonder and emotional charge missing from what is, in essence, nothing more than a bloated TV episode. 🖳

William Shatner *Admiral James T Kirk* • DeForest Kelley *Dr Leonard "Bones" McCoy* • James Doohan *Scotty* • Walter Koenig *Chekov* • Nichelle Nichols *Uhura* • Christopher Lloyd *Kruge* • Robin Curtis *Lieutenant Saavik* • Merritt Butrick *David Marcus* • James B Sikking *Captain Styles* • Mark Lenard *Ambassador Sarek* ■ *Dir* Leonard Nimoy • *Scr* Harve Bennett, from the TV series created by Gene Roddenberry

Star Trek IV: the Voyage Home ★★★★ ⑫

Science-fiction adventure   1986 · US · Colour · 117mins

After three impressive but rather po-faced adventures, the *Enterprise* regulars got the chance to let their hair (what was left of it) down a little for this hugely enjoyable trek. The chaps have to travel back to eighties San Francisco to free a couple of whales that can save the Earth from a destructive space probe. William Shatner gets to romance whale expert Catherine Hicks, although his comic double act with Nimoy is a lot more fun, and, while there is little in the way of traditional sci-fi spectacle, the crew clearly relish the opportunity to poke fun at the idiosyncrasies of modern-day California. Contains swearing. 🖳

William Shatner *Captain James T Kirk* • Leonard Nimoy *Spock* • Catherine Hicks *Dr Gillian Taylor* • DeForest Kelley *Dr Leonard "Bones" McCoy* • James Doohan *Scotty* • George Takei *Sulu* • Walter Koenig *Chekov* • Nichelle Nichols *Commander Uhura* • Majel Barrett *Dr Christine Chapel* • Jane Wyatt *Amanda, Spock's mother* • Mark Lenard *Sarek* • Robin Curtis *Lieutenant Saavik* ■ *Dir* Leonard Nimoy • *Scr* Harve Bennett, Steve Meerson, Peter Krikes, Nicholas Meyer, from a story by Leonard Nimoy, Harve Bennett, from the TV series created by Gene Roddenberry

Star Trek V: the Final Frontier ★★★ ⑫

Science-fiction fantasy   1989 · US · Colour · 102mins

With William Shatner in the director's chair, this lacks the wit and panache of its predecessor, but still makes for an enjoyable romp. A messianic figure (Laurence Luckinbill) is holding a distant planet hostage but, in reality, wants to lay his hands on the ageing *Enterprise* and its even creakier crew. Aiming for a more mystical plane than usual, the plot is embarrassingly trite at times. In the end it just about gets by, thanks to the delightful interplay between Shatner, Nimoy and DeForest

Kelley, and a typically action-packed finale. Contains swearing. 🖳

William Shatner *Captain James T Kirk* • Leonard Nimoy *Mr Spock* • DeForest Kelley *Dr Leonard "Bones" McCoy* • James Doohan *Scotty* • Walter Koenig *Chekov* • Nichelle Nichols *Lieutenant Uhura* • George Takei *Sulu* • Laurence Luckinbill *Sybok* • David Warner *St John Talbot* ■ *Dir* William Shatner • *Scr* David Loughery, from a story by William Shatner, Harve Bennett, David Loughery, from the TV series created by Gene Roddenberry

Star Trek VI: the Undiscovered Country ★★★★ ⑫

Science-fiction adventure   1991 · US · Colour · 108mins

The *Star Trek* movie series goes supernova with an outstanding episode directed by Nicholas Meyer, who also directed *The Wrath of Khan*. Mirroring world news events of the time (the Soviet Union's dissolution), Meyer crafts a near perfect blend of humanistic messages, affectionate lampooning, epic visuals and fairy-tale imagination as the classic *Enterprise* crew encounters treachery during prospective peace negotiations with the Klingons. Clever Shakespearean touches heighten the dramatic agony and ecstasy. 🖳

William Shatner *Captain James T Kirk* • Leonard Nimoy *Spock* • DeForest Kelley *Dr Leonard "Bones" McCoy* • James Doohan *Montgomery "Scotty" Scott* • Walter Koenig *Pavel Chekov* • Nichelle Nichols *Nytoba Uhuru* • George Takei *Captain Hikaru Sulu* • Kim Cattrall *Lieutenant Valeris* • Mark Lenard *Sarek* • Christopher Plummer *General Chang* • Iman *Martia* • David Warner *Chancellor Gorkon* • Christian Slater *Excelsior crewman* ■ *Dir* Nicholas Meyer • *Scr* Nicholas Meyer, Denny Martin Flinn, from a story by Leonard Nimoy, Lawrence Konner, Mark Rosenthal, from the TV series created by Gene Roddenberry

Star Trek: Generations ★★★★ ⑫

Science-fiction adventure   1994 · US · Colour · 113mins

Some of the old *Star Trek* cast, led by William Shatner, unite with the *Next Generation* crew, commanded by Patrick Stewart, to stop mad scientist Malcolm McDowell tapping into an intergalactic energy source that can bring one's most desired fantasies to life. If you can stay with the multi-layered and self-referential plot, this fun science-fiction saga builds up to warp speed for an exciting climax. This special-effects laden adventure shamelessly trades in fan sentiment and nostalgia as the two-much loved generations of space folk heroes merge into one space/time continuum. Stewart brings all his dignity to bear as the commander of the famous starship and makes *The Next Generation*'s transition from small to big screen an effective and winning one. 🖳

Patrick Stewart *Captain Jean-Luc Picard* • Jonathan Frakes *Commander William T Riker* • Brent Spiner *Lt Commander Data* • Levar Burton *Lt Commander Geordi La Forge* • Michael Dorn *Lt Worf* • Gates McFadden *Dr Beverly Crusher* • Marina Sirtis *Counselor Deanna Troi* • Malcolm McDowell *Soran* • James Doohan *Scotty* • Walter Koenig *Chekov* • William Shatner *Captain James T Kirk* • Whoopi Goldberg *Guinan* ■ *Dir* David Carson • *Scr* Ronald D Moore, Brannon Braga, from a

story by Brannon Braga, Ronald D Moore, Rick Berman, from characters created by Gene Roddenberry

Star Trek: First Contact

★★★★★ 12

Science-fiction adventure
1996 · US · Colour · 106mins

The Borg travel back in time to sabotage that pivotal moment in Earth's destiny when we first made contact with an alien race. What else can Captain Picard do except follow and sort things out? The *Next Generation* crew reassemble for the best film adventure yet. Epic in scope, grandiose in emotional sweep, and featuring orgasmic special effects, this is packed with ideas, thrills, in-jokes and tense action. Director Jonathan Frakes (Commander Riker) has a keen visual eye and inherent understanding of the series's history. ▣

Patrick Stewart *Captain Jean-Luc Picard* • Jonathan Frakes *Commander William Riker* • Brent Spiner *Lt Commander Data* • LeVar Burton *Lt Commander Geordi La Forge* • Michael Dorn *Lt Commander Worf* • Gates McFadden *Dr Beverly Crusher* • Marina Sirtis *Counselor Deanna Troi* • Alice Krige *Borg Queen* • James Cromwell *Zefram Cochrane* • Alfre Woodard *Lily Sloane* • Dwight Schultz *Lt Barclay* • Robert Picardo *Holographic doctor* ■ *Dir* Jonathan Frakes • *Scr* Brannon Braga, Ronald D Moore, from a story by Rick Berman, Brannon Braga, Ronald D Moore, from the TV series created by Gene Roddenberry

Star Trek: Insurrection

★★★ PG

Science-fiction adventure
1998 · US · Colour · 98mins

Ethnic cleansing gets the *Trek* workout in the ninth feature, which is aimed squarely at the fans. Travelling where *Star Trek* has boldly gone before, with the light-hearted tale of a planet of perpetual youth and the two races who are struggling for the right to use it, there's nothing new in this proficient cocktail of predictable space heroics and *Lost Horizon* homages. Visually impressive (marking the first use of entirely digital effects for the spaceships), the film also features F Murray Abraham as an unusual villain with his face-lifted-to-death look, while Donna Murphy is affecting as Captain Picard's latest love interest. ▣

Patrick Stewart *Captain Jean-Luc Picard* • Jonathan Frakes *Riker* • Brent Spiner *Lt Commander Data* • LeVar Burton *Lt Commander Geordi La Forge* • Michael Dorn *Lt Commander Worf* • Gates McFadden *Beverly Crusher* • Marina Sirtis *Troi* • F Murray Abraham *Ru'afo* • Donna Murphy *Anij* • Anthony Zerbe *Dougherty* ■ *Dir* Jonathan Frakes • *Scr* Michael Piller, from a story by Rick Berman, Michael Piller, from the TV series created by Gene Roddenberry

Star Wars Episode IV: A New Hope

★★★★★ U

Science-fiction fantasy adventure
1977 · US · Colour · 119mins

Director George Lucas's spectacular space opera is a timeless good versus evil fable cosmically dressed up with ground-breaking special effects, a dazzling array of intergalactic characters and stirring adventure. After buying two servant robots, Luke Skywalker accidentally triggers Princess

Leia's holographic distress signal from one of the droids. Thus Luke's whirlwind quest, bringing meaning to his aimless life while clarifying the mysteries of his past, begins as it means to go on with breathless excitement and wide-eyed wonder. Combining winning performances from "unknowns" Mark Hamill, Carrie Fisher and Harrison Ford with thrilling visuals, Lucas forged a new style of classic science fiction from the shimmering childhood memories of his B-movie serial past. ▣

Mark Hamill *Luke Skywalker* • Harrison Ford *Han Solo* • Carrie Fisher *Princess Leia Organa* • Peter Cushing *Grand Moff Tarkin* • Alec Guinness *Ben (Obi-Wan) Kenobi* • Anthony Daniels *See Threepio (C3PO)* • Kenny Baker (1) *Artoo-Detoo (R2D2)* • Peter Mayhew *Chewbacca* • Dave Prowse *Darth Vader* • James Earl Jones *Darth Vader* ■ *Dir/Scr* George Lucas • *Cinematographer* Gilbert Taylor • *Music* John Williams • *Art Director* John Barry

Star Wars Episode I: the Phantom Menace ★★★ U

Science-fiction action adventure
1999 · US · Colour · 132mins

The second coming of director George Lucas's mythic brainchild lacks that vital sense of wonder. Instead, Lucas provides a welter of incident, cosmic dilemmas, cryptic forebodings and idiotic dialogue; absolutely phenomenal on the visual front, the film is completely mindless in the story department as characters are placed in position to explain what we already know from his middle trilogy. Forget the overworked plot about Queen Amidala (Natalie Portman) trying to stop the Trade Federation invading her peaceful planet with help from Jedi Knights Qui-Gon Jinn (Liam Neeson) and Obi-Wan Kenobi (Ewan McGregor). Thrill instead at the state-of-the-art technical wizardry and just enough fizzing action (the truly exciting pod race) to keep nostalgic wistfulness at bay. Only Neeson gives this schematic ever-vending space opera – sadly trapped by its own legacy – what little emotional gravitas it contains. ▣

Liam Neeson *Qui-Gon Jinn* • Ewan McGregor *Obi-Wan Kenobi* • Natalie Portman *Queen Amidala/Padmé* • Jake Lloyd *Anakin Skywalker* • Ian McDiarmid *Senator Palpatine* • Pernilla August *Shmi Skywalker* • Oliver Ford Davies *Sio Bibble* • Frank Oz *Yoda* • Anthony Daniels *C-3PO* • Kenny Baker (1) *R2-D2* • Terence Stamp *Chancellor Valorum* • Brian Blessed *Boss Nass* • Ray Park *Darth Maul* • Celia Imrie *Fighter Pilot Bravo 5* • Samuel L Jackson *Jedi Knight Mace Windu* • Sofia Coppola *Saché* • Greg Proops *Fode* • Scott Capurro *Beed* • Lindsay Duncan *TC-14* ■ *Dir/Scr* George Lucas • *Music* John Williams

Stardust ★★ 15

Musical drama 1974 · UK · Colour · 106mins

Singer David Essex reprises his role as Jim MacLaine, the working class boy who wanted to become a pop star in this dated but enjoyable sequel to *That'll Be The Day*. In this follow-up he becomes the biggest rock star in the world – so you just know it's going to all go horribly wrong. Most interesting here – apart from Essex's lame attempts at acting – is the supporting cast of sixties warblers, including

Adam Faith (as MacLaine's roadie) and Marty Wilde. ▣

David Essex *Jim MacLaine* • Adam Faith *Mike* • Larry Hagman *Porter Lee Austin* • Ines Des Longchamps *Danielle* • Rosalind Ayres *Jeanette* • Marty Wilde *Colin Day* • Edd Byrnes *Television interviewer* • Keith Moon *JD Clover* • Dave Edmunds *Alex* • Paul Nicholas *Johnny* ■ *Dir* Michael Apted • *Scr* Ray Connolly

Stardust Memories

★★★★ 15

Comedy 1980 · US · BW · 84mins

Woody Allen vents his spleen against critics and audiences in this heavily autobiographical comedy. He plays Sandy Bates, a director remarkably like Allen, who wants to break out of the comedy mould and make "serious" movies. Attending a weekend film festival of his work, he runs the gauntlet of fans and critics, and muses on his complicated love life with Charlotte Rampling and Jessica Harper. This two-fingered salute to audiences deserves marks for audacity but nothing for charity. Compared with later works like the delightful *Everyone Says I Love You*, this exudes narcissism – more like *Everyone Knows I Love Me*. Contains sexual references and some swearing. ▣

Woody Allen *Sandy Bates* • Charlotte Rampling *Dorrie* • Jessica Harper *Daisy* • Marie-Christine Barrault *Isobel* • Tony Roberts *Tony* • Helen Hanft *Vivian Orkin* • John Rothman *Jack Abel* ■ *Dir/Scr* Woody Allen

Starflight One ★★★ U

Futuristic adventure
1983 · US · Colour · 109mins

Director Jerry Jameson specialised in this type of jeopardy movie in the seventies and eighties, with gems like *Terror on the 40th Floor* and *The Deadly Tower*. Here, Lee Majors deals with a new-fangled jetliner in crisis, having been inadvertently chucked into outer space on its maiden flight. Naturally there's a sturdy cast of watchables on board, while the special effects are courtesy of *Star Wars* wizard John Dykstra, former head of Industrial Light & Magic. ▣

Lee Majors *Capt Cody Briggs* • Hal Linden *Josh Gilliam* • Ray Milland *QT Thornwell* • Gail Strickland *Nancy Gilliam* • Lauren Hutton *Erika Hansen* • George DiCenzo *Bowdish* • Robert Englund ■ *Dir* Jerry Jameson • *Scr* Robert Malcolm Young, from a story by Gene Warren, Peter R Brooke

Stargate ★★★★ PG

Science-fiction adventure
1994 · US · Colour · 115mins

Aliens colonised ancient Egypt through a space-time portal, according to this derivative yet hugely enjoyable cosmic adventure. James Spader is terrific as the code-cracking archaeologist who accompanies soldier Kurt Russell across the universe to fight galactic tyrant Jaye Davidson, who's clearly wearing the frocks *The Crying Game* couldn't afford. Simple in execution, yet classic in the nostalgic way it evokes the feel of vintage forties' serials, director Roland Emmerich successfully combines plot strands from literature and other films of the genre, with some imaginative special effects and impressive visuals. One of

the film's best achievements is its depiction of being hurtled across the universe at the speed of light. Contains swearing and violence. ▣ *DVD*

Kurt Russell *Col Jonathan "Jack" O'Neil* • James Spader *Dr Daniel Jackson* • Jaye Davidson *Ra* • Viveca Lindfors *Catherine* • Alexis Cruz *Skaara* • Mili Avital *Sha'uri* • Leon Rippy *General West* • John Diehl *Lieutenant Kawalsky* ■ *Dir* Roland Emmerich • *Scr* Roland Emmerich, Dean Devlin • *Cinematographer* Karl Walter, Lindenlaub • *Production Designer* Holger Gross

Starlight ★

Musical drama 1989 · US · Colour · 78mins

Clearly intended as a sort of "Fame's Summer Vacation", this musical drama will have you cringeing within minutes. It's set in a country camp where a bunch of aspiring city kids brush up their entertainment skills under the tutelage of a venerable vaudevillian. When he takes his final curtain call, however, the school gets a far less sympathetic principal and even these budding troupers begin to wonder whether the show will go on. This show shouldn't have got off the ground in the first place.

Kario Salem *Arthur Hall* • Jean Taylor *Mary* • Pamela Payton-Wright *Louise* • Ciro Barbaro *Dewey* • Kathryn Eames *Evelyn Ruth* • Robert Earl Jones *Joe* • William Hickey *Billy Davis* • *Dir* Orin Wechsberg • *Scr* MJ Wells, from a story by Orin Wechsberg, Daniel Gualtieri

Starlight Hotel ★★★ PG

Drama 1987 · NZ · Colour · 93mins

This would-be "rites of passage" drama is a rather cheery, benign but muddle-headed affair. It's the Depression: cue much wearing of depressing undergarments, and young Greer Robson and Peter Phelps tramping the countryside in search of a crust. And that's all there is here apart from some nice shots of New Zealand and a certain winsome charm.

Greer Robson *Kate Marshall* • Peter Phelps *Patrick "Pat" Dawson* • Marshall Napier *Detective Wallace* • The Wizard [Ian Brackenbury Channell] *Spooner* ■ *Dir* Sam Pillsbury • *Scr* Grant Hinden Miller, from the novel *The Dream Monger* by Grant Hinden Miller

The Starmaker ★★★ 18

Comedy drama 1994 · It · Colour · 102mins

Giuseppe Tornatore (*Cinema Paradiso*) returns to similarly nostalgic territory with this drama set in the fifties. Roving conman Sergio Castellitto poses as a movie talent scout who persuades Sicilian villagers to pay for their own screen tests and promises them a bright future. This is a smashing idea – intrinsically funny and flexible enough to combine the dreams and crushed hopes of any number of budding actors who stare into the camera and tell us their life stories. But the film is oddly repetitive, and Tornatore's humanitarian heart and the touristy photography are a bit much after a while. In Italian with English subtitles. ▣

Sergio Castellitto *Joe Morelli* • Tiziana Lodato *Beata* • Franco Scaldati *Brigadiere Mastropaolo* • Leopoldo Trieste *Mute* ■ *Dir*

Giuseppe Tornatore • *Scr* Giuseppe Tornatore, Fabio Rinaudo, from a story by Giuseppe Tornatore

Starman ★★★★ PG

Science-fiction romance
1984 · US · Colour · 110mins

A curious alien responds to the *Voyager* spacecraft's invitation to visit Earth, lands in Wisconsin and takes the form of Karen Allen's late husband in a romantic road movie with a cosmic twist. John Carpenter's religious sci-fi parable has as much heart and emotion as it does special effects, and gives Oscar-nominated Jeff Bridges a real chance to stretch his acting talent as the extraterrestrial eager to learn about the pleasures and pain of human existence. Funny, suspenseful and moving (have those tissues ready for the heart-rending climax), this engaging space odyssey is one of Carpenter's best efforts. Contains swearing and violence.

Jeff Bridges *Starman* • Karen Allen *Jenny Hayden* • Charles Martin Smith *Mark Shermin* • Richard Jaeckel *George Fox* • Stefan Phalen *Major Bell* • Tony Edwards *Sergeant Lemon* ■ *Dir* John Carpenter • *Scr* Bruce A Evans, Raynold Gideon

Stars ★★★★

Drama   1959 · E Ger/Bul · BW · 93mins

The first East German film to find favour abroad was written by a Bulgarian Jew and directed by a Red Army veteran. The combination of their experiences and a refusal to indulge in easy sentimentality enables director Konrad Wolf and screenwriter Anzel Wagenstein to impart realism, abhorrence and faint optimism in the story of the German soldier who falls in love while transporting Greek Jews from a Bulgarian detention centre. The dramatic onus rests on Jürgen Frohriep, as he realises the enormity of the Nazis' crimes and deserts to join the Partisans, but his scenes with Sascha Krusharska have poignance. In German with English subtitles.

Sascha Krusharska *Ruth* • Jürgen Frohriep *Walter* • Erik S Klein *Kurt* • Stefan Peichev *Uncle Petko* • Georgi Naumov *Blazhe* • Ivan Kondov *Ruth's father* ■ *Dir* Konrad Wolf, Rangel Vulchanov • *Scr* Angel Wagenstein

Stars and Bars ★ 15

Comedy   1988 · US · Colour · 90mins

It would be nice to recommend this picture and on paper it promises much: Daniel Day-Lewis and Harry Dean Stanton in the main roles, based on a novel by William Boyd and directed by Pat O'Connor, who made *Cal*. Sadly, something went horribly wrong with this comedy about an Englishman's misadventures in the American Deep South. What was quite funny in the novel becomes, in Boyd's script, trite and embarrassing, and O'Connor's heavy hand mires the film in an excess of all-American tack.

Daniel Day-Lewis *Henderson Dores* • Harry Dean Stanton *Loomis Gage* • Laurie Metcalf *Melissa* • Martha Plimpton *Bryant* • Kent Broadhurst *Sereno* • Maury Chaykin *Freebom Gage* • Matthew Cowles *Beckman Gage* • Joan Cusack *Irene Stein* ■ *Dir* Pat O'Connor • *Scr* William Boyd, from his novel

Stars and Stripes Forever ★★★ U

Musical biography
1952 · US · Colour · 89mins

March king John Philip Sousa is waspishly incarnated by Clifton Webb, who portrays a composer desperate to write ballads, not marches. It may or may not be true, but who cares when his fabulous compositions are dispersed through the movie in superb Alfred Newman arrangements? Ruth Hussey makes a tolerant Mrs Sousa, and upcoming Fox stars Robert Wagner and Debra Paget seem to enjoy themselves as the youngsters. Lovers of uniforms, parades and military brass bands shouldn't miss this.

Clifton Webb *John Philip Sousa* • Debra Paget *Lily* • Robert Wagner *Willie* • Ruth Hussey *Jennie* • Finlay Currie *Colonel Randolph* • Benay Venuta *Madame Bernsdorff-Mueller* ■ *Dir* Henry Koster • *Scr* Lamar Trotti, Ernest Vajda, from the autobiography *Marching Along* by John Philip Sousa

The Stars Fell on Henrietta ★★★

Drama   1995 · US · Colour · 105mins

Barely released, this Depression-era drama stars Robert Duvall as a Texan oilman who has struck lucky for others but never himself. Actor/director James Keach creates a fine Dust Bowl atmosphere from the desolate panhandle landscape and elicits some good performances as well. Duvall is excellent, as are Aidan Quinn and Frances Fisher as the poor couple whose farmland arouses lodger Duvall's radar instinct for locating oil. Fisher was the one-time partner of the film's producer, Clint Eastwood, and their child Francesca Ruth plays one of Fisher's daughters in the story.

Robert Duvall *Mr Cox* • Aidan Quinn *Don Day* • Frances Fisher *Cora Day* • Brian Dennehy *Big Dave* • Lexi Randall *Beatrice Day* • Kaytlyn Knowles *Pauline Day* • Francesca Ruth Eastwood *Mary Day* ■ *Dir* James Keach • *Scr* Philip Railsback

Stars in My Crown ★★★

Period religious drama
1950 · US · BW · 89mins

Always upstanding but never a major star, Joel McCrea gives another sterling performance as the new parson appointed to a small Southern town. He proves to be of stern stuff as he encounters epidemics and the menace of the Ku Klux Klan, while shattering the superstitious illusions of the populace. Director Jacques Tourneur was better known for eerie horrors (*Cat People*) and brooding *films noirs* (*Build My Gallows High*), but he neatly blends genre convention with period nostalgia to explore themes rarely tackled in the average B-western.

Ellen Drew *Harriet Gray* • Dean Stockwell *John Kenyon* • Alan Hale *Jed Isbell* • Lewis Stone *Dr DK Harris Sr* • James Mitchell *Dr DK Harris Jr* • Amanda Blake *Faith Radmore Samuels* • Ed Begley *Lon Backett* • Jim Arness [James Arness] *Rufe Isbell* ■ *Dir* Jacques Tourneur • *Scr* Margaret Fitts, from the novel by Joe David Brown

The Stars Look Down ★★★★ PG

Drama   1939 · UK · BW · 94mins

Carol Reed's well-crafted drama is based on AJ Cronin's novel about life in an English mining town. Michael Redgrave tops the bill as the upwardly mobile son of a miner, while Margaret Lockwood is the woman he marries. The film is strong on detail in its portrayal of mining life, though it was eclipsed at the box office by the warmer *How Green Was My Valley*, made in 1941. It creaks with age in parts, but remains a powerful movie. Graham Greene rated it as one of the best British movies he'd ever seen.

Michael Redgrave *David Fenwick* • Margaret Lockwood *Jenny Sunley* • Emlyn Williams *Joe Gowan* • Nancy Price *Martha Fenwick* • Allan Jeayes *Richard Barras* • Edward Rigby *Robert Fenwick* ■ *Dir* Carol Reed • *Scr* JB Williams, from the novel by AJ Cronin

Stars on Parade ★★ U

Musical   1944 · US · BW · 62mins

The fact that the leads were the relatively unknown and uninteresting Larry Parks and Lynn Merrick, and that no one else in the cast, except for the Nat King Cole Trio, is anyone you've ever heard of, makes the title a misnomer. The almost invisible plot has a group of struggling entertainers putting on a show to prove to Hollywood producers that there is talent in their own back yard. It was made a couple of years before Parks hit the big time as Al Jolson in *The Jolson Story* and Senator McCarthy ruined his life and career.

Larry Parks *Danny Davis* • Lynn Merrick *Dorothy Dean* • Ray Walker *Billy Blake* • Jeff Donnell *Mary Brooks* • Robert Williams *Jerry Browne* • Selmer Jackson *JL Carson* • Edythe Elliott *Mrs Dean* • Mary Currier *Nan McNair* ■ *Dir* Lew Landers • *Scr* Monte Brice

Starship Troopers ★★★★ 18

Science-fiction action
1997 · US · Colour · 124mins

Director Paul Verhoeven's ultra-violent adaptation of science-fiction writer Robert A Heinlein's classic 1959 novel – a saga about Earth versus alien bugs – is popcorn exploitation at its lip-smacking, blood-spattered best. Whether portraying the chilling spectacle of millions of ugly giant insects swarming over the planet or the astonishing intergalactic battles, the digitally-created special effects are simply outstanding. It's when Verhoeven cuts to the teenage romance – which the young leads clearly don't have the emotional depth or acting ability to handle – that his sensational cartoon carnage comes unstuck. But the dull bits are never long enough to really matter or do too much damage to one's sheer enjoyment of Verhoeven's absurdly apocalyptic satire. Contains violence and some swearing. DVD

Casper Van Dien *Johnny Rico* • Dina Meyer *Dizzy Flores* • Denise Richards *Carmen Ibanez* • Jake Busey *Ace Levy* • Neil Patrick Harris *Carl Jenkins* • Clancy Brown *Sergeant Zim* • Michael Ironside *Jean Rasczak* ■ *Dir* Paul Verhoeven • *Scr* Edward Neumeier, from the novel by Robert A Heinlein

Start Cheering ★★★

Musical comedy   1938 · US · BW · 78mins

Slight but bright and entertaining musical comedy about a Hollywood actor who tires of starring in college films and decides to enrol as a student in a real university, much to the lament of his manager, who schemes to get him expelled. The cast includes an array of vaudeville names, including the Three Stooges and, above all, Jimmy Durante as the manager's sidekick, who steals the show and the best laughs with a high-energy performance. It's not exactly *West Side Story*, but for fans of broad comedy it's still a lot of fun.

Jimmy Durante *Willie Gumbatz* • Walter Connolly *Sam Lewis* • Joan Perry *Jean Worthington* • Charles Starrett *Ted Crosley* • Raymond Walburn *Dean Worthington* • Broderick Crawford *Biff Gordon* ■ *Dir* Albert S Rogell • *Scr* Eugene Solow, Richard E Wormser, Philip Rapp, from the short story *College Hero* by Corey Ford in *The Saturday Evening Post*

Start the Revolution without Me ★★★★ PG

Period farce   1970 · US · Colour · 86mins

In 18th-century France, two sets of identical twins get scrambled at birth thanks to an incompetent doctor, resulting in double helpings of Donald Sutherland and Gene Wilder. One pair of brothers grow up rich and privileged, while their less fortunate counterparts are peasants. Confused? You will be when the mismatched twins find themselves on opposing sides during some Revolutionary skirmishes. There's a *Monty Python* quality to some of the humour, and director Bud Yorkin places the verbal fireworks when and where they are most needed.

Gene Wilder *Claude Coupé/Philippe Di Sisi* • Donald Sutherland *Charles Coupé/Pierre Di Sisi* • Hugh Griffith *King Louis XVI* • Jack MacGowran *Jacques Cabriolet* • Billie Whitelaw *Queen Marie Antoinette* • Victor Spinetti *Duke d'Escargot* • Orson Welles *Narrator* ■ *Dir* Bud Yorkin • *Scr* Fred Freeman, Lawrence J Cohen, from the story *Two Times Two* by Fred Freeman

Starting Again ★★

Biographical drama
1994 · US · Colour · 97mins

Comedienne, chat-show regular and, nowadays, queen of home shopping television, Joan Rivers has not had an easy time of it. However, what undermines this often tragic biopic is the fact that both Rivers and her daughter Melissa play themselves. Rather than heightening the drama, these real-life impersonations serve only to cheapen it, and any sympathy we have for the pair as they struggle to cope with Joan's husband's suicide is lost by the sham re-creation of once genuine emotions. While you can understand Rivers's need to share her troubles, her triumph over adversity comes across as smug. Revelations of this kind are best told in print.

Joan Rivers • Melissa Rivers ■ *Dir* Oz Scott • *Scr* Susan Rice

Starting Over ★★★ 15

Romantic comedy
1979 · US · Colour · 101mins

Get those tissues out for this romantic comedy in which a non-mustachioed Burt Reynolds – in one of his most sensitive performances – stars as a man coping with his wife (Candice Bergen) leaving him to pursue a singing career. There are some funny – and moving – moments to be had as he consults his pals (who happen to be psychiatrists) and even joins a divorced men's group. There's also much hilarity from Bergen's eye-wincingly awful singing. Nice support from Jill Clayburgh, too, as the commitment-shy teacher with whom Burt attempts a relationship. ▭

Burt Reynolds *Phil Potter* • Jill Clayburgh *Marilyn* • Candice Bergen *Jessica* • Charles Durning *Michael* • Frances Sternhagen *Marva* • Austin Pendleton *Paul* • Mary Kay Place *Marie* • MacIntyre Dixon *Dan Ryan* ■ *Dir* Alan J Pakula • *Scr* James L Brooks, from the novel by Dan Wakefield

State Fair ★★★ U

Comedy 1933 · US · BW · 99mins

A day out at the Iowa state fair with the Frake family is the fulcrum for this folksy, good-humoured, idealised and beautifully performed piece of period Americana. Abel Frake (the much-loved Will Rogers) is hoping his prize pig will win the Blue Ribbon; his wife, Louise Dresser, has entered her pickles and mincemeat. The young ones, meanwhile, are alive to romance, with daughter Janet Gaynor finding true love with newspaper reporter Lew Ayres and son Norman Foster faring less well in a fling with too-knowing girl Sally Eilers. Delightful and innocent, it was a major hit of 1933.

Will Rogers *Abel Frake* • Janet Gaynor *Margy Frake* • Lew Ayres *Pat Gilbert* • Sally Eilers *Emily Joyce* • Norman Foster *Wayne Frake* • Louise Dresser *Melissa Frake* ■ *Dir* Henry King • *Scr* Paul Green, Sonya Levien, from the novel by Phil Stong

State Fair ★★★★ U

Musical 1945 · US · BW · 96mins

The second and probably best of the three Hollywood movies inspired by Phil Stong's popular novel of country folk and their simple ways, set in the American Midwest. It takes the same story of pickles, pigs and boy-meets-girl at the country fair, as told in the 1933 movie, but sets it to music with some topnotch numbers by Rodgers and Hammerstein, including *That's for Me* and *It Might As Well Be Spring*, which bagged the Oscar for best song. Wholesome and entertaining fare. ▭

Jeanne Crain *Margy Frake* • Dana Andrews *Pat Gilbert* • Dick Haymes *Wayne Frake* • Vivian Blaine *Emily Joyce* • Charles Winninger *Abel Frake* • Fay Bainter *Melissa Frake* • Donald Meek *Hippenstahl* • Frank McHugh *McGee* • Percy Kilbride *Miller* ■ *Dir* Walter Lang • *Scr* Oscar Hammerstein II, Sonya Levien, Paul Green, from the novel by Phil Stong

State Fair ★★ U

Musical 1962 · US · Colour · 118mins

A major disappointment, this remake of a much-loved 1945 musical is shackled by the leaden direction of José Ferrer. Even the legendary Alice Faye, returning to the screen after an absence of 17 years, seems dispirited. The Rodgers and Hammerstein songs are still wonderful, though the five new ones added by Rodgers alone are merely serviceable. Ann-Margret performs a torrid dance number which would have scandalised 1945 audiences, and there is some interest in seeing Pat Boone and the talented Bobby Darin, both pop idols of the time.

Pat Boone *Wayne Frake* • Bobby Darin *Jerry Dundee* • Pamela Tiffin *Margie Frake* • Ann-Margret *Emily Porter* • Alice Faye *Melissa Frake* • Tom Ewell *Abel Frake* • Wally Cox *Hipplewaite* • David Brandon *Harry* ■ *Dir* José Ferrer • *Scr* Richard L Breen, from the 1945 film, from the novel by Phil Stong

State of Emergency ★★★

Medical drama 1994 · US · Colour · 89mins

Joe Mantegna headlines this scathing portrait of the state of the American health service. It's basically the day-to-day life of the casualty ward of a crisis-ridden hospital, seen mainly through the eyes of patient Paul Dooley and the lead doctor Mantegna. The latter is as riveting as ever, but this is an ensemble piece and there are excellent supporting turns from the likes of Lynn Whitfield, Robert Beltran and Richard Beymer. Fans of *Casualty* and *ER* will love it.

Joe Mantegna *Doctor John Novelli* • Lynn Whitfield *Dehlia Johnson* • Melinda Dillon *Betty Anderson* • Paul Dooley *John Anderson* • Richard Beymer *Doctor Ronald Frames* • Jay O Sanders *Doctor Jeffrey Forrest* • Robert Beltran *Raoul Hernandez* ■ *Dir* Lesli Linka Glatter • *Scr* Susan Black, Lance Gentile

State of Grace ★★★★ 18

Crime thriller 1990 · US · Colour · 128mins

Set in New York's Irish quarter, this glowering thriller makes so many blatant bids to be bracketed with the mob movies of Martin Scorsese that it could justifiably be nicknamed *O'GoodFellas*. While not up to the Scorsese standard, this is still a cracking crime movie, with gutsy performances from Sean Penn, the under-rated Ed Harris and that master of manic malevolence, Britain's own Gary Oldman. Penn's off-screen partner (now wife) Robin Wright gets slightly lost in the mêlée and director Phil Joanou might have kept the running time down, but it's violent, vibrant and very impressive. Contains swearing, violence, drug abuse and nudity. ▭

Sean Penn *Terry Noonan* • Gary Oldman *Jackie Flannery* • Ed Harris *Frankie Flannery* • Robin Wright [Robin Wright Penn] *Kathleen Flannery* • John Turturro *Nick* • John C Reilly *Stevie* • Burgess Meredith *Finn* ■ *Dir* Phil Joanou • *Scr* Dennis McIntyre

State of Siege ★★★ 15

Political thriller
1972 · Fr/US/It/W Ger · Colour · 115mins

Although set in an unnamed state, this is clearly a film about the abduction by Uruguay's Tupamaro guerillas of Daniel Mitrione. Mitrione was a member of the US Agency for International Development, whose traffic control brief provided a front for his expertise in the interrogation and torture of political prisoners. There was widespread criticism of the casting of the iconic Yves Montand as the villain, while others complained that the director's sympathies overtly lay with the kidnappers. Either way, despite re-using the reportage techniques he had employed on *Z*, Costa-Gavras was less successful in condensing his ideas into the conspiracy thriller format. A French language film. ▭

Yves Montand *Santore* • Renato Salvatori *Lopez* • OE Hasse *Ducas* • Jacques Weber *Hugo* • Jean-Luc Bideau *Este* • Evangeline Peterson *Mrs Santore* ■ *Dir* Constantin Costa-Gavras [Costa-Gavras] • *Scr* Constantin Costa-Gavras [Costa-Gavras], Franco Solinas

State of the Union ★★★★

Political drama 1948 · US · BW · 121mins

Adapted from a play by Howard Lindsay and Russel Crouse, starring Spencer Tracy and Katharine Hepburn, and directed by Frank Capra, this one could hardly miss. Originally released in the year of a presidential campaign, it concerns a millionaire industrialist (Tracy) running for the highest office and unwittingly putting himself and his integrity at the mercy of other people's unprincipled ambition. When the candidate's estranged wife (Hepburn) is persuaded to return for a public reunion, there are unexpected consequences. Enthralling and astringently witty, the film boasts top-class supporting performances from Adolphe Menjou, Van Johnson and Angela Lansbury, while the star duo fires on all cylinders.

Spencer Tracy *Grant Matthews* • Katharine Hepburn *Mary Matthews* • Van Johnson *Spike McManus* • Angela Lansbury *Kay Thorndyke* • Adolphe Menjou *Jim Conover* • Lewis Stone *Sam Thorndyke* ■ *Dir* Frank Capra • *Scr* Anthony Veiller, Myles Connolly, from a play by Howard Lindsay, Russel Crouse

The State of Things ★★★★

Drama 1982 · US/Por/W Ger · BW · 121mins

Shot contemporaneously with the interminable production of *Hammett*, Wim Wenders's treatise on the uneasy relationship between the European art film and Hollywood was dubbed by its director as the last of the B-movies. The shifts between narrative and dissertation are superbly achieved, as the cast and crew of a poverty-stricken sci-fi remake are stranded in Portugal and left to cogitate on the ironies of life and illusion as their producer heads for the States in search of funds. Despite dividing the critics (who found it either cold and cynical or astute and acerbic), this cameo-packed film won the Golden Lion award at the Venice Film Festival.

Patrick Bauchau *Friedrich "Fritz" Munro, the director* • Isabelle Weingarten *Anna* • Allen Goorwitz [Allen Garfield] *Gordon* • Samuel Fuller *Joe Corby, the cameraman* • Viva Auder *Kate, the scriptgirl* • Jeffrey Kime *Mark* • Paul Getty III *Dennis, the writer* • Roger Corman *Lawyer* ■ *Dir* Wim Wenders • *Scr* Wim Wenders, Robert Kramer

State Secret ★★★ U

Thriller 1950 · UK · BW · 100mins

A serviceable thriller from Frank Launder and Sidney Gilliat that borrows its blend of comedy and suspense from their own spy caper *Night Train to Munich*. Douglas Fairbanks Jr stars as a surgeon lured to the Balkan state of Vosnia after its dictator is wounded in an assassination attempt. When his patient dies, Fairbanks has to take to the hills with plucky Glynis Johns at his side. Vosnia is straight out of an A-Z of clichés, but Gilliat directs with plenty of panache and the location photography is stunning. ▭

Douglas Fairbanks Jr *Dr John Marlowe* • Glynis Johns *Lisa* • Jack Hawkins *Colonel Galcon* • Herbert Lom *Karl Theodor* • Walter Rilla *General Niva* • Karel Stepanek *Dr Revo* • Carl Jaffe *Janovik Prada* ■ *Dir* Sidney Gilliat • *Scr* Sidney Gilliat, from the novel *Appointment with Fear* by Roy Huggins • *Producer* Frank Launder

Static ★★★ 15

Satirical drama 1985 · US · Colour · 90mins

In this decidedly odd drama, Keith Gordon plays a guy who invents a TV that can supposedly tune in to heaven. It can't, of course, and simply shows static. But try telling that to spiritually isolated people who desperately need to believe in something bigger and better. By turns moving and amusing, but also drawn-out and dreary, *Static* displays an obvious intelligence and will appeal to fans of the surreal films of David Lynch. ▭

Keith Gordon *Ernie Blick* • Amanda Plummer *Julia Purcell* • Bob Gunton *Frank* • Lily Knight *Patty* • Barton Heyman *Sheriff William Orling* • Reathel Bean *Fred Savins* • Jane Hoffman *Emily Southwick* ■ *Dir* Mark Romanek • *Scr* Keith Gordon, Mark Romanek

A Station for Two ★★★ PG

Romantic drama
1983 · USSR · Colour · 133mins

Shades of 1954's *Indiscretion of an American Wife* colour this exceedingly mild satire from the usually acerbic Eldar Ryazanov. Yet, considering the restrictions placed on Soviet film-makers, this is still an acute analysis of the moral and material problems then facing the USSR, with the queues, delays, shortages, drunkenness and racketeering that provide the back story clearly serving a microcosmic purpose. The narrative itself has allegorical undertones, as one-time concert pianist Oleg Basilashvili is released from the gulag where he's serving a sentence for manslaughter in order to visit his wife. However, a chance encounter with waitress Lyudmila Gurchenko alters everything. A Russian language film.

Oleg Basilashvili *Platon* • Lyudmila Gurchenko *Vera* • Nikita Mikhalkov *Vera's boyfriend* • Nonna Mordyukova *Waitress* ■ *Scr* Emil Braginsky, from a story by Eldar Ryazanov

Station Six-Sahara ★★★★

Drama 1962 · UK/W Ger · BW · 101mins

Eroticism isn't something that the British cinema tackles very often, but this 1962 offering does. It's set on an oil pipeline in the middle of the Sahara where the blokes are muscular, sweaty and bad-tempered. Their frustration is palpable. Then out of the blue comes *Baby Doll* herself, a provocative, unbuttoned Carroll Baker. Directed by former editor Seth Holt and co-written by Bryan Forbes, it makes the most of an intrinsically ridiculous situation, relishing the clichés, laying on the impudent symbolism and wringing out

as much sexual tension as possible. A real collector's item.

Carroll Baker *Catherine* • Peter Van Eyck *Kramer* • Ian Bannen *Fletcher* • Denholm Elliott *Macey* • Hansjörg Felmy *Martin* • Mario Adorf *Santos* • Biff McGuire *Jimmy* • Harry Baird *Sailor* ■ *Dir* Seth Holt • *Scr* Bryan Forbes, Brian Clemens, from the play *Men without a Past* by Jacques Maret

Station West ★★★

Western 1948 · US · BW · 92mins

Former crooner Dick Powell had just carved out a new career for himself as a tough guy in such taut thrillers as *Farewell My Lovely* (1945) and *Johnny O'Clock* (1947) and so brought a new, darker image to this cleverly scripted RKO western, based on a Luke Short tale about an army investigator trying to sort out a series of gold heists. A little *noir* knowledge might not come amiss if you're planning on finding the baddie along with our hero. Jane Greer makes a feisty sparring partner, but what really gives this movie some distinction is the use of clever one-liners, courtesy of writers Frank Fenton and Winston Miller.

Dick Powell *Haven* • Jane Greer *Charlie* • Agnes Moorehead *Mrs Caslon* • Burl Ives *Hotel clerk* • Tom Powers *Captain Iles* • Gordon Oliver *Prince* • Steve Brodie *Stellman* • Guinn Williams *Mick* • Raymond Burr *Mark Bristow* • Regis Toomey *Goddard* ■ *Dir* Sidney Lanfield • *Scr* Frank Fenton, Winston Miller, from a novel by Luke Short

Stavisky ★★★★

Political drama
1974 · Fr/It · Colour · 117mins

With Jean-Paul Belmondo in the lead, a famous scandal as its subject, atmospheric art deco sets and a memorable Stephen Sondheim score, this is Alain Resnais's most commercial picture. Yet, with its temporal shifts and deft blend of fact, memory and fallacy, it also serves as a perfect vehicle for Resnais's trademark preoccupations, as he explores the legend grown up around a financial swindle that had the most sinister political implications. It's a technically accomplished film too, with Resnais using filters to approximate thirties Technicolor hues and restricting himself to angles only extant in the period. In French with English subtitles.

Jean-Paul Belmondo *Stavisky* • Charles Boyer *Baron Raoul* • François Périer *Albert Borelli* • Anny Duperey *Arlette Stavisky* • Michel Lonsdale *Dr Mezy* • Claude Rich *Bonny* ■ *Dir* Alain Resnais • *Scr* Jorge Semprun • *Cinematographer* Sacha Vierny

Stay Hungry ★★★★ 18

Drama 1976 · US · Colour · 98mins

Before Arnold Schwarzenegger found muscleman fame and Robert Englund became Elm Street's Freddy, they turned up as characters in Bob Rafelson's culture-clash tale about what happens when Alabama heir Jeff Bridges infiltrates a downtown gym for real-estate reasons and falls for Sally Field. Totally laid-back, this all seems pointlessly unstructured, until you realise that's the way it's supposed to be: an endearing look at barbell bums who may never win through, but have lots of fun trying. Contains violence, swearing and nudity.

Jeff Bridges *Craig Blake* • Sally Field *Mary Tate Farnsworth* • Arnold Schwarzenegger *Joe Santo* • RG Armstrong *Thor Erickson* • Robert Englund *Franklin* • Helena Kallianiotes *Anita* • Roger E Mosley *Newton* • Scatman Crothers *Butler* ■ *Dir* Bob Rafelson • *Scr* Bob Rafelson, Charles Gaines, from the novel by Charles Gaines

Stay Tuned ★★ PG

Comedy fantasy 1992 · US · Colour · 84mins

The central conceit is quite clever: TV-obsessed John Ritter sells his soul to the devil (Jeffrey Jones) and finds himself literally trapped in the box with wife Pam Dawber. However, the execution is all wrong, and the result is a string of rather lame send-ups of popular television shows. Jones is as reliable as ever and there are supporting turns from the likes of Eugene Levy and Salt-N-Pepa. But the two leads are bland and, apart from a spiffing animation sequence (directed by Chuck Jones), Peter Hyams never really gets a handle on the project.

John Ritter *Roy Knable* • Pam Dawber *Helen Knable* • Jeffrey Jones *Spike* • Eugene Levy *Crowley* • David Tom *Darryl Knable* • Heather McComb *Diane Knable* • Salt-N-Pepa ■ *Dir* Peter Hyams • *Scr* Tom S Parker, Jim Jennewein, from a story by Tom S Parker, Jim Jennewein, Richard Siegel

Staying Afloat ★

Spy thriller 1993 · US · Colour

Sometimes producers do the critics' work for them by giving their films titles that beg damning puns. Larry Hagman must shoulder the blame in this instance, for he was one of the executive producers of this leaky thriller that quickly starts shipping water before sinking without a trace. Hagman also stars, playing a former millionaire whose cash-flow problems force him into operating as a secret agent from his yacht moored off the Florida coast. The intention was clearly to emulate the suave derring-do of such playboy adventurers as the Saint and the Falcon, but this TV movie drifts way off course.

Larry Hagman *Alexander Turnball Hollingsworth Iii* • Eric Christmas *Ryder* • Gregg Henry *Ed Smith* • Claire Yarlett *Lauren Morton* • Antoni Corone *Carlos* • Dakin Matthews *Henry Ashley* ■ *Dir* Eric Laneuville • *Scr* Michael Sadowski, Bob Shayne, from a story by Bob Shayne, Glen A Larson

Staying Alive ★★ PG

Drama 1983 · US · Colour · 92mins

Not quite a career low for John Travolta (*Two of a Kind* was still to come), but one he nevertheless would probably love to forget. The idea of doing a sequel to the film that launched his career (*Saturday Night Fever*) was a good one, but the warning bells should have started ringing over the involvement of Sylvester Stallone, who co-wrote and directed this clunker. The slim plot focuses on Travolta, now a professional dancer, being torn between two women as he prepares for a big show. Stallone, however, largely gives us a retread of *Rocky*, while brother Frank, who was responsible for much of the music, is certainly no Bee Gee. Contains swearing.

John Travolta *Tony Manero* • Cynthia Rhodes *Jackie* • Finola Hughes *Laura* • Steve Inwood *Jesse* • Julie Bovasso *Mrs Manero* • Charles Ward *Butler* ■ *Dir* Sylvester Stallone • *Scr* Sylvester Stallone, Norman Wexler, from characters created by Nik Cohn

Staying Together ★★★ 15

Comedy drama 1989 · US · Colour · 87mins

A sentimental, if well-intentioned little movie about a small-town family facing radical upheavals. The McDermotts own a fried chicken business and the three boys believe that is where their future lies. But when dad Jake sells the restaurant and dies, the boys have to rethink. This character-driven movie doesn't sound like much, but the plot and characters are surprisingly engrossing thanks to sensitive direction from actress Lee Grant.

Sean Astin *Duncan McDermott* • Stockard Channing *Nancy Trainer* • Melinda Dillon *Eileen McDermott* • Jim Haynie *Jake McDermott* • Levon Helm *Denny Stockton* • Dinah Manoff *Lois Cook* • Dermot Mulroney *Kit McDermott* • Tim Quill *Brian McDermott* ■ *Dir* Lee Grant • *Scr* Monte Merrick

The Steal ★★ PG

Crime comedy 1994 · UK · Colour · 90mins

This has a strong cast, but it's the uninspired direction and script that leave the talented players floundering. Alfred Molina and Helen Slater are the amateur crooks out to rob a City firm who get mixed up in an increasingly hysterical series of misadventures. The leads give of their best and there are enthusiastic turns from the likes of Jack Dee, Stephen Fry, Dinsdale Landen and Peter Bowles, yet it must go down as another missed opportunity. Contains some swearing.

Alfred Molina *Cliff* • Helen Slater *Kim* • Peter Bowles *Lord Childwell* • Dinsdale Landen *Sir Wilmot* • Heathcote Williams *Jeremiah* • Stephen Fry *Wimborne* • Bryan Pringle *Cecil, bank doorman* • Jack Dee *Wilmot's servant* ■ *Dir* John Hay • *Scr* John Hay

Steal Big, Steal Little ★★ 12

Action comedy 1995 · US · Colour · 108mins

This misguided comedy tale of greed and corruption stars Andy Garcia as the identical twin brothers – Ruben and Robert – battling over the estate left by their adoptive mother. As you would expect, one's a really nice guy and the other is a scheming rat. What sounds like a simple tale is in reality a confusing mess of too many plot strands and supporting characters.

Andy Garcia *Ruben Partida Martinez/Robert Martin* • Alan Arkin *Lou Perilli* • Rachel Ticotin *Laura Martinez* • Joe Pantoliano *Eddie Agopian* • Holland Taylor *Mona Rowland-Downey* • Ally Walker *Bonnie Martin* • David Ogden Stiers *Judge Winton Myers* ■ *Dir* Andrew Davis • *Scr* Andrew Davis, Lee Blessing, Jeanne Blake, Terry Kahn, from a story by Teresa Tucker-Davies, Frank Ray Perilli, Andrew Davis

Stealing Beauty ★★ 15

Romantic drama
1995 · It/ UK/ Fr · Colour · 113mins

It's sad to see such an accomplished director as Bernardo Bertolucci stumble into bathos with this small-scale romantic drama. Liv Tyler stars as the American teenager who, after her mother's suicide, takes a summer holiday with an expatriate family in Tuscany. Anxious to lose her virginity and discover the identity of her biological father, she encounters a range of eccentric house guests, including Jeremy Irons as a terminally-ill playwright and Jean Marais as an art dealer. It all rings pretentiously false. Contains swearing and sex scenes.

Sinead Cusack *Diana Grayson* • Jeremy Irons *Alex Parrish* • Jean Marais *Monsieur Guillaume* • Donal McCann *Ian Grayson* • DW Moffett *Richard Reed* • Stefania Sandrelli *Noemi* • Rachel Weisz *Miranda Fox* • Liv Tyler *Lucy Harmon* ■ *Dir* Bernardo Bertolucci • *Scr* Susan Minot, from a story by Bernardo Bertolucci

Stealing Heaven ★★ 15

Historical romance
1988 · UK/Yug · Colour · 110mins

The true story of medieval star-crossed lovers Abelard and Heloise gets an unsubtle and highly erotic treatment in director Clive Donner's soap-opera confection. Philosophy scholar Abelard, who is supposed to remain celibate, falls for the aristocratic Heloise and they flout both religion and society as they wend their romantic way towards inevitable tragedy. Despite the efforts of a good cast, that includes Denholm Elliott and Bernard Hepton, the film remains resolutely ordinary.

Derek De Lint *Abelard* • Kim Thomson *Heloise* • Denholm Elliott *Canon Fulbert* • Bernard Hepton *Bishop Martin* • Kenneth Cranham *Vice Chancellor Suger* • Patsy Bryne *Agnes* ■ *Dir* Clive Donner • *Scr* Chris Bryant, from the novel by Marion Meade

Stealing Home ★★★★ 15

Drama 1988 · US · Colour · 93mins

Here's a rarity; not shown at cinemas in the UK, this should be seen if only for future double Oscar-winner Jodie Foster's fine performance as the wild Katie, whose death evokes troubled memories and regrets among her young contemporaries, Billy and Alan. Told in flashback, this movie is the cinematic autobiography of its two writer/directors (Steven Kampmann and Will Aldis) and, as such, was really too earnest and personal to achieve a wide release. Mark Harmon plays the grown-up Billy, fixated on baseball, with John Shea terrific as his fanatical father, and watch for Harold Ramis in a small but tellingly funny role as the adult Alan. Contains swearing.

Mark Harmon *Billy Wyatt as an adult* • Jodie Foster *Katie Chandler* • Blair Brown *Ginny Wyatt* • Jonathan Silverman *Alan Appleby as a teenager* • Harold Ramis *Alan Appleby as an adult* • John Shea *Sam Wyatt* • William McNamara *Billy Wyatt as a teenager* ■ *Dir/ Scr* Steven Kampmann, Will Aldis

Steamboat Bill, Jr ★★★★★ U

Silent comedy 1928 · US · BW · 69mins

The last of Keaton's fully independent films, made just before he signed with MGM and went into a precipitous decline. The story concerns two rival steamboat operators and Keaton, of course, plays the saphead son of one of them, arriving fresh from college and falling in love with the rival's daughter. Keaton achieves an authentic, Mark Twain-style look, although the film was made entirely in

California rather than the Deep South. As well as a series of wonderful gags, he also produces the most spectacular and dangerous sequence of his entire career – a cyclone that sweeps up everything in its path. This culminates in an entire house collapsing on our hero, who saves himself by escaping through a tiny upstairs window. ▭

Buster Keaton *Steamboat Bill Jr* • Ernest Torrence *Steamboat Bill* • Tom Lewis *His first mate* • Tom McGuire *John James King, his rival* • Marion Byron *Mary King, his daughter* • Joe Keaton *Barber* ■ *Dir* Charles Reisner • *Scr* Carl Harbaugh

Steamboat round the Bend ★★★ U

Drama 1935 · US · BW · 81mins

A warm-hearted Will Rogers vehicle, released after his tragic death in a plane crash. With the distance of time, this may require tolerance from the viewer, but it's still fascinating to watch a riverboat battle between America's two folk philosophers of the time, Rogers himself and the garrulous Irvin S Cobb. Director John Ford was always prone to sentimentalise, and this is no exception. But he achieves a sweet, elegiac feel for a more gentle, romantic past that's difficult to re-create on screen. The only fly in the ointment is a racial stereotype from Stepin Fetchit – sadly, par for the course in those days.

Will Rogers *Dr John Pearly* • Anne Shirley *Fleety Belle* • Eugene Pallette *Sheriff Rufe Jeffers* • John McGuire *Duke* • Berton Churchill *New Moses* • Stepin Fetchit *Jonah* ■ *Dir* John Ford • *Scr* Dudley Nichols, Lamar Trotti, from the novel by Ben Lucian Burman

Steamboat Willie ★★★★★

Animation 1928 · US · BW · 7mins

Walt Disney's third Mickey Mouse cartoon has Mickey as the captain of a steamboat sailing up the Mississippi, and demonstrates Disney's use of music and sound to give additional weight to a production's narrative and structure. (This was the first animated film with sound.) In one memorable moment, a cow's teeth are played like a xylophone, while its udder is used as a bagpipe! The term "Mickey Mouse Music" – with the soundtrack covering all visual events – undoubtedly came from this cartoon, which was the first notable example of the audio-visual orchestration that would be used so effectively in later Disney successes.

Walt Disney *Mickey Mouse* ■ *Dir* Walt Disney • *Scr* Walt Disney, Ub Iwerks • *Music* Carl Stalling • *Animator* Ub Iwerks

Steaming ★★★★ 18

Drama 1985 · UK · Colour · 91mins

If you liked Nell Dunn's breast-beating play about an all-women group at the local Turkish baths, you'll love Joseph Losey's movie, which sticks rigidly to text and scene. It is a tightly drawn, multi-charactered, often insightful look at the female condition, with a last, wonderful performance from Diana Dors as the surrogate mum in charge of the towels. If women wittily waxing about men and periods is not your scene, avoid. But it is still both achingly sad and funny in equal turns. Contains nudity. ▭

Vanessa Redgrave *Nancy* • Sarah Miles *Sarah* • Diana Dors *Violet* • Patti Love *Josie* • Brenda Bruce *Mrs Meadows* • Felicity Dean *Dawn Meadows* • Sally Sagoe *Celia* • Anna Tzelniker *Mrs Goldstein* ■ *Dir* Joseph Losey • *Scr* Patricia Losey, from the play by Nell Dunn

Steel ★★ 15

Drama 1980 · US · Colour · 97mins

There are elements of *The Fountainhead*, *The Towering Inferno* and *Dallas* in this melodrama about the race to complete the top nine floors of a skyscraper before the banks close in. Lee Majors stars (and produces) as the construction leader and George Kennedy as the company owner whose early departure leads to his daughter Jennifer O'Neill taking over, worrying the banks in the process and giving the story a sexist slant. Like the skyscraper itself, production in Lexington, Kentucky was dogged by problems, including the death of stuntman AJ Bakunis to whom the picture is dedicated. It's a pity the movie itself is so ordinary. ▭

Lee Majors *Mike Catton* • Jennifer O'Neill *Cass Cassidy* • Art Carney *Pignose Moran* • Harris Yulin *Eddie Cassidy* • George Kennedy *Lew Cassidy* • Roger E Mosley *Lionel* • Albert Salmi *Tank* ■ *Dir* Steve Carver • *Scr* Leigh Chapman, from a story by Rob Ewing, Peter S Davis, William N Panzer

Steel ★★ PG

Action fantasy 1997 · US · Colour · 92mins

Loosely based on the DC Comics superhero of the same name, former basketball star Shaquille O'Neal suits up in a metal overcoat and butts heads with street gangs armed with super-weapons. As an actor, Shaq makes a great basketball player, and one suspects that he finds remembering all those pesky lines of dialogue as hard as making free throw shots consistently. As portrayed in this movie, Steel resembles nothing so much as what would happen if Batman went to RoboCop's tailor. ▭

Shaquille O'Neal *Steel/John Henry Irons* • Annabeth Gish *Susan Sparks* • Judd Nelson *Nathaniel Burke* • Richard Roundtree *Uncle Joe* • Irma P Hall *Grandma Odessa* • Ray J Martin • Charles Napier *Colonel David* ■ *Dir* Kenneth Johnson • *Scr* Kenneth Johnson, from a character created by Jon Bogdanove, Louise Simonson

The Steel Bayonet ★★

Second World War drama 1957 · UK · BW · 82mins

A British war movie, made by Michael Carreras, whose father Sir James owned Hammer Film Studios. Carreras directs rather in the style of an American platoon picture – the title is reminiscent of a Sam Fuller movie – as it deals with Leo Genn and his battle-worn men who are ordered to hold a farmhouse during the Allied assault on Tunis. As in American movies, the men embody a variety of attitudes towards the morality of war – heroic, cynical and all points in between – but, this being a British movie, it all comes down to class attitudes and whether your accent is posh or working-class.

Leo Genn *Major Gerrard* • Kieron Moore *Captain Mead* • Michael Medwin *Lieutenant Vernon* • Robert Brown *Sergeant Major Gill* •

Michael Ripper *Private Middleditch* • John Paul *Lieutenant Colonel Derry* • Michael Caine ■ *Dir* Michael Carreras • *Scr* Howard Clewes

The Steel Helmet ★★★

War drama 1951 · US · BW · 84mins

The first in a long line of Samuel Fuller war movies has Gene Evans as a seasoned sergeant in the thick of the Korean War. He survives a massacre, is saved by an orphan and injects a deep-rooted cynicism into the platoon he adopts as his own. Shot in a mere ten days and sometimes looking like it took only five, the movie has a combustible energy that is so typical of its director. Bringing up the rear of the cast list is Lynn Stalmaster, who later gained fame as Hollywood's most sought-after casting agent.

Gene Evans *Sgt Zack* • Robert Hutton *Pvt "Conchie" Bronte* • Richard Loo *Sgt "Buddhahead" Tanaka* • Steve Brodie *Lt Driscoll* • James Edwards *Cpl "Medic" Thompson* • Sid Melton *Joe, 2nd GI* • Richard Monahan *Pvt Baldy* • William Chun *"Short Round"* • Lynn Stalmaster *2nd Lieutenant* ■ *Dir/Scr* Samuel Fuller

Steel Justice ★ PG

Science-fiction 1992 · US · Colour · 86mins

Set some time in the next century, the action in this TV movie centres on a cop who follows the advice of a time traveller and transforms his son's toy robot into a fire-breathing, villain-crunching dinosaur. More "Roboflop" than *Robocop*, this might have worked had it been played for laughs, but this pilot for a TV series that never took off is directed with no sense of its own ludicrousness by Christopher Crowe. ▭

Robert Taylor (2) *Lieutenant David Nash* • JA Preston *Jeremiah Jonas* • Joan Chen *Nicole Robbins* • Season Hubley *Gina Morelli* • John Finn *Lt Aaron Somes* ■ *Dir* Christopher Crowe • *Scr* John Hill, Christopher Crowe

The Steel Key ★★ U

Spy drama 1953 · UK · BW · 70mins

Just five years after playing Laertes in Laurence Olivier's *Hamlet*, Terence Morgan found himself fronting uninspired B-movies like this one. He's effective enough as Johnny O'Flynn, trying to rescue a scientist and his formula for super-hardened steel from the clutches of enemy agents. But the brisk pace can't disguise either the potholes in the plot or the phoneyness of the dialogue. Director Robert Baker and his production partner, Monty Berman, would have more luck with small-screen espionage in the sixties with Roger Moore as *The Saint*.

Terence Morgan *Johnny O'Flynn* • Joan Rice *Doreen Wilson* • Raymond Lovell *Insp Forsythe* • Dianne Foster *Sylvia Newman* • Hector Ross *Beroni* • Colin Tapley *Dr Crabtree* • Arthur Lovegrove *Gilchrist* ■ *Dir* Robert S Baker • *Scr* John Gilling, from a story by Roy Chanslor

Steel Magnolias ★★★★ PG

Comedy drama 1989 · US · Colour · 113mins

Expanded from his own play by Robert Harling, *Steel Magnolias* provided juicy roles for some of Hollywood's leading ladies at a time when muscle-bound action heroes still held sway at the box office. Sally Field, Daryl Hannah,

Olympia Dukakis and Julia Roberts interact so beautifully as they discuss men, the menopause, manicures and marriage in Dolly Parton's kitsch small-town beauty salon that it was something of a surprise that only Roberts scooped an Oscar nomination. A little too dependent on sassy one-liners and awash with sentiment by the end, this is still wonderful entertainment. Contains mild swearing. ▭

Sally Field *M'Lynn Eatenton* • Dolly Parton *Truvy Jones* • Shirley MacLaine *Ouiser Boudreaux* • Daryl Hannah *Annelle Dupuy Desoto* • Julia Roberts *Shelby Eatenton Latcherie* • Olympia Dukakis *Clairee Belcher* • Tom Skerritt *Drum Eatenton* • Dylan McDermott *Jackson Latcherie* • Sam Shepard *Spud Jones* ■ *Dir* Herbert Ross • *Scr* Robert Harling, from his play

The Steel Trap ★★★ U

Crime comedy 1952 · US · Colour · 84mins

Assistant bank manager Joseph Cotten steals money from his employer and attempts to flee to Brazil where there is no extradition treaty, but finds his plans thwarted when he misses his flight. Cotten and Teresa Wright, the uncle and niece from Hitchcock's *Shadow of a Doubt*, are reunited here as husband and wife, and both are excellent. The film is directed from his own screenplay by Andrew L Stone, who would go on to specialise in well-made suspense tales.

Joseph Cotten *Jim Osborne* • Teresa Wright *Laurie Osborne* • Eddie Marr *Ken* • Aline Towne *Gail* • Bill Hudson *Raglin* ■ *Dir* Andrew Stone [Andrew L Stone] • *Scr* Andrew Stone

Steelyard Blues ★★★ 15

Comedy 1973 · US · Colour · 89mins

Whatever happened to director Alan Myerson, who announced himself as an offbeat original with this comic irreverence? Perhaps he was swallowed up one dark night by the American establishment on which this film is an attack, albeit an affectionate one. Strung out attractively between dotty humour and period paranoia, this concerns a bunch of square pegs who plan to revive an abandoned seaplane and escape to a better life. The humour, never a matter of contrived gags, emerges naturally from the situation. Contains swearing. ▭

Donald Sutherland *Jesse Veldini* • Jane Fonda *Iris Caine* • Peter Boyle *Eagle Throneberry* • Howard Hesseman *Frank Veldini* • Garry Goodrow *Duval Jacks* • John Savage *The Kid* • Richard Schaal *Zoo official* ■ *Dir* Alan Myerson • *Scr* David S Ward

Stella ★★★

Comedy mystery 1950 · US · BW · 75mins

Based on a novel by whodunit author Doris Miles Disney, this frantic black comedy feels like an inversion of *The Trouble with Harry*, as all the fun stems from an accidental death and the burial of a body. Victor Mature gives a sportingly self-ridiculing performance as the insurance investigator attempting to make sense of the ramblings of Ann Sheridan's eccentric kin as they seek to pass off any old corpse to get their hands on a $20,000 pay-out, while barking nephew David Wayne tries to recall where he interred his detested uncle.

Ann Sheridan *Stella* • Victor Mature *Jeff De Marco* • David Wayne *Carl Granger* • Randy Stuart *Claire Granger* • Marion Marshall *Mary* • Frank Fontaine *Don* • Leif Erickson *Fred Anderson* • Evelyn Varden *Flora Bevins* ■ *Dir* Claude Binyon • *Scr* Claude Binyon, from the novel *Family Skeleton* by Doris Miles Disney

Stella ★★★

Drama   1955 · Gr · BW · 94mins

Michael Cacoyannis's second feature made an instant star of its debuting lead, Melina Mercouri. Gleefully flouting patriarchal notions of marriage, possession and pride, Mercouri's hall singer is the Greek equivalent of Carmen, as she inflames passions with her smouldering availability and tempestuous spirit. Yet she herself only has eyes for footballer George Foundas – until, that is, she begins to perceive marriage as a trap and not a declaration of love. Despite bringing a raw realism to his depiction of backstreet Athens, Cacoyannis allows Mercouri too much latitude and her exuberance unbalances the insubstantial narrative. A Greek language film.

Melina Mercouri *Stella* • George Foundas *Milto* • Alekos Alexandrakis *Aleko* • Sophia Vembo *Maria* • Voula Zoumboulaki *Anneta* ■ *Dir* Michael Cacoyannis • *Scr* Michael Cacoyannis, from the play *Stella with the Red Gloves* by Iakovos Kabanellis

Stella ★★15

Melodrama   1990 · US · Colour · 104mins

Battling Bette Midler takes on the old Barbara Stanwyck role of working-class mother Stella Dallas and loses. Not only does her character (here renamed Stella Claire) seem horribly politically incorrect in her efforts to get illegitimate daughter Trini Alvarado married to an upper-crust beau, but Midler is also far too feisty for this out-of-date melodrama. Even a starry cast that includes John Goodman, Eileen Brennan and Marsha Mason is defeated by this over-sentimental stodge. Contains swearing, drug abuse and brief nudity. ▭

Bette Midler *Stella Claire* • John Goodman *Ed Munn* • Trini Alvarado *Jenny Claire* • Stephen Collins *Stephen Dallas* • Marsha Mason *Janice Morrison* • Eileen Brennan *Mrs Wilkerson* • Linda Hart *Debbie Whitman* • Ben Stiller *Jim Uptegrove* ■ *Dir* John Erman • *Scr* Robert Getchell, from the novel *Stella Dallas* by Olive Higgins Prouty

Stella Dallas ★★★★

Silent drama   1925 · US · BW · 108mins

Small-town Stella (Belle Bennett) marries out of her class. When her husband Ronald Colman leaves their hopeless marriage and returns to New York, she lavishes love on their daughter Lois Moran, but later sacrifices the girl to a better life with her father and marriage to Douglas Fairbanks Jr. Down-at-heel Bennett, watching the wedding through a window with tears streaming down her face, gave the cinema of weepy melodrama one of its most famous and enduring images. Played beautifully by Bennett and remarkably by Moran, who carries off the young adult Laurel with aplomb, this silent

tear-jerker was directed with taste and sensitivity by Henry King.

Ronald Colman *Stephen Dallas* • Belle Bennett *Stella Dallas* • Alice Joyce *Helen Morrison* • Jean Hersholt *Ed Munn* • Beatrix Pryor *Mrs Grovesnor* • Lois Moran *Laurel Dallas* • Douglas Fairbanks Jr *Richard Grovesnor* • Vera Lewis *Miss Tibbets* ■ *Dir* Henry King • *Scr* Frances Marion, from the novel by Olive Higgins Prouty

Stella Dallas ★★★★U

Melodrama   1937 · US · BW · 101mins

The magnificent Barbara Stanwyck never won a performance Oscar, the Academy making its usual reparation by presenting her with an honorary award in 1981. *Stella Dallas* is the movie for which she deserved the best actress Oscar, but that year the honour went to Luise Rainer in Sidney Franklin's *The Good Earth*. Stella Dallas, the heroine of Olive Higgins Prouty's popular novel, is the ultimate soap-opera queen, a woman who, quite literally, sacrifices everything for her daughter's happiness, and this movie is the definitive version of the tale. Stanwyck is brilliant, her own upbringing as a Brooklyn orphan giving added resonance to the story: the famous scene as she watches through a window while her daughter (Anne Shirley) gets married is one of the highlights of movie melodrama. ▭

Barbara Stanwyck *Stella Martin Dallas* • John Boles *Stephen Dallas* • Anne Shirley *Laurel Dallas* • Barbara O'Neil *Helen Morrison* • Alan Hale *Ed Munn* • Marjorie Main *Mrs Martin* • Edmund Elton *Mr Martin* • Tim Holt *Richard* ■ *Dir* King Vidor • *Scr* Sarah Y Mason, Victor Heerman, from the play by Harry Wagstaff Gribble, Gertrude Purcell, from the novel by Olive Higgins Prouty

Stella Does Tricks ★★★18

Drama   1997 · UK · Colour · 94mins

A bittersweet little story about teenage prostitution from director Coky Giedroyc that is well-intentioned but ends up being rather voyeuristic. *Trainspotting*'s Kelly Macdonald is excellent as the feisty young girl working for creepy pimp James Bolam who wants to stop working the streets and go away with drug addict Hans Matheson. Inspired by a documentary series, the film is not exactly heartening but remains somehow compelling, mainly due to Macdonald's winning performance. Unfortunately, the general grubbiness of the film is trying and AL Kennedy's script is somewhat clichéd. Such a sensitive subject deserves better treatment than this. Contains drug abuse, swearing and violence. ▭

Kelly Macdonald *Stella McGuire* • James Bolam *Mr Peters* • Hans Matheson *Eddie* • Ewan Stewart *McGuire* • Andy Serkis *Fitz* ■ *Dir* Coky Giedroyc • *Scr* AL Kennedy

Stella Maris ★★★★

Silent drama   1918 · US · BW · 84mins

"Two Marys for the price of one!" gloated the poster for this weepie starring "America's Sweetheart", Mary Pickford, in a dual role. As Stella Maris she is a pretty and pampered invalid, and as Unity Blake she is a less attractive orphan girl. Both are in love with Conway Tearle. In order to ensure some sort of happy ending, it's the homely Unity who sacrifices herself for

the happiness of the ringleted Stella. Director Marshall A Neilan pumped the tears without mercy, helped by a realistically successful double portrayal by Pickford. Box-office figures proved it to be one of the most successful movies of the time – a wonderful escapist route from thoughts of the First World War battlefields.

Mary Pickford *Stella Maris/Unity Blake* • Conway Tearle *John Risca* • Marcia Manon *Louise Risca* • Ida Waterman *Lady Blount* • Herbert Standing *Sir Oliver Blount* ■ *Dir* Marshall A Neilan [Marshall Neilan] • *Scr* Frances Marion, from the novel by William J Locke

Step Lively ★★★U

Musical comedy   1944 · US · BW · 84mins

Frank Sinatra's last film before his move to MGM is a musical remake of the comedy *Room Service* – also the basis for a Marx Brothers movie. Under the tutelage of Gene Kelly, Sinatra would finally prove that he was more than just the king of the bobbysoxers, but here he occasionally looks a little lost when he's not given some crooning to do. George Murphy is wildly over the top as a theatrical producer who's initially interested in Sinatra's cash rather than his voice. There's solid support from Adolphe Menjou and Walter Slezak and – of course – a handful of hummable tunes from Sammy Cahn and Jule Styne. ▭

Frank Sinatra *Glen* • George Murphy *Miller* • Adolphe Menjou *Wagner* • Gloria DeHaven *Christine* • Walter Slezak *Gribble* • Eugene Pallette *Jenkins* • Wally Brown *Binion* • Alan Carney *Harry* ■ *Dir* Tim Whelan • *Scr* Warren Duff, Peter Milne, from the play *Room Service* by John Murray, Allen Boretz • *Music/Lyrics* Sammy Cahn, Jule Styne

Step Lively, Jeeves ★★

Comedy   1937 · US · BW · 69mins

This sequel to *Thank You, Jeeves* commits the ultimate heresy of featuring the world's most resourceful gentleman's gentleman without the young master himself, one Bertie Wooster. Owing nothing to the genius of creator PG Wodehouse, this is an amiable affair, but too much of the action centres on a couple of American con men (Alan Dinehart and George Givot) who trick Jeeves into believing he has come into a fortune. Arthur Treacher, who spent the majority of his career playing butlers, is again superb in the title role, but the film could do with a silly ass or two.

Arthur Treacher *Jeeves* • Patricia Ellis *Patricia Westley* • Robert Kent *Gerry Townsend* • Alan Dinehart *Hon Cedric B Cromwell* • George Givot *Prince Boris Caminov* • Helen Flint *Babe Ross* • John Harrington *Barney Ross* ■ *Dir* Eugene Forde • *Scr* Frank Fenton, from a story by Lynn Root, Frances Hyland, from characters created by PG Wodehouse

A Step toward Tomorrow ★★★

Drama   1996 · US · Colour

This weepie drama stars Judith Light as the divorced mother who moves her family across the country so that her paralysed son can be treated by a top neurosurgeon. This could have been a predictable and rather gushy TV movie, but a good cast, including Christopher

Reeve, Alfre Woodard and Brad Dourif, make it a moving experience.

Judith Light *Anna Lerner* • Christopher Reeve *Denny Gabriel* • Alfre Woodard *Dr Sandlin* • Tom Irwin *Dr Decker* • Kendall Cunningham *Georgie* • Tim Redwine *Ben* • Brad Dourif *Kirby* ■ *Dir* Deborah Reinisch • *Scr* Tom Nursall, Harris Goldberg

The Stepfather ★★★★18

Horror   1986 · US · Colour · 85mins

A sardonic and unerringly frightening B-movie classic that strips down the American Dream to its maggot-ridden gory glory. Shelley Hack and Jill Schoelen play a widow and her daughter who gradually come to realise that the charming, affable man of the house is actually a multiple murderer obsessed with middle-class values and establishing the perfect home. Their failure to live up to his pure vision of domestic bliss earmarks them as additions to his ever-growing list of victims. The acting is uniformly fine, with Terry O'Quinn unforgettable as the maniacal patriarch whose psychotic mood swings tighten the suspense screws. Joseph Ruben's faultless direction sets the mayhem against an unsettling backdrop of painfully mundane normality. ▭

Terry O'Quinn *Jerry Blake/Henry Morrison/Bill Hodgkins* • Jill Schoelen *Stephanie Maine* • Shelley Hack *Susan Blake* • Stephen Shellen *Jim Ogilvie* • Robyn Stevan *Karen* ■ *Dir* Joseph Ruben • *Scr* Donald E Westlake, from a story by Carolyn Lefcourt, Brian Garfield, Donald E Westlake

Stepfather II ★★18

Horror   1989 · US · Colour · 87mins

The psychotic super-dad (Terry O'Quinn) escapes from a Washington State mental institution, sets himself up as a marriage counsellor and has another go at perfect family life with real-estate agent Meg Foster in this lacklustre sequel. O'Quinn is as good as ever, yet even he can't make the jokey dialogue seem believable. The bloody wedding ceremony is fun, but nothing comes close to the intense power of the first episode. ▭

Terry O'Quinn *The Stepfather* • Meg Foster *Carol Grayland* • Caroline Williams *Matty Crimmins* • Jonathan Brandis *Todd Grayland* • Henry Brown *Dr Joseph Danvers* • Mitchell Laurance *Phil Grayland* ■ *Dir* Jeff Burr • *Scr* John Auerbach, from characters created by Carolyn Lefcourt, Brian Garfield, Donald E Westlake

The Stepford Children ★★15

Science-fiction thriller   1987 · US · Colour · 95mins

A dull sequel to Bryan Forbes's genuinely creepy *The Stepford Wives*, this time with the focus on the robotic offspring. Familiar TV faces Barbara Eden and Don Murray are the new family in town who begin to worry that the atmosphere in Stepford is just too good to be true in particular how worryingly responsible the teenagers are. It's an interesting premise but director Alan J Levi fails to find any black humour in the piece and the result is a suspense chiller devoid of both suspense and chills. ▭

Don Murray *Steven Harding* • Barbara Eden *Laura Harding* • Randall Batinkoff *David*

U = SUITABLE FOR ALL   Uc = SUITABLE FOR ALL, ESPECIALLY FOR YOUNG CHILDREN (VIDEO ONLY)   PG = PARENTAL GUIDANCE

Harding • Tammy Lauren *Mary Harding* • Richard Anderson *Lawrence Danton* • Dick Butkus *Tim Wilcox* ■ *Dir* Alan J Levi • *Scr* William Bleich

The Stepford Husbands ★★
Science-fiction thriller   1996 · US · Colour

Or a case of "Men Behaving Too Nicely". In a desperate attempt to breathe new life into a now predictable concept, this second made-for-TV sequel to 1975's *The Stepford Wives* finds women very much in control of the sinister Connecticut town. Donna Mills is the long-suffering wife trying to make a new start with her petulant husband Michael Ontkean, a novelist with writer's block. He quickly becomes suspicious of the locals' apparent contentment; Mills, meanwhile, starts to wonder if there may be something in the town's revolutionary psychiatric scheme for stroppy males. The performances are bland, as is the scare-free direction of Fred Walton.

Donna Mills *Jodi Davison* • Michael Ontkean *Mick Davison* • Sarah Douglas *Dr Frances Borzage* • Louise Fletcher *Mariam Benton* • Cindy Williams *Caroline Knox* • Joe Inscoe *Dennis Knox* • Jeffrey Pillars *Gordon Hayes* • Caitlin Clarke *Lisa Hayes* ■ *Dir* Fred Walton • *Scr* Ken Wheat, Jim Wheat

The Stepford Wives ★★★ 15
Science-fiction thriller
1975 · US · Colour · 114mins

Intelligent scripting and thoughtful direction by Bryan Forbes turn Ira Levin's bestseller about surburban housewives becoming obedient robots into an intriguing frightener highlighting society's increasing obsession with perfection. It unfolds at a measured pace so the suspenseful mystery can exert a chilling grip before it ultimately appals, and Katharine Ross and Paula Prentiss shine as the nonconformist women fighting their animatronic fate. You'll be looking at those Nanette Newman washing-up liquid commercials in a different light after this. Contains swearing and some violence. ▱

Katharine Ross *Joanna* • Paula Prentiss *Bobby* • Peter Masterson *Walter* • Nanette Newman *Carol* • Patrick O'Neal *Dale Coba* • Tina Louise *Charmaine* • Carol Rosson *Dr Fancher* ■ *Dir* Bryan Forbes • *Scr* William Goldman, from the novel by Ira Levin

Stephen King's The Night Flier ★★★
Horror thriller   1997 · US · Colour · 95mins

Based on one of Stephen King's most peculiar short stories, this involves a vampire who pilots a Cessna plane and leaves a trail of bodies in his wake. Sleazy tabloid reporter Miguel Ferrer and young rival Julie Entwisle pursue the mysterious killer. Director Mark Pavia does wonders on a small budget, making the atmosphere genuinely tense and mysterious, and gruesome when it needs to be. However, a number of questions remain unanswered, and Pavia seems content to focus on Ferrer's utterly obnoxious character.

Miguel Ferrer *Richard Dees* • Julie Entwisle *Katherine Blair* • Dan Monahan *Merton Morrison* • Michael H Moss *Dwight Renfield* • John Bennes *Ezra Hannon* • Beverly Skinner

Selida McCamon ■ *Dir* Mark Pavia • *Scr* Mark Pavia, Jack O'Donnell, from the short story by Stephen King

Stephen King's Thinner ★ 18
Horror   1996 · US · Colour · 88mins

Director Tom Holland's totally banal and pedestrian horror movie is the "thinner" end of the wedge as far as adaptations of Stephen King's books go. Robert John Burke is the grossly overweight lawyer cursed by the King of the Gypsies to fade away to nothing after killing a Romany in a hit-and-run car accident. Nothing convinces in this latex-heavy bust where the nightmare twists cause more yawns than terror. Joe Mantegna adds acting weight to the scrawny scares, but he's too little, too late. Contains swearing and violence. ▱

Robert Burke *Billy Halleck* • Joe Mantegna *Richie Ginelli* • Lucinda Jenney *Heidi Halleck* • Joy Lenz *Linda Halleck* • Time Winters *Prosecutor* • Howard Erskine *Judge Phillips* ■ *Dir* Tom Holland • *Scr* Michael McDowell, Tom Holland, from the novel by Richard Bachman [Stephen King]

Stepmom ★★★ 12
Drama   1998 · US · Colour · 119mins

Despite its unappealing title, this is an touching and sophisticated film about post-divorce family life. As the girlfriend of divorcee Ed Harris, ambitious fashion photographer Julia Roberts starts off on the wrong foot when she meets his family. Attempting to woo his two children she finds herself competing with their "perfect" mother Susan Sarandon. However, when Sarandon falls seriously ill, the women must reappraise their priorities. Strong performances, which are not afraid to be unsympathetic, and unpredictable narrative twists make this far from your average sentimental family drama and viewing requires a large quantity of tissues. ▱ **DVD**

Julia Roberts *Isabel Kelly* • Susan Sarandon *Jackie Harrison* • Ed Harris *Luke Harrison* • Jena Malone *Anna Harrison* • Liam Aiken *Ben Harrison* • Lynn Whitfield *Dr Sweikert* ■ *Dir* Chris Columbus • *Scr* Gigi Levangie, Jessie Nelson, Steven Rogers, Karen Leigh Hopkins, Ron Bass, from a story by Gigi Levangie

Steppenwolf ★★
Drama   1974 · US · Colour · 107mins

Since 1927, Herman Hesse's novel has sold millions of copies and is regarded as an intensely personal work in its portrait of the intellectual and emotional crises facing a man nudging 50. Inevitably, the response to director Fred Haines's treatment of a seemingly unfilmable book has concentrated on the success in translating it to the screen, but for most people it will emerge as a very striking film visually (belying a fairly small budget) dominated by Max von Sydow's fine performance as the questioning man. Other points of interest are the intercut animation and the spirited appearance by Pierre Clémenti, made shortly after his release from prison.

Max von Sydow *Harry* • Dominique Sanda *Hermine* • Pierre Clémenti *Pablo* • Carla Romanelli *Maria* • Roy Bosier *Aztec* • Alfred Baillou *Goethe* ■ *Dir* Fred Haines • *Scr* Fred Haines, from the novel by Hermann Hesse • *Cinematographer* Tomaslav Pinter

Stepping Out ★★★ PG
Musical drama
1991 · Can/US · Colour · 104mins

Lewis Gilbert's rather humdrum hymn to tap and shuffle, with Liza Minnelli – in a role that contains definite shades of *Cabaret's* Sally Bowles – as a Broadway hoofer attempting to transform a bunch of near-hopeless amateurs into a crack dancing troupe. All stereotypes are firmly in place, including Julie Walters as a germ-obsessed housewife and Shelley Winters as the cantankerous pianist, who rolls her eyes at every missed step. What you expect is precisely what you get from Gilbert, but, despite its obviousness, this has pockets of fun. Contains some swearing. ▱

Liza Minnelli *Mavis Turner* • Shelley Winters *Mrs Fraser* • Julie Walters *Vera* • Ellen Greene *Maxine* • Sheila McCarthy *Andy* • Bill Irwin *Geoffrey* • Carol Woods *Rose* • Robyn Stevan *Sylvia* • Jane Krakowski *Lynne* ■ *Dir* Lewis Gilbert • *Scr* Richard Harris, from his play

Stepping Razor – Red X ★★★ 18
Documentary
1992 · Can · Colour and BW · 99mins

Canadian filmmaker Nicholas Campbell does for murdered reggae star Peter Tosh what Oliver Stone did for JFK: he deconstructs his death and puts intriguing new perspectives on it. Officially Tosh, former sidekick to Bob Marley and one of reggae's undisputed greats, was killed by criminals. Campbell reckons the murder may have been politically motivated. It's intriguing stuff, marred occasionally by Campbell's contrived visuals. ▱

Dir/Scr Nicholas Campbell

The Stepsister ★ 12
Thriller   1997 · US/Can · Colour · 87mins

This preposterous TV movie makes Cinderella's family seem like *The Brady Bunch*. Newcomer Rena Sofer stars as the young heroine, a psych major who suspects her new, seemingly sweet stepmother (Linda Evans) and her seductive stepsister (Bridgette Wilson) of killing her wealthy father. When her stepmother is later found dead, her evil sibling frames her for the murder. This is a mediocre, contrived thriller with few thrills, but there's some camp fun to be had. ▱

Rena Sofer *Darcy Canfield* • Bridgette Wilson *Melinda Shaw* • Linda Evans *Joan Shaw* • Alan Rachins *Derick Canfield* ■ *Dir* Charles Correll • *Scr* Matt Dorff

Steptoe and Son ★★★ PG
Comedy   1972 · UK · Colour · 93mins

One of the better sitcom spin-offs, with regular writers Ray Galton and Alan Simpson contributing a script that not only has a half-decent story, but also gags that, while not out of the top drawer, would not have disgraced the original TV series. Wilfrid Brambell and Harry H Corbett reprise their celebrated roles to good effect, with Albert typically derisive of Harold's endearingly oafish attempts to better himself. However, here he has a stern adversary in Carolyn Seymour, Harold's new stripper-bride, whose mercenary intentions threaten the future of the

rag-and-bone yard. Not vintage, but far from a failure. ▱

Wilfrid Brambell *Albert Steptoe* • Harry H Corbett *Harold Steptoe* • Carolyn Seymour *Zita* • Arthur Howard *Vicar* • Victor Maddern *Chauffeur* • Fred Griffiths *Barman* ■ *Dir* Cliff Owen • *Scr* Ray Galton, Alan Simpson, from their TV series

Steptoe and Son Ride Again ★★ PG
Comedy   1973 · UK · Colour · 94mins

This second movie featuring the nation's favourite junkmen is very much a rags-and-bones affair, with the material stretched to fraying point to justify the running time. Apart from the unnecessary crudeness of its humour, the main problem here is the dilution of the intense, disappointed fondness that made the pair's TV relationship so engaging, in order to squeeze in a handful of sketchily-drawn characters whose sole purpose is to lend the action a big-picture feel. Wilfrid Brambell and Harry H Corbett spark occasionally, but Ray Galton and Alan Simpson's weak script finally gets the better of them. ▱

Wilfrid Brambell *Albert Steptoe* • Harry H Corbett *Harold Steptoe* • Diana Dors *Woman in flat* • Milo O'Shea *Doctor Popplewell* • Neil McCarthy *Lennie* • Bill Maynard *George* • George Tovey *Percy* • Sam Kydd *Claude* ■ *Dir* Peter Sykes • *Scr* Ray Galton, Alan Simpson, from their TV series

Stereo ★★
Science-fiction   1969 · Can · BW · 65mins

In the near future, experiments in telepathic exchange are being conducted by the Canadian Academy for Erotic Inquiry. The idea is to remove a group of volunteers' power of speech, increase their latent telepathic powers, give them aphrodisiac drugs and ultimately expose sexuality for its "polymorphous perversity". The tests result in antagonism and violence. This was David Cronenberg's directorial debut and it's a confused, distanced, but quietly disturbing cautionary tale, which introduced some of the major themes of his more mature work.

Ronald Mlodzik • Iain Ewing • Jack Messinger • Clara Mayer • Paul Mulholland • Arlene Mlodzik ■ *Dir/Scr* David Cronenberg

The Sterile Cuckoo ★★★
Romantic comedy drama
1969 · US · Colour · 107mins

An Oscar-nominated performance by Liza Minnelli, playing the sort of character who puts the "kook" into cuckoo. She's an insecure near-nutter who ropes a hapless college student into her neurotically self-centred world. Predictably, his grades go all to pot in the process. Wendell Burton beautifully plays the boy; curiously, he's been little heard of since. No such obscurity for Alan J Pakula, here making his directorial debut. The movie was released as *Pookie* in the UK – the name of Minnelli's character.

Liza Minnelli *Pookie Adams* • Wendell Burton *Jerry* • Tim McIntire *Charlie Schumacher* • Elizabeth Harrower *Landlady* • Austin Green *Pookie's father* • Sandra Faison [Sandy Faison] *Nancy Putnam* • Chris Bugbee *Roe* •

Jawn McKinley *Helen Upshaw* ▪ *Dir* Alan J Pakula • *Scr* Alvin Sargent, from the novel by John Nichols

Stevie ★★★ 15
Biographical drama
1978 · UK · Colour · 101mins

Glenda Jackson is typically terrific in this play-derived drama about a poetess living with her doting but dotty maiden aunt (Mona Washbourne, who gives Glenda a run for her money in the scene-stealing stakes). Trevor Howard narrates and co-stars. Not much happens and, as a film, *Stevie* never quite escapes its obvious stage origins. But it's an intriguing character study, and worth watching by the more culturally-inclined for the quality of the performances alone. ▫

Glenda Jackson *Stevie Smith* • Mona Washbourne *Aunt* • Alec McCowen *Freddy* • Trevor Howard *The Man* • Emma Louise Fox *Stevie as a child* ▪ *Dir* Robert Enders • *Scr* Hugh Whitmore, from his play and the works of Stevie Smith

Stick ★ 18
Crime thriller 1985 · US · Colour · 104mins

Elmore Leonard adapted his own novel about a flamboyant ex-con who goes down the vengeance trail after his best buddy is rubbed out. Set in the now familiar Leonard world of loan sharks, drug dealers and Palm Beach slimeballs with terrible taste in shirts and wallpaper, it squanders everything for the sake of making star/director Burt Reynolds a handsome, loveable rogue. Apparently, Reynolds took all the guts out of the book and reshot the ending but the result was still a critical pasting and disaster at the box-office. George Segal and Charles Durning play their parts as though auditioning for *La Cages aux Folles*. ▫

Burt Reynolds *Stick* • Candice Bergen *Kyle* • George Segal *Barry* • Charles Durning *Chucky* • Jose Perez *Rainy* • Richard Lawson *Cornell* • Castulo Guerra *Nestor* ▪ *Dir* Burt Reynolds • *Scr* Elmore Leonard, Joseph C Stinson, from the novel by Elmore Leonard

Sticky Fingers ★★★ 15
Comedy 1988 · US · Colour · 84mins

There is a wonderful air of naive debauchery and jangling nerves about this story of two flat-sharing musicians who are left holding $91,000 in a holdall. Piles of designer clothes and plentiful wild parties later, the hoods are on their trail. The film boasts lovely performances from Helen Slater and Melanie Mayron and a gloriously zany overview of immaturity and neurosis from director Catlin Adams, whose impressive first feature this was. Contains some swearing. ▫

Helen Slater *Hattie* • Melanie Mayron *Lolly* • Eileen Brennan *Stella* • Loretta Devine *Diane* • Christopher Guest *Sam* • Carol Kane *Kitty* • Stephen McHattie *Eddie* ▪ *Dir* Catlin Adams • *Scr* Catlin Adams, Melanie Mayron

The Sticky Fingers of Time ★★ 15
Science-fiction thriller
1997 · US · Colour and BW · 82mins

The basic premise of Hilary Brougher's first feature is intriguing enough, with

fifties sci-fi novelist Terumi Matthews finding her work taking her in an unexpected direction – 40 years into the future. There she meets fellow writer Nicole Zaray, who shares her mysterious time-travelling abilities and some other disturbing symptoms. However, Brougher's recurring shifts between monochrome and colour, an excess of expository chat and the introduction of other (malevolent) time-travellers make it almost impossible to maintain a grip on the plot. Clearly the intention is profundity, but the overall impression is pretension. ▫

Terumi Matthews *Tucker* • Nicole Zaray *Drew* • Belinda Becker *Ofelia* • James Urbaniak *Isaac* • Amanda Vogel *Girl in window* • Leo Marks *Dex* • Samantha Buck *Gorge* ▪ *Dir/Scr* Hilary Brougher

Stiff Upper Lips ★★★★ 15
Period drama parody
1997 · UK · Colour · 95mins

A parody (long overdue, some might feel) of the "white flannel" school of British film-making that produced the likes of *Brideshead Revisited*, *Chariots of Fire* and *Gandhi*, which are all amusingly ridiculed here by co-writer/director Gary Sinyor. Prunella Scales is delightful as the aristocratic Aunt Agnes, who takes her soppy family on a Grand Tour, during which many awful mishaps occur. A genuinely witty script, and locations in Italy and India, make one forget that the joke could have been made in a three-minute television sketch. A marvellous cast does not include producer Ismael Merchant, who refused a part – as a merchant.

Peter Ustinov *Horace* • Prunella Scales *Aunt Agnes Ivory* • Georgina Cates *Emily Ivory* • Samuel West *Edward Ivory* • Sean Pertwee *George* • Brian Glover *Eric* • Frank Finlay *Hudson Junior* ▪ *Dir* Gary Sinyor • *Scr* Paul Simpkin, Gary Sinyor

Stigmata ★★★ 18
Supernatural thriller
1999 · US · Colour · 102mins

The Exorcist meets *Carrie* in this dumb but fun religious horror. Patricia Arquette is the atheist hairdresser who suddenly starts suffering from vicious stigmata – wounds identical to the ones Christ received on the cross – which, understandably, hinder her ability to give a good cut and blow-dry. When Vatican priest Gabriel Byrne is sent to investigate, he realises there are more to her gory wounds than meets the eye – especially when she starts spouting a strange tongue which may be the true language of Christ. A booming soundtrack (from Billy Corgan of the Smashing Pumpkins), flashy images and pop video-style direction by Rupert Wainwright add to the film's frenetic feel, while diverting us from some of the less plausible plot twists. Silly, loud and gruesome, yet strangely entertaining. ▫ *DVD*

Patricia Arquette *Frankie Paige* • Gabriel Byrne *Father Andrew Kiernan* • Jonathan Pryce *Cardinal Daniel Houseman* • Nia Long *Donna Chadway* • Thomas Kopache *Father Durning* • Rade Sherbedgia *Marion Petrocelli* • Enrico Colantoni *Father Dario* • Dick Latessa *Father Gianni Delmonico* ▪ *Dir* Rupert Wainwright • *Scr* Tom Lazarus, Rick Ramage, from a story by Tom Lazarus

Still Crazy ★★★★ 15
Comedy 1998 · US/UK · Colour · 91mins

Fans of the superb rockumentary *This Is Spinal Tap* will chortle at this nineties British take on the theme. Ageing rockers Jimmy Nail, Timothy Spall, Stephen Rea and Bill Nighy (along with roadie Billy Connolly) reform the successful seventies group Strange Fruit to go on the road one more time. There are all the clashing egos, old grudges and bad rock numbers you'd expect, plus a deft script from comedy writers Dick Clement and Ian La Frenais, but the true plaudits should go to the performances from Nighy (as the narcissistic lead singer) and Bruce Robinson (writer/director of *Withnail and I*) in a strangely moving cameo role. Contains swearing. ▫ *DVD*

Stephen Rea *Tony Costello* • Billy Connolly *Hughie* • Jimmy Nail *Les Wickes* • Timothy Spall *Beano Baggot* • Bill Nighy *Ray Simms* • Juliet Aubrey *Karen Knowles* • Bruce Robinson *Brian Lovell* • Phil Daniels *Neil Gaydon* • Frances Barber *Woman in black* • Phil Davis [Philip Davis] *Limo driver* • Zoë Ball *Zoë* ▪ *Dir* Brian Gibson • *Scr* Dick Clement, Ian La Frenais

Still Not Quite Human ★★
Science-fiction comedy
1992 · US · Colour · 90mins

This is the third installment of a low-tech Disney trilogy about a scientist father (Alan Thicke) and his android son. In this chapter, the son must join forces with other androids to free his eccentric father from an evil industrialist who has kidnapped him. Although there's nothing particularly memorable here, and it's arguably the weakest of the three *Not Quite Human* movies, there's probably enough solid light entertainment to amuse an adolescent audience.

Alan Thicke *Dr Jonas Carson/Bonus* • Jay Underwood *Chip* • Betsy Palmer *Aunt Mildred* • Christopher Neame *Dr Frederick Berrigon* • Sheelah Megill *Miss Prism* • Rosa Nevin *Officer Kate Morgan* ▪ *Dir/Scr* Eric Luke

Still of the Night ★★★★
Thriller 1982 · US · Colour · 90mins

Occasionally as tense as *Jagged Edge*, with dramatic moments reminiscent of medium-grade Hitchcock, this nonetheless never quite cuts the mustard as true suspense. On-the-move Meryl Streep stays still just long enough to enthral psychiatrist Roy Scheider, one of whose patients winds up dead, in director Robert Benton's moral tale, which proclaims doctors should not mix business and pleasure. For all its flaws in plotting, it's a sleekly crafted movie with acting to suit its literacy, and style to match both. Contains some violence. ▫

Roy Scheider *Sam Rice* • Meryl Streep *Brooke Reynolds* • Jessica Tandy *Grace Rice* • Joe Grifasi *Joe Vitucci* • Sara Botsford *Gail Phillips* • Josef Sommer *George Bynum* • Irving Metzman *Murray* ▪ *Dir* Robert Benton • *Scr* Robert Benton, from a story by David Newman, Robert Benton

Stillwatch ★★ 15
Supernatural thriller
1987 · US · Colour · 93mins

This entertaining supernatural mystery, based on the novel by genre queen Mary Higgins Clark, stars the always watchable Angie Dickinson and ex-Wonder Woman Lynda Carter. The two women – TV reporter Carter and the senator she is profiling – get involved in spooky doings in the journalist's Washington flat, the site of an old murder. This well-worn formula is given a fresh feel thanks to taut direction by Rod Holcomb and campy performances by the lady leads. Despite a hokey ending, it's a fun TV movie. ▫

Angie Dickinson *Senator Abigail Winslow* • Lynda Carter *Patricia Traymore* • Don Murray *Sam Kingsley* • Barry Primus *Toby Wilson* • Louise Latham *Lila Thatcher* • Stuart Whitman *Luther Pelham* ▪ *Dir* Rod Holcomb • *Scr* Laird Koenig, David Peckinpah, from the novel by Mary Higgins Clark

The Sting ★★★★★ PG
Comedy drama 1973 · US · Colour · 123mins

These things rarely come off, but the reteaming of *Butch Cassidy and the Sundance Kid* stars Paul Newman and Robert Redford with its director George Roy Hill proved to be a glorious triumph. The period romp raced away with seven Oscars. Newman and Redford are the two con men who, after the death of an old chum, set about fleecing dangerous mobster Robert Shaw out of a fortune. The sting itself is as audacious as it is elaborate, but the real pleasure comes from the easy, charismatic playing of the two leads, the lovingly created thirties settings and Marvin Hamlisch's inspired reworking of Scott Joplin's music. The excellent supporting cast includes Charles Durning, Eileen Brennan and Ray Walston. Contains some swearing. ▫ *DVD*

Paul Newman *Henry Gondorff* • Robert Redford *Johnny Hooker* • Robert Shaw *Doyle Lonnegan* • Charles Durning *Lt William Snyder* • Ray Walston *JJ Singleton* • Eileen Brennan *Billie* • Harold Gould *Kid Twist* • John Heffernan *Eddie Niles* ▪ *Dir* George Roy Hill • *Scr* David S Ward • *Costume Designer* Edith Head • *Cinematographer* Robert Surtees • *Art Director* Henry Bumstead • *Music* Scott Joplin

The Sting II ★★ PG
Comedy 1983 · US · Colour · 97mins

Proof that lightning never strikes twice (except in the case of *The Godfather, Part II*), this was the belated and unnecessary sequel to George Roy Hill's multi-Oscar-winning hit. Robert Redford and Paul Newman's scam on gangster Robert Shaw is reprised as a boxing set-up, with Jackie Gleason and Mac Davis as their inadequate replacements. Despite the presence of Oliver Reed and Karl Malden, it's Teri Garr who wins on all counts. ▫

Jackie Gleason *Gondorff* • Mac Davis *Hooker* • Teri Garr *Veronica* • Karl Malden *Macalinski* • Oliver Reed *Lonnegan* ▪ *Dir* Jeremy Paul Kagan • *Scr* David S Ward

Stir Crazy ★★★ 15
Comedy 1980 · US · Colour · 106mins

As Sidney Poitier's direction and a firm script all but vanish beneath the clowning, Richard Pryor and Gene

Wilder (again playing the cynic and the innocent) are, according to your taste, either highly creative or contrived, witty or noisy, inspired or tedious. Relying more on mugging than acting (especially in the second half), they play a couple of goons who leave New York for California and are wrongly imprisoned for a bank robbery en route. To give the film its due, prison clichés are cleverly lampooned and Pryor's chicken scene is one that will last. Contains some violence and swearing.

Gene Wilder *Skip Donahue* • Richard Pryor *Harry Monroe* • Georg Stanford Brown *Rory Schultebrand* • JoBeth Williams *Meredith* • Miguel Angel Suarez *Jesus Ramirez* • Craig T Nelson *Deputy Ward Wilson* • Barry Corbin *Warden Walter Beatty* • Charles Weldon *Blade* ■ *Dir* Sidney Poitier • *Scr* Bruce Jay Friedman

Stir of Echoes ★★★ 15

Supernatural thriller
1999 · US · Colour · 99mins

In the US, David Koepp's creepy supernatural tale was completely overshadowed by *The Sixth Sense*. However, while it isn't as smart or satisfying, it delivers a handful of extremely frightening moments and a credible performance from Kevin Bacon as a man haunted by startling visions. Using jolting cuts and stylised camerawork to evoke fear rather than contemporary, effects-driven shocks, Koepp immerses the audience in an atmospheric mystery involving hypnotism, psychic powers, a dead girl and Bacon's son, who seems to share his "gift". The film's biggest flaw is an overcooked final half hour, as Bacon's obsessive, destructive hunt for answers becomes slightly ludicrous. The last scene is a real chiller, though.

Kevin Bacon *Tom Witzky* • Kathryn Erbe *Maggie Witzky* • Illeana Douglas *Lisa* • Liza Weil *Debbie Kozac, the babysitter* • Kevin Dunn *Frank McCarthy* • Conor O'Farrell *Harry Damon* • Jenny Morrison *Samantha* ■ *Dir* David Koepp • *Scr* David Koepp, from the novel by Richard Matheson

A Stitch in Time ★★ U

Comedy 1963 · UK · BW · 90mins

Norman Wisdom relives a little of his youth in this hopelessly sentimental comedy, as his first job at just 13 was as a delivery boy. This was his final film in black and white and also his last big starring success at the box office, for he belonged to a more innocent age. The script sticks closely to the winning Wisdom formula and he knots his cap in confused shyness in his attempts to declare his love for a pretty nurse. Stalwart stooges Edward Chapman (Mr Grimsdale, of course) and Jerry Desmonde prove once more that straight men can often be much funnier than the comics.

Norman Wisdom *Norman Pitkin* • Edward Chapman *Grimsdale* • Jeannette Sterke *Janet Haskell* • Jerry Desmonde *Sir Hector Hardcastle* • Jill Melford *Lady Brinkley* • Glyn Houston *Welsh* • Hazel Hughes *Matron* ■ *Dir* Robert Asher • *Scr* Jack Davies, Norman Wisdom, Henry Blyth, Eddie Leslie

Stock Car ★ U

Drama 1955 · UK · BW · 66mins

At various stages during his career Wolf Rilla proved himself to be a highly competent director, notably with his chilling version of *Village of the Damned*. That makes this road smash of a picture all the more disappointing. It packs in every kind of quota quickie cliché, as plucky garage owner Rona Anderson turns to dashing driving ace Paul Carpenter to help her repulse the threat of a charlatan creditor. The mediocrity is unrelenting, with the race sequences every bit as hackneyed as the risible melodrama.

Paul Carpenter *Larry Duke* • Rona Anderson *Katie Glebe* • Harry Fowler *Monty Albright* • Paul Whitsun-Jones *Turk McNeil* • Susan Shaw *Gina* • Robert Rietty *Roberto* • Alma Taylor *Nurse Sprott* ■ *Dir* Wolf Rilla • *Scr* AR Rawlinson, Victor Lyndon

Stockade ★★★ 15

Drama 1991 · US · Colour · 93mins

Sheen family projects tend to be more serious fare than usual (think of 1996's *The War at Home*) and this is no exception. In this gripping but talky drama, dad Martin is in the director's chair and also has a co-starring role, alongside son Charlie. There's even a part for a less well-known member of the family, Ramon Estevez. Sheen Jr plays a reluctant soldier sentenced to a term in a military stockade, where he gets locked into a dangerous battle of wills with a cruel NCO, played by Sheen Sr. This is solid if slightly familiar entertainment. Contains swearing and violence.

Charlie Sheen *Franklin Bean Jr* • Martin Sheen *Sergeant Otis V McKinney* • Larry Fishburne [Laurence Fishburne] *Stokes* • Blu Mankuma *Spoonman (Bryce)* • Michael Beach *Webb* • Harry Stewart *Sweetbread (Crane)* • John Toles-Bey *Lawrence* • James Marshall *Lamar* • Ramon Estevez *Gessner* • F Murray Abraham *Garcia* ■ *Dir* Martin Sheen • *Scr* Dennis Schryack, Martin Sheen, from the novel *Count a Lonely Cadence* by Gordon Weaver

Stolen Babies ★★★ PG

Drama based on a true story
1993 · US · Colour · 90mins

Former *St Elsewhere* actor Eric Laneuville directed this often gripping fact-based tale about a woman who tried to expose an illegal adoption ring in the forties. Lea Thompson (*Back to the Future*) is the Memphis welfare worker looking after abused and neglected children, who's introduced to a respected woman (Mary Tyler Moore) who runs an adoption agency with a hidden secret. Although Thompson is impressive, it is Moore who steals the show, proving that not only has she left her dippy sixties' image behind, but her mesmerising, hard-as-nails performance in *Ordinary People* was not a one-off.

Lea Thompson *Annie Beales* • Mary Tyler Moore *Georgia Tann* • Kathleen Quinlan *Bekka Stern* • Mary Nell Santacroce *Judge Camille Kelley* • Tom Nowicki *Bascom Stern* • Sam Waterston *Governor Gordon Browning* ■ *Dir* Eric Laneuville • *Scr* Sharon Elizabeth Doyle

The Stolen Children ★★★★ 15

Drama 1992 · It/Fr/Swe · Colour · 110mins

This heart-warming if occasionally sentimental story was inspired by a newspaper headline. In addition to highlighting a range of social issues, director Gianni Amelio also coaxes a quite remarkable performance from Valentina Scalici, as an 11-year-old Sicilian girl who is sent to an orphanage after her desperate mother sells her into prostitution in Milan. Enrico Lo Verso is equally impressive as the inexperienced cop escorting the girl and her younger brother, making his growing affection for them seem inevitable when it could so easily have looked contrived. In Italian with English subtitles.

Enrico Lo Verso *Antonio* • Valentina Scalici *Rosetta* • Giuseppe Ieracitano *Luciano* • Renato Carpentieri *Marshal* • Vitalba Andrea *Antonio's sister* • Fabio Alessandrini *Grignani* ■ *Dir* Gianni Amelio • *Scr* Sandro Petraglia, Stefano Rulli, Gianni Amelio

Stolen Face ★★

Drama 1952 · UK · BW · 71mins

Take this early Hammer melodrama with a ton of salt and you may enjoy its wild fantasy about sexual obsession and the incredible achievements of plastic surgery. Two forties stars, past their prime, were dragged to Britain to boost international sales. Surgeon Paul Henreid falls in love with pianist Lizabeth Scott. Thwarted in his desire, he gives Scott's face to a woman convict (not a good move). Scott has fun playing both *femme* roles, one good, one bad but fans may detect in this tosh the themes that director Terence Fisher later developed in his *Frankenstein* films.

Paul Henreid *Dr Philip Ritter* • Lizabeth Scott *Alice Brent/Lilly* • André Morell *David* • Mary Mackenzie *Lilly* • John Wood *Dr Jack Wilson* • Susan Stephen *Betty* • Arnold Ridley *Dr Russell* ■ *Dir* Terence Fisher • *Scr* Martin Berkeley, Richard Landau

Stolen Hearts ★★ 15

Romantic comedy
1996 · US · Colour · 91mins

Sandra Bullock has little to do in this romantic comedy caper but look gorgeous, leaving her co-star, American stand-up comedian Denis Leary, with the lion's share of the movie. Unfortunately, Leary's trademark put-downs are not enough to carry the film. He's a petty thief who steals a Matisse painting and goes on the run with his girlfriend (Bullock), holing up in a rich New England neighbourhood where the white-trash twosome stand out like sore thumbs. The film shows some glimmers of sarcastic potential and makes the point that art's often more to do with money than talent, but co-writer Leary's ego ultimately gets in the way. Contains swearing.

Denis Leary *Frank* • Sandra Bullock *Roz* • Stephen Dillane *Evan Marsh* • Yaphet Kotto *O'Malley* • Mike Starr *Fitzie* • Jonathan Tucker *Todd* • Wayne Robson *Beano* • Michael Badalucco *Quinn* ■ *Dir* Bill Bennett • *Scr* Denis Leary, Mike Armstrong, from a story by Denis Leary, Mike Armstrong, Ann Lembeck

Stolen Hours ★★ U

Drama 1963 · UK/US · Colour · 96mins

This glossy British remake of *Dark Victory* is a pale imitation of the Bette Davis classic. Susan Hayward – no stranger to screen hardship – is an American socialite with a terminal illness who falls for her doctor (Michael Craig). It's a worthy production, but the Davis original is too indelible to forget. Cult jazz trumpeter Chet Baker makes a brief appearance, playing himself.

Susan Hayward *Laura Pember* • Michael Craig *Dr John Carmody* • Diane Baker *Ellen Pember* • Edward Judd *Mike Bannerman* • Paul Rogers *Dr Eric McKenzie* • Robert Bacon *Peter* • Chet Baker ■ *Dir* Daniel Petrie • *Scr* Jessamyn West, Joseph Hayes, from the play *Dark Victory* by George Brewer Jr, Bertram Block

Stolen Kisses ★★★★★

Romantic comedy 1968 · Fr · Colour · 90mins

After *The 400 Blows* and the *Antoine et Colette* episode of *Love at Twenty*, Truffaut catches up with Antoine Doinel as he leaves the army and becomes a private eye. Hired by shoeshop owner Michel Lonsdale to find out why the employees hate him, Doinel falls madly in love with Lonsdale's wife (Delphine Seyrig), while trying to remain faithful to his girlfriend (Claude Jade). Once again, Doinel is played to perfection by Jean-Pierre Léaud. The scene in which he sits in front of a mirror and chants the names of the two women in his life is a wonderful image of romantic obsession. Add some engaging subplots and a bit of Hitchcockian mischief with a man in a raincoat, and you have one of Truffaut's greatest movies, a slight but utterly magical romantic comedy set in the Paris of our dreams. A French language film.

Jean-Pierre Léaud *Antoine Doinel* • Delphine Seyrig *Fabienne Tabard* • Claude Jade *Christine Darbon* • Michel Lonsdale *Monsieur Tabard* • Harry-Max *Monsieur Henri* • André Falcon *Monsieur Blady* ■ *Dir* François Truffaut • *Scr* François Truffaut, Claude de Givray, Bernard Revon

A Stolen Life ★★★

Melodrama 1946 · US · BW · 107mins

The great Bette Davis sometimes struggled to find vehicles worthy of her talent, but even in this relatively creaky melodrama, which is the only film she ever produced, she conveys the marvellous sense of the dramatics that made her a Hollywood great. Her star quality is particularly evident as she plays twins (one good, one bad), but unfortunately the men in the cast aren't up to her standard. Although one of America's most popular stars after playing opposite Rita Hayworth in the same year's *Gilda*, Glenn Ford is callow and uninteresting. Both Dane Clark and Bruce Bennett offer period good looks and suits, and do what little the script allows them to do well. But, frankly, a Warner Bros studio-bound New England fools nobody, and neither does this plot.

Bette Davis *Kate Bosworth/Pat Bosworth* • Glenn Ford *Bill Emerson* • Dane Clark *Karnock* • Walter Brennan *Eben Folgor* • Charles Ruggles *Freddie Lindley* • Bruce Bennett *Jack Talbot* • Peggy Knudsen *Diedra* ■ *Dir* Curtis Bernhardt • *Scr* Catherine Turney, Margaret Buell Wilder, from the novel by Karel J Benes

Stompin' at the Savoy ★★★ PG

Drama 1992 · US · Colour · 91mins

No, not London's grand hotel but Harlem's Savoy Ballroom, where four black domestic workers in the late thirties spend time dancing their troubles away. Loosely based around the lives of scriptwriter Beverly M Sawyer's mother and her sisters, who left North Carolina for New York's glittering pavements, it's a TV movie with more dramatic charm than most. □

Lynn Whitfield *Esther Tolbert* • Vanessa L Williams *Pauline Richardson* • Vanessa Bell Calloway *Dorothy Fanroy* • Jasmine Guy *Alice Nichols* • Mario Van Peebles *Walter* • Michael Warren *Calvin Hunter* ■ *Dir* Debbie Allen • *Scr* Beverly M Sawyer

The Stone Boy ★★★★

Drama 1984 · US · Colour · 93mins

Robert Duvall, Frederic Forrest and Glenn Close head the terrific cast of this powerful rural drama. Young Arnold Hillerman (Jason Presson) accidentally shoots and kills his older brother (played by TV Superman Dean Cain), then has to cope alone with the trauma of it after his farming family retreat into their own private grief. This is one of those rare films that seems quietly and accurately to convey the emotions of true tragedy. However, it's rarely shown these days, maybe because it's deemed a bit too downbeat for audiences who want uplifting escapism. It remains a fine ensemble piece and well worth watching out for.

Robert Duvall *Joe Hillerman* • Jason Presson *Arnold Hillerman* • Frederic Forrest *Andy Jansen* • Glenn Close *Ruth Hillerman* • Wilford Brimley *George Jansen* • Gail Youngs *Lu Jansen* • Cindy Fisher *Amalie* • Dean Cain *Eugene Hillerman* ■ *Dir* Christopher Cain • *Scr* Gina Berriault, from her novel

Stone Cold ★★ 18

Action thriller 1991 · US · Colour · 88mins

Former football player Brian Bosworth started his new thespian career in this bubble-brained action movie that required some cuts before obtaining an R rating in the US. There is still more than enough violence and mayhem to satisfy action fans, though its frequent heavy-handedness and perversely cruel tone may cause some misgivings. Bosworth is a cop, working undercover with the FBI to infiltrate Lance Henriksen's biker/white militant gang. He seems to be taking it all very seriously, but viewers may find they need to suspend their critical faculties to enjoy this one.

Brian Bosworth *Joe Huff/John Stone* • Lance Henriksen *Chains Cooper* • William Forsythe *Ice* • Arabella Holzbog *Nancy* • Sam McMurray *Lance* • Richard Gant *Cunningham* ■ *Dir* Craig R Baxley • *Scr* Walter Doniger

Stone Cold Dead ★

Thriller 1980 · Can · Colour · 97mins

An inert TV thriller, this stars Richard Crenna as the cop investigating the serial killing of prostitutes, whose photograph is taken as they die. Directed by George Mendeluk, from Hugh Garner's novel *The Sin Sniper*, it has occasional moments of invention, but on the whole possesses all the vitality of a corpse.

Richard Crenna *Detective Sgt Boyd* • Paul Williams *Julius Kurtz* • Linda Sorenson *Monica Page* • Belinda J Montgomery *Sandy Macauley* • Charles Shamata [Chuck Shamata] *Sgt Tony*

Colabre ■ *Dir* George Mendeluk • *Scr* George Mendeluk, from the novel *The Sin Sniper* by Hugh Garner

The Stone Killer ★★ 18

Action thriller 1973 · US · Colour · 91mins

A Michael Winner film starring Charles Bronson immediately conjures up an image of violence. Both men live up to expectations in this nasty movie. Bronson plays a former New York cop now working in LA, who is almost indistinguishable from the killers he's trying to track down. As usual, he's notionally on the side of the good guys, but an unknowing audience could easily be fooled. The only thing this film has going for it is the rather bizarre plot, involving gangsters hiring combat-trained Vietnam veterans to settle a long-standing Mafia feud. Stomach-churning and predictable. Contains swearing, violence and nudity. □

Charles Bronson *Detective Lou Torrey* • Martin Balsam *Al Vescari* • David Sheiner *Detective Guido Lorenz* • Norman Fell *Detective Les Daniels* • Ralph Waite *Detective Mathews* • Eddie Firestone *George Armitage, the junkie* • Walter Burke *JD* ■ *Dir* Michael Winner • *Scr* Gerald Wilson, from the novel *A Complete State of Death* by John Gardner

Stone Pillow ★★

Drama 1985 · US · Colour · 100mins

The most noteworthy aspect of this TV movie is that it features famed comedian Lucille Ball in a rare dramatic role as an elderly New York City bag lady. Ball befriends a social worker (Daphne Zuniga), who's posing as a homeless person herself, and teaches her about life on the streets. While the film deals with an important issue, it is given somewhat superficial treatment, not enhanced by Ball who – despite the rags, bags, and ratty dark hair – has trouble overcoming her image as the loveable funny Lucy. Director George Schaefer does the best he can with an average script.

Lucille Ball *Florabelle* • Daphne Zuniga *Carrie Lang* • William Converse-Roberts *Max* • Stephen Lang *Tim* • Susan Batson *Ruby* • Anna Maria Horsford *Collins* ■ *Dir* George Schaefer • *Scr* Rose Leiman Goldemberg

Stones for Ibarra ★★★★ PG

Drama 1988 · US · Colour · 96mins

Based on the bestselling novel by Harriett Doerr, this is a thoughtful and often moving drama about a San Francisco couple who move to a small Mexican village to reopen a copper mine, only to have their dreams turn sour when the husband learns he is suffering from cancer. Glenn Close and Keith Carradine give restrained and touching performances; they are well supported by co-star Alfonso Arau, now better known as the director of *Like Water for Chocolate* and *A Walk in the Clouds*. Simple but poignant stuff. Contains violence. □

Glenn Close *Sara Everton* • Keith Carradine *Richard Everton* • Alfonso Arau *Chuy Santos* • Ray Oriel *Domingo Garcia* • Trinidad Silva *Basilio Garcia* ■ *Dir* Jack Gold • *Scr* Ernest Kinoy, from the novel by Harriett Doerr

Stonewall ★★ 15

Drama 1995 · UK · Colour · 94mins

The credentials for this film couldn't have been better, with co-producer Christine Vachon already responsible for the independent hits *Swoon* and *Go Fish*, and director Nigel Finch having made a string of imaginative TV documentaries. However, the decision to introduce a fictional love story into this re-creation of the infamous 1969 riot at the Stonewall Inn in Greenwich Village was a serious misjudgement. It constantly clouds the issue and deflects from the more serious purpose of examining the penalties and prejudices suffered by the gay community in those pre-liberation days. The cast looks good but, sadly, lacks the necessary acting ability. Contains swearing. □

Guillermo Diaz *La Miranda* • Frederick Weller *Matty Dean* • Brendan Corbalis *Ethan* • Duane Boutté *Bostonia* • Bruce MacVittie *Vinnie* • Peter Ratray *Burt* • Dwight Ewell *Helen Wheels* ■ *Dir* Nigel Finch • *Scr* Rikki Beadle Blair, from the book by Martin Duberman

A Stoning in Fulham County ★★

Drama 1988 · US · Colour · 96mins

Although he is as able to evoke the cultural and religious detail of the Amish as Peter Weir did in *Witness*, director Larry Elikann lacks Weir's dynamism and so sadly keeps his characters and ideas at arm's length in this TV movie. As a result, despite decent acting, the drama never really begins to bite. There is, however, a certain fascination in the intricacies of Amish morality. After an infant is killed, no one will testify against those responsible, secular courts being a no-go zone for the Amish community.

Ken Olin *Jim Sandler* • Jill Eikenberry *Susan Sandler* • Ron Perlman *Jacob Shuler* • Maureen Mueller *Sarah Shuler* • Olivia Burnette *Rachel Shuler* • Peter Michael Goetz *Homer Keller* • Gregg Henry *Sheriff Steve Woodman* ■ *Dir* Larry Elikann • *Scr* Jud Kinberg, Jackson Gillis, from a story by Jackson Gillis

The Stooge ★★★ U

Musical comedy 1951 · US · BW · 100mins

This clever and perhaps prescient Dean Martin and Jerry Lewis vehicle sees Martin showing a marked antipathy to his partner – the titular stooge. Not a natural comedy, this movie was filmed in 1951 but released some time later, when Paramount realised they had no need for damage limitation as far as their money-spinning top comedy team was concerned. There's also a brilliant character study from Eddie Mayehoff, while Polly Bergen proves an attractive foil. With hindsight, it looks as though reality was intruding on the popular comedy team, as the Dino character learns how important his stooge is to his career. It wasn't until until after *Pardners* that the paying public became aware of the truth.

Dean Martin *Bill Miller* • Jerry Lewis *Ted Rogers* • Polly Bergen *Mary Turner* • Marion Marshall *Frecklehead Tait* • Eddie Mayehoff *Leo Lyman* • Richard Erdman *Ben Bailey* ■ *Dir*

Norman Taurog • *Scr* Fred F Finklehoffe, Martin Rackin, Elwood Ullman, from a story by Fred F Finklehoffe, Sid Silvers

Stop at Nothing ★★★ 15

Drama 1991 · US · Colour · 94mins

Hill Street Blues star Veronica Hamel heads the cast of this superior TV movie, as a woman inspired by her own childhood experiences to rescue victims of abuse. Seeking to prevent her from returning a young girl to her mother is private eye Lindsay Frost, who has been hired by the child's father. With the exception of Aline Issermann's *A Shadow of Doubt*, few films have tackled the topic of child abuse with the necessary tact and insight, but director Chris Thomson steers clear of sensationalism, as he seeks to show that abuse cases are not always cut and dried. □

Veronica Hamel *Nettie Forbes* • Lindsay Frost *Parrish* • Annabella Price *Glenna Howard* • Robert Desiderio *Sgt Jake Morris* • Joseph Hacker *James Howard* • Caroline McWilliams *AJ Parkes* • Lou Beatty Jr *Sergeant Wade* ■ *Dir* Chris Thomson • *Scr* Stephen W Johnson

Stop Making Sense ★★★★ PG

Concert documentary
1984 · US · Colour · 87mins

Building from an image of a single pair of white sneakers into a sublime, almost surreal display of cerebral rock, this is simply one of the finest concert films ever made. Yet this enviable achievement isn't down to the understated direction of Jonathan Demme or the subtle photography of *Blade Runner* cameraman Jordan Cronenweth. What makes this such a memorable experience is the ingenuity of Talking Heads front man David Byrne. In addition to writing and giving a mesmerising performance of the 16 songs on the soundtrack, he also designed the show, which includes some wonderfully atmospheric shadow mime sequences, played out on a triptych screen behind the minimalist stage. □ *DVD*

Dir Jonathan Demme • *Scr* David Byrne

Stop! or My Mom Will Shoot ★ PG

Action comedy 1992 · US · Colour · 83mins

The comedy that finally seemed to convince Sylvester Stallone that he wasn't really very funny; after this he was back to the action-adventure genre with *Cliffhanger*. This is an inane, woefully joke-free example of Hollywood conceptualising and very little else. Stallone is the tough detective whose life is ruined when his fussy, dotty mother Estelle Getty turns up to stay with him. Director Roger Spottiswoode once looked set for great things, but he makes a mess of the uneasy mixture of comedy and action here – although the dire script hardly helps. Contains swearing. □

Sylvester Stallone *Joe Bomowski* • Estelle Getty *Tutti* • JoBeth Williams *Gwen Harper* • Roger Rees *Parnell* • Martin Ferrero *Paulie* • Gailard Sartain *Munroe* • John Wesley *Tony* • Al Fann *Lou* ■ *Dir* Roger Spottiswoode • *Scr* Blake Snyder, William Osborne, William Davies

Stop the World, I Want to Get Off ★★

Musical 1966 · UK · Colour and BW · 99mins

"What kind of fool am I?" bawls Tony Tanner, and what kind of musical is this, you might ask. It's a listless version of the Broadway and West End hit by Anthony Newley and Leslie Bricusse, which goes all allegorical as it recounts the ups and downs of its everyman hero Littlechap (Tanner), and is only kick-started into some sort of life by the delectable Millicent Martin. Too self-pitying for long-term tolerance, it was remade in 1978 as *Sammy Stops the World*, with Sammy Davis Jr. Contains swearing.

Tony Tanner *Littlechap* • Millicent Martin *Evie/ Anya/Ara/Ginnie* • Leila Croft *Susan* • Valerie Croft *Jane* • Neil Hawley *Little Littlechap* • Graham Lyons *Father-in-law* ■ *Dir* Philip Saville • *Scr* Anthony Newley, Leslie Bricusse, David Donable, Al Ham, Marilyn Bergman, Alan Bergman, from the play by Anthony Newley, Leslie Bricusse

Stop, You're Killing Me ★★★

Musical comedy 1952 · US · Colour · 86mins

No studio remade its product more frequently than Warner Bros, invariably only changing the setting, or adding colour and songs. This is an update of a marvellous Damon Runyon/Howard Lindsay play called *A Slight Case of Murder*, which in 1938 became one of Edward G Robinson's most popular film vehicles. Broderick Crawford, though personable, is no substitute for Edward G, who could easily have reprised his original role in this remake. The film certainly doesn't need its musical moments. Nevertheless, the basic plot premise is still amusing and there's a nice piece of casting in the wonderful Margaret Dumont as the unlucky discoverer of the body at the climax.

Broderick Crawford *Remy Marko* • Claire Trevor *Nora Marko* • Virginia Gibson *Mary Marko* • Bill Hayes *Chance Whitelaw* • Margaret Dumont *Mrs Whitelaw* • Howard St John *Mahoney* • Charles Cantor *Mike* ■ *Dir* Roy Del Ruth • *Scr* James O'Hanlon, from the play *A Slight Case of Murder* by Damon Runyon, Howard Lindsay

Stopover Forever ★

Thriller 1964 · UK · BW · 59mins

This amateur-hour B-movie stars Ann Bell as an air hostess who becomes convinced that she's the target for a killer when she swaps flights at the last moment and her replacement is murdered. Wandering round Sicily, she suspects in turn: her married lover; a cop whose wife she killed in a car crash; a pilot; and an American millionaire and whips herself up into a paranoid frenzy in the process. Director Frederic Goode takes some nice holiday snaps of Sicily's beaches, ancient ruins and bustling carnival, but the acting is distinctly ropey and the final twist can't save a woeful story.

Ann Bell *Sue Chambers* • Anthony Bate *Trevor Graham* • Conrad Phillips *Eric Cunningham* • Bruce Boa *Freddie* • Julian Sherrier *Captain Carlos Mordente* ■ *Dir* Frederic Goode • *Scr* David Osborne

Stopover Tokyo ★★ U

Spy drama 1957 · US · Colour · 100mins

Screenwriter Richard Breen co-wrote the Oscar-winning script for 1953's *Titanic* and directed just one picture, this spy drama about double- and triple-crossing in Tokyo. Robert Wagner is likeable but also a bit lightweight as the counter-espionage agent who may – or may not – be protecting the US Ambassador. He finds time for a romance with Joan Collins but things get rather hard to follow without much compensation in the acting or the action. [video]

Robert Wagner *Mark Fannon* • Joan Collins *Tina* • Edmond O'Brien *George Underwood* • Ken Scott *Tony Barrett* • Reiko Oyama *Koko* • Larry Keating *High Commissioner* ■ *Dir* Richard L Breen • *Scr* Richard L Breen, Walter Reisch, from the novel by John P Marquand

Storefront Hitchcock ★★★ 12

Concert movie 1998 · US · Colour · 77mins

A mix of alfresco music and off-the-wall musings from eccentric British songster Robyn Hitchcock. The film is directed by Jonathan Demme, of *The Silence of the Lambs* fame. He's a big Robyn Hitchcock fan, and patently regarded this small-scale spot of whimsy as a welcome change from the high-pressure world of big-bucks Hollywood film-making. Incidentally, new-ager Hitchcock is also one of the UK's leading authorities on ancient stone circles, ley lines and the like.

Dir Jonathan Demme

The Stork Club ★★★ U

Musical comedy 1945 · US · BW · 98mins

A lightweight frivolity that is at once a major plug for the legendary Manhattan nightspot, and a showcase for the energetic talents of Betty Hutton, who sings half-a-dozen made-to-order numbers. The plot has Stork Club hat-check girl Hutton saving a shabby tramp (Barry Fitzgerald) from drowning and being rewarded for her good deed when he turns out to be a millionaire. He sets her up in luxury, which causes a problem with her musician boyfriend (Don DeFore) when he returns from a trip. Don't expect any plot twists, just go along with this easy-going ride.

Betty Hutton *Judy Peabody* • Barry Fitzgerald *JB Bates* • Don DeFore *Danny Wilton* • Robert Benchley *Tom Curtis* • Bill Goodwin *Sherman Billingsley* • Iris Adrian *Gwen* • Mikhail Rasumny *Coretti* • Mary Young *Mrs Edith Bates* ■ *Dir* Hal Walker • *Scr* BG De Sylva, John McGowan

The Storm ★★

Drama 1938 · US · BW · 75mins

Formula storytelling has Charles Bickford as the burly ship's radio operator who looks out for Tom Brown as his kid brother and gets the wrong idea about his girl, played by Nan Grey. Barton MacLane is the reckless skipper who lets Bickford's pal, Preston Foster, die at sea. It's a short trip, but in its favour, the film is never dull – with brawls, fires, shipwrecks, storms and an emergency appendectomy following each other in quick succession.

Charles Bickford *Bob Roberts* • Barton MacLane *Captain Cogswell* • Preston Foster *Jack Stacey* • Tom Brown *Jim Roberts* • Nan Grey *Peggy Phillips* • Andy Devine *Hansen* • Frank Jenks *Peter Carey* • Samuel S Hinds *Captain Kenny* ■ *Dir* Harold Young • *Scr* Daniel Moore, Hugh King, Theodore Reeves, George Yohalem, from a story by Daniel Moore, Hugh King

Storm and Sorrow ★★★ U

Drama based on a true story
1990 · US · Colour · 91mins

This TV movie is based on the exploits of young mountaineer Molly Higgins, who became a last-minute stand-in for another American climber on a 1974 international expedition to the Hindu Kush. Director Richard A Colla had shown a flair for location work with the aerial shots in *The Great Balloon Adventure* and his mountain views (with the Hungarian and Austrian peaks standing in for the Pamir Mountains) are often spectacular. However, the personal tensions between the climbers are long on chat and short on interest, though Lori Singer shows some spark as the outsider who overcomes opposition and survives tragedy. Contains swearing. [video]

Lori Singer *Molly Higgins* • Todd Allen *Gary Ullin* • Agnes Banfalvy *Elvira* • Steven Anderson *Sam Fairbanks* • John David Bland *Doug Lavery* • Jay Baker *Jeff Lowe* ■ *Dir* Richard A Colla • *Scr* Leigh Chapman, from the book *Storm and Sorrow in the High Pamirs* by Robert Craig

Storm Boy ★★★

Drama 1976 · Ausl · Colour · 88mins

Shot off the coast of South Australia, Henri Safran's movie debut is a kind of *Kes* with pelicans. His handling of the bird sequences and the stunning views of the island seascape cannot be faulted, but Safran has misjudged the pacing of his tale and, fascinating and beautiful though the natural history footage often is, it prevents the narrative from flowing. Greg Rowe gets under your skin as the neglected boy who is befriended by a pelican chick and by an Aboriginal outsider – David Gulpilil, giving his customary sound performance.

Greg Rowe *Mike* • Peter Cummins *Hide-Away Tom* • David Gulpilil *Fingerbone Bill* • Judy Dick *Miss Walker* • Tony Allison *Ranger* • Michael Moody *Boat master* ■ *Dir* Henri Safran • *Scr* Sonia Berg, from the novel by Colin Thiele

Storm Center ★★★

Drama 1956 · US · BW · 85mins

This is a tremendously courageous subject for its period that is still relevant today, as librarian Bette Davis is fired for refusing to remove a book on communism from the shelves. Unfortunately, the movie is directed by one of the screenwriters (Daniel Taradash) and it lapses too often into cliché and sentiment. Although the theme deserved more than this melodramatic treatment, it's also likely that a better movie would still have met with an uninterested public. Davis is watchable, as are Brian Keith and the excellent and underused Kim Hunter, but, if ever a subject was let down by its director, it's this one.

Bette Davis *Alicia Hull* • Brian Keith *Paul Duncan* • Kim Hunter *Martha Lockridge* • Paul Kelly *Judge Robert Ellerbe* • Kevin Coughlin *Freddie Slater* • Joe Mantell *George Slater* • Sallie Brophy *Laura Slater* • Howard Wierum *Mayor Levering* ■ *Dir* Daniel Taradash • *Scr* Daniel Taradash, Elick Moll

Storm in a Teacup ★★★

Comedy 1937 · UK · BW · 88mins

When the authoritarian provost of a small Scottish town (Cecil Parker) orders an old lady's dog to be confiscated because she hasn't paid her fines, reporter Rex Harrison picks up the story and creates a national scandal. The furious provost institutes legal proceedings against the journalist, but his daughter Vivien Leigh, who is in love with the young man, intervenes. Well directed by Victor Saville, the film is an oh-so-English, pre-Second World War relic, that's sweet and funny. Parker is splendidly pompous, and the youthful Leigh and Harrison make a good-looking and charming couple.

Vivien Leigh *Victoria Gow* • Rex Harrison *Frank Burden* • Sara Allgood *Mrs Hegarty* • Cecil Parker *Provost Willie Gow* • Ursula Jeans *Lisbet Skirving* • Gus McNaughton *Horace Skirving* ■ *Dir* Victor Saville, Ian Dalrymple • *Scr* Ian Dalrymple, Donald Bull, from James Bridie's adaptation of the play *Sturm in Wasserglas* by Bruno Frank

Storm over Asia ★★★★★ PG

Classic silent drama
1928 · USSR · BW · 93mins

The summit of Soviet cinema was reached in the twenties with the films of Dovzhenko, Eisenstein and Pudovkin, whose last great silent film this was. It concerns nomadic fur-trapper, Bair, who is set up as a puppet monarch by the occupying British interventionist forces in Mongolia in 1918. But, realising his national identity, and believing himself to be a descendent of Genghis Kahn, he rouses the Asian hordes against their oppressors. The film ends with an impressive storm symbolising the force of revolution. A film of great visual beauty, dynamic montage, humour and compassion, it also has an ethnographic quality in the detailed depiction of the life of the Mongolian herdsmen. A new version with a sound track was released some 20 years later under Vsevolod Pudovkin's supervision. [video]

Valeri Inkishinov *Blair, a mongol huntsman* • I Inkishinov *Blair's father* • A Chistyakov *Commander of a partisan detachment* • A Dedintsev *Commander of the occupation forces* ■ *Dir* Vsevolod I Pudovkin • *Scr* Osip Brik, from a story by I Novokshenov

Storm over the Nile ★★ U

Adventure 1955 · UK · Colour · 102mins

Zoltan Korda makes little effort to disguise the fact that this is a remake of his 1939 classic *The Four Feathers*. The script is the same RC Sherriff, Lajos Biro and Arthur Wimperis adaptation of AEW Mason's classic adventure novel, while some of the original location footage is also included, distorted to fit the new picture's CinemaScope format. Co-director Terence Young helps bring a touch of pizzazz to the action sequences, yet the story, of an officer who's branded a coward but who proves to have more pluck than his pals, has dated badly. 🎞

Laurence Harvey *John Durrance* • Anthony Steel *Harry Faversham* • James Robertson-Justice *General Burroughs* • Geoffrey Keen *Dr Sutton* • Ronald Lewis *Peter Burroughs* • Ian Carmichael *Tom Willoughby* • Michael Hordern *General Faversham* • Jack Lambert *Colonel* • Mary Ure *Mary Burroughs* • Christopher Lee *Karaga Pasha* ■ *Dir* Zoltan Korda, Terence Young • *Scr* RC Sherriff, Lajos Biró, Arthur Wimperis, from the novel *The Four Feathers* by AEW Mason

Storm over Wyoming ★ U

Western   1950 · US · BW · 60mins

One of seven Tim Holt B-westerns cranked out by RKO during 1950 (when such pictures were beginning to lose money), this has more action than most but no other distinguishing features. Tim and his Mexican-Irish sidekick Richard Martin rescue a cowboy from being strung up by sheepherders and are rewarded with jobs as ranch hands. Noreen Nash has an active role as the sheep rancher whose crooked foreman is causing most of the trouble. The man rescued from the necktie party is former cowboy star Tom Keene, now working as a character player under the name of Richard Powers.

Tim Holt *Dave* • Richard Martin *Chito Rafferty* • Noreen Nash *Chris Marvin* • Richard Powers *Tug Caldwell* • Betty Underwood *Ruby* • Bill Kennedy *Rawlins* • Kenneth MacDonald *Scott* • Leo McMahon *Zeke* • Richard Kean *Watson* • Don Haggerty *Marshal* ■ *Dir* Lesley Selander • *Scr* Earl Repp

Storm Warning ★★

Drama   1950 · US · BW · 89mins

Fashion model Ginger Rogers decides to visit her sister (Doris Day), in a small southern town. Arriving at night, she witnesses a Klan murder, and soon realises that one of the perpetrators is her brother-in-law, Steve Cochran. DA Ronald Reagan asks her to testify as a witness to the killing, leading to an agonising clash of loyalties for Rogers. A punchy and intriguing little social conscience effort from Warner Bros, convincingly acted all round, is ruined by its ultimate descent into crudely obvious melodrama. It does, however, hold the interest throughout.

Ginger Rogers *Marsha Mitchell* • Ronald Reagan *Burt Rainey* • Doris Day *Lucy Rice* • Steve Cochran *Hank Rice* • Hugh Sanders *Charlie Barr* • Lloyd Gough *Cliff Rummel* • Raymond Greenleaf *Faulkner* ■ *Dir* Stuart Heisler • *Scr* Daniel Fuchs, Richard Brooks, from their story *Storm Center*

Stormy ★★ U

Western   1935 · US · BW · 66mins

Noah Beery Jr may take the lead in this western melodrama about a thoroughbred colt that's lost after a train wreck, but his thunder is stolen by the horse in the title role, no less than Rex the Wonder Horse. Among the other supporting humans, J Farrell MacDonald, as the wonderfully named Trinidad Dorn, emerges with dignity and Jean Rogers makes a pert heroine. A year after *Stormy*, director Louis Friedlander changed his name to

Lew Landers and continued in a prolific low-budget career.

Noah Beery Jr *Stormy* • Jean Rogers *Kerry Dorn* • J Farrell MacDonald *Trinidad Dorn* • Walter Miller *Craig* • James P Burtis *Greasy* • Charles Hunter *The Arizona Wrangler* ■ *Dir* Louis Friedlander [Lew Landers] • *Scr* George H Plympton, Ben G Kohn, from a story by Cherry Wilson

Stormy Monday ★★★ 15

Romantic thriller 1987 · UK · Colour · 88mins

Mike Figgis marked himself out as a director to watch out for with this assured debut, which successfully transplants *film noir* to the unlikely surroundings of Newcastle upon Tyne. Sean Bean is the young innocent who falls for visiting American Melanie Griffith and gets caught between the machinations of sinister American developer Tommy Lee Jones and local jazz club owner Sting. It doesn't always convince, but Figgis summons up a melancholy air of menace, and the performances, particularly Jones's, are memorable. Contains violence, swearing, sex scenes and nudity. 🎞

Melanie Griffith *Kate* • Tommy Lee Jones *Cosmo* • Sting *Finney* • Sean Bean *Brendan* • James Cosmo *Tony* • Mark Long *Patrick* • Brian Lewis *Jim* ■ *Dir/Scr* Mike Figgis

Stormy Waters ★★★★

Romantic drama   1941 · Fr · BW · 90mins

Jacques Prévert co-wrote the screenplay, based on Roger Vercel's popular novel of doomed love, *Remorques*, in which tugboat captain Jean Gabin rescues Michèle Morgan from the sea and falls in love with her. The picture was begun in 1939, but the Nazi Occupation held up production. It was eventually completed in the studio, although director Jean Gremillon had managed earlier to film a number of realistic sea scenes on location at Brest. A perceptive but gloomy study of passion and fidelity, the film benefits from the masterly performances of its trio of top stars. In French with English subtitles.

Jean Gabin *André Laurent* • Michèle Morgan *Catherine* • Madeleine Renaud *Yvonne Laurent* • Charles Blavette *Gabriel Tanguy* ■ *Dir* Jean Grémillon • *Scr* Roger Vercel, Charles Spaak, Jacques Prévert, André Cayatte, from the novel *Remorques* by Roger Vercel

Stormy Weather ★★★ U

Musical   1943 · US · BW · 77mins

Little more than an excuse to feature some of the finest black American performers, this expertly made extravaganza may well seem tasteless today. Try to ignore the parade of grinning racial stereotypes, and concentrate instead on the star turns. Here's the great Bill Robinson, and a zoot-suited Cab Calloway, with Coleman Hawkins in his line-up. Here's the flamboyant Fats Waller performing *Ain't Misbehavin'*, the sensational Nicholas Brothers and, best of all, lovely Lena Horne performing the title number and a wondrous *I Can't Give You Anything but Love, Baby*. But the sight of black comedians "blacking up" with burnt cork is hard to watch, and the virtually nonexistent plot is trite, with the Horne-Robinson sudden

and clinchless romance particularly unbelievable. 🎞

Lena Horne *Selina Rogers* • Bill Robinson *Corky* • Cab Calloway • Katherine Dunham • Fats Waller • Ada Brown • Dooley Wilson *Gabe* ■ *Dir* Andrew Stone [Andrew L Stone] • *Scr* Frederick Jackson, Ted Koehler, HS Kraft, from a story by Jerry Horwin, Seymour B Robinson

Stormy Weathers ★★★ PG

Comedy adventure
1992 · US · Colour · 91mins

After attracting criticism in her early film career, which was transformed by the TV series *Moonlighting*, Cybill Shepherd was confident enough to help back this starring vehicle in which she's a private eye searching for the missing relative of an Italian aristocrat. There is nothing memorable in this TV movie, but it features a decent enough performance from Shepherd. 🎞

Cybill Shepherd *Samantha "Sam" Weathers* • Robert Beltran *Lorenzo "Gio" Giovanni De Zaccagnini* • Charlie Schlatter *Squirrel* • Kurt Fuller *Detective Horshak* • Diane Salinger *Bogey* • Roy Thinnes *Andrew Chase* • Mimi Kuyzk *Congresswoman Gloria Chase* ■ *Dir* Will Mackenzie • *Scr* Stephan Blom-Cooper, V Phipps-Wilson, Gerald Ayres, from a story by Stephan Blom-Cooper, V Phipps-Wilson

The Story Lady ★★★

Drama   1991 · US · Colour · 96mins

This winning drama about a sprightly pensioner forging a new career as a TV presenter was tailor-made for Jessica Tandy. She is in typically top form, but the digs against the exploitative nature of television lack bite and TV-movie specialist Larry Elikann struggles to keep sickly sentiment at bay. There's fine support from a splendid cast, which includes Ed Begley Jr, Charles Durning and Richard Masur.

Jessica Tandy *Grace McQueen* • Stephanie Zimbalist *Julie Pollard* • Lisa Jakub *Alexandra Pollard* • Christopher Gartin *Scott* • Tandy Cronyn *Meg* • Ed Begley Jr *Otis* • Richard Masur *Norm* • Charles Durning *Judge* ■ *Dir* Larry Elikann • *Scr* Robert Zeschin

The Story of a Cheat ★★★★★

Comedy drama   1936 · Fr · BW · 83mins

Though very much a man of the stage who only occasionally made films, Sacha Guitry was still capable of being highly cinematic. Here, for example, the entire story is enacted visually, with only Guitry's voiceover and Adolphe Borchard's score for accompaniment – although countess Marguerite Moreno does speak in a café scene. An under-acknowledged influence on the New Wave, this is a bravura auteurist exhibition, as Guitry not only stars in this self-scripted picaresque about a cardsharp convinced that fortune can be seduced by deception, but also manipulates time and space with a masterly ease that perfectly complements the action's witty amorality. A French language film.

Sacha Guitry *The cheat* • Jacqueline Delubac *Young woman* • Rosine Deréan *The jewel thief* • Marguerite Moreno *The countess* ■ *Dir* Sacha Guitry • *Scr* Sacha Guitry, from the novel *Memoires d'un Tricheur* by Sacha Guitry

Story of a Love Story ★★

Romantic fantasy drama
1973 · Fr · Colour · 110mins

Give director John Frankenheimer a hard-hitting melodrama or a bruising action film and he'll produce a polished picture. However, when confronted with a romantic drama he's likely to be confounded by his own pretensions.That is exactly what has happened here: the film is so preoccupied with the fact or fiction game that the adulterous affair between author Alan Bates and Dominique Sanda is almost secondary. It looks great, but sometimes that's just not enough. Contains nudity.

Alan Bates *Harry* • Dominique Sanda *Nathalie* • Evans Evans *Elizabeth* • Lea Massari *Woman* • Michael Auclair [Michel Auclair] *Georges* • Laurence De Monaghan *Cleo* ■ *Dir* John Frankenheimer • *Scr* Nicholas Mosley

The Story of Alexander Graham Bell ★★ U

Biographical drama 1939 · US · BW · 98mins

Intended by 20th Century-Fox to rival the hefty Warner Bros biographies of famous personages (Louis Pasteur, Emile Zola), this biopic of the man who invented the telephone is too straightforward, sentimental and slow to compete. Don Ameche, then known as a light comedian and debonair leading man, tried to gain gravitas in the role as he teaches the deaf to communicate, while pioneering his research into transmitting speech over the telegraph wires. Loretta Young plays his girlfriend and his loyal assistant, who is Henry Fonda, who is far more convincing as a visionary than the miscast Ameche.

Don Ameche *Alexander Graham Bell* • Loretta Young *Mrs Bell* • Henry Fonda *Tom Watson* • Charles Coburn *Gardner Hubbard* • Spring Byington *Mrs Hubbard* • Gene Lockhart *Thomas Sanders* ■ *Dir* Irving Cummings • *Scr* Lamar Trotti, from a story by Ray Harris

The Story of Dr Wassell ★★

Second World War drama
1944 · US · Colour · 136mins

Having won an Oscar as the First World War hero in *Sergeant York*, Gary Cooper played another real-life hero, Dr Corydon Wassell, who managed to evacuate nine wounded men from Java and get them safely to Australia, dodging Japanese bombs all the way. Wassell himself was awarded the Navy Cross and was commended in Presidential radio broadast. He was reluctant to give his co-operation to Cecil B DeMille's movie, which is overlong, sentimental, self-important and cliché-ridden.

Gary Cooper *Dr Corydon M Wassell* • Laraine Day *Madeline* • Signe Hasso *Bettina* • Dennis O'Keefe *"Hoppy" Hopkins* • Carol Thurston *Trematini* • Carl Esmond *Lt Dirk Van Daal* ■ *Dir* Cecil B DeMille • *Scr* Alan LeMay, Charles Bennett, James Hilton, from the stories by Dr Corydon M Wassell, James Hilton

The Story of Esther Costello ★★★

Drama   1957 · UK · BW · 104mins

Melodrama in the grand Hollywood tradition as wealthy socialite Joan Crawford adopts an Irish girl (Heather

Sears) who has lost her sight, speech and hearing as a result of an accident. Unfortunately, Crawford's estranged husband (Rossano Brazzi) turns her charitable deed into a shameless exploitation racket. Crawford adds high emotional gloss to a tailor-made role that successfully tugs the heartstrings and holds the interest.

Joan Crawford *Margaret Landi* • Rossano Brazzi *Carlo Landi* • Heather Sears *Esther Costello* • Lee Patterson *Harry Grant* • Ron Randell *Frank Wenzel* • Fay Compton *Mother Superior* • John Loder *Paul Marchant* • Denis O'Dea *Father Devlin* • Sidney James *Ryan* ∎ *Dir* David Miller • *Scr* Charles Kaufman, from the novel by Nicholas Monsarrat

The Story of GI Joe ★★★★
Biographical Second World War drama
1945 · US · BW · 109mins

Similar to *A Walk in the Sun*, this salute to the ordinary, anonymous foot soldier is based on the memoirs of war correspondent Ernie Pyle, who is played by Burgess Meredith. Dealing with the guys who yomped it all the way from North Africa to Rome via Sicily, it was hailed at the time as one of the most authentic war movies ever made. Like Spielberg's *Saving Private Ryan* – which owes a lot to this movie – it's crudely manipulative yet often very moving, mainly due to Robert Mitchum's star-building, Oscar-nominated performance as the GI who rises to become the platoon's commander.

Burgess Meredith *Ernie Pyle* • Robert Mitchum *Lt Bill Walker* • Freddie Steele *Sgt Steve Warnicki* • Wally Cassell *Pvt Dondaro* • Jimmy Lloyd *Pvt Spencer* • Jack Reilly *Pvt Robert "Wingless" Murphy* • Bill Murphy *Pvt Mew* • William Self *"Gawky" Henderson* ∎ *Dir* William A Wellman • *Scr* Leopold Atlas, Guy Endore, Philip Stevenson, from the books *Here Is Your War* and *Brave Men* by Ernie Pyle

The Story of Gilbert and Sullivan ★★★ U
Biographical musical drama
1953 · UK · Colour · 111mins

Splendidly Technicolored, though slow-moving, this is a British account of the Tim Rice and Andrew Lloyd Webber team of their day, incarnated by Robert Morley (a rare top-billed appearance as the volatile Gilbert) and Maurice Evans (a rather bloodless Sullivan). Chunks of the comic operettas are ladled out among the petty squabblings that constitute the plot, and music fans will enjoy Martyn Green in an acting role, plus Owen Brannigan and Webster Booth. The movie is stolen by the urbane Peter Finch as the equally urbane Richard D'Oyly Carte.

Robert Morley *WS Gilbert* • Maurice Evans *Arthur Sullivan* • Eileen Herlie *Helen Lenoir* • Martyn Green *George Grossmith* • Peter Finch *Richard d'Oyly Carte* • Dinah Sheridan *Grace Marston* • Isabel Dean *Mrs Gilbert* • Wilfrid Hyde White *Mr Marston* ∎ *Dir* Sidney Gilliat • *Scr* Sidney Gilliat, Leslie Bailey, Vincent Korda, from the book *The Gilbert and Sullivan Book* by Leslie Bailey

The Story of Louis Pasteur
★★★
Biography 1936 · US · BW · 87mins

Paul Muni won an Oscar and established a formula for Warner Bros biopics with his performance in the

lead role of Louis Pasteur. The trick that Sheridan Gibney and Pierre Collings's Oscar-winning script pulls is to make scientific research into sterilisation and rabies interesting, and director William Dieterle pulls another trick by keeping a firm check on the running time. There's some minor love interest, of course, but it's Muni's picture – though today his acting style and the general hagiographic approach seem very old-fashioned.

Paul Muni *Louis Pasteur* • Josephine Hutchinson *Mme Pasteur* • Anita Louise *Annette Pasteur* • Donald Woods *Jean Martel* • Fritz Leiber *Dr Charbonnet* • Henry O'Neill *Roux* ∎ *Dir* William Dieterle • *Scr* Sheridan Gibney, Pierre Collings, from a story by Sheridan Gibney, Pierre Collings

The Story of Mankind ★ U
Historical fantasy drama
1957 · US · Colour · 99mins

Future disaster-movie king Irwin Allen (*The Poseidon Adventure*, *The Towering Inferno*) made this portentous rubbish in which the question of whether or not the human race should be allowed to survive is debated in front of a heavenly tribunal. Ronald Colman (in his last film) is the Spirit of Man, advancing the argument in favour of human kind; Vincent Price gleams with wicked delight as the Devil. Based on Hendrik Van Loon's bestseller, this is generally, and rightly, acknowledged as one of the worst films ever made, but for those who can tolerate it, it is absolutely hilarious.

Ronald Colman *Spirit of Man* • Hedy Lamarr *Joan of Arc* • Groucho Marx *Peter Minuit* • Harpo Marx *Isaac Newton* • Chico Marx *Monk* • Virginia Mayo *Cleopatra* • Agnes Moorehead *Queen Elizabeth* • Vincent Price *Devil* ∎ *Dir* Irwin Allen • *Scr* Irwin Allen, Charles Bennett, from the book by Hendrik Willem Van Loon

The Story of O ★★★ 18
Erotic drama
1975 · Fr/W Ger · Colour · 96mins

This tale of a woman who becomes a willing slave to the men she loves was banned in the UK for 25 years, though it's a toss-up these days as to what's more shocking – Corinne Cléry's sexual subservience or Udo Kier's flared Cerruti trousers. It's based on the controversial S&M classic by Pauline Réage and *Emmanuelle* director Just Jaeckin takes a dreamy, soft-focus, shampoo commercial approach to his film's still eye-opening sexual content. The addition of then-fashionable feminism – by withstanding all the pain and humiliation her lovers dish out, O proves herself stronger than they are – barely excuses the exploitation tableaux. However, Jaeckin's often unintentionally funny erotic epic remains a seventies landmark. A French language film.

Corinne Cléry *O, a photographer* • Udo Kier *René* • Anthony Steel *Sir Stephen H* • Jean Gaven *Pierre, O's valet* • Christiane Minazzoli *Anne-Marie* • Martine Kelly *Thérèse* • Jean-Pierre Andréani *Eric, Master III* ∎ *Dir* Just Jaeckin • *Scr* Sébastien Japrisot, from the novel *Histoire d'O* by Pauline Réage [Anne Desclos]

The Story of Qiu Ju
★★★★★ 15
Drama 1992 · HK/Chi · Colour · 96mins

Scooping both the Golden Lion and the best actress award at Venice, this is an impeccable piece of film-making by Zhang Yimou. Gong Li gives an exceptional performance as the tenacious woman who is prepared to go to any lengths to secure justice after her husband is assaulted by the village elder. Exposing the flaws in the Communist legal system and the chasm between urban and rural living standards, this is Yimou's first study of contemporary China. As ever, the engrossing drama, which is underpinned throughout with bitter humour, is tightly handled and the use of colour and landscape is exhilarating. In Mandarin with English subtitles.. 📺

Gong Li *Wan Qiu Ju* • Liu Peiqi *Wan Qing Lai* • Yang Liuchun *Meizi* • Lei Laosheng *Wang Shantang, village chief* • Ge Zhijun *Officer Li* ∎ *Dir* Zhang Yimou • *Scr* Liu Heng, from the story *Wanjia Susong* by Chen Yuanbin

The Story of Robin Hood and His Merrie Men ★★★ U
Adventure 1952 · UK · Colour · 83mins

This may not hold a candle to the Errol Flynn version, but at around 80 minutes and boasting authentic English locations and fine Technicolor photography, it's among the best of all Robin Hood films and excellent family entertainment. Richard Todd enjoys himself as the famous outlaw, but is up against strong competition, with Peter Finch as the wicked Sheriff and the delightful Hubert Gregg cast against type as the evil King John. There's light-hearted humour, a tuneful Allan-a-Dale and some lively swordfights. Produced by Walt Disney, who later made a cartoon version, it's briskly directed by the highly professional Ken Annakin.

Richard Todd *Robin Hood* • Joan Rice *Maid Marian* • Peter Finch *Sheriff of Nottingham* • James Hayter *Friar Tuck* • James Robertson-Justice *Little John* • Martita Hunt *Queen Eleanor* • Hubert Gregg *Prince John* • Bill Owen *Stutely* • Reginald Tate *Hugh Fitzooth* ∎ *Dir* Ken Annakin • *Scr* Lawrence E Watkin

The Story of Ruth ★★ U
Biblical drama 1960 · US · Colour · 131mins

Twentieth Century-Fox was the studio behind this Hollywood makeover of the Old Testament. It's a lengthy and colourful but ultimately static version of the Sunday School favourite. Elana Eden plays Ruth, who renounces false gods in order to worship the true faith of her husband. Familiar faces Stuart Whitman and Tom Tryon are the men in her life. The clichés are strung together by scriptwriter Norman Corwin (*Lust for Life*).

Stuart Whitman *Boaz* • Tom Tryon *Mahlon* • Viveca Lindfors *Eleilat* • Peggy Wood *Naomi* • Jeff Morrow *Tob* • Elana Eden *Ruth* • Thayer David *Hedak* ∎ *Dir* Henry Koster • *Scr* Norman Corwin

The Story of Seabiscuit ★★ U
Sports drama 1949 · US · Colour · 92mins

Shirley Temple co-stars with the famous American racehorse Seabiscuit in a fictionalised account of its racing success. Temple plays the niece of Seabiscuit's dedicated trainer, Barry Fitzgerald, and her romantic interest is provided by jockey Lon McCallister. Racing historians will enjoy the documentary footage of the great horse in action.

Shirley Temple *Margaret O'Hara* • Barry Fitzgerald *Shawn O'Hara* • Lon McCallister *Ted Knowles* • Rosemary De Camp *Mrs Charles S Howard* • Donald MacBride *George Carson* • Pierre Watkin *Charles S Howard* ∎ *Dir* David Butler • *Scr* John Taintor Foote, from his story

The Story of the Beach Boys: Summer Dreams
★★ 15
Biographical drama
1990 · US · Colour · 92mins

The sixties' sunned and surfed purveyors of classic teen hits were an odd bunch beneath their seemingly clean-cut bonhomie, but drummer Dennis Wilson, on whom this hagiography is based, was not the most talented, interesting or indeed most troubled member of the group. Hence this major whitewash job, which glosses over his brother Brian's bouts of depression, presenting instead a tantalising glimpse of talent here and a modicum of insight there, with the end result adding up to very little indeed. Great tunes, though. Contains drug abuse and nudity.

Bruce Greenwood *Dennis Wilson* • Greg Kean *Brian Wilson* • Bo Foxworth *Carl Wilson* • Casey Sander *Mike Love* • Andrew Myler *Al Jardine* • Arlen Dean Snyder *Murry* ∎ *Dir* Michael Switzer • *Scr* Charles Rosin, from the book *Heroes and Villains: the True Story of the Beach Boys* by Steven Gaines

Story of the Late Chrysanthemums ★★★★★
Period melodrama 1939 · Jap · BW · 142mins

Widely regarded as director Kenji Mizoguchi's finest accomplishment, this costume drama is notable for its humanist insight into the role of women in Japanese society. Composed in depth and shot primarily in stately long takes, the story follows the selfless trials of servant Kakuko Mori, as she tries to help the son of a wealthy family achieve his ambition of becoming a kabuki artist. While painting a harsh portrait of life in the 1880s, Mizoguchi warms the heart with his attention to detail and the understated way in which female impersonator Shotaro Hanayagi comes to appreciate his wife's sacrifice. Quite beautiful. In Japanese with English subtitles.

Shotaro Hanayagi *Kikunosuke Onoe* • Kakuko Mori *Otoku* • Kokichi Takada *Fukusuke Nakamura* • Gonjuro Kawarazaki *Kikugoro Onoe V* • Yoko Umemura *Osato, Kikugoro Onoe's wife* ∎ *Dir* Kenji Mizoguchi • *Scr* Yoshikata Yoda, Matsutaro Kawaguchi, from a story by Shofu Muramatsu

The Story of Three Loves ★★★ U

Portmanteau romantic drama
1953 · US · Colour · 121mins

A beautifully shot portmanteau romance, filmed by MGM with all stops out, featuring a marvellously starry cast, impossibly romantic situations and a particularly fine score from Miklos Rozsa. The mood is bittersweet throughout, and the attitudes and settings resolutely Hollywood European, with wonderful resonances for film fans. Here's James Mason as a ballet impresario, touched by *Red Shoes* ballerina Moira Shearer, dancing to Rachmaninov à la Frederick Ashton. Here's Kirk Douglas playing a trapeze artist, partnered by tragic Pier Angeli as a girl who has lost her will to live. Best of all, in the weakest segment, is young Ricky Nelson, transformed by magic into Farley Granger.

Moira Shearer *Paula Woodward* • James Mason *Charles Coudray* • Agnes Moorehead *Aunt Lydia* • Miklos Rozsa *Conductor* • Ethel Barrymore *Mrs Pennicott* • Leslie Caron *Mademoiselle* • Farley Granger *Thomas Campbell Jr* • Ricky Nelson *Tommy, aged 12* • Pier Angeli *Nina* • Kirk Douglas *Pierre Narval* ■ *Dir* Gottfried Reinhardt, Vincente Minnelli • *Scr* John Collier, Jan Lustig, George Froeschel, John Collier, Jan Lustig, George Froeschel, from the stories by Arnold Phillips, Ladislas Vajda, Jacques Maret

The Story of Us ★★ 15

Romantic comedy
1999 · US · Colour · 95mins

Director Rob Reiner tries to make another *When Harry Met Sally*-style romantic comedy, but clearly forgot to hire someone capable of turning in a funny or moving script. Bruce Willis and Michelle Pfeiffer do their best as an unhappily married couple who opt for a temporary separation when their kids go off to summer camp. However, what could have been a sweet and amusing tale of mid-marriage crisis is a rather one-sided affair.

Michelle Pfeiffer *Katie Jordan* • Bruce Willis *Ben Jordan* • Rita Wilson *Rachel* • Julie Hagerty *Liza* • Paul Reiser *Dave* • Tim Matheson *Marty* • Colleen Rennison *Erin aged 10* • Jake Sandvig *Josh aged 12* • Red Buttons *Arnie* ■ *Dir* Rob Reiner • *Scr* Alan Zweibel, Jessie Nelson

The Story of Vernon and Irene Castle ★★★★ U

Musical biography 1939 · US · BW · 89mins

This was the last RKO teaming of its incomparable dance duo of Fred Astaire and Ginger Rogers. They are cleverly cast as their great predecessors the Castles, the foremost dance partners of the early 20th century, in a tale that took on new resonances at the outbreak of the Second World War. The finale is almost unbearably moving, but to reveal more would give away the ending. The period songs are spot on, though the ever-sophisticated Astaire and Rogers look nothing like the bunny-hugging Castles (Irene was critical of Ginger's impersonation). The scripting leaves something to be desired, but despite its flaws, Ginger looks swell and Fred dances divinely. ▭

Fred Astaire *Vernon Castle* • Ginger Rogers *Irene Castle* • Edna May Oliver *Maggie Sutton* • Walter Brennan *Walter* • Lew Fields • Etienne Girardot *Papa Aubel* • Janet Beecher *Mrs Foote* • Rolfe Sedan *Emile Aubel* ■ *Dir* HC Potter • *Scr* Richard Sherman, Oscar Hammerstein, Dorothy Yost, from the books *My Husband* and *My Memories of Vernon Castle* by Irene Castle

Story of Women ★★★

Second World War drama
1988 · Fr · Colour · 110mins

Isabelle Huppert won the best actress prize at the Venice Film Festival for her portrayal of a mother whose struggle to survive the Nazi Occupation brought her into conflict with the Vichy authorities. Before becoming the last woman in France to be guillotined, Marie Latour performs abortions with a detachment that causes many to label her a monster. But Claude Chabrol refuses to take sides, adopting Jean Renoir's famous maxim that everyone has their reasons, as he dispassionately reconstructs the bleak realities of the early forties. In French with English subtitles.

Isabelle Huppert *Marie* • François Cluzet *Paul* • Marie Trintignant *Lulu/Lucie* • Nils Tavernier *Lucien* ■ *Dir* Claude Chabrol • *Scr* Claude Chabrol, Colo Tavernier O'Hagan, from the novel *Une Affaire de Femmes* by Francis Szpiner

Storybook ★

Fantasy adventure
1995 · US · Colour · 88mins

This is a dreadfully botched attempt to create a world of wonder similar to CS Lewis's Narnia. Everything about Lorenzo Doumani's film is either derivative or third rate. Set during the Second World War, the story concerns a young boy who is transported to a mythical kingdom through the pages of a magic book, where he teams up with a woodsman, an owl and a boxing kangaroo to wrest the throne from the evil Swoozie Kurtz. The acting of eight-year-old Sean Fitzgerald leaves a lot to be desired, but his adult co-stars are little better. If only the script had encouraged as many laughs as the puppets and the special effects.

Sean Fitzgerald *Brandon* • Swoosie Kurtz *Queen Evilia* • Richard Moll *Woody* • William McNamara *Arthur* • Milton Berle *Illuzor* • Gary Morgan *Pouch* ■ *Dir* Lorenzo Doumani • *Scr* Susan Bowen, Lorenzo Doumani

Storyville ★★★ 15

Mystery drama 1992 · US · Colour · 113mins

Mark Frost, David Lynch's unsung partner on the cult TV series *Twin Peaks*, made his directorial debut with this nasty story of dark deeds in the Deep South. As if adultery, corruption, blackmail and murder weren't enough, Frost throws in a little video voyeurism and an upcoming election to keep the plot simmering. James Spader disappoints as the politically ambitious lawyer at the centre of events, but there are some choice performances from Jason Robards, Joanne Whalley-Kilmer and Piper Laurie. Engagingly offbeat, but the action loses its way towards the end. Contains violence, sex scenes and swearing. ▭

James Spader *Cray Fowler* • Joanne Whalley-Kilmer [Joanne Whalley] *Natalie Tate* • Jason Robards [Jason Robards Jr] *Clifford Fowler* • Charlotte Lewis *Lee* • Michael Warren *Nathan Lefleur* • Michael Parks *Michael Trevallian* • Chuck McCann *Pudge Herman* • Charles Haid *Abe Choate* • Woody Strode *Charlie Sumpter* ■ *Dir* Mark Frost • *Scr* Mark Frost, Lee Reynolds, from the book *Juryman* by Frank Galbally, Robert Macklin

Stowaway ★★★★ U

Musical comedy 1936 · US · BW · 86mins

A prime vehicle for talented child star Shirley Temple. She plays the daughter of a slain Chinese missionary's who stows away on a playboy's yacht. This is one of Temple's best, with an excellent cast, just enough plot and some splendid musical moments. She sings, dances and, in one memorable, sequence impersonates not only Al Jolson and Eddie Cantor, but also Ginger Rogers. Alice Faye, on the brink of major stardom, introduces one of her trademark songs, Mack Gordon and Harry Revel's ballad *Goodnight, My Love*. Shirley even converses in Chinese in this entertaining movie, which was one of the biggest box-office hits of its year. ▭

Shirley Temple *Ching-Ching, daughter of missionaries* • Robert Young *Tommy Randall* • Alice Faye *Susan Parker* • Eugene Pallette *The Colonel* • Helen Westley *Mrs Hope* • Arthur Treacher *Atkins* • J Edward Bromberg *Judge Booth* ■ *Dir* William A Seiter • *Scr* William Conselman, Arthur Sheekman, Nat Perrin, from the story by Samuel G Engel

La Strada ★★★★ PG

Drama 1954 · It · BW · 103mins

This Fellini classic about a brutal circus strong man and a childlike woman was dismissed in Italy on release but hailed abroad as a masterpiece, making Fellini's reputation as a Great Artist and consigning Anthony Quinn to life as a Greek/Italian/Arab/Eskimo. Today, despite the touching performance by Fellini's wife Giulietta Masina, the movie seems crudely sentimental, its love story between a human animal and a simple waif hardly able to contain all the messages and symbols about humanity that the Italian maestro tosses at it. Combining the neorealism of Fellini's early career and the outright fantasies of his later work, this is well worth seeing, if only for its historical impact and striking influence. In Italian with English subtitles. ▭

Anthony Quinn *Zampano* • Giulietta Masina *Gelsomina* • Richard Basehart *Il Matto/"The Fool"* • Aldo Silvani *Il Signor Giraffa* ■ *Dir* Federico Fellini • *Scr* Federico Fellini, Tullio Pinelli, Ennio Flaiano

Straight out of Brooklyn ★★★ 15

Drama 1991 · US · Colour · 82mins

With its firm grasp of the realities of Brooklyn street life and its uncompromising use of realistic language and violence, this bruising account of what it's like to be black in urban America is all the more remarkable considering its debuting writer/director, Matty Rich, was only 19 when he completed it. There are jagged edges, but, like the rawness of the performances, they only add to the power of the picture. Rich's acting too readily recalls Spike Lee's Mars Blackmon in *She's Gotta Have It*, but Lawrence Gilliard Jr excels as the teenager who resorts to crime as a way out of the environment that condemned his parents. Contains violence, swearing, sex scenes and drug abuse. ▭

George T Odom *Ray Brown* • Ann D Sanders *Frankie Brown* • Lawrence Gilliard Jr [Larry Gilliard Jr] *Dennis Brown* • Barbara Sanon *Carolyn Brown* • Reana E Drummond *Shirley* • Matty Rich *Larry Love* • Mark Malone *Kevin* • Ali Shahid Abdul Wahha *Luther* ■ *Dir/Scr* Matty Rich

Straight Shooting ★★★

Silent western 1917 · US · BW · 75mins

Long believed to be lost until it was rediscovered in a Czech film archive in the sixties, this very early western is part of a series that starred Harry Carey as Cheyenne Harry under the direction of John Ford. During production it crept up to five reels, becoming Ford's first feature. It develops a cattlemen versus homesteaders conflict, with Cheyenne Harry changing sides. Ford's visual style is already often striking. Harry Carey's gesture of one arm grasping the other would be repeated as a homage by John Wayne at the end of Ford's *The Searchers*.

Harry Carey *Cheyenne Harry* • Duke Lee *Thunder Flint* • George Berrell *Sweetwater Sims* • Molly Malone *Joan Sims* • Ted Brooks *Tom Sims* • Hoot Gibson *Danny Morgan* ■ *Dir* Jack Ford [John Ford] • *Scr* George Hively

The Straight Story ★★★★★ U

Biographical road movie
1999 · US/Fr/UK · Colour · 107mins

Following the excesses of *Lost Highway*, David Lynch is in mellower mood with this whimsical road movie that, nevertheless, slyly dissects middle American mores with disarming precision. Exhibiting dignified self-assurance, Richard Farnsworth gives an Oscar-nominated performance as the Iowa farmer travelling by lawnmower to visit his dying brother in Wisconsin. There's selfless support from Sissy Spacek, as his traumatised daughter, and the various eccentrics he meets en route. It's hard to imagine a gentler film, yet Lynch fully exploits the stately pace to gaze fondly upon life's rich pageant. He also slips in a crane shot of such monumental inconsequence that it borders on the brilliant. ▭ DVD

Richard Farnsworth *Alvin Straight* • Sissy Spacek *Rose Straight* • Harry Dean Stanton *Lyle Straight* • Everett McGill *Tom the John Deere dealer* • John Farley *Thorvald Olsen* • Kevin Farley *Harald Olsen* • Jane Galloway Heitz *Dorothy* • Joseph A Carpenter *Bud* ■ *Dir* David Lynch • *Scr* John Roach, Mary Sweeney • *Cinematographer* Freddie Francis • *Music* Angelo Badalamenti

Straight Talk ★★★★ PG

Romantic comedy
1992 · US · Colour · 86mins

Both Dolly Parton and James Woods are perfectly cast as the bogus radio agony aunt and the sleazy reporter investigating her in this fun romantic comedy, which was filmed on location in Chicago. Woods's reporter wants to expose Parton as a sham, but soon finds he wants to get her into bed

along the way. What makes this work so well is the sparring double act of the two leads, especially Woods, who by now has honed his grumpy cynic role to perfection. Contains some swearing. ▭

Dolly Parton *Shirlee Kenyon* • James Woods *Jack Russell* • Griffin Dunne *Alan Riegert* • Michael Madsen *Steve Labell* • Deirdre O'Connell *Lily* • John Sayles *Guy Girardi* • Teri Hatcher *Janice* • Spalding Gray *Dr Erdman* • Jerry Orbach *Milo Jacoby* ■ *Dir* Barnet Kellman • *Scr* Craig Bolotin, Patricia Resnick

Straight Time ★★★ 18

Crime drama   1978 · US · Colour · 109mins

This terrific if sordid little opus was originally begun with the film's star Dustin Hoffman directing himself, but he handed the reins over to Broadway veteran Ulu Grosbard when the strain of juggling both tasks got too much for him. Hoffman is brilliant as petty hood Max Dembo, and there are marvellous supporting performances from the lowlife likes of M Emmet Walsh, Gary Busey and Harry Dean Stanton. Never a popular movie, this has been re-evaluated in the light of *Reservoir Dogs*, which featured this story's original author, Edward Bunker, in an acting role. Contains violence, swearing and nudity. ▭

Dustin Hoffman *Max Dembo* • Theresa Russell *Jenny Mercer* • Harry Dean Stanton *Jerry Schue* • Gary Busey *Willy Darin* • M Emmet Walsh *Earl Frank* • Sandy Barron *Manny* • Kathy Bates *Selma Darin* ■ *Dir* Ulu Grosbard • *Scr* Alvin Sargent, Edward Bunker, Jeffrey Boam, from the novel *No Beast So Fierce* by Edward Bunker

Straight to Hell ★ 15

Spoof spaghetti western
1987 · UK · Colour · 82mins

An awful spoof spaghetti western by *Sid and Nancy* director Alex Cox who took all his pop star friends to Spain to shoot what is essentially an expensive home movie. Sy Richardson, Joe Strummer and Dick Rude play desperadoes on the run after a bank robbery. The Pogues are the MacMahon Gang who want them out of the one-horse town they control. Grace Jones, Elvis Costello and Courtney Love also appear but even then they can't make the action less stilted or the improvised/drunken/nonsensical dialogue any less boring. ▭

Sy Richardson *Norwood* • Joe Strummer *Simms* • Dick Rude *Willy* • Courtney Love *Velma* • Zander Schloss *Karl* • Del Zamora *Poncho* • Luis Contreras *Sal* • Dennis Hopper *IG Farben* • Elvis Costello *Hives, the butler* • Grace Jones *Sonya* ■ *Dir* Alex Cox • *Scr* Alex Cox, Dick Rude

Strait-Jacket ★★★

Horror   1963 · US · BW · 92mins

"When the axe swings, the excitement begins!" screamed the original poster for William Castle's showy horror tale. But you'll be screaming louder with laughter watching trampy Joan Crawford playing a rehabilitated convicted murderess who may, or may not, be returning to her old head-severing habits. Scripted by *Psycho's* Robert Bloch, it was the writer's favourite because it was filmed intact. Castle aimed to encourage audiences for this seminal stalk-and-slash thriller

by providing restrictive seat belts in cinemas, plus free cardboard axes to wave during the head-rolling mayhem. But history has proved Crawford to be the best gimmick of all.

Joan Crawford *Lucy Harbin* • Diane Baker *Carol* • Leif Erickson *Bill Cutler* • Howard St John *Raymond Fields* • John Anthony Hayes *Michael Fields* • Rochelle Hudson *Emily Cutler* • George Kennedy *Leo Krause* ■ *Dir* William Castle • *Scr* Robert Bloch

The Straits of Love and Hate ★★★

Drama   1937 · Jap · BW · 88mins

Inspired by Tolstoy's novel *Resurrection*, yet bearing the visual imprint of Josef von Sternberg's 1928 film *The Docks of New York*, this is a typically sympathetic study of a woman *in extremis* from master director Kenji Mizoguchi. However, Fumiko Yamaji, who plays the servant who is impregnated by an innkeeper's feckless son and who runs away to join a band of second-rate strolling players, must have felt oppressed herself, as Mizoguchi reportedly made her rehearse one scene 700 times. Yet, the stress was apparently worthwhile, as there is touching resignation in her decision to foreswear romance and settle for the minor consolations of life on the road. In Japanese with English subtitles.

Fumiko Yamaji *Ofumi* • Seizaburo Kawazu *Yoshitaro* • Masao Shimizu *Kenkichi* • Haruo Tanaka *Hirose* • Kumeko Urabe ■ *Dir* Kenji Mizoguchi • *Scr* Yoshikata Yoda, Kenji Mizoguchi, Matsutaro Kawaguchi, from the novel *Resurrection* by Leo Tolstoy

Stranded ★★ 15

Science-fiction drama
1987 · US · Colour · 77mins

Friendly aliens crash-land and establish contact with an old woman and her granddaughter in a rural area, but the usual movie misunderstandings occur and the local authorities rush in to make a mess of things. Add an alien assassin and some feisty locals into the mix and you've got 80 minutes of science-fiction fun starring Joe Morton as the Sheriff. It looks pretty good and Maureen O'Sullivan adds a nice touch as a grandma, but it takes a long time to go anywhere. ▭

Ione Skye *Deirdre* • Joe Morton *Sheriff McMahon* • Maureen O'Sullivan *Grace Clark* • Susan Barnes *Helen Anderson* • Cameron Dye *Lieutenant Scott* • Michael Greene *Vernon Burdett* • Brendan Hughes *Prince* ■ *Dir* Tex Fuller • *Scr* Alan Castle

Stranded ★★ 15

Supernatural thriller
1989 · Can · Colour · 87mins

Deborah Wakeham and Ryan Michael play an unhappily married couple in a lightweight chiller that only delivers a modicum of suspense and mystery. Suspecting that Michael is having an affair, Wakeham books a break on a secluded island in a bid to patch up their relationship, but they soon find themselves at the mercy of the island's violent past. The two leads are bland and director Paul Tucker, saddled with an unremarkable script, struggles to inject any style into the

proceedings. Contains some violence and swearing. ▭

Deborah Wakeham *Lynn* • Ryan Michael *Paul* • Stephen E Miller *Boyd* ■ *Dir* Paul Tucker • *Scr* Boon Collins, Dan Vining, from a story by Daniel D Williams

The Strange Affair ★★★

Crime drama   1968 · UK · Colour · 104mins

Failed student Michael York becomes a policeman and immediately gets entangled with bent cops, drug dealing and lustful Susan George. Like David Greene's previous film, *Sebastian*, this film's swinging London trappings – Indian mystics, flower people, garish decor, circular beds, touristy locations – tend to work against the more traditional underworld elements and one is never quite sure if York has corruption in his genes or if he's just a berk. On the plus side are some diverting supporting performances and flashes of quirky humour.

Michael York *Peter Strange* • Jeremy Kemp *Detective Sgt Pierce* • Susan George *Frederika "Fred" March* • Jack Watson *Daddy Quince* • George A Cooper *Superintendent Kingley* • Barry Fantoni *Charley Small, informer* ■ *Dir* David Greene • *Scr* Stanley Mann, from the novel by Bernard Toms

A Strange Affair ★★★

Drama   1981 · Fr · Colour · 100mins

There's a Capraesque feel to this psychological drama, which begins with an air of despondent realism only to suddenly soar into flights of inexplicable fantasy. The reason for this sudden change in the fortunes of Gérard Lanvin is Michel Piccoli, who not only takes over the shop where he works, but also insinuates himself into other areas of his life. But such is the lightness of Pierre Granier-Deferre's touch that this transformation has a disarming stealth that prevents the action from becoming tacky or twee. Piccoli enjoys himself as the mysterious stranger, and much depends on the underplaying of Lanvin and Nathalie Baye, as his wife. French dialogue dubbed into English.

Michel Piccoli *Bertrand Malair* • Nathalie Baye *Nina Coline* • Gérard Lanvin *Louis Coline* • Jean-Pierre Kalfon *François Lingre* • Jean-François Balmer *Paul Belais* • Madeleine Cheminat *Yette* ■ *Dir* Pierre Granier-Deferre • *Scr* Christopher Frank, Pierre Granier-Deferre

A Strange Affair ★★ 12

Romantic drama   1995 · US · Colour · 88mins

Judith Light may not be TV-movie royalty, but she has certainly been good value in such pictures as the enjoyable sixties girl-band comedy, *My Boyfriend's Back*. She holds together this dubious story with some conviction, as the wife whose plans to leave her husband of 23 years are shattered when he has a stroke. This in itself would have made for fascinating drama, but writer Daniel Freudenberger couldn't leave matters there and introduces a lover, who rapidly becomes the sick man's best friend. Unlikely, to say the least, but slick, nevertheless. ▭

Judith Light *Lisa McKeever* • William Russ *Art Maskin* • Jay Thomas *Eric McKeever* ■ *Dir* Ted Kotcheff • *Scr* Daniel Freudenberger

The Strange Affair of Uncle Harry ★★ 15

Mystery drama   1945 · US · BW · 77mins

Released as plain *Uncle Harry* in the USA, this Broadway-based thriller stars George Sanders as a textile designer who lives with his two spinster sisters. When he falls in love with Ella Raines, one of the sisters is consumed with jealousy. While Sanders gives an excellent, multi-layered performance, the dreadful studio-imposed ending precipitated the resignation of the producer, Joan Harrison, a regular associate of Hitchcock.

George Sanders *Harry Melville Quincy* • Geraldine Fitzgerald *Lettie Quincy* • Ella Raines *Deborah Brown* • Sara Allgood *Nona* • Moyna MacGill *Hester Quincy* • Samuel S Hinds *Dr Adams* ■ *Dir* Robert Siodmak • *Scr* Stephen Longstreet, Keith Winter, from the play *Uncle Harry* by Thomas Job

Strange Alibi ★★

Police drama   1941 · US · BW · 63mins

Arthur Kennedy proved to be a consummate character actor but early in his screen career, under a standard Warner Bros contract, he was tried out as leading man material in some B-pictures. In this one he's the cop who consorts with crooks and deliberately gets a bad reputation in the hope of exposing the mysterious head of a crime syndicate, only to be found out, framed and put behind bars. Blonde and bland leading lady Joan Perry wisely gave up acting soon after this picture and married Columbia production chief Harry Cohn.

Arthur Kennedy *Joe Geary* • Joan Perry *Alice Delvin* • Jonathan Hale *Chief Sprague* • John Ridgely *Tex* • Florence Bates *Katie* • Charles Trowbridge *Governor Phelps* • Cliff Clark *Capt Reddick* • Stanley Andrews *Lt Detective Pagle* ■ *Dir* D Ross Lederman • *Scr* Kenneth Gamet, Fred Nibolo Jr, from the story *Give Me Liberty* by Leslie T White

The Strange and Deadly Occurrence ★

Thriller   1974 · US · Colour · 74mins

Vera Miles and Robert Stack's remote new home isn't proving to be very peaceful. Is it really haunted by occult demons or is someone playing tricks and engineering the "unexplainable" accidents? Initial interest in this doggedly old-fashioned TV movie soon flags, thanks to the static narrative and ponderous direction by horror veteran John Llewellyn Moxie. Not so strange, but certainly deadly.

Robert Stack *Michael Rhodes* • Vera Miles *Christine Rhodes* • Margaret Willock *Melissa Rhodes* • LQ Jones *Sheriff Berlinger* • Herbert Edelman *Felix Festinger* • Dena Dietrich *Audrey* • Bill McKinney *Pratt* ■ *Dir* John Llewellyn Moxey • *Scr* Sandor Stern

Strange Bedfellows ★★★

Comedy   1965 · US · Colour · 98mins

Executive Rock Hudson and his Italian wife Gina Lollobrigida have been separated for five years. When they come across each other in London, it is obvious there is still a spark between them, but after one passionate night they start bickering all over again. Their plans to part are complicated by Gig Young, a PR man determined to keep them together for the sake of Hudson's firm. Old hand Melvin Frank here turns in another smooth but unexceptional romantic comedy, enlivened by the talents of Terry-Thomas and Arthur Haynes.

Rock Hudson *Carter Harrison* • Gina Lollobrigida *Toni* • Gig Young *Richard Bramwell* • Edward Judd *Harry Jones* • Terry-Thomas *Assistant Mortician* • Arthur Haynes *Carter's taxi driver* • Howard St John *JL Stevens* • David King *Toni's taxi driver* ■ *Dir* Melvin Frank • *Scr* Melvin Frank, Michael Pertwee, from a story by Norman Panama, Melvin Frank

Strange Boarders ★★★
Comedy thriller   1938 · UK · BW · 74mins

The spy thriller meets the bedroom farce in this sprightly British suspense comedy. Tom Walls plays an investigator called away from his honeymoon with Renée Saint-Cyr to discover which of the guests at Irene Handl's boarding house has stolen some top-secret blueprints. While he mingles with a tiptoeing maid, a Boer War colonel, an Argentinian meat merchant, a travelling salesman, a dotty old dear and a sinister blind man, Saint-Cyr books into the establishment, suspecting him of adultery. Walls was never the most understated of screen performers, but he keeps this enjoyable mystery bright and breezy.

Tom Walls *Tommy Blythe* • Renée Saint-Cyr *Louise Blythe* • Googie Withers *Elsie* • Ronald Adam *Barstow* • CV France *Colonel Anstruther* • Nina Boucicault *Mrs Anstruther* • Leon M Lion *Luke* • C Denier Warren *Fry* • Irene Handl *Mrs Dewar* ■ *Dir* Herbert Mason • *Scr* Ar Rawlinson, Sidney Gilliat, from the novel *The Strange Boarders of Paradise Crescent* by E Phillips Oppenheim

Strange Brew ★★ PG
Comedy   1983 · US · Colour · 86mins

This is of interest chiefly because it marked the first starring role for Rick Moranis, who also shares directorial duties with comic partner Dave Thomas. The film is built around a pair of characters the duo originally created for a Canadian TV sketch show and, consequently, is episodic and a little uneven. However, Moranis and Thomas make an endearing pair of numbskulls and Max von Sydow has fun as the mad man who is putting something strange in a brewery's beer. ▭

Dave Thomas (1) *Doug McKenzie* • Rick Moranis *Bob McKenzie* • Max von Sydow *Brewmeister Smith* • Paul Dooley *Claude Elsinore* • Lynne Griffin *Pam Elsinore* • Angus MacInnes *Jean Larose* • Tom Harvey *Inspector* ■ *Dir* Dave Thomas (1), Rick Moranis • *Scr* Dave Thomas, Rick Moranis, Steven DeJarnatt

Strange Cargo ★★★
Drama   1940 · US · BW · 113mins

Clark Gable and Joan Crawford's eighth and last picture together is mighty peculiar, a jungle adventure that turns into a religious parable about redemption. The sweatily pectoral Gable, plus Paul Lukas and Peter Lorre, hack their way through the jungle together with Ian Hunter, Christ's even creepier disciple in French Guiana, in a bid to escape from Devil's Island. Crawford, meanwhile, turns in another Sadie Thompson routine as a "dancer". As with Gable's

earlier essay in lust, *Red Dust*, the Catholic Legion of Decency took umbrage and condemned it as blasphemous. Recommended for connoisseurs of studio foliage and general crankiness.

Clark Gable *Andre Verne* • Joan Crawford *Julie* • Ian Hunter *Cambreau* • Peter Lorre *Cochon* • Paul Lukas *Hessler* • Albert Dekker *Moll* • J Edward Bromberg *Flaubert* • Eduardo Ciannelli *Telez* ■ *Dir* Frank Borzage • *Scr* Lawrence Hazard, Lesser Samuels, Anita Loos (adaptation), from the book *Not Too Narrow... Not Too Deep* by Richard Sale

Strange Days ★★★★ 18
Science-fiction action thriller
1995 · US · Colour · 139mins

Ralph Fiennes is a dealer in virtual reality clips that replicate sensory perceptions in director Kathryn Bigelow's dazzling sci-fi thriller. As New Year's Eve 1999 approaches, he tries to track down a killer recording his crimes for the ultimate "snuff" experience. A fascinating look at the dangers of advanced technology and their moral implications, this is controversial, highly imaginative and inventively staged. Using subjective camerawork to place the viewer in the voyeuristic frame, Bigelow cleverly reinvents *film noir* for audiences raised on *Terminator 2*, while presenting a dark vision on where cinema for pure sensation's sake could be heading. Contains violence and swearing. ▭

Ralph Fiennes *Lenny Nero* • Angela Bassett *Lornette "Mace" Mason* • Juliette Lewis *Faith Justin* • Tom Sizemore *Max Peltier* • Michael Wincott *Philo Gant* • Vincent D'Onofrio *Burton Steckler* • Glenn Plummer *Jeriko One* ■ *Dir* Kathryn Bigelow • *Scr* James Cameron, Jay Cocks, from a story by James Cameron

The Strange Door ★★ U
Horror   1951 · US · BW · 80mins

A contrived melodrama is heightened in stature by the presence of Boris Karloff and Charles Laughton. The latter is a sadistic French nobleman who imprisons his brother in the basement for marrying a woman they both loved. It's when Laughton tries to marry his brother's daughter to an infamous brigand in revenge that manservant Karloff rebels and the "crushing room" is called into torture service. Florid direction by Joseph Pevney and Laughton over-playing the madness make the proceedings more histrionic than horror historic.

Charles Laughton *Sire Alan de Maletroit* • Boris Karloff *Voltan* • Sally Forrest *Blanche de Maletroit* • Richard Stapely *Denis de Beaulieu* • Michael Pate *Talon* • Paul Cavanagh *Edmond de Maletroit* ■ *Dir* Joseph Pevney • *Scr* Jerry Sackheim, from the story *The Sire de Maletroit's Door* by Robert Louis Stevenson

Strange Holiday ★
Second World War drama
1942 · US · BW · 61mins

One of the more bizarre artefacts to have survived from the Second World War, this propaganda piece was financed by General Motors and stars Claude Rains, who returns from a holiday in the backwoods to find America transformed into a Nazi dictatorship. Not quite an American version of *It Happened Here*, it was made in 1942 and shelved until 1945

when Rains himself arranged its limited release. Writer/director Arch Oboler was a maverick talent who started on radio and was best known for the 3-D feature *Bwana Devil*.

Claude Rains *John Stevenson* • Bobbie Stebbins *John Jr* • Barbara Bates *Peggy Lee* • Paul Hilton *Woodrow Jr* • Gloria Holden *Mrs Jean Stevenson* • Milton Kibbee *Sam Morgan* ■ *Dir/Scr* Arch Oboler

Strange Impersonation ★★
Drama   1946 · US · BW · 62mins

Director Anthony Mann had his work cut out here to make a halfway decent picture from such a ridiculous story, on a miniscule budget. Brenda Marshall is a the research scientist, badly scarred in a fire, who returns after plastic surgery with a new identity, seeking to regain her fiancé from the rival who caused the blaze. The director draws good performances from his cast, which includes Hillary Brooke as the bad girl, and builds an atmosphere of oppressive tension. But it doesn't have the right cameraman or sufficient time to give it a true *film noir* look.

Brenda Marshall *Nora Goodrich* • William Gargan *Dr Stephan Lindstrom* • Hillary Brooke *Arline Cole* • George Chandler *JW Rinse* • Ruth Ford *Jane Karaski* • HB Warner *Dr Mansfield* ■ *Dir* Anthony Mann • *Scr* Mindret Lord, from a story by Anne Wigton, Lewis Herman

Strange Interlude ★★★★
Melodrama   1932 · US · BW · 109mins

Norma Shearer, distraught at the death of her beloved in war, makes a self-sacrificing marriage to Alexander Kirkland, but she is forced by circumstance to have her child by Clark Gable and falls in love with him. Another significant man in her life is her childhood friend Ralph Morgan, who is also in love with her. MGM's attempt to film Eugene O'Neill's complex five-hour long Pulitzer Prize-winning play was either foolhardy or a brave bid for intellectual respectability. Critics were sharply divided over the merits of the play and few people liked (or saw) the lavish film, which is a heightened, experimental delve into the torment of an idealistic and highly-strung, but strong, woman and the three weak men around her. Indeed, watching it is hard work, but brings rich rewards. Shearer again demonstrates the versatility that made her the queen of MGM, while Gable (sporting a moustache for the first time) is splendid in a serious role.

Norma Shearer *Nina Leeds* • Clark Gable *Ned Darrell* • Alexander Kirkland *Sam Evans* • Ralph Morgan *Charlie Marsden* • Robert Young *Gordon, as a young man* • May Robson *Mrs Evans* • Maureen O'Sullivan *Madeleine* • Henry B Walthall *Prof Leeds* ■ *Dir* Robert Z Leonard • *Scr* Bess Meredyth, C Gardner Sullivan, from the play by Eugene O'Neill

Strange Invaders ★★★★ 12
Science-fiction   1983 · US · Colour · 89mins

An affectionate parody of fifties' alien invasion B-movies, this film's deceptively simple premise evokes memories of *It Came from Outer Space*, with co-writer/director Michael Laughlin bringing the genre bang up to date courtesy of the marvellous special

effects, warmly comic overtones and a sharply observed script. This recaptures exactly the heady atmosphere and demented imagery of its major inspirations. The second in a loose trilogy Laughlin began in 1981 with *Strange Behaviour* but never completed, this is an almost flawless piece of science-fiction fun. Contains swearing. ▭

Paul LeMat *Charles Bigelow* • Nancy Allen *Betty Walker* • Diana Scarwid *Margaret* • Michael Lerner *Willie Collins* • Louise Fletcher *Mrs Benjamin* • Wallace Shawn *Earl* • Fiona Lewis *Waitress/Avon Lady* • Kenneth Tobey *Arthur Newman* ■ *Dir* Michael Laughlin • *Scr* William Condon, Michael Laughlin

Strange Lady in Town ★★★ U
Western   1955 · US · Colour · 111mins

Greer Garson is Dr Julia Winslow Garth, peddling pills to the good citizens of Santa Fe in the late 19th century. Glossily shot by Harold Rosson, this is more melodrama than western, with Garson having trouble with her outcast brother Cameron Mitchell as well as confronting the usual ignorance and prejudice amongst her patients. As with many of director Mervyn LeRoy's later films, this is polished stuff, but obviously paste rather than a real gem. Greer glows with goodness, but Dana Andrews looks a mite peeved to be so completely upstaged.

Greer Garson *Dr Julia Winslow Garth* • Dana Andrews *Rork O'Brien* • Cameron Mitchell *David Garth* • Lois Smith *Spurs O'Brien* • Walter Hampden *Father Gabriel* ■ *Dir* Mervyn LeRoy • *Scr* Frank Butler

The Strange Love of Martha Ivers ★★★★★ PG
Film noir   1946 · US · BW · 115mins

A critical and commercial hit for Barbara Stanwyck, Van Heflin and, making his debut, Kirk Douglas, this high-voltage portrait of evil and greed remains blissfully absorbing and entertaining. Stanwyck, only just avoiding chewing the scenery, is millionairess Martha, married to Douglas. A weak-willed DA with (understandably) a drinking problem, he allowed an innocent man to be convicted for a murder his wife committed years before. Enter a nemesis from the past in the form of Van Heflin, and the fun begins. ▭

Barbara Stanwyck *Martha Ivers* • Van Heflin *Sam Masterson* • Kirk Douglas *Walter O'Neil* • Lizabeth Scott *Toni Marachek* • Judith Anderson *Mrs Ivers* • Roman Bohnen *Mr O'Neil* • Ann Doran *Secretary* ■ *Dir* Lewis Milestone • *Scr* Robert Rossen, from the story *Love Lies Bleeding* by Jack Patrick

The Strange Love of Molly Louvain ★★
Melodrama   1932 · US · BW · 70mins

Ann Dvorak, abandoned in childhood to the wrong side of the tracks but determined to be respectable, is courted by a wealthy young man. He deserts her, leaving her pregnant. She boards out her daughter, but her liaison with a scumbag (Leslie Fenton) implicates her in a murder. In hiding with Richard Cromwell, long in love with her, she falls for fast-talking

U = SUITABLE FOR ALL   Uc = SUITABLE FOR ALL, ESPECIALLY FOR YOUNG CHILDREN (VIDEO ONLY)   PG = PARENTAL GUIDANCE

newspaperman Lee Tracy who is unaware she's the fugitive. A minor credit on director Michael Curtiz's filmography, this is clichéd and unbelievable, but not uninvolving.

Ann Dvorak *Molly Louvain* • Lee Tracy *Scottie Cornell* • Richard Cromwell *Jimmy Cook* • Guy Kibbee *Pop* • Leslie Fenton *Nicky Grant* • Frank McHugh *Skeets* ■ *Dir* Michael Curtiz • *Scr* Erwin Gelsey, Brown Holmes, from the play *Tinsel Girl* by Maurine Dallas Watkins

The Strange One ★★

Drama 1957 · US · BW · 99mins

A hard-nosed, pulls-no-punches drama for its time. It's about life at a US military academy, ruled by a sadistic cadet leader played by Ben Gazzara, who revels in the name of Jocko De Paris. A sort of landlocked *Caine Mutiny*, it doubtless seems preachy and stagey today, and only James Olson and George Peppard register as Jocko's punching bags.

Ben Gazzara *Jocko De Paris* • Pat Hingle *Harold Knoble* • Mark Richman [Peter Mark Richman] *Cadet Colonel Corger* • Arthur Storch *Simmons* • Paul Richards (1) *Perrin McKee* • Larry Gates *Major Avery* • James Olson *Roger Gatt* • Julie Wilson *Rosebud* • George Peppard *Robert Marquales* ■ *Dir* Jack Garfein • *Scr* Calder Willingham, from his novel and play *End as a Man*

A Strange Place to Meet ★★ PG

Drama 1988 · Fr · Colour · 93mins

Catherine Deneuve's enthusiasm provided the impetus behind this minimalist roadside drama, and ultimately earned her a producer's credit on the film. Having impressed with a series of shorts and documentaries, François Dupeyron took something of a risk with his debut feature, as there is precious little story and plenty of inconsequential dialogue involved in the chance encounter between an unworldly doctor attempting to mend his car and a woman who has been dumped in a layby by her exasperated husband. It's intriguing trying to pick the facts from the fibs and fantasies, but it hardly makes for compulsive viewing. ▭

Catherine Deneuve *France* • Gérard Depardieu *Charles* • André Wilms *Georges* • Nathalie Cardone *Sylvie* • Jean-Pierre Sentier *Pierrot* ■ *Dir* François Dupeyron • *Scr* François Dupeyron, Dominique Faysse

Strange Planet ★★★ 15

Romantic comedy
1999 · Ausl · Colour · 96mins

An episodic romantic comedy from Australia about a year in the love lives of six men and women. Perceptive and engaging, Emma-Kate Croghan's follow-up to *Love and Other Catastrophes* features a trio of delightful performances from career girl Claudia Karvan, sweet but insecure Naomi Watts and quirky Alice Garner. The male characters are incredibly dull and self-absorbed in comparison. The film loses its perky momentum after a cracking first half, culminating in a matchmaking climax that's way too convenient. Luckily, the infectious energy – backed by a wonderful dance soundtrack – papers over most of the

cracks in the script. Contains swearing, drug abuse and sex scenes.

Claudia Karvan *Judy* • Naomi Watts *Alice* • Alice Garner *Sally* • Tom Long *Ewan* • Aaron Jeffrey *Joel* • Felix Williamson *Neil* • Hugo Weaving *Steven* • Rebecca Frith *Amanda* ■ *Dir* Emma-Kate Croghan • *Scr* Stavros Kazantzidis, Emma-Kate Croghan

The Strange Vengeance of Rosalie ★

Drama 1972 · US · Colour · 107mins

A pointless, ill-conceived and painfully contrived thriller that revives the old chestnut of the kidnapped falling in love with the kidnapper. In this instance it's travelling salesman Ken Howard who is abducted by young native American girl Bonnie Bedelia under the guise of driving to her grandfather's ranch in New Mexico. But the ranch turns out to be a remote shack, her grandfather is dead and she's there to protect a stash of gold that local layabout Anthony Zerbe wants to steal. After she nobbles Howard when he tries to escape, the dumb plot descends into mass confusion.

Bonnie Bedelia *Rosalie* • Ken Howard *Virgil* • Anthony Zerbe *Fry* ■ *Dir* Jack Starrett • *Scr* Anthony Greville-Bell, John Kohn

Strange Voices ★★★ 15

Drama 1987 · US · Colour · 92mins

The strange voices in this depressing drama are tormenting teenager Nancy McKeon, who is diagnosed as suffering from schizophrenia, forcing her worried parents Valerie Harper and Stephen Macht to seek medical help. Mental illness is a tricky subject to deal with and, although it's handled sensitively here, one can't help but wish the tale offered more insights. Though it makes a good stab at providing more than just a catalogue of events, it's not a patch on the similarly themed, Emmy Award-winning *Sybil*, in which Sally Field starred as a young woman suffering from multiple personality disorder. ▭

Valerie Harper *Mrs Glover* • Nancy McKeon *Nikki Glover* • Stephen Macht *Mr Glover* • Millie Perkins *Helen* • Robin Morse *Jenny* ■ *Dir* Arthur Allan Seidelman • *Scr* Donna Dottley Powers, Wayne Powers, from a story by Roberta Dacks, Nancy Geller

The Strange Woman ★★★

Period melodrama 1946 · US · BW · 101mins

This is a rare examples of ace cult director Edgar G Ulmer (*Detour*, *Bluebeard*) working with major stars and he coaxes what is possibly a career-best performance from Hedy Lamarr. Lamarr stars as a social-climbing beauty who ensnares boring Gene Lockhart, suave George Sanders and gauche Louis Hayward during her rise from a deprived childhood. It's highly enjoyable tosh, glamorous to look at and played to perfection by its stars. A B-movie that successfully masquerades as an A.

Hedy Lamarr *Jenny Hager* • George Sanders *John Evered* • Louis Hayward *Ephraim Poster* • Gene Lockhart *Isaiah Poster* • Hillary Brooke *Meg Saladine* • Rhys Williams *Deacon Adams* • June Storey *Lena Tempest* ■ *Dir* Edgar G Ulmer • *Scr* Herb Meadow, from the novel by Ben Ames Williams

The Strange World of Planet X ★★

Science-fiction thriller 1957 · UK · BW · 0mins

Perhaps because the hysterical levels of fifties Cold War paranoia that swept America did not reach the same heights here, Britain never really went for big insect movies. However, the odd ones did slip out and here Forrest Tucker is the obligatory square-jawed imported American out to stop irradiated bugs taking over the world. Cheap and cheerful fun.

Forrest Tucker *Gil Graham* • Gaby André *Michele Dupont* • Martin Benson *Smith* • Hugh Latimer *Jimmy Murray* • Wyndham Goldie *Brigadier Cartwright* • Alec Mango *Dr Laird* ■ *Dir* Gilbert Gunn • *Scr* Paul Ryder, Joe Ambor, from a story by Gene Ray

The Stranger ★★★ PG

Thriller 1946 · US · BW · 94mins

Orson Welles was said to have had little time for this thriller about the search for a Nazi war criminal in small-town America, but it helped put him back on the Hollywood map after a series of box-office failures. There are some of his characteristic directorial touches on view, as well as some of the actorly excesses that typified the performances he gave when he was jobbing to fund his more personal projects. Stars Edward G Robinson and Loretta Young are impressive, but the eye always alights on the imposing figure of the third-billed Welles. Russell Metty's stylish, shadowy black-and-white photography are so superb, it beggars belief the film was also released in a colourised version. ▭

Edward G Robinson *Wilson* • Loretta Young *Mary Longstreet* • Orson Welles *Professor Charles Rankin/Franz Kindler* • Philip Merivale *Judge Longstreet* • Richard Long *Noah Longstreet* • Byron Keith *Dr Jeff Lawrence* • Billy House *Potter* ■ *Dir* Orson Welles • *Scr* Anthony Veiller, John Huston (uncredited), Orson Welles, from a story by Victor Trivas, Decla Dunning

The Stranger ★★

Drama 1967 · Alg/Fr/It · Colour · 104mins

Despite the insistence of the author's widow, Luchino Visconti was totally the wrong director to adapt Albert Camus's stark, existential tale of the outsider whose irrational act of murder lands him on death row. His visuals are too ornate, his grasp of thirties Franco-Algerian politics too tenuous and his sympathy for the alienated killer too superficial. Yet, he still succeeds in drawing an undervalued performance from Marcello Mastroianni, in which he captures the emotional inertia that prevents Arthur Meursault from crying at his mother's funeral and thus gives credence to the accusations of calculating malice. Fascinating, but a failure nonetheless. An Italian language film.

Marcello Mastroianni *Arthur Meursault* • Anna Karina *Marie Cardona* • Georges Wilson *Examining magistrate* • Bertrand Blier *Defense counsel* • Pierre Bertin *Judge* • Georges Geret *Raymond* • Bruno Cremer *Priest* ■ *Dir* Luchino Visconti • *Scr* Suso Cecchi D'Amico, Georges Conchon, Emmanuel Robles, Luchino Visconti, from the novel *L'Etranger* by Albert Camus • *Producer* Dino De Laurentiis • *Cinematographer* Giuseppe Rotunno

The Stranger ★★★

Psychological thriller
1987 · US/Arg · Colour and BW · 89mins

One thing strikes you about this film immediately, and that's how good it looks. But what this intriguing memory-loss thriller gains in style, it loses in construction, as Argentinian director Adolfo Aristarain overdoes the black-and-white flashbacks and too often allows the tension to slacken. However, Bonnie Bedelia (*Die Hard*) is highly convincing as an amnesiac witness to murder, and Peter Riegert chips in with a decent turn as the doctor she believes she can trust (but can she?). Contains brief nudity.

Bonnie Bedelia *Alice Kildee* • Peter Riegert *Dr Harris Kite* • Barry Primus *Sergeant Drake* • David Spielberg *Hobby* • Marcos Woinski *Macaw* • Julio De Grazia *Jay* • Cecilia Roth *Anita* ■ *Dir* Adolfo Aristarain • *Scr* Dan Gurskis • *Cinematographer* Horacio Maira

The Stranger ★★

Drama 1991 · Ind · Colour · 118mins

Influenced by the writings of Claude Lévi-Strauss (and with a nod towards the story of Martin Guerre), this was Satyajit Ray's final film, but still very much a minor work. Utpal Dutt is suitably ambiguous as the returning prodigal who may or may not be the uncle Mamata Shankar has not seen since 1955. While Ray handles the awkward civilities of the homecoming in his typically unassuming manner, he fails to build the tension as Shankar's husband (Dipankar De) decides to put the stranger to the test. Subtly satirical, allegorically autobiographical, yet disappointingly formal. In Bengali with English subtitles.

Dipankar De *Sudhindra Bose* • Mamata Shankar *Anila Bose* • Bikram Bhattacharya *Satyaki/Bablu* • Utpal Dutt *Manmohan Mitra* • Dhritiman Chatterjee *Prithwish Sen Gupta* ■ *Dir/Scr* Satyajit Ray

A Stranger among Us ★★ 15

Crime drama 1992 · US · Colour · 104mins

Released in British cinemas as *Close to Eden*, this is a flop under any name, with Melanie Griffith woefully miscast as a cop investigating a murder in New York's tightknit Hasidic community. Throw in a romantic interest in the form of Eric Thal and you have an uneven thriller from director Sidney Lumet, who has certainly had his share of career ups and downs. Contains some violence and swearing. ▭

Melanie Griffith *Emily Eden* • Eric Thal *Ariel* • John Pankow *Levine* • Tracy Pollan *Mara* • Lee Richardson *Rebbe* • Mia Sara *Leah* • Jamey Sheridan *Nick Kemp* ■ *Dir* Sidney Lumet • *Scr* Robert J Avrech

Stranger at My Door ★★★ U

Western 1956 · US · BW · 84mins

This western adventure stars Skip Homeier as Clay Anderson, a dangerous outlaw who learns that there is more to life than stealing and killing when he seeks shelter in the home of preacher Hollis Jarret (Macdonald Carey). Good characterisation and plenty of action make this fine family entertainment.

Macdonald Carey *Hollis Jarret* • Patricia Medina *Peg Jarret* • Skip Homeier *Clay*

Anderson • Stephen Wootton *Dodie Jarret* • Louis Jean Heydt *Sheriff John Tatum* • Howard Wright *Doc Parks* • Slim Pickens *Ben Silas, horse trader* ■ *Dir* William Witney • *Scr* Barry Shipman, from his story

The Stranger beside Me

★★★

Drama based on a true story
1995 · US · Colour

This true-life TV movie is set in San Diego and chronicles the horrific discoveries made by a navy wife when her husband is accused of being a Peeping Tom. Director Sandor Stern is on very different territory from his earlier *Amityville Horror* movies and *Glitz*, but he presents each new revelation with some skill, piecing together a portrait of a serial rapist without the tabloid touch that blights so many TV movies. Tiffani-Amber Thiessen gives a controlled performance in the lead, offering a credible impression of hurt innocence as her husband's crimes are uncovered.

Tiffani-Amber Thiessen *Jennifer Moore* • Eric Close *Chris Gallagher* • Lorrie Morgan *Nancy Halloran* • Gerald McRaney *Dave Morgan* • Steven Eckholdt *Detective Bill Rounder* ■ *Dir* Sandor Stern • *Scr* Bruce Miller

A Stranger Came Home ★

Crime mystery   1954 · UK · BW · 80mins

Paulette Goddard gave up her screen career (apart from one Italian job ten years later) after being reduced to this dreary non-thriller for Hammer Films – a long fall from her first British picture, *An Ideal Husband*, six years earlier. Supposedly irresistible as the wife of a vanished businessman, she is favoured by Hollywood-style soft-focus close-ups. Her husband, played by William Sylvester, reappears with a bad case of amnesia, seeking to find out which of three former associates had tried to kill him. Suave character actor George Sanders didn't really write the book on which this film is based and wisely refrained from appearing in it.

Paulette Goddard *Angie* • William Sylvester *Philip Vickers* • Patrick Holt *Job Crandall* • Paul Carpenter *Bill Saul* • Alvys Maben *Joan Merrill* • Russell Napier *Inspector Treherne* • David King-Wood *Sessions* ■ *Dir* Terence Fisher • *Scr* Michael Carreras, from the novel *Stranger at Home* by George Sanders

Stranger from Venus ★ U

Science-fiction   1954 · UK · BW · 74mins

A low budget British remake (although uncredited) of *The Day the Earth Stood Still* and starring the same lead Patricia Neal, this is directed by Burt Balaban, who adds a mere hint of American zip to the stiff upper lip atmosphere and limited public house setting. After crashing her car, Neal meets mysterious Helmut Dantine who has travelled from Venus to persuade mankind to abandon their nuclear power experiments. A spaceship arrives to increase the pressure, but the dying Dantine sends it away as he disappears in a puff of smoke. Lacklustre and too restrained.

Patricia Neal *Susan North* • Helmut Dantine *The Stranger* • Derek Bond *Arthur Walker* • Cyril Luckham *Dr Meinard* • Willoughby Gray *Tom* • Marigold Russell *Gretchen* • Arthur

Young *Scientist* • Kenneth Edwards *Charles Dixon* ■ *Dir* Burt Balaban • *Scr* Hans Jacoby, from a story by Desmond Leslie

A Stranger in My Arms ★★

Melodrama   1959 · US · BW · 88mins

June Allyson plays a war widow whose husband has been killed in Korea in this not-so-classic melodrama from Ross Hunter, producer of many of Douglas Sirk's best films. She has to deal with her difficult mother-in-law (Mary Astor), a woman ruthlessly intent on seeing that her adored son is posthumously honoured, and with the air force officer (Jeff Chandler) asked to testify to the dead man's heroism. Turns out he was actually a coward, but June has Jeff to console her. Neither the drama nor the romance catch light in this dull and portentous film. The earnest stars lack the charisma to lift the material, leaving the polished veteran Astor to provide what little spark there is.

June Allyson *Christina Beasley* • Jeff Chandler *Pike Yarnell* • Sandra Dee *Pat Beasley* • Charles Coburn *Vance Beasley* • Mary Astor *Mrs Beasley* • Peter Graves (1) *Donald Beasley* • Conrad Nagel *Harley Beasley* • Hayden Rorke *Marcus Beasley* • Reita Green *Bessie Logan* ■ *Dir* Helmut Käutner • *Scr* Peter Berneis, from the novel *And Ride a Tiger* by Robert Wilder • *Cinematographer* William H Daniels [William Daniels] • *Producer* Ross Hunter

Stranger in My Bed ★★

Drama based on a true story
1986 · US · Colour · 96mins

The title shrieks the melodramatic intent of this TV movie, which is, like so many of its kind, based on a true story. Lindsay Wagner stars as Beverly Slater, the devoted mother who experiences a total personality change after she is involved in a car accident. You know you're always going to get a foot-to-the-floor performance from Wagner and she doesn't disappoint, taking amnesia, mood swings, illicit love and regret in her stride before the inevitably happy ending. Armand Assante is among those left with little to do but stand by and admire.

Lindsay Wagner *Beverly Slater* • Armand Assante *Hal Slater* • Douglas Sheehan [Doug Sheehan] *Roger Hammond* • Allison Court *Joan Slater* • Gabriel Damon *Stuart Slater* ■ *Dir* Larry Elikann • *Scr* Audrey Davis Levin

Stranger in My Home ★★ 15

Thriller   1997 · US · Colour · 87mins

Also known as *Brother's Keeper*, this TV movie revisits the premise that has been fuelling films from the Barbara Stanwyck vehicle *No Man of Her Own* to Agnieszka Holland's *Olivier Olivier*. This time, the focus is on the person taken in by the stranger who claims to be a long-lost relative, with Victoria Hamel giving a steady performance as the lawyer who believes the client she is defending for murder is the brother their impoverished mother had to give away. As such stories can only end in one of two ways, it's hardly a suspense shocker. However it is solidly staged. Contains violence and some swearing. 🖵

Veronica Hamel *Jennifer Richmond* • Joe Penny *Ned Covington* • Daniel Hugh-Kelly *Doug Martin* • Leigh Taylor-Young *Margot* •

Robert Curtis-Brown *Blake* • Michael Angarano *Drew* • Betsy Beard *Lauretta* ■ *Dir* Farhad Mann • *Scr* Robert Hamilton

Stranger in the Family

★★ PG

Drama   1991 · US · Colour · 95mins

It's amnesia again, this time involving the teenage victim of a car crash having to learn how to do everything all over again. Glum stuff, not mitigated by the earnest and tortuous family saga woven around the sorrowful central theme. Talented Teri Garr is wasted here, but nonetheless is excellent, as are all the cast. But did it all have to be so strained? The family members experience the whole gamut of emotions and crises: guilt, anger, interdependency. It's all very American, and maybe a little too intense for UK palates. 🖵

Neil Patrick Harris *Steve Thompson* • Teri Garr *Randi Thompson* • Randle Mell *Alan Thompson* • Sierra Samuel *Shari Thompson* • Kathryn Dowling *Dr Webb* • Cully Fredricksen *Principal Kadinski* • Mag Ruffman *Mrs Kessler* ■ *Dir* Donald Wrye • *Scr* Hal Sitowitz

Stranger in the House

★★ 15

Mystery melodrama
1967 · UK · Colour · 90mins

Also known as *Cop-Out*, the highlight of this melodrama is a solid performance from James Mason as a depressed, drunken ex-barrister who comes out of retirement for a seemingly hopeless murder case involving his daughter's boyfriend. Simenon's novel had already been filmed in an intelligent French version starring Raimu, but this adaptation makes an uneasy transfer to sleepy Hampshire. Nevertheless reliable British performers such as Yootha Joyce, Moira Lister and Rita Webb are worth picking out in small parts. 🖵

James Mason *John Sawyer* • Geraldine Chaplin *Angela Sawyer* • Bobby Darin *Barney Teale* • Paul Bertoya *Jo Christophorides* • Ian Ogilvy *Desmond Flower* • Bryan Stanyon *Peter Hawkins* • Pippa Steel *Sue Phillips* • Clive Morton *Col Flower* • Moira Lister *Mrs Flower* • Yootha Joyce *Girl at shooting range* • Rita Webb *Mrs Plaskett* ■ *Dir* Pierre Rouve • *Scr* Pierre Rouve, from the novel *Les Inconnus dans la Maison* by Georges Simenon

A Stranger in the Mirror

★★ 15

Melodrama   1993 · US · Colour · 94mins

Another slice of overwrought hokum adapted from the prolific pen of novelist Sidney Sheldon, which aspires, unsuccessfully, to be *A Star Is Born*, but will undoubtedly be lapped up by fans of kitsch melodrama. Perry King plays the ambitious comedian who begins swimming with the Hollywood sharks with predictable results. Christopher Plummer is ripely over the top as King's agent, and another familiar face in the supporting cast is that of Juliet Mills (sister of Hayley, daughter of John). Director Charles Jarrott surprisingly manages to keep a straight face throughout. 🖵

Perry King *Toby Temple* • Lori Loughlin *Josephine Czinski/Jill Castle* • Christopher Plummer *Clifton Lawrence* • Geordie Johnson *David Kenyon* • Juliet Mills *Alice Tanner* •

Paula Shaw *Mrs Czinski* • Janie Woods-Morris *Mrs Kenyon* • George Touliatos *Sam Winters* ■ *Dir* Charles Jarrott • *Scr* Stirling Silliphant, from the novel by Sidney Sheldon

A Stranger in Town ★★★

Drama   1995 · US · Colour

A nerve-jangling TV movie based on Kenneth Zunder's play *Higher Laws*. While some of the claustrophobic intensity of the stage production has been lost in the transfer to the small screen, this is still an uncomfortable thriller thanks to the solid performances of Jean Smart, as the mother of a sickly child, and Gregory Hines as the stranger who fetches up on her doorstep. Director Peter Levin, perhaps best known for the less than distinguished *Royal Romance of Charles and Diana*, lets slip the revelations about Smart with enough guile to keep you glued to the end.

Jean Smart *Kay Tarses* • Gregory Hines *Barnes* • Jeffrey Nordling *Larry* • Lucinda Jenney *Jeanine* ■ *Dir* Peter Levin • *Scr* Ara Watson, Sam Blackwell, from the play *Higher Laws* by Kenneth Zunder

Stranger on Horseback

★★★ U

Western   1955 · US · Colour · 65mins

Joel McCrea brings his calm authority to this strong but unusually brief western, playing the circuit judge who dares to arrest Kevin McCarthy, the spoiled killer son of the local land baron (John McIntire) and then has to coax witnesses to testify. The film was shot in Mexico using an unsatisfactory colour process. However, highly capable director Jacques Tourneur draws effective performances from the cast, which also includes Emile Meyer as the intimidated local sheriff, John Carradine as a corrupt attorney, and the young Czech-born Miroslava, a star of Mexican cinema who killed herself just as this film was released.

Joel McCrea *Rick Thorne* • Miroslava *Amy Lee Bannerman* • Kevin McCarthy *Tom Bannerman* • John McIntire *Josiah Bannerman* • Nancy Gates *Caroline Webb* • John Carradine *Colonel Streeter* • Emile Meyer *Sheriff Nat Bell* ■ *Dir* Jacques Tourneur • *Scr* Herb Meadow, Don Martin, from a story by Louis L'Amour

Stranger on My Land

★★★ 15

Action drama   1988 · US · Colour · 92mins

This is an intelligent, moving drama, ably directed by TV-movie specialist Larry Elikann. Tommy Lee Jones is the head of a stubborn rural family locked in battle with the government who want to take their land for military use. As well as the star, there are equally good supporting turns from Dee Wallace Stone and that accomplished picture stealer, Ben Johnson. Certainly worth a look. Contains some violence. 🖵

Tommy Lee Jones *Buddy Whitman* • Dee Wallace Stone *Annie Whitman* • Ben Johnson *Vern Whitman* • Terry O'Quinn *Connie Priest* • Pat Hingle *Judge Munson* • Michael Paul Chan *Eliot Song* ■ *Dir* Larry Elikann • *Scr* Edward Hume, IC Rappaport

Stranger on the Run ★★★

Western 1967 · US · Colour · 97mins

This intelligent western drama features Henry Fonda as a ragged-drunk who, having drifted into a bleak railroad town, finds himself arrested for murder. A perverse deputy (Michael Parks) decides to keep the manhunt going, and releases the innocent man into the desert to be chased by his brutal railway posse. Based on a story by Reginald Rose – whose *Twelve Angry Men* also dealt with one man against the mob – this TV movie has a strong cast (including Anne Baxter and Sal Mineo), workmanlike direction by Don Siegel and an intelligent script that lifts it above the average.

Henry Fonda *Ben Chamberlain* • Anne Baxter *Valverda Johnson* • Michael Parks *Vince McKay* • Dan Duryea *OE Hotchkiss* • Sal Mineo *George Blaylock* • Lloyd Bochner *Mr Gorman* • Michael Burns *Matt Johnson* • Tom Reese *Leo Weed* ■ *Dir* Don Siegel • *Scr* Dean E Riesner, from a story by Reginald Rose

Stranger on the Third Floor ★★★

Thriller 1940 · US · BW · 62mins

Although John Huston's *The Maltese Falcon* is usually regarded as the first authentic *film noir*, this gripping thriller from RKO came out a year earlier. All the requisite *noir* elements are present: the fatalistic, paranoid mood, the corkscrew murder plot and bug-eyed Peter Lorre as the "stranger". The violent story, including knifings and capital punishment, is remarkably compressed by Boris Ingster's direction. But the star of the show is the expressionistic camerawork of Nicholas Musuraca, the maestro who would later shoot *Cat People* and *Build My Gallows High*.

Peter Lorre *The Stranger* • John McGuire *Michael Ward* • Margaret Tallichet *Jane* • Elisha Cook Jr *Joe Briggs* • Charles Waldron *District attorney* • Charles Halton *Meng* • Ethel Griffies *Mrs Kane* • Cliff Clark *Martin* ■ • *Scr* Frank Partos, from his story • *Cinematographer* Nicholas Musuraca

Stranger than Paradise ★★★★ 15

Drama 1984 · US · BW · 85mins

Developed from a 30-minute short and made for a mere $120,000, this chilled-out road movie could be seen as the first slacker picture. Shot in long takes, each ending with a dawdling fade to black, the action (if that's the word) centres on Hungarian immigrant John Lurie, his cousin Eszter Balint and his mate Richard Edson, and their driftings between Cleveland and Florida. The winner of the Caméra d'Or at Cannes, this is a unique and irresistible film, which warned us all that the only thing to expect from Jim Jarmusch is the unexpected. It's superbly shot by Tom DiCillo, who went on to direct the magnificent *Living in Oblivion*. Contains swearing. ▭

John Lurie *Willie* • Eszter Balint *Eva* • Richard Edson *Eddie* • Cecillia Stark *Aunt Lottie* • Danny Rosen *Billy* • Sara Driver *Girl with hat* ■ *Dir/Scr* Jim Jarmusch

A Stranger to Love ★★

Drama based on a true story
1996 · US · Colour

Pam Dawber – of *Mork and Mindy* fame – finds love with amnesiac Beau Bridges, but then he discovers that his idyllic life with her has merely been an accidental diversion from his real existence. Based on a true story, this TV movie might have been unbearably sentimental. That it isn't is down to the interplay between Dawber and Bridges; their performances are matched by Tess Harper, as the wife who never stopped believing her husband was alive. Contains violence and some swearing.

Beau Bridges *Allan Grant* • Pam Dawber *Andi Stanton* • Tess Harper *Linda Grant* ■ *Dir* Peter Levin • *Scr* Richard Leder

A Stranger Waits ★ 15

Thriller 1987 · US · Colour · 89mins

In this trashy thriller, Suzanne Pleshette goes slumming as a rich widow who hires a new caretaker for her seaside estate, and takes him to bed not knowing he plans to murder her. There is some suspense, since the handsome stud's intentions are telegraphed early on and we know our wealthy heroine is in danger, but this woman-in-jeopardy film makes us feel as we've seen it all before. It's creaky and derivative – and really not worth the wait. ▭

Suzanne Pleshette *Kate Bennington* • Justin Deas *Mike Webber* • Kenneth Welsh *Richard Miller* • Tom Atkins *Sheriff Burke Collier* ■ *Dir* Robert Lewis • *Scr* Durrell Royce Crays, from a story by Bruce Lansbury

The Stranger Within ★★★ 18

Psychological thriller
1990 · US · Colour · 89mins

This thriller centres on a child who may not be all he seems. When Rick Schroder (looking suitably sinister) meets Kate Jackson, he claims to be her son who was abducted 16 years previously. But is he? A surprisingly tense psychological film, helped by the increasingly unhinged performance of Jackson, it's also one of the few TV movies of this type where you can't guess the ending straight away. Contains violence and some swearing. ▭

Rick Schroder *Mark* • Kate Jackson *Mare* • Chris Sarandon *Dan Vance* • Clark Sandford *Captain Bender* • Peter Breitmayer *Phil Bender* • Pamela Danser *Emma* ■ *Dir* Tom Holland • *Scr* John Pielmeier

The Stranger Wore a Gun ★★ U

Western 1953 · US · Colour · mins

A strong cast comes to the aid of this implausible Randolph Scott western, originally released in 3-D in the United States. One-eyed director Andre De Toth (*House of Wax*) stages a fiery climax in a blazing saloon, that made 3-D audiences feel the heat. Scott plays the man protecting gold shipments from hold-ups, and his adversaries include the ever-hissable George Macready, Alfonso Bedoya's beaming Mexican bandit, and two gunmen played by Lee Marvin and Ernest Borgnine early in their careers.

The two women vying for Randy's affections are the worldly Claire Trevor (splendid as always) and the respectable Joan Weldon (pallid and anodyne). ▭

Randolph Scott *Jeff Travis* • Claire Trevor *Josie Sullivan* • Joan Weldon *Shelby Conroy* • George Macready *Jules Mourret* • Alfonso Bedoya *Degas* • Lee Marvin *Dan Kurth* • Ernest Borgnine *Bull Slager* ■ *Dir* Andre De Toth • *Scr* Kenneth Gamet, from the novel *Yankee Gold* by John M Cunningham

Strangers All ★★

Drama 1935 · US · BW · 68mins

The strangers are the members of a family, each so different from the other as to have no common ground. Shopkeeper and family breadwinner Preston Foster is at loggerheads with brothers William Bakewell, an egotistical aspiring actor, and James Bush, a naive socialist radical; daughter Florine McKinney dumps her fiancé and marries another without telling the family; and mother May Robson tries to hold her bickering brood together. Director Charles Vidor tries to keep control with no more than passable results, thanks to an unintegrated mishmash of domestic drama and comedy.

May Robson *"Mom"* Anna Carter • Preston Foster *Murray Carter* • Florine McKinney *Lily Carter* • William Bakewell *Dick Carter* • James Bush *Lewis Carter* • Samuel S Hinds *Mr Green* • Clifford Jones *Pat Gruen* ■ *Dir* Charles Vidor • *Scr* Milton Krims, from the play *Strangers All: or, Separate Lives* by Marie M Bercovici

The Stranger's Hand ★★★ U

Spy thriller 1953 · It/UK · BW · 85mins

Written by Guy Elmes from an uncompleted story by Graham Greene, this intriguing Cold War thriller is most memorable for director Mario Soldati's inspired use of the magic and mystery of Venice. Combining both wide-eyed wonder and growing fear, Richard O'Sullivan impresses as the young boy who goes in search of his kidnapped father, receiving sympathetic support from unlikely hero Richard Basehart and hotel receptionist Alida Valli. Trevor Howard appears all too briefly as the missing major, but the author himself contributes a cameo, as the hand untying the mooring rope of one of the gondolas.

Trevor Howard *Maj Court* • Alida Valli *Roberta* • Richard Basehart *Joe Hamstringer* • Eduardo Ciannelli *Dr Vivaldi* • Richard O'Sullivan *Roger Court* ■ *Dir* Mario Soldati • *Scr* Guy Elmes, Giorgio Bassani, from the story by Graham Greene

Strangers in the City ★★★

Drama 1962 · US · BW · 83mins

An interesting example of early sixties' independent cinema, this highlights the plight of a Puerto Rican family struggling to make a life for themselves on the mean streets of Manhattan. Camilo Delgado is the disaffected father unable to adapt to life in the States; when he loses his job, his children (Robert Gentile and Rosita de Triana) head out in search of work, only to encounter a world of crime and prejudice. As directed by Rick Carrier, the film tends towards the overblown, with the tragedy escalating

to near-Jacobean proportions by the film's climax. But there are still some powerful moments, and it's certainly ahead of its time in depicting the hardships faced by America's ever-expanding Latino population.

Robert Gentile *Felipe Alvarez* • Camilo Delgado *José Alvarez* • Rosita de Triana *Antonia Alvarez* • Creta Margos *Elena Alvarez* • Robert Corso *Caddy* • Bob O'Connell *Dan* ■ *Dir* Rick Carrier • *Scr* Rick Carrier, from a story by Rick Carrier, Elgin Ciampi

Strangers Kiss ★★★★ 15

Romantic drama
1983 · US · Colour and BW · 93mins

With *Slow Burn* and *Heart of Midnight* to his credit, as well as this cleverly conceived and well-executed drama, Matthew Chapman should be a better known director. The obvious inspiration for this movie about film-making is Stanley Kubrick's *Killer's Kiss*, but, without that film's steely black-and-white photography, Mikhail Suslov's colour shots are more akin to the lush melodramas that Douglas Sirk used to make for producer Ross Hunter. Peter Coyote is outstanding as the obsessive director prepared to endanger the life of his star (Victoria Tennant) to complete his picture. Intricate, astute and very classy.

Peter Coyote *Stanley* • Victoria Tennant *Carol Redding* • Blaine Novak *Stevie Blake* • Dan Shor *Farris* • Richard Romanus *Frank Silva* • Linda Kerridge *Shirley* • Carlos Palomino *Estoban* ■ *Dir* Matthew Chapman • *Scr* Blaine Novak, Matthew Chapman, from a story by Blaine Novak

Strangers May Kiss ★★★

Romantic drama 1931 · US · BW · 83mins

Passionately in love with foreign correspondent Neil Hamilton, Norma Shearer is heartbroken when he goes off on an assignment. She dallies with a series of lovers in Europe and finally decides to go home and marry her faithful suitor Robert Montgomery, whereupon Hamilton reappears, unleashing suicidal despair in Shearer with his reaction to her behaviour in his absence. Shearer, photographed by Garbo's favourite William Daniels, and directed by George Fitzmaurice, holds the screen in the kind of role she came to play almost peerlessly countless times – and more than once with Montgomery as the fall guy with a penchant for the bottle. An archetypal thirties romantic drama, this is very good if not quite the very best.

Norma Shearer *Lisbeth Corbin* • Robert Montgomery *Steve* • Neil Hamilton *Alan* • Marjorie Rambeau *Geneva* • Irene Rich *Celia* • Hale Hamilton *Andrew* ■ *Dir* George Fitzmaurice • *Scr* John Meehan, from the novel by Ursula Parrott • *Cinematographer* William H Daniels [William Daniels]

Stranger's Meeting ★

Crime thriller 1957 · UK · BW · 63mins

A circus acrobat (Peter Arne), convicted of killing his partner but innocent of the crime, escapes and sets out to clear his name and find the real culprit. Directed by Robert Day – later to make a career in television on both sides of the Atlantic – and co-starring Delphi Lawrence and Barbara Archer, this is an example of the British film industry at its worst. It's inconceivable

that this pathetically feeble, clumsy and uninteresting film could have been made – even as a programme filler, which it is – as late as 1957.

Peter Arne *Harry Belair* • Delphi Lawrence *Margot Sanders* • Conrad Phillips *David Sanders* • Barbara Archer *Rosie Foster* • David Ritch *Giovanni* • David Lodge *Fred* ■ *Dir* Robert Day • *Scr* David Gordon

Strangers on a Train
★★★★★ PG

Classic thriller   1951 · US · BW · 96mins

Although not Alfred Hitchcock's best film, this splendid thriller is testimony to the director's mastery of technique and his ability to turn even the most unpromising material into a gripping movie. After nearly a dozen writers had turned down the chance to adapt Patricia Highsmith's novel, Raymond Chandler stepped into the breach, only to disagree with Hitch on several key scenes and suffer the ignominy of having his dialogue polished by Czenzi Ormonde, a staff writer. Hitchcock was also underwhelmed by Farley Granger in a role he felt cried out for William Holden. Nevertheless, he turns the murderous bargain between eccentric playboy Robert Walker and tennis champ Granger into a nail-biter, with the two fairground scenes outstanding. He approved of one casting decision, however – his daughter Patricia plays Ruth Roman's suspicious sister. 🖵

Farley Granger *Guy Haines* • Ruth Roman *Anne Morton* • Robert Walker *Bruno Antony* • Leo G Carroll *Senator Morton* • Patricia Hitchcock *Barbara Morton* • Laura Elliott *Miriam* • Marion Lorne *Mrs Antony* • Jonathan Hale *Mr Antony* ■ *Dir* Alfred Hitchcock • *Scr* Raymond Chandler, Czenzi Ormonde, Whitfield Cook, from the novel by Patricia Highsmith

The Stranger's Return ★★ U

Drama   1933 · US · BW · 87mins

Having left her husband, Miriam Hopkins goes to live with her grandfather Lionel Barrymore on his farm in the Midwest, where she becomes passionately involved with married man and father Franchot Tone. Meanwhile, in between dispensing advice to Hopkins and expressing his disapproval of the affair, Barrymore, who is facing approaching death, has to fend off the grasping relatives who are trying to get their clutches on his land. King Vidor directed this dour drama which, despite its excellent cast, remains unappealing.

Lionel Barrymore *Grandpa Storr* • Miriam Hopkins *Louise Storr* • Franchot Tone *Guy Crane* • Stuart Erwin *Simon, farmhand* • Irene Hervey *Nettie Crane* • Beulah Bondi *Beatrice* ■ *Dir* King Vidor • *Scr* Brown Holmes, Phil Stong, from the novel by Phil Stong

Strangers When We Meet ★★★ 15

Romantic drama
1960 · US · Colour · 112mins

A sophisticated study of compulsive marital infidelity starring Kirk Douglas and Kim Novak, beautifully acted and glamorously photographed, this is marred only by a syrupy music score that undermines the bittersweet pathos of the events portrayed. Director Richard Quine's use of landscape and roadside assignations

works well, and the supporting cast is exemplary, especially Barbara Rush as Douglas's wife, Walter Matthau as a lecherous friend, and rnie Kovacs as the writer for whom architect Douglas builds a house. Despite censorship limitations at the time, Evan Hunter's adaptation of his own novel has the ring of truth to it and makes satisfying, though uncomfortable, viewing. 🖵

Kirk Douglas *Larry Coe* • Kim Novak *Maggie Gault* • Ernie Kovacs *Roger Altar* • Barbara Rush *Eve Coe* • Walter Matthau *Felix Anders* • Virginia Bruce *Mrs Wagner* • Kent Smith *Stanley Baxter* ■ *Dir* Richard Quine • *Scr* Evan Hunter, from his novel

The Strangler ★★

Crime drama   1964 · US · BW · 88mins

Released to capitalise on the Boston Strangler frenzy of the time, this racy black-and-white thriller is better than most exploitation features. Young Boston nurses have been murdered, but the chief suspect, a solitary lab technician obsessed with dolls (played with relish by a creepy Victor Buono), seems to have an iron-clad alibi, which even a lie-detector test can't shake. Ellen Corby (Grandma Walton) plays his possessive and hated mother.

Victor Buono *Leon Kroll* • David McLean *Lt Benson* • Diane Sayer *Barbara* • Davey Davison *Tally* • Ellen Corby *Mrs Kroll* • Baynes Barron *Sgt Clyde* • Michael Ryan *Posner* ■ *Dir* Burt Topper • *Scr* Bill S Ballinger

Strapless ★★★ 15

Romantic drama   1988 · UK · Colour · 95mins

A rather jarring and unconvincing look at romance from writer/director David Hare (*Plenty*). Blair Brown is the fortysomething doctor who re-evaluates her life when she is wooed by charming but unreliable Bruno Ganz, who turns out to be not the man she first thought he was. More believable is the relationship between Brown and her younger, freer – and pregnant – sister played by Bridget Fonda. But ultimately this drama suffers from stilted dialogue and direction and an overall condescending attitude towards female independence. 🖵

Blair Brown *Lillian Hempel* • Bridget Fonda *Amy Hempel* • Bruno Ganz *Raymond Forbes* • Alan Howard *Mr Cooper* • Michael Gough *Douglas Brodie* • Hugh Laurie *Colin* • Suzanne Burden *Romaine Salmon* • Rohan McCullough *Annie Rice* ■ *Dir/Scr* David Hare

Strategic Air Command ★★★ U

Drama   1955 · US · Colour · 113mins

James Stewart and June Allyson star as a baseball player and his wife for the second time in their careers in this unconvincing combination of domestic melodrama and high-flying flag-waving. Paramount's biggest money-spinner of 1955, the film is most effective during the thrilling aerial sequences, which were skilfully shot by cinematographers William Daniels and Tom Tutwiler although the crash-landing on Greenland is also impressively staged. Director Anthony Mann seems more at home with the male-bonding between Stewart and his fellow trainee pilots, but Allyson still makes an impact in a role less saccharine than usual.

James Stewart *Lieutenant Colonel Robert "Dutch" Holland* • June Allyson *Sally Holland* • Frank Lovejoy *General Ennis C Hawkes* • Barry Sullivan *Lieutenant Colonel Rocky Samford* • Alex Nicol *Ike Knowland* • Bruce Bennett *General Espy* • Jay C Flippen *Doyle* ■ *Dir* Anthony Mann • *Scr* Valentine Davies, Beirne Lay Jr, from a story by Beirne Lay Jr

The Stratford Adventure ★★★ U

Documentary   1954 · Can · Colour · 44mins

This Oscar-nominated documentary chronicles the sterling efforts of Stratford, Ontario, to stage an annual festival of Shakespeare. The local bigwigs get together, raise enough for a shoestring budget and persuade Tyrone Guthrie to produce the plays. Guthrie in turn persuades Alec Guinness to star in *All's Well That Ends Well* and *Richard III*, with a cast that also includes Irene Worth (who later starred with Guinness in *The Scapegoat*). Theatre fans won't want to miss this chance to see snatches of Guinness in these classic plays; they should also read his marvellous account of the festival in his 1985 memoir *Blessings in Disguise*.

Dir Morten Parker • *Scr* Gudrun Parker

The Stratton Story ★★★ U

Biographical sports drama
1949 · US · BW · 106mins

Douglas Morrow won a best original story Oscar for this biopic of Monty Stratton, the impoverished southern cotton picker who became a baseball star with the Chicago White Sox until a freak hunting accident threatened his career. James Stewart is typically affable in the lead, but he also does a good job of conveying Stratton's post-injury bitterness. In the first of a trio of collaborations with Stewart, June Allyson is just a tad too perfect as the sports star's devoted wife, although the scene in which she discovers her husband has been taking secret dance lessons is very sweet.

James Stewart *Monty Stratton* • June Allyson *Ethel Stratton* • Frank Morgan *Barney Wile* • Agnes Moorehead *Ma Stratton* • Bill Williams *Eddie Dibson* • Bruce Cowling *Ted Lyons* • Cliff Clark *Josh Higgins* ■ *Dir* Sam Wood • *Scr* Douglas Morrow, Guy Trosper, from a story by Douglas Morrow

Straw Dogs ★★★★ 18

Thriller   1971 · UK · Colour · 116mins

Mild-mannered maths teacher Dustin Hoffman finds his manhood tested when, after he moves to a Cornish village, the local toughs viciously rape his wife, Susan George, and threaten his home. One of the key movies in the controversial seventies debate about unacceptable screen violence, director Sam Peckinpah's cynical parable virtually states that all pacifists are cowardly thugs under their liberal exteriors. Reprehensible and disturbing in equal measure, this pitch black revenge drama remains potent and shocking, particularly the much-discussed and questionable rape scene – filmed as though George is unconsciously "asking for it". 🖵

Dustin Hoffman *David* • Susan George *Amy* • Peter Vaughan *Tom Hedden* • TP McKenna *Major Scott* • Del Henney *Venner* • Ken

Hutchison *Scutt* • Colin Welland *Reverend Hood* • Jim Norton *Cawsey* ■ *Dir* Sam Peckinpah • *Scr* David Zelag Goodman, Sam Peckinpah, from the novel *The Siege of Trencher's Farm* by Gordon M Williams

Strawberry and Chocolate
★★★ 18

Comedy   1993 · Cub · Colour · 105mins

Considering that America tries to prevent the worldwide distribution of Cuban films, it is remarkable that the island's first gay movie should have been nominated for the best foreign film Oscar. It was co-directed by Juan Carlos Tabío and Tomás Gutiérrez Alea, the latter perhaps the most gifted of all Cuban film-makers. What should have been a witty and subversive aside on Cuban socio-sexual politics has become, in fact, a showy, rather obvious film that can't make up its mind whether to be Almodóvar-like kitsch, *Educating Rita* or *Kiss of the Spiderwoman*. In Spanish with English subtitles. Contains sex scenes and nudity.

Jorge Perugorria *Diego* • Mirta Ibarra *Nancy* • Francisco Gattorno *Miguel* • Joel Angelino *German* • Marilyn Solaya *Vivian* ■ *Dir* Tomás Gutiérrez Alea, Juan Carlos Tabío • *Scr* Senel Paz, from his story *El Lobo, El Bosque y el Hombre Nuevo*

The Strawberry Blonde ★★★★ U

Romantic comedy   1941 · US · BW · 94mins

Dentists don't often get to play romantic leads in the movies, but James Cagney does his bit by playing a struggling tooth-doctor in this forties' remake of the 1933 Gary Cooper movie *One Sunday Afternoon*. Scripted by Julius and Philip Epstein, who helped write *Casablanca* the following year, this is an agreeable comedy, set in turn-of-the-century New York. The action flashes back to tell of Cagney's enduring passion for Rita Hayworth (in the title role), but his ultimate discovery is that, in nice, sweet Olivia de Havilland, he has married the right woman all along. 🖵

James Cagney *Biff Grimes* • Olivia de Havilland *Amy Lind* • Rita Hayworth *Virginia Brush* • Alan Hale *Old Man Grimes* • Jack Carson *Hugo Barnstead* • George Tobias *Nicholas Pappalas* • Una O'Connor *Mrs Mulcahey* ■ *Dir* Raoul Walsh • *Scr* Julius J Epstein, Philip G Epstein, from the play *One Sunday Afternoon* by James Hogan

The Strawberry Statement ★★★

Political drama   1970 · US · Colour · 108mins

Easy Rider showed studio executives that there was a huge, untapped youth audience out there, running riot on the nation's campuses to protest against the Vietnam war. So Hollywood quickly came over all radical with movies such as *Getting Straight* and *The Strawberry Statement*, in which student Simon (Bruce Davison) is turned into a militant and free love advocate by fellow student Kim Darby. It all ends with a frenzied riot and a stand-off with the National Guard while John Lennon sings *Give Peace a Chance*. Time capsule stuff.

Bruce Davison *Simon* • Kim Darby *Linda* • Bud Cort *Elliot, the coxswain* • Murray

MacLeod *George* ■ *Dir* Stuart Hagmann • *Scr* Israel Horovitz, from the novel *The Strawberry Statement: Notes of a College Revolutionary* by James Simon Kunen

Stray Dog ★★★

Crime drama 1949 · Jap · BW · 122mins

As is often the case with Akira Kurosawa, this is a film in which a quest results in self-discovery. Here, rookie detective Toshiro Mifune has his pistol stolen on a crowded bus and begins painstakingly tracking down the culprit as the gun is used in a series of crimes. Kurosawa gives the action an authentic feel by shooting in the more rundown areas of Tokyo, emphasising the sticky summer heat and Mifune's sense of self-loathing. But he is also at pains to convey the essential goodness of ordinary people and the beauty of the world. Inspired by actual events, this is a minor but compelling work. In Japanese with English subtitles.

Toshiro Mifune *Murakami* • Takashi Shimura *Sato* • Ko Kimura [Isao Kimura] *Yuro* • Keiko Awaji *Harumi* • Reisaburo Yamamoto *Hondo* ■ *Dir* Akira Kurosawa • *Scr* Ryuzo Kikushima, Akira Kurosawa, from a novel by Akira Kurosawa

Strays ★★ 15

Horror 1991 · US · Colour · 79mins

What a shocker! No, not the movie (though it's not brilliant), but the very thought that anyone could see horror potential in a concept about mean kitties. Co-producer/writer Shaun Cassidy (David's half-brother) did and this anaemic *Arachnophobia* clone is the result. *Apollo 13's* Kathleen Quinlan and *thirtysomething's* Timothy Busfield are the yuppie couple living in the country, unaware that their attic and cellar are infested with psychotic moggies. It's as daft as it sounds, with the ferocious felines jumping out of the woodwork during a climactic thunderstorm and scaring no one but the dutiful cast. Contains violence. ▭

Timothy Busfield *Paul Jarrett* • Kathleen Quinlan *Lindsey Jarrett* • Claudia Christian *Claire Lederer* ■ *Dir* John McPherson • *Scr* Shaun Cassidy

Streamers ★★★ 18

Drama 1983 · US · Colour · 113mins

Up close and personal animosity comes to the boil in the one-set locality of an army barracks dormitory. Director Robert Altman developed the film from its original stage context, in much the same way as he did with his earlier offering, *Come Back to the Five and Dime, Jimmy Dean, Jimmy Dean.* The screenplay is an adaptation by David Rabe of his own Broadway venture and its claustrophobic tensions are expanded thanks to fine acting – especially from Matthew Modine and Michael Wright. ▭

Matthew Modine *William "Billy" Wilson* • Michael Wright *Carlyle* • Mitchell Lichtenstein *Richard "Richie" Douglas* • David Alan Grier *Roger Hicks* • Guy Boyd *Sergeant Rooney* • George Dzundza *Sergeant Cokes* ■ *Dir* Robert Altman • *Scr* David Rabe, from his play

Street Angel ★★

Silent drama 1928 · US · BW · 102mins

At the first Academy Awards, Janet Gaynor was voted best actress Oscar-winner for three films: director Frank Borzage's *Seventh Heaven* and *Street Angel* and, best of all, FW Murnau's *Sunrise.* The least of these is *Street Angel,* a turgidly sentimental melodrama that reunited Gaynor with her *Seventh Heaven* co-star, Charles Farrell. It's the tale of a Neapolitan slum girl who resorts to illegal means to procure medicine for her sick mother. She temporarily avoids arrest by joining a circus, where artist Farrell paints her as the Madonna. Although contemporary audiences seemed unworried by the more "icky" elements, the film is now little more than a barely tolerable collector's item. Principally silent, it includes some sound sequences.

Janet Gaynor *Angela* • Charles Farrell *Gino* • Alberto Rabagliati *Policeman* • Gino Conti *Policeman* • Guido Trento *Neri, police sergeant* ■ *Dir* Frank Borzage • *Scr* Marion Orth, Katherine Hilliker (titles), HH Caldwell (titles), Philip Klein, Henry Roberts Symonds, from the novel *Cristilinda* by Monckton Hoffe • *Cinematographer* Ernest Palmer • *Art Director* Harry Oliver

Street Angel ★★★★

Romance 1937 · Chi · BW · 100mins

Having debuted with the political musical *Cityscape* (1935), Yuan Muzhi reaffirmed his left-wing credentials with this socially critical, yet warmly human drama, which proved to be his final feature. Both a tribute to the spirit of the poor and an indictment of Shanghai's post-colonial indifference, it is, essentially, a moving love story in which naive musician Zhao Dan attempts to rescue Manchurian exile Zhou Xuan from prostitution. However, with its frank discussion of contentious issues, its roots in traditional Chinese art and its stylistic debt to Hollywood and Soviet cinema, it merits its reputation as a proto-neorealist study of life being lived. In Mandarin with English subtitles.

Zhao Dan *Chen Shaoping* • Wei Heling *Wang, newspaper seller* • Zhou Xuan *Xiao Hong, little singer* • Zhao Huishen *Xiao Yun* ■ *Dir* Yuan Muzhi • *Scr* Yuan Muzhi

Street Fighter ★★ 12

Action adventure 1994 · US · Colour · 97mins

Jean-Claude Van Damme and Kylie Minogue team up for a movie adaptation of the popular video game. If that unlikely pairing isn't enough to put you off, the simple-minded plot will. It concerns an Allied Nations forces assignment to overthrow General Bison (Raul Julia in his last role), the dictator of a mythical Asian territory. Despite some neat production design – the camouflage costumes are particularly natty – there's little to get excited about in this laughably bad action adventure. Contains violence and some swearing. ▭ *DVD*

Jean-Claude Van Damme *Colonel William F Guile* • Raul Julia *Bison [Wen Ming-Na]* *Chun-Li* • Damian Chapa *Ken* • Kylie Minogue *Cammy* • Simon Callow *An official* • Roshan Seth *Dhalsim* • Wes Studi *Sagat* ■ *Dir/Scr* Steven E de Souza

Street of Crocodiles ★★★ PG

Animation 1986 · UK · Colour and BW · 20mins

A puppet warily explores the darkened rooms of a deserted lecture hall and finds other dolls acting in strange ways in a typical stop-motion animation production from the idiosyncratic Brothers Quay. This is gloomy, creepy and quite unsettling – Stephen and Timothy Quay tap into the nether regions of our worst childhood nightmares and the claustrophobic end result couldn't be further from the colourful fantasy of Ray Harryhausen. Screws twist out of objects, mechanical cogs turn, junk comes alive and one female doll exposes her breasts in this relentlessly downbeat and unique nightmare, which continuously offers up one startling image after another to jolt you back from Disneyland. ▭

Dir Stephen Quay, Timothy Quay • *Scr* Brothers Quay [Stephen Quay, Timothy Quay], from the short story collection *Ulica Krokodyli* by Bruno Schulz

Street of Dreams ★★ 15

Thriller 1988 · US · Colour · 90mins

Based on a book by Timothy Harris, this is an average thriller from director William A Graham, who probably best known for the abysmal *Return to the Blue Lagoon.* This TV movie is marginally better, although Morgan Fairchild is miscast as the down-on-her-luck *femme fatale,* who drags private eye Ben Masters into a Hollywood murder case. It's mildly interesting, especially if you want to see the seamier side of Tinseltown. ▭

Ben Masters *Thomas Kyd* • Morgan Fairchild *Laura Cassidy* • Diane Salinger *Ann Kepler* • Michael Cavanaugh *Lieutenant Marcus* • Alan Autry *Morris Field* • Gerald Hiken *Dix* ■ *Dir* William A Graham

Street of Shadows ★★★ PG

Thriller 1953 · UK · BW · 80mins

They used to churn out these pseudo *noir* thrillers by the van load in the early fifties with varying degrees of success. This one moves along at a brisk trot, but basically there is little else to commend it, apart from a workmanlike performance by Cesar Romero as a casino owner madly in love with (the consistently under-rated) Kay Kendall. Kendall often had a strange luminescent quality on screen and this film shows it to moody advantage. If only the script were better. ▭

Cesar Romero *Luigi* • Kay Kendall *Barbara Gale* • Edward Underdown *Inspector Johnstone* • Victor Maddern *Limpy* • Simone Silva *Angele Abbe* • Liam Gaffney *Fred Roberts* • Robert Cawdron *Sergeant Hadley* • John Penrose *Captain Gerald Gale* • Bill Travers *Nigel Langley* ■ *Dir* Richard Vernon • *Scr* Richard Vernon, from the novel *The Creaking Chair* by Lawrence Meynall

Street of Shame ★★★★

Drama 1955 · Jap · BW · 85mins

Set in Dreamland, in Tokyo's Yoshiwara red-light district, this study of oppressed womanhood was the final feature of Kenji Mizoguchi. Denied the chance to shoot on location in docudramatic style, he nevertheless manages to expose the exploitation and hypocrisy of bordello life with such power that the film was credited with swaying the Diet during its debates on prostitution. The tone is signature Mizoguchi in its sympathetic approach to the women's plight, with the most impressive performance coming from Machiko Kyo as the flint-hearted hooker, who mercilessly denounces the father whose excesses have condemned her to unrelenting misery. Not the great director's most accomplished picture, but a fitting swansong nonetheless. In Japanese with English subtitles.

Machiko Kyo *Miki* • Ayako Wakao *Yasumi* • Michiyo Kogure *Hanae* • Aiko Mimasu *Yumeko* • Kenji Sugawara *Eiko* ■ *Dir* Kenji Mizoguchi • *Scr* Masashige Narusawa, from the story *Susaki no Onna* by Yoshiko Shibaki

Street Scene ★★★★

Drama 1931 · US · BW · 80mins

Adapted by Elmer Rice from his play and directed by King Vidor, the film covers the events of a night and morning in the lives of tenement dwellers during a stifling Manhattan summer. It centres on young Sylvia Sidney and her unhappy mother's illicit affair, which leads to tragedy. Dated, and sometimes stagey, this is nonetheless riveting as an early attempt to capture a slice of tenement life and as an evocation of New York's melting pot of immigrants. It was a step on the way to stardom for Sidney, young, beautiful and demonstrating the poignant quality that became her trademark. Many of the rest came from the original Broadway cast, among them Beulah Bondi.

Sylvia Sidney *Rose Maurrant* • William Collier [William Collier Jr] *Sam Kaplan* • Estelle Taylor *Anna Maurrant* • Beulah Bondi *Emma Jones* • Max Montor *Abe Kaplan* • David Landau *Frank Maurrant* • Matt McHugh *Vincent Jones* ■ *Dir* King Vidor • *Scr* Elmer Rice, from his play

Street Smart ★★ 18

Thriller based on a true story 1987 · US · Colour · 92mins

Journalistic ethics come under rather fuzzy scrutiny in a tepid thriller based on a true story. Christopher Reeve plays a struggling magazine writer who finds his career taking off after the publication of his fictional exposé of Manhattan prostitution. Despite his success, Reeve soon discovers that his story has some very deadly consequences in a slow-moving melodrama sparked into sporadic life by Morgan Freeman's Oscar-nominated portrayal of a low-life pimp. ▭

Christopher Reeve *Jonathan Fisher* • Morgan Freeman *Fast Black* • Kathy Baker *Punchy* • Mimi Rogers *Alison Parker* • Jay Patterson *Leonard Pike* • Andre Gregory *Ted Avery* ■ *Dir* Jerry Schatzberg • *Scr* David Freeman

Street Song ★★

Musical 1935 · UK · BW · 64mins

The release of *The Ghost Camera* on video did much to reawaken interest in Bernard Vorhaus, the British director who had his career ruined in the early fifties by the evidence of his fellow film-makers during the Hollywood communist witch-hunt. There's a rather ominous ring, therefore, to the plotline of this creaky musical melodrama, directed and co-written by Vorhaus, in which singer John Garrick is sacked from his radio slot after being accused of a crime he didn't commit.

John Garrick *Tom Tucker* • René Ray *Lucy* • Lawrence Hanray *Tuttle* • Wally Patch *Wally* • Johnny Singer *Billy* ■ *Dir* Bernard Vorhaus • *Scr* Bernard Vorhaus, Paul Gangelin

A Street to Die ★★ PG

Drama 1985 · Ausl · Colour · 92mins

A brave drama about the effect on humans of the defoliant Agent Orange used during the Vietnam War. When an Australian ex-soldier with leukaemia discovers many of his fellow veterans are also afflicted with the condition, he initiates a lawsuit against the authorities. Well made and well acted (particularly by Chris Haywood), it's a sympathetic demonstration of the hidden casualties of war.

Chris Haywood *Col Turner* • Jennifer Cluff *Lorraine Turner* • Peter Hehir *Peter Townley* • Arianthe Galani *Dr Walsea* • Peter Kowitz *Craig* ■ *Dir/Scr* Bill Bennett

Street War ★★★ 15

Police drama 1992 · US · Colour · 88mins

Also known as *Urban Crossfire*, this is one of the *In the Line of Duty* series of US TV movies based on real-life police cases. Mario Van Peebles and Ray Sharkey both rise above the material to give superb performances, in a tale about two cops fighting drugs on the streets of New York. Based on a *New York Daily News* article, this is an often interesting crime drama, although even at its best moments it still doesn't rate as highly as an episode of *NYPD Blue*. ▣

Ray Sharkey *Victor Tomasino* • Mario Van Peebles *Raymond Williamson* • Peter Boyle *Dan Reilly* • Michael Boatman *Robert Dayton* • Courtney B Vance *John "Justice" Butler* • Morris Chestnut *Carl "Prince" Franklin* • Laurie Morrison *Cynthia* • Merlin Santana *Mikey* ■ *Dir* Dick Lowry • *Scr* Thomas S Cook, Mark Kreigel, from the *New York Daily News* article *Living Large*

The Street with No Name ★★★★

Crime thriller 1948 · US · BW · 90mins

When, in his screen debut in *Kiss of Death*, Richard Widmark giggled as he pushed an old lady in a wheelchair down the stairs, 20th Century-Fox knew it had a star on its books. In the same vein, this follow-up casts him as a psychotic hypochondriac, always snorting on an inhaler and beating his wife. Not many screen villains looked nastier than Widmark in those days, his thin-lipped mouth and bony face epitomising the look of a man with antisocial tendencies. FBI agent Mark Stevens is the nominal hero of this *noir*ish thriller, but he's no match for Widmark, even though the script demands that justice must be seen to be done.

Mark Stevens *Cordell* • Richard Widmark *Alec Stiles* • Lloyd Nolan *Inspector Briggs* • Barbara Lawrence *Judy Stiles* • Ed Begley *Chief Harmatz* • Donald Buka *Shivvy* • Joseph Pevney *Matty* • John McIntire *Cy Gordon* ■ *Dir* William Keighley • *Scr* Harry Kleiner

A Streetcar Named Desire ★★★★★ 15

Classic melodrama 1951 · US · BW · 119mins

This is the legendary Marlon Brando at the height of his powers, right at the start of his career, playing the brutal Stanley Kowalski. His confrontational relationship with his sister-in-law – Southern belle Blanche DuBois (Vivien Leigh) – is at the mind-splitting core of Tennessee Williams's memorable melodrama. The play's homosexual references were cut to comply with censorship rules of the day, though Blanche's implied violation and references to her sordid past remain. This classic drama won four Oscars – awards for Kazan, Leigh, Kim Hunter (as Brando's wife) and Karl Malden, but Brando missed out to Humphrey Bogart (for *The African Queen*). ▣

Vivien Leigh *Blanche DuBois* • Marlon Brando *Stanley Kowalski* • Kim Hunter *Stella Kowalski* • Karl Malden *Mitch* • Rudy Bond *Steve Hubbell* • Nick Dennis *Pablo Gonzales* • Peg Hillias *Eunice Hubbell* ■ *Dir* Elia Kazan • *Scr* Tennessee Williams, Oscar Saul (adaptation), from the play by Tennessee Williams • *Cinematographer* Harry Stradling • *Art Director* Richard Day • *Set Designer* George James Hopkins

The Streetfighter ★★★ 15

Action drama 1975 · US · Colour · 89mins

This marvellously evocative tough-as-nails Depression era drama has a sanguine James Coburn managing unsmiling brute Charles Bronson, who's well cast as a slugger of mythical dimensions. Debut director Walter Hill takes an elliptical, almost existential, route in telling his story, which means that the overall impact is dissipated quite early on. Nevertheless, there's much to admire, particularly the combination of cinematographer Phil Lathrop's Panavision photography and editor Roger Spottiswoode's handling of the fight sequences. Strother Martin is particularly good as Bronson's junkie second, but it's hard to care about any of the characters. ▣

Charles Bronson *Chaney* • James Coburn *Spencer "Speed" Weed* • Jill Ireland *Lucy Simpson* • Strother Martin *Poe* • Maggie Blye *Gayleen Schoonover* • Michael McGuire *Gandil* • Robert Tessier *Jim Henry* ■ *Dir* Walter Hill • *Scr* Walter Hill, Bryan Gindorff, Bruce Henstell • *Cinematographer* Philip Lathrop • *Editor* Roger Spottiswoode

Streets ★★★ 18

Thriller 1990 · US · Colour · 80mins

The fourth of Katt Shea Ruben's films for Roger Corman's New World Productions is a gritty, often gripping drama about teen runaways in LA. *Married With Children* star Christina Applegate is Dawn, a 14-year-old junkie prostitute. David Mendenhall plays Sy, a clean-cut suburban boy who arrives in LA with the vague idea of becoming a rock star and saves Dawn from a violent punter. The movie follows the couple as Dawn gives Sy a tour of the world she inhabits, while the psychotic punter tries to track them down. Neither tub-thumping nor slick, the movie says what it has to say without sentimentalising or toning down the violence, with a great performance from Applegate. ▣

Christina Applegate *Dawn* • David Mendenhall *Sy* • Eb Lottimer *Lumley* • Patrick Richwood *Bob* • Kady Tran *Dawn's blonde roommate* • Mel Castelo *Elf* ■ *Dir* Katt Shea Ruben • *Scr* Katt Shea Ruben, Andy Ruben

Streets of Fire ★★★ 15

Action romance 1984 · US · Colour · 89mins

Director Walter Hill obviously had fun with this violent rock-fuelled fantasy shot in a sort of youth culture neverland. Viewers will have fun spotting the faces of future stars such as Rick Moranis, Willem Dafoe, Amy Madigan, Bill Paxton, Diane Lane and Robert Townsend, although for Michael Paré, who plays the brooding loner hero, this was probably his career high spot. Paré arrives back in town just in time to gather up a posse of old friends and rescue his rock-star ex-girlfriend from the clutches of a merciless biker gang. Scored by the peerless Ry Cooder, the music also comes courtesy of retro-rockers the Blasters. ▣

Michael Paré *Tom Cody* • Diane Lane *Ellen Aim* • Rick Moranis *Billy Fish* • Willem Dafoe *Raven* • Amy Madigan *McCoy* • Deborah Van Valkenburgh *Reva* • Bill Paxton *Clyde* • Lee Ving *Greer* • Robert Townsend *Lester* ■ *Dir* Walter Hill • *Scr* Walter Hill, Larry Gross

Streets of Gold ★★ 15

Sports drama 1986 · US · Colour · 89mins

Distinguished Austrian actor Klaus Maria Brandauer (*Mephisto*) often looks as if he's about to cry this boxing drama, perhaps because he's been asked to be as monosyllabic, gruff and sweaty as Sly Stallone. Furthermore, he'd swapped meaningful European cinema for big American clichés. However, he still manages to bring detail and a hint of depth to his role of Soviet champ turned dishwasher turned trainer, in a thrusting but dull outing that lacks the innocent gung-ho spirit of the *Rocky* films. Contains swearing. ▣

Klaus Maria Brandauer *Alek Neuman* • Wesley Snipes *Roland Jenkins* • Adrian Pasdar *Timmy Boyle* • Angela Molina *Elena Gitman* • Elya Baskin *Klebanov* ■ *Dir* Joe Roth • *Scr* Heywood Gould, Richard Price,Tim Cole, from a story by Dezso Magyar

Streets of Laredo ★★★ U

Western 1949 · US · Colour · 92mins

This is an inferior remake of King Vidor's splendid 1936 western *The Texas Rangers* (the one about the three outlaw pals who go their separate ways, with two becoming lawmen chasing the third) but this time round there are no Indians in the tale. Nevertheless, there is a fine star-making performance from a deceptively casual William Holden, whose burgeoning screen presence forces attention, especially when dull co-star Macdonald Carey is on screen. The stunning Technicolor photography is really what gives this western its distinction – unsurprising since it's by colour expert Ray Rennahan, an Oscar winner for *Gone with the Wind*.

William Holden (1) *Jim Dawkins* • Macdonald Carey *Lorn Reming* • Mona Freeman *Rannie Carter* • William Bendix *Wahoo Jones* • Stanley Ridges *Major Bailey* • Alfonso Bedoya

Charley Calico ■ *Dir* Leslie Fenton • *Scr* Charles Marquis Warren, from a story by Louis Stevens, Elizabeth Hill

Streetwise ★★★ 18

Documentary 1985 · US · Colour · 96mins

An Academy Award-nominated documentary about the nightmare flip side of the American dream. Martin Bell's "shock doc" focuses on the teenagers who live rough on the streets of Seattle, where they earn what passes for a living as prostitutes, pimps, muggers and petty drug dealers. The film passes no judgements and offers no answers. Sad and depressing, this litany of lost souls is tough, sobering viewing. ▣

Dir Martin Bell • *Scr* from the article *Streets of the Lost* in *LIFE,magazine* by Mary Ellen Mark, Cheryl McCall • *Editor* Nancy Baker • *Music* Tom Waits

Strictly Ballroom ★★★★★ PG

Romantic comedy drama 1992 · Ausl · Colour · 90mins

Feel-good movies don't come any better than this Australian smash hit, which is an exuberant joy from sequined start to feathered finish. *Come Dancing* meets *Dirty Dancing* when rebel ballroom star Paul Mercurio hesitantly teams up with ugly duckling novice Tara Morice for an important contest. He wants to perform his own Latin routine, however, rather than the boring steps set by the conservative dancing federation. Will love be in the air? What do you think! Kitsch and as corny as anything, this hilariously heart-warming "Last Tango Down Under" is the ideal pick-me-up. Bright, breezy and strictly fabulous. Contains swearing. ▣ **DVD**

Paul Mercurio *Scott Hastings* • Tara Morice *Fran* • Bill Hunter *Barry Fife* • Pat Thomson *Shirley Hastings* • Gia Carides *Liz Holt* • Peter Whitford *Les Kendall* • Barry Otto *Doug Hastings* • John Hannan *Ken Railings* • Sonia Kruger *Tina Sparkle* ■ *Dir* Baz Luhrmann • *Scr* Baz Luhrmann, Craig Pearce, from a story by Baz Luhrmann, Andrew Bovell, from an original idea by Baz Luhrmann and the NIDA stage production

Strictly Business ★★ 15

Romantic comedy 1991 · US · Colour · 79mins

This so-so comedy sees an upwardly mobile corporate middle runger turning to a wise-ass office boy for help in de-yuppifying his image so that he can woo a pretty showbiz wannabe. Strictly silly, it's not without the occasional laugh and some neat playing. Director Kevin Hooks enjoyed slightly greater success with *Passenger 57*. Contains swearing and some violence. ▣

Tommy Davidson *Bobby Johnson* • Joseph C Phillips *Waymon Tinsdale III* • Halle Berry *Natalie* • David Marshall Grant *David* • Anne-Marie Johnson *Diedre* • Jon Cypher *Drake* • Paul Butler *Leroy Halloran* • James McDaniel *Roland Halloran* • Sam Rockwell *Gary* • Samuel L Jackson *Monroe* ■ *Dir* Kevin Hooks • *Scr* Pam Gibson, Nelson George

Strike ★★★★ 12

Silent political drama 1924 · USSR · BW · 86mins

Sergei Eisenstein's debut feature was an electrifying testament to the

dramatic and intellectual power of cinema. It chronicles the suppression of a 1912 factory uprising after one of the workers had committed suicide. The bold decision to focus on collective heroism invests the film with a scale and energy that is intensified by the brilliance of Eisenstein's rhythmic editing of Edouard Tissé's starkly realistic visuals. Juxtaposing images to give them satirical, metaphorical or emotional weight (the massacre being intercut with slaughterhouse scenes), Eisenstein transformed the "kino-eye" footage into the "kino-fist" he hoped would inspire revolutionary endeavour. ▭

Grigori Alexandrov *Factory foreman* • Aleksandr Antonov [Aleksander Antonov] *Member of strike committee* • Yduif Glizer *Queen of Thieves* • Mikhail Gomorov *Worker* • I Ivanov *Chief of police* ■ *Dir* Sergei Eisenstein • *Scr* Sergei Eisenstein, Grigori Alexandrov, V Pletniev, I Kravtchunovsky

Strike! ★★ 🔢
Comedy drama
1998 · US/Can · Colour · 93mins

The girls of St Trinian's meet the *Dead Poets Society* in this sharp, witty tale of pupil power set in an exclusive American school in the early sixties. Kirsten Dunst (*Drop Dead Gorgeous*) and Gaby Hoffmann (*American Beauty*) are two of the students waging a campaign to prevent male pupils from being admitted to their beloved school. Rachael Leigh Cook (*She's All That*) and Lynn Redgrave are among the strong supporting cast. Contains sexual references. ▭

Kirsten Dunst *Verena Von Stefan* • Gaby Hoffmann *Odette Sinclair* • Lynn Redgrave *Miss McVane* • Rachael Leigh Cook *Abby* • Thomas Guiry "*Frosty*" *Frost* • Vincent Kartheiser *Snake* ■ *Dir/Scr* Sarah Kernochan

Strike Force ★★ 🔢
Detective drama 1975 · US · Colour · 84mins

This routine TV movie is notable mainly for the presence of a very young Richard Gere – a couple of years before his breakthrough in *Looking for Mr Goodbar*. He plays a raw, inexperienced trooper called in to help track down a gang of drug dealers, but the nominal star is sixties Broadway sensation Cliff Gorman. Interesting as a curiosity piece for Gere completists, but otherwise rather dull. ▭

Cliff Gorman *Detective Joey Gentry* • Richard Gere *Trooper Walter Spenser* • Marilyn Chris *Faye Stone* • Donald Blakely *Agent Jerome Ripley* • Edward Grover *Captain Peterson* ■ *Dir* Barry Shear • *Scr* Roger O Hirson, from a story by Sonny Grosso

Strike It Rich ★
Romantic comedy
1990 · US · Colour · 81mins

Leads Robert Lindsay and Molly Ringwald demonstrate a distinct shortage of sexual chemistry in this dire adaptation of Graham Greene's *Loser Takes All* from director James Scott. They play a fifties couple inveigled into a honeymoon they can't afford by Lindsay's boss John Gielgud. Left by Gielgud in one of Monte Carlo's most expensive hotels, the newlyweds have to "strike it rich" in order to pay the bill. Ringwald looks ridiculous in period costume and sounds worse,

and Lindsay is more father figure than lover.

Molly Ringwald *Cary Porter* • Robert Lindsay *Ian Bertram* • John Gielgud *Herbert Dreuther* • Frances de la Tour *Mrs De Vere* • Max Wall *Bowles* • Simon de la Brosse *Philippe* • Margi Clarke *Bowles's nurse* ■ *Dir* James Scott • *Scr* James Scott, from the novel *Loser Takes All* by Graham Greene

Strike Me Pink ★★★ 🅤
Musical comedy 1936 · US · Colour · 95mins

The last, but by no means least, of the six films Eddie Cantor made for Samuel Goldwyn is a wacky comedy with songs that allegedly utilised many more writers than those credited. Cantor is a mild tailor who, inspired by a book called *Man or Mouse: What Are You?*, agrees to run an amusement park that gangsters have targeted for their slot-machine business. The farcical consequences become surreal at times – tough guy Edward Brophy breaks into a ballet routine in one priceless sequence. ▭

Eddie Cantor *Eddie Pink* • Ethel Merman *Joyce Lenox* • Sally Eilers *Claribel Hayes* • Parkyakarkus [Harry Einstein] *Harry Parke* • William Frawley *Copple* • Helen Lowell *Ma Carson* • Gordon Jones *Butch Carson* • Brian Donlevy *Vance* • Edward Brophy *Killer* ■ *Dir* Norman Taurog • *Scr* Frank Butler, Walter DeLeon, Francis Martin, Philip Rapp, from the novel *Dreamland* by Clarence Buddington Kelland • *Choreographer* Robert Alton

Strike Up the Band ★★★★ 🅤
Musical 1940 · US · BW · 119mins

"Let the music play... ". This is one of the great MGM Judy Garland/Mickey Rooney collaborations, a super Busby Berkeley-directed heart-warmer with a major bonus in a fine score. Very much of its period, from a time when band contests on radio were the peak of public entertainment and Paul Whiteman (here playing himself) was the "King of Jazz", this vehicle creates several marvellous moments for the two leads. Rooney demonstrates what a fine drummer he was (and still is), while Garland, who has never looked lovelier, breaks your heart with her plaintive rendering of *Our Love Affair*. The movie never palls during its long running time, and, despite the rubber-boned June Preisser, it's never unwatchable, avoiding the sentimentality that so often ruins these "let's put on a show" plots.

Mickey Rooney *Jimmy Connors* • Judy Garland *Mary Holden* • June Preisser *Barbara Frances Morgan* • William Tracy *Phillip Turner* • Ann Shoemaker *Mrs Connors* • Larry Nunn *Willie Brewster* • George Lessey *Mr Morgan* • Phil Silvers *Pitch man* ■ *Dir* Busby Berkeley • *Scr* John Monks, Fred F Finklehoffe, Herbert Fields (uncredited), Kay Van Riper (uncredited)

Striking Distance ★★★ 🔢
Crime thriller 1993 · US · Colour · 97mins

The river police are not usually known for their on-screen heroics, but this ripsnorting Bruce Willis vehicle (or perhaps boat would be more accurate) certainly puts them on the map. Willis is his usual hard-nosed loner, who finds himself relegated to the unfashionable water cops (and partnered with *Sex and the City's* Sarah Jessica Parker) when he breaks

ranks and testifies against a policeman who also happens to be a member of his family. However, a serial killer with an unhealthy interest in Willis's life offers the chance of redemption. The aptly named Rowdy Herrington ensures the action roars along and that the set pieces are suitably big and brash. Contains swearing, violence, sex scenes and nudity. ▭ *DVD*

Bruce Willis *Tom Hardy* • Sarah Jessica Parker *Jo Christman* • Dennis Farina *Nick Detillo* • Tom Sizemore *Danny Detillo* • Brion James *Detective Eddie Eiler* • Robert Pastorelli *Jimmy Detillo* • Timothy Busfield *Tony Sacco* • John Mahoney *Vince Hardy* ■ *Dir* Rowdy Herrington • *Scr* Rowdy Herrington, Martin Kaplan

Stripes ★★★ 🔢
Comedy 1981 · US · Colour · 101mins

This was the breakthrough film for Bill Murray, whose sleazy charisma helps disguise the formulaic "you're in the army now" plotting. Layabout Murray and chum Harold Ramis (also co-writer) are conned into joining up (by an unbilled Harry Dean Stanton, in a neat cameo). Murray's sparring with the obligatory hard-nosed NCO (Warren Oates, in one of his last film roles), is a constant delight. A surprise hit, this comedy also provided early high profile roles for Judge Reinhold, John Candy and Sean Young. ▭

Bill Murray *John* • Harold Ramis *Russell* • Warren Oates *Sergeant Hulka* • PJ Soles *Stella* • Sean Young *Louise* • John Candy *Ox* • John Larroquette *Captain Stillman* • Judge Reinhold *Elmo* ■ *Dir* Ivan Reitman • *Scr* Len Blum, Dan Goldberg, Harold Ramis

The Stripper ★★★
Melodrama 1963 · US · BW · 94mins

Politely retitled *Woman of Summer* in Britain, this is an atmospheric drama about a woman from small-town Kansas who, having failed as a movie actress, returns home as part of a sleazy dance troupe. There she gets involved with Claire Trevor's teenage son (Richard Beymer). Joanne Woodward is beautifully cast as the woman whose life resembles a never-ending car crash, though she's more self-reliant than wallowing in self-pity. The story is based on a play by William Inge and is fairly restrained compared to his other Deep South melodramas. The film marked the directing debut of Franklin J Schaffner who went on to win an Oscar for *Patton*.

Joanne Woodward *Lila Green* • Richard Beymer *Kenny Baird* • Claire Trevor *Helen Baird* • Carol Lynley *Miriam Caswell* • Robert Webber *Ricky Powers* • Louis Nye *Ronnie Cavendish* • Gypsy Rose Lee *Madame Olga* ■ *Dir* Franklin J Schaffner • *Scr* Meade Roberts, from the play *A Loss of Roses* by William Inge

Stripper ★★★ 🔢
Documentary 1985 · US · Colour · 86mins

This documentary is a brave attempt to come up with a non-exploitative insight into the world of stripping. Against the backdrop of the first annual convention for the trade, Janette Boyd, Sara Costa and Kimberly Holcomb are among the dancers who speak frankly about the job, while director Jerome Gary keeps the actual scenes of stripping down to a minimum. The soundtrack is from

ace composer Jack Nitzsche, who was responsible for the music for films such as *The Exorcist* and *One Flew over the Cuckoo's Nest*. Contains swearing and nudity. ▭

Dir Jerome Gary

Striptease ★★ 🔢
Crime comedy 1996 · US · Colour · 112mins

When devoted mother Demi Moore loses custody of her child to her lowlife erstwhile husband Robert Patrick because she's unemployed, she takes a job as a stripper in a Florida topless bar to earn money and get the child back. She becomes the object of several men's lust, notably that of oily, corrupt politician Burt Reynolds, and finds herself involved in murder and blackmail. Andrew Bergman's screenplay is a mess, pulling its punches on the sleaze, while combining tear-jerking sentimentality and inadequate humour with the drama. However, Bergman as director makes it good-looking enough and Moore does well in a difficult role. Contains violence, swearing and nudity. ▭ *DVD*

Demi Moore *Erin Grant* • Armand Assante *Al Garcia* • Ving Rhames *Shad* • Robert Patrick *Darrell Grant* • Burt Reynolds *Congressman Dilbeck* • Paul Guilfoyle *Malcolm Moldovsky* • Jerry Grayson *Orly* • Rumer Willis *Angela Grant* ■ *Dir* Andrew Bergman • *Scr* Andrew Bergman, from the novel by Carl Hiaasen

Stroker Ace ★ 🅿🅖
Comedy 1983 · US · Colour · 90mins

Burt Reynolds and his then wife-to-be Loni Anderson star in a lame comedy centred around the larger-than-life exploits of racing car driver Stroker Ace (Reynolds). Stroker is successful at his sport, but he isn't impressed by the loony promotional work (such as dressing up as a giant chicken) that he is forced to do by his sponsor (Ned Beatty), who is the owner of a chain of fried chicken shops. The clash between the two loud personalities forms the core of the film. Reynolds's career has swung between fine movies and mere timepassers, but this one's the pits. ▭

Burt Reynolds *Stroker Ace* • Ned Beatty *Clyde Torkle* • Jim Nabors *Lugs* • Parker Stevenson *Aubrey James* • Loni Anderson *Pembrook Feeney* • Bubba Smith *Arnold* • John Byner *Doc Seegle* ■ *Dir* Hal Needham • *Scr* Hal Needham, Hugh Wilson, from the novel *Stand On It* by William Neely, Robert K Ottum

Stromboli ★★ 🅿🅖
Drama 1950 · It · BW · 101mins

When Ingrid Bergman abandoned her husband (and Hollywood) for Italian director Roberto Rossellini, she found herself at the centre of the first major showbiz scandal of the postwar era. Denounced by religious groups, blacklisted by the studios and called "Hollywood's apostle of degradation" by a US senator, Bergman made this film with Rossellini (whom she soon married). Launched with a fanfare, it flopped noisily. It's easy to see why: Bergman is ill at ease as the refugee who marries an Italian fisherman, while the island of Stromboli's volcano simmers symbolically in the background. Part melodrama, part neorealist exercise with amateur performers, it never jells. An Italian language film.

Ingrid Bergman *Karin Bjiorsen* • Mario Vitale *Antonio* • Renzo Cesana *Priest* • Mario Sponza *Lighthouse keeper* ■ *Dir* Roberto Rossellini • *Scr* Roberto Rossellini, Art Cohn, Renzo Cesana, Sergio Amedei, CP Callegari

Strong Hands ★★★
Political thriller 1997 · It · Colour · 92mins

Linking the 1974 terrorist bombing of the Piazza del Loggia in Brescia with the Bosnian conflict, this conspiracy thriller makes intriguing, if laboured use of its factual foundation. Director Franco Bernini builds the suspense effectively enough, as he moves forward 20 years to the consultation between psychoanalyst Francesca Neri (who lost a sister in the atrocity) and war correspondent Claudio Amendola, who convinces her of government involvement in the blast. The final time shift, to a court case in the present, cranks up the melodrama rather than the tension, but you'll want to linger long enough to see how it all turns out. An Italian language film.

Francesca Neri *Claudia* • Claudio Amendola *Tancredi* • Enzo De Caro *Giulio* • Toni Bertorelli *Judge Consoli* • Massimo De Francovich *Professor Sembriani* • Bruno Armando *Captain Landino* ■ *Dir* Franco Bernini • *Scr* Franco Bernini, Maura Nuccetelli

Strong Language ★
Comedy drama 1998 · UK · Colour · 75mins

First-timer Simon Rumley is to be congratulated for his persistence in making this talking-heads scrapbook for a hard-earned £30,000. However, his portrait of nineties London twentysomethings is often as disappointingly contrived as its visual style is simple. Had the voices been authentic, then the diversity of opinions expressed might have carried some weight. But, in the mouths of a largely inexperienced cast, Rumley's ruminations sound self-conscious and too obviously scripted. Touching on everything from racists to Oasis and Ecstasy to HIV, this parochial vox pop says more about the director and his milieu than the nation's youth.

David Groves *Narrator* • Al Nedjari *Pete, unemployed* • Paul Tonkinson *Danny, lift attendant* • Julie Rice *Tatty, astrologer & tarot card reader* • Charlie De'Ath *Stuart, video director* • Kelly Marcel *Philippa, magazine production assistant* ■ *Dir/Scr* Simon Rumley

The Strong Man ★★★ U
Silent comedy 1926 · US · BW · 73mins

Of the four great silent comedians, Harry Langdon is virtually forgotten – though, in popularity terms, he once stood beside Chaplin, Keaton and Harold Lloyd. The puny, sad-faced clown plays a Belgian immigrant who tours America with circus strong man Zandow (Arthur Thalasso), while searching for his pen pal, who turns out to be a blind girl. It's not as sentimental as it sounds, and the sequences with Langdon being ravished by Gertrude Astor and labouring under the effects of a heavy cold are superb. As much a social drama about the immigrant experience as a comedy, this was Langdon's best

movie and gave Frank Capra his first official directorial credit.

Harry Langdon *Paul Bergot* • Priscilla Bonner *Mary Brown* • Gertrude Astor *"Gold Tooth"* • William V Mong *Parson Brown* • Robert McKim *Roy McDevitt* • Arthur Thalasso *Zandow the Great* ■ *Dir* Frank Capra • *Scr* Arthur Ripley, Frank Capra, Hal Conklin, Robert Eddy, Reed Heustis (titles), from the story by Arthur Ripley

The Strongest Man in the World ★★★ U
Comedy 1975 · US · Colour · 88mins

This was Kurt Russell's third outing as Disney's super-teen Dexter Riley. This time his misadventures begin when he acquires phenomenal strength from chemicals accidentally added to his favourite breakfast cereal. While he goes on to win a weightlifting contest, the unscrupulous Cesar Romero and Phil Silvers try to steal the formula from Eve Arden. Russell is amiable enough, but the real fun comes from the film's seasoned stars, who expertly manage to wring smiles out of some pretty tired gags.

Kurt Russell *Dexter Riley* • Joe Flynn *Dean Higgins* • Eve Arden *Aunt Harriet Crumply* • Cesar Romero *Aj Arno* • Phil Silvers *Kinwood Krinkle* • Dick Van Patten *Harry* • Harold Gould *Dietz* ■ *Dir* Vincent McEveety • *Scr* Herman Groves, Joseph L McEveety

Strongroom ★★
Crime drama 1961 · UK · BW · 80mins

This low-budget thriller has all the mystery and tension of a shelved *Thunderbirds* episode. Two petty crooks discover their consciences after their accomplice dies in a hit-and-run accident, and they decide to break back into the bank they have just robbed, to prevent the manager and his secretary from suffocating in the safe. If the anxious expressions and banal utterances of the villains aren't bad enough, there are glutinous exchanges between the stuffy boss and his assistant, as they find love. Director Vernon Sewell sets up this improbable story quite neatly, but it's hardly breathless entertainment.

Derren Nesbitt *Griff* • Colin Gordon *Mr Spencer* • Ann Lynn *Rose Taylor* • John Chappell *John Musgrove* • Keith Faulkner *Len* ■ *Dir* Vernon Sewell • *Scr* Max Marquis, Richard Harris, from an idea by Richard Harris

Struck by Lightning ★★★ 15
Comedy drama 1990 · Ausl · Colour · 91mins

While not of the calibre of the remarkable 1996 film *The Eighth Day*, this Australian drama nevertheless takes a refreshing and honest look at the subject of Down's syndrome. Director Jerzy Domaradzki refuses to wallow in sentimentality and draws lively performances from his Down's syndrome cast. There's also solid work from Garry McDonald and Brian Vriends, as the senior teachers at a special school who come into conflict. It's a shame their rivalry has to take in a romantic triangle, as they compete for the affections of social worker Catherine McClements. Compassionate but never corny, this is highly rewarding. Contains swearing.

Garry McDonald *Ollie Rennie* • Brian Vriends *Pat Cannizzaro* • Catherine McClements *Jill*

McHugh • Jocelyn Betheras *Jody* • Dick Tomkins *Donald* • Roger Haddad *Peter* ■ *Dir* Jerzy Domaradzki • *Scr* Trevor Farrant

The Struggle ★★
Drama 1931 · US · BW · 77mins

Blaming his recent failures on a lack of independence, DW Griffith, the once-great director, decided to produce his final film quickly and cheaply himself. The title, which accurately reflects the last decade of Griffith's working life, refers to a millworker's struggle to give up the demon drink. Anita Loos and her husband John Emerson meant their screenplay, reminiscent of Emile Zola's *The Drunkard*, to be humorous, but Griffith turned it into a rather maudlin and naive morality tale – though it didn't merit the hostile reviews that it initially received.

Hal Skelly *Jimmie Wilson* • Zita Johann *Florrie Wilson* • Charlotte Wynters *Nina* • Evelyn Baldwin *Nan Wilson* • Jackson Halliday *Johnnie Marshall* ■ *Dir* DW Griffith • *Scr* Anita Loos, John Emerson

Stryker ★ 18
Science-fiction adventure
1983 · US · Colour · 80mins

What would the exploitation industry have done without *Mad Max*? Here's another quickie clone, directed by the all-too-prolific Filipino schlock merchant Cirio H Santiago. Cowboy-hatted Steve Sandor is the road warrior battling over water with various weirdly dressed tribes, including an army of midgets, in this corny futuristic mess. Nothing looks real, everything seems daft and Sandor engenders zero sympathy in a poorly constructed apocalyptic fantasy failure. Contains violence, swearing and nudity.

Steve Sandor *Stryker* • Andria Savio *Delha* • William Ostrander *Bandit* • Michael Lane [Mike Lane] *Kardis* • Julie Gray *Laurenz* ■ *Dir* Cirio H Santiago • *Scr* Howard R Cohen, from a story by Leonard Hermes

Stuart Little ★★★ U
Fantasy 1999 · US · Colour · 84mins

Based on the much-loved novel by EB White, this half-digital, half-analogue charmer owes more to the mouse-mat maestros than the word processors. For while the animation is pixel-perfect, the narrative is short on inspiration and awash with sentiment. Both Stuart the orphan mouse and Snowbell, his feline nemesis, are expertly realised and superbly voiced by Michael J Fox and Nathan Lane respectively. But the human cast are awkward interlopers, with Geena Davis and Hugh Laurie overeager and Jonathan Lipnicki lacking his *Jerry Maguire* cuteness. Visually it's vibrant, inventive and inviting, but overall it's less adorable than the delightful *Babe*.

Michael J Fox *Stuart Little* • Geena Davis *Mrs Little* • Hugh Laurie *Mr Little* • Jonathan Lipnicki *George Little* • Nathan Lane *Snowbell* • Jennifer Tilly *Camille Stout* • Chazz Palminteri *Smokey* • Jeffrey Jones *Uncle Crenshaw* • Steve Zahn *Monty* ■ *Dir* Rob Minkoff • *Scr* M Night Shyamalan, Greg Brooker, from the novel by EB White

Stuart Saves His Family ★★★ 12
Comedy 1995 · US · Colour · 93mins

This feature-length adaptation of Al Franken's Stuart Smalley sketches from TV's *Saturday Night Live* didn't deserve the critical and commercial panning it received on its release. The problem lies with the movie's attempt to combine serious drama with the mocking of neurotic TV host Stuart Smalley. Stuart's interactions with his equally neurotic friends on and off his self-help TV show are realistic, yet amusing all the same. The second half of the movie brings a change of pace, with Stuart rejoining his estranged and extremely dysfunctional family, prompting a number of heartbreaking confessions and outbursts.

Al Franken *Stuart Smalley* • Laura San Giacomo *Julia* • Vincent D'Onofrio *Donnie* • Shirley Knight *Stuart's mom* • Harris Yulin *Stuart's dad* • Lesley Boone *Jodie* • John Link Graney *Kyle* ■ *Dir* Harold Ramis • *Scr* Al Franken, from his book

Stuck with Each Other ★★
Comedy 1989 · US · Colour · 96mins

A mildly original plot is greatly enhanced by the magnetic combination of *Cagney & Lacey*'s Tyne Daly and Richard Crenna. They have great fun in this caper comedy, which is crisply directed by Daly's former husband, Georg Stanford Brown. Salesman Crenna and secretary Daly discover a million dollars of dirty money in the open safe of their recently deceased boss. They make off with the loot to have the time of their lives, but are pursued by two equally greedy and buffoonish thugs. This romantic romp offers a welcome change from the usual dramatic fare of TV films.

Richard Crenna *Bert Medwick* • Tyne Daly *Sylvia Cass* • Roscoe Lee Browne • Eileen Heckart • Michael J Pollard • Bubba Smith ■ *Dir* Georg Stanford Brown • *Scr* Harold Jack Bloom, Howard Albrecht

The Stud ★★ 18
Sex drama 1978 · US · Colour · 91mins

The Jackie Collins novel about jet-set sex in swinging London was updated for this celebrated (for all the wrong reasons) example of disco and sexploitation, but it still looked coy and old-fashioned in 1978. Jackie's sister Joan revived her career as the rich bitch whose toy boy (Oliver Tobias) makes fruitless attempts to escape her clutches. The shallow plot and paper-thin characterisations matter little today, compared to the kitsch appeal of the Collins sisters and the dodgy disco milieu. However it was one of the most successful of its ilk and spawned a sequel, *The Bitch*.

Joan Collins *Fontaine Khaled* • Oliver Tobias *Tony Blake* • Emma Jacobs *Alex Khaled* • Sue Lloyd *Vanessa* • Walter Gotell *Ben Khaled* ■ *Dir* Quentin Masters • *Scr* Jackie Collins, Humphries Dave, Christopher Stagg, from the novel by Jackie Collins

Student Bodies ★ 15
Horror spoof 1981 · US · Colour · 81mins

A largely unsuccessful attempt to lampoon the *Halloween/Friday the 13th* slasher trend, this horror spoof

has a masked killer, The Breather, cutting a swathe through his sassy classmates using an inventive array of sharp school supplies. The rare amusing moments include one victim being paper-clipped to death and the "producer" putting in an on-screen appearance to apologise for the lack of gore and then swearing to make up for it in ratings terms. The actual producer was renowned Hollywood director Michael Ritchie, who used the infamous Alan Smithee credit to cover his humiliation. ▭

Kristen Riter *Toby* • Matthew Goldsby *Hardy* • Richard Brando *The Breather* • Joe Flood *Mr Dumpkin* • Joe Talarowski *Principal Peters* • Mimi Weddell *Miss Mumsley* • Carl Jacobs *Dr Sigmund* • Peggy Cooper *Ms Van Dyke* ■ *Dir/ Scr* Mickey Rose

Student Exchange ★ PG

Comedy   1987 · US · Colour · 85mins

A dire Disney comedy about a couple of teens who are ignored by their classmates until they reinvent themselves as foreign exchange students visiting the school. Daft in the extreme, this is only worth watching for the cameo appearances by Lisa Hartman, Bionic Woman Lindsay Wagner and the now infamous OJ Simpson, who got a much larger audience for his televised trial than this ever would. ▭

Viveka Davis *Carol* • Todd Field *Neil* • Gavin Macleod *Vice-principal Durfner* • Maura Tierney *Kathy* • Mitchell Anderson *Rod* • Lisa Hartman • OJ Simpson ■ *Dir* Mollie Miller • *Scr* William Davies, William Osborne

The Student Prince ★★★ U

Musical   1954 · US · Colour · 106mins

This was to have starred romantic tenor Mario Lanza as the prince who falls for a barmaid, only Lanza grew too obese to wear the period costumes, economically handed over from MGM's *The Prisoner of Zenda* remake. While his voice remains on the rousing soundtrack, he was replaced in the film by stiff Edmund Purdom, who in the same year had also replaced a difficult Marlon Brando in *The Egyptian*, but whose star was to fall as quickly as it rose. The film sounds magnificent and looks sumptuous, and the plot about the duties of royalty has resonances today.

Ann Blyth *Kathie* • Edmund Purdom *Prince Karl* • John Ericson *Count Von Asterburg* • Louis Calhern *King of Karlsburg* • Edmund Gwenn *Professor Juttner* • John Williams *Lutz* • SZ Sakall *Joseph Ruder* • Betta St John *Princess Johanna* • Mario Lanza *Prince Karl's singing voice* ■ *Dir* Richard Thorpe • *Scr* William Ludwig, Sonya Levien, from the operetta by Dorothy Donnelly, Sigmund Romberg and the novel and play by William Meyer-Förster • *Music* Sigmund Romberg

The Student Prince in Old Heidelberg ★★★

Silent romantic comedy
1927 · US · BW · 102mins

This is a silent screen version of a play and a popular operetta about a Ruritanian prince, studying at Heidelberg university, who falls for the local innkeeper's pretty niece. Norma Shearer and "Latin lover" Ramon Novarro star in this early example of

MGM in lavish mode. The absence of sound is well compensated for by the great Ernst Lubitsch's direction, with him stylishly extracting every ounce of charm and wistful romance from the piece and its stars. MGM remade it as a musical, *The Student Prince*, in 1954. This is better.

Ramon Novarro *Prince Karl Heinrich* • Norma Shearer *Kathi* • Jean Hersholt *Dr Juttner* • Gustav von Seyffertitz *King Karl VII* • Philippe De Lacy *Heir apparent* ■ *Dir* Ernst Lubitsch • *Scr* Hans Kräly, Marian Ainslee (titles), Ruth Cummings (titles), from the operetta *The Student Prince* by Dorothy Donnelly, Sigmund Romberg and the play *Alt Heidelberg (Old Heidelberg)* by Wilhelm Meyer-Förster

Studs Lonigan ★★★

Drama   1960 · US · BW · 95mins

Made on an inadequate budget, this ambitious and flawed study of restless teenagers in Chicago in the twenties is highly imaginative visually (Haskell Wexler is credited as photographic adviser), with some inventive links between scenes courtesy of the editing experience of director Irving Lerner. But newcomer Christopher Knight makes a hash of the central character – a pity when Warren Beatty was originally envisaged and a young actor called Jack Nicholson had to be content with playing one of Studs's pals. Heavily cut before release and taking some liberties with James T Farrell's classic novel, this drama nevertheless views its young characters' foibles with sympathy and insight.

Christopher Knight (1) *Studs Lonigan* • Frank Gorshin *Kenny Killarney* • Venetia Stevenson *Lucy Scanlon* • Carolyn Craig *Catherine Banahan* • Jack Nicholson *Weary Reilly* • Robert Casper *Paulie Haggerty* • Dick Foran *Patrick Lonigan* ■ *Dir* Irving Lerner • *Scr* Philip Yordan, from the novel by James T Farrell • *Editor* Verna Fields

A Study in Terror ★★★★ 15

Mystery thriller
1965 · UK/W Ger · Colour · 90mins

No fictional character has been portrayed more often on screen than Sherlock Holmes, but of the scores of actors to tackle the role, few deserved a second outing beneath the famous deerstalker more than John Neville. In this neatly plotted, at times gruesome, picture, he gives a stylish performance as Baker Street's most famous tenant – a portrayal which is all the more impressive for the lack of acting or sleuthing support he receives from Donald Houston as Watson. Director James Hill re-creates the Whitechapel of the Jack the Ripper era with evident relish, and the solution is a corker. ▭

John Neville *Sherlock Holmes* • Donald Houston *Dr John Watson* • John Fraser *Lord Edward Carfax* • Anthony Quayle *Dr Murray* • Robert Morley *Mycroft Holmes* • Barbara Windsor *Annie Chapman* • Adrienne Corri *Angela* • Frank Finlay *Inspector Lestrade* • Judi Dench *Sally* ■ *Dir* James Hill • *Scr* Derek Ford, Donald Ford, from a novel by Ellery Queen [Frederic Dannay, Manfred Lee], from the characters created by Sir Arthur Conan Doyle

The Stuff ★★★ 15

Comedy horror   1985 · US · Colour · 82mins

Director Larry Cohen has one of the quirkiest minds in the fantasy genre

and this gory junk-food horror satire is one of his best ever ideas. For here's a monster movie where the monster doesn't eat, you eat it! "The Stuff" is a delicious new fast-food dessert that becomes a marketing sensation. But the bubbly goo turns out to be a living substance, a killer product that turns the nation into crazed, foaming addicts. A blackly comic attack on American consumerism, the military and the advertising world, this *Blob* in reverse is a fun shocker chock full of spoof ingredients and food for thought. Contains swearing. ▭

Michael Moriarty *David "Mo" Rutherford* • Andrea Marcovicci *Nicole* • Garrett Morris *"Chocolate Chip" Charlie* • Paul Sorvino *Colonel Spears* • Scott Bloom *Jason* • Danny Aiello *Vickers* • Patrick O'Neal *Fletcher* • James Dixon *Postman* ■ *Dir/Scr* Larry Cohen

The Stunt Man ★★★★

Drama   1980 · US · Colour · 130mins

Peter O'Toole soars off the overacting scale as a film director trying to make a war movie and hiring the fugitive Vietnam veteran who killed his chief stunt man. O'Toole later claimed that he based his character on the intimidating, ruthless perfectionist David Lean – and he got an Oscar nomination for it. If you can see through the smokescreen of O'Toole's performance, you'll find a slightly subversive, long and rather ramshackle satire about movies, illusion and politics. A lot of the filming was done at the Hotel del Coronado in San Diego, famous as the location for *Some Like it Hot*.

Peter O'Toole *Eli Cross* • Barbara Hershey *Nina Franklin* • Steve Railsback *Cameron* • Sharon Farrell *Denise* • John Garwood *Gabe* • Allen Goorwitz [Allen Garfield] *Sam* • Alex Rocco *Jake* ■ *Dir* Richard Rush • *Scr* Lawrence B Marcus, Richard Rush (adaptation), from the novel by Paul Brodeur

Stunts ★★★

Action thriller   1977 · US · Colour · 83mins

Predating the Burt Reynolds stunt-man movie *Hooper* by a year, this amiable film within a film cleverly exploits the public's fascination for stunts, while at the same time presenting an intriguing little murder mystery. Robert Forster is the man investigating the mysterious death of his stunt-man brother and discovering that there's a maniac stalking the film set. Mark L Lester (not the one in *Oliver!*), provides slick direction in the bruising action scenes. One nice touch has the crew hands all sporting T-shirts saying "To hell with dialogue – let's wreck something". Fiona Lewis's reporter is the token female in the all-male group. The film also features an early score by Michael Kamen, today one of Hollywood's top composers.

Robert Forster *Glen Wilson* • Fiona Lewis *BJ Parswell* • Joanna Cassidy *Patti Johnson* • Darrell Fetty *Dave* • Bruce Glover *Chuck Johnson* • James Luisi *Blake* • Richard Lynch *Pete* ■ *Dir* Mark L Lester • *Scr* Dennis Johnson, Barney Cohen, from a story by Raymond Lofaro, from an idea by Robert Shaye, Michael Harpster

The Stupids ★★ PG

Comedy   1995 · US · Colour · 89mins

This misfiring comedy is a sad reflection of how far director John Landis has fallen since *Trading Places*. There are faint echoes of *The Brady Bunch Movie*, as Tom Arnold gives his all as the head of a family unable to cope with life in the nineties. Thanks to the energetic efforts of the cast, this is not a total disaster, and there are even occasional moments of pleasing surrealism. But, for the most part, this is a loosely linked collection of crass slapstick gags. Bizarrely, several film-makers, including David Cronenberg, Costa-Gavras and Norman Jewison have cameo roles. ▭

Tom Arnold *Stanley Stupid* • Jessica Lundy *Joan Stupid* • Bug Hall *Buster Stupid* • Alex McKenna *Petunia Stupid* • Scott Kraft *Policeman* • Christopher Lee *Evil Sender* • David Cronenberg *Postal supervisor* • Norman Jewison *TV director* • Costa-Gavras *Gas station guy* ■ *Dir* John Landis • *Scr* Brent Forrester, from the characters created by James Marshall, Harry Allard

Sub Down ★★ PG

Action thriller   1997 · US · Colour · 87mins

Despite a promising set-up, this submarine disaster outing offers only low-key undersea thrills. Tom Conti, Stephen Baldwin and Gabrielle Anwar are research scientists on nuclear sub the USS *Portland* on a mission below the Polar icecap. The trouble starts when their mini-sub causes a Russian sub to collide with the *Portland*, sending it plunging to the ocean floor. The budgetary restraints show. ▭

Stephen Baldwin *Rick Postley* • Gabrielle Anwar *Laura Dyson* • Tom Conti *Harry Rheinhardt* • Chris Mulkey *Commander John Kirsch* • Tony Plana *Lieutenant Commander Melges* • Joe Dain [Joseph Dain] *Sonar Chief Fleck* • Kevin Connolly *Petty Officer Holliday* ■ *Dir* Alan Smithee [Gregg Champion] • *Scr* Howard Chesley, from a story by Silvio Muraglia, Daniel Sladek, Howard Chesley

The Subject Was Roses ★★★★

Drama   1968 · US · Colour · 108mins

Based on Frank D Gilroy's Pulitzer Prize-winning Broadway play about a young Second World War veteran's troubled relationship with his parents, this is famous as the movie comeback of Patricia Neal after a near-fatal stroke, and her Oscar-nominated performance is all the more affecting with this knowledge. Martin Sheen plays the returning serviceman in only his second film role. The action is a trifle enclosed and theatrical, but this actually enhances the emotional punch of the drama. It's a film that requires work, but if you can stay the course, it's hugely rewarding.

Patricia Neal *Nettie Cleary* • Jack Albertson *John Cleary* • Martin Sheen *Timmy Cleary* • Don Saxon *Nightclub master of ceremonies* • Elaine Williams *Woman* • Grant Gordon *Man in a restaurant* ■ *Dir* Ulu Grosbard • *Scr* Frank D Gilroy, from his play

Submarine Patrol ★★★

First World War action adventure
1938 · US · BW · 95mins

This is directed by the great John Ford, but it sure doesn't look like a John

Ford movie. The director had been underwater before, for the submarine drama *Men without Women*, and this film about sub searchers contains several themes from the earlier tale. There is a love interest this time, with captain's daughter Nancy Kelly falling for playboy sailor Richard Greene. Before they set sail, there's a fair amount of those good-natured high jinks that tend to irritate Ford's detractors, involving Ford regulars such as Ward Bond and John Carradine. But, once they cast off, suspense abounds and the well-handled climax is full of action.

Richard Greene *Perry Townsend III* • Nancy Kelly *Susan Leeds* • Preston Foster *Lieutenant John C Drake* • George Bancroft *Captain Leeds* • Slim Summerville *Ellsworth "Spotts" Ficketts* • Joan Valerie *Anne* • John Carradine *McAllison* • Ward Bond *Olaf Swanson* ■ *Dir* John Ford • *Scr* Rian James, Darrell Ware, Jack Yellen, from the novel *The Splinter Fleet* by John Milholland

Submarine Seahawk ★ 🆄

Second World War drama
1959 · US · BW · 83mins

Spencer Gordon Bennet was a stuntman who acted in silent movies and became a prolific director of movie serials. Towards the end of his career, he made cheap B-features, which closely resembled the serial format, with shoddy sets, hackneyed plots and casts of unknowns and has-beens. Such trashy tales now have a cult following, and this feeble war drama is no exception. Unfortunately, unlike Bennet's genuinely batty *Atomic Submarine*, which was filmed on the same sets – sorry, set – this has little to recommend it.

John Bentley *Paul Turner* • Brett Halsey *David Shore* • Wayne Heffley *Dean Stoker* • Steve Mitchell *Andy Flowers* • Henry McCann *Ellis* • Frank Gerstle *Captain Boardman* • Paul Maxwell *Bill Hallohan* ■ *Dir* Spencer Gordon Bennet • *Scr* Lou Rusoff, Owen Harris

Submarine X-1 ★★★ 🆄

Second World War drama
1967 · UK · Colour · 89mins

One of the few cinema features made by prolific TV-movie director William Graham, this Second World War action film would never win any prizes for originality. But the story of a mini-sub raid on a German battleship is decently acted by James Caan and a supporting cast of British and American second-stringers. The Scottish loch scenes – in which the crews prepare for their mission to the Norwegian fjords – lack the thrill of the aerial sequences in *633 Squadron*, but Graham brings an unexpected tension to the underwater finale, in spite of having to accommodate virtually every submarine cliché in the book.

James Caan *Lt Commander Bolton* • Rupert Davies *Vice-Admiral Redmayne* • Norman Bowler *Sub-Lt Pennington* • David Sumner *Lt Davies* • William Dysart *Lt Gogan* • Brian Grellis *CPO Barquist* ■ *Dir* William Graham [William A Graham] • *Scr* Donald S Sanford, Guy Elmes, from a story by John C Champion, Edmund H North

The Substitute ★★★ 15

Thriller 1993 · US · Colour · 83mins

Anyone who witnessed Amanda Donohoe's vampiric antics in *The Lair of the White Worm* should have no problem accepting her as a replacement teacher prepared to go to any lengths to protect her guilty secret, in this predictable but curiously compelling TV movie. The sinister mood is slickly generated by director Martin Donovan, who made the equally atmospheric thriller *Apartment Zero* (and should not be confused with the American actor of the same name). Mark Wahlberg makes his movie debut as one of the class lumbered with the teacher from hell. ▣

Amanda Donohoe *Laura Ellington/Gayle Richards* • Dalton James *Josh Wyatt* • Eugene Robert Glazer *Ben Wyatt* • Mark Wahlberg *Ryan Westerberg* • Natasha Gregson Wagner *Jenny* • Brigitta Dau *Margo* ■ *Dir* Martin Donovan • *Scr* Cynthia Verlaine

The Substitute ★★ 18

Action drama 1996 · US · Colour · 109mins

When his teacher girlfriend, Diane Venora, is savagely beaten up by one of her disgruntled students, ex-soldier of fortune Tom Berenger takes over her job at Columbus High School and uses mercenary tactics to nail the drug gang responsible. Supposedly a gritty look at a social problem, director Robert Mandel's contemporary *Blackboard Jungle* meets *Rambo* nudges towards mindless camp far too often to be taken as anything but trashy exploitation. Berenger, doing a poor Steven Seagal impression, doesn't help and by the time a rocket launcher is set up in the school corridors for the brainless climax, unintentional humour has overtaken any serious intent. Contains violence, swearing and brief nudity. ▣

Tom Berenger *Shale* • Ernie Hudson *Principal Claude Rolle* • Diane Venora *Jane Hetzko* • Glenn Plummer *Darryl Sherman* • Marc Anthony *Juan* • Raymond Cruz *Joey Six* • William Forsythe *Hollan* • Luis Guzman *Rem* ■ *Dir* Robert Mandel • *Scr* Alan Ormsby, Roy Frumkes, Rocco Simonelli

The Substitute 2: School's Out ★ 18

Action drama 1997 · US · Colour · 86mins

What was a minor guilty pleasure in the first period has become redundant over recess, teaching nothing new to the viewer. Tom Berenger is gone in this made-for-video sequel to *The Substitute*, which asks us to believe another mercenary (Treat Williams) also fakes his credentials and enters an inner city school to find those responsible for hurting a loved one. In this excursion it's Williams's murdered brother. Aside from changing the hero and the motive, it pretty much plays like a rewrite of the original. Williams's "nice" demeanour also makes him a poor choice to play a professional soldier who kills for money. ▣

Treat Williams *Thomasson* • BD Wong *Drummond* • Angel David *Joey Six* • Michael Michele *Kara* • Larry Gilliard Jr *Dontae* ■ *Dir* Steven Pearl • *Scr* Roy Frumkes, Rocco Simonelli, from their characters

The Substitute Wife ★★★ 15

Period drama 1994 · US · Colour · 88mins

Farrah Fawcett gives a powerful performance in this period piece. She plays a hard-bitten prostitute in the 19th-century American west, who becomes a surrogate wife and mother to Peter Weller's family. It makes for great weepie material, and the leads, including Lea Thompson as Weller's dying wife, milk it for all it's worth. Director Peter Werner sometimes lets the sentimentality get out of hand, but he nevertheless scores in his gritty re-creation of the harshness of life on the frontier.

Farrah Fawcett *Pearl Hickson* • Lea Thompson *Amy Hightower* • Peter Weller *Martin Hightower* • Karis Bryant [Karis Paige Bryant] *Jessica Hightower* ■ *Dir* Peter Werner • *Scr* Stan Daniels

The Subterraneans ★★

Drama 1960 · US · Colour · 88mins

A former graduate and sportsman abandons himself to looking for the meaning of life in San Francisco and takes up with acolytes of the Beat generation. He has an affair with a free-spirited member of the group and, when she becomes pregnant, they decide to rejoin conventional society. Starring George Peppard and Leslie Caron, this unsatisfying bowdlerisation of Jack Kerouac's novel entirely misses the point of Beat philosophy. As directed by Ranald MacDougall and photographed by Joseph Ruttenberg, it does at least offer an evocative atmosphere, along with a generous helping of jazz, largely composed by André Previn.

Leslie Caron *Mardou Fox* • George Peppard *Leo Percepied* • Janice Rule *Roxanne* • Roddy McDowall *Yuri Gligoric* • Anne Seymour *Charlotte Percepied* • Jim Hutton *Adam Moorad* • Scott Marlowe *Julien Alexander* • Ruth Storey *Analyst* ■ *Dir* Ranald MacDougall • *Scr* Robert Thom, from the novel by Jack Kerouac

Suburban Commando ★★★ PG

Comedy adventure
1991 · US · Colour · 86mins

The appeal of Hulk Hogan may seem bewildering unless you enjoy seeing chaps pretending to throw each other around a wrestling ring, but at least he is well aware of his limitations when it comes to films. This is one of Hogan's more enjoyable efforts, in which he is the alien warrior who lands on Earth and struggles to blend in with Christopher Lloyd's puzzled family. Hogan makes Arnold Schwarzenegger look like an actor of great subtlety, but there are some nice one-liners and director Burt Kennedy ropes in a classy supporting cast. Contains swearing and violence. ▣

Hulk Hogan *Shep Ramsey* • Christopher Lloyd *Charlie Wilcox* • Shelley Duvall *Jenny Wilcox* • Larry Miller *Adrian Beltz* • William Ball *General Suitor* • JoAnn Dearing *Margie Tanen* • Jack Elam *Colonel Dustin "Dusty" McHowell* ■ *Dir* Burt Kennedy • *Scr* Frank Cappello

subUrbia ★★★ 15

Comedy drama 1996 · US · Colour · 115mins

Richard Linklater, king of the slacker movie here brings a perfect slacker-type story to the screen. It's based the stage play by Eric Bogosian, the controversial talk-show host who was the subject of Oliver Stone's film *Talk Radio*, and the story is inspired by his early life. Set in a parking lot during one long night, it's an ensemble piece about a group of aimless twentysomethings and their meeting with old friend Pony (Jayce Bartok) who's gone on to become a successful rock star. Indie queen Parker Posey turns in another fine performance as his publicist, in this dark and absorbing work. Contains swearing, sexual references and some violence. ▣

Giovanni Ribisi *Jeff* • Steve Zahn *Buff* • Amie Carey *Sooze* • Ajay Naidu *Nazeer* • Jayce Bartok *Pony* • Nicky Katt *Tim* • Parker Posey *Erica* ■ *Dir* Richard Linklater • *Scr* Eric Bogosian, from his play

Subway ★★★★ 15

Thriller 1985 · Fr · Colour · 97mins

Christopher Lambert goes underground in director Luc Besson's chic cult classic. He's a safe-cracker who falls in love with Isabelle Adjani while turning over her husband's strongbox and finds refuge from the authorities amongst the oddballs inhabiting the shady world of the Paris metro. Besson's darkly humorous script and spiky style, combined with the starkly depressing environment and weird subculture, give this New Wave suspense thriller a delightful edginess and unique look. If you like Besson's movies (*The Big Blue*, *Leon*), you'll love this dazzler. In French with English subtitles. ▣

Isabelle Adjani *Helena* • Christopher Lambert *Fred* • Richard Bohringer *Florist* • Michel Galabru *Commissioner Gesberg* • Jean-Hugues Anglade *The Roller Skater* • Jean-Pierre Bacri *Batman* • Jean Reno *Drummer* ■ *Dir* Luc Besson • *Scr* Luc Besson, Pierre Jolivet, Alain Le Henry, Marc Perrier, Sophie Schmit • *Art Director* Alexandre Trauner

Subway in the Sky ★★★

Crime drama 1958 · UK · BW · 86mins

Though not highly regarded on its release, thanks to its cast, subject matter and director, this crime drama bears re-evaluation today. It's set in postwar Germany and features two particularly watchable stars, both of whom have done better work. Ageing bobby-sox idol Van Johnson is a better actor than is generally acknowledged. He had a propensity for worried, introverted heroes and here he's hiding from the authorities in the flat of cabaret singer Hildegarde Neff. Director Muriel Box was one of the few English women directors to have had a successful screen career, but she struggles to conceal the stage origins of the material.

Van Johnson *Major Baxter Grant* • Hildegarde Neff *Lilli Hoffman* • Albert Lieven *Carl von Schecht* • Cec Linder *Captain Carson* • Katherine Kath *Anna Grant* • Vivian Matalon *Stefan* • Carl Jaffe *Adler* ■ *Dir* Muriel Box • *Scr* Jack Andrews, from a play by Ian Main

🆄 = SUITABLE FOR ALL   🆄🅢 = SUITABLE FOR ALL, ESPECIALLY FOR YOUNG CHILDREN (VIDEO ONLY)   PG = PARENTAL GUIDANCE

Subzero ★★★ PG
Animated action adventure
1998 · US · Colour · 63mins

Spinning off from the animated *Batman* TV show, this direct-to-video feature has the Dynamic Duo out to stop villain Mr Freeze, who's reappeared in order to continue his endless quest to find a cure for his cryogenically frozen wife. The animation may not be particularly fluid, but the Fleischer-like art design is a wonder to behold. The script captures the wham-bam flavor of a comic book, while avoiding the pitfall of aiming strictly at a juvenile audience. Some thought has been given to these characters, especially the villain, who comes across as a tragic figure and actually generates some sympathy. 🖭

Kevin Conroy *Batman/Bruce Wayne* • Michael Ansara *Mr Freeze/Dr Victor Fries* • Loren Lester *Robin/Dick Grayson* • Efrem Zimbalist Jr *Alfred* • George Dzundza *Dr Gregory Belson* ■ *Dir* Boyd Kirkland • *Scr* Randy Rogel, Boyd Kirkland, from characters created by Bob Kane

Success Is the Best Revenge ★★★ 15
Drama   1984 · UK/Fr · Colour · 85mins

Following *Moonlighting*, director Jerzy Skolimowski continued his theme of Polish exiles in London. Very much a family affair, in terms of the plot and the filming, it was shot at Skolimowski's Kensington home and co-written by his son, Michael Lyndon, who also appears in a main role. A Polish theatre director (Michael York) becomes totally absorbed with the play he is staging, to the point where his family feel alienated by his behaviour. The film suffers from being slightly unfocused, with the plot going off in too many directions, but visually and cinematically there is much to admire. 🖭

Michael York *Alex Rodak* • Joanna Szerzerbic *Wife* • Michael Lyndon *Adam* • Michel Piccoli *French official* • Anouk Aimée *Monique de Fontaine* • John Hurt *Dino Montecurva* ■ *Dir* Jerzy Skolimowski • *Scr* Michael Lyndon, Jerzy Skolimowski • *Cinematographer* Mike Fash

A Successful Calamity ★★★
Comedy   1932 · US · BW · 72mins

In his later years, British theatre actor George Arliss unexpectedly became a major Hollywood film star, usually playing an upper-class or royal role. Here he is a millionaire who returns home after a prolonged business trip in Europe to find his self-centered family are taking their money for granted. To teach them a lesson he feigns bankruptcy, sparking several amusing scenes. Based on the 1917 play by Clare Kummer, this is a deft morality tale which, while somewhat dated, still has much to recommend it.

George Arliss *Henry Wilton* • Mary Astor *Emmie Wilton* • Evalyn Knapp *Peggy Wilton* • Grant Mitchell *Connors* • David Torrence *Partington* • William Janney *Eddie Wilton* • Hardie Albright *George Struthers* • Hale Hamilton *John Belden* ■ *Dir* John G Adolfi • *Scr* Austin Parker, Maude Howell, Julien Josephson, from the play by Clare Kummer

Such a Long Journey ★★★ 15
Drama   1998 · Can/UK · Colour · 113mins

Adapted from the Booker-nominated novel by Rohinton Mistry, this allegorical study of India's socio-political problems in the early seventies is held together by a performance of muddled idealism and dignified pride from Roshan Seth, as a Parsi bank clerk whose world begins to crumble after he agrees to do a favour for a friend in the secret service. This slowly simmering story is handled with care by director Sturla Gunnarsson, who exploits the contrasting colours and moods of Bombay to heighten the authenticity of what could so easily have become an overloaded melodrama Contains swearing and sexual situations.

Roshan Seth *Gustad Noble* • Om Puri *Ghulam* • Soni Razdan *Dilnavaz Noble* • Naseeruddin Shah *Jimmy Bilimoria* • Sam Dastor *Dinshawji* • Vrajesh Hirjee *Sohrab Noble* ■ *Dir* Sturla Gunnarsson • *Scr* Sooni Taraporevala, from the novel by Rohinton Mistry

Such Good Friends ★★★★
Black comedy   1971 · US · Colour · 101mins

This witty and adroit Otto Preminger film (one of the director's last), gives Dyan Cannon her best screen role to date. She's the wife of a hospitalised New Yorker (Laurence Luckinbill) who discovers an awful lot about her hubby while he's in care. Sexy and clever by turns, the screenplay is by a pseudonymous Elaine May. The film contains one of the great telephone scenes, as Dyan prepares to "service" James Coco solicitously while he's engaged in conversation. Very funny and about as black as black comedies get – its ultra-sophisticated subtext bears repeated reviewings.

Dyan Cannon *Julie Messenger* • James Coco *Dr Timmy Spector* • Jennifer O'Neill *Miranda Graham* • Ken Howard *Cal Whiting* • Nina Foch *Mrs Wallman* • Laurence Luckinbill *Richard Messenger* • Burgess Meredith *Bernard Kalman* • Louise Lasser *Marcy Berns* ■ *Dir* Otto Preminger • *Scr* Esther Dale [Elaine May], David Shaber, from the novel by Lois Gould

Sudden Death ★★★★ 18
Action thriller 1995 · US · Colour · 105mins

Despite its mundane title, this is one of Jean-Claude Van Damme's best thrillers. As a fire officer at an ice hockey stadium, he is given the task of thwarting the deliciously menacing Powers Boothe, who plans to blow up the spectators – among them Van Damme's kids and the US vice president. Who can resist a movie in which the Muscles from Brussels has to fight an assassin dressed as a penguin? Although plausibility isn't its strongest suit, it moves at a rollicking pace and never takes itself too seriously. This is one not just for Van Damme devotees, but for all action fans, right up to its explosively exciting climax. 🖭 *DVD*

Jean-Claude Van Damme *Darren McCord* • Powers Boothe *Joshua Foss* • Raymond J Barry *Vice President* • Whittni Wright *Emily McCord* • Ross Malinger *Tyler McCord* • Dorian Harewood *Hallmark* • Jophery Brown *Wootton* ■ *Dir* Peter Hyams • *Scr* Gene Quintano, from a story by Karen Baldwin

Sudden Fear ★★★
Thriller   1952 · US · BW · 110mins

Joan Crawford has a splendid opportunity to suffer agonies in this contrived but lively thriller in which she accidentally discovers her husband is plotting to kill her. The woman's whirlwind passion for someone as sinister as Jack Palance does strain credulity, although her career as a playwright serves to explain why she devises her own scheme to trap Palance and his grasping girlfriend, Gloria Grahame, rather than calling in the police. Dramatically photographed by Charles Lang Jr and forcefully acted under the direction of David Miller, the film is always a visual treat.

Joan Crawford *Myra Hudson* • Jack Palance *Lester Blaine* • Gloria Grahame *Irene Neves* • Bruce Bennett *Steve Kearney* • Touch Connors [Mike Connors] *Junior Kearney* ■ *Dir* David Miller • *Scr* Lenore Coffee, Robert Smith, from the novel by Edna Sherry

Sudden Fury ★★ 15
Comedy based on a true story
1993 · US · Colour · 88mins

Neil Patrick Harris attempts to ditch his nice kid *Doogie Howser, MD* image in this intense and unsettling TV-movie drama, inevitably based on a true story. He is surprisingly convincing as one of three adopted children who fall under suspicion when their parents are murdered. There's a solid supporting cast, including Gregory Harrison and Lisa Banes, but Craig R Baxley's direction is unspectacular. 🖭

Neil Patrick Harris *Brian Hannigan* • Johnny Galecki *Daniel Hannigan* • Linda Kelsey *Maureen Hannigan* • John M Jackson *Joe Hannigan* • Gregory Harrison *Tom Kelley* • Lisa Banes *Barbara Forester* ■ *Dir* Craig R Baxley • *Scr* Matthew Bombeck, from the book by Leslie Walker

Sudden Impact ★★★ 18
Crime thriller   1983 · US · Colour · 112mins

This fourth outing for Clint Eastwood's magnum enforcer, "Dirty Harry" Callahan has the big man with the big gun hunting a woman who's systematically tracking down and terminating the sickos who raped her and her sister. Sondra Locke, Eastwood's partner at the time, plays the ladykiller. More down and dirty than previous *Harrys*, it won't disappoint series fans, even if the formula is starting to wear a little thin. Incidentally, this is the film in which Eastwood delivers his much quoted "Go ahead, make my day" quip. Contains violence, swearing and sexual references. 🖭

Clint Eastwood *Inspector Harry Callahan* • Sondra Locke *Jennifer Spencer* • Pat Hingle *Chief Jannings* • Bradford Dillman *Captain Briggs* • Paul Drake *Mick* • Audrie J Neenan *Ray Parkins* ■ *Dir* Clint Eastwood • *Scr* Joseph C Stinson, from a story by Earl E Smith, Charles B Pierce, from characters created by Harry Julian Fink, RM Fink

Suddenly ★★★ PG
Crime thriller   1954 · US · BW · 72mins

Withdrawn from distribution for years because star Frank Sinatra found out Lee Harvey Oswald had watched it only days before assassinating President Kennedy, *Suddenly* is a must-see

rarity, if for that reason alone. Ol' Blue Eyes is the gun crazy killer who holds a family hostage in the hick town of Suddenly, California, as part of a plot to kill the US President, who's passing through on a fishing holiday. Sinatra plays this tough tension-laden thriller to the hilt, and he's given top-notch support by Sterling Hayden as the local sheriff and James Gleason as the retired secret service agent whose house is taken over by the would-be assassin. 🖭

Frank Sinatra *John Baron* • Sterling Hayden *Sheriff Tod Shaw* • James Gleason *Pop Benson* • Nancy Gates *Ellen Benson* • Kim Charney *Pidge Benson* • Paul Frees *Benny Conklin* • Christopher Dark *Bart Wheeler* ■ *Dir* Lewis Allen • *Scr* Richard Sale

Suddenly ★★
Drama   1996 · US · Colour · 96mins

Comedy actress Kirstie Alley took a wrong turn at dramatic acting when she chose to portray an outgoing but acerbic waitress whose life is suddenly shattered by an accident that leaves her a paraplegic. Abandoned by her fiancé, she becomes bitter and angry, numbing her emotional pain with booze and pills. While well intentioned, this over-the-top melodrama offers nothing new to the well-worn "accident victim overcoming life tragedy" theme. Director Robert Allan Ackerman might have saved this runaway rollercoaster ride of emotions if only he could have reined in Alley – but she was also this soapy TV movie's executive producer.

Kirstie Alley *Marty Doyle* • Jason Beghe *Joe Mulvey* • Jason Bernard *Louie* • Colleen Camp *Jude* • Nancy Cartwright *Dell* ■ *Dir* Robert Allan Ackerman • *Scr* David Kinghorn

Suddenly It's Spring ★★★
Romantic comedy   1947 · US · BW · 88mins

Paulette Goddard returns from the war as an officer to find that her lawyer husband, Fred MacMurray, has found someone else and wants a divorce, which she refuses. A woman's place is usually at the centre of director Mitchell Leisen's movies, and role-reversal is a constant theme. The gender switch is about the only novelty in this pleasantly familiar, lightweight romantic comedy with two agreeable leads. Given that the "other" man and woman are played by the not very interesting Macdonald Carey and Arleen Whelan, it doesn't take a genius to guess who will be with whom at the end.

Paulette Goddard *WAC Captain Mary Morely/ "Captain Lonelyhearts"* • Fred MacMurray *Peter Morely* • MacDonald Carey [Macdonald Carey] *Jack Lindsay* • Arleen Whelan *Gloria Fay* • Lilian Fontaine *Mary's mother* • Frank Faylen *Harold Michaels* ■ *Dir* Mitchell Leisen • *Scr* Claude Binyon, PJ Wolfson, from the story *Sentimental Journey* by PJ Wolfson

Suddenly, Last Summer ★★★★ 15
Drama   1959 · UK · BW · 109mins

This wonderfully overheated drama by Tennessee Williams, who wrote the screenplay with Gore Vidal, is animated by two ultra-powerful performances by Elizabeth Taylor and Katharine Hepburn. Taylor is the niece about to be committed to a mental

instituton by southern matriarch Hepburn after witnessing the violent death of a homosexual cousin. Montgomery Clift is the neurosurgeon called in to assess the girl's sanity rating before a possible lobotomy. Director Joseph L Mankiewicz makes it a class act all round. 🖦

Elizabeth Taylor *Catherine Holly* • Montgomery Clift *Dr John Cukrowicz* • Katharine Hepburn *Mrs Violet Venable* • Albert Dekker *Dr Hockstader* • Mercedes McCambridge *Mrs Holly* • Gary Raymond *George Holly* • Mavis Villiers *Mrs Foxhill* • Patricia Marmont *Nurse Benson* • Joan Young *Sister Felicity* ■ *Dir* Joseph L Mankiewicz • *Scr* Gore Vidal, Tennessee Williams, from the play by Tennessee Williams • *Production Designer* Oliver Messel, William Kellner • *Set Designer* Scott Slimon

Sudie and Simpson ★★★

Drama 1990 · US · Colour · 95mins

This is a beautifully judged tale of innocence and prejudice set in forties' Georgia. Louis Gossett Jr and Sara Gilbert are outstanding as the elderly black man and the 12-year-old tomboy, whose unlikely friendship outrages the local community. Frances Fisher leads a strong supporting cast, while Mario DiLeo's filming of the gorgeous rural views stand in stark contrast to the ugly emotions of the populace. Following *Cold Sassy Tree*, this provides further proof of former choreographer Joan Tewkesbury's abilities as a sensitive and assured director.

Louis Gossett Jr *Simpson* • Sara Gilbert *Sudie Harrigan* • John Jackson [John M Jackson] *Dr Stubbs* • Paige Dannahy *Mary Agnes* • Frances Fisher *Miss Marge* • Ken Strong *Clay Harrigan* • Robby Preddy *Mrs Harrigan* • Larry Black *Mr Ethridge* ■ *Dir* Joan Tewkesbury • *Scr* Ken Koser, Sara Flanigan Carter, from the novel *Sudie* by Sara Flanigan Carter

Suez ★★★

Biographical drama 1938 · US · BW · 104mins

Twentieth Century-Fox was marvellously adept high-budget biopics. But one of the most unlikely candidates for Fox screen canonisation must surely have been 19th-century French engineer Ferdinand de Lesseps, who was the force behind the construction of the Suez Canal. Fox turned his story into a slice of romantic hokum for their contractee, popular matinée idol Tyrone Power, and the whole saga became a rattlingly entertaining melodrama under the expert direction of Allan Dwan and Otto Brower.

Tyrone Power *Ferdinand de Lesseps* • Loretta Young *Empress Eugenie* • Annabella *Toni* • J Edward Bromberg *Said* • Joseph Schildkraut *La Tour* • Henry Stephenson *Count de Lesseps* • Sidney Blackmer *du Brey* • Maurice Moscovich *Mohammed Ali* • Sig Rumann [Sig Ruman] *Sergeant Fellerin* ■ *Dir* Allan Dwan, Otto Brower • *Scr* Philip Dunne, Julien Josephson, from a story by Sam Duncan

Suffering Bastards ★★★

Comedy 1989 · US · Colour · 89mins

A provocative title for a well-crafted but chat-heavy comedy in which a guy regales a girl he meets in a bar with tall tales about his hard-luck past. Are they fact or fiction? And does it matter if they're just a weapon in his chat-up arsenal? Eric Bogosian and Gina

Gershon star, with John C McGinley at the top of a talented support cast. McGinley also wrote the piece, which sounds and looks a little better suited to the stage than the cinema screen.

Eric Bogosian *Mr Leech* • Gina Gershon *Sharnetta* • John C McGinley *Buddy Johnson* • David Warshofsky *Al Johnson* • Michael Wincott *Chazz* ■ *Dir* Bernard McWilliams • *Scr* John C McGinley

Sugar Hill ★★★ 18

Crime thriller 1993 · US · Colour · 118mins

While so many films about inner-city New York centre on the violence of drug-related crime, this multi-layered drama instead focuses on the actual human toll. In particular, director Leon Ichaso is keen to explore the difficulties involved in quitting the ghetto and starting over. As the dealer determined to leave behind the trade that has destroyed his family, Wesley Snipes is convincingly torn between a romance with well-heeled Theresa Randle and his loyalty to his brother (Jeffrey Wright), who's in thrall to gangster Abe Vigoda. However, the wordiness of Barry Michael Cooper's script detracts from the film's authenticity. Contains violence, swearing, drug abuse and nudity. 🖦

Wesley Snipes *Roemello Skuggs* • Michael Wright *Raynathan Skuggs* • Theresa Randle *Melissa* • Clarence Williams III *Ar Skuggs* • Abe Vigoda *Gus Molino* • Larry Joshua *Harry Molino* • Ernie Hudson *Lolly* ■ *Dir* Leon Ichaso • *Scr* Barry Michael Cooper

Sugarbaby ★★★ 15

Romantic comedy
1985 · W Ger · Colour · 85mins

Infinitely better than Ricki Lake's 1989 remake *Babycakes*, Percy Adlon's unconventional romantic comedy was rightly hailed as a triumph for its star, Marianne Sägebrecht. She excels as the generously proportioned Munich mortuary assistant whose obsession with a married underground train driver (Eisi Gulp) inspires a scheme to seduce him. However, this is also a skilfully directed film, with the candified neon colour schemes suggesting a fairy-tale atmosphere that is reinforced by the wicked witch-like appearance of Gulp's wife, Manuela Denz. Mischievous, fair-minded and slick. In German with English subtitles.

Marianne Sägebrecht *Marianne* • Eisi Gulp *Eugen Huber* • Toni Berger *Funeral parlor boss* • Manuela Denz *Huber's wife* • Will Spindler *1st train driver* ■ *Dir* Percy Adlon • *Scr* Percy Adlon, Gwendolyn von Ambesser, from a story by Percy Adlon • *Cinematographer* Johanna Heer

Sugarfoot ★★ U

Western 1951 · US · Colour · 79mins

An undistinguished Warner Bros western, this pairs rugged Randolph Scott with suave Raymond Massey as his nemesis, a combination that worked to better effect a year later in the same studio's *Carson City*. It is better remembered today as one of the first western TV series based on a feature film. This is very average, and really only for fans of the implacable Scott, though the super fifties Technicolor gives it a certain class and

Adele Jergens is a stand-out, singing a nifty Sammy Cahn number.

Randolph Scott *Sugarfoot* • Adele Jergens *Reva Cairn* • Raymond Massey *Jacob Stint* • SZ Sakall *Don Miguel* • Robert Warwick *JC Crane* • Arthur Hunnicutt *Fly-up-the-creek Jones* • Hugh Sanders *Asa Goodhue* ■ *Dir* Edwin L Marin • *Scr* Russell Hughes, from a novel by Clarence Budington

The Sugarland Express
★★★ PG

Action adventure based on a true story
1974 · US · Colour · 104mins

Truncated for general release in this country, this is the complete version of this marvellously constructed chase movie from a young Steven Spielberg, based on truth, about a young couple heading for Sugarland, Texas, pursued by the police as they race across the state. As written, the couple are not particularly likeable, but as played by Goldie Hawn and William Atherton they're funny and sympathetic, even when they capture patrolman Michael Sacks and hold him hostage. The set pieces are beautifully handled and grizzled veteran Ben Johnson is watchable as the head cop on their tail. Early proof of Spielberg's talent. Contains violence and swearing. 🖦

Goldie Hawn *Lou Jean Poplin* • Ben Johnson *Captain Tanner* • Michael Sacks *Officer Maxwell Slide* • William Atherton *Clovis Poplin* • Gregory Walcott *Officer Mashburn* • Steve Kanaly *Jessup* • Louise Latham *Mrs Looby* ■ *Dir* Steven Spielberg • *Scr* Hal Barwood, Matthew Robbins, from a story by Steven Spielberg, Hal Barwood, Matthew Robbins

Sugartime ★★ 18

Period drama 1995 · US · Colour · 106mins

The love affair between mobster Sam Giancana and rising singer Phyllis McGuire was a big scandal that damaged their careers, though this retelling of their story, for the most part, neglects to tell us why. This low-key HBO movie re-creates the period quite nicely, but it seems to start at a later point than it should have, beginning and proceeding with characters we know little about. As the famous couple, John Turturro and Mary-Louise Parker try, but they have no chemistry and their sudden evolution from casual acquaintances to lovers is unbelievable. 🖦

John Turturro *Sam Giancana* • Mary-Louise Parker *Phyllis McGuire* • Elias Koteas *Butch Blasi* • Maury Chaykin *Tony Accardo* • Louis Del Grande *Chuckie English* • Deborah Duchene *Christine McGuire* • Larissa Lapchinski *Dorothy McGuire* ■ *Dir* John N Smith • *Scr* Martyn Burke, from the non-fiction book *Roemer: Man Against the Mob* by William F Roemer Jr

Suicide Battalion ★★ U

Second World War adventure
1958 · US · BW · 78mins

This static Second World War action adventure is directed by Edward L Cahn, who managed to churn out roughly ten similarly uninspired films a year during this period. Not that the executives at AIP cared particularly about quality. This was drive-in fodder, made to support a horror or beach party flick and featuring actors who would appeal to the teenage market. Here, Michael Connors and John

Ashley break into a captured American base to destroy some secret papers. For fans only.

Michael Connors [Mike Connors] *Major Matt McCormack* • John Ashley *Tommy Novello* • Jewell Lian *Elizabeth Ann Mason* • Russ Bender *Harry Donovan* • Bing Russell *Lt Chet Hall* • Scott Peters *Wally Skilzowski* ■ *Dir* Edward L Cahn • *Scr* Lou Rusoff

Suicide Kings ★★★ 15

Comedy thriller 1997 · US · Colour · 102mins

Despite the tortuous plot, this black comedy provides a rewarding mix of amoral laughs and suspense. Christopher Walken – who can do this sort of thing in his sleep – stars as a mob boss kidnapped by a group of youngsters who need to raise their own ransom to rescue one of their girlfriends. However, Walken quickly realises that one of the kidnappers has a hidden agenda and begins to play them off against each other. The youngsters, who include Henry Thomas, Jay Mohr and Sean Patrick Flanery, more than hold their own with the experienced Walken, and there's also a nice turn from Denis Leary. A little too clever for its own good, this still holds the attention. Contains swearing and violence. 🖦

Christopher Walken *Charles Barrett* • Denis Leary *Lono Vecchio* • Sean Patrick Flanery *Max Minot* • Johnny Galecki *Ira Reder* • Jay Mohr *Brett Campbell* • Jeremy Sisto *TK* ■ *Dir* Peter O'Fallon • *Scr* Josh McKinney, Wayne Rice, Gina Goldman, from the story *The Hostage* by Don Stanford

Suite 16 ★★★ 18

Erotic drama
1994 · UK/Bel/Neth · Colour · 106mins

A wealthy paraplegic offers sanctuary to a fleeing felon in return for his aiding him with his erotic fantasies. Pete Postlethwaite is the dirty old man, Antonie Kamerling his hunky helper, in an intriguing if somewhat pretentious piece that was badly mismarketed as soft-core porn by most of its distributors. Unsurprisingly, it underwhelmed the dirty-mac brigade, and has been little seen since. Considering the presence of Postlethwaite and the co-scripting of *The Fast Show*'s Charlie Higson, it deserves a little more attention. In English and French with subtitles. Contains swearing, sex scenes and violence. 🖦

Pete Postlethwaite *Glover* • Antonie Kamerling *Chris* • Geraldine Pailhas *Helen* • Tom Jansen *Paul* • Bart Slegers *Rudy* ■ *Dir* Dominique Deruddere • *Scr* Charles Higson, Lise Mayer

Sullivan's Travels ★★★★★

Satirical comedy 1941 · US · BW · 90mins

A sparkling satire from writer/director Preston Sturges this centres on the age-old Hollywood dilemma of art versus entertainment. Giving perhaps his best performance, Joel McCrea plays a hugely successful slapstick comedy director who yearns to make a serious movie. So he hits the road, disguised as a tramp, in a concerted attempt to find out what it means to suffer. With Veronica Lake in a star-making turn as McCrea's travelling companion, the plot veers from inspired insight to corny contrivance at

U = SUITABLE FOR ALL Uc = SUITABLE FOR ALL, ESPECIALLY FOR YOUNG CHILDREN (VIDEO ONLY) PG = PARENTAL GUIDANCE

such a rattling pace the sheer vigour of the action carries you along. This classic comedy should leave you in no doubt where Sturges thought a movie's first duty lay, yet it's also one of the few films that manages to strike a winning balance between the horns of its own dilemma.

Joel McCrea *John L Sullivan* • Veronica Lake *The girl* • William Demarest *Mr Jones* • Robert Warwick *Mr Lebrand* • Franklin Pangborn *Mr Casalais* • Porter Hall *Mr Hadrian* • Robert Greig *Sullivan's butler* • Eric Blore *Sullivan's valet* • Arthur Hoyt *Preacher* • Preston Sturges *Man in film studio* ■ *Dir/Scr* Preston Sturges

The Sum of Us ★★★ 15
Comedy   1995 · Ausl · Colour · 95mins

Although set against the familiar landmarks of Sydney, this well-meaning plea for sexual tolerance never quite escapes its theatrical origins. Too many stagey lines and matey nods to camera intrude upon widower Jack Thompson's eager efforts to make plumber son Russell Crowe feel at home with his homosexuality. Yet, such is the geniality of Thompson's one-man assault on Aussie macho culture that it's easy to forgive the many contrivances, if not the glutinous resolution to the rift that follows Crowe's separation from his deeply suspicious boyfriend (John Polson). Warm and witty, this is nonetheless never as poignant or hilarious as it thinks. Contains swearing. ▦

Jack Thompson *Harry Mitchell* • Russell Crowe *Jeff Mitchell* • John Polson *Greg* • Deborah Kennedy *Joyce Johnson* • Joss Morony *Young Jeff* • Mitch Mathews *Gran* • Julie Herbert *Mary* ■ *Dir* Kevin Dowling, Geoff Burton • *Scr* David Stevens, from his play

Summer and Smoke ★★
Drama   1961 · US · Colour · 118mins

Tennessee Williams's play, spanning several years in the life of the timid, sexually repressed and neurotic daughter of a minister in a small Southern town, won Geraldine Page plaudits and fame in the 1952 Broadway production. She repeated it on screen under the direction of Peter Glenville, who had staged the play in the West End. Laurence Harvey co-stars as the wild young doctor for whom Page harbours a passion, with Rita Moreno as the dance-hall girl who's much more his cup of tea. However, the material – never the playwright's best – simply fails to ignite and is worth enduring only for Page's performance. She was Oscar-nominated, along with Una Merkel and Elmer Bernstein for his score.

Geraldine Page *Alma Winemiller* • Laurence Harvey *John Buchanan* • Una Merkel *Mrs Winemiller* • Rita Moreno *Rosa Zacharias* • John McIntyre *Dr Buchanan* ■ *Dir* Peter Glenville • *Scr* James Poe, Meade Roberts, from the play by Tennessee Williams

A Summer at Grandpa's ★★★★ PG
Drama   1984 · Tai · Colour · 97mins

Such is the mastery of Hou Hsiao-Hsien that he takes a situation ripe for sentimentalising and fills it with small moments of truth and insight into how kids relate to grown-ups. There's an Ozu-like feel about the action, with its

subtle contrasts between town and country, youth and age, success and failure. But as Wang Qiguang and his younger sister witness the rivalry between their grandpa and uncle, it's the innocent immediacy of children's preoccupations that is most keenly observed. This is rite-of-passage film, without the easy lessons and cosy resolutions – and all the more charming and effective for it. In Mandarin with English subtitles.

Wang Qiguang *Tung-Tung* • Gu Jun *Grandpa* • Mei Fang *Grandma* • Lin Xiuling *Pi-Yun* • Edward Yang ■ *Dir* Hou Hsiao-Hsien • *Scr* Zhu Tianwen, Hou Hsiao-Hsien

A Summer by the River ★★★
Period drama   1998 · Fin · Colour · 86mins

Evoking the popular outdoor adventures of the mid-1950s, Markku Polonen's period drama could easily have collapsed into mawkish nostalgia, as a widower rediscovers his self-esteem and grows closer to his 10-year-old son in the course of a single summer of tree felling. However, there's a touch of grit about his progress from mockable townie novice to respected logger; even his romance with a free-thinking blonde isn't all soft-centred. Making the most of his striking locations, Polonen achieves a genuine bond between Pertti Koivula and Imo Kontio, who is much more than the adorable moppet he'd be in a Hollywood equivalent. A Finnish language film.

Imo Kontio *Topi* • Esko Nikkari *Hannes* • Anu Palevaara *Hilkka* • Peter Franzen *Kottarainen* • Pertti Koivula *Tenbo* ■ *Dir/Scr* Markku Polonen

Summer Holiday ★★★
Musical comedy   1948 · US · Colour · 92mins

This musical version of Eugene O'Neill's play *Ah, Wilderness* is a spirited, if low-key, MGM production with little of lasting value, unless you warm to the brash Mickey Rooney in the lead and the film's highlight, a song about the family car called *The Stanley Steamer*. Co-star Gloria DeHaven is certainly mouthwatering, but the film is largely in the hands of veterans Walter Huston, Frank Morgan and Agnes Moorehead, whose professionalism is impressive but just not compelling. It does, however, look superb and has the potential to be an acquired taste.

Mickey Rooney *Richard Miller* • Gloria DeHaven *Muriel McComber* • Walter Huston *Nat Miller* • Frank Morgan *Uncle Sid* • Jackie "Butch" Jenkins *Tommy Miller* • Marilyn Maxwell *Belle* • Agnes Moorehead *Cousin Lily* ■ *Dir* Rouben Mamoulian • *Scr* Frances Goodrich, Albert Hackett, Irving Brecher, Jean Holloway, from the play *Ah, Wilderness* by Eugene O'Neill

Summer Holiday ★★★ U
Musical comedy   1962 · UK · Colour · 103mins

Cliff Richard is still making hit records nearly 40 years after this high-spirited romp. It's unlikely that his knighthood was awarded solely on the strength of this wholesome road movie (the less than august debut of director Peter Yates), in which four youths cross Europe in a London Transport double-

decker bus. But there are plenty of fondly remembered songs, some splendid scenery and a willing supporting cast. ▦

Cliff Richard *Don* • Lauri Peters *Barbara* • Melvyn Hayes *Cyril* • Una Stubbs *Sandy* • Teddy Green *Steve* • Pamela Hart *Angie* • Jeremy Bulloch *Edwin* ■ *Dir* Peter Yates • *Scr* Peter Myers, Ronald Cass

Summer Interlude ★★★★ PG
Drama   1950 · Swe · BW · 91mins

This is the picture that established Ingmar Bergman's international reputation. Although it still deals with the theme of young love that dominated his earliest films, it contains the first intimations of the dramatic intensity and structural complexity that would characterise his more mature work. As the world-weary ballerina recalling her teenage affair with timid student Birger Malmsten, Maj-Britt Nilsson gives a performance of such sensitivity that one is at a loss to explain why Bergman dropped her from his stock company after *Secrets of Women* a couple of years later. Gunnar Fischer and Bengt Jarnmark's shimmering images of the sunny Swedish countryside further enhance this subtle, moving film. In Swedish with English subtitles. ▦

Maj-Britt Nilsson *Marie* • Birger Malmsten *Henrik* • Alf Kjellin *David Nystrom* • Georg Funkquist *Uncle Erland* • Mimi Pollak *Aunt Elizabeth* ■ *Dir* Ingmar Bergman • *Scr* Ingmar Bergman, Herbert Grevenius, from a story by Ingmar Bergman

Summer Lovers ★★ 18
Erotic comedy   1982 · US · Colour · 98mins

After 1980's *The Blue Lagoon*, director Randal Kleiser chose another, equally exotic, location for this slightly more grown-up tale of young romance. The setting this time is a sun-drenched Greek island, where poor old Peter Gallagher finds himself torn between Daryl Hannah and Valerie Quennessen. It looks great, but there's more depth in a teen magazine picture story than in this empty-headed nonsense, though it's interesting to see the now-familiar Gallagher in such an early role. Contains sex scenes and nudity. ▦

Peter Gallagher *Michael Papas* • Daryl Hannah *Cathy Feathererst* • Valerie Quennessen *Lina* • Barbara Rush *Jean Feathererst* • Carole Cook *Barbara Foster* • Hans Van Tongeren *Jan Tolin* ■ *Dir/Scr* Randal Kleiser

Summer Magic ★★★ U
Period comedy   1963 · US · Colour · 109mins

This cheerful remake of *Mother Carey's Chickens* was co-produced by Walt Disney himself, with Hayley Mills stepping into the shoes occupied by Anne Shirley in the 1938 adaptation of Kate Douglas Wiggin's popular novel. Mills is not at her effervescent best, but she's still suitably fresh-faced, as she finds time for a little innocent romance while helping widowed mother Dorothy McGuire raise her brothers. Director James Neilson lovingly re-creates the atmosphere of 1900s Maine, but the highlight is Burl Ives's rendition of *The Ugly Bug Ball*. ▦

Hayley Mills *Nancy Carey* • Burl Ives *Osh Popham* • Dorothy McGuire *Margaret Carey* • Deborah Walley *Cousin Julie* • Eddie Hodges

Gilly Carey • Jimmy Mathers *Peter Carey* • Michael J Pollard *Digby Popham* • Wendy Turner *Lallie Joy Popham* • Una Merkel *Maria Popham* ■ *Dir* James Neilson • *Scr* Sally Benson, from the book *Mother Carey's Chickens*, by Kate Douglas Wiggin

The Summer My Father Grew Up ★★
Drama   1991 · US · Colour · 97mins

British director Michael Tuchner has had an eventful career since his debut with *Villain* in 1971. In addition to working on the movie of *Whatever Happened to the Likely Lads?* and *Mr Quilp*, the musical adaptation of Dickens's *The Old Curiosity Shop*, he's directed over a dozen TV movies, including the Anthony Hopkins version of *The Hunchback of Notre Dame*. If only he was on that sort of form with this thoroughly predictable tale, in which John Ritter tries to build bridges with his son following a divorce.

John Ritter *Dr Paul Saunders* • Matthew Lawrence *Timmy Sanford* • Joe Spano *Louis* • Margaret Whitton *Naomi* • Karen Young *Chandelle Sanford* ■ *Dir* Michael Tuchner • *Scr* Sandra Jennings, from the play *Tooth of the Lion* by Robert Elswit

The Summer of Aviya ★★ PG
Drama   1988 · Is · Colour · 95mins

The Holocaust may have ended, but its effects linger on in this moving, semi-autobiographical tale from Israeli writer Eli Cohen. Set shortly after the end of the Second World War, Cohen's heart-tugging film tells of a disturbed and disturbing summer when the relationship between a young girl and her traumatised mother reaches a crisis point. Up close and personal.

Gila Almagor *Gila Almagor's mother* • Kaipo Cohen • Eli Cohen ■ *Dir* Eli Cohen • *Scr* Eli Cohen, Gila Almagor, Haim Buzaglo

The Summer of Ben Tyler ★★★
Wartime drama   1996 · US · Colour · 134mins

Two-time Emmy-winner James Woods delivers a stirring performance as an ethical attorney who rocks a small southern town when he chooses to take in the mentally slow teenage son of his recently deceased black housekeeper. Set during the Second World War, this highly emotional production eloquently illuminates the nature of racial prejudice and intolerance. It's poignant television drama with superb performances by Woods and a stunning supporting cast that includes Elizabeth McGovern and newcomer Charles Mattocks. A must-see, if only for Mattocks's sensitive portrayal and the provocative subject.

James Woods *Temple Rayburn* • Elizabeth McGovern *Celia Rayburn* • Charles Mattocks *Ben Tyler* • Len Cariou *Spencer Maitland* • Julia McIlvaine *Nell Rayburn* ■ *Dir* Arthur Allan Seidelman • *Scr* Robert Inman

Summer of '42 ★★ 15
Wartime drama   1971 · US · Colour · 99mins

Robert Mulligan's surprisingly popular rite-of-passage picture is so shrouded in nostalgia that it immediately arouses your suspicions. Home-front life in the year after America entered the Second World War simply couldn't have been this good – the sun shines too brightly, teenagers and adults alike are just too darn nice and Michel Legrand's score is almost nauseatingly lush. But there is something undeniably touching about 15-year-old Gary Grimes's relationship with war bride Jennifer O'Neill, which almost atones for the adolescent humour and the cosiness of the period detail. A sequel, *Class of '44*, was even less convincing. Contains swearing, violence and sex scenes.

Jennifer O'Neill *Dorothy* • Gary Grimes *Hermie* • Jerry Houser *Oscy* • Oliver Conant *Benjie* • Katherine Allentuck *Aggie* • Christopher Norris *Miriam* • Lou Frizzell *Druggist* • Robert Mulligan *Narrator* ■ *Dir* Robert Mulligan • *Scr* Herman Raucher

Summer of Sam ★★ 18

Drama   1999 · US · Colour · 136mins

Full marks to Spike Lee for tackling a movie where all the main characters are white, but *Summer of Sam* remains a deeply flawed effort. The year is 1977, and New York is being terrorised by David Berkowitz, the serial killer dubbed "Son of Sam". However, the focus here is on the troubled marriage of John Leguizamo and Mira Sorvino, and the rather seedy life of fledgling punk rocker and part-time male hooker Adrien Brody. The main problem is that the characters are largely caricatures. Not only are they a pretty dislikeable bunch; they also look as if they have wandered in from a second-rate version of *GoodFellas*. On the plus side, the scenes involving Berkowitz are disturbingly creepy, while Lee successfully evokes the seedy side of the late seventies. ▦ **DVD**

John Leguizamo *Vinny* • Adrien Brody *Ritchie* • Mira Sorvino *Dionna* • Jennifer Esposito *Ruby* • Michael Rispoli *Joey T* • Saverio Guerra *Woodstock* • Brian Tarantino *Bobby Del Fiore* • Al Palagonia *Anthony* • Ben Gazarra *Luigi* • Spike Lee *John Jeffries* • John Turturro *Harvey the black dog* ■ *Dir* Spike Lee • *Scr* Victor Colicchio, Michael Imperioli, Spike Lee

Summer of the Colt ★★ U

Drama   1989 · Can/Arg · Colour · 96mins

Having already contributed to the award-winning *The Dog Who Stopped the War* (1984) and the box-office smash *Bach and Broccoli* (1986) to producer Rock Demers's *Tales for All* franchise, André Melançon lost his way with this mediocre co-production. Though it stars two of Argentina's most respected stars, Hector Alterio and China Zorrilla, they spend too much time in the wings during this sentimental story of three Buenos Aires kids who head for their grandfather's pampas farm for the holidays. For once, the series' blend of stirring adventure and spirited youth misfires, although the scenery and the horses are awesomely beautiful. Spanish dialogue dubbed into English.

Hector Alterio *Federico* • China Zorrilla *Ana* • Alexandra London-Thompson *Laura* • Juan de Benedictis *Daniel* • Santiago Gonzalez *Martin* • Mariano Bertolini *Felipe* • Gabriela Felperin *Manuela* ■ *Dir* André Melançon • *Scr* Geneviève Lefebvre, André Melançon, Rodolfo Otero, from a story by Rodolfo Otero

A Summer Place ★★★

Melodrama   1959 · US · Colour · 129mins

A lush assemblage of sexual matters – teenage awakenings, adultery, pregnancy, divorce – dominate Delmer Daves's adaptation of Sloan Wilson's steamy bestseller about the middle-classes at play on the beaches of New England. From the same stable of would-be "shockers" as *Peyton Place*, this glossy affair was quite outspoken for its time and cleaned up at the box office. The youthful focus is on pretty-boy Troy Donahue's romance with Sandra Dee, while the adult coupling mainly involves married Dorothy McGuire and her lover Richard Egan. The soapy score and the hit title song, composed by Max Steiner, contribute greatly to the attractions of this enjoyable trash.

Richard Egan *Ken Jorgenson* • Dorothy McGuire *Sylvia Hunter* • Sandra Dee *Molly Jorgenson* • Arthur Kennedy *Bart Hunter* • Troy Donahue *Johnny Hunter* • Constance Ford *Helen Jorgenson* ■ *Dir* Delmer Daves • *Scr* Delmer Daves, from the novel by Sloan Wilson

Summer Rental ★★ PG

Comedy   1985 · US · Colour · 83mins

Harassed and overworked air-traffic controller Jack Chester (John Candy) badly needs a vacation and takes his family away to holiday on a beach. But almost from the moment they arrive, things start to go wrong and the supposedly restful trip turns into a nightmare every bit as stressful as Jack's job. The combined talents of John Candy and Carl Reiner should have ensured a better end product than this thin comedy which, despite some good moments, fails to fully exploit its promising premise. ▦

John Candy *Jack Chester* • Richard Crenna *Al Pellet* • Karen Austin *Sandy* • Rip Torn *Scully* • Kerri Green *Jennifer* • Joey Lawrence *Bobby* • John Larroquette *Don Moore* ■ *Dir* Carl Reiner • *Scr* Jeremy Stevens, Mark Reisman

Summer School ★★★ 15

Comedy   1987 · US · Colour · 92mins

A surprisingly genial teen comedy with *St Elsewhere's* Mark Harmon as the teacher who reluctantly agrees to cancel his vacation and teach English to a class of misfits over the summer holidays. It's a bit of a disappointment when you realise it was directed by Carl Reiner (who made *All of Me* and *The Jerk* with Steve Martin), but Harmon and co-star Kirstie Alley are funny and they are ably abetted by the teenage supporting cast. Contains swearing and violence. ▦

Mark Harmon *Freddy Shoop* • Kirstie Alley *Robin Bishop* • Robin Thomas *Phil Gills* • Dean Cameron *Francis "Chainsaw" Gremp* • Gary Riley *Dave Frazier* • Shawnee Smith *Rhonda Altobello* • Courtney Thorne-Smith *Pam House* ■ *Dir* Carl Reiner • *Scr* Jeff Franklin, from a story by Stuart Birnbaum, David Dashev, Jeff Franklin

Summer Stock ★★★★ U

Musical   1950 · US · Colour · 108mins

Better known in the UK as *If You Feel like Singing*, this was Judy Garland's last MGM feature and, despite rather obvious scene-by-scene weight fluctuations stemming from her

attempts to withdraw from drug dependency, she managed to deliver another wonderful musical. Pure joy from beginning to end, this quintessential "let's put on a show in a barn" movie contains moments that are among the career highlights of the film's two stars. Gene Kelly's newspaper dance is a treat and Garland's *Get Happy* finale became an instant classic. There's a fabulous rapport between the two leads and the whole is wrapped up in that sumptuous MGM Technicolor.

Judy Garland *Jane Falbury* • Gene Kelly *Joe D Ross* • Eddie Bracken *Orville Wingait* • Gloria DeHaven *Abigail Falbury* • Marjorie Main *Esme* • Phil Silvers *Herb Blake* • Ray Collins *Jasper G Wingait* • Nita Bieber *Sarah Higgins* ■ *Dir* Charles Walters • *Scr* George Wells, Sy Gomberg, from a story by Sy Gomberg

Summer Storm ★★★

Historical romantic drama   1944 · US · BW · 106mins

Based on Anton Chekhov's story *The Shooting Party*, this offering from director Douglas Sirk stars George Sanders, Linda Darnell and Edward Everett Horton (supplying the humour, though his role is more serious than usual). Darnell is Olga, the wife of the manager of his country estate, whose affair with local judge Sanders leads to murder, injustice and disintegration. Events take place both before and after the Russian Revolution in this interesting – if only partially successful – attempt to venture away from the Hollywood mainstream into character- and conversation-driven European-style drama.

George Sanders *Fedor Petroff* • Linda Darnell *Olga* • Anna Lee *Nadina* • Edward Everett Horton *Count Volsky* • Hugo Haas *Urbenin* • Lori Lahner *Clara* • John Philliber *Polycarp* • Sig Ruman *Kuzma* ■ *Dir* Douglas Sirk • *Scr* Rowland Leigh, Douglas Sirk, Robert Thoeren, from the story *The Shooting Party* by Anton Chekhov

A Summer Story ★★★★ 15

Romantic period drama   1987 · UK · Colour · 92mins

A beautifully filmed turn-of-the-century romance, based on John Galsworthy's tale *The Apple Tree*. James Wilby is the lawyer who falls for Devon country girl Imogen Stubbs while recuperating from an accident. When he has to leave, he promises to take her with him, but things don't go as planned. Wilby and Stubbs are ideally cast, and director Piers Haggard manages to keep the sentiment in check, so it never wanders into Mills and Boon territory. ▦

Imogen Stubbs *Megan David* • James Wilby *Frank Ashton* • Kenneth Colley *Jim* • Sophie Ward *Stella Halliday* • Susannah York *Mrs Narracombe* • Jerome Flynn *Joe Narracombe* • Lee Billett *Nick Narracombe* • Oliver Perry *Rick Narracombe* ■ *Dir* Piers Haggard • *Scr* Penelope Mortimer, from the short story *The Apple Tree* by John Galsworthy • *Cinematographer* Kenneth MacMillan

Summer Vacation: 1999 ★★★★ 15

Drama   1988 · Jap · Colour · 89mins

Following the Japanese stage tradition of "Takurazuka" in which girls play the story's teenaged boys, this is a

dreamlike study of the adolescent agonies that arise from the pangs of first love. After one of their number seems to commit suicide on account of unrequited passion, three sexually awakening boarding school students are thrown into confusion by the arrival of another youth who bears an eerie resemblance to their friend. Both a gay ghost story and a hymn to lost innocence, Shusuke Kaneko's unique film combines disarmingly androgynous performances with lush visuals to hauntingly romantic effect. In Japanese with English subtitles.

Eri Miyajima *Yu/Kaoru/Last new boy* • Tomoko Otakara *Kazuhiko* • Miyuki Nakano *Naoto* • Rie Mizuhara *Norio* ■ *Dir* Shusuke Kaneko • *Scr* Rio Kishida

Summer Wishes, Winter Dreams ★★

Drama   1973 · US · Colour · 88mins

When Joanne Woodward rails about her disappointing life to Martin Balsam, her patient, desperately dull husband and then concludes "I had no business inflicting all of this on you", audiences are likely to concur. This serious, well-intentioned drama is believably written, capably directed and beautifully acted (with Sylvia Sidney, making a comeback after 17 years, as Woodward's aged mother) and it isn't particularly long, but it fails to make these characters anything but tedious. Nevertheless, Woodward and Sidney received Oscar nominations for their performances.

Joanne Woodward *Rita Walden* • Martin Balsam *Harry Walden* • Sylvia Sidney *Mrs Pritchett, Rita's mother* • Dori Brenner *Anna* • Win Forman *Fred Goody* • Tresa Hughes *Betty Goody* ■ *Dir* Gilbert Cates • *Scr* Stewart Stern

Summer with Monika ★★★★★ PG

Drama   1952 · Swe · BW · 91mins

The last of Ingmar Bergman's studies of young love and the alienating effects of city life, this is a masterpiece of contrasting images and emotions. The brilliant, sunlit scenes set on the isolated islands perfectly capture the joy and innocence of summer love, as sassy teenager Harriet Andersson and adoring Lars Ekborg splash in the dappled water and kiss beneath the stars. But Gunnar Fischer's stifling shots of Stockholm are perhaps more impressive, as he sets the visual tone for the gradual drift into disillusionment and desertion. At once idyllic and tragic, this is clearly the work of a master. In Swedish with English subtitles.

Harriet Andersson *Monika* • Lars Ekborg *Harry* • John Harryson *Lelle* • Georg Skarstedt *Harry's father* • Dagmar Ebbesen *Harry's aunt* ■ *Dir* Ingmar Bergman • *Scr* Per-Anders Fogelstrom, Ingmar Bergman

Summerfield ★★★

Mystery   1977 · Ausl · Colour · 95mins

Sunday Too Far Away remains director Ken Hannam's best known and most loved movie, but this thriller, which pays homage to many Hollywood movies of the genre, is an entertaining and atmospheric later work. A new

schoolteacher arrives in a small Australian town, following the disappearance of his predecessor and soon realises there is more to the place and the inhabitants than meets the eye. Hannam successfully handles the suspense so that each new development is a surprise, and, thankfully, the finale cannot be predicted half an hour before the end.

Nick Tate *Simon Robinson* • John Waters *David Abbott* • Elizabeth Alexander *Jenny Abbott* • Michelle Jarman *Sally Abbott* • Charles Tingwell *Doctor Miller* • Geraldine Turner *Betty Tate* • Max Cullen *Jim Tate* • Barry Donnelly *Sgt Potter* ■ *Dir* Ken Hannam • *Scr* Cliff Green

A Summer's Tale ★★★★ U
Romantic comedy
1996 · Fr · Colour · 109mins

Like his earlier films, *Claire's Knee* and *Pauline at the Beach*, this is a sunny treatise on the agonies of holiday romance from director Eric Rohmer. This time, however, there's a male protagonist, with Melvil Poupaud torn between his love of music and his infatuations with girlfriend Aurélia Nolin, vacation waitress Amanda Langlet and her friend Gwenaëlle Simon. His prevarications are as natural as they are frustrating, as comic as they are suspenseful. Displaying again Rohmer's gift for capturing the vernacular and behaviour of youth, this third instalment of his *Tales of the Four Seasons* series is an absolute delight. In French with English subtitles. ▭

Melvil Poupaud *Gaspard* • Amanda Langlet *Margot* • Aurélia Nolin *Léna* • Gwenaëlle Simon *Solène* ■ *Dir/Scr* Eric Rohmer

Summertime ★★★★ PG
Romantic drama 1955 · US · Colour · 98mins

This was the movie that whetted director David Lean's appetite for location filming with international stars. Katharine Hepburn, in a piece of unlikely casting (she's too damn smart), is the spinster on holiday in Venice and Rossano Brazzi the object of her affection in this touching adaptation of Arthur Laurents's play *The Time of the Cuckoo*, later musicalised by Stephen Sondheim. Venice looks fabulous, thanks to cameraman Jack Hildyard, and Katharine Hepburn really does take that plunge into a canal. Lean's love of train sequences is on show and the whole is perfect matinée fare. ▭

Katharine Hepburn *Jane Hudson* • Rossano Brazzi *Renato Di Rossi* • Isa Miranda *Signora Fiorina* • Darren McGavin *Eddie Jaeger* • Mari Aldon *Phyl Jaeger* • Jane Rose *Mrs McIlhenny* • Macdonald Parke *Mr McIlhenny* • Gaitano Audiero *Mauro* ■ *Dir* David Lean • *Scr* David Lean, He Bates, from the play *The Time of the Cuckoo* by Arthur Laurents

The Sun Also Rises ★★★★
Drama 1957 · US · Colour · 130mins

An expansive version of Ernest Hemingway's great "lost generation" novel, with a slightly too old Tyrone Power in the leading role of Jake Barnes, the impotent wartime flier adrift in Paris. Ava Gardner is Lady Brett Ashley, a dissolute sensualist roaming Europe, and Errol Flynn is simply magnificent as the alcoholic Mike Campbell, a character that he could clearly identify with. Also particularly fine are Mel Ferrer and Eddie Albert as Power's cronies, and take note of the swarthy actor playing Gardner's bullfighter lover – Robert Evans, future producer of *Chinatown*.

Tyrone Power *Jake Barnes* • Ava Gardner *Lady Brett Ashley* • Mel Ferrer *Robert Cohn* • Errol Flynn *Mike Campbell* • Eddie Albert *Bill Gorton* • Gregory Ratoff *Count Mippipopolous* • Juliette Greco *Georgette* • Robert Evans *Pedro Romero* ■ *Dir* Henry King • *Scr* Peter Viertel, from the novel by Ernest Hemingway

The Sun Shines Bright ★★★ PG
Drama 1953 · US · BW · 100mins

Charles Winninger inherits the role of Judge Priest from Will Rogers, who played him in Ford's 1934 movie *Judge Priest*. This time the benevolent judge is standing for re-election in Fairfield, Kentucky, in 1905, but he has some serious competition. There are comic and romantic strands to the story as well as serious subplots involving rape and racism – a mix that modern audiences may find naive or offensive, or both. Whatever the views of the critics or the public, Ford cited this as one of his personal favourites, and his feeling for the story and the period is easy to see. ▭

Charles Winninger *Judge Priest* • Arleen Whelan *Lucy Lee Lake* • John Russell *Corwin* • Stepin Fetchit *Jeff Poindexter* • Russell Simpson *Dr Lewt Lake* • Ludwig Stössel *Herman Felsburg* • Francis Ford *Feeney* ■ *Dir* John Ford • *Scr* Laurence Stallings, from stories by Irvin S Cobb

The Sun, the Moon and the Stars ★★★
Romantic comedy 1995 · Ire · Colour · 92mins

The heavenly bodies of the title are three tarot cards belonging to an occult-obsessed teenager who attempts to reunite her separated parents. After her mother walks out of her job, they go on a family vacation, where they meet eccentric Angie Dickinson and park keeper Jason Donovan. Not an Irish *Parent Trap*, but whimsical enough to be watchable.

Angie Dickinson *Abbie* • Jason Donovan *Pat* • Gina Moxley *Monica* • Elaine Cassidy *Shelley* ■ *Dir/Scr* Geraldine Creed

Sun Valley Serenade ★★★ U
Musical 1941 · US · BW · 82mins

The blonde-haired, blue-eyed Norwegian ice-skating champion Sonja Henie returned to the screen after a two-year absence for this smash hit. However the movie's success was doubtless helped by the presence of Glenn Miller in one of only two films he made, and the Mack Gordon/Harry Warren score. The characteristic candy-floss plot – Miller's star pianist (John Payne) is assigned to take care of refugee Henie – is only an excuse on which to hang the numbers, including a breathtaking finale that has Henie skating on black ice before she skis off into the sunset with Payne. ▭

Sonja Henie *Karen Benson* • John Payne *Ted Scott* • Glenn Miller *Phil Carey* • Milton Berle

Nifty Allen • Lynn Bari *Vivian Dawn* • Joan Davis *Miss Carstairs* • Dorothy Dandridge *Vocalist* ■ *Dir* H Bruce Humberstone • *Scr* Robert Ellis, Helen Logan, from a story by Art Arthur, Robert Harari • *Choreographer* Hermes Pan • *Cinematographer* Edward Cronjager • *Music Director* Emil Newman

Sunburn ★★★
Detective comedy
1979 · US · Colour · 99mins

Those more inclined to swallow the idea of detective Charles Grodin and Farrah Fawcett (as the model he hires to pose as his wife) falling in love while investigating an insurance case in Mexico may enjoy this otherwise forgettable mystery romp. Fawcett is actually one of the better aspects of the movie, giving a likeable rendering of her reasonably intelligent character. She and the rest of the cast (including Art Carney) are unfortunately saddled with a story that has little mystery and little else going on for it.

Farrah Fawcett-Majors [Farrah Fawcett] *Ellie Morgan* • Charles Grodin *Jake Dekker* • Art Carney *Al Marcus* • Joan Collins *Nera* • William Daniels *Crawford* • John Hillerman *Webb* • Eleanor Parker *Mrs Thoren* • Keenan Wynn *Mark Elmes* ■ *Dir* Richard C Sarafian • *Scr* John Daly, Stephen Oliver, James Booth, from the novel *The Bind* by Stanley Ellin

Sunchaser ★★ 15
Road movie 1996 · US · Colour · 117mins

Directed by Michael Cimino, whose overblown *Heaven's Gate* all but destroyed United Artists, this is an over-egged pudding that ambitiously seeks to mix elements of road and male-bonding movies, and to toss in some native American mysticism for good measure. Jon Seda is impressive as a teen hoodlum dying of cancer. After breaking out of prison, he takes passing doctor Woody Harrelson hostage and forces him to drive to a mystical lake that, according to legend, has healing properties. Though well intentioned, it's somewhat pretentious and Harrelson is miscast. Contains swearing and some violence. ▭

Woody Harrelson *Dr Michael Reynolds* • Jon Seda *Brandon "Blue" Monroe* • Anne Bancroft *Dr Renata Baumbauer* • Alexandra Tydings *Victoria Reynolds* • Matt Mulhern *Dr Chip Byrnes* ■ *Dir* Michael Cimino • *Scr* Charles Leavitt

Sunday ★★★
Drama 1997 · US · Colour · 93mins

Winner of the Grand Jury Prize at the Sundance Film Festival, this is a fascinating look at being lonely, and the lengths we'll go to to kid ourselves we're not. Spanning a single day, this quality character study stars David Suchet as a downsized executive, now homeless, who pretends to be a famous art-film director to woo washed-up actress Lisa Harrow. The pretence becomes an intrinsic part of their day's mating rituals. The film is a little arty and won't appeal to everyone, but there's much here to admire, not least the performances of the two leads.

David Suchet *Oliver/Matthew* • Lisa Harrow *Madeleine Vesey* • Jared Harris *Ray* • Larry Pine *Ben Vesey* • Joe Grifasi *Scottie Elster* • Arnold Barkus *Andy* • Bahman Soltani *Abram* ■ *Dir* Jonathan Nossiter • *Scr* James Lasdun, Jonathan Nossiter

Sunday, Bloody Sunday ★★★★ 15
Drama 1971 · UK · Colour · 105mins

Divorced Glenda Jackson shares bisexual Murray Head with gay Peter Finch in John Schlesinger's ground-breaking exploration of heterosexual and homosexual relationships. Only made because Schlesinger had broken taboos, both critically and commercially, with *Midnight Cowboy*, this seventies moral tale caused shock waves thanks to Finch and Head sharing one of the first all-male on-screen kisses. Finch steals the acting honours with a sympathetic performance amongst the tangled web of verbalised angst about the real meaning of communication, sexual and otherwise, as symbolised by telephone wires linking the busy eternal triangle's lives together. ▭

Glenda Jackson *Alex Greville* • Peter Finch *Dr Daniel Hirsh* • Murray Head *Bob Elkin* • Peggy Ashcroft *Mrs Greville* • Maurice Denham *Mr Greville* • Vivian Pickles *Alva Hodson* • Frank Windsor *Bill Hodson* • Thomas Baptiste *Professor Johns* • Tony Britton *Mr Harding* ■ *Dir* John Schlesinger • *Scr* Penelope Gilliatt

Sunday Dinner for a Soldier ★★★ U
Romantic drama 1944 · US · BW · 86mins

Some find this period whimsy charming, others glutinous, but in its day it chimed perfectly with popular taste, as lovely Anne Baxter yearned for just what it says – a GI to bring home for lunch on Sunday. Handsome John Hodiak turns up just in time. Expertly made Hollywood schmaltz, this is one of those movies about impoverished people who don't actually suffer from being poor, but just get all philosophical with a foxy twinkle in their eye. Those not put off by the patently phoney studio backdrops might find themselves watching with a gentle smile on their faces.

Anne Baxter *Tessa Osborne* • John Hodiak *Eric Moore* • Charles Winninger *Grandfather Osborne* • Anne Revere *Agatha* • Connie Marshall *Mary Osborne* • Chill Wills *Mr York* ■ *Dir* Lloyd Bacon • *Scr* Wanda Tuchock, Melvin Levy, from the story by Martha Cheavens

Sunday Drive ★★ U
Comedy adventure
1986 · US · Colour · 89mins

Carrie Fisher probably wouldn't regard this as a career highlight but, as the title implies, it will keep the kids entertained on a Sunday afternoon. The plot involves six people, a dog and the confusion that ensues when two groups drive off in each other's cars. It's wildly implausible, but harmless enough and the actors – not to mention the dog – seem to be enjoying themselves. Tony Randall (one half of TV's *The Odd Couple*) co-stars. ▭

Tony Randall *Uncle Bill* • Carrie Fisher *Franny Jessup* • Audra Lindley *Aunt Joan* • Hillary Wolf *Christine Franklin* • Raffi Digiura *John-Elliot Franklin* • Claudia Cron *Susan* ■ *Dir* Mark Cullingham • *Scr* Larry Brand

Sunday in New York ★★★
Comedy 1963 · US · Colour · 104mins

One of those early sixties' capers in which provincial innocents, in this case

a young Jane Fonda, head for the big city and fall madly in love with life in the fast lane. This is a delightfully skittish romp in the Big Apple, showing off Fonda's youthful charisma to best advantage and ably assisted by Peter Nero's memorable score. A film that harks back to those curiously winsome days when sex came tiptoeing out of the celluloid closet and everyone thought they were being madly daring. It all seems rather innocent now.

Cliff Robertson *Adam Tyler* • Jane Fonda *Eileen Tyler* • Rod Taylor *Mike Mitchell* • Robert Culp *Russ Wilson* • Jo Morrow *Mona Harris* • Jim Backus *Flight dispatcher* • Peter Nero ■ *Dir* Peter Tewksbury • *Scr* Norman Krasna, from his play

Sunday in the Country
★★ 18

Crime thriller   1975 · Can · Colour · 87mins

Ernest Borgnine plays a farmer in the backwoods of America who takes the law into his own hands when three dangerous fugitives attempt to take him and his granddaughter hostage. John Trent's decidedly cruel and violent crime drama is distinguished by Borgnine's performance as the calm countryman who coolly exacts a terrible revenge against Michael J Pollard and his cronies. The whole premise is questionable, and those of a nervous disposition won't relish the torture scenes. 🖵

Ernest Borgnine *Adam Smith* • Michael J Pollard *Leroy* • Hollis McLaren *Lucy* • Louis Zorich *Dinelli* • Cec Linder *Ackerman* • Vladimir Valenta *Luke* • Al Waxman *Sergeant* ■ *Dir* John Trent • *Scr* Robert Maxwell, John Trent, from a story by David Main

Sunday in the Country
★★★★ U

Drama   1984 · Fr · Colour · 90mins

Adapted from Pierre Bost's novella, this lyrical conversation piece deservedly won Bertrand Tavernier the best director award at Cannes. Beautifully evoking a balmy Sunday afternoon in the late summer of 1912, the film eavesdrops on the subtly charged encounters between an ageing painter (Louis Ducreux), his beloved but unreliable daughter (Sabine Azéma) and his married son (Michel Aumont). All the performances are impeccable and Tavernier alights on such topics as Impressionism, family allegiances and the purpose of life with a light but restless touch. Bruno de Keyzer's gorgeous photography makes this serene drama quite irresistible. In French with English subtitles. 🖵

Louis Ducreux *Monsieur Ladmiral* • Sabine Azéma *Irène* • Michel Aumont "*Gonzague*" *Edouard* • Geneviève Mnich *Marie-Thérèse* • Monique Chaumette *Mercédès* • Claude Winter *Madame Ladmiral* ■ *Dir* Bertrand Tavernier • *Scr* Bertrand Tavernier, Colo Tavernier, from the novella *Monsieur Ladmiral Va bientôt Mourir* by Pierre Bost

Sunday Too Far Away
★★★★

Drama   1974 · Ausl · Colour · 94mins

A real brawler set in the Australian outback. Life as a sheep-shearer can be rather monotonous, but hard man Jack Thompson has enough star power to keep us watching this tale of rivalry

and hardship. He's chief shearer and troubleshooter, calling the men out on strike when the bosses try to introduce non-union labour. There's real integrity in Ken Hannam's direction, as he takes us right into the heart of a world very like that of the Wild West where rivalries are fuelled by booze and life is a real struggle. Men at work have rarely been so convincingly portrayed. Contains some swearing.

Jack Thompson *Foley* • Phyllis Ophel *Ivy* • Peter Cummins "*Black*" *Arthur* • Reg Lye *Old Garth* • John Charman *Barman* • Gregory Apps *Michael Simpson* • Max Cullen *Tim King* • Ken Shorter *Frankie Davis* ■ *Dir* Ken Hannam • *Scr* John Dingwall

Sundays and Cybèle
★★★

Drama   1962 · Fr · BW · 110mins

Debutant director Serge Bourguignon won the Oscar for best foreign language film with this self-promoting, arty affair. Hardy Kruger is the amnesiac German pilot who forges a friendship with pre-teen orphan Patricia Gozzi. There is an undeniable tenderness in their relationship, even though there's an inevitability about the consequences of their innocent Christmas sojourn in the woods. Cinematographer Henri Decaë's compositions, though elegant, strain too hard for lyrical effect, while the film's surface intelligence means that such key themes as identity and conformity are given only a cursory examination. A French language film.

Hardy Kruger *Pierre* • Nicole Courcel *Madeleine* • Patricia Gozzi *Françoise/Cybèle* • Daniel Ivernel *Carlos* • Michel de Re *Bernard* • André Oumansky *Nurse* ■ *Dir* Serge Bourguignon • *Scr* Antoine Tudal, Serge Bourguignon, Bernard Eschassériaux, from the novel *Les Dimanches de Ville D'Avray* by Bernard Eschassériaux

Sunday's Children
★★★★

Drama   1992 · Swe · Colour · 118mins

It's apt that this study of fathers and sons (the second part of the autobiographical trilogy scripted by Ingmar Bergman) should be directed by Bergman's own son, Daniel. Recalling the summer of 1926, when the young Ingmar tried to become closer to his strict father (a chaplain to the Swedish royal family), *Sunday's Children* is such an assured film that it could easily have been directed by the master himself. The sunlit country picnics and cycle rides are joyous evocations of past times, but they also make the darker moments of doubt and the confrontations between Thommy Berggren and Henrik Linnros all the more dramatic and powerful. In Swedish with English subtitles.

Henrik Linnros *Pu* • Thommy Berggren *Pu's father* • Börje Ahlstedt *Uncle Carl* ■ *Dir* Daniel Bergman • *Scr* Ingmar Bergman, from his autobiography *The Magic Lantern*

Sundown
★★★

Wartime adventure   1941 · US · BW · 90mins

Gene Tierney's sultry looks are used to good effect in this Second World War yarn set in Africa, where a band of Nazis are supplying weapons to tribesmen in the hope that they will rise up against the British. Commissioner Bruce Cabot befriends

the locals (including a young Dorothy Dandridge), while English major George Sanders wrestles with his distrust of Arabs. Tierney is the lynchpin, working undercover for the Allies but arousing Sanders's suspicions as she romances Cabot. The film is well photographed and rattles along efficiently enough, even if it doesn't quite reach the heights it aspires to.

Gene Tierney *Zia* • Bruce Cabot *Captain Bill Crawford* • George Sanders *Major Coombes* • Cedric Hardwicke *Bishop Coombes* • Harry Carey *Dewey* • Joseph Calleia *Pallini* • Reginald Gardiner *Lt Turner* • Dorothy Dandridge *Kipsang's bride* ■ *Dir* Henry Hathaway • *Scr* Barre Lyndon, Charles G Booth, from a story by Barre Lyndon • *Cinematographer* Charles Lang

The Sundowners
★★★ U

Western   1950 · US · Colour · 85mins

An agreeable western, filmed entirely on location in Texas, that rests on the roguish charm of Robert Preston and the superb Technicolor photography by Winton Hoch. The film introduces John Barrymore Jr who is unexceptional as the teenage kid idolising Preston as his bad outlaw brother. Robert Sterling plays the more conventional middle brother and ex-accountant Jack Elam makes an early film appearance as a scared murder witness. Leading western novelist Alan LeMay (*The Searchers*) produced and scripted this adaptation of one of his early pieces, *Thunder in the Dust*, as well as appearing uncredited as Preston's companion.

Robert Preston *Kid Wichita* • Robert Sterling *Tom Cloud* • Chill Wills *Sam Beard* • John Litel *John Gaul* • Cathy Downs *Kathleen Boyce* • Jack Elam *Earl Boyce* • Don Haggerty *Elmer Gaul* • John Barrymore Jr [John Drew Barrymore] *Jeff Cloud* ■ *Dir* George Templeton • *Scr* Alan LeMay

The Sundowners
★★★★ U

Adventure   1960 · US · Colour · 124mins

A marvellously authentic family epic from Warner Bros, set in Australia and containing superb performances (and moderately believable Australian accents) from Robert Mitchum and Deborah Kerr. Backing up the two leads in this sheep-shearing saga is a strong cast and excellent technical credits, notably the striking Technicolor photography from Jack Hildyard and an atmospheric Dimitri Tiomkin score, with a main theme featuring mouth-organist Tommy Reilly. The film earned five Oscar nominations, a tribute to its co-producer/director, the late Fred Zinnemann, whose exquisite handling of the personal drama proves once again what a fine film-maker he was.

Deborah Kerr *Ida Carmody* • Robert Mitchum *Paddy Carmody* • Peter Ustinov *Venneker* • Michael Anderson Jr *Sean* • Glynis Johns *Mrs Firth* • Dina Merrill *Jean Halstead* • Ewen Solon *Bob Halstead* • Chips Rafferty *Quinlan* ■ *Dir* Fred Zinnemann • *Scr* Isobel Lennart, from the novel by Jon Cleary

Sunflower
★★ 15

Drama   1969 · It/Fr · Colour · 102mins

Co-screenwriter Cesare Zavattini and director Vittorio De Sica were two of the key figures in the neorealist movement that dominated Italian cinema in the postwar era. But there is

little evidence of their celebrated humanism in this preposterous nonsense in which Sophia Loren goes to the USSR in search of missing husband Marcello Mastroianni only to find him married to Lyudmila Savelyeva and blissfully ignorant of her existence. It gets worse when he recovers his memory and heads for Italy, where a rude shock awaits him. If the leads are as embarrassed as they should be, they don't let it show. In Italian with English subtitles. 🖵

Sophia Loren *Giovanna* • Marcello Mastroianni *Antonio* • Lyudmila Savelyeva *Mascia* ■ *Dir* Vittorio De Sica • *Scr* Tonino Guerra, Cesare Zavattini, Gheorgi Mdivani

Sunny
★★ PG

Romance   1941 · US · BW · 136mins

Producer/director Herbert Wilcox remade this hit Broadway musical for his wife, the oh-so-charming, restrained English actress Anna Neagle. Wilcox reworked the original book, cutting out most of the (admittedly silly) plot, and leaving a thin tale about a bareback-riding circus performer (Neagle) who marries a New Orleans aristocrat (John Carroll), despite his stiff-necked family's disapproval. 🖵

Anna Neagle *Sunny O'Sullivan* • Ray Bolger *Bunny Billings* • John Carroll *Larry Warren* • Edward Everett Horton *Henry Bates* • Grace Hartman *Juliet Runnymede* • Paul Hartman *Egghead* • Frieda Inescort *Elizabeth Warren* • Helen Westley *Aunt Barbara* ■ *Dir* Herbert Wilcox • *Scr* Sid Herzig, from a play by Otto Harbach, Oscar Hammerstein II • *Music* Jerome Kern

Sunny Side Up
★★★

Musical comedy   1929 · US · BW and Tinted · 80mins

A charming but creaky musical comedy from the early days of the talkies, this is a lightweight offering from 20th Century-Fox. It stars popular screen sweethearts Janet Gaynor (hot from winning the first ever best actress Oscar) and the loveable Charlie Farrell. It's almost a singing version of their standard tenement-girl-falls-for-Farrell plot, but who cares when the songs are such fabulous De Sylva, Henderson and Brown classics as the title number, *I'm a Dreamer (Aren't We All?)*, and the apt *If I Had a Talking Picture of You*.

Janet Gaynor *Molly Carr* • Charles Farrell *Jack Cromwell* • El Brendel *Eric Swenson* • Marjorie White *Bee Nichols* • Frank Richardson *Eddie Rafferty* • Sharon Lynne *Jane Worth* • Mary Forbes *Mrs Cromwell* • Joe E Brown *Joe Vitto* ■ *Dir* David Butler • *Scr* Buddy De Sylva, Ray Henderson, Lew Brown, David Butler

Sunnyside
★★★★

Silent satirical drama   1919 · US · BW · 41mins

In this pastoral fairy tale, Charlie Chaplin is a farm hand in love with Edna Purviance (again!). Chaplin said the production of *Sunnyside* was "like pulling teeth", and he must have appreciated the great ballet dancer Vaslav Nijinsky telling him that the dance with four nymphs was "pure delight".

Charlie Chaplin [Charles Chaplin] *Handyman* • Edna Purviance *Woman* • Tom Wilson *Boss* • Henry Bergman *Father* ■ *Dir* Charles Chaplin • *Scr* Charles Chaplin, from his story

Sunrise ★★★★★ U

Silent drama 1927 · US · BW · 90mins

Janet Gaynor won the first ever best actress Oscar for her work in this exquisite silent feature, subtitled *A Song of Two Humans*. Emigré director FW Murnau, best known for *Nosferatu the Vampire*, has reduced a tale of threatened marriage to its bare essentials, as, in one visit to the city, the marriage renews itself. It is hard to convey briefly the wonder of imagery on display here, as Murnau both wittily and stylistically uses every aspect of visual storytelling, even making imaginative use of the back projection itself. Perspective design and stunning photography (by Charles Rosher and Karl Struss) help immeasurably. The tale is timeless, the setting nameless and the mood resolutely central European, though it was filmed in America. Big George O'Brien brings a distinctively American presence to the romantically tortured hero, and Gaynor is simply perfection. 🎞

George O'Brien *The Man* • Janet Gaynor *The Wife* • Bodil Rosing *Maid* • Margaret Livingston *Woman from the city* • J Farrell MacDonald *Photographer* ■ *Dir* Friedrich W Murnau [FW Murnau] • *Scr* Carl Mayer, from the novel *Die Reise nach Tilsit* by Hermann Sudermann

Sunrise at Campobello ★★★ U

Biographical drama 1960 · US · Colour · 143mins

Adapted from his own Broadway success by Dore Schary, and directed by Vincent J Donehue who had supervised it on stage, this is an interesting and moving account of Franklin D Roosevelt's life during his battle with polio. Although the film at times betrays its theatrical origins, it remains enthralling despite being long. It also leaves posterity a record of Ralph Bellamy's extraordinary stage performance, re-created here. Curiously, the Oscar nomination went to Greer Garson as Roosevelt's wife, Eleanor – a decent performance for which, no doubt in the interests of authenticity, she wore protruding false teeth. The supporting cast, notably Hume Cronyn, is first class.

Ralph Bellamy *Franklin Delano Roosevelt* • Greer Garson *Eleanor Roosevelt* • Hume Cronyn *Louis Howe* • Jean Hagen *Missy Le Hand* • Ann Shoemaker *Sara Roosevelt* • Alan Bunce *Al Smith* • Tim Considine *James Roosevelt* ■ *Dir* Vincent J Donehue • *Scr* Dore Schary, from his play

Sunset ★★ 15

Comedy thriller 1988 · US · Colour · 102mins

As with many of Blake Edwards's films, the concept is great, but the execution disastrous. Set in silent-era Hollywood, this would-be comedy thriller finds the film industry's first western star Tom Mix (Bruce Willis) joining forces with the ageing Wyatt Earp (James Garner) to solve a murder involving corrupt studio chiefs. Edwards's direction clumsily fails to blend the comic and action elements of the plot, while Willis irritates in the lead role. What makes it worth a look is Garner, easily rising above the substandard material. Contains violence, swearing and nudity. 🎞

Bruce Willis *Tom Mix* • James Garner *Wyatt Earp* • Malcolm McDowell *Alfie Alperin* • Mariel Hemingway *Cheryl King* • Kathleen Quinlan *Nancy Shoemaker* • Jennifer Edwards *Victoria Alperin* • Patricia Hodge *Christina Alperin* • Richard Bradford *Captain Blackworth* • M Emmet Walsh *Chief Dibner* • Joe Dallesandro *Dutch Kieffer* ■ *Dir* Blake Edwards • *Scr* Blake Edwards, from a story by Rod Amateau

Sunset Beat ★★ 15

Drama 1990 · US · Colour · 94mins

George Clooney is probably eternally grateful that this TV movie, a pilot for a proposed TV series, didn't come to anything. Had he been stuck in this California cop show, he might not have been free to take on his star-making role in *ER*. Careers are full of such ifs, but the word here should surely be "why?". Even an eager young hopeful must have realised that this tale of officers going undercover as bikers had little mileage in it. Contains some violence. 🎞

George Clooney *Chic Chesbro* • Michael DeLuise *Tim Kelly* • Markus Flanagan *Bradley Coolidge* • Erik King *Tucson Smith* • James Tolkan *Captain Ray Parker* ■ *Dir* Sam Weisman • *Scr* Patrick Hasburgh

Sunset Boulevard ★★★★★ PG

Drama 1950 · US · BW · 105mins

The title is a savage pun, the tone unremittingly dark, the whole a stark and deeply satisfying, brilliantly constructed witty work of original cinematic genius from master director Billy Wilder, a Hollywood satire that is both canny and knowing about the film industry itself and affectionate towards those souls unfortunate enough to be caught up in the fiscal and emotional jungle that is motion picture-making. This is a terrific film, greatly aided by superb casting, notably silent-screen siren Gloria Swanson as former movie queen Norma Desmond and the excellent William Holden, replacing original choices Gene Kelly and Montgomery Clift, as doomed writer Joe Gillis. 🎞

William Holden (1) *Joe Gillis* • Gloria Swanson *Norma Desmond* • Erich von Stroheim *Max Von Mayerling* • Nancy Olson *Betty Schaefer* • Fred Clark *Sheldrake* • Lloyd Gough *Morino* • Jack Webb *Artie Green* ■ *Dir* Billy Wilder • *Scr* Billy Wilder, Charles Brackett, DM Marshman Jr, from the story *A Can of Beans* by Charles Brackett, Billy Wilder • *Costume Designer* Edith Head • *Cinematographer* John F Seitz • *Music* Franz Waxman

Sunset Grill ★★ 18

Thriller 1992 · US · Colour · 99mins

A weary LA private detective gets more than he bargained for when he attempts to avenge the murder of his wife. For he uncovers a sinister conspiracy revolving around Mexicans being killed and sold for their body parts. Directed by former horror veteran Kevin Connor, this decidedly odd thriller is an equal mix of the bizarre and the mundane. No great shakes – the deliberate genre confusion ends up being just that – but *Robocop*'s Peter Weller does bring some variety to his clichéd role as the drunken private eye stuck in an old-fashioned rut, while Stacy Keach is suitably menacing as a sadistic tycoon.

Contains swearing, violence, sex scenes and nudity. 🎞

Peter Weller *Ryder Hart* • Lori Singer *Loren Duquesne* • Stacy Keach *Harrison Shelgrove* • Michael Anderson Jr *Carruthers* • Alexandra Paul *Anita* • John Rhys-Davies *Stockton* • Pete Koch *Christian* ■ *Dir* Kevin Connor • *Scr* Marcus Wright, Faruque Ahmed

Sunset Heights ★★ 15

Science-fiction thriller 1996 · UK/Ire · Colour · 91mins

Set in the near future, this flawed but intriguing thriller presents a nightmare vision of life in Northern Ireland. Two ruthless gangs now police their communities using fear and violence. Caught between the two is Toby Stephens, whose child is believed to be latest victim of a serial killer known as The Preacher. The gangs believe they have found the killer – but is he really guilty? The plotting is confused but there are strong performances from the cast, and director Colm Villa displays some stylish visual touches. Contains violence. 🎞

Toby Stephens *Luke* • Jim Norton *Sam Magee* • Patrick O'Kane *Friday Knight* • Joe Rea *Victor* • James Cosmo *MacDonald* ■ *Dir/Scr* Colm Villa

Sunset Park ★★ 15

Sports comedy drama 1996 · US · Colour · 99mins

A rare lead outing for Rhea Perlman, this is an uneasy amalgam of comedy and ghetto drama. The former *Cheers* star plays a basketball novice who reluctantly becomes the unlikely trainer to a struggling team from a deprived, inner city high school. Of course, it's not long before she is won over. It's a familiar enough tale, enthusiastically played, but the laughs are dampened by regular waves of unwelcome sentimentality. 🎞

Rhea Perlman *Phyllis Saroka* • Fredro Starr *Shorty* • Carol Kane *Mona* • Terrence Dashon Howard *Terrence Howard* *Spaceman* • Camille Saviola *Barbara* • De'Aundre Bonds *Busy-Bee* • James Harris *Butter* • Anthony Hall [Anthony C Hall] *Andre* ■ *Dir* Steve Gomer • *Scr* Seth Zvi Rosenfeld, Kathleen McGhee-Anderson

Sunshine ★★★★ 15

Epic romantic drama 1999 · Hun/Ger/Can/Aus · Colour · 179mins

This sprawling epic is a glorious summation of the themes that have preoccupied Istvan Szabo over the last 20 years. Just as Klaus Maria Brandauer portrayed three victims of ambition and treachery in *Mephisto*, *Colonel Redl* and *Hanussen*, so Ralph Fiennes essays a trio of flawed ancestors whose personal tragedies are enacted against the great events of the 20th century. Passing through Hungary's imperial, fascist and communist phases, the action chronicles the history of a Jewish family whose bid to belong is undermined by successive generations' susceptibility to passion, vanity and lust for power. Occasionally protracted, but always majestic and masterly.

Ralph Fiennes *Ignatz Sonnenschein/Adam Sors/Ivan Sors* • Rosemary Harris *Valerie Sors* • Rachel Weisz *Greta Sors* • Jennifer Ehle *Valerie Sonnenschein* • Deborah Kara Unger *Major Carole Kovacs* • Molly Parker

Hannah Wippler • James Frain *Gustave Sonnenschein* • David De Keyser *Emmanuel Sonnenschein* • William Hurt *Andor Knorr* ■ *Dir* Istvan Szabo • *Scr* Istvan Szabo, Israel Horovitz, from a story by Istvan Szabo

The Sunshine Boys ★★★★ PG

Comedy 1975 · US · Colour · 106mins

George Burns, who died just a cigar length past his 100th birthday, made his big-screen comeback in this Neil Simon-scripted comedy about two ageing, rival vaudevillians. Burns stepped in when Jack Benny died and found himself co-starring with the best scene-stealer in the business, Walter Matthau, as heavily made-up as he was for his crotchety grandfather role in Jack Lemmon's *Kotch*. As with many of Simon's confections, it's a New York Jewish odd couple sort of story, overtly sentimental but played to perfection. Richard Benjamin also makes an impact as Matthau's nephew and agent, who tries to reconcile the two old boys. Contains some swearing. 🎞

Walter Matthau *Willy Clark* • George Burns *Al Lewis* • Richard Benjamin *Ben Clark* • Lee Meredith *Nurse in sketch* • Carol Arthur *Doris* • F Murray Abraham *Mechanic* • Howard Hesseman *Commercial director* ■ *Dir* Herbert Ross • *Scr* Neil Simon, from his play

The Sunshine Boys ★★★ U

Comedy 1997 · US · Colour · 85mins

The words Woody Allen and TV movie were once mutually exclusive. But, just a year after he directed and starred in a made-for-television version of his own play *Don't Drink the Water*, he was back as a jobbing actor in this update of Neil Simon's classic comedy. Woody takes on the role that won George Burns an Oscar, while Peter Falk steps into Walter Matthau's shoes, as the struggling entertainer who calls on his now-detested partner to revive his fortunes. Simon's acerbic wit is as amusing as ever and he neatly turns nephew Richard Benjamin into niece Sarah Jessica Parker. It's a good try, but the original is unsurpassable. 🎞

Woody Allen *Al Lewis* • Peter Falk *Willie Clark* • Sarah Jessica Parker *Nancy* ■ *Dir* John Erman • *Scr* Neil Simon, from his play

Sunstroke ★★ 15

Thriller 1992 · US · Colour · 86mins

There are some cynics who say that if a film's got Jane Seymour in it somewhere, then approach with extreme caution. To be fair, she is not entirely hammy in this curious tale of a woman, who has been linked to a murder, travelling through Arizona in search of her missing daughter. There are a lot of sand, flies, pokey petrol stations and dreary diners, but little explanation of how she got into this terrible pickle in the first place. Contains violence. 🎞

Jane Seymour *Teresa Blake* • Stephen Meadows *Greg Foster* • Steve Railsback *Tyler Biggs* • Ray Wise *Larry Winters* • Don Ameche *Jake* • Mark Davenport *Lovell* ■ *Dir* James Keach • *Scr* Duane Poole

Sunstruck ★ U

Comedy drama
1972 · Ausl/UK · Colour · 91mins

This star vehicle for singer and comedian Harry Secombe was made Down Under back in the days when the Welsh warbler used to summer there. Daft and dated, even at the time, the slight tale has Secombe playing a dimwit Welsh schoolteacher who emigrates to the Aussie outback. The simple-minded humour derives from his patent unsuitability for the new way of life. Donald Houston pops up to lend pal Secombe moral support, but, thankfully, it's the sort of film they don't make any more.

Harry Secombe *Stanley Evans* • Maggie Fitzgibbon *Shirley Marshall* • John Meillon *Mick Cassidy* • Dawn Lake *Sal Cassidy* • Peter Whittle *Pete Marshall* • Dennis Dennis Jordan *Steve Cassidy* • Donald Houston ■ *Dir* James Gilbert • *Scr* James Grafton, Stan Mars

The Super ★★★ 15

Comedy   1991 · US · Colour · 85mins

Joe Pesci's Oscar for *GoodFellas*, as well as his appearances in blockbusters such as *Home Alone*, earned him the opportunity to become an unlikely leading man, but he enjoys mixed success here in his first such role. On paper it sounds great: Pesci plays a sleazy New York landlord who is taken to court and sentenced to living in one of his own rat-filled apartments. The star is fine, and there's good support from Rubén Blades and Vincent Gardenia, but director Rod Daniel indulges in too much soppy moralising, and the film veers uncomfortably between comedy and drama. Contains swearing. 🖵

Joe Pesci *Louie Kritski* • Vincent Gardenia *Big Lou Kritski* • Madolyn Smith Osborne [Madolyn Smith] *Naomi Bensinger* • Rubén Blades *Marlon* • Stacey Travis *Heather* • Carole Shelley *Irine Kritski* ■ *Dir* Rod Daniel • *Scr* Sam Simon

The Super Cops ★★★ 15

Detective comedy drama
1973 · US · Colour · 90mins

A fine telling of the true story of two cops, nicknamed "Batman and Robin", who used unconventional crime-busting techniques to stop drug dealing in the Bedford-Stuyvesant area of New York's Brooklyn. A sort of *French Connection* with more laughs, the film is fast, furious, and often very funny, and it benefits from using the actual locations where real-life events occurred. Ron Leibman and David Selby play super cops David Greenberg and Robert Hantz, with the bona fide detectives popping up in bit parts. Coincidentally, the screenplay was by Lorenzo Semple Jr, who also scripted the 1966 *Batman* movie. 🖵

Ron Leibman *Greenberg* • David Selby *Hantz* • Sheila Frazier *Sara* • Pat Hingle *Lieutenant Novick* • Dan Frazer *Krasna* • Joseph Sirola *Lieutenant O'Shaughnessy* • Arny Freeman *Judge Kellner* ■ *Dir* Gordon Parks • *Scr* Lorenzo Semple Jr, from the non-fiction book by LH Whittemore

Super Mario Bros ★★ PG

Fantasy adventure
1993 · US · Colour · 99mins

How do you turn a popular interactive video game into an equally engaging and exciting movie? Not like this, you don't! This awkward fantasy contains few trace elements from the "Super Mario Land" games themselves, thereby instantly betraying the very audience it was made for. Bob Hoskins and John Leguizamo try their best as the two plumbers adrift in a parallel dinosaur dimension, but it isn't super, amusing or thrilling by any stretch of the imagination. Contains swearing and violence.

Bob Hoskins *Mario Mario* • Dennis Hopper *King Koopa* • John Leguizamo *Luigi Mario* • Samantha Mathis *Daisy* • Fisher Stevens *Iggy* • Richard Edson *Spike* • Fiona Shaw *Lena* ■ *Dir* Rocky Morton, Annabel Jankel • *Scr* Parker Bennett, Terry Runté, Ed Solomon, from the characters created by Shigeru Miyamoto, Takashi Tezuka

Super-Sleuth ★★

Comedy mystery 1937 · US · BW · 65mins

Jack Oakie fans will enjoy his skilful clowning as an egotistical movie star in this brightly written comedy. Portraying a specialist in screen sleuthing, Oakie sets out to show up the LA police, represented by Edgar Kennedy, by catching a mysterious killer of celebrities. After receiving a death threat himself, along with a complaint over the quality of his last film, he seeks advice from Eduardo Ciannelli's amateur criminologist. Ann Sothern sparkles as the studio publicity head and there are entertaining glimpses of film-making on the RKO lot and on location.

Jack Oakie *Willard "Bill" Martin* • Ann Sothern *Mary Strand* • Eduardo Ciannelli *Professor Horman* • Alan Bruce *Larry Frank* • Edgar Kennedy *Lt Garrison* • Joan Woodbury *Doris Dunne* • Bradley Page *Ralph Waring* • Paul Guilfoyle *Gibbons* ■ *Dir* Ben Stoloff [Benjamin Stoloff] • *Scr* Gertrude Purcell, Ernest Pagano, from a play by Harry Segall

Superdad ★★ U

Comedy   1974 · US · Colour · 91mins

Bob Crane is overprotective of his daughter, Kathleen Cody and tries to prevent her from spending time with a group of friends he considers unsuitable by sending her to far away Huntington College. Cody learns of the ruse and turns into an even bigger rebel, eventually getting engaged to a hippy artist and political agitator (Joby Baker). When her former boyfriend Kurt Russell returns to the scene, her father is more than happy to embrace him as one of the family. Twee, sickly Disney family comedy with few redeeming factors. 🖵

Bob Crane *Charlie McCready* • Barbara Rush *Sue McCready* • Kurt Russell *Bart* • Joe Flynn *Cyrus Hershberger* • Kathleen Cody *Wendy McCready* • Bruno Kirby *Stanley* • Joby Baker *Klutch* • Dick Van Patten *Ira Hershaw* ■ *Dir* Vincent McEveety • *Scr* Joseph L McEveety, from a story by Harlan Ware

Superfly ★★★ 18

Blaxploitation 1972 · US · Colour · 88mins

By 1972 the conventions of the blaxploitation genre were well established and this notorious film exploited them to the hilt. The anti-hero, played by supercool martial artist Ron O'Neal, is a cocaine pusher who plans one last deal before retirement; but things don't go as he planned. The black men are little more than robots, the white men are crooked and the women (black and white) are sex objects. In the US, black activists picketed screenings, turning the film into a huge box-office hit. Today, this success is hard to understand. Its cult status, however, makes it required viewing for fans of the crazy seventies. O'Neal directed the even worse sequel *Superfly TNT*. Contains swearing, violence and sex scenes. 🖵

Ron O'Neal *Youngblood Priest* • Carl Lee *Eddie* • Sheila Frazier *Georgia* • Julius Harris *Scatter* • Charles McGregor *Fat Freddie* • Nate Adams *Dealer* • Polly Niles *Cynthia* ■ *Dir* Gordon Parks Jr • *Scr* Phillip Fenty

Supergirl ★★ PG

Adventure   1984 · UK · Colour · 111mins

A disastrous attempt to extend the *Superman* series by bringing the Man of Steel's comic book cousin (played here by Helen Slater) to Earth, to retrieve a vital power source that has fallen into the hands of the evil Faye Dunaway. The story is pretty daft, the special effects merely ordinary and Slater is a rather weak superheroine. Dunaway attempts to get into the spirit of things with a wildly over-the-top performance, but British actors Peter O'Toole and Peter Cook simply look embarrassed.

Helen Slater *Kara, Supergirl/Linda Lee* • Faye Dunaway *Selena* • Peter O'Toole *Zaltar* • Mia Farrow *Alura* • Brenda Vaccaro *Bianca* • Peter Cook *Nigel* • Simon Ward *Zor-El* ■ *Dir* Jeannot Szwarc • *Scr* David Odell

The Supergrass ★★ 15

Comedy   1985 · UK · Colour · 93mins

In a so-so comedy, a spin-off from *The Comic Strip* TV series, Ade Edmondson poses as a drug dealer to impress a girlfriend. However he finds that the pretence also fools the police, who pressure him into grassing on his nonexistent drugs ring. There's strong support from Dawn French, Jennifer Saunders and Peter Richardson, who also co-wrote and directed, but this is small-screen stuff that doesn't stand up to big-screen scrutiny. 🖵

Adrian Edmondson *Dennis* • Jennifer Saunders *Lesley* • Peter Richardson *Harvey Duncan* • Dawn French *Andrea* • Keith Allen *Wong* • Nigel Planer *Gunter* • Robbie Coltrane *Troy* ■ *Dir* Peter Richardson • *Scr* Pete Richens, Peter Richardson

Superman ★★★★ PG

Fantasy adventure
1978 · US · Colour · 137mins

This big-budget, epic scale version of the Man of Steel legend is irresistible, fabulous entertainment. The elegiac opening – from the destruction of Krypton to Clark Kent's arrival at the *Daily Planet* in Metropolis – turns more traditional comic book when Clark falls for Lois Lane, before a bright and breezy confrontation with comedic criminal Lex Luthor. The deliberate clash of styles generates much excitement and, yes, you'll believe a man can fly. Christopher Reeve is perfectly cast (though Dean Cain fans may now disagree) and as a spectacle it's a highly satisfying confection. 🖵

Christopher Reeve *Clark Kent/Superman* • Gene Hackman *Lex Luthor* • Margot Kidder *Lois Lane* • Marlon Brando *Jor-El* • Ned Beatty *Otis* • Jackie Cooper *Perry White* • Glenn Ford *Pa Kent* • Trevor Howard *First Elder* • Terence Stamp *General Zod* • Susannah York *Lara* • Larry Hagman *Major* ■ *Dir* Richard Donner • *Scr* Mario Puzo, David Newman, Leslie Newman, Robert Benton, from the story by Mario Puzo, from the comic strip by Jerry Siegel, Joe Shuster • *Cinematographer* Geoffrey Unsworth • *Music* John Williams • *Production Designer* John Barry

Superman II ★★★★ PG

Fantasy adventure
1980 · UK/US · Colour · 127mins

Purists may not agree, but this is probably the best segment of the *Superman* saga in terms of plot, free from the occasionally po-faced seriousness of the first and the rampant silliness of the remaining two. Director Richard Lester delivers a knowing, knockabout cartoon with Superman (Christopher Reeve) finding out that he is no longer the toughest guy around when three baddies are exiled from his home planet and arrive on Earth. The effects are equal to the first film and there's a strong supporting cast, including an irascible Gene Hackman and the excellent Terence Stamp. 🖵

Christopher Reeve *Clark Kent/Superman* • Gene Hackman *Lex Luthor* • Margot Kidder *Lois Lane* • Terence Stamp *General Zod* • Ned Beatty *Otis* • Sarah Douglas *Ursa* • Jack O'Halloran *Non* • Valerie Perrine *Eve Teschmacher* • Susannah York *Lara* • Jackie Cooper *Perry White* ■ *Dir* Richard Lester • *Scr* Mario Puzo, David Newman, Leslie Newman, from the story by Mario Puzo, from the characters created by Jerry Siegel, Joe Shuster

Superman III ★★ PG

Fantasy adventure
1983 · US · Colour · 119mins

Director Richard Lester injected a much needed irreverence into *Superman II*, but he lost his way badly with this third instalment of "the man from Krypton" saga. There are a few nice touches, such as when Christopher Reeve turns nasty, but this proved to be the beginning of the end for the series. The attempt to up the laughter quotient by introducing Richard Pryor doesn't work, and neither he nor Robert Vaughn prove to be an adequate replacement for Gene Hackman's Lex Luthor. Margot Kidder wanted little to do with this sequel and must have been thankful only to get a look-in as Lois Lane. Still, for die-hard fans of the superhero, this is adequate entertainment. 🖵

Christopher Reeve *Superman/Clark Kent* • Richard Pryor *Gus Gorman* • Jackie Cooper *Perry White* • Margot Kidder *Lois Lane* • Annette O'Toole *Lana Lang* • Annie Ross *Vera Webster* • Pamela Stephenson *Lorelei Ambrosia* • Robert Vaughn *Ross Webster* ■ *Dir* Richard Lester • *Scr* David Newman, Leslie Newman, from the characters created by Jerry Siegel, Joe Shuster

U = SUITABLE FOR ALL   Uc = SUITABLE FOR ALL, ESPECIALLY FOR YOUNG CHILDREN (VIDEO ONLY)   PG = PARENTAL GUIDANCE

Superman IV: the Quest for Peace ★★ PG

Fantasy adventure
1987 · US · Colour · 88mins

Despite the return of Gene Hackman as the evil Lex Luthor, this creaky, tired third sequel sounded the final death knell for the *Superman* saga. In this one, Christopher Reeve's man in tights has finally brought about peace in our time, but soon finds himself up against Luthor (now a budding arms baron), his irritating nephew (Jon Cryer) and a powerful new foe called Nuclear Man, while his bespectacled alter ego Clark Kent has to fight off predatory publisher's daughter Mariel Hemingway. However, the enthusiastic hamming can't hide the clunking direction by Sidney J Furie and the poor special effects. 📼

Christopher Reeve *Superman/Clark Kent* • Gene Hackman *Lex Luthor* • Jackie Cooper *Perry White* • Marc McClure *Jimmy Olsen* • Jon Cryer *Lenny* • Sam Wanamaker *David Warfield* • Mark Pillow *Nuclear Man* • Mariel Hemingway *Lacy Warfield* • Margot Kidder *Lois Lane* ■ *Dir* Sidney J Furie • *Scr* Lawrence Konner, Mark Rosenthal, from a story by Christopher Reeve, Lawrence Konner, Mark Rosenthal, from characters created by Jerry Siegel, Joe Shuster

Supernatural ★

Mystery melodrama 1933 · US · BW · 65mins

Heiress Carole Lombard becomes involved with fake medium Alan Dinehart, who says he can put her in touch with her dead brother. Of course, he's only after her money. The extraordinarily convoluted plot then sees Lombard possessed by the spirit of a dead murderess as she threatens to exact revenge on the fraudulent Dinehart. This is a disappointing vehicle for the talents of the lovely Lombard, though it remains a collectable curiosity for her fans.

Carole Lombard *Roma Courtney* • Randolph Scott *Grant Wilson* • Vivienne Osborne *Ruth Rogen* • Alan Dinehart *Paul Bavian* • HB Warner *Dr Houston* • Beryl Mercer *Madame Gourjan* • William Farnum *Robert Hammond* ■ *Dir* Victor Halperin • *Scr* Harvey Thew, Brian Marlow, from the story by Garnett Weston

Supernova ★ 15

Science-fiction adventure
2000 · US · Colour · 90mins

Begun by *Romper Stomper* director Geoffrey Wright, finished by *48 HRS* director Walter Hill, re-edited against his wishes by Francis Ford Coppola and then partly re-shot by *The Hidden* director Jack Sholder. It's no wonder this drag of a science-fiction adventure is an incomprehensible mess. Credited to a bogus name – Thomas Lee, the new century's friendlier-sounding Alan Smithee replacement – this relentlessly mediocre *Alien* rip-off at least looks good, as it shambles through the familiar conventions of the genre. A medical crew in deep space answer a distress call and take on board the only survivor of a mysterious mining accident. James Spader and Angela Bassett try in vain to soften the ridiculous impact of such clumsy space-opera theatrics, while the rest of the cast do little but disrobe.

James Spader *Nick Vanzant* • Angela Bassett *Kaela Evers* • Robert Forster *AJ Marley* • Lou

Diamond Phillips *Yerzy Penalosa* • Peter Facinelli *Karl Larson* • Robin Tunney *Danika Lund* • Wilson Cruz *Benj Sotomejor* • Eddy Rice Jr *Flyboy* ■ *Dir* Thomas Lee [Walter Hill] • *Scr* David Campbell Wilson, from a story by William Malone

Superstar ★★ 12

Comedy 1999 · US · Colour · 95mins

Calling this particular *Saturday Night Live* spin-off a cut above their usual product isn't exactly a compliment. It does have its moments, but it sometimes has to go wildly out of its way to get to them. Molly Shannon's character is a nerdy Catholic high-school girl is determined not to let her dizzy nature or her snotty classmates stop her from becoming a star. The supporting characters are underused, and much of the action is generally lame. However, the non-stop attempts at humour do manage to induce a mild chuckle every few minutes.

Molly Shannon *Mary Katherine Gallagher* • Will Ferrell *Sky Corrigan/Jesus* • Elaine Hendrix *Evian* • Harland Williams *Slater* • Mark McKinney *Father Ritley* • Glynis Johns *Grandma* • Jason Blicker *Howard* • Gerry Bamman *Father John* ■ *Dir* Bruce McCulloch • *Scr* Steven Wayne Koren, from the character created by Molly Shannon

Superstar: the Karen Carpenter Story ★★★★

Experimental biographical fantasy
1987 · US · Colour · 43mins

Years before *Velvet Goldmine*, director Todd Haynes explored the opposite end of the musical spectrum with this notorious short about seventies pop duo The Carpenters. Making unauthorised use of their music, Haynes presents a surreal re-enactment of the ill-fated life and career of singer Karen Carpenter and her brother Richard, using Barbie dolls instead of actors. Despite the superficially camp treatment, there's a serious message behind Haynes's portrayal of the doomed Karen, as she battles with overnight success, family pressures and the anorexia nervosa that would cause her death. Contemporary newsreel and TV-show footage provides the background to this bizarre yet moving examination of the dark side of seventies pop culture.

Gwen Kraus *Voice* • Bruce Tuthill *Voice* ■ *Dir* Todd Haynes • *Scr* Todd Haynes, Cynthia Schneider

Superstar: the Life and Times of Andy Warhol ★★★★

Documentary 1991 · US · Colour · 87mins

An absorbing documentary made three years after the death of pop artist and film-maker Warhol. Extremely well researched and well put together by Chuck Workman, it includes interviews with Warhol's relatives and famous friends, fascinating footage from the Warhol Factory, and clips from early films that many may not have seen. Paul Morrissey, who directed Warhol's biggest hits, is noticeably absent, and there is a tendency to eulogise rather than analyse, but anyone interested in the zeitgeist of the Sixties will not be disappointed. 📼

Dir/Scr Chuck Workman • *Cinematographer* Burleigh Wartes

Supervixens ★★★★ 18

Sex comedy drama
1975 · US · Colour · 104mins

Cult sexploiter Russ Meyer cranked up to overdrive his giddy formula of fast pacing, breathless editing and weird camera angles with this exaggerated cartoon romp, complete with a ''That's all, folks!'' ending. The convoluted plot, detailing the sexual misadventures of a man on the run for a murder he didn't commit, includes escaped Nazis and psycho cops alongside the usual bevy of well-proportioned fantasy females. Numerous characters pop up from Meyer's own back catalogue in this delightfully manic roller-coaster ride through the sexual mores of mid-seventies Americana, laced with outrageous comedy and extreme violence. The dynamite climax is exactly that. Contains violence, swearing, sex scenes and nudity. 📼

Shari Eubank *Superangel/Supervixen* • Charles Pitts *Clint Ramsey* • Charles Napier *Harry Sledge* • Uschi Digard *Supersoul* • Henry Rowland *Martin Bormann* • Christy Hartburg *Superlorna* • Sharon Kelly *Supercherry* ■ *Dir/Scr* Russ Meyer

Support Your Local Gunfighter ★★★★ U

Comedy western 1971 · US · Colour · 88mins

Amiable James Garner polished up his TV *Maverick* persona for a wonderfully witty pair of cowboy satires directed by Burt Kennedy, who had secured his spurs by writing a cycle of Randolph Scott westerns. This isn't exactly a sequel to *Support Your Local Sheriff!*, except perhaps in tone, but is equally funny, as con man Garner passes himself off as a deadly gunman. Bumbling Jack Elam walks away with the movie as Garner's buddy and delivers one of the funniest last lines in American screen comedy. The rest of the cast is handpicked, ranging from WC Fields's put-upon stooge Grady Sutton to TV's *The Rifleman* himself, Chuck Connors. One to cherish, a genuine side-splitting treat. 📼

James Garner *Latigo Smith* • Suzanne Pleshette *Patience Barton* • Jack Elam *Jug May* • Joan Blondell *Jenny* • Harry Morgan *Taylor Barton* • Marie Windsor *Goldie* • Henry Jones *Ez* • John Dehner *Colonel Ames* • Chuck Connors *Swifty Morgan* • Grady Sutton *Storekeeper* ■ *Dir* Burt Kennedy • *Scr* James Edward Grant

Support Your Local Sheriff! ★★★★ PG

Comedy western 1969 · US · Colour · 89mins

This is one of a pair of priceless comedy gems (*Support Your Local Gunfighter* followed in 1971) from director Burt Kennedy, which spoof the western genre with great affection and provide marvellous roles for James Garner. Here he utilises his easy-going, wry charm as a put-upon lawman. Western fans will enjoy the clever casting. Walter Brennan virtually reprises the role of Ike Clanton in *My Darling Clementine*, only this time for laughs, and there's Joan Hackett from *Will Penny*. Jack Elam and Bruce Dern

are both hysterically funny, especially Elam as Garner's useless deputy. Even if you don't care for westerns, this is well worth a look for a good laugh. 📼

James Garner *Jason McCullough* • Joan Hackett *Prudy Perkins* • Walter Brennan *Pa Danby* • Harry Morgan *Mayor Olly Perkins* • Jack Elam *Jake* • Bruce Dern *Joe Danby* • Henry Jones *Preacher Henry Jackson* • Walter Burke *Fred Johnson* ■ *Dir* Burt Kennedy • *Scr* William Bowers

Suppose They Gave a War and Nobody Came? ★★★ 15

Satirical comedy drama
1970 · US · Colour · 112mins

A commander of a US army base in the American South hopes to foster good will with the nearby town by organising a dance. All seems well at first, but when army sergeant Tony Curtis is caught canoodling with local beauty Suzanne Pleshette, the resulting fracas leads to war breaking out between the town and the military. Sometimes farcical, sometimes satirical, it's a crazy sprawling mess of a comedy that manages to entertain, despite its many flaws. 📼

Brian Keith *Nace* • Tony Curtis *Shannon Gambroni* • Ernest Borgnine *Sheriff Harve* • Ivan Dixon *Sergeant Jones* • Suzanne Pleshette *Ramona* • Tom Ewell *Billy Joe Davis* • Bradford Dillman *Captain Myerson* • Don Ameche *Colonel Flanders* ■ *Dir* Hy Averback • *Scr* Don McGuire, Hal Captain, from a story by Hal Captain

Sur ★★★★ 15

Drama 1987 · Arg/Fr · Colour · 118mins

Following his treatise on physical exile, *Tangos, Exilo de Gardel* (1985), Argentinian director Fernando E Solanas (himself heading home after a prolonged absence) explores the pain of the prisoner in this vibrant, lyrical, political and poignant study of national transition and individual turmoil. Consciously employing a theatrical style, he uses tango, poetry and song to counterpoint the jumble of emotions, memories, hopes and fears that beset newly released Miguel Angel Sola, as he returns to his Buenos Aires neighbourhood. However, his wife, Susu Pecoraro, also has to readjust, having turned to close friend Philippe Léotard for solace in her isolation. A Spanish language film.

Susu Pecoraro *Rosi Echegoyen* • Sola Miguel Angel *Floreal Echegoyen* • Philippe Léotard *Roberto* • Lito Cruz *El Negro* • Ulises Dumont *Emilio* ■ *Dir/Scr* Fernando E Solanas

Sure Fire ★★★

Drama 1990 · US · Colour · 83mins

Arrogant real-estate salesman Tom Blair embarks on a crooked scheme to sell vacation homes in Utah to wealthy Californians in micro-budget master Jon Jost's experimental 16mm gem. But as the scam collapses, so does Blair's family life, and he and his estranged wife start fighting for the loyalties of their teenage son. The resolution of this power struggle is tragic and haunting. Moody music, extended takes and innovative narrative mechanisms combine to lay bare a dark and disturbing portrait of warped politics and ethical values. A funny and frightening gaze into the heart of Reagan's legacy.

Tom Blair *Wes* • Kristi Hager *Bobbi* • Robert Ernst *Larry* • Kate Dezina *Ellen* • Phillip R Brown *Phillip* • Dennis R Brown *Dennis* ■ *Dir/Scr* Jon Jost

The Sure Thing ★★★★ 15

Comedy 1985 · US · Colour · 90mins

This delightful comedy from director Rob Reiner should have made John Cusack a star. He's superb as a beer-guzzling, sex-obsessed freshman who travels from his eastern college to California during the holidays to meet up with a beautiful girl who's a "sure thing". However, during a series of misadventures he ends up on the road with clean-living Daphne Zuniga, and that's where the fun really begins. Both the leads are enjoyable to watch, and this seems like a virtual blueprint for Reiner's later *When Harry Met Sally...* , but with even more charm. Watch out for a young Tim Robbins as the driver with whom no one should ever hitch a ride. Contains some swearing. ▭

John Cusack *Walter "Gib" Gibson* • Daphne Zuniga *Alison Bradbury* • Anthony Edwards *Lance* • Boyd Gaines *Jason* • Lisa Jane Persky *Mary Ann* • Viveca Lindfors *Professor Taub* • Nicollette Sheridan *The Sure Thing* • Tim Robbins *Gary* ■ *Dir* Rob Reiner • *Scr* Steven L Bloom, Jonathan Roberts

Surf Nazis Must Die ★ 18

Futuristic satire 1987 · US · Colour · 78mins

This is one of cinema's most notoriously titled movies and a typical release from Troma – the studio that gave us *Rabid Grannies* and *The Toxic Avenger* – featuring bad acting, a nonexistent budget and a ludicrous plotline. It's set in a future California, where a devastating earthquake has left millions homeless and the beaches have turned into battlegrounds, as rival surf gangs vie for control. Not as much fun as it could have been, and it takes itself way too seriously. ▭

Barry Brenner *Adolf* • Gail Neely *Mama Washington* • Michael Sonye *Mengele* • Dawn Wildsmith *Eva* • Jon Ayre *Narrator* ■ *Dir* Peter George • *Scr* Jon Ayre

Surf Ninjas ★ PG

Comedy adventure
1993 · US · Colour · 83mins

Isn't it amazing that, in the midst of the nineties ninja craze, with "kid ninja" movies being made every other year, not one of them had a decent martial arts sequence or a single line of decent dialogue? This one has the audacity to include both Rob Schneider and Leslie Nielsen for its odious comic relief. Polynesian brothers Ernie Reyes Jr and Nicholas Cowan discover that they are the royal heirs to an island nation, which was overthrown by evil warlord Colonel Chi (Nielsen). So the kids decide to kick some bad guy butt and reclaim their country. Even children will roll their eyes. ▭

Ernie Reyes Jr *Zatch* • Ernie Reyes Jr *Johnny* • Nicholas Cowan *Adam* • John Karlen *Mac* • Rob Schneider *Iggy* • Leslie Nielsen *Colonel Chi* ■ *Dir* Neal Israel • *Scr* Dan Gordon

Surrender ★★★ PG

Romantic comedy
1987 · US · Colour · 91mins

A light courtship comedy about a confused woman caught in two minds about the men in her life. Sally Field is Little Miss Muddle; Michael Caine and Steve Guttenberg (what happened to him?) are the twin objects of her affections. Though the film is trite and contrived at times, strong performances, in particular from the two male leads, just about carry it through. ▭

Sally Field *Daisy Morgan* • Michael Caine *Sean Stein* • Steve Guttenberg *Marty Caesar* • Peter Boyle *Jay Bass* • Julie Kavner *Ronnie* • Jackie Cooper *Ace Morgan* • Louise Lasser *Joyce* • Iman *Hedy* ■ *Dir/Scr* Jerry Belson

The Surrogate ★★ 12

Thriller 1995 · US · Colour · 88mins

This overheated, logic-defying drama explores the somewhat murky world of child surrogacy. Alyssa Milano plays the financially strapped art student who agrees to become a surrogate for a nice, childless couple (Connie Sellecca and David Dukes). All goes swimmingly to start with, but soon Milano begins to suspect that they are not quite the ideal parents-to-be they make out. It's competently played, but director Jan Egleson struggles to escape the straitjacket of the TV-movie format. ▭

Alyssa Milano *Amy Winslow* • Connie Sellecca *Joan Quinn* • David Dukes *Stuart Quinn* ■ *Dir* Jan Egleson • *Scr* Raymond Hartung, from a story by Raymond Hartung, Elisa Bell

Survival on the Mountain ★★

Adventure based on a true story
1996 · US · Colour

Although it bears the stamp of Francis Ford Coppola as one of the executive producers (Billy Crystal was another!), this is a no-more-than-formulaic made-for-TV adventure. Dennis Boutsikaris (who played Woody Allen in the 1995 TV mini-series *Love and Betrayal: The Mia Farrow Story*) and Markie Post are the American couple hiking in the Himalayas who get caught up in an avalanche. The settings are spectacular, but the "against all odds" struggle never really grips and the direction is predictable.

Dennis Boutsikaris *Ron Plotkin* • Markie Post *Debbie Plotkin* • Hiro Kanagawa *Ang* ■ *Dir* John Patterson • *Scr* Dennis Turner

Survival Run ★ 18

Action crime drama
1979 · US · Colour · 93mins

Vincent Van Patten and five other teens get stranded in the middle of the desert, reacting to their situation by drinking beer, having sex, and singing badly around the campfire. When they stumble onto the camp of drug dealers Peter Graves and Ray Milland (looking very uncomfortable in the heat), the hunt begins and they must fight back. There's never any sense of danger or tension on the part of the teens and the limp fighting can barely be considered action sequences. Contains swearing, sex scenes and violence.

Peter Graves (1) • Ray Milland • Vincent Van Patten • Pedro Armendariz Jr • Susan Pratt O'Hanlon ■ *Dir* Larry Spiegel • *Scr* Larry Spiegel, GM Cahill, from a story by GM Cahill

Survive the Savage Sea ★★★ U

Drama based on a true story
1992 · US · Colour · 87mins

Shot around the Great Barrier Reef, this is the true story of the Carpenter family, who spent 37 days at sea waiting to be rescued after their boat was capsized by whales. It's an incredible tale of human endurance and those involved were clearly remarkable people, but, translated into TV drama and aimed at a family audience, their experiences end up looking rather clichéd. Don't expect cinema-standard special effects, because the budget obviously wasn't there. However, seasoned actors Robert Urich and Ali MacGraw show the necessary strength of character and they're backed up by some spirited performances from the younger members of the cast. ▭

Robert Urich *Jack Carpenter* • Ali MacGraw *Claire Carpenter* • Danielle Von Zerneck *Susan* • Mark Ballou *Gary* • David Franklin *Wally* • Ryan Urich *Brian* • John Heywood *Commander* • Gus Mercurio *Mr Haines* ■ *Dir* Kevin James Dobson • *Scr* Scott Swanton, Fred Haines, Dougal Robertson, from the book by Dougal Robertson

Surviving ★★★ 15

Drama 1985 · US · Colour · 137mins

An often fascinating and powerful movie about the devastating consequences of thwarted teenage romance. Zach Galligan and Molly Ringwald are the young lovers, driven to desperate measures when their parents oppose their relationship. A strong cast includes Ellen Burstyn and Marsha Mason as the mothers confronting this teenage angst and struggling to deal with their own feelings of guilt. ▭

Ellen Burstyn *Tina Morgan* • Len Cariou *David Morgan* • Zach Galligan *Rick Morgan* • Marsha Mason *Lois Carlson* • Molly Ringwald *Lonnie Carlson* • Paul Sorvino *Harvey Carlson* • River Phoenix *Philip Morgan* • Heather O'Rourke *Sarah Morgan* ■ *Dir* Waris Hussein • *Scr* Joyce Eliason

Surviving Desire ★★★ PG

Drama 1989 · US · Colour · 52mins

Independent film-maker Hal Hartley made this short movie for the small screen. The semi-improvised film tells of a professor of literature (Martin Donovan) who's obsessed with Dostoyevsky and then becomes infatuated with one of his students (Mary Ward). Though containing some sharp dialogue, at its centre are Hartley's usual themes of trust and betrayal – a condensation of ideas made all the more palatable by its brevity. ▭

Martin Donovan *Jude* • Matt Malloy *Henry* • Rebecca Nelson *Katie* • Julie Sukman *Jill* • Mary Ward [Mary B Ward] *Sophie* ■ *Dir/Scr* Hal Hartley

Surviving Picasso ★★★★ 15

Biographical drama
1996 · US · Colour · 120mins

James Ivory directs Anthony Hopkins in a vision of Picasso's life that argues his passion for women equalled his passion for painting. His objects of desire are all stunning – Natascha McElhone, Julianne Moore, Susannah Harker – but which of them will prove a match for him? Hopkins is excellent as the walking ego and McElhone makes a very impressive impact in her first major role. As ever Ivory directs with flair and aesthetic insight, but the subject matter may be too eclectic for many people's taste and there's very little of Picasso's actual work on offer, so fans of his paintings will be disappointed. Contains some swearing and a sex scene.

Anthony Hopkins *Pablo Picasso* • Natascha McElhone *Françoise* • Julianne Moore *Dora Maar* • Joss Ackland *Henri Matisse* • Jane Lapotaire *Olga Koklova* • Joseph Maher *Kahnweiler* • Bob Peck *Françoise's father* • Diane Venora *Jacqueline Rocque* • Joan Plowright *Françoise's grandmother* • Susannah Harker *Marie-Thérèse* ■ *Dir* James Ivory • *Scr* Ruth Prawer Jhabvala, from the non-fiction book *Picasso: Creator and Destroyer* by Arianna Stassinopoulos Huffington

Surviving the Game ★★ 15

Action thriller 1994 · US · Colour · 92mins

Another variant on the shopworn manhunt premise, best exhibited back in the thirties with *The Most Dangerous Game*. This time, rapper-cum-thespian Ice T is a homeless derelict conned out of the city and into the wilderness to act as prey for a bunch of thrill-seeking high rollers including Gary Busey's ex-CIA agent, F Murray Abraham's Wall Street executive and Rutger Hauer. Well, what would a film of this type be without good old Rutger? Former Spike Lee cinematographer Ernest R Dickerson brings technical bravado to the proceedings, but the whole premise of wealthy whites hunting homeless blacks is morally tasteless. ▭

Ice T [Ice-T] *Jack Mason* • Rutger Hauer *Burns* • Charles S Dutton *Cole* • Gary Busey *Hawkins* • F Murray Abraham *Wolf Sr* • John C McGinley *Griffin* • William McNamara *Wolf Jr* • Jeff Corey *Hank* ■ *Dir* Ernest R Dickerson • *Scr* Eric Bernt

The Survivor ★★ 15

Thriller 1981 · Ausl · Colour · 82mins

Robert Powell puts on that martyred look he keeps handy in lieu of acting as a pilot, the sole survivor of a crashed jet, who is prey to visions of dead passengers. Jenny Agutter simpers while Powell whimpers in this Australian oddity directed by David Hemmings, a would-be thriller that's sadly lacking in suspense. Perhaps former actor Hemmings, star of Michelangelo Antonioni's *Blow Up* back in the sixties, just got stuck with the wrong cast. Joseph Cotten also appears in the sad twilight of a distinguished career. Contains violence and swearing. ▭

Robert Powell *Keller* • Jenny Agutter *Hobbs* • Joseph Cotten *Priest* • Angela Punch McGregor *Beth Rogan* • Ralph Cotterill *Slater*

U = SUITABLE FOR ALL   Uc = SUITABLE FOR ALL, ESPECIALLY FOR YOUNG CHILDREN (VIDEO ONLY)   PG = PARENTAL GUIDANCE

• Peter Sumner *Tewson* ■ *Dir* David Hemmings • *Scr* David Ambrose, from the novel by James Herbert

The Survivors ★★ 15
Comedy   1983 · US · Colour · 98mins

What starts as a promising social satire soon descends into coarse slapstick and manic babble as Robin Williams and Walter Matthau come to terms with life after foiling a crime, but being identified by the miscreant. Williams is transformed from mild-mannered executive into gun-toting survivalist by his intervention in a diner robbery, while his fellow hero Matthau (who has already seen his garage go up in flames) manages to stay cynically calm. The clash of these eccentric characters should have provided the impetus for some acerbic asides on modern living, but director Michael Ritchie lets the picture and his stars run out of control. Contains some swearing and violence. ▭

Walter Matthau *Sonny Paluso* • Robin Williams *Donald Quinelle* • Jerry Reed *Jack Locke* • James Wainwright *Wes Huntley* • Kristen Vigard *Candice Paluso* • Annie McEnroe *Doreen* • Anne Pitoniak *Betty* ■ *Dir* Michael Ritchie • *Scr* Michael Leeson

Susan and God ★★★
Comedy drama   1940 · US · Colour · 115mins

Shallow and narcissistic society wife and mother Joan Crawford, whose disregard is alienating her husband Fredric March, returns from a European trip with a new fad – religion. Her verbal zealotry and pious interference in other people's lives causes havoc and drives her husband to drink. An unusual drama, written by Anita Loos from a play by Rachel Crothers and directed by George Cukor, who draws a persuasive performance from Crawford.

Joan Crawford *Susan Trexel* • Fredric March *Barry Trexel* • Ruth Hussey *Charlotte* • John Carroll *Clyde Rochester* • Rita Hayworth *Leonora Stubbs* • Nigel Bruce *Hutchins Stubbs* • Bruce Cabot *Michael O'Hara* ■ *Dir* George Cukor • *Scr* Anita Loos, from a play by Rachel Crothers

Susan Lenox: Her Fall and Rise ★★★
Romantic melodrama
1931 · US · BW · 76mins

Based on the notorious novel by David Graham Phillips, the British film censor was having none of it, lopping out several key seconds and changing the title to *The Rise of Helga*. The whole steamy movie is tame today, save for the undeniable sexual magnetism between Greta Garbo and Clark Gable in their only screen pairing. She insisted on newcomer Gable as co-star, and their early country scenes make it easy to see why. Gable is too physically strong to crash so quickly downhill as the plot dictates. Garbo is magic, though, and this movie is but a prologue to the greatness to come.

Greta Garbo *Susan Lenox* • Clark Gable *Rodney* • Jean Hersholt *Ohlin* • John Miljan *Burlingham* • Alan Hale *Mondstrum* • Hale Hamilton *Mike Kelly* • Hilda Vaughn *Astrid* • Russell Simpson *Doctor* ■ *Dir* Robert Z Leonard • *Scr* Wanda Tuchock, Zelda Sears, Leon Gordon, Edith Fitzgerald, from the novel by David Graham Phillips

Susan Slade ★
Melodrama   1961 · US · Colour · 116mins

The daughter of a respectable engineer falls pregnant by a handsome mountaineer who is promptly killed in an accident. After hiding in South America, she returns to California with her illegitimate baby and has to deal with the consequences of her father's unexpected death. Produced, written and directed by Delmer Daves, possibly in a bid to recapture the magic of thirties melodrama, this glossy nonsense is turgid, unconvincing and boring.

Troy Donahue *Hoyt Brecker* • Connie Stevens *Susan Slade* • Dorothy McGuire *Leah Slade* • Lloyd Nolan *Roger Slade* • Brian Aherne *Stanton Corbett* • Grant Williams *Conn White* ■ *Dir* Delmer Daves • *Scr* Delmer Daves, from the novel *The Sin of Susan Slade* by Doris Hume • *Music* Max Steiner

Susan Slept Here ★★★
Comedy   1954 · US · Colour · 97mins

This super-sophisticated farce is as funny and risqué now as it was back in 1954, and Debbie Reynolds is simply terrific in one of her rare naughty-but-nice roles as a sexy teenage delinquent foisted on screenwriter Dick Powell. The Hollywood scene is well observed by director Frank Tashlin, and the humour is peppered with in-jokes. (The narrator is an Oscar statuette!) The Technicolor is particularly rich, and the Oscar-nominated theme song went to number one in the charts. (Remember *Hold My Hand* by Don Cornell?) A film for fifties freaks.

Dick Powell *Mark Christopher* • Debbie Reynolds *Isabella* • Anne Francis *Isabella* • Alvy Moore *Virgil* • Glenda Farrell *Maude* • Horace McMahon *Maizel* ■ *Dir* Frank Tashlin • *Scr* Alex Gottlieb, from the play *Susan* by Alex Gottlieb, Steve Fisher

Susana ★★
Melodrama   1951 · Mex · BW · 82mins

Shot on a miniscule budget, Luis Buñuel considered this the low point of his career. Released in the States as *The Devil and the Flesh*, it was the first film he made after his stunning comeback feature, *Los Olvidados*. While not one of his best efforts, it is still a stinging assault on Mexico's rich and religious, in particular their indolence and hypocrisy. Rosita Quintana tries hard in the title role, showing suitable humility as she begs God for a miraculous release from jail, yet revealing aN irresistible sensuality as she seduces every man on Fernando Soler's ranch. In Spanish with English subtitles.

Fernando Soler *Don Guadalupe* • Rosita Quintana *Susana* • Victor Manuel Mendoza *Jesus* • Matilde Palou *Carmen* ■ *Dir* Luis Buñuel • *Scr* Jaime Salvador, Luis Buñuel

Susannah of the Mounties ★★★ U
Adventure   1939 · US · BW · 79mins

Count your blessings you are watching this Shirley Temple vehicle in Britain, for the chances are you would have to endure a grotesque colourised version if you were tuning in anywhere in the United States. Having survived a tribal massacre, little Miss Curly Top is

taken in by Mountie Randolph Scott and duly helps him get both his man (the truly villainous Victor Jory) and his woman (Margaret Lockwood, making her Hollywood debut). There's some toned-down action and a teeth-grinding sequence in which Scott is taught to tap dance, but it's mostly harmless.

Shirley Temple *Susannah Sheldon* • Randolph Scott *Inspector Angus ''Monty'' Montague* • Margaret Lockwood *Vicky Standing* • Martin Good Rider *Little Chief* • J Farrell MacDonald *Pat O'Hannegan* • Maurice Moscovich *Chief Big Eagle* • Victor Jory *Wolf Pelt* ■ *Dir* William A Seiter • *Scr* Robert Ellis, Helen Logan, from a story by Fidel La Barba, Walter Ferris, from the novel *Susannah, a Little Girl of the Mounties* by Muriel Denison

Susan's Plan ★★★ 18
Comedy   1998 · US · Colour · 84mins

A contrived, complex and intermittently hilarious comedy from John Landis, the director of *Animal House*, *The Blues Brothers* and *Trading Places*. This isn't in the same league, but marks something of a return to form by Landis, who's lost his way in recent years. Nastassja Kinski plays Susan, who's desperate to bump off her reprehensible ex-hubby for cash and hires a string of bumbling hit men to do it. Routine stuff, elevated above the ordinary by a cracking cast including Billy Zane, Lara Flynn Boyle and Dan Aykroyd. Contains swearing, violence and nudity.

Nastassja Kinski *Susan* • Billy Zane *Sam* • Michael Biehn *Bill* • Dan Aykroyd *Bob* • Lara Flynn Boyle *Betty* • Rob Schneider *Steve* • Adrian Paul *Paul* ■ *Dir/Scr* John Landis

The Suspect ★★★
Period thriller   1944 · US · BW · 85mins

Directed by German émigré Robert Siodmak, this Edwardian drama stars Charles Laughton in the kind of role in which he excelled. He plays a decent, ordinary shopkeeper whose life is made a misery by his deeply unpleasant wife Rosalind Ivan. Smitten with pretty stenographer Ella Raines, he beats his wife to death with a cane, but gets away with claiming she died in an accidental fall. He marries Raines and all is well until his blackmailing neighbour Henry Daniell begins to suspect the truth. Modest, suspenseful and absorbing, with the added frisson of claiming our sympathies entirely for the murderer.

Charles Laughton *Philip Marshall* • Ella Raines *Mary Gray* • Dean Harens *John Marshall* • Stanley C Ridges [Stanley Ridges] *Inspector Huxley* • Henry Daniell *Mr Gilbert Simmons* • Rosalind Ivan *Cora Marshall* • Molly Lamont *Mrs Edith Simmons* • Raymond Severn *Merridew* ■ *Dir* Robert Siodmak • *Scr* Bertram Millhauser, Arthur T Hormen, from the novel *This Way Out* by James Ronald

Suspect ★★
Spy drama   1960 · UK · BW · 80mins

Frankly, you expect better from the Boulting brothers. Written by Nigel Balchin, Jeffrey Dell and Roy Boulting from Balchin's own novel, *A Sort of Traitors*, this story of spies at a chemical research lab betrays its secret through casting. Nominal stars Tony Britton and Virginia Maskell are awful, and you soon wish splendid supports Peter Cushing, Donald

Pleasence, Raymond Huntley and Ian Bannen had more to do. The Boultings fail to create the claustrophobia that might have intensified the climate of suspicion, and the casting of Spike Milligan in an espionage drama is the only real talking point.

Tony Britton *Bob Marriott* • Virginia Maskell *Lucy Byrne* • Peter Cushing *Professor Sewall* • Ian Bannen *Alan Andrews* • Raymond Huntley *Sir George Gatling* • Thorley Walters *Mr Prince* • Donald Pleasence *Brown* • Spike Milligan *Arthur* ■ *Dir* Roy Boulting, John Boulting • *Scr* Nigel Balchin, Jeffrey Dell, Roy Boulting, from the novel *A Sort of Traitors* by Nigel Balchin

Suspect ★★ 15
Courtroom thriller
1987 · US · Colour · 116mins

An early Hollywood role for Liam Neeson, playing a deaf-mute Vietnam veteran accused of murder. Cher is his lawyer and Dennis Quaid is the jury member who provides a glimmer of hope in a seemingly hopeless case. Director Peter Yates winds up the courtroom tension to some effect, but any sympathy for Neeson's plight soon gets lost as suspicion shifts to a higher legal authority and the plot becomes too far-fetched. Contains violence and swearing. ▭

Cher *Kathleen Riley* • Dennis Quaid *Eddie Sanger* • Liam Neeson *Carl Wayne Anderson* • John Mahoney *Judge Matthew Helms* • Joe Mantegna *Charlie Stella* • Philip Bosco *Paul Gray* • E Katherine Kerr *Grace Comisky* • Fred Melamed *Morty Rosenthal* ■ *Dir* Peter Yates • *Scr* Eric Roth

Suspect Device ★ 18
Science-fiction thriller
1995 · US · Colour · 90mins

King of the drive-ins Roger Corman was behind this sci-fi tale of bullets, bodies and bombs. Committed fans of the genre will adore the fast-paced action, but those looking for in-depth character development and a plausible plot will be disappointed. The story revolves around US intelligence employee Dan Jericho, adequately portrayed by C Thomas Howell, who inadvertently opens a top-secret file and instantly becomes a wanted man hunted by assassins. Fleeing to New Mexico, he learns that he's a cyborg marked for elimination.

C Thomas Howell *Dan Jericho* • Stacey Travis *Jessica* • Jed Allen *Artemus* • John Beck *CIA director* ■ *Dir* Rick Jacobson • *Scr* Alex Simon, from a story by Rob Kerchner

Suspended Alibi ★ U
Crime drama   1956 · UK · BW · 64mins

Innocuous British crime drama, only to be commended for its brevity. Patrick Holt is the newspaperman convicted of the murder of his best friend. Honor Blackman plays his loyal wife, Naomi Chance his mistress, Valentine Dyall the plodding police inspector and Andrew Keir the crime reporter who digs out the truth. The least ambitious feature made by film union ACT's production subsidiary, it served its purpose as a time-filler.

Patrick Holt *Paul Pearson* • Honor Blackman *Lynn Pearson* • Valentine Dyall *Inspector Kayes* • Naomi Chance *Diana* • Lloyd Lamble *Waller* • Andrew Keir *Sandy Thorpe* ■ *Dir* Alfred Shaughnessy • *Scr* Kenneth R Hayles

Suspicion ★★★★ U
Psychological thriller
1941 · US · BW · 96mins

A marvellous Hitchcock thriller, with timid Joan Fontaine in mortal fear of being bumped off by her husband, amoral Cary Grant. Fontaine won the best actress Oscar for her pouting female-in-trouble portrayal, though some believe it was to compensate her for not winning the award for *Rebecca* the previous year. It all begins well enough, with Grant's bounder Johnnie Aysgarth a most unlikeable cad. But the film is hopelessly crippled by the censorship of the time, and is ultimately both predictable and implausible. Nevertheless, there's much to enjoy, not least a totally phoney Hollywood England and sterling support from British expatriates Nigel Bruce and Cedric Hardwicke. 🖭

Cary Grant *Johnnie Aysgarth* • Joan Fontaine *Lina McLaidlaw* • Cedric Hardwicke *General McLaidlaw* • Nigel Bruce *Gordon Cochran "Beaky" Thwaite* • Dame May Whitty *Mrs McLaidlaw* • Isabel Jeans *Mrs Newsham* ■ *Dir* Alfred Hitchcock • *Scr* Samson Raphaelson, Joan Harrison, Alma Reville, from the novel *Before the Fact* by Frances Iles [Anthony Berkeley Cox]

Suspicious Agenda ★★★ 18
Crime thriller
1994 · Can/US · Colour · 96mins

Recovering from the death of his partner, hostage negotiator Richard Grieco gets involved in the hunt for the imaginatively named "Lead Killer", a maniac vigilante bumping off those who've slipped through the clutches of justice with the aid of some molten lead. Grieco, one of the more reliable stars of the straight-to-video industry, puts teen movies behind him to star in this nasty crime thriller, directed with an eye for the grotesque by Clay Borris. Contains swearing, violence and nudity. 🖭

Richard Grieco *Tony Castagne* • Nick Mancuso *Jimmy Davane* • Jim Byrnes *Lt Rayburn* ■ *Dir* Clay Borris • *Scr* Kevin Rockdate

Suspicious Minds ★★ 18
Thriller
1997 · US · Colour · 90mins

An erotic thriller, spiced up with some environmental red herrings, that is classier than most and boosted by a top-line cast headed up by Patrick Bergin. He plays a former detective turned private eye who is hired by a wealthy businessman to track his beautiful young wife (Jayne Heitmeyer) who he suspects is having an affair. Bergin duly completes his job but things get complicated when the woman's lover turns up murdered and he gets involved in an environmental battle being waged by greenie terrorist Gary Busey. 🖭

Patrick Bergin *Jack Ramsey* • Gary Busey *Vic Mulvey* • Jayne Heitmeyer *Isabelle Whitmore* • Daniel Pilon *Richard Whitmore* ■ *Dir* Alain Zaloum • *Scr* Alain Zaloum, Brenda Newman

Suspiria ★★★★ 18
Supernatural horror
1976 · It · Colour · 94mins

Jessica Harper goes to a German ballet school where zombie witches prowl the corridors in the first horror fantasy epic from Dario Argento, the Italian Hitchcock. An absolutely stunning combination of menacing *Grand Guignol* atmosphere, dazzling colours, gory violence and lush décor, the famous opening 20 minutes is an unforgettable experience. Argento's gruesomely Gothic confection is a landmark in cinematic shock sensation and spawned the similarly themed *Inferno*. 🖭 **DVD**

Jessica Harper *Susy Bannion* • Joan Bennett *Madame Blanc* • Alida Valli *Miss Tanner* • Udo Kier *Frank* • Flavio Bucci *Daniel* • Stefania Casini *Sara* • Miguel Bose *Mark* • Rudolf Schundler *Professor Milius* ■ *Dir* Dario Argento • *Scr* Dario Argento, Dario Nicolodi

Suture ★★★ 15
Thriller
1993 · US · BW · 91mins

Great things were predicted for Scott McGehee and David Siegel after they debuted with this ultra-stylised *film noir*. However, they didn't work together again until they teamed on *Lush*. Borrowing freely from Hiroshi Teshigahara's *The Face of Another* and John Frankenheimer's *Seconds*, this postmodern monochrome melodrama delights in disorientating the viewer. At the centre of the confusion are half-brothers Dennis Haysbert and Michael Harris, whose racial and physical dissimilarity is turned into a mischievous lookalike gag on which depends the plot's dastardly game of interchangeable identities. 🖭

Dennis Haysbert *Clay Arlington* • Mel Harris *Dr Renee Descartes* • Sab Shimono *Dr Max Shinoda* • Dina Merrill *Alice Jameson* ■ *Dir/Scr* Scott McGehee, David Siegel

Suzhou River ★★★★
Romantic tragedy
2000 · Chi/Ger · Colour · 83mins

With an unseen videographer giving the action an intriguingly subjective viewpoint, Lou Ye's teasing treatise on perspective and identity irresistibly recalls Alfred Hitchcock's *Rear Window* and *Vertigo*. Hired by a vodka racketeer to chaperone his daughter Zhou Xun, motorcycle courier Jia Hongsheng connives at her kidnapping, only to be jailed for murder when she seems to commit suicide. On his release, Jia becomes besotted with an aquarium mermaid (Zhou again), with tragic consequences. With its world-weary narration, oppressive cityscapes and dangerous passions, this blend of *film noir* and psychological drama is as edgy as it's engrossing. In Mandarin with English subtitles.

Zhou Xun *Meimei/Moudan* • Jia Hongshen *Mardar* • Yao Anlian *Boss* • Nai An *Mada* ■ *Dir* Lou Ye • *Scr* Lou Ye

Suzy ★★★
Romantic melodrama
1936 · US · BW · 99mins

In London, penniless American chorus girl Jean Harlow marries Irish would-be inventor Franchot Tone but flees to a cabaret job in Paris after she believes him shot dead by a female spy. When the First World War breaks out, she marries French flying ace Cary Grant. Drama escalates when Tone, not dead after all, turns up in uniform… George Fitzmaurice directs this rather curious but effective and fast-moving piece that begins as romantic comedy (Dorothy Parker contributed to the script) and switches to espionage thriller. Harlow is ingenuous and charming, Tone an attractive hero and Grant, unusually, a cad undone by his shameless womanising.

Jean Harlow *Suzy Trent* • Cary Grant *André Charville* • Franchot Tone *Terry Moore* • Benita Hume *Mme Diane Eyrelle* • Lewis Stone *Baron Charville* ■ *Dir* George Fitzmaurice • *Scr* Dorothy Parker, Alan Campbell, Horace Jackson, Lenore Coffee, from the novel by Herbert Gorman

Svengali ★★
Drama
1931 · US · BW · 76mins

George du Maurier's famous Victorian novel, *Trilby*, tells of a beautiful young girl whose singing teacher uses hypnotism to turn her into a great opera singer. This version shifts the novel's emphasis on to Svengali himself, played in his most uninhibited, histrionic style by John Barrymore, while Marian Marsh is the artist's model who falls under his spell. Apart from the Oscar-nominated cinematography and the historical interest of watching Barrymore in action, there's not much of interest in this melodrama, which lacks the horror of *The Phantom of the Opera*.

John Barrymore *Svengali* • Marian Marsh *Trilby* • Bramwell Fletcher *Billee* • Donald Crisp *The Laird* • Lumsden Hare *Taffy* ■ *Dir* Archie Mayo • *Scr* J Grubb Alexander, from the novel *Trilby* by George du Maurier • *Cinematographer* Barry McGill

Svengali ★★
Drama
1954 · UK/US · Colour · 82mins

George du Maurier's novel *Trilby*, on which this film is based, was notorious in the late Victorian era for its overblown sexuality, telling the story of a manipulative music teacher/hypnotist called Svengali and a beautiful Irish artist's model called Trilby O'Ferrall who falls under his baleful spell. Set in Paris, it's a story of sexual jealousy that, in this version, conforms to censorship demands of the time and is less suggestive than the 1931 John Barrymore film (itself a remake of a 1915 silent). However, it's worth seeing for Donald Wolfit hamming away for all he's worth as the menacing Svengali.

Hildegarde Neff *Trilby O'Ferrall* • Donald Wolfit *Svengali* • Terence Morgan *Billy Bagot* • Derek Bond *The Laird* • Paul Rogers *Taffy* • David Kossoff *Gecko* • Alfie Bass *Carrell* • Harry Secombe *Barizel* ■ *Dir* Noel Langley • *Scr* Noel Langley, from the novel *Trilby* by George du Maurier

Svengali ★★
Drama
1983 · US · Colour · 96mins

Two-time Oscar winner Jodie Foster is woefully miscast in this TV movie, as the singer who rises to stardom under the guidance of voice coach Peter O'Toole. Director Anthony Harvey (best known for directing O'Toole in *The Lion in Winter*) manages to throw in every cliché in the book in what was the second reworking of the 1931 John Barrymore movie. This might be worth sitting through just to catch an early performance from Holly Hunter, another best actress Oscar winner. Peter O'Toole *Anton Bosnyak* • Jodie Foster *Zoe Alexander* • Elizabeth Ashley *Eve Swiss* • Larry Joshua *Johnny Rainbow* • Pamela Blair *Trish* • Barbara Byrne *Mrs Burns-Rizzo* • Ronald Weyand *Hypnotist* • Holly Hunter *Leslie* ■ *Dir* Anthony Harvey • *Scr* Frank Cucci, from a story by Sue Grafton

Swallows and Amazons ★★★ U
Adventure
1974 · UK · Colour · 88mins

Lovingly photographed by Denis Lewiston, this is an engaging, if hardly enthralling adaptation of the Arthur Ransome novel. Director Claude Whatham clearly revels in the innocence of this twenties summer, when the four swallows and two amazons embarked upon their adventures, and he makes the most of the beautiful Lake District scenery. But the story stubbornly refuses to come to life, and few modern youngsters will relate to such old-fashioned game-playing. 🖭

Virginia McKenna *Mrs Walker* • Ronald Fraser *Uncle Jim* • Brenda Bruce *Mrs Dixon* • Jack Woolgar *Old Billy* • John Franklyn-Robbins *Young Billy* • Simon West *John* • Zanna Hamilton *Susan* • Sophie Neville *Titty* ■ *Dir* Claude Whatham • *Scr* David Wood, from the novel by Arthur Ransome

Swamp Thing ★★ 15
Horror
1982 · US · Colour · 84mins

Wes Craven's terminally campy adaptation of the eco-friendly DC comic book character is a trivial pursuit into juvenile territory for the horror director. Dr Alec Holland (Ray Wise) is transformed into the half-man/half-slime creature after an accident with a plant growth stimulant and battles evil genius Arcane (Louis Jourdan), who sees the formula as a way to gain world domination. Adrienne Barbeau goes way beyond the call of duty as the vague heroine valiantly getting knocked around, falling in dirty swamp water and losing her clothes. Elsewhere the tacky special effects, cheap budget and banal dialogue doom this *Incredible Hulk* meets *Southern Comfort* affair. 🖭

Louis Jourdan *Arcane* • Adrienne Barbeau *Alice Cable* • Ray Wise *Dr Alec Holland* • David Hess *Ferret* • Nicholas Worth *Bruno* • Don Knight *Ritter* • Al Ruban *Charlie* • Dick Durock *Swamp Thing* ■ *Dir/Scr* Wes Craven

Swamp Water ★★
Melodrama
1941 · US · BW · 89mins

Like other European émigrés, the gifted French director Jean Renoir went to Hollywood to escape the Nazi occupation. But this, the first of his American films, was a disappointment. He was plunged in at the deep end in the isolated setting of the Georgia swampland, where escaped convict Walter Brennan hides and befriends trapper Dana Andrews. It's a story that needs more explanation than was given by the usually fine scriptwriter Dudley Nichols and a deeper understanding from Renoir himself.

Walter Brennan *Tom Keefer* • Walter Huston *Thursday Ragan* • Anne Baxter *Julie* • Dana Andrews *Ben Ragan* • Virginia Gilmore *Mabel Mckenzie* • John Carradine *Jesse Wick* • Mary Howard *Hannah* • Eugene Pallette *Jeb McKane* ■ *Dir* Jean Renoir • *Scr* Dudley Nichols, from a story by Vereen Bell

U = SUITABLE FOR ALL   Uc = SUITABLE FOR ALL, ESPECIALLY FOR YOUNG CHILDREN (VIDEO ONLY)   PG = PARENTAL GUIDANCE

The Swan ★★★ U

Romantic drama
1956 · US · Colour · 107mins

Best known today as Grace Kelly's final Hollywood production (it was released before *High Society*, though made after it), this features the star soon to become a princess playing a very MGM version of a princess in a lavish adaptation of a hoary old play by Ferenc Molnar, which had been filmed at least twice previously. You know the score: the beautiful Kelly is in love with handsome tutor Louis Jourdan, but she's officially betrothed to prince Alec Guinness. Director Charles Vidor understands this glossy tosh and films it beautifully, but Guinness (in his first American film) is miscast, and the whole thing rather falls to pieces in its slow second half.

Grace Kelly *Princess Alexandra* • Alec Guinness *Prince Albert* • Louis Jourdan *Dr Nicholas Agi* • Agnes Moorehead *Queen Maria Dominika* • Jessie Royce Landis *Princess Beatrix* • Brian Aherne *Father Hyacinth* • Leo G Carroll *Caesar* • Estelle Winwood *Symphorosa* ■ *Dir* Charles Vidor • *Scr* John Dighton, from the play by Ferenc Molnar

The Swan Princess ★★★ U

Animated musical
1994 · US · Colour · 85mins

A brave bid to produce a Disneyesque feature on a fraction of the budget, this politically correct fairy tale is entertaining enough, but it lacks the sparkle of the films it's trying to emulate. Director Richard Rich and character designer Steve Gordon, both Disney old boys, know the formula, but some rather uninspired artwork and the feeble songs undercut the neat reworking of *Swan Lake*. Jack Palance makes a booming Rothbart, while John Cleese is great fun as a French frog called Jean-Bob. Odette is good and feisty, but Prince Derek is a bit of a drip. ■ *DVD*

Jack Palance *Rothbart* • Howard McGillin *Prince Derek* • Michelle Nicastro *Princess Odette* • John Cleese *Jean-Bob* • Steven Wright *Speed* ■ *Dir* Richard Rich • *Scr* Brian Nissen, from a story by Richard Rich, Brian Nissen • *Animator* Steven E Gordon

The Swan Princess: The Secret of the Castle ★★ U

Animated fantasy 1997 · US · Colour · 71mins

Although the animation is serviceable, insufficient attention has been paid either to the plot or the comic relief, with the result that genuine wit and excitement are replaced merely by volume and pace. Younger viewers will probably still enjoy the third-rate pop songs that accompany Derek, Odette and their animal friends as they seek to prevent the evil Clavius from taking control of the all-powerful Black Arts. ■

Michelle Nicastro *Odette* • Douglas Sills *Derek* • Jake Williamson *Clavius* • Christy Landers *Uberta* • Donald Sage MacKay *Jean-Bob* • Doug Stone *Speed* ■ *Dir* Richard Rich • *Scr* Brian Nissen, from a story by Richard Rich, Brian Nissen

Swanee River ★★ U

Musical biography
1939 · US · Colour · 86mins

Don Ameche plays composer Stephen Foster (*Beautiful Dreamer*) in 20th Century-Fox's unintentionally camp biopic, in which every cliché uttered becomes a cue for a song. Naturally enough, he wants to pen symphonies, but finds he can't stop drowning his sorrows. Andrea Leeds is his luckless spouse, but the surprise casting of the movie is the great Al Jolson himself as EP Christy, the forerunner of the black-faced minstrels. Unfortunately, Fox's garish Technicolor makes him look as though he's fallen into a tub of boot polish. As you've gathered, the film's not high on taste, but fun if you're in a tolerant mood.

Don Ameche *Stephen Foster* • Al Jolson *EP Christy* • Andrea Leeds *Jane* • Felix Bressart *Henry Kleber* • Chick Chandler *Bones* • Russell Hicks *Andrew McDowell* • George Reed *Old Joe* ■ *Dir* Sidney Lanfield • *Scr* John Taintor Foote, Philip Dunne

Swann ★★★★ 15

Drama 1996 · Can/UK · Colour · 91mins

An elegant, passionate meditation on feminism. Bestselling author Miranda Richardson arrives at a small Canadian town to prepare a biography of local poet, Mary Swann, murdered by her husband. Brenda Fricker is Mary's closest friend and the film examines Richardson's growing relationship with her as she unravels the secrets of Swann's tragic death. Adapted from a novel by Carol Shields and directed by Anna Benson Gyles, it's a small film of great impact. ■

Miranda Richardson *Sarah Maloney* • Brenda Fricker *Rose Hindmarch* • Michael Ontkean *Stephen* • David Cubitt *Brownie* • John Neville *Cruzzi* • Sean McCann *Homer* • Sean Hewitt *Morton Jimroy* ■ *Dir* Anna Benson Gyles • *Scr* David Young, from the novel by Carol Shields

Swann in Love ★★ 18

Drama 1984 · Fr/W Ger · Colour · 105mins

Jeremy Irons makes a pig's ear out of Proust's novel *Un Amour de Swann* from *Remembrance of Things Past*. As the French aristocrat, Irons scampers after working-class totty Ornella Muti through the scummy streets of Paris. His lust is fulfilled, but he remains lovelorn, troubled by the fact that he genuinely cares for her. Alain Delon is more charismatic as the gay, butch Baron and Muti is suitably smutty and sexy, but this is an awkward affair that lacks any true passion. ■

Jeremy Irons *Charles Swann* • Ornella Muti *Odette de Crecy* • Alain Delon *Baron de Charlus* • Fanny Ardant *Duchesse de Guermantes* • Marie-Christine Barrault *Mrs Vedurin* • Anne Bennent *Chloe* • Nathalie Juvent *Madame Cottard* ■ *Dir* Volker Schlöndorff • *Scr* Peter Brook, Jean-Claude Carrière, Marie-Hélène Estienne, Volker Schlöndorff, from the novel *Un Amour de Swann* by Marcel Proust

The Swarm ★ 12

Disaster 1978 · US · Colour · 148mins

African killer bees are moving west and threatening to engulf Houston, Texas. Quick, call on entomologist Michael Caine and a hive of Hollywood has-beens to out-ham each other while reciting terrible dialogue and getting stung by coloured Styrofoam pellets! Producer/director Irwin Allen added new meaning to his "master of disaster" title with this bumbled B-movie, considered one of the worst ever made by popular consensus. However, there's tons to enjoy precisely because it is so awful. ▭

Michael Caine *Brad Crane* • Katharine Ross *Helena* • Richard Widmark *General Slater* • Richard Chamberlain *Dr Hubbard* • Olivia de Havilland *Maureen Schuster* • Ben Johnson *Felix* • Lee Grant *Anne MacGregor* • José Ferrer *Dr Andrews* • Patty Duke Astin [Patty Duke] *Rita Bard* • Fred MacMurray *Clarence* ■ *Dir* Irwin Allen • *Scr* Stirling Silliphant, from the novel by Arthur Herzog

Swashbuckler ★★★ PG

Swashbuckling adventure
1976 · US · Colour · 96mins

Unfairly dismissed at the time, this was a genuine attempt by Universal to re-create the kind of adventure film it used to deliver by the dozen: the good-natured pirate romp. Originally retitled *The Scarlet Buccaneer* for the UK, it evoked fond memories of its star's foray into similar territory on TV: a generation will recall a pre-*Jaws* Robert Shaw as swashbuckling Dan Tempest in the fifties series *The Buccaneers*. Shaw does well here, romancing lovely Genevieve Bujold and swapping riddles with James Earl Jones, but there was no audience for this kind of derring-do in the seventies. ▭

Robert Shaw *Ned Lynch* • James Earl Jones *Nick Debrett* • Peter Boyle *Lord Durant* • Geneviève Bujold *Jane Barnet* • Beau Bridges *Major Folly* • Geoffrey Holder *Cudjo* • Avery Schreiber *Polonski* • Anjelica Huston *Woman of Dark Visage* ■ *Dir* James Goldstone • *Scr* Jeffrey Bloom, from a story by Paul Wheeler

Swedenhielms ★★★

Drama 1935 · Swe · BW · 92mins

Directed by the great Gustav Molander, this was Ingrid Bergman's third film and, while she gives a wholehearted performance as an heiress hoping to marry into the family of a talented but poor scientist, the critics of the day considered her no more than "feelingful". Nevertheless, it's fascinating to see a legend in the making. The real star of the show, however, is Gösta Ekman as scientist Rolf Swedenhielm, who would go on to play opposite Bergman in her breakthrough picture *Intermezzo*. Karin Swanstrom also impresses as the sister-in-law who averts a scandal that would have jeopardised Ekman's chances of winning the Nobel Prize. In Swedish with English subtitles.

Gösta Ekman (1) *Rolf Swedenhielm* • Karin Swanstrom *Marta Boman* • Bjorn Berglund *Rolf Swedenhielm Jr* • Hakan Westergren *Bo Swedenhielm* • Tutta Rolf *Julia Swedenhielm* • Ingrid Bergman *Astrid* ■ *Dir* Gustaf Molander • *Scr* Stina Bergman, Gustaf Molander, from the play by Hjalmar Bergman

Sweeney! ★★★ 18

Crime drama 1976 · UK · Colour · 92mins

Not in the same manor as the legendary TV series, this spin-off is a reasonable reminder of what made John Thaw and Dennis Waterman as Regan and Carter the icons of seventies law enforcement.

Screenwriter Ranald Graham's unfamiliarity with the characters occasionally brings the action to a screeching halt. However, he cranks out a typically abrasive plot, which sees the boys investigating a suicide only to find themselves knee-deep in vice, blackmail and corruption. Thaw and Waterman are solid as rocks, although the guests brought in to give the project class (including Ian Bannen, Colin Welland and Barry Foster) try a little too hard. Contains violence and swearing. ▭

John Thaw *Detective Inspector Regan* • Dennis Waterman *Detective Sergeant Carter* • Barry Foster *McQueen* • Ian Bannen *Baker* • Colin Welland *Chadwick* • Diane Keen *Bianca* • Brian Glover *Mac* • Lynda Bellingham *Janice* ■ *Dir* David Wickes • *Scr* Ranald Graham, from the TV series by Ian Kennedy Martin

Sweeney 2 ★★ 18

Police drama 1978 · UK · Colour · 103mins

A dated-looking spin-off from the popular seventies TV series has flying-squadders Regan and Carter tackling upper-bracket bank robbers who fly in for each job to maintain their Mediterranean lifestyle. John Thaw and Dennis Waterman play the two tough 'tecs, struggling with material that would have barely filled a 50-minute television slot, let alone a full-length cinema feature. However it's certainly more violent than its small-screen cousin. Familiar faces to watch out for in the support cast include Denholm Elliott and Nigel Hawthorne. ▭

John Thaw *Detective Inspector Jack Regan* • Dennis Waterman *Detective Sergeant George Carter* • Denholm Elliott *Jupp* • David Casey *Goodyear* • Ken Hutchison *Hill* • Nigel Hawthorne *Dilke* • John Flanagan *Willard* • Derrick O'Connor *Llewellyn* ■ *Dir* Tom Clegg • *Scr* Troy Kennedy Martin, from the TV series by Ian Kennedy Martin

Sweeney Todd, the Demon Barber of Fleet Street ★★★

Horror 1936 · UK · BW · 66mins

Tod Slaughter was billed as "the Horror Man of Europe" for his forays into early chiller territory with titles like *Murder in the Red Barn* and *Crimes at the Dark House*. As the legendary throat-slitting barber, the aptly-named Slaughter turns in what every genre historian agrees is a quintessential performance. He's at his highly theatrical, villainous best in this dainty slice of British horror and, if you can ignore the creaks, this film is melodramatic fun.

Tod Slaughter *Sweeney Todd* • Eve Lister *Johanna* • Bruce Seton *Mack* • Davina Craig *Nan* • DJ Williams *Stephen Oakley* • Jerry Verno *Pearley* ■ *Dir* George King • *Scr* Frederick Hayward, HF Maltby, from the play by George Dibdin-Pitt

Sweepers ★★ 15

Action 1999 · US · Colour · 92mins

In a standard action movie that has a veneer of political correctness, Dolph Lundgren plays a landmine clearance expert who disappears into the Angolan wilderness after his young son is killed. Lundgren is found by bomb squad boffin Clare Stansfield and recruited to track down the lethal new A6 super-mine that's in the hands of terrorists. The impressive explosions help to overcome any humanitarian leanings the movie may have begun with as Lundgren picks off the bad guys. Another video favourite, Bruce Payne, offers solid support. 🖵

Dolph Lundgren *Christian Erickson* • Claire Stansfield *Michelle Flynn* • Bruce Payne *Cecil Hopper* • Ian Roberts *Yager* • Fats Bookholane *Old Mo* • Sifiso Maphanga *Arthur* ■ *Dir* Darby Black [Keoni Waxman] • *Scr* Darby Black [Keoni Waxman], Kevin Bernhardt

Sweet Adeline ★★

Period musical   1935 · US · BW · 87mins

A sweet-as-honey Irene Dunne takes the title role in this period (late 19th-century) musical, set in Hoboken, New Jersey where Adeline is adored by all the men who frequent her father's lovely beer garden. Spoilt for choice, she finally settles for songwriter Donald Woods. Directed by Mervyn LeRoy with dances staged by Bobby Connolly, this otherwise unremarkable, overly winsome and somewhat dull movie is partly redeemed by the Jerome Kern-Oscar Hammerstein II songs, which include *Why Was I Born?*, *Don't Ever Leave Me* and *Here Am I*.

Irene Dunne *Adeline Schmidt* • Donald Woods *Sid Barnett* • Hugh Herbert *Rupert Rockingham* • Ned Sparks *Dan Herziq* • Joseph Cawthorn *Oscar Schmidt* ■ *Dir* Mervyn LeRoy • *Scr* Irwin S Gelsey, from a musical by Jerome Kern, Oscar Hammerstein II

Sweet and Lowdown ★★

Musical   1944 · US · BW · 76mins

An aspiring trombone player (James Cardwell) who works in a factory is given his chance by Benny Goodman and goes on the road with the orchestra. But his youthful arrogance and swollen head almost put him back where he started. A minor entry from Fox, this moral tale-cum-romance with a fairytale outcome – directed by journeyman Archie Mayo – co-stars Jack Oakie as Goodman's loyal road manager, Lynn Bari as the band's predatory, cradle-snatching vocalist and Linda Darnell as the rich girl in love with Cardwell. Anodyne entertainment but with enough music to please fans of Goodman, who plays himself.

Linda Darnell *Trudy Wilson* • James Cardwell *Johnny Birch* • Lynn Bari *Pat Sterling* • Jack Oakie *Popsy* • Allyn Joslyn *Lester Barnes* • John Campbell *Dixie Zang* • Roy Benson *Skeets McCormick* • Dickie Moore *General Carmichael* • Benny Goodman ■ *Dir* Archie Mayo • *Scr* Richard English, from a story by Richard English, Edward Haldeman

Sweet and Lowdown
★★★★ PG

Period comedy drama
1999 · US · Colour · 95mins

After the disappointing *Celebrity*, Woody Allen bounds back with a sparkling biography of a fictional thirties jazzman whose life only makes sense when he's playing guitar. Sean Penn is Emmet Ray, a kleptomaniac musical genius whose idea of a good time is to watch trains, shoot rats and seduce women – though not necessarily in that order. Happiness comes in a sweetly fulfilling relationship with mute innocent Hattie (Samantha Morton), though the

feckless Ray is soon up to his old tricks with society gal Blanche (Uma Thurman). A host of jazz experts, including Allen himself, deliver straight-faced tributes to Ray's gift, while the costumes and production design are splendidly opulent. But it's British actress Morton who steals the show, getting her revenge after Penn breaks her heart by silently breaking ours.

Sean Penn *Emmet Ray* • Samantha Morton *Hattie* • Uma Thurman *Blanche* • Brian Markinson *Bill Shields* • Anthony LaPaglia *Al Torrio* • Gretchen Mol *Ellie* • Vincent Guastaferro *Sid Bishop* • John Waters *Mr Haynes* • Woody Allen ■ *Dir/Scr* Woody Allen • *Cinematographer* Zhao Fei • *Production Designer* Santo Loquasto

Sweet Angel Mine ★ 18

Psychological drama
1996 · UK/Can · Colour · 85mins

Shocking secrets are revealed when city teen Oliver Milburn goes to the bleak Canadian backwoods looking for his long-lost father. For barmy mother Alberta Watson kills any man lusting after her daughter Margaret Langrick and buries the victims in her "garden of dead roses". Director Curtis Radcliffe can't decide what sort of film he's making here – an exploitation horror movie complete with graphic gore, or a showy slice of arthouse surrealism taking an academic look at the taboo subjects of incest and child abuse. A pretentious psychological study that proves too schizophrenic to have any real point. 🖵

Oliver Milburn *Paul Davis* • Margaret Langrick *Rauchine* • Anna Massey *Mother* • Alberta Watson *Megan* • John Dunsworth *Billy Lee Davis* • Mike Crimp *Sergeant Taylor* ■ *Dir* Curtis Radcliffe • *Scr* Sam Maheu, Tim Willocks

Sweet Bird of Youth
★★★ 15

Melodrama   1962 · US · Colour · 115mins

The ingredients of Tennessee Williams's original stage play (racism, substance abuse, male prostitution, castration) are present, if muted in this bleak entertainment. The play, directed by Elia Kazan, starred Paul Newman and Geraldine Page. The movie, directed by Richard Brooks, retained the original leads and toned down the text for audiences in the conservative American Midwest. Despite obvious flaws, it's a polished production, with fine supporting performances from Rip Torn and Ed Begley, who won the best supporting actor Oscar.

Paul Newman *Chance Wayne* • Geraldine Page *Alexandra Del Lago* • Ed Begley *"Boss" Finley* • Shirley Knight *Heavenly Finley* • Rip Torn *Thomas J Finley Jr* • Mildred Dunnock *Aunt Nonnie* • Madeleine Sherwood *Miss Lucy* • Philip Abbott *Dr George Scudder* ■ *Dir* Richard Brooks • *Scr* Richard Brooks, from the play by Tennessee Williams

Sweet Bird of Youth ★★★

Drama   1989 · US · Colour

This TV-movie version of Tennessee Williams's celebrated play is perhaps more significant for academic reasons than cinematic ones. Based on screenwriter Gavin Lambert's exhaustive research, it's less a remake than a reinvention that draws

on a range of Williams's writings to reinterpret several key scenes. Elizabeth Taylor, something of a Williams specialist after *Cat on a Hot Tin Roof* and *Suddenly, Last Summer*, does well enough in the role made famous by Geraldine Page, while Rip Torn (who has been involved with the play on stage, cinema and TV) shows he knows the material inside out. Studious rather than steamy, and somewhat staid. Contains nudity.

Elizabeth Taylor *Alexandra Del Lago* • Mark Harmon *Chance Wayne* • Rip Torn *Tom Finley* • Valerie Perrine *Miss Lucy* • Kevin Geer *Tom Jr* • Seymour Cassel *Hatcher* • Cheryl Paris *Heavenly* ■ *Dir* Nicolas Roeg • *Scr* Gavin Lambert, from the play by Tennessee Williams

Sweet Charity ★★★ PG

Musical   1968 · US · Colour · 142mins

Dancer, theatre director and choreographic genius Bob Fosse made his film directing debut when he brought his Broadway hit to the screen. Based on Fellini's *Nights of Cabiria*, the musical was transposed to New York and chronicles the sad life of a dance-hall hostess whose sleazy experiences fail to dampen her belief in fairy-tale romance. Though it's jam-packed with stunning numbers – *Hey, Big Spender*, *Rhythm of Life*, *If They Could See Me Now* and more – the film is brash, gaudy and overheated and lacks the sophisticated edge and sharp impact of the stage original, with Shirley MacLaine's turbine-powered Charity substituting energy for subtlety. However Sammy Davis Jr, Chita Rivera and Paula Kelly are as electrifying as Fosse's choreography. 🖵

Shirley MacLaine *Charity Hope Valentine* • Sammy Davis Jr *Big Daddy* • Ricardo Montalban *Vittorio Vitale* • John McMartin *Oscar* • Chita Rivera *Nickie* • Paula Kelly *Helene* • Stubby Kaye *Herman* ■ *Dir* Bob Fosse • *Scr* Peter Stone, from the musical by Neil Simon, Cy Coleman, Dorothy Fields, from the film *Nights of Cabiria* by Federico Fellini, Ennio Flaiano, Tullio Pinelli

Sweet Dreams ★★★ 15

Biographical drama
1985 · US · Colour · 109mins

Having already produced the Loretta Lynn biopic *Coal Miner's Daughter*, Bernard Schwartz here turned his attention to her friendly rival for the Queen of Country title, Patsy Cline. The result is a film packed with fine acting and superb singing (provided, via record, by Cline herself). Unfortunately, the life story is pretty unremarkable, at least in the hands of writer Robert Getchell and director Karel Reisz. Consequently, the sparks between Jessica Lange and Ed Harris ignite nothing but their scenes together, giving the action a disappointingly staccato rhythm. Ultimately it does tug at the heartstrings, but not as much as it should. 🖵

Jessica Lange *Patsy Cline* • Ed Harris *Charlie Dick* • Ann Wedgeworth *Hilda Hensley* • David Clennon *Randy Hughes* • James Staley *Gerald Cline* • Gary Basaraba *Woodhouse* • John Goodman *Otis* • PJ Soles *Wanda* ■ *Dir* Karel Reisz • *Scr* Robert Getchell

Sweet Dreams ★

Mystery thriller   1996 · US · Colour

Beverly Hills 90210 bad girl Tiffani-Amber Thiessen should never have left her postcode to star in this nightmare about a business woman affected by amnesia who's rescued by a kindly cop when she is found half-drowned. As she struggles to recover and reclaim her past, married psychiatrist David Newsom offers his help, claiming they were once lovers. You'll wish you not only had amnesia, but were also in a coma after sitting through this made-for-TV nonsense.

Tiffani-Amber Thiessen *Alison Sullivan* • A Martinez *Doug Harrison* • David Newsom *Jack Renault* • Amy Yasbeck *Laura Renault* • Conchata Ferrell *Dr Kate Lowe* ■ *Dir* Jack Bender • *Scr* Bruce Miller

Sweet Emma Dear Böbe
★★★★ 18

Drama   1992 · Hun · Colour · 77mins

Best known for his insights of the nation's past, István Szabó demonstrates a sure grasp of contemporary reality in this despondent study of the newly liberated Hungary. Forced to abandon their careers as Russian teachers on the fall of Communism, Johanna Ter Steege and Enikö Börcsök personify the options open to a society emerging from decades of oppression. Reining in his fondness for stylistic flourish – yet barely suppressing his anger – Szabó struggles to find the light at the end of this dark passage of transition, as Ter Steege pursues a hopeless affair with her tyrannical headmaster and Börcsök flirts with rich foreign tourists. A Hungarian language film. 🖵

Johanna Ter Steege *Emma* • Enikö Börcsök *Böbe* • Peter Andorai *Stefanics* • Éva Kerekes *Sleepy* ■ *Dir* István Szabó • *Scr* István Szabó, from an idea by Andrea Veszits

Sweet Hearts Dance
★★★ 15

Comedy drama   1988 · US · Colour · 96mins

Don Johnson and Susan Sarandon are high school sweethearts who've been married for 15 years and have three children. Then Johnson realises he doesn't love his wife any more, just as his best buddy, Jeff Daniels, gets himself a new girlfriend. Scripted by Ernest Thompson, writer of *On Golden Pond*, this is a slightly ponderous study of marital angst, often warm and witty but lacking real bite. There are good performances, though, and one of the kids is played by Justin Henry from *Kramer vs Kramer*. Set in leafy Vermont, it somehow finds time for a comic and scenic Caribbean interlude. Contains swearing and nudity. 🖵

Don Johnson *Wiley Boon* • Susan Sarandon *Sandra Boon* • Jeff Daniels *Sam Manners* • Elizabeth Perkins *Adie Nims* • Kate Reid *Pearne Manners* • Justin Henry *Kyle Boon* • Holly Marie Combs *Debs Boon* • Heather Coleman *BJ Boon* ■ *Dir* Robert Greenwald • *Scr* Ernest Thompson

   U = SUITABLE FOR ALL   **Uc** = SUITABLE FOR ALL, ESPECIALLY FOR YOUNG CHILDREN (VIDEO ONLY)   **PG** = PARENTAL GUIDANCE

The Sweet Hereafter
★★★★ 15

Psychological drama
1997 · Can · Colour · 107mins

Atom Egoyan won the Grand Jury prize at Cannes and was also Oscar nominated for his direction and adaptation of Russell Banks's novel about the impact of a schoolbus crash (which kills 14 children) on a small Canadian community. Although the Pied Piper analogy is overemphasised, this is still an intricate and involving drama, in which the town's guilty secrets are slowly revealed as ambulance-chasing lawyer Ian Holm tries to persuade the bereaved to sue for damages. With Sarah Polley outstanding as a survivor paralysed by the accident, this is an intense, atmospheric and deeply moving experience. Contains some swearing and nudity. ▭

Ian Holm *Mitchell Stephens* • Sarah Polley *Nicole Burnell* • Bruce Greenwood *Billy Ansell* • Tom McCamus *Sam Burnell* • Gabrielle Rose *Dolores Driscoll* • Arsinée Khanjian *Wanda Otto* • Alberta Watson *Risa Walker* • Maury Chaykin *Wendell Walker* ■ *Dir* Atom Egoyan • *Scr* Atom Egoyan, from the novel by Russell Banks

Sweet Hostage
★★ 15

Drama　1975 · US · Colour · 90mins

Unsurprisingly hard to cast after her performance in *The Exorcist* two years earlier, Linda Blair was a natural choice for this wordy TV version of author Nathaniel Benchley's *Welcome to Xanadu*, as the illiterate farm girl kidnapped by a demented psychopath. Since this is TV movie land, the ingredients of the original tale have been considerably diluted, though Blair is very good. So is Martin Sheen, who becomes not just kidnapper but also teacher and ultimately lover. Pretty tasteless stuff, and Lee Philips, better known as an actor in *Peyton Place*, directs with little flair or style. ▭

Linda Blair *Doris Mae Withers* • Martin Sheen *Leonard Hatch* • Jeanne Cooper *Mrs Withers* • Bert Remsen *Mr Withers* • Lee DeBroux *Sherriff Emmet* • Dehl Berti *Harry Fox* ■ *Dir* Lee Philips • *Scr* Edward Hume, from the novel *Welcome to Xanadu* by Nathaniel Benchley

Sweet Hunters
★★★★

Drama　1969 · Pan · Colour · 100mins

A resolutely arty effort about an American who lives with his wife and son on a private island. The arrival of the professor's sister-in-law starts to upset the already delicate balance of relationships. Then – instead of the anticipated migratory birds – an escaped convict lands on the island. Some viewers may tire of this soul-searching drama after 20 minutes, but others will find it riveting, mainly due to Sterling Hayden's performance in which all of the actor's physical power and emotional weakness, as well as his troubled history, is laid open like a festering wound. Carl Orf's music provides a suitably mythic context for the allegorical drama.

Sterling Hayden *Allan* • Maureen McNally *Clea* • Susan Strasberg *Lis* • Andrew Hayden *Bob* • Stuart Whitman *Prisoner* ■ *Dir* Ruy Guerra • *Scr* Ruy Guerra, Philippe Dumarçay, Gérard Zingg

Sweet Justice
★★★ 15

Martial arts crime drama
1992 · US · Colour · 90mins

Finn Carter is a feisty kickboxer who returns to her small home town following the mysterious death of her estranged sister Suzanne, who was the local mayor. Discovering that Suzanne's business partner (Frank Gorshin) was up to no good, Carter decides to dispense her own brand of justice. Clichéd but at least not boring, it also features B-movie favourite Marc Singer. Fans of female action films will find the all-woman Special Forces team of particular interest. ▭

Marc Singer *Steve* • Finn Carter *Sunny Justice* • Frank Gorshin *Rivas* • Mickey Rooney ■ *Dir* Allen Plone • *Scr* Allen Plone, Jim Tabilio

Sweet Liberty
★★★ 15

Comedy　1986 · US · Colour · 101mins

Compared with *The Player*, this is little more than a mild nip at the movie world. However, there are still plenty of laughs to be had as small-town college professor Alan Alda (writer/director/star) gets sucked into the ego-ridden lives of a movie crew when they make a film based on his American War of Independence novel. Michael Caine steals the show as the womanising lead, but there is handsome support from Michelle Pfeiffer, Bob Hoskins and Saul Rubinek. Overall, though, the requisite bite is missing. Contains some swearing and brief nudity. ▭

Alan Alda *Michael Burgess* • Michael Caine *Elliott James* • Michelle Pfeiffer *Faith Healy* • Bob Hoskins *Stanley Gould* • Lise Hilboldt *Gretchen Carlsen* • Lillian Gish *Cecelia Burgess* • Saul Rubinek *Bo Hodges* • Lois Chiles *Leslie* ■ *Dir/Scr* Alan Alda

Sweet Nothing
★★ 18

Drama　1995 · US · Colour · 85mins

Released just after Mira Sorvino won her Oscar for *Mighty Aphrodite* (the cynical may believe the two events are linked), this grim drama is about a white-collar worker who gets dragged into drug addiction. Michael Imperioli persuades his reluctant wife to agree to a three-month limited term of dealing crack in order to provide money for his family. Three years later and they're both hooked: he to the drug, his wife to the money. His predictable descent to rock-bottom is portrayed without mercy to either the characters or the audience. Contains swearing and some violence. ▭

Michael Imperioli *Angel* • Mira Sorvino *Monika* • Paul Calderon *Raymond* • Patrick Breen *Greg* • Richard Bright *Jack the Cop* • Billie Neal *Rio* ■ *Dir* Gary Winick • *Scr* Lee Drysdale

Sweet November
★★

Comedy drama　1968 · US · Colour · 112mins

Suffering from a chronic case of the cutes, Sandy Dennis and Anthony Newley star here in director Robert Ellis Miller's oddly effective, but undoubtedly eccentric tragicomedy. She's doing her best, as an amateur sex therapist, to take a lover a month to rid them of their inhibitions. Trouble is that November's lodger, tycoon Newley, wants to claim her permissive life all to himself. The idea works surprisingly well at first, but both stars

seem to be in competition, trying to make irritating ad libs out of Herman Raucher's script. It all becomes exasperatingly coy, and to make matters worse the largely unknown support cast makes little impact.

Sandy Dennis *Sara Deever* • Anthony Newley *Charlie Blake* • Theodore Bikel *Alonzo* • Burr DeBenning *Clem Batchman* • Sandy Baron *Richard* • Marj Dusay *Carol* • Martin West *Gordon* ■ *Dir* Robert Ellis Miller • *Scr* Herman Raucher

Sweet Poison
★★★ 18

Thriller　1991 · US · Colour · 96mins

Steven Bauer is the sexy criminal who escapes from custody and takes a married couple hostage. He's soon getting passionate with the wife (played by Patty Healy), and together they decide to dispose of her husband (Edward Herrmann) in this predictable thriller. It's a passable cross between *The Postman Always Rings Twice* and *The Desperate Hours*, but it's not as good as either. Bauer, though, isn't bad, and one wonders why his film career hasn't been more successful. Contains violence and swearing. ▭

Edward Herrmann *Henry Odell* • Steven Bauer *Bobby Stiles* • Patty Healy *Charlene Odell* • Pruitt Taylor Vince *Coyle* • Lyman Ward *Metz* • Noble Willingham *Clemens* • John Hawkes *Jimmy* • Eric Bruskotter *JJ* ■ *Dir* Brian Grant • *Scr* Wally Klenhard

Sweet Revenge
★★ PG

Romantic comedy
1990 · US/Fr · Colour · 84mins

This mildly amusing romantic comedy has a clever plot that never quite leaves the starting blocks despite the efforts of its stars Rosanna Arquette and Carrie Fisher. Basically the plot revolves around a divorce settlement that goes haywire when attorney Carrie Fisher finds that she must pay alimony to her ex-husband John Sessions, a struggling writer, until he remarries. In desperation, she recruits actress Rosanna Arquette to lure him into matrimony. This tepid tale does try hard with a cute plot twist, but ultimately it fails to be nothing more than standard TV movie fluff. ▭

Rosanna Arquette *Kate Williams* • Carrie Fisher *Linda Michaels* • John Sessions *John Michaels* • John Hargreaves *Jim Harris* • François-Eric Gendron *Frank Marsh* • Myriam Moszko *Ruth* ■ *Dir* Charlotte Brandstrom • *Scr* Janet Brownell

The Sweet Ride
★★

Drama　1967 · US · Colour · 109mins

Jacqueline Bisset fans covet this picture about the beach culture of southern California. It was Bisset's first major role in a Hollywood picture, coming just before *The Detective* and *Bullitt*, but it's a good deal more revealing than those. Yes, one does miss Frankie Avalon, Fabian and Annette Funicello, but this is much more grown-up stuff that even alludes to the Vietnam War. Bisset plays a TV soap star who drops her producer for an affair with Michael Sarrazin, a tennis hustler who appears to like Bisset's penchant for rough trade.

Tony Franciosa [Anthony Franciosa] *Collie Ransom* • Michael Sarrazin *Denny McGuire* • Jacqueline Bisset *Vicki Cartwright, actress* •

Bob Denver *Choo-Choo Burns, jazz pianist* • Michael Wilding *Mr Cartwright* • Michele Carey *Thumper* • Norma Crane *Mrs Cartwright* ■ *Dir* Harvey Hart • *Scr* Tom Mankiewicz, from the novel by William Murray

Sweet Rosie O'Grady
★★★ U

Musical comedy　1943 · US · Colour · 75mins

An extremely entertaining 20th Century-Fox Technicolor musical and a vehicle for Betty Grable; for many that's recommendation enough. It's all about a burlesque queen and an inquisitive reporter, and if that sounds a mite familiar, that's because it is. Fox is up to its old tricks again with this remake of 1937's *Love Is News*, itself remade again in 1948 as *That Wonderful Urge*. Both versions starred Tyrone Power as the newspaper man; here the character is played by Robert Young, presumably because Power was off fighting in the Second World War. Anyway, this time the plot is set in late-19th century London, and Adolphe Menjou is particularly watchable as the editor of the *Police Gazette*.

Betty Grable *Madeleine Marlowe* • Robert Young *Sam MacKeever* • Adolphe Menjou *Morgan* • Reginald Gardiner *Duke Charles* • Virginia Grey *Edna Van Dyke* • Phil Regan *Composer* • Sig Rumann [Sig Ruman] *Joe Flugelman* • Alan Dinehart *Arthur Skinner* ■ *Dir* Irving Cummings • *Scr* Ken Englund, from a story by William R Lipman, Frederick Stephani, Edward Van Every

Sweet Smell of Success
★★★★★ PG

Drama　1957 · US · BW · 92mins

Not a box-office success in its day, this mordant satire has rightly picked up admirers over the years, and is at long last recognised for the classic that it is. It contains key career highs for Burt Lancaster, as the vicious Broadway columnist JJ Hunsecker, and Tony Curtis as Sidney Falco, the hustling press agent totally under Hunsecker's all-powerful thumb. Lancaster's relationship with his sister Susan Harrison is particularly perverse, and provides the plot thrust for the Faustian pact, which is still relevant in an era of dubious media ethics. Diamond-hard photography from the great James Wong Howe and a sizzling Clifford Odets screenplay contribute immeasurably to this film's brutal quality, and it remains a milestone tribute to its canny British director Alexander Mackendrick.

Burt Lancaster *JJ Hunsecker* • Tony Curtis *Sidney Falco* • Susan Harrison *Susan Hunsecker* • Martin Milner *Steve Dallas* • Sam Levene *Frank D'Angelo* • Barbara Nichols *Rita* • Jeff Donnell *Sally* • Joseph Leon *Robard* ■ *Dir* Alexander Mackendrick • *Scr* Clifford Odets, Ernest Lehman, from the short story *Tell Me About It* by Ernest Lehman

Sweet Sweetback's Baad Asssss Song
★★★★ 18

Blaxploitation　1971 · US · Colour · 92mins

An important feature in the history of black film-making in the States, this is an angry riposte to the stereotypical characters that exist in both mainstream and blaxploitation pictures. Written, directed, edited and scored by its star, Melvin Van Peebles, it's a film that couldn't care less if it makes any friends. It can be loosely labelled a road movie, yet the relentless stream of sex, violence and prejudice, described with a mixture of realism, artifice and grim humour, isn't supposed to entertain, but rather incite. Still astonishing 30 years after its controversial release. Contains swearing and nudity.

Melvin Van Peebles *Sweetback* • Simon Chuckster *Beetle* • Hubert Scales *Mu-Mu* • John Dullaghan *Commissioner* • Rhetta Hughes *Old girlfriend* ■ *Dir/Scr* Melvin Van Peebles

Sweet Temptation ★★
Erotic drama 1996 · US · Colour

A melodramatic erotic drama in which Beverly D'Angelo finds herself on a collision course with her teenage daughter when the latter falls for her toyboy fiancé. D'Angelo is fine and there are capable supporting turns from TV regulars such as *Melrose Place*'s Rob Estes and *Knots Landing*'s Ted Shackelford. However, the direction and script for this TV movie are strictly by numbers. Contains swearing and violence.

Beverly D'Angelo *Jesse Larson* • Rob Estes *Billy Stone* • Ted Shackelford *Les* ■ *Dir* Ron Lagomarsino • *Scr* Joyce Eliason

Sweet Torture ★★
Drama 1971 · Fr · Colour · 90mins

Expanded from a one-act play by Georges Arnaud, this could have been a sobering exposé of police brutality and corrupt detective practices. However, Edouard Molinaro overcooks the interrogation of Marc Porel, who is prepared to shop his partner – he killed a ticket clerk during a raid on a visiting circus – in order to marry his loyal girlfriend, Caroline Cellier. But sadistic inspectors Philippe Noiret and Roger Hanin aren't content with simple snitching and try to beat a self-incriminating confession out of him. For all the melodramatic fireworks, Molinaro doesn't seem interested in either theme or character and only Noiret emerges with any credit. French dialogue dubbed into English.

Philippe Noiret *Chief Inspector* • Roger Hanin *Insp Borelli* • Marc Porel *Dubreuilh* • Caroline Cellier *Catherine* ■ *Dir* Edouard Molinaro • *Scr* JF Hauduroy, Edouard Molinaro, from a play by Georges Arnaud

Sweet William ★★
Drama 1980 · UK · Colour · 91mins

A rather languid drama, adapted from her own novel by Beryl Bainbridge and directed by Claude Whatham, who made *That'll Be the Day* and the film of Arthur Ransome's *Swallows and Amazons*. Sam Waterston plays a Scot with a bevy of ex-wives and girlfriends; Jenny Agutter falls for him and lives to regret it. Despite the presence of a decent cast (Anna Massey, Tim Pigott-Smith, Geraldine James), this portrait of a rather unpleasant cad lacks a real cutting edge. Contains some swearing and nudity.

Sam Waterston *William McClusky* • Jenny Agutter *Ann Walton* • Anna Massey *Edna* • Geraldine James *Pamela* • Daphne Oxenford *Mrs Walton* • Rachel Bell *Mrs Kershaw* •

David Wood *Vicar* • Tim Pigott-Smith *Gerald* ■ *Dir* Claude Whatham • *Scr* Beryl Bainbridge, from her novel

Sweetheart of the Campus ★
Musical 1941 · US · BW · 64mins

This small-scale clanger of a campus musical marked both the return to the screen after a three-year absence of Ruby Keeler and (with the exception of a forgotten cameo) her permanent exit remarriage and retirement. The one-note, boring plot has something to do with bandleader Ozzie Nelson and his troupe involved with attempts to encourage intake at a college when student enrolment has dropped. Seven uninspired musical numbers serve only as sporadic fillers for the gaping hole that is the script. What Edward Dmytryk was doing in the director's chair is anybody's guess.

Ruby Keeler *Betty Blake* • Ozzie Nelson *Ozzie Norton* • Harriet Hilliard *Harriet Hale* • Gordon Oliver *Terry Jones* • Don Beddoe *Sheriff Denby* • Charles Judels *Victor Demond* • Kathleen Howard *Mrs Minnie Sparr* • Alan Hale Jr *Football player* ■ *Dir* Edward Dmytryk • *Scr* Robert D Andrews, Edmann Hartmann, from a story by Robert D Andrews

Sweethearts ★★★
Musical comedy 1938 · US · Colour · 120mins

As the first-ever MGM feature filmed wholly in three-strip Technicolor (*The Wizard of Oz* was part colour, part sepia), this musical comedy has historical significance, though that same process tends to overshadow the popular star team of Jeanette MacDonald and Nelson Eddy. They warble through the Victor Herbert score and struggle through a brand new Dorothy Parker-Alan Campbell screenplay, but much of their thunder is stolen by dance-whiz Ray Bolger. The Broadway to Hollywood plot was well worn even then, but the production value more than compensate.

Jeanette MacDonald *Gwen Marlowe* • Nelson Eddy *Ernest Lane* • Frank Morgan *Felix Lehman* • Ray Bolger *Hans the dancer* • Florence Rice *Kay Jordan* • Mischa Auer *Leo Kronk* • Fay Holden *Hannah the dresser* ■ *Dir* WS Van Dyke II [WS Van Dyke] • *Scr* Dorothy Parker, Alan Campbell, from the operetta by Harry B Smith, Fred DeGresac, Robert B Smith, Victor Herbert

Sweetie ★★★★ 15
Comedy drama 1989 · Ausl · Colour · 95mins

Although better known for her critically acclaimed 1993 hit *The Piano*, director Jane Campion's first film for the cinema, *Sweetie*, is a far more quirky and original movie that quickly established her as one of the most interesting directors working today. Part comedy, part drama, it follows the lives of two eccentric sisters and their equally unstable lovers when they come together under one roof. Like David Lynch's *Blue Velvet*, the film shows us the surreal side of suburbia, where even the most ordinary person is not what he or she seems. Funny, affecting and wonderful. Contains swearing and nudity.

Genevieve Lemon *Dawn, "Sweetie"* • Karen Colston *Kay* • Tom Lycos *Louis* • Jon Darling *Gordon* • Dorothy Barry *Flo* • Michael Lake

Bob • André Pataczek *Clayton* ■ *Dir* Jane Campion • *Scr* Gerard Lee, Jane Campion, from an idea by Jane Campion

Swell Guy ★★
Melodrama 1946 · US · BW · 86mins

The ironic title refers to a war correspondent (Sonny Tufts) who returns home to his brother and sister-in-law in a small town where he is fêted as a celebrity. But he is in fact a manipulative, dishonest bad apple who wreaks havoc on his brother's marriage, dishonours a wealthy local girl (Ann Blyth) and cons the citizenry. Adapted by Richard Brooks from a play, *The Hero*, the film as directed by Frank Tuttle is solid in all departments, but winds up as disappointingly aimless and unrevealing.

Sonny Tufts *Jim Duncan* • Ann Blyth *Marian Tyler* • Ruth Warrick *Ann Duncan* • William Gargan *Martin Duncan* • John Litel *Arthur Tyler* • Thomas Gomez *Dave Vinson* • Millard Mitchell *Steve* • Mary Nash *Sarah Duncan* ■ *Dir* Frank Tuttle • *Scr* Richard Brooks, from the play *The Hero* by Gilbert Emery

Swept Away... by an Unusual Destiny in the Blue Sea of August ★★
Comedy drama 1974 · It · Colour · 120mins

Predictable sparks fly when dismissive Milanese socialite Mariangela Melato and communist sailor Giancarlo Giannini wash up on a desert island during a yachting trip. Forced back to nature, their class differences crumble in an *Admirable Crichton* sort of way, with Melato seemingly thrilled by Giannini's increasingly macho posturing. However, in defending her film against a feminist backlash, Lina Wertmuller claimed that everyone had got it wrong and that Melato symbolised bourgeois male arrogance rather than submissive womanhood. Nice try, but for all its lushness and actorly commitment, this lacks the ironic wit to be that incisive. An Italian language film.

Giancarlo Giannini *Gennarino Carunchio* • Mariangela Melato *Raffaella Lanzetti* • Riccardo Salvino *Raffaela's husband* ■ *Dir/Scr* Lina Wertmuller

The Swimmer ★★★★ PG
Fantasy drama 1968 · US · Colour · 90mins

If you've seen that jeans advertisement where a hunk takes a dip in a dozen pools to the strains of *Mad about the Boy*, check out *The Swimmer*, for this is the original. Based on a story by cult writer John Cheever, it stars Burt Lancaster as a washed-up suburban man who decides to swim home, using all the pools in his neighbourhood. This is not only healthy (and Lancaster looks terrific in his trunks); it's also a metaphor for alienation from affluence, sexual desire and Vietnam. Not to everyone's taste, this weird picture now seems an oddly powerful companion piece to *The Graduate*.

Burt Lancaster *Ned Merrill* • Janet Landgard *Julie Hooper* • Janice Rule *Shirley Abbott* • Tony Bickley *Donald Westerhazy* • Marge Champion *Peggy Forsburgh* • Nancy Cushman *Mrs Halloran* • Bill Fiore *Howie Hunsacker* ■ *Dir* Frank Perry • *Scr* Eleanor Perry, from the short story by John Cheever

The Swimming Pool ★★
Drama 1968 · Fr/It · Colour · 119mins

A pool in St Tropez provides the setting for this sexual roundelay. The men are two of France's biggest stars – Alain Delon and Maurice Ronet – and the women are Romy Schneider and Jane Birkin, in her first major role following brief appearances in *The Knack* and *Blow Up*. It's a case of he fancies her, she fancies him and round and round they go, until someone ends up in the deep end. A bit too long and the plot doesn't really get anywhere, but the glam trappings have a certain retro appeal. French dialogue dubbed into English.

Alain Delon *Jean-Paul* • Romy Schneider *Marianne* • Maurice Ronet *Harry* • Jane Birkin *Penelope* ■ *Dir* Jacques Deray • *Scr* Jean-Emmanuel Conil, Jean-Claude Carrière, Jacques Deray

Swimming to Cambodia ★★★ 18
Satirical monologue 1987 · US · Colour · 77mins

Spalding Gray described his experiences filming *The Killing Fields* in a one-man stage show, here condensed into a shorter film by director Jonathan Demme. Covering the same ground – the appalling conflict and atrocities which happened in Cambodia – Gray basically delivers a monologue to camera, explaining his experiences in the film from casting to finding out about the Khmer Rouge. Criticised for being a self-aggrandising attempt to capitalise on his small role in the film, Gray insisted that he was trying to show how his experiences as an actor helped him understand the nature of war. He succeeds in his objective, making the horror of war clearer to the audience too.

Spalding Gray • Sam Waterston *Sydney Schanberg* • Ira Wheeler *Ambassador Wade* ■ *Dir* Jonathan Demme • *Scr* Spalding Gray, from his play

Swimming with Sharks ★★★ 15
Comedy 1994 · US · Colour · 89mins

While not in the same class as *The Player*, this savage Tinseltown satire from director George Huang is often hilarious in between its bouts of numbingly bleak cynicism. Unfolding its story in a series of flashbacks, it features Frank Whaley as the hapless assistant of heartless Hollywood mogul Kevin Spacey, who enjoys exercising his power right down to the brand of sweetener he wants in his coffee. Spacey's dazzling portrayal of the acid-tongued executive is the most memorable facet of this tar-black comedy, which is heavy on industry in-jokes and vicious put-downs. Contains swearing and violence.

Kevin Spacey *Buddy Ackerman* • Frank Whaley *Guy* • Michelle Forbes *Dawn Lockard* • Benicio Del Toro *Rex* • TE Russell *Foster Kane* • Roy Dotrice *Cyrus Miles* • Matthew Flynt *Manny* ■ *Dir/Scr* George Huang

Swimsuit ★
Comedy 1989 · US · Colour · 95mins

The TV-movie industry has thrown up some rubbish over the years, but

nothing can compare to this dismal comedy, in which William Katt tries to revive the fortunes of his clothing company by inviting suggestions for a new range of swimwear. Little more than an excuse to parade a good deal of flesh, this unforgivable mess was directed by Chris Thomson, whose peekaboo style and inability to time even the most straightforward gag will have you wincing with embarrassment.

William Katt *Brian* • Catherine Oxenberg *Jade* • Cyd Charisse *Mrs Allison* • Nia Peeples *Maria* • Cheryl A Pollak [Cheryl Pollak] *Rosy* ■ *Dir* Chris Thomson • *Scr* Robin Schiff

The Swindle ★★★
Crime drama   1955 · Fr/It · BW · 117mins

The fabled prospect of Federico Fellini directing Humphrey Bogart haunts this biting tragicomedy, although Broderick Crawford still makes a decent fist of playing alongside Richard Basehart and Franco Fabrizi as the provincial con men out to fleece the desolate, the devout and the disabled. Having posed as priests and petty bureaucrats, the gang disperses, only for Crawford to hook up with new confrères and be undone by a fatal pang of conscience. Determined to bury his neorealist past, Fellini achieves a cynical authenticity here that even undermines the faint optimism of his calculatedly ambiguous finale. Minor, but equally delicious and malicious. An Italian language film.

Broderick Crawford *Augusto* • Richard Basehart *Picasso* • Franco Fabrizi *Roberto* • Giulietta Masina *Iris* • Lorella De Luca *Patrizia* ■ *Dir* Federico Fellini • *Scr* Federico Fellini, Ennio Flaiano, Tullio Pinelli, from a story by Federico Fellini, Ennio Flaiano

Swing ★★★★
Drama   1983 · W Ger · Colour · 130mins

Based on a 1934 autobiographical novel by Annette Kolb, Percy Adlon's warmly nostalgic, almost carelessly episodic study of an unconventional family's eccentric adventures, has a zest one rarely associates with costume dramas. Although every bit as punctilious in its period detail as his Proust memoir, *Céleste* (1981), the endless round of garden parties, recitals, balls, theatre visits and encounters with royalty and celebrity sweeps along the willing imagination and evokes a glorious sense of the *joie de vivre* of childhood that contrasts so mischievously with the stiffness of singing teacher Christine Kaufmann and court gardener Rolf Illig, the disapproving Prussian neighbours. A German language film.

Anja Jaenicke *Mathias Lautenschlag* • Joachim Bernhard *Otto Lautenschlag* • Lena Stolze *Gervaise Lautenschlag* • Rolf Illig *Herr Lautenschlag* • Christine Kaufmann *Mme Lautenschlag* ■ *Dir* Percy Adlon • *Scr* Percy Adlon, from the novel *Die Schaukel* by Annette Kolb

Swing ★★ 15
Musical comedy drama
1998 · UK · Colour · 93mins

In a piece of uninspired casting, singer Lisa Stansfield plays – you guessed it – a singer in this run-of-the-mill Liverpudlian romantic comedy. She's the ex-girlfriend of ex-con Hugo Speer, who joins his swing band against the

wishes of her policeman husband (Danny McCall). It's predictable but likeable fare, with a nice performance (and even better vocals) from Stansfield, and peppered with fun supporting turns from the likes of Alexei Sayle and what seems to be half the cast of *Brookside*. The biggest surprise, however, is the appearance by Bruce Springsteen's saxophonist Clarence Clemons, who adds much-needed class to the proceedings as the sax-playing philosopher with whom Speer shares a jail cell. Contains swearing. ▭

Hugo Speer *Martin Luxford* • Lisa Stansfield *Joan Woodcock* • Tom Bell *Sid Luxford* • Rita Tushingham *Mags Luxford* • Alexei Sayle *Mighty Mac* • Paul Usher *Liam Luxford* • Danny McCall *Andy* • Clarence Clemons *Jack* ■ *Dir* Nick Mead • *Scr* Nick Mead, from a story by Su Lim, Nick Mead

Swing Fever ★★
Musical sports comedy
1943 · US · BW · 80mins

Bespectacled, sophomoronic bandleader Kay Kyser, instead of remaining behind his baton where he belonged, was asked to carry it for this silly MGM second feature. As a hick composer who also knows how to hypnotise people, Kyser uses his skill on a boxer in order to fix a fight. On the plus side, Marilyn Maxwell plays a scheming blonde, and Lena Horne sings *You're So Indifferent*. Ava Gardner, still two years away from stardom, is seen briefly as a receptionist

Kay Kyser *Lowell Blackford* • Marilyn Maxwell *Ginger Gray* • William Gargan *"Waltzy" Malone* • Nat Pendleton *"Killer" Kennedy* • Lena Horne • Ava Gardner *Receptionist* ■ *Dir* Tim Whelan • *Scr* Nat Perrin, Warren Wilson, from a story by Matt Brooks, Joseph Hoffman

Swing High, Swing Low
★★★
Drama   1937 · US · BW · 92mins

Originally a hit play called *Burlesque*, this was filmed in 1929 as a tearjerking backstage drama, *The Dance of Life*, with Nancy Carroll and Hal Skelly, and would surface again in 1948 as the musical *When My Baby Smiles at Me* with Betty Grable and Dan Dailey. Here, comedy is effectively mixed in to the drama about a newly married showbiz couple who come unstuck when he, a trumpeter, gets a job in a New York nightclub and is seduced by the singer (Dorothy Lamour). Mitchell Leisen is in full command of the material.

Carole Lombard *Maggie King* • Fred MacMurray *Skid Johnson* • Charles Butterworth *Harry* • Jean Dixon *Ella* • Dorothy Lamour *Anita Alvarez* • Harvey Stephens *Harvey Howel* • Anthony Quinn *The Don* ■ *Dir* Mitchell Leisen • *Scr* Virginia Van Upp, Oscar Hammerstein Ii, from the play *Burlesque* by George Manker Watters, Arthur Hopkins

Swing Kids ★★ 15
Drama   1993 · US · Colour · 109mins

Set in Germany during the Nazi uprising, this film poses an interesting dilemma. A group of youngsters, led by Robert Sean Leonard and Christian Bale, are torn between the rise of Hitler Youth and the popularity of

American Swing music and dance. The premise, however, is muted by a lack of directorial punch from Thomas Carter and though the actors are appealing, lack of period detail and overly long sequences of swing dull down a good idea. The best bit is Kenneth Branagh's appearance as a nasty SS officer. ▭

Robert Sean Leonard *Peter* • Christian Bale *Thomas* • Frank Whaley *Arvid* • Barbara Hershey *Frau Muller* • Kenneth Branagh *SS official* • Tushka Bergen *Evey* • David Tom *Willi* • Julia Stemberger *Frau Linge* ■ *Dir* Thomas Carter • *Scr* Jonathan Marc Feldman

Swing Shift ★★★★ PG
Romantic drama   1984 · US · Colour · 99mins

Directed by Jonathan Demme before he became known for movies such as *The Silence of the Lambs* and *Philadelphia*, this is a small but often delightful romantic drama that went by largely unnoticed on its limited cinema release in Britain. Goldie Hawn is the unassuming housewife who goes to work in a factory during the Second World War while her husband (Ed Harris) is away fighting, and it is there that she meets free spirit Christine Lahti and cool trumpeter Kurt Russell. It was allegedly during filming that Hawn and Russell fell in love in real life, and they are certainly convincing as the two poles-apart lovers drawn together in a wartorn world. Funny and moving, this film also boasts early roles for Holly Hunter and singer Belinda Carlisle. Contains swearing.

Goldie Hawn *Kay Walsh* • Kurt Russell *Lucky Lockhart* • Christine Lahti *Hazel Zanussi* • Fred Ward *Biscuits Toohey* • Ed Harris *Jack Walsh* • Holly Hunter *Jeannie Sherman* • Belinda Carlisle *Jamboree singer* ■ *Dir* Jonathan Demme • *Scr* Rob Morton

Swing Shift Maisie ★★ U
Comedy   1943 · US · BW · 86mins

It's the Second World War and Maisie (Ann Sothern) is out in the cold when her latest cabaret act folds. Without a dime to her name, she talks her way into an aircraft-building factory, falls for test pilot James Craig and saves him from the scheming clutches of her roommate (Jean Rogers) Although the background was topical, this entry in the continuing adventures of the one and only Maisie strains for content and is really rather tedious.

Ann Sothern *Maisie Ravier* • James Craig *Brian B "Breezy" McLaughlin* • Jean Rogers *Iris Reed* • Connie Gilchrist *Maw Lustvogel* • John Qualen *Horatio Curley* • Fred Brady *Judd Evans* ■ *Dir* Norman Z McLeod • *Scr* Mary C McCall Jr, Robert Halff, from the character created by Wilson Collison

Swing Time ★★★★★ U
Musical   1936 · US · BW · 103mins

Top Hat might have been more popular, but this is actually the finest of the Fred Astaire/Ginger Rogers movies. Working with a major director in George Stevens, Fred and Ginger achieve such heights that to single out a particular instance might seem invidious. But the climactic *Never Gonna Dance* seems to provide the perfect example of the effortless style Astaire was able to convey, and the dialogue scene between the pair that

precedes the dance is among their most poignant. The plot? Who cares, when the Jerome Kern score includes *The Way You Look Tonight*, *A Fine Romance*, *Pick Yourself Up* and *Bojangles of Harlem*? ▭

Fred Astaire *John "Lucky" Garnett* • Ginger Rogers *Penelope "Penny" Carrol* • Victor Moore *Dr Cardetti, "Pop"* • Helen Broderick *Mabel Anderson* • Eric Blore *Mr Gordon* • Betty Furness *Margaret Watson* • George Metaxa *Ricardo Romero* ■ *Dir* George Stevens • *Scr* Howard Lindsay, Allan Scott, from a story by Erwin Gelsey • *Choreographer* Hermes Pan

The Swinger ★★
Romantic comedy
1966 · US · Colour · 80mins

This sixties sex tale was designed to exploit the pneumatic charms of Swedish-American starlet Ann-Margret. Here she's Kelly Olsson, a writer of love stories who is frustrated when saucy magazine *Girl-Lure* turns down her work for being too innocent. Determined to prove them wrong, she steals sleazy material from lurid paperbacks and passes it off as semi-autobiographical material, thus piquing the interest of editor Anthony Franciosa and his seedy boss Robert Coote. Of course, her attempts to live up to such a bacchanalian lifestyle backfire.

Ann-Margret *Kelly Olsson* • Anthony Franciosa *Ric Colby* • Robert Coote *Sir Hubert Charles* • Yvonne Romain *Karen Charles* • Nydia Westman *Aunt Cora* • Craig Hill *Sammy Jenkins* • Milton Frome *Mr Olsson* • Mary LaRoche *Mrs Olssen* ■ *Dir* George Sidney • *Scr* Lawrence Roman

Swingers ★★★★ 15
Comedy drama   1996 · US · Colour · 92mins

An honest exploration of male friendship based on lead actor Jon Favreau's autobiographical script about his first years in Hollywood. He, and three other out-of-work buddies, bar hop around LA's hip watering holes, bitch nonstop, continually try to pick up women and wait endlessly by the phone for that all important call. A highly original and entertaining delight using hilariously side-splitting situations to illuminate male neuroses in an uncompromising way. Complete with discussions on the various merits of Martin Scorsese and Quentin Tarantino, with affectionate direction by Doug Liman to match those two masters, this independent labour of love carries the solid ring of truth and a superb performance by Vince Vaughn. Contains swearing. ᴅᴠᴅ

Jon Favreau *Mike* • Vince Vaughn *Trent* • Ron Livingston *Rob* • Patrick Van Horn *Sue* • Alex Desert *Charles* • Heather Graham *Lorraine* • Deena Martin *Christy* ■ *Dir* Doug Liman • *Scr* Jon Favreau • *Cinematographer* Doug Liman

The Swiss Conspiracy ★★ 15
Thriller   1975 · US/W Ger · Colour · 85mins

Jack Arnold, more at home with sci-fi horror movies such as *It Came from Outer Space* and *Creature from the Black Lagoon*, directed this dismal thriller in which David Janssen is hired to protect high-class Swiss banking customers, at the same time proving you can still be a star with a face that completely lacks expression. At least John Ireland and Ray Milland display a few emotions, but they come across as too inhuman to elicit any sympathy. Perhaps Arnold was the right director after all. ▣

David Janssen *David Christopher* • Senta Berger *Denise Abbott* • John Ireland *Dwight McGowan* • John Saxon *Robert Hayes* • Ray Milland *Johann Hurtil* • Elke Sommer *Rita Jensen* • Anton Diffring *Franz Benninger* ■ Dir Jack Arnold • Scr Norman Klenman, Philip Saltzman, Michael Stanley, from the novel by Michael Stanley

Swiss Family Robinson
★★★ **U**

Period adventure   1940 · US · BW · 93mins

A modest film version of Johann David Wyss's once popular novel about a family, shipwrecked during the Napoleonic wars, who set about building a house and a new life on a desert island. Four-square and agreeably old-fashioned "family" entertainment with a mild message about values, the film boasts the rich voice of Orson Welles as its narrator and a good cast headed by Thomas Mitchell as William Robinson and child star Freddie Bartholomew on loan from MGM. Inexplicably, the production was a box-office disaster for RKO.

Orson Welles *Narrator* • Thomas Mitchell *William Robinson* • Edna Best *Elizabeth Robinson* • Freddie Bartholomew *Jack Robinson* • Terry Kilburn *Ernest Robinson* • Tim Holt *Fritz Robinson* • Baby Bobby Quillan *Francis Robinson* ■ Dir Edward Ludwig • Scr Walter Ferris, Gene Towne, Graham Baker, from the novel by Johann David Wyss

Swiss Family Robinson
★★★★ **U**

Period adventure
1960 · US · Colour · 126mins

John Mills and Dorothy McGuire leading their family in a chorus of *Oh, Christmas Tree* (in an impossibly luxurious desert island tree house) is, for many, an abiding memory of childhood cinema-going. Viewed many moons later, Disney's lavish (if overlong) version of Johann Wyss's novel lost little of its appeal. British director Ken Annakin shot the film on the West Indian island of Tobago and keeps the action brisk and breezy. Compared to state-of-the-art sequences in modern action adventures, though, the shipwreck, the raft rescue and the pirate raid are perhaps not as thrilling as they once seemed. ▣ **DVD**

John Mills *Father Robinson* • Dorothy McGuire *Mother Robinson* • James MacArthur *Fritz Robinson* • Janet Munro *Roberta* • Sessue Hayakawa *Pirate chief* • Tommy Kirk *Ernst* • Kevin Corcoran *Francis* • Cecil Parker *Captain Moreland* ■ Dir Ken Annakin • Scr Lowell S Hawley, from the novel by Johann David Wyss

Swiss Miss
★★ **U**

Comedy   1938 · US · BW · 64mins

The loveable Laurel and Hardy are still watchable, even in their weaker movies. Here they're a couple of mousetrap salesmen, plying their trade in Switzerland. There are enough gags to sustain the interest in this Alpine caper, in spite of some painfully laboured musical interludes. ▣

Stan Laurel *Stan* • Oliver Hardy *Ollie* • Della Lind *Anna Hoeful Albert* • Walter Woolf King

---

Victor Albert • Eric Blore *Edward* ■ Dir John G Blystone • Scr James Parrott, Felix Adler, from a story by Jean Negulesco, Charles Rogers, Stan Laurel

Switch
★★ **15**

Comedy   1991 · US · Colour · 98mins

A rather disappointing and decidedly lewd gender-swap tale from Blake Edwards. Perry King is the ladykiller, killed by ladies and reincarnated as Ellen Barkin. It's a story that has a lot going for it, but it cops out as soon as lesbianism rears its alternative head. Barkin has proved herself worthy of much better material than this with her roles in *The Big Easy* and *Sea of Love*, but here she made a grave mistake in putting her faith in Edwards's slapstick brand of humour. Contains swearing and brief nudity. ▣

Ellen Barkin *Amanda Brooks* • Jimmy Smits *Walter Stone* • JoBeth Williams *Margo Brofman* • Lorraine Bracco *Sheila Faxton* • Tony Roberts *Arnold Freidkin* • Perry King *Steve Brooks* • Bruce Martyn Payne [Bruce Payne] *Devil* • Lysette Anthony *Liz* ■ Dir/Scr Blake Edwards

The Switch
★★★★ **PG**

Drama based on a true story
1993 · US · Colour · 91mins

Presumably because of Tinseltown prejudice against the television movie, there are perfectly decent actors who have practically no life beyond the small screen. Gary Cole and Craig T Nelson are a case in point. They have no trouble bringing an emotional and psychological authenticity to their respective roles of a seriously injured biker who wants to die and a DJ who is his political, and personal, opposite. Issues of life and death, responsibility and freedom are woven in with some style. ▣

Gary Cole *Larry McAfee* • Craig T Nelson *Russ Fine* • Beverly D'Angelo *Dee Fine* • Kathleen Nolan *Amelia McAfee* • Chris Mulkey *Bill* • L Scott Campbell *Mrs Linson* • Max Gail *Judge Johnson* ■ Dir Bobby Roth • Scr Thomas S Cook, from a story by Thomas S Cook, Ron Schultz

Switchback
★★★ **15**

Action thriller   1997 · US · Colour · 113mins

A refreshingly different variation on the overused serial killer plot, cutting between Dennis Quaid's miserable FBI man on the trail of the killer he believes has kidnapped his son, and travelling companions Danny Glover and Jared Leto – both of whom are just suspicious enough to be the culprit. Writer/director Jeb Stuart (co-writer of *Die Hard* and *The Fugitive*) is confident enough to make the "suspects" more interesting than the hero, although his shaky plotting throws up its share of unlikely contrivances. Still, fine performances and a couple of pulsating action sequences warrant a view. Contains violence, nudity and swearing. ▣

Dennis Quaid *Agent Frank LaCrosse* • Danny Glover *Bob Goodall* • Jared Leto *Lane Dixon* • Ted Levine *Nate Booker* • R Lee Ermey *Sheriff Buck Olmstead* ■ Dir/Scr Jeb Stuart

---

Switchblade Sisters
★★ **18**

Crime action adventure
1975 · US · Colour · 86mins

Quentin Tarantino tried re-releasing this exploitation cheapie in 1999, though it still didn't really find an audience. Indeed, the movie has dated in a way that makes it more tacky than actually hilarious, and though a director known for campy exploitation movies was at the helm, the very low budget results in the characters providing more "attitude" and arguments than violence or sexual material. Still, this saga of the trials and battles of an all-girl gang does have its moments, not just with the expected women in prison sequence, but a roller rink massacre and a surprisingly big-scale climactic street war that includes a tank. Contains violence and drug abuse. ▣

Robbie Lee *Lace* • Joanne Nail *Maggie* • Monica Gayle *Patch* • Asher Brauner *Dominic* • Chase Newhart *Crabs* • Marlene Clark *Muff* • Kitty Bruce *Donut* • Janice Karman *Bunny* ■ Dir Jack Hill • Scr FX Maier, from a story by FX Maier, Jack Hill, John Prizer

Switching Channels ★★★ **PG**

Romantic comedy
1987 · US · Colour · 100mins

After three screen versions of *The Front Page* set in a newspaper office (including the best of them all, *His Girl Friday*), it was only a matter of time before someone brought the story into the TV age. Canadian director Ted Kotcheff never quite comes to grips with the pace of either the story or the humour, and his uncertain handling hampers his more than capable cast. Burt Reynolds keeps threatening to match two of his predecessors in the role, Cary Grant and Walter Matthau, but Kathleen Turner and Christopher Reeve leave you longing for Rosalind Russell and Ralph Bellamy. Contains swearing. ▣

Kathleen Turner *Christy Colleran* • Burt Reynolds *John L Sullivan IV* • Christopher Reeve *Blaine Bingham* • Ned Beatty *Roy Ridnitz* • Henry Gibson *Ike Roscoe* • George Newbern *Siegenthaler* • Al Waxman *Berger* ■ Dir Ted Kotcheff • Scr Jonathan Reynolds, from the play *The Front Page* by Ben Hecht, Charles MacArthur

Switching Parents   ★★★ **PG**

Drama based on a true story
1992 · US · Colour · 88mins

First Drew Barrymore tried to divorce parents Ryan O'Neal and Shelley Long in the 1984 comedy *Irreconcilable Differences*, and now we have this more serious look at the subject, which is actually based on a true story. Gregory Kingsley (Joseph Gordon-Levitt) is the 12-year-old who is tired of being shunted between his estranged parents and foster homes. His solution is to take his family to court so he can "divorce" them and be formally adopted by his foster parents. Director Linda Otto tells this potentially sensational story without lapsing into melodrama. ▣

Joseph Gordon-Levitt *Gregory Kingsley* • Daniel De Santo *Jeremiah Kingsley* • Brian Cook *Zachary Kingsley* • Kathleen York *Rachel Kingsley* • Robert Joy *Ralph Kingsley* ■ Dir Linda Otto • Scr Sharon Elizabeth Doyle

---

Swoon
★★★ **18**

Crime drama   1992 · US · BW · 93mins

Overly arty and surrealistic it might be, but writer/director Tom Kalin's take on the famous Leopold and Loeb murder case is still provocative, gripping and chilling, raising clever contemporary issues within its period confines. Using monochrome melodrama, archive footage and experimental narrative, Kalin starkly examines with haunting effectiveness the homophobia behind the conviction of the two wealthy gay Chicago college kids who killed a schoolboy for kicks in 1924. Although the police ignore them as likely suspects at first, it's the duo's snobby sense of superiority that's their downfall. Contains swearing. ▣

Daniel Schlachet *Richard Loeb* • Craig Chester *Nathan Leopold Jr* • Ron Vawter *State's Attorney Crowe* • Michael Kirby *Detective Savage* • Michael Stumm *Doctor Bowman* • Valda Z Drabla *Germaine Reinhardt* • Natalie Stanford *Susan Lurie* • Paul Connor *Bobby Franks* ■ Dir/Scr Tom Kalin

The Sword and the Cross
★★

Biblical drama   1958 · It · Colour · 93mins

The success of such films as MGM's *Quo Vadis* and *Ben-Hur* must have left a lot of props and costumes in the scene docks at Cinecittà studios, Rome. A whole sub-genre arose utilising existing materials with quasi-religious plots, invariably importing a Hollywood name to add international lustre. This one finds Yvonne De Carlo, caught in a mid-career slide, visiting "Hollywood on the Tiber" to skulk about as Mary Magdalene in a fictional romance set during the last days of Christ. It's not unwatchable, but don't expect taste. Italian dialogue dubbed into English..

Yvonne De Carlo *Mary Magdalene* • Jorge Mistral *Caius Marcellus* • Rossana Podesta *Marthe* • Philippe Hersent *Pontius Pilate* • Mario Girotti [Terence Hill] *Lazarus* ■ Dir Carlo L Bragaglia [Carlo Bragaglia]

The Sword and the Rose
★★ **U**

Historical drama   1952 · US · Colour · 87mins

In days of old when knights were bold and painted scenery was a cutting-edge special effect, this Disney costume drama would have had children in raptures. Nowadays, it's grandparents who will get the most enjoyment out of this corny romp, in which Michael Gough pantomimically wicked lord stands between Glynis Johns's winsome Mary Tudor and true happiness. Gleefully dispensing with historical fact, it's all simply an excuse for Richard Todd to prance about in brightly coloured tights (again), while James Robertson-Justice demonstrates what a Scottish Henry VIII might have sounded like. ▣

Richard Todd *Charles Brandon* • Glynis Johns *Princess Mary Tudor* • James Robertson-Justice *King Henry VIII* • Michael Gough *Duke of Buckingham* • Jane Barrett *Lady Margaret* • Peter Copley *Sir Edwin Caskoden* • Rosalie Crutchley *Queen Catherine of Aragon* ■ Dir Ken Annakin • Scr Lawrence E Watkin, from the novel *When Knighthood Was in Flower* by Charles Major

The Sword and the Sorcerer ★★ 18

Fantasy adventure
1982 · US · Colour · 95mins

This unexciting and overly bloody fantasy excursion was an attempt to jump on the sword-and-sorcery bandwagon that was kick-started by the success of Schwarzenegger's *Conan the Barbarian*. Much chewing of scenery is in evidence here as Errol Flynn-wannabe Lee Horsley and his merry band of mercenaries do battle with evil king Richard Lynch to rescue an enslaved kingdom. Directorial debutante Albert Pyun commits the three cardinal sins for a fantasy movie: being confusing, unimaginative and dull. The only novelty here is the hero's three-bladed sword, and that soon overstays its welcome. Contains violence. ▭

Lee Horsley *Talon* • Kathleen Beller *Alana* • Simon MacCorkindale *Mikah* • George Maharis *Machelli* • Richard Lynch *Cromwell* • Richard Moll *Xusia* ■ *Dir* Albert Pyun • *Scr* Albert Pyun, John Stuckmeyer, Tom Karnowski

The Sword in the Stone ★★★ U

Animated adventure
1963 · US · Colour · 76mins

Disney's feature-length cartoon account of young King Arthur's magical misadventures may feature unmemorable songs by the Sherman brothers, but the film makes good use of its limited animation techniques (Disney was on a cost-cutting drive at the time) in relating the legend of Arthur, here nicknamed Wart, and the valuable life lessons taught to him by wizard Merlin. Memorable sequences include Wart's transformation into a fish to witness the wonders of the underwater world (shades of *The Little Mermaid* to come) before pulling Excalibur from the stone and claiming his rightful inheritance. ▭ **DVD**

Rickie Sorenson *Wart* • Sebastian Cabot *Sir Ector* • Karl Swenson *Merlin, the magician* • Junius Matthews *Archimedes* • Norman Alden *Sir Pelinore* • Martha Wentworth *Mad Madame Mim/Granny Squirrel* • Alan Napier *Sir Pelinore* ■ *Dir* Wolfgang Reitherman • *Scr* Bill Peet, from the book by TH White

Sword of Gideon ★★★ 15

Action adventure
1986 · UK/Can · Colour · 148mins

The massacre of Israeli athletes at the 1972 Munich Olympics is the starting point for this TV action movie from director Michael Anderson (*Logan's Run, The Quiller Memorandum*). Steven Bauer is the commando, assigned to head an anti-terrorist squad to avenge the murders, and the strong supporting cast includes Michael York as an explosives expert and Colleen Dewhurst as prime minister Golda Meir. As entertainment it works well, though inevitably it will leave audiences divided on the morality of these revenge killings. ▭

Steven Bauer *Avner* • Rod Steiger *Mordechai Samuels* • Michael York *Robert* • Colleen Dewhurst *Golda Meir* • Leslie Hope *Shoshana* • Robert Joy *Hans* • Lino Ventura *Papa* ■ *Dir* Michael Anderson • *Scr* Chris Bryant, from the novel *Vengeance* by George Jonas

The Sword of Monte Cristo ★★ U

Period swashbuckling adventure
1951 · US · Colour · 79mins

Some vigorous swordplay, handsome settings and lavish costumes fail to make up for the convoluted plot and general shortcomings of this second-rate action adventure tale, very loosely inspired by Alexandre Dumas's classic novel. George Montgomery is merely adequate as the loyal French officer who helps save Napoleon III from the treachery of his tyrannical chief minister, and this sort of Gallic swashbuckler has been done far better many times before and since.

George Montgomery *Captain Renault* • Paula Corday [Rita Corday] *Lady Christiane* • Berry Kroeger *Minister Charles La Roche* • William Conrad *Major Nicolet* • Rhys Williams *Major of Varonne* • Steve Brodie *Sergeant* • Robert Warwick *Marquis de Montableau* • David Bond *Louis Napoleon III* ■ *Dir* Maurice Geraghty • *Scr* Maurice Geraghty, from the novel *The Count of Monte Cristo* by Alexandre Dumas

Sword of Sherwood Forest ★★ U

Adventure drama 1960 · UK · Colour · 76mins

To many, ex-Brylcreem boy Richard Greene was the definitive Robin Hood, ushering in ITV in a cleverly cast (though cheaply made) TV series with a remarkably catchy theme tune. Here's the feature, co-produced by Greene for Hammer Films. Alan Wheatley makes way for Peter Cushing as the villainous Sheriff of Nottingham, and the film is directed by Cushing's Hammer colleague, Terence Fisher. Technicolor adds some scale, but this is really a cheap and cheerful affair. ▭

Richard Greene *Robin Hood* • Peter Cushing *Sheriff of Nottingham* • Niall MacGinnis *Friar Tuck* • Sarah Branch *Maid Marian Fitzwalter* • Richard Pasco *Earl Of Newark* • Nigel Green *Little John* • Jack Gwillim *Archbishop of Canterbury, Hubert Walter* ■ *Dir* Terence Fisher • *Scr* Alan Hackney

Sword of the Valiant ★ PG

Fantasy adventure
1984 · UK · Colour · 97mins

This is tantamount to a star-studded remake of Stephen Weeks's low-budget 1973 film *Gawain and the Green Knight*. He has made little improvement on his own original, however. Miles O'Keeffe is quite dreadful in the role of the squire Gawain, challenged by Sean Connery's Green Knight to answer a riddle within a year or risk having his head chopped off. Barely on screen, Trevor Howard and Peter Cushing are shamefully wasted, as are the locations.

Miles O'Keeffe *Gawain* • Cyrielle Claire *Linet* • Leigh Lawson *Humphrey* • Sean Connery *Green Knight* • Trevor Howard *King Arthur* • Peter Cushing *Seneschal* • Ronald Lacey *Oswald* • Lila Kedrova *Lady of Lyonesse* ■ *Dir* Stephen Weeks • *Scr* Stephen Weeks, Philip M Breen, Howard C Pen

The Swordsman of Siena ★★

Swashbuckling drama
1962 · Fr/It · Colour · 96mins

British actor Stewart Granger flails around with sabre and rapier in this Italian swashbuckler, set in the 16th century. Our hero plays a soldier of fortune who gets caught up in a struggle between a brutal nobleman and a rebel underground movement. He also gets to stretch his romantic muscles in dallying with Sylva Koscina and Tony Curtis's ex-wife, Christine Kaufmann. There's plenty of colourful costumes and sword fights, but the plot is as predictable as a calendar. Granger is also looking too long in the tooth to this sort of thing. Italian dialogue dubbed into English.

Stewart Granger *Thomas Stanwood* • Sylva Koscina *Orietta Arconti* • Christine Kaufman *Serenella Arconti* • Riccardo Garrone *Don Carlos* • Tullio Carminati *Father Giacomo* ■ *Dir* Etienne Perier, Baccio Bandini • *Scr* Michael Kanin, Fay Kanin, Alec Coppel, Sandro Continenza, Dominique Fabre, from a story by Anthony Marshall

Sworn to Silence ★★★ 15

Courtroom drama 1987 · US · Colour · 94mins

This thought-provoking TV movie benefits from the sure hand of veteran director Peter Levin and an outstanding cast that includes Peter Coyote and Dabney Coleman, with Liam Neeson in an uncharacteristic role as a sadistic killer. The intricate plot centres on the dilemma of two small-town lawyers who face a quandary when they discover the man they've been assigned to defend is guilty of several vicious crimes. The issues of lawyer/client confidentiality and ''privileged information'' are explored with balanced integrity and absorbing emotional tension. ▭

Peter Coyote *Sam Fischetti* • Dabney Coleman *Martin Costigan* • Liam Neeson *Vincent Cauley* • Caroline McWilliams *Maureen Fischetti* • David Spielberg *Aaron Goodman* ■ *Dir* Peter Levin • *Scr* Robert L Joseph, from the novel *Privileged Information* by Tom Alibrandi, Frank H Armani

Sworn to Vengeance ★★ 18

Police thriller 1993 · US · Colour · 89mins

Set in Carson City, Nevada, this TV movie is inspired by the remarkable true story of a psychic who joined forces with a lone police sergeant to track down the killer of a trio of innocent teenagers. Robert Conrad turns in a dogged performance as the cop who decides to investigate the brutal slayings despite the indifference of his colleagues, and Sharon Farrell is equally effective as his visionary sidekick. But it's William McNamara who steals the show as the psychotic exhibitionist who likes nothing better than to boast about his crimes. Contains violence and swearing. ▭

Robert Conrad *Sergeant Jack Stewart* • William McNamara • Gary Bayer • Sharon Farrell ■ *Dir* Peter H Hunt • *Scr* David Epstein, John Carlen

Sylvester ★★★ PG

Drama 1985 · US · Colour · 99mins

Early film from director Tim Hunter, who two years later would make disturbing cult film *River's Edge*. Melissa Gilbert stars as the tomboy who rides her horse Sylvester to victory in the Olympics three-day event at Lexington, Kentucky. The plot superficially resembles *National Velvet*, but Hunter brings a darker touch to the proceedings by making Gilbert's character rather unlikeable. Veteran Richard Farnsworth gives a fine performance as Charlie's tipsy but tough mentor. ▭

Richard Farnsworth *Foster* • Melissa Gilbert *Charlie* • Michael Schoeffling *Matt* • Constance Towers *Muffy* • Pete Kowanko *Harris* ■ *Dir* Tim Hunter • *Scr* Carol Sobieski

Sylvia ★★★★

Detective drama 1964 · US · BW · 114mins

Hollywood's sex siren in residence – the one and only Carroll Baker – is about to marry a millionaire, so he hires a private detective to shed some light on her past. She's a champion rose grower and a published poet, so there shouldn't be too many surprises. But then comes the bad news: after being abused as a child, she became a prostitute and fell in with some very bad company indeed. As prurient and lurid as a mainstream Hollywood movie could be in 1965, this is a Harold Robbins epic in all but name, superbly filmed and with a whole line of feeble, emasculated or disturbed men to trample over Sylvia's eventful life. What makes the film seem so authentic and compelling is Baker's own love-hate relationship with her *Baby Doll* screen image.

Carroll Baker *Sylvia West* • George Maharis *Alan Macklin* • Joanne Dru *Jane Philips* • Peter Lawford *Frederick Summers* • Viveca Lindfors *Irma Olanski* • Edmond O'Brien *Oscar Stewart* • Aldo Ray *Jonas Karoki* • Ann Sothern *Mrs Argona* ■ *Dir* Gordon Douglas • *Scr* Sidney Boehm, from the novel by EV Cunningham

Sylvia ★★★ PG

Drama 1984 · NZ · Colour · 94mins

Moving biopic from the fledgling days of New Zealand cinema which recounts the early life of acclaimed novelist Sylvia Ashton-Warner, who, before finding fame as a writer, pioneered a radical new teaching programme to help Maori children. Eleanor David shines in the lead role, and there is sterling support from Tom Wilkinson (*The Full Monty*) and Nigel Terry (*Excalibur*). Director Michael Firth admirably evokes the conservatism and prejudices of post-Second World War New Zealand. ▭

Eleanor David *Sylvia Henderson* • Nigel Terry *Aden* • Tom Wilkinson *Keith Henderson* • Mary Regan *Opal* • Martyn Sanderson *Inspector Gulland* • Terence Cooper *Inspector Bletcher* • David Letch *Inspector Scragg* ■ *Dir* Michael Firth • *Scr* Michael Quill, F Fairfax, Michael Firth, from the books *Teacher* and *I Pass This Way* by Sylvia Ashton-Warner

Sylvia Scarlett ★★ U

Comedy drama 1936 · US · BW · 86mins

Petty fraudster Edmund Gwenn and his daughter Katharine Hepburn (disguised as a boy to fool pursuing cops) join forces in England with cockney jewel thief Cary Grant. Their picaresque escapades and emotional entanglements defeat the script and George Cukor's direction. A bemused public gave the thumbs down to this sprawling and tedious account of Compton Mackenzie's novel, and the film hasn't improved with age.

However, it has its moments, and Hepburn, giving her all and flamboyantly sporting drag, makes Sylvia something of a cult figure in this age of sexual ambivalence. 🔲

Katharine Hepburn *Sylvia Scarlett* • Cary Grant *Jimmy Monkley* • Brian Aherne *Michael Fane* • Edmund Gwenn *Henry Scarlett* • Natalie Paley *Lily* • Dennie Moore *Maudie Tilt* ■ *Dir* George Cukor • *Scr* Gladys Unger, John Collier, Mortimer Offner, from the novel *The Early Life and Adventures of Sylvia Scarlett* by Compton Mackenzie

La Symphonie Pastorale ★★★★★

Drama	1946 · Fr · BW · 107mins

A blind orphan girl (Michèle Morgan) is brought up by a pastor (Pierre Blanchar) and his wife in a small mountain village, where the pastor teaches his sightless charge to understand the world as a place of beauty and serenity. However, he and his son (Jean Desailly) both fall in love with her, and the latter, hopeful of marriage, arranges an operation to restore her sight. Adapted from André Gide's painfully sad novella and filmed against a background of exquisite visuals, the film won the Grand Prix at Cannes in 1946, while the ravishing Morgan's miraculously profound and expressive performance saw her voted best actress. A French gem, redolent with beauty and despair. In French with English subtitles.

Michèle Morgan *Gertrude* • Pierre Blanchar *Pastor Jean Martin* • Line Noro *Amélie Martin* • Jacques Louvigny *Casteran* • Jean Desailly *Jacques Martin* • Andrée Clément *Piette Casteran* ■ *Dir* Jean Delannoy • *Scr* Pierre Bost, Jean Aurenche, Jean Delannoy, from the novel by André Gide

Symphony of Six Million ★★★

Drama	1932 · US · BW · 85mins

Based on a story by Fannie Hurst, the era's most prolific purveyor of three-handkerchief weepies, and directed by the efficient Gregory La Cava, the movie concerns a doctor of humble origins (Ricardo Cortez) who sells out his high ideals for money and status, only to fail in performing an operation on his own father (Gregory Ratoff). He redeems himself, however, by saving the woman he loves (Irene Dunne). Max Steiner's emotive score heightens the drama without disguising Cortez's wooden acting, but the film, complete with then rare scenes of surgical procedure, is a good wallow.

Ricardo Cortez *Dr Felix Klauber* • Irene Dunne *Jessica* • Anna Appel *Hannah Klauber* • Gregory Ratoff *Meyer "Lansman" Klauber* ■ *Dir* Gregory La Cava • *Scr* Bernard Schubert, J Walter Ruben, James Seymour, from a story by Fannie Hurst

Syncopation ★★★ 🅄

Period drama	1942 · US · BW · 88mins

Eleven musical numbers and the participation of Benny Goodman, Harry James, Gene Krupa, Charlie Barnet and Joe Venuti are the only possible reasons to sit through this dreary tale of a young trumpeter from Chicago (Jackie Cooper) and a New Orleans girl (Bonita Granville) who share an obsession with jazz and Walt Whitman.

Top-billed Adolphe Menjou barely figures as Granville's architect father. German-born William Dieterle directed and produced the film for his own company and RKO, but was unable to make something that justified his move into unfamiliar territory.

Adolphe Menjou *George Latimer* • Jackie Cooper *Johnnie* • Bonita Granville *Kit Latimer* • George Bancroft *Mr Porter* • Ted North *Paul Porter* • Todd Duncan *Rex Tearbone* • Connee Boswell *Café singer* ■ *Dir* William Dieterle • *Scr* Philip Yordan, Frank Cavett, from the story *The Band Played On* by Valentine Davies

The System ★★★

Romantic drama	1964 · UK · BW · 92mins

Once upon a time, teenage boys used to go to the unromantic English seaside to pick up their girls, before cheap air travel to the Costa Brava was introduced. This quaint period romp provides a mirror of those not-so-innocent times, elegantly photographed in black-and-white by cinematographer Nicolas Roeg and oozing early sixties charm from Peter Draper's clever screenplay. The young, talented cast is headed by Oliver Reed, Jane Merrow, Barbara Ferris and Julia Foster, and watch closely for director Michael Winner in shot on the platform as the train arrives at Torquay.

Oliver Reed *Tinker* • Jane Merrow *Nicola* • Barbara Ferris *Suzy* • Julia Foster *Lorna* • Harry Andrews *Larsey* • Ann Lynn *Ella* • David Hemmings *David* • John Alderton *Nidge* ■ *Dir* Michael Winner • *Scr* Peter Draper

TC 2000 ★ 18

Science-fiction action thriller	1993 · US · Colour · 90mins

In the future, a depleted ozone layer has made living on the surface of the earth almost impossible; the rich have retreated to an underground city, while the less fortunate stay on the surface. Billy Blanks plays one of the defenders of the city, soon finding himself on the surface and allying with Bolo Yeung when he stumbles onto the inevitable conspiracy. Blanks and Yeung are as imposing as ever, though all the script gives them is a succession of not particularly exciting fight sequences. At least Yeung's part plays to his strengths by not overburdening him with dialogue. 🔲

Billy Blanks *Jason Storm* • Bobbie Phillips *Zoey Kinsella* • Bolo Yeung *Sumai* • Jalal Merhi *Niki Picasso* • Matthias Hues *Bigalow* ■ *Dir* TJ Scott • *Scr* TJ Scott, from a story by J Stephen Maunder

T-Force ★ 18

Science-fiction action adventure	1995 · US · Colour · 89mins

The T-Force of the title is the *Termination Force*, an anti-terrorist squad composed entirely of a form of android called cybernauts. This may excuse the lamentable acting by the main characters, but even the human characters are atrociously played. Really long action sequences are broken up only by half-brained ponderings on whether or not robots are truly sentient beings. Jack Scalia plays the human cop who has to stop T-Force. 🔲

Jack Scalia *Jack* • Erin Gray *Mayor Pendleton* • Vernon Wells *Samuel Washington* • Bobby Johnston *Cain* • Evan Lurie *Adam* ■ *Dir* Richard Pepin • *Scr* Jacobsen Hart

THX 1138 ★★★★ 15

Science-fiction fantasy	1971 · US · Colour · 82mins

The debut feature from *Star Wars* maestro George Lucas is a bleak, claustrophobic affair which is light years away from the straightforward heroics of Luke Skywalker and co. The always excellent Robert Duvall takes the title role as a man quietly rebelling against a repressive world where everyone has to have Yul Brynner haircuts, and the police are as frighteningly bland as a McDonald's assistant. The obtuse script doesn't help, but it looks wonderful and Lucas conjures up a genuinely chilling air. 🔲

Robert Duvall *THX 1138* • Donald Pleasence *SEN 5241* • Don Pedro Colley *SRT* • Maggie McOmie *LUH 3417* • Ian Wolfe *PTO* • Sid Haig *NCH* • Marshall Efron *TWA* • John Pearce

DWY • Johnny Weissmuller Jr *Chrome Robot* ■ *Dir* George Lucas • *Scr* George Lucas, Walter Murch, from a story by George Lucas

T-Men ★★★★

Film noir	1947 · US/UK · BW · 92mins

The "T" refers to Treasury Agents, as opposed to G-Men (FBI), and the picture is a real humdinger, one of director Anthony Mann's early works. It's a key *film noir* and a testament to the brilliance of cameraman John Alton, whose lighting can make a concrete wall as expressive as a Turner landscape. The story is hardly original – agents are assigned to smash a counterfeiting racket – but Mann's inventive telling belies the bargain-basement budget. Audiences at the time marvelled at Dennis O'Keefe's performance as one of the agents, a startling change from his early musicals.

Dennis O'Keefe *Dennis O'Brien* • Alfred Ryder *Tony Genaro* • Mary Meade *Evangeline* • Wallace Ford *Schemer* • June Lockhart *Mary Genaro* • Charles McGraw *Moxie* • Jane Randolph *Diana* • Art Smith *Gregg* ■ *Dir* Anthony Mann • *Scr* John C Higgins, from a story by Virginia Kellogg

Ta Dona ★★

Drama	1991 · Mali · Colour · 100mins

The clash between traditional rituals and the environmental realities of a changing world are explored in this slow-moving drama from Mali. Raising issues that have currency across Africa, including post-colonial neglect, poor standards of education, and the gulf between urban and rural communities, Adama Drabo openly sides with the peasant farmers who are even exploited by corrupt government officials in times of drought. Shot through with Bambara myths and superstitions, from burning crop residue before sewing, and sacrificing bulls, to placing faith in the magical power of the poisonous cenari plant, the film has few answers to the intractable questions it poses. In French with English subtitles.

Balamoussa Keita [Balla Moussa Keita] • Diarrah Sanogo • Arouna Diarra ■ *Dir/Scr* Adama Drabo

Taal ★★★ 🅄

Romantic melodrama	1999 · Ind · Colour · 179mins

This masala melodrama has the distinction of being the first Bollywood production to make it into the top 20 of the US box office. Director Subhash Ghai (*Pardes*) (1997), borrows liberally from such recent blockbusters as *Dil Se*, *Bombay* and *Dil To Pagal Hai* to fashion this star-crossed romance, which features Akshaye Khanna as a millionaire's son who teams up with his loyal friend Anil Kapoor to defy class prejudice and the ruthless materialism of modern society in order to win the heart of folk singer, Aishwarya Rai. In Hindi with English subtitles.

Anil Kapoor *Vikrant Kapoor aka Kapu* • Aishwarya Rai *Manasi* • Akshaye Khanna *Manav Mehta* • Alok Nath *Tara Babu* • Amrish Puri *Jagmohan* ■ *Dir/Scr* Subhash Ghai

🅄 = SUITABLE FOR ALL   🆄ᶜ = SUITABLE FOR ALL, ESPECIALLY FOR YOUNG CHILDREN (VIDEO ONLY)   🅿🅶 = PARENTAL GUIDANCE

Table for Five ★★★ PG
Drama　　1983 · US · Colour · 116mins

Hankies at the ready for this sentimental *Kramer vs Kramer*-style heartstring-tugger. Jon Voight stars as the divorced dad who takes his kids on a Mediterranean holiday, only to learn while they are away that his ex-wife has died and her husband may want custody of the children. While admittedly gushy towards the finale, this is best enjoyed for the earlier scenes of Voight trying to get to know his children all over again. ▭

Jon Voight *JP Tannen* • Richard Crenna *Mitchell* • Marie-Christine Barrault *Marie* • Millie Perkins *Kathleen* • Roxana Zal *Tilde* • Robby Kiger *Truman-Paul* ■ *Dir* Robert Lieberman • *Scr* David Seltzer

Tabu ★★★ U
Silent drama　　1931 · US · BW · 76mins

After creative differences caused him to leave WS Van Dyke to complete *White Shadows in the South Seas* (1928), the father of the documentary film, Robert Flaherty, found the same thing happening to him with his collaborator on another Polynesian project, the great German expressionist, FW Murnau. Overruled in his bid to promote the ethnographical aspect above the film's melodramatic storyline, he left Murnau and Oscar-winning cameraman Floyd Crosby to tell the tale of forbidden love and tyrannical superstition, which they did with lyrical integrity. ▭

Reri [Anna Chevalier] *The girl* • Matahi *The boy* • Robert J Flaherty [Robert Flaherty] *Narrator* ■ *Dir* FW Murnau • *Scr* from the story *Turia* by FW Murnau, Robert J Flaherty [Robert Flaherty]

Taffin ★★ 18
Action thriller 1988 · US/UK · Colour · 92mins

Dull thriller, with Pierce Brosnan as a tough-guy debt collector confronting unscrupulous developers who want to build a chemical plant in a quiet Irish town. Brosnan's watchable, but displays little of the charisma that he'd bring years later to Bond. A rock-solid support cast includes Patrick Bergin, Alison Doody and Ray McAnally. ▭

Pierce Brosnan *Mark Taffin* • Ray McAnally *O'Rourke* • Alison Doody *Charlotte* • Jeremy Child *Martin* • Dearbhla Molloy *Mrs Martin* • Jim Bartley *Conway* • Patrick Bergin *Mo Taffin* ■ *Dir* Francis Megahy • *Scr* David Ambrose, from a novel by Lyndon Mallett

Tagget ★★ 15
Spy thriller　　1991 · US · Colour · 85mins

A TV movie outing for one of the principals of *Hill Street Blues*. Daniel J Travanti stars as a disabled Vietnam veteran who discovers that he is not the only one with old scores to settle when he seeks out the spies responsible for his injuries. It would appear that another couple of script conferences, at the very least, were needed to tidy up this sloppy plot, which seems to have baffled director Richard T Heffron. Contains violence.

Daniel J Travanti *John Tagget* • Roxanne Hart *Annie Harris* • William Sadler *Uri Chelenkoff* • Stephen Tobolowsky *Al Hentz* • Peter Michael Goetz *Alexander Howell* • Lyman Ward *William*

Schiller • Vincent Guastaferro *Pete Alcantara* • Sarah Douglas *Mrs Sands* ■ *Dir* Richard T Heffron • *Scr* Peter SS Fischer, Richard T Heffron, Janis Diamond, from the novel by Irving A Greenfield

Tai-Pan ★ 18
Historical adventure drama
1986 · US · Colour · 121mins

Inept and lengthy adaptation of James Clavell's bestseller about the 19th-century European trader who establishes his headquarters in Hong Kong, despite opposition from and frequent attacks by rivals. Bryan Brown is the hero we're supposed to like but don't, while Joan Chen adds a touch of Oriental elegance to the sprawling plot over which director Daryl Duke seems to have no control. ▭

Bryan Brown *Dirk Struan/Tai-Pan* • John Stanton *Brock* • Joan Chen *May-May* • Tim Guinee *Culum* • Bill Leadbitter *Gorth* • Russell Wong *Gordon* • Katy Behean *Mary* • Kyra Sedgwick *Tess* ■ *Dir* Daryl Duke • *Scr* John Briley, Stanley Mann, from the novel by James Clavell

Tail Lights Fade ★★
Comedy road movie
1999 · Can · Colour · 87mins

The evocative title and strong youth cast of this indie cinema fare flatter to deceive, in what turns out to be a comedy road movie misfire. Young hipsters like Jake Busey (*Starship Troopers*), Denise Richards (*The World Is Not Enough*), Elizabeth Berkley (*The First Wives Club*) and Breckin Meyer (*The Craft*) fail to breathe much life into the story of a cross-country hot rod race to reach a marijuana stash abandoned by a busted friend before the cops find it.

Denise Richards *Wendy* • Breckin Meyer *Cole* • Jake Busey *Bruce* • Tanya Allen *Angie* • Elizabeth Berkley *Eve* • Jaimz Woolvett *Ben* ■ *Dir* Malcolm Ingram • *Scr* Matt Gissing

Tail of a Tiger ★★
Adventure fantasy drama
1984 · Ausl · Colour · 84mins

Amazingly, the director of the wondrously bizarre *Bad Boy Bubby* (1993) was also at the controls of this wonderless and doggedly traditional kidpic. Rolf De Heer keeps threatening to get this Sydney-based tale of individualism versus peer pressure off the ground, only to allow it to plummet back into old-fashioned mediocrity. The concept of ghostly airmen returning to repair a clapped out Tiger Moth is intriguing and original, but De Heer would rather concentrate on nerdy Grant Navin's rivalry with flashy flyboy Peter Feeley and his mawkish relationship with Gordon Poole, the plane's rejuvenated alcoholic owner.

Grant Navin *Orville Ryan* • Gordon Poole *Harry* • Caz Lederman *Lydia Ryan* • Gayle Kennedy *Beryl* ■ *Dir/Scr* Rolf De Heer

Tails You Live, Heads You're Dead ★★ 15
Detective mystery thriller
1995 · US · Colour · 87mins

Ordinary lives are turned upside-down in this devilishly effective thriller. Businessman Ted McGinley (*Married... with Children*) encounters serial killer

---

Corbin Bernsen (*LA Law*) in a bar, and discovers that he has been chosen as the next victim. After he and his family are threatened, the businessman hires private detective Tim Matheson in an effort to outwit the psychotic assassin. A well-plotted cat-and-mouse battle between hunter and prey is enlivened by Bernsen's credible and sinister turn as the homicidal stalker. Sharp direction by co-star Matheson makes this TV movie a surprisingly taut suspenser. ▭

Corbin Bernsen *Mr Jones/Netter* • Ted McGinley *Jeffrey Quint* • Tim Matheson *Detective McKinley* • Maria Del Mar *Melanie* • Jeff Pustil *Phil Wiseman* • John White *Kevin* ■ *Dir* Tim Matheson • *Scr* Miguel Tejada-Flores, from the short story *Liar's Dice* by Bill Pronzini

Tainted Blood ★ 15
Thriller　　1993 · US · Colour · 82mins

An adopted teenager's murder of his parents leads reporter Raquel Welch on a search for his "lost" twin sister, who may be genetically programmed to kill her foster family. She narrows the suspects down to teenagers Natasha Gregson Wagner and Kerri Green. Forget genetically modified food, this kind of rubbish is the real threat to society, doomed by Welch's inept performance, a ludicrous script and Matthew Patrick's leaden, dim-witted direction. Despite an energetic, dignified performance by Wagner, this film is fatally tainted from beginning to end. ▭

Raquel Welch *Elizabeth* • Alley Mills *Mrs Jane Pattersen* • Kerri Green *Tori Pattersen* • Natasha Gregson Wagner *Lissa Drew* ■ *Dir* Matthew Patrick • *Scr* Kathleen Rowell, from a story by Ginny Cerrella

Taipei Story ★★★★
Romantic drama　　1984 · Tai · Colour

Edward Yang confirmed his place in the vanguard of New Taiwanese Cinema with this episodic insight into the consumerist erosion of traditional values and the role of women in an increasingly emasculated patriarchal society. Caught between duty and doubt, Cai Qin gradually comes to realise that she's being exploited by her reckless father and self-centred sister and has nothing in common with her fiancé Hou Hsiao-Hsien, as he subsists on nostalgia for his days as a baseball star and his relationship with a newly returned old flame. Played against harsh neon cityscapes, this is an uncompromising study of urban alienation and wasted lives. In Mandarin with English subtitles.

Cai Qin *Chin* • Hou Xiaoxian [Hou Hsiao-Hsien] *Lon* • Ke Suyuan *Gwan* • Wu Hinnan *Chin's Father* • Lin Xiuling *Ling* • Wu Nianchen *Kim* ■ *Dir* Edward Yang • *Scr* Edward Yang, Hou Xiaoxian, Zhu Tianwen

The Take ★★
Action crime drama
1974 · US · Colour · 91mins

Routine action pic, distinguished, if anything, by its eclectic cast, which includes Billy Dee Williams – who enjoyed a flash of fame in the seventies – Eddie Albert, Vic Morrow and, in a fine turn as a cheap hood, bleach-blanketed pop phenomenon Frankie Avalon. Williams stars as

---

corrupt cop who plays a dangerous double-game with mob boss Morrow, taking bribes while at the same time trying to take him down in order to impress his superiors.

Billy Dee Williams *Sneed* • Eddie Albert *Chief Berrigan* • Frankie Avalon *Danny James* • Sorrell Booke *Oscar* • Tracy Reed *Nancy* • Albert Salmi *Dolek* • Vic Morrow *Manso* • A Martinez *Tallbear* ■ *Dir* Robert Hartford-Davis • *Scr* Del Reisman, Franklin Coen, from the novel *Sir, You Bastard* by GF Newman

The Take ★★ 18
Crime thriller　　1990 · US · Colour · 86mins

Even that normally energetic actor Ray Sharkey looks drained by this meandering movie, which is defeated by its underdeveloped script. As a result, the parade of macho thrills in Miami has no discernible shape, and director Leon Ichaso appears to have lost control of the proceedings. What's worse, he's failed to make good use of a reasonable cast, including R Lee Ermey and Lisa Hartman. Contains violence and swearing.

Ray Sharkey *Detective Dennis Delaney* • R Lee Ermey *Detective Tony Weller* • Larry Manetti *Barry Shaw* • Joe Lala *Detective Eddie Suarez* • Lisa Hartman *Sally Delaney* ■ *Dir* Leon Ichaso • *Scr* Edward Anhalt, Handel Glassberg, from the novel by Eugene Izzi

Take a Giant Step ★★★
Drama　　1959 · US · BW · 99mins

A black boy (Johnny Nash), sent to a white New England school in order to give him a better chance in life, has his adolescence complicated by the racial discrimination and hostility he encounters. He finds comfort with black maid Ruby Dee and wise counsel from his grandmother Estelle Hemsley. Adapted, and watered down, from his own play, by Louis S Peterson, this modest film represents an earnest attempt to confront the race issue before it was fashionable to do so. It's very well played by Nash, and certainly worth watching, but lacks both incisiveness of approach and depth of feeling.

Johnny Nash *Spencer Scott* • Ruby Dee *Christine the maid* • Estelle Hemsley *Grandma* • Frederick O'Neal *Lem Scott* • Ellen Holly *Carol* • Pauline Meyers *Violet* ■ *Dir* Philip Leacock • *Scr* Louis S Peterson, Julius J Epstein, from a play by Louis S Peterson

Take a Girl Like You ★★ 15
Comedy drama　　1970 · UK · Colour · 94mins

Kingsley Amis's novel about a northern girl who teaches in a London grammar school was published in 1960 and fed off the fifties atmosphere of frugality and furtive sex. Filmed at the tail end of sixties, it seemed dated on release, with Hayley Mills valiantly trying to remain virginal despite the best efforts of Labour councillor and landlord John Bird and art teacher Oliver Reed, who of course is a bit of a Bohemian. It's directed with an uncertain feeling by Jonathan Miller. ▭

Noel Harrison *Julian Ormerod* • Oliver Reed *Patrick Standish* • Hayley Mills *Jenny Bunn* • Sheila Hancock *Martha Thompson* • John Bird *Dick Thompson* • Aimi MacDonald *Wendy* • Ronald Lacey *Graham* • Geraldine Sherman *Anna* ■ *Dir* Jonathan Miller • *Scr* George Melly, from the novel by Kingsley Amis

Take a Hard Ride ★★

Western 1975 · US/It · Colour · 102mins

As the spaghetti western was on its last legs in the mid-seventies, the Hollywood blaxploitation industry cavalry arrived to prolong its demise. This violent example of genre crossbreeding has cowboy Jim Brown on a mission to deliver $86,000 to his dying boss's wife and teaming up with gambler Fred Williamson. Unfortunately word gets around about the money and they become the target of bounty hunter Lee Van Cleef's ruthless posse. Williamson gives a nicely laconic performance in journeyman Italian exploitation director Antonio Margheriti's Canary Islands shot shoot-em-up, where deft humour rides uncomfortable side-saddle with hosts of bloody corpses.

Jim Brown *Pike* • Lee Van Cleef *Kiefer* • Fred Williamson *Tyree* • Catherine Spaak *Catherine* • Jim Kelly *Kashtok* • Barry Sullivan *Sheriff Kane* • Dana Andrews *Morgan* • Harry Carey Jr *Dumper* ■ *Dir* Anthony M Dawson [Antonio Margheriti] • *Scr* Eric Bercovici, Jerry Ludwig

Take a Letter, Darling ★★★

Comedy 1942 · US · BW · 93mins

Rosalind Russell replaced Claudette Colbert in this agreeable romantic comedy in which Russell portrays the sort of career woman with whom she became identified and brilliantly gets laughs from occasionally thin material. As a high-flying advertising executive, she hires Fred MacMurray as a private secretary and escort to keep wolves at bay, but what ensues is not as predictable as it may sound. This is certainly not in the same league as director Mitchell Leisen's *Midnight, Remember the Night* or *Arise, My Love*, but it is good fun, expertly played, with all the trappings – gorgeous costumes, lush settings – of Hollywood escapism.

Rosalind Russell *AM MacGregor* • Fred MacMurray *Tom Verney* • Macdonald Carey *Jonathan Caldwell* • Constance Moore *Ethel Caldwell* • Robert Benchley *GB Atwater* • Charles Arnt *Fud Newton* • Cecil Kellaway *Uncle George* • Kathleen Howard *Aunt Minnie* ■ *Dir* Mitchell Leisen • *Scr* Claude Binyon, from a story by George Beck

Take Care of Your Scarf, Tatjana ★★★★

Comedy 1994 · Fin · BW · 65mins

Novelist and radio writer Peter Tinniswood and Finnish director Aki Kaurismäki could be soulmates. Tinniswood's Uncle Mort would be perfectly at home in a Kaurismäki film, delighting in the drab Finnish landscapes and the dreariness of daily life. Set in the early sixties, this road movie is a brilliant study of sexual and cultural unease expressed almost exclusively in pregnant pauses and meaningful gestures, as a pair of morose music-loving Finns give a couple of Russian women a lift, against a soundtrack of suitably miserable rhythm and blues music. Kaurismäki regulars Kati Outinen and Matti Pellonpää give what amount to masterclasses in comic understatement. In Finnish with English subtitles.

Kati Outinen *Tatjana* • Matti Pellonpää *Reino* • Kirsi Tykkyläinen *Klavdia* • Mato Valtonen •

Valto • Elina Salo *Hotel manageress* • Irma Junnilained *Valto's mother* • Veikko Lavi *Vepe* • Pertti Husu *Vepe* • The Regals • The Renegades ■ *Dir* Aki Kaurismäki • *Scr* Aki Kaurismaki, Sakke Jarvenpaa

Take Down ★★★ PG

Sports drama 1978 · US · Colour · 106mins

English teacher Edward Herrmann grudgingly agrees to coach the wrestling team at his down-and-out high school and inspires the deadbeat students to greater glory in this warmly sentimental sports saga. The one major team hope is Lorenzo Lamas (in his first big movie role). But does the graduation no-hoper, also saddled with an alcoholic father, have the grit to succeed against all the odds? Medium range melodrama to be sure, yet Herrmann is highly engaging and Lamas impresses with a vulnerable and sensitive performance. 🎬

Edward Herrmann *Ed Branish* • Kathleen Lloyd *Jill Branish* • Lorenzo Lamas *Nick Kilvitus* • Maureen McCormick *Brooke Cooper* • Nicolas Beauvy *Jimmy Kier* • Stephen Furst *Randy Jensen* • Kevin Hooks *Jasper Macgruder* ■ *Dir* Kieth Merrill • *Scr* Kieth Merrill, Eric Hendershot

Take Her, She's Mine ★★★

Comedy 1963 · US · Colour · 97mins

James Stewart is the doting but conservative father who goes into panic mode when his maturing teenage daughter Sandra Dee, exhibits the traits of her generation by supporting ban the bomb and espousing the hippie ethos. The situation is aggravated when the girl goes to Paris to study art and gets involved with painter Philippe Forquet. Dad arrives to take charge and gets himself into numerous scrapes... A pleasing, if now dated, family comedy, which takes a light-hearted approach to the political and cultural upheavals of the sixties. Dee is charming; Stewart effortlessly extracts maximum mileage from his role.

James Stewart *Frank Michaelson* • Sandra Dee *Mollie Michaelson* • Audrey Meadows *Anne Michaelson* • Robert Morley *Pope-Jones* • Philippe Forquet *Henri Bonnet* • John McGiver *Hector G Ivor* ■ *Dir* Henry Koster • *Scr* Nunnally Johnson, from a play by Phoebe Ephron, Henry Ephron

Take It Easy ★★

Comedy 1971 · Fr · Colour · 90mins

The third of Alain Delon's nine outings under the direction of Jacques Deray lacks the class of their previous year's collaboration, *Borsalino*. Delon plays a priest who discovers that the wife he presumed long dead (real ex, Nathalie) is not only very much alive, but has also seen the light and plans to give up prostitution to enter a convent. Despite playing on his temptable worldliness, Delon misjudges the film's comic tone, unlike Paul Meurisse, who steals the show as an irascible bishop with pre-Reformation views on the spiritual status of women. French dialogue dubbed into English.

Alain Delon *Simon Médieu* • Paul Meurisse *Bishop* • Nathalie Delon *Rita* • Julien Guiomar *Francisco* • Paul Preboist *L'Abbé de Coeur* ■ *Dir* Jacques Deray • *Scr* Pascal Jardin

Take Me High ★ U

Musical 1973 · UK · Colour · 86mins

Cliff Richard ended a five-year hiatus to star in this indigestible offering. He plays a bank manager who recaptures his fast-departing youth by helping a failing restaurant become the most talked-about eatery in the West Midlands by launching the Brumburger. The songs are confined to the soundtrack, while the "comedy" plods along with all the zip of Spaghetti Junction at rush hour. Cliff does his amiable best, but if old pros like Hugh Griffith, George Cole and Richard Wattis can't raise a smile, what chance does he have? 🎬

Cliff Richard *Tim Matthews* • Debbie Watling *Sarah* • Hugh Griffith *Sir Harry Cunningham* • George Cole *Bert Jackson* • Anthony Andrews *Hugo Flaxman* • Richard Wattis *Sir Charles Furness* • Madeline Smith *Vicki* ■ *Dir* David Askey • *Scr* Christopher Penfold

Take Me Home Again ★★★ PG

Drama 1994 · US · Colour · 87mins

Writer Ernest Thompson won an Oscar for *On Golden Pond* and he transfers its theme of child-parent reconciliation to the open road in this entertaining TV movie. Kirk Douglas revels in the role of the retired travelling salesman who decides to embark on one last adventure before he dies. However, he's prevented from dominating the film by Craig T Nelson, who digs deep to convince as the wayward son who goes along for the ride. With able support from Eileen Brennan and Bess Armstrong, this is a funny, provocative and touching tale. 🎬

Kirk Douglas *Ed Reece* • Craig T Nelson *Larry Reece* • Eileen Brennan *Sada* • Bess Armstrong *Connie* • Bonnie Bartlett *Sylvia Reece* • Richard Gilliland *Russ Reece* ■ *Dir* Tom McLoughlin • *Scr* Ernest Thompson, from the novel *The Lies Boys Tell* by Lamar Herrin

Take Me Out to the Ball Game ★★★★ U

Musical 1949 · US · Colour · 89mins

A wonderful MGM musical with super songs, ravishing Technicolor and extraordinary talent both behind and in front of the camera. This is really a practice run for *On the Town* and, eventually, the great *Singin' in the Rain*, with star Gene Kelly and director Stanley Donen providing the original story, and taking over both choreography and some directing chores from ailing veteran Busby Berkeley. The movie's enchanting, not just for Kelly's great all-stops-out Irish solo, nor for the fabulous trio of Kelly, Frank Sinatra and the under-rated Jules Munshin, but also for a delightfully no-nonsense Esther Williams as the girl who inherits a baseball team. 🎬

Frank Sinatra *Dennis Ryan* • Esther Williams *KC Higgins* • Gene Kelly *Eddie O'Brien* • Betty Garrett *Shirley Delwyn* • Edward Arnold *Joe Lorgan* • Jules Munshin *Nat Goldberg* • Richard Lane *Michael Gilhuly* • Tom Dugan *Slappy Burke* ■ *Dir* Busby Berkeley • *Scr* Harry Tugend, George Wells (uncredited), Harry Crane, from a story by Gene Kelly, Stanley Donen

Take Me to Town ★★ U

Musical comedy adventure
1953 · US · Colour · 80mins

Ann Sheridan is Vermilion O'Toole, a saloon singer with a past who takes refuge from the law in a remote lumber-jacking community where woodsman Sterling Hayden is also the local preacher. His three young sons decide that Vermilion would make them a perfect mom, but the locals are hostile. Needless to say, she wins them – and Hayden – over. Folksy, saccharine-coated gloop, directed by Douglas Sirk and hard to swallow.

Ann Sheridan *Vermilion O'Toole* • Sterling Hayden *Will Hall* • Philip Reed *Newton Cole* • Phyllis Stanley *Mrs Stoffer* • Larry Gates *Ed Daggett* • Lee Patrick *Rose* • Forrest Lewis *Ed Higgins* ■ *Dir* Douglas Sirk • *Scr* Richard Morris, from his story *Flame of the Timberline*

Take My Daughters, Please ★★

Comedy 1988 · US · Colour · 96mins

Misplaced parental pride and concern form the basis for this TV movie comedy. Desperate mother Rue McClanahan (*The Golden Girls*) conspires to marry off her eligible – but rapidly ageing – brood of daughters before it's too late to find them suitable husbands. It's not exactly *Pride and Prejudice*, but this pleasant nonsense about romance and good-natured sibling rivalry co-stars Susan Ruttan (*LA Law*) and *NYPD Blue's* Kim Delaney as two of the unmarried sisters.

Rue McClanahan *Lilah Page* • Stefanie Kramer *Jess Page* • Susan Ruttan *Courtney Page* • Deidre Hall *Nell Page* • Kim Delaney *Evan Page* • Charles Frank *Marc* ■ *Dir* Larry Elikann • *Scr* Lindsay Harrison

Take My Life ★★★★ PG

Murder mystery 1947 · UK · BW · 75mins

An impressive directorial debut from British cinematographer Ronald Neame, who would go on to be responsible for such major works as *Tunes of Glory*, *The Prime of Miss Jean Brodie* and *The Poseidon Adventure*. Hugh Williams is accused of murder and his opera singer wife Greta Gynt is determined to find out who really did it. This was the kind of intelligent thriller that Hollywood directors could churn out in their sleep and it is to Neame's credit that he makes it clever, convincing and, above, all stylish. 🎬

Hugh Williams *Nicholas Talbot* • Greta Gynt *Philippa Bentley* • Marius Goring *Sidney Flemming* • Francis L Sullivan *Prosecuting counsel* • Henry Edwards *Inspector Archer* • Rosalie Crutchley *Elizabeth Rusman* • Marjorie Mars *Mrs Newcombe* • Maurice Denham *Defending counsel* ■ *Dir* Ronald Neame • *Scr* Winston Graham, Valerie Taylor, Margaret Kennedy, from a story by Winston Graham, Valerie Taylor

Take the Money and Run ★★★ PG

Comedy 1969 · US · Colour · 81mins

After years of writing for TV and doing his own stand-up routine, Woody Allen finally made his debut as co-writer, director and star with this ambitious cod documentary. Nicely joshing the "Voice of Doom" style of narration and

such Hollywood movies as *The Defiant Ones*, the film gets off to a flying start, with public enemy Virgil Starkwell's childhood remaining among the funniest things Allen has ever done. The inspiration slowly ebbs away though, and the last ten minutes are something of a chore. Allen's co-author was Mickey Rose, who did the same for *Bananas*. 🎞

Woody Allen *Virgil Starkwell* • Janet Margolin *Louise* • Marcel Hillaire *Fritz* • Jacquelyn Hyde *Miss Blaire* • Lonny Chapman *Jake* • Jan Merlin *Al* • James Anderson *Chain gang warden* ■ *Dir* Woody Allen • *Scr* Woody Allen, Mickey Rose

Take This Job and Shove It
★★ **PG**

Comedy   1981 · US · Colour · 95mins

This big business comedy stars Robert Hays as Frank Macklin, a decent chap, who is sent by his firm back to his home town to increase the efficiency of the local brewery. His appointment is met with some hostility by the employees (many of whom he knows personally) but he soon proves his worth – only to make the brewery so profitable that it may be put up for sale. Named after the hit song performed by Johnny Paycheck, this well-meaning comedy features an uneasy mix of sloppy slapstick and toothless satire.

Robert Hays *Frank Macklin* • Barbara Hershey *JM Halstead* • David Keith *Harry Meade* • Tim Thomerson *Ray Binkowski* • Eddie Albert *Samuel Ellison* • Penelope Milford *Lenore Meade* • Art Carney *Charlie Pickett* • Martin Mull *Dick Ebersol* • David Allan Coe *Mooney* ■ *Dir* Gus Trikonis • *Scr* Barry Schneider, from a story by Jeffrey Bernini, Barry Schneider, from a song by David Allen Coe

Take Your Best Shot
★★

Romantic comedy
1982 · US · Colour · 96mins

Robert Urich stars as a struggling thespian who agrees to give it all up for his wife Meredith Baxter Birney and open a restaurant, but then he's offered a prized role in a major New York play. This interesting dilemma is presented as a rather soulless TV movie by people who, frankly, should know better. For a supposed romantic comedy, this is far too melodramatic and unreal.

Robert Urich *Jess Marriner* • Meredith Baxter Birney [Meredith Baxter] *Carol Marriner* • Jeffrey Tambor *Alden Pepper* • Jack Bannon *Dr Barry Richardson* ■ *Dir* David Greene • *Scr* Richard Levinson, William Link

Taken Away
★★ **12**

Drama based on a true story
1996 · US · Colour · 85mins

Since making their names in *LA Law*, real-life married couple Michael Tucker and Jill Eikenberry have regularly teamed up in TV movies. Here, Eikenberry plays a kidnap victim with a heart condition who has been left bound and gagged in her car; Tucker is her frantic husband who's desperately trying to locate her. The two leads turn in believable performances and, although it hardly taxes the brain, this is an intriguing enough time-passer. Contains some strong language. 🎞

Michael Tucker *Mark Hale* • Jill Eikenberry *Jan Hale* • James Marsden *Michael Galler* • Shane Meier *David Rattray* • Robert Wisden *Chief Ben Alpert* • Michael MacRae *Special Agent Grey* ■ *Dir* Jerry Jameson • *Scr* Ronald Parker

The Takeover
★ **18**

Crime action drama
1995 · US · Colour · 87mins

Mob boss wannabe Billy Drago leads reinforcements for his ongoing drugs war with club owner Nick Mancuso. Unwillingly drawn into the battle is ex-con David Amos, who lost both his restaurant and his girlfriend to Mancuso. The focus here is more on the characters than action, and the latter is directed in a more realistic fashion. The level of acting is generally substandard, possibly due to the fact nobody really does much except sit down and make plans after shooting off their guns. 🎞

Billy Drago *Danny Stein* • John Savage *Greg* • Nick Mancuso *Anthony Vilachi* • Eric DaRe *Venokur* • David Amos *Jonathan Fitzsimmons* • Gene Mitchell *Mickey Lane* • Cali Timmins *Kathy* ■ *Dir* Troy Cook • *Scr* Gene Mitchell

Taking Back My Life
★★ **15**

Drama based on a true story
1992 · US · Colour and BW · 90mins

Patricia Wettig plays rape victim Nancy Ziegenmeyer, whose accounts of her harrowing experience and her problematic recovery were covered in lurid detail by the press. The sadly familiar tale makes much of its factual basis and features two fine actresses in supporting roles: Ellen Burstyn, best remembered for her Oscar-winning role in *Alice Doesn't Live Here Anymore*, and Joanna Cassidy.

Patricia Wettig *Nancy Ziegenmeyer* • Stephen Lang *Steven Ziegenmeyer* • Ellen Burstyn *Wilma* • Eileen Brennan *Vicki Martin* • Shelley Hack *Nan Horvat* • Joanna Cassidy *Geneva Overholser* • Gina Hecht *Deanne* ■ *Dir* Harry Winer • *Scr* April Smith, from articles in the *Des Moines Register*

Taking Care of Business
★★ **15**

Comedy   1990 · US · Colour · 103mins

Originally shown at British cinemas as *Filofax*, this is a rather slight *Trading Places* rip-off with James Belushi as the prisoner on the run who finds wealthy Charles Grodin's Filofax and proceeds to steal his identity. The talented Belushi doesn't have enough good material here, while the usually excellent Grodin forfeits some of his substantial charm to the demands of the over-frenetic comedy. This is too uneven to be the riproaring entertainment it intends, but it's still harmless fun. Contains swearing. 🎞

James Belushi *Jimmy Dworski* • Charles Grodin *Spencer Barnes* • Anne DeSalvo *Debbie* • Loryn Locklin *Jewel* • Stephen Elliott *Walter Bentley* • Hector Elizondo *Warden* • Veronica Hamel *Elizabeth Barnes* ■ *Dir* Arthur Hiller • *Scr* Jill Mazursky, Jeffrey Abrams

The Taking of Beverly Hills
★★ **15**

Action crime thriller
1991 · US · Colour · 90mins

Routine action film, in which crook Robert Davi fakes a toxic spill so that his men can loot the homes of LA's rich and famous during the evacuation. Predictably, die-hard hero Ken Wahl rumbles the ruse, and tosses several spanners in the works. It's a promising plot, indifferently handled by director Sidney J Furie, who directed *The Ipcress File* back in the mid-sixties. 🎞

Ken Wahl *Terry "Boomer" Hayes* • Harley Jane Kozak *Laura Sage* • Matt Frewer *Ed Kelvin* • Tony Ganios *EPA Man* • Robert Davi *Robert "Bat" Masterson* • Lee Ving *James [Lee Ving] Varney* • Branscombe Richmond *Benitez* ■ *Dir* Sidney J Furie • *Scr* Rick Natkin, David Fuller, David J Burke, from a story by Sidney J Furie, Rick Natkin, David Fuller

The Taking of Flight 847
★★★ **15**

Drama based on a true story
1988 · US · Colour · 95mins

A convincing performance from the "bionic" Lindsay Wagner anchors this true story of flight attendant Uli Derickson's heroism during the 1985 hijacking of a TWA airliner. Norman Morrill's dramatic torn-from-the-headlines script, Paul Wendkos's taut direction and Wagner's subtle performance convey the anguish of the hostage situation. Eli Danker is equally credible as the head terrorist who goes nose-to-nose with Derickson over the precarious fate of the passengers. 🎞

Lindsay Wagner *Uli Derickson* • Eli Danker *Castro* • Sandy McPeak *John Testrake* • Ray Wise *Phil Maresca* • Leslie Easterbrook *Audrey* • Laurie Walters *Jane* ■ *Dir* Paul Wendkos • *Scr* Norman Morrill

The Taking of Pelham One Two Three
★★★★ **15**

Thriller   1974 · US · Colour · 100mins

Gerald Greenberg and Robert Q Lovett are the "stars" of this tough and compelling thriller about the hijack of a New York subway train. They are the film editors whose superb sense of rhythm and pace brings real tension to the radio exchanges between villain Robert Shaw and transport cop Walter Matthau, who tries to prevent Shaw and his gang from killing hostages while waiting for the payment of a $1 million ransom. Frankly, this motley collection of clichéd passengers doesn't deserve to be rescued, but, fortunately, director Joseph Sargent keeps the focus firmly on his leads. Shaw is admirably fanatical, and the world-weary, wisecracking Matthau is magnificent. Contains swearing. 🎞

Walter Matthau *Lieutenant Garber* • Robert Shaw *Blue* • Martin Balsam *Green* • Hector Elizondo *Grey* • Earl Hindman *Brown* • James Broderick *Denny Doyle* • Dick O'Neill *Correll* • Lee Wallace *Mayor* • Tom Pedi *Caz Dolowicz* • Jerry Stiller *Lieutenant Rico Patrone* ■ *Dir* Joseph Sargent • *Scr* Peter Stone, from the novel by John Godey

Taking Off
★★★★ **18**

Comedy drama   1971 · US · Colour · 88mins

Director Milos Forman's (*Amadeus*, *One Flew over the Cuckoo's Nest*) first American movie is a comedy of manners. Like the Czech quasi-comedies that brought him international acclaim, it's charming, sexy, bittersweet, and, in truth, a trifle plotless, but, like them it contains gems of observation and a wondrous understanding of human nature. This is very much a post-hippy, pot-smoking period piece, dealing with a dropout teenager's effect on her parents. Buck Henry, who co-wrote *The Graduate*, plays the runaway's father, getting out of his depth in the permissive society. Watch out for a nascent Carly Simon in one of the quick cuts of the devastatingly well-edited (by John Carter) audition number. 🎞

Lynn Carlin *Lynn Tyne* • Buck Henry *Larry Tyne* • Linnea Heacock *Jeannie Tyne* • Georgia Engel *Margot* • Tony Harvey *Tony* • Audra Lindley *Ann Lockston* • Paul Benedict *Ben Lockston* • Vincent Schiavelli *Schiavelli* • Ike Turner • Tina Turner • Carly Simon *Audition singer* ■ *Dir* Milos Forman • *Scr* Milos Forman, John Guare, Jean-Claude Carriere, John Klein

Tale of a Vampire
★★ **18**

Horror   1992 · UK/Jap · Colour · 97mins

Melancholic bloodsucker Julian Sands prowls suburban London searching for the double of his lost lover, Virginia, in this arty postmodern Hammer homage. When Sands eventually finds her in the guise of librarian Suzanna Hamilton (giving a dreadful performance) he must battle occult historian Kenneth Cranham for his spirit. Depressingly ordinary, despite a few oriental flourishes, this Mills and Boon vampire romance is far too low-key to make any lasting impression. 🎞

Julian Sands *Alex* • Suzanna Hamilton *Anne/Virginia* • Kenneth Cranham *Edgar* • Marian Diamond *Denise* • Michael Kenton *Magazine man* • Catherine Blake *Virginia, aged 5* ■ *Dir* Shimako Sato • *Scr* Shimako Sato, Jane Corbett, from a story by Shimako Sato, from the poem *Annabel Lee* by Edgar Allan Poe

A Tale of Springtime
★★★★ **U**

Romance   1989 · Fr · Colour · 102mins

"Tales of the Four Seasons" is the third series of films made by Eric Rohmer. This first entry shows that the keen intelligence, insight into the emotions of youth and unrivalled genius for chamber drama that made "Six Moral Tales" and "Comedies and Proverbs" so irresistible remained undimmed as the director entered his seventies. As ever in Rohmer's features, we feel we are eavesdropping on real people, with their behaviour, conversation and sheer unpredictability the very stuff of human nature. Deftly handled and effortlessly played, particularly by Anne Teyssèdre and Hugues Quester, this tale of matchmaking and friendship is utterly beguiling. In French with English subtitles. 🎞

Anne Teyssèdre *Jeanne* • Hugues Quester *Igor* • Florence Darel *Natasha* • Eloise Bennett *Eve* • Sophie Robin *Gaelle* ■ *Dir/Scr* Eric Rohmer

The Tale of Sweeney Todd ★★

Period horror drama
1998 · US/Ire · Colour · 92mins

The umpteenth telling of the tale of the demon barber of Fleet Street, and of the cutthroat sideline that led to the sale of London's finest fingernail pies. Riper than a month-old avocado, the film is directed by the versatile John Schlesinger, and stars Oscar-winner Ben Kingsley as Sweeney Todd, and Joanna Lumley as his pie-making partner in crime. Hardly the most subtle and sophisticated film ever made, it's nonetheless an entertaining enough romp.

Ben Kingsley *Sweeney Todd* • Joanna Lumley *Mrs Lovett* • Campbell Scott *Ben Carlyle* • Selina Boyack *Alice* • John Kavanagh *Rutledge* • Katharine Schlesinger *Lucy* • David Wilmot *Tom* ■ *Dir* John Schlesinger • *Scr* Peter Buckman, from a story by Peter Shaw

The Tale of the Fox ★★★★

Satirical fantasy 1931 · Fr · BW · 65mins

Adapted from Johann Wolfgang von Goethe's fable, *Renard the Fox*, Ladislaw Starewicz's only feature contains 100 different puppet characters and took a decade to prepare and 18 months to film. The story of the mischievous fox who is called to the court of the Lion King to explain his pranks works well as a children's film, thanks to the superbly judged blend of animal and human traits and the painstaking attention to natural detail. But it's also a subtle political satire that simmers with a deliciously naughty sexual tension. A French language film.

Dir Ladislaw Starewicz, Irène Starewicz • *Scr* Wladyslaw Starewicz, Irène Starewicz, Roger Richebé, Jean Nohain, Antoinette Nordmann, from the story *Die Reineke Fuchs* by Johann Wolfgang von Goethe • *Animator* Ladislaw Starewicz, Irene Starewicz

The Tale of Tsar Saltan ★★★

Animation 1984 · USSR · Colour

Animator I Ivanov-Vano rounded off a wonderful career with this stylised adaptation of Pushkin's delightful fairy tale. Having been cast adrift in a barrel with his mother, Prince Guildon befriends a white swan. The swan subsequently assists the prince's journey home and his struggle against the wicked aunts who have gained control over his unsuspecting father. The story might be a tad slow and repetitive for today's kids, but its beauty should win them over. Russian dialogue dubbed into English.

Dir I Ivanov-Vano, L Milchin • *Scr* I Ivanov-Vano, L Milchin, from a novel by Alexander Pushkin • *Animator* I Ivanov-Vano, L Milchin

A Tale of Two Cities

★★★★★ U

Historical drama 1935 · US · BW · 120mins

And it's a (Charles) Dickens of a tale told with all the verve and confidence of MGM in the thirties. Ronald Colman is convincingly noble as lawyer Sydney Carton, a victim of unrequited love, who finds purpose in an act of self-sacrifice during the ruthless period of

the French Revolution. The other actors – Elizabeth Allan, Basil Rathbone and Edna May Oliver – are at the mercy of some massive crowd scenes, for which thousands of extras were recruited. The featured players survive very well through a magnificent storming of a rather flimsy Bastille, while the cut-off point of the final scene with Madame La Guillotine and Sydney Carton will bring tears to your eyes. It is a far, far better movie of the classic than they were to make thereafter with Dirk Bogarde. ▭

Ronald Colman *Sydney Carton* • Elizabeth Allan *Lucie Manette* • Edna May Oliver *Miss Pross* • Blanche Yurka *Mme Defarge* • Reginald Owen *Stryver* • Basil Rathbone *Marquis St Evremonde* • Henry B Walthall *Dr Manette* • Donald Woods *Charles Darnay* ■ *Dir* Jack Conway • *Scr* WP Lipscomb, SN Behrman, from the novel by Charles Dickens

A Tale of Two Cities ★★★ U

Historical drama 1957 · UK · BW · 112mins

Dirk Bogarde gives a good account of himself in this Rank remake of Dickens's French Revolution novel. TEB Clarke, who scripted many of the best Ealing comedies, was perhaps an odd choice for such a prestigious project and, in striving for dramatic weight, he is occasionally guilty of being both pompous and ponderous. Nevertheless, director Ralph Thomas brings the best out of his cast, with Dorothy Tutin making a fetching Lucie Manette and Christopher Lee a truly hissable Marquis St Evremonde. ▭

DVD

Dirk Bogarde *Sydney Carton* • Dorothy Tutin *Lucie Manette* • Cecil Parker *Jarvis Lorry* • Stephen Murray *Dr Manette* • Athene Seyler *Miss Pross* • Christopher Lee *Marquis St Evremonde* • Donald Pleasence *John Barsad* • Rosalie Crutchley *Madame Defarge* ■ *Dir* Ralph Thomas • *Scr* TEB Clarke, from the novel by Charles Dickens

A Tale of Two Cities ★★ U

Animated drama
1984 · Ausl · Colour · 75mins

The best that makers of animated classics can hope for is that the film will not be denounced as a travesty that dishonours the original text. This Australian adaptation of Dickens's tale of selfless heroism set at the time of the French Revolution certainly has its faults, not least the atrocious accents. But the animation and the sense of fear generated by the Reign of Terror is rather well captured. As ever, the villains are better drawn than the goodies, with Evremonde and Madame DeFarge thoroughly nasty pieces of work. ▭

Dir Warwick Gilbert • *Scr* Russell Thornton, from the novel by Charles Dickens

Talent for the Game ★★★ PG

Sports drama 1991 · US · Colour · 87mins

A modest but watchable entry in the baseball genre. Edward James Olmos is the baseball scout who discovers a brilliant young pitcher in an Idaho backwater, but watches in dismay as he is ruthlessly exploited by his club. Olmos delivers a typically gutsy performance and, although the story is slight, director Robert M Young handles the proceedings

commendably. Larry Ferguson, who co-wrote such hits as *Highlander* and *The Hunt for Red October*, had a hand in the script. Contains some strong language. ▭

Edward James Olmos *Virgil Sweet* • Lorraine Bracco *Bobbie Henderson* • Jamey Sheridan *Tim Weaver* • Terry Kinney *Gil Lawrence* • Jeff Corbett *Sammy Bodeen* • Tom Bower *Reverend Bodeen* • Janet Carroll *Rachel Bodeen* ■ *Dir* Robert M Young • *Scr* David Himmelstein, Tom Donnelly, Larry Ferguson

The Talented Mr Ripley

★★★★ 15

Drama 1999 · US · Colour · 133mins

Director Anthony Minghella follows his award-winning *The English Patient* with this absorbing thriller, based on the novel by Patricia Highsmith. Matt Damon plays the eponymous Ripley, a young opportunist who seeks out Dickie Greenleaf (Oscar-nominated Jude Law), an American playboy living it up in Europe. Ripley becomes friends with Dickie, but gradually comes to covet his carefree lifestyle and glamorous girlfriend (Gwyneth Paltrow). A compelling idea that benefits from Minghella's classy direction and a zeitgeist cast. ▭

Matt Damon *Tom Ripley* • Gwyneth Paltrow *Marge Sherwood* • Jude Law *Dickie Greenleaf* • Cate Blanchett *Meredith Logue* • Philip Seymour Hoffman *Freddie Miles* • Jack Davenport *Peter Smith-Kingsley* • James Rebhorn *Herbert Greenleaf* • Philip Baker Hall *Alvin MacCarron* ■ *Dir* Anthony Minghella • *Scr* Anthony Minghella, from the novel by Patricia Highsmith

Tales from a Hard City

★★★★

Documentary drama
1994 · UK/Fr · Colour · 80mins

The glorious British documentary tradition is alive and well and living in Sheffield. Director Kim Flitcroft spent a year with his subjects, and what a quartet they are: Glen the karaoke car thief; Paul the thespian boxer; Wayne the wannabe media mogul; and Sarah the star-in-the-making Wayne wants to promote. Fact repeatedly proves more bizarre than fiction throughout the film and, while the foursome are sometimes hard to live with, they are certainly never dull.

Dir Kim Flitcroft • *Scr* Geoffrey Beattie (story consultant)

Tales from the Crypt

★★★ 18

Horror 1972 · UK · Colour · 91mins

An excellent anthology of scares-with-a-smile stories drawn from EC horror comics, with Ralph Richardson as the crypt keeper revealing a quintet of fearsome futures to a veteran British cast of terror troupers. Peter Cushing returns from the grave, Patrick Magee is a victimised blind man, Joan Collins battles a psychotic Santa Claus, Richard Greene does a variation on *The Monkey's Paw* and Ian Hendry can't get used to being dead in this faithful re-creation of EC's grim-and-grin formula. Ace direction by genre favourite Freddie Francis adeptly leavens the vivid horror with seriocomic interludes. ▭

Ralph Richardson *Crypt keeper* • Geoffrey Bayldon *Guide* • Joan Collins *Joanne Clayton* • Ian Hendry *Carl Maitland* • Nigel Patrick *William Rogers* • Patrick Magee *George Carter* • Peter Cushing *Grimsdyke* • Richard Greene *Ralph Jason* • Roy Dotrice *Charles Gregory* ■ *Dir* Freddie Francis • *Scr* Milton Subotsky, from stories from the comic books *Tales from the Crypt* and *The Vault of Horror,*, by Al Feldstein, Johnny Craig, William Gaines

Tales from the Crypt: Demon Knight ★★ 18

Horror fantasy 1995 · US · Colour · 88mins

Not an anthology in the fondly remembered tradition of the original *Tales from the Crypt*, just one duff story ripped off from *Night of the Living Dead*. Billy Zane is the evil force who hounds an assortment of misfits trapped in a Texas motel in his search for an ancient talisman containing the blood of Jesus Christ. Crude sight gags and slimy schlock are accented over mordant humour in director Ernest R Dickerson's eager-to-please but flimsy fright-fest. Contains swearing and violence. ▭

Billy Zane *The Collector* • William Sadler *Brayker* • Jada Pinkett [Jada Pinkett Smith] *Jeryline* • Brenda Bakke *Cordelia* • CCH Pounder *Irene* • Dick Miller *Uncle Willy* ■ *Dir* Ernest R Dickerson • *Scr* Ethan Reiff, Cyrus Voris, Mark Bishop

Tales from the Crypt Presents: Bordello of Blood ★★ 18

Horror comedy 1996 · US · Colour · 82mins

This barely competent B-movie gross-out is tedious, tawdry and tiresome. Stand-up comedian Dennis Miller is the detective hired by Erika Eleniak to find her wayward punk brother Corey Feldman, who has disappeared after patronising a brothel-cum-funeral home run by ancient vampire queen Angie Everhart. The brains behind the whorehouse is Reverend Chris Sarandon who not only gets to rid the world of lust-crazed sinners, but also funds his evangelical cable channel by selling their belongings. The blood-letting is pretty rudimentary, with the CGI topless babe explosions looking particularly cheesy. For undemanding horror anoraks only. Contains swearing and violence. ▭

John Kassir *Crypt Keeper* • Dennis Miller *Rafe Guttman* • Erika Eleniak *Katherine Verdoux* • Angie Everhart *Lilith* • Chris Sarandon *Reverend Current* • Corey Feldman *Caleb Verdoux* • Aubrey Morris *McCutcheon* • Whoopi Goldberg ■ *Dir* Gilbert Adler • *Scr* Gilbert Adler, AL Katz, from a story by Bob Gale, Robert Zemeckis

Tales from the Darkside: the Movie ★★★ 18

Horror 1991 · US · Colour · 89mins

A 3,000-year-old mummy, a malignant moggy and a gruesome gargoyle take their monstrous turns in a taut, tight and fun trio of terror tales drawn from the work of authors Sir Arthur Conan Doyle and Stephen King. High on creepy atmosphere, low on boring exposition, this well-crafted movie version of its duff namesake TV series is an agreeably ambitious and solidly shocking outing. Watch out for Christian Slater in shorts, Debbie Harry

U = SUITABLE FOR ALL   Uc = SUITABLE FOR ALL, ESPECIALLY FOR YOUNG CHILDREN (VIDEO ONLY)   PG = PARENTAL GUIDANCE

as a housewife from hell and, especially, the jolting *Cat from Hell* episode! Contains violence and swearing. 🖵

Deborah Harry *Betty* • David Forrester *Priest* • Matthew Lawrence *Timmy* • Christian Slater *Andy* • Steve Buscemi *Edward Bellingham* • Julianne Moore *Susan* • Micheal Deak *Mummy* • David Johansen *Halston* • William Hickey *Drogan* • James Remar *Preston* • Rae Dawn Chong *Carola* ■ *Dir* John Harrison • *Scr* Michael McDowell, George Romero, from the story *Lot 249* by Sir Arthur Conan Doyle, from the story *Cat from Hell* by Stephen King

Tales from the Hood   ★★

Horror   1995 · US · Colour · 101mins

Spike Lee was the executive producer of this horror anthology that attempts to comment on an aspect of the African-American experience in each of its stories – with uneven results.The first story (a rookie cop encounters brutal and bigoted colleagues) is flat and predictable, and the third story (a racist politician struck by an old slave curse) seems like a rip-off of *Trilogy of Terror's* Zuni fetish doll segment. Much better are the second story (a boy and the ''monster'' that appears in his room at night), and the instant classic *Clockwork Orange*-inspired fourth story, concerning the attempted reform of a gang member. An amusing Clarence Williams III plays the ghoulish mortician linking the four stories.

Clarence Williams III *Mr Simms* • Joe Torry *Stack* • Wings Hauser *Strom* • Anthony Griffith *Clarence* • Michael Massee *Newton* • Tom Wright *Martin Moorehouse* ■ *Dir* Rusty Cundieff • *Scr* Rusty Cundieff, Darin Scott

The Tales of Beatrix Potter   ★★★ Ⓤ

Dance fantasy   1971 · UK · Colour · 85mins

A big 1971 hit that slips into ballet slippers to tell the lovely stories of Beatrix Potter, set in their original Lakeland landscape. Ballet maestro Frederick Ashton choreographs and makes an outstanding appearance as a fussy Mrs Tiggy-Winkle The *corps de ballet* comes with realistic-looking mouse heads, Mrs Puddleduck is a treat and there's a midnight *pas de deux* between two piglets. But the noteworthy costumes tend toward the bulky with a rather smothering effect, and though intended for children, its Peter Rabbit charm is too manipulative and humdrum to urge many balletomane stirrings. 🖵

Frederick Ashton *Mrs Tiggy-Winkle* • Alexander Grant *Pigling Bland/Peter Rabbit* • Julie Wood *Mrs Tittlemouse* • Keith Martin *Johnny Town Mouse* • Ann Howard *Jemima Puddle-Duck* • Robert Mead *Fox* • Wayne Sleep *Tom Thumb/Squirrel Nutkin* ■ *Dir* Reginald Mills • *Scr* Richard Goodwin, Christine Edzard, from the stories by Beatrix Potter • *Costume Designer* Christine Edzard

The Tales of Hoffmann   ★★★★ Ⓤ

Opera   1951 · UK · Colour · 119mins

Three years after the success of *The Red Shoes*, Michael Powell and Emeric Pressburger returned to the world of ballet at the behest of Sir Thomas Beecham for this irresistible confection. With Moira Shearer and Frederick Ashton dancing superbly and Hein Heckroth's art design and costumes worthy of their Oscar nominations, this sumptuous adaptation of Offenbach's opera is a visual delight. But with the Sadler's Wells Chorus backing singers of the calibre of Robert Rounseville and Ann Ayars, it sounds pretty good, too. Indeed, only the slightly muddled structure detracts from what is otherwise an audacious cinematic experiment. 🖵

Robert Rounseville *Hoffmann* • Moira Shearer *Stella/Olympia* • Robert Helpmann *Lindorff/Coppelius/Dapertutto* • Pamela Brown *Nicklaus* • Frederick Ashton *Kleinzack/Cochenille* • Leonide Massine *Spalanzani* • Ludmilla Tcherina *Giulietta* • Ann Ayars *Antonia* • John Ford *Nathaniel* ■ *Dir/Scr* Michael Powell, Emeric Pressburger

Tales of Manhattan   ★★★

Portmanteau comedy
1942 · US · BW · 118mins

That title is really an awkward pun: the ''tales'' are those of a tail coat, and this charming all-star portmanteau comedy is a collection of playlets about the coat's adventures. Very much of its time and less than charming today, the episode involving the great Paul Robeson looks quite racist in its Uncle Remus sort of way, and one wonders why it wasn't deleted, instead of the notoriously missing WC Fields sequence. Edward G Robinson has a splendid moment, as does Charles Laughton at Carnegie Hall, and Rita Hayworth looks simply ravishing in the first story, but if ever a movie was a curate's egg it's this one.

Charles Boyer *Paul Orman* • Rita Hayworth *Ethel Halloway* • Ginger Rogers *Diane* • Henry Fonda *George* • Cesar Romero *Harry Wilson* • Charles Laughton *Charles Smith* • Elsa Lanchester *Elsa Smith* • Edward G Robinson *Larry Browne* • George Sanders *Williams* • Paul Robeson *Luke* • Ethel Waters *Esther* ■ *Dir* Julien Duvivier • *Scr* Ben Hecht, Ferenc Molnar, Donald Ogden Stewart, Samuel Hoffenstein, Alan Campbell, Ladislas Fodor, Laszlo Vadnai, Laslo Gorog, Lamar Trotti, Henry Blankford, Ed Beloin, Bill Morrow

Tales of Ordinary Madness   ★ ⑱

Drama   1981 · It/Fr · Colour · 97mins

Italian director Ferreri – infamous for his rejection of bourgeois morality, notably in *La Grande Bouffe* – has adapted this film from the autobiographical writings of the alcoholic beat poet Charles Bukowski. Set mainly in Los Angeles, it stars Ben Gazzara as the disillusioned, womanising poet and he certainly gives a remarkable performance. But what might be wonderful pronouncements on paper, in prose or poetry, certainly don't come across on screen and the effect is pretentious, tedious and very dated. Contains violence, nudity, sex scenes, drug abuse and swearing 🖵

Ben Gazzara *Charles Serking* • Ornella Muti *Cass* • Susan Tyrrell *Vera* • Tanya Lopert *Vicky* • Roy Brocksmith *Barman* ■ *Dir* Marco Ferreri • *Scr* Sergio Amidei, Marco Ferreri, Anthony Foutz, from the short story collection *Erections, Ejaculations, Exhibitions and General Tales of Ordinary Madness* by Charles Bukowski

Tales of Terror   ★★★ ⑮

Horror   1962 · US · Colour · 84mins

One of cult director Roger Corman's classier productions, helped by ace genre writer Richard Matheson's skilled if loose adaptations of three Edgar Allan Poe stories. Ranging between macabre *Grand Guignol* and preposterously broad comedy, this cheerfully chilling collection is further boosted by the memorable teaming of Vincent Price and Peter Lorre, the latter in excellent scene-stealing form. 🖵

Vincent Price *Locke/Fortunato/Valdemar* • Maggie Pierce *Lenora* • Leona Gage *Morella* • Peter Lorre *Montresor* • Joyce Jameson *Annabel* • Basil Rathbone *Carmichael* • Debra Paget *Helene* ■ *Dir* Roger Corman • *Scr* Richard Matheson, from the stories *Morella* , *The Black Cat*, *The Facts in the Case of M Valdemar* and *The Cask of Amontillado* by Edgar Allan Poe

Tales That Witness Madness   ★★ ⑱

Portmanteau horror
1973 · UK · Colour · 86mins

This portmanteau of four horror stories was mysteriously shelved for years, eventually turning up on TV in the eighties. Director Freddie Francis had previously done better examples of the genre, notably *Torture Garden*. Here the most effective segments are the first (although derivative of Ray Bradbury's story *The Veldt*) and the last (quite gruesome). An interesting cast includes Kim Novak, in a part intended for Rita Hayworth, Jack Hawkins, in his final film, and Joan Collins, seen rather startlingly doing the vacuuming. 🖵

Jack Hawkins *Nicholas* • Donald Pleasence *Dr Tremayne* • Russell Lewis *Paul* • Peter McEnery *Timothy* • Joan Collins *Bella* • Michael Jayston *Brian* • Kim Novak *Auriol* • Michael Petrovitch *Kimo* • Mary Tamm *Ginny* ■ *Dir* Freddie Francis • *Scr* Jennifer Jayne

Talk of Angels   ★★ ⑫

Period romantic drama
1998 · US · Colour · 93mins

Though it's pretty to look at and finely acted, there is something missing from this rather insubstantial romantic tale, set in the thirties. Polly Walker plays a young Irish woman who leaves her Civil War-torn homeland for Spain, which is, er, on the brink of Civil War. She is employed to look after the young daughters of a wealthy but liberal doctor (Franco Nero), but her life becomes complicated when she catches the eye of his idealistic (and married) young son, Vincent Perez. Despite the strong cast – look out for Frances McDormand in particular – this is neither a gushy love story or a political epic. 🖵

Polly Walker *Mary Lavelle* • Vincent Perez *Francisco Areavaga* • Franco Nero *Dr Vicente Areavaga* • Marisa Paredes *Dona Consuelo* • Leire Berrocal *Milagros* • Penelope Cruz *Pilar* • Frances McDormand *Conlon* • Ruth McCabe *O'Toole* ■ *Dir* Nick Hamm • *Scr* Ann Guedes, Frank McGuinness, from the novel *Mary Lavelle* by Kate O'Brien

The Talk of the Town   ★★★★ Ⓤ

Comedy drama   1942 · US · BW · 113mins

The eternal triangle – two men besotted by the same woman who is attracted to both – is the central ingredient of this classy, intelligent and witty romantic comedy. However, skilfully interwoven into the mix is an examination of hypocrisy, the inequities of the law and a measure of suspense. Cary Grant, a politically reformist factory worker, is wrongfully accused of murder and hides out in Jean Arthur's house, where he becomes friends with Ronald Colman, a distinguished legal academic and Supreme Court judge lodging there. Ideas are exchanged and both fall for their hostess. Story, script and picture were Oscar-nominated, the stars deserved to be. 🖵

Cary Grant *Leopold Dilg* • Jean Arthur *Nora Shelley* • Ronald Colman *Michael Lightcap* • Edgar Buchanan *Sam Yates* • Glenda Farrell *Regina Bush* • Charles Dingle *Andrew Holmes* • Emma Dunn *Mrs Shelley* • Rex Ingram *Tilney* ■ *Dir* George Stevens • *Scr* Irwin Shaw, Sidney Buchman, Dale Van Every, from a story by Sidney Harmon

Talk Radio   ★★★★ ⑱

Drama   1988 · US · Colour · 104mins

A gripping picture, which dates from the time when director Oliver Stone made good films rather than sensational headlines, featuring a tour de force performance from Eric Bogosian. The basic plot recalls Clint Eastwood's *Play Misty for Me*, but there all similarities end as DJ Bogosian lets fly with a series of blistering diatribes against the callers to his late night radio show. The subplots rather get in the way of the monologues, which are delivered with such power and passion that one can only wonder why Bogosian's career has gone nowhere since. Contains swearing and violence. 🖵

Eric Bogosian *Barry Champlain* • Alec Baldwin *Dan* • Ellen Greene *Ellen* • Leslie Hope *Laura* • John C McGinley *Stu* • John Pankow *Dietz* • Michael Wincott *Kent* • Linda Atkinson *Sheila Fleming* ■ *Dir* Oliver Stone • *Scr* Eric Bogosian, Oliver Stone, from the play by Eric Bogosian, Ted Savinar, from the non-fiction book *Talked to Death: the Life and Murder of Alan Berg* by Stephen Singular

Talkin' Dirty after Dark   ★★★ ⑱

Comedy   1991 · US · Colour · 86mins

A comedy about comedians. Set around John Witherspoon's LA comedy club where stand-up acts rub shoulders with the equally crazy staff of the late night cabaret venue. Admid the joke-telling there is a complex web of romantic entanglements and sexual liaisons. A good showcase for a bunch of young comedians, the film particularly highlights the amiable, fast-talking Martin Lawrence who plays newcomer Terry, who wins over the crowd with blue routines about sex. The dirty talking seems to be what the crowd likes best. A profane, undisciplined romp which triumphs through some truly funny sequences.

Martin Lawrence *Terry* • John Witherspoon *Dukie* • Jedda Jones *Rubie Lin* • ''Tiny''Lister

Jr [Tom "Tiny" Lister Jr] *Bigg* • Phyllis Yvonne Stickney *Aretha* • Renee Jones *Kimmie* • Darryl Sivad *Percy* • Yolanda King *Mother* ■ *Dir/Scr* Topper Carew

The Tall Blond Man with One Black Shoe ★★★ PG

Spy comedy 1972 · Fr · Colour · 85 mins

Physical French comedy, for those who like physical French comedies, and highly rated by those who do. This farce stars Pierre Richard as a bumbling innocent whose life becomes hectic when he is mistaken for a spy by rival groups of secret agents. Easy to watch, and surprisingly action-packed, with Richard showing himself to be a talented slapstick comic. The film spawned one French sequel, *The Return Of...*, two years later, and was oddly retitled *The Man With One Red Shoe* for the US remake. A French language film.

Pierre Richard *François* • Bernard Blier *Milan* • Jean Rochefort *Toulouse* • Mireille Darc *Christine* • Jean Carmet *Maurice* • Colette Castel *Paulette* • Jean Obe *Botrel* ■ *Dir* Yves Robert • *Scr* Yves Robert, Francis Veber

Tall, Dark and Deadly ★★ 15

Thriller 1995 · US · Colour · mins

This predictable, formulaic TV thriller starts off decently, but it's a cheap attempt to cash in on the success of films like *Sleeping with the Enemy*. Kim Delaney (*NYPD Blue*) is a successful female architect, who should know better, but falls under the spell of a charming stranger (Jack Scalia). Naturally, he turns out to be an obsessive nut, and she finds herself running for her life. This is a creaky and derivative package that should be renamed *Dull, Stark, and Deadly*!

Jack Scalia *Roy Calvin* • Kim Delaney *Maggie Springer* • Todd Allen *Sam* • Gina Mastrogiacomo *Gloria Bowers* • Ely Pouget *Toni* ■ *Dir* Kenneth Fink • *Scr* MaryAnne Kasica, Michael Scheff

The Tall Guy ★★★ 15

Romantic comedy
1989 · UK · Colour · 88mins

Now that she's regarded as one of Hollywood's leading thespians, it's unlikely that you'll ever see Emma Thompson like this again. So make the most of this often hilarious comedy directed by Mel Smith and written pre-*Four Weddings and a Funeral* by Richard Curtis particularly the brilliant knockabout love scene with the gangling Jeff Goldblum. They work well together throughout the film, with her deadpan approach and his neuroses perfectly matched. The musical version of *The Elephant Man* is a master stroke and Rowan Atkinson's knowing send-up of his own image is both funny and generous. The plot wanders a little towards the end, but this is cosy, feel-good, if rather naive, fun. Contains swearing and nudity.

Jeff Goldblum *Dexter King* • Emma Thompson *Kate Lemon* • Rowan Atkinson *Ron Anderson* • Geraldine James *Carmen* • Emil Wolk *Cyprus Charlie* • Kim Thomson *Cheryl* • Harold Innocent *Timothy* • Anna Massey *Mary* ■ *Dir* Mel Smith • *Scr* Richard Curtis

Tall in the Saddle ★★★ U

Western 1944 · US · BW · 87mins

If ever there was a title made for Big John Wayne, this is it. However, the Duke barely gets a look-in, as in reality it's more of a vehicle for his tempestuous co-star Ella Raines, who goes a-gunning for the Duke in order to woo him. George "Gabby" Hayes is in there, too, in a complex plot in which Wayne is framed for murder as he discovers Ward Bond's crooked plans to steal Audrey Long's ranch. But none of this matters, really. Edwin L Marin's direction is fast-moving, there are two terrific fist fights, and, for those of you who wondered exactly what Wayne got up to during the Second World War, this will answer your question.

John Wayne *Rocklin* • Ella Raines *Arly Harolday* • Audrey Long *Clara Cardell* • George "Gabby" Hayes *Dave* • Elisabeth Risdon *Miss Martin* • Ward Bond *"Judge" Garvey* • Don Douglas *Mr Harolday* • Paul Fix *Bob Clews* ■ *Dir* Edwin L Marin • *Scr* Michael Hogan, Paul P Fix, from a story by Gordon Ray Young

Tall Man Riding ★★ U

Western 1955 · US · Colour · 81mins

Randolph Scott returns to town to avenge a bullwhipping he received for daring to court a cattle baron's daughter, some years earlier, and finds that she has married another. Her father, meanwhile, is now almost blind and about to lose his spread. With outlaws and landgrabbers stirring up trouble, Scott has his hands full. Dorothy Malone plays the girl he left behind, with Peggie Castle as the usual contrast, a saloon singer hooked up with the bad guys. Not a great western, but there are many worse.

Randolph Scott *Larry Madden* • Dorothy Malone *Corinna Ordway* • Peggie Castle *Reva* • Bill Ching [William Ching] *Rex Willard* • John Baragrey *Cibo Pearlo* • Robert Barrat *Tucker "Tuck" Ordway* • John Dehner *Ames Luddington* • Paul Richards (1) *Peso Kid* ■ *Dir* Lesley Selander • *Scr* Joseph Hoffman, from a novel by Norman A Fox

The Tall Men ★★★★ U

Western 1955 · US · Colour · 122mins

Clark Gable rarely ventured out West, but on the evidence of this impressive picture he should have done so more often. Few directors understood the man of action better than Raoul Walsh, who draws bristling performances from both Gable and Robert Ryan in a tough trail-driving tale. Jane Russell is also on top form, giving as good as she gets as the boys bid for her affections. Walsh stages the action sequences with typical bravado and handles the more intimate moments with great finesse. Superbly photographed by Leo Tover, this is one of the genre's most unjustly overlooked films.

Clark Gable *Ben Allison* • Jane Russell *Nella Turner* • Robert Ryan *Nathan Stark* • Cameron Mitchell *Clint Allison* • Juan Garcia *Luis* • Harry Shannon *Sam* • Emile Meyer *Chickasaw* ■ *Dir* Raoul Walsh • *Scr* Sydney Boehm, Frank Nugent, from a novel by Clay Fisher

Tall Stories ★★★

Drama 1990 · Por · Colour · 92mins

Shot in under 20 days, Joachim Pinto's rites of passage picture may be set alongside the sunlit Portuguese coast, but there are plenty of dark secrets lurking in the boarding house where most of the action takes place. Sent to stay with his aunt for the summer, impressionable 12-year-old Bruno Leite hero worships wastrel Manuel Lobao, who spends much of his time boasting of his sexual conquests. However, the truth about his proclivities emerges after doctor Luis Miguel Cintra checks in and the flighty maid seeks revenge for her wrongful dismissal. An assured investigation into adolescent angst. A Portuguese language film.

Bruno Leite *Miguel* • Manuel Lobao *Joao* • Isabel De Castro *Dona Marta* • Luis Miguel Cintra *Dr Fernando* ■ *Dir/Scr* Joachim Pinto

The Tall Stranger ★★ PG

Western 1957 · US · Colour · 79mins

A very routine western that's mainly of interest for reuniting the stars of Raoul Walsh's *Colorado Territory*, Joel McCrea and Virginia Mayo. This was one of the movies that Allied Artists (formerly the poverty row studio Monogram) made to consolidate its A-feature reputation. However, despite the spurious grandeur achieved by filming in CinemaScope, the two leads look too old and Thomas Carr's direction is resolutely B-western.

Joel McCrea *Ned Bannon* • Virginia Mayo *Ellen* • Barry Kelley *Hardy Bishop* • Michael Ansara *Zarata* • Whit Bissell *Judson* • James Dobson *Dud* • George Neise [George N Neise] *Harper* ■ *Dir* Thomas Carr • *Scr* Christopher Knopf, from a story by Louis L'Amour

The Tall T ★★★★ U

Western 1957 · US · Colour · 76mins

Randolph Scott plays the very ordinary cowpoke who stumbles into the hands of kidnappers, carefully biding his time to turn the tables and free their captive, the rich man's wife played by Maureen O'Sullivan. The outlaws are finely etched in Burt Kennedy's screenplay as both ruthless and human, and skilfully portrayed by Henry Silva, Skip Homeier and, especially, Richard Boone as their leader, a lonely, intelligent figure who cannot escape his nature. It is superbly filmed, almost entirely outdoors, by director Budd Boetticher, and the vivid, desolate landscape greatly enhances the drama.

Randolph Scott *Pat Brennan* • Richard Boone *Usher* • Maureen O'Sullivan *Doretta Mims* • Arthur Hunnicutt *Ed Rintoon* • Skip Homeier *Billy Jack* • Henry Silva *Chink* ■ *Dir* Budd Boetticher • *Scr* Burt Kennedy, from the story *The Captives* by Elmore Leonard

Tall Tale: the Unbelievable Adventures of Pecos Bill ★★★ PG

Western adventure
1994 · US · Colour · 99mins

Jeremiah Chechik, who directed the disappointing movie version of *The Avengers*, also made this amiable, feel-good family western for Disney. Patrick Swayze has a lot of fun portraying the folk hero Pecos Bill, who, with two companions, helps a family battle a greedy land agent (Scott Glenn in enjoyably pantomimic form). Children will lap up this updated version of good old-fashioned western action and Chechik certainly seems at home on the range.

Patrick Swayze *Pecos Bill* • Oliver Platt *Paul Bunyan* • Roger Aaron Brown *John Henry* • Nick Stahl *Daniel Hackett* • Scott Glenn *JP Stiles* • Stephen Lang *Jonas Hackett* • Jared Harris *Head Thug Pug* • Catherine O'Hara *Calamity Jane* ■ *Dir* Jeremiah Chechik • *Scr* Steven L Bloom, Robert Rodat

The Tall Target ★★★★ U

Drama 1951 · US · BW · 77mins

This ingeniously plotted, moody period thriller is a hidden nugget of gold among a great deal of early fifties' tosh. An exemplary Dick Powell plays Abraham Lincoln's bodyguard, a lone cop searching for an assassin as the newly elected president travels to Baltimore aboard a train in 1861. Director Anthony Mann's beautifully paced, atmospherically shot movie hums with intelligent intrigue and some neatly paced performances, particularly from Powell, who shines as the determined maverick with a mission.

Dick Powell *John Kennedy* • Paula Raymond *Ginny Beaufort* • Adolphe Menjou *Colonel Caleb Jeffers* • Marshall Thompson *Lance Beaufort* • Ruby Dee *Rachel* • Will Geer *Homer Crowley* • Richard Rober *Lieutenant Coulter* • Florence Bates *Charlotte Alsop* • Victor Kilian *John K Gannon* ■ *Dir* Anthony Mann • *Scr* Art Cohn, George Worthington Yates, from a story by George Worthington Yates, Geoffrey Homes [Daniel Mainwaring]

Talos the Mummy ★★★ 15

Horror adventure thriller
1997 · US/Lux · Colour · 114mins

A "me-too" Mummy quickie that cashed in on video while the Brendan Fraser blockbuster was cleaning up at the box office. The film is inventively cast, with martial arts star Jason Scott Lee popping up as a gun-toting detective and Louise Lombard from TV's *House of Eliott* providing the glamour. The strong pre-title sequence features horror great Christopher Lee. The story follows traditional bandaged lines as the remains of Talos, a very bad ancient Egyptian indeed, are disturbed by archaeologists, resulting in mayhem in modern-day London.

Jason Scott Lee *Riley* • Louise Lombard *Samantha Turkel* • Sean Pertwee *Bradley Cortese* • Lysette Anthony *Dr Claire Mulrooney* • Michael Lerner *Professor Marcus* • Jack Davenport *Detective Bartone* • Honor Blackman *Captain Shea* • Christopher Lee *Sir Richard Turkel* • Shelley Duvall *Edith Butros* ■ *Dir* Russell Mulcahy • *Scr* John Esposito, Russell Mulcahy, from a story by Keith Williams, Russell Mulcahy

Tamahine ★★

Comedy 1963 · UK · Colour · 95mins

Back in the 18th century, Captain Cook brought to England a Tahitian named Omai who caused considerable cultural uproar and became a sexual magnet for ladies of wealth and discrimination. Transposed to an English boys' public school in 1963 with Nancy Kwan playing a desirous Tahitian, the cultural collision doesn't have quite the same impact. Even so, the dusky, demure and scantily clad Miss Kwan drives everyone into a lather, including art master Derek Nimmo, posh pupil James Fox and supercilious headmaster Dennis Price. The ending,

1396

U = SUITABLE FOR ALL Uc = SUITABLE FOR ALL, ESPECIALLY FOR YOUNG CHILDREN (VIDEO ONLY) PG = PARENTAL GUIDANCE

though telegraphed, is pure South Seas fantasy, shot on the island of Bora Bora.

Nancy Kwan *Tamahine* • John Fraser *Richard* • Dennis Price *Poole* • Coral Browne *Madam Becque* • Dick Bentley *Storekeeper* • Derek Nimmo *Clove* • Justine Lord *Diana* • Michael Gough *Cartwright* • Allan Cuthbertson *Housemaster* • James Fox *Oliver* ■ *Dir* Philip Leacock • *Scr* Denis Cannan, from the novel by Thelma Nicklaus

Tamanna ★★★★ PG

Drama based on a true story
1997 · Ind · Colour · 124mins

This is the tale of a daughter who learns the horrifying truth about how she was left to die as a baby because of her gender. Boasting convincing performances from Pooja Bhatt as Tamanna, and Paresh Rawal as her kindly adoptive father, this is a lively and intelligent film that moves on with tremendous pace, and provides an effective and probing look at the controversial issue of infanticide. In Hindi with English subtitles. 📼

Paresh Rawal *Tikku* • Pooja Bhatt *Tamanna* ■ *Dir* Mahesh Bhatt • *Scr* Tanuja Chandra, Mahesh Bhatt, Yadar Rajt

The Tamarind Seed ★★★ 15

Romantic thriller
1974 · UK · Colour · 119mins

"I am a man and I want you," Omar Sharif says to Julie Andrews. "I know we are dialectically opposed to each other, but we must keep materialist thinking out of it." Julie thinks for a minute, maybe of England, and then says, "Are you trying to enrol me in the KGB or are you really defecting?" Omar is the most gorgeous spy in the Soviet bloc and Julie is the prettiest foreign office employee, so why shouldn't the Iron Curtain melt? There are occasional hints that Blake Edwards saw this as a satire on all those spy melodramas, but mostly it's tosh, lusciously shot in Barbados, Paris and London. 📼

Julie Andrews *Judith Farrow* • Omar Sharif *Feodor Sverdlov* • Anthony Quayle *Jack Loder* • Sylvia Syms *Margaret Stephenson* • Daniel O'Herlihy [Dan O'Herlihy] *Fergus Stephenson* • Oscar Homolka *Gen Golitsyn* • Bryan Marshall *George MacLeod* ■ *Dir* Blake Edwards • *Scr* Blake Edwards, from the novel by Evelyn Anthony

The TAMI Show ★★★★★

Music concert documentary
1964 · US · BW · 113mins

The third best concert movie ever made, after *Woodstock* and *Monterey Pop*, because it captures practically every significant chart act of the day at the height of their explosive performance powers. Filmed at the Santa Monica Civic Auditorium on 24 October 1964, the Teenage Awards Music International show begins with hosts Jan and Dean introducing Chuck Berry with Gerry and the Pacemakers and ends with the Rolling Stones whipping the crowd into an hysterical frenzy. In between, The Supremes and Lesley Gore boast huge hairdos, Billy J. Kramer sings Lennon and McCartney, The Beach Boys surf through their California Sound and James Brown struts his funky stuff.

Fabulous talent in an amazingly witty and vivacious time capsule.
Dir Steve Binder

The Taming of the Shrew ★★

Comedy   1929 · US · BW · 63mins

Shakespeare's comedy has been much-filmed, perhaps most popularly in the musical version as *Kiss Me Kate*. This version co-stars the King and Queen of Hollywood, Douglas Fairbanks and Mary Pickford, paired for the first and last time. Unfortunately, working together revealed severe differences in temperament and approach – the battle between Shakespeare's lovers carried on and off the screen and ended their marriage. The Bard's verse takes second place to the stars' energetic mugging, and is done little service by their vocal deficiencies. But the supporting players are good, and as a curiosity and a piece of Hollywood history it's fairly entertaining.

Mary Pickford *Katherine* • Douglas Fairbanks *Petruchio* • Edwin Maxwell *Baptista* • Joseph Cawthorn *Gremio* • Clyde Cook *Grumio* ■ *Dir* Sam Taylor • *Scr* Sam Taylor, from the play by William Shakespeare

The Taming of the Shrew ★★★★ U

Comedy   1967 · US/It · Colour · 116mins

Made at the height of one of their own violent love affairs, Richard Burton and Elizabeth Taylor breathe their own personal life into Shakespeare's not so politically correct tale of Petruchio subduing his shrewish wife. It's a lush version in which director Franco Zeffirelli – who would return to the Bard with *Romeo and Juliet* (1968) and *Hamlet* (1990) – opts for colourful action rather than well-wrought articulation. It's certainly a feast for the eye – ravishing photography, impressive sets and costumes – and benefits from the ebullient performances of one of moviedom's greatest couples. 📼

Richard Burton *Petruchio* • Elizabeth Taylor *Katharina* • Michael Hordern *Baptista* • Cyril Cusack *Grumio* • Michael York *Lucentio* • Alfred Lynch *Tranio* • Natasha Pyne *Bianca* • Alan Webb *Gremio* • Victor Spinetti *Hortensio* ■ *Dir* Franco Zeffirelli • *Scr* Paul Dehn, Suso Cecchi D'Amico, Franco Zeffirelli, from the play by William Shakespeare • *Cinematographer* Oswald Morris, Luciano Trasatti • *Costume Designer* Irene Sharaff, Danilo Donati

Tammy and the Bachelor ★★★ U

Comedy   1957 · US · Colour · 89mins

Something of a surprise smash hit in its day, this modest but utterly charming piece of whimsy started a series featuring the guileless heroine, who came from the backwoods to charm Louisiana society. Debbie Reynolds is endearingly energetic as the heroine with a talent for sorting out problems (something of a teenage Shirley Temple), and wistfully sings the song *Tammy*, that was to top the Hit Parade in both the USA and UK.

Debbie Reynolds *Tammy Tyree* • Leslie Nielsen *Peter Brent* • Walter Brennan *Grandpa* • Mala Powers *Barbara* • Sidney Blackmer

Professor Brent • Mildred Natwick *Aunt Renie* • Fay Wray *Mrs Brent* ■ *Dir* Joseph Pevney • *Scr* Oscar Brodney, from the novel *Tammy out of Time* by Cid Ricketts Sumner

Tammy and the Doctor ★★ U

Comedy   1963 · US · Colour · 88mins

Quintessential fifties cutie Sandra Dee takes on the Debbie Reynolds mantle for the second time as the country girl among city folk, falling hook, line and sinker for handsome white-coated doctor Peter Fonda, here making his screen debut. This is truly a slight piece, but not without charm thanks to Universal's shrewd casting of a horde of veterans for those who would swiftly tire of the winsome Dee and the gauche Fonda – watch out for Beulah Bondi, Reginald Owen, and onetime leading man Macdonald Carey. This was Tammy's last big-screen outing.

Sandra Dee *Tammy Tyree* • Peter Fonda *Dr Mark Cheswick* • Macdonald Carey *Dr Wayne Bentley* • Beulah Bondi *Mrs Call* • Margaret Lindsay *Rachel Coleman, Head Nurse* • Reginald Owen *Jason Tripp* • Adam West *Dr Eric Hassler* ■ *Dir* Harry Keller • *Scr* Oscar Brodney, from characters created by Cid Ricketts Sumner

Tampopo ★★★★ 18

Satire   1986 · Jap · Colour · 109mins

While *Dim Sum: a Little Bit of Heart* and *Eat Drink Man Woman* might have whetted the appetite, they rather left you wanting cinematically. Juzo Itami's busy satire not only gives hungry viewers more than their fill of delicious food, but also satisfies the film gourmet. In addition to homages to *Shane*, *Seven Samurai* and *Death in Venice*, this story of a trucker (Tsutomu Yamazaki), who turns a roadside noodle bar owned by Nobuko Miyamoto (Itami's wife and regular star) into Tokyo's finest restaurant, is packed with parodies of westerns, samurai pictures and Japanese gangster and porn films. In Japanese with English subtitles. 📼

Tsutomu Yamazaki *Goro* • Nobuko Miyamoto *Tampopo* • Koji Yakusho *Gangster* • Ken Watanabe *Gun* ■ *Dir/Scr* Juzo Itami

Tan-Badan ★★ 18

Melodrama   1986 · Ind · Colour · 123mins

The prodigal son is a staple theme in Bollywood and it's linked here to an exploration of wealth, duty and loyalty that is supposed to stand as a metaphor for the state of Indian society and the decline of her traditional industries. A rich man's son is more interested in the good life than running the family business. The story is pure melodrama, with the indolent man frittering away his inheritance while leaving to his devious manager the care of both his disabled millionaire father and a diehard family friend the factory that made his fortune. In Hindi with English subtitles. 📼

Govinda • Khushboo Jyoti Patel • Sharat Saxena • Satyen Kappu • Raj Mehra ■ *Dir* Anand

Tanganyika ★★ U

Adventure drama 1954 · US · Colour · 81mins

In East Africa around 1900, murderer Jeff Morrow is exerting an evil influence over the warlike Nakumbi natives, thus endangering the lives of white settlers in the colony. A safari, led by Van Heflin and including Morrow's decent brother Howard Duff, sets off on a manhunt to catch the renegade. A bizarre combination of jungle adventure and thriller, this is absolute piffle, as evidenced by the presence of schoolteacher Ruth Roman and a couple of children in the hunting party, but it's awful enough to be quite entertaining.

Van Heflin *John Gale* • Ruth Roman *Peggy Merion* • Howard Duff *Dan Harder* • Jeff Morrow *Abel McCracken* • Joe Comadore *Andolo* • Gregory Marshall *Andy Merion* • Noreen Corcoran *Sally Merion* ■ *Dir* Andre De Toth • *Scr* William Sackheim, Richard Alan Simmons, from a story by William R Cox

Tangier ★★

Thriller   1982 · UK · Colour · 82mins

When American Ronny Cox is arrested by UK customs, he is sent to North Africa to replace a British spy whom he resembles, in order to flush out an enemy bugging expert. This British thriller has the gloss of a mini-series, but it also has the kind of plot twists, oddball characters and glib one-liners that were old hat in forties B-pictures, while the traitor is hardly as unobtrusive as a camel in a kasbah. Billie Whitelaw provides some backbone as Cox's old flame, but Glynis Barber as his new lover is reduced to playing Glynis Barbie.

Ronny Cox • Billie Whitelaw • Glynis Barber • Ronald Fraser ■ *Dir* Michael E Briant • *Scr* Michael Russell, from the novel by Nicholas Luard

Tango ★★★ 15

Black comedy   1993 · Fr · Colour · 86mins

That it mocks its audience rather than satirises its characters is the main problem with this vulgar road movie about an unsavoury wife-murdering trio. After the humanity of *Monsieur Hire* and the quirkiness of *The Hairdresser's Husband*, hopes were high for this freewheeling black comedy from Patrice Leconte, which he promised would rock the politically correct back on their self-righteous feet. But despite a quality cast that includes Philippe Noiret and Jean Rochefort, Leconte lacks the restraint and wit that could have made this a minor masterpiece. In French with English subtitles. 📼

Philippe Noiret *The Elegant Man (L'Elegant)* • Richard Bohringer *Vincent* • Thierry Lhermitte *Paul* • Miou-Miou *Marie* • Judith Godreche *Madeleine* • Michèle Laroque *Helene Baraduc* • Maxime Leroux *Mariano Escobar* • Jean Rochefort ■ *Dir* Patrice Leconte • *Scr* Patrice Leconte, Patrice Dewolf

Tango ★★ 12

Dance drama
1998 · Arg/Sp/Fr/Ger · Colour · 115mins

There's something about the tango that seems to bring out the introverted, arty and pretentious in film-makers: witness Sally Potter's self-indulgent *The Tango Lesson*. Here writer/director Carlos Saura's moody but monotonous tale of Mario, an Argentinian theatre director, strives to give the tango some sort of social significance. His efforts at integrating rhythms and visuals gradually come to mirror Mario's mid-life crisis, his troubles with women, even his feelings of political repression. Fifteen years earlier, Saura's *Carmen* had attempted something similar, but had blended its rhythms and blues more successfully. In Spanish with English subtitles.

Miguel Angel Sola *Mario Suarez* • Cecilia Narova *Laura Fuentes* • Mia Maestro *Elena Flores* • Juan Carlos Copes *Carlos Nebbia* • Carlos Rivarola *Ernesto Landi* ■ *Dir/Scr* Carlos Saura

Tango and Cash ★★★ 18
Action thriller   1989 · US · Colour · 99mins

Sylvester Stallone and Kurt Russell get the opportunity to show off who has the best fitness trainer in this hugely silly, hugely enjoyable action thriller. The main twist in this buddy caper is that Stallone is actually quite sophisticated (he even wears glasses at times), while Russell is the no-brain, all-brawn thug. The plot follows two bickering detectives who become reluctant partners when they are framed by evil drugs baron Jack Palance.Teri Hatcher provides the glamour, while Russian director Andrei Konchalovsky produces lots of big explosions, but this is really all about Stallone and Russell doing their utmost to out-macho each other. Contains swearing, violence and nudity. ▭ *DVD*

Sylvester Stallone *Ray Tango* • Kurt Russell *Gabe Cash* • Jack Palance *Yves Perret* • Teri Hatcher *Kiki* • Michael J Pollard *Owen* • Brion James *Requin* • Geoffrey Lewis *Police captain* • James Hong *Quan* • Robert Z'Dar *Face* ■ *Dir* Andrei Konchalovsky • *Scr* Randy Feldman

Tango Bar ★★★
Dance documentary
1988 · P Ric/Arg · Colour · 90mins

The tango is so inextricably woven into the fabric of Argentinian history that any socio-cultural overview is bound to have political implications. Thus, the live numbers performed by the Tango Argentino troupe and the film clips revealing how the dance has been depicted down the years are pregnant with a significance that is reinforced by the tense relationship between piano player Raul Julia, long-exiled bandoneonist Ruben Juarez and their mutual mistress, singer Valeria Lynch. Tango aficionados will revel in the performances, although film fans will be more intrigued by the juxtaposed clips of Rudolph Valentino, Abbott and Costello, Gene Kelly and Fred Flintstone. In Spanish with English subtitles.

Raul Julia *Ricardo* • Valeria Lynch *Elena* • Ruben Juarez *Antonio* ■ *Dir* Marcos Zurinaga • *Scr* Marcos Zurinaga, Juan Carlos Codazzi, Jose Pablo Feinman

The Tango Lesson ★★ PG
Dance drama
1997 · UK/Fr · BW and Colour · 97mins

Supreme self-indulgence on the part of British writer/director Sally Potter. She plays herself, taking a break from

writing her latest screenplay to attend a tango exhibition. So struck is she by the super-sexy rhythms, that she reshapes her film around the dance and the man who teaches it. This is the film about that film. The idea of dispensing with the distinction between life and art is interesting, if not exactly original. This film, also made with funding from Argentina, Japan and Germany, looks good, and moves well, but you're still left thinking of a certain emperor and his new clothes. In English, French and Spanish with subtitles. ▭

Sally Potter *Sally* • Pablo Veron *Pablo* • Gustavo Naveira *Gustavo* • Fabian Salas *Fabian* • David Toole *Fashion designer* • Carolina Iotti *Pablo's partner* • Carlos Copello *Carlos* ■ *Dir/Scr* Sally Potter

Tangos, Exilo de Gardel ★★★

Drama   1985 · Arg/Fr · Colour

One of the founders of Third Cinema, Argentinian director Fernando E Solanas explores the agony of exile in this politically charged variation on the "putting on a show" theme. Taking as his subject the life of tango star Carlos Gardel, who was killed in 1935, playwright Miguel Angel Sola smuggles the manuscript out of Buenos Aires to compatriots, who sacrifice both personal and national identities as they eke out their enforced absence in Paris. Very much a patchwork of emotions, events and ideas, the film leavens its melancholic melodrama with sublime moments of symbolic music. In Spanish with English subtitles.

Marie Laforêt • Philippe Léotard • Miguel Angel Sola • Marina Vlady ■ *Dir/Scr* Fernando E Solanas

Tank ★★ PG
Comedy drama   1984 · US · Colour · 110mins

A Sherman tank is the unlikely vehicle of choice in this unusual road movie. Soon-to-retire sergeant major James Garner has spent 15 years painstakingly restoring an army tank. A clash with corrupt local lawman GD Spradlin results in the sheriff framing Garner's son and demanding money for his release from a prison camp. Garner is double-crossed and so takes his tank cross country to free his son from the camp. This leaden comedy is enlivened only by the consistent James Garner.

James Garner *Sergeant Major Zack Carey* • Shirley Jones *LaDonna Carey* • C Thomas Howell *Billy Carey* • Mark Herrier *Elliott* • Sandy Ward *General Hubik* • Jenilee Harrison *Sarah* • James Cromwell *Deputy Euclid* • GD Spradlin *Sheriff Buelton* ■ *Dir* Marvin J Chomsky • *Scr* Dan Gordon

Tank Girl ★★ 15
Science-fiction comedy
1995 · US · Colour · 99mins

This gets nowhere near the sassy black spark of the original comic strip, yet those unfamiliar with its source will find it goofy, undemanding fare. Lori Petty is the Tank Girl of the title, demonstrating an early manifestation of "girl power" as she takes on evil Malcolm McDowell in a water-starved post-apocalyptic world. Director Rachel

Talalay never quite gets a handle on the mix of comedy and futuristic action, but Petty is surprisingly credible in the lead and McDowell is suitably over the top as the villain. However, the most fun comes from watching hip rapper Ice-T playing a poetry-loving half-man/half-kangaroo. Contains violence and swearing.

Lori Petty *Rebecca Buck/Tank Girl* • Ice T [Ice-T] *T-Saint* • Malcolm McDowell *Kesslee* • Naomi Watts *Jet Girl* • Don Harvey *Sergeant Small* • Jeff Kober *Booga* ■ *Dir* Rachel Talalay • *Scr* Tedi Sarafian, from the comic strip by Alan Martin, Jamie Hewlett

Tap ★★ PG
Drama   1989 · US · Colour · 106mins

If the title had not already worked against this dull movie, then the improbable story certainly would have. Burglar Gregory Hines plays the nimble-footed Max Washington, the son of a legendary dancer, who's released from prison faced with two options. He can either join mentor Little Mo (Sammy Davis Jr) at his tap dancing club or regroup with his old partners in crime for one last job, a jewel heist. Tap dance fanatics may well adore the film but few will be engaged by its assembly of clichéd characters. On the plus side are the swansong performance by the ailing Davis Jr, and the dazzling manoeuvrings of Gregory Hines ▭

Gregory Hines *Max Washington* • Suzzanne Douglas *Amy* • Sammy Davis Jr *Little Mo* • Savion Glover *Louis* • Joe Morton *Nicky* • Dick Anthony Williams *Francis* • Sandman Sims *Sandman* • Bunny Briggs *Bunny* ■ *Dir/Scr* Nick Castle

Tapeheads ★★ 15
Comedy   1988 · US · Colour · 87mins

John Cusack and Tim Robbins are a comedy combo in this lightweight offering from former video director Bill Fishman. The two play ex-security guards trying to make it as music video producers and setting their sights on becoming MTV's finest. Given that the film credits every bigwig in the music industry one expects more than this sub-*Wayne's World* series of skits with Cusack and Robbins going from disaster to success. It has a surprisingly dated feel to it, and given the calibre of the two leads makes for very average viewing. ▭

John Cusack *Ivan Alexeev* • Tim Robbins *Josh Tager* • Mary Crosby *Samantha Gregory* • Clu Gulager *Norman Mart* • Katy Boyer *Belinda Mart* • Jessica Walter *Kay Mart* • Sam Moore *Billy Diamond* • Junior Walker *Lester Diamond* • Doug McClure *Sid Tager* • Connie Stevens *June Tager* ■ *Dir* Bill Fishman • *Scr* Bill Fishman, Peter McCarthy, from a story by Ryan Rowe, Jim Herzfeld, Bill Fishman, Peter McCarthy

Taps ★★★ PG
Drama   1981 · US · Colour · 121mins

This marked Tom Cruise's first impact in the movies, Sean Penn's debut, and Timothy Hutton's follow-up to his Oscar-winning role in *Ordinary People*. They play cadets who take over their military academy when it's threatened with redevelopment, in Harold Becker's fascinating film which parallels *if . . . .* It sometimes gets hysterical and loses

its narrative way, but the bright young stars and George C Scott as the iron-jawed commander see it through. ▭

George C Scott *General Harlan Bache* • Timothy Hutton *Brian Moreland* • Ronny Cox *Colonel Kerby* • Sean Penn *Alex Dwyer* • Tom Cruise *David Shawn* • Brendan Ward *Charlie Auden* • Evan Handler *Edward West* • John P Navin Jr *Derek Mellott* ■ *Dir* Harold Becker • *Scr* Darryl Ponicsan, Robert Mark Kamen, from the story *Father Sky* by Devery Freeman, James Lineberger

Tarana ★★★ PG
Drama   1951 · Ind · BW · 137mins

Although it's best known for its spectacular masala musicals, Bollywood also has a social conscience. Director Ram Daryani was renowned for the intelligence with which he tackled controversial issues, without ever losing sight of the central story. Here, he passes some pointed observations on arranged marriages, the class divide and the struggle between progress and tradition, but most eyes will be on regular co-stars Madhubala and Dilip Kumar as the star-crossed lovers whose path to happiness is strewn with prejudice. In Hindi with English subtitles.

Madhubala *Tarana* • Dilip Kumar • Kumar Shyama • Jeevan ■ *Dir* Ram Daryani

Tarang ★★★ 15
Drama   1983 · Ind · Colour · 163mins

A far cry from the razzle-dazzle of the Bollywood musical, this epic melodrama belongs to the tradition of social protest cinema made familiar to western audiences by the work of such directors as Satyajit Ray and Shyam Benegal. Kumar Shahani has neither Ray's humanity nor Benegal's political passion, but he packs his tale with plenty of incident and makes a number of telling points about India's industrial future. The family feuds might resemble *Dallas* at times, but the discussion of union activism and the acceptance of foreign investment gives the film a cutting edge. A Hindi language film. ▭

Smita Patil • Amol Palekar ■ *Dir* Kumar Shahani • *Scr* Kumar Shahani, Roshan Shahani

Tarantula ★★★
Science-fiction   1955 · US · BW · 80mins

Although inspired by *Them!*, director Jack Arnold's big bug shocker is a classic in its own right due to excellent special effects and the potent use of haunting desert locations. Scientist Leo G Carroll is working in an isolated laboratory trying to solve world famine and injects a spider with special nutrients that cause it to grow to enormous size. The giant arachnid eventually escapes, first to decimate cattle and then to eat people as it crawls towards a fiery climax. The stillness of the desert allows Arnold to impeccably mount the tension in between the compelling spectacle of a spider on the rampage. Clint Eastwood has a bit part as a jet pilot in this model creature feature.

John Agar *Dr Matt Hastings* • Mara Corday *Stephanie Clayton* • Leo G Carroll *Prof Gerald Deemer* • Nestor Paiva *Sheriff Jack Andrews* • Ross Elliott *Joe Burch* • Edwin Rand *Lt John*

U = SUITABLE FOR ALL   Uc = SUITABLE FOR ALL, ESPECIALLY FOR YOUNG CHILDREN (VIDEO ONLY)   PG = PARENTAL GUIDANCE

Nolan • Raymond Bailey *Townsend* • Hank Patterson *Josh* • Clint Eastwood *First pilot* ■ *Dir* Jack Arnold • *Scr* Robert M Fresco, Martin Berkeley, from a story by Jack Arnold, Robert M Fresco • *Special Effects* Clifford Stine, David S Horsley

Taras Bulba ★★ U

Historical epic 1962 · US · Colour · 123mins

This very watchable junk was ostensibly based on the novel by Nikolai Gogol, but with a screenplay that would have made him weep. The locations are indeed impressive, as is the score by the distinguished Franz Waxman, but the casting is ludicrous and the art direction positively cardboard. Director J Lee Thompson fails to find the necessary scale, and the film isn't bad enough to enjoy as a romp. Of the leads Tony Curtis and Yul Brynner as Cossack son and father the less said the better, though, for connoisseurs of such things, there is a particularly effective hand-lopping-off scene.

Tony Curtis *Andrei Bulba* • Yul Brynner *Taras Bulba* • Christine Kaufmann *Natalia Dubrov* • Sam Wanamaker *Filipenko* • Brad Dexter *Shilo* • Guy Rolfe *Prince Grigory* • Perry Lopez *Ostap Bulba* • George Macready *Governor* ■ *Dir* J Lee Thompson • *Scr* Waldo Salt, Karl Tunberg, from the novel by Nikolai Gogol

Target ★★ 15

Spy thriller 1985 · US · Colour · 112mins

Arthur Penn has had an indifferent directorial career since the glories of the sixties and seventies. This early take on the *True Lies* concept – family man hides the fact that he's a secret agent – ultimately disappoints, even though it reunites him with *Bonnie and Clyde* star Gene Hackman. The latter plays a seemingly ordinary American businessman who gets drawn into Cold War intrigue when his wife Gayle Hunnicutt is kidnapped in Paris. At the same time he has to rebuild a relationship with his surly adolescent son Matt Dillon and, sadly, Penn never successfully marries the two conflicting elements. Contains violence, swearing and nudity. ▭

Gene Hackman *Walter Lloyd* • Matt Dillon *Chris Lloyd* • Gayle Hunnicutt *Donna Lloyd* • Victoria Fyodorova *Lise* • Ilona Grubel *Carla* • Herbert Berghof *Schroeder* • Josef Sommer *Barney Taber* • Guy Boyd *Clay* ■ *Dir* Arthur Penn • *Scr* Howard Berk, Don Petersen, from a story by Leonard Stern

Target Eagle ★★ PG

Action adventure
1982 · Sp/Mex · Colour · 94mins

Clever casting injects some life into a predictable action thriller centred around mercenaries hired to smash a smuggling ring. George Peppard, better known for his good guy TV roles in *Banacek* and *The A-Team*, relishes the chance to be the chief baddie, and Max von Sydow is also unusually cast as a police chief. ▭

George Peppard *Ronald* • Jorge Rivero *Andrea* • Maud Adams *Anne* • Chuck Connors *Fisher* • Susana Dosamantes *Laura* • Max von Sydow *Spanish police chief* ■ *Dir/Scr* J Anthony Loma

Target Earth ★★

Science-fiction drama 1998 · US · Colour

Extraterrestrials are up to their usual tricks in this made-for-TV sci-fi adventure. When a man goes insane and a little girl is kidnapped, a small-town Illinois cop realizes something is terribly wrong. Soon, he finds himself battling insidious aliens who have implanted devices to control the minds of humans, from local citizens to government agents. Writer Michael Vickerman and director Peter Markle have taken every 1950s space-invader cliché and fed them into a blender, producing this silly, banal, painting-by-numbers tale.

Christopher Meloni *Sam Adams* • Marcia Cross *Karen* • John C McGinley *Agent Naples* ■ *Dir* Peter Markle • *Scr* Michael Vickerman

Target: Harry ★★ 18

Crime drama 1968 · US · Colour · 81mins

Vic Morrow is caught up in some James Bond-style international intrigue in this made-for-TV movie from cult director Roger Corman (under the pseudonym Harry Neill), that was shelved for several years. The plot involves engraving plates stolen from the British Mint, and Suzanne Pleshette provides the glamour. ▭

Vic Morrow *Harry Black* • Suzanne Pleshette *Diane Reed* • Victor Buono *Mosul Rashi* • Cesar Romero *Lieutenant George Duval* • Stanley Holloway *Jason Carlyle* • Charlotte Rampling *Ruth Carlyle* • Michael Ansara *Major Miles Segora* ■ *Dir* Harry Neill [Roger Corman] • *Scr* Bob Barbash

Target of Suspicion ★★

Thriller 1994 · US · Colour

Bob Swaim, director of the rugged Gallic *policier La Balance*, brings more class than is deserved to this hand-me-down Parisian TV thriller. Tim Matheson is the married businessman who makes the mistake of getting involved with a beautiful model. When she is murdered, Matheson must prove his innocence.

Tim Matheson *Nick Matthews* • Lysette Anthony *Jennifer Matthews* • Noemie Kocher *Julie Dormoy* ■ *Dir* Bob Swaim • *Scr* Brian Ross, from a story by Christian Biegalski, Benedicte Popper

Targets ★★★★

Crime thriller 1968 · US · Colour · 89mins

The stunning feature debut of film critic-turned-writer/director Peter Bogdanovich is graced by a marvellous valedictory performance from Boris Karloff. Karloff plays Byron Orlok, an ageing horror star who finds himself in the gun sights of that scourge of contemporary America, a random sniper, chillingly portrayed by Tim O'Kelly. This is a compulsive thriller, based on the real-life killing spree of Charles Whitman in 1966. It is genuinely disturbing and immaculately crafted, with themes that are still relevant today. With Karloff originally only available for two days' shooting, would-be production schedulers might care to observe how cleverly Bogdanovich builds around his star. The cinematography, by debuting émigré Laszlo Kovacs, is superb.

Boris Karloff *Byron Orlok* • Tim O'Kelly *Bobby Thompson* • Nancy Hsueh *Jenny* • James Brown (2) *Robert Thompson* • Sandy Baron *Kip Larkin* • Arthur Peterson *Ed Loughlin* • Mary Jackson *Charlotte Thompson* • Tanya Morgan *Ilene Thompson* • Monty Landis [Monte Landis] *Marshall Smith* • Peter Bogdanovich *Sammy Michaels* ■ *Dir* Peter Bogdanovich • *Scr* Peter Bogdanovich, from a story by Polly Platt, Peter Bogdanovich

Tarka the Otter ★★★ PG

Adventure 1978 · UK · Colour · 87mins

Author Henry Williamson refused to allow Disney to film his much-loved wildlife novel. Instead, he entrusted the story of Tarka to director David Cobham, who co-wrote the script with Gerald Durrell. Cobham not only remained fairly faithful to the best-selling original, but, in collaboration with cameraman John McCallum, also painted a glorious picture of the Devon countryside. Although the action is occasionally deflected by a nature ramble approach, Tarka's adventures, particularly his run-in with Deadlock the otter hound, are skilfully staged and vividly brought to life by Peter Ustinov's narration. ▭ *DVD*

Peter Bennett *Master of the otter hounds* • Edward Underdown *Hibbert* • Brenda Cavendish *Lucy* • John Leeson *Hunt secretary* • Reg Lye *Farmer* • Peter Ustinov *Narrator* ■ *Dir* David Cobham • *Scr* Gerald Durrell, David Cobham, from the novel by Henry Williamson

The Tarnished Angels ★★★★

Adventure drama 1957 · US · BW · 90mins

Here's a re-teaming of three of the principals from Douglas Sirk's successful melodrama *Written on the Wind*, as journalist Rock Hudson joins ace barnstorming pilot Robert Stack and his sexy wife Dorothy Malone. Hudson's character is embarrassingly underwritten, but he manages to make his newshound eminently watchable, and the film never looks less than splendid in black-and-white CinemaScope. Shallow but well made, this melodrama fails to disguise the innate misanthropy of its literary source, William Faulkner's *Pylon*, though many have found much to admire in its sleazy bitterness.

Rock Hudson *Burke Devlin* • Robert Stack *Roger Shumann* • Dorothy Malone *Laverne Shumann* • Jack Carson *Jiggs* • Robert Middleton *Matt Ord* • Alan Reed *Colonel Fineman* • Alexander Lockwood *Sam Hagood* • Chris Olsen *Jack Shumann* • Robert J Wilke *Hank* • Troy Donahue *Frank Burnham* ■ *Dir* Douglas Sirk • *Scr* George Zuckerman, from the novel *Pylon* by William Faulkner

Tarnished Lady ★★

Drama 1931 · US · BW · 80mins

The film that marked the talkie debut of the already legendary, husky-voiced stage star Tallulah Bankhead, who returned to Hollywood after several years as the toast of London's West End stage. Sadly, Tallulah's exotic, erotic charms failed to make much impact on the camera. Despite glossy production, a Donald Ogden Stewart screenplay and direction by George Cukor, this tale of a Park Avenue girl who grows bored with marriage and leaves her husband (Clive Brook) to

seek a more interesting life, is no more than an efficient plod.

Tallulah Bankhead *Nancy Courtney* • Clive Brook *Norman Cravath* • Phoebe Foster *Germaine Prentiss* • Alexander Kirkland *DeWitt Taylor* • Osgood Perkins *Ben Sterner* • Elizabeth Patterson *Mrs Courtney* • Eric Blore *Jewelry counter clerk* ■ *Dir* George Cukor • *Scr* Donald Ogden Stewart, from his story *New York Lady*

Tarzan ★★★ U

Animation 1999 · US · Colour · 88mins

Despite some visually arresting action scenes, the first ever cartoon based on the classic jungle hero falls way short of Disney's recent output. With weak comic relief provided by assorted "Animalz N the Hood", this is a frenetic mix of *George of the Jungle* and *Gorillas in the Mist*, with constant bouts of animated mayhem to keep the kids amused. Heaven forbid there should be any quiet, reflective moments as Tarzan (voiced by Tony Goldwyn) decides whether to stay in Africa or return to England with Jane (Minnie Driver). Lacking the epic sweep of *Mulan* or *The Lion King*, and laced with feeble background songs from Phil Collins (inexplicably awarded an Oscar), this King of the Swingers may be merchandise-friendly, but it's no jungle VIP.

Brian Blessed *Clayton* • Glenn Close *Kala* • Minnie Driver *Jane* • Tony Goldwyn *Tarzan* • Nigel Hawthorne *Professor Porter* • Lance Henriksen *Kerchak* ■ *Dir* Chris Buck, Kevin Lima • *Scr* Tab Murphy, Bob Tzudiker, Noni White, David Reynolds, from characters created by Edgar Rice Burroughs

Tarzan and His Mate ★★★★ U

Adventure 1934 · US · BW · 90mins

Generally regarded as the best of the Johnny Weissmuller MGM *Tarzans*, this is notable for being extremely raunchy, even by present-day standards, since it predates Hollywood's notorious censorship code. Cavorting semi-naked among the studio undergrowth is the lovely Maureen O'Sullivan as Jane. After this, the loincloths grew less revealing, but Weissmuller still cut a fine figure as the Lord of the Jungle. And, that yell!

Johnny Weissmuller *Tarzan* • Maureen O'Sullivan *Jane Parker* • Neil Hamilton *Harry Holt* • Paul Cavanagh *Martin Arlington* • Forrester Harvey *Beamish* • William Stack *Tom Pierce* • Desmond Roberts *Henry Van Ness* ■ *Dir* Cedric Gibbons • *Scr* Howard Emmett Rogers, Leon Gordon, from a story by James Kevin McGuinness, from characters created by Edgar Rice Burroughs

Tarzan and the Amazons ★★ U

Adventure 1945 · US · BW · 75mins

It's not very good, and the Sol Lesser production values are decidedly cheesy, but any movie proffering tiny Maria Ouspenskaya as the queen of the Amazons has camp appeal – if little else. This reintroduced Jane, in the lacklustre person of Brenda Joyce, with Johnny Sheffield on hand as Boy, so it's down to a tired Johnny Weissmuller to make this tosh bearable. Fun of sorts, though, and certainly ecologically sound.

Johnny Weissmuller *Tarzan* • Johnny Sheffield *Boy* • Brenda Joyce *Jane* • Henry Stephenson *Henderson* • Maria Ouspenskaya *Amazon queen* • Barton MacLane *Ballister* ■ *Dir* Kurt Neumann, Sol Lesser • *Scr* Hans Jacoby, Marjorie L Pfaelzer, from characters created by Edgar Rice Burroughs

Tarzan and the Great River
★★ U

Adventure   1967 · US/Swi · Colour · 88mins

The Lord of the Jungle swings into action when an old zoo curator friend is murdered by a vicious cult of Leopard Men. Journeying up river towards the leader's hideout, accompanied by his trusty chimp and lion, Tarzan helps the local doctor to halt an epidemic. Not one of the best Tarzan adventures, but Mike Henry makes a decent job of the eponymous hero, and the Brazilian locations are watchable.

Mike Henry *Tarzan* • Jan Murray *Captain Sam Bishop* • Manuel Padilla Jr *Pepe* • Diana Millay *Dr Ann Phillips* ■ *Dir* Robert Day • *Scr* Bob Barbash, from a story by Bob Barbash, Lewis Reed, from characters created by Edgar Rice Burroughs

Tarzan and the Green Goddess
★★

Adventure   1938 · US · BW · 72mins

This feature is one of two culled from episodes of *The New Adventures of Tarzan*. It combines some previously unseen material with footage edited from the last ten reels of the 1935 serial. Its star was Herman Brix, but he changed his name to Bruce Bennett and enjoyed a long career, albeit not as the ape man. The story is as evergreen as the jungle, with Tarzan out to protect civilisation from evil men who want a secret explosive formula hidden in a Mayan idol called the Green Goddess. Our hero battles everything from raging torments to roaring lions.

Herman Brix [Bruce Bennett] *Tarzan* • Ula Holt *Ula Vale* • Frank Baker *Major Martling* • Don Castello *Raglan* ■ *Dir* Edward Kull • *Scr* Charles F Royal, from characters created by Edgar Rice Burroughs

Tarzan and the Huntress
★★ U

Adventure   1947 · US · BW · 72mins

The greatest Tarzan of them all, Johnny Weissmuller, was looking old and tired by this 11th film in his series. After *Tarzan and the Mermaids* the role of King of the Jungle passed to Lex Barker. Here, Brenda Joyce as Jane and Johnny Sheffield as Boy have more of a part to play than usual, as evil zoologist Patricia Morison plots to spirit animals into her private menagerie. It's all ecologically interesting, and certainly never boring. It's let down by the RKO production values, which just look cheap and shoddy, underlining that the great days of Weissmuller's reign, which began at MGM, were well and truly over.

Johnny Weissmuller *Tarzan* • Johnny Sheffield *Boy* • Brenda Joyce *Jane* • Patricia Morison *Tanya* • Barton MacLane *Weir* • John Warburton *Marley* • Wallace Scott *Smithers* • Charles Trowbridge *King Farrod* ■ *Dir* Kurt

Neumann • *Scr* Jerry Gruskin, Rowland Leigh, from characters created by Edgar Rice Burroughs

Tarzan and the Jungle Boy
★★ U

Adventure   1968 · US/Swi · Colour · 90mins

Mike Henry made an engaging Tarzan, but he couldn't take the pace. Indeed, declining health while filming (including a chimp bite!) prompted him to sue the producer. Tarzan is asked by a journalist to enter unknown and hostile territory to rescue a boy who has been lost for seven years. The area is dominated by an angry tribe whose dying chief is choosing which of his two sons – one bad, one good – should succeed him. The plot holds few surprises, but at least the location photography means that the movie looks good.

Mike Henry *Tarzan* • Rafer Johnson *Nagambi* • Alizia Gur *Myrna Claudel* • Ed Johnson *Buhara* • Ronald Gans *Ken* • Steven Bond [Steve Bond] *Erik* ■ *Dir* Robert Gordon • *Scr* Stephen Lord, from characters created by Edgar Rice Burroughs

Tarzan and the Leopard Woman
★★ U

Adventure   1946 · US · BW · 72mins

Murder cults aren't a subject to be treated light-heartedly these days, but back in the mid-forties they could still be wheeled out as a plot device. Here Tarzan, hindered and aided by Jane and Boy (Brenda Joyce and Johnny Sheffield), does what he can to destroy the titular villain, splendidly incarnated by Acquanetta. It's all jolly silly, and mercifully short, but Johnny Weissmuller was getting a bit old for the role.

Johnny Weissmuller *Tarzan* • Johnny Sheffield *Boy* • Brenda Joyce *Jane* • Acquanetta *Lea* • Edgar Barrier *Lazar* • Tommy Cook *Kimba* ■ *Dir* Kurt Neumann • *Scr* Carroll Young, from characters created by Edgar Rice Burroughs

Tarzan and the Lost Safari
★★★ U

Adventure   1956 · UK · Colour · 81mins

One of the best fifties episodes in the jungle saga brought a welcome mid-period lift to the series by being the first to venture into CinemaScope and Technicolor. Gordon Scott rescues the members of a safari team – stranded after a plane crash – from the evil clutches of a white hunter (Robert Beatty). Thankfully, old stock footage was discarded and the movie was actually filmed on location in Africa, though studio scenes were shot in England with the likes of Wilfrid Hyde White and Yolande Donlan in the supporting cast.

Gordon Scott *Tarzan* • Robert Beatty "Tusker" *Hawkins* • Yolande Donlan *Gamage Dean* • Betta St John *Diana* • Wilfrid Hyde White "Doodles" *Fletcher* • George Coulouris *Carl Kraski* ■ *Dir* H Bruce Humberstone • *Scr* Montgomery Pittman, Lillie Hayward, from characters created by Edgar Rice Burroughs

Tarzan and the Lost City
★★ PG

Action adventure
1998 · Ausl/US · Colour · 80mins

Casper Van Dien dons the famous loincloth in this unambitious but enjoyable family adventure. Tarzan, now Lord Greystoke, has been fully integrated into British high society and is set to wed the beautiful Jane (Jane March). However, after experiencing a disturbing vision of the destruction of his childhood home, he's soon back swinging through the trees in his beloved Africa. Youngsters won't be disappointed. ▭

Casper Van Dien *Tarzan* • Jane March *Jane* • Steven Waddington *Nigel Ravens* • Winston Ntshona *Mugambi* • Rapulana Seiphemo *Kaya* • Ian Roberts *Captain Dooley* ■ *Dir* Carl Schenkel • *Scr* Bayard Johnson, J Anderson Black, from characters created by Edgar Rice Burroughs

Tarzan and the Mermaids
★★ U

Adventure   1948 · US · BW · 67mins

Filmed in Mexico (mainly Acapulco) with an ambitious music score by Dimitri Tiomkin, this is less of a jungle adventure than most Tarzan films, as water and swimming sequences dominate. The spectacular scenery is the film's main asset as the story is a slow-moving affair in which Tarzan helps a native girl (Linda Christian) from being forced into marriage to a phoney island god. During the shooting of the breathtaking cliff diving sequence, Johnny Weissmuller's double, Angel Garcia, was killed. This was Weissmuller's 12th and last screen portrayal of Tarzan.

Johnny Weissmuller *Tarzan* • Brenda Joyce *Jane* • Linda Christian *Mara* • George Zucco *Palanth* • Andrea Palma *Luana* • Fernando Wagner *Varga* • Edward Ashley *Commissioner* ■ *Dir* Robert Florey • *Scr* Carroll Young, from characters created by Edgar Rice Burroughs

Tarzan and the She-Devil
★★ U

Adventure   1953 · US · BW · 75mins

Despite the exotic title and a great villain in Raymond Burr, this is a standard tale of ivory-seeking elephant hunters being stymied by the king of the jungle. Tarzan spends a good deal of the film in tied-up captivity, and director Kurt Neumann allows the pace to slacken too often before the climactic elephant stampede. The film's abrupt climax suggests production problems – producer Sol Lesser had already padded the film with scenes from explorer Frank Buck's 1934 film *White Cargo*. This was the fifth and final Tarzan film for Lex Barker.

Lex Barker *Tarzan* • Joyce Mackenzie *Jane* • Raymond Burr *Vargo* • Monique Van Vooren *Lyra* • Tom Conway *Fidel* • Henry Brandon *M'Tara* • Michael Granger *Lavar* ■ *Dir* Kurt Neumann • *Scr* Karl Kamb, Carroll Young, from characters created by Edgar Rice Burroughs

Tarzan and the Slave Girl
★★ U

Adventure   1950 · US · BW · 74mins

The plotting of this adventure is exceptionally fanciful, as Jane is kidnapped by a tribe of lion worshippers who are being decimated by a strange malady and want to repopulate their civilisation. Tarzan finds himself fighting a native tribe called the Waddies, who disguise themselves as bushes, and also fighting off the advances of a seductive nurse (Denise Darcel). Vanessa Brown is the first of several actresses to play Jane after the departure of Brenda Joyce.

Lex Barker *Tarzan* • Vanessa Brown *Jane* • Robert Alda *Neil* • Hurd Hatfield *Prince* • Arthur Shields *Dr Campbell* • Tony Caruso [Anthony Caruso] *Sengo* • Denise Darcel *Lola* ■ *Dir* Lee Sholem • *Scr* Hans Jacoby, Arnold Belgard, from characters created by Edgar Rice Burroughs

Tarzan and the Trappers   ★

Adventure   1958 · US · BW · 70mins

The theme of white hunters searching for a lost city – said to be full of untold treasure – is so overworked that it needs the sort of production and cast that is totally missing in this compilation of three television episodes made for a series that failed to happen. Gordon Scott and Eve Brent are an acceptable Tarzan and Jane, but other elements on display are under par. A successful Tarzan television series was ultimately made in 1966, starring Ron Ely.

Gordon Scott *Tarzan* • Eve Brent *Jane* • Rickie Sorenson *Boy* ■ *Dir* Charles Haas, Sandy Howard • *Scr* Frederick Schlick, Robert Leach, from characters created by Edgar Rice Burroughs

Tarzan and the Valley of Gold
★★ U

Adventure   1966 · US/Swi · Colour · 89mins

Mike Henry was poached from US pro football for this better than average jungle romp, which gives more than a nod to James Bond's *Goldfinger*. A gold-obsessed archvillain, played with gusto by goateed David Opatoshu, kidnaps a boy, believing he holds the secret to a lost civilisation of gold. Enter a more gentlemanly Tarzan (by aircraft), who is persuaded to strip off his groovy suit, don a loincloth and re-enter the jungle to sort it all out. There's plenty of modern (well, sixties) weaponry, kinky situations and grandiose settings, but those expecting a standard ape man adventure will be surprised by the sharp script and playful tone.

Mike Henry *Tarzan* • Nancy Kovack *Sophia Renault* • David Opatoshu *Vinaro* • Manuel Padilla Jr *Ramel* • Don Megowan *Mr Train* • Enrique Lucero *Perez* • Eduardo Noriega *Talmadge* • John Kelly *Voss* ■ *Dir* Robert Day • *Scr* Clair Huffaker, from characters created by Edgar Rice Burroughs

Tarzan Escapes   ★★★

Adventure   1936 · US · BW · 95mins

The third entry in MGM's legendary jungle series was easily the most problematic, with a number of scenes being reshot from scratch. Much to the

U = SUITABLE FOR ALL   Uc = SUITABLE FOR ALL, ESPECIALLY FOR YOUNG CHILDREN (VIDEO ONLY)   PG = PARENTAL GUIDANCE

disgust of director Richard Thorpe, studio boss Louis B Mayer insisted that the more violent action be considerably toned down. Yet this is still a full-blooded adventure, as Johnny Weissmuller resists John Buckler's attempts to exhibit him as a freak of nature back in Britain. Maureen O'Sullivan's husband, future director John Farrow, was among the scriptwriters.

Johnny Weissmuller *Tarzan* • Maureen O'Sullivan *Jane Parker* • John Buckler *Captain Frye* • Benita Hume *Rita Parker* • William Henry *Eric Parker* • Herbert Mundin *Herbert Henry Rawlins* • EE Clive *Masters* ■ *Dir* Richard Thorpe • *Scr* Cyril Hume, John Farrow, Karl Brown, from characters created by Edgar Rice Burroughs

Tarzan Finds a Son! ★★★ U
Adventure   1939 · US · BW · 82mins

One of the splendid MGM Tarzans, starring the popular Johnny Weissmuller as the ape man and lovely Maureen O'Sullivan as Jane. Forbidden to produce children outside wedlock by the new film censorship code, the couple find a boy whose parents were killed in a plane crash, and begin a jungle version of a custody battle! It's a cleverly scripted and generally satisfying tale for young and old alike. "Boy" was played by tousle-haired Johnny Sheffield, who later starred in a movie series of his own, starting in 1949 with *Bomba the Jungle Boy*.

Johnny Weissmuller *Tarzan* • Maureen O'Sullivan *Jane* • John Sheffield [Johnny Sheffield] *Boy* • Ian Hunter *Austin Lancing* • Henry Stephenson *Sir Thomas Lancing* • Frieda Inescort *Mrs Lancing* • Henry Wilcoxon *Mr Sande* • Laraine Day *Mrs Richard Lancing* ■ *Dir* Richard Thorpe • *Scr* Cyril Hume, from characters created by Edgar Rice Burroughs

Tarzan Goes to India
★★★ U
Adventure   1962 · UK · Colour · 86mins

After playing a villain to Gordon Scott's King of the Jungle in *Tarzan the Magnificent*, former stunt man and western heavy Jock Mahoney took over the title role. This episode lifts the material out of its familiar rut by sending the hero to India for an elephant-rescuing operation, during which he encounters a company of Indians as well as Gajendra, King of the Elephants. More "Elephant Boy" than jungle adventure, but it serves its purpose.

Jock Mahoney *Tarzan* • Mark Dana *O'Hara* • Jai *Jai the Elephant Boy* • Simi *Princess Kamara* • Leo Gordon *Bryce* ■ *Dir* John Guillermin • *Scr* Robert Hardy Andrews, John Guillermin, from characters created by Edgar Rice Burroughs

Tarzan in Manhattan ★★ PG
Action adventure 1989 · US · Colour · 93mins

A change of location doesn't mean much of a change of pace for the rainforest swinger (this time played by the fairly anonymous Joe Lara): Tarzan treats the skyscraper jungle just like his own, pursuing Jan-Michael Vincent, who has kidnapped Cheetah in this tree-top home, in this lacklustre TV movie. Tony Curtis is in there somewhere as modern-day Jane, Kim Crosby's father, but the idea has

clocked up too many sequels to produce any surprises. ▣

Joe Lara *Tarzan* • Kim Crosby *Jane* • Jan-Michael Vincent *Brightmore* • Joe Seneca *Joseph* • Tony Curtis *Archimedes Porter* ■ *Dir* Michael Schultz • *Scr* Anna Sandor, Bill Gough

Tarzan of the Apes ★★★
Silent adventure   1918 · US · BW · 55mins

The first of the adventures of the jungle swinger, this has a rather wan Elmo Lincoln as the stranded aristocrats' child reared by the apes. Years later, explorer Jane (Enid Markey) comes looking for the Greystoke heir, prompting some heroics from the smitten Tarzan. The series didn't really get going until Johnny Weissmuller donned the loincloth, but, as a curiosity, and in view of what was to come, this is well worth seeing. Existing versions of the film run at less than half the length of the original 130 minute running time. ▣

Elmo Lincoln *Tarzan* • Enid Markey *Jane Porter* • Gordon Griffith *Tarzan as a child* • True Boardman *Lord Greystoke* • Kathleen Kirkham *Lady Greystoke* ■ *Dir* Scott Sidney • *Scr* William E Wing, from the novel by Edgar Rice Burroughs

Tarzan, the Ape Man ★★★★
Adventure   1932 · US · BW · 99mins

This is the first, and classiest, movie in the series starring Olympic swimming champion Johnny Weissmuller as the jungle swinger. Directed by WS Van Dyke, with a skill to confirm his nickname of "One-Take Woody", the tale introduces the ape-reared boy to future partner Jane (Maureen O'Sullivan), daughter of huffing-and-puffing C Aubrey Smith, who's searching for an elephant graveyard. Fighting a variety of big cats, armed with only a knife, may look unrealistic – as does some of the in-cut library material – but the fun at the expense of city dwellers on safari and the atmosphere of studio fantasy make it a museum piece that still lives and breathes.

Johnny Weissmuller *Tarzan* • Maureen O'Sullivan *Jane Parker* • Neil Hamilton *Harry Holt* • C Aubrey Smith *James Parker* • Doris Lloyd *Mrs Cutten* • Forrester Harvey *Beamish* • Ivory Williams *Riano* ■ *Dir* WS Van Dyke • *Scr* Cyril Hume, Ivor Novello, from characters created by Edgar Rice Burroughs

Tarzan, the Ape Man ★★ U
Adventure   1959 · US · Colour · 81mins

Twenty-seven years after MGM unveiled (literally) the now-legendary Johnny Weissmuller in the film of the same title, the studio had the temerity to remake it with one of the most lacklustre of all Tarzans, Denny Miller, in his only outing in the role. Since the company owned the original they tinted some footage from that and, apparently, even earlier silent Tarzan films. Nothing helped and the story of the white hunter and his daughter who discover the ape man in the jungle makes for conventional fare.

Denny Miller *Tarzan* • Joanna Barnes *Jane Parker* • Cesare Danova *Holt* • Robert Douglas *Col Parker* • Thomas Yangha *Riano* ■ *Dir* Joseph M Newman • *Scr* Robert J Hill, from characters created by Edgar Rice Burroughs

Tarzan, the Ape Man ★ 15
Adventure   1981 · US · Colour · 107mins

A legendary turkey, with Bo Derek traipsing through the greenery looking for excuses to disrobe more often than Edgar Rice Burroughs's jungle king himself. Directed by Bo's husband, John Derek, this actionless soft-core spectacular is a demented vanity production on such an epic scale that all you can do is stare in disbelief. Wooden Miles O'Keeffe must be the worst screen Tarzan ever, in a slice of pretentious exotica rating a minus 10 on the "Bo-rometer". Contains some swearing and nudity. ▣

Bo Derek *Jane Parker* • Richard Harris *James Parker* • John Phillip Law *Harry Holt* • Miles O'Keeffe *Tarzan* • Akushula Selayah *Nambia, "Africa"* • Steven Strong *Ivory King* • Maxime Philoe *Riano* • Leonard Bailey *Feathers* • Wilfrid Hyde White *Club member* ■ *Dir* John Derek • *Scr* Tom Rowe, Gary Goddard, from characters created by Edgar Rice Burroughs

Tarzan the Fearless ★★ U
Adventure   1933 · US · BW · 85mins

Made by independent producer Sol Lesser just after MGM had released its first Tarzan blockbuster with Johnny Weissmuller, this starred the equally muscular Buster Crabbe, and followed MGM's portrayal of Tarzan as a grunting ape man rather than the educated hero of the original stories. Made simultaneously as a serial, this feature version is episodic and crudely edited. Crabbe's athleticism is fine, but his acting consists mainly of showing his teeth in an inane smile. Jacqueline Wells (later to become better known as Julie Bishop) is the heroine seeking her father in the jungle, but deciding at the film's end to stay with Tarzan. ▣

Buster Crabbe [Larry "Buster" Crabbe] *Tarzan* • Jacqueline Wells [Julie Bishop] *Mary Brooks* • E Alyn Warren *Dr Brooks* • Edward Woods *Bob Hall* • Philo McCollough *Jeff Herbert* • Mischa Auer *High Priest* ■ *Dir* Robert F Hill • *Scr* Basil Dickey, George H Plympton, Ford Beebe, Walter Anthony, from characters created by Edgar Rice Burroughs

Tarzan the Magnificent ★★★ U
Adventure   1960 · UK · Colour · 86mins

Recalling the James Stewart/Robert Ryan western *The Naked Spur*, this was the last of Gordon Scott's five outings as Edgar Rice Burroughs's jungle hero. His adversary here, Jock Mahoney, would succeed him two years later in *Tarzan Goes to India*. The real star of the show, however, is veteran John Carradine, who throws restraint to the wind as the head of Mahoney's clan intent on ambushing the ape man before he can turn him over for trial. Betta St John also scores as the wife of weedy Lionel Jeffries who falls for the villain's charms.

Gordon Scott *Tarzan* • Jock Mahoney *Coy Banton* • Betta St John *Fay Ames* • John Carradine *Abel Banton* • Lionel Jeffries *Ames* • Alexandra Stewart *Laurie* ■ *Dir* Robert Day • *Scr* Berne Giler, Robert Day, from characters created by Edgar Rice Burroughs

Tarzan Triumphs ★★★
Second World War adventure
1943 · US · BW · 76mins

The first of the RKO Tarzan movies, produced by Sol Lesser, pits our hero, still in the brawny form of Johnny Weissmuller, against a topical German foe. The plot this time has Nazi paratroopers landing in a lost city and, sadly, leaves no room for Jane. Instead there's a fabulous performance from Cheetah, who here gets a super coda as he does something quite ingenious with the Nazis' short-wave radio – so it's worth sitting tight until the very end. The princess of the lost city is played by the sublime, perpetually under-rated Frances Gifford, star of Republic's *Jungle Girl* serial.

Johnny Weissmuller *Tarzan* • Johnny Sheffield *Boy* • Frances Gifford *Zandra* • Stanley Ridges *Col Von Reichart* • Rex Williams *Schmidt* • Sig Ruman *Sergeant* • Pedro De Cordoba *Patriarch* ■ *Dir* William Thiele • *Scr* Carroll Young, Roy Chanslor, from a story by Carroll Young, from characters created by Edgar Rice Burroughs

Tarzan's Deadly Silence
★★ U
Adventure   1970 · US · Colour · 87mins

Routine outing for the loin-clothed ape man, cobbled together from two episodes of the *Tarzan* TV series. Ron Ely is the biggest swinger in town, here battling a crazed soldier whose private army is threatening an African village. The supporting cast includes a former Tarzan, Jock Mahoney. TV values, no real cinematic merit. Incidentally, do you know Tarzan's famous last words? "Who greased that viiiiiiiiiiiiiiiiine?"

Ron Ely *Tarzan* • Jock Mahoney *The Colonel* • Manuel Padilla Jr *Jai* • Woody Strode *Marshak* • Rudolph Charles *Officer* • Nichelle Nichols *Ruana* ■ *Dir* Robert L Friend, Lawrence Dobkin • *Scr* Lee Erwin, Jack A Robinson, John Considine, Tim Considine, from characters created by Edgar Rice Burroughs

Tarzan's Desert Mystery
★★★ U
Spy adventure   1943 · US · BW · 69mins

Johnny Weissmuller's second jungle adventure for RKO is energetic hokum, a piece of lively wartime propaganda directed with zip by William Thiele. With Jane absent, the heroine is a chirpy showgirl (Nancy Kelly) with a secret message for a sheik, warning of foreign spies in his midst. The fast-moving action incorporates prehistoric monsters, man-eating plants and a totally unconvincing yet still gruesome giant spider which nearly devours Boy before turning its attention to the nasty Nazis. One of the most entertaining of the series.

Johnny Weissmuller *Tarzan* • Johnny Sheffield *Boy* • Nancy Kelly *Connie Bryce* • Otto Kruger *Paul Hendrix* • Joe Sawyer *Karl Straeder* • Lloyd Corrigan *Sheik Abdul El Khim* ■ *Dir* William Thiele • *Scr* Edward T Lowe, from a story by Carroll Young, from characters created by Edgar Rice Burroughs

Tarzan's Fight for Life ★ U
Adventure   1958 · US · Colour · 86mins

In the third of six films in which he starred as Tarzan, former lifeguard

Gordon Scott gets a new Jane, Eve Beck, and wrestles a live python in the film's best sequence. Otherwise it is business as usual when Tarzan's friendship with a doctor running a hospital in the jungle brings him into conflict with a tribal witch doctor and his superstitious followers.

Gordon Scott *Tarzan* • Eve Brent *Jane* • Rickie Sorensen *Tartu* • James Edwards *Futa* • Carl Benton Reid *Dr Sturdy* ■ *Dir* H Bruce Humberstone • *Scr* Thomas Hal Phillips, from characters created by Edgar Rice Burroughs

Tarzan's Greatest Adventure ★★★ U

Adventure   1959 · UK · Colour · 84mins

One of the best Tarzan movies, actually filmed on authentic African locations, with a fine plot and reliable direction from John Guillermin (*The Towering Inferno* and *The Blue Max*). Gordon Scott is Tarzan, with a greatly increased vocabulary compared with his predecessors, and the British co-stars are impressive, with such venerable names as Anthony Quayle and Niall MacGinnis among them. This is a splendid romp, beautifully photographed and edited, and it may even convert non-Tarzan fans. Watch out for Sean Connery as the diamond hunter.

Gordon Scott *Tarzan* • Anthony Quayle *Slade* • Sara Shane *Angie* • Niall MacGinnis *Kruger* • Sean Connery *O'Bannion* • Al Mulock *Dino* • Scilla Gabel *Toni* ■ *Dir* John Guillermin • *Scr* John Guillermin, Berne Giler, from a story by Les Crutchfield, from characters created by Edgar Rice Burroughs

Tarzan's Hidden Jungle ★★ U

Adventure   1955 · US · BW · 72mins

Gordon Scott – a former GI and fireman – makes his debut as Tarzan, opposing white hunters who are posing as United Nations photographers. Filmed in California with bought-in footage of African wildlife, this lacks wit and pace, but Scott went on to star in several more Tarzan adventures. He also married his co-star, Vera Miles, who plays a nurse he saves from restless natives.

Gordon Scott *Tarzan* • Vera Miles *Jill Hardy* • Peter Van Eyck *Dr Celliers* • Jack Elam *Burger* • Charles Fredericks *DeGroot* • Richard Reeves *Reeves* ■ *Dir* Harold Schuster • *Scr* William Lively, from characters created by Edgar Rice Burroughs

Tarzan's Magic Fountain ★★★ U

Adventure   1949 · US · BW · 72mins

The first film Lex Barker made as Tarzan is also his best. The narrative, dealing with an elixir of youth, is intriguing and gripping with a neat mixture of humour and suspense. Evelyn Ankers, one of the screen's great B-movie heroines, is an aviatrix who crashed in the jungle 20 years earlier and still looks youthful, and Albert Dekker is a convincingly duplicitous villain who sights a fortune in marketing the secret of eternal youth. Brenda Joyce, considered second only to Maureen O'Sullivan as an effective "Jane", retired from the screen after this movie. Elmo Lincoln,

the screen's first Tarzan in 1918, has a bit part in this movie.

Lex Barker *Tarzan* • Brenda Joyce *Jane* • Albert Dekker *Trask* • Evelyn Ankers *Gloria James* • Charles Drake *Dodd* • Alan Napier *Douglas Jessup* ■ *Dir* Lee Sholem • *Scr* Curt Siodmak, Harry Chandlee, from characters created by Edgar Rice Burroughs

Tarzan's New York Adventure ★★★ U

Adventure   1942 · US · BW · 70mins

One of the best-loved and best-remembered of all the MGM Johnny Weissmuller *Tarzans*, this might not seem quite so original today in the wake of both *Jungle 2 Jungle* and *George of the Jungle*, and perhaps it owed more than a little to *King Kong* even then. Still, Tarzan's confrontation with interior plumbing is still mightily amusing, funny enough to make you forget the nastiness of the abduction plot, as Boy is snatched from his ersatz jungle "parents" by unscrupulous circus folk. Sadly, this was the last time the lovely Maureen O'Sullivan played Jane.

Johnny Weissmuller *Tarzan* • Maureen O'Sullivan *Jane* • Johnny Sheffield *Boy* • Chill Wills *Manchester Mountford* • Paul Kelly *Jimmie Shields* • Charles Bickford *Buck Rand* • Virginia Grey *Connie Beach* • Cy Kendall *Colonel Ralph Sargent* ■ *Dir* Richard Thorpe • *Scr* William R Lipman, Myles Connolly, from a story by Myles Connolly, from characters created by Edgar Rice Burroughs

Tarzan's Peril ★★★ U

Adventure   1951 · US · BW · 78mins

Filmed largely in Africa, this is one of the better Tarzan films, with fascinating shots of wildlife and plenty of action in its tale of gun-runners attempting to start a war between tribes. Though Virginia Huston is ineffectual as Jane, there is a striking performance by Dorothy Dandridge, in a small role as a jungle queen who wants peace, and George Macready, one of the screen's most hissable villains, proves a worthy adversary for hero Tarzan. The film was also supposed to be the first of the series in colour, but after much of the colour footage was destroyed in an accident, it was decided to switch to black and white.

Lex Barker *Tarzan* • Virginia Huston *Jane* • George Macready *Radijek* • Douglas Fowley *Trask* • Glenn Anders *Andrews* • Dorothy Dandridge *Melmendi* ■ *Dir* Byron Haskin • *Scr* Samuel Newman, Francis Swann, John Cousins, from characters created by Edgar Rice Burroughs

Tarzan's Revenge ★

Adventure   1938 · US · BW · 70mins

This has the dubious distinction of being a contender for the worst Tarzan adventure ever made. Decathlon champion of the 1936 Olympics Glenn Morris co-stars with champion backstroke swimmer Eleanor Holm, but neither of them can act. The plot has Morris rescuing Holm from becoming part of a sultan's harem, and the film is directed by B-movie specialist D Ross Lederman with no style whatsoever.

Glenn Morris *Tarzan* • Eleanor Holm *Eleanor* • George Barbier *Roger* • C Henry Gordon *Ben Alleu Bey* • Hedda Hopper *Penny* • George

Meeker *Nevin* ■ *Dir* D Ross Lederman • *Scr* Robert Lee Johnson, Jay Vann, from characters created by Edgar Rice Burroughs

Tarzan's Savage Fury ★★ U

Adventure   1952 · US · BW · 80mins

This was the first movie to be directed by Cyril "Cy" Endfield in Britain, after he became one of the blacklisted Hollywood exiles. Not surprisingly, this routine adventure does not compare with his stunning offerings like *The Sound of Fury*, but it was the beginning of a long career in Britain where his most famous film proved to be *Zulu*. Lex Barker becomes caught up in a typical adventure when his cousin, visiting him in Africa to obtain his help for Britain's military security, is killed. Plenty of action helps the story along.

Lex Barker *Tarzan* • Dorothy Hart *Jane* • Patric Knowles *Edwards* • Charles Korvin *Rokov* • Tommy Carlton *Joey* ■ *Dir* Cyril Endfield [Cy Endfield] • *Scr* Cyril Hume, Hans Jacoby, Shirley White, from characters created by Edgar Rice Burroughs

Tarzan's Secret Treasure ★★ U

Adventure   1941 · US · BW · 81mins

High production values can't compensate for a ridiculous plot, but there is a certain perverse delight in watching Johnny Weissmuller's ape man and Maureen O'Sullivan's Jane cohabit in a tree house the like of which only the MGM art department could provide. There's a slew of rather more dignified character players than you'd expect in this type of tosh, including Reginald Owen and Barry Fitzgerald, plus George Sanders's elder brother Tom Conway. They all looking worried, as well they might; after all, they 're trying to fool Tarzan into helping them find gold. He may be big, but he certainly ain't stupid.

Johnny Weissmuller *Tarzan* • Maureen O'Sullivan *Jane* • Johnny Sheffield *Boy* • Reginald Owen *Professor Elliot* • Barry Fitzgerald *O'Doul* • Tom Conway *Medford* • Philip Dorn *Vandermeer* ■ *Dir* Richard Thorpe • *Scr* Myles Connolly, Paul Gabeglin, from characters created by Edgar Rice Burroughs

Tarzan's Three Challenges ★★ U

Adventure   1963 · US · Colour · 92mins

The producers dropped some Tarzan staples, such as Jane and Cheetah, in this episode of the jungle-fresh franchise, added Far Eastern locations and spent some money – all to good effect. A wise Oriental ruler is near death, and Tarzan has to prove himself a worthy minder to take the shrewd boy successor safely to the throne. On location, Jock Mahoney, in his second outing as the ape man, lost lots of weight during several bouts of illness; his constantly changing body is one of this able picture's incidental pleasures.

Jock Mahoney *Tarzan* • Woody Strode *Khan/ Tarim* • Tsu Kobayashi *Cho San* • Earl Cameron *Mang* ■ *Dir* Robert Day • *Scr* Berne Giler, Robert Day, from characters created by Edgar Rice Burroughs

Task Force ★★ U

Action drama
1949 · US · BW and Colour · 116mins

This long-winded account of the struggle to persuade the American navy to develop aircraft carriers opens with Gary Cooper as the retiring admiral looking back on his days as an early advocate of their use, arguing with politicians, newspaper proprietors and stubborn navy bigwigs. Only as the film bursts into colour towards the end, to work in documentary footage from the Second World War and demonstrate the carriers' worth in the Battle of Okinawa, does writer/director Delmer Daves's picture achieve lift-off.

Gary Cooper *Jonathan L Scott* • Jane Wyatt *Mary Morgan Scott* • Wayne Morris *McKinney* • Walter Brennan *Pete Richard* • Julie London *Barbara McKinney* • Bruce Bennett *McCluskey* • Jack Holt *Reeves* ■ *Dir/Scr* Delmer Daves

A Taste for Killing ★★ 15

Thriller   1992 · US · Colour · 83mins

In this formulaic thriller from director Lou Antonio, Jason Bateman and Henry Thomas star as college friends who find work on an oil rig to earn some money over the summer. Shunned by most of the crew, they are befriended by Michael Biehn, who turns out to be a sociopath. Biehn (*The Terminator*, *Aliens*, and *The Abyss*) is a persuasive bad guy, while Bateman and Thomas (Elliott in *ET*) make the most of their leading roles. Contains violence. ▭

Jason Bateman *Blaine Stoddard III* • Henry Thomas *Cary Sloan* • Michael Biehn *Bo Landry* • Helen Cates *Tess Kennedy* • Blue Deckert *Elray Phelps* • Fred Lerner *Duane* • Dan Ammerman *Mr Stoddard* • Richard Dillard *Mr Sloan* • Diane Perella *Mrs Sloan* • Renee Zellweger *Mary Lou* ■ *Dir* Lou Antonio • *Scr* Dan Bronson, from a story by Allen Rucker, Hudson Marquez

A Taste of Cherry ★★★★ PG

Drama   1997 · Iran · Colour · 94mins

Sharing the Palme d'Or at Cannes with Shohei Imamura's *The Eel*, Abbas Kiarostami's unconventional road movie is as much about the filmic process as morality, mortality or modern Iran. World-weary, middle-aged Homayoon Irshadi cruises the suburbs of Tehran in search of someone willing to transgress Islamic law by burying him after his suicide. Each person he propositions has symbolic significance, including a Kurdistani soldier and an Afghan seminary student, before he finally finds a taxidermist, who accepts the reward to pay his son's medical bills. Endlessly fascinating, with the subtle shifts in landscape and palette quite masterly. In Farsi with English subtitles. ▭

Homayoon Irshadi *Mr Badiei* • Abdol Hossain Bagheri *Mr Bagheri, taxidermist in Natural History Museum* • Afshin Khorshid Bakhtiari *Worker* • Safar Ali Moradi *Soldier from Kurdistan* • Mir Hossain Nouri *Clergyman* ■ *Dir/Scr* Abbas Kiarostami

A Taste of Evil ★★

Psychological thriller
1971 · US · Colour · 73mins

Veteran Hammer scriptwriter Jimmy Sangster updated his 1961 psychological shocker *Scream of Fear* for this early Aaron Spelling produced

TV movie thriller – with mixed results. Overfamiliarity dogs the *Les Diaboliques*-inspired plot in which rape victim Barbara Parkins is either going crazy or the victim of a fiendish scheme. Barbara Stanwyck is good value in the role originally played by Ann Todd, with Roddy McDowall, William Windom and Arthur O'Connell keeping the suspense going, as the other possible suspects.

Barbara Stanwyck *Miriam Jannings* • Barbara Parkins *Susan Wilcox* • Roddy McDowall *Dr Michael Lomas* • William Windom *Harold Jannings* • Arthur O'Connell *John* • Bing Russell *Sheriff* ■ *Dir* John Llewellyn Moxey • *Scr* Jimmy Sangster

A Taste of Honey ★★★★★ 15
Drama   1961 · UK · BW · 96mins

A ground-breaking movie of its time, with the mousy Rita Tushingham in her screen debut as the unwanted teenage daughter of Dora Bryan, a hilariously vulgar Salford lass who is being courted by a flash and pimpish Robert Stephens. Our Rita is saved from her living hell by two social exiles – a black sailor, who makes her pregnant, and a homosexual who makes her happy, until the poverty trap snaps shut around her. Set in dank bedsits, amid the grimy smokestacks, polluted canals and the tacky prom at Blackpool, this movie – a romance of sorts, and a comedy – survives as a priceless barometer of England and English attitudes in 1961.

Rita Tushingham *Jo* • Dora Bryan *Helen* • Murray Melvin *Geoffrey* • Robert Stephens *Peter* • Paul Danquah *Jimmy* • David Boliver *Bert* • Moira Kaye *Doris* ■ *Dir* Tony Richardson • *Scr* Shelagh Delaney, Tony Richardson, from the play by Shelagh Delaney

Taste the Blood of Dracula ★★★ 15
Horror   1969 · UK · Colour · 87mins

Three Victorian gentlemen get more than they bargained for when they indulge in Satanism for fun with the assistance of Ralph Bates. They inadvertently resurrect Count Dracula (Christopher Lee), who sends their sons and daughters on a killing spree. Although Lee is given little to do apart from look suavely menacing, he does metamorphose into a caped hero battling the hypocrisy of Victorian family values in this flamboyantly romantic grim fairy tale, with a genuinely imaginative, cut-glass ending. [cc]

Christopher Lee *Dracula* • Geoffrey Keen *William Hargood* • Gwen Watford *Martha Hargood* • Linda Hayden *Alice Hargood* • Ralph Bates *Lord Courtley* • Peter Sallis *Samuel Paxton* • Anthony Corlan *Paul Paxton* • Roy Kinnear *Weller* ■ *Dir* Peter Sasdy • *Scr* John Elder [Anthony Hinds], from the character created by Bram Stoker

Tatie Danielle ★★ 15
Black comedy   1990 · Fr · Colour · 107mins

Having mauled the middle-classes in *Life Is a Long Quiet River*, Etienne Chatiliez gives them an even more torrid time here at the hands of the auntie from hell, Tsilla Chelton. Relishing every little torture she inflicts upon Catherine Jacob and her dull, but decent family, Chelton gives a

wonderfully malicious performance, but what began as a wicked satire ends up getting lost in the darkness of its own comedy, and we become increasingly drawn to the put-upon relatives. In French with English subtitles. Contains swearing and nudity. [cc]

Tsilla Chelton *Auntie Danielle* • Catherine Jacob *Catherine Billard* • Isabelle Nanty *Sandrine* • Neige Dolsky *Odile* • Eric Pratt *Jean-Pierre Billard* • Laurence Février *Jeanne Billard* • Virginie Pradal *Madame Lafosse* • Mathieu Foulon *Jean-Marie Billard* ■ *Dir* Etienne Chatiliez • *Scr* Florence Quentin, Etienne Chatiliez

Tattoo ★★ 18
Drama   1980 · US · Colour · 98mins

Bruce Dern kidnaps model Maud Adams in a sleazy psycho-drama. Written by Joyce Buñuel, daughter of Luis, it's supposed to be an insightful study of psychopathic behaviour; tattoo artist Dern's enforced needlework on Bond girl Adams is presented as a rape substitute. But, while it may have been Buñuel's intention to shower her controversial material in allegorical significance, former commercials director Bob Brooks isn't up to the job, dismally failing to invest the film with any style or artistry and reducing it to peepshow level. Contains swearing and nudity. [cc]

Bruce Dern *Karl Kinsky* • Maud Adams *Maddy* • Leonard Frey *Halsey* • Rikke Borge *Sandra* • John Getz *Buddy* • Peter Iacangelo *Dubin* • Alan Leach *Customer* • Cynthia Nixon *Cindy* ■ *Dir* Bob Brooks • *Scr* Joyce Buñuel, from a story by Bob Brooks

Tawny Pipit ★★★ U
Comedy   1944 · UK · BW · 77mins

It was almost unthinkable in wartime that a British picture should criticise officialdom and poke fun at the eccentricities of national life. In Bernard Miles's independently produced feature, the only problem is that the satire is so gentle and the humour so whimsical that it makes *The Last of the Summer Wine* look like a searing social statement. However, the story about rare birds that nest in a field outside a Cotswolds village is not without its charm, the excellent cast is a pleasure to watch and the photography is quite exquisite. [cc]

Bernard Miles *Colonel Barton-Barrington* • Rosamund John *Hazel Broome* • Niall MacGinnis *Jimmy Bancroft* • Jean Gillie *Nancy Forester* • Lucie Mannheim *Russian sniper* • Christopher Steele *Reverend Kingsley* ■ *Dir* Bernard Miles, Charles Saunders • *Scr* Bernard Miles, Charles Saunders, from a story by Bernard Miles

Taxi! ★★★
Crime melodrama   1932 · US · BW · 70mins

This is a fast-paced, tough-as-nails Warner Bros melodrama with crackling dialogue, starring the great James Cagney as the New York cabby involved in some inter-taxi-company rivalry. The opening sequence is a real surprise, with Cagney speaking fluent Yiddish, learned during his East Side childhood. Loretta Young is the perky heroine, and there's some early fancy footwork from George Raft, who, like Cagney, was better known as a screen gangster than for what was his real forte – hoofing.

James Cagney *Matt Nolan* • Loretta Young *Sue Riley* • George E Stone *Skeets* • Guy Kibbee *Pop Riley* • David Landau *Buck Gerard* • Ray Cooke *Danny Nolan* • Leila Bennett *Ruby* • Dorothy Burgess *Marie Costa* • Matt McHugh *Joe Silva* • George Raft *William "Willie" Kenny* ■ *Dir* Roy Del Ruth • *Scr* Kubec Glasmon, John Bright, from the play *The Blind Spot* by Kenyon Nicholson

Taxi ★★
Comedy drama   1953 · US · BW · 77mins

Directing his first movie in three years, Gregory Ratoff is deserted by the sure touch that persuaded 20th Century-Fox to entrust him with so many minor A features during the Second World War. Too many cooks were involved in concocting a script with little flavour of the New York streets which force Dan Dailey into emotional overdrive. Playing a world-weary cabby, he has to shrug off the loan sharks on his tail to help vulnerable Irish immigrant Constance Smith who's trying to locate her errant husband.

Dan Dailey *Ed Nielson* • Constance Smith *Mary* • Neva Patterson *Miss Millard* • Blanche Yurka *Mrs Nielson* • Geraldine Page *Florence Albert* • Rex O'Malley *Butler* • John Cassavetes *Cab driver* ■ *Dir* Gregory Ratoff • *Scr* DM Marshman Jr, Daniel Fuchs, Alex Joffe, Jean Paul Le Chanois, from the story *Sans Laisser d'Adresse* by Hans Jacoby, Fred Brady

Taxi ★★ 15
Action drama   1998 · Fr · Colour · 89mins

The fancy automobile stunts are everything in this puerile, paper-thin comedy-thriller scripted by Luc Besson (*The Fifth Element*). Speed-freak taxi driver Samy Naceri and timid cop Frédéric Diefenthal team up to catch a slick bunch of bank robbers, leading to much squealing of tyres through the streets of Marseilles. Had it been played seriously (à la *Ronin*), this might have been a cracker. Unfortunately, director Gérard Pirès adds feeble *Carry On*-style stabs at slapstick humour as the couple screw up the case and the bumbling Diefenthal attempts to woo a ludicrously statuesque police officer (supermodel Emma Sjöberg). In French with English subtitles. Contains swearing and drug abuse.

Samy Naceri *Daniel* • Frédéric Diefenthal *Émilien* • Marion Cotillard *Lilly* • Emma Sjöberg *Petra* • Manuela Gourary *Camille* ■ *Dir* Gérard Pirès • *Scr* Luc Besson

Taxi 2 ★★★
Action drama   2000 · Fr · Colour · 85mins

Just as hi-octane as its commercially successful 1998 predecessor, this harum scarum sequel reteams daredevil Marseilles taxi driver Samy Naceri and laconic cop Frédéric Diefenthal, in another screenplay by Luc Besson. However, it benefits considerably from the snappier direction of Gérard Krawczyk, who not only keeps the plot ticking over, but also invests a Hollywood gusto into the action sequences (including one in which the ultra-customised cab sprouts wings). There's even some efficiently staged chop socky by way of variation, as a gang of ruthless ninjas kidnap a prominent Japanese politician and Diefenthal's statuesque partner, Emma

Sjöberg. Fast, furious and fun. A French/Japanese language film.

Samy Naceri *Daniel* • Frédéric Diefenthal *Émilien* • Emma Sjöberg *Petra* • Bernard Farcy *Chief Inspector Gibert* • Marion Cotillard *Lilly* ■ *Dir* Gérard Krawczyk • *Scr* Luc Besson

Taxi Blues ★★★
Drama   1990 · Fr/USSR · Colour · 110mins

Despite the visual excesses of a debutant, Pavel Lounguine won the best director prize at Cannes for this pioneering allegory on Russia at the crossroads. Alcoholic Jewish saxophonist Pyotr Nikolajevitch Mamonov epitomises the liberated intellectualism of the new era, while conservative Muscovite cabby Piotr Zaitchenko represents the hard-pressed proletariat. The film can hardly be said to be subtle in its symbolism, especially once their unlikely camaraderie is soured by sudden wealth and romantic rivalry. But Lounguine is less interested in them than in the crime, sexploitation, squalor and corruption unleashed by the collapse of communism. Courageous, but too aware of its own significance. In Russian with English subtitles. ■

Pyotr Nikolajevitch Mamonov *Liocha* • Piotr Zaitchenko *Schlikov* • Vladimir Kachpour *Old Netchiporenko* • Natalia Koliakanova *Christina* • Hal Singer ■ *Dir/Scr* Pavel Lounguine

Taxi Driver ★★★★★ 18
Drama   1976 · US · Colour · 109mins

Robert De Niro is mesmerising as the Vietnam veteran spiralling into one of director Martin Scorsese's most frightening circles of hell, as he seeks a twisted redemption by saving the soul of New York child prostitute Jodie Foster. This time the bustling helter-skelter of Scorsese's *Mean Streets* gives way to a measured, chilly calm and cinematographer Michael Chapman ensures the Big Apple glistens with barely concealed menace. It's De Niro's show, but the supporting players (Foster, Harvey Keitel, Cybill Shepherd) are almost as good, and there's a genuinely scary cameo from Scorsese himself. This deeply disturbing modern masterpiece established Scorsese as a major figure in world cinema, and it has not lost any of its power to shock. Contains violence and swearing. DVD

Robert De Niro *Travis Bickle* • Cybill Shepherd *Betsy* • Jodie Foster *Iris* • Peter Boyle *Wizard* • Leonard Harris *Charles Palantine* • Harvey Keitel *Sport* • Albert Brooks *Tom* • Martin Scorsese *Passenger* ■ *Dir* Martin Scorsese • *Scr* Paul Schrader • *Cinematographer* Michael Chapman

A Taxing Woman ★★★★ 18
Comedy drama   1987 · Jap · Colour · 127mins

The sharpest critic of Japanese mores in the 1980s, Juzo Itami focuses on the national obsession with all things material in this supremely controlled satire. His wife, Nobuko Miyamoto, is hilariously tenacious as the demure tax inspector whose slavish attention to detail is rewarded when she's given a pop at seedy motel mobster Tsutomu Yamazaki, whose flair for embezzlement matches her own devotion to duty. With an unlikely

romance and flashes of humanity intruding upon the relentless pursuit of success, this blend of Yakuza comedy and procedural thriller is both socially revealing and slyly entertaining. In Japanese with English subtitles.

Nobuko Miyamoto *Ryoko Itakura* • Tsutomu Yamazaki *Hideki Gondo* • Masahiko Tsugawa *Assistant Chief Inspector Hanamura* • Eitaro Ozawa *Tax accountant* ■ *Dir/Scr* Juzo Itami

Taza, Son of Cochise ★★ U

Western   1954 · US · Colour · 79mins

A belated attempt to redress the portrayal of native Americans started by *Broken Arrow*, this western starts with an uncredited Jeff Chandler making a brief, brief appearance as the wise warrior chief Cochise, passing on the pipe of peaceful co-existence to his son, played rather stiffly by Rock Hudson. Unfortunately, a dissenting Geronimo and others stir up some predictable trouble. Shot entirely on location in Utah, it's vigorously staged by director Douglas Sirk whose main interest lay in exploring tribal lore.

Rock Hudson *Taza* • Barbara Rush *Oona* • Gregg Palmer *Captain Burnett* • Bart Roberts [Rex Reason] *Naiche* • Morris Ankrum *Gray Eagle* • Gene Iglesias [Eugene Iglesias] *Chato* • Robert Burton *General Cook* ■ *Dir* Douglas Sirk • *Scr* George Zuckerman, Gerald Grayson Adams, from a story by Gerald Grayson Adams

Tea and Sympathy ★★★★

Drama   1956 · US · Colour · 121mins

''So the boy think's he's homosexual and the teacher's wife seduces him to prove he isn't, so what's the problem?'', a perplexed French producer once said to director, Vincente Minnelli. But in its day *Tea and Sympathy* was notorious, the play banned in the UK and the film ''X'' certificated. Re-creating their Broadway roles, Deborah Kerr (pronounced ''car''), John Kerr (pronounced ''cur'', no relation) and Leif Erickson, are all superbly cast, though the honesty of their performances is slightly threatened by the gloss in which MGM has almost drowned the tale. Today, this movie may seem tame, but its dialogue was groundbreaking 40 years ago.

Deborah Kerr *Laura Reynolds* • John Kerr *Tom Robinson Lee* • Leif Erickson *Bill Reynolds* • Edward Andrews *Herb Lee* • Darryl Hickman *Al* • Norma Crane *Ellie Martin* • Dean Jones *Ollie* • Jacqueline de Wit *Lilly Sears* ■ *Dir* Vincente Minnelli • *Scr* Robert Anderson, from his play

Tea for Two ★★ U

Musical comedy   1950 · US · Colour · 93mins

Though popular enough in its day, this Technicolored Doris Day vehicle is not one of her better musicals, suffering greatly from lacklustre direction and an astoundingly stupid plotline. It's a loose remake of *No, No, Nanette*, in which the heroine has to reply ''no'' to every question asked of her in an otherwise uneventful weekend in order to fulfil a bet. Seasoned troupers like Gene Nelson, Billy De Wolfe and SZ ''Cuddles'' Sakall do their best, but this is a daft tale that's not even cute enough to be camp. Still, it's cheerful and harmless enough, and the period

songs make it quite a sweet time-passer. ⬚

Doris Day *Nanette* • Gordon MacRae *Jimmy* • Gene Nelson *Tommy* • Eve Arden *Pauline* • Billy De Wolfe *Larry* • SZ Sakall *Max* • Patrice Wymore *Beatrice* • Bill Goodwin *William Early* ■ *Dir* David Butler • *Scr* Harry Clork, from the musical play *No, No, Nanette* by Frank Mandel, Otto Harbach, Vincent Youmans, Emil Nyitray

Tea with Mussolini ★★★ PG

Period comedy drama
1998 · It · Colour · 116mins

Franco Zeffirelli (*Hamlet* and *The Taming Of The Shrew*) here turns his camera on to his own life as a young boy growing up in Mussolini's Italy of the 1930s. Following his mother's death, the young Luca is rescued from the prospect of life in an orphanage by an eccentric group of expatriate women dubbed ''Scorpioni''. Luca is not the central character of the film – rather the eyes through which we see these corseted and costumed women. Judi Dench, Joan Plowright, Maggie Smith, Lily Tomlin and Cher give boisterously strong performances as the gaggle of women who gather over tea to gossip and act as unofficial minders and teachers to Luca. Later, the movie focuses more on conventional wartime dramas than on the relationships between the women, ultimately turning this into an interesting anecdote rather than a rich character piece. Contains some strong language. ⬚

Cher *Elsa* • Judi Dench *Arabella* • Joan Plowright *Mary* • Maggie Smith *Lady Hester* • Lily Tomlin *Georgie* • Baird Wallace *Luca* ■ *Dir* Franco Zeffirelli • *Scr* John Mortimer, Franco Zeffirelli, from an autobiography by Franco Zeffirelli

Teachers ★★ 15

Comedy   1984 · US · Colour · 102mins

Nick Nolte is Alex, a cynical teacher at the overcrowded and indisciplined John F Kennedy High School. When a graduating student is found to be illiterate, his family sue the school causing Vice Principal Judd Hirsch to rally the staff in defence of their teaching methods. The prosecuting lawyer, JoBeth Williams, turns out to have been a student at the school, and her situation is further complicated when she starts to fall for Alex... A by-the-numbers story of a good teacher managing to inspire the kids others ignore. Predictable, but enjoyable for those who like this sort of thing. ⬚

Nick Nolte *Alex* • JoBeth Williams *Lisa* • Judd Hirsch *Roger* • Ralph Macchio *Eddie* • Lee Grant *Dr Burke* • Richard Mulligan *Herbert* • Allen Garfield *Rosenberg* • Royal Dano *Ditto* • Laura Dern *Diane* • Crispin Glover *Danny* • Morgan Freeman *Lewis* ■ *Dir* Arthur Hiller • *Scr* WR McKinney

Teacher's Pet ★★★★ U

Comedy   1958 · US · BW · 119mins

A delightful comedy, with Clark Gable as a crusty, hard-bitten newspaper editor who, instead of lecturing to Doris Day's journalism class, decides to enrol as a pupil. And, of course, his initial disdain for reporters who learn from books is swayed by his attraction to the teacher. Fay and Michael Kanin's screenplay becomes thin by

the end, but Gable and Day fill it out with boisterous enthusiasm, possibly realising what upstaging opposition they've got from the great Gig Young, who was Oscar-nominated for his performance as Doris's other beau.

Clark Gable *James Gannon* • Doris Day *Erica Stone* • Gig Young *Dr Hugo Pine* • Mamie Van Doren *Peggy DeFore* • Nick Adams *Barney Kovac* • Peter Baldwin *Harold Miller* • Charles Lane (1) *Roy* • Harry Antrim *Lloyd Crowley* ■ *Dir* George Seaton • *Scr* Fay Kanin, Michael Kanin

Teaching Mrs Tingle ★★★★

Black comedy thriller
1999 · US · Colour · 94mins

An awesome central performance by Helen Mirren and a diamond cut sparkling script packed with bitchy one-liners turn *Scream* scribe Kevin Williamson's directorial debut into a hugely entertaining black comedy in the sly Hitchcock tradition. Mirren is the eponymous teacher, doing her damnedest to stop Leigh Ann Watson (Katie Holmes) winning a scholarship. The tables turn when Holmes and two friends hold their nemesis hostage in her own house after being caught looking at exam papers in advance. An ingenious postmodern fairy tale and capriciously cool comic chiller, overflowing with the bitter and twisted ironies of life.

Helen Mirren *Mrs Tingle* • Katie Holmes *Leigh Ann Watson* • Jeffrey Tambor *Coach Wenchell* • Barry Watson *Luke Churner* • Marisa Coughlan *Jo Lynn Jordan* • Liz Stauber *Trudie Tucker* • Michael McKean *Principal Potter* • Molly Ringwald *Miss Banks* ■ *Dir/Scr* Kevin Williamson

The Teahouse of the August Moon ★★★ U

Comedy   1956 · US · Colour · 122mins

Marlon Brando stars as the Japanese interpreter who comes into conflict with Glenn Ford, as the latter attempts to bring American democracy and materialism to the Japanese island of Okinawa. As a satire on the culture clash it has some teeth, though not quite as lethal-looking as those worn by Brando as part of his hilarious make-up. Brando made the film partly to raise money to make a documentary about the UN's role in Asia – an interest that led to his 1963 feature *The Ugly American* – but he disliked *Teahouse*.

Marlon Brando *Sakini* • Glenn Ford *Captain Fisby* • Machiko Kyo *Lotus Blossom* • Eddie Albert *Captain McLean* • Paul Ford *Colonel Purdy* • Jun Negami *Mr Seiko* • Henry Morgan [Harry Morgan] *Sgt Gregovich* ■ *Dir* Daniel Mann • *Scr* John Patrick, from the play by John Patrick and the novel by Vern J Sneider

Teamster Boss: the Jackie Presser Story ★★★

Biographical drama
1992 · US · Colour · 111mins

Brian Dennehy gives a no-holds-barred performance as the tough-talking union man who works his crooked way to the top, in this compelling TV drama. He's more than ably supported by a topnotch cast including Jeff Daniels, Maria Conchita Alonso and Eli Wallach, though Alastair Reid's direction is inevitably constrained by the TV-movie

format. And, if the deals Presser strikes with the mob and the way he manipulates the FBI seem a little larger than life, just remember that this is based on the true story of one of the most powerful US labour leaders of the Reagan era.

Brian Dennehy *Jackie Presser* • Jeff Daniels *Tom Noonan* • Maria Conchita Alonso *Carmen* • Eli Wallach *Bill Presser* • Robert Prosky *Maisha Rockman* • Tony LoBianco *Alan Dorfman* • Al Waxman *Alan Friedman* • Frank Pellegrino *Tony Provensano* • Val Avery *Fat Tony Salerno* ■ *Dir* Alastair Reid • *Scr* Abby Mann, from the book *Mobbed Up* by James Neff

Teaserama ★★ 15

Cult burlesque review
1955 · US · Colour · 62mins

Tempest Storm was one of the last of the classic strippers of the burlesque era. In this poverty-row record of her revue, she's joined by other disrobing artists, dancing girls and comedians, including, in one legendary mistress/maid scenario, queen of the fifties pin-ups, Betty Page. Shot (saying directed would give completely the wrong impression!) with a single, static camera by mail-order sleaze king Irving Klaw, this ''adults only'' antique is so coy and innocent by today's standards it's hard to believe it was ever considered controversial or racy. Contains semi-nudity.

Tempest Storm • Betty Page • Honey Baer • Cherry Knight • Chris LaChris • Vicki Lynn • Joe E Ross • Dave Starr • Trudy Wayne • Twinnie Wallen ■ *Dir* Irving Klaw

The Teckman Mystery ★★ U

Thriller   1954 · UK · BW · 89mins

There's more than a hint of *The Third Man* in this passable thriller, co-written by Francis Durbridge from his own BBC serial. John Justin looks suitably bemused as an author who discovers that the dead air ace whose biography he's been commissioned to write may not have perished after all. Director Wendy Toye makes a reasonable fist at keeping the pace up and the clues hidden, but she's no Carol Reed.

Margaret Leighton *Helen Teckman* • John Justin *Philip Chance* • Roland Culver *Inspector Harris* • Michael Medwin *Martin Teckman* • George Coulouris *Garvin* • Duncan Lamont *Inspector Hilton* • Raymond Huntley *Maurice Miller* ■ *Dir* Wendy Toye • *Scr* Francis Durbridge, James Matthews, from the TV serial *The Teckman Biography* by Francis Durbridge

Tecumseh: the Last Warrior ★★ 12

Historical drama   1995 · US · Colour · 90mins

The Native American perspective of history is the focus of this ambitious TV movie. Shawnee warrior Tecumseh (Jesse Borrego) tries to unite the tribes against the white settlers threatening to take over Indian lands. He and his followers find themselves confronted by governor – and later US president – William Henry Harrison (David Clennon), whose mission it is to defeat them at all costs. Clennon is splendid as the now obscure Harrison, but despite its good intentions and exciting, energetic battle scenes, this movie cannot overcome its

U = SUITABLE FOR ALL   Uc = SUITABLE FOR ALL, ESPECIALLY FOR YOUNG CHILDREN (VIDEO ONLY)   PG = PARENTAL GUIDANCE

occasionally confusing storyline, talky script and preachy tone. Contains some violence. ▭

Jesse Borrego *Tecumseh* • David Morse *Galloway* • Tantoo Cardinal *Turtle Mother* • David Clennon *Harrison* • Douglas Spain *Teen Tecumseh* • Holt McCallany *Blue Jacket* • August Schellenberg *Black Hoof* ■ *Dir* Larry Elikann • *Scr* PF Edwards, from the book *Panther in the Sky* by James Alexander Thom

Ted & Venus   ★★ 18

Romantic comedy drama
1991 · US · Colour · 95mins

An offbeat romance from Bud Cort, directing here but maybe better known as an actor in cult favourite *Harold and Maude*. Cort stars too, playing a poet whose obsession with dream-girl Kim Adams forces him to ever wilder efforts to attract her attention. Funny at times, but maybe it needed more of the endearing wackiness of Cort's most famous film to make it really work. The quality support cast includes James Brolin, Carol Kane, Rhea Perlman and an early appearance by Woody Harrelson.

Bud Cort *Ted Whitley* • James Brolin *Max Waters* • Kim Adams *Linda Turner* • Carol Kane *Colette/Colette's twin sister* • Pamella D'Pella *Gloria* • Brian Thompson *Herb* • Rhea Perlman *Grace* • Woody Harrelson *Homeless Vietnam veteran* • Timothy Leary *Poetic judge* ■ *Dir* Bud Cort • *Scr* Paul Ciotti, Bud Cort, from a story by Paul Ciotti

The Ted Kennedy Jr Story   ★★

Biographical drama
1986 · US · Colour · 100mins

This TV movie tackles another Kennedy family tragedy, this time focusing on the Massachusetts senator's 12-year-old son, who lost his leg to cancer, and valiantly struggled to resume a normal life. Part disease-of-the-week, part biography, this could have been an exercise in mawkish melodrama, but instead manages to be quite tender. Craig T Nelson (*The Devil's Advocate*) plays the senator and Susan Blakely (*The Towering Inferno*) is his wife, Joan.

Craig T Nelson *Senator Edward Kennedy* • Susan Blakely *Joan Kennedy* • Kimber Shoop *Ted Kennedy Jr* • Michael J Shannon *Senator John Tunney* • Dennis Creaghan *Dr Bill Reed* • Jeff Harding *Joe Wright* • Christopher Connolly *Patrick Kennedy* ■ *Dir* Delbert Mann • *Scr* Roger O Hirson

Teen Agent   ★★★ PG

Spy comedy   1991 · US · Colour · 84mins

Gadgets, glamour, gold and girls. No, it's not another James Bond rerun, just swarthy Richard Grieco in a fun spy spoof laced with sly Ian Fleming references and 007-inspired gimmicks. Former TV star Grieco is mistaken for an undercover CIA agent when he flies to Paris for French lessons, and, armed by MI5 with suction sneakers, X-ray specs and a tank-cum-sports car, is sent to investigate Roger Rees, a megalomaniac in high camp *Goldfinger* mode. Although predictable every step of the way, this will leave you enjoyably shaken and pleasantly stirred. ▭

Richard Grieco *Michael Corben* • Linda Hunt *Ilsa Grunt* • Roger Rees *Augustus Steranko* • Robin Bartlett *Mrs Grober* • Gabrielle Anwar

---

Mariska • Geraldine James *Vendetta Galante* • Michael Siberry *Richardson* • Roger Daltrey *Blade* ■ *Dir* William Dear • *Scr* Darren Star, from a story by Fred Dekker

Teen Kanya   ★★★ U

Comedy drama   1961 · Ind · BW · 114mins

Satyajit Ray filmed two of Tagore's stories on the centenary of the author's birth. Both are charming tales about the difficulties faced by young women in love. In *The Postmaster* an orphaned girl becomes attached to her employer, who repays her affection by helping with her education. A young man rejects an arranged marriage in *The Conclusion*, but finds that his own choice of bride resents being forced into matrimony. The film's success is due as much to the gifted playing and Ray's observant eye, as to Tagore's skills as a storyteller. In Bengali with English subtitles.

Anil Chatterjee *Nandalal* • Chandana Bannerjee *Ratan* • Aparna Das Gupta *Mrinmoyee* • Soumitra Chatterjee *Amulya* ■ *Dir* Satyajit Ray • *Scr* Satyajit Ray, from the stories *The Postmaster* and *The Conclusion* by Rabindranath Tagore

Teen Witch   ★★ PG

Fantasy comedy   1989 · US · Colour · 88mins

On learning that she will become a witch on her 16th birthday, un-hip student Robin Lively uses her magic powers to become the most popular girl in school, get back at her uncaring teachers and snare a hunky boyfriend. Fortune teller Zelda Rubinstein guides her through the spell-casting until she discovers, the hard way, to be careful what she wishes for. Lightweight fare, with zero special effects, but a few MTV-style musical dance numbers punctuating the pallid pace. ▭

Robyn Lively *Louise* • Dick Sargent *Frank* • Zelda Rubinstein *Serena* • Dan Gauthier *Brad* • Joshua Miller *Richie* • Shelley Berman *Mr Weaver* ■ *Dir* Dorian Walker • *Scr* Robin Menken, Vernon Zimmerman

Teen Wolf   ★★★ PG

Comedy   1985 · US · Colour · 91mins

Likeable, if lightweight comedy about a teenager who longs to be a little less ordinary. Then he discovers a family curse that kicks in when the moon is full. Beneath the facial fur, this is just another instalment of growing pains, although it does feature cinema's only werewolf slam dunk sports sequence and the engaging Fox doing what he does best – turning a loser into a winner. Jason Bateman took over in the needless sequel *Teen Wolf Too*. ▭

Michael J Fox *Scott Howard* • James Hampton *Harold Howard* • Susan Ursitti *Lisa "Boof" Marconi* • Jerry Levine *Stiles* • Matt Adler *Lewis* • Lorie Griffin *Pamela* • Jim MacKrell [James Mackrell] *Mr Thorne* • Mark Arnold *Mick McAllister* • Jay Tarses *Coach Finstock* ■ *Dir* Rod Daniel • *Scr* Joseph Loeb III, Matthew Weisman

Teenage Caveman   ★★ U

Fantasy adventure   1958 · US · BW · 65mins

Cult director Roger Corman's prehistoric *Rebel without a Cause* is justly famous for its catchpenny title, cheap dinosaurs (borrowed from *One*

Million BC), the "stuffed deer" scene and lead actor Robert Vaughn in his pre-*Man from UNCLE* days. He's the titular boy who breaks tribal rules and ventures into the "forbidden land", where he learns his violent society is really a post-apocalyptic one. Vaughn calls this "one of the best-worst films of all time": he's right, but its tackiness is engaging and Corman imbues it with a naive charm.

Robert Vaughn *Boy* • Leslie Bradley *Symbol Maker* • Darrah Marshall *Maiden* • Frank De Kova *Villain* ■ *Dir* Roger Corman • *Scr* R Wright Campbell

Teenage Gang Debs   ★★

Crime drama   1966 · US · BW · 77mins

Two years after *The Beautiful, the Bloody and the Bare*, New York film-maker Sande N Johnsen turned to the brutal world of street gangs in this uncompromising slice of inner-city exploitation. *West Side Story* this isn't, as Diana Conti persuades the leader of the Manhattan-based Golden Falcons into battle against John Batis and his Brooklyn Rebels. The rumble involving the sadistic Aliens and the skin-carving finale are alarmingly authentic. There's also plenty of crucially unhip jive talk and one of the worst dance routines you are ever likely to see.

Diana Conti *Terry* • Linda Gale *Angel* • Eileen Scott *Ellie* • Sandra Kane *Annie* • Robin Nolan *Maria* • Linda Cambi *Shirley* • Sue McManus *Sally* • John Batis *Johnny* ■ *Dir* Sande N Johnsen • *Scr* Hy Cahl

Teenage Monster   ★

Science-fiction horror
1958 · US · BW · 65mins

This ho-hum science-fiction horror movie was titled *Meteor Monster* until the success of *I Was a Teenage Werewolf* caused every horror film to jump on the same bandwagon. In a plot that drags western clichés into its juvenile delinquent mix, teenager Gilbert Perkins is infected by rays from a weird meteor and slowly turns into a rampaging murderous hairy monster. His protective mother, Anne Gwynne, tries to hide him in the cellar, but it's not too long before the local sheriff becomes suspicious. ▭

Anne Gwynne *Ruth Cannon* • Gloria Castillo *Kathy North* • Stuart Wade *Sheriff Bob* • Gilbert Perkins *Charles Cannon* • Charles Courtney *Marv Howell* ■ *Dir* Jacques Marquette • *Scr* Ray Buffum

Teenage Mutant Ninja Turtles   ★★★ PG

Fantasy adventure
1990 · US · Colour · 87mins

Those kickboxing Teletubbies of yesteryear made their feature debut in this uneven comic-strip fantasy directed by pop-video whiz kid Steve Barron. In case you'd forgotten, the awesome foursome are pizza-munching, kung-fu fighting, sewer-dwelling super-reptiles who, in this mindless adventure, help perky TV reporter Judith Hoag solve a Manhattan crime spree masterminded by the Shredder, a Darth Vader-voiced rogue ninja master. Elias Koteas scores as a mock turtle vigilante, but little else in this garish affair hits the

---

target, despite Barron covering the cracks with fast editing and cartoon violence. Contains violence. ▭

Judith Hoag *April O'Neil* • Elias Koteas *Casey Jones* • Josh Pais *Raphael* • Michelan Sisti *Michaelangelo* • Leif Tilden *Donatello* • David Forman *Leonardo* • Michael Turney *Danny Pennington* • Jay Patterson *Charles Pennington* ■ *Dir* Steve Barron • *Scr* Todd W Langen, Bobby Herbeck, from a story by Bobby Herbeck, from characters created by Kevin Eastman, Peter Laird

Teenage Mutant Ninja Turtles II: the Secret of the Ooze   ★★ PG

Fantasy adventure
1991 · US · Colour · 84mins

Nothing to do with Ivan Ooze (who posed a few problems for the Power Rangers), but the nasty stuff that caused our heroes to live underground, shout "cowabunga" and gorge themselves on bizarre flavoured pizzas in the first place. Seeking once more to stamp out the Foot clan, the turtles team up with reporter Paige Turco and gormless delivery boy Ernie Reyes. The human characters (even scientist David Warner) are pretty pointless, however, as this is all about the latex quartet and monsters like Rahzar and Tokka. Less abrasive than its predecessor and considerably less successful at the box office. ▭

Paige Turco *April O'Neil* • David Warner *Professor Jordan Perry* • Michelan Sisti *Michaelangelo* • Leif Tilden *Donatello* • Kenn Troum *Raphael* • Mark Caso *Leonardo* • Kevin Clash *Splinter* • Ernie Reyes Jr *Keno* • François Chau *Shredder* • Toshishiro Obata *Tatsu* ■ *Dir* Michael Pressman • *Scr* Todd W Langen, from characters created by Kevin Eastman, Peter Laird

Teenage Mutant Ninja Turtles III   ★★ PG

Fantasy adventure
1992 · US · Colour · 91mins

A second sequel but, by this stage, a largely irrelevant one, as the equally irritating Power Rangers had succeeded the Pizza-loving amphibians in the children's popularity stakes. Writer/director Stuart Gillard tries to inject some life into the project by including some tongue-in-cheek scenes in 17th-century Japan, but it quickly degenerates into half-hearted cartoonish action. Stuart Wilson and Elias Koteas are the best known names in the cast and manage to keep a reasonably straight face through it all. Contains some violence. ▭

Elias Koteas *Casey Jones/Whit Whitley* • Paige Turco *April O'Neil* • Stuart Wilson *Captain Dirk Walker* • Sab Shimono *Lord Norinaga* • Vivian Wu *Princess Mitsu* • Mark Caso *Leonardo* • Matt Hill *Raphael* • Jim Raposa *Donatello* • David Fraser *Michaelangelo* • James Murray *Splinter* ■ *Dir* Stuart Gillard • *Scr* Stuart Gillard, from characters created by Kevin Eastman, Peter Laird

Teenage Rebel   ★★

Comedy drama   1956 · US · BW · 94mins

A misleading title for a mediocre family picture about teenager Betty Lou Keim who, having lived with her father for some years after her parents' divorce,

---

is sent back to her mother Ginger Rogers when dad decides to remarry. Initially resentful of both maternal control and her stepfather Michael Rennie, she gradually warms to her new surroundings. Entirely forgettable despite Oscar nominations for costume, art direction and set decoration.

Ginger Rogers *Nancy Fallon* • Michael Rennie *Jay Fallon* • Mildred Natwick *Grace Hewitt* • Betty Lou Keim *Dodie* • Warren Berlinger *Dick Hewitt* • Rusty Swope *Larry Fallon* ■ *Dir* Edmund Goulding • *Scr* Walter Reisch, Charles Brackett, from the play *A Roomful of Roses* by Edith Sommer

Teenager ★★ 18

Drama   1974 · US · Colour · 86mins

A low-budget director (looking like cult icon Roger Corman), gets the cast of his latest Hell's Angels biker flick to invade a small town for real for docu-drama veracity. Death results as the townspeople fight back. Meanwhile, a local girl (the teenager of the misleading title) and the star actor fall in love. A cross between Dennis Hopper's *The Last Movie* and Corman's own *The Wild Angels*, this hopelessly hippy drive-in delight features Sue Bernard from *Faster, Pussycat! Kill! Kill!* A real collector's item for die hard schlock watchers. ▭

Joe Warfield • Andrea Cagan • Reid Smith • Sue Bernard ■ *Dir* Gerald Seth Sindell

Teesri Kasam ★★★ U

Musical   1966 · Ind · BW · 148mins

Raj Kapoor reprises one of his most popular roles, as Hiraman, the bullock-cart driver. But this study of the oppression of women in general and the sexual exploitation of dancers in particular ultimately lacks the courage of its convictions. Director Basu Bhattacharya was making his feature debut, but he isn't helped by a script that can't decide whether its primary aim is to inform or to entertain. However, Kapoor's songs and Waheeda Rehman's dance numbers provide a charming and effective distraction from the film's many flaws. In Hindi with English subtitles. ▭

Raj Kapoor *Hiraman* • Waheeda Rehman *Hirabai* ■ *Dir* Basu Bhattacharya • *Scr* Nabendu Ghosh

Telefon ★★★ PG

Spy thriller   1977 · US · Colour · 98mins

This is far from director Don Siegel's best work, but it's a more than acceptable thriller with a nifty plot and a couple of cracking performances. Charles Bronson is solid enough as a KGB troubleshooter sent to the USA to prevent "sleeping" agents from carrying out their missions, and Lee Remick is typically assured as his contact. But the film belongs to Donald Pleasence as a crazed Stalinist spymaster and Tyne Daly as a sharp-tongued CIA computer boffin. Contains violence. ▭

Charles Bronson *Grigori Borzov* • Lee Remick *Barbara* • Donald Pleasence *Nicolai Dalchimsky* • Tyne Daly *Dorothy Putterman* • Alan Badel *Colonel Malchenko* • Patrick Magee *General Strelsky* • Sheree North *Marie*

Wills ■ *Dir* Don Siegel • *Scr* Peter Hyams, Stirling Silliphant, from the novel by Walter Wager

The Telegraph Trail ★★ U

Western   1933 · US · BW · 51mins

One of a short series of B-westerns that John Wayne shot for Warner Bros, this features him as a Indian-hating US army scout who routs the redskins after they've interrupted the construction of the telegraph wire across the plains. The impressive climax, with its shots of an Indian war dance, was lifted from the silent Ken Maynard western, *The Red Raiders*. The comic relief from Frank McHugh and Otis Harlan is a distinct minus. ▭

John Wayne *John Trent* • Marceline Day *Alice Ellis* • Frank McHugh *Sgt Tippy* • Otis Harlan *Zeke Keller* • Albert J Smith *Gus Lynch* • Yakima Canutt *"High Wolf"* ■ *Dir* Tenny Wright • *Scr* Kurt Kempler

The Telephone ★ 15

Comedy drama   1988 · US · Colour · 78mins

Poor Whoopi Goldberg has been involved in a number of dubious big screen projects in her time (*Fatal Beauty, Theodore Rex*) but this plumbs new depths. With a script by the unlikely pairing of musician Harry Nilsson and Terry Southern (co-writer of *Easy Rider*), and direction by dependable character actor Rip Torn (*The Larry Sanders Show*), an intriguing project was on the cards. But it wasn't to be. This is virtually a one-woman show with Whoopi as Vashti Blue, a "resting" actress constantly talking on the phone or ranting to her pet owl. And that's it! ▭

Whoopi Goldberg *Vashti Blue* • Severn Darden *Max* • Elliott Gould *Rodney* • John Heard *Telephone man* • Amy Wright *Honey Boxe/Irate neighbor/Jennifer, answering machine voice* • Ronald J Stallings *Saxophone player* ■ *Dir* Rip Torn • *Scr* Terry Southern, Harry Nilsson

Tell It to the Judge ★★

Romantic comedy   1949 · US · BW · 85mins

Co-stars Rosalind Russell and Robert Cummings have to employ all their considerable skill as *farceurs* to keep this lightweight comedy afloat. The plot concerns the attempts of lawyer Cummings to get back with his ex-wife Russell, but the cause of their split – dumb blonde Marie McDonald – is the key witness in a case Cummings is working on. Every time he woos back his wife, up pops the blonde in a compromising situation. Admittedly it's thin stuff, but Russell allows herself to be put through some undignified slapstick in pursuit of laughs.

Rosalind Russell *Marsha Meredith* • Robert Cummings *Peter Webb* • Gig Young *Alexander Darvac* • Marie McDonald *Ginger Simmons* • Harry Davenport *Judge Meredith* • Fay Baker *Valerie Hobson* • Katharine Warren *Kitty Lawton* • Douglass Dumbrille *George Ellerby* ■ *Dir* Norman Foster • *Scr* Nat Perrin, Roland Kibbee, from a story by Devery Freeman

Tell Me a Riddle ★★★

Drama   1980 · US · Colour · 90mins

Unaware that the illness from which she is suffering is terminal, elderly Lila

Kedrova, who has been locked in mutually unsatisfying 40-year-marriage to Melvyn Douglas, visits her granddaughter Brooke Adams in San Francisco. There, she reflects on her unfulfilled life and, before her death, finds reconciliation with her husband. Marking the directorial debut of Oscar-winning actress Lee Grant (*Shampoo*), this is a truthful, perceptive and intelligent film, that is well-made and well-acted, but perhaps too sad and sombre to hold a broad appeal.

Melvyn Douglas *David* • Lila Kedrova *Eva* • Brooke Adams *Jeannie* • Lili Valenty *Mrs Mays* • Dolores Dorn *Vivi* • Bob Elross *Sammy* • Jon Harris *Mathew* • Zalman King *Paul* ■ *Dir* Lee Grant • *Scr* Joyce Eliason, Alev Lytle, from a novel by Tillie Olsen

Tell Me Lies ★★

Drama   1967 · UK · Colour and BW · 116mins

Following the disturbing film version of Peter Weiss's *Marat/Sade*, theatre director Peter Brook and Glenda Jackson reteamed for another all-out assault on the senses with this satirical swipe at the Vietnam War. This time, however, the chaotic structure (it's a mixture of sketches, music and news footage) fails to hold the attention and now seems self-indulgent rather than radical. Worth a look, though, if only for the eclectic cast which includes novelist Kingsley Amis, Patrick Wymark and Paul Scofield.

Mark Jones *Mark* • Pauline Munro *Pauline* • Robert Lloyd *Bob* • Kingsley Amis • Peggy Ashcroft • Glenda Jackson • Paul Scofield • Patrick Wymark • James Cameron • Ian Hogg ■ *Dir* Peter Brook • *Scr* Denis Cannan, Michael Kustow, Michael Scott, from the play *US* by Denis Cannan

Tell Me No Lies ★★

Drama   1991 · US · Colour · 96mins

Families and their secrets have become a popular subject for American TV movies. Here the realistic depiction of the psychological and emotional strains of modern family life (where a husband tries to adopt his late wife's son) helps offset any contrivance in the plot, while a decent sense of drive helps to make up for the perfunctory performances (Katherine Helmond apart), which add too little weight to the characters' motivations.

Steven Weber *Terry Milner* • Katherine Helmond *Genna* • Robert Hy Gorman *Jay* • Mary Page Keller *Amanda Milner* • Ben Kronen *Mr Grundel* • Wendy Bowers *Teacher* ■ *Dir* Sandor Stern • *Scr* Sandor Stern, from a story by Kandy Stern

Tell Me No Secrets ★★★

Mystery thriller   1996 · US · Colour

This convoluted but watchable courtroom thriller bucks the trend of most made-for-TV fare by coming up with a good twist at the end. Lori Loughlin stars as an ambitious lawyer who gets personally entangled in a rape case in which her ex-husband, played by Bruce Greenwood, is the opposing attorney. Loughlin and Greenwood are excellent, as is the script by Warren Taylor.

Lori Loughlin *Jess Koster* • Bruce Greenwood *Don Shaw* • Joe Flanigan *Adam Stiles* • Tracey Walter ■ *Dir* Bobby Roth • *Scr* Warren Taylor, from a novel by Joy Fielding

Tell Me That You Love Me, Junie Moon ★★

Comedy drama   1970 · US · Colour · 112mins

After establishing himself as one of Hollywood's most incisive, intelligent and provocative directors, by the end of the 1960s Otto Preminger had seemingly lost his grip. His judgement and objectivity had been replaced by trendy issues and glutinous sentimentality. A wildly over-emotional Liza Minnelli is Junie Moon while non-names Robert Moore and Ken Howard are her co-stars in this account of a facially disfigured young woman, a wheelchair-bound homosexual and an epileptic drop-out who, together, leave the hospital where they've been sheltering their neuroses, and set up home together. It should be inspiring, but it isn't.

Liza Minnelli *Junie Moon* • Ken Howard *Arthur* • Robert Moore *Warren* • James Coco *Mario* • Kay Thompson *Miss Gregory* • Ben Piazza *Jesse* ■ *Dir* Otto Preminger • *Scr* Marjorie Kellogg, from her novel

Tell Them Willie Boy Is Here ★★★ 15

Western   1969 · US · Colour · 93mins

A sombre, allegorical western written and directed by Abraham Polonsky, a victim of the McCarthy anti-communist witch-hunts. The film may seem too arty and introspective for today's tastes since the main thread of the story a traditional pursuit across fine landscapes is frequently broken for homilies on life and liberty. Even so, Robert Redford is excellent as the deputy sheriff chasing the Indian who's killed his prospective father-in-law. Robert Blake, as the fugitive, and Katharine Ross (from *The Graduate*), as his girlfriend, are less impressive in their heavy make-up. ▭

Robert Redford *Christopher Cooper* • Katharine Ross *Lola Boniface* • Robert Blake *Willie Boy* • Susan Clark *Dr Elizabeth Arnold* • Barry Sullivan *Ray Calvert* • Charles McGraw *Frank Wilson* • John Vernon *Hacker* ■ *Dir* Abraham Polonsky • *Scr* Abraham Polonsky, from the book *Willie Boy* by Harry Lawton

Telling Lies in America ★★★★ 15

Period drama   1997 · US · Colour · 97mins

This sweet and subtle coming-of-age story was written by Joe Eszterhas, who is more noted for steamy material like *Basic Instinct* and *Showgirls*. Partly autobiographical, the film tells of an immigrant Hungarian kid (Brad Renfro) who falls under the spell of Kevin Bacon's charismatic but ethic-free radio DJ. When Bacon is accused of taking record company backhanders, Renfro has to decide whether to jeopardise his father's citizenship assessment by lying for a friend. Terrific performances from Bacon and Renfro, and solid support from Maximilian Schell and *Ally McBeal's* Calista Flockhart. Contains swearing and sexual references. ▭

Kevin Bacon *Billy Magic* • Brad Renfro *Karchy Jonas* • Maximilian Schell *Dr Istvan Jonas* • Calista Flockhart *Diney Majeski* • Paul Dooley *Father Norton* • Luke Wilson *Henry* ■ *Dir* Guy Ferland • *Scr* Joe Eszterhas

The Temp ★★ 15
Thriller 1993 · US · Colour · 92mins

There was the nanny from hell in *The Hand That Rocks the Cradle* and the lodger from hell in *Pacific Heights* now it's time to meet Satan's secretary in this lesser take on the same theme. Lara Flynn Boyle (*Wayne's World* and *Twin Peaks*) is the shorthand expert wanting to make her way to the top no matter who stands in her way in this at times rather ludicrous thriller. Unfortunately, this film is neither as scary nor as funny as its predecessors, and serves only to embarrass a usually competent cast that includes Timothy Hutton, *The A-Team's* Dwight Schultz and Faye Dunaway. Contains swearing, sex scenes and violence.

Timothy Hutton *Peter Derns* • Lara Flynn Boyle *Kris Bolin* • Dwight Schultz *Roger Jasser* • Oliver Platt *Jack Hartsell* • Steven Weber *Brad Montroe* • Colleen Flynn *Sara Meinhold* • Faye Dunaway *Charlene Towne* ■ *Dir* Tom Holland • *Scr* Kevin Falls, from a story by Kevin Falls, Tom Engelman

Tempest ★★
Drama 1959 · It/Yug/Fr · Colour · 120mins

Producer Dino de Laurentiis's attempt to do cinematically for Pushkin what his *War and Peace* did for Tolstoy (ie: make a fortune and render the work accessible to movie audiences). While the spectacle (Technicolor and Technirama photography by the great Aldo Tonti) certainly passes muster, the direction by former Italian neo-realist Alberto Lattuada seems to presage and belong to another, later era, when poor-dubbing and cheap spectacle would suffice on a Saturday night out in Rome. Here, some thought has gone into the retelling of the overthrow of Russia's Catherine the Great, and Viveca Lindfors makes a striking Empress, with assorted costumed thesps like Van Heflin, Agnes Moorehead and Vittorio Gassman in support, but the whole is undermined by a trashy, sexy subplot involving gauche Geoffrey Horne and an over-ripe Silvana Mangano (producer Dino's wife). Italian, Serbo Croat and French dialogue dubbed into English.

Silvana Mangano *Masha* • Van Heflin *Pugacev* • Viveca Lindfors *Catherine II* • Geoffrey Horne *Peter Griniev* • Robert Keith *Captain Mironov* • Agnes Moorehead *Vassilissa* • Oscar Homolka *Savelic* • Helmut Dantine *Svabrin* • Vittorio Gassman *Prosecutor* • Fulvia Franco *Palaska* • Finlay Currie *Count Griniev* ■ *Dir* Alberto Lattuada • *Scr* Alberto Lattuada, Ivo Perilli, from stories by Alexander Pushkin

The Tempest ★★★ 15
Drama 1979 · UK · Colour · 87mins

Derek Jarman's version of Shakespeare's play is really just a skit, though Jarman's fans claim that he preserves the soul of the play, while stripping away the flesh. Heathcote Williams is Prospero, Toyah Willcox a punk Miranda and Christopher Biggins is just very slightly camp. At the end,

opera diva Elisabeth Welch, accompanied by a shipload of pretty sailor boys, drops anchor and sings "Stormy Weather".

Heathcote Williams *Prospero* • Karl Johnson *Ariel* • Toyah Willcox *Miranda* • Peter Bull *Alonso* • Richard Warwick *Antonio* • Elisabeth Welch *Goddess* • Jack Birkett *Caliban* • Ken Campbell *Gonzalo* • Christopher Biggins *Stephano* • David Meyer *Ferdinand* • Neil Cunningham *Sebastian* ■ *Dir* Derek Jarman • *Scr* Derek Jarman, from the play by William Shakespeare

Tempest ★★ 15
Fantasy drama 1982 · US · Colour · 136mins

Director Paul Mazursky's transposition of Shakespeare's play into a modern setting is a lengthy, self-indulgent folly. As the architect who seeks solace on a Greek island, John Cassavetes introduces an unexpected conviction to an otherwise uninspired story, which, for all the beauty of Donald McAlpine's seascapes, is nothing more than another study in Manhattan angst. The Shakespearean links are clumsily forged, and the whole conceit is made to seem faintly ridiculous by the zealous significance of the performances, with only Gena Rowlands and Molly Ringwald approximating real people. Contains swearing and nudity.

John Cassavetes *Phillip* • Gena Rowlands *Antonia* • Susan Sarandon *Aretha* • Vittorio Gassman *Alonzo* • Raul Julia *Kalibanos* • Molly Ringwald *Miranda* • Sam Robards *Freddy* ■ *Dir* Paul Mazursky • *Scr* Paul Mazursky, Leon Capetanos, from the play by William Shakespeare

Temptation ★★
Period melodrama 1946 · US · BW · 98mins

A striking Victorian beauty (strikingly beautiful Merle Oberon, fittingly gowned by Orry-Kelly) deserts her dreary husband (dreary George Brent) – an Egyptologist – for flashing-eyed Egyptian (an over-the-top Charles Korvin). A mistake – as was the film, which resembles an attempt to revive the dodo in returning to an old novel and play, already made as a silent called *Bella Donna* with Pola Negri in 1923. Directed at sleepwalking pace by Irving Pichel, it's almost idiotic enough to be mildly enjoyable.

Merle Oberon *Ruby Chepstow Armine* • George Brent *Nigel Armine* • Charles Korvin *Mahmoud Baroudi* • Paul Lukas *Sir Meyer Isaacson* • Lenore Ulric *Marie* • Arnold Moss *Ahmed* • Robert Capa *Hamza* • Aubrey Mather *Dr Harding* ■ *Dir* Irving Pichel • *Scr* Robert Theoron, from the novel *Bella Donna* by Robert Smythe Hichens, from the play *Bella Donna* by James Bernard Fagan

The Temptress ★★★
Silent drama 1926 · US · BW · 117mins

A Parisian aristocrat "sells" his not inexperienced wife Greta Garbo to a banker to secure himself a life of material luxury. She falls madly in love with Antonio Moreno, an Argentinian engineer who leaves her when he learns she is married. Following him to Argentina, Garbo inflames the passions of several men en route to a climactic fall-out that leads her back to Paris and a life of degradation. Begun under the direction of Garbo's Swedish mentor Mauritz Stiller, who was

replaced by Fred Niblo, this raging inferno of lust, love and degeneracy was her second American film and it attracted ecstatic reviews.

Greta Garbo *Elena* • Antonio Moreno *Robledo* • Roy D'Arcy *Manos Duros* • Marc MacDermott *M Fontenoy* • Lionel Barrymore *Canterac* • Virginia Brown Faire *Celinda* ■ *Dir* Fred Niblo • *Scr* Dorothy Farnum, Mauritz Stiller, Marian Ainslee, from the novel *La Tierra de Todos* by Vicente Blasco-Ibañez, Leo Ongley (translation)

Temptress ★★ 18
Erotic thriller 1995 · US · Colour · 89mins

This lavishly produced erotic chiller is a class above the usual soft-core fare. *NYPD Blue's* Kim Delaney is transformed into the bad girl of the title after being possessed by the goddess Kali on a trip to India. There are sound supporting turns from the likes of Chris Sarandon, Corbin Bernsen and Ben Cross, and director Lawrence Lanoff brings at least a hint of style to the usual genre clichés. Contains swearing, sex scenes and nudity.

Kim Delaney *Karin Swann* • Chris Sarandon *Matthew Christianson* • Corbin Bernsen *Nick* • Dee Wallace Stone *Allison Mackie* • Ben Cross *Dr Samudaya* • Jessica Walter *Dr Phyllis Evergreen* ■ *Dir* Lawrence Lanoff • *Scr* Melissa Mitchell

Temptress Moon ★★★ 15
Romantic period drama 1996 · HK/Chi · Colour · 115mins

Following its indifferent reception at Cannes, Chen Kaige's visually stunning period piece suffered substantial cuts and the imposition of gutsier subtitles. But this remains an overwrought melodrama from a director much more at home with the stoic reactions of individuals than with momentous events of history. Complete with operatic emotions, two-dimensional performances (even from Gong Li and Leslie Cheung) and fumbling attempts to depict passion, the tale of a country boy caught up in both the aftermath of the 1911 Revolution and the opium-induced decline of his Shanghai family is a tantalising disappointment. In Manadrin with English subtitles. Contains some swearing and sexual situations.

Leslie Cheung *Yu Zhongliang* • Gong Li *Pang Ruyi* • Kevin Lin *Pang Duanwu* • He Saifei [He Caifei] *Yu Xiuyi, Zhongliang's sister* • Zhang Shi *Li Niangyui* • Lin Lianqun *Pang An* • Ge Xiangting *Elder Qi* ■ *Dir* Chen Kaige • *Scr* Shu Kei, from a story by Chen Kaige, Wang Anyi

10 ★★★★ 18
Comedy 1979 · US · Colour · 117mins

If George Segal hadn't walked off the set of this Blake Edwards film, would Dudley Moore be a movie star today? Desperately sexist in hindsight, this acerbic look at Los Angeles in a goldfish bowl is still relentlessly funny, mixing satire and observation together with some really rude gags. Ravel's *Bolero* will never be the same after you see what our Dud and Bo Derek get up to during its strains. As dated as Derek's hair plaits, but still very perceptive, occasionally vulgar and a lot of fun. Contains swearing, sex scenes and nudity.

Dudley Moore *George* • Julie Andrews *Sam* • Bo Derek *Jenny* • Robert Webber *Hugh* • Dee Wallace [Dee Wallace Stone] *Mary Lewis* • Sam Jones *David* • Brian Dennehy *Bartender* ■ *Dir/Scr* Blake Edwards

The Ten Commandments ★★★★
Silent biblical epic 1923 · US · BW and Colour · 146mins

Cecil B DeMille's first silent version marked his emergence as an epic (in both senses) showman. Despite its odd combination of two unconnected tales, ancient and modern, the film is a "must see" combination of interesting curiosity, historical document, lavish spectacle and entertaining melodrama. The first section covers Old Testament episodes that include, naturally, Moses receiving the Commandments, the worship of the Golden Calf, and the Israelites crossing the Red Sea. The modern story is a parable of two brothers, bad Rod La Rocque and good Richard Dix. Among other dastardly deeds, Rod cheats on his wife (Leatrice Joy) with Nita Naldi who, unbeknown to him, has escaped from a leper colony… It's all done with full-blooded conviction and panache.

Theodore Roberts *Moses* • Charles De Roche *Rameses* • Estelle Taylor *Miriam* • Julia Faye *Pharaoh's wife* • Terrence Moore *Pharaoh's son* • James Neill *Aaron* • Lawson Butt *Dathan* • Edythe Chapman *Mrs Martha McTavish* • Richard Dix *John McTavish* • Rod La Rocque *Dan McTavish* • Leatrice Joy *Mary Leigh* ■ *Dir* Cecil B DeMille • *Scr* Jeanie Macpherson

The Ten Commandments ★★★★ U
Biblical epic 1956 · US · Colour · 219mins

This masterpiece of heroic vulgarity represents the Hollywood epic at the peak of its all-American powers. Cecil B DeMille's remake of his 1923 silent movie, about the life of Moses and his leadership of the Israelites in their exodus from Egypt, adds over an hour to his first telling of the story, but, with untypical restraint, sticks to the original total of just ten commandments. It's a movie to savour, less for the sparkle of its dialogue or the complexity of its characterisations, than for the sheer magnificence of its set pieces and its casual deployment of 25,000 extras at the drop of a tablet.

Charlton Heston *Moses* • Yul Brynner *Rameses* • Anne Baxter *Nefretiti* • Edward G Robinson *Dathan* • Yvonne De Carlo *Sephora* • Debra Paget *Lilia* • John Derek *Joshua* • Nina Foch *Bithiah* • John Carradine *Aaron* • Vincent Price *Elder* • Cedric Hardwicke *Sethi* ■ *Dir* Cecil B DeMille • *Scr* Aeneas MacKenzie, Jesse L Lasky Jr, Jack Gariss, Frederick M Frank, from the novel *The Prince of Egypt* by Dorothy Clarke Wilson, from the novel *Pillar of Fire* by Rev JH Ingraham, from the novel *On Eagle's Wings* by Rev GE Southon

Ten Days in Paris ★★
Mystery spy drama 1939 · UK · BW · 81mins

This is a modest little British programme filler with a lot to be modest about. Basedon Bruce Graeme's novel *The Disappearance of Roger Tremayne*, it finds amnesiac

crash victim Rex Harrison waking up in Paris to be told he's a spy. As an example of gentlemanly espionage it has no suspense, and even the charismatic Harrison exhibits little of his usual flair. 💬

Rex Harrison *Robert Stevens* • Karen Verne [Kaaren Verne] *Diane De Guermantes* • CV France *General De Guermantes* • Leo Genn *Lanson* • Joan Marion *Denise* • Antony Holles *François* ■ *Dir* Tim Whelan • *Scr* James Curtis, John Meehan Jr, from the novel *The Disappearance of Roger Tremayne* by Bruce Graeme

Ten Days' Wonder ★★★

Mystery drama   1971 · Fr · Colour · 108mins

Orson Welles plays Theo Van Horn, representing God no less, in Claude Chabrol's portentous and enigmatic theological thriller, in which the ten days of the action represent each of the Ten Commandments. Chabrol shifted the action from a drab American town to a magnificent private estate in Alsace where Welles, as an old patriarch, dictates to his child bride (Marlène Jobert) and adopted son (Anthony Perkins). The film was shot in a virtuoso, high-gothic style, possibly influenced by the eminent presence of Welles, while Perkins gives a typically nervous, agitated performance which the restless camera mirrors. French dialogue dubbed into English.

Orson Welles *Theo Van Horn* • Marlène Jobert *Helene Van Horn* • Michel Piccoli *Paul Regis* • Anthony Perkins *Charles Van Horn* • Guido Alberti *Ludovic* ■ *Scr* Paul Gardner, Paul Gégauff, Eugene Archer, from a novel by Ellery Queen [Frederic Dannay, Manfred B Lee]

Ten Gentlemen from West Point ★★🅤

Drama   1942 · US · BW · 103mins

Not quite the *Top Gun* of its day, though very gung ho, this propagandist frolic from 20th Century-Fox charts the founding in 1802 of West Point military academy. Directed by action maestro Henry Hathaway, it stars George Montgomery as one of the cadets and Maureen O'Hara, who appears for no other reason than to provide some romance and respite from all the scenes of men training. Too episodic and contrived, it ends with a tribute to the academy as the place where military top brass Grant, Sherman and MacArthur learned their jobs.

George Montgomery *Dawson* • Maureen O'Hara *Carolyn Bainbridge* • John Sutton *Howard Shelton* • Laird Cregar *Major Sam Carter* • John Shepperd [Shepperd Strudwick] *Henry Clay* • Victor Francen *Florimond Massey* • Harry Davenport *Bane* • Ward Bond *Scully* • Douglass Dumbrille *General William Henry Harrison* ■ *Dir* Henry Hathaway • *Scr* Richard Maibaum, George Seaton, from a story by Malvin Ward

Ten Little Indians ★★🅸🅴

Thriller   1965 · UK · BW · 95mins

This is the second film version of Agatha Christie's ever-popular whodunit, complete with a hugely irritating "guess-the-killer" break. Co-writer Harry Alan Towers enjoyed the experience so much that he went on to make the picture twice more in 1975 and 1989. It's hard to think of Dame Agatha as the originator of the serial

killer thriller, but that's essentially what this ingenious mystery is. The cast of fading British stars doesn't seem particularly enthralled, while director George Pollock might have injected the film with a little more enthusiasm. 💬

Hugh O'Brian *Hugh Lombard* • Shirley Eaton *Ann Clyde* • Fabian *Mike Raven* • Leo Genn *General Mandrake* • Stanley Holloway *William Blore* • Wilfrid Hyde White *Judge Cannon* • Daliah Lavi *Ilona Bergen* • Dennis Price *Dr Armstrong* ■ *Dir* George Pollock • *Scr* Peter Yeldham, Dudley Nichols, Peter Welbeck [Harry Alan Towers], from the novel and play *Ten Little Niggers* by Agatha Christie

The 10 Million Dollar Getaway ★★★🅸🅵

Crime thriller   1991 · US · Colour · 89mins

Based on a notorious robbery, this well executed TV film stars John Mahoney (*Frasier*) as Jimmy "the Gent" Burke who, with his gang of colourful New York hoodlums, plans and executes a $10 million heist at Kennedy airport – with surprising results. The script is tight, the direction is well-paced, and everyone involved seems to have a real feel for the shady underworld depicted here. 💬

John Mahoney *Jimmy "the Gent" Burke* • Tony LoBianco *Tony "Ducks" Carallo* • Tom Noonan *Mr Y* • Karen Young *Theresa* ■ *Dir* James A Contner • *Scr* Christopher Canaan, from a book by Doug Feiden

Ten North Frederick ★★★★

Drama   1958 · US · BW · 101mins

One of those fabulous extended soapy dramas based on the kind of bestselling doorstop novel that 20th Century-Fox seemed to specialise in during the early CinemaScope period. Gary Cooper stars as a successful lawyer, shoved into the political big time by grasping wife Geraldine Fitzgerald, who finds brief solace in the arms of ex-model Suzy Parker. Former *Peyton Place* star Diane Varsi excels as Coop's daughter, and another newcomer shows signs of star quality Stuart Whitman, who plays Varsi's trumpet-playing love. Sit back and enjoy a good wallow.

Gary Cooper *Joe Chapin* • Diane Varsi *Ann Chapin* • Suzy Parker *Kate Drummond* • Geraldine Fitzgerald *Edith Chapin* • Tom Tully *Slattery* • Ray Stricklyn *Joby* • Philip Ober *Lloyd Williams* • John Emery *Paul Donaldson* • Stuart Whitman *Charley Bongiorno* ■ *Dir* Philip Dunne • *Scr* Philip Dunne, from the novel by John O'Hara

10 Rillington Place ★★★★★🅸🅵

Biographical crime drama
1970 · UK · Colour · 106mins

Three years after Timothy Evans went to the gallows for the murder of his wife and daughter, John Reginald Christie, the family's landlord and a wartime special constable, was convicted of this and six other crimes. Based on the book by Ludovic Kennedy that helped secure Evans's posthumous pardon in 1966, Richard Fleischer's film is nowhere near as visually audacious as his *Boston Strangler* two years previously. But it does contain an acting tour de force from Richard Attenborough as the

seedy killer, who boasted openly of his ability to perform "minor operations". Superbly re-creating the atmosphere of late-forties' London, this is a chilling study of an evil mind. Contains swearing. 💬

Richard Attenborough *John Reginald Christie* • Judy Geeson *Beryl Evans* • John Hurt *Timothy John Evans* • Pat Heywood *Mrs Ethel Christie* • Isobel Black *Alice* • Miss Riley *Baby Geraldine* • Phyllis McMahon *Muriel Eady* ■ *Dir* Richard Fleischer • *Scr* Clive Exton, from the book by Ludovic Kennedy

Ten Seconds to Hell ★★

Drama   1959 · US · BW · 93mins

A typically catchpenny title for a typically brash Robert Aldrich movie about German bomb-disposal experts in postwar Berlin coming to explosive blows over Martine Carol, who was ahead of Jeanne Moreau and Brigitte Bardot as a French sex symbol in the fifties. Jack Palance and Jeff Chandler rant eloquently enough, but it's too stridently contrived for any credibility. Aldrich's film is a dampish squib when compared with the great Powell-Pressburger film on the same subject, *The Small Back Room*.

Jeff Chandler *Karl Wirtz* • Jack Palance *Eric Koertner* • Martine Carol *Margot Hofer* • Robert Cornthwaite *Loeffler* • Dave Willock *Tillig* • Wesley Addy *Sulke* • Jimmy Goodwin *Globke* • Virginia Baker *Frau Bauer* • Richard Wattis *Major Haven* ■ *Dir* Robert Aldrich • *Scr* Robert Aldrich, Teddi Sherman, from the novel *The Phoenix* by Lawrence P Bachmann

Ten Tall Men ★★★🅤

Comedy adventure
1951 · US · Colour · 96mins

Dr Kildare's veteran writer/director Willis Goldbeck fashioned a more-than-passable film from this robust tale of the Foreign Legion, but *Beau Geste* isn't. Nevertheless, with Burt Lancaster at the peak of his teeth-and-glory years in the lead, and tough hombres Gilbert Roland and Kieron Moore in support, this comedy adventure is well worth catching, especially since it's in sharp fifties Technicolor. Unfortunately, leading lady Jody Lawrance is rather uninteresting and those phoney night studio interiors show up badly on TV, revealing the desert sky as nothing more than a royal blue cyclorama.

Burt Lancaster *Sergeant Mike Kincaid* • Jody Lawrance *Mahla* • Gilbert Roland *Corporal Luis Delgado* • Kieron Moore *Corporal Pierre Molier* • George Tobias *Londos* • John Dehner *Jardine* • Nick Dennis *Mouse* • Mike Mazurki *Roshko* ■ *Dir* Willis Goldbeck • *Scr* Roland Kibbee, Frank Davis, from a story by James Warner Bellah, Willis Goldbeck

10 Things I Hate about You ★★★★🅸🅲

Romantic comedy
1999 · US · Colour · 97mins

Shakespeare's *The Taming of the Shrew* gets updated *Clueless*-style to high-school America for this engaging romantic comedy from debut director Gil Junger. Kat (Julia Stiles) is the sulky teen who doesn't like anybody. This causes a problem for her hormonally-charged younger sister Bianca (Larisa Oleynik), who has been told by their dad that she can't date until Kat does. Newcomer Heath Ledger (who remarkably like Jim

Morrison) plays the unfortunate lad picked to introduce Kat to the dating scene, while the rest of the cast is peppered with equally good-looking youngsters, including *Third Rock from the Sun's* Joseph Gordon-Levitt as Bianca's sweet but nerdy admirer. Smartly paced, fun and funny, this is just as enjoyable for adults as it is for its intended teenage market. Contains some sexual references. 💬 **DVD**

Heath Ledger *Patrick Verona* • Julia Stiles *Katarina Stratford* • Joseph Gordon-Levitt *Cameron James* • Larisa Oleynik *Bianca Stratford* • David Krumholtz *Michael Eckman* • Andrew Keegan *Joey Donner* • Susan May Pratt *Mandella* ■ *Dir* Gil Junger • *Scr* Karen McCullah Lutz, Kirsten Smith

10:30 PM Summer ★

Drama   1966 · US/Sp · Colour · 84mins

French novelist Marguerite Duras and director Jules Dassin adapted the former's novel as a vehicle for the latter's wife, Melina Mercouri. She brings her strident Greek passion to the role of a wife, holidaying in Spain with her husband Peter Finch and best friend Romy Schneider. While troubled with erotic and alarming dreams – or, being Duras, perhaps it's reality – about hubby and friend getting together, she wanders the streets and meets a runaway Spaniard (Julian Mateos) who has killed his wife and her lover. Intensely irritating, hysteria-ridden drivel with little entertainment value.

Melina Mercouri *Maria* • Romy Schneider *Claire* • Peter Finch *Paul* • Julian Mateos *Rodrigo Palestra* • Isabel Maria Perez *Judith* • Beatriz Savon *Rodrigo's wife* ■ *Dir* Jules Dassin • *Scr* Jules Dassin, Marguerite Duras, from a novel by Marguerite Duras

Ten Thousand Bedrooms ★★🅤

Musical comedy 1957 · US · Colour · 114mins

Millionaire hotel owner Dean Martin visits Rome to check out his latest acquisition and becomes romantically entangled with four Italian sisters, particularly the eldest, Eva Bartok. Anna Maria Alberghetti, Lisa Montell and Lisa Gaye are the other girls in a large cast, which also includes Walter Slezak as the girls' Italian papa. A witless and interminable romantic comedy, this was Martin's first film without Jerry Lewis and, despite a generous number of songs tacked on to the unfunny proceedings, it's salad without the dressing.

Dean Martin *Ray Hunter* • Anna Maria Alberghetti *Nina Martelli* • Eva Bartok *Maria Martelli* • Dewey Martin *Mike Clark* • Walter Slezak *Papa Vittorio Martelli* • Paul Henreid *Anton* • Lisa Montell *Diana Martelli* • Lisa Gaye *Anna Martelli* ■ *Dir* Richard Thorpe • *Scr* Laslo Vadnay, Art Cohn, William Ludwig, Leonard Spigelgass

10 to Midnight ★★🅸🅱

Thriller   1983 · UK · Colour · 95mins

Selecting the worst Charles Bronson film of the eighties provides an embarrassment of riches. Not only are all of them pretty awful, but the plots are often strikingly similar. This nasty thriller, for example, could just have easily been an entry in the *Death Wish* series. This time Bronson plays cop

Leo Kessler, who's supposed to be tracking down a serial killer of women. When orthodox methods fail, he's reduced to planting evidence and then stalking the murderer himself. ▭

Charles Bronson *Leo Kessler* • Lisa Eilbacher *Laurie Kessler* • Andrew Stevens *Paul McAnn* • Gene Davis *Warren Stacey* • Geoffrey Lewis *Dave Dante* • Wilford Brimley *Captain Malone* • Iva Lane *Bunny* • Ola Ray *Ola* ■ *Dir* J Lee Thompson • *Scr* William Roberts

Ten Who Dared ★★PG
Historical adventure
1960 · US · Colour · 92mins

Set in the 19th century, this Disney production is based on the real-life diary chronicling the adventures of Major John Wesley Powell, an explorer/geologist/botanist who lost his arm in the Civil War but undaunted traversed nearly a thousand miles of the American west. The film features John Beal as Powell and Brian Keith as William Dunn negotiating uncharted territories. Opting for a plodding, dutifully episodic approach, veteran Hollywood director William Beaudine – here at the tail end of a 50-year career – fails to translate a scientific expedition into entertainment. ▭

Brian Keith *William Dunn* • John Beal *Major John Wesley Powell* • James Drury *Walter Powell* • RG Armstrong *Oramel Howland* • Ben Johnson *George Bradley* • LQ Jones *Billy Hawkins* • Dan Sheridan *Jack Sumner* ■ *Dir* William Beaudine • *Scr* Lawrence Edward Watkin, from the journal of Major John Wesley Powell

The Tenant ★★★18
Psychological thriller
1976 · Fr · Colour · 119mins

Roman Polanski directs a male take on the themes of paranoia and delusion that he explored from a female perspective in *Repulsion* ten years earlier. Polanski also stars, playing an expatriate Pole in Paris who comes to believe that the tenants of his apartment block are devilishly conspiring to drive him to suicide. Melvyn Douglas and Shelley Winters co-star in a puzzling and absorbing thriller that, on occasions, recalls not just *Repulsion* but also has vague echoes of *Rosemary's Baby*. ▭

Roman Polanski *Trelkovsky* • Isabelle Adjani *Stella* • Melvyn Douglas *Mr Zy* • Jo Van Fleet *Madame Dioz* • Bernard Fresson *Scope* • Lila Kedrova *Madame Gaderian* • Shelley Winters *Concierge* ■ *Dir* Roman Polanski • *Scr* Roman Polanski, Gerard Brach, from the novel *Le Locataire Chimérique* by Roland Topor

Tender Comrade ★★★U
Second World War drama
1943 · US · BW · 102mins

On the surface, a harmless enough tale about women living together while their menfolk are off at war, but this slight drama had serious repercussions. Ginger Rogers's mother objected to her daughter uttering the sentiment "Share and share alike" in the film, and four years later writer Dalton Trumbo and director Edward Dmytryk were hauled before the House Un-American Activities Committee and imprisoned as "unfriendly" witnesses and alleged communists all because the women lived and worked communally in the movie!

Ginger Rogers *Jo Jones* • Robert Ryan *Chris Jones* • Ruth Hussey *Barbara* • Patricia Collinge *Helen Stacey* • Mady Christians *Manya* • Kim Hunter *Doris* • Jane Darwell *Mrs Henderson* • Mary Forbes *Jo's mother* ■ *Dir* Edward Dmytryk • *Scr* Dalton Trumbo, from his story

Tender Hooks ★★★
Drama
1988 · Ausl · Colour · 95mins

Talk about life in the raw. This is the remarkable feature debut of the Australian film-maker Mary Callaghan and it packs more squalor, indolence and misfortune into its running time than you would believe possible. Yet the characters who inhabit this part of Sydney's Kings Cross district are bursting with life, even though that life consists of botched robberies, prostitution, drug addiction and prison. Jo Kennedy is hugely impressive as the hairdresser whose world is turned upside down by her encounter with waster Nique Needles. But it's Callaghan's realistic touches that make this sobering film so fulfilling.

Jo Kennedy *Mitch* • Nique Needles *Rex Reeson* • Anna Phillips *Gaye* • Robert Menzies *Yawn* • John Polson *Tony* • Ian Mortimer *Vic* ■ *Dir/Scr* Mary Callaghan

Tender Is the Night ★★
Drama
1961 · US · Colour · 146mins

This adaptation of Scott Fitzgerald's semi-autobiographical novel fails to achieve a coherent film from the complex, opaque material. Jason Robards and Jennifer Jones are Dick and Nicole Diver, the "beautiful people" of the 1920s, squandering their lives on a hedonistic existence among the Jazz Age jet set on the French Riviera. Robards as former psychiatrist Diver, and a too-old Jones as his ex-patient, now his wife, make a good stab at their roles and the enormous cast includes Joan Fontaine, Tom Ewell and Jill St John in the major supporting parts. There is some vicarious entertainment to be had from watching the unstable, amoral, idle rich playing and disintegrating – in Robards's case into alcoholism – but to date the book remains unfilmable.

Jason Robards Jr *Dick Diver* • Jennifer Jones *Nicole Diver* • Joan Fontaine *Baby Warren* • Jill St John *Rosemary Hoyt* • Tom Ewell *Abe North* • Cesare Danova *Tommy Barban* • Paul Lukas *Dr Dohmer* • Carole Mathews *Mrs Hoyt* ■ *Dir* Henry King • *Scr* Ivan Moffat, from the novel by F Scott Fitzgerald

Tender Is the Night ★★
Drama
1992 · Ven · Colour

Littered with references to the films of Luis Buñuel and touching on everything from urban alienation to cultural colonialism, this is a visually audacious, but intellectually undisciplined offering from the Venezuelan director, Leonardo Henriquez. Juxtaposing scenes of sexual gratification, emotional stagnation and political inarticulacy, the action centres around the crumbling relationship between Constanza Giner and Diego Risquez, who sit in different parts of a Caracas bar and bemoan their lot. Footage of natural disasters, combat zones and trashy TV conspire to suggest deep-set significance, but the film's resolute

obscurantism keeps even the most willing viewer at a distance. In Spanish with English subtitles.

Constanza Giner • Diego Risquez • Victor Cuica • Mariangelica Ayala ■ *Dir* Leonardo Henriquez

Tender Mercies ★★★★PG
Drama
1982 · US · Colour · 87mins

A spare, lean performance from spare, lean Robert Duvall won him an Oscar. Duvall wakes up, after a drunken binge, in a Texan motel owned by religious widow Tess Harper and her young son Allan Hubbard. Having failed once in both his life and career as a country singer (Duvall sings his own songs) he hesitatingly tries again with Harper. Australian director Bruce Beresford shows a sympathetic connection to the hot dusty Texan locations for his first Hollywood film and screenwriter Horton Foote (who also won an Oscar) provides a realistic pace. This episodic and atmospheric story is a poignant portrayal of redemption. ▭

Robert Duvall *Mac Sledge* • Tess Harper *Rosa Lee* • Allan Hubbard *Sonny* • Betty Buckley *Dixie* • Ellen Barkin *Sue Anne* • Wilford Brimley *Harry* • Michael Crabtree *Lewis Menefee* • Lenny Von Dohlen *Robert Dennis* ■ *Dir* Bruce Beresford • *Scr* Horton Foote

The Tender Trap ★★★★
Comedy
1955 · US · Colour · 110mins

Director Charles Walters was responsible for some terrific musicals *Good News*, *Easter Parade*, *High Society* and some sophisticated comedies like this one. A single swinger – the perfectly cast Frank Sinatra – falls into marriage (that's the "trap" of the title), but it's the wit and style of the ensemble playing that gives the film such charm. Debbie Reynolds co-stars, and Celeste Holm and David Wayne are the other principals, with Wayne's morning-after scene a particular joy to watch. The pre-titles sequence is especially memorable, as in a single take Sinatra a "dot on the map" casually saunters towards the audience singing the title song, which became an instant hit.

Frank Sinatra *Charlie Y Reader* • Debbie Reynolds *Julie Gillis* • David Wayne *Joe McCall* • Celeste Holm *Sylvia Crewes* • Jarma Lewis *Jessica Collins* • Lola Albright *Poppy Matson* • Carolyn Jones *Helen* • Howard St John *Sam Sayers* ■ *Dir* Charles Walters • *Scr* Julius J Epstein, from the play by Max Shulman, Robert Paul Smith

The Tender Years ★★★U
Period drama
1947 · US · BW · 79mins

In a rural American community around 1870, a young boy (Richard Lyon) tries to save a local dog from his abusive owner, who also stages canine duels inside his barn. As the religious minister seeking to outlaw dog-fighting in response to his small son's love for an errant pooch, wide-mouthed comedian Joe E Brown takes it all veryseriously. A determinedly schmaltzy movie that wearsitsheart all too obviously on its platitudinous sleeve.

Joe E Brown *Rev Will Norris* • Richard Lyon *Ted Norris* • Noreen Nash *Linda* • Charles Drake *Bob Wilson* • Josephine Hutchinson *Emily Norris* • James Millican *Kit Barton* • Griff

Barnett *Senator Cooper* • Jeanne Gail *Jeanie* ■ *Dir* Harold Schuster • *Scr* Jack Jungmeyer Jr, Arnold Belgard, Abel Finkel, from a story by Jack Jungmeyer Jr

Tenebrae ★★★18
Horror thriller
1982 · It · Colour · 96mins

One of the best psycho-thrillers from Dario Argento, the Italian Hitchcock, full of stylish camerawork, kinky flashbacks, impressive gore and an ace electronic soundtrack. Novelist Anthony Franciosa visits Rome to promote his latest bestseller, only to find a murderer is copying the killings in his book. It's enormous fun sifting out the red herrings in this ultra-violent Agatha Christie-style whodunit, and the twist ending really is twisted. Argento demonstrates his unparalleled technical virtuosity in the famous roof-glide scene, where the camera prowls over and through an apartment building in which a murder will be committed, before witnessing the break-in – all in one long, continuous take. Italian dialogue dubbed into English. Contains violence, sex scenes and some swearing. ▭ *DVD*

John Saxon *Bullmer* • Anthony Franciosa *Peter Neal* • Christian Borromeo *Gianni* • Mirella D'Angelo *Tilde* • Veronica Lario *Jane* • Ania Pieroni *Elsa* ■ *Dir/Scr* Dario Argento

Tennessee Champ ★★U
Sports drama
1954 · US · Colour · 72mins

Daniel, a religious young Southern boxer (Dewey Martin), gets his break when he is taken up by fight manager Willy Wurble (Keenan Wynn), but is horrified to learn that Wurble is fixing a match. Preaching his own message about morality and God, Daniel changes Wurble's wicked ways and gets a clean fight with Sixty Jubel (Charles Buchinsky). With Shelley Winters as Wynn's wife, this sentimental minor entry from MGM doesn't exactly compel one's attention. Buchinsky, of course, would do rather more as Charles Bronson.

Shelley Winters *Sarah Wurble* • Keenan Wynn *Willy Wurble* • Dewey Martin *Daniel Norson* • Earl Holliman *Happy Jackfield* • Dave O'Brien *Luke MacWade* • Charles Buchinsky [Charles Bronson] *Sixty Jubel* ■ *Dir* Fred M Wilcox • *Scr* Art Cohn, from the story *The Lord in His Corner*,and other stories by Eustace Cockrell

Tennessee's Partner ★★
Western
1955 · US · Colour · 85mins

Routine western with John Payne as a gambler, Rhonda Fleming running a gold rush saloon and cowboy Ronald Reagan arriving to marry his sweetheart (Coleen Gray) who turns out to be a "loose woman". More of a melodrama than a shoot-'em-up, the picture was made by RKO to rival Fox's new CinemaScope process. However, it's clumsily shot, with a hand-me-down look, and was one of many disappointing pictures from the late career of veteran director Allan Dwan.

John Payne *Tennessee* • Ronald Reagan *Cowpoke* • Rhonda Fleming *Duchess* • Coleen Gray *Goldie* • Anthony Caruso *Turner* • Morris Ankrum *Judge* • Leo Gordon *Sheriff* ■ *Dir* Allan Dwan • *Scr* Milton Krims, DD Beauchamp, Graham Baker, Teddi Sherman, from a story by Bret Harte

Tension ★★★

Crime drama   1949 · US · BW · 90mins

A title to take seriously, as in this case the film does pile on the suspense. Cyd Charisse is out of her ballet shoes for a low-budgeter, in which she plays the girl who falls for troubled Richard Basehart while he is trying to establish a new identity after plotting the murder of his wife's lover. Director John Berry was one of the best of the period's B-picture craftsmen until a group of directors, Edward Dmytryk among them, "named" him as a communist and Berry was blacklisted.

Richard Basehart *Warren Quimby* • Audrey Totter *Claire Quimby* • Cyd Charisse *Mary Chanler* • Barry Sullivan *Lieutenant Collier Bonnabel* • Lloyd Gough *Barney Deager* • Tom D'Andrea *Freddie* • William Conrad *Lieutenant Edgar Gonsales* • Tito Renaldo *Narco* ■ *Dir* John Berry • *Scr* Allen Rivkin, from a story by John Klorer

Tension at Table Rock ★★★ U

Western   1956 · US · Colour · 93mins

Charles Marquis Warren was the creative force behind such great TV western shows as *Gunsmoke*, *Rawhide* and *The Virginian*. These programmes plundered B-movies and serials for their ideas, and here Warren rustled the plotlines from two classics of the genre, *High Noon* and *Shane*, for this tale of smoking guns and smouldering passions. In an era when action men were second-class citizens in Hollywood, Richard Egan never quite made the big time, but here he gives a sterling and convincing performance alongside Dorothy Malone and lawman Cameron Mitchell.

Richard Egan *Wes Tancred* • Dorothy Malone *Lorna Miller* • Billy Chapin *Jody Barrows* • Cameron Mitchell *Sheriff Miller* • Joe De Santis *Ed Barrows* • Royal Dano *Jameson* • Edward Andrews *Kirk* • DeForest Kelley *Breck* • Angie Dickinson *Cathy Murdock* ■ *Dir* Charles Marquis Warren • *Scr* Winston Miller, from the novel *Bitter Sage* by Frank Gruber

Tentacles ★★

Horror   1977 · It · Colour · 101mins

The Italian answer to *Jaws*, from Ovidio G Assonitis, director of *Beyond the Door*, which was the Italian answer to *The Exorcist*. A giant octopus goes on a murderous rampage during a resort's annual yacht race. John Huston is the reporter trying to get to the ecological bottom of why the scary squid is acting so nasty. Shelley Winters is Huston's sister whose son nearly goes missing during one attack. A lively enough rip-off featuring direct lifts from the Spielberg shock handbook all wrapped up in a gorgeous Euro-pop score by Stelvio Cipriani. Someone should have pointed out early on though that an octopus just isn't that frightening. Some dialogue dubbed into English.

John Huston *Ned Turner* • Shelley Winters *Tillie Turner* • Bo Hopkins *Will Gleason* • Henry Fonda *Mr Whitehead* • Delia Boccardo *Vicky Gleason* • Cesare Danova *John Corey* • Alan Boyd *Mike* • Claude Akins *Captain Robards* ■ *Dir* Ovidio G Assonitis • *Scr* Jerome Max, Tito Carpi, Steve Carabatsos, Sonia Molteni

The Tenth Man ★★★ PG

Drama   1988 · US/UK · Colour · 94mins

During the war, Graham Greene had a contract with MGM where he wrote what he later remembered as a two-page treatment for a movie that was never made. When the treatment was discovered some 40 years later, it turned out to be a 60,000 word novel set in France after the Liberation, which tells the story of a once wealthy lawyer who gave away his fortune in exchange for his life. The book was published in 1985, and this TV-movie version is impeccably directed by Jack Gold. Joining Anthony Hopkins in the starry cast, Kristin Scott Thomas, Derek Jacobi and Cyril Cusack keep the somewhat convoluted tale on the rails. 🖵

Anthony Hopkins *Jean Louis Chavel* • Derek Jacobi *Imposter* • Kristin Scott Thomas *Therese* • Cyril Cusack *Parish priest* • Brenda Bruce *Madame Mangeot* • Timothy Watson *Michel Mangeot* • Paul Rogers *Breton* ■ *Dir* Jack Gold • *Scr* Lee Langley, from the novel by Graham Greene

The Tenth Victim ★★★

Science-fiction thriller
1965 · It · Colour · 92mins

Famous now as one of the inspirations for *Austin Powers* (Ursula Andress wore the first bullet-firing bra as sported by the "fembots"), this erratically engrossing science-fiction thriller has a fabulous sixties pop art look. In the 21st century, war has been replaced with a legalised game in which the participants are licensed-to-kill assassins, and anyone reaching the score of ten victims hits the financial jackpot. Andress is assigned to kill a cropped blond Marcello Mastroianni, but he falls in love with his huntress in this convincing futuristic satire that still pleases the eye even when it habitually falls through cracks in the weak script. Italian dialogue dubbed into English.

Ursula Andress *Caroline Meredith* • Marcello Mastroianni *Marcello Polletti* • Elsa Martinelli *Olga* • Salvo Randone *Professor* • Massimo Serato *Lawyer* • Evi Rigano *Victim* ■ *Dir* Elio Petri • *Scr* Elio Petri, Tonino Guerra, Giorgio Salvioni, Ennio Flaiano, from the novel *The Seventh Victim* by Robert Sheckley

Tenue de Soirée ★★★ 18

Comedy   1986 · Fr · Colour · 84mins

Although this scurrilous comedy reunited Bertrand Blier with the co-stars of *Les Valseuses*, Miou-Miou and Gérard Depardieu, it was the newcomer, Michel Blanc, who stole the picture and won himself the best actor prize at Cannes. Smugly iconoclastic, gleefully picaresque, hopelessly misogynistic and outrageously funny are all descriptions that could aptly be applied to the menage that develops between Depardieu's larger-than-life bisexual crook, Blanc's timid husband and Miou-Miou's opportunistic wife. But while the performances are so out there they're almost heroic, Blier is intent solely on shocking and, consequently, the swipes at the indolent bourgeoisie and his risible resolution are ultimately damaging to a very funny film. In French with English subtitles.

Gérard Depardieu *Bob* • Michel Blanc *Antoine* • Miou-Miou *Monique* • Bruno Cremer *Art collector* • Jean-Pierre Marielle *Depressed man* • Caroline Sihol *Depressed woman* ■ *Dir/Scr* Bertrand Blier

Tequila Sunrise ★★★ 15

Thriller   1988 · US · Colour · 110mins

A straight whiskey sour about loyalty becomes a confused cocktail about nothing much, when narcotics cop Kurt Russell tries to persuade his friendly neighbourhood drug dealer Mel Gibson not to go in for one last big trade-off. But both are too distracted by Michelle Pfeiffer to tackle their buddy-buddy differences head-on. Writer/director Robert Towne has done better work, but as scriptwriter only on movies such as *Chinatown*, for example. Here, his wordiness gets between the viewer and the rather unappealing characters, which may not be a bad thing. Contains swearing, drug abuse and nudity. 🖵 **DVD**

Mel Gibson *Dale McKussic* • Michelle Pfeiffer *Jo Ann Vallenari* • Kurt Russell *Lieutenant Nick Frescia* • Raul Julia *Carlos/Commandante Escalante* • JT Walsh *Maguire* • Arliss Howard *Gregg Lindroff* • Ann Magnuson *Shaleen* ■ *Dir/Scr* Robert Towne

Teresa ★★★

Romantic drama   1951 · US · BW · 101mins

Director Fred Zinnemann's tale of an imported GI bride was a courageously topical subject, and indicative of a now-forgotten trend at MGM to confront burning contemporary issues, most famously, slum education in *The Blackboard Jungle*. Lovely Italian actress Pier Angeli brings great honesty and truth to the title role, and there are echoes of her own real-life plight in the plot, as she encounters small-town bigotry in the role of GI John Ericson's girl. As her psychiatrist, young Rod Steiger makes an impressive movie debut. Frankly, Ericson is weak and over-extended in the lead, but Zinnemann's documentary-style treatment is winning, and the Stewart Stern script doesn't shirk the issues. A slight film, but a sincere and genuinely tender one.

Pier Angeli *Teresa* • John Ericson *Philip Quas* • Patricia Collinge *Philip's mother* • Richard Bishop *Philip's father* • Peggy Ann Garner *Susan* • Ralph Meeker *Sergeant Dobbs* • Rod Steiger *Frank* ■ *Dir* Fred Zinnemann • *Scr* Stewart Stern, from the story by Stewart Stern, Alfred Hayes

Term of Trial ★★★★

Drama   1962 · UK · BW · 138mins

Made at the height of the "kitchen sink" boom in British cinema, this rather neglected drama boasts one of Laurence Olivier's most uncharacteristic and under-rated performances. As the teacher at an inner city school who is looked down upon by everyone from blowsy wife Simone Signoret to class bully Terence Stamp, he conveys a sense of both seedy decency and wounded resignation that makes his prosecution for molestation and persecution by Signoret all the more painful to endure. In her screen debut, Sarah Miles is superb as the scorned teenager and Thora Hird bristles with back-street indignation as her grasping mother.

Laurence Olivier *Graham Weir* • Simone Signoret *Anna Weir* • Sarah Miles *Shirley Taylor* • Hugh Griffith *O'Hara* • Terence Stamp *Mitchell* • Roland Culver *Trowman* • Thora Hird *Mrs Taylor* ■ *Dir* Peter Glenville • *Scr* Peter Glenville, from the novel by James Barlow

Terminal Bliss ★★ 18

Drama   1990 · US · Colour · 87mins

A sluggish, downbeat story of whiney, party-going rich kids who get stoned a lot and indulge themselves excessively on consumer goodies. But angst is the order of their day as they pop pills, shaft pals, swap gals, and generally OD on bourgeois ennui. It is hard to feel sympathy for such unpleasant, over-privileged under-achievers. *Beverly Hills 90210* heart-throb Luke Perry was already in the process of perfecting his mean and moody "son of Dean" persona. 🖵

Luke Perry *John Hunter* • Timothy Owen *Alex Golden* • Estee Chandler *Stevie Bradley* • Sonia Curtis *Kirsten Davis* • Micah Grant *Bucky O'Connell* • Alexis Arquette *Craig Murphy* • Brian Cox *Dream Surgeon* ■ *Dir/Scr* Jordan Alan

Terminal Choice ★★★ 18

Medical thriller   1983 · Can · Colour · 94mins

Suspenseful little chiller about a hospital that plays it less by the book than by the bookie. The staff lay wagers as to when patients will pop their clogs, and aren't above manipulating the odds in their favour. Rather bloodier than it needs to be, the film still manages to generate surprising tension, partly because of taut and economic direction, and partly because it's played dead straight by its high-calibre cast of Joe Spano, Diane Venora, David McCallum and a young Ellen Barkin. 🖵

Joe Spano *Dr Frank Holt* • Diane Venora *Anna Lang* • David McCallum *Dr Dodson* • Robert Joy *Dr Harvey Rimmer* • Don Francks *Chauncey Rand* • Nicholas Campbell *Henderson* • Ellen Barkin *Mary O'Connor* ■ *Dir* Sheldon Larry • *Scr* Neal Bell, from a story by Peter Lawrence

Terminal Entry ★★ 15

Thriller   1988 · US · Colour · 93mins

Competent and mildly exciting variant on the *War Games* theme, with three kids hacking into what they think is a hot new video game. But the game is no game: it's a genuine computer programme, part of the US's hi-tech defence system. And the kids, unknowingly, are playing key roles in a real-life US anti-terrorist strike. The still-topical subject matter should appeal to kids. 🖵

Edward Albert *Capt Danny Jackson* • Kabir Bedi *Terrorist commander* • Yaphet Kotto *Styles* • Heidi Helmer *Chris* • Patrick Labyorteaux *Bob* • Tracy Brooks Swope *Dominique* ■ *Dir* John Kincade • *Scr* David Mickey Evans, Mark Sobel, from a story by Mark Sobel

Terminal Force ★ 15

Crime action adventure
1987 · US · Colour · 86mins

More poverty-row thrills and spills from shoestring budget director Fred Olen Ray. Eurotrash action star Richard Harrison plays a cop on suspension

forced to protect an underworld grass after a gangster's daughter is kidnapped. Former teen idol Troy Donahue lends a certain camp value; video *femme fatale* Michelle Bauer adds the sex appeal; but neither can make up for the total deficiency of plot, action or sense. Terminal bore would be a better title! 🎞

Richard Harrison *Nick Tyree* • Troy Donahue *Slim* • Dawn Wildsmith *Delilah* • Jay Richardson *Johnny Ventura* • Michelle Bauer ■ *Dir* Fred Olen Ray • *Scr* Ernest D Farino

Terminal Island ★

Futuristic prison drama
1973 · US · Colour · 87mins

A crummy exploitation pic – terminal in all departments – about a future offshore prison colony where California's killers are sent because the death penalty has been abolished. The arrival of women prisoners results in their being treated as sex slaves. No prizes for guessing the extent to which this "Calcatraz" becomes a scene of mayhem and violence. The sole point of interest is an early screen appearance by Tom Selleck, popping up here in pre-*Magnum PI* days.

Phyllis Davis *Joy Lang* • Don Marshall *AJ Thomas* • Ena Hartman *Carmen Sims* • Marta Kristen *Lee Phillips* • Tom Selleck *Dr Milford* ■ *Dir* Stephanie Rothman • *Scr* Jim Barnett, Charles S Swartz, Stephanie Rothman

Terminal Justice ★★ 🔞

Science-fiction thriller
1996 · US · Colour · 90mins

Mildly entertaining futuristic nonsense featuring Lorenzo Lamas as a digitally-enhanced cop – he lost his eye in the Russian Cartel war of 2002! – on the trail of Chris Sarandon's ambitious crime king. Cheap 'n' cheesy, but more creative than many of its ilk, with a plot that somehow takes in virtual reality sex, self-cloning and a deadly miniature helicopter. It would be a more enjoyable movie without Chippendale lookalike Lamas, whose acting talents don't even extend to a convincing swagger. 🎞

Peter Coyote *Vivyan* • Lorenzo Lamas *Bobby Chase* • Chris Sarandon *Matthews* • Kari Salin [Kari Wuhrer] *Pamela Travis* • Barry Yourgrau *Brady* ■ *Dir* Rick King • *Scr* Wynne McLaughlin, Frederick Bailey

The Terminal Man ★★★★ 🔞

Science-fiction 1974 · US · Colour · 99mins

An extraordinarily intense performance from the usually laid-back George Segal nicely matches the desolation of this futuristic thriller, in which a scientist has a computer implant connected to his brain and becomes addicted to its killer vibes. Adapted from a novel on the *Frankenstein* theme by Michael Crichton, writer/director Mike Hodges brilliantly creates a high-tech parable in which meddling scientists get a moral comeuppance. The film was only patchily shown in cinemas on its original release, but deserved better: its implications are as thought-provoking as they are scary. Contains some violence. 🎞

George Segal *Harry Benson* • Joan Hackett *Dr Janet Ross* • Richard A Dysart [Richard Dysart] *Dr John Ellis* • Jill Clayburgh *Angela Black* • Donald Moffat *Dr Arthur Mcpherson* • Matt

Clark *Gerhard* • Michael C Gwynne *Dr Robert Morris* • Normann Burton [Norman Burton] *Detective Captain Anders* • William Hansen *Dr Ezra Manon* ■ *Dir* Mike Hodges • *Scr* Mike Hodges, from the novel by Michael Crichton

Terminal Velocity ★★ 🔞

Action adventure 1994 · US · Colour · 97mins

Terminal stupidity, more like it. The second in a brief Hollywood flirtation with skydiving movies – *Drop Zone* came out in the same year – this is a big, dumb action thriller that exhilarates when airborne, but drags dangerously when on solid ground. Charlie Sheen is the dogged parachuting instructor investigating the death of a pupil, who gets mixed up with Russian gangsters. It's good to see Nastassja Kinski back on the screen, but it's hard to take Sheen seriously as an action hero, and the film lacks premier league baddies. Contains violence, swearing and nudity. 🎞 **DVD**

Charlie Sheen *Ditch Brodie* • Nastassja Kinski *Chris Morrow* • James Gandolfini *Ben Pinkwater* • Christopher McDonald *Kerr* • Gary Bullock *Lex* • Hans R Howes [Hans Howes] *Sam* • Melvin Van Peebles *Noble* • Suli McCullough *Robocam* • Cathryn De Prume *Karen* • Richard Sarafian Jr *Dominic* ■ *Dir* Deran Sarafian • *Scr* David Twohy

Terminal Virus ★★

Science-fiction erotic thriller
1995 · US/Phil · Colour · 74mins

A vaguely distasteful slice of soft porn wrapped up in the flimsiest of sci-fi plots. It's set in a clichéd post-apocalyptic world where a deadly disease makes sexual intercourse a definite no-no. A couple of intrepid chaps come up with a possible cure, but of course they need some consenting couples to try it out. James Brolin is the only recognisable face in the cast, and he should have known better. Contains violence and sex scenes.

Bryan Genesse *Joe Knight* • James Brolin *McCabe* • Richard Lynch *Calloway* • Craig Judd *Rieger* • Kehli O'Byrne *Shara* ■ *Dir* Dan Golden • *Scr* Joe Sprosty, Jeff Pulce, Daniella Purcell

Terminal Voyage ★★★

Science-fiction thriller 1994 · US · Colour

This is the closest we've been to an Agatha Christie mystery in space. Echoes of *Ten Little Indians* abound in this slickly produced TV sci-fi thriller, as a multinational team of astronauts awakens from a century of cryogenic slumber to discover that one of them is a killer. Ex-*Dynasty* star Emma Samms is a standout as the government agent with a hidden agenda, and there's admirable support from Steven Bauer and Ming-Na Wen (who voiced the lead in Disney's *Mulan*). Contains violence, swearing and drug abuse.

Emma Samms *Becker* • Steven Bauer *Reese* • Gregory McKinney *Major Hollis* • Alan Rachins *Lieutenant Jammad* • Brenda Bakke *Zinovitz* • Wen Ming-Na *Han* ■ *Dir* Rick Jacobson • *Scr* Mark Evan Schwartz

The Terminator ★★★★★ 🔞

Science-fiction action thriller
1984 · US · Colour · 102mins

Arnold Schwarzenegger said "I'll be back," and he was, seven years later. But the success of the sequel should not undermine the powerhouse strengths of James Cameron's original high-tech nightmare, with violent cyborg Arnie time-warped from the future to alter the nuclear war-torn course of history. Generating maximum excitement from the first frame, the dynamic thrills are maintained right up to the nerve-jangling climax. Wittily written with a nice eye for sharp detail, it's hard sci-fi action all the way, and Linda Hamilton shines as the bewildered waitress who unwittingly becomes the saviour of the human race. Contains swearing, violence, a sex scene and nudity. 🎞

Arnold Schwarzenegger *Terminator* • Michael Biehn *Kyle Reese* • Linda Hamilton *Sarah Connor* • Paul Winfield *Traxler* • Lance Henriksen *Vukovich* • Rick Rossovich *Matt* • Bess Motta *Ginger* • Earl Boen *Silberman* • Dick Miller *Pawn shop clerk* • Shawn Schepps *Nancy* ■ *Dir* James Cameron • *Scr* James Cameron, Gale Anne Hurd, William Wisher Jr

Terminator 2: Judgment Day ★★★★★ 🔞

Science-fiction action thriller
1991 · US · Colour · 145mins

Director James Cameron piles on the gutsy grit, hard-edged humour and rollercoaster action in a worthy sequel to his own 1984 horror fantasy classic. Adrenalin junkies get epic value for money in this version, which includes extra footage not seen in cinemas in this country, as android Arnie Schwarzenegger comes back from the future to save our world from the T-1000 super cyborg, whose liquid metal shape-changing abilities set a new cinematic standard for stunning computer graphic special effects. Linda Hamilton turns in another marvellous performance as the fiercely committed heroine who puts a necessary human face on Cameron's hi-decibel mayhem and pyrotechnical bravura. Contains swearing and violence. 🎞

Arnold Schwarzenegger *The Terminator* • Linda Hamilton *Sarah Connor* • Edward Furlong *John Connor* • Robert Patrick *T-1000* • Earl Boen *Dr Silberman* • Joe Morton *Miles Dyson* • S Epatha Merkerson *Tarissa Dyson* • Castulo Guerra *Enrique Salceda* • Michael Biehn *Kyle Reese* ■ *Dir* James Cameron • *Scr* James Cameron, William Wisher

Terms of Endearment ★★★★ 🔞

Drama 1983 · US · Colour · 131mins

Showered with Oscars (it won five, and was nominated for a further seven), this is American mainstream movie-making at its best. Director James L Brooks (*Broadcast News*) succeeds in keeping sticky sentiment largely at bay in this story (based on *Last Picture Show* writer Larry McMurtry's novel) of the often strained mother-daughter relationship between Shirley MacLaine and Debra Winger. Jack Nicholson delivers one of his effortless scene-stealing supporting roles, and other familiar faces include Danny DeVito, Jeff Daniels and John Lithgow. Contains swearing.

Shirley MacLaine *Aurora Greenway* • Debra Winger *Emma Horton* • Jack Nicholson *Garrett Breedlove* • Danny DeVito *Vernon Dahlart* • Jeff Daniels *Flap Horton* • John Lithgow *Sam Burns* • Lisa Hart Carroll *Patsy Clark* • Betty R King *Rosie Dunlop* • Huckleberry Fox *Teddy Horton* • Troy Bishop *Tommy Horton* ■ *Dir* James L Brooks • *Scr* James L Brooks, from the novel by Larry McMurty

La Terra Trema ★★★★ 🆄

Drama 1947 · It · BW · 153mins

Inspired by a 19th-century novel by Giovanni Verga and intended as the first instalment of a trilogy on the exploitation of Sicilian labour (the other parts were to have focused on farmers and miners), this is much more of a neorealist document than Luchino Visconti's previous picture, *Ossessione*. Shooting without a script and using only non-professionals, he explores the trials of the fishermen of Aci Trezza as they are fleeced by worldly wholesalers and middlemen. Yet, despite the fact that the film was partially funded by the Communist Party, it still has an operatic realism, thanks to Visconti's editing of Graziati Aldo's meticulously composed vistas. In Italian with English subtitles. 🎞

Luchino Visconti *Narrator* • Antonio Pietrangeli *Narrator* • Antonio Arcidiacono *Narrator* ■ *Dir* Luchino Visconti • *Scr* Luchino Visconti, from the novel *I Malavoglia* by Giovanni Verga

A Terrible Beauty ★★ 🆄

Second World War drama
1960 · UK · BW · 90mins

Set during the Second World War, stressing dramatic cliché, racial stereotyping and local colour over any kind of political analysis, this is a typical Hollywood yarn. Robert Mitchum is a reluctant recruit to the IRA, who finds leaving rather more difficult after the discovery that his new colleagues are collaborating with the Nazis to defeat the British. Made in Dublin, mainly on a studio set, with Mitchum well cast and ably supported by Richard Harris in one of his early roles, and Cyril Cusack.

Robert Mitchum *Dermot O'Neill* • Anne Heywood *Neeve Donnelly* • Dan O'Herlihy *Don McGinnis* • Cyril Cusack *Jimmy Hannafin* • Richard Harris *Sean Reilly* • Marianne Benet *Bella O'Neill* • Niall MacGinnis *Ned O'Neill* • Harry Brogan *Patrick O'Neill* • Eileen Crowe *Kathleen O'Neill* ■ *Dir* Tay Garnett • *Scr* Robert Wright Campbell, from the novel by Arthur Roth

The Territorians ★★

Thriller 1996 · Ausl · Colour

Odd couple cop movies are a dime a dozen, but at least this gutsy Australian TV thriller has the novelty of a hard-bitten Sydney detective partnered by an Aboriginal rookie. Making the most of the inhospitable countryside around Darwin, director Michael Offer deftly trades off Steven Vidler's rule-book sleuthing and Aaron Pedersen's more intuitive methods, as the duo trail the psychopath responsible for brutal camp-site killings. Scoring its cultural points without undue emphasis, and with a slowly building subplot – involving Vidler's family making a cross-country journey – adding to the tension, this is surprisingly effective viewing. Contains violence, swearing and nudity.

Aaron Pedersen *Constable Tom Daly* • Steven Vidler *Robert McCabe* • Peter Adams *Sarge Kennedy* • Susan Lyons *Ann* • Jamie Croft *Josh* ■ *Dir* Michael Offer • *Scr* Ted Roberts

The Terror ★★15

Horror   1963 · US · Colour · 72mins

More famous for being made in three days with leftover actors and sets from *The Raven* than anything else, cult director Roger Corman's impromptu ghost story is an incomprehensible shocker. Lost Napoleonic soldier Jack Nicholson follows spectral Sandra Knight (Nicholson's wife at the time) to a cliff top mansion owned by the demented Boris Karloff where mysterious things are going on – so mysterious in fact, neither the filmmakers nor the audience can work out what's happening! Although Corman took the overall credit, scenes were also directed by Francis Ford Coppola, Monte Hellman, Jack Hill, Dennis Jacob and Nicholson (all uncredited). A legendary tale of Hollywood economy, and an equally legendary mess. ▭

Boris Karloff *Baron von Leppe* • Jack Nicholson *Lt André Duvalier* • Sandra Knight *Hélène* • Richard Miller *[Dick Miller] Stefan* • Dorothy Neumann *Old woman* ■ *Dir* Roger Corman • *Scr* Leo V Gordon, Jack Hill

Terror at Deception Ridge ★★★15

Action thriller   1994 · US · Colour · 89mins

This gutsy thriller will have you checking out your fellow passengers very carefully next time you board a bus. Newly sprung from jail, Michael O'Keefe could be forgiven for thinking his troubles were over. But they're just about to begin, because his travelling companion is crooked bank manager Ed Begley Jr, who has stolen the ransom money demanded by his wife's kidnappers and they will stop at nothing to retrieve it. This may be *Die Hard* at *Speed*, but director John McPherson eschews slam-bam action to build the tension with skill. ▭

Michael O'Keefe *Jack Bolder* • Ed Begley Jr *Jack Davis* • Linda Purl *Helen Davis* • Michelle Johnson *Natalie Harris* • Colleen Flynn *Lianne Melrose* • Miguel Ferrer *Ray Hayes* ■ *Dir* John McPherson • *Scr* Randy Kornfield

Terror by Night ★★★U

Murder mystery   1946 · US · BW · 60mins

Short, but neat, Sherlock Holmes thriller that moves fast enough to skim over the potholes in the plot. Basil Rathbone and Nigel Bruce are hired to safeguard a gem called the Star of Rhodesia. Three murders later, Holmes has cracked the mystery, and Dennis Hoey has overdone his comic act as Inspector Lestrade to an irritating degree. Years before, Alan Mowbray had appeared in the Clive Brook and Reginald Owen movies about Holmes, but he wrote that Rathbone's version of the sleuth was the best. ▭

Basil Rathbone *Sherlock Holmes* • Nigel Bruce *Dr John H Watson* • Alan Mowbray *Major Duncan Bleek* • Dennis Hoey *Inspector Lestrade* • Renee Godfrey *Vivian Vedder* •

Skelton Knaggs *Sands* ■ *Dir* Roy William Neill • *Scr* Frank Gruber, from a story by Sir Arthur Conan Doyle

Terror from the Year 5,000 ★

Science-fiction horror
1958 · US · Colour · 66mins

Actually, it's a terror from the year 1958! This unbelievable claptrap features a hideously deformed sex kitten who materialises through a time machine to mate and save the future of mankind. The mutant cat with four eyes is a laugh, but not much else is in this brazenly clumsy cheapie, which, amazingly does have something of a cult following. More famous to horror film buffs these days because part of the soundtrack was later used in the classic *Night of the Living Dead*.

Ward Costello *Robert Hedges* • Joyce Holden *Claire Erling* • John Stratton *Victor* • Frederic Downs *Professor Erling* • Fred Herrick *Angelo* • Beatrice Furdeaux *Miss Blake* • Salome Jens *AD 5000 woman* ■ *Dir/Scr* Robert J Gurney Jr

Terror in a Texas Town ★★PG

Western   1958 · US · BW · 77mins

This B-western from talented, minor director Joseph H Lewis (*Gun Crazy* and *The Big Combo*) has built up a cult following over the years. It is an extraordinary work, with two actors who were prominent during the McCarthy anti-Communist witch-hunts, squaring up to each other in a truly remarkable climax, as star Sterling Hayden wields a harpoon against the symbolically black-clad gunman Ned Young. Many hardened western admirers consider the contrivances of this movie and its elegiac camera style phoney and theatrical, but there's no denying its originality of form given the obvious constraints of plot and budget. Hayden makes a genuinely formidable and complex character of the wrathful returning Swede. ▭

Sterling Hayden *George Hansen* • Sebastian Cabot *Ed McNeil* • Carol Kelly *Molly* • Eugene Martin *Pepe Mirada* • Ned Young *[Nedrick Young] Johnny Crale* • Victor Millan *José Mirada* ■ *Dir* Joseph H Lewis • *Scr* Ben L Perry

Terror in the City ★★

Drama   1963 · US · BW · 86mins

Indie director Allen Baron doesn't so much pay homage to his French New Wave heroes, as slavishly imitate them. The story focuses on a child who runs away to Manhattan, where he falls in with tribes of street urchins, petty criminals, ethnic gangs and a prostitute played by Lee Grant. Made for less than $200,000 and released under the title *Pie in the Sky*, it was shot entirely on location in the Times Square area of New York using the hand-held, semi-documentary techniques that brought Godard and Truffaut international acclaim.

Lee Grant *Suzy* • Richard Bray *Brill* • Michael Higgins *Carl* • Roberto Marsach *Paco* • Robert Allen *Brill's father* ■ *Dir/Scr* Allen Baron

Terror in the Family ★★

Drama   1996 · US · Colour · 86mins

A compulsive, if somewhat distasteful, look at an American family hitting the auto-destruct button behind its façade of normality. Joanna Kerns and Dan Lauria are the parents trying to cope with a teenage daughter who makes Beavis and Butt-head seem like adolescent role models. What starts off as a bad case of the sulks eventually sparks off the almost total disintegration of the family. The playing is commendable, but director Gregory Goodell backs away from making it truly nasty. Contains violence, swearing, sex scenes and nudity.

Joanna Kerns *Cynthia Marten* • Dan Lauria *Todd Marten* • Hilary Swank *Deena Marten* • Andy Kavovit *Garret* • Kathleen Wilhoite *Judith* ■ *Dir/Scr* Gregory Goodell

Terror in the Mall ★★

Action thriller
1998 · US/ Ger · Colour · 85mins

A depressingly ordinary TV movie, in which the phrase "shop till you drop" takes on a new meaning when a group of people find themselves trapped in a shopping mall after a dam bursts. It's notable mainly for providing a rare screen role for *Starsky and Hutch* star David Soul, while *Melrose Place*'s Robert Estes is the other familiar face in the largely unknown cast.

Rob Estes *Glen Savoy* • Shannon Sturges *Dr Sheri Maratos* • Angeline Ball *Suzanne Price* • George Anton *Tom* • David Soul *Roger Carey* ■ *Dir* Norberto Barba • *Scr* John Mandel, Dan Gordon, from a story by Dan Gordon

Terror in the Sky ★★

Adventure   1971 · US · Colour · 90mins

This serviceable TV movie remake of *Zero Hour* (1957) was rushed out to capitalise on the success of *Airport*. There's no Dean Martin here, but a cut-price version in the form of Doug McClure as an ex-helicopter pilot with personal problems who summons the courage to land a plane when the crew are struck down by food poisoning. Lame material given more than it deserves by a game cast.

Doug McClure *George Spencer* • Lois Nettleton *Janet Turner* • Roddy McDowall *Dr Ralph Baird* • Leif Erickson *Marty Treleavan* • Keenan Wynn *Milton* • Kenneth Tobey *Captain Wilson* ■ *Dir* Bernard L Kowalski • *Scr* Richard Nelson, Elinor Karpf, Stephen Karpf

Terror in the Wax Museum ★★

Horror   1973 · US · Colour · 93mins

Exhibits apparently come to life and commit murder in a very ordinary variation on the wax museum theme, with a mundane explanation for all the creepy goings-on. Poor scripting and direction doom the pedestrian plot further, although the cast – studded with an amazing array of intrepid old-timers – is enough of an attraction in itself to make this tired *House of Wax* retread worth watching.

Ray Milland *Harry Flexner* • Broderick Crawford *Amos Burns* • Elsa Lanchester *Julia Hawthorn* • Maurice Evans *Inspector Daniels* • Shani

Wallis *Laurie Mell* • John Carradine *Claude Dupree* ■ *Dir* Georg Fenady • *Scr* Jameson Brewer, from a story by Andrew Fenady

The Terror Inside ★★

Psychological thriller   1996 · US · Colour

Also known as *Shattered Mind* and *Dead Suzy*, this psychological TV thriller provides drama series regular Heather Locklear, with the opportunity to show that she's capable of rather more than just looking glamorous. It has obvious similarities to the Sally Field movie *Sybil*, as Locklear plays a woman suffering from the effect of her multiple personalities. Locklear convincingly veers from feisty hooker and abrasive teen to vulnerable child and suicidal victim, but Thomas Baum's script is so confused that the schizophrenic manifestations exist in something of a dramatic vacuum, and director Stephen Gyllenhaal seems incapable of making her struggle to regain control of her life seem credible.

Heather Locklear *Suzy Mitchell* • Brett Cullen *Sean* • Eric Silver *Caroline Kava Martha Tremayne* ■ *Dir* Stephen Gyllenhaal • *Scr* Thomas Baum

Terror Is a Man ★★

Horror   1959 · US/Phil · BW · 76mins

This commendable rehash of *Island of Lost Souls* (1932) was shot in the Philippines on a low budget, that could only extend to one "manimal" mutant instead of the usual pack. Francis Lederer is the mad doctor conducting experiments on a remote island, enabling him to turn a jungle cat into something resembling a human. His horrified wife Greta Thyssen confides in shipwreck victim Richard Derr, until the monster kidnaps her and sets in motion the tragic cliff-top finale. Originally an on-screen buzzer was the warning signal for the faint-hearted to look away from the gruesome operation footage.

Francis Lederer *Dr Charles Girard* • Greta Thyssen *Frances Girard* • Richard Derr *William Fitzgerald* • Peyton Keesee *Tiago* • Oscar Keesee *Walter* • Flory Carlos *Beast-Man* ■ *Dir* Gerry DeLeon • *Scr* Harry Paul Harber

Terror of Mechagodzilla ★★★15

Monster horror   1975 · Jap · Colour · 79mins

Practically all of Godzilla's enemies from Ghidorah to Rodan are assembled in this 20th anniversary production. So what else could alien powers do in yet another world domination scheme, except build a nasty robot version of the loveable T-Rex? But the old fire-snorter hits back and bangs his tail in suitable disdain at this outrageous ploy to upstage him with a pile of shiny junk. Talking of piles of shiny junk, veteran Godzilla creator Inoshiro Honda directs this monster mishmash with a lurid comic-strip style replete with engagingly daffy visual spectacle. Japanese dialogue dubbed into English.. ▭

Dir Inoshiro Honda • *Scr* Katsuhiko Sasaki

Terror on Highway 91 ★★15

Police drama   1989 · US · Colour · 89mins

Ricky Schroder isn't the first child star to discover that the going gets tough

U = SUITABLE FOR ALL   **Uc** = SUITABLE FOR ALL, ESPECIALLY FOR YOUNG CHILDREN (VIDEO ONLY)   **PG** = PARENTAL GUIDANCE

when you grow up, and despite his plucky efforts, he looks out of his depth in this TV thriller. He plays an idealistic young policeman in the Deep South who rebels against the corrupt ways of his colleagues, led by the supremely sleazy George Dzundza and Brad Dourif. Look out for a bland early appearance from Lara Flynn Boyle as Schroder's girlfriend.

Ricky Schroder [Rick Schroder] *Clay Nelson* • George Dzundza *Jesse Barton* • Matt Clark *Jim Warren* • Lara Flynn Boyle *Laura Taggart* • Brad Dourif *Keith Evans* ■ *Dir* Jerry Jameson • *Scr* Stuart Schoffman, from the book by Steven Sellers

Terror on Track 9 ★★
Thriller 1992 · US · Colour · 96mins

It isn't exactly *Inspector Morse*, but these made-for-television thrillers must have found an audience somewhere – this is the fifth movie in the series featuring Richard Crenna as detective Frank Janek. This time around Crenna and his faithful sidekick Cliff Gorman are called in to catch a killer haunting New York's Central Station whose victims include the niece of a senior police officer. As usual, Crenna is as solid as a rock, and there's also a better than average supporting cast.

Richard Crenna *Lieutenant Frank Janek* • Cliff Gorman *Sergeant Aaron Greenberg* • Joseph Campanella *Chief Mleczko* • Swoosie Kurtz *Marcia Hobbs* • Joan Van Ark *Leslie Renner* ■ *Dir* Robert Iscove • *Scr* Monte Stettin, from a character created by William Bayer

Terror Train ★★ 18
Horror 1980 · Can · Colour · 92mins

Several years after participating in a cruel fraternity initiation that backfired and traumatised the victim, scream queen Jamie Lee Curtis and her college buddies rent a train for a party, with conductor Ben Johnson and young magician David Copperfield along for the ride. It doesn't take long for one of the many masked party-goers on board to start bumping people off. The script doesn't stray far from the standard eighties stalk-and-slash formula, though director Roger Spottiswoode generates a noticeable amount of atmosphere, making the most of the superior production values (including some excellent night photography) and the talented cast.

Ben Johnson *Carne* • Jamie Lee Curtis *Alana* • Hart Bochner *Doc Manley* • David Copperfield *Magician* • Derek MacKinnon *Kenny Hampson* • Sandee Currie *Mitchy* ■ *Dir* Roger Spottiswoode • *Scr* TY Drake

The Terror Within ★ 18
Science-fiction horror
1988 · US · Colour · 84mins

One of producer Roger Corman's countless imitations of *Alien*. The futuristic setting is not a spaceship, but an underground lab, where Andrew Stevens and George Kennedy are among the few survivors of a holocaust that has left the planet virtually uninhabitable. Trouble arrives when a pregnant woman gives birth to a monster. The rubber-suited mutant is an embarrassment to watch, but looks good compared to the set design that seems to recycle the same hallway

and room for all parts of the underground complex.

George Kennedy *Hal* • Andrew Stevens *David* • Starr Andreeff *Sue* • Terri Treas *Linda* • John Lafayette *Andre* • Tommy Hinchley *Neil* • Yvonne Saa *Karen* ■ *Dir* Thierry Notz • *Scr* Thomas M Cleaver

The Terroriser ★★★ 15
Drama 1986 · Tai · Colour · 108mins

Edward Yang was one of the driving forces of Taiwanese cinema's New Wave in the late eighties and early nineties, with his *A Brighter Summer Day*. Here, he demonstrates a complete mastery of theme, narrative and technique as he weaves together episodes from the lives of characters bound together by mischievous phone calls. Exploring the nature of truth in fiction, film and photography, this complex picture demands your full attention: the stylish visuals and committed performances, notably from Cora Miao as a novelist suffering from writer's block and Wang An as the telephone terror, are the reward. In Mandarin with English subtitles.

Cora Miao *Zhou Yufen [miu Qianren]* • Li Liqun *Li Lizhong* • Jin Shijie *Ah Shen* • Gu Baoming *Lao Gu* ■ *Dir* Edward Dechang Yang • *Scr* Li Yuan [Ye Xiao], Yang Dechang [Edward Yang]

TerrorVision ★★ 15
Science-fiction comedy
1986 · US · Colour · 81mins

This supposed satire on the media-obsessed, suburban middle classes is in fact a toe-curlingly embarrassing *Poltergeist* rip-off featuring a cartoonishly dysfunctional family. A new satellite dish accidentally beams an alien into the Putterman's living room. Unfortunately he turns out to be voracious rather than cute, gobbling up everyone in his path. Writer/director Ted Nicolaou intentionally parodies those Z-grade monster movies of the fifties, but ironically has produced something of which Ed Wood would be proud.

Diane Franklin *Suzy Putterman* • Gerrit Graham *Stanley Putterman* • Mary Woronov *Raquel Putterman* • Chad Allen *Sherman Putterman* • Jonathan Gries *O D* • Jennifer Richards *Medusa* • Alejandro Rey *Spiro* • Bert Remsen *Grampa* ■ *Dir/Scr* Ted Nicolaou

Tess ★★★★ PG
Drama 1979 · Fr/UK · Colour · 165mins

Roman Polanski's now classic adaptation of Hardy's black and ironic tragedy is not as good as the novel, but still has much to recommend it, not least the evocative Oscar-winning photography. Nastassja Kinski rocketed to stardom after her starring role as the country girl, whose disastrous sexual encounters with her rakish cousin come back to haunt her when she finally finds love in the arms of Angel Clare (Peter Firth). Devastating and powerful, Polanski achieves the requisite pathos and shoots a stunning denouement against the backdrop of Stonehenge. The movie also won Oscars for costumes and art direction.

Nastassia Kinski [Nastassja Kinski] *Tess* • Leigh Lawson *Alec d'Urberville* • Peter Firth *Angel Clare* • John Collin *John Durbeyfield* •

David Markham *Rev Mr Clare* • Rosemary Martin *Mrs Durbeyfield* • Richard Pearson *Vicar of Marlott* • Carolyn Pickles *Marian* ■ *Dir* Roman Polanski • *Scr* Roman Polanski, Gerard Brach, John Brownjohn, from the novel by Thomas Hardy • *Cinematographer* Geoffrey Unsworth, Ghislain Cloquet • *Music* Philippe Sarde • *Production Designer* Pierre Guffroy • *Costume Designer* Anthony Powell

Tess of the Storm Country ★★
Silent drama 1922 · US · BW · 137mins

This second adaptation of Grace Miller White's novel stars Mary Pickford – who'd starred in the 1914 original – as a fisherman's daughter who comes to the rescue of a woman about to be ostracised for her illegitimate baby. Pickford claims the baby as her own, admirably deflecting scorn away from the other woman. Naturally, it all comes right in the end. Pickford, a screen veteran at 21, acquired her top star status in the earlier version for Famous Players, and now bought back the rights for $50,000 to do it all over again. Ten years later, Fox rather pointlessly remade it for Janet Gaynor and Charles Farrell, and updated it in 1960 for Diane Baker.

Mary Pickford *Tessibel Skinner* • Lloyd Hughes *Frederick Graves* • Gloria Hope *Teola Graves* • David Torrence *Elias Graves* • Forrest Robinson *Daddy Skinner* • Jean Hersholt *Ben Letts* ■ *Dir* John S Robertson • *Scr* Elmer Harris, from the novel by Grace Miller White

Tess of the Storm Country ★★ U
Romantic melodrama
1960 · US · Colour · 84mins

Amazingly, the fourth screen version of the popular Grace Miller White family novel about a Scottish girl growing up among the Pennsylvania Dutch. Beautifully shot on location in CinemaScope by 20th Century-Fox as a vehicle for Diane Baker, who became a successful producer and in-demand character actress. Trouble is, time hasn't been kind to this sentimental tale, and, although it worked twice for Mary Pickford (in 1914 and again in 1922), the sixties found this good-looking opus reduced to being released as a supporting feature.

Diane Baker *Tess Maclean* • Jack Ging *Peter Graves* • Lee Philips *Eric Thorson* • Archie Duncan *Hamish Maclean* • Nancy Valentine *Teola Graves* • Bert Remsen *Mike Foley* • Wallace Ford *Fred Thorson* ■ *Dir* Paul Guilfoyle • *Scr* Charles Lang, Rupert Hughes, from the novel by Grace Miller White

Test Pilot ★★★★
Drama 1938 · US · Colour · 118mins

A topnotch MGM Clark Gable vehicle, teaming him with ace director Victor Fleming, a year before the pair made history for producer David O Selznick with *Gone with the Wind*. This is one of those flying movies based on the work of pioneering pilot-turned-writer Frank "Spig" Wead whose own courageous story was filmed in *The Wings of Eagles* and, like many such films, this rings true in the skies, but less so on the ground. Still, Gable's belle is sparky Myrna Loy and his mechanic pal is Spencer Tracy, so whatever the weaknesses in the action, it's certainly watchable. Acting honours, though, are

stolen by crusty Lionel Barrymore as an aeronautic tycoon, and his performance in this film was much mimicked by Mickey Rooney. Despite not being one of Gable's most famous films, *Test Pilot* was one of the movie events of its year and it still looks pretty damn good today.

Clark Gable *Jim Lane* • Myrna Loy *Ann Barton* • Spencer Tracy *Gunner Sloane* • Lionel Barrymore *Howard B Drake* • Samuel S Hinds *General Ross* • Arthur Aylesworth *Frank Barton* • Claudia Coleman *Mrs Barton* ■ *Dir* Victor Fleming • *Scr* Vincent Lawrence, Waldemar Young, Howard Hawks (uncredited), from a story by Frank Wead.

Testament ★★★★ PG
Disaster drama 1983 · US · Colour · 85mins

A sobering movie detailing with chilling accuracy how a typical family copes after an unspecified nuclear attack devastates America. There are no fancy special effects, just a shocking interruption during *Sesame Street*, followed by a blinding flash. In the aftermath, Jane Alexander (giving a stunning performance) must cope with situations she has always dreaded – mourning her missing husband, burying her children and coming to terms with the stark reality that she too will eventually die of radiation sickness. But although she tries, she can't commit suicide – and that is her testament in the life-affirmation stakes. Director Lynne Littman accomplishes so much without hammering home the points or preaching. This is one of the best films ever made about the futility of nuclear war.

Jane Alexander *Carol Wetherly* • William Devane *Tom Wetherly* • Ross Harris [Rossie Harris] *Brad Wetherly* • Roxana Zal *Mary Liz Wetherly* • Lukas Haas *Scottie Wetherly* • Philip Anglim *Hollis* • Lilia Skala *Fania* • Leon Ames *Henry Abhart* • Rebecca De Mornay *Cathy Pitkin* • Kevin Costner *Phil Pitkin* ■ *Dir* Lynne Littman • *Scr* John Secret Young, from the story *The Last Testament* by Carol Amen

Testament ★★ PG
Political drama 1988 · UK · Colour · 79mins

It's no accident that TV journalist Tania Rogers returns to her Ghanaian homeland in search of Werner Herzog on the set of *Cobra Verde*, as no one has explored the impact of environment on the psyche more effectively than the visionary German director. Working under the auspices of the Black Audio Film Collective, writer/director John Akomfrah demonstrates admirable control in leaking fragments of information that enable us to piece together the horrifying experience that scarred Rogers during the fall of the Nkrumah regime. But, in order to achieve this "War Zone of Memories", Akomfrah is occasionally obscure and inconsequential.

Tania Rogers *Abena* • Evans Hunter *Rashid* • Emma Francis Wilson *Danso* • Frank Parkes *Mr Parkes* ■ *Dir/Scr* John Akomfrah

Le Testament d'Orphée ★★★★
Experimental drama 1960 · Fr · BW · 79mins

Testament to Jean Cocteau's influence on the New Wave, his final feature was partly financed and produced by François Truffaut. But, while he exhorts the younger generation to bear his legacy, Cocteau is more interested here in looking back, with a potent mix of nostalgia and disillusionment, to the worlds and characters he created. No wonder this ragbag of references to his gloriously diverse artistic output is subtitled "Don't Ask Me Why". Anyone coming to this poetic sojourn seeking revelation is going to be disappointed, as it's strictly for aficionados, although the uninitiated might enjoy spotting such acolytes as Yul Brynner, Brigitte Bardot and Pablo Picasso. In French with English subtitles.

Jean Cocteau *Jean Cocteau, the Poet* • Jean-Pierre Léaud *The Schoolboy* • Edouard Dermit *Cegeste* • Henri Cremieux *The Professor* • Françoise Christophe *The Nurse* • Maria Casarès *The Princess* • Jean Marais *Oedipus* • Pablo Picasso • Charles Aznavour • Roger Vadim • Brigitte Bardot • Yul Brynner ■ *Dir/Scr* Jean Cocteau

The Testament of Dr Mabuse ★★★★

Classic horror   1932 · Ger · BW · 88mins

Fritz Lang always liked to boast that the second part of his celebrated crime trilogy was such a calculated insult to the Nazis, that he feared for his life. Always one to embroider his own legend, Lang was nevertheless correct in claiming that the depiction of a master criminal who hypnotised people into doing his evil bidding was a bit near the knuckle for Goebbels, who had the film banned. Yet Lang's wife and co-scenarist, Thea von Harbou, was a committed Nazi who refused to follow her husband into French exile. Whatever the motivational truth, this is still a dark tale, told with atmospheric panache.

Rudolf Klein-Rogge *Dr Mabuse* • Otto Wernicke *Insp Karl Lohmann* • Oskar Beregi *Professor Baum* • Gustav Diessl *Thomas Kent* • Wera Liessem *Lilli* ■ *Dir* Fritz Lang • *Scr* Thea von Harbou, Fritz Lang, from characters created by Norbert Jacques

The Testament of Dr Cordelier ★★★★

Horror drama   1959 · Fr · BW · 72mins

Jean Renoir was one of the first great directors to make a film using television methods. The shooting of this updated free adaptation of Robert Louis Stevenson's *Dr Jekyll and Mr Hyde* took around ten days at the Radio-Télévision Française studios. The use of multiple cameras gives the film the fluid, rough-edged spontaneous appeal of a live TV play. The switch between the cheap-looking studio interiors and the streets of Paris produces an appropriate sense of displacement and schism. Jean-Louis Barrault is extraordinary as the jaunty, twitching, shaggy, prancing, bestial Monsieur Opale, the evil alter ego of the silver-haired, dignified and respectable Dr Cordelier. Shot in 1959, the film had to wait at least two years for a release. In French with English subtitles.

Jean-Louis Barrault *Dr Cordelier/Opale* • Teddy Bilis *Maitre Joly* • Michel Vitold *Dr Severin* • Jean Topart *Désiré* • Micheline Gary *Marguerite* • Jean Renoir *Narrator* ■ *Dir* Jean Renoir • *Scr* Jean Renoir, from the novel *Dr Jekyll and Mr Hyde* by Robert Louis Stevenson • *Cinematographer* Georges Leclerc

Testimony ★★ PG

Biographical drama
1987 · UK · BW and Colour · 150mins

This heavy and long-winded biopic of the Russian composer Dmitri Shostakovich, was directed by one of the *enfants terribles* of eighties UK cinema and television, Tony Palmer. Ben Kingsley brings his customary excellence to the leading role, but he can't quite compensate for a dull narrative, and for the film's ponderous overemphasis on Shostakovich's clashes with the Soviet authorities. A plus though, is the excellent photography, mainly black and white but with bursts of colour.

Ben Kingsley *Dmitri Shostakovich* • Sherry Baines *Nina Shostakovich* • Magdalen Asquith *Galya* • Mark Asquith *Maxim* • Terence Rigby *Stalin* • Ronald Pickup *Tukhachevksy* • John Shrapnel *Zhdanov* • Frank Carson *Carnival fat man* • Chris Barrie *Carnival thin man* ■ *Dir* Tony Palmer • *Scr* David Rudkin, Tony Palmer, from the memoirs *The Memoirs of Dmitri Shostakovich* by Dmitri Shostakovich

Tetsuo ★★ 18

Science-fiction fantasy
1989 · Jap · BW · 67mins

This is one of those movies which leaves you with the feeling that you're not quite sure what it was about. The basic plot of a Japanese businessman, apparently involved in a road accident, who suddenly finds himself turning into a metallic mutant monster, is merely an excuse for cult Japanese director Shinya Tsukamoto to bombard the viewer with surreal and nightmarish images. He not only directed but also wrote, filmed and played one of the leads, and has obviously read too many adult comic books. Employing grainy black-and-white photography, minimal dialogue and a pounding techno soundtrack this will either be seen as pretentious rubbish or a classy art movie. A sequel followed in 1991. In Japanese with English subtitles.

Tomoroh Taguchi *Salaryman* • Kei Fujiwara *Salaryman's girlfriend* • Nobu Kanaoka *Woman in glasses* • Shinya Tsukamoto *Young metals fetishist* ■ *Dir/Scr* Shinya Tsukamoto

Tetsuo II: Body Hammer ★★★ 18

Science-fiction horror
1991 · Jap · Colour · 78mins

Not so much a sequel to Shinya Tsukamoto's cult movie *Tetsuo*, as a radical reworking of that "body horror" study in mutant machine madness. Don't try and make sense of the story as bizarre experiments turn people into weapons, just savour the shiny images as Tsukamoto highlights "the beauty in destruction", in retina-scorching metallic hues. The central body-machine melding a frenzy of post-modern *Alien* and David Lynch industrial design is well worth waiting for in this homo- and sado-erotic avant-garde abstraction. In Japanese with English subtitles.

Tomoroh Taguchi *Taniguchi* • Nobu Kanaoka *Kana* • Shinya Tsukamoto *Yatsu* • Keinosuke Tomioka *Minori* ■ *Dir/Scr* Shinya Tsukamoto

Tex ★★★★ PG

Drama   1982 · US · Colour · 98mins

Early roles for Matt Dillon, Meg Tilly and Emilio Estevez in a terrific coming-of-age yarn, based on a book by SE Hinton. It focuses on the trials and tribulations of teenager Dillon and his elder brother, growing up footloose and parent-free in Oklahoma. Director Tim Hunter draws great performances from relatively inexperienced kids. Five years later he'd do it again with the even more highly-rated *River's Edge* and a cast that included a young Keanu Reeves.

Matt Dillon *Tex McCormick* • Jim Metzler *Mason McCormick* • Meg Tilly *Jamie Collins* • Bill McKinney *Pop McCormick* • Frances Lee McCain *Mrs Johnson* • Ben Johnson *Cole Collins* • Emilio Estevez *Johnny Collins* ■ *Dir* Tim Hunter • *Scr* Charlie Haas, Tim Hunter, from a novel by SE Hinton

Tex and the Lord of the Deep ★★★

Western   1985 · It · Colour

Having already brought the Ringo Kid and Zorro to the screen, Duccio Tessari plundered the Tex Willer comic strips for this refreshingly unselfconscious Western. What starts off as a routine outlaw tale, as Giuliano Gemma's Tex is called in to investigate an attack on an army weapons convoy, turns into a far more sinister case when he is confronted by Riccardo Petrazzi's vicious Lord of Deep. Enthusiastic support is provided by Carlo Mucari as Tiger Jack and William Berger as Kit Carson and die-hard comic fans will recognise Giovanni Luigi Bonelli (who created the strip in 1948) as the witch doctor. Italian dialogue dubbed into English.

Giuliano Gemma *Tex Willer* • Carlo Mucari *Tiger Jack* • William Berger *Kit Carson* • Isabel Russinova *Tulac* • Flavio Bucci *Kanas* • Riccardo Petrazzi *Lord of the Deep* • Giovanni Luigi Bonelli *Witch doctor* ■ *Dir* Duccio Tessari • *Scr* Gianfranco Clerici

The Texan ★★

Western   1930 · US · BW · 72mins

One of Gary Cooper's first starring vehicles, this Paramount western presents him as Quico, the Llano Kid, a cocky bandit who is persuaded to impersonate the missing son of wealthy aristocrat Emma Dunn. Predictably, his innate good nature rebels at the deception, especially when he falls for one of the family, the lovely Fay Wray. Directed by John Cromwell from O Henry's story *The Double-Dyed Deceiver*, it has one of the celebrated storyteller's twists – a mild one – at the end, and bears a striking resemblance to the same studio's later Alan Ladd western, *Branded*.

Gary Cooper *Enrique "Quico", The Llano Kid* • Fay Wray *Consuelo* • Emma Dunn *Señora Ibarra* • Oscar Apfel *Thacker* • James Marcus *John Brown* • Donald Reed *Nick Ibarra* ■ *Dir* John Cromwell • *Scr* Daniel N Rubin, Oliver HP Garrett, from the story *The Double-Dyed Deceiver* by O Henry

The Texans ★★★

Western   1938 · US · BW · 92mins

There's nothing really special here, but this would-be epic from Paramount is still interesting to watch for its period setting and a fine cast. A remake of the far superior silent *North of '36*, it tells the tale of the opening up of the West, including the formation of the Ku Klux Klan and the first cattle drive along the Chisholm Trail. Randolph Scott is the grim-faced trail boss, but he's second-billed to Joan Bennett (in her only western), who gives the impression that she would rather be somewhere else. Three-time Academy Award winner Walter Brennan is the trail cook, a role he would immortalise ten years later in *Red River*.

Joan Bennett *Ivy Preston* • Randolph Scott *Kirk Jordan* • May Robson *Granna* • Walter Brennan *Chuckawalla* • Robert Cummings *Captain Alan Sanford* • Raymond Hatton *Cal Tuttle* • Robert Barrat *Isaiah Middlebrack* ■ *Dir* James Hogan • *Scr* Bertrand Millhauser, Paul Sloane, William Wister Haines, from the story *North of '36* by Emerson H Hough

Texas ★★★ PG

Western   1941 · US · BW · 89mins

Here's a classy western from Columbia, teaming two matinée idols (and drinking buddies) William Holden and Glenn Ford, competing for the love of *Stagecoach's* Claire Trevor. To be appreciated today it really needs colour, but it stems from the period when you didn't waste your budget if you had stars who would attract an audience nevertheless. And without such films, the resonances Holden brought to *The Wild Bunch* or Ford to *3:10 to Yuma* and *The Fastest Gun Alive* would be nonexistent, and cinema would be the poorer. George Marshall directs like a man who knows his territory, and turns out a satisfying and well-crafted movie.

William Holden (1) *Dan Thomas* • Glenn Ford *Tod Ramsey* • Claire Trevor *"Mike" King* • George Bancroft *Windy Miller* • Edgar Buchanan *Doc Thorpe* • Don Beddoe *Sheriff* ■ *Dir* George Marshall • *Scr* Horace McCoy, Lewis Meltzer, from his story Lewis Meltzer

Texas across the River ★★ PG

Comedy western 1966 · US · Colour · 96mins

An amiable comedy western, pairing likeable Dean Martin with French heart-throb Alain Delon, in the first of a series of interesting, but failed attempts to turn Delon into a Hollywood star. There are simplistic pleasures to be had there, though not if you're a die-hard western fan. Others will delight in the performance of Rat Pack member Joey Bishop as a deadpan Indian, and there's super cinematography by the great Russell Metty. However, the talented director Michael Gordon, best known for the 1950 version of *Cyrano de Bergerac* and *Pillow Talk*, seems an odd choice for this material.

Dean Martin *Sam Hollis* • Alain Delon *Don Andrea Baldasar* • Rosemary Forsyth *Phoebe Ann Taylor* • Joey Bishop *Kronk* • Tina Marquand *Lonetta* • Peter Graves (1) *Captain Stimpson* ■ *Dir* Michael Gordon • *Scr* Wells Root, Harold Greene, Ben Star

Texas Adios ★★★ 15
Spaghetti western
1966 · US · Colour · 88mins

This spaghetti western lacks the stylisation and darkly comic touches that characterised the films of Italian western supremos Sergio Leone or Sergio Corbucci, with whom Franco Nero, the hero of this film, would team later in the same year for the cult classic *Django*. Without ever matching the charisma of the coffin-hauling, killing machine character of that movie, Nero plays a dutiful son who sets about avenging his father's death (indeed, the film was released as *The Avenger* in the States). But director Ferdinando Baldi's script lacks an innovative set piece that might have enlivened the all-too-familiar plotline, and the film lacks the explosive punch of the best of its kind. Italian dialogue dubbed into English. ▭

Franco Nero *Burt Sullivan* • Cole Kitosch *Jim* • Jose Suarez *Cisco Delgado* • Elisa Montes *Girl* ■ *Dir* Ferdinando Baldi • *Scr* Ferdinando Baldi, Franco Rossette

The Texas Chain Saw Massacre ★★★★ 18
Horror
1974 · US · Colour · 79mins

Time has not dimmed the shock value of director Tobe Hooper's seminal classic, based on the same real-life case that inspired *Psycho*. The scream-filled chiller, which was finally granted a certificate from the British Board of Film Classification for its 25th anniversary re-release, finds five lost Texans breaking down in their mini-van and encountering a demented family of murderous cannibals who use human meat in their special recipe sausages. Cleverly making his audience identify with animals in a slaughterhouse, Hooper has innocent victims hung on meat hooks, sliced into chunks, sledge-hammered and put in freezers. Another directorial masterstroke is his use of a documentary-style realism, coupled with the true horror of anticipation and suggestion, taking the terror factor into stunning and disturbing areas. Low on gore (the three sequels made up for it), the film was made on a micro-budget, which only adds to the harsh, gritty and creepy tone, and sears this razor-sharp nightmare into the brain for ever. Contains violence and swearing. ▭

Marilyn Burns *Sally* • Allen Danziger *Jerry* • Paul A Partain *Franklin* • William Vail *Kirk* • Teri McMinn *Pam* • Edwin Neal *Hitchhiker* • Jim Siedow *Old man* • Gunnar Hansen *Leatherface* ■ *Dir* Tobe Hooper • *Scr* Kim Henkel, Tobe Hooper, from their story

The Texas Chainsaw Massacre Part 2 ★★★★
Horror comedy
1986 · US · Colour · 95mins

A masterful sequel by director Tobe Hooper to his own seminal shriek masterpiece that's wilder, weirder, funnier, gorier and one of the most harrowing movies ever made. Evangelical ex-Texas Ranger Dennis Hopper is determined to bring the demented cannibal family to justice after the disappearance of his nephew (the wheelchair victim in the original). He's helped by DJ Caroline Williams who's taped one of their atrocities

during a live phone-in. Bursting with style, energy and inventive satire and with its power to shock, outrage and disturb still intact, this rich slice of unrelenting American Gothic is as much a true horror classic as Hooper's 1974 original. Contains violence and swearing.

Dennis Hopper *Lieutenant "Lefty" Enright* • Caroline Williams *Vanita "Stretch" Brock* • Bill Johnson *Leatherface* • Jim Siedow *Drayton Sawyer the Cook* • Bill Moseley *Chop-Top* ■ *Dir* Tobe Hooper • *Scr* LM Kit Carson

Texas Lady ★★ U
Western
1955 · US · Colour · 81mins

A routine western, made mesmerisingly watchable by the sheer force of its star, Claudette Colbert, playing a crusading journalist in town to take over her father's newspaper against all odds. She looks splendid, and is well supported by goodies Barry Sullivan and John Litel, and baddies Ray Collins and Walter Sande. The Technicolor's nice, but then the cinematographer was *Gone with the Wind's* Ray Rennahan, one of Hollywood's finest. ▭

Claudette Colbert *Prudence Webb* • Barry Sullivan *Chris Mooney* • Gregory Walcott *Jess Foley* • Ray Collins *Ralston* • Walter Sande *Sturdy* • James Bell *Cass Gower* ■ *Dir* Tim Whelan • *Scr* Horace McCoy

The Texas Rangers ★★★★
Western
1936 · US · BW · 75mins

Released to coincide with the Lone Star state's centennial celebrations, this roistering good-natured adventure had the commercial effect of bringing the western back into public favour, rescuing it from poverty row B-movie obscurity. Allegedly based on official Texas Rangers records, this is a loosely woven tale about three buddies; Fred MacMurray, Jack Oakie and baddie Lloyd Nolan, who fall out. Director King Vidor has an especially firm grasp on the action sequences, and, despite the absence of colour, this Paramount offering is as satisfying a western as you're likely to see.

Fred MacMurray *Jim Hawkins* • Jack Oakie *Wahoo Jones* • Jean Parker *Amanda Bailey* • Lloyd Nolan *Sam Mcgee* • Edward Ellis *Major Bailey* • Bennie Bartlett *David* • Frank Shannon *Captain Stafford* ■ *Dir* King Vidor • *Scr* Louis Stevens, from a story by King Vidor, Elizabeth Hill Vidor, from the book by Walter Prescott Webb

Texas Rangers Ride Again ★★ U
Western
1940 · US · BW · 68mins

A misfiring sequel to director King Vidor's rollicking *Texas Rangers*, with a dull John Howard, best remembered as Bulldog Drummond, and a ludicrously over-the-top Akim Tamiroff (poor substitutes for Fred MacMurray and Jack Oakie in the original). Still, Ellen Drew as the feisty heroine, Robert Ryan (early in his career) and May Robson (near the end of hers) make this worth a look, despite the contemporary setting and James Hogan's routine direction.

Ellen Drew *Ellen "Slats" Dangerfield* • John Howard (1) *Jim Kingston* • Akim Tamiroff *Mio Pio* • May Robson *Cecilia Dangerfield* • Broderick Crawford *Mace Townsley* • Charley

Texas Terror ★★ U
Western
1935 · US · BW · 50mins

In the mid-thirties, John Wayne was busy releasing a string of movies, many of them B westerns that were made for producer Paul Malvern at Monogram Pictures, a poverty row outfit known for such westerns and the Bowery Boys series. Wayne was their workhorse and *Texas Terror* sticks to the formula, with Lucile Brown, plus his regular collaborator in these movies, famed stuntman Yakima Canutt, who later co-directed the chariot race in the remake of *Ben-Hur*, and an actor named Buffalo Bill Jr – he was not related to William Cody at all. The surprising thing is that these B westerns, none more than 70 minutes, were released as single features in Arizona, New Mexico and Texas where they made huge profits, because few of the major studios at the time were producing western features in any numbers. ▭

John Wayne *John Higgins* • Lucile Brown *Beth Matthews* • Leroy Mason *Joe Dickson* • George Hayes [George "Gabby" Hayes] *Sheriff Williams* • Buffalo Bill Jr *Blackie* ■ *Dir/Scr* Robert N Bradbury

Texasville ★ 15
Comedy drama
1990 · US · Colour · 120mins

The Last Picture Show was one of the icon movies of early seventies America, and its director Peter Bogdanovich was inevitably going to be drawn to novelist Larry McMurtry's 1987 sequel. The book was disappointing, but no one could have envisaged that the film version was going to be so mind-numbingly bad. The out-of-form Bogdanovich simply tries too hard, spending the first part of the picture debunking the original and longing despairingly for past glories in the cloying closing stages. The members of the cast were either too polite to say anything or, heaven forbid, having fun. ▭

Jeff Bridges *Duane Jackson* • Cybill Shepherd *Jacy Farrow* • Annie Potts *Karla Jackson* • Timothy Bottoms *Sonny Crawford* • Cloris Leachman *Ruth Popper* • Randy Quaid *Lester Marlow* • Eileen Brennan *Genevieve* ■ *Dir* Peter Bogdanovich • *Scr* Peter Bogdanovich, from the novel by Larry McMurtry

Thank God He Met Lizzie ★★★ 15
Romantic comedy
1997 · Ausl · Colour · 86mins

This quirky Australian comedy, starring a pre-*Elizabeth* Cate Blanchett, is no skeleton in the closet. Instead, it's a charming, amusingly eccentric affair, which tracks the romantic dilemmas of loner Richard Roxburgh (who co-starred with Blanchett in *Oscar and Lucinda*), who has last-minute reservations on the day of his wedding to Blanchett. There's good work, too, from Frances O'Connor, now better known for her role in *Madame Bovary*. ▭

Richard Roxburgh *Guy Jamieson* • Cate Blanchett *Lizzie O'Hara* • Frances O'Connor *Jenny Follett* • Linden Wilkinson *Poppy O'Hara*

• John Gaden *Dr O'Hara* • Genevieve Mooy *Mrs Jamieson* • Michael Ross *Mr Jamieson* ■ *Dir* Cherie Nowlan • *Scr* Alexandra Long

Thank God It's Friday ★★★ 15
Musical
1978 · US · Colour · 85mins

Here's what disco was really like circa 1978. The flipside of *Saturday Night Fever*, director Robert Klane's exploitative movie doesn't carry any message as it focuses on different people assembling at the Zoo disco in Hollywood for that pop movie staple – a dance contest. But using a non-stop soundtrack of disco hits, it expertly communicates the exciting, buzzy, hip and happening atmosphere of seventies clubland. More fun than it pretends to be, Jeff Goldblum and Debra Winger make early movie appearances as disco queen Donna Summer belts out the Oscar-winning song *Last Dance*. Contains swearing. ▭

Donna Summer *Nicole Sims* • Valerie Landsburg *Frannie* • Terri Nunn *Jeannie* • Chick Vennera *Marv Gomez* • Ray Vitte *Bobby Speed* • Mark Lonow *Dave* • Andrea Howard *Sue* • Jeff Goldblum *Tony* • Robin Menken *Maddy* • Debra Winger *Jennifer* ■ *Dir* Robert Klane • *Scr* Barry Armyan Bernstein

Thank You and Good Night! ★★★
Documentary
1991 · US · Colour · 85mins

Moving documentary, about the physical decline and ultimate death of film-maker Jan Oxenberg's Jewish grandmother, Mae Joffe. This isn't just a conventional documentary though, as Oxenberg experiments freely with various styles and techniques, from using cut-out characters to home movie and outright fantasy sequences. Apart from the loss of a grandparent, there's a wider message here about family relationships and dealing with illness and bereavement. But the various elements combine beautifully in an offbeat movie, that's also tenderhearted and touching.

Dir/Scr Jan Oxenberg

Thank You, Jeeves ★★
Comedy
1936 · UK · BW · 57mins

Jeeves and Wooster have been firm favourites with readers and TV audiences for many years, but their antics have yet to be brought to the big screen with any degree of success. There is only the faintest echo of the Wodehouse wit and brio in this silly story about industrial espionage and gunrunning. Arthur Greville Collins's well-meaning adaptation has the fortune to have Arthur Treacher as the fish-eating valet for whom no crisis is insurmountable, but David Niven (in his first Hollywood starring role) is far too suave and knowing to convince as that prize ass, Bertie Wooster.

David Niven *Bertie Wooster* • Arthur Treacher *Jeeves* • Virginia Field *Marjorie Lowman* • Lester Matthews *Elliott Manville* • Colin Tapley *Tom Brock* • John Graham Spacey *Jack Stone* ■ *Dir* Arthur Greville Collins • *Scr* Joseph Hoffman, Stephen Gross, from the story by PG Wodehouse

Thank You, Mr Moto ★★★

Crime mystery   1937 · US · BW · 66mins

The second series entry featuring Peter Lorre as John P Marquand's Japanese sleuth, is perhaps the least tangled and most enjoyable, although the atmosphere is surprisingly sinister for a B-movie. The picture opens with Moto, disguised as a Gobi nomad, trying to infiltrate a gang preying on the desert's ancient treasure troves. The clues bring him into contact with a Chinese prince, his overprotective mother and some ruthless gangsters, determined to collect the seven scrolls that will lead them to the treasure of Genghis Khan. Lorre bustles around to good effect, and John Carradine is excellent as a shady antiques dealer.

Peter Lorre *Mr Moto* • Thomas Beck *Tom Nelson* • Pauline Frederick *Madame Chung* • Jayne Regan *Eleanor Joyce* • Sidney Blackmer *Eric Koerger* • Sig Rumann [Sig Ruman] *Colonel Tchernov* • John Carradine *Pereira* ■ *Dir* Norman Foster • *Scr* Norman Foster, Willis Cooper, from a story by John P Marquand

Thank Your Lucky Stars ★★★★ Ⓤ

Musical   1943 · US · BW · 122mins

One of the most enjoyable of Hollywood's patriotic, star-studded wartime concoctions, is a joy from start to finish, as Eddie Cantor takes us on a magic carpet ride through show-biz land. Here are unlikely and delightful songbirds Errol Flynn and Bette Davis singing, respectively, *That's What You Jolly Well Get* and *They're Either Too Young or Too Old*; and there's also super work from Ann Sheridan and Dinah Shore, and a particularly fine production number involving Hattie McDaniel. Watch also for tough palookas John Garfield and Humphrey Bogart sending themselves up. It's virtually plotless, so wherever you join it you'll have a terrific time. 🎞

Eddie Cantor *Joe Sampson/Himself* • Joan Leslie *Pat Dixon* • Dennis Morgan *Tommy Randolph* • Dinah Shore • SZ Sakall *Dr Schlenna* • Edward Everett Horton *Farnsworth* ■ *Dir* David Butler • *Scr* Norman Panama, Melvin Frank, James V Kern, from a story by Everett Freeman, from a story by Arthur Schwartz

Thanks a Million ★★

Musical comedy   1935 · US · BW · 85mins

Minor, but nevertheless enjoyable, musical comedy from 20th Century-Fox, effectively a star vehicle for crooner Dick Powell, with some interesting, but now dated sideswipes at political chicanery. Radio comedian Fred Allen has some moments as the troubled wisecracking manager pushing Powell for governor, and there's splendid period music from Paul Whiteman and his band and the Yacht Club Boys. Interestingly, this was remade as *If I'm Lucky*, with Edgar Buchanan in the Fred Allen role and Carmen Miranda instead of Paul Whiteman!

Dick Powell *Eric Land* • Ann Dvorak *Sally Mason* • Fred Allen *Ned Lyman* • Patsy Kelly *Phoebe Mason* • Raymond Walburn *Hugh Culliman* • David Rubinoff *Orchestra Leader* • Benny Baker *Tammany* ■ *Dir* Roy Del Ruth • *Scr* Nunnally Johnson, from a story by Melville Crossman [Darryl F Zanuck]

Thanks for Everything ★★★

Comedy   1938 · US · BW · 70mins

Henry Smith (Haley) is an unexceptional chap who wins a radio competition to find "Mr Average American". Unscrupulous advertising men Barcourt (Menjou) and Brady (Oakie), seize the opportunity to exploit Smith using his very averageness to sell any number of items. Their plans falter however, when Smith falls in love. Fast paced satire on the advertising world benefits from the strong playing of veterans Menjou and Oakie, who shine amongst a worthy cast. Better than average fun.

Adolphe Menjou *JB Harcourt* • Jack Oakie *Brady* • Jack Haley *Henry Smith* • Arleen Whelan *Madge Raines* • Binnie Barnes *Kay Swift* ■ *Dir* William A Seiter • *Scr* Harry Tugend, Curtis Kenyon, Art Arthur, from a story by Gilbert Wright

The Thanksgiving Promise ★★

Drama   1986 · US · Colour · 90mins

The Fabulous Baker Boys brought Beau Bridges and brother Jeff together on the big screen, but this TV movie (directed by Beau) seems to feature the whole Bridges clan, including father Lloyd, mother Dorothy, and Beau's own son Jordan. It's a slightly sickly, but sweet tale of a boy who becomes rather attached to the goose he's supposed to be fattening up for Thanksgiving, so expect lots of cute close-ups of the starring goose, and some heart-wrenching (and sometimes stomach-turning) family moments.

Beau Bridges *Hank Tilby* • Millie Perkins *Lois Tilby* • Courtney Thorne-Smith *Sheryl* • Ed Lauter *Coach Gruniger* • Anne Haney *Mrs Sudsup* • Beau Dremann *Alec* • Jordan Bridges *Travis Tilby* • Lloyd Bridges *Stewart Larson* • Dorothy Dean Bridges *Aggie Larson* ■ *Dir* Beau Bridges • *Scr* Glenn L Anderson, Peter N Johnson, Blaine M Yorgason and Craig Holyoak from the novel *Chester, I Love You* by Blaine M and Brenton Yorgason

That Certain Age ★★★

Musical comedy   1938 · US · BW · 95mins

In her fourth feature, 17-year-old Deanna Durbin was allowed a boyfriend (Jackie Cooper, who was the same age), but no kiss yet. This amiable comedy, written by Billy Wilder, Charles Brackett and Bruce Manning, has Deanna temporarily neglecting Cooper while developing a crush on her parents' houseguest, man-of-the-world journalist Melvyn Douglas. She also finds time to warble six songs, ranging from Jimmy McHugh and Harold Adamson's title song to selections from Charles Gounod and Leo Delibes. Former silent film star Irene Rich plays Deanna's mother.

Deanna Durbin *Alice Fullerton* • Melvyn Douglas *Vincent Bullitt* • Jackie Cooper *Ken* • Irene Rich *Mrs Fullerton* • Nancy Carroll *Grace Bristow* • John Halliday *Mr Fullerton* • Jackie Searl [Jackie Searl] *Tony* • Charles Coleman *Stephens* • Peggy Stewart *Mary Lee* ■ *Dir* Edward Ludwig • *Scr* Bruce Manning, Billy Wilder

That Certain Feeling ★★

Comedy   1956 · US · Colour · 102mins

A romantic comedy that is neither romantic nor funny, this does at least offer the bizarre combination of George Sanders and Bob Hope competing for the favours of Sanders' fiancée, Eva Marie Saint, who happens to be Hope's ex-wife. The complications ensue when top cartoonist Sanders loses his touch and hires bumbling artist Hope to "ghost" his strip. Also involved in this inferior offering from the Melvin Frank–Norman Panama stable, is the splendid Pearl Bailey as Sanders' maid and Hope's ally.

Bob Hope *Francis X Dignan* • Eva Marie Saint *Dunreath Henry* • George Sanders *Larry Larkin* • Pearl Bailey *Gussie* • David Lewis *Joe Wickes* • Al Capp • Jerry Mathers *Norman Taylor* ■ *Dir* Norman Panama, Melvin Frank • *Scr* Norman Panama, Melvin Frank, IAL Diamond, William Altman

That Certain Woman ★★★

Melodrama   1937 · US · BW · 91mins

An example of a movie remade by its original director, this is a new version of the 1929 Gloria Swanson early talkie *The Trespasser*, with a simmering Bette Davis as the gangster's widow trying to go straight. Director Edmund Goulding has less luck with Bette than he did with Gloria in this overblown melodrama, though a young and gauche Henry Fonda does impress as a playboy, vying with lawyer Ian Hunter for Davis's affections. Despite a rather disappointing finale, this is still fun to watch today, especially for its wonderful array of Warner Bros supporting players.

Bette Davis *Mary Donnell* • Henry Fonda *Jack Merrick* • Ian Hunter *Lloyd Rogers* • Anita Louise *Flip* • Donald Crisp *Mr Merrick Sr* • Hugh O'Connell *Virgil Whitaker* • Katherine Alexander *Mrs Rogers* ■ *Dir* Edmund Goulding • *Scr* Edmund Goulding, from the film *The Trespasser* by Edmund Goulding

That Championship Season ★★★ 15

Drama   1982 · US · Colour · 104mins

Jason Miller is probably best known for his role as Father Karras in *The Exorcist* and for being the father of Jason Patric. But Miller was really a playwright who dabbled in acting, and this movie marked his sole effort as a director, adapting his own Pulitzer Prize-winning play which also won a Tony Award and the New York Drama Critics' Award in 1972. It's the story of four former basketball players and their coach, who have a reunion and engage in the sort of bonding dialogue and down home wisdom, beloved of American playwrights. Some may find it smug and a bit too wordy, but four actors barely into middle age are obviously enjoying themselves trading juicy lines with Robert Mitchum. 🎞

Bruce Dern *George Sitkowski* • Stacy Keach *James Daley* • Robert Mitchum *Coach Delaney* • Martin Sheen *Tom Daley* • Paul Sorvino *Phil Romano* • Arthur Franz *Macken* • Michael Bernosky *Jacks* • Joseph Kelly *Malley* ■ *Dir* Jason Miller • *Scr* Jason Miller, from his play

That Championship Season ★★

Drama   1999 · US · Colour · 126mins

Based on the Pulitzer prize-winning play by Jason Miller, Paul Sorvino (*Goodfellas*) headlines this lethargic TV adaptation, in which four former high school basketball stars and their coach, reunite to celebrate the anniversary of their team's state championship season, 20 years earlier. Everyone appears happy to be at the reunion, but slowly an ugly undercurrent of bigotry, suspicion, fear and jealousy begins to destroy everything that once united these basketball heroes. In spite of a stellar cast, including Gary Sinise (*Ransom*), Terry Kinney (*Sleepers*), and Vincent D'Onofrio (*Ed Wood*), this version fails to ignite, as the players never seem to get off the bench, dramatically.

Vincent D'Onofrio *Phil Romano* • Terry Kinney *James Daley* • Tony Shalhoub *Mayor George Sitkowski* • Gary Sinise *Tom Daley* • Paul Sorvino *Coach* ■ *Dir* Paul Sorvino • *Scr* Jason Miller, from his play

That Cold Day in the Park ★★★

Psychological drama   1969 · US/Can · Colour · 113mins

Early Robert Altman, with the brilliant Sandy Dennis as an emotionally disturbed spinster who becomes infatuated with a young man she meets in the park, and takes him home to live with her. But her possessive jealousy soon renders him more prisoner than partner. The main theme of this rather disturbing film is repressed sexuality, but there are also odd hints of things darker and more taboo. Altman directs with customary aplomb, a film that's a sort of switched-sex companion piece to *The Collector*.

Sandy Dennis *Frances Austen* • Michael Burns *Boy* • Susanne Benton *Nina* • Luana Anders *Sylvie* • John Garfield Jr *Nick* ■ *Dir* Robert Altman • *Scr* Gillian Freeman, from a novel by Richard Miles

That Darn Cat! ★★ Ⓤ

Comedy   1965 · US · Colour · 111mins

Lively, if overlong, Disney caper in which all the pieces slot together with ease. Yet, while it makes efficient entertainment, the film is not as much fun as it should be, bearing in mind its exceptional cast. The cat steals the show by a whisker from nosey neighbours William Demarest and Elsa Lanchester. Hayley Mills is perky enough as the cat's owner, but it's a dull role compared to those of Dean Jones as the FBI agent with a cat allergy and Roddy McDowall as a drip whose ducks are the frisky feline's favourite playmates. 🎞

Hayley Mills *Patti Randall* • Dean Jones *Zeke Kelso* • Roddy McDowall *Gregory Benson* • Dorothy Provine *Ingrid Randall* • Neville Brand *Dan* • Elsa Lanchester *Mrs MacDougall* • William Demarest *Mr MacDougall* ■ *Dir* Robert Stevenson • *Scr* Gordon Gordon, Mildred Gordon, Bill Walsh, from the novel *Undercover Cat* by Gordon Gordon, Mildred Gordon

That Darn Cat ★★ Ⓤ

Comedy   1997 · US · Colour · 85mins

Not the 1965 original, but a once-more-with feline remake which stars Christina Ricci in the role originally played by Hayley Mills. The story stays much the same as Ricci and rookie FBI agent Doug E Doug team up with the meandering moggy to pussyfoot after

some kidnappers. It's watchable enough, especially for anyone unfamiliar with original. But a lack of anything new and improved makes one wonder why Disney bothered rehashing something that wasn't a standout in the first place. There's a cameo from the original film's male lead, Dean Jones. 🎬 **DVD**

Christina Ricci *Patti* • Doug E Doug *Zeke Kelso* • Dean Jones *Mr Flint* • George Dzundza *Boetticher* • Peter Boyle *Pa* • Michael McKean *Peter Randall* • Bess Armstrong *Judy Randall* • Dyan Cannon *Mrs Flint* • John Ratzenberger *Dusty* • Estelle Parsons *Old Lady McCracken* ■ *Dir* Bob Spiers • *Scr* LA Karaszewski [Larry Karaszewski], SM Alexander [Scott Alexander], from the novel *Undercover Cat* by Mildred Gordon, Gordon Gordon, from the film *That Darn Cat!* by Bill Walsh, Mildred Gordon, Gordon Gordon

That Eye, the Sky ★★★

Fantasy drama 1994 · Ausl · Colour · 105mins

A far cry from the black comedy of *Death in Brunswick*, John Ruane's second feature is a mystical melodrama, adapted from a novel by Tim Winton. Occasionally recalling Robert Mitchum in *Night of the Hunter*, Peter Coyote gives a memorable performance as the mysterious wandering evangelist who comes to the aid of a crisis-stricken farming family, though never quite assuaging the doubts of teenager Amanda Douge. With Lisa Harrow also impressive as the tether's-end wife taken by the stranger's charm and Jamie Croft as her impressionable son, this is a film that will either enchant or infuriate.

Peter Coyote *Henry Warburton* • Lisa Harrow *Alice Flack* • Amanda Douge *Tegwyn Flack* • Jamie Croft *Ort* • Paul Sonkkila *Mr Cherry* • Louise Silversen *Mrs Cherry* ■ *Dir* John Ruane • *Scr* Jim Barton, John Ruane, from the novel by Tim Winton

That Funny Feeling ★★

Romantic comedy
1965 · US · Colour · 93mins

One of those familiar romantic comedies in which the leads continually cross each other's path before they get together. This time, pleasant performances from Bobby Darin and his real-life wife Sandra Dee distract attention from the coincidences. Dee is an aspiring actress who entertains rich publisher Darin in an apartment that she doesn't own, but works in as a maid. Unbeknown to her, it's his apartment. It sounds daft, but you've seen worse.

Sandra Dee *Joan Howell* • Bobby Darin *Tom Milford* • Donald O'Connor *Harvey Granson* • Nita Talbot *Audrey* • Larry Storch *Luther* • James Westerfield *Officer Brokaw* • Leo G Carroll *O'Shea* ■ *Dir* Richard Thorpe • *Scr* David R Schwartz, from a story by Norman Barasch, Carroll Moore

That Gang of Mine ★★★

Sports comedy 1940 · US · BW · 62mins

Another trip out with the East Side Kids, which evolved from the Bowery Boys, which was a hangover from the far more serious Dead End Kids. This time Muggs (Leo Gorcey) is trying to be a jockey of thoroughbreds, though what distinction it does have comes from being directed by Joseph H Lewis – a

cult film-maker who revs up the action a treat.

Bobby Jordan *Danny Dolan* • Leo Gorcey *Muggs Maloney* • Clarence Muse *Ben* • Dave O'Brien *Knuckles Dolan* • Joyce Bryant *Louise* • Donald Haines *Skinny* • David Gorcey *Peewee* • "Sunshine Sammy" Morrison *Scruno* ■ *Dir* Joseph H Lewis • *Scr* William Lively, from a story by Alan Whitman

That Hamilton Woman
★★★ PG

Drama 1941 · UK · BW · 124mins

"You cannot make peace with dictators," says Laurence Olivier as Lord Nelson, "You have to destroy them, wipe them out!" Audiences being bombed in London in 1941 caught the drift immediately and it was rumoured that Churchill not only urged Alexander Korda to make the film, but that he also wrote Nelson's maiden speech in the House of Lords. As propaganda, the picture is as single-minded as Olivier's later *Henry V*. But this is mainly a turgid love story, with Vivien Leigh as Lady Hamilton, whose adulterous affair with the naval hero was just as newsworthy as Napoleon's campaigns. With Leigh fresh from the success of *Gone with the Wind* and newly married to Olivier, the picture, which was made in Hollywood, reaped a mint of money. 🎬

Vivien Leigh *Emma Hart Hamilton* • Laurence Olivier *Lord Horatio Nelson* • Alan Mowbray *Sir William Hamilton* • Sara Allgood *Mrs Cadogan-Lyon* • Gladys Cooper *Lady Nelson* • Henry Wilcoxon *Captain Hardy* ■ *Dir* Alexander Korda • *Scr* Walter Reisch, RC Sherriff • *Set Designer* Vincent Korda, Julia Heron

That Kind of Woman ★★

Romantic drama 1959 · US · Colour · 94mins

Sophia Loren, the mistress of millionaire George Sanders, meets a group of GIs during a train trip and ends up spending the night with Tab Hunter, one of their number. To her, it's a one-night stand, but for him it's love eternal: he proposes marriage, thus presenting her with the conflict of choice between a fresh new life and her old one. No prizes for guessing who wins. Directed by Sidney Lumet, the movie can hardly fail to be competently made, but is actually an embarrassingly miscast and unconvincing bucketful of soap.

Sophia Loren *Kay* • Tab Hunter *Red* • George Sanders *The Man* • Barbara Nichols *Jane* • Jack Warden *Kelly* ■ *Dir* Sidney Lumet • *Scr* Walter Bernstein

That Lady ★★

Historical drama
1955 · UK · Colour · 100mins

Once mooted as a comeback vehicle for the great Garbo, it fell to an ill-cast Olivia de Havilland to portray the lusty one-eyed Princess of Eboli in this would-be spectacular 16th-century Spanish epic. Gilbert Roland is splendid, though, as de Havilland's lover, and King Philip II is played with intelligence by Paul Scofield, making his movie debut. Unfortunately, the film was among the first to be made using CinemaScope and the novelty of the process seems to have reduced director Terence Young to providing little more than a series of tableaux.

Olivia de Havilland *Ana De Mendoza, Princess Of Eboli* • Gilbert Roland *Antonio Perez* • Paul Scofield *Philip II* • Françoise Rosay *Bernadina* • Dennis Price *Mateo Vasquez* • Robert Harris *Cardinal* • Christopher Lee *Captain* ■ *Dir* Terence Young • *Scr* Anthony Veiller, Sy Bartlett, from a novel by Kate O'Brien

That Lady in Ermine ★★★ U

Musical 1948 · US · Colour · 89mins

A richly Technicolour Betty Grable fantasy musical with a genuinely mythic sense to it, remembered more today for the fact that it was, sadly, the last movie of the great Ernst Lubitsch. The director famed for the stylish wit of his "Lubitsch Touch" died after only eight days shooting and was replaced by another notable European exile, Otto Preminger. The transition was seamless, but one can't help wondering whether Preminger coarsened the original wafer-thin material, which revolves around a 19th-century European army officer billeting his men in a castle with a past. Nevertheless, the result is very entertaining, if not particularly memorable, with Douglas Fairbanks Jr and Cesar Romero immensely likeable in support.

Betty Grable *Francesca/Angelina* • Douglas Fairbanks Jr *Colonel Teglash/The Duke* • Cesar Romero *Mario* • Walter Abel *Major Horvath/benvenuto* • Reginald Gardiner *Alberto* • Harry Davenport *Luigi* ■ *Dir* Ernst Lubitsch, Otto Preminger • *Scr* Samson Raphaelson, from an operetta by Rudolph Schanzer, Ernest Welisch

That Lucky Touch ★★ PG

Romantic comedy 1975 · UK · Colour · 89mins

Roger Moore and Susannah York team up again after *Gold* and attempt to re-create something of the sexual chemistry that Rock Hudson and Doris Day cooked up a decade earlier. The setting is Brussels and a NATO war games event, with Moore as an arms dealer and York a leftie *Washington Post* journalist. It breezes along nicely, has some barbed comments about American imperialism and a federal Europe, and Moore and York are attractive and relaxed. In his final screen role, Lee J Cobb adds some much-needed class playing an American general married to Shelley Winters, who sets everyone's teeth on edge. 🎬

Roger Moore *Michael Scott* • Susannah York *Julia Richardson* • Shelley Winters *Diana Steedeman* • Lee J Cobb *General Steedeman* • Jean-Pierre Cassel *Leo* • Raf Vallone *General Peruzzi* • Sydne Rome *Sophie* • Donald Sinden *General Armstrong* ■ *Dir* Christopher Miles • *Scr* John Briley, from a idea by Moss Hart

That Man Bolt ★★ 18

Blaxploitation martial arts drama 1973 · US · Colour · 98mins

A violent action movie with Fred Williamson as martial arts specialist Jefferson Bolt, who agrees to deliver one-million dollars of syndicate money, only to find himself involvedin a catalogue of attemptson his life. Car chases, girls and acupuncture torture all figure in the escapist plot, which also weaves in Teresa Graves singing a rendition of Tom Jones's *She's a Lady*. It'sanunwieldy chop-socky story

that required two directors. One would have been enough, if he had been talented. 🎬

Fred Williamson *Jefferson Bolt* • Byron Webster *Griffiths* • Miko Mayama *Dominique* • Teresa Graves *Samantha Nightingale* • Satoshi Nakamura *Kumada* • John Orchard *Carter* ■ *Dir* Henry Levin, David Lowell Rich • *Scr* Quentin Werty, Charles Johnson

That Man from Rio ★★★★ U

Crime comedy adventure 1964 · Fr/It · Colour · 112mins

How many other James Bond spoofs received an Oscar nomination for their screenplay? Moreover, how many could call upon Jean-Paul Belmondo in this kind of form – as a French air force pilot who spends his eight-day leave traversing the Atlantic and the Brazilian mainland, in a frantic bid to rescue feisty girlfriend Françoise Dorléac from the Amazon natives intent on finding a horde of lost jungle treasure. With Philippe de Broca roaring through the set-pieces (which just get gleefully more preposterous) and exploiting every one of his exotic locations, this is hectic, hilarious and more than a match for Indiana Jones. In French with English subtitles.

Jean-Paul Belmondo *Adrien Dufourquet* • Françoise Dorléac *Agnes* • Jean Servais *Professor Catalan* • Simone Renant *Lola* • Milton Ribeiro *Tupac* • Ubiracy De Oliveira *Sir Winston* • Adolfo Celi *Senor De Castro* ■ *Dir* Philippe de Broca • *Scr* Philippe de Broca, Jean-Paul Rappeneau, Ariane Mnouchkine, Daniel Boulanger

That Man George ★★

Crime adventure 1965 · Fr/It/Sp · Colour · 90mins

French director Jacques Deray proved himself deft at underworld movie shenanigans, particularly in the splendid 1970 film *Borsalino*. Known in America as *That Man George!*, this is the type of colourful thriller that kept international audiences entertained throughout the sixties, but generally didn't play too well in English-speaking territories owing to wholesale dubbing of the bulk of the cast. American lead George Hamilton lets his tan do the acting as he romances Claudine Auger, the lovely Bond girl from *Thunderball*, and combats assorted other villains as he takes a shipment of gold bullion across Morocco. Mindless, fast-moving and uninvolving, although there's a nice twist at the end. French dialogue dubbed into English..

George Hamilton *George* • Claudine Auger *Lila* • Alberto de Mendoza *Travis* • Daniel Ivernel *Vibert* • Tiberio Murgia *Jose* ■ *Dir* Jacques Deray • *Scr* Henri Lanoë, Jose Giovanni, Suzanne Arduini, Jacques Deray, from the novel *The Heisters* by Robert Page Jones

That Midnight Kiss ★★★ U

Romantic musical
1949 · US · Colour · 97mins

Not the best of MGM's musicals, but noteworthy as the feature debut of Mario Lanza, the star who brought opera to the movies and became the first tenor since Caruso to achieve massive worldwide popularity. This is virtually his biography, as Philadelphia opera patroness Ethel Barrymore has problems with the male lead of daughter Kathryn Grayson's stage debut, then Grayson discovers that local truck driver Lanza can more than hold his own with an aria. Glossy nonsense, helped along by co-stars Keenan Wynn and the wonderful Jules Munshin. Director Norman Taurog later worked regularly with a great fan of Lanza, Elvis Presley.

Kathryn Grayson *Prudence Budell* • José Iturbi *Himself* • Ethel Barrymore *Abigail Budell* • Mario Lanza *Johnny Donnetti* • Keenan Wynn *Artie Glenson* • J Carrol Naish *Papa Donnetti* • Jules Munshin *Michael Pemberton* • Thomas Gomez *Guido Betelli* ■ *Dir* Norman Taurog • *Scr* Bruce Manning, Tamara Hovey

That Night ★★★ 🔟

Drama
1992 · US/Jap/Ger/Fr · Colour · 85mins

An affectionate portrait of adolescent nostalgia from first-time director Craig Bolotin, previously best known as the co-writer of Ridley Scott's *Black Rain*. The setting is the uneventful Long Island suburbia of the early sixties, where impressionable youngster Eliza Dushku becomes the fascinated witness to a generation-gap battle between her neighbours – daughter Juliette Lewis and mum Helen Shaver. The story is very slight, but the young Dushku is a revelation, and Lewis and C Thomas Howell, Lewis's unsuitable beau, also deliver convincing performances. Contains swearing and sexual references.

C Thomas Howell *Rick* • Juliette Lewis *Sheryl* • Helen Shaver *Ann* • Eliza Dushku *Alice Bloom* • John Dossett *Larry Bloom* • J Smith-Cameron *Carol Bloom* • Katherine Heigl *Kathryn* ■ *Dir* Craig Bolotin • *Scr* Craig Bolotin, Alice McDermott

That Night in Rio ★★★

Musical comedy 1941 · US · Colour · 90mins

''I-yi-yi-yi-yi I like you vairy much'' sings Carmen Miranda in, arguably, her greatest screen musical. This remake of *Folies Bergère*, later itself remade as *On the Riviera* (20th Century-Fox was renowned for recycling it's plots) is really a vehicle for Don Ameche, in a dual role, and Alice Faye. But, from the opening, it's Miranda who runs away with the film. Whether chanting *Chica Chica Boom Chic* or romancing Ameche, she's the bee's knees. By the way, if you're lusting for Rio, this movie never leaves the back lot.

Alice Faye *Baroness Cecilia Duarte* • Don Ameche *Larry Martin/Baron Duarte* • Carmen Miranda *Carmen* • SZ Sakall *Arthur Penna* • J Carrol Naish *Machado* • Curt Bois *Felicio Salles* • Leonid Kinskey *Pierre Dufont* • Frank Puglia *Pedro, the valet* • Maria Montez *Inez* ■ *Dir* Irving Cummings • *Scr* George Seaton, Bess Meredyth, Hal Long, Samuel Hoffenstein, Jessie Ernst, from a play by Rudolph Lothar, Hans Adler

That Obscure Object of Desire ★★★★★ 🔞

Drama 1977 · Fr/Sp · Colour · 99mins

Luis Buñuel's final film, is a fitting end to a dazzling career. A witty, ironic and barbed morality tale, it follows the increasingly desperate attempts of wealthy businessman Fernando Rey to seduce his maid, unaware that his world is collapsing around his ears. Buñuel only hit upon the intriguing idea of casting two actresses in the role of Conchita after Maria Schneider walked

off the set, but it proved to be a creative masterstroke, as the switches between Carole Bouquet and Angela Molina teasingly suggest the indecision in Rey's mind as he searches for the elusive woman of his dreams. In French with English subtitles. 🎬

Fernando Rey *Mathieu* • Carole Bouquet *Conchita* • Julien Bertheau *Edouard/ d'Oleargues* • André Weber *Martin* • Piéral [Pierre Piéral] *Psychology professor* • Bernard Musson *Police inspector* ■ *Dir* Luis Buñuel • *Scr* Luis Buñuel, Jean-Claude Carrière, from the novel *La Femme et le Pantin* by Pierre Loüys

That Old Feeling ★ 🔟

Romantic comedy
1997 · US · Colour · 100mins

More schmaltz than the average person can stomach. Bette Midler and Dennis Farina play feuding divorcees, meeting up at their daughter's wedding to a politician who trades on his squeaky clean image. It's not too long before they realise they still fancy each other. Alhough there's a nice quick-fire repartee between Midler and Farina, they aren't exactly in the Astaire and Rogers class when it comes to bickering. You'll probably be able to guess the outcome five minutes into the proceedings. One to watch out the corner of one eye only. Contains sexual references and swearing. 🎬

Bette Midler *Lilly Leonard* • Dennis Farina *Dan De Mora* • Paula Marshall *Molly De Mora* • Gail O'Grady *Rowena* • David Rasche *Alan* • Jamie Denton *Keith Marks* • Danny Nucci *Joey Donna* ■ *Dir* Carl Reiner • *Scr* Leslie Dixon

That Riviera Touch ★★ 🔞

Comedy 1966 · UK · Colour · 93mins

Sacked from a chocolate factory, Morecambe and Wise head for the south of France in what starts out looking like a customised remake of the old Laurel and Hardy comedy *Saps at Sea*. But Eric and Ernie's regular writers, Sid Green and Dick Hills, quickly run into the problem that blighted all three of their movies; the pair's relaxed, intimate style might have been perfect for the sketch format of their TV show, but it was totally wrong for sustaining narratives. Jewel heists, speed-boat chases and a cliffhanging finale are all there, but there aren't many laughs. 🎬

Eric Morecambe *Eric* • Ernie Wise *Ernie* • Suzanne Lloyd *Claudette* • Paul Stassino *Le Pirate* • Armand Mestral *Inspector Duval* ■ *Dir* Cliff Owen • *Scr* Sidney C Green, Richard M Hills, Peter Blackmore

That Secret Sunday ★★ 🔞

Crime drama 1986 · US · Colour · 89mins

James Farantino stars as an investigative reporter in this moody TV film about police corruption, in which an apparent serial-killing victim may actually have died in a shady incident involving some undercover cops. Farantino does an admirable job as the journalist who leads an eager group of young associates in his risky business. But, at the end of the day, there's nothing particularly special about this crime story, whose good intentions don't justify what amounts to a rather manipulative melodrama. 🎬

James Farentino *Gerald Remson* • Parker Stevenson *Scott Dennis* • Daphne Ashbrook *Collie Sherwood* • William Lucking *Detective Bernie Hodges* • Michael Lerner *Mario Pinelli* ■ *Dir* Richard Colla [Richard A Colla] • *Scr* Al Martinez, Philip Saltzman

That Sinking Feeling ★★★ 🅿🅶

Drama 1979 · UK · Colour · 85mins

Scottish cinema has certainly come a long way since Bill Forsyth made his directorial debut with this thin, but still enjoyable, comedy. Can you imagine these teenagers inhabiting the world of *Trainspotting*? This established the Forsyth style: underplayed humour and seemingly irrelevant gags, with a subtle pay-off and the quirky use of the local idiom. The theft of a consignment of sinks is planned with the intricacy of a *Rififi*-like heist, but, as in so many caper movies, it just couldn't go smoothly. Many of the cast, who were then members of the Glasgow Youth Theatre, would return in *Gregory's Girl*. 🎬

Robert Buchanan *Ronnie* • John Hughes *Vic* • Billy Greenlees *Wal* • Douglas Sannachan *Simmy* • Alan Love *Alec* • Danny Benson *Policeman* • Eddie Burt *Van Driver* • Tom Mannion *Doctor* • Eric Joseph *The Wee Man* • Gordon John Sinclair [John Gordon-Sinclair] *Andy* ■ *Dir/Scr* Bill Forsyth

That Summer of White Roses ★★ 🔞

Drama 1989 · UK/Yug · Colour · 98mins

Set in 1944 in a Yugoslavian backwater miraculously untouched by the ravages of the Second World War, Rajko Grlic's drama rapidly becomes muddled and unfocused as simple-minded lifeguard Tom Conti marries widow Susan George to shield her from the Nazis. There is a warmth here that touches the heart, even if it doesn't engage the mind. If the movie misses out on the tragedy of the idea, it still arouses compassion. Contains swearing. 🎬

Tom Conti *Andrija Gavrilovic* • Susan George *Ana* • Rod Steiger *Martin* • Nitzan Sharron *Danny* • Alun Armstrong *Zemba* • John Gill *Doctor* • John Sharp *Mayor* ■ *Dir* Rajko Grlic • *Scr* Borislav Pekic, Kajko Grlic, Simon MacCorkindale, from the novel *Defense and the Last Days* by Borislav Pekic

That Thing You Do! ★★★★ 🅿🅶

Musical comedy 1996 · US · Colour · 103mins

Tom Hanks's directorial debut is an immensely likeable pop fable about the meteoric rise and fall of the Wonders, an all-American small-town mythical rock 'n' roll band. Set in a period-perfect 1964, and featuring a marvellously evocative soundtrack of cod-Golden Oldies, Hanks deliberately emphasises the *Forrest Gump*-style feelgood nostalgia, rather than making any hard-hitting statement about the price of fame. Hanks also plays the group's opportunistic manager, but it's sweet-natured Tom Everett Scott who registers strongest as the drumming driving force behind the aspiring Beatles, with Liv Tyler equally affecting as the band mascot. 🎬

Tom Everett Scott *Guy Patterson* • Liv Tyler *Faye* • Johnathon Schaech *Jimmy* • Steve Zahn *Lenny* • Ethan Embry *The Bass Player* • Tom Hanks *Mr White* • Charlize Theron *Tina* • Chris Isaak *Uncle Bob* • Kevin Pollak *Boss Vic Koss* ■ *Dir/Scr* Tom Hanks

That Touch of Mink ★★★ 🅄

Romantic comedy
1962 · US · Colour · 94mins

A very popular Doris Day vehicle from her post-*Pillow Talk* second coming, in which she co-stars with Cary Grant. The movie only works if you accept that Day won't sleep with Grant, which might have made sense back in 1962 (the year before the Beatles) but hardly makes any sense at all now: after all, these are two of the best-looking and most sophisticated people in the world. But that's the plot – will she or won't she, and we know she won't. This is quintessential Day fluff, complete with quite unnecessary heavily-gauzed close-ups, and Grant can barely disguise the fact that he's getting a little too long in the tooth for such foolishness. Still, there's much charm, and if you accept the premise, this is a lot of fun. 🎬

Cary Grant *Philip Shayne* • Doris Day *Cathy Timberlake* • Gig Young *Roger* • Audrey Meadows *Connie* • Alan Hewitt *Dr Gruber* • John Astin *Beasley* • John McKee *Collins, chauffeur* ■ *Dir* Delbert Mann • *Scr* Stanley Shapiro, Nate Monaster

That Uncertain Feeling ★★★

Romantic comedy 1941 · US · BW · 81mins

Ernst Lubitsch directed this remake of *Kiss Me Again* (1925), one of his best silent pictures, with that uncertain touch. Something was lost when sound was added, although the screenplay crackled wittily for the first quarter of the picture – based on a French boudoir comedy – afterwards it becomes ever sillier and more desperate. Still, Lubitsch was able to ring some clever comic changes out of the central triangle theme. Merle Oberon gets recurring hiccups after six years of marriage to insurance salesman Melvyn Douglas, and her psychiatrist diagnoses marriage trouble. She then has a brief flirtation with Burgess Meredith, as another patient who claims to be the greatest pianist in the world. The latter has the best zany moments in the film.

Merle Oberon *Jill Baker* • Melvyn Douglas *Larry Baker* • Burgess Meredith *Alexander Sebastian* • Alan Mowbray *Dr Vengard* • Olive Blakeney *Margie* • Harry Davenport *Jones* • Eve Arden *Sally Aikens* ■ *Dir* Ernst Lubitsch • *Scr* Donald Ogden Stewart, Walter Reisch, from the play *Divorçons* by Victorien Sardou, Emile de Najac

That Was Then... This Is Now ★★★ 🔞

Drama 1985 · US · Colour · 97mins

Emilio Estevez's directorial career has been largely undistinguished (*Wisdom*, *Men at Work*), but when he scripted this respectful adaptation of the SE Hinton novel, it seemed he might well have a career behind as well as in front of the camera. He and Craig Sheffer take the roles of two troubled adolescents whose friendship is threatened when romance rears its head. Estevez's screenplay is faithful to its source and, although it is a little downbeat, it remains a moving drama

🅄 = SUITABLE FOR ALL   🅄c = SUITABLE FOR ALL, ESPECIALLY FOR YOUNG CHILDREN (VIDEO ONLY)   🅿🅶 = PARENTAL GUIDANCE

about the traumas of growing up. The strong supporting cast includes Kim Delaney and, in a small role, Morgan Freeman. Contains swearing and violence. ▣

Emilio Estevez *Mark Jennings* • Craig Sheffer *Bryon Douglas* • Kim Delaney *Cathy Carlson* • Jill Schoelen *Angela Shepard* • Barbara Babcock *Mrs Douglas* • Frank Howard *"M & M/Carlson* • Frank McCarthy *Mr Carlson* • Larry B Scott *Terry Jones* • Morgan Freeman *Charlie Woods* ■ *Dir* Christopher Cain • *Scr* Emilio Estevez, from the novel

That Woman Opposite ★★
Murder mystery   1957 · UK · BW · 83mins

Don't expect too much of this modest film, based on John Dickson Carr's thriller *The Emperor's Snuffbox*, and you'll be agreeably entertained by an efficiently directed work graced by many recognisable faces. The setting is a small French town where an English antique dealer is found murdered. An inconsequential plot of intrigue and romance follows, as a private detective (Dan O'Herlihy) attempts to solve the mystery. American actress Phyllis Kirk was imported to play the romantic lead, although Petula Clark, William Franklin and Wilfred Hyde White will be more familiar to British audiences.

Phyllis Kirk *Eve* • Dan O'Herlihy *Dermot Kinross* • Wilfrid Hyde White *Sir Maurice Lawes* • Petula Clark *Janice* • Jack Watling *Toby* • William Franklyn *Ned* ■ *Dir* Compton Bennett • *Scr* Compton Bennett, from the novel *The Emperor's Snuffbox* by John Dickson Carr

That Wonderful Urge ★★★
Comedy   1948 · US · BW · 81mins

Tyrone Power is a cocky and insistent reporter who ridicules heiress Gene Tierney. To get her own back, she declares to the world that he has married her for money. The plot was familiar to those who remembered the earlier version called *Love Is News* (1937). Although suitably witty and slick, the remake is less good, mainly because Power, reprising his role, was more palatable at 24 than at 35, Loretta Young was more lively in the role of the heiress than Tierney, and had a far better supporting cast.

Tyrone Power *Thomas Jefferson Tyler* • Gene Tierney *Sara Farley* • Reginald Gardiner *Count Andre de Guyon* • Arleen Whelan *Jessica Woods* • Lucile Watson *Aunt Cornelia* • Gene Lockhart *Judge* • Lloyd Gough *Duffy* • Porter Hall *Attorney Ketchell* ■ *Dir* Robert B Sinclair • *Scr* Jay Dratler, from the story *Love Is News* by William R Lipman, Frederick Stephani

That'll Be the Day ★★★ 🔞
Musical drama   1973 · UK · Colour · 87mins

Now there's one to have the critics at each other's throats. In the blue corner, those who consider this dose of rock 'n' roll to be a nostalgic delight, while in the red we have those who think it's a glam sham, viewing the fifties through glitter-tinted spectacles. No matter where your sympathies lie, it's hard to avoid the fact that the film is beginning to show its age, but David Essex brings a certain swagger to the character of Jim MacLaine, while Ringo Starr and Billy Fury score in key cameos. Contains swearing. ▣

David Essex *Jim MacLaine* • Ringo Starr *Mike* • Rosemary Leach *Mrs MacLaine* • James Booth *Mr MacLaine* • Billy Fury *Stormy Tempest* • Keith Moon *JD Clover* • Rosalind Ayres *Jeanette* • Robert Lindsay *Terry Sutcliffe* ■ *Dir* Claude Whatham • *Scr* Ray Connolly

That's Carry On ★★★ 🅿🅶
Comedy compilation   1977 · UK · Colour and BW · 91mins

You can almost guarantee that your favourite *Carry On* clip will be missing from this compilation, which sticks to all the obvious moments that had already been aired on the TV "best of" series. Kenneth Williams and Barbara Windsor shot a few linking scenes that contain some of the biggest laughs, but there's more than a ring of truth in Williams's contention that the later films scripted by Talbot Rothwell were overly dependent on smut and lacked the sharpness of his earlier efforts. With a little more imagination and discrimination, this could have been a cracking collection, but it's still well worth a watch. ▣

Kenneth Williams • Barbara Windsor ■ *Dir* Gerald Thomas • *Scr* Tony Church

That's Dancing! ★★★★ 🅤
Dance compilation   1985 · US · Colour and BW · 100mins

Top-of-the-range tappers are featured in this all-dancing spectacular from Jack Haley Jr, who also made the *That's Entertainment!* films. And exhilarating fun it is, too, featuring not just tap-dancing, but many other forms of dance, from early Busby Berkeley extravaganzas to Michael Jackson, via ballet and acrobatics. Like those earlier compilation films, the movie is essentially the best bits of numerous musicals, but within the limitations of the format, it's highly enjoyable. Unlike *That's Entertainment!*, it doesn't rely exclusively on the MGM archives, so look out for Fred Astaire and Ginger Rogers, who made their thirties films with RKO. A splendid array of Hollywood talent. ▣

Dir/Scr Jack Haley Jr

That's Entertainment! ★★★★★ 🅤
Compilation   1974 · US · BW and Colour · 122mins

A lovingly assembled MGM compilation of its greatest triumphs, in a field that it had made its own: the musical. Here, wittily discussed and cleverly edited, are some of the Crown Jewels of Hollywood, linked by a superb cast of comperes, including Frank Sinatra, Elizabeth Taylor and Liza Minnelli, whose tribute to her mother Judy Garland is both exquisite and moving. This is entertainment on a grand scale, the snippets making you ache to see the originals. Two sequels followed, but this was the great forerunner, and a big box-office hit. ▣

Dir Jack Haley Jr

That's Entertainment, Part II ★★★★ 🅤
Compilation   1976 · US · Colour and BW · 123mins

The first film was a hard act to follow, but director Gene Kelly's sequel is satisfying and includes a memorable sequence of new material featuring the ageing Kelly dancing again with the great Fred Astaire. There's also a witty Saul Bass title sequence: watch how the graphics mirror the artists' names. Although this MGM compilation is not as powerful as its unique predecessor, for those unfamiliar with the output of the greatest studio of them all it is mandatory viewing. For others, it's a chance to recapture the lovely golden glow that watching an MGM musical can bring. ▣

Gene Kelly • Fred Astaire ■ *Dir* Gene Kelly

That's Entertainment! III ★★★★ 🅤
Compilation   1994 · US · Colour and BW · 108mins

There may be the suspicion that MGM was scraping the barrel for this third compilation from its vaults, but it's a gold plated barrel! It also provides an answer for all those who thought the 1946 musical comedy *The Harvey Girls* lacked a third act number – it's here, as Judy Garland belts out *March of the Dogies*, in a restored and remixed version. Another highlight is Garland performing Irving Berlin's *Mr Monotony*, which was cut from 1948's *Easter Parade*. There's much more, including some sentimental reminiscing from the great names of the era, and a last, sad, sight of the great Gene Kelly. Mickey Rooney doesn't look at his best, either, but Debbie Reynolds and Ann Miller still display all the qualities that made them such shining stars. Beautifully assembled and immaculately edited. ▣

Dir Bud Friedgen, Michael J Sheridan

That's Life ★★★ 🔞
Comedy drama   1986 · US · Colour · 101mins

Failing to realise that smug, affluent Californians are of interest mainly to themselves, Blake Edwards invites us to share in their every tiny worry, their every waking moment. Stepping into the shoes of another mid-life neurotic, Jack Lemmon succeeds in making him both sympathetic and irksome. Meanwhile his introspection has blinded him to the more pressing needs of his wife (Julie Andrews). Shot in the Malibu home of director Edwards and his real-life wife Andrews, the cast includes members of their family as well as appearances from Lemmon's wife Felicia Farr and son Chris. ▣

Jack Lemmon *Harvey Fairchild* • Julie Andrews *Gillian Fairchild* • Sally Kellerman *Holly Parrish* • Robert Loggia *Father Baragone* • Jennifer Edwards *Megan Fairchild Bartlet* • Chris Lemmon *Josh Fairchild* • Felicia Farr *Madame Carrie* ■ *Dir* Blake Edwards • *Scr* Milton Wexler, Blake Edwards

That's My Boy ★★ 🅤
Comedy   1951 · US · BW · 98mins

A college football caper redesigned as a vehicle for Dean Martin and Jerry Lewis. Lewis is the son of a wealthy college alumnus father, who wants his unathletic student son to play for his own old football team, and hires fellow-student and pigskin star Martin to train him. After the requisite number of struggles, Jerry triumphs by scoring the winning goal in the climactic game of the season. The movie, sparse on laughs, is even less amusing to those with no understanding of the intricacies of American football.

Dean Martin *Bill Baker* • Jerry Lewis *"Junior" Jackson* • Ruth Hussey *Ann Jackson* • Eddie Mayehoff *"Jarring Jack" Jackson* • Marion Marshall *Terry Howard* • Polly Bergen *Betty Hunter* • Hugh Sanders *Coach Wheeler* • John McIntire *Benjamin Green* ■ *Dir* Hal Walker • *Scr* Cy Howard, from his story

That's Right – You're Wrong ★★★ 🅤
Musical comedy   1939 · US · Colour · 94mins

The first – and best – of an increasingly inane series of comedy musicals starring popular radio bandleader Kay Kyser. Here, Kyser makes his screen debut with his musicians and his nonsensical "Kollege of Musical Knowledge" quiz. The plot involves a reluctant Kyser being lured to Hollywood, where producer Adolphe Menjou is under orders to star him in a hit. Chaos and confusion ensue when the scriptwriters, confronted with the nondescript, bespectacled Kyser, are unable to come up with a plot. Directed by David Butler, this is a mix of childish rubbish with a nice spoof on Hollywood studio execs and methods.

Kay Kyser *With Kay Kyser*, Adolphe Menjou, Lucille Ball and May Robson. Kay • Adolphe Menjou *Delmore* • Lucille Ball *Sandra Sand* • May Robson *Grandma* • Dennis O'Keefe *Chuck Deems* ■ *Dir* David Butler • *Scr* William Conselmann, James V Kern, from a story by David Butler, William Conselmann

That's Your Funeral ★
Comedy   1972 · UK · Colour · 81mins

In all its long years, the Hammer House of Horror never churned out anything as gruesome as this abysmal comedy. The original TV sitcom only ran for one six-part series, so why anyone thought it was worth making a feature version is beyond comprehension. Bill Fraser sledgehammers his way through gags that should have been allowed to rest in peace years ago, while even the usually reliable Raymond Huntley struggles to raise a smile. The plot was dead on its feet when Laurel and Hardy used it in 1942's *A-Haunting We Will Go*, but at least they spared us the embarrassing hearse chase. Contains swearing and drug abuse.

Bill Fraser *Basil Bulstrode* • Raymond Huntley *Emanuel Holroyd* • David Battley *Percy* • John Ronane *Mr Smallbody* • Sue Lloyd *Miss Peach* • Dennis Price *Mr Soul* • Roy Kinnear *Mr Purvis* ■ *Dir* John Robins • *Scr* Peter Lewis

Theatre of Blood ★★★★
Horror   1973 · UK · Colour · 102mins

The magnum opus of Vincent Price's film career, this stylish, witty comedy horror boasts an irresistible premise, an inspired ensemble cast, fabulous

music and first-rate production values. In a part he was born to play, Price is classically trained actor Edward Lionheart, who murders theatre critics using famous death scenes from Shakespeare's plays as payback for being dismissive of his talents. Aided by his faithful daughter Edwina (Diana Rigg) and a group of tramps, Lionheart plans each killing with elaborate inventiveness and cunning disguise. Price does a superior job portraying an inferior actor and mines every nuance of tragedy and comedy with triumphant brilliance and delicious gusto. Enormously enjoyable.

Vincent Price *Edward Lionheart* • Diana Rigg *Edwina Lionheart* • Ian Hendry *Peregrine Devlin* • Harry Andrews *Trevor Dickman* • Coral Browne *Chloe Moon* • Robert Coote *Oliver Larding* • Jack Hawkins *Solomon Psaltery* • Michael Hordern *George Maxwell* • Arthur Lowe *Horace Sprout* • Robert Morley *Meredith Merridrew* • Dennis Price *Hector Snipe* ■ *Dir* Douglas Hickox • *Scr* Anthony Greville-Bell

Theatre of Death ★★★

Horror   1966 · UK · Colour · 89mins

Is Christopher Lee, the obsessive director of a *Grand Guignol* theatre, responsible for a series of vampire-like killings terrorising Paris? It's fearful fun finding out in this odd horror whodunit (shot at the old Lyric in London), played out against a neatly realised backdrop of fake gore, backstage seediness and macabre motives. Long revered by Lee cultists as a showcase for one of the actor's best performances, this baroque, moody, murder mystery also features a rare screen role for thirties musical comedy star Evelyn Laye, and is impressively photographed by Gilbert Taylor who later worked on *Star Wars*.

Christopher Lee *Philippe Darvas* • Lelia Goldoni *Dani Cirreaux* • Julian Glover *Charles Marquis* • Evelyn Laye *Madame Angele* • Jenny Till *Nicole Chapel* ■ *Dir* Samuel Gallu • *Scr* Ellis Kadison, Roger Marshall, from a story by Ellis Kadison

The Theft of the Mona Lisa ★★

Romantic comedy
1965 · Fr/It · Colour · 98mins

Coming between *Is Paris Burning?* and *The Young Girls of Rochefort*, this was the second of three films that George Chakiris made in France in the mid-sixties. It's a humdrum period caper movie that has none of the ingenuity or intensity of *Rififi* and even less of the bravura that made the gallery sequences in the remake of *The Thomas Crown Affair* so entertaining. However, it does have the advantage of being based on a true story, as Leonardo's masterpiece was lifted from the Louvre in 1911 and not returned for two years. French dialogue dubbed into English.

George Chakiris *Vincent* • Marina Vlady *Nicole* • Jean Lefebvre *Guard* • Margaret Lee *Titina* • Paul Frankeur *Boss* ■ *Dir* Michel Deville

Their First Mistake ★★★★ U

Comedy   1932 · US · BW · 20mins

Brilliant Laurel and Hardy short, featuring a non-stop array of gags around the subject of the boys and a baby. Ollie's wife is angry that he spends so little time with her and so much time with Stan. The boys come to the conclusion that if she had a baby, she wouldn't have time to harangue Ollie. So they adopt a child, only to find, when they return home, that the wife has left, leaving the lads holding the baby. Terrific stuff.

Stan Laurel *Stan* • Oliver Hardy *Ollie* • Mae Busch *Mrs Arabella Hardy* • Billy Gilbert *Process server* • George Marshall *Neighbour* ■ *Dir/Scr* George Marshall

Thelma & Louise ★★★★★ 15

Drama   1991 · US · Colour · 124mins

Oscar-winning scriptwriter Callie Khourie puts women in the driver's seat when Geena Davis and Susan Sarandon are two friends who go on a weekend spree to escape from the boredom of their small-town routines and the dissatisfaction with their respective relationships. On their first night of freedom, Louise (Sarandon) kills a man trying to rape Thelma (Davis). They flee and thus begins the voyage of self-discovery. Ridley Scott's hugely entertaining film is also provoking – it's impossible to watch the plight of Thelma and Louise without feeling indignation. The film was also something of a watershed for three of the supporting cast, Brad Pitt, Michael Madsen and Harvey Keitel, who all went on to bigger things. Contains swearing, violence. 📺 DVD

Susan Sarandon *Louise Sawyer* • Geena Davis *Thelma Dickinson* • Harvey Keitel *Hal Slocombe* • Michael Madsen *Jimmy* • Christopher McDonald *Darryl* • Stephen Tobolowsky *Max* • Brad Pitt *J D* • Timothy Carhart *Harlan* • Lucinda Jenney *Lena, Waitress* • Jason Beghe *State Trooper* • Sonny Carl Davis *Albert* • Ken Swofford *Major* ■ *Dir* Ridley Scott • *Scr* Callie Khouri

Thelonious Monk: Straight No Chaser ★★★ PG

Music documentary
1988 · US · BW and Colour · 89mins

Jazz buff Clint Eastwood acted as executive producer on this documentary about the great jazz pianist and composer of standards like *Round Midnight*. Director Charlotte Zwerin uses concert footage of Monk on tour in the late sixties, shot by Christian Blackwood with new interviews and biographical material about Monk, who died in 1982. Eastwood's own homage to Charlie Parker, *Bird*, was released in 1988.

Samuel E Wright *Narration* ■ *Dir* Charlotte Zwerin • *Cinematographer* Christian Blackwood

Them! ★★★★★ PG

Science-fiction   1954 · US · BW · 88mins

The best of the giant bug movies of the fifties is a science-fiction classic. Spawned by atomic radiation, mutant ants arrive in Los Angeles from the New Mexico desert and infest the sewer system in a taut, atmospheric and totally convincing shocker laden with clever visual and verbal puns. Terrific special effects, noble humanitarian sentiments, involving performances and a first-class script make for monster thrills. 📺

James Whitmore *Sgt Ben Peterson* • Edmund Gwenn *Dr Harold Medford* • Joan Weldon *Dr Patricia Medford* • James Arness *Robert Graham* • Onslow Stevens *Brig Gen O'Brien* • Leonard Nimoy *Sergeant* ■ *Dir* Gordon Douglas • *Scr* Ted Sherdeman, Russell Hughes, by George Worthing Yates

Them ★★

Science-fiction thriller   1996 · US · Colour

Not a remake of the fifties sci-fi B-movie about massive mutant ants, but an even lower-key affair about the strange goings-on in a town at the foot of the Sierra Nevada mountains. The prologue, in which scientist Scott Patterson claims to have witnessed the arrival of aliens, sets the scene for yet another reworking of the *Body Snatchers* scenario; folk disappearing, others behaving like zombies and everyone else a potential suspect. Hindered by some indifferent special effects, this was the pilot for a proposed TV series, and it's not hard to see why the option wasn't picked up. Contains violence.

Scott Patterson *Simon Trent* • Tony Todd *Berlin* • Clare Carey *Kelly Black* • Dustin Voigt *Jake Trent* ■ *Dir* Bill L Norton • *Scr* Charles Grant Craig, from an idea by Charles Grant Craig, Patrick Gilmore

Them Thar Hills! ★★★★ U

Comedy   1934 · US · BW · 18mins

Stan Laurel believed that he and Ollie should have "stayed in the short film category" and watching gems like this one can understand his reluctance to milk a comic situation beyond a perfectly realised twenty minutes. Oliver has been told to take it easy, so the duo head for the hills and a caravan site where, in a tender scene, he is shown as blissfully happy. From such contentment, disaster can only follow and so it does when bootleggers fill the nearby well with moonshine whisky. A camper's wife joins the boys and by the time her husband arrives the trio are plastered. The inevitable destructive tit-for-tat routine follows. A lesser sequel with the same couple followed the next year, actually called *Tit-for-Tat*. 📺

Stan Laurel *Stan* • Oliver Hardy *Ollie* • Billy Gilbert *Doctor* • Charlie Hall *Motorist who runs out of gas* • Mae Busch *Motorist's wife* ■ *Dir* Charles Rogers • *Scr* Stan Laurel, HM Walker

The Theme ★★★★

Drama   1979 · USSR · Colour · 99mins

This was among the first films to benefit from the thawing of Soviet cinema in the Gorbachev era. Michael Ulyanov stars as a pulp novelist whose subservience to the Party line has led to his advancement in Moscow's literary circles. Seeking inspiration, he travels to the country where he becomes infatuated with Inna Churikova, a suppressed artist who shames him for his compromises. The winner of the Golden Bear at the 1987 Berlin Film Festival, Gleb Panfilov's searching study of artistic integrity and freedom of movement is not an easy watch, but it rewards the effort. In Russian with English subtitles.

Mikhail Ulyanov *Esenin* • Inna Churikova *Sasa Nikolaeva* ■ *Dir* Gleb Panfilov • *Scr* Gleb Panfilov, Aleksander Cervinski

Theodora Goes Wild ★★★★

Comedy   1936 · US · BW · 94mins

Wonderful, madcap comedy from the genre's golden period, with Irene Dunne utterly enchanting in her first comic starring role as the author of the *Peyton Place* of its day, who hits the big city and falls for the book's illustrator, debonair Melvyn Douglas. They make a delightful couple, for a while, and that's the main theme of Sidney Buchman's clever, twist-laden screenplay. There's excellent support from a fabulous array of Columbia character actors, notably disapproving aunts Elisabeth Risdon and Margaret McWade, and Stanislavsky-trained émigré director Richard Boleslawski has the good sense to sit back and let the cast get on with it.

Irene Dunne *Theodora Lynn* • Melvyn Douglas *Michael Grant* • Thomas Mitchell *Jed Waterbury* • Thurston Hall *Arthur Stevenson* • Rosalind Keith *Adelaide Perry* • Spring Byington *Rebecca Perry* • Elisabeth Risdon *Aunt Mary* • Margaret McWade *Aunt Elsie* ■ *Dir* Richard Boleslawski • *Scr* Sidney Buchman, from a story by Mary E McCarthy

Theodore Rex ★★ PG

Comedy fantasy 1995 · US · Colour · 87mins

Only the threat of litigation kept Whoopi Goldberg on board this turkey and it is to her credit that she does her best to make it fly. But she clearly didn't regard being teamed with a doltish detective (who just happens to be a tyrannosaurus) as one of the highlights of her career. Writer/director Jonathan Betuel has problems making us believe in a world in which dinosaurs have been revived, and he needs someone more menacing than mad scientist Armin Mueller-Stahl to distract us from the woeful special effects. Children might enjoy it, but grown-ups should ensure that they are busy elsewhere when it's on. Contains violence and swearing.

Whoopi Goldberg *Katie Coltrane* • Armin Mueller-Stahl *Dr Edgar Kane* • Juliet Landau *Dr Shade* • Bud Cort *Spinner* • Stephen McHattie *Edge* • Richard Roundtree *Commissioner Lynch* • Peter Mackenzie *Alex Summers* • Peter Kwong *Toymaker* • George Newbern *Theodore Rex* • Carol Kane *Molly Rex* ■ *Dir/Scr* Jonathan Betuel

Theorem ★★★★ 15

Drama   1968 · It · Colour · 94mins

Pier Paolo Pasolini found himself on an obscenity charge for this adaptation of his own novel, in which a handsome stranger seduces every member of a wealthy household before departing abruptly. They then have to deal with the irrevocable impact he's had on their lives. Oblivious to whether Terence Stamp's intruder was messiah or demon, the Italian government banned the film, recognising that in its blend of Marxism and religion, Pasolini had created a scathing indictment of the sexually repressed bourgeoisie of which even Buñuel would have been proud. Laura Betti won the best actress prize at Venice for her performance as the skittish maid, but it's Stamp's ethereal presence that dominates proceedings. In Italian with English subtitles. 📺

Terence Stamp *Visitor* • Silvana Mangano *Mother* • Massimo Girotti *Father* • Anne

Wiazemsky *Daughter* • Laura Betti *Maid* • Andrés José Cruz *Son* ■ *Dir* Pier Paolo Pasolini • *Scr* Pier Paolo Pasolini, from his novel

The Theory of Flight
★★★★ 15

Romantic drama
1998 · UK/US · Colour · 101mins

Like *Truly Madly Deeply*, what was originally made as a BBC film for TV was later reconsidered for theatrical release. And rightly so. This is a very tender and honest depiction of human fallibility – mental and physical. Kenneth Branagh plays a man re-inventing the aeroplane, a futile expression of his lack of emotional freedom. After a flight attempt off a public building lands him on probation, he is assigned to take care of motor neurone disease patient Helena Bonham Carter. In many ways less disabled than Branagh as a person, Bonham Carter is determined to lose her virginity before she dies. And together the two pursue their dreams of sexual and literal flight. What could have been an excruciatingly silly tale is handled with the sensitivity to make this a very touching film. Contains swearing and sexual references.

Kenneth Branagh *Richard* • Helena Bonham Carter *Jane Hatchard* • Gemma Jones *Anne* • Holly Aird *Julie* • Ray Stevenson *Gigolo* ■ *Dir* Paul Greengrass • *Scr* Richard Hawkins

There Are No Children Here
★★★ 15

Drama
1993 · US · Colour · 90mins

Mothers battling to keep their kids away from drugs and crime are usually relegated to the background in the street films of ''new black'' cinema. However, the maternal viewpoint is very much to the fore in this crusading film, in which Oprah Winfrey plays a Chicago mother determined to keep her brood on the straight and narrow. Winfrey proved with her Oscar-nominated turn in *The Color Purple* that she is no mean actress, and she comes across as a tower of strength here. But the TV-movie format serves to draw some of the sting from the story. Contains violence. 🎞

Oprah Winfrey *Lajoe Rivers* • Keith David *John Paul Rivers* • Mark Lane *Lafeyette Rivers* • Norman Golden II [Norman D Golden II] *Pharoah Rivers* • Maya Angelou *Lelia Mae* • Vonte Sweet *Craig* ■ *Dir* Anita Addison • *Scr* Bobby Smith Jr, from the novel by Alex Kotlowitz

There Goes My Baby
★★★

Drama
1994 · US · Colour · 98mins

If imitation is the sincerest form of flattery, *American Graffiti* must be feeling very flattered indeed. This is one of the many attempts to recapture its teen angst, and it's better than some. Set in 1965, the film focuses on a clichéd bunch of senior High School students as they prepare to enter the real world. The characters are stereotypes, running the familiar gamut from surfer dude and hippy chick to Vietnam draft dodger and school swot. But the quality of the film's ensemble cast just about brings them to life. Faces in the cast include Dermot Mulroney and *ER*'s Noah Wyle.

Dermot Mulroney *Pirate* • Rick Schroder *Stick* • Kelli Williams *Sunshine* • Noah Wyle *Finnegan* • Jill Schoelen *Babette* • Kristin Minter *Tracy* • Lucy Deakins *Mary Beth* • Kenny Ransom *Calvin* ■ *Dir/Scr* Floyd Mutrux

There Goes My Heart
★★

Romantic comedy
1938 · US · BW · 81mins

Fredric March stars as a newspaperman trying to interview heiress Virginia Bruce, in this comedy directed by Norman Z McLeod. Unfortunately she's escaped the control of her department store-owner grandfather and decamped to New York. Sound familiar? Clearly lost for inspiration, the unbelievably convoluted plot sees Bruce adopting an alias, rooming with salesgirl Patsy Kelly and ending up as one herself in grandpa's department store, before March discovers her true identity. It draws on *It Happened One Night* and *The Richest Girl in the World*, and several other movies for ideas. The result, though it's well done, is a predictable echo of all of them.

Fredric March *Bill Spencer* • Virginia Bruce *Joan Butterfield/Joan Baker* • Patsy Kelly *Peggy O'Brien* • Alan Mowbray *Pennypepper E Pennypepper* • Nancy Carroll *Dorothy Moore* ■ *Dir* Norman Z McLeod • *Scr* Eddie Moran, Jack Jevne, from a story by Ed Sullivan

There Goes the Bride
★ PG

Farce
1979 · UK · Colour · 86mins

On the day of his daughter's wedding in Florida, an advertising executive takes a couple of accidental bumps on the head – each of which, in the time-honoured tradition of this sort of thing, cause embarrassing and supposedly hilarious hallucinations. By the time the third blow brings him to his senses, the couple have already slept together. An unamusing Ray Cooney farce with a curious mélange of British and US actors, all presumably wondering what their agents were playing at. Contains poor jokes. 🎞

Tom Smothers *Timothy Westerby* • Twiggy *Polly Perkins* • Sylvia Syms *Ursula Westerby* • Michael Witney *Bill Shorter* • Martin Balsam *Elmer Babcock* • Phil Silvers *Psychiatrist* ■ *Dir* Terence Marcel [Terry Marcel] • *Scr* Ray Cooney, Terence Marcel, John Chapman, from a play by Ray Cooney

There Goes the Groom
★★

Comedy
1937 · US · BW · 64mins

''Here comes the groom'' might have been a more appropriate title for this marginally screwball romantic comedy about a family with financial problems, hoping to solve them by hooking a wealthy son-in-law for their elder daughter Louise Henry. Enter her old high-school sweetheart Burgess Meredith, back from a successful foray in the Alaskan goldfields, but directing his attention to the younger daughter Ann Sothern. The cast, including the perennial Hollywood mother-figure Mary Boland, keep this good-natured but unmemorable movie just about intact in the face of its paper-thin plot.

Ann Sothern *Bettina ''Betty'' Russell* • Burgess Meredith *Derek ''Dick'' Mathews* • Mary Boland *Mrs Genevieve Pearson Russell* • Onslow Stevens *Dr Joel Becker* • William Brisbane *Potter Russell* • Louise Henry *Janet*

Russell ■ *Dir* Joseph Santley • *Scr* SK Lauren, Dorothy Yost, Harold Kusell, from the short story *Let Freedom Swing* by David Garth

There Is Another Sun
★★

Crime thriller
1951 · UK · BW · 97mins

This seedy tale of greed and betrayal among funfair folk focuses on a stunt rider and a boxer, who put aside their rivalries to steal the boss's life savings. There's nothing new in the story and the performances of Maxwell Reed and Laurence Harvey have little to commend them. But director Lewis Gilbert's prying camera finds many dark corners behind the twinkling lights of the carnival stalls, and it's the thoroughly nasty atmosphere conjured up in a place dedicated to enjoyment that makes this unusually effective British movie worth watching. Its alternative title, *Wall of Death* (often used for TV screenings), dates from a 1953 reissue.

Maxwell Reed *Racer* • Susan Shaw *Lillian* • Laurence Harvey *Maguire* • Hermione Baddeley *Gypsy Sarah* • Meredith Edwards *Bratcher* • Robert Adair *Sarno* • Leslie Dwyer *Foley* ■ *Dir* Lewis Gilbert • *Scr* Guy Morgan, from a story by James Raisin

There Must Be a Pony
★★

Melodrama
1986 · US · Colour · 95mins

Soapy melodrama, with Liz Taylor as a fallen star, who's had psychiatric problems and is now attempting a comeback. At the same time a risky romance with a hunky stranger angers her son. So-so material is elevated by a strong cast which also includes Robert Wagner and James Coco. The storyline sounds like it might have been specially written for Liz, but was actually adapted from the novel by James Kirkwood Jr.

Elizabeth Taylor *Marguerite Sydney* • Robert Wagner *Ben Nichols* • James Coco *Merwin Trellis* • William Windom *Lee Hertzig* • Edward Winter *David Hollis* • Ken Olin *Jay Savage* • Dick O'Neill *Det Roy Clymer* • Mickey Rooney *Mickey Rooney* • Chad Lowe *Josh Sydney* ■ *Dir* Joseph Sargent • *Scr* Mart Crowley, from the novel by James Kirkwood Jr

There Was a Crooked Man
★★★★ U

Comedy
1960 · UK · BW · 106mins

Even some of those generally left cold by clown Norman Wisdom, admit that this is one of his best films. Made on loan-out from his usual studio, Rank, this comedy allowed him to show more versatility, although he holds fast to his ''poor but honest'' persona, inspired by Chaplin. An unwitting accomplice to a robbery, Norman teams up with the gang of crooks who get him imprisoned to outwit the venal mayor of a seaside town. Three sequences (a bank robbery, a battle with factory machinery, and Brian Oulton taking a shower unaware that Norman is in the stall with him) are among the funniest things Wisdom did. Alfred Marks as the gang boss and Andrew Cruickshank as the mayor, are excellent foils.

Norman Wisdom *Davy Cooper* • Alfred Marks *Adolf Carter* • Andrew Cruickshank *McKillup* • Reginald Beckwith *Station master* • Susannah York *Ellen* • Jean Clarke *Freda* • Timothy

Bateson *Flash Dan* ■ *Dir* Stuart Burge • *Scr* Reuben Ship, from the play *The Odd Legend of Schultz* by James Birdie

There Was a Crooked Man...
★★★ 15

Western
1970 · US · Colour · 118mins

Kirk Douglas and Henry Fonda – actors as different in style and persona as could be – are pitted against each other in this period crime movie with a western flavour. Douglas is a tough uncompromising outlaw who escapes from jail and goes in search of his hidden booty; Fonda is the gentle sheriff-turned-prison warden who patiently pursues Douglas in the hope of rehabilitating him. With a screenplay by Robert Benton and David Newman (*Bonnie and Clyde*), direction by veteran Joseph L Mankiewicz and two major stars, the movie promises much, but delivers little. 🎞

Kirk Douglas *Paris Pitman Jr* • Henry Fonda *Woodward Lopeman* • Hume Cronyn *Dudley Whinner* • Warren Oates *Floyd Moon* • Burgess Meredith *The Missouri Kid* • John Randolph *Cyrus McNutt* • Arthur O'Connell *Mr Lomax* ■ *Dir* Joseph L Mankiewicz • *Scr* David Newman, Robert Benton, from the story *Prison Story* by David Newman, Robert Benton

There Was a Little Boy
★★★

Drama
1993 · US · Colour

Cybill Shepherd gets the chance to sink her teeth into a grittier role than usual in this moving made-for-TV drama. She plays a mother-to-be who is haunted by memories of her first child who disappeared 15 years earlier. The ever-reliable John Heard is superb as her husband and Shepherd is almost as good, helped by a largely unknown, though fine supporting cast. The drama is handled with sympathy by *Deep Impact* director Mimi Leder.

Cybill Shepherd *Julie Warner* • John Heard *Greg Warner* • Scott Bairstow *Jesse* • Elaine Kagan *Esperanza* • Vondie Curtis-Hall *Danforth* ■ *Dir* Mimi Leder • *Scr* Wesley Bishop, from the novel by Claire R Jacobs

There Was Once a Cop
★★★

Crime drama
1969 · Fr · Colour · 95mins

The enduring partnership of director Georges Lautner and the dazzling Mireille Darc dashed off another slick comedy thriller with this often hilarious tale of the bachelor cop who takes on a fake family to help nail Nice's biggest drugs-ring. But what are gangsters, corrupt cops, the CIA and the Mafia when there's a little horror like Hervé Hillien to contend with? He is brattishly brilliant as Darc's lawless son and his exchanges with Michel Constantin (who is already out of his depth both with the case and his feelings for Darc) are astutely scripted and briskly played. French dialogue dubbed into English.

Michel Constantin *Inspector* • Mireille Darc ''*Wife*'' • Hervé Hillien ''*Son*'' • Michel Lonsdale ■ *Dir* Georges Lautner • *Scr* Georges Lautner, Francis Veber, from a book by Richard Caron

Theremin: an Electronic Odyssey ★★★★
Music documentary
1993 · US · Colour · 78mins

An informative and absorbing documentary, charting the life of Russian emigré Leon Theremin – inventor of the musical instrument used to make the eerie noises on such films as *The Day the Earth Stood Still*, *Spellbound* and *It Came from Outer Space* – and how it influenced the course of popular culture. Beach Boy Brian Wilson talks about the creation of the pop hit *Good Vibrations*, Robert Moog (inventor of the Moog synthesizer) credits him with launching the era of electronic music in 1920, and virtuoso player Clara Rockmore (Theremin's protégée) demonstrates the range of the instrument in performance. Director Steven M Martin hits the right notes of whimsy and dramatic insight as he spans two continents, and takes the viewer through the roaring Twenties, the Lenin and Stalin eras and beyond, revealing political secrets from Theremin's life and the profound impact his other inventions also had on society. A must-see curio about a fascinating subject.
Dir/Scr Steven M Martin

There's a Girl in My Soup ★★ 15
Comedy   1970 · UK · Colour · 91mins
Adapted by Peter Kortner and Terence Frisby (from his stage play), this is a very tame version of a sex comedy that ran and ran on both sides of the Atlantic. Roy Boulting directs without much enthusiasm for his tale of womanising TV celebrity Peter Sellers, who is knocked off his stride by a chance encounter with dippy waif Goldie Hawn. Content to cruise through his meagre helping of wisecracks, the miscast Sellers still teams surprisingly well with Hawn, who also has some funny scenes with ditched boyfriend Nicky Henson. Contains swearing. ▭
Peter Sellers *Robert Danvers* • Goldie Hawn *Marion* • Tony Britton *Andrew Hunter* • Nicky Henson *Jimmy* • John Comer *John* • Diana Dors *John's wife* • Gabrielle Drake *Julia Halforde-Smythe* • Geraldine Sherman *Caroline* • Judy Campbell *Lady Heather* • Nicola Pagett *Clare* ■ *Dir* Roy Boulting • *Scr* Terence Frisby, Peter Kortner, from a play by Terence Frisby

There's Always a Woman ★★★
Detective crime comedy
1938 · US · BW · 82mins
Private eye Melvyn Douglas is hired by Mary Astor for a routine investigation that soon escalates into a murder case. His wife, Joan Blondell, an enthusiastic and charmingly meddlesome amateur sleuth, involves herself and beats her husband to the solution. Directed by Alexander Hall from a delightfully zany script, with Blondell the stand-out in an excellent cast., this was planned as the first part of a series. But Blondell withdrew and the idea petered out after *There's That Woman Again*, a disappointing follow-up with Douglas and Virginia Bruce.

Joan Blondell *Sally Reardon* • Melvyn Douglas *William Reardon* • Mary Astor *Lola Fraser* • Frances Drake *Anne Calhoun* • Jerome Cowan *Nick Shane* • Rita Hayworth *Ketterling's secretary* ■ *Dir* Alexander Hall • *Scr* Gladys Lehman, Joel Sayre, Philip Rapp, Morrie Ryskind, from a short story by Wilson Collison

There's Always Tomorrow ★★
Melodrama   1956 · US · BW · 84mins
Fred MacMurray is the model husband who feels that he is taken for granted by his family. The reappearance of old flame Barbara Stanwyck revitalises him and he dreams of starting a new life with her. His wife Joan Bennett remains blissfully unaware of the situation, but it's not long before his children sense that something is going on. The moral message is loud and clear. Douglas Sirk directs and Stanwyck is terrific, but the soap opera fails to ignite due to the lack of heat in a dull screenplay.
Barbara Stanwyck *Norma Miller* • Fred MacMurray *Clifford Groves* • Joan Bennett *Marion Groves* • Pat Crowley *Ann* • William Reynolds *Vinnie Groves* • Gigi Perreau *Ellen Groves* • Judy Nugent *Frankie Groves* ■ *Dir* Douglas Sirk • *Scr* Bernard C Schoenfeld, from a story by Ursula Parrott

There's No Business like Show Business ★★★★ U
Musical   1954 · US · Colour · 112mins
The title was so long it filled the CinemaScope screen and that was exactly what 20th Century-Fox intended, to show off its new (and then virtually exclusive) letterbox screen process. Fox also crammed this musical with as many stars as possible, adding zest to its hokey old "Broadway family" plot. The story rarely matters in this kind of film, though this does take a dive when "Prince of Wails" Johnnie Ray, shows a serious inclination towards the priesthood. As the title suggests, this is the Irving Berlin songbook, and a fine one it is, though the censor interfered with *Heat Wave* by insisting on a change from "seat" to "feet" and, since it's sung by Marilyn Monroe, it simply doesn't make sense. Neither does Marilyn hanging out with Donald O'Connor for that matter, but it's that kind of movie. Ethel Merman, Dan Dailey and Mitzi Gaynor are all in good voice, and that garish Fox style is displayed to full effect. ▭
Ethel Merman *Molly Donahue* • Donald O'Connor *Tim Donahue* • Marilyn Monroe *Vicky* • Dan Dailey *Terrance Donahue* • Johnnie Ray *Steve Donahue* • Mitzi Gaynor *Katy Donahue* • Richard Eastham *Lew Harris* • Hugh O'Brian *Charles Gibbs* ■ *Dir* Walter Lang • *Scr* Phoebe Ephron, Henry Ephron, from a story by Lamar Trotti

There's One Born Every Minute ★★ U
Comedy   1942 · US · BW · 59mins
Veteran comic actors Hugh Herbert, Guy Kibbee and Edgar Kennedy get what mileage they can from a plot which has Herbert as a small-town pudding manufacturer whose secret ingredient, Vitamin Z, puts "Zumph" into his product and gets him elected mayor. The Universal production's one claim to cinematic fame is that it was the screen debut of ten-year-old Elizabeth Taylor, who was training as a singer at the time and warbles a duet with former *Our Gang* star Carl "Alfalfa" Switzer. The studio dropped Taylor shortly afterwards and its casting director spent the rest of his life living down his verdict on the young star: "The kid has nothing."
Hugh Herbert *Lemuel P Twine/Ghost of Abner Twine/Ghost of Claudius Twine* • Peggy Moran *Helen Barbara Twine* • Tom Brown *Jimmie Hanagan* • Guy Kibbee *Lester Cadwalader Sr* • Catharine Doucet *[Catherine Doucet] Minerva Twine* • Elizabeth Taylor *Gloria Ann Twine* • Carl "Alfalfa"Switzer *[Carl Switzer] Junior Twine* ■ *Dir* Harold Young • *Scr* Robert B Hunt, Brenda Weisberg, from the story *Man or Mouse* by Robert B Hunt

There's Something about Mary ★★★★ 15
Romantic comedy
1998 · US · Colour · 114mins
Those kings of bad taste Peter and Bobby Farrelly (*Dumb and Dumber*, *Kingpin*) surpassed themselves with this defiantly non-PC but wickedly funny Hollywood smash. Ben Stiller plays a writer (Ted Stroehmann) who, 13 years later, is still obsessed by his prom date, Cameron Diaz, even though the occasion ended in disaster. The problem is that a queue of fellow misfits have also fallen under her spell, including British comic Lee Evans and a seedy private eye (Matt Dillon) Stiller hired to find her. With gags about the mentally and physically disabled, dead dogs and serial killers, not to mention the now infamous "hair gel" scene, this is unwholesome entertainment for older members of the family. The hapless Stiller uncovers a previously unseen gift for slapstick, although none of the cast can be faulted in this area. There's also an inspired musical commentary from American cult singer–songwriter Jonathan Richman. Contains swearing, sexual references. ▭ **DVD**
Cameron Diaz *Mary Jenson* • Matt Dillon *Pat Healy* • Ben Stiller *Ted Stroehmann* • Lin Shaye *Magda* • Lee Evans *Tucker* • Chris Elliott *Dom* • Jonathan Richman *himself* • Jeffrey Tambor *Sully* • Markie Post *Mary's mom* ■ *Dir* Peter Farrelly, Bobby Farrelly • *Scr* Peter Farrelly, Bobby Farrelly, Ed Decter, John J Strauss, from a story by Ed Decter, John J Strauss

Thérèse ★★★★ PG
Drama   1986 · Fr · Colour · 91mins
Taking a leaf out of Robert Bresson's stark book, director Alain Cavalier has created a film that has the purity and simplicity of its subject – the devout life of Thérèse Martin spent as a Carmelite nun in the convent at Lisieux. Thérèse, who was canonised in 1924, is serenely played by stage actress Catherine Mouchet from the age of 15 until her death of TB, aged 24, in 1897. Cavalier presents the story in a series of tableaux that recount, with little dialogue and action, the everyday existence of the nuns, without preaching or religiosity. The film went on to win six Cesars. A French language film.
Catherine Mouchet *Thérèse Martin* • Aurore Prieto *Celine* • Sylvia Habault *Pauline* •

Ghislaine Mona *Marie* • Hélène Alexandridis *Lucie* ■ *Dir* Alain Cavalier • *Scr* Alain Cavalier, Camille de Casabianca

Thérèse Desqueyroux ★★★★
Drama   1962 · Fr · BW · 107mins
Emmanuelle Riva won the Best Actress prize at Venice for her controlled portrayal of a bored provincial poisoner in this faithful adaptation of François Mauriac's novel. Director Georges Franju was attacked by contemporary critics for adhering so closely to the text, even though it touches on such perennial themes as atheism, solitude and inarticulation. Yet with its stately pace, flashback structure, steely detachment, enigmatic characterisation and minimalist performances, this is an unnerving Bressonian study in both the ennui that sets Riva against her husband, Philippe Noiret, and the unquestioning charity that prompts his family to forgive her. In French with English subtitles.
Emmanuelle Riva *Thérèse Desqueyroux* • Philippe Noiret *Bernard Desqueyroux* • Edith Scob *Anne de la Trave* • Sami Frey *Jean Azevedo* • Renée Devillers *Mme de la Trave* • Richard Saint-Bris *Hector de la Trave* • Lucien Nat *Jerome Larroque* ■ *Dir* Georges Franju • *Scr* Georges Franju, Claude Mauriac, François Mauriac, from his novel

Thérèse Raquin ★★★★
Crime drama   1953 · Fr · BW · 100mins
Breaking with Jacques Feyder's now lost 1928 version of Emile Zola's dark psychological novel, Marcel Carné elected to update the action and relocate it to the backstreets of Lyons. However, all the naturalistic intensity of the original has been retained, as frustrated housewife Simone Signoret and trucker Raf Vallone suffer much more than pangs of conscience after they murder her husband. The deterioration of their relationship is charted with a lyrical realism that often approaches vintage Carné, but surpassing the gallant efforts of the leads is Sylvie – superb as the mute mother-in-law, watching their torment with malicious satisfaction. In French with English subtitles.
Simone Signoret *Thérèse Raquin* • Raf Vallone *Laurent* • Jacques Duby *Camille Raquin* • Roland Lesaffre *The sailor* • Sylvie *Mme Raquin* ■ *Dir* Marcel Carné • *Scr* Charles Spaak, Marcel Carné, from the novel by Emile Zola

These Foolish Things ★★★★ PG
Drama   1990 · Fr · Colour · 102mins
Nicely underplayed domestic drama from top French director Bertrand Tavernier, maker of *The Watchmaker of St Paul*, *'Round Midnight* and *Mississippi Blues*. Jane Birkin plays a screenwriter who returns home to re-establish her interrupted relationship with her dying dad (Dirk Bogarde). The film follows them as they work out their differences, reminisce about times past, and restore mutual respect and understanding. Smashing stuff, very moving, with terrific performances from the two leads. A French language film. ▭

U = SUITABLE FOR ALL   Uc = SUITABLE FOR ALL, ESPECIALLY FOR YOUNG CHILDREN (VIDEO ONLY)   PG = PARENTAL GUIDANCE

Dirk Bogarde *Daddy* • Jane Birkin *Caroline* • Odette Laure *Miche* • Emmanuelle Bataille *Juliette* • Charlotte Kady *Barbara* ■ *Dir* Bertrand Tavernier • *Scr* Colo Tavernier

These Thousand Hills ★★

Western 1959 · US · Colour · 95mins

Lacking the grandeur of other A B Guthrie Jr adaptations like *The Big Sky* or *The Way West* (both coincidentally starring Kirk Douglas), this is a solid 20th Century-Fox western featuring a long list of contract players, the film having been made toward the end of the studio contract system. The fifties' would-be icons on show include Don Murray, Richard Egan and Stuart Whitman, in a long-winded saga about a cowboy's loyalties and responsibilities. The women, Lee Remick and Patricia Owens, actually show more *cojones* than the men, and talented director Richard Fleischer seems at a loss as to how to present the story with any degree of dynamism. Still, it's not unintelligent, just dull.

Don Murray *Lat Evans* • Richard Egan *Jehu* • Lee Remick *Callie* • Patricia Owens *Joyce* • Stuart Whitman *Tom Ping* • Albert Dekker *Conrad* • Harold J Stone *Ram Butler* ■ *Dir* Richard Fleischer • *Scr* Alfred Hayes, from the novel by AB Guthrie Jr

These Three ★★★ U

Drama 1936 · US · BW · 88mins

Time hasn't been kind to this fine adaptation of Lillian Hellman's play *The Children's Hour*. Deprived of its original sinister title, and with all references to lesbianism removed by the censors of the day, this still offers a stronger impact than the 1961 remake with Audrey Hepburn and Shirley MacLaine, which was also directed by William Wyler. What keeps this tale riveting is the superbly skilled portrayal by child actress Bonita Granville as the little horror who spreads the initial lie, and the well-matched teaming of Merle Oberon and Miriam Hopkins as the schoolteachers involved. As the man in the scandal, Joel McCrea is bland and was easily outshone by James Garner in the remake, although the role here is more pivotal, since the plot was changed to incorporate a male-female affair. [video]

Miriam Hopkins *Martha Dobie* • Merle Oberon *Karen Wright* • Joel McCrea *Dr Joseph Cardin* • Catherine Doucet *Mrs Lily Mortar* • Alma Kruger *Mrs Tilford* • Bonita Granville *Mary Tilford* ■ *Dir* William Wyler • *Scr* Lillian Hellman, from her play *The Children's Hour*

These Wilder Years ★★

Drama 1956 · US · BW · 90mins

A shame that two such powerful performers as Barbara Stanwyck and James Cagney met so late in their careers on such a mushy little picture. Directed with dull restraint by Roy Rowland, this old-fashioned weepie has unmarried millionaire Cagney trying to persuade Stanwyck, the head of a children's home, to reveal the whereabouts of the illegitimate son he handed over for adoption years before.

James Cagney *Steve Bradford* • Barbara Stanwyck *Ann Dempster* • Walter Pidgeon *James Rayburn* • Betty Lou Keim *Suzie* • Don Dubbins *Mark* • Edward Andrews *Mr Spottsford* • Basil Ruysdael *Judge* • Dean Jones *Hardware clerk* • Tom Laughlin *Football player* ■ *Dir* Roy Rowland • *Scr* Frank Fenton, from a story by Ralph Wheelwright

They All Kissed the Bride ★★ U

Comedy 1942 · US · BW · 87mins

An unexceptional and rather long-winded Joan Crawford comedy – no, she isn't the bride, that's kid sister Helen Parrish – in which she spends much of the time arguing with, and ultimately romancing, reporter Melvyn Douglas. Crawford copes well enough with her bossy-boots role, but her character isn't likeable, and as a result the film isn't very watchable, despite sterling support from the likes of Roland Young and Billie Burke. Director Alexander Hall does what he can, but this is no *Philadelphia Story*, to which it rather obviously aspires.

Joan Crawford *Margaret J Drew* • Melvyn Douglas *Michael Holmes* • Roland Young *Marsh* • Billie Burke *Mrs Drew* • Allen Jenkins *Johnny Johnson* • Andrew Tombes *Crane* ■ *Dir* Alexander Hall • *Scr* PJ Wolfson, Andrew P Solt, Henry Altimus, from a original by Gina Kaus, Andrew P Solt

They All Laughed ★★★

Comedy 1981 · US · Colour · 115mins

A stylish and splendidly wacky comedy about detectives who can't help getting involved with the women they are tailing. It's important as a late Audrey Hepburn entry, and she looks as lovely as ever, co-starring here with Ben Gazzara on wonderfully evocative New York locations (shades of *Breakfast at Tiffany's*). Director Peter Bogdanovich, seriously under-rated these days, pulls it all together with great élan, aided by a quirky cast, out of which Blaine Novak and lovely Patti Hansen shine. There's a morbid interest, though, in watching murdered centrefold Dorothy Stratten, directed by lover Bogdanovich. She died before the film came out.

Audrey Hepburn *Angela Niotes* • Ben Gazzara *John Russo* • John Ritter *Charles Rutledge* • Colleen Camp *Christy Miller* • Patti Hansen *Deborah "Sam" Wilson* • Dorothy Stratten *Dolores Martin* ■ *Dir/Scr* Peter Bogdanovich

They Call Me Bruce ★★★

Martial arts action comedy
1982 · US · Colour · 86mins

A naive chinese cook in Los Angeles, is unaware that the restaurant in which he works is run by the local mafia. Modelling himself on his hero Bruce Lee, whom he is often mistaken for, the lad enrols in a local kung fu school and makes headlines when he defeats a gang of thieves in a fight. Noting his prowess, his gangster bosses dupe him into becoming a drug courier. This is a likeable martial-arts/ganster movie spoof, with Johnny Yune excellent as Bruce. A superior example of its type, it spawned an equally smart sequel, *They Still Call Me Bruce*, in 1987, once again with Yune as Bruce.

Johnny Yune *Bruce* • Bill Capizzi *Lil Pete* • Martin Azarow *Big Al* • Tony Brande *Boss of Bosses* • Ralph Mauro *Freddy* • Pam Huntington *Anita* • John Fujioka *Master* • Margaux Hemingway *Karmen* • Bill Kirchenbauer *Polish Killer* ■ *Dir* Elliott Hong • *Scr* Johnny Yune, Elliott Hong, Tim Clawson, David Randolph

They Call Me Mister Tibbs! ★★★

Police thriller 1970 · US · Colour · 107mins

With the emphasis on the Mister, it's Sidney Poitier, back again as the black detective after his love-hate relationship with sheriff Rod Steiger worked so well in *In the Heat of the Night*. This time he's investigating the killing of a hooker who was close to his friend Martin Landau, and the usual clichés about a cop's fraught domestic life form a counterpoint to the main action. Poitier is impressive in his ruthless integrity, but the film misses the character contrast of the original. Steiger, where art thou?

Sidney Poitier *Virgil Tibbs* • Martin Landau *Reverend Logan Sharpe* • Barbara McNair *Valerie Tibbs* • Anthony Zerbe *Rice Weedon* • Jeff Corey *Captain Marden* • David Sheiner *Herbert Kenner* • Juano Hernandez *Mealie* • Norma Crane *Marge Garfield* • Edward Asner [Ed Asner] *Woody Garfield* ■ *Dir* Gordon Douglas • *Scr* Alan R Trustman, James R Webb, from a story by Alan R Trustman, from the character created by John Ball

They Came from beyond Space ★★

Science-fiction thriller
1967 · UK · Colour · 85mins

A pallid attempt by Hammer rivals Amicus, to rehash some of the thematic lines from the *Quatermass* series. Astral invaders take over a Cornish factory to enslave earthlings so they'll repair a spaceship that has crashed on the moon. Fortunately, astrophysicist Robert (*The Slime People*) Hutton has a metal plate in his head, which makes him immune from alien control, and he single-handedly combats the evil extraterrestrials, led by stalwart genre icon Michael Gough.

Robert Hutton *Dr Curtis Temple* • Jennifer Jayne *Lee Mason* • Michael Gough *Monj* • Zia Mohyeddin *Dr Farge* • Geoffrey Wallace *Alan Mullane* • Bernard Kay *Richard Arden* • John Harvey *Bill Trethowan* • Diana King *Mrs Trethowan* ■ *Dir* Freddie Francis • *Scr* Milton Subotsky, from the novel *The Gods Hate Kansas* by Joseph Millard

They Came to Cordura ★★★★ PG

Drama 1959 · US · Colour · 118mins

A grim but satisfying drama, in which a gaunt Gary Cooper stars as an army major accused of cowardice during an expedition against Pancho Villa in 1916 Mexico. Cooper can only avoid disgrace if he recommends five men from his regiment who are worthy of receiving the Congressional Medal of Honor. There's a magnificent line-up of co-stars, including Rita Hayworth, but none of the characters they portray emerges with much credit as director Robert Rossen examines issues of bravery and cowardice. The location photography (by *Bonnie and Clyde's* Burnett Guffey) is stunning and the overall effect richly rewarding. [video]

Gary Cooper *Major Thomas Thorn* • Rita Hayworth *Adelaide Geary* • Van Heflin *Sergeant John Chawk* • Tab Hunter *Lieutenant William Fowler* • Richard Conte *Corporal Milo Trubee* • Michael Callan *Private Andrew Hetherington* ■ *Dir* Robert Rossen • *Scr* Ivan Moffat, Robert Rossen

They Came to Rob Las Vegas ★★

Action thriller
1968 · It/Sp/ Fr/W Ger · Colour · 99mins

After his brother is killed during a Las Vegas heist, Gary Lockwood plans to do the job right. With a little help from Elke Sommer, he robs a heavily armoured truck, but agent Jack Palance is soon on his trail. Although let down slightly by some stiff dialogue, the film boasts a rock-solid cast and is a slick and ingenious computer-age thriller with a suggestion of humanity versus technology.

Gary Lockwood *Tony* • Elke Sommer *Anne* • Lee J Cobb *Skorsky* • Jack Palance *Douglas* • Jean Servais *Gino* • Roger Hanin *Boss* • Georges Geret *Leroy* ■ *Dir* Antonio Isasi • *Scr* Antonio Isasi, J Eisinger, L Comeron, J Illa

They Can't Hang Me ★★

Spy drama 1954 · UK · BW · mins

A minor Cold War thriller, directed by Val Guest from a novel by Leonard Mosley, the themes of atomic secrets and double agents may have lost some of their resonance, but Guest puts a neat spin on events by having a condemned killer (Andre Morell) strike a death row deal with cop Terence Morgan , to deliver a treacherous scientist in return for leniency. Naturally, things don't go according to plan. The back-up cast is as solid as a rock, with Guest's wife Yolande Donlan putting in an effective appearance.

Terence Morgan *Inspector Brown* • Yolande Donlan *Jill* • André Morell *Robert Pitt* • Ursula Howells *Antonia Pitt* • Anthony Oliver *Newcome* • Reginald Beckwith *Harold* ■ *Dir* Val Guest • *Scr* Val Guest, Val Valentine, from a novel by Leonard Mosley

They Died with Their Boots On ★★★★ U

Western 1941 · US · BW · 134mins

A rip-roaring biopic with Errol Flynn as General George Armstrong Custer, who works his way up the ranks and dies heroically at the battle of the Little Bighorn. History is cast to the wind as Flynn's hero becomes sympathetic to the Indian cause, while Mrs Custer (Olivia de Havilland, still playing Melanie from *Gone with the Wind*) fusses about trying to get her husband to settle down. Cast as Custer's chief adversary Crazy Horse is none other than Anthony Quinn, who said of his director, Raoul Walsh, "He was the least technical director I knew, but he relished the process with such a fire that I could almost taste it with him." [video]

Errol Flynn *George Armstrong Custer* • Olivia de Havilland *Elizabeth Bacon Custer* • Arthur Kennedy *Ned Sharp* • Charley Grapewin *California Joe* • Gene Lockhart *Samuel Bacon* • Anthony Quinn *Crazy Horse* • Stanley Ridges *Major Romulus Taipe* • John Litel *General Philip Sheridan* ■ *Dir* Raoul Walsh • *Scr* Wally Klein, Aeneas MacKenzie

They Drive by Night ★★★★

Drama 1940 · US · BW · 93mins

A rip-roaring Warner Bros melodrama with a knockout cast in a "love and glory" saga of life among long-distance truck drivers on the Frisco road. The movie neatly snaps into two

thematically linked halves, the first; a tale of perils on the road, the latter; a virtual reworking of Warners' earlier *Bordertown*, with George Raft and Ida Lupino in the old Paul Muni/Bette Davis roles. Co-stars Humphrey Bogart and sizzling Ann Sheridan also draw the attention in a crackingly directed film from Raoul Walsh, though it's a shame Walsh didn't swap Bogie and Raft: the latter becomes disastrously tedious as the movie progresses. Lupino, though, is superb, and the Jerry Wald/Richard Macaulay dialogue is as crisp as it comes. A real goodie, made in classic Warner style, at a time when no other studio's product hit the same heights.

George Raft *Joe Fabrini* • Ann Sheridan *Cassie Hartley* • Ida Lupino *Lana Carlsen* • Humphrey Bogart *Paul Fabrini* • Gale Page *Pearl Fabrini* • Alan Hale *Ed J Carlsen* • Roscoe Karns *Irish McGurn* ■ *Dir* Raoul Walsh • *Scr* Jerry Wald, Richard Macaulay, from the novel *The Long Haul* by Al Bezzerides

They Flew Alone ★★★ U

Biographical drama 1941 · UK · BW · 107mins

Called *Wings and the Woman* on its American release, which just about sums up producer/director Herbert Wilcox's version of the life of pioneer female flyer Amy Johnson. A popular personality in newsreels of the thirties, Amy's all vim and vigour here, as portrayed by Mrs Wilcox, Anna Neagle. Unfortunately, marriage to pilot Jim Mollison (who himself had a drink problem) wasn't always harmonious. That much is probably true. What certainly never happened was Amy Johnson coming back from beyond the grave to deliver a patriotic wartime sermon to cinema audiences of the forties. Shame on you, Mr Wilcox!

Anna Neagle *Amy Johnson* • Robert Newton *Jim Mollison* • Edward Chapman *Mr Johnson* • Joan Kemp-Welch *Mrs Johnson* • Nora Swinburne *ATA commandant* ■ *Dir* Herbert Wilcox • *Scr* Miles Malleson, from the story by Lord Castlerosse

They Gave Him a Gun ★★★

Drama 1937 · US · BW · 93mins

A young First World War recruit (Franchot Tone), so sickened by the idea of killing a man wants to go AWOL. But, propped up by his friend (Spencer Tracy), he turns into a gun-happy hero. Later he carries the weaponry and new attitude into civilian life to become a mobster. W S Van Dyke directs this interesting melodrama with a pacifist and anti-crime message, and a love story that involves both men committed to the same girl (Gladys George). Very nicely acted, and quite absorbing, despite a few credibility gaps and a too-convenient resolution.

Spencer Tracy *Fred Willis* • Gladys George *Rose Duffy* • Franchot Tone *Jimmy Davis* • Edgar Dearing *Sgt Meadowlark* • Mary Lou Treen [Mary Treen] *Saxe* • Cliff Edwards *Laro* ■ *Dir* WS Van Dyke II [WS Van Dyke] • *Scr* Cyril Hume, Richard Maibaum, Maurice Rapf, from the novel by William Joyce

They Got Me Covered

★★★ U

Comedy 1943 · US · BW · 89mins

Only Bing Crosby was missing from this wartime flag-waver that might otherwise have been called "The Road to Victory". Bob Hope zings his way through a generous ration of wisecracks, as he and Dorothy Lamour root out Nazi Otto Preminger and his cohorts. Screenwriter Harry Kurnitz, who was something of a dab hand at both comedies and thrillers, adeptly judges the mix of suspense and silliness, leaving director David Butler with little to do but keep up the tempo and show off Sam Goldwyn's typically lavish sets. Eduardo Ciannelli and Donald Meek are the pick of the supporting cast. 🔲

Bob Hope *Robert Kittredge* • Dorothy Lamour *Christina Hill* • Lenore Aubert *Mrs Margo Vanescu* • Otto Preminger *Otto Fauscheim* • Eduardo Ciannelli *Baldanacco* • Marion Martin *Gloria, The "Glow Girl"* • Donald Meek *Little old man* • Phyllis Ruth *Sally* ■ *Dir* David Butler • *Scr* Harry Kurnitz, from a story by Leonard Q Ross, Leonard Spigelgass

They Had to See Paris ★★★

Comedy 1929 · US · BW · 96mins

When a simple, hardworking Oklahoma family man (Will Rogers) unexpectedly strikes oil and comes into a great deal of money, his wife (Irene Rich) develops delusions of grandeur. She drags the family to Paris, buys a chateau, tries to marry off her daughter (Marguerite Churchill) to a title, and battles to transform her husband from hick to gentleman. Rogers, America's favourite homespun philosopher and wit, entered talkies in this comedy, with director Frank Borzage proving he could press the laughter buttons as well as the tear ducts, for which he is best known.

Will Rogers *Pike Peters* • Irene Rich *Mrs Peters* • Owen Davis Jr *Ross Peters* • Marguerite Churchill *Opal Peters* • Fifi D'Orsay *Claudine* ■ *Dir* Frank Borzage • *Scr* Sonya Levien, from a novel by Homer Croy

They Knew What They Wanted ★★

Drama 1940 · US · BW · 88mins

Charles Laughton probably wouldn't win any plaudits from Messrs Scorsese or Coppola with his portrayal of Italian-American winemaker Tony Patucci. He cons pen pal waitress Carole Lombard into marriage by sending her a picture not of himself, but of his beefcake employee, William Gargan. The plan backfires when Lombard falls in love with Gargan. It's like a French farce transplanted to the Napa Valley – except that it isn't played for laughs. Laughton apparently behaved like a tyrant on the set, but the story gave him a weird accent to play with, and fed his obsession with his physical appearance.

Carole Lombard *Amy Peters* • Charles Laughton *Tony Patucci* • William Gargan *Joe* • Harry Carey *Doctor* • Frank Fay *Father McKee* • Joe Bernard [Joseph Bernard] *RF D* • Janet Fox *Mildred* • Lee Tung-Foo *Ah Gee* • Karl Malden *Red* ■ *Dir* Garson Kanin • *Scr* Robert Ardrey, from the play by Sidney Howard

They Live ★★★ 18

Science-fiction thriller
1988 · US · Colour · 90mins

A return to his B-movie roots for John Carpenter, this is a cheerful knockabout salute to the alien invasion sci-fi movies of the fifties. Wrestler-turned-actor Roddy Piper is the working-class hero who, on finding a special pair of sunglasses, discovers that alien-like creatures appear to have taken over Los Angeles and are controlling the remaining human residents with subliminal advertising. There's a nicely relaxed feel to Carpenter's direction and he keeps the action roaring along, stopping only to take a few satirical swipes at yuppy life. Piper handles the action scenes better than he deals with dialogue, but he is well supported by Keith David and Meg Foster. Contains violence, swearing. 🔲

Roddy Piper *Nada* • Keith David *Frank* • Meg Foster *Holly Thompson* • George "Buck" Flower *Drifter* • Peter Jason *Gilbert* • Raymond St Jacques *Street preacher* • Jason Robards III *Family man* ■ *Dir* John Carpenter • *Scr* Frank Armitage [John Carpenter], from the short story *Eight O'Clock in the Morning* by Ray Nelson

They Live by Night ★★★★

Film noir romance 1949 · US · BW · 95mins

Nicholas Ray made his directorial debut with this Depression era drama of young lovers on the run from the law, who find themselves staring into the abyss. Cathy O'Donnell and Farley Granger are the misfits who meet in the aftermath of a prison break-out. They fall in love and marry, but Granger is unable to shake off his criminal associations, leaving little prospect of a happy ending. There are superficial similarities with later films like *Bonnie and Clyde* and *Badlands*, but this is a poignant story of idealism and romanticism betrayed by corruption. Ray's later films like *Johnny Guitar* and *Rebel without a Cause* enjoy a cult following, but this was a stunning debut. Edward Anderson's novel *Thieves Like Us* was remade by Robert Altman in the seventies under its original title.

Farley Granger *Bowie* • Cathy O'Donnell *Keechie* • Howard Da Silva *Chickamaw* • Jay C Flippen *T- Dub* • Helen Craig *Mattie* • Will Wright *Mobley* • Marie Bryant *Singer* • Ian Wolfe *Hawkins* ■ *Dir* Nicholas Ray • *Scr* Charles Schnee, Nicholas Ray, from the novel *Thieves Like Us* by Edward Anderson

They Made Him a Criminal ★★

Political drama 1980 · It/USSR · Colour

This was the last feature completed by the Soviet director Grigori Chukrai, whose reputation rests on the wartime drama, *Ballad of a Soldier* (1959). As someone used to living under a totalitarian regime, he quickly creates the oppressive atmosphere that characterised Portugal under the Salazaar dictatorship. But the plot is far too convoluted to be engrossing, as taxi-driver Giancarlo Giannini first becomes involved with revolutionary waitress Ornella Muti and then heads a prison break after enduring sadistic torture. The background is fascinating, but the treatment is dull. Italian and Russian dialogue dubbed into English.

Giancarlo Giannini *Antonio* • Ornella Muti *Maria* • Stefano Madia *Paco* • Eugenj Lebediev *Rostao* ■ *Dir* Grigorij Ciukhrai [Grigori Chukrai]

They Made Me a Criminal ★★★ PG

Drama 1939 · US · BW · 87mins

John Garfield stars as a hard-boiled boxing champion on the run from what he believes is a murder rap in this rollicking tale which goes at breakneck pace throughout and contains strong, well-played performances from the likes of Gloria Dickson, May Robson, Claude Rains and Ann Sheridan. Essentially, it's an ensemble piece, with everyone getting a fair stab at the limelight. Not to everyone's taste, but admirable for its impudent tone.

John Garfield *Johnny Bradfield/"Jack Dorney"* • Gloria Dickson *Peggy* • Claude Rains *Detective Monty Phelan* • Ann Sheridan *Goldie* • May Robson *Gramma* • Billy Halop *Tommy* • Bobby Jordan *Angel* • Leo Gorcey *Spit* • Huntz Hall *Dippy* ■ *Dir* Busby Berkeley • *Scr* Sid Herzig, from the book by Bertram Millhauser, Beulah Marie Dix

They Made Me a Fugitive ★★★

Crime thriller 1947 · UK · BW · 99mins

Alberto Cavalcanti was a Brazilian-born, Swiss-educated architect and lawyer, who went on to direct such praised British films as *Dead of Night* (the ventriloquist's dummy episode) and *Went the Day Well?*, while also turning out this grim, but largely absorbing example of British *film noir*. Trevor Howard leads a strong cast in the story of an ex-RAF pilot for whom things go from bad to worse.

Trevor Howard *Clem Morgan* • Sally Gray *Sally* • Griffith Jones *Narcey* • René Ray *Cora* • Mary Merrall *Aggie* • Vida Hope *Mrs Fenshawe* ■ *Dir* Alberto Cavalcanti • *Scr* Noel Langley, from the novel *A Convict Has Escaped* by Jackson Budd

They Met in Bombay ★★★ U

Comedy adventure 1941 · US · BW · 91mins

Rosalind Russell and Clark Gable are rival thieves, both after a priceless necklace belonging to an English duchess in a movie that combines comedy with wartime flag-waving. They work well together in the sophisticated comedy that makes up the first half of the action. The second half isn't so good, with Gable going all heroic and winning the Victoria Cross after impersonating a British army officer. The script was co-authored by Anita Loos, who had worked on earlier Gable vehicles *Saratoga* and *San Francisco*.

Clark Gable *Gerald Meldrick* • Rosalind Russell *Anya Von Duren* • Peter Lorre *Captain Chang* • Jessie Ralph *Duchess Of Beltravers* • Reginald Owen *General* • Matthew Boulton *Inspector Cressney* • Leslie Vincent *Lt Ashley* ■ *Dir* Clarence Brown • *Scr* Edwin Justus Mayer, Anita Loos, Leon Gordon, from a story by John Kafka

They Met in the Dark ★★ U

Mystery spy thriller 1943 · UK · BW · 91mins

Framed by Nazi agents, navy commander Richard Heritage (James

Mason) loses his job for accidentally revealing secret information. Determined to clear his name, he goes in search of the woman who set him up, only to find her dead. Joining forces with visiting Canadian Laura Verity (Joyce Howard), they set out to unmask theatrical agent Tom Walls whose business is a front for Nazi spies. An old-fashioned, run-of-the-mill and unlikely espionage thriller, topical during the Second World War years, but it's rather unrewarding now. ▭

James Mason *Comdr Richard Heritage* • Joyce Howard *Laura Verity* • Tom Walls *Christopher Child* • Phyllis Stanley *Lily Bernard* • Edward Rigby *Mansel* • Ronald Ward *Carter* • Ian Fleming ■ *Dir* Karel Lamac • *Scr* Anatole de Grunwald, Miles Malleson, Basil Bartlett, Victor McClure, James Seymour, from the novel *The Vanished Corpse* by Anthony Gilbert

They Might Be Giants
★★★ U

Mystery drama 1971 · US · Colour · 85mins

This curio features George C Scott as a New Yorker who thinks he's Sherlock Holmes. Donning the deerstalker, puffing on the pipe and adopting a quizzical look, Scott encounters a psychiatrist, Dr Watson, who declares him to be suffering from classic paranoia. And since this Dr Watson is played by Joanne Woodward, the tale also gains a weird romantic angle. Written by James Goldman and directed by Antony Harvey – the editor of Stanley Kubrick's *Lolita* and *Dr Strangelove* – this isn't for everyone. Some may find it silly and sentimental, others a captivating romantic fantasy. Studio cuts certainly don't help matters, but it remains a rarity of some distinction.

George C Scott *Justin Playfair* • Joanne Woodward *Dr Mildred Watson* • Jack Gilford *Peabody* • Lester Rawlins *Blevins Playfair* • Rue McClanahan *Daisy* ■ *Dir* Anthony Harvey • *Scr* James Goldman

They Only Kill Their Masters
★★★

Crime mystery 1972 · US · Colour · 97mins

Police chief James Garner has a tough case on his hands: the death of a local divorcee and a suspect who's a dog, a doberman called Murphy. Despite the presence of the amiable Garner and the dog, however, this isn't a cutesy Disney movie, but a rather clever thriller about the sexual shenanigans that go on in a tightly knit coastal community. What's more, it has a cast that is guaranteed to make older film fans happy.

James Garner *Police Chief Abel Marsh* • Katharine Ross *Kate* • Hal Holbrook *Watkins* • Harry Guardino *Capt Streeter, sheriff* • June Allyson *Mrs Watkins* • Christopher Connelly *John, cop* • Tom Ewell *Walter, cop* • Peter Lawford *Campbell* • Ann Rutherford *Gloria* ■ *Dir* James Goldstone • *Scr* Lane Slate

They Passed This Way ★★ U

Western 1948 · US · BW · 89mins

A surprisingly low-key western from the short-lived independent Liberty production unit, releasing through Eagle-Lion, co-starring the bland (and married) star couple Joel McCrea and Frances Dee. Veteran Charles Bickford steals the acting honours as the

lawman searching for McCrea, but Alfred E Green's direction seems in no hurry to advance the plot. This is almost a "western noir" in style, not unlike Raoul Walsh's *Pursued* the previous year, but without that film's peculiar intensity.

Joel McCrea *Ross McEwen* • Frances Dee *Fay Hollister* • Charles Bickford *Pat Garrett* • Joseph Calleia *Monte Maqruez* • William Conrad *Sheriff Egan* • Martin Garralaga *Florencio* ■ *Dir* Alfred E Green • *Scr* Graham Baker, Teddi Sherman, from the novel *Paso Por Aqui* by Eugene Manlove Rhodes, adapted by William Brent, Milarde Brent

They Rode West
★★★ U

Western 1954 · US · Colour · 84mins

This exciting western reunites the popular lovers from *The Caine Mutiny*, handsome Robert Francis and lovely May Wynn. The story deals with medical ethics, as medical officer Francis uses his skill to help the Kiowa Indians, to the disgust of the soldiers at his fort. It's directed with skill by cult favourite Phil Karson, and also stars Donna Reed, the year after she received her best supporting actress Oscar for *From Here to Eternity*. Francis, a contemporary of James Dean, was tragically killed at the age of 25 in a plane crash soon after this film was released.

Robert Francis *Doctor Allen Seward* • Donna Reed *Laurie MacKaye* • May Wynn *Manyi-ten* • Phil Carey *[Philip Carey]* *Captain Peter Blake* • Onslow Stevens *Colonel Ethan Waters* ■ *Dir* Phil Karlson • *Scr* DeVallon Scott, Frank Nugent, from a story by Leo Katcher

They Shall Have Music
★★★ U

Musical drama 1939 · US · BW · 97mins

Producer Samuel Goldwyn fought a long, losing battle to make classical music popular on the big screen, but it certainly wasn't through lack of trying. Here, Archie Mayo directs a tale that finds room for top-billed virtuoso Jascha Heifetz to play no less than five violin pieces. In the story, tough youngster Gene Reynolds (later to produce the TV series *MASH*) takes up the violin after hearing Heifetz perform, enrolling in music classes as a way out of the slums. It's a bit like *Dead End* with music, and, also on hand is that film's star, Joel McCrea. One of Reynolds's prodigious fellow students is played by debuting Dolly Loehr, later to find a measure of teen stardom as Diana Lynn.

Jascha Heifetz *Jascha Heifetz* • Joel McCrea *Peter McCarthy* • Walter Brennan *Professor Lawson* • Andrea Leeds *Ann Lawson* • Gene Reynolds *Frankie* • Terry Kilburn *Dominick* • Tommy Kelly *Willie* ■ *Dir* Archie Mayo • *Scr* Irmgard von Cube, John Howard Lawson, Robert Presnell and Anthony Veiller, from the novel by Charles L Clifford

They Shoot Horses, Don't They?
★★★ 15

Drama 1969 · US · Colour · 119mins

Portraying the dance-marathon craze that swept America during the Depression in the thirties, director Sydney Pollack gives us plenty of cause for compassion in this hard-hitting adaptation of Horace McCoy's novel. Jane Fonda and Michael

Sarrazin are among the partners wearily dragging themselves beyond the end of their tethers, spurred on by the monstrous master of ceremonies (an Oscar-winning Gig Young). It's too tunnel-visioned to work as the intended microcosm of America and the flash-forward narrative is peculiar, but the photography is suitably sickly hued and the performances are wittily authentic. Contains violence, swearing and sex scenes. ▭

Jane Fonda *Gloria Beatty* • Michael Sarrazin *Robert Syverton* • Susannah York *Alice* • Gig Young *Rocky* • Red Buttons *Sailor* • Bonnie Bedelia *Ruby* • Michael Conrad *Rollo* • Bruce Dern *James* • Al Lewis *Turkey* ■ *Dir* Sydney Pollack • *Scr* James Poe, Robert E Thompson, from the novel by Horace McCoy

They Watch
★★

Supernatural drama 1993 · US · Colour · 100mins

An intriguing gothic tale, adapted from a Rudyard Kipling short story, about a man obsessed by the spirit of his dead child. Patrick Bergin is well cast as the architect who puts his career before his family, only to be overcome with guilt when his young daughter dies. In desperation he turns to a blind medium, played by Vanessa Redgrave, who seems to have established contact with her. The two leads turn in impeccable performances and, although the material is slight, director John Korty summons up a suitably doomladen, disturbing atmosphere.

Patrick Bergin *Mark Samuels* • Vanessa Redgrave *Florence Latimer* • Valerie Mahaffey *Chris Samuels* • Nancy Moore Atchison *Nikki Samuels* • Rutanya Alda *Sue Madehurst* ■ *Dir* John Korty • *Scr* Edith Swensen, from the short story by Rudyard Kipling

They Were Expendable
★★★★ U

Second World War drama 1945 · US · BW · 129mins

During the war, John Ford served in the navy and made several documentaries, including the classic *The Battle of Midway*. When the war looked like being won, he enlisted with MGM to make *They Were Expendable*, a drama about buying time for the navy after the disaster of Pearl Harbor. It is an epic – long, reflective, bursting with incident – and contains fine performances from Robert Montgomery, John Wayne, Donna Reed and members of Ford's stock company. Amazingly, fellow director Lindsay Anderson discovered that Ford himself had never seen it : "I was ordered to do it," he told Anderson, "I didn't put a goddamned thing into that picture … I never saw a goddamned foot of it." Anderson rated the film as one of Ford's finest and urged the director to give it a try. He later received a cable from Ford saying: "Have seen *Expendable*. You were right. Ford." ▭

Robert Montgomery *Lt John Brickley* • John Wayne *Lt RG "Rusty" Ryan* • Donna Reed *Lt Sandy Davyss* • Jack Holt *General Martin* • Ward Bond *"Boats" Mulcahey* • Marshall Thompson *Ensign Snake Gardner* • Paul Langton *Ensign Andy Andrews* ■ *Dir* John Ford, Robert Montgomery • *Scr* Frank W Wead, from the book by William L White

They Were Not Divided ★★

Second World War drama 1950 · UK · BW · 101mins

There's not much evidence in this stiff-upper-lipped Second World War drama to suggest that Terence Young would go on to direct three of the best Bond movies in the early sixties. The action is almost totally reliant on the sort of gung-ho camaraderie that was characteristic of the recruiting propaganda that filled British screens in the first days of the conflict. Edward Underdown's Guards officer and Ralph Clanton's have-a-go Yank are nothing more than caricatures, but contemporary audiences queued round the block to see their exploits as they drove the Nazis back to Berlin. They weren't divided, but they weren't very interesting, either.

Edward Underdown *Philip* • Ralph Clanton *David* • Helen Cherry *Wilhelmina* • Stella Andrews *Jane* • Michael Brennan *Smoke O'Connor* • Michael Trubshawe *Major Bushy Noble* • John Wynn *45 Jones* ■ *Dir/Scr* Terence Young

They Were Sisters ★★★ U

Drama 1945 · UK · BW · 109mins

A quintessential Gainsborough melodrama following the marriages of three sisters, whose husbands, it turns out, range from the tolerant to the tyrannical. The sisters are played by three splendid actresses whose looks (and diction) epitomise a long-gone era: Phyllis Calvert, Dulcie Gray and Anne Crawford. Today, though, the main interest is in the character of Geoffrey, a no-good sadist who causes untold misery to Gray's sweet Charlotte: he's played by a young James Mason, giving a performance every bit as vicious as his work in *The Seventh Veil* and *The Man in Grey*. ▭

Phyllis Calvert *Lucy* • James Mason *Geoffrey* • Hugh Sinclair *Terry* • Anne Crawford *Vera* • Peter Murray Hill *William* • Dulcie Gray *Charlotte* • Barrie Livesey *Brian* ■ *Dir* Arthur Crabtree • *Scr* Roland Pertwee, Katherine Strueby, from the novel by Dorothy Whipple

They Who Dare ★★★ U

Second World War drama 1953 · UK · Colour · 103mins

Considering director Lewis Milestone was responsible for those combat classics *All Quiet on the Western Front* and *A Walk in the Sun*, this is a very disappointing account of an Allied commando raid on Rhodes. Ordered to knock out a couple of airfields, Dirk Bogarde and Denholm Elliott spend as much time squabbling with each other as they do confronting the enemy. Akim Tamiroff, Gérard Oury and Eric Pohlmann are far more watchable, but not even they can atone for the sloppy dialogue (much of which was improvised) and the throwaway finale. The action sequences are convincing enough, but Milestone was capable of so much better. ▭

Dirk Bogarde *Lieutenant Graham* • Denholm Elliott *Sergeant Corcoran* • Akim Tamiroff *Captain George One* • Gérard Oury *Captain George Two* • Eric Pohlmann *Captain Papadopoulos* • Alec Mango *Patroklis* • Kay Callard *Nightclub singer* ■ *Dir* Lewis Milestone • *Scr* Robert Westerby

They Won't Believe Me
★★★

Crime drama   1947 · US · BW · 95mins

Robert Young sheds his good guy image to play a heel on trial for murder. He's cheated on his wealthy wife(Rita Johnson). He's been involved with a young writer (Jane Greer) and then with a gold-digging secretary (Susan Hayward). One has died in a car accident, one has committed suicide, but can Young persuade the jury that he didn't kill anybody? Told as a long flashback, this is written by crime novelist Jonathan Latimer, produced by Hitchcock associate Joan Harrison, and directed by former actor Irving Pichel. It's slick and artificial but still engrossing.

Robert Young *Larry Ballentine* • Susan Hayward *Verna Carlson* • Jane Greer *Janice Bell* • Rita Johnson *Gretta Ballentine* • Tom Powers *Trenton* • George Tyne *Lt Carr* ■ *Dir* Irving Pichel • *Scr* Jonathan Latimer, from a story by Gordon McDonell

They Won't Forget
★★★

Drama   1937 · US · BW · 95mins

Directed by Mervyn LeRoy, this was Warner Bros's answer to MGM's *Fury*, which in turn was Fritz Lang's searing indictment of lynch law and mob rule. Starring Claude Rains as a Deep South DA, the story spins on the murder of a student (Lana Turner) and the suspicion that falls on a black janitor and a college lecturer. When the politically ambitious Rains clears the janitor and condemns the lecturer, a smart-aleck lawyer arrives to defend him, leading us into a courtroom drama in which the real defendant is bigotry. With strong performances and a deal of moralising, this can be favourably compared to the 1996 adaptation of John Grisham's *A Time to Kill.*

Claude Rains *Andrew J Griffin* • Gloria Dickson *Sybil Hale* • Edward Norris *Robert Paerry Hale* • Otto Kruger *Michael Gleason* • Allyn Joslyn *William P Brock* • Lana Turner *Mary Clay* • Linda Perry *Imogene Mayfield* • Elisha Cook Jr *Joe Turner* ■ *Dir* Mervyn LeRoy • *Scr* Robert Rossen, Aben Kandel, from the novel *Death in the Deep South* by Ward Greene

They're a Weird Mob
★ U

Romantic comedy
1966 · Ausl · Colour · 112mins

An utterly dire, and rightly neglected, Michael Powell/Emeric Pressburger collaboration, a far cry from the days of their greatest films, such as *The Red Shoes*, *Black Narcissus* and *A Matter of Life and Death*. Pressburger contributed only the screenplay here, under the pseudonym of Richard Imrie, but even that is nothing to be proud of. This lacklustre would-be comedy derives most of its laughs from Italian immigrant Walter Chiari (best remembered for once having an affair with Ava Gardner) battling with the Aussie dialect, while trying to locate his female cousin. All performances, with the honourable exception of Australian veteran Chips Rafferty as the cousin's dad, are deplorable, verging on the amateur, and the whole simply doesn't come off.

Walter Chiari *Nino Culotta* • Clare Dunne *Kay Kelly* • Chips Rafferty *Harry Kelly* • Alida Chelli *Giuliana* • Ed Devereaux *Joe* ■ *Dir* Michael Powell • *Scr* Richard Imrie [Emeric Pressburger], from the novel by Nino Culotta

They're Playing With Fire ★

Crime horror   1984 · US · Colour · 96mins

Sexy professor Sybil Danning seduces student Eric Brown and begs him to help her carry out a money-making murder scheme. Meanwhile, a masked maniac is on the loose, killing people with an axe. A preposterous thriller which rapidly descends into slasher territory and doesn't convince in either area. Fans of sex siren Danning won't mind though, as she cavorts alot naked. Contains nudity.

Sybil Danning *Diane Stevens* • Eric Brown *Jay Richards* • Andrew Prine *Michael Stevens* • Paul Clemens *Martin "Bird" Johnson* • KT Stevens *Lillian Stevens* ■ *Dir* Howard Avedis • *Scr* Howard Avedis, Marlene Schmidt

Thicker than Blood ★★ PG

Drama based on a true story
1993 · US · Colour · 89mins

The agony of a father who is not only torn from his son when his girlfriend leaves him, but also has to face up to the fact that the boy he has come to adore is not his own. Peter Strauss could so easily have poured syrup all over this role, but instead he produces a credible blend of anger, affection and determination as he battles for custody of the child. Rachel Ticotin also avoids the easy characterisation, playing the mother as someone at the end of her tether rather than a selfish monster. 📺

Peter Strauss *Larry McLinden* • Rachel Ticotin *Diane Middleton* • Bob Dishy *Glen Schwartz* • Brenda Bazinet *Mary* ■ *Dir* Michael Dinner • *Scr* Judson Klinger

Thicker than Blood ★★ 12

Drama   1998 · US · Colour · 92mins

Based on the Bill Cain play, *Stand-Up Tragedy*, this TV film features Hollywood bad boy Mickey Rourke in an uncharacteristic turn as a priest and mentor to a former student (Dan Futterman), who returns to teach at Rourke's inner-city mission school. The two come into conflict over Futterman's devotion to one particularly promising student. It's a story with emotional appeal, strengthened by a good cast and steady direction by Richard Pearce. There is not a lot of action, and its roots as a play too often show but, in spite of being predictable, it is surprisingly palatable. Contains swearing and violence. 📺

Mickey Rourke *Father Frank Larkin* • Dan Futterman *Griffin Bryne* • Carlo Alban *Lee Cortez* • Lauren Velez *Camilla Lopez* • Josh Mostel *Burke Kendall* • Peter Maloney *Mitch James* ■ *Dir* Richard Pearce • *Scr* Bill Cain, from his play *Stand-Up Tragedy*

Thicker than Water ★★★ U

Comedy   1935 · US · BW · 20mins

The last ever Laurel and Hardy short, in which the pair squander their family savings on a grandfather clock. Though not as brilliant as some of their earlier shorts, this still has some rib-tickling moments. After 1935, the duo concentrated on feature-length movies, although they did make a cameo appearance in the 1936 Charley Chase short, *On the Wrong Trek*. 📺

Stan Laurel *Stan* • Oliver Hardy *Ollie* • Daphne Pollard *Mrs Daphne Hardy* • James Finlayson *Auction operator* • Harry Bowen *Auctioneer* • Charlie Hall *Bank teller* ■ *Dir* James W Horne • *Scr* from a story by Stan Laurel, HM Walker, Charles Rogers

The Thief
★★

Spy drama   1952 · US · BW · 86mins

If you've ever cringed at the ridiculous dialogue in many Hollywood movies, this one may provide some relief. Ray Milland stars in a spy drama that features no dialogue at all, relying instead on narration, sound effects, creating the right ambience, and the intelligence of the audience. Milland is a nuclear physicist who turns traitor for the Russians, but then finds himself under investigation by the FBI and forced to go into hiding. The gimmick isn't entirely successful as it leaves Milland's motivation unclear, but it's worth a look.

Ray Milland *Allan Fields* • Martin Gabel *Mr Bleek* • Rita Gam *The girl* • Harry Bronson *Harris* • John McKutcheon *Dr Linstrum* • Rita Vale *Miss Philips* ■ *Dir* Russell Rouse • *Scr* Clarence Greene, Russell Rouse

Thief
★★★★ 18

Crime drama   1981 · US · Colour · 117mins

Director Michael Mann's auspicious feature debut pins its story of a professional jewel thief (James Caan), to a near-abstract idea about the criminal's urge to self-destruct – despite the meticulous way he plans his life. The terrific opening sequence – a diamond robbery set to the music of Tangerine Dream – sets the mood and style for a crime drama that's almost too intellectual for its own genre. Nevertheless, one to see from a director who would later make the epic *The Last of the Mohicans* and the thriller *Heat*. Contains swearing, violence and nudity. 📺

James Caan *Frank* • Tuesday Weld *Jessie* • Willie Nelson *Okla* • James Belushi *Barry* • Robert Prosky *Leo* • Tom Signorelli *Attaglia* • Dennis Farina *Carl* ■ *Dir* Michael Mann • *Scr* Michael Mann, from the book *The Home Invaders* by Frank Hohimer

The Thief
★★★★ 15

Drama   1997 · Rus/Fr · Colour · 93mins

Echoing his father Grigori's socialist realist masterpiece, *Ballad of a Soldier* (1960), Pavel Chukrai's Oscar-nominated drama, chronicles the crimes of a very different type of trooper. Seen through the eyes of her six year-old son, Ekaterina Rednikova's abrupt romance with Vladimir Mashkov is both intimidating and bewildering, as the threesome flits between provincial towns exploiting Mashkov's Red Army respectability. Contrasting the conditions of postwar austerity with the post-Communist present, this allegory on Yeltsin's Russia is stylishly composed and superbly acted, particularly by the son, whose gradual conversion to hero worship, eventually has tragic ramifications. In Russian with English subtitles.. Contains sex, swearing, violence. 📺

Vladimir Mashkov *Tolian* • Ekaterina Rednikova *Katia* • Misha Filipchuk *Sania, aged six* • Amaliia Mordvinova *Doctor's wife* • Dima Chigarev *Sania, aged 12* • Iurii Beliaev *Sania, aged 48* ■ *Dir/Scr* Pavel Chukrai

The Thief of Bagdad
★★★★ U

Silent action fantasy
1924 · US · BW · 210mins

A grinning, bare-chested Douglas Fairbanks shimmies up a rope and enters a room in the palace, intending to steal a casket of baubles. Instead, his eyes fall on Princess Julanne Johnston, and he swears there and then to be worthy of her and take her for a ride on a magic carpet. Of such things movie myths are made, effortlessly embodied by Fairbanks in one of his most famous roles. Maybe it dawdles in some sections and some performances are distinctly wobbly, but even those, like the special effects, have a charm all their own. William Cameron Menzies, who later designed *Things to Come* and *Gone With the Wind*, provided the memorable sets, a clever combination of real structures and shots which utilised painted pieces of glass placed right next to the camera lens. 📺

Douglas Fairbanks *The Thief of Bagdad* • Snitz Edwards *His evil associate* • Charles Belcher *The holy man* • Julanne Johnston *The princess* • Anna May Wong *The Mongol slave* • Winter Blossom *The slave of the lute* • Etta Lee *The slave of the sand board* • Brandon Hurst *The caliph* ■ *Dir* Raoul Walsh • *Scr* Lotta Woods, from a story by Elton Thomas [Douglas Fairbanks] • *Cinematographer* Arthur Edeson • *Costume Designer* Mitchell Leisen

The Thief of Bagdad
★★★★ U

Fantasy adventure
1940 · UK · Colour · 101mins

A wonderfully atmospheric *Arabian Nights* adventure for children of all ages, particularly young lads who can identify with Sabu singing ''I want to be a bandit, can't you understand it?'' part of a marvellous score by Miklos Rozsa, which, incidentally, was the first ever to be committed to record. Producer and co-director Alexander Korda spared no expense to bring the magic to the screen, undeterred by the outbreak of war which necessitated decamping from England to Hollywood, not to mention using five other directors! Oscar-winning Technicolor photography and sumptuous art direction make this the definitive movie of this particular tale. With a giant genie, flying carpets, magical mechanical horses, a beautiful princess, Sabu himself, and a wickedly wicked grand vizier in the person of Conrad Veidt, what more could any adventure-seeker ask for? 📺

Conrad Veidt *Jaffar* • Sabu *Abu* • June Duprez *Princess* • John Justin *Ahmad* • Rex Ingram *Djinni* • Miles Malleson *Sultan* • Morton Selten *King* • Mary Morris *Halima* • Hay Petrie *Astrologer* ■ *Dir* Ludwig Berger, Michael Powell, Tim Whelan, Zoltan Korda, William Cameron Menzies, Alexander Korda • *Scr* Lajos Biro, Miles Malleson • *Cinematographer* Georges Périnal, Osmond Borradaile • *Art Director* Vincent Korda

U = SUITABLE FOR ALL   Uc = SUITABLE FOR ALL, ESPECIALLY FOR YOUNG CHILDREN (VIDEO ONLY)   PG = PARENTAL GUIDANCE

The Thief of Baghdad ★ U

Fantasy adventure
1978 · UK/Fr · Colour · 96mins

The fourth screen version of the *Arabian Nights* fantasy, filmed in France and using the Zoptic system also featured in *Superman*, for the flying scenes. Otherwise, the effects are not special at all, and the whole enterprise has a listless air. Enjoyment depends on one's tolerance of Peter Ustinov's ad-libbing sprees and Roddy McDowall's tendency to camp everything up. Former ballerina Marina Vlady, best known as the hooker-housewife in Godard's *Two or Three Things I Know about Her*, behaves like a zombie. 🖭

Roddy McDowall *Hasan* • Peter Ustinov *Caliph* • Kabir Bedi *Prince Taj* • Terence Stamp *Wazir Jaudur* • Frank Finlay *Abu Bakar* • Marina Vlady *Perizadah* • Pavla Ustinov *Princess Yasmine* • Ian Holm *Gatekeeper* ■ *Dir* Clive Donner • *Scr* AJ Carothers

Thief of Damascus ★★★ U

Adventure 1952 · US · Colour · 78mins

A light-hearted *Arabian Nights* cock-up featuring Paul Henreid, Robert Clary and Lon Chaney Jr as Abu Andar, Aladdin and Sinbad. The band members pool their magical talents in order to rescue Princess Elena Verdugo from the nasty likes of desert mogul John Sutton. Despite its hotch-potch pantomime, it's really quite likeable.

Paul Henreid *Abu Andar* • John Sutton *Khalid* • Jeff Donnell *Sheherazade* • Lon Chaney Jr *Sinbad* • Elena Verdugo *Neela* • Robert Clary *Aladdin* • Edward Colmans *Sultan Raudah* • Nelson Leigh *Ben Jammal* • Philip Van Zandt *Ali Baba* ■ *Dir* Will Jason • *Scr* Robert E Kent

Thief of Hearts ★★★ 18

Thriller 1984 · US · Colour · 96mins

A slick and sensual psychological drama, with Steven Bauer as a burglar who breaks into a married woman's home and steals a diary detailing her innermost sexual fantasies. He then uses them to woo the woman, who hasn't the faintest idea that he's acting on inside information. Sounds sleazy, and up to a point it is. But it's well-made with strong performances from Bauer and Barbara Williams, and fairly subtle use of its sex scenes. Spicier ones were reportedly added for the film's video release. Watch out for an early support appearance by David Caruso. 🖭

Steven Bauer *Scott Muller* • Barbara Williams *Mickey Davis* • John Getz *Ray Davis* • David Caruso *Buddy Calamara* • Christine Ebersole *Janie Pointer* • George Wendt *Marty Morrison* ■ *Dir/Scr* Douglas Day Stewart

The Thief of Paris ★★★★

Period comedy drama
1967 · Fr/It · Colour · 120mins

A melancholy, even pessimistic work from the fine French director, Louis Malle, set in and around 1900. Jean-Paul Belmondo stars as Georges, a wealthy young Parisian whose uncle squanders his fortune , then marries off the cousin he loves to a rich neighbour. Georges steals the jewels of the neighbour's family and obsessed by the notion of revenge against bourgeois society and its hypocrisies, embarks on a life of crime as a master thief. Enriched by warm colour photography and a marvellous sense of period, Malle was evidently influenced by the great French director Robert Bresson – he had worked as his assistant – and by *Pickpocket*, his definitive study of a thief alienated from society. A French language film.

Jean-Paul Belmondo *Georges Randal* • Geneviève Bujold *Charlotte* • Marie Dubois *Geneviève* • Françoise Fabian *Ida* • Julien Guiomar *Lamargelle* • Paul Le Person *Roger La Honte* ■ *Dir* Louis Malle • *Scr* Louis Malle, Jean-Claude Carrière, Daniel Boulanger, from a story by Georges Darien

The Thief Who Came to Dinner ★★★ 15

Crime comedy drama
1973 · US · Colour · 100mins

Written by Walter Hill (later to direct blockbuster movies like *The Driver* and *48 HRS*), this has moments of originality, but is otherwise a tepid, episodic comedy thriller. Ryan O'Neal is the computer analyst-turned-jewel thief, with Jacqueline Bisset as his girl. But it's support actors Warren Oates, playing a bemused insurance investigator, and Austin Pendleton, as an exasperated editor, who make the most of the predictable plot. 🖭

Ryan O'Neal *Webster Mcgee* • Jacqueline Bisset *Laura Keaton* • Warren Oates *Dave Reilly* • Jill Clayburgh *Jackie* • Charles Cioffi *Henderling* • Ned Beatty *Deams* • Austin Pendleton *Zukovsky* • George Morfogen *Rivera* • Gregory Sierra *Dynamite* • Michael Murphy *Ted* ■ *Dir* Bud Yorkin • *Scr* Walter Hill, from the novel by Terence Lore Smith

Thieves ★★ PG

Romantic comedy
1977 · US · Colour · 90mins

Herb Gardner's Broadway play was transferred virtually line-for-line to the screen, retaining the play's lead actress, Marlo Thomas, who co-stars with Charles Grodin, director of the original stage production. It's about life in New York, how hard it is, and how the marriage of Thomas and Grodin, both teachers, runs into problems. It was roasted by the critics at the time – "Dull, dated, downbeat" said *Variety* – but supporting roles by throaty Mercedes McCambridge and seedy Hector Elizondo perk it up. Watch out, too, for a brief cameo from Broadway's hottest director, Bob Fosse. 🖭

Marlo Thomas *Sally Cramer* • Charles Grodin *Martin Cramer* • Irwin Corey *Joe Kaminsky* • Hector Elizondo *Man below* • Mercedes McCambridge *Street lady* • John McMartin *Gordon* • Gary Merrill *Street man* • Bob Fosse *Mr Day* ■ *Dir* John Berry, Al Viola • *Scr* Herb Gardner, from his play

Thieves' Highway ★★★★

Thriller 1949 · US · BW · 92mins

A superb 20th Century-Fox melodrama from a great *film noir* period, about a tough soldier out to get the racketeer who ruined his dad while he was away fighting in the Second World War. This is a committed socialist work from director Jules Dassin, with a fine cast that includes Lee J Cobb and the great Morris Carnovsky. The screenplay, from his novel *Thieves' Market*, is by the gifted Al Bezzerides, best remembered for *Kiss Me Deadly* and *They Drive by Night*. American cinema at its most exciting, absorbing European influences and spitting them out in a tough, unsparing, uniquely American way. This movie makes Quentin Tarantino look like Noddy.

Richard Conte *Nick Garcos* • Valentina Cortesa [Valentina Cortese] *Rica* • Lee J Cobb *Mike Figlia* • Barbara Lawrence *Polly Faber* • Jack Oakie *Slob* • Millard Mitchell *Ed* • Joseph Pevney *Pete* • Morris Carnovsky *Yanko Garcos* ■ *Dir* Jules Dassin • *Scr* Ai Bezzerides, from the novel *Thieves' Market* by Al Bezzerides

Thieves' Holiday ★★★

Crime biography 1946 · US · BW · 99mins

Sometimes known as *Scandal in Paris*, this diversion utilises the suave persona and polished style of George Sanders in the unusual guise of an 18th-century Parisian. Drawing its story from the memoirs of Eugene Vidocq, a thief who mended his ways to become Prefect of Police and first chief of the Sûreté, the movie concerns his relationship with a cabaret entertainer (Carole Landis) for whom he steals a bejewelled garter, his imprisonment, and his reformation under the influence of Signe Hasso. A light mix of drama and romantic comedy directed by Douglas Sirk and easy to digest.

George Sanders *Eugene-François Vidocq* • Signe Hasso *Thérèse* • Carole Landis *Loretta* • Akim Tamiroff *Emile Vernet* • Gene Lockhart *Chief of Police Richet* • Jo Ann Marlowe *Mimi* ■ *Dir* Douglas Sirk • *Scr* Ellis St Joseph, from a memoir by François Eugene Vidocq

Thieves like Us ★★★★ 15

Crime drama 1974 · US · Colour · 117mins

Robert Altman's remake of Nicholas Ray's doom-laden *film noir They Live by Night*, has Altman regular Shelley Duvall and Keith Carradine convincing and touching as the young lovers adrift in the poverty-stricken Deep South. Set in the thirties and shot in Mississippi, the picture is classically made, lacking the "innovations" that were Altman's trademarks. Louise Fletcher, later an Oscar winner for *One Flew over the Cuckoo's Nest*, appears in her screen debut. Contains nudity. 🖭

Keith Carradine *Bowie* • Shelley Duvall *Keechie* • John Schuck *Chicamaw* • Bert Remsen *T-dub* • Louise Fletcher *Mattie* • Ann Latham *Lula* • Tom Skerritt *Dee Mobley* ■ *Dir* Robert Altman • *Scr* Calder Willingham, Joan Tewkesbury, Robert Altman, from the novel by Edward Anderson

The Thin Blue Line ★★★★★ 15

Documentary 1988 · US · Colour · 97mins

In 1976 a Dallas policeman, Robert Wood, routinely stopped a car and was shot dead. Later, a known delinquent, 16-year-old David Harris, was arrested after boasting about the murder. Under questioning, Harris protested his innocence and blamed a hitch-hiker he had picked up, Randall Adams. Adams was tried and sentenced to death, later commuted to life imprisonment. Twelve years after the crime, documentary film-maker Errol Morris re-opened the case and produced this stunning film, an unsurpassed blend of interviews and reconstruction. Our journey into the case is also Morris's, as he slowly uncovers a symphony of doubt and a miscarriage of justice. The sense of unease, heightened by an enthralling collection of witnesses, accumulates so that a random murder in Dallas, puts all of America under the microscope. The picture earned its ultimate prize – not an Oscar but a retrial and, in the end, Adams's release. 🖭

Dir/Scr Errol Morris • *Music* Philip Glass

Thin Ice ★★

Romantic musical comedy
1937 · US · BW · 78mins

This lightweight trifle stretches Norwegian skating star Sonja Henie's acting ability more than a little, as she plays an ice-skating coach who falls in love with a prince (Tyrone Power). His sly, knowing performance suggests that the plot is not exactly coincidental – in the heady days of the romance between Edward VIII and divorcee Mrs Simpson. For this opus, 20th Century-Fox constructed a special camera rig to follow Henie's movements on the ice, but it could be argued that the expense was hardly justified, since the real highlight is not the dimpled skater but the wonderfully raucous comedienne Joan Davis, best-remembered over here for her TV series *I Married Joan*, performing the arch ballad *I'm Olga from the Volga*.

Sonja Henie *Lili Heiser* • Tyrone Power *Rudolph* • Arthur Treacher *Nottingham* • Raymond Walburn *Uncle Dornic* • Joan Davis *Orchestra Leader* • *Dir* Sidney Lanfield • *Scr* Boris Ingster, Milton Sperling, from the play *Der Komet* by Attila Obok

Thin Ice ★ 15

Drama 1994 · UK · Colour · 85mins

Scarcely believable on any level, director Fiona Cunningham Reid's hopelessly naive, same-gender romance feels like it has come from another dim and distant era. Every cliché is stumbled into as a white heterosexual ice skater teams up with a black lesbian partner and enters the Gay Games in New York. Leads Charlotte Avery and Sabra Williams skate on thin ice in more ways than one. 🖭

Charlotte Avery *Natalie* • Sabra Williams *Steffi* • James Dreyfus *Greg* • Clare Higgins *Fiona* • Ian McKellen • Guy Williams *Charles* • Barbara New *Felicity* • Martha Freud *Cosima* ■ *Dir* Fiona Cunningham Reid • *Scr* Fiona Cunningham Reid, Geraldine Sherman

A Thin Line between Love and Hate ★ 18

Comedy thriller 1996 · US · Colour · 103mins

A feeble *Fatal Attraction* clone from comedian Martin Lawrence, who has no one else to blame considering he's the executive producer, director, co-writer and star. He plays a vulgar Casanova with limited ambitions, who gets his comeuppance after romancing glamorous real estate tycoon Lynn Whitfield and dumping her for his true love, Regina King. Whitfield is the victim of an abusive marriage, and doesn't take too lightly to being jilted in this unfunny, uncouth comedy thriller which toes a very thin line between bad and awful before stumbling irrevocably into the latter. 🖭

Martin Lawrence *Darnell* • Lynn Whitfield *Brandi* • Regina King *Mia* • Bobby Brown *Tee*

• Della Reese *Ma Wright* • Malinda Williams *Erica* • Daryl Mitchell *Earl* • Roger E Mosley *Smitty* ■ *Dir* Martin Lawrence • *Scr* Martin Lawrence, Bentley Kyle Evans, Kenny Buford, Kim Bass, from a story by Martin Lawrence

The Thin Man ★★★★
Classic detective comedy
1934 · US · BW · 93mins
The first in a popular series, based on Dashiell Hammett's characters, with William Powell and Myrna Loy as Nick and Nora Charles, amateur sleuths and the epitome of thirties style and sophistication. Hammett had written a thriller, but MGM turned it into a screwball comedy, with Powell and Loy making a sizzling couple – forerunners to Cary Grant and Katharine Hepburn in *Bringing Up Baby*. Their excessive drinking and other shocking habits (the characters are based on Hammett and Lillian Hellman) delighted audiences 60 years ago and still do today, even if the pacing now seems rather slow.
William Powell *Nick Charles* • Myrna Loy *Nora Charles* • Maureen O'Sullivan *Dorothy Wynant* • Nat Pendleton *Lieutenant John Guild* • Minna Gombell *Mimi Wynant* • Porter Hall *MacCauley* • Henry Wadsworth *Tommy* ■ *Dir* WS Van Dyke • *Scr* Albert Hackett, Frances Goodrich, from the novel by Dashiell Hammett

The Thin Man Goes Home ★★★
Detective comedy drama
1944 · US · BW · 100mins
Fifth in the Dashiell Hammett-inspired series that began with *The Thin Man* in 1934. William Powell plays Nick Charles, a man aided by a sharp mind, several dry martinis and a glamorous wife Nora – usually in that order. In this film he's on a visit to his home town and as usual, the amateur sleuths and Asta the dog are up to their elegant necks in solving a murder mystery. Audiences would not have it any other way.
William Powell *Nick Charles* • Myrna Loy *Nora Charles* • Lucile Watson *Mrs Charles* • Gloria De Haven [Gloria DeHaven] *Laura Ronson* • Anne Revere *Crazy Mary* • Harry Davenport *Dr Bertram Charles* • Helen Vinson *Helena Draque* • Lloyd Corrigan *Dr Bruce Clayworth* ■ *Dir* Richard Thorpe • *Scr* Robert Riskin, Dwight Taylor, from a story by Robert Riskin, from a story by Harry Kurnitz, from characters created by Dashiell Hammett

The Thin Red Line ★★
Second World War drama
1964 · US · BW · 95mins
Admirers of Terrence Malick's excellent 1998 version of James Jones' epic Second World War novel may find this disappointing. But this well-acted picture takes a more conventional approach, focusing on the spiky relationship between veteran first sergeant Jack Warden and raw private Keir Dullea. In the bitter conflict in Guadalcanal in the Pacific, the two men's loathing for each other develops into mutual respect. The combat sequences are first class, without war being glorified.
Keir Dullea *Private Doll* • Jack Warden *1st Sgt Welsh* • James Philbrook *Colonel Tall* • Ray Daley *Captain Stone* ■ *Dir* Andrew Marton • *Scr* Bernard Gordon, from the novel by James Jones

The Thin Red Line ★★★★★15
Second World War drama
1998 · US · Colour · 163mins
After twenty years in the wilderness – that is to say, not talking to the press and finding better things to do than making movies – Terrence Malick launched his belated third feature – this magnificent account of the battle for Guadalcanal in the South Pacific. Based on James Jones's novel, first filmed in 1964, it's a long, discursive and deeply philosophical evocation of war, beautifully shot by cameraman John Toll in Queensland and on Guadalcanal itself. Although the film boasts an all-star cast, big names like Travolta and Clooney have only brief appearances, while Sean Penn as a cynical sergeant and Nick Nolte as a mad, Kilgore-like colonel make deeper impressions, the major role goes to the unknown Jim Caviezel as an ordinary Joe. But it is Malick himself who provides the real star turn with his extraordinary direction. Malick's war is not only between the US Marines and the Japanese, it is a war with our own natures and with nature itself – the vast plains of high grass, the rain forest and the reptiles, birds and insects within it – as well as the Melanesian islanders, who walk past a platoon without noticing them. A modern masterpiece. Contains swearing, violence.
Sean Penn *1st Sgt Welsh* • Jim Caviezel [James Caviezel] *Private Witt* • John Cusack *Captain Gaff* • Ben Chaplin *Private Bell* • Nick Nolte *Lt Colonel Tall* • Woody Harrelson *Keck* • Elias Koteas *Captain "Bugger" Staros* • John Travolta *Qintard* • George Clooney *Bosche* ■ *Dir* Terrence Malick • *Scr* Terrence Malick, from the novel by James Jones

The Thing ★★★★18
Science-fiction thriller
1982 · US · Colour · 103mins
John Carpenter's remake of Howard Hawks and Christian Nyby's influential 1951 creature feature, is a special-effects extravaganza of the highest order. In fact, the updated screenplay by Bill Lancaster (son of Burt) sticks more closely to the plot of the classic John W Campbell short story that inspired the original, as the occupants of a polar research station are menaced by an alien with the ability to change its shape and impersonate its enemies. Carpenter stresses the slimy ET at the expense of characterisation, mood and practically everything else, yet it's precisely this one grisly facet that makes it such compelling science fiction. Even *Alien* can't hold a candle to the nightmarish images on offer here, so be warned. Contains violence and swearing. *DVD*
Kurt Russell *Macready* • Wilford Brimley *Blair* • TK Carter *Nauls* • David Clennon *Palmer* • Keith David *Childs* • Richard Dysart *Dr Cooper* • Charles Hallahan *Norris* • Peter Maloney *Bennings* • Richard Masur *Clark* ■ *Dir* John Carpenter • *Scr* Bill Lancaster, from the story *Who Goes There?* by John W Campbell Jr

The Thing Called Love ★★15
Drama 1993 · US · Colour · 109mins
Peter Bogdanovich directs River Phoenix in one of his final roles, in this run-of-the-mill drama about love and fame amongst a group of aspiring country singers. Phoenix is fine as the young singer trying to make a name for himself in Nashville, and he's backed up by a competent young cast which includes Samantha Mathis, Dermot Mulroney and Sandra Bullock, as well as a handful of bona fide country singers. But despite the authenticity of the music and winning performances, it never really kicks into gear and ends up as a brief footnote to Phoenix's promising career.
River Phoenix *James Wright* • Samantha Mathis *Miranda Presley* • Dermot Mulroney *Kyle Davidson* • Sandra Bullock *Linda Lue Linden* • KT Oslin *Lucy* • Anthony Clark *Billy* • Webb Wilder *Ned* ■ *Dir* Peter Bogdanovich • *Scr* Carol Heikkinen

The Thing from Another World ★★★★12
Science-fiction thriller
1951 · US · BW · 82mins
A pioneering science-fiction movie emphasising suspense and atmosphere, rather than the shock special effects of John Carpenter's 1982 remake, in a tense story of Arctic scientists trying to cope with the first of Hollywood's Cold War aliens. Credited as being only produced by Howard Hawks, it's suspiciously full of his signature flourishes (camaraderie in the face of ambush, for instance) and director Christian Nyby never made anything half as good again.
Kenneth Tobey *Captain Patrick Hendry* • Margaret Sheridan *Nikki* • Robert Cornthwaite *Dr Carrington* • Douglas Spencer *Scotty* • James Young *Lt Eddie Dykes* • Dewey Martin *Crew Chief* • James Arness *The "Thing"* ■ *Dir* Christian Nyby • *Scr* Charles Lederer, from the story *Who Goes There?* by John Wood Campbell Jr [Don A Stuart]

The Thing with Two Heads ★★
Blaxploitation horror
1972 · US · Colour · 87mins
Probably the most lunatic blaxploitation horror film ever made, and also the genre's biggest missed opportunity to say something profound. Bigoted brain surgeon Ray Milland learns he's dying of cancer, so needs to transplant his head on to a healthy body. Unfortunately, racist Milland wakes to find his head next to that of condemned black-killer Rosey Grier, who is intent on clearing his name. With each head trying to seek control of Grier's body, the jokes should have been funnier, the racist allegory more up-front and the pacing more breakneck to cover the absolute idiocy of the premise. It's hard to figure out what's the dumbest stunt of all – the dummy heads substituted for action shots, or the two actors' necks unconvincingly bandaged together. A year before this, AIP also released the equally idiotic *The Incredible Two-Headed Transplant*.
Ray Milland *Dr Maxwell Kirshner* • Rosey Grier *Jack Moss* • Don Marshall *Dr Fred Williams* • Roger Perry *Dr Philip Desmond* • Chelsea Brown *Lila* • Kathy Baumann [Katherine Baumann] *Patricia* • John Dullaghan *Thomas* • John Bliss *Donald* ■ *Dir* Lee Frost • *Scr* Lee Frost, James Gordon White, Wes Bishop

Things Are Tough All Over ★★15
Comedy 1982 · US · Colour · 86mins
Double act "Cheech" Marin and Tommy Chong became (in)famous for their drug-related comedy routines that seemed perfectly suited to the American youth subculture of the seventies. Here, the duo eschew the pharmaceutical theme for a more-or-less straight farce about the adventures of two musicians employed by some arabs to drive a limousine full of money from Chicago to Vegas. The boys try hard (doubling as the Arabs and appearing in drag) and even rope in their real-life wives, but to little avail. Low comedy, as opposed to their normal "high" standards.
Richard "Cheech" Marin *Richard "Cheech" Marin/Mr Slyman* • Tommy Chong *Tommy Chong/Prince Habib* • Shelby Fiddis *1st French Girl* • Rikki Marin *2nd French Girl* • Evelyn Guerrero *Donna* • John Steadman *Oldtimer* • Rip Taylor ■ *Dir* Thomas K Avildsen • *Scr* Richard "Cheech" Marin, Thomas Chong [Tommy Chong]

Things Change ★★★★PG
Crime comedy 1988 · US · Colour · 96mins
After *House of Games*, playwright and stage director David Mamet cast veteran Hollywood star Don Ameche as an ageing shoeshine man in this charming tale. Ameche is persuaded to take the rap for a Mafia murder, in return for the fulfillment of his lifelong dream of owning a fishing boat. Mamet regular Joe Mantegna is the well-meaning minder who's assigned to take care of him, and decides to allow his charge one final fling of freedom. Trouble starts when Ameche is mistaken for a real Family man. A lovely film, beautifully crafted, and full of characters you'll care about.
Don Ameche *Gino* • Joe Mantegna *Jerry* • Robert Prosky *Joseph Vincent* • JJ Johnston *Frankie* • Ricky Jay *Mr Silver* • Mike Nussbaum *Mr Green* ■ *Dir* David Mamet • *Scr* David Mamet, Shel Silverstein

The Things of Life ★★★
Drama 1969 · Fr/It/Swi · Colour · 89mins
An opening car crash, spectacularly filmed, sends this glossy marital drama into flashback mode, in which Michel Piccoli vacillates between estranged wife Lea Massari and mistress Romy Schneider. Questions are raised: will Piccoli end up with Massari or Schneider, or will he end up dead? A movie of shifting moods and shifting allegiances rather than substance, well acted by the three leads although Piccoli is too rough-edged to be a sympathetic hero and the fact that he's an architect is a bit of a cliché – building for a living, his life falls apart. It was a huge hit in France and was remade in 1994 as *Intersection* with Sharon Stone and Richard Gere. French dialogue dubbed into English.
Michel Piccoli *Pierre Berard* • Romy Schneider *Hélène* • Lea Massari *Catherine Berard* • Gérard Lartigau *Bertrand Berard* • Jean Bouise *François* • Herve Sand *Truck driver* ■ *Dir* Claude Sautet • *Scr* Paul Guimard, Jean-Loup Dabadie, Claude Sautet, from the novel *Les Choses de la Vie* by Paul Guimard

Things to Come ★★★★ 🅿🅶
Science-fiction   1936 · UK · BW · 89mins

Although a classic slice of British sci-fi, Alexander Korda's elaborate production of HG Wells's prophetic novel is weakened by a prevailing air of over-theatricality and naivety. Spanning almost 100 years from 1940 to 2036, it begins during a world war and goes through plague and a technological revolution, ending with everyone living in an enormous Art Deco underground city run by Raymond Massey. Awesome sets and magnificent design make this hugely ambitious antique vision of the future, Britain's answer to *Metropolis*. Amazingly, Wells actually visited the studio while it was being made. ▭

Raymond Massey *John Cabal/Oswald Cabal* • Edward Chapman *Pippa Passworthy/raymond Passworthy* • Ralph Richardson *The Boss* • Margaretta Scott *Roxana/rowena* • Cedric Hardwicke *Theotocopulos* • Maurice Braddell *Dr Harding* • Sophie Stewart *Mrs Cabal* • Derrick de Marney *Richard Gordon* • Ann Todd *Mary Gordon* • George Sanders *Pilot* ■ *Dir* William Cameron Menzies • *Scr* HG Wells, Lajos Biró, from the book *The Shape of Things to Come* by HG Wells • *Cinematographer* Georges Périnal • *Production Designer* Vincent Korda

Things to Do in Denver When You're Dead ★★★★ 🔞
Crime drama   1995 · US · Colour · 110mins

The comparisons to Quentin Tarantino's work are inevitable, but Gary Fleder's witty, hip take on the gangster movie marked him out as an individual talent to watch. Andy Garcia plays a former mobster who is called in by his wheelchair-bound, former boss, Christopher Walken, to carry out one more job. When it goes badly wrong, Garcia and his associates find themselves on the hit list. The vivid splashes of violence are ably handled by Fleder, but he also delights in the rich dialogue of his oddball collection of characters, warmly brought to life by an eclectic cast that includes William Forsythe, Steve Buscemi, Christopher Lloyd and Treat Williams, who gives a career-reviving performance as an ex-boxer who works out on the corpses at a funeral parlour. Contains violence, swearing and sex scenes. ▭

Andy Garcia *Jimmy "The Saint" Tosnia* • Christopher Lloyd *Pieces* • William Forsythe *Franchise* • Bill Nunn *Easy Way* • Treat Williams *Critical Bill Dooley* • Jack Warden *Joe Heff* • Steve Buscemi *Mr Shhh* • Fairuza Balk *Lucinda* • Gabrielle Anwar *Dagney* • Christopher Walken *The Man with the Plan* ■ *Dir* Gary Fleder • *Scr* Scott Rosenberg

Think Big ★ 🅿🅶
Action comedy   1990 · US · Colour · 86mins

What is to be said about a movie where Richard Kiel ("Jaws" from the Bond films) manages to be boring as a villain? Only that his lacklustre performance seems to come from a realisation of the stupidity of the storyline, in which two dumb truck drivers (twins David and Peter Paul) are caught in a conspiracy to transport toxic waste. Still, as Cheech and Chong are to drugs, the Paul brothers are the only ones who could have delivered the few laughs there are with this material, including the chant,

"Chicken bone! Chicken bone! Lucky, lucky chicken bone!" ▭

Peter Paul *Vic* • David Paul *Rafe* • Martin Mull *Dr Bruekner* • David Carradine *John Sweeney* • Richard Kiel *Irving* • Claudia Christian *Dr Irene Marsh* ■ *Dir* Jon Turteltaub • *Scr* Edward Kovach, Jon Turteltaub, David Tausik, from a story by Jim Wynorski, RJ Robertson

Think Fast, Mr Moto ★★★
Crime mystery   1937 · US · BW · 66mins

The first in the eight-strong series featuring Peter Lorre as Mr Moto, the master of blindingly obvious disguises. Here, the Japanese sleuth is on the track of diamond smugglers operating out of San Francisco. Starting with the discovery of a body in an antique shop during Chinese New Year and transporting us, via a murderous ocean cruise, to the gambling joints of Shanghai, the story rapidly becomes impenetrable, with virtually every character acting shiftily. But, thanks to director Norman Foster and a wholehearted cast, the film has an irresistible momentum.

Peter Lorre *Mr Moto* • Virginia Field *Gloria Danton* • Thomas Beck *Bob Hitchings* • Sig Rumann [Sig Ruman] *Nicholas Marloff* • Murray Kinnell *Mr Joseph Wilkie* • Lotus Long *Lela Liu* • John Rogers *Carson* • George Cooper *Muggs Blake* ■ *Dir* Norman Foster • *Scr* Norman Foster, Howard Ellis Smith, from the novel by John P Marquand

The Third Day ★★★
Drama   1965 · US · Colour · 102mins

Despite some lapses in the screenplay, this amnesia thriller works well as a psychodrama. There are convincing leading performances from George Peppard and Elizabeth Ashley, and an eclectic cast that includes Roddy McDowall, Mona Washbourne and Herbert Marshall. Director Jack Smight would take the drama up a notch the following year with Paul Newman in *The Moving Target*.

George Peppard *Steve Mallory* • Elizabeth Ashley *Alexandria Mallory* • Roddy McDowall *Oliver Parsons* • Arthur O'Connell *Dr Wheeler* • Mona Washbourne *Catherine Parsons* • Herbert Marshall *Austin Parsons* ■ *Dir* Jack Smight • *Scr* Burton Wohl, Robert Presnell Jr, from the novel by Joseph Hayes

Third Finger, Left Hand ★★ 🆄
Comedy   1940 · US · BW · 96mins

A perky Myrna Loy vehicle with a bogglingly unbelievable plot, this is pleasant, but undemanding. Loy could be gloriously funny in the right role (*The Thin Man*) and here, as Melvyn Douglas's reluctant fiancée, she shines with her usual panache. But the script is thin and what starts out as a moderately pleasing soufflé, falls flat well before the final reel. The humour is childish at best, squirmingly embarrassing at worst. A dud in some books, but Loy and Douglas fans may still find some pleasure in it.

Myrna Loy *Margot Sherwood Merrick* • Melvyn Douglas *Jeff Thompson* • Raymond Walburn *Mr Sherwood* • Lee Bowman *Philip Booth* • Bonita Granville *Vicky Sherwood* • Felix Bressart *August Winkel* ■ *Dir* Robert Z Leonard • *Scr* Lionel Houser

The Third Generation ★★★
Black comedy   1979 · W Ger · Colour · 105mins

Not one of Rainer Werner Fassbinder's best films, but still an interesting depiction of middle-class urban radicals, dealing with a group of Berlin terrorists whose conflicts are gradually eating away at their nucleus. The director, who constantly ran out of money during the film's making, called it "a comedy in six parts", and it is played as political farce. It provoked violent controversy in Germany, where it was attacked by the left and right – the latter for glorifying terrorists and the former for betraying the heirs of the Baader-Meinhof Gang. In German with English subtitles.

Volker Spengler *August Brem* • Bulle Ogier *Hilde Krieger* • Hanna Schygulla *Susanne Gast* • Harry Baer *Rudolf Mann* • Vitus Zeplichal *Bernhard von Stein* • Udo Kier *Edgar Gast* • Margit Carstensen *Petra Vielhaber* • Günther Kaufmann *Franz Walsch* • Eddie Constantine *Peter Lurz* ■ *Dir/Scr* Rainer Werner Fassbinder

The Third Man ★★★★★ 🅿🅶
Classic thriller   1949 · UK · BW · 99mins

Developed by Graham Greene from an idea jotted down on the flap of an envelope, this virtually flawless feature is one of the best British films of all time. Set in postwar occupied Vienna, the plot is a corker, littered with memorable bits and played to perfection by an unforgettable cast, led with distinction by Orson Welles and Joseph Cotten. A master of place, angle and shade, director Carol Reed (helped by his Oscar-winning cinematographer Robert Krasker) fashions a city in which menace lurks around every corner, while Anton Karas's jaunty zither music uniquely echoes the wit and drama of this dark, yet daringly light, picture. ▭

Joseph Cotten *Holly Martins* • Orson Welles *Harry Lime* • Alida Valli *Anna Schmidt* • Trevor Howard *Major Calloway* • Paul Hoerbiger *Harry's porter* • Ernst Deutsch *"Baron" Kurtz* • Erich Ponto *Dr Winkel* • Siegfried Breuer *Popescu* • Bernard Lee *Sergeant Paine* • Geoffrey Keen *British policeman* • Wilfrid Hyde White *Crabbin* ■ *Dir* Carol Reed • *Scr* Graham Greene

Third Man on the Mountain ★★★ 🆄
Adventure   1959 · US · Colour · 100mins

Well-made and enjoyable Disney adventure, with youngster James MacArthur determined to scale the Alpine peak that claimed his father's life. However, when an early attempt ends in embarrassment, MacArthur is forced to seek training, transforming from callow youth to responsible adolescent along the way. MacArthur is a convincing lead, ably supported by familliar faces such as Janet Munro and Herbert Lom. This is life-affirming stuff with a clear moral purpose, and the location footage of the Swiss Alps is breath-taking.

Michael Rennie *Captain John Winter* • James MacArthur *Rudi Matt* • Janet Munro *Lizbeth Hempel* • James Donald *Franz Lerner* • Herbert Lom *Emil Saxo* • Laurence Naismith *Teo Zurbriggen* ■ *Dir* Ken Annakin • *Scr* Eleanore Griffin, from the book *Banner in the Sky* by James Ramsey Ullman

The Third Secret ★★★
Drama   1964 · UK · BW · 105mins

A psychiatrist is found shot dead. Did he kill himself or is something sinister going on? This psychological thriller, directed by Charles Crichton, is never as clever as it thinks it is, though the cast is outstanding: Richard Attenborough, Jack Hawkins, Diane Cilento, Rachel Kempson and Judi Dench, but the star of the show, as one of the dead shrink's patients trying to establish the truth, is Stephen Boyd, an Irish actor who, notwithstanding a riveting performance as Messala in *Ben-Hur*, never quite made it to the top.

Stephen Boyd *Alex Stedman* • Jack Hawkins *Sir Frederick Belline* • Richard Attenborough *Alfred Price-gorham* • Diane Cilento *Anne Tanner* • Pamela Franklin *Catherine Whitset* • Paul Rogers *Dr Milton Gillen* ■ *Dir* Charles Crichton • *Scr* Robert L Joseph

Third Time Lucky ★★
Drama   1949 · UK · BW · 90mins

What a difference it would have made had this routine British drama been produced in Hollywood. A gambler doesn't realise that he loves his lucky mascot until the chips are down. Dermot Walsh and Glynis Johns just don't set the screen alight and similarly, Gordon Parry (in fairness, directing only his second feature) fails to capture the seedy world of gambling dens and backstreet drinking joints. The corny, moralising ending, however, is pure Hollywood.

Glynis Johns *Joan* • Dermot Walsh *Lucky* • Charles Goldner *Flash* • Harcourt Williams *Doc* • Yvonne Owen *Peggy* • Helen Haye *Old Lady* ■ *Dir* Gordon Parry • *Scr* Gerald Butler, from his novel *They Cracked Her Glass Slipper*

The Third Voice ★★★★
Thriller   1960 · US · BW · 78mins

Extraordinarily stylish thriller by writer/director Hubert Cornfield, from Charles Williams's novel, *All the Way*, in which a woman kills her wealthy lover and an accomplice impersonates him through some financial processes. Edmond O'Brien, Laraine Day and Julie London form a suspenser-à-trois which lends credibility to an artificial situation.

Edmond O'Brien *The Voice* • Laraine Day *Marian Forbes* • Julie London *Corey Scott* • Ralph Brooks *Harris Chapman* • Roque Ybarra *Fisherman* • Ruben Moreno *Fisherman* ■ *Dir* Hubert Cornfield • *Scr* Hubert Cornfield, from the novel *All the Way* by Charles Williams

Third World Cop ★★★ 🆕
Crime   1999 · Jam · Colour · 98mins

Dirty Harry, Jamaican style. A rogue cop with a big gun and a disdain for conventional police procedure is withdrawn from rural duties and transferred to Kingston, the island's front line of crime. There his maverick approach to policing brings him into conflict with a former best buddy who's now right hand man to a vicious gunrunner. Produced by the same team behind the 1997 hit *Dancehall Queen*, *Third World Cop* is filmed in the flashy fashion of a Hong Kong martial arts movie. Neatly directed and solidly acted by an all-black cast, it breaks no new ground, but treads familiar territory with some skill and style. Non-attuned ears, though, may require a crash course in Jamaican patois to decipher much of the dialogue.

Paul Campbell *Capone* • Mark Danvers *Ratty* • Carl Bradshaw *Wonie* • Audrey Reid *Rita* ■ *Dir* Chris Browne • *Scr* Suzanne Fenn, Chris Browne, Chris Salewicz

Thirst ★★★

Drama   1949 · Swe · BW · 83mins

Produced at a time of marital crisis, the most commercially successful of Ingmar Bergman's early films is also something of an artistic watershed, as it weaves flashbacks, dreams and subplots into an engaging dramatic whole, which places a new emphasis on the female perspective. Travelling in a train compartment that symbolises her confinement in a non-communicative marriage, former ballerina Eva Henning recalls the affair that left her unable to conceive. Juxtaposed with this is the sequence of events that drove art historian Birger Malmsten's first wife, Birgit Tengroth, to suicide. (Tengroth also wrote the source stories.) A bittersweet taste of things to come. In Swedish with English subtitles.

Eva Henning *Rut* • Birger Malmsten *Bertil* • Birgit Tengroth *Viola* • Hasse Ekman *Dr Rosengren* • Mimi Nelson *Valborg* • Bengt Eklund *Raoul* ■ *Dir* Ingmar Bergman • *Scr* Herbert Grevenius, from short stories by Birgit Tengroth

Thirst ★★ 18

Horror   1979 · Ausl · Colour · 90mins

This intriguing modern-day vampire parable is set in a hospital in Australia's outback, where the hapless patients are "milked" for their blood by a secret society that believes its consumption bestows upon them great power. Sadly, Rod Hardy plays the whole thing totally deadpan, as if he's directing Chekhov. More ironic humour might have lent the outrageous premise more effectiveness. Still, there are some nice touches, such as having the blood stored in bottles, Unigate-style. Moreover, the film includes some solid performances, notably by Chantal Contouri as a woman whom the sect believe to be descended from their founder, Countess Bathory – a real-life Hungarian noblewoman who cooked human flesh and bathed in virgin blood. ▭

Chantal Contouri *Kate Davis* • David Hemmings *Dr Fraser* • Henry Silva *Dr Gauss* • Max Phipps *Hodge* • Shirley Cameron *Mrs Barker* • Rod Mullinar *Derek* • Robert Thompson *Sean* • Walter Pym *Dichter* ■ *Dir* Rod Hardy • *Scr* John Pinkney

Thirst ★★

Disaster movie 1998 · US · Colour · 120mins

While *Jaws* may have made you afraid to go into the water, this TV movie will make you pause before drinking it. During a withering heat wave, deadly parasites infect a town's water supply, filling the hospitals and forcing the community to be quarantined. Water filtration engineer Adam Arkin (*Chicago Hope*) struggles to a find a way to kill the pernicious microbe before everyone dies of dehydration. Mirroring actual events in the American Midwest, this

film is kept vividly believable by John Mandel's purposeful script, Bill L Norton's taut direction and understated performances by Arkin, Joely Fisher (*Ellen*) and Giancarlo Esposito (*The Usual Suspects*).

Adam Arkin *Bob Miller* • Joely Fisher *Susan Miller* • Giancarlo Esposito *Dr Carver* • Ken Jenkins *Lou Wolford* • Phyllis Lyons *Allison* • Michael Cudlitz *Andy* ■ *Dir* Bill L Norton • *Scr* John Mandel, Paul A Kaufman

Thirteen at Dinner ★★★ U

Murder mystery 1985 · US · Colour · 90mins

Peter Ustinov gives another performance as Hercule Poirot in this second screen version of Agatha Christie's *Lord Edgware Dies*. He is troubled by the murder of a peer and becomes convinced that, in spite of the evidence of the guests at a dinner party, the peer's wife may have committed the crime. As the police turn their attention to her, a second killing occurs to prevent Poirot discovering some vital information. It's glossy, efficient entertainment, with a highly contrived denouement, but Ustinov is fine and Faye Dunaway holds back nothing as the suspected widow. Contains swearing. ▭

Peter Ustinov *Hercule Poirot* • Faye Dunaway *Jane Wilkinson/Carlotta Adams* • David Suchet *Inspector Japp* • Jonathan Cecil *Arthur Hastings* • Bill Nighy *Ronald Marsh* • Diane Keen *Jenny Driver* • John Stride *Film director* • Benedict Taylor *Donald Ross* ■ *Dir* Lou Antonio • *Scr* Rod Browning, from the novel *Lord Edgware Dies* by Agatha Christie

13 East Street ★

Crime thriller 1952 · UK · BW · 70mins

Quota-quickie expert John Gilling scripted this tiresome affair, in which cop Patrick Holt poses as a jewel thief on the run in order to infiltrate a gang of warehouse breakers. Although moll Sandra Dorne convinces the boss to trust him, it's only a matter of time before one of the crooks remembers where he's seen Holt before, and he's sent on a suicidal raid on a fur store near St Paul's. Dora Bryan is good value as a nosy neighbour who taunts Holt's wife Sonia Holm with rumours that he's having an affair, but that's little compensation.

Patrick Holt *Detective Fraser/Gerald Blake* • Sandra Dorne *Judy* • Robert Ayres *Larry Conn* • Sonia Holm *Joan* • Dora Bryan *Valerie* • Michael Balfour *Joey Long* • Michael Brennan *George Mack* ■ *Dir* Robert S Baker • *Scr* John Gilling, from a story by Robert S Baker

13 Rue Madeleine ★★ U

Second World War drama
1946 · US · BW · 95mins

This is one of several documentary-style dramas made by 20th Century-Fox in the forties, produced by Louis de Rochemont and adopting the stentorian style of the *March of Time* newsreels he co-created. A narrator intones, the images look snatched from real-life... and a Hollywood star gives the game away. In this case it's James Cagney, slightly miscast as an American agent training spies for service in occupied Europe. The cloak-and-dagger dramatics are brightened by the presence of pretty French actress Annabella, known to art-house audiences as the lead in René Clair's

1931 film *Le Million*. Directed by that notorious on-set bully Henry Hathaway, the picture was shot in New England and Quebec, which was, as far as Hollywood was concerned, halfway to France. ▭

James Cagney *Bob Sharkey* • Annabella *Suzanne de Bouchard* • Richard Conte *Bill O'Connell* • Frank Latimore *Jeff Lassiter* • Walter Abel *Charles Gibson* • Melville Cooper *Pappy Simpson* ■ *Dir* Henry Hathaway • *Scr* John Monks Jr, Sy Bartlett

The Thirteenth Floor ★★ 18

Science-fiction film noir thriller
1999 · US · Colour · 86mins

Computer technician Craig Bierko finds himself the main suspect when his boss – the mastermind behind a computer simulation of 1937 Los Angeles populated with programmed inhabitants who are oblivious to their actual origin – is found murdered. Though Bierko's subsequent investigation uncovers plenty of twists and turns, most viewers will have a pretty good idea of the final explanation by the end of the first third of the movie. Predictable as it is, this still retains some interest. The computer simulation of the thirties world perfectly re-creates the era, the performances are acceptable, and the script makes each sequence play out in an intelligent and plausible fashion. ▭ *DVD*

Craig Bierko *Douglas Hall* • Armin Mueller-Stahl *Hannon Fuller* • Gretchen Mol *Jane Fuller* • Vincent D'Onofrio *Whitney/Ashton* • Dennis Haysbert *Detective Larry McBain* • Steven Schub *Zev Bernstein* • Jeremy Roberts *Tom* ■ *Dir* Josef Rusnak • *Scr* Josef Rusnak, Ravel Centeno-Rodriguez, from the novel *Simulacron 3* by Daniel Galouye

The Thirteenth Guest ★★

Murder mystery comedy
1932 · US · BW · 69mins

In this low-budget ensemble mystery story from the tiny Monogram studio, 13 guests – who were all present 13 years earlier at a dinner that saw the sudden death of their host – reassemble, and find themselves under collective threat from a mysterious, hooded killer. Ginger Rogers, soon to become a major and versatile star, is the leading lady of this old-fashioned but quite entertaining comedy thriller, loosely – and very badly – remade, also by Monogram, as *The Mystery of the Thirteenth Guest* in 1943.

Ginger Rogers *Marie Morgan/Lela* • Lyle Talbot *Phil Winston* • J Farrell MacDonald *Capt Ryan* • James C Eagles *Harold "Bud" Morgan* • Eddie Phillips *Thor Jensen* • Erville Alderson *John Adams* • Robert Klein *John Barksdale* • Crauford Kent *Dr Sherwood* ■ *Dir* Albert Ray • *Scr* Frances Hyland, Arthur Hoerl, Armitage Trail, from the novel by Armitage Trail

The 13th Letter ★★★

Film noir mystery drama
1951 · US · BW · 85mins

Using a mixed French and American cast (along with Englishman Michael Rennie), producer/director Otto Preminger turned to Henri-George Clouzot's masterly French thriller, *Le Corbeau* (*The Raven*), for this tale about a series of poison-pen letters that cause havoc in a provincial

French-Canadian town. Charles Boyer as a doctor, Constance Smith as his wife, Rennie – also a doctor, and the object of Smith's unwelcome attentions – and Linda Darnell, as a woman whose beauty is marred by a club foot, all convince in the central roles. A little melodramatic aaand not in the same class as Clouzot's film, this is still suspenseful entertainment.

Linda Darnell *Denise* • Charles Boyer *Dr Laurent* • Michael Rennie *Dr Pearson* • Constance Smith *Cora Laurent* • Françoise Rosay *Mrs Sims* • Judith Evelyn *Sister Marie* • Guy Sorel *Robert Helier* ■ *Dir* Otto Preminger • *Scr* Howard Koch, from the story *Le Corbeau* by Louis Chavance

The 13th Warrior ★★★ 15

Period action adventure
1999 · US · Colour · 102mins

The *Vikings* meets *Congo* in *Die Hard*-director John McTiernan's old-fashioned horror adventure, based on Michael Crichton's early novel *Eaters of the Dead*. Antonio Banderas looks decidedly uncomfortable as a 922AD Middle Eastern emissary abducted by Norsemen to fight the barbaric cannibals who are terrorising their countrymen. How the Arab adapts to a totally alien culture and uncovers the secrets of the feared "spirits in the mist" makes for a visually arresting, if half-baked, saga, though the initially promising fantasy mystique soon evaporates into a rather mundane reality. The film is never boring – there are numerous epic battle sequences and graphic scenes of slaughter – but it's not really that exciting either and shows clear signs of production difficulties. Jerry Goldsmith's marvellously stirring soundtrack is a major plus, however. Contains violence. ▭

Antonio Banderas *Ahmed Ibn Fahdlan* • Diane Venora *Queen Weilew* • Dennis Storhoi *Herger/Joyous* • Vladimir Kulich *Buliwyf* • Omar Sharif *Melchisidek* • Anders T Andersen *Wigliff, King's son* • Richard Bremmer *Skeld/Superstitious* • Tony Curran *Weath, musician* ■ *Dir* John McTiernan • *Scr* William Wisher, Warren Lewis, from the novel *Eaters of the Dead* by Michael Crichton

–30– ★★★ U

Drama   1959 · US · BW · 96mins

Jack Webb brought the deadpan *Dragnet* style to a select number of cinema features as producer, director and star. This one provides a documentary-like treatment of the few hours before a Los Angeles newspaper reaches its deadline. (The American title refers to the traditional sign for the end of a reporter's copy – in Britain, the film was retitled *Deadline Midnight*.) A story is breaking: a three-year-old girl and her dog have disappeared. It turns out she is lost down a storm drain and a massive search is launched. Ex-reporter William Bowers wrote the excellent script, with Webb (as the night editor) and a cast of little-known actors bringing the characters vividly to life in the single setting of the newsroom.

Jack Webb *Sam Gatlin* • William Conrad *Jim Bathgate* • David Nelson *Earl Collins* • Whitney Blake *Peggy Gatlin* • Louise Lorimer *Bernice Valentine* • James Bell *Ben Quinn* • Nancy Valentine *Jan Price* ■ *Dir* Jack Webb • *Scr* William Bowers

Thirty-Day Princess ★★★

Romantic comedy 1934 · US · BW · 73mins

Sylvia Sidney, in a rare break from the usual suffering heroines she portrays, stars in a dual role here. She's a foreign princess, in New York for a series of public appearances to raise money, and a down-on-her-luck actress and lookalike, hired to impersonate the royal visitor when the latter gets mumps. Cary Grant is an upper-crust newspaper publisher and the romantic interest, Edward Arnold the banker behind the deception. This small-scale romantic comedy overcomes its well-worn plot, thanks to the performances, the Paramount house-style and a charming script – written by a committee of four, but clearly benefiting from the witty contributions of Preston Sturges.

Sylvia Sidney *Nancy Lane/Princess "Zizzi" Catterina* • Cary Grant *Porter Madison III* • Edward Arnold *Richard Gresham* • Henry Stephenson *King Anatole XII* ■ *Dir* Marion Gering • *Scr* Sam Hellman, Edwin Justus Mayer, Frank Partos, from the story by Clarence Budington Kelland

30 Is a Dangerous Age, Cynthia ★★★

Romantic comedy 1967 · US · Colour · 85mins

One of those sixties oddities, with everyone rushing around being breezily neurotic as nightclub musician Dudley Moore panics at the thought of imminently turning 30. Moore basically plays himself, even fronting his real-life jazz trio, and it works enjoyably enough, with Suzy Kendall suitably kooky and charming as the girl he chases. Not a movie that has aged with any dignity, but there are considerably worse examples of "swinging" celluloid than this.

Dudley Moore *Rupert Street* • Eddie Foy Jr *Oscar* • Suzy Kendall *Louise* • John Bird *Herbert Greenslade* • Harry Towb *Mr Woolley* • Patricia Routledge *Mrs Woolley* ■ *Dir* Joseph McGrath • *Scr* Dudley Moore, Joseph McGrath, John Wells

The 39 Steps ★★★★★ U

Classic thriller 1935 · UK · BW · 82mins

Robert Donat plays Richard Hannay, handcuffed for much of the time to Madeleine Carroll, who moves in a north-by-northwesterly direction to Scotland to uncover a spy ring and Peggy Ashcroft in a rare film role. These early Hitchcock thrillers – including his first version of *The Man Who Knew Too Much* and *The Lady Vanishes* – are fondly regarded, even if they lack the complexity of his later work in Hollywood and creak like a much-loved antique bedstead. Based on John Buchan's novel, this masterwork brims with typical set pieces, most notably, the climax in a music hall where Mr Memory is asked "What are the 39 Steps?". If you haven't seen the film 39 times, you probably won't remember. ▣ **DVD**

Robert Donat *Richard Hannay* • Madeleine Carroll *Pamela* • Lucie Mannheim *Miss Smith* • Godfrey Tearle *Professor Jordan* • Peggy Ashcroft *Crofter's wife* • John Laurie *Crofter* • Helen Haye *Mrs Jordan* ■ *Dir* Alfred Hitchcock • *Scr* Charles Bennett, Alma Reville, Ian Hay, from the novel by John Buchan

The Thirty-Nine Steps ★★ U

Spy drama 1959 · UK · Colour · 94mins

Alfred Hitchcock cast a long and large shadow, leaving many a director in debt to a master film-maker. But this remake of his 1935 classic thriller is totally overwhelmed by the original. Kenneth More battles bravely to take on the role of Richard Hannay that Robert Donat made so very suavely his own, but succumbs to a bout of overplayed bravado. The Hitchcock impetus still pulses through some of the action, but director Ralph Thomas should have been ashamed.

Kenneth More *Richard Hannay* • Taina Elg *Fisher* • Brenda de Banzie *Nellie Lumsden* • Barry Jones *Professor Logan* • Reginald Beckwith *Lumsden* • Faith Brook *Nannie* • Michael Goodliffe *Brown* • James Hayter *Mr Memory* ■ *Dir* Ralph Thomas • *Scr* Frank Harvey, from the novel by John Buchan

The Thirty-Nine Steps ★★★ PG

Thriller 1978 · UK · Colour · 98mins

The third film of John Buchan's novel goes back to its source, setting the story in its original date (1914) and laying on a little too much period colour along the way. Robert Powell has the bearing but not the charm as hero Richard Hannay, chased across the Highlands by foreign agents for a notebook. The sinister mystery at the beginning and the famous climax, involving a Harold Lloyd-like stunt atop Big Ben, are good, exciting fun in the best daredevil tradition. Unfortunately the middle sags, and this is where one becomes all too aware of the shortcomings of the 1914 setting. ▣

Robert Powell *Richard Hannay* • David Warner *Appleton* • Eric Porter *Chief Supt Lomas* • Karen Dotrice *Alex Mackenzie* • John Mills *Scudder* • George Baker *Sir Walter Bullivant* • Ronald Pickup *Bayliss* • Donald Pickering *Marshall* ■ *Dir* Don Sharp • *Scr* Michael Robson, from the novel by John Buchan

Thirty Seconds over Tokyo ★★★ U

Second World War drama 1944 · US · BW · 132mins

Overlong but impressively-staged war drama that depicts America's first secret bombing raid over Tokyo, just four months after Pearl Harbor. Apart from the inevitable "woman's angle" – scenes with Van Johnson's wife back home – the first part of the film concentrates on military planning, led by Spencer Tracy as the real-life Lt Col James Doolittle. Later, it follows the tensions aboard the *Ruptured Duck* bomber as it flies above the Pacific and crashes off the coast of China, where Van Johnson loses a leg. The script, by future blacklistee Dalton Trumbo, is full of heroic speeches, and the special effects won an Oscar. ▣

Spencer Tracy *Lt Col James H Doolittle* • Van Johnson *Capt Ted W Lawson* • Robert Walker *David Thatcher* • Phyllis Thaxter *Ellen Jones Lawson* • Tim Murdock *Dean Davenport* • Scott McKay *Davey Jones* • Robert Mitchum *Bob Gray* ■ *Dir* Mervyn LeRoy • *Scr* Dalton Trumbo, from the novel by Capt Ted W Lawson, Robert Considine

36 Chowringhee Lane ★★★

Drama 1982 · Ind · Colour · 112mins

Produced by Bollywood superstar Shashi Kapoor, Aparna Sen's directorial debut has the chintzy feel of an early Merchant-Ivory picture. Yet it also contains several elements that go against the general atmosphere of post-colonial purdah and regret, notably a surreal dream sequence and some extravagant editing. Jennifer Kendal is magnificent as the sixty-something teacher who seizes upon the presence of writer Dhritiman Chatterjee and his lover, Debashree Roy, in her Calcutta apartment as a release from a life tinged with sadness and disappointment. Melancholic and melodramatic, yet quite affecting.

Jennifer Kendal *Miss Violet Stoneham* • Dhritiman Chatterjee *Samaresh Moitra* • Geoffrey Kendal *Eddie Stoneham* ■ *Dir/Scr* Aparna Sen

36 Hours ★★★★

Second World War spy thriller 1964 · US · BW · 114mins

An American intelligence officer is kidnapped by Nazi agents who want him to reveal the D-day invasion plans in this ingeniously scripted film that was a substantial hit in the UK. It's often remembered more for its plot than its title – there can't be many movie buffs around who haven't at one time or another been asked: "What was the name of that film where James Garner is captured by the Germans and told that he's spent the last six years in an amnesiac state?" Well, it's this one, in all its black-and-white splendour, a cleverly-mounted opus from writer/director George Seaton with a particularly persuasive Rod Taylor as a Nazi major.

James Garner *Major Jefferson Pike* • Rod Taylor *Major Walter Gerber* • Eva Marie Saint *Anna Hedler* • Werner Peters *Otto Schack* • John Banner *Ernst* • Russell Thorson *Gen Allison* ■ *Dir* George Seaton • *Scr* George Seaton, from a story by Carl K Hittleman, Luis H Vance and the story *Beware of the Dog* by Roald Dahl

36 Hours to Die ★★ 18

Crime thriller 1999 · US/Can · Colour · 90mins

Recuperating from a heart attack, brewery owner Treat Williams learns that his brother has managed to embroil them in a deadly, mob-run extortion scheme. His family and business are suddenly threatened, and he finds he has only 36 hours to fend off the gangsters. While the ending of this arthouse wannabe – which plays like an episode of *The Sopranos* – is never much in doubt, the script by Robert Rodat contains enough twists and idiosyncrasies to make it seem fresh. Combined with intense performances by Williams, Kim Cattrall and Saul Rubinek, this is a violent but fascinating trip into the underworld. ▣

Treat Williams *Noah Stone* • Kim Cattrall *Kim Stone* • Carroll O'Connor *Uncle Jack O'Malley* • Saul Rubinek *Morano* • Alain Goulem *Frank Stone* • Barbara Eve Harris *Barbara Woods* ■ *Dir* Yves Simoneau • *Scr* Robert Rodat

Thirty Two Short Films about Glenn Gould ★★★★★ U

Biographical drama 1993 · Can · Colour · 93mins

It's too close to say which is the better pianist biopic: this exceptional Canadian film inspired by Bach's *Goldberg Variations* or *Shine*, Scott Hicks's outstanding feature on the life of Australian David Helfgott. The key to François Girard's picture is that he leaves Gould an enigma, allowing us to draw our own conclusions from the 32 vignettes that range from childhood to his sudden decision to quit the concert hall and concentrate on recording. Colm Feore's performance is remarkable, while Girard's use of sound is as masterly as his visual ingenuity and his sense that the minor episode is often as revealing as a major turning point. ▣

Colm Feore *Glenn Gould* • Derek Keurvorst *Gould's father* • Katya Ladan *Gould's mother* • Devon Anderson *Glenn aged 3* • Joshua Greenblatt *Glenn aged 8* • Sean Ryan *Glenn aged 12* • Kate Hennig *Chambermaid* ■ *Dir* François Girard • *Scr* François Girard, Don McKellar, Nick McKinney

This above All ★★★

Second World War drama 1942 · US · BW · 109mins

A soapy wartime drama, produced by 20th Century-Fox with all the patriotic stops out and starring Tyrone Power as an unlikely working-class British soldier, who romances upper-class WAAF Joan Fontaine while struggling with pacifist urges. There's a marvellous supporting cast of British expats, and director Anatole Litvak does so well by RC Sherriff's script (based on a popular novel by Eric Knight) that even the most cynical might be reaching for the tissues.

Tyrone Power *Clive Briggs* • Joan Fontaine *Prudence Cathaway* • Thomas Mitchell *Monty* • Henry Stephenson *General Cathaway* • Nigel Bruce *Ramsbottom* • Gladys Cooper *Iris* • Philip Merivale *Dr Roger Cathaway* • Alexander Knox *Rector* ■ *Dir* Anatole Litvak • *Scr* RC Sherriff, from the novel by Eric Knight

This Angry Age ★★★

Drama 1957 · It/US · Colour · 111mins

Shot by French director René Clement on an island off Thailand with a cast that included Italians Silvana Mangano and Alida Valli and Americans Jo Van Fleet and Anthony Perkins playing French colonials in Indochina, the film suffered from its hybrid parentage and over-melodramatic moments. Nevertheless, it caught the rich hues of the tropics in Technirama, and was an absorbing enough study of a colonial family. The script obliquely suggests an incestuous relationship between siblings Mangano and Perkins, the latter in a role conceived for James Dean, killed 18 months earlier, and they have a sensuous dance number called "the Crawl".

Anthony Perkins *Joseph Dufresne* • Silvana Mangano *Suzanne Dufresne* • Richard Conte *Michael* • Jo Van Fleet *Madame Dufresne* • Nehemiah Persoff *Albert* • Alida Valli *Claude* ■ *Dir* René Clément • *Scr* Irwin Shaw, Rene Clement, from the novel *Un Barrage contre le Pacifique (Sea Wall)* by Marguerite Duras

This Boy's Life ★★★★ 15
Biographical drama
1993 · US · Colour · 110mins

Anyone sceptical about Leonardo DiCaprio's acting abilities should check out this moving coming-of-age drama. In this troubling tale set in Seattle in the fifties, Leo plays the rebellious teenage son of working mum Ellen Barkin who finds himself locked in a battle of wills with bullying stepfather Robert De Niro. After the lightweight antics of his first American movie, *Doc Hollywood*, British director Michael Caton-Jones relishes the opportunity to try out meatier material and makes the most of Robert Getchell's largely unsentimental adaptation of Tobias Wolff's acclaimed autobiography. Contains violence, swearing, sex scenes and nudity. ▣

Robert De Niro *Dwight Hansen* • Ellen Barkin *Caroline Wolff* • Leonardo DiCaprio *Toby* • Jonah Blechman *Arthur Gayle* • Eliza Dushku *Pearl* • Chris Cooper *Roy* • Carla Gugino *Norma* • Tobey Maguire *Chuck Bolger* ■ *Dir* Michael Caton-Jones • *Scr* Robert Getchell, from the autobiography by Tobias Wolff

This Can't Be Love ★★★
Romantic drama
1994 · US · Colour · 100mins

After six years away from the screen, the early nineties proved a busy time for Katharine Hepburn. In between the TV movie *The Man Upstairs* and *Love Affair*, she managed to squeeze in this TV production that reunited her with Anthony Harvey, who directed her to an Oscar in *The Lion in Winter*. Heroically overcoming the effects of a neurological disorder, the 86-year-old Hepburn shows she has lost none of her ability to command the screen as she plays a reclusive actress who rekindles an old romance with the 78-year-old Anthony Quinn.

Katharine Hepburn *Marion Bennette* • Anthony Quinn *Michael Reyman* • Jason Bateman *Grant Landis* • Jami Gertz *Sarah Wells* • Maxine Miller *Wilma* ■ *Dir* Anthony Harvey • *Scr* Duane Poole

This Child Is Mine ★★ PG
Drama
1985 · US · Colour · 92mins

A teenage mother faces a heartbreaking decision and a childless couple confront the pitfalls of adoption in this frank TV movie. Seventeen-year-old unwed mother Nancy McKeon gives her baby up for adoption only to change her mind later. She finds herself embroiled in a bitter legal and emotional battle with the adoptive parents, Lindsay Wagner and Chris Sarandon. There's nothing particularly new or surprising about this sentimental drama, but mothers everywhere may still find themselves reaching for the tissues. ▣

Lindsay Wagner *Bonnie Wilkerson* • Chris Sarandon *Craig Wilkerson* • Nancy McKeon *Kimberly Downs* • Michael Lerner *Abe Rosenberg* • Scotch Byerley *Dr Greevey* ■ *Dir* David Greene • *Scr* Charles Rosin

This Could Be the Night ★★★ U
Romantic comedy 1957 · US · BW · 104mins

Virginal New England college graduate Jean Simmons, teaching school in Manhattan, takes a night job as secretary to a club owner with underworld connections (Paul Douglas), clashes with his aggressive partner (Anthony Franciosa) and affects the lives of everybody connected with the establishment. A romantic comedy drama, directed by Robert Wise, with Simmons excellent in a role that has Audrey Hepburn written all over it. Douglas is terrific as the gentlemanly rough diamond who takes her to his heart, and the rest of the cast, which includes Julie Wilson as the club's star singer and a veteran Joan Blondell, live up to the principals. A charming and lively case of wishful thinking.

Jean Simmons *Anne Leeds* • Paul Douglas *Rocco* • Anthony Franciosa *Tony Armotti* • Julie Wilson *Ivy Corlane* • Neile Adams *Patsy St Clair* • Joan Blondell *Crystal St Clair* ■ *Dir* Robert Wise • *Scr* Isobel Lennart, from stories by Cordelia Baird Gross

This Day and Age ★
Crime drama 1933 · US · BW · 82mins

Cecil B DeMille offers an extreme right-wing solution to the problem of the American gangster. When the law can't convict a known killer, a group of decent high school kids, led by Richard Cromwell, step in to kidnap him and extract a confession by dangling him over a pit full of rats. The gangster is so broken by the experience that he signs a confession before the authorities. Writer Bartlett Cormack made some amends for this hysterical and dangerous film when he later worked on *Fury*, which showed mob rule from the point of view of an innocent victim.

Charles Bickford *Louis Garrett* • Richard Cromwell *Steve Smith* • Judith Allen *Gay Merrick* • Harry Green *Herman* • Bradley Page *Toledo* • Eddie Nugent [Edward Nugent] *Don Merrick* ■ *Dir* Cecil B DeMille • *Scr* Bartlett Cormack

This Earth Is Mine ★★★
Drama 1959 · US · Colour · 123mins

A melodrama on an epic scale, this immensely enjoyable tosh provides ideal, undemanding matinée fare. Top-billed are two great movie stars of the period, Rock Hudson and Jean Simmons, both of whom barely flex their acting muscles but look superb. The real acting comes from Dorothy McGuire and Claude Rains, who virtually steal this Prohibition-era saga of uproar in the Napa Valley vineyards from their co-stars. Although his eye for landscape never falters, veteran director Henry King has problems pulling together the sprawling script and its many disparate elements. However, students of bootlegging should check this one out.

Rock Hudson *John Rambeau* • Jean Simmons *Elizabeth* • Dorothy McGuire *Martha* • Claude Rains *Philippe Rambeau* • Kent Smith *Francis Fairon* ■ *Dir* Henry King • *Scr* Casey Robinson, from the novel *The Cup and the Sword* by Alice Tisdale Hobart

This Gun for Hire ★★★
Crime drama 1942 · US · BW · 80mins

Predating *film noir*, Frank Tuttle's wartime thriller, adapted from Graham Greene's novel, nonetheless has several *noir* elements. It is a tale involving ruthless fifth columnists, the cold-blooded hit man they hire and then try to dispose of, and the cabaret entertainer who gets caught up in the ensuing mess. Billed below Robert Preston, Laird Cregar and Veronica Lake, the movie rocketed the unknown Alan Ladd to stardom on the strength of his performance as the loner-killer. It also began his popular teaming with Lake, whose combination of blonde cool and touching vulnerability clicked into box-office chemistry with the laconic and charismatic actor.

Veronica Lake *Ellen Graham* • Robert Preston *Michael Crane* • Laird Cregar *Willard Gates* • Alan Ladd *Philip Raven* • Tully Marshall *Alvin Brewster* ■ *Dir* Frank Tuttle • *Scr* Albert Maltz, WR Burnett, from the novel *A Gun For Sale* by Graham Greene

This Gun for Hire ★★ 15
Crime drama 1991 · US · Colour · 85mins

The 1942 Alan Ladd original – an exercise in menacing *film noir* – followed the Graham Greene novel *A Gun for Sale* on which it was based fairly closely, while the 1957 film *Short Cut to Hell* (a second attempt at the text) was a rather limp re-run, despite being directed by James Cagney. This version, a TV movie featuring Robert Wagner, certainly comes complete with alluring *noir* visuals, for which New Orleans is a perfect setting. Yet, in trying to give space to its characters, it sometimes slows down to the point of blandness. Wagner, as the lethal gunman who's been double-crossed, just can't equal Ladd's detailed performance. ▣

Robert Wagner *Raven* • Nancy Everhard *Anne* • John Harkins *Boyton* • Frederic Lehne [Fredric Lehne] *Mather* • Kristina Loggia *Cynthia* ■ *Dir* Lou Antonio • *Scr* Nevin D Schreiner, from the film by Albert Maltz, WR Burnett, from the novel *A Gun for Sale* by Graham Greene

This Happy Breed ★★★★★ U
Drama 1944 · UK · Colour · 105mins

The second of David Lean's four collaborations with Noël Coward provides a fascinating picture of the way we were. The action is largely confined to an unremarkable but lovingly re-created Clapham home, but such is the ebb and flow of events (both domestic and historical) that the two hours it takes to cover the 20 inter-war years seem to fly by. Celia Johnson is superb as the eminently sensible suburban housewife, while Kay Walsh gives a spirited performance as her mouthy daughter. But the best scenes belong to neighbours Robert Newton and Stanley Holloway, as a couple of very British chroniclers of their times. ▣ DVD

Robert Newton *Frank Gibbons* • Celia Johnson *Ethel Gibbons* • John Mills *Billy Mitchell* • Kay Walsh *Queenie Gibbons* • Stanley Holloway *Bob Mitchell* • Amy Veness *Mrs Flint* • Alison Leggatt *Aunt Sylvia* • Laurence Olivier *Narrator* ■ *Dir* David Lean • *Scr* David Lean, Ronald Neame, Anthony Havelock-Allan, Noël Coward, from the play by Noël Coward

This Happy Feeling ★★ U
Romantic comedy
1958 · US · Colour · 92mins

Hoping to repeat the success of the previous year's *Tammy and the Bachelor*, producer Ross Hunter put Debbie Reynolds in the path of another unsuspecting swain in this over-eager comedy, written and directed by Blake Edwards. But we're never quite caught up in the fun as Debbie tilts her cap at retired film star Curt Jurgens. Nor are we ever totally convinced by the arch quirkiness of such supporting characters as Estelle Winwood's tipsy cook. Alexis Smith and Troy Donahue enjoy themselves as a failed starlet and a moody actor, but we're never really in on those jokes either.

Debbie Reynolds *Janet Blake* • Curt Jurgens *Preston Mitchell* • John Saxon *Bill Tremaine* • Alexis Smith *Nita Hollaway* • Mary Astor *Mrs Tremaine* ■ *Dir* Blake Edwards • *Scr* Blake Edwards, from the play *For Love or Money* by F Hugh Herbert

This Is Elvis ★★ PG
Biography
1981 · US · Colour and BW · 143mins

Not in the same league as John Carpenter's faithful biopic starring Kurt Russell, but an engaging failure, nevertheless. Writers/directors Malcolm Leo and Andrew Solt blend in real footage with the staged scenes but, for all their efforts, do little more than scratch the surface of the myth behind the king of rock 'n' roll. The lack of familiar faces among the cast doesn't help. Contains swearing. ▣

Paul Boensch III *Elvis aged 10* • David Scott *Elvis aged 18* • Dana Mackay *Elvis aged 35* • Johnny Harra *Elvis aged 42* • Lawrence Koller *Vernon Presley* • Rhonda Lyn *Priscilla Presley* ■ *Dir/Scr* Malcolm Leo, Andrew Solt

This Is My Affair ★★★
Crime drama 1937 · US · BW · 99mins

A catchpenny title, since stars Robert Taylor and Barbara Stanwyck were alleged to be ''that way'' about each other. But don't be deterred from watching this cracking crime story, set in the early 1900s. The ''affair'' turns out to be Taylor's mission: he's been sent to the Midwest by President McKinley to root out bank robbers. Stanwyck is absolutely wonderful in an atypical role as a saloon singer, and it's easy to see how Taylor fell for her. They married for real two years later.

Robert Taylor (1) *Lieutenant Richard L Perry* • Barbara Stanwyck *Lil Duryea* • Victor McLaglen *Jock Ramsey* • Brian Donlevy *Batiste Duryea* • Sidney Blackmer *President Theodore Roosevelt* • John Carradine *Ed* • Alan Dinehart *Doc Keller* ■ *Dir* William A Seiter • *Scr* Allen Rivkin, Lamar Trotti, from the novel *The McKinley Case* by Melville Crossman

This Is My Father ★★★
Romantic drama
1998 · Ire/Can · Colour · 120mins

Compelling drama, with teacher James Caan learning a life lesson when a photo from his mother's past causes him to wonder about the identity of his father. This search for truth takes him to Ireland, where details of an unsuspected past romance emerge. Written and directed by Paul Quinn, and starring brother Aidan, James Caan, Stephen Rea, John Cusack and a who's who of Irish supporting actors.

Aidan Quinn *Kieran O'Day* • Moya Farrelly *Fiona Flynn* • Stephen Rea *Father Quinn* • John Cusack *Eddie Sharp, the pilot* • James

U = SUITABLE FOR ALL, Uc = SUITABLE FOR ALL, ESPECIALLY FOR YOUNG CHILDREN (VIDEO ONLY), PG = PARENTAL GUIDANCE

Caan *Kieran Johnson* • Jacob Tierney *Jack, Kieran Johnson's nephew* • Colm Meaney *Seamus* ■ *Dir/Scr* Paul Quinn

This Is My Life ★★★ 15

Comedy drama 1992 · US · Colour · 89mins

The formidable Nora Ephron made her directorial debut with this tale of single mum Julie Kavner trying to pursue a career in the world of stand-up comedy. Her daughters (Gaby Hoffmann and Samantha Mathis) soon find that their increasingly absentee mother is using their experiences as material for her act. The cast is certainly a treat (Carrie Fisher, Dan Aykroyd), while Ephron's writing is at her sharpest. Quite why the whole fails to gel is a great mystery, but there is definitely too much slack around the middle. A more experienced hand was probably needed on the tiller. [video]

Julie Kavner *Dottie Ingels* • Samantha Mathis *Erica Ingels* • Gaby Hoffmann *Opal Ingels* • Carrie Fisher *Claudia Curtis* • Dan Aykroyd *Arnold Moss* • Bob Nelson *Ed* • Marita Geraghty *Mia Jablon* ■ *Dir* Nora Ephron • *Scr* Nora Ephron, Delia Ephron, from the novel *This Is Your Life* by Meg Wolitzer

This Is My Street ★★

Drama 1963 · UK · BW · 102mins

The street of the title is a rather grim one in London's Battersea, before the place became gentrified, wherein a womanising lodger (Ian Hendry) seduces overburdened mother (June Ritchie). She becomes infatuated with him, but he dumps her for her sister. A well-written, nicely shot squalor fest, based on Nan Maynard's novel. Fascinating fact: Mike Pratt and Annette Andre later starred together in the original TV series, *Randall and Hopkirk (Deceased)*.

Ian Hendry *Harry King* • June Ritchie *Margery Graham* • John Hurt *Charlie* • Avice Landone *Lily* • Meredith Edwards *Steve* • Madge Ryan *Kitty* • Annette Andre *Jinny* • Mike Pratt *Sid* ■ *Dir* Sidney Hayers • *Scr* Bill MacIlwraith, from the novel by Nan Maynard

This Is Spinal Tap ★★★★★ 15

Satire 1984 · US · Colour · 79mins

A brilliantly crafted and completely on-target satire of the rock 'n' roll industry. Filmed in mock documentary style as director Rob Reiner follows a fictitious British heavy metal band on tour, every rock music cliché is savagely lampooned for maximum hilarity. The Stonehenge-inspired production number is a showstopping highlight, but there's also immense pleasure to be had in the details, particularly the unbelievably crass song lyrics. Christopher Guest and Michael McKean are perfect as the group's incredibly stupid lead guitarist and singer. A cult classic and a pop send-up landmark. [video] DVD

Christopher Guest *Nigel Tufnel (lead guitar)* • Michael McKean *David St Hubbins (lead guitar)* • Harry Shearer *Derek Smalls (bass)* • RJ Parnell *Mick Shrimpton (drums)* • David Kaff *Viv Savage (keyboards)* • Rob Reiner *Marti DiBergi* • Bruno Kirby *Tommy Pischedda* • Anjelica Huston *Designer* • Billy Crystal *Mime artist* ■ *Dir* Rob Reiner • *Scr* Christopher Guest, Michael McKean, Harry Shearer, Rob Reiner

This Is the Army ★★★ U

Musical revue 1943 · US · Colour · 116mins

Mainly of historical interest, this filmed record of Irving Berlin's patriotic forties stage revue is performed partly by amateur military personnel supported by a flock of Warner Brothers contract players, including hoofer and future Republican senator George Murphy bizarrely playing the father of actor and future US president Ronald Reagan (Murphy was nine years Reagan's senior). Also in the cast is world heavyweight champion Joe Louis, and Berlin himself singing *Oh, How I Hate To Get Up In The Morning*. It isn't over until fat lady Kate Smith sings *God Bless America*.

Irving Berlin • George Murphy *Jerry Jones* • Joan Leslie *Eileen Dibble* • George Tobias *Maxie Twardofsky* • Alan Hale *Sgt McGee* • Charles Butterworth *Eddie Dibble* • Rosemary DeCamp *Ethel* • Kate Smith • Ronald Reagan *Johnny Jones* • Joe Louis ■ *Dir* Michael Curtiz • *Scr* Casey Robinson, Capt Claude Binyon, Philip G Epstein, Julius G Epstein, from the play by Irving Berlin

This Is the Night ★★★

Romantic comedy 1932 · US · BW · 78mins

Fifth-billed Cary Grant plays his first featured role at Paramount as an Olympic javelin champion and husband of Thelma Todd, who arrives at her Paris hotel with her lover Roland Young in tow, to find Grant unexpectedly there. The three of them, plus Young's pal Charlie Ruggles and Lily Damita, an actress hired to pose as Young's nonexistent wife, go to Venice where the male trio are captivated by Damita. This romantic comedy is unmistakeably Lubitsch territory, as emphasised by the casting of Young and Ruggles, although it's hardly a masterpiece. Nonetheless, directed with brio by Frank Tuttle, it's mildly risqué, sophisticated and entertaining.

Lili Damita *Germaine* • Charlie Ruggles [Charles Ruggles] *Bunny West* • Roland Young *Gerald Gray* • Thelma Todd *Claire* • Cary Grant *Stephen* ■ *Dir* Frank Tuttle • *Scr* Benjamin Glazer, George Marion, from the plays *Naughty Cinderella* by Avery Hopwood and *Pouche* by Rene Peter, Henri Falk

This Is the Sea ★★ 15

Drama 1996 · Ire/UK/US · Colour · 103mins

It's hard on well-intentioned films with good moments to condemn them with faint praise, but that's the case with this *Romeo and Juliet* story set in Ireland just after the 1994 ceasefire. Somehow the timeliness of the film and its background seem less compelling now, though the film's chief merit is in the young performers. Samantha Morton plays Hazel, a protestant much sheltered by her mother. When she goes to Belfast she meets Malachy (McDade), a Catholic with ties to the Irish Republican Army. The duo make the best of their parts, emerging unscathed by the heavy-duty acting which surrounds them in a film which is both honest and non-partisan. Contains swearing.

Richard Harris *Old Man Jacobs* • Gabriel Byrne *Rohan* • John Lynch *Padhar McAliskey* • Dearbhla Molloy *Ma Stokes* • Ian McIlhinney *Da Stokes* • Samantha Morton *Hazel Stokes* • Ross McDade *Malachy McAliskey* • Rick Leaf *Pastor Lamthorn* ■ *Dir/Scr* Mary McGuckian

This Island Earth ★★★★ PG

Science-fiction adventure
1955 · US · Colour · 82mins

This intelligent slice of fifties sci-fi ranks among the best and most cleverly conceived of the genre. Really it's a film of two parts. A talky earthbound section finds brainy boffins being recruited by the otherworldly Jeff Morrow to save his distant homeland from destruction by interplanetary warfare. That's followed by a full-blooded space opera featuring astounding surrealistic landscapes on the planet Metaluna and fearsome insect-like mutations with huge bulbous craniums. Hokey at times for sure, but its message is clear: the more advanced the technology, the greater the scope for destruction. [video]

Jeff Morrow *Exeter* • Faith Domergue *Dr Ruth Adams* • Rex Reason *Dr Cal Meacham* • Lance Fuller *Brack* • Russell Johnson *Steve Carlson* • Richard Nichols *Joe Wilson* • Karl Lindt *Engelborg* • Douglas Spencer *Monitor* ■ *Dir* Joseph M Newman • *Scr* Franklin Coen, Edward G O'Callaghan, from the novel *The Alien Machine* by Raymond F Jones

This Land Is Mine ★★

Second World War drama
1943 · US · BW · 103mins

Throughout the Second World War, Hollywood failed to capture the fear and suspicion that pervaded occupied Europe. This tale of a cowardly schoolteacher, Charles Laughton, who is inspired to heroism by his love for a Resistance fighter, Maureen O'Hara, is no exception. Jean Renoir's inability to re-create the atmosphere of Vichy France is partly excused by the fact that he had been living in exile from his homeland since 1940 after the Nazis placed him on a death list for his socialist sympathies. This bland picture, directed with virtually no enthusiasm for its clichéd villagers and hysterical Nazis, had little dramatic or propagandist value.

Charles Laughton *Albert Lory* • Maureen O'Hara *Louise Martin* • George Sanders *George Lambert* • Walter Slezak *Major Erich von Keller* • Kent Smith *Paul Martin* ■ *Dir* Jean Renoir • *Scr* Dudley Nichols

This Love of Ours ★★

Melodrama 1945 · US · BW · 90mins

Merle Oberon and Charles Korvin star in this banal, third-rate romantic melodrama about a jealous husband who unjustly deserts his wife. Years later, he discovers her in a Chicago nightclub, assisting Claude Rains in his act, and begs her forgiveness. He takes her home where, of course, their daughter, who believes her dead, rejects her... Director William Dieterle, given a budget of $2 million, expertly attempts to extract every ounce of drama he can from his low-voltage cast and the pitiful script, recycled in 1956 as *Never Say Goodbye* with Rock Hudson and Cornell Borchers.

Merle Oberon *Karin Touzac/Florence Hale* • Charles Korvin *Michel Touzac* • Claude Rains *Dr Joseph Targel* • Carl Esmond *Uncle Robert* • Sue England *Susette Touzac* • Jess Barker *Chadwick* • Harry Davenport *Dr Jerry Wilkerson* ■ *Dir* William Dieterle • *Scr* Bruce Manning, John Klorer, Leonard Lee, from the play *Come Prima Meglio de Prima* by Luigi Pirandello

This Man Can't Die ★★

Spaghetti western 1970 · It · Colour · 90mins

Director Giancarlo Baldanello reheats the familiar recipe in this violent, no-surprises spaghetti western which isn't a patch on the ones that Sergio Leone used to make. Set during the American Civil War, it's a tired tale of revenge, with Guy Madison as the soldier of fortune determined to mete out his own kind of justice to the affluent town boss who had his parents killed. Having seen his Hollywood career collapse in the late fifties, Madison spent much of the sixties making low-budget action movies in Europe. Italian dialogue dubbed into English.

Guy Madison *Martin Benson* • Peter Martell *Tony Guy* • Rik Battaglia *Vic Graham* • Lucienne Bridou *Susy Benson* • Steve Merrick *Daniel Benson* • Rosalba Neri *Jenny Benson* • John Bartha *Melin* ■ *Dir* Giancarlo Baldanello • *Scr* Luigi Emmanuele, Gino Mangini, from a story by Luigi Emmanuele

This Man Is Mine ★★

Drama 1934 · US · BW · 75mins

RKO and director John Cromwell surrounded the lovely Irene Dunne with all the elegant accoutrements – sets, clothes and a Max Steiner score – that her fans would expect, but neglected to give her a convincing script or a sufficiently attractive leading man. The plot has Dunne battling to keep the affections of her philandering husband (Ralph Bellamy) when he falls into the ruthlessly seductive clutches of Constance Cummings, who has no problems about stealing him away. Wafer-thin and disappointingly dull, but it's all over swiftly.

Irene Dunne *Tony Dunlap* • Ralph Bellamy *Jim Dunlap* • Constance Cummings *Francesca "Fran" Harper* • Kay Johnson *Bee McCrea* • Charles Starrett *Jud McCrea* • Sidney Blackmer *Mort Holmes* ■ *Dir* John Cromwell • *Scr* Jane Murfin, from the play *Love Flies in the Window* by Anne Morrison Chapin

This Man Stands Alone ★★

Drama based on a true story
1979 · US · Colour · 78mins

Was it the content or just the original length that caused American television bosses to dismember this movie, so that the end product has an uncomfortable stop-start structure? At any rate, Louis Gossett Jr (an Oscar-winner for his supporting role in *An Officer and a Gentleman*) successfully manages to push such flaws to the side by combining fire with sensitivity. Gossett is occasionally electrifying as a black civil rights campaigner who, galvanised by the assassination of Martin Luther King, decides to stand for sheriff against a much-favoured segregationist. Further concentration on the issues might have helped an otherwise messy film.

Louis Gossett Jr *Tom Hayward* • Clu Gulager *Marvin Tayman* • Mary Alice *Minnie Hayward* • Barry Brown *Fred Tayman* • Barton Heyman *George Tayman* ■ *Dir/Scr* Jerrold Freedman

This Man's Navy ★★ U

Wartime comedy drama
1945 · US · BW · 99mins

The appeal of Wallace Beery can be hard to fathom now, but he was one of MGM's most reliable draws for nearly

20 years. In this piece of sentimental twaddle, he's the airship pilot who boasts of a nonexistent son, then finds young Tom Drake to play the part. After the boy also becomes a flyer, the two have their differences but are reunited behind Japanese lines during the Second World War. A flyer himself, director William A Wellman must have been attracted by the location shooting at naval dirigible bases.

Wallace Beery *Ned Trumpet* • Tom Drake *Jess Weaver* • James Gleason *Jimmy Shannon* • Jan Clayton *Cathey Cortland* • Selena Royle *Maude Weaver* • Noah Beery Sr [Noah Beery] *Joe Hodum* ■ *Dir* William A Wellman • *Scr* Borden Chase, Allen Rivkin, from a story by Borden Chase, from an idea by Comdr Herman E Halland

This Other Eden ★★ U

Comedy 1959 · UK · BW · 80mins

A curious film for Leslie Phillips to find himself in, this is an overwrought tale about the emotions that erupt when the statue of a long-dead IRA hero is blown up in the square of a sleepy Irish village. Phillips is fine as the son of the Black and Tan who shot the gunman, and who is blamed for the explosion. He is adequately supported by Audrey Dalton as his lover and Norman Rodway as the terrorist's seminarian son, but the film lacks the power of such Hollywood lynch dramas as Fritz Lang's *Fury* or William A Wellman's *The Ox-Bow Incident*.

Audrey Dalton *Maire McRoarty* • Leslie Phillips *Crispin Brown* • Niall MacGinnis *Devereaux* • Geoffrey Golden *McRoarty* • Norman Rodway *Conor Heaphy* • Milo O'Shea *Pat Tweedy* ■ *Dir* Muriel Box • *Scr* Patrick Kirwan, Blanaid Irvine, from the play by Louis d'Alton

This Property Is Condemned ★★★★ 15

Drama 1966 · US · Colour · 105mins

This adaptation of Tennessee Williams's one-act play was to have starred Elizabeth Taylor with Richard Burton to direct. Francis Ford Coppola was one of the screenwriters, but though his name appears on the credits he had little to do with the film that was eventually made. The setting is a boarding house during the Depression where the landlady exploits her daughter Alva's charms to attract custom. But Alva – gorgeous Natalie Wood – has her eye on nice Robert Redford, who has arrived in town to lay off the railroad men. The beautiful camerawork of James Wong Howe, the fresh performances and Sydney Pollack's assured direction keep this impressive film from overheating in the usual Williams manner. [video]

Natalie Wood *Alva Starr* • Robert Redford *Owen Legate* • Charles Bronson *JJ Nichols* • Kate Reid *Hazel Starr* • Mary Badham *Willie Starr* • Alan Baxter *Knopke* • Robert Blake *Sidney* • John Harding *Johnson* • Dabney Coleman *Salesman* ■ *Dir* Sydney Pollack • *Scr* Francis Ford Coppola, Fred Coe, Edith Sommer, from the play by Tennessee Williams

This Rebel Breed ★

Crime drama 1960 · US · BW · 92mins

Rita Moreno is the best thing about this crude and exploitative story of racial strife among teenage gangs of black, white and Latin Americans. She has some affecting moments as the Mexican girl whose white boyfriend has died in a gang fight. She then takes up with black Latino Mark Damon, not knowing that he is an undercover police officer seeking to stem the supply of drugs to high school kids. A brief lecture at the end by a police officer hardly overcomes the relish with which the final riot is staged or the general air of sensationalism.

Rita Moreno *Lola* • Mark Damon *Frank* • Gerald Mohr *Lt Brooks* • Jay Novello *Papa* • Eugene Martin *Rudy* • Tom Gilson *Muscles* • Richard Rust *Buck* • Douglas Hume *Don* • Diane Cannon [Dyan Cannon] *Wiggles* ■ *Dir* Richard L Bare • *Scr* Morris Lee Green, from the story *All God's Children* by William Rowland, Irma Berk

This Reckless Age ★★★

Comedy 1932 · US · BW · 63mins

Family problems arise Charles "Buddy" Rogers and Frances Dee). whose parents have sacrificed themselves to a life of hardship to give them every advantage, turn out ungratefully self-absorbed and shallow. They rather unconvincingly come good over the course of a film that otherwise successfully treads a fine line between seriousness and humour, and demonstrates that the "generation gap" is nothing new. The sympathetic parents are well played by Broadway veterans Richard Bennett and Frances Starr, and the screenplay came from the pen of future writer/director Joseph L Mankiewicz.

Charles "Buddy" Rogers *Bradley Ingals* • Richard Bennett *Donald Ingals* • Peggy Shannon *Mary Burke* • Charles Ruggles *Goliath Whitney* • Frances Dee *Lois Ingals* • Frances Starr *Eunice Ingals* ■ *Dir* Frank Tuttle • *Scr* Joseph L Mankiewicz, from the play *The Goose Hangs High* by Lewis Beach

This Sporting Life ★★★★★ 15

Drama 1963 · UK · BW · 128mins

Director Lindsay Anderson's first feature film is his best, giving Richard Harris and Rachel Roberts the roles of their lives. Harris is the miner turned ruthless professional rugby player; Roberts is the repressed, widowed landlady with whom he can only communicate through violence. Adapted from David Storey's novel, it includes some remarkable confrontation sequences – one particular quarrel between the two is painfully honest – and the northern town where it all takes place is as clearly defined as was the setting in *Saturday Night and Sunday Morning* (which producer Karel Reisz directed). This numbers among the early ripples of the British New Wave. [video] DVD

Richard Harris *Frank Machin* • Rachel Roberts *Mrs Hammond* • Alan Badel *Weaver* • William Hartnell *Johnson* • Colin Blakely *Maurice Braithwaite* • Vanda Godsell *Mrs Weaver* • Arthur Lowe *Slomer* • Anne Cunningham *Judith* • Jack Watson *Len Miller* ■ *Dir* Lindsay Anderson • *Scr* David Storey, from his novel

This Thing Called Love ★★★

Romantic comedy 1940 · US · BW · 94mins

A film that not only acknowledged the existence of sex as a component of love and marriage but actually built its jokes on that fact of life was so unusual in the pre-permissive climate of 1940 that the Legion of Decency actually banned this otherwise innocuous offering. The story concerns Rosalind Russell's belief that marriages are best cemented on a celibate start, and her decision to keep her groom, Melvyn Douglas, waiting three months for her favours. When she's finally ready to succumb, he falls ill. Bright romantic farce, elegantly played by its attractive stars.

Rosalind Russell *Ann Winters* • Melvyn Douglas *Tice Collins* • Binnie Barnes *Charlotte Campbell* • Allyn Joslyn *Harry Bertrand* • Gloria Dickson *Florence Bertrand* • Lee J Cobb *Julio Diestro* • Gloria Holden *Genevieve Hooper* ■ *Dir* Alexander Hall • *Scr* George Seaton, Ken Englund, PJ Wolfson, from the play by Edwin Burke

This Wife for Hire ★★

Comedy drama 1985 · US · Colour · 97mins

Mork and Mindy's Pam Dawber is the wife who creates all sorts of predictable problems with hubby when she decides to go out to work as a housekeeper. This might have worked as an episode of a half hour sitcom, but as a movie it's mildly amusing and completely missable. Only worth watching so you can see what Sam J Jones looks like when he's not in his *Flash Gordon* costume.

Pam Dawber *Marsha Harper* • Robert Klein *Alan Harper* • Ann Jillian *Valerie Roberts* • Laraine Newman *Louise Bellini* • Dick Gautier *Howard Greer* • Sam J Jones [Sam Jones] *Tommy Sellers* ■ *Dir* Jim Drake • *Scr* Phil Margo, Don Segall

This Woman Is Dangerous ★★

Melodrama 1952 · US · BW · 97mins

Not here she isn't, as ageing movie queen Joan Crawford nears the end of her glory days at Warner Bros. This was her last movie for the studio, and, though two of her following films *Sudden Fear* and *Johnny Guitar* were moderately successful, we're a full decade away here from her splendid comeback in *What Ever Happened to Baby Jane?*. Of course, Crawford in full flow is always watchable, but this vehicle strains credibility as the star assists at operations, cares for the daughter of widower doctor Dennis Morgan and tries to free herself from the clutches of gangster boyfriend David Brian. The kind of movie that gives Hollywood a bad name.

Joan Crawford *Beth Austin* • Dennis Morgan *Dr Ben Halleck* • David Brian *Matt Jackson* • Richard Webb *Franklin* • Mari Alden *Ann Jackson* • Philip Carey *Will Jackson* • Ian MacDonald *Joe Grossland* ■ *Dir* Felix Feist • *Scr* Geoffrey Holmes, George W Yates, from the story *Stab of Pain* by Bernard Girard

This World, Then the Fireworks ★★★ 18

Crime drama 1996 · US · Colour · 95mins

A contrived but decent stab at contemporary *film noir*, with *Titanic* baddie Billy Zane as an investigative reporter forced to hide out at the home of his sister, Gina Gershon. Following a childhood trauma, Zane and his sibling enjoy a relationship that extends beyond the warm and loving. Soon they embark on a scam aimed at conning a pretty local policewoman out of her beach-front home. Predictably, it all ends in tears. *This World* may not produce true fireworks, but it's no damp squib either. Contains swearing, violence and sex scenes. [video]

Billy Zane *Marty Lakewood* • Gina Gershon *Carol Lakewood-Wharton* • Sheryl Lee *Patrolwoman Lois Archer* • Rue McClanahan *Mom Lakewood* • Seymour Cassel *Detective Harris* • William Hootkins *Jake Krutz, private investigator* • Will Patton *Police Lt Morgan* ■ *Dir* Michael Oblowitz • *Scr* Larry Gross, from the story by Jim Thompson

This Year's Love ★★★ 18

Romantic comedy
1999 · UK · Colour · 104mins

Writer/director David Kane tries hard to tap into the "Cool Britannia" zeitgeist with this breezy romantic comedy, set in and around funky Camden Lock and filled to bursting with homegrown stars of the future. However, while Catherine McCormack, Douglas Henshall and Dougray Scott deliver spunky, dynamic performances, the episodic script gives them little to work with. Charting three years in the lives of six London dropouts, the film recalls *La Ronde* with its constant swapping of sexual partners. Sadly, the schematic plotting soon becomes yawningly predictable. Kathy Burke's "fat bird" and Ian Hart's loner come off best, though Jennifer Ehle beggars belief as a dreadlocked single mother. Contains drug abuse, swearing and sex scenes. [video]

Kathy Burke *Marey* • Jennifer Ehle *Sophie* • Ian Hart *Liam* • Douglas Henshall *Danny* • Catherine McCormack *Hannah* • Dougray Scott *Cameron* • Emily Woof *Alice* • Sophie Okonedo *Denise* ■ *Dir/Scr* David Kane

The Thomas Crown Affair ★★★ PG

Crime drama 1968 · US · Colour · 97mins

Wound up by its irritatingly wistful, Oscar-winning song, *The Windmills of Your Mind*, this is a work of clockwork precision by director Norman Jewison and cameraman Haskell Wexler, who give what is essentially a caper movie an unnecessarily reverent sheen. Steve McQueen is the businessman organising a bank heist out of boredom, while Faye Dunaway is the insurance investigator who falls for the bad guy. You can take or leave the story, but the style is something else, though the split screens don't come across on TV all that effectively. It's written by Alan R Trustman, a business attorney whose first movie this was. Wish fulfilment, perhaps? Contains some violence. [video]

Steve McQueen *Thomas Crown* • Faye Dunaway *Vicky Anderson* • Paul Burke *Eddy Malone* • Jack Weston *Erwin Weaver* • Biff McGuire *Sandy* • Yaphet Kotto *Carl* • Todd Martin *Benjy* • Sam Melville *Dave* ■ *Dir* Norman Jewison • *Scr* Alan R Trustman • *Music* Michel Legrand

The Thomas Crown Affair ★★★★ 15

Romantic heist caper
1999 · US · Colour · 113mins

This loose remake of the 1968 Steve McQueen/Faye Dunaway caper has current 007 Pierce Brosnan as the millionaire who steals art in his spare time, and Rene Russo as the sultry insurance investigator with an unusually close interest in his extracurricular activities. It's considerably steamier than the original as Russo goes topless on a beach and shimmies in a diaphanous dress that leaves nothing to the imagination, and the pair get extremely hot and heavy on the stairs of Brosnan's mansion. Yet it's all stylishly done by *Die Hard* director John McTiernan, and it's far more enjoyable than *Entrapment*. The fact that Brosnan and Russo are a sexy and believable match is just one of the factors (along with a taut script and good support from Denis Leary and Dunaway herself) that make this cat-and-mouse thriller worth catching. Contains swearing, sex scenes and nudity. ▭ **DVD**

Pierce Brosnan *Thomas Crown* • Rene Russo *Catherine Banning* • Denis Leary *Detective Michael McCann* • Ben Gazzara *Andrew Wallace* • Frankie Faison *Detective Paretti* • Fritz Weaver *John Reynolds* • Charles Keating *Golchan* • Faye Dunaway *Psychiatrist* ■ *Dir* John McTiernan • *Scr* Leslie Dixon, Kurt Wimmer, from a story by Alan R Trustman

Thomas the Imposter
★★★★

First World War fantasy
1964 · Fr · BW · 94mins

Partly inspired by his own experiences with an ambulance unit during the First World War, Jean Cocteau's 1923 novel explored both the horrors of war and the creation of a personal myth. Drawing comparisons between combat and theatre, Georges Franju plays heavily on the notion of illusion, both in his baroque visuals (notably in the fantasy dream sequences) and in presenting teenager Fabrice Rouleau's deceptions as a morally inspired sleight of hand when he poses as a famous general's nephew to help Polish-French princess Emmanuelle Riva's ambulance service return to Paris. However, harsh reality intrudes in the no-man's-land finale. In French with English subtitles.

Emmanuelle Riva *Princess de Bormes* • Jean Servais *Pesquel-Duport* • Fabrice Rouleau *Guillaume Thomas* • Sophie Darès *Henriette* • Michel Vitold *Dr Vernes* • Rosy Varte *Mme Valiche* • Bernard Lavalette *Dr Gentil* ■ *Dir* Georges Franju • *Scr* Jean Cocteau, Georges Franju, Michel Worms, Raphael Cluzel, from the novel by Jean Cocteau

Thompson's Last Run
★★★ PG

Thriller   1986 · US · Colour · 94mins

Star vehicles were getting thinner for Robert Mitchum in his later years, despite the fact that he looked better as time went by. His craggy features are well suited to TV, and here the great man emerges with credit, his dignity unruffled. He's paired opposite Wilford Brimley, a comparative youngster, as one-time buddies now on opposite sides of the law. The two are watchable, certainly, but the whole isn't really up to much, and the flat lighting and simplistic shooting that characterise TV movies of this period don't flatter either star. Not, of course, that Mitchum ever cared how he looked, and we must be grateful for

another chance to watch him at work. ▭

Robert Mitchum *John Thompson* • Wilford Brimley *Red Haines* • Kathleen York *Louise* • Guy Boyd *James Warner* • Royce Wallace *Mary* • Susan Tyrrell *"Pookie"* • Daniel McDonald *Tyrrell* • Benjamin Gregory *Little John* ■ *Dir* Jerrold Freedman • *Scr* John Carlen

Thoroughbreds Don't Cry
★★

Sports comedy drama
1937 · US · BW · 80mins

A young jockey (17-year-old Mickey Rooney) is hired to ride a dead cert for visiting English aristocrat C Aubrey Smith. He is forced by his no-good father, however, to lose the race, setting in motion a train of events that sees him barred from riding but cheering Smith's nephew to victory with a clear conscience. Directed by Alfred E Green for MGM, this otherwise undistinguished little racetrack tale is remembered for the first joint appearance of Rooney and Judy Garland, the latter as his friend and niece of Sophie Tucker (who runs the boarding house where Rooney lodges). Garland also sings two songs.

Judy Garland *Cricket West* • Mickey Rooney *Tim Donahue* • Sophie Tucker *Mother Ralph* • C Aubrey Smith *Sir Peter Calverton* • Ronald Sinclair *Roger Calverton* • Forrester Harvey *Wilkins* ■ *Dir* Alfred E Green • *Scr* Lawrence Hazard, from a story by Eleanore Griffin, J Walter Ruben

Thoroughly Modern Millie
★★★ U

Musical   1967 · US · Colour · 138mins

A popular but thoroughly overlong vehicle for Julie Andrews that succeeds despite a confusing plot and a screenplay that never seems to know when to say "enough". But there's still much to enjoy, not least the bizarre appearances by Broadway divas Beatrice Lillie and Carol Channing, of whom a little goes an awfully long way. The real delight is co-star James Fox, dancing and romancing as if to the musical born, plus the utterly delectable Mary Tyler Moore, whose natural good-naturedness proves a fine counterpoint to Andrews's studied brittleness. Director George Roy Hill lacks both the lightness of touch and the surety of style that this movie desperately needs, and although the production values are sumptuous, *Millie* now looks sadly dated.

Julie Andrews *Millie Dillmount* • Mary Tyler Moore *Dorothy Brown* • Beatrice Lillie *Mrs Meers* • James Fox *Jimmy Smith* • John Gavin *Trevor Graydon* • Carol Channing *Muzzy Van Hossmere* ■ *Dir* George Roy Hill • *Scr* Richard Morris • *Music* Elmer Bernstein

Those Bedroom Eyes ★★ 18

Thriller   1993 · US · Colour · 87mins

Mimi Rogers is the best reason to watch this run-of-the-mill drama about a Harvard professor (Tim Matheson) who becomes involved with a mysterious woman on a train. But soon he realises she may not be all she seems. Instead of the woman of his dreams, she may just be his worst nightmare, a killer who murders wealthy men. This "is she/isn't she" psychotic killer plot has been done

many times before, and there's nothing really new here. But at least Rogers shows once again that she's a talent to reckon with. ▭

Tim Matheson *William Tauber* • Mimi Rogers *Ali Broussard* • William Forsythe *Mike Stoller* • Carlos Gomez *Hector Morales* • Carroll Baker *Mrs Graham* ■ *Dir* Leon Ichaso • *Scr* Deborah Dalton

Those Calloways
★★★ PG

Drama   1964 · US · Colour · 125mins

A trapper (Brian Keith) spends his savings on some land by a lake in Maine to establish a sanctuary and protect the geese, and moves there with his wife (Vera Miles) and 19-year-old son (Brandon de Wilde). The family's idealistic ambitions are beset with problems and danger, and Keith has to fend off the attentions of a fake conservationist who wants to develop the land for goose-hunters. A family film from Disney that peddles the right values and, while way too long and suffering from too many plot strands, is sensitively made, well-acted and entertaining. ▭

Brian Keith *Cam Calloway* • Vera Miles *Liddy Calloway* • Brandon de Wilde *Bucky Calloway* • Walter Brennan *Alf Simes* • Ed Wynn *Ed Parker* • Linda Evans *Bridie Mellot* • Philip Abbott *Dell Fraser* • John Larkin *Jim Mellot* • Tom Skerritt *Whit Turner* ■ *Dir* Norman Tokar • *Scr* Louis Pelletier, from the novel *Swiftwater* by Paul Annixter

Those Endearing Young Charms
★★

Romance   1945 · US · BW · 82mins

Many wartime romances have a certain endearing, if not enduring charm, and this is no exception. Shop assistant Laraine Day has to choose between army officer Robert Young, who is a bit of a heel, and nice but dull Bill Williams (in his film debut) from back home. There is no doubt who is the more attractive for her, despite the warnings of her sensible mother, played beautifully by Ann Harding.

Robert Young *Hank* • Laraine Day *Helen* • Ann Harding *Mrs Brandt* • Marc Cramer *Capt Larry Stowe* • Anne Jeffreys *Suzanne* ■ *Dir* Lewis Allen • *Scr* Jerome Chodorov, from a play by Edward Chodorov

Those Glory, Glory Days
★★★ PG

Biographical drama
1983 · UK · Colour · 90mins

Written by *The Observer*'s football correspondent, Julie Welch, this amusing slice of pre-Swinging Sixties nostalgia was originally shown on Channel 4's *First Love* series: it enjoyed a brief theatrical run, following some glowing reviews by the nation's TV critics. Zoe Nathenson gives a wholehearted performance as the teenager obsessed with Tottenham Hotspur and their Northern Irish skipper, Danny Blanchflower (who crops up in a cameo). Some of the freshness might have worn off, but this is still an unusual and enjoyable story.

Zoe Nathenson *Julia, "Danny"* • Sara Sugarman *Toni* • Cathy Murphy *Tub* • Liz Campion *Jailbird* • Amelia Dipple *Petrina* • Elizabeth Spriggs *School mistress* • Julia McKenzie *Mrs Herrick* • Peter Tilbury *Mr Herrick* ■ *Dir* Philip Saville • *Scr* Julie Welch

Those Lips, Those Eyes
★★★★

Romance comedy drama
1980 · US · Colour · 107mins

Michael Pressman – best known for directing *To Gillian on Her 37th Birthday* (1996) and TV hits *The Practice* and *Chicago Hope* – directs this cute little movie about the lessons a young student (Tom Hulce) learns when he spends one summer in the 1950s working for a theatre company. There's love, of course, with the older leading lady (Glynnis O'Connor), but the best lines and performance come from Frank Langella as the troupe's ageing leading man. Not far removed from John Duigan's romantic comedy drama *The Leading Man* with Jon Bon Jovi and Thandie Newton, but much better.

Frank Langella *Harry Crystal* • Glynnis O'Connor *Ramona* • Tom Hulce *Artie Shoemaker* • George Morfogen *Sherman Spratt* • Jerry Stiller *Mr Shoemaker* • Rose Arrick *Mrs Shoemaker* • Herbert Berghof *Dr Julius Fuldauer* ■ *Dir* Michael Pressman • *Scr* David Shaber

Those Magnificent Men in Their Flying Machines
★★★★ U

Comedy   1965 · UK · Colour · 126mins

A fabulous excuse for a host of international comedians to don period garb, climb aboard wondrously ramshackle aircraft and dominate the screen over top-billed stars Stuart Whitman and Sarah Miles. Co-writer and director Ken Annakin keeps the action rattling along at a rate of knots, never slowing the pace for the romance, and allocates equal screen time to the different nationalities competing in the race. The glorious photography will inevitably be diminished on TV, but the wonderfully British robustness of the wacky premise can never be affected. ▭

Sarah Miles *Patricia Rawnsley* • James Fox *Richard Mays* • Stuart Whitman *Orvil Newton* • Alberto Sordi *Count Emilio Ponticelli* • Robert Morley *Lord Rawnsley* • Gert Frobe *Colonel Manfred Von Holstein* • Jean-Pierre Cassel *Pierre Dubois* • Eric Sykes *Courtney* • Terry-Thomas *Sir Percival Ware-Armitage* • Tony Hancock *Harry Popperwell* • Benny Hill *Fire Chief Perkins* • Flora Robson *Mother Superior* ■ *Dir* Ken Annakin • *Scr* Jack Davies, Ken Annakin • *Cinematographer* Christopher Challis

Those Secrets
★★

Drama   1991 · US · Colour · 100mins

Blair Brown and Arliss Howard add a little class to a mind-boggling TV movie. They play a seemingly happy couple who have been storing a few secrets from each other: Howard has had an affair while Brown used to be a prostitute. Once the truth is out of the bag, both their lives begin to spiral out of control. If you believe the sequence of events here you'll believe anything, but it nevertheless remains gripping in a curious sort of way. Former Bratpacker Mare Winningham turns up in support. Contains swearing and sex scenes.

Blair Brown *Nielle* • Arliss Howard *Simon Banesh* • Paul Guilfoyle *Leonard Sellars* •

Louis Giambalvo *Kobe* • Barbara Howard *Beth* • Mare Winningham *Faye* ■ *Dir* David Manson • *Scr* Lauren Currier

Those She Left Behind ★★ 15

Drama 1989 · US · Colour · 90mins

Gary Cole struggles with the pressures of being a father in this uninspired TV movie. Admittedly the death of his wife in childbirth has left him with the weighty responsibility of caring for their baby daughter. Despite help from his mother-in-law (Colleen Dewhurst) and his late wife's best friend (Joanna Kerns), Cole considers offering his child up for adoption. Though Michael O'Hara's script and Waris Hussein's direction are full of serious intent, they cannot compensate for this film's arid, emotionless tone, which never extends beyond the inconveniences of single-parenting and a pat ending.

Gary Cole *Scott Grimes* • Joanna Kerns *Diane Pappas* • Mary Page Keller *Sue Grimes* • Colleen Dewhurst ■ *Dir* Waris Hussein • *Scr* Michael O'Hara

Those Were the Days ★★★ U

Comedy 1934 · UK · BW · 80mins

Anxious to show he was capable of more than just the bumbling teacher from his famous music-hall skit, *The Fourth Form at St Michael's*, Will Hay played a Victorian magistrate in this enjoyable adaptation of Arthur Wing Pinero's brisk stage farce, *The Magistrate*. Making his feature debut, Hay doesn't look totally at ease, having not yet mastered playing down for the camera. But no one could do pompous bemusement quite like him and his scenes with teenage stepson John Mills (actually 26 at the time) are good value. Venerators of vaudeville will also delight in seeing several star turns going through their paces.

Will Hay *Brutus Poskett* • Iris Hoey *Agatha Poskett* • Angela Baddeley *Charlotte* • Claud Allister *Captain Horace Vale* • George Graves *Colonel Alexander Lukyn* • John Mills *Bobby* • Jane Carr (1) *Minnie Taylor* ■ *Dir* Thomas Bentley • *Scr* Fred Thompson, Frank Miller, Frank Launder, Jack Jordan, from the play *The Magistrate* by Arthur Wing Pinero

Those Who Love Me Can Take the Train ★★★★ 15

Drama 1998 · Fr · Colour · mins

As in *La Reine Margot* (1994), Patrice Chéreau explores the dysfunctional dynamic between the members of a crumbling family and its immediate entourage. Shooting initially with handheld cameras on a Limoges-bound train, he bewilders with the sheer number of people heading for a once-great artist's funeral and the complexity of their relationships. But the skeletons and revelations soon fall into place as marriages, pregnancies, addictions, gay affairs, sex changes and all manner of ambitions and delusions are dragged into the open. What follows is soap opera of a sophistication even Douglas Sirk would have envied. In French with English subtitles.

Pascal Greggory *François* • Jean-Louis Trintignant *Lucien* • Valéria Bruni-Tedeschi *Claire* • Charles Berling *Jean-Marie* • Bruno Todeschini *Louis* • Sylvian Jacques *Bruno* • Vincent Perez *Viviane* ■ *Dir* Patrice Chéreau • *Scr* Danièle Thompson, Patrice Chéreau, Pierre Trividic

Thou Shalt Not Kill ★★

Courtroom drama
1961 · Fr/It/Yug · BW · 128mins

Director Claude Autant-Lara made successful and critically esteemed films, but the arrival of the French New Wave and a more freewheeling style of cinema rendered them unfashionable. This film – made 40 years after his entry into films – was eventually shot as a co-production in Yugoslavia, but for political reasons the French and Italian authorities proved reluctant to have it shown. Set in 1949, it follows the trial of both a French conscientious objector and a German priest who, under orders, has killed a member of the Resistance. The young Frenchman is condemned for "evading" his duty, while the priest is condemned for "doing" his duty. Sadly the execution of this sturdy, overlong movie is less compelling than the narrative suggests. In French with English subtitles.

Laurent Terzieff *Jean-François Cordier* • Horst Frank *Adler* • Suzanne Flon *Mme Cordier* ■ *Dir* Claude Autant-Lara • *Scr* Claude Autant-Lara, Jean Aurenche, Pierre Bost, from a story by Jean Aurenche

A Thousand Acres ★★★ 15

Drama 1997 · US · Colour · 100mins

This modern reworking of *King Lear*, based on Jane Smiley's Pulitzer Prize-winning novel, is an anti-men melodrama given weight and class by its three female leads – Michelle Pfeiffer, Jessica Lange and Jennifer Jason Leigh. They play the sisters who fall out over some family land that is to be divided up by their gruff father Jason Robards. Their conflict, and their relationships with the men in their lives, form the centre of the film. While relentlessly downbeat thanks to Jocelyn Moorhouse's pedestrian direction, this is nonetheless a rare showcase for three of Hollywood's best actresses, and it also features accomplished performances from Colin Firth, Kevin Anderson and Keith Carradine. Contains some swearing, sexual references and violence.

Michelle Pfeiffer *Rose Cook Lewis* • Jessica Lange *Ginny Cook Smith* • Jason Robards [Jason Robards Jr] *Larry Cook* • Jennifer Jason Leigh *Caroline Cook* • Colin Firth *Jess Clark* • Keith Carradine *Ty Smith* • Kevin Anderson *Peter Lewis* • Pat Hingle *Harold Clark* ■ *Dir* Jocelyn Moorhouse • *Scr* Laura Jones, from the novel by Jane Smiley

A Thousand and One Nights ★★★ U

Fantasy comedy adventure
1945 · US · Colour · 89mins

A high-spirited Columbia comedy that pokes gentle fun at the *Arabian Nights* genre, with a singing Cornel Wilde quite dashing as Aladdin. Wilde is well supported by a genial Phil Silvers and canny genie Evelyn Keyes. Rex Ingram, the "real" genie from the immortal 1940 movie *The Thief of Bagdad*, makes a knowing guest appearance. Much of this is genuinely spectacular, while director Alfred E Green proves *The Jolson Story* was no fluke. Fun for all ages, and keep a look-out for a young Shelley Winters (billed, as she was in her early career, as Winter).

Cornel Wilde *Aladdin* • Evelyn Keyes *Genie* • Phil Silvers *Abdullah* • Adele Jergens *Princess Armina* • Dusty Anderson *Novira* • Dennis Hoey *Sultan Kamar Al-Kir/Prince Hadji* • Philip Van Zandt *Grand Wazir Abu-Hassan* • Rex Ingram *Giant* • Shelley Winter [Shelley Winters] *Handmaiden* ■ *Dir* Alfred E Green • *Scr* Wilfred H Pettitt, Richard English, Jack Henley, from a story by Wilfred H Pettitt

A Thousand Clowns ★★★ U

Comedy drama 1965 · US · BW · 115mins

Jason Robards, a free-spirited writer, quits his job on the kid's TV series *Chuckles the Chipmunk*, mainly due to a personality clash with the show's star, Gene Saks. Robards is guardian to his precocious 12-year-old nephew Barry Gordon, but this arrangement is threatened by his unemployed status. Barbara Harris, from the child welfare board, checks the situation out and soon finds herself falling for Robards. Adapted by Herb Gardner from his own stage play, this is a thoughtful, intriguing comedy with much to recommend it. The film was nominated for four Oscars, with Martin Balsam winning as best supporting actor for his role as Robard's brother.

Jason Robards Jr *Murray Burns* • Barbara Harris *Sandra* • Martin Balsam *Arnold Burns* • Barry Gordon *Nick* • Gene Saks *Leo* • William H Daniels [William Daniels] *Albert* ■ *Dir* Fred Coe • *Scr* Herb Gardner, from his play

Thousand Eyes ★★

Drama 1984 · W Ger · Colour · 85mins

This rather unsavoury offering from writer/director Hans-Christoph Blumenberg has Barbara Rudnik as a respectable marine biologist who lives with her parents in a cosy part of Hamburg. However, when she's not listening to taped messages from her lover in Australia, she's on display at a peep show trying to earn the money for her ticket Down Under. Blumenberg directs with such earnestness that, although the film shares many of the themes of Ken Russell's *Crimes of Passion*, it seems closer to a bleeding heart TV movie than a provocative piece of cinema. The usually excellent Armin Mueller-Stahl (*Music Box*) sadly descends here to the standard level of the rest of the cast. German dialogue, dubbed into English.

Barbara Rudnik *Gabriele* • Armin Mueller-Stahl *Arnold* • Karin Baal *Vera* • Peter Kraus *Schirmer* • Vera Tschechowa *Victoria* ■ *Dir/Scr* Hans-Christoph Blumenberg

The Thousand Eyes of Dr Mabuse ★★★

Crime drama
1960 · W Ger/It/Fr · BW · 103mins

Resisting offers to rework *The Nibelungen* or *Metropolis* or make a musical version of *Destiny*, Fritz Lang returned to the criminal underworld for his swansong feature. The narrative owes much to the serials of yesteryear; the imagery is shot through with expressionist leitmotifs and the gadgetry (banks of TV sets, exploding phones and two-way mirrors) is high kitsch rather than high-tech. But the emphasis was very much on the extent to which the Nazi ethos, symbolised by Wolfgang Preiss's sinister mastermind, still pervaded contemporary Berlin. Critics detested it, but there are enough flashes of mastery to engross. In German with English subtitles.

Dawn Addams *Marion Menil* • Peter Van Eyck *Henry B Travers* • Wolfgang Preiss *Dr Jordan* • Gert Fröbe *Inspector Krass* • Werner Peters *Hieronymous P Mistelzweig* • Andrea Checchi *Inspector Berg* • Howard Vernon *"No 12"* ■ *Dir* Fritz Lang • *Scr* Heinz Oskar Wuttig, Fritz Lang, from an idea by Jan Fethke, from characters created by Norbert Jacques • *Cinematographer* Karl Löb

A Thousand Heroes ★★ PG

Drama based on a true story
1992 · US · Colour · 87mins

If the success of a disaster movie is measured by the number of people who fail to make it through, then here's one to be counted a near-miss. That's because hundreds survive this made-for-TV drama based on a real-life incident. A jumbo jet flight from Denver to Chicago crashes in a cornfield after several engine explosions – not good for the passengers aboard, but a great opportunity for special effects. Despite the best efforts of Richard Thomas and James Coburn, though, it only comes across convincingly when Charlton Heston's around.

Charlton Heston *Captain Al Haynes* • Richard Thomas *Gary Brown* • James Coburn *Jim Hathaway* • Leon Russom *Bob Hamilton* • John M Jackson *Lt Col Dennis Nielsen* • Tom O'Brien *Chris Porter* • Philip Baker Hall *Sam Gochenour* • Tom Everett *Dan Bennett* ■ *Dir* Lamont Johnson • *Scr* Harve Bennett

Thousand Pieces of Gold ★★

Historical drama
1990 · US · Colour and BW · 105mins

Imposing modern attitudes on a period piece can sometimes corrupt the authenticity of the material, and that's pretty much the case with this adaptation of Ruthanne Lum McCunn's fact-based book. From the moment she is sold by her Manchurian father to an American marriage broker, Rosalind Chao is driven by fierce self-esteem (not feminist idealism) to resist the evils of prostitution, slavery and racial prejudice. Director Nancy Kelly re-creates the hardships of frontier life without resorting to western clichés and draws superior performances from Chao and Chris Cooper, the one man to show her charity. Yet her message is somewhat over-stressed.

Rosalind Chao *Lalu Nathoy* • Dennis Dun *Jim Chao* • Michael Paul Chan *Hong King* • Chris Cooper *American gambler* ■ *Dir* Nancy Kelly • *Scr* Anne Makepeace, from the novel by Ruthanne Lum McCunn

Thousands Cheer ★★★ U

Second World War musical
1943 · US · Colour · 125mins

Pianist/conductor José Iturbi made his film debut in this blockbusting wartime musical romance, whose witless script is the excuse for a grand finale ostensibly staged for the boys at an army camp, compered by Mickey Rooney and parading a host of MGM stars in songs, dances and sketches. Among the many: Judy Garland, Lena

Horne, Frank Morgan, Red Skelton, Ann Sothern, Lucille Ball and tiny Margaret O'Brien. The nominal stars are Kathryn Grayson and Gene Kelly. She's a singer who, while visiting her colonel father, organises the show, falls for private Kelly, a circus aerialist (cue trapeze act), and tries to bring her long-separated parents (John Boles, Mary Astor) together again.

Kathryn Grayson *Kathryn Jones* • Gene Kelly *Eddie Marsh* • Mary Astor *Hyllary Jones* • José Iturbi • John Boles *Col Bill Jones* • Dick Simmons *Captain Fred Avery* ■ *Dir* George Sidney • *Scr* Paul Jarrico, Richard Collins

Thrashin' ★ 15

Action drama romance
1986 · US · Colour · 88mins
Josh Brolin (son of James) stars in yet another *Romeo and Juliet* retread – this time on skateboards. Brolin falls for Pamela Gidley, little sister of rival skater gang leader Robert Rusler. It's the same old story, which should come as no surprise from director David Winters, who played A-Rab in *West Side Story*. The acting is terrible, the story is worse, and the film is only notable for the appearance of rock group the Red Hot Chili Peppers.

Josh Brolin *Corey Webster* • Robert Rusler *Tommy Hook* • Pamela Gidley *Chrissy* • Brooke McCarter *Tyler* • Brett Marx *Bozo* • Josh Richman *Radley* • David Wagner *Little Stevie* • Sherilyn Fenn *Velvet* ■ *Dir* David Winters • *Scr* Paul Brown, Alan Sacks

Three ★★★★

Portmanteau war drama
1965 · Yug · BW · 79mins
Aleksandar Petrovic emerged as the inspiration behind "Novi Film" with this ethically challenging, subtly symbolic yet grimly realistic portmanteau. In the first segment, young Velimir Bata Zivojinovic watches helplessly as an innocent man is summarily executed at the urging of a crowd of compatriots. He has joined the Partisans by the second episode, in which he is powerless to prevent a sadistic death of a fellow guerilla, who is immolated and riddled with Nazi bullets. Finally, Zivojinovic is an army officer supervising the postwar execution of collaborators and Chetniks and allows a pretty girl to die, despite taking pity on her. A Serbo-Croat language film.

Velimir Bata Zivojinovic [Bata Zivojinovic] *Milos* ■ *Dir* Aleksandar Petrovic • *Scr* Antonije Isakovic, Aleksandar Petrovic, from the book *Paprit i Vatra* by Antonije Isakovic

Three ★★

Drama   1969 · UK · Colour · 104mins
A modish but offbeat adult drama about two American guys on a European tour who find their friendship strained when they become attracted to sexy Charlotte Rampling, who joins them on their trip. The story could easily have strayed into soap opera, but a mature script keeps the cast's heads above water.

Charlotte Rampling *Marty* • Robie Porter *Bert* • Sam Waterston *Taylor* • Pascale Roberts *Claude* • Edina Ronay *Liz* ■ *Dir* James Salter • *Scr* James Salter, from the story *Then There Were Three* by Irwin Shaw

Three Ages ★★★★

Silent comedy   1923 · US · BW · 55mins
Buster Keaton's delightful parody of DW Griffith's epic, *Intolerance*, tells the same story intercut between different time periods, with Buster as the hero, Wallace Beery as the villain and Margaret Leahy as the girl. In the Stone Age, there's a mortal combat for love; in Roman times it is a battle to the death in the arena; while the Present Day sees a play off on the football field. The first of three full-length features for Metro, it was a box-office investment they never regretted.

Buster Keaton *The hero* • Margaret Leahy *The girl* • Wallace Beery *The villain* • Joe Roberts *The father* • Horace Morgan *The emperor* • Lillian Lawrence *The mother* • Oliver Hardy • *Dir* Buster Keaton, Eddie Cline [Edward Cline] • *Scr* Clyde Bruckman, Jean Havez, Joseph Mitchell

¡Three Amigos! ★★★ PG

Comedy western 1986 · US · Colour · 98mins
Originally conceived as a vehicle for Chevy Chase, Steve Martin and John Belushi, this enjoyably indulgent comedy hit the big screen with another *Saturday Night Live* regular, Martin Short, in place of Belushi, who died in 1982. The leads play stars of silent westerns who end up in Mexico on what they think is a publicity tour, only to discover that they are expected to defend a village from an evil group of bandits. It's nowhere near as funny as it should have been given the talent on show, but the chemistry between the stars and the gentle digs at the western genre make for a diverting enough entertainment. Contains swearing.

Chevy Chase *Dusty Bottoms* • Steve Martin *Lucky Day* • Martin Short *Ned Nederlander* • Patrice Martinez *Carmen* • Philip Gordon *Rodrigo* • Michael Wren *Cowboy* • Fred Asparagus *Bartender* ■ *Dir* John Landis • *Scr* Steve Martin, Lorne Michaels, Randy Newman

3 Bad Men ★★★★

Silent western   1926 · US · BW · 92mins
The second of John Ford's epic silent westerns after *The Iron Horse* (1924) had its contemporary appeal dented by the director's insistence on giving the prominent outlaw roles to grizzled character actors – J Farrell MacDonald, Tom Santschi and Frank Campeau. He did have the popular but bland George O'Brien as the young settler and Olive Borden as his sweetheart, both of whom are protected by the wanted threesome from a crooked sheriff and his gang as they take part in the Cherokee Strip land rush. Ford shot much of the film on remote locations but re-created the spectacular land rush near Los Angeles, where the memorable shot of a baby being snatched to safety was done with a real infant. Ford did not go west again until *Stagecoach* (1939).

George O'Brien *Dan O'Malley* • Olive Borden *Lee Carlton* • Lou Tellegen *Layne Hunter* • J Farrell MacDonald *Mike Costigan* • Tom Santschi *Bull Stanley* • Frank Campeau *Spade Allen* ■ *Dir* John Ford • *Scr* John Stone, Ralph Spence (titles), Malcolm Stuart Boylan (titles)

Three Bites of the Apple ★★

Comedy   1967 · US · Colour · 98mins
David McCallum took time off from his hit TV series *The Man from UNCLE* to star in this travelogue comedy set on the Italian Riviera. McCallum plays Stanley Thrumm, an English travel courier whose life is changed one night when he goes to a casino in search of an American who has strayed from his tour. Cajoled into gambling, McCallum hits a winning streak and makes a small fortune. He is observed by the sexy Sylva Koscina, who contrives to meet him and then connives with her ex-husband, Domenico Modugno, to fleece the Englishman of his winnings. Good scenery, but the lacklustre script wastes the on-screen talent.

David McCallum *Stanley Thrumm* • Sylva Koscina *Carla Moretti* • Tammy Grimes *Angela Sparrow* • Harvey Korman *Harvey Tomlinson* • Domenico Modugno *Remo Romano* • Avril Angers *Gladys Tomlinson* ■ *Dir* Alvin Ganzer • *Scr* George Wells

Three Brave Men ★★

Drama   1956 · US · BW · 88mins
This drama is a curious relic of the Cold War, showing how a civilian employee of the US Navy is suspended and investigated for being a security risk. In fact, it soon becomes clear that the man isn't a spy at all and that the whole exercise is simply that – a test case to prove the Navy's ability to deal with the threat of espionage. As the unfortunate sap, Ernest Borgnine has the requisite physical presence and wide-eyed innocence he gave to his Oscar-winning turn as Marty. What this story needs, though, is a savage twist or surprise; instead it's just an exercise in moral righteousness and a veiled attack on McCarthyism.

Ray Milland *Joe DiMarco* • Ernest Borgnine *Bernie Goldsmith* • Frank Lovejoy *Captain Winfield* • Nina Foch *Lieutenant McCoy* • Dean Jagger *Rogers* • Virginia Christine *Helen Goldsmith* • Edward Andrews *Major Jensen* ■ *Dir* Philip Dunne • *Scr* Philip Dunne, from articles by Anthony Lewis

Three Brothers ★★★

Drama   1980 · It/Fr · Colour · 111mins
Returning to their hilltop village for the funeral of their mother, a Roman judge (Philippe Noiret), a teacher of underprivileged Neapolitan children (Vittorio Mezzogiorno) and a Turin mechanic with marital problems (Michele Placido) end up discussing how they've drifted apart and try to renew ties with their ageing father (Charles Vanel). Adapted from Platonov's story, *The Third Son*, this is a laboured, if unexpectedly lyrical allegory on the social, cultural and political antagonisms that divide modern Italy. However, director Francesco Rosi isn't prepared to rest there and also explores such weighty topics as the age gap, terrorism and death. Overloaded, but emotive. In Italian with English subtitles.

Philippe Noiret *Raffaele Giuranna* • Michele Placido *Nicola Giuranna* • Vittorio Mezzogiorno *Rocco Giuranna/Young Donato* • Charles Vanel *Donato Giuranna* • Andrea Ferreol

Raffael's wife ■ *Dir* Francesco Rosi • *Scr* Tonino Guerra, Francesco Rosi, from the story *The Third Son* by A Platonov

The Three Caballeros ★★★ U

Part-animated fantasy
1944 · US · Colour · 84mins
This wonderful slice of richly-Technicolored magic from Walt Disney was a follow-up to the short *Saludos Amigos*, a product of the US "Good Neighbour" policy towards Latin America. Combining live-action and animation in a series of fun-filled episodes, it stars Joe Carioca, his friend Panchito and Donald Duck himself enjoying a musical spree which gives vent to a marvellously creative burst of cartoon energy. There's more wizardry as Donald gets tied up with the soundtrack and falls in love with Carmen Miranda's sister Aurora. Bear with the coy opening scenes; this is a real treat that deserves to be better known.

Dir Norman Ferguson, Clyde Geronimi, Jack Kinney, Bill Roberts, Harold Young • *Scr* Homer Brightman, Ernest Terrazzas, Ted Sears, Bill Peet, Ralph Wright, Elmer Plymmer, Roy Williams, William Cottrell, Del Connell, James Bodrero

Three Came Home ★★★★

Second World War drama
1950 · US · BW · 105mins
Intensely moving and superbly acted adaptation of a true story, with magnificent performances from Claudette Colbert and Sessue Hayakawa as a Second World War internee and a cultured Japanese officer respectively. Generally under-rated, if remembered at all today, this is a particularly fine example of postwar cinema, dealing with moral issues raised by the war itself. Although the Borneo setting is clearly a Hollywood soundstage, director Jean Negulesco creates a totally believable environment, and former silent star Hayakawa's performance prompted David Lean to cast him in *The Bridge on the River Kwai*.

Claudette Colbert *Agnes Newton Keith* • Patric Knowles *Harry Keith* • Florence Desmond *Betty Sommers* • Sessue Hayakawa *Colonel Suga* • Sylvia Andrew *Henrietta* • Mark Keuning *George* • Phyllis Morris *Sister Rose* ■ *Dir* Jean Negulesco • *Scr* Nunnally Johnson, from the autobiography by Agnes Newton Keith

Three Cases of Murder ★★★

Portmanteau murder mystery
1954 · UK · BW · 88mins
A compendium of three tales of the not-entirely-unexpected variety, which is notable mainly for a typically larger-than-life performance from a visiting Orson Welles. He gets his teeth into the role of an aristocratic politician who undergoes a disturbing penance for a wrong-doing he perpetuated on a colleague. The other stories feature able performances from a reliable British cast.

Alan Badel *Mr X* • Hugh Pryse *Jarvis* • John Salew *Mr Rooke* • Emrys Jones *George Wheeler* • John Gregson *Edgar Curtain* • Elizabeth Sellars *Elizabeth* • Orson Welles

Lord Mountdrago • Alan Badel *Owen* • Helen Cherry *Lady Mountdrago* ■ *Dir* Wendy Toye, David Eady, George More O'Ferrall • *Scr* Donald Wilson, Sidney Carroll, Ian Dalrymple, from stories by Roderick Wilkinson, Brett Halliday, W Somerset Maugham

Three Coins in the Fountain ★★★★ U

Romantic comedy
1954 · US · Colour · 97mins

Twentieth Century-Fox's stand-by plot was the one involving three assorted girls in any location, and here they're in Rome, throwing money for wishes into the Fountain of Trevi. Their wishes are granted, of course, by Clifton Webb, Louis Jourdan and Rossano Brazzi. Milton Krasner's cinematography won an Oscar, as did the (uncredited) Frank Sinatra title song, even though lyricist Sammy Cahn resorted to the meaningless coda "Make it mine, make it mine, make it mine" when he was unable to rhyme "fountain" with anything sensible. It sold a million! In its day, the movie's dialogue was considered quite risqué, and the clothes and performances were the epitome of sophisticated chic. Sit next to the Kleenex. ▭

Clifton Webb *Shadwell* • Dorothy McGuire *Miss Francis* • Jean Peters *Anita* • Louis Jourdan *Prince Dino Di Cessi* • Maggie McNamara *Maria* • Rossano Brazzi *Georgio* • Howard St John *Burgoyne* • Kathryn Givney *Mrs Burgoyne* • Cathleen Nesbitt *Principessa* ■ *Dir* Jean Negulesco • *Scr* John Patrick, from the novel by John H Secondari • *Music* Victor Young

Three Colours Blue ★★★★★ 15

Drama 1993 · Fr/Swi/Pol · Colour · 93mins

Polish director Krzysztof Kieslowski already had the sublime and unsurpassable *Dekalog* series to his credit when he embarked upon this trilogy, named after the colours of the French flag and derived from the Revolutionary principles of liberty, equality and fraternity. Juliette Binoche gives an intense yet sensitive performance as the survivor of a crash which killed her family, who discovers that, no matter how great her pain, she doesn't have the freedom to give up life. The process by which she deals with her grief is minutely observed, yet Kieslowski's direction is never intrusive, and his use of Zbigniew Preisner's score is inspired. In French with English subtitles. Contains some nudity. ▭

Juliette Binoche *Julie* • Benoît Régent *Olivier* • Florence Pernel *Sandrine* • Charlotte Véry *Lucille* • Hélène Vincent *Journalist* • Philippe Volter *Estate agent* ■ *Dir* Krzysztof Kieslowski • *Scr* Krzysztof Piesiewicz, Krzysztof Kieslowski, Agnieszka Holland, Edward Zebrowski, Slawomir Idziak

Three Colours Red ★★★★★ 15

Drama 1994 · Fr/Swi/Pol · Colour · 99mins

Earning Krzysztof Kieslowski Oscar nominations for both script (co-written by Krzysztof Piesiewicz) and direction, the concluding part of his tricolor trilogy has much in common with his earlier *The Double Life of Véronique*. Not only does it reunite him with Irène

Jacob, but it also explores the theme that people are bound together by fraternal ties that they can never anticipate or fully understand. Gloriously shot on location in Geneva by Oscar-nominated cinematographer Piotr Sobocinski, the film's use of colour and sound is unparalleled in nineties cinema, while the intricate plot linking model Jacob with snooping judge Jean-Louis Trintignant is spellbinding. The concluding sequence is a masterstroke. In French with English subtitles. Contains sex scenes and nudity.

Irène Jacob *Valentine Dussaut* • Jean-Louis Trintignant *Judge Joseph Kern* • Frédérique Feder *Karin* • Jean-Pierre Lorit *Auguste Bruner* • Samuel Lebihan *Photographer* • Marion Stalens *Veterinary surgeon* • Teco Celio *Barman* ■ *Dir* Krzysztof Kieslowski • *Scr* Krzysztof Piesiewicz, Krzysztof Piesiewicz

Three Colours White ★★★★ 15

Comedy drama
1993 · Fr/Swi/Pol · Colour · 91mins

The second film in Krzysztof Kieslowski's trilogy inspired by the ideals of the French Revolution is the slightest of the series, yet there is still much to admire in a movie intended as a tribute to Charlie Chaplin. Although a comedy, *White* is an examination of the aftermath of the Communist regime in Poland under which everyone was supposed to be equal. The picture painted of democratic Warsaw, with its shady deals and run-down streets, is both unflattering and affectionate, providing an animated backdrop to this droll story of love on the rocks. Zbigniew Zamachowski excels as the jilted hairdresser determined never to feel inferior again. In Polish and French with English subtitles. Contains violence and nudity.

Zbigniew Zamachowski *Karol Karol* • Julie Delpy *Dominique* • Janusz Gajos *Mikolaj* • Jerzy Stuhr *Jurek* • Grzegorz Warchol *Elegant man* • Jerzy Nowak *Old farmer* ■ *Dir* Krzysztof Kieslowski • *Scr* Krzysztof Piesiewicz, Krzysztof Kieslowski

Three Comrades ★★★

Drama 1938 · US · BW · 100mins

Three Germans who fought in the First World War run a repair shop and all are in love with the same girl – Margaret Sullavan – who just happens to have terminal tuberculosis. This overblown melodrama was intended to make American audiences cry buckets yet, at the same time, comprehend Hitler's Reich, though the word "Nazi" was *verboten*. One of MGM's hired hacks, F Scott Fitzgerald, received credit for the script, though it was extensively rewritten by Joseph L Mankiewicz after Sullavan protested that Fitzgerald's dialogue was unplayable. Many now find its naff poetic meanderings unwatchable, though it needs to be seen in the context of 1938.

Robert Taylor (1) *Erich Lohkamp* • Margaret Sullavan *Pat Hollmann* • Franchot Tone *Otto Koster* • Robert Young *Gottfried Lenz* • Guy Kibbee *Alfons* • Lionel Atwill *Franz Breuer* • Henry Hull *Dr Heinrich Becker* • George Zucco *Dr Plauten* ■ *Dir* Frank Borzage • *Scr* F Scott Fitzgerald, Edward Paramore [Edward E Paramore Jr], from the novel by Erich Maria Remarque

Three Days of the Condor ★★★★

Thriller 1975 · US · Colour · 116mins

Conspiracy theories abounded in Hollywood in the seventies, as film-makers began to explore the nation's dark underside in the wake of Vietnam and Watergate. Directed by Sydney Pollack and starring Robert Redford, this tense thriller suffers in comparison with *All the President's Men*, in which Redford appeared the following year. But it is still a polished piece of work, as Redford holds photographer Faye Dunaway hostage while he tries to ascertain Max von Sydow's role in the murder of his undercover colleagues. The excellent cast makes up for Pollack's occasional lapses in pacing. Contains violence and some swearing.

Robert Redford *Turner* • Faye Dunaway *Kathy Hale* • Cliff Robertson *Higgins* • Max von Sydow *Joubert* • John Houseman *Mr Wabash* • Addison Powell *Atwood* • Walter McGinn *Sam Barber* • Tina Chen *Janice* ■ *Dir* Sydney Pollack • *Scr* Lorenzo Semple Jr, David Rayfiel, from the novel *Six Days of the Condor* by James Grady

The Three Faces of Eve ★★★ PG

Psychological drama 1957 · US · BW · 87mins

An Oscar-winning performance from Joanne Woodward is the highlight of writer/director Nunnally Johnson's uneven film. Woodward is Eve, a young wife and mother who has three split personalities – insecure housewife, irresponsible floozy and educated woman. Her husband (David Warner) is sceptical, but a psychiatrist (Lee J Cobb) soon sees all three personalities and takes on the task of trying to merge them into one again. Alistair Cooke adds some weight as the narrator, but despite the fact that it's based on a real case history, the movie falters when Woodward interacts with anyone except her doctor. ▭

Joanne Woodward *Eve* • David Wayne *Ralph White* • Lee J Cobb *Dr Luther* • Edwin Jerome *Dr Day* • Alena Murray *Secretary* • Nancy Kulp *Mrs Black* • Douglas Spencer *Mr Black* • Terry Ann Ross *Bonnie* • Alistair Cooke *Narrator* ■ *Dir* Nunnally Johnson • *Scr* Nunnally Johnson, from a book by Corbett H Thigpen, Hervey M Cleckley

Three Faces West ★★ U

Drama 1940 · US · BW · 75mins

One of John Wayne's first pictures at his home studio, Republic, after he'd become a hot box-office draw thanks to *Stagecoach*, this modern western attempted to cash in on John Ford's *The Grapes of Wrath* by featuring the plight of Dust Bowl farmers as well as being a story of refugees from Nazi Germany settling in America. Wayne arranges for Charles Coburn's eminent Viennese surgeon and his daughter, played by Norwegian actress Sigrid Gurie, to move away from the doomed farming area and settle in Oregon. Preaching self-help and optimism, the film shows no sign of a left-wing viewpoint, though the director, Bernard Vorhaus, and one of the writers, Samuel Ornitz, were later blacklisted. ▭

John Wayne *John* • Sigrid Gurie *Leni* • Charles Coburn *Dr Braun* • Spencer Charters *Nunk* •

Helen MacKellar *Mrs Welles* • Roland Varno *Eric* • Sonny Bupp *Billy Welles* ■ *Dir* Bernard Vorhaus • *Scr* Frederick Hugh Herbert [F Hugh Herbert], Samuel Ornitz, Doris Anderson, Joseph Moncure March

Three for the Road ★★

Drama 1975 · US · Colour · 78mins

No, not the Charlie Sheen teen movie about the senator's troublesome daughter, but a pilot for a TV series that never got off the ground. Alex Rocco (still best known as Moe Greene in *The Godfather*) stars as a widowed photographer who packs his sons into their camper and sets off around the States in search of scoops. Boris Sagal, who directed Charlton Heston in *The Omega Man*, does what he can with the patchy plot, and Rocco and sons Vince Van Patten and Leif Garrett try to inject some life, but this is eminently forgettable stuff.

Alex Rocco *Pete Karras* • Vincent Van Patten *John Karras* • Leif Garrett *Endy Karras* ■ *Dir* Boris Sagal • *Scr* Perry Grant, Jerry McNeely, William Kelley, Sid Dorfman, Jack Turley, Arnold Peyser, Lois Peyser

Three for the Road ★★ 15

Drama 1987 · US · Colour · 87mins

Even after *Platoon*, Charlie Sheen was demonstrating his unerring ability to pick turkeys, and this would-be road movie was never released in cinemas over here. Sheen and the under-rated Alan Ruck (the pair had appeared together the year before in *Ferris Bueller's Day Off*) bite off more than they can chew when they are asked to escort the rebellious daughter of a politician to a reform school, and laughs remain thin on the road. ▭

Charlie Sheen *Paul Tracy* • Kerri Green *Robin Kitteridge* • Alan Ruck *Tommy, "TS"* • Sally Kellerman *Blanche* • Blair Tefkin *Missy* • Raymond J Barry *Senator Kitteridge* • Alexa Hamilton *Virginia* • Bert Remsen *Stu* ■ *Dir* BWL Norton [Bill L Norton] • *Scr* Richard Martini, Tim Metcalfe, Miguel Tejada-Flores, from a story by Richard Martini

Three for the Show ★★★

Musical 1955 · US · Colour · 91mins

This is the one about the girl who, believing her husband dead, has remarried only for him to reappear and confront her with a dilemma. It was a successful romantic comedy as *Too Many Husbands* in 1940, and would resurface in reverse – James Garner playing a husband with two wives – as *Move Over, Darling* in 1963. Here, showgirl Betty Grable is caught between returning Jack Lemmon and incumbent Gower Champion in a lively musical version of the tale, in which her friend (Marge Champion) is waiting in the wings for whoever Betty decides to sacrifice. Good choreography and ace dancing from the Champions.

Betty Grable *Julie* • Marge Champion *Gwen Howard* • Gower Champion *Vernon Lowndes* • Jack Lemmon *Marty Stewart* • Myron McCormick *Mike Hudson* • Paul Harvey *Colonel Wharton* • Robert Bice *Sergeant O'Hallihan* ■ *Dir* HC Potter • *Scr* Edward Hope, Leonard Stern [Leonard B Stern], from the play *Too Many Husbands* by W Somerset Maugham

U = SUITABLE FOR ALL   Uc = SUITABLE FOR ALL, ESPECIALLY FOR YOUNG CHILDREN (VIDEO ONLY)   PG = PARENTAL GUIDANCE

Three Fugitives ★★★ 15

Crime comedy   1989 · US · Colour · 92mins

French director Francis Veber makes his Hollywood debut with this enjoyable remake of his own 1986 French odd-couple farce, *Les Fugitifs*. Nick Nolte and Martin Short were not destined to become one of the great comic double acts, but Nolte does well enough as the armed robber out on parole, while Short gets plenty of slapstick laughs as the incompetent bank robber who drags the unwilling Nolte into his bungled caper. The action gets off to a good start, and, despite sentimental moments, keeps up a fair pace, with a healthy ration of laughs en route. Contains violence and swearing. ▭

Nick Nolte *Daniel Lucas* • Martin Short *Ned Perry* • Sarah Rowland Doroff *Meg Perry* • James Earl Jones *Detective Dugan* • Alan Ruck *Tener* • Kenneth McMillan *Horvath* ■ *Dir/Scr* Francis Veber

Three Godfathers ★★★ U

Western   1948 · US · Colour · 102mins

The first half-hour of this western ranks among the very best of ace director John Ford's work. But then the plot starts, and the film turns out to be a western precursor of *Three Men and a Baby*, only here the trio is on the run from sheriff Ward Bond. Excellent though the three leads are, all have done far better work for Ford (John Wayne in *Stagecoach*, Pedro Armendariz in *The Fugitive*, and Harry Carey Jr in *Wagonmaster*). They manage to keep their own embarrassment at bay, but the sheer daftness of the whole exercise, plus its bizarre religious and allegorical connotations, mean it's far from being among director Ford's best films. ▭

John Wayne *Robert Hightower* • Pedro Armendariz *Pete* • Harry Carey Jr *Kid* • Ward Bond *''Buck'' Perley Sweet* • Mae Marsh *Mrs Perley Sweet* • Mildred Natwick *Mother* • Jane Darwell *Miss Florie* • Guy Kibbee *Judge* ■ *Dir* John Ford • *Scr* Laurence Stallings, Frank S Nugent, from the story by Peter B Kyne

Three Hats for Lisa ★★ U

Musical   1965 · UK · Colour · 95mins

In the same year that the Beatles made *Help!* and the Dave Clark Five challenged fans to *Catch Us If You Can*, Joe Brown starred in this trite tosh about a docker, a cabby and a foreign film star. Not even the presence of the great Sidney James can elevate this story of Sophie Hardy's search for three typically English hats. The script, co-written by *Carry On* regular Talbot Rothwell, raises a few smiles, but the songs signified a new low in screen pop. However, someone thought Sidney Hayers (a capable horror director) had a way with musicals, as he landed Cliff Richard's *Finders Keepers* the following year. ▭

(2) Joe Brown *Johnny Howjego* • Sophie Hardy *Lisa Milan* • Sidney James *Sid Marks* • Una Stubbs *Flora* • Peter Bowles *Sammy* • Seymour Green *Signor Molfino* • Josephine Blake *Miss Penny* ■ *Dir* Sidney Hayers • *Scr* Leslie Bricusse, Talbot Rothwell, from a story by Leslie Bricusse

Three Hours to Kill ★★

Western   1954 · US · Colour · 76mins

A strange little western, one of dozens influenced by *High Noon's* emphasis on ticking clocks, in which Dana Andrews has three hours to find the man who killed his fiancée's brother. Having escaped a lynch mob and finding, three years later, that his lady love (Dianne Foster) is unhappily married to a former friend, Andrews is in a hurry to clear his name and give us a happy ending. Andrews is well cast, and the story rattles along in B-movie fashion, with mild tension and an agreeable lack of pretension.

Dana Andrews *Jim Guthrie* • Donna Reed *Laurie Mastin* • Dianne Foster *Chris Plumber* • Stephen Elliott *Ben East* • Richard Coogan *Niles Hendricks* • Laurence Hugo *Marty Lasswell* • James Westerfield *Sam Minor* ■ *Dir* Alfred Werker • *Scr* Richard Alan Simmons, Roy Huggins, Maxwell Shane, from a story by Alex Gottlieb

The 300 Spartans ★★★ PG

Historical adventure   1962 · US · Colour · 113mins

At a time when the ''sword and sandal'' epic was flourishing in Italy, 20th Century-Fox went to Greece to shoot this antiquarian adventure about the stalwart defence of Thermopylae in 480 BC. With most of the studio's resources diverted to the making of *The Longest Day* and *Cleopatra*, the production looks a little threadbare, but the locations are intelligently used by director Rudolph Maté, who also manages to stage the battle sequences on a reasonably convincing scale. Less authentic, however, is the dialogue, which defeats an actor of the calibre of Ralph Richardson, and gives an animated statue like Richard Egan no chance at all. ▭

Richard Egan *King Leonidas of Sparta* • Ralph Richardson *Themistocles of Athens* • Diane Baker *Ellas* • Barry Coe *Phylon* • David Farrar *Xerxes* • Donald Houston *Hydarnes* • Anna Synodinou *Gorgo* • Kieron Moore *Ephialtes* ■ *Dir* Rudolph Maté • *Scr* George St George, from a story by Ugo Liberatore, Remigio Del Grosso, Giovanni D'Eramo, Gian Paolo Callegari

300 Year Weekend ★★

Drama   1971 · US · Colour · 84mins

An ambitious but unsuccessful attempt at a ''big idea'', this movie tells the different stories of a group of patients encountered by doctor Michael Tolan over the course of a single day. Nowadays, it's the sort of thing done on TV every week by *Casualty*, *ER* and other shows. The script was co-written by actor William Devane, who also appears in a small role.

Michael Tolan *Dr Marshall* • Sharon Laughlin *Nancy* • Roy Cooper *Hal* • Gabriel Dell *Wynter* • Mel Dowd *Carole* • Bernard Ward *Rockne* • Dorothy Lyman *Jean* • William Devane *Tom* ■ *Dir* Victor Stoloff • *Scr* Victor Stoloff, William Devane, Jerome Alden

Three in the Attic ★

Sex comedy drama   1968 · US · Colour · 90mins

Considering this film was made by a veteran director who had worked on Orson Welles's early classics and who made the cracking *Al Capone* (1959),

this Swinging Sixties wish-fulfilment fantasy may come as something of a letdown. When three women discover they have been seeing the same man, they decide to take revenge. Tying him up in the attic, they try to kill him with constant sex. What a way to go!

Christopher Jones *Paxton Quigley* • Yvette Mimieux *Tobey Clinton* • Judy Pace *Eulice* • Maggie Thrett *Jan* • Nan Martin *Dean Nazarin* ■ *Dir* Richard Wilson • *Scr* Stephen H Yafa

Three into Two Won't Go ★★★

Drama   1969 · UK · Colour · 93mins

Seminal sixties sex drama, with Rod Steiger as a salesman who picks up sexy hitchhiker Judy Geeson, has a fling with her, and then finds his marriage to Claire Bloom under threat when the girl brazenly moves in with them. Directed by Peter Hall, and written by Edna O'Brien from an Andrea Newman novel, this has obvious class. But passing time and changing moral values have done it no favours. Considered quite shocking in its day, it's now hard to see what all the fuss was about.

Rod Steiger *Steve Howard* • Claire Bloom *Frances Howard* • Judy Geeson *Ella Patterson* • Peggy Ashcroft *Belle* • Paul Rogers *Jack Roberts* • Lynn Farleigh *Janet* • Elizabeth Spriggs *Marcia* ■ *Dir* Peter Hall • *Scr* Edna O'Brien, from a novel by Andrea Newman

Three Kings ★★★★ 15

Wartime action adventure   1999 · US · Colour · 115mins

A superb – though very violent – mix of comedy, drama and action, set at the end of the Gulf War. Hearing a rumour that Saddam Hussein has stashed stolen gold in Kuwaiti bunkers, US soldiers George Clooney, Ice Cube and Mark Wahlberg embark on a secret field trip with the help of a map they find concealed about an Iraqi soldier's person (you don't want to know where). It seems simple enough: grab the bullion and be rich for the rest of their lives. However, when they encounter Kuwaitis being tortured by Saddam's men, the guys reluctantly agree to help them. Wittily scripted by director David O Russell, this boasts terrific performances (from Clooney and Cube especially) while taking some well-aimed stabs at the late 20th-century phenomenon of war waged on television. The end result is reckless, gripping and unmissable.

George Clooney *Major Archie Gates* • Mark Wahlberg *Sergeant Troy Barlow* • Ice Cube *Staff Sergeant Chief Elgin* • Nora Dunn *Adriana Cruz* • Jamie Kennedy *Walter Wogaman* • Mykel T Williamson *Colonel Horn* • Cliff Curtis *Amir Abdulah* ■ *Dir* David O Russell • *Scr* David O Russell, from a story by John Ridley

Three Little Girls in Blue ★★★ U

Musical   1946 · US · Colour · 90mins

A light and chirpy musical remake of 1938's *Three Blind Mice* (the plot was later rehashed for *How to Marry a Millionaire* in 1953). The story could scarcely be simpler: take three girls, bored with life down on the chicken farm, and each wanting to find a rich husband. Cut to the big city, add a

handful of musical numbers, some frisky hoofing and lavish period art direction. Stir gently and end up with an agreeable movie that is unmomentous but entertaining.

June Haver *Pam Charters* • George Montgomery *Van Damm Smith* • Vivian Blaine *Liz Charters* • Celeste Holm *Miriam Harrington* • Vera-Ellen *Myra Charters* • Frank Latimore *Steve Harrinton* • Charles Smith *Mike Bailey* • Charles Halton *Hoskins* ■ *Dir* H Bruce Humberstone • *Scr* Valentine Davies, Brown Holmes, Lynn Starling, Robert Ellis, Helen Logan, from the play by Stephen Powys

Three Little Words ★★★★ U

Biographical musical   1950 · US · Colour · 102mins

Another fanciful Hollywood biopic of popular composers used as an excuse for a string of good numbers, though this has more plot than usual. Bert Kalmar and Harry Ruby bore as much resemblance to Fred Astaire and Red Skelton as the story bears to their lives. But with Astaire in three dances, two with Vera-Ellen (the romantic *Thinking of You* and the witty *Mr And Mrs Hoofer at Home*) and Skelton, funny but more restrained than usual, it cannot miss as light entertainment. In her third film, Debbie Reynolds has a cameo as Helen Kane, the ''Boop-Boop-a-Doop'' girl in *I Wanna Be Loved By You*. Other songs include *Who's Sorry Now*, *You are My Lucky Star* and Groucho Marx's theme *Hooray for Captain Spaulding*.

Fred Astaire *Bert Kalmar*, ''Kendall the Great'' • Red Skelton *Harry Ruby* • Vera-Ellen *Jessie Brown Kalmar* • Arlene Dahl *Eileen Percy* • Keenan Wynn *Charlie Kope* • Gale Robbins *Terry Lordel* • Gloria DeHaven *Mrs Carter DeHaven* • Debbie Reynolds *Helen Kane* ■ *Dir* Richard Thorpe • *Scr* George Wells, from an autobiography by Bert Kalmar, Harry Ruby

Three Lives and Only One Death ★★★★

Fantasy comedy drama   1996 · Fr · Colour · 124mins

The genius of Marcello Mastroianni illuminates this amusing and highly accessible diversion from Raúl Ruiz. He plays four different roles in a seemingly disconnected quartet of stories: a travelling salesman who surprises his ex-wife and her new husband; a Sorbonne professor who takes up with a similarly detached prostitute; a sinister butler trying to poison his employers; and a tycoon with a tendency to panic in a crisis. The aim of this delicious mêlée of running gags and visual puns is to question the validity of a single European culture. But it works equally well as a dark comedy A French language film.

Marcello Mastroianni *Mateo Strano/Georges Vickers/Butler/Luc Allamand* • Anna Galiena *Tania* • Marisa Paredes *Maria* • Melvil Poupaud *Martin* • Chiara Mastroianni *Cecile* • Arielle Dombasle *Helene* • Feodor Atkine *André* • Jean-Yves Gautier *Mario* ■ *Dir* Raúl Ruiz • *Scr* Raúl Ruiz, Pascal Bonitzer

The Three Lives of Karen ★★ 12

Psychological drama   1997 · US · Colour · 85mins

An unsuspected double life is the dilemma confronted by the heroine of

this predictable TV movie. A woman, unknowingly suffering from amnesia, is confronted by a stranger who shows up with conclusive proof that she is his wife. She returns home with him and soon begins to uncover the painful secrets of her past. There's nothing new or shocking in this "who am I?" tale, which relies too heavily on the preposterous contrivance of repressed memories. Gail O'Grady is credible as the forgetful wife, but David Burton Morris's flat direction fails to make any impression. The good thing about this movie is that it is quickly forgotten. Contains some strong language and violence.

Gail O'Grady *Karen/Emily/Cindy* • Dennis Boutsikaris *Paul Riggs* • Tim Guinee *Matt* • Bonnie Johnson *Lois* • Monica Bugajski *Jessica* ■ *Dir* David Burton Morris • *Scr* David Chisolm

The Three Lives of Thomasina ★★★ U

Period fantasy
1963 · US/UK · Colour · 94mins

Patrick McGoohan is superb in this British-made Disney fantasy about a veterinary surgeon whose decision to destroy his daughter's ailing cat leads to magical encounters with a mysterious stranger. McGoohan is nicely supported by Susan Hampshire and Finlay Currie, but the adult leads are no match for the delightful Karen Dotrice as McGoohan's daughter and a very scene-stealing feline. Director Don Chaffey would go on to direct McGoohan in the cult British television series *The Prisoner*.

Patrick McGoohan *Andrew MacDhui* • Susan Hampshire *Lori MacGregor* • Karen Dotrice *Mary MacDhui* • Laurence Naismith *Reverend Angus Peddie* • Jean Anderson *Mrs MacKenzie* • Finlay Currie *Grandpa Stirling* ■ *Dir* Don Chaffey • *Scr* Robert Westerby, from the novel *Thomasina, the Cat Who Thought She Was God* by Paul Gallico

Three Loves ★★★

Silent romantic thriller 1929 · Ger · BW

In this strange, dreamlike, threatening and romantic story, young Frenchman Uno Henning, who has married for money rather than love, meets the intriguing Marlene Dietrich on his honeymoon. He falls in love with her, and she begs him to save her from sinister Fritz Kortner she is with and of whom she is obviously terrified. A German silent, directed by Kurt (later Curtis) Bernhardt, this is the film that first gained American attention for Dietrich, with *Variety* drawing comparisons to Garbo and pronouncing the German star "a strong contender for international honours".

Marlene Dietrich *Stascha* • Fritz Kortner *Dr Karoff* • Frida Richard *Frau Leblanc* • Oskar Sima *Charles Leblanc* • Uno Henning *Henry Leblanc* ■ *Dir* Kurt Bernhardt [Curtis Bernhardt] • *Scr* Ladislaus Vajda, from the novel *Die Frau, nach der Man sich Sehnt* by Max Brod

Three Loves Has Nancy ★

Romantic comedy 1938 · US · BW · 69mins

Janet Gaynor, a naive and irritating girl from a hick town down South, comes to New York to look for her missing fiancé, and seeks refuge with novelist Robert Montgomery whom she'd met earlier. Her presence, cooking and homespun simplicity cause general mayhem for Montgomery and his drunken friend, neighbour and publisher Franchot Tone. A misplaced attempt at screwball comedy, so extreme in its absurdity as to defy any attempt to convince. The stars, however, do a valiant job in attempting to keep the nonsense afloat, with Gaynor embracing her idiotic role wholeheartedly.

Janet Gaynor *Nancy Briggs* • Robert Montgomery *Malcolm Niles* • Franchot Tone *Robert Hansen* • Guy Kibbee *Pa Briggs* • Claire Dodd *Vivian Herford* • Reginald Owen *Valet* • Cora Witherspoon *Mrs Herford* ■ *Dir* Richard Thorpe • *Scr* Bella Spewack, Sam Spewack, George Oppenheimer, David Hertz, from a story by Lee Loeb, Mort Braus

Three Men and a Baby ★★★★ PG

Comedy 1987 · US · Colour · 98mins

The title says it all – bachelors Ted Danson, Steve Guttenberg and Tom Selleck are left holding the baby abandoned on their doorstep, and it's not long before they are knee-deep in bottles, nappies and gooey moments. The three leads look suitably harassed as they adapt to changing, feeding and burping duties, and director Leonard Nimoy (Mr Spock himself) keeps the comedy and entertainment coming thick and fast. Based on the French film *Trois Hommes et un Couffin*, this is thoroughly enjoyable family fare. Contains swearing.

Tom Selleck *Peter Mitchell* • Steve Guttenberg *Michael Kellam* • Ted Danson *Jack Holden* • Nancy Travis *Sylvia* • Margaret Colin *Rebecca* • Celeste Holm *Jack's mother* • Philip Bosco *Det Melkowitz* ■ *Dir* Leonard Nimoy • *Scr* James Orr, Jim Cruickshank, from the film *Trois Hommes et un Couffin* by Coline Serreau

3 Men and a Cradle ★★★★ PG

Comedy 1985 · Fr · Colour · 105mins

Former actress Coline Serreau hit the jackpot as a writer/director with this box-office smash about three die-hard bachelors who have to look after a freshly hatched baby girl. The plot centres around the allegation that one of the men is the baby's father. There's also a stash of drugs hidden in the cradle that attracts the attentions of the underworld and the cops. Smartly paced and engagingly acted by the relatively unknown cast, it's a sweet little satire about the demolition of the male ego in the era of feminism. Hollywood snapped up the remake rights and made the monster hit *Three Men and a Baby*. French dialogue dubbed into English.

Roland Giraud *Pierre* • Michel Boujenah *Michel* • André Dussollier *Jacques* • Philippine Leroy-Beaulieu *Sylvia* • Gwendoline Mourlet *First Marie* • Jennifer Moret *Second Marie* • Dominique Lavanant *Madame Rapons* ■ *Dir/Scr* Coline Serreau

Three Men and a Little Lady ★★ PG

Comedy 1990 · US · Colour · 99mins

Casting British actors to perform as if they were retarded eccentrics in an imaginary England of the fifties seems almost contemptuous, in this decidedly lacklustre comedy sequel to *Three Men and a Baby*. Tom Selleck, Steve Guttenberg and Ted Danson travel to London to try and prevent their adopted daughter from being sent to (horror of horrors!) boarding school. As a national insult it would have been more effective if it had been better made. Count it as another example of Hollywood's quaint and unrealistic view of the British way of life. DVD

Tom Selleck *Peter Mitchell* • Steve Guttenberg *Michael Kellam* • Ted Danson *Jack Holden* • Nancy Travis *Sylvia Bennington* • Robin Weisman *Mary Bennington* • Christopher Cazenove *Edward* • Sheila Hancock *Vera* • Fiona Shaw *Miss Lomax* • John Boswall *Barrow* ■ *Dir* Emile Ardolino • *Scr* Charlie Peters, from a story by Sara Parriott, Josann McGibbon

Three Men in a Boat ★★★★ U

Comedy 1956 · UK · Colour · 94mins

The nostalgic appeal of Jerome K Jerome's Victorian trio is undimmed – and perhaps even enhanced – by a rather childish approach to their messing about on the Thames with a scene-stealing dog. Despite a pretend feud between Jimmy Edwards and Laurence Harvey, kept up throughout filming for publicity purposes, the ensemble, including David Tomlinson, is amiability itself, while the parasol-toting girls (Shirley Eaton, Jill Ireland, Lisa Gastoni) are as radiant as the golden days of yesteryear. It was made at a time when British studios could turn out frivolous material like this and know that audiences would love it.

Laurence Harvey *George* • Jimmy Edwards *Harris* • David Tomlinson *J* • Shirley Eaton *Sophie Clutterbuck* • Jill Ireland *Bluebell Porterhouse* • Lisa Gastoni *Primrose Porterhouse* • Martita Hunt *Mrs Willis* • Campbell Cotts *Ambrose Porterhouse* • Joan Haythorne *Mrs Porterhouse* ■ *Dir* Ken Annakin • *Scr* Hubert Gregg, Vernon Harris, from the novel by Jerome K Jerome

Three Men in White ★★ U

Medical drama 1944 · US · BW · 84mins

The 1942 departure of its title star, Lew Ayres, ended the popular series of *Dr Kildare* films. However, with Lionel Barrymore still on hand, MGM segued into the *Dr Gillespie* series, focusing on the crusty old wheelchair-bound physician for six increasingly feeble movies, which finally put paid to Blair Hospital in 1947. This one has Gillespie seeking a new assistant and having to choose between Van Johnson and Keye Luke, each of whom is assigned a test case. Directed by Willis Goldbeck, it has Ava Gardner on hand to raise the temperature.

Lionel Barrymore *Dr Leonard Gillespie* • Van Johnson *Dr Randall Adams* • Marilyn Maxwell *Ruth Edley* • Keye Luke *Dr Lee Wong How* • Ava Gardner *Jean Brown* • Alma Kruger *Molly Byrd* ■ *Dir* Willis Goldbeck • *Scr* Martin Berkeley, Harry Ruskin, from the characters created by Max Brand

Three Men on a Horse ★★

Comedy 1936 · US · BW · 88mins

Frank McHugh is the timid author of greetings card verses who has an uncanny knack for picking winning horses, which leads to him falling into the bad company of racetrack touts. In making this mildly enjoyable film version of a Broadway smash hit, Warners and director Mervyn LeRoy commendably avoided using big stars so that it remained a character piece played by character actors. It introduced to the screen Sam Levene from the original cast (but passed over Shirley Booth and Millard Mitchell). McHugh came from the studio contract list, along with his co-star Joan Blondell, Guy Kibbee, Allen Jenkins and Eddie "Rochester" Anderson.

Frank McHugh *Erwin Trowbridge* • Joan Blondell *Mabel* • Carol Hughes *Audrey Trowbridge* • Allen Jenkins *Charley* • Guy Kibbee *Mr Carver* • Sam Levene *Patsy* • Teddy Hart *Frankie* • Edgar Kennedy *Harry* • Eddie "Rochester" Anderson *Moses* ■ *Dir* Mervyn LeRoy • *Scr* Laird Doyle, from the play by John Cecil Holm, George Abbott

Three Men to Destroy ★★★

Crime thriller 1980 · Fr · Colour · 90mins

Yet another Alain Delon crime thriller, this one reunites him (for the seventh time) with Jacques Deray, who directed him in the cult classic *Borsalino*. Stopping to help an accident victim, Delon finds himself caught up in a bungled underworld hit and becomes the target of ruthless mobster Pierre Dux. However, when he turns himself into an efficient killing machine, the pursuit takes on a very different nature. Based on a novel by Jean-Patrick Manchette, this is a dark, almost Darwinian treatise on our potential for violence. Edgily directed, it's played with plenty of steel by the dourly dashing Delon. French dialogue dubbed into English.

Alain Delon *Michel Gerfaut* • Dalila DiLazzaro *Bea* • Pierre Dux *Emmerich* • Michel Auclair *Leprince* ■ *Dir* Jacques Deray • *Scr* Jacques Deray, Christopher Franck, from the novel by Jean-Patrick Manchette

The Three Musketeers ★★★★ U

Silent swashbuckling adventure
1921 · US · BW · 131mins

This was the first major screen version of Alexandre Dumas's literary romp, though it had been filmed several times since 1911. Douglas Fairbanks had himself dipped a toe in the Dumasian sea in 1917 with *A Modern Musketeer*, in which he played D'Artagnan of Kansas. But in 1921 it was all stops out, with lavish sets, slavish attention to detail and knavish behaviour on the screen. Producer/star Fairbanks and director Fred Niblo were fresh from *The Mark of Zorro* and they made this swordfest just as exuberantly entertaining. It was a smash hit everywhere and remained the definitive version until Richard Lester's two-parter of 1973.

Douglas Fairbanks *D'Artagnan* • Leon Barry *Athos* • George Siegmann *Porthos* • Eugene Pallette *Aramis* • Boyd Irwin *De Rocheford* • Thomas Holding *George Villiers, Duke of Buckingham* • Sidney Franklin *Bonacieux* • Charles Stevens *Planchet, D'Artagnan's lackey* • Nigel De Brulier *Cardinal Richelieu* • Willis Robards *Capt de Treville* • Adolphe Menjou *Louis XIII, King of France* ■ *Dir* Fred Niblo • *Scr* Edward Knoblock, Lotta Woods, from the novel by Alexandre Dumas

1440 U = SUITABLE FOR ALL Uc = SUITABLE FOR ALL, ESPECIALLY FOR YOUNG CHILDREN (VIDEO ONLY) PG = PARENTAL GUIDANCE

The Three Musketeers ★

Swashbuckling adventure
1935 · US · BW · 90mins

The first talkie version of the Dumas classic was slated at the time and remains a catastrophe, due mainly to the unappealing cast. What one needs is a convincing action hero like Fairbanks or even Clark Gable. The hangdog Walter Abel, who was imported from Broadway with much fanfare to play D'Artagnan, seems hopelessly lost, as do his equally uncharismatic cohorts. The imposing thespian playing the villainous Cardinal Richelieu, Nigel de Brulier, played the same role in the 1921 Douglas Fairbanks version.

Walter Abel *D'Artagnan* • Paul Lukas *Athos* • Margot Grahame *Milady de Winter* • Heather Angel *Constance* • Ian Keith *De Rochefort* • Moroni Olsen *Porthos* • Onslow Stevens *Aramis* • Rosamond Pinchot *Queen Anne* • Nigel De Brulier *Cardinal Richelieu* ■ *Dir* Rowland V Lee • *Scr* Dudley Nichols, Rowland V Lee, from the novel by Alexandre Dumas

The Three Musketeers ★★ U

Swashbuckling comedy
1939 · US · BW · 73mins

People sometimes assume – wrongly – that the MGM *Three Musketeers* of 1948 must be a musical, if only because Gene Kelly plays D'Artagnan. This 1939 effort does almost count as a musical (it was retitled *The Singing Musketeer* in Britain), though Dumas's story remains essentially unchanged. Don Ameche stars as D'Artagnan, Binnie Barnes is Milady and the Ritz Brothers (Fox's answer to the Marxes) are three slapstick lackeys. Songs include *My Lady, Song of the Musketeers* and *Viola*. Veteran director Allan Dwan also directed the 1917 Douglas Fairbanks picture *A Modern Musketeer*.

Don Ameche *D'Artagnan* • Binnie Barnes *Milady de Winter* • Lionel Atwill *De Rochefort* • Gloria Stuart *Queen* • Pauline Moore *Lady Constance* • Joseph Schildkraut *King* • John Carradine *Naveau* • Miles Mander *Cardinal Richelieu* • Douglas Dumbrille [Douglas Dumbrille] *Athos* ■ *Dir* Allan Dwan • *Scr* MM Musselman, William A Drake, Sam Hellman, Sid Kuller, Ray Golden, from the novel by Alexandre Dumas

The Three Musketeers ★★★ U

Swashbuckling adventure
1948 · US · Colour · 120mins

This glamorous MGM version of Alexandre Dumas's novel, directed in glorious Technicolor by under-rated maestro George Sidney, has a marvellously athletic Gene Kelly as D'Artagnan. This film paved the way for Sidney's later and greater swashbuckler, *Scaramouche*. Until that production, however, this movie contained the longest-ever screen fencing sequences, and they are indeed the highlight of what is a rather overlong and relentlessly Americanised version of the classic tale. In order not to offend American Catholics, Richelieu (endearingly overacted by Vincent Price) is no longer a cardinal and all internecine court wrangling is played down. Nevertheless, Lana Turner, top-billed over Kelly, is a ravishingly

beautiful Countess de Winter and, among the all-star cast, Van Heflin makes a suitably morose Athos, though he seems to have strayed in from another movie. 🎬

Lana Turner *Milady, Countess Charlotte de Winter* • Gene Kelly *D'Artagnan* • June Allyson *Constance Bonacieux* • Van Heflin *Athos* • Angela Lansbury *Queen Anne* • Frank Morgan *King Louis XIII* • Vincent Price *Richelieu* ■ *Dir* George Sidney • *Scr* Robert Ardrey, from the novel by Alexandre Dumas

The Three Musketeers ★★★★ U

Swashbuckling comedy adventure
1973 · Pan · Colour · 102mins

Scripted by George MacDonald Fraser (of *Flashman* fame) with close reference to the Alexandre Dumas classic, this is a sparkling version of the famous duel between the all-for-one quartet and Cardinal Richelieu and his scheming accomplice, Milady. Michael York gives D'Artagnan a clever twist of yokel to contrast him with his more worldly companions, played with wit and charm by Oliver Reed, Richard Chamberlain and Frank Finlay. The action has all the pace and unpredictability one has come to expect from director Richard Lester, while the villainous intrigue is done to a crisp by Charlton Heston and Faye Dunaway. Fast, furious and fun. 🎬

Michael York *D'Artagnan* • Raquel Welch *Constance Bonacieux* • Oliver Reed *Athos* • Richard Chamberlain *Aramis* • Frank Finlay *Porthos* • Charlton Heston *Cardinal Richelieu* • Faye Dunaway *Milady de Winter* • Christopher Lee *Rochefort* • Spike Milligan *M Bonacieux* • Roy Kinnear *Planchet* ■ *Dir* Richard Lester • *Scr* George MacDonald Fraser, from the novel by Alexandre Dumas

The Three Musketeers ★★ PG

Swashbuckling comedy adventure
1993 · US · Colour · 101mins

Richard Lester's knockabout, anarchic 1973 take on Alexandre Dumas's classic is unlikely to be surpassed, and this version for the grown-up Brat Pack is misconceived from start to finish. Kiefer Sutherland, Charlie Sheen and Oliver Platt are the swashbuckling trio, Chris O'Donnell is the idealistic D'Artagnan who joins their cause and Rebecca De Mornay the sinister Milady. The aim looks to have been a sort of "Young Swords", but the Americanisms constantly jar and the action set pieces are clumsily handled by director Stephen Herek. 🎬

Charlie Sheen *Aramis* • Kiefer Sutherland *Athos* • Chris O'Donnell *D'Artagnan* • Oliver Platt *Porthos* • Tim Curry *Cardinal Richelieu* • Rebecca De Mornay *Milady* • Gabrielle Anwar *Queen Anne* • Michael Wincott *Rochefort* • Paul McGann *Girad/Jussac* • Julie Delpy *Constance* • Hugh O'Connor *King Louis* ■ *Dir* Stephen Herek • *Scr* David Loughery, from the novel by Alexandre Dumas

3 Ninja Kids ★★★ PG

Martial arts action
1992 · US/S Kor · Colour · 84mins

Also known as *3 Ninjas*, this was the first of a series of four films featuring Victor Wong's high-kicking grandchildren. Disney certainly didn't churn out this kind of thing when most of today's parents were young, but

their children will probably revel in this pre-teen chop-socky adventure. As anyone who's seen *Home Alone* knows, the last thing villains should do is take on resourceful kids, especially when their dad is an FBI agent and grandpa is a martial arts master. But that's what the henchmen of an evil arms dealer do here – so they really were asking for trouble.

Victor Wong *Grandpa* • Michael Treanor *Rocky* • Max Elliott Slade *Colt* • Chad Power *Tum Tum* • Rand Kingsley *Snyder* • Alan McRae *Sam Douglas* ■ *Dir* Jon Turteltaub • *Scr* Edward Emanuel, from the story by Kenny Kim

3 Ninjas Kick Back ★★ U

Martial arts adventure
1994 · US/Jap · Colour · 88mins

The second film in the series about three children with formidable martial arts skills finds the boys faced with a conundrum. Should they go to Japan with Grandpa (Victor Wong), or play in the little league baseball championships? There wouldn't be much of a story if they didn't go to Japan, where they become embroiled in a standard *Goonies*-style hunt for hidden treasure. This film might please those who thought *Home Alone* was the ultimate comedy. 🎬

Victor Wong *Grandpa* • Max Elliott Slade *Colt* • Sean Fox *Rocky* • Evan Bonifant [J Evan Bonifant] *Tum Tum* • Caroline Junko King *Miyo* • Dustin Nguyen *Glam* • Alan McRae *Sam* ■ *Dir* Charles T Kanganis • *Scr* Mark Saltzman, from a screenplay by Simon Sheen

3 Ninjas Knuckle Up ★ PG

Martial arts adventure
1995 · US · Colour · 82mins

In this, their third film, the three diminutive ninjas and their grandpa (Victor Wong) end up on an American Indian reservation, which is under siege by a polluting corporation and a gang of bikers. The fights seem to get longer and less inspired in each film, and the dust bowl setting smacks of a shrinking budget. Throw in some typical "We are all brothers" Indian wisdom for ambiance and you have below-par children's entertainment. 🎬

Victor Wong *Grandpa* • Charles Napier *Jack* • Michael Treanor *Rocky* • Max Elliott Slade *Colt* • Chad Power *Tum Tum* • Crystle Lightning *Jo* • Patrick Kilpatrick *JJ* • Donald L Shanks [Don Shanks] *Charlie* ■ *Dir* Sang Okk Sheen

Three O'Clock High ★★ 15

Comedy
1987 · US · Colour · 85mins

Director Phil Joanou (*U2 Rattle and Hum*, *Final Analysis*) here turns his hand to a teen comedy, which is effectively a rip-off of *High Noon* but in a familiar high school setting. Casey Siemaszko is student Jerry Mitchell, facing up to a showdown with a fearsome teen rival in this lightweight fare, which is only slightly redeemed by the sterling performances of the cast, including Anne Ryan and Richard Tyson. Aaron Spelling, purveyor of the ultimate nineties teen series – *Beverly Hills 90210* – was one of the executive producers. 🎬

Casey Siemaszko *Jerry Mitchell* • Anne Ryan *Franny Perrins* • Richard Tyson *Buddy Revell* • Stacey Glick *Brei Mitchell* • Jonathan Wise *Vincent Costello* • Jeffrey Tambor *Mr Rice* •

Philip Baker Hall *Detective Mulvahill* • John P Ryan *Mr O'Rourke* ■ *Dir* Phil Joanou • *Scr* Richard Christian Matheson, Thomas Szollosi

Three of Hearts ★★ 18

Romantic comedy drama
1992 · US · Colour · 105mins

A romantic tale with a twist. Kelly Lynch and Sherilyn Fenn play a gay couple who contrive to split up by the end of the opening credits. A devastated Lynch then hires stud and gigolo William Baldwin to escort her to a wedding. Baldwin suggests a plan to win Fenn back which involves him wooing her and then breaking her heart. Original and feisty initially, the film descends into more conventional territory when Baldwin falls for Fenn – with predictable complications. Strong performances from the leads make this a watchable piece, but the weight of an "alternative" premise isn't enough to raise it above the average. 🎬

William Baldwin *Joe Casella* • Kelly Lynch *Connie* • Sherilyn Fenn *Ellen* • Joe Pantoliano *Mickey* • Gail Strickland *Yvonne* • Cec Verrell *Allison* • Claire Callaway *Isabella* • Marek Johnson *Gail* ■ *Dir* Yurek Bogayevicz • *Scr* Adam Greenman, Mitch Glazer, from a story by Adam Greenman

Three on a Couch ★★★ U

Comedy
1966 · US · Colour · 108mins

In an art competition, Jerry Lewis wins F30,000 and a commission to paint a prestigious mural in Paris. His fiancée, psychiatrist Janet Leigh, is reluctant to go with him, however, as she is in the middle of delicate therapy with three women who have suffered at the hands of thoughtless men. Lewis takes the drastic step of trying to cure the women himself, by befriending them in the guise of their ideal man. The ruse works and the women improve dramatically, their faith in men seemingly restored – but at what cost? The idiosyncratic Jerry Lewis is more restrained than normal in this clumsy comedy that nonetheless contains moments of genius.

Jerry Lewis *Christopher Pride/Warren/Ringo/Rutherford/Heather* • Janet Leigh *Dr Elizabeth Acord* • Mary Ann Mobley *Susan Manning* • Gila Golan *Anna Jacque* • Leslie Parrish *Mary Lou Mauve* • James Best *Dr Ben Mizer* • Kathleen Freeman *Murphy* • Buddy Lester *Drunk* • Scatman Crothers ■ *Dir* Jerry Lewis • *Scr* Bob Ross, Samuel A Taylor, from a story by Arne Sultan, Marvin Worth

Three on a Match ★★★

Drama
1932 · US · BW · 63mins

The bizarre title of this tale, later remade with the much less obtuse title *Broadway Musketeers*, hides an intelligent little movie about friendships and new rivalries. A suspenseful atmosphere pervades throughout and director Mervyn LeRoy makes good use of external locations to develop the theme of encroaching tragedy. Watch out for Humphrey Bogart, not yet a superstar, in a cast that plays a well honed script to the hilt. Not a masterpiece, but well worth the effort.

Joan Blondell *Mary Keaton* • Warren William *Henry Kirkwood* • Ann Dvorak *Vivian Revere* • Bette Davis *Ruth Westcott* • Lyle Talbot *Mike Loftus* • Humphrey Bogart *Harve the Mug* •

Patricia Ellis *Linda* ■ *Dir* Mervyn LeRoy • *Scr* Lucien Hubbard, Kubec Glasmon, John Bright, from the story by Kubec Glasmon, John Bright

Three Ring Circus ★★

Drama　　1954 · US · Colour · 103mins

Just what Dean Martin and Jerry Lewis saw in each other is beside the point, it's what audiences at the time saw in them. This film is typical of their routine mix of slapstick and schmaltz, with the pair playing discharged servicemen joining a circus. It's not to everyone's taste, but it was certainly popular with the public in the fifties, with Martin's role as cynical smoothie more appealing to some than Lewis's rather less sophisticated interpretation of his character.

Dean Martin *Pete Nelson* • Jerry Lewis *Jerry Hotchkiss* • Joanne Dru *Jill Brent* • Zsa Zsa Gabor *Saadia* • Wallace Ford *Sam Morley* • Sig Ruman *Fritz Schlitz* • Gene Sheldon *Puffo* • Elsa Lanchester *Bearded lady* ■ *Dir* Joseph Pevney • *Scr* Don McGuire

Three Sailors and a Girl ★★★ U

Musical　　1953 · US · Colour · 95mins

This Warner Bros romp is, amazingly, based on a stage play by Pulitzer Prize-winning author George S Kaufman. There's little trace of its source as likeable Gordon MacRae, hoofer Gene Nelson and winsome Jane Powell get involved in one of those staple musical plots about raising the money to put on a show. Sam Levene and vaudevillian Jack E Leonard provide seasoned support, but basically this is predictable stuff, pleasant but not particulary inspiring.

Jane Powell *Penny Weston* • Gordon MacRae *Choir Boy Jones* • Gene Nelson *Twitch* • Sam Levene *Joe Woods* • George Givot *Rossi* • Veda Ann Borg *Faye Foss* • Archer MacDonald *Webster* • Raymond Greenleaf *Morrow* ■ *Dir* Roy Del Ruth • *Scr* Roland Kibbee, Devery Freeman, from the play *The Butter and Egg Man* by George S Kaufman

Three Seasons ★★★ 12

Drama　　1999 · US/Viet · Colour · 108mins

Striking in its imagery but disappointingly cosy in its themes, Tony Bui's feature debut is the first American film to be made in Vietnam since the war. There's an element of bridge-building here, particularly in the plot strand concerning ex-GI Harvey Keitel's search for the daughter he's never seen. Yet Bui is more interested in depicting the beauty of his homeland and the warm-hearted simplicity of its people. Other threads follow a young woman (Nguyen Ngoc Hiep) who learns to balance tradition and progress while picking flowers in a lotus garden and cyclo driver Don Duong, whose love for prostitute Zoë Bui is an object lesson in forgiving and forgetting the past. Contains sexual references and nudity. 🔲

Don Duong *Hai* • Nguyen Ngoc Hiep *Kien An* • Tran Manh Cuong *Teacher Dao* • Harvey Keitel *James Hager* • Zoe Bui *Lan* • Nguyen Huu Duoc *Woody* • Minh Ngoc *Truck driver* ■ *Dir* Tony Bui • *Scr* Tony Bui, Timothy Linh Bui

Three Secrets ★★

Drama　　1950 · US · BW · 97mins

With a less talented director and actresses, this weepy could have drowned in its own tears. But Robert Wise keeps the drama on course and Eleanor Parker, Patricia Neal and Ruth Roman are splendid as the three mothers who wait together in a mountain cabin for news after a plane crash. Considerable emotion is derived from an admittedly contrived situation in which a five-year-old boy is the sole survivor of the crash. The news that the crash happened on his birthday and that he was given up for adoption unites the women, each of whom made a sacrifice years previously and believe the child may be theirs. But which one is the mother?

Eleanor Parker *Susan Chase* • Patricia Neal *Phyllis Horn* • Ruth Roman *Ann Lawrence* • Frank Lovejoy *Bob Duffy* • Leif Erickson *Bill Chase* • Ted De Corsia *Del Prince* • Larry Keating *Mark Harrison* ■ *Dir* Robert Wise • *Scr* Martin Rackin, Gina Kaus, from their story *Rock Bottom*

Three Secrets ★★

Weepie　　1999 · US · Colour · 89mins

TV-movie queen Jaclyn Smith stars in this dawdling telefilm, a remake of the 1950 movie. A plane crash strands an eight-year-old orphan boy in the wilderness. Frenzied media coverage of the ensuing search causes three disparate women to reluctantly come forward, each believing herself to be the boy's biological mother. Deft performances by an excellent cast – including Katy Boyer (*Trapped*) and Nicole Forester – fail to compensate for a fatal lack of suspense in the script and in Marcus Cole's direction. This impressive looking but contrived and unconvincing story of redemption brought on by near tragedy should be strictly for devoted fans of its star.

Jaclyn Smith *Diane Caulfeld* • Katy Boyer *Cassie Hopper* • Nicole Forester *Kelly Thomas* • Scott Plank *Gil* • Jason Brooks *Garrett* • Tyne Daly *Shelley* ■ *Dir* Marcus Cole • *Scr* Victoria Jennings Arch, Joseph M Slowensky [Joe Slowensky], from the film by Martin Rackin, Gina Kaus

The Three Sisters ★★

Period drama　　1966 · US · BW · 166mins

A filmed version of Lee Strasberg's Actors Studio production that ran comfortably on Broadway during the mid-sixties, this version of Chekhov's turn-of-the-century play doesn't quite come off, but it's certainly different. Three unhappy women for whom city life in Moscow is the centre of their universe search for a meaningful life in a Russian village. Though it may be interesting for students of the Method and/or fans of offbeat experiments with the classics, this black-and-white theatrical transcription may be an irritant to some viewers, despite a cast that includes Geraldine Page, Shelley Winters and Sandy Dennis.

Gerald Hiken *Andrei* • Shelley Winters *Natalya* • Geraldine Page *Olga* • Kim Stanley *Masha* • Sandy Dennis *Irina* • Albert Paulsen *Kulygin* • Kevin McCarthy *Vershinin* • James Olson *Baron Tuzenbach* • Robert Loggia *Solyony* • Luther Adler *Chebutikin* ■ *Dir* Paul Bogart • *Scr* from the play by Anton Chekhov

Three Sisters ★★ U

Period drama　　1970 · UK · Colour · 155mins

Though of value to biographers and theatre historians, this is a negligible cinematic experience, this is a record of Olivier's National Theatre production. Apart from two added sequences, there is no attempt to make this a "movie" in the way that earlier Chekhov adaptations were, such as the Soviet film *The Lady with the Little Dog*. Olivier is simply content to have Geoffrey Unsworth's camera rooted to its tripod as it records some admittedly fine performances from the actors portraying the three sisters who grow bored with provincial life and yearn for dashing men and the glamour of Tsarist Moscow. 🔲

Jeanne Watts *Olga* • Joan Plowright *Masha* • Louise Purnell *Irina* • Derek Jacobi *Andrei* • Alan Bates *Colonel Vershinin* • Kenneth Mackintosh *Kulighin* • Sheila Reid *Natasha* • Laurence Olivier *Chebutikin* • Ronald Pickup *Tusenbach* ■ *Dir* Laurence Olivier, John Sichel • *Scr* Moura Budber, from the play by Anton Chekhov

Three Sisters ★★★ 12

Drama　　1988 · It/Fr/W Ger · Colour · 112mins

Also known as *Paura e Amore*, this reworking of Chekhov's play sees the action transported from Russia to the chilly Italian town of Pavia. The story has been updated, with Greta Scacchi unhappily married to a TV comic and the threat of the arms race hanging over the proceedings. Yet director Margarethe von Trotta has retained the subtle complexities of the original play in order to explore such themes as sibling rivalry, fidelity, ambition and the nature of love. In a dual role, Scacchi acquits herself well in an international cast, including Fanny Ardant and Valeria Golino, but the achingly beautiful visuals can't quite atone for the over-deliberate pacing. In Italian, French and German with English subtitles.

Fanny Ardant *Velia* • Greta Scacchi *Maria/ Maria's mother* • Valeria Golino *Sandra* • Peter Simonischek *Massimo* • Sergio Castellitto *Roberto* • Agnes Soral *Sabrina* • Paolo Hendel *Federico* • Jan-Paul Biczycki *Cecchini* ■ *Dir* Margarethe von Trotta • *Scr* Dacia Maraini, Margarethe von Trotta

Three Smart Girls ★★★

Romantic musical comedy　　1937 · US · BW · 86mins

Three young daughters (Nan Grey, Barbara Read and Deanna Durbin) of divorced parents determine to stop the remarriage of their mega-rich Wall Street financier father Charles Winninger to young gold-digger Binnie Barnes, and reunite their parents. The driving force is the youngest sister, a precocious and irrepressible hoyden with an opera singer's voice. This is the comedy that made Durbin a huge star and established the formula for her subsequent clutch of moneymakers (two of which, *Three Smart Girls Grow up* and *Hers to Hold* were sequels to this). Oscar-nominated for best picture and script, it's complete nonsense from start to finish and, as played by a splendid cast, which includes Alice Brady as Barnes's monster mother and a young Ray Milland, is thoroughly delightful.

Deanna Durbin *Penny Craig* • Binnie Barnes *Donna Lyons* • Alice Brady *Mrs Lyons* • Ray Milland *Lord Michael Stuart* • Charles Winninger *Judson Craig* • Mischa Auer *Count Arisztid* • Nan Grey *Joan Craig* • Barbara Read *Kay Craig* • Franklin Pangborn *Jeweler* ■ *Dir* Henry Koster • *Scr* Adele Comandini, Austin Parker, from a story by Adele Comandini

The Three Stooges Go around the World in a Daze ★★ U

Adventure farce　　1963 · US · BW · 93mins

As the epitome of crazed and meaningless slapstick comedy, the Three Stooges are not to everyone's taste. However, this relentlessly silly homage to *Around the World in 80 Days* is chucklesome in spots. Phileas Fogg's great-grandson is challenged by a dastardly con man to re-create his ancestor's famous journey. Alas, he decides to take his servants, the Stooges, along for the ride.

Moe Howard • Larry Fine • Joe De Rita • Jay Sheffield *Phileas Fogg III* • Joan Freeman *Amelia* • Walter Burke *Lory Filch* • Peter Forster *Vickers Cavendish* • Maurice Dallimore *Crotchet* ■ *Dir* Norman Maurer • *Scr* Elwood Ullman, from a story by Norman Maurer

The Three Stooges in Orbit ★★ U

Science-fiction comedy
1962 · US · BW · 87mins

After many, many years of tweaking, thumping, poking and brawling, the Stooges were moving into weirder and weirder areas. Here they're battling a pair of Martian invaders Ogg (George N Neise) and Zogg (Rayford Barnes) who are plotting to steal the secret plans of a super-vehicle invented by the eccentric Professor Danforth (Emil Sitka). Not one of the boys' best efforts, but there's plenty of the usual flesh-slapping antics once so beloved of small boys and a not insignificant number of their fathers.

Moe Howard • Larry Fine • Joe De Rita • Carol Christensen *Carol* • Edson Stroll *Capt Tom Andrews* • Emil Sitka *Prof Danforth* • George N Neise *Ogg* • Rayford Barnes *Zogg* ■ *Dir* Edward Bernds • *Scr* Elwood Ullman, from a story by Norman Maurer

The Three Stooges Meet Hercules ★★ U

Comedy　　1962 · US · BW · 88mins

After creating the expected havoc with the soda fountain, drug store clerks Moe, Larry, and "Curly" Joe are accidentally transported back to ancient Greece with their wimpy scientist friend when his new time machine malfunctions. When they meet Hercules (who is a villain here), the Stooges decide to get their friend to stand up for himself and become more of a man. Those who are familiar with the Stooges's love-it-or-hate-it brand of humour will pretty much know right away whether they will enjoy the movie. In this instance, though, detractors may even find it tolerable, since there is less head-bashing and eye-poking than usual.

Moe Howard • Larry Fine • Joe De Rita • Vicki Trickett *Diane Quigley* • Quinn Redeker *Schuyler Davis* • George N Neise *Ralph Dimsal/Odius* • Samson Burke *Hercules* •

U = SUITABLE FOR ALL　　**Uc** = SUITABLE FOR ALL, ESPECIALLY FOR YOUNG CHILDREN (VIDEO ONLY)　　**PG** = PARENTAL GUIDANCE

Mike McKeever *Ajax* • Marlin McKeever *Argo* ■ *Dir* Edward Bernds • *Scr* Elwood Ullman, from a story by Norman Maurer

Three Strangers ★★★

Drama   1946 · US · BW · 92mins

A New Year's Eve pact between three strangers culminates in each signing a sweepstake ticket, which they hope will bring a change in their fortunes. Instead a combination of embezzlement, adultery and murder brings misery to all three. This story was dreamed up by John Huston who pitched it to Alfred Hitchcock who, though enthusiastic, was unable to take it on. Huston subsequently worked on the screenplay, but although he had since become a director in his own right, war intervened and Jean Negulesco eventually took over the project. Sydney Greenstreet is his usual imperious self, Peter Lorre is bug-eyed and shifty and the third member of the triumvirate is Geraldine Fitzgerald, one of Warners's most belligerent contract players.

Sydney Greenstreet *Arbutney* • Peter Lorre *Johnny West* • Geraldine Fitzgerald *Crystal* • Joan Lorring *Icy* • Robert Shayne *Fallon* • Marjorie Riordan *Janet* • Arthur Shields *Prosecutor* ■ *Dir* Jean Negulesco • *Scr* John Huston, Howard Koch, from the story *Three Men and a Girl* by John Huston

3:10 to Yuma ★★★★★ PG

Western   1957 · US · BW · 88mins

Unquestionably one of the finest westerns ever made, this is a gripping and truly suspenseful tale. It features consummate performances from Glenn Ford, as the cocksure baddie, and Van Heflin, as the farmer pledged to hold Ford in check until the titular train arrives. Director Delmer Daves makes superior use of camera cranes and bleak horizons, and the screenplay (based on an Elmore Leonard original) is an object lesson in scripting for the screen. The scenes between Ford and bar girl Felicia Farr are exceptionally fine. The superb whole is boosted by a marvellous Frankie Laine theme song.
▭

Glenn Ford *Ben Wade* • Van Heflin *Dan Evans* • Felicia Farr *Emmy* • Leora Dana *Alice Evans* • Henry Jones *Alex Potter* • Richard Jaeckel *Charlie Prince* • Robert Emhardt *Mr Butterfield* ■ *Dir* Delmer Daves • *Scr* Halsted Welles, from the story by Elmore Leonard

Three Texas Steers ★★ U

Western   1939 · US · BW · 55mins

Any time the girl in a Hollywood B-movie inherits a circus, you can be sure of a swarm of villains plotting to take it away from her. But "The Three Mesquiteers" (John Wayne, Ray Corrigan, Max Terhune) are on hand to help her get back on her feet, after the bad guys have caused a series of accidents and reduced her circus to one cage and a trailer. Wayne had already made *Stagecoach*, but was temporarily back in B westerns. Playing the heiress is the talented Carole Landis at the start of her brief career, while the leading heavy is former star Ralph Graves.

John Wayne *Stony Brooke* • Ray Corrigan *Tucson Smith* • Max Terhune *Lullaby Joslin* • Carole Landis *Nancy Evans* • Ralph Graves

George Ward • Roscoe Ates *Sheriff Brown* ■ *Dir* George Sherman • *Scr* Betty Burbridge, Stanley Roberts, from the characters created by William Colt MacDonald

Three the Hard Way ★★★

Blaxploitation action adventure
1974 · US · Colour · 90mins

This above-average blaxploitation flick teams a triumvirate of black action stars – Jim Brown, Fred (*Black Caesar*) Williamson and ex karate champion Jim (*Enter the Dragon*) Kelly. The preposterous plot involves a bunch of neo-Nazis attempting to infect the water supply of several US cities with a serum that kills only black people. Director Gordon Parks Jr (*Superfly*) just about keeps a straight face amid the numerous shoot-outs and bouts of kung fu fighting. Gloriously over the top, this was itself spoofed in *I'm Gonna Git You Sucka*, Keenen Ivory Wayans's hilarious send-up of the blaxploitation genre, which also starred Jim Brown.

Jim Brown *Jimmy Lait* • Fred Williamson *Jagger Daniels* • Jim Kelly *Mister Keyes* • Sheila Frazier *Wendy Kane* • Jay Robinson *Monroe Feather* • Charles McGregor *Charley* • Howard Platt *Keep* • Richard Angarola *Dr Fortrero* ■ *Dir* Gordon Parks Jr • *Scr* Eric Bercovici, Jerry Ludwig

Three to Tango ★★★ 12

Romantic comedy
1999 · US · Colour · 98mins

This sweet, if somewhat politically incorrect, romantic comedy barely made a dent at the US box office, possibly because audiences could catch all the stars (*Friends*'s Matthew Perry, *The Practice*'s Dylan McDermott and *Party of Five*'s Neve Campbell) on their TVs for free. It's worth seeking out, however, for a nice performance from Perry and a hilarious one from Oliver Platt, who seems to be making a career of being the best and funniest thing in average movies. The plot is simple. Big businessman McDermott thinks Perry is gay, so he asks him to watch over his mistress (Campbell), little realising that Perry is falling for her. Cute rather than uproariously funny, this is still proof that Perry could make it on the big screen – if only he had sharper material.

Matthew Perry *Oscar Novak* • Neve Campbell *Amy Post* • Dylan McDermott *Charles Newman* • Oliver Platt *Peter Steinberg* • Cylk Cozart *Kevin Cartwright* • John C McGinley *Strauss* • Bob Balaban *Decker* • Deborah Rush *Lenore* ■ *Dir* Damon Santostefano • *Scr* Rodney Vaccaro, Aline Brosh McKenna, from a story by Rodney Vaccaro

Three Tough Guys ★★

Action crime drama
1974 · US/It · Colour · 91mins

This unusual Italian buddy movie features a two-fisted renegade ex-con priest, who's in Chicago to investigate a bank robbery. (Give it its due: bet you haven't seen that before). The cleric teams up with (*South Park*'s Chef) Isaac Hayes who, besides turning in a well-judged performance, supplies a pretty listenable soundtrack. The dubbing detracts somewhat from the dialogue, but it's fast moving and efficient. Italian dialogue dubbed into English. Contains some violence.

Lino Ventura *Father Charlie* • Isaac Hayes *Lee Stevens* • Fred Williamson *Joe Snake* • Paula Kelly *Fay Collins* • William Berger *Captain Ryan* • Luciano Salce *Bishop* • Vittorio Sanipoli *Mike Petralia* • Jacques Herlin *Tequila* ■ *Dir* Duccio Tessari • *Scr* Luciano Vincenzoni, Nicola Badalucco

Three Violent People ★★

Western   1956 · US · Colour · 99mins

"They've got a saying in Texas – the Rio Grande changes its course, the Saunders don't." Charlton Heston is the inflexible Colt Saunders, the rancher who marries Anne Baxter's Southern woman on an impulse and throws her out on when he learns about her unsavoury past. Tom Tryon is the one-armed Cinch Saunders who falls out with his brother Colt. And then there's the post-Civil War adminstration making iniquitous tax demands. It ought to add up to highly combustible entertainment but the characters are one-dimensional and, frankly, you couldn't give a damn.

Charlton Heston *Colt Saunders* • Anne Baxter *Lorna Hunter Saunders* • Gilbert Roland *Innocencio* • Tom Tryon *Cinch Saunders* • Forrest Tucker *Cable, deputy commissioner* • Bruce Bennett *Harrison* • Elaine Stritch *Ruby LaSalle* • Barton MacLane *Yates* ■ *Dir* Rudolph Maté • *Scr* James Edward Grant, from a story by Leonard Praskins, Barney Slater

Three Wise Girls ★★

Drama   1932 · US · BW · 66mins

Three girls (Mae Clarke, Jean Harlow, and Marie Prevost) leave their one-horse town for jobs, excitement and romance in the Big Apple. One, not so wisely, becomes a kept Park Avenue mistress; another settles happily for an agreeable chauffeur; and a third becomes a store mannequin. The last is Harlow who has to deal with the fact her lover is married – should she go or should she stay? The blonde bombshell's wisdom prevailed off-screen – after this routine tale, she left her career doldrums behind at Columbia and joined MGM.

Jean Harlow *Cassie Barnes* • Mae Clarke *Gladys Kane* • Walter Byron *Jerry Dexter* • Marie Prevost *Dot* • Andy Devine *Chauffeur* • Natalie Moorhead *Ruth* • Jameson Thomas *Arthur Phelps* ■ *Dir* William Beaudine • *Scr* Agnes Christine Johnston, Robert Riskin, from the story *Blonde Baby* by Wilson Collison

Three Wishes ★★ PG

Fantasy drama   1995 · US · Colour · 110mins

Director Martha Coolidge made the similarly themed *Rambling Rose*, in which a stranger comes into the family fold and changes everyone's life. Here Patrick Swayze is the said stranger. A bum with a dog on a string, he may be an angel sent to help them cope with the potential loss of their father, reported missing in action in the Korean War, and with one son's cancer. All of this culminates in the granting of three wishes. Clumsily structured as a flashback to the fifties, the story is both daft and sentimental but, as family fare goes, its OK and the kids might enjoy it. ▭

Patrick Swayze *Jack McCloud* • Mary Elizabeth Mastrantonio *Jeanne Holman* • Joseph Mazzello *Tom Holman* • Seth Mumy *Gunny Holman* • David Marshall Grant *Phil* • Jay O

Sanders *Coach Schramka* • Michael O'Keefe *Adult Tom* • John Diehl *Leland's dad* ■ *Dir* Martha Coolidge • *Scr* Elizabeth Anderson, from a story by Ellen Green, Clifford Green

3 Women ★★★★

Drama   1977 · US · Colour · 123mins

This very personal Robert Altman movie based on a dream is as enthralling as it is entertaining, with keen insights into feminine psychology. An enigmatic chamberwork, as opposed to the orchestrations of the original *MASH* or his masterpiece, *Nashville*, this is about the transference of personality. Shelley Duvall is vapidly splendid as the gossip therapist into whose flat moves the adoring Sissy Spacek, while tongue-tied Janice Rule is the painter formulating fears of male aggression into mythic murals. This is the kind of allusive spellbinder that only cinema can achieve. "Every time I make a movie, it's like jumping off a cliff," Altman says. Be there to pick up the miraculous pieces.

Shelley Duvall *Millie Lammoreaux* • Sissy Spacek *Pinky Rose* • Janice Rule *Willie Hart* • Robert Fortier *Edgar Hart* • Ruth Nelson *Mrs Rose* • John Cromwell *Mr Rose* • Sierra Pecheur *Mr Bunweill* ■ *Dir/Scr* Robert Altman

Three Women in Love ★★★ 18

Comedy drama
1988 · W Ger · Colour · 83mins

Littered with classical allusions, Rudolf Thome's metaphysical satire provides a deceptively sharp insight into the arrogance of even the most unworldly males in setting their expectations of women so low. Totally wrapped up in the minor success of his book on Heraclitus, academic Johannes Herrschmann is vain enough to believe that shopgirls Franziska, Beate and Martha are adoring acolytes content to minister to his every need, instead of semi-divine agents of time using him as a messenger (his surname is Hermes) for their more ethereal pensées. Garrulous in places, this is astute in its sexual and intellectual assertions. In German with English subtitles.

Johannes Herrschmann *Georg Hermes* • Adriana Altaras *Franziska* • Friederike Tiefenbacher *Beate* • Claudia Matschulla *Martha* • Jürgen Wink *Franziska's lover* • Werner Gerber *Martha's lover* • Anton Rey *Beate's lover* ■ *Dir/Scr* Rudolf Thome

The Three Worlds of Gulliver ★★★ U

Fantasy adventure
1959 · UK · Colour · 94mins

In spite of the title, Kerwin Mathews spends most of his time among the giants of Brobdingnag and the little people of Lilliput in this loose adaptation of Jonathan Swift's timeless classic novel. Playing down the satire in favour of family adventure, director Jack Sher benefits from the expertise of a mostly British supporting cast that includes June Thorburn and Basil Sydney. But it's the Superdynamation work of effects maestro Ray Harryhausen that gives the action its fantastical feel. Equally impressive is Bernard Herrmann's soundtrack, written a year before his score for *Psycho*.

Kerwin Mathews *Dr Lemuel Gulliver* • Jo Morrow *Gwendolyn* • June Thorburn *Elizabeth* • Lee Patterson *Reldresal* • Grégoire Aslan *King Brobdingnag* • Basil Sydney *Emperor of Lilliput* • Charles Lloyd Pack *Makovan* ■ *Dir* Jack Sher • *Scr* Arthur Ross, Jack Sher, from the novel *Gulliver's Travels* by Jonathan Swift

The Threepenny Opera
★★★★

Musical black comedy
1931 · Ger/US · BW · 113mins

That master of early German cinema, GW Pabst, seemed the ideal choice for this reworking of Bertolt Brecht's play, itself an adaptation of John Gay's *The Beggar's Opera*. But Brecht was furious with the film's toning down of his play's anti-capitalist content and sued the German production company. Several of Brecht and Kurt Weill's original songs are missing, but Weill's wife, Lotte Lenya, mesmerisingly re-creates her legendary stage role of Jenny, and Rudolf Forster makes a roguish Mackie Messer. What's more, the film is a triumph of visual stylisation, thanks to Andre Andreiev's evocative sets and Fritz Arno Wagner's superb photography. A German language film.

Rudolf Forster *Mackie Messer* • Carola Neher *Polly Peachum* • Reinhold Schünzel *Tiger-Brown* • Fritz Rasp *Peachum* • Valeska Gert *Mrs Peachum* • Lotte Lenya *Jenny* • Hermann Thimig *Vicar* ■ *Dir* GW Pabst • *Scr* Leo Lania, Ladislaus Vadja, Béla Balász, from the play by Bertolt Brecht, from the play *The Beggar's Opera* by John Gay

Three's a Crowd
★★★

Romantic comedy
1969 · US · Colour · 57mins

Larry Hagman and Jessica Walter work well together in a breezy little comedy about an airline pilot who finds it a touch tricky keeping a brace of wives in two separate cities. There are shades here of the Cary Grant/Irene Dunne classic *My Favourite Wife*, although even Hagman's most fervent admirers would have to admit that he lacks Grant's sardonic charm. Still, he manages to keep the movie bouncing along, albeit a touch too knowingly.

Larry Hagman *Jim Carson* • Jessica Walter *Jessica Carson* • EJ Peaker *Ann Carson* • Harvey Korman *Dr Pike* • Norman Fell *Norman* • Stu Gilliam *Ralph Wilcox* • Mickey Deems *Drunk* • Farrah Fawcett *Hitchhiker* ■ *Dir* Harry Falk • *Scr* Harry Winkler, Nate Monaster, from a story by Nate Monaster

Threesome
★★

Romantic drama   1984 · US · Colour · 97mins

In this TV movie, wealthy Stephen Collins is instrumental in getting his former girlfriend Deborah Raffin together with his friend Joel Higgins, but he later decides he wants her back in his life. This boasts glittering New York locations and a cast that's easy on the eye, and veteran TV director Lou Antonio makes good use of both. It's diverting if routine stuff for lovers of romantic drama.

Stephen Collins *Peter Hatten* • Deborah Raffin *Barbara Jones* • Joel Higgins *Dan Shaper* • Susan Hess *Gloria* • Addison Powell *Mr Jones*

• Dana Delany *Laura Shaper* ■ *Dir* Lou Antonio • *Scr* Lawrence B Marcus, from the novel *Salt* by Herbert Gold

Threesome
★★★ 18

Romantic comedy
1994 · US · Colour · 89mins

A clerical error puts student Lara Flynn Boyle in the same digs as jock Stephen Baldwin and sensitive Josh Charles, in writer/director Andrew Fleming's appealing, if contrived, look at teenage sexual identity. The romantic triangle that develops between the three is sometimes handled intelligently (gay Charles's coming out, for example), but for the most part the writing lacks both reality and conviction. Baldwin in particular acquits himself well in a difficult role. But this remains a prime example of Hollywood being just too tasteful with "controversial" material, and the end result is mawkish rather than truthful. Contains swearing, drug abuse, sex scenes and nudity. ▣

Lara Flynn Boyle *Alex* • Stephen Baldwin *Stuart* • Josh Charles *Eddy* • Alexis Arquette *Dick* • Martha Gehman *Renay* • Mark Arnold *Larry* • Michele Matheson *Kristen* ■ *Dir/Scr* Andrew Fleming

Threshold
★★★ PG

Drama   1981 · Can · Colour · 92mins

American distributors ignored this dramatically persuasive fictional Canadian story of the world's first artificial-heart transplant for two years – until speculative fiction became headline fact. One of the side effects of the publicity that accompanied the real-life operation was an airing for this surprisingly low-key account of the effect on people of such revolutionary surgery. It's a pity that some commanding performances – Donald Sutherland as the surgeon, Jeff Goldblum as the artificial heart's inventor and Mare Winningham as the worried recipient – were left in the dark for so long. ▣

Donald Sutherland *Dr Thomas Vrain* • John Marley *Edgar Fine* • Sharon Acker *Tilla Vrain* • Mare Winningham *Carol Severance* • Jeff Goldblum *Dr Aldo Gehring* • Michael Lerner *Henry De Vici* • Allan Nicholls *Dr Basil Rents* ■ *Dir* Richard Pearce • *Scr* James Salter

Thrill
★★

Thriller   1996 · US · Colour

Sam Pillsbury made his name in his native New Zealand with such pleasingly quirky items as *The Scarecrow* and *Starlight Hotel*. Of late, however, he has found himself stranded in TV-movie land and here he struggles to break free from the straitjacket of the genre. TV-movie veteran Stepfanie Kramer is the amusement park owner plagued by a terrorist, who threatens to blow up one of her rides. The supporting cast includes Antonio Sabato Jr from *Melrose Place* and *ER*'s Christine Harnos, but this is nowhere near as much fun as the seventies disaster flick *Rollercoaster*.

Antonio Sabato Jr *Jack Coulson* • Stepfanie Kramer *Theresa Coulson* • Christine Harnos *Anne Simon* • Ted Marcoux *Carl Paster* ■ *Dir* Sam Pillsbury • *Scr* Betty Goldberg, from a story by Joel Steiger, from the novel by Robert Byrne

Thrill of a Romance
★★★

Musical   1945 · US · Colour · 103mins

Another of the trite, vacuous musical romances dreamed up for MGM's human mermaid, Esther Williams. This one has romance blossoming in a mountain resort between Esther, who swims, and soldier on leave Van Johnson, who sings. The numbers include hits *I Should Care* and *Please Don't Say No, Say Maybe*, the latter memorable for being belted out by famous Wagnerian opera tenor Lauritz Melchior, making his film debut in the first of several such frivolities. Tommy Dorsey and Xavier Cugat, with their orchestras, further enliven the proceedings.

Esther Williams *Cynthia Glenn* • Van Johnson *Major Thomas Milvaine* • Frances Gifford *Maude Bancroft* • Henry Travers *Hobart Glenn* • Spring Byington *Nona Glenn* • Lauritz Melchior *Nils Knudsen* ■ *Dir* Richard Thorpe • *Scr* Richard Connell, Gladys Lehman

The Thrill of It All
★★★

Romantic comedy
1963 · US · Colour · 107mins

An enjoyably wacky satire on the world of advertising, this pairied Doris Day with the immensely likeable James Garner for the first time. It's the one in which Day becomes a star of soap commercials, much to the annoyance of her gynaecologist husband Garner, and contains the memorable scene in which Garner drives the family convertible into a swimming pool that wasn't there when he left for work in the morning. There's lots to chuckle over in the clever Carl Reiner screenplay, not least the super cameo he wrote in for himself. It may seem a bit dated now, but back in the sixties this irreverent and glossy comedy was considered strong, anarchic stuff.

Doris Day *Beverly Boyer* • James Garner *Dr Gerald Boyer* • Arlene Francis *Mrs Fraleigh* • Edward Andrews *Gardiner Fraleigh* • Reginald Owen *Old Tom Fraleigh* • ZaSu Pitts *Olivia* • Elliott Reid *Mike Palmer* • Carl Reiner ■ *Dir* Norman Jewison • *Scr* Carl Reiner, from a story by Carl Reiner, Larry Gelbart

Thrillkill
★★ 15

Thriller   1984 · Can · Colour · 86mins

One of those fairly nondescript movies that suffers for having no stars, no big-name director and no big budget to back it up. The only thing it does have going for it is a plot with potential. A female computer expert, who invents video games for a living and hacks into corporate bank accounts, is murdered, and her sister, a police officer, investigates. Unfortunately, despite the valiant efforts of directors Anthony Kramreither and Anthony D'Andrea, the story doesn't really come to anything and the end result is disappointing. Contains swearing and violence. ▣

Robin Ward *Frank* • Gina Massey *Bobbie* • Joy Boushel *Maggie* • Diana Reis *Carly* • Kurt Reis *Scholfield* • Eugene Clark *Grissom* ■ *Dir* Anthony Kramreither, Anthony D'Andrea • *Scr* Anthony D'Andrea

Throne of Blood
★★★★★ PG

Drama   1957 · Jap · BW · 104mins

TS Eliot considered this the finest film ever made, though several critics have attacked this loose adaptation of

Shakespeare's *Macbeth* for the one-dimensionality of the characters. Whatever faults there may be in the dramatic structure, there's no denying the power of the atmosphere director Akira Kurosawa builds up through his majestic use of camera movement and the eerie sets that earned the film its alternative title, *Cobweb Castle*. At the centre of these Noh tableaux stands Toshiro Mifune, as the villain so much at the mercy of fate and the elements that all you can feel at his death is pity. In Japanese with English subtitles. Contains violence. ▣

Toshiro Mifune *Taketoki Washizu* • Isuzu Yamada *Asaji* • Takashi Shimura *Noriyasu Odagura* • Minoru Chiaki *Yoshiaki Miki* ■ *Dir* Akira Kurosawa • *Scr* Hideo Oguni, Shinobu Hashimoto, Ryuzo Kikushima, Akira Kurosawa, from the play *Macbeth* by William Shakespeare

Through a Glass Darkly
★★★★ 15

Drama   1961 · Swe · BW · 85mins

The first part of Ingmar Bergman's "religious" trilogy, this unrelenting drama took the Oscar for best foreign film of 1961. Set on a remote Baltic island, it charts the descent into madness of Harriet Andersson, while her father Gunnar Björnstrand and husband Max von Sydow look on with a mix of morbid curiosity and utter helplessness. Gone are the optimistic symbols Bergman usually associates with summer and in their place come some of the bleakest and most searching images of his career. Andersson is outstanding in an impossible role. One of the films that earned Bergman his reputation as a harbinger of doom, it is gripping nonetheless. In Swedish with English subtitles. ▣

Harriet Andersson *Karin* • Gunnar Björnstrand *David* • Max von Sydow *Martin* • Lars Passgard *Minus* ■ *Dir/Scr* Ingmar Bergman • *Cinematographer* Sven Nykvist

Through the Eyes of a Killer
★★ 18

Mystery thriller   1992 · US · Colour · 94mins

Adapted from a short story called *The Master Builder*, this made-for-TV thriller definitely has nothing to do with the Ibsen play of the same name. Marg Helgenberger stars as a designer whose new romance with builder Richard Dean Anderson coincides with a spate of neighbourhood killings. The big question is whether her new beau or her jilted ex-lover (Joe Pantoliano) is responsible. It's hardly a nail-biter, and director Peter Markle (*Wagons East!*) relies on tired voyeuristic tricks to generate tension. Tippi Hedren, once Alfred Hitchcock's favourite actress, is wasted in a cameo role. ▣

Marg Helgenberger *Laurie Fisher* • Richard Dean Anderson *Ray Bellano* • Joe Pantoliano *Jerry Tarlton* • David Marshall Grant *Max Campbell* • Melinda Culea *Alison Rivers* • Tippi Hedren *Renata Bellano* • Monica Parker *Dorothy* ■ *Dir* Peter Markle • *Scr* John Pielmeier, Solomon Isaacs, from the short story *The Master Builder* by Christopher Fowler

Through the Olive Trees
★★★★ U

Drama   1994 · Iran/Fr · Colour · 99mins

The final part of Abbas Kiarostami's "friendship" trilogy centres on the production of the second episode, *And Life Goes On...*, which was itself a revisitation of the first film, *Where is my Friend's House?*. Blurring the lines between life and art, Kiarostami pokes fun at the filming process, as his *cinéma vérité* project turns into an off-screen melodrama, after orphan student Tahereh Ladania stops speaking to her leading man, stonemason Hossein Rezai, because she considers his marriage proposal insulting. But besides the self-reflection, this is also a tribute to the hardy inhabitants of Iran's earthquake-ravaged northlands. In Farsi with English subtitles. 🖳

Hossein Rezai *Hossein* • Tahereh Ladania *Tahereh* • Mohammad Ali Keshavarz *Film Director* • Zarifeh Shiva *Mrs Shiva* • Farhad Kheradmand *Farhad* • Mahbanou Darabi ■ *Dir/Scr* Abbas Kiarostami

Throw Momma from the Train
★★★★ 15

Comedy   1987 · US · Colour · 83mins

Danny DeVito, stepping out impressively as a director, also stars in this comedy. As an actor, even in his familiar pop-eyed, wired persona, he clearly has the ability to build in a lot of rich character detail. As a director, he focuses on the vitality of his characters and the wonderfully creative dialogue, rather than overheating the barminess of the central situation. Asked by his writing teacher Billy Crystal to view Hitchcock's *Strangers on a Train*, DeVito, who wants rid of his monstrous bully of a mother (played by Oscar-nominated Anne Ramsey), is inspired by the murder-swap idea to make changes in his own – and his teacher's – life. Chaos and spiky black comedy ensue. 🖳

Danny DeVito *Owen Lift* • Billy Crystal *Larry Donner* • Anne Ramsey *Momma* • Kim Greist *Beth* • Kate Mulgrew *Margaret* • Branford Marsalis *Lester* • Rob Reiner *Joel* • Bruce Kirby *Detective DeBenedetto* • Oprah Winfrey ■ *Dir* Danny DeVito • *Scr* Stu Silver

Thumb Tripping
★ 18

Road movie   1972 · US · Colour · 90mins

Before producers Irwin Winkler and Robert Chartoff scored a hit with *Rocky*, and director Quentin Masters created a career-defining role for Joan Collins in *The Stud*, they were all involved in this strained counterculture road movie that nobody, not even the *Easy Rider* hippies was aimed at, went to see. That's mainly because its a jangling mess, with Meg Foster and Michael Burns hitching their way through California and coming into contact with various unhinged characters: switchblade-wielding Bruce Dern; lust-crazed trucker Mike Conrad; and nymphomaniac housewife Mariana Hill. The Friends of Distinction soundtrack is as dull as the loopy concept. 🖳

Michael Burns *Gary* • Meg Foster *Chay* • Mariana Hill [Marianna Hill] *Lynn* • Burke Burns *Jack* • Mike Conrad *Diesel* • Bruce

Dern *Smitty* • Larry Hankin *Simp* • Joyce Van Patten *Mother* ■ *Dir* Quentin Masters • *Scr* Don Mitchell, from his novel

Thumbelina
★★★ U

Animated adventure
1994 · US/Ire · Colour · 63mins

This is ex-Disney animator Don Bluth's cartoon version of Hans Christian Andersen's tale about the tiniest of tots who is parted from her fairy prince to suffer the attentions of Berkeley Beetle, a troupe of toads and an elderly, unsuitable mole. The song *Follow Your Heart*, co-written by Barry Manilow, adds more sweetener to an already saccharine story, while the animation is rather lifeless. That won't stop little girls from agonising along with this most miniature of princesses, though. 🖳 **DVD**

Jodi Benson *Thumbelina* • Gino Conforti *Jacquimo* • Barbara Cook *Mother* • Will Ryan *Hero* • June Foray *Queen Tabitha* • Kenneth Mars *King Colbert* • Gary Imhoff *Prince Cornelius* • Joe Lynch *Grundel* ■ *Dir* Don Bluth, Gary Goldman • *Scr* Don Bluth, from the fairy tale by Hans Christian Anderson

Thunder Afloat
★★ U

War drama   '   1939 · US · BW · 94mins

This was intended as a straightforward First World War yarn, with Wallace Beery as a hard-nosed tugboat skipper – not a million miles away from his celebrated Long John Silver in the 1934 *Treasure Island* – joining the US Navy to get revenge on the German submarines that sank his ship. However the advent of the Second World War lent the film unexpected topicality, as Hitler once more pressed the dreaded U-boats into service in the Atlantic. Action adventures such as this one seem incredibly creaky by today's standards, but this rattles along efficiently enough, with Beery dependably gruff and Chester Morris good value as Beery's civilian rival, who ends up busting his chops as his senior officer in the fleet.

Wallace Beery *Jon Thorson* • Chester Morris *"Rocky" Blake* • Virginia Grey *Susan Thorson* • Douglass Dumbrille *District commander* • Carl Esmond *U-boat Captain* • Clem Bevans *"Cap" Finch* • John Qualen *Milt* • Regis Toomey *Ives* ■ *Dir* George B Seitz • *Scr* Wells Root, Harvey Haislip, from a story by Ralph Wheelwright, Harvey Haislip

Thunder Alley
★ 15

Sports drama   1967 · US · Colour · 90mins

This uninspired drama has one-time heart-throb Fabian as a former driver who joins a low-rent stock-car circus after a blackout destroys his racing career. Tension builds when he get the chance to run a 500-mile race, as his protégé and partner (Warren Berlinger) tries to take the lead against orders. Car aficionados might enjoy the stock footage of crashes, which pepper the picture. Love interest and songs are provided by Annette Funicello, another fondly remembered teen idol of the pre-Beatles period. 🖳

Annette Funicello *Francie Madsen* • Fabian *Tommy Callahan* • Diane McBain *Annie Blaine* • Warren Berlinger *Eddie Sands* • Jan Murray *Pete Madsen* • Stanley Adams *Mac Lunsford* • Maureen Arthur *Babe* ■ *Dir* Richard Rush • *Scr* Sy Salkowitz

Thunder and Lightning
★★ 15

Adventure   1977 · US · Colour · 94mins

This is a so-so action film about amiable moonshiners keeping one car chase ahead of the law. David Carradine and Kate Jackson play the spirited leads, and they're an attractive pairing. In terms of originality of plot, though, the film is anything but 100 per cent proof. But it's okay viewing if you're a *Smokey and the Bandit* or *Dukes of Hazzard* fan – and if your idea of action is a neat car pursuit followed by a pile-up.

David Carradine *Harley Thomas* • Kate Jackson *Nancy Sue Hunnicutt* • Roger C Carmel *Ralph Junior Hunnicutt* • Sterling Holloway *Hobe Carpenter* • Eddie Barth *Rudi Volpone* • Ron Feinberg *Bubba* • George Murdock *Jake Summers* ■ *Dir* Corey Allen • *Scr* William Hjortsberg

Thunder Bay
★★ U

Adventure drama
1953 · US · Colour · 102mins

James Stewart and partner Dan Duryea drill for oil off the Louisiana coast and threaten the local shrimp industry in a disappointing Universal adventure. "They wanted a picture with Jimmy Stewart and we concocted one," Stewart said later of this heavily contrived effort that isn't a patch on the great series of westerns he made with the same director, Anthony Mann. It's the sort of movie that's made by numbers. There's a bit of action, a bit of romance, a bit of capitalist conflict and – when that gets monotonous – the weather turns bad.

James Stewart *Steve Martin* • Joanne Dru *Stella Rigaud* • Dan Duryea *Johnny Gambi* • Gilbert Roland *Teche Bossier* • Marcia Henderson *Francesca Rigaud* • Robert Monet *Phillipe Bayard* • Jay C Flippen *Kermit MacDonald* ■ *Dir* Anthony Mann • *Scr* Gil Doud, John Michael Hayes

Thunder In Paradise
★★ 15

Action adventure
1993 · US · Colour · 104mins

Hulk Hogan flexes his acting chops as a good-hearted mercenary who, after marrying the owner of a luxury hotel, becomes involved in a treasure hunt to help her keep the hotel out of the clutches of her greedy uncle (Patrick Mcnee). Think that's confusing? Try figuring out why Sam Jones is tossed into the mix as the villain, or why we should care about all of the bickering that goes on during the treasure hunt. At least there are some pretty pictures of the beach. This is the low-budget pilot of a short-lived American television series. 🖳

Hulk Hogan *RJ "Hurricane" Spencer* • Chris Lemmon *Martin "Bru" Brubaker* • Felicity Waterman *Megan Whitaker* • Carol Alt *Kate LaRew* • Robin Weisman *Jessie Whitaker* • Patrick Macnee *Edward Whitaker* ■ *Dir* Douglas Schwartz • *Scr* Michael Berk

Thunder in the City
★★★

Satirical comedy drama
1937 · UK · BW · 76mins

Seeing Edward G Robinson and Ralph Richardson acting their respective socks off is the juicy prospect offered by this comedy proving the old adage of America and England being two

countries separated by a common language. Robinson is the hotshot Yank who arrives in London aiming to raise a million dollars to finance a mine in Africa; Richardson is the rather staid establishment banker he must win over. Nigel Bruce does a Dr Watson as Robinson's guide through the minefields of British class and etiquette. Robinson made this highly enjoyable film specifically to escape his screen image as a mobster.

Edward G Robinson *Dan Armstrong* • Luli Deste *Lady Patricia* • Nigel Bruce *The Duke of Glenavon* • Constance Collier *The Duchess of Glenavon* • Ralph Richardson *Henry Graham Manningdale* • Annie Esmond *Lady Challoner* • Arthur Wontner *Sir Peter Challoner* • Elizabeth Inglis *Dolly* ■ *Dir* Marion Gering • *Scr* Akos Tolnay, Aben Kandel, Robert E Sherwood, Walter Hackett, from a story by Robert E Sherwood, Aben Kandel

Thunder in the Sun
★★ U

Western   1959 · US · Colour · 80mins

Susan Hayward is saddled with a ridiculous, almost incomprehensible accent as the wife of a Basque leader, who falls for handsome wagon-train scout Jeff Chandler, in a movie that can't make up its mind whether it's a western or the story of the beginning of California's Napa Valley wine industry. Not that anybody cares – the pace is too sluggish and the plot totally mind-numbing. There's a super Indian ambush sequence photographed by the great Stanley Cortez, but basically this film is an insult to Basques – and everyone else.

Susan Hayward *Gabrielle Dauphin* • Jeff Chandler *Lon Bennett* • Jacques Bergerac *Pepe Dauphin* • Blanche Yurka *Louise Dauphin* • Carl Esmond *Andre Dauphin* • Fortunio Bonanova *Fernando Christophe* • Bertrand Castelli *Edmond Dauphin* • Veda Ann Borg *Marie* ■ *Dir* Russell Rouse • *Scr* Russell Rouse, Stewart Stern, from a story by Guy Trosper, James Hill

Thunder Island
★★ U

Thriller   1963 · US · BW · 64mins

This fast-moving thriller finds professional assassin Gene Nelson forcing an American couple to help him murder a dictator exiled on a Latin American island. The job proves more difficult that the hitman intended, leading to an exciting chase in Puerto Rico's El Morro castle. An efficient and occasionally gripping movie, this has Jack Nicholson credited as co-screenwriter.

Gene Nelson *Billy Poole* • Fay Spain *Helen Dodge* • Brian Kelly *Vincent Dodge* • Miriam Colon *Anita Chavez* • Art Bedard *Ramon Alou* • Evelyn Kaufman *Jo Dodge* • Antonio Torres Martino *Col Cepeda* • Stephanie Rifkinson *Linda Perez* ■ *Dir* Jack Leewood • *Scr* Don Devlin, Jack Nicholson

A Thunder of Drums
★★★

Western   1961 · US · Colour · 96mins

This well-made western was inspired by the same source material as John Ford's great cavalry trilogy, the short stories of *Saturday Evening Post* writer James Warner Bellah, who wrote the screenplay. It stars Richard Boone, fresh from his TV series *Have Gun Will Travel*, as a growling fort commander, and the dashing George Hamilton as a conscience-stricken lieutenant. Richard

Chamberlain – whose popularity was about to soar with his starring role in TV's *Dr Kildare* – features down the cast. Also on parade are Charles Bronson, Slim Pickens and that maestro of the twangy guitar, Duane Eddy. *The Big Circus* director Joseph M Newman is clever enough to know how to get the most out of this familiar stuff.

Richard Boone *Capt Stephen Maddocks* • George Hamilton *Lt Curtis McQuade* • Luana Patten *Tracey Hamilton* • Arthur O'Connell *Sgt Rodermill* • Charles Bronson *Trooper Hanna* • Richard Chamberlain *Lt Porter* • Duane Eddy *Trooper Eddy* • James Douglas *Lt Gresham* • Slim Pickens *Trooper Erschick* ■ *Dir* Joseph M Newman • *Scr* James Warner Bellah

Thunder on the Hill ★★
Mystery melodrama 1951 · US · BW · 84mins
Claudette Colbert, one of Hollywood's most sparkling queens of sophisticated comedy, dons a nun's habit in this dramatic thriller, set in a convent presided over by Mother Superior Gladys Cooper. When, during a flood, a distraught Ann Blyth – who's accused of murder and under guard – arrives to take refuge from the storm, Sister Claudette sets out to prove she's innocent by unearthing the real killer. It's adapted from the once-fashionable West End play, *Bonaventure*, and director Douglas Sirk maintains a sense of atmosphere. But it's uneventful, despite the complicated plot denouement.

Claudette Colbert *Sister Mary Bonaventure* • Ann Blyth *Valerie Carns* • Robert Douglas *Dr Jeffreys* • Anne Crawford *Isabel Jeffreys* • Philip Friend *Sidney Kingham* • Gladys Cooper *Mother Superior* ■ *Dir* Douglas Sirk • *Scr* Oscar Saul, Andrew Solt, from the play *Bonaventure* by Charlotte Hastings

Thunder over Arizona ★★ U
Western 1956 · US · Colour · 74mins
George Macready (*Gilda*, *Paths of Glory*) is the town tyrant who evokes the arcane Apex Rule whereby, if a mineral vein runs through his land, the owners of the territory containing the head of the vein have to surrender their rights. Of course, he's not going to get away with that. Unfortunately, he fails to recognise that his hired gun, Skip Homeier (*Tomorrow the World*), isn't actually the killer he thinks he is. A pacey, colourful B-western from Republic, this is shot in their cheap widescreen process, Naturama, and directed with conviction by house hack Joe Kane.

Skip Homeier *Tim Mallory* • Kristine Miller *Fay Warren* • George Macready *Ervin Plummer* • Wallace Ford *Hal Styles* • Jack Elam *Slats* • Nacho Galindo *Pancho* • Gregory Walcott *Mark* • George Keymas *"Shotgun" Kelly* ■ *Dir* Joe Kane [Joseph Kane] • *Scr* Sloan Nibley

Thunder over the Plains ★★ U
Western 1953 · US · Colour · 82mins
It's Texas just after the Civil War, as the state comes under the exploitative influence of northern carpetbaggers. Randolph Scott is the native Texan who, as a captain in the Union army of occupation, has the tricky job of enforcing law and order despite his sympathy for Charles McGraw's defiant

band of vigilantes. A contrast in villainy is offered by Elisha Cook Jr's corrupt tax assessor and Lex Barker's West Point captain, who lusts after Scott's wife (Phyllis Kirk) while he's away. Andre De Toth's direction keeps the complicated story on the move but he can't create any real tension.

Randolph Scott *Captain David Porter* • Lex Barker *Captain Bill Hodges* • Phyllis Kirk *Norah* • Charles McGraw *Ben Westman* • Henry Hull *Lt Col Chandler* • Elisha Cook Jr *Standish* • Fess Parker *Kirby* ■ *Dir* Andre De Toth • *Scr* Russell Hughes

Thunder Pass ★★ U
Western 1954 · US · BW · 78mins
Don't expect *Stagecoach* – despite the presence of two of that film's cast members Andy Devine and John Carradine – as this is just another plodding Indian wars outing. It's directed without flourish by Frank McDonald, who spins a standard tale of pioneer settlers menaced by wily tribesmen.

Dane Clark *Storm* • Dorothy Patrick *Murdock* • Andy Devine *Injun* • Raymond Burr *Tulsa* • John Carradine *Bergstrom* • Mary Ellen Kay *Charity* • Raymond Hatton *Ancient* ■ *Dir* Frank McDonald • *Scr* Tom Hubbard, Fred Eggers, from a story by George Van Marter

Thunder Rock ★★★★
Fantasy drama 1942 · UK · BW · 111mins
Without ever breaking entirely free from its theatrical origins, this propagandist allegory nevertheless succeeds in creating an atmosphere that is at once haunting, mournful and inspiring. As the writer disillusioned by the world's complacent response to fascism, Michael Redgrave gives one of his most complex and tormented performances. He regains his crusading spirit as a result of his encounters with the victims of a shipwreck that occurred years before on the rocks near the lighthouse he now tends. With a bullish contribution from James Mason and truly touching support from Lilli Palmer, as a ghostly émigrée, this is one of the Boulting brothers' finest achievements.

Michael Redgrave *David Charleston* • Barbara Mullen *Ellen Kirby* • James Mason *Streeter* • Lilli Palmer *Melanie Kurtz* • Finlay Currie *Captain Joshua* • Frederick Valk *Dr Kurtz* • Frederick Cooper *Ted Briggs* ■ *Dir* Roy Boulting • *Scr* Jeffrey Dell, Bernard Miles, from the play by Robert Ardrey

Thunder Run ★ 15
Action thriller 1986 · US · Colour · 86mins
A homage to the *Mad Max* movies would be a polite way of describing this film, but, more accurately, it's a shameless and conspicuously inferior rip-off. It amounts to little more than one long and largely unthrilling chase sequence across the Nevada and Arizona deserts, as a veteran trucker battles to bring a cargo of plutonium through in the face of fiendish opposition. The film is chiefly of interest as the last feature made by Forrest Tucker, the star of umpteen Hollywood action pictures of the forties and fifties, who died shortly afterwards. Contains swearing and nudity. ▭

Forrest Tucker *Charlie Morrison* • John Ireland *George Adams* • John Shepherd *Chris* • Jill

Whitlow *Kim* • Wally Ward *Paul* • Cheryl M Lynn *Jilly* ■ *Dir* Gary Hudson • *Scr* Charles Davis, Carol Heyer, from a story by Carol Lynn, Clifford Wenger Sr

Thunderball ★★★ PG
Spy adventure 1965 · UK · Colour · 125mins
The Bond series went well and truly comic strip with this gadget-filled extravaganza that too often cuts plotline corners to squeeze in all the high-tech hardware. Playing 007 for the fourth time, Sean Connery is still getting a kick out of the part, but he's less the suave spy and more the man of action than in previous outings. Adolfo Celi makes a worthy opponent, but Claudine Auger is one of the least memorable of the Bond girls. Director Terence Young never quite solves the pacing problems posed by filming underwater, but John Stears's Oscar-winning special effects more than compensate. ▭

Sean Connery *James Bond* • Claudine Auger *Domino Derval* • Adolfo Celi *Emilio Largo* • Luciana Paluzzi *Fiona Volpe* • Rik Van Nutter *Felix Leiter* • Bernard Lee *"M"* • Martine Beswick *Paula Caplan* • Guy Doleman *Count Lippe* • Molly Peters *Patricia Fearing* • Desmond Llewelyn *"Q"* • Lois Maxwell *Moneypenny* ■ *Dir* Terence Young • *Scr* Richard Maibaum, John Hopkins, from the story by Kevin McClory, Jack Whittingham, Ian Fleming, from the characters created by Ian Fleming

Thunderbirds ★
Second World War drama 1952 · US · BW · 98mins
The late John Derek will always be remembered for his beautiful wives – Ursula Andress and Bo Derek in particular – and it's easy to forget that he was once famous in his own right. As a handsome, if slightly wooden, leading man in the Errol Flynn mould, he starred in a string of action-adventure flicks during the fifties. This routine Second World War drama is spiced up by the square-jawed heroics of Derek and John Drew Barrymore (father of Drew) as raw recruits becoming men on the battlefields of Europe. Watch out for a young Slim Pickens among the privates on parade.

John Derek *Gil Hackett* • John Barrymore Jr [John Drew Barrymore] *Tom McCreery* • Mona Freeman *Lt Ellen Henderson* • Gene Evans *Mike Braggart* • Eileen Christy *Mary Caldwell* • Ward Bond *Sgt Logan* • Barton MacLane *Sgt Durkee* ■ *Dir* John H Auer • *Scr* Mary C McCall Jr, from a story by Kenneth Gamet

Thunderbolt ★★★★
Crime drama 1929 · US · BW · 91mins
Before Josef von Sternberg made Marlene Dietrich into a star, the very different George Bancroft was his favourite actor. In the fourth and last of his films with Sternberg, Bancroft, in the title role, plays a gangster, as he did in *Underworld* (1927). While on death row he plots to kill his moll's lover, falsely imprisoned in the same jail. Although the quality of the sound recording is primitive — it was Sternberg's first talkie — the director uses it as atmospherically as he does the camera. The moll is played by Fay Wray, who had just gained star status in *The Wedding March* (1928), directed

by another Viennese-born director, Erich von Stroheim.

George Bancroft *Thunderbolt Jim Lang* • Fay Wray *"Ritzy"* • Richard Arlen *Bob Morgan* • Tully Marshall *Warden* • Eugenie Besserer *Mrs Morgan* • James Spottswood *Snapper O'Shea* • Fred Kohler *Bad Al Frieberg* ■ *Dir* Josef von Sternberg • *Scr* Jules Furthman, Herman J Mankiewicz, from a story by Jules Furthman, Charles Furthman • *Cinematographer* Henry Gerrard

Thunderbolt and Lightfoot ★★★★ 18
Crime drama 1974 · US · Colour · 109mins
Here's a rattlingly good adventure movie, the directing debut of Michael Cimino, (*The Deer Hunter*, *Heaven's Gate*). Clint Eastwood is the crook who teams up with drifter Jeff Bridges and, with George Kennedy and Geoffrey Lewis (father of Juliette) in pursuit, goes on a hapless quest for hidden loot. Eastwood takes a bit of a back seat, letting the other three walk away with the acting honours. Bridges is terrific, but it's the manic Lewis you will remember. The scenery is mighty handsome, and the roll call of technicians would later feature in some of Eastwood's own fine work as a director. If you can ignore its rather tasteless sense of humour, this is enormously enjoyable. Contains violence, swearing and nudity. ▭

Clint Eastwood *John "Thunderbolt" Doherty* • Jeff Bridges *"Lightfoot"* • Geoffrey Lewis *Goody* • Catherine Bach *Melody* • Gary Busey *Curly* • George Kennedy *Red Leary* • Burton Gilliam *Welder* ■ *Dir/Scr* Michael Cimino

Thundercrack! ★★★
Underground sex melodrama 1975 · US · BW · 158mins
Underground film-maker George Kuchar – lover of Hollywood melodrama, especially *film noir* – had many acolytes, the best-known of which was Curt McDowell, the director of this insane parody of *The Old Dark House*. It sounds and looks like Kuchar's work because Kuchar wrote it (indulgently) and lit it (often strikingly). He's also the actor inside the gorilla suit. As in the 1932 James Whale film, strangers seeking shelter from a nasty storm stumble upon an isolated house. Unaware of some serious peephole activity, the characters lounge and talk (and talk) and eventually get around to (unsimulated) sex. As the rather odd lady of the house, Marion Eaton compensates deliriously for her amateur peers. And while the mock soap-opera dialogue is banal and the shock of the outlandish sex scenes is insufficient for the two-and-a-half-hour running time, this is genuinely a one-off.

Marion Eaton *Mrs Gert Hammond* • George Kuchar *Bing* • Melinda McDowell *Sash* • Mookie Blodgett *Chandler* • Moira Benson *Roo* • Rick Johnson *Toydy* • Ken Scudder *Bond* • Maggie Pyle *Willene* ■ *Dir* Curt McDowell • *Scr* George Kuchar, from a story by Mark Ellinger, Curt McDowell

Thunderhead – Son of Flicka ★★★ U
Drama 1945 · US · Colour · 76mins
Roddy McDowall, Preston Foster and Rita Johnson return for this eventful

sequel to *My Friend Flicka*. Once again the horses are shown in all their glory as Thunderhead overcomes the injury that forced him to quit racing, in order to drive away his own father, a rogue stallion that is troubling the herds of neighbouring ranchers. Pacier and more action-packed than the original, the film's highlight is undoubtedly the ferocious fight sequence, though the finale in which horse and boy bid a fond farewell will have many a lip quivering.

Roddy McDowall *Ken McLaughlin* • Preston Foster *Rob McLaughlin* • Rita Johnson *Nelle* • James Bell *Gus* • Diana Hale *Hildy* • Carleton Young *Major Harris* • Ralph Sanford *Mr Sargent* • Robert Filmer *Tim* ■ *Dir* Louis King • *Scr* Dwight Cummins, Dorothy Yost, from a novel by Mary O'Hara

Thunderhead ★★★★ 15
Thriller 1992 · US · Colour · 114mins

In this intelligent, gripping thriller, set in the seventies and loosely based on real events, Val Kilmer plays an FBI agent who, having long ago denied his native American heritage, is sent to investigate a murder on a reservation. Director Michael Apted treats the subject matter with some sensitivity and there are powerful supporting turns from Sam Shepard, Fred Ward and Graham Greene. Look out, too, for an appearance by rock musician David Crosby. This was one of the first projects undertaken by Robert De Niro's production house. Contains violence and swearing. ▭

Val Kilmer *Ray Levoi* • Sam Shepard *Frank Coutelle* • Graham Greene *Walter Crow Horse* • Fred Ward *Jack Milton* • Fred Dalton Thompson *William Dawes* • Sheila Tousey *Maggie Eagle Bear* • Chief Ted Thin Elk *Grandpa Sam Reaches* ■ *Dir* Michael Apted • *Scr* John Fusco

Thursday ★★★★ 18
Comedy crime drama
1998 · US · Colour · 84mins

This Tarantino-esque movie relates the blackly comic tale of ex-criminal Thomas Jane (*Deep Blue Sea*), who has now taken the path of respectability, with all its suburban trappings. Cue 24 hours of hell on his doorstep. A relatively short film, but a densely packed one, this combines action (often culminating in murder), with luscious dialogue and a first-rate cast. Jane and old buddy Aaron Eckhart (*Erin Brockovich*) are fine, but both are overshadowed by Paulina Porizkova, as the slinkiest, sexiest heroine in years – to call her and Jane's memorable sexual encounter "subversive" is an understatement. Sick and sadistic, but in a fun way. Contains swearing and violence. ▭

Thomas Jane *Casey Wells* • Aaron Eckhart *Nick* • Paulina Porizkova *Dallas* • James LeGros *Billy Hilly* • Paula Marshall *Christine Wells* • Michael Jeter *Doctor Jarvis* • Glenn Plummer *Rasta Man* • Mickey Rourke *Kasarov* • *Dir/Scr* Skip Woods

Thursday's Game ★★★
Comedy 1971 · US · Colour · 100mins

Gene Wilder and Bob Newhart play poker with the guys every Thursday. When their buddies call it quits, Wilder and Newhart decide to keep Thursday as a wife-free zone and instead indulge in all sorts of weekly shenanigans, while letting their spouses (Ellen Burstyn and Cloris Leachman) believe they are still playing poker. Unsurprisingly, the wives soon discover the ruse. Originally conceived as a theatrical feature, this 1971 star-studded comedy was inexplicably shelved and only saw the light of day in 1974, when it premiered on US TV. With its good cast and cute script, it's well worth a look.

Gene Wilder *Harry Evers* • Bob Newhart *Marvin Ellison* • Ellen Burstyn *Lynne Evers* • Cloris Leachman *Lois Ellison* • Martha Scott *Mrs Reynolds* • Nancy Walker *Miss Bender* • Valerie Harper *Ann Menzenne* • Rob Reiner *Joel Forrest* • Norman Fell *Mel Leonard* ■ *Dir* Robert Moore • *Scr* James L Brooks

Tiara Tahiti ★★ PG
Drama 1962 · UK · Colour · 96mins

Director Ted Kotcheff's feature debut (he's billed as William T Kotcheff) is an adequate showcase for the talents of James Mason and John Mills. Nobody can smarm like Mason and he breezes through the picture, as a cultured crook who sees Mills's arrival on Tahiti to negotiate a hotel deal as the chance to pay him back for his being cashiered at the end of the war. Mills occasionally struggles to convince in the more difficult role, not always managing to keep the lid on his histrionics. Cinematographer Otto Heller gives the island a travel-brochure look, but it's the interplay between the leads that catches the imagination. ▭

James Mason *Captain Brett Aimsley* • John Mills *Lt Colonel Clifford Southey* • Claude Dauphin *Henri Farengue* • Herbert Lom *Chong Sing* • Rosenda Monteros *Belle Annie* • Jacques Marin *Marcel Desmoulins* • Libby Morris *Adele Franklin* • Madge Ryan *Millie Brooks* • Roy Kinnear *Captain Tom Enderby* ■ *Dir* William T Kotcheff [Ted Kotcheff] • *Scr* Geoffrey Cotterell, Ivan Foxwell, Mordecai Richler, from the novel by Geoffrey Cotterell

The Tichborne Claimant ★★★ PG
Period drama 1998 · UK · Colour · 98mins

Based on a true tale of Victorian fortune-hunting, this period piece is more televisual than filmic, and sadly lacking in originality. In the all-too-familiar *Martin Guerre* scenario, manservant John Kani sets out to the seas in search of lost aristocrat and heir Sir Roger Tichborne. He returns to Blighty with a coarse alcoholic in Tichborne's place and the pair are initially successful, but soon get embroiled in a legal battle. It all becomes rather ridiculous, as the claimant seeks backing by appealing to the working man and selling shares in the aristocracy. The presence of Stephen Fry, Robert Hardy and Sir John Gielgud adds class, but that isn't enough to make this good cinema. Contains sexual references and some strong language.

John Kani *Andrew Bogle* • Robert Pugh *The claimant* • John Gielgud *Cockburn* • Stephen Fry *Hawkins* • Robert Hardy *Lord Rivers* • Rachael Dowling *Mary Anne* • Paola Dionisotti *Dowager* • Charles Gray *Arundell* ■ *Dir* David Yates • *Scr* Joe Fisher

The Ticket ★★ 12
Action thriller 1997 · US · Colour · 84mins

A plane crashlands in a snowy wasteland. On board are a family en route to Denver to collect a multi-million-dollar lottery prize. They discover their (borrowed) plane was sabotaged and find themselves pursued by the father's unscrupulous employers, who will stop at nothing to get their hands on the winning ticket. Fans may root for the villains to catch Hollywood bad girl Shannen Doherty (*Charmed*), who plays against type in this familiar family-in-jeopardy thriller, as the damsel in distress. James Marshall (*Twin Peaks*) provides stalwart support as her resourceful husband, while Heidi Swenberg and John Tench are effective as the deadly schemers.

Shannen Doherty *CeeCee Reicker* • James Marshall *Keith Reicker* • Phillip Van Dyke *Eric Reicker* • Heidi Swedberg *Rita Martin* • John Tench *Chuck Martin* ■ *Dir* Stuart Cooper • *Scr* David Alexander

The Ticket of Leave Man ★★
Crime melodrama 1937 · UK · BW · 71mins

Villainous Victorians were Tod Slaughter's stock in trade, and this film is no exception. Based on a 1918 silent, it's the story of a murderer who tries to drag criminals even further into a life of crime. Even in the thirties, Slaughter's films were seen as old-fashioned melodrama, hysterically overacted. Now they're cherished as collector's items in the "so bad, they're good" category. The cast always seems to be having great fun hamming it up but, of course, we're laughing at the film, not with it.

Tod Slaughter *Tiger Dalton* • Marjorie Taylor *May Edwards* • John Warwick *Bob Brierly* • Robert Adair *Hawkshaw* • Frank Cochran *Melter Moss* • Peter Gawthorne *Joshua Gibson* ■ *Dir* George King • *Scr* HF Maltby, AR Rawlinson, from a play by Tom Taylor

Ticket to Heaven ★★★
Drama 1981 · Can · Colour · 107mins

A powerful drama about religious cults. Nick Mancuso is on top form as a man on the rebound from a bad relationship, who's brainwashed into becoming a "heavenly child" by a fanatical sect. The top-notch support cast includes Meg Foster, Saul Rubinek and Kim Cattrall (*Sex and the City*), but the most memorable performance comes from the obscure RH Thomson as a pragmatic cult deprogrammer. It's no barrel of laughs, but there are flashes of humour to lighten the load.

Nick Mancuso *David* • Saul Rubinek *Larry* • Meg Foster *Ingrid* • Kim Cattrall *Ruthie* • RH Thomson *Linc Strunk* • Jennifer Dale *Lisa* • Guy Boyd *Eric* ■ *Dir* Ralph L Thomas • *Scr* Ralph L Thomas, Anne Cameron, from the novel *Moonwebs* by Josh Freed

A Ticket to Tomahawk ★★★ U
Comedy western 1950 · US · Colour · 90mins

Western spoofs were rare in the earnest early fifties, but this colourful 20th Century-Fox romp sends up the old "stagecoach versus incoming railroad" plot to grand effect. It's helped by a witty screenplay by director Richard Sale and his then wife, the novelist and playwright Mary Loos, and superb Technicolor photography from Harry Jackson. Amiable Dan Dailey is the travelling salesman who teams up with sharp-shootin' Anne Baxter, while slimy Rory Calhoun uses every means he can to stop the railroad from gettin' through to Colorado, including Indians, bandits and dancers. Look closely at the actress on Dan Dailey's right-hand side in the big production number: that's Marilyn Monroe and you can't keep your eyes off her. Neither could agent Johnny Hyde; he got Monroe her next film, *The Asphalt Jungle*.

Dan Dailey *Johnny Behind-the-Deuces* • Anne Baxter *Kit Dodge Jr* • Rory Calhoun *Dakota* • Walter Brennan *Terence Sweeney* • Charles Kemper *Chuckity* • Connie Gilchrist *Madame Adelaide* • Arthur Hunnicutt *Sad Eyes* • Will Wright *US Marshal Dodge* ■ *Dir* Richard Sale • *Scr* Mary Loos, Richard Sale

Tickets for the Zoo ★★★
Drama 1991 · UK · Colour · 90mins

This was director Brian Crumlish's first feature. His background in documentaries and experience of working with the homeless are clearly evident in this hard-hitting portrait of teen alienation and despair in 1990s Edinburgh. Alice Bree and Mickey MacPherson are utterly convincing as the brother and sister forced to fend for themselves after they outgrow their orphanage. There are unmistakeable shades of Ken Loach and Mike Leigh in Christeen Winford's script, but this stark story, based on workshops with kids from city squats and hostels, has a gritty character all of its own.

Alice Bree *Carol Forbes* • Tom Smith *George* • Mickey MacPherson *Pogo* ■ *Dir* Brian Crumlish • *Scr* Christeen Winford

Tickle Me ★ U
Musical comedy 1965 · US · Colour · 86mins

Judging by the improbable situation and silly set pieces, it is unsurprising to discover that a pair of ex-Three Stooges writers scripted this unengaging Elvis Presley vehicle. An ex-rodeo rider falls in love when he gets a job in a health spa (for women only, of course), and becomes involved in a hunt for hidden treasure. Elvis is watchable (just), but it's one for fans of the King only. ▭

Elvis Presley *Lonnie Beale* • Jocelyn Lane *Pam Merritt* • Julie Adams *Vera Radford* • Jack Mullaney *Stanley Potter* • Merry Anders *Estelle Penfield* • Connie Gilchrist *Hilda* • Edward Faulkner *Brad Bentley* • Bill Williams *Deputy Sturdivant* ■ *Dir* Norman Taurog • *Scr* Elwood Ullman, Edward Bernds

A Ticklish Affair ★★ U
Romantic comedy
1963 · US · Colour · 87mins

This pleasant if unadventurous romantic comedy concerns US naval commander Gig Young, who investigates a false alarm set off by a child, and falls in love with the boy's widowed mother Shirley Jones. Initially, she's unwilling to remarry, as her first husband was a Navy man, too, and she wants a stable home life for her three kids. One of them (Billy Mumy, who played Will Robinson in TV's *Lost in Space*) saves the day.

Shirley Jones *Amy Martin* • Gig Young *Cmdr Key Weedon* • Red Buttons *Flight Officer Simon Shelley* • Carolyn Jones *Tandy Martin* • Edgar Buchanan *Gramps Martin* • Peter Robbins *Grover Martin* • Billy Mumy [Bill Mumy] *Alex Martin* • Bryan Russell *Luke Martin* ■ *Dir* George Sidney • *Scr* Ruth Brooks Flippen, from the story *Moon Walk* by Barbara Luther

Ticks ★★ 🔞

Horror   1993 · US · Colour · 81mins

This affectionate homage to the big monster movies of the fifties, such as *Them!*, spoofs the typical moments of the genre while adding gore and dark humour for the nineties audience. A marijuana farmer in a mountain village concocts a special fertiliser for his plants, but his leaky machine spills it on to some tick eggs, causing massive mutation and mayhem. It's then up to a group of troubled teenagers at a mountain retreat to save the day and escape. Several plot holes and narrative gaps indicate that the movie was shortened from a longer – and presumably more coherent – cut. Ultimately the level of gore and slime is so extreme, it becomes comical instead of disgusting. Contains violence and swearing. ▭

Peter Scolari *Charles Danson* • Rosalind Allen *Holly Lambert* • Ami Dolenz *Dee Dee Davenport* • Alfonso Ribeiro *Darrel "Panic" Lumley* • Ray Oriel *Rome Hernandez* • Seth Green *Tyler Burns* • Virginya Keehne *Melissa Danson* ■ *Dir* Tony Randel • *Scr* Brent V Friedman

Tidal Wave: No Escape ★★

Drama   1997 · US · Colour · 120mins

A so-so splice of the disaster movie and the political thriller, this TV movie has boffin Corbin Bernsen being called in to find out whether a lethal series of tidal waves are man-made or a natural phenomenon. The former *LA Law* star is as reliable as ever, there are useful supporting performances from Julianne Phillips and Lawrence Hilton-Jacobs and director George Miller (the *Andre* rather than the *Mad Max* one) does his best to conceal the limitations of the budget.

Corbin Bernsen *John Wahl* • Julianne Phillips *Dr Jessica Weaver* • Harve Presnell *Stanley Schiff* • Gene Wolande *Dr Jules Bernard* • Lawrence Hilton-Jacobs *Marlan Clark* • Wendy Schenker *Jan Richards* ■ *Dir* George Miller (1) • *Scr* Teddy Sarafian, George Malko

Tie Me Up! Tie Me Down! ★★ 🔞

Black comedy drama
1990 · Sp · Colour · 97mins

Actress and former porn star Victoria Abril is kidnapped by Antonio Banderas, who's recently been released from psychiatric care. He hopes that she'll eventually fall in love with him and start the family he's always wanted, in Pedro Almodóvar's unfocused and lurid tale of kinky sex and bondage. The fact that Abril does indeed fall for her captor makes this darkly orgiastic comedy of terrors and errors one of the more controversial entries in the Spanish wunderkind's cult camp canon. It's distressingly

superficial and the disquieting knotty romance fails to convince, despite the incendiary chemistry between the two leads. In Spanish with English subtitles. ▭

Victoria Abril *Marina* • Antonio Banderas *Ricky* • Francisco Rabal *Maximo Espejo* • Loles Leon *Lola* • Julieta Serrano *Alma* ■ *Dir/Scr* Pedro Almodóvar

The Tie That Binds ★★★ 🔞

Thriller   1995 · US · Colour · 94mins

Debut director Wesley Strick delivers a double whammy of emotional manipulation in this tug-of-love movie. Six-year-old Janie (Julia Devin) is abandoned by criminal couple Daryl Hannah and Keith Carradine, and adopted by yuppies Vincent Spano and Moira Kelly. When her parents returns to claim her, the traumatised child is caught between the two families. *The Tie That Binds* isn't concerned with issues of nature versus nurture but with gulp-in-the-throat tear-jerking. As such, it works. But it could have been so much better. Contains swearing and violence. ▭

Daryl Hannah *Leann Netherwood* • Keith Carradine *John Netherwood* • Moira Kelly *Dana Clifton* • Vincent Spano *Russell Clifton* • Julia Devin *Janie* • Ray Reinhardt *Sam Bennett* • Barbara Tarbuck *Jean Bennett* ■ *Dir* Wesley Strick • *Scr* Michael Auerbach

Tierra ★★★ 🔞

Romantic drama 1995 · Sp · Colour · 117mins

It all seems so simple. A stranger named Angel arrives to delouse a vineyard and falls for a free-spirited local girl. But he also has eyes for a farmer's put-upon wife. Julio Medem delights in dazzling and disorienting the viewer. The camera is his co-conspirator, constantly shifting its perspective as it roams across the dusty landscape, prowls through bedrooms and even peers deep down into the soil. But don't let the fractured logic of the narrative, the enigmatic acting and the elusiveness of the symbolism deter you. There is tremendous satisfaction to be gained from rising to the picture's not inconsiderable challenges. A Spanish language film. Contains sex scenes and swearing. ▭

Carmelo Gomez *Angel Bengoelxeo* • Emma Suarez *Angela* • Karra Elejalde *Patricio* • Silke Klein *Mari* • Nancho Novo *Alberto* • Txema Blasco *Tomas* ■ *Dir/Scr* Julio Medem

Tiffany Jones ★ 🔞

Comedy   1973 · UK · Colour · 86mins

Made in the days of dolly birds and psychedelia, this pathetic attempt to produce an *Avengers* clone, but with more nudity, is adapted from a newspaper's comic strip and has Anouska Hempel helping a denim-clad prince regain his throne from a wicked dictator. At least Ray Brooks has the talent to seem embarrassed, but nothing can faze director Peter Walker, who was to go on to co-direct the even kinkier *House of Whipcord*. Contains swearing and nudity. ▭

Anouska Hempel *Tiffany Jones* • Ray Brooks *Guy* • Susan Sheers *Jo* • Damien Thomas *Salvador* • Eric Pohlmann *President Jabal* • Richard Marner *Vorjak* • Ivor Salter *Karatik* •

Lynda Baron *Anna Karekin* ■ *Dir* Peter Walker • *Scr* Alfred Shaughnessy, from the comic strip by Pat Tourret, Jenny Butterworth

The Tiger and the Pussycat ★★

Comedy drama
1967 · US/It · Colour · 108mins

This US/Italian co-production makes almost nothing of either country's qualities, though it's filmed in Rome. Vittorio Gassman is a 45-year-old engineer and family man experiencing an early mid-life crisis. Approaching American art student Ann-Margret to blame her for his spurned son's suicide attempt, he finds himself attracted to her. Determined to be with her, he jeopardises his work, home and reputation. The film wastes several opportunities, though it has a certain box-office gloss.

Vittorio Gassman *Francesco Vincenzini* • Ann-Margret *Carolina* • Eleanor Parker *Esperia* • Caterina Boratto *Delia* • Eleonora Brown *Luisella* • Antonella Steni *Pinella* ■ *Dir* Dino Risi • *Scr* Agenore Incrocci, Furio Scarpelli, from a story by Agenore Incrocci, Furio Scarpelli, Dino Risi

Tiger Bay ★★★ 🔞

Thriller   1959 · UK · BW · 102mins

Making her film debut, Hayley Mills gives an astonishing performance as a young girl who befriends murderous sailor Horst Buchholz and hinders the investigation of detective John Mills at every turn. The "kid and the killer" plot had cropped up regularly during the fifties and this variation has nothing new to say on the subject. But J Lee Thompson (always a fine director of children) breathes new life into it, not only with his astute handling of the 12-year-old Hayley, but also by surrounding her with totally credible characters and by capturing faithfully the sights and sounds of Cardiff's docklands. ▭

John Mills *Superintendent Graham* • Horst Buchholz *Korchinsky* • Hayley Mills *Gillie* • Yvonne Mitchell *Anya* • Megs Jenkins *Mrs Phillips* • Anthony Dawson *Barclay* • George Selway *Det Sgt Harvey* ■ *Dir* J Lee Thompson • *Scr* John Hawkesworth, Shelley Smith from the novel *Rodolphe et le Revolver* by Noel Calef

Tiger by the Tail ★

Thriller   1955 · UK · BW · 82mins

Another trudge through the lowest depths of British movie-making, in the company of quota quickie specialist John Gilling. Larry Parks stars in this, one of his British movies, made after he was driven out of Hollywood at the height of his career during the McCarthy witch-hunts of the fifties. This experience drained him of the zest he displayed in pictures such as *The Jolson Story*, as he plods dispiritedly through a tatty little tale about a journalist threatened by hoodlums. A completely thrill-free thriller.

Larry Parks *John Desmond* • Constance Smith *Jane Claymore* • Lisa Daniely *Anna Ray* • Cyril Chamberlain *Foster* • Ronan O'Casey *Nick* • Donald Stewart *Macaulay* ■ *Dir* John Gilling • *Scr* John Gilling, Willis Goldbeck, from the novel by John Mair

Tiger by the Tail ★★★

Mystery melodrama
1970 · US · Colour · 99mins

This is one of the first melodramas to use the aftermath of Vietnam as a context for its thrills. When veteran Christopher George is wrongly accused of killing his brother, his socialite girlfriend (Tippi Hedren) seeks to help him out. It's a neat little film, which director RG Springsteen contrives to make quite watchable.

Christopher George *Steve Michaelis* • Tippi Hedren *Rita Armstrong* • Dean Jagger *Top Polk* • John Dehner *Sheriff Chancey Jones* • Charo *Darlita* • Lloyd Bochner *Del Ware* • Glenda Farrell *Sarah Harvey* • Alan Hale [Alan Hale Jr] *Billy Jack Whitehorn* ■ *Dir* RG Springsteen • *Scr* Charles A Wallace

Tiger from the River Kwai ★★

Martial arts drama   1975 · It · Colour

Abandon all thoughts of railway bridges, this has nothing to do with British PoWs or sadistic Japanese guards. It is, in fact, a martial arts adventure in the mould of the TV movie that launched the hit series *Kung Fu*. Krung Srivilan stars as a young Thai who promises his dying American friend that he will take his money and few possessions to his family back home. Only his quick fists see him through a series of unremarkable adventures that reveal America to be anything but the paradise that he imagined.

George Eastman • Krung Srivilan ■ *Dir* Franco Lattanzi

Tiger in the Smoke ★★★

Crime drama   1956 · UK · BW · 92mins

Margery Allingham's source novel provides a distinctly offbeat, metaphysical edge to this thriller, in which male lead Donald Sinden spends most of his time gagged and bound. Meanwhile Tony Wright's personification of evil terrorises his fiancée (Muriel Pavlow) and her clergyman father (Laurence Naismith) in his search for a treasure that proves to be worth more than he could ever have imagined. From its opening image of street musicians in the London fog, the film builds up a compelling atmosphere of strangeness under Roy Baker's able direction.

Donald Sinden *Geoffrey Levett* • Muriel Pavlow *Meg Elgin* • Tony Wright *Jack Havoc* • Bernard Miles *Tiddy Doll* • Alec Clunes *Asst Commissioner Oates* • Laurence Naismith *Canon Avril* • Christopher Rhodes *Chief Inspector Luke* ■ *Dir* Roy Baker [Roy Ward Baker] • *Scr* Anthony Pelissier, from the novel by Margery Allingham • *Cinematographer* Geoffrey Unsworth

The Tiger Makes Out ★★

Comedy   1967 · US · Colour · 94mins

Mailman Eli Wallach is full of the brooding resentment that seems to infect many of those working for the US Mail. He decides to exact revenge for his crummy life by "freeing the tiger" within himself. Wallach plots to make a dramatic and symbolic gesture by kidnapping a pretty girl, but in anger he snatches the wrong party. His victim Ann Jackson is a suburban

housewife with as many frustrations as Wallach himself. Murray Schisgal adapted his own stage two-hander *The Tiger* into this much grander movie. Unfortunately, the expansion serves only to obscure the finer points of the original idea. Watch out for a young Dustin Hoffman.

Eli Wallach *Ben Harris* • Anne Jackson *Gloria Fiske* • Bob Dishy *Jerry Fiske* • John Harkins *Leo* • Ruth White *Mrs Kelly* • Roland Wood *Mr Kelly* • Dustin Hoffman ■ *Dir* Arthur Hiller • *Scr* Murray Schisgal, from his play *The Tiger*

The Tiger of Eschnapur
★★★

Adventure drama
1959 · W Ger/Fr/It · Colour · 101mins

With his career nearing its end, Fritz Lang returned from Hollywood to Germany for a script that he had written over 30 years earlier for an adventure directed by Joe May. The first of a two-part story (completed by *The Indian Tomb*, 1959) it uses many real Indian locations and creates a world that is both fabulous and authentic. The story of persecuted lovers fleeing a jealous maharajah has a comic-strip nature, and the acting is rather stilted, but Lang's use of colour and decor provides some pleasure. Both features were brutally re-edited for release as a single 95-minute film in the USA and the UK as *Journey to the Lost City*. In German with English subtitles.

Debra Paget *Seeta* • Walter Reyer *Chandra* • Paul Hubschmid *Harald Berger* • Claus Holm *Dr Walter Rhode* • Sabine Bethmann *Irene Rhode* • Valery Inkijinoff *Yama* • René Deltgen *Prince Ramigani* • Jochen Brockmann *Padhu* ■ *Dir* Fritz Lang • *Scr* Fritz Lang, Werner Jörg Lüddecke, from an idea by Thea von Harbou, from a novel by Richard Eichberg

Tiger of the Seven Seas
★★ U

Action adventure 1962 · It · Colour · 89mins

Gianna Maria Canale returns as the feisty sea dog's daughter in this so-so sequel to *Queen of the Pirates*. Here she takes command of her father's ship and later has to uncover the identity of her murderer and clear her lover Anthony Steel of the crime. Italian film-makers have always had a penchant for costume pictures, and director Luigi Capuano manages to convey period atmosphere without ever persuading us we are anywhere but in a film studio. He stages the action sequences with gusto, but, in trying to coax animated performances out of Canale and Steel, he was fighting a losing battle. Italian dialogue dubbed into English.

Gianna Maria Canale *Consuelo* • Anthony Steel *William* • Grazia Maria Spina *Anna Da Cordoba* • Ernesto Calindri *Inigo Da Cordoba* • Andrea Aureli *Laura* ■ *Dir* Luigi Capuano • *Scr* Arpad De Riso, Luigi Capuano, Ottavio Poggi, from a story by Nino Battiferri

Tiger Shark
★★★

Drama 1932 · US · BW · 80mins

Rumoured to be an inspiration for *Jaws* and pre-dating that blockbuster by a few decades, this efficient little melodrama features Edward G Robinson as a tuna-fishing Captain Hook – he lost a hand to the sharks –

who is involved in a vicious triangle with wife Zita Johann and Richard Arlen. An early film by Howard Hawks, it is, for all its tabloid theatricality, typically well crafted, as the encircling sharks echo the passions of the humans.

Edward G Robinson *Mike Mascarena* • Richard Arlen *Pipes Boley* • Zita Johann *Quita Silva* • Leila Bennett *Muggsey* • Vince Barnett *Engineer* • J Carrol Naish *Tony* • William Ricciardi *Manuel Silva* • Edwin Maxwell *Doctor* ■ *Dir* Howard Hawks • *Scr* Wells Root, from the story *Tuna* by Houston Branch

Tiger Town
★★★ U

Sports adventure 1983 · US · Colour · 73mins

Having been Oscar-nominated for his performance as the little lad in *Kramer vs Kramer*, Justin Henry went on to play slightly bigger little lads in TV movies such as this one from Disney. He stars as a wide-eyed fan who joins with ageing baseball star Roy Scheider to revive the fortunes of a Detroit team. Films about American sports have a poor track record with young British movie-watchers, as the box-office failure of *The Mighty Ducks* and *Angels* proves, and a lack of familiarity with the rules of baseball may mean many will be bored long before the exciting climax.

Roy Scheider *Billy Young* • Justin Henry *Alex* • Ron McLarty *Buddy* • Bethany Carpenter *Nancy* • Noah Moazezi *Eddie* • Mary Wilson *Soloist* ■ *Dir/Scr* Alan Shapiro

A Tiger Walks
★★ U

Drama 1964 · US · Colour · 84mins

A couple of years after making *The Lion* on location in Africa, child actor Pamela Franklin has a go at something similar for Disney, only this time it's an escaped tiger that's loose in small-town America. The tone is unusually downbeat for Disney, with the film's sense of provincial politics owing more to Ibsen than Burbank. Studio director Norman Tokar isn't really up to the job, and Brian Keith and Vera Miles, although reliable, aren't strong enough screen presences to carry the drama (John Wayne and Maureen O'Hara would have been splendid). The cast also includes one-time "Elephant Boy" Sabu in his last movie role.

Brian Keith *Sheriff Pete Williams* • Vera Miles *Dorothy Williams* • Pamela Franklin *Julie Williams* • Sabu *Ram Singh* • Edward Andrews *Governor* • Peter Brown *Vern Goodman* • Kevin Corcoran *Tom Hadley* • Theodore Marcuse [Theo Marcuse] *Josef Pietz* ■ *Dir* Norman Tokar • *Scr* Lowell S Hawley, from the novel by Ian Niall

Tiger Warsaw
★ 15

Drama 1988 · US · Colour · 88mins

Fifteen years after he shot and wounded his father during a violent family argument, Patrick Swayze returns to his home town to try to make peace with his nearest and dearest. He finds it a long and slow struggle, as will anyone watching this movie, which is filled with both pointless scenes and no explanation of key details. There's always a sense that there's a good story dealing with forgiveness and reliving painful memories waiting to break out. But from the acting (including Swayze) to

the production values, it's strictly amateur night for this independent production.

Patrick Swayze *Chuck "Tiger" Warsaw* • Lee Richardson *Mitchell Warsaw* • Piper Laurie *Frances Warsaw* • Mary McDonnell *Paula Warsaw* • Barbara Williams *Karen* • Bobby DiCicco *Tony* • Jenny Chrisinger *Val* • James Patrick Gillis *Roger* ■ *Dir* Amin Q Chaudhri • *Scr* Roy London

The Tiger Woods Story
★★ PG

Biographical sports drama
1998 · US · Colour · 98mins

A suspiciously sanitised made-for-television biopic of the man who is one of the biggest names in golf today. The film focuses on the 1997 triumph by Woods, confidently played by Khalil Kain, in the US Masters. Flashbacks fill in the details of his life story, going right back to when his pushy dad Keith David met his Thai mother (Freda Foh Shen) while he was serving in the army in South East Asia. As a young player, Tiger's startling abilities on the links become quickly apparent, but he must battle racism and jealousy from other competitors before he establishes himself as the star he is now. There a few hints of petulance and egotism, but director LeVar Burton (best known for his role in the later *Star Trek* movies) keeps the mood upbeat.

Khalil Kain *Tiger Woods, aged 16 to 21* • Keith David *Earl Woods* • Freda Foh Shen *Tida Woods* • Roger Twibell *Masters Announcer No 1* • John Schroeder *Masters Announcer No 2* ■ *Dir* LeVar Burton • *Scr* Takashi A Bufford, from the book *Tiger* by John Strege

Tigers in Lipstick
★

Erotic comedy 1979 · It · Colour · 83mins

Four continental sex symbols gamely strut their stuff in this limp throwback to the fluffy Italian sex comedies that were popular in the sixties. The seven-segment anthology revolves around women being the more assertive sex and begins with a half-dressed Ursula Andress walking down the street and causing car crashes, because of her deal with a repair garage. In another episode, busy Laura Antonelli tries to arrange love sessions with an orchestra conductor – with chaotic results. Monica Vitti and Sylvia Kristel are sandwiched in the middle in even more inconsequential episodes. The tame material is blandly directed by Luigi Zampa, the dubbing into English is atrocious, and fans of the leading ladies will be disappointed and frustrated by the insubstantial feel of each sketch. A young Roberto Benigni appears in a cameo. An Italian language film.

Ursula Andress • Laura Antonelli • Sylvia Kristel • Monica Vitti • Orazio Orlando • Michele Placido • Roberto Benigni ■ *Dir* Luigi Zampa • *Scr* Tonino Guerra, Giorgio Salvioni

A Tiger's Tale
★★ 15

Romantic comedy
1987 · US · Colour · 93mins

Another of Kirk Douglas's sons, Peter, made his directorial debut with this self-penned effort, which tries to be too many things at once and ends up being very little at all. The age-gap romance between C Thomas Howell

and his girlfriend's mother, Ann-Margret, is vaguely credible, especially once she becomes pregnant. But too many other aspects smack of contrivance – Howell's pet tiger and Ann-Margret's penchant for kimonos most readily springing to mind. Moreover, the peripheral characters are also poorly drawn – Howell's ex-girlfriend, Kelly Preston, is depicted as a brat and his dad, Charles Durning, as a bumpkin, – and the humour is tastelessly patronising.

Ann-Margret *Rose Butts* • C Thomas Howell *Bubber Drumm* • Charles Durning *Charlie Drumm* • Kelly Preston *Shirley Butts* • Ann Wedgeworth *Claudine* • William Zabka *Randy* ■ • *Scr* Peter Vincent Douglas [Peter Douglas], from the novel *Love and Other Natural Disasters* by Allen Hannay III

The Tigger Movie
★★★ U

Animation 2000 · US · Colour · 77mins

Winnie the Pooh's striped sidekick takes centre stage for the first *Pooh* picture to hit cinemas in nearly two decades. The voice artists have changed, but otherwise it's the same formula as before, with a down-in-the-dumps Tigger bouncing off in search of his family and his pals mounting a rescue mission when he fails to return. This Disney offering is pitched at pre-school, nursery and younger kids. Accompanying adults, however, may pooh-pooh at the sluggish pace, silly songs and simplistic moralising.

Jim Cummings *Tigger/Winnie the Pooh* • Nikita Hopkins *Roo* • Ken Sansom *Rabbit* • John Fiedler *Piglet* • Peter Cullen *Eeyore* • Andre Stojka *Owl* • Kath Soucie *Kanga* • Tom Attenborough *Christopher Robin* • John Hurt *Narrator* ■ *Dir* Jun Falkenstein • *Scr* Jun Falkenstein, from a story by Eddie Guzelian, from the characters created by AA Milne

Tight Spot
★★★ PG

Film noir 1955 · US · BW · 92mins

Ginger Rogers stars as the wisecracking moll who's afraid to give evidence against a big-time gangster played by Lorne Greene. Edward G Robinson co-stars as the attorney seeking her co-operation and Brian Keith is the cop in charge of her safety. This highly capable cast has the benefit of a well worked-out script (by William Bowers from a play by Lenard Kantor) and of tight direction (by Phil Karlson) that makes the most of the confined setting of a hotel room. The result is a gripping thriller, quite the best of Ginger's later films.

Ginger Rogers *Sherry Conley* • Edward G Robinson *Lloyd Hallett* • Brian Keith *Vince Striker* • Lorne Greene *Benjamin Costain* • Katherine Anderson *Mrs Willoughby* • Allen Nourse *Marvin Rickles* • Peter Leeds *Fred Packer* • Doye O'Dell *Mississippi Mac* ■ *Dir* Phil Karlson • *Scr* William Bowers, from the play *Dead Pigeon* by Leonard Kantor

Tightrope
★★★★ 18

Thriller 1984 · US · Colour · 109mins

One of Clint Eastwood's greatest strengths is that he has been willing to explore the darker side of his film persona. In this under-rated thriller, he portrays a flawed and at times disturbing extension of his Dirty Harry character. Once again he is the maverick detective on the trail of a serial killer, only this time he is

worried that both he and the man he is hunting share the same sexual tastes. Writer/director Richard Tuggle is either unwilling or unable to fully develop the theme, but he does make good use of the New Orleans settings and secures a powerful performance from Geneviève Bujold as a rape counsellor. One just wonders what Eastwood the director would have achieved with the same material. Contains violence and swearing.

Clint Eastwood *Wes Block* • Geneviève Bujold *Beryl Thibodeaux* • Dan Hedaya *Detective Molinari* • Alison Eastwood *Amanda Block* • Jennifer Beck *Penny Block* • Marco St John *Leander Rolfe* • Rebecca Perle *Becky Jacklin* ■ *Dir/Scr* Richard Tuggle

Tigrero: a Film That Was Never Made ★★★

Documentary
1994 · Fin/Bra/Ger · Colour · 75mins

Hollywood history is littered with failed projects, but the dirt on them rarely sees the light of day – which makes Mika Kaurismäki's documentary all the more revelatory and valuable. Set in Brazil's Mato Grosso, *Tigrero* was a jungle adventure that was slated to star John Wayne, Tyrone Power and Ava Gardner, before 20th Century-Fox mogul Darryl F Zanuck. wrote it off as an insurance risk. Escorted by Jim Jarmusch, director Sam Fuller returns to the jungle village of Karaja for the first time since he scouted locations back in the fifties, offering his attentive protégé a colourful version of the truth as well as plentiful insights into his larger-than-life personality.

Dir/Scr Mika Kaurismäki • *Cinematographer* Jacques Cheuiche

'Til Death ★★★

Crime drama   1993 · Mex · Colour · 90mins

This is a surprisingly assured feature debut by Mexican director Fernando Sarinana. Alternating between the capital and the northern region around Tijuana, the film follows the attempts of two friends to raise the money they need to open a dog training school in the USA. In addition to presenting a disturbing picture of city life, the director explores the hardships facing the *cholos* (the border people). Although he can't resist the odd stylistic flourish, Sarinana convincingly combines violence, romance and humour, while also drawing fine performances from his young cast. In Spanish with English subtitles.

Demian Bichir *Mauricio* • Juan Manuel Bernal *El Boy* • Veronica Merchant *Victoria* • Dolores Beristain *Chenta* ■ *Dir* Fernando Sarinana • *Scr* Marcela Fuentes Berain

'Til There Was You ★★12

Romantic comedy
1997 · US · Colour · 109mins

The woeful miscasting of Jeanne Tripplehorn sabotages this romantic comedy, as two people who are destined to meet contrive to keep missing each other. Tripplehorn fumbles in all her attempts at comedy – particularly frustrating in a movie that features Sarah Jessica Parker (*Sex and the City*) and Jennifer Aniston (*Friends*) in supporting roles. Dylan McDermott fares better as the man she will one

day meet and fall for, but, in true movie style, he's actually on the opposing side of her fight to save her historic home. At least director Scott Winant handles this with a refreshing lack of sentimentality. Contains some swearing and sexual references.

Jeanne Tripplehorn *Gwen Moss* • Dylan McDermott *Nick Dawkan* • Sarah Jessica Parker *Francesca Lanfield* • Jennifer Aniston *Debbie* • Craig Bierko *Jon* ■ *Dir* Scott Winant • *Scr* Winnie Holzman

'Til We Meet Again ★★★

Romance   1940 · US · BW · 99mins

One of the greatest of all shipboard romances, this was definitively filmed in 1932 with Kay Francis and William Powell as the doomed lovers. The remake isn't at all bad, but George Brent's savoir-faire always seemed assumed,and it's awfully hard to care whether Merle Oberon actually succumbs to her fatal disease or not. Nevertheless, the setting is superb and director Edmund Goulding (*Grand Hotel*) certainly knows how to keep the romance simmering. Frank McHugh plays the role he took in the earlier version again – and he's just as unfunny.

Merle Oberon *Joan Ames* • George Brent *Dan Hardesty* • Pat O'Brien *Steve Burke* • Geraldine Fitzgerald *Bonny Coburn* • Binnie Barnes *Countess Liz de Bresac* • Frank McHugh *Rockingham T Rockingham* • Eric Blore *Sir Harold Pinckard* ■ *Dir* Edmund Goulding • *Scr* Warren Duff, from a story by Robert Lord • *Cinematographer* Tony Gaudio

Tilaï ★★★★PG

Drama
1990 · Burkina Faso/Swi/Fr · Colour · 78mins

Set in an isolated village in the scrublands of Burkina Faso, this is a compelling tale of filial disobedience and fraternal loyalty from Idrissa Ouedraogo. Deftly handling the complexities of the plot and making expert use of the colours and vistas of the landscape, director Ouedraogo courageously questions an array of tribal customs, including the "tilaï", the ancient law that insists that incest is punishable by death. The stately pace (so typical of much sub-Saharan cinema) and the glowing photography enhance the power of the drama, which is enacted within an admirable naturalism by a largely non-professional cast. In the African language More with English subtitles.

Rasmane Ouedraogo *Saga* • Ina Cisse *Nogma* • Roukietou Barry *Kuilga* • Assane Ouedraogo *Kougri* • Sibidou Sidibe *Poko* • Moumouni Ouedraogo *Tenga* • Mariam Barry *Bore* ■ *Dir/Scr* Idrissa Ouedraogo

Till Death Us Do Part ★★PG

Comedy   1968 · UK · Colour · 95mins

One of the great strengths of the original TV series of *Till Death Us Do Part* was the loose, discursive nature of each episode and the topicality of many of the Alf Garnett character's diatribes about politics, race, religion and royalty. Obviously, the feature format precluded the use of a similar structure and writer Johnny Speight's decision to opt for a *Millions like Us* account of family fortunes from the

thirties to contemporary times only partly comes off. There are highlights, such as Alf at the 1966 World Cup final, but not many, and they're not up to the television standard.

Warren Mitchell *Alf Garnett* • Dandy Nichols *Else Garnett* • Anthony Booth *Mike* • Una Stubbs *Rita Garnett* • Liam Redmond *Mike's Father* • Bill Maynard *Bert* • Brian Blessed *Sergeant* • Sam Kydd *Fred* ■ *Dir* Norman Cohen • *Scr* Johnny Speight, from his TV series

Till the Clouds Roll By ★★★★U

Musical biography
1946 · US · Colour · 135mins

MGM's lush tribute to Jerome Kern was intended as a straightforward biography, but Kern's death in 1945 turned this biopic into a most moving celebration, as the studio's full roster of stars perform the composer's greatest numbers, climaxing with a ridiculously boyish looking Frank Sinatra crooning *Ol' Man River*. The film features a potted version of *Show Boat*, with Lena Horne as Julie, and has some marvellous highlights. These include a sequence featuring Judy Garland as Broadway star Marilyn Miller, directed by Garland's then-husband Vincente Minnelli. The dramatic stuff, though, is heavily handled by former actor Richard Whorf, and Robert Walker is not ideally cast as Kern, though his moments with pal Van Heflin and daughter Lucille Bremer are occasionally touching. Watch this for the MGM talent on display, and the dazzling array of production numbers.

Robert Walker *Jerome Kern* • Van Heflin *James I Hessler* • Judy Garland *Marilyn Miller* • Lucille Bremer *Sally* • Joan Wells *Sally as a girl* • Paul Langton *Oscar Hammerstein II* • Dorothy Patrick *Mrs Jerome Kern* • Mary Nash *Mrs Muller* • Frank Sinatra ■ *Dir* Richard Whorf • *Scr* Myles Connolly, Jean Holloway, George Wells (adaptation), from a story by Guy Bolton

Till the End of Time ★★★

Romantic drama   1946 · US · BW · 105mins

Overshadowed by the similarly plotted *The Best Years of Our Lives*, released the same year, this melodrama about three returning Second World War veterans was a successful vehicle for heart-throb Guy Madison. Top-billed Dorothy McGuire is endearingly sympathetic as a war widow, a role that could have become cloying in other hands, and a youthful-looking Robert Mitchum provides a tough contrast to Madison's lightweight leading man. The theme song, adapted from Chopin's *Polonaise in A Flat Major*, was a massive hit in its day for Perry Como.

Dorothy McGuire *Pat Ruscomb* • Guy Madison *Cliff Harper* • Robert Mitchum *William Tabeshaw* • Bill Williams *Perry Kincheloe* • Tom Tully *CW Harper* • William Gargan *Sgt Gunny Watrous* • Jean Porter *Helen Ingersoll* • Johnny Sands *Tommy* ■ *Dir* Edward Dmytryk • *Scr* Allen Rivkin, from the novel *They Dream of Home* by Niven Busch

Till There Was You ★PG

Romantic thriller
1990 · Ausl · Colour · 90mins

A plotless, pointless mystery film, the sole purpose of which seems to be to

promote tourism to Vanuatu, the South Seas island paradise on which it's set. Charisma-free Mark Harmon plays a saxophonist who visits the island at his brother's behest, only to find his sibling has been murdered and Harmon has to solve his death. He finds time to bungee jump with the natives, romance Deborah Unger and tootle a few bluesy tunes on his horn.

Mark Harmon *Frank Flynn* • Jeroen Krabbé *Viv* • Deborah Unger [Deborah Kara Unger] *Anna* • Shane Briant *Rex* ■ *Dir* John Seale • *Scr* Michael Thomas

Till We Meet Again ★★★

First World War romantic thriller
1936 · US · BW · 71mins

A largely forgotten, if beautifully made, First World War spy romance, with distinguished Herbert Marshall (who himself lost a leg during the 1914–18 conflict) quite brilliant as an actor from England who falls in love with German actress Gertrude Michael, only to lose contact with her when war breaks out. As spies, and enemies, they find each other again. Marshall's clever underplaying is extremely moving, with Michael also excellent, and their performances are surprisingly believable. Director Robert Florey understands passion and was seldom allowed this kind of material or budget. A vintage Paramount picture, luminously photographed by the great Victor Milner, it's very touching.

Herbert Marshall *Alan Barclay* • Gertrude Michael *Elsa Durany* • Lionel Atwill *Ludwig* • Rod La Rocque *Carl Schrottle* • Guy Bates Post *Captain Minton* • Vallejo Gantner *Vogel* • Torben Meyer *Kraus* ■ *Dir* Robert Florey • *Scr* Edwin Justus Meyer, Brian Marlow, Alfred Davis, Morton Barteaux, from the play *The Last Curtain* by Alfred Davis

Till We Meet Again ★★

Second World War drama
1944 · US · BW · 88mins

Director Frank Borzage has a reputation for being one of the great romantic movie storytellers, but his actual output is rather patchy, ranging from sublime Janet Gaynor silents such as *Seventh Heaven* to sentimental tosh such as this routine wartime drama. A French nun (B-movie regular Barbara Britton) helps a flier (a bored-looking Ray Milland) get back behind Allied lines. Of course, there was a market for films like this at the time, especially in an America untouched by enemy action, and Milland was a big star, but, sadly, this simply isn't very good.

Ray Milland *John* • Barbara Britton *Sister Clothilde* • Walter Slezak *Mayor Vitrey* • Lucile Watson *Mother Superior* • Konstantin Shayne *Major Krupp* • Vladimir Sokoloff *Cabeau* • Marguerite D'Alvarez [Margarita D'Alvarez] *Madame Sarroux* • Mona Freeman *Elise* ■ *Dir* Frank Borzage • *Scr* Lenore Coffee, from the play by Alfred Maury

Tillie and Gus ★★

Comedy   1933 · US · BW · 58mins

The first of four films that infant Baby LeRoy (who retired from the screen aged four) made with on-screen child-hater WC Fields. This rather haphazard comedy, directed by Francis Martin, has Fields as a card-sharp married to a

U = SUITABLE FOR ALL   Uc = SUITABLE FOR ALL, ESPECIALLY FOR YOUNG CHILDREN (VIDEO ONLY)   PG = PARENTAL GUIDANCE

landlady from Alaska (the then 70-year-old Alison Skipworth), who helps to foil a con man who is fleecing Skipworth's niece and her husband. Fields has strong competition from his very funny leading lady, but the laughs occur in the context of a somewhat hazy plot.

WC Fields *Augustus Q Winterbottom* • Alison Skipworth *Tillie Winterbottom* • Baby LeRoy The "King" Sheridan • Jacqueline Wells [Julie Bishop] *Mary Blake Sheridan* • Clifford Jones *Tom Sheridan* • Clarence Wilson *Phineas Pratt* • George Barbier *Capt Fogg* • Barton MacLane *Commissioner McLennan* ■ *Dir* Francis Martin • *Scr* Walter De Leon, Francis Martin, from a story by Rupert Hughes

Tillie's Punctured Romance ★★★★★ U

Silent comedy   1914 · US · BW · 74mins

America's first feature-length comedy (six reels) had Charles Chaplin in its cast – but Marie Dressler was the lead because she was the star of the stage musical comedy *Tillie's Nightmare*, famous because of its song, *Heaven Help The Working Girl*. Tillie (Dressler) is believed to be a recent heiress to Chaplin and Mabel Normand, and he rushes her into marriage. However, she realises love's deception and she and Normand soon regard themselves as victims of male treachery. Directed by Mack Sennett, it now appears crude and clumsy, but it was a ground-breaker for its time, as well as being a box-office sensation – and it made Chaplin a star. ▭

Marie Dressler *Tillie Banks, country girl* • Charles Chaplin *Charlie, city slicker* • Mabel Normand *Mabel, his girl friend* • Charles Bennett *Douglas Banks, Tillie's millionaire uncle* • Mack Swain *John Banks, Tillie's father* • Chester Conklin *Mr Whoozis, friend of John Banks* ■ *Dir* Mack Sennett • *Scr* Hampton Del Ruth, from the play *Tillie's Nightmare* by Edgar Smith

Tilt ★★ 15

Drama   1978 · US · Colour · 106mins

Three years after the ultimate pinball wizardry of *Tommy*, came this rather plodding but detailed account of another pinball performer, Brooke Shields. She teams up with budding rock star Ken Marshall, and their freewheeling adventures lead to a showdown with pinball ace Charles Durning. The camerawork from inside the machines brings tension to the long-running contest, but this isn't the pinball equivalent of *The Hustler*. Donald Cammell continued his disappointing career post-*Performance* by co-writing the screenplay. ▭

Brooke Shields *Tilt* • Ken Marshall *Neil Gallagher* • Charles Durning *The Whale* • John Crawford *Mickey* • Harvey Lewis *Henry Bertolino* • Robert Brian Berger *Replay* ■ *Dir* Rudy Durand • *Scr* Rudy Durand, Donald Cammell, from a story by Rudy Durand

Tim ★★★★

Drama   1979 · Ausl · Colour · 90mins

Mel Gibson starred in this low-profile weepie in between the first two *Mad Max* movies. It couldn't be further from the murder and mayhem of those action favourites. Gibson plays a trusting simpleton who tumbles into a relationship with the wary older woman (Piper Laurie) who is teaching him to

read. The sexual tensions between this odd couple keep sentiment at bay, and Gibson's performance as the wide-eyed innocent alerted audiences to the fact that there was more to the man than just action movies. *Tim* is adapted from the first novel by Colleen McCullough, author of *The Thorn Birds*.

Piper Laurie *Mary Horton* • Mel Gibson *Tim Melville* • Alwyn Kurts *Ron Melville* • Pat Evison *Emily Melville* • Peter Gwynne *Tom Ainsley* • Deborah Kennedy *Dawn Melville* • David Foster *Mick Harrington* • Margo Lee *Mrs Harrington* • James Condon *John Harrington* ■ *Dir* Michael Pate • *Scr* Michael Pate, from the novel by Colleen McCullough

Tim Burton's The Nightmare before Christmas ★★★★★ PG

Animated musical drama 1993 · US · Colour · 73mins

Only the deliciously demented imagination of *Batman* director Tim Burton could have come up with such a dark vision of the holiday season. Producing here, Burton called on the services of innovative animation director Henry Selick and composer Danny Elfman (a regular Burton collaborator who wrote the ten surreal songs and lends his singing voice to the lead character) for this wonderfully weird fable that's packed with scary spooks, gags and dazzling décor. It enchants with every busy frame as spindly Jack Skellington, the mastermind behind Halloween, hijacks Christmas out of boredom, becoming a frightening Santa delivering nasty surprises instead of presents to terrified children. A delightful breath of fresh scare, its affectionate trashing of Christmas traditions is conceptually cunning and clever enough to please every generation. ▭ **DVD**

Danny Elfman *Jack Skellington (singing)* • Chris Sarandon *Jack Skellington (speaking)* • Catherine O'Hara *Sally/Shock* • William Hickey *Evil scientist* • Glenn Shadix *Mayor* • Paul Reubens *Lock* • Ken Page *Oogie Boogie* • Ed Ivory *Santa* ■ *Dir* Henry Selick • *Scr* Caroline Thompson, from a story and characters created by Tim Burton

Timberjack ★★ U

Western   1955 · US · Colour · 92mins

In this average western drama, Sterling Hayden seeks revenge for the murder of his father and pits the family timber business against powerful competitor David Brian, who's also his rival for Vera Ralston's saloon keeper. Some fresh scenery and details (such as Chinese bartenders and servants) count for little against routine plotting and brawling and, while veteran Adolphe Menjou revels in his flowery dialogue, the songs by a dubbed Ralston and Hoagy Carmichael are dreary. Hayden reputedly received a bonus to co-star with Ralston (wife of the Republic studio head) and it makes a change to see men fight over a less attractive woman.

Sterling Hayden *Tim Chipman* • Vera Ralston *Lynne Tilton* • David Brian *Croft Brunner* • Adolphe Menjou *Swiftwater Tilton* • Hoagy Carmichael *Jingles* • Chill Wills *Steve Riika* • Jim Davis *Poole* ■ *Dir* Joseph Kane • *Scr* Allen Rivkin, from the novel by Dan Cushman

Timbuktu ★★ U

Wartime western adventure
1959 · US · BW · 91mins

These days anyone can fly to Timbuktu in central Mali, but the word still has a mythological ping that evokes a mystical place, somewhere at the very end of the earth. Victor Mature is the sort of beefcake actor who feels at home in Timbuktu – and in rubbishy action movies like this one. He's a trader and adventurer who sides with the French Foreign Legion over their skirmishes with the local Tuareg raiders, who gorge themselves on sheep's eyes and vultures' tongues. Mature also fancies the French commander's wife, Yvonne De Carlo, who just melts in his arms.

Victor Mature *Mike Conway* • Yvonne De Carlo *Natalie Dufort* • George Dolenz *Colonel Dufort* • John Dehner *Emir* • Marcia Henderson *Jeanne Marat* • James Foxx *Lieutenant Marst* • Leonard Mudie *Mohamet Adani* • Paul Wexler *Suleyman* ■ *Dir* Jacques Tourneur • *Scr* Anthony Veiller, Paul Dudley

Time after Time ★★★★ 15

Science-fiction crime thriller
1979 · US · Colour · 107mins

In Nicholas Meyer's splendid literary conceit, the novelist HG Wells (Malcolm McDowell) follows Jack the Ripper (David Warner) from Victorian London to contemporary San Francisco in his time machine. It's a sometimes gruesome experience, but it's wittily aware of anachronisms, as the blood-steeped Ripper, warped in nature as well as time, becomes gratefully aware that the present day has many more killing devices. That's an advancement Wells was always pessimistically aware of when contemplating the future, and it's a point he would have relished being made in a film that never down-markets his genius even though it up-markets the action. Contains violence and swearing. ▭

Malcolm McDowell *Herbert G Wells* • David Warner *Dr John Lesley Stevenson* • Mary Steenburgen *Amy Robbins* • Charles Cioffi *Lieutenant Mitchell* • Laurie Main *Inspector Gregson* • Andonia Katsaros *Mrs Turner* • Patti D'Arbanville *[Patti D'Arbanville-Quinn] Shirley* • Keith McConnell *Harding* • Geraldine Baron *Carol* • James Garrett *Edwards* ■ *Dir* Nicholas Meyer • *Scr* Nicholas Meyer, from a story by Karl Alexander, Steve Hayes

Time Bandits ★★★★ PG

Fantasy comedy 1981 · UK · Colour · 111mins

Before Terry Gilliam found success in the US with *The Fisher King* and *Twelve Monkeys*, he made a series of wondrously inventive fantasies, of which this was one of the best. Its story of a schoolboy accompanying a group of outlaw dwarves on a jolting trip through time has some astonishing sequences, while the marvellous cast includes John Cleese as Robin Hood, Sean Connery as a Greek warrior king and Ralph Richardson as God. Ex-Python Gilliam is one of the great conjurers of cinema, and this film is proof of his ample and unpredictable talent. Contains some violence and swearing. ▭

John Cleese *Robin Hood* • Sean Connery *King Agamemnon* • Craig Warnock *Kevin* • Shelley Duvall *Pansy* • Katherine Helmond *Mrs Ogre* •

Ian Holm *Napoleon* • Michael Palin *Vincent* • Ralph Richardson *Supreme Being* ■ *Dir* Terry Gilliam • *Scr* Michael Palin, Terry Gilliam

Time Bomb ★★

Crime action thriller
1991 · US · Colour · 96mins

Avi Nesher is one of those directors who is only as strong as his script, because of his reliance on pyrotechnics and action sequences to carry a movie. The first half hour of this effort is well done. Michael Biehn plays a sympathetic, bookish watch repairer who experiences strange and violent flashbacks, and who is repeatedly attacked by mysterious people trying to kill him. He hires psychiatrist Patsy Kensit to unlock his mind, neither of them knowing what it will trigger. After this intriguing setup, Biehn's character quickly becomes grating and unlikeable, and the unfolding mystery becomes progressively sillier. Superior action sequences keep the proceedings watchable, but no more.

Michael Biehn *Eddie Kay* • Patsy Kensit *Dr Anna Nolmar* • Richard Jordan *Colonel Taylor* • Tracy Scoggins *Ms Blue* • Billy Blanks *Mr Brown* • Jim Maniaci *Mr Grey* • Steven J Oliver *Mr Redd* • Ray "Boom Boom" Mancini [Ray Mancini] *Mr Black* ■ *Dir/Scr* Avi Nesher

Time Flies ★★★ U

Fantasy comedy   1944 · UK · BW · 84mins

The time travel comedy was big in Britain in 1944, for not only did *ITMA* radio series star Tommy Handley take this trip to Elizabethan England, but Tommy Trinder also ventured back to Ancient Rome in *Fiddlers Three*. This is easily the superior picture, with Handley's regular radio writer Ted Kavanagh as part of the team serving up a generous portion of period gags, such as Handley pipping Sir Walter Raleigh to tobacco and a spot of cloak laying, and George Moon singing a music-hall song at the Globe. Some of the jokes have travelled less well and it falls flat in places, but it's a thoroughly entertaining romp. ▭

Tommy Handley *Tommy* • Evelyn Dall *Susie Barton* • George Moon *Bill Barton* • Felix Aylmer *Professor* • Moore Marriott *Soothsayer* • Graham Moffatt *Nephew* • John Salew *William Shakespeare* • Leslie Bradley *Walter Raleigh* • Olga Lindo *Queen Elizabeth* ■ *Dir* Walter Forde • *Scr* Howard Irving Young, JOC Orton, Ted Kavanagh

A Time for Dying ★★ PG

Western   1971 · US · Colour · 69mins

This was the final film of director Budd Boetticher and actor/producer Audie Murphy, who reprises the role of Jesse James from 1950's *Kansas Raiders*. Boetticher's cult status was founded on the westerns he made with Randolph Scott but, sadly, this just isn't in the same league. It's a blend of western and youth movie as teenager Richard Lapp becomes a bounty hunter known for his love of animals (he saves a rabbit from a snake), the ladies (he saves a girl from a bordello) and quick-draw gunfights. The script hints at deep themes, but it's cheap-looking and was clearly made in a hurry. ▭

Richard Lapp *Cass* • Anne Randall *Nellie Winters* • Audie Murphy *Jesse James* • Victor Jory *Judge Roy Bean* • Beatrice Kay *Mamie* ■ *Dir/Scr* Budd Boetticher

A Time for Loving ★★
Portmanteau romantic drama
1971 · UK · Colour · 103mins

A British-made portmanteau film that echoes the structure of the same year's *Plaza Suite* by setting a series of romantic episodes in the same Parisian apartment. Directed by Christopher Miles from a script by French playwright Jean Anouilh and with theme music by Michael Legrand, it features an international cast including Mel Ferrer, Joanna Shimkus and Britt Ekland. Unfortunately, without Neil Simon's comic gifts or a sufficiently skilled or attractive cast, the intended soufflé falls flat more often than it rises.

Mel Ferrer • Joanna Shimkus • Britt Ekland • Philippe Noiret • Susan Hampshire • Mark Burns • Lila Kedrova • Robert Dhery ■ *Dir* Christopher Miles • *Scr* Jean Anouilh

Time Gentlemen Please! ★★🅤
Comedy   1952 · UK · BW · 85mins

One of the few pictures produced by the ill-fated low-budget Group 3 company, this feeble film attempts to reproduce the whimsy of the Ealing comedies and succeeds only in being snobbish, predictable and dull. Eddie Byrne overplays his hand as the rascal who is the blot on a village's 100-percent employment record and threatens to ruin its chances of national publicity. As usual, Sid James scores as the pub landlord who is also running a crooked campaign for the parish council, but the plot is contrived and inconsequential.

Eddie Byrne *Dan Dance* • Hermione Baddeley *Emma Stebbins* • Raymond Lovell *Sir Digby Montague* • Jane Barrett *Sally* • Dora Bryan *Peggy Stebbins* • Robert Brown *Bill Jordan* • Thora Hird *Alice Crouch* • Sidney James *Eric Hace* ■ *Dir* Lewis Gilbert • *Scr* Peter Blackmore, Val Guest, from the novel *Nothing to Lose* by RJ Minney

The Time Guardian ★★★🅿🅶
Science-fiction action adventure
1987 · Aus · Colour · 83mins

Carrie Fisher isn't the only reason why this time-travel saga will seem familiar. *Mad Max* and *The Terminator* have been thrown into the blender along with *Star Wars*, for a reasonably exciting fantasy set in Australia. The quite complicated plot begins in the year 4039. Earth has been destroyed by a cyborg master race called the Jen-Diki. Escaping ruler Dean Stockwell sends warriors Fisher and Tom Burlinson back in time to 1988 to engineer another future battle with the killer robots before they become too strong. In the outback, the two culture-clash soldiers meet loner Nikki Coghill, who helps them fight the corrupt Aussie police. Good special effects, a quick pace and non-stop action disguise plot holes you could fly a spaceship through. ▭

Tom Burlinson *Ballard/The Time Guardian* • Nikki Coghill *Annie* • Dean Stockwell *Boss* • Carrie Fisher *Petra* • Peter Merrill *Zuryk* • Tim

Robertson *Sergeant McCarthy* • John Clark • Jimmy James ■ *Dir* Brian Hannant • *Scr* Brian Hannant, John Baxter

Time in the Sun ★★★
Documentary drama
1939 · US/Mex · BW · 60mins

In 1931, Sergei Eisenstein spent some months in Mexico shooting his semi-documentary *Que Viva Mexico!*. After fighting bureaucracy and trying to obtain money to keep the film going, the great Russian director had to return to the USSR. However, his producer, the American novelist Upton Sinclair, never sent him the reels to edit. Instead he sold them to producer Sol Lesser, who assembled some of the raw material into a crude film called *Thunder over Mexico* (1933). Later Eisenstein's first biographer Marie Seton edited the reels to make this version, a superior travelogue with banal narration. Though not quite as Eisenstein envisaged, it still retains much of his bizarre humour and homoeroticism, and its magnificent photography.

Charles Frederick Lindsley *Narrator* • William Royal *Narrator* • Ponce Espino *Narrator* • Carlos Tarin *Narrator* ■ *Dir* Sergei Eisenstein • *Scr* Grigori Alexandrov, Marie Seton, Paul Burnford, Anita Breener, Franz Blom, Samuel A Datlowe

Time Limit ★★★
Wartime courtroom drama
1957 · US · BW · 96mins

An engrossing, if stagey court-martial drama, this is the only film to have been directed by actor Karl Malden. It's set during the Korean War and deals with an American major (Richard Baseheart) charged with collaboration with the enemy during his time as a PoW. Basehart pleads guilty but the investigating officer digs deeper and discovers a terrible secret. Essentially a drama about the nature of truth rather than the morality of war, it owes as much to *Rashomon* as to traditional courtroom dramas such as *12 Angry Men*. The cast, led by Richard Widmark, are in uniform – and are uniformly excellent, especially the undervalued Basehart.

Richard Widmark *Colonel William Edwards* • Richard Basehart *Major Harry Cargill* • Dolores Michaels *Corporal Jean Evans* • June Lockhart *Mrs Cargill* • Carl Benton Reid *General Connors* • Martin Balsam *Sergeant Baker* • Rip Torn *Lieutenant George Miller* • Alan Dexter *Mike* ■ *Dir* Karl Malden • *Scr* Henry Denker, from the play by Ralph Berkey, Henry Denker

Time Lock ★★★
Drama   1957 · UK · BW · 72mins

Shot on a shoestring at the old Beaconsfield Studios but set in Canada, this nail-biting thriller was based on a TV play by Arthur Hailey, who went on to find huge success as the writer of blockbuster novels such as *Airport* and *Hotel*. It's a race against time to free a small boy from a bank vault before he suffocates. Written and produced by Peter Rogers and directed by Gerald Thomas, this drama is hardly what you expect from the team that devised the *Carry On* series, but Thomas builds the tension adroitly enough and gets a fine

performance out of young Vincent Winter. It provided Sean Connery with his first speaking role, as a welder.

Robert Beatty *Peter Dawson* • Betty McDowall *Lucille Walker* • Vincent Winter *Steven Walker* • Lee Patterson *Colin Walker* • Sandra Francis *Evelyn Webb* • Alan Gifford *George Foster* • Robert Ayres *Inspector Andrews* • Victor Wood *Howard Zeeder* • Sean Connery *Welder* ■ *Dir* Gerald Thomas • *Scr* Peter Rogers, from a TV play by Arthur Hailey

The Time Machine ★★★★🅿🅶
Science-fiction fantasy
1960 · UK/US · Colour · 98mins

HG Wells's marvellous novel is superbly brought to life in this charming and stylish adaptation directed by *The War of the Worlds* producer George Pal. Leaving his comfortable Victorian life behind, inventor Rod Taylor hops aboard his ingenious time contraption to explore the horrors of the future and speeds through two World Wars and atomic destruction (in 1966!) towards the eventual enslavement of the human race by subterranean cannibals. A richly speculative science-fiction classic that both stimulates and entertains, this imaginative film deservedly won an Oscar for special effects. ▭

Rod Taylor *George* • Alan Young *David Filby/James Filby* • Yvette Mimieux *Weena* • Sebastian Cabot *Dr Philip Hillyer* • Tom Helmore *Anthony Bridewell* • Whit Bissell *Walter Kemp* • Doris Lloyd *Mrs Watchett* ■ *Dir* George Pal • *Scr* David Duncan, from the novel by HG Wells

A Time of Destiny ★★🄸🄵
Second World War drama
1988 · US · Colour · 112mins

A portentous title for an overblown melodrama, in which the significant talents of William Hurt and Timothy Hutton are diminished by the pseudo-operatic approach take by husband-and-wife film-making team Gregory Nava and Anna Thomas (*El Norte*). Hurt is the revenge-driven son determined to kill Hutton, whom he believes caused the death of his Basque father. The two become best buddies during the Second World War and find themselves in mortal danger before Hurt hits the vengeance trail again. If you believe this plot, you'll believe anything. Contains swearing and violence. ▭

William Hurt *Martin* • Timothy Hutton *Jack* • Melissa Leo *Josie* • Francisco Rabal *Jorge* • Concha Hidalgo *Sebastiana* • Stockard Channing *Margaret* ■ *Dir* Gregory Nava • *Scr* Gregory Nava, Anna Thomas

The Time of His Life ★★★🅤
Comedy   1955 · UK · BW · 73mins

Richard Hearne's enduring creation Mr Pastry delighted audiences for over 25 years. The youthful Hearne's impersonation of an incident-prone old man was popular not just in the UK and the US, but all across Europe. The character made a record number of appearances on *The Ed Sullivan Show* and was a favourite of comedy superstar Buster Keaton. In this film, Mr Pastry is an ex-con paying an unwanted visit to his daughter, who has made something of herself in society. Though not a patch on

Pastry's many TV shows, it's still a nostalgic treat.

Richard Hearne *Charles Pastry* • Ellen Pollock *Lady Florence* • Richard Wattis *Edgar* • Robert Moreton *Humphrey* • Frederick Leister *Sir John* • Peter Sinclair *Kane* • John Downing *Simon* • Anne Smith *Penelope* ■ *Dir* Leslie Hiscott • *Scr* Leslie Hiscott, Richard Hearne, from the story by Leslie Hiscott, Brock Williams

Time of Miracles ★★★
Drama   1990 · Yug · Colour · 98mins

Clumsy in its symbolism, but still possessing the power to provoke, Goran Paskaljevic's historical allegory caused a storm of protest when it was released in a Yugoslavia on the brink of civil implosion, even though the swift passage of events somewhat undermined its political relevance. Set during the immediate aftermath of the Second World War, when the nation was similarly divided, the story concerns the appearance of a mysterious messianic figure who not only frustrates the mayor's attempts to put a small-town church to a more utilitarian use, but also resurrects a much-loved schoolteacher after his suspicious death. In Serbo-Croat with English subtitles.

Predrag Miki Manojlovic [Miki Manojlovic] *Nicodemus* • Dragan Maksimovic *Lazarus* ■ *Dir* Goran Paskaljevic • *Scr* Goran Paskaljevic, Borislav Pekik, from a novel by Borislav Pekik

Time of the Gypsies ★★★★★🄸🄵
Drama   1989 · Yug · Colour · 136mins

Sarajevo-born Emir Kusturica is a firm favourite at Cannes, having taken Palmes d'Or in 1985 for *When Father Was Away on Business* and in 1995 for *Underground*. He was awarded the best director prize in 1989 for this astonishing blend of romance, realism and raw humour. Using both trained and non-professional performers, he reveals the divisions, deprivations and dreams of the Romany people through this true story set in Milan and in the breathtaking, but severe, countryside of the former Yugoslavia. Davor Dujmovic gives a remarkable performance as the gypsy with telekinetic powers who is prepared to sacrifice everything to win the hand of his beloved. At once epic and intimate, this is the work of a master film-maker. In Romany and Serbo-Croat with English subtitles. Contains violence and nudity. ▭

Davor Dujmovic *Perhan* • Bora Todorovic *Ahmed Dzida* • Ljubica Adzovic *Grandmother* • Husnija Hasmovic *Uncle Merdzan* • Elvira Sali *Danira* ■ *Dir* Emir Kusturica • *Scr* Emir Kusturica, Gordan Mihic

The Time of Their Lives ★★🅤
Period comedy fantasy
1946 · US · BW · 81mins

Between 1941 and the early 1950s, the comedy duo of Abbott and Costello were a national institution and earned around $800,0000 a year – a fantastic sum for actors in black-and-white B movies. One of their films, *Buck Privates*, grossed 20 times its cost. But in 1945, they temporarily fell out over a domestic matter and did not speak for months. Reunited, they

🅤 = SUITABLE FOR ALL   🅤🄴 = SUITABLE FOR ALL, ESPECIALLY FOR YOUNG CHILDREN (VIDEO ONLY)   🅿🄶 = PARENTAL GUIDANCE

made this "thriller" in which they did not work as a team but as individual characters. The plot involved two revolutionary ghosts haunting a country house – a phenomenon investigated with predictably comic results.

Bud Abbott Ralph Greenways/Cuthbert Greenways • Lou Costello Horatio Prim • Marjorie Reynolds Melody Allen • Binnie Barnes Mildred "Millie" Dean • John Shelton Sheldon "Shelly" Gage • Jess Barker Tom Danbury • Gale Sondergaard Emily ■ Dir Charles Barton • Scr Val Burton, Walter De Leon, Bradford Ropes, John Grant

The Time of Your Life
★★★★

Comedy drama   1948 · US · BW · 109mins

Produced by William Cagney for Cagney Productions and starring brother James, this faithful rendering of William Saroyan's play, for which the author won, but refused, the 1940 Pulitzer Prize, is set entirely in a San Francisco waterfront bar run by gruff but kindly William Bendix. Here, a bunch of eccentrics, failures and wannabes live on dreams past and present, acutely and understandingly observed by a mysterious Cagney, part tough guy, part altruist. They include the simpleton sidekick he rescued from the gutter (Wayne Morris), a washed-up hooker (Jeanne Cagney) and a colorful fantasist of the Old West (former vaudevillian James Barton). Although leisurely, talky, too long and characterised by sentimental philosophising, it's extremely well acted and well directed (by HC Potter), with some terrific tap-dancing from Paul Draper.

James Cagney Joe • William Bendix Nick • Wayne Morris Tom • Jeanne Cagney Kitty Duval • Broderick Crawford Krupp, a bewildered cop • Ward Bond McCarthy • Paul Draper Harry ■ Dir HC Potter • Scr Nathaniel Curtis, from the play by William Saroyan

Time Regained
★★★★ 18

Drama   1999 · Fr/It · Colour · 162mins

Such is the dazzling complexity of Marcel Proust's masterpiece, it requires a film-maker of rare imagination to convey its multiple levels of meaning. As time elapses from the optimistic 1880s to the depressed 1920s, Chilean director Raul Ruiz calls on all manner of technical strategies to blend narrative, memory, emotion and dream into a sublime cinematic experience. Surrounded by such luminaries as Catherine Deneuve and John Malkovich, Marcello Mazzarella proves pivotal as Marcel, the writer whose life among the aristocracy becomes his art. Handsomely staged and acutely scripted, this triumph of technique and intellect is one of the finest literary adaptations of recent years. A French language film.

Catherine Deneuve Odette • Emmanuelle Béart Gilberte • Vincent Perez Morel • Pascal Greggory Saint-Loup • Marcello Mazzarella Narrator • Chiara Mastroianni Albertine • Marie-France Pisier Madame Verdurin • John Malkovich Baron de Charlus ■ Dir Raul Ruiz • Scr Raul Ruiz, Gilles Taurand, from the novel Le Temps Retrouvé by Marcel Proust

Time Runner
★ 15

Science-fiction action adventure
1993 · Can · Colour · 92mins

Fans of Mark Hamill will be embarrassed to see their idol miserably failing in an attempt to emulate Michael Biehn's character from *The Terminator*. How far he has fallen since *Star Wars*. Hamill's 21st-century character travels back to 1992 in order to warn Earth of a future alien invasion, but the invaders are already secretly in place and are out to stop him. Appallingly cheap and dull, with a time-jumping script and dim-witted characters, this makes no sense. The only interest comes in seeing how the landscape in the interior of British Columbia (where this was filmed) looks strikingly like southern California. 📺

Mark Hamill Michael Raynor • Rae Dawn Chong Karen • Brion James Neila • Marc Baur Colonel Freeman • Gordon Tipple Arnie ■ Dir Michael Mazo • Scr Greg Derochie, Ron Tarrant, Ian Bray, Christopher Hyde, Michael Mazo, from a story by John A Curtis

Time to Die
★★★

Western   1985 · Col/Cuba · Colour · 98mins

Gabriel Garcia Marquez originally wrote the screenplay for *Time to Die* in 1965, when it was filmed as a western by Mexican Arturo Ripstein. Having already overseen a TV-movie remake in 1984, Czech-trained Columbian director Jorge Ali Triana fluently reworked it for the big screen. Anyone familiar with Francesco Rosi's *Chronicle of a Death Foretold* will instantly recognise the story. Exploring the juggernaut nature of fate and the futility of macho honour codes, the action follows Gustavo Angarita as he returns home 18 years after he killed a man, knowing that local custom dictates he must die at the hands of his victim's sons. In Spanish with English subtitles.

Gustavo Angarita Juan Sayago • Sebastian Ospina Julian Moscote • Jorge Emilio Salazar Pedro Moscote • Maria Eugenia Davila Mariana • Lina Botero Sonia ■ Dir Jorge Ali Triana • Scr Gabriel Garcia Marquez

A Time to Die
★ 18

Crime drama   1991 · US · Colour · 89mins

Former porn star Traci Lords has hampered her attempt to become a serious actress by appearing in too many sleazy B-movies. Baby-faced and with pouty lips, Lords is completely miscast here as an unfairly convicted photographer, whose community service involves promoting the good name of the police department. She soon finds herself in danger when she photographs a murder by the cop who had arrested her earlier. This PM Entertainment production has the company's trademark superior cinematography, but its star further hampers the slow-moving story. It's also time for co-star Richard Roundtree (*Shaft*) to place a moratorium on playing any more chief of police roles. 📺

Traci Lords Jackie Swanson • Jeff Conaway Frank • Robert Miano Eddie • Jesse Thomas Kevin • Nitchie Barrett Sheila • Richard Roundtree Captain Ralph Phipps ■ Dir/Scr Charles T Kanganis

A Time to Kill
★★★★ 15

Thriller   1996 · US · Colour · 143mins

This dramatisation of John Grisham's first novel cleaned up at the box office, probably because Joel Schumacher wisely doesn't deviate too much from a proven formula – an attractive lead, a starry supporting cast and an even mix of action thrills and courtroom barnstorming. The one difference here is the casting of then-unknown Matthew McConaughey. He plays an inexperienced southern lawyer defending a working-class black man (Samuel L Jackson) who publicly murdered the white trash who abducted and raped his ten-year-old daughter. Sandra Bullock plays the law student who offers to help McConaughey. In the redneck corner is politically ambitious district attorney Kevin Spacey and most of the small town of Clanton, Mississippi. McConaughey makes a pretty good fist of the lead role, but, as with most Grisham adaptions, the real strength is in the supporting turns – Spacey, Jackson, Donald and Kiefer Sutherland, and Oliver Platt are all superb. Contains violence and swearing. 📺 *DVD*

Matthew McConaughey Jack Brigance • Sandra Bullock Ellen Roark • Samuel L Jackson Carl Lee Hailey • Kevin Spacey Rufus Buckley • Oliver Platt Harry Rex Vonner • Charles S Dutton Sheriff Ozzie Walls • Brenda Fricker Ethel Twitty • Donald Sutherland Lucien Wilbanks • Kiefer Sutherland Freddie Cobb ■ Dir Joel Schumacher • Scr Akiva Goldsman, from the novel by John Grisham

A Time to Live
★★★ PG

Drama based on a true story
1985 · US · Colour · 91mins

Making her TV-movie debut, Liza Minnelli reveals surprising depths in this affecting drama based on Mary-Lou Weisman's bestseller *Intensive Care*, which chronicles her son's decade-long battle with muscular dystrophy. With a script that rises well above the average "disease of the week" TV movie, this isn't simply a series of mawkish episodes depicting the boy's gradual decline, as director Rick Wallace leavens the action with examples of genuine courage and moments of humour. Jeffrey DeMunn and Corey Haim provide intelligent support as Minnelli's husband and son, while TV-movie regular Swoosie Kurtz plays another loyal-friend role. 📺

Liza Minnelli Mary-Lou Weisman • Jeffrey DeMunn Larry Weisman • Corey Haim Peter Weisman • Scott Schwartz Adam Weisman • Swoosie Kurtz Patricia • Janine Manatis Mangie ■ Dir Rick Wallace • Scr John McGreevey, from the book Intensive Care by Mary-Lou Weisman

The Time to Live and the Time to Die
★★★★ PG

Drama   1985 · Tai · Colour · 136mins

A fond evocation of life in Taiwan after the mainland revolution offering a shrewd insight into the pain of fumbling towards adolescent understanding, this is Hou Hsiao-Hsien's most autobiographical film. Passing from trusting youth to wannabe delinquent, more interested in acquiring teen-gang street-cred than

filial duty, You Anshun gives a fine performance. Convincingly portraying this time of turbulent emotions, he reinforces the allegorical aspects of the story, which sees his siblings rally round to survive the familial and financial crisis attending the death of their father. Steadily directed, it features typical flashes of gentle wit and deep humanity. In Mandarin and Hokkien with English subtitles.

You Anshun • Tian Feng • Tang Ruyun • Xiao Ai ■ Dir Hou Hsiao-Hsien • Scr Zhu Tianwen

A Time to Love and a Time to Die
★★

Second World War romance
1958 · US · Colour · 132mins

Adapted from the novel by Erich Maria Remarque, who wrote the First World War drama *All Quiet on the Western Front*, so memorably filmed by Universal in 1930, this covers similarly compassionate territory without anything like the same impact. Set during the Second World War, it is essentially the tale of a young German soldier (John Gavin) who marries a girl (Lilo Pulver) during his leave, but still returns to the Russian front. The film fails to convince, with Gavin and his fellow soldiers so strongly American it's impossible to relate to them as Germans. The inadequate Pulver is the genuine article, as are the German small-part players, but this overlong CinemaScope movie belongs more to Universal's archive of soap operas than its serious war pictures.

John Gavin Ernst Graeber • Lilo Pulver [Liselotte Pulver] Elizabeth Kruse • Jock Mahoney Immerman • Don DeFore Boettcher • Keenan Wynn Reuter • Erich Maria Remarque Professor Pohlmann • Dieter Borsche Captain Rahe • Thayer David Oscar Binding • Klaus Kinski George Lieutenant ■ Dir Douglas Sirk • Scr Orin Jannings, from the novel by Erich Maria Remarque

A Time to Triumph
★★

Drama based on a true story
1986 · US · Colour · 96mins

Great things were predicted for the 16-year-old Patty Duke after she won an Oscar as Helen Keller in *The Miracle Worker*. A quarter of a century later, she was going nowhere fast in unremarkable TV movies like this true-life tale. Here she plays Concetta Hassan, whose response to the family problems that follow her husband's heart attack is to become an army helicopter pilot. In her first role after she divorced John Astin and became president of the Screen Actors Guild, Duke does a passable job. But the movie was more of a personal hit, as she later married the sergeant who acted as technical adviser.

Patty Duke Concetta Hassan • Joseph Bologna Chuck Hassan • Julie Bovasso Jackie • Denise Mickelbury Sergeant Martin • Dara Modglin Raye Loudin • Jackie Welch Frances • Keith Colbert Frankie ■ Dir Noel Black • Scr Lavina Dawson, George Yanok

Time Trackers
★★ U

Science-fiction adventure
1989 · US · Colour · 81mins

In 2033, evil scientist Lee Bergere commanders a time tunnel and uses the device to go back in history so he can claim the credit for inventing it. Unfortunately, he ends up in medieval England where a Robin Hood-type hero is the nemesis of villains everywhere. Produced on the cheap by Roger Corman, this sci-fi adventure is most successful on the humour front, thanks to Ned Beatty's sparkling turn as a contemporary cop in hot pursuit of Bergere through the centuries. Bergere and co-star Kathleen Beller previously appeared together in *Dynasty*. ▣

Ned Beatty *Harry* • Wil Shriner *Charles* • Kathleen Beller *RJ* • Bridget Hoffman *Madeline* • Alex Hyde-White *Edgar* • Lee Bergere *Zandor* ■ *Dir/Scr* Howard R Cohen

Time without Pity ★★★

Crime drama 1957 · UK · BW · 89mins

After years of dodging the Hollywood blacklist by releasing films under pseudonyms or crediting them to other film-makers, Joseph Losey was able to put his own name to this adaptation of Emlyn Williams's stage play *Someone Waiting*. Although the story of a father trying to save his son from the gallows is supposed to be a thriller, Losey places so much emphasis on the capital punishment angle that the social theme too often swamps the suspense. Michael Redgrave is solid, however, as the alcoholic dad fighting against time, and Freddie Francis's photography enhances the sense of desperation. Though muddled, it's undeniably provocative.

Michael Redgrave *David Graham* • Ann Todd *Honor Stanford* • Leo McKern *Robert Stanford* • Peter Cushing *Jeremy Clayton* • Alec McCowen *Alec Graham* • Renee Houston *Mrs Harker* • Paul Daneman *Brian Stanford* • Lois Maxwell *Vicky Harker* ■ *Dir* Joseph Losey • *Scr* Ben Barzman, from the play *Someone Waiting* by Emlyn Williams

Timecop ★★★ 18

Science-fiction adventure 1994 · US · Colour · 93mins

The Muscles from Brussels encounters his younger self – and sports a silly hairdo – when he's sent back in time to catch a sinister senator who is trying to change the past for his own monetary ends. If you can follow the time-travel logic, which everyone seems to be making up as they go along, then director Peter Hyams's gleaming comic-strip action adventure is dumb fun, with good old Jean-Claude causing as much futuristic Van Dammage as possible. Most sci-fi fans, however, will find it desperately outdated. Best exchange Jean-Claude: ''He read my mind.'' Jean-Claude's wife: ''With your English, I'm not surprised.'' Contains swearing, violence, sex scenes and nudity. ▣ *DVD*

Jean-Claude Van Damme *Max Walker* • Mia Sara *Melissa* • Ron Silver *McComb* • Bruce McGill *Matuzak* • Gloria Reuben *Fielding* • Scott Bellis *Ricky* • Jason Schombing *Atwood* ■ *Dir* Peter Hyams • *Scr* Mark Verheiden, from a story by Mark Verheiden, Mark Richardson, from their comic book series

The Times of Harvey Milk ★★★★ 15

Documentary 1983 · US · Colour · 34mins

Using TV news footage and a host of fascinating interviews, this absorbing Oscar-winning documentary outlines the brief, but shining, political career of the charismatic Harvey Milk, America's first openly gay politician. Elected as a San Francisco Supervisor in 1977, Milk was assassinated the following year alongside Mayor George Moscone. The murders provoked storms of protest, especially when the killer, an ex-policeman, was given a light sentence (he pleaded temporary insanity induced by junk food!), and were commemorated with a very moving candle-lit vigil. Eloquent, insightful, this documentary narrated by *Torch Song Trilogy*'s Harvey Fierstein. Contains swearing.

Harvey Fierstein *Narrator* ■ *Dir* Robert Epstein

Times Square ★ 15

Comedy drama 1980 · US · Colour · 106mins

This overblown and laughable attempt by Hollywood to do for punk what *Saturday Night Fever* did for disco came at least three years too late. Poor little rich girl Trini Alvarado runs away to Manhattan. There she meets punkette Robin Johnson, who first inducts her into the New Wave scene and then turns them both into the cult singing sensations The Sleaze Sisters. It's fatuous, glossy rubbish that strenuously avoids any issue that could get in the way of its upbeat message. The soundtrack includes music by the Pretenders, the Ramones, the Patti Smith Group and Lou Reed. Johnson performs *Flowers in the City* with real New York Doll David Johansen. ▣

Tim Curry *Johnny Laguardia* • Trini Alvarado *Pamela Pearl* • Robin Johnson *Nicky Marotta* • Peter Coffield *David Pearl* • Herbert Berghof *Dr Huber* • David Margulies *Dr Zymabsky* • Anna Maria Horsford *Rosie Washington* ■ *Dir* Allan Moyle • *Scr* Jacob Brackman, from a story by Allan Moyle, Leanne Unger

Timescape ★★★ 15

Science-fiction drama 1991 · US · Colour · 89mins

Jeff Daniels stars as a widower whose battered guest house becomes a rendezvous for time travellers from the next century. Daniels carries the film with a characteristically engaging performance, but veers toward the comically bug-eyed when he discovers that the visitors have in fact turned up to witness an impending disaster. Writer/director David N Twohy brings enough invention to the plot to flesh out the imaginative premise, while the impressive special effects are by Oscar-winner John Dykstra (*Star Wars*). Contains some swearing. ▣

Jeff Daniels *Ben Wilson* • Ariana Richards *Hillary Wilson* • Emilia Crow *Reeve* • Jim Haynie *Oscar* • Nicholas Guest *Spall* ■ *Dir* David N Twohy • *Scr* David N Twohy, from the novella *Vintage Season* by CL Moore, Lawrence O'Donnell Jr

Timeslip ★★

Science-fiction thriller 1955 · UK · BW · 93mins

In this quaint British science-fiction oddity, a radiation overdose propels an atomic scientist seven seconds into the future. Numerous muddled plotlines intertwine, with gangsters and spies trying to exploit his reaction to events before they happen, but nothing too interesting is done with the nifty premise taken from Charles Eric Maine's novel *The Isotope Man*. Ken Hughes, who later directed big movies such as *Cromwell* and *Chitty Chitty Bang Bang*, slows the action down even further with small-scale thrills and utterly conventional direction.

Gene Nelson *Mike Delaney* • Faith Domergue *Jill Friday* • Joseph Tomelty *Inspector Cleary* • Donald Gray *Maitland* • Vic Perry *Vasquo* • Peter Arne *Stephen Maitland* • Launce Maraschal *Editor* • Charles Hawtrey *Scruffy* ■ *Dir* Ken Hughes • *Scr* Charles Eric Maine, Ken Hughes, from the novel *The Isotope Man* by Charles Eric Maine

Timestalkers ★★★ PG

Science-fiction adventure 1987 · US · Colour · 90mins

Science fiction comes to the Wild West in this sharply told TV time-travel adventure. College professor William Devane, a collector of Old West artefacts, travels back in time to the American frontier with mysterious Lauren Hutton, to track down evil gunslinger Klaus Kinski, who has appropriated modern technology for his murderous spree. Thanks to an inventive, well-plotted script by Brian Clemens, and Michael Schultz's fast-paced direction, it all makes eminent sense as the action hurtles toward its gripping conclusion. ▣

William Devane *Scott McKenzie* • Lauren Hutton *Georgia Crawford* • Klaus Kinski *Dr Joseph Cole* • John Ratzenberger *General Joe Brodsky* • Forrest Tucker *Texas John Cody* • James Avery *Blacksmith* ■ *Dir* Michael Shultz • *Scr* Brian Clemens, from the unpublished novel *The Tintype* by Ray Brown

Timetable ★★

Crime drama 1956 · US · BW · 80mins

First there's the ingenious robbery on a train, then there's the investigation by insurance man Mark Stevens and cop King Calder. A twist 25 minutes into the picture puts a new complexion on the case. As producer, director and star, Stevens tries to create an intelligent, out-of-the-rut thriller – but too many events happen off screen before the standard chase and final shoot-out in Mexico. The staging is unexceptional and Stevens's own performance is dull. However, he extracts bright work from his supporting cast, which includes Felicia Farr as one of the gang and Jack Klugman as a minor hood.

Mark Stevens *Charlie* • King Calder *Joe* • Felicia Farr *Linda* • Marianne Stewart *Wife* • Wesley Addy *Brucker* • Alan Reed *Wolfe* • Jack Klugman *Frankie* ■ *Dir* Mark Stevens • *Scr* Aben Kandel, from a story by Robert Angus

Tin Cup ★★★★ 15

Romantic sports comedy 1996 · US · Colour · 129mins

This is an immensely likeable romantic comedy with Kevin Costner playing cute and, maybe surprisingly for some, playing golf. Reunited with his *Bull Durham* director Ron Shelton, Costner, perhaps hoping for another *Field of Dreams*-like bonanza, plays Roy ''Tin Cup'' McAvoy, the drunken, down-at-heel pro of a driving range in the back of beyond. Then one day in walks Rene Russo – '' pretty girl, ugly swing'' – who wants Roy to teach her how to play. He is smitten and since she turns out to be a therapist, she can help rid him of his inner demons. She is also the girlfriend of his long-standing, more successful rival, Don Johnson. As a means of getting the girl and regaining his own self-respect, Roy enters the US Open. You don't need to be a golfer to enjoy it. Contains swearing and brief nudity. ▣ *DVD*

Kevin Costner *Roy McAvoy* • Rene Russo *Dr Molly Griswold* • Don Johnson *David Simms* • Richard ''Cheech'' Marin *Romeo Posar* • Linda Hart *Doreen* • Dennis Burkley *Earl* • Rex Linn *Dewey* ■ *Dir* Ron Shelton • *Scr* Ron Shelton, John Norville

The Tin Drum ★★★★ 15

Wartime drama 1979 · W Ger/Fr/Yug/Pol · Colour · 135mins

The winner of the Palme d'Or at Cannes and an Oscar for best foreign film, Volker Schlöndorff's adaptation of Gunter Grass's allegorical novel compensates for diminishing the original's thematic complexity with some supreme visual bravado. Even more laudable is the performance of David Bennent, as the young Danziger, who decides at the age of three to stop growing and express his disgust at the folly of the adults, so casually treading the path to Nazism, by emitting glass-shattering screams and thumping his beloved tin drum. Although occasionally over-reliant on expressionist excess, it's a film that still manages to be both powerful and memorable. In German with English subtitles. ▣

David Bennent *Oskar* • Mario Adorf *Alfred Matzerath* • Angela Winkler *Agnes Matzerath* • Daniel Obrychski *Jan Bronski* • Katharina Thalbach *Maria Matzerath* • Charles Aznavour *Sigismund Markus* ■ *Dir* Volker Schlöndorff • *Scr* Jean-Claude Carriere, Franz Seitz, Volker Schlöndorff, from the novel by Gunter Grass

Tin Men ★★★★ 15

Comedy drama 1987 · US · Colour · 107mins

Director Barry Levinson (*Rain Man*) is much sought after in Hollywood, but his smaller personal projects remain the most fun. This, along with *Diner*, is one of his best. Danny DeVito and Richard Dreyfuss are the rival aluminium cladding salesmen who fall out after a car accident and become locked in an ever-escalating feud. The two leads spark off each other superbly and they are ably supported by the likes of Barbara Hershey, John Mahoney, Bruno Kirby and JT Walsh. The sixties' settings are lovingly re-created and Levinson wonderfully captures the hustling banter of the reps. In spite of the laughs, there's a bittersweet undercurrent running throughout and the tone is one of regret rather than warm nostalgia. Contains swearing. 🖵

Richard Dreyfuss *Bill "BB" Babowsky* • Danny DeVito *Ernest Tilley* • Barbara Hershey *Nora Tilly* • John Mahoney *Moe* • Jackie Gayle *Sam* • Stanley Brock *Gil* • Seymour Cassel *Cheese* • Bruno Kirby *Mouse* • JT Walsh *Wing* ■ *Dir/Scr* Barry Levinson

Tin Pan Alley ★★★ U

Musical   1940 · US · BW · 94mins

One of the most attractive and popular of all the vehicles Alice Faye made for 20th Century-Fox. She's cast here with upcoming starlet Betty Grable, dynamic Jack Oakie and handsome but boring John Payne, in one of those stand-by plots about struggling songwriters. There are still plenty of highlights to enjoy, however, including a navel-less (thanks to the censors) *Sheik of Araby* confection with Billy Gilbert, and a glimpse of the knockout Nicholas Brothers, but these days, despite Alfred Newman's Oscar-winning soundtrack, this movie's mainly for nostalgia lovers.

Alice Faye *Katie Blane* • Betty Grable *Lily Blane* • Jack Oakie *Harry Calhoun* • John Payne *Skeets Harrigan* • Allen Jenkins *Sergeant Casey* • Esther Ralston *Nora Bayes* • Ben Carter *Boy* • John Loder *Reggie Carstair* ■ *Dir* Walter Lang • *Scr* Robert Ellis, Helen Logan, from a story by Pamela Harris

The Tin Soldier ★★

Fantasy drama   1995 · US · Colour · 90mins

Academy Award-winner Jon Voight (*Coming Home*) takes on one of his most unusual roles in this updated adaptation of a Hans Christian Andersen story. A toy tin soldier (Voight) comes to life to help a ten-year-old boy (Trenton Knight), who's troubled by his father's recent death and trying to cope with his family's move into a tough, gang-infested Los Angeles neighbourhood. Voight's debut as director of this flimsy fantasy is an overly precious effort. Young Knight's descent into the gang world is equally improbable, and not even the staunch support of Ally Sheedy as his strong, but disbelieving mother can make this march in step.

Jon Voight *Yarik* • Trenton Knight *Billy McClusky* • Ally Sheedy *Billy's mom* • Dom DeLuise *Mr Fallon* ■ *Dir* Jon Voight • *Scr* Patrick J Clifton, from the story *The Steadfast Tin Soldier* by Hans Christian Andersen

The Tin Star ★★★★★ U

Western   1957 · US · BW · 92mins

Here's a *real* western. It's a sturdy, finely wrought work from masters of the genre in their prime, with lawman turned bounty hunter Henry Fonda helping young sheriff Anthony Perkins to hold down his job in a town ravaged by outlaws. Written by Dudley Nichols (*Stagecoach*) and Oscar-nominated for best story and screenplay, it's directed by maestro Anthony Mann, who takes a linear, classic and deliberately underemphatic approach, allowing the setting and characters to tell the story. Mann eschews false *High Noon* ethics and really understands the essence of heroism. This is an under-rated must-see experience.

Henry Fonda *Morg Hickman* • Anthony Perkins *Sheriff Ben Owens* • Betsy Palmer *Nona Mayfield* • Michel Ray *Kip Mayfield* • Neville Brand *Bart Bogardus* • John McIntire *Dr McCord* • Mary Webster *Millie Parker* • Lee Van Cleef *Ed McGaffey* ■ *Dir* Anthony Mann • *Scr* Dudley Nichols, from the story *The Tin Badge* by Barney Slater, Joel Kane

Tina: What's Love Got to Do with It ★★★★ 18

Biographical drama
1993 · US · Colour · 112mins

As you would expect of a film based on the autobiography *I, Tina* and on which Tina Turner herself acted as on-set adviser, this is hardly the most objective showbiz biopic of all time. While Angela Bassett should be applauded for her beautifully observed portrait of the singing superstar, perhaps greater credit should be given to Laurence Fishburne for his warts-and-all performance as Ike, the man who, for all his faults, did put Tina in the spotlight. Both stars deserved their Oscar nominations for virtually carrying a picture that looks and sounds great, but is dramatically a little oversimplified. Contains violence and swearing. 🖵 **DVD**

Angela Bassett *Tina Turner* • Laurence Fishburne *Ike Turner* • Vanessa Bell Calloway *Jackie* • Jenifer Lewis *Zelma Bullock* • Phyllis Yvonne Stickney *Alline Bullock* • Khandi Alexander *Darlene* ■ *Dir* Brian Gibson • *Scr* Kate Lanier, from the autobiography *I, Tina* by Tina Turner, Kurt Loder

The Tingler ★★★★ 15

Horror   1959 · US · BW · 78mins

One of the best examples of the work of the great horror producer/director William Castle, the king of gimmick cinema, whose shockers always shouted "Boo!" with lurid style. Here, doctor Vincent Price discovers that fear creates a parasite, which grows on the spine unless the victim screams. Price isolates one of the large insect-like creatures and it escapes. Immensely enjoyable hokum, it was originally shown with the legendary stunt "Percepto" – selected cinema seats wired to administer mild electric shocks. This is a mini-classic, with a ripe Price performance, bizarre chills and goofy psychedelic imagery.

Vincent Price *Dr William Chapin* • Judith Evelyn *Mrs Higgins* • Darryl Hickman *David Morris* • Patricia Cutts *Isabel Chapin* • Pamela Lincoln *Lucy Stevens* • Philip Coolidge *Ollie Higgins* ■ *Dir* William Castle • *Scr* Robb White

Tinpis Run ★★★

Drama   1991 · Bel/Fr/PNG · Colour · 90mins

Directed by Pengau Nengo, the first indigenous feature produced in Papua New Guinea is a freewheeling combination of road movie, anthropological treatise, political satire and family melodrama. The action centres around Gerard Gabud, a village chief who divides his time between running a taxi service and coping with the caprices of his rebellious daughter, Rhoda Selan. With Leo Konga striving to keep Gabud out of trouble as he traverses the island's narrow winding roads, ferries corrupt politicians, tackles cardsharps and car thieves, and even encounters a tribal war, it's

an ill-disciplined rattlebag of incidents and ideas, but the energy is infectious.

Gerard Gabud *Village chief* • Rhoda Selan *Chief's daughter* ■ *Dir* Pengau Nengo • *Scr* John Barre, Séverin Blanchet, Martin Maden, Pengau Nengo

Tintin and the Lake of Sharks ★★★ U

Animated adventure
1973 · Bel/Fr · Colour · 76mins

After numerous books and several TV serials, Tintin finally graduated to feature-length films, including this rousing encounter with his arch-enemy, Rastapopoulos. Die-hard fans of Hergé's blond-quiffed troubleshooter may not be bowled over by this animated adventure, but the action rattles along apace, as Tintin, Snowy, Captain Haddock and the inimitable Thomson and Thompson investigate skulduggery in Syldavia. Spooky villas, artificial lakes, mysterious professors and missing artefacts crop up at every turn, as well as two new pals Niko and Nouchka, who fall into the clutches of the world's most dastardly villain. 🖵

Dir Raymond Le Blanc

Tintorera ★★

Adventure drama
1977 · UK/Mex · Colour · 88mins

It's *Jaws* with sex! This is one of several international rip-offs rushed out following the success of Spielberg's film. Several naked starlets (among them Susan George, who must have signed the contract purely for the Mexican holiday) frolic on board a yacht and in the sea and, almost incidentally, are menaced by a tiger shark. The views are pretty, but the direction by Rene Cardona Jr, son of the man responsible for *Survive!*, is atrocious.

Susan George *Gabriella* • Hugo Stiglitz *Esteban* • Andres Garcia *Miguel* ■ *Dir* Rene Cardona Jr • *Scr* Ramon Bravo

Tip on a Dead Jockey ★★

Crime drama   1957 · US · BW · 98mins

At one point, Orson Welles was lined up to direct this melodrama. Sadly, however, it ultimately ended up in the dull hands of Richard Thorpe. Welles might have shaken up this tepid piece based on a magazine story by Irwin Shaw, in which Robert Taylor's war-weary pilot mopes around Madrid, having lost his nerve for flying and all interest in his wife Dorothy Malone. She eventually stirs him up enough for him to take a smuggling job and then the film sputters briefly to life, as Taylor takes a moral stand on the difference between moving currency and moving drugs.

Robert Taylor *Lloyd Tredman* • Dorothy Malone *Phyllis Tredman* • Gia Scala *Paquita Heldon* • Martin Gabel *Bert Smith* • Marcel Dalio *Toto del Aro* • Jack Lord *Jimmy Heldon* ■ *Dir* Richard Thorpe • *Scr* Charles Lederer, from a story by Irwin Shaw

The Tit and the Moon ★★ 18

Comedy drama 1994 · Sp/Fr · Colour · 86mins

While thankfully less testosterone driven than *Jamon Jamon* or *Golden Balls*, this is the least persuasive of

Bigas Luna's recent movies. Having set up his central relationships, the director becomes so besotted with both Mathilda May's body and his own symbolic imagery that the film becomes as tedious as it is unfathomable. The young Biel Duan is appealing enough and Gérard Darmon makes the impotent *pétomane* (professional farter) surprisingly sympathetic, but the focus is so firmly on May that they struggle to make sufficient impact. José Luis Alcaine's delicious photography is wasted on such prurient nonsense as this. In Catalan, Spanish and French with English subtitles. Contains nudity. 🖵

Biel Duan *Tete* • Mathilda May *Estrellita "La Gabacha"* • Gérard Darmon *Maurice "El Gabacho"* • Miguel Poveda *Miquel "El Charmego"* • Abel Folk *Father* • Genis Sanchez *Stallone* • Laura Mañá *Mother* • Victoria Lepori *She of the Breasts* ■ *Dir* Bigas Luna • *Scr* Cuca Canals, Bigas Luna

Tit for Tat ★★★★ U

Comedy   1934 · US · BW · 19mins

In *Them Thar Hills* (1934) a health trip turned into an escalating battle, as Laurel and Hardy clashed over irascible Charlie Hall over a misunderstanding involving the latter's wife (Mae Busch) and a well full of bootlegged liquor. In this Oscar-nominated sequel, the two factions revive their feud when they find themselves as neighbouring shopkeepers – a situation that gives them plenty of painful props with which to abuse one another. A classic and hilarious example of the team's peculiar brand of patient, methodical aggression. 🖵

Stan Laurel *Stanley* • Oliver Hardy *Oliver* • Mae Busch *Grocer's wife* • Charlie Hall *Grocer* • James C Morton *Policeman* ■ *Dir* Charles Rogers • *Scr* Stan Laurel

Titan AE ★★★★ PG

Animated science-fiction adventure
2000 · US · Colour · mins

Talk about starting with a bang. Don Bluth (*An American Tail*) kicks off this animated spectacular with nothing less than the blowing-up of the Earth, forcing survivors Cale (voiced by Matt Damon) and Akima (Drew Barrymore) to put one over on the offending aliens by reactivating a hidden supercraft, The Titan. Three parts *Star Wars* to one part *Star Trek III*, *Titan AE* (After Earth, in case you're wondering), the film imaginatively blends top-quality cel and digital animation, resulting in something well beyond mere eye candy for kids. A particularly glorious scene in which ephemeral space "angels" ride the bow wakes of a spaceship in the same way as dolphins ride the bow waves of boats inspired two of my kiddie companions to respond with "Cool".

Matt Damon *Cale* • Drew Barrymore *Akima* • Bill Pullman *Korso* • John Leguizamo *Gune* • Nathan Lane *Preed* • Janeane Garofalo *Stith* • Ron Perlman *Prof Sam Tucker* • Alex D Linz *Young Cale* ■ *Dir* Don Bluth, Gary Goldman • *Scr* Ben Edlund, John August, JossWhedon, from a story by Hans Bauer, Randall McCormick • *Animation director* Len Simon

Titanic ★★★ PG
Drama   1953 · US · BW · 93mins

An impressively staged, all-star 20th Century-Fox account of the great 1912 luxury liner disaster. It's well mounted and well played, despite being markedly inferior to its 1997 namesake – the writers of this movie did pick up their own Oscar – and to a superb British version made five years later, Rank's *A Night to Remember*. Barbara Stanwyck and Clifton Webb are top-billed as a couple trapped in a doomed marriage, and a young Robert Wagner romances the couple's daughter, Audrey Dalton. ▦

Clifton Webb *Richard Sturges* • Barbara Stanwyck *Julia Sturges* • Robert Wagner *Giff Rogers* • Audrey Dalton *Annette Sturges* • Thelma Ritter *Mrs Maude Young* • Brian Aherne *Captain EJ Smith* ■ *Dir* Jean Negulesco • *Scr* Charles Brackett, Walter Reisch, Richard Breen

Titanic ★★★★★ 12
Epic romantic drama
1997 · US · Colour · 186mins

There are two love stories here: one is between James Cameron and a ship; the other is between society girl Kate Winslet and third-class passenger Leonardo DiCaprio. Cameron's script wouldn't have sustained Clark Gable and Vivien Leigh for 80 minutes, but, somehow and his magical cast revive that old-style studio gloss for three riveting hours. *Titanic* is a sumptuous and surprisingly witty assault on the emotions, with a final hour that fully captures the horror and the freezing, paralysing fear of the moment. And there are single shots, such as an awesome albatross-like swoop past the steaming ship, when you sense Cameron hugging himself with the fun of it all. At a cost of over $200 million, it's the most expensive movie ever made. It grossed nearly two billion dollars at the box office – a record – and it won 11 Oscars, equalling *Ben-Hur*'s haul of Academy Awards. ▦ **DVD**

Leonardo DiCaprio *Jack Dawson* • Kate Winslet *Rose DeWitt Bukater* • Billy Zane *Cal Hockley* • Kathy Bates *Molly Brown* • Frances Fisher *Ruth DeWitt Bukater* • Gloria Stuart *Old Rose* • Bill Paxton *Brock Lovett* • Bernard Hill *Captain EJ Smith* ■ *Dir/Scr* James Cameron • *Cinematographer* Russell Carpenter • *Music* James Horner • *Editor* Conrad Buff, James Cameron, Richard A Harris

Titanic Town ★★★ 15
Comedy drama
1998 · UK/Ger/Fr · Colour · 97mins

Based on a semi-autobiographical novel by Mary Costello, this woman's view of Belfast at the height of the Troubles in 1972 makes a change from the customary depiction of Northern Ireland as the land of revenge and martyrdom, although its broad – sometimes slapstick – humour is hard to adjust to. Julie Walters (almost the only Brit in a mostly local cast) is Catholic housewife Bernie, who adopts a grassroots approach to bringing peace to the region. Her fans will not be disappointed by her barnstorming performance. Others may still be intrigued by this little-known film made by Roger Michell, who went on to

direct *Notting Hill*. Contains swearing. ▦

Julie Walters *Bernie McPhelimy* • Ciaran Hinds *Aidan McPhelimy* • Ciaran McMenamin *Dino/Owen* • Nuala O'Neill *Annie McPhelimy* • Lorcan Cranitch *Tony* • Oliver Ford Davies *George Whittington* ■ *Dir* Roger Michell • *Scr* Anne Devlin, from a novel by Mary Costello

The Titfield Thunderbolt ★★★ U
Comedy   1952 · UK · Colour · 79mins

Although it gives off an undeniably warm glow, this tale of the rescue of a much-loved branch line clearly shows that the Ealing comedy express was beginning to run out of steam. Only in this rather too cosy world could social protest be undertaken on behalf of the forelock-tugging lower classes by squires, bishops, vicars, bumbling town clerks and amiable drunks. Despite a patronising tone and writer TEB Clarke's failure to realise the full potential of the satire, this is still an entertaining piece, thanks to director Charles Crichton's formidable talent and the highly polished playing of a practised cast. ▦

Stanley Holloway *Valentine* • George Relph *Reverend Weech* • Naunton Wayne *Blakeworth* • John Gregson *Gordon* • Godfrey Tearle *Bishop* • Hugh Griffith *Dan* • Gabrielle Brune *Joan* • Sidney James *Hawkins* ■ *Dir* Charles Crichton • *Scr* TEB Clarke

Title Shot ★
Crime drama   1979 · Can · Colour · 96mins

There have been several classic boxing movies, but this is not one of them. In fact, it's a contender for the title of worst pug pic ever made. Weighing in at well over his matinée idol poundage, Tony Curtis is beaten before he starts with this story of a crooked fight manager whose boxer is too dumb to take the dive that will earn them both a fortune. Saddled with a dismal script and the inadequate support of Richard Gabourie, Curtis mugs shamelessly in a desperate bid to both raise a laugh and retain his credibility.

Tony Curtis *Frank Renzetti* • Richard Gabourie *Blake* • Susan Hogan *Sylvia* • Allan Royal *Dunlop* • Robert Delbert *Rufus Taylor* • Natsuko Ohama *Terry* ■ *Dir* Les Rose • *Scr* John Saxton, from a story by Richard Gabourie

Tito and Me ★★★★
Comedy drama
1992 · Yug/Fr · Colour · 105mins

With its blend of proletarian comedy and political allegory, could any film have been more fitting to be the last bearer of the imprint "Made in Yugoslavia" than this one? Exploding the cult of personality and poking fun at the socialist realist style that dominated Eastern Bloc cinema, Goran Markovic's semi-autobiographical rite-of-passage picture is set in 1954 and chronicles 10-year-old foodaholic Dimitrie Vojnov's bid to win the heart of classmate Milena Vukosav. But in attempting to prove his unswerving loyalty to his hero, Marshall Tito, he finds himself on a ghastly cross-country ramble led by the sadistic Lazar Ristovski. A Serbo-Croatian language film.

Dimitrie Vojnov *Zoran* • Lazar Ristovski *Raja* • Anica Dobra *Mother* • Pedrag Manojlovic [Miki

Manojlovic] *Father* • Ljiljana Dragutinovic *Aunt* • Milena Vukosav *Jasna* • Vojislav Brajovic *Marshall Tito* ■ *Dir/Scr* Goran Markovic

Titus ★★★ 18
Drama   1999 · US · Colour · 162mins

Julie Taymor wowed Broadway with her musical version of Disney's *The Lion King* and this epic retelling of Shakespeare's gory tragedy, based on another stage production, has a similar knockout impact. It's a shame that the attention lavished on the visual elements wasn't equalled by that given to the performances. These range from the gruff (Anthony Hopkins's wronged Roman general, Titus) and the camp (Alan Cumming's Hitler-esque emperor, Saturninus) to the downright bizarre (Jessica Lange's Amazonian warrior queen, Tamora). Still, there are enough jaw-dropping scenes here to excuse the extravagant running time and Taymor's decision to give her elaborate design concept precedence over the Bard's verse. ▦

Anthony Hopkins *Titus Andronicus* • Jessica Lange *Tamora* • Alan Cumming *Saturninus* • Harry Lennix [Harry J Lennix] *Aaron* • Colm Feore *Marcus* • Angus MacFadyen *Lucius* • Jonathan Rhys-Meyers *Chiron* • Matthew Rhys *Demetrius* • Laura Fraser *Lavinia* ■ *Dir* Julie Taymor • *Scr* Julie Taymor, from the play *Titus Andronicus* by William Shakespeare

To Be or Not to Be ★★★★ U
Second World War satire
1942 · US · BW · 94mins

"So they call me Concentration Camp Ehrhardt?... ''. There's good taste, and there's this fabulously funny and original wartime comedy from director Ernst Lubitsch, which transcends taste. Witty and cleverly satirical by turns, this movie avoids giving offence by its magnificent casting, with Jack Benny as "that great, great actor Joseph Tura" and the wonderful comedian Carole Lombard, in her final film. Don't miss the opening, a hysterical gag concerning Hitler. There's poignancy, too, and a terrific running joke involving Lombard's admirer, played by the young Robert Stack. Mel Brooks starred in an audacious remake of this story, but the immutable style of this classic original proved impossible to re-create. ▦

Carole Lombard *Maria Tura* • Jack Benny *Joseph Tura* • Robert Stack *Lt Stanislav Sobinski* • Felix Bressart *Greenberg* • Lionel Atwill *Rawitch* • Stanley Ridges *Professor Siletsky* • Sig Rumann [Sig Ruman] *Colonel Ehrhardt* • Tom Dugan *Bronski* ■ *Dir* Ernst Lubitsch • *Scr* Edwin Justus Mayer, from a story by Ernst Lubitsch, Melchior Lengyel

To Be or Not to Be ★★★ PG
Comedy   1983 · US · Colour · 102mins

The coarse-grained humour makes one long for the sublime Ernst Lubitsch 1942 original, but this update is still a cracking comedy. Director Alan Johnson does remarkably well to keep the ebullient Mel Brooks in check, as the hammy head of a theatrical troupe who becomes involved in the Polish Resistance's fight against the Nazis. Co-starring with husband Brooks for the first time, Anne Bancroft is tremendous fun in a role that will for ever be associated with Carole Lombard. But what was the Academy

thinking of when it nominated Charles Durning for his shocking performance as "Concentration Camp Erhardt"? ▦

Mel Brooks *Frederick Bronski* • Anne Bancroft *Anna Bronski* • Tim Matheson *Lieutenant Andre Sobinski* • Charles Durning *Colonel Erhardt* • José Ferrer *Professor Siletski* • Christopher Lloyd *Captain Schultz* ■ *Dir* Alan Johnson • *Scr* Thomas Meehan, Ronny Graham, from the film *To Be or Not to Be* by Edwin Justus Mayer, from a story by Ernst Lubitsch, Melchior Lengyel

To Brave Alaska ★★
Drama based on a true story
1996 · US · Colour · 89mins

In this drama based on a true story, Alyssa Milano and Cameron Bancroft play a young couple whose romantic illusions about goldmining in Alaska are rudely shattered when they find themselves stranded without food in the grip of increasingly fierce storms. Bruce Pittman successfully evokes the wintry landscapes (it was actually filmed in Canada), but there are no real surprises in the story.

Alyssa Milano *Denise Harris* • Cameron Bancroft *Roger Lewis* • Duncan Fraser *Wylie Bennett* • Winston Rekert *Bill Decreeft* • Barbara Tyson *Barbara Decreeft* ■ *Dir* Bruce Pittman • *Scr* Carol Mendelsohn

To Catch a King ★★ PG
Second World War spy thriller
1984 · US · Colour · 97mins

Club owner Robert Wagner and singer Teri Garr star in this unimpressive spy thriller with a far-fetched plot – they uncover a Nazi scheme to kidnap royalty in the form of the Duke and Duchess of Windsor. Considering that the film was based on a novel by Harry Patterson – the pen name of Jack Higgins, *The Eagle Has Landed* – it should have been much more convincing. Wagner and Garr manage to keep it fairly watchable and there are a number of British TV alumni in the cast to pique the interest too. ▦

Robert Wagner *Joe Jackson* • Teri Garr *Hannah Winter* • Horst Janson *General Walter Schellenberg* • John Standing *Duke of Windsor* • Barbara Parkins *Duchess of Windsor* • Marcel Bozzuffi *Colonel da Cunha* • Jane Lapotaire *Irene Neumann* • Barry Foster *Max Winter* • Peter Egan *Heydrich* ■ *Dir* Clive Donner • *Scr* Roger O Hirson, from the novel by Harry Patterson [Jack Higgins]

To Catch a Thief ★★★ PG
Romantic mystery
1955 · US · Colour · 102mins

Always regarded as a minor work in the Hitchcock canon, *To Catch a Thief* hasn't aged very well and is undermined by some ugly, eye-jarring colour photography and back projection. Cary Grant plays a retired jewel thief who lives on the French Riviera and looks frankly ridiculous in his matelot T-shirt and grey flannels. Grace Kelly, as an heiress with too many jewels, is really just "her serene highness in waiting", since it was while making this movie that she met her future husband Prince Rainier. The famous scene in which she and Grant speed along the mountain road where Kelly eventually met her tragic death is distressing to watch. ▦

Cary Grant *John Robie* • Grace Kelly *Frances Stevens* • Jessie Royce Landis *Mrs Stevens* •

U = SUITABLE FOR ALL   Uc = SUITABLE FOR ALL, ESPECIALLY FOR YOUNG CHILDREN (VIDEO ONLY)   PG = PARENTAL GUIDANCE

John Williams *HH Hughson* • Charles Vanel *Bertani* • Brigitte Auber *Danielle* • Jean Martinelli *Foussard* ■ *Dir* Alfred Hitchcock • *Scr* John Michael Hayes, from the novel by David Dodge • *Costume Designer* Edith Head • *Cinematographer* Robert Burks

To Catch a Yeti ★★

Comedy adventure
1993 · US/UK · Colour · 95mins

It's impossible to fathom what the singer Meat Loaf hoped to achieve by starring in this goofy children's tale. He plays a big game hunter whose expedition to the Himalayas results in the discovery that the yeti is, in fact, a cuddly pet with the killing capacity of a Care Bear. Naturally, the little fella gets transported to New York and is befriended by a small child. This is all harmless fun, but could the man who sang *Bat out of Hell* really be outwitted by a frozen Mogwai?

Meat Loaf *Big Jake Grizzly* • Chantallese Kent [Chantellese Kent] *Amy* • Richard Howland *Blubber* ■ *Dir* Bob Keen • *Scr* Paul Adam, Lionel Shenken

To Dance with the White Dog ★★★ U

Drama 1993 · US · Colour · 99mins

Hume Cronyn and Jessica Tandy were one of Broadway and Hollywood's great couples. Married for 52-years until Tandy's death in 1994. In this movie, directed by the reliable Glenn Jordan and made for the Hallmark greetings card company, they are an elderly couple whose marriage, ends when Tandy passes on. This leaves Cronyn devastated until a white dog appears and gives him companionship. Since no one else can see the dog, everyone thinks he's lost his mind. A thick slice of whimsy recommendable to fans of its two stars. ▭

Hume Cronyn *Sam Peek* • Jessica Tandy *Cora Peek* • Christine Baranski *Kate* • Amy Wright *Carrie* • Frank Whaley *James Peek* • Harley Cross *Bobby* • Esther Rolle *Neelie* ■ *Dir* Glenn Jordan • *Scr* Susan Cooper, from the novel by Terry Kay

To Die For ★★ 15

Fantasy comedy 1994 · UK · Colour · 96mins

The ghost of a drag queen who has died from an Aids-related illness, returns to haunt his promiscuous boyfriend and to force him to mourn properly. It's a ponderously well-meaning, lightweight, fantasy comedy with a cast of British television personalities including Jean Boht and Tony Slattery. It's heart is in the right place, but nothing else really is. ▭

Thomas Arklie *Simon* • Ian Williams *Mark* • Tony Slattery *Terry* • Dillie Keane *Siobhan* • Jean Boht *Mrs Downs* • John Altman *Dogger* • Caroline Munro *Mrs Pignon* • Gordon Milne *Drop Dead Gorgeous* • Nicholas Harrison *Siobhan's first lover* • Ian McKellen *Quilt documentary narrator* • Sinitta *Quilt documentary narrator* ■ *Dir* Peter Mackenzie Litten • *Scr* Johnny Byrne, from a story by Paul McEnvoy, Pater Litten

To Die For ★★★★★ 15

Satirical crime drama
1995 · US · Colour · 102mins

Nicole Kidman gives the best performance of her career in director Gus Van Sant's brilliantly acerbic satire

on fame and the American Dream. Sharply scripted by Buck Henry from Joyce Maynard's best-selling novel – inspired by true events – Kidman plays shallow, suburban princess Suzanne Stone, whose entire life has been devoted to becoming a television celebrity. But when the gorgeous ice maiden marries Larry Maretto (Matt Dillon), everyone expects her to quash her ambitions and become the dutiful wife and mother. Instead, she talks her way into a job at the local TV station, quickly becomes the weathergirl and starts working her way up the corporate ladder. Trouble is, Larry keeps getting in the way. How the driven Suzanne schemes to murder her husband, with the help of besotted fan Joaquin Phoenix, comprises the rest of this razor-sharp anecdote. Fine support comes from Illeana Douglas, who gets to end this delightful satire with a marvellously cynical cutting-edge climax. Contains violence, swearing, sex, and drug abuse. ▭

Nicole Kidman *Suzanne Stone* • Matt Dillon *Larry Maretto* • Joaquin Phoenix *Jimmy Emmett* • Casey Affleck *Russell Hines* • Illeana Douglas *Janice Maretto* • Alison Folland *Lydia Mertz* • David Cronenberg *Man at lake* ■ *Dir* Gus Van Sant • *Scr* Buck Henry, from the novel by Joyce Maynard

To Die in Madrid ★★

Documentary 1963 · Fr · BW · 85mins

A much-admired documentary, narrated by John Gielgud and Irene Worth, which offers a wealth of unusual archive footage on the Spanish Civil War. The rise of Franco and the coming of the Second World War is humanly rendered. The film was nominated for a documentary Oscar in 1965, but though it lost to *The Eleanor Roosevelt Story*, it received wide distribution around the world. Originally titled *Mourir à Madrid*.

John Gielgud *Narration* • Irene Worth *Narration* ■ *Dir* Frédéric Rossif

To Dorothy, a Son ★★ U

Comedy 1954 · UK · BW · 88mins

Having made her name as both a playwright and screenwriter, Muriel Box turned director in 1952. Coming between *Both Sides of the Law* and *The Beachcomber*, she struggles to make something of a story short on credibility and atmosphere. Shelley Winters stars as a vengeful divorcée trying to keep her mitts on a fortune by preventing her successor from producing a male heir. Co-stars John Gregson and Peggy Cummins have more trouble coping with Winters's overplaying than her evil schemes.

Shelley Winters *Myrtle La Mar* • John Gregson *Tony Rapallo* • Peggy Cummins *Dorothy Rapallo* • Wilfrid Hyde White *Mr Starke* • Mona Washbourne *Nurse Appleby* • Hal Osmond *Livingstone Potts* • Hartley Power *Cy Daniel* ■ *Dir* Muriel Box • *Scr* Peter Rogers, from the play by Roger MacDougall

To Each His Own ★★★★

Melodrama 1946 · US · BW · 123mins

After two years' absence from the screen, while she conducted – and won – a court case against Warners' draconian contractual regulations, Olivia de Havilland returned to star for

Paramount in this example of a "woman's picture" at its best, and won the best actress Oscar. Impeccably directed by Mitchell Leisen, the movie has de Havilland as an unmarried mother haunted by regrets at having given up her baby for adoption during the First World War. Come the Second World War and she, now a wealthy cosmetics tycoon, encounters a young American serviceman (John Lund) in London, who turns out… Well, we didn't tell you! A satisfying contribution to a long and honourable tradition.

Olivia de Havilland *Jody Norris* • John Lund *Capt Cosgrove/Gregory Piersen* • Mary Anderson *Corinna Sturges Piersen* • Roland Culver *Lord Desham* • Phillip Terry *Alex Piersen* • Bill Goodwin *Mac Tilton* • Virginia Welles *Liz Lorimer* ■ *Dir* Mitchell Leisen • *Scr* Charles Brackett, Jacques Thery, from a story by Charles Brackett

To Each His Own Hell ★★★

Thriller 1977 · Fr · Colour · 100mins

André Cayatte first explored the sombre subject of a child's murder in *Two Are Guilty*. However, the suspense of that *policier* is replaced here with an emotional intensity that is often painful to watch. As the cop whose daughter is kidnapped, Annie Girardot is distressingly credible, both as she consoles her husband and son before delivering the ransom and, then, as she seeks the perpetrator with a stern tenacity. With its unflinching attention to detail and a shocking conclusion, this is grimly realistic and a relentlessly harrowing affair. French dialogue dubbed into English.

Annie Girardot *Madeleine* • Bernard Fresson *Bernard* • Hardy Krüger *Inspector* • Fernand Ledoux *Grandad* ■ *Dir* André Cayatte • *Scr* Jean Curtelin and André Cayatte

To Face Her Past ★★

Drama based on a true story
1996 · US · Colour · 120 mins

A gloriously sudsy true story that manages to combine a number of staples of the genre – serious disease, long-buried secrets, teenage pregnancy – in one painfully melodramatic confection. Patty Duke plays a mother who is forced to seek out the child she abandoned as a teenager, in order to get a transplant for her daughter, who has been diagnosed as having leukaemia. Duke milks her role for all its worth, soundly supported by such familiar faces as David Odgen Stiers, James Brolin and Gabrielle Carteris.

Patty Duke *Beth Bradfield* • Tracey Gold *Lori Molina* • James Brolin *Greg Hollander* • David Ogden Stiers *Ken Bradfield* • Gabrielle Carteris *Megan Hollander* • Francis X McCarthy *Vic Hollander* • Susan Brown *Kate Hollander* ■ *Dir* Steven Schachter • *Scr* Renee Longstreet, from an article by Jane Kesner Ardmore

To Gillian on Her 37th Birthday ★★★ 15

Romantic drama 1996 · US · Colour · 88mins

The spectre of *Ally McBeal* creator David E Kelley looms over this tear-jerker, with Peter Gallagher as a widower still haunted not just by the memory of his dead wife, but by apparitions of her. Kelley wrote the screenplay and co-produced, while the

deceased Gillian is played by his wife, Michelle Pfeiffer. Claire Danes is the daughter Gallagher emotionally neglects in consequence, and Kathy Baker and Bruce Altman try to bring him to his senses during a celebration to mark what would have been his Gillian's 37th birthday. Sentimental tosh, but it will no doubt appeal to those who enjoy Kelley's unique insights into the female psyche. Contains swearing and sexual references. ▭

Peter Gallagher *David Lewis* • Michelle Pfeiffer *Gillian Lewis* • Claire Danes *Rachel Lewis* • Laurie Fortier *Cindy Bayles* • Wendy Crewson *Kevin Dollof* • Bruce Altman *Paul Wheeler* • Kathy Baker *Esther Wheeler* ■ *Dir* Michael Pressman, Michael Pressman • *Scr* David E Kelley, from the play by Michael Brady

To Have and Have Not ★★★★★ PG

Second World War drama
1944 · US · BW · 96mins

When producer/director Howard Hawks accepted the drunken challenge of filming Ernest Hemingway's "unfilmable" novel, neither of the two reprobates could have foreseen this as the outcome. One of Hollywood's most satisfying romantic melodramas, this Hawksian version of *Casablanca* features Humphrey Bogart in one of his best roles, as a reluctant patriot who falls for sultry Lauren Bacall (in her movie debut), and the two leads created an on-screen chemistry that resulted in a lifetime's love affair: "If you want me, just whistle. You know how to whistle, don't you Steve?". This is a gloriously witty, wonderfully enjoyable movie. ▭

Humphrey Bogart *Harry Morgan* • Walter Brennan *Eddie* • Lauren Bacall *Marie Browning "Slim"* • Dolores Moran *Helene De Bursac* • Hoagy Carmichael *Crickett* • Walter Molnar *Paul De Bursac* • Sheldon Leonard *Lieutenant Coyo* ■ *Dir* Howard Hawks • *Scr* Jules Furthman, William Faulkner, from the novel by Ernest Hemingway

To Have and to Hold ★★

Drama 1951 · UK · BW · 66mins

A British programme-filler about a man (Patrick Barr) who, crippled in a riding accident and discovering that he has only a short time left to live, devotes himself to ensuring the security and happiness of his wife and daughter (Avis Scott, Eunice Gayson). His concern becomes obsessive to the point where he encourages his wife's so-far only friendly and affectionate relationship with another man. A non-starry but well-played little drama.

Avis Scott *June De Winter* • Patrick Barr *Brian Harding* • Robert Ayres *Max* • Eunice Gayson *Peggy Harding* • Ellen Pollock *Roberta* • Richard Warner *Cyril* • Harry Fine *Robert* ■ *Dir* Godfrey Grayson • *Scr* Reginald Long from a play by Lionel Brown

To Have & to Hold ★ 18

Romantic thriller
1996 · Ausl · Colour · 95mins

The second feature film from Australian award-winner John Hillcoat (*Ghosts… of the Civil Dead*) is an uninteresting and unpleasant yarn about the destructive obsession of lovers (Tcheky Karyo and Rachel Griffiths) in the Papua New Guinea

jungle. Great photography can't disguise a feeble plot, in which Karyo's ongoing obsession with his dead wife (Anni Finsterer) threatens his sanity and Griffiths's life. Contains swearing, sex scenes and violence. ▭

Tcheky Karyo *Jack* • Rachel Griffiths *Kate Henley* • Steve Jacobs *Sal* • Anni Finsterer *Rose* • David Field *Stevie* ■ *Dir* John Hillcoat • *Scr* Gene Conkie, from a story by John Hillcoat, Gene Conkie

To Heal a Nation ★★ U

Drama based on a true story
1988 · US · Colour · 95mins

This worthy drama tells the true story of former soldier Jan C Scruggs (Eric Roberts, brother of Julia) who, on his return from Vietnam, set about building a memorial to the troops who died during the conflict. While occasionally lurching into melodrama, its heart is in the right place, and director Michael Pressman manages to press most of the right emotional buttons. On the downside, Roberts is too mannered in the lead role, and he's given little help by the lightweight support cast. ▭

Eric Roberts *Jan Scruggs* • Glynnis O'Connor *Becky Scruggs* • Marshall Colt *Jack Wheeler* • Scott Paulin *Bob Doubek* • Laurence Luckinbill *Senator Bob Mathias* • Linden Chiles *Senator John Warner* ■ *Dir* Michael Pressman • *Scr* Jan C Scruggs and Joel L Swerdlow

To Hell and Back ★★★ PG

Biographical war drama
1955 · US · Colour · 101mins

Cowboy star Audie Murphy was America's most decorated hero in the Second World War, winning 24 decorations and killing 240 enemy soldiers, and this is the movie version of his life, based on his autobiography. This was a relatively big movie for Murphy and Universal. Filmed in early CinemaScope with authentically re-created battle scenes, Murphy is a likeable lead. His subsequent career was confined almost solely to westerns and he died in an air crash after battles with alcoholism and the scandal of an attempted murder charge. ▭

Audie Murphy *Audie Murphy* • Marshall Thompson *Johnson* • Charles Drake *Brandon* • Gregg Palmer *Lt Manning* • Jack Kelly *Kerrigan* • Paul Picerni *Valentino* • Susan Kohner *Maria* ■ *Dir* Jesse Hibbs • *Scr* Gil Doud, from Audie Murphy's autobiography

To Joy ★★★

Drama
1949 · Swe · BW · 95mins

Only a minor entry in the Ingmar Bergman canon, but no film by him is without interest. Several themes that were to recur throughout his career are touched upon: notably the fragility of marital bliss and the conflict between artistic creativity and personal contentment. Gunnar Fischer's subtle cinematography reinforces the claustrophobia of the chamber drama, which is played with an occasionally overcooked intensity by Stig Olin and Maj-Britt Nilsson, as the musicians whose sterile marriage is torn apart by his affair with a married woman. Legendary director Victor Sjöstrom impresses in a cameo as an orchestra conductor. In Swedish with English subtitles.

Stig Olin *Stig* • Maj-Britt Nilsson *Martha* • Victor Sjöstrom *Sonderby* ■ *Dir/Scr* Ingmar Bergman

To Kill a Clown ★

Drama
1972 · US · Colour · 83mins

This unremarkable effort is a strange mix of domestic drama and psycho-thriller. A couple whose marriage is on the rocks spends their make-or-break time together on a remote New England island, but then find themselves trapped and at the mercy of a crackpot Vietnam vet played, believe it or not, by a pre-*M*A*S*H* Alan Alda. Gwyneth Paltrow's mum, Blythe Danner, co-stars with Alda and they ensure one or two quality acting moments. But, overall, one suspects this isn't a movie featured too prominently on their CVs.

Alan Alda *Major Ritchie* • Blythe Danner *Lily Frischer* • Heath Lamberts *Timothy Frischer* • Eric Clavering *Stanley* ■ *Dir* George Bloomfield • *Scr* George Bloomfield, IC Rapoport, from the story *Master of the Hounds* by Algis Budrys

To Kill a Mockingbird
★★★★★ PG

Classic drama
1962 · US · BW · 123mins

A beautifully crafted and faithful screen adaptation (by playwright Horton Foote, who won an Oscar) of the now-classic Harper Lee novel about a lawyer in the Deep South and the effect of a rape trial on his children. Gregory Peck won the best actor Oscar as Atticus Finch, but in truth he's ill-cast – if ever a role was meant for Henry Fonda it was this one. Robert Duvall, making his screen debut as the disturbed Boo Radley, is excellent, as are the children, while Robert Mulligan's direction is quietly impressive (even if the film's a shade overlong). The book was once considered strong stuff, but is now taught in schools everywhere. ▭

Gregory Peck *Atticus Finch* • Mary Badham *Scout Finch* • Phillip Alford *Jem Finch* • John Megna *Dill Harris* • Frank Overton *Sheriff Heck Tate* • Rosemary Murphy *Miss Maudie Atkinson* • Brock Peters *Tom Robinson* • Estelle Evans *Calpurnia* • Ruth White *Mrs Dubose* • Robert Duvall *Boo Radley* ■ *Dir* Robert Mulligan • *Scr* Horton Foote, from the novel by Harper Lee

To Kill a Priest ★★ 18

Political religious drama
1988 · Fr/US · Colour · 112mins

Chrisopher Lambert heads a strong cast, including Ed Harris, Joss Ackland, Tim Roth and Pete Postlewaite, in this biographical film about a radical priest in Poland in the early eighties. Ed Harris is the militia man charged with finding and eliminating Solidarity supporter Father Alek (Lambert), before his fervent opposition to the government spreads any further. Despite the compelling subject matter, the film moves from convoluted scene to convoluted scene. Lambert is bland and miscast and it's Harris as his would-be killer who (wrongly) becomes far more empathetic. It's a bit of a "Europudding", which takes itself far too seriously and evokes laughter in some very inappropriate places. ▭

Christopher Lambert *Father Alek* • Ed Harris *Stefan* • Joanne Whalley *Anna* • Joss Ackland

Colonel • David Suchet *Bishop* • Tim Roth *Feliks* • Pete Postlethwaite *Joseph* • Timothy Spall *Igor* • Cherie Lunghi *Halina* • Gregor Fisher *Father Irek* • Brian Glover *Minister* ■ *Dir* Agnieszka Holland • *Scr* Agnieszka Holland, Jean-Yves Pitoun, from a story by Agnieszka Holland

To Kill a Rat ★★★★

Crime thriller
1977 · Fr · Colour · 118mins

With 135-plus films to his credit, Michel Audiard was one of France's most prolific and versatile screenwriters. Based on a novel by Raf Vallet, this was the eighth of his 13 collaborations with Georges Lautner and must rank among the best. Essaying another laconic loner, Alain Delon becomes the target of a cabal of corrupt politicians after his friend (Maurice Ronet) tips him off to the whereabouts of an incriminating notebook. With seemingly everyone having something to hide, the suspense never lets up for a second, as Delon and Ronet's girlfriend, Ornella Muti, try to separate the devious from the deadly. A French language film.

Alain Delon *Xavier "Xav" Maréchal* • Ornella Muti *Valérie* • Stéphane Audran *Christiane Dubaye* • Mireille Darc *Francoise* • Maurice Ronet *Philippe Dubaye* • Klaus Kinski *Nicolas Tomsky* • Michel Aumont *Morot* ■ *Dir* Georges Lautner • *Scr* Georges Lautner, Michel Audiard, from a novel by Raf Vallet

To Live ★★★★ 12

Epic drama
1994 · Chi · Colour · 126mins

While it might lack the visual splendour of *Red Sorghum* or the dramatic intensity of *Raise the Red Lantern*, this is still a superbly realised piece of work, combining the historical sweep of an epic with the finely etched characterisations of a chamber drama. Although it incurred the wrath of the authorities, the film isn't a condemnation of the errors of Mao, but a tribute to the spirit of the Chinese people who survived them. Gong Li seems to be incapable of giving a bad performance, but she's more than matched by Ge You, who won the best actor award at Cannes. In Mandarin with English subtitles. Contains violence. ▭

Ge You *Xu Fugui* • Gong Li *Jiazhen* • Niu Ben *Town Chief Niu* • Guo Tao *Chunsheng* • Wu Jiang *Wan Erxi* ■ *Dir* Zhang Yimou • *Scr* Lu Wei, from the novel *Lifetimes* by Yu Hua

To Live and Die in LA ★★★ 18

Crime thriller
1985 · US · Colour · 110mins

Although merely a rehash of *The French Connection* in many respects, director William Friedkin's cult high-tech thriller features excitingly kinetic car chases through the City of Angels and hi-energy gun battles choreographed to a pounding uptempo rock score. Treasury agents William Petersen and John Pankow go to extraordinary lengths by bending their Federal rule book to crack the operation of sadistic counterfeiter Willem Dafoe, in a raw tale laced with *Miami Vice* visuals and brutal raunch. Dafoe is a suitably slimy adversary in the maverick director's exercise in

nihilistic *noir*. Contains violence and swearing. ▭

William L Petersen [William Petersen] *Richard Chance* • Willem Dafoe *Eric Masters* • John Pankow *John Vukovich* • Debra Feuer *Bianca Torres* • John Turturro *Carl Cody* • Darlanne Fluegel *Ruth Lanier* • Dean Stockwell *Bob Grimes* • Steve James *Jeff Rice* • Robert Downey Sr *Thomas Bateman* • Michael Greene *Jim Hart* ■ *Dir* William Friedkin • *Scr* William Friedkin, Gerald Petievich, from the novel by Gerald Petievich

To Live and Die in Tsimshatsui ★★★ 18

Action thriller
1994 · HK · Colour · 96mins

Aware of the large number of Hong Kong residents involved with the Triads, director Lau Wai Keung here sets out to show that many of them were drawn into crime because of their dire circumstances, rather than inveterate evil. Indeed, the crooks get the best press in this high-octane drama, as cop Jacky Cheung goes undercover and discovers his adversaries are, in many ways, more human than his superiors. Complete with a romantic subplot featuring Wu Chien-lien, playing against type as a gangster's unpredictable sister, this is a provocative study of the difference between social and legal justice. In Cantonese with English subtitles. Contains violence, swearing. ▭

Jacky Cheung *Ah Lik* • Roy Cheung *Hung Tai* • Wu Chien-lien ■ *Dir* Lau Wai Keung

To My Daughter ★★ PG

Drama
1990 · US · Colour · 90mins

A disease-of-the-week has unexpected repercussions in this TV movie based on a true story. Obsessed mother Rue McClanahan is consumed with grief following the death of her favourite daughter Julie (Michele Green). She completely ignores her other children, until she finds solace completing Julie's unfinished book. This is an inflated piece of TV melodrama disguised as a cautionary tale about parental favouritism. Ty Miller and Samantha Mathis are convincing as McClanahan's surviving children and the final scene packs a considerable punch, but there's a lack of believable, sustained drama. ▭

Rue McClanahan *Laura Carlston* • Michele Green *Julie Carlston* • Samantha Mathis *Anne Carlston* • Ty Miller *Bobby Carlston* • George Coe *Frank Parsons* ■ *Dir* Larry Shaw • *Scr* William A Schwartz

To My Daughter with Love ★★

Drama
1994 · US · Colour

Rick Schroder turns in a sensitive performance as a recently widowed young man struggling with the demands of caring for his six-year-old daughter and holding down a job. At the insistence of wealthy in-laws Linda Gray and Lawrence Pressman, he agrees to let them raise the child, believing they can give her more. Of course he realises he's made a terrible mistake and tries to prove to his daughter that together they can build a new life. Director Kevin Hooks keeps the melodramatic contrivances to a minumum in this TV movie, but the one-note performances of the

supporting cast seldom transcend the well-worn formula.

Rick Schroder *Joey Cutter* • Linda Gray *Eleanor Monroe* • Lawrence Pressman *Arthur Monroe* • Megan Gallivan *Alice Cutter* • Ashley Malinger *Emily Cutter* • Keith Amos *Tim* ■ *Dir* Kevin Hooks • *Scr* Michael de Guzman

To Our Loves ★★★★ 15
Drama   1984 · Fr · Colour · 99mins

Three years after shocking audiences with Isabelle Huppert's adulterous pursuit of the boorish Gérard Depardieu in *Loulou*, Maurice Pialat explored the theme of teenage promiscuity in this equally controversial picture. Pialat draws a disturbingly authentic performance from Sandrine Bonnaire, whose confused relationship with her absentee father (Pialat) prompts her to adopt an increasingly reckless attitude towards sex. The violent slanging matches with her brother are grimly arresting, but less revealing than the still naive 15-year-old's excruciating encounters with the father whose love she craves. In French with English subtitles.

Sandrine Bonnaire *Suzanne* • Dominique Besnéhard *Robert* • Maurice Pialat *The father* • Evelyne Ker *The mother* ■ *Dir* Maurice Pialat • *Scr* Maurice Pialat, Arlette Langmann

To Paris with Love ★★★
Romantic comedy
1954 · UK · Colour · 78mins

An amiable, light-hearted exercise in post-war "naughtiness", with Alec Guinness and Vernon Gray as father and son, each planning amorous adventures for the other. The ensuing complications are enlivened by Guinness's engaging performance, reunited as he is with *Kind Hearts and Coronets* director Robert Hamer, and a screenplay of sweet charm from Warner Bros veteran Robert Buckner. Both the leading lady, Odile Versois, and Paris itself are delightful in mid-fifties' Technicolor, and this movie is often shamefully under-rated.

Alec Guinness *Colonel Sir Edgar Fraser* • Odile Versois *Lisette Marconnet* • Vernon Gray *Jon Fraser* • Jacques François *Victor de Colville* • Elina Labourdette *Sylvia Gilbert* • Austin Trevor *Leon de Colville* ■ *Dir* Robert Hamer • *Scr* Robert Buckner

To Please a Lady ★★★ U
Romantic sports drama
1950 · US · BW · 91mins

Clark Gable and Barbara Stanwyck star for veteran MGM director Clarence Brown in an efficient, straightforward movie that combines motor-racing action with drama and romance. Gable is a champion midget-car driver, hated by the crowds after the death of another driver in an accident for which he is held responsible. Journalist Stanwyck tries to get his side of the story, but he won't talk. After she witnesses another fatal on-track accident in which he's involved, she bad-mouths him in the press. Needless to say, neither the action nor their relationship stops there.

Clark Gable *Mike Brannan* • Barbara Stanwyck *Regina Forbes* • Adolphe Menjou *Gregg* • Will Geer *Jack Mackay* • Roland Winters *Dwight*

Barrington • William C McGaw *Joie Chitwood* ■ *Dir* Clarence Brown • *Scr* Barré Lyndon, Marge Decker, from their story

To Protect and Serve ★★ 18
Thriller   1992 · Swi · Colour · 88mins

An intriguing spin on the "bent coppers" scenario, which focuses on an investigation into why corrupt lawmen are turning up dead. The evidence points inexplicably to a young policeman (C Thomas Howell) but is he being set up? Although Howell struggles to carry off his leading role, the film does benefit from a strong supporting cast, which includes a rare appearance by Richard Romanus, one of the forgotten stars of Martin Scorsese's breakthrough film *Mean Streets*. Contains swearing, violence, sex scenes and drug abuse.

C Thomas Howell *Egan* • Lezlie Deane *Harriet* • Richard Romanus *Captain Maloul* • Joe Cortese *Kazinsky* • Steve Ganon *Lieutenant Burton* • Jessie Lawrence Ferguson *Becker* ■ *Dir* Eric Weston • *Scr* Darren Dalton, Kent Perkins, Eric Weston, Freeman King

To Save the Children ★★ 15
Crime drama   1994 · US · Colour · 90mins

The depressingly familiar culture of violence in America is the subject of this TV drama, based on events that took place in Wyoming in 1986. Richard Thomas (*The Waltons*) is cast effectively gainst type as deranged ex-cop David Young, who holds a school hostage with a home-made bomb. Wendy Crewson plays Young's devoted, but equally insane wife, but veteran TV hero Robert Urich is inexplicably wasted as a passive teacher. John Boy Walton, wait till Mama hears about this!

Richard Thomas *David Young* • Robert Urich *Jake Downey* • Wendy Crewson *Dorsie Young* • Jessica Steen *Kathi Davidson* • Joseph Ziegler *Matt Eckhardt* ■ *Dir* Steven Hilliard Stern • *Scr* James S Henerson, from the book *When Angels Intervene* by Hartt Wixom, Judene Wixom

To See Such Fun ★★★★ U
Comedy compilation
1977 · UK · Colour and BW · 90mins

A compilation of some of the funniest and most memorable sequences from over a score of British film comedies. Originally intended for theatrical release, this loving exercise in comic nostalgia immediately ran into all sorts of copyright problems, which may explain why its first appearance was as a Christmas day special on British television (LWT) in 1977. However, it has always been trimmed for TV transmissions and is best seen in its video release form. A cornucopia of comical clips compiled by writer/performer Dick Vosburgh and hosted by comedy aficionado Frank Muir.

Frank Muir *Host* ■ *Dir* Jon Scoffield

To Sir, with Love ★★★ PG
Drama   1967 · UK · Colour · 100mins

After snarling his way through a New York education as a student in *The Blackboard Jungle* 12 years earlier, Sidney Poitier moved nearer the chalk-face to be a new teacher in London's East End motivating less surly pupils

to be responsible citizens. Director James Clavell's adaptation of ER Braithwaite's novel is a soft-centred affair, though Poitier does punch Christian Roberts just to prove he's boss. Lulu sings the title song, while Judy Geeson develops a credible and poignant crush on her teacher. Naive it may have been, but it became one of the year's top box-office hits. Contains swearing. **DVD**

Sidney Poitier *Mark Thackeray* • Christian Roberts *Denham* • Judy Geeson *Pamela Dare* • Suzy Kendall *Gillian Blanchard* • Lulu *Barbara Pegg* • Faith Brook *Mrs Evans* • Geoffrey Bayldon *Weston* • Edward Burnham *Florian* • Gareth Robinson *Tich* • Grahame Charles *Femman* • Patricia Routledge *Clinty* ■ *Dir* James Clavell • *Scr* ER Braithwaite

To Sir with Love 2 ★★
Drama   1996 · US · Colour · 92mins

Belated and rather pointless sequel to the 1967 original, with a well-preserved Sidney Poitier reprising his role as the teacher, whose quiet dignity instills respect and self-belief in a rowdy class of slum kids. The action is transposed from London to the US, putting teach in touch with a clichéd classload of stereotypical hoodlums. Peter Bogdanovich directs with skill, but no great distinction. Poitier looks like he could sleepwalk through this sort of stuff, and probably did.

Sidney Poitier *Mark Thackeray* • Christian Payton *Wilsie Carrouthers* • Dana Eskelson *Evie Hillis* • Fernando Lopez *Danny Lombardi* • Michael Gilio *Frankie Davanon* ■ *Dir* Peter Bogdanovich • *Scr* Philip Rosenberg

To Sleep with Anger ★★★★ 12
Drama   1990 · US · Colour · 101mins

Charles Burnett's story of a black family settled in Los Angeles from the South, is an engrossing study of conflicts in Black America. Danny Glover has never been better, playing a seductive charmer from the past whose storytelling moves from the comic to the sinister, a domestic demagogue who stirs up nightmare tensions the family never knew existed. Contains swearing.

Danny Glover *Harry Mention* • Paul Butler *Gideon* • Mary Alice *Suzie* • Carl Lumbly *Junior* • Vonetta McGee *Pat* • Richard Brooks *Babe Brother* ■ *Dir/Scr* Charles Burnett

To the Devil a Daughter ★★ 18
Horror   1976 · UK/W Ger · Colour · 88mins

The penultimate Hammer film to date, is a muddled mixture of post-*Exorcist* shock and the more traditional House of Horror style. Based on Dennis Wheatley's occult bestseller (he hated it), the plot has satanist Christopher Lee coercing nubile nun Nastassja Kinski into having the Devil's offspring, while Richard Widmark, a writer specialising in the supernatural, tries to foil his plan. Although skilfully directed by Peter Sykes with a firm tendency towards a trendy fragmented narrative and explicit exploitation, this misguided attempt to update Hammer's image is more likely to be remembered for teen Kinski's unashamed early performance than

anything else. Contains violence, swearing and nudity.

Richard Widmark *John Verney* • Christopher Lee *Father Michael Raynor* • Honor Blackman *Anna Fountain* • Denholm Elliott *Henry Beddows* • Michael Goodliffe *George De Grass* • Nastassia Kinski [Nastassja Kinski] *Catherine Beddows* • Anthony Valentine *David* ■ *Dir* Peter Sykes • *Scr* Chris Wicking, from the novel by Dennis Wheatley

To the Four Winds ★★★
Historical drama   1987 · Sp · Colour

Inspired by events leading to the destruction of Guernica, this is a sobering reminder of the human cost of the Spanish Civil War. Although the focus falls on the romance between a poet who becomes a major in the Republican army and a well-heeled British aid worker, there's nothing novelettish about director Jose A Zorrilla's approach to their relationship. Nor does he sentimentalise the plight of the children they seek to escort to safety. However, he does make some interesting points about the way the conflict was reported by the foreign press. A Spanish language film.

Xavier Elorriaga *Esteban Urkiaga* • Anne Louise Lambert *Georgina* • Jean-Claude Bouillaud *Baldie* • Peter Leeper *Steer* • Antonio Passy *Guillaume* • Ramon Barea *Genaro* • Ramon Aguirre *Jose A Aguirra* • Miguel Munarriz *Beldarrain* ■ *Dir* Jose A Zorrilla • *Scr* Jose A Zorrilla, Xabier Elorriaga, A Urretavizcaya [Arantxa Urretavizcaya]

To the Shores of Tripoli ★★ U
Second World War drama
1942 · US · Colour · 85mins

20th Century-Fox's salute to the Marines, the title coming from the military song. There isn't much of a plot – merely the training of the blokes, their patriotism, the tough sergeant, the girl back home, winsome nurse... you know the drill. Much of it was shot at the Marines' major Pacific base in San Diego, though apparently Fox also had a second unit in Honilulu photographing background footage when the Japanese struck Pearl Harbor. In full Technicolor, a rarity for 1942 since most Second World War movies were in black-and-white, only changing to colour in 1944 when victory was assured.

John Payne *Chris Winters* • Maureen O'Hara *Mary Carter* • Randolph Scott *Sgt Dixie Smith* • Nancy Kelly *Helene Hunt* • William Tracy *Johnny Dent* • Maxie Rosenbloom *Okay Jones* • Henry Morgan [Harry Morgan] *Mouthy* ■ *Dir* Bruce Humberstone [H Bruce Humberstone] • *Scr* Lamar Trotti, from a story by Steve Fisher

To the Starry Island ★★★★
Historical drama
1994 · S Kor · Colour · 99mins

An affecting and superbly observed study of the impact of war on village life. A poet returns to his island to discover that the locals are unwilling to bury his friend's father because of past events. Revisiting familiar places, he recalls the characters that inhabited his childhood and the moment when the Korean War turned everybody into strangers. Demonstrating a mastery of flashback and a keen insight into human interaction, Park Kwang-Su excels himself in the scene where the locals betray each other to invading troops, which boasts an unbearable tension and a startling climax. In Korean with English subtitles.

Moon Sung-Keun *Moon Duk-bae/moon Chae-ku* • Ahn Sung-Kee *Kim Senior/kim Shul* ■ *Dir* Park Kwang-Su • *Scr* Park Kwang-Su, Lee Chang-Dong, Im Chulwoo

To Trap a Spy ★★★

Spy comedy drama
1966 · US · Colour · 92mins

The first movie spin-off from the highly successful TV spy show *The Man from UNCLE* also stands as one of the best. Comprising footage from the pilot episode, it contains additional new scenes which focused on turning Napoleon Solo, played with devilish charm by Robert Vaughn, into a playboy about town. Poor old David McCallum as sidekick Illya Kuryakin hardly gets a look in. The *femme fatale* quota was also enhanced to spice up the box office, in this case Luciana Paluzzi's cold-hearted vamp, a role she played to perfection in the Bond epic *Thunderball*. Patricia Crowley is fun too as a housewife-cum-spy. Never mind the thin plot – UNCLE agents must protect a visiting African diplomat from assassination – just feel the nostalgia.

Robert Vaughn *Napoleon Solo* • David McCallum *Illya Kuryakin* • Patricia Crowley [Pat Crowley] *Elaine May Donaldson* • Fritz Weaver *Vulcan* • Luciana Paluzzi *Angela* • William Marshall *Ashumen* • Will Kuluva *Mr Allison* ■ *Dir* Don Medford • *Scr* Sam Rolfe

To Walk Again ★★ PG

Drama based on a true story
1994 · US · Colour · 87mins

There's no doubting the courage of Eddie Keating, the US marine who defied the doctors who told him he would never walk again after he was accidentally shot in the head during a routine training exercise. Cameron Bancroft pulls out all the stops in this TV movie to convey the pain of rehabilitation, but the over-cooked performances of Blair Brown and Ken Howard as his ever-loving parents clearly devalue the drama. Director Randall Zisk's sole intention is to bring lumps to throats, but surely such heroic courage deserves a more intelligent approach? ▭

Blair Brown *Carole Keating* • Ken Howard *Ed Keating Sr* • Cameron Bancroft *Eddie Keating* • Carmen Argenziano *Dr Cantore* • Joely Collins *Kelly* • Gabrielle Miller *Karen* ■ *Dir* Randall Zisk • *Scr* George Eckstein

To Walk with Lions ★★★★ 12

Biographical drama
1999 · Can · Colour · 109mins

Grittier and less sentimental than the original, this fine follow-up to *Born Free* stars Richard Harris as an ageing George Adamson, long separated from wife Joy, but still enjoying life with the lions despite the predations of poachers and the grudging tolerance of the Kenyan government. The story is seen through the eyes of an English backpacker (John Michie), who chronicles Adamson's life up to his brutal killing by poachers in 1989. The leonine-looking Harris delivers a towering lead performance – like good

wine, he matures with age – and there's solid support from Kerry Fox, Honor Blackman, Ian Bannen and Geraldine Chaplin.

Richard Harris *George Adamson* • John Michie *Tony Fitzjohn* • Ian Bannen *Terence Adamson* • Kerry Fox *Lucy Jackson* • Hugh Quarshie *Maxwell* • Honor Blackman *Joy Adamson* • Geraldine Chaplin *Victoria Andrecelli* ■ *Dir* Carl Schultz • *Scr* Sharon Buckingham, Keith Ross Leckie

To Wong Foo, Thanks for Everything, Julie Newmar ★★★ PG

Comedy   1995 · US · Colour · 103mins

America's riposte to *The Adventures of Priscilla, Queen of the Desert* is a good concept in search of a plot. The concept? Dress macho movie stars Patrick Swayze and Wesley Snipes in evening gowns, sit back, and watch the camp laughs roll in. And sometimes they do. The plot? Three New York drag queens on the road to Hollywood get stuck in small-town America. Cue the culture clash messages about tolerance, Aids awareness and sexual freedom. Although sentimentally shallow and nowhere near as gutsy as *Priscilla*, Beeban Kidron's frock opera is diverting enough with the hugely underrated John Leguizamo giving an amazing performance as Chi Chi Rodriguez, the cha-cha queen from hell. Contains swearing. ▭

Wesley Snipes *Noxeema Jackson* • Patrick Swayze *Vida Boheme* • John Leguizamo *Chi Chi Rodriguez* • Stockard Channing *Carol Ann* • Blythe Danner *Beatrice* • Arliss Howard *Virgil* • Jason London *Bobby Ray* • Chris Penn [Christopher Penn] *Sheriff Dollard* • Melinda Dillon *Merna* • Beth Grant *Loretta* ■ *Dir* Beeban Kidron • *Scr* Douglas Carter

The Toast of New Orleans ★★★ U

Musical drama   1950 · US · Colour · 96mins

Chubby tenor Mario Lanza's second starring role, the first was in the previous year's *That Midnight Kiss*, again teams him with glamorous co-star Kathryn Grayson. This was the film that helped him become a household name, belting out the momentous *Be My Love* at every possible opportunity, as he portrays a singing fisherman discovered by suave impresario David Niven. Grayson may be top-billed, but 19-year-old Rita Moreno, later to win an Oscar in *West Side Story*, steals the honours in a super dance number . Lanza's next film was the smash hit *The Great Caruso*, and the seeds of both his stardom and his self-destruction were duly sown.

Kathryn Grayson *Suzette Micheline* • Mario Lanza *Pepe Abellard Duvalle* • David Niven *Jacques Riboudeaux* • J Carrol Naish *Nicky Duvalle* • James Mitchell *Pierre* • Richard Hageman *Maestro P Trellini* ■ *Dir* Norman Taurog • *Scr* Sy Gomberg, George Wells

The Toast of New York ★★★ U

Biographical drama 1937 · US · BW · 104mins

Rotund character actor Edward Arnold makes a strong fist of the leading role of the American 19th-century entrepreneur John Fisk, but the

thunder (and there's quite a lot of that!) is stolen from Arnold by juvenile leads Cary Grant and Frances Farmer. Farmer in particular being exceptionally lively. Grant glides through the role of Fisk's partner, revealing that graceful quality that would serve him well, but he seems far too contemporary for this biopic, which, as Hollywood has a tendency to do, plays fast and loose with the known facts. ▭

Edward Arnold *Jim Fisk* • Cary Grant *Nick Boyd* • Frances Farmer *Josie Mansfield* • Jack Oakie *Luke* • Donald Meek *Daniel Drew* • Thelma Leeds *Fleurique* • Clarence Kolb *Cornelius Vanderbilt* ■ *Dir* Rowland V Lee • *Scr* Dudley Nichols, John Twist, Joel Sayre, from the book *Book of Daniel Drew* by Bouck White, from the story *Robber Barons* by Matthew Josephson

Tobacco Road ★★★

Drama   1941 · US · BW · 84mins

Erskine Caldwell's novel was a solid sensation in its day, uncovering the (literal) dirt on a Georgia backwoods community, and went on to become an amazingly long-running Broadway success. When 20th Century-Fox filmed the piece, it wisely retained Charley Grapewin to repeat his role as Jeeter Lester, head of a clan beset by financial woes and seemingly incapable of sorting out its problems. He's terrific, but the studio settings look uncomfortably phony today, and Fox's resident beauty Gene Tierney looks strained and out of place. However, this quaint material still fascinates, and John Ford retains the darkly comic elements of Caldwell's novel – this is not a meditation on the nobility of the poor and uneducated. A real curio.

Charley Grapewin *Jeeter Lester* • Marjorie Rambeau *Sister Bessie* • Gene Tierney *Ellie May Lester* • William Tracy *Duke Lester* • Elizabeth Patterson *Ada Lester* • Dana Andrews *Dr Tim* ■ *Dir* John Ford • *Scr* Nunnally Johnson, from the play by Jack Kirkland, from the novel by Erskine Caldwell

Tobe Hooper's Night Terrors ★ 18

Erotic horror   1994 · Is · Colour · 93mins

Tobe Hooper's Night Terrors may very well be the worst horror film made during the nineties. In present day Cairo, a young woman (Zoe Trilling) is seduced into a life of debauchery by a descendant of the Marquis De Sade (Robert Englund). This slim plot is interrupted every now and then by bizarre visions (a naked man on a horse, a snake lady) and by flashbacks to the original De Sade being tortured to death. Totally bereft of entertainment value, the only point here, is the one on England's pneumatic stabbing tool. ▭

Robert Englund *Marquis de Sade/Paul Chevalier* • Zoe Trilling *Genie* • Chandra West *Beth* ■ *Dir* Tobe Hooper • *Scr* Daniel Mattmoor, Rom Globus

Tobruk ★★★ PG

Second World War adventure drama
1966 · US · Colour · 104mins

Rock Hudson in a decidedly Hollywood backlot North Africa, surrounded by assorted British war-film veterans including Norman Rossington and Percy Herbert, having a go at blowing

up Rommel's fuel lines. While director Arthur Hiller – on his way to *Love Story* and *Plaza Suite* – makes it heavy going, it's just about watchable, thanks to the interesting screenplay by actor Leo V Gordon (who also appears in the film). The action scenes were used again in the Richard Burton action adventure *Raid on Rommel*, in which you can easily identify many of the actors from *Tobruk*. ▭

Rock Hudson *Major Donald Craig* • George Peppard *Captain Kurt Bergman* • Nigel Green *Colonel John Harker* • Guy Stockwell *Lieutenant Max Mohnfeld* • Jack Watson *Sergeant Major Tyne* • Norman Rossington *Alfie* • Percy Herbert *Dolan* ■ *Dir* Arthur Hiller • *Scr* Leo V Gordon

Toby Tyler, or Ten Weeks with a Circus ★★ Uc

Adventure   1960 · US · Colour · 90mins

Disney regular Kevin Corcoran is the young lad who succeeds in doing what most children dream of: swap life at home for the excitement of the circus. It's an easy-going if dated adventure, but the performances are pleasing and the youngsters will lap it up. ▭

Kevin Corcoran *Toby Tyler* • Henry Calvin *Ben Cotter* • Gene Sheldon *Sam Treat* • Bob Sweeney *Harry Tupper* • Richard Eastham *Colonel Sam Castle* • James Drury *Jim Weaver* • Barbara Beaird *Mademoiselle Jeanette* ■ *Dir* Charles Barton • *Scr* Bill Walsh, Lillie Hayward, from the novel by James Otis Kaler

Today It's Me... Tomorrow You! ★★★ 15

Spaghetti western 1968 · It · Colour · 90mins

Although better known as one of the masters of "yellow" (giallo) horror, Dario Argento was no mug when it came to spaghetti westerns (after all, he co-wrote Sergio Leone's *Once upon a Time in the West*). Here, with director Tonino Cervi, he has concocted a rattling tale of revenge, deception and greed, that looks superb and ceaselessly commands attention. Brett Halsey (here billed as Montgomery Ford) stars as an ex-jailbird who hires a gunslinging quartet to hunt the man who framed him. But he is outshone by Bud Spencer, who, adrift from regular co-star Terence Hill, represses most of his comic instincts to give a performance of polished villainy. Italian dialogue dubbed into English. ▭

Montgomery Ford [Brett Halsey] *Bill Kiowa* • Bud Spencer *O'Bannion* • William Berger *Colt Moran* • Tatsuya Nakadai *Elfrego* • Wayde Preston *Jeff Milton* ■ *Dir* Tonino Cervi • *Scr* Dario Argento, Tonino Cervi

Today We Live ★★★

First World War romance
1933 · US · BW · 110mins

A First World War drama in which Joan Crawford, deeply attached to her brother Franchot Tone and engaged to her childhood sweetheart Robert Young, falls in love with Gary Cooper. All four end up on active service in France where, between air battles (using some spare footage from *Hell's Angels*) and tragedy, the complicated emotional triangle is played out. Co-scripted by William Faulkner and directed by Howard Hawks, this is surely one of the weirdest films ever made. The plot defies credibility at almost every turn, and the intimate scenes of high drama between the protagonists are written and spoken in a curiously clipped, semi-poetical shorthand. That we are asked to believe in three of the stars as members of the English upper crust is the least of the problems in this drawn-out and stilted work. And yet the dreamlike, almost surreal atmosphere and strangely theatrical style is grimly compelling. A real oddity, but an interesting one.

Joan Crawford *Diana Boyce-Smith* • Gary Cooper *Richard Bogard* • Robert Young *Claude* • Franchot Tone *Ronnie Boyce-Smith* • Roscoe Karns *McGinnis* • Louise Closser Hale *Applegate* • Rollo Lloyd *Major* • Hilda Vaughn *Eleanor* ■ *Dir* Howard Hawks • *Scr* Edith Fitzgerald, Dwight Taylor, William Faulkner, from the story *Turn About* by William Faulkner

The Todd Killings ★★
Crime drama 1971 · US · Colour · 90mins

Director Barry Shear followed the satirical *Wild in the Streets* with this provocative study of another sort of teen ''idol''. Here, it's a young man in a small American town, adored by the girls, who despises the world that he sees and becomes a serial killer. Robert F Lyons plays this unremorseful character as coolly (or blandly) as possible while Shear's direction is thrustingly energetic. Although there's interest in a cast that includes Barbara Bel Geddes, Gloria Grahame and a pre-*Waltons* Richard Thomas, their supporting roles give them little scope.

Robert F Lyons *Skipper Todd* • Richard Thomas *Billy Roy* • Belinda J Montgomery *Roberta* • Barbara Bel Geddes *Mrs Todd* • Sherry Miles *Amata* • Joyce Ames *Haddie* • Holly Near *Norma* • James Broderick *Sam* • Gloria Grahame *Mrs Roy* • Fay Spain *Mrs Mack* • Edward Asner [Ed Asner] *Fred Reardon* ■ *Dir* Barry Shear • *Scr* Dennis Murphy, Joel Oliansky, from a story by Mann Rubin

Together Again ★★★
Romantic comedy 1944 · US · BW · 99mins

The title unashamedly refers to the reteaming of Irene Dunne and Charles Boyer, the hit duo of *Love Affair* and *When Tomorrow Comes*, but this time eschewing the tempestuous storms of romantic melodrama for the shenanigans of romantic comedy. She plays the widowed mayoress of a New England town; he is a New York sculptor commissioned, at the suggestion of Dunne's cupid-playing father-in-law Charles Coburn, to cast a new statue of her late husband, the former mayor. Naturally they fall in love, but not before multiple misunderstandings. Charles Vidor directs, the cast gleams and the movie is featherweight fun.

Irene Dunne *Anne Crandall* • Charles Boyer *George Corday* • Charles Coburn *Jonathan Crandall Sr* • Mona Freeman *Diana Crandall* • Jerome Courtland *Gilbert Parker* • Elizabeth Patterson *Jessie* • Charles Dingle *Morton Buchman* • Walter Baldwin *Witherspoon* ■ *Dir* Charles Vidor • *Scr* Virginia Van Upp, F Hugh Herbert, from a story by Stanley Russell, Herbert Biberman

Tokyo Cowboy ★★★
Comedy 1994 · Can · Colour and BW · 94mins

A festival favourite in its native Canada, this charming tale of movie

mania and cross-cultural confusion sees Hiromoto Ida as the Japanese fast-food employee who quits his dead-end existence, for a chance to emulate his cowboy heroes in the backwoods home of his Canadian penpal. However, while his enthusiasm amuses Christianne Hirt, it infuriates her girlfriend, Janne Mortil, and the stage is set for a showdown. Neatly played, this warm, funny film owes its greatest debt to director Kathy Garneau and photographer Kenneth Hewlett, who stage Ida's black-and-white western daydreams with considerable skill.

Hiromoto Ida *No Ogawa* • Christianne Hirt *Kate Beatty* • Janne Mortil *Shelly* • Alec Willow *Postman* • Anna Ferguson *Kate's mother* ■ *Dir* Kathy Garneau • *Scr* Caroline Anderson

Tokyo Drifter ★★★★ 12
Cult action thriller
1966 · Jap · Colour and BW · 80mins

Coming between *Elegy to Violence* and *Branded to Kill*, this deliriously contrived yakuza flick earned director Seijun Suzuki a cult following outside a less receptive Japan. Combining elements from hard-boiled pulp, the spaghetti western and the Hollywood musical, this cartoon-like parody of the platitudes and attitudes of the gangster movie also makes spectacular use of colour, stylised decor and an ambiguous narrative. At the centre of the often surreal mayhem is Tetsuya Watari, whose ambition to quit the rackets is frustrated by his inability to shake either his dark past or the dogged attentions of hit man Hideaki Nitani. In Japanese with English subtitles. ▭

Tetsuya Watari *Hondo Tetsuya* • Chieko Matsubara *Chiharu* • Hideaki Nitani *Aizawa Kenji* • Ryuji Kita *Kurata* • Tsuyoshi Yoshida *Keiichi* • Hideaki Esumi *Otsuka* ■ *Dir* Seijun Suzuki • *Scr* Yasunori Kawauchi

Tokyo Fist ★★★★ 18
Action horror drama
1995 · Jap · Colour · 83mins

Extraordinarily oppressive, raw and gore-drenched Japanese tale of the mental and physical transformation of a wimpy insurance salesman (director Shinya Tsukamoto, who also produced, wrote, shot and edited!), his disturbed girlfriend and an old school friend turned rival, a professional boxer. Shot on darting hand-held camera, Tsukamoto demonstrates mesmerising mastery of light, colour and sound as the trio conflict outside and inside the fight ring in some of the most punishing, bloody fight scenes since *Raging Bull*. Like Tsukamoto's *Tetsuo* movies, this is certainly not for those with a delicate stomach. By the end you'll feel as battered and bruised as the film's enraged protagonists. In Japanese with English subtitles. Contains swearing, violence and sex scenes. ▭

Kahori Fujii *Hizuru* • Kohji Tsukamoto *Kojima Takuji* • Shinya Tsukamoto *Tsuda Yoshiharu* • Naoto Takenaka *Ohizumi, trainer* ■ *Dir* Shinya Tsukamoto • *Scr* Shinya Tsukamoto, from a story by Hisashi Saito, Shinya Tsukamoto

Tokyo Joe ★★★
Melodrama 1949 · US · BW · 88mins

Humphrey Bogart is running a bar in an exotic location and trying to win back his ex-wife Florence Marly, who's gone off and married dull Alexander Knox. It's as uninvolving as it sounds, and dates from that awkward period in Bogart's career between his public recantation that he had no communist tendencies, and his public and industry return to favour with *The African Queen*. The main weakness is the casting of Marly, a totally uncharismatic Franco-Czech actress and the authentic Tokyo backdrops only serve to underline the phoniness of the venture, but Bogey plays everything for real, and is, as ever, compulsively watchable.

Humphrey Bogart *Joe Barrett* • Alexander Knox *Mark Landis* • Florence Marly *Trina* • Sessue Hayakawa *Baron Kimura* • Jerome Courtland *Danny* • Gordon Jones *Idaho* • Teru Shimada *Ito* ■ *Dir* Stuart Heisler • *Scr* Cyril Hume, Bertram Millhauser, Walter Doniger, from a story by Steve Fisher

Tokyo Olympiad ★★★★
Documentary 1965 · Jap · Colour · 154mins

The Tokyo Games of 1964 were preserved as a tribute to human athleticism and endurance in this lyrical documentary. Employing 164 camera units, many of which were equipped with especially-devised telephoto and night-vision lenses, Kon Ichikawa was only interested in winners and losers, if they exemplified the spirit of competition. Consequently, he focused on the last-minute preparations of sprinters, the watering techniques of marathon runners and the progress of the Olympic torch.

Dir Kon Ichikawa • *Scr* Kon Ichikawa, Natto Wada, Yoshio Shiraska, Shuntaro Tanikawa

Tokyo Pop ★★★ 18
Comedy drama 1988 · US · Colour · 98mins

Engaging teen romance that takes some very gentle pot-shots at the differences between East and West. Carrie Hamilton (daughter of actress Carol Burnett), is the impulsive budding singer who swaps New York for Tokyo and finds romance with band leader Yutaka Tadokoro. Fran Rubel Kuzui breathes fresh life into the clichéd story line and directs the proceedings with style, while the two leads turn in winning performances.

Carrie Hamilton *Wendy Reed* • Yutaka Tadokoro *Hiro Yamaguchi* • Taiji Tonoyama *Grandfather* • Tetsuro Tanba *Dota* • Masami Harukawa *Mother* • Toki Shiozawa *Mama-san* • Hiroshi Mikami *Seki* ■ *Dir* Fran Rubel Kuzui • *Scr* Fran Rubel Kuzui, Lynn Grossman, from a story by Fran Rubel Kuzui

Tokyo Story ★★★★★ U
Drama 1953 · Jap · BW · 129mins

A moving story, simply and beautifully told. Yasujiro Ozu was a master film-maker, who specialised in the kind of middle-class family melodrama known in Japanese as *shomin-geki* and this one of his finest achievements. Chishu Ryu and Chieko Higashiyama give performances of great dignity as the disappointed parents who are rejected by their thankless children. Setsuko

Hara, playing the widow of their favourite son, is the epitome of gentleness as the only relative to show them any kindness. Ryu and Hara were regular members of Ozu's acting troupe, and Hara retired from films when the director died in 1963. In Japanese with English subtitles. ▭

Chishu Ryu *Shukishi Hirayama* • Chieko Higashiyama *Tomi Hirayama* • Setsuko Hara *Noriko* • So Yamamura *Koichi* • Haruko Sugimura *Shige Kaneko* ■ *Dir* Yasujiro Ozu • *Scr* Kogo Noda, Yasujiro Ozu

Tol'able David ★★★★
Silent melodrama 1921 · US · BW · 118mins

One of the best of Henry King's simple, nostalgic evocations of rural and small town America, the film gave 26-year-old Richard Barthelmess, his finest role. He plays a gentle mailman living happily in Greenstream Valley until his idyll is disturbed by a family of fugitives from justice. He defends the community, becomes a hero and wins the girl. Beautifully shot on location in the Virginia mountains.

Richard Barthelmess *David Kinemon* • Gladys Hulette *Esther Hatburn* • Walter P Lewis *Iscah Hatburn* • Ernest Torrence *Luke Hatburn* • Ralph Yearsley *Luke's brother* • Forrest Robinson *Grandpa Hatburn* ■ *Dir* Henry King • *Scr* Edmund Goulding, Henry King, from the short story by Joseph Hergesheimer • *Cinematographer* Henry Cronjager

Tol'able David ★★
Melodrama 1930 · US · BW · 65mins

What worked through the inspired casting and eloquent direction of the 1921 silent masterpiece, fails to make a similar impression in this fairly close talkie re-make. Adding spoken dialogue to the dramatic story of feuding families in rural America, only makes it seem more old-fashioned and obvious. New discovery Richard Cromwell has the earnestness, but not the expressive qualities of Richard Barthelmess as he takes over the role of the boy who is branded a coward, but proves himself a hero in the end. Noah Beery is no match in villainy for Ernest Torrence.

Richard Cromwell *David Kinemon* • Noah Beery Sr [Noah Beery] *Luke* • Joan Peers *Esther Hatburn* • Henry B Walthall *Amos Hatburn* • George Duryea [Richard Powers] *Tom Keene* • Alan Kinemon *Edmund Breese* • Barbara Bedford *Rose Kinemon* • Helen Ware *Mrs Kinemon* ■ *Dir* John Blystone [John G Blystone] • *Scr* Benjamin Glazer, from a story by Joseph Hergesheimer

Tollbooth ★★★★
Comedy drama 1994 · US · Colour · 108mins

A bona-fide ''sleeper'' of a movie, which all but disappeared after making quite a splash at Cannes 1994. In this dark, comic fable of Florida roadside life, Fairuza Balk is Doris, who has been waiting 20 years for her father, a cab driver, to return home. Her mother, Louise Fletcher, also awaits his return, though it transpires he was quite an unsavoury character. Balk's boyfriend, Lenny Von Dohlen, is a tollbooth attendant who takes snapshots of every cab to pass through the booth, determined to locate her father. The story, however, is secondary to the quirky style of the piece and director Salome Breziner, taking her cue from

David Lynch, serves up a sizzling slice of dysfunctional life.

Fairuza Balk *Doris* • Lenny Von Dohlen *Jack* • Will Patton *Dash* • Louise Fletcher *Lillian* • Seymour Cassel *Larry/Leon* • James Wilder *Vic* • William Katt *Waggy* • Roberta Hanley *Twyla* ■ *Dir/Scr* Salome Breziner

Tom and Huck ★★★ PG

Adventure 1995 · US · Colour · 88mins

Stephen Sommers clearly has an affinity for Mark Twain. Not only did write and direct *The Adventures of Huck Finn*, but he also co-scripted this retelling of the story of the Missouri scamps who witness a graveyard killing and save the wrongfully accused Muff Potter by ensnaring the murderous Injun Joe. Fresh from his success in *The Client*, Brad Renfro is a suitably mischievous Huck, but it's Jonathan Taylor Thomas who makes the better impression as the more responsible Tom Sawyer. Disney take typical care with the trappings, but Norman Taurog's 1938 version remains the best one to date.

Jonathan Taylor Thomas *Tom Sawyer* • Brad Renfro *Huck Finn* • Eric Schweig *Injun Joe* • Charles Rocket *Judge Thatcher* • Amy Wright *Aunt Polly* • Micheal McShane *Muff Potter* • Marian Seldes *Widow Douglas* • Rachael Leigh Cook *Becky Thatcher* ■ *Dir* Peter Hewitt • *Scr* Stephen Sommers, David Loughery, from the novel by Mark Twain

Tom and Jerry: the Movie ★★ U

Animation 1992 · US · Colour · 80mins

Having starred in 161 cartoons, won numerous Oscars and danced with Gene Kelly and Esther Williams, surely Tom and Jerry deserved more respect than this. Director Phil Roman and writer Dennis Marks should have Spike the bulldog set upon them for making the now-talking duo become friends in adversity. The whole point of those marvellous shorts was the comic mayhem, not the tacky bonhomie. Children who are not familiar with the original cartoons may find some enjoyment here – f they can get past the ghastly songs.

Richard Kind *Tom* • Dana Hill *Jerry* • Anndi Lynn McAfee *Robyn Starling* • Charlotte Rae *Aunt Figg* • Tony Jay *Lickboot* • Henry Gibson *Dr Applecheek* ■ *Dir* Phil Roman • *Scr* Dennis Marks, from characters created by William Hanna, Joseph Barbera

Tom & Viv ★★★ 15

Biographical drama
1994 · US/UK · Colour · 119mins

Willem Dafoe stars as Tom, otherwise known as the poet TS Eliot, and Miranda Richardson plays Viv, the society girl who marries him and ends up in a lunatic asylum. While she lets rip with a suitable display of madness, Dafoe behaves quietly and poetically, before locking her up and getting out his pen. It often looks and sounds like a play, which it was. Problem is, you have to believe that the characters are who they say they are. If not, who cares? Contains swearing.

Miranda Richardson *Vivienne Haigh-Wood* • Willem Dafoe *TS "Tom" Eliot* • Tim Dutton *Maurice Haigh-wood* • Nickolas Grace *Bertrand Russell* • Clare Holman *Louise Purdon* • Rosemary Harris *Rose Haigh-wood* • Philip Locke *Charles Haigh-wood* • Joanna McCallum *Virginia Woolfe* ■ *Dir* Brian Gilbert • *Scr* Michael Hastings, Adrian Hodges, from the play by Michael Hastings

Tom Brown's Schooldays ★★ U

Drama 1940 · US · BW · 81mins

Rugby School relocates to the Bowery for this RKO adaptation of Thomas Hughes's novel. This is more about taming street urchins than reforming the iniquities of 19th-century public schooling, a fact confirmed by the presence of Dead End Kid Billy Halop as Flashman. Oozing with liberal sentimentality, the script emphasises the saintly deeds of Cedric Hardwicke's Dr Arnold, rather than the suffering of our hero. Of the boys, Freddie Bartholomew is less Fauntleroyish than usual as East, while Jimmy Lydon is clearly out of his depth as Tom. The Robert Newton remake is infinitely superior.

Cedric Hardwicke *Dr Thomas Arnold* • Freddie Bartholomew *East* • Jimmy Lydon [James Lydon] *Tom Brown* • Josephine Hutchinson *Mrs Arnold* • Billy Halop *Flashman* ■ *Dir* Robert Stevenson • *Scr* Walter Ferris, Frank Cavett, Gene Towne, Graham Baker, Robert Stevenson, from the novel by Thomas Hughes

Tom Brown's Schooldays ★★★ U

Drama 1951 · UK · BW · 94mins

Shot on location at Rugby School, this is a reverential, if rather lacklustre, rendition of Thomas Hughes's famous portrait of public school life. Having just chewed the scenery as Long John Silver in *Treasure Island*, Robert Newton gives a performance of almost saintly sincerity as the headmaster intent on ridding his school of class prejudice and bullying. John Howard Davies (who had suffered at the hands of Newton in David Lean's *Oliver Twist*) does a nice line in smiling through the tears as Tom Brown, but the film belongs squarely to John Forrest, who, as Flashman, is the epitome of vicious snobbery.

John Howard Davies *Tom Brown* • Robert Newton *Doctor Arnold* • Diana Wynyard *Mrs Arnold* • Hermione Baddeley *Sally Harrowell* • Kathleen Byron *Mrs Brown* • James Hayter *Old Thomas* • John Charlesworth *East* • John Forrest *Flashman* • Michael Hordern *Wilkes* • Max Bygraves *Coach guard* ■ *Dir* Gordon Parry • *Scr* Noel Langley, from the novel by Thomas Hughes

Tom, Dick and Harry ★★★★ U

Comedy 1941 · US · BW · 82mins

Here, Ginger Rogers is choosing between the three characters of the title, but her character's rather mercenary nature makes her ultimately hard to like, so we don't really care who she ends up with, or whether she marries for love or money or both. In fact, the bloke we end up rooting for is Phil Silvers's obnoxious ice-cream man, a clear precursor of Sergeant Bilko. With hindsight, perhaps writer Paul Jarrico, was trying to make some pertinent points about capitalism (he was later blacklisted), but director Garson Kanin just keeps the pace fast and the laughter flowing.

Ginger Rogers *Janie* • George Murphy *Tom* • Alan Marshal *Dick Hamilton* • Burgess Meredith *Harry* • Joe Cunningham *Pop* • Jane Seymour (2) *Ma* • Leonore Lonergan *Babs* • Vicki Lester *Paula* • Phil Silvers *Ice Cream Man* ■ *Dir* Garson Kanin • *Scr* Paul Jarrico

Tom Horn ★★★ 15

Western 1980 · US · Colour · 93mins

When Steve McQueen knew that his cancer was terminal, he swiftly made two features (the other was *The Hunter*) after a long period of chosen inactivity. This western is a good deal better than it deserves to be, given that McQueen fell out with the credited, relatively inexperienced director William Wiard (whose previous work included a number of episodes of *The Rockford Files* TV series), and the shoot was ramshackle, with pages of the script discarded daily. Nevertheless, this is extremely well photographed (by John Alonzo), with stunning landscapes, and McQueen captures the grim, realistic mood perfectly. Contains swearing.

Steve McQueen *Tom Horn* • Linda Evans *Glendolene Kimmel* • Richard Farnsworth *John Coble* • Billy Green Bush *Joe Belle* • Slim Pickens *Sam Creedmore* ■ *Dir* William Wiard • *Scr* Thomas McGuane, Bud Shrake

Tom Jones ★★★★ PG

Period comedy adventure
1963 · UK · Colour · 116mins

This massively popular period romp carted off four Oscars, including best picture and best direction. It was always arch, overlong and uncertain of tone, but nevertheless very funny and extraordinarily bawdy, especially in the notorious eating scene between Albert Finney (as Tom) and Joyce Redman. Technically, the film was massively influential and the desaturated colour, speeded-up action and lewd narration characterised the sixties' "Swinging England" cinema, and attracted all of the Hollywood majors to come and make movies here.

Albert Finney *Tom Jones* • Susannah York *Sophie Western* • Hugh Griffith *Squire Western* • Edith Evans *Miss Western* • Diane Cilento *Molly Seagrim* • George Devine *Squire Allworthy* • David Warner *Blifil* • Lynn Redgrave *Susan* ■ *Dir* Tony Richardson • *Scr* John Osborne, from the novel by Henry Fielding

Tom Sawyer ★★★

Adventure 1930 · US · BW · 85mins

The first of several sound versions of Mark Twain's novel – it was filmed as a silent in 1917 with Mary Pickford's brother, Jack, in the title role. In this version, Jackie Coogan plays Tom and at the age of only sixteen it marked his screen comeback, for he had not made a film for three years. Huck Finn is played by Junior Durkin and both lads starred in the sequel, *Huckleberry Finn*, the following year. Off the set they were firm friends, but tragedy struck in 1935 when Durkin was killed in a car crash and Coogan was the only survivor.

Jackie Coogan *Tom Sawyer* • Junior Durkin *Huckleberry Finn* • Mitzi Green *Becky Thatcher* • Lucien Littlefield *Teacher* • Tully Marshall *Muff Potter* • Clara Blandick *Aunt Polly* • Mary Jane Irving *Mary* • Ethel Wales *Mrs Harper* • Jane Darwell *Widow Douglass* ■ *Dir* John Cromwell • *Scr* Sam Mintz, Grover Jones, William Slavens McNutt, from the novel *The Adventues of Tom Sawyer* by Mark Twain

Tom Sawyer ★★★★ U

Musical period adventure
1973 · US · Colour · 102 mins

Co-financed by *Reader's Digest*, this is a simply marvellous children's version of Mark Twain's oft-filmed classic about two orphaned chillun – Tom and his pal, Huckleberry Finn – and life on the Mississippi riverbanks. All the famous scenes – like Tom's painting of the picket fence, the nocturnal body-snatching, the gluttonous "Widder" Douglas and her cat and the courtroom drama are filmed just as they are described in the book. There are some dispensable songs, but what counts is the beautifully evocative photography, two nicely modulated juvenile performances and Warren Oates enjoying himself as the local drunkard, Muff Potter.

Johnny Whitaker *Tom Sawyer* • Celeste Holm *Aunt Polly* • Warren Oates *Muff Potter* • Jeff East *Huckleberry Finn* • Jodie Foster *Becky Thatcher* • Kunu Hank *Injun Joe* • Lucille Benson *Widder Douglas* • Henry Jones *Mr Dobbins* ■ *Dir* Don Taylor • *Scr* Robert B Sherman, Richard M Sherman, from the novel *The Adventures of Tom Sawyer* by Mark Twain • *Cinematographer* Frank Stanley

tom thumb ★★★ U

Fantasy musical
1958 · US/UK · Colour · 95mins

The endearing, and enduring, MGM musical fantasy version of the Brothers Grimm fairy tale, made by Noveltoon puppet king and special effects wizard George Pal, and partly shot at MGM's British studios. Technically this is a treat, with wonderfully acrobatic dancer Russ Tamblyn – already familiar from 1954's *Seven Brides for Seven Brothers* – perfectly cast as the minuscule hero who brings joy to his elderly parents (Bernard Miles and Jessie Matthews). The production sequences *The Yawning Song* and the title number, where the toys come to life, are splendid entertainment for children of all ages, and Peter Sellers and Terry-Thomas make a very hissable pair of pantomime villains. Only Alan Young seems out of place, uncomfortable in fairyland. The effects won an Oscar.

Russ Tamblyn *Tom Thumb* • Alan Young *Woody the Piper* • Terry-Thomas *Ivan* • Peter Sellers *Tony* • Jessie Matthews *Anna* • June Thorburn *Forest Queen* • Bernard Miles *Jonathan* • Ian Wallace *Cobbler* • Peter Butterworth *Kapellmeister* ■ *Dir* George Pal • *Scr* Ladislas Foder, from the story by the Brothers Grimm

The Tomb of Ligeia ★★★★

Horror 1964 · UK · Colour · 81mins

Stunningly photographed by Arthur Grant at an ancient Norfolk abbey, the last in Roger Corman's celebrated Edgar Allan Poe cycle is unquestionably one of the best. Set in England in the 1820s, the film departs somewhat from Poe's original tale, but there's a distinct chill in the air as Vincent Price believes his new bride has been possessed by the evil spirit of his late first wife (both played by Elizabeth Shepherd). With more than a nod in

the direction of Hitchcock's *Vertigo* (both in terms of theme and denouement), this stylish picture also marked Corman's temporary retirement as a horror director until *Frankenstein Unbound* in 1990.

Vincent Price *Verden Fell* • Elizabeth Shepherd *Lady Ligeia Fell/Lady Rowena Trevanion* • John Westbrook *Christopher Gough* • Oliver Johnston *Kenrick* • Derek Francis *Lord Trevanion* • Richard Vernon *Dr Vivian* ■ *Dir* Roger Corman • *Scr* Robert Towne, from the story *Ligeia* by Edgar Allan Poe

Tomboy ★ 15

Drama   1985 · US · Colour · 90mins

A dire *Flashdance*-style drama without the hit soundtrack, *Tomboy* is the tale of a female garage mechanic who finds her feminine side when she falls in love, but displays her macho tendencies when she decides to compete in the Daytona 500 in a car of her own design. When she's not revving up the engine, she's revving up her boyfriend, while Eric Douglas (son of Kirk, brother of Michael), as the villain of the piece, proves he has inherited none of his family's talent for acting. A movie designed to fulfil every teenage boy's fantasy: if a scene doesn't have a topless girl in it, rest assured it will have a cool car. Contains swearing and nudity.

Betsy Russell *Tommy Boyd* • Jerry Dinome *Randy Starr* • Kristi Somers *Seville Ritz* • Richard Erdman *Chester* • Ben Douglas *Ernie Leeds Jr* ■ *Dir* Herb Freed • *Scr* Ben Zelig, from a idea by Mark Tenser

Tomboy and the Champ ★★ U

Comedy drama   1961 · US · Colour · 76mins

Expect all meat-eating youngsters to go off their burgers for a while after seeing this touching kidpic about a lonely child and her pet cow, especially after hearing such heart-tugging ditties as *Who Says Animals Don't Cry*. Candy Moore turns in a willing performance as the 13-year-old Texan girl who befriends a calf while recovering from polio on Uncle's (Ben Johnson) farm. However, there are also a few hard facts of country life to be learned after their victory at the Chicago International Exposition attracts the wrong kind of attention. Perhaps unsurprisingly, Francis D Lyon directs with shameless sentimentality.

Candy Moore *Tommy Jo* • Ben Johnson *Uncle Jim* • Jesse White *Windy Skiles* • Jess Kirkpatrick *Model T Parson* • Christine Smith *Aunt Sarah* • Paul Bernath *Jaspar Stockton* • Norman Sherry *Fowler Stockton* ■ *Dir* Francis D Lyon • *Scr* Virginia M Cooke, from a story by Tommy Reynolds, William Lightfoot

Tombstone ★★★★ 15

Western
1993 · US · Colour and BW · 124mins

Right from the dazzling opening of Robert Mitchum narrating over silent, black-and-white western footage accompanied by Bruce Broughton's expectant score, before the screen explodes into colour, this take on the Wyatt Earp legend never shifts out of top gear. This is very much a traditional western (well, post-spaghetti and post-Peckinpah) and far preferable to the rather self-important and

overlong Kevin Costner version, *Wyatt Earp*, released later the same year. Kurt Russell makes a satisfyingly equivocal hero, while Val Kilmer has a field day in the showier role as the consumptive Doc Holliday. Cameo appearances by Charlton Heston and Harry Carey Jr add to the general feeling of a saddleworn genre being paid the most viscerally thrilling and generous of tributes. The film was sharply scripted by Kevin Jarre, who was abruptly sacked as director and replaced by George Pan Cosmatos, a man of no reputation who suddenly came up smelling of roses. Contains swearing and violence. *DVD*

Kurt Russell *Wyatt Earp* • Val Kilmer *Doc Holliday* • Sam Elliott *Virgil Earp* • Bill Paxton *Morgan Earp* • Powers Boothe *Curly Bill Brocius* • Michael Biehn *Johnny Ringo* • Charlton Heston *Henry Hooker* • Jason Priestley *Deputy Sheriff Billy Breckenridge* • Robert Mitchum *Narrator* ■ *Dir* George Pan Cosmatos • *Scr* Kevin Jarre

Tommy ★★★★ 15

Musical   1975 · UK · Colour · 106mins

The Who's rock opera, about "a deaf, dumb and blind kid" who becomes an exploited "pinball wizard", gets the inimitable Ken Russell treatment, which is no more than it deserves. For, while eye-popping excess – what's done to Ann-Margret is unforgivable – keeps us watching, the story is as absurd as the grotesque nature of its telling. Stridency, both vocal and visual, is all, and Roger Daltrey's Tommy is flattened by the weight of celebrity (Eric Clapton, Keith Moon, Jack Nicholson and Tina Turner). Elton John has the best of it, thumping away on a piano as though trying to prove something, rather like Ken Russell himself. Worth watching, though, just for its reputation as a must-see for a generation.

Roger Daltrey *Tommy Walker* • Oliver Reed *Frank Hobbs* • Ann-Margret *Nora Walker Hobbs* • Elton John *Pinball Wizard* • Eric Clapton *Preacher* • Keith Moon *Uncle Ernie* • Jack Nicholson *Specialist* • Robert Powell *Group Captain Walker* • Paul Nicholas *Cousin Kevin* • Tina Turner *Acid Queen* ■ *Dir* Ken Russell • *Scr* Ken Russell, from the rock opera by Pete Townshend and The Who • *Cinematographer* Dick Bush, Ronnie Taylor

Tommy Boy ★★★ 12

Comedy   1995 · US · Colour · 93mins

Chris Farley's tragic career closely mirrored that of John Belushi's: fame on *Saturday Night Live*, an aversion to healthy pursuits and a young death at the age of 33. But he never had the *Blues Brothers* or *Animal House*-style success of his more famous contemporary, and most of his films disappeared quickly from view. This is about the best of the bunch: a big, dumb comedy about Farley's attempts to save the family business from gold-digger Bo Derek. His *Saturday Night Live* partner David Spade is an ideal foil, there's a helping hand from Belushi's old chum Dan Aykroyd and Rob Lowe again sends himself up (à la *Wayne's World*). Subtle it ain't, but there are enough gross moments to raise a few laughs.

Chris Farley *Tommy* • David Spade *Richard* • Brian Dennehy *Big Tom* • Bo Derek *Beverly* •

Dan Aykroyd *Zalinsky* • Julie Warner *Michelle* • Rob Lowe *Paul* ■ *Dir* Peter Segal • *Scr* Bonnie Turner, Terry Turner, Fred Wolf

The Tommy Steele Story ★★ U

Musical biography
1957 · UK · Colour · 77mins

Who else would have been able to carry the life story (such as it was after 21 years) of Britain's first rock'n'roll star, Tommy Steele, but the Bermondsey boy himself? Following young Tommy Hicks from his humble beginnings, through his days at sea to the contract with Decca and that breakthrough single *Rock with the Caveman*, this is an unremarkable meteoric rise story, not made any easier to swallow by Steele's swaggering performance. A must for fans nearly 40 years ago, but it hasn't worn well.

Tommy Steele *Tommy Steele* • Patrick Westwood *Brushes* • Hilda Fenemore *Tommy's mother* • Charles Lamb *Tommy's father* • Peter Lewiston *John Kennedy* ■ *Dir* Gerard Bryant • *Scr* Norman Hudis

Tommy the Toreador ★★★ U

Musical comedy   1959 · UK · Colour · 83mins

Perky pop star Tommy Steele, a former seaman himself, plays the part of a sailor in this lively and likeable musical comedy. The film concerns Steele's adventures after he saves the life of a bullfighter while on leave in Spain. Comic consequences include Tommy having to take the toreador's place and confronting a ferocious bull in the ring. The amusing events (concocted by five different writers) are interspersed with a nice variety of songs, including the novelty hit *Little White Bull*. Ill-fated Janet Munro (she died at the age of 38) makes a pert heroine.

Tommy Steele *Tommy* • Janet Munro *Amanda* • Sidney James *Cadena* • Bernard Cribbins *Paco* • Kenneth Williams *Vice Consul* • Eric Sykes *Martin* • Warren Mitchell *Waiter* • Charles Gray *Gomez* ■ *Dir* John Paddy Carstairs • *Scr* Nicholas Phipps, Sid Colin, Talbot Rothwell, from a story by George H Brown, Patrick Kirwan

Tommy Tricker and the Stamp Traveller ★ U

Fantasy   1988 · Can · Colour · 101mins

Sponsored not only by Canada Post, but also by a major Canadian snack food producer, this children's film has more than its share of product plugs. After classmate Tommy Tricker swindles him into trading his father's rare stamp, a boy sets off on a magical journey halfway around the world to find a replacement using a magic spell that enables him to travel on stamps. More than half of this excruciatingly slow movie goes by before the journey actually starts, and the on-location shooting in China and Australia is remarkably uninspired. Even for such a young cast, the acting is remarkably poor, and the film-makers seem to have no idea how children act or speak in real life.

Lucas Evans *Ralph* • Anthony Rogers *Tommy* • Jill Stanley *Nancy* • Andrew Whitehead *Albert* ■ *Dir* Michael Rubbo • *Scr* Michael Rubbo

Tomorrow ★★★★

Drama   1972 · US · BW · 103mins

Has Robert Duvall ever made a truly bad film? If so, this isn't it. Instead, it's Duvall firing on all cylinders in a fine adaptation of a lesser-known William Faulkner story. He plays a handyman who falls for, a pregnant woman who mysteriously turns up at his place of work. The girl is played equally brilliantly by Olga Bellin, who seems to have since vanished without trace. Like her, the film is rarely seen, but worth seeking out.

Robert Duvall *Jackson Fentry* • Olga Bellin *Sarah Eubanks* • Sudie Bond *Mrs Hulie* • Richard McConnell *Isham Russell* • Peter Masterson *Lawyer* • William Hawley *Papa Fentry* ■ *Dir* Joseph Anthony • *Scr* Horton Foote, from a story by William Faulkner

Tomorrow at Ten ★★★

Crime drama   1962 · UK · BW · 80mins

A modest little thriller that managed to secure a grade A cast, but was still released as a B feature. Rank regular John Gregson is the cop sorting out a nasty child kidnapping case involving a psychotic bomber. The bad guy is *Jaws*'s Robert Shaw (before he became an international star), while theatre actor Alec (father of Martin) Clunes plays the father of the kidnap victim. Veteran British director Lance Comfort expertly translates the workmanlike script, and the support cast contains many familiar faces, including: William Hartnell (the first Doctor Who); Alan Wheatley, who played the Sheriff in *The Adventures of Robin Hood* in the fifties; and Kenneth Cope Hopkirk in the *Randall and Hopkirk (Deceased)* TV series.

John Gregson *Inspector Parnell* • Robert Shaw *Marlow* • Alec Clunes *Anthony Chester* • Alan Wheatley *Bewley* • Kenneth Cope *Sergeant Grey* • Ernest Clark *Doctor Towers* • Piers Bishop *Jonathan* • Helen Perry *Robbie* • William Hartnell *Freddy* ■ *Dir* Lance Comfort • *Scr* Peter Millar, James Kelly

Tomorrow Is Forever ★★

Drama   1945 · US · BW · 103mins

This hackneyed melodrama, directed at a deadly tempo by Irving Pichel, stars Claudette Colbert as a Baltimore chemist who, after her husband Orson Welles is reported killed in the First World War, is taken in by her boss George Brent, whom she eventually marries. Many years later, when Brent imports a limping, heavily-bearded scientist from Austria to work for him, guess who he turns out to be? The most interesting aspect of this below average "woman's picture" is the early appearance of six-year-old Natalie Wood as Colbert's daughter.

Claudette Colbert *Elizabeth MacDonald Hamilton* • Orson Welles *John MacDonald/ Erich Kessler* • George Brent *Larry Hamilton* • Lucile Watson *Aunt Jessie Hamilton* • Richard Long *John Andrew "Drew" Hamilton* • Natalie Wood *Margaret* ■ *Dir* Irving Pichel • *Scr* Lenore Coffee, from a novel by Gwen Bristow

The Tomorrow Man ★★

Science-fiction drama
1995 · US · Colour · 85mins

A shape-shifting android is sent from the virtually annihilated 26th century to change the present in order to protect

the future, in a poor man's *Terminator 2* crossed with *Quantum Leap*. This feature-length pilot for a proposed TV series is clichéd sci-fi stuff centred around a surprisingly appealing performance from Julian Sands as Ken, the super cyborg masquerading as a fashion model. Computer expert Giancarlo Esposito offers strong support as his comic foil, friend and mentor and, despite its predictability and feel-good *Star Trek* slant, the film's sufficiently upbeat to pass the time as light-hearted entertainment.

Julian Sands *Kenn* • Giancarlo Esposito *Jonathan Driscoll* • Craig Wasson *Doctor Galloway* ■ *Dir* Bill D'Elia • *Scr* Alan Spencer

Tomorrow Never Comes ★★★ 15

Crime drama
1977 · Can/UK · Colour · 86mins

A violent thriller, in which Stephen McHattie discovers his former girlfriend (Susan George) is seeing another man and takes her hostage. Oliver Reed is the police lieutenant given the job of breaking the siege. Peter Collinson directed with a cute eye for the unsavoury detail, while Pinewood writing stalwarts Sydney Banks, David Pursall and Jack Seddon plumb the depths of seediness rather than character. But, at least, it gives us a chance to witness the hefty presence of Raymond Burr away from his judicial guise as Perry Mason. *DVD*

Oliver Reed *Jim Wilson* • Susan George *Janie* • Raymond Burr *Burke* • John Ireland *Captain* • Stephen Mchattie *Frank* • Donald Pleasence *Dr Todd* • Paul Koslo *Willy* • John Osborne *Lyne* ■ *Dir* Peter Collinson • *Scr* David Pursall, Jack Seddon, Sydney Banks

Tomorrow Never Dies ★★★★ 12

Spy adventure
1997 · US/UK · Colour · 114mins

For the first hour or so, this 18th Bond movie is up there with the best of them: it has terrific pace, Pierce Brosnan has romantic and rough-house appeal, Teri Hatcher is a match for him, and the post-Cold War story has grip and even plausibility. Sadly, the second half doesn't quite sustain the momentum: the story moves from Europe to Asia (back to the locations of *The Man with the Golden Gun*) and Jonathan Pryce's media mogul makes a pathetically unthreatening villain whose motto is "There's no news like bad news". Flaws aside, this is still the best Bond movie since the days of Mr Connery. Contains violence, swearing and sex. *DVD*

Pierce Brosnan *James Bond* • Jonathan Pryce *Elliot Carver* • Michelle Yeoh *Wai Lin* • Teri Hatcher *Paris Carver* • Judi Dench *"M"* • Desmond Llewelyn *"Q"* • Samantha Bond *Miss Moneypenny* • Gotz Otto *Stamper* • Joe Don Baker *Jack Wade* • Ricky Jay *Henry Gupta* • Geoffrey Palmer *Admiral Roebuck* • Colin Salmon *Robinson – Chief of Staff* ■ *Dir* Roger Spottiswoode • *Scr* Bruce Feirstein, from characters created by Ian Fleming

Tomorrow the World! ★★★

Drama
1944 · US · BW · 85mins

Based on a play by James Gow and Arnaud D'Usseau, this wartime drama eerily prefigures Maxwell Anderson's

The Bad Seed, in its portrayal of a nightmarish youngster on the loose in picket-fence America. Fresh from his stage success, 14-year-old Skippy Homeier reprises his role as the orphaned Hitler Youth member, sent to live with his liberal uncle (Frederic March) in the States. He soon begins spreading hatred and seeking recruits to his cause, until March is forced to adopt some strong-arm tactics of his own. The ending's pat and Liverpool-born director Leslie Fenton doesn't do enough to open out the source material, but the central idea still retains its power to disturb.

Fredric March *Mike Frame* • Betty Field *Leona Richards* • Agnes Moorehead *Jessie Frame* • Skippy Homeier [Skip Homeier] *Emil Bruckner* • Joan Carroll *Pat Frame* • Edit Angold *Frieda* • Rudy Wissler *Stan* • Boots Brown *Ray* ■ *Dir* Leslie Fenton • *Scr* Ring Lardner Jr, Leopold Atlas, from a play by James Gow, Arnaud D'Usseau

Tomorrow We Live ★★★ U

Spy melodrama
1942 · UK · BW · 87mins

In the darkest days of the Second World War, dashing John Clements gets mixed up with French freedom fighters, and two women: Greta Gynt, seemingly pro-Nazi, and waitress Judy Kelly, who actually is hustling for the occupying forces. *Casablanca* this isn't: it is, however, packed with action, and Clements is excellent in what today seems like a rather obvious piece of propaganda – unsurprising, really, since it was produced by British Aviation Films. Watch for a young Herbert Lom way down in the cast.

John Clements *Jean Batiste* • Godfrey Tearle *The Mayor* • Hugh Sinclair *Major Von Kleist* • Greta Gynt *Marie Duschen* • Judy Kelly *Germaine* • Yvonne Arnaud *Madame Labouche* • Karel Stepanek *Seitz* ■ *Dir* George King, George King • *Scr* Anatole de Grunwald, from a story by Dorothy Hope

Tom's Midnight Garden ★★

Fantasy adventure
1998 · UK · Colour · 107mins

Just who writer/director Willard Carroll hoped would enjoy this is a mystery. Clocking in at a hundred-plus minutes, it is unlikely to sustain the interests of children, while adults are unlikely see it as anything other than a twee fable. Singer Anthony Way stars as a teenager who, during a summer stay with his childless aunt and uncle, discovers that at midnight, the ugly area around the building turns into a magical garden inhabited by a lonely orphan from the previous century. Sadly the scenes between the children are unengaging, while the adults, including James Wilby and Greta Scacchi, add no lustre to a pretty, but overlong effort from a director who's no stranger to children's films.

Greta Scacchi *Aunt Gwen* • James Wilby *Uncle Alan Kitson* • Joan Plowright *Mrs Bartholomew* • Anthony Way *Tom* • David Bradley (1) *Abel* • Penelope Wilton *Aunt Melbourne* • Nigel Le Vaillant *Tom Long, as adult* • Liz Smith *Mrs Willows* • Florence Hoath *Hatty at 12* ■ *Dir* Willard Carroll • *Scr* Willard Carroll, from the novel by Philippa Pearce

Tongues Untied ★★★

Documentary
1989 · US · Colour · 55mins

"If in America, a black is the lowest of the low, what is a gay black?" asks one of the characters in Marlon T Riggs's personal, positive and impassioned plea for an end to homophobia and racism. Combining poetry, testimony, mime, rap, voiceovers and archival footage in a manner that's simultaneously abrasive, compassionate, inelegant and articulate, Riggs makes his case for increased tolerance and "brother to brother" unity with wit and autobiographical frankness. It's poetic, chaotic, controversial and a fitting tribute to a film-maker who died from Aids in 1994, aged 37.

Marlon T Riggs ■ *Dir* Marlon T Riggs • *Scr* Joseph Bream, Craig Harris, Essex Hemphill, Reginald Jackson, Steve Langley, Alan Miller, Donald Woods

Toni ★★★★

Romantic crime drama
1935 · Fr · BW · 90mins

Itself inspired by Marcel Pagnol's *Angèle*, Jean Renoir's fact-based tale of marital angst, was a key influence on neorealism, via the impact it made on one of his young assistants, Luchino Visconti. Shooting fluently and exclusively on location in the Midi, with a predominantly non-professional cast, Renoir succeeds in marrying character and environment in a way that not only emphasises their human nature and the authenticity of everyday existence, but also defuses the potentially melodramatic aspects of the plot – Italian quarry worker Charles Blavette takes the blame for his beloved's crime of passion. Disarmingly simple, simmeringly sensual and woefully undervalued. A French language film.

Charles Blavette *Antonio "Toni" Canova* • Celia Montalvan *Josepha* • Jenny Helia *Marie* • Edouard Delmont *Fernand* ■ *Dir* Jean Renoir • *Scr* Jean Renoir, Carl Einstein, Jacques Mortier [Jacques Levert]

Tonight and Every Night ★★★ U

Wartime romance
1945 · US · Colour · 88mins

This *London Can Take It*-style wartime romance was supposedly a tribute to Soho's Windmill theatre (here, called the Music Box), which claimed it never closed during the Blitz. Actually, it was more famous for its nude revues, although here the showgirls, including Rita Hayworth, keep well covered (in fact, it was the first time Hayworth worked with Jean Louis, her favourite dress designer). Hayworth falls for pilot Lee Bowman and Janet Blair for dancer Marc Platt; a weak actor but a good dancer (here he has a bizarre number in which he mimes to one of Hitler's speeches). The title number (by Jule Styne and Sammy Cahn) uses a trick of having the performers walking out of a film onto the stage.

Rita Hayworth *Rosalind "Roz" Bruce* • Lee Bowman *Paul Lundy* • Janet Blair *Judy Kane* • Marc Platt *Tommy Lawson* • Leslie Brooks *Angela* • Shelley Winters *Bubbles* ■ *Dir* Victor Saville • *Scr* Lesser Samuels, Abem Finkel, from the play *Heart of the City* by Lesley Storm

Tonight for Sure ★★★

Erotic comedy western
1961 · US · Colour · 69mins

Francis Ford Coppola's first movie – made while he was studying at UCLA – is a piece of audacity forgivable because of his youth, about Don Kenney, who spies on women, and Karl Schanzer, who imagines nude women everywhere. The Catholic principle rules. Not much evidence of Coppola's later talents, but interesting because of what is to come.

Don Kenney • Karl Schanzer • Virginia Gordon • Marli Renfro ■ *Dir/Scr* Francis Ford Coppola

Tonight We Sing ★★★ U

Musical biography
1953 · US · Colour · 109mins

Sol Hurok used his exceptional appreciation of musical talent to become the most famously dedicated, ambitious and successful of the American impresarios. What possessed 20th Century-Fox to cast the bloodless David Wayne as Hurok in this biopic, though, is something only the studio's late chiefs must know. The script, cobbled together from bits and pieces of Hurok's memoirs, is a similarly feeble affair, and Mitchell Leisen's direction is uncharacteristically leaden. Fortunately, however, the film remains a feast of opera and boasts a violin solo from Isaac Stern (as Eugene Ysaye) and the sight of Tamara Toumanova (as Anna Pavlova) dancing *The Dying Swan*.

David Wayne *Sol Hurok* • Ezio Pinza *Feodor Chaliapin* • Roberta Peters *Elsa Valdine* • Tamara Toumanova *Anna Pavlova* • Anne Bancroft *Emma Hurok* • Isaac Stern *Eugene Ysaye* ■ *Dir* Mitchell Leisen • *Scr* Harry Kurnitz, George Oppenheimer, from a book by Sol Hurok, Ruth Goode

Tonite Let's All Make Love in London ★★★

Documentary
1967 · UK · BW and Colour · 69mins

Director Peter Whitehead turns his camera on Swinging London – the era when Carnaby Street was the centre of the universe and even *Time* magazine featured it on the front cover. This documentary features some fascinating interviews with sixties trendsetters like Mick Jagger, Julie Christie, Michael Caine and David Hockney. No real conclusions are drawn, apart from Caine's prediction: "All this dolly-bird stuff won't matter a damn in ten years' time. It's on the way out already."

Dir/Scr Peter Whitehead

Tonka ★★★ U

Period adventure 1958 · US · Colour · 92mins

Also known as *A Horse Called Comanche*, this adventure set against the Sioux War arrived at a time when Hollywood was trying to make amends for its various injustices. Here Disney reverses a tendency towards negative portrayals of native American Indians, by casting Sal Mineo as a young Sioux tribesman who tames a wild, white horse he calls Tonka, only then for it to be taken away from him and sold to the cavalry, where it is renamed Comanche. After a series of attempts to win the horse back, the pair are reunited. Aimed at children, who should revel in it. 🖭

Sal Mineo *White Bull* • Philip Carey *Captain Miles Keogh* • Jerome Courtland *Lieutenant Henry Nowlan* • Rafael Campos *Strong Bear* • HM Wynant *Yellow Bull* • Joy Page *Prairie Flower* • Britt Lomond *General George Armstrong Custer* • Herbert Rudley *Captain Benteen* ■ *Dir* Lewis R Foster • *Scr* Lewis R Foster, Lillie Hayward, from the novel *Comanche* by David Appel

Tony Draws a Horse ★★

Comedy   1950 · UK · BW · 90mins

When eight-year-old Tony Fleming draws a sexually explicit horse, his parents are divided over the right way to deal with the situation. The resulting fall out sees psychiatrist Clare Fleming (Anne Crawford), leaving her doctor husband Howard (Cecil Parker) and returning to the bosom of her family. Once there she takes off to France with her sister's fiancé, kick-starting a chain of farcical events. Prolific comedy director John Paddy Carstairs turns in a workmanlike, but nevertheless likeable, adaptation of Lesley Storm's stage play.

Cecil Parker *Dr Howard Fleming* • Anne Crawford *Clare Fleming* • Derek Bond *Tim Shields* • Barbara Murray *Joan Parsons* • Mervyn Johns *Alfred Parsons* • Barbara Everest *Mrs Parsons* • Edward Rigby *Grandpa* ■ *Dir* John Paddy Carstairs • *Scr* Brock Williams, from the play by Lesley Storm

Tony Rome ★★★

Mystery thriller 1967 · US · Colour · 109mins

Frank Sinatra always wanted to be Bogart, and in this adaptation of Marvin Albert's novel *Miami Mayhem*, he successfully takes on his mantle of hard-boiled private eye à la Philip Marlowe or Sam Spade. This tough and nasty Miami-set thriller is a classy act, with searing dialogue, a fine Billy May score and topnotch support from the likes of Richard Conte and Gena Rowlands. Director Gordon Douglas manages to cleverly mask the fact that the plot is no great shakes, though it does bear comparison with *The Big Sleep*. Sinatra reprised his character here in *Lady in Cement*.

Frank Sinatra *Tony Rome* • Jill St John *Ann Archer* • Richard Conte *Lt Santini* • Gena Rowlands *Rita Kosterman* • Simon Oakland *Rudolph Kosterman* • Jeffrey Lynn *Adam Boyd* • Lloyd Bochner *Vic Rood* • Robert J Wilke *Ralph Turpin* • Rocky Graziano *Packy* ■ *Dir* Gordon Douglas • *Scr* Richard L Breen, from the novel *Miami Mayhem* by Marvin Albert

Too Bad She's Bad ★★

Comedy   1955 · It · BW · 103mins

Vittorio De Sica is a pickpocket who cajoles his beautiful daughter Sophia Loren, into acting as his assistant. Complications arise when Loren, acting as a honey trap for a couple of crooks out to rob an honest cabbie, finds her own feelings start to stir when the taxi driver, Marcello Mastroianni, falls for her. A modest romantic comedy at best, it's notable as the first-time pairing of Loren and Mastroianni, and as the film where Loren first showed a penchant for comedy. Italian dialogue dubbed into English.

Sophia Loren *Lina* • Vittorio De Sica *Stroppiani* • Marcello Mastroianni *Paolo* • Umberto Melnati *Man whose wallet is stolen* •

Margherita Bagni *His wife* ■ *Dir* Alessandro Blasetti • *Scr* Suso Cecchi D'Amico, Ennio Flaiano, Alessandro Continenza, from a story by Alberto Moravia

Too Good to Be True ★★15

Thriller   1988 · US · Colour · 95mins

Loni Anderson unsuccessfully attempts to ditch her dizzy blonde image with this lifeless updated version of the 1945 Gene Tierney melodrama *Leave Her to Heaven*. Anderson is the beauty who snares mournful widower Patrick Duffy and then reveals a psychopathic nature when anyone tries to get between her and her man. The main problem here is the two leads, who are just too bland for this sort of stuff, and it's left to the likes of James B Sikking and Julie Harris to try and inject some real feeling into an otherwise routine thriller. 🖭

Patrick Duffy *Richard Harland* • Loni Anderson *Ellen Berent* • Neil Patrick Harris *Danny* • Glynnis O'Connor *Ruth Berent* • Julie Harris *Margaret Berent* • James B Sikking *Russell Quinton* ■ *Dir* Christian I Nyby II • *Scr* Timothy Bradshaw

Too Hot to Handle ★★★★

Comedy adventure 1938 · US · BW · 105mins

A hugely enjoyable three-hander from Clark Gable, Myrna Loy and Walter Pidgeon, in which Gable and Pidgeon play devil-may-care newsreel photographers vying for the attentions of feisty aviatrix Ms Loy. Gable is in his element – charming, wry, raffish and risk-taking – and his spoof bombing raid into China is the film's *pièce de résistance*. Everything gels in this movie: the stars, the action scenes and a stylish, witty script ably stands the test of time.

Clark Gable *Chris Hunter* • Myrna Loy *Alma Harding* • Walter Pidgeon *Bill Dennis* • Walter Connolly *Gabby MacArthur* • Leo Carrillo *Joselito* • Virginia Weidler *Hulda Harding* • Henry Kolker *Pearly Todd* • Marjorie Main *Miss Wayne* ■ *Dir* Jack Conway • *Scr* Laurence Stallings, John Lee Mahin, from a story by Len Hammond

Too Hot to Handle ★★15

Comedy drama 1991 · US · Colour · 111mins

Originally released as *The Marrying Man*, this Kim Basinger/Alec Baldwin comedy is a clunker under any name. The rumours of on-set battles between the leads and the producers were far more interesting than the story itself, which follows the on-off love affair between nightclub singer/gangster's moll Basinger and millionaire playboy Baldwin in the forties. Unfortunately, neither lead is a deft hand at comedy although Basinger did a nice cameo turn later in *Wayne's World 2*, and the humour in the script is not that strong either – despite the fact that the writer is none other than Neil Simon. Disappointing, but worth a look for the two glamorous stars who have since become husband and wife. Contains violence and swearing. 🖭

Kim Basinger *Vicki Anderson* • Alec Baldwin *Charley Pearl* • Robert Loggia *Lew Horner* • Elisabeth Shue *Adele Horner* • Armand Assante *Bugsy Siegel* • Paul Reiser *Phil* • Fisher Stevens *Sammy* • Peter Dobson *Tony Madden* ■ *Dir* Jerry Rees • *Scr* Neil Simon

Too Late Blues ★★★

Musical drama   1962 · US · BW · 103mins

Director John Cassavetes, who had struck creative gold with the improvisational *Shadows*, tries to shoehorn his energy into a more conventional, plot-driven film. In this story about jazz pianist John ''Ghost'' Wakefield (Bobby Darin), notions about artistic commitment aren't fully explored. However, in the muso's brittle relationship with a neurotic aspiring singer (Stella Stevens) and his deteriorating relations with his band, the essential Cassavetes comes fully alive. The music, by the way (blasted out by the likes of Benny Carter and Red Mitchell), is a five-star treat.

Bobby Darin *John ''Ghost'' Wakefield* • Stella Stevens *Jess Polanski* • Cliff Carnell *Charlie* • Seymour Cassel *Red* • Bill Stafford *Shelly* • Richard Chambers *Pete* • Nick Dennis *Nick* ■ *Dir* John Cassavetes • *Scr* John Cassavetes, Richard Carr

Too Late the Hero ★★★15

Second World War drama
1970 · US · Colour · 133mins

An exciting and violent, but rather too long macho action tale from director Robert Aldrich. Early on he delivered the stark, lean *Attack!*, but middle-career spread began with the immensely successful (and long) *The Dirty Dozen*, and he never looked back. At over two hours, this tale about male bonding is typical Aldrich, as soldiers Michael Caine and Cliff Robertson are dispatched on a suicide mission in the Pacific arena during the Second World War. Contains violence. 🖭

Michael Caine *Private Tosh Hearne* • Cliff Robertson *Lieutenant Lawson* • Ian Bannen *Thornton* • Harry Andrews *Lt Col Thompson* • Denholm Elliott *Captain Hornsby* • Ronald Fraser *Campbell* • Lance Percival *Corporal Mclean* • Percy Herbert *Johnstone* • Henry Fonda *Captain Nolan* • Ken Takakura *Major Yamaguchi* ■ *Dir* Robert Aldrich • *Scr* Robert Aldrich, Lukas Heller, from the story by Robert Aldrich, Robert Sherman

Too Many Crooks ★★★U

Comedy   1958 · UK · BW · 81mins

The cast is a who's who of British comedy and the script is by Michael Pertwee, but this picture never lives up to its billing, largely owing to the cack-handed direction of Mario Zampi. This is all the more surprising bearing in mind the Italian exile had been responsible for such comedy classics as *Laughter in Paradise* and *The Naked Truth*. Terry-Thomas gives a priceless performance as the wheeler-dealer unconcerned whether he sees abducted wife Brenda de Banzie ever again, but George Cole, Sid James and the gang overdo the ''cor blimey'' criminality. 🖭

Terry-Thomas *Billy Gordon* • George Cole *Fingers* • Brenda de Banzie *Lucy* • Bernard Bresslaw *Snowdrop* • Sidney James *Sid* • Joe Melia *Whisper* • Vera Day *Charmaine* • Delphi Lawrence *Beryl, secretary* • John Le Mesurier *Magistrate* • Nicholas Parsons *Tommy* ■ *Dir* Mario Zampi • *Scr* Michael Pertwee, from the story by Jean Nery, Christiane Rochefort

Too Many Girls ★★★U

Musical comedy   1940 · US · BW · 84mins

A terrific version of the Broadway hit show, retaining many of the original cast and directed for the screen by the grand old man of Broadway himself, George Abbott. It's geared as a vehicle for Lucille Ball, who, incidentally, met future husband and business partner Desi Arnaz while on set. Also having fun with what's left of the Rodgers and Hart score are Frances Langford and Ann Miller, and the movie also marks the debuts of stars-to-be Van Johnson and Eddie Bracken. The songs aren't vintage, and today some of them may seem a little tasteless, but there's no denying the sheer verve of the piece.

Lucille Ball *Connie Casey* • Richard Carlson *Clint Kelly* • Ann Miller *Pepe* • Eddie Bracken *Jojo George* • Frances Langford *Eileen Eilers* • Desi Arnaz *Manuelito* • Van Johnson *Chorus boy* ■ *Dir* George Abbott • *Scr* John Twist, from the stage musical by George Marion Jr, Richard Rodgers, Lorenz Hart

Too Many Husbands ★★★

Comedy   1940 · US · BW · 81mins

Mistakenly believed to have drowned in a shipwreck, Fred MacMurray finds his way home to discover that his wife (Jean Arthur) is now remarried. The two men vie for the right to ''their'' wife, who encourages and relishes their attentions, until the matter of where she belongs must be decided in court. Slight but neat romantic comedy, tailor-made for its star trio and directed with his habitual flair for such material by Wesley Ruggles. Remade as a musical, *Three for the Show*, with Betty Grable in 1955, but the idea was used in reverse – one husband, two wives – in *My Favorite Wife* (Irene Dunne, Cary Grant in 1940) and *Move Over, Darling* (Doris Day, James Garner in 1963).

Jean Arthur *Vicky Lowndes* • Fred MacMurray *Bill Cardew* • Melvyn Douglas *Henry Lowndes* • Harry Davenport *George* • Dorothy Peterson *Gertrude Houlihan* • Melville Cooper *Peter* • Edgar Buchanan *McDermott* ■ *Dir* Wesley Ruggles • *Scr* Claude Binyon, from the play by W Somerset Maugham

Too Many Lovers ★★

Romantic comedy   1957 · Fr · Colour

Club singer Zizi Jeanmaire has high standards when it comes to men, so why has she saddled herself with so many losers? In addition to a rich slob, she has a punch-drunk boxer, an argumentative thief and a married man whose wife refuses to divorce him. Amidst all this mediocrity, a mystery man keeps sending her flowers. It's not hard to guess who has an account at the florists in this dim-witted romantic comedy. With the exception of Gert Fröbe as the wealthy wolf, the suitors are all bores and Jeanmaire is hardly a ball of fire herself. French dialogue dubbed into English.

Zizi Jeanmaire *Lulu* • Daniel Gelin *Alain* • Henri Vidal *Jo* • Gil Vidal *Max* • François Périer *Robert* • Marie Daems *Germaine* ■ *Dir* Henri Decoin • *Scr* Charles Spaak

Too Much ★U

Comedy   1987 · US · Colour · 85mins

A kiddie clone of the previous year's *Short Circuit* that lives up to its title in saccharine sweetness and nauseating cuteness. Lonely little Bridgette Andersen lives in Japan, where she is given a prototype robot to befriend. When the evil Professor Finkel and his stupid henchmen try and steal the experimental cyborg (looking suspiciously like R2D2 from *Star Wars*), the duo go on the run and have uninvolving misadventures. A banal fantasy that even children will find syrupy beyond redemption. ▣

Bridgette Andersen *Suzy* • Masato Fukazama *Too Much* • Hiroyuki Watanabe *Tetsuro* • Char Fontana *Professor Finkel* • Uganda *Bernie* ■ *Dir/Scr* Eric Rochat

Too Much Sun ★ 18

Comedy 1990 · US · Colour · 93mins

Robert Downey Sr directs Junior in a totally tasteless farce about a multimillionaire, whose offspring must compete to produce an heir and inherit his fortune. The hitch is that the brother and sister are gay – cue much tasteless humour. This is laugh-an-hour stuff despite the best efforts of a cast which, in addition to Ralph (*The Karate Kid*) Macchio and Hollywood veteran Howard Duff.

Robert Downey Jr *Reed Richmond* • Eric Idle *Sonny Rivers* • Andrea Martin *Bitsy Rivers* • Jim Haynie *Father Seamus Kelly* • Laura Ernst *Susan Connor* • Leo Rossi *George Bianco* • Ralph Macchio *Frank Della Rocca Jr* • Howard Duff *OM Rivers* ■ *Dir* Robert Downey • *Scr* Robert Downey, Laura Ernst, Al Schwartz

Too Much, Too Soon ★★

Biographical drama 1958 · US · BW · 101mins

The Barrymores were known as The Royal Family of Broadway, but the second generation did much to tarnish the reputation as this lacklustre biopic of Diana Barrymore reveals. Dorothy Malone is suitably downbeat as the daughter destroyed by the drinking of her famous father John, who is played with disturbing authenticity by Errol Flynn (who considered the "The Great Profile" among his key influences). Flynn makes the most of a disappointing script, but it was a sad farewell to Warners, the studio where he had once been the king of the swashbucklers.

Dorothy Malone *Diana Barrymore* • Errol Flynn *John Barrymore* • Efrem Zimbalist Jr *Vincent Bryant* • Ray Danton *John Howard* • Neva Patterson *Michael Strange* • Murray Hamilton *Charlie Snow* • Martin Milner *Lincoln Forrester* ■ *Dir* Art Napoleon • *Scr* Art Napoleon, Jo Napoleon, from the autobiography by Diana Barrymore, Gerold Frank

Too Outrageous! ★

Comedy drama 1987 · Can · Colour · 100mins

The very disappointing sequel to *Outrageous* (1977) picks up the story of female impersonator Robin Turner (played with camp aplomb once more by Craig Russell), now a smash on the New York drag queen circuit, who must decide between mainstream success or remaining true to his art. Where director Richard Benner's first movie was fresh, smart and funny, his follow-up is a hackneyed and boring affair with few laughs. And most of those come from Russell's ever brilliant impersonations of such obvious gay

icons as Barbra Streisand and Mae West.

Craig Russell *Robin Turner* • Hollis McLaren *Liza Connors* • David McIlwraith *Bob* • Ron White *Luke* • Lynne Cormack *Betty Treisman* • Michael J Reynolds *Lee Sturges* • Timothy Jenkins *Rothchild* ■ *Dir/Scr* Richard Benner

Too Scared to Scream ★★ 18

Psychological thriller 1982 · US · Colour · 94mins

The spectre of *Psycho* looms large over *Honeymoon Killers* actor-turned-director Tony LoBianco's first-time slasher thriller as New York cops Mike Connors and Anne Archer investigate murders in a high-rise apartment block. Prime suspect is doorman Ian McShane, a bitter ex-actor eager to recite Shakespeare at the drop of a knife, who lives with his invalid mother Maureen O'Sullivan. Obvious red herrings defy the slow-building suspense but the cast brings a much needed zing to events.

Mike Connors *Lieutenant Dinardo* • Anne Archer *Kate* • Leon Isaac Kennedy *Frank* • Ian McShane *Hardwick* • Ruth Ford *Irma* • John Heard *Lab technician* • Carrie Nye *Graziella* • Maureen O'Sullivan *Mother* ■ *Dir* Tony LoBianco • *Scr* Glenn Leopold, Neal Barbera

Too Soon to Love ★★★

Drama 1960 · US · BW · 89mins

The first film directed by Richard Rush – one of a group of independent film-makers who formed an American version of the *Nouvelle Vague* – this tale of two teenage sweethearts driven by uncomprehending parents into a saga of unwanted pregnancy, abortion, robbery and attempted suicide, is better than it sounds and as a social document of its time has been compared to *Rebel without a Cause*. Stars Jennifer West and Richard Evans had less than sparkling careers, but playing the hero's buddy (called "Buddy") was none other than Jack Nicholson.

Jennifer West *Cathy Taylor* • Richard Evans *Jim Mills* • Warren Parker *Mr Taylor* • Ralph Manza *Hughie Wineman* • Jack Nicholson *Buddy* • Jacqueline Schwab *Irene* • Billie Bird *Mrs Jefferson* ■ *Dir* Richard Rush • *Scr* Laszlo Gorog, Richard Rush

Too Young the Hero ★★ 15

Second World War adventure 1988 · US · Colour · 92mins

An unconvincing performance by former child star Ricky Schroder is the weak link in this otherwise intriguing TV movie. The subject matter is fascinating – a young teen manages to enlist in the US Navy during the Second World War – and within the constraints of the genre, the film doesn't pull any punches in depicting the brutality of both the conflict and the armed forces themselves. ▣

Ricky Schroder [Rick Schroder] *Calvin Graham* • Jon DeVries *Captain Gatch* • Rick Warner *Holbrook* • Mary-Louise Parker *Pearl* • Debra Mooney *Calvin's mother* ■ *Dir* Buzz Kulik • *Scr* David J Kinghorn, from a story by Calvin Graham, Gary Thomas

Too Young to Die? ★★★ 18

Drama based on a true story 1990 · US · Colour · 88mins

In *Cape Fear*, Juliette Lewis proved she could transfix an audience with the same scorching intensity as her co-stars, Robert De Niro and Nick Nolte. In this earlier drama, her startling professional maturity is just as clear in the portrayal of a 15-year-old jailbird. The film tends towards the episodic but is considerably lit up by the presence of Lewis and Brad Pitt, who teamed up again three years later in *Kalifornia*. Contains violence, swearing and nudity. *DVD*

Juliette Lewis *Amanda Sue Bradley* • Michael Tucker *Buddy Thorton* • Brad Pitt *Billy Canton* • Michael O'Keefe *Mike Medwicki* • Yvette Heyden *Annie Meechan* ■ *Dir* Robert Markowitz • *Scr* David Hill, George Rubino, from a story by David Hill

Toothless ★★★

Fantasy 1997 · US · Colour · 82mins

A well-worn concept is given a new spin in this delightful fantasy. Killed in a freak accident, mean-spirited dentist Kirstie Alley finds herself in limbo. Condemned to the role of Tooth Fairy, she must perform her duties – dispensing coins and wisdom in exchange for baby teeth – before she can get into heaven. She eventually helps a lonely young boy Ross Malinger (*Sleepless in Seattle*), whose widowed father (Dale Midkiff) hasn't had time for his son. This TV film sparkles with warmth, eccentric characters and a vivid depiction of God's waiting room.

Kirstie Alley *Dr Katherine Lewis/The Tooth Fairy* • Lynn Redgrave *Ms Rogers* • Ross Malinger *Bobby Jameson* • Dale Midkiff *Thomas Jameson* • Daryl "Chill" Mitchell [Daryl Mitchell] *Raul* • Melanie Mayron *Mindy* • Kathryn Zaremba *Carrie* • Eileen Brennan *Joe* ■ *Dir* Melanie Mayron • *Scr* Mark S Kaufman

Tootsie ★★★★ 15

Comedy 1982 · US · Colour · 111mins

One of the highlights of Dustin Hoffman's illustrious career, this cross-dressing comedy drama avoids all the obvious pitfalls and manages to make some pertinent comments on the role of women within both showbiz and society. Hoffman's Dorothy Michaels is a wonderfully realised creation and testament to the actor's painstaking preparation for a part. Director Sydney Pollack judges the shifts of tone to perfection, but special mention should be made of his clever pastiche of daytime soaps. Nominated for ten Oscars, the film landed only one – a best supporting statuette for Jessica Lange. ▣

Dustin Hoffman *Michael Dorsey/Dorothy Michaels* • Jessica Lange *Julie* • Teri Garr *Sandy* • Dabney Coleman *Ron* • Charles Durning *Les* • Bill Murray *Jeff* • Sydney Pollack *George Fields* • George Gaynes *John Van Horn* • Geena Davis *April* ■ *Dir* Sydney Pollack • *Scr* Larry Gelbart, Murray Schisgal, Elaine May (uncredited), from a story by Don McGuire, Larry Gelbart

Top Banana ★★★

Musical comedy 1953 · US · Colour · 103mins

The immortal Phil Silvers (Sgt Bilko), enjoyed a distinguished career before

his small screen triumph. Undoubtably his biggest pre-Bilko success was in the Tony Award-winning Broadway musical comedy *Top Banana*. Silvers is brilliant as fast-talking TV comic Jerry Biffle, the "Top Banana" of the title (ie headlining comedian of a show) and his performance, along with the authentic burlesque routines on offer, make this rewarding viewing. Originally made in 3-D, a gimmick which was undergoing a boom at the time.

Phil Silvers *Jerry Biffle* • Rose Marie *Betty Dillon* • Danny Scholl *Cliff Lane* • Judy Lynn *Sally Peters* • Jack Albertson *Vic Davis* • Johnny Coy *Tommy Phelps* • Joey Faye *Pinky* • Herbie Faye *Moe* ■ *Dir* Alfred E Green • *Scr* Gene Towne, from the musical by Hy Kraft, Johnny Mercer

Top Dog ★★ 12

Action comedy 1995 · US · Colour · 89mins

Chuck Norris's tough-cop persona is teamed with the police force's most cavalier canine to solve the murder of the dog's former partner. Someone should tell Norris not to partner with actors more dynamic than he is – the mutt is superior in every way. Parents should note that there is some violence and innuendo here, although the kids will probably love the dog's antics. Similarly, action fans should be warned about the saccharine dog angle. ▣ *DVD*

Chuck Norris *Jake Wilder* • Clyde Kusatsu *Captain Callahan* • Michele Lamar Richards *Savannah Boyette* • Peter Savard Moore *Karl Koller* • Erik Von Detten *Matthew Swanson* • Carmine Caridi *Lou Swanson* ■ *Dir* Aaron Norris • *Scr* Ron Swanson, from a story by Aaron Norris, Tim Grayem

Top Gun ★★★ 15

Action drama 1986 · US · Colour · 105mins

Quentin Tarantino's vigorous assertion in *Sleep with Me* that this is the ultimate gay fantasy movie rather pulls the carpet from under the feet of reviewers of this slavish tribute to flash fly boys and their high-tech toys. There is no denying the quality and entertainment value of the flying sequences, which effortlessly blend mile-high footage with state-of-the-art modelwork, but the rivalry between Tom Cruise and Val Kilmer, and Cruise's tempestuous affair with Kelly McGillis are pure bunk. Yet, with the shameful exception of McGillis, all emerged with reputations enhanced, particularly director Tony Scott, who takes all the credit for preventing this mindless macho daydream from nose-diving. Contains swearing, and a sex scene. ▣

Tom Cruise *Pete "Maverick" Mitchell* • Kelly McGillis *Charlotte "Charlie" Blackwood* • Val Kilmer *Tom "Iceman" Kazansky* • Anthony Edwards *Nick "Goose" Bradshaw* • Tom Skerritt *Commander Mike Metcalf, "Viper"* • Michael Ironside *Dick "Jester" Wetherly* • John Stockwell *Bill "Cougar" Cortell* • Barry Tubb *Henry "Wolfman" Ruth* • Rick Rossovich *Ron "Slider" Kerner* • Tim Robbins *Sam "Merlin" Wills* ■ *Dir* Tony Scott • *Scr* Jim Cash, Jack Epps Jr

Top Hat ★★★★★ U

Romantic musical 1935 · US · BW · 93mins

The quintessential Fred Astaire–Ginger Rogers movie; *Swing Time* may be more sophisticated, but there's no

question that this fabulous production was more popular. The mistaken identity plot actually works, and the casting is simply flawless. Astaire consolidates his image with the title number *Top Hat, White Tie and Tails* and the Irving Berlin score is a constant delight. Also terrific are *Cheek to Cheek*, *Isn't This a Lovely Day (To Be Caught in the Rain)?* and the fabulous *Piccolino* finale. Good-natured, warm-hearted and very witty (especially the hansom cab scene), this is a movie to treasure for its sumptuous Art-Deco design and the pairing of its principal players.

Fred Astaire *Jerry Travers* • Ginger Rogers *Dale Tremont* • Edward Everett Horton *Horace Hardwick* • Helen Broderick *Madge Hardwick* • Erik Rhodes *Alberto Beddini* • Eric Blore *Bates* ■ *Dir* Mark Sandrich • *Scr* Dwight Taylor, Allan Scott, from the musical *The Gay Divorcee* by Dwight Taylor, Cole Porter, from the play *The Girl Who Dared* by Alexander Farago, Aladar Laszlo

The Top of His Head ★★★

Drama 1988 · Can · Colour and BW · 110mins

You may notice a few superficial similarities between this quirky Canadian drama and Jim Carrey's *The Cable Guy*. In Carrey's film, it was a cable guy who turned an innocent bystander's world upside down, while here it's a satellite dish salesman who's on the receiving end. However, Stephen Ouimette is more than willing to have his vertical hold knocked out of kilter by wacky performance artist Christie MacFadyen, as he's tired of missing out on the big picture. There's more than a hint of Atom Egoyan's preoccupation with perception in this offbeat brew, which isn't totally surprising as writer/director Peter Mettler once served as his cinematographer.

Stephen Ouimette *Gus Victor* • Christie MacFadyen *Lucy Ripley* • Gary Reineke *Policeman* • David Fox • Julie Wildman • John Paul Young ■ *Dir/Scr* Peter Mettler

Top of the World ★ 18

Thriller 1997 · US · Colour · 94mins

This bottom of the barrel cop thriller wastes a good cast in a weak heist plot and surrounds them with botched action and bad special effects. Ex-cop Peter Weller leaves prison after serving time for a pension fund scam only to find himself in the centre of a Las Vegas casino robbery planned by stereotypical baddie Dennis Hopper. So sloppy in places it defies belief – a helicopter shot down at night lands a few seconds later in broad daylight – this patched together formula flick gives new meaning to the word lacklustre. Contains swearing and violence. DVD

Peter Weller *Ray Mercer* • Dennis Hopper *Charles Atlas* • Tia Carrere *Rebecca Mercer* • David Alan Grier *Detective Augustus* • Cary-Hiroyuki Tagawa *Captain Hefter* • Joe Pantoliano *Vince Castor* ■ *Dir* Sidney J Furie • *Scr* Bart Madison

Top Secret! ★★★ 15

Spy spoof 1984 · US · Colour · 86mins

The *Airplane!* team brings you, well, something not quite as funny, a Cold War spoof with an Elvis Presley-style musical grafted on. No Leslie Nielsen this time; instead there is Val Kilmer as a rock idol who plays East Berlin and gets pulled into a plot to bring down the Wall and reunite Germany. Things get progressively sillier, what with people dressing up as cows, re-enacting *The Great Escape* and clay-pigeon-shooting surfers, and the guest spots mount up Peter Cushing, Jeremy Kemp and, hilariously, Omar Sharif. Contains swearing.

Val Kilmer *Nick Rivers* • Omar Sharif *Cedric* • Jeremy Kemp *General Streck* • Warren Clarke *Colonel von Horst* • Lucy Gutteridge *Hillary Flammond* • Michael Gough *Dr Flammond* • Tristram Jellinek *Major Crumpler* • Peter Cushing *Bookstore proprietor* ■ *Dir* Jim Abrahams, David Zucker, Jerry Zucker • *Scr* Jim Abrahams, David Zucker, Jerry Abrahams, Martyn Burke

Top Secret Affair ★★★ U

Comedy 1957 · US · BW · 99mins

The chemistry is missing between stars Kirk Douglas and Susan Hayward in this rather heavy-handed frolic, maybe because they were old buddies in real life who went to school together back in New York before Hollywood beckoned. Comedy was never really Douglas's forte, and his dimpled grimacing doesn't help this adaptation of John P Marquand's satire. Hayward, however, positively sizzles as the publisher who's trying to discredit newly-appointed diplomat Douglas. Despite the welcome presence of Jim Backus and Paul Stewart, the movie really needed a dash more production gloss to really work.

Kirk Douglas *Major General Melville Goodwin* • Susan Hayward *Dottie Peale* • Paul Stewart *Bentley* • Jim Backus *Colonel Gooch* • John Cromwell *General Grimshaw* • Michael Fox *Lotzie* • Frank Gerstle *Sergeant Kruger* • Roland Winters *Senator Burwick* ■ *Dir* HC Potter • *Scr* Roland Kibbee, Allan Scott, from the novel *Melville Goodwin, USA* by John P Marquand

Topaz ★★ PG

Spy thriller 1969 · US · Colour · 120mins

Leon Uris adapted his own bestseller for this lacklustre spy story. Alfred Hitchcock, who had no real enthusiasm for the project, eventually asked for a rewrite by Samuel Taylor (*Vertigo*), but there was still far too much plot, too many explanations, and not enough character depth to bring this Cold War thriller to life. The action centres on a Cuban revolutionary and the presence of double agents in the French secret service. Hitchcock was so at odds with his material that he reportedly shot three different endings for perhaps the poorest film of his Hollywood career.

John Forsythe *Michael Nordstrom* • Frederick Stafford *André Devereaux* • Dany Robin *Nicole Devereaux* • John Vernon *Rico Parra* • Karin Dor *Juanita de Cordoba* • Michel Piccoli *Jacques Granville* • Philippe Noiret *Henri Jarre* • Claude Jade *Michele Picard* • Michel Subor *François Picard* • Roscoe Lee Browne *Philippe Dubois* ■ *Dir* Alfred Hitchcock • *Scr* Samuel Taylor, from the novel by Leon Uris

Topaze ★★★★

Comedy drama 1933 · US · BW · 78mins

John Barrymore's wonderfully-timed and sympathetic study, as the honest but hugely naive schoolmaster, lights up this Ben Hecht version of Marcel Pagnol's play. After losing his job in a private school, Topaze (Barrymore) is inveigled into a scheme to sell designer mineral water, organised by a crooked Baron (Reginald Mason). Myrna Loy plays Mason's lover, who is attracted by Barrymore's transformation from timid dupe into a confident man of substance. The story was later re-made by Peter Sellers as *Mr Topaze* (1961).

John Barrymore *Auguste Topaze* • Myrna Loy *Coco* • Albert Conti *Henri* • Luis Alberni *Dr Bomb* • Reginald Mason *Baron de Latour-Latour* • Jobyna Howland *Baroness de Latour-Latour* • Jackie Searle *Charlemagne de Latour-Latour* • Frank Reicher *Dr Stegg* ■ *Dir* Harry d'Abbadie D'Arrast • *Scr* Ben Hecht, Benn W Levy, from the play by Marcel Pagnol

Topaze ★★★

Satire 1951 · Fr · BW · 136mins

Despite the fact that Marcel Pagnol had already failed once in his bid to outdo Louis J Gasnier's 1932 adaptation of his own stage hit, the playwright-turned-director embarked upon this second remake, with Fernandel this time seeking to surpass Louis Jouvet's original performance. Proving that behind every cynic there's a lapsed idealist, the horse-faced comic is superb as the bashful schoolmaster unable to declare his feelings for headmaster's daughter Jacqueline Pagnol. However, Jouvet is much less convincing as the fast-learning political dupe who not only outwits his corrupt master, Jacques Morel, but also steals his mistress, Hélène Perdrière. A French language film.

Fernandel *Topaze* • Hélène Perdrière *Suzy Courtois* • Jacqueline Pagnol *Ernestine Muche* • Yvette Etiévant *Secretary* • Jacques Morel *Régis Castel-Vergnac* ■ *Dir* Marcel Pagnol • *Scr* Marcel Pagnol, from his play

Topkapi ★★★★ U

Comedy thriller 1964 · US · Colour · 114mins

In spoofing his own intricate heist classic, *Rififi*, Jules Dassin pioneered one of the most popular sub-genres of the sixties, the comic crime caper. Deliciously scripted by one-time Ealing alumnus Monja Danischewsky, it combines sparkling dialogue with moments of unbearable tension, most notably during the prolonged heist on an Istanbul museum in a bid to purloin a priceless dagger. The band of misfits hired by Melina Mercouri and Maximilian Schell are effectively played, but it was the showy performance of Peter Ustinov that caught the eye and earned him a best supporting actor Oscar.

Melina Mercouri *Elizabeth Lipp* • Peter Ustinov *Arthur Simpson* • Maximilian Schell *William Walter* • Robert Morley *Cedric Page* • Akim Tamiroff *Geven* • Gilles Segal *Giulio* • Jess Hahn *Fischer* • Titos Wandis [Titos Vandis] *Harback* • Ege Ernart *Major Tufan* ■ *Dir* Jules Dassin • *Scr* Monja Danischewsky, from the novel *The Light of Day* by Eric Ambler

El Topo ★★★ 18

Surreal spaghetti western
1971 · Mex · Colour · 119mins

There's plenty to offend everyone here. Shot in Mexico by the Chilean-born actor/writer/director Alexandro Jodorowsky, *El Topo* which translates as *The Mole* is the cult film fan's cult film. A brief description would do scant justice to the bewildering array of images – some witty, some bleak and some so obscure that only Jodorowsky himself can have the foggiest idea what they actually mean. But, given the knowledge that the references range from Fellini and Buñuel to Marcel Marceau and the Bible, you will get a better idea of just how eclectic this western (yes, western!) really is. In Spanish with English subtitles. Contains violence and sex scenes.

Alexandro Jodorowsky *El Topo* • Brontis Jodorowsky *Brontis (as a child)* • Mara Lorenzio *Mara* • David Silva *Colonel* • Paula Romo *Woman in black* ■ *Dir/Scr* Alexandro Jodorowsky

Topper ★★★★

Fantasy comedy 1937 · US · BW · 98mins

An excellent whimsical comedy with Cary Grant and Constance Bennett as the rich couple who drive their streamlined automobile into a tree. Surviving as ghosts, they harass Mr Topper (Roland Young), their starchy, hen-pecked bank manager, who has regarded them – his major stockholders – as irresponsible and trivial, which is exactly what they are. The idea is that in life Grant and Bennett have disgusted Young but in death they liberate him – the movie aims for a soft subversiveness. A huge hit in 1937, it gave Bennett her best role and Grant was rarely more elegant.

Cary Grant *George Kerby* • Constance Bennett *Marion Kerby* • Roland Young *Cosmo Topper* • Billie Burke *Mrs Topper* • Alan Mowbray *Wilkins* • Eugene Pallette *Casey* • Arthur Lake *Elevator boy* • Hedda Hopper *Mrs Stuyvesant* ■ *Dir* Norman Z McLeod • *Scr* Jack Jevne, Eric Hatch, Eddie Moran, from the novel *The Jovial Ghosts* by Thorne Smith

Topper Returns ★★★

Fantasy comedy 1941 · US · BW · 88mins

The spooky slapstick series of three Topper pictures ended with this old dark house spoof. All the ingredients are here, including wall panels, hidden passages and disappearing bodies. The film begins with the killing of Joan Blondell, who then returns in phantom form to solve her own murder. There are quite a few laughs, but the movie is but a ghost of *Topper* (1937) and *Topper Takes a Trip* (1939), although Roland Young was his wonderfully bemused self again in the title role.

Roland Young *Cosmo Topper* • Joan Blondell *Gail Richards* • Carole Landis *Ann Carrington* • Billie Burke *Mrs Topper* • Dennis O'Keefe *Bob* • Patsy Kelly *Maid* • HB Warner *Henry Carrington/Walter Harberg* ■ *Dir* Roy Del Ruth • *Scr* Jonathan Latimer, Gordon Douglas, from characters created by Thorne Smith

Topper Takes a Trip ★★★ U

Fantasy comedy 1939 · US · BW · 80mins

The sequel to the original *Topper* (1937), with Roland Young again playing hen-pecked banker Cosmo Topper, now being sued for divorce by Billie Burke. For no real reason, the action shifts to Europe where the spectral Constance Bennett – the reason for the divorce proceedings – works to save the marriage when Burke eyes a Riviera fancy boy. Cary Grant appears only in a flashback to the first film but his role as Constance's constant companion is taken by a yapping dog. It's all very silly, but oddly sophisticated, too.

Constance Bennett *Marion Kerby* • Roland Young *Cosmo Topper* • Billie Burke *Clara Topper* • Alan Mowbray *Wilkins* • Verree Teasdale *Mrs Parkhurst* • Franklin Pangborn *Louis, hotel manager* • Alexander D'Arcy [Alex D'Arcy] *Baron de Rossi* • Armand Kaliz *Clerk* ■ *Dir* Norman Z McLeod • *Scr* Eddie Moran, Jack Jevne, Corey Ford, from the novel *Topper Takes a Trip* by Thorne Smith

Topsy-Turvy ★★★★★ 12
Biographical comedy drama
1999 · UK/US · Colour · 160mins

After Laurel and Hardy, the most notable odd couple in show business is probably British operetta writers Gilbert and Sullivan. Director Mike Leigh here celebrates their collaborative genius, using the construction of *The Mikado* to show that their casual virtuosity was really painstaking craft. The newly-knighted Arthur Sullivan (Allan Corduner), a musician, lecher and dandy, met his literary match in William Schwenck Gilbert (Jim Broadbent), whose taste for the absurd extended to his librettos. Sullivan, whose solo work was corrupted by sentimentality, thought he was better than Gilbert's whimsy, but Leigh skilfully convinces us that their separate talents spoke with one voice. Contains one nude scene.

Jim Broadbent *William Schwenck Gilbert* • Allan Corduner *Arthur Sullivan* • Timothy Spall *Richard Temple* • Lesley Manville *Lucy "Kitty" Gilbert* • Ron Cook *Richard D'Oyly Carte* • Wendy Nottingham *Helen Lenoir* • Kevin McKidd *Durward Lely* • Shirley Henderson *Leonora Braham* • Alison Steadman *Madame Leon* ■ *Dir/Scr* Mike Leigh

Tora! Tora! Tora! ★★★ U
Second World War drama
1970 · US/Jap · Colour · 136mins

A meticulous account of the preparations for and execution of the Japanese attack on the US naval base at Pearl Harbor on 7 December 1941. With Richard Fleischer staging the American segments and Toshio Masuda and Kinji Fukasaku directing events from the Japanese perspective, the film bends over backwards to show that patriotism, courage and commitment were present on both sides, and therein lies its weakness. The battle sequences are magnificent, but the production's magnanimity makes it impossible to judge the true impact of the happenings on either nation. In Japanese and English with subtitles. ▭

Martin Balsam *Admiral Husband E Kimmel* • Soh Yamamura [So Yamamura] *Admiral Isoroku Yamamoto* • Jason Robards Jr *General Walter C Short* • Joseph Cotten *Henry L Stimson* • Tatsuya Mihashi *Commander Minoru Genda* • EG Marshall *Lieutenant Colonel Rufus S Bratton* • Takahiro Tamura *Lieutenant Commander Fuchida* • James Whitmore *Admiral William F Halsey* ■ *Dir* Richard Fleischer, Toshio Masuda, Kinji Fukasaku • *Scr* Larry Forrester, Hideo Oguni,

Ryuzo Kikushima, from the book by Gordon W Prange and the book *The Broken Seal* by Ladislas Farago

Torch Song ★★
Romantic drama 1953 · US · Colour · 90mins

There's camp, and there's *Torch Song*. Joan Crawford (far too old) is an unhappy Broadway star, and Michael Wilding is a blind pianist who falls in love with her and nearly ruins his Hollywood career. Fortunately, his character can't see Crawford perform *Two-Faced Woman* in blackface, but, alas, we can. Director Charles Walters appears as Crawford's dancing partner in the opening number, but don't blame him for this cliché-upon-cliché farrago: he knew exactly what to do with this kind of material. Sit back and prepare to chortle.

Joan Crawford *Jenny Stewart* • Michael Wilding *Tye Graham* • Gig Young *Cliff Willard* • Marjorie Rambeau *Mrs Stewart* • Henry Morgan [Harry Morgan] *Joe Denner* • Dorothy Patrick *Martha* • James Todd *Philip Norton* ■ *Dir* Charles Walters • *Scr* John Michael Hayes, Jan Lustig, from the story *Why Should I Cry?* by IAR Wylie

Torch Song Trilogy ★★★★ 15
Drama 1988 · US · Colour · 114mins

The driving force behind this splendid gay romantic comedy drama is Harvey Fierstein, who repeats his Tony award-winning stage performance in this screen version of his own hit play. Although it occasionally lapses into soppiness, the script is a finely judged mix of sass and schmaltz. Gravel-voiced, camp and desperately vulnerable, Fierstein is tremendous, while Anne Bancroft does the best of her string of Jewish mama routines. The surprise is Matthew Broderick, who is perfect, playing against type, as Harvey's lover.

Harvey Fierstein *Arnold Becker* • Anne Bancroft *Ma* • Matthew Broderick *Alan* • Brian Kerwin *Ed* • Karen Young *Laurel* • Eddie Castrodad *David* • Ken Page *Murray* • Charles Pierce *Bertha Venation* ■ *Dir* Paul Bogart • *Scr* Harvey Fierstein, from his play

Torchlight ★★ 18
Drama 1984 · US · Colour · 88mins

This "holier than thou" take on the dangers of cocaine addiction fails to be anything other than black and white. Artist Pamela Sue Martin meets construction boss Steve Railsback and, after a whirlwind romance, they marry. Their domestic bliss is shattered by the arrival of cocaine dealer Ian McShane. After a night of debauchery together, Martin decides she can't stand "charlie" but Railsback is hooked, and with the sleazy McShane a regular house visitor, trouble lies ahead. Director Tom Wright's morality tale may be a useful deterrent for teenagers, but adult audiences are likely to be unimpressed. ▭

Pamela Sue Martin *Lillian Gregory* • Steve Railsback *Jake Gregory* • Ian McShane *Sidney* • Al Corley *Al* • Rita Taggart *Rita* • Arnie Moore *Richard* ■ *Dir* Tom Wright • *Scr* Eliza Moorman, Pamela Sue Martin

Torment ★★★ 12
Drama 1944 · Swe · BW · 96mins

This sombre work was the first big international Swedish success for more than two decades. It was rightly acclaimed at the time for its marvellous performances especially from Mai Zetterling, and the clever sustained direction of Alf Sjöberg. Today, however, this study of schoolboy Alf Kjellin's affair with Zetterling, the mistress of his despised, despotic teacher (Stig Jarrel), is mainly of interest because its screenplay is by the young Ingmar Bergman, who would go on to become a giant of world cinema. In Swedish with English subtitles. ▭

Alf Kjellin *Jan-Erik* • Mai Zetterling *Bertha* • Stig Jarrel *Caligula* • Olof Winnerstrand *School Principal* • Gosta Cederlund *Pippi* ■ *Dir* Alf Sjöberg • *Scr* Ingmar Bergman

Torn Apart ★★
Romantic drama 1990 · US · Colour · 95mins

So much care has been taken not to offend anyone, that this adaptation of Chayym Zeldis's Romeo and Juliet novel, *A Forbidden Love*, offers few worthwhile insights into the extent to which the Middle East conflict affects everyday life. It also doesn't help casting a couple of photogenic Americans in the key roles of the Israeli soldier and his Arab girlfriend, even though both Adrian Pasdar and Cecilia Peck turn in creditable performances. Overladen with good intentions, but dramatically a non-starter.

Adrian Pasdar *Ben Arnon* • Cecilia Peck *Laila Malek* • Barry Primus *Arie Arnon* • Machram Huri *Mahmoud Malek* • Arnon Zadok *Professor Mansour* • Margrit Polak *Ilana Arnon* ■ *Dir* Jack Fisher • *Scr* Marc Kristal, from the novel *A Forbidden Love* by Chayym Zeldis

Torn between Two Lovers ★★ PG
Romantic drama 1979 · US · Colour · 95mins

Lee Remick is torn between husband Joseph Bologna and George Peppard, the divorced architect she meets at an airport and has an affair with. The talented Remick is wasted in this stereotypical role, and viewers may not find her choice between Bologna and Peppard particularly enviable either. Director Delbert Mann – who won an Oscar for his first film, *Marty*, in 1955 – keeps a thin layer of crustiness over the slush. The movie was inspired by a treacly seventies ballad. ▭

Lee Remick *Diane Conti* • George Peppard *Paul Rassmussen* • Joseph Bologna *Ted Conti* • Derrick Jones *Andy Conti* • Murphy Cross *Nina Dworski* • Molly Cheek *Sherry Sanders* ■ *Dir* Delbert Mann • *Scr* Doris Silverton, from a story by Doris Silverton, Rita Lakin

Torn Curtain ★★★ 15
Spy thriller 1966 · US · Colour · 122mins

What looked in its day to be a failure and a disappointment to fans of Alfred Hitchcock does, at least, contain one of the maestro's most compelling sequences. "I wanted to show how difficult it is to kill someone", Hitch said, and, in a prolonged scene involving Paul Newman played without dialogue he certainly does. It's the

high spot in a remarkably ridiculous Cold War thriller, very much of its period, with phoney locations, phonier back projection, and, phoniest of all, the casting of Newman and Julie Andrews (particularly Andrews) as an American defector and his fiancée. If there was any chemistry between the stars, it certainly doesn't show on the screen. Still, Hitchcock fans won't mind, and shouldn't miss it. ▭

Paul Newman *Professor Michael Armstrong* • Julie Andrews *Sarah Sherman* • Lila Kedrova *Countess Kuchinska* • Hansjörg Felmy *Heinrich Gerhard* • Tamara Toumanova *Ballerina* • Wolfgang Kieling *Hermann Gromek* • Gunter Strack *Professor Manfred* • Ludwig Donath *Professor Lindt* ■ *Dir* Alfred Hitchcock • *Scr* Brian Moore, from his story

Tornado! ★★
Action adventure 1996 · US · Colour · 82mins

With the blockbuster *Twister* giving audiences a taste for the forces of nature, it was inevitable that the cash-ins wouldn't be too far behind. This one at least boasts a decent enough cast: *Ghostbusters* co-star Ernie Hudson is the scientist looking to perfect a machine that can detect lethal tornados, while *The Evil Dead's* Bruce Campbell is his dashing, risk-taking chum. Shannon Sturges provides the love interest as the grumpy accountant who finally succumbs to Campbell's charms. The action breezes along, but lacks the budget to get anywhere near to reproducing *Twister's* extraordinary visual effects. Contains swearing.

Bruce Campbell *Jake Thorne* • Shannon Sturges *Sam Callen* • Ernie Hudson *Dr Branson* ■ *Dir* Noel Nosseck • *Scr* John Logan

Torpedo Run ★★★ U
Second World War drama
1958 · US · Colour · 95mins

Long before *Crimson Tide* and *The Hunt for Red October*, there was a similar fifties' vogue, typified by *Run Silent, Run Deep*, *The Enemy Below* and this excellent MGM drama. Claustrophobically made, the film boasts a tense plot as commander Glenn Ford accidentally blows up a Japanese prison ship with his own family on board. The chase is then on to find the enemy aircraft carrier which used the ship as a shield. This is from the most successful period in Ford's career, between *The Blackboard Jungle* and the end of his MGM contract, and his nervy, tense performance is mesmerising. Director Joseph Pevney had made the enjoyable war drama *Away All Boats*, but here the pacing is a shade too slow.

Glenn Ford *Lieutenant Commander Barney Doyle* • Ernest Borgnine *Lieutenant Archer Sloan* • Diane Brewster *Jane Doyle* • Dean Jones *Lieutenant Jake "Fuzz" Foley* • LQ Jones *"Hash" Benson* • Philip Ober *Admiral Samuel Setton* • Richard Carlyle *Commander Don Adams* ■ *Dir* Joseph Pevney • *Scr* Richard Sale, William Wister Haines, from stories by Richard Sale

The Torrent ★★★★
Silent romantic drama
1926 · US · BW · 68mins

Vicente Blasco-Ibáñez was one of the most adapted novelists of the silent era, and it was his potboiler *Among the Orange Trees* that provided Greta Garbo with her Hollywood entrance. Starring opposite MGM's very own Latin lover, Ricardo Cortez, she was somewhat improbably cast as a provincial Spanish girl, who recovers from their parting by becoming a famous Parisian diva. But despite the efforts of his scheming mother, Martha Mattox, their paths keep crossing. Even at the age of 20, Garbo's genius is apparent in the small, slow, seductive movements that reveal the psychological intensity that would become her trademark.

Ricardo Cortez *Don Rafael Brull* • Greta Garbo *Leonora* • Gertrude Olmsted *Remedios* • Edward Connelly *Pedro Moreno* • Lucien Littlefield *Cupido* • Martha Mattox *Dona Bernarda Brull* ■ *Dir* Monta Bell • *Scr* Katherine Hilliker (titles), HH Caldwell (titles), Dorothy Farnum, from the novel *Entre Naranjos (Among the Orange Trees)* by Vicente Blasco-Ibañez

Torrents of Spring ★★ PG

Period romantic drama
1989 · Fr/It · Colour · 97mins

Seeking to emulate Nikita Mikhalkov's success with Chekhov's *Dark Eyes*, Jerzy Skolimowski has badly misjudged the tone of Turgenev's novel and turned a stifling chamber drama into a dreamily sunlit travelogue. Instead of being driven to distraction by his love for German baker's daughter Valeria Golino, and his passion for married noblewoman Nastassja Kinski, Timothy Hutton merely looks alternately moon-faced and peevish. There are picturesque scenes of glorious inconsequence such as the balloon trip and the Venice finale, which add nothing to our understanding of the underdrawn characters. But then neither do the supposedly revelatory duel, the excruciating dinner party and the library tryst. ▣

Timothy Hutton *Dimitri Sanin* • Nastassja Kinski *Maria Nikolaevna Polozov* • Valeria Golino *Gemma Rosselli* • Francesca De Sapio *Signora Rosselli –Gemma's mother* • William Forsythe *Polozov* • Urbano Barberini *Von Doenhof* • Jacques Herlin *Pantaleone* ■ *Dir* Jerzy Skolimowski • *Scr* Jerzy Skolimowski, Arcangelo Bonaccorso, from the novel *Spring Torrents* by Ivan Turgenev

Torrid Zone ★★★

Adventure
1940 · US · BW · 93mins

Not the title of a late-night Channel 4 season, but a James Cagney movie in which the combustible star sports a pencil-thin moustache and a sneer. Pat O'Brien, Cagney's boss, runs an export business in Central America and saloon singer Ann Sheridan, then known as the "Oomph Girl", competes with Helen Vinson for Cagney's attention. Always reminiscent of Clark Gable and Jean Harlow's sexy melodrama *Red Dust*, this sweaty piece of tropical torpor was never that torrid, but is still enjoyable.

James Cagney *Nick Butler* • Pat O'Brien *Steve Case* • Ann Sheridan *Lee Donley* • Andy Devine *Wally Davis* • Helen Vinson *Gloria Anderson* • George Tobias *Rosario* • Jerome Cowan *Bob Anderson* ■ *Dir* William Keighley • *Scr* Richard Macaulay, Jerry Wald

Tortilla Flat ★★★ U

Drama   1942 · US · BW · 105mins

Off-screen machinations marked the transition from page to screen of John Steinbeck's novel. John Garfield was keen to star as the newly wealthy Danny, but MGM had to pull out all the stops in their efforts to persuade Warner Bros to release him. Spencer Tracy and Akim Tamiroff have plum roles as a couple of freeloaders talking Garfield into letting them have one of the houses he's inherited. Hedy Lamarr had the best part of her career as the strong-minded object of Garfield's affections in this amiable drama that was a bigger hit with critics than public on its initial release.

Spencer Tracy *Pilon* • Hedy Lamarr *Dolores "Sweets" Ramirez* • John Garfield *Danny* • Akim Tamiroff *Pablo* • Frank Morgan *Pirate* • Sheldon Leonard *Tito Ralph* • John Qualen *Jose Maria Corcoran* • Donald Meek *Paul D Cummings* ■ *Dir* Victor Fleming • *Scr* John Lee Mahin, Benjamin Glaser, from the novel by John Steinbeck

Torture Garden ★★★ 15

Horror   1967 · UK · Colour · 96mins

A group of fairground visitors are shown their futures by the strange Dr Diabolo (Burgess Meredith) in one of the better compendium chillers from Amicus, Hammer's main British horror rival. Robert (*Psycho*) Bloch's skilful script which includes cannibal cats, haunted pianos, eternal Hollywood life and the reincarnation of Edgar Allan Poe, gives director Freddie Francis imaginative opportunities to indulge in stylish camerawork for maximum gothic effect. Jack Palance is particularly good as the crazed Poe fanatic. ▣

Jack Palance *Ronald Wyatt* • Beverly Adams *Carla Haynes* • Burgess Meredith *Dr Diabolo* • Peter Cushing *Lancelot Canning* • Michael Bryant *Colin Williams* • Maurice Denham *Colin's uncle* • John Standing *Leo* • Robert Hutton *Paul* ■ *Dir* Freddie Francis • *Scr* Robert Bloch, from his stories *Enoch* , *Terror Over Hollywood*, *Mr Steinway*, *The Man Who Collected Poe*

The Total Balalaika Show ★★★★

Concert documentary
1994 · Fin · Colour · 56mins

The Leningrad Cowboys and the Red Army Choir might not sound like the perfect combination, but as Aki Kaurismäki's joyous concert movie proves, they are a match made in musical heaven. Considering they were once the self-proclaimed worst band in the world, the Cowboys belt out terrific versions of the Turtles's *Happy Together* and ZZ Top's *Gimme All Your Lovin'*, while the Army renditions of *Volga Boatmen*, *Kalinka* (complete with Cossack-dancing Cowboys) and *Dark Eyes* are sublime. Totally capturing the euphoric atmosphere of the event, this is quite an experience. An English/Russian language film.

Dir Aki Kaurismäki

Total Eclipse ★★ 18

Biographical drama
1995 · UK/Fr/Bel · Colour · 106mins

Female *Titanic* fanatics will probably want to catch this film because it

features teen heart-throb Leonardo DiCaprio in the buff, but apart from that they are likely to be disappointed. Director Agnieszka Holland (*Europa, Europa*) and writer Christopher Hampton (*Dangerous Liaisons*) have produced a stodgy biopic that focuses on the more lurid aspects of the (sadomasochistic) relationship between 19th-century poets Verlaine (David Thewlis) and Rimbaud (DiCaprio). DiCaprio gave better early performances in films like *What's Eating Gilbert Grape* and *This Boy's Life*. ▣

Leonardo DiCaprio *Arthur Rimbaud* • David Thewlis *Paul Verlaine* • Romane Bohringer *Mathilde Verlaine* • Dominique Blanc *Isabelle Rimbaud* • Nita Klein *Rimbaud's mother* • Christopher Hampton *The judge* ■ *Dir* Agnieszka Holland • *Scr* Christopher Hampton

Total Recall ★★★★ 18

Science-fiction thriller
1990 · US · Colour · 108mins

This rip-roaring slice of sci-fi excess remains Arnold Schwarzenegger's most satisfying film since his breakthrough hit *The Terminator*. Director Paul Verhoeven, armed with a smart script loosely based on a short story by cult novelist Philip K Dick, cuts loose with a gloriously over-the-top mix of black humour, ultra-violence and spectacular effects. The result was a massive worldwide hit. Schwarzenegger is the dull construction worker on a futuristic Earth, who is drawn into a conspiracy on the planet Mars when a virtual reality holiday awakens long-dormant memories. Ronny Cox delivers another villainous performance, and is ably assisted by Michael Ironside. However, the real find turned out to be Sharon Stone, whose performance led to her ground-breaking role in Verhoeven's next movie, *Basic Instinct*. Contains violence, swearing and nudity. ▣

Arnold Schwarzenegger *Douglas Quaid* • Rachel Ticotin *Melina* • Sharon Stone *Lori Quaid* • Ronny Cox *Cohaagen* • Michael Ironside *Richter* • Marshall Bell *George/Kuato* • Mel Johnson Jr *Benny* • Michael Champion *Helm* • Roy Brocksmith *Dr Edgemar* • Ray Baker *McClane* ■ *Dir* Paul Verhoeven • *Scr* Ronald Shusett, Dan O'Bannon, Gary Goldman, from a story by Ronald Shusett, Dan O'Bannon, Jon Povill, from the short story *We Can Remember It for You Wholesale* by Philip K Dick

Totally F***ed Up ★★★ 18

Comedy drama   1993 · US · Colour · 75mins

In 15 numbered chapters, six gay and lesbian LA teenagers divulge every minute detail about how screwed up their disenfranchised lives are. There's the slacker, the would-be film-maker, his artist boyfriend, the skateboarder, and two lesbians who dream of having a baby. Edgy, moody, humorous and containing some immensely powerful moments, this is a penetrating look at what it means to be young, gay and terminally bored. Director Gregg Araki continued his Teen Apocalypse trilogy in *The Doom Generation* and completed it with *Nowhere*. ▣

James Duval *Andy* • Roko Belic *Tommy* • Susan Behshid *Michele* • Jenee Gill *Patricia* • Gilbert Luna *Steven* • Lance May *Deric* • Alan Boyce *Ian* • Craig Gilmore *Brendan* ■ *Dir/Scr* Gregg Araki

Toto Le Héros ★★★★ 15

Drama   1991 · Bel/Fr/ Ger · Colour · 87mins

Former circus performer Jaco Van Dormael made an outstanding start to his directorial career with this remarkable film that is both a beguiling portrait of childhood and a touching treatise on unrealised dreams. Effortlessly slipping between past and present through a sequence of stylish flashbacks, Van Dormael traces the lifelong resentment of Thomas, who has waited 60 years to avenge himself on Alfred, a business tycoon, with whom Thomas believes he was switched shortly after birth. The three actors who play Toto are all superb, but it's the atmosphere, dark humour and narrative complexity that make this so enthralling. In French with English subtitles. Contains violence and nudity. ▣

Michel Bouquet *Old Thomas* • Jo de Backer *Adult Thomas* • Thomas Godet *Young Thomas* • Gisela Uhlen *Old Evelyne* • Mireille Perrier *Adult Evelyne* • Sandrine Blancke *Alice* • Peter Böhlke *Old Alfred* • Didier Ferney *Adult Alfred* ■ *Dir/Scr* Jaco Van Dormael

The Touch ★★★ 15

Drama   1971 · US/Swe · Colour · 107mins

On the surface, this appears to be one of Ingmar Bergman's lesser chamber dramas. In the Swedish master's first English-language film, Elliott Gould (of all people!) appears uncomfortable playing the Jewish archaeologist who embarks on an affair with Bibi Andersson. But despite awakening a whole new side of her personality through this unexpected passion, the security offered by her doctor husband, Max von Sydow still beckons. Yet, the film takes on deeper meaning when we realise it is a meditation on the troubled marriage of Bergman's parents, with the photograph Andersson shows Gould of her mother actually depicting Karin Bergman. ▣

Bibi Andersson *Karin Vergerus* • Elliott Gould *David Kovac* • Max von Sydow *Andreas Vergerus* • Sheila Reid *Sara* • Staffan Hallerstram *Anders Vergerus* • Maria Nolgard *Agnes Vergerus* ■ *Dir/Scr* Ingmar Bergman

Touch ★★★ 15

Comedy drama   1996 · US · Colour · 96mins

Director Paul Schrader's first feature after a long lay-off is a quizzical adaptation of bestselling author Elmore Leonard's atypical novel. Deftly skirting supernatural satire, this uncommonly sophisticated and amusing comic fable focuses on Skeet Ulrich, an ex-monk with curative abilities, whose gift is seen by opportunist Christopher Walken as media gold. Loaded with fine performances (Tom Arnold is fabulous as a wannabe Christian martyr) and acute observations on media manipulation and right wing religious extremists, Schrader's deliciously oddball movie is highly individual and wonderfully eccentric.

Bridget Fonda *Lynn Faulkner* • Gina Gershon *Debra Lusanne* • LL Cool J • Christopher Walken *Bill Hill* • Skeet Ulrich *Juvenal* • Tom Arnold *August Murray* • Paul Mazursky *Artie* • Janeane Garofalo *Kathy Worthington* ■ *Dir* Paul Schrader • *Scr* Paul Schrader, from the novel by Elmore Leonard

Touch and Go ★ U

Comedy 1955 · UK · Colour · 81mins

A depressing wallow in the sort of whimsy that Ealing foisted upon the world as British Realism. This clumsy clash of ancient and modern revolves around the furniture designer Jack Hawkins's decision to emigrate to Australia when his latest efforts are deemed too futuristic by his stick-in-the-mud employer. Had his family pointed to sneak previews of life on Ramsay Street or in Summer Bay, one could have understood their resistance, but surely one would have swum all the way to escape such dreary friends and limited opportunities?

Jack Hawkins *Jim Fletcher* • Margaret Johnston *Helen Fletcher* • June Thorburn *Peggy Fletcher* • John Fraser *Richard Kenyon* • Roland Culver *Reg Fairbright* • Alison Leggatt *Alice Fairbright* ■ *Dir* Michael Truman • *Scr* William Rose, from a story by Tania Rose, William Rose

Touch and Go ★ 15

Romantic comedy drama
1986 · US · Colour · 97mins

Comedian Michael Keaton tries flexing his dramatic muscle for the first time in a formula romance that, despite its violent conclusion, remains grounded in TV movie sentiment. He plays a Chicago hockey star who becomes involved with single mother Maria Conchita Alonso after her son has tried to mug him. The usual relationship problems ensue, which never hit any note of truth and stick essentially to sitcom parameters. Keaton barely rises to the challenge and wouldn't make the successful mainstream crossover until *Clean and Sober* in 1988. 📼

Michael Keaton *Bobby Barbato* • Maria Conchita Alonso *Denise DeLeon* • Ajay Naidu *Louis DeLeon* • John Reilly *Jerry Pepper* • Maria Tucci *Dee Dee* ■ *Dir* Robert Mandel • *Scr* Alan Ormsby, Bob Sand, Harry Colomby

A Touch of Adultery ★ 15

Romantic comedy 1992 · It · Colour · 98mins

The teaming of perennial *Mary Poppins* virgin Julie Andrews with Italian heart-throb Marcello Mastroianni must have looked good on paper. But both stars are ill-served by a vacuous script, based on the warhorse play *Tchin Tchin*, about two recently divorced strangers finding solace and companionship with each other. Leaden direction by Gene Saks doesn't help. 📼

Julie Andrews *Pamela Picquet* • Marcello Mastroianni *Cesareo Gramaldi* • Ian Fitzgibbon *Bobby Picquet* • Jean-Pierre Castaldi *Marcel* • Jean-Jacques Dulon *Dr Noiret* • Maria Marchado *Miss Knudson* ■ *Dir* Gene Saks • *Scr* Ronald Harwood, from the play *Tchin Tchin* by François Billetdoux

A Touch of Class ★★★★★

Romantic comedy
1973 · UK · Colour · 105mins

Classy stuff, indeed, as married American George Segal becomes an emotional prisoner of Glenda Jackson, a divorcee designer whose British barbs sink home painfully as Segal attempts a series of romantic passes. Co-writer (with Jack Rose)/director Melvin Frank hones the script to a cutting edge to ensure that sentimentality does not oversweeten the romance, and succeeds in keeping the piece ironically humorous rather than schmaltzily corny, which it so easily could have become. Jackson won an Oscar for this one, though Segal's harassed stud should have received an award for unbuttoned bewilderment. Contains swearing.

George Segal *Steve Blackburn* • Glenda Jackson *Vicki Allessio* • Paul Sorvino *Walter Menkes* • Hildegard Neil *Gloria Blackburn* • Cec Linder *Wendell Thompson* • K Callan *Patty Menkes* • Mary Barclay *Martha Thompson* ■ *Dir* Melvin Frank • *Scr* Melvin Frank, Jack Rose

Touch of Evil ★★★★★ 12

Classic film noir 1958 · US · Colour · 104mins

It was star Charlton Heston (improbably cast as a Mexican) who persuaded Universal to hire Orson Welles to direct this crime thriller. In so doing, he secured not only Welles's most magnificent late character creation (as corrupt corpulent cop Hank Quinlan), but also the film that virtually capped a style the great Welles himself had helped create: you could say that the span of *film noir* started with *Citizen Kane* and ended with this movie. It's a byzantine and disturbingly brilliant melodrama that rivets an audience from its now justly-famed opening title sequence to its grisly finale. In composition, in dialogue and character, and in sheer style, this is what cinema can and should be capable of, and it took the genius of Orson Welles to turn the cheap novel *Badge of Evil* into this terrifically entertaining study in depravity. 📼

Orson Welles *Hank Quinlan* • Charlton Heston *Ramon Miguel (Mike) Vargas* • Janet Leigh *Susan Vargas* • Joseph Calleia *Pete Menzies* • Akim Tamiroff *"Uncle Joe" Grandi* • Joanna Moore *Marcia Linnekar* • Ray Collins *Adair* • Dennis Weaver *Night Man* • Marlene Dietrich *Tanya* • Zsa Zsa Gabor *Strip joint owner* ■ *Dir* Orson Welles • *Scr* Orson Welles, from the novel *Badge of Evil* by Whit Masterson • *Cinematographer* Russell Metty

A Touch of Larceny ★★★ U

Comedy 1959 · UK · BW · 94mins

James Mason was never anything less than a suave and sophisticated performer. However, comedy was not really his forte, even when it was as gentle as in this urbane tale of treachery and libel. Adapted from Andrew Garve's novel *The Megstone Plot*, the film benefits from the polished presence of that other silky screen smoothie, George Sanders, and willing support from Vera Miles, whose fortunes took a significant upswing the following year when she co-starred in Alfred Hitchcock's *Psycho*.

James Mason *Commander Max Easton* • George Sanders *Sir Charles Holland* • Vera Miles *Virginia Killain* • Oliver Johnston *Minister* • Robert Flemyng *Larkin* ■ *Dir* Guy Hamilton • *Scr* Roger MacDougall, Paul Winterton, Ivan Foxwell, Guy Hamilton, from the novel *The Megstone Plot* by Andrew Garve

A Touch of Love ★★ 15

Drama 1969 · UK · Colour · 102mins

Margaret Drabble adapted her novel, *The Millstone*, for this capable and well-made social drama. An unwed student (Sandy Dennis, in one of her most effective performances) loses her virginity and becomes pregnant. The rest of the cast is also strong, including Ian McKellen's sharp television announcer, the unwitting father of the child. 📼

Sandy Dennis *Rosamund Stacey* • Ian McKellen *George* • Eleanor Bron *Lydia* • John Standing *Roger* • Michael Coles *Joe* • Rachel Kempson *Sister Harvey* • Margaret Tyzack *Sister Bennett* ■ *Dir* Waris Hussein • *Scr* Margaret Drabble, from her novel *The Millstone*

A Touch of Scandal ★★ 15

Comedy 1984 · US · Colour · 88mins

You can guess the plot from the title of this one – Angie Dickinson's political career is threatened when a few skeletons pop out her closet. Unfortunately, we've heard all this before, and even the experienced and personable cast (Tom Skerritt, Don Murray, Robert Loggia) and director Ivan Nagy can't save this from being just another run-of-the-mill drama. 📼

Angie Dickinson *Katherine Gilvey* • Tom Skerritt *Father Dwelle* • Jason Miller *Reverend Locke* • Don Murray *Benjamin Gilvey* • Robert Loggia *Paul Avakian* • Stephen Shellen *Billy Podovsky* • Lois Foraker *Polly* ■ *Dir* Ivan Nagy • *Scr* Richard A Guttman

Touch of Truth ★★★ 15

Drama based on a true story
1994 · US · Colour · 89mins

Echoing the theme of child abuse found in *Sleepers*, this is an emotionally exhausting TV movie with so many plot threads that you are scarcely allowed to recover from one trauma before you are enmeshed in an even more stressful one. Melissa Gilbert and Patty Duke give earnest performances as, respectively, the mother of an autistic child and the teacher who tries to develop his life skills. Their feud over the boy's welfare is convincingly depicted, but his courtroom ordeal is even more harrowing. Sure, it's manipulative, but it's a vast improvement on most TV movies. 📼

Patty Duke *Terry Walser* • Melissa Gilbert *Karen Barth* • Bradley Pierce *Michael Barth* • Markus Flanagan *Roger Barth* ■ *Dir* Michael Switzer • *Scr* Robert Inman

A Touch of Zen ★★★★

Martial arts action drama
1969 · Tai · Colour · 175mins

King Hu was one of the masters of the *wu xia* or swordplay film, yet this labyrinthine epic is much more than a simple action flick. The first in the "Buddhist" trilogy (completed by *Raining in the Mountain* and *Legend in the Mountain*), *A Touch of Zen* is at the same time a study of rural life, a ghost story, a discussion of philosophical ideas and a thrilling fight film, with each element being handled with rare skill by Hu, a director whose love of Chinese opera and classical art is clearly evident in every frame. In Mandarin with English subtitles.

Hsu Feng *Yang* • Chun Shih *Ku* • Pai Ying *Shih* • Tien Peng *Ou-Yang* • Hsueh Han *Lu* ■ *Dir/Scr* King Hu

Touchdown ★★ 15

Drama 1981 · US · Colour · 86mins

Co-director Silvio Narizzano made *Georgy Girl* in 1966, so he can be forgiven for foisting this preachy slice of high-school angst on an unsuspecting public. A boy, crazy about football and music, goes into an emotional tailspin after being diagnosed as partially deaf, falling in with a bad lot who rampage through the school. The film was released on video five years later, for those who wanted to see Demi Moore making her movie debut. 📼

Paul Carafotes *John Carluccio* • Victor French *Gary Carluccio* • Lelia Goldoni *Jean Carluccio* • Val Avery *Coach Rizo* • Dennis Patrick *Dr Bowers* • Demi Moore *Corri* ■ *Dir* Silvio Narizzano, Rami Alon • *Scr* Rami Alon

Touched by Love ★★★ U

Drama 1979 · US · Colour · 93mins

Also known as *To Elvis, With Love* (a title which tends to give away the plot), this moving if somewhat sentimental drama is based on a true story. It's a tale of a child with cerebral palsy who becomes more open and communicative after a nursing trainee (Deborah Raffin) encourages her to write a letter to Elvis Presley. Raffin gives a competent performance as Lena Canada (she received a Golden Globe nomination) but it is a young Diane Lane who steals the film and successfully tugs at the heartstrings as Karen, the girl lucky enough to become The King's pen pal.

Deborah Raffin *Lena Canada* • Diane Lane *Karen* • Michael Learned *Dr Bell* • John Amos *Tony* • Cristina Raines *Amy* • Mary Wickes *Margaret* • Clu Gulager *Don Fielder* ■ *Dir* Gus Trikonis • *Scr* Hesper Anderson, from the book *To Elvis, with Love* by Lena Canada

Tough Enough ★ 15

Melodrama 1982 · US · Colour · 101mins

Forgettable attempt by Richard Fleischer to explore the ugly world of the "Tough Man" fighting circuit in America. Dennis Quaid struggles as the failing singer turned fighter and the storyline is barely worthy of lasting the first round, let alone going the distance. 📼

Dennis Quaid *Art Long* • Carlene Watkins *Caroline Long* • Warren Oates *James Neese* • Stan Shaw *PT Coolidge* • Pam Grier *Myra* • Bruce McGill *Tony Fallon* • Wilford Brimley *Bill Long* • Fran Ryan *Gert Long* ■ *Dir* Richard O Fleischer [Richard Fleischer] • *Scr* John Leone

Tough Guys ★★★ 15

Comedy 1986 · US · Colour · 99mins

To watch Kirk Douglas and Burt Lancaster use their combined star power to rescue a ropey script is to witness celebrity at its most intense and endearing. As the perpetrators of America's last train robbery, they are released from prison, elderly and bewildered, into an ageist world, so they mount their own grey offensive. Douglas's athletic and sexual prowess is a show-off embarrassment, but Lancaster retains a dignity and poise which confronts the dilemma of age with enormous poignancy. Both, though, spark an on-screen magic that has as much to do with their past

charisma as their roles here. Contains some violence and swearing. ⎕

Burt Lancaster *Harry Doyle* • Kirk Douglas *Archie Long* • Charles Durning *Deke Yablonski* • Alexis Smith *Belle* • Dana Carvey *Richie Evans* • Darlanne Fluegel *Skye Foster* • Eli Wallach *Leon B Little* • Monty Ash *Vince* ■ *Dir* Jeff Kanew • *Scr* James Orr, Jim Cruickshank

Tough Guys Don't Dance
★★ 18

Black comedy 1987 · US · Colour · 104mins

Bizarre black comedy with *film noir* flourishes, written and directed by Norman Mailer as an exercise in experimental movie-making. Ryan O'Neal plays a downtrodden would-be writer who may have committed a murder – but can't quite remember. Yes, it's that sort of film, with lots of weird people running around in a weird manner, saying weird things. The movie seeks to send up Raymond Chandler, but only works intermittently. A strong supporting cast includes Isabella Rossellini, Lawrence Tierney and Wings Hauser. ⎕

Ryan O'Neal *Tim Madden* • Isabella Rossellini *Madeline* • Debra Sandlund *Patty Lareine* • Wings Hauser *Regency* • John Bedford Lloyd *Wardley Meeks III* • Clarence Williams III *Bolo* • Lawrence Tierney *Dougy Madden* ■ *Dir/Scr* Norman Mailer

The Toughest Man in the World
★ PG

Drama 1984 · US · Colour · 94mins

A horribly misconceived vehicle for *The A-Team's* Mr T. He plays a brute with a heart of gold who finds himself responsible for troubled kids from a youth centre and sets them on the straight and narrow. A mind-numbing amalgam of cartoonish action and syrupy sentimentality. Incidentally, Renaissance man Mr T also gets to sing the theme song.

Mr T *Bruise Brubaker* • Dennis Dugan *Dick* • John P Navin Jr *Billy* • Peggy Pope *Esther* • Lynne Moody *Leslie* • Joe Greco *Matty* • Tom Milanovich *Tanker* ■ *Dir* Dick Lowry • *Scr* Jimmy Sangster, Richard A Guttman, from a story by Vincent Bono

Tourist Trap
★★ 15

Horror 1979 · US · Colour · 89mins

Take *House of Wax*, season with *The Texas Chainsaw Massacre*, add a soupçon of *Carrie* and leave for 20 minutes, or preferably for the rest of your waking life. Suspense is a rare commodity in this low-budget horror flick focusing on a group of teens – including future Charlie's Angel and Bond girl Tanya Roberts – who get marooned in the desert when their jeep breaks down. Unluckily for them it's near a museum housing a collection of wax models controlled by nutty Chuck Connors. It's tempting to say that the dummies give the best performances.

Chuck Connors *Slausen* • Jon Van Ness *Jerry* • Jocelyn Jones *Molly* • Robin Sherwood *Eileen* • Tanya Roberts *Becky* • Keith McDermott *Woody* ■ *Dir* David Schmoeller • *Scr* David Schmoeller, J Larry Carroll

Tourist Trap
★★

Comedy adventure
1998 · US · Colour · 95mins

The wacky side of history is the focus of this family TV movie. Disillusioned banker Daniel Stern decides to put some fire in his life by taking his reluctant family on a motor-home vacation which involves retracing the steps of a Civil War ancestor. Calamity and chaos ensue, as they encounter bizarre characters and the old soldier's ghost (Paul Giamatti). It's lightweight fun, filled with harmless, nearly non-stop action sequences and Julie Hagerty is wonderful playing straight-woman to Stern's appropriately goofy patriarch.

Daniel Stern *George Piper* • Julie Hagerty *Bess Piper* • David Rasche *Derek Early* • Paul Giamatti *Jeremiah Piper* • Margot Finley *Rachel Piper* • Blair Slater *Josh Piper* • Ryan Reynolds *Wade Early* ■ *Dir* Richard Benjamin • *Scr* Andy Breckman

Tous les Matins du Monde
★★★★ 15

Historical drama 1992 · Fr · Colour · 109mins

The winner of seven Césars (the French equivalent to the Oscars), this majestic historical costume drama is a delight for both eyes and ears. Jean-Pierre Marielle is outstanding as 17th-century composer Sainte Colombe, while on his debut Guillaume Depardieu is splendidly dashing as his sole pupil, Marin Marais. Guillaume's father Gérard Depardieu has a choice cameo as the older Marais, who becomes Louis XIV's musical director, looking back with regret on his reckless youth, when he betrayed Sainte Colombe's daughter and only half learned the lessons of the master. Director Alain Corneau captures the period perfectly and the baroque viola da gamba music is magnificent. In French with English subtitles. Contains sex scenes and nudity. ⎕

Jean-Pierre Marielle *Monsieur De Sainte Colombe* • Gérard Depardieu *Marin Marais* • Anne Brochet *Madeleine* • Guillaume Depardieu *Young Marin Marais* • Caroline Sihol *Mme de Sainte Colombe* • Carole Richert *Toinette* ■ *Dir* Alain Corneau • *Scr* Pascal Quignard, Alain Corneau, from the novel by Pascal Quignard

Tout Va Bien
★★★ 18

Experimental political drama
1972 · Fr/It · Colour · 91mins

After four years of making 16mm and video movies, Marxist co-directors Jean-Luc Godard and Jean-Pierre Gorin returned to ''commercial'' film-making by casting Jane Fonda and Yves Montand in the leading roles. But audiences didn't exactly flock to see this depiction of workers occupying their factory and holding their bosses prisoner. Fonda plays an American journalist and Montand – her lover – a former New Wave director now forced to make TV ads for a living, as Godard himself had done. There is a lot of serious talk, a splendid composite set and a few jokes, but it is now a dated monument to the revolutionary spirit of 1968. In French with English subtitles. ⎕

Jane Fonda *Susan* • Yves Montand *Jacques* • Vittorio Capprioli *Factory manager* • Pierre

Oudry *Frédéric* • Jean Pignol *CGT delegate* • Elizabeth Chauvin *Geneviève* ■ *Dir/Scr* Jean-Luc Godard, Jean-Pierre Gorin

Tovarich
★★★

Comedy 1937 · US · BW · 92mins

Claudette Colbert and Charles Boyer, anticipating the Russian Revolution, are the aristocrats who escape to Paris, where they deposit the tsar's billions in a Paris bank and, unwilling to spend the cash, set themselves up as a maid and butler in a grand French home. Inevitably, they are found out, leading to a farcical comedy of disguise. While not nearly as entertaining or as politically astute as the later *Ninotchka*, Colbert and Boyer make a suave and witty couple, ably supported by an imperious Basil Rathbone.

Claudette Colbert *The Grand Duchess Tatiana Petrovna/Tina Dubrovsky* • Charles Boyer *Prince Mikail Alexandrovitch Ouratieff/Michel* • Basil Rathbone *Gorotchenko* • Anita Louise *Helen Dupont* • Melville Cooper *Charles Dupont* • Isabel Jeans *Fernande Dupont* • Maurice Murphy *Georges Dupont* ■ *Dir* Anatole Litvak • *Scr* Casey Robinson, Robert E Sherwood, from the play by Jacques Deval

Toward the Unknown
★★ U

Drama 1956 · US · Colour · 114mins

Called *Brink of Hell* in the UK, this dour drama remains unexciting under any title, as stressed pilot William Holden tries to regain the respect of his men. Dating from that pre-space age era when nearly every studio made a patriotic airborne drama, the flight sequences here probably looked spectacular at the time, and the action grinds to a halt when the planes are on the ground. Co-star Virginia Leith, in her short movie career, performed a similar function at Fox looking after pilot Guy Madison in *On the Threshold of Space*, and her close-ups in this film are virtually identical. A young James Garner makes his film debut.

William Holden (1) *Major Lincoln Bond* • Lloyd Nolan *Brigadier General Bill Banner* • Virginia Leith *Connie Mitchell* • Charles McGraw *Colonel ''Mickey'' McKee* • Murray Hamilton *Major ''Bromo'' Lee* • Paul Fix *Major General Bryan Shelby* • LQ Jones *Lieutenant Sweeney* • James Garner *Major Joe Craven* ■ *Dir* Mervyn LeRoy • *Scr* Beirne Lay Jr

Towed in a Hole
★★★★ U

Comedy 1932 · US · BW · 20mins

The best Stan and Ollie movie is the one you are watching, although some masterpieces are so ingenious in their destructive comedy that they linger in the mind. The springboard here is Stanley's suggestion that they should not just sell fish, but catch it as well – thus doubling their income. A boat is found and its refit becomes an orgy of misfortune. Memorable jokes include Stanley, confined below, getting his head stuck behind the mast. Oliver is up a ladder painting it. Stanley finds a saw... Anticipation is more than half the pleasure with this duo – the most endearing and inventive comedians in cinema history. ⎕

Stan Laurel *Stan* • Oliver Hardy *Ollie* • Billy Gilbert *Joe, junkyard owner* ■ *Dir* George Marshall • *Scr* HM Walker, Stan Laurel

The Tower
★ 15

Science-fiction thriller
1992 · US · Colour · 86mins

There's a tower block, right? And it's controlled by this state-of-the-art computer. And the owners are dead chuffed with it. You'll never guess what happens... the computer goes haywire and only one man can stop it? Oh, you've seen it? If not, you've seen countless films like it. This has to be one of the most derivative plotlines ever concocted. ⎕

Paul Reiser *Tony Minot* • Roger Rees *Mr Littlehill* • Susan Norman *Linda Furillo* • Annabelle Gurwitch *Sally* • Dee Dee Rescher *Gretchen* • Charmaine Cruise *Secretary* ■ *Dir* Richard Kletter • *Scr* John Riley, Richard Kletter, from a story by John Riley

Tower of Evil
★★ 18

Horror 1972 · UK · Colour · 89mins

A series of killings and some buried treasure lure detective Bryant Halliday and a group of unusually attractive, pot-smoking, sex-starved archaeologists to the archetypal accursed isle. It isn't long before further frenzied murders start to reduce their number. Terrible dialogue and not much suspense, but the nudity, violence, and Robin Askwith are very seventies, and this has found a new generation of fans. ⎕

Bryant Halliday *Det Brent* • Jill Haworth *Rose* • Anthony Valentine *Dr Simpson* • Anna Palk *Nora* • Jack Watson *Hamp* • Mark Edwards *Adam* • Derek Fowlds *Dan* • Robin Askwith *Des* ■ *Dir* Jim O'Connolly • *Scr* Jim O'Connolly, from a story by George Baxt

The Tower of Lies

Silent drama 1925 · US · BW

Swedish director Victor Sjöström (aka Seastrom) had made such masterpieces as *The Wind* (1928), and this dour and miscast MGM drama reunited him with Norma Shearer and Lon Chaney stars of *He Who Gets Slapped* (1924). Chaney plays a Swedish farmer about to lose his livelihood to unbalanced landowner Ian Keith; Shearer is Chaney's daughter who goes to the city to raise money, resorts to prostitution, and returns home in disgrace before being rescued by her childhood sweetheart (William Haines). No prints exist of this lost film.

Norma Shearer *Glory* • Lon Chaney *Jan* • Ian Keith *Lars* • Claire McDowell *Katrina* • William Haines *August* • David Torrence *Eric* ■ *Dir* Victor Seastrom [Victor Sjöström] • *Scr* Agnes Christine Johnston, Max Marcin, Marian Ainslee (titles), Ruth Cummings (titles), from the novel *Kejsarn av Portugallien; en Värmlandsberättelse* by Selma Ottiliana Lovisa Lagerlöf

Tower of London
★★★

Historical drama 1939 · US · BW · 92mins

Universal, having hit pay dirt with their fictitious monsters, here turned their attentions to British history, producing a highly fanciful account of the Duke of Gloucester's machinations to seize the throne as Richard III. The Duke of Clarence is drowned in a wine barrel, but most of the rest, involving Gloucester and royal executioner Mord dispatching all and sundry, is fabrication, grim but too often

plodding. The chief appeal is the fruity performances of Basil Rathbone, Boris Karloff, Vincent Price and Leo G Carroll.

Basil Rathbone *Richard, Duke of Gloucester* • Boris Karloff *Mord* • Barbara O'Neil *Queen Elizabeth* • Ian Hunter *King Edward IV* • Vincent Price *Duke of Clarence* • Nan Grey *Lady Alice Barton* • John Sutton *John Wyatt* • Leo G Carroll *Hastings* ■ *Dir* Rowland V Lee • *Scr* Robert N Lee

Tower of London ★★

Horror 1962 · US · BW · 79mins

Roger Corman's film about Richard III keeps the basic structure of the better 1939 film of the same title, as the Duke of Gloucester murders everyone who blocks his path to the throne. This is more of a spook film, as Gloucester is troubled, like Macbeth, by the ghosts of his victims. Vincent Price, who played the Duke of Clarence in the earlier film, makes a formidable if camp Gloucester, and the script is unusually intelligent, but the action is studio-bound – grim without being chilling. This is one of Corman's lesser-known films, not made for his usual studio, AIP.

Vincent Price *Richard of Gloucester* • Michael Pate *Sir Ratcliffe* • Joan Freeman *Lady Margaret* • Robert Brown *Sir Justin* • Justice Watson *Edward IV* • Sarah Selby *Queen Elizabeth* • Richard McCauly *Clarence* • Eugene Martin *Edward V* ■ *Dir* Roger Corman • *Scr* Leo V Gordon, F Amos Powell, James B Gordon, from a story by Leo V Gordon, F Amos Powell

Tower of Terror ★★

Fantasy 1997 · US · Colour · 89mins

The happiest haunted house on earth is the locale for this Disney TV movie. Tabloid reporter Steve Guttenberg investigates the mysterious long-ago disappearance of five guests from a Hollywood hotel elevator on Halloween night, 1939. The fact that this film is aimed at the younger set inevitably robs it of any real thrills or suspense; in the end, the dreadful dialogue is more frightening than the ghosts, who are more cuddly than creepy.

Steve Guttenberg *Buzzy Crocker* • Nia Peeples *Jill* • Micheal McShane *Chris "Q"Todd* • Amzie Strickland *Abigail Gregory* • Melora Hardin *Claire Poulet* ■ *Dir/Scr* DJ MacHale

The Towering Inferno

★★★★ 15

Disaster movie 1974 · US · Colour · 158mins

It took two major studios Fox and Warner Bros pooling resources and two similar novels *The Tower* and *The Glass Inferno* to make disaster movie maestro Irwin Allen's triple-Oscar-winning hit. The fun comes from guessing which superstars will get fried to a crisp in the burning San Francisco skyscraper, ignited during the opening ceremony, and who will be saved by daring fire chief Steve McQueen. The big-name cast plays second fiddle to the blazing special effects, but the mounting suspense and outlandish rescue attempts fan the consistently entertaining flames. Contains swearing and harrowing scenes.

Steve McQueen *Fire Chief Michael O'Hallorhan* • Paul Newman *Doug Roberts* • William Holden (1) *Jim Duncan* • Faye Dunaway *Susan*

Franklin • Fred Astaire *Harlee Claiborne* • Susan Blakely *Patty Simmons* • Richard Chamberlain *Roger Simmons* • Jennifer Jones *Lisolette Mueller* • OJ Simpson *Security Chief Jernigan* • Robert Vaughn *Senator Gary Parker* • Robert Wagner *Dan Bigelow* ■ *Dir* John Guillermin, Irwin Allen • *Scr* Stirling Silliphant, from the novels *The Tower* by Richard Martin Stern and *The Glass Inferno* by Thomas N Scortia, Frank M Robinson

The Town Bully ★★

Drama 1988 · US · Colour · 95mins

Noel Black who won critical acclaim for his 1968 drama *Pretty Poison*, with Tuesday Weld here directs a so-so tale of a prosecutor (Bruce Boxleitner) attempting to arrest the vigilante who killed a criminal accused of intimidating a town. Expect lots of "You can't just go round killing people..." speeches and an underplayed performance from Boxleitner, who unfortunately looks like he'd prefer to be toting a gun than a legal dictionary.

Bruce Boxleitner *Bobby Doniger* • Pat Hingle *Charlie King* • David Graf *Raymond West* ■ *Dir* Noel Black • *Scr* Jonathan Rintels

A Town Called Hell ★★

Spaghetti western 1971 · UK/Sp · Colour · 97mins

Although shot in Spain, this western also known as *A Town Called Bastard* is one of the few British ventures into the genre. Set in 1895 in Mexico, it is a brutal affair, in which Stella Stevens seeks to discover who killed her husband a decade earlier, while Martin Landau threatens to reveal that his brother, Robert Shaw, is not a priest but a ruthless bandit. The cast nearly compensates for a slackness in Robert Parrish's direction, as the movie lurches from tightly shot moments of brooding tension to frantic outbursts of stylised violence.

Robert Shaw *Priest* • Telly Savalas *Don Carlos* • Stella Stevens *Alvira* • Michael Craig *Paco* • Martin Landau *Colonel* • Dudley Sutton *Spectre* • Fernando Rey *Old blind farmer* ■ *Dir* Robert Parrish • *Scr* Richard Aubrey

A Town Has Turned to Dust

★★ 18

Science-fiction drama 1998 · US · Colour · 87mins

Based on a Rod Serling script dusted off from his *Twilight Zone* heyday, this cable movie combines thoughtful storytelling with above average acting. Set in a futuristic desert hamlet, ruthless town boss Ron Perlman lynches an innocent native American, setting the scene for a revolt by the murdered teenager's brother, Frankie Avina, and a clash with drunken sheriff, Stephen Lang. The movie's message – that age-old problems such as racism and oppression are timeless – may be a little dated, and some scenes are awkwardly disjointed, but its heart is in the right place even if the special effects aren't up to scratch. Contains violence.

Ron Perlman *Jerry Paul* • Stephen Lang *Harvey Denton* • Judy Collins *Ree* • Gabriel Olds *Hannify* • Babara Jane Reams *Maya* • Frankie Avina *Tooth* ■ *Dir* Rob Nilsson • *Scr* Rod Serling

A Town like Alice ★★★ PG

War drama 1956 · UK · BW · 111mins

Director Jack Lee's documentary background is evident in this earnest adaptation of Nevil Shute's celebrated wartime novel about a group of women route-marched across Malaya by the invading Japanese. While he has little difficulty setting his scene, he struggles to prevent some episodes contained in the rather underwhelming script from lapsing into overwrought melodrama. The cast members keep their heads above water, with sympathetic guard Tagaki, Jean Anderson later one of the stars of the BBC PoW drama *Tenko* and Renee Houston offering stout support to Virginia McKenna, whose romantic interludes with Peter Finch provide some charming relief from the trials of the trek. *DVD*

Virginia McKenna *Jean Paget* • Peter Finch *Joe Harman* • Takagi *Japanese Sergeant* • Tran Van Khe *Captain Sugaya* • Jean Anderson *Miss Horsefall* • Marie Lohr *Mrs Dudley Frost* • Maureen Swanson *Ellen* • Renee Houston *Ebbey* ■ *Dir* Jack Lee • *Scr* WP Lipscomb, Richard Mason, from the novel by Nevil Shute

Town on Trial ★★

Crime mystery 1956 · UK · BW · 96mins

A very British whodunit sees Scotland Yard man John Mills called in to investigate unsavoury goings on in an English town. A woman with a dubious reputation is found dead on club property and there's no shortage of suspects for Mills to grill, all of whom seem to have a dodgy past. This modest mystery offers a modicum of tension, though the title would have us believe that Home Counties morality is open to question.

Charles Coburn *Dr John Fenner* • John Mills *Supt Mike Halloran* • Barbara Bates *Elizabeth Fenner* • Derek Farr *Mark Roper* • Alec McCowen *Peter Crowley* • Elizabeth Seal *Fiona Dixon* ■ *Dir* John Guillermin • *Scr* Robert Westerby, Ken Hughes

Town Rat, Country Rat ★★★★

Silent animation 1923 · Fr · Tinted · 13mins

Ladislaw Starewicz demonstrates his cinematic ingenuity and a fondness for slapstick, as well as his genius for puppetry, in this spicily satirical retelling of the familiar fable of the country rat overwhelmed by the pace and danger of city life. Starting with a mischievous use of back projection, as the town rat motors out of Paris, the film also includes iconic cartoon dialogue, a segment combining live-action and animation (as a curious kitten chases the rodentine revellers at a cabaret soirée) and an intricate superimposition flashback, as the country rat recalls the wine and the women that enlivened his adventure.

Dir Ladislaw Starewicz • *Scr* Ladislaw Starewicz, from a fable by Jean de La Fontaine

A Town Torn Apart ★★ PG

Drama based on a true story 1992 · US · Colour · 86mins

Husband-and-wife team Michael Tucker and Jill Eikenberry (TV's *LA Law*), star in this tepid TV movie directed by

Daniel Petrie. Usually school movies are about dedicated teachers struggling to impart a little knowledge into delinquent teens, but here the problem lies with the parents in a small town who disapprove of city slicker Tucker's modern methods. You'll find more controversy and drama on one of those TV "confessions" shows. Contains some swearing.

Michael Tucker *Dennis Littky* • Carole Galloway *Sheila Bennett* • Jill Eikenberry *Ellen Kreiger* • Linda Griffiths *Hallie* • Bernard Behrens *Angus Maclean* ■ *Dir* Daniel Petrie • *Scr* Deena Goldstone, from the non-fiction book *Doc* by Susan Kammeraad-Campbell

Town without Pity ★★ 15

Courtroom drama 1961 · US/W Ger/Swi · BW · 99mins

Kirk Douglas has often been drawn to roles in which he can express self-disgust. Here he stars as an army officer defending four American servicemen on a charge of raping a young girl in Germany (played by Christine Kaufmann). As the case progresses, Douglas reluctantly sullies the girl's reputation to save the men from a death sentence. Filmed in Germany, this comes across as crude and loud, revelling in its sensational aspects.

Kirk Douglas *Major Steve Garrett* • Christine Kaufmann *Karin Steinhof* • EG Marshall *Major Jerome Pakenham* • Robert Blake *Jim* • Richard Jaeckel *Bidie* • Frank Sutton *Chuck* ■ *Dir* Gottfried Reinhardt • *Scr* Silvia Reinhardt, George Hurdalek, Jan Lustig, from the novel *The Verdict* by Manfred Gregor

The Toxic Avenger ★★★ 18

Spoof horror 1985 · US · Colour · 75mins

After years of churning out teen comedies that weren't very funny, Troma Films hit the big time with this outrageously tacky superhero spoof. Weedy janitor Mark Torgl is transformed into good-guy monster the Toxic Avenger (Mitchell Cohen) after being dumped into a barrel of toxic goo by a gang of thugs. Toxie (as he's known to his friends) is very nice to his blind girlfriend but metes out violent punishment to local criminals. Loaded with infantile slapstick, amateurish acting, teen-orientated erotica and extreme gore (trimmed considerably in this country) this is B-movie making at its crudest and purest. *DVD*

Andree Maranda *Sara* • Mitchell Cohen *Toxic Avenger* • Jennifer Baptist *Wanda* • Cindy Manion *Julie* • Robert Prichard *Slug* • Gary Schneider *Bozo* • Mark Torgl *Melvin* • Marisa Tomei *Health club girl* ■ *Dir* Michael Herz, Samuel Weil • *Scr* Joe Ritter, Lloyd Kaufman, Gay Partington Terry, Stuart Strutin

The Toxic Avenger, Part II

★★ 18

Spoof horror 1988 · US · Colour · 90mins

Fans of Troma Films' most celebrated creation had to wait three years for the inevitable follow-up. In the meantime their hero had achieved near iconic status, but even his most die-hard fans had trouble finding anything to enjoy in this wholesale debacle which sees Toxie, travelling to Japan to save the planet's ecosystem from an evil industrial conglomerate. Shot back-to-back with the even more lamentable

Part III, this was co-directed by Lloyd Kaufman, the founder of Troma, who have since given the world such masterpieces as *Surf Nazis Must Die* and *Cannibal! The Musical.* 🎞 **DVD**

Ron Fazio *The Toxic Avenger* • John Altamura *The Toxic Avenger* • Phoebe Legere *Claire* • Rick Collins *Apocalypse Inc Chairman* • Rikiya Yasuoka *Big Mac* ■ *Dir* Lloyd Kaufman, Michael Herz • *Scr* Gay Partington Terry, from a story by Lloyd Kaufman

The Toy ★★ 🅿🅶

Comedy 1982 · US · Colour · 97mins

Richard Pryor, a journalist fallen on hard times, is working as a janitor at the Bates department store. His slapstick incompetence at dealing with an inflatable toy is watched by nine-year-old Eric, the spoiled heir to the Bates empire. Eric is allowed to visit his father (Jackie Gleason) at work once every year and to have anything he chooses for that week. Eric chooses to have Jack as a human "toy". An adaptation of Francis Veber's 1976 French film *Le Jouet*, this version has some fine moments (especially at the start) but soon degenerates into a mawkish message movie. 🎞

Richard Pryor *Jack Brown* • Jackie Gleason *US Bates* • Ned Beatty *Morehouse* • Scott Schwartz *Eric Bates* • Teresa Ganzel *Fancy Bates* • Wilfrid Hyde White *Barkley* • Annazette Chase *Angela* ■ *Dir* Richard Donner • *Scr* Carol Sobieski, from the film *Le Jouet* by Francis Veber

Toy Soldiers ★★ 🅸🅵

Action thriller 1991 · US · Colour · 107mins

A dopey action story that blends *Animal House* antics with Rambo-ish heroics to risible effect. Sean Astin and Wil Wheaton are the teenage pranksters who lead their classmates in a fight back when nasty South American mobsters take over their school. Louis Gossett Jr and Denholm Elliott provide a few memorable moments and manage to keep straight faces throughout the brattish posturing of the younger members of the cast, but the sheer silliness of the concept doomed this project right from the start. Contains violence. 🎞

Sean Astin *Billy Tepper* • Wil Wheaton *Joey Trotta* • Keith Coogan *Snuffy Bradberry* • Andrew Divoff *Luis Cali* • R Lee Ermey *General Kramer* • Mason Adams *Deputy Director Brown* • Denholm Elliott *Headmaster* • Louis Gossett Jr *Dean Parker* ■ *Dir* Daniel Petrie Jr • *Scr* Daniel Petrie Jr, David Koepp, from the novel by William P Kennedy

Toy Story ★★★★★ 🅿🅶

Animated comedy adventure 1995 · US · Colour · 88mins

The first completely computer-generated animation feature is a masterpiece from director John Lasseter, with voice-overs by Tom Hanks, Tim Allen, Don Rickles and others rounding out convincing characterisations. Woody, an old-fashioned pullstring cowboy, is his owner Andy's favourite toy, and lords it benevolently over Mr Potato Head, Bo-Peep and Rex the Dinosaur. Until, that is, the arrival of newcomer Buzz Lightyear, a high-tech space-ranger. Only when the two heroes are united against the evil boy next door is there

a reconciliation. It's a great adventure story as well as a jokey parable. An instant classic of a unique kind. 🎞

Tom Hanks *Woody* • Tim Allen *Buzz Lightyear* • Don Rickles *Mr Potato Head* • Jim Varney *Slinky Dog* • Wallace Shawn *Rex* • John Ratzenberger *Hamm* • Annie Potts *Bo Peep* • *Dir* John Lasseter • *Scr* Joss Whedon, Andrew Stanton, Joel Cohen, Alec Sokolow, from a story by John Lasseter, Pete Docter, Andrew Stanton, Joe Ranft • *Music* Randy Newman • *Animator* Pete Docter, Rich Quade, Ash Brannon

Toy Story 2 ★★★★★ 🆄

Animated comedy adventure 1999 · US · Colour · 94mins

Originally intended as a 60-minute, straight-to-video project, this was a work in progress right up to its release – complete with last-minute additions to the cast. Product opportunism, perhaps. Yet who can be wholly cynical about a film that not only manages to surpass its predecessor, but also restores credibility to that much-debased term, "family entertainment"? Buzz Lightyear's bid to rescue Woody the cowboy from the clutches of a sleazy toy collector will keep the youngsters on the edge of their seats. However, it's the little touches that will delight the grown-ups, most notably the in-jokes at the expense of *Star Wars* and *Jurassic Park*, and the charming re-creation of a fifties TV puppet show. Nigh-on perfect.

Tom Hanks *Woody* • Tim Allen *Buzz Lightyear* • Joan Cusack *Jessie* • Kelsey Grammer *Prospector* • Don Rickles *Mr Potato Head* • Jim Varney *Slinky Dog* • Wallace Shawn *Rex* • John Ratzenberger *Hamm* • Annie Potts *Bo Peep* ■ *Dir* John Lasseter, Lee Unkrich, Ash Brannon • *Scr* Andrew Stanton, Rita Hsiao, Doug Chamberlin, Chris Webb, from a story by John Lasseter, Pete Docter, Ash Brannon, Andrew Stanton

The Toy Wife ★★ 🆄

Period romantic drama 1938 · US · BW · 95mins

Returned from Europe to the family seat in Louisiana, Luise Rainer throws off her beau Robert Young and steals her sister's fiancé, Melvyn Douglas. They marry and have a child, but she proves incapable of meeting the demands of her position. This overheated period melodrama did no favours to the career of Rainer, holder of two consecutive Oscars for *The Great Ziegfeld* and *The Good Earth*. Inhabiting the same territory as *Jezebel* and *Gone with the Wind*, but displaying the dramatic quality of neither, it was considered arthritically old-fashioned in its day, and now has little to offer other than high-class sets and costumes.

Luise Rainer *Gilberta "Frou Frou" Brigard* • Melvyn Douglas *Georges Sartoris* • Robert Young *André Vallaire* • Barbara O'Neil *Louise Brigard* • HB Warner *Victor Brigard* • Alma Kruger *Mme Vallaire* • Libby Taylor *Suzanne* ■ *Dir* Richard Thorpe • *Scr* Zoe Akins

Toys ★★★ 🅿🅶

Comedy fantasy 1992 · US · Colour · 116mins

Director Barry Levinson's fragile fable about war-addicted general Michael Gambon inheriting his brother's toy factory is monumentally self-indulgent and hopelessly naive. Robin Williams,

playing the nephew trying to stop Gambon manufacturing only war games, tanks and guns, is surprisingly low-key and this anti-war fantasy satire greatly misses a core crowd-pleasing performance from the ad-lib master. You'll gasp in sheer amazement at the magnificent sets and decor, but they are the only real reasons for watching this cult flop. Contains some violence. 🎞

Robin Williams *Leslie Zevo* • Michael Gambon *The General* • Joan Cusack *Alsatia Zevo* • Robin Wright [Robin Wright Penn] *Gwen* • LL Cool J *Patrick* • Donald O'Connor *Kenneth Zevo* • Arthur Malet *Owens Owens* • Jack Warden *Zevo Sr* ■ *Dir* Barry Levinson • *Scr* Valerie Curtin, Barry Levinson

Toys in the Attic ★★

Melodrama 1963 · US · BW · 90mins

Lillian Hellman's play is the basis for this steamy though softened drama about bizarre goings-on in a fading New Orleans family. Dean Martin is good as the ne'er-do-well who brings his young bride home to visit his poverty-stricken spinster sisters (Wendy Hiller and Geraldine Page), while hiding his ill-gotten riches. But one of the sisters is obsessively in love with him, and tries to force him to stay. Not quite Tennessee Williams, but engrossing none the less.

Dean Martin *Julian Berniers* • Geraldine Page *Carrie Berniers* • Yvette Mimieux *Lily Prine Berniers* • Wendy Hiller *Anna Berniers* • Gene Tierney *Albertine Prine* • Nan Martin *Charlotte Warkins* • Larry Gates *Cyrus Warkins* ■ *Dir* George Roy Hill • *Scr* James Poe, from the play by Lillian Hellman

Traces of Red ★★ 🅸🅵

Mystery thriller 1992 · US · Colour · 100mins

It's shades of *Sunset Boulevard*, as the newly-killed corpse of cop James Belushi narrates the story of a serial killer with a penchant for Yves Saint Laurent lipstick and bad poetry. Unfortunately the similarity ends there, as the increasingly convoluted and implausible plot is interspersed with the standard mixture of soft-core porn and violence. A fair-quality cast includes Tony Goldwyn as Belushi's partner, and a sexually ravenous Lorraine Bracco.

James Belushi *Jack Dobson* • Lorraine Bracco *Ellen Schofield* • Tony Goldwyn *Steve Frayn* • William Russ *Michael Dobson* • Faye Grant *Beth Frayn* • Michelle Joyner *Morgan Cassidy* ■ *Dir* Andy Wolk • *Scr* Jim Piddock

Track of the Cat ★★★★

Western drama 1954 · US · Colour · 102mins

A strange and brooding western melodrama, distinguished by its unique sense of design. Although filmed in CinemaScope and colour, the whole film is art directed, costumed, and lit for black-and-white – only occasional flashes of colour breaking up the wintery landscape. Although rather ponderous, there are fine performances from lead Robert Mitchum and, particularly, from Beulah Bondi as the family matriarch. There are some parallels with *Long Day's Journey into Night* in terms of the family travails, and the structure, which here involves a very symbolic hunt for a wild cat.

Robert Mitchum *Curt Bridges* • Teresa Wright *Grace Bridges* • Diana Lynn *Gwen Williams* • Tab Hunter *Harold "Hal" Bridges* • Beulah Bondi *Ma Bridges* • Philip Tonge *Pa Bridges* • William Hopper *Arthur* • Carl "Alfalfa" Switzer [Carl Switzer] *Joe Sam* ■ *Dir* William A Wellman • *Scr* Al Bezzerides, from a novel by Walter Van Tilburg Clark

Track 29 ★★★ 🅸🆁

Fantasy melodrama 1988 · UK · Colour · 86mins

Surrealist director Nicolas Roeg joins arcane writer Dennis Potter for a well constructed Freudian psychodrama about cloaking sexual unfulfilment behind easy nostalgia. Taking its title from the song Chattanooga Choo-Choo, housewife Theresa Russell finds her erotic fantasies triggered by stranger Gary Oldman, while her dowdy husband plays with his model railway in the attic. However, Oldman's multiple-identity crisis means he could also be her adopted son. Shockingly original, amusingly chilling and occasionally inaccessible, this study in self-delusion seldom goes off the rails. Contains swearing, violence and nudity. 🎞

Theresa Russell *Linda Henry* • Gary Oldman *Martin* • Christopher Lloyd *Dr Henry Henry* • Sandra Bernhard *Nurse Stein* • Colleen Camp *Arlanda* • Seymour Cassel *Dr Bernard Fairmont* • Leon Rippy *Trucker* ■ *Dir* Nicolas Roeg • *Scr* Dennis Potter

Trackdown ★★ 🅸🆁

Thriller 1976 · US · Colour · 93mins

Montana cowboy James Mitchum (son of Robert) goes to Los Angeles in pursuit of his sister, Karen Lamm, who has drifted into high class prostitution after being gang-raped and sold to Beverly Hills pimp Vince Cannon. Director Richard T Heffron choreographs the rooftop and elevator mayhem well in this little-seen vigilante thriller, but the sleazy subject matter and violence won't appeal to some. 🎞

Jim Mitchum [James Mitchum] *Jim Calhoun* • Karen Lamm *Betsy Calhoun* • Anne Archer *Barbara* • Erik Estrada *Chucho* • Cathy Lee Crosby *Lynn* • Vince Cannon *Johnny Dee* ■ *Dir* Richard T Heffron • *Scr* Paul Edwards, from a story by Ivan Nagy

Trackdown: Finding the Goodbar Killer ★★

Crime thriller based on a true story 1983 · US · Colour · 86mins

The true story that was fictionalised as *Looking For Mr Goodbar*, with Richard Gere, is reprised with a more factual slant in this TV movie. George Segal is the cop who is determined to track down the murderer of a New York schoolteacher. It's an interesting story, but unfortunately is handled here in the most boring way possible, as Segal plods through his investigation like Dixon of Dock Green.

George Segal *John Grafton* • Shelley Hack *Logan Gay* • Alan North *Lieutenant Walter Belden* • Barton Heyman *Alan Cahill* • Steve Allie Collura *Steve Miscelli* • Shannon Presby *John Charles Turner* • Jean Debaer *Betty Grafton* • Tracy Pollan *Eileen Grafton* ■ *Dir* Bill Persky • *Scr* Albert Ruben

Tracks ★

Drama 1977 · US · Colour · 91mins

An unwatchable mess from Hollywood's most pretentious independent director, Henry Jaglom. Dennis Hopper plays a Vietnam veteran with problems, principally the dead body of a buddy he's transporting across the US for burial. Jaglom's slick symbolism and Hopper's "Hey man, like, real heavy" dialogue puts this into a time capsule that should be buried real deep, man. The project was originally written by Jaglom for Jack Nicholson and director Bob Rafelson. Contains swearing, sex scenes and nudity.

Dennis Hopper *Sergeant Jack Falen* • Taryn Power *Stephanie* • Dean Stockwell *Mark* • Topo Swope *Chloe* • Michael Emil *Emile* ■ *Dir/Scr* Henry Jaglom

Trade-Off ★★

Thriller 1995 · US · Colour · 92mins

For some reason, Theresa Russell is a much better actress under the guidance of husband Nicolas Roeg than she is with any other director. She smoulders effectively enough in this steamy thriller, but she produces none of the intensity or intelligence she's capable of. This blatant rip-off of Alfred Hitchcock's *Strangers on a Train* teams her with Adam Baldwin (who isn't a brother of Alec and William), but, apart from a little nookie, it adds nothing to the familiar story of murder without motives. Barry Primus plays the cop on their trail. Contains violence, swearing and sex scenes.

Theresa Russell *Jackie Daniels* • Adam Baldwin *Thomas Hughes* • Megan Gallagher *Karen Hughes* • Barry Primus *Detective Gold* • Pat Skipper *Kirk Daniels* ■ *Dir* Andrew Lane • *Scr* Paul Koval, Ed Fitzgerald

Trade Winds ★★

Detective comedy drama
1938 · US · BW · 93mins

Director Tay Garnett justified a tax-deductible sailing trip around the world by taking a cinematographer to record the sights and writing a story en route. The footage provided the backdrop for this lightweight tale of detective Fredric March's pursuit of high-class murder suspect Joan Bennett. The stars never had to leave the studio, as the film used a record amount of back projection. Predictably, this contributed to an air of tedium that was relieved only by some bright lines attributable to Dorothy Parker being one of the film's screenwriters.

Fredric March *Sam Wye* • Joan Bennett *Kay Kerrigan* • Ralph Bellamy *Ben Blodgett* • Ann Sothern *Jean Livingstone* • Sidney Blackmer *Thomas Bruhme II* • Thomas Mitchell *Commissioner Blackton* • Robert Elliott *Capt George Faulkiner* ■ *Dir* Tay Garnett • *Scr* Dorothy Parker, Alan Campbell, Frank R Adams, from a story by Tay Garnett

Trader Horn ★★★★

Adventure 1931 · US · BW · 123mins

The first film to be made on location in Africa, the troubles that beset the production almost outweighed the life-and-death struggle of the title character (Harry Carey) and his young companion (Duncan Renaldo) as they venture among dangerous animals, and even more dangerous tribes, engaged in a search for the white daughter of missionaries abducted 20 years earlier. They find her, of course, in the beautiful, blonde guise of Edwina Booth. The film was almost abandoned when the studio saw the rag-bag of footage assembled by director WS Van Dyke, but another year's work in Hollywood and Mexico eventually earned it a best picture Oscar nomination. While some sequences are horribly over-extended, the actual filming (especially of animal behaviour) is impressive and beautiful by any standards, especially those of 1931. An interesting, historic and, on the whole, entertaining film.

Harry Carey *Aloysius "Trader" Horn* • Edwina Booth *Nina Trent* • Duncan Renaldo *Peru* • Mutia Omoolu *Renchero* • Olive Golden *Edith Trent* • C Aubrey Smith *Trader* ■ *Dir* WS Van Dyke II [WS Van Dyke] • *Scr* Richard Schayer, Cyril Hume, Dale Van Every, John Thomas Neville, from the novel by Alfred Aloysius Horn, Ethelreda Lewis • *Cinematographer* Clyde de Vinna

Trading Hearts ★★★

Romantic comedy
1988 · US · Colour · 88mins

Raul Julia is the dumped baseball player who hooks up with singer Beverly D'Angelo in this fifties-set drama. The action flits between a light-hearted romance and a legal battle when D'Angelo is threatened with court action by her ex-husband who wants custody of their child. It's well played with some nice period details, but it's not exactly original. Contains swearing.

Raul Julia *Vinnie* • Beverly D'Angelo *Donna* • Jenny Lewis *Yvonne* • Parris Buckner *Robert* • Robert Gwaltney *Ducky* ■ *Dir* Neil Leifer • *Scr* Frank Deford

Trading Places ★★★★ 15

Comedy 1983 · US · Colour · 111mins

A blatant, unacknowledged reworking of *The Prince and the Pauper*, this rattling comedy showcases the unique talents of Eddie Murphy and Dan Aykroyd, who have never recaptured the form shown here. However, there is no question that the acting honours go to the veterans Don Ameche and Ralph Bellamy, as the mischievous business bigwigs whose wager brings about the respective rise and fall of the stars. Director John Landis tends to pull his satirical punches against yuppydom, and it's a shame he settles for a brash slapstick finale after so many fresh, immaculately timed comic situations, but this is still entertaining if slightly familiar fare. Contains swearing and nudity.

Eddie Murphy *Billy Ray Valentine* • Dan Aykroyd *Louis Winthorpe III* • Jamie Lee Curtis *Ophelia* • Ralph Bellamy *Randolph Duke* • Don Ameche *Mortimer Duke* • Denholm Elliott *Coleman* • Paul Gleason *Beeks* • Bo Diddley *Pawnbroker* • Jim Belushi [James Belushi] *King Kong* • Kristin Holby *Penelope* ■ *Dir* John Landis • *Scr* Timothy Harris, Herschel Weingrod

Traffic ★★★★

Comedy 1972 · US · Colour · 96mins

Any number of things could go wrong as Monsieur Hulot takes the vehicle of the future to an Amsterdam motor show. The fact that not many did bothered the critics, who wanted something more spectacular than some loosely linked observations on motoring and modernity. But Jacques Tati's final feature is filled with astute musings and wry ruminations about, for example, the way owners resemble their cars or have windscreen wipers in tune with their personalities. The nose-picking sequence and the grotesque ballet of the pile-up reinforce his thesis that life is increasingly lived in isolation and that progress is a highly relative term. In French with English subtitles.

Jacques Tati *Monsieur Hulot* • Maria Kimberly *Maria* • Marcel Fravel *Truck driver* ■ *Dir* Jacques Tati • *Scr* Jacques Tati, Jacques Lagrange

Traffic in Souls ★★★★

Silent drama 1913 · US · BW · 74mins

A landmark in the history of the American cinema, miraculously preserved for posterity, this was remarkable in its time for both its subject matter and its length. Focusing on the white slave traffic that was obsessing America and its moral reformers, the plot sets a lily-white heroic cop (Matt Moore) against a corrupt organisation of traffickers led by publicly respectable "pillar" of New York society (William Welsh), who kidnap Moore's fiancée's sister (Ethel Grandin) for purposes of prostitution. The cunning methods of seducing and then kidnapping the girls are revealed in parallel plotting with the "business" end of the operation, the police action, and the domestic lives of the key protagonists. With its histrionic style, the film raises the occasional giggle, but it's acted with absolute commitment, photographed with wonderful depths of texture and edited for maximum suspense.

Jane Gail *Mary Barton* • Ethel Grandin *Lorna Barton* • William Turner *Isaac Barton* • Matt Moore *Officer Larry Burke* • William Welsh *William Trubus* • Mrs Hudson Lyston *Mrs Trubus* • Irene Wallace *Alice Trubus* • William Cavanaugh *Bill Bradshaw* ■ *Dir* George Loane Tucker • *Scr* Walter MacNamara, George Loane Tucker

The Tragedy of a Ridiculous Man ★★★

Drama 1981 · It · Colour · 116mins

Ugo Tognazzi plays a rich cheese manufacturer who has to decide whether to sell everything to raise a ransom for his kidnapped son. The twist is that his offspring may be one of the gang, radicals dedicated to the overthrow of capitalism. It works as both a thriller and a black comedy, tuning in to then-current topics of kidnapping and Red Brigade terrorism. Interesting rather than exciting, this lacks the stylistic flourishes one expects of director Bernardo Bertolucci. Tognazzi, though, is Italy's answer to Anthony Quinn – he's big, expansive, a paterfamilias, a nice slice of Parma ham. In Italian with English subtitles.

Ugo Tognazzi *Primo* • Anouk Aimée *Barbara* • Laura Morante *Laura* • Victor Cavallo *Adelfo* • Olimpia Carlisi *Chiromant* • Vittorio Caprioli *Marshal* ■ *Dir/Scr* Bernardo Bertolucci

The Tragedy of Flight 103: the Inside Story ★★★

Drama based on a true story
1990 · US · Colour · 89mins

The ever-present spectre of international terrorism is explored in this TV movie about the bombing of Pan Am flight 103 over Lockerbie in December 1988. Instead of the usual manipulative melodrama, the film meticulously examines the circumstances which led to the deaths of 270 people. The real participants in the disaster are skilfully portrayed by a superb cast including Ned Beatty, Peter Boyle and Timothy West, as the film details the minute-by-minute events that resulted in catastrophe.

Ned Beatty *C Edward Acker* • Peter Boyle *Fred Ford* • Harry Ditson *Martin Shugrue* • Vincent Gardenia *Harry Pizer* • Timothy West *Col Wood* • Michael Wincott *Ulrich Weber* ■ *Dir* Leslie Woodhead • *Scr* Michael Eaton

The Trail Beyond ★★ U

Western 1934 · US · BW · 54mins

With a bigger budget than John Wayne was used to at his home-from-home, Monogram Studios, this Lone Star western was the first talkie version of popular cowboy novel *The Wolf Hunters*. The extra cash gave the Duke the benefit of both Noah Beery Sr and Noah Beery Jr in support, plus more location shooting, but the screenplay by future western producer Lindsley Parsons errs seriously on the side of melodrama. The cameraman was the great Archie Stout, who would later photograph Wayne on John Ford's *Fort Apache* and *The Quiet Man*.

John Wayne *Rod Drew* • Noah Beery Sr [Noah Beery] *George Newsome* • Noah Beery Jr *Wabi* • Verna Hillie *Felice Newsome* • Iris Lancaster *Marie* • Robert Frazer *Jules Larocque* • Earl Dwire *Benoit* • Eddie Parker *Ryan, the Mountie* ■ *Dir* Robert N Bradbury • *Scr* Lindsley Parsons, from the novel *The Wolf Hunters* by James Oliver Curwood

Trail of Tears ★★ PG

Drama 1995 · US · Colour · 87mins

Katey Sagal is something of a cult icon thanks to her wife-from-hell role as Peggy Bundy in the wonderful sitcom *Married with Children*. Here, disappointingly, she is playing it straight, along with another American sitcom star, *Mork and Mindy's* Pam Dawber. They play two mothers who team up to rescue their kids who have been kidnapped by their ex-partners. It's a typically over-ripe slice of drama.

Pam Dawber *Cheryl* • Katey Sagal *Annie* ■ *Dir* Donald Wrye • *Scr* Matthew Bombeck

The Trail of the Lonesome Pine ★★★

Drama 1936 · US · Colour · 102mins

Becky Sharp may have been first but it was this drama that really sold 1930s audiences on the new three-strip Technicolor process through the beauty of outdoor settings filmed on Californian locations by cameraman W Howard Greene. The tale of a long-running feud between two mountain clans was an old favourite, filmed twice before, but a young director – Henry Hathaway – and youthful stars –

Fred MacMurray, Henry Fonda, Sylvia Sidney – gave it a fresh look. Fonda's performance is supposed to have been the inspiration for Al Capp's *Li'l Abner*.

Sylvia Sidney *June Tolliver* • Fred MacMurray *Jack Hale* • Henry Fonda *Dave Tolliver* • Fred Stone *Judd Tolliver* • Nigel Bruce *Mr Thurber* • Beulah Bondi *Melissa* • Robert Barrat *Buck Falin* ■ *Dir* Henry Hathaway • *Scr* Grover Jones, Harvey Thew, Horace McCoy, from the novel by John Fox Jr

Trail of the Pink Panther
★ PG

Comedy 1982 · US · Colour · 92mins

This purported tribute to the genius of Peter Sellers is exploitation at its most shameless. Released two years after Sellers's death, the film is a crudely assembled compilation of unremarkable out-takes and dismally unfunny new footage involving TV reporter Joanna Lumley descending on Clouseau's friends and foes to piece together a picture (if you will) of the Inspector after he vanishes on a case. Director Blake Edwards proceeded to direct two more *Pink Panther* movies, which hit new lows of taste and quality. 🖭

Peter Sellers *Inspector Clouseau* • David Niven *Sir Charles Litton* • Herbert Lom *Dreyfus* • Richard Mulligan *Clouseau Sr* • Joanna Lumley *Marie Jouvet* • Capucine *Lady Litton* • Robert Loggia *Bruno* • Harvey Korman *Professor Balls* • Burt Kwouk *Cato* • Graham Stark *Hercule* ■ *Dir* Blake Edwards • *Scr* Frank Waldman, Tom Waldman, Blake Edwards, Geoffrey Edwards, from a story by Blake Edwards

Trail of the Vigilantes ★★ U

Comedy western 1940 · US · BW · 74mins

A harmless enough western with one of those "undercover man infiltrates outlaws" plots, given some novelty by the casting of urbane Franchot Tone as the easterner out west. Classy Warren William is the gang leader, and Broderick Crawford and Andy Devine are good value as his chubby henchmen. Veteran director Allan Dwan keeps the action moving, resulting in a brisk, bright, comedy western, with even Mischa Auer thrown in for good value.

Franchot Tone *"Kansas" Tim Mason* • Warren William *Mark Dawson* • Broderick Crawford *Swanee* • Andy Devine *Meadows* • Mischa Auer *Dmitri Bolo* • Porter Hall *Sheriff Corley* • Peggy Moran *Barbara Thornton* ■ *Dir* Allan Dwan • *Scr* Harold Shumate

Trail Street ★★★ U

Western 1947 · US · BW · 84mins

This bustling western has a nicely belated entry by star Randolph Scott as legendary lawman "Bat" Masterson, summoned to a Kansas town to stop the cattlemen from trampling wheat farmers underfoot. Though briskly directed by Ray Enright, it's over-stuffed with familiar ingredients, including the saloon singer played by Anne Jeffreys and the contrasting nice girl played by Madge Meredith, but its subplot of discovering a heat-resistant strain of wheat is based on fact. Its worst feature is the tiresome anecdotes of the aptly nicknamed George "Gabby" Hayes.

Randolph Scott *"Bat" Masterson* • Robert Ryan *Allen Harper* • Anne Jeffreys *Ruby Stone* • George "Gabby" Hayes *Billy* • Madge Meredith *Susan Pritchett* • Steve Brodie *Logan Maury* • Billy House *Carmody* • Virginia Sale *Hannah* • Jason Robards *Jason* ■ *Dir* Ray Enright • *Scr* Gene Lewis, from the novel *Golden Horizon* by William Corcoran

The Train ★★★★ PG

Second World War drama
1964 · Fr/It/US · BW · 127mins

An absolutely marvellous war movie, with Burt Lancaster superb as the railwayman attempting to stop demented Nazi officer Paul Scofield from pillaging art treasures from France in the dying days of the Second World War. The technically flawless direction is by John Frankenheimer, who took over at short notice from Arthur Penn, and the sheer excitement of using real trains is palpable – no models or digital effects here! The French locations are exceptionally well used, and Jeanne Moreau and the great Michel Simon contribute tellingly authentic portrayals. The film also raises an interesting moral issue: is any work of art ever worth a person's life? 🖭

Burt Lancaster *Labiche* • Paul Scofield *Colonel von Waldheim* • Jeanne Moreau *Christine* • Michel Simon *Papa Boule* • Suzanne Flon *Miss Villard* • Wolfgang Preiss *Herren* • Richard Munch *Von Lubitz* • Albert Remy *Didont* ■ *Dir* John Frankenheimer • *Scr* Franklin Coen, Frank Davis, Walter Bernstein, from the novel *Le Front de l'Art* by Rose Valland

Train of Dreams ★★★★

Documentary drama
1987 · Can · Colour · 89mins

A gritty, powerful docudrama about a wayward 17-year-old Montreal hoodlum and his descent into a life of professional crime and violence. He ends up in a correctional facility where a teacher attempts to bring poetry and music into his life. This is a thought-provoking movie which packs a tremendous emotional punch. There is a realistic feel to the piece which makes its no-holds-barred impact all the more startling. A largely unknown cast brilliantly brings Montreal's less salubrious side to extraordinary life. Contains swearing, substance abuse and nudity.

Jason St Amour *Tony Abruzzi* • Marcella Santa Maria *Mrs Abruzzi* • Fred Ward *Teacher* • Christopher Neil *Nicky Abruzzi* • David Linesky *Tony's lawyer* • Milton Hartman *Crown attorney* ■ *Dir* John N Smith • *Scr* John N Smith, Sally Bochner, Sam Grana

Train of Events ★★★

Portmanteau drama 1949 · UK · BW · 88mins

As the night express from Euston to Liverpool is about to career off the rails, the movie also lurches into flashback, showing why various passengers were making the fated journey. There's the engine driver; a philandering orchestra conductor; an actor who's killed his wife; and a girl in love with an escaped German PoW. Rehashing 1933's *Friday the 13th*, which was set aboard a doomed bus, this portmanteau effort is inevitably uneven, though the cast of stalwarts is worth watching.

Jack Warner *Jim Hardcastle* • Gladys Henson *Mrs Hardcastle* • Susan Shaw *Doris Hardcastle* • Patric Doonan *Ron Stacey* ■ *Dir* Sidney Cole, Basil Dearden, Charles Crichton • *Scr* Basil Dearden, TEB Clarke, Ronald Millar, Angus Macphail

Train of Life ★★★ 12

Second World War comedy adventure
1999 · Fr/Bel · Colour · 102mins

Following *Life Is Beautiful*, this raucous co-production (made with funding from Romania and the Netherlands) attempts to cast comic light over the nightmare experienced by Europe's Jews during the Second World War. The central premise is undeniably inventive, but having the inhabitants of an isolated village pose as a trainload of prisoners and their escorts in an audacious bid to reach Palestine leaves Radu Mihaileanu's film wide open to questions of taste. Whether celebrating the Yiddish spirit or caricaturing the Nazi threat, the action just manages to retain its equilibrium. But, after so much risky ingenuity, the ending can only be considered a misjudgement. A French language film.

Lionel Abelanski *Schlomo* • Rufus *Mordechai* • Clément Harari *Le Rabbi* • Michel Muller *Yossi* • Bruno Abraham-Kremer *Yankele* • Agathe de la Fontaine *Esther* ■ *Dir/Scr* Radu Mihaileanu

The Train Robbers ★★★ U

Western 1973 · US · Colour · 88mins

This rather overlooked western is a typical example of director Burt Kennedy's rumbustious view of frontier life. The Duke stars as a no-nonsense old-timer hired by grieving widow Ann-Margret to retrieve the gold stolen by her late husband. Wayne still cuts an imposing figure during the action sequences and shows again that he was a better actor than even he gave himself credit for, while ruminating on the gory glory days with Ben Johnson. 🖭

John Wayne *Lane* • Ann-Margret *Mrs Lowe* • Rod Taylor *Grady* • Ben Johnson *Wil Jesse* • Christopher George *Calhoun* • Bobby Vinton *Ben Young* • Jerry Gatlin *Sam Turner* • Ricardo Montalban *Pinkerton man* ■ *Dir/Scr* Burt Kennedy

Train to Pakistan ★★★

Drama 1997 · Ind/UK · Colour · 108mins

This thought-provoking drama is set in the period immediately after the partition of India. Like Deepa Mehta's controversial *Earth*, the emphasis is on the tensions that arose between the subcontinent's various ethnic groups following independence in 1947. In this case, writer/director Pamela Rooks concentrates on the events that spark gang warfare between the dominant Sikhs and the Muslim minority in the small Punjabi town of Mano Majra. The politics isn't always easy to follow, but the cast members, led by Mohan Agashe, turn in committed performances. In Hindi and Punjabi with English subtitles. Contains violence.

Mohan Agashe *Hukum Chand* • Nirmal Pandey *Jagga* • Rajit Kapur *Jailor* • Smriti Mishra *Nimmo* ■ *Dir* Pamela Rooks • *Scr* Pamela Rooks, from the novel by Khushwant Singh

Trainspotting ★★★★★ 18

Drama 1995 · UK · Colour · 89mins

Irvine Welsh's controversial bestseller is brought to the screen as a dazzling assault on the senses, thanks to director Danny Boyle's cinematic imagination and invention. Deliberately summoning up comparisons with *A Clockwork Orange*, this nonetheless fiercely original and provocative shocker focuses on the disintegrating friendship of four Edinburgh lads as they embark on an endless drugs and petty-crime bender heading seemingly towards self-destruction. The harrowing and bleak subject matter is presented as a hilariously funny walk on the wild side, with no moral stance taken or punches pulled. The action and emotions are expertly choreographed to a soundtrack by the likes of Blur and Pulp, but the most galvanising sequence is Ewan McGregor's overdose backed by Lou Reed's song *Perfect Day*. McGregor is absolutely brilliant as the smart-aleck junkie Renton – his nightmare trip through a toilet bowl is once seen, never forgotten. High praise, too, for *The Full Monty*'s Robert Carlyle, who gives a stunning performance as the violent Begbie. A savagely sophisticated work and a landmark British classic. Contains violence, swearing, sex scenes, drug abuse and nudity. 🖭

DVD

Ewan McGregor *Mark Renton* • Ewen Bremner *Daniel "Spud"* • Jonny Lee Miller *Simon "Sick Boy"* • Kevin McKidd *Tommy* • Robert Carlyle *Begbie* • Kelly Macdonald *Diane* • Peter Mullan *Swanney* • James Cosmo *Mr Renton* • Eileen Nicholas *Mrs Renton* • Susan Vidler *Allison* ■ *Dir* Danny Boyle • *Scr* John Hodge, from the novel by Irvine Welsh

The Traitor ★★

Spy drama 1957 · UK · BW · 87mins

Nuance was not Donald Wolfit's strong suit, but he had presence and power in spades. He totally dominates this story with a bluster and conviction that keeps an uninspiring tale of the hunt for a Second World War traitor from falling flat on its face. Writer/director Michael McCarthy had a splendid sense of place, but no talent whatsoever for generating and sustaining suspense. It was a smart move casting Wolfit, Christopher Lee and Anton Diffring as a trio of shifty-looking suspects, but it all too quickly becomes clear in which direction the finger is pointing.

Donald Wolfit *Colonel Price* • Robert Bray *Major Shane* • Jane Griffiths *Vicki Toller* • Carl Jaffe *Professor Toller* • Anton Diffring *Joseph Brezzini* • Oscar Quitak *Thomas Rilke* • Rupert Davies *Clinton* • John Van Eyssen *Lt Grant* • Christopher Lee ■ *Dir/Scr* Michael McCarthy

The Tramp ★★★ U

Silent comedy 1915 · US · BW · 24mins

Having saved Edna Purviance from larcenous hobos, Charlie Chaplin is rewarded with a job on her farm. However, any romantic aspirations he has are frustrated by the arrival of her fiancé. Almost halfway through his Essanay contract, Chaplin here began to refine the "Little Fellow" who remains the most recognisable figure of the silent era. The pugnacious approach to bullies, the gentility

around women and the balletic feuding with inanimate objects are all present and correct. So, unfortunately, is the pathos that many feel undermines his comic genius, manifesting itself in the first appearance of that trademark sashay down a dusty road.

Charles Chaplin *Tramp* • Edna Purviance *Farmer's daughter* • Bud Jamison *Tramp* • Leo White *Tramp* • Lloyd Bacon *Lover* ■ *Dir/Scr* Charles Chaplin

Tramp, Tramp, Tramp
★★★★ **U**

Silent comedy   1926 · US · BW · 64mins

Whey-faced clown Harry Langdon, known as "The Wonderful Baby", made a number of shorts for Mack Sennett before his first feature, directed by Harry Edwards and co-written by Frank Capra, who developed Langdon's innocent film persona. Although some of the gags are reminiscent of those performed by Buster Keaton and Harold Lloyd, there are many that belong to Langdon alone – watch how he throws rocks at a cyclone to persuade it to go away. The film is a series of amusing exploits he has while competing in a cross-country walk in order to win the heart of Joan Crawford, then an up-and-coming 22-year-old flapper.

Harry Langdon *Harry* • Joan Crawford *Betty Burton* • Edwards Davis *John Burton* • Carlton Griffin *Roger Caldwell* ■ *Dir* Harry Edwards • *Scr* Frank Capra, Tim Whelan, Hal Conklin, J Frank Holliday, Gerald Duffy, Murray Roth

Trancers
★★★ **15**

Science-fiction fantasy thriller
1985 · US · Colour · 73mins

Tim Thomerson is a 23rd-century cop who goes back in time to capture his arch-nemesis who is planning to change the past in order to control the future with his zombie henchmen ("trancers"). *Blade Runner* French connects with *The Terminator* in a nail-biting quickie from minor cult director Charles Band. Thomerson gives a wonderfully high-flying Dirty Harry-goes-cyber-punk portrayal and 1997 best actress Oscar winner Helen Hunt makes an early appearance as his innocent sidekick in present day LA.

Tim Thomerson *Jack Deth/Philip Dethon* • Helen Hunt *Leena* • Michael Stefani *Martin Whistler/Lt Wiesling* • Art LaFleur *McNulty* • Telma Hopkins *Engineer Raines* • Richard Herd *Chairman Spencer* • Anne Seymour *Chairman Ashe* ■ *Dir* Charles Band • *Scr* Danny Bilson, Paul De Meo

Trancers II: The Return of Jack Deth
★★ **15**

Science-fiction action
1991 · US · Colour · 84mins

Tim Thomerson returns as the no-nonsense Jack Deth, a cop from the future stuck in modern day Los Angeles, in Charles Band's belated sequel to his own mid-eighties cult hit. Once again pitted against zombie-like creatures (trancers), Thomerson's engagingly laconic Deth also has to deal with a convoluted love life – two wives in different centuries. And yes, that's a pre-*As Good As It Gets* Helen Hunt as one of the spouses. Look out also for two-time Bond girl and

Hammer starlet Martine Beswick. Not nearly as much fun as its predecessor, but that didn't stop the makers from churning out yet more sequels.

Tim Thomerson *Jack Deth* • Helen Hunt *Lena Deth* • Megan Ward *Alice Stillwell* • Biff Manard *Hap Ashby* • Martine Beswick *Nurse Trotter* • Jeffrey Combs *Doctor Pyle* • Alyson Croft *McNulty* • Telma Hopkins *Raines* ■ *Dir* Charles Band • *Scr* Jackson Barr, from a story by Charles Band, Jackson Barr

Transformers – The Movie
★ **U**

Animated adventure
1986 · US · Colour · 84mins

The feature-length version of the cartoon TV series is based on the popular toy's that mutate into hi-tech weaponry and vehicles. The fighting cyborgs must save the universe from the planet Unicron – voiced by Orson Welles – and its intergalactic army led by the evil Megatron. Other top voice talent includes Leonard Nimoy, Robert Stack, Judd Nelson and Eric Idle. The usual mind-numbing blitz of cheap graphics, marginally vulgar dialogue and nasty violence means parents with impressionable children should take heed.

Leonard Nimoy *Galvatron* • Robert Stack *Ultra Magnus* • Eric Idle *Wreck Gar* • Judd Nelson *Hot Rod/Rodimus Prime* • Lionel Stander *Kup* • John Moschitta *Blurr* • Orson Welles *Planet Unicron* ■ *Dir* Nelson Shin • *Scr* Ron Friedman

Transylvania 6-5000
★ **PG**

Comedy horror   1985 · US · Colour · 94mins

A ridiculous horror comedy, this pitiful imitation of Mel Brooks' *Young Frankenstein* was written and directed by one of his former associates. Jeff Goldblum and Ed Begley Jr are cringingly unfunny as journalists sent to Transylvania, where they encounter a werewolf, a mummy and other classic movie monsters. With a cast that includes such comic notables as Carol Kane, Jeffrey Jones and Michael (*Seinfeld*) Richards, you would expect a fair quota of laughs, but the American and Yugoslav cast tiresomely overplay a surfeit of unoriginal gags. Geena Davis surely won't want reminding of her role as a nymphomaniac vampire.

Jeff Goldblum *Jack Harrison* • Joseph Bologna *Dr Malavaqua* • Ed Begley Jr *Gil Turner* • Carol Kane *Lupi* • Jeffrey Jones *Lepscu* • John Byner *Radu* • Geena Davis *Odette* • Michael Richards *Fejos* ■ *Dir/Scr* Rudy DeLuca

Transylvania Twist
★★★ **15**

Horror parody   1989 · US · Colour · 78mins

Think *Carry On Screaming* meets *Airplane* and you'll have a pretty good idea of the merits of this better-than-average horror spoof. Terminally silly for sure, but enough of the gags hit their target to keep you watching as youngsters search for a fabled book with the power to raise evil spirits, hidden in a spooky castle. Director Jim Wynorski's misspent youth watching scary movies is ploughed onto the screen as he lampoons genre clichés, institutions such as *The Exorcist* and fright icons Jason and Leatherface. Veteran Robert Vaughn also gets in on the act hamming it up like a trooper as

a Dracula-style bloodsucker. Horror legend Boris Karloff also makes an appearance – two decades after his death – courtesy of some clever use of out-takes from Roger Corman's *The Terror*. An undiscovered minor treat for horror buffs that's well worth catching.

Robert Vaughn *Lord Byron Orlock* • Teri Copley *Marissa Orlock* • Steve Altman *Dexter Ward* • Ace Mask *Van Helsing* • Angus Scrimm *Stefan* • Stu Nathan *Sports announcer* • Monique Gabrielle *Patricia* ■ *Dir* Jim Wynorski • *Scr* RJ Robertson

The Trap
★

Murder mystery   1947 · US · BW · 68mins

After nine years and 22 films in the role, Sidney Toler was to bow out of this increasingly bankrupt series. Better known for his work on William Boyd's Hopalong Cassidy pictures, Howard Bretherton directs with little sense of the genre and resorts to such horror clichés as creeping around in the dark, as Charlie and "Number Two Son" Victor Sen Yung head for Malibu Beach to expose the killer in an acting troupe. Mantan Moreland returns as the perpetually petrified chauffeur, but the most interesting piece of casting is that of Kirk Alyn, cinema's original Superman, as the cop on the case.

Sidney Toler *Charlie Chan* • Mantan Moreland *Birmingham* • Victor Sen Yung *Jimmy Chan* • Tanis Chandler *Adelaide* • Larry Blake *Rick Daniels* • Kirk Alyn *Sgt Reynolds* ■ *Dir* Howard Bretherton • *Scr* Miriam Kissinger, from a character created by Earl Derr Biggers

The Trap
★★★ **15**

Romantic adventure
1966 · UK/Can · Colour · 101mins

Made at the height of the Swinging Sixties, this surprisingly moving drama was a distinct change of pace for stars Oliver Reed and Rita Tushingham. Set in Canada in the 1880s, it traces the relationship of fur trapper Reed and the waif-like Tushingham, a mute he purchases at a wife auction. Acting almost solely with her enormous eyes, Tushingham gives a genuinely affecting performance and, as impatience turns to understanding and ultimately affection, Reed also demonstrates a mellow side that he too rarely allows us to see. Director Sidney Hayers makes their bloodcurdling adventures wholly believable, and ultimately the tragedy of the tale is heartrending. Cinematographer Robert Krasker's views of the snowy mountains are often majestic. DP

Rita Tushingham *Eve* • Oliver Reed *Jean La Bete* • Rex Sevenoaks *Trader* • Barbara Chilcott *Trader's wife* • Linda Goranson *Trader's daughter* • Blain Fairman *Clerk* • Walter Marsh *Preacher* ■ *Dir* Sidney Hayers • *Scr* David Osborn

The Trap
★★★ **18**

Thriller   1975 · Fr · Colour · 96mins

Positively bristling with malice, this unrelentingly nasty thriller from Pierre Granier-Deferre makes *The War of the Roses* look like an advertisement for marriage guidance counselling. Ingrid Thulin and Lino Ventura are equally despicable and in revenge for his casting her aside for a younger woman, she incarcerates him . Armed

with the tricks she picked up from translating detective novels, the once downtrodden Thulin is more than a match for the ruthless Ventura, and it's to Granier-Deferre's credit that the resolution of this sordid game of cat and mouse is always in doubt. In French with English subtitles.

Lino Ventura *Julien* • Ingrid Thulin *Helene* • Sophie *Secretary* • William Sabatier • Dominique Zardi *Postman* ■ *Dir* Pierre Granier-Deferre • *Scr* Pascal Jardin, Pierre Granier-Deferre, from the play *La Cage* by Jack Jacquine

Trapeze
★★★ **U**

Drama   1956 · US · Colour · 101mins

Shot at the Cirque d'Hiver in Paris, this simmering melodrama was something of a departure for director Carol Reed after two decades of typically British topics and central European thrillers. However, Reed always knew where to place his camera and he achieves some of the finest ever big-top shots thanks to the high-flying work of Robert Krasker, the cinematographer responsible for those stunning angles in *The Third Man*, also directed by Reed. Burt Lancaster, an acrobat before he entered films, is perfectly cast as the only person to have completed the triple somersault, while Tony Curtis gives a good account of himself as both Lancaster's pupil and his rival for the affections of tumbler Gina Lollobrigida.

Burt Lancaster *Mike Ribble* • Tony Curtis *Tino Orsini* • Gina Lollobrigida *Lola* • Katy Jurado *Rosa* • Thomas Gomez *Bouglione* • Johnny Puleo *Max the dwarf* • Minor Watson *John Ringling North* • Sidney James *Snake Charmer* ■ *Dir* Carol Reed • *Scr* James R Webb, Liam O'Brien, from the novel *The Killing Frost* by Max Catto

Trapped
★★ **15**

Thriller   1973 · US · Colour · 83mins

James Brolin became a TV actor straight after college and has never managed to transcend his own good looks, spending much of his career marooned by mediocrity. These days, of course, he's better known as Mr Barbra Streisand. In this TV movie he is ill-served by a director who, starting from a promising idea – a man is trapped in department store with salivating guard dogs – is unable to develop it into an interesting movie.

James Brolin *Chuck Brenner* • Susan Clark *Elaine Moore* • Earl Holliman *David Moore* • Robert Hooks *Sgt Connaught* • Ivy Jones *Connie Havenmeyer* • Bob Hastings *Bartender* • Tammy Harrington *Carrie* ■ *Dir* Frank De Felitta • *Scr* Frank DeFelitta

Trapped
★★★ **15**

Thriller   1989 · US · Colour · 88mins

Kathleen Quinlan puts up a game performance of part abject terror and part gutsy fortitude, as a woman trapped in her high-rise eyrie playing cat and mouse with a killer. This is a suspenseful thriller with obvious nods to *Die Hard* as Quinlan hares around managing to appear ultra-glamorous in the face of various escapades that would make your average heroine look decidedly the worse for wear. But this is Hollywood and, though utterly

U = SUITABLE FOR ALL   **Uc** = SUITABLE FOR ALL, ESPECIALLY FOR YOUNG CHILDREN (VIDEO ONLY)   **PG** = PARENTAL GUIDANCE

unbelievable, the movie grips from start to finish. Contains violence. ▭
Kathleen Quinlan *Marianne* • Bruce Abbott *John* • Ben Loggins *Killer* • Katy Boyer *Renni* • Tyress Allen *Danny* ■ *Dir* Fred Walton • *Scr* Fred Walton, Steve Feke

Trapped and Deceived
★★ 12
Drama 1994 · US · Colour · 88mins
Beverly Hills 90210 meets *One Flew over the Cuckoo's Nest* in this well-meaning but rather bland made-for-TV tale. Jennie Garth is the rebellious high school student sent to a supposed therapy centre by her parents, who cannot cope with her antisocial behaviour. However, she is shocked to discover that the centre is actually closer to a borstal than a hospital. Presumably, it is a subject close to the teen soap star's heart as she also serves as executive producer, but she does little to extend her usual range of sulky looks. Luckily, there's a strong supporting cast in the shape of LA Law's Jill Eikenberry, Helen Shaver and, especially, Paul Sorvino – GoodFellas and Mira Sorvino's dad – as the bad guy. Contains violence. ▭
Jennie Garth *Laura* • Jill Eikenberry *Michelle* • Tom Irwin *Robert* ■ *Dir* Robert Iscove • *Scr* Tim Kring

Trapped in Paradise ★★★ PG
Comedy 1994 · US · Colour · 106mins
One from the days before Nicolas Cage reinvented himself as an action star, this is a slight, but engaging festive offering. Cage is the hapless good guy who is roped into a yuletide robbery by his brothers (Dana Carvey and Jon Lovitz), when they find themselves trapped by the weather in possibly the nicest small town in America. Carvey and Lovitz grab the best lines, but Cage is a commendable straight man. Writer/director George Gallo can't resist laying on the Christmas sentiment at the end but, for the most part, he keeps the story moving in amiable fashion. Contains swearing. ▭
Nicolas Cage *Bill Firpo* • Dana Carvey *Alvin Firpo* • Jon Lovitz *Dave Firpo* • Mädchen Amick *Sarah Collins* • Vic Mazzucci *Vic Manni* • Florence Stanley *Ma Firpo* • Richard Jenkins *Shaddus Peyser* • Donald Moffat *Clifford Anderson* • Angela Patton *Hattie Anderson* • Richard B Shull *Father Ritter* ■ *Dir/Scr* George Gallo

Trapped in Silence
★
Drama 1986 · US · Colour · 94mins
Teenager Kiefer Sutherland, suffers from elective mutism – inability to speak due to emotional trauma – in this manipulative psychological melodrama that pretends to be a mindbender, but ends up just being a mindnumber. Marsha Mason stars as a well-meaning psychologist determined to get to the bottom of his problems, but isn't given much to work with here. She later teamed up again with co-star John Mahoney to play his girlfriend Sherry in TV's *Frasier*.
Marsha Mason *Jennifer Hubbell* • Kiefer Sutherland *Kevin Richter* • Ron Silver *Dr Jeff Tomlinson* • John Mahoney *Dr Winslow* • Stephen Pearlman *Dr Rosenthal* • Amy Wright

Dana Wendolowski ■ *Dir* Michael Tuchner • *Scr* Pat E Victor, from a non-fiction book by Torey Hayden

Trapped in Space ★★★ 15
Science-fiction drama
1994 · US · Colour · 83mins
Based on the Arthur C Clarke short story *Breaking Strain*, this minor science-fiction gem could be described as Hitchcock's *Lifeboat* in space. A cargo spaceship is hit by a meteor and the astronauts find themselves condemned to a lingering death in an airless craft. The devastating effect this has on the once-friendly crew members is shown using plenty of nerve-jangling shocks and suspenseful surprise, and there's a completely unexpected resolution. Tautly and teasingly directed by Arthur Allan Seidelman, this efficient no-nonsense exercise in chilling claustrophobia and fragmented fear is a real discovery. ▭
Jack Wagner *Chief Engineer Mcneil* • Jack Coleman *Second Mate Grant* • Craig Wasson *Bosun Palmer* • Sigrid Thornton *Engineer Cadet Isaacs* • Kay Lenz *Gillings* • Kevin Colson *Captain Howard* ■ *Dir* Arthur Allan Seidelman • *Scr* Arlington Hughes, Melinda M Snodgrass, from the short story *Breaking Strain* by Arthur C Clarke

Traps ★★★
Period drama 1994 · Ausl · Colour · 98mins
Actress Pauline Chan adapts Kate Grenville's novel *Dreamhouse*, changing the Tuscan setting to Vietnam in the fifties. The disturbances in the nation become a metaphor for the disintegrating marriage of visiting photographer Saskia Reeves, and her journalist husband Robert Reynolds. He refuses to see the country's unrest, but Reeves picks up on the volatile political situation, as communist guerrillas protest against French occupation. Their complicated relationship with plantation owner Sami Frey and his daughter brings matters to head. Reeves is excellent, though the film loses its way at the end.
Saskia Reeves *Louise Duffield* • Robert Reynolds *Michael Duffield* • Sami Frey *Daniel Renouard* • Jacqueline McKenzie *Viola Renouard* • Kiet Lam *Tuan* ■ *Dir* Pauline Chan • *Scr* Pauline Chan, Robert Carter, from the novel *Dreamhouse* by Kate Grenville

Trash ★★★ 18
Comedy drama 1970 · US · Colour · 103mins
This was arguably the first product from the Warhol studio to resemble a mainstream film. It has a conventional narrative, with actors playing parts as opposed to themselves, and it is "properly" edited. The story of a heroin addict rendered impotent carries a clear anti-drugs message, but this did not impress the British censor, who originally cut a shooting up scene. As the junkie, Joe Dallesandro enjoyed his finest hour, although he and others still stumble over their lines and have trouble sustaining their characters. Transvestite Holly Woodlawn, playing Dallesandro's roommate, has the funniest scenes. Too long, but too startling to be boring. ▭
Joe Dallesandro *Joe* • Holly Woodlawn *Holly* • Jane Forth *Jane* • Michael Sklar *Welfare investigator* • Geri Miller *Go-go dancer* •

Andrea Feldman *Rich girl* • Bruce Pecheur *Jane's husband* • Johnny Putnam *Boy from Yonkers* • Bob Dallesandro *Boy on street* ■ *Dir/Scr* Paul Morrissey • *Producer* Andy Warhol

Trauma ★
Horror 1962 · US · BW · 93mins
Lorrie Richards here makes the reluctant return to a musty mansion, in an attempt to recall the traumatic events that have ruined her life. This is the kind of picture that Roger Corman used to rattle out with cheerful abandon, but Robert M Young, at the start of an undistinguished career, shuns the tongue-in-cheek approach that might have enlivened proceedings. Richards has clearly forgotten how to act (if she ever knew how) and it is sad to see the likeable Lynn Bari down among the Z-movies.
John Conte *Warren Clyner* • Lynn Bari *Helen Garrison* • Lorrie Richards *Emmaline Garrison* • David Garner *Craig Schoonover* • Warren Kemmerling *Luther* ■ *Dir* Robert Malcolm Young [Robert M Young] • *Scr* Robert Malcolm Young

Trauma ★★
Thriller 1983 · W Ger · Colour · 103mins
A bizarre story that writer/director Gabi Kubach fails to handle with much conviction. The plot revolves around the search for a missing wife, but the confusing behaviour of Birgit Doll, as a detective's assistant involved in the hunt, becomes an irritating distraction. Even Armin Mueller-Stahl, so good in *Music Box* and *Shine*, can't enliven the proceedings. German dialogue dubbed into English.
Birgit Doll *Anna* • Lou Castel *Lemaitre* • Armin Mueller-Stahl *Sam* • Hanne Wieder *Anna's Mother* • Janna Marangosoff *Christina* • Eva Maria Hagen *Christina's Mother* ■ *Dir/Scr* Gabi Kubach

Trauma ★★ 18
Horror thriller 1993 · US/It · Colour · 101mins
Even fans of horror director Dario Argento are likely to find this Italian/American co-production boring. Asia Argento (Dario's daughter) plays a troubled young woman who may have the key to a killer's identity, but her semi-romantic involvement with a journalist just slows the movie down. It's still an Argento film, what with the psycho on the loose who shows a fondness for decapitating his victims with an electric saw, but *Trauma* features less of the fluid camerawork and over-the-top gore effects one expects from his best work. However, unlike some of his earlier movies, the mainly American cast – *Carrie*'s Piper Laurie, *Child's Play*'s Brad Dourif – at least gives the maestro some acting muscle to play with. Contains swearing, violence, nudity, drug abuse. ▭
Christopher Rydell *David* • Asia Argento *Aura Petrescu* • Laura Johnson *Grace* • James Russo *Captain Travis* • Brad Dourif *Dr Lloyd* • Frederic Forrest *Dr Judd* • Piper Laurie *Adriana Petrescu* ■ *Dir* Dario Argento • *Scr* Dario Argento, T ED Klein, from a story by Franco Ferrini, from a story by Giovanni Romoli, from a story by Dario Argento

The Traveling Executioner ★★
Black comedy 1970 · US · Colour · 95mins
A strange tale of a live-wire ex-carnival man who, in 1918, travels around America with his portable electric chair, executing convicted criminals for $100. Events take a shocking turn in Alabama, when he falls for the surviving half of death-sentenced siblings. The story line intrigues on paper, but falls rather flat in, erm, execution, the result of rather dull direction. Played as some sort of fable, it also suffers from some corny acting, even by its star, the usually dependable Stacy Keach. Could have been better in quirkier, defter hands. ▭
Stacy Keach *Jonas Candide* • Marianna Hill *Gundred Herzallerliebst* • Bud Cort *Jimmy* • Graham Jarvis *Doc Prittle* • James J Sloyan [James Sloyan] *Piquant* • M Emmet Walsh *Warden Brodski* ■ *Dir* Jack Smight • *Scr* Garrie Bateson

Traveling Man ★★★ 15
Comedy 1989 · US · Colour · 100mins
The Empire Strikes Back director Irvin Kershner here returns to earth with a comedy drama that is reliant on performances, rather than state-of-the-art special effects. John Lithgow is the burned out travelling salesman who has to take a young upstart (Jonathan Silverman) on the road with him, unaware that his new colleague is after his business. Lithgow hasn't been this good since *The World According to Garp*, and it is his performance that makes what could have been a depressing drama, entertaining. Actress/singer Chynna Phillips, who has since married *Backdraft* star William Baldwin, puts in an appearance. Contains swearing. ▭
John Lithgow *Ben Cluett* • Jonathan Silverman *Billy Fox* • John Glover *Chick Beeler* • Margaret Colin *Joanna Reath* • Chynna Phillips *Mona Voight* ■ *Dir* Irvin Kershner • *Scr* David Taylor

The Traveller ★★★★
Drama 1974 · Iran · BW
Having made some 20 shorts at the Institute for the Intellectual Development of Children and Young Adults, Abbas Kiarostami made his feature film debut with this bittersweet story that demonstrates the enduring legacy of neo-realism. Footie-mad Hassan Darabi is the epitome of rapscallion innocence, as he wheels, deals and steals his way to the money that buys him a ticket to Teheran for a big World Cup game. But it's the way Kiarostami sees through the boy's wide eyes each petty frustration and perceived injustice, as well as the awe-inspiring city sites, that makes this traveller's tale so shrewd, amusing and, ultimately, heartbreaking. In Farsi with English subtitles.
Hassan Darabi *Ghassem Joulai* ■ *Dir* Abbas Kiarostami • *Scr* Abbas Kiarostami, from a short story by Hassan Rafi'ie

Traveller ★★★ 18
Drama 1997 · US · Colour · 96mins
Highly watchable buddy movie, set against the backdrop of the US's

nomadic Irish-American community, with its rigid rules, intense distrust of outsiders, and almost Mob-style hierarchy. Bill Paxton (*A Simple Plan*, *Apollo 13*) plays a veteran traveller and scamster. Mark Wahlberg (*Boogie Nights*) is the young semi-outsider who teams up with him to learn the ropes. The plot switches from character-driven to action-driven when Paxton cons cash from a crook to pay the medical bills of the new lady in his life (*ER*'s Julianna Margulies). Boasting strong performances and a solid plot, this also looks terrific, courtesy of first-time director Jack Green's former incarnation as cinematographer on *Unforgiven* and *Twister*. Contains swearing and one violent scene. ▭

Bill Paxton *Bokky* • Mark Wahlberg *Pat* • Julianna Margulies *Jean* • James Gammon *Double D* • Luke Askew *Boss Jack* • Nikki Deloach *Kate* • Danielle Wiener *Shane* ■ *Dir* Jack Green • *Scr* Jim McGlynn

Travelling North ★★★★ 15

Comedy drama 1986 · Ausl · Colour · 93mins
Film-makers have rarely been able to refrain from revealing the soft centres of grumpy old men. However, David Williamson's splendid adaptation of his stage hit resists the temptation and, by keeping Leo McKern's retired engineer cantankerous to the last, he presents us with a totally believable human being. In his first film in his native Australia, McKern gives an outstanding performance as a short-tempered know-all trying the patience of his new neighbours, and Julia Blake is equally impressive as the middle-aged divorcee who shares his new life. Carl Schultz imaginatively opens out the play and keeps the sentiment in check. Contains swearing. ▭

Leo McKern *Frank* • Julia Blake *Frances* • Graham Kennedy *Freddie* • Henri Szeps *Saul* • Michele Fawdon *Helen* • Diane Craig *Sophie* ■ *Dir* Carl Schultz • *Scr* David Williamson, from his play

The Travelling Players
★★★★

Epic political drama
1975 · Gr · Colour · 230mins
The central instalment in director Theo Angelopoulos's "trilogy of history" that also includes *Days of '36* (1972) and *The Hunters* (1977), this epic exploration of post-Civil War Greece (which won international acclaim and a number of awards when it was first released) was partially made in secret during the military junta of 1967-74. Sprawling to nearly four hours, it makes extensive use of lingering long takes as a troupe of itinerant players and their (constantly interrupted) interpretation of a rustic idyll entitled *Golfo the Shepherdess* traverse 12 years of political turmoil (1939-52). With its stately pace and obscure references to mythology and contemporary events, the film requires patience. But its power and intelligence more than repay the effort. In Greek with English subtitles.

Eva Kotamanidou *Electra* • Aliki Georgoulis *Mother* • Stratos Pachis *Agamemnon* • Maris Vassiliou *Clytemnestra* • Vaneglis Kazan *Aegisthos* • Grigoris Evangelatos *Poet* ■ *Dir*

Theodoros Angelopoulos [Theo Angelopoulos] • *Scr* Theodoros Angelopoulos [Theo Angelopoulos]

Travels with Anita ★★

Romantic comedy
1978 · It · Colour · 125 mins
Fresh from *Foul Play* and with *Private Benjamin* in the pipeline, this dark Italian comedy seems an odd role for Goldie Hawn, as the script is third-rate and the dubbing process robs her of that trademark ditziness. The story line is also unremarkable, as Goldie's American tourist hooks up with a banker (Giannini) en-route to his father's funeral, only for him to forget to mention, during the course of their fractious adventures, that he is married. Italian dialogue dubbed into English.

Goldie Hawn *Anita* • Giancarlo Giannini *Guido* • Claudine Auger *Elisa* • Aurore Clément *Cora* • Renzo Montagnani *Omero* ■ *Dir* Mario Monicelli • *Scr* Leo Benvenuti, Piero De Bernardi, Tullio Pinelli, Paul Zimmerman, Mario Monicelli

Travels with My Aunt ★★★

Comedy 1972 · US · Colour · 109mins
This adaptation of Graham Greene's novel had a lot going for it – an Oscar-nominated turn from Maggie Smith, strong support from the likes of Alec McCowen and Robert Stephens, and direction from Hollywood veteran George Cukor. McCowen plays timid bank manager Henry Pulling, who meets his "aunt" (Smith) at his mother's cremation and is persuaded to accompany her on some freewheeling travels. The previously inhibited Henry soon finds himself drawn into various bizarre adventures, involving ransom demands, smuggling, dope smoking and his aunt's string of exotic lovers. Smith overdoes the eccentricity a bit and the plot obviously strains credibility, but it's colourful fun and one of the lighter and more entertaining screen versions of Greene's work.

Maggie Smith *Aunt Augusta* • Alec McCowen *Henry Pulling* • Louis Gossett Jr *Wordsworth* • Robert Stephens *Visconti* • Cindy Williams *Tooley* • Valerie White *Madame Dambreuse* ■ *Dir* George Cukor • *Scr* Jay Presson Allen, from the novel by Graham Greene

La Traviata ★★★★ U

Opera 1982 · It · Colour · 105mins
Director Franco Zeffirelli's version of the classic opera with vocal heavyweights Placido Domingo and Teresa Stratas is entirely successful and even stronger than his Shakespeare adaptations, *Romeo and Juliet*, and *Hamlet*. Unlike most translations, this version of the Dumas, Piave and Verdi opera hammers home the tragedy of the consumptive courtesan Violetta and her doomed love for Alfredo. Sumptuous, indulgent and cinematic, even an opera-resistant audience will find this accessible, and it is one of the few truly great filmed operas. In Italian with English subtitles. ▭

Teresa Stratas *Violetta* • Placido Domingo *Alfredo* • Cornell MacNeil *Germont* • Alan Monk *Baron* • Axelle Gall *Flora* ■ *Dir* Franco Zeffirelli

Treacherous Beauties ★★

Crime thriller 1994 · US · Colour · 90mins
Harlequin is America's version of Mills and Boon, but this glossy melodrama in the Harlequin series has more in common with the "sex and shopping" genre than the British company's chaste romances. In seeking her brother's killer, Emma Samms goes head to head with Catherine Oxenberg, who just might have been his secret lover. Sparks also fly between Samms and Oxenberg's brother, Bruce Greenwood, but is he innocent? Tippi Hedren has a cameo, but it's the *Dynasty* old girls who hold centre stage. Contains sex scenes and nudity.

Emma Samms *Anne Marie Kerr* • Catherine Oxenberg *Simone Hollister* • Bruce Greenwood *Jason Hollister* • Mark Humphrey *Brent Hollister* • Tippi Hedren ■ *Dir* Charles Jarrott • *Scr* Naomi Janzen, Jim Henshaw

Tread Softly ★

Musical murder mystery comedy
1952 · UK · BW · 70mins
Awesomely bad musical comedy thriller, offering only the melancholy spectacle of a once great star on her uppers. American Frances Day, a bubbly singer/comedienne in Britain from the twenties, was fading fast by the time she made this senseless second-feature about a company of actors trying to stage a revue in a haunted theatre. The film is reminiscent of, but even cheaper than, the earlier *Murder at the Windmill*. Day disappeared in 1965 and was a recluse until her death in 1984.

Frances Day *Madeleine Peters* • Patricia Dainton *Tangye Ward* • John Bentley *Keith Gilbert* • John Laurie *Angus Mcdonald* • Olaf Olsen *Philip Defoe* • Nora Nicholson *Isobel Mayne* ■ *Dir* David MacDonald • *Scr* Gerald Verner, from his radio serial *The Show Must Go On*

Tread Softly Stranger ★★ PG

Crime drama 1958 · UK · BW · 91mins
The big question here is, what on earth were Diana Dors, Terence Morgan and George Baker doing in such a dreary little film? Director Gordon Parry was capable of making involving pictures, but here he insists on his cast delivering each line as if it had the dramatic weight of a Russian novel, which is more than a little preposterous for a petty melodrama about criminal brothers falling for the same girl. The intention was to cash in on the vogue for "it's grim up north" movies, but the result is a bumper collection of unintentional laughs. ▭

Diana Dors *Calico* • George Baker *Johnny Mansell* • Terence Morgan *Dave Mansell* • Patrick Allen *Paddy Ryan* • Jane Griffiths *Sylvia* • Maureen Delany *Mrs Finnegan* • Betty Warren *Flo* ■ *Dir* Gordon Parry • *Scr* George Minter, Denis O'Dell, from the play *Blind Alley* by Jack Popplewell

Treasure Hunt ★★★ U

Comedy 1952 · UK · Colour · 82mins
Artist/novelist/screenwriter John Paddy Carstairs had a long and busy career, much of it in the world of comedy. He directed 10 films between 1950 and 1955 and formed a successful partnership with Norman Wisdom. Here

he adapted Farrell and Perry's hit stage play, managing to capture much of the eccentric charm of the piece. An extended Irish family have mislaid their fortune and take in lodgers to make ends meet. Wild chaos ensues. A first class cast headed by Jimmy Edwards, here turning in another larger than life performance in two roles.

Jimmy Edwards *Sir Roderick* • Martita Hunt *Aunt Anna Rose* • Naunton Wayne *Eustace Mills* • Athene Seyler *Consuelo Howard* • June Clyde *Mrs Cleghorn-Thomas* • Miles Malleson *Mr Walsh* • Susan Stephen *Mary O'Leary* ■ *Dir* John Paddy Carstairs • *Scr* Anatole de Grunwald, from a play by MJ Farrell, from a play by John Perry

Treasure Island ★★★ U

Adventure 1934 · US · BW · 98mins
The first sound version of Robert Louis Stevenson's ripping yarn, directed by Victor Fleming who later made *Gone with the Wind* with all the resources of MGM behind him. Wallace Beery is well cast as Long John Silver (though not, perhaps, as memorably as Robert Newton in 1950), Lionel Barrymore is Billy Bones and young Jackie Cooper plays "Aaargh, Jim lad". More than 60 years on, a certain amount of woodworm has infested the foremasts, so what was always a rather ponderous adventure may seem even more so today. ▭

Wallace Beery *Long John Silver* • Jackie Cooper *Jim Hawkins* • Lionel Barrymore *Billy Bones* • Otto Kruger *Dr Livesey* • Lewis Stone *Capt Alexander Smollett* • Nigel Bruce *Squire Trelawney* • Charles "Chic" Sale *Ben Gunn* • William V Mong *Pew* • Charles McNaughton *Black Dog* ■ *Dir* Victor Fleming • *Scr* John Lee Mahin, Leonard Praskins, John Howard Lawson, from the novel by Robert Louis Stevenson

Treasure Island ★★★ U

Adventure 1950 · UK · Colour · 95mins
A live-action Disney adventure that owes its reputation to just one thing: Robert Newton's performance as Long John Silver. Here is the original, the one and only "Aargh, Jim lad," croaked by the extraordinary Newton whose body lurches drunkenly and whose piglet eyes have the twinkle of gin. Newton did not have to act this way; he was pickled much of the time and this dedication to naturalism caused him to return to the part in a television series and a sequel, *Long John Silver* (1955). Apart from some pretty camerawork by Freddie Young, the rest of this production isn't much to shout about, and as Jim Hawkins, Bobby Driscoll is the worst sort of precocious American child star who, in real life, was headed for a very un-Disney future of drug addiction, poverty and an early death. ▭ *DVD*

Bobby Driscoll *Jim Hawkins* • Robert Newton *Long John Silver* • Basil Sydney *Capt Smollett* • Walter Fitzgerald *Squire Trelawney* • Denis O'Dea *Dr Livesey* • Ralph Truman *George Merry* • Finlay Currie *Billy Bones* • John Laurie *Blind Pew* ■ *Dir* Byron Haskin • *Scr* Lawrence E Watkin, from the novel by Robert Louis Stevenson

Treasure Island ★★ PG

Adventure
1972 · UK/Sp/Fr/W Ger · Colour · 84mins

On the face of it, a reasonably entertaining canter through the oft-filmed pages of Robert Louis Stevenson, with Orson Welles delivering a monstrously fat and fruity performance as Long John Silver. Although Welles gets a co-writer's credit, he actually initiated this project in 1966, having previously adapted the story into a radio show in the thirties. He wrote the screenplay and started directing it back-to-back with his Shakespearian rumination, *Chimes at Midnight*. But the usual Welles gremlins and health problems forced him to abandon *Treasure Island* until his Spanish producer brought in another director, John Hough, to take over the reins. The result is an outright children's film with Welles's performance only sometimes suggesting darker goings on. 🎞

Orson Welles *Long John Silver* • Kim Burfield *Jim Hawkins* • Walter Slezak *Squire Trelawney* • Lionel Stander *Billy Bones* • Paul Muller *Blind Pew* • Maria Rohm *Mrs Hawkins* • Angel del Pozo *Dr Livesey* • Michel Garland *Merry* ■ *Dir* John Hough • *Scr* Wolf Mankowitz, Orson Welles, from the novel by Robert Louis Stevenson

Treasure Island ★★★ PG

Adventure
1990 · US · Colour · 126mins

Robert Louis Stevenson's classic adventure gets the lavish telemovie treatment under Fraser C Heston's direction. His father Charlton is Long John Silver and *Empire of the Sun* star Christian Bale is Jim Hawkins. Shot on the same ship used for *Mutiny on the Bounty* (1962), the lush Caribbean locations make the familiar thrills easy on the eye. 🎞

Charlton Heston *Long John Silver* • Christian Bale *Jim Hawkins* • Oliver Reed *Capt Billy Bones* • Christopher Lee *Blind Pew* • Richard Johnson *Squire Trelawney* • Julian Glover *Doctor Livesey* • Michael Thoma *Hunter* ■ *Dir* Fraser C Heston • *Scr* Fraser C Heston, from the novel Robert Louis Stevenson

Treasure Island ★

Adventure
1991 · Fr/US · Colour · 115mins

Surely not the last version of *Treasure Island* ever made, but probably the weirdest. Experimental, expatriate Chilean director Raúl Ruiz is far too clever to make your everyday adaptation; he has to make a film *about* a film *about* Treasure Island. This egg-head non-version, with its in-jokes, allusions and analysis of Stevenson's classic, sometimes looks and sounds like a Godard anti-movie and, indeed, Godard actors like Anna Karina and Jean-Pierre Léaud make brief appearances in dual roles. Kids will probably switch off after three minutes. Most adults might not even last that long. Released, sort of, in 1991, but made in 1986.

Vic Tayback *Silver* • Melvil Poupaud *Jonathan* • Martin Landau *Old Captain* • Lou Castel *Doctor/Father* • Jeffrey Kime *Timothy* • Anna Karina *Mother* ■ *Dir* Raúl Ruiz • *Scr* Raúl Ruiz, from the novel by Robert Louis Stevenson

Treasure of Lost Canyon ★★ U

Adventure
1952 · US · Colour · 81mins

After being conned out of his inheritance by a dubious San Francisco attorney, an orphaned lad (Tommy Ivo) is given a home by a kindly small-town doctor (William Powell) who helps him track down a treasure chest. Directed by former cameraman Ted (*Notorious*) Tetzlaff and loosely based on a story by Robert Louis Stevenson, this is a mediocre adventure movie for children. The only point of interest for adult movie fans is to ponder the mystery of William Powell's presence in it.

William Powell *Doc Brown* • Tommy Ivo *David* • Rosemary De Camp *Samuella* • Henry Hull *Lucius* • Julia Adams [Julie Adams] *Myra Wade* • Charles Drake *Jim Anderson* • Chubby Johnson *Baltimore Dan* ■ *Dir* Ted Tetzlaff • *Scr* Brainerd Dullfield, Emerson Crocker, from the story *The Treasure of Franchard* by Robert Louis Stevenson

Treasure of Matecumbe ★★ U

Adventure
1976 · US · Colour · 110mins

This movie is a typical example of a well-intentioned Disney family crowd-pleaser. An overlong, simplistic tale along the lines of *The Adventures of Tom Sawyer* about two boys looking for treasure, helped by a useless batch of character actors, it was made during that period, roughly between Walt's death and *The Little Mermaid*, when the studio seemed to have lost touch with its audience's needs. Surprisingly star-billed alongside Peter Ustinov is the little-known Robert Foxworth, who simply can't carry the movie, despite sterling (and hammy) support from baddie Vic Morrow (Jennifer Jason Leigh's dad). Location shooting on the Florida Keys is a plus, but the whole interminable mess looks no better than a TV pilot.

Peter Ustinov *Dr Snodgrass* • Robert Foxworth *Jim* • Joan Hackett *Lauriette* • Vic Morrow *Spangler* • Johnny Doran *Davie* • Billy Attmore *Thad* • Jane Wyatt *Aunt Effie* ■ *Dir* Vincent McEveety • *Scr* Don Tait, from the novel *A Journey to Matecumbe* by Robert Lewis Taylor

The Treasure of Monte Cristo ★★★

Adventure
1960 · UK · Colour · 79mins

An interesting adventure involving buried treasure on the famous island, with Hollywood exile Rory Calhoun providing the muscle and Italy's Gianna Maria Canale the glamour. This is really only double-bill material, though there's plenty of action and thrills, plus a certain low-budget style that's rather endearing. The British contingent headed by genteel Patricia Bredin and slimy Peter Arne does what is required efficiently enough.

Rory Calhoun *Captain Adam Corbett* • Patricia Bredin *Pauline Jackson* • John Gregson *Renato* • Gianna Maria Canale *Lucetta* • Peter Arne *Count Boldini* • Sam Kydd *Albert* ■ *Dir* Monty Berman, Robert S Baker • *Scr* Leon Griffiths

The Treasure of Pancho Villa ★★ U

Western
1955 · US · Colour · 95mins

Though this western set during the Mexican Revolution of the 1910s is rather lethargic, it nevertheless has a potentially interesting premise – cynical mercenary Rory Calhoun clashes with idealists Gilbert Roland and Shelley Winters en route to deliver a shipment of gold to legendary rebel leader Villa. But director George Sherman struggles under the gravitas of his theme, and what should have been an action-packed scenario, falters thanks to the excessive war of words between the leads.

Rory Calhoun *Tom Bryan* • Shelley Winters *Ruth Harris* • Gilbert Roland *Juan Castro* • Joseph Calleia *Pablo Morales* • Carlos Mosquiz *Commandant* • Fanny Schiller *Laria Morales* ■ *Dir* George Sherman • *Scr* Niven Busch, from a story by J Robert Bren, Gladys Atwater

The Treasure of San Teresa ★★★

Drama
1959 · UK/W Ger · BW · 81mins

One of those "hunt for the wartime treasure" movies, cheerfully put together with an attractive international cast, headed by Eddie Constantine at his most rugged and Dawn Addams at her most gorgeous. The eclectic supporting cast includes double-dealing Marius Goring, Christopher Lee, Nadine Tallier and Clive Dunn, no less. Despite the diversity of nationalities, director Alvin Rakoff manages to hold all the accents together (not to mention the complexities of the plot). Co-feature fodder, but fun.

Eddie Constantine *Larry Brennan* • Dawn Addams *Hedi von Hartmann* • Gaylord Cavallaro *Mike Jones* • Marius Goring *Rudi Siebert* • Nadine Tallier *Zizi* • Willie White *General von Hartmann* • Walter Gotell *Inspector* • Christopher Lee *Jaeger* ■ *Dir* Alvin Rakoff • *Scr* Jack Andrews, from a story by Jeffrey Dell

Treasure of the Golden Condor ★★★ U

Adventure
1953 · US · Colour · 92mins

If this all seems a mite familiar, that's because it's yet another example of 20th Century-Fox recycling its favourite plots: this time it's the Tyrone Power Pacific island-set tale *Son of Fury* relocated in Central America, and with Cornel Wilde seeking his fortune. *Son of Fury* was a movie that cried out for Technicolor and here Fox remedied that error, even stressing colour in the title. To movie fans, the female members of the cast are the most interesting: although the lead is lacklustre Constance Smith, there's also *King Kong's* Fay Wray and a very young Anne Bancroft on the way up. Director Delmer Daves, better known later for dramas such as *A Summer Place*, and westerns such as *3:10 to Yuma* and *The Last Wagon*, cut his teeth on tosh like this.

Cornel Wilde *Jean-Paul* • Constance Smith *Clara* • Finlay Currie *MacDougal* • Walter Hampden *Pierre* • Anne Bancroft *Marie* • George Macready *Marquis* • Fay Wray *Marquise* • Leo G Carroll *Dondel* ■ *Dir* Delmer Daves • *Scr* Delmer Daves, from the novel *Benjamin Blake* by Edison Marshall

The Treasure of the Sierra Madre ★★★★★ PG

Western adventure
1948 · US · BW · 121mins

An enduringly popular classic about a trio of losers trying to find a crock of gold in bandit-infested Mexico. Humphrey Bogart turns in a memorable performance as drifter Fred C Dobbs, who latches on to gnarled old prospector Walter Huston, while Tim Holt plays a young lad with ideals. Pitched as an updated biblical fable about greed and human despair, the movie has a superb opening, some portentous passages and a thunderous score by Max Steiner. Subtle it isn't, and the ending, often imitated (most notably in Sam Peckinpah's *The Wild Bunch*), is, frankly, embarrassing, but director/writer John Huston still persuades you this is a great movie. The movie won Oscars for direction, screenplay and best supporting actor. 🎞

Humphrey Bogart *Dobbs* • Walter Huston *Howard* • Tim Holt *Curtin* • Bruce Bennett *Cody* • Barton MacLane *McCormick* • Alfonso Bedoya *"Gold Hat"* • A Soto Rangel *Presidente* • Manuel Donde *El Jefe* • Jose Torvay *Pablo* • John Huston *"White Suit"* ■ *Dir* John Huston • *Scr* John Huston, from the novel by B Traven • *Cinematographer* Ted McCord

Treasure of the Yankee Zephyr ★★

Adventure
1981 · Ausl/NZ · Colour · 90mins

Actor David Hemmings (*Blow Up*) directed this muddled and messy adventure with Donald Pleasence and Ken Wahl competing with George Peppard to recover a fortune from a Second World War plane wreck. It's not just the map to the treasure that gets lost, but also the plot. Lesley Ann Warren is the only guiding star.

Ken Wahl *Barney* • Lesley Ann Warren *Sally* • Donald Pleasence *Gibbie* • George Peppard *Theo Brown* • Bruno Lawrence *Barker* • Grant Tilly *Collector* ■ *Dir* David Hemmings • *Scr* Everett de Roche

The Treasure Seekers ★★ U

Adventure
1977 · US · Colour · 96mins

Rod Taylor wrote this story about the search for pirate Henry Morgan's sunken treasure as his own vehicle. That was the first mistake. The second was to have it made so turgidly with co-star Stuart Whitman. Despite the elfin femininity of Elke Sommer, it never succeeds in being anything other than a clone of so many movies about searchers for illusory riches. 🎞

Rod Taylor *Marion Casey* • Stuart Whitman *Stack Baker* • Jeremy Kemp *Reginald Landers* • Elke Sommer *Ursula* • Keenan Wynn *"Meat Cleaver" Stewart* • Jennie Sherman *Debbie* • Bob Phillips *Joe* • Keith Foote *Lincoln* ■ *Dir* Henry Levin • *Scr* Rod Taylor

A Tree Grows in Brooklyn ★★★★

Melodrama
1945 · US · BW · 128mins

The debut feature of celebrated director Elia Kazan (who went on to win Oscars for best director for *Gentleman's Agreement* and *On the Waterfront*) is set in early 1900s New York. Dorothy McGuire is excellent as the stoic Ma Nolan, whose efforts to keep her family together are hampered by an alcoholic husband (James Dunn) and the arrival of a third baby. Peggy Ann Garner received a special Academy Award for her role as the daughter, who dreams of a better life, and for whom the titular tree is a symbol of hope. Stick with this one for the initial dull 30 minutes – it will reward your patience.

Dorothy McGuire *Katie* • Joan Blondell *Aunt Sissy* • James Dunn *Johnny Nolan* • Lloyd Nolan *McShane* • Peggy Ann Garner *Francie Nolan* • Ted Donaldson *Neeley Nolan* • James Gleason *McGarrity* • Ruth Nelson *Miss McDonough* ■ *Dir* Elia Kazan • *Scr* Tess Slesinger, Frank Davis, from the novel by Betty Smith

A Tree Grows in Brooklyn
★★

Period drama 1974 · US · Colour · 90mins

Not Elia Kazan's 1945 classic about family values at risk, but a TV-movie remake that labours to make the same points. There are fine performances, however, from Diane Baker, as the Mother Courage of the lower orders, and Cliff Robertson as the alcoholic head of the family and occasional breadwinner. Unfortunately, there's not much of the original's flair.

Cliff Robertson *Johnny Nolan* • Diane Baker *Katie Nolan* • James Olson *McShane* • Pamelyn Ferdin *Francie Nolan* • Nancy Malone *Aunt Sissy* ■ *Dir* Joseph Hardy • *Scr* Blanche Hanalis, Tess Slesinger, from the novel by Betty Smith, Frank Davis

Tree of Hands
★★ 18

Thriller 1988 · UK · Colour · 85mins

Novelist Ruth Rendell's psychological thriller is turned into a rather messy and distinctly underwhelming movie, with Helen Shaver as the woman whose own child dies and who then takes on a child kidnapped by her mother, played by Lauren Bacall. The parents of the kidnapped child bring one set of problems, while Shaver herself is being blackmailed. Lacklustre direction and a schlock-horror script are the major weaknesses. ⌨

Helen Shaver *Benet Archdale* • Lauren Bacall *Marsha Archdale* • Malcolm Stoddard *Dr Ian Raeburn* • Peter Firth *Terence* • Paul McGann *Barry* • Kate Hardie *Carol* • Tony Haygarth *Kostas* • Phyllida Law *Julia* • David Schofield *Detective Inspector* ■ *Dir* Giles Foster • *Scr* Gordon Williams, from the novel by Ruth Rendell

The Tree of Wooden Clogs
★★★★

Drama 1978 · It · Colour · 186mins

Following in the tradition of Georges Rouquier's *Farrebique*, Ermanno Olmi's sprawling study of peasant life in Lombardy at the end of the 19th century, is one of the last great neo-realist films. Shot on 16mm and using only non-professional players, this pseudo-documentary epic finds drama in the changing of the seasons and the everyday tasks of the farm. Acting as his own cameraman, Olmi opts for muted colours that suggest both the period and the simplicity of the lifestyle. However, he is somewhat less subtle in emphasising the Marxist message, which he neatly conveys by

means of religious, as well as traditional, rural imagery. In Italian with English subtitles.

Luigi Ornaghi *Batisti* • Francesca Moriggi *Batistina* • Omar Brignoli *Minek* • Antonio Ferrari *Tuni* ■ *Dir/Scr* Ermanno Olmi

Trees Lounge
★★★★ 15

Comedy drama 1996 · US · Colour · 91mins

Steve Buscemi once claimed he'd have been a bar bum had his acting career failed. This is indie film-making à la John Cassavetes rather than Quentin Tarantino, with the humour being understated, the drama credible, the dialogue having an everyday ring and the performances ideally suited to a world of regrets and whiskey chasers. If the camerawork is occasionally prone to showiness, the atmosphere of both the neighbourhood Buscemi prowls in his ice-cream van and the Trees Lounge itself is totally authentic. Contains drug abuse, swearing, violence. ⌨

Steve Buscemi *Tommy* • Carol Kane *Connie* • Mark Boone Junior *Mike* • Chloë Sevigny *Debbie* • Bronson Dudley *Bill* • Anthony LaPaglia *Rob* • Michael Buscemi *Raymond* • Elizabeth Bracco *Theresa* ■ *Dir/Scr* Steve Buscemi

Tremors
★★★★★ 15

Comedy horror 1989 · US · Colour · 91mins

The spirit of the "Killer Bs" is gloriously resurrected in this, the ultimate story of the worm that turned. Kevin Bacon and Fred Ward are a sort of "Simple and Simpler", an endearingly goofy pair of handymen who discover that huge underground worms have broken through the Earth's surface and are now swallowing up everything in their path. Director Ron Underwood keeps both the action and laughs roaring along at a tremendous pace and there is a string of entertaining cameos, most notably from Michael Gross the father in TV's *Family Ties* and country star Reba McEntire as an unlikely pair of survivalists. Add to that a refreshingly tough and intelligent female lead (Finn Carter) and the result is the sharpest, funniest monster movie in years. Contains swearing. ⌨

Kevin Bacon *Valentine McKee* • Fred Ward *Earl Basset* • Finn Carter *Rhonda LeBeck* • Michael Gross *Burt Gummer* • Reba McEntire *Heather Gummer* • Bobby Jacoby *Melvin Plug* • Charlotte Stewart *Nancy* • Tony Genaro *Miguel* • Ariana Richards *Mindy* • Richard Marcus *Nestor* ■ *Dir* Ron Underwood • *Scr* SS Wilson and Brent Maddock, from a story by Wilson, Maddock, Underwood

Tremors 2: Aftershocks
★★★ 12

Science-fiction horror comedy 1995 · US · Colour · 95mins

Surprisingly entertaining made-for-video sequel to Ron Underwood's monster movie classic. The giant worms are munching in Mexico, so Fred Ward is called in along with Christopher Gartin. Sharply written and engagingly performed, this stays true to the jokey spirit of the original, whilst adding a new breed of overground "graboids" to literally chew the scenery. Although it lacks the frantic pace and sprightly camera work of the original, it's

smarter and more fun than many cinema follow-ups and Michael Gross is again hilarious as fearless gun-nut Burt. ⌨

Fred Ward *Earl Bassett* • Michael Gross *Burt Gummer* • Helen Shaver *Kate White Reilly* • Marcelo Tubert *Senor Ortega* • Christopher Gartin *Grady Hoover* ■ *Dir* SS Wilson • *Scr* SS Wilson, Brent Maddock

The Trench
★★ 15

First World War drama 1999 · UK/Fr · Colour · 98mins

William Boyd's directorial debut is a sincere, but stagey attempt to explore the psychological pressures weighing on diverse tommies awaiting their first day on the Somme. Although the camera restlessly suggests the cramped, primitive conditions, Tony Pierce-Roberts's glassy photography too often highlights the atmospheric shortcomings of the sets. Similarly, the cast rallies to the colours, but their commitment can't disguise the fact that the script is populated solely by stock combat characters: the naive private, chirpy cockney, gritty sergeant and spineless officer. There have been many examples that portrayed a similar situation so much better, and even *Blackadder Goes Forth* showed sharper insight. Contains swearing, violence.

Paul Nicholls *Billy MacFarlane* • Daniel Craig *Sgt Telford Winter* • Julian Rhind-Tutt *Ellis Harte* • Danny Dyer *Victor Dell* • James D'Arcy *Colin Daventry* • Tam Williams *Eddie MacFarlane* • Antony Strachan *Horace Beckwith* ■ *Dir/Scr* William Boyd

Trenchcoat
★★ PG

Comedy mystery 1983 · US · Colour · 87mins

A chirpy adventure in which an aspiring author finds herself drawn into a convoluted plot that seems to have leapt from the pages of her favourite fiction. Although the Maltese locations are easy on the eye and the conspiracy storyline scurries along without making too many demands on the imagination, the chief interest lies in the willing performances of Margot Kidder and Robert Hays. Both are no doubt relieved to escape from typecasting as *Superman's* Lois Lane and *Airplane!* pilot Ted Striker respectively. ⌨

Margot Kidder *Mickey Raymond* • Robert Hays *Terry Leonard* • David Suchet *Inspector Stagnos* • Gila Von Weitershausen *Eva Werner* • Daniel Faraldo *Nino Tenucci* • Ronald Lacey *Princess Aida* • John Justin *Marquis Depina* ■ *Dir* Michael Tuchner • *Scr* Jeffrey Price, Peter Seaman

Trenchcoat in Paradise
★★ PG

Mystery thriller 1989 · US · Colour · 89mins

The usually reliable director Martha Coolidge (*Lost in Yonkers*, *Rambling Rose*) strays into TV detective territory – without success. Dirk Benedict is a private eye who, in one of those fish-out-of-water scenarios beloved of TV writers, moves from New Jersey to the "paradise" that is Hawaii. Of course, instead of peace and tranquility, he's soon pitched into murder and mayhem. Despite credible performances from Benedict and Bruce Dern this is a dull hotchpotch of a movie, with characters

introduced and swept away – seemingly on a whim. ⌨

Dirk Benedict *Eddie Mazda* • Bruce Dern *John Hollander* • Catherine Oxenberg *Lisa Duncan* • Kim Zimmer *Claire Hollander* • Sydney Walsh *Mona Williams* • Michelle Phillips *Susanna Hollander* ■ *Dir* Martha Coolidge • *Scr* Tom Dempsey

Trent's Last Case
★★★ U

Crime mystery 1952 · UK · BW · 86mins

E C Bentley's diverting detective story was the prototype for the modern whodunit. This is the best of the three screen adaptations, even though the 1929 version was made by Howard Hawks – still learning his craft at the time. Michael Wilding stars as the shrewd sleuth of the title investigating the suspicious death of tycoon Orson Welles, who, in just a few flashbacks, masterfully creates a victim who was simply begging to be bumped off. Herbert Wilcox sprinkles the clues and red herrings with a steady hand, while John McCallum and Margaret Lockwood stand out among the suspects. ⌨

Margaret Lockwood *Margaret Manderson* • Michael Wilding *Philip Trent* • Orson Welles *Sigsbee Manderson* • John McCallum *John Marlowe* • Miles Malleson *Burton Cupples* • Hugh McDermott *Calvin C Bunner* • Sam Kydd *Inspector Murch* • Jack McNaughton *Martin* ■ *Dir* Herbert Wilcox • *Scr* Pamela Bower, from the novel by EC Bentley

Trespass
★★ 18

Thriller 1992 · US · Colour · 96mins

Whatever happened to director Walter Hill? The man who matched an understanding of the male psyche with a pumping, muscular style of direction in films such as *The Long Riders* and *Southern Comfort* seems to have lost his touch with the years. It's as if he's remembered the window-dressing, but forgotten the soul. Here, an unlikely premise (two firemen discover a map that points to a cache of gold in a disused factory) is buoyed up by a merely efficient set of thrills, which are sometimes funny, but veer towards the hysterical as the film approaches its tough finale. Contains violence, swearing. ⌨

Bill Paxton *Vince* • Ice T [Ice-T] *King James* • William Sadler *Don* • Ice Cube *Savon* • Art Evans *Bradlee* • De'Voreaux White *Lucky* • Bruce A Young *Raymond* • Glenn Plummer *Luther* • Stoney Jackson *Wickey* • TE Russell *Video* • Tiny Lister [Tom "Tiny" Lister Jr] *Cletus* ■ *Dir* Walter Hill • *Scr* Bob Gale, Robert Zemeckis

The Trespasser
★★★

Drama 1929 · US · BW · 91mins

Silent-screen drama queen Gloria Swanson produced, took a hand in the screenplay, and starred in this, her first talkie, making herself $1 million at the box office. She plays a secretary whose marriage to Robert Ames, the son of a multi-millionaire, is destroyed by Ames' father. She is left with their baby, he remarries an invalid (England's Kay Hammond), but years later... A romantic melodrama on the familiar theme of mother love and self-sacrifice, the movie would not hold much interest now if it were not for the always mesmerising presence of la Swanson, who earned the film an

Oscar nomination. Director/ screenwriter Edmund Goulding rewrote and redirected it in 1937 as *That Certain Woman* with Bette Davis. 🖵

Gloria Swanson *Marion Donnell* • Robert Ames *Jack Merrick* • Purnell Pratt *Hector Ferguson* • Henry B Walthall *Fuller* • Wally Albright Jr [Wally Albright] *Jackie* • William Holden (2) *John Merrick Sr* • Blanche Frederici *Miss Potter* • Kay Hammond *Catherine "Flip" Merrick* ■ *Dir/Scr* Edmund Goulding

Trial ★★★★

Drama   1955 · US · BW · 108mins

This gut-wrenching MGM drama was Glenn Ford's follow-up to his superb performance in *Blackboard Jungle*. Scripted by Don Mankiewicz from his own novel, this is a powerful study of courtroom justice, and one of the few movies to deal with the influence of Communism on US politics. Here, it's in open discussion as it impinges on the case of a Mexican youth (*Blackboard Jungle's* Rafael Campos) on trial for murder. The film is also the first to feature an African-American judge, played by Juano Hernandez. The Oscar-nominated Arthur Kennedy and the under-rated Dorothy McGuire provide excellent support, but this is Ford's movie, and what a screen presence he is – a rare combination of movie star and actor.

Glenn Ford *David* • Dorothy McGuire *Abbe* • Arthur Kennedy *Barney* • John Hodiak *John J. Armstrong* • Katy Jurado *Mrs Chavez* • Rafael Campos *Angel Chavez* • Juano Hernandez *Judge Theodore Motley* • Robert Middleton *AS "Fats" Sanders* ■ *Dir* Mark Robson • *Scr* Don Mankiewicz, from his novel

The Trial ★★★★ PG

Drama   1962 · Fr/It/W Ger · BW · 113mins

Orson Welles's film of Franz Kafka's novel is everything one expects: audacious, weird and impish, filled with references to Welles's own life as well as to *Citizen Kane*. Anthony Perkins is another citizen K, Joseph K, who is arrested and put on trial for no obvious reason in some strange autocratic state. Welles's use of locations (notably the Gare D'Orsay in Paris) is spellbinding, creating a dark labyrinth with the slenderest of resources. While Perkins is brilliantly paranoid, Jeanne Moreau and Romy Schneider are mysteriously exotic. Welles himself plays the Advocate, the ringmaster of this nightmare comedy. 🖵

Orson Welles *The Advocate* • Anthony Perkins *Joseph K* • Jeanne Moreau *Miss Burstner* • Romy Schneider *Leni* • Elsa Martinelli *Hilda* • Akim Tamiroff *Bloch* • Arnoldo Foà *Inspector A* • William Kearns *First Asst Inspector* • Jess Hahn *Second Asst Inspector* • Suzanne Flon *Miss Pittl* • Michael Lonsdale *(Michel Lonsdale) Priest* ■ *Dir* Orson Welles • *Scr* Orson Welles, from the novel by Franz Kafka

The Trial ★★ 15

Drama   1993 · UK/It · Colour · 115mins

Kyle MacLachlan and Anthony Hopkins star in director David Jones's version of Kafka's classic novel about an innocent man accused. Unlike Orson Welles's 1963 version – and despite this version's scripting from Harold Pinter – this is seriously lacking the necessary dramatic darkness. MacLachlan is bland as Josef K, arrested and struggling to uncover the

reason why, and Hopkins manages to steal the film completely with his very brief appearance as the priest who helps Josef. The novel is marvellous, Welles's film is fantastic, but this is simply a very poor imitation of a great original. Go back to the novel. 🖵

Kyle MacLachlan *Josef K* • Anthony Hopkins *The Priest* • Jason Robards Jr *Dr Huld* • Jean Stapleton *Landlady* • Juliet Stevenson *Fraulein Burstner* • Polly Walker *Leni* • Alfred Molina *Titorelli* ■ *Dir* David Jones • *Scr* Harold Pinter, from the novel by Franz Kafka

Trial and Error ★★★ U

Comedy   1962 · UK · BW · 75mins

Also known as *The Dock Brief*, this neat little comedy was adapted from a radio play by John Mortimer (of *Rumpole* fame). The amusing storyline pits failed barrister Peter Sellers against Richard Attenborough's henpecked husband, who confounds all Sellers's ploys to have him acquitted on a charge of murdering his wife. Sellers does a nice line in comic despair, but this is not one of his most memorable characterisations and he is easily outflanked by Attenborough, who seems to be having a marvellous time playing the role of an unrepentant killer. 🖵

Peter Sellers *Morgenhall/Doctor* • Richard Attenborough *Fowle/Judge/Jury foreman/Member of public/Character witness* • Beryl Reid *Doris* • David Lodge *Bateson* • Frank Pettingell *Tuppy Morgan* • Eric Woodburn *Judge Banter* ■ *Dir* James Hill • *Scr* Pierre Rouve, from the radio play by John Mortimer

Trial & Error ★★★ 15

Courtroom thriller   1992 · US · Colour · 90mins

Tim Matheson revels in the role of an election candidate forced to choose between admitting that the murder conviction that made his name as a lawyer, is less reliable than a politician's promise, or see his wife fall victim to the real killer, who is still very much at large. If you can ignore the more obvious plot contrivances, this is a slick study of a man reckoning what price is worth paying for power. Contains violence.

Tim Matheson *Peter Hudson* • Helen Shaver *Katherine Woodfield* • Sean Mccann *Albert Grant* • Page Fletcher *Ken Norwich* • Michael J Reynolds *Governor Nelson* • Ian D Clark *Randi Kirby* ■ *Dir* Mark Sobel • *Scr* Rick Way, Jim Lindsay, Nevin Schreiner, from a story by Andrew Marin

Trial and Error ★★ 12

Comedy   1997 · US · Colour · 94mins

Seinfeld star Michael Richards (the eccentric Kramer) has been trying to find the right outlet for his considerable comedic talents outside the cult TV show, and unfortunately this isn't it. He does provide the few laughs that are here, as the pal of lawyer Jeff Daniels, who agrees to impersonate him in court when Daniels is indisposed – with supposedly hilarious results. While director Jonathan Lynn has shown a deft hand at comedy (*My Cousin Vinny*, *The Whole Nine Yards*), he's let down here by a lumpen script – a shame when he has such a talented cast, including Charlize Theron and Rip Torn. 🖵

Michael Richards *Richard Rietti* • Jeff Daniels *Charles Tuttle* • Charlize Theron *Billie Tyler* • Jessica Steen *Elizabeth Gardner* • Austin Pendleton *Judge Paul Z Graff* • Rip Torn *Benny Gibbs* ■ *Dir* Jonathan Lynn • *Scr* Sara Bernstein, Gregory Bernstein, from a story by Cliff Gardner, Sara Bernstein, Gregory Bernstein

Trial by Combat ★★

Comedy   1976 · UK · Colour · 89mins

Initially released as *Choice of Arms*, this is an idiotic fantasy about a secret society calling itself the Knights of Avalon, whose members dress up in medieval armour and act as a lynch mob, murdering dangerous criminals to make up for what they believe is an ineffective justice system. Seemingly inspired by *The Avengers* TV show, it has some nice touches, though it's not as funny or stylish as the original; nor is it in any way subversive. Just a fancy dress party, really. Contains violence, swearing.

John Mills *Bertie Cook* • Donald Pleasence *Sir Giles Marley* • Barbara Hershey *Marion Evans* • Margaret Leighton *Ma Gore* • Brian Glover *Sidney Gore* • David Birney *Sir John Gifford* • Peter Cushing *Sir Edward Gifford* ■ *Dir* Kevin Connor • *Scr* Julian Bond, Steve Rossen, Mitchell Smith, from a story by Fred Weintraub, Paul Heller

Trial by Fire ★ 15

Courtroom drama   1995 · US · Colour · 92mins

Teacher Gail O'Grady must clear her name when one of her students commits suicide after claiming she had an affair with him. This lachrymose melodrama is nothing more than a standard "Issue of the Week" TV movie, with few surprises. Director Alan Metzger is a TV-movie specialist, but even his experience counts for nothing in this very sorry production. Contains brief nudity. 🖵

Gail O'Grady *Paulette Gill* • Keith Carradine *Owen Turner* • Michael Bowen *Roger Gill* • Ken Lerner *Earl Cleaver* • Mariangela Pino *Evie Bauchmoyer* • Devon Odessa *Patsy Thurman* ■ *Dir* Alan Metzger • *Scr* Richard Lawton

Trial by Jury ★★ 15

Thriller   1994 · US · Colour · 102mins

Jury tampering is a subject ripe with potential, yet both this film and *The Juror*, which followed two years later, never really make the most of it. In this one, Joanne Whalley-Kilmer is the woman who stands up against flamboyant mobster Armand Assante, who wants to ensure his court case goes his way. Director Heywood Gould does his best, but the plotting gets sillier by the minute and the erratic performances from the starry cast; Assante wildly over the top, William Hurt low key and sleazy as a bent ex-cop, don't help, either. Contains sexual references, swearing, violence. 🖵

Joanne Whalley-Kilmer [Joanne Whalley] *Valerie Aston* • Armand Assante *Rusty Pirone* • Gabriel Byrne *Daniel Graham* • William Hurt *Tommy Vesey* • Kathleen Quinlan *Wanda* • Margaret Whitton *Jane Lyle* • Ed Lauter *John Boyle* • Richard Portnow *Leo Greco* ■ *Dir* Heywood Gould • *Scr* Jordan Katz, Heywood Gould

The Trial of Billy Jack ★

Drama   1974 · US · Colour · 170mins

The cult half-breed ex-Green Beret is on trial for murder while fighting corrupt White House officials and the usual unappreciative rednecks, in this third entry in the hippy-dippy *Billy Jack* series which began in 1967 with *The Born Losers*. Delores Taylor narrates the suspect "peace through violence" story of this stunningly pretentious and overlong vanity production from all-round auteur Tom Laughlin. Drawing on real issues as political markers in the stodgy conspiracy theory/martial arts laden script, Laughlin indulges in Vietnam flashbacks and ludicrous psychedelic spirit encounters, while stumbling towards a yawn-making kung-fu finale. Trivia fans should note the appearance from Sacheen Littlefeather, the native American who accepted Marlon Brando's best actor Oscar for *The Godfather*.

Tom Laughlin *Billy Jack* • Delores Taylor *Jean Roberts* • Victor Izay *Doc* • Teresa Laughlin *Carol* • William Wellman Jr *National Guardsman* ■ *Dir* Tom Laughlin • *Scr* Tom Laughlin, Delores Taylor, Teresa Christina

The Trial of Mary Dugan ★★

Crime melodrama   1941 · US · BW · 89mins

It started as a sensational Broadway courtroom melodrama of 1927, about a woman who lived in sin to help her brother through law college and is defended by him when she murders her lover. It became a huge hit as MGM's first all-talkie with Norma Shearer. This is a dull and sanitised remake with new star Laraine Day making little impression as a dull but decent stenographer and Robert Young playing a mere boyfriend, rather than her sibling.

Laraine Day *Mary Dugan* • Robert Young *Jimmy Blake* • Tom Conway *Edgar Wayne* • Frieda Inescort *Mrs Wayne* • Henry O'Neill *Galway* • John Litel *Mr West* • Marsha Hunt *Agatha Hall* ■ *Dir* Norman Z McLeod • *Scr* Bayard Veiller, from his play

The Trial of the Incredible Hulk ★★ PG

Science-fiction adventure   1989 · US · Colour · 95mins

Surely after three TV movies and a four-year series, the Hulk would have vented all his anger and stopped going through his supply of shirts so rapidly? Well, no. Bill Bixby steps behind the camera to bring yet another instalment of the comic-book hero's adventures to the screen, and it bears all the hallmarks of an idea that has run out of steam. Bixby went on to direct yet another helping of this tame action fare. 🖵

Bill Bixby *Doctor David Banner* • Lou Ferrigno *The Hulk* • Rex Smith *Matt Murdoch/Daredevil* • John Rhys-Davies *Wilson Fisk* • Marta Dubois *Ellie Mendez* • Nancy Everhard *Christa Klein* • Nicholas Hormann *Edgar* • Joseph Mascolo *Tendelli* • Richard Cummings Jr *Al Pettiman* ■ *Dir* Bill Bixby • *Scr* Gerald DiPego

Trial on the Road ★★★

Drama   1971 · USSR · BW · 97mins

Evocatively shot in lustrous widescreen monochrome, Alexei German's directorial debut was banned in the

USSR for 15 years, primarily because the character played by Vladimir Zamanski is a Red Army deserter returning to the fold after collaborating with the Nazis. However, German is equally audacious in his presentation of Anatoli Solonitsyn's stiffly sadistic major (a chillingly pragmatic Stalinist) and Rolan Bykov's partisan commander, who operates according to instinct and humanity rather than dogma. Counter-stereotypes aside, though, this exercise in the "poetics of courage" actually adheres quite closely, in terms of structure and resolution, to the tenets of the socialist realist war movie. A Russian language film.

Rolan Bykov • Anatoli Solonitsyn • Vladimir Zamanskii • Oleg Borisov ■ *Dir* Alexei German • *Scr* Eduard Volodarsky, from the book by Yuri German

The Trials of Oscar Wilde ★★★★

Drama 1960 · UK · Colour · 123mins

Released in America as *The Man with the Green Carnation*, this is a moving account of the fall from grace of the finest playwright of the Victorian era. Although Peter Finch looks nothing like Wilde, he gives an assured, poignant and Bafta-winning performance, excelling particularly during his courtroom jousts with James Mason as the abrasive Sir Edward Carson. John Fraser makes an admirably self-centred Lord Alfred Douglas, while Lionel Jeffries plays impressively against type as the irascible Marquis of Queensberry, who first publicly accused Wilde of homosexuality. Gregory Ratoff's black-and-white picture, *Oscar Wilde* starring Robert Morley, was released almost simultaneously.

Peter Finch *Oscar Wilde* • James Mason *Sir Edward Carson* • Yvonne Mitchell *Constance Wilde* • Nigel Patrick *Sir Edward Clarke* • John Fraser *Lord Alfred Douglas* • Lionel Jeffries *Marquis Of Queensberry* • Maxine Audley *Ada Leverson* • James Booth *Alfred Wood* ■ *Dir* Ken Hughes • *Scr* Ken Hughes, from the play *The Stringed Lute* by John Furnell and the book by Montgomery Hyde

Tribute ★★

Drama 1980 · Can · Colour · 125mins

Having enjoyed a Broadway triumph with this over-ripe and tragi-comic role in the original play, it was inevitable that Jack Lemmon would be invited to immortalise his character on screen. Adapted by the original author, it comes across as talkative and maudlin with Lemmon – as a glib theatrical press agent – encouraged to give a very mannered performance. Better acting comes from Lee Remick as his estranged wife and Robby Benson as the son who returns to discover his father has a fatal illness. If anything, it shows what a loss Benson was to the screen when he turned to directing and teaching.

Jack Lemmon *Scottie Templeton* • Robby Benson *Jud Templeton* • Lee Remick *Maggie Stratton* • Colleen Dewhurst *Gladys Petrelli* • John Marley *Lou Daniels* • Kim Cattrall *Sally Haines* • Gale Garnett *Hilary* • Teri Keane *Evelyn* ■ *Dir* Bob Clark • *Scr* Bernard Slade, from his play

Tribute to a Bad Man ★★★★ PG

Western 1956 · US · Colour · 91mins

A fine MGM western, well directed by Robert Wise with a genuine feel for life on the frontier, and beautifully shot by the great cinematographer Robert Surtees (*Ben-Hur*, *The Last Picture Show*). It's dominated by a larger-than-life performance from James Cagney as a ruthless cattle baron, taking over at the last minute from Spencer Tracy. Irene Papas is the imported co-star, and her relationship with gruff Cagney forms the tough centre of the movie. The two leads are backed up by a knockout cast of western faces, including Lee Van Cleef and Royal Dano.

James Cagney *Jeremy Rodock* • Don Dubbins *Steve Miller* • Irene Papas *Jocasta Constantine* • Stephen McNally *McNulty* • Vic Morrow *Lars Peterson* • James Griffith *Barjack* • Lee Van Cleef *Fat Jones* ■ *Dir* Robert Wise • *Scr* Michael Blankfort, from a short story by Jack Schaefer

Les Tricheurs ★★★

Drama 1984 · Fr/W Ger · Colour · 95mins

A continental offering from director Barbet Schroeder, it dates from the period before his move to English-language pictures (*Barfly*). This is set within the glossy jetset gambling scene, where Jacques Dutronc and Kurt Raab concoct an ingenious scheme to beat the roulette wheel (the title translates as *The Cheaters*). As Dutronc's lucky charm, Bulle Ogier is especially effective and the casino sequences show a great attention to detail. However, the characters are as shallow as the world they inhabit – then again, perhaps that's the point. A French language film.

Jacques Dutronc *Elric* • Bulle Ogier *Suzie* • Kurt Raab *Jorg* • Virgilio Teixeira *Toni* ■ *Dir* Barbet Schroeder • *Scr* Barbet Schroeder, Pascal Bonitzer, Steve Baes

Trick ★★★ 15

Romantic comedy 1999 · US · Colour · 89mins

From the same school of gay film-making as *Billy's Hollywood Screen Kiss*, Jim Fall's unassuming romantic comedy pokes gentle fun at such stereotypes as the bitchy drag queen and the disco stud. Christian Campbell could hardly be more cherubic as the struggling musical composer whose chance to make it with a hunky stripper, J P Pitoc, is frustrated by a lack of privacy and a wealth of conflicting advice. Yet it's the much-maligned Tori Spelling's animated performance as a motor-mouthed off-Broadway wannabe that leaves the deepest impression. A huge hit on the festival circuit, this has "date movie" stamped all over it.

Christian Campbell *Gabriel* • JP Pitoc *Mark* • Tori Spelling *Katherine Lambert* • Lorri Bagley *Judy* • Brad Beyer *Rich* • Steve Hayes *Perry* ■ *Dir* Jim Fall • *Scr* Jason Schafer

Trick or Treat ★★ 18

Comedy horror 1986 · US · Colour · 93mins

Evil Kiss-type rock star Sammi Curr (Tony Fields) returns from the dead when one of his biggest fans, Marc Price, plays his last unreleased album backwards. At first Price caters to every murderous whim the shock rocker's spirit demands, until he realises he's being duped by the Devil. A tedious and adolescent heavy metal comedy-horror it features head-bangers Ozzy Osbourne and Gene Simmons in cameo roles and is perfunctorily directed by Charles Martin Smith, the nerd in *American Graffiti*. There's the obligatory ludicrous rubber demons and a killer toilet! Yes, a killer toilet!

DVD

Tony Fields *Sammi Curr* • Marc Price *Eddie Weinbauer* • Lisa Orgolini *Leslie Graham* • Doug Savant *Tim Hainey* • Elaine Joyce *Angie Weinbauer* • Ozzy Osbourne *Reverend Aaron Gilstrom* • Gene Simmons *Nuke* ■ *Dir* Charles Martin Smith • *Scr* Rhet Topham, Michael S Murphey, Joel Soisson, from a story by Rhet Topham

Trick or Treats ★★

Horror 1982 · US · Colour · 91mins

No-budget horror rip-off, about a girl who agrees to babysit a spoiled brat on Halloween. Jackelyn Giroux looks a bit too old to play the terrorised sitter, but there's solid support from Carrie Snodgress and David Carradine, and director Paul Bartel plays a wino. Otherwise there's little to recommend this film, though movie buffs may like to note that director Gary Graver was the cameraman on some of Orson Welles's later films.

Jackelyn Giroux *Linda* • Peter Jason *Malcolm* • Chris Graver *Christopher* • David Carradine *Richard* • Carrie Snodgress *Joan* • Jillian Kesner *Andrea* • Paul Bartel *Wino* ■ *Dir/Scr* Gary Graver

Tricks ★★

Drama 1997 · US · Colour · 96mins

A rather gloomy star vehicle for the ex-Mrs Tom Cruise, Mimi Rogers, who also produced this made-for-TV tale. She plays a former Las Vegas dancer who turns to prostitution in order to raise money for a college education. Rogers, cast against type, is believable enough in the title role and there is solid support from Tyne Daly and Ray Walston. However, the direction from Kenneth Fink is undistinguished.

Mimi Rogers *Jackie Simpson* • Tyne Daly *Sarah* • Ray Walston *Big Sam* • Callum Keith Rennie *Adam* • Ron Halder *Tommy* • Kevin McNulty *Henry* ■ *Dir* Kenneth Fink • *Scr* Deborah Amelon

Tricks of the Trade ★★★ 15

Comedy thriller 1988 · US · Colour · 91mins

Director Jack Bender, here succeeds in balancing comedy and suspense in a lively enough thriller. It's a female buddy-buddy film of the most eccentric kind, concerning the joint efforts of a wife and a prostitute, in whose flat the wife's husband has just died, to find the killer. Bender is, however, occasionally over-ambitious when he should be keeping the story tight. Star Cindy Williams is best remembered as Shirley in *Laverne and Shirley*. ▦

Cindy Williams *Catherine* • Markie Post *Marla* • Scott Paulin *Catherine's friend* • James Whitmore Jr *Detective* • Chris Mulkey *Detective* • Susan Davis *Edith* ■ *Dir* Jack Bender • *Scr* Noreen Stone

The Trigger Effect ★★★ 15

Thriller 1996 · US · Colour · 90mins

A massive power failure causes panic among the inhabitants of a well-to-do US suburb. There's a parallel with *Lord of the Flies* in this stark reminder of the thin veneer that disguises our more savage instincts. Director David Koepp, screenwriter on both *Jurassic Park* movies, handles the mounting chaos with some aplomb, despite his reduction of most characters to disaster-movie stereotypes. He's helped by a high calibre cast which includes Kyle MacLachlan, Elisabeth Shue and Dermot Mulroney. Contains swearing, sexual references, violence. ▦

Kyle MacLachlan *Matthew* • Elisabeth Shue *Annie* • Dermot Mulroney *Joe* • Richard T Jones *Raymond* • Bill Smitrovich *Steph* • Michael Rooker *Gary* ■ *Dir/Scr* David Koepp

Trigger Happy ★★★★ 15

Crime comedy 1996 · US · Colour · 92mins

Originally known as *Mad Dog Time*, this is a quirky gangster comedy featuring hilarious turns from an impressive all-star cast. Richard Dreyfuss is Vic, the mob boss in a mental institution. Meanwhile, his associates and rivals battle over who takes control of his business and his girlfriend. Jeff Goldblum, Ellen Barkin, Diane Lane, Gabriel Byrne, Kyle MacLachlan and Gregory Hines are just some of the mobsters and their molls scattering the odd little film written and directed by Larry Bishop, which may puzzle more conventional Mafia movie fans, but will delight those with a more skewed sense of humour. ▦

Larry Bishop *Nick* • Richard Dreyfuss *Vic* • Gabriel Byrne *Ben London* • Ellen Barkin *Rita Everly* • Jeff Goldblum *Mickey Holliday* • Diane Lane *Grace Everly* • Gregory Hines *Jules Flamingo* • Kyle MacLachlan *Jake Parker* • Burt Reynolds *"Wacky" Jacky Jackson* ■ *Dir/Scr* Larry Bishop

Trilogy of Terror II ★★ 15

Horror thriller 1996 · US · Colour · 86mins

It took Dan Curtis two decades to finally get around to making a sequel to his excellent made-for-television horror anthology. Again he employed the writing talents of genre master Richard Matheson (*Duel* and *The Incredible Shrinking Man*), but this time with uneven results. Lysette Anthony, the personification of the English rose, performs the same duty as Karen Black did in the 1974 original, that of appearing in all three stories. The first involves a pair of lovers who murder the woman's husband. The second is a suspenseful tale about a mother who summons her son back from the dead. But as usual with such fare, the best tale is served up last as an African tribal doll comes to life and embarks upon a murderous rampage. A satisfying treat if you don't expect too much. Contains violence, some swearing and a sex scene. ▦

Lysette Anthony *Laura/Alma/Ellen* • Geraint Wyn Davies *Ben* • Matt Clark *Ansford* • Geoffrey Lewis *Stubbs* ■ *Dir* Dan Curtis • *Scr* William F Nolan, Dan Curtis, Richard Matheson, from the short story *The Graveyard Rats* by Henry Kuttner, from the short story *Prey* by Richard Matheson

Trio ★★★
Portmanteau drama
1950 · UK/US · BW · 91mins

Sandwiched between *Quartet* and *Encore*, this is the second of Gainsborough's Somerset Maugham portmanteau pictures. Considering the writing talent involved and the quality of the performances, it seems slightly strange that the only Oscar-nomination the picture received was for best sound. Ken Annakin directs the first two stories, *The Verger*, with James Hayter and Kathleen Harrison on sparkling form, and *Mr Knowall*, with cheeky chappy supreme Nigel Patrick. The final half of the film contains Harold French's sentimental *Sanatorium*, starring Jean Simmons and Michael Rennie, to send you off with a tear in your eye.

James Hayter *Albert Foreman* • Kathleen Harrison *Emma Brown* • Felix Aylmer *Bank manager* • Michael Hordern *Vicar* • Nigel Patrick *Max Kelada "Mr Know-All"* • Anne Crawford *Mrs Ramsay* • Wilfrid Hyde White *Mr Gray* • Jean Simmons *Evie Bishop* • Roland Culver *Ashenden* • Michael Rennie *George Templeton* ■ *Dir* Ken Annakin, Harold French • *Scr* W Somerset Maugham, RC Sherriff, Noel Langley, from the short stories by W Somerset Maugham • *Sound* Gordon McCallum, CC Stevens, J Mitchell

The Trip ★★★
Drama 1967 · US · Colour · 76mins

"Feel Purple, Taste Green" screamed the posters for cult director Roger Corman's highly controversial drugs epic in which hippy Bruce Dern guides confused commercials director Peter Fonda through his first LSD acid trip. After scoring from Dennis Hopper (who else?) it's back to a luxury LA pad where Fonda digs an orange's aura, experiences good and bad vibes, has psychedelic visions of sex, death and dancing girls, grooves to washing machines in a laundromat and wanders through sets leftover from Corman's own Edgar Allen Poe movies. Part exploitation flick, part non-preachy message picture, this fractured love-in, scripted by Jack Nicholson and told almost entirely through rapid-fire visuals, is a fascinating period piece.

Peter Fonda *Paul Groves* • Susan Strasberg *Sally Groves* • Bruce Dern *John* • Dennis Hopper *Max* • Salli Sachse *Glenn* • Katherine Walsh *Lulu* • Barboura Morris *Flo* • Caren Bernsen *Alexandra* • Dick Miller *Cash* ■ *Dir* Roger Corman • *Scr* Jack Nicholson • *Cinematographer* Arch R Dalzell

The Trip to Bountiful ★★★★ U
Drama 1985 · US · Colour · 103mins

Geraldine Page's superb, Oscar-winning performance is the showpiece of this classy, intelligent, affecting and enjoyable drama, adapted with much skill by Horton Foote from his own stage and TV play. John Heard and Carlin Glynn give fine support as the son and peevish daughter-in-law of an elderly Texan woman (Page), who sets off from their Houston apartment on a journey of escape and returns to the small town of Bountiful where she was born. This makes the film a variety of road movie, but as far from a conventional one as it is possible to imagine. Not to be missed. Contains swearing. ▭

Geraldine Page *Carrie Watts* • John Heard *Ludie Watts* • Carlin Glynn *Jessie Mae* • Richard Bradford *Sheriff* • Rebecca De Mornay *Thelma* • Kevin Cooney *Roy* ■ *Dir* Peter Masterson • *Scr* Horton Foote, from his TV play

Triple Bogey on a Par Five Hole ★★★★
Comedy 1991 · US · BW and Colour · 88mins

The Levy's, a pair of married crooks who specialise in robbing people on golf courses, are both shot dead by one of their would-be victims. Thirteen years later screenwriter Remy Gravelle (played by underground film maker Eric Mitchell) is hired to research the story of the Levy's three children who endlessly circle Manhattan on a luxury yacht ironically called the *Triple Bogey*. When he meets the Levy children, Mitchell tries to remain dispassionate, but gradually gets drawn in to their complex world. Fascinating comedy drama shot mostly in atmospheric black and white. Screenwriter and indie film maker Amos Poe here delivers a mesmerising, haunting film far removed from typical Hollywood fare.

Eric Mitchell *Remy Gravelle* • Daisy Hall *Amanda Levy* • Angela Goethals *Bree Levy* • Jesse McBride *Satch Levy* • Alba Clemente *Nina Baccardi* • Robbie Coltrane *Steffano Baccardi* • Philip Seymour Hoffman *Klutch* ■ *Dir* Amos Poe • *Scr* Amos Poe

Triple Cross ★★
Biographical Second World War drama
1966 · Fr/UK · Colour · 141mins

Christopher Plummer is in jail in Jersey when the Nazis invade. He promptly secures a job in the Intelligence Service, leaving viewers to wonder if he's a traitor. Plummer makes the most of his enigmatic character and he's joined by heavyweights like Yul Brynner as a German with a monocle and brutal accent, Trevor Howard as a Jerseyman through-and-through, and the stunningly beautiful Romy Schneider as the requisite countess. Stuffed with plot and counterplot, it's based on the allegedly true exploits and autobiography of Eddie Chapman.

Christopher Plummer *Eddie Chapman* • Romy Schneider *The Countess* • Trevor Howard *Distinguished civilian* • Gert Fröbe *Col Steinhager* • Yul Brynner *Baron von Grunen* • Claudine Auger *Paulette* • Georges Lycan *Leo* ■ *Dir* Terence Young • *Scr* René Hardy, William Marchant, from the autobiography *The Eddie Chapman Story* by Eddie Chapman, Frank Owen

The Triple Echo ★★★
Drama 1972 · UK · Colour · 94mins

Adapted from a novel by H E Bates and set on a remote farm in 1942, this unlikely drama might have provoked a few unintentional smirks if it hadn't been so sensitively played by Glenda Jackson and Brian Deacon. Michael Apted's careful direction makes the ruse of disguising deserter Deacon as Jackson's sister seem almost credible, while his re-creation of the tranquil wartime countryside makes the abrupt intrusion of vulgar sergeant Oliver Reed all the more foreboding. Contains swearing, violence.

Glenda Jackson *Alice Charlesworth* • Oliver Reed *Sergeant* • Brian Deacon *Barton* • Anthony May *Subaltern* • Gavin Richards *Stan* • Jenny Lee Wright *Christine* • Ken Colley [Kenneth Colley] *Corporal* • Daphne Heard *Shopkeeper* ■ *Dir* Michael Apted • *Scr* Robin Chapman, from the novel by HE Bates

Triplecross ★★
Crime thriller 1995 · US · Colour · 95mins

This TV movie attempts the tricky task of interweaving three plot strands into a convincing whole. Jeno Hodi's film is vaguely compelling violent, abusive and blatantly titillating, but still worth sticking with. As he tries to resolve the relationships between jewel thief Patrick Bergin, girlfriend Ashley Laurence, ex-partner Michael Paré and unhinged FBI agent Billy Dee Williams, the action hurtles towards a rash of obvious twists and overneat endings. A Pity, really. Contains violence, swearing, sex scenes and nudity.

Michael Paré *Teddy* • Billy Dee Williams *Oscar Pierce* • Ashley Lauren [Ashley Laurence] *Julia* • Patrick Bergin *Jimmy Ray* ■ *Dir* Jeno Hodi • *Scr* JA Rosen

Trippin' ★★
Comedy 1999 · US · Colour · 94mins

High school student "G" (Deon Richmond) is faced with a number of problems. He has no date and no money for the prom, he hasn't even started applying for college, and is too shy to approach the prettiest girl in school. Instead of confronting his problems, he constantly daydreams about how he'd like his life to be. The movie never finds a constant tone, constantly switching back and forth from a refreshingly believable look at African-American life to being immature, preachy, or even violent. Some funny moments and the likeability of Richmond's character make it a tolerable way to pass time, despite the fact we've seen everything here many times before.

Deon Richmond *Gregory Reed* • Donald Adeosun Faison *June* • Guy Torry *Fish* • Maia Campbell *Cinny Hawkins* • Aloma Wright *Louise Reed* • Harold Sylvester *Willie Reed* • Cleavon McClendon *Jamal* • Bill Henderson *Gramps* ■ *Dir* David Raynr [David Hubbard] • *Scr* Gary Hardwick

Tristana ★★★★★ PG
Drama 1970 · Sp/It/Fr · Colour · 94mins

The last film that Luis Buñuel shot in his native Spain, is not only a searing indictment of the Franco regime, but also an attack on the Spanish people as a whole for allowing their country to be consumed by corruption and decay. Set in Toledo in the late twenties, the film explores the relationship between a depraved nobleman and his ward, who is determined to avenge the seduction that ruined her life. Revelling in his sins, Fernando Rey is superb as the pitiless Don Lope, while Catherine Deneuve is at her chilling best as the victim turned tormentor. It's bitter, biting and brilliant. In Spanish with English subtitles. ▭

Catherine Deneuve *Tristana* • Fernando Rey *Don Lope* • Franco Nero *Horacio* • Lola Gaos *Saturna* • Antonio Casas *Don Cosme* • Jesús Fernández *Saturno* • Vicente Soler *Don*

Ambrosio ■ *Dir* Luis Buñuel • *Scr* Luis Buñuel, Julio Alejandro, from the novel by Benito Perez Galdos

Triumph of the Heart ★★★ U
Drama based on a true story
1991 · US · Colour · 93mins

A tear-jerker about the friendship between an all-American football star and a young disabled boy based on a story that one might call melodramatic – f it weren't true. Mario Van Peebles, son of the even more implausibly named director Melvin Van Peebles, gives a competent performance as the caring jock, while Lane Davis does justice to the part of the boy whom he befriends. ▭

Mario Van Peebles *Ricky Bell* • Lane Davis *Ryan Blankenship* • Susan Ruttan *Carol Blankenship* • Polly Holliday *Ruth Weidner* • Lynn Whitfield *Natala Bell* • Woody Watson *Larry Blankenship* ■ *Dir* Richard Michaels • *Scr* Jeff Andrus

Triumph of the Spirit ★★★ 15
Second World War drama
1989 · US · Colour · 115mins

In this powerful fact-based Holocaust drama filmed on location at the Auschwitz-Birkenau death camp, Willem Dafoe portrays a Jewish boxer who's forced, literally, to fight for his life, and for the lives of his family. Sensibly, it's a work of some restraint, preferring to forgo the familiar shock-horror Holocaust imagery, and opting instead to mirror the monstrosities in people's reactions to them. Dafoe, incidentally, shed 20 pounds to play the part, and looks suitably skeletal. Edward James Olmos and Robert Loggia provide quality support in a film that's maybe not everyone's idea of entertainment, but is still grimly hard-hitting in both senses of the phrase. ▭

Willem Dafoe *Salamo Arouch* • Wendy Gazelle *Allegra* • Robert Loggia *Father Arouch* • Edward James Olmos *The Gypsy* • Kelly Wolf *Elena* • Costas Mandylor *Avram Arouch* ■ *Dir* Robert M Young • *Scr* Laurence Heath, Andrzej Krakowski, Robert M Young, Arthur Coburn, Millard Lampell, Shimon Arama, Zion Haen

Triumph of the Will ★★★★
Classic propaganda
1935 · Ger · BW · 120mins

Personally selected by Hitler, Leni Riefenstahl was given unlimited financial resources, the full co-operation of the Nazi hierarchy and a crew of more than a hundred to make a record of the 1934 Nuremberg Party rally. Special ramps, elevators, tracks and platforms were constructed so that every detail of Albert Speer's meticulously choreographed spectacle could be captured and used to convey the might and universality of Nazism and the messianic aura of the Führer. Taking eight months to edit, this remains one of the most potent pieces of propaganda ever produced, with Riefenstahl's mastery of her medium ensuring the total success of a pernicious project. In German with English subtitles.

Dir Leni Riefenstahl • *Scr* Walter Ruttmann (subtitles) • *Editor* Leni Riefenstahl •

Cinematographer Sepp Allgeier, Karl Attenberger, Werner Bohne • *Music* Herbert Windt

Triumph over Disaster: the Hurricane Andrew Story ★★

Drama based on a true story
1993 · US · Colour · 120mins

In August 1992, Hurricane Andrew wiped out sizeable chunks of southern Florida, with winds of over 150mph causing $20 billion worth of damage. Shot on location in Miami and using actual footage of the disaster, this TV movie follows the trail of destruction, detailing many stories of heroism as residents fought to triumph over disaster. Dwarfed by noise and the scale of destruction, a virtually unknown cast performs efficiently.

Ted Wass *Bryan Norcross* • Brynn Thayer *Sandra Channing* • John Getz *Doug Hulin* • Arnetia Walker *Paulette Rickles* • Brian McNamara *Cal Kessler* • George Grizzard *Dr Sheets* • Eileen Heckart *Shelley* ■ *Dir* Marvin J Chomsky • *Scr* Casey Kelly

Triumphs of a Man Called Horse ★ 15

Adventure   1983 · US/Mex · Colour · 85mins

Fans of the previous two *Horse* films will be disappointed by the relatively brief appearance of Richard Harris as the ageing Sioux leader. This lame sequel finds him joining with son Koda (Michael Beck) and an army captain (Vaughn Armstrong) to protect the tribe against settlers drawn by the gold rush. One would never believe that Kubrick's loyal cameraman, John Alcott, shot it. 🎞

Richard Harris *Man Called Horse* • Michael Beck *Koda* • Ana De Sade *Redwing* • Vaughn Armstrong *Capt Cummings* • Anne Seymour *Elk woman* • Buck Taylor *Sgt Bridges* • Simon Andreu *Gance* • Lautaro Murua *Perkins* ■ *Dir* John Hough • *Scr* Ken Blackwell, Carlos Aured, from a story by Jack DeWitt, from a character created by Dorothy M Johnson

Trog ★ 15

Science-fiction melodrama
1970 · UK · Colour · 87mins

Indescribable nonsense with anthropologist Joan Crawford battling Michael Gough over the fate of a recently discovered prehistoric caveman. Will Joan teach the Missing Link all about life in the 20th century before Gough calls in the army to destroy him? You won't care either way in this painful dud directed by Freddie Francis, the usually reliable veteran horror master. Intercut footage from *The Animal World* serves as Trog's memories in Joan's last feature film. 🎞

Joan Crawford *Dr Brockton* • Michael Gough *Sam Murdock* • Bernard Kay *Inspector Greenham* • Kim Braden *Anne* • David Griffin *Malcolm* • John Hamill *Cliff* • Thorley Walters *Magistrate* • Jack May *Dr Selbourne* ■ *Dir* Freddie Francis • *Scr* Aben Kandel, from a story by Peter Bryan, John Gilling

Trojan Eddie ★★★ 15

Drama   1996 · Ire/UK · Colour · 99mins

The totally different styles of bully-boy Richard Harris and hangdog Stephen Rea mesh to advantage in this slow-moving Irish fable. Rea is loser Eddie,

a peddler forced by circumstances to fetch and carry for Harris, godfather to the local travellers. The Irish landscape has never looked so beautiful and there's plenty of time to observe it, but the depiction of the mentality of the people is as idiotic as it is idealistic. Contains violence, swearing. 🎞

Richard Harris *John Power* • Stephen Rea *Trojan Eddie* • Brendan Gleeson *Ginger Power* • Sean McGinley *Raymie* • Angeline Ball *Shirley* • Brid Brennan *Betty* • Stuart Townsend *Dermot* ■ *Dir* Gillies MacKinnon • *Scr* Billy Roche

The Trojan War ★★ U

Period action adventure
1961 · Fr/It · Colour · 103mins

In this routinel, but watchable sword-and-sandal epic set a decade into the eponymous conflict, Trojan ruler Paris becomes jealous of people's champion Aeneas (Steve Reeves) and denounces him. Meanwhile, the Greeks plan their wooden horse trick. Very spectacular and the action moves along excitingly enough. Also known as *The Trojan Horse*. An Italian language film.

Steve Reeves *Aeneas* • John Drew Barrymore *Ulysses* • Warner Bentivegna *Paris* • Juliette Mayniel *Creusa* • Lydia Alfonsi *Cassandra* • Arturo Dominici *Achilles* ■ *Dir* Giorgio Ferroni • *Scr* Giorgio Stegani, Ugo Liberatore, Federico Zardi

Trojan War ★★ 12

Comedy   1997 · US · Colour · 79mins

Will Friedle plays a horny youth who gets the chance to bed the girl of his dreams, though he must first find a condom. What starts out as a five-minute trip to find one, quickly turns into a kind of *After Hours* experience, as the hapless hero encounters one disaster after another in his pursuit of a prophylactic. If the direction and editing had been less frenzied, chances are it would have been funnier. It still has its moments, particularly with some hilarious cameos by Lee Majors and Anthony Michael Hall. Warner Bros sent this comedy straight to video. Contains swearing, sexual references. 🎞

Will Friedle *Brad* • Jennifer Love Hewitt *Leah* • Marley Shelton *Brooke* • Jason Marsden *Josh* • Danny Masterson *Seth* • David Patrick Kelly *The Bagman* • Eric Balfour *Kyle* ■ • *Scr* Andy Burg, Scott Myers

The Trojan Women ★

Drama   1971 · Gr/US · Colour · 111mins

This is as dull as counting sheep in a fog, despite the presence of such luminaries as Katharine Hepburn, Vanessa Redgrave and – surprise, surprise – Irene Papas. Directed by Michael Cacoyannis – for several years after *Zorba the Greek*, Hollywood just tossed drachmas at him – it's the story of Helen, Hecuba and that sassy seer Cassandra. Brian Blessed seems to be competing in the Anthony Quinn "River of Life" contest, but loses out to Patrick Magee who seems on the verge of imploding. All in all, a dire affair.

Katharine Hepburn *Hecuba* • Geneviève Bujold *Cassandra* • Vanessa Redgrave *Andromache* • Irene Papas *Helen* • Brian Blessed *Tathybius*

• Patrick Magee *Menelaus* ■ *Dir* Michael Cacoyannis • *Scr* Michael Cacoyannis, from the play by Euripides

Troll ★ 15

Fantasy horror   1986 · US · Colour · 79mins

One of the Band family's strangest movies during their short-lived Empire Pictures enterprise seems to have been planned as a horror movie for both kids, and those who don't really watch this type of film. So it isn't surprising that the proceedings are not that scary; the movie's best moments generate a kind of a peculiar feeling that's hard to pinpoint (mild indigestion, possibly?). Michael Moriarty and Shelley Hack move into a new apartment building, and a mysterious troll possesses their little girl. The troll in his new guise then starts mutating the building's residents into creatures, or into forests as is the case with resident Sonny Bono. Whatever his actions are, the common factor is cheesiness. 🎞

Noah Hathaway *Harry Potter Jr* • Michael Moriarty *Harry Potter Sr* • Shelley Hack *Anne Potter* • Jennifer Beck *Wendy Potter* • Sonny Bono *Peter Dickinson* • Phil Fondacaro *Malcolm Malory/Torok* • Julia Louis-Dreyfus *Jeanette Cooper* ■ *Dir* John Carl Buechler • *Scr* Ed Naha

The Trollenberg Terror ★★

Horror   1958 · UK · BW · 82mins

A Swiss ski resort is terrorised by tentacled monsters from outer space in an efficiently suspenseful British cheapie marred by awful special effects. Two bits of cotton wool stuck on a mountain photo make do for the cloudy snowscapes in veteran Hammer scriptwriter Jimmy Sangster's screen version of the BBC TV series. Forrest Tucker is miscast as the hero, and Janet Munro is affecting as the telepathic heroine the aliens seize as their mouthpiece.

Forrest Tucker *Alan Brooks* • Laurence Payne *Philip Truscott* • Janet Munro *Anne Pilgrim* • Jennifer Jayne *Sarah Pilgrim* • Warren Mitchell *Professor Crevett* • Frederick Schiller *Klein* ■ *Dir* Quentin Lawrence • *Scr* Jimmy Sangster, from the BBC TV series by Peter Key

Tromeo & Juliet ★ 18

Erotic spoof   1996 · US · Colour · 102mins

The Troma team's take on *Romeo and Juliet* looked like a refreshing distraction from the over-rated Leonard DiCaprio version when they simultaneously hit the video stores. However, it is unremittingly awful. With Motorhead's Lemmy as narrator, this vaguely follows the original Shakespeare storyline, but mainly serves as an excuse to string together a series of loathsome and resolutely unfunny set-pieces. The performances, too, are quite appalling and even Troma devotees will find little to chortle about. Contains swearing, sex scenes, violence. 🎞

Jane Jensen *Juliet Capulet* • Will Keenan *Tromeo Que* • Valentine Miele *Murray Martini* • Maximillian Shaun *Cappy Capulet* • Steve Gibbons *London Arbuckle* • Sean Gunn *Sammy Capulet* ■ *Dir* Lloyd Kaufman • *Scr* James Gunn, Lloyd Kaufman

Tron ★★★ PG

Science-fiction adventure
1982 · US · Colour · 92mins

The road to Disney's current smash *Toy Story* began here, in its dazzling electronic *Fantasia*. Once computer genius Jeff Bridges entered cyberspace to prove himself the rightful inventor of stolen game patents, director Steven Lisberger broke cinematic territory by using, and inventing, state-of-the-art digital graphics to depict a bizarre video nether world. The Light Cycle race where machines create solid walls of colour behind them as they speed around a grid is the highlight of a complex, but lighthearted, adventure. Video game enthusiasts will love it. 🎞

Jeff Bridges *Kevin Flynn/Clu* • David Warner *Ed Dillinger/Sark* • Bruce Boxleitner *Alan Bradley/Tron* • Cindy Morgan *Lora/Yori* • Barnard Hughes *Dr Walter Gibbs/Dumont* • Dan Shor *Ram* • Peter Jurasik *Crom* ■ *Dir* Steven Lisberger • *Scr* Steven Lisberger, from a story by Steven Lisberger, Bonnie MacBird

Troop Beverly Hills ★★ PG

Comedy   1989 · US · Colour · 101mins

In this airy comedy, a bunch of moneyed little misses strive to be hits as Wilderness Girls (a Girl Guide-type group), but a resentful area troop leader resolves to make them fail. Neatly made and hard to hate, stars Shelley Long and Craig T Nelson bring their customary professionalism to the movie. 🎞

Shelley Long *Phyllis Nefler* • Craig T Nelson *Freddy Nefler* • Betty Thomas *Velda Plendor* • Mary Gross *Annie Herman* • Stephanie Beacham *Vicki Sprantz* • Audra Lindley *Frances Temple* • Edd Byrnes *Ross Coleman* • Ami Foster *Claire Sprantz* ■ *Dir* Jeff Kanew • *Scr* Pamela Norris, Margaret Grieco Oberman, from a story by Ava Ostern Fries

Trooper Hook ★★

Western   1957 · US · BW · 82mins

This western, the sixth and last pairing of Barbara Stanwyck and Joel McCrea, should have amounted to much more, being based on a superb story by Jack Schaefer, the author of *Shane*. Stanwyck gives an intelligent performance as the rescued captive of the Apaches who won't give up the son she had by an Indian chief, but McCrea is not quite tough enough as the cavalry sergeant who escorts her back to her rancher husband. There's a fatal lack of subtlety in the supporting characters, while the direction of Charles Marquis Warren is often clumsy, and Tex Ritter's title song soon becomes tiresome.

Joel McCrea *Sgt Hook* • Barbara Stanwyck *Cora Sutliff* • Earl Holliman *Jeff Bennett* • Edward Andrews *Charlie Travers* • John Dehner *Fred Sutliff* • Susan Kohner *Consuela* • Royal Dano *Trude* • Terry Lawrence *Quito* ■ *Dir* Charles Marquis Warren • *Scr* Charles Marquis Warren, David Victor, Herbert Little Jr, from a story by Jack Schaefer

Trop Belle pour Toi ★★★★ 18

Comedy   1989 · Fr · Colour · 87mins

Director Bertrand Blier can never be accused of shying away from controversy. He was accused of sexism in many quarters for this tale

🅤 = SUITABLE FOR ALL   🅤ᶜ = SUITABLE FOR ALL, ESPECIALLY FOR YOUNG CHILDREN (VIDEO ONLY)   PG = PARENTAL GUIDANCE

of a successful car dealer who abandons his statuesque wife for a plain, older secretary. Yet, thanks to the wholehearted performances of Gérard Depardieu and Josiane Balasko, this is a genuinely touching love story. Blier can't resist mocking the sexual repression and social hypocrisy of the middle classes in a manner that recalls the later satires of Luis Buñuel. His film is a touch short of stamina, but the blend of earthy drama and surrealist fantasy is thrilling. In French with English subtitles. Contains swearing, nudity. 🖵

Gérard Depardieu *Bernard Barthélémy* • Josiane Balasko *Colette Chevassu* • Carole Bouquet *Florence Barthélémy/colette's Neighbour* • Roland Blanche *Marcello* • François Cluzet *Pascal Chevassu* • Didier Benureau *Léonce* • Philippe Loffredo *Tanguy* • Sylvie Orcier *Marie-Catherine* ■ *Dir/Scr* Bertrand Blier

Trottie True ★★ 🆄
Romantic comedy
1949 · UK · Colour · 92mins
Had it been made by 20th Century-Fox with Betty Grable in the lead, this film might have fulfilled its potential as a nostalgic romp through an age when every stage door johnny was a milord, waiting to sweep a chorus girl off to a life of luxury. However, in the hands of perpetual underachiever Brian Desmond Hurst, it becomes a cheap exercise in gold-digging set against backdrops that, in spite of the rich Technicolor, look second-hand rather than antique. Yet Jean Kent is plucky enough as she falls for trouper Bill Owen, balloonist Andrew Crawford and aristocrat James Donald. 🖵

Jean Kent *Trottie True* • James Donald *Lord Digby Landon* • Hugh Sinclair *Maurice Beckenham* • Lana Morris *Bouncie Barrington* • Andrew Crawford *Sid Skinner* • Bill Owen *Joe Jugg* • Harcourt Williams *Duke of Wellwater* • Michael Medwin *Marquis Monty* • Hattie Jacques *Daisy Delaware* ■ *Dir* Brian Desmond Hurst • *Scr* C Denis Freeman, from the play by Caryl Brahms, SJ Simon

Le Trou ★★★★
Prison drama   1959 · Fr/It · BW · 123mins
Released the same week as Jean-Luc Godard's mould-breaking *Breathless*, Jacques Becker's final feature marks a significant stylistic departure from his previous pictures. Shot with an austerity that reinforces the grimly claustrophobic story of an attempted prison break, and made with a non-professional cast, it has inevitably been compared to Robert Bresson's *A Man Escaped*. But, the influence of Jean Renoir and John Huston ensures that this is more a study in psychology than spirituality. There's also a hint of Jules (*Rififi*) Dassin in the painstaking attention to the finger-numbing mechanics of digging a tunnel with makeshift tools. Physically exhausting, emotionally searing, yet deeply humanistic. A French language film.

Michel Constantin *Geo* • Philippe Leroy *Manu* • Marc Michel *Gaspard* • Raymond Meunier *Monseigneur* • Jean Keraudy *Oldtimer* ■ *Dir* Jacques Becker • *Scr* Jacques Becker, Jean Aurel, Jose Giovanni

Trouble along the Way ★★★ 🆄
Comedy drama   1953 · US · BW · 105mins
John Wayne as a divorcee trying to retain custody of daughter Sherry Jackson. The director, unusually, is Warner Bros workhorse genius Michael Curtiz, who directed the classic *Casablanca*. This comedy drama seems to be a personal project for both Wayne and the Hungarian-born Curtiz, a debt Wayne would later repay by ensuring that the terminally ill director be hired for what was to be his last movie, Wayne's 1961 western *The Comancheros*. There's a lot of religiosity on hand, which some may find hard to take, and a school football team makes an uncomfortable metaphor for teamwork at home. Still, Donna Reed shines, and the whole is, if not entirely entertaining, at least quite fascinating. 🖵

John Wayne *Steve Aloysius Williams* • Donna Reed *Alice Singleton* • Charles Coburn *Father Burke* • Tom Tully *Father Malone* • Sherry Jackson *Carole Williams* • Marie Windsor *Anne McCormick* • Tom Helmore *Harold McCormick* ■ *Dir* Michael Curtiz • *Scr* Melville Shavelson, Jack Rose, from the story *It Figures* by Douglas Morrow, Robert H Andrews

Trouble at Midnight ★★
Western   1937 · US · BW · 68mins
Universal turned out a series of features starring likeable Noah Beery Jr, better known today for TV's *The Rockford Files*, but in truth audiences didn't warm to him as a leading man. Here, he plays a rancher in a daft mystery about rustling that can't seem to make up its mind whether it's a gangster flick, a western or a comedy. Ironically, Beery himself became a rancher when his career didn't pan out as planned and cited his favourite career role as a cattle rancher in Howard Hawks's great western *Red River*.

Noah Beery Jr *Kirk Cameron* • Catherine Hughes *Catherine Benson* • Larry Blake *Tony Michaels* • Bernadene Hayes *Marion* • Louis Mason *Elmer* ■ *Dir* Ford Beebe • *Scr* Ford Beebe, Maurice Geraghty, from the story *Night Patrol* by Kimball Herrick, from the story *Midnight Raiders* by Maurice Geraghty

Trouble Bound ★★★ 🔞
Action crime comedy
1993 · US · Colour · 85mins
Under-rated Michael Madsen (Mr Blonde in *Reservoir Dogs*) plays an out-of-luck gambler who sets off across country with a dead body in the boot of a car he's just won. But it quickly proves the least of his problems as he then hooks up with winsome waitress Patricia Arquette, who's out to avenge the murder of her Mafia grandfather. Of course, this curious couple end up being pursued. With the requisite amount of car chases, gun battles and misunderstandings, this is tongue-in-cheek, if violent, entertainment. Contains violence, swearing, nudity. 🖵

Michael Madsen *Harry Talbot* • Patricia Arquette *Kit Califano* • Florence Stanley *Granny* • Seymour Cassel *Santino* • Sal Jenco *Danny* • Paul Ben-Victor *Zand* • Darren Epton *Raphael* • Billy Bob Thornton *Coldface* ■ *Dir* Jeffrey Reiner • *Scr* Darrell Fetty, Francis Delia

Trouble Brewing ★★★ 🆄
Comedy   1939 · UK · BW · 86mins
George Formby as a printer with a detective fixation, intent on capturing a gang of counterfeiters to impress fellow journo Googie Withers. It hardly takes Sherlock Holmes to figure out who is the master criminal, but the red herrings that pad out the story are amusing. Anthony Kimmins sets the action brisk, but like all Formby directors he makes a stilted hash of the saucy songs.

George Formby *George Gullip* • Googie Withers *Mary Brown* • Gus McNaughton *Bill Pike* • Garry Marsh *AG Brady* • Joss Ambler *Lord Redhill* • Ronald Shiner *Bridgewater* • Martita Hunt *Madame Berdi* ■ *Dir* Anthony Kimmins • *Scr* Anthony Kimmins, Angus McPhail, Michael Hogan

Trouble for Two ★★★
Comedy   1936 · US · BW · 75mins
You'd never guess from the title, but this is MGM's version of Robert Louis Stevenson's ''Suicide Club'' stories. It's an expertly made, glossily produced oddity, pairing the excellent Robert Montgomery, playing an unlikely 19th-century prince, with an unusually mysterious Rosalind Russell (they were reunited the following year in *Night Must Fall*). The theme is interesting: members of an anarchic London club set Montgomery a series of life-threatening tasks before he can marry his beloved, Russell. A wayward, off-the-wall product of the studio system that deserved greater recognition.

Robert Montgomery *Prince Florizel* • Rosalind Russell *Miss Vandeleur* • Frank Morgan *Colonel Geraldine* • Reginald Owen *Dr Franz Noel* • Louis Hayward *Young man with cream tarts* • EE Clive *King* • Walter Kingsford *Malthus* • Ivan Simpson *Collins* • Tom Moore *Major O'Rock* ■ *Dir* J Walter Ruben • *Scr* Manuel Seff, Edward E Paramore Jr, from the stories *Suicide Club* by Robert Louis Stevenson

Trouble in Mind ★★★★ 🔞
Futuristic crime thriller
1985 · US · Colour · 107mins
An intelligent yet not wholly successful attempt by Alan Rudolph to re-create the kind of futuristic *film noir* pioneered by Jean-Luc Godard in *Alphaville*. Kris Kristofferson stars as an ex-cop just out of jail for murder, whose hopes for a fresh start with diner owner Geneviève Bujold are sidetracked by his involvement with Lori Singer and her violent partner, Keith Carradine, a petty crook whose behaviour and appearance grow increasingly bizarre and violent as he becomes entangled with Rain City crime boss, Divine. It's engrossing stuff and if the romance falls flat, the use of comedy to map Carradine's decline is inspired. 🖵 **DVD**

Kris Kristofferson *John Hawkins* • Keith Carradine *Coop* • Lori Singer *Georgia* • Geneviève Bujold *Wanda* • Joe Morton *Solo* • Divine *Hilly Blue* • George Kirby *Lieutenant Gunther* • John Considine *Nate Nathanson* ■ *Dir/Scr* Alan Rudolph

Trouble in Paradise 🌟🌟🌟🌟🌟
Romantic comedy   1932 · US · BW · 81mins
Two expert European thieves (Miriam Hopkins and Herbert Marshall)

masquerading as aristocrats meet in Venice, fall in love and team up professionally. Their elaborate plans almost come unstuck when, in the guise of secretaries, they infiltrate the household of a wealthy and glamorous Parisienne (Kay Francis) whose charms extend beyond her jewellery collection. Made by Ernst Lubitsch, whose famous ''touch'' is everywhere evident, this is arguably the most highly sophisticated romantic comedy ever to emerge from Hollywood. Brilliantly scripted, flawlessly stylish and faultlessly acted, it's a masterpiece, as well as being wonderfully good fun.

Miriam Hopkins *Lily Vautier* • Kay Francis *Mariette Colet* • Herbert Marshall *Gaston Monescu, ''LuValle''* • Charlie Ruggles [Charles Ruggles] *Major* • Edward Everett Horton *François Filiba* • C Aubrey Smith *Giron* • Robert Greig *Jacques the butler* ■ *Dir* Ernst Lubitsch • *Scr* Grover Jones, Samson Raphaelson, from the play *A Becsuletes Megtalalo (The Honest Finder)* by Aladar Laszlo • *Cinematographer* Victor Milner

Trouble in Paradise ★★★ 15
Comedy adventure
1989 · US · Colour · 92mins
Raquel Welch, looking stunning well into middle age, here stars as a widow travelling by sea to America who finds herself on a deserted island with an Australian sailor (Jack Thompson) when their ship is wrecked in a typhoon. It's kind of *The Admirable Crichton* meets *Gilligan's Island*, but Welch is well cast as the elegant woman cast adrift. 🖵

Raquel Welch *Rachel Baxley* • Jack Thompson *Jake La Fontaine* • Nicholas Hammond *Arthur* • Anthony Wong *Ringe* • Ralph Cotterill *Hughes* ■ *Dir* Di Drew • *Scr* Robert Sherman, Ben Marshall, from a story by Robert Sherman

Trouble in Store ★★★ 🆄
Comedy   1953 · UK · BW · 82mins
This was Norman Wisdom's film debut and, according to some, it was all downhill from here. It's certainly one of his best outings, largely because the sentimentality that became almost unbearable in his later films is rigorously kept in check here by director John Paddy Carstairs. Wisdom is as willing and as hopeless as ever, but he still manages to take time off from his hectic schedule of driving store boss Jerry Desmonde to the brink of distraction to find romance with Lana Morris. Desmonde's comic fury is a joy to watch, as is Margaret Rutherford's twittery performance as a shoplifter. 🖵

Norman Wisdom *Norman* • Margaret Rutherford *Miss Bacon* • Moira Lister *Peggy* • Derek Bond *Gerald* • Lana Morris *Sally* • Jerry Desmonde *Freeman* • Megs Jenkins *Miss Gibson* • Joan Sims *Edna* ■ *Dir* John Paddy Carstairs • *Scr* John Paddy Carstairs, Maurice Cowan, Ted Willis

Trouble in Texas ★
Western drama   1937 · US · BW · 97mins
Made on the cheap for the independent Grand National company, this was one of the first westerns to star singer Tex Ritter and one of the last in which a young Rita Cansino appeared before changing her name to Rita Hayworth. Tex is the rodeo star and Rita the federal agent working

undercover as a saloon singer to solve the deaths of rodeo contestants and a series of robberies. Ritter's voice and Rita's looks are some compensation for the lame plot and obvious insertion of stock rodeo footage. The picture was later reissued giving Rita top billing under her new name.

Tex Ritter *Tex Masters* • Rita Cansino [Rita Hayworth] *Carmen* • Earl Dwire *Barker* • Yakima Canutt *Squint* • Dick Palmer *Duke* • Hal Price *G-Man* ■ *Dir* RN Bradbury [Robert N Bradbury] • *Scr* Robert Tansey, from a story by Lindsey Parsons

Trouble in the Glen ★ U

Comedy 1954 · UK · Colour · 91mins

Margaret Lockwood enjoyed great success as an ingénue then as Britain's leading actress during much of the forties. But films such as this contributed to her virtual retirement from the screen when barely 40. Directed by Herbert Wilcox, it involved American talent in what purports to be an amusing comedy. Co-star Orson Welles helps turn it into something nearer tragicomedy with his dodgy wig and even dodgier Scottish accent, a bad hangover from his 1948 version of *Macbeth*. Shot in a terrible process called Trucolor, you are advised not to adjust your sets.

Margaret Lockwood *Marissa* • Orson Welles *Sanin Mengues/Sandy Menzies* • Forrest Tucker *Jim "Lance" Lancing* • Victor McLaglen *Parlan* • John McCallum *Malcolm* • Eddie Byrne *Dinny Sullivan* • Archie Duncan *Nolly Dukes* • Ann Gudrun *Dandy Dinmont* ■ *Dir* Herbert Wilcox • *Scr* Frank S Nugent, from a story by Maurice Walsh

Trouble Man ★

Blaxploitation crime thriller
1972 · US · Colour · 99mins

Twentieth Century-Fox's answer to the black action cycle initiated by MGM's *Shaft* was this crude and violent underworld melodrama. In the hope of reproducing the success of the Richard Roundtree character, Fox even employed *Shaft's* producer, Joel Freeman, and one of its writers, John DF Black. In a one-note role as Mr T, a supercool LA private eye drawn into a gangland feud, Robert Hooks is out-acted by Paul Winfield (as a double-crossing racketeer) and Julius Harris (as a rival hood) but then they do have slightly more varied characters to play.

Robert Hooks *Mr T* • Paul Winfield *Chalky* • Ralph Waite *Pete* • William Smithers *Captain Joe Marks* • Paula Kelly *Cleo* • Julius Harris *Big* • Bill Henderson *Jimmy* ■ *Dir* Ivan Dixon • *Scr* John DF Black

Trouble Shooters: Trapped beneath the Earth ★★ PG

Action drama 1993 · US · Colour · 88mins

Despite the decent direction of Bradford May, and even with the popular singer turned actor Kris Kristofferson starring, this disaster-adventure film about an earthquake in southern Utah falls short. The picture centres around the efforts of a family-run search and rescue operation attempting to save survivors trapped underneath a collapsed building. Realistic special effects add to the tension and drama, but the cumbersome family-feud subplot distracts the audience from what could have been a taut rescue movie and turns it into a hokey soap opera. [video]

Kris Kristofferson *Stan Mather* • David Newsom *Cody Mather* • Leigh McCloskey *Frank Mather* • Caitlin Dulany *Claudia* ■ *Dir* Bradford May • *Scr* Dave Alan Johnson, Michael Pavone, from a story by Wesley Strick

The Trouble with Angels ★★★ U

Comedy drama 1966 · US · Colour · 110mins

Best known for her acting in hard-bitten melodramas, Ida Lupino may seem a curious choice to direct this convent comedy. Yet she brings a much-needed hint of steel to what might otherwise have become another predictable journey down the road from rebellion to reformation. Hayley Mills is naughtier than in her Disney days, but much of her thunder is stolen by the debuting June Harding as her mousey friend. Mother Superior Rosalind Russell similarly walks away with every scene she's in, but not even the dependable support of Binnie Barnes and Mary Wickes can atone for the cosiness of the conclusion.

Rosalind Russell *Mother Superior* • Hayley Mills *Mary Clancy* • June Harding *Rachel Devery* • Binnie Barnes *Sister Celestine* • Camilla Sparv *Sister Constance* • Gypsy Rose Lee *Mrs Phipps* ■ *Dir* Ida Lupino • *Scr* Blanche Hanalis, from the novel *Life with Mother Superior* by Jane Trahey

Trouble with Eve ★ U

Comedy 1959 · UK · BW · 66mins

The idea that a cosy country tearoom could become a den of vice is pretty hard to swallow at the best of times, but here it's as indigestible as a week-old rock cake in this dismal comedy from director Francis Searle. Hy Hazell is the proprietor whose activities are called into question when the local inspector is caught with his pants down. Unfunny from start to finish, and no amount of tittle-tattling neighbours, shrewish daughters or late-life romance is going to alter that fact.

Robert Urquhart *Brian Maitland* • Hy Hazell *Louise Kingston* • Garry Marsh *Roland Axbridge* • Vera Day *Daisy* • Sally Smith *Eve* • Tony Quinn *Bellchambers* • Denis Shaw *George* ■ *Dir* Francis Searle • *Scr* Brock Williams, from the play *Widows Are Dangerous* by June Garland

The Trouble with Girls ★ U

Comedy drama 1969 · US · Colour · 95mins

It's 1927, and Elvis Presley brings his mobile "chautauqua" show (an entertainment born out of the popular adult educational movement of the previous century), to Iowa, where he battles with Marilyn Mason as she tries to organise a performers' union. This love-hate scenario is disrupted when the local chemist is found dead, and Elvis has to persuade the murderer to confess on stage. The unusual phenomenon of the chautauqua could have provided an unusual backdrop for a film, but in this joyless vehicle it's used ineffectively, wasting a supporting cast which includes Vincent Price and John Carradine, and providing only a handful of numbers for its star. [video]

Elvis Presley *Walter Hale* • Marilyn Mason *Charlene* • Nicole Jaffe *Betty* • Sheree North *Nita Bix* • Edward Andrews *Johnny* • John Carradine *Mr Drewcolt* • Anissa Jones *Carol* • Vincent Price *Mr Morality* ■ *Dir* Peter Tewksbury • *Scr* Arnold Peyser, Lois Peyser, from a story by Mauri Grashin

The Trouble with Harry ★★★★★ PG

Black comedy 1955 · US · Colour · 94mins

The poster advertising this delicious black comedy bore the tagline "The unexpected from Hitchcock!". It was the best Paramount could do with a picture that it had no idea how to promote, and it was no surprise that it flopped at the box office. But the director was mighty proud of this adaptation of Jack Trevor Story's novel, always naming it among his personal favourites. There's the odd suspenseful moment, but this is primarily a masterpiece of wry humour and dramatic understatement, as John Forsythe, Shirley MacLaine, Edmund Gwenn and Mildred Natwick decide in the most matter-of-fact way what to do with the body of a man three of them think they might have murdered. The acting is perfection, with MacLaine (in her debut) quite wonderful. [video]

Edmund Gwenn *Captain Albert Wiles* • John Forsythe *Sam Marlowe, the painter* • Shirley MacLaine *Jennifer Rogers, Harry's wife* • Mildred Natwick *Miss Graveley* • Mildred Dunnock *Mrs Wiggs* • Jerry Mathers *Arnie Rogers, Harry's Son* • Royal Dano *Calvin Wiggs* • Parker Fennelly *Millionaire* ■ *Dir* Alfred Hitchcock • *Scr* John Michael Hayes, from the novel by Jack Trevor Story

The Trouble with Spies ★★ PG

Spy spoof 1987 · US · Colour · 85mins

In this cheerful but anorexic spy spoof, Donald Sutherland plays a bumbling agent whose missions are so secret, everyone knows about them. He's sent to Ibiza to obtain the secret recipe for a truth serum but spends the time avoiding numerous attempts on his life. Fortunately for Sutherland, he has a cast of noted actors such as Ned Beatty, Ruth Gordon and Michael Horden to support him. (They at least can share in the humiliation of being in this piffle.) Unfortunately, the direction by Burt Kennedy is just inept. [video]

Donald Sutherland *Appleton Porter* • Ned Beatty *Harry Lewis* • Ruth Gordon *Mrs Arkwright* • Lucy Gutteridge *Mona Smith* • Michael Hordern *Jason Lock* • Robert Morley *Angus Watkins* • Gregory Sierra *Captain Sanchez* ■ *Dir* Burt Kennedy • *Scr* Burt Kennedy, Marc Lovell

The Troublemaker ★★

Crime comedy 1964 · US · BW · 81mins

Based on a story by Buck Henry, whose specialisation in the lives of earnest young innocents led to the later brilliance of *The Graduate*, this is a dated and very tame comedy about the adventures of a yokel (Tom Aldredge) at large in New York. It's made no better by being improvised by a group called "The Premise", which included the director Theodore J Flicker and Henry himself, presumably there to guard the few words he had written. This is where the Swinging Sixties came to a juddering halt.

Tom Aldredge *Jack Armstrong* • Joan Darling *Denver James* • Theodore Flicker *Crime Commissioner* • James Frawley *Sol/Sal/Judge Kelly* • Buck Henry *Tr Kingston* ■ *Dir* Theodore Flicker • *Scr* Theodore J Flicker, Buck Henry, from a story by Buck Henry

The Truce ★★★

Biographical drama
1997 · It/Fr/Swi/Ger · Colour · 117mins

A prize-winning director, known initially for his uncompromising social realism, Francesco Rosi gained a reputation in his later career for literary adaptations. While less imposing than his sprawling version of Carlo Levi's *Christ Stopped at Eboli*, this faithful account of Primo Levi's postwar journey from Auschwitz back to Italy still has the power to provoke and move. However, whereas we can identify with Gian Maria Volonté's outsider as he slowly comes to terms with his exile in Eboli, here John Turturro's need to push through the chaos around him prevents us from fully empathising with either his tortured memories or his response to freedom. In Italian with English subtitles. Contains swearing.

John Turturro *Primo* • Massimo Ghini *Cesare* • Rade Serbedzija *The Greek* • Stefano Dionisi *Daniele* • Teco Celio *Colonel Rovi* ■ *Dir* Francesco Rosi • *Scr* Francesco Rosi, Stefano Rulli, Sandro Petraglia, Tonino Guerra, from the novel by Primo Levi

Truck Stop Women ★★★

Action 1974 · US · Colour · 87mins

Here's a cult movie that really delivers in terms of raucous exploitation. Lieux Dressler plays the boss of a robbery and prostitution ring who has to fight off efforts by the mob to take over her operation, based in a highway truck stop. Director Mark L Lester slams everything at us in terms of action – road crashes, sexual shenanigans, the denting of macho morale – while Dressler, *Playboy* playmate Claudia Jennings and Gene Drew are cast well enough to be in a Russ Meyer movie. Seeing the well-endowed Jennings sporting a machine-gun makes you wonder just how much of an inspiration this was on the *Chicks Who Love Guns* sequence in *Jackie Brown*.

Claudia Jennings *Rose* • Lieux Dressler *Anna* • John Martino *Smith* • Dennis Fimple *Curly* • Dolores Dorn *Trish* • Gene Drew *Mac* ■ *Dir* Mark L Lester • *Scr* Mark L Lester, Paul Deason, from a story by Paul Deason

Truck Turner ★★ 18

Blaxploitation 1974 · US · Colour · 87mins

Apart from providing the voice for *South Park's* Chef, soul brother Isaac Hayes is probably better known for his Oscar-winning *Shaft* theme than for his acting. Here he makes a credible hero in a typical seventies blaxploitation action movie in the mould of *Black Caesar* and *Superfly*. Hayes plays the title character, a ruthless bounty hunter whose targets are pimps and pushers. Director Jonathan Kaplan, who went on to make *The Accused* and once studied film under Martin Scorsese, provides the no-frills, in-your-face action, while also eliciting an outrageous performance from *Star Trek's* Nichelle Nichols as a foul-mouthed brothel madam. [video]

1486 U = SUITABLE FOR ALL Uc = SUITABLE FOR ALL, ESPECIALLY FOR YOUNG CHILDREN (VIDEO ONLY) PG = PARENTAL GUIDANCE

Isaac Hayes *Truck Turner* • Yaphet Kotto *Harvard Blue* • Alan Weeks *Jerry* • Annazette Chase *Annie* • Paul Harris *Gator* • Nichelle Nichols *Dorinda* • Sam Laws *Nate* ■ *Dir* Jonathan Kaplan • *Scr* Leigh Chapman, Oscar Williams, Michael Allin, from a story by Jerry Wilkes

True as a Turtle ★ 🆄

Comedy   1956 · UK · Colour · 92mins

Director Wendy Toye was all at sea with this tiresome cross-Channel version of *Genevieve*, in which John Gregson and June Thorburn fall out over the juvenile jealousies and petty pomposities of the seafaring fraternity while honeymooning on board Cecil Parker's yacht. Their bliss is further blighted by the discovery that they have become involved with a counterfeit gaming chip racket centred in a French casino and by the tensions that arise during a return voyage in a pea-soup fog. However, the only thing truly indiscernible in this crass caper is why anyone bothered to make it. 🖭

John Gregson *Tony Hudson* • June Thorburn *Jane Hudson* • Cecil Parker *Dudley* • Keith Michell *Harry Bell* • Elvi Hale *Anne* • Avice Landone *Valerie* ■ *Dir* Wendy Toye • *Scr* Jack Davies, John Coates, Nicholas Phipps, from the novel by John Coates

True Betrayal ★★★ 🆂

Murder mystery   1990 · US · Colour · 93mins

An oddball thriller and unsuccessful TV pilot that never quite manages to find its feet, although star Mare Winningham acts the socks off hers trying. Winningham is a private investigator new to the job who decides to become chummy with a prime murder suspect in the hope of trapping him. It's a familiar theme and unfortunately this film fails to supply anything new. The story was based on the true experiences of celebrated Houston investigator Kim Paris, a woman of some respect and notoriety among her peers, and the general consensus was that *True Betrayal* did not do her or the genre justice. Contains violence. 🖭

Mare Winningham *Kim Paris* • Peter Gallagher *David West* • Caroline Williams *Sammi* • Tom O'Brien *Tom* • GW Bailey *Halsey* • M Emmet Walsh *Clyde Wilson* ■ *Dir* Roger Young • *Scr* Alan Sharp

True Blue ★★ 🆂

Sports drama based on a true story
1996 · UK · Colour · 110mins

There's an intriguing story of macho rivalries and treacheries trying to get out of this account of events leading up to the 1987 Boat Race, when experienced American oarsmen were drafted into the Oxford team. But the potentially fascinating tale of modern sporting endeavour versus unmoving Oxbridge tradition fights a losing battle with director Ferdinand Fairfax's laborious scene-setting and Brian Tufano's painterly photography, while talented young actors such as Johan Leysen and Dominic West get caught in a backwash of bathos in which one anticlimax follows another. Contains swearing and brief nudity. 🖭 **DVD**

Johan Leysen *Daniel Topolski* • Dominic West *Donald Macdonald* • Dylan Baker *Michael Suarez* • Geraldine Somerville *Ruth Macdonald* • Josh Lucas *Dan Warren* • Brian McGovern

Rick Ross • Ryan Bollman *Morrison Black* • Andrew Tees *John Smythson* ■ *Dir* Ferdinand Fairfax • *Scr* Rupert Walters, from the non-fiction book by Daniel Topolski, Patrick Robinson

True Colors ★★ 🆂

Drama   1991 · US · Colour · 105mins

It's perfectly clear from the outset of this by-the-numbers drama what will happen when two law students graduate and go their own ways, one to the Justice Department where spotless behaviour is seemingly the norm, the other into the moral sewer of politics. It's a pity that fine actors like John Cusack and James Spader are defeated by the all-too-obvious plot, yet both leads bring enough energy and detail to their roles to provide some interest. Contains swearing. 🖭

John Cusack *Peter Burton* • James Spader *Tim Garrity* • Imogen Stubbs *Diana Stiles* • Mandy Patinkin *John Palmeri* • Richard Widmark *Senator James B Stiles* • Dina Merrill *Joan Stiles* • Philip Bosco *Senator Steubens* • Paul Guilfoyle *John Lawry* ■ *Dir* Herbert Ross • *Scr* Kevin Wade

True Confections ★★★

Drama   1990 · Can · Colour · 95mins

With a title like that, this would seem ripe for some sort of spoof of TV-movie true stories. Actually, it's a winningly offbeat little charmer from Canada in which Leslie Hope keeps slipping into her own fantasy world, as her Jewish parents browbeat her for not settling down with a nice young man. The familiar Jewish neuroses get another airing, but are enlivened by some nicely surreal touches from director Gail Singer and the Walter Mittyesque daydreaming of the heroine. The performances from the largely unknown cast are also spot-on.

Leslie Hope • Kyle McCulloch • Jill Riley • Judah Katz ■ *Dir/Scr* Gail Singer

True Confession ★★★

Comedy mystery   1937 · US · BW · 84mins

Fred MacMurray and Carole Lombard co-star as a highly moral attorney and his wife, a compulsive liar. When she's had up for murdering her boss, her husband gets her off on grounds of self-defence. Of course she's innocent, as her husband discovers when John Barrymore turns up to blackmail her. A romantic screwball farce, directed by Wesley Ruggles and played with sufficient expertise to disguise some of the weaker aspects of the script, which declines to explain why Lombard is incapable of telling the truth. The movie spirals from mad to madder and is extremely funny. Remade in 1946 as the much less appealing *Cross My Heart* with Betty Hutton.

Carole Lombard *Helen Bartlett* • Fred MacMurray *Kenneth Bartlett* • John Barrymore *Charley Jasper* • Una Merkel *Daisy McClure* • Porter Hall *Prosecutor* • Edgar Kennedy *Darsey* • Hattie McDaniel *Ella* ■ *Dir* Wesley Ruggles • *Scr* Claude Binyon, from the play *Mon Crime* by Louis Verneuil, Georges Berr

True Confessions ★★★ 🆂

Drama   1981 · US · Colour · 103mins

Do you remember all those priests-versus-the-law movies of the thirties with Pat O'Brien and James Cagney? This is an update (though it's set in the forties), with Robert Duvall as a Los Angeles cop who suspects that his brother, a priest played by Robert De Niro, is linked with the murder of a prostitute. These two great actors, bowed by such a major theme as the human conscience, furrow their brows and speak as if they can't do joined-up writing. Despite many arid passages and generally stolid direction from Ulu Grosbard (more usually a stage director and a chum of De Niro's), it's worth seeing if only to appreciate how major stars do not a movie make. Contains violence and swearing. 🖭

Robert De Niro *Des Spellacy* • Robert Duvall *Tom Spellacy* • Charles Durning *Jack Amsterdam* • Kenneth McMillan *Frank Crotty* • Ed Flanders *Dan T Campion* • Burgess Meredith *Seamus Fargo* • Cyril Cusack *Cardinal Danaher* ■ *Dir* Ulu Grosbard • *Scr* John Gregory Dunne, Joan Didion, from the novel by John Gregory Dunne

True Crime ★★★ 🆇

Crime thriller   1999 · US · Colour · 127mins

Clint Eastwood directs and stars as a grizzled journalist with 12 hours to prove a prisoner on San Quentin's Death Row is innocent in this solid adaptation of Andrew Klavan's anti-capital punishment novel. Alternately tautly gripping and ridiculously facile, this suspense thriller at times resembles a big-budget episode of *Murder, She Wrote* (hokey plot contrivances and clues undiscovered by the police instantly found by Eastwood), yet retains its "beat the clock" shape mainly because the superstar director accents character issues and details above the mechanics of the whodunit material. Driven by a rich vein of sympathetic humanity, Eastwood turns in one of the most thoughtful and perceptive performances of his career. Contains swearing. 🖭 **DVD**

Clint Eastwood *Steve Everett* • Isaiah Washington *Frank Beachum* • Denis Leary *Bob Findley* • Lisa Gay Hamilton *Bonnie Beachum* • James Woods *Alan Mann* • Bernard Hill *Warden Luther Plunkitt* • Michael Jeter *Dale Porterhouse* ■ *Dir* Clint Eastwood • *Scr* Stephen Schiff, Paul Brickman, Larry Gross, from the novel by Andrew Klavan

True Grit ★★★★ 🅿🅶

Western   1969 · US · Colour · 127mins

Big John Wayne finally won peer group recognition, taking the best actor Oscar for his portrayal of Reuben J "Rooster" Cogburn, a cantankerous, one-eyed, drunken old reprobate hired by Mattie Ross (the excellent Kim Darby) to avenge her father's death at the hands of thoroughly nasty Tom Chaney (Jeff Corey). This movie has acquired a reputation for being a rollicking fun western, but actually it is extraordinarily violent for its era and is not really suitable for family viewing, despite its strong moral theme. Glen Campbell is ineffective as Texas Ranger La Boeuf (a role first offered to Elvis Presley, to whom Wayne wouldn't take second billing), but it doesn't

really matter. It's still a film of many memorable moments, not least of which is Cogburn's final shoot-out in a Colorado clearing. 🖭

John Wayne *Reuben J "Rooster" Cogburn* • Glen Campbell *La Boeuf* • Kim Darby *Mattie Ross* • Jeff Corey *Tom Chaney* • Robert Duvall *Ned Pepper* • Jeremy Slate *Emmett Quincy* • Dennis Hopper *Moon* ■ *Dir* Henry Hathaway • *Scr* Marguerite Roberts, from the novel by Charles Portis

True Identity ★★★ 🆂

Comedy thriller   1991 · US · Colour · 89mins

British comic Lenny Henry stars as a struggling actor who crosses the path of mobster Frank Langella, and decides he has to take a different identity so he can't be found. Naturally, Lenny's make-up artist pal turns our hero into a white man so he can avoid the wrath of the mob. The script doesn't do justice to the star's talent as a comedian, but the transformation is extremely impressive, and Henry does a good job of turning every duff line and situation into a rib-tickling one. Contains violence and swearing. 🖭

Lenny Henry *Miles Pope* • Frank Langella *Frank Luchino/Leland Carver* • Charles Lane (3) *Duane* • JT Walsh *Craig Houston* • Anne-Marie Johnson *Kristi Reeves* • Andreas Katsulas *Anthony* • Michael McKean *Harvey Cooper* ■ *Dir* Charles Lane (3) • *Scr* Andy Breckman, Will Osborne, Will Davies, from a sketch by Andy Breckman

True Lies ★★★★ 🆂

Action comedy   1994 · US · Colour · 134mins

Until the arrival of *GoldenEye*, this comedy spy thriller from the *Terminator* team of Arnold Schwarzenegger and director James Cameron was the nearest thing in years to a great James Bond movie. Arnie's the unshaken, unstirred secret agent, always saving the world in time to get home for dinner with his wife and kids, who are blissfully unaware of his dangerous job. Aside from the truly spectacular action, there's exceptional comedy support from Tom Arnold and a winning performance from Jamie Lee Curtis, who transforms from timid housewife to confident heroine. It may be wildly implausible and a trifle misogynistic, but, on the pure excitement level, Cameron's blockbuster is unbeatable. Contains swearing and violence. 🖭

Arnold Schwarzenegger *Harry Tasker* • Jamie Lee Curtis *Helen Tasker* • Tom Arnold *Gib* • Bill Paxton *Simon* • Tia Carrere *Juno* • Art Malik *Aziz* • Eliza Dushku *Dana* • Charlton Heston *Spencer Trilby* ■ *Dir* James Cameron • *Scr* James Cameron, from a screenplay by Claude Zidi, Simon Michael, Didier Kaminka

True Love ★★★★ 🆂

Comedy drama   1989 · US · Colour · 100mins

All imminent newlyweds should avoid this like the plague, because this is a film about the kind of doubts that can bring that thundering juggernaut known as your wedding day to a screeching halt. Directed with admirable insight by the debuting Nancy Savoca (who also co-wrote with husband Richard Guay), this is comedy so close to the bone that it's often wincingly painful to watch. Annabella Sciorra is perfectly cast as the Italian/American who suddenly discovers dipsomanic Ron

Eldard isn't the man of her dreams. A witty throwback to the days when Hollywood could do this kind of thing blindfold. Contains swearing.

Annabella Sciorra *Donna* • Ron Eldard *Michael* • Star Jasper *JC* • Aida Turturro *Grace* • Roger Rignack *Dom* • Michael J Wolfe *Brian* • Kelly Cinnante *Yvonne* ■ *Dir* Nancy Savoca • *Scr* Nancy Savoca, Richard Guay

True Romance   ★★★★ 18
Black comedy thriller
1993 · US · Colour · 116mins

Movie-obsessed comic store worker Christian Slater meets hooker Patricia Arquette. After getting married then accidentally stealing a fortune in cocaine from her pimp Gary Oldman, they hit the rocky road to possible oblivion. Scriptwriter Quentin Tarantino blends Hong Kong gangster movie clichés, *film noir* revisionism, slick but ultra-heavy violence and a host of great star cameos to create an acid cocktail. Director Tony Scott's superb visual style is the icing on the cake. Contains swearing, drug abuse, nudity, sex scenes and violence. ▦ *DVD*

Christian Slater *Clarence Worley* • Patricia Arquette *Alabama Whitman* • Dennis Hopper *Clifford Worley* • Val Kilmer *Mentor* • Gary Oldman *Drexl Spivey* • Brad Pitt *Floyd* • Christopher Walken *Vincenzo Coccetti* ■ *Dir* Tony Scott • *Scr* Quentin Tarantino, Roger Avary (uncredited)

True Stories   ★★★ PG
Comedy   1986 · US · Colour · 85mins

Not so much a movie as a feature-length rock video held together by a kooky storyline, with former Talking Head David Byrne strolling through the eccentric lives of the common, but secretly colourful, folk of the fictional community of Virgil, Texas as they prepare for their annual "Celebration of Specialness". Alternately intriguing and condescending, Byrne's ironic detachment ultimately wears out its welcome, though the soundtrack, as you would expect, is consistently entertaining. The members of the brilliant ensemble cast including John Goodman, Spalding Gray and Swoosie Kurtz give heart to a group of characters inspired by tabloid newspaper and magazine stories. ▦

David Byrne *Narrator* • John Goodman *Louis Fyne* • Swoosie Kurtz *Miss Rollings, the laziest woman in the world* • Spalding Gray *Earl Culver* • Alix Elias *Cute woman* • Annie McEnroe *Kay Culver* ■ *Dir* David Byrne • *Scr* David Byrne, Beth Henley, Stephen Tobolowsky

The True Story of Jesse James   ★★ U
Western   1957 · US · Colour · 91mins

Perhaps better known by its British title *The James Brothers*, this is anything but the "true story" of the notorious outlaw. Bolstered by a fine score from the neglected Leigh Harline, the movie is seriously undermined by an unnecessary flashback structure and by the crippling use of contemporary Fox contractees. While attractive to watch, juvenile stars Robert Wagner and Jeffrey Hunter are wholly inadequate as Jesse and Frank James. Director Nicholas Ray was one of the finest Hollywood film-makers,

and in the classic *Rebel without a Cause* showed a fine understanding of the connection between crime and adolescent angst. But here he quite fails to grasp the tale's potential, and in his own words made "a very ordinary movie". Shame.

Robert Wagner *Jesse James* • Jeffrey Hunter *Frank James* • Hope Lange *Zee* • Agnes Moorehead *Mrs Samuel* • Alan Hale Jr *Cole Younger* • Alan Baxter *Remington* • John Carradine *Reverend Jethro Bailey* • Rachel Stephens *Anne* ■ *Dir* Nicholas Ray • *Scr* Walter Newman, from the film *Jesse James* by Nunnally Johnson

The True Story of Lynn Stuart   ★★
Crime thriller   1957 · US · BW · 76mins

In this gritty crime drama, dope smugglers are brought to book by a resourceful housewife. Although a minor production, Betsy Palmer gives an intelligent performance as the woman who cuddles up to Jack Lord's hoodlum in order to avenge the death of her dope-addicted nephew. It may sound far-fetched, but it's actually based on real-life events. Burnett Guffey's photography, largely done on location, adds a touch of class to Lewis Seiler's competent direction.

Betsy Palmer *Phyllis Carter* • Jack Lord *Willie Down* • Barry Atwater *Hagan* • Kim Spalding *Ralph Carter* • Karl Lukas *Hal Bruck* • Casey Walters *Eddie Dine* • Harry Jackson *Husband Officer* ■ *Dir* Lewis Seiler • *Scr* John H Kneubuhl, from articles by Pat Michaels

True to Life   ★★★ U
Comedy   1943 · US · BW · 93mins

Audiences were confused to find that a film starring singers Dick Powell and Mary Martin was not a musical, especially as there are three incidental songs by Hoagy Carmichael and Johnny Mercer, including *The Old Music Master*. Nevertheless, the movie is an engaging comedy in which Powell plays a radio writer who looks for a "typical" American family from which he can obtain material for his soap opera, but instead finds a household full of eccentrics. Although these include the irritating comic actor Victor Moore, Martin, in one of her few "straight" roles, is charming.

Mary Martin *Bonnie Porter* • Franchot Tone *Fletcher Marvin* • Dick Powell *Link Ferris* • Victor Moore *Pop Porter* • Mabel Paige *Mom Porter* • William Demarest *Jake* • Clarence Kolb *Mr Huggins* • Yvonne De Carlo *Girl* ■ *Dir* George Marshall • *Scr* Don Hartman, Harry Tugend, from a story by Ben Barzman, Bess Taffel, Sol Barzman

Truly Madly Deeply   ★★★★ PG
Drama   1990 · UK · Colour · 102mins

The British *Ghost*, but a far more witty and incisive affair, topped off with glorious performances from Alan Rickman as the dearly departed who returns and Juliet Stevenson as his grief-stricken partner struggling to come to terms with his loss. The strengths of this movie are numerous, most notably an emotional integrity in every scene and director Anthony Minghella's ability to inject the pathos with well-aimed humour. In many ways, the success of this film in America

paved the way for a wider distribution for *Four Weddings and a Funeral* and Minghella's later triumph *The English Patient*. Contains swearing. ▦

Juliet Stevenson *Nina* • Alan Rickman *Jamie* • Bill Paterson *Sandy* • Michael Maloney *Mark* • Deborah Findlay *Claire* • Christopher Rozycki *Titus* • David Ryall *George* • Jenny Howe *Burge* ■ *Dir/Scr* Anthony Minghella

Truman   ★★★★ PG
Biographical drama
1995 · US · Colour · 133mins

This outstanding Emmy winner, based on the Pulitzer Prize-winning biography by David McCullough, stars the incomparable Gary Sinise as Harry S Truman, the 33rd President of the United States. Insightful direction by Frank Pierson and a tour de force performance by Sinise enliven the intelligent script by Tom Rickman (*Coal Miner's Daughter*). An authentic re-creation of the period along with an effective supporting cast that includes Diana Scarwid and Richard Dysart, this captivating biopic is not just for history buffs but for all those who enjoy fine film-making. ▦

Gary Sinise *Harry S Truman* • Diana Scarwid *Bess Wallace Truman* • Richard Dysart *Henry L Stimson* • Colm Feore *Charlie Ross* • James Gammon *Sam Rayburn* • Tony Goldwyn *Clark Clifford* • Pat Hingle *Thomas Joseph Pendergast* ■ *Dir* Frank Pierson • *Scr* Tom Rickman, from the biography by David McCullough

The Truman Show ★★★★★ PG
Satirical comedy drama
1998 · US · Colour · 98mins

An ingenious concept (scripted by *Gattaca's* director/screenwriter Andrew Niccol), flawlessly executed by director Peter Weir. From audacious start to poignant finale, Weir's science-fiction comedy drama is both dazzling and sophisticated. Truman Burbank (Jim Carrey) is the star of the world's most popular television show – only he doesn't know it! Although he thinks he lives in the idyllic island community of Seahaven, it's just an elaborate set housed in a vast Hollywood studio, and all his family and friends are really actors. How that realisation slowly dawns and spurs him on to find out what's real and what's fake in his emotionally confused universe is the stuff of ambitious cinematic brilliance. With superlative support from Ed Harris as the show's creator Christof and Laura Linney as Truman's "wife" Meryl, Carrey reveals his dramatic range in a compelling fable about media omnipotence. ▦

Jim Carrey *Truman Burbank* • Laura Linney *Meryl* • Noah Emmerich *Marlon* • Natascha McElhone *Lauren/Sylvia* • Holland Taylor *Truman's mother* • Brian Delate *Truman's father* • Ed Harris *Christof* ■ *Dir* Peter Weir • *Scr* Andrew Niccol

Trust   ★★★ 15
Drama   1990 · UK/US · Colour · 101mins

Dangerous things happen in this tragicomedy from independent film-maker Hal Hartley. Teenager Adrienne Shelly breaks the news of her pregnancy to her parents, causing dad to suffer a heart attack. Elsewhere, a baby is abducted and the antihero (Martin Donovan) carries a hand grenade

around in case of emergency. This was Hartley's second feature, but such is the deadpan approach that you're never totally involved, just intrigued. His arms-length style earned him critical plaudits, and he went on to direct lead actor Donovan in several films, including *Flirt* and *Amateur*. A movie with a flavour all its own. ▦

Adrienne Shelly *Maria Coughlin* • Martin Donovan *Matthew Slaughter* • Merritt Nelson *Jean Coughlin* • John MacKay *Jim Slaughter* • Edie Falco *Peg Coughlin* • Gary Sauer *Anthony* ■ *Dir/Scr* Hal Hartley

Trust in Me   ★★
Police thriller   1994 · US/Can · Colour

This uncompromising TV crime drama centres on an unlikely alliance between a Vancouver cop and a leather-clad biker. But the pursuit of a gang of gunrunners turns nasty when an ambush leaves the cop grievously wounded and the biker apparently dead – or is he? The versatile Bill Corcoran directs with plenty of pace, which is just as well considering the unlikely plot, and Currie Graham and Stacy Keach turn in sufficiently bullish performances, with the latter particularly revelling in his nickname, "The Reverend". Contains swearing.

Currie Graham • Stacy Keach • Sandra Nelson • Ian Tracey ■ *Dir* Bill Corcoran • *Scr* Hart Hanson, Matt Macleod

Trust Me   ★★ 15
Comedy thriller 1989 · US · Colour · 85mins

Despite winning a meaty role in *The Equalizer*, Adam Ant has never managed to shake off his Prince Charming/Dandy Highwayman pop image. Here he stars as an art gallery owner in debt who decides the only way out is to promote a respected artist and then kill him so the work increases in value. A daft idea, and the acting isn't much better as Mr Ant moves through each scene looking as if he's in search of a pop interlude. Contains swearing. ▦

Adam Ant *James Callendar* • David Packer *Sam Brown* • Talia Balsam *Catherine Walker* • William Deacutis *Billy Brawthwaite* • Joyce Van Patten *Nettie Brown* • Barbara Bain *Mary Casal* ■ *Dir* Bobby Houston • *Scr* Bobby Houston, Gary Rigdon

The Truth about Cats and Dogs   ★★★★ 15
Romantic comedy
1996 · US · Colour · 96mins

An adorable and very funny romantic comedy with Janeane Garofalo stealing the film as the radio talk show veterinary surgeon whom listener Ben Chaplin falls for. Garofalo is convinced Chaplin will be disappointed when he actually meets her, so she sends lovely but dim Uma Thurman in her place. Numerous romantic complications ensue as both women fall for the lucky fellow. It all zips along merrily against a sunny Santa Monica background, with Garofalo once again proving her skill as a comedian, while Thurman shows a previously unseen talent for comedy herself. One phone sex scene may be a bit risqué for younger viewers, but otherwise this will appeal to all ages. It marked a return to form for director Michael Lehmann,

whose highs have included *Heathers*, but whose lows unfortunately include the teeth-grindingly awful *My Giant*. ▣

Uma Thurman *Noelle* • Janeane Garofalo *Abby* • Ben Chaplin *Brian* • Jamie Foxx *Ed* • James McCaffrey *Roy* • Richard Coca *Eric* • Stanley DeSantis *Mario* ■ *Dir* Michael Lehmann • *Scr* Audrey Wells

The Truth about Spring

★★★ U

Adventure   1964 · UK · Colour · 102mins

John Mills teams with daughter Hayley for the third time in this fanciful adventure that might well have passed for children's entertainment in the mid-sixties, but probably won't appeal to today's more sophisticated youngsters. Sir John hams it up as a crusty sea captain whose brush with smugglers lands tomboy Hayley in the arms of a young James MacArthur (pre-*Hawaii Five-O*). Lionel Jeffries, David Tomlinson and Harry Andrews go right overboard in support and Richard Thorpe directs at a fair clip, but too little happens to stir the imagination and it's hard to see many kids revelling in the romance.

Hayley Mills *Spring Tyler* • John Mills *Tommy Tyler* • James MacArthur *William Ashton* • Lionel Jeffries *Cark* • Harry Andrews *Sellers* • Niall MacGinnis *Cleary* • Lionel Murton *Simmons* • David Tomlinson *Skelton* ■ *Dir* Richard Thorpe • *Scr* James Lee Barrett, from the story *Satan: a Romance of the Bahamas* by Henry de Vere Stacpoole

The Truth about Women ★★

Comedy   1958 · UK · Colour · 106mins

A bizarre charade in which Laurence Harvey plays a sort of Don Juan character, recalling his amorous, exotic adventures in Arabia, Paris, London, New York, the First World War and beyond. The moral is that one's first love is the only love that matters – aaah! – but the problem here is that Harvey is also something of a cold fish, brilliant as the man on the make in *Room at the Top* but not overly furnished with plain, old-fashioned charm. The women make the most of their extended cameos, servicing the hero (so to speak) and posing in their Cecil Beaton costumes.

Laurence Harvey *Sir Humphrey Tavistock* • Julie Harris *Helen Cooper* • Diane Cilento *Ambrosine Viney* • Mai Zetterling *Julie* • Eva Gabor *Louise* • Michael Denison *Rollo* • Derek Farr *Anthony* • Elina Labourdette *Comtesse* ■ *Dir* Muriel Box • *Scr* Sydney Box, Muriel Box

Truth or Consequences, NM

★★★ 18

Comedy thriller   1997 · US · Colour · mins

For his feature directing debut Kiefer Sutherland might have chosen something just a little bit more original than the routine heist-goes-wrong scenario and someone a little more capable than the writer of *Body of Evidence* to bring it to life. Vincent Gallo is the ex-con setting up one last robbery with former cell-mate Sutherland, a trigger-happy sociopath. Naturally things don't go to plan and the gang end up taking hostages and falling foul of Rod Steiger's Las Vegas mobster and fruitcake Martin Sheen. This pulp mixture of *Reservoir Dogs* and *Natural Born Killers* is violently

played out among the scenic mountains and deserts of Utah and expertly played by a solid cast, while Sutherland proves a safe pair of hands behind the lens. ▣

Kiefer Sutherland *Curtis Freley* • Grace Phillips *Donna Moreland* • Vincent Gallo *Raymond Lembecke* • Kim Dickens *Addy Monroe* • Rod Steiger *Tony Vago* • Kevin Pollak *Gordon Jacobson* • Martin Sheen *Sir* ■ *Dir* Kiefer Sutherland • *Scr* Brad Mirman

The Trygon Factor   ★★ 15

Crime drama   1967 · UK · Colour · 83mins

Fake nuns set up a million-dollar heist in this farcical British crime drama. Stewart Granger is the Scotland Yard detective called in to investigate a convent situated on the grounds of Cathleen Nesbitt's stately home; Susan Hampshire is her photographer daughter. Blackly comic at best, the film boasts a cast of British stalwarts including Robert Morley and James Robertson-Justice, but they just end up milling around in the hope of being directed by Cyril Frankel. Unfortunately for them, and us, he never gets to grip with that task. ▣

Stewart Granger *Supt Cooper-Smith* • Susan Hampshire *Trudy Emberday* • Robert Morley *Hubert Hamlyn* • Cathleen Nesbitt *Livia Emberday* • Brigitte Horney *Sister General/Mrs Hamlyn* • Sophie Hardy *Sophie* • James Robertson-Justice *Sir John* ■ *Dir* Cyril Frankel • *Scr* Derry Quinn, Stanley Munro, from a story by Derry Quinn

Tryst   ★★

Erotic thriller   1994 · US · Colour · 101mins

A so-called erotic thriller, this is about as steamy as the inside of a fridge. Barbara Carrera vamps it up as the bored wife who seduces the young son of one of her domestic staff, much to the distress of millionaire husband (David Warner going through the motions). Director Peter Foldy makes some ham-fisted nods towards *film noir* greats, but it doesn't deserve to be mentioned in the same breath as any of them, as it is neither titillating nor suspenseful. Contains swearing, violence and nudity.

Barbara Carrera *Julia Germaine* • Louise Fletcher *Maggie Tyler* • David Warner *Jason Germaine* • Steve Bond *Parkinson* • Johnny LaSpada *Todd Barker* ■ *Dir/Scr* Peter Foldy

Tuck Everlasting   ★★★★

Animation   1981 · US · Colour · 114mins

In an utterly beguiling fable, a woods-dwelling family who are impervious to pain, ageing and death are stumbled upon by an inquisitive 12-year-old girl. Based on Natalie Babbit's award-winning novel, this independently-produced animation is almost as well-kept a secret as the family's immortality. But hunt it out: family entertainment doesn't come much better than this.

Fred A Keller *Angus Tuck* • James McGuire *Man in yellow suit* • Paul Flessa *Jesse Tuck* • Margaret Chamberlain *Winnie* • Sonia Raimi *Mary Tuck* • Bruce D'Aurio *Miles Tuck* ■ *Dir* Frederick King Keller • *Scr* Stratton Rawson, Fred A Keller, Frederick King Keller, from the novel by Natalie Babbit

Tucker: the Man and His Dream   ★★ PG

Biographical drama
1988 · US · Colour · 105mins

Under the directorial auspices of Francis Ford Coppola, Jeff Bridges stars as Preston Tucker, a real-life innovative car designer whose career was gunned down by his big business competitors. Also a loyal family man, the portrayal of his home life with wife Joan Allen nevertheless just plays like a bad sitcom. Preston meanwhile creates a production line for the definitive American automobile and stirs up a storm of PR, but sadly very little in the viewer. Coppola was fascinated by the Tucker mobile and indeed the car is the star here. But unless you share the director's enthusiasm, you'll be calling out the AA to haul you out of your seat. Beautiful to look at though, thanks to the scintillating work of master cameraman Vittorio Storaro. ▣

Jeff Bridges *Preston Tucker* • Joan Allen *Vera Tucker* • Martin Landau *Abe Karatz* • Frederic Forrest *Eddie Dean* • Mako *Jimmy Sakuyama* • Dean Stockwell *Howard Hughes* • Lloyd Bridges *Senator Homer Ferguson* • Elias Koteas *Alex Tremulis* • Christian Slater *Junior* ■ *Dir* Francis Ford Coppola • *Scr* Arnold Schulman, David Seidler • *Executive Producer* George Lucas

Tudawali   ★★★

Drama   1987 · Ausl · Colour

This TV movie is an intriguing oddity from Australia which transcends its novelty value because of the performance of Ernie Dingo (who gave a marvellously comic turn in Paul Hogan's *Crocodile Dundee II*) as the eponymous hero, Robert Tudawali, the first Aboriginal film star. Inevitably, the star was torn between the simplicities of his native life and the cynical values of the whites, a conflict from which he was released by his mysterious death in 1967 at the age of 38.

Ernie Dingo *Robert Tudawali* • Peter Fisher *Harry* • Jedda Cole *Peggy* • Frank Wilson *Charles Chauvel* ■ *Dir* Steve Jodrell • *Scr* Alan Seymour

Tudor Rose   ★★★

Historical drama   1936 · UK · BW · 80mins

The short life and even shorter reign of Lady Jane Grey is given some poignancy by Nova Pilbeam, and heraldic significance and atmosphere by director Robert Stevenson. This is a Tudor story in which Elizabeth scarcely makes an appearance, but a mainly British cast – including Cedric Hardwicke and John Mills – make the "prithees" sound convincing. The American title, *Nine Days a Queen*, was an adequate description of the film's storyline.

John Mills *Lord Guildford Dudley* • Sir Cedric Hardwicke [Cedric Hardwicke] *Earl of Warwick* • Felix Aylmer *Edward Seymour* • Leslie Perrins *Thomas Seymour* • Frank Cellier *Henry VIII* • Desmond Tester *Edward VI* • Sybil Thorndike *Ellen* ■ *Dir* Robert Stevenson • *Scr* Robert Stevenson, Miles Malleson

Tuff Turf   ★★ 18

Drama   1984 · US · Colour · 106mins

Unremarkable teen drama, with new kid in town James Spader falling for streetwise local girl Kim Richards. Trouble looms in the shape of her hot-tempered lover (Paul Mones), who doesn't take too kindly to Spader muscling in on his turf. Despite vague undertones of *West Side Story*, this is worth watching solely for Spader in his pre-*sex, lies and videotape* days, and for a brief, early appearance by Robert Downey Jr. ▣

James Spader *Morgan Hiller* • Kim Richards *Frankie Croyden* • Paul Mones *Nick Hauser* • Robert Downey Jr *Jimmy Parker* • Matt Clark *Stuart Hiller* • Claudette Nevins *Page Hiller* • Olivia Barash *Ronnie* ■ *Dir* Fritz Kiersch • *Scr* Jette Rinck, from a story by Greg Collins O'Neill, Murray Michaels

Tugboat Annie   ★★★

Comedy drama   1933 · US · BW · 87mins

A ramshackle vehicle (in all senses of the word) reuniting the popular star team of the 1930 hit *Min and Bill*, loveable Marie Dressler and gruff Wallace Beery. It was based on Norman Reilly Raine's *Saturday Evening Post* stories about Annie Brennan and her no-good hubby Terry, who never hit Annie "'cept in self-defence". When this was made, Oscar-winner Dressler was number one at the box office; a year later she was dead from cancer. Tugboat Annie survived in two more screen incarnations (Marjorie Rambeau and Jane Darwell) and a 1957 TV series. Annie's tugboat, the *Narcissus*, was sailed again by Beery in 1941's *Barnacle Bill*.

Marie Dressler *Annie Brennan* • Wallace Beery *Terry Brennan* • Robert Young *Alec Brennan* • Maureen O'Sullivan *Pat Severn* • Willard Robertson *Red Severn* • Tammany Young *Shif'less* ■ *Dir* Mervyn LeRoy • *Scr* Zelda Sears, Eve Green, Norman Reilly Raine, from stories by Norma Reilly Raine

Tulsa   ★★

Drama   1949 · US · Colour · 90mins

Films about the search for oil helped fill Hollywood's own financial pipeline on occasion, and this was the biggest since MGM's *Boom Town*. The addition of rich Technicolor not only enhanced the blazing climax but also the red curls of fiery leading lady Susan Hayward. It's she who builds an empire out of the black gold with the help of Robert Preston's geologist and enters into an unholy partnership with oil baron Lloyd Gough. Producer Walter Wanger throws a conservation angle into this otherwise formula-bound entertainment as oil pollutes the traditional grazing lands of her native American friend, Pedro Armendariz.

Susan Hayward *Cherokee "Cherry" Lansing* • Robert Preston *Brad "Bronco" Brady* • Pedro Armendariz *Jim Redbird* • Chill Wills *Pinky Jimpson* • Harry Shannon *Nelse Lansing* • Ed Begley *"Crude" Johnny Brady* • Jimmy Conlin *Homer Triplette* ■ *Dir* Stuart Heisler • *Scr* Frank Nugent, Curtis Kenyon, from a story by Richard Wormser

Tumbleweed   ★★ U

Western   1953 · US · Colour · 78mins

A very average Universal western starring its resident cowboy, Audie

Murphy, who this time out is accused of deserting a wagon train during an Indian raid. There are lots of familiar western faces on hand, including Chill Wills and Lee Van Cleef, but perhaps it's worth mentioning that the title role goes to a horse. Leading lady Lori Nelson was little more than an ingénue at this stage of her career, before she met up with the Creature from the Black Lagoon in the sequel *Revenge of the Creature*. In the US this was originally double-billed on release with imported British thriller *The Net*. Contains violence.

Audie Murphy *Jim Harvey* • Lori Nelson *Laura* • Chill Wills *Sheriff Murchoree* • Roy Roberts *Nick Buckley* • Russell Johnson *Lam* • KT Stevens *Louella Buckley* • Madge Meredith *Sarah* • Lee Van Cleef *Marv* ■ *Dir* Nathan Juran • *Scr* John Meredyth Lucas, from the novel *Three Were Renegades* by Kenneth Perkins

Tumbleweeds ★★★

Silent western epic 1925 · US · BW · 82mins

The first real cowboy star – just a gallop ahead of Tom Mix – and a major influence on the development of the western during the silent era, the upright, unsmiling hero figure of William S Hart made his final appearance in what is probably the best-known of his films. The plot has Hart vanquishing the lawless with the aid of his sharpshooting, playing protector to pioneer settler Barbara Bedford. Simple, formula stuff to be sure, but with an authentic flavour of the Old West and a famous land-rush action sequence. Despite the film's huge success, Hart sued UA for negligence in distribution and won a sizeable sum. In 1939, the star reissued *Tumbleweeds* with sound effects and a prologue, spoken by himself, about how the West had changed.

William S Hart *Don Carver* • Barbara Bedford *Molly Lassiter* • Lucien Littlefield *Kentucky Rose* • J Gordon Russell *Noll Lassiter* • Richard R Neill *Bill Freel* • Jack Murphy *Bart Lassiter* ■ *Dir* King Baggot • *Scr* C Gardner Sullivan, from a story by Hal G Evarts

Tumbleweeds ★★★ 12

Drama 1999 · US · Colour · 100mins

Janet McTeer gives an Oscar-nominated performance as a spirited, flirty floozy who drags her 12-year-old daughter (newcomer Kimberley J Brown) out west in search of a better life. This funny, tender and predictably tear-stained slice of life echoes other parent-and-child road movies, from *Alice Doesn't Live Here Anymore* to the Susan Sarandon/Natalie Portman vehicle, *Anywhere but Here*. Yet it has a sassy charm all its own, with McTeer's unself-conscious sexuality providing a vivid contrast to Brown's unaffected innocence. Writer/director Gavin O'Connor (whose ex-wife Angela Shelton based the story on her own mother) also appears as McTeer's truck-driving lover.

Janet McTeer *Mary Jo Walker* • Kimberly J Brown *Ava Walker* • Jay O Sanders *Dan* • Gavin O'Connor *Jack Ranson* • Michael J Pollard *Mr Cummings* • Laurel Holloman *Laurie Pendleton* • Lois Smith *Ginger* ■ *Dir* Gavin O'Connor • *Scr* Gavin O'Connor, Angela Shelton

The Tune ★★★ PG

Animated musical comedy 1992 · US · Colour · 66mins

The earliest experiments in matching music and animation were conducted in the thirties by such avant-garde masters as Oskar Fischinger and Len Lye. Bill Plympton's feature debut pays homage to these collages of image and rhythm, as a failed songwriter tries his hand at a variety of musical styles in order to relaunch his career. The action occasionally becomes a little mushy, as the inhabitants of the fantasy world of Flooby Nooby try to teach their guest to write from the heart, but there is undoubted beauty in the 30,000 pencil-and-watercolour drawings that comprise this highly entertaining film. ▣

Daniel Nieden *Del* • Maureen McElheron *Didi* • Marty Nelson *Mayor/Mr Mega/Mrs Mega* • Emily Bindiger *Dot* ■ *Dir* Bill Plympton • *Scr* Bill Plympton, Maureen McElheron, PC Vey

Tunes of Glory ★★★★ PG

Drama 1960 · UK · Colour · 106mins

John Mills won best actor at the Venice film festival for his priggish performance in this stiff-upper-lipped military drama, but few critics would have had any complaints but he shared the prize with his co-star Alec Guinness. Mills is the blue-blooded Pacific veteran who's determined to make his new regiment fit for the demands of peacetime, while Guinness is the time-serving Alamein hero who remains stubbornly obsessed with past glories. James Kennaway's rather bombastic script, adapted from his own novel, was Oscar-nominated, and, if Ronald Neame's direction is occasionally stodgy, the central conflict between Mills and Guinness remains as compelling as its resolution is shocking. ▣

Alec Guinness *Lieutenant Colonel Jock Sinclair* • John Mills *Lieutenant Colonel Basil Barrow* • Dennis Price *Major Charlie Scott* • Susanna York *Morag Sinclair* • John Fraser *Corporal Piper Fraser* • Allan Cuthbertson *Captain Eric Simpson* • Kay Walsh *Mary* • John MacKenzie *Pony Major* • Gordon Jackson *Captain Jimmy Cairns* ■ *Dir* Ronald Neame • *Scr* James Kennaway, from his novel

The Tunnel ★★ U

Science-fiction drama 1935 · UK · BW · 88mins

Michael Balcon produced this Gaumont-British remake of a German film, *Der Tunnel*. It was heavily geared towards the American market with Hollywood stars including Richard Dix as the engineering genius behind the scheme for a railway tunnel under the Atlantic, Walter Huston (seen only briefly) as the US President, Helen Vinson as the daughter of an American millionaire backer, and Madge Evans as Dix's anxious wife. Leslie Banks leads the British contingent, while George Arliss matches Huston as Britain's prime minister. The massive drilling operations which bring the team into explosive contact with volcanic lava are far more impressive than the human story. ▣

Richard Dix *McAllan* • Leslie Banks *Robbie* • Madge Evans *Ruth McAllan* • Helen Vinson *Varlia* • C Aubrey Smith *Lloyd* • Basil Sydney *Mostyn* • Henry Oscar *Grellier* • Walter Huston

President of the United States • George Arliss Prime Minister ■ Dir Maurice Elvey • Scr L Du Garde Peach, Kurt Siodmak [Curt Siodmak], from the novel by Bernhard Kellermann

The Tunnel of Love ★★

Comedy 1958 · US · BW · 98mins

This film marked the first time Gene Kelly had directed a picture which he was not in, and though he makes an efficient job of transcribing the Broadway comedy by Joseph Fields, Peter De Vries and the blacklisted Jerome Chodorov, it comes out as one of those plays that convulsed theatre audiences in New York and London but seems only mildly amusing on screen. Doris Day and Richard Widmark (the latter in a rare comedy role) play a married couple forced to battle through all sorts of bureaucratic formalities in order to adopt a child. Shot in only three weeks on virtually one set, the film still lost money – Day later blamed its failure on a poor script.

Doris Day *Isolde Poole* • Richard Widmark *Augie Poole* • Gig Young *Dick Pepper* • Gia Scala *Estelle Novick* • Elisabeth Fraser *Alice Pepper* • Elizabeth Wilson *Miss MacCracken* • Vikki Dougan *Actress* ■ *Dir* Gene Kelly • *Scr* Joseph Fields, Jerome Chodorov (uncredited), Peter De Vries, from their play

Tunnel Vision ★★ 18

Thriller 1994 · Ausl · Colour · 90mins

After a couple of American B-features, Patsy Kensit continued her globetrotting career with this so-so Australian thriller. She and Robert Reynolds play two detectives on the trail of an artistically minded serial killer. To complicate things further, Reynolds finds himself a suspect in a separate case when the man he suspects of sleeping with his wife turns up dead. The leads are no more than competent, but at least Kensit doesn't make any wince-inducing attempts at an accent, and there are some nifty twists in the plot. It's also good to see Hammer favourite Shane Briant back on the screen. Contains swearing and nudity. ▣

Patsy Kensit *Kelly Wheatstone* • Robert Reynolds *Frank Yanovitch* • Rebecca Rigg *Helena Martelli* • Gary Day *Steve Docherty* • Shane Briant *Kevin Bosey* ■ *Dir/Scr* Clive Fleury

Tunnelvision ★★

Comedy 1976 · US · Colour · 67mins

There are more misses than hits in this satire on what television, allegedly, would deliver in the future with a series of themed sketches not unlike the similiarly anarchic *Kentucky Fried Movie*, but none nearly as clever or, more importantly, as funny. This is one of those collectors-only items like *The Gong Show Movie* or *National Lampoon Goes to the Movies* that is of less interest for what's actually on the screen than for who shows up in the relentlessly unfunny and crass sketches. Here there's a chance to catch Chevy Chase, *Reversal of Fortune*'s Ron Silver and *Private Parts* director Betty Thomas. Also along for the ride is a clutch of *National Lampoon* and *Saturday Night Live* future alumni. It's interesting, but it's crudely made and just isn't funny.

Phil Proctor *Christian A Broder* • Howard Hesseman *Senator McMannus* • Ernie Anderson *Quant O'Neil* • Edwina Anderson *Melanie Edwards* • Chevy Chase • Laraine Newman *Sonja* • Rick Hurst *Father Phaser Gun* ■ *Dir* Brad Swirnoff, Neal Israel • *Scr* Neal Israel, Michael Mislove

Turbulence ★★★ 18

Action thriller 1997 · US · Colour · 96mins

In one of the more manic of the countless *Die Hard* imitations, Ray Liotta stars as a psycho who hijacks a Christmas Eve flight transporting him to prison. Lauren Holly plays the plucky flight attendant who has to beat off Liotta's advances and attempt to land the aircraft safely. This is far from sophisticated adult entertainment, but it's so ludicrously overblown that it's hard not to be entertained by the sheer enthusiasm and abandonment of logic and credibility. Veteran director Robert Butler is an old hand when it comes to this kind of airborne nonsense, having made the 1976 TV movie *Mayday at 40,000 Feet!*. Contains swearing and violence. ▣

DVD

Ray Liotta *Ryan Weaver* • Lauren Holly *Teri Halloran* • Brendan Gleeson *Stubbs* • Hector Elizondo *Detective Aldo Hines* • Rachel Ticotin *Rachel Taper* • Jeffrey DeMunn *Brooks* • John Finn *Sinclair* • Ben Cross *Captain Bowen* ■ *Dir* Robert Butler • *Scr* Jonathan Brett

Turk 182! ★★ 15

Comedy drama 1985 · US · Colour · 92mins

An off-target shot at Capraesque "feel good" by Bob Clark, the man who gave the world *Porky's*. Timothy Hutton plays a New York graffiti artist who uses his talent to shame mayor Robert Culp after the city fathers fail to compensate his fireman brother, injured in an off-duty rescue. Hutton is seriously miscast as the spray-can vigilante, while Peter Boyle, Darren McGavin and Paul Sorvino are wasted in minor roles. The presence of Robert Urich as Hutton's brother and Kim Cattrall as his girlfriend tips us off that this is strictly B-movie fare. ▣

Timothy Hutton *Jimmy Lynch* • Robert Urich *Terry Lynch* • Kim Cattrall *Danny Boudreau* • Robert Culp *Mayor Tyler* • Darren McGavin *Detective Kowalski* • Steven Keats *Jockamo* • Paul Sorvino *Paul Sorvino* • Peter Boyle *Detective Ryan* ■ *Dir* Bob Clark • *Scr* James Gregory Kingston, Denis Hamill, John Hamill, from a story by James Gregory Kingston

Turkey Shoot ★★★ 18

Futuristic action thriller 1981 · Ausl · Colour · 83mins

In this gore-drenched futuristic version of *The Most Dangerous Game* set in the Australian outback, social deviants (freedom fighter Steve Railsback, shoplifter Olivia Hussey, prostitutes et al) are sent to barbaric concentration camps, supposedly for re-education. But in reality it's to provide human prey for warden Michael Craig to indulge his sadistic predilection for extreme blood sports. Convincingly mounted and violent (with explosive arrows and machetes put to very nasty use), this cynical political allegory may be transparent exploitation, but it sure does deliver a high shock quotient. ▣

Steve Railsback *Paul Anders* • Olivia Hussey *Chris Walters* • Michael Craig *Charles*

Thatcher • Carmen Duncan *Jennifer* • Noel Ferrier *Mallory* • Lynda Stoner *Rita Daniels* • Roger Ward *Ritter* • Michael Petrovitch *Tito* • Gus Mercurio *Red* ■ *Dir* Brian Trenchard-Smith • *Scr* Jon George, Neill Hicks, from a story by George Schenck, Robert Williams, David Lawrence

The Turkish Bath ★★★ 15

Drama 1996 · It/Tur/Sp · Colour · 98mins

Winner of a brace of Golden Globes, this atmospheric drama slowly draws you into the back streets of Istanbul and even more deeply into the lives of their inhabitants. The Turkish cast is admirable, but the focus falls firmly on Alessandro Gassman, as the Italian businessman who inherits a bath-house from an aunt and whose independent lifestyle eventually leads to tragedy. Director Ferzan Ozpetek's sunny cityscapes are striking, but it's the evocative interiors (with their haunting light and architectural beauty) that give this search for cultural and sexual identity its extraordinary sense of serenity and fulfilment. In Italian and Turkish with English subtitles. Contains sex scenes, violence and some swearing.

Alessandro Gassman *Francesco* • Francesca D'Aloja *Marta* • Mehmet Gunsur *Mehmet* • Carlo Cecchi *Oscar* • Halil Ergun *Osman* ■ *Dir* Ferzan Ozpetek • *Scr* Ferzan Ozpetek, Stefano Tummolini

Turkish Delight ★★★★

Erotic drama 1973 · Neth · Colour · 101mins

Dutch director Paul Verhoeven burst onto the international film scene with this truly bizarre and shocking romance featuring unprecedented amounts of frontal nudity, graphic sex and scatological behaviour. It also shot star Rutger Hauer to fame. He plays a sex-obsessed artist/sculptor whose exhibitionism is fuelled by an intense relationship with suburban Monique van de Ven. But whereas his carnal conduct is more about affronting respectable society with revolutionary values, hers has a darker base in mental imbalance due to a brain tumour. Told in flashback, the main thrust of this memorable Dutch treat is how their sad, stormy and erotic affair turned out to be the passionate pinnacle in Hauer's empty life. A surprisingly tender and touching tale that sticks with you long after the credits have rolled. Dutch dialogue dubbed into English. 📺

Monique van de Ven *Olga* • Rutger Hauer *Eric* • Tonny Huurdeman *Mother* • Dolf de Vries *Paul* ■ *Dir* Paul Verhoeven • *Scr* Gerard Soeteman, from the novel *Turks Fruit* by Jan Wolkers

Turn Back the Clock ★

Drama 1933 · US · BW · 80mins

Simply dreadful cringe-athon, with cigar store owner Lee Tracy run over by a car and dreaming how he might have lived a better life, been nicer to his wife, fought better in the First World War and warned President Woodrow Wilson about European policy. He also wonders what life might have been like if he was rich. In 1933, when the Depression was ripping through lives like a tornado, this sugary sort of thing went down a treat.

Lee Tracy *Joe Gimlet* • Mae Clarke *Mary Gimlet* • Otto Kruger *Ted Wright* • George Barbier *Pete Evans* • Peggy Shannon *Elvina Wright* • C Henry Gordon *Mr Holmes* • Clara Blandick *Mrs Gimlet* ■ *Dir* Edgar Selwyn • *Scr* Edgar Selwyn, Ben Hecht

Turn Back the Clock ★★ PG

Thriller 1989 · US · Colour · 90mins

A warmed-over remake of the 1947 film *Repeat Performance*, this has *Hotel* star Connie Sellecca asking for a second chance after she shoots her husband and getting her wish: her life restarts a year before the fateful event. Unfortunately, nothing that subsequently happens holds the interest of the viewer, despite good supporting performances from David Dukes and *North and South* actress Wendy Kilbourne, and you'll wish you could turn back the clock to the moment before you decided to watch this plodding tale.

Connie Sellecca *Sheila Powers* • David Dukes *Barney* • Jere Burns *William Hawkins* • Wendy Kilbourne *Tracy Alexander* • Gene Barry *John Forrester* • Dina Merrill *Maureen Dowd* ■ *Dir* Larry Elikann • *Scr* Lee Hutson, Lindsay Harrison

The Turn of the Screw ★ 18

Supernatural horror
1992 · UK/US/Fr · Colour · 91mins

Yet another adaptation of Henry James's classic horror novel, and yet another adaptation which falls short of the original 1961 film version *The Innocents*. Director Rusty Lemorande has gone at the material and stripped it of all subtlety, which includes adding superfluous narration from Marianne Faithful and updating the context to 1960s England. Patsy Kensit is also sadly inadequate as the young governess whose charges appear possessed by their former manservant and governess and who seeks to save their souls. 📺

Patsy Kensit *Jenny* • Julian Sands *Mr Cooper* • Stéphane Audran *Mrs Grose* • Clare Szekeres *Flore* • Olivier Debray *Quint* • Joseph England *Miles* • Bryony Brind *Miss Jessel* • Marianne Faithfull *Narrator* ■ *Dir* Rusty Lemorande • *Scr* Rusty Lemorande, from the novella by Henry James

Turn the Key Softly ★★

Drama 1953 · UK · BW · 81mins

Worthy intentions are still discernible beneath this superficial social melodrama essaying 24 hours in the lives of three women (played by Yvonne Mitchell, Joan Collins and Kathleen Harrison) released from Holloway prison. In her first starring role, Mitchell makes a silk purse out of a sow's ear, but the rest of the cast go with the caricatures they're given. Extensive location work shows London in the grip of postwar austerity. Film-maker Richard Massingham, who starred in his own documentaries, is glimpsed as a bystander.

Joan Collins *Stella Jarvis* • Yvonne Mitchell *Monica Marsden* • Kathleen Harrison *Mrs Quilliam* • Terence Morgan *David* • Thora Hird *Landlady* • Dorothy Alison *Joan* • Glyn Houston *Bob* • Geoffrey Keen *Gregory* ■ *Dir* Jack Lee • *Scr* Maurice Cowan, Jack Lee, John Brophy, from a novel by John Brophy

Turnabout ★★

Comedy 1940 · US · Colour · 83mins

Producer Hal Roach – better known for his association with Laurel and Hardy – directed few films and we can see why with this one. Adapted from a sex fantasy by Thorne Smith (who also wrote *Topper*), this tells of the marital role-reversal of businessman John Hubbard and housewife Carole Landis through the magical powers of an Indian statue. Whatever satirical sting the idea might might have had is withdrawn by the cuteness and the inadequacy of the direction. A pity, as Roach was a good producer.

Adolphe Menjou *Phil Manning* • Carole Landis *Sally Willows* • John Hubbard *Tim Willows* • William Gargan *Joel Clare* • Verree Teasdale *Laura Bannister* • Mary Astor *Marion Manning* ■ *Dir* Hal Roach • *Scr* Mickell Novack, Berne Giler, John McClain, Rian James, from a novel by Thorne Smith

Turner & Hooch ★★★ PG

Comedy 1989 · US · Colour · 95mins

An enjoyable comedy vehicle for Tom Hanks, starring as dapper California detective Scott Turner, who teams up with slob-dog Hooch to solve a drug-related murder. While the script is sometimes short on laughs, British director Roger Spottiswoode keeps the action jogging along, giving Hanks room to display the kind of comic timing that established his Hollywood reputation in films like *Splash!* and *The Money Pit*. Hanks is well-served by his canine co-star, but Mare Winningham is sadly wasted. Contains swearing and violence. 📺 **DVD**

Tom Hanks *Scott Turner* • Mare Winningham *Emily Carson* • Craig T Nelson *Police Chief Hyde* • Reginald VelJohnson *Detective David Sutton* • Scott Paulin *Zack Gregory* • JC Quinn *Walter Boyett* • John McIntire *Amos Reed* • David Knell *Ernie* ■ *Dir* Roger Spottiswoode • *Scr* Dennis Shryack, Michael Blodgett, Daniel Petrie Jr, Jim Cash, Jack Epps Jr, from a story by Dennis Shryack, Michael Blodgett, Daniel Petrie Jr

The Turning ★ 18

Drama 1992 · US · Colour · 87mins

A 20-year old skinhead returns to his rural home town to torment his parents, who have recently decided to divorce. In an attempt to reconcile the family, he takes his dad's new girlfriend hostage. This movie, based on a stage play, would have deservedly languished in total obscurity if not for the fact that Gillian Anderson of *The X Files* fame made her motion picture debut here. Other than that, there's no reason to watch. 📺

Karen Allen *Glory* • Raymond J Barry *Mark Harnish* • Michael Dolan *Cliff Harnish* • Tess Harper *Martha Harnish* • Gillian Anderson *April Cavanaugh* ■ *Dir* Lou Puopolo • *Scr* Lou Puopolo, from the play *Home Fires Burning* by Chris Ceraso

The Turning Point ★★★

Crime 1952 · US · BW · 85mins

This powerful, well-cast Hollywood crime drama was one of several suggested by the Kefauver hearings on organised crime in the early fifties. It builds considerable tension as Edmond O'Brien's crimebusting lawyer heads an investigation into a city's

racketeering and is slowly exposed to the depth of corruption and villainy involved. William Holden is astutely cast as the cynical reporter who finds himself helping O'Brien. Director William Dieterle creates a consistent visual style to convey a dark world in which a villain will burn down an occupied tenement block in order to cover his tracks.

William Holden (1) *Jerry McKibbon* • Edmond O'Brien *John Conroy* • Alexis Smith *Amanda Waycross* • Tom Tully *Matt Conroy* • Ed Begley *Eichelberger* • Dan Dayton *Ackerman* ■ *Dir* William Dieterle • *Scr* Warren Duff, from the story *Storm in the City* by Horace McCoy

The Turning Point ★★★ PG

Drama 1977 · US · Colour · 114mins

A woman's movie in the guise of a ballet film, which was nominated for 11 Oscars but astonishingly won none, and has as its central dynamic the opposing forces of home and career. The American Ballet Theatre stops off in Oklahoma reuniting two former colleagues: Anne Bancroft, now prima ballerina in the company, and Shirley MacLaine, who opted for marriage and children. In the course of the movie both wonder whether they made the right decision, finally coming to terms with their lives and futures through the fate of MacLaine's daughter Leslie Browne. Much of the same ground was covered by that other box-office ballet favourite, Powell and Pressburger's *The Red Shoes*, but here the dancing is relegated to second place behind the drama. Nevertheless, the dancing is splendid and intoxicating – featuring many of the stars of the day including Baryshnikov and Sibley – which more than makes up for Bancroft's obvious lack of Terpsichorean skill. 📺

Shirley MacLaine *Deedee Rodgers* • Anne Bancroft *Emma Jacklin* • Mikhail Baryshnikov *Kopeikine* • Leslie Browne *Emilia* • Tom Skerritt *Wayne* • Martha Scott *Adelaide* • Antoinette Sibley *Sevilla* • Alexandra Danilova *Dahkarova* • Starr Danias *Carolyn* ■ *Dir* Herbert Ross • *Scr* Arthur Laurents

Turtle Beach ★★ 15

Political drama 1992 · US · Colour · 84mins

A strong subject – the plight of the Vietnamese boat people – is squandered by this movie in which everything except the scenery looks shoddy. Greta Scacchi plays an Australian journalist who heads for Malaysia to cover events as the locals hack the refugees to pieces. Scacchi's friend (Joan Chen) is a former prostitute married to the Australian High Commissioner (the script goes in for nifty coincidences like this) and domestic strife breaks out back home because Scacchi has seemingly abandoned her children. Preview responses were so bad that the film was drastically shortened, though it still bombed everywhere. The most dramatic event occurred off screen when Scacchi was hospitalised after being hit on the head by a falling coconut. Contains violence and sex scenes. 📺

Greta Scacchi *Judith Wilkes* • Joan Chen *Lady Minou Hobday* • Jack Thompson *Ralph Hamilton* • Art Malik *Kanan* • Norman Kaye *Sir Adrian Hobday* • Victoria Longley *Sancha*

Hamilton • Martin Jacobs *Richard* ■ *Dir* Stephen Wallace • *Scr* Ann Turner, from the novel by Blanche d'Alpuget

Turtle Diary ★★★ PG

Comedy drama 1985 · UK · Colour · 91mins

An odd two-hander from Glenda Jackson and Ben Kingsley as a pair of lonely liberals desperate to liberate the turtles in a zoo from what they see as their cruel plight. As you would expect, the acting is subtle and intelligent, with John Irvin's direction giving the film a stately but oversimplified pace. The movie's main problem is that it fails to bring out the great insights on Britain and the Brits which distinguish Russell Hoban's insightful novel from other stabs at the genre. ▭

Glenda Jackson *Neaera Duncan* • Ben Kingsley *William Snow* • Richard Johnson *Mr Johnson* • Michael Gambon *George Fairbairn* • Rosemary Leach *Mrs Inchcliff* • Eleanor Bron *Miss Neap* • Harriet Walter *Harriet* • Jeroen Krabbé *Sandor* • Nigel Hawthorne *Publisher* ■ *Dir* John Irvin • *Scr* Harold Pinter, Bill Darrid, from the novel by Russell Hoban

The Tuskegee Airmen
★★★★ PG

Wartime drama based on a true story
1995 · US · Colour · 101mins

In the tradition of *Glory*, this TV movie recalls the exploits of the first black aerial combat unit sent into action during the Second World War. Billeted at the Tuskegee air base, the "Fighting 99th" was formed to boost the civil rights cause, although the recruits were subjected to endless racial abuse from the top brass down. While the emphasis is on Hannibal Lee (played with some distinction by Laurence Fishburne), this is very much an ensemble piece, with Courtney B Vance, Cuba Gooding Jr and John Lithgow providing solid support. Contains swearing. ▭

Laurence Fishburne *Hannibal Lee* • Cuba Gooding Jr *Billy Roberts* • Allen Payne *Walter Peoples* • Malcolm-Jamal Warner *Leroy Cappy* • Courtney B Vance *Lieutenant Jeffrey Glenn* • AndréBraugher *Lieutenant Colonel Benjamin O Davis* • John Lithgow *Senator Conyers* ■ *Dir* Robert Markowitz • *Scr* Paris H Qualles, Ron Hutchinson, Trey Ellis, from a story by Robert Williams, TS Cook

The Tuttles of Tahiti ★★★ U

Comedy 1942 · US · BW · 91mins

A South Sea island comedy starring Charles Laughton, based on a novel by the authors of *Mutiny on the Bounty*, Charles Nordhoff and James Norman Hall. Laughton's performance here is far removed from his memorable Captain Bligh, but he evidently has fun as the idler who engages in a verbal battle with the formidable Florence Bates, while Bates's daughter Peggy Drake makes eyes at Laughton's son, the hunky Jon Hall. Mindless nonsense, but skilfully handled by director Charles Vidor, and the literate screenplay (co-written by James Hilton, author of *Lost Horizon*) makes this eminently watchable.

Charles Laughton *Jonas* • Jon Hall *Chester* • Peggy Drake *Tamara* • Victor Francen *Dr Blondin* • Florence Bates *Emily* • Gene Reynolds *Ru* • Curt Bois *Jensen* • Adeline De Walt Reynolds *Mama Ruau* ■ *Dir* Charles

Vidor • *Scr* S Lewis Meltzer, Robert Carson, James Hilton, from the novel *No More Gas* by Charles Nordhoff, James Norman Hall

Twelfth Night ★★★ U

Comedy 1996 · UK/US · Colour · 128mins

Beautifully designed in a pre-Raphaelite sort of way by Sophie Becher and with rich autumnal photography by Clive Tickner, this is an undeniably handsome version of Shakespeare's cruellest comedy. Yet, considering Trevor Nunn spent so long with the Royal Shakespeare Company, he brings surprisingly little to the play. The film skirts around virtually all of the social and sexual themes raised by the various misunderstandings and alliances that follow the storm-tossed arrival of Imogen Stubbs and brother Steven Mackintosh on the shores of Illyria. Notwithstanding the conservative direction, the performances, particularly of Helena Bonham Carter, Nigel Hawthorne and Richard E Grant, are highly polished. ▭

Helena Bonham Carter *Olivia* • Imogen Stubbs *Viola* • Nigel Hawthorne *Malvolio* • Richard E Grant *Sir Andrew Aguecheek* • Ben Kingsley *Feste* • Mel Smith *Sir Toby Belch* • Imelda Staunton *Maria* • Toby Stephens *Orsino* • Steven Mackintosh *Sebastian* • Nicholas Farrell *Antonio* ■ *Dir* Trevor Nunn • *Scr* Trevor Nunn, from the play by William Shakespeare

12 Angry Men ★★★★★ 12

Classic courtroom drama
1957 · US · BW · 112mins

Based on a television play by Reginald Rose about a lone juror holding out for a not guilty verdict with the remaining 11 ready to convict, this marvellous movie has become part of life's currency: there's no courtroom in the world where *12 Angry Men* is not either invoked or recalled. Henry Fonda stars as juror eight (no characters have names), and he also co-produced the movie. Although acclaimed as an instant classic, the film made no money on release, and Fonda wasn't able to pay himself his deferred acting fee. Fonda's integrity illuminates the film, which benefits immeasurably from debut director Sidney Lumet's masterly sense of cinema: the action takes place on a single claustrophobic set (an actual New York jury room), yet Lumet finds an infinite variety of visual set-ups and angles within the confines. Few films can genuinely be called brilliant, but this is one of them. ▭

Henry Fonda *Juror eight* • Lee J Cobb *Juror three* • Ed Begley *Juror ten* • EG Marshall *Juror four* • Jack Warden *Juror seven* • Martin Balsam *Juror one* • John Fiedler *Juror two* • Jack Klugman *Juror five* • Edward Binns *Juror six* • Joseph Sweeney *Juror nine* • George Voskovec *Juror 11* • Robert Webber *Juror 12* ■ *Dir* Sidney Lumet • *Scr* Reginald Rose, from his TV play

Twelve Angry Men ★★★★

Courtroom drama
1997 · US · Colour · 117mins

Writer Reginald Rose updated his original 1954 Emmy-winning TV play and 1957 feature screenplay for this classy made-for-cable remake. An all-star cast including George C Scott and Jack Lemmon headline this absorbing drama that centres around 12 jurors who, having been charged by the judge

to deliver a verdict, retire to the jury room to deliberate. It seems to be an open-and-shut case of an inner-city boy accused of murdering his father – except for one juror (Lemmon) who believes the youth to be innocent on grounds of "reasonable doubt". Thus begins a running war of words and actions that uncover prejudices and personal agendas which ultimately decide the fate of the young offender. Under William Friedkin's skilful direction, Lemmon gives a brilliant performance, as do the distinguished supporting cast of Hume Cronyn, Tony Danza, Ossie Davis, Edward James Olmos and Armin Mueller-Stahl.

Jack Lemmon *Juror No 8* • Courtney B Vance *Juror No 1* • Ossie Davis *Juror No 2* • George C Scott *Juror No 3* • Armin Mueller-Stahl *Juror No 4* • Dorian Harewood *Juror No 5* • James Gandolfini *Juror No 6* • Tony Danza *Juror No 7* • Hume Cronyn *Juror No 9* • Mykel T Williamson *Juror No 10* • Edward James Olmos *Juror No 11* • William Petersen *Juror No 12* ■ *Dir* William Friedkin • *Scr* Reginald Rose, from his TV play

The Twelve Chairs ★★★ U

Black comedy 1970 · US · Colour · 89mins

Russian bureaucrat Ron Moody learns that his mother is dying and races home, only to be told that she has hidden the family fortune in one of 12 dining chairs left in their ancestral home. He hurries home, only to find the chairs have gone to the Ministry of Housing to be relocated. Moody teams up with a young con man (Frank Langella) and the pair go off in search of the chairs. Mel Brooks's second feature (following *The Producers*) is a sustained laugh-fest with a much more disciplined plot than his later works. An old story perhaps, and primitive in parts, but there is still much to enjoy here. ▭

Ron Moody *Ippolit Vorobyaninov* • Frank Langella *Ostap Bender* • Dom DeLuise *Father Fyodor* • Mel Brooks *Tikon* • Bridget Brice *Young woman* • Robert Bernal *Curator* • David Lander *Engineer Bruns* • Diana Coupland *Madame Bruns* ■ *Dir* Mel Brooks • *Scr* Mel Brooks, from a story by Ilya Ilf, Yevgeny Petrov

Twelve Monkeys ★★★★ 15

Science-fiction thriller
1995 · US/UK/Ger/Jap/Fr · Colour · 123mins

Inspired by Chris Marker's acclaimed 1962 short film, *La Jetée*, this labyrinthine sci-fi thriller was penned by the co-writer of *Blade Runner*, David Webb Peoples, and his wife, Janet. Yet it's very much the work of Monty Python alumnus Terry Gilliam, who imposes his own pseudo-poetic vision onto a world that is doomed to viral annihilation unless time traveller Bruce Willis can prevent the disaster. Although it was Brad Pitt who landed the Oscar nomination for his twitchy performance as the leader of the Army of the Twelve Monkeys, it's Willis's anguished introvert who holds this gripping, hauntingly atmospheric film together. Contains swearing, violence and nudity. ▭ *DVD*

Bruce Willis *James Cole* • Madeleine Stowe *Dr Kathryn Railly* • Brad Pitt *Jeffrey Goines* • Christopher Plummer *Dr Goines* • Joseph Melito *Young Cole* • Jon Seda *Jose* • David Morse *Dr Peters* • Frank Gorshin *Dr Fletcher*

■ *Dir* Terry Gilliam • *Scr* David Peoples, Janet Peoples, from the film *La Jetée* by Chris Marker • *Cinematographer* Roger Pratt

12:01 ★★★★ 15

Science-fiction thriller
1993 · US · Colour · 90mins

Whereas *Groundhog Day* used the idea of living the same day over and over again for laughs, director Jack Sholder takes the same premise (from Richard Lupoff's 1973 novella) and goes for dynamic action to craft a clever thriller. Engaging Jonathan Silverman is the clerk caught in a time-loop involving an associate's murder, who tries to prevent the killing from taking place by changing incidental details each time the same day dawns. A neatly cut and highly polished gem, the tale is never contrived, continuously engrossing and has a gut-wrenching climax. ▭

Jonathan Silverman *Barry Thomas* • Helen Slater *Lisa Fredericks* • Martin Landau *Dr Thadius Moxley* • Jeremy Piven *Howard Richter* • Robin Bartlett *Ann Jackson* • Nicholas Surovy [Nicolas Surovy] *Robert Denk* ■ *Dir* Jack Sholder • *Scr* Philip Morton, from a short film by Jonathan Heap, Hillary Ripps, from the short story *12:01 PM* by Richard Lupoff

Twelve O'Clock High
★★★★ U

Second World War drama
1949 · US · BW · 132mins

To watch Gregory Peck crack under the strain of high command (he's in charge of a pressure-cooked American bomber unit based in England during the Second World War) is as alarming as the collapse of the Statue of Liberty: he's such a monument to liberal integrity. However, although he was nominated for an Oscar for his performance here, it was Dean Jagger who won the award for best supporting actor. It's all a wonderful example of ensemble acting, so any trophies are a bit redundant, though no doubt they were gratefully received. ▭

Gregory Peck *General Frank Savage* • Hugh Marlowe *Lieutenant Colonel Ben Gately* • Gary Merrill *Colonel Keith Davenport* • Dean Jagger *Major Harvey Stovall* • Millard Mitchell *General Pritchard* • Robert Arthur *Sergeant McIlhenny* • Paul Stewart *Captain "Doc" Kaiser* • John Kellogg *Major Cobb* ■ *Dir* Henry King • *Scr* Sy Bartlett, Beirne Lay Jr, from their novel

Twelve plus One ★★

Comedy 1969 · It/Fr · Colour · 95mins

There are 13 salon chairs, one of which contains a hidden fortune in jewels. Mel Brooks made a movie out of Ilf and Petrov's story in the same year, though neither version achieved much of a release anywhere. If Brooks's version is marginally the better film, this version is far more watchable due to the chocolate-box assortment of stars on show, including the positively sofa-like Orson Welles, ageing Italian heart-throb Vittorio Gassman and eccentric Englishman Terry-Thomas. Hollywood starlet Sharon Tate makes her final appearance before her murder. The same Russian story also formed the basis of two earlier British films – *Keep Your Seats, Please* (1936) and *The Fifth Chair* (1945) – as well as Cuban and Russian versions.

U = SUITABLE FOR ALL   Uc = SUITABLE FOR ALL, ESPECIALLY FOR YOUNG CHILDREN (VIDEO ONLY)   PG = PARENTAL GUIDANCE

Vittorio Gassman *Mike* • Orson Welles *Markau* • Mylene Demongeot *Judy* • Sharon Tate *Pat* • Terry-Thomas *Albert* • Tim Brooke-Taylor *Jackie* • Vittoria De Sica *Di Seta* ■ *Dir* Luciano Lucignani • *Scr* Nicolas Gessner, Marc Benham, from a story by Ilya Ilf, Yevgeny Petrov

The 12 Tasks of Asterix
★★★★ U

Animated comedy 1975 · Fr · Colour · 78mins
Written especially for the screen by René Goscinny and Albert Uderzo, this is the best of the Asterix cartoons, if only because something of the wit and ingenuity of the original books shines through. Determined to rid himself of the indomitable Gauls once and for all, Caesar sets Asterix and Obelix a Herculean quota of seemingly impossible tasks. But crocodiles, ghosts, Greek sprinters, German wrestlers and Egyptian sorcerers prove no match for our intrepid heroes, who even manage to get an A38 permit out of Rome's notoriously gnarled bureaucracy. Graphically on the conservative side, but otherwise brisk, slick and hugely entertaining.
Dir René Goscinny, Albert Uderzo • *Scr* René Goscinny, Albert Uderzo

Twentieth Century ★★★★★ U

Comedy 1934 · US · BW · 88mins
The title refers to the express train which ran between New York and Chicago, where movie producers and stars changed for the connection to Los Angeles. Aboard this deliriously enjoyable trip is a Broadway impresario (John Barrymore) and a recalcitrant Hollywood star (Carole Lombard). She is his protégé, but after several flops he's trying to lure her back to Broadway. Hecht and MacArthur's script, directed at supersonic speed by Howard Hawks, is a stream of acidic barbs, offering the stars ample scope for grandiose caricature. In fact, the arch theatricality of the piece functions as a comment on movie-making and the edgy relationship between Hollywood and Broadway in the early years of the talkies. First class all the way.
John Barrymore *Oscar Jaffe* • Carole Lombard *Lily Garland* • Walter Connolly *Webb* • Roscoe Karns *O'Malley* • Charles Levison [Charles Lane (1)] *Jacobs* • Etienne Girardot *Clark* • Dale Fuller *Sadie* ■ *Dir* Howard Hawks • *Scr* Charles Macarthur, Ben Hecht, from their play, from the play *Napoleon on Broadway* by Charles Bruce Millholland

Twenty Bucks ★★★ 15

Comedy drama 1993 · US · Colour · 87mins
An erratic but pleasing ensemble piece that follows the fortunes of a $20 note as it changes hands. This simple premise allows director Keva Rosenfeld to tell a bundle of stories – some funny, some downbeat – involving an eclectic cast that includes Brendan Fraser, Elisabeth Shue, Steve Buscemi, Christopher Lloyd, Linda Hunt and even soul diva Gladys Knight. Amazingly, despite the sprawling concept, Rosenfeld maintains a narrative thread for most of the film. Originated in 1935 by writer/producer Endre Bohem (who died in 1990), it was brought up to date by his son

Leslie (formerly one half of the Sparks pop duo), who also scripted the volcano disaster movie *Dante's Peak*.
Linda Hunt *Angeline* • Brendan Fraser *Sam* • Melora Walters *Stripper* • Gladys Knight *Mrs McCormac* • Elisabeth Shue *Emily Adams* • Steve Buscemi *Frank* • Christopher Lloyd *Jimmy* • William H Macy *Property Clerk* ■ *Dir* Keva Rosenfeld • *Scr* Endre Bohem, Leslie Bohem

28 Days ★★ 15

Drama 2000 · US · Colour · 109mins
Sandra Bullock is the Manhattan wild child forced into rehab after hijacking a limo at her sister's wedding and driving it into a house. Refusing to admit she has a drink problem, Sandy slowly comes to terms with her addiction with help from tough-but-fair guidance counsellor Steve Buscemi and the usual round of kooky Hollywood misfits. Directed by Betty Ford... sorry, Thomas, *28 Days* is the kind of touchy-feely, sentimental hogwash that's more likely to drive people to drink than keep them off it. From Viggo Mortensen's womanising sports star to Dominic West's irresponsible English drunkard, it's also notable for containing not a single sympathetic male character. 28 days? More like a life sentence.
Sandra Bullock *Gwen Cummings* • Viggo Mortensen *Eddie Boone* • Dominic West *Jasper* • Diane Ladd *Bobbie Jean* • Elizabeth Perkins *Lily* • Steve Buscemi *Cornell* • Alan Tudyk *Gerhardt* • Michael O'Malley *Oliver* • Marianne Jean-Baptiste *Roshanda* ■ *Dir* Betty Thomas • *Scr* Susannah Grant

The 25th Hour ★★

Second World War comedy drama 1967 · Fr/It/Yug · Colour · 118mins
A lavishly made, episodic war epic with Anthony Quinn as a Romanian peasant who is accused of being Jewish and condemned to slave labour. Shunned by the Jewish prisoners he becomes essentially stateless and thus a walking, talking metaphor. He changes sides and becomes a German soldier, all the time searching for his wife, Virna Lisi, who has been raped by the godless Russians. British, French, Italians and many others will have someone to root for in the United Nations cast. Turkish-born, French-domiciled director Henri Verneuil and Quinn immediately made another war movie together, *Guns for San Sebastian*. A French language film.
Anthony Quinn *Johann Moritz* • Virna Lisi *Suzanna Moritz* • Grégoire Aslan *Nicolai Dobresco* • Michael Redgrave *Defense counsel* • Serge Reggiani *Trajan Koruga* • Marcel Dalio *Strul* • Marius Goring *Col Müller* • Alexander Knox *Prosecutor* • John Le Mesurier *Magistrate* ■ *Dir* Henri Verneuil • *Scr* Henri Verneuil, François Boyer, Wolf Mankowitz, from the novel *La Vingt-Cinquieme Heure* by Constantin Virgil Gheorghiu

The 24 Hour Woman ★★

Comedy drama 1999 · US · Colour · 93mins
There are shades of the Diane Keaton vehicle *Baby Boom* in this comedy about a morning television show producer (Rosie Perez) who attempts to juggle between career and baby. While the film does have some funny moments, it's mainly due to a bitchy

supporting turn from Patti LuPone (as Perez's calculating boss) rather than Perez's screechy performance or the script from director Nancy Savoca. A disappointment, especially when you consider Savoca was the talented helmer of *Dogfight* and *True Love*.
Marianne Jean-Baptiste *Madeline Labelle* • Rosie Perez *Grace Santos* • Patti LuPone *Joan Marshall* • Margo Lynn *Karen Duffy* • Diego Serrano *Eddie Diaz* • Wendell Pierce *Roy Labelle* ■ *Dir* Nancy Savoca • *Scr* Nancy Savoca, Richard Guay

24 Hours to Midnight ★ 18

Martial arts action 1992 · US · Colour · 83mins
Martial arts actor Cynthia Rothrock has never had an American-made vehicle that's approached her work in Hong Kong. This particular effort is so bad, it's not surprising it was shelved until English-speaking audiences knew her better. When the gang he was going to testify against kills Rothrock's husband, she puts on her ninja outfit and picks off the gang one by one. It's bargain basement in every aspect, from the crumbling locations to the lamely choreographed fight sequences. It also contains one of the most obvious body doubles ever, provided for the nudity-shy Rothrock.
Cynthia Rothrock *Devon Grady* • Stack Pierce *"White Powder" Chan* • Bernie Pock *Lester McQueen* • Myra Lee Ann Jackson • Leo T Fong *Mr Big* ■ *Dir/Scr* Leo T Fong

20 Million Miles to Earth
★★★ PG

Science-fiction horror 1957 · US · BW · 79mins
A spaceship returning from an expedition to Venus crashes near Sicily, releasing a fast-growing reptilian beast that rampages through Rome in one of animation master Ray Harryhausen's best fantasy films, and his own personal favourite. The snake-tailed giant Ymir monster is also one of Harryhausen's finest creations: it has a well-defined personality and manages to evoke sympathy for its bewildered plight. The Ymir's fight with an elephant and the Roman locations add unique touches to this minor classic.
William Hopper *Calder* • Joan Taylor *Marisa* • Frank Puglia *Dr Leonardo* • John Zaremba *Dr Judson Uhl* • Thomas B Henry [Thomas Browne Henry] *General AD McIntosh* • Tito Vuolo *Police commissioner* ■ *Dir* Nathan Juran • *Scr* Bob Williams, Christopher Knopf, from a story by Charlott Knight, Ray Harryhausen

29 Acacia Avenue ★★★

Comedy 1945 · UK · BW · 84mins
The film version of the West End success about a couple who return home unexpectedly after a holiday and surprise their teenage offspring fails to fully disguise its theatrical origins. It nevertheless makes for pleasant period entertainment, with particularly likeable performances from British veterans Gordon Harker and Betty Balfour as the parents. Today, though, the problems encountered seem relatively trivial, but it's nice to see stars like Jimmy Hanley and Dinah Sheridan (once husband and wife) in

their youth. Unusually, this seemingly quintessential English piece was actually released in the US as *The Facts of Love*. Wonder what the Americans made of the accents?
Gordon Harker *Mr Robinson* • Betty Balfour *Mrs Robinson* • Jimmy Hanley *Peter* • Carla Lehmann *Fay* • Hubert Gregg *Michael* • Jill Evans *Joan* • Henry Kendall *Mr Wilson* • Dinah Sheridan *Pepper* ■ *Dir* Henry Cass • *Scr* Muriel and Sydney Box, from the play by Denis Constanduros, Mabel Constanduros

29th Street ★★★ 15

Comedy drama 1991 · US · Colour · 97mins
Frank Pesce Jr is a remarkable character. Cursed with a lucky streak that constantly seems to work against him, the garrulous New Yorker crops up in a cameo and also had a hand in the writing of this breezy comedy based on his win on the state lottery that ended up being more trouble than it was worth. Speaking Brooklynese like a native, Australian-born Anthony LaPaglia gives a spirited performance as Pesce, while Danny Aiello makes a splendid sparring partner as his opinionated father. But it's Lainie Kazan as Pesce's endearingly dotty mother who steals the show. Shame about the silly ending, though.
Danny Aiello *Frank Pesce Sr* • Lainie Kazan *Mrs Pesce* • Anthony LaPaglia *Frank Pesce Jr* • Robert Forster *Sergeant Tartaglia* • Frank Pesce *Vito Pesce* • Donna Magnani *Madeline Pesce* • Ron Karabatsos *Philly the Nap* ■ *Dir* George Gallo • *Scr* George Gallo, from a story by Frank Pesce Jr, James Franciscus

Twenty-One ★★★ 15

Drama 1991 · UK · Colour · 101mins
Before Patsy Kensit became better known as Mrs Liam Gallagher she had a long list of movies to her name, but it has to be said that most were forgettable. This, though, is one of her more commendable efforts: a brave, breezy twentysomething comedy drama, with Kensit discovering the dating game is not all that it is cracked up to be. With her straight-to-camera observations, Kensit has a lot of weight to carry, but generally convinces as a sparky, independent young woman. There are plenty of familiar faces in the supporting cast, including Rufus Sewell, Patrick Ryecart and Susan Wooldridge.
Patsy Kensit *Katie* • Jack Shepherd *Kenneth* • Patrick Ryecart *Jack* • Maynard Eziashi *Baldie* • Rufus Sewell *Bobby* • Sophie Thompson *Francesca* • Susan Wooldridge *Janet* • Robert Bathurst *Mr Metcalfe* ■ *Dir* Don Boyd • *Scr* Don Boyd, Zoe Heller, from a story by Don Boyd

21 Days ★★★ PG

Melodrama 1937 · UK · BW · 71mins
Here's a classy pedigree: Graham Greene co-wrote the screenplay of this Alexander Korda production based on a John Galsworthy West End hit. The story, about two lovers who spend precious time together before the man is tried for murder, features a well-cast Laurence Olivier making a dashing leading man, but it's his later real-life wife, the top-billed Vivien Leigh, who positively sparkles. Also on hand is Leslie Banks as Olivier's brother. Robert Newton and old-timers Esme Percy and Hay Petrie round off the

stage-drawn cast in this rather wordy but still worthy adaptation. ▢

Vivien Leigh *Wanda* • Laurence Olivier *Larry Durrant* • Leslie Banks *Keith Durrant* • Francis L Sullivan *Mander* • Hay Petrie *John Aloysius Evans* • Esme Percy *Henry Walenn* • Robert Newton *Tolly* • Victor Rietti *Antonio* ∎ *Dir* Basil Dean • *Scr* Graham Greene, Basil Dean, from the play *The First and the Last* by John Galsworthy

The 27th Day ★★★ U

Science-fiction 1957 · US · BW · 75mins

A quite extraordinary anti-communist tract masquerading as naive science fiction. An alien gives five people from five different countries a box of capsules capable of destroying life on their continent if opened. The capsules become harmless after 27 days or on the owner's death. Suicide or destruction is the choice until the Russian emissary is ordered to annihilate the western world. A real Cold War curio with an equally bizarre pay-off despite pedestrian direction by William Asher, who graduated to helming *Beach Party* movies.

Gene Barry *Jonathan Clark* • Valerie French *Eve Wingate* • George Voskovec *Professor Klaus Bechner* • Arnold Moss *The Alien* • Stefan Schnabel *Leader* • Ralph Clanton *Mr Ingram* • Friedrich Ledebur *Dr Karl Neuhaus* • Paul Birch *Admiral* ∎ *Dir* William Asher • *Scr* John Mantley, from his novel

20,000 Leagues under the Sea ★★★

Silent adventure 1916 · US · BW

Captain Nemo (Allan Holubar) and his crew of the submarine *Nautilus* journey through the ocean depths to a tropical island to rescue Nemo's daughter, encountering challenges such as a fight with an octopus. Written and directed by Stuart Paton, this is an impressive achievement for so early a film. The pioneering Williamson brothers built an underwater camera for the production, which cost Universal founder Carl Laemmle such a fortune that even the film's popularity was unable to yield a profit. ▢

Allan Holubar *Captain Nemo/Prince Daaker* • Jane Gail *A child of nature/Princess Daaker* • Dan Hanlon *Professor Aronnax* • Edna Pendleton *Aronnax's daughter* • Curtis Benton *Ned Land* • Matt Moore *Lt Bond* • Howard Crampton *Cyrus Harding* ∎ *Dir* Stuart Paton • *Scr* Stuart Paton, from the novel by Jules Verne

20,000 Leagues under the Sea ★★★★ U

Science-fiction adventure 1954 · US · Colour · 121mins

A marvellously designed and fabulously cast retelling of Jules Verne's fantasy saga about Captain Nemo and his submarine, *Nautilus*. Kirk Douglas gives a bravura performance as a harpoonist Ned Land, even using his own voice for the song *A Whale of a Tale*, but it's James Mason's Nemo that gives the film its strength. Peter Lorre adds comic relief, while Paul Lukas and especially the under-rated Robert J Wilke bring dignity to the proceedings. Director Richard Fleischer makes the most of the action sequences, notably a sensational

battle with a giant squid. A treat for grown-ups and children alike. ▢

Kirk Douglas *Ned Land* • James Mason *Captain Nemo* • Paul Lukas *Professor Aronnax* • Peter Lorre *Conseil* • Robert J Wilke *Mate on the Nautilus* • Carleton Young *John Howard* • Ted De Corsia *Captain Farragut* ∎ *Dir* Richard Fleischer • *Scr* Earl Felton, from the novel by Jules Verne

20,000 Years in Sing Sing ★★★

Prison drama 1933 · US · Colour · 81mins

One of Warners' torrid crime melodramas, allegedly "torn from today's headlines", filmed in a quasi-documentary style and providing gutsy entertainment in the guise of moral enlightenment. Spencer Tracy is a jailed gangster taking on the prison authorities, and Bette Davis is his moll. The movie wears its social conscience on its sleeve (*Happy Days Are Here Again* is on the soundtrack when the national grid has a sudden surge of demand), but it also remains solid enough, with good performances from the two stars and sleek direction from Hollywood's finest workhorse, Michael Curtiz.

Spencer Tracy *Tom Connors* • Bette Davis *Fay* • Lyle Talbot *Bud* • Arthur Byron *Warden Long* • Grant Mitchell *Dr Ames* • Warren Hymer *Hype* • Louis Calhern *Joe Finn* • Sheila Terry *Billie* ∎ *Dir* Michael Curtiz • *Scr* Courtney Terrett, Robert Lord, Wilson Mizner, Brown Holmes, from the book by Warden Lewis E Lawes

23 Paces to Baker Street ★★★★ U

Thriller 1956 · US · Colour · 102mins

Between appearing in melodramatic Graham Greene and Georges Simenon adaptations, former musical star Van Johnson seemed determined to confirm his acting versatility in this cracking London-set thriller, starring as a blind playwright who overhears dastardly doings. Londoners will enjoy seeing director Henry Hathaway's skewwhiff city geography, and there's a fair amount of on-screen fog. However, despite the clichés, the suspense is kept taut, the English support cast is faultless, and American import Vera Miles is notably sympathetic. One of a series of 20th Century-Fox British-set movies made in the fifties, which also included hits like *The Man Who Never Was* and *Sink the Bismarck!*.

Van Johnson *Phillip Hannon* • Vera Miles *Jean Lennox* • Cecil Parker *Bob Matthews* • Patricia Laffan *Miss Alice MacDonald* • Maurice Denham *Inspector Grovening* • Estelle Winwood *Barmaid* • Liam Redmond *Mr Murch/Joe* ∎ *Dir* Henry Hathaway • *Scr* Nigel Balchin, from the novel *A Warrant for X* by Philip MacDonald

TwentyFourSeven ★★★ 15

Comedy drama 1997 · UK · BW · 92mins

The first full-length feature from rising British director Shane Meadows provides the often under-used Bob Hoskins with his best role in years. Hoskins plays an amiable former boxer who sets up a council-estate fight club as a focus for the unharnessed energies of local youth. It's well-intentioned, but things don't always run smoothly. Performances, many of

them from first-time actors, pack a punch, and Meadows brings a genuine feel-of-the-real to proceedings via his decision to shoot it all in black and white. Well worth going a few rounds with. Contains violence and swearing. ▢

Bob Hoskins *Alan Darcy* • Mat Hand *Fagash* • Sun Hand *Jordan* • Sarah Thom *Louise* • Sammy Pasha *Jimmy* • Gina Aris *Sharon* • James Corden *Tonka* • Danny Nussbaum *Tim* • Bruce Jones *Geoff, Tim's dad* ∎ *Dir* Shane Meadows • *Scr* Shane Meadows, Paul Fraser

Twice Dead ★★ 18

Thriller 1988 · US · Colour · 83mins

When a family moves into a creaky old mansion, the ghost of a long-dead movie star is disturbed by their skirmishes with a gang of local thugs. This is a strictly by-the-numbers offering from the less than prolific director Bert L Dragin, who went on to make only one other movie, and adds nothing new to the mothballed haunted house genre. Nevertheless, there are a few effective mood swings as light relief suddenly gives way to violent death – the punks are initially scared off using bogus horror props and then brutally dispatched for real. On the whole, though, it's one to avoid. ▢

Tom Breznahan *Scott* • Jill Whitlow *Robin/Myrna* • Jonathan Chapin *Crip/Tyler* • Christopher Burgard *Silk* • Sam Melville *Harry* • Brooke Bundy *Sylvia* • Joleen Lutz *Candy* • Todd Bridges *Petie* ∎ *Dir* Bert L Dragin • *Scr* Bert L Dragin, Robert McDonnell

Twice in a Lifetime ★★★★ 15

Drama 1985 · US · Colour · 106mins

A fine drama in which the cast and production team use their considerable experience to good effect. Colin Welland, who won an Oscar for his *Chariots of Fire* screenplay, was responsible for the script, which tells an all-too-common story of a family being torn apart when the husband strays, in this case with a local barmaid on the eve of his 50th birthday. The well-judged performances by Gene Hackman as the blue-collar husband, Ellen Burstyn as his quietly despairing wife and Ann-Margret as the other woman help make Bud Yorkin's film a moving, and at times riveting, experience. ▢

Gene Hackman *Harry Mackenzie* • Ann-Margret *Audrey Minnelli* • Ellen Burstyn *Kate Mackenzie* • Amy Madigan *Sunny* • Ally Sheedy *Helen Mackenzie* • Stephen Lang *Keith* • Darrell Larson *Jerry Mackenzie* ∎ *Dir* Bud Yorkin • *Scr* Colin Welland

Twice round the Daffodils ★★ PG

Comedy 1962 · UK · BW · 85mins

Oh dear, a watered-down *Carry On Nurse* set (tastefully) in a male tuberculosis ward, with nurse Juliet Mills running the show. The *Carry On* producer/director team of Peter Rogers and Gerald Thomas would occasionally make these forays away from their popular series, but would invariably use a similar cast. Here's Joan Sims and Kenneth Williams again, plus those students from *Doctor in the House* (made by Gerald Thomas's brother Ralph), Donalds Sinden and

Houston, chasing nurses Jill Ireland and Nanette Newman. This obsession with nurses continued in *Nurse on Wheels* (also with Mills and the excellent Ronald Lewis). ▢

Juliet Mills *Catty* • Donald Sinden *Ian Richards* • Donald Houston *John Rhodes* • Kenneth Williams *Harry Halfpenny* • Ronald Lewis *Bob White* • Andrew Ray *Chris Walker* • Joan Sims *Harriet Halfpenny* • Jill Ireland *Janet* ∎ *Dir* Gerald Thomas • *Scr* Norman Hudis, from the play *Ring for Catty* by Patrick Cargill, Jack Beale

Twice Told Tales ★★

Horror 1963 · US · Colour · 119mins

United Artists borrowed AIP's successful *Tales of Terror* omnibus formula, and its star Vincent Price, for this crudely creepy anthology which failed to give horror writer Nathaniel Hawthorne the same box-office cred already achieved by Edgar Allan Poe. Given the sparse production values and varying degrees of horror and atmosphere, it's not difficult to see why, despite the fine source material. In *Dr Heidegger's Experiment*, Price discovers the elixir of eternal youth, while as a Paduan scientist in *Dr Rappaccini's Daughter*, he tragically injects his beloved offspring with a potion that makes her lethal to the touch. Buried treasures, warlocks and ancestral karma are at the devilish heart of *The House of Seven Gables*. Directed by Sydney Salkow, the film still offers enough lush photography and great ensemble acting to make it a chocolate box fantasy horror that works more often than not.

Vincent Price *Alex Medbourne/Dr Rappaccini/Gerald Pyncheon* • Sebastian Cabot *Dr Carl Heidegger* • Mari Blanchard *Sylvia Ward* • Brett Halsey *Giovanni Guastconti* • Abraham Sofaer *Prof Pietro Baglioni* • Joyce Taylor *Beatrice Rappaccini* • Beverly Garland *Alice Pyncheon* • Richard Denning *Jonathan Maulle* • Jacqueline de Wit *Hannah* ∎ *Dir* Sidney Salkow • *Scr* Robert E Kent, from stories by Nathaniel Hawthorne

Twice Two ★★★ U

Comedy 1933 · US · BW · 20mins

Laurel and Hardy reached their creative peak in the thirties with films that ranged from the sublime (*The Music Box*) to the ordinary. This oddity falls in between and revives a gimmick from *Brats* (1930), where they played their own sons. That film used elaborate sets and trick photography, but here they tackle four roles utilising clever editing. Stanley and Oliver have each married the other's twin sisters. They share a house and the "boys" work together. The nub of the story is a celebratory dinner during which the "girls" chaotically fall out. The female voices were dubbed with the duo in drag. ▢

Stan Laurel *Stan/Mrs Hardy* • Oliver Hardy *Ollie/Mrs Laurel* • Baldwin Cooke *Soda jerk* • Charlie Hall *Delivery boy* • Ham Kinsey *Passer-by outside store* • Carol Tevis *Mrs Hardy* • Mae Wallace *Mrs Laurel* ∎ *Dir* James Parrott • *Scr* Stanley Laurel

Twice upon a Time ★★★ U

Animated fantasy adventure
1983 · US · Colour · 75 mins

A little-seen and neglected animation feature, executive produced by George

Lucas, and using the old-fashioned Lumage technique of photographing miniature cut-outs through glass. Ralph the All-Purpose Animal and his sidekick Mum (who only speaks in noises) heroically fight Synonamess Botch, the tyrannical ruler of the Murkworks Nightmare Factory, when he uses his maniacal powers to invade the sweet dreams of the gentle Rushers of Din with horrific and scary images. The unusual animation and sophisticated humour make director John Korty and Charles Swenson's unique flight of fancy a treat for older children and discerning adults.

Lorenzo Music *Ralph* • Judith Kaham Kampmann *Fairy Godmother* • Marshall Efron *Synonamess Botch* • James Cranna *Rod Rescueman Scuzzbopper* • Julie Payne *Flora Fauna* • Hamilton Camp *Greensleeves* ■ *Dir* John Korty, Charles Swenson • *Scr* John Korty, Charles Swenson, Suella Kennedy, Bill Couturie, from a story by John Korty, Suella Kennedy, Bill Couturie

Twice Upon a Time ★★
Romantic fantasy   1998 · US · Colour

Molly Ringwald, once queen of the Brat Pack but now all grown-up in TV movie limbo, stars as an unhappy television producer in this silly little fantasy in which a wish on a turkey wishbone transports her to an alternate universe. In this new place she is married to her ex-beau Rob Youngblood, a handsome sports celebrity, and producing a hit show. However, when her current boyfriend George Newbern falls for her arch-nemesis, she soon regrets her wish and searches for a way to return to her old life. Ringwald is fine as the lost-in-space malcontent but the cumbersome plot and trite dialogue leave her little to work with. The old "be careful what you wish for" adage is definitely in play here but you still might regret watching this wishy-washy comedy.

Molly Ringwald *Beth Sager* • Ellen Crawford *Peg Sager* • George Newbern *Joe Townsend* • Melora Walters *Alana Merribon* • Shawnee Smith *Martie Fowler* • Rob Youngblood *Nick Fowler* ■ *Dir* Thom Eberhardt • *Scr* Scott Fifer

Twilight ★★★ 15
Detective drama 1998 · US · Colour · 90mins

It's always a pleasure to see Gene Hackman, Susan Sarandon and Paul Newman at work, and this low-key detective drama that harks back to the heyday of *film noir* is no exception. Newman stars as a private eye who lives with cancer-stricken actor Hackman and his wife Sarandon. Asked to deliver blackmail money, Newman finds himself resurrecting a 20-year-old murder case involving Sarandon's ex-husband. Newman as a seventysomething is still convincing in both action and love scenes, but the overall pace of the film tends towards the sluggish and its reflective mood explains why it didn't make it big at the box office. Contains swearing, violence and sex scenes. ▭

Paul Newman *Harry Ross* • Susan Sarandon *Catherine Ames* • Gene Hackman *Jack Ames* • Stockard Channing *Verna* • Reese Witherspoon *Mel Ames* • Giancarlo Esposito *Reuben* • James Garner *Raymond Hope* • Liev Schreiber *Jeff Willis* ■ *Dir* Robert Benton • *Scr* Robert Benton, Richard Russo

Twilight Avengers ★★
Spaghetti western   1970 · It · Colour

Director Adalberto Albertini was shrewd enough to realise that several masters of the spaghetti western appended English pseudonyms to their films: Sergio Corbucci took Stanley Corbett, Enzo Barboni used EB Clucher and Antonio Margheriti masqueraded as Anthony B Dawson. The fact that Albertini chose to call himself Al Albert is symptomatic of the creative poverty that blights this tame tale. Set against the backdrop of the great Californian gold rush, it grimly follows the tried and trusted formula, and not even the pitting of a troupe of travelling players against the desperadoes peps it up. Italian dialogue dubbed into English.

Tony Kendall • Helen Parker • Peter Thorrys • Robert Widmark ■ *Dir* Al Albert [Adalberto Albertini]

Twilight for the Gods ★★
Drama   1958 · US · Colour · 118mins

A love story between Rock Hudson and the *Cannibal*, a sailing ship that's rotten to the timbers and threatens to sink with the usual assortment of passengers – a call girl, suicidal businessman and refugees from communism. Filmed in and around Hawaii, it gave Hudson a well-earned break from his romantic melodramas and the chance to play a disgraced, drunken wreck not unlike Humphrey Bogart in *The Caine Mutiny*.

Rock Hudson *Captain David Bell* • Cyd Charisse *Charlotte King* • Arthur Kennedy *Ramsay* • Leif Erickson *Hutton* • Charles McGraw *Yancy* • Ernest Truex *Butterfield* • Richard Haydn *Wiggins* • Judith Evelyn *Ethel* ■ *Dir* Joseph Pevney • *Scr* Ernest K Gann, from his novel

Twilight of Honor ★★★
Drama   1963 · US · BW · 104mins

This is something of a *déjà vu* melodrama. Richard Chamberlain – on sabbatical from *Dr Kildare* – plays a small-town, small-time lawyer who takes on the defence of a young hooligan (Oscar nominee Nick Adams) aided by the sage advice of veteran attorney Claude Rains. Not exactly a star-making turn for Chamberlain but it's directed with some style by Boris Sagal, though we've seen it all before.

Richard Chamberlain *David Mitchell* • Joey Heatherton *Laura Mae Brown* • Nick Adams *Ben Brown* • Claude Rains *Art Harper* • Joan Blackman *Susan Harper* • James Gregory *Norris Bixby* • Pat Buttram *Cole Clinton* • Jeanette Nolan *Amy Clinton* ■ *Dir* Boris Sagal • *Scr* Henry Denker, from the novel by Al Dewlen

The Twilight of the Golds ★★
Drama   1996 · US · Colour · 91mins

There is a lot of screaming in this TV movie based on the stage play by Jonathan Tolins. Husband Jon Tenney and wife Jennifer Beals learn through prenatal testing that their unborn son has the genetic makeup for homosexuality. As Beals's brother (Brendan Fraser) is gay, this is a sensitive subject. Years of underlying feelings between her brother and her parents (Faye Dunaway, Garry

Marshall) come to the surface. Director Ross Marks must think that having his actors yelling their lines will make the audience understand them better, and the overwrought performances ruin an interesting premise.

Jennifer Beals *Suzanne Stein* • Faye Dunaway *Phyllis Gold* • Garry Marshall *Walter Gold* • Brendan Fraser *David Gold* • Jon Tenney *Rob Stein* • Rosie O'Donnell *Jackie* • John Schlesinger *Adrian Lodge* • Patrick Bristow *Brandon* ■ *Dir* Ross Kagan Marks • *Scr* Seth Bass, Jonathan Tolins, from the play by Jonathan Tolins

The Twilight of the Ice Nymphs ★★★
Drama   1997 · Can · Colour · 91mins

Cult Canadian director Guy Maddin is one of the most challenging and idiosyncratic talents of contemporary cinema, but his work is something of an acquired taste. Extrapolating from the bizarre stylisation of 1992's *Careful*, Maddin here fashions another opaque exercise in eccentric melodrama and obscure film references. He's helped by a cast of notables which includes Shelley Duvall, Frank Gorshin and Alice Krige, all of whom seem in tune with their director's weirdness. However, the film's leading man, Nigel Whitmey, had his name removed from the credits after Maddin redubbed his dialogue.

Pascale Bussières *Juliana Kossel* • Shelley Duvall *Amelia Glahn* • Frank Gorshin *Cain Ball* • Alice Krige *Zephyr Eccles* • RH Thomson *Dr Issac Solti* • Ross McMillan *Matthew Eccles* ■ *Dir* Guy Maddin • *Scr* George Toles

Twilight on the Prairie ★★ U
Western   1944 · US · BW · 61mins

An enjoyable musical, featuring Johnny Downs and Vivian Austin, but distinguished by the presence of both Australian-born comic Leon Errol and the great Jack Teagarden and his Orchestra. It contains such fabulous musical numbers as *I Got Mellow in the Yellow of the Moon*, *The Sip Nip Song* and *Where the Prairie Meets the Sky*, all sadly forgotten today. Very pleasant for fans of obscure forties musical westerns; others should give it a miss by a mile!

Johnny Downs *Bucky Williams* • Vivian Austin *Sally Barton* • Leon Errol *Cactus Barton* • Connie Haines *Ginger Lee* • Eddie Quillan *Phil Travers* ■ *Dir* Jean Yarbrough • *Scr* Clyde Bruckman, from a story by Warren Wilson

Twilight People ★★ 15
Horror   1973 · Phil · Colour · 75mins

After *Terror Is a Man*, *Beast of Blood* and *The Mad Doctor of Blood Island*, the fourth unofficial reworking of HG Wells's *The Island of Dr Moreau* from Filipino fright-master Eddie Romero is the funniest of the lot. John Ashley is transported to a remote South Pacific island where a crazed doctor is creating the usual half human/half animal rebellious menagerie. The nice line in crude monsters includes a flying bat man, an antelope man and blaxploitation icon Pam Grier as the Panther woman. Roger Corman handled executive producer chores on this silly yet quite gory exploiter. ▭

John Ashley *Matt Farrell* • Pat Woodell *Neva Gordon* • Pam Grier *Panther woman* ■ *Dir* Eddie Romero • *Scr* Eddie Romero, Jerome Small

Twilight Zone: Rod Serling's Lost Classics ★★ 12
Supernatural thriller
1994 · US · Colour · 88mins

A bit of a misnomer, this one. A couple of unfilmed scripts (not intended for *The Twilight Zone* TV series) were found by creator Rod Serling's widow, Carol, and turned into a television movie. The first segment stars Amy Irving in a lacklustre tale called *The Theatre*. The second feature-length story is called *Where the Dead Are*, and stars Patrick Bergin and Jack Palance. Basically a homage to HG Wells, the plot has Bergin as a Boston surgeon who treks to a mysterious island. There he finds mad doctor Palance experimenting with human tissue regeneration. It's more a period horror tale than a weird *Twilight Zone* segment, and the pedestrian direction and lacklustre atmosphere make this a strictly routine affair, despite screenplay involvement by veteran sci-fi writer Richard Matheson. Contains some swearing. ▭

Amy Irving *Melissa Sanders* • Gary Cole *James* • Heidi Swedberg *Joanie* • Patrick Bergin *Dr Benjamin Ramsey* • Jack Palance *Jeremy Wheaton* • Jenna Stern *Susan Wheaton* • Julia Campbell *Maureen* • Peter McRobbie *Dr Ames* ■ *Dir* Robert Markowitz • *Scr* Richard Matheson, Rod Serling

Twilight Zone: the Movie ★★★ 15
Cult supernatural drama
1983 · US · Colour · 96mins

Despite the involvement of Hollywood major league directors Steven Spielberg, John Landis and Joe Dante, it was Australian George Miller, responsible for cult hit *Mad Max* and its sequel, who produced the one truly scary section of this feature-length stab at Rod Serling's classic TV series. In Miller's tale, paranoid passenger John Lithgow is the only person on a plane who can see a creature gnawing away at the wings. The rest of the stories are a mixed bag: the Spielberg oldies' story is pure slush; Dante's wickedly cruel mixture of animation and live action eventually goes the same way; while Landis's contribution remains overshadowed by the controversial death of star Vic Morrow during filming. Contains violence and swearing. ▭

Burgess Meredith *Narrator* • Dan Aykroyd *Passenger* • Albert Brooks *Driver* • Vic Morrow *Bill* • Doug McGrath *Larry* • Charles Hallahan *Ray* • Bill Quinn *Conroy* ■ *Dir* John Landis, Steven Spielberg, Joe Dante, George Miller (2) • *Scr* John Landis, George Clayton Johnson, Josh Rogan, Richard Matheson

Twilight's Last Gleaming ★★★★★ 15
Political thriller
1977 · US/W Ger · Colour · 137mins

If Colonel Kurtz from *Apocalypse Now* had survived, he might have ended up like Burt Lancaster in this absolutely riveting thriller. Lancaster, a brilliant, medal-heavy war hero, decides to force the US government to come clean about why it fought in Vietnam. He does this by hijacking a nuclear missile silo and periodically raises the temperature by pushing the right buttons. While President Charles Durning sweats, Richard Widmark and the army gathers outside Lancaster's underground bunker. As with Lancaster's 1964 movie *Seven Days in May*, this is a clever, plausible and subversive movie that capitalised on President Carter's avowed policy of open government. Contains some swearing and violence. ▭

Burt Lancaster *Lawrence Dell* • Richard Widmark *Martin MacKenzie* • Charles Durning *President Stevens* • Melvyn Douglas *Zachariah Guthrie* • Paul Winfield *Willis Powell* • Burt Young *Augie Garvas* • Joseph Cotten *Arthur Renfrew* ■ *Dir* Robert Aldrich • *Scr* Ronald M Cohen, Edward Huebsch, from the novel *Viper Three* by Walter Wager

Twin Beds ★★★ U

Comedy 1942 · US · Colour · 83mins

This fast, furious and often funny bedroom farce has George Brent and Joan Bennett as newlyweds who never seem able to be alone together because their apartment keeps being invaded by two other couples. When they all decide to move away from each other, they find they have all moved to the same apartment block. As the two other women are played by the delightful Una Merkel and Glenda Farrell, we can only be pleased. The film refers to the war obliquely, but the only battle is the battle of the sexes.

George Brent *Mike Abbott* • Joan Bennett *Julie Abbott* • Mischa Auer *Nicolai Cherupin* • Una Merkel *Lydia* • Glenda Farrell *Sonya Cherupin* • Ernest Truex *Larky* • Margaret Hamilton *Norah* ■ *Dir* Tim Whelan • *Scr* Curtis Kenyon, Kenneth Earl, E Edwin Moran, from a play by Margaret Mayo, Salisbury Field

Twin Detectives ★★

Thriller 1976 · US · Colour · 78mins

The whole point of this TV movie was to persuade executives to award a series to Lillian Gish, the veteran actress who began her career with pioneering director DW Griffith back in 1912. However, this tale of twin detectives who take on the gang behind a fake psychic racket lacks the invention to sustain its intriguing premise. More to the point, real-life twins Jim and Jon Hager simply don't have the screen presence to carry the action, despite the valiant efforts of director Robert Day to hide their inadequacies.

Jim Hager *Tony Thomas* • Jon Hager *Shep Thomas* • Lillian Gish *Billy Jo Haskins* • Patrick O'Neal *Leonard Ranier* ■ *Dir* Robert Day • *Scr* Robert Specht, from a story by Robert Specht, Robert Carrington, Everett Chambers

Twin Dragons ★★★ PG

Action comedy 1992 · HK · Colour · 99mins

Guying Jean-Claude Van Damme's *Double Impact*, this sprightly chopsocky comedy once again has Jackie Chan combining the styles of Bruce Lee and Charlie Chaplin to entertaining effect. As twins separated at birth, Chan keeps both girlfriends Maggie Cheung and Nina Chi Li and a

gangster's gormless henchmen guessing through a series of slick set pieces. Such is the pace of the action that it's impossible to detect the seams between the scenes handled by co-directors Tsui Hark and Ringo Lam. Unfortunately, the matte work that allows Chan to act with himself is not nearly so invisible. Cantonese dialogue dubbed into English. ▭

Jackie Chan *Boomer/John Ma* • Cheung Man-Yuk [Maggie Cheung] *Barbara* • Nina Chi Li *Tammy* • Anthony Chan *Hotel staffer* • Philip Chan *Hotel manager* • John Wu [John Woo] *Priest* ■ *Dir* Lam Ling-Tung [Ringo Lam], Tsui Hark • *Scr* Barry Wong, Tsui Hark, Cheung Tung Jo, Yik Wong, Val Kuklowsky, Rod Dean

Twin Falls Idaho ★★

Drama 1999 · US · Colour · 110mins

Screenwriters and real-life brothers Mark and Michael Polish take a page from David Lynch in this bizarre movie. They also play the parts of Siamese twins holed up in a seedy hotel who are eventually befriended by hooker Michele Hicks. It starts off well, promising to be darkly funny, tragic and a fascinating look at the nature of twins. After Hicks's initially shocked character takes an active interest in the two, the movie's momentum comes to a dead halt and doesn't revive until the last 20 minutes. Certainly unforgettable and haunting at times, but it's mostly much ado about nothing.

Michele Hicks *Penny* • Teresa Hill *Sissy* • Robert Beecher *D'Walt* • Michael Polish *Francis Falls* • Mark Polish *Blake Falls* • Patrick Bauchau *Miles* • Lesley Ann Warren *Francine* ■ *Dir* Michael Polish • *Scr* Michael Polish, Mark Polish

Twin Peaks: Fire Walk with Me ★★★★ 18

Cult drama 1992 · US · Colour · 129mins

The exploding TV set at the beginning is the tip-off that David Lynch's deeply meaningful, horrific and disturbing descent into Laura Palmer's private hell, which begins seven days before she's found wrapped in plastic, will pursue dark introspective themes that his landmark pseudo-psychic maxi-series dared only hint at. Undervalued on cinema release, the Sultan of Strange's Rubik cube glorification of the terror-filled magic of life is a spaced-out odyssey of extraordinary obsession and power. As one hypnotic sequence follows another (the strobe-lit disco degradation perturbs the most), Lynch's startling contemplation on our unfair universe is a must for *Twin Peaks* freaks. Contains swearing, drug abuse and nudity. ▭

Sheryl Lee *Laura Palmer* • Ray Wise *Leland Palmer* • Moira Kelly *Donna Hayward* • David Bowie *Phillip Jeffries* • Chris Isaak *Special Agent Chester Desmond* • Harry Dean Stanton *Carl Rodd* • Kyle MacLachlan *Special Agent Dale Cooper* • Mädchen Amick *Shelly Johnson* ■ *Dir* David Lynch • *Scr* David Lynch, Robert Engels • *Cinematographer* Ronald Victor Garcia • *Music* Angelo Badalamenti

Twin Sisters ★★ 15

Drama 1992 · Can/US · Colour · 88mins

A glossy but laughably melodramatic TV movie that features two unconvincing performances from

Stepfanie Kramer. She stars as twins, one of whom is caught up in a murderous intrigue when she foolishly tries to find out what has happened to her wayward sister. James Brolin sleepwalks through his supporting role while third-billed Frederic Forrest is clearly slumming. Sadly, this would-be thriller is fatally short of both suspense and surprises. Contains violence and nudity. ▭

Stepfanie Kramer *Lynn/Carole* • Susan Almgren *Sophie* • Frederic Forrest *Delvaux* • James Brolin *Michael* • Larry Dane *Boone* • Richard Zeman *Carson* • Vlasta Vrana *Reeves* • Robert Morelli *Jarrett* ■ *Dir* Tom Berry • *Scr* David Preston, from a story by Jean-Marc Paland, from an idea by André Koob

Twin Sisters of Kyoto ★★★★

Melodrama 1963 · Jap · Colour · 107mins

Taken from the novel by Yasunari Kawabata, this Oscar-nominated class drama concerns sisters who were abandoned at birth because twins were reputed to bring bad luck. Now the daughter of a wealthy merchant, Chieko goes in search of her sibling, only for their contentment to be short-lived as she becomes convinced Naeko is attempting to steal her beau. Appearing in over 100 films, Shima Iwashita worked many times with Yasujiro Ozu and her husband, Masahiro Shinoda. But nothing surpasses her dual performance in this affecting study of identity and self-image which is handled with tact and insight by Noboru Nakamura. In Japanese with English subtitles.

Shima Iwashita *Chieko/Naeko* • Seiji Miyaguchi *Takichiro Sada* • Teruo Yoshida *Ryusuke Mizuki* • Tamotsu Hayakawa *Shinichi Mizuki* ■ *Dir* Noboru Nakamura • *Scr* Toshihide Gondo, from the novel *Koto* by Yasunari Kawabata

Twin Town ★★ 18

Black comedy 1997 · UK · Colour · 95mins

Described by some as a Welsh *Trainspotting*, this muddled, Swansea-set black comedy does share some superficial law-breaking similarities, but has none of the style, energy or invention of that movie. Real-life brothers Llyr Evans and Rhys Ifans (*Notting Hill*) are manic, moral-free young criminals who exact revenge when their builder father is refused compensation for an accident at work. There's no shortage of candid sex, drugs and rock 'n' roll (from top Welsh bands, naturally), but the fun soon drains away and the tone turns really nasty, bumping off men, woman and pets in the pursuit of a fashionably dark morality. Contains sex scenes and drug abuse. ▭

Llyr Evans *Julian Lewis* • Rhys Ifans *Jeremy Lewis* • Dorien Thomas *Greyo* • Dougray Scott *Terry Walsh* • Biddug Williams *Mrs Mort* • Ronnie Williams *Mr Mort* • Huw Ceredig *Fatty* ■ *Dir* Kevin Allen • *Scr* Kevin Allen, Paul Durden

The Twinkle in God's Eye ★★ U

Western 1955 · US · BW · 72mins

In this personally produced project, Mickey Rooney plays a former wild boy who turns over a new leaf to become a

parson and brings religion to a frontier mining town. Rooney was so keen on the project he also wrote the title song (but refrains from singing it). In actual fact, Rooney's self-assurance suits the part and he converts the toughest of hombres as well as the dancing girls in the saloon. Coleen Gray co-stars as one of the floozies with Hugh O'Brian as the gambling hall proprietor.

Mickey Rooney *Reverend Macklin* • Coleen Gray *Laura* • Hugh O'Brian *Marty* • Joey Forman *Ted* • Don "Red" Barry [Donald Barry] *Dawson* • Touch Connors [Mike Connors] *Lou* • Jill Jarmyn *Millie* • Kem Dibbs *Johnny* ■ *Dir* George Blair • *Scr* PJ Wolfson

Twinky ★ 15

Romantic drama
1969 · UK/It · Colour · 94mins

Before he hit paydirt with *The Omen* and (later) the *Lethal Weapon* franchise, director Richard Donner churned out this abysmal relic from Swinging London that not even its distinguished supporting cast can salvage. Twinky is Susan George, a 16-year-old schoolgirl who elopes with an American novelist played by Charles Bronson. Both sets of parents, on both sides of the Atlantic, are appalled and most viewers will be too as dear mini-skirted, rapidly maturing Twinky participates in street demos and sets her sights on a career as a hippy. The overall tone suggests a sort of *Carry On Lolita*, replete with songs by *Carry On* regular Jim Dale. ▭

Charles Bronson *Scott Wardman* • Susan George *Lola Twinky Londonderry* • Trevor Howard *Grandfather* • Honor Blackman *Mrs Londonderry* • Michael Craig *Mr Londonderry* • Robert Morley *Judge Roxburgh* • Jack Hawkins *Judge Millington-Draper* • Lionel Jeffries *Mr Creighton* • Orson Bean *Hal* ■ *Dir* Richard Donner • *Scr* Norman Thaddeus Vane

Twins ★★★★ PG

Comedy 1988 · US · Colour · 102mins

One of those rare things: a one-joke comedy that actually works. Danny DeVito is the dim-witted scuzzball who discovers naive, intelligent Arnold Schwarzenegger is his genetically engineered brother. Comic moments abound as the odd couple team up to find their long-lost mom, including Arnie's first awkward attempts at romance with Kelly Preston (now Mrs John Travolta). DeVito is on form and Arnie shows he can handle comedy, although, when the pair teamed up again for *Junior*, the result wasn't quite as successful. Contains swearing. ▭

DVD

Arnold Schwarzenegger *Julius Benedict* • Danny DeVito *Vincent Benedict* • Kelly Preston *Marnie Mason* • Chloe Webb *Linda Mason* • Bonnie Bartlett *Mary Ann Benedict* • Marshall Bell *Webster* • Trey Wilson *Beetroot McKinley* • David Caruso *Al Greco* ■ *Dir* Ivan Reitman • *Scr* William Davies, William Osborne, Timothy Harris, Herschel Weingrod

Twins of Evil ★★★ 18

Horror 1971 · UK · Colour · 83mins

Hammer ransacked J Sheridan Le Fanu's classic terror tale *Carmilla* for the last time in this completion of its trilogy following *The Vampire Lovers* and *Lust for a Vampire*. Mary and Madeleine Collinson, *Playboy* magazine's first twin centrefolds, play ''which one's the vampire?'' in a streamlined, if predictable, period piece laced with the usual quota of heaving bosoms, blood-red lipstick, lesbianism and gory decapitations. Touches of ethereal Gothic atmosphere and a neat funereal flamboyancy lift this slick shock package. 📼

Peter Cushing *Gustav Weil* • Kathleen Byron *Katy Weil* • Dennis Price *Dietrich* • Madeleine Collinson *Freda Gellhorn* • Mary Collinson *Maria Gellhorn* • Damien Thomas *Count Karnstein* • David Warbeck *Anton Hoffer* • Isobel Black *Ingrid Hoffer* ■ • Scr Tudor Gates, from characters created by J Sheridan Le Fanu

The Twist ★★
Comedy 1976 · Fr · Colour · 105mins

When he's good he's exceptional, but when he's off form even the most devoted fan is hard pressed to explain the appeal of Claude Chabrol. Although at his best with thrillers, he has produced a number of incisive character studies, but even specialists like Ingmar Bergman, Claude Sautet or Woody Allen would have struggled to separate the poignant from the pretentious in this languid study of the infidelities and prejudices of diverse bourgeois couples. Shamefully throwing away a top-drawer Franco-American cast, this will appeal only to the most ardent Chabrol devotees.

Bruce Dern *William Brandeis* • Stéphane Audran *Claire Brandeis* • Sydne Rome *Nathalie* • Jean-Pierre Cassel *Jacques Lalovet* • Ann-Margret *Charlie Minerva* • Curd Jürgens [Curt Jurgens] *Jeweller* • Charles Aznavour *Dr Lartigue* ■ • Dir Claude Chabrol • Scr Claude Chabrol, Norman Enfield, Ennio De Concini, Maria Pafusto, from a novel by Licie Faure

Twist ★★★
Documentary 1992 · Can · Colour · 78mins

Whatever happened to dance crazes? There was a time when anybody not knowing the steps to the charleston or the carioca was squarer than square. This entertaining Canadian documentary charts the ups and downs of the twist, which had hips swinging across the world in the early sixties. Revealing that the song itself was a forgotten B-side written and recorded by Hank Ballard before Chubby Checker re-recorded it, the film shows that it was far more than a dance-hall phenomenon, catching on when other dances like the watusi sank without trace.

Dir Ron Mann

Twist and Shout ★★★
Drama 1985 · Den · Colour · 100mins

Bille August's sequel to his 1983 teenpic *Zappa* is also adapted from novelist Bjarne Reuter's acclaimed rites-of-passage trilogy. Turning their attention from rebellion to rock and romance, Adam Tonsberg and Lars Simonsen find life no easier. Tonsberg's Beatle-mad drummer has to repay a debt to old flame Ulrikke Juul Bondo after getting Camilla Soeberg pregnant, while Simonsen tries to prevent his abusive father from committing his depressive mother to an asylum. Refusing to rely on easy nostalgia, August captures the energy of Copenhagen in the just-Swinging

Sixties, but also highlights the realities attendant on this new-found freedom. A Danish language film.

Adam Tonsberg *Bjorn* • Lars Simonsen *Erik* • Ulrikke Juul Bondo *Kirsten* • Camilla Soeberg *Anna* ■ • Dir Bille August • Scr Bille August, Bjarne Reuter, from a novel by Bjarne Reuter

Twisted Nerve ★★★
Thriller 1968 · UK · Colour · 117mins

In its day, this was a highly controversial and, to some, tasteless thriller. One would expect nothing less from Leo Marks, writer of *Peeping Tom*. But this time round, the story of a seemingly nice young man, who is in fact a homicidal maniac, went too far by implying a link between Down's syndrome and psychosis. Film-makers the Boulting Brothers had to add a disclaimer to the front of the film. The wholesome young stars of *The Family Way*, Hayley Mills and Hywel Bennett, are ludicrously miscast, and suspense is not comedy director Roy Boulting's forte, but the bizarre story is still gripping, and the murders, though a long time coming, provide a suitably ghastly climax. 📼

Hayley Mills *Susan Harper* • Hywel Bennett *Martin Durnley/Georgie Clifford* • Billie Whitelaw *Joan Harper* • Phyllis Calvert *Enid Durnley* • Frank Finlay *Henry Durnley* • Barry Foster *Gerry Henderson* • Timothy West *Superintendent Dakin* ■ • Dir Roy Boulting • Scr Leo Marks, Roy Boulting, from a story by Roger Marshall, from an idea by Roger Marshall, Jeremy Scott

Twister ★★ 15
Drama 1989 · US · Colour · 89mins

Nothing remotely to do with Jan De Bont's epic about whirling weather. Instead, this is an irritating ''crazy gang'' comedy about a bunch of batty siblings who find themselves trapped with their dotty old dad in the family mansion during a freak weather storm. Harry Dean Stanton plays the dad, while Suzy Amis and the genuinely odd Crispin Glover (*River's Edge*) are among the offspring in a film that sorely mistakes being way-out for being remotely interesting. 📼

Harry Dean Stanton *Eugene Cleveland* • Suzy Amis *Maureen Cleveland* • Crispin Glover *Howdy Cleveland* • Dylan McDermott *Chris* • Jenny Wright *Stephanie* ■ • Dir Michael Almereyda • Scr Michael Almereyda, from the novel *Oh!* by Mary Robison

Twister ★★★ PG
Action adventure 1996 · US · Colour · 108mins

Speed director Jan De Bont takes destruction to new levels in this daft but breathtaking adventure, a salute to the daredevil meteorologists who chase the tornados that plague America's Midwest. Here, Bill Paxton stars as a TV weatherman who is drawn back to his dangerous former profession as a storm-chaser to help estranged wife Helen Hunt place a tornado-measuring invention in the eye of a storm. Don't worry about the laboured storyline or the lack of chemistry between Paxton and Hunt; just sit back and gape at the wondrous effects that allow cars, houses and even the odd farm animal to be sent spiralling through the air. Contains some swearing. 📼 *DVD*

Bill Paxton *Bill Harding* • Helen Hunt *Jo Harding* • Jami Gertz *Melissa* • Cary Elwes *Dr Jonas Miller* • Lois Smith *Aunt Meg* • Alan Ruck *Dusty* • Philip Seymour Hoffman *Rabbit* ■ • Dir Jan De Bont • Scr Michael Crichton, Anne-Marie Martin

Two against the Law ★★★★
Crime drama 1973 · Fr/It · Colour · 100mins

Trying to go straight after serving ten years for robbery, Alain Delon falls back on the support of Jean Gabin's social worker when his wife is killed in a car crash. However, a new romance with bank clerk, Mimsy Farmer, coincides with the escape of his former buddy, Victor Lanoux, and suspicious cop Michel Bouquet begins to turn up the heat. With its unforgettable final scene, the third and last collaboration between the iconic Gabin and young pretender Delon not only makes for a fascinating contrast between their acting styles, but also provides some penetrating insights into the problems facing released prisoners. French and Italian dialogue dubbed into English.

Alain Delon *Gino* • Mimsy Farmer *Lucy* • Michel Bouquet *Goitreau* • Victor Lanoux *Mariel* • Ilaria Occhini *Sophie* • Jean Gabin *Germain* ■ • Dir/Scr José Giovanni

2 ½ Dads ★★ U
Comedy 1986 · US · Colour · 44mins

Household fun and frolics as a bachelor and two single dads join forces under one roof with their youngsters. A Disney presentation following the *Brady Bunch* formula, it's all very sweet, but the mayhem is predictable. A world away from two of star George Dzundza's other movies: he featured in *The Deer Hunter* and *Basic Instinct*. Tony Bill went on to direct the Christian Slater-Marisa Tomei tear-jerker *Untamed Heart*. 📼

George Dzundza *Pete Seltzer* • Richard Young *Frank Manley* • Sal Viscuso *Chick Leone* • Lenore Kasdorf *Arlene* • Mary Kohnert *Kathleen* • Bill Warlock [Billy Warlock] *Danny Seltzer* ■ • Dir Tony Bill • Scr Gordon Farr

Two and Two Make Six ★★ U
Romantic comedy drama 1961 · US · BW · 50mins

Ace cinematographer Freddie Francis made his directorial debut with this trifle about a US Air Force deserter who rides off on his motorbike and falls in love with his pillion passenger. George Chakiris takes a leading film role for the first time having been plucked from the London stage version of *West Side Story*, and Janette Scott co-stars. Francis seemed happier with later horror fare and eventually went back behind the camera for such movies as David Lynch's *The Elephant Man* and Martin Scorsese's *Cape Fear*.

George Chakiris *Larry Curado* • Janette Scott *Irene* • Alfred Lynch *Tom* • Jackie Lane *Julie* • Athene Seyler *Aunt Phoebe* • Bernard Braden *Sgt Sokolow* • Malcolm Keen *Harry Stoneham* • Ambrosine Philpotts *Lady Smith-Adams* ■ • Dir Freddie Francis • Scr Monja Danischewsky

Two Arabian Knights ★★★
Silent romantic comedy 1927 · US · BW · 92mins

Relative newcomer Lewis Milestone won an Oscar for best comedy direction (the only time this award was given) at the first Academy Awards ceremony. It tells of the rivalry between a tough sergeant (Louis Wolheim) and a smart private (William Boyd, the future Hopalong Cassidy) who seem to hate each other more than the enemy. But when they are captured by the Germans, they make their escape disguised as Arabs, and rescue a maiden (Mary Astor) from an evil bey. This profitable and amusing farce was only the second production of the 22-year-old Howard Hughes.

William Boyd *Pvt W Daingerfield Phelps* • Mary Astor *Anis Bin Adham* • Louis Wolheim *Sgt Peter McGaffney* • Michael Vavitch *Emir of Jaffa* • Ian Keith *Shevket* • Boris Karloff *Purser* ■ • Dir Lewis Milestone • Scr James T O'Donohue, Wallace Smith, George Marion Jr (titles)

Two Bits ★★★
Period drama 1995 · US · Colour · 93mins

Displaying ingenuity in adversity, a Depression-era kid concocts all manner of schemes to make the money he needs to attend the opening of a new movie theatre. Newcomer Jerry Barone is terrific as the tyke. Al Pacino is as excellent as ever as the kid's inspirational but dying grandad, and there's good support from Mary Elizabeth Mastrantonio as Barone's mum. Director James Foley's previous credits include less wholesome fare like *Glengarry Glen Ross* and *After Dark, My Sweet* while the screenplay is by Joseph Stefano (*Psycho*). With such a crack cast and crew, this family-orientated film can hardly fail.

Mary Elizabeth Mastrantonio *Luisa* • Al Pacino *Grandpa* • Jerry Barone *Gennaro* • Patrick Borriello *Tullio* • Andy Romano *Dr Bruna* • Donna Mitchell *Mrs Bruna* ■ • Dir James Foley • Scr Joseph Stefano

Two-Bits and Pepper ★★
Comedy 1995 · US · Colour · 90mins

A rather dire – though undeniably quirky – *Home Alone* rip-off, with Joe Piscopo starring in a dual role as a pair of burglars who kidnap a couple of girls and decide to hold them for ransom. It gets decidedly weird when the girls outwit their captors with the help of two Mr Ed-like talking horses. While funny in places, this is too uneven and downright silly to work for its entire running time, despite the presence of deft comedian Piscopo (*Johnny Dangerously*) and the more serious Dennis Weaver (best known as the terrorised driver in *Duel*).

Joe Piscopo *Spider/Zike* • Lauren Eckstrom *Tyler* • Rachel Crane *Katie* • Perry Stephens *Roger* • Kathrin Lautner *Carla* • Dennis Weaver *Sheriff Pratt* • Shannon Gallant *Monica* ■ • Dir Corey Michael Eubanks • Scr Corey Michael Eubanks

2by4 ★★★
Drama 1998 · US · Colour · 90mins

With a rough edge to shame even the rawest indie movie, Jimmy Smallhorne's scowling investigation into the lingering effects of child abuse

has an authenticity and immediacy that makes for deeply uncomfortable, if utterly compelling viewing. Also taking the part of the Bronx-Irish construction worker whose laddish lifestyle is increasingly disturbed by harrowing nightmares, Smallhorne admirably conveys the sexual confusion that alienates his girlfriend, Kimberly Topper, and draws him ever closer to Aussie street hustler, Bradley Fitts. Chris O'Neill is also impressive as the uncle with the darkest of secrets.

Jimmy Smallhorne *Johnnie Maher* • Chris O'Neill *Uncle Trump* • Bradley Fitts *Christian* • Joe Holyoake *Joe* • Terrence McGoff *Billy* • Ronan Carr *Brains* • Leo Hamill *Paddy* ■ *Dir* Jimmy Smallhorne • *Scr* Jimmy Smallhorne, Terry McGoff, Fergus Tighe, from a screenplay by Jimmy Smallhorne, Terry McGoff

Two Came Back ★★★

Thriller   1997 · US · Colour · 120mins

The title is a bit of a giveaway, but this is still an admirably grim story of survival on the high seas. TV regulars Jonathan Brandis from *Seaquest DSV* and *Sabrina, the Teenage Witch's* Melissa Joan Hart (showing she can handle serious stuff as well as her usual lightweight fluff) play a couple of young sailors who are brought together with three others to deliver a yacht to its owners. When a storm hits, the youngsters find themselves in a desperate battle for survival. There are plucky performances from the cast and TV-movie veteran Dick Lowry keeps the direction on an even keel.

Melissa Joan Hart *Susan Clarkson* • Jonathan Brandis *Jason O'Donnel* • David Gail *Matt* • Jon Pennell *Rick* • Susan Walters *Stacy* • Susan Sullivan *Patrica Clarkson* ■ *Dir* Dick Lowry • *Scr* Raymond Hartung, from the book *Albatross* by Deborah Scaling-Kiley, Meg Noonan

2 Days in the Valley ★★★ 18

Comedy thriller 1996 · US · Colour · 100mins

An interestingly quirky and occasionally steamy comedy drama which tips its hat at Tarantino's *Pulp Fiction* and Robert Altman's *Short Cuts*. Danny Aiello, James Spader, Teri Hatcher, Jeff Daniels and then-unknown Charlize Theron (who has gone on to make an impact in *The Cider House Rules* and Woody Allen's *Celebrity*) play just some of the unusual characters who inhabit the strange environs of LA in this amoral and often bizarre tale. Writer/director John Herzfeld is better known for less hip fare, including TV movies like *Casualties of Love: The "Long Island Lolita" Story* and *Don King: Only in America*. Contains swearing, violence and sex scenes. ▣

Danny Aiello *Dosmo Pizzo* • Greg Cruttwell *Allan Hopper* • Jeff Daniels *Alvin Strayer* • Teri Hatcher *Becky Foxx* • Glenne Headly *Susan Parish* • Marsha Mason *Audrey Hopper* • Charlize Theron *Helga Svelgen* • James Spader *Lee Woods* ■ *Dir/Scr* John Herzfeld

Two Deaths ★★★ 18

Drama   1994 · UK · Colour · 98mins

Director Nicolas Roeg and screenwriter Allan Scott have shifted the scene from Chile to Romania for this adaptation of Stephen Dobyns's novel *The Two Deaths of Senora Puccini*. This set-bound drama could be

situated anywhere, however, and it would still have the same resonance. There's no escaping the theatricality of the piece, but the story that unfolds over dinner is both compelling and disturbing. Michael Gambon effortlessly conveys pride and regret as he reveals how he has mistreated his housekeeper, Sonia Braga, whose statuesque dignity masks a burning desire for revenge. Far from Roeg's best, but still a solid professional job. Contains violence, a sex scene and nudity. ▣

Michael Gambon *Daniel Pavenic* • Sonia Braga *Ana Puscasu* • Patrick Malahide *George Buscan* • Ion Caramitru *Carl Dalakis* • Nickolas Grace *Marius Vernescu* • Lisa Orgolini *Young Ana* • Niall Refoy *Young Pavenic* ■ *Dir* Nicolas Roeg • *Scr* Allan Scott, from the novel *The Two Deaths of Senora Puccini* by Stephen Dobyns

Two Evil Eyes ★★★ 18

Horror   1990 · It/US · Colour · 114mins

Masters of horror George A Romero and Dario Argento joined forces to create this double bill based on a pair of Edgar Allan Poe stories. Romero's contribution is *The Facts in the Case of M Valdemar*, in which a man is mesmerised at the moment of death but with awful consequences. Poe's slim story is stretched to no avail, and the new material is handled in a conventional TV style. Argento's version of *The Black Cat* is more successful. The adaptation, a radical update involving Harvey Keitel as a photographer who goes mad and murders his girlfriend, is again overlong but builds to a mad and bloody climax. Note the (pointless) homage to *Psycho*, with Martin Balsam walking up an identical staircase to the one in the Bates house. ▣

Adrienne Barbeau *Jessica Valdemar* • EG Marshall *Steven Pike* • Bingo O'Malley *Ernest Valdemar* • Harvey Keitel *Rod Usher* • Madeleine Potter *Annabel* • John Amos Legrand • Sally Kirkland *Eleonora* • Martin Balsam *Mr Pym* • Kim Hunter *Mrs Pym* ■ *Dir* George A Romero, Dario Argento • *Scr* George A Romero, Dario Argento, Franco Ferrini, from the stories *The Facts in the Case of M Valdemar* and *The Black Cat* by Edgar Allan Poe • *Music* Pino Donaggio

Two-Faced Woman ★★★

Romantic drama   1941 · US · BW · 93mins

Greta Garbo's last movie is nowhere near as bad as contemporary reviews would have you believe, and certainly didn't warrant the most fabulous female screen face of all opting for a retirement that would last until her death almost 50 years later. True, MGM's attempt to Americanise her doesn't quite come off, but there's much to enjoy in this sophisticated comedy, especially Garbo dancing the "Chica-Chocka". The risqué material led to the Catholic League of Decency condemning the movie, and it was actually banned in Australia, factors that didn't help Garbo's image. Today we can appreciate it for what it is: a well-performed piece of froth.

Greta Garbo *Karin Borg Blake/Katherine Borg* • Melvyn Douglas *Larry Blake* • Constance Bennett *Griselda Vaughn* • Roland Young *OO Miller* • Robert Sterling *Dick Williams* • Ruth Gordon *Miss Ellis* • George Cleveland *Sheriff* • George P Huntley Jr [GP Huntley Jr] *Mr Wilson*

■ *Dir* George Cukor • *Scr* SH Behrman, Salka Viertel, George Oppenheimer, from the play by Ludwig Fulda

The Two Faces of Dr Jekyll ★★

Erotic horror   1960 · UK · Colour · 88mins

Hammer's flop version of the overworked Robert Louis Stevenson classic grafts on Oscar Wilde's *The Picture of Dorian Gray* for extra literacy amid the tired Gothic chills. This time the old and weak Jekyll (Paul Massie) transforms into a dashing and virile playboy with an eye for London's cancan girls. Christopher Lee lends his usual excellent support as the lecherous best friend, crushed to death by a python when found in the arms of Jekyll's wife (Dawn Addams).

Paul Massie *Dr Jekyll/Mr Hyde* • Dawn Addams *Kitty* • Christopher Lee *Paul Allen* • David Kossoff *Litauer* • Francis De Wolff *Inspector* • Norma Marla *Maria* • Magda Miller *Sphinx girl* • Oliver Reed *Beau* ■ *Dir* Terence Fisher • *Scr* Wolf Mankowitz, from the novel by Robert Louis Stevenson

Two Fathers' Justice ★★ PG

Drama   1985 · US · Colour · 95mins

A creaky buddy vehicle for seventies stars Robert Conrad and George Hamilton which passes the time amiably enough even if it never really convinces. The two stars play two mismatched dads – one blue-collar, the other a pampered businessman – who team up as unlikely vigilantes to gain revenge on the gangsters responsible for the accidental death of their two kids who were about to be married. Look out for Lolita Davidovich in only her second movie. ▣

Robert Conrad *Stack* • George Hamilton *Bradley* • Brooke Bundy *Moe* • Catherine Corkill *Janice* • Whitney Kershaw *Karen* • Greg Terrell *John* • Bo Kaprall *Andy* ■ *Dir* Rod Holcomb • *Scr* David J Kinghorn, Brown Meggs, from a story by Brown Meggs

Two Fathers: Justice for the Innocent ★★

Action drama   1993 · US · Colour · 91mins

Old TV hands George Hamilton and Robert Conrad spark off each other nicely in this otherwise uninspired variation on the vigilante theme. They are the two fathers of the title – one a wealthy city type, the other a blue collar worker – who find a common cause when their children are murdered by a drug dealer. When, years later, the dealer escapes from prison, Hamilton and Conrad reunite to try and track him down. The fact that the two stars have nothing in common with Charles Bronson is a bonus, but both the direction and script could have done with a little more zip.

Robert Conrad *Stackhouse* • George Hamilton *Trent Bradley* • Danny Goldring *Special Agent Larkin* • Ned Schmitke *Madigan* • Gary Houston *Leonard Kapskin* ■ *Dir* Paul Krasny • *Scr* Stephen Zito, from characters created by Brown Meggs

Two Flags West ★★★ U

Historical western drama
1950 · US · BW · 91mins

It took a lot of nerve for anyone but John Ford to make cavalry westerns,

but writer/producer Casey Robinson and director Robert Wise gave it a good try with this dramatic story built on the fact that Confederate prisoners were allowed to serve in Union army posts out west during the Civil War. Jeff Chandler makes a strong impression as an embittered commanding officer; Joseph Cotten is the Confederate leader plotting to escape; Cornel Wilde is a Union captain; while Linda Darnell is the army widow coveted by all three men. There's more talk and less action than in most westerns, but director Wise brings the fort setting to life and stages the final Indian attack with considerable vigour.

Joseph Cotten *Col Clay Tucker* • Linda Darnell *Elena Kenniston* • Jeff Chandler *Maj Henry Kenniston* • Cornel Wilde *Capt Mark Bradford* • Dale Robertson *Lem* • Jay C Flippen *Sgt Terrance Duffy* • Noah Beery [Noah Beery Jr] *Cy Davis* • Harry Von Zell *Ephraim Strong* ■ *Dir* Robert Wise • *Scr* Casey Robinson, from a story by Frank S Nugent, Curtis Kenyon

Two for Texas ★★ 15

Western   1998 · US · Colour · 92mins

Going over familiar historical territory, this made-for-cable western is a high quality, pacy retelling of the war between the fledgling United States and Mexico over who gets to own Texas. This time around, though, the valiant last stand of Davy Crockett and company at the Alamo is only one part of the story, with director Rod Hardy opting to look at the aftermath as well. Tom Skerritt (as Sam Houston) and Peter Coyote (Jim Bowie) are among the real-life luminaries, although the story itself is seen from the perspective of two escaped convicts, Kris Kristofferson and Scott Bairstow, who inadvertently find themselves caught up in the making of history. Contains violence. ▣

Kris Kristofferson *Hugh Allison* • Scott Bairstow *Son Holland* • Tom Skerritt *Sam Houston* • Peter Coyote *Jim Bowie* • Irene Bedard *Sana* • Victor Rivers *Emile Landry* • Rodney A Grant *Iron Jacket* ■ *Dir* Rod Hardy • *Scr* Larry Brothers, from the novel by James Lee Burke

Two for the Road ★★★★ PG

Comedy drama
1967 · UK/US · Colour · 110mins

The relationship of a couple (Audrey Hepburn and Albert Finney), from the youthful idyll of their love affair and early years of marriage through the stages of disillusion to the brink of collapse, is told in a series of sometimes confusing flashbacks and flash-forwards. Directed by Stanley Donen with his customary flair, the comedy drama is played out in glossy French locations as the couple make a series of road trips across the country over a period of 12 years. Frederic Raphael's Oscar-nominated screenplay is a quintessentially Swinging Sixties piece, reflecting both the strengths and weakness of the period. Hepburn (then 37) effortlessly ages backwards to a young student and, freed from her Givenchy-clad image, evinces a range of emotions with controlled subtlety and incisiveness. Finney is excellent, and there's a memorable cameo from Eleanor Bron. ▣

U = SUITABLE FOR ALL   **Uc** = SUITABLE FOR ALL, ESPECIALLY FOR YOUNG CHILDREN (VIDEO ONLY)   **PG** = PARENTAL GUIDANCE

Audrey Hepburn *Joanna Wallace* • Albert Finney *Mark Wallace* • Eleanor Bron *Cathy Manchester* • William H Daniels [William Daniels] *Howard Manchester* • Claude Dauphin *Maurice Dalbret* • Nadia Gray *Françoise Dalbret* ■ *Dir* Stanley Donen • *Scr* Frederic Raphael

Two for the Seesaw ★★

Romantic comedy drama
1962 · US · BW · 218mins

Jewish dancer Shirley MacLaine befriends Robert Mitchum, a sultry out-of-towner who arrives in New York after his marriage breaks up. Based on a fifties Broadway play, it's really an extended conversation piece about the moral climate of the time, with the camera anchored to the spot while the stars wade through the reams of dialogue. It looks tame today, but the British censor thought all this "adult" talk worthy of an X-rating. There's also a party scene in Greenwich Village that was probably very trendy at the time but now dates the film terribly.

Robert Mitchum *Jerry Ryan* • Shirley MacLaine *Gittel Mosca* • Edmon Ryan *Taubman* • Elisabeth Fraser *Sophie* • Eddie Firestone *Oscar* • Billy Gray *Mr Jacoby* ■ *Dir* Robert Wise • *Scr* Isobel Lennart, from the play by William Gibson

Two Friends ★★

Drama
1986 · Ausl · Colour · 76mins

The first feature film from Jane Campion, director of *The Piano*, *Portrait of a Lady* and *Holy Smoke*. Made for Australian television, the film traces the diverging career and life paths taken by two high school girls (Emma Coles and Kris Bidenko). Campion has evolved into an accomplished filmmaker. This, though, with its strange mix of styles and wayward direction, smacks more of a craft-learning exercise than a polished product.

Emma Coles *Louise* • Kris Bidenko *Kelly* • Kris McQuade *Janet, Louise's mother* • Deborah May *Chris, Kelly's mother* • Peter Hehir *Malcolm, Kelly's stepfather* • Tony Barry *Charlie, Kelly's father* ■ *Dir* Jane Campion • *Scr* Helen Garner

Two Gentlemen Sharing ★★

Melodrama
1969 · UK · Colour · 106mins

One of the many daring, if trendy attacks on racial prejudice and class barriers that sixties television and cinema specialised in. Ted Kotcheff's film of David Stuart Leslie's novel focuses on the love lives of a white, aristocratic advertising executive and a black Jamaican lawyer – both Oxford graduates – sharing a flat in London. There are few surprises on offer, but the film is competently acted, particularly by flatmates Robin Philips and Hal Frederick and love interest Judy Geeson.

Robin Phillips *Roddy* • Judy Geeson *Jane* • Hal Frederick *Andrew* • Esther Anderson *Caroline* • Norman Rossington *Phil* • Hilary Dwyer *Ethne* • Rachel Kempson *Mrs Ashby-Kydd* ■ *Dir* Ted Kotcheff • *Scr* Evan Jones, from the novel by David Stuart Leslie

Two Girls and a Guy ★★★★ 18

Comedy drama   1997 · US · Colour · 82mins

Robert Downey Jr gives a superb performance as the egotistical struggling actor who is confronted by his two girlfriends – neither of whom knew the other existed – when he returns to his New York home following a trip. The film takes place almost entirely in the apartment, as Heather Graham and Natasha Gregson Wagner battle it out for the man both believed was perfect but whom they've discovered is anything but. More like a riveting performance piece than a narrative film, writer/director James Toback's darkly comic story of infidelity is every actor's dream and a fascinating experiment for the audience. Contains swearing and a sex scene. ▭

Robert Downey Jr *Blake Allen* • Natasha Gregson Wagner *Lou* • Heather Graham *Carla* • Angel David *Tommy* • Frederique Van Der Wal *Carol* ■ *Dir/Scr* James Toback

Two Girls and a Sailor ★★★ U

Musical   1944 · US · Colour · 124mins

Not to be confused with the 1953 film *Three Sailors and a Girl*, this overlong MGM extravaganza is rewarding if you feel inclined to stick with it. But, frankly, with the limitations of the small screen it's only worth dipping into for its highlights, which include Jimmy Durante in his bizarre prime and Lena Horne singing *Paper Doll*. As for the two girls of the title, who are a wartime nightclub song-and-dance act, June Allyson seems too knowing, but the always under-rated Gloria DeHaven charms, while Van Johnson gives a delightful, easy-going performance of great charisma. Nostalgia enthusiasts will need no persuasion; others may enjoy spotting a very young Ava Gardner in support.

June Allyson *Patsy Deyo* • Gloria DeHaven *Jean Deyo* • Van Johnson *John "Johnny" Dyckman Brown III* • Tom Drake *Sgt Frank Miller* • Henry Stephenson *John Dyckman Brown I* • Henry O'Neill *John Dyckman Brown II* • Ben Blue *Ben* • Carlos Ramírez *Carlos* • Jimmy Durante *Billy Kipp/"Junior" Kipp* ■ *Dir* Richard Thorpe • *Scr* Richard Connell, Gladys Lehman

Two Guys from Milwaukee ★★★

Comedy   1946 · US · BW · 90mins

Despite its plot's regal connections this is just another Warner Bros programme filler with Dennis Morgan as a young Balkan prince travelling incognito and making friends with talkative cab driver Jack Carson. Joan Leslie is the girl who catches the prince's eye and IAL Diamond, who went on to great things with Billy Wilder, co-wrote the script. Of its kind, a diverting entertainment; look out for cameos from Humphrey Bogart and Lauren Bacall.

Dennis Morgan *Prince Henry* • Joan Leslie *Connie Read* • Jack Carson *Buzz Williams* • Janis Paige *Polly* • SZ Sakall *Count Oswald* • Patti Brady *Peggy Evans* • Rosemary DeCamp *Nan Evans* • Lauren Bacall • Humphrey Bogart ■ *Dir* David Butler • *Scr* Charles Hoffman, IAL Diamond

The Two-Headed Spy ★★★ U

Second World War spy drama
1958 · UK · BW · 93mins

A taut little wartime spy saga, directed by the one-eyed Andre De Toth, with Jack Hawkins as the Englishman who has been planted by British intelligence into Germany since the end of the First World War. By the time the Second World War breaks out, Hawkins has a senior admin job in Berlin and passes information to his contact, a clockmaker, and then to a singer played by Gia Scala. The emphasis is on Hawkins's character and his refusal to become romantically involved with anyone and therefore vulnerable. Kenneth Griffith appears briefly as Hitler, a young Michael Caine exhibits his flair for foreign accents playing a Gestapo agent, and there's also a chance to see British stage actor Walter Hudd, who was cast as Lawrence of Arabia for a Korda project in the thirties.

Jack Hawkins *Gen Alex Schottland* • Gia Scala *Lili Geyr* • Erik Schumann *Lt Reinisch* • Alexander Knox *Gestapo leader Mueller* • Felix Aylmer *Cornaz* • Walter Hudd *Adm Canaris* • Kenneth Griffith *Adolf Hitler* • Michael Caine *2nd Gestapo agent* • Donald Pleasence *Gen Hardt* ■ *Dir* Andre De Toth • *Scr* James O'Donnell, from a story by J Alvin Kugelmass

200 Cigarettes ★★ 15

Romantic comedy
1999 · US · Colour · 97mins

What looks very promising – a twentysomething comedy starring top Hollywood young guns – is almost immediately disappointing. Ben Affleck and brother Casey, Courtney Love, Jay Mohr and Christina Ricci are all angst-ridden young adults trying to get their lives in gear on New Year's Eve, 1981. But we've seen these relationship and insecurity problems played out ad infinitum and sadly this has a feel of a sitcom not worthy of the silver screen. The beginning and end are both crisp and engaging but like an unsuccessful soufflé Risa Bramon Garcia's film sags terribly in the middle. Contains swearing and sex scenes. ▭

Ben Affleck *Bartender* • Casey Affleck *Tom* • Angela Featherstone *Caitlyn* • Janeane Garofalo *Ellie* • Kate Hudson *Cindy* • Courtney Love *Lucy* • Jay Mohr *Jack* • Martha Plimpton *Monica* • Christina Ricci *Val* • Paul Rudd *Kevin* ■ *Dir* Risa Bramon Garcia • *Scr* Shana Larsen

200 Motels ★★★

Music documentary
1971 · US · Colour · 98mins

Taking a leaf out of the cute anarchy of *A Hard Day's Night*, directors Frank Zappa and Tony Palmer invest Zappa's own music (performed by the Mothers of Invention) with animation, sketches and jokes, much of it skewed towards a comic critique of touring, rock-band style. As with Zappa's own brand of guitar hysteria, many of the interludes are imaginative, funny or mad (sometimes all three) and depend on the viewer having some knowledge of the fab world of pop. Zappa was the one rock star who could make noise fun. His libretto, by the way, was declared obscene, and so what was conceived as a live show became this film instead. Contains swearing.

Ringo Starr *Larry the dwarf* • Frank Zappa • Theodore Bikel *Rance Muhammitz* • Don Preston *Bif Debris* • Jimmy Carl Black *Cowboy Burtram* • Keith Moon *Hot Nun* ■ *Dir* Frank Zappa, Tony Palmer • *Scr* Frank Zappa, Tony Palmer, from a story by Frank Zappa

The Two Jakes ★★★ 15

Detective thriller
1990 · US · Colour · 131mins

If Robert Towne and Roman Polanski fell out over *Chinatown*, worse happened during this sequel. With Towne directing, shooting was cancelled after the first day when Robert Evans – the producer of the first film – was fired in the role of the villain, the other Jake. Shooting resumed four years later with Jack Nicholson as director/star and Harvey Keitel as his co-star, and Towne and Nicholson haven't spoken since. The result was crushing disappointment, even anger at the wasted opportunity. The second in Towne's planned trilogy about land deals in Los Angeles in the late forties, it evokes eerie echoes of the first story, but is muddled and lacks the epic perspectives of the original. But some scenes stand out and Nicholson has a sharp, sardonic eye for the trash culture of southern California. Contains violence and swearing. ▭

Jack Nicholson *Jake Gittes* • Harvey Keitel *Jake Berman* • Meg Tilly *Kitty Berman* • Madeleine Stowe *Lillian Bodine* • Eli Wallach *Cotton Weinberger* • Rubén Blades *Mickey Nice* • Frederic Forrest *Chuck Newty* • David Keith *Loach* • Richard Farnsworth *Earl Rawley* ■ *Dir* Jack Nicholson • *Scr* Robert Towne

Two-Lane Blacktop ★★★

Road movie drama
1971 · US · Colour · 102mins

Existential road movie that takes its cue from *Easy Rider* and features Beach Boys' drummer Dennis Wilson and seventies singer/songwriter James Taylor in their first straight leading roles. They play drifters cruising the American Southwest in their souped-up 1955 Chevrolet, who challenge old-timer Warren Oates (a career-best performance) and his GTO Pontiac to a cross-country race with car ownership as the prize. Monte Hellman's intense direction and quirky charm compensate for a low-key script, and there are nice supporting turns from Laurie Bird and Harry Dean Stanton as hitchhikers.

Warren Oates *GTO* • James Taylor *Driver* • Dennis Wilson *Mechanic* • Laurie Bird *Girl* • HD Stanton [Harry Dean Stanton] *Oklahoma hitchhiker* • David Drake *Needles station attendant* • Richard Ruth *Needles station mechanic* • Jaclyn Hellman *Driver's girl* ■ *Dir* Monte Hellman • *Scr* Rudy Wurlitzer, Will Corry, from a story by Will Corry

Two Left Feet ★★★ 15

Comedy   1963 · UK · BW · 89mins

In this adult comedy about adolescent sexual complications, Alan (Michael Crawford) is an unworldly 19-year-old who goes out on a date to a jazz club with older waitress Eileen (Nyree Dawn Porter). At the club Eileen ignores him, instead flirting with two other guys. Alan in turn meets Beth (Julia Foster) with whom he seems far happier. Misunderstandings and frustrations complicate the situation, with Alan at

the centre of the crossed relations. A stark look at sixties sexual mores with fine performances, especially from Crawford and Porter.

Michael Crawford *Alan Crabbe* • Nyree Dawn Porter *Eileen* • Julia Foster *Beth Crowley* • Michael Craze *Ronnie* • David Hemmings *Brian* • Dilys Watling *Mavis* • David Lodge *Bill* • Bernard Lee *Mr Crabbe* ■ *Dir* Roy Baker [Roy Ward Baker] • *Scr* Roy Baker [Roy Ward Baker], John Hopkins, from the novel *In My Solitude* by David Stuart Leslie

The Two Little Bears   ★★ U

Fantasy drama   1961 · US · BW · 84mins

An ursine caper of very little consequence. When two young brothers receive instructions from a gypsy on how to transform themselves into bears, they perform the trick for their school principal father (Eddie Albert), whose sanity is called into serious question by the local education board when he attempts to spread word of the miracle. Astonishingly enough, his wife doesn't believe him either. Neither would Goldilocks – and she had a fairy tale to support.

Eddie Albert *Harry Davis* • Jane Wyatt *Anne Davis* • Brenda Lee *Tina Davis* • Soupy Sales *Officer Pat McGovern* • Donnie Carter *Timmy Davis* • Butch Patrick *Billy Davis* • Jimmy Boyd *Tina's boyfriend* • Nancy Kulp *Miss Wilkins* ■ *Dir* Randall F Hood • *Scr* George W George, from a story by Judy George

The Two Lives of Carol Letner   ★★

Crime drama   1981 · US · Colour · 96mins

Originally shown as *Dial 911*, this TV movie is a long way short of films such as *The Little Kidnappers* and *The Spanish Gardener*, which director Philip Leacock made in Britain in the fifties. Instead, it's a slick but empty made-for-TV entertainment that takes an age to tell its trite tale. The ubiquitous Meredith Baxter Birney is miscast as the eponymous heroine, a former prostitute turned college student who returns to the streets to help round up a money-laundering gang. A pre-*Miami Vice* Don Johnson is scarcely more convincing as the cop who falls for her. One life would have been enough.

Meredith Baxter Birney [Meredith Baxter] *Carol Letner* • Don Johnson *Bob Howard* • Dolph Sweet *Lt Ron Vance* • Salome Jens *Dr Miller* ■ *Dir* Philip Leacock • *Scr* Annie Scott, from a story by Albert R Lagrus

Two Loves   ★

Drama   1961 · US · Colour · 99mins

Retitled *The Spinster* in the UK, this bizarre melodrama stars Shirley MacLaine as a teacher in New Zealand who may or may not be frigid but who drinks brandy for breakfast, burns on a short fuse and is probably bonkers. Her pupils love her. So does teaching colleague Laurence Harvey, a bit mad himself, but his amorous attentions are snubbed. Jack Hawkins is the terribly British school inspector who is divorcing his wife and also falls for MacLaine. Meanwhile, who's got Shirley's young Maori assistant pregnant? This hotbed of emotion in prim, middle-class New Zealand might have made an interesting Michael Powell movie with Deborah Kerr or Jean Simmons, but MGM bungles

everything about it and makes it laughable in quite the wrong way.

Shirley MacLaine *Anna Vorontosov* • Laurence Harvey *Paul Lathrope* • Jack Hawkins *WWJ Abercrombie* • Nobu McCarthy *Whareparita* • Ronald Long *Headmaster Reardon* • Norah Howard *Mrs Cutter* • Juano Hernandez *Rauhuia* • Edmund Vargas *Matawhero* ■ *Dir* Charles Walters • *Scr* Ben Maddow, from the novel *Spinster* by Sylvia Ashton-Warner

Two Men in Manhattan   ★★★

Crime   1959 · Fr · BW · 100mins

Having been forced to abandon two projects following *Bob Le Flambeur*, Jean-Pierre Melville somewhat understandably took a hands-on approach to this study in journalistic ethics. In addition to scripting, directing and starring, he also shot a good deal of the New York location footage himself, capturing the seedy underside of the city, while still managing to give it an irresistible allure. Melville's reporter teams with scoop-chasing photographer Pierre Grasset, to track down a missing UN diplomat, only to fall out when they discover his corpse. Recalling John Huston's *The Asphalt Jungle*, this is a hard-nosed, cynical film with an unexpectedly poetic heart. In English and French with subtitles.

Jean-Pierre Melville *Moreau* • Pierre Grasset *Delmas* • Michèle Bailly • Jean Darcante ■ *Dir/Scr* Jean-Pierre Melville

Two-Minute Warning   ★★

Drama   1976 · US · Colour · 115mins

The recipient of an Oscar nomination for its editing, this interminable drama has all the character sophistication of a disaster movie. In a cast littered with guest stars, everyone is a loser of sorts, unlike the sniper at the NFL play-off and his police pursuer, who are both psychopaths. While the acting styles of John Cassavetes and Charlton Heston clash like cymbals, director Larry Peerce preoccupies himself with grandstanding camerawork that does little to heighten tension or make us care for the potential targets. Contains violence and swearing.

Charlton Heston *Captain Peter Holly* • John Cassavetes *Sergeant Chris Button* • Martin Balsam *Sam McKeever* • Beau Bridges *Mike Ramsay* • Marilyn Hassett *Lucy* • David Janssen *Steve* • Jack Klugman *Stu Sandman* • Gena Rowlands *Janet* • Walter Pidgeon *Pickpocket* ■ *Dir* Larry Peerce • *Scr* Edward Hume, from the novel by George La Fountaine • *Editor* Walter Hanneman, Eve Newman

Two Moon Junction   ★★ 18

Erotic drama   1988 · US · Colour · 100mins

Another soft porn flick from the stable of director Zalman King. As with *Wild Orchid* and *Lake Consequence*, a poor plot forms an excuse for various pornographic encounters, but it's naff fun nevertheless. Sherilyn Fenn rejects her educated past to run off with hunk Richard Tyson. The couple are chased by her family and local law enforcers intent on stopping their adventures both above and between the sheets. Watch out for supermodel and future *Joan of Arc* star Milla Jovovich in one of her first acting attempts. ▣

Sherilyn Fenn *April Delongpre* • Kristy McNichol *Patti-Jean* • Richard Tyson *Perry* • Louise Fletcher *Belle* • Burl Ives *Sheriff Earl Hawkins* • Martin Hewitt *Chad Douglas Fairchild* • Millie Perkins *Mrs Delongpre* • Don Galloway *Senator Delongpre* ■ *Dir* Zalman King • *Scr* Zalman King, from a story by Zalman King, MacGregor Douglas

Two Mothers for Zachary   ★★

Drama based on a true story
1996 · US · Colour

Vanessa Redgrave in combative mood is the prime reason for watching this TV movie about the tug of war between a grandmother and her daughter (Valerie Bertinelli) for custody of the latter's son. Overly tinged with melodrama, the film nevertheless touches on a range of contentious issues from child abuse (by Redgrave's boyfriend) to the suitability of lesbian partners in the raising of a small boy. Although litigation plays a key role in the proceedings, it's disappointing that director Peter Werner couldn't have found a more interesting way to convey the facts than an endless series of courtroom encounters.

Valerie Bertinelli *Jody Ann Shaffell* • Vanessa Redgrave *Nancy Shaffell* • Randy Means *Harlan* • Colleen Flynn *Maggie Fergus* ■ *Dir* Peter Werner • *Scr* Linda Voorhees

The Two Mrs Carrolls   ★★★ PG

Crime drama   1945 · US · BW · 94mins

The only teaming of two great movie icons, Humphrey Bogart and Barbara Stanwyck, this sordid tale about a wife-killer leaves much to be desired, and falls way behind similar plottings like *Gaslight* and *Suspicion*. Today, this nasty old tosh is resolutely entertaining, though you can still understand why Warners kept it on the shelf for a couple of years after it was filmed in 1945. Bogie is seriously miscast as the psychopathic artist murderer, and Stanwyck is equally under-used as his intended victim. The whole betrays its stage origins, and although Martin Vale's play was a West End hit the film never really won an audience. ▣

Humphrey Bogart *Geoffrey Carroll* • Barbara Stanwyck *Sally Morton Carroll* • Alexis Smith *Cecily Latham* • Nigel Bruce *Dr Tuttle* • Isobel Elsom *Mrs Latham* • Pat O'Moore *Charles Fennington* ■ *Dir* Peter Godfrey • *Scr* Thomas Job, from the play by Martin Vale

Two Much   ★★ PG

Romantic comedy
1995 · Sp/US · Colour · 113mins

Making a good screwball comedy is an exact science, but unfortunately director Fernando Treuba (who made the far more impressive *Belle Epoque*) fumbles with every aspect of this one, ultimately producing a stupid movie which most of the cast members are sure to omit from their CVs. Antonio Banderas comes off worst as the art dealer who romances socialite Melanie Griffith but then falls for her sister Daryl Hannah, causing him to pretend he actually has an identical twin. Cue lots of ridiculous situations and Banderas looking increasingly ill-at-ease, while a more accomplished

supporting cast (Danny Aiello, Joan Cusack) embarrassingly look on. ▣

Antonio Banderas *Art Dodge* • Melanie Griffith *Betty Kerner* • Daryl Hannah *Liz Kerner* • Danny Aiello *Gene Paletto* • Joan Cusack *Gloria* • Eli Wallach *Sheldon* • Gabino Diego *Manny* ■ *Dir* Fernando Trueba • *Scr* Fernando Trueba, David Trueba, Donald E Westlake

Two Much Trouble   ★★

Comedy   1995 · US · Colour · 88mins

Beverly D'Angelo plays an ex-con who babysits the spoilt kids of wealthy Ed Begley Jr and Carol Kane in this lacklustre, occasionally saccharine retread of that favourite Hollywood theme: little brats running rings around uncaring adults. The relentlessly juvenile script defeats the combined talents of the eclectic cast, and even children may find it is a little beneath them. Keep an eye out for future *Friends* star Lisa Kudrow and former John Waters regular Mink Stole. Contains swearing.

Beverly D'Angelo *Edie* • Brady Bluhm *Jason Van Arsdale* • Rachel Duncan *Bea Van Arsdale* • Ed Begley Jr *Paul Van Arsdale* • Carol Kane *Treva Van Arsdale* ■ *Dir/Scr* Michael James McDonald

Two Mugs from Brooklyn   ★

Comedy   1942 · US · Colour · 73mins

One of Hal Roach's cheaply-made, light comedies, which he called "streamliners", with generally unknown names in the leads. Here William Bendix (who had made his screen debut the year previously, making an impression as a vicious thug in *The Glass Key*) shows his gentle dumb-ox side as a Brooklyn cabbie opposite Joe Sawyer, another simpleton. The plot, such as it is, has the two mugs trying to keep their taxi business going while keeping their demanding wives happy.

William Bendix *Tim* • Joe Sawyer *Eddie* • Grace Bradley *Sadie* ■ *Dir* Kurt Neumann

Two Mules for Sister Sara   ★★★★ 15

Comedy western
1970 · US · Colour · 100mins

Clint Eastwood stars in one of his rare quizzical, slightly bemused roles as a heroic cowboy in this immensely enjoyable Don Siegel caper, co-starring Shirley MacLaine as an unusual nun. The main players bounce off each other, and MacLaine in particular turns in a great comic performance as her ill-fitting habit begins to slip. Siegel keeps the tension and pace roaring along as he pitches them in the middle of the Mexican Revolution. A great script infuses a joyous movie. ▣

Clint Eastwood *Hogan* • Shirley MacLaine *Sister Sara* • Manolo Fabregas *Colonel Beltran* • Alberto Morin *General LeClaire* • Armando Silvestre *1st American* • John Kelly *2nd American* • Enrique Lucero *3rd American* • David Estuardo *Juan* ■ *Dir* Don Siegel • *Scr* Albert Maltz, from a story by Budd Boetticher

Two O'Clock Courage   ★

Murder mystery   1945 · US · BW · 66mins

It starts promisingly, with a bloodied Tom Conway staggering forward to lean on a signpost at a deserted city crossroads. But it goes downhill rapidly and stays there after Ann Rutherford's wisecracking cabbie picks him up and improbably decides to help Conway solve his case of amnesia. Anthony Mann's alert staging tries to bring some life to the verbose story, but it's beyond resuscitation. Jane Greer makes her screen debut as a drunken cutie, billed as Bettejane Greer.

Tom Conway *Man* • Ann Rutherford *Patty Mitchell* • Richard Lane *Haley* • Lester Matthews *Mark Evans* • Roland Drew *Steve Maitland* • Emory Parnell *Inspector Bill Brenner* • Bettejane Greer [Jane Greer] *Helen Carter* ■ *Dir* Anthony Mann • *Scr* Robert E Kent, from a novel by Gelett Burgess

Two of a Kind ★★ PG
Fantasy romantic comedy
1983 · US · Colour · 83mins

Five years on from *Grease*, John Travolta and Olivia Newton-John re-teamed for a fantasy romance about a couple used as guinea pigs by God in an experiment to prove that not all mortals are irredeemably corrupt. Played as a screwball comedy, it has its stupid moments, and its endearing ones, but not enough of them. True fans of John and Livvy will probably quite like it. Others will view it more as a wet weekend in Blackpool than a fortnight in *Grease*. ▣

John Travolta *Zach Melon* • Olivia Newton-John *Debbie Wylder* • Charles Durning *Charlie* • Oliver Reed *Beazley* • Beatrice Straight *Ruth* • Scatman Crothers *Earl* • Richard Bright *Stuart* ■ *Dir/Scr* John Herzfeld

The Two of Us ★★★★ U
Second World War drama
1967 · Fr · BW · 86mins

Michel Simon won the best actor prize at Berlin for his work in Claude Berri's autobiographical tale about a Catholic, Pétain-supporting anti-Semite who unknowingly forms a close friendship with a young Jewish refugee. This is a superlative performance, as Simon humanises the curmudgeonly fascist who never lets up for a second in his attempt to indoctrinate the boy with his hideous views. It's also a courageous and selfless piece of acting, as he allows young Alain Cohen to steal scene after scene as the irrepressible eight year-old who delights in deflating his host. Touching, but never sentimental or trite. In French with English subtitles.

Michel Simon *Pépé* • Alain Cohen *Claude* • Luce Fabiole *Granny Mémé* • Roger Carel *Victor* • Paul Preboist *Maxime* ■ *Dir* Claude Berri • *Scr* Claude Berri, Gérard Brach, Michel Rivelin

Two on a Guillotine ★★
Mystery
1965 · US · BW · 107mins

To claim her magician father's estate, a woman (Connie Stevens, who also plays her deceased mother) has to spend a week in his scary mansion. A quintessential haunted house picture, produced and directed by TV's *Cannon* William Conrad. Cesar Romero has a lot of camp fun with better than average material.

Connie Stevens *Melinda Duquesne/Cassie Duquesne* • Dean Jones *Val Henderson* • Cesar Romero *John "Duke" Duquesne* • Parley Baer *"Buzz" Sheridan* • Virginia Gregg

---

Dolly Bast • Connie Gilchrist *Ramona Ryerdon* ■ *Dir* William Conrad • *Scr* Henry Slesar, John Kneubuhl, from a story by Henry Slesar

Two or Three Things I Know about Her ★★★★★
Experimental drama
1966 · Fr · Colour · 95mins

Inspired by an article on high-rise prostitution and shot simultaneously with *Made in USA*, this is according to Jean-Luc Godard "a sociological essay in the form of a novel, written not with words, but with notes of music". Marina Vlady stars as the housewife hooker who turns tricks to survive in an increasingly consumerist society. But the real "Her" of the title is Paris, which cinematographer Raoul Coutard captures with a symphonic energy that matches Godard's audacious combination of ideas, images and sounds as he touches on everything from coffee to Vietnam. A tad dated, but still daring. In French with English subtitles.

Marina Vlady *Juliette Janson* • Anny Duperey *Marianne* • Roger Montsoret *Robert Janson* • Jean Narboni *Roger* • Christophe Bourseiller *Christophe* • Marie Bourseiller *Solange* • Raoul Lévy *The American* • Jean-Luc Godard *Narrator* ■ *Dir* Jean-Luc Godard • *Scr* Jean-Luc Godard, from the article *Les Etoiles Filantes* by Catherine Vimenet

Two People ★
Romance
1973 · US · Colour · 100mins

After directing such splendid prestige productions as *West Side Story*, *The Sound of Music*, *The Sand Pebbles* and *The Andromeda Strain*, Robert Wise unwisely dived into the "youth market" with this romance between guilt-ridden draft dodger Peter Fonda and unhappy fashion model Lindsay Wagner. There's far too much "hey man" soul-searching and a rush of domestic crises that would occupy a TV soap for months. Wise's direction also seems to have been influenced by the worst excesses of the French New Wave and the intellectualism of Michelangelo Antonioni. Nice locations but it just appears dated now.

Peter Fonda *Evan Bonner* • Lindsay Wagner *Deirdre McCluskey* • Estelle Parsons *Barbara Newman* • Alan Fudge *Fitzgerald* • Philippe March *Gilles* • Frances Sternhagen *Mrs McCluskey* • Brian Lima *Marcus McCluskey* ■ *Dir* Robert Wise • *Scr* Richard DeRoy

Two Rode Together ★★★ PG
Western
1961 · US · Colour · 104mins

A rather slow-moving late John Ford western, pairing James Stewart and Richard Widmark, who both seem slightly ill at ease in underwritten roles as a cynical sheriff and a gallant cavalry officer out to rescue victims of Comanche raids. Still, *Elmer Gantry's* Shirley Jones and *The Alamo's* Linda Cristal are well at home on the range, and keep an eye open for Henry Brandon, Chief Scar from Ford's classic *The Searchers*. The Stewart character has most of the dialogue but none of the answers, and neither, one suspects, has director Ford. ▣

James Stewart *Guthrie Mccabe* • Richard Widmark *Lieutenant Jim Gary* • Shirley Jones *Marty Purcell* • Linda Cristal *Elena De La Madriaga* • Andy Devine *Sergeant Darius P*

Posey • John McIntire *Major Frazer* • Paul Birch *Edward Purcell* ■ *Dir* John Ford • *Scr* Frank Nugent, from the novel *Comanche Captives* by Will Cook

Two Sisters from Boston ★★★
Musical romantic comedy
1946 · US · BW · 112mins

Boston blue-blood Kathryn Grayson works as the belle of a Bowery nightspot to finance her opera studies. She conceals the fact from her family with the help of her initially outraged younger sister June Allyson and her boss Jimmy Durante, and achieves her ambitions. From the team of producer Joe Pasternak and director Henry Koster, who gave the world the Deanna Durbin movies, this period musical comedy is a sort of Durbin-type vehicle for grown-ups. Sometimes very funny, and with some cute touches – along with famous tenor Lauritz Melchior strutting his stuff, and a very young and pretty Peter Lawford contributing to the romance – it's a charming dose of heavenly nonsense.

Kathryn Grayson *Abigail Chandler* • June Allyson *Martha Canford Chandler* • Lauritz Melchior *Olstrom* • Jimmy Durante *"Spike"* • Peter Lawford *Lawrence Patterson Jr* • Ben Blue *Wrigley* • Isobel Elsom *Aunt Jennifer* • Harry Hayden *Uncle Jonathan* ■ *Dir* Henry Koster • *Scr* Myles Connolly, James O'Hanlon, Harry Crane, Charles Previn, William Wymetal

Two Small Bodies ★
Crime drama
1993 · Ger · Colour · 85mins

There are some movies that you can tell instantly were made from stage plays. This unpleasant film only has two actors, Fred Ward and Suzy Amis. Amis plays a hostess in a strip joint whose two small children have disappeared, and Ward is the cop who conducts his interviews at her home. It's not really a mystery (the fate of the kids is discovered off camera), as the emphasis is on the psychosexual relationship that develops between the two characters. Fred Ward erotic? Didn't the director see *Henry and June*?

Suzy Amis *Eileen Mahoney* • Fred Ward *Lieutenant Brann* ■ *Dir* Beth B • *Scr* Beth B, from the play by Neal Bell

Two Stage Sisters ★★★★★
Period melodrama
1964 · Chi · Colour · 114mins

Denounced for a formalism that supposedly undermined its political value, Xie Jin's period musical drama is one of the glories of pre-Cultural Revolution cinema. Rarely have colour, camera movement and composition been so harmoniously combined for what is, essentially, a backstage melodrama. Showgirls Fang Xie and Yindi Cao drift apart in wartime Shanghai, with the latter marrying in pursuit of material comfort, while the former begins to see the political light. Feminist tract, political thesis and nationalist paean it may be, but this is also an impeccably realised film that succeeds equally as art, propaganda and entertainment. A Mandarin language film.

Xie Fang *Chunhua* • Cao Yindi *Yuehong* • Feng Ji *Xing* • Gao Yuansheng *Jiang Bo* • Shen Fengjuan *Xiao Xiang* ■ *Dir* Xie Jin • *Scr* Lin Gu, Xu Jin, Xie Jin

The Two Tars ★★★★★ U
Silent comedy
1928 · US · BW · 21mins

As an example of what Stan called "reciprocal destruction", this is one of the greatest of Laurel and Hardy's early silents. It features them as two sailors on leave from the USS *Oregon*, doing the kind of comic damage only they are capable of – from wrecking a gum machine to causing a traffic jam of mutilated cars. The girls they pick up on the way – Thelma Hill and Ruby Blaine – are only too happy to get a lift in the rented Model T, but they sneak off quickly when things get tough and bad-tempered characters such as Edgar Kennedy appear. This has the classic final shot in which Stan and Ollie's tin lizzie has an argument with a train and slims down considerably. "Everybody follow them sailors," shouts an irate traffic cop. For years audiences have delighted in following that order. ▣

Stan Laurel *Stan* • Oliver Hardy *Ollie* • Thelma Hill *Brunette coquette* • Ruby Blaine *Blonde coquette* • Charley Rogers *Man whose fenders are ripped back* • Edgar Kennedy *Family motorist* ■ *Dir* James Parrott • *Scr* Leo MaCarey, HM Walker (titles)

2001: a Space Odyssey ★★★★★ U
Science-fiction epic
1968 · UK/US · Colour · 135mins

Stanley Kubrick's seminal sci-fi work is now considered by many to be less a supreme piece of cinema than an interesting, innovative product of the sixties. But the memorable celluloid images still strongly resonate, like the giant, vulnerable fetus floating through space and the tribe of apes painfully putting two and two together. It is Kubrick's haunting, stylised combination of music and visuals which gives *2001* its eerie, mesmerising quality, but even its most devoted disciples are hard pressed to tell you what it's actually about, and, as a slice of philosophy on how we all got started and where we ultimately go, the movie has little credence. However, it's a must-see if you never have, even though its visual impact is seriously hampered by the small screen. ▣

Keir Dullea *Dave Bowman* • Gary Lockwood *Frank Poole* • William Sylvester *Dr Heywood Floyd* • Daniel Richter *Moonwatcher* • Leonard Rossiter *Smyslov* • Margaret Tyzack *Elena* • Robert Beatty *Halvorsen* • Sean Sullivan *Michaels* ■ *Dir* Stanley Kubrick • *Scr* Stanley Kubrick, Arthur C Clarke, from the short story *The Sentinel* by Arthur C Clarke

2010 ★★★ PG
Science-fiction
1984 · US · Colour · 111mins

Based on the novel by Arthur C Clarke, writer/director Peter Hyams' earnest script unites Soviets and Americans to discover why astronaut Bowman vanished. Some spectacular special effects (the space walk transference) are the highlights of this unnecessary sequel to the monumental *2001: a Space Odyssey*, which quickly runs out of rocket fuel after a bright start. The

---

Black Monolith is back, but there is little of Stanley Kubrick's epic sense or masterfully ambiguous myths and mysteries. Instead, director Peter Hyams replaces them with banal over-explicitness and a simplified religious ending. ▣

Roy Scheider *Heywood Floyd* • John Lithgow *Walter Curnow* • Helen Mirren *Tanya Kirbuk* • Bob Balaban *R Chandra* • Keir Dullea *Dave Bowman* • Douglas Rain *Voice of Hal 9000* • Madolyn Smith *Caroline Floyd* • Dana Elcar *Dimitri Moisevitch* ■ *Dir* Peter Hyams • *Scr* Peter Hyams, from the novel *2010: Odyssey Two* by Arthur C Clarke

Two Thousand Maniacs!
★★ 18

Horror　　　　1964 · US · Colour · 79mins

After the notorious *Bloodfeast*, the second best-known splatter shocker from trashmeister Herschell Gordon Lewis is a macabre and ultra-gory update of *Brigadoon*. Just outside the southern town of Pleasant Valley, whose citizens were massacred by Union troops during the Civil War, the dead villagers reappear to wreak horrific revenge on six northern tourists. Lewis mainstays Thomas Wood and the equally wooden Connie Mason are two of the Yankees treated to such southern discomfort as dismemberment, barbecuing, thumb-cutting and being mashed to a pulp in a barrel full of spikes. While as badly acted and technically inept as any Lewis drive-in exploiter, the cheaply graphic effects still carry a potent charge and this "ghastly beyond belief" tale was the nearest the agony auteur ever got to a crossover success. ▣

Connie Mason *Terry Adams* • Thomas Wood [William Kerwin] *Tom White* • Jeffrey Allen *Mayor Buckman* • Ben Moore *Lester* • Shelby Livingston *Bea Miller* • Gary Bakeman *Rufe* • Jerome Eden *John Miller* • Michael Korb *David Wells* ■ *Dir* Herschell G Lewis • *Scr* Herschell G Lewis [Herschell Gordon Lewis], from his story

Two Thousand Women
★★★ PG

Second World War drama
1944 · UK · BW · 92mins

Frank Launder made some of the best films of his career during the Second World War. While not a patch on *Night Train to Munich*, *The Young Mr Pitt* or *Millions like Us*, this was still an effective piece of propaganda, with an uplifting plot (co-written by Launder and Sidney Gilliat) a celebration of British pluck, a healthy spot of Nazi bashing and a dash of gallows humour. However, while this was just what Churchill ordered in 1944, it weighs a little heavily today. Fortunately, among the 2,000 of the title are some of the finest actresses of the time. ▣

Phyllis Calvert *Freda Thompson* • Flora Robson *Miss Manningford* • Patricia Roc *Rosemary Brown* • Renee Houston *Maud Wright* • Anne Crawford *Margaret Long* • Jean Kent *Bridie Johnson* • Reginald Purdell *Alec Harvey* • James McKechnie *Jimmy Moore* ■ *Dir* Frank Launder • *Scr* Frank Launder, Sidney Gilliat, from a story by Frank Launder, Michael Pertwee

Two Tickets to Broadway
★★★ U

Musical comedy 1951 · US · Colour · 106mins

An immensely likeable Technicolor musical with a super cast and a nice line in satire, sending up the then-new medium of television, and featuring a terrific Bob Crosby mickey-take on his famous brother Bing. The girls are particularly scintillating: Janet Leigh, Gloria DeHaven and Ann Miller in one movie, and in Busby Berkeley-choreographed routines too. Tony Martin is a bit of a pudding in the lead, but amiable sidekick Eddie Bracken more than compensates. Lawyer turned director James V Kern wisely stands back and lets the musical numbers and comedy skits work for themselves, a technique that certainly suits the great vaudeville comic headliners Smith and Dale, making a rare movie appearance.

Tony Martin *Dan Carter* • Janet Leigh *Nancy Peterson* • Gloria DeHaven *Hannah Holbrook* • Eddie Bracken *Lew Conway* • Ann Miller *Joyce Campbell* • Barbara Lawrence *"Foxy" Rogers* ■ *Dir* James V Kern • *Scr* Sid Silvers, Hal Kanter, from a story by Sammy Cahn

Two Way Stretch　★★★★ U

Comedy　　　　1960 · UK · BW · 83mins

Fans of Peter Sellers rate this unselfconscious British venture as one of the best things he did: a prison comedy predating *Porridge* and with a snarling stand-off between cocky convict Sellers and paranoid warden Lionel Jeffries. The plot of trying to break back into prison after a heist is wonderfully developed, and the cameos along the way (Irene Handl, Wilfrid Hyde White, Bernard Cribbins) are a delight.

Peter Sellers *Dodger Lane* • Wilfrid Hyde White *Reverend Basil "Soapy" Fowler* • David Lodge *Jelly Knight* • Bernard Cribbins *Lennie Price* • Maurice Denham *Cmdr Horatio Bennet, the prison governor* • Lionel Jeffries *Sidney Crout* • Irene Handl *Mrs Price* • Liz Fraser *Ethel* • Beryl Reid *Miss Pringle* ■ *Dir* Robert Day • *Scr* John Warren, Len Heath, Alan Hackney, from the story by John Warren

Two Weeks in Another Town
★★★★

Melodrama　　1962 · US · Colour · 106mins

If you think film-makers are unstable, this overwrought but convincing fable about Hollywood has-beens will confirm it. Kirk Douglas is the on-the-skids actor in Rome for a small part in a low-budget movie directed by the equally struggling Edward G Robinson, but he's hampered by ex-wife Cyd Charisse and jet-set corruption. It's extraordinarily well acted, and the tricksy style suits the devious characters. Director Vincente Minnelli had, ten years before, made one of the best movies about Hollywood – *The Bad and the Beautiful* also starring Douglas. This concentrates on the "bad" with a look at the soul-destroying insecurity that goes with celebrity. "Beautiful" is only the way they look on screen.

Kirk Douglas *Jack Andrus* • Edward G Robinson *Maurice Kruger* • Cyd Charisse *Carlotta* • George Hamilton *Davie Drew* • Dahlia Lavi *Veronica* • Claire Trevor *Clara Kruger* • James Gregory *Brad Byrd* • Rosanna

Schiaffino *Barzelli* • Joanna Roos *Janet Bark* ■ *Dir* Vincente Minnelli • *Scr* Charles Schnee, from the novel by Irwin Shaw

Two Women　　　　★★★ 15

Second World War drama
1960 · It/Fr · BW · 99mins

Two Women marked the graduation of Sophia Loren from pouting sex-kitten to major league actress as she and her daughter experience the ravages of war, the desolation of being refugees and the horror of rape following the Allied bombing of Rome. Filmed in the neo-realist style of De Sica's earlier classic, *Bicycle Thieves*, the picture earned Loren an Oscar – the first ever awarded to a non-American actor or actress performing in a foreign language. It was a feat not repeated until Roberto Benigni won in 1999 for *Life is Beautiful*. An Italian language film. Contains violence and some swearing. ▣

Sophia Loren *Cesira* • Jean-Paul Belmondo *Michele* • Raf Vallone *Giovanni* • Eleanor Brown *Rosetta* • Renato Salvatori *Florindo* • Carlo Ninchi *Michele's father* • Andrea Checchi *Fascist* ■ *Dir* Vittorio De Sica • *Scr* Cesare Zavattini, Vittorio De Sica, Alberto Moravia

Two Years before the Mast
★★★

Drama　　　　1946 · US · BW · 97mins

They say worse things happen at sea, and they don't come any worse than serving under Howard Da Silva's martinet of a captain in this grim saga of 19th-century seafaring based on a classic book which aimed at reforming sailors' working conditions. Alan Ladd is the shipowner's son, shanghaied into serving under Da Silva and soon stripped to the waist for a flogging. Director John Farrow had a real-life passion for the sea and this lavishly staged and strongly cast production (with William Bendix, Barry Fitzgerald and Brian Donlevy as members of the crew) is the best of Farrow's several maritime adventures, its box-office success eventually prompting his reunion with Ladd for another rough voyage in *Botany Bay* (1952).

Alan Ladd *Charles Stewart* • Brian Donlevy *Richard Henry Dana* • William Bendix *Amazeen* • Howard Da Silva *Captain Francis Thompson* • Barry Fitzgerald *Dooley* • Esther Fernandez *Maria Dominguez* • Albert Dekker *Brown* ■ *Dir* John Farrow • *Scr* Seton I Miller, George Bruce, from the novel by Richard Henry Dana Jr

Twogether　　　　　★★ 18

Drama　　　1994 · US · Colour · 117mins

A pun as bad as this is usually enough to set alarm bells ringing, but this wry look at modern love is not quite as trite as the title suggests. Written and directed by Andrew Chiaramonte, it's a twist on the old "morning after the night before" story, as artist Nick Cassavetes and environmental activist Brenda Bakke get drunk, get married, conceive and get divorced – although not necessarily in that order. Poking none-too-subtle fun at nineties hedonism, this study of adult adolescence could have done with less lust and a few more laughs. ▣

Damian London *Mark Saffron* • Nick Cassavetes *John Madler* • Brenda Bakke *Allison McKenzie* • Jennifer Bassey *Mrs McKenzie* • Jeremy Piven *Arnie* • Jim Beaver *Oscar* ■ *Dir/Scr* Andrew Chiaramonte

Tycoon　　　　　　★★★ U

Drama　　　1947 · US · Colour · 123mins

John Wayne may seem unlikely casting as a railroad engineer in this epic saga, but he's actually very good at conveying steely determination, the mainstay of his character's make-up here. This is a satisfying hunk of Hollywood tosh, with particularly convincing love scenes, perhaps because the Duke and lovely co-star Laraine Day were (allegedly) secretly involved with each other at the time. A stronger director than studio hack Richard Wallace might have made something of that on screen, but nevertheless Wayne and Day are supported by a very distinguished supporting cast, including Sir Cedric Hardwicke, Dame Judith Anderson (Mrs Danvers in *Rebecca*), and a mean Anthony Quinn. ▣

John Wayne *Johnny Munroe* • Laraine Day *Maura Alexander* • Cedric Hardwicke *Frederick Alexander* • Judith Anderson *Miss Braithwaite* • James Gleason *Pop Mathews* • Anthony Quinn *Ricky* • Grant Withers *Fog Harris* ■ *Dir* Richard Wallace • *Scr* Borden Chase, John Twist, from a novel by CE Scoggins

Typhoon　　　　　　　★★★

Adventure romance
1940 · US · Colour · 70mins

After Sam Goldwyn borrowed Dorothy Lamour and had a huge hit with *The Hurricane*, the star's contract studio, Paramount, tried to go one better with *Typhoon*, photographing their famous "Sarong Girl" in glorious Technicolor. It's set on an island in the Pacific and the irretrievably silly plot and screenplay has Lamour as a castaway since childhood who's discovered by a couple of sailors. The rest of the action involves the stock ingredients of a South Seas romantic adventure, with Robert Preston as Lamour's amour. Naturally the film's *raison d'être* is the typhoon, with a forest fire thrown in for good measure. It's OK, but *The Hurricane* was better.

Dorothy Lamour *Dea* • Robert Preston *Johnny Potter* • Lynne Overman *Skipper Joe* • J Carrol Naish *Mekaike* ■ *Dir* Louis King • *Scr* Allen Rivkin, from a story by Steve Fisher

Tyson　　　　　　　★★ 15

Biographical drama
1995 · US · Colour · 105mins

The tempestuous life of boxing champion Mike Tyson sounds like ideal material for a TV movie. Sadly, this glossy biopic only scratches the surface as it follows Tyson from his crime-ridden childhood in Brooklyn, through his rehabilitation as a boxer and his rise to the top of the ranks, to his downfall when he is charged with rape. While Michael Jai White is passable as Tyson, he is overshadowed by veterans George C Scott as Tyson's beloved coach and Paul Winfield as promoter Don King. Director Uli Edel does well in his depiction of the young Tyson's life, but struggles as the story develops. In the end, it is no more revealing than a

U = SUITABLE FOR ALL　Uc = SUITABLE FOR ALL, ESPECIALLY FOR YOUNG CHILDREN (VIDEO ONLY)　PG = PARENTAL GUIDANCE

newspaper feature. Contains swearing, violence and sex scenes. 📺

George C Scott *Cus D'Amato* • Paul Winfield *Don King* • Michael Jai White *Mike Tyson* • James B Sikking *Bill Cayton* • Malcolm-Jamal Warner *Rory Holloway* • Tony LoBianco *Jimmy Jacobs* • Clark Gregg *Kevin Rooney* • Kristen Wilson *Robin Givens* ■ *Dir* Uli Edel • *Scr* Robert Johnson, from the biography *Fire and Fear* by Jose Torres

U-571
★★★ 12

Second World War action thriller
2000 · US · Colour · 116mins

This rip-roaring throwback to the wartime adventures of old finds Matthew McConaughey as a rookie submarine skipper in charge of a crippled U-boat after a secret plot to steal an Enigma code machine from the Nazis goes pear-shaped in the middle of the Atlantic. Since it was British sailors who got hold of the Enigma, it's a tad galling to see the likes of Bill Paxton, Harvey Keitel and Jon Bon Jovi take the credit. But all gripes are forgotten as McConaughey tries to outsmart a German destroyer with just a handful of torpedoes and a leaking sub. Not a patch on Wolfgang Petersen's seminal *Das Boot*, Jonathan Mostow's film does at least deliver its fair share of undemanding popcorn entertainment.

Matthew McConaughey *Lt Andrew Tyler* • Bill Paxton *Lt Commander Mike Dahlgren* • Harvey Keitel *Chief Klough* • Jon Bon Jovi *Lt Peter Emmett* • David Keith *Marine Major Coonan* ■ *Dir* Jonathan Mostow • *Scr* Jonathan Mostow, Sam Montgomery, David Ayer, from a story by Jonathan Mostow

UHF
★★ PG

Parody   1989 · US · Colour · 92mins

This comedy can't decide whether to be another *Kentucky Fried Movie* (in its many parodies of TV shows and movies), or another take on the old "small company versus big heartless corporation" formula. Comic musician "Weird Al" Yankovic (who co-wrote the script) plays a slacker who takes over the management of a failing TV station, and is soon producing bizarre yet top-rated shows, raising the ire of rival TV station manager Kevin McCarthy. Michael Richards gives a side-splittingly funny performance as simple-minded janitor Stanley Spadowski, and the occasional laughs found in the samples of the TV programming make this fun for those willing to put their brain in neutral. 📺

"Weird Al" Yankovic *George Newman* • Victoria Jackson *Teri* • Kevin McCarthy *RJ Fletcher* • Michael Richards *Stanley Spadowski* • David Bowe *Bob* • Stanley Brock *Uncle Harvey* • Anthony Geary *Philo* • Trinidad Silva *Raul Hernandez* ■ *Dir* Jay Levey • *Scr* Al Yankovic ["Weird Al" Yankovic], Jay Levey

US Marshals
★★

Action thriller   1998 · US · Colour · 105mins

Not so much a sequel to *The Fugitive* as a rehash, this has Tommy Lee Jones reprising his Oscar-winning role as US Marshal Samuel Gerard. In place of Harrison Ford, we have Wesley Snipes and in place of a murdered wife, we have a corkscrew plot about

the CIA. Former editor Stuart Baird keeps the action rolling along in a rather monotonous manner and characterisation is limited to the odd one-liner before the next big bang. It wasn't the hit everyone clearly expected, but die-hard fans of mindless action won't be bored. 📺 *DVD*

Tommy Lee Jones *Chief Deputy Marshal Samuel Gerard* • Wesley Snipes *Mark Sheridan* • Robert Downey Jr *John Royce* • Joe Pantoliano *Deputy Marshal Cosmo Renfro* • Daniel Roebuck *Deputy Marshal Biggs* • Tom Wood *Deputy Marshal Newman* • LaTanya Richardson *Deputy Marshal Cooper* • Irène Jacob *Marie* • Kate Nelligan *US Marshal Walsh* ■ *Dir* Stuart Baird • *Scr* John Pogue, from the characters created by Roy Huggins

U Turn
★★★★ 18

Black comedy thriller
1997 · US/Fr · Colour · 119mins

After the information overload of *Nixon* and the controversy of *Natural Born Killers*, Oliver Stone directed this low-budget, compact thriller. It's a rarity from the normally serious director – a surreal black comedy sometimes worthy of Buñuel that pays passing tribute to *Red Rock West* and the pulp fiction of Jim Thompson. Sean Penn stars as the mysterious drifter who arrives in Superior, Arizona, and becomes involved in a small-town conspiracy involving local flirt Jennifer Lopez and her husband Nick Nolte. Lending practised support are Powers Boothe and Billy Bob Thornton, while Jon Voight is almost unrecognisable as a blind native American. As a sustained mood piece, the movie is a triumph. Contains swearing, violence and sex scenes. 📺 *DVD*

Sean Penn *Bobby Cooper* • Jennifer Lopez *Grace McKenna* • Nick Nolte *Jake McKenna* • Powers Boothe *Sheriff Potter* • Claire Danes *Jenny* • Joaquin Phoenix *Toby N Tucker* • Billy Bob Thornton *Darrell* • Jon Voight *Blind man* • Julie Hagerty *Flo* • Bo Hopkins *Ed* • Liv Tyler *Girl in bus station* ■ *Dir* Oliver Stone • *Scr* John Ridley, from his novel *Stray Dogs*

U2 Rattle and Hum
★★★ 15

Concert documentary
1988 · US · Colour and BW · 94mins

After the very wonderful *This Is Spinal Tap*, it's hard to take any "rockumentary" seriously these days, particularly one about the ever sincere U2. In fact, the Irish band even make a very moving visit to Gracelands during their 1987-88 North American tour. That said, this is stylishly shot in a mixture of grainy black and white and colour by Phil Joanou, there's a scene-stealing performance from blues legend BB King and the concert footage is stunning. 📺

Dir Phil Joanou • *Cinematographer* Robert Brinkmann, Jordan Cronenweth

UFOria
★★★ PG

Science-fiction comedy
1980 · US · Colour · 89mins

Grocery store cashier and born-again Christian Cindy Williams awaits the appearance of a flying saucer, which she believes will bring salvation. Her boyfriend (Fred Ward) works for a phoney evangelist (Harry Dean Stanton) who intends to exploit the "God is an astronaut" phenomenon

for all that it's worth. Made in 1980 but shelved until the mid-eighties, this is an amiable, oddball movie that, on its eventual release, picked up quite a few admirers. The acting is fine throughout and the piece, while undisciplined in places, has undeniable charm. 📺

Cindy Williams *Arlene* • Harry Dean Stanton *Brother Bud* • Fred Ward *Sheldon* • Robert Gray *Emile* • Darrell Larson *Toby* • Harry Carey Jr *George Martin* • Hank Worden *Colonel* ■ *Dir/Scr* John Binder

Ugetsu Monogatari
★★★★★ PG

Period melodrama   1953 · Jap · BW · 92mins

Drawing on two stories by Akinari Ueda and one by Guy de Maupassant, this ethereal *jidai-geki* (Japanese period drama) won a top prize at Venice and confirmed Kenji Mizoguchi's reputation in the west. Set during the 16th-century civil wars, the story concerns two peasants whose weakness spells disaster for their wives. Farmer Sakae Ozawa's dream of becoming a samurai precipitates the rape of Mitsuko Mito, while potter Masayuki Mori's obsession with the ghostly Machiko Kyo results in the death of Kinuyo Tanaka. In exploring the transience of happiness and the injustice of patriarchal society, Mizoguchi makes lyrical use of gliding long takes that reinforce his material and mystical themes. It's a work of sheer genius. A Japanese language film. 📺

Machiko Kyo *Lady Wakasa* • Masayuki Mori *Genjuro* • Kinuyo Tanaka *Miyagi* • Sakae Ozawa *Tobei* • Mitsuko Mito *Ohama* ■ *Dir* Kenji Mizoguchi • *Scr* Matsutaro Kawaguchi, Yoshikata Yoda, from the stories *Asaji Ga Yado* and *Jasei No In* from *Ugetsu Monogatari* by Akinari Ueda and from the story *Décoré!* by Guy de Maupassant • *Cinematographer* Kazuo Miyagawa

The Ugly
★★ 18

Horror   1996 · NZ · Colour · 89mins

Kiwi Scott Reynolds's first feature revolves around a male psycho being interviewed by a female shrink and was cheekily dubbed by one wag "The Silence of the New Zealand Lambs". It's all style (for some reason the colour scheme is almost entirely blue and red) and not enough content. The complex flashback structure is deliberately disorienting, as you're never sure which are real events and which are those that the killer (Paolo Rotondo, in his screen debut) remembers happening. This and lots of gory bloodletting make for a disturbing, but rarely pulse-pounding, experience. Contains swearing and violence. 📺

Paolo Rotondo *Simon Cartwright* • Rebecca Hobbs *Dr Karen Shumaker* • Roy Ward *Dr Marlowe* • Vanessa Byrnes *Julie, aged 25* • Sam Wallace *Simon, aged 13* • Paul Glover *Phillip* ■ *Dir/Scr* Scott Reynolds

The Ugly American
★★★ PG

Political drama   1963 · US · Colour · 115mins

Marlon Brando stars in one of his least-known roles, as the American ambassador to Sarkhan, an Asian state divided between north and south, capitalist and communist. Brando intended this as a hard-hitting critique of American foreign policy and a movie that supported the work of the UN – he even cast his sister, Jocelyn, as a UN aid worker. But as usual with Brando, things got rather muddled, the studio interfered and no one could make a decision about anything – least of all the director, who shot it in Thailand. But despite its obvious flaws and bungled scenes, it's eerily prophetic about the Vietnam war, which Kennedy and Johnson were in the process of escalating. ▣

Marlon Brando *Harrison Carter MacWhite* • Eiji Okada *Deong* • Sandra Church *Marion MacWhite* • Pat Hingle *Homer Atkins* • Arthur Hill *Grainger* • Jocelyn Brando *Emma Atkins* • Kukrit Pramoj *Prime Minister Kwen Sai* ■ *Dir* George Englund • *Scr* Stewart Stern, from the novel by William J Lederer, Eugene Burdick

The Ugly Dachshund ★★★ 🅤

Comedy   1966 · US · Colour · 89mins

Ideal entertainment for dog lovers everywhere, this Disney story is about a Great Dane called Brutus who's brought up with dachshunds and, thereafter, thinks he's one of them – however tall he gets. Dean Jones and Suzanne Pleshette are the human stars having to face up to the havoc caused in this charming family fare. Barking mad, maybe, but delightfully so. ▣

Dean Jones *Mark Garrison* • Suzanne Pleshette *Fran Garrison* • Charlie Ruggles [Charles Ruggles] *Dr Pruitt* • Kelly Thordsen *Officer Carmody* • Parley Baer *Mel Chadwick* • Robert Kino *Mr Toyama* • Mako *Kenji* • Charles Lane (1) *Judge* ■ *Dir* Norman Tokar • *Scr* Albert Aley, from the book *Dogs in an Omnibus* by Gladys Bronwyn Stern

Ulee's Gold   ★★★★ 🅸🅵

Drama   1997 · US · Colour · 108mins

The winner of a Golden Globe (though denied a best actor Oscar), Peter Fonda returned from years in the cinematic wilderness to give the best performance of his career in this slow-burning southern drama. Fonda meticulously builds up the character of the Florida beekeeper and Vietnam veteran who has to interrupt his strict routine to rescue his estranged daughter-in-law and tackle the villains double-crossed by his jailed son. Wisely, director Victor Nunez devotes considerable time to watching Fonda tending his hives, for this not only tells us so much about Ulysses Jackson's approach to life, but also sets the pace of the action, which rolls languorously like Tupelo honey dripping off a comb. With so much empty entertainment around, this is a rare treat. Contains some swearing, sexual references and violence. ▣ **DVD**

Peter Fonda *Ulysees "Ulee" Jackson* • Patricia Richardson *Connie Hope* • Jessica Biel *Casey Jackson* • J Kenneth Campbell *Sheriff Bill Floyd* • Christine Dunford *Helen Jackson* • Steven Flynn *Eddie Flowers* • Dewey Weber *Ferris Dooley* ■ *Dir/Scr* Victor Nunez

Ultimate Betrayal   ★★★ 🅸🅵

Drama based on a true story
1994 · US · Colour · 93mins

Donald Wrye's film is a well-acted, thoughtful and harrowing tale about the abuse lurking beneath the surface of a seemingly stable American family, when the youngest daughter (Ally Sheedy) sues her father (Henry Czerny)

who, she alleges, molested his children when they were young. However, not all the siblings are keen to see their past raked over in public. There are moving performances from Marlo Thomas, Mel Harris and Sheedy in the leading roles and Wrye's direction is level-headed, even though it does occasionally tip into overwrought melodrama. But it doesn't quite have the courage of its deeply held convictions. ▣

Marlo Thomas *Sharon Rodgers* • Mel Harris *Susan Rodgers* • Ally Sheedy *Mary Rodgers* • Kathryn Dowling *Beth Rodgers* • Eileen Heckart *Sarah McNeil* ■ *Dir* Donald Wrye • *Scr* Gregory Goodell

Ultimate Lie   ★★

Drama based on a true story
1996 · US · Colour · 97mins

This juicy slice of made-for-TV drama manages to stir both adultery and teenage prostitution into a deliciously over-the-top confection. Blair Brown is the proud mum who is more than a little disturbed to discover that: a) her young daughter (*Sex and the City*'s Kristin Davis) is a call girl; and b) her husband (Michael Murphy) uses the same call-girl service. That's the cue for much weeping, wailing and hand-wringing as the family begins to self destruct. It's good fun if you can manage to keep a straight face.

Kristin Davis *Claire McGrath* • Blair Brown *Joan McGrath* • Michael Murphy *Malcolm McGrath* • George Eads *Ben McGrath* • Gregory Itzin *Richard Levine* • Jane Marla Robbins *Elise Levine* • Nicolette Scorsese *Eileen* ■ *Dir* Larry Shaw • *Scr* Rob Fresco

The Ultimate Warrior
★★★★ 🅸🅵

Science-fiction thriller
1975 · US · Colour · 89mins

Ecological catastrophes have left New York in ruins and under Max von Sydow's ruthless leadership. Yul Brynner is the "street fighter" who guides his own posse of survivors to a better life away from such post-Armageddon tyranny. This is exciting, intelligent stuff from Robert Clouse (*Enter the Dragon*) and strangely prophetic of John Carpenter's 1981 movie *Escape from New York*. Loads of ingenious details and chilling moments make this under-rated science-fiction adventure a cut above the rest, with the final chase out of the city a model of gripping suspense. Contains swearing. ▣

Yul Brynner *Carson* • Max von Sydow *The Baron* • Joanna Miles *Melinda* • William Smith *Carrot* • Richard Kelton *Cal* • Stephen McHattie *Robert* • Darrell Zwerling *Silas* ■ *Dir/Scr* Robert Clouse

Ulysses   ★★★ 🅤

Adventure   1954 · It · Colour · 99mins

Several Italians plus classy Hollywood hacks Ben Hecht and Irwin Shaw laboured on this film of Homer's *Odyssey*. Whenever the actors open their mouths the movie loses its credibility (and the dubbing doesn't help). However, an actor such as Kirk Douglas has tremendous presence – even barefoot and in a mini-skirt – on the long commute home from the Trojan wars and going in to battle with

mythical beasties such as the Cyclops, sultry Sirens and Anthony Quinn. The special effects are cheap and wonky but the movie has an élan that makes it hard to resist. Italian dialogue dubbed into English. ▣

Kirk Douglas *Ulysses* • Silvana Mangano *Penelope/Circe* • Anthony Quinn *Antinous* • Rossana Podesta *Nausicaa* • Sylvie *Euriclea* • Daniel Ivernel *Euriloco* • Jacques Dumesnil *Alicinous* ■ *Dir* Mario Camerini • *Scr* Franco Brusati, Mario Camerini, Ennio De Concini, Hugh Gray, Ben Hecht, Ivo Perilli, Irwin Shaw, from the poem *The Odyssey* by Homer

Ulysses   ★★★ 🅸🅵

Fantasy drama
1967 · US/UK · Colour · 126mins

If ever a great novel was unfilmable, this is it – James Joyce's sublime chronicle of Dublin Jew Leopold Bloom's long night's journey into day. Milo O'Shea is poignant as everyman Bloom and Barbara Jefford is superb as his rancid, randy wife Molly, but the enthusiasm of producer/director/co-writer Joseph Strick just isn't enough to lift Joyce's classic work from the pages and bring it to life. A flawed enterprise, the film is partly salvaged by the use of genuine Dublin locations and the marvellous performances of the mainly Irish cast. ▣

Barbara Jefford *Molly Bloom* • Milo O'Shea *Leopold Bloom* • Maurice Roëves *Stephen Dedalus* • TP McKenna *Buck Mulligan* • Martin Dempsey *Simon Dedalus* • Sheila O'Sullivan *May Goulding Dedalus* ■ *Dir* Joseph Strick • *Scr* Joseph Strick, Fred Haines, from the novel by James Joyce

Ulysses' Gaze   ★★★ 🅿🅶

Epic drama 1995 · Gr/Fr/It · Colour · 173mins

Harvey Keitel stars as a Greek film-maker who goes in search of his Balkan roots in director Theodoros Angelopoulos's lengthy but ultimately haunting political fable. Clearly based on Angelopoulos's own experiences (Keitel's character is called "A"), the film slips between past and present, with both classical and personal allusion, until, by the end of a bleak odyssey of self-discovery, the film-maker has learned more than he ever wanted to know about his former home. An ironic final passage complements the heightened atmosphere of reality, giving this gently unfolding epic drama an assurance that's matched by its audacious courage. In English and Greek with subtitles. ▣

Harvey Keitel *A* • Maia Morgenstern *Woman* • Erland Josephson *Preserver* • Thanassis Vengos *Chauffeur* • Yorgos Michalakopoulos *Correspondant* • Dora Volonaki *Old woman (Athens)* ■ *Dir* Theodoros Angelopoulos • *Scr* Theodoros Angelopoulos, Tonino Guerra, Petro Markaris

Ulzana's Raid   ★★★★ 🅸🅱

Western   1972 · US · Colour · 96mins

This was attacked by some for being a reactionary return to the depiction of native Americans as bloodthirsty savages and mocked by others for its attempts to combine violent action with diatribes about racial prejudice. Yet Robert Aldrich's powerful seventies western also has many champions, who see it as both a bold Vietnam allegory and an attempt to restore a

semblance of historical accuracy to events coloured by decades of horse-opera exploitation and liberal revisionism. Burt Lancaster is superb as the scout saddened by conflict, while Alan Sharp's script and Joseph Biroc's cinematography are first class. Contains violence, some swearing and brief nudity. ▣

Burt Lancaster *McIntosh* • Bruce Davison *Lt Garnett Debuin* • Jorge Luke *Ke-Ni-Tay* • Richard Jaeckel *Sergeant* • Joaquin Martinez *Ulzana* • Lloyd Bochner *Captain Gates* • Karl Swenson *Rukeyser* ■ *Dir* Robert Aldrich • *Scr* Alan Sharp

Umberto D   ★★★★★ 🅿🅶

Drama   1952 · It · BW · 84mins

"The ideal film," wrote Cesare Zavattini, the theoretical father of neorealism, "would be 90 minutes in the life of a man to whom nothing happens." Shot on location, with a non-professional cast and an attention to detail that allows the viewer to discover the emotional or dramatic content of a scene, Vittorio De Sica's poignant study of an ageing civil servant, ostracised by the society he'd so faithfully served, comes close to fulfilling that vision. Fighting despair with dignity, Carlo Battisti is outstanding, whether coddling his devoted dog, Flike, or relishing his chats with pregnant maid, Maria-Pia Casilio. A sublime piece of humanist, observational cinema. An Italian language film. ▣

Carlo Battisti *Umberto Domenico Ferrari* • Maria-Pia Casilio *Maria* • Lina Gennari *Landlady* • Alberto Albani Barbieri *Fiancé* • Elena Rea *Sister* • Ileana Simova *Surprised woman in the bedroom* • Memmo Carotenuto *Voice of light for Umberto in hospital* ■ *Dir* Vittorio De Sica • *Scr* Cesare Zavattini, Vittorio De Sica, from a story by Cesare Zavattini

The Umbrellas of Cherbourg   ★★★★★ 🅤

Musical   1964 · Fr/W Ger · Colour · 86mins

Everything is sung – even the most mundane dialogue – in director Jacques Demy's enchanting French throwback to the Hollywood musicals of the late twenties. The stunning design (Cherbourg citizens allowed their buildings to be painted pink and red) and Catherine Deneuve's ethereal performance add to the fairy-tale qualities of the haunting love story between a shop girl and a garage attendant. It's when he leaves her pregnant to fight in the Algerian War that Demy's tuneful heartbreaker reaches the dizzy romantic heights. Michel Legrand's gorgeous score includes the standard *I Will Wait for You* and *Watch What Happens*. Absolutely beguiling. In French with English subtitles. ▣

Catherine Deneuve *Geneviève Emery* • Nino Castelnuovo *Guy Foucher* • Anne Vernon *Madame Emery* • Ellen Farner *Madeleine* • Marc Michel *Roland Cassard* • Mireille Perrey *Aunt Elise* • Jean Champion *Aubin* • Harald Wolff *Dubourg* ■ *Dir/Scr* Jacques Demy

Unabomber   ★★ 🅸🅵

Drama based on a true story
1996 · US · Colour · 85mins

Hollywood wasted no time in rushing this headline-making news story onto

the air only five months after Ted Kaczynski was captured. This particular slice of exploitation chronicles the massive manhunt for the Unabomber, the mysterious terrorist who, over the course of 18 years, sent 16 deadly home-made bombs to university professors and business executives. Robert Hays (*Airplane*) adequately conveys the emotional torment that David Kaczynski went through when he realised that his brother was the crazed bomber. Tobin Bell as Ted Kaczynski and Dean Stockwell, as a determined postal inspector, do their best for this cheap production, which ultimately offers little insight.

Tobin Bell *Ted Kaczynski* • Robert Hays *David Kaczynski* • Dean Stockwell *Ben Jeffries* • Victoria Mallory *Linda Kaczynski* ■ *Dir* Jon Purdy • *Scr* John McGreevey

The Unbearable Lightness of Being ★★★ 18
Romantic political drama
1988 · US · Colour · 165mins

The problem of coming to terms with reality is the simplest explanation for this blatant, European-style art film directed by American Philip Kaufman. Lengthily elaborated from Milan Kundera's bestseller, it concerns a womanising surgeon (Daniel Day-Lewis) whose main loves are sacred (Juliette Binoche) and profane (Lena Olin), and how their involvement collides with the communist authorities in Czechoslovakia. Some wonderful atmospherics of a besieged culture don't make up for the fact that, at nearly three hours, it runs out of important things to say. Contains swearing and sex scenes.

Daniel Day-Lewis *Tomas* • Juliette Binoche *Tereza* • Lena Olin *Sabina* • Derek De Lint *Franz* • Erland Josephson *The Ambassaador* • Pavel Landowsky *Pavel* • Donald Moffat *Chief Surgeon* ■ *Dir* Philip Kaufman • *Scr* Philip Kaufman, Jean-Claude Carrière, from the novel by Milan Kundera

Unbecoming Age ★★★
Fantasy comedy 1992 · US · Colour · 90mins

In a thought-provoking family film, a downtrodden mum who's just turned 40 is finally able to stick two fingers up to her bullying hubby after a magic bubble grants her deepest desire, and she finds she can no longer remember her age. Renewed "youthfulness" leads to changes in appearance, personality and permissiveness. Diane Salinger and John Calvin star, but the main cast interest resides in an early film appearance by George Clooney. Good for grown-ups and older kids – though smaller children will probably miss some of the film's finer subtleties.

Diane Salinger *Julia* • John Calvin *Charles* • Priscilla Pointer *Grandma* • George Clooney *Mac* • Colleen Camp *Deborah* • Wallace Shawn *Dr Block* • Shera Danese *Letty* ■ *Dir* Deborah Ringel, Alfredo Ringel • *Scr* Meridith Baer, Geoff Prysirr

The Unbelievable Truth ★★★ 15
Drama 1989 · US · Colour · 86mins

Although it has echoes of a popular soap opera in its celebration of the mundane, Hal Hartley's feature debut

(shot in just 11 days) is the closest thing yet to a suburban western – a sort of *Shane* on Long Island. Robert Burke is suitably terse and mysterious as the man in black (is he a killer or a priest?) who gives discontented Adrienne Shelly something more to think about than parental suffocation, nuclear holocaust and teenage romance. Full of quirky conversations and eccentric characters, the film riddles its small-town idyll with well-aimed pot shots. The ending feels forced, however, and Hartley's direction is occasionally overintrusive. Contains swearing.

Adrienne Shelly *Audry Hugo* • Robert John Burke [Robert Burke] *Josh Hutton* • Christopher Cooke [Chris Cooke] *Vic Hugo* • Julia McNeal *Pearl* • Katherine Mayfield *Liz Hugo* • Gary Sauer *Emmet* • Mark Bailey *Mike* • David Healy *Todd Whitbread* • Edie Falco *Jane, a waitress* ■ *Dir/Scr* Hal Hartley

The Unborn ★★ 18
Horror 1991 · US · Colour · 80mins

This schlocky killer-foetus film has a young wife convinced that her doctor has inseminated her with mutant sperm. She's proved right when the offspring avoids abortion and slithers off and goes on the rampage. The film earns a second star simply for the earnestness of some of the actors, who must have realised what twaddle they were in, but put a brave face on things anyway. Aptly, the film gave birth to a sequel three years later.

Brooke Adams *Virginia Marshall* • Jeff Hayenga *Brad Marshall* • James Karen *Dr Richard Meyerling* • K Callan *Martha* • Jane Cameron *Beth* • Lisa Kudrow *Louisa* ■ *Dir* Rodman Flender • *Scr* Henry Dominic

The Uncanny ★ 15
Portmanteau horror
1977 · Can/UK · Colour · 84mins

Petrified Peter Cushing has written a book proving that cats are planning world domination and tries to persuade Ray Milland to publish it on the strength of a trio of creepy tales. In the first, Simon Williams and Susan Penhaligon try to cheat Joan Greenwood's cats out of their inheritance, while in the second an orphan shrinks her evil cousin and uses her as a cat toy. Mercifully it gets no worse because Donald Pleasence and Samantha Eggar put some vim into their *Pit and the Pendulum* pastiche. Overall, however, this dismal portmanteau picture induces more cringes than chills.

Peter Cushing *Wilbur Gray* • Ray Milland *Frank Richards* • Susan Penhaligon *Janet* • Joan Greenwood *Miss Malkin* • Alexandra Stewart *Mrs Joan Blake* • Donald Pleasence *Valentine De'Ath* • Samantha Eggar *Edina Hamilton* ■ *Dir* Denis Héroux • *Scr* Michel Parry

Uncensored ★★ U
Second World War drama
1942 · UK · BW · 106mins

The problem with this wartime movie is that it's too polite. There's no sense of menace or danger in the Belgian setting, where the Nazis are in occupation. That's partly the fault of the screenplay (by three distinguished writers including Terence Rattigan, a regular collaborator with director Anthony Asquith) and Asquith, who

hadn't the temperament for such a story. The central characters are Eric Portman, an entertainer, and Phyllis Calvert. Together they revive a patriotic underground newspaper, *La Libre Belgique*, only to be betrayed. However, the outcome is a far cry from the real likely result of such resistance in 1942.

Eric Portman *Andre Delange* • Phyllis Calvert *Julie Lanvin* • Griffith Jones *Father de Gruyte* • Raymond Lovell *Von Koerner* • Peter Glenville *Charles Neels* • Frederick Culley *Victor Lanvin* • Irene Handl *Frau von Koerner* ■ *Dir* Anthony Asquith • *Scr* Wolfgang Wilhelm, Terence Rattigan, Rodney Ackland

Uncertain Glory ★★★ U
Second World War drama
1944 · US · BW · 97mins

Only too obviously typecast, Errol Flynn plays a philandering criminal in Second World War-ravaged Europe who gives his life, hoping to redeem himself. Though rather talky for a Raoul Walsh-directed movie, it features fine performances by Flynn, Paul Lukas and Jean Sullivan.

Errol Flynn *Jean Picard* • Paul Lukas *Marcel Bonet* • Jean Sullivan *Marianne* • Lucile Watson *Mme Maret* • Faye Emerson *Louise* • James Flavin *Captain of the Guard Mobile* • Douglas Dumbrille [Douglas Dumbrille] *Police commissioner* ■ *Dir* Raoul Walsh • *Scr* Laszlo Vadnay, Max Brand, from a story by Joe May, Laszlo Vadnay

Unchained ★★ U
Prison drama 1955 · US · BW · 75mins

This well-intentioned, serious study of an actual experiment in penal reform is a little dull compared with the average Hollywood prison picture, although its theme song *Unchained Melody* was a huge hit. It was filmed at an actual prison without bars, with veteran star Chester Morris playing the real-life originator of the scheme and blond football star Elroy "Crazylegs" Hirsch in the lead role of an inmate who is tempted to escape. It was made by the independent writer/producer/director Hall Bartlett who had previously produced the film of Hirsch's life story, *Crazylegs*.

Elroy "Crazylegs" Hirsch *Steve Davitt* • Barbara Hale *Mary Davitt* • Chester Morris *Kenyon J Scudder* • Todd Duncan *Bill Howard* • Johnny Johnston *Eddie Garrity* • Peggy Knudsen *Elaine* • Jerry Paris *Joe Ravens* • John Qualen *Leonard Haskins* ■ *Dir* Hall Bartlett • *Scr* Hall Bartlett, from the book *Prisoners Are People* by Kenyon J Scudder

The Uncle ★★★★
Drama 1964 · UK · BW · 89mins

This little charmer caused controversy by being denied a release for two years, during which time the film was slightly re-edited against its director's wishes. But *The Uncle* is one of the cinema's most inventive and perceptive portraits of childhood. It's about a seven year-old boy named Gus who becomes an uncle rather suddenly. The shock of the birth catapults him into an emotional crisis, leading to isolation from his family and school friends. Filmed in and around Plymouth, it's a touching story, beautifully performed by young Robert Duncan and Rupert Davies (the star of the sixties TV series *Maigret*).

Rupert Davies *David* • Brenda Bruce *Addie* • Robert Duncan *Gus* • William Marlowe *Wayne* • Ann Lynn *Sally* • Barbara Leake *Emma* • Helen Fraser *Mary* ■ *Dir* Desmond Davis • *Scr* Desmond Davis, Margaret Abrams, from a novel by Margaret Abrams

Uncle Benjamin ★★★
Swashbuckling comedy
1969 · Fr · Colour · 91mins

The name of Edouard Molinaro will forever be associated with *La Cage aux Folles* . All the good taste and restraint that made that picture an Oscar winner for best foreign language film are gleefully absent in this rollicking piece of costume bawdiness, which comes over as a cross between a Henry Fielding novel and a Hollywood swashbuckler. Jacques Brel is solid enough as the 18th-century country doctor of the title, but veteran actor Bernard Blier steals the picture as a coarse, cruel aristocrat. French dialogue dubbed into English..

Jacques Brel *Benjamin Rathery* • Claude Jade *Manette* • Rosy Varte *Bettine* • Robert Dalban *Aubergiste* • Bernard Blier *Cambyse* • Armand Mestral *Machecourt* ■ *Dir* Edouard Molinaro • *Scr* André Couteaux, Jean-François Hauduroy, from a story by Claude Tillier

Uncle Buck ★★★ 15
Comedy 1989 · US · Colour · 95mins

This movie marked writer/director John Hughes's move away from adolescence, after films such as *The Breakfast Club* and *Ferris Bueller's Day Off*, and return to childhood. Despite the fact that this was also the film that unleashed Macaulay Culkin on to the world at large, there is still much to enjoy. John Candy makes the most of his starring role as the loveable slob who is pressed into looking after his brother's children and Hughes stages some neat comic set pieces. Only the sentimental moralising strikes a false note. Contains swearing.

John Candy *Buck Russell* • Macaulay Culkin *Miles Russell* • Jean Louisa Kelly *Tia Russell* • Gaby Hoffman *Maizy Russell* • Amy Madigan *Chanice Kobolowski* • Elaine Bromka *Cindy Russell* • Garrett M Brown *Bob Russell* • Laurie Metcalf *Marcie Dahlgren-Frost* • Jay Underwood *Bug* ■ *Dir/Scr* John Hughes

Uncle Sam ★★ 18
Comedy horror 1997 · US · Colour · 85mins

Controversial director William Lustig has created an unusually comic-tinged horror movie that tries to mix in some serious moments. The problem with the Larry Cohen screenplay is its contradictions – on the one hand it attempts to criticise the American military and its more recent wars, on the other it attacks "undesirable" citizens (including draft dodgers) who undermine the country. Wherever the viewpoint is in the course of the film, it never seems to fit with the main story concerning a dead Gulf War veteran who comes back to life, dresses in an Uncle Sam costume and kills various unpatriotic people in his home town. Better special effects might have helped. Contains violence, nudity and drug abuse.

Leslie Neale *Sally Baker* • Christopher Ogden *Jody Baker* • David "Shark" Fralick *Sam Harper* • Robert Forster *Congressman*

Cummings • Timothy Bottoms *Donald Crandall* • Isaac Hayes *Jed Crowley* • Bo Hopkins *Sgt Twining* ■ *Dir* William Lustig • *Scr* Larry Cohen

Uncle Silas ★★★
Chiller 1947 · UK · BW · 102mins

Though dated, this melodrama is distinguished by a glowing performance from the lovely Jean Simmons, as the teenage ward sent to live with creepy old Uncle Silas (Derrick de Marney) in his ramshackle mansion. Atmospherics abound, with the nightmarish feel superbly sustained by the cinematography of Robert Krasker and Nigel Huke, and helped by the over-the-top performances of de Marney and Greek actress Katina Paxinou (*For Whom the Bell Tolls*). It's one of those tales in which Simmons finally realises de Marney is trying to do her in, which today seems a bit laughable. But throw yourself into its steamy, manic moodiness and you'll enjoy it all the same.

Jean Simmons *Caroline Ruthyn* • Katina Paxinou *Madame De La Rougierre* • Derrick de Marney *Uncle Silas* • Derek Bond *Lord Richard Ilbury* • Sophie Stewart *Lady Monica Waring* • Manning Whiley *Dudley Ruthyn* • Esmond Knight *Dr Bryerly* • Reginald Tate *Austin Ruthyn* ■ *Dir* Charles Frank • *Scr* Ben Travers, from the novel by Sheridan Le Fanu

Uncle Tom's Cabin ★★★ PG
Drama 1987 · US · Colour · 108mins

This is a fine adaptation of Harriet Beecher Stowe's classic novel, which follows the plight of two slaves, Tom and Eliza, in the pre-Civil War South as they make their separate and very different ways through the evil system of slavery. Avery Brooks as Uncle Tom gives great pathos to his portrayal of the humble slave, while Edward Woodward is chilling as the venomous overseer, Simon Legree. Phylicia Rashad and Bruce Dern round out a strong cast artfully directed by Stan Lathan, and there's a pre-stardom appearance from Samuel L Jackson. Though it was written over 100 years ago, there is nothing dated about this timeless story.

Avery Brooks *Uncle Tom* • Phylicia Rashad *Eliza* • Bruce Dern *St Clare* • Edward Woodward *Simon Legree* • George Coe *Shelby* • Jenny Lewis *Little Eva* • Troy Beyer *Emmeline* • Paula Kelly *Cassy* • Samuel Jackson [Samuel L Jackson] *George* ■ *Dir* Stan Lathan • *Scr* John Gay, from the novel by Harriet Beecher Stowe

Uncommon Valor ★★★ 15
Action drama 1983 · US · Colour · 100mins

Gene Hackman is incapable of giving a bad performance, although he hasn't always worked on the best of films. This action tale is a case in point, as he brings an unusual psychological depth to the part of an embittered father leading a hand-picked platoon into Laos to find his son, reported missing in action ten years before in Vietnam. Joe Gayton's script would win no prizes for originality or political correctness, and the direction of Ted Kotcheff only just passes muster. However, co-producer John Milius knows how to put on a show. Contains violence and swearing.

Gene Hackman *Colonel Rhodes* • Robert Stack *MacGregor* • Fred Ward *Wilkes* • Reb

Brown *Blaster* • Randall "Tex" Cobb *Sailor* • Patrick Swayze *Scott* • Harold Sylvester *Johnson* • Tim Thomerson *Charts* ■ *Dir* Ted Kotcheff • *Scr* Joe Gayton

Unconquered ★★★
Historical adventure 1947 · US · Colour · 146mins

Cecil B DeMille's vast western epic stars Paulette Goddard, as the cockney murderess transported to slavery in colonial America, where Gary Cooper saves her from the clutches of fur trapper Howard Da Silva. As if that wasn't enough, there's savage tribesmen, shooting the rapids and being burned at the stake to contend with, too. With all that to get through, it's hardly surprising this adventure seems to last forever. Fortunately, DeMille keeps the moralising to a minimum and just seems anxious to pack as much passion, drama, and colour into it as the budget will allow. A real galumpher of a movie – Cooper is as dull as ditchwater, but Goddard shows she's a real trouper.

Paulette Goddard *Abby Hale* • Gary Cooper *Capt Chris Holden* • Howard Da Silva *Martin Garth* • Boris Karloff *Guyasuta* • Cecil Kellaway *Jeremy Love* • Ward Bond *John Fraser* • Katherine DeMille *Hannah* • Henry Wilcoxon *Capt Steele* • C Aubrey Smith *Lord Chief Justice* ■ *Dir* Cecil B DeMille • *Scr* Charles Bennett, Frederic M Frank, Jesse Lasky Jr, from the novel *The Judas Tree* by Neil H Swanson

Unconquered ★★★★ PG
Drama based on a true story 1989 · US · Colour · 113mins

This TV movie combines an uplifting true story of individual sporting success against the odds with an illuminating study of racial hatred in the American South at the time of Martin Luther King. The worthy cast is headed by Peter Coyote as a progressive senator and Dermot Mulroney as his athlete son, coping with both the prejudice against his father and his own physical disabilities. The result is an above-average effort that could be described as *Chariots of Fire* with a social conscience.

Peter Coyote *Richmond Flowers Sr* • Dermot Mulroney *Richmond Flowers Jr* • Tess Harper *Mary Flowers* • Jenny Robertson *Cindy Shiver* • Frank Whaley *Arnie Woods* • Bob Gunton *George Wallace* • Larry Riley *Martin Luther King* • RD Call *Floyd Petrie* • Noble Willingham *Bear Bryant* ■ *Dir* Dick Lowry • *Scr* Pat Conroy, from a story by Martin Chitwood

The Undead ★★★ 15
Horror 1957 · US · BW · 71mins

Cult director Roger Corman's first "real" horror movie – albeit one with sci-fi overtones – was this quickie reincarnation tale that cashed in on the "previous existence" craze of the fifties. Filmed in a derelict supermarket (hence the strangely effective, claustrophobic atmosphere), the film has Pamela Duncan as a hapless hooker who, hypnotised by her psychiatrist, returns to medieval times where she's condemned as a witch. The super-low budget stretched to rampaging knights in armour, a neat metamorphosis of witch to cat, and even an appearance by the Devil. A

textbook example of cut-price Corman.

Pamela Duncan *Helene/Diana* • Richard Garland *Pendragon* • Allison Hayes *Livia* • Val Dufour *Quintus* • Mel Welles *Smolkin* • Dorothy Neuman *Meg Maud* • Billy Barty *The Imp* ■ *Dir* Roger Corman • *Scr* Charles Griffith, Mark Hanna

The Undeclared War ★★★★
Documentary 1992 · Fr · Colour · 240mins

Gleaned from 50-odd hours of interviews with 28 conscripted veterans of the battle for Algeria (1954–62), Bertrand Tavernier's documentary broke a silence that had existed since a divided France ceded what to many was less a colony than an integral part of *La Patrie*. Employing personal photos and establishing shots of the north African desert and the city of Grenoble (home to the interviewees and site of one of the most ferocious antiwar demonstrations), Tavernier allows the men to explore their own memories and emotions. While some deliver impenitent diatribes, others simply break down. Harrowing, revelatory and invaluable. In French with English subtitles.

Dir Bertrand Tavernier

The Undefeated ★★ PG
Western 1969 · US · Colour · 113mins

The title could well refer to the film's two stars, both, alas, well past their sell-by dates. A late western, this is undistinguished but beautifully photographed, in Panavision, by veteran cameraman William Clothier. A toupeed, paunchy John Wayne is a Union colonel on his way to Mexico, who confronts mustachioed Confederate colonel Rock Hudson. The theme of post-Civil War reconciliation ensures that no sparks fly between the two main characters; nor is there any real chemistry between the stars. Director Andrew V McLaglen seems to have had problems establishing the right tone for this tale. US football fans might relish the casting of gridiron stars Roman Gabriel and Merlin Olsen, while lovers of the genre might recall the glory days of those members of John Ford's repertory company present here – Ben Johnson and Harry Carey Jr.

John Wayne *Colonel John Henry Thomas* • Rock Hudson *Colonel James Langdon* • Tony Aguilar *General Rojas* • Roman Gabriel *Blue Boy* • Marian McCargo *Ann Langdon* • Ben Johnson *Short Grub* • Harry Carey Jr *Webster* ■ *Dir* Andrew V McLaglen • *Scr* James Lee Barrett, from a story by Stanley L Hough

Under California Stars ★★ U
Western 1948 · US · Colour · 69mins

In this minor late entry in the career of self-styled "king of the cowboys" Roy Rogers, much of the pleasure is provided by B-musical star Jane Frazee, the former radio singer best known for swingin' and swayin' in movies such as *Kansas City Kitty* and *Hellzapoppin'*. She provides a watchable alternative to Trigger, as Rogers once again manages to avoid damage to his cowboy outfits, despite fisticuffs and some hard riding. Rogers's movies

with Republic director Joseph Kane (44 in all) were a good deal more fun than the grittier later ones, directed by William Witney, who tried to toughen up Roy's image from 1946 onwards. For fans only.

Roy Rogers *Roy Rogers* • Jane Frazee *Caroline Maynard* • Andy Devine *Cookie Bullfincher* • George H Lloyd [George Lloyd] *Jonas "Pop" Jordan* • Wade Crosby *Lye McFarland* • Michael Chapin *Ted Conover* • House Peters Jr *Ed* ■ *Dir* William Witney • *Scr* Sloan Nibley, Paul Gangelin, from a story by Paul Gangelin

Under Capricorn ★★★ PG
Period melodrama 1949 · UK · Colour · 112mins

Although this is one of Alfred Hitchcock's oddest movies, the master's hand is firmly in evidence. A melodrama with strong echoes of *Rebecca* and *Suspicion* set in 19th-century Australia, it stars Ingrid Bergman as a rich woman coming to terms with her marriage to stablehand and transported convict Joseph Cotten. The production was troubled by the start of Bergman's infamous love affair with Roberto Rossellini and by Hitchcock's eagerness to finish the film quickly to avoid paying British taxes. Fresh from *Rope*, with its experimental single-take technique, Hitchcock intended to shoot *Under Capricorn* in a similar style. This idea was quickly abandoned, though you may notice some shots that run for more than five minutes without a cut, contributing to the film's heady, half-baked romanticism. A terrible flop on release, it has, like many other Hitchcock films, been re-evaluated in recent years.

Ingrid Bergman *Lady Henrietta Flusky* • Joseph Cotten *Sam Flusky* • Michael Wilding *Charles Adare* • Margaret Leighton *Milly* • Cecil Parker *Governor* • Denis O'Dea *Corrigan* • Jack Watling *Winter* ■ *Dir* Alfred Hitchcock • *Scr* James Bridie, Hume Cronyn, from the play by John Colton, Margaret Linden and from the novel by Helen Simpson

Under Fire ★★★★ 15
Political drama 1983 · US · Colour · 122mins

This exceptional political thriller, part morality tale and part action adventure, has three journalists (Nick Nolte, Gene Hackman and Joanna Cassidy) covering the Nicaraguan revolution and becoming involved in the violent struggle. Director Roger Spottiswoode has brilliantly realised the electric atmosphere generated by rubble-strewn streets, above which snipers lurk and in which people die just because they get in the way. The three stars stand out and Jean-Louis Trintignant is credibly creepy as a French double agent. What's most intriguing, though, is the way the journalists try to stay aloof, yet still find themselves forced to take sides. It's hard to keep your cool when all around are losing theirs. Contains swearing.

Nick Nolte *Russell Price* • Ed Harris *Oates* • Gene Hackman *Alex Grazier* • Joanna Cassidy *Claire Stryder* • Alma Martinez *Isela* • Holly Palance *Journalist* • Jean-Louis Trintignant *Marcel Jazy* ■ *Scr* Ron Shelton, Clayton Frohman, from a story by Clayton Frohman

U = SUITABLE FOR ALL Us = SUITABLE FOR ALL, ESPECIALLY FOR YOUNG CHILDREN (VIDEO ONLY) PG = PARENTAL GUIDANCE

Under Investigation ★★
Murder mystery 1993 · US · Colour · 94mins
This erotic thriller has the usual mix of fall-guys and *femmes fatales*, portrayed by actors who really should know better. Former *LA Law* star Harry Hamlin plays the world-weary detective who gets mixed up with Joanna Pacula, his prime suspect in a murder investigation. There's a better than average supporting cast (Ed Lauter, Richard Beymer), but both the plotting and the direction lack imagination. Contains volence, sex scenes, swearing and nudity.
Harry Hamlin *Detective Harry Keaton* • Joanna Pacula *Abbey Jane Strong* • Ed Lauter *Captain Maguire* • Richard Beymer *Dr Jerry Parsons* ■ *Dir/Scr* Kevin Meyer

Under Milk Wood ★★★ 15
Drama 1971 · UK · Colour · 87mins
Dylan Thomas's celebrated 1954 radio play was a complex blend of dream, reality and poetry, which dealt with life, love and liquid refreshment in the mythical Welsh fishing village of Llaregyub. Richard Burton, who plays "First Voice" – the narrator – knew Thomas well and had performed the play on radio. He's joined here by his then-wife Elizabeth Taylor as the childhood sweetheart of Captain Cat, the blind seafarer played by Peter O'Toole. There's a fascinating cast and Thomas's dialogue remains exceptionally vivid – especially with Burton's voice driving much of it. Andrew Sinclair's direction sensibly avoids any divertionary fireworks. ▭
Richard Burton *First Voice* • Elizabeth Taylor *Rosie Probert* • Peter O'Toole *Captain Cat* • Glynis Johns *Myfanwy Price* • Vivien Merchant *Mrs Pugh* • Sian Phillips *Mrs Ogmore-Pritchard* • Victor Spinetti *Mog Edwards* ■ *Dir* Andrew Sinclair • *Scr* Andrew Sinclair, from the radio play by Dylan Thomas

Under Oath ★★
Crime drama 1996 · US · Colour
There are shades of the under-rated cinema release *Gang Related* in this determinedly cynical TV movie about police corruption. Here Jack Scalia and Eddie Velez are two bitter detectives who decide to swindle a suspected gun dealer. But they do not realise that their intended victim is actually an undercover agent and, when he is accidentally killed, all hell breaks loose. The supporting cast isn't bad (Richard Lynch, James Russo) and the action bustles along at a nice pace. Contains violence.
Jack Scalia *Nick Hollit* • Eddie Velez *Ray Ramirez* • James Russo *Chief Erickson* • Richard Lynch *Daniel Saltarelli* ■ *Dir* Dave Payne • *Scr* Scott Sandin

Under Pressure ★★★
Thriller 1997 · US · Colour · 88mins
Charles Sheen – the artist formerly known as Charlie – plays a fireman who wins a bravery medal. But because his wife leaves him he turns into the neighbour from hell, menacing little kids whose model plane breaks his window, killing repair men and generally behaving badly. The plot has elements of both *Backdraft* and *Falling Down* and while Sheen gives a fine performance, the direction is a mite too mild-mannered to make this thriller as chilling as it should have been. ▭
Charles Sheen [Charlie Sheen] *Lyle Wilder* • Mare Winningham *Catherine Braverton* • David Andrews *Reese Braverton* • Noah Fleiss *Zach Braverton* • Chelsea Russo *Marcie Braverton* • John Ratzenberger *Al Calavito* • Dawnn Lewis *Sandy Tierra* ■ *Dir* Craig R Baxley • *Scr* Betsy Giffen Nowrasteh

Under Satan's Sun ★★★★
Religious drama 1987 · Fr · Colour · 98mins
Since Robert Bresson had already adapted two Georges Bernanos novels, *Diary of a Country Priest* and *Mouchette*, it was logical that Maurice Pialat should elect to emulate his stark authenticity in relating Bernanos's tale of the village cleric who comes to see Satan as the world's controlling force. Yet, this is clearly the work of an atheist, who considers that Father Gérard Depardieu's relentless self-flagellation is as much an act of pride as saintliness. The elliptical structure brings an intellectual rigour to the emotive exchanges, while the performances of Depardieu and Sandrine Bonnaire, as a pregnant teenage killer, are riveting in their intensity. In French with English subtitles.
Gérard Depardieu *Donissan* • Sandrine Bonnaire *Mouchette* • Maurice Pialat *Menou-Segrais* • Alain Artur *Cadignan* • Yann Dedet *Gallet* • Brigitte Legendre *Mouchette's mother* • Jean-Claude Bourlat *Malorthy* ■ *Dir* Maurice Pialat • *Scr* Sylvie Danton, Maurice Pialat, from a novel by Georges Bernanos

Under Siege ★★ 15
Political thriller 1986 · US · Colour · 138mins
Not the Steven Seagal film, but a TV movie about terrorism in America, which culminates in an attack on the buildings of power in Washington DC. The ever-dependable Peter Strauss stars with Hal Holbrook, Lew Ayres and Paul Winfield, but even these considerable talents can't overcome a slow-moving plot. One of the many scriptwriters on the film was none other than journalist Bob Woodward, of Watergate fame. ▭
Peter Strauss *John Garry* • Hal Holbrook *President Monroe* • EG Marshall *Harold Sloan* • Paul Winfield *Andrew Simon* • Lew Ayres *John Pace* • Frederick Coffin *Dan Murphy* • Mason Adams *Geoffrey Wiggins* • Fritz Weaver *Bernard Hughes* ■ *Dir* Roger Young • *Scr* Bob Woodward, Christian Williams, Richard Harwood, Alfred Sole, from a story by Bob Woodward, Christian Williams, Richard Harwood

Under Siege ★★★★ 15
Action adventure 1992 · US · Colour · 98mins
After a string of routine action thrillers, Steven Seagal hit gold with this slick nautical spin on the *Die Hard* concept. Portraying possibly the unlikeliest cook in the history of cinema, Seagal is the US Navy's only hope when a crack squad of terrorists, led by Tommy Lee Jones, hijacks his ship. Seagal lacks natural charisma, but at least he's marginally less wooden than the likes of Chuck Norris, and a flamboyant performance from Jones, plus some sterling work from fellow baddies Gary Busey and Colm Meaney, more than compensate for his deficiencies. Former *Baywatch* babe Erika Eleniak has little to do but pop out of a cake and scream a lot, but provides the requisite slice of glamour. Like Seagal, director Andrew Davis earned his spurs with mainly straight to video fodder, but here he never misses a beat and stages some awesome set pieces. Contains swearing and violence, with a nude scene. ▭ *DVD*
Steven Seagal *Casey Ryback* • Tommy Lee Jones *William Strannix* • Gary Busey *Commander Krill* • Erika Eleniak *Jordan Tate* • Patrick O'Neal *Captain Adams* • Damian Chapa *Tackman* • Troy Evans *Granger* • David McKnight *Flicker* • Colm Meaney *Daumer* ■ *Dir* Andrew Davis • *Scr* JF Lawton

Under Siege 2 ★★ 18
Action thriller 1995 · US · Colour · 93mins
The original *Under Siege* was a hugely entertaining affair, thanks mainly to the sheer scale of the destruction and its top-drawer cast of cartoon villains. This sequel sadly falls down in both departments. Basically, it's the same story – this time set on a train. Steven Seagal is a chef who finds himself up against another gang of international terrorists, led by the faintly ludicrous mad professor Eric Bogosian. New Zealand director Geoff Murphy gives it his all, but there is a second-hand feel to the increasingly outlandish action stunts. Contains swearing and violence. ▭ *DVD*
Steven Seagal *Casey Ryback* • Eric Bogosian *Travis Dane* • Katherine Heigl *Sarah Ryback* • Morris Chestnut *Bobby Zachs* • Everett McGill *Penn* • Kurtwood Smith *General Stanley Cooper* • Nick Mancuso *Tom Breaker* • Andy Romano *Admiral Bates* ■ *Dir* Geoff Murphy • *Scr* Richard Hatem, Matt Reeves, from the characters created by JF Lawton

Under Suspicion ★★★ 18
Thriller 1991 · US/UK · Colour · 95mins
An intriguing if not entirely successful attempt to create a home-grown *noir* thriller, this stars Liam Neeson as a cynical private eye caught up in a tortuous murder plot involving *femme fatale* Laura San Giacomo. The fifties Brighton setting is suitably seedy and, as with other films of its ilk, there's plenty of twists and turns. However the story is a little far-fetched and Neeson never really convinces as the hard-boiled private detective. ▭
Liam Neeson *Tony Aaron* • Laura San Giacomo *Angeline* • Kenneth Cranham *Frank* • Maggie O'Neill *Hazel* • Alan Talbot *Powers* • Malcolm Storry *Waterston* • Martin Grace *Colin* • Kevin Moore *Barrister* ■ *Dir/Scr* Simon Moore

Under Ten Flags ★★ U
Second World War drama 1960 · US/It · BW · 113mins
"An inexplicably dreadful piece of multilingual nonsense about the war", wrote Charles Laughton's biographer, Simon Callow, of this naval drama. Produced in Italy by Dino De Laurentiis with an Italian director and crew, it stars Laughton as a British bulldog admiral and Van Heflin as a German skipper, playing cat and mouse with each other. While Van Heflin is not your usual card-carrying Nazi, just a clever tactician, Laughton goes for the full Churchillian effect. A derisory love story with French import Mylene Demongeot is thrown in but just slows things down considerably.
Van Heflin *Reger* • Charles Laughton *Adm Russell* • Mylene Demongeot *Zizi* • John Ericson *Krueger* • Liam Redmond *Windsor* • Alex Nicol *Knoche* • Grégoire Aslan *Master of Abdullah* • Cecil Parker *Col Howard* ■ *Dir* Duilio Coletti • *Scr* Vittoriano Petrilli, Duilio Coletti, Ulrich Mohr, Leonardo Bercovici (uncredited), William Douglas Home, from the diaries of Bernhard Rogge

Under the Boardwalk ★ 15
Comedy 1988 · US · Colour · 98mins
This update of Shakespeare's *Romeo and Juliet* is set on the beaches of California. Here members of rival surf teams fall in love during a weekend of fierce competition at an annual surf-off. Weirdly, this teen romance is narrated by a character from the future, but even this oddity fails to add spark to what is a lucklustre story hampered further by cheap production values. ▭
Keith Coogan *Andy* • Danielle Von Zerneck *Allie* • Richard Joseph Paul *Nick Rainwood* • Steve Monarque *Reef* • Roxana Zal *Gitch* • Brian Avery *Hap Jordan* • Hunter Von Leer *Midas* ■ *Dir* Fritz Kiersch

Under the Cherry Moon ★ 15
Musical romance 1986 · US · BW · 100mins
Even ardent fans of the "artist formerly known as Prince" will scoff at this monumentally pretentious ego trip, in which His Purpleness plays a piano-playing gigolo on the French Riviera, wooing rich Kristin Scott Thomas against her father's wishes. In a gob-smacking black-and-white exercise in narcissistic posturing, Prince endlessly compares wardrobes with Jerome Benton, makes love on a bed of rose petals, and finally dies (thank goodness!). The soundtrack – which is among the star's best work – is reduced to the level of background music. It's a vanity venture, not even worth watching for kitsch value. Contains some violence and swearing. ▭
Prince *Christopher Tracy* • Jerome Benton *Tricky* • Kristin Scott Thomas *Mary Sharon* • Steven Berkoff *Mr Sharon* • Francesca Annis *Mrs Wellington* • Emmanuelle Sallet *Katy* • Alexandra Stewart *Mrs Sharon* ■ *Dir* Prince • *Scr* Becky Johnston

Under the Doctor ★ 18
Comedy 1976 · UK · Colour · 81mins
Such was the state of British screen comedy in the 1970s that even its stalwarts were reduced to accepting roles as nudie cuties. Indeed, Liz Fraser did nothing but peek-a-boo fluff in the middle of the decade, managing to retain her dignity while all else were losing their clothes. She's joined here by Barry Evans, who gets to play four different roles, the most significant being an amorous psychiatrist coping with a clientele made up exclusively of sexually frustrated females. ▭
Barry Evans *Colin/Dr Boyd/Mr Johnson/Lt Cranshaw* • Liz Fraser *Sandra* • Hilary Pritchard *Lady Victoria* • Penny Spencer *Marion* • Jonathan Cecil *Rodney Harrington-Harrington/Lord Woodbridge* ■ *Dir* Gerry Poulson • *Scr* Ron Bareham

Under the Hula Moon ★★★

Comedy thriller   1995 · US · Colour · 96mins

Reminiscent of *Raising Arizona*, this is an eccentric romantic comedy about a trailer-park couple who have only their dream of moving to Hawaii to sustain them. Their dream is put on the backburner when the husband's convict brother escapes from prison and comes a-calling. Stephen Baldwin and Christopher Penn play the male leads. But any British interest resides in the film's leading lady, Emily Lloyd, the bright young actress whose career rapidly went from wishing she was here to wishing she was anywhere. She's good, proving that she only needs the right film to re-establish herself. Unfortunately this obviously wasn't it, watchable though she is. Contains violence and swearing.

Stephen Baldwin *Buzz* • Emily Lloyd *Betty* • Christopher Penn *Turk* • Musetta Vander *Maya Gundinger* • Pruitt Taylor Vince *Bob* ■ *Dir* Jeff Celantano • *Scr* Jeff Celantano, Gregory Webb

Under the Influence   ★★

Drama   1986 · US · Colour · 100mins

Andy Griffith (*Matlock*) plays an alcoholic who denies his addiction and drives his wife and two of his four kids into their own battle with substance abuse. After he suffers a heart attack, the whole family is forced to face the reality of their dysfunctional lives. Griffith, Joyce Van Patten, Season Hubley, Dana Andersen and Keanu Reeves are excellent as the self-destructive family. Sharply directed by Thomas Carter (*Miami Vice*), this TV movie offers a sobering portrait of a middle-class family in crisis. An important social issue drama done with style and intelligence.

Andy Griffith *Noah Talbot* • Season Hubley *Ann Talbot Simpson* • Paul Provenza *Stephen Talbot* • Keanu Reeves *Eddie Talbot* • Dana Andersen *Terri Talbot* • Kario Salem *John Simpson* ■ *Dir* Thomas Carter • *Scr* Joyce Rebeta-Burditt

Under the Piano   ★★★ 15

Drama   1995 · Can · Colour · 87mins

One of the world's leading opera stars takes centre stage in this heart-rending Canadian melodrama. As the faded diva who is too wrapped up in her own woes to recognise the talent of her autistic savant daughter, Teresa Stratas sweeps through every scene with imperious disdain. Strong performances from Megan Follows and Amanda Plummer maintain the balance, however, with Follows particularly impressive as she battles both her condition and her domineering mother to fulfil her musical potential. Based on the true story of sisters Dolly and Henrietta Giardini, this is a thoughtful and powerfully played variation on the *Rain Man* theme. 🖵

Amanda Plummer *Franny* • Megan Follows *Rosetta* • Teresa Stratas *Regina* • James Carroll *Nick* • John Juliani *Frank* • Jackie Richardson *Mrs Syms* • Richard Blackburn *Dr Banman* • Dan Lett *Dr Harkness* ■ *Dir* Stefan Scaini • *Scr* Blair Ferguson

Under the Rainbow   ★ PG

Comedy   1981 · US · Colour · 93mins

Despite the presence of the great Eve Arden, a former Ziegfeld girl and put-down queen of screwball comedies, this strange attempt at a comedy set in Hollywood's golden era is a grotesque misfire. Chevy Chase and Carrie Fisher are a talent scout and FBI agent respectively who uncover a Nazi plot in a hotel over-run with scores of oddball eccentrics from the cast of *The Wizard of Oz*. A yellow brick road to nowhere – and certainly not to any form of entertainment. 🖵

Chevy Chase *Bruce Thorpe* • Carrie Fisher *Annie Clark* • Billy Barty *Otto Kriegling* • Eve Arden *Duchess* • Joseph Maher *Duke* • Robert Donner *Assassin* • Mako *Nakamuri* • Cork Hubbert *Rollo Sweet* ■ *Dir* Steve Rash • *Scr* Pat McCormick, Harry Hurwitz, Martin Smith, Pat Bradley, Fred Bauer, from a story by Pat Bradley, Fred Bauer

Under the Red Robe   ★★

Swashbuckling drama
1937 · UK · BW · 80mins

Victor Sjöström was the director of many silent classics in his native Sweden and, most famously, *The Wind*, made in Hollywood and *The Divine Woman*, the sole Garbo film lost to history. Also a fine actor, he retired from directing in 1930, then returned to the megaphone for this final movie, made for Alexander Korda. It's a swashbuckler, set in 17th-century France, with Conrad Veidt as a gambler condemned to be executed, who's then given a deadly mission by Cardinal Richelieu (Raymond Massey). It has the odd moment, but was not to be the crowning glory of Sjöström's career; that came in 1957 with his performance in Bergman's masterpiece *Wild Strawberries*.

Conrad Veidt *Gil de Berault* • Annabella *Lady Marguerite* • Raymond Massey *Cardinal Richelieu* • Romney Brent *Marius* • Sophie Stewart *Elise, Duchess of Foix* • Wyndham Goldie *Edmond, Duke of Foix* • Lawrence Grant *Father Joseph* ■ *Dir* Victor Seastrom [Victor Sjöström] • *Scr* Lajos Biro, Philip Lindsay, JL Hodson, Arthur Wimperis, from the play by Edward E Rose and the novel by Stanley J Weyman

Under the Skin   ★★★★ 18

Drama   1997 · UK · Colour · 79mins

A heart-rending examination of unresolved grief, and how it can be a destructive force, is brought unflinchingly to life in a shattering performance by Samantha Morton. When their mother (Rita Tushingham) dies, two Liverpool sisters react differently to the bereavement. Claire Rushbrook, who is pregnant, cries a lot but gets on with her life, whereas the younger, wilder Morton starts a downward moral spiral of sordid sex and alcohol binges. Although it's reminiscent of *Breaking the Waves*, this quest for emotional fulfilment in tragic times may lack the overall polish and expertise of that grandiose epic. But with its *cinéma vérité* style, this is equally wrenching, thanks to Morton's raw and riveting portrayal. Contains swearing and sex scenes. 🖵

Samantha Morton *Iris Kelley* • Claire Rushbrook *Rose* • Rita Tushingham *Mum* • Christine Tremarco *Veronica/"Vron"* • Stuart

Under the Volcano   ★★★ 15

Drama   1984 · UK · Colour · 107mins

Malcolm Lowry's 1947 novel is a cult classic about an alcoholic British consul adrift in Mexico with his unfaithful ex-wife and his half-brother, a journalist just back from the Spanish Civil War. Local religious festivals and simmering volcanoes contribute to the consul's self-destruction. John Huston long cherished a movie version and – as with *Moby Dick* – it proved to be a daunting task, since the novel is a stream of consciousness, a river of booze and a mountain of poetic symbolism. Albert Finney gives the drunk act to end all drunk acts and rather overshadows the stunningly beautiful Jacqueline Bisset – one can readily imagine Richard Burton and Ava Gardner doing it for Huston 20 years earlier. 🖵

Albert Finney *Geoffrey Firmin* • Jacqueline Bisset *Yvonne Firmin* • Anthony Andrews *Hugh Firmin* • Ignacio Lopez Tarso *Dr Vigil* • Katy Jurado *Señora Gregoria* • James Villiers *Brit* • Dawson Bray *Quincey* ■ *Dir* John Huston • *Scr* Guy Gallo, from the novel by Malcolm Lowry • *Cinematographer* Gabriel Figueroa

Under the Yum Yum Tree
   ★★

Comedy   1963 · US · Colour · 109mins

With *The Apartment*, Jack Lemmon defined the urbanised, neurotic, sexually insecure American male. Thus typecast, Lemmon drifted through a series of movies including this "sex comedy". Nowadays it seems hopelessly dated, but in the ghetto of Beverly Hills in 1963 it was probably regarded as deeply subversive. Lemmon plays a lecherous landlord who starts to lust after one of his tenants, Carol Lynley, who is living with her boyfriend (Dean Jones). Lemmon always has his precious moments and those make this comedy of frustration worth watching – just. It was a big hit and led to a companion effort from Lemmon and co-writer/director Swift called *Good Neighbor Sam*.

Jack Lemmon *Hogan* • Carol Lynley *Robin* • Dean Jones *David* • Edie Adams *Irene* • Imogene Coca *Dorkus* • Paul Lynde *Murphy* • Robert Lansing *Charles* ■ *Dir* David Swift • *Scr* Lawrence Roman, David Swift, from the play by Lawrence Roman

Under Two Flags   ★★★

Action adventure   1936 · US · BW · 110mins

This Foreign Legion saga, already filmed twice in the silent era, stars Ronald Colman and Victor McLaglen, as the desert-based soldiers, and Claudette Colbert and Rosalind Russell as zee women in zee kasbah. Frank Lloyd, exhausted by *Mutiny on the Bounty*, directed the talkie bits, Otto Brower the battles, which look like afterthoughts since the real battle is between the sexes and between two Oxford graduates, Colman and Arab chieftain Onslow Stevens. It's *Boys' Own* stuff, with Colman often caught posing for the camera if not acting and

Townsend *Tom* • Matthew Delamere *Gary* • Mark Womack *Frank* • Clare Francis *Elana* ■ *Dir/Scr* Carine Adler • *Cinematographer* Barry Ackroyd

Colbert tossing aside her usual chic and letting her hair down.

Ronald Colman *Corporal Victor* • Claudette Colbert *Cigarette* • Victor McLaglen *Major Doyle* • Rosalind Russell *Lady Venetia* • J Edward Bromberg *Colonel Ferol* • Nigel Bruce *Captain Menzies* • Herbert Mundin *Rake* • Gregory Ratoff *Ivan* ■ *Dir* Frank Lloyd, Otto Brower • *Scr* WP Lipscomb, Walter Ferris, from the novel by Ouida

Under Western Skies   ★★ U

Musical western   1945 · US · BW · 56mins

A programme filler about a vaudeville singer, played by Martha O'Driscoll, who fetches up in an Arizona town and gets involved in all sorts of trouble. There are some funny moments and it's always good to see popular comedians of the time, such as Leon Errol, but this is very slight indeed, though the songs are pleasant enough. Aficionados of *The Rockford Files* might get a kick out of seeing Noah Beery Jr (Jim Rockford's dad in the long-running TV series) as a romantic lead, while those old enough to remember the early TV series *The Cisco Kid* will recognise Leo Carrillo (he played Pancho) in support.

Martha O'Driscoll *Katie* • Noah Beery Jr *Tod* • Leo Carrillo *King Randall* • Leon Errol *Willie* • Irving Bacon *Sheriff* • Ian Keith *Prof Moffet* • Jennifer Holt *Charity* ■ *Dir* Jean Yarbrough • *Scr* Stanley Roberts, Clyde Bruckman, from a story by Stanley Roberts

Under Your Hat   ★ U

Musical comedy   1940 · UK · BW · 79mins

Jack Hulbert and Cicely Courtneidge are an acquired taste and you really needed to have been there at the time to appreciate the humour in this woeful comedy of errors. Wartime audiences were so grateful to see just about anything that they were willing to forgive even the most dismal movies – particularly morale-boosting flagwavers. The lowest of many dips below zero is the scene in which Courtneidge poses as French maid to catch hubby Hulbert with Leonora Corbett, unaware they are both spies on the track of a new aero-carburettor.

Jack Hulbert *Jack Millett* • Cicely Courtneidge *Kay Millett* • Austin Trevor *Boris Vladimir* • Leonora Corbett *Carole Markoff* • Cecil Parker *Sir Geoffrey Arlington* • Tony Hayes *George* • Charles Oliver *Carl* • HF Maltby *Colonel Sheepshanks* ■ *Dir* Maurice Elvey • *Scr* Rodney Ackland, Anthony Kimmins, L Green, Jack Hulbert, from the play by Jack Hulbert, Archie Menzies, Geoffrey Kerr, Arthur Macrae

Undercover   ★

Second World War drama
1943 · UK · BW · 88mins

Ealing came of age during the Second World War, with inspired pictures such as *Went the Day Well?* and *San Demetrio, London*. Released in the same year as the latter, this Resistance drama aims for a similarly docudramatic feel. But realism was outside the range of such starchy actors as John Clements, Michael Wilding and Tom Walls and the result is, frankly, embarrassing. Director Sergei Nolbandov took his cast to Wales to add authenticity to a tale of Partisans and Nazis. But he only succeeded in raising morale by getting laughs in all the wrong places.

U = SUITABLE FOR ALL   Uc = SUITABLE FOR ALL, ESPECIALLY FOR YOUNG CHILDREN (VIDEO ONLY)   PG = PARENTAL GUIDANCE

John Clements *Milosh Petrovitch* • Tom Walls *Kossan Petrovitch* • Mary Morris *Anna Petrovitch* • Godfrey Tearle *General Von Staengel* • Michael Wilding *Constantine* • Niall MacGinnis *Dr Jordan* • Robert Harris *Colonel Von Brock* • Rachel Thomas *Maria Petrovitch* ■ *Dir* Sergei Nolbandov • *Scr* John Dighton, Monja Danischewsky, Sergei Nolbandov, Milos Sokulich, from a story by George Slocombe

Undercover ★★

Period comedy drama
1983 · Ausl · Colour · 87mins

Directed by David Stevens, this light-hearted period drama recalls the rise of that upstanding institution, the House of Burley, with an uneasy mix of fact and whimsy. Launched in the twenties after extensive research, the company's range of underwear became one of the first Australian products to corner an international market. The supporting cast (particularly the stylish Sandy Gore) is admirable. But, unfortunately, Stevens allows himself to be distracted from his fascinating story and spends too much time wondering whether country girl Genevieve Picot will plump for old-fashioned salesman Peter Phelps or his go-ahead American rival, Michael Paré. Contains swearing.

Genevieve Picot *Libby McKenzie* • John Walton *Fred Burley* • Michael Paré *Max Wylde* • Sandy Gore *Nina* • Peter Phelps *Theo Finch* • Barry Otto *Professor Henckel* ■ *Dir* David Stevens • *Scr* Miranda Downes

Undercover Blues ★★★15

Comedy thriller 1993 · US · Colour · 86mins

An amiable if minor throwback to the comedy spy caper so popular at the end of the sixties. Dennis Quaid and Kathleen Turner are super spies on leave in New Orleans with their infant, who are called back into service to help foil a plot to sell off top secret weapons. Quaid and Turner make charismatic leads and are surrounded by a talented support cast: Fiona Shaw is enjoyably over-the-top as a villain; Stanley Tucci excels as a hapless thug; and there are engaging turns from Tom Arnold and Larry Miller. Herbert Ross's direction is suitably light and, even if it isn't as funny as some in the cast appear to think it is, the film is still undemanding fun. Contains some swearing. ▭

Kathleen Turner *Jane Blue* • Dennis Quaid *Jeff Blue* • Fiona Shaw *Novacek* • Stanley Tucci *Muerte* • Larry Miller *Detective Sergeant Halsey* • Tom Arnold *Vern Newman* ■ *Dir* Herbert Ross • *Scr* Ian Abrams

Undercover Girl ★★★

Crime 1950 · US · BW · 82mins

Policewoman Alexis Smith joins forces with plain-clothes policeman Scott Brady and is sent undercover to pose as a drug buyer in order to nail a narcotics ring. Which, of course, she does, but not before having to escape from numerous threatening situations. This is a routine fifties programme filler, but no less entertaining for that, and it's refreshing to have a glamorous woman at the centre of the rough stuff. Gladys George, the superb star of the 1937 version of *Madame X*, turns up in director Joseph Pevney's supporting cast.

Alexis Smith *Christine Miller/"Sal Willis"* • Scott Brady *Lt Mike Trent* • Richard Egan *Jess Taylor* • Gladys George *Liz Crow* • Edmon Ryan *Doc Holmes* • Gerald Mohr *Reed Menig* • Royal Dano *Moocher* ■ *Dir* Joseph Pevney • *Scr* Harry Essex, from a story by Robert Hardy Andrews, Francis Rosenwald

Undercover Girl ★★

Crime drama 1958 · UK · BW · 76mins

This cheap British B-movie was a support filler and has the regulation glamourous leading lady and the obligatory North American (in this case Canadian) leading man. Former band crooner Paul Carpenter is an amiable, but fairly dreary, star of sorts and co-star Kay Callard *West of Suez* has a passable second-string leading lady quality – though a few acting lessons wouldn't have gone amiss. The real interest lies in the appearance in an "acting" role of Jackie Collins, now better known for writing raunchy novels. Carpenter's second wife, Kim Parker, is also on view, as a maid.

Paul Carpenter *Johnny Carter* • Kay Callard *Joan Foster* • Monica Grey *Evelyn King* • Bruce Seton *Ted Austin* • Jackie Collins *Peggy Foster* • Maya Koumani *Miss Brazil* • Kim Parker *Maid* ■ *Dir* Francis Searle • *Scr* Bernard Lewis, Bill Luckwell, from a story by Bernard Lewis

Undercover Maisie ★★★

Comedy 1947 · US · BW · 90mins

Ann Sothern and Maisie finally bowed out with this tenth entry in the series, pairing her with Barry Nelson as the last of the men in her life. Falling victim to con tricksters in Los Angeles, Maisie goes to the police. While there, she's spotted by detective Nelson as an ideal undercover girl. He puts her through a crash course in the Police Academy and sends her out on a job that leads to her kidnapping and near-murder. Maisie ends as she began – with a flourish – and even manages some realistically tense situations before her ingenuity triumphs.

Ann Sothern *Maisie Ravier* • Barry Nelson *Lt Paul Scott* • Mark Daniels *Chip Dolan* • Leon Ames *Amor* • Clinton Sundberg *Guy Canford* • Dick Simmons *Gilfred I Rogers* • Charles D Brown *Captain Mead* ■ *Dir* Harry Beaumont • *Scr* Thelma Robinson

The Undercover Man ★★★

Crime drama 1949 · US · BW · 84mins

An entertaining co-feature from cult director Joseph H Lewis, best known for his remarkable thriller *Gun Crazy*. Produced by *The Hustler's* Robert Rossen, it's based on the real-life entrapment of gangster Al Capone for tax evasion, a tale beloved of Hollywood scriptwriters. The story is economically filmed and driven at a fine pace, and there are terrific performances by leads Glenn Ford, Nina Foch and James Whitmore, making his screen debut. The crisp images of *Bonnie and Clyde* cinematographer Burnett Guffey are also a major plus.

Glenn Ford *Frank Warren* • Nina Foch *Judith Warren* • James Whitmore *George Pappas* • Barry Kelley *Edward O'Rourke* • David Wolfe *Stanley Weinburg* • Frank Tweddell *Inspector Herzog* • Howard St John *Joseph S Horan* • Leo Penn *Sidney Gordon* ■ *Dir* Joseph H

Lewis • *Scr* Sydney Boehm, Malvin Wald, Jerry Rubin, from the article *Undercover Man: He Trapped Capone* by Frank J Wilson

Undercurrent ★★★15

Spy drama 1946 · US · BW · 115mins

With a knockout cast – Hepburn, Taylor, Mitchum – a director hitting his creative stride and MGM – the Rolls-Royce of studios near its prime – how can you go wrong? Easy. By having a moth-eaten cardboard script, obvious studio interiors, a cast that doesn't care and a director plagued by domestic problems. What should have been a rip-roaring melodrama on the lines of *Suspicion* fizzles flatly on the screen. It's over-written, overwrought and overlength – a fine welcome back for MGM's matinee idol Robert Taylor, playing a psychopath, after his military service in the Second World War. Nevertheless, sheer star power saves the day, and the three principals manage to make this daft nonsense mesmerisingly watchable. ▭

Katharine Hepburn *Ann Hamilton* • Robert Taylor (1) *Alan Garroway* • Robert Mitchum *Michael Garroway* • Edmund Gwenn *Prof Dink Hamilton* • Marjorie Main *Lucy* • Vincente Minnelli • *Scr* Edward Chodorov, Marguerite Roberts, George Oppenheimer, from the novel *You Were There* by Thelma Strabel

Underground ★★

Second World War drama adventure
1941 · US · BW · 94mins

This anti-Nazi propaganda piece still retains some of its didactic power thanks to its unconventional staging – within the realms of the Third Reich. Jeffrey Lynn and Philip Dorn play German brothers Kurt and Eric Franken, the former immersed in Hitler's doctrine, the latter struggling to resist his homeland's ill-fated trajectory. Unsurprisingly, it's Dorn's viewpoint that triumphs, and the wayward Lynn manages to see the error of his ways in time for the melodramatic denouement. Functional rather than inspired, the film at least manages to engage the brain, even if the *sturm und drang* of the Nazi milieu is slightly overplayed.

Jeffrey Lynn *Kurt Franken* • Philip Dorn *Eric Franken* • Kaaren Verne *Sylvia Helmuth* • Mona Maris *Fräulein Gessner* • Peter Whitney *Alex* ■ *Dir* Vincent Sherman • *Scr* Charles Grayson, from a story by Oliver HP Garrett, Edwin Justus Mayer

Underground ★★★15

Epic Second World War comedy
1995 · Fr/Ger/Hun · Colour · 163mins

Although it won Emir Kusturica a second Palme d'Or at Cannes, this bittersweet dramatisation of the decline of Yugoslavia so angered critics in his native Bosnia (for failing to condemn Serbian aggression) that he threatened to abandon cinema altogether. Beneath the black farce – Second World War partisans take refuge in a cellar, which becomes their home for decades – there are traces of nostalgia for the illusory union of Tito's Yugoslavia, even though Kusturica acknowledges that this regime relied on indoctrinating people into accepting the imperative to perpetuate the wartime spirit of resistance. With much of the action taken at a frantic pace,

to the accompaniment of brass or gypsy bands, this is as breathless as it's perplexing. A Serbo-Croatian language film. ▭

Miki Manojlovic *Marko* • Lazar Ristovski *Petar Popara "Blacky"* • Mirjana Jokovic *Natalija* • Slavko Stimac *Ivan* • Ernst Stotzner *Franz* • Srdjan Todorovic *Jovan* • Mirjana Karanovic *Vera* ■ *Dir* Emir Kusturica • *Scr* Emir Kusturica, from a story by Dusan Kovacevic

Underground ★★★★18

Crime thriller 1998 · UK · Colour · 93mins

This gritty, ultra low-budget, British thriller is about teen drug-dealer Rat (Billy Smith), who makes deliveries around the clock. When he wanders into another supplier's patch, the film follows him as he spends a long night of hide and seek. Writer/director Paul Spurrier (who also performed just about every technical role) does an exceptional job. The naturalistic performances – including cameos from Chrissie Cotterill and Ian Dury as Mum and Dad – are good and the music soundtrack is comparable to most major releases. Amazingly, it was shot in a fortnight and the hairy, climactic car chase was filmed entirely without permission or stunt drivers. Quite an achievement, given its sparse resources. Contains swearing. ▭

Billy Smith *Rat* • Zoe Smale *Skye* • Ian Dury *Rat's dad* • Chrissie Cotterill *Rat's mum* • Nick Sutton *Raymond* • Alison Lintott *Debbie* ■ *Dir/Scr* Paul Spurrier

The Underground Orchestra ★★★

Documentary 1998 · Neth · Colour · 108mins

Heddy Honigmann's documentary about the multinational band of buskers who perform on the streets and trains of the French capital not only provides a diverse musical education, but also a sobering insight into the penury and humiliation they're forced to endure. This is despite her rather naive and intrusive insistence on trying to make political capital out of both her subjects and the supposedly sophisticated Parisians who either watch or ignore them. Drawn from trouble spots around the world, these latter-day troubadours have long ceased to play for pleasure, but their artistry and integrity still shine through. A Dutch language film.

Dir Heddy Honigmann • *Scr* Heddy Honigmann, Nosh van der Lely • *Cinematographer* Eric Guichard

The Underneath ★★★15

Crime thriller 1995 · US · Colour · 94mins

Peter Gallagher takes on the Burt Lancaster role in director Steven Soderbergh's intriguing remake of the 1949 *film noir* Criss Cross. Playing the black sheep, Gallagher returns home to Texas to look for his ex-lover Alison Elliott and plan a bank heist. The problem is she's taken up with a small-time hood and his envious policeman brother wants her too. Soderbergh mixes erotic duplicity, sibling rivalry and sizzling suspense into an increasingly corkscrew plot with a surprise pay-off. Despite a few style inconsistencies, and a gradual build-up that may prove too slow for the impatient, this is a tautly constructed thriller making pertinent points about sexual jealousy and cynical manipulation. 🔲

Peter Gallagher *Michael Chambers* • Alison Elliott *Rachel* • William Fichtner *Tommy Dundee* • Adam Trese *David Chambers* • Joe Don Baker *Clay Hinkle* • Paul Dooley *Ed Dutton* • Elisabeth Shue *Susan* ■ *Dir* Steven Soderbergh • *Scr* Sam Lowry, Daniel Fuchs, from the film *Criss Cross* by Daniel Fuchs, from the novel by Don Tracy

Undertow ★★

Thriller　　1996 · US · Colour · 92mins

Eric Red and Kathryn Bigelow's previous collaborations include the cult classic *Near Dark* and the equally good *Blue Steel*; Red also wrote the wonderful *The Hitcher*. Given their record in keeping us on the edge of our seats, this TV movie – a virtual three-hander – is a disappointment. Lou Diamond Phillips finds himself trapped in a house with an unhinged Charles Dance and his silent wife (Mia Sara) after he is involved in a car accident. To make matters worse, a hurricane is approaching. Despite the plot, there is very little in the way of suspense, and Dance and Phillips seem to be locked in some sort of overacting competition.

Lou Diamond Phillips *Jack Ketchum* • Charles Dance *Lyle Yates* • Mia Sara *Willie Yates* ■ *Dir* Eric Red • *Scr* Eric Red, Kathryn Bigelow

Underwater! ★★★ 🅤

Adventure　　1955 · US · Colour · 94mins

The most remarkable thing about this Jane Russell movie was not that it was the first film in SuperScope, nor that it was started by cult director Nicholas Ray, but that its world premiere was held underwater in a headline-grabbing stunt organised by ace publicist Russell Birdwell (the man who once engineered the search for Scarlett O'Hara). The star of the premiere was not the buxom Miss Russell, but a young and then-unknown starlet called Jayne Mansfield, who proved that she could fill a swimsuit even better than Russell. Mansfield wasn't even in the movie and ended up with a Warner Bros contract. The film itself is interesting enough. John Sturges eventually took over the directorial reins, resulting in some fine sub-aqua photography, but not even he could do much with the routine plot. 🔲

Jane Russell *Theresa* • Richard Egan *Johnny* • Gilbert Roland *Dominic* • Lori Nelson *Gloria* • Robert Keith *Father Cannon* • Joseph Calleia *Rico* • Eugene Iglesias *Miguel* ■ *Dir* John Sturges • *Scr* Walter Newman, from the story *The Big Rainbow* by Hugh King, Robert B Bailey

Underworld ★★★★

Silent crime melodrama
1927 · US · BW · 75mins

Considered by some critics to be the first gangster picture, the model for a prolific genre, this silent film was based on an original story by Ben Hecht who, as a reporter, had witnessed several of the elements incorporated into the film. However, Hecht wanted his name taken off the credits because he felt that director Josef von Sternberg had distorted his intentions – though that didn't prevent

him picking up his Oscar. It was only Sternberg's third solo feature and already his strong visual sense and eye for detail was evident. The plot, which ends with an exciting shootout, involves a racketeer (George Bancroft), his moll (Evelyn Brent) and an alcoholic lawyer (Clive Brook), but it's less important than the atmosphere created.

George Bancroft *"Bull" Weed* • Clive Brook *"Rolls Royce"* • Evelyn Brent *"Feathers"* • Larry Semon *"Slippy" Lewis* • Fred Kohler *"Buck"Mulligan* • Helen Lynch *Mulligan's girl* ■ *Dir* Josef von Sternberg • *Scr* Robert N Lee, Charles Furthman, from a story by Ben Hecht, George Marion Jr • *Cinematographer* Bert Glennon • *Set Designer* Hans Dreier

Underworld ★★★ 🔞

Comedy crime thriller
1996 · US · Colour · 95mins

Comedian-cum-actor Denis Leary stars in this violent gangster thriller as an ex-con who has to confront his past before looking to his future. That means killing the men who put his dad in a coma. Rooted in the idea of revenge as therapy, the film is solidly directed by Roger Christian (*Nostradamus*, *The Sender*), and evidently owes something to both *Pulp Fiction* and *The Usual Suspects*. However, spirited acting, from a quality cast that includes Joe Mantegna and Annabella Sciorra, prevents familiarity breeding too much contempt. Contains violence, swearing and sex scenes. 🔲

Denis Leary *Johnny Crown/Johnny Alt* • Joe Mantegna *Frank Gavilan/Richard Essex* • Annabella Sciorra *Dr Leah* • Larry Bishop *Ned Lynch* • Abe Vigoda *Will Cassady* • Robert Costanzo *Stan* • Traci Lords *Anna* • Jimmie F Skaggs *Smilin' Phil Fox/Todd Streeb* ■ *Dir* Roger Christian • *Scr* Larry Bishop

The Underworld ★★

Thriller　　1997 · US · Colour

The writer of *The Usual Suspects* and one of its stars joined forces as two of the executive producers on this TV movie, only to prove that lightning rarely strikes twice. Despite the efforts of writer Christopher McQuarrie and star Kevin Pollak, there's plenty of action but little substance to this tale of a master criminal whose determination to go straight could cost him his life. Pollak contributes a typically pugnacious performance and there's committed support from Felicity Huffman as a bent cop, but Chris Sarandon's mobster and Josh Charles's hotshot district attorney are too thinly drawn to hold our attention. Contains violence and swearing.

Kevin Pollak *Charlie Dire* • Lucy Webb *Judge Virginia Rhinehart* • Chris Sarandon *Johnny Hospidore* • Robert Rusler *Dick Goznia* • Josh Charles *William Ehrlich* • Felicity Huffman *Maria Mostello* • Gina Torres *Amanda Coogan* • Geoffrey Lewis *Joe Haaksman* ■ *Dir* Rod Holcomb • *Scr* Christopher McQuarrie

The Underworld Story ★★★

Crime drama　　1950 · US · BW · 90mins

This tough-as-nails crime drama from *Zulu* director Cy Endfield was made before he fell foul of the Hollywood blacklist and moved to Britain. A co-feature about a crusading reporter who uncovers small-town corruption, it's

given muscle by rugged Dan Duryea as the hero and suave Herbert Marshall as the villain, while Gale Storm is intriguingly cast as a *femme fatale*. As you watch this, it becomes clear how Endfield's heartfelt liberalism made him such an easy target during the communist witch-hunts.

Dan Duryea *Mike Reese* • Herbert Marshall *Stanton* • Gale Storm *Cathy* • Howard Da Silva *Durham* • Michael O'Shea *Munsey* • Mary Anderson *Molly* • Gar Moore *Clark* • Melville Cooper *Major Radford* ■ *Dir* Cy Endfield • *Scr* Henry Blankfort, Cy Endfield, from a story by Craig Rice

Underworld USA ★★★★

Crime drama　　1961 · US · BW · 98mins

What sets this apart from other revenge movies is Cliff Robertson's brooding, stricken presence as a man seeking vengeance upon the four gangsters who, when he was young, killed his father. Sam Fuller's writing and direction substantiate the authenticity of the theme of sin without salvation and – unusually for a Fuller movie – women get a look in in this macho world. Dolores Dorn is a credibly sympathetic girlfriend and Beatrice Kay a redoubtable pillar of compassion.

Cliff Robertson *Tolly Devlin* • Dolores Dorn *Cuddles* • Beatrice Kay *Sandy* • Paul Dubov *Gela* • Robert Emhardt *Conners* • Larry Gates *Driscoll* • Richard Rust *Gus* ■ *Dir* Samuel Fuller • *Scr* Samuel Fuller, from articles in the *Saturday Evening Post* by Joseph F Dinneen

The Undying Monster ★★★

Chiller　　1942 · US · BW · 62mins

Made in the wake of the success of *The Wolf Man* the previous year, this Holmesian affair about a cursed English family places the emphasis on brooding atmosphere rather than horrific effects. Director John Brahm made his name with shadowy costume melodramas such as *Hangover Square*. This thoughtful, if stolid, outing is one of his best – particularly for the brilliant striking-clock opening, which sets the gloomy tone.

James Ellison *Bob Curtis* • Heather Angel *Helga Hammond* • John Howard (1) *Oliver Hammond* • Bramwell Fletcher *Dr Geoffrey Covert* • Heather Thatcher *Christy* • Aubrey Mather *Inspector Craig* ■ *Dir* John Brahm • *Scr* Lillie Hayward, Michael Jacoby, from the play by Jessie Douglas Kerruish

The Unearthly ★

Horror　　1957 · US · BW · 68mins

Mad scientist John Carradine and his research assistant Marilyn Buferd discover a new gland containing the secret of youth and, in their crazed efforts to achieve immortality, end up with a cellar full of grotesque monsters. Poorly scripted, crudely directed and overacted by Carradine to a distracting degree, this cheap fear fodder is somewhat similar to the previous year's *The Black Sleep*. Potential victim Allison Hayes starred in the cult classic *Attack of the 50 Foot Woman* and Tor Johnson, playing the manservant Lobo who turns on Carradine, appeared in the awful *Plan 9 from Outer Space*.

John Carradine *Professor Charles Conway* • Allison Hayes *Grace Thomas* • Myron Healey

Mark Houston • Sally Todd *Natalie* • Marilyn Buferd *Dr Sharon Gilchrist* • Arthur Batanides *Danny Green* • Tor Johnson *Lobo* • Harry Fleer *Harry Jedrow* ■ *Dir* Boris Petroff • *Scr* Geoffrey Dennis [John DF Black], Jane Mann, from a story by Jane Mann

An Unexpected Family ★★ 🅟🅖

Drama　　1996 · US · Colour · 88mins

This gooey TV movie is saved only by the energetic performance of veteran actress Stockard Channing. She plays an independent career woman who finds her life drastically changed when her younger, irresponsible sister leaves her two children on her doorstep. During the course of a year she reluctantly bonds with the kids but trouble ensues when her thoughtless sister eventually returns and demands to have her brood back. It's all a bit tedious as this tear-jerker covers no new ground. Stephen Collins is pleasing as the sensible widower and best friend but it's all about those sweet little kids. 🔲

Stockard Channing *Barbara Whitney* • Stephen Collins *Sam* • Christine Ebersole *Ruth Whitney* • Noah Fleiss *Matt Whitney* ■ *Dir* Larry Elikann • *Scr* Lee Rose

An Unexpected Life ★★ 🅟🅖

Drama　　1998 · US · Colour · 88mins

A drippy sequel to the 1996 cable TV movie *An Unexpected Family*. Stockard Channing plays a die-hard New Yorker, who leaves with her nephew and niece, over whom she has legal custody, and settles in a small town. While trying to adjust to her new life, she discovers she is pregnant. She marries her boyfriend (Stephen Collins), has the baby and faces the fears of being a new mother. The family peace is shaken when her wayward sister re-petitions the court for joint custody of the kids, who don't want to return to their mother's care. While Channing is always a treat, this inflated piece of melodrama is all-too predictable. 🔲

Stockard Channing *Barbara Whitney* • Stephen Collins *Sam Sadwich* • Christine Ebersole *Ruth Whitney* • Noah Fleiss *Matt Whitney* • Chelsea Russo *Megan Whitney* ■ *Dir* David Jones • *Scr* Lee Rose

The Unexpected Mrs Pollifax ★★

Spy drama　　1999 · US · Colour

Venerable stage and screen actress Angela Lansbury gives a plucky performance as the silver-haired secret agent Emily Pollifax, who, recently widowed, pursues her lifelong ambition to become a spy. In a case of mistaken identity, she is hired by the CIA and sent to Morocco to pick up a book containing an encrypted message. When the CIA send an agent to protect her, they are both taken hostage, but the feisty senior uses her wit and wisdom to outsmart the bad guys. Based on a Dorothy Gilman novel, and filmed on location in Ireland, Paris and Morocco, this slick production is fast-paced and fun. Solid support from actors Thomas Ian Griffith and Ed Bishop make this diverting TV movie an unexpected pleasure.

Angela Lansbury *Mrs Pollifax* • Thomas Ian Griffith *Farrell* • Ed Bishop *Carstairs* • Joseph

Long *Alekseiyagoda* • Paul Birchard *Bishop* ■ *Dir* Anthony Shaw • *Scr* Robert T Megginson, from the novel *A Palm for Mrs Pollifax* by Dorothy Gilman

The Unfaithful ★★★
Melodrama 1947 · US · BW · 108mins

Seven years after Bette Davis and Herbert Marshall starred so effectively in an adaptation of Somerset Maugham's *The Letter* for Warner Bros, the studio returned to the material, rearranging it, but retaining the central plot. Ann Sheridan is the woman who, having been unfaithful to her husband (Zachary Scott) during his absence on war duty, suffers genuine remorse over her infidelity and finds herself implicated in the murder of her erstwhile lover. Director Vincent Sherman, well in control, elicits a strong central performance from Sheridan and delivers an altogether respectable remake of a classic of stage and screen.

Ann Sheridan *Chris Hunter* • Lew Ayres *Larry Hannaford* • Zachary Scott *Bob Hunter* • Eve Arden *Paula* • Jerome Cowan *Prosecuting attorney* • Steven Geray *Martin Barrow* • John Hoyt *Detective-Lt Reynolds* • Peggy Knudsen *Claire* ■ *Dir* Vincent Sherman • *Scr* David Goodis, James Gunn, from a play by W Somerset Maugham (uncredited)

Unfaithfully Yours ★★★★
Comedy 1948 · US · BW · 105mins

A perfect slice of director Preston Sturges's tangy acidic humour, *Unfaithfully Yours* is a highly amusing look at suspicion and revenge. Rex Harrison plays the celebrated and egocentric conductor, who believes his wife is adulterous. This has great wit and flair, and Sturges fashions his many attempts to humiliate her with a dash of strychnine in the mix. Linda Darnell is sublime as Harrison's clever, duplicitous wife and the dramatic swathes of Rossini, Tchaikovsky and Wagner add to the dark atmosphere.

Rex Harrison *Sir Alfred de Carter* • Linda Darnell *Daphne de Carter* • Barbara Lawrence *Barbara Henshler* • Rudy Vallee *August Henshler* • Kurt Kreuger *Anthony* • Lionel Stander *Hugo Standoff* • Edgar Kennedy *Detective Sweeney* ■ *Dir/Scr* Preston Sturges

Unfaithfully Yours ★★★ 15
Comedy 1983 · US · Colour · 92mins

Dudley Moore gives one of his better performances in this gently diverting and broadly satisfactory remake of the 1948 Preston Sturges comedy about a symphony orchestra conductor who suspects his young wife of making beautiful music with a handsome violinist. Indeed, as both a comedian and musician, Moore could hardly have better credentials for the role of a jealous conductor, originally played by Rex Harrison, while Nastassja Kinski is suitably coquettish as his flirting spouse. A slighter film than the original, this is also a pacier one, with some entertaining helpings of slapstick. ▭

Dudley Moore *Claude Eastman* • Nastassja Kinski *Daniella Eastman* • Armand Assante *Maximillian Stein* • Albert Brooks *Norman Robbins* • Cassie Yates *Carla Robbins* • Richard Libertini *Giuseppe* • Richard B Shull

Jess Keller ■ *Dir* Howard Zieff • *Scr* Valerie Curtin, Barry Levinson, Robert Klane, from the film by Preston Sturges

An Unfinished Affair ★★
Drama thriller 1996 · US · Colour

Few films have been more imitated in recent years than *Fatal Attraction*. This TV movie adds a new twist to the well-worn revenge plot by having the errant husband play just as dirty as his jilted mistress. Having had a fling with Jennie Garth during his wife's illness, Tim Matheson tries to have her deported as an illegal immigrant after she refuses to return a priceless painting belonging to his father-in-law. It's a shame that the story takes the easy option of having Garth threaten Matheson's son as all the vitriol drains out to be replaced by cheap shocks and cosy reconciliations.

Jennie Garth *Sheila Hart* • Tim Matheson *Alex Connor* • Leigh Taylor-Young *Cynthia Connor* • Peter Facinelli *Rick Connor* ■ *Dir* Rod Hardy • *Scr* Rama Laurie Stagner, Dan Witt

Unfinished Business ★★★
Drama 1983 · Can · Colour · 99mins

In *Nobody Waved Goodbye* (1964), Don Owen introduced us to Peter (Peter Kastner), an impulsive adolescent who ran away from his overbearing bourgeois parents and descended into petty crime before marrying Julie Biggs. Now, some 20 years later, they are divorced and struggling to maintain control over their own teenage daughter (Isabelle Mejias). Here was a golden opportunity to explore the way in which the flower-power generation handled the concerns of the free-thinking kids of the nuclear age. But, instead, Owen concentrates on heredity and allows issues such as unemployment, political indolence and impending holocaust to be sidetracked by domestic melodrama.

Isabelle Mejias *Izzy Marks* • Peter Spence *Jesse* • Leslie Toth *Matthew* • Peter Kastner *Peter Marks* • Julie Biggs *Julie Marks* • Chuck Shamata *Carl* ■ *Dir/Scr* Don Owen

Unfinished Business ★★★
Comedy drama 1985 · Ausl · Colour · 78mins

Having impressed with his scripts for Paul Cox's *Man of Flowers* and *My First Wife*, Bob Ellis made his directorial debut with this acerbic comedy of sexual manners. But while his screenplay contains the odd pertinent insight and some choice banter, his pacing and shot selection leave much to be desired. John Clayton and Michele Fawdon do, however, rise to the occasion as the old flames who embark on a clandestine relationship to provide her childless marriage with issue. Clayton is particularly perceptive, as the swaggering, yet tetchy middle-aged lothario trying to haul in the waistline and turn back the clock.

John Clayton *Geoff* • Michele Fawdon *Maureen* • Norman Kaye *George* • Bob Ellis *Geoff's Flatmate* • Andrew Lesnie *Telegraph Boy* ■ *Dir/Scr* Bob Ellis

Unfinished Business... ★★
Drama 1987 · US · Colour · 65mins

Great things were predicted for Swedish actress Viveca Lindfors when she first arrived in Hollywood in 1946. Though she married director Don Siegel, things didn't work out and she returned to Europe. In 78 films she never really found a role to showcase her talents and so she wrote one for herself. Based on her relationship with the playwright George Tabori (with whom she had a son, actor Kristoffer Tabori), the story concerns an actress deliberating whether to renew an affair with the Hungarian lover who hurt her so badly 15 years earlier.

Viveca Lindfors *Helena* • Peter Donat *Ferenzy* • Gina Hecht *Vickie* • James Morrison *Jonathan* • Anna Deavere Smith *Anna* • Hayley Taylor-Block *Kristina* ■ *Dir/Scr* Viveca Lindfors

An Unfinished Piece for Mechanical Piano ★★★★ U
Romantic drama 1976 · USSR · Colour · 97mins

The cryptic title refers to Anton Chekhov's early unfinished play *Platanov*, which the director Nikita Mikhalkov, who also plays the drunken doctor, has skilfully adapted for the screen. At times a tragic farce, this is set in 1910. The atmosphere of the lazy summer's day at widow Antonina Shuranova's country estate is beautifully captured, although the film's pace too often reflects the lethargy of the characters and the aesthetics distract from the text. However, the ensemble acting is superb. A Russian language film. ▭

Aleksandr Kalyagin *Platonov* • Elena Solovei *Sophia* • Evgenia Glushenko *Sasha* • Antonina Shuranova *Anna Petrovna* • Yuri Bogatyriov *Sergei* ■ *Dir* Nikita Mikhalkov • *Scr* Nikita Mikhalkov, Aleksander Adabashyan, from the play *Platonov* by Anton Chekhov

The Unfinished Symphony ★★★
Musical biographical drama 1934 · Aus/UK · BW · 83mins

Hans Jaray plays Franz Schubert in a lush account of the composer's life and the story behind his failure to finish his most famous work. Filmed in Vienna and given a lush production rich in romantic atmosphere, the film benefits greatly from the Vienna Philharmonic Orchestra playing the composer's great works, with the chorus of the State Opera providing a stirring rendition of the *Ave Maria*. Heroine Marta Eggerth was an operetta star in Germany and Austriain the thirties before a brief Hollywood career.

Helen Chandler *Emmie Passenter* • Marta Eggerth *Caroline Esterhazy* • Hans Jaray *Franz Schubert* • Ronald Squire *Count Esterhazy* • Beryl Laverick *Mary* • Hermine Sterler *Princess Kinsky* • Cecil Humphreys *Salieri* ■ *Dir* Willy Forst, Anthony Asquith • *Scr* Benn W Levy, from a story by Walter Reisch

Unforgettable ★★ 15
Thriller 1996 · US · Colour · 112mins

In order to find his wife's killer, police medical examiner Ray Liotta injects himself with the secret memory-transfer formula of researcher Linda Fiorentino, together with the brain fluid

of his wife, in order to "see" her last memories. Amazingly, this outrageous premise manages never to come across as the least bit goofy, but that's where the problem lies. The film is so solemn and serious that it never gets a chance to be exciting and mysterious, making it into a long 112-minute slog. Fiorentino is good under the circumstances, but Liotta is not convincing as a man who is supposed to be completely obsessed with solving the case. Contains swearing. ▭

Ray Liotta *Dr David Krane* • Linda Fiorentino *Dr Martha Briggs* • Peter Coyote *Don Bresler* • Christopher McDonald *Stewart Gleick* • David Paymer *Curtis Avery* • Duncan Fraser *Michael Stratton* • Caroline Elliott *Cara Krane* ■ *Dir* John Dahl • *Scr* Bill Geddie

Unforgivable ★★ 15
Drama based on a true story 1995 · US · Colour · 87mins

Known for directing pretty hopeless thrillers such as *Still Life* and *Man in the Attic*, Graeme Campbell was perhaps an odd choice for this family melodrama. Based on a true story, it centres on a compulsive wife-beater's attempts to save his marriage by undergoing counselling. John Ritter is perhaps not everyone's idea of an abusive thug, but he nevertheless turns in a creditable performance, and he's neatly supported by Harley Jane Kozak. While it raises several important issues and could offer some solace to those in a similar situation, this slice of sensationalism dressed as sincerity will fool no one. Contains violence. ▭

John Ritter *Paul Hegstrom* • Harley Jane Kozak *Judy Hegstrom* • Kevin Dunn *Milt Steiner* • Susan Gibney *Beth* • Gina Phillips [Gina Philips] *Tammy Hegstrom* ■ *Dir* Graeme Campbell • *Scr* Dan Levine, AR Simoun, from a story by AR Simoun

The Unforgiven ★★★★ PG
Western 1960 · US · Colour · 116mins

This handsome Texas-set western from director John Huston is based on a novel by Alan LeMay, whose more famous *The Searchers* tells the flipside of this tale. Both share stunning homestead-under-siege sequences. Huston is particularly well served by Burt Lancaster and an unusually interesting support cast, including two *Duel in the Sun* veterans, Lillian Gish and Charles Bickford, and an excellent Audie Murphy (in a rare big-budget feature). Only Audrey Hepburn, unusually, lacks credibility. Superbly photographed on location by Franz Planer, with a fine Dimitri Tiomkin score, this film deserves to be better known. The racial issues it deals with are no less comfortable now than they were at both the time of the historical events and when the movie was made. ▭

Burt Lancaster *Ben Zachary* • Audrey Hepburn *Rachel Zachary* • Audie Murphy *Cash Zachary* • John Saxon *Johnny Portugal* • Charles Bickford *Zeb Rawlins* • Lillian Gish *Mattilda Zachary* • Albert Salmi *Charlie Rawlins* ■ *Dir* John Huston • *Scr* Ben Maddow, from the novel by Alan LeMay

Unforgiven ★★★★★ 15

Western 1992 · US · Colour · 125mins

Winner of four Oscars, including best picture and best director, Clint Eastwood's western is one of the finest films made in the genre. Exploring the harsh realities of frontier life, he depicts the west as an unforgiving place. It's clear from the fevered manner in which Saul Rubinek's dime novelist character gathers his Wild West stories that an era is about to pass into legend. Screenwriter David Webb Peoples reinforces this shift in attitudes through the film's understated feminism and its assertion that what once passed for law and order often had little to do with justice. Eastwood's own world-weary performance as the retired gunslinger, forced to strap on the six-shooters one last time to feed his children, is exemplary. The support playing of Morgan Freeman as his former partner, Richard Harris as a vain killer and Oscar-winning Gene Hackman as the vicious Sheriff Daggett is unsurpassable. It's easy to see why Eastwood dedicated the film to Sergio Leone and Don Siegel – this is both a testament and a riposte to his work with them. Contains violence and swearing. DVD

Clint Eastwood *William Munny* • Gene Hackman *Sheriff "Little Bill" Daggett* • Morgan Freeman *Ned Logan* • Richard Harris *English Bob* • Jaimz Woolvett *"Schofield Kid"* • Saul Rubinek *WW Beauchamp* • Frances Fisher *Strawberry Alice* • Anna Thomson [Anna Levine] *Delilah Fitzgerald* ■ *Dir* Clint Eastwood • *Scr* David Webb Peoples

The Unholy ★★ 18

Horror 1988 · US · Colour · 97mins

In a misguided and ultimately tedious attempt at a theologically-themed horror movie, Ben Cross is the priest who, after surviving a drop from a five-storey building, becomes the "Chosen One" and is assigned to rid a church of a demonic presence that's seducing and killing clergymen. Good location work in New Orleans and a sterling supporting cast, which includes Hal Holbrook and Trevor Howard, do their utmost but Camilo Vila's slow-paced direction kills this one stone dead. Even the suitably gruesome effects cannot save what is just another diluted take on *The Exorcist*. It was co-written by Philip Yordan, who is more noted for his work on sixties epics such as *El Cid* and *55 Days at Peking*.

Ben Cross *Father Michael* • Ned Beatty *Lieutenant Stern* • William Russ *Luke* • Jill Carroll *Millie* • Hal Holbrook *Archbishop Mosley* • Trevor Howard *Father Silva* • Peter Frechette *Claude* ■ *Dir* Camilo Vila • *Scr* Philip Yordan, Fernando Fonseca

The Unholy Garden ★★ U

Crime drama 1931 · US · BW · 71mins

This decidedly creaky Samuel Goldwyn production stars Ronald Colman and Fay Wray in a tale of desert intrigue. It was the first original screenplay written for Hollywood by the New York theatre team of Ben Hecht and Charles MacArthur, who quickly devised the plot (a den of thieves, a beautiful girl, etc) in return for an astronomical $25,000 and a slice of the profits. Goldwyn thought he had a bargain and the writers thought they had struck gold by peddling brass. Set in a Sahara that only a Hollywood soundstage could produce, it was slightly unfairly trashed by the critics and ended up losing $200,000.

Ronald Colman *Barrington Hunt* • Fay Wray *Camille de Jonghe* • Estelle Taylor *Eliza Mowbray* • Tully Marshall *Baron de Jonghe* • Ulrich Haupt [Ullrich Haupt] *Colonel Von Axt* • Henry Armetta *Nick the Goose* • Lawrence Grant *Dr Shayne* ■ *Dir* George Fitzmaurice • *Scr* Ben Hecht, Charles MacArthur

Unholy Partners ★★

Crime drama 1941 · US · BW · 94mins

Edward G Robinson and Mervyn LeRoy made one of the first and best of the crusading newspaper movies, *Five Star Final*, in 1931. But this similarly themed story, set just after the First World War, isn't in the same league – though Robinson is incapable of delivering a boring performance. He plays an idealistic editor whose paper is bankrolled by racketeeer Edward Arnold. The story of their feud features too many ridiculous contrivances and familiar melodramatics.

Edward G Robinson *Bruce Corey* • Laraine Day *Miss Cronin* • Edward Arnold *Merrill Lambert* • Marsha Hunt *Gail Fenton* • William T Orr *Tommy Jarvis* • Don Beddoe *Mike Reynolds* • Charles Dingle *Clyde Fenton* • Charles Cane *Insp Brody* ■ *Dir* Mervyn LeRoy • *Scr* Earl Baldwin, Bartlett Cormack, Lesser Samuels

The Unholy Rollers ★★★

Sports action drama
1972 · US · Colour · 88mins

A funky and very funny cult classic from the Roger Corman production line, this stars the wonderful Claudia Jennings, the late *Playboy* model-turned-action heroine. She hits the *Rocky* road to fame as a single-minded factory worker desperate for glory in the roller-derby ring. How she overcomes the usual slew of obstacles – vicious rivals, bitchy opponents and domestic problems – is brilliantly marshalled with zip, zing and charm by director Vernon Zimmerman in this effervescent blue-collar odyssey. Inspirational, stimulating and exciting, it's also a great companion piece to Raquel Welch's similarly themed *Kansas City Bomber*.

Claudia Jennings *Karen* • Louis Quinn *Stern* • Betty Anne Rees *Mickey* • Roberta Collins *Jennifer* • Alan Vint *Greg* • Candice Roman *Donna* ■ *Dir* Vernon Zimmerman • *Scr* Howard R Cohen, from a story by Vernon Zimmerman, Howard R Cohen

The Unholy Three ★★★★

Silent crime drama 1925 · US · BW · 86mins

A midget who masquerades as a baby, a giant strongman and a cross-dressing ventriloquist (Lon Chaney) become a crime syndicate in miniature in director Tod Browning's strangely affecting silent melodrama. This is a serious and imaginative presentation of diabolical deeds, cruel vindictiveness and ghoulish humour. Genre creator Browning fashions unique thrills from the sheer novelty value of the freak-show outlaw story and highlights the twisted scenario with a wealth of deft cinematic touches. Browning was a founding father of movie horror and this sensational shocker is one of his, and Chaney's, finest achievements.

Lon Chaney *Professor Echo/Granny O'Grady* • Harry Earles *Tweedledee* • Victor McLaglen *Hercules* • Mae Busch *Rosie O'Grady* • Matt Moore *Hector McDonald* • Matthew Betz *Regan* • William Humphreys *Defense attorney* ■ *Dir* Tod Browning • *Scr* Waldemar Young, from the story *The Terrible Three* by Clarence Aaron "Tod" Robbins

The Unholy Three ★★

Crime drama 1930 · US · BW · 75mins

The success of the 1925 version of Clarence Aaron "Tod" Robbins's story about a triumvirate of circus exiles becoming master criminals led to this remake, cashing in on the novelty of sound. It's Lon Chaney's first talkie and his last picture ever as he died from throat cancer straight afterwards. Chaney reprises his role as a ventriloquist disguised as the female owner of a pet shop. But director Jack Conway is clearly not in the same class as *auteur* Tod Browning and his quick refit is far inferior to the original.

Lon Chaney *Prof Echo* • Lila Lee *Rosie O'Grady* • Elliott Nugent *Hector McDonald* • Harry Earles *Midget* • John Miljan *Prosecuting attorney* • Ivan Linow *Hercules* • Clarence Burton *Regan* • Crauford Kent *Defense attorney* ■ *Dir* Jack Conway • *Scr* JC Nugent, Elliott Nugent, from the story *The Terrible Three* by Clarence Aaron "Tod" Robbins

The Unholy Wife ★★

Crime drama 1957 · US · Colour · 94mins

Diana Dors's Hollywood sojourn yielded two RKO programme fillers, this crime melodrama and the dreadful *I Married a Woman*, in which she clearly proved she had what it takes to become an international star. Unfortunately for Dors, there were just too many starlets in the studio system, and she couldn't compete with the likes of Marilyn Monroe and Jayne Mansfield. Rod Steiger manages to chew less scenery than usual in his role as Dors's cuckolded husband, but overall this has few memorable moments.

Rod Steiger *Paul Hochen* • Diana Dors *Phyllis Hochen* • Tom Tryon *San* • Beulah Bondi *Emma Hochen* • Marie Windsor *Gwen* • Arthur Franz *Reverend Stephen Hochen* • Luis Van Rooten *Ezra Benton* • Joe De Santis *Gino Verdugo* ■ *Dir* John Farrow • *Scr* Jonathan Latimer, from a story by William Durkee

Unhook the Stars ★★★ 15

Comedy drama 1996 · Fr · Colour · 100mins

Nick Cassavetes (son of actor/director John) directs his mother Gena Rowlands ina comedy drama, which also features a pre-*Phantom Menace* appearance from Jake Lloyd. Marisa Tomei gives a nice performance as the young mother who disrupts the life of neighbour Rowlands while looking for a babysitter for her son. However, Rowlands unsurprisingly steals the film from not only Tomei, but also male co-star Gérard Depardieu, who seems slightly ill at ease throughout. Nonetheless, it's an interesting and character-driven film which once again confirms what a superb acting treasure America has in Rowlands. Contains swearing and sexual references.

Gena Rowlands *Mildred* • Marisa Tomei *Monica* • Gérard Depardieu *Big Tommy* • Jake Lloyd *JJ* • Moira Kelly *Ann Mary Margaret* • David Sherrill *Ethan* ■ *Dir* Nick Cassavetes • *Scr* Nick Cassavetes, Helen Caldwell

The Uninvited ★★★★★

Horror 1944 · US · BW · 98mins

The *Casablanca* of horror, it's a potential programme filler in which all the elements came together to produce a classic of the genre. Brother and sister Ray Milland and Ruth Hussey buy a house in Cornwall and find it haunted. Though containing what are now narrative clichés (a mysterious room, sinister housekeeper) and strained humour, this is an ingenious ghost story. Aided by Charles Lang's photography and Victor Young's score, it still sends shivers up the spine. This was the first film by British director Lewis Allen who failed to re-create the formula in his follow-up, *The Unseen*, and was soon lost to American television.

Ray Milland *Roderick Fitzgerald* • Ruth Hussey *Pamela Fitzgerald* • Donald Crisp *Comdr Bench* • Cornelia Otis Skinner *Miss Holloway* • Dorothy Stickney *Miss Hird* • Barbara Everest *Lizzie Flynn* • Alan Napier *Dr Scott* • Gail Russell *Stella Meredith* ■ *Dir* Lewis Allen • *Scr* Dodie Smith, Frank Partos, from a novel by Dorothy Macardle

Union City ★★ 15

Drama 1980 · US · Colour · 81mins

Blondie singer Debbie Harry plays the plain, frustrated wife of a meek businessman (Dennis Lipscomb) whose obsession with catching a petty thief leads to murder. Based on the Cornell Woolrich story *The Corpse Next Door* (because a body is hidden in an adjacent apartment) director Mark Reichert plays it too offbeat, arty and tricksy for it to emerge as another classic from the writer's work such as *Rear Window* and *The Bride Wore Black*. Most of the opportunities for smart black comedy are blown by the relentlessly downbeat tone and Reichert's fudged aim for Fassbinder-esque European irony. But Harry acquits herself well.

Dennis Lipscomb *Harlan* • Deborah Harry *Lillian* • Irina Maleeva *Mrs Gofka – the Contessa* • Everett McGill *Larry Longacre* • Sam McMurray *Young vagrant* • Terina Lewis *Evelyn – secretary* • Pat Benatar *Jeanette* ■ *Dir* Mark Reichert • *Scr* Mark Reichert, from the story *The Corpse Next Door* by Cornell Woolrich

Union Depot ★★★

Comedy drama 1932 · US · BW · 75mins

Completely overshadowed by MGM's *Grand Hotel* to which it is often and stupidly compared, this modest offering from First National, set amid the bustle of a major train station, is a snappy and appealing entertainment. Douglas Fairbanks Jr stars as a young hobo who finds some money, decks himself out as a gentleman, and falls for a broke dancer (Joan Blondell) who needs $64 to get to Salt Lake City. Matters are complicated by a stolen pawn ticket, a violin case crammed with counterfeit money, and the arrest of Doug and Joan. Quite silly, but the stars are charming and attractive and the supporting players excellent.

1512 U = SUITABLE FOR ALL Uc = SUITABLE FOR ALL, ESPECIALLY FOR YOUNG CHILDREN (VIDEO ONLY) PG = PARENTAL GUIDANCE

Douglas Fairbanks Jr *Chic Miller* • Joan Blondell *Ruth* • Guy Kibbee *Scrap Iron* • Alan Hale *Baron* • Frank McHugh *Drunk* • George Rosener *Bernardi* • Dickie Moore *Little Boy* ■ *Dir* Alfred E Green • *Scr* Kenyon Nicholson, Walter De Leon, John Bright, Kubec Glasmon, from the play by Gene Fowler, Douglas Durkin, Joe Laurie

Union Pacific ★★★ U

Western   1939 · US · BW · 134mins

This epic about the construction of the first transcontinental railroad was a smash hit in 1939. It stars Joel McCrea as the overseer for Union Pacific, fighting local tribesman and saboteurs on the way to linking up with the Central Pacific line. Barbara Stanwyck is a tomboy postmistress and Robert Preston (in his first big role) impresses as a likeable gambler. As usual, producer/director Cecil B DeMille stages too many scenes in the comfort of a sound stage, relying on obvious back projection, and it is the outdoor footage, including the raid on the train, that provides the film's most memorable moments.
Barbara Stanwyck *Mollie Monahan* • Joel McCrea *Jeff Butler* • Akim Tamiroff *Fiesta* • Robert Preston *Dick Allen* • Lynne Overman *Leach Overmile* • Brian Donlevy *Sid Campeau* • Lon Chaney Jr *Dollarhide* ■ *Dir* Cecil B DeMille • *Scr* Walter DeLeon, C Gardner Sullivan, Jesse Lasky Jr, Jack Cunningham, from the novel *Trouble Shooters* by Ernest Haycox

Union Station ★★

Crime thriller   1950 · US · BW · 80mins

Considered a real nailbiter in its day, this competent police thriller benefits from the real location of the concourse, platforms and threatening bowels of a bustling Art Deco station. Here, a millionaire is instructed to deliver the ransom for his kidnapped blind daughter. William Holden, tight-jawed and efficient, is in charge of the on-the-spot manhunt, Barry Fitzgerald is the kindly police chief and Nancy Olson the necessary feminine interest. Ace cinematographer-turned-director Rudolph Maté extracts maximum mileage from the settings, and wrings tension from the simple plot.
William Holden (1) *Lt William Calhoun* • Nancy Olson *Joyce Willecombe* • Barry Fitzgerald *Insp Donnelly* • Lyle Bettger *Joe Beacom* • Jan Sterling *Marge Wrighter* • Allene Roberts *Lorna Murcall* • Herbert Heyes *Henry Murcall* • Don Dunning *Gus Hadder* ■ *Dir* Rudolph Maté • *Scr* Sydney Boehm, from the story *Nightmare in Manhattan* by Thomas Walsh

Universal Soldier ★★★ 18

Futuristic action thriller
1992 · US · Colour · 99mins

Part *Terminator*, part *Robocop*, all dumb fun: *Independence Day* director Roland Emmerich's earlier sci-fi potboiler is a by-the-numbers affair, with dialogue you'd swear appears in comic balloons. But as no one takes the ultimate warrior premise seriously, the unpretentious pandering to the action-plus brigade is a likeable strength, not a jarring weakness. The Muscles from Brussels (Jean-Claude Van Damme) has the edge over the Swedish Meatball (Dolph Lundgren) in every respect, from his showcase kick boxing to his send-up nude scene, in this OTT jeopardy jackpot, where what you see is exactly what you get. Contains violence and swearing ▭
Jean-Claude Van Damme *Luc Devreux* • Dolph Lundgren *Andrew Scott* • Ally Walker *Veronica Roberts* • Ed O'Ross *Colonel Perry* • Jerry Orbach *Dr Gregor* • Leon Rippy *Woodward* • Tico Wells *Garth* • Ralph Moeller *GR76* ■ *Dir* Roland Emmerich • *Scr* Richard Rothstein, Christopher Leitch, Dean Devlin

Universal Soldier – the Return ★ 18

Futuristic action thriller
1999 · US · Colour · 83mins

An insultingly awful big-screen follow-up to the 1992 Jean-Claude Van Damme hit (which has already spawned two straight-to-video tales featuring Matt Battaglia in place of the original star). Van Damme's nice guy terminator is now a technical adviser on the secret government project that turns dead soldiers into killing machines. Naturally, they go on the rampage, leading to much thrill-free punching, kicking and riddling with bullets. Thinly plotted and painfully clichéd even by genre standards, this moronic mess doesn't even have the benefit of crowd-pleasing action sequences. Contains violence. ▭ **DVD**
Jean-Claude Van Damme *Luc* • Michael Jai White *SETH* • Heidi Schanz *Erin* • Xander Berkeley *Dylan Cotner* • Justin Lazard *Captain Blackburn* • Kiana Tom *Maggie* • Daniel Von Bargen *General Radford* • James Black *Sergeant Morrow* ■ *Dir* Mic Rodgers • *Scr* William Malone, John Fasano, from the characters created by Richard Rothstein, Christopher Leitch, Dean Devlin

The Unkissed Bride ★

Comedy   1966 · US · Colour · 82mins

The term "unkissed" is a rather polite euphemism: the person struggling here to fulfil his wedding night sexual obligations with Anne Helm is former Disney juvenile lead Tommy Kirk (*The Shaggy Dog*). To cure his condition, Kirk has LSD sprayed on him while he sleeps, so his dreamy fairy-tale fantasies become real, and that's why this mindless opus never passed the British censor. Contains drug abuse.
Tom Kirk [Tommy Kirk] *Ted* • Anne Helm *Margie* • Jacques Bergerac *Jacques Phillipe* • Danica d'Hondt *Doctor Marilyn Richards* • Robert Ball *Ernest Sinclair* ■ *Dir/Scr* Jack H Harris

The Unknown ★★★★

Silent drama   1927 · US · BW · 50mins

Single-minded in its brutality, perversity and odd shock value, Tod Browning's Freudian nightmare is the most accomplished and morbid melodrama the Master of Silent Macabre ever directed. Lon Chaney straps his arms down with a painful harness as Alonzo the Armless Wonder, a circus performer who throws knives with his feet. It's when he falls in love with Joan Crawford who has a fear of being touched that murder, amputation and obsession come under the dark carnival spotlight. A fascinating silent classic, it still appals because of its sadomasochistic and devious tone – two Browning staples brought powerfully to the foreground in this perfectly crafted and warped passion play. Contains violence
Lon Chaney *Alonzo* • Norman Kerry *Malabor* • Joan Crawford *Estrellita* • Nick De Ruiz *Zanzi* • John George *Cojo* • Frank Lanning *Costra* ■ *Dir* Tod Browning • *Scr* Waldemar Young, from a story by Tod Browning

The Unknown Guest ★★ U

Mystery drama   1943 · US · BW · 64mins

A script by Philip Yordan and a score by Dmitri Tiomkin add to the unnerving atmosphere of this curious country chiller in which the arrival of renegade Victor Jory coincides with the disappearance of his aged aunt and uncle from their hotel. Director Kurt Neumann puts an interesting slant on small-town life and cleverly plays on Jory's sinister screen persona to keep you guessing, while also coaxing a brassy performance from Pamela Blake as the maid who's unsure of Jory's intentions.
Victor Jory *Chuck Williams* • Pamela Blake *Julie* • Veda Ann Borg *Helen* • Harry Hayden *Nadroy* • Nora Cecil *Martha Williams* • Lee White *Joe Williams* • Paul Fix *Fats* ■ *Dir* Kurt Neumann • *Scr* Philip Yordan, from a story by Maurice Franklin

The Unknown Soldier ★★★★ 15

War drama   1983 · Fin · Colour · 149mins

Edvin Laine's 1955 adaptation of Väinö Linna's autobiographical novel caused a political scandal. Having lost land to the USSR in the "Winter War" of 1939–40, Finland briefly allied with Hitler during the so-called "Continuation War" of 1941–44, when 80,000 men were lost in a counterattack for which the Finnish forces were singularly unprepared. The implications of that alliance were still a source of shame, but Rauni Mollberg's epic, unflinchingly realistic remake is more concerned with the emotions of the teenage conscripts who were sent on what amounted to a suicide mission. A Finnish language film. Contains some swearing, sexual references and violence. ▭
Risto Tuorila *Koskela* • Pirkka-Pekka Petelius *Hietanen* • Paavo Liski *Rokka* • Mika Mäkelä *Rahikainen* • Pertti Koivula *Lahtinen* ■ *Dir* Rauni Mollberg • *Scr* Rauni Mollberg, Veikko Aaltonen, from a novel by Väinö Linna

Unknown World ★ U

Science-fiction adventure
1951 · US · BW · 74mins

Scientists bore into the Earth aboard a half tank/half submarine mole ship, dubbed a "cyclotram", to find a subterranean safe haven from atomic war. Unfortunately, the peaceful centre proves harmful to human reproduction in a highly moral sci-fi quickie containing a wordy script, plodding direction, dinky special effects and not even an occasional thrill. After a fun start, this low-cal effort will probably bore you too!
Victor Kilian *Dr Jeremiah Morley* • Bruce Kellogg *Wright Thompson* • Otto Waldis *Dr Max A Bauer* • Marilyn Nash *Joan Lindsey* • Jim Bannon *Andy Ostengaard* ■ *Dir* Terrell O Morse [Terry Morse] • *Scr* Millard Kaufman

Unlawful Entry ★★★ 18

Thriller   1992 · US · Colour · 106mins

After the evil nanny in *The Hand That Rocks the Cradle* and the creepy flatmate in *Single White Female*, meet the psychotic cop – so unbalanced that you see him unravelling before your eyes. He's portrayed with credibility by Ray Liotta, who never reduces his character to caricature. As he targets innocent couple Kurt Russell and Madeleine Stowe, his insecurities become unnervingly mixed in with his charm. Sadly, there are yawning gaps in the plot, and the *Fatal Attraction*-style climax is so overcooked you can't help but laugh. Contains violence, swearing and nudity. ▭ **DVD**
Kurt Russell *Michael Carr* • Ray Liotta *Officer Pete Davis* • Madeleine Stowe *Karen Carr* • Roger E Mosley *Officer Roy Cole* • Ken Lerner *Roger Graham* • Deborah Offner *Penny* • Carmen Argenziano *Jerome Lurie* ■ *Dir* Jonathan Kaplan • *Scr* Lewis Colick, from a story by George D Putnam, John Katchner, Lewis Colick

Unlawful Passage ★★

Drama   1994 · US · Colour

Imagine a cross between *Dead Calm* and *Yojimbo*, in which an architect and his soap-star wife are baled out by a Mexican banana vendor called Paco and you have some idea of what to expect from this ocean-going thriller. Lee Horsley and Felicity Waterman are totally out of their depth as the stylish couple whose luxury yacht is commandeered by drug smugglers. Waterman has her moments, using her charms to befuddle her kidnappers, but Horsley is less than convincing as the architect turned action hero. Contains violence, swearing, sex scenes and nudity. ▭
Lee Horsley *Peter Browning* • Felicity Waterman *Gale Browning* • William Zabka *Howie* ■ *Dir* Camilo Vila • *Scr* Peter L Dixon

Unlikely Suspects ★★ 15

Drama   1996 · US · Colour · 86mins

A worthy drama about sexual harassment, in which members of an American high school's football team, led by Lochlyn Munro, are accused of molesting the cheerleaders. Sarah Chalke is the student who decides to tell all, with the help of her mother Shanna Reed. There's no doubting the film's good intentions, but the air-brushed performances and direction weaken the message somewhat. Contains violence. ▭
Shanna Reed *Anne Wilson* • Josh Taylor *Ted Wilson* • Sarah Chalke *Krista Wilson* • Lochlyn Munro *Josh Rieber* • Brigitte Dau *Ruth Gayle* • Gwynyth Walsh *Vicky Cooke* ■ *Dir* Joseph L Scanlan • *Scr* Natalie Chaidez

Unman, Wittering and Zigo ★★★★

Mystery   1971 · UK · BW · 101mins

No surprise that this creepy script by Giles Cooper moved from medium to medium (a radio play in 1957, then a TV play in 1965, and then this 1971 film) as it is a truly nightmarish scenario. Teacher David Hemmings is informed by his pupils at a boys' public school that they murdered his predecessor and will bump him off as well if he doesn't follow orders. Hemmings conveys very well the terror of being at the mercy of a class of delinquents, and the suspense is marred only by occasionally fussy camerawork. The conclusion, though, is somewhat unsatisfactory. One of the boys is played by ex-*EastEnder*Michael Cashman.

David Hemmings *John Ebony* • Douglas Wilmer *Headmaster* • Anthony Haygarth [Tony Haygarth] *Cary Farthingale* • Carolyn Seymour *Silvia Ebony* • Hamilton Dyce *Mr Winstanley* • Barbara Lott *Mrs Winstanley* • Michael Cashman *Terhew* ∎ *Dir* John Mackenzie • *Scr* Simon Raven, from the play by Giles Cooper

An Unmarried Woman
         ★★★★ 18

Romantic comedy
1978 · US · Colour · 119mins

Jill Clayburgh produces an assured and sensitive portrayal of wounded Big Apple womanhood when her privileged Manhattan lifestyle is undermined by her husband leaving her. Director Paul Mazursky has a sharp eye for New York detail – lots of vacuous parties, sweaty aerobics and a perceptive parade of Clayburgh's self-obsessed beaux. As her character inches towards feminism, Clayburgh truly comes into her own as the movie's second half gains neat pace and momentum. It doesn't matter that it all looks a little dated at times. ▣

Jill Clayburgh *Erica* • Alan Bates *Saul* • Michael Murphy *Martin* • Charlie • Pat Quinn *Sue* • Kelly Bishop *Elaine* • Lisa Lucas *Patti* • Linda Miller *Jeannette* • Andrew Duncan *Bob* ∎ *Dir/Scr* Paul Mazursky

The Unnamable
         ★ 18

Horror   1988 · US · Colour · 83mins

A tedious haunted house tale that ransacks the ingeniously twisted work of HP Lovecraft to little horrific effect. A demon pursues four Miskatonic University students through an old mansion sealed years before by a priest. Lots of annoying false scares, fake tree monsters and bloody decapitations lead to the climactic entrance of a daft female monster with wings, hooves and horns. This musty menace complete with its inane love song is, sadly, unwatchable. Contains violence. ▣

Charles King *Howard Damon* • Mark Kinsey Stephenson *Randolph Carter* • Alexandra Durrell *Tanya Heller* • Katrin Alexandre *The Creature* • Laura Albert *Wendy Barnes* • Delbert Spain *Joshua Winthrop* ∎ *Dir* Jean-Paul Ouellette • *Scr* Jean-Paul Ouellette, from the story by HP Lovecraft

The Unnamable Returns
★ 18

Horror   1992 · US · Colour · 99mins

...but whatever for? Literally picking up the story on exactly the same night the uninspired original ended, this sequel features Maria Ford as an ancient monster's beautiful alter ego who can't stop her beastly half gorily killing off more Arkham County inhabitants. After indulging in some limp *Splash*-inspired culture clashing, complete with gratuitous nudity, the winged creature she eventually becomes turns into a chair! While marginally better than its predecessor (this one actually has a budget), and managing to raise a few

decent scares, this is not only unnamable, but unnecessary. Contains swearing. ▣

Mark Kinsey Stephenson *Randolph Carter* • Charles Klausmeyer *Eliot Damon Howard* • Maria Ford *Alyda Winthrop* • John Rhys-Davies *Professor Harley Warren* • David Warner *Chancellor Thayer* • Richard Domeier *Officer Malcolm Bainbridge* • Siobhan McCafferty *Officer Debbie Lesh* ∎ *Dir* Jean-Paul Ouellette • *Scr* Jean-Paul Ouellette, from the stories *The Statement of Randolph Carter* and *The Unnamable* by HP Lovecraft

Unnatural Causes: the Agent Orange Story ★★★ 15

Drama based on a true story
1986 · US · Colour · 95mins

The Last American Hero director Lamont Johnson and director/ screenwriter John Sayles (*Eight Men Out*) are the men behind this interesting tale about a counsellor (Alfre Woodard) and a sick Vietnam veteran (John Ritter) trying to prove that the latter's disease was caused by Agent Orange. Woodard as true-life crusader Maude DeVictor is superb, and she's matched by Ritter, who's best known for comic roles in films like *Skin Deep* and the TV series *Three's Company*. ▣

John Ritter *Frank Coleman* • Alfre Woodard *Maude DeVictor* • Patti Labelle *Jeanette Thompson* • John Vargas *Fernando "Nando" Sanchez* • Frederick Allen *Kid* • Richard Anthony Crenna *Soldier* • Frank Pellegrino *Raul* • Jonathan Welsh *Dr Lester* • John Sayles *Lloyd* ∎ *Dir* Lamont Johnson • *Scr* John Sayles, from story by Martin M Goldstein, Stephen Doran, Robert Jacobs

An Unremarkable Life ★★

Drama   1989 · US · Colour · 98mins

A melodramatic talk-fest about two elderly cohabiting sisters who fall out when one decides to start dating, thus upsetting the duo's finely balanced equilibrium. This is a cue for much bickering and even more reminiscing. There are quality performances from Hollywood veterans Patricia Neal and Shelley Winters, but their efforts are wasted on a script that needed to be sharper and wittier.

Patricia Neal *Frances McEllany* • Shelley Winters *Evelyn McEllany* • Mako *Max Chin* ∎ *Dir* Amin Q Chaudhri • *Scr* Marcia Dinneen

Les Uns et les Autres ★★★

Historical drama   1981 · Fr · Colour · 185mins

As a bloated, all-stops-out melodrama this effort from Claude Lelouch takes some beating, though an hour may be enough for the majority of viewers. Starting in 1936, it chronicles the lives of four couples (played by actors in multiple roles) – American, Russian, French and German – and takes them through the obstacle race and marathon that is that thing called life. There is the Second World War, the Holocaust, the Cold War, Algeria and Vietnam. There is race relations, car smashes, cancer, the works. But most of all there is music which links everyone together in a sort of hey-ho, let's-go medley. Exhausting yet somehow amazing. In French with English subtitles.

James Caan *Glenn Sr/Glenn Jr* • Robert Hossein *Simon Meyer/Robert Prat* • Nicole

Garcia *Anne* • Geraldine Chaplin *Suzan/Sarah Glenn* • Daniel Olbrychski *Karl* • Jacques Villeret *Jacques* ∎ *Dir/Scr* Claude Lelouch

The Unseen ★★★

Murder mystery   1945 · US · BW · 81mins

Although co-scripted by Raymond Chandler, this has none of the sawn-off dialogue he was famous for. But it is nevertheless full of an atmosphere of foreboding as governess Gail Russell starts to believe that dark deeds were done in a neighbouring house and Joel McCrea's children had something to do with them. There is a mood of authentic creepiness that was obviously meant to follow in the same year's *The Uninvited*, which was also directed by Lewis Allen.

Joel McCrea *David Fielding* • Gail Russell *Elizabeth Howard* • Herbert Marshall *Dr Charles Evans* • Richard Lyon *Barnaby Fielding* • Nona Griffith *Ellen Fielding* • Phyllis Brooks *Maxine* • Isobel Elsom *Marian Tygarth* • Norman Lloyd *Jasper Goodwin* ∎ *Dir* Lewis Allen • *Scr* Raymond Chandler, Hagar Wilde, Ken Englund, from the novel *Her Heart in Her Throat* by Ethel Lina White

The Unsinkable Molly Brown ★★★★ U

Musical   1964 · US · Colour · 123mins

One of the last gasps of the great MGM musical, this has much to recommend it, particularly the no-holds-barred leading performance of the Oscar-nominated Debbie Reynolds. Maestro director Charles Walters (*Easter Parade* and *High Society*), does what he can with a substandard score by *The Music Man's* Meredith Willson, but is helped by a sparkling cast, especially Jack Kruschen and *grande dame* Martita Hunt, revelling in their roles. The Colorado scenery (filmed on location) is splendid, as is leading man Harve Presnell. Musical fans and children won't be worried by its length, and others will delight in its cautionary tale, unless they've an aversion to red that is... ▣

Debbie Reynolds *Molly Brown* • Harve Presnell *Johnny Brown* • Ed Begley *Shamus Tobin* • Jack Kruschen *Christmas Morgan* • Hermione Baddeley *Mrs Grogan* • Vassili Lambrinos *Prince Louis De Laniere* • Fred Essler *Baron Karl Ludwig Von Ettenburg* • Martita Hunt • Harvey Lembeck *Polak* ∎ *Dir* Charles Walters • *Scr* Helen Deutsch, from the musical by Meredith Willson, Richard Morris

Unspeakable Acts ★★★ 18

Drama based on a true story
1990 · US · Colour · 94mins

Based on the transcripts from a child abuse trial in Miami in 1984, this is a well-played TV drama that follows the efforts of a husband-and-wife team of psychologists (played by Jill Clayburgh and Brad Davis of *Midnight Express* fame) to gather incriminating evidence from their child witnesses. An often disturbing but well-meaning film. ▣

Jill Clayburgh *Dr Laurie Braga* • Brad Davis *Dr Joseph Braga* • Gregory Sierra *Frank Fuster* • Bess Meyer *Iliana Fuster* • James Handy *Jeff Samek* • Jenny Gago *Christina Royo* ∎ *Dir* Linda Otto • *Scr* Alan Landsburg, from the book by Jan Hollingsworth

The Unspoken Truth ★★ 15

Drama based on a true story
1995 · US · Colour · 87mins

Lea Thompson (*Caroline in the City*) is a wife who is so loyal to her abusive husband (James Marshall of *Twin Peaks* fame) that she agrees to share the blame for a murder he has committed. If that isn't sensational enough, the drama then switches to her bid to retain custody of her daughter and her sister's determination to leak a dark family secret to secure her release. This outlandish melodrama is so full of unlikely events and resistible characters that it could only have been based on a true story. Contains some violence. ▣

Lea Thompson *Brianne Hawkins* • Patricia Kalember *Margaret Trainor* • James Marshall *Clay Hawkins* • Dick O'Neill *Thomas Cleary* • Karis Paige Bryant *Lily Hawkins* ∎ *Dir* Peter Werner • *Scr* JA Mitty

Unstrung Heroes ★★★★ PG

Comedy drama   1995 · US · Colour · 89mins

A charming little comedy drama from actress/director Diane Keaton (who remains behind the camera for this one. Nathan Watt plays the little boy who grows up under the influence of his quirky father (John Turturro, superb) and his even wackier uncles (Maury Chaykin and *Seinfeld*'s Michael Richards) when his mother (Andie MacDowell, in her best performance to date) becomes seriously ill. Keaton capably handles the mix of humour and sadness, delivering a superbly performed, moving and very funny tale about growing up and the weirdness of families. A film which can make you cry both tears of joy and sadness. ▣

Andie MacDowell *Selma Lidz* • John Turturro *Sid Lidz* • Michael Richards *Danny Lidz* • Maury Chaykin *Arthur Lidz* • Nathan Watt *Steven/Franz Lidz* • Kendra Krull *Sandy Lidz* ∎ *Dir* Diane Keaton • *Scr* Richard LaGravenese, from the book by Franz Lidz

An Unsuitable Job for a Woman ★★★ 15

Mystery   1981 · UK · Colour · 90mins

The original film adaptation of PD James's bestseller (later a TV series with Helen Baxendale). Pippa Guard is quietly efficient as Cordelia Gray, who takes over a detective agency after her partner commits suicide. There's certainly nothing straightforward about her first case she's hired to investigate the "suicide" of a businessman's son in a picturesque cottage. Making only his second feature, director Christopher Petit casts a moody pall over traditional whodunit country and scatters clues with tantalising skill. An expert cast, which includes Billie Whitelaw, helps boost the enjoyment no end. ▣

Billie Whitelaw *Elizabeth Leaming* • Pippa Guard *Cordelia Gray* • Paul Freeman *James Callender* • Dominic Guard *Andrew Lunn* • Elizabeth Spriggs *Miss Markland* • David Horovitch *Sergeant Maskell* • Dawn Archibald *Isobel* • James Gilbey *Boy* ∎ *Dir* Christopher Petit • *Scr* Elizabeth McKay, Brian Scobie, Christopher Petit, from the novel by PD James

The Unsuspected ★★★★

Crime drama 1947 · US · BW · 102mins

A virtually unknown but highly underrated suspense thriller, it's impeccably directed by the great Michael Curtiz and features the urbane Claude Rains as a radio star performer specialising in spine-shivering broadcasts. This was actually intended as a starring vehicle for one Michael North, a Curtiz discovery who didn't work out, and the subsequent revoicing of North and the minimising of his role creates a truly unsettling feeling throughout the film. The period insights into the workings of radio are deftly done, as are the action sequences, but the clever scripting is the real bonus, aided by co-stars Audrey Totter as a nymphomaniac and Hurd Hatfield as a drunk. Adult fare indeed.

Claude Rains *Victor Grandison* • Joan Caulfield *Matilda Frazier* • Audrey Totter *Althea Keane* • Constance Bennett *Jane Moynihan* • Hurd Hatfield *Oliver Keane* • Michael North *Steven Francis Howard* • Fred Clark *Richard Donovan* • Jack Lambert *Mr Press* ■ *Dir* Michael Curtiz • *Scr* Ranald MacDougall, Bess Meredyth, from a novel by Charlotte Armstrong

Untamed ★★★

Romantic adventure
1955 · US · Colour · 108mins

A splendid early CinemaScope melodrama, with the then-new widescreen process deployed effectively in a South Africa-located tale of a trek across the veldt. Passions flare and Zulus attack the wagon train in this lusty adaptation of a bodice-ripper of a novel by Helga Moray. Featuring two of 20th Century-Fox's finest (handsome Tyrone Power and fiery redhead Susan Hayward), this is one of the last examples of this type of imperialist tosh. There's fine support from rising stars Richard Egan and Rita Moreno, and Britain's own John Justin makes a convincing Boer. Agnes Moorehead, as ever, steals every scene she's in, but the real star is that stunning photography.

Tyrone Power *Paul Van Riebeck* • Susan Hayward *Katie O'Neill* • Richard Egan *Kurt Hout* • John Justin *Shawn Kildare* • Agnes Moorehead *Aggie* • Rita Moreno *Julia* • Hope Emerson *Maria De Groot* ■ *Dir* Henry King • *Scr* Talbot Jennings, Frank Fenton, William A Bacher, Michael Blankfort, from the novel by Helga Moray

Untamed Frontier ★★

Western 1952 · US · Colour · 75mins

A routine range war western, despite talented Argentine director Hugo Fregonese's attempts to make something more of the territorial theme, and despite the valiant efforts of a cast headed by Joseph Cotten and Shelley Winters. There's certainly nothing in the script worthy of attention. Even western fans may feel that this is as much of a chore to watch as the cast and crew obviously felt it was to make.

Joseph Cotten *Kirk Denbow* • Shelley Winters *Jane Stevens* • Scott Brady *Glenn Denbow* • Suzan Ball *Lottie* • Minor Watson *Matt Denbow* • Katherine Emery *Camilla Denbow* • Lee Van Cleef *Dave Chittun* ■ *Dir* Hugo Fregonese • *Scr* Gerald Drayson Adams, John Bagni, Polly James, Gwen Bagni, from a story by Houston Branch, Eugenia Night

Untamed Heart ★★★ 15

Romantic drama 1993 · US · Colour · 97mins

Marisa Tomei and Christian Slater both work hard to wring every ounce of uplift and emotion from director Tony Bill's well-meaning, if slightly contrived, romance. Slater is the shy kitchen guy with a congenital heart defect who saves waitress Tomei from some thugs, an event that leads the bruised souls to embark on a hesitant relationship. Everyone says it can't last especially delicious Rosie Perez in another of her trademark sassy, wisecracking roles but, although the outcome is fairly predictable, there's enough here to engage and amuse. Contains some violence, swearing and nudity. [video]

Christian Slater *Adam* • Marisa Tomei *Caroline* • Rosie Perez *Cindy* • Kyle Secor *Howard* • Willie Garson *Patsy* • Claudia Wilkens *Mother Camilla* ■ *Dir* Tony Bill • *Scr* Tom Sierchio

Untamed Love ★★★ 12

Drama based on a true story
1994 · US · Colour · 91mins

An affecting and compassionate look at child abuse through the true story of a six-year-old girl and her special education teacher. The Americans do this kind of TV movie in two ways, as either embarrassingly mawkish or thoughtful and mature. *Untamed Love* is in the latter category, with good performances from Cathy Lee Crosby and Ashlee Lauren as the determined teacher and her hapless pupil respectively. This is sometimes hard to take, but it rewards greatly as the delicate story unfolds. [video]

Cathy Lee Crosby *Maggie Bernard* • John Getz *Chad* • Gary Frank *Mr Eldridge* • Ashlee Lauren *Caitlin Eldridge* • Jaime P Gomez [Jaime Gomez] *Miguel* • Mel Winkler *Sam Powers* ■ *Dir* Paul Aaron • *Scr* Peter Nelson, from the book *One Child* by Torey Hayden

Until September ★★ 15

Romantic drama 1984 · US · Colour · 92mins

Director Richard Marquand had a maddeningly brief and erratic career before his death in 1987: one moment he was thrilling audiences with the likes of *Return of the Jedi* and *Jagged Edge*, the next it was on to mush like *Hearts of Fire* and this ill-conceived romantic drama. Karen Allen is the Yank visiting France who misses her flight home and then falls for dashing Thierry Lhermitte (*Le Cop*). The international cast does its best, but no-one's heart really seems to be in it. Contains swearing and nudity. [video]

Karen Allen *Mo Alexander* • Thierry Lhermitte *Xavier de la Perouse* • Christopher Cazenove *Philip* • Marie Catherine Conti *Isabelle* • Hutton Cobb *Andrew* • Michael Mellinger *Colonel Viola* ■ *Dir* Richard Marquand • *Scr* Janice Lee Graham

Until the End of the World ★★ 15

Science-fiction road movie
1991 · Ger/Fr/Ausl · Colour · 151mins

This misbegotten epic shows how an arthouse director can blow $23 million and still emerge with a three-hour film that's less than perfect. Thus Wim Wenders, admired for his bleak thrillers and general coolness in movies including *Paris, Texas* and *Wings of Desire*, took William Hurt, Max von Sydow, Sam Neill and others to eight countries without a script, assuming that sheer genius was enough. All they had was an idea about a nuclear satellite crashing to Earth in 1999 and a cluster of unrelated subplots. Hurt is given a not very interesting love interest and seems bored out of his mind. It's nicely shot, though, partly in the Australian outback, but then, so are car advertisements. Contains violence, swearing and nudity. [video]

William Hurt *Trevor McPhee/Sam Farber* • Solveig Dommartin *Claire Tourneur* • Sam Neill *Eugene Fitzpatrick* • Max von Sydow *Henry Farber* • Rüdiger Vogler *Philip Winter* • Ernie Dingo *Burt* • Jeanne Moreau *Edith Farber* ■ *Dir* Wim Wenders • *Scr* Wim Wenders, Peter Carey, from the story by Wim Wenders, Solveig Dommartin

Until They Sail ★★★

Second World War drama
1957 · US · BW · 94mins

A marvellously overwrought war drama, brought to the screen with a superb cast: Joan Fontaine, Jean Simmons, Piper Laurie and Sandra Dee as sisters, getting emotionally wrapped up with American servicemen, with murder and melodrama as the result. Superbly directed by ace craftsman Robert Wise (*West Side Story* and *The Sound of Music*), this also features a handsome Paul Newman and the excellent pre-Disney Dean Jones. No great shakes, but a jolly good matinée weepie, and compulsively viewable thanks to its cast.

Jean Simmons *Barbara Leslie Forbes* • Joan Fontaine *Anne Leslie* • Paul Newman *Captain Jack Harding* • Piper Laurie *Delia Leslie* • Charles Drake *Captain Richard Bates* • Sandra Dee *Evelyn Leslie* • Wally Cassell *"Shiner" Phil Friskett* • Alan Napier *Prosecution* • Dean Jones ■ *Dir* Robert Wise • *Scr* Robert Anderson, from a story by James A Michener

The Untouchables ★★★★★ 15

Crime drama 1987 · US · Colour · 114mins

Brian De Palma's riveting take on the old TV show with Kevin Costner in a star-making performance as Eliot Ness, the quiet Treasury agent and family man who picks up a pump-action rifle in order to rid Chicago of bootlegger Al Capone. Always a showman, De Palma lets loose with a barrage of bloody set pieces, notably the climax at the railway station a nod to the famous Odessa steps sequence in *The Battleship Potemkin* in which time literally stands still. David Mamet's dialogue crackles, Ennio Morricone's music sings and the production design sparkles. Andy Garcia joins the team, and a plumped-up Robert De Niro plays Capone, yet for many the main attraction is Sean Connery's Oscar-winning performance as the veteran, philosophical Irish cop who shows Costner the ropes. Contains violence and swearing. [video]

Kevin Costner *Eliot Ness* • Sean Connery *Jim Malone* • Andy Garcia *George Stone* • Robert De Niro *Al Capone* • Charles Martin Smith *Oscar Wallace* • Richard Bradford *Mike* • Jack Kehoe *Payne* • Brad Sullivan *George* • Billy Drago *Frank Nitti* ■ *Dir* Brian De Palma • *Scr* David Mamet, suggested by the TV series and from the works of Oscar Fraley, with Eliot Ness, Paul Robsky • *Cinematographer* Stephen H Burum • *Production Designer* Patrizia von Brandenstein

Unzipped ★★★★ 15

Documentary
1995 · US · Colour and BW · 73mins

Hugely enjoyable documentary that follows New York fashion designer Isaac Mizrahi as he plans his 1994 show featuring an "Eskimo" look inspired by another documentary, *Nanook of the North*. Mizrahi performs very amusingly for the camera, and his supermodels (Campbell, Crawford, Moss et al) also seem to know exactly how to behave for maximum effect. Not surprisingly, director Douglas Keeve is an ex-fashion photographer. Black-and-white footage contrasts strikingly with the colour shots used for the clothes sequences. Despite the artifice, this is a far more revealing portrait of the world of haute couture than Altman's farcical *Prêt-à-Porter*.

Dir Douglas Keeve

Up ★★★ 18

Sex comedy 1976 · US · Colour · 78mins

The penultimate movie from the notorious Russ Meyer, stars the inexplicably named Raven De La Croix as a woman who revenges herself against the man who raped her. It's one of his best and most outrageous, typically overflowing with outsize bosoms, cartoon violence and bible-thumbing morality that ensures wrongdoers get their just deserts. The Meyer sense of humour is also intact, one shot takes place inside a man's trousers as his flies are unzipped. Other highlights include an outdoor grope-fest and a chain saw battle. From a story co-written by celebrated US film critic Roger Ebert, this is likely to offend most fragile sensibilities, feminists especially. Contains strong sex scenes and violence. [video]

Robert McLane *Paul* • Edward Schaaf *Adolph Schwartz* • Mary Gavin *Headsperson* • Elaine Collins *Ethiopian chief* • Su Ling *Limehouse* • Linda Sue Ragsdale *Gwendolyn* • Janet Wood *Sweet Li'l Alice* • Raven De La Croix *Margo Winchester* ■ *Dir* Russ Meyer • *Scr* B Callum [Russ Meyer], from a story by Russ Meyer, Reinhold Timme [Roger Ebert], Jim Ryan

Up at the Villa ★★★★ 12

Period romantic thriller
1998 · US · Colour · 115mins

The dark forces of fascism invade idyllic Tuscany in this charismatic thirties drama. Kristin Scott Thomas, a penniless aristocrat on the verges of colonial society, is befriended by countess Anne Bancroft and pursued by a stalwart James Fox. In a matter of hours her world is turned upside down by two chance encounters: one with a refugee that results in murder, the other with a rakish Sean Penn whose appearance sparks mutual passion. The chemistry between the two leads is tangible, while Philip Haas directs with an energy that makes his film very compelling indeed.

Kristin Scott Thomas *Mary Panton* • Sean Penn *Rowley Flint* • Anne Bancroft *Princess San Ferdinando* • James Fox *Sir Edgar Swift* • Jeremy Davies *Karl Richter* • Derek Jacobi *Lucky Leadbetter* • Dudley Sutton *Harold*

Atkinson ■ Dir Philip Haas • Scr Belinda Haas, from a novella by W Somerset Maugham

Up Close & Personal
★★★ 15

Romantic drama
1996 · US · Colour · 119mins

Robert Redford and Michelle Pfeiffer star in this romantic drama set in a Miami television newsroom. Redford plays the veteran former White House correspondent who takes small-town girl Pfeiffer under his wing, helping her overcome stage fright and seeing her career as a television journalist take off as his idles. It's all tosh, of course, but its Star Is Born theme of male self-sacrifice is finely manipulated by director Jon Avnet so, as a three-hankie movie, it's not to be sniffed at. Sadly, the talents of Stockard Channing and Kate Nelligan are wasted in relatively minor roles as hard-bitten rival news anchors. Contains swearing and violence. 🔲 DVD

Robert Redford Warren Justice • Michelle Pfeiffer Tally "Sallyanne" Atwater • Stockard Channing Marcia McGrath • Joe Mantegna Bucky Terranova • Kate Nelligan Joanna Kennelly • Glenn Plummer Ned Jackson • James Rebhorn John Merino • Scott Bryce Rob Sullivan • Dedee Pfeiffer Luanne Atwater ■ Dir Jon Avnet • Scr Joan Didion, John Gregory Dunne, from the book Golden Girl by Alanna Nash

Up from the Beach
★★★ U

War drama
1965 · US · BW · 98mins

Cliff Robertson gives his usual distinguished performance as an American army sergeant who becomes involved with Resistance civilians after the D-Day landings. Slow-moving, but it has its gripping moments, especially with Francoise Rosay playing an elderly peasant-woman whom you just don't know whether to trust or not. Director Robert Parrish just about controls the action, but takes it all at too steady a pace.

Cliff Robertson Sgt Edward Baxter • Red Buttons Pfc Harry Devine • Irina Demick Lili Rolland • Marius Goring German Commandant • Slim Pickens Artillery Colonel • James Robertson-Justice British Beachmaster • Broderick Crawford US MP Major • Françoise Rosay Lili's grandmother ■ Dir Robert Parrish • Scr Stanley Mann, Claude Brulé, Howard Clewes, from the novel Epitaph For an Enemy by George Barr

Up Goes Maisie
★★ U

Comedy
1946 · US · BW · 88mins

After a gap in 1945, Maisie (Ann Sothern) returned for her penultimate adventure which, for the only time in the series, co-starred her with the same leading man for the second time. He's George Murphy (Ringside Maisie), this time as an inventor working on a new helicopter design, with Maisie as his assistant, in which capacity she foils his nefarious rivals and gets to pilot the helicopter. She got the plane up, but the series was spiralling down.

Ann Sothern Maisie Ravier • George Murphy Joe Morton • Hillary Brooke Barbara Nuboult • Horace McNally [Stephen McNally] Tim Kingby • Ray Collins Mr Hendrickson • Jeff York

Elmer Saunders ■ Dir Harry Beaumont • Scr Thelma Robinson, from the character created by Wilson Collison

Up in Arms
★★★ U

Musical comedy 1944 · US · Colour · 105mins

This first starring vehicle for Danny Kaye has dated badly, its wartime theme about a hypochondriac who's drafted into the army seeming faintly distasteful today, and the obvious studio settings aren't enhanced by the garish forties Technicolor. Nevertheless, former Broadway comedian Kaye proves to be far superior to his surroundings, aided by some wonderful material, most notably in the movie's highlight, a now-classic comedy monologue set in the lobby of a movie theatre. Dinah Shore and Constance Dowling both look ravishing in forties get-up, and there's also excellent support from Dana Andrews and Louis Calhern. Owen Davis's play The Nervous Wreck, was previously made in 1930 as an Eddie Cantor vehicle called Whoopee!. 🔲

Danny Kaye Danny Weems • Constance Dowling Mary Morgan • Dinah Shore Virginia Merrill • Dana Andrews Joe Nelson • Louis Calhern Colonel Ashley • George Mathews Blackie • Benny Baker Butterball • Elisha Cook Jr Info Jones ■ Dir Elliott Nugent • Scr Don Hartman, Allen Boretz, Robert Pirosh, from the play The Nervous Wreck by Owen Davis

Up in Central Park
★★★

Musical comedy 1948 · US · BW · 86mins

A disappointing adaptation of the Broadway success, dealing with the unlikely subject of city hall corruption, revolving around New York's notoriously crooked statesman Boss Tweed, played effectively by Vincent Price. Turned here into a vehicle for Deanna Durbin, the film loses most of the original Sigmund Romberg score, though Dick Haymes makes a likeable enough leading man (he's the reporter who exposes the corruption). The film needed a more expensive production, but Durbin fans will cherish this, her penultimate movie before her retirement.

Deanna Durbin Rosie Moore • Dick Haymes John Matthews • Vincent Price Boss Tweed • Albert Sharpe Timothy Moore • Tom Powers Regan • Hobart Cavanaugh Mayor Oakley • Thurston Hall Governor Motley ■ Dir William A Seiter • Scr Karl Tunberg, from the play by Dorothy Fields, Herbert Fields, Sigmund Romberg

Up in Mabel's Room
★★

Farce 1944 · US · BW · 76mins

The marital bliss of newly married Gary and Geraldine Ainsworth (Dennis O'Keefe, Marjorie Reynolds) is shattered when Gary's friendship with Mabel (glamorous Gail Patrick), the fiancée of his business partner Arthur (Lee Bowman), is misinterpreted by Geraldine and Arthur. A standard bedroom farce, it's directed by Allan Dwan and boasts Mischa Auer, Charlotte Greenwood and Binnie Barnes in the supporting line-up. Originally a play, and filmed as a silent in 1926, it's good-natured but uninterestingly tame.

Dennis O'Keefe Gary Ainsworth • Marjorie Reynolds Geraldine Ainsworth • Gail Patrick

Mabel Essington • Mischa Auer Boris • Charlotte Greenwood Martha • Lee Bowman Arthur Weldon • John Hubbard Jimmy Larchmont • Binnie Barnes Alicia Larchmont ■ Dir Allan Dwan • Scr Tom Reed, Isobel Dawn, from a play by Wilson Collison, Otto Harbach, from the story Oh Chemise by Wilson Collison

Up in the Cellar
★★★★

Comedy 1970 · US · Colour · 93mins

Wes Stern is a hapless student whose life is turned upside down when his poetry scholarship is annulled by a rogue computer. He finds himself a puppet in a battle between David Arkin a wealthy student with ideas of revolution and the monstrous college president Maurice Camber (a pre-JR Larry Hagman). Using sex as a weapon, Stern tries to get at Hagman through the women in his life. Director Theodore J Flicker's follow-up to his magnificent satire The President's Analyst is another effervescent comedy overflowing with great ideas and cunning twists. Although the subject matter is dated, the craft of the piece still shines through.

Wes Stern Colin Slade • Joan Collins Pat Camber • Larry Hagman Maurice Camber • Nira Barab Tracy Camber • Judy Pace Harlene Jones • David Arkin Hugo ■ Dir Theodore Flicker • Scr Theodore J Flicker, from the novel The Late Wonder Boy by Angus Hall

Up in the World
★★ U

Comedy 1956 · UK · BW · 86mins

This tacky comedy gave notice that Norman Wisdom's winning formula was already beginning to wear thin. Here he plays a window cleaner who befriends a lonely boy millionaire, much to the annoyance of sniffy guardian Jerry Desmonde. The slapstick inevitably centres around ladders and broken windows, the sentiment around Michael Caridia and a hamster called Harold. But the worst aspect of this maudlin mishmash is that Wisdom gets to warble so often. No wonder he ends up in prison. 🔲

Norman Wisdom Norman • Maureen Swanson Jeannie • Jerry Desmonde Major Willoughby • Ambrosine Philpotts Lady Banderville • Colin Gordon Fletcher Hetherington • Michael Caridia Sir Reginald Banderville • Michael Ward Maurice ■ Dir John Paddy Carstairs • Scr Jack Davies, Henry E Blyth, Peter Blackmore

Up 'n' Under
★★ 12

Sports comedy 1997 · UK · Colour · 98mins

A top line-up of British sitcom stars take to the rugby field in a mildly diverting by-the-numbers sports comedy. Gary Olsen bets his house on a ridiculous wager with smug rival Tony Slattery and naturally, Olsen's team is the least enthusiastic and skilful in the land. Very, very predictable fare, but it pushes some of the right buttons. Seasoned comic performers Olsen and Neil Morrissey are joined by Griff Rhys Jones in an amusing commentator cameo, and Samantha Janus taking a gratuitous shower. Contains swearing. 🔲

Gary Olsen Arthur Hoyle • Richard Ridings Frank • Samantha Janus Hazel Scott • Ralph Brown Phil • Neil Morrissey Steve • Adrian Hood Tommy • David MacCreedy Tony • Tony

Slattery Reg Welch • Griff Rhys Jones Ray Mason ■ Dir John Godber • Scr John Godber, from his play

Up Periscope
★★★ U

War drama 1959 · US · Colour · 99mins

Warner Bros knew the box-office value of a good submarine flick, having produced Destination Tokyo. Here the ever-economic studio reworked the sets from the previous year's Alan Ladd vehicle The Deep Six to showcase its new star, TV's Maverick James Garner, in a nail-biting Second World War drama. This also benefits from the skill of veteran director Gordon Douglas, and from stalwart Edmond O'Brien in support. More recently, The Hunt for Red October and Crimson Tide have proved that the submarine genre is alive and well, but do they really have to say "Dive! Dive! Dive!" in every one of these films?

James Garner Ken Braden • Edmond O'Brien Stevenson • Andra Martin Sally • Alan Hale Jr Malone • Carleton Carpenter Carney • Frank Gifford Mount • William Leslie Doherty ■ Dir Gordon Douglas • Scr Richard Landau, from the novel by Robb White

Up Pompeii
★★ 15

Comedy 1971 · UK · Colour · 86mins

Frankie Howerd dons a toga for a film version of his TV series based on the life of Roman slave Lurcio. Unfortunately, the blatantly obvious Carry On-style formula (the cast even features Carry On regular Bernard Bresslaw) only works sporadically. There's more interest in trying to put names to the plethora of familiar British faces in the cast, among them Patrick Cargill as the Emperor Nero and Michael Hordern as the unfortunate Ludicrus Sextus. 🔲

Frankie Howerd Lurcio • Patrick Cargill Nero • Michael Hordern Ludicrus • Barbara Murray Ammonia • Lance Percival Bilius • Bill Fraser Prosperus • Adrienne Posta Scrubba • Julie Ege Voluptua • Bernard Bresslaw Gorgo • Roy Hudd MC ■ Dir Bob Kellett • Scr Sid Colin, from an idea by Talbot Rothwell

Up the Academy
★★ 15

Comedy 1980 · US · Colour · 83mins

Trying to emulate the success of National Lampoon, Mad magazine got into the movie business with this irreverent, bad-taste saga of high jinks at a military academy. Star Ron Leibman, presumably unhappy with the finished product, succeeded in getting his name taken off the credits and later even Mad magazine itself, disowned the movie. Despite this unfavourable background, the film does have a crude energy and some sparky moments. 🔲

Ron Leibman Major • Wendell Brown Ike • Tom Citera Hash • J Hutchinson Oliver • Ralph Macchio Chooch • Harry Teinowitz Ververgaert • Tom Poston Sisson • Ian Wolfe Commandant Caseway ■ Dir Robert Downey • Scr Tom Patchett, Jay Tarses

Up the Chastity Belt
★★ PG

Period comedy 1971 · UK · Colour · 89mins

A glance at the credits – produced by Ned Sherrin, script by Sid Colin, Ray Galton and Alan Simpson, score by Carl Davis – raises one's hopes for

this medieval incarnation of Frankie Howerd's TV hit *Up Pompeii*. But, sadly, expectations are soon dashed as it becomes clear that Lurkalot is a pale imitation of his ancient ancestor Lurcio, and that there are few comic highlights to brighten these "dark ages". As dependent as he was on handcrafted material, Howerd looks very ordinary beside the infinitely more versatile supporting cast of top character comics. 🔲

Frankie Howerd *Lurkalot/King Richard The Lionheart* • Graham Crowden *Sir Coward de Custard* • Bill Fraser *Sir Braggart de Bombast* • Roy Hudd *Nick the Pick* • Hugh Paddick *Robin Hood* • Anna Quayle *Lady Ashfodel* • Lance Percival *Reporter* • Godfrey Winn *Archbishop of All England* • Eartha Kitt *Scheherazade* ■ *Dir* Bob Kellett • *Scr* Sid Colin, Ray Galton, Alan Simpson

Up the Creek ★★★ U

Comedy 1958 · UK · BW · 82mins

Veteran writer/director Val Guest and an experienced cast of *farceurs*, including Peter Sellers, enliven this British naval farce with its timeworn story of an incompetent officer pitted against the wily lower ranks. (The exposition is that of *Oh, Mr Porter!*, also written by Guest.) Silly, accident-prone David Tomlinson is given the command of an ancient destroyer, where Sellers controls the rackets. The chaos when an admiral Wilfrid Hyde White arrives for an inspection is extremely funny. The film's success inspired a sequel, *Further up the Creek*, and probably the radio series *The Navy Lark*.

David Tomlinson *Lt Humphrey Fairweather* • Peter Sellers *Bosun Docherty* • Wilfrid Hyde White *Admiral Foley* • Vera Day *Lily* • Liliane Sottane *Susanne* • Tom Gill *Flag Lieutenant* • Michael Goodliffe *Nelson* • Reginald Beckwith *Publican* ■ *Dir* Val Guest • *Scr* Val Guest, Len Heath, John Warren

Up the Down Staircase ★★

Drama 1967 · US · Colour · 123mins

Having successfully brought *To Kill a Mockingbird* to the screen, director Robert Mulligan makes a fair attempt to do the same with Bel Kaufman's highly entertaining but fragmentary novel. Sandy Dennis plays a young, novice teacher who has her ideals severely tested in an underfunded, bureaucratic inner-city school. Much of the movie is shot on location but, even though the kids perform well, the adult characters are a little too pat for the film to be totally convincing. Imagine *To Sir, With Love*, set in New York, without Sidney Poitier, and you won't be far wrong.

Sandy Dennis *Sylvia Barrett* • Patrick Bedford *Paul Barringer* • Eileen Heckart *Henrietta Pastorfield* • Ruth White *Beatrice Schracter* • Jean Stapleton *Sadie Finch* • Sorrell Booke *Dr Bester* ■ *Dir* Robert Mulligan • *Scr* Tad Mosel, from the novel by Bel Kaufman

Up the Front ★ PG

Comedy 1972 · UK · Colour · 84mins

The final film to be spun off from TV's *Up Pompeii* leaves Frankie Howerd stranded in the middle of no man's land with nothing more than a tattoo to cover his blushes. Not even Morecambe and Wise's regular writer Eddie Braben could do anything to pep

up Sid Colin's desperate script and you end up feeling sorry for the likes of Stanley Holloway, Zsa Zsa Gabor and Hermione Baddeley, even though their lacklustre performances really merit reproach. 🔲

Frankie Howerd *Lurk* • Zsa Zsa Gabor *Mata Hari* • Bill Fraser *Groping* • Lance Percival *Von Gutz* • Stanley Holloway *Vincento* • Madeline Smith *Fanny* • Hermione Baddeley *Monique* • William Mervyn *Lord Twithampton* • Dora Bryan *Cora Crumpington* • Bob Hoskins *Recruiting Sergeant* ■ *Dir* Bob Kellett • *Scr* Sid Colin, Eddie Braben

Up the Junction ★★

Drama 1967 · UK · Colour · 118mins

When Ken Loach adapted Nell Dunn's provocative novel *Up the Junction* for TV in the sixties, it shocked the nation. Director Peter Collinson's big screen version was more polished, and therein lay its undoing. Loach's semi-documentary style gave Battersea the suitably bleak look that made the central character's decision to move there from Chelsea seem both politically significant and socially courageous. Collinson, however, offers a working-class wonderland and has Suzy Kendall play the girl as a cross between a sixties' supermodel and a melodramatic sob sister. A badly dated curio.

Suzy Kendall *Polly* • Dennis Waterman *Peter* • Adrienne Posta *Rube* • Maureen Lipman *Sylvie* • Michael Gothard *Terry* • Liz Fraser *Mrs McCarthy* • Hylda Baker *Winny* • Alfie Bass *Charlie* • Linda Cole *Pauline* ■ *Dir* Peter Collinson • *Scr* Roger Smith, from the book by Nell Dunn

Up the River ★★

Prison comedy 1930 · US · BW · 92mins

A major movie for collectors of screen debuts since no lesser personages than Spencer Tracy and Humphrey Bogart made their start in features right here. It started out as a prison drama but when MGM's *The Big House* cornered that market it was quickly transformed into a comedy. Bogart plays an upper-class convict who is in love with fellow jailbird, Claire Luce. Tracy is an escaped con who voluntarily returns to help his prison win a crucial ball game. Director John Ford called it "a piece of junk", but you can't deny the novelty of two of Hollywood's finest beginning their careers in such an offbeat comedy.

Spencer Tracy *St Louis* • Warren Hymer *Dannemora Dan* • Humphrey Bogart *Steve* • Claire Luce *Judy* • William Collier Sr *Pop* • Joan Lawes *Jean* • Sharon Lynn [Sharon Lynne] *Edith La Verne* ■ *Dir* John Ford • *Scr* Maurine Watkins, John Ford, William Collier Sr

Up the Sandbox ★★★ 15

Comedy 1972 · US · Colour · 93mins

A genuinely charming performance by Barbra Streisand redeems this awkward yet fitfully touching theatrical account of being alone in a crowded and thoughtless New York. Babs has any number of fantasies – including one that involves being seduced by Fidel Castro! – and director Irvin Kershner cleverly manages to integrate them into the main narrative. New York actors David Selby (as Barbra's husband) and Jane Hoffman (as a Jewish mom) are particularly good. Not

a success at the time, this now has more than a little period appeal. Contains some violence, swearing, nudity and a sex scene. 🔲

Barbra Streisand *Margaret Reynolds* • David Selby *Paul Reynolds* • Jane Hoffman *Mrs Yussim* • John C Becher *Mr Yussim* • Jacobo Morales *Fidel Castro* • Ariane Heller *Elizabeth* ■ *Dir* Irvin Kershner • *Scr* Paul Zindel, from the novel by Anne Richardson Roiphe

Up to His Ears ★★★ U

Comedy 1965 · Fr/It · Colour · 96mins

An updated version of a Jules Verne novel, this is one of several comic adventure movies Philippe de Broca made with the energetic Jean-Paul Belmondo in a daredevil role. Belmondo is a millionaire, bored with life, who hires a hit man to assassinate him, but changes his mind after meeting the statuesque Ursula Andress, who is as easy on the eye as the Far Eastern locations. But, filmed at a frenzied pace, it loses much of its initial humour and impetus along the way. A French language film.

Jean-Paul Belmondo *Arthur* • Ursula Andress *Alexandrine* • Jean Rochefort *Leon* • Maria Pacôme *Suzy* • Valérie Lagrange *Alice* ■ *Dir* Philippe de Broca • *Scr* Philippe de Broca, Daniel Boulanger, from a novel by Jules Verne

Uphill All the Way ★ PG

Western comedy adventure 1985 · US · Colour · 82mins

It might have seemed a good idea at the time to team country music stars Roy Clark and Mel Tillis in a *Smokey and the Bandit*-style chase movie, but it's a cryin' shame nobody bothered to find out if they could act. They can't, and, despite being surrounded by such notables as big Burl Ives, Glen (*Wichita Lineman*) Campbell, and even Burt Reynolds, this unintentional farce is a total non-starter, even for fans of the "good ole boys" themselves. 🔲

Roy Clark *Ben Hooker* • Mel Tillis *Booger Skaggs* • Glen Campbell *Captain Hazleton* • Trish Van Devere *Widow Quinn* • Richard Paul *Dillman* • Burt Reynolds *Poker Player* • Elaine Joyce *Miss Jesse* • Jacque Lynn Colton *Lucinda* • Burl Ives *Sheriff John Catledge* • Frank Gorshin *Pike* ■ *Dir/Scr* Frank Q Dobbs

Upkaar ★★ 15

Melodrama 1967 · Ind · Colour · 161mins

A decade after making his acting bow, Manoj Kumar turned director with a film he described as "a 16,000-foot-long celluloid flag of India". He's not kidding, either, as this musical melodrama is so strident an affirmation of patriotic fervour as often to be embarrassing to watch. Kumar also stars as a hard-working farmer, who sacrifices everything to put brother Prem Chopra through college. However, Chopra becomes a gangster and Kumar throws himself into the war against Pakistan, where he confounds the family nemesis, Madan Puri, and falls for life-saving surgeon, Asha Parekh. Imposing, but its overt nationalism borders on the fanatical. A Hindi language film. 🔲

Asha Parekh • Manoj Kumar • Pran • Kamini Kaushal • Prem Chopra • Madan Puri ■ *Dir/Scr* Manoj Kumar

Upper World ★★★

Crime melodrama 1934 · US · BW · 72mins

A fine Warner Bros melodrama, based on a Ben Hecht story, about a romance across the tracks between a dancer, Ginger Rogers, and a married businessman, suave Warren William, whose socialite ("upper world") wife is impeccably played by Mary Astor. When the burlesque girl is found dead, the cops are loathe to incriminate William, and thereby hangs a terrific tale, unhindered in its day by the new censorship code that movies like this one encouraged. There's a whole range of tough performances to savour, and look out for a very young Mickey Rooney.

Warren William *Alexander Stream* • Mary Astor *Hettie Stream* • Ginger Rogers *Lilly Linder* • Theodore Newton *Rocklen* • Andy Devine *Oscar, the Chauffeur* • Dickie Moore *Tommy Stream* • J Carrol Naish *Lou Colima* • Robert Barrat *Commissioner Clark* • Mickey Rooney *Jerry* ■ *Dir* Roy Del Ruth • *Scr* Ben Markson, from a story by Ben Hecht

Ups and Downs of a Handyman ★ 18

Sex comedy 1975 · UK · Colour · 85mins

This is another cheap-and-cheerful sex comedy in the vein of Timothy Lea's naughty bestsellers. Barry Stokes brings a certain cheeky charm to the title role, while Gay Soper, Sue Lloyd and Valerie Leon find him plenty to do around the house. What little comedy there is comes from Benny Hill stalwart Bob Todd, as the local magistrate, and Chic Murray, as a harassed bobby. Derrick Slater's script is one long smutty gag, while the direction is perfunctory at best. Contains nudity. 🔲

Barry Stokes *Bob* • Gay Soper *Maisie* • Sue Lloyd *The blonde* • Bob Todd *Squire Bullsworthy* • Chic Murray *PC Knowles* • Robert Dorning *Newsagent* • Valerie Leon *Redhead* • Penny Meredith *Margaretta* ■ *Dir* John Sealey • *Scr* Derrick Slater

Upstairs and Downstairs ★★★

Comedy 1959 · UK · Colour · 100mins

It must have been very frustrating for the cast of accomplished British comedy performers, let alone for international stars Claudia Cardinale and Mylene Demongeot, to have watched all their efforts being frittered away by such dull leads as Michael Craig and Anne Heywood. As the newlyweds searching for the perfect servant, they are the weak link in every scene. But you can still enjoy seeing Cardinale as a man-mad maid, Joan Hickson as a secret tippler, Joan Sims as a timid Welsh nanny, Sid James as a put-upon bobby and Demongeot as a Pollyanna-like au pair.

Michael Craig *Richard Barry* • Anne Heywood *Kate Barry* • Mylene Demongeot *Ingrid Gunnar* • James Robertson-Justice *Mansfield* • Claudia Cardinale *Maria* • Sidney James *PC Edwards* • Joan Hickson *Rosemary* • Joan Sims *Blodwen* • Joseph Tomelty *Arthur Farringdon* • Nora Nicholson *Mrs Edith Farringdon* • Daniel Massey *Wesley Cotes* ■ *Dir* Ralph Thomas • *Scr* Frank Harvey, from the novel by Ronald Scott Thorne

Uptown Saturday Night
★★★ PG

Comedy   1974 · US · Colour · 99mins

Sidney Poitier directs and stars in this comedy about a pair of buddies (Poitier and Bill Cosby) who become involved with the criminal underworld when they try to retrieve a stolen winning lottery ticket. There's a very funny Harry Belafonte as a black godfather – Brando-style – and such undeniable comic talents as Richard Pryor and Flip Wilson. Sociologists might argue that these amiable romps did less than nothing to advance African-American cinema, but audiences at the time didn't care, and this hit spawned two sequels. Contains swearing. 🖵

Sidney Poitier *Steve Jackson* • Bill Cosby *Wardell Franklin* • Harry Belafonte *Geechie Dan Beauford* • Flip Wilson *The Reverend* • Richard Pryor *Sharp Eye Washington* • Rosalind Cash *Sarah Jackson* • Roscoe Lee Browne *Congressman Lincoln* ■ *Dir* Sidney Poitier • *Scr* Richard Wesley

The Upturned Glass   ★★★

Crime   1947 · UK · BW · 86mins

In his last British film before taking off for Hollywood, James Mason returned to the kind of brooding figure that female audiences had adored in *The Seventh Veil* and *Odd Man Out*. He's the brilliant brain surgeon who concocts an elaborate revenge on the shrewish figure responsible for the death of the married woman he loved. The murderess is played by Pamela Kellino (Mason's wife, who co-scripted) while his great love is Rosamund John. The plot is heavily contrived, but Mason's performance and Lawrence Huntington's directorial flair keep you hooked.

James Mason *Michael Joyce* • Rosamund John *Emma Wright* • Pamela Kellino *Kate Howard* • Ann Stephens *Ann Wright* • Morland Graham *Clay* ■ *Dir* Lawrence Huntington • *Scr* John P Monaghan, Pamela Kellino, from a story by John P Monaghan

Upworld   ★★ PG

Comedy thriller   1993 · US · Colour · 87mins

Another variation on the mismatched cops scenario sees a detective paired with a leftover from *The Lord of the Rings*. Unsurprisingly, it's an idea that never caught on and this went straight to video in the UK. Detective Anthony Michael Hall discovers that the only witness to an undercover assignment that goes wrong is a furry little creature from the depths of the Earth who has been sent to the surface to recharge a magical stone that provides power for his subterranean world. Kids would love the Ewok-style capers; most parents will probably marvel at the sheer stupidity of the concept. 🖵

Anthony Michael Hall *Casey Gallagher* • Claudia Christian *Samantha Kennedy* • Jerry Orbach *Stan Walton* • Mark Harelik *Derek Kaminsky* • Eli Danker *Zadar* • Robert Z'Dar *Reggie* • Joseph R Sicari *Lou Ferril* ■ *Dir* Stan Winston • *Scr* Pen Densham, John Watson, from a story by Pen Densham

Uranus   ★★★ 15

Historical drama   1990 · Fr · Colour · 99mins

Cinema has rarely explored the tumult of recrimination that seized postwar

France. So this adaptation of Marcel Aymé's 1948 novel, with its scrupulously balanced refusal to reopen old wounds, has to be considered something of a missed opportunity. It also has to be ranked as high melodrama. For while the topic of political expediency (whether it's collaboration with Berlin or Moscow) is as compelling as it is troubling, the shading in Claude Berri's dour reconstruction of a bitter, self-flagellatory period is a bit too black and white. Moreover, the inhabitants of the small Provençal village, despite being well played by a bevy of stars, are largely caricatures. A French language film.

Phillipe Noiret *Watrin* • Gérard Depardieu *Léopold* • Jean-Pierre Marielle *Archambaud* • Michel Blanc *Gaigneux* • Michel Galabru *Monglat* • Gérard Desarthe *Maxime Loin* • Fabrice Luchini *Jourdan* • Daniel Prévost *Rochard* ■ *Dir* Claude Berri • *Scr* Claude Berri, Arlette Langmann, from the novel by Marcel Aymé

Urban Cowboy   ★★★ 15

Drama   1980 · US · Colour · 128mins

A steamy romance between Texas oil worker John Travolta and strong-willed Debra Winger is played out against the backdrop of honky-tonk dancing and mechanical rodeos in an uneven country-and-western soap opera. Packed with music from the likes of the Eagles, the Charlie Daniels Band and Linda Ronstadt, director James Bridges's overlong portrait of American manhood in the early eighties was an effort to re-promote Travolta as the nightclub macho man of *Saturday Night Fever* fame. In a Tammy Wynette way, it sort of works. Contains some violence and swearing. 🖵

John Travolta *Bud Davis* • Debra Winger *Sissy Davis* • Scott Glenn *Wes Hightower* • Madolyn Smith *Pam* • Barry Corbin *Uncle Bob* • Brooke Alderson *Aunt Corene* • Cooper Huckabee *Marshall* ■ *Dir* James Bridges • *Scr* James Bridges, Aaron Latham

Urban Legend   ★★ 18

Horror thriller   1998 · US · Colour · 95mins

One of the weaker examples of the late nineties resurgence in stalk 'n' slash movies, it sees attractive teenagers being dispatched in the form of – you've guessed it – urban legends (an apparent stalker is actually trying to warn a girl about the axeman hiding in car). The gimmicky murders are the film's sole stab at innovation (anyone heard of *Scream*?), although some of the later "legends" seem made up for the purposes of the plot. The pedestrian direction, bland cast and a ludicrous final unmasking don't add up to much, even with a pointed cameo from Robert "Freddy Krueger" Englund. Contains strong violence. 🖵 *DVD*

Jared Leto *Paul* • Alicia Witt *Natalie* • Rebecca Gayheart *Brenda* • Michael Rosenbaum *Parker* • Loretta Devine *Reese* • Joshua Jackson *Damon* • Robert Englund *Professor Wexler* • Brad Dourif *Gas station attendant* ■ *Dir* Jamie Blanks • *Scr* Silvio Horta

Urga   ★★★★ PG

Drama   1990 · Fr/USSR · Colour · 114mins

The winner of the Golden Lion at the Venice Film Festival, this is a visually

stunning parable on the dubious benefits of progress. Alternating between the rolling expanses of the steppe and the homely clutter of a shepherd's tent, director Nikita Mikhalkov manages to make both the traditional lifestyle of the Mongolian family and the trappings of consumerism seem attractive, while at the same time pointing out their pitfalls. Vladimir Gostukhin is superb as the coarse Russian truck driver, while Badema and Bayaertu are quietly impressive as the couple who give him shelter. At once rustic and subtle, boisterous and contemplative, this is a magnificent film. In Russian and Mongolian with English subtitles. 🖵

Badema *Pagma* • Bayaertu *Gombo* • Vladimir Gostukhin *Sergei* • Babushka *Grandma* • Larissa Kuznetsova *Marina* • Jon Bochinski *Stanislas* • Bao Yongyan *Bourma* ■ *Dir* Nikita Mikhalkov • *Scr* Roustam Ibraguimbekov, from a short story by Roustam Ibraguimbekov, Nikita Mikhalkov

Used Cars   ★★★★ 15

Comedy   1980 · US · Colour · 107mins

Tasteless, risqué, outrageous and amoral, this early offering from director Robert Zemeckis is all these things and more. But it's also one of the funniest ruminations on American values, as the car showroom becomes a warped microcosm of society. Revealing Kurt Russell's under-utilised talent as a first-rate comedian, it's a good-natured, if highly eccentric, wisecracker, finding untold amounts of amusement in the misfortunes and embarrassment of others. Contains swearing. 🖵

Kurt Russell *Rudy Russo* • Jack Warden *Roy L Fuchs/Luke Fuchs* • Gerrit Graham *Jeff* • Frank McRae *Jim the Mechanic* • Deborah Harmon *Barbara Fuchs* • Joseph P Flaherty *Sam Slaton* • David L Lander *Freddie Paris* • Michael McKean *Eddie Winslow* ■ *Dir* Robert Zemeckis • *Scr* Robert Zemeckis, Bob Gale

Used People   ★★★ 15

Comedy drama   1992 · US · Colour · 111mins

One of those huge "feel good" ensemble pieces where the sheer size and quality of the cast help explain the lack of substance. The fact that this was Italian star Marcello Mastroianni's first true Hollywood movie was the main talking point on the film's release, and he delivers a typically charming performance as he courts the recently widowed Shirley MacLaine. Kathy Bates, Jessica Tandy and Marcia Gay Harden provide first-class support, and British director Beeban Kidron also making her Hollywood debut orchestrates the proceedings with confidence. Contains sex scenes and swearing. 🖵

Shirley MacLaine *Pearl Berman* • Marcello Mastroianni *Joe Meledandri* • Kathy Bates *Bibby* • Jessica Tandy *Frieda* • Sylvia Sidney *Becky* • Marcia Gay Harden *Norma* • Bob Dishy *Jack Berman* ■ *Dir* Beeban Kidron • *Scr* Todd Graff, from his play *The Grandma Plays*

The Usual Suspects
★★★★★ 18

Crime thriller   1995 · US · Colour · 101mins

What made this audacious but unheralded thriller the must-see film of 1995? Was it because it gave the

world the criminal mastermind Keyzer Soze? Maybe it was the intricacy of the flashback-packed script and the deft sleights of hand executed by its fledgling director. Perhaps everyone admired the outstanding ensemble acting. Yes, Kevin Spacey stole the show and fully merited the best supporting actor Oscar for his mesmerising performance, but everyone in that rogues' gallery played their part to perfection, not to mention the mysterious Pete Postlethwaite and confused cops Dan Hedaya and Chazz Palminteri. Or was it simply that noticeboard that kept coming back to haunt everyone? Whatever the reason, this is a film that demands to be watched repeatedly – a good old-fashioned pulp fiction told in the slickest nineties style. A true modern classic. Contains violence and swearing. 🖵 *DVD*

Gabriel Byrne *Dean Keaton* • Kevin Spacey *Roger "Verbal" Kint* • Chazz Palminteri *Dave Kujan* • Benicio Del Toro *Fred Fenster* • Stephen Baldwin *Michael McManus* • Kevin Pollak *Todd Hockney* • Pete Postlethwaite *Kobayashi* • Suzy Amis *Edie Finneran* • Giancarlo Esposito *Jack Baer* • Dan Hedaya *Sergeant Jeff Rabin* • Paul Bartel *Smuggler* ■ *Dir* Bryan Singer • *Scr* Christopher McQuarrie

Utilities   ★★ 15

Romantic comedy
1981 · Can · Colour · 89mins

Canadian comedy featuring *Airplane!'s* Robert Hays as Bob, a well-meaning social worker, who, fed up with their business practices and profiteering, rallies against the phone, gas and electric companies. Brooke Adams plays Marion, a cop with divided loyalties – determined to curb Hays's activities on the one hand, but at the same time harbouring romantic feelings towards him. Some nice scenes and some unexpected crude humour, but overall another case of wasted potential. 🖵

Robert Hays *Bob Hunt* • Brooke Adams *Marion Edwards* • John Marley *Roy Blue* • James Blendick *Kenneth Knight* ■ *Dir* Harvey Hart • *Scr* David Greenwalt, M James Kouf Jr [Jim Kouf], from a story by Carl Manning

Utu   ★★★★ 15

Action drama   1983 · NZ · Colour · 99mins

Owing something to Fred Schepisi's *Chant of Jimmie Blacksmith*, this is a powerful drama which plays like a New Zealand "western". A Maori serving with the colonial British Army finds his family massacred by some of its rogue elements and vows "utu", Maori for "retribution". He then raises a rebel army and goes in for a spot of payback. Action-packed yet poignant, the film was made by Geoff Murphy, director of the equally excellent *Quiet Earth*, and of efficient sequels *Under Siege 2* and *Young Guns 2*. 🖵

Anzac Wallace *Te Wheke* • Bruno Lawrence *Williamson* • Wi Kuki Kaa *Wiremu* • Tim Elliott *Colonel Elliott* • Ilona Rodgers *Emily Williamson* • Tania Bristowe *Kura* • Maerata Mita *Matu* ■ *Dir/Scr* Geoff Murphy

Utz   ★★★ 12

Mystery drama
1992 · UK /Ger/It · Colour · 93mins

With an award-winning performance from Armin Mueller-Stahl, *Utz* is a

U = SUITABLE FOR ALL   **Uc** = SUITABLE FOR ALL, ESPECIALLY FOR YOUNG CHILDREN (VIDEO ONLY)   **PG** = PARENTAL GUIDANCE

complex character study of an obsessive Czech collector of fine porcelain figures who's understandably distraught when the country's then-communist government decrees his collection actually belongs to the State. Along with Mueller-Stahl, Peter Riegert, Paul Scofield and Brenda Fricker head a top-notch cast in a film that's as fine and detailed as the figures Utz collects, though it may be too dry for some tastes. Director George Sluizer made the classic Dutch chiller *The Vanishing* and its subsequent US remake. ▨

Armin Mueller-Stahl *Baron Kaspar Joachim von Utz* • Brenda Fricker *Marta* • Peter Riegert *Marius Fischer* • Paul Scofield *Doctor Vaclav Orlik* • Miriam Karlin *Grandmother Utz* ■ *Dir* George Sluizer • *Scr* Hugh Whitemore, from the novel by Bruce Chatwin

The VIPs ★★
Drama   1963 · UK · Colour · 119mins

Made principally to cash in on the Richard Burton/Elizabeth Taylor romance, *The VIPs* is glossy, but as tedious as the delay at Heathrow that the story depicts. Only Margaret Rutherford's deliriously dotty, Oscar-winning duchess and Orson Welles's movie mogul fleeing the taxman breathe life into the bottomless pit of clichés. Other celebrities we now include Maggie Smith and even David Frost.

Elizabeth Taylor *Frances Andros* • Richard Burton *Paul Andros* • Louis Jourdan *Marc Champselle* • Elsa Martinelli *Gloria Gritti* • Margaret Rutherford *Duchess of Brighton* • Maggie Smith *Miss Mead* • Rod Taylor *Les Mangrum* • Linda Christian *Miriam Marshall* • Orson Welles *Max Buda* • Dennis Price *Commander Millbank* ■ *Dir* Anthony Asquith • *Scr* Terence Rattigan

VI Warshawski ★★🔞
Crime mystery   1991 · US · Colour · 85mins

One of those movies which looks good on paper but is sunk by a lousy script. A rasping, sassy Kathleen Turner stars as the spiky, difficult, liberal-feminist private eye VI "Vic" Warshawski. But here the investigator becomes a man-fearing, baseball-obsessed pain in the rear, in a film that's sunk by its plot – a lame piece of fluff about a 13-year-old and a dodgy inheritance. Only worth watching for Turner, who desperately attempts to inject some grit into the proceedings, but this first in a hastily abandoned series drags perceptibly throughout. Contains violence and swearing. ▨

Kathleen Turner *Victoria I Warshawski* • Jay O Sanders *Murray Ryerson* • Charles Durning *Lieutenant Mallory* • Angela Goethals *Kat Grafalk* • Nancy Paul *Paige Grafalk* • Frederick Coffin *Horton Grafalk* • Charles McCaughan *Trumble Grafalk* ■ *Dir* Jeff Kanew • *Scr* Edward Taylor, David Aaron Cohen, Nick Thiel, from a story by Edward Taylor, from novels by Sara Paretsky

Vacas ★★★
Historical drama   1992 · Sp · Colour · 96mins

Translating as *Cows* and described as a negative comedy (whatever that is), Julio Medem's directorial debut is a difficult film to like. Yet the standard of its imaginative camerawork, its playful shifts from reality to fantasy and the assuredness with which the narrative strands have been woven together have to be admired. Following the sometimes bleak fortunes of two Basque families between the civil wars of 1875 and 1936, the four stories have something of a fairy-tale quality and are interesting enough, but the lack of character depth prevents total

involvement and the thematic significance often eludes the uninitiated. Contains violence.

Emma Suarez *Cristina* • Carmelo Gomez *Manuel/Ignacio/Peru* • Ana Torrent *Catalina* • Karra Elejalde *Ilegorri/Lucas* • Klara Badiola *Madalen* • Txema Blasco *Manuel* • Kandido Uranga *Carmelo/Juan* • Pilar Barden *Paulina* ■ *Dir* Julio Medem • *Scr* Julio Medem, Michel Gaztambide, from a story by Julio Medem

The Vagabond ★★★★ 🅄
Silent comedy drama
1916 · US · BW · 25mins

The short that fully confirmed Charlie Chaplin as the Little Tramp – with tarnished bowler hat, holey baggy pants and jaunty cane. He plays a fiddling busker who rescues Edna Purviance from the clutches of the ever-villainous and even-more-mountainous Eric Campbell. Shameless sentiment in a timeless world, this effort prefers straight drama to belly laughs, but that's not to say it doesn't entertain. ▨

Charles Chaplin *Street musician* • Edna Purviance *Girl stolen by gypsies* • Eric Campbell *Gypsy chieftain* • Leo White *Old Jew/Gypsy woman* ■ *Dir* Charles Chaplin • *Scr* Charles Chaplin, Vincent Bryan

Vagabond ★★★★
Mystery drama   1985 · Fr · Colour · 106mins

Opening with the discovery of Sandrine Bonnaire's body, this is less an investigation into the personality and problems of the teenage drifter than a penetrating examination of the society that was culpable for her demise. Combining eye-witness testimonies with reconstructions of Bonnaire's peripatetic final days, director Agnès Varda reveals a cold, alienated individual who reflects the prejudices and fears of those she encounters, including liberal academic Macha Méril, who finds herself uncomfortably fascinated by her. Shot with spartan poetry and solemnly played by a largely non-professional cast, this is a cheerless study of displacement, waste and collective responsibility. In French with English subtitles.

Sandrine Bonnaire *Mona Bergeron* • Macha Méril *Madame Landier* • Yolande Moreau *Yolande* • Stéphane Freiss *Jean-Pierre* • Marthe Jarnais *Aunt Lydie* • Joël Fosse *Paulo* ■ *Dir/Scr* Agnès Varda

The Vagabond King ★★★ 🅄
Musical   1956 · US · Colour · 87mins

"Remember the Name, You'll Never Forget the Voice", screamed the posters, touting Maltese baritone Oreste "Kirkop" as beggar-rogue poet François Villon in the third screen outing of Rudolf Friml's operetta. Sadly, though a pleasant personality and singer, both the star's name and voice have been forgotten, as this was his only movie. It was also the last film appearance of soprano Kathryn Grayson. Familiar and old-fashioned, it still has some good songs such as *Love Me Tonight*, as well as new ones composed by Friml himself.

Kathryn Grayson *Catherine de Vaucelles* • Oreste "Kirkop" *Francois Villon* • Rita Moreno *Huguette* • Sir Cedric Hardwicke [Cedric Hardwicke] *Tristan* • Walter Hampden *King Louis XI* • Leslie Nielsen *Thibault* • William

Prince Rene • Jack Lord *Ferrebone* ■ *Dir* Michael Curtiz • *Scr* Ken Englund, Noel Langley, from the musical by Rudolf Friml, Brian Hooker, William H Post, from the play *If I Were King* by Justin Huntly McCarthy, from a novel by RH Russell

The Vagrant ★★ 🔞
Comedy horror   1992 · US/Fr · Colour · 87mins

A brave but flawed attempt at a genuinely nasty black comedy and the ultimate yuppy nightmare to boot. Bill Paxton, unwisely cast against type, is the ordinary middle-class professional who finds himself the target for homeless derelict Marshall Bell, who proceeds to make his life a living hell. Chris Walas (*The Fly II*) directs with flamboyance and the cast, including Michael Ironside as an investigating police officer, certainly hams it up enthusiastically. However, ultimately the film is undone by a script lacking in depth and bite. Contains swearing, violence and sex scenes. ▨

Bill Paxton *Graham Krakowski* • Michael Ironside *Lieutenant Ralf Barfuss* • Marshall Bell *The vagrant* • Mitzi Kapture *Edie Roberts* • Colleen Camp *Judy Dansig* • Patrika Darbo *Doatti* • Marc McClure *Chuck* ■ *Dir* Chris Walas • *Scr* Richard Jeffries

The Valachi Papers ★★🔞
Crime drama   1972 · It/Fr · Colour · 119mins

Based on the true story of famed mob informant Joe Valachi, and with Charles Bronson playing Valachi, this study of early 20th-century gangster life should have had more of an impact. Instead, it views Valachi's rise and fall, and the intricacies of rules and roles in the Mafia in a rather casual fashion. The almost European look of the movie – Italian producer Dino De Laurentiis chose British pro Terence Young to helm – also dilutes the gritty feel the movie tries to generate. The 50-year-old Bronson is good, but isn't convincing in the flashback scenes of his character as a young man. ▨

Charles Bronson *Joseph Valachi* • Lino Ventura *Vito Genovese* • Jill Ireland *Maria Valachi* • Walter Chiari *Dominic "The Gap" Petrilli* • Joseph Wiseman *Salvatore Maranzano* • Gerald S O'Loughlin *Ryan* • Amedeo Nazzari *Gaetano Reina* • Fausto Tozzi *Albert Anastasia* ■ *Dir* Terence Young • *Scr* A Maiuri [Dino Maiuri], Massimo De Rita, Stephen Geller, from the book by Peter Maas

The Valdez Horses ★★★🔞
Western   1973 · It/Sp/Fr · Colour · 92mins

Charles Bronson gives one of his best performances in this little-known European western. He looks very relaxed and comfortable as Chino, a half-breed cowboy who takes in a young runaway (Vincent Van Patten) on his small ranch, even smiling and laughing out loud several times. Chino's character is more complex than the typical western loner; he's not always sympathetic and handles the local racists in an atypical way for both the genre and for Bronson. The screenplay itself is quite loose, even taking occasional breaks from the main story to show local colour or attempt humour. ▨

Charles Bronson *Chino Valdez* • Jill Ireland *Louise* • Vincent Van Patten *Jamie Wagner* • Marcel Bozzuffi *Maral* • Melissa Chimenti

Indian Girl • Fausto Tozzi *Cruz* ■ *Dir* John Sturges • *Scr* Dino Maiuri, Massimo De Rita, Clair Haffaker, from the novel by Lee Hoffman

Valdez Is Coming ★★
Western   1971 · US · Colour · 90mins

A western notable only for a performance of immense dignity from the great Burt Lancaster as a Mexican-American lawman bent on justice. An unlikely debut for Broadway theatre director Edwin Sherin, who fails to get the most out of the material and quite clearly has no cinema technique. The film is crucially under-cast, with a far stronger screen presence than Jon Cypher required as Lancaster's nemesis. Only Richard Jordan manages to register among the supports. Contains violence, swearing and sex scenes.

Burt Lancaster *Bob Valdez* • Susan Clark *Gay Erin* • Jon Cypher *Frank Tanner* • Barton Heyman *El Segundo* • Richard Jordan *RI Davis* • Frank Silvera *Diego* • Hector Elizondo *Mexican rider* • Phil Brown *Malson* ■ *Dir* Edwin Sherin • *Scr* Ronald Kibbee, David Rayfiel, from the novel by Elmore Leonard

Valentina ★★★
Romantic wartime drama
1982 · Sp · Colour · 85mins

This appealing account of the making of a hero is told from a French prison camp at the end of the Spanish Civil War by a defeated Republican volunteer. Set in a small north-eastern Spanish town in 1911, it follows eight-year-old Jorge Sanz, as he is inspired in his pursuit of his pretty neighbour, Paloma Gomez, by the local priest's tales of the champions, saints and poets of days past. Drawing fine performances from both his young cast and Hollywood veteran Anthony Quinn, writer/director Antonio J Betancor bathes the action in an uplifting nostalgic glow. Spanish dialogue dubbed into English.

Anthony Quinn *Mosen Joaquin* • Jorge Sanz *Jose Garces (boy)* • Paloma Gomez *Valentina* • Saturno Cerra *Don Jose* • Conchita Leza *Dona Luisa* • Alfredo Lucchetti *Don Arturo* ■ *Dir* Antonio J Betancor [Antonio Jose Betancor] • *Scr* Antonio J Betancor, Carlos Escobedo, Antonio José, Javier Moro, Lautano Murua, from the novel *Days of Dawn* by Ramon J Sender

Valentine's Day ★ 18
Crime thriller   1998 · US · Colour · 90mins

Mario Van Peebles is in hot water in this derivative crime thriller, playing a cop assigned to protect mysterious mob witness Zerha Leverman and finding himself falling in love with her. Although packaged as an action adventure, it's actually more like *Basic Instinct*, though with less emphasis on sex. The few sex scenes, while explicit, aren't titillating anyway. Even those who haven't seen *Basic Instinct* will find each step of the plot very familiar, with characters and even lines of dialogue lifted straight out of your typical TV cop show. Contains swearing, sex scenes and some violence. ▭ **DVD**

Mario Van Peebles *Jack Valentine* • Randy Quaid *Phil* • Rae Dawn Chong *Sally* • Ben Gazzara *Joe Buddha* • Zerha Leverman *Alma* ■ *Dir* Duane Clark • *Scr* Norman Snider

Valentino ★★
Romantic drama
1951 · US · Colour · 104mins

It probably seemed a good idea to film the life of Hollywood's most famous Latin lover, but unfortunately the tale proved impossible to cast. Newcomer Anthony Dexter was unveiled in a welter of publicity, hair brilliantined and duly parted in the middle, but unfortunately he had no personal charisma whatsoever. Despite being paired with ravishing redhead Eleanor Parker, the screen stubbornly refused to ignite. Anyway, the true story of the "Pink Powder Puff" and his lesbian lover could never be told in the censor-bound fifties. The film, though good-looking enough in Technicolor, sank without trace.

Anthony Dexter *Rudolph Valentino* • Eleanor Parker *Joan Carlisle* • Richard Carlson *William King* • Patricia Medina *Lila Reyes* • Joseph Calleia *Luigi Verducci* • Dona Drake *Maria Torres* • Otto Kruger *Mark Towers* ■ *Dir* Lewis Allen • *Scr* George Bruce

Valentino ★★★ 18
Biographical drama
1977 · UK · Colour · 122mins

Director Ken Russell seems to have approached the life story of Rudolph Valentino with no particular aim, and structures it simply as a series of flashbacks spinning out of the silent star's funeral. Much of what is depicted is probably far from the truth. But Russell obviously had fun re-creating (in London) New York and Hollywood in the 1920s. Valentino's conflicts with power-crazy moguls and totally crazy actresses are irresistibly entertaining. There is also the endless fascination of watching Rudolf Nureyev (in his screen acting debut) attempt the role of the Great Lover. ▭

Rudolf Nureyev *Rudolph Valentino* • Leslie Caron *Alla Nazimova* • Michelle Phillips *Natasha Rambova* • Carol Kane *"Fatty"'s girl* • Felicity Kendal *June Mathis* • Seymour Cassel *George Ullman* • Peter Vaughan *Rory O'Neil* • Huntz Hall *Jesse Lasky* • Ken Russell *Rex Ingram* ■ *Dir* Ken Russell • *Scr* Ken Russell, Mardik Martin, from the book *Valentino: An Intimate Exposé of the Sheik* by Brad Steiger, Chaw Mank

Valentino Returns ★★★ 15
Romantic drama   1987 · US · Colour · 91mins

No, Rudy hasn't risen from his grave. Instead, "Valentino Returns" turns out to be the pet name for the pink Cadillac purchased by small-town boy Barry Tubb, who hopes it will prove a big girl-puller, like the real Rudy was. The film has a nice feeling for its time and place – fifties California – but it lacks focus, meandering along too many backroads when it should have stuck to life's highways. Good performances, though, from both Tubb and Frederic Forrest as his ne'er-do-well dad. ▭

Barry Tubb *Wayne Gibbs* • Frederic Forrest *Sonny Gibbs* • Veronica Cartwright *Pat Gibbs* • Jenny Wright *Sylvia Fuller* • Macon McCalman *Leroy Fuller* • Seth Isler *Harry Ames* ■ *Dir* Peter Hoffman • *Scr* Leonard Gardner, from his story

Valerie ★★★
Western courtroom drama
1957 · US · BW · 82mins

With the ghost of *Rashomon* hovering over its approach, this mix of western and courtroom drama, although manoeuvred in and out of flashback skilfully enough by director Gerd Oswald, inevitably suffers by comparison. Sterling Hayden, a former Civil War hero and now a respected member of a ranching community, is on trial for murdering wife Anita Ekberg's parents and violently assaulting her. The man's character – or lack of it – emerges through the conflicting testimonies and viewpoints of various witnesses. A curious little drama with a melodramatic and unconvincing climax, but not without interest.

Sterling Hayden *John Garth* • Anita Ekberg *Valerie* • Anthony Steel *Reverend Blake* • Peter Walker *Herb Garth* • John Wengraf *Louis Horvat* • Iphigenie Castiglioni *Mrs Horvat* • Jerry Barclay *Mingo* ■ *Dir* Gerd Oswald • *Scr* Leonard Heideman, Emmett Murphy

Valiant Is the Word for Carrie ★★★
Melodrama   1936 · US · BW · 109mins

The undervalued actress Gladys George is best remembered now for the final scene in *The Roaring Twenties*, as she cradles James Cagney and utters the closing line, "He used to be a big shot''. But three years earlier she had been nominated for a best actress Oscar for her performance in this uninhibited melodrama, a quintessential four-handkerchief weepie. As the town trollop who selflessly devotes herself to caring for two orphans, George suffers with style and was unlucky to lose the Oscar to Luise Rainer for *The Great Ziegfeld*.

Gladys George *Carrie Snyder* • Arline Judge *Lady* • John Howard (1) *Paul Darnley* • Dudley Digges *Dennis Ringrose* • Harry Carey *Phil Yonne* • Isabel Jewell *Lili Eipper* ■ *Dir* Wesley Ruggles • *Scr* Claude Binyon, from the novel by Barry Benefield

The Valley ★★★
Erotic road movie
1972 · Fr · Colour · 114mins

The second movie by Barbet Schroeder to use the music of Pink Floyd (the first was *More*), this hippy epic has dropout Bulle Ogier and friends travelling through New Guinea looking for a mythical Eden-like valley where they can freely indulge their alternative lifestyles. The professional actors interact with the primitive tribesman, and even join in with their stripped-down rituals to fascinating and hyper-exotic effect, highlighted by the trance-like Floyd score. Strangely compelling and enigmatic, it was the height of radical chic to have seen this unusual rarity in the seventies. In French with English subtitles.

Jean-Pierre Kalfon *Gaetan* • Bulle Ogier *Viviane* • Michael Gothard *Olivier* • Valérie Lagrange *Hermine* • Jerome Beauvarlet *Yann* ■ *Dir/Scr* Barbet Schroeder

Valley Girl ★★★★ 15
Romantic comedy
1983 · US · Colour · 98mins

Bright and breezy teen film, about the barrier-crossing romance between an upscale San Fernando Valley suburbanite (Deborah Foreman) and an out-there Hollywood punk (the out-there Nicolas Cage). Funny, sexy and almost impossible to dislike, *Valley Girl* is widely rated as one of the top teen romances. Why? Maybe it's the female touch of director Martha Coolidge, bringing some much-needed class to the normally male-made genre.

Nicolas Cage *Randy* • Deborah Foreman *Julie* • Elizabeth Daily *Loryn* • Michael Bowen *Tommy* • Cameron Dye *Fred* • Heidi Holicker *Stacey* • Michelle Meyrink *Suzie* ■ *Dir* Martha Coolidge • *Scr* Wayne Crawford, Andrew Lane

The Valley of Decision ★★★
Drama   1945 · US · BW · 118mins

Greer Garson is the daughter of Irish steel worker Lionel Barrymore in Pittsburgh, who goes to work as a maid in the household of mill owner Donald Crisp and becomes indispensable to his family. Although loved by one of the mill owner's sons (Gregory Peck), the possibility of their marriage is thwarted by industrial strife between Barrymore and Crisp that ends in tragedy. The winning warmth of Garson won the actress her fifth consecutive Oscar nomination and Peck climbed higher in the star stakes, while the film, a tear-stained period drama packed with a starry cast, grossed nearly $6 million on its first release. A bit plodding, but it still provides a nice wallow for a rainy afternoon.

Gregory Peck *Paul Scott* • Greer Garson *Mary Rafferty* • Donald Crisp *William Scott* • Lionel Barrymore *Pat Rafferty* • Preston Foster *Jim Brennan* • Gladys Cooper *Clarissa Scott* • Marsha Hunt *Constance Scott* • Reginald Owen *McCready* ■ *Dir* Tay Garnett • *Scr* John Meehan, Sonya Levien, from the novel by Marcia Davenport

Valley of Eagles ★★ U
Crime drama   1951 · UK · BW · 85mins

There are really three films here: a wildlife adventure; a cold war thriller; and a standard issue cop yarn complete with Jack Warner. The story concerns a boffin's wife who absconds to Lapland with her husband's invention and his assistant, played by Anthony Dawson. The husband, the policeman and two children set off in pursuit and, after being attacked by bears en route, meet the Laplanders who hunt with eagles. Ambitious for what is really a B-movie. Directed by Terence Young, who later made *Dr No* with Dawson as its sub-villain.

Jack Warner *Inspector Petersen* • John McCallum *Dr Nils Ahlen* • Nadia Gray *Kara Niemann* • Anthony Dawson *Sven Nystrom* • Mary Laura Wood *Helga Ahlen* • Christopher Lee *First Detective* ■ *Dir/Scr* Terence Young

Valley of Fire ★★ U
Western   1951 · US · BW · 62mins

A minor Gene Autry programme filler, featuring the singing cowboy star in the kind of B-flick guaranteed to satisfy fans and the occasional Saturday children's matinée audience, but which

really offers very little to anyone else. Not, of course, that Autry cared: he knew his audience well, and shrewd manipulation of his career and investments made him one of Hollywood's richest men. This was one of Autry's six theatrical releases in 1951, but he and his trusty steed Champion (the Wonder Horse) would find television more lucrative and more secure.

Gene Autry • Pat Buttram *Breezie Larrabee* • Gail Davis *Laurie* • Russell Hayden *Steve Guilford* • Christine Larson *Bee Laverne* • Harry Lauter *Tod Rawlings* • Terry Frost *Grady McKean* ■ *Dir* John English • *Scr* Gerald Geraghty, from a story by Earle Snell

The Valley of Gwangi ★★ 12

Fantasy adventure 1969 · US · Colour · 91mins

An unsuccessful touring circus encounters a forbidden valley full of prehistoric animals, and captures its massive allosaurus leader. Guess what – it escapes to terrorise the cast. A very watchable fantasy adventure, though as with other films Ray Harryhausen had a hand in, the stop-motion special effects put the flat characters and routine plot in the shade. [video]

James Franciscus *Tuck Kirby* • Gila Golan *TJ Breckenridge* • Richard Carlson *Champ Connors* • Laurence Naismith *Prof Horace Bromley* • Freda Jackson *Tia Zorina* • Gustavo Rojo *Carlos Dos Orsos* ■ *Dir* James O'Connolly [Jim O'Connolly] • *Scr* William E Bast, Julian More, from the story by William E Bast

Valley of Mystery ★

Adventure 1967 · US · Colour · 93mins

This lacklustre effort contains a bunch of second division film stars – Richard Egan, Peter Graves, Fernando Lamas, among others – trying to salvage what's left of their careers by appearing in a plane-crash drama originally made for television. Ending up in the South American jungle, the survivors are made up of familiar screen characters – has-been comedian, escaped killer, famous singer, novelist on a quest. The poor souls then get mixed up with a mad missionary and his yen for human sacrifice. Like the plane after the crash, it's a pile of junk though it still managed to get a cinema release.

Richard Egan *Wade Cochran* • Peter Graves (1) *Ben Barstow* • Joby Baker *Pete Patton* • Lois Nettleton *Rita Brown* • Harry Guardino *Danny O'Neill* • Julie Adams *Joan Simon* • Fernando Lamas *Francisco Rivera* ■ *Dir* Joseph Leytes • *Scr* Richard Neal, Lowell Barrington, from a story by Lawrence B Marcus, Richard Neal

Valley of Song ★★ U

Comedy 1953 · UK · BW · 74mins

War breaks out amongst a bickering group of Welsh choristers preparing for a major concert in this engaging little comedy, scripted by Phil Park and Cliff Gordon from the latter's radio play. There's no Harry Secombe but look out for Rachel Roberts and Kenneth Williams in early screen roles.

Mervyn Johns *Minister Griffiths* • Clifford Evans *Geraint Llewellyn* • Maureen Swanson *Olwen Davies* • John Fraser *Cliff Lloyd* • Rachel Thomas *Mrs Lloyd* • Betty Cooper *Mrs Davies* • Rachel Roberts *Bessie Lewis* • Hugh Pryse *Lloyd, the undertaker* • Edward Evans *Davies, the shopkeeper* • Kenneth Williams *Lloyd, the haulage man* ■ *Dir* Gilbert Gunn • *Scr* Cliff Gordon, Phil Park, from the radio play *Choir Practice* by Cliff Gordon

Valley of the Dolls ★★ 15

Melodrama 1967 · US · Colour · 118mins

Three young women, led by Barbara Parkins, have their illusions shattered as they try to make it in the corrupt world of show business. Unsurprisingly, Hollywood drew back from portraying the full depravity of Jacqueline Susann's archetypal sex and ambition novel, and the drug abuse subplot (the "dolls" of the title are barbiturates) could have been handled more sensitively. But Susan Hayward gives it all she's got as an appalling yet appealing Broadway megastar, and there's a certain camp appeal about the whole thing. [video]

Barbara Parkins *Anne Welles* • Patty Duke *Neely O'Hara* • Sharon Tate *Jennifer North* • Paul Burke *Lyon Burke* • Tony Scotti *Tony Polar* • Martin Milner *Mel Anderson* • Charles Drake *Kevin Gilmore* • Alexander Davion *Ted Casablanca* • Lee Grant *Miriam* • Susan Hayward *Helen Lawson* • Jacqueline Susann *Reporter* ■ *Dir* Mark Robson • *Scr* Helen Deutsch, Dorothy Kingsley, from the novel by Jacqueline Susann

Valley of the Kings ★★ U

Romantic adventure 1954 · US · Colour · 85mins

Apart from the majestic musical score by Miklos Rozsa, there's not much to recommend this archaeological adventure. Set in 1900, Robert Taylor is the rough, tough treasure hunter who's persuaded by old flame Eleanor Parker to go on an expedition to the ancient tombs of Egypt. Of course, feelings are rekindled but Parker is now married to Carlos Thompson. Into this romantic mix can be added a band of tomb robbers, including sinister Kurt Kasznar (*Land of the Giants*), and some attractive locations but that's all there is to this tomb with a view.

Robert Taylor (1) *Mark Brandon* • Eleanor Parker *Ann Mercedes* • Carlos Thompson *Philip Mercedes* • Kurt Kasznar *Hamed Bachkour* • Victor Jory *Taureg Chief* • Leon Askin *Valentine Arko* ■ *Dir* Robert Pirosh • *Scr* Robert Pirosh, Karl Tunberg, from the book *Gods, Graves and Scholars* by CW Ceram

Valley of the Sun ★★★ U

Western 1942 · US · BW · 78mins

Director George Marshall, who had made a great job of combining the conventions of comedy with those of the western in *Destry Rides Again*, was hauled in to repeat the trick here but clearly mislaid his magic wand. The nub of the story concerns rivalry and conflict between an army scout (James Craig) and a nasty Indian agent (Dean Jagger), both after the same girl (Lucille Ball). The former also objects to the latter's treatment of the Indians – who include Geronimo (Tom Tyler) and Cochise (one-time Latin lover Antonio Moreno). Violent action and imbecilic farce simply fail to mix here.

Lucille Ball *Christine Larson* • James Craig *Jonathan Ware* • Sir Cedric Hardwicke [Cedric Hardwicke] *Warrick* • Dean Jagger *Jim Sawyer* • Tom Tyler *Geronimo* • Antonio Moreno *Chief Cochise* ■ *Dir* George Marshall • *Scr* Horace McCoy, from a story by Clarence Budington Kelland

Valmont ★★★★ 15

Period drama 1989 · Fr/UK · Colour · 136mins

Coming hot on the heels of *Dangerous Liaisons*, this opulent reworking of the notorious Choderlos de Laclos novel plays on the emotions in the same way that Stephen Frears's film teased the intellect. Director Milos Forman is more concerned with the perils of pursuing your desires than in the machinations of the indolent and, consequently, the characters take as much pleasure in the act of seduction as in its art. It's impossible to resist comparing the two productions, but while Frears's is truer to the calculating spirit of the book and boasts the showier cast, Forman's has greater human interest and the more heartfelt performances.

Colin Firth *Vicomte de Valmont* • Annette Bening *Marquise de Merteuil* • Meg Tilly *Madame de Tourvel* • Fairuza Balk *Cécile de Volanges* • Sian Phillips *Madame de Volanges* • Jeffrey Jones *Gercourt* • Henry Thomas *Danceny* • Fabia Drake *Madame de Rosemonde* • TP McKenna *Baron* • Isla Blair *Baroness* ■ *Dir* Milos Forman • *Scr* Jean-Claude Carrière, from the novel *Les Liaisons Dangereuses* by Choderlos de Laclos

Les Valseuses ★★★★ 18

Drama 1974 · Fr · Colour · 112mins

Also known as *Making It* and *Going Places*, Bertrand Blier's often shocking film was named after the French slang word for "testicles". As the grotesque, joy-riding delinquents who tend to think with that part of their anatomy, Gérard Depardieu and Patrick Dewaere are the personification of ignorance, indulgence and insensitivity. Their sexual encounters with newly sprung jailbird Jeanne Moreau and drifting thrill-seeker Miou-Miou manage to be both repellent and compelling. But the film loses its bite after Depardieu and Dewaere go on the run, although the sequence with a young Isabelle Huppert has a dark fascination. In French with English subtitles. [video]

Gérard Depardieu *Jean-Claude* • Patrick Dewaere *Pierrot* • Miou-Miou *Marie-Ange* • Jeanne Moreau *Jeanne* • Jacques Chailleux *Jacques* • Michel Peurilon *Surgeon* • Brigitte Fossey *Young mother* • Isabelle Huppert *Jacqueline* ■ *Dir* Bertrand Blier • *Scr* Bertrand Blier, Philippe Dumarcay, from the novel by Bertrand Blier

Value for Money ★★

Comedy 1955 · UK · Colour · 93mins

Take one bluff, penny-wise Yorkshireman and a blowsy, blonde showgirl, exaggerate every regional characteristic and then whisk them together into a romantic froth. Season with a couple of quaint cameos and you have *Value for Money*. Forget the mediocre on-screen antics of John Gregson and Diana Dors (neither of whom are on form) and take a look instead at the backroom boys who helped assemble this featherweight comedy. Popular novelist RF Delderfield has a hand in the script, the cinematographer is the peerless Geoffrey Unsworth and the composer is Malcolm Arnold. It just goes to show that the finest ingredients don't always result in a tasty dish.

John Gregson *Chayley Broadbent* • Diana Dors *Ruthine West* • Susan Stephen *Ethel* • Derek Farr *Duke Popplewell* • Frank Pettingell *Higgins* • Jill Adams *Joy* • Charles Victor *Lumm* • James Gregson *Oldroyd* • Ernest Thesiger *Lord Dewsbury* • Donald Pleasence *Limpy* ■ *Dir* Ken Annakin • *Scr* RF Delderfield, William Fairchild, from the novel by Derrick Boothroyd

Vamp ★★ 18

Horror comedy 1986 · US · Colour · 89mins

Grace Jones oozes animal sexuality and danger as the sensual vampire of the title, but even she can't save this botched attempt to mix *Animal House* laughs with kinky horror. Chris Makepeace and Robert Rusler are the college students who stumble upon a den of strippers with serious dental problems, but the one good gag is lifted directly from the far superior *An American Werewolf in London*. [video]

Grace Jones *Katrina* • Chris Makepeace *Keith* • Robert Rusler *AJ* • Sandy Baron *Vic* • Dedee Pfeiffer *Amaretto* • Gedde Watanabe *Duncan* ■ *Dir* Richard Wenk • *Scr* Richard Wenk, from a story by Donald P Borchers, Richard Wenk

Vampira ★★ 15

Comedy horror 1975 · UK · Colour · 84mins

David Niven dons the cloak of Dracula in this long-in-the-tooth vampire comedy well past its Swinging Sixties sell-by-date. The Count, who has turned his castle into a Playboy-style tourist resort, is searching for a rare blood type donor to revive his wife Vampira. The stale gag is that she's eventually reincarnated as black babe Teresa Graves. Niven adds a touch of class to the ridiculously old-fashioned proceedings and is the only reason for watching this dire farce from director Clive Donner. [video]

David Niven *Count Dracula* • Teresa Graves *Countess Vampira* • Peter Bayliss *Maltravers* • Jennie Linden *Angela* • Nicky Henson *Marc* • Linda Hayden *Helga* ■ *Dir* Clive Donner • *Scr* Jeremy Lloyd

The Vampire Bat ★ PG

Horror 1933 · US · BW · 60mins

A series of small-town murders turn out to be the work of scientist Lionel Atwill who drains his victims of blood in order to nourish a flesh parasite he has created. A standard-issue mad doctor tale, it was evidently made to cash-in on the success of Universal's *Dracula* with frightened Fay Wray and hero Melvyn Douglas lending limp support to the hopelessly outdated proceedings. [video]

Lionel Atwill *Dr Otto von Niemann* • Fay Wray *Ruth Bertin* • Melvyn Douglas *Karl Brettschneider* • Maude Eburne *Gussie Schnappmann* • George E Stone *Kringen* • Dwight Frye *Herman Gleib* ■ *Dir* Frank R Strayer • *Scr* Edwart T Lowe

Vampire Circus ★★★ 18

Horror 1971 · UK · Colour · 83mins

This isn't the Hammer freak show its title might suggest, but a vampire horror that conjures up a fairy-tale atmosphere at first, as the arrival of a circus in an isolated 19th-century town in central Europe coincides with an outbreak of plague. Adrienne Corri's intense beauty shines like a beacon in the murky atmosphere, but the delicacy of mood collapses into blood-spurting horrifics towards the end. ⬚

Adrienne Corri *Gypsy woman* • Laurence Payne *Professor Mueller* • Thorley Walters *Burgermeister* • John Moulder-Brown *Anton Kersh* • Lynne Frederick *Dora Mueller* ■ *Dir* Robert Young • *Scr* Judson Kinberg, from a story by George Baxt, Wilbur Stark

Vampire Hunter D   ★★★🔢

Animated science-fiction horror
1985 · Jap · Colour · 80mins

An adventurous manga animation melange of JRR Tolkien, Sergio Leone, Hammer horror and mainstream sci-fi. Far off in the 13th millennium, D is hired by village beauty Doris to save her from Count Magnus Lee's clutches. Having sampled her jugular, the ancient giant now wants Doris for his bride and D must infiltrate his mountain fortress in order to halt his plans. Director Toyoo Ashida uses a wildly eclectic palate of styles and astonishing depth to achieve his helter-skelter imagery in one of the best Japanese cartoons in the *Akira* tradition. ⬚

Dir Toyoo Ashida, Carl Macek • *Scr* Yasuhi Hirano

Vampire in Brooklyn ★★★🔢

Horror   1995 · US · Colour · 97mins

Eddie Murphy's streetwise persona is often at odds here with director Wes Craven's more explicit, doom-laden beastliness, and the intended comedy becomes lost in the horror. Murphy stars as suave Caribbean vampire Maximillian, a master of disguise, who comes to America to find his soulmate – NYPD cop Angela Bassett, who is unaware that she is Murphy's bride-to-be. There are some good moments – Murphy as an alcoholic preacher and as an Italian gangster stand out – but too often Craven puts on the frighteners so heavily that the chuckles get squeezed out. ⬚

Eddie Murphy *Maximillian/Preacher Pauley/Guido* • Angela Bassett *Rita* • Allen Payne *Justice* • Kadeem Hardison *Julius* • John Witherspoon *Silas* • Zakes Mokae *Dr Zeko* • Joanna Cassidy *Dewey* • Simbi Khali *Nikki* ■ *Dir* Wes Craven • *Scr* Charles Murphy, Christopher Parker, Michael Lucker, from a story by Charles Murphy, Eddie Murphy, Vernon Lynch Jr

Vampire in Venice   ★★🔢

Horror   1987 · It · Colour · 89mins

Returning to the role of Dracula, Klaus Kinski is here confronted with vampire hunter Christopher Plummer as he wearily inducts a princess and her eager sister into the ranks of the undead. Kinski gives a demonstration of melancholic malevolence that is every bit as impressive as his performance in Werner Herzog's *Nosferatu*. But, Augusto Caminito relies too much on Venetian splendour and close-ups of Kinski's eyes to conjure up atmosphere and the result is languor, not horror. Italian dialogue dubbed into English. Contains violence and sexual content. ⬚

Klaus Kinski *Nosferatu* • Barbara De Rossi *Helietta Canins* • Christopher Plummer *Paris Catalano* • Yorgo Voyagis *Giuseppe Barnabo* •

Clara Colosimo *Medium* • Maria C Cumani *Matilde Canins* • Donald Pleasence *Exorcist* ■ *Dir/Scr* Augusto Caminito

The Vampire Lovers   ★★

Horror   1970 · UK · Colour · 90mins

The first of Hammer's three Karnstein chillers (based on Sheridan LeFanu's *Carmilla*) is an atmospheric and erotic undead tale detailing the life of lesbian vampire Mircalla, voluptuously played by Ingrid Pitt. Peter Cushing lends a greater credibility to the sensuality-heavy production than the repetitious script would normally warrant. Inventive direction by Roy Ward Baker conspires to make this brazenly exploitative horror hokum better than it deserves to be. *Lust for a Vampire* and *Twins of Evil* followed. ⬚

Ingrid Pitt *Mircalla/Marcilla/Carmilla Karnstein* • Peter Cushing *General Spielsdorf* • Madeline Smith *Emma* • Jon Finch *Carl* • Pippa Steele *Laura Spielsdorf* • George Cole *Morton* • Dawn Addams *Countess* • Douglas Wilmer *Baron Hartog* • Kate O'Mara *Mme Perrodot* • Ferdy Mayne *Doctor* ■ *Dir* Roy Ward Baker • *Scr* Tudor Gates, from the story *Carmilla* by J Sheridan Le Fanu, adapted by Harry Fine, Michael Style

Vampirella   ★★

Science-fiction horror
1996 · US · Colour · 90mins

It would be an overstatement to say that wooden Talisa Soto brings Forrest J Ackerman's comic book heroine to life, but she does at least portray Vampirella in three dimensions. The plot has something to do with Vampirella coming to Earth from her home planet of Drakulon in order to kill Dracula. But you'll forget all that when you realise that ageing rocker Roger Daltrey is playing the big vampiric cheese, and that Drac's new persona is a Lestat-like rock star named Jamie Blood. Not as much fun as it ought to be. Contains nudity, violence and swearing.

Talisa Soto *Vampirella* • Roger Daltrey *Vlad/Jamie Blood* • Richard Joseph Paul *Adam Van Helsing* • Angus Scrimm *High Elder* • Corrina Harney *Sallah* ■ *Dir* Jim Wynorski • *Scr* Gary Gerani, from a story by Forrest J Ackerman

Vampires in Havana   ★★

Comic animation
1985 · Cub · Colour · 80mins

Vampirism is equated to the Mafia in a delightfully stylised, if sometimes crudely drawn, Cuban cartoon feature combining Hammer horror, gangster movies, James Bond and Latin American history. Professor Von Dracula and his nephew Joseph Amadeus become the focus of a war between the undead of Chicago and Düsseldorf, thanks to Vampisol, a sun-block drug that allows vampires to walk around in daylight. Light-hearted fun with surprisingly little political comment. In Spanish with English subtitles.

Dir/Scr Juan Padron

Vampire's Kiss   ★🔢

Horror comedy   1988 · US · Colour · 99mins

Yuppie Nicolas Cage gets bitten by sexy vampire Jennifer Beals, but when he doesn't turn into a vampire, he

fakes it and becomes a mixed-up psycho wearing plastic fangs and prowling discos for victims. Falling between horror comedy and a serious study of mental illness, director Robert Bierman's wretched farrago is hideously unfunny, witless and offensively stupid. Cage is so over the top as the pathetic loser, he's just ridiculous. Contains violence. ⬚

Nicolas Cage *Peter Loew* • Maria Conchita Alonso *Alva Restrepo* • Jennifer Beals *Rachel* • Elizabeth Ashley *Dr Glaser* • Kasi Lemmons *Jackie* • Bob Lujan *Emilio* • Jessica Lundy *Sharon* • John Walker *Donald* ■ *Dir* Robert Bierman • *Scr* Joseph Minion

Vampyr   ★★★★★

Horror   1932 · Fr/Ger · BW · 62mins

Based on *Carmilla*, Carl Theodor Dreyer's hypnotic psychological chiller, this also borrows from other stories contained in J Sheridan Le Fanu's collection, *In a Glass Darkly*. The film's visual ethereality was an accident caused by the fogging of a lens, but the dreamlike structure (with its shifting perspectives, unexpected juxtapositions and defiance of logic) was a conscious attempt to keep the viewer disorientated. Shot on location in France, this was Dreyer's first talkie and is a singular masterwork. In German with English subtitles. ⬚

Julian West *David Gray* • Maurice Schutz *Lord of the Manor* • Rena Mandel *Gisèle* • Sybille Schmitz *Léone* • Jan Hieronimko *The village doctor* • Henriette Gérard *Marguerite Chopin* • Albert Bras *The old servant* ■ *Dir* Carl Theodor Dreyer • *Scr* Carl Theodor Dreyer, Christen Jul, from the short story *Carmilla* by J Sheridan Le Fanu • *Cinematographer* Rudolph Maté, Louis Née

The Van   ★★🔢

Comedy drama
1996 · Ire/UK · Colour · 95mins

It's been a case of diminishing returns as far as the cinematic adaptations of Roddy Doyle's Barrytown trilogy are concerned. Following the soulful success of Alan Parker's *The Commitments*, Stephen Frears struggled to bring much bite to *The Snapper*, and in this concluding episode he stalls in the opening scene and then refuses to get out of first gear. The flashes of the Republic of Ireland's achievements at the 1990 World Cup are wonderfully evocative, but the tale of unemployed scalliwags Colm Meaney and Donal O'Kelly and their clapped-out "chipper" van feels forced and lacks a sense of place. Contains swearing. ⬚

Colm Meaney *Larry* • Donal O'Kelly *Bimbo* • Ger Ryan *Maggie* • Caroline Rothwell *Mary* • Neili Conroy *Diane* • Ruaidhri Conroy *Kevin* • Brendan O'Carroll *Weslie* • Stuart Dunne *Sam* ■ *Dir* Stephen Frears • *Scr* Roddy Doyle, from his novel

Van Gogh   ★★★★🔢

Biographical drama
1991 · Fr · Colour · 151mins

Vincente Minnelli, Paul Cox and Robert Altman have all made films about the tortured life of Vincent Van Gogh, but Maurice Pialat's superbly photographed account of his last few months is by far the most compelling. Creating the atmosphere of Auvers-sur-Oise with great care, he builds up his portrait

through a wealth of tiny details rather than the broader brush strokes of Minnelli or Altman. Gaunt, withdrawn and acting on impulses that are terrifying in their suddenness and ferocity, Jacques Dutronc is magnificent in the title role. In French with English subtitles. ⬚

Jacques Dutronc *Vincent Van Gogh* • Alexandra London *Marguerite Gachet* • Gerard Sety *Doctor Gachet* • Bernard Le Coq *Theo Van Gogh* • Corinne Bourdon *Jo* • Elsa Zylberstein *Cathy* ■ *Dir/Scr* Maurice Pialat • *Cinematographer* Gilles Henry, Emmanuel Machuel

Van Nuys Blvd   ★★

Comedy drama   1979 · US · Colour · 93mins

A raunchy late seventies B-movie about drag racing, with Bill Adler as the country boy who heads for the Californian town of Van Nuys in search of the fast-lane. He's rapidly inducted into a ludicrously drawn subculture of cheeseburgers, chicks and cars, cars, cars, pushing himself and his beloved automobile to the limit, before opting for the charms of former *Playboy* Playmate Cynthia Wood. A meaningless exercise in male wish-fulfilment, it's tacky but kind of enjoyable, too.

Bill Adler *Bobby* • Cynthia Wood *Moon* • Dennis Bowen *Greg* • Melissa Prophet *Camille* • David Hayward *Chooch* • Tara Strohmeier *Wanda* • Dana Gladstone *Al Zass* ■ *Dir/Scr* William Sachs

Vanessa, Her Love Story   ★

Melodrama   1935 · US · BW · 74mins

Unaware that her husband is suffering from inherited insanity, unhappily married Helen Hayes takes a lover (Robert Montgomery), who later loses an arm while on military duty with the British army in Egypt. All ends happily for the lovers when Hayes's husband dies. Although the film was co-adapted by Hugh Walpole from the last of his *Herries Chronicles* novels and features a quality supporting cast, this is a really deathly soap opera which goes straight to the bottom of the heap. Hayes, not surprisingly, returned to Broadway immediately afterwards and stayed there for 16 years.

Helen Hayes *Vanessa* • Robert Montgomery *Benjie* • Otto Kruger *Ellis* • May Robson *Judith* • Lewis Stone *Adam* • Henry Stephenson *Barney* • Violet Kemble-Cooper *Lady Herries* ■ *Dir* William K Howard • *Scr* Lenore Coffee, Hugh Walpole, from the novel by Hugh Walpole

Vanished without a Trace   ★★★🔢

Drama based on a true story
1993 · US · Colour · 89mins

When it comes to TV movies based on true stories, Hollywood relishes the chance to exploit the unsettling and horrid goings-on in the trim gardens of tiny-town America. Here, a father imaginative kidnapping involving 26 children, their bus driver and three rich-kid criminals causes ructions in the setting of Chowchilla, California. The suspense is ably sustained by director Vern Gillum, and Karl Malden, as the driver, enlivens the proceedings with his trademark mix of doggedness and decency. ⬚

Karl Malden *Edward Ray* • Tim Ransom *Fred Woods Iv* • Travis Fine *Rick Schoenfeld* • Tom Hodges *Jim Schoenfeld* • Julie Harris *Odessa Ray* • Bobby Zameroski *Tim Pearson* ■ *Dir* Vern Gillum • *Scr* David Eyre Jr, from the book *Why Have They Taken Our Children* by Jack W Baugh, Jefferson Morgan

The Vanishing ★★★★ 15

Psychological thriller
1988 · Neth/Fr · Colour · 101mins

George Sluizer's chilling tale of premeditation, abduction and obsession, sees an unassuming family man infatuated with the perfect kidnap. Bernard-Pierre Donnadieu emerges as one of the screen's most chilling, calculating and conceited psychotics, and the quiet satisfaction with which he explains his technique to the victim's boyfriend, Gene Bervoets, is unnerving in the extreme. From the moment we realise Johanna Ter Steege is in danger to the final shocking twist, Sluizer inexorably, expertly draws us deeper into the mystery, exposing our own morbid curiosity in the process. In Dutch and French with English subtitles. Contains violence. ▭

Bernard-Pierre Donnadieu *Raymond Lemorne* • Gene Bervoets *Rex Hofman* • Johanna Ter Steege *Saskia Wagter* • Gwen Eckhaus *Lienexe* • Bernadette Le Saché *Simone Lemorne* • Tania Latarjet *Denise* ■ *Dir* George Sluizer • *Scr* Tim Krabbé, George Sluizer (adaptation), from the novel *The Golden Egg* by Tim Krabbé

The Vanishing ★★ 15

Thriller   1993 · US · Colour · 105mins

Hollywood has a fine tradition of trampling over foreign classics, but this rankles more than most, mainly because the director of the outstanding original European version, Dutchman George Sluizer, is also behind the lens this time. Kiefer Sutherland is the troubled holidaymaker whose girlfriend vanishes without a trace at a service station. His obsessive search for her leads him to eccentric teacher Jeff Bridges, who may or may not hold the key to the mystery. Although Sluizer doesn't deviate far from the original story except in the travesty of the ending, he fails to sustain the icy air of menace of the first film, and the movie is further unhinged by a bizarre, over-the-top performance from the normally reliable Bridges. Contains swearing and violence. ▭

Jeff Bridges *Barney Cousins* • Kiefer Sutherland *Jeff Harriman* • Nancy Travis *Rita Baker* • Sandra Bullock *Diane Shaver* • Park Overall *Lynn* • Maggie Linderman *Denise Cousins* • Lisa Eichhorn *Helene* • George Hearn *Arthur Bernard* ■ *Dir* George Sluizer • *Scr* Todd Graff, from the novel *The Golden Egg* by Tim Krabbé

Vanishing Act ★★★ PG

Thriller   1986 · US · Colour · 93mins

A case of *déjà vu*, as this was the third film to be based on Robert Thomas's play *The Trap for a Lonely Man* about a bride going missing on her honeymoon. Mike Farrell, of TV's *M*A*S*H* fame, plays the puzzled husband, and a strong cast also boasts *Superman*'s Margot Kidder and Elliott Gould. This is a smartly

produced, compelling mystery thriller. ▭

Mike Farrell *Harry Kenyon* • Margot Kidder *Chris Kenyon* • Elliott Gould *Police Lieutenant Rudameyer* • Fred Gwynne *Father Macklin* • Graham Jarvis *Dr Demarco* ■ *Dir* David Greene • *Scr* Richard Levinson, William Link, from the play *The Trap for a Lonely Man* by Robert Thomas

The Vanishing Corporal ★★★★

Second World War comedy drama
1962 · Fr · BW · 106mins

Jean-Pierre Cassel is the vanishing corporal, a prisoner of war who dedicates himself to escape, but all his attempts fail and he is sent to detention camps for punishment. Finally, he and his buddy (Claude Brasseur) get back to Paris where they vow to join the Resistance. Set in a German PoW camp, like his masterpiece *La Grande Illusion*, though this time in the Second World War, Jean Renoir approaches the subject as comedy and he manages to suggest the grimmer reality beneath the surface. A French language film.

Jean-Pierre Cassel *The Corporal* • Claude Brasseur *Pater* • Claude Rich *Ballochet* • OE Hasse *Drunk traveller* • Jean Carmet *Emile* ■ *Dir* Jean Renoir • *Scr* Jean Renoir, Guy Lefranc, from the novel *Le Caporal Epinglé* by Jacques Perret

Vanishing Frontier ★★★

Western   1932 · US · BW · 65mins

Former American football hero Johnny Mack Brown made a major impact in the title role of MGM's 1930 *Billy the Kid*, but an alleged affair with William Randolph Hearst's mistress Marion Davies cost him true stardom. This Paramount romp was one of his last major movies, though he continued to headline in popular programme-fillers throughout the next three decades. At least here he has a half-decent role, playing a kind of Robin Hood of the west. There's fine support, too, from veterans ZaSu Pitts and Raymond Hatton.

Johnny Mack Brown *Kirby Tornell* • Evelyn Knapp *Carol Winfield* • ZaSu Pitts *Aunt Sylvia* • Raymond Hatton *Waco* • J Farrell MacDonald *Hornet* • Wallace Macdonald *Capt Kearney* ■ *Dir* Phil Rosen • *Scr* Stuart Anthony

Vanishing Point ★★★ 18

Road movie   1971 · US · Colour · 94mins

In Denver, Barry Newman climbs into a Dodge Challenger, switches on the ignition, puts his foot down and aims to be in California in 15 hours, stopping only for fuel (petrol for the car and amphetamines for him). This road movie followed in the wake of *Easy Rider* and it sets out to be a similar essay in alienation, taking in the expected hippy colonies, Hell's Angels and bigoted cops ▭

Barry Newman *Kowalski* • Cleavon Little *Super Soul* • Dean Jagger *Prospector* • Victoria Medlin *Vera* • Paul Koslo *Young cop* • Robert Donner *Older cop* ■ *Dir* Richard C Sarafian • *Scr* Guillermo Cain, from a story outline by Malcolm Hart

Vanishing Point ★★

Adventure   1997 · US · Colour · 92mins

A remake of the 1971 cult classic, Viggo Mortensen plays a racing driver who learns that his wife's (*ER*'s Christine Elise) pregnancy is life threatening, so he races across four states in a super-charged car to be by her side. Through a series of misunderstandings he becomes a wanted man, with the police and FBI in hot pursuit. Writer/director Charles Robert Carner revs up the action, but eventually runs out of gas, despite a good cast and scenic desert locations.

Viggo Mortensen *James Kowalski* • Christine Elise *Raphinia* • Keith David *Taftley* • Steve Railsback *Sergeant Preston* • Rodney A Grant *Native American spiritualist* • Jason Priestley *The Voice* ■ *Dir* Charles Robert Carner • *Scr* Charles Robert Carner, from the 1971 film

The Vanquished ★★★ U

Portmanteau drama   1953 · It · BW · 86mins

A collection of stories exploring the moral turpitude of postwar Europe. In the opening episode, French pupils kill a classmate for cash; an Italian college student becomes involved with the black market in the second, while an English poet seeks to profit from the death of an apparently respectable woman in the third. Censorship problems dogged the picture, but the director's genius for linking the inner self and environment is well established. An Italian language film.

Jean-Pierre Mocky *Pierre* • Etchika Choureau *Simone* • Franco Interlenghi *Claudio* • Anna-Maria Ferrero *Marina* • Evi Maltagliati *Claudio's Mother* • Eduardo Ciannelli *Claudio's Father* • Peter Reynolds *Aubrey* • Fay Compton *Mrs Pinkerton* • Patrick Barr *Kent Watton* ■ *Dir* Michelangelo Antonioni • *Scr* Michelangelo Antonioni, Suso Cecchi D'Amico, Giorgio Bassani, Diego Fabbri, Turi Vasile, Roger Nimier

Vanya on 42nd Street ★★★ U

Drama   1994 · US · Colour · 115mins

Three directors on different continents took on Anton Chekhov's *Uncle Vanya* within the space of two years. Michael Blakemore staged his version of the play *Country Life* in the Australian outback, while Anthony Hopkins located his interpretation called *August* in North Wales. But only Louis Malle could have thought of setting the play in a dilapidated New York theatre, with the action being performed by a rehearsing cast sitting around a table in their day clothes. Wallace Shawn is excellent in the title role, but, while Malle's approach allows us to concentrate on the text and offers an insight into the acting process, his final film marks a slightly disappointing end to an exceptional career. ▭

Wallace Shawn *Vanya* • Julianne Moore *Yelena* • Andre Gregory • George Gaynes *Serebryakov* • Brooke Smith *Sonya* • Larry Pine *Dr Astrov* • Phoebe Brand *Nanny* • Lynn Cohen *Maman* • Jerry Mayer *Waffles* • Madhur Jaffrey *Mrs Chao* ■ *Dir* Louis Malle • *Scr* David Mamet, from the play *Uncle Vanya* by Anton Chekhov

Variety Girl ★★ U

Musical   1947 · US · BW and Colour · 86mins

Yet another entry in the seemingly interminable string of studio star cavalcades of which Paramount seemed to be particularly fond. The characteristic non-plot has two hopefuls (Mary Hatcher, Olga San Juan) arriving at the studio in search of a future. Here, they encounter a roster of names ranging from Bing Crosby and Bob Hope (in a very funny golfing sketch), through Barbara Stanwyck, Gary Cooper, Burt Lancaster and Pearl Bailey, to William Holden, Cecil B DeMille and Spike Jones and His City Slickers.

Mary Hatcher *Catherine Brown* • Olga San Juan *Amber La Vonne* • DeForest Kelley *Bob Kirby* • Bing Crosby • Gary Cooper • Ray Milland • Paulette Goddard • Barbara Stanwyck • Bob Hope • William Holden (1) *William Holden* • Veronica Lake • Burt Lancaster • Pearl Bailey *Specialty* • Cecil B DeMille ■ *Dir* George Marshall • *Scr* Edmund Hartmann, Frank Tashlin, Robert Welch, Monte Brice

Variety Jubilee ★★★ U

Musical   1942 · UK · BW · 92mins

This simple, nostalgic tribute to the British music hall tradition begins with two former variety artists who become partners in running a vaudeville venue at the dawn of the 20th century. One of their sons is then killed in the First World War, before a grandson takes over the family enterprise and makes it a success again. The film consists largely of musical variety acts performed by numerous forgotten old-timers of a bygone era. Wonderful!

Reginald Purdell *Joe Swan* • Ellis Irving *Kit Burns* • Lesley Brook *Evelyn Vincent* • Marie Lloyd Jr *Marie Lloyd* • Tom E Finglass *Eugene Stratton* • John Rorke *Gus Elen* • Betty Warren *Florrie Forde* • Charles Coborn ■ *Dir* Maclean Rogers • *Scr* Kathleen Butler, from a story by Mabel Constanduros

Variety Time ★★★ U

Compilation   1948 · US · BW · 58mins

Long before *That's Entertainment!*, studios would assemble clips from past productions into compilations. RKO made this, shooting new footage of Jack Paar as MC to link the songs, sketches and two comedy shorts (both very funny) that comprised the bill. As several of the song-and-dance numbers are from B-movies which are hard to see nowadays, musical fans will find a look worthwhile.

Jack Paar *MC* ■ *Dir* Hal Yates

Varsity Blues ★★★ 15

Comedy drama   1999 · US · Colour · 104mins

New hunk on the block James Van Der Beek (*TV's Dawson's Creek*) is the high-school football player who challenges the authority of his control-freak coach (Jon Voight giving another hilariously over-the-top performance) when he becomes the team's star quarterback. This teenage drama is basically a nineties throwback to eighties' sports movies such as *Youngblood* and *All the Right Moves*: the usual mix of sports action, drinking and girls with the odd moral tale thrown in. Predictable stuff for grown-ups, which may go over the heads of non-American football aficionados. Contains swearing and nudity. 🔲

James Van Der Beek *Jonathan "Mox" Moxon* • Jon Voight *Coach Bud Kilmer* • Paul Walker *Lance Harbor* • Ron Lester *Billy Bob* • Scott Caan *Tweeter* • Richard Lineback *Joe Harbor* • Tiffany C Love *Collette Harbor* ■ *Dir* Brian Robbins • *Scr* W Peter Iliff

Vassa ★★★★ PG

Drama   1983 · USSR · Colour · 136mins

Gleb Panfilov directed Maxim Gorky's play as a vehicle for his wife Inna Churikova, and depicts her as the last bastion of strength in a morass of corruption, indolence and perversion. Her husband is charged with child molestation, her drunken brother is accused of impregnating the maid, her daughters are insane and nymphomaniac, and then her detested daughter-in-law arrives with news of her son's terminal illness. It's soap operatic, but the pre-Revolutionary trappings are sumptuous and the political subtext is intelligently underplayed. In Russian with English subtitles.

Inna Churikova *VassaZheleznova* • Vadim Medvedev *Sergei* • Nikolai Skorobogatov *Prokhor, Vassa's brother* • Valentina Telichkina *Anna, Vassa's secretary* • Valentina Yakunina *Rachel* ■ *Dir* Gleb Panfilov • *Scr* Gleb Panfilov, from the play *Vassa Zheleznova* by Maxim Gorky

Vatel ★★

Comedy drama
2000 · Fr/US · Colour · 117mins

All the ingredients seem right – a screenplay co-written by Tom Stoppard, an Ennio Morricone score and Gérard Depardieu as François Vatel, the backstreet urchin whose culinary expertise and genius for baroque entertainments enchanted the court of Louis XIV. But under Roland Joffé's undistinguished direction, what emerges is a disappointing romp, where sexual and political intrigue intersperse with misfiring spectacle and inconsequential banter. Failing to exploit the grandeur of the period and wasting an ill-at-ease cast which includes Uma Thurman, Tim Roth and Julian Sands, this is both extravagant and unappetising.

Gérard Depardieu *François Vatel* • Uma Thurman *Anne de Montausier* • Tim Roth *Marquis de Lauzun* • Julian Glover *Prince de Conde* • Julian Sands *King Louis XIV* • Timothy Spall *Gourville* ■ *Dir* Roland Joffé • *Scr* Jeanne Labrune, Tom Stoppard (English adaptation)

Vaudeville ★★★★

Silent melodrama   1925 · Ger · BW · 57mins

EA Dupont was handed this assignment after producer Erich Pommer felt FW Murnau was approaching it with too little enthusiasm. However, the dazzling display of visual artistry that transformed this otherwise humdrum showbiz melodrama was fashioned not by the director, but by his cinematographer Karl Freund. His bravura use of chiaroscuro lighting, subjective camera, overlapping dissolves and expressionist montage is quite masterly and demonstrates the pictorial sublimity of silent cinema. The

story of the trapeze artist who murders his rival in love was much butchered for its US release to remove its moral ambiguities, although both versions have their merits.

Emil Jannings *Boss Huller* • Lya de Putti *Bertha-Marie* • Warwick Ward *Artinelli* • Charles Lincoln *Actor* ■ *Dir* EA Dupont • *Scr* EA Dupont, Leo Birinksi, from the novel *Der Eid des Stephan Huller* by Felix Holländer

Vault of Horror ★★

Horror   1973 · UK · Colour · 86mins

Five men trapped in a mysterious basement room following a journey in an elevator, tell each other their recurring nightmares in this formulaic horror movie. The film was adapted from William Gaines's terror comics, which would account for such bizarre section titles as *Midnight Mess* and *This Trick'll Kill You*. This was the sixth horror compendium made by Amicus, for a time Hammer's most formidable rival. British actors such as Terry-Thomas and Daniel Massey bring a touch of class to an otherwise pedestrian production.

Daniel Massey *Rogers* • Anna Massey *Donna* • Michael Craig *Maitland* • Edward Judd *Alex* • Curt Jurgens *Sebastian* • Dawn Addams *Inez* • Terry-Thomas *Critchit* • Glynis Johns *Eleanor* • Marianne Stone *Jane* • Tom Baker *Alex Moore* • Denholm Elliott *Diltant* ■ *Dir* Roy Ward Baker • *Scr* Milton Subotsky, from the comic magazines *The Vault of Horror* and *Tales from the Crypt* by Al Feldstein, William Gaines

Vegas Vacation ★ PG

Comedy   1997 · US · Colour · 90mins

The hapless Chevy Chase and long-suffering wife Beverly D'Angelo head for Las Vegas and get mixed up in a series of unamusing misadventures, in yet another Lampoon venture. Randy Quaid, as Chase's trailer trash cousin, fares the best, but laughs are pretty much thin on the ground. Not even a talented supporting cast (Wallace Shawn, Sid Caesar) can do much to rescue this. 🔲

Chevy Chase *Clark W Griswold* • Beverly D'Angelo *Ellen Griswold* • Randy Quaid *Cousin Eddie* • Ethan Embry *Rusty Griswold* • Marisol Nichols *Audrey Griswold* • Wayne Newton ■ *Dir* Stephen Kessler • *Scr* Elisa Bell, from a story by Bob Ducsay

Vegas Vice ★★

Erotic thriller   1994 · US · Colour · 86mins

As John Travolta was busy reinventing himself in *Pulp Fiction*, his brother Joey, also an actor, was branching out in new directions, debuting behind the camera with this bog-standard erotic thriller. The plot's a disposable number about cops hunting a serial killer, and the film is notable solely for the fact that genre queen Shannon Tweed is, for once, overshadowed in the nudity department, courtesy of co-star Rebecca Ferratti. Contains violence, swearing, sex scenes and nudity.

Sam Jones *Joe Owens* • Shannon Tweed *Andrea Thompson* • James Gammon *Dan Bronski* • Miguel A Nunez [Miguel A Nunez Jr] *Bugs* • Tom Fridley *Mike* • Rebecca Ferratti *Allison* ■ *Dir* Joey Travolta • *Scr* Rich Dillon, Joey Travolta

Velvet Goldmine ★★ 15

Musical drama
1998 · UK/US · Colour · 118mins

Todd Haynes (*Safe*) is an imaginative and original director, and he employs both these qualities here but, sadly, they fail to make this mish-mash of a movie work. Ewan MacGregor and Jonathan Rhys-Meyers star as a couple of cultish singers over-indulging on sex, drugs and rock'n'roll, and failing to make their lives function. A thinly disguised tribute to Iggy Pop and Bowie's Ziggy Stardust, the action is seen as a montage through the eyes of investigative journalist Christian Bale. The duo's rise and fall is charted in all its bottom-flashing, cocaine-snorting glory and it looks great and has tons of atmosphere, but this is a soulless, unstructured piece of film-making and at the end of the day, you don't really care about the characters or their downfall. Contains swearing, nudity, sex scenes and violence. 🔲
DVD

Ewan McGregor *Curt Wild* • Jonathan Rhys-Meyers *Brian Slade* • Toni Collette *Mandy Slade* • Christian Bale *Arthur Stuart* • Eddie Izzard *Jerry Devine* • Emily Woof *Shannon* • Janet McTeer *Female narrator* ■ *Dir* Todd Haynes • *Scr* Todd Haynes, from a story by James Lyons, Todd Haynes

The Velvet Touch ★★

Crime drama   1948 · US · BW · 97mins

Rosalind Russell and her husband, producer Frederick Brisson played safe with this mechanical and lifeless melodrama, for which she specially hired top cinematographer Joseph Walker to ensure she looked her best in dresses by Travis Banton. She plays the Broadway star who kills her former lover in an argument and lets another actress, take the blame. The brightest move was the casting of portly Sydney Greenstreet as a theatre-loving police captain in awe of Russell. Not so bright was the casting of stolid Leo Genn as her English boyfriend.

Rosalind Russell *Valerie Stanton* • Leo Genn *Michael Morrell* • Claire Trevor *Marion Webster* • Sydney Greenstreet *Captain Danbury* • Leon Ames *Gordon Dunning* • Frank McHugh *Ernie Boyle* • Walter Kingsford *Peter Gunther* • Dan Tobin *Jeff Trent* • Lex Barker *Paul Banton* ■ *Dir* John Gage • *Scr* Leo Rosten, Walter Reilly, from a story by William Mercer, from a story by Annabel Ross

The Velvet Vampire ★★★

Erotic horror   1971 · US · Colour · 79mins

A strange vampire tale which is given an interesting feminist slant by Stephanie Rothman, one of the few female directors to work in the genre. After their dune buggy breaks down, Michael Blodgett and Sherry Miles accept an invitation to spend the weekend at Celeste Yarnall's Mojave desert ranch, unaware that she is an undead descendant of *Carmilla* author Sheridan Le Fanu (the influential horror writer). But Yarnall, who wears protective clothing in daylight, is more interested in Miles than her husband and, after drinking Blodgett dry, focuses her lesbian attentions on the remaining victim. An offbeat and comedy-laced psychedelic shocker.

Michael Blodgett *Lee Ritter* • Sherry Miles *Susan Ritter* • Celeste Yarnall *Diane LeFanu* •

Paul Prokop *Cliff* • Gene Shane *Carl Stoker* • Jerry Daniels *Juan* • Sandy Ward *Amos* ■ *Dir* Stephanie Rothman • *Scr* Maurice Jules, Charles S Swartz, Stephanie Rothman

Vendetta ★★ 18

Period drama based on a true story
1999 · US · Colour · 112mins

The downtrodden Sicilian labourers on the docks and wharfs of 1890s New Orleans form the background to this well made, but dour TV drama. Since the abolition of slavery, the local dock owners have been importing cheap labour from Sicily, then several immigrant men are framed for the murder of a policeman and their fight for justice inflames the city. Contains violence. 🔲

Christopher Walken *James Houston* • Clancy Brown *Chief Hennessy* • Bruce Davison *Thomas Semmes* • Luke Askew *William Parkerson* • Alessandro Colla *Gaspare Marchesi* • Andrew Connolly *Sheriff Bill Villere* ■ *Dir* Nicholas Meyer • *Scr* Timothy Prager

The Venetian Affair ★★

Spy thriller   1966 · US · Colour · 92mins

Evidently made by MGM to cash in on the popularity of Robert Vaughn in *The Man from UNCLE*, this thriller is a gritty exploration of the murky world of espionage. Vaughn is an ex-agent who's brought in from the cold to investigate the death of a diplomat at a Venetian peace conference. The involvement of Elke Sommer – his ex-wife and the reason he was sacked in the first place – only complicates matters further. An unremarkable affair apart from a welcome bit of menace from Boris Karloff.

Robert Vaughn *Bill Fenner* • Elke Sommer *Sandra Fane* • Felicia Farr *Claire Connor* • Karlheinz Böhm *Robert Wahl* • Luciana Paluzzi *Giulia Almeranti* • Boris Karloff *Dr Pierre Vaugiroud* • Roger C Carmel *Mike Ballard* • Edward Asner [Ed Asner] *Frank Rosenfeld* ■ *Dir* Jerry Thorpe • *Scr* E Jack Neuman, from the novel by Helen MacInnes

Venetian Bird ★★

Crime drama   1952 · UK · BW · 95mins

Borrowing liberally from *The Third Man*, this is a tolerable time-passer, although a little lightweight in the suspense department. Director Ralph Thomas offers some pretty postcard views of Venice, but he only fully exploits his fascinating location during the ingenious final chase sequence, which culminates in a Hitchcockian use of a famous landmark. Richard Todd is below par as the detective dispatched to uncover information about an air-raid victim who might be a war hero, a master criminal or both. The supporting cast is adequate, but John Gregson is simply dreadful.

Richard Todd *Edward Mercer* • Eva Bartok *Adriana* • John Gregson *Cassana* • George Coulouris *Spadoni* • Margot Grahame *Rosa Melitus* • Walter Rilla *Count Boria* • Sidney James *Bernardo* ■ *Dir* Ralph Thomas • *Scr* Victor Canning, from his novel

Vengeance ★

Police crime drama
1937 · US/Can · BW · 57mins

Lyle Talbot stars as a policeman, a crack target shooter, who can't bring himself to fire at a human being – not

even when he's fleeing a bank robber (Marc Lawrence). In disgrace, Talbot assumes a new identity and infiltrates the gang, not fluffing the next opportunity to shoot down his man. Wendy Barrie does heroine duties in this dismal B-feature that, though made in Canada, is indistinguishable from Hollywood's dross.

Lyle Talbot *"Dynamite" Hogan/Tom Connors* • Wendy Barrie *Polly Moore* • Marc Lawrence *Pete Brower* • Eddie Acuff *Tex McGirk* • Lucille Lund *Babe Foster* • Robert Rideout *Slim Ryan* • Reginald Hincks *Inspector Blair* ■ *Dir* Del Lord • *Scr* JP McGowan

Vengeance Is Mine ★★★

Biographical crime drama
1979 · Jap · Colour · 128mins

A constant feeling of uneasiness is to be found in this telling of the true story of Iwao Enokizu (played here by Ken Ogata), a Japanese serial killer who went on a murder and robbery spree lasting over two months. Shohei Imamura provides no easy answers to Enokizu's motivations, simply showing his life and actions. Yet this simple presentation works, as it encourages the viewer to find some answer somewhere. It also gives the opportunity to highlight aspects of the Japanese psyche – citizens are seen recognising the wanted Enokizu, but doing nothing. In Japanese with English Subtitles.

Ken Ogata *Iwao Enokizu* • Rentaro Mikuni *Shizuo Enokizu* • Chocho Mikayo *Kayo Enokizu* • Mitsuko Baisho *Kazuko Enokizu* ■ *Dir* Shohei Imamura • *Scr* Masaru Baba, from a book by Ryuzo Saki

The Vengeance of Fu Manchu ★★ PG

Crime drama
1967 · UK/W Ger/HK/Ire · Colour · 87mins

The inscrutable Oriental arch villain forces a surgeon to create a killer clone of his Scotland Yard nemesis, Nayland Smith, in the third Fu Manchu tale starring Christopher Lee. Don Sharp's light direction in the original *The Face of Fu Manchu* is sorely missed here, and director Jeremy Summers half-heartedly trys to patch a lacklustre, and surprisingly, actionless affair together out of plodding material. Only Tsai Chin as the infamous criminal's daughter rises to the occasion. ▭

Christopher Lee *Fu Manchu* • Tony Ferrer *Inspector Ramos* • Tsai Chin *Lin Tang* • Douglas Wilmer *Nayland Smith* • Wolfgang Kieling *Dr Lieberson* • Suzanne Roquette *Maria Lieberson* • Howard Marion-Crawford *Dr Petrie* ■ *Dir* Jeremy Summers • *Scr* Peter Welbeck [Harry Alan Towers], from characters created by Sax Rohmer

The Vengeance of She ★★ PG

Fantasy adventure
1968 · UK · Colour · 97mins

Czechoslovakian beauty Olinka Berova is taken for the reincarnation of novelist H Rider Haggard's Ayesha (as immortalised by Ursula Andress) in this mediocre sequel to *She* (1965). Scripted by Peter O'Donnell, the creator of *Modesty Blaise*, and once again starring John Richardson as Killikrates, the lover of "She Who Must

Be Obeyed", director Cliff Owen piles on the close-ups of Ms Berova in a Lost City fantasy adventure with reliable Hammer production values and colourful exotica. ▭

John Richardson *King Killikrates* • Olinka Berova *Carol* • Edward Judd *Philip Smith* • Colin Blakely *George Carter* • Derek Godfrey *Men-Hari* • Jill Melford *Sheila Carter* • George Sewell *Harry Walker* ■ *Dir* Cliff Owen • *Scr* Peter O'Donnell, from characters created by H Rider Haggard

Vengeance: the Demon ★★ 18

Horror   1988 · US · Colour · 82mins

Lance Henriksen stars as a farmer in the back woods, trying to make ends meet with his young son. City folk arrive to run over the boy with their motorcycles – accidentally, of course. The anguished Henriksen then enlists the help of the local witch woman to summon Pumpkinhead, an unstoppable demon with one objective: revenge. The long-anticipated directorial debut of make-up and special effects master Stan Winston owes more than a little to his previous work on *Aliens*. Unfortunately the result is little more than an average monster flick, with the scary moments sabotaged by a lame script. ▭

Lance Henriksen *Ed Harley* • Jeff East *Chris* • John DiAquino *Joel* • Kimberly Ross *Kim* • Joel Hoffman *Steve* • Cynthia Bain *Tracy* • Kerry Remsen *Maggie* • Tom Woodruff Jr *Pumpkinhead* ■ *Dir* Stan Winston • *Scr* Mark Patrick Carducci, Gary Gerani, from a story by Mark Patrick Carducci, Stan Winston, Richard C Weinman, from a poem by Ed Justin

Vengeance: the Story of Tony Cimo ★★★ 15

Drama based on a true story
1986 · US · Colour · 84mins

A routine, but rugged vigilante thriller, which provides an early role for Frances McDormand, who won an Oscar for her performance in *Fargo*. Brad Davis is the blue-collar worker who decides to become judge and jury when he loses patience with the legal system following the murder of his parents. Director Marc Daniels successfully avoids most of the clichés of the genre and is rewarded with good performances from a better-than-average cast: along with Davis and McDormand, there are solid turns from the likes of Michael Beach, Roxanne Hart and Brad Dourif. ▭

Brad Davis *Tony Cimo* • Roxanne Hart *Jan Cimo* • William Conrad *Jim Dunn* • Brad Dourif *Lamar Sands* • Michael Beach *Rudolf Tyner* • Chuck Patterson *Leroy Skelton* • Cass Morgan *Rene Moon Benton* • Frances McDormand *Brigette Moon* ■ *Dir* Marc Daniels • *Scr* James Lee Barrett

Vengeance Valley ★★★ PG

Western   1951 · US · Colour · 82mins

A decent psychological western with Burt Lancaster as the rancher's adopted son who always takes the wrap for his foster-brother, played by snivelling, sneering Robert Walker. A woman comes between them – gets pregnant – and we're into Eugene O'Neill territory or a Wild West spin on Cain and Abel. It's nicely shot in the Rocky Mountains and western buffs

will quickly note that you get two Wyatt Earps for your money here: Lancaster played him in the classic *Gunfight at the OK Corral* while further down the cast list is Hugh O'Brian who played Earp in a long-running TV series. ▭

Burt Lancaster *Owen Daybright* • Robert Walker *Lee Strobie* • Joanne Dru *Jen Strobie* • Ray Collins *Arch Strobie* • Sally Forrest *Lily Fasken* • John Ireland *Hub Fasken* • Hugh O'Brian *Dick Fasken* ■ *Dir* Richard Thorpe • *Scr* Irving Ravetch, from the novel by Luke Short

Venice/Venice ★

Comedy drama 1992 · US · Colour · 108mins

Exasperating and self-indulgent exercise from director Henry Jaglom, the wannabe art-house Woody Allen. After taking his latest movie to Venice, Italy, for the annual film festival and baring his soul to journalists (while being annoyingly ignored by John Landis, his friend on the critics' jury), it's back to Venice, California, for some embarrassing sexual guru posturing as desperate women fawn around the navel-gazing film-maker. Nothing more than an elaborate home movie and, despite some scathing showbiz truths and a neat turn by David Duchovny (as the star of Jaglom's festival offering), just as intolerable to watch.

Nelly Alard *Jeanne* • Henry Jaglom *Dean* • Suzanne Bertish *Carlotta* • Daphna Kastner *Eve* • David Duchovny *Dylan* • Suzanne Lanza *Dylan's girlfriend* • Vernon Dobtcheff *Alexander* • John Landis ■ *Dir/Scr* Henry Jaglom

Venom ★★★ 15

Thriller   1982 · UK · Colour · 88mins

Enjoyable thriller, based on Alan Scholefield's novel, which looks as though it was dreamed up during an extremely drunken weekend. Kidnappers plus child are holed up in a house with a deadly black mamba snake. The script may be weak in places, but prepare to shriek when the serpent slithers up wicked Oliver Reed's trouser leg. Remarkably, director Piers Haggard is also responsible for witchcraft shocker *Satan's Skin* and TV classic *Pennies from Heaven*. ▭

Klaus Kinski *Jacmel* • Oliver Reed *Dave* • Nicol Williamson *Commander William Bulloch* • Sarah Miles *Dr Marion Stowe* • Sterling Hayden *Howard Anderson* • Cornelia Sharpe *Ruth Hopkins* • Lance Holcomb *Philip Hopkins* • Susan George *Louise* ■ *Dir* Piers Haggard • *Scr* Robert Carrington, from a novel by Alan Scholefield

Vent d'Est ★★★

Political essay
1969 · Fr/It/W Ger · Colour · 92mins

Hailed as the first Marxist western, this is the fourth of the six anti-movies that Jean-Luc Godard made under the auspices of the Dziga-Vertov Group. He sought to bring down what he considered to be the crumbling edifice of traditional filmic language by constructing a political argument out of pure sounds and images. However, as this resolutely non-narrative essay reveals, the very act of articulating a statement or creating an impression is impossible without betraying a degree of subjectivity. Among Godard's co-conspirators are directors Marco Ferreri

and Glauber Rocha, themselves no strangers to cinematic controversy. In French with English subtitles.

Gian Maria Volonté *Soldier* • Anne Wiazemsky *Whore* ■ *Dir* Jean-Luc Godard • *Scr* Jean-Luc Godard, Daniel Cohn-Bendit

Le Vent de la Nuit ★★★

Romantic drama 1999 · Fr · Colour · 95mins

Desire, doubt and disillusion dominate this intense character study from the under-rated Philippe Garrel. Art student Xavier Beauvois vacillates between an unsatisfactory liaison with a possessive housewife and a dream job with a celebrated architect (Daniel Duval). Catherine Deneuve gives a brittle performance as the mistress racked by fears that Beauvois is only interested in her money. However, she is matched all the way by Duval's blend of ruthless professionalism and personal pain, as he remains haunted by both his wife's suicide and the electroshock therapy he endured after his participation in the 1968 Paris riots. In French with English subtitles.

Catherine Deneuve *Hélène* • Daniel Duval *Serge* • Xavier Beauvois *Paul* • Jacques Lasalle *Hélène's husband* ■ *Dir* Philippe Garrel • *Scr* Xavier Beauvois, Marc Cholodenko, Arlette Lagmann

Venus Beauty ★★★ 15

Comedy drama 1998 · Fr · Colour · 106mins

Vanity and fear of rejection underlie this French variation on the *Steel Magnolias* theme. The action takes its tone from the emotional state of its central character (Nathalie Baye), a beautician who seeks casual sex to numb the sense of loneliness she feels when not working at prudish Bulle Ogier's Paris salon. But, while Baye's brittle performance holds the film together, the eccentric collection of clients and co-workers undoubtedly adds intrigue to Tonie Marshall's disarmingly frank study of modern woman and what she'll do to remain true to her self-image. In French with English subtitles. Contains swearing and sex scenes.

Nathalie Baye *Angèle Piana* • Bulle Ogier *Nadine* • Samuel LeBihan [Samuel Lebihan] *Antoine Dumont* • Jacques Bonnaffé *Jacques* ■ *Dir* Tonie Marshall • *Scr* Tonie Marshall, Jacques Audiard, Marion Vernoux

Venus Peter ★★ 12

Drama   1989 · UK · Colour · 92mins

After many fine performances, Ray McAnally deserved a more distinguished swan song than this muddled piece of mysticism and malarkey. Recalling Michael Powell's *The Edge of the World* and John Sayles's *The Secret of Roan Inish* (and inferior to both), this view of Orkneys' life in the late forties brims o'er with eccentric characters and meaningless dialogue. Debuting director Ian Sellar throws in some haunting seascapes, but little of interest happens to disturb the endless flow of words. Contains nudity.

Ray McAnally *Grandfather* • David Hayman *Kinnear* • Sinead Cusack *Miss Balsilbie* • Gordon R Strachan *Peter* • Sam Hayman *Baby Peter* • Caroline Paterson *Mother* • Alex

McAvoy *Beadle* ■ *Dir* Ian Sellar • *Scr* Ian Sellar, Christopher Rush, from the book *A Twelvemonth and a Day* by Christopher Rush

Vera Cruz ★★★★ PG

Western 1954 · US · Colour · 89mins

Splendid *Boys' Own* stuff as two of the cinema's greatest icons slug it out down Mexico way. Gary Cooper is top-billed, but co-star Burt Lancaster is the man to watch in this terrific adventure. Produced by Lancaster's own company and directed by Robert Aldrich, who would collaborate out west once more with Lancaster in *Ulzana's Raid*, the movie has a rattling pace and a fine sense of style that's hard to top. The supporting cast includes Ernest Borgnine and Charles Bronson (still being billed here as Buchinsky), well before they teamed up with Aldrich again for *The Dirty Dozen*. ▭

Gary Cooper *Benjamin Trane* • Burt Lancaster *Joe Erin* • Denise Darcel *Countess Marie Duvarre* • Cesar Romero *Marquis De Labordere* • Sarita Montiel *Nina* • George Macready *Emperor Maximilian* • Ernest Borgnine *Donnegan* • Morris Ankrum *General Aguilar* • Henry Brandon *Danette* • Charles Buchinsky [Charles Bronson] *Pittsburgh* ■ *Dir* Robert Aldrich • *Scr* Roland Kibbee, James R Webb, from the story by Borden Chase

Verboten! ★★ PG

Thriller 1959 · US · BW · 86mins

This high-flown melodrama is much beloved by fans of maverick director Samuel Fuller, though other viewers may think it's hardly worth passing the time of day with. James Best brings dignity to a rare leading role as the GI uncovering a neo-Nazi conspiracy in postwar Germany, but Susan Cummings is woefully inadequate as his romantic interest. There's an underlying naive subtext that's either quite disturbing, or enjoyable, depending on your point of view; there's also a rather painful theme song recorded by then top star Paul Anka. ▭

James Best *Sgt David Brent* • Susan Cummings *Helga Schiller* • Tom Pittman *Bruno Eckart* • Paul Dubov *Capt Harvey* • Harold Daye *Franz Schiller* • Dick Kallman *Helmuth* ■ *Dir/Scr* Samuel Fuller

The Verdict ★★★

Crime mystery 1946 · US · BW · 86mins

Dirty Harry director Don Siegel's first feature marked the last reteaming of Sydney Greenstreet and Peter Lorre, the dynamic duo from *The Maltese Falcon*, where a Scotland Yard superintendent Greenstreet is forced to resign, only to become embroiled in another murder case. A little dusty maybe, but still the best of the three movie versions of Israel Zangwill's macabre novel *The Big Bow Mystery*.

Sydney Greenstreet *George Edward Grodman* • Peter Lorre *Victor Emmric* • Joan Lorring *Lottie* • George Coulouris *Superintendent Buckley* • Rosalind Ivan *Mrs Benson* • Paul Cavanagh *Clive Russell* • Arthur Shields *Reverend Holbrook* • Morton Lowry *Arthur Kendall* ■ *Dir* Don Siegel • *Scr* Peter Milne, from the novel *The Big Bow Mystery* by Israel Zangwill

Verdict ★★★

Drama 1974 · Fr/It · Colour · 97mins

André Cayatte's tasteless shocker (also known as *Jury of One*) is a far cry from such crusading classics as his *Justice Est Faite*. In his penultimate picture, the great Jean Gabin gives a typically gutsy performance as a judge whose diabetic wife is abducted by a besotted mother, determined to have her student son acquitted when he's charged with rape and murder. Less sure-footed is Sophia Loren, who overdoes the eye-rolling as the kidnapper, and Cayatte also betrays his limitations in the scenes outside the courtroom. In French with English subtitles. Contains violence.

Sophia Loren *Térésa Léoni* • Jean Gabin *Président Leguen* • Henri Garcin *Maître Lannelonge* • Julien Bertheau *Advocate General Verlac* • Michel Albertini *AndréLéoni* • Gisèle Casadesus *Nicole Leguen* • Muriel Catala *Annie Chartier* ■ *Dir* André Cayatte • *Scr* André Cayatte, Henri Coupon, Pierre Dumayet, Paul Andreota

The Verdict ★★★ 15

Courtroom drama
1982 · US · Colour · 123mins

A return to court for Sidney Lumet, director of the masterly *12 Angry Men*. Paul Newman was widely (and wrongly) tipped to win his first Oscar for his portrayal of an alcoholic lawyer on the skids, who fights to redeem himself when a medical malpractice case pits him against the power of the Catholic Church. Scripted by David Mamet, it's a compelling, if wordy, piece, rooted in liberalism and stubbornly refusing to deliver the promised fireworks. Newman's character's self-disgust also becomes a little heavy-going in places. Charlotte Rampling and James Mason are in the fine supporting cast. Contains swearing. ▭

Paul Newman *Frank Galvin* • Charlotte Rampling *Laura Fischer* • Jack Warden *Mickey Morrissey* • James Mason *Ed Concannon* • Milo O'Shea *Judge Hoyle* • Lindsay Crouse *Kaitlin Costello Price* • Edward Binns *Bishop Brophy* • Julie Bovasso *Maureen Rooney* ■ *Dir* Sidney Lumet • *Scr* David Mamet, from the novel by Barry Reed

La Vérité ★★★

Thriller 1960 · Fr/It · BW · 125mins

Henri-Georges Clouzot earned his reputation as one of the darkest French film-makers with such classics as *The Wages of Fear* and *Les Diaboliques* (remade as *Diabolique* starring Sharon Stone). Here, he strays into the courtroom territory usually associated with André Cayatte and rather loses his way in a maze of flashbacks. Brigitte Bardot digs deep into her acting resources as the young girl accused of murdering her sister's trendy boyfriend, but, although she breezes through certain scenes, it's hard to escape the suspicion that the role is beyond her talents. This is intriguing rather than compelling viewing. In French with English subtitles.

Brigitte Bardot *Dominique Marceau* • Charles Vanel *Maitre Guerin, defence attorney* • Paul Meurisse *Eparvier, prosecuting attorney* • Sami Frey *Gilbert Tellier* • Marie-José Nat *Annie Marceau* • Louis Seigner *President of the Court* ■ *Dir* Henri-Georges Clouzot • *Scr*

Henri-Georges Clouzot, Simone Drieu, Michèle Perrein, Jérôme Géronimi, Christiane Rochefort, Simone Marescat, Vera Clouzot

Veronika Voss ★★★ 12

Drama 1982 · W Ger · BW · 100mins

The concluding part of Rainer Werner Fassbinder's trilogy is inspired by the tragic life of Sybille Schmitz, "the German Garbo", whose death eerily presages the director's own, later in the year. As ever, exploiting the conventions of Hollywood melodrama, he draws parallels between the worlds promised by politicians and film-makers alike, as he sets sports writer Hilmar Thate the impossible task of saving faded Nazi star Rosel Zech – from herself and her coterie. With the piercing monochrome conveying both the period and a noirish sense of doom, this is essentially *Sunset Boulevard* on downers. A German language film. ▭

Rosel Zech *Veronika Voss* • Hilmar Thate *Robert Krohn* • Cornelia Froboess *Henriette* • Annemarie Düringer *Dr Marianne Katz* • Doris Schade *Josefa* • Erik Schumann *Dr Edel* ■ *Dir* Rainer Werner Fassbinder • *Scr* Rainer Werner Fassbinder, Peter Marthesheimer, Pea Fröhlich

Vertigo ★★★★★ PG

Classic psychological thriller
1958 · US · Colour · 122mins

This is one of the truly great Hitchcocks, with retired cop James Stewart, who has a terror of heights, hired by Tom Helmore to follow his suicidal wife (Kim Novak). Stewart falls in love with her but can't stop her falling to her death. Some months later he spots a woman (also played by Novak) who bears an uncanny resemblance to the dead woman, but fear of falling plunges him into a complex web of deceit. Novak gives her greatest performance, while the darker side of Stewart shatters his all-American Mr Nice Guy persona. It's a hallucinatory movie, of dreamlike revelations in its glistening San Francisco locations, and it displays Hitchcock's own obsession – love as a fetish that degrades women and deranges men. ▭ *DVD*

James Stewart *John "Scottie" Ferguson* • Kim Novak *Madeleine/Judy* • Barbara Bel Geddes *Midge* • Tom Helmore *Gavin Elster* • Henry Jones *Coroner* • Raymond Bailey *Doctor* • Ellen Corby *Manageress* • Konstantin Shayne *Pop Leibel* • Paul Bryar *Captain Hansen* • Margaret Brayton *Saleswoman* • William Remick *Jury foreman* • Julian Petruzzi *Flower vendor* ■ *Dir* Alfred Hitchcock • *Scr* Alex Coppel, Samuel Taylor, from the novel *D'entre les Morts* by Pierre Boileau, Thomas Narcejac • *Cinematographer* Robert Burks

Very Bad Things ★★★★ 18

Black comedy 1998 · US · Colour · 100mins

This very black comedy, which marked the directorial debut of actor/writer Peter Berg (acclaimed for his role in *The Last Seduction*), is certainly not for the easily-offended. Berg brings together a cool cast – Christian Slater, Jeremy Piven, Daniel Stern, Leland Orser, Jon Favreau – for a twisted and hilarious tale of mayhem that begins when bridegroom Favreau and his pals embark on a stag weekend in Las Vegas, before his marriage to the beautiful but ruthless Cameron Diaz.

Their booze and drug-fuelled party goes awry, however, when an unfortunate accident leaves them with a dead stripper on their hands. Before long, friends are pitted against friends and the body count rises. This gruesome tale is propelled by a sharp script and topnotch performances. Those with a warped sense of humour should be enthralled. ▭

Christian Slater *Robert Boyd* • Cameron Diaz *Laura Garrety* • Daniel Stern *Adam Berkow* • Jeanne Tripplehorn *Lois Berkow* • Jon Favreau *Kyle Fisher* • Jeremy Piven *Michael Berkow* • Leland Orser *Charles Moore* • Lawrence Pressman *Mr Fisher* ■ *Dir/Scr* Peter Berg

A Very Brady Christmas ★★

Comedy 1988 · US · Colour · 94mins

Only die-hard fans of the seventies popular TV sitcom will want to sit though this sappy reunion movie starring all but one of the original cast members. Well, the kids are all grown and return to the family homestead for the Yuletide season. They all have problems, but this being the Brady Bunch, everything is neatly resolved in the end. It's no holiday classic, but it's mindless fun for everyone and Florence Henderson and Robert Reed still look great in polyester.

Florence Henderson *Carol Brady* • Robert Reed *Mike Brady* • Ann B Davis *Alice Nelson* • Maureen McCormick *Marcia* • Eve Plumb *Jan* • Jennifer Runyon *Cindy Brady* • Barry Williams *Greg Brady* • Christopher Knight (2) *Peter Brady* ■ *Dir* Peter Baldwin • *Scr* Sherwood Schwartz, Lloyd J Schwartz, from the TV series by Sherwood Schwartz

A Very Brady Sequel ★★★ 12

Comedy 1996 · US · Colour · 85mins

The second trip to the cinema for American TV's insufferably cheery family of the early seventies is more savagely satirical than its predecessor. Yet the movie still has great affection for its characters, which are wonderfully played by the cast, especially Shelley Long and Gary Cole as parental know-it-alls Carol and Mike Brady. Still stuck in a seventies time warp in the nineties, the Bradys are stunned by the appearance of Carol's former husband, who was previously thought dead. With the subtext getting more than a stir, the narrative hits on drugs, kidnapping, and mutual romantic attraction between step-siblings (Marcia and Greg), all of it bleached and starched by that innocent Brady charm. ▭

Shelley Long *Carol Brady* • Gary Cole *Mike Brady* • Christopher Daniel Barnes *Greg Brady* • Christine Taylor *Marcia Brady* • Paul Sutera *Peter Brady* • Jennifer Elise Cox *Jan Brady* • Jesse Lee *Bobby Brady* • Olivia Hack *Cindy Brady* ■ *Dir* Arlene Sanford • *Scr* Harry Elfont, Deborah Kaplan, James Berg, Stan Zimmerman, from the characters created by Sherwood Schwartz

The Very Edge ★

Drama 1962 · UK · Colour · 89mins

Another British cheapie that hoped to lure audiences into auditoriums with the sort of sensationalist story found in their Sunday papers. Here, we have sexual pervert Jeremy Brett's obsession with pregnant Anne

U = SUITABLE FOR ALL **Uc** = SUITABLE FOR ALL, ESPECIALLY FOR YOUNG CHILDREN (VIDEO ONLY) **PG** = PARENTAL GUIDANCE

Heywood passing from harassment to assault, with the result that she loses her baby. In spite of police insistence that they handle the case, her husband (Richard Todd) takes the law into his own hands. No longer a bankable star, Todd bases his dispirited perfomance in his stock quality of stuffy indignation.

Anne Heywood *Tracey Lawrence* • Richard Todd *Geoffrey Lawrence* • Jack Hedley *McInnes* • Nicole Maurey *Helen* • Jeremy Brett *Mullen* • Barbara Mullen *Dr Shaw* • Maurice Denham *Crawford* ■ *Dir* Cyril Frankel • *Scr* Elizabeth Jane Howard, from a story by Vivian Cox, Leslie Bricusse, Raymond Stross

Very Important Person ★★★ U

Comedy   1961 · UK · BW · 93mins

The key to this winning comedy is a witty script by Jack Davies and Henry Blyth, which cleverly lampoons many of the conventions and stereotypes of the prisoner-of-war pictures that had been one of the staples of the British film industry for over a decade. Stanley Baxter gives one of his best film performances as a camp inmate posing as a high-ranking Nazi in a bid to spring scientist James Robertson-Justice, while the deft comic support from Leslie Phillips, Eric Sykes and the deliciously deadpan Richard Wattis is of a very high order.

James Robertson-Justice *Sir Ernest Pease* • Leslie Phillips *Jimmy Cooper* • Stanley Baxter *Everett/Major Stampel* • Eric Sykes *Willoughby* • Richard Wattis *Woodcock* ■ *Dir* Ken Annakin • *Scr* Jack Davies, Henry Blyth

A Very Private Affair ★★★

Drama   1962 · Fr/It · Colour · 93mins

Brigitte Bardot plays a movie star, an idolised sex symbol, suffering from the pressures of stardom and seeking love. She finds it in Marcello Mastroianni, an intellectual theatre director. There is some fascination in seeing Bardot playing a role that is modelled on herself to some degree, but both she and Mastroianni cannot overcome the shallowness of the screenplay and plot. One of Louis Malle's least distinguished movies, it does have some superb camerawork by Henri Decaë with splendid views of Lake Geneva and Spoleto, where the film's dramatic finale takes place. In French with English subtitles.

Brigitte Bardot *Jill* • Marcello Mastroianni *Fabio* • Gregor von Rezzori *Gricha* • Eléonore Hirt *Cecile* ■ *Dir* Louis Malle • *Scr* Louis Malle, Jean-Paul Rappeneau, Jean Ferry

A Very Special Favor ★★★

Comedy   1965 · US · Colour · 104mins

In the mid-sixties, Rock Hudson made a whole string of farces in which he was coupled with the most seductive actresses Europe had to offer. The aim was to titillate mildly, then vacillate, with Hudson playing his own secret games of sexual deception. In this effort, Hudson is an oil zillionaire, with an eye only for a balance sheet who starts to romance lawyer Charles Boyer's daughter, a psychiatrist played by Caron. The plots of two Billy Wilder-Audrey Hepburn films – *Sabrina Fair* and *Love in the Afternoon* – have been

grafted together and the result is very dated in its general tone.

Rock Hudson *Paul Chadwick* • Leslie Caron *Lauren Boullard* • Charles Boyer *Michel Boullard* • Walter Slezak *Etienne, proprietor* • Dick Shawn *Arnold Plum* • Larry Storch *Harry, taxi driver* ■ *Dir* Michael Gordon • *Scr* Stanley Shapiro, Nate Monaster

The Very Thought of You ★★

Drama   1944 · US · BW · 98mins

Very much of its period, not just in title but also in wartime content, this tale of romance and marriage falls flat due to bland Dennis Morgan. He is seriously undercast as the male lead opposite volatile (and ever underrated these days) Eleanor Parker, whose hairstyle alone makes this worth watching. Skilled director Delmer Daves, almost as well-known for his melodramas as he was for his westerns, doesn't seem to bring too much to the table here, but Dane Clark convinces in a gritty sub-John Garfield sort of way.

Dennis Morgan *Sgt Dave Stewart* • Eleanor Parker *Janet Wheeler* • Dane Clark *"Fixit"* • Faye Emerson *Cora* • Beulah Bondi *Mrs Wheeler* ■ *Dir* Delmer Daves • *Scr* Alvah Bessie, Delmer Daves, from a story by Lionel Wiggam

Vessel of Wrath ★★★★

Comedy drama   1938 · UK · BW · 86mins

The story (by Somerset Maugham) of a spinster missionary and her attempts to reform a drunken beach bum, has obvious similarities to *The African Queen*, and happily this is nearly in the same league as that classic. Elsa Lanchester and Charles Laughton are delightful as the mismatched pair, the quirky Lanchester having her largest (and favourite) screen role. The only film directed by the legendary European producer Erich Pommer, it was a box-office failure, but is a real gem. Robert Newton, who has a supporting role in this version, starred with Glynis Johns in a fair remake titled *The Beachcomber* in 1954.

Charles Laughton *Ginger Ted* • Elsa Lanchester *Martha Jones* • Tyrone Guthrie *Owen Jones, M D* • Robert Newton *Controleur* • Dolly Mollinger *Lia* • Rosita Garcia *Kati* ■ *Dir* Erich Pommer, Bartlett Cormack • *Scr* Bartlett Cormack, B Van Thal, from the short story by W Somerset Maugham

Vestige of Honor ★★★ PG

Drama based on a true story   1990 · US · Colour · 89mins

America wrestles with its conscience over its involvement in Vietnam and Oliver Stone, in particular, has successfully captured the raw, pointless power of the war. This TV movie was tucked away in the American schedules, but it is no less praiseworthy for that. It tells the real-life tale of a US serviceman who returns to Southeast Asia 17 years after the end of the war to see if he can help the Montagnard tribespeople, who had supported the US forces, but were subsequently abandoned to the North Vietnamese. The film's insights into this dark corner of the conflict are sometimes moving, and there are some key moments of suspense. 🖵

Michael Gross *Don Scott* • Gerald McRaney *Chuck Phelan* • Season Hubley *Marilyn Scott* • Kenny Lao *Bryn Scott* • Harsh Nayyar *Ha-Doi* • Cliff Gorman *Sanderson* • Jason Scott Lee *Ha-kuhn* ■ *Dir* Jerry London • *Scr* Steve Brown

La Veuve de Saint-Pierre ★★★ 15

Period romantic drama   2000 · Fr · Colour · mins

Set in 1850, Patrice Leconte's sombre tragedy unfolds against the austere backdrop of Saint-Pierre, a small French island off the Canadian coast. A drunken drifter (played by Yugoslavian film director Emir Kusturica) is found guilty of murder and is sentenced to death. There being neither guillotine nor executioner on the isle, the condemned man is placed in the custody of captain Daniel Auteuil and his wife, Juliette Binoche, who become attached to their prisoner and plot his escape. It's an unusual story, told with empathy and precision, while Binoche and Auteuil are well-matched as the couple who risk all in a selfless and ultimately self-destructive act of compassion. A French language film.

Juliette Binoche *Madame La* • Daniel Auteuil *The Captain* • Emir Kusturica *Neel Auguste* • Michel Duchaussoy *The Governor* • Philippe Magnan *President Venot* ■ *Dir* Patrice Leconte • *Scr* Claude Faraldo

Vibes ★ PG

Adventure comedy
1988 · US · Colour · 95mins

This attempt to launch an acting career for singer Cyndi Lauper, of *Girls Just Want to Have Fun* fame was a disaster. (That song was the inspiration for a 1985 film.) Lauper and Jeff Goldblum play rent-a-psychics hired by Peter Falk to find a legendary lost city of gold. Goldblum survived the debacle. Lauper made *Life with Mikey* and *Off and Running*, but has rarely been seen on screen since. The only vibes you'll get from this fiasco are bad ones. 🖵

Cyndi Lauper *Sylvia Pickel* • Jeff Goldblum *Nick Deezy* • Julian Sands *Dr Harrison Steele* • Googy Gress *Ingo Swedlin* • Peter Falk *Harry Buscafusco* • Michael Lerner *Burt Wilder* • Ramon Bieri *Eli Diamond* • Elizabeth Pena *Consuela* ■ *Dir* Ken Kwapis • *Scr* Lowell Ganz, Babaloo Mandel, from a story by Babaloo Mandel, Deborah Blum, Lowell Ganz

The Vicar of Bray ★★

Period drama   1937 · UK · BW · 66mins

Making extravagantly expansive gestures and projecting to hit the rear of the music hall stalls, Stanley Holloway shows why it took so long for him to establish himself as a screen performer. Here he plays the Irish clergyman who is hired to tutor the future Charles II and finds himself matchmaking in an English Civil War version of *Romeo and Juliet*. The songs are ghastly and the period trappings cheap and inaccurate, but Felix Aylmer and Garry Marsh go some way to atoning.

Stanley Holloway *Bray* • Hugh Miller *King Charles I* • K Hamilton Price *Prince Charles Stuart* • Felix Aylmer *Earl of Brendon* • Margaret Vines *Lady Norah Brendon* • Garry Marsh *Sir Richard Melross* • Esmond Knight *Dennis Melross* • Martin Walker *Sir Patrick*

Condon • Eve Gray *Meg Clancy* • Kitty Kirwan *Molly* ■ *Dir* Henry Edwards • *Scr* H Fowler Mear, from the story by Anson Dyer

Vice Squad ★★

Crime drama   1953 · US · BW · 88mins

A day in the life of a Los Angeles cop, played by Edward G Robinson, and co-starring Paulette Goddard as the owner of an escort agency. Semi-documentary in style and owing much to the earlier and far superior *Detective Story* with Kirk Douglas, it lurches from one murder to the next. It's serious and slightly dull, and Robinson and Goddard have few opportunities to display their talents. Spaghetti western fans should watch for Lee Van Cleef as a heavy. The title was regarded as too racy for Britain so it was renamed *The Girl in Room 17*.

Edward G Robinson *Captain Barnaby* • Paulette Goddard *Mona* • KT Stevens *Ginny* • Porter Hall *Jack Hartrampf* • Adam Williams *Marty Kusalich* • Edward Binns *Al Barkis* • Lee Van Cleef *Pete* ■ *Dir* Arnold Laven • *Scr* Lawrence Roman, from the novel *Harness Bull* by Leslie T White

Vice Squad ★★ 18

Crime thriller   1982 · US · Colour · 86mins

This is the movie that made Wings Hauser a star, deservedly bringing him critical raves as a psychotic pimp who brutally murders one of his prostitutes when she tries to walk out on him. When hooker Season Hubley is forced by police into taking part in a sting operation that results in Hauser's arrest, he plans to catch and kill her when he subsequently escapes custody. It's unusual that an exploitation movie set in the world of prostitution has no nudity or real sex, with more chitchat than action in or out of the bedroom. However, Hauser is a really nasty piece of work, and whenever he's in a scene, the energy level immediately shoots up. 🖵

Season Hubley *Princess* • Gary Swanson *Tom Walsh* • Wings Hauser *Ramrod* • Pepe Serna *Pete Mendez* • Beverly Todd *Louise Williams* • Joseph DiGirolama *Kowalski* • Maurice Emmanuel *Edwards* ■ *Dir* Gary A Sherman [Gary Sherman] • *Scr* Sandy Howard, Robert Vincent O'Neil, Kenneth Peters

Vice Versa ★★★ U

Comedy   1947 · UK · BW · 111mins

This is a wonderful treat, even funnier now than when it first came out and much better than its 1988 Judge Reinhold remake (though inferior to *Big*, which is substantially the same F Anstey tale revisited). Under Peter Ustinov's nimble direction, father and son Roger Livesey and Anthony Newley swap places, and succeed in outraging all and sundry. There are some lovely supporting performances, especially from a bemused, schoolmasterly James Robertson-Justice. Ustinov himself adapted the novel, and in the early days of TV this film was often shown split into segments. This is the way to see it, complete.

Roger Livesey *Paul Bultitude* • Kay Walsh *Mrs Verlayne* • David Hutcheson *Marmaduke Paradine* • Anthony Newley *Dick Bultitude* • James Robertson-Justice *Dr Grimstone* • Petula Clark *Dulcie Grimstone* • Patricia Raine

Alice • Joan Young *Mrs Grimstone* ■ *Dir* Peter Ustinov • *Scr* Peter Ustinov, from the novel by F Anstey

Vice Versa ★★★ PG

Comedy   1988 · US · Colour · 94mins

Although it lacks the charm of the 1947 British film of the same name, this is a better-than-average body-swap movie. Most of it is down to the inspired playing of Judge Reinhold and *The Wonder Years'* Fred Savage, who learn that their respective lives are not quite as enjoyable as they imagine when they switch bodies. The two leads are fresh and convincing in both their personae, and, although sentimentality occasionally raises its head, director Brian Gilbert keeps the action flowing at a pleasing rate. Contains swearing. 🖵

Judge Reinhold *Marshall Seymour* • Fred Savage *Charlie Seymour* • Corinne Bohrer *Sam* • Swoosie Kurtz *Tina* • David Proval *Turk* • Jane Kaczmarek *Robyn* • Gloria Gifford *Marcie* • William Prince *Avery* • Beverly Archer *Mrs Luttrell* • James Hong *Kwo* ■ *Dir* Brian Gilbert • *Scr* Dick Clement, Ian La Frenais

The Vicious Circle ★★

Crime drama   1957 · UK · BW · 84mins

Adapting his own serial, *The Brass Candlestick*, Francis Durbridge was evidently over-attached to his material as there is simply too much plot. John Mills has a fair stab at the Hitchcockian "wrong man", playing a respectable London doctor desperate to discover who is trying to frame him for the murder of an actress whose body has fetched up in his flat. *Carry On* stalwart Gerald Thomas directs with a surprising affinity for the whodunit.

John Mills *Dr Howard Latimer* • Derek Farr *Ken Palmer* • Noelle Middleton *Laura James* • Wilfrid Hyde White *Robert Brady* • Roland Culver *Inspector Dane* • Mervyn Johns *Dr George Kimber* • René Ray *Mrs Ambler* • Lionel Jeffries *Geoffrey Windsor* ■ *Dir* Gerald Thomas • *Scr* Francis Durbridge, from his TV series *The Brass Candlestick*

Victim ★★★ 15

Drama   1961 · UK · BW · 95mins

A ground-breaker in its depiction of homosexuality, this film marks Dirk Bogarde's brave bid to break free of his matinée idol image. He plays a homosexual barrister whose former lover commits suicide after he's arrested to protect Bogarde's name. Bogarde can either say nothing or "come out", putting a strain on his marriage to Sylvia Syms and possibly ending his career. By today's standards the film is tame, and director Basil Dearden insisted that homosexuals should be called "inverts". However, the movie refuses to glamorise its subject, depicting homosexuality in every sidestreet, every Rolls-Royce and every club in town, stopping short only at Downing Street. Contains swearing. 🖵

Dirk Bogarde *Melville Farr* • Sylvia Syms *Laura Farr* • Dennis Price *Calloway* • Anthony Nicholls *Lord Fullbrook* • Peter Copley *Paul Mandrake* • Norman Bird *Harold Doe* • Peter McEnery *Jack Barrett* • Donald Churchill *Eddy Stone* ■ *Dir* Basil Dearden • *Scr* Janet Green, John McCormick

Victim of Beauty ★★★ 15

Thriller based on a true story
1991 · US · Colour · 86mins

There are two TV movies with this title and they were both made in 1991, but this isn't the one starring Jennifer Rubin. Instead, it's an above average true-life tale, set in South Carolina, that tells the story of a bold attempt to rescue a diabetic teenager held hostage by a serial killer. The film is held together by a solid performance from William Devane as the local sheriff forced into using the hostage's beauty-queen sister (*Star Trek: Voyager*'s Seven of Nine, Jeri Lynn Ryan) as bait, and by Roger Young's steady direction, which keeps , sensationalism at bay. Contains violence and nudity. 🖵

William Devane *Sheriff Jim Metts* • Jeri Lynn Ryan [Jeri Ryan] *Dawn Smith* • Michele Abrams *Shari Smith* • Butch Slade *Larry Gene Bell* • Linda Pierce *Hilda Smith* ■ *Dir* Roger Young • *Scr* John Robert Bensink

Victim of Beauty ★★ 15

Thriller   1991 · US · Colour · 93mins

Otherwise known as *Drop Dead Gorgeous*, this is yet another thriller set in and around the world of modelling. Jennifer Rubin is the glamorous girl whose dates all meet various grisly ends, but, unfortunately, co-stars Sally Kellerman and Michael Ironside are the only convincing players in this predictable and low-on-thrills TV fare. Contains violence and nudity. 🖵

Jennifer Rubin *Allie Holton* • Peter Outerbridge *Dylan Wiatt* • Sally Kellerman *Evelyn Ash* • Michael Ironside • Stephen Shellen *Shelby Voit* ■ *Dir* Paul Lynch • *Scr* Thomas Baum, Bill Wells, Mimi Rothman Schapiro, from a story by Harriet Steinberg

Victim of Innocence ★★★

Drama   1990 · US · Colour · 96mins

Anthony John Denison stars as a family man, happily married to Cheryl Ladd, who reads a magazine article and becomes convinced that a familiar-looking picture is that of his daughter, the result of an affair with a Vietnamese woman when he was stationed there during the war. The girl comes to America and Denison's marriage begins to crack. This is a tough, angst-ridden tale, and director Mel Damski manages to keep sentimentality at bay.

Cheryl Ladd *Laura Huntoon* • Anthony John Denison *Barry Huntoon* • Julia Nickson-Soul *Nhung* • Melissa Chan *Tuyet Mai* • Joe Spano *Jim* • Nancy Grahn *Jann* ■ *Dir* Mel Damski • *Scr* Audrey Davis Levin

Victim of Love ★★★ 15

Thriller   1991 · US · Colour · 88mins

Current 007 Pierce Brosnan stars in a role that's far removed from the suave and sophisticated secret agent. He plays a British professor who, following the recent death of his wife, charms his way into the life of psychologist JoBeth Williams, who is unaware that he has a rather sinister side to him. Directed by Jerry London who made the mini-series *Shogun*, this has a fair quota of tense moments, and Brosnan is perfect as the villain. Contains swearing, nudity. 🖵

Pierce Brosnan *Paul Tomlinson* • JoBeth Williams *Tess Palmer* • Virginia Madsen *Carla Simmons* • Georgia Brown *Emma Walters* • Murphy Cross *Roz Fleisher* • Ruben Pla *Carousel Attendant* ■ *Dir* Jerry London • *Scr* James J Desmarais, Alison Rosenfeld Desmarais

Victim of Love: the Shannon Mohr Story ★★ PG

Crime drama based on a true story
1993 · US · Colour · 88mins

Amazingly, this seemingly wildly fictional TV movie is based on a series of true events. In 1980, a woman was killed during a horse-riding accident. Her parents insisted she was murdered by her new husband for the insurance money, and ten years later the story was aired on the US TV series *Unsolved Mysteries*. The husband was ultimately brought to justice. This rendition plays true to the known facts, but is, alas, rather uninspiringly told. 🖵

Dwight Schultz *Dave Davis* • Bonnie Bartlett *Lucille Mohr* • Andy Romano *Bob Mohr* • Sally Murphy *Shannon Mohr Davis* • Dennis Boutsikaris *Jack Mandel* • Gregg Henry *Detective Don Brooks* ■ *Dir* John Cosgrove • *Scr* Bryce Zabel

Victim of Rage ★★ 18

Drama based on a true story
1994 · US · Colour · 90mins

The plotline of the good woman falling for the bad man, is one of cinema's oldest stand-bys. As its alternative title *Cries Unheard: the Donna Yaklich Story* suggests, this revenge drama is based on the true story of a Los Angeles woman for whom a blind date is the start of a nightmare. Jaclyn Smith suffers glamorously, while Brad Johnson chews the scenery as the husband whose body-building pills turn him into a maniac. Yet more proof that the truth doesn't always make great drama. Contains violence. 🖵

Jaclyn Smith *Donna Yaklich* • Brad Johnson *Dennis Yaklich* • David Lascher *Denny Yaklich* • Hilary Swank ■ *Dir* Armand Mastroianni • *Scr* Christopher Canaan

Victim of the Haunt ★★ 15

Horror   1996 · US · Colour · 88mins

Suburbanites get drawn into supernatural events in this fair-to-middling spin on the now familiar *Poltergeist* theme. Sharon Lawrence plays a woman recovering from a nervous breakdown after a miscarriage, who discovers that her new home is possessed by an evil spirit, but husband Beau Bridges and her doctor are convinced she is suffering a relapse. Both the cast and the effects are better than average and director Larry Shaw works hard to sustain the chill factor. 🖵

Beau Bridges *Charley* • Sharon Lawrence *Patricia* ■ *Dir* Larry Shaw • *Scr* Karen Clark

Victor Frankenstein ★★

Horror   1977 · Ire/Swe · Colour · 92mins

Elegantly photographed, but dull European co-production of Mary Shelley's classic tale of terror directed by American ex-pat Calvin Floyd, was promoted as being the most faithful version ever committed to film. Too melodramatic and psychologically straightforward to qualify as authentic, Per Oscarsson plays The Creature as a juvenile delinquent, brutally railing against his experimental creator, Leon Vitali, and society in general. This pretentious reading was a festival favourite, but not an audience one.

Leon Vitali *Victor Frankenstein* • Per Oscarsson *Monster* • Nicholas Clay *Henry* • Stacy Dorning *Elisabeth* • Jan Ohlsson *William* • Olof Bergström *Father* ■ *Dir* Calvin Floyd • *Scr* Calvin Floyd, Yvonne Floyd, from the novel *Frankenstein* by Mary Shelley • *Cinematographer* Tony Forsberg

Victor/Victoria ★★★ 15

Comedy   1982 · UK · Colour · 128mins

Julie Andrews as a bloke? Although this decision earns it an honourable mention in the hall of fame for monumental pieces of miscasting, this typically crude Blake Edwards comedy remains quite a hoot. Andrews is the struggling singer who leaps to fame and fortune in thirties Paris when she decides to impersonate a man impersonating a woman. James Garner is the very heterosexual American troubled by his attraction to him/her. There are a few songs to keep more traditional Andrews fans happy, plus an outrageously camp turn from Robert Preston and some fine supporting performances from Lesley Ann Warren, John Rhys-Davies and, in particular, Alex Karras. 🖵

Julie Andrews *Victor/Victoria* • James Garner *King Marchan* • Robert Preston *Carroll "Toddy" Todd* • Lesley Ann Warren *Norma* • Alex Karras *Squash* • John Rhys-Davies *André Cassell* • Graham Stark *Waiter* ■ *Dir* Blake Edwards • *Scr* Blake Edwards, from the film *Viktor und Viktoria* by Reinhold Schünzel • *Music* Henry Mancini

Victoria the Great ★★★ U

Historical biographical drama
1937 · UK · BW and Colour · 105mins

When Laurence Housman first wrote his play *Victoria Regina*, it was banned by the Lord Chamberlain as, in 1935, the royal family could not be shown on the British stage. But the play was a hit on Broadway and such was the enthusiasm of King Edward VIII, he commissioned producer and director Herbert Wilcox to make it into a film to commemorate the centenary of Victoria's accession to the throne. Anna Neagle takes Victoria from girlhood to old age, and the drama concentrates on her personal relationship with Prince Albert (Anton Walbrook). It's all fairly tame, and a long way from the rough ride given to the royals of today. Yet Neagle's sympathy for the monarch shines through, and the final reel, which bursts into glorious Technicolor for the Diamond Jubilee, is a delightful piece of patriotic pomp. 🖵

Anna Neagle *Queen Victoria* • Anton Walbrook *Prince Albert* • Walter Rilla *Prince Ernest* • Mary Morris *Duchess of Kent* • HB Warner *Lord Melbourne* • Grete Wegener *Baroness Lehzen* • CV France *Archbishop of Canterbury* • James Dale *Duke of Wellington* • Charles Carson *Sir Robert Peel* • Hubert Harben *Lord Conyngham* • Felix Aylmer *Lord Palmerston* ■ *Dir* Herbert Wilcox • *Scr* Miles Malleson, Charles de Grandcourt, from the play *Victoria Regina* by Laurence Housman

U = SUITABLE FOR ALL   Uc = SUITABLE FOR ALL, ESPECIALLY FOR YOUNG CHILDREN (VIDEO ONLY)   PG = PARENTAL GUIDANCE

The Victors ★★★
War epic   1963 · US/UK · BW · 175 mins

After writing *The Bridge on the River Kwai* and writing-producing *The Guns of Navarone*, Carl Foreman was ready to make his big statement as a director. The result is one of the most ambitious war movies ever made, shot in black-and-white with an all-star cast and designed to show how war degrades people on all sides. A shot of victors and vanquished – both exhausted and looking like vagrants – rams home the point. Subtlety was never on Foreman's agenda and three hours of episodic hectoring and ironic twists of fate do get a bit wearisome. However, there are some stunning sequences such as a firing squad in the snow with Frank Sinatra's *Have Yourself a Merry Christmas* on the soundtrack.

George Hamilton *Cpl Trower* • George Peppard *Cpl Chase* • Jeanne Moreau *Frenchwoman* • Romy Schneider *Regine* • Melina Mercouri *Magda* • Eli Wallach *Sgt Craig* • Vincent Edwards [Vince Edwards] *Baker* • Rosanna Schiaffino *Maria* • Maurice Ronet *French Lt Cohn* • Peter Fonda *Weaver* • Senta Berger *Trudi* • Elke Sommer *Helga* • Albert Finney *Russian soldier* ■ *Dir* Carl Foreman • *Scr* Carl Foreman, from the novel *The Human Kind: a Sequence* by Alexander Baron

Victory ★★
Drama   1940 · US · BW · 78mins

Fredric March is Hendrik Heyst, the perpetual exile who lives on an island in the Malay archipelago, contentedly detached from life until he rescues an English girl and has to cope with three rogues sent by local strongman Sig Ruman. Time and time again, Joseph Conrad's deeply metaphysical dramas prove tough nuts to crack, though in this case the studio-imposed restriction on length doomed everyone to failure before the cameras started rolling.

Fredric March *Hendrik Heyst* • Betty Field *Alma* • Sir Cedric Hardwicke [Cedric Hardwicke] *Mr Jones* • Jerome Cowan *Martin Ricardo* • Sig Rumann [Ruman Sig] *Mr Schomberg* • Margaret Wycherly *Mrs Schomberg* ■ *Dir* John Cromwell • *Scr* John L Balderston, from the novel by Joseph Conrad

Victory ★★ 15
Period romance
1995 · UK/Fr/Ger · Colour · 94mins

Sluggish screen version of the Joseph Conrad novel, which focuses on a Dutch East Indies recluse who rescues a woman from bothersome baddies and offers her refuge on his remote island. Unfortunately, the island obviously isn't remote enough, and their troubles soon come looking for them. Although Willem Dafoe, Sam Neill, Irène Jacob and Rufus Sewell comprise an attractive cast, they're given little to get their teeth into by a film that's long on steamy languor, but short on characterisation. Contains violence and nudity. ▭

Willem Dafoe *Axel Heyst* • Sam Neill *Mr Jones* • Irène Jacob *Alma* • Rufus Sewell *Martin Ricardo* • Jean Yanne *Schomberg* • Ho Yi *Wang* • Bill Paterson *Captain Davidson* ■ *Dir* Mark Peploe • *Scr* Mark Peploe, from the novel by Joseph Conrad

Victory at Entebbe ★
Drama based on a true story
1976 · US · Colour · 118mins

In June 1976, Palestinian and German terrorists hijacked an Air France airbus and flew to Idi Amin's Uganda. After six days, an Israeli commando unit stormed the airport at Entebbe to free the hostages. Within five months two lousy movies had been made – *Raid on Entebbe* and this one, both for American TV, but released in cinemas elsewhere. The movie reduces everything to the level of a daytime soap opera, but with an all-star cast.

Kirk Douglas *Hershel Vilnofsky* • Burt Lancaster *Shimon Peres* • Elizabeth Taylor *Edra Vilnofsky* • Anthony Hopkins *Yitzhak Rabin* • Richard Dreyfuss *Colonel Yonatan "Yonni" Netanyahu* • Helen Hayes *Mrs Wise* • Theodore Bikel *Yakov Shlomo* • Julius Harris *President Idi Amin* • Linda Blair *Chana Vilnofsky* • Harris Yulin *General Dan Shomron* • Helmut Berger *German terrorist* ■ *Dir* Marvin J Chomsky • *Scr* Ernest Kinoy

The Victory of Women ★★★
Drama   1946 · Jap · Colour · 80mins

Returning to the director's chair for the first time after the Second World War, Kenji Mizoguchi's innate sympathy for the plight of women in Japanese society again came to the fore in this indictment of the prejudicial legal system and the sinister legacy of old-style militarism. Kinuyo Tanaka gives a typically feisty performance as the lawyer defending a poverty-stricken mother who killed her baby in a desperate fit of grief following the death of her husband. Intriguingly, the verdict is never revealed. In Japanese with English subtitles.

Kinuyo Tanaka *Hiroko Hosokawa* • Michiko Kuwano *Michiko* • Mitsuko Miura *Moto Asakura* • Shin Tokudaiji *Keita Yamaoka* • Toyoko Takahashi *Mother* • Yoshihira Matsumoto [Katsuhira Matsumoto] *Prosecutor Kono* ■ *Dir* Kenji Mizoguchi • *Scr* Kogo Noda, Kaneto Shindo

Victory through Air Power ★★★ U
Part-animated wartime documentary
1943 · US · Colour · 65mins

Along with the Donald Duck cartoon, *Der Fuehrer's Face*, this is the best known of the many propaganda and training films produced by the Disney studio during the Second World War. Although it begins with a comic history of aviation, the real purpose of the picture was to convince the top brass of the viability of Major Alexander de Seversky's theories on strategic long-range bombing and how it could disrupt enemy weapons production and supply lines, as well as demoralise the civilian population. The mix of live action, knockabout cartooning and serious graphics worked on wartime audiences and remains surprisingly powerful today.

Dir Clyde Geronimi, Jack Kinney, James Algar • *Scr* Perce Pearce, from the non-fiction book by Major Alexander de Seversky

Videodrome ★★★★ 18
Horror thriller   1982 · Can · Colour · 83mins

With its subject matter of screen violence, this remains one of David Cronenberg's most personal, complex and disturbing films, even if it doesn't always make a lot of sense. James Woods is the amoral cable programmer who gets drawn to a sickening sadomasochistic channel called "Videodrome", which turns out to have a much more sinister purpose. Cronenberg uses this framework to explore his favourite themes (new technology fusing with the human body, voyeurism, the links between sex and violence) and, although the plot begins to unravel, the startling imagery and Woods's fierce performance make for a deeply unsettling experience. The supporting cast includes Blondie singer Debbie Harry as Woods's girlfriend. Contains swearing and graphic and disturbing images. ▭

James Woods *Max Renn* • Sonja Smits *Bianca O'Blivion* • Deborah Harry *Nicki Brand* • Peter Dvorsky *Harlan* • Les Carlson *Barry Convex* • Jack Creley *Brian O'Blivion* • Lynne Gorman *Masha* ■ *Dir/Scr* David Cronenberg

Vidheyan ★★★
Drama   1993 · Ind · Colour · 112mins

Novelist Zachariah objected to this adaptation of his story, but it remains a powerful indictment of political indolence. Having already excelled in Adoor Gopalakrishnan's previous two pictures, *Anantaram* and *The Walls*, Mammooty gives a towering performance as the tyrannical village landlord, who not only enslaves the timid Gopha Kumar (a Christian immigrant from Kerala), but also compels him to participate in the murder of his kindly wife, Tanvi Azmi, and the prostitution of Kumar's own bride, Sabita Anand. Commenting on the tinderbox situation in South Karnataka, this is stirring good versus evil melodrama, even if you're not *au fait* with the historical background. A Malayalam language film.

Mammooty *Bhaska Patelar* • Gopha Kumar *Thommie* • Tanvi Azmi *Sarojakka* • Sabita Anand *Omana* ■ *Dir* Adoor Gopalakrishnan • *Scr* Adoor Gopalakrishnan, from a story by Zachariah

La Vie de Château ★★★★
Wartime comedy drama
1965 · Fr · BW · 92mins

A gripping and extremely evocative comedy drama about the French Resistance set in the crumbling Normandy manor house owned by the staid Philippe Noiret and his beautiful wife, Catherine Deneuve. Into their midst arrives a Free French agent on a mission from England to prepare for D-Day. Deneuve falls in love with him and things are further complicated by the Germans who suddenly take over the château. Part wartime thriller, part marital drama, it's about the bravery and heroism that lies dormant in everyone. Three of the writers were directors but this marked Jean-Paul Rappeneau's debut, who would go on to make *Cyrano de Bergerac* in 1990. A French language film.

Catherine Deneuve *Marie* • Philippe Noiret *Jerome* • Pierre Brasseur *Dimanche* • Mary Marquet *Charlotte* • Henri Garcin *Julien* • Carlos Thompson *Klopstock* ■ *Dir* Jean-Paul Rappeneau • *Scr* Jean-Paul Rappeneau, Alain Cavalier, Claude Sautet, Daniel Boulanger

La Vie de Jésus ★★★
Drama   1996 · Fr · Colour · 96 mins.

Although the title for this pseudo-Bressonian study of teenage ennui was borrowed from philologist Ernest Renan's 1863 historical contextualising of the gospels, the action was inspired by debuting director Bruno Dumont's time as a teacher of similarly disaffected small-town kids. Despite looking older, David Douche is the skinheaded 19-year-old leader of a scooter gang in Bailleul, northern France. His relationship with cashier Marjorie Cottreel is based on perfunctory sex and he responds to her interest in Arab teenager Kader Chaatouf with a violence that's both proprietorial and racist. As surly a study of spiritual humanism as cinema has seen. In French with English subtitles. Contains violence.

David Douche *Freddy* • Marjorie Cottreel *Marie* • Kader Chaatouf *Kader* • Sébastien Delbaere *Gégé* • Samuel Boidin *Michou* • Steve Smagghe *Robert* • Sébastien Bailleul *Quinquin* • Geneviève Cottreel *Yvette, Freddy's mother* ■ *Dir/Scr* Bruno Dumont

La Vie Est à Nous ★★★
Propaganda   1936 · Fr · BW · 62mins

Although Jean Renoir was never a member of the French Communist Party, he was asked by them to supervise this propaganda film of sketches, newsreels and political speeches. Despite the fact that there were eight directors on the project, including the great still photographer Henri Cartier-Bresson, with the styles ranging from French naturalism to Russian Socialist Realism, the collaborative effort has the stamp of Renoir on it. An interesting and uneven document of the day, it glows with enthusiasm and optimism (the Popular Front had just won a victory in the Spanish election). Banned soon after, it resurfaced after May 1968. In French with English subtitles.

Julien Bertheau *Unemployed worker* • Marcel Duhamel *Garage owner* • O'Brady *Washer* • Jean Dasté *Schoolteacher* • Emile Drain *Worker* • Jean Renoir *Bistro owner* ■ *Dir* Jean Renoir, Jean-Paul Le Chanois, Jacques Becker, André Zwobada, Pierre Unik, Henri Cartier-Bresson, P Vaillant-Couturier, Jacques Brunius • *Scr* Jean Renoir, Jean-Paul Le Chanois, Jacques Becker, André Zwobada, Pierre Unik, P Vaillant-Couturier, Henri Cartier-Bresson, Jacques Brunius

La Vie Est Belle ★★★ PG
Comedy musical
1987 · Bel/Fr/Zaire · Colour · 82mins

Papa Wemba leaves his village for Kinshasa to pursue his ambition to become a recording star, only to have to work as a houseboy. He falls in love with Bibi Krubwa, a girl who gives him the money to form a band, but her mother forces an end to the relationship until a witch doctor intervenes to help the unhappy Kourou. Co-written and co-directed by Belgian-born Benoit Lamy and Zaire's Ngangura Mweze, this is an interesting insight into an unfamiliar culture. It's charming, cheerful and well-played, particularly by Wemba, a Paris-based international pop star. In French with English subtitles.

Papa Wemba *Kourou* • Bibi Krubwa *Kabibi* • Landu Nzunzimbu Matshia *Mamou* • Kanku Kasongo *Nvouandou* • Lokinda Mengi Feza *Nzazi* • Kalimazi Lombume *Mongali* ■ *Dir* Benoit Lamy, Ngangura Mweze • *Scr* Benoit Lamy, Maryse Léon, Ngangura Mweze

The View from Pompey's Head ★★

Drama 1955 · US · Colour · 96mins

Major stars weren't available for this film version of a popular novel by Hamilton Basso, so writer/producer/director Philip Dunne attempted to create one out of little-known British actress Dana Wynter and promoted action player Richard Egan to the male lead. Wynter is highly proficient as a Southern belle but lacks that extra something. Egan is monotonous as the successful lawyer returning to his home town and his old love. Their rekindled passion proves less interesting than the revelation of a deep secret in the past of Sidney Blackmer's elderly novelist.
Richard Egan *Anson Page* • Dana Wynter *Dinah* • Cameron Mitchell *Mickey Higgins* • Sidney Blackmer *Garvin Wales* • Marjorie Rambeau *Lucy Wales* • Rosemarie Bowe *Kit* ■ *Dir* Philip Dunne • *Scr* Philip Dunne, from a novel by Hamilton Basso

A View to a Kill ★★★〔PG〕

Spy adventure 1985 · UK · Colour · 125mins

A below-average Bond movie, with Roger Moore as 007 for the seventh and final time. His smoothness is now a bit tired, but there's still some action and excitement to be had. The baddies are headed by Christopher Walken and his accomplice, girlfriend Grace Jones, and, while both can look pretty scary, you don't get the impression that they're particularly evil. Patrick Macnee, of TV's *The Avengers* fame, fares a lot better as Bond's right-hand man, and Tanya Roberts does what Bond girls do pretty well. But the plot doesn't really convince, perhaps because we've seen it or something similar so many times before. 〔▭〕
Roger Moore *James Bond* • Christopher Walken *Max Zorin* • Tanya Roberts *Stacey Sutton* • Grace Jones *May Day* • Patrick Macnee *Tibbett* • David Yip *Chuck Lee* • Fiona Fullerton *Pola Ivanova* • Willoughby Gray *Dr Carl Mortner* • Desmond Llewelyn *"Q"* • Robert Brown *"M"* • Lois Maxwell *Miss Moneypenny* • Walter Gotell *General Gogol* ■ *Dir* John Glen • *Scr* Richard Maibaum, Michael G Wilson, from characters created by Ian Fleming

Vigil ★★★〔15〕

Drama 1984 · NZ · Colour · 86mins

An early film from Vincent Ward, director of the excellent *The Navigator – a Medieval Odyssey* and *Map of the Human Heart*, and the ghastly *What Dreams May Come*. Ward's noted for his visual style, and there's plenty on which to feast the eyes in this attractive tale of a New Zealand farm girl struggling to adapt when a young drifter fills the family place vacated by her recently-dead dad. Absorbing. 〔▭〕
Penelope Stewart *Elizabeth Peers* • Frank Whitten *Ethan Ruir* • Fiona Kay *Lisa Peers, "Toss"* • Bill Kerr *Birdie* • Gordon Shields *Justin Peers* ■ *Dir* Vincent Ward • *Scr* Vincent Ward, Graeme Tetley, Fiona Lindsay

Vigil in the Night ★★★

Medical melodrama 1940 · US · BW · 95mins

Well adapted from an AJ Cronin novel, this exciting melodrama features the marvellous Carole Lombard as a committed nurse who takes the blame for a fatal mistake made by her sister Anne Shirley. The RKO studio's re-creation of England is, unusually for a Hollywood film of this period, remarkably convincing, and the British support cast headed by handsome doctor Brian Aherne is also excellent. (Watch out for a very young Peter Cushing.) Director George Stevens would go on to make bigger and more prestigious movies like *Shane* and *Giant*, but his skill at storytelling was honed at RKO, and this is a good example of his earlier work. His straightforward, no-nonsense cinematic style makes this very satisfying.
Carole Lombard *Anne Lee* • Anne Shirley *Lucy Lee* • Brian Aherne *Dr Prescott* • Julien Mitchel *Matthew Bowley* • Robert Coote *Dr Caley* • Rita Page *Glennie* • Peter Cushing *Joe Shand* ■ *Dir* George Stevens • *Scr* Fred Guiol, PJ Wolfson, Rowland Leigh, from the novel by AJ Cronin

Vigilante Cop ★★★〔15〕

Thriller based on a true story 1991 · US · Colour · 90mins

Also known as *Shoot First: a Cop's Vengeance*, this tough TV movie relates the true story of a rogue police officer who, in 1979, took the law into his own hands in the Texas town of San Antonio. There have been dozens of films made about buddies who find themselves in deadly confrontation and director Mel Damski has nothing new to say on the subject. However, he does generate a sinister lawless atmosphere and coaxes energetic performances from Alex McArthur as the death-wish cop and Dale Midkiff as the police academy pal faced with ending his reign of terror. 〔▭〕
Alex McArthur *Stephen Smith* • Dale Midkiff *Farrell Tucker* • Lucinda Jenny *Beth Tucker* • Loryn Locklin *Lea* • GD Spradlin *Chief Hogan* • Terry O'Quinn *Sgt Ray Nicholas* ■ *Dir* Mel Damski • *Scr* Joe Gunn, Gary Michael White

Vigilante Force ★★〔18〕

Adventure drama 1975 · US · Colour · 85mins

Kris Kristofferson is the Vietnam vet brought in by his brother (Jan-Michael Vincent) to fight off lawless oil workers in a booming California town in this awkward combination of western and war genres from director George Armitage. Highlighting male bonding and nasty violence above a cohesive story, at heart it's a self-conscious retelling of the Cain and Abel saga. But Kristofferson acquits himself well, as does Bernadette Peters in a barnstorming portrayal as a down-at-heel cabaret artist. It also marked one of the last feature film roles for future *Dallas* star and TV-movie regular Victoria Principal, who plays Vincent's girlfriend. Contains violence and swearing. 〔▭〕
Kris Kristofferson *Aaron Arnold* • Jan-Michael Vincent *Ben Arnold* • Victoria Principal *Linda Christopher* • Bernadette Peters *Little Dee* • Brad Dexter *Mayor Bradford* • Judson Pratt *Harry Lee* ■ *Dir/Scr* George Armitage

The Vigilantes Return ★★〔U〕

Western 1947 · US · Colour · 66mins

A pretty average western, with marshal Jon Hall hiding his true identity to trap villain Robert Wilcox, whose saloon is the front for an outlaw lair. Nothing special, but efficiently done, and notable for appearances from throaty, rotund *Stagecoach* character actor Andy Devine and, in one of his earliest roles, terrific baddie Jack Lambert. The girl, Margaret Lindsay, is in cahoots with the baddies, but since she's an old flame of our hero's, you can guess what happens.
Jon Hall *Johnnie Taggart* • Margaret Lindsay *Kitty* • Paula Drew *Louise Holden* • Andy Devine *Andy* • Robert Wilcox *Clay Curtwright* • Jonathan Hale *Judge Holden* • Arthur Hohl *Sheriff* ■ *Dir* Ray Taylor • *Scr* Roy Chanslor

Vigo: Passion for Life ★★〔15〕

Biographical drama 1997 · UK/Jap/Fr/Sp/Ger · Colour · 103mins

Sadly, this filmic essay on the tragic life of thirties French film director Jean Vigo fails to improve on director Julien Temple's earlier efforts (*Absolute Beginners* and *Earth Girls Are Easy*). Though imaginatively shot, this is ultimately a depressing, dragging tale of Vigo and his wife Lydu's terminal tuberculosis and how the couple wrestle to love and live under feelings of acute mortality. Though lifted by earnest and endearing performances from leads James Frain and Romane Bohringer, the film fails to convey the revolutionary legacy Vigo left behind him; he died at 29, having already made classics *Zéro de Conduite* and *L'Atalante*. Try to see those films rather than this one. Contains swearing and sex scenes.
Romane Bohringer *Lydu Lozinska* • James Frain *Jean Vigo* • Diana Quick *Emily* • William Scott-Masson *Marcel* • James Faulkner *Dr Gerard* • Jim Carter *Bonaventure* • Paola Dionisotti *Marie* • Lee Ross *Oscar Levy* ■ *Dir* Julien Temple • *Scr* Peter Ettedgui, Anne Devlin, Julien Temple, from the play *Love's a Revolution* by Chris Ward, from the biography *Jean Vigo* by Paulo Emilio Salles Gomes

The Viking Queen ★

Historical adventure 1967 · UK · Colour · 91mins

There's only one reason for catching this risible offering from Hammer and that's the chance to spot the Viking wearing a wristwatch! Otherwise, there's little pleasure to be gained from watching such seasoned performers as Niall MacGinnis, Donald Houston and Adrienne Corri making fools of themselves in a story that would struggle to get a pass grade in GCSE English. The romance between Roman governor Don Murray and tribal queen Carita is silly enough, but her feuds with the local druids are so po-faced you'll either nod off or double up with laughter. Thank goodness they don't make 'em like this any more.
Don Murray *Justinian* • Carita *Salina* • Donald Houston *Maelgan* • Andrew Keir *Octavian* • Adrienne Corri *Beatrice* • Niall MacGinnis *Tiberion* • Wilfrid Lawson *King Priam* • Nicola Pagett *Talia* • Patrick Troughton *Tristram* ■ *Dir* Don Chaffey • *Scr* Clarke Reynolds, from a story by John Temple-Smith

The Viking Sagas ★★★〔15〕

Historical adventure 1995 · Ice/US · Colour · 79mins

An entertaining mix of utter tosh and surprising historical accuracy, this American-Icelandic co-production opens with an explicit death sequence that has to be seen to be disbelieved. The story focuses on an warrior prince who vows vengeance when his father is murdered and his people are run off their land. The action scenes are exciting, but performances are dreary in comparison and the pacing is rather pedestrian. It looks good, however, perhaps because director Michael Chapman was cinematographer on such Martin Scorsese films as *Taxi Driver* and *Raging Bull*. 〔▭〕
Ralph Moeller *Kjartan* • Sven-Ole Thorsen *Gunnar* • Ingibjorg Stefansdottir *Gudrun* • Thorir Waagfjord *Bolli* ■ *Dir* Michael Chapman • *Scr* Paul R Gurian, Dale Herd

Viking Women and the Sea Serpent ★

Adventure 1957 · US · BW · 65mins

A rock-bottom Roger Corman entry that was an attempt to set a standard escape story in a distinct historical time period. Unfortunately the paltry budget meant all Norse fact had finally to be ignored and enough cheap fantasy tossed in to please the horror crowd. Hence the last minute appearance of the cheesy sea monster. Badly lit, ultra-phoney (the cast members all wear blond wigs) and with dialogue mostly consisting of "Huh", this is a seldom-seen Corman quickie. You'll soon realise why.
Abby Dalton *Desir* • Susan Cabot *Enger* • Brad Jackson *Vedric* • June Kenney *Asmild* • Richard Devon *Stark* ■ *Dir* Roger Corman • *Scr* Lawrence Goldman, from a story by Irving Block

The Vikings ★★★★★〔PG〕

Historical epic 1958 · US · Colour · 110mins

This tremendously exciting, albeit gory, adventure epic was a huge hit for independent producer/star Kirk Douglas, who generously changed the title of Edison Marshall's novel *The Viking* in order to include his friends Tony Curtis as Eric the Viking, Janet Leigh (Mrs Curtis) as the lovely Princess Morgana, and Ernest Borgnine as King Ragnar. Jack Cardiff's location photography is superb (real fjords!), and Harper Goff's splendid art direction gives a remarkably authentic sense of period. There is a fine feel of lusty enjoyment pervading this movie, and it's hard to see how it could have been made any better. That uncredited title narration, by the way, is by Orson Welles. Contains violence. 〔▭〕
Tony Curtis *Eric* • Kirk Douglas *Einar* • Ernest Borgnine *Ragnar* • Janet Leigh *Morgana* • James Donald *Egbert* • Alexander Knox *Father Godwin* • Frank Thring *Aella* ■ *Dir* Richard Fleischer • *Scr* Calder Willingham, Dale Wasserman, from the novel *The Viking* by Edison Marshall

Villa! ★★

Western 1958 · US · Colour · 71mins

A rattling, far-from-accurate account of Pancho Villa's conversion to the Mexican revolutionary cause. As played

〔U〕 = SUITABLE FOR ALL, 〔Uc〕 = SUITABLE FOR ALL, ESPECIALLY FOR YOUNG CHILDREN (VIDEO ONLY) 〔PG〕 = PARENTAL GUIDANCE

by Rodolfo Hoyos, Villa is more of a rogue than a rebel, chasing money and women in equal measure; but the focus here is on gun-runner Brian Keith, moved by the suffering of the peasants around him to take sides with Hoyos against the oppressive regime. Editor turned director James B Clark keeps the action moving, but there's little here – the charms of Cesar Romero aside – to distinguish this from similar run-of-the-mill fare.
Brian Keith *Bill Harmon* • Cesar Romero *Fierro Lopez* • Margia Dean *Julie North* • Rodolfo Hoyos *Pancho Villa* • Rosenda Monteros *Mariana* • Carlos Muzquiz *Cabo* • Elisa Loti *Manuela* • Enrique Lucero *Tenorio* ■ *Dir* James B Clark • *Scr* Louis Vittes

Villa Rides ★★ 15
Western   1968 · US · Colour · 116mins

A paella western, with Yul Brynner wearing a wig and a sadistic sneer as the Mexican folk hero. The original script was written by Sam Peckinpah, who hoped to direct it; but Brynner objected to Peckinpah's story. A TV director (Buzz Kulik) was brought in and Robert Towne who later wrote *Chinatown* gave the script a make-over. The result is a botched job, watchable only for a few rousing action scenes and for Robert Mitchum's sleepy-eyed gun-runner who literally flies in and out of the story. Contains violence and swearing.
Yul Brynner *Pancho Villa* • Robert Mitchum *Lee Arnold* • Maria Buccella [Grazia Buccella] *Fina Gonzalez* • Charles Bronson *Fierro* • Robert Viharo *Urbina* • Frank Wolff *Captain Francisco Ramirez* • Herbert Lom *General Huerta* • Alexander Knox *President Francisco Madero* • Fernando Rey *Colonel Fuentes* ■ *Dir* Buzz Kulik • *Scr* Robert Towne, Sam Peckinpah, from the book *Pancho Villa* by William Douglas Lansford

Village in the Mist ★★★
Drama   1983 · S Kor · Colour · 90mins

Im Kwon-taek had already directed more than 70 films by the time he made this startlingly graphic commercial success, which many critics have cited as a South Korean take on *Straw Dogs*. Dark secrets lurk beneath the surface calm of the remote village to which Chong Yun-hee is dispatched as a supply teacher, but they begin to emerge after she's raped by a sinister outsider, Ahn Sung-kee. As ever Im's preoccupation is with the way in which tradition and culture impact upon modern society, although the main focus of this technically dazzling film is on the status of women within the Confucian morality system. In Korean with English subtitles.
Ahn Sung-kee *Sinister outsider* • Chong Yun-hee *Teacher* ■ *Dir* Im Kwon-taek • *Scr* Song Kil-han, from the book *Island without a Name* by I Mun-yol

Village of the Damned ★★★★
Science-fiction horror
1960 · UK · BW · 77mins

Twelve women give birth to blond alien offspring after a strange force puts their community into a 24-hour trance, in this remarkably faithful adaptation of John Wyndham's novel *The Midwich Cuckoos*. In a film that is compelling,

creepy and often unbearably tense, an icy George Sanders becomes their teacher and then tries to halt their world domination plans. Superbly acted, with the human/family side of the horror unusually explored more than the fantasy elements, this British near-classic is a sci-fi treat and remains so. Contains violence.
George Sanders *Gordon Zellaby* • Barbara Shelley *Anthea Zellaby* • Martin Stephens *David* • Michael Gwynn *Major Alan Bernard* • Laurence Naismith *Dr Willers* • Richard Warner *Harrington* • Jenny Laird *Mrs Harrington* • Sarah Long *Evelyn Harrington* ■ *Dir* Wolf Rilla • *Scr* Wolf Rilla, Stirling Silliphant, George Barclay, from the novel *The Midwich Cuckoos* by John Wyndham

Village of the Damned ★★ 15
Science-fiction horror
1995 · US · Colour · 93mins

Those blond alien youngsters return to wreak havoc in a small town in cult director John Carpenter's pointless update of the 1960 British sci-fi near-classic based on John Wyndham's famous novel *The Midwich Cuckoos*. Despite the setting being transferred to California, superior special effects heightening the nastiness (Kirstie Alley's hard-to-watch self-autopsy) and Christopher Reeve (the film was released in the States just prior to his tragic riding accident) giving a nicely heroic performance, the end result forgoes the touches and stylish atmosphere you might expect from Carpenter for a bland TV movie-style sheen, relieved only by hints of comedy. Stick with the original. Contains violence.
Christopher Reeve *Alan Chaffee* • Kirstie Alley *Dr Susan Verner* • Linda Kozlowski *Jill McGowan* • Michael Paré *Frank McGowan* • Meredith Salenger *Melanie Roberts* • Mark Hamill *Reverend George* • Pippa Pearthree *Mrs Sarah Miller* ■ *Dir* John Carpenter • *Scr* David Himmelstein, from the 1960 film, from the novel *The Midwich Cuckoos* by John Wyndham

Village of the Giants ★★ PG
Science-fiction comedy drama
1965 · US · Colour · 77mins

Producer Bert I Gordon was a master of crude productions with gimmicky titles, such as *The Amazing Colossal Man* and *Empire of the Ants*, and this improbable but fun tale about a boy genius (Ron Howard) who invents a food that causes growth to gigantic proportions is down to his usual standard. However, it's enjoyable hokum, supposedly based on an HG Wells original, which gets by on pure brio.
Tommy Kirk *Mike* • Johnny Crawford *Horsey* • Beau Bridges *Fred* • Ronny Howard [Ron Howard] *Genius* • Joy Harmon *Merrie* • Bob Random *Rick* • Tisha Sterling *Jean* ■ *Dir* Bert I Gordon • *Scr* Alan Caillou, by Bert I Gordon, from the novel *The Food of the Gods* by HG Wells

Villain ★★★ 18
Crime drama   1971 · UK · Colour · 93mins

Made the same year as *Get Carter* with Michael Caine, *Villain* stars Richard Burton as vicious East End gangster Vic Dakin, who rules by fear and the cut-throat razor. Clearly

inspired, if that's the word, by the career of the Kray twins, the picture is one of unrelieved ugliness, from the run-down locations to the run-down bulk of Burton himself: overweight, shabby, self-loathing. Adored by his mother, he's a homosexual with a toy-boy lover, a Labour voter who worries about OAPs. Wavering uneasily between horror, black comedy and sentimentality, it's held together by Burton's performance, a brave attempt to escape the straitjacket of being the world's highest paid movie star. Contains violence and swearing.
Richard Burton *Vic Dakin* • Ian McShane *Wolfe Lissner* • Nigel Davenport *Bob Matthews* • Donald Sinden *Gerald Draycott* • Fiona Lewis *Venetia* • TP McKenna *Frank Fletcher* • Joss Ackland *Edgar Lowis* • Cathleen Nesbitt *Mrs Dakin* • Colin Welland *Tom Binney* ■ *Dir* Michael Tuchner • *Scr* Dick Clement, Ian La Frenais, Al Lettieri, from the novel *The Burden of Proof* by James Barlow

The Villain Still Pursued Her ★★★
Comedy   1940 · US · BW · 65mins

There are some clumsily carved slices of ham in this spoof on old-time melodrama, directed by Edward Cline, former creative aide to Buster Keaton and other silent clowns. Buster makes a guest appearance in this tale of villainous landlord Alan Mowbray, who terrorises the sweet-natured Margaret Hamilton and her attractive daughter Anita Louise. Boos and hisses are encouraged but it doesn't work as it should and audiences generally sit silent and baffled. It deserves marks for trying, though.
Hugh Herbert *Frederick Healy* • Anita Louise *Mary Wilson* • Alan Mowbray *Cribbs* • Buster Keaton *William Dalton* • Joyce Compton *Hazel Dalton* • Richard Cromwell *Edward Middleton* • Billy Gilbert *Announcer* • Margaret Hamilton *Mrs Wilson* ■ *Dir* Edward F Cline [Edward Cline] • *Scr* Elbert Franklin, from the play *The Fallen Saved*

Vincent and Me ★★★
Fantasy drama
1990 · Can/Fr · Colour · 100mins

Having already made *Tommy Tricker and the Stamp Traveller* and *The Peanut Butter Solution*, Michael Rubbo directed the eleventh entry in Rock Demers's *Tales for All* series, which has now amassed over 100 awards at festivals around the world. Produced to mark the centenary of Vincent Van Gogh's death, the film was shot in Arles and Amsterdam, as well as Montreal, where 13-year-old painter Nina Petronzio dreams of emulating her hero. However, when she magically gets to meet him (a sensitive performance from Tcheky Karyo), he urges her to follow her own artistic instincts. Warm, wise and visually inspired. A French language film.
Nina Petronzio *Jo* • Christopher Forrest *Felix* • Paul Klerk *Joris* • Matthew Mabe *Tom Mainfield* • Anna-Maria Giannotti *Gran* • Tcheky Karyo *Vincent Van Gogh* ■ *Dir/Scr* Michael Rubbo

Vincent and Theo ★★★ 15
Biographical drama
1990 · UK/Fr/US · Colour · 133mins

Outlining the last years of painter Vincent Van Gogh (Tim Roth), as seen

through the eyes of his brother Theodore (Paul Rhys), this is a haunting study in loneliness, obsession and the tough quest for validation in the blinkered art world. Unusual direction by Robert Altman and an intense performance by Roth as the tortured genius make this intimate biopic a thought-provoking look at the schizophrenic nature of the creative impulse as it impacts on family life.
Tim Roth *Vincent Van Gogh* • Paul Rhys *Theodore Van Gogh* • Bernadette Giraud *Marguerite Gachet* • Adrian Brine *Uncle Cent* • Jip Wijngaarden *Sien Hoornik* • Johanna Ter Steege *Jo Bonger* • Wladimir Yordanoff *Paul Gauguin* ■ *Dir* Robert Altman • *Scr* Julian Mitchell

Vincent, François, Paul and the Others ★★★
Comedy drama   1974 · It/Fr · Colour · 118mins

The lives, loves and midlife crises of a group of middle-class Parisians, principally a doctor, a writer and a factory owner who are all fiftysomethings and looking for something better. Surrounding them are the "others" – friends, wives, mistresses – and they all interact with ingenious timing and often witty results. As in all authentically French movies, coffee is sipped, cigarettes smoked and philosophy explored, but Claude Sautet's film is really just an extremely glossy soap opera made eminently watchable by its heavyweight cast. A French language film.
Yves Montand *Vincent* • Michel Piccoli *Francois* • Serge Reggiani *Paul* • Gérard Depardieu *Jean* • Stéphane Audran *Catherine* • Marie Dubois *Lucie* • Antonella Lualdi *Julia* ■ *Dir* Claude Sautet • *Scr* Jean-Loup Dabadie, Claude Néron, Claude Sautet, from the novel *La Grande Marrade* by Claude Néron

Vincent: the Life and Death of Vincent Van Gogh ★★★ PG
Biographical drama
1987 · Ausl · Colour · 95mins

This is a film closer in spirit to documentary than Vincente Minnelli's *Lust for Life* or Robert Altman's *Vincent and Theo*. Paul Cox's essay uses the artist's letters (sensitively read by John Hurt) to both examine the sources of his creative inspiration and reassess his mental state during those tormented final years, when he not only painted at a furious rate, but also suffered an anguish that finally crushed his ferocious resolve to remain sane. The film also traces the development of Van Gogh's style from the earliest line drawings to the powerfully emotive canvases of his Arles period. Enthralling and informative.
John Hurt *Reader* ■ *Dir* Paul Cox • *Scr* Paul Cox, from the letters of Vincent Van Gogh

Vintage Wine ★★
Comedy   1935 · UK · BW · 81mins

Despite his grand age, Seymour Hicks, head of a wine dynasty, refuses to slow down and maintains a boisterous life with his new young wife, Claire Luce. Scandalised by his behaviour, the other members of his family descend on his home allowing his wife to discover that he is actually 20 years older than he led her to believe. A flowery farce based on Alexander Engel's play *Der Ewige Jungeling* and starring the great British stage actor Sir Seymour Hicks, a reliable purveyor of such comedy. Dated but affable.

Seymour Hicks *Charles Popinot* • Claire Luce *Nina Popinot* • Eva Moore *Josephine Popinot* • Judy Gunn *Blanche Popinot* • Miles Malleson *Henri Popinot* • Kynaston Reeves *Benedict Popinot* ■ *Dir* Henry Edwards • *Scr* Seymour Hicks, Ashley Dukes, H Fowler Mear, from the play *Der Ewige Jungeling (The Eternal Youth)* by Alexander Engel

Vinyl ★★
Satire   1965 · US · BW · 70mins

One of several films Andy Warhol made with playwright Ronald Tavel during 1965. The quasi-script, reputedly based on Anthony Burgess's novel *A Clockwork Orange*, focuses on sado-masochism and features a lot of bondage and torture. The dialogue in the second reel is inaudible because there are records playing in another part of the studio. Finally the cast (including Warhol regulars Gerard Malanga, Edie Sedgwick and Ondine) get stoned on amyl nitrate, and an orgy begins. Dedicated cineastes may retain a modicum of interest.

Gerard Malanga *Victor* • Edie Sedgwick *Woman on trunk* • John MacDermott *Detective* • Ondine ■ *Dir* Andy Warhol • *Scr* Ronald Tavel, from the novel *A Clockwork Orange* by Anthony Burgess

Violent City ★★
Crime action drama
1970 · Fr/It · Colour · 99mins

Following his compelling appearance as a stone-faced mystery man in Leone's *Once upon a Time in the West*, Charles Bronson then moved on to this French/Italian thriller and played a stone-faced hit man. Do you sense the beginning of a pattern? The plot owes much to John Boorman's *Point Blank* as Bronson is out to avenge the double-cross by Telly Savalas which put him in prison. To make matters worse, Savalas is now with the ex-con's girlfriend (Jill Ireland). Inevitably, with Mr Bronson on the case, the body count is high. It's a pity the same can't be said for the tension in what is a predictably frayed affair.

Charles Bronson *Jeff* • Jill Ireland *Vanessa* • Umberto Orsini *Steve* • Telly Savalas *Weber* • Michel Constantin *Killian* • George Savalas *Shapiro* ■ *Dir* Sergio Sollima • *Scr* Sauro Scavolini, Gianfranco Calligarich, Lina Wertmuller

Violent Cop ★★★★ 🔞
Thriller   1989 · Jap · Colour · 98mins

Although he was already a massive star in Japan, this brooding thriller made actor/first-time director Takeshi "Beat" Kitano the hip name to drop in film circles over here. The plot itself could have come from any mainstream blockbuster: a tough, unconventional cop (Kitano) and his new, inexperienced partner find themselves up against their fellow officers when investigating a drugs case. However, the usual Hollywood clichés are turned on their head by Kitano's highly stylised direction, the splashes of

quirky black humour and sudden jolts of extreme violence. On the screen, Kitano's charismatic performance is riveting. In Japanese with English subtitles.. 🖳

"Beat" Takeshi [Takeshi Kitano] *Detective Azuma* • Maiko Kawakami *Akari* • Haku Ryu *Kiyohiro, hit man* • Makoto Ashikawa *Kikuchi, rookie* • Shiro Sano *Police Chief Yoshinari* • Shigeru Hiraizumi *Detective Iwaki* ■ *Dir* Takeshi Kitano • *Scr* Hisashi Nozawa

The Violent Enemy ★★ 🅤
Political thriller   1969 · UK · Colour · 93mins

Based on the novel *A Candle for the Dead* by Hugh Marlowe (aka Jack Higgins), this downbeat thriller stars Tom Bell as an IRA man on the run, who is reluctantly recruited to blow up a British-owned power station. It's efficiently made, if unsurprising, and familiar American actor Ed Begley is worth watching as the fanatical Irish mastermind behind the scheme.

Tom Bell *Sean Rogan* • Susan Hampshire *Hannah Costello* • Ed Begley *Colum O'More* • Jon Laurimore *Austin* • Michael Standing *Fletcher* • Noel Purcell *John Michael Leary* • Philip O'Flynn *Inspector Sullivan* ■ *Dir* Don Sharp • *Scr* Edmund Ward, from the novel *A Candle For The Dead* by Hugh Marlowe [Jack Higgins]

The Violent Men ★★★ 🅿🅶
Western   1955 · US · Colour · 91mins

This well cast but under-scripted western reunites two of the *Double Indemnity* stars, as wheelchair-bound land baron Edward G Robinson discovers that his venal wife Barbara Stanwyck is in love with his own brother, played by the ever-excellent Brian Keith. Into this positively seething morass of emotion walks rancher Glenn Ford, intent on pacifying the townsfolk who've turned against the unscrupulous empire-building Robinson. There's real star power on display here, and Ford is superb, but the whole isn't quite as good as the sum of its parts. 🖳

Glenn Ford *John Parrish* • Barbara Stanwyck *Martha Wilkison* • Edward G Robinson *Lew Wilkison* • Dianne Foster *Judith Wilkison* • Brian Keith *Cole Wilkison* • May Wynn *Caroline Vail* • Caroline Vail *May Wynn* • Warner Anderson *Jim McCloud* ■ *Dir* Rudolph Maté • *Scr* Harry Kleiner, from the novel *Rough Company* by Donald Hamilton

The Violent Ones ★★★
Crime drama   1967 · US · Colour · 87mins

Actor Fernando Lamas directed himself stylishly in this grim drama about three Anglo-American strangers implicated in the rape and murder of a girl in a small Mexican town. Lamas plays the sheriff who has to protect the Mexican-hating suspects – including Aldo Ray and David Carradine – from a lynch mob spurred on by the dead girl's father. Not particularly original in its examination of prejudice, the movie nevertheless does all it needs to convince and contains an exciting desert-chase climax.

Fernando Lamas *Manuel Vega* • Aldo Ray *Joe Vorzyck* • Tommy Sands *Mike Marain* • David Carradine *Lucas Barnes* • Lisa Gaye *Dolores* • Melinda Marx *Juanita* ■ *Dir* Fernando Lamas • *Scr* Doug Wilson, Charles Davis, from a story by Fred Freiberger, Herman Miller

Violent Playground ★★
Crime drama   1958 · UK · BW · 107mins

From the producing/directing team of Michael Relph and Basil Dearden, a drearily predictable but well-handled slice of dour British realism, set in Liverpool. Stanley Baker is a policeman who, after unsuccessfully investigating an outbreak of arson, is transferred to the job of juvenile liaison officer in a depressed area. He falls in love with Anne Heywood, only to discover that her young brother David McCallum is the arsonist. The film finally catches alight, too, in a dramatic climax where young McCallum gets a gun and holds his siblings hostage.

Stanley Baker *Sgt Truman* • Anne Heywood *Cathie Murphy* • David McCallum *Johnny Murphy* • Peter Cushing *Priest* • John Slater *Sgt Walker* • Clifford Evans *Heaven Evans* • Moultrie Kelsall *Superintendent* • George A Cooper *Chief Inspector* ■ *Dir* Basil Dearden • *Scr* James Kennaway, from his novel

Violent Road ★ 🅤
Drama   1958 · US · BW · 77mins

Obviously indebted to the French thriller *The Wages of Fear*, this very ordinary Hollywood picture shows three pairs of drivers taking trucks full of highly dangerous rocket fuel along a rough mountain road. The journey is full of contrived incidents and, naturally, not everyone makes it – but it's hard to care one way or the other. Brian Keith stars as the tough leader whose recruits include Dick Foran's war veteran and Efrem Zimbalist Jr's engineer with a secret.

Brian Keith *Mitch* • Dick Foran *Sarge* • Efrem Zimbalist Jr *George Lawrence* • Merry Anders *Carrie* • Sean Garrison *Ken Farley* • Joanna Barnes *Peg Lawrence* • Perry Lopez *Manuelo* • Ann Doran *Edith* ■ *Dir* Howard W Koch • *Scr* Richard Landau, from a story by Don Martin

Violent Saturday ★★★★
Crime drama   1955 · US · Colour · 89mins

A well-made, tense and exciting study of the preparations for a bloody and daring bank raid in a small Arizona town, filmed on actual locations by talented director Richard Fleischer, who made a couple of other crime studies for 20th Century-Fox, *Compulsion* and *The Boston Strangler*. The assembled cast is impressive: a pre-stardom Lee Marvin, Stephen McNally and J Carrol Naish are the baddies, and there's back-up from the likes of Victor Mature and Ernest Borgnine. Veteran Sylvia Sidney is a welcome addition to any cast, but the real star of the film is its superb climax.

Victor Mature *Shelley Martin* • Richard Egan *Boyd Fairchild* • Stephen McNally *Harper* • Virginia Leith *Linda* • Tommy Noonan *Harry Reeves* • Lee Marvin *Dill* • Margaret Hayes *Emily* • J Carrol Naish *Chapman* • Sylvia Sidney *Elsie* • Ernest Borgnine *Stadt* ■ *Dir* Richard Fleischer • *Scr* Sydney Boehm, from the novel by William L Heath

Violent Summer ★★
Thriller   1961 · Fr · BW · 84mins

A French film from director Michel Boisrond concerns the mysterious and sinister events that befall an author (Henri-Jacques Huet) while a house guest of a wealthy widow (Martine

Carol) on the Riviera, where she lives with her doctor lover (Jean Desailly) and two children. Sex, murder, a strong atmosphere and a proficient cast promise a good thriller, but the screenplay appears to run out of ideas halfway through, leaving the film to limp to a weak and unsatisfying conclusion. A French language film.

Martine Carol *Georgina* • Jean Desailly *Francis* • Daliah Lavi *Marie* • Geneviève Grad *Sylvie* • Henri-Jacques Huet *Michel* ■ *Dir* Michel Boisrond • *Scr* Annette Wademant

Violets Are Blue ★★★ 🅿🅶
Romance   1986 · US · Colour · 82mins

There are some great performances in this strong romantic drama, with Kevin Kline and Sissy Spacek leading the way playing former high-school sweethearts. Since graduation Kline has settled down and become a family man and Spacek has grasped a career and is now a world famous photographer. When she returns to her home town and encounters him, he welcomes her into his family fold until it becomes clear to the small community that these two have unfinished business. This is a subtle and sophisticated handling of difficult choices that avoids being trite and schmaltzy. The result makes for compelling and mature viewing. 🖳

Sissy Spacek *Gussie Sawyer* • Kevin Kline *Henry Squires* • Bonnie Bedelia *Ruth Squires* • John Kellogg *Ralph Sawyer* • Jim Standiford *Addy Squires* • Augusta Dabney *Ethel Sawyer* ■ *Dir* Jack Fisk • *Scr* Naomi Foner

Violette Nozière ★★★
Historical crime drama
1977 · Fr · Colour · 123mins

Based on a sensational 1930s murder case, this film is every bit as mixed-up as its heroine; for while Claude Chabrol teases us with extravagant ellipses, he actually tells the story of the Parisienne who murdered her father in a highly traditional, typically sub-Hitchcockian manner. Isabelle Huppert won the best actress prize at Cannes for her work as the demure teenager whose wild nights in the Latin Quarter result in syphilis and the opportunity to poison Jean Carmet and the more durable Stéphane Audran. But her icily nuanced performance is heavily reliant on Chabrol's incisive re-creation of her stifling bourgeois environment. A French language film.

Isabelle Huppert *Violette Noziere* • Stéphane Audran *Germaine Noziere* • Jean Carmet *Baptiste Noziere* ■ *Dir* Claude Chabrol • *Scr* Odile Barski, Herve Bromberger, Frederic Grendel, from a non-fiction book by Jean-Marie Fitere

The Virgin and the Gypsy ★★★
Drama   1970 · UK · Colour · 95mins

Published posthumously, DH Lawrence's novella explored many of the sexual and social themes that recurred so often in his work. In this film version, Joanna Shimkus plays the curious innocent, whose strict upbringing drives her to sample the forbidden temptations offered by traveller Franco Nero. Even though both give decent performances, their sex scenes won't raise many pulse

rates. So rejoice instead in the accomplished playing of the supporting cast, which boasts such stalwarts as Fay Compton (as the tyrannical grandmother), Kay Walsh (as Aunt Cissie) and Maurice Denham as Shimkus's reverend father. Director Christopher Miles captures the period well, but the film smoulders when it should catch fire. Contains nudity.

Joanna Shimkus *Yvette Saywell* • Franco Nero *Gypsy* • Honor Blackman *Mrs Fawcett* • Mark Burns *Major Eastwood* • Maurice Denham *Rector* • Fay Compton *Grandma* • Kay Walsh *Aunt Cissie* • Harriet Harper *Lucille Saywell* ■ *Dir* Christopher Miles • *Scr* Alan Plater, from the novella by DH Lawrence

Virgin Island ★★ U

Romantic drama 1958 · UK · Colour · 98mins

Perfect English rose Virginia Maskell is cruising the Virgin Islands when archaeologist John Cassavetes sweeps her off her feet. Within a few days they are married, and they subsequently have a baby and become tediously contented. Even Maskell's mum, Isabel Dean, seems happy, despite the fact that Cassavetes, an inwardly seething method actor, is hardly romantic leading man material. Nothing more than a travelogue with silly dialogue, it's bland and pleasant, though it's likely that if Sidney Poitier ever saw his performance as a shifty native, he would die of embarrassment.

John Cassavetes *Evan* • Virginia Maskell *Tina* • Sidney Poitier *Marcus* • Isabel Dean *Mrs Lomax* • Colin Gordon *The Commissioner* • Howard Marion-Crawford *Prescott* • Edric Connor *Captain Jason* ■ *Dir* Pat Jackson • *Scr* Philip Rush, Pat Jackson, from the novel *Our Virgin Island* by Robb White

Virgin Machine ★★★

Drama 1988 · W Ger · BW · 85mins

Updating the medieval quest for courtly love to the California of sex lines, S&M and lipstick lesbians, Monika Treut has created a picaresque satire that not only explores the nature of gender orientation, but also modern morality and the cultural gulf between Europe and America. Quitting Hamburg to go in search of her mother, Ina Blum soon forgets her book on romance as she encounters a number of women prepared to give her a practical insight into her sexual identity. Elfi Mikesch's sensuous monochrome photography is outstanding, as it conveys both the thrill of Blum's awakening and the different atmospheres of her contrasting environments. In German with English subtitles.

Ina Blum *Dorothee Müller* • Marcelo Uriona *Bruno* • Gad Klein *Heinz* • Peter Kern *Hormone specialist* • Dominique Gaspar *Dominique* • Susie Bright *Susie Sexpert* ■ *Dir/Scr* Monika Treut

The Virgin Queen ★★★ U

Historical drama 1955 · US · Colour · 87mins

Sixteen years after she played Elizabeth I in *The Private Lives of Elizabeth and Essex*, Bette Davis reprised the role of the last Tudor in this colourful but rather tepid melodrama. She gets to chew a little scenery as she realises that Richard Todd's Walter Raleigh is in love with lady-in-waiting Joan Collins, but the history lesson script keeps her on a short leash. Todd comes across as a sulky boy who isn't allowed to play in the Americas rather than an ambitious man of action, and his romance with the demure Collins is soggier than a cloak over a puddle. [video]

Bette Davis *Queen Elizabeth I* • Richard Todd *Sir Walter Raleigh* • Joan Collins *Beth Throgmorton* • Jay Robinson *Chadwick* • Herbert Marshall *Lord Leicester* • Dan O'Herlihy *Lord Derry* • Robert Douglas *Sir Christopher Hatton* ■ *Dir* Henry Koster • *Scr* Harry Brown, Mindret Lord

The Virgin Soldiers ★★★ 15

War comedy drama 1969 · UK · Colour · 90mins

Leslie Thomas's first novel went straight to the top of the bestseller charts in 1966 and this movie version quickly tried to capitalise on its success. Thomas wrote about his national service experiences in Singapore, where manhood was discovered through "sex" and military action during the Malayan Emergency. In one sense the movie, written by John Hopkins, Ian La Frenais and John McGrath, is just *Private's Progress* with a touch of *Carry On Sergeant*, but the vivid action scenes and the probability of getting shot give it a blacker dramatic edge. Hywel Bennett is the hero, Lynn Redgrave the RSM's comely daughter and Tsai Chin plays an Oriental tart called Juicy Lucy. [video]

Hywel Bennett *Private Brigg* • Lynn Redgrave *Phillipa Raskin* • Nigel Davenport *Sergeant Driscoll* • Nigel Patrick *Regimental Sergeant Major Raskin* • Rachel Kempson *Mrs Raskin* • Jack Shepherd *Sergeant Wellbeloved* • Tsai Chin *Juicy Lucy* • Christopher Timothy *Corporal Brook* ■ *Dir* John Dexter • *Scr* John Hopkins, John McGrath, Ian La Frenais, from the novel by Leslie Thomas

The Virgin Spring ★★★★ 15

Historical drama 1960 · Swe · BW · 85mins

Winner of the 1960 Oscar for best foreign film, Ingmar Bergman's stark study of the cruelty and superstition of the Middle Ages positively drips with symbolism. However, it also works as a powerful revenge tragedy, as Max von Sydow encounters the men who raped and murdered his daughter after she'd been cursed by her half-sister. Often considered one of Bergman's bleakest films, the story has a miraculous ending that dispels his doubts about the presence of God. The acting has an all-too-rare intensity and the photography of Sven Nykvist (working with Bergman for the first time) is a joy to behold. In Swedish with English subtitles. Contains violence. [video]

Max von Sydow *Herr Tore* • Birgitta Valberg *Mareta Tore* • Gunnel Lindblom *Ingeri* • Birgitta Pettersson *Karin Tore* • Axel Duberg *Thin herdsman* • Tor Isedal *Mute herdsman* ■ *Dir* Ingmar Bergman • *Scr* Ulla Isaksson, from the 14th-century ballad *Tores Dotter I Vange*

The Virgin Suicides ★★ 15

Drama 1999 · US · Colour · 96mins

You've got to admire Sofia Coppola's courage. After the critical pasting she received for her ill-judged appearance in *The Godfather Part III*, you'd have understood if she never went near a movie set for the rest of her days. But here she is again, behind the camera this time, scripting and directing a black comedy about group suicide. The film focuses on five sublime sisters (Kirsten Dunst among them) and the impact on family, friends and community when they simultaneously kill themselves. The brightly coloured look contrasts nicely with the dark subject matter, and there are neat performances from Kathleen Turner and James Woods as the girls' ultra-repressive parents. Overall, though, there's not enough substance to match the undoubted style, and you're left strangely unaffected by events that should move you deeply.

James Woods *Mr Lisbon* • Kathleen Turner *Mrs Lisbon* • Kirsten Dunst *Lux Lisbon* • Josh Hartnett *Trip Fontaine* • Hanna Hall *Cecilia Lisbon* • Chelse Swain *Bonnie Lisbon* • AJ Cook *Mary Lisbon* • Leslie Hayman *Therese Lisbon* • Danny DeVito *Dr Hornicker* ■ *Dir* Sofia Coppola • *Scr* Sofia Coppola, from the novel by Jeffrey Eugenides

Virginia City ★★★ U

Western 1940 · US · BW · 120mins

You'd expect more from this follow-up to the splendid *Dodge City*, but Warner Bros failed to provide star Errol Flynn and director Michael Curtiz with the same back-up: they even stinted on colour. Still, any Warners film from this period is worth a look, especially when it's such a badly miscast western, set during the American Civil War. Humphrey Bogart, on the cusp of stardom, plays the most unlikely snarling Mexican bandit you'll ever see, and it's hard to believe in prissy Miriam Hopkins, not a hair out of place, as a Confederate spy posing as a dance-hall girl. Nevertheless, the scale is lavish, the camerawork is professional, and Flynn and Randolph Scott are very watchable.

Errol Flynn *Kerry Bradford* • Miriam Hopkins *Julia Hayne* • Randolph Scott *Vance Irby* • Humphrey Bogart *John Murrell* • Frank McHugh *Mr Upjohn* • Alan Hale *Olaf "Moose" Swenson* • Guinn "Big Boy" Williams [Guinn Williams] *"Marblehead"* • John Litel *Marshal* ■ *Dir* Michael Curtiz • *Scr* Robert Henry Buckner [Robert Buckner], Norman Reilly Raine (uncredited), Howard Koch (uncredited)

The Virginian ★★★★

Western 1929 · US · BW · 92mins

This early talkie (with clear recording) retains its bite even though so many of its details have since become clichés. Gary Cooper is splendid as the Virginian, a ranch foreman forced into a romantic rivalry with his weak friend Richard Arlen. The object of their affection is Mary Brian's priggish schoolmarm who tries to restrain Cooper, like Grace Kelly in *High Noon*, from shooting it out with Walter Huston's rustler villain. Besides its celebrated line, "If you want to call me that... smile!", there's also the first voicing of "This town ain't big enough for the both of us". Most surprising is the successful introduction of broad comedy but Victor Fleming's direction is assured and at times imaginative.

Gary Cooper *The Virginian* • Walter Huston *Trampas* • Richard Arlen *Steve* • Mary Brian *Molly Wood* • Chester Conklin *Uncle Hughey* • Eugene Pallette *Honey Wiggin* • EH Calvert *Judge Henry* • Helen Ware *Ma Taylor* • Victor Potel *Nebraskey* ■ *Dir* Victor Fleming • *Scr* Howard Estabrook, Edward E Paramore Jr, Grover Jones, Keene Thompson, Joseph L Mankiewicz, from the play by Owen Wister, Kirk La Shelle, from the novel by Owen Wister

The Virginian ★★ U

Western 1946 · US · Colour · 86mins

"If you want to call me that, smile." Not the great Gary Cooper in the 1929 version of author Owen Wister's classic western, nor James Drury in the long-running (but dull) sixties television series, but this time around it's poker-faced Joel McCrea warning off Brian Donlevy as the villainous Trampas. The rich Technicolor helps the aged tale, but overall there's nothing particularly special about the story any more, and the direction (by former editor Stuart Gilmore) is quite unremarkable. You'll watch wanting more, although Sonny Tufts delivers one of his best performances as a good guy turned rustler.

Joel McCrea *The Virginian* • Brian Donlevy *Trampas* • Sonny Tufts *Steve Andrews* • Barbara Britton *Molly Wood* • Fay Bainter *Mrs Taylor* • Henry O'Neill *Mr Taylor* • Bill Edwards *Sam Bennett* ■ *Dir* Stuart Gilmore • *Scr* Frances Goodrich, Albert Hackett, Edward E Paramore Jr, Howard Estabrook, from the play by Owen Wister, Kirk La Shelle, from the novel by Owen Wister

Viridiana ★★★★★ 15

Drama 1961 · Mex/Sp · BW · 86mins

Luis Buñuel's most scathing attack on the Catholic Church and the depravity of the modern world was filmed with the uncomprehending approval of Franco's fascist cinema supremos. Later they unsuccessfully tried to withdraw the picture after nominating it as Spain's official entry at Cannes. *Viridiana* traces the moral decline of a saintly girl who inadvertently drives her lascivious uncle to suicide and is then brutally exploited by the outcasts she shelters on his estate. The apex of Buñuel's satire is a mocking pastiche of Leonardo da Vinci's *Last Supper*. The Vatican censured the film as "an insult to Christianity" but it still ended up winning the Cannes Golden Palm. In Spanish with English subtitles. [video]

Silvia Pinal *Viridiana* • Francisco Rabal *Jorge* • Fernando Rey *Don Jaime* • Margarita Lozano *Ramona* • Victoria Zinny *Lucia* • Teresa Rabal *Rita* ■ *Dir* Luis Buñuel • *Scr* Luis Buñuel, Julio Alajandro, from a story by Luis Buñuel

Virtual Sexuality ★★★ 15

Fantasy comedy 1999 · UK · Colour · 89mins

Justine (Laura Fraser) is the lovelorn teenage girl who is accidentally transformed into her ideal man in this *Weird Science*-style British comedy scripted by former agony uncle Nick Fisher. Smartly written and aimed firmly at young girls, this has an attractive cast (Marcelle Duprey as Justine's best friend, Luke de Lacey as her nerdy pal, Rupert Penry-Jones as the mega-hunk Justine morphs into) and zips along merrily to a fun conclusion. Possibly a bit slight for anyone over the age of 18, but perfect low-budget fun for *Just Seventeen* readers. [video]

Laura Fraser *Justine* • Rupert Penry-Jones *Jake* • Luke de Lacey *Chas* • Kieran O'Brien

Alex • Marcelle Duprey *Fran* • Natasha Bell *Hoover* • Steve John Shepherd *Jason* ■ *Dir* Nick Hurran • *Scr* Nick Fisher

Virtuosity ★★★ 15

Science-fiction thriller
1995 · US · Colour · 101mins

Cyberspace wizardry covers the yawning gaps in this soulless thriller where the loose ends mount up faster than the body count, despite expert performances by the two commanding leads. If disgraced cop turned convict Denzel Washington can eliminate the computer-generated serial killer Sid 6.7 (played by Russell Crowe) – with just under 200 separate homicidal tendencies, including those of Hitler and Manson, to his personality – he'll be gratefully pardoned in director Brett Leonard's spasmodically entertaining high-tech fantasy adventure. But because Sid can rejuvenate himself out of any predicament (and these sequences are the film's visual highlights), there's basically no suspense generated and Leonard's virtual reality collection of hand-me-down bytes never recovers from this fatal flaw. ▣

Denzel Washington *Parker Barnes* • Kelly Lynch *Madison Carter* • Russell Crowe *Sid 6.7* • Stephen Spinella *Lindenmeyer* • William Forsythe *William Cochran* • Louise Fletcher *Elizabeth Deane* ■ *Dir* Brett Leonard • *Scr* Eric Bernt

The Virtuous Sin ★★

Romantic drama   1930 · US · BW · 80mins

A drawn-out drama revolving around the efforts of Kay Francis in 1917 Russia to save her bacteriologist husband Kenneth MacKenna, a military misfit, from having to go to war by seducing his commanding officer Walter Huston. Matters are complicated when she falls in love with the officer. The Russian setting and characters are of no visible benefit to this forgotten offering from Paramount, which marked George Cukor's second directing effort, shared with Louis Gasnier and giving no indication of his future prominence.

Walter Huston *Gen Gregori Platoff* • Kay Francis *Marya Ivanovna* • Kenneth MacKenna *Lt Victor Sablin* ■ *Dir* George Cukor, Louis Gasnier • *Scr* Martin Brown, Louise Long, from the novel *A Tábornok (The General)* by Lajos Zilahy

Virus ★★ PG

Disaster fantasy
1980 · Jap · Colour · 102mins

One of Japan's biggest budgeted movies, though it seems much of the cash went to the all-star (and mostly American) cast than on the special effects, many of which belong in the cheaper Godzilla movies. Possibly to try to attract a wide audience, the movie is not content to focus on the few survivors of a worldwide plague but packs in everything else under the sun, from forced prostitution to nuclear holocaust. The results don't completely make sense, especially in prints that cut about an hour from the running time. Some striking visuals and badly cast stars provide the main curiosity value. ▣

Sonny Chiba *Dr Yamauchi* • Chuck Connors *Captain MacCloud* • Stephanie Faulkner *Sarah*

Baker • Glenn Ford *Richardson* • Stuart Gillard *Dr Mayer* • Olivia Hussey *Marit* • George Kennedy *Admiral Conway* • Ken Ogata *Professor Tsuchiya* • Edward James Olmos *Captain Lopez* • Henry Silva *Garland* ■ *Dir* Kinji Fukasaku • *Scr* Koji Takada, Gregory Knapp, Kinji Fukasaku, from a novel by Sakyo Komatsu

Virus ★★ 18

Science-fiction horror
1998 · US · Colour · 99mins

Oscar-winning visual effects artist/James Cameron protégé John Bruno terminally accents effects over plot in his dreary feature-directing debut and adds insult to injury by making those effects merely tarnished knock-offs of *The Terminator*, *The Abyss* and *Aliens*. A sinking tugboat crew take refuge on a deserted Russian science vessel during a typhoon only to find it harbouring an alien energy force. Derivative of everything from *Leviathan* to *Deep Rising*, Bruno's hybrid mass of genre clichés simply joins the dots and doesn't even entertain on a schlock level. Jamie Lee Curtis, William Baldwin and Donald Sutherland give career-worst performances in this lame-brained terror tripe, with the final robot monster looking more like a mobile junkyard than anything truly scary. Contains strong violence. ▣

Jamie Lee Curtis *Kit Foster* • William Baldwin *Steve Baker* • Donald Sutherland *Captain Everton* • Joanna Pacula *Nadia* • Marshall Bell *JW Woods Jr* • Julio Oscar Mechoso *Squeaky* • Sherman Augustus *Richie* • Cliff Curtis *Hiko* ■ *Dir* John Bruno • *Scr* Chuck Pfarrer, Dennis Feldman, from the comic books by Chuck Pfarrer

Vision Quest ★ 15

Sports drama   1985 · US · Colour · 107mins

This is one movie that Matthew Modine and Linda Fiorentino would rather forget. Modine stars as an overly thin high school wrestling champ, whose obsession with his sport is confused by a growing infatuation with his father's lodger (Fiorentino). As "the older woman" she wraps him round her little pinkie, but of course this gives him the confidence to confront his biggest competitor in the ring. Wrestling is a strange sport and, as a subject, makes for an even stranger movie. Fiorentino is as strong as ever and Modine just about holds his own, given the appalling script and risible storyline. Madonna appears briefly to sing the hit song *Crazy For You*.

Matthew Modine *Louden Swain* • Linda Fiorentino *Carla* • Michael Schoeffling *Kuch* • Ronny Cox *Loudon's father* • Harold Sylvester *Tanneran* • Charles Hallahan *Coach* • JC Quin *Elmo* • Daphne Zuniga *Margie Epstein* • Forest Whitaker *Bulldozer* ■ *Dir* Harold Becker • *Scr* Darryl Ponicsan, from a novel by Terry Davis

Visions of Eight ★★★

Sports documentary
1973 · US · Colour · 105mins

It was hoped that having eight directors from different nationalities working on the official film of the 1972 Munich Olympics would be symbolic of the internationalism of the sportsmen and women themselves. However, the result was a spoiled broth that gave

neither statistics nor expressed any of the excitement of the events. Instead we are given a series of arty, tricksy and often spectacular moments created in a vacuum. The killing of eleven members of the Israeli team by Palestinian guerilas, the subject of the Oscar-winning documentary *One Day in September*, is touched upon only with the memorial service. Among the more amusing episodes is Mai Zetterling's view of the weightlifters.

Dir Yuri Ozerov, Mai Zetterling, Arthur Penn, Michael Pfleghar, Kon Ichikawa, Claude Lelouch, Milos Forman, John Schlesinger • *Scr* Deliara Ozerova, David Hughes, Arthur Penn, Michael Pfleghar, Shuntaro Tanikawa, Claude Lelouch, John Schlesinger

Visions of Light ★★★★ PG

Documentary
1992 · US/Jap · Colour and BW · 90mins

This fascinating documentary pays handsome tribute to the forgotten artists of film, the cinematographers. Passing with regrettable speed over silent geniuses like Billy Bitzer, who truly sculpted with light, the film sings the praises of black-and-white photography and reveals how some of the most memorable images ever shot in Hollywood were achieved. The work of such master craftsmen as George Barnes, Gregg Toland, William Daniels and John Alton is illustrated with well-chosen clips and heartfelt praise from the leading lighting cameramen of today. If you've ever marvelled at an image and wondered how they did it, this is for you. ▣

Todd McCarthy *Narrator* ■ *Dir* Arnold Glassman, Todd McCarthy, Stuart Samuels • *Scr* Todd McCarthy

Visions of Terror ★★

Supernatural thriller
1994 · US · Colour · 91mins

New Zealand director Sam Pillsbury's debut feature, the black comedy *The Scarecrow*, marked him out as a talent to watch, but a move to the USA did not prove as productive as it did for compatriots like Roger Donaldson (*No Way Out*) and Geoff Murphy (*Freejack*), and he has often found himself working on routine TV fare, such as this ordinary psychic thriller. Barbara Eden is the police psychologist with visions of murder who gets drawn into a world of corruption when a policeman is killed. Eden isn't overly convincing in the leading role, there are no big names among the supporting cast and Pillsbury's direction is pedestrian.

Barbara Eden *Jesse Newman* • Steven Anthony Jones *Captain Armstrong* • Missy Crider *Kimberly* • Michael Nouri *David Zaccariah* • Joan Pringle *Gwen Singleton* • Ted Marcoux *Tony Carpelli* ■ *Dir* Sam Pillsbury • *Scr* Duane Poole

The Visit ★★

Drama 1964 · W Ger/Fr/It/US · BW · 100mins

In an adaptation of the Dürrenmatt play, Ingrid Bergman is the richest woman in the world who returns to her impoverished home village. On arriving she promises the peasants riches but only if they execute Anthony Quinn – her former lover and the father of her dead child who, to save his own skin, forced her into exile and prostitution.

This is a good dramatic story that might have made a western, though the original play was set in Switzerland, as is this movie version. Hollywood changed – that is, softened – the ending and made a stodgy German-Franco-Italian pudding out of it that Quinn (who also produced) and Bergman can't quite bring to life.

Ingrid Bergman *Karla Zachanassian* • Anthony Quinn *Serge Miller* • Irina Demick *Anya* • Paolo Stoppa *Doctor* • Hans Christian Blech *Capt Dobrick* • Romolo Valli *Town painter* • Valentina Cortese *Mathilda Miller* ■ *Dir* Bernhard Wicki • *Scr* Ben Barzman, from the play by Maurice Valency, from the play *Der Besuch der alten Dame* by Friedrich Dürrenmatt

Visit to a Small Planet ★★ U

Fantasy comedy   1960 · US · BW · 85mins

Jerry Lewis is Kreton, an unemotional alien visitor who comes to a small Virginian town and encounters the all too emotional inhabitants – including Ellen Spelding (Joan Blackman) who manages to capture Kreton's heart. Based on Gore Vidal's satirical stage play, this was another failed attempt to capture the genius of Jerry Lewis on screen. Vidal despised the movie and contemporary critics were less than enthusiastic; time has added a certain period charm, though it's still pretty wide of the mark.

Jerry Lewis *Kreton* • Joan Blackman *Ellen Spelding* • Earl Holliman *Conrad* • Fred Clark *Major Roger Putnam Spelding* • Lee Patrick *Rheba Spelding* • Gale Gordon *Bob Mayberry* • Ellen Corby *Mrs Mayberry* ■ *Dir* Norman Taurog • *Scr* Edmund Beloin, Henry Garson, from the play by Gore Vidal

Les Visiteurs ★★★★ 15

Comedy   1993 · Fr · Colour · 102mins

A bawdy riposte to French cinema's propensity for intellectual navel-gazing, this time-travelling farce smashed box-office records on its original release. Celebrating the enduring appeal of *café théâtre* (the Gallic cousin of music-hall), the slapstick adventures of a medieval nobleman and his squire who wind up in nineties France will strike many as a sort of *Carry On Blackadder*. But there's also a mischievous social subtext here, as Jean Reno and Christian Clavier's search for a book of spells brings them into contact with various bourgeois caricatures. The humour is decidedly lavatorial, but it's difficult not to enter into the spirit of this gleefully irreverent romp. In French with English subtitles. ▣

Christian Clavier *Jacquouille La Fripouille/Jacquart* • Jean Reno *Godefroy de Montmirail* • Valérie Lemercier *Frénégonde de Pouille/Béatrice* • Marie-Anne Chazel *Ginette la clocharde* ■ *Dir* Jean-Marie Poiré • *Scr* Jean-Marie Poiré, Christian Clavier

Les Visiteurs 2: Les Couloirs du Temps ★★★

Fantasy comedy   1998 · Fr · Colour · 116mins

The French have never been particularly prone to sequelitis, but Jean-Marie Poiré succumbed on this occasion and made a pretty fair job of re-creating both the madcap comedy and commercial success of the original. Opening with a neat illuminated manuscript reprise, the action darts back and forth through time, as 12th-century knight Jean Reno returns to the future to avert a curse on his forthcoming marriage. Just as Reno doubles up as a long-lost playboy, so Christian Clavier alternates between playing his mischievous vassal and a prissy estate manager, beset by wolves and the inquisition. Patchy, but energetically played and anarchic. A French language film.

Jean Reno *Godefroy de Montmirail* • Christian Clavier *Jacquouille/Jacquart* • Muriel Robin *Béatrice/Frénégonde* • Marie-Anne Chazel *Ginette* • Christian Bujeau *Jean-Pierre* ■ *Dir* Jean-Marie Poiré • *Scr* Jean-Marie Poiré, Christian Clavier

Les Visiteurs du Soir ★★★★

Romantic fantasy 1942 · Fr · BW · 122mins
Forced by the German Occupation to make "escapist" films, the director/writer team of Marcel Carné and Jacques Prévert went back to the 15th century for this rather stilted and whimsical fairytale. Alain Cuny and Arletty play servants of the Devil disguised as minstrels. They arrive at a wedding of a baron's daughter with the intention of causing mischief. It was seen by many of the French audiences at the time as an allegory of their situation with the Devil as Hitler (Jules Berry). In French with English subtitles.

Maria Déa *Anne* • Jules Berry *The Devil* • Arletty *Dominique* • Fernand Ledoux *Baron Hughes* • Alain Cuny *Gilles* • Marcel Herrand *Renaud* ■ *Dir* Marcel Carné • *Scr* Jacques Prévert, Pierre Laroche

Visiting Hours ★★ 18

Horror thriller 1982 · Can · Colour · 99mins
ER it isn't, as a scalpel-wielding psycho stalks the wards and hallways of a major metropolitan hospital. *Star Trek*'s William Shatner, who should have beamed himself up from this one, plus fellow Canadian film regulars Michael Ironside and Lee Grant, star in a solid, if sick, slasher movie that lingers a little too lovingly on its dirty deeds. Scalpels aren't just slid into bodies – they're slid in and twisted. And all in glorious close-up. 🖵

Michael Ironside *Colt Hawker* • Lee Grant *Deborah Ballin* • Linda Purl *Sheila Munroe* • William Shatner *Gary Baylor* • Lenore Zann *Lisa* • Harvey Atkin *Vinnie Bradshaw* • Helen Hughes *Louise Shepherd* ■ *Dir* Jean-Claude Lord • *Scr* Brian Taggert

The Visitor ★ 18

Horror 1980 · It/US · Colour · 97mins
From opportunist producer Ovidio G Assonitis, the man responsible for the Italian *Exorcist*, *Beyond the Door*, and the Italian *Jaws*, *Tentacles*, comes the Italian *Omen* souped up with reheated sci-fi and horror leftovers from every success in the genre. A rich occultist tries to father a devil child in this incoherent mess complete with odd special effects, weird camera angles and religious mumbo jumbo. Directors Sam Peckinpah and John Huston also appear in baffling cameo roles in this triumph of artlessness and bad taste. 🖵

Mel Ferrer *Dr Walker* • John Huston *Jersey Colsowitz, the visitor* • Glenn Ford *Jake* • Lance Henriksen *Raymond* • Paige Conner *Katie Collins* • Joanne Nail *Barbara Collins* • Shelley Winters *Jane Phillips* • Sam Peckinpah *Sam* ■ *Dir* Michael J Paradise [Giulio Paradisi] • *Scr* Lou Comici, Robert Mundi, from a story by Michael J Paradise [Giulio Paradisi], Ovidio G Assonitis

The Visitors ★★★ 15

Drama 1972 · US · Colour · 102mins
Elia Kazan self-financed this drama on a shoestring, shooting it in and around his own New England home from a script by his son, Chris. It deals with Vietnam and uses the same real-life story basis as Brian De Palma's masterly *Casualties of War*, showing how a GI accuses two of his confrères of raping and murdering a Vietnamese girl. After the war, the two ex-GIs show up looking for vengeance. Barely released anywhere – it had a controversial screening at Cannes, mainly because jury president Joseph Losey had a long-standing feud with Kazan over the McCarthy witch-hunts – it has many flaws, but should be seen for its treatment of a complex theme and for the feature-film debut of James Woods. 🖵

Patrick McVey *Harry Wayne* • Patricia Joyce *Martha Wayne* • James Woods *Bill Schmidt* • Chico Martinez *Tony Rodriguez* • Steve Railsback *Mike Nickerson* ■ *Dir* Elia Kazan • *Scr* Chris Kazan

Visitors of the Night ★★ 12

Science-fiction drama 1995 · US · Colour · 90mins
Did Markie Post's daughter get abducted by aliens when she disappeared for a few hours one night? Post believes the same thing happened to her when she was a girl, so is history repeating itself? A lightweight addition to the *Communion* school of science fiction. Contains some violence, strong language. 🖵

Markie Post *Judith* • Candace Cameron *Katie* • Dale Midkiff *Sheriff Marcus Ashley* • Stephen McHattie *Bryan English* • Pam Hyatt *Judith's mother* • Susan Hogan *Dr Dillard* • Allan Royal *Dr Geary* ■ *Dir* Jorge Montesi • *Scr* Michael J Murray

Vital Signs ★★ 15

Drama 1990 · US · Colour · 98mins
A routine hospital drama, neither especially dire nor especially memorable, about a bunch of third-year med students living and loving their way through training. Packed with all the usual medical clichés, from ward emergencies to quickies in the linen cupboard, the film is flattered by a cast that includes Adrian Pasdar, Diane Lane and Laura San Giacomo. A pre-*NYPD Blues* Jimmy Smits is especially good as the instructing surgeon. 🖵

Adrian Pasdar *Michael Chatham* • Diane Lane *Gina Wyler* • Jack Gwaltney *Kenny Rose* • Laura San Giacomo *Lauren Rose* • Jane Adams *Suzanne Maloney* • Jimmy Smits *Dr David Redding* • Tim Ransom *Bobby Hayes* ■ *Dir* Marisa Silver • *Scr* Larry Ketron, Jeb Stuart, from a story by Larry Ketron

I Vitelloni ★★★★ PG

Drama 1953 · It/Fr · BW · 103mins
Federico Fellini was trying to greenlight *La Strada* when he devised this portrait of the reckless vitelloni (large slabs of veal) he'd known during his youth in Rimini. Sketched with satirical insight, this tale focuses on five boys who are gradually forced to confront their bleak futures. At the centre of the action is a carnival, in which the buddies' costumes, masks and grotesque pranks are symbolically linked to the alienation and sexual frustration rife in early 1950s Italy. Fellini claimed that this alienation and sexual frustration, coupled with the national tendency towards farcical anarchy and psychological anguish, contributed to the rise of Fascism. An Italian language film.

Franco Interlenghi *Moraldo* • Franco Fabrizi *Fausto* • Alberto Sordi *Alberto* • Leopoldo Trieste *Leopoldo* • Riccardo Fellini *Riccardo* • Elenora Ruffo *Sandra* ■ *Dir* Federico Fellini • *Scr* Federico Fellini, Ennio Flaiano, Tullio Pinelli, from a story by Federico Fellini, Ennio Flaiano, Tullio Pinelli

Viva Italia! ★★★

Portmanteau black comedy 1978 · It · Colour · 115mins
A portmanteau black comedy, consisting of nine episodes designed to show that the typical Italian male is a monster. Some segments run less than five minutes while others last nearly fifteen, adding up to a breezy, but distinctly uneven ninety in all, linked by a surprise ending. Three of Italy's biggest stars – Vittorio Gassman, Alberto Sordi and Ugo Tognazzi – seize their chances, either tossing food all over the kitchen, giving a lift to a crime victim in a Rolls-Royce and then chucking him out after he bleeds over the leather, or breaking a wife's legs to try to revive her fading singing career. In Italian with English subtitles.

Ugo Tognazzi *The Husband* • Vittorio Gassman *The Cardinal* • Ornella Muti *The Hitchhiker* • Orietta Berti *The Singer* ■ *Dir* Mario Monicelli, Dino Risi, Ettore Scola • *Scr* Agenore Incrocci, Ruggero Maccari, Giuseppe Moccia, Ettore Scola, Bernardino Zapponi

Viva Knievel! ★★★ PG

Action thriller 1977 · US · Colour · 99mins
This amazingly kitsch one-off stars the man himself Evel Knievel, a non-actor if ever there was one, in a movie so absurd it simply has to be seen to be believed. Directed by veteran Gordon Douglas and featuring Lauren Hutton, Gene Kelly, Cameron Mitchell and Leslie Nielson among the cast, this is vanity cinema with a vengeance: the opening sequence involving Knievel and a group of orphans is truly amazing. However, there is a real and perverse pleasure to be gained from watching the work of true professionals such as Douglas and Kelly, as they manage to turn this sow's ear into something vaguely resembling a purse. 🖵

Evel Knievel *Evel Knievel* • Gene Kelly *Will Atkins* • Lauren Hutton *Kate Morgan* • Red Buttons *Ben Andrews* • Leslie Nielsen *Stanley Millard* • Frank Gifford *Himself* • Sheila Allen

Sister Charity • Cameron Mitchell *Barton* ■ *Dir* Gordon Douglas • *Scr* Antonio Santillan, Norman Katkov, from a story by Santillan

Viva Las Vegas ★★★★ U

Musical comedy drama 1964 · US · Colour · 81mins
This is one of the last great MGM musicals, retitled *Love in Las Vegas* when it was originally shown in the UK. For once, the fabulous Elvis Presley found himself in the hands of a good director, *Kiss Me Kate*'s George Sidney, and teamed with a worthy and equally volatile co-star, the vivacious Ann-Margret, who had starred in Sidney's musical comedy hit from the previous year, *Bye Bye Birdie*. Especially fine are Elvis and Ann-Margret's workout to *Come On, Everybody* and the gentle rock ballad *The Lady Loves Me*. There's also a terrific version of Ray Charles's *What'd I Say*. Choreography is by *West Side Story*'s David Winters, there's wonderful Panavision cinematography by Joseph Biroc (who was camera operator on all the Astaire/Rogers musicals) and the whole glossy package is far and away Elvis's best post-*Blue Hawaii* movie. It's a shame he missed MGM's musical heyday by at least a decade.

Elvis Presley *Lucky Jackson* • Ann-Margret *Rusty Martin* • Cesare Danova *Count Elmo Mancini* • William Demarest *Mr Martin* • Nicky Blair *Shorty Farnsworth* • Robert B Williams *Swanson* • Bob Nash *Big Gus Olson* • Roy Engel *Baker* ■ *Dir* George Sidney • *Scr* Sally Benson

Viva Maria! ★★★

Comedy 1965 · Fr/It · Colour · 120mins
The pairing of Brigitte Bardot and Jeanne Moreau created enough excitement in 1965 for this to be an art-house blockbuster. Bardot was France's reigning sex symbol and so was Moreau, but in artier movies, here they're singers who tussle with a typically disorganised Mexican revolution. Both actresses seem to be enjoying the occasion, as does a perfectly cast George Hamilton. Georges Delerue's songs are pleasing, and the photography is ravishingly beautiful, but the picture's two hour length has it running out of steam by the end.

Jeanne Moreau *Maria I* • Brigitte Bardot *Maria II* • George Hamilton *Florès* • Gregor von Rezzori *Diogène* ■ *Dir* Louis Malle • *Scr* Louis Malle, Jean-Claude Carrière

Viva Max! ★★★ U

Comedy 1969 · US · Colour · 92mins
It's virtually impossible to ignore Peter Ustinov. But try to let your eye drift away from the master scene-stealer and on to John Astin (Gomez in TV's *The Addams Family*) who gives an admirably understated comic performance as his doltish sidekick. His twitchy idiocy stands in stark contrast to Ustinov's heavily-accented showboating, as the Mexican general who leads a ramshackle band across the border in a bid to retake the Alamo. Adapted from a novel by James Lehrer, this buoyantly played, but sloppily directed comedy was mostly shot at Cinecittà in Rome.

Peter Ustinov *General Maximilian Rodrigues de Santos* • Pamela Tiffin *Paula Whitland* • Jonathan Winters *General Billy Joe Hallson* • John Astin *Sgt Valdez* • Keenan Wynn *General Barney LaComber* • Harry Morgan *Chief of Police George Sylvester* • Alice Ghostley *Hattie Longstreet Daniel* • Kenneth Mars *Dr Sam Gillison* ■ *Dir* Jerry Paris • *Scr* Elliot Baker, from a novel by James Lehrer.

Viva Villa! ★★★

Biographical drama 1934 · US · BW · 115mins

An intelligently crafted, David O Selznick-produced MGM adventure epic, credited to director Jack Conway (also responsible for the Ronald Colman version of *A Tale of Two Cities*), but actually started by Howard Hawks. Some obvious studio-bound sequences mar enjoyment, and the whole thing is a tad overlong, but with some excellent supporting performances, notably from Stuart Erwin (a last-minute substitute for Lee Tracy) as a US reporter. Beery plays Villa, the Mexican revolutionary, warts and all. The crowd scenes are particularly well handled (the assistant director, John Waters, received an Oscar) and the scale is undeniably epic. If you like Beery, or have never seen him, this is one of his best. If you can't stand the sight of his brand of mugging, stay away.

Wallace Beery *Pancho Villa* • Fay Wray *Teresa* • Stuart Erwin *Johnny Sykes* • Leo Carillo *Sierra* • Donald Cook *Don Felipe* • George E Stone *Chavito* • Joseph Schildkraut *General Pascal* ■ *Dir* Jack Conway • *Scr* Ben Hecht, from the book by Edgcumb Pinchon, OB Stade

Viva Zapata! ★★★ PG

Biographical drama 1952 · US · BW · 108mins

Marlon Brando stars as Mexican revolutionary leader Emiliano Zapata in director Elia Kazan's celebrated drama. When the movie was first planned, producer Darryl Zanuck wanted Tyrone Power for the lead, but Kazan, who had just made *A Streetcar Named Desire*, finally persuaded him to go with Brando, while Jean Peters was preferred to Julie Harris for the heroine role. This remains a strong, exciting and heavily politicised picture, the script (by John Steinbeck) won Anthony Quinn an Oscar, playing Brando's brother and revolutionary colleague. There's also decent support from Joseph Wiseman, later famous as Dr No, the villain in the first Bond film. 🎦

Marlon Brando *Emiliano Zapata* • Jean Peters *Josefa Espejo* • Anthony Quinn *Eufemio Zapata* • Joseph Wiseman *Fernando Aguirre* • Arnold Moss *Don Nacio* • Alan Reed *Pancho Villa* • Margo *La Soldadera* • Harold Gordon *Don Francisco Madero* ■ *Dir* Elia Kazan • *Scr* John Steinbeck, from the novel *Zapata the Unconquered* by Edgcumb Pichon

Vivacious Lady ★★★ U

Comedy drama 1938 · US · BW · 90mins

Professor James Stewart tries to tell his conservative dad, the wonderfully irascible Charles Coburn, that he has married showgirl Ginger Rogers in this sparkling screwball comedy, directed by the great George Stevens. It's a funny idea, and you don't really notice that it's a one-joke movie. Super support actors include Beulah Bondi,

playing slightly against type as Stewart's mum, Franklin Pangborn and Grady Sutton, and, very early in their careers, lively Jack Carson and loveable Hattie McDaniel. 🎦

Ginger Rogers *Frances Brent* • James Stewart *Peter Morgan* • James Ellison *Keith Beston* • Charles Coburn *Doctor Morgan* • Beulah Bondi *Mrs Morgan* • Frances Mercer *Helen* • Phyllis Kennedy *Jenny* • Alec Craig *Joseph* • Franklin Pangborn *Apartment manager* ■ *Dir* George Stevens • *Scr* PJ Wolfson, Ernest Pagano, by I AR Wylie

Vivre pour Vivre ★

Romantic drama 1967 · Fr · Colour · 130mins

This follow up to *A Man and a Woman* from director Claude Lelouch is risible. Despite the talents of Yves Montand and Candice Bergen, this sun-saturated, overstylised and poorly scripted film couldn't be worse. Montand plays a TV reporter who, despite being married to Annie Girardot, is unable to resist the charms of super-glamorous model Bergen. Cue an all too familiar love triangle with lashings of sex and tears, accompanied by a terrible soundtrack. In French with English subtitles.

Yves Montand *Robert Colomb* • Candice Bergen *Candice* • Annie Girardot *Catherine Colomb* • Irène Tunc *Mireille* • Anouk Ferjac *Jacqueline* ■ *Dir* Claude Lelouch • *Scr* Claude Lelouch, Pierre Uytterhoeven

Vixen ★★★★ 18

Cult sex comedy 1968 · US · Colour · 70mins

The one genuinely erotic movie made by cult director Russ Meyer. A huge box-office hit, it led him to mainstream Hollywood and his stunning trash satire *Beyond the Valley of the Dolls*. Pneumatic Erica Gavin is the Canadian nymphomaniac of the title, a pun on the then popular lesbian drama *The Fox*, who makes love with her bush pilot husband, her brother, a black draft-dodger, a Mountie and another woman while deciding if she really wants to fly to Cuba or not. Meyer got his explosive sexual cocktail past the censors of the day (not in Britain, though!) by cleverly incorporating the hot contemporary issues of racism, communism and Vietnam into his histrionic mix. As the uninhibited sexual healer of Meyer's crazed fable, Gavin rises to the occasion with a truthful abandon and conviction rarely seen in the soft-core genre. Contains swearing, sex scenes.

Erica Gavin *Vixen Palmer* • Harrison Page *Niles* • Garth Pillsbury *Tom Palmer* • Michael Donovan O'Donnell *O'Bannion* • Vincene Wallace *Janet King* • Jon Evans *Jud* • Robert Aitken *Dave King* ■ *Dir* Russ Meyer • *Scr* Robert Rudelson, from a story by Russ Meyer, Anthony James Ryan

Vladimir et Rosa ★★★

Experimental political drama 1970 · Fr/W Ger/US · Colour · 103mins

Ostensibly, this one of Jean-Luc Godard and Jean-Pierre Gorin's Dziga-Vertov experiments, is a reconstruction of the Chicago Seven conspiracy trial. But Godard's main purpose is to explore the film-making process, from the technical and artistic choices involved in the compromises that inevitably have to be made. Comprising peeks at the off-stage lives of the

characters and tactical discussions between the directors, the film alights on everything from the Black Panthers to radical feminism. In French with English subtitles.

Jean-Luc Godard *Jean-Luc Godard/Vladimir Lenin* • Jean-Pierre Gorin *Jean-Pierre Gorin/ Karl Rosa (after Rosa Luxemburg)* • Anne Wiazemsky *Ann, women's liberation militant* • Juliet Berto *Juliet/Weatherwoman/Hippie* • Yves Alfonso *Yves, revolutionary student from Berkeley* ■ *Dir/Scr* Jean-Luc Godard, Jean-Pierre Gorin

Vogues ★★★

Musical comedy 1937 · US · Colour · 108mins

A breathtaking and, unusually, blonde Joan Bennett stars as an impoverished debutante who ditches a hateful millionaire (Alan Mowbray) at the altar and goes to work as a model in New York's top fashion house, only to fall for its owner, Warner Baxter. However, the plot; involving dirty tricks from a rival designer (Mischa Auer) and romantic complications, is totally unimportant to a film whose *raison d'être* is high fashion. And what fashion it is – an extravaganza of magnificent clothes donned by America's top models of the time, plus a pageant of outrageous costumes worn by Park Avenue matrons at the Seven Arts Ball. A must-see for Bennett fans, fashion freaks and colour enthusiasts.

Warner Baxter *George Curson* • Joan Bennett *Wendy Van Klettering* • Helen Vinson *Mary Curson* • Mischa Auer *Prince Muratory* • Alan Mowbray *Henry Morgan* • Jerome Cowan *Mr Brockton* • Alma Kruger *Sophie Miller* • Marjorie Gateson *Mrs Lemke* • Hedda Hopper *Mrs Van Klettering* ■ *Dir* Irving Cummings • *Scr* Bella Spewack, Samuel Spewack • *Cinematographer* Ray Rennahan • *Costume Designer* Helen Taylor

Voice in the Mirror ★★★

Drama 1958 · US · BW · 102mins

This second cousin to the screen's classic study of alcoholism, *The Lost Weekend* (1945), charts the decline of successful LA commercial artist Richard Egan who, after his daughter dies, takes refuge in the bottle, despite the support and sympathy of his wife Julie London and his doctor Walter Matthau. Why and how he finally regenerates himself provides the movie's rather wafty and sentimental message, but this modest and non-starry movie does fine in the wake of its hard-hitting predecessor.

Richard Egan *Jim Burton* • Julie London *Ellen Burton* • Walter Matthau *Dr Leon Karnes* • Arthur O'Connell *William Tobin* • Ann Doran *Mrs Devlin* • Bart Bradley *Gene Devlin* • Hugh Sanders *Mr Hornsby* ■ *Dir* Harry Keller • *Scr* Larry Marcus

Voice of Merrill ★★

Mystery 1952 · UK · BW · 66mins

A complex and, ultimately, rather dull British suspenser, with Valerie Hobson and James Robertson-Justice as a husband and wife under suspicion for murdering a blackmailer. A talent much stronger than John Gilling's (who both wrote and directed this tosh) was needed to bring off this tale of murder among the plummy voices, but these days there's pleasure to be gained just from watching the elegant cast go

through their preposterous paces. Called *Murder Will Out* in the US.

Valerie Hobson *Alycia Roach* • Edward Underdown *Hugh Allen* • James Robertson-Justice *Jonathan Roach* • Henry Kendall *Ronald Parker* ■ *Dir* John Gilling • *Scr* John Gilling, from a story by Gerald Landeau, Terence Austin

Voices ★★ 15

Drama 1979 · US · Colour · 101mins

A rock-singer story with an idea so far-fetched it has jet lag. Michael Ontkean is the wannabe rocker who falls in love with deaf Amy Irving who – perhaps because of her deafness – falls in love with him. A story as silly as this requires more careful direction than it gets from Robert Markowitz. 🎦

Michael Ontkean *Drew Rothman* • Amy Irving *Rosemarie Lemon* • Alex Rocco *Frank Rothman* • Barry Miller *Raymond Rothman* ■ *Dir* Robert Markowitz • *Scr* John Herzfeld

Voices of Sarafina! ★★★

Documentary 1988 · US · Colour · 85mins

The hit musical *Sarafina!* charts the political awakening of a black schoolgirl growing up in a seventies South African township and was filmed in 1992 with Whoopi Goldberg. This documentary goes behind the scenes of the original Broadway production and talks to the young black South African actors involved about the oppression they experience in their homeland. Urged by the show's writer/director Mbongeni Ngema, the schoolchildren show a passionate commitment to being international ambassadors for black South Africa and give frank and often harrowing testimonies. But it is the infectious joy of the youngsters' invigorating singing and dancing that reveals itself as their most potent means of self-expression and their strongest weapon against the evils of apartheid.

Dir Nigel Noble • *Scr* Mbongeni Ngema • *Music* Hugh Masekela • *Costume Designer* Irene, Omar Kiam

Volcano ★★

Drama 1950 · It · BW · 106mins

William Dieterle was a German-born Hollywood director best known for *The Hunchback of Notre Dame* and biopics of Emile Zola and Louis Pasteur. In the early fifties he was tainted – but never officially blacklisted – by the McCarthy witch-hunts, so he fled to Europe and made this drama in the neorealist style of *La Terra Trema* and *Stromboli*, which it closely resembles as it was shot in the same location. Anna Magnani stars as a Naples prostitute, sentenced by the courts to return to her village on a volcanic island where life is as harsh as a prison sentence. Rossano Brazzi, a man with a past and not much of a future, arrives and upsets the apple cart. An Italian language film.

Anna Magnani *Maddalena Natoli* • Rossano Brazzi *Donato* • Geraldine Brooks *Maria* • Eduardo Ciannelli *Giulio* ■ *Dir* William Dieterle • *Scr* Piero Tellini, Victor Stoloff, Erskine Caldwell, from a story by Renzo Avanzo

Volcano ★★★ 12

Disaster thriller 1997 · US · Colour · 99mins

Emergency chief Tommy Lee Jones saves Los Angeles from being covered by molten lava in a taut, 1990's redefinition of the disaster movie. Using the simple suspense device of cross-cutting, the blissfully unaware main players go about their daily activities with ominous subterranean magma heaving, the digital special effects come into their own when the city streets become rivers of fire and the urban destruction goes on overdrive. A gripping and spectacular action fantasy in which MacArthur Park does indeed melt in the dark. ▦

DVD

Tommy Lee Jones *Mike Roark* • Anne Heche *Dr Amy Barnes* • Gaby Hoffman *Kelly Roark* • Don Cheadle *Emmit Reese* • Jacqueline Kim *Dr Jaye Calder* • Keith David *Lieutenant Ed Fox* • John Corbett *Norman Calder* • Michael Rispoli *Gator Harris* ■ *Dir* Mick Jackson • *Scr* Jerome Armstrong, from a story by Billy Ray

Volcano: Fire on the Mountain ★★

Disaster thriller 1997 · US · Colour · 88mins

Volcanologists had been pretty thin on the ground in the cinema until 1996 when they suddenly seemed to be everywhere you looked. Just as Pierce Brosnan predicted dire events in Roger Donaldson's *Dante's Peak*, so Dan Cortese keeps himself busy warning the residents of a chic Californian ski resort that its bumper season is going to end in disaster. Because this was a TV movie, director Graeme Campbell has nowhere near the special effects budget that Donaldson had, so he wisely concentrates on the various human dramas precipitated by the impending disaster rather than on rivers of molten lava and crumbling masonry.

Dan Cortese *Peter Slater* • Cynthia Gibb *Kelly Adams* • Don Davis [Don S Davis] *Mayor Hart* • Lynda Boyd *Maureen* • Brian Kerwin *Buck Adams* • Colin Cunningham *Stan* ■ *Dir* Graeme Campbell • *Scr* Craig Spector, Steve Womack, from a story by Donna Ebbs, Merrill Karpf, Scott Weinstein

Volere, Volare ★★★★ 15

Part-animated romantic fantasy 1991 · It · Colour · 91mins

Even though Maurizio Nichetti and Guido Manuli ingeniously combine live-action and animated footage in this endlessly inventive comedy, it's the noises that linger in the memory. As the exacting sound editor who begins to turn into a cartoon on encountering kinky hooker Angela Finocchiaro, Nichetti combines slapstick and psychological humour to great effect. Things get off to a sluggish start, but once animated animals and Nichetti's pornographer brother start interfering in his love life, the action becomes increasingly amusing and audacious. In Italian with English subtitles. Contains nudity. ▦

Angela Finocchiaro *Martina* • Maurizio Nichetti *Maurizio* • Mariella Valentini *Loredana* • Patrizio Roversi *Patrizio* • Remo Remotti *Professor Bambino* ■ *Dir* Maurizio Nichetti, Guido Manuli, Walter Cavazutti, Walter Cavazutti • *Scr* Maurizio Nichetti, Guido Manuli

Les Voleurs ★★ 18

Thriller 1996 · Fr · Colour · 111mins

By shuffling perspectives and alternating time frames, André Téchiné makes a bold assault here on the structure of the traditional police drama. But in seeking to show that truth is often fragmentary, he concentrates too much on technique, with too little emotion expended on his characters. Flashing back from the murder of young Julien Rivière's father, the action centres primarily on the relationship between tomboy shoplifter Laurence Côte, Daniel Auteuil (a cop in a family of thieves) and lesbian philosophy teacher Catherine Deneuve. With performances as detached as the direction, this is an intellectual exercise bereft of humanity. In French with English subtitles. Contains sex scenes, swearing, violence. ▦

Catherine Deneuve *Marie* • Daniel Auteuil *Alex* • Laurence Côte *Juliette* • Benoît Magimel *Jimmy* • Fabienne Babe *Mireille* • Didier Bezace *Ivan* • Julien Rivière *Justin* ■ *Dir* André Téchiné • *Scr* André Téchiné, Gilles Taurand, Michel Alexandre, Pascal Bonitzer

Volpone ★★★

Comedy 1940 · Fr · BW · 94mins

Made before the outbreak of war, this handsome version of Ben Jonson's classic comedy was released during the occupation of France. It starred the great French actor Harry Baur in the title role, who had a Jewish wife and had played Jewish roles since the silent days. In 1943 after the film was shown, he was arrested, strenuously tortured by the Gestapo and died a few days later. Directed by Maurice Tourneur (father of Jacques), the film altered the central characterisation but otherwise acknowledged its origins with stylish visuals and memorable performances. In French with English subtitles.

Harry Baur *Volpone* • Louis Jouvet *Mosca* • Fernand Ledoux *Corvino* • Marion Dorian *Canina* • Jean Temerson *Voltore* • Alexandre Rignault *Leone* ■ *Dir* Maurice Tourneur • *Scr* Jules Romains, from the play by Ben Jonson

Volunteers ★★ 15

Comedy 1985 · US · Colour · 102mins

Tom Hanks is reunited with his *Splash* co-star John Candy for this clumsy, but occasionally amusing outing. Hanks plays the arrogant heir running away from his gambling debts who joins the Peace Corps in the early sixties and gets caught up with Asian warlords, communist guerrillas and the CIA. Candy steals the show playing an earnest patriot brainwashed into becoming a Maoist revolutionary, but director Nicholas Meyer plays down the satirical opportunities of the plot in the search for easy laughs. Contains violence, swearing. ▦

Tom Hanks *Lawrence Bourne III* • John Candy *Tom Tuttle From Tacoma* • Rita Wilson *Beth Wexler* • Tim Thomerson *John Reynolds* • Gedde Watanabe *At Toon* • George Plimpton *Lawrence Bourne Jr* • Ernest Harada *Chung Mee* ■ *Dir* Nicholas Meyer • *Scr* Ken Levine, David Isaacs, from a story by Keith Critchlow

Von Richthofen and Brown ★★ PG

War action drama 1971 · US · Colour · 92mins

Also known as *The Red Baron*, this aerial epic was released in the slipstream of *The Blue Max* and though it's often cheap and tawdry, it also looks more like an A movie than anything else made by B-movie supremo, Roger Corman. The legendary German flying ace von Richthofen is played by John Phillip Law (the angel from *Barbarella*) and his Canadian rival, Brown, is played by Don Stroud. One has a phony German accent, the other doesn't and both are conceived as *Boys' Own* cardboard cut-outs. Memories of *Wings* and *Hell's Angels* are hardly ever stirred and after this costly flop, Corman didn't direct another film for nearly two decades. ▦

John Phillip Law *Baron von Richthofen* • Don Stroud *Roy Brown* • Barry Primus *Hermann Goering* • Karen Huston *Ilse* • Corin Redgrave *Hawker* • Hurd Hatfield *Fokker* • George Armitage *Wolff* • Steve McHattie *Voss* ■ *Dir* Roger Corman • *Scr* John William Corrington, Joyce Hooper Corrington

Von Ryan's Express ★★★ PG

Second World War drama 1965 · US · Colour · 111mins

A rattlingly exciting Second World War escape adventure, following on from the box-office success of *The Great Escape*, with a well cast Frank Sinatra as Colonel Joseph L Ryan, a tough PoW who seizes a German train delivering Allied prisoners. Sinatra delivers one of his best performances, director Mark Robson uses his camera skilfully, and the support cast is exceptionally well chosen: co-star Trevor Howard is always excellent in confrontation roles, and a nod to *The Great Escape* finds John Leyton (who had a number one hit with *Johnny Remember Me* in 1961) as a British lieutenant. The eagle-eyed should note Hollywood restaurateur Michael Romanoff as an Italian noble. The film was a major commercial success in its day. ▦

Frank Sinatra *Col Joseph L Ryan* • Trevor Howard *Major Eric Fincham* • James Brolin *Private Ames* • Raffaela Carra *Gabriella* • Brad Dexter *Sergeant Bostick* • Sergio Fantoni *Captain Oriani* • John Leyton *Orde* • Edward Mulhare *Costanzo* • Wolfgang Preiss *Major von Klemment* ■ *Dir* Mark Robson • *Scr* Wendell Mayes, Joseph Landon, from a novel by David Westheimer

Voodoo ★★ 18

Supernatural thriller 1995 · US · Colour · 88mins

Former eighties teen heart-throb Corey Feldman still can't act, but at least in this supernatural thriller he has lost his former obnoxiousness. After transferring to a new college, Feldman is quickly accepted into a fraternity eager to have him. He soon finds out his frat buddies are voodoo practitioners, and that he is the key for the upcoming ceremony that will give them immortality. Surprisingly suspenseful, the unique Keith Bilderbeck score (more sounds than actual music) generates its own share of the atmosphere. If the characters weren't so clichéd, their fates and actions not so predictable, it could have been a genuine sleeper. Contains swearing, strong violence, nudity. ▦

Corey Feldman *Andy Chadway* • Sarah Douglas *Prof Conner* • Jack Nance *Lewis* • Joel Edwards *Marsh* • Diana Nadeau *Rebecca* • Ron Melendez *Erik* ■ *Dir* Rene Eram • *Scr* Brian Dimuccio, Dino Vindeni

Voodoo Man ★

Horror 1944 · US · BW · 62mins

Bela Lugosi continued his downward career trend in this Monogram mediocrity as mad Dr Marlowe, the lunatic occultist who kidnaps women to transfer their souls into his comatose wife, who has been in a permanent trance for over twenty years. Sixty two minutes of this chronic schlock ordeal would make anyone equally catatonic.

Bela Lugosi *Dr Richard Marlowe* • John Carradine *Toby* • George Zucco *Nicolas* • Tod Andrews [Michael Ames] *Ralph Dawson* • Wanda McKay *Betty Benton* • Ellen Hall *Mrs Evelyn Marlowe* ■ *Dir* William Beaudine • *Scr* Robert Charles

Voodoo Woman ★ PG

Horror 1957 · US · BW · 67mins

A cheap and cheerful slice of horror with a mad professor carrying out horrible experiments on a young (and beautiful, of course) woman. The stilted acting and dialogue will probably raise a laugh for some fans of this sort of cult nonsense, but one thing is for sure, no one will be remotely frightened by it. ▦

Marla English *Marilyn Blanchard* • Tom Conway *Dr Roland Gerard* • Touch Connors [Mike Connors] *Ted Bronson* • Lance Fuller *Rick/Harry* • Mary Ellen Kaye *Susan* • Paul Dubov *Marcel the Innkeeper* ■ *Dir* Edward L Cahn • *Scr* Russell Bender, VI Voss

Vote for Huggett ★★ U

Comedy 1948 · UK · BW · 81mins

The endearing Huggett family first appeared as characters in *Holiday Camp*. Three films, of which this was the second, followed their progress and later a long-running radio series ensured their popularity. Here, Joe is standing for election as a councillor but runs into trouble when he proposes a war memorial site on land part-owned by his wife – she won't sell. Chaos follows when niece Diana forges her aunt's signature and puts her uncle in a pickle. Jack Warner and Kathleen Harrison are wonderful as mum and dad and yes, that's a young Diana Dors as the troublesome niece. ▦

Jack Warner *Joe Huggett* • Kathleen Harrison *Ethel Huggett* • Susan Shaw *Susan* • Petula Clark *Pet Huggett* • David Tomlinson *Harold Hinchley* • Diana Dors *Diana* • Peter Hammond *Peter Hawtrey* • Amy Veness *Grandma* ■ *Dir* Ken Annakin • *Scr* Mabel Constanduros, Denis Constanduros, Allan Mackinnon

A Vow to Kill ★★ PG

Thriller 1995 · US · Colour · 87mins

Former teenage heart-throb Richard Grieco is the smooth con man who whisks away heiress Julianne Phillips to a honeymoon on an isolated island. But, unbeknown to her, Grieco is already demanding a ransom from her rich father. Phillips is landed with a thankless, empty-headed role, while Grieco is wildly over the top as the scheming gigolo. The anonymous direction is from Harry S Longstreet. ▣

Richard Grieco *Eric Lewis* • Julianne Phillips *Rachel Evans* • Gordon Pinsent *Frank Evans* • Peter MacNeill *Sam Flowers* • Tom Cavanagh *Andy Neiman* • Nicole Oliver *Linda Mason* ■ *Dir* Harry S Longstreet • *Scr* Sean Silas, Renee Longstreet, Harry S Longstreet

The Voyage ★★
Drama 1974 · It · Colour · 101mins

Dreary and ill-cast commercial disaster based upon Pirandello's tale of two lovers – not allowed to marry – who find themselves destroyed by fate. Neither Sophia Loren nor Richard Burton seem comfortable here, and it's depressing to discover that it was directed by the once-great neo-realist genius Vittorio De Sica, who previously steered Loren to her Oscar in *Two Women*. There's effective support from Ian Bannen, but the dubbing of the Italian supports leaves much to be desired. Burton and Loren didn't have much luck together with their next vehicle, the ill-conceived and dreadful TV version of *Brief Encounter*, which played some theatrical dates solely on the strength of their names. Italian dialogue dubbed into English.

Sophia Loren *Adriana* • Richard Burton *Cesar* • Ian Bannen *Antonio* • Renato Pinciroli *Doctor* • Daniele Pitani *Notary* • Barbara Pilavin *Mother* • Sergio Bruni *Armando Gill* ■ *Dir* Vittorio De Sica • *Scr* Diego Fabbri, Massimo Franciosa, Luisa Montagnana, from a play by Luigi Pirandello

The Voyage ★★★ 15
Political satire
1991 · Arg/Fr · Colour · 133mins

After celebrating the return of democracy to Argentina, Fernando E Solanas embarked on this pessimistic odyssey through Latin America, which laments not only the lingering legacy of oppression and neglect, but also the intrusive and exploitative presence of the United States. Travelling by bicycle from the world's southernmost city, Ushaia, in search of his anthropologist father, Walter Quiroz responds to such sights as flooded valleys, remote Andes villages, rickety gold mines and jungle outposts with a suitable mix of awe and disillusion. But, for all its arresting imagery, the film lacks thematic and dramatic focus. In Spanish with English subtitles. ▣

Walter Quiroz *Martin* • Soledad Alfaro *Vidala* • Ricardo Bartis *Monitor* • Cristina Becerra *Violeta* • Marc Berman *Nicolás* • Chiquinho Brandao *Paizinho* • Franklin Caicedo *Rower* ■ *Dir/Scr* Fernando E Solanas

Voyage ★★ 15
Drama 1993 · US · Colour · 85mins

Rutger Hauer sleepwalks his way through this routine straight-to-video thriller, which unsuccessfully attempts to cash in on the success of *Dead Calm*. Hauer and Karen Allen play a couple who rather unwisely decide to repair their marriage by taking a sea cruise with charming, but psychotic Eric Roberts and his girlfriend, Connie

Nielsen. Despite the quality cast, there's little in the way of suspense, and it's hard to believe that the film is directed by John Mackenzie (*The Long Good Friday*). Contains violence, sex scenes, swearing. ▣

Rutger Hauer *Morgan Norvell* • Eric Roberts *Gil Freeland* • Karen Allen *Catherine "Kit" Norvell* • Connie Nielsen *Ronnie Freeland* ■ *Dir* John Mackenzie • *Scr* Mark Montgomery, from a story by Mark Montgomery, Khris Baxter

Voyage of Terror ★★ 15
Thriller 1998 · US · Colour · 174mins

Outbreak meets *The Poseidon Adventure* in this silly, but fun disaster movie. TV icon Lindsay Wagner is a scientist on a cruise who discovers the flu bug that is sweeping the ship is, in fact, the lethal ebola virus. In true disaster movie style there is a starry cast including such luminaries as Martin Sheen, Brian Dennehy and Michael Ironside.

Lindsay Wagner *Dr Stephanie Tauber* • Michael Ironside *McBride* • Martin Sheen *Henry Northcutt* • Brian Dennehy *President of the United States* ■ *Dir* Brian Trenchard-Smith • *Scr* Mel Frohman

Voyage of Terror: the Achille Lauro Affair ★★
Drama based on a true story
1990 · US/W Ger/Fr/It · Colour

In 1985, four Palestinians hijacked an Italian cruise ship, torturing and killing a passenger. This Italian-made TV movie, originally a two-part mini-series based on the headline news event, relates the shocking facts in a highly engrossing manner. Hollywood stars Burt Lancaster and Eva Marie Saint play Leon and Marilyn Klinghoffer in the frightening tale, but most memorable is Joseph Nasser as the politically-driven head hijacker who'll stop at nothing to achieve his goal.

Burt Lancaster *Leon Klinghoffer* • Eva Marie Saint *Marilyn Klinghoffer* • Robert Culp *General Davies* • Renzo Nontagnani *Captain de Rosa* • Dominique Sanda *Margot* • Bernard Fresson *Pierre* • Gabriele Ferzetti *Annichiarico* • Joseph Nasser *Molqi* ■ *Dir* Alberto Negrin • *Scr* Sergio Donati, Alberto Negrin

Voyage of the Damned ★★ PG
Drama 1976 · UK · Colour · 174mins

An ark story that emerged several years before Schindler's, Stuart Rosenberg's film is based on the voyage of the *SS St Louis*, which set sail for Cuba in 1939 with 937 Jewish refugees on board, only to be forced back to Europe when it was refused a berth. As the ship's captain, Max von Sydow brings some much needed gravitas to the proceedings, but the script is desperate and the direction's unbearably ponderous. The odds against so many star names giving such bad performances in the same film are incalculable. A miserable memorial to a tragic event. ▣

Faye Dunaway *Denise Kreisler* • Max von Sydow *Captain Gustav Schroeder* • Oskar Werner *Dr Egon Kreisler* • Malcolm McDowell *Max* • James Mason *Dr Juan Remos* • Orson Welles *Jose Estedes* • Katharine Ross *Mira Hauser* • Ben Gazzara *Morris Troper* • Lee Grant *Lili Rosen* • Sam Wanamaker *Carl*

Rosen* • Lynne Frederick *Anna Rosen* • Julie Harris *Alice Feinchild* ■ *Dir* Stuart Rosenberg • *Scr* Steve Shagan, David Butler, from the book by Max Morgan-Witts, Gordon Thomas

Voyage to the Bottom of the Sea ★★★ U
Science-fiction adventure
1961 · US · Colour · 100mins

Walter Pidgeon and Joan Fontaine are top billed in this entertaining sci-fi outing, but the real star is the submarine *Seaview*. Accounting for $400,000 of the picture's budget, the glass-fronted nuclear sub went on to star in its own TV series following its exploits here, as admiral Pidgeon fires its missiles into the Van Allen radiation belt and saves Earth from meltdown. Fontaine is totally out of her depth, but Peter Lorre and the rest of the cast are splendid. Co-writer/producer/director Irwin Allen went on to become the king of the disaster movie in the early seventies, as the creative force behind such films as *The Poseidon Adventure* and *The Towering Inferno*. ▣

Walter Pidgeon *Admiral Harriman Nelson* • Joan Fontaine *Dr Susan Hiller* • Barbara Eden *Cathy Connors* • Peter Lorre *Commodore Lucius Emery* • Robert Sterling *Capt Lee Crane* • Michael Ansara *Miguel Alvarez* • Frankie Avalon *Chip Romano* • Regis Toomey *Dr Jamieson* ■ *Dir* Irwin Allen • *Scr* Irwin Allen, Charles Bennett, from a story by Allen

Voyage to the Planet of Prehistoric Women ★
Science-fiction fantasy
1966 · US · Colour · 78mins

Following *Voyage to the Prehistoric Planet*, this also recycles special effects highlights from the 1962 Russian science-fiction spectacle *Planeta Burg*. A disorienting dog's dinner of a movie with new footage shot by Peter Bogdanovich, it features fifties' sex bomb Mamie Van Doren as the leader of a tribe of bikini-clad alien maidens who lie around a beach and worship a pterodactyl god, while telepathically communicating with lost astronauts. None of the new scenes really match in this tortuously repackaged exploiter.

Mamie Van Doren *Moana* • Mary Mark • Paige Lee ■ *Dir* Derek Thomas [Peter Bogdanovich] • *Scr* Henry Ney

Voyage to the Prehistoric Planet ★
Fantasy 1965 · US · Colour · 80mins

Roger Corman used cannibalised footage from the 1962 Russian space epic *Planeta Burg* and incorporated new material shot by director Curtis Harrington. A spaceship crew crash-land on a planet and relay their encounters with robot men and dinosaurs to a space platform orbiting above them. As was often the case with Corman quickies of the sixties, the story behind the movie is more interesting than the movie itself.

Basil Rathbone *Professor Hartman* • Faith Domergue *Marcia* ■ *Dir* John Sebastian [Curtis Harrington] • *Scr* John Sebastian [Curtis Harrington]

Voyager ★★★ 15
Drama
1991 · Ger/Fr/Gr · Colour and BW · 108mins

A complex drama with the always impressive Sam Shepard as a Unesco worker and compulsive traveller who drifts through Europe and across the Atlantic on an ocean liner in search of love and the meaning of life. He's haunted by an affair from his past and a new romance with a young woman only takes him further back in time. Director Volker Schlöndorff cleverly conveys the mood of postwar Europe, and, even though the locations veer far and wide, eventually coming to rest in Greece, the main aim of the story is to journey inside Shepard's head. Contains sex scenes. ▣

Sam Shepard *Walter Faber* • Julie Delpy *Sabeth* • Barbara Sukowa *Hannah* • Dieter Kirchlechner *Herbert Hencke* • Deborra-Lee Furness *Ivy* • Traci Lind *Charlene* • August Zirner *Joachim* ■ *Dir* Volker Schlöndorff • *Scr* Rudy Wurlitzer, from the novel *Homo Faber* by Max Frisch

Vroom ★★ 15
Road movie drama
1988 · UK · Colour · 84mins

David Thewlis and Clive Owen hope to fulfil their dreams by hitting the open road in a classic American car they have lovingly restored. Unfortunately, they also take along a sultry divorcée, and soon the libidos and tensions begin to rise. Although nothing more than a formulaic road movie with a few quirky twists, the acting from the two headliners alone make it worthwhile. ▣

Clive Owen *Jake* • David Thewlis *Ringe* • Diana Quick *Susan* • Jim Broadbent *Donald* • Philip Tan *Shane* ■ *Dir* Beeban Kidron • *Scr* Jim Cartwright

W ★★★ **15**

Thriller 1974 · US · Colour · 91mins

This humdrum thriller is something of a comedown for director Richard Quine, (*The Solid Gold Cadillac* and *Bell, Book and Candle*). Former fashion model Twiggy (in her second film role) plays an amnesiac recovering from an abusive first marriage, but then her new marriage is disrupted when she is pursued by a mysterious attacker known only as "W". Naturally, her first husband (Dirk Benedict) is the prime suspect. Her second husband here is played by Michael Witney, who later became her first husband in real life. If Twiggy could have acted, some note of plausibility might have been struck but, as it is, it's just one of many pursued girl movies. ▣

Twiggy *Katie Lewis* • Michael Witney *Ben Lewis* • Eugene Roche *Charles Jasper* • Dirk Benedict *William Caulder* • John Vernon *Arnie Felson* • Michael Conrad *Lt Whitfield* • Alfred Ryder *Investigator* • Carmen Zapata *Betty* ■ *Dir* Richard Quine • *Scr* Gerald Di Pego, James Kelly, from the story *Chance for a Killing* by Ronald Shusett

WB, Blue and the Bean ★★ **15**

Action comedy 1988 · US · Colour · 84mins

W B stands for a character nicknamed "White Bread" in this uneven comedy, written and directed by former stuntman Max Kleven. *Baywatch* star David Hasselhoff plays the loaf in question, a charming, fast-living tennis coach moonlighting as a bail bondsman, who gets the hassle-free clients – until his boss posts a million-dollar bond for heiress Linda Blair. The woeful plot is no more than a means for Kleven to stage a series of action sequences; so line up the six-pack and leave your mind outside the door. ▣

David Hasselhoff *White Bread* • Linda Blair *Nettie* • Tony Brubaker *Blue* • Tom Rosales *Bean* • John Vernon *Mr Ridgeway* • Charles Brill *Haronian* • Gregory Scott Cummins *Zalazar* ■ *Dir/Scr* Max Kleven

WC Fields and Me ★★★

Biographical drama
1976 · US · Colour · 111mins

Lambasted on release for taking liberties with the truth, Arthur Hiller's biopic of famed tippler comedian Fields (Rod Steiger) remains impressive in its own right. Covering the life of the vaudevillian-turned-film-star from the perspective of lover Carlotta Monti, there's a feel of the real in its re-creation of the Hollywood of long ago. Like Fields, Steiger never lets you forget he's the star. But there are sterling support performances too,

from Valerie Perrine and Bernadette Peters among others.

Rod Steiger *WC Fields* • Valerie Perrine *Carlotta Monti* • John Marley *Studio Head Bannerman* • Jack Cassidy *John Barrymore* • Bernadette Peters *Melody* • Dana Elcar *Agent Dockstedter* • Paul Stewart *Florenz Ziegfeld* • Billy Barty *Ludwig* ■ *Dir* Arthur Hiller • *Scr* Bob Merrill, from the book by Carlotta Monti, Cy Rice • *Music* Henry Mancini

WUSA ★★★★

Drama 1970 · US · Colour · 114mins

A clutch of famous faces – Paul Newman, Joanne Woodward, Laurence Harvey – are upstaged by Anthony Perkins in this dark drama. Newman stars as a cynical disc jockey at a right-wing New Orleans radio station; Perkins is the liberal conscience whose confrontations with the station are so raw and relevant they sideline the brittle affair between Woodward and Newman. Despite such dramatic imbalance, there are enough insights here to make this one of the more important movies about the state of America in the seventies.

Paul Newman *Rheinhardt* • Joanne Woodward *Geraldine* • Anthony Perkins *Rainey* • Laurence Harvey *Farley* • Pat Hingle *Bingamon* • Cloris Leachman *Philomene* • Don Gordon *Bogdanovich* ■ *Dir* Stuart Rosenberg • *Scr* Robert Stone, from his novel *A Hall of Mirrors*

WW and the Dixie Dancekings ★★★

Comedy 1975 · US · Colour · 90mins

An amiable redneck dirt-kickin' romp from the days when genial Burt Reynolds could do no wrong, and when John G Avildsen was a director of promise, long before *Rocky V* and the *Karate Kids*. The "Dixie Dancekings" of the title are a hokey country-and-western outfit fronted by genuine country star Jerry Reed (who wrote the hit *Guitar Man* for Elvis Presley). There are those who think Burt is laconic, sexy and utterly loveable, and others who remain convinced that Mr Reynolds basically plays Mr Reynolds. His attempts to propel the band onwards and upwards are amusing and the easy charm that became his trademark makes this pleasant viewing. Contains some violence and swearing.

Burt Reynolds *WW Bright* • Conny Van Dyke *Dixie* • Jerry Reed *Wayne* • Ned Beatty *Country Bull* • James Hampton *Junior* • Don Williams *Leroy* • Richard D Hurst *Butterball* • Art Carney *Deacon Gore* ■ *Dir* John G Avildsen • *Scr* Thomas Rickman

Waati ★★

Political drama 1995 · Fr · Colour · 140mins

Souleymane Cissé, Mali's best-known film-maker, was acclaimed for *Yeelen*, his 1987 study of the clash between modern values and traditional tribal magic. Here, he turns his focus on apartheid, telling the story of a young South African girl who flees to the Ivory Coast after she kills a policeman in revenge for the murder of her family – shot for walking on a "whites only" beach. Four cinematographers worked on this sprawling drama to give each location a fresh feel, but even those impressed by the film's power and intensity will find it a little hard going

at times. In Zulu, Sotho, Afrikaans, French and English with subtitles. Contains violence, swearing.

Lineo Tsolo • Sidi Yaya • Mary Twala • Eric Meyeni ■ *Dir/Scr* Souleymane Cissé

Wabash Avenue ★★★

Musical 1950 · US · Colour · 92mins

One of Betty Grable's most popular and well-remembered musical vehicles, this Technicolor frolic is the one where she sings *I Wish I Could Shimmy like My Sister Kate*, among the 26 song standards propping up the soundtrack, and where hunk Victor Mature and casino owner Phil Harris vie for her favours. Sounds familiar? Of course. Twentieth Century-Fox simply remade Grable's 1943 hit *Coney Island* virtually in its entirety, moving the cast to 1890s Chicago. Still, it doesn't matter a jot, as director Henry Koster injects pace and overall brightness into a likeable and quaintly vulgar venture. It's well worth watching, especially if you harbour an aversion to the usual witless and mindless Fox musicals of this period.

Betty Grable *Ruby Summers* • Victor Mature *Andy Clark* • Phil Harris *Uncle Mike* • Reginald Gardiner *English Eddie* • James Barton *Hogan* • Barry Kelley *Bouncer* • Margaret Hamilton *Tillie Hutch* ■ *Dir* Henry Koster • *Scr* Harry Tugend, Charles Lederer

The Wackiest Ship in the Army ★★ **U**

Comedy 1961 · US · Colour · 95mins

A broken-down boat is used as a decoy in the Second World War, but the tone is uncertain: is it meant to be funny, or isn't it? As a screenwriter, Richard Murphy worked on some really interesting films, including *Broken Lance* and *Compulsion*. But here, he proves not to be the ideal director of his own material, despite a cast headed by the genial Jack Lemmon and teen idol Ricky Nelson, for whom underplaying is no real substitute for acting ability. The support cast is full of welcome faces but, overall, even though it later spawned a TV series, the film simply doesn't work. ▣

Jack Lemmon *Lt Rip Crandall* • Ricky Nelson *Ensign Tommy Hanson* • John Lund *Commander Vandewater* • Chips Rafferty *Patterson* • Tom Tully *Capt McClung* • Joby Baker *Josh Davidson* • Warren Berlinger *Sparks* • Patricia Driscoll *Maggie* ■ *Dir* Richard Murphy • *Scr* Richard Murphy, Herbert Margolis, William Raynor, from a story by Herbert Carlson

Wacko ★★★

Spoof horror 1981 · US · Colour · 80mins

A sloppy but quite lively and funny *Airplane!*-style spoof of *Halloween* and other famous horror movies. Whoever had the idea of casting Joe Don Baker as the world's sloppiest and most dirty-minded cop deserves a medal for his brilliance. His policeman character is in pursuit of the "Lawnmower Killer", who has left signs that he'll strike again 13 years to the day from when he first appeared. The best gags involve the skewering of the countless clichés found in slasher movies, though there are plenty of sight gags, puns and other amusing attempts at humour, and the movie keeps up the

hilarity until almost the very end. Appearances by famous (and yet to be famous) cult stars are the icing on the cake.

Joe Don Baker *Dick Harbinger* • Stella Stevens *Marg Graves* • George Kennedy *Dr Graves* • Julia Duffy *Mary Graves* • Scott McGinnis *Norman Bates* • Andrew Clay [Andrew Dice Clay] *Tony* • Elizabeth Daily *Bambi* • Michele Tobin *Rosie* • Anthony James *Zeke* ■ *Dir* Greydon Clark • *Scr* Dana Olsen, Michael Spound, M James Kauf Jr, David Greenwalt

Waco ★★

Western 1966 · US · Colour · 71mins

Despite the starring presence of Howard Keel, this is not a musical, but a run-of-the-mill, second-rung western. While the local citizenry is being terrorised by a gang of lawless thugs, Keel – a gunslinger with a hot reputation – is cooling his heels behind bars until somebody has the bright idea that he is the man to drive out the desperados. Released for the purpose, he does what's expected of him, with glamorous Jane Russell – whose costumes were designed by Edith Head – on hand for encouragement.

Howard Keel *Waco* • Jane Russell *Jill Stone* • Brian Donlevy *Ace Ross* • Wendell Corey *Preacher Sam Stone* • Terry Moore *Dolly* • John Smith *John Agar George Gates* • Gene Evans *Deputy Sheriff O'Neill* • DeForest Kelley *Bill Rile* ■ *Dir* RG Springsteen • *Scr* Steve Fisher, from the novel *Emporia* by Harry Sanford, Max Lamb

Wadi 1981-1991 ★★★

Drama 1991 · Is · Colour · 97mins

In 1981, Amos Gitai explored the daily reality of the Arab-Israeli conflict in *Wadi*, a revealing talking-head documentary. Returning to the scrubland of Wadi Rushmia, near Haifa, Gitai discovers that much has changed in the decade since his original documentary about the difficulties of co-existence in Israel's disputed territories. The main focus this time is on a couple of Russian immigrants, one of whom has fallen in love with a Galilean woman, while the other lives in isolation with his animals, having been shunned by this perpetual tinderbox of a community.

Dir/Scr Amos Gitai

Wag the Dog ★★★★ **15**

Satirical comedy 1997 · US · Colour · 92mins

Just before an election, the US President is accused of molesting a teenage girl in the Oval Office. Keen to divert interest away from the scandal, he orders his spin doctors to come up with something quickly. In consultation with a Hollywood producer, they invent a war against Albania. Of course, this is pure fiction – things like that don't happen in real life, do they? Yet, *Wag the Dog* suddenly found itself mentioned every night on the news as Clinton fought against the mire of Monica and Milosevic. Robert De Niro is creepily effective as the tweedy, faceless spin doctor hired by Anne Heche of the White House PR machine, but best of all is Dustin Hoffman, who gives a hilarious performance as the tanned Hollywood mogul. Shot by Barry Levinson in a mere 29 days, this satire on the media and politics is a joy from start to finish. Contains some swearing and sexual references. ▭ **DVD**

Dustin Hoffman *Stanley Motss* • Robert De Niro *Conrad Brean* • Anne Heche *Winifred Ames* • Denis Leary *Fad King* • Willie Nelson *Johnny Green* • Andrea Martin *Liz Butsky* • Kirsten Dunst *Tracy Lime* • William H Macy *Mr Young* • Craig T Nelson *Senator Neal* • Woody Harrelson *Sergeant William Schumann* • Jim Belushi [James Belushi] *Jim Belushi* ■ *Dir* Barry Levinson • *Scr* David Mamet, Hilary Henkin, from the novel *American Hero* by Larry Beinhart

The Wages of Fear
★★★★★ PG

Adventure   1953 · Fr · BW · 147mins

The tension is unbearable as two truckloads of nitroglycerin traverse 300 miles of inhospitable Latin American terrain in order to help extinguish an oilfield fire. But, for all it says about courage and endurance, this is also a grindingly cynical study of human nature, with each member of the expatriate quartet willing to sacrifice the others for a bigger payoff. In bringing Georges Arnaud's novel to the screen, Henri-Georges Clouzot wisely spends time shading in the background detail that intensifies the excitement of the action by drenching it in a sweaty, anti-Hawksian spirit of rivalry. Unusually winning top prizes at both Cannes and Berlin, this is cinema's most suspenseful condemnation of capitalism. In English and French with subtitles. ▭

Yves Montand *Mario* • Charles Vanel *Jo* • Vera Clouzot *Linda* • Folco Lulli *Luigi* • Peter Van Eyck *Bimba* • William Tubbs *O'Brien* • Dario Moreno *Hernandez* ■ *Dir* Henri-Georges Clouzot • *Scr* Henri-Georges Clouzot, Jérome Géronimi, from the novel *Le Salaire de la Peur* by Georges Arnaud

Wagner
★★ 15

Epic biographical drama
1983 · UK/Hun/Aus · Colour · 488mins

This biopic of the composer was conceived by maverick director Tony Palmer on a very grand scale indeed. It was shot in six countries with Richard Burton in the title role; Olivier, Gielgud and Richardson on screen together; and a supporting cast of thousands including the Hungarian army. Wagner's music is played by three orchestras, conducted by Georg Solti. The first cut, nine hours long, premiered in London in 1983 to mixed reviews. Palmer declared that he would never cut it, but shorter versions emerged later. Wagnerians hoping for new insight into the obsessions of a highly complex mind will find instead an epic folly of the old school, very nice to look at, thanks to cameraman Vittorio Storaro. ▭

Richard Burton *Richard Wagner* • Vanessa Redgrave *Cosima* • Gemma Craven *Minna Wagner* • Laszlo Galffi *Ludwig II* • John Gielgud *Pfistermeister* • Ralph Richardson *Pforden* • Laurence Olivier *Pfeufer* • Ekkehard Schall *Franz Liszt* ■ *Dir* Tony Palmer • *Scr* Charles Wood • *Cinematographer* Vittorio Storaro

Wagonmaster
★★★★ PG

Western   1950 · US · BW · 85mins

One of the greatest and most warmly human of the series of westerns made by the master of the genre, John Ford, this time a simplistic plot about two young itinerant cowboys who help lead a Mormon wagon train to Utah. As youths, Harry Carey Jr and Ben Johnson reveal a callow expectancy of what life has in store, and are profoundly moving as they exchange stanzas when deciding to "fall in 'hind the wagon train". Many sequences are beautifully filmed, particularly a difficult river crossing, and it is interesting to see Ward Bond on hand, later to play the lead in *Wagon Train*, the TV series inspired by the movie. ▭

Ben Johnson *Travis* • Ward Bond *Wiggs* • Joanne Dru *Denver* • Harry Carey Jr *Sandy* • Charles Kemper *Uncle Shiloh* • Alan Mowbray *Dr Locksley Hall* • Jane Darwell *Sister Ledyard* • James Arness *Floyd Clegg* ■ *Dir* John Ford • *Scr* Frank S Nugent [Frank Nugent], Patrick Ford, from a story by John Ford • *Cinematographer* Bert Glennon • *Music* Richard Hageman

Wagons East!
★ PG

Comedy western
1994 · US · Colour · 102mins

It's always a shame when a star dies young, but it seems doubly unfair that someone as likeable and talented as John Candy should have bowed out part-way through the production of this stinker. The idea of having a bunch of lily-livered pioneers quit the Wild West and head home is essentially a good one. Yet director Peter Markle buries it in a quagmire of comic incompetence, which can't have been helped by the loss of his lead. Candy and John C McGinley are shamefully wasted as the spotlight falls continuously on the painfully unfunny Richard Lewis, although not even he can be blamed for the dismal slapstick. Contains swearing. ▭

John Candy *James Harlow* • Richard Lewis *Phil Taylor* • John C McGinley *Julian* • Ellen Greene *Belle* • Robert Picardo *Ben Wheeler* • Ed Lauter *John Slade* • William Sanderson *Zeke* • Rodney A Grant *Little Feather* ■ *Dir* Peter Markle • *Scr* Matthew Carlson, from a story by Jerry Abrahamson

The Wagons Roll at Night
★★

Crime drama   1941 · US · BW · 83mins

In this Warner Bros reworking of their own movie *Kid Galahad*, Humphrey Bogart is the owner of a seedy carnival, intent on protecting his convent-educated young sister, Joan Leslie, from his rough life. Meanwhile, when a lion escapes, he fires his tamer (Sig Ruman) and takes on Eddie Albert instead, who proceeds to fall for Leslie. It's extraordinary to think that this melodramatic farrago, which so ill-befits its star, was made in the same year as the Bogart classic *The Maltese Falcon*.

Humphrey Bogart *Nick Coster* • Sylvia Sidney *Flo Lorraine* • Eddie Albert *Matt Varney* • Joan Leslie *Mary Coster* • Sig Rumann [Sig Ruman] *Hoffman the Great* • Cliff Clark *Doc* ■ *Dir* Ray Enright • *Scr* Fred Niblo Jr, Barry Trivers, from the novel *Kid Galahad* by Francis Wallace

Waikiki Wedding
★★★

Musical comedy   1937 · US · BW · 88mins

This good-natured sun-drenched musical, characteristic of the period, is set in a Paramount studio version of Hawaii. Here, amid the grass skirts and exotic scenery, pineapple growers' PR man Bing Crosby is masterminding a Miss Pineapple beauty contest. Bing, of course, falls for the winner, Shirley Ross, and croons his way through several "South Seas" numbers, including Oscar-winning mega-hit *Sweet Leilani*, while his sidekick Bob Burns tangles with motor-mouthed Martha Raye to supply the comedy. The hula-hula-style choreography by LeRoy Prinz picked up an Oscar nomination.

Bing Crosby *Tony Marvin* • Bob Burns *Shad Buggle* • Martha Raye *Myrtle Finch* • Shirley Ross *Georgia Smith* • George Barbier *JP Todhunter* • Leif Erickson *Dr Victor Quimby* • Anthony Quinn *Kimo* ■ *Dir* Frank Tuttle • *Scr* Frank Butler, Don Hartman, Walter DeLeon, Frances Martin, from a story by Frank Butler, Don Hartman • *Choreographer* LeRoy Prinz

Wait 'til the Sun Shines, Nellie
★★★ U

Drama   1952 · US · Colour · 107mins

Produced by vaudeville legend George Jessel, this is a polished and thoroughly professional piece of period melodrama that demonstrates the virtue of that old-fashioned concept – a story with a beginning, a middle and an end. David Wayne gives his finest screen performance as the homely small-town barber who accepts the joys and trials of life with equal grace. Director Henry King shows the same sure grasp of bygone America that had made his *In Old Chicago* and *Alexander's Ragtime Band* so special, and, while this isn't in the same class, it's still finely crafted entertainment.

David Wayne *Ben Halper* • Jean Peters *Nellie* • Hugh Marlowe *Ed Jordan* • Albert Dekker *Lloyd Slocum* • Helene Stanley *Eadie Jordan* • Tommy Morton [Tom Morton] *Ben Halper Jr, aged 20* • Joyce MacKenzie *Bessie Jordan* • Alan Hale Jr *George Oliphant* ■ *Dir* Henry King • *Scr* Allan Scott, Maxwell Shane, from the novel *I Heard Them Sing* by Ferdinand Reyher

Wait till Your Mother Gets Home!
★★★

Comedy based on a true story
1983 · US · Colour

Starsky and Hutch star Paul Michael Glaser here gets to do his *Mr Mom* impersonation in this blatant TV movie rip-off of the Michael Keaton comedy. Despite the familiarity of the plot (butch man has to stay home and look after the house and kiddies while wife Dee Wallace goes to work), Glaser manages to make the movie amiable enough, and, although he doesn't have the comic timing and manic expressions of Keaton, he still injects considerable charm into the proceedings.

Paul Michael Glaser *Bob Peters* • Dee Wallace [Dee Wallace Stone] *Pat Peters* • Peggy McCay *Cynthia Peters* • David Doyle *Herman Ohme* • Ray Buktenica *Fred* • Lynne Moody *Marion* • Rita Taggart *Mrs Walt Johnson* ■ *Dir* Bill Persky • *Scr* Bill Persky, David Eyre Jr

Wait until Dark
★★★★

Thriller   1967 · US · Colour · 108mins

A powerful piece of theatre can often seem very flat on film because the screen distances the viewer from the immediacy and intimacy of the stage performance. Terence Young's version of Frederick Knott's Broadway hit is a magnificent exception. Oscar-nominated Audrey Hepburn is quite superb as the blind woman who keeps her wits about her when drug dealers break into her apartment to recover a doll full of heroin. Alan Arkin pulls out all the psychotic stops as the leader of the gang, and Young never lets the suspense drop. Contains violence.

Audrey Hepburn *Susy Hendrix* • Alan Arkin *Roat* • Richard Crenna *Mike Talman* • Efrem Zimbalist Jr *Sam Hendrix* • Jack Weston *Carlino* • Samantha Jones *Lisa* • Julie Herrod *Gloria* • Frank O'Brien *Shatner* ■ *Dir* Terence Young • *Scr* Robert Carrington, Jane-Howard Carrington, from the play by Frederick Knott • *Cinematographer* Charles Lang

Wait until Spring, Bandini
★★

Drama 1989 · Bel/Fr/It/US · Colour · 100mins

Too little is asked of a fine cast in this handsome, but uninspiring adaptation of John Fante's autobiographical novel. Belgian director Dominique Deruddere brings a keen outsider's eye to the Colorado setting, but his grasp of the twenties atmosphere is less assured. Joe Mantegna offers a typically bullish performance, as the unemployed bricklayer with a penchant for gambling and a deep-seated loathing of his mother-in-law, Renata Vanni. But neither Ornella Muti, as his put-upon wife, nor Faye Dunaway, as a seductive neighbour make much of an impact, although Michael Bacall registers as the movie-mad son who cannily saves his parents' marriage.

Joe Mantegna *Svevo Bandini* • Ornella Muti *Maria Bandini* • Faye Dunaway *Mrs Effie Hildegarde* • Burt Young *Rocco Saccone* • Michael Bacall *Arturo Bandini* • Renata Vanni *Donna Toscana, Maria's mother* ■ *Dir* Dominique Deruddere • *Scr* Dominique Deruddere, from the novel by John Fante

Waiting
★★★ 15

Drama   1990 · Ausl · Colour · 93mins

A domestic drama from down under, about an artist who agrees to be a surrogate mum to a childless couple's baby. The film follows the girl and her friends through the pregnancy, with events taking a dramatic turn when she starts having second thoughts about giving the baby up. Noni Hazlehurst plays the lady who waits while her co-stars include Deborra-Lee Furness, the bike-riding avenger in cult Aussie movie *Shame*.

Noni Hazlehurst *Clare* • Deborra-Lee Furness *Diane* • Frank Whitten *Michael* • Helen Jones *Sandy* • Denis Moore *Bill* • Fiona Press *Therese* • Ray Barrett *Frank* • Noga Bernstein *Rosie* ■ *Dir/Scr* Jackie McKimmie

Waiting for Guffman
★★★ 15

Comedy   1996 · US · Colour · 80mins

Straight-faced "mockumentary" that sends up am-dram pretentiousness and middle American values in equal

measure. Directed by and starring Christopher Guest (*Spinal Tap*), the film's spot-on spoofery focuses on a smalltown "auteur" and his ambitious plan to stage a musical review to mark the town's 150th anniversary. The results are far funnier than the film's inability to secure UK distribution might suggest (it earned merely a low-key video release), and a strong support cast includes Catherine O'Hara and Parker Posey. ▣

Christopher Guest *Corky St Clair* • Eugene Levy *Dr Allan Pearl* • Fred Willard *Ron Albertson* • Catherine O'Hara *Sheila Albertson* • Parker Posey *Libby Mae Brown* • Bob Balaban *Lloyd Miller* • Lewis Arquette *Clifford Wooley* ■ *Dir* Christopher Guest • *Scr* Christopher Guest, Eugene Levy • *Music/Lyrics* Michael McKean, Harry Shearer, Christopher Guest

Waiting for Michelangelo
★★
Romantic comedy drama
1995 · Can/Swi · Colour · 93mins

Typical! You wait ages for a bloke and then two come along at once. That's the situation in which single mother and TV journalist Renée Coleman finds herself in this amiable romantic comedy. The two men who match her identikit ideal are a Swiss gallery owner and a successful writer, but which one is as perfect as Michelangelo's David? Coleman holds things together nicely, although the story is a little too familiar and the characters a touch too contrived to engross.

Renée Coleman *Kelly Hildon* • Roy Dupuis *Thomas Schumacher* • Rick Roberts *Jonathan* • Jeremy Chance *Peter* • Michael Adam *Austin Hildon* • Ruth Marshall *Evelyn* ■ *Dir* Curt Truninger • *Scr* Margrit Ritzmann, Curt Truninger

Waiting for the Light
★★★ **PG**
Comedy drama 1989 · US · Colour · 90mins

In her later years Shirley MacLaine has specialised in portrayals of eccentric ladies of a certain age. This is one of her best – a former circus performer, now children's entertainer, whose behaviour brings trouble to her niece Teri Garr, who has taken on a diner in a small town in Washington State. It's pleasant enough, but director Chris Monger's debut feature has little rhyme or reason. MacLaine gives a polished performance and the surface sheen makes for enjoyable viewing, but underneath there's little of substance. Contains some swearing. ▣

Shirley MacLaine *Aunt Zena* • Teri Garr *Kay Harris* • Colin Baumgartner *Eddie Harris* • Hillary Wolf *Emily Harris* • Clancy Brown *Joe* • Vincent Schiavelli *Mullins* • John Bedford Lloyd *Reverend Stevens* • Jeff McCracken *Charlie* ■ *Dir/Scr* Christopher Monger

Waiting for the Moon
★
Biographical drama
1987 · US · Colour · 88mins

Linda Bassett and Linda Hunt play one of the 20th century's most interesting couples, author Gertrude Stein and cookery writer Alice B Toklas. The infamous pair lived together in Paris for over twenty years and played host to artists from Hemingway to Picasso. Sadly, this great story is still waiting to be told well as Jill Godmilow's film only skims the surface. There is no apparent depth to the relationship between these women despite the talent of the two actresses.

Linda Hunt *Alice B Toklas* • Linda Bassett *Gertrude Stein* • Andrew McCarthy *Henry Hopper* • Bernadette Lafont *Fernande Olivier* • Bruce McGill *Ernest Hemingway* • Jacques Boudet *Guillaume Apollinaire* ■ *Dir* Jill Godmilow • *Scr* Mark Magill, from a story by Jill Godmilow, Mark Magill

Waiting to Exhale
★★★ **15**
Drama 1995 · US · Colour · 118mins

No matter what problems confront the female quartet in this crowd-pleasing melodrama, the most pressing concern always seems to be the shortage of good men. Like that woman's picture extraordinaire *Thelma & Louise*, it's directed by a man – marking the directorial debut of Forest Whitaker. There's a patronising tone of indulgence pervading the film that manifests itself in the smart one-liners, the minor triumphs designed to elicit high-fives among the audience and the tear-jerking feelgood of the finale. Expertly acted by a cast that includes Whitney Houston and Angela Bassett, this owes little to life and a bit too much to glossy magazine aspirations. ▣

Whitney Houston *Savannah* • Angela Bassett *Bernadine* • Loretta Devine *Gloria* • Lela Rochon *Robin* • Gregory Hines *Marvin* • Dennis Haysbert *Kenneth* • Mykel T Williamson *Troy* • Michael Beach *John Sr* ■ *Dir* Forest Whitaker • *Scr* Terry McMillan, Ronald Bass, from the novel by Terry McMillan

Waiting Women
★★★
Comedy 1952 · Swe · BW · 94mins

This episodic drama from Ingmar Bergman continued his fascination with exploring the battle of the sexes from the female perspective. Waiting for their partners to join them for the summer, three sisters-in-law describe key moments in their relationships. Anita Björk talks about an extra-marital affair and the effect it had on her husband; Maj-Britt Nilsson recalls the pregnancy that led her to marry painter Birger Malmsten; and Eva Dahlbeck alights on a night stuck in a lift with her pompous spouse, Gunnar Björnstrand. It's a patchy anthology, but the comic finale is splendid. In Swedish with English subtitles.

Anita Björk *Rakel* • Eva Dahlbeck *Karin* • Maj-Britt Nilsson *Marta* • Karl Arne Holmsten *Eugen* • Jarl Kulle *Kaj* • Birger Malmsten *Martin* • Gunnar Björnstrand *Fredrik* ■ *Dir/Scr* Ingmar Bergman

Wake Island
★★★★
Second World War drama
1942 · US · BW · 87mins

A major Second World War movie, made at a time when America was beginning to realise what the conflict was about and that some mothers' sons wouldn't be coming home. Director John Farrow achieves an almost documentary-style realism, even though the film is relentlessly Hollywood in style and features that well-known studio platoon consisting entirely of stereotypes. News of the heroic December 1941 defence of Wake, a Pacific island lost to the Japanese, was barely off the presses when filming began, and a grim gung-ho mood is apparent throughout the feature. It received four Oscar nominations, including best picture, best director and best supporting actor for William Bendix, who, along with Brian Donlevy, gives a particularly fine performance. The ending is very moving and extraordinarily patriotic.

Brian Donlevy *Major Geoffrey Caton* • Macdonald Carey *Lieutenant Cameron* • Robert Preston *Joe Doyle* • William Bendix *Smacksie Randall* • Albert Dekker *Shad McClosky* • Walter Abel *Commander Roberts* • Mikhail Rasumny *Probenzky* • Don Castle *Private Cunkel* ■ *Dir* John Farrow • *Scr* WR Burnett, Frank Butler

Wake Me when It's Over
★★ **U**
Comedy 1960 · US · Colour · 125mins

It's hard to credit while viewing this lacklustre adaptation of Howard Singer's novel that only five years earlier Mervyn LeRoy had co-directed that classic portrait of service life, *Mister Roberts*. Dick Shawn assumes the Bilko-like mantle from Jack Lemmon, as he cashes in on the clerical error that drafted him by setting up a luxury hotel on an isolated Japanese island. There's a good chemistry between Shawn and Ernie Kovacs, the platoon captain whose men are the joint's most dedicated patrons, but the dialogue could do with a little more snap, especially in the court-martial sequences.

Ernie Kovacs *Captain Stark* • Margo Moore *Lt Nora McKay* • Jack Warden *Doc Farrington* • Nobu McCarthy *Ume* • Dick Shawn *Gus Brubaker* • Don Knotts *Sgt Warren* ■ *Dir* Mervyn LeRoy • *Scr* Richard L Breen, from a novel by Howard Singer • *Cinematographer* Leon Shamroy

Wake of the Red Witch
★★★ **PG**
Adventure 1949 · US · BW · 102mins

A John Wayne seafaring action adventure from Republic studios. It would have benefited from colour, but still provides reasonable entertainment. Gail Russell is the girl Wayne and rival ship owner Luther Adler are fighting over, and the South Seas setting is very studio-bound. The *Red Witch* herself was used again in 1953's *Fair Wind to Java*, and now resides in the Hollywood Wax Museum on Hollywood Boulevard. Incidentally, Wayne named his film production company, Batjac, after the fictional shipping line in this movie. ▣

John Wayne *Captain Ralls* • Gail Russell *Angelique Desaix* • Gig Young *Sam Rosen* • Luther Adler *Mayrant Ruysdaal Sidneye* • Adele Mara *Teleia Van Schreeven* • Paul Fix *Antonio "Ripper" Arrezo* • Eduard Franz *Harmenszoon Van Schreeven* ■ *Dir* Edward Ludwig • *Scr* Harry Brown, Kenneth Gamet, from the novel by Garland Roark

Wake Up and Live
★★★
Musical comedy 1937 · US · BW · 91mins

Alice Faye's beautiful rendition here of *There's a Lull in My Life* should be more than enough for most of her fans. But this Faye vehicle (one of four she made the same year) also has a fast and furious plot involving a feud between band leader Ben Bernie and arch-columnist and broadcaster Walter Winchell, no less. There's some nice clowning, too, from Jack Haley as a performer with a phobia about microphones, two years before he played the Tin Man in *The Wizard of Oz*. Former jazz musician Sidney Lanfield provides the pacy direction for this fine example of Hollywood taking revenge on its then-current rival, radio.

Walter Winchell • Ben Bernie • Alice Faye *Alice Huntley* • Patsy Kelly *Patsy Kane* • Ned Sparks *Steve Cluskey* • Jack Haley *Eddie Kane* • Grace Bradley *Jean Roberts* ■ *Dir* Sidney Lanfield • *Scr* Harry Tugend, Jack Yellen, from a story by Curtis Kenyon, from the book by Dorothea Brande

Waking Ned
★★★★ **PG**
Comedy 1998 · UK/Fr · Colour · 87mins

An utterly charming gem of a film from first-time director Kirk Jones, which was a surprise hit Stateside thanks to an imaginative marketing effort. Set on a tiny Irish island, two old men become hysterical when they discover an anonymous local has won the lottery. Their attempts to uncover the lucky so-and-so involve bribery and much false nicety until success results in them orchestrating a complex lie which involves the entire community. Ian Bannen stars with David Kelly as the avaricious OAPs in a tale that is both laugh out loud funny and extremely touching.

Ian Bannen *Jackie O'Shea* • David Kelly *Michael O'Sullivan* • Fionnula Flanagan *Annie O'Shea* • Susan Lynch *Maggie* • James Nesbitt *Pig Finn* • Maura O'Malley *Mrs Kennedy* • Robert Hickey *Maurice* • Paddy Ward *Brendy* ■ *Dir/Scr* Kirk Jones

Walk a Crooked Mile
★★
Spy drama 1948 · US · BW · 90mins

Dennis O'Keefe of the FBI and Louis Hayward of Scotland Yard join forces to investigate a trail of murders concealing a plot to smuggle atom bomb plans from America to London. One of the original Cold War spy yarns, the urgent documentary style of this thriller reflects the political climate of the time, with the communists cast as stage villains and respectful nods to the post-war "special relationship" between America and Britain. Although South African-born Hayward acquits himself well in the English detective role, it's a pity the budget didn't stretch to importing Jack Warner.

Louis Hayward *Philip Grayson* • Dennis O'Keefe *Daniel O'Hara* • Louise Allbritton *Dr Toni Neva* • Carl Esmond *Dr Ritter Van Stolb* • Onslow Stevens *Igor Braun* • Raymond Burr *Krebs* • Art Baker *Dr Frederick Townsend* ■ *Dir* Gordon Douglas • *Scr* George Bruce, from a story by Bertram Millhauser

Walk a Crooked Path
★★
Drama 1969 · UK · Colour · 85mins

Tenniel Evans is an embittered boarding school housemaster who, passed over for promotion, plans to murder his rich, alcoholic wife (Faith Brook) and live with his mistress (Patricia Haynes). Bizarrely, he does this by paying a student (Clive Endersby) to claim that he was homosexually abused by Evans, thus humiliating Brook so badly that she commits suicide. A year after Lindsay Anderson took the public school system apart in *if....*, this seems rather straightforwardly sordid, like an X-rated *Goodbye, Mr Chips*, but the plot is quite clever, revealed in flashbacks and sudden twists and revelling in the rather risqué elements.

Tenniel Evans *John Hemming* • Faith Brook *Elizabeth Hemming* • Christopher Coll *Bill Colman* • Patricia Haines *Nancy Colman* • Clive Endersby *Philip Dreaper* • Georgina Simpson *Elaine* • Georgina Cookson *Imogen Dreaper* ■ *Dir* John Brason • *Scr* Barry Perowne

Walk, Don't Run ★★★ U

Romantic comedy
1966 · US · Colour · 113mins

Cary Grant is as magically urbane as ever playing a British industrialist in this, his final movie, but sadly leaves the romance to the youngsters in a so-so comedy set during the 1964 Tokyo Olympic Games. Samantha Eggar is the embassy secretary with whom Grant lodges and Jim Hutton the member of the American Olympic squad he introduces into her life. A remake of the 1943 film *The More the Merrier*, it's lower on laughs but notable for Grant's sleek charm.

Cary Grant *Sir William Rutland* • Samantha Eggar *Christine Easton* • Jim Hutton *Steve Davis* • Miiko Taka *Aiko Kurawa* • Ted Hartley *Yuri Andreyovitch* • Ben Astar *Dimitri* • George Takei *Police Captain* ■ *Dir* Charles Walters • *Scr* Sol Saks, from the story of *The More the Merrier,(1943)* by Robert Russell, Frank Ross • *Cinematographer* Harry Stradling

Walk East on Beacon ★ U

Spy thriller 1952 · US · BW · 97mins

Totally inept "red scare" thriller, with George Murphy trailing communist agents across a paranoid free world. The script is based on a *Reader's Digest* article called *The Crime of the Century* written by the then head of the FBI, J Edgar Hoover. The whole picture (and many others of its ilk) seems to be bankrolled by the FBI as both a recruitment advertisement and a dire warning to ordinary Americans about the dangers of communism. Look out for George Roy Hill in a minor role, before he became famous for directing such films as *Butch Cassidy and the Sundance Kid*.

George Murphy *Inspector Belden* • Finlay Currie *Professor Kafer* • Virginia Gilmore *Millie* • Karel Stepanek *Alex* • Louisa Horton *Elaine* • Peter Capell *Gino* • Bruno Wick *Danzig* ■ *Dir* Alfred Werker • *Scr* Leo Rosten, Virginia Shaler, Emmett Murphy, Leonard Heidemann, from the magazine article *The Crime of the Century* by J Edgar Hoover

A Walk in the Clouds ★★ PG

Romantic drama 1995 · US · Colour · 98mins

Speed star Keanu Reeves slows down to near-stasis in this cliché-ridden, forties-set romantic drama – the American debut of Mexican director Alfonso Arau following his success with *Like Water for Chocolate*. Returning from the Second World War to be reunited with his unfaithful wife, travelling salesman Reeves meets a pregnant girl during a business trip and

agrees to pose as her husband to protect her from the wrath of her strict vineyard-owning family in California. Until a well-staged fire, happy peasants frolic among the grapes and, in Zorba mode, grandpa Anthony Quinn overacts as if only he can make up for Reeves's wooden performance. Sadly, despite its pretentions, this is merely a prettily filmed trudge through a romanticised past. Contains some sexual references. ▣

Keanu Reeves *Paul Sutton* • Aitana Sanchez-Gijon *Victoria Aragon* • Anthony Quinn *Don Pedro Aragon* • Giancarlo Giannini *Alberto Aragon* • Angelica Aragon *Marie Jose Aragon* • Evangelina Elizondo *Guadelupe Aragon* • Freddy Rodriguez *Pedro Aragon Jr* • Debra Messing *Betty Sutton* ■ *Dir* Alfonso Arau • *Scr* Robert Mark Kamen, Mark Miller, Harvey Weitzman, from the 1942 film *Quatro Passi fra le Nuvole* by Piero Tellini, Cesare Zavattini, Vittorio De Benedetti

A Walk in the Spring Rain ★

Romantic melodrama
1970 · US · Colour · 98mins

The bored, middle-aged wife (Ingrid Bergman) of a bored, middle-aged college professor (Fritz Weaver), while vacationing in Tennessee mountain country meets a local farmer (Anthony Quinn) who is the polar opposite of her husband. Although he, too, is married, his wife is a shrew and they fall in love (or is it lust?). One of far too many films which marked the nadir of Bergman's post-Rossellini career, this turgid rubbish, whose stars make a frankly incredible duo, is also not helped by a lack of distinction in every department, from the uninspired screenplay through the irritating secondary characters to the pedestrian direction. Those who worship at the Bergman shrine may find it tolerable.

Anthony Quinn *Will Cade* • Ingrid Bergman *Libby Meredith* • Fritz Weaver *Roger Meredith* • Katherine Crawford *Ellen Meredith* • Tom Fielding *Boy Cade* • Virginia Gregg *Ann Cade* • Mitchell Silberman *Bucky* ■ *Dir* Guy Green • *Scr* Stirling Silliphant, from the novella by Rachel Maddux

A Walk in the Sun ★★★★

Second World War drama
1945 · US · BW · 117mins

Lewis Milestone, who directed the classic *All Quiet on the Western Front*, creates the model for all those platoon pictures that followed, from his own *Pork Chop Hill* to Kubrick's first feature *Fear and Desire*, to *Platoon* itself and *The Thin Red Line*. The story is simple: a ragbag of foot-slogging GIs are part of the invasion force in Italy and chase the Germans north to eventual defeat. The excellent but unstarry cast means no John Wayne or Clark Gable-style heroics, but they all "talk the talk" in a way that seems completely authentic and most of the time they are just coping with boredom, exhaustion and the probability of sudden death. There are mercifully no overt "war is hell" messages.

Dana Andrews *Sgt Tyne* • Richard Conte *Rivera* • John Ireland *Windy* • George Tyne *Friedman* • Lloyd Bridges *Sgt Ward* • Sterling Holloway *McWilliams* • Herbert Rudley *Sgt Porter* • Norman Lloyd *Archimbeau* • Steve Brodie *Judson* • Huntz Hall *Carraway* ■ *Dir* Lewis Milestone • *Scr* Robert Rossen, from a story by Harry Brown

Walk like a Dragon ★★

Western 1960 · US · BW · 94mins

James Clavell was known primarily as a writer but also produced and directed a couple of his screenplays including this well-intentioned and fairly successful western drama with a central theme of racial conflict. Jack Lord (later of *Hawaii Five-O* fame and fortune) plays an American who rescues a young Chinese woman (Nobu McCarthy) from slavery and the prospect of enforced prostitution. When he takes her to his home in San Francisco, he is faced by prejudice from westerners in general and one oriental (James Shigeta) in particular. Watch out for the great singer/composer Mel Tormé as a bible-punching gunman.

Jack Lord *Line Bartlett* • Nobu McCarthy *Kim Sung* • James Shigeta *Cheng Lu* • Mel Tormé *The Deacon* • Josephine Hutchinson *Ma Bartlett* ■ *Dir* James Clavell • *Scr* James Clavell, Daniel Mainwaring

Walk like a Man ★★ PG

Comedy 1987 · US · Colour · 82mins

Howie Mandel, excellent as both a stand-up comic and as Dr Fiscus in TV series *St Elsewhere*, has never quite made the transition to the big screen, and this one-joke comedy is a good example why. He plays a man raised by wolves who returns to civilisation just in time to make life extremely difficult for his brother, Christopher Lloyd. Most of the jokes revolve around slobbering and other social faux pas, and it becomes painful to watch a comic talent such as Mandel (and the rest of the cast for that matter) reduced to dire material like this. ▣

Howie Mandel *Bobo Shand* • Christopher Lloyd *Reggie Henry* • Cloris Leachman *Margaret Shand* • Colleen Camp *Rhonda Shand* • Amy Steel *Penny* • Stephen Elliott *Walter Welmont* • George DiCenzo *Bub Downs* • John McLiam *HP Truman* ■ *Dir* Melvin Frank • *Scr* Robert Klane

A Walk on the Moon ★★ 15

Romantic comedy
1999 · US · Colour · 107mins

Woodstock and "one giant leap for mankind" form a life-changing backdrop to this run-of-the-mill holiday of discovery. Diane Lane and Anna Paquin are on great form, as an unfulfilled wife succumbing to a campsite affair and her confused teenage daughter respectively. The script is very mundane, though, and is hampered by predictable plotting and meagre dramatic moments that never really catch fire. The reconstruction of Woodstock, where the normally reserved Lane abandons her inhibitions with the aid of drugs, feels completely unlikely and damages the credibility of the whole movie. Some flavourful period details aside – the whole camp transfixed by the TV transmission of Neil Armstrong's monumental moonwalk, for example – this is a small step for independent cinema. Contains swearing and sex scenes. ▣

Diane Lane *Pearl Kantrowitz* • Viggo Mortensen *Walker Jerome* • Liev Schreiber *Marty Kantrowitz* • Anna Paquin *Alison Kantrowitz* • Tovah Feldshuh *Lilian Kantrowitz*

• Bobby Boriello *Daniel Kantrowitz* • Stewart Bick *Neil Leiberman* • Jess Platt *Herb Fogler* ■ *Dir* Tony Goldwyn • *Scr* Pamela Gray

Walk on the Wild Side ★★★ 15

Melodrama 1962 · US · BW · 109mins

Although purporting to be a frank exploration of prostitution and lesbianism, Edward Dmytryk's adaptation of Nelson Algren's racy novel pulls its punches in virtually every scene. Too much time is spent in the company of dull Texan Laurence Harvey as he searches for his runaway lover, Capucine, and helps Anne Baxter and Jane Fonda to see the error of their ways. Far more interesting is madame Barbara Stanwyck's obsession with Capucine, but both script and direction keep the action at a gentle simmer rather than pressing on to boiling point. Saul Bass's title credits are rightly renowned as classic examples of the art. ▣

Laurence Harvey *Dove Linkhorn* • Jane Fonda *Kitty Twist* • Capucine *Hallie* • Barbara Stanwyck *Jo Courtney* • Anne Baxter *Teresina Vidaverri* • Richard Rust *Oliver* • Joanna Moore *Miss Precious* • Karl Swenson *Schmidt* • Donald Barry *Dockery* ■ *Dir* Edward Dmytryk • *Scr* John Fante, Edmund Morris, from the novel by Nelson Algren

Walk Proud ★★ 15

Drama 1979 · US · Colour · 93mins

A mixed-race *Romeo and Juliet*, with Robby Benson as a chicano who falls for a white girl at his high school. The relationship is put to the test when Benson's gang buddies disapprove of him dating outside his race, and he has to choose between following his heart and following his friends. Like Benson's character, the film proves to have its heart in the right place, if perhaps not its art. The whole thing lacks pace and punch, though there's a good performance from Benson who was tipped for the top back in the late seventies and early eighties, but never quite made it off the B-list. ▣

Robby Benson *Emilio* • Sarah Holcomb *Sarah* • Henry Darrow *Mike* • Pepe Serna *Cesar* • Trinidad Silva *Dagger* ■ *Dir* Robert Collins • *Scr* Evan Hunter

Walk the Proud Land ★★ U

Biographical western
1956 · US · Colour · 84mins

A splendidly titled Audie Murphy western, with the baby-faced war hero cast in a true-life tale as John Philip Clum, the Indian agent responsible for liaising with the captured Apache warrior Geronimo – a role taken for the third time on screen by Jay Silverheels, best known for playing Tonto in TV's *The Lone Ranger*. This potentially powerful story of conflict is rather spoiled by the emphasis on Clum's domestic troubles. Nevertheless, Murphy is convincing, and both Pat Crowley and Anne Bancroft are excellent in supporting roles. ▣

Audie Murphy *John P Clum* • Anne Bancroft *Tianay* • Pat Crowley *Mary Dennison* • Charles Drake *Tom Sweeney* • Tommy Rall *Taglito* • Robert Warwick *Eskiminzin* • Jay Silverheels *Geronimo* ■ *Dir* Jesse Hibbs • *Scr* Gil Doud, Jack Sher, from the biography *Apache Agent* by Woodworth Clum

U = SUITABLE FOR ALL, Uc = SUITABLE FOR ALL, ESPECIALLY FOR YOUNG CHILDREN (VIDEO ONLY) PG = PARENTAL GUIDANCE

A Walk with Love and Death ★

Historical drama 1969 · US · Colour · 90mins

John Huston got the worst notices of his long career for this fiasco and he was vilified for casting his own daughter, Anjelica, in the leading role of the nobleman's daughter caught up in the Hundred Years' War. As her suitor, Huston rejected actors and cast Assaf Dayan, the son of Moshe Dayan, the warrior defence minister of Israel. It was a crazy project from the start, born of nepotism, egotism and the flower-power movement of the sixties. It is one of the stupidest movies ever made, so it's a testimony to Anjelica's talent and determination that her career ever took off.

Anjelica Huston *Lady Claudia* • Assaf Dayan *Heron of Foix* • Anthony Corlan *Robert* • John Hallam *Sir Meles of Bohemia* • Eileen Murphy *Gypsy girl* • Anthony Nicholls *Father Superior* ■ *Dir* John Huston • *Scr* Dale Wasserman, from the novel by Hans Koningsberger • *Music* Georges Delerue

Walkabout ★★★★★ 12

Drama 1970 · Ausl/US · Colour · 96mins

Nicolas Roeg's second film as director is an atmospheric masterpiece of sexual tension, with Jenny Agutter and Lucien John as the children stranded in the Australian outback when their father commits suicide. As the youngsters are guided by an Aborigine youth (David Gulpilil), who teaches them to live off the seemingly arid land, the film examines the relationship between the youth and the girl – one that has to span a chasm of misunderstandings caused by cultural differences and the innocence of childhood. Roeg conjures up a tale as dazzling as the shimmering landscape against which it is set. Contains nudity. ▭

Jenny Agutter *Girl* • Lucien John [Luc Roeg] *Brother* • David Gulpilil *Aborigine* • John Meillon *Father* • Peter Carver *No-hoper* • John Illingsworth *Husband* ■ *Dir* Nicolas Roeg • *Scr* Edward Bond, from the novel *The Children* by James Vance Marshall • *Music* John Barry

Walker ★★ 18

Period biographical drama 1987 · US · Colour · 90mins

Made only three years after *Repo Man*, this highly stylised film from director Alex Cox shows him as only a shadow of his former self, with the stiffly told story of American mercenary William Walker who, backed by a tycoon, took over as President of Nicaragua in the mid-19th century. Toting slogans such as ''One must act with severity or perish!'', Walker was eventually hoisted with his own petard when the natives decided they'd had enough of his ''ordered discipline''. Ed Harris is bombastically charismatic, though the anti-American rant, which may have been justified, proves too one-sided for real drama. Contains some swearing. ▭

Ed Harris *William Walker* • Peter Boyle *Cornelius Vanderbilt* • Richard Masur *Ephraim Squier* • René Auberjonois *Major Siegfried Henningson* • Marlee Matlin *Ellen Martin* • Sy Richardson *Captain Hornsby* ■ *Dir* Alex Cox • *Scr* Rudy Wurlitzer

Walker: Texas Ranger ★★

Martial arts drama 1997 · US · Colour

Bad guys don't stand a chance in this action-packed TV pilot – it would lead to a spinoff series – starring martial arts expert Chuck Norris. He plays a tough, kickboxing Texas Ranger who teams up with his former martial arts student (Jimmy Wlcek), now an instructor, to pursue a serial cop-killer whose next target is Walker's childhood pal. High-energy and a strong sense of morality infuse this entertaining cop thriller, sharply directed by Chuck's brother Aaron. Fans of traditional martial arts films might be disappointed in the low body count but an interesting plot and credible characters at least compensate for its lack of mindless, gratuitous violence. Predictable but surprisingly palatable.

Chuck Norris *Cordell Walker* • Jimmy Wlcek *Trent Malloy* • Clarence Gilyard *James Trivette* • Sheree J Wilson *Alex Cahill* • Noble Willingham *CD Parker* ■ *Dir* Aaron Norris • *Scr* Bob Gookin, Aaron Norris

Walking and Talking ★★★ 15

Comedy drama 1996 · UK/US · Colour · 85mins

Writer/director Nicole Holofcener makes an impressive debut with this New York-based tale of fantasy, angst and desire, which had her somewhat cynically dismissed as a young Woody Allen. Sharply scripted and smartly cast, this comedy of discontent is inhabited by credible characters who have something approximating real conversations. As the longtime friends whose lives begin to unravel when marriage rears its head, Catherine Keener and Anne Heche are both fresh and funny. However, they do have nearly all the best lines, as the chaps are less well defined although Kevin Corrigan's geeky video clerk is hilarious. Contains swearing.

Catherine Keener *Amelia* • Anne Heche *Laura* • Todd Field *Frank* • Liev Schreiber *Andrew* • Kevin Corrigan *Bill* • Randall Batinkoff *Peter* ■ *Dir/Scr* Nicole Holofcener

The Walking Dead ★★★

Horror 1936 · US · BW · 66mins

Boris Karloff is framed for murder and sent to the electric chair. A mad doctor electronically revives him, however, to wreak vengeance on the gangsters responsible for his fate, in a moving and macabre variation on the *Frankenstein* theme. Benefiting enormously from Karloff's first-rate turn as the hollow-eyed zombie with a penchant for the piano, director Michael Curtiz keeps predictability at bay with a slick style and some marvellously expressionistic lighting. A few steps down the poignancy ladder from *Frankenstein*, admittedly, but still a weird Karloff classic.

Boris Karloff *John Ellman* • Ricardo Cortez *Nolan* • Warren Hull *Jimmy* • Robert Strange *Merritt* • Joseph King *Judge Shaw* • Edmund Gwenn *Dr Evan Beaumont* • Marguerite Churchill *Nancy* • Barton MacLane *Loder* • Henry O'Neill *Warner* • Paul Harvey *Blackstone* ■ *Dir* Michael Curtiz • *Scr* Ewart Adamson, Peter Milne, Robert Andrews, Lillie Hayward, from a story by Ewart Adamson, Joseph Fields

The Walking Dead ★★★

War drama 1995 · US · Colour · 89mins

An ambitious project, with an excellent cast, especially the under-used Joe Morton as Sergeant Barkley, the leader of a group of black soldiers in Vietnam on what, unbeknownst to them, is a suicide mission. When the impossible nature of their mission becomes apparent, the soldiers go through fluctuations in their loyalty to Barkley, who harbours a dark secret in his own past. Good direction and convincing set pieces can't save the script, which is a bit too contrived and predictable to be enjoyable.

Allen Payne *Pfc Cole Evans* • Eddie Griffin *Pvt Hoover Blanche* • Joe Morton *Sgt Barkley* • Vonte Sweet *Pfc Joe Brooks* • Roger Floyd *Cpl Pippins* • Ion Overman *Shirley Evans* ■ *Dir/Scr* Preston A Whitmore II

The Walking Hills ★★★

Western 1949 · US · BW · 78mins

Nine men and one woman look for buried treasure in the desert. Partly filmed in Death Valley, it's an old story with the usual assortment of incompatible characters but cleverly written by western novelist Alan LeMay, smartly directed by a young John Sturges, and ably cast: Randolph Scott is his usual incorruptible self, John Ireland a detective with William Bishop as his quarry, and Edgar Buchanan a wily old prospector, while Arthur Kennedy plays a drifter as shifty as the sand dunes. The setting is made to count and there's a memorable sandstorm in which a fight with shovels occurs. The sole woman among the dunes and dudes is Ella Raines.

Randolph Scott *Jim Carey* • Ella Raines *Chris Jackson* • William Bishop *Shep* • Edgar Buchanan *Old Willy* • Arthur Kennedy *Chalk* • John Ireland *Frazee* ■ *Dir* John Sturges • *Scr* Alan LeMay, Virginia Roddick

The Walking Stick ★★★★

Drama 1970 · UK · Colour · 101mins

This bittersweet romance, charmingly played by David Hemmings and Samantha Eggar and set in lovely Hampstead, develops unexpectedly. Disabled businesswoman Eggar is courted by mysterious artist Hemmings, but is quite inhibited. However the love story (old-fashioned for its time with bedroom scenes dissolving to the next morning) gradually switches gear into another genre with surprising ease. Director Eric Till, who has a fine eye for detail, did nothing else as interesting as this – with the exception of his debut movie *Hot Millions*. A distinguished supporting cast – Emlyn Williams and Phyllis Calvert included – certainly helps.

David Hemmings *Leigh Hartley* • Samantha Eggar *Deborah Dainton* • Emlyn Williams *Jack Foil* • Phyllis Calvert *Erica Dainton* • Ferdy Mayne *Douglas Dainton* • Francesca Annis *Arabella Dainton* • Bridget Turner *Sarah Dainton* ■ *Dir* Eric Till • *Scr* George Bluestone, from the novel by Winston Graham

Walking Tall ★★ 18

Crime drama based on a true story 1973 · US · Colour · 119mins

The influence of *Dirty Harry* can be felt in every stride of Tennessee county sheriff Buford Pusser, as he declares war on the various low-lifes who pollute his jurisdiction. During the course of his campaign – which harks back to the days of Wyatt Earp – he's widowed and nearly bludgeoned to death. Based on the story of a real-life character, the picture muddles any moral argument and instead piles on the skull-crushing violence, relishing the crude stereotypes on both sides. As the bat-wielding Pusser, Joe Don Baker certainly fills the screen, the role making him a minor star. He wisely opted out of the two sequels. Contains violence. ▭

Joe Don Baker *Buford Pusser* • Elizabeth Hartman *Pauline Pusser* • Gene Evans *Sheriff Thurman* • Noah Beery Jr *Grandpa Pusser* • Brenda Benet *Luan* • John Brascia *Prentiss* • Bruce Glover *Grady Coker* • Arch Johnson *Buel Jaggers* ■ *Dir* Phil Karlson • *Scr* Mort Briskin

Wall of Silence ★★★

Drama 1993 · Arg · Colour · 102mins

Set seven years after the collapse of the junta, Lita Stantic's poised study of the scars tearing apart the newly democratic Argentina would have been more effective had it focused on why the survivors preferred to forget the military tyranny they endured. Instead it explores the problems faced by a film-maker whose project is foundering because of their reticence. Nevertheless, Ofelia Medina gives a subtle performance as the widow who slowly comes to suspect that her activist husband is alive after all. Vanessa Redgrave is more mannered as the visiting documentarist, but she gives the picture a certain political credibility. In English and Spanish with subtitles.

Vanessa Redgrave *Kate Benson* • Ofelia Medina *Silvia* ■ *Dir* Lita Stantic • *Scr* Graciela Maglie, Lita Stantic, Gabriela Massuh

Wall Street ★★★★ 15

Drama 1987 · US · Colour · 120mins

Oliver Stone opted for a change of direction following his Vietnam War drama *Platoon* with this stylish morality tale about insider trading – a topical subject at the time. Charlie Sheen gives a believable performance as the gullible broker who's prepared to break the law in pursuit of riches, and he's matched by his father Martin (also playing his screen father) as the blue-collar union representative who takes a dim view of his son's wheeler-dealing. Stealing the show, however, is Oscar-winner Michael Douglas, who is memorable as ruthless corporate raider Gordon Gekko. Unusually, Stone's trademark neurotic camera movements actually seem appropriate here as the film details the titanic struggle for good over greed. ▭

Michael Douglas *Gordon Gekko* • Charlie Sheen *Bud Fox* • Martin Sheen *Carl Fox* • Daryl Hannah *Darien Taylor* • Terence Stamp *Sir Larry Wildman* • Sean Young *Kate Gekko* • James Spader *Roger Barnes* • Hal Holbrook *Lou Mannheim* • Saul Rubinek *Harold Salt* • Sylvia Miles *Sylvie Drimmer* ■ *Dir/Scr* Oliver Stone • *Cinematographer* Robert Richardson

Waller's Last Walk ★★★

Drama 1989 · W Ger · Colour · 100mins

Three years in the making and mournfully played by Rolf Illig, Christian Wagner's film is set in the director's childhood home of Allgäu in Bavaria. The story centres on an old railway inspector, as he makes his final journey down the condemned track that has been his life. Cleverly littering this steady progress with flashbacks to fond recollections, much-missed friends and events best forgot (most notably the line's usage during the Second World War), Wagner also shows the track becoming increasingly overgrown and dilapidated, as time catches up with memory. In German with English subtitles.

Rolf Illig *Waller* • Sibylle Canonica *Rosina* • Franz Boehm *Stumpf* • Volker Prechtel *Karg* • Herbert Knaup *Waller as a young man* • Crescentia Dünsser *Angelika Heindl* ■ *Dir* Christian Wagner • *Scr* Christian Wagner, from the novel *Die Strecke* by Gerhard Kopf

Walls ★★★ 18

Drama based on a true story
1984 · Can · Colour · 84mins

Based on a true story, this is a solidly mounted account of the kidnap of a Canadian prison officer-cum-reformer and her colleagues by a killer driven to breaking point by a prolonged stretch in solitary confinement. Comparisons with the Kevin Bacon/Christian Slater starrer *Murder in the First* are inevitable, as here, too, a liberal lawyer attempts to bring to wider attention the fact that a prison regime is as much responsible for a prisoner's actions as his so-called criminal mentality. While lacking the performance power of Marc Rocco's film, this modest, sometimes violent atmospheric production still leaves you with plenty to think about. ▣

Andrée Pelletier *Joan Tremblay* • Winston Rekert *Danny Baker* • Alan Scarfe *Ron Simmons* • John Wright *Curt Willis* • John Lord *Louis Martin* ■ *Dir* Thomas Shandell • *Scr* Christian Bruyere, from his play

Walls of Glass ★★★ 15

Drama 1985 · US · Colour · 82mins

As odd as its title, this likeable independent one-off gives the opportunity of a lifetime to character actor Philip Bosco, a face you'll certainly recognise even if the name doesn't ring any bells. He plays a Shakespeare-spouting New York cabby, which is pretty apt for an actor whose career includes notable seasons with Shakespeare companies. Unfortunately, this quirky drama failed to turn Bosco into a well-known movie star, and, despite a distinguished cast including Oscar-winners Geraldine Page and Olympia Dukakis, the public didn't respond to this winning tale. Contains swearing. ▣

Philip Bosco *James Flanagan* • Geraldine Page *Mama* • Linda Thorson *Andrea* • William Hickey *Papa* • Olympia Dukakis *Mary* • Brian Bloom *Danny* • Steven Weber *Sean* ■ *Dir* Scott Goldstein [Scott D Goldstein] • *Scr* Edmond Collins, Scott Goldstein

Walpurgis Night ★★★★

Drama 1935 · Swe · BW · 82mins

Hailed on its release as one of the best films ever made in Sweden, this sensationalist melodrama packed a powerful social punch of the kind that few pictures made anywhere else in the world could match. Tackling both adultery and abortion, Gustaf Edgren's film focuses on the unhappy marriage between Lars Hanson and his vain wife Karin Kavli. While both give earnest performances, the film belongs to Ingrid Bergman as Hanson's devoted lover and to Victor Sjöström – one of Europe's leading silent directors but perhaps best known as the professor in Ingmar Bergman's *Wild Strawberries* – as her father, a crusading editor leading a campaign to boost the birth rate. In Swedish with English subtitles.

Lars Hanson *Johan Borg* • Karin Kavli *Clary Borg* • Victor Seastrom [Victor Sjöström] *Fredrik Bergstrom* • Ingrid Bergman *Lena* • Erik Berglund *Gustav Palm* • Sture Lagerwall *Svenson* ■ *Dir* Gustaf Edgren • *Scr* Oscar Rydqvist, Gustaf Edgren

A Walton Easter ★★★

Drama 1997 · US · Colour · 96mins

This beautifully realised drama reunites the original cast of the beloved American TV series. It's now 1970, and reporter John-Boy Walton (Richard Thomas) and his pregnant spouse return to the Blue Ridge Mountains to help commemorate his parents' (Ralph Waite, Michael Learned) 40th wedding anniversary. As the clan plans a party, Ma and Pa just want to slip away to Virginia Beach. Meanwhile John-Boy begins to yearn for the simple country life but his wife can't wait to get back to New York City. Yes, it's sentimental and sweet but it doesn't hurt to see a little caring and sharing for a change.

Richard Thomas *John-Boy Walton* • Ralph Waite *John Walton* • Michael Learned *Olivia Walton* • Jon Walmsley *Jason Walton* • Judy Norton [Judy Norton-Taylor] *Mary Ellen* • Mary Beth McDonough *Erin* • Eric Scott *Ben Walton* • David Harper [David W Harper] *Jim-Bob* ■ *Dir* Bill Corcoran • *Scr* Julie Sayres, from characters created by Earl Hamner

A Walton Thanksgiving Reunion ★★

Seasonal drama 1993 · US · Colour · 96mins

The original *Waltons* cast members are back for this heart-warming TV film, based on the Emmy award-winning series. In 1963, the close-knit Virginia family gathers together to celebrate Thanksgiving at the old homestead. Their own personal problems are soon put on hold as the clan reacts to the assassination of President Kennedy, whose death changes the lives of many in the family. If you're not a fan of the popular series then there is no reason to sit through this one, but if you are, then there is fun to be had in seeing the familiar faces all grown up.

Richard Thomas *John-Boy Walton* • Michael Learned *Olivia Walton* • Ralph Waite *John Walton* • Ellen Corby *Grandma Walton* • Kami Cotler *Elizabeth Walton* • David Harper [David W Harper] *Jim-Bob Walton* • Mary Beth McDonough *Erin Walton* • Judy Norton-Taylor *Mary Ellen* • Jon Walmsley *Jason* ■ *Dir* Harry Harris • *Scr* Rod Peterson, Claire Whitaker, from characters created by Earl Hamner

A Walton Wedding ★★

Drama 1995 · US · Colour · 120mins

The second reunion movie to star the original cast of the popular series. In the mid-sixties, the Walton clan from Virginia gathers once more at the old homestead when John-Boy (Richard Thomas) decides to marry his ritzy, New York fashion editor girlfriend (Kate McNeil). Plans go awry when her busybody aunt tries to arrange a posh do that the newlyweds don't want. While all this is going on, Olivia (Michael Learned) is returning to college and John (Ralph Waite) is embroiled in local politics. Fans of the Walton brood should find much to celebrate in this one. ▣

Richard Thomas *John-Boy Walton* • Michael Learned *Olivia Walton* • Ralph Waite *John Walton* • Ellen Corby *Grandma Walton* • Kami Cotler *Elizabeth Walton* • David Harper [David W Harper] *Jim-Bob Walton* • Mary Beth McDonough *Erin* • Judy Norton [Judy Norton-Taylor] *Mary Ellen Walton* • Kate McNeil *Janet Gilchrist* ■ *Dir* Robert Ellis Miller • *Scr* Rod Peterson, Claire Whitaker, from characters created by Earl Hamner

Waltz across Texas ★★

Romantic drama 1982 · US · Colour · 99mins

Anne Archer co-wrote the story, co-produced and starred in this tired romantic drama in 1982 with her husband Terry Jastrow. Archer is a geologist, Jastrow is a businessman, and both have designs on a piece of oil-rich land that could make their respective fortunes; needless to say, love intervenes. Archer has gone on to greater things since this pot-boiler, working with the likes of Gene Hackman, Harrison Ford and John Travolta during the nineties.

Anne Archer *Gail Weston* • Terry Jastrow *John Taylor* • Mary Kay Place *Kit Peabody* • Richard Farnsworth *Frank Walker* • Noah Beery [Noah Beery Jr] *Joe Locker* • Josh Taylor *Luke Jarvis* • Ben Piazza *Bill Wrather* ■ *Dir* Ernest Day • *Scr* Bill Svanoe, from a story by Terry Jastrow, Anne Archer

Waltz of the Toreadors ★★★★ 15

Comedy 1962 · UK · Colour · 100mins

In one of his most impressive performances, Peter Sellers plays retired General Leo Fitzjohn, unhappily married to Emily (Margaret Leighton) and given a second chance at fulfilment with old flame Ghislaine (Dany Robin). French playwright Jean Anouilh, from whose comedy the movie is derived, made despair glossily fashionable in the sixties and director John Guillermin and writer Wolf Mankowitz transform bleak emotional undercurrents into a seductively bittersweet proposition. ▣

Peter Sellers *General Leo Fitzjohn* • Dany Robin *Ghislaine* • Margaret Leighton *Emily Fitzjohn* • John Fraser *Robert* • Cyril Cusack *Doctor Grogan* • Prunella Scales *Estella* • Denise Coffey *Sidonia* • Jean Anderson *Agnes* • John Le Mesurier *Vicar* ■ *Dir* John Guillermin • *Scr* Wolf Mankowitz, from the play *La Valse des Toréadors* by Jean Anouilh

Waltzing Regitze ★★★

Drama 1989 · Den · Colour · 85mins

A superbly acted chronicle of a durable, if often tempestuous

marriage. Alternating between a celebratory garden party and events long passed, Kaspar Rostrup clearly has Ingmar Bergman's *Scenes from a Marriage* in mind, but he brings considerably greater warmth to the story of the wartime lovers, who defy convention by not only living together unmarried, but also refusing to baptise their son. Rikke Bendsen and Ghita Norby excel playing the free-spirited wife, a woman as likely to invite a tramp to Christmas dinner as set upon the local headmaster, while Mikael and Frits Helmuth look on with bemusement and pride. A Danish language film.

Frits Helmuth *Karl Age* • Mikael Helmuth *Karl Age, as a young man* • Ghita Norby *Regitze* • Rikke Bendsen *Regitze, as a young woman* • Henning Moritzen *Borge* • Michael Moritzen *Borge, as a young man* ■ *Dir* Kaspar Rostrup • *Scr* Kaspar Rostrup, from a novel by Martha Christensen

Wanda ★★★★

Crime drama 1971 · US · Colour · 102mins

The winner of the International Critics' Prize at Venice, Barbara Loden's charming film also earned her the distinction of being the first woman director to have her debut feature awarded a cinema release since Ida Lupino's *Not Wanted* in 1949. Based on a true story and shot in 16mm, it is an unsentimental hard luck tale, in which Loden also stars as an outsider who agrees to act as a getaway driver for her neurotic lover, Michael Higgins. Loden, who was married to Elia Kazan, is totally believable. ▣

Barbara Loden *Wanda* • Michael Higgins *Mr Dennis* • Charles Dosinan *Dennis's father* • Frank Jourdano *Soldier* • Valerie Manches *Girl in roadhouse* ■ *Dir/Scr* Barbara Loden

Wanda Nevada ★★

Romantic western
1979 · US · Colour · 105mins

Notable solely for being the only film to feature father and son Henry and Peter Fonda together, this western, set in the fifties, has Fonda Jr as a poker-faced card player who wins orphaned Brooke Shields as his jackpot and takes her gold prospecting in the Grand Canyon. The whimsicality of the piece is sometimes hard to take and Miss Shields, then aged 14, lacks the quirkiness of, say, Tatum O'Neal in *Paper Moon*, a film director Peter Fonda is evidently trying to emulate. Fonda Sr appears late in the picture as a grizzled, bewhiskered prospector.

Peter Fonda *Beaudray Demerille* • Brooke Shields *Wanda Nevada* • Fiona Lewis *Dorothy Deerfield* • Luke Askew *Ruby Muldoon* • Ted Markland *Strap Pangburn* • Severn Darden *Merlin Bitterstix* • Paul Fix *Texas Curly* • Henry Fonda *Old Prospector* • Fred Ashley *Barber* ■ *Dir* Peter Fonda • *Scr* Dennis Hackin

The Wanderer ★★

Period romantic drama
1967 · Fr · Colour · 103mins

One of the great delights of Alain Fournier's 1913 novel, *Le Grand Meaulnes*, is that the rational world and the realm of childlike dreams seem able to co-exist without straining credibility. Unfortunately, director Jean-Gabriel Albicocco was unable to reproduce that delicate balance, even

U = SUITABLE FOR ALL   Uc = SUITABLE FOR ALL, ESPECIALLY FOR YOUNG CHILDREN (VIDEO ONLY)   PG = PARENTAL GUIDANCE

though his screenplay was co-written by the novelist's sister, Isabelle Rivière. Instead, this adaptation is shot through with false poetry and a visual flamboyance that owes little either to the book or life in rural France in the 1890s. Brigitte Fossey stars as the object of Jean Blaise's lifelong passion, but his odyssey lacks enchantment away from the page. In French with English subtitles.

Jean Blaise *Augustin Meaulnes* • Brigitte Fossey *Yvonne de Galais* • Alain Libolt *François Seurel* • Alain Noury *Frantz de Galais* • Juliette Villard *Valentine Blondeau* • Christian de Tilière *Ganache* • Marcel Cuvelier *M Seurel* ■ Dir Jean-Gabriel Albicocco • Scr Jean-Gabriel Albicocco, Isabelle Rivière, from the novel *Le Grand Meaulnes* by Alain Fournier

The Wanderers ★★★ 18

Drama 1979 · US/Neth · Colour · 112mins

An early film from Philip Kaufman who went on to direct the likes of *The Right Stuff* and *The Unbearable Lightness of Being.* Though less lauded than the broadly similar *American Graffiti,* and more variable in its tone and quality (it's a bit episodic), this tale of the high-school life of a bunch of Italian-American kids in New York's Bronx in the early sixties remains thoroughly entertaining. Of its stars (Ken Wahl, Karen Allen, John Friedrich), only Allen really went on to bigger if not necessarily better things, playing the love interest in *Raiders of the Lost Ark* and *Starman.* ▭ **DVD**

Ken Wahl *Richie* • John Friedrich *Joey* • Karen Allen *Nina* • Toni Kalem *Despie Galasso* • Alan Rosenberg *"Turkey"* • Jim Youngs *Buddy* • Tony Ganios *Perry* • Linda Manz *"Peewee"* ■ Dir Philip Kaufman • Scr Rose Kaufman, Philip Kaufman, from the novel by Richard Price • Cinematographer Michael Chapman

Wanted Dead or Alive ★★ 18

Action adventure 1986 · US · Colour · 102mins

Rutger Hauer stars as a former CIA agent turned bounty hunter – referred to as the grandson of Steve McQueen's character from the identically named fifties TV show – with a reputation for hauling in the toughest criminals. However he has his hands full when Arab terrorists, led by Kiss front man Gene Simmons acting as if he were starring in a *Spiderman* cartoon, start a bombing campaign in downtown LA. Hauer excels as an action man, but the daft plot and excessive violence do him no favours with someone being noisily shot or blown up every few minutes. ▭

Rutger Hauer *Nick Randall* • Robert Guillaume *Philmore Walker* • Gene Simmons *Malak Al Rahim* • Mel Harris *Terry* • William Russ *Danny Quintz* • Susan McDonald *Louise Quintz* • Jerry Hardin *John Lipton* ■ Dir Gary Sherman • Scr Michael Patrick Goodman, Brian Taggert, Gary Sherman

Wanted for Murder ★★★

Crime thriller 1946 · UK · BW · 102mins

Eric Portman is on fine form in this chilling thriller as the descendant of a public hangman who strangles young women in London's open spaces, creating a tragic figure of a man who can't help his inherited impulses. Roland Culver is a skilful adversary as the Scotland Yard inspector who slowly

and patiently closes in on his man. Co-written by Emeric Pressburger and directed by Lawrence Huntington, it makes superb use of London backgrounds and has a memorable climax near the Serpentine in Hyde Park, which has the cold grip of nightmare about it.

Eric Portman *Victor Colebrooke* • Dulcie Gray *Anne Fielding* • Derek Farr *Jack Williams* • Roland Culver *Inspector Conway* • Stanley Holloway *Sgt Sullivan* • Barbara Everest *Mrs Colebrooke* • Kathleen Harrison *Florrie* • Bonar Colleano *Corporal Mappolo* ■ Dir Lawrence Huntington • Scr Emeric Pressburger, Rodney Ackland, Maurice Cowan, from the play by Percy Robinson, Terence de Marney

Waqt ★★★★ 15

Drama 1965 · Ind · Colour · 163mins

A major box-office success, this lavish *masala* melodrama is so full of plot that there is scarcely room for the songs, many of which went on to become popular hits. Beginning with an earthquake and a family tragedy, the film ends with a nail-biting courtroom sequence, when a lawyer has to defend his thief brother, who has been framed for murder. Superstar Sunil Dutt is splendid as the lawyer and there is sterling support from rascally Raaj Kumar and Sadhana as the girl for whose affections they both vie. Director Yash Chopra juggles drama, comedy and spectacle with great aplomb. In Hindi with English subtitles. ▭

Sunil Dutt • Raaj Kumar • Sadhana • Sharmila Tagore • Shashi Kapoor ■ Dir Yash Chopra • Scr Akhtar-ul-Iman

The War ★★ 12

Drama adventure 1994 · US · Colour · 119mins

Had this slender tale of childhood in the seventies simply focused on the feud between neighbourhood kids from different sides of the tracks, it would have engrossed younger viewers and proved most instructive for their parents. But no one bought either the heavy-handed pacifism or the Pollyanna morality that Jon Avnet felt were essential. With both Kevin Costner and Mare Winningham straying the wrong side of earnestness, it's left to Elijah Wood, LaToya Chisholm and the rest of the junior cast to provide the dramatic impetus. ▭

Elijah Wood *Stu* • Kevin Costner *Stephen* • Mare Winningham *Lois* • Lexi Randall *Lidia* • LaToya Chisholm *Elvadine* • Christopher Fennell *Billy* • Donald Sellers *Arliss* • Leon Sills *Leo* • Will West *Lester Lucket* ■ Dir Jon Avnet • Scr Kathy McWorter

The War against Mrs Hadley ★★★ U

Second World War drama 1942 · US · BW · 85mins

When the Second World War comes to America with the bombing of Pearl Harbor, the spoiled, wealthy, snobbish and stubborn Mrs Hadley, widow of a Washington newspaper magnate, regards it as a personal affront that her needs are ignored, and learns a lot of hard lessons about life and herself. Starring the splendid middle-aged character actress Fay Bainter, this is a cunning mix of family drama,

psychological study, moral fable and patriotic wartime propaganda.

Edward Arnold *Elliott Fulton* • Fay Bainter *Stella Hadley* • Richard Ney *Theodore Hadley* • Jean Rogers *Patricia Hadley* • Sara Allgood *Mrs Michael Kirkpatrick* • Spring Byington *Cecilia Talbot* • Van Johnson *Michael Fitzpatrick* ■ Dir Harold S Bucquet • Scr George Oppenheimer

War and Peace ★★★ U

Historical drama 1956 · It/US · Colour · 199mins

No less than four versions of Tolstoy's epic novel were planned by Hollywood in the mid-fifties, one of which was to have been produced by Mike Todd, directed by Fred Zinnemann and starring Audrey Hepburn as Natasha. But producer Dino De Laurentiis moved faster than anyone else: he hired King Vidor to direct, he hired the Italian army and, crucially, he hired Hepburn. As a spectacle, it's still impressively humane, though not particularly Russian, and the casting is decidedly odd: Henry Fonda as Pierre, Mel Ferrer (Hepburn's then husband) as Prince Andrei, plus John Mills, Herbert Lom and the amazing Anita Ekberg. The vast battle scenes were later dwarfed by the six-hour Soviet version. ▭

Audrey Hepburn *Natasha Rostov* • Henry Fonda *Pierre Bezukhov* • Mel Ferrer *Prince Andrei Bolkonsky* • Vittorio Gassman *Anatole Kuragin* • John Mills *Platon Karatsev* • Herbert Lom *Napoleon* • Oscar Homolka *General Mikhail Kutuzov* • Anita Ekberg *Helene* • Helmut Dantine *Dolokhov* ■ Dir King Vidor • Scr Bridget Boland, Robert Westerby, King Vidor, Mario Camerini, Ennio De Concini, Ivo Perilli, Irwin Shaw, from the novel by Leo Tolstoy • Cinematographer Jack Cardiff

War and Peace ★★★★ PG

Epic 1966 · USSR · Colour · 399mins

All the resources of the Soviet film industry and the Red Army were put at Sergei Bondarchuk's disposal to make what was intended to be an expression of Soviet pride – designed to be premiered in instalments at international film festivals – and to dwarf anything turned out by capitalist Hollywood. The sumptuous ballroom scenes match those in Visconti's *The Leopard* while the battle scenes are awesome in their scope – like oil paintings come to life – and filmed with overhead cameras which glide over thousands of extras as they fight Napoleon's army at Austerlitz and Borodino. Just how Sergei Bondarchuk directed all this while also playing the major role of Pierre is anyone's guess. Avoid the edited English-dubbed version at all costs; the original version, though extremely patchy, is still masterly in parts but always fascinating to watch. ▭

Lyudmila Savelyeva *Natasha Rostov* • Sergei Bondarchuk *Pierre Bezuhov* • Vyacheslav Tikhonov *Prince Andrei Bolkonsky* • Viktor Stanitsyn *Ilya Andreevich Rostov* • Kira Golovko *Countess Rostova* • Oleg Tabakov *Nikolay Rostov* • Norman Rose *Narrator* ■ Dir Sergei Bondarchuk • Scr Sergei Bondarchuk, Vasily Solovyov, from the novel by Leo Tolstoy

War Arrow ★★ U

Western 1953 · US · Colour · 78mins

Jeff Chandler and Maureen O'Hara make a spirited pair in this innocuous

western. He's the cavalry major who over-rides the opposition of fort commander John McIntire and recruits friendly native American Seminoles to help defeat hostile Kiowas. O'Hara plays the feisty wife of a missing captain who's as good as any man in action at wielding a rifle or putting out a dynamite charge. Handsomely photographed in Technicolor and adequately directed by B-western veteran George Sherman, it's assembly line stuff, lacking in any extra dimension.

Maureen O'Hara *Elaine Corwin* • Jeff Chandler *Major Howell Brady* • Suzan Ball *Avis* • John McIntire *Colonel Jackson Meade* • Charles Drake *Luke Schermerhorn* • Dennis Weaver *Pino* • Noah Beery Jr *Augustus Wilks* • Henry Brandon *Maygro* ■ Dir George Sherman • Scr John Michael Hayes

The War at Home ★★ 18

Drama 1996 · US · Colour · 118mins

Emilio Estevez directs and stars in this leaden tale of a young Vietnam vet finding it impossible to readjust to family life. We've seen this sort of emotion-drenched scenario dozens of times before and with far more success. Its trump cards are the always brilliant Kathy Bates as Estevez's mum and real-life dad Martin Sheen as… you've guessed it, but James Duff's script is long on clichés, short on characterisation and becomes less plausible as it goes along. The film's main handicap though, is Estevez. His embittered, one-note performance is less than believable and his direction never more than workmanlike. Contains some swearing and violence. ▭

Emilio Estevez *Jeremy Collier* • Kathy Bates *Maurine Collier* • Martin Sheen *Bob Collier* • Kimberly Williams *Karen Collier* • Corin Nemec *Donald* • Ann Hearn *Music teacher* • Carla Gugino *Melissa* ■ Dir Emilio Estevez • Scr James Duff, from his play *Homefront*

The War between Men and Women ★★★

Comedy drama 1972 · US · Colour · 105mins

Based on the cartoons of James Thurber, this sounds like a comedy but it's more of a mawkish drama with funny bits about a cynical cartoonist (Jack Lemmon) who is going blind and the divorced mother of three whom he marries. When her ex-husband shows up – the excellent Jason Robards as a war photographer – their emotionally disturbed children become even more of a problem and then Lemmon's eye operation doesn't work. Lemmon does his usual neurotic schtick but Barbara Harris matches him scene for scene. However, the real embodiment of Thurber's sense of the ridiculous is their pregnant dog which all but steals the show.

Jack Lemmon *Peter Wilson* • Barbara Harris *Terry Kozlenko* • Jason Robards [Jason Robards Jr] *Stephen Kozlenko* • Herbert Edelman *Howard Mann* • Lisa Gerritsen *Linda Kozlenko* • Moosie Drier *David Kozlenko* • Severn Darden *Doctor Harris* ■ Dir Melville Shavelson • Scr Melville Shavelson, Danny Arnold, from writings and drawings by James Thurber

The War between Us ★★★

Drama 1995 · Can · Colour · 93mins

Apart from Alan Parker's *Come See the Paradise*, surprisingly few films have been made about the experiences of Japanese people in North America during the Second World War. Rather than exploring the subject in any great depth, this film from Canadian director Anne Wheeler uses it as the backdrop for the friendship that develops between a Japanese woman who has to leave behind everything she has worked for in the city and a housewife who knows little of life beyond her mining town in the wastes of British Columbia. Sensibly directed and uncloyingly played by Mieko Ouchi and Shannon Lawson. Contains swearing.

Shannon Lawson *Peg Parnham* • Mieko Ouchi *Aya Kawashima* • Robert Wisden *Ed Parnham* • Ian Tracey *Jig Parnham* • Juno Ruddell *Marg Parnham* • Edmond Kato *Mrs Kawashima* • Robert Ito *Mr Kawashima* ■ *Dir* Anne Wheeler • *Scr* Sharon Gibbon

The War Game ★★★★

Documentary drama 1965 · UK · BW · 44mins

Such was the power of *The War Game* that the BBC, which produced it, refused to transmit Peter Watkins's film, leaving it to sit on the shelf, gathering dust and notoriety, before a cinema release in 1966. Watkins had already made a name for himself with the savage *Culloden* and he used the same documentary-style techniques to create an image of England in the moments before a nuclear attack. It's a nightmarish blend of Ealing comedy, *Dad's Army* and wartime Ministry of Information. View it in the context of 1965 when the Cold War was at its hottest and when the youth of the world awoke each day thinking they would be vaporised at any minute.

Michael Aspel *Commentator* • Dick Graham *Commentator* ■ *Dir* Peter Watkins, Derek Ware • *Scr* Peter Watkins • *Cinematographer* Peter Bartlett

War Hunt ★★

War drama 1962 · US · BW · 82mins

One of the most enduring actor-director partnerships has been that of Robert Redford and Sydney Pollack, resulting in such films as *Jeremiah Johnson*, *The Way We Were* and *Out of Africa*. This is where they first met, both making their screen debuts as actors in this low-budget, rapidly shot platoon drama set in the Korean War. Redford is a private and Pollack a sergeant and they are both disturbed by the psychotic behaviour of John Saxon, a knife-wielding private who relishes hand-to-hand combat with "the commies" and has an adoring, orphaned Korean boy as some sort of mascot. It's all rather pretentious and oddly reminiscent of Kubrick's illusive first feature *Fear and Desire*.

John Saxon *Pvt Raymond Endore* • Robert Redford *Pvt Roy Loomis* • Charles Aidman *Capt Wallace Pratt* • Sydney Pollack *Sgt Van Horn* • Gavin MacLeod *Pvt Crotty* • Tommy Matsuda *Charlie* • Tom Skerritt *Corporal Showalter* ■ *Dir* Denis Sanders • *Scr* Stanford Whitmore

War Italian Style ★★

Second World War comedy
1966 · It · Colour · 74mins

A feeble Italian Second World War satire featuring comedy double-act Franco Franchi and Ciccio Ingrassia. The Italian comics play a pair of incompetent spies in a piece that would be forgettable if it wasn't for the fact that it features one of Buster Keaton's last screen roles. The genius of silent comedy died later in the year. Sadly there's little to recommend in this film, miles away in quality from his golden age comedies and the later good work on US television. An English/Italian language film.

Buster Keaton *General Von Kassler* • Franco Franchi *Frank* • Ciccio Ingrassia *Joe* • Martha Hyer *Lieut Inge Schultze* • Fred Clark *General Zacharias* ■ *Dir* Luigi Scattini • *Scr* Franco Castellano, Pipolo, from an idea by Fulvio Lucisano

The War Lord ★★★★

Historical epic 1965 · US · Colour · 122mins

A sombre, beautifully photographed historical epic with feudal warlord Charlton Heston exerting his *droit du seigneur* – the knight's right to spend the night with any new wife-to-be he chooses. On this occasion he selects blushing bride Rosemary Forsyth but Heston only takes her reluctantly since he's delirious from a wound and – against all reason – he seems influenced by pagan tradition and the druid fertility symbols that litter the landscape of 11th-century Normandy. While Heston's savage haircut is a definite distraction, the way the movie subverts his epic *El Cid* persona makes this a fascinating and rather disturbing excursion into the past.

Charlton Heston *Chrysagon* • Richard Boone *Bors* • Rosemary Forsyth *Bronwyn* • Maurice Evans *Priest* • Guy Stockwell *Draco* • Niall MacGinnis *Odins* • James Farentino *Marc* ■ *Dir* Franklin Schaffner [Franklin J Schaffner] • *Scr* John Collier, Millard Kaufman, from the play *The Lovers* by Leslie Stevens • *Cinematographer* Russell Metty

The War Lover ★★★ PG

War drama 1962 · US/UK · BW · 101mins

Steve McQueen is a US bomber pilot based in East Anglia, boasting of his prowess in the air over Germany and in bed with the local crumpet. But it's McQueen's much more sensitive friend, Robert Wagner, who wins Shirley Anne Field's heart and their love affair is set beside McQueen's love for war and his big, powerful and seemingly invincible Flying Fortress. Philip Leacock easily twists McQueen's charisma to bring out the psychopathic qualities of his character, for whom war is a convenience and not a crime. 🎬

Steve McQueen *Buzz Rickson* • Robert Wagner *Ed Bolland* • Shirley Ann Field [Shirley Anne Field] *Daphne Caldwell* • Gary Cockrell *Lynch* • Michael Crawford *Junior Sailen* • Billy Edwards [Bill Edwards] *Brindt* • Chuck Julian *Lamb* • Robert Easton *Handown* ■ *Dir* Philip Leacock • *Scr* Howard Koch, from the novel by John Hersey

War of the Buttons ★★★

Comedy drama 1962 · Fr · BW · 93mins

Louis Pergaud's novel is brought to the screen with an irresistible mix of nostalgia, satire and adolescent high jinks. But there's a pronounced sentimental streak undermining Yves Robert's account of the rivalry between two gangs of French schoolboys which results in their leaders, André Treton and Michel Isella, being sent to a reformatory. The most famous sequence is undoubtedly the nude attack made by Treton's gang to prevent their buttons and belts being captured as war trophies, which exemplifies the editorial pace and youthful exuberance of the film. In French with English subtitles.

Martin Lartigue *Tigibus* • André Treton *Lebrac* • Michel Isella *Aztec* • Jacques Dufilho *Aztec's father* • Pierre Trabaud *Teacher* ■ *Dir* Yves Robert • *Scr* François Boyer, Yves Robert, from the novel *La Guerre des Boutons* by Louis Pergaud

War of the Buttons ★★ PG

Comedy 1993 · UK/Fr · Colour · 90mins

Producer David Puttnam and writer Colin Welland, Oscar winners both for *Chariots of Fire*, teamed up again for this remake of the 1962 French movie in which gangs of boys from rival villages stalk the forests and steal each other's buttons, forcing them to fight stark naked. Transplanted to Ireland – the picture was shot at Union Hall and Castletownshend in County Cork – the story retains its whimsy as well as its hints at allegory – "Lords of the Fly Buttons", perhaps. Sadly, energetic performances from the kids and well-paced direction from debutant John Roberts didn't prevent a box-office disaster. 🎬

Gregg Fitzgerald *Fergus* • Gerard Kearney *Big Con* • Daragh Naughton *Boffin* • Brenda McNamara *Tim* • Kevin O'Malley *Fishy* • John Cleere *Peter* • John Coffey *Geronimo* • Colm Meaney *Geronimo's dad* ■ *Dir* John Roberts • *Scr* Colin Welland, from the novel *La Guerre des Boutons* by Louis Pergaud

War of the Colossal Beast ★ PG

Cult science-fiction
1958 · US · BW and Colour · 68mins

The Amazing Colossal Man didn't die! He turned up in Mexico with a disfigured face and a gigantic appetite in a "what have we done to deserve this" sequel from trash-master supremo, Bert I Gordon. The producer/director's initials are the only thing that is BIG about this fourth division science-fiction dud, though. Far funnier than the original, if that counts for anything. 🎬

Sally Fraser *Joyce Manning* • Dean Parkin [Duncan "Dean" Parkin] *Colonel Glenn Manning* • Roger Pace *Major Baird* • Russ Bender *Dr Carmichael* • Charles Stewart *Captain Harris* • George Becwar *Swanson* • Robert Hernandez *Miguel* • Rico Alaniz *Sgt Luis Murillo* • George Alexander *Army officer* • George Navarro *Mexican doctor* • John McNamara *Neurologist* ■ *Dir* Bert I Gordon • *Scr* George Worthing Yates, from a story by Bert I Gordon

War of the Gargantuas ★★

Science-fiction monster horror
1970 · Jap/US · Colour · 92mins

Intended as the sequel to *Frankenstein Conquers the World*, the American re-edited version of director Inoshiro Honda's wackily conceived continuation obscures all reference to the original only to emerge as one of the funniest monster extravaganzas ever. No point trying to make sense of the deconstructed plot – scientist Russ Tamblyn blaming himself for an epic battle between a furry brown giant monster and his evil green-hued twin which destroys Tokyo – just thrill along to the spectacular effects (the motorway destruction is particularly well done), a silly giant octopus and the night-club song *The Words Get Stuck in My Throat*.

Russ Tamblyn *Dr Paul Stewart* • Kumi Mizuno *His assistant* • Kipp Hamilton *Singer* • Yu Fujiki *Army commander* ■ *Dir* Inoshiro Honda • *Scr* Inoshiro Honda, Kaoru Mabuchi

The War of the Roses ★★★★ 15

Black comedy 1989 · US · Colour · 111mins

A blistering black comedy from Danny DeVito that is less an assault on marriage than on the acquisitiveness of Reaganite America. Suggesting that hell is not other people, but other people's possessions, the film rapidly escalates into a frenzy of comic viciousness. Trading slyly on their coy relationship in *Romancing the Stone*, Michael Douglas and Kathleen Turner hurl themselves into their parts, tainting expressions of vengeful glee with real bile. The scene in which Douglas seasons the fish stew is a standout among several wickedly excessive incidents that raise laughs as well as hackles thanks to DeVito's bravura direction. Contains violence and swearing. 🎬

Michael Douglas *Oliver Rose* • Kathleen Turner *Barbara Rose* • Danny DeVito *Gavin D'Amato* • Marianne Sägebrecht *Susan* • Peter Donat *Larrabee* • Sean Astin *Josh, aged 17* • Heather Fairfield *Carolyn, aged 17* • GD Spradlin *Harry Thurmont* ■ *Dir* Danny DeVito • *Scr* Michael Leeson, from the novel by Warren Adler

War of the Satellites ★ U

Science-fiction 1958 · US · BW · 66mins

Within months of the first Russian Sputnik being launched into space, cult director Roger Corman had this cash-in released in cinemas. Aliens threaten the destruction of Earth unless the planet's space programme is terminated. Scientist Richard Devon's dead body is taken over by the aliens to sabotage further intergalactic explorations in Corman's excruciatingly dull, over-talkative and rambling exploiter.

Dick Miller *Dave Royer* • Susan Cabot *Sybil Carrington* • Richard Devon *Dr Van Pander* • Eric Sinclair *Dr Lazar* • Michael Fox *Akad* • Roger Corman *Ground control* ■ *Dir* Roger Corman • *Scr* Lawrence Louis Goldman, from the story by Irving Block, Jack Rabin • *Special Effects* Jack Rabin, Irving Block, Louis DeWitt

U = SUITABLE FOR ALL, Uc = SUITABLE FOR ALL, ESPECIALLY FOR YOUNG CHILDREN (VIDEO ONLY) PG = PARENTAL GUIDANCE

War of the Wildcats ★★ U

Western 1943 · US · BW · 97mins

Having made *In Old California*, John Wayne followed it with *In Old Oklahoma*, though it reverted to its working title *War of the Wildcats* two years after its original release. In any case, the title was virtually immaterial as the film was shot in Utah. The story concerns Wayne's efforts to drill for oil and win the hand of Martha Scott from rival Albert Dekker. Political matters enter the fray when Wayne starts fighting for the rights of American Indians – the "little fellers" as he calls them. Reputedly, this caused consternation in Washington where it was thought the implication that native Americans had been treated badly by the government would create a negative image of America which could be exploited by the Nazis. Republic made the changes asked of them and made a box-office hit, too.

John Wayne *Daniel Somers* • Martha Scott *Catherine Allen* • Albert Dekker *James E Gardner* • George "Gabby" Hayes *Desprit Dean* • Marjorie Rambeau *Bessie Baxter* • Dale Evans *Cuddles Walker* • Grant Withers *Richardson* • Sidney Blackmer *Teddy Roosevelt* ■ *Dir* Albert S Rogell • *Scr* Ethel Hill, Eleanor Griffin, from a story by Thomson Burtis

The War of the Worlds ★★★★ PG

Science-fiction adventure 1953 · US · Colour · 81mins

Although it never comes close to reproducing the panic generated by Orson Welles's famous 1938 radio broadcast, this is a splendid version of HG Wells's sci-fi classic. When the "meteor" that lands in southern California turns out to be the mothership of a Martian invasion, the governments of the world unleash their most potent weapons in a counterproductive attempt to stem the tide of destruction. The miraculous deliverance is clumsily staged, but it scarcely matters. Director Byron Haskin enhances the impact of the Oscar-winning special effects by ensuring that his extras convey a genuine sense of terror as civilisation collapses around them. Contains violence.

Gene Barry *Dr Clayton Forrester* • Ann Robinson *Sylvia Van Buren* • Les Tremayne *General Mann* • Robert Cornthwaite *Doctor Pryor* • Sandro Giglio *Doctor Bilderbeck* • Lewis Martin *Pastor Collins* • William Phipps *Wash Perry* • Paul Birch *Alonzo Hogue* • Cedric Hardwicke *Narrator* ■ *Dir* Byron Haskin • *Scr* Barré Lyndon, from the novel by HG Wells • *Cinematographer* George Barnes

War Party ★★★ 18

Action 1988 · US · Colour · 93mins

An alternative take on the western, with modern-day white folk and native Americans taking opposite sides for a town's centennial re-creation of an old cowboy/Injun fight. But old wounds are reopened, and old prejudices reignited, when someone starts using live ammunition. A potentially intriguing idea, but it's exhausted in the first 20 minutes. The film then becomes just an underdeveloped variant on the traditional western. There are good performances, though, from a Brat-Pack cast that includes Kevin Dillon and Billy Wirth, and it's directed by a Briton, Franc Roddam, of *Quadrophenia* fame.

Billy Wirth *Sonny Crowkiller* • Kevin Dillon *Skitty Harris* • Tim Sampson *Warren Cutfoot* • Jimmy Ray Weeks [Jimmie Ray Weeks] *Jay Stivic* • Kevyn Major Howard *Calvin Morrisey* ■ *Dir* Franc Roddam • *Scr* Spencer Eastman

War Requiem ★★★ PG

Experimental documentary drama
1988 · UK · BW and Colour · 88mins

Benjamin Britten's *War Requiem*, written in 1962 for the dedication of the new Coventry Cathedral, is visualised as an elongated music video by director Derek Jarman. Laurence Olivier, in his last work on film before his death, plays a disabled veteran Second World War soldier whose memories and reflections accompany the highly acclaimed Britten opus. Newsreel footage of the Great War and atomic explosions are intercut with sequences featuring Owen Teale (as the Unknown Soldier) and Tilda Swinton (a battlefield nurse) looking powerlessly on at all the devastation and wasted lives. Jarman's ultimately inspiring, negative statement on war matches the intense emotions of Britten's music to perfection.

Nathaniel Parker *Wilfred Owen* • Tilda Swinton *Nurse* • Laurence Olivier *Old Soldier* • Patricia Hayes *Mother* • Rohan McCullough *Enemy Mother* • Nigel Terry *Abraham* • Owen Teale *Unknown Soldier* • Sean Bean *German Soldier* ■ *Dir* Derek Jarman • *Scr* Derek Jarman, from the original music to oratorio *War Requiem* by Benjamin Britten and the original libretto to oratorio *War Requiem* by Wilfred Owen • *Music* Benjamin Britten • *Cinematographer* Richard Greatrex

The War Room ★★★★

Political documentary
1993 · US · Colour · 90mins

Over three decades after he collaborated on that classic of Direct Cinema, *Primary* (which followed JFK's assault on the White House), DA Pennebaker hit the campaign trial again in this Oscar-nominated account of the 1992 election. The focus is less on Bill Clinton than the contrasting temperaments of his chief spin-doctors – plain-speaking campaign boss James Carville and suave press spokesman George Stephanopoulos – as they seek to counter allegations of adultery, dope-smoking and draft-dodging. There are also fascinating insights into the in-fighting within the Democratic camp and the romantic liaison between Carville and George Bush's senior aide, Mary Matalin.

Dir DA Pennebaker, Chris Hegedus • *Cinematographer* Nick Doob, DA Pennebaker, Kevin Rafferty

The War Wagon ★★★ U

Western 1967 · US · Colour · 96mins

Westerns starring John Wayne and Kirk Douglas approached the genre from very different directions. It's not surprising, therefore, that there's an uneasy tension behind the pair's bonhomie in this rugged comedy adventure. Yet nobody was better at directing this kind of romp than Burt Kennedy, who not only exploits the rivalry between his stars, but also gets superior supporting performances from Bruce Cabot, Keenan Wynn and Howard Keel (cunningly cast as an acerbic American Indian). The action might have been a little more robust, but the wagon itself (with its swivelling turret and machine gun) is a real scene-stealer.

John Wayne *Taw Jackson* • Kirk Douglas *Lomax* • Howard Keel *Levi Walking Bear* • Robert Walker [Robert Walker Jr] *Billy Hyatt* • Keenan Wynn *Wes Catlin* • Bruce Cabot *Frank Pierce* • Valora Noland *Kate Catlin* • Joanna Barnes *Lola* • Bruce Dern *Hammond* ■ *Dir* Burt Kennedy • *Scr* Clair Huffaker, from his novel *Badman* • *Cinematographer* William H Clothier [William Clothier] • *Music* Dimitri Tiomkin [Dmitri Tiomkin]

The War Zone ★★★★★ 18

Drama 1999 · UK/It · Colour · 98mins

Actor Tim Roth makes a stunning directorial debut with a distressingly believable story of incest within a close-knit family. Adapted by Alexander Stuart from his acclaimed novel, this bleak drama elicits supremely natural performances from young newcomers Freddie Cunliffe and Lara Belmont, while Ray Winstone portrays their abusive father as no *Nil by Mouth* monster, but as a loving parent. Roth also makes inspired, emotive use of the stark, jagged Devon landscapes, whose grey-hued coldness seems to mirror Belmont's pain and turns an already uncomfortable experience into a devastating one. Contains swearing and nudity. DVD

Ray Winstone *Dad* • Lara Belmont *Jessie* • Freddie Cunliffe *Tom* • Tilda Swinton *Mum* • Annabelle Apsion *Nurse* • Kate Ashfield *Lucy* • Colin J Farrell *Nick* • Aisling O'Sullivan *Carol* ■ *Dir* Tim Roth • *Scr* Alexander Stuart, from his novel

WarGames ★★★★ PG

Drama 1983 · US · Colour · 108mins

Whiz kid Matthew Broderick accidentally hacks into a Pentagon computer and starts playing a game called Global Thermonuclear War, only to discover he's inadvertently pushing the world toward destruction for real. This is an inventive nail-biter that's consistently entertaining and worryingly thought-provoking, laced by director John Badham with just the right amount of invigorating humour. Great edge-of-the-seat suspense is generated as defence specialist Dabney Coleman desperately tries to avert the impending holocaust, while preachy sentiment is kept to a minimum. Contains swearing. DVD

Matthew Broderick *David Lightman* • Dabney Coleman *John McKittrick* • John Wood *Professor Falken* • Ally Sheedy *Jennifer Mack* • Barry Corbin *General Beringer* • Juanin Clay *Pat Healy* • Dennis Lipscomb *Lyle Watson* • Kent Williams *Arthur Cabot* • Joe Dorsey *Colonel Conley* • Irving Metzman *Richter* ■ *Dir* John Badham • *Scr* Lawrence Lasker, Walter F Parkes

Warlock ★★★ U

Western 1959 · US · Colour · 120mins

An impressive psychological western, with Henry Fonda on magnificent form as a former gunfighter, aching with regret for a passing age and a wasted life, whose success as a lawman means that his corrupt regime is tolerated by the locals. The gradual disintegration of Fonda's friendship with gambler Anthony Quinn is deftly handled by director Edward Dmytryk, allowing the stars' contrasting acting styles to define their characters. With Richard Widmark surprisingly restrained and glamour provided by Dorothy Malone, this deserves to be better known.

Richard Widmark *Johnny Gannon* • Henry Fonda *Clay Blaisdell* • Anthony Quinn *Tom Morgan* • Dorothy Malone *Lilly Dollar* • Dolores Michaels *Jessie Marlow* • Wallace Ford *Judge Holloway* • Tom Drake *Abe McQuown* • Richard Arlen *Bacon* • DeForest Kelley *Curley Burne* • Regis Toomey *Skinner* ■ *Dir* Edward Dmytryk • *Scr* Robert Alan Aurthur, from the novel by Oakley Hall

Warlock ★★★ 15

Horror 1989 · US · Colour · 97mins

Richard E Grant's great central performance as a witchfinder elevates this gory "bell, book and candle" tale to convincing heights. He's hunting warlock Julian Sands who, having escaped through a 1691 time portal to present-day LA, is looking for a Satanic bible to help him destroy the world. Slasher veteran Steve Miner's assured direction keeps everything exciting while unusual plot twists maintain a level of constant surprise. A kind of necromantic *Highlander* with superior special effects that's both bewitching and absorbing, it spawned a couple of lame sequels.

Richard E Grant *Giles Redferne* • Julian Sands *The Warlock* • Lori Singer *Kassandra* • Kevin O'Brien *Chas* • Mary Woronov *Channeller* • Richard Kuss *Mennonite* ■ *Dir* Steve Miner • *Scr* David Twohy • *Music* Jerry Goldsmith

Warlock: the Armageddon ★★ 18

Horror 1993 · US · Colour · 94mins

Julian Sands returns for the second time as the titular warlock, emerging fully grown, if you please, from a woman recently impregnated. He's on a quest to track down six magical runestones, which hold the power to herald the second coming of his satanic master, or dad as he likes to call him. Horror veteran Anthony Hickox knows it's a load of old tosh so directs with total disregard for the boundaries of taste or style. At one point Sands, whose sardonic portrayal of evil incarnate is a huge plus, dispatches an irksome art collector by turning him into his own abstract Picasso masterpiece! Never boring, mind you, just dumb. Contains violence and swearing

Julian Sands *Warlock* • Chris Young *Kenny Travis* • Paula Marshall *Samantha Ellison* • Joanna Pacula *Paula Dare* • Steve Kahan *Will Travis* • RG Armstrong *Franks* • Charles Hallahan *Ethan Larson* • Bruce Glover *Ted Ellison* ■ *Dir* Anthony Hickox • *Scr* Kevin Rock, Sam Bernard

Warlords of Atlantis ★★★ PG

Action adventure 1978 · UK · Colour · 92mins

It may be small beer compared with the monster movies of the computer age, but this is still a decent romp from director Kevin Connor, and it's far better paced than *The Lost World: Jurassic Park*. Doug McClure is the clean-cut Hollywood hero (and about as

Victorian as skateboards) who discovers the fabled city (ruled, would you believe, by Cyd Charisse and Daniel Massey) and its monstrous menagerie of sundry sea beasties – including a giant octopus. The sets and the creatures are as wobbly as the script and the performances, but that's just part of the charm. 🖭

Doug McClure *Greg Collinson* • Peter Gilmore *Charles Aitken* • Shane Rimmer *Captain Daniels* • Lea Brodie *Delphine Briggs* • Michael Gothard *Atmir* • Hal Galili *Grogan* • John Ratzenberger *Fenn* • Cyd Charisse *Atsil* • Daniel Massey *Atraxon* ■ *Dir* Kevin Connor • *Scr* Brian Hayles

A Warm December ★★

Drama 1973 · UK · Colour · 100mins
This mawkish affair begins as a thriller and ends up as a romance. Sidney Poitier (making his second film as director) stars as an American widower, a doctor who falls for the supposedly hounded niece (Esther Anderson) of an African diplomat, only to discover that the people who are following her are doing it for her own good – she has sickle-cell anaemia. This is tough all round, especially for audiences.

Sidney Poitier *Doctor Matt Younger* • Esther Anderson *Catherine* • Yvette Curtis *Stefanie Younger* • George Baker *Henry Barlow* • Earl Cameron *Ambassador George Oswandu* • Johnny Sekka *Myomo* • Hilary Crane *Marsha Barlow* ■ *Dir* Sidney Poitier • *Scr* Lawrence Roman

Warm Nights on a Slow Moving Train ★★★ 18

Drama 1987 · Ausl · Colour · 87mins
Covering similar ground to Ken Russell's much-maligned *Crimes of Passion* (but with less sensationalism and considerably more intelligence), this intriguing Australian tale of dual personality was withheld from release after its completion in 1986. However, director Bob Ellis's simmering thriller deserves a wider showing. As the mousey Catholic school art teacher who works as a train-board prostitute by night to help her morphine-addicted, paraplegic brother, Wendy Hughes gives a performance that is as subtle and sensitive as it is dark and disturbing. Colin Friels also does well as the client who draws her into a dangerous liaison. 🖭

Wendy Hughes *Girl* • Colin Friels *Man* • Norman Kaye *Salesman* • John Clayton *Football coach* • Lewis Fitz-Gerald *Girl's brother* • Rod Zuanic *Soldier* • Steve J Spears *Singer* • Grant Tilly *Politician* ■ *Dir* Bob Ellis • *Scr* Bob Ellis, Denny Lawrence

Warming Up ★★★

Comedy 1983 · Ausl · Colour · 94mins
Without ever quite striking the right balance between the satirical and the downright silly, this is, nevertheless, an entertaining comedy, in which the worlds of ballet and Australian Rules football meet head on. Barbara Stephens is hugely impressive as the no-nonsense dance instructor whose refusal to accept the ''men only'' regime in the backwater town of Wilgunyah prompts her to train the Wombats football team behind the back of their coach and her nemesis,

cop Henri Szeps. Director Bruce Best stages the training sequences very well, but the matches themselves are less convincing. Never uproariously funny, but there are plenty of smiles.

Barbara Stephens *Juliet Cavanagh-Forbes* • Henri Szeps *Peter Sullivan* • Queenie Ashton *Mrs Marsh* • Adam Fernance *Randolph Cavanagh-Forbes* • Lloyd Morris *Ox* • Tim Grogan *Snoopy* • Ron Blanchard *Lennie* ■ *Dir* Bruce Best • *Scr* James Davern

Warning Shot ★★★★

Crime thriller 1967 · US · Colour · 99mins
David Janssen was at the height of his fame from playing the title role in TV's long-running series *The Fugitive* when he starred in this pacey and entertaining thriller about a policeman's bid to clear his name – not unlike the Fugitive himself – of killing an apparently unarmed and upstanding medic. In the process, he encounters not just plenty of drama and excitement but also an all-star cast, including Lillian Gish, Carroll O'Connor, Walter Pidgeon, Sam Wanamaker and our very own Joan Collins in a brief appearance as Janssen's wife.

David Janssen *Sergeant Tom Valens* • Ed Begley *Captain Roy Klodin* • Keenan Wynn *Sergeant Ed Musso* • Sam Wanamaker *Frank Sanderman* • Lillian Gish *Alice Willows* • Stefanie Powers *Liz Thayer* • Eleanor Parker *Mrs Doris Ruston* • George Grizzard *Walt Cody* • George Sanders *Calvin York* • Steve Allen *Perry Knowland* • Carroll O'Connor *Paul Jerez* • Joan Collins *Joanie Valens* • Walter Pidgeon *Orville Ames* ■ *Dir* Buzz Kulik • *Scr* Mann Rubin, from the novel *711 – Officer Needs Help* by Whit Masterson

Warning Sign ★★★ 15

Science-fiction thriller 1985 · US · Colour · 94mins
Although derivative of a dozen other mind-melt movies, from *The China Syndrome* to *The Andromeda Strain*, Hal Barwood's thriller is engrossing action all the way with its bacterial twists and brain-damaged turns. The excellent acting lifts it way above the norm, although mouth-foaming maniac Richard Dysart delivers some stupidly inspired dialogue about rage being beautiful. But you'll be sorry when the curtain finally falls on this exciting, high-tech tale. 🖭

Sam Waterston *Cal Morse* • Kathleen Quinlan *Joanie Morse* • Yaphet Kotto *Major Connolly* • Jeffrey DeMunn *Dan Fairchild* • Richard Dysart *Dr Nielsen* • GW Bailey *Tom Schmidt* • Jerry Hardin *Vic Flint* ■ *Dir* Hal Barwood • *Scr* Hal Barwood, Matthew Robbins

Warpath ★★ U

Western 1951 · US · Colour · 95mins
A sobering pre-revisionist western, a reminder of a Hollywood where Red Indians were treated like dirt, this Paramount caper is actually dedicated to the Seventh Cavalry. Using events leading up to the battle of Little Bighorn as a background for a stark revenge plot, Edmond O'Brien (too chubby for a western hero) rides out to avenge his slaughtered fiancée. In the hands of director Byron Haskin, it's a perfectly functional time-passer, but if John Ford had filmed this, it would have been a different movie altogether.

Still, the Indian attack is well photographed in Technicolor.

Edmond O'Brien *John Vickers* • Dean Jagger *Sam Quade* • Charles Stevens *Courier* • Forrest Tucker *Sergeant O'Hara* • Harry Carey Jr *Captain Gregson* • Polly Bergen *Molly Quade* • James Millican *General Custer* • Wallace Ford *Private Potts* • Paul Fix *Private Fiore* ■ *Dir* Byron Haskin • *Scr* Frank Gruber • *Cinematographer* Ray Rennahan

Warrendale ★★★

Documentary 1967 · Can · BW · 102mins
A cause célèbre after it was rejected by the Canadian Broadcasting Corporation on account of its four-letter content, Allan King's ''Direct Cinema'' documentary still makes for disconcerting viewing. Priding itself on allowing its residents as much latitude as possible, Warrendale was a hostel for emotionally disturbed adolescents run by one Dr Brown on the outskirts of Toronto. Observing the kids at leisure, in therapy and (most tellingly) in shock after the death of their beloved cook, King provides no commentary and resists editorial intrusion to present a graphic and frequently shocking picture of a generation with little self-respect and even less hope.

Dir Allan King

The Warrior and the Sorceress ★★ 18

Martial arts action adventure 1983 · US · Colour · 74mins
Part samurai movie, part western and part fantasy, in the end this fumbling affair comes across as nothing more than a blatant rip-off of Akira Kurosawa's *Yojimbo*, which also formed the basis for *A Fistful of Dollars*. David Carradine plays a holy warrior, in all but name his television *Kung Fu* character, who arrives in an impoverished village where two rival gangs vie for control over a water well. It's not long before Carradine is playing each side against the other. Exotic Maria Socas, cast as the sorceress, spends the entire movie topless. Maybe the budget was so small they could only afford half her costume! 🖭

David Carradine *Kain* • Luke Askew *Zeg* • Maria Socas *Naja* • Anthony DeLongis *Kief* • Harry Townes *Bludge* ■ *Dir* John C Broderick • *Scr* John C Broderick, from a story by William Stout, John C Broderick

Warrior Queen ★ 18

Period exploitation drama 1986 · US · Colour · 67mins
Silliness, thy name is *Warrior Queen*. Sybil Danning stars as the titular Queen Berenice, an attractive but deadly woman who arrives in Pompeii for a festival and to negotiate with the city's ruler, Clodius. Donald Pleasence leaves no bit of scenery unchewed as the self-indulgent mayor, so it's no wonder his wife wants to hook up with an attractive young gladiator. Calamity results, ending with the death of several major characters as Pompeii is destroyed by the nearby volcano. The film lifts footage from the superior *The Last Days of Pompeii* (1960) with Steve Reeves. 🖭

Sybil Danning *Berenice* • Donald Pleasence *Clodius* • Richard Hill *Marcus* • Josephine

Jacqueline Jones *Chloe* • Tally Chanel *Vespa* • Stasia Micula [Samantha Fox] *Philomena/Augusta* • Suzanna Smith *Veneria* ■ *Dir* Chuck Vincent • *Scr* Rick Marx, from a story by Harry Alan Towers

The Warriors ★★★★ 18

Action drama 1979 · US · Colour · 88mins
Essentially, this vivid and violent gangland thriller is an urban western: a New York gang battles its way back to home turf following the murder of a rival gang leader during a ceasefire meeting. Despite the gritty storyline and locations, there's a doomed, romantic feel to the film and a poetic quality to the exhilarating fight scenes. Walter Hill sketches the characters with some sympathy and is rewarded with excellent performances from the largely unknown cast. 🖭

Michael Beck *Swan* • James Remar *Ajax* • Thomas Waites [Thomas G Waites] *Fox* • Dorsey Wright *Cleon* • Brian Tyler *Snow* • David Harris *Cochise* • Tom McKitterick *Cowboy* • Mercedes Ruehl *Policewoman* ■ *Dir* Walter Hill • *Scr* Walter Hill, David Shaber, from the novel by Sol Yurick • *Cinematographer* Andrew Laszlo

Warriors of Virtue ★ PG

Action adventure 1997 · US · Colour · 98mins
Plenty of warriors, but very little virtue in this slice of kids codswallop, about an Earth boy who's sucked down some sort of intergalactic plughole, and winds up aiding kangaroo-style furred friendlies against the evil overlord who's taken over their world. Younger kids may appreciate the fight scenes, handled by Hong Kong action director Ronny Yu, and might also identify with the half-pint hero. Older kids will quite rightly suggest that the film copies its ''kangaroos'' and hops it. Ranks with *Tank Girl* as the worst super-marsupials movie ever made. 🖭

Angus MacFadyen *Komodo* • Mario Yedidia *Ryan Jeffers* • Marley Shelton *Elysia* • Dennis Dun *Ming* • Tom Towles *General Grillo* • Michael Anderson [Michael J Anderson] *Mudlap* • Adrienne Corcoran *Tsun* • Doug Jones *Yee* ■ *Dir* Ronny Yu • *Scr* Michael Vickerman, Hugh Kelly, from characters created by Dennis Law, Ronald Law, Christopher Law, Jeremy Law

Washington Merry-Go-Round ★★

Political melodrama 1932 · US · BW · 78mins
Lee Tracy finds himself on the trail of corruption in high places in this creaky ode to the American way. Although it touches on many of the points later raised in *Mr Smith Goes to Washington*, James Cruze's half-hearted picture lacks the sharpness of the Frank Capra classic, and Tracy (more at home in his familiar role as a fast-talking reporter) is no James Stewart. Alan Dinehart badly fumbles the part of the treacherous statesman, while the enthusiastic Constance Cummings is given too little to do as Tracy's Girl Friday.

Lee Tracy *Button Gwinnett Brown* • Constance Cummings *Alice Wylie* • Alan Dinehart *Norton* • Walter Connolly *Senator Wylie* • Clarence Muse *Clarence, the Valet* • Arthur Vinton *Beef Brannigan* • Frank Sheridan *Kelleher* ■ *Dir* James Cruze • *Scr* Jo Swerling, from a story by Maxwell Anderson

U = SUITABLE FOR ALL Uc = SUITABLE FOR ALL, ESPECIALLY FOR YOUNG CHILDREN (VIDEO ONLY) PG = PARENTAL GUIDANCE

Washington Square ★★★ PG

Romantic drama
1997 · US · Colour · 111mins

Previously filmed as *The Heiress* in 1949, this romantic drama reverts to novelist Henry James's original title, with Jennifer Jason Leigh as the dowdy spinster in 19th century America, whose chance of marriage is cruelly denied her by her domineering father, Albert Finney. It starts promisingly as director Agnieszka Holland sets the scene with a breathtaking camera swoop from above the treetops to a bedroom where a beautiful woman has just died, bloodily, in childbirth. From then on, however, Holland is less assured and the film ultimately fails to live up to its early promise. Finney has real menace as the unforgiving father and Ben Chaplin acquits himself well as the gold-digging Morris Townsend, but, whereas Olivia de Havilland won an Oscar for her crushed violet in William Wyler's ersion, Leigh is far too mannered for sympathy. ▭

Jennifer Jason Leigh *Catherine Sloper* • Albert Finney *Dr Austin Sloper* • Ben Chaplin *Morris Townsend* • Maggie Smith *Aunt Lavinia Penniman* • Judith Ivey *Aunt Elizabeth Almond* • Betsy Brantley *Mrs Montgomery* • Jennifer Garner *Marian Almond* • Peter Maloney *Jacob Webber/Notary* • Robert Stanton *Arthur Townsend* • Arthur Laupus *Mr Almond* ■ *Dir* Agnieszka Holland • *Scr* Carol Doyle, from the novel by Henry James

The Wasp Woman ★★

Science-fiction horror
1959 · US · BW · 62mins

Cosmetics boss Susan Cabot uses wasp enzymes for a rejuvenation formula and turns into a blood-lusting bug-eyed monster in cult director Roger Corman's ironic rip-off of *The Fly*. For a film of barely an hour, it's pretty slow, and more ridiculous than frightening. However, Cabot's coolly professional performance makes up for the cheapness of the production (the first to be made by Corman's own company, Filmgroup) and helps paper over the weak scripting by beefy character actor Leo Gordon.

Susan Cabot *Janice Starlin* • Fred Eisley [Anthony Eisley] *Bill Lane* • Barboura Morris *Mary Dennison* • Michael Marks *Dr Eric Zinthrop* • William Roerick *Arthur Cooper* • Frank Gerstle *Hellman* ■ *Dir* Roger Corman • *Scr* Leo Gordon

Watch It ★★★ 15

Comedy drama 1992 · US · Colour · 98mins

Just like the twentysomething males it satirises, this wry drama shirks its reponsibilities by seeking refuge in a childish prank just when it needs to show a little maturity. Perpetual students Jon Tenney, John C McGinley and Tom Sizemore live for the eponymous game they've played since college, largely because they can't cope with life in the raw. Consequently, they're much less interesting than Tenney's cousin, Peter Gallagher, who tires of the jokes after he falls for vet Suzy Amis. Smartly written by director Tom Flynn, this will be a source of discomfort to lads everywhere as they recognise their less attractive traits. Contains swearing and brief nudity. ▭

Peter Gallagher *John* • John C McGinley *Rick* • Suzy Amis *Anne* • Lili Taylor *Brenda* • Jon Tenney *Michael* • Cynthia Stevenson *Ellen* • Tom Sizemore *Danny* ■ *Dir/Scr* Tom Flynn

Watch It, Sailor! ★★ U

Comedy 1961 · UK · BW · 83mins

The path of true love never runs smooth, which is handy for makers of romantic comedies. Here it's the courtship between naval lieutenant Dennis Price and his bride-to-be Liz Fraser which is in danger of running aground when Price is served with a paternity suit. A host of familiar British comedy talent fill out the cast including Irene Handl, Miriam Karlin and Frankie Howerd. Based on the stage play of the same name, this is unexceptional, though some enjoyment can be found watching the old pros go through their paces.

Miriam Karlin *Mrs Lack* • Dennis Price *Lt Cmdr Hardcastle* • Liz Fraser *Daphne* • Irene Handl *Edie Hornett* • Graham Stark *Carnoustie Bligh* • Vera Day *Shirley Hornett* • Marjorie Rhodes *Emma Hornett* • Cyril Smith *Mr Hornett* • John Meillon *Albert Tufnell* • Frankie Howerd *Organist* ■ *Dir* Wolf Rilla • *Scr* Falkand Cary, Philip King, from the play by Falkand Cary, Philip King

Watch on the Rhine ★★★★★ U

Drama 1943 · US · BW · 107mins

Lillian Hellman's hit 1941 play came to the screen directed by Herman Shumlin, responsible for the Broadway production, and retained much of its original stage cast. One of the most powerful and impassioned pleas for resistance to fascism in modern drama, the action takes place before the outbreak of the Second World War and involves a German (Paul Lukas), his American wife (Bette Davis) and their children, who, while staying with Davis's mother (Lucille Watson), encounter a dispossessed Rumanian count (George Coulouris). The count discovers Lukas's true identity as an anti-Nazi resistance worker and prepares to sell the information to the Germans. The film combines politics, heroism, poignancy, suspense and sophisticated wit to gripping effect. Lukas won the best actor Oscar, with picture, screenplay and Watson nominated. ▭

Bette Davis *Sara Muller* • Paul Lukas *Kurt Muller* • Geraldine Fitzgerald *Marthe de Brancovis* • Lucile Watson *Fanny Farrelly* • Beulah Bondi *Anise* • George Coulouris *Teck de Brancovis* • Donald Woods *David Farrelly* • Henry Daniell *Phili von Ramme* ■ *Dir* Herman Shumlin • *Scr* Dashiell Hammett, Lillian Hellman, from the play by Lillian Hellman • *Music* Max Steiner • *Cinematographer* Hal Mohr

Watch the Birdie ★★ U

Comedy 1950 · US · BW · 70mins

Although red-haired comic Red Skelton was one of MGM's top comedians, the studio executives never quite knew what to do with him, as this dreary remake of Buster Keaton's *The Cameraman* (1928) shows. In it, photographer Skelton inadvertently films a private conversation revealing a crooked scam and saves rich girl Arlene Dahl from financial ruin. Skelton insisted on also playing the roles of

his father and grandfather, which was not a good idea.

Red Skelton *Rusty Cammeron/Pop Cammeron/Grandpop Cammeron* • Arlene Dahl *Lucia Corlane* • Ann Miller *Miss Lucky Vista* • Leon Ames *Grantland D Farns* • Pam Britton [Pamela Britton] *Mrs Shanway* • Richard Rober *Mr Hugh Shanway* • Dick Wessel *Man who undresses* ■ *Dir* Jack Donohue • *Scr* Ivan Tors, Devery Freeman, Harry Ruskin, from a story by Marshall Neilan Jr

Watch Your Stern ★★ PG

Comedy 1960 · UK · BW · 84mins

Directed by Gerald Thomas, produced by Peter Rogers and starring such regulars as Kenneth Connor, Leslie Phillips, Joan Sims and Hattie Jacques, this is a *Carry On* in all but name. There aren't actually all that many laughs as twitchy tar Connor assumes a range of disguises to cover up a blunder over torpedo plans. But the by-play between the characters is slick and there is some amusing slapstick involving admiral Noel Purcell's bicycle. Moreover, who would pass up the sight of chief petty officer Sid James in a beard? The team found their sea legs two years later in *Carry On Cruising*. ▭

Kenneth Connor *Ordinary Seaman Blissworth* • Eric Barker *Captain David Foster* • Leslie Phillips *Lieutenant Commander Fanshawe* • Joan Sims *Ann Foster* • Hattie Jacques *Agatha Potter* • Spike Milligan *Dockyard mate* • Eric Sykes *Dockyard mate* • Sidney James *Chief Petty Officer Mundy* • Ed Devereaux *Commander Phillips* • David Lodge *Security sergeant* ■ *Dir* Gerald Thomas • *Scr* Alan Hackney, Vivian A Cox, from the play *Something about a Sailor* by Earle Couttie

Watched ★★★ 15

Psychological drama
1974 · US · Colour · 92mins

The old chestnut of a government agent going underground is given some spark by the acting of Stacy Keach as a man who stalked dope addicts. Mentally unstable, he's now at odds with Harris Yulin, head of the narcotics department. Some social relevancies put a tighter spin on the usual procedures as customary. ▭

Stacy Keach *Mike Mandell/Sonny* • Harris Yulin *Gordon Pankey* • Bridget Pole *Informer* • Turid Aarsted *Blonde* • Valeri Parker *Hitchhiker* ■ *Dir/Scr* John Parsons

The Watcher in the Woods ★★★

Supernatural horror
1982 · US/UK · Colour · 83mins

Disney attempted to shake its kiddie popcorn image with this tale of a composer's family moving into a mysterious cottage owned by sinister Bette Davis. But the psychic alien time-warp plot is too silly for adults and not daft enough to make it a proper children's treat. Director John Hough knows how to use atmosphere, though, and sustains it quite well, despite ex-ice skater Lynn-Holly Johnson's bland central performance. However, his decision to go the soft gothic horror route and then suddenly leave the horror out is a mistake, and the movie never recovers. Disney in fact changed the climax after a disastrous test screening. Bette Davis

completists won't want to miss it, though.

Bette Davis *Mrs Aylwood* • Carroll Baker *Helen Curtis* • David McCallum *Paul Curtis* • Lynn-Holly Johnson *Jan Curtis* • Kyle Richards *Ellie Curtis* • Ian Bannen *John Keller* • Richard Pasco *Tom Colley* • Frances Cuka *Mary Fleming* • Benedict Taylor *Mike Fleming* ■ *Dir* John Hough, Vincent McEveety • *Scr* Brian Clemens, Harry Spalding, Rosemary Anne Sisson, from the novel by Florence Engel Randall

Watchers ★ 18

Science-fiction horror
1988 · Can · Colour · 86mins

Horror novelist Dean R Koontz was extremely unhappy with this adaptation of his work, though he had plenty of warning with bargain-basement producers Roger Corman and Damian Lee attaching themselves to the project. All hope of redemption disappeared with Corey Haim cast as the teen hero who finds an extremely intelligent dog, not knowing that it is the result of a government experiment that also produced a pursuing Sasquatch-like animal (or is it a guy in a gorilla suit?). Once again Michael Ironside, playing the usual government agent who comes in to try to cover things up, manages to give a stereotyped and poorly written character some menace and personality. Dark, murky and unexciting. ▭

Corey Haim *Travis* • Barbara Williams *Nora* • Michael Ironside *Lem* • Lala Sloatman *Tracey* • Duncan Fraser *Sheriff Gaines* ■ *Dir* Jon Hess • *Scr* Bill Freed, Damian Lee, from the novel by Dean R Koontz

The Watchmaker of St Paul ★★★★ PG

Crime drama 1973 · Fr · Colour · 100mins

Bertrand Tavernier made his feature debut with this reworking of Georges Simenon's US-set novella *L'Horloger d'Everton*. The fact that it was co-scripted by veterans Jean Aurenche and Pierre Bost betrays Tavernier's desire to produce a literate picture in the "Tradition of Quality" mode. But there's no studio-bound realism here, as Tavernier captures the authentic Lyonnais atmosphere and uses his own birthplace as the setting for several key scenes. Philippe Noiret is superb as the watchmaker questioning both his bourgeois beliefs and his paternal value on learning of his son's involvement in a political killing. Equally impressive is Jean Rochefort's quietly dignified cop. In French with English subtitles.

Philippe Noiret *Michel Descombes* • Jean Rochefort *Inspector Guiboud* • Jacques Denis *Antoine* • Yves Afonso *Inspector Bricard* ■ *Dir* Bertrand Tavernier • *Scr* Bertrand Tavernier, Jean Aurenche, Pierre Bost, from the novel *L'Horloger d'Everton* by Georges Simenon

Water ★ 15

Comedy 1985 · UK · Colour · 93mins

One of the disasters that sank the British film company HandMade, *Water* stars Michael Caine as a British diplomat on a West Indian island awash with Communist insurrection and Americans dredging mineral water – a kind of sparkling Castreau?

Intended as a satire on the Falklands and Grenada, it falls flat in all departments, mainly because co-writers Dick Clement (who also directs) and Ian La Frenais couldn't sustain a narrative over their usual 30-minute sitcom ration. Valerie Perrine and Brenda Vaccaro are irritating, Billy Connolly embarrassing and Maureen Lipman sadly miscast as a Mrs Thatcher figure. Only the marvellous Leonard Rossiter raises a smile. Contains swearing.

Michael Caine *Baxter Thwaites* • Valerie Perrine *Pamela* • Brenda Vaccaro *Dolores* • Leonard Rossiter *Sir Malcolm Leveridge* • Billy Connolly *Delgado* • Dennis Duggan *Rob* • Fulton Mackay *Eric* • Jimmie Walker *Jay Jay* • Dick Shawn *Deke Halliday* • Fred Gwynne *Spender* ■ *Dir* Dick Clement • *Scr* Dick Clement, Ian La Frenais, Bill Persky, from a story by Bill Persky

The Water Babies ★ U

Part-animated fantasy adventure
1978 · UK/Pol · Colour · 81mins

Combining cartoon and live action, this is a ghastly adaptation of the Charles Kingsley classic. Admittedly, director Lionel Jeffries had to revert to animation to tell his tale of a young chimney sweep who rescues a group of underwater children from a tyrannical shark. But the cartooning is bland, the voicing of the sea creatures and the water babies too cute and the songs are a disgrace. Compounding the disappointment, the opening section (in which shifty sweep James Mason and his dimwitted assistant Bernard Cribbins plot to burgle a country manor) shows promise.

James Mason *Grimes* • Billie Whitelaw *Mrs Doasyouwouldbedoneby* • Tommy Pender *Tom* • Bernard Cribbins *Masterman* • Joan Greenwood *Lady Harriet* • David Tomlinson *Sir John* • Samantha Gates *Ellie* • Paul Luty *Sladd* ■ *Dir* Lionel Jeffries • *Scr* Michael Robson, from the novel by Charles Kingsley

The Water Engine ★★★

Drama 1992 · US · Colour · 100mins

A made-for-cable version of a typically intense David Mamet stage play, adapted by Mamet himself. It's an ingenious transposition to thirties Chicago of the classic Ealing satire *The Man in the White Suit*. William H Macy attempts to patent a water-powered engine, but falls foul of conniving attorney Joe Mantegna, whose machinations drive Macy to try and conceal his blueprints, with tragic consequences. Director Steven Schachter opts to retain a stagey atmosphere and is rewarded by powerful performances from the talented cast, but some of Mamet's literary devices – overheard conversations, a sinister chain letter – serve only to baffle rather than enhance the drama.

William H Macy *Charles Lang* • John Mahoney *Mason Gross* • Joe Mantegna *Lawrence Oberman* • Patti LuPone *Rita* • Mike Nussbaum *Mr Wallace* • Treat Williams *Dave Murray* • Tim Farrell *Bernie* • Charles Durning *Museum guide* • Joanna Miles *Mrs Varec* ■ *Dir* Steven Schachter • *Scr* David Mamet

The Waterboy ★★★★ 12

Sports comedy 1998 · US · Colour · 86mins

Incredibly dumb but equally infectious, this comedy reunites *Wedding Singer* director Frank Coraci with his star Adam Sandler as a water-boy who dispenses H_2O to sweaty college footballers, whose great joy is hurling abuse at the not-too-bright lad. One day, their mean words (this time about his beloved Cajun mum, Kathy Bates) are just too much and he strikes back by charging one of the players, so impressing the coach that he ends up on the team. Featuring great performances from Bates and The Fonz himself, Henry Winkler (as the bewildered coach), this popular hit allows Sandler to put his modest comedic talent to good use. DVD

Adam Sandler *Bobby Boucher* • Kathy Bates *Mama Boucher* • Henry Winkler *Coach Klein* • Fairuza Balk *Vicki Vallencourt* • Jerry Reed *Red Beaulieu* • Larry Gilliard Jr *Derek Wallace* • Blake Clark *Farmer Fran* • Peter Dante *Gee Grenouille* ■ *Dir* Frank Coraci • *Scr* Tim Herlihy, Adam Sandler

The Waterdance ★★★ 15

Drama 1991 · US · Colour · 102mins

A gritty, syrup-free movie about a disparate group of young men attempting to come to terms with the fact that they will be paralysed for the rest of their lives. As a young novelist who has an accident on a hiking holiday and slowly puts his life back together, Eric Stoltz is excellent in the lead, and Wesley Snipes and William Forsythe, both more usually associated with action roles, are equally good as two fellow paraplegics. Evoking distant memories of Marlon Brando in *The Men*, but shorn of its war associations, *The Waterdance* is a well-acted, moving and often witty tour through a variety of fears and neuroses. Co-director/scriptwriter Neal Jimenez is himself confined to a wheelchair following an accident. Contains some violence, swearing and nudity.

Eric Stoltz *Joel Garcia* • Wesley Snipes *Raymond Hill* • William Forsythe *Bloss* • Helen Hunt *Anna* • Elizabeth Pena *Rosa* • William Allen Young *Les* • Henry Harris *Mr Gibson* ■ *Dir* Neal Jimenez, Michael Steinberg • *Scr* Neal Jimenez

Waterfront ★★★

Drama 1950 · UK · BW · 80mins

Having co-directed *Private Angelo*, Michael Anderson went solo with this sobering portrait of Liverpool in the Depression. Adapted from the novel by John Brophy, the film is undeniably melodramatic. Yet it has a surprisingly raw naturalism that suggests the influence of both Italian neorealism and the proud British documentary tradition. As the seaman whose drunken binges mean misery for his family and trouble for his shipmates, Robert Newton reins in his tendency for excess, and he receives solid support from the ever-dependable Kathleen Harrison and a young Richard Burton, in only his third feature.

Robert Newton *Peter McCabe* • Kathleen Harrison *Mrs McCabe* • Richard Burton *Ben Satterthwaite* • Avis Scott *Nora McCabe* • Susan Shaw *Connie McCabe* • Robin Netscher *George Alexander* • Kenneth Griffith *Maurice Bruno* ■ *Dir* Michael Anderson • *Scr* John Brophy, Paul Soskin, from the novel by John Brophy

Waterhole #3 ★★★ 15

Western farce 1967 · US · Colour · 91mins

Where else would you expect a western about deception, ambition and naked greed to be set but Integrity, Arizona? James Coburn becomes the hero of this comedy tale by dint of the fact that he is marginally less repellent than his rivals, all scouring this particular desert watering hole for the proceeds of a gold robbery. The ever-vivacious Joan Blondell is on sparkling form as an avaricious madam, while Carroll O'Connor hams up a storm as a sheriff with some highly personal views on upholding the law. Produced by Blake Edwards's company, this is rough'n'ready entertainment along the lines of *Cat Ballou*.

James Coburn *Lewton Cole* • Carroll O'Connor *Sheriff John Copperud* • Margaret Blye [Maggie Blye] *Billee Copperud* • Claude Akins *Sgt Henry Foggers* • Timothy Carey *Hilb* • Joan Blondell *Lavinia* • Robert Cornthwaite *George* • Bruce Dern *Deputy Sheriff* • James Whitmore *Captain Shipley* ■ *Dir* William Graham [William A Graham] • *Scr* Joseph T Steck, Robert R Young

Waterland ★★ 15

Drama 1992 · UK · Colour · 90mins

Based on Graham Swift's Booker Prize-winning novel, this was very much a pet project of Jeremy Irons who stars with his wife, Sinead Cusack. The story charts the emotional collapse of a teacher and his wife who grew up on the flat marshlands of the East Anglian fens. This landscape, superbly captured, serves to underline the characters as they flash back and forward through the bleak wreckage of their lives, all for the benefit of Irons's American students (convenient for production finance) who get this grim story in lieu of history lessons. It's earnest, unpleasant and more often tedious than engrossing. Contains swearing and nudity.

Jeremy Irons *Tom Crick* • Sinead Cusack *Mary Crick* • Ethan Hawke *Mathew Price* • Grant Warnock *Young Tom* • Lena Headey *Young Mary* • David Morrissey *Dick Crick* • John Heard *Lewis Scott* • Callum Dixon *Freddie Parr* ■ *Dir* Stephen Gyllenhaal • *Scr* Peter Prince, from the novel by Graham Swift

Waterloo ★★★★ U

Historical drama
1970 · It/USSR · Colour · 126mins

Rod Steiger gives a magnificent performance as Napoleon – all hot rages and cool calculation – as he heads for his destiny in Belgium in Ukrainian director Sergei Bondarchuk's epic history lesson. Steiger even manages to upstage the thousands of Soviet soldiers recruited as extras for the battle scenes, yet he's nearly outshone by Christopher Plummer as the Duke of Wellington, whose arrogance shows his contempt for lower-class cannon-fodder. Bondarchuk filmed in Italy and the Ukraine, and the result is a mightily credible reconstruction of a crunch-point that changed the course of western history. It's the two major performances, though, that lift it out of the textbooks and give it humanity. DVD

Rod Steiger *Napoleon Bonaparte* • Orson Welles *Louis XVIII* • Virginia McKenna *Duchess of Richmond* • Michael Wilding *Sir William Ponsonby* • Donal Donnelly *Private O'Connor* • Christopher Plummer *Duke of Wellington* • Jack Hawkins *General Thomas Picton* • Dan O'Herlihy *Marshal Michel Ney* • Terence Alexander *Lord Uxbridge* ■ *Dir* Sergei Bondarchuk • *Scr* HAL Craig, Sergei Bondarchuk, Vittorio Bonicelli

Waterloo Bridge ★★★★ PG

Romantic melodrama
1940 · US · BW · 104mins

This was the second version of Robert E Sherwood's celebrated stage play of star-crossed lovers to make it to the screen, and MGM director Mervyn LeRoy went for an unashamedly tear-jerking approach, even though the Hollywood prudishness of the day forced him to draw some of the sting from the story. In her first film role after her Oscar-winning Scarlett O'Hara in *Gone with the Wind*, Vivien Leigh gives a heartbreaking performance as the ballerina who falls in love with army captain Robert Taylor during a First World War air raid, only to be driven on to the streets after she is misinformed of his death. Taylor was never more handsome, and there's sterling support from Hollywood's British colony, especially Virginia Field who excels as Leigh's loyal friend.

Vivien Leigh *Myra Lester* • Robert Taylor (1) *Captain Roy Cronin* • Lucile Watson *Lady Margaret Cronin* • Virginia Field *Kitty* • Maria Ouspenskaya *Mme Olga Kirowa* • C Aubrey Smith *Duke* • Janet Shaw *Maureen* • Janet Waldo *Elsa* • Steffi Duna *Lydia* • Virginia Carroll *Sylvia* • Leda Nicova *Marie* ■ *Dir* Mervyn LeRoy • *Scr* SN Behrman, Hans Rameau, George Froeschel, from the play by Robert E Sherwood

Waterloo Road ★★

Wartime drama 1944 · UK · BW · 75mins

Best remembered today as the wartime movie with a terrific fist-fighting climax as tiny John Mills beats up his wife's lover, six-foot-plus spiv Stewart Granger. If you believe that, you'll probably believe in the rest of this atypically stodgy Sidney Gilliat production. Told in a rather woolly flashback structure by Alastair Sim's kindly philosophising doctor, the plot is nevertheless extremely realistic for its day – many soldiers received that dread "Dear John" letter – and it's fascinating to watch the star-making performance from Granger. But Arthur Crabtree's stark photography fails to disguise the cramped studio interiors used for much of the film.

John Mills *Jim Colter* • Stewart Granger *Ted Purvis* • Alastair Sim *Dr Montgomery* • Joy Shelton *Tillie Colter* • Beatrice Varley *Mrs Colter* • Alison Leggatt *Ruby* • Leslie Bradley *Mike Duggan* ■ *Dir* Sidney Gilliat • *Scr* Val Valentine, from a story by Sidney Gilliat • *Cinematographer* Arthur Crabtree

Watermelon Man ★★★

Comedy drama 1970 · US · Colour · 99mins

Bigoted white insurance salesman Godfrey Cambridge wakes up one morning to find he has turned black overnight. The transformation, which baffles doctors, sees Cambridge being

1550 U = SUITABLE FOR ALL Uc = SUITABLE FOR ALL, ESPECIALLY FOR YOUNG CHILDREN (VIDEO ONLY) PG = PARENTAL GUIDANCE

ostracised by his friends and family, and having to seek a new life in the black community. Melvin Van Peebles's savage satire may have dated but its message (hammered home in Herman Raucher's script) is still potent. Comedian Godfrey Cambridge is marvellous in the lead, squeezing out laughs even when the situation becomes grim.

Godfrey Cambridge *Jeff Gerber* • Estelle Parsons *Althea Gerber* • Howard Caine *Mr Townsend* • D'Urville Martin *Bus driver* • Mantan Moreland *Counterman* • Kay Kimberly *Erica* • Kay E Kuter *Dr Wainwright* • Scott Garrett *Burton Gerber* • Erin Moran *Janice Gerber* ∎ *Dir* Melvin Van Peebles • *Scr* Herman Raucher • *Music* Melvin Van Peebles

The Watermelon Woman
★★ 15

Comedy drama 1996 · US · Colour · 80mins

It might have won the Teddy Bear for the best gay film at the 1996 Berlin festival, but Cheryl Dunye's fictional documentary is too inward-looking for its own good. Hollywood's denial of opportunity to black (let alone gay and lesbian) performers in the thirties and forties is certainly a topic worthy of discussion. But Dunye's pursuit of the "watermelon woman", a character actress she keeps spotting in old Hollywood movies, gets tangled up too often in her relationships with her closest friend and a new white lover. Moreover, the camerawork is fussy and the satire is too self-congratulatory. However, there is an insightful glimpse of controversial academic Camille Paglia in action. ▦

Cheryl Dunye *Cheryl* • Guinevere Turner *Diana* • Valerie Walker *Tamara* • Lisa Marie Bronson *Fae "The Watermelon Woman" Richards* • Irene Dunye *Herself* • Brian Freeman *Lee Edwards* • Ira Jeffries *Shirley Hamilton* • Camille Paglia ∎ *Dir/Scr* Cheryl Dunye

Watership Down
★★★ U

Animation 1978 · UK · Colour · 87mins

Martin Rosen inherited this adaptation of Richard Adams's cult novel – about the adventures of a diverse group of rabbits – after John Hubley, who helped animate many Disney classics of the forties, had departed owing to "creative differences". The visual and vocal characterisations are of variable quality, but it's hard to see what Hubley could have done to improve on Rosen's respectable version of what is a very difficult book to translate to the screen, especially when you take into account that animation for adults is still somewhat uncharted territory. One for fans and first-timers only, this isn't your average cuddly bunny movie, and contains scenes that may be disturbing for children. ▦

John Hurt *Hazel* • Richard Briers *Fiver* • Michael Graham-Cox *Bigwig* • John Bennett *Captain Holly* • Ralph Richardson *Chief Rabbit* • Simon Cadell *Blackberry* • Terence Rigby *Silver* • Roy Kinnear *Pipkin* • Hannah Gordon *Hyzenthlay* • Zero Mostel *Kehaar* • Michael Hordern *Frith* ∎ *Dir* Martin Rosen • *Scr* Martin Rosen, from the novel by Richard Adams

Waterworld
★★★★ 12

Futuristic adventure
1995 · US · Colour · 129mins

Declared dead in the water owing to escalating costs, nightmare production problems and clashing egos, Kevin Reynolds's lavish *Mad Max* on jet-skis emerged as a spectacular and thrilling sci-fi fantasy. In the far future, the polar icecaps have melted, covering the entire planet in water and making dirt the most valuable commodity. Only the enigmatic loner Mariner (Kevin Costner) offers a ray of hope to Helen (Jeanne Tripplehorn) and Enola (Tina Majorino), the latest victims of a Smoker sea raid, as he battles the bandits responsible (led by Dennis Hopper) and continues his search to find the one piece of mythical Dryland. Offering plenty of comic-book heroics and spectacular stunts, Costner gives one of his finest performances as the half man/half amphibian whose steely character holds the whole full-blooded epic adventure together. Contains violence and swearing. ▦ **DVD**

Kevin Costner *Mariner* • Dennis Hopper *Deacon* • Jeanne Tripplehorn *Helen* • Tina Majorino *Enola* • Michael Jeter *Gregor* • Gerard Murphy *Nord* • RD Call *Enforcer* ∎ *Dir* Kevin Reynolds • *Scr* Peter Rader, David Twohy, Joss Whedon • *Cinematographer* Dean Semler

Wattstax
★★

Documentary 1972 · US · Colour · 101mins

A filmed record of the 1972 benefit concert held at the Los Angeles Coliseum to raise money for the Watts community on the seventh anniversary of the violent riots. Amusingly emceed by Richard Pryor, the impressive roster of black soul and R&B acts includes the Dramatics, the Staple Singers, Carla Thomas, William Bell, Kim Weston and the Bar-Kays. The highlights are Isaac Hayes belting out *Shaft*, Rufus Thomas doing the *Funky Chicken* and the Reverend Jesse Jackson singing *I Am Somebody*.

Dir Mel Stuart

Wavelength
★★ 15

Science-fiction thriller
1983 · US · Colour · 83mins

The title comes from psychic Cherie Currie being able to mentally "hear" the cries of aliens who were shot down and then imprisoned by the government in a secret desert facility. She enlists the aid of singer Robert Carradine and prospector Keenan Wynn to help her break the visitors out before they're put under the knife. The three actors are very likeable in their roles, and the excellently creepy score by Tangerine Dream generates a decent amount of atmosphere. Somewhat slow, but the main problem is its low budget, which among other things results in the aliens being played by bald African-American children with no makeup. ▦

Robert Carradine *Bobby Sinclaire* • Cherie Currie *Iris Longacre* • Keenan Wynn *Dan* • Cal Bowman *General Milton Ward* • James Hess *Colonel James MacGruder* ∎ *Dir/Scr* Mike Gray • *Music* Tangerine Dream

Wax Mask
★★ 18

Horror 1997 · It · Colour · 94mins

A nostalgic salute to vintage Hammer horror by way of *House of Wax* and souped up with extra gore and kinky sex, this car-boot-sale chiller from special-effects man turned director Sergio Stivaletti is a luridly engaging if shoddy shocker. Robert Hossein is the Roman wax museum owner hiding dark secrets and a scarred face behind interchangeable masks that allow him to masquerade as every other cast member in the convoluted whodunit plot. Produced by Dario Argento, this was originally crafted to mark Lucio Fulci's mainstream comeback, but the splatter maestro died just a few weeks before shooting and Stivaletti took over the panicked production. All that disarray shines through the hair-raising fakery even if it doesn't get in the way of comfortable enjoyment. An Italian language film. Contains violence, sex scenes and swearing. ▦

Robert Hossein *Boris* • Romina Mondello *Sonia* • Riccardo Serventi Longhi *Andrea* • Gabriella Giogelli *Francesca* • Umberto Balli *Alex* ∎ *Dir* Sergio Stivaletti • *Scr* Lucio Fulci, Daniele Stroppa, from a story by Dario Argento, from the novel *The Wax Museum* by Gaston Leroux

Waxwork
★★ 18

Horror 1988 · US · Colour and BW · 92mins

When a mysterious waxworks museum appears overnight in a small anonymous town, its sinister owner invites a group of teens, including Zach Galligan (*Gremlins*), to a special midnight showing. "Stop on by and give afterlife a try" was the film's tagline, and that's precisely what happens when each of the youngsters are sucked into the wax tableaux to meet a grisly doom. Director Anthony Hickox certainly has tongue firmly in cheek, but his pastiches of old-time movie monsters such as Dracula and the Mummy lack the necessary wit and soon border on repetitiveness. Veterans Patrick Macnee and David Warner give knowingly camp performances that add to the overall comic-book tone, spoilt only by the maker's penchant for unnecessary unpleasantness. ▦

Zach Galligan *Mark* • Deborah Foreman *Sarah* • Michelle Johnson *China* • Dana Ashbrook *Tony* • Miles O'Keeffe *Count Dracula* • Patrick Macnee *Sir Wilfred* • David Warner *Mr Lincoln* • John Rhys-Davies *Anton Weber* ∎ *Dir/Scr* Anthony Hickox

Waxwork II: Lost in Time
★★

Horror comedy
1992 · US · Colour and BW · 104 mins

A dull and dumber sequel reuniting the star and director of an original which wasn't all that great. This picks up directly where the first one left off with Zach Galligan surviving the apocalyptic end of the deadly waxwork museum only to be propelled into various time periods – all recognisable horror settings – to defeat evil. This ploy enables Anthony Hickox to once again prove his uninspired talent for spoofing various genre movies, this time ranging from *Nosferatu* to *The Haunting*. An eclectic cast includes cameos from

Drew Barrymore and *Evil Dead*'s Bruce Campbell. Even *EastEnders* regular Martin Kemp pops up as Baron Frankenstein. Enjoyable for horror buffs in the right mood.

Zach Galligan *Mark Loftmore* • Sophie Ward *Eleanore Pratt* • Patrick Macnee *Sir Wilfred* • Alexander Godunov *Scarabus* • Martin Kemp *Baron Frankenstein* • Monika Schnarre *Sarah* • Bruce Campbell *John Wright* • David Carradine *Beggar* • Marina Sirtis *Gloria* • John Ireland *King Arthur* • Drew Barrymore *Vampire victim* ∎ *Dir/Scr* Anthony Hickox

Waxworks
★★★★

Silent gothic horror 1924 · Ger · BW · 93mins

Paul Leni's last film in Germany before continuing on his chilly way to America is also one of his best, and gives us a chance to see four of Germany's finest actors in their earlier days. Wilhelm Dieterle, who was to become a renowned Hollywood director, plays a young poet who tells three stories behind three exhibits in a wax museum: Haroun-al-Raschid (Emil Jannings), Ivan the Terrible (Conrad Veidt) and Jack the Ripper (Werner Krauss). The expressionist lighting and designs are symbolic of character and plot, creating a haunting atmosphere.

Wilhelm Dieterle [William Dieterle] *Young poet/Assad/Groom* • Emil Jannings *Haroun-al-Raschid* • Conrad Veidt *Ivan the Terrible* • Werner Krauss *Jack the Ripper, "Spring Heeled Jack"* • Olga Belajeff *Showman's daughter/Zarah/Bride* • John Gottwot *Showman* ∎ *Dir* Paul Leni • *Scr* Henrik Galeen • *Cinematographer* Helmar Lerski • *Art Director* Paul Leni, Fritz Maurischat

The Way Ahead
★★★★ U

Second World War drama
1944 · UK · BW · 109mins

One of the finest "in this together" flag-wavers produced in Britain during the Second World War. From Eric Ambler and Peter Ustinov's script, director Carol Reed, who had earned a reputation for social realism in the mid-thirties and had spent part of the war making army documentaries, creates a totally believable world in which a squad of raw recruits becomes an integral part of the local community as they go through basic training. David Niven is top-billed, but he generously enters into the ensemble spirit that makes this beautifully observed drama as uplifting today as in 1944. ▦

David Niven *Lieutenant Jim Perry* • Raymond Huntley *Davenport* • Billy Hartnell [William Hartnell] *Sergeant Fletcher* • Stanley Holloway *Brewer* • James Donald *Lloyd* • John Laurie *Luke* • Leslie Dwyer *Beck* • Hugh Burden *Parsons* • Jimmy Hanley *Stainer* • Renee Ascherson [Renée Asherson] *Marjorie Gillingham* ∎ *Dir* Carol Reed • *Scr* Eric Ambler, Peter Ustinov, from a story by Eric Ambler

Way Down East
★★★★★

Silent melodrama
1920 · US · BW Tinted · 145mins

Lillian Gish, at her most lovely and moving, is the innocent and trusting young country girl tricked into a fake marriage by wealthy, womanising wastrel Lowell Sherman, who leaves her pregnant. The baby dies and the destitute girl finds employment with fanatically religious farmer Burr McIntosh, whose son Richard

Barthelmess falls in love with Gish. A twenties melodrama with elements of tragedy, DW Griffith's film offers a happy ending that is nothing less than a coup given what has gone before. Although uncomfortably extended in length by some extraneous and jarring ''yokel'' comedy, *Way Down East* is a miracle of visual composition, brilliantly acted, with Gish giving one of the most eloquent performances of the silent screen. Justly celebrated for the climactic sequence where Gish, drifting unconscious on a raft of ice in a storm, is rescued by Barthelmess, the film offers many less obvious moments that are just as memorable.

Lillian Gish *Anna Moore* • Richard Barthelmess *David Bartlett* • Mrs David Landau *Anna's mother* • Lowell Sherman *Lennox Sanderson* • Burr McIntosh *Squire Bartlett* • Josephine Bernard *Mrs Tremont* • Mrs Morgan Belmont *Diana Tremont* • Norma Shearer *Barn dancer* ■ *Dir* DW Griffith • *Scr* Anthony Paul Kelly, from the play *Annie Laurie* by Lottie Blair Parker, as elaborated in the play by Joseph R Grismer • *Cinematographer* GW Bitzer [Billy Bitzer], Hendrik Sartov, Paul H Allen

Way Down East ★★
Melodrama   1935 · US · BW · 84mins

A prime example of Hollywood's all-too-frequent attempts to remake a masterpiece when there's little possibility of equalling, let alone improving, the original. Fifteen years after the silent collaboration of DW Griffith and Lillian Gish, Fox handed a sound version to Henry King and Rochelle Hudson (replacing the more suitable Janet Gaynor who dropped out), with Henry Fonda in the Richard Barthelmess role. King's work is all right, especially his re-creation of the ice-river climax, but Hudson is no match for Gish, leaving the honours to Fonda in a much smaller role. The major problem though, lies in the material which, by the mid-thirties, played as outmoded period melodrama, needing a genius to rescue it.

Rochelle Hudson *Anna Moore* • Henry Fonda *David Bartlett* • Slim Summerville *Constable Seth Holcomb* • Edward Trevor *Lennox Sanderson* • Margaret Hamilton *Martha Perkins* • Andy Devine *Hi Holler* • Russell Simpson *Squire Bartlett* • Spring Byington *Mrs Bartlett* ■ *Dir* Henry King • *Scr* Howard Estabrook, William Hurlbut, from the 1920 film by Anthony Paul Kelly, from the play *Annie Laurie* by Lottie Blair Parker, as elaborated in the play by Joseph R Grismer

Way of a Gaucho ★★★ Ⓤ
Western   1952 · US · Colour · 90mins

Director Jacques Tourneur was a dab hand at many styles of film-making, bringing a little extra something to *films noirs* and westerns, swashbucklers and horrors. Out West, he responded to the landscape with a natural eye, turning out this clever but forgotten Argentinian-set western for 20th Century-Fox. Although not ideally cast, Rory Calhoun does well as the disaffected gaucho of the title, who greets the arrival of civilisation on the pampas by organising outlaw resistance. Richard Boone is sent to apprehend him, and Philip Dunne's moralistic screenplay has Calhoun capitulate and win Gene Tierney as a

reward. It's an interesting concept, and Tourneur's direction is striking.

Rory Calhoun *Martin* • Gene Tierney *Teresa* • Richard Boone *Salinas* • Hugh Marlowe *Miguel* • Everett Sloane *Falcon* • Enrique Chaico *Father Fernandez* ■ *Dir* Jacques Tourneur • *Scr* Philip Dunne, from the novel by Herbert Childs

The Way of All Flesh ★★★★
Silent drama   1927 · US · BW · 90mins

The great German actor Emil Jannings, in his first American film, stars as a respectable bank clerk – a model husband and father of six – who, en route to delivering a package of bonds in Chicago, is conned by a girl and her criminal boyfriend. The latter is killed by a passing train. Jannings changes places with the dead man and then disappears, an act which leads to his steady descent into the gutter. Jannings won the first ever Oscar jointly for his full-blooded performances in this and *The Last Command*. Directed by Victor Fleming, it was also nominated for best picture. But if it all seems over the top now, it's nonetheless an engrossing drama, with a poignant denouement. 🎬

Emil Jannings *August Schiller* • Belle Bennett *Mrs Schiller* • Phyllis Haver *Mayme* • Donald Keith *August Jr* • Fred Kohler *The Tough* ■ *Dir* Victor Fleming • *Scr* Jules Furthman, Lajos Biró, Julian Johnson (titles) • *Cinematographer* Victor Milner

The Way of All Flesh ★★
Melodrama   1940 · US · BW · 85mins

Louis King directs and Akim Tamiroff stars in this pointless remake of the 1927 film. Stripped of the more awesomely melodramatic aspects that proved effective in the silent version, this tale of a respectable bank cashier who goes to the dogs in the big city, leaving his wife (the wonderful Gladys George) and family to nurse their memories, is competent, but dated and all-too predictable. Tamiroff, a character actor better known for his succession of often sinister foreigners, does fine but lacks star punch.

Akim Tamiroff *Paul Kriza Sr* • Gladys George *Anna Kriza* • William Henry *Paul Jr* • John Hartley *Victor Kriza* • Marilyn Knowlden *Julie Kriza* • Betty McLaughlin *Mitzi Kriza* ■ *Dir* Louis King • *Scr* Lenore Coffee, from the 1927 film by Jules Furthman, Lajos Biró

The Way of the Dragon ★★★
Martial arts adventure
1973 · HK · Colour · 98mins

Made before Bruce Lee's international breakthrough in *Enter the Dragon*, this Hong Kong effort finds the martial arts superstar at the peak of his powers. The plot – gangsters threaten a Chinese restaurant owner in Rome – is instantly forgettable (scriptwriting clearly wasn't one of Lee's fortes) and there is a travelogue feel to some of the Italian sequences. However, Lee the director stages some stunning fight set pieces, most memorably a clash at the Colosseum with Chuck Norris (not a star in his own right in those days). The film was also released as *The Return of the Dragon*.

Bruce Lee *Tang Lung* • Chuck Norris *Colt* • Nora Miao *Chen Ching Hua* • Wang Chung

Hsin *Uncle Wang* • Ti Chin *Ah K'ung* • Jon T Benn *Boss* • Robert Wall *Robert* ■ *Dir/Scr* Bruce Lee

Way Out West ★★★★★ Ⓤ
Classic comedy   1937 · US · BW · 63mins

Stan Laurel and Oliver Hardy get to sing their hit song *Trail of the Lonesome Pine* as they go west to deliver a mine-deed inheritance to prospector's daughter Rosina Lawrence. However they are waylaid by crooked saloon owner James Finlayson and his moll, Sharon Lynne. This inspired western parody contains some of the duo's most memorable routines, making it one of those films you can watch umpteen times and still come back for more. 🎬

Stan Laurel *Stan* • Oliver Hardy *Ollie* • Sharon Lynne *Lola Marcel* • James Finlayson *Mickey Finn* • Rosina Lawrence *Mary Roberts* • Stanley Fields *Sheriff* ■ *Dir* James W Horne • *Scr* Charles Rogers, Felix Adler, James Parrott, from a story by Jack Jevne, Charles Rogers

The Way to the Gold ★★ Ⓤ
Adventure drama   1957 · US · BW · 94mins

Ex-con Jeffrey Hunter sets out to uncover loot buried 30 years before by a now-deceased villain, only to discover the treasure site covered by an artificial lake. Barry Sullivan, Walter Brennan and Neville Brand feature as the rivals on his trail, but act like self-pitying automata. Only Sheree North, as Hunter's girlfriend, seems to bring a touch of life to her role.

Jeffrey Hunter *Joe Mundy* • Sheree North *Hank Clifford* • Barry Sullivan *Marshal Hannibal* • Walter Brennan *Uncle George* • Neville Brand *Little Brother Williams* • Jacques Aubuchon *Clem Williams* • Ruth Donnelly *Mrs Williams* ■ *Dir* Robert D Webb • *Scr* Wendell Mayes, from the novel by Wilbur Daniel Steele

The Way to the Stars ★★★★ Ⓤ
Second World War drama
1945 · UK · BW · 104mins

A well judged piece of Second World War stiff-upper-lipped drama concerning the activities of an RAF squadron and its members' relationships with their loved-ones and the flashy flyboys who have recently arrived from America. The first joint project of director Anthony Asquith, producer Anatole de Grunwald and writer Terence Rattigan, this perfectly captures the spirit of Britain at a moment when loss was perhaps even more agonising, simply because victory was so close at hand. Michael Redgrave and Rosamund John are straight out of the Noël Coward school of British bourgeoisie, but John Mills and Renée Asherson are closer to reality as the couple dallying over a wartime wedding. 🎬 *DVD*

Michael Redgrave *David Archdale* • John Mills *Peter Penrose* • Rosamund John *Miss Toddy Todd* • Douglass Montgomery *Johnny Hollis* • Stanley Holloway *Mr Palmer* • Trevor Howard *Squadron Leader Carter* • Renée Asherson *Iris Winterton* • Felix Aylmer *Rev Charles Moss* ■ *Dir* Anthony Asquith • *Scr* Terence Rattigan, Anatole de Grunwald, from a story by Terence Rattigan, from a story by Richard Sherman

Way... Way Out ★★
Comedy   1966 · US · Colour · 104mins

When Russian astronomer Anita Ekberg claims she was attacked by a US astronaut on a jointly run moonbase, US Lunar Division chief Robert Morley decrees that in future all US moonbase personnel will be married couples. Consequently Jerry Lewis, next in line to staff the moonbase, hastily has to arrange a wedding to fellow worker Connie Stevens in order to fulfil his mission. This was yet another uncomfortable vehicle for Lewis who was finding it increasingly difficult to find suitable material and collaborators. Thankfully, old pros Morley and Brian Keith provide some amusing substance to the lunatic proceedings.

Jerry Lewis *Peter* • Connie Stevens *Eileen* • Robert Morley *Quonset* • Dennis Weaver *Hoffman* • Howard Morris *Schmidlap* • Brian Keith *General Hallenby* • Dick Shawn *Igor* • Anita Ekberg *Anna* ■ *Dir* Gordon Douglas • *Scr* William Bowers, Laslo Vadnay

The Way We Were ★★★★ ᴾᴳ
Romantic drama
1973 · US · Colour · 113mins

A glossy romance between ugly duckling Barbra Streisand and glamorous Robert Redford. She's poor, jittery, Jewish and a radical, and he's rich, self-assured, Gentile and conservative: the ideal odd couple. Set against the backdrop of a changing America, including the McCarthy witch-hunts, every scene seems dreamed up by a dating-agency computer, though the sheer professionalism of the picture and the performances can't fail to touch you. Redford, as a character seemingly hewn from the pages of F Scott Fitzgerald (he's a writer to boot), is perfectly cast and Streisand is simply Streisand. Watch out for James Woods in an early role. Contains swearing. 🎬 *DVD*

Barbra Streisand *Katie Morosky* • Robert Redford *Hubbell Gardiner* • Bradford Dillman *JJ* • Lois Chiles *Carol Ann* • Patrick O'Neal *George Bissinger* • Viveca Lindfors *Paula Reisner* • Allyn Ann McLerie *Rhea Edwards* • Murray Hamilton *Brooks Carpenter* • Herbert Edelman *Bill Verso* • Diana Ewing *Vicki Bissinger* ■ *Dir* Sydney Pollack • *Scr* Arthur Laurents, from his novel

The Way West ★★★★
Western   1967 · US · Colour · 122mins

A spectacular western directed by Andrew V McLaglen from the Pulitzer Prize-winning novel by AB Guthrie Jr. It boasts a magnificent leading trio of Kirk Douglas, Robert Mitchum and Richard Widmark, in roles they were born to play – Mitchum, in particular, is remarkably good as a trail scout. The scale is impressive as politician Douglas leads a wagon train along the hazardous Oregon trail to California, while Bronislau Kaper's outstanding score deserves to be better known. Watch out for a young Sally Field in her movie debut.

Kirk Douglas *Senator William J Tadlock* • Robert Mitchum *Dick Summers* • Richard Widmark *Lije Evans* • Lola Albright *Rebecca Evans* • Michael Witney *Johnnie Mack* • Michael McGreevey *Brownie Evans* • Sally Field *Mercy McBee* • Katherine Justice *Amanda Mack* • Stubby Kaye *Sam Fairman*

Ⓤ = SUITABLE FOR ALL   Ⓤc = SUITABLE FOR ALL, ESPECIALLY FOR YOUNG CHILDREN (VIDEO ONLY)   ᴾᴳ = PARENTAL GUIDANCE

Jack Elam *Preacher Wetherby* ■ *Dir* Andrew V McLaglen • *Scr* Ben Maddow, Mitch Lindemann, from the novel by AB Guthrie Jr • *Cinematographer* William H Clothier [William Clothier]

Wayne's World ★★★★ PG

Comedy   1992 · US · Colour · 90mins

This spin-off from the TV show *Saturday Night Live* brought "teen speak" to a new level. Mike Myers and Dana Carvey are Wayne and Garth, whose low-budget public access cable show is transformed into a national TV phenomenon by sleazy producer Rob Lowe. Along the way, Myers falls in love with rock chick Tia Carrere and, along with Carvey, gets to meet their idol Alice Cooper. Aiming for the unashamedly moronic, director Penelope Spheeris nevertheless manages to sneak in some sly satiric jibes and it benefits from inspired casting: Myers and Carvey are excellent, Lowe and Lara Flynn Boyle, as Myers's mad ex-girlfriend, are both nicely cast against type, and there is a neat cameo from *Terminator 2* villain Robert Patrick. Contains swearing and sex scenes.

Mike Myers *Wayne Campbell* • Dana Carvey *Garth Algar* • Rob Lowe *Benjamin Oliver* • Tia Carrere *Cassandra* • Brian Doyle-Murray *Noah Vanderhoff* • Lara Flynn Boyle *Stacy* • Michael DeLuise *Alan* ■ *Dir* Penelope Spheeris • *Scr* Mike Myers, Bonnie Turner, Terry Turner, from characters created by Mike Myers

Wayne's World 2 ★★★ PG

Comedy   1993 · US · Colour · 90mins

Wayne and Garth return for another goofy pop culture delve into suburban Americana. This time Mike Myers's cleverly conceived alter ego is searching for meaning in his life and decides to mount a "Waynestock" rock concert. The gleeful party atmosphere conjured up by the first and funnier movie continues here with silly gags, daft catch phrases ("schwing"), surprising cameos and hip in-jokes. But it's a sloppy hit-and-miss affair that's very much a case of diminishing returns despite the odd hysterical highlight such as Myers's kung-fu battle with James Hong. Contains some swearing.

Mike Myers *Wayne Campbell* • Dana Carvey *Garth Algar* • Tia Carrere *Cassandra* • Christopher Walken *Bobby Cahn* • Ralph Brown *Del Preston* • Olivia D'Abo *Betty Jo* • Kim Basinger *Honey Hornée* • James Hong *Mr Wong* • Heather Locklear ■ *Dir* Stephen Surjik • *Scr* Mike Myers, Terry Turner, Bonnie Turner, from characters created by Mike Myers

The Wayward Bus ★★

Drama   1957 · US · BW · 88mins

A *Grand Hotel* type story from a novel by John Steinbeck about a group of people whose lives are changed on a bus trip in California, this is a patchy affair with an interesting cast that deserved a better script. Jayne Mansfield gives a touching performance as a stripper who wants to become a "real actress", and there are good performances by Dan Dailey as a travelling salesman and Joan Collins as the driver's tipsy wife, but the superficial characterisation and pat situations leave them, like the bus on which they travel, on rocky ground.

Joan Collins *Alice* • Jayne Mansfield *Camille* • Dan Dailey *Ernest Horton* • Rick Jason *Johnny Chicoy* • Betty Lou Keim *Norma* • Dolores Michaels *Mildred Pritchard* • Larry Keating *Pritchard* ■ *Dir* Victor Vicas • *Scr* Ivan Moffat, from the novel by John Steinbeck

We All Loved Each Other So Much ★★★★

Romantic drama

1974 · It · BW and Colour · 136mins

With guest appearances by Vittorio De Sica and Federico Fellini, a wealth of clips from the likes of Rossellini, Visconti and Antonioni, and impudent pastiches of some classic scenes, this cinematic rattlebag will prove an endless delight for fans of postwar Italian film. However, the casual viewer is also catered for, as Ettore Scola chronicles the 30-year friendship between political activist Nino Manfredi, radical cinéaste Stefano Satta Flores and self-made bourgeois, Vittorio Gassman, who not only share a common history, but also a mutual passion for the ravishing Stefania Sandrelli. Alternately broad and sentimental, inspired and contrived, but always sympathetic and amusing. An Italian language film.

Nino Manfredi *Antonio* • Vittorio Gassman *Gianni* • Stefania Sandrelli *Luciana* • Stefano Satta Flores *Nicola* • Vittorio De Sica • Federico Fellini • Giovanna Ralli *Elide* ■ *Dir* Ettore Scola • *Scr* Age [Agenore Incrocci], Furio Scarpelli, Ettore Scola

We Are Not Alone ★★

Drama   1939 · US · BW · 105mins

A Hollywood melodrama set in one of those quiet English villages where dark passions flow just as strongly as the Earl Grey. Paul Muni is the local doctor, Flora Robson is his fearsome wife and Jane Bryan the dancer with whom he falls in love. The story seldom rises above Mills and Boon levels of cliché and predictability, and owes its inspiration to the case of Dr Crippen. But the setting at the outbreak of the First World War, with Britain close to panic meant much to audiences in 1939 when it seemed as if we were "alone" again.

Paul Muni *Dr David Newcome* • Jane Bryan *Leni-Krafft* • Flora Robson *Jessica Newcome* • Raymond Severn *Gerald Newcome* • Una O'Connor *Susan* • Alan Napier *Archdeacon* • James Stephenson *Sir William Clintock* • Montagu Love *Major Millman* • Henry Daniell *Sir Ronald Dawson* ■ *Dir* Edmund Goulding • *Scr* James Hilton, Milton Krims, from the novel by James Hilton

We Dive at Dawn ★★★ U

Second World War drama

1943 · UK · BW · 92mins

This tense British study of submarine warfare, directed by Anthony Asquith, is packed with incident (as a determined crew pursues a Nazi battleship across the Baltic) and credible characters, played by the likes of John Mills and Eric Portman, who remain human for all their quiet heroism. **DVD**

Eric Portman *James Hobson* • John Mills *Lt Freddie Taylor* • Reginald Purdell *CPO Dicky Dabbs* • Niall MacGinnis *PO Mike Corrigan* • Joan Hopkins *Ethel Dabbs* • Josephine Wilson *Alice Hobson* ■ *Dir* Anthony Asquith • *Scr* JP Williams, Frank Launder, Val Valentine

We Don't Want to Talk about It ★★★★ PG

Drama   1993 · Arg/It · Colour · 93mins

This is essentially a touching parable on the blindness of love, though some will find the romance between an ageing Casanova and a fabulously cultured dwarf rather hard to take. Yet the only dubious character in this intriguing flashback to an imaginary Latin American town in the thirties is scheming widow Luisina Brando, whose motives for pairing Marcello Mastroianni with her daughter, Alejandra Podesta, are not exactly selfless. Flirting occasionally with lapses in taste and the lazy deceits of magic realism, this curiously uplifting tale is kept on track by the excellence of the performances. In Spanish with English subtitles. Contains nudity.

Marcello Mastroianni *Ludovico D'Andrea* • Luisina Brando *Leonor* • Alejandra Podesta *Charlotte* • Betiana Blum *Madama* • Roberto Carnaghi *Padre Aurelio* • Alberto Segado *Dr Blanes* • Jorge Luz *Alcalde* ■ *Dir* Maria Luisa Bemberg • *Scr* Maria Luisa Bemberg, Jorge Goldenberg, from a short story by Julio Llinas

We Joined the Navy ★★ U

Comedy   1962 · UK · Colour · 109mins

A modestly amusing service comedy with Kenneth More as a blithering idiot ordered to train navy cadets at Dartmouth College. Making a hash of that billet, More is transferred to the American fleet in the Med, thus allowing Hollywood hero Lloyd Nolan to help the film at the box-office in America. It's really little more than *Doctor in the House* in uniform, with More using his comic persona in that film to send up his earlier screen career as a Second World War warrior, and Dirk Bogarde reprising his own *Doctor in the House* role in a cameo.

Kenneth More *Lieutenant Commander Badger aka "Bodger"* • Lloyd Nolan *Admiral Ryan* • Joan O'Brien *Carol Blair* • Mischa Auer *Colonel/President* • Jeremy Lloyd *Dewberry* • Dinsdale Landen *Bowles* • Derek Fowlds *Carson* • Denise Warren *Collette* • John Le Mesurier *Dewberry Senior* • Lally Bowers *Mrs Dewberry* • Laurence Naismith *Admiral Blake* • Andrew Cruickshank *Admiral Filmer* • Brian Wilde *Petty Officer Gibbons* • Esma Cannon *Consul's Wife* • Dirk Bogarde *Dr Simon Sparrow* • Michael Bentine *Psychologist* • Sidney James *Dancing instructor* ■ *Dir* Wendy Toye • *Scr* Arthur Dales [Howard Dimsdale], from a novel by John Winton

We Live Again ★★★ PG

Melodrama   1934 · US · BW · 78mins

The Russian answer to the Swedish Garbo, Anna Sten, was exceptionally well cast opposite dashing Fredric March in this uncredited adaptation of Tolstoy's *Resurrection*, but the public never really warmed to her. Today, this movie is an impressive work, beautifully photographed by Gregg Toland (*Citizen Kane*), and impressively condensed into 80-odd minutes, in part by newcomer Preston Sturges. Director Rouben Mamoulian's sense of scale is awesome, from the opening scenes on the steppes, and including a detailed Russian Orthodox Easter Mass. Incidentally, listen closely to the latter: the music was erroneously recorded backwards!

Fredric March *Prince Dmitri* • Anna Sten *Katusha Maslova* • Jane Baxter *Missy Kortchagin* • C Aubrey Smith *Prince Kortchagin* • Sam Jaffe *Gregory Simonson* • Ethel Griffies *Aunt Maria* • Gwendolyn Logan *Aunt Sophia* • Mary Forbes *Mrs Kortchagin* ■ *Dir* Rouben Mamoulian • *Scr* Maxwell Anderson, Leonard Praskins, Preston Sturges, from the novel *Resurrection* by Leo Tolstoy

We of the Never Never ★★★ U

Adventure drama

1982 · Ausl · Colour · 127mins

Influential Aussie drama, one of the first to really register in the UK. Angela Punch McGregor packs her middle name as a gutsy high-society girl who marries a cattle-station manager, and leaves for an outback life among macho men who regard women as a liability. Handsomely mounted and impeccably played.

Angela Punch McGregor *Jeannie Gunn* • Arthur Dignam *Aeneas Gunn* • Tony Barry *Mac* • Tommy Lewis *Jackeroo* • Lewis FitzGerald *Jack* • Martin Vaughan *Dan* • John Jarratt *Dandy* • Tex Morton *Landlord* ■ *Dir* Igor Auzins • *Scr* Peter Schreck, from an autobiography by Jane Taylor Gunn

We Still Kill the Old Way ★★★

Crime drama   1967 · It · Colour · 99mins

Adapted from a novel by Leonardo Sciascia, this is perhaps the least effective of director Elio Petri's collaborations with screenwriter Ugo Pirro. Less ferocious than *Investigation of a Citizen Under Suspicion*, the film uses a murder mystery to comment on contemporary Italian society from a distinctly left-wing perspective. Gian Maria Volonté gives a typically steady performance as the teacher convinced that two friends have fallen foul of a poison pen campaign. But Irene Papas overplays the widow for whom he falls, despite her suspicious involvement with a local dignitary. An Italian language film.

Gian Maria Volonté *Paolo Laurana* • Irene Papas *Luisa Roscio* • Gabriele Ferzetti *Rosello* • Salvo Randone *Professor Roscio* • Luigi Pistilli *Arturo Manno* • Mario Scaccia *Priest* • Laura Nucci *Paulo's mother* ■ *Dir* Elio Petri, • *Scr* Elio Petri, Ugo Pirro, from the novel *A ciascuno il suo* by Leonardo Sciascia

We the Jury ★★★

Courtroom drama   1996 · US · Colour

A gripping TV movie drama in the same vain as *Twelve Angry Men* but without the distinguished acting talent. The story centres on the sensational murder trial of talk-show hostess (Lauren Hutton) charged with killing her philandering husband, and how it takes its toll on the 12 sequestered jurors. Although the defendant confesses to the shooting, the jury must decide to what extent she's culpable. Hostility and prejudices surface as they wrestle to reach a verdict. Kelly McGillis gives a subtle performance as a prim jury member, and Christopher Plummer shines as a slick defense lawyer. Sturla Gunnarsson's sharp direction keeps the pace taut while deft writing delivers an emotional punch.

Kelly McGillis *Alyce Bell* • Christopher Plummer *Wilfred Fransiscus* • Lauren Hutton

Wynne Atwood • Janet Wright *Gladys Mackenzie* • Anais Granofsky *Naomi Buddin* • Nicky Guadagni *Beryl Granger* • Karen Robinson *Evelyn Harris* ■ *Dir* Sturla Gunnarsson • *Scr* Philip Rosenberg

We the Living ★★★★

Political drama 1942 · It · BW · 270mins

Director Goffredo Alessandrini's splendid film version of Ayn (*The Fountainhead*) Rand's novel stars Alida Valli and Rossano Brazzi, both first-class and at the peak of their youthful beauty, as Kira, a student in love with anti-Communist aristocrat Leo in 1920s Russia. To help Leo, who is suffering from TB but being denied medical treatment, Kira engages in an affair with an influential member of the secret police (Fosco Giachetti), setting the rest of the action in motion. After a successful run in Italy, the film was withdrawn on political grounds by the Mussolini-era authorities and disappeared until 1988, when Rand's legal advisers tracked down a copy and restored it. In Italian with English subtitles, when re-released in 1986.

Alida Valli *Kira Argounova* • Rossano Brazzi *Leo Kovalensky* • Fosco Giachetti *Andrei Taganov* • Giovanni Grasso *Tishenko* • Emilio Cigoli *Pavel Syerov* • Cesrina Gheraldi *Comrade Sonia* ■ *Dir* Goffredo Alessandrini • *Scr* Anton Giulio Majano, from the novel by Ayn Rand, adapted by Corrado Alvaro, Orio Vergani

We Think the World of You ★★★ PG

Comedy drama 1988 · UK · Colour · 94mins

Tackling homosexual prejudice in fifties Britain, Alan Bates is a civil servant with an ongoing passion for bad boy Gary Oldman. In return, Oldman plays Bates for his money and when he is sent to prison, Oldman's wife continues the scrounging. Aware he is being taken for a ride but helpless in his unrequited passion, Bates projects all his feelings about the younger man onto Oldman's Alsatian dog, his fight to love and protect the animal an obvious metaphor for his feelings for another man. Not an easy film, this is masterfully intelligent and understated with spot on performances from Oldman, Bates and a very lovely hound.

Alan Bates *Frank Meadows* • Gary Oldman *Johnny Burney* • Frances Barber *Megan* • Liz Smith *Millie Burney* • Max Wall *Tom Burney* • Kerry Wise *Rita* • Ivor Roberts *Harry* ■ *Dir* Colin Gregg • *Scr* Hugh Stoddart, from a novel by Joseph R Ackerley

We Were Strangers ★★★

Adventure drama 1949 · US · BW · 105mins

The charismatic John Garfield, nearing the end of a career destroyed by the McCarthy blacklist, stars in this sombre political drama set in the early thirties and well directed by John Huston. Garfield plays a Cuban-born American who returns to the country of his birth to help with a revolutionary group's elaborate plan to assassinate some government ministers. Things don't go according to plan, but there's time for an obligatory romance (with Jennifer Jones). Even though it dissipates its serious political theme with too much mechanical detail, the film is still tense and atmospheric.

Jennifer Jones *China Valdes* • John Garfield *Tony Fenner* • Pedro Armendariz *Armando Ariete* • Gilbert Roland *Guillermo Mantilla* • Ramon Novarro *Chief* • Wally Cassell *Miguel* ■ *Dir* John Huston • *Scr* Peter Viertel, John Huston, from the episode *China Valdez* in the novel *Rough Sketch* by Robert Sylvester

The Weak and the Wicked ★★★ PG

Prison drama 1953 · UK · BW · 83mins

The title says it all. This is one of those riveting women's prison pictures full of sneering warders and snarling, sulky inmates that alternates alarmingly between enlightening social comment and overloaded melodrama. A robust cast that contains all the usual suspects (we have the expected fine performance from a shy, retiring Diana Dors) provides a meaty glimpse behind the clanging doors. Within such fifties dramas lies the genesis of a more humane, compassionate treatment of social issues, that would be explored in the sixties.

Glynis Johns *Jean Raymond* • Diana Dors *Betty* • John Gregson *Michael* • Jane Hylton *Babs* • Sidney James *Sid Baden* • AE Matthews *Harry Wicks* • Anthony Nicholls *Chaplain* ■ *Dir* J Lee Thompson • *Scr* J Lee Thompson, Anne Burnaby, Joan Henry, from the book *Who Lie in Gaol* by Joan Henry

The Weaker Sex ★★ U

Second World War drama
1948 · UK · BW · 84mins

A marvellous British cast play out this nostalgic and very human story of the latter war years, leading up to D-Day. The central character is Martha (Ursula Jeans), who adds to her housewife duties with stints as a canteen worker and fire watcher. Her son is away fighting and her two daughters are Wrens living at home. With two navy men billeted at the house, Martha's life is full as she waits for the war's end and a family reunion. Based on a successful play, *No Medals*, this gentle film was given a nicely ironic title for the sentimental screen version.

Ursula Jeans *Martha Dacre* • Cecil Parker *Geoffrey Radcliffe* • Joan Hopkins *Helen Dacre* • Derek Bond *Nigel* • Lana Morris *Lolly Dacre* • John Stone *Roddy* • Thora Hird *Mrs Gaye* ■ *Dir* Roy Baker [Roy Ward Baker] • *Scr* Esther McCracken, Paul Soskin, from the play *No Medals* by Esther McCracken

Weapons of Mass Distraction ★★ 15

Satirical comedy drama
1997 · US · Colour · 92mins

Gifted writer and producer Larry Gelbart of *M*A*S*H* TV series fame tried to re-create the powerful black comedy of his *Barbarians at the Gate*, but he bombed on this one. Shamelessly torn from the headlines, this cable TV film charts the blind ambition of rival media moguls who attempt to purchase the same professional football team and embark on a vicious campaign of blackmail, political intrigue and tabloid mud-slinging that culminates in the near destruction of both of them. Gabriel Byrne and Ben Kingsley are wicked as the Rupert Murdoch and Ted Turner-like titans, as are Mimi Rogers and Kathy Baker in supporting roles. At times, the film is clever, but it's so often over the top, it almost borders on absurdity – which is too bad as the moral message gets lost in the madness. Contains swearing, sex scenes and some violence.

Gabriel Byrne *Lionel Powers* • Ben Kingsley *Julian Messenger* • Mimi Rogers *Ariel Powers* • Jeffrey Tambor *Alan Blanchard* • Illeana Douglas *Rita Pascoe* • Paul Mazursky *Dr Cummings* • Chris Mulkey *Jerry Pascoe* • Kathy Baker *Margo Powers* ■ *Dir* Stephen Surjik • *Scr* Larry Gelbart

The Web ★★★

Film noir thriller 1947 · US · BW · 87mins

In an exceptionally well-scripted thriller, Vincent Price stands out as the wealthy New York businessman who twice uses Edmond O'Brien's young bodyguard to dispose of his adversaries and almost gets away with it. Ella Raines makes a spirited secretary – as she did in the 1944 *Phantom Lady* – who helps O'Brien clear himself while William Bendix is the police lieutenant who's not as dumb as he looks. This was the first major film directed by Michael Gordon who makes the most of the taut screenplay by William Bowers and Bertram Milhauser.

Ella Raines *Noel Faraday* • Edmond O'Brien *Bob Regan* • William Bendix *Lt Damico* • Vincent Price *Andrew Colby* • Maria Palmer *Martha Kroner* • John Abbott *Murdock, Charles* • Fritz Leiber *Leopold Kroner* • Howland Chamberlin *James Nolan* ■ *Dir* Michael Gordon • *Scr* William Bowers, Bertram Milhauser, from a story by Harry Kurnitz

Web of Deceit ★★★

Thriller 1994 · US · Colour · 93mins

This is a more than adequate made-for-TV thriller starring Corbin Bernsen and Amanda Pays as a couple (the pair are married in real-life) whose relationship is stretched to breaking point when their baby vanishes. Post-natal depression has taken its toll, but do those blood stains really mean Pays committed murder? The tension is admirably sustained by director Bill Corcoran.

Corbin Bernsen *Mark Elshant* • Amanda Pays *Catherine Elshant* • Albert Schultz *Bernie* • Mimi Kuzyk *Laura* • Neve Campbell *Beth* • Al Waxman *Herb* ■ *Dir* Bill Corcoran • *Scr* Raymond Hartung, from a story by Raymond Hartung, Joe Broido

Web of Passion ★★★

Mystery drama 1959 · Fr · Colour · 108mins

This adaptation of Stanley Ellin's novel *The Key to Nicholas Street* marked Claude Chabrol's entry into the full-colour, big-budget mainstream. Yet the detachment that would undermine several future projects is already in evidence, as he prioritises technique over dialogue and character. However, the influence of Hitchcock and Lang is also felt in this astute blend of thriller and social drama, in which Chabrol takes savage delight (another nascent trademark) in dissecting Jacques Dacqmine's dysfunctional bourgeois household. Madeleine Robinson won the best actress prize at Venice as Dacqmine's shrewish wife, but it's Jean-Paul Belmondo's coarse Hungarian catalyst who catches the eye. A French language film.

Madeleine Robinson *Thérèse Marcoux* • Jacques Dacqmine *Henri Marcoux* • Jean-Paul Belmondo *Laszlo Kovacs* • Bernadette Lafont *Julie* • Antonella Lualdi *Léda* ■ *Dir* Claude Chabrol • *Scr* Paul Gégauff, from the novel *The Key to Nicholas Street* by Stanley Ellin

A Wedding ★★★★ 15

Comedy drama 1978 · US · Colour · 119mins

Not so much a nuptial mass as a marital massacre, as Robert Altman sets his sights on a high-society wedding with his scatter-shot technique, as two families collide, booze floats Sunday-best appearances out of the window, and skeletons rattle out of cupboards. The performers – Carol Burnett, Paul Dooley, Mia Farrow, Vittorio Gassman and Lillian Gish among them – are marvellous enough in isolation, but Altman's splintering style slides them into a mosaic as comic as it is dramatic as it is poignant. Contains swearing.

Carol Burnett *Tulip Brenner, mother of the bride* • Paul Dooley *Snooks Brenner, father of the bride* • Amy Stryker *Muffin Brenner, the bride* • Mia Farrow *Buffy Brenner, the bride's sister* • Dennis Christopher *Hughie Brenner, the bride's brother* • Lillian Gish *Nettie Sloan, the groom's grandmother* • Geraldine Chaplin *Rita Billingsley, wedding co-ordinator* • Desi Arnaz Jr *Dino Corelli, the groom* • Nina Van Pallandt *Regina Corelli, the groom's mother* • Vittorio Gassman *Luigi Corelli, the groom's father* ■ *Dir* Robert Altman • *Scr* John Considine, Patricia Resnick, Allan Nicholls, Robert Altman, from a story by John Considine, Robert Altman

The Wedding Banquet ★★★★ 15

Comedy 1993 · Tai/US · Colour · 103mins

The clash between eastern and western cultures is adeptly wrung for marvellously rich comedy and pathos in Ang Lee's refreshing look at the marriage-go-round that occurs when gay Winston Chao decides to wed for convenience. Unfortunately, his thrilled parents decide to hop over from Taiwan for the ceremony and that's when the hilarious complications really start in the absorbing efforts to hide his real sexuality, nonconformist lifestyle and boyfriend. Sharply observed and never once striking a false note, this sweet and sour rib-tickler is a real treat. In English and Mandarin with subtitles. Contains sex scenes and nudity.

Winston Chao *Gao Wai-Tung* • May Chin *Wei-Wei* • Ah-Leh Gua *Mrs Gao* • Lung Sihung *Mr Gao* • Mitchell Lichtenstein *Simon* • Neal Huff *Steve* • Ang Lee *Wedding guest* ■ *Dir* Ang Lee • *Scr* Ang Lee, Neil Peng, James Schamus

Wedding Bell Blues ★★★

Comedy 1996 · US · Colour · 111mins

Three single women go to Las Vegas in order to get sham marriages so their families will get off their backs. The concept may sound like a bad sitcom, but the film scores points thanks to a cast that includes Illeana Douglas, Paulina Porizkova, and Julie Warner. Most of the stereotypical Las Vegas elements show up, such as Elvis impersonators and a cameo by a casino lounge star (Debbie Reynolds in this case), but *Wedding Bell Blues* makes you take an interest in the fates of the main characters.

Illeana Douglas *Jasmine* • Paulina Porizkova *Tanya* • Julie Warner *Micki* • John Corbett *Cary* • Jonathan Penner *Matt* • Charles Martin Smith *Oliver* • Stephanie Beacham *Tanya's mother* • Debbie Reynolds ■ *Dir* Dana Lustig • *Scr* Annette Goliti Gutierrez, from a story by Dana Lustig, Annette Goliti Gutierrez

Wedding in Galilee ★★★ 12

Drama   1987 · Bel/Fr · Colour · 111mins

Set in the occupied West Bank at a time of martial law, Palestinian director Michel Khleifi's debut feature is an impassioned, if naive, plea for tolerance. An elder is intent on giving his son a traditional Arab wedding, and must enlist the help of the local Israeli governor. Maintaining a documentarist's distance, he establishes a potential flashpoint situation – only to defuse it by concentrating on the human interaction of these implacable foes. Performed by a largely non-professional cast, the film combines detailed ritual with a discussion of the region's colonial past and successfully contrasts political tension with the undeniable sexual frisson between the guests. An Arabic/Hebrew/Turkish language film. Contains some nudity.

Ali Mohammed El Akili *The Mukhtar* • Nazih Akleh *The Groom* • Bushra Karaman *The mother* • Anna Achdian *Bride* ■ *Dir/Scr* Michel Khleifi

Wedding in White ★★★

Drama   1972 · Can · Colour · 106mins

Set during the Second World War, this award-winning Canadian feature is a powerful study of patriarchy gone mad, directed and written by William Fruet from his own stage play. Donald Pleasence is on top form playing the uptight ex-soldier who discovers his teenage daughter (Carol Kane) has been raped by an army colleague of his son. The drama plays out the consequences of the girl's subsequent pregnancy, as Pleasence concocts a bizarre and ultimately horrific scheme to preserve the family honour. But there's a serious point being made behind the macabre atmosphere, and Pleasence is truly riveting.

Carol Kane *Jeannie* • Donald Pleasence *Jim* • Doris Petrie *Mary* • Leo Phillips *Sandy* • Christine Thomas *Sarah* • Paul Bradley *Jimmie* ■ *Dir* William Fruet • *Scr* William Fruet, from his play

The Wedding March ★★★★★

Silent melodrama
1928 · US · BW and Colour · 113mins

A flawlessly restored version of the silent masterpiece by the great Erich von Stroheim, who also stars as a dissolute Viennese aristocrat falling in love with a peasant girl. The complex combination of cynicism, irony and genuine romanticism elevates this work to great cinematic art, and it contains many truly startling sequences, not least of which is the astounding scene where Stroheim's mother virtually seduces her own son into marrying for money, or the one where the respective fathers seal the wedding pact in a brothel. There is a remarkable pageant scene in early

Technicolor, replete with robust reds, and the whole is enhanced by a new score by Carl Davis that impertinently interweaves Mendelssohn with *Deutschland über Alles*. But the real glory is in the casting – to watch Stroheim and the lovely Fay Wray flirt and fall in love during the feast of Corpus Christi is simply transcendental.

Erich von Stroheim *Prince Nicki* • Fay Wray *Mitzi Schrammell* • Matthew Betz *Schani Eberle* • ZaSu Pitts *Cecelia Schweisser* • Hughie Mack *Anton Eberle, Schani's father* • George Fawcett *Prince Ottokar von Wildeliebe-Rauffenburg* • Maude George *Princess Maria von Wildeliebe-Rauffenburg* • George Nichols *Fortunat Schweisser* • Dale Fuller *Katerina Schrammell* • Cesare Gravina *Martin Schrammel* ■ *Dir* Erich von Stroheim • *Scr* Erich von Stroheim, Harry Carr • *Cinematographer* Hal Mohr, B Sorenson, Ben Reynolds • *Set Designer* Richard Day, Erich von Stroheim

The Wedding Night ★★ PG

Drama   1935 · US · BW · 79mins

The third, and last, of producer Samuel Goldwyn's attempts to turn his Russian protégée Anna Sten into a new Garbo. Although charismatic in her European films, Sten seemed hard and unlikeable in English; and here, despite being well cast as a Polish tobacco-grower's daughter in an interesting and original story, and supported by an endearing Gary Cooper performance, the public didn't take to her at all. Sten continued to appear in American movies, though not in star vehicles, for another 25 years. Coop's wife (Helen Vinson), who has to fight Sten for his love, is the better-written character and rightly dominates the film. Furthermore, the moody photography by Gregg Toland (*Citizen Kane*) is first-rate, though the film now has dated rather poorly.

Gary Cooper *Tony Barrett* • Anna Sten *Manya Nowak* • Ralph Bellamy *Fredrik Sobieski* • Helen Vinson *Dora Barrett* • Siegfried Rumann [Ruman Sig] *Jan Nowak* • Esther Dale *Kaise Nowak* • Leonid Snegoff *Mr Sobieski* • Eleanor Wesselhoeft *Mrs Sobieski* ■ *Dir* King Vidor • *Scr* Edith Fitzgerald, from a story by Edwin Knopf

The Wedding Party ★★

Comedy   1966 · US · BW · 90mins

Brian De Palma's directorial first was actually shot in 1964, completed in 1966 and released, even then only briefly, in 1969. It's a comedy drama about an impending wedding, with the groom getting cold feet once he discovers what boors his fiancée and her family are. Made wholly in collaboration with a teacher and fellow student from De Palma's college days, the film is a curiosity for its debutante appearances by both Jill Clayburgh and Robert De Niro, amusingly credited here as Robert DeNero.

Jill Clayburgh *Josephine Fish* • Charles Pfluger *Charlie* • Valda Setterfield *Mrs Fish* • Jennifer Salt *Phoebe* • Raymond McNally *Mr Fish* • John Braswell *Reverend Oldfield* • Judy Thomas *Celeste, organist* • Robert DeNero [Robert De Niro] *Cecil* ■ *Dir/Scr* Cynthia Munroe, Brian De Palma, Wilford Leach

Wedding Rehearsal ★★ U

Comedy   1932 · UK · BW · 75mins

Grandmother Kate Cutler is going to curtail bachelor marquis Roland Young's allowance if he doesn't marry one of her chosen wedding candidates, but he falls for his mother's secretary, who believe it or not turns out to be beautiful without her glasses. Unsurprising, since she's lovely Merle Oberon (and incidentally the future wife of the film's director Alexander Korda). Unfortunately, no one in this creaky comedy, except for leading man Young, seems able to act their way out of a paper bag, and the sight of Lady Tree, John Loder and Maurice Evans attempting to convince is totally unappealing. As a period piece, though, this is undeniably fascinating.

Roland Young *Reggie, Marquis of Buckminster* • George Grossmith *Lord Stokeshire* • John Loder *"Bimbo"* • Maurice Evans *"Tootles"* • Wendy Barrie *Lady Mary Rose Wroxbury* • Joan Gardner *Lady Rosemary Wroxbury* • Merle Oberon *Miss Hutchinson* • Lady Tree *Lady Stokeshire* ■ *Dir* Alexander Korda • *Scr* Arthur Wimperis, Helen Gordon, from a story by Lajos Biro, George Grossmith

The Wedding Singer ★★★★ 12

Romantic comedy
1998 · US · Colour · 92mins

Sweet and screamingly funny, Adam Sandler is pitch-perfect as a hopelessly romantic cabaret wedding singer who falls in love with waitress Drew Barrymore at a nuptial function and then discovers she's engaged to someone else. The chemistry between the two stars works like a charm and director Frank Coraci has enormous fun with the music, fashions and fads of the mid-eighties setting. A good-natured romp with a knowing sense of the ridiculous and a great soundtrack. Contains sexual references and some swearing. *DVD*

Adam Sandler *Robbie Hart* • Drew Barrymore *Julia* • Christine Taylor *Holly* • Allen Covert *Sammy* • Matthew Glave *Glenn* • Ellen Albertini Dow *Rosie* • Angela Featherstone *Linda* • Alexis Arquette *George* ■ *Dir* Frank Coraci • *Scr* Tim Herlihy

The Wedding Tackle ★★ 15

Comedy   2000 · UK · Colour · 92mins

Take a comedy of errors, toss in some soap-opera crises and lace with innuendo, and the result would be this glorified British sitcom. The ensemble cast gives it everything, but their characters feel like dismally uncool outcasts from *This Life*, with each infantile, groin-motivated male trying to squirm out of (or wriggle into) the affections of their marginally more mature female counterparts. Skeletons fall out of the stag-night cupboard with alarming regularity, but the brash self-obsession of the revellers makes Rami Dvir's film difficult to warm to.

Adrian Dunbar *Mr Mac* • James Purefoy *Hal* • Tony Slattery *Little Ted* • Neil Stuke *Salt* • Leslie Grantham *George* • Victoria Smurfit *Clodagh* • Susan Vidler *Vinni* • Amanda Redman *Petula* • Sara Stockbridge *Felicity* ■ *Dir* Rami Dvir • *Scr* Nigel Horne

Wedlock ★ 18

Futuristic action adventure
1991 · US · Colour · 98mins

Rutger Hauer's presence in this silly sci-fi excursion is understandable – he's been hard up for a decent job for years. But why is Mimi Rogers slumming as a prisoner in a high-tech jail? The inmates wear explosive collars, designed to detonate if ever two matching ones get too far from each other. This supposedly keeps the convicts from escaping, since they don't know who their "deadlock" partner is. But guess which two movie stars figure it out? Why the warden doesn't just set the collars to explode when cons wander too far from the prison itself is a mystery. Contains violence and swearing.

Rutger Hauer *Frank Warren* • Mimi Rogers *Tracy Riggs* • Joan Chen *Noelle* • James Remar *Sam* • Stephen Tobolowsky *Warden Holliday* ■ *Dir* Lewis Teague • *Scr* Broderick Miller

Wee Willie Winkie ★★★

Comedy drama   1937 · US · BW · 103mins

The film that caused 20th Century-Fox and Shirley Temple to sue novelist Graham Greene for libel, after he alluded to the sexual precocity of the nine-year-old star in his review of the film for *Night and Day*. Temple stars as yet another cute moppet in this sickly sweet reworking of Rudyard Kipling's vigorous tale of military life during the Raj. It is prevented from lapsing into unbearable sentimentality by the firm but sympathetic hand of western maestro John Ford, the polished reserve of C Aubrey Smith as Temple's malleable grandpa and the gruff good nature of sergeant Victor McLaglen.

Shirley Temple *Priscilla Williams* • Victor McLaglen *Sergeant MacDuff* • C Aubrey Smith *Colonel Williams* • June Lang *Joyce Williams* • Michael Whalen *Lieutenant "Coppy" Brandes* • Cesar Romero *Khoda Khan* ■ *Dir* John Ford • *Scr* Ernest Pascal, Julien Josephson, from the story by Rudyard Kipling

Weeds ★★★ 18

Drama   1987 · US · Colour · 113mins

Nick Nolte is the prisoner at San Quentin who forms a theatre group with his fellow convicts in this drama, loosely based on a true story. While Nolte and his worthy co-stars (William Forsythe, Joe Mantegna) give strong performances, they are bogged down by a script that can't decide whether to be light-hearted or deadly serious. Contains violence and swearing.

Nick Nolte *Lee Umstetter* • Lane Smith *Claude* • William Forsythe *Burt the Booster* • John Toles-Bey *Navarro* • Joe Mantegna *Carmine* • Ernie Hudson *Bagdad* • Rita Taggart *Lillian Bingington, newspaper critic* ■ *Dir* John Hancock • *Scr* Dorothy Tristan, John Hancock

Weekend ★★★★★ 18

Drama   1967 · Fr · Colour · 98mins

Jean-Luc Godard's nightmare vision of the collapse of western capitalism has lost none of its blistering power. Hurling traditional narrative methods to the winds, Godard sends Mireille Darc and Jean Yanne on a journey to her mother's during the course of which they encounter such diverse characters

as Emily Brontë dressed as Alice in Wonderland, the French Revolutionary Saint-Just and a cell of Maoist cannibals who persuade Darc to join them. The most audacious moment in this film of ceaseless invention is the lengthy traffic jam tracking shot, in which increasingly disturbing images are recorded with an unchanging lack of passion. In French with English subtitles. ▣

Mireille Darc *Corinne* • Jean Yanne *Roland* • Jean-Pierre Kalfon *Leader of the FLSO* • Valérie Lagrange *His moll* • Jean-Pierre Léaud *Saint-Just/Young man in phone booth* • Yves Beneyton *Member of FLSO* • Paul Gégauff *Pianist* ■ *Dir/Scr* Jean-Luc Godard

Weekend at Bernie's
★★★ **15**

Comedy   1989 · US · Colour · 94mins

OK, it's a one joke movie and, yes, the gags are largely moronic, but this is still pretty good fun. Andrew McCarthy and Jonathan Silverman are the two junior executives who are forced to pretend their crooked boss (Terry Kiser) is still alive over a weekend in which he is to host a swinging party at the beach. It's a lot more tasteless than you would expect from Hollywood and, in fact, from usually reliable but dull Ted Kotcheff but Kiser makes it all worthwhile in a scene-stealing performance as the much put-upon corpse. Actually, he is probably too good: it's hard to avoid typecasting as an actor and there are few major roles as dead people. ▣ *DVD*

Andrew McCarthy *Larry Wilson* • Jonathan Silverman *Richard Parker* • Catherine Mary Stewart *Gwen Saunders* • Don Calfa *Paulie, the "Iceman"* • Catherine Parks *Tina* • Eloise Broady *Tawny* • Terry Kiser *Bernie Lomax* ■ *Dir* Ted Kotcheff • *Scr* Robert Klane

Weekend at Bernie's II ★ **PG**
Comedy   1992 · US · Colour · 85mins

The central idea – 101 uses for a corpse – was barely substantial enough to sustain the first movie, but, unbelievably, most of the original team - including stars Andrew McCarthy and Jonathan Silverman, and writer Robert Klane – were talked into this rather foolish sequel. The now jobless McCarthy and Silverman use the hapless Bernie (Terry Kiser), who's been turned into a walking zombie through voodoo, in a bid to locate the money he stole from their old company. Kiser selflessly endures indignity after indignity, but the slapstick is laboured and decent gags are thin on the ground. ▣

Andrew McCarthy *Larry Wilson* • Jonathan Silverman *Richard Parker* • Terry Kiser *Bernie Lomax* • Troy Beyer *Claudia* • Barry Bostwick *Hummel* • Tom Wright *Charles* ■ *Dir/Scr* Robert Klane

Week-End at the Waldorf
★★★

Portmanteau comedy drama
1945 · US · BW · 129mins

Borrowing the idea from its more famous *Grand Hotel*, MGM came up with this star-studded portmanteau movie covering nefarious goings-on and various romances during a weekend at Manhattan's glitzy Waldorf Astoria. Robert Benchley provides a narrative link between the stories, which feature Edward Arnold, Lana Turner, Van Johnson, Keenan Wynn and, centrally, the romantic comedy entanglement between Ginger Rogers as a famous movie star and Walter Pidgeon as a famous war correspondent. A largely diverting, but slightly heavy-handed and overlong movie.

Ginger Rogers *Irene Malvern, the actress* • Lana Turner *Bunny Smith, the stenographer* • Walter Pidgeon *Chip Collyer, the war correspondent* • Van Johnson *Capt James Hollis, the flyer* • Edward Arnold *Martin X Edley, the promoter* • Keenan Wynn *Oliver Webson, the cub reporter* • Robert Benchley *Randy Morton, the columnist* • Phyllis Thaxter *Cynthia Drew* ■ *Dir* Robert Z Leonard • *Scr* Sam Spewack, Bella Spewack, Guy Bolton (adaptation, from the play *Menschen im Hotel (Grand Hotel)* by Vicki Baum

Weekend in Havana ★★★
Musical   1941 · US · Colour · 80mins

Having sent Betty Grable to fall in love with Don Ameche in Argentina, then similarly despatching Alice Faye to Rio, this characteristic entry in the series of anodyne, colourful Fox musicals of the period packed Alice off to Havana as a department store assistant who goes on a trip to the Cuban hot spot and falls in love with shipping official John Payne. As in all these movies, Carmen Miranda is on hand as a nightclub entertainer, showcasing her outrageously ebullient Latin-American flavoured dance routines and camp, exotic headgear. Agreeable nonsense.

Alice Faye *Nan Spencer* • Carmen Miranda *Rosita Rivas* • John Payne *Jay Williams* • Cesar Romero *Monte Blanca* • Cobina Wright Jr *Terry McCracken* • George Barbier *Walter McCracken* • Sheldon Leonard *Boris* • Leonid Kinskey *Rafael* ■ *Dir* Walter Lang • *Scr* Karl Tunberg, Darrell Ware

A Weekend in the Country
★★★

Romantic comedy
1996 · US · Colour · 94mins

In a well-cast ensemble comedy, a motley bunch of New York neurotics descend on California's Napa Valley for a soul-searching weekend of angst and enlightenment. Pitched somewhere between the "group" comedies of Woody Allen and "group" dramas of Henry Jaglom, the production stems from the writing team of Ken Branagh's *Peter's Friends*. However things don't gel quite so well, despite the efforts of a cracking cast which includes Jack Lemmon, Dudley Moore, Christine Lahti and Rita Rudner.

Richard Lewis *Bobby Stein* • Christine Lahti *Ruth Oakely* • Rita Rudner *Sally Shelton* • Jack Lemmon *Bud Bailey* • Dudley Moore *Simon Farrell* • Faith Ford *Susan Kaye* • John Shea *Michael* ■ *Dir* Martin Bergman • *Scr* Rita Rudner, Martin Bergman

Weekend of Shadows ★★★
Action drama   1978 · Ausl · Colour · 94mins

John Waters, star of this action drama set in pre-war Australia, must be tired of explaining to folk that he is not the John Waters who is Baltimore's most celebrated cult auteur, but the John Waters who has appeared in some of the landmark films of Australian cinema, including *Breaker Morant* and *The Getting of Wisdom*. This film is not up to their standard, but still allows Waters to give another convincing performance as a member of a posse chasing a Polish immigrant suspected of murder who's forced to question his values. ▣

John Waters *Rabbit* • Melissa Jaffer *Vi* • Wyn Roberts *Sergeant Caxton* • Barbara West *Helen Caxton* • Graham Rouse *Ab Nolan* • Graeme Blundell *Bernie Collins* • Bill Hunter *Bosun* • Keith Lee *David Wayne* ■ *Dir* Tom Jeffrey • *Scr* Peter Yeldham, from the novel *The Reckoning* by Hugh Atkinson

Weekend Pass ★ **18**
Comedy   1984 · US · Colour · 85mins

In this inane sex comedy, four navy men fresh out of boot camp go wild on leave in Los Angeles. There they have the usual drunken brawls and meet a bevy of strippers. Their weekend comes to an end sooner for them than this mild exploitation picture does for the viewer. ▣

DW Brown *Paul Fricker* • Peter Ellenstein *Lester Gidley* • Patrick Hauser *Webster Adams* • Chip McAllister *Bunker Hill* ■ *Dir* Lawrence Bassoff • *Scr* Lawrence Bassoff, from a story by Mark Tenser

Weekend Reunion ★★★
Comedy   1990 · US · Colour · 96mins

A lightweight comedy about a high school reunion, and the problems Christopher Rich has when he finds himself caught between two of his ex-girlfriends. This isn't exactly mind-bending stuff, but all the performances are likeable enough. It's also an early role for Lauren Holly, who featured in *Dumb and Dumber*.

Christopher Rich *Archie Andrews* • Lauren Holly *Betty Cooper* • Karen Kopins *Veronica Lodge* • Sam Whipple *Jughead* • Gary Kroeger *Reggie Mantle* • David Doyle *Mr Weatherbee* ■ *Dir* Dick Lowry • *Scr* Evan Katz, from the characters from the comic *Archie*

Weekend Warriors ★★
Comedy   1986 · US · Colour · 85mins

In 1961, a group of Hollywood wannabe actors and singers join the National Guard to avoid the draft. Initially the ruse works and they have an easy time of it but the plan backfires when some top brass descend on the camp and threaten to send them away on active service. The boys decide to stage a show to prove that they would be more use as entertainers than fighters. This strained comedy stars Chris Lemmon (Jack Lemmon's son) and Lloyd Bridges (father of Jeff and Beau) who plays a colonel.

Chris Lemmon *Vince Tucker* • Lloyd Bridges *Colonel Archer* • Vic Tayback *Sergeant Burge* • Graham Jarvis *Congressman Balljoy* • Daniel Greene *Phil McCracken* ■ *Dir* Bert Convy • *Scr* Bruce Belland, Roy M Rogosin

Weekend with Father ★★★
Romantic comedy   1951 · US · BW · 83mins

Van Heflin and Patricia Neal, usually unsmiling in downbeat dramas, manage to display a lighter touch in this modest family comedy-romance directed by Douglas Sirk, before he gained his reputation for rich and ripe Technicolor melodramas. Heflin plays a widower with two daughters, and Neal is a widow with two sons. They meet while taking their respective children to summer camp, and naturally fall in love. Naturally there are complications with the kids when they decide to marry. Predictable and cosy it may be, but it's harmless and amusing.

Van Heflin *Brad Stubbs* • Patricia Neal *Jean Bowen* • Gigi Perreau *Anne Stubbs* • Virginia Field *Phyllis Reynolds* • Richard Denning *Don Adams* • Jimmy Hunt *Gary Bowen* • Janine Perreau *Patty Stubbs* • Tommy Rettig *David Bowen* ■ *Dir* Douglas Sirk • *Scr* Joseph Hoffman, from a story by George F Slavin, George W George

Weird Science ★★ **15**
Comedy fantasy   1985 · US · Colour · 89mins

The worst of John Hughes's early comedies, but still a cut above most teen fodder of the time. Hughes regular Anthony Michael Hall and Ilan Mitchell-Smith are the sex-obsessed high-tech anoraks who summon up the computer-generated woman of their dreams (Kelly LeBrock). Hughes remains a sharp observer of teenage woes but this time around there is a crassness to much of the humour and far too much time is spent leering. The best performance comes from Bill Paxton as Mitchell-Smith's fascist brother, and look out, too, for an early role for Robert Downey Jr. Contains swearing and brief nudity. ▣

Anthony Michael Hall • Ilan Mitchell-Smith *Wyatt* • Kelly LeBrock *Lisa* • Bill Paxton *Chet* • Suzanne Snyder *Deb* • Judie Aronson *Hilly* • Robert Downey Jr *Ian* • Robert Rusler *Max* ■ *Dir/Scr* John Hughes

Welcome Home ★★★ **15**
Drama   1989 · US · Colour · 88mins

Or not, as the case may be, when Kris Kristofferson, a Vietnam veteran, is shipped home after 17 years living contentedly with his Cambodian wife and children. His American wife, JoBeth Williams, is now remarried and cut the yellow ribbon years ago. This is a partially successful attempt to examine familial strife and the consequences of rising from the dead, but it's exceptionally mushy stuff. Sam Waterston, as Williams's husband number two, gives a sterling portrayal of compassion and understanding. Contains swearing and brief nudity. ▣ *DVD*

Kris Kristofferson *Jake* • JoBeth Williams *Sarah* • Sam Waterston *Woody* • Brian Keith *Harry* • Thomas Wilson Brown *Tyler* • Trey Wilson *Colonel Barnes* • Ken Pogue *Senator Camden* • Kieu Chinh *Leang* • Matthew Beckett *Kim* • Jessica Ramien *Siv* ■ *Dir* Franklin J Schaffner • *Scr* Maggie Kleinman

Welcome Home, Bobby ★★
Drama   1986 · US · Colour

The story of a working-class father who turns his back on his teenage son when he discovers he's been frequenting the gay red light district. What prevents this TV movie from packing the intended punch is the overloading of the plot (by having the boy arrested for drug dealing) and the unrestrained barnstorming of Tony LoBianco as the irate father. Timothy Williams is rather more believable as the tormented son.

Tony LoBianco *Joe Cavalero* • Gisela Caldwell *Rose Cavalero* • Nan Woods *Beth Lund* • Adam Baldwin *Cleary Biggs* • Stephen James *Mark Reed* • John Karlen *Mr Geffin* ■ Dir Herbert Wise • Scr Conrad Bromberg

Welcome Home, Roxy Carmichael ★★★ 15

Comedy   1990 · US · Colour · 91mins

Airplane! and *Hot Shots!* director Jim Abrahams is the rather odd choice for this subtle comedy starring Winona Ryder, which relies heavily on her performance and that of co-star Jeff Daniels. Ryder plays a 15-year-old misfit (much like her characters in *Mermaids* and *Heathers*) who is awaiting the return to the town of legendary local Roxy Carmichael, who she believes is her real mother. Predictable in places, the plot surrounding Ryder hasn't been fully developed, but once again the young actress gives a winning performance. Contains some nudity. 📟

Winona Ryder *Dinky Bossetti* • Jeff Daniels *Denton Webb* • Laila Robins *Elizabeth Zaks* • Thomas Wilson Brown *Gerald Howells* • Joan McMurtrey *Barbara Webb* • Graham Beckel *Leo Bossetti* • Frances Fisher *Rochelle Bossetti* • Robby Kiger *Beannie Billings* ■ Dir Jim Abrahams • Scr Leigh Hopkins

Welcome Home, Soldier Boys ★★

Drama   1971 · US · Colour · 90mins

A wildly over-the-top action film, rooted in the hoary old movie myth that all Vietnam veterans are damaged goods. The film centres on four former Green Berets who celebrate their return to "the world" by taking over and terrorising a town. Cue much nastiness and wham-bam-thank-you-ma'am mayhem. This mindless tosh is done slickly enough, but you'd be desperate to waste 90 minutes of your life on it.

Joe Don Baker *Danny* • Paul Koslo *Shooter* • Alan Vint *Kid* • Elliott Street *Fatback* • Jennifer Billingsley *Broad* • Billy Green Bush *Sheriff* ■ Dir Richard Compton • Scr Guerdon Trueblood

Welcome Stranger ★★

Medical comedy drama
1947 · US · BW · 107mins

Paramount scored a massive box-office hit with *Going My Way* (1944), in which Barry Fitzgerald and Bing Crosby co-starred as, respectively, a crusty old priest and a new young assistant who, eventually, form a heart-warming relationship. In this flagrant rerun of the formula, the pair are doctors, running a clinic and adored by their patients. Bing bursts into song on several occasions, romances blonde schoolteacher Joan Caulfield, and saves curmudgeonly old Barry's life, much as he saved his church in the earlier film.

Bing Crosby *Dr Jim Pearson* • Joan Caulfield *Trudy Mason* • Barry Fitzgerald *Dr Joseph McRory* • Wanda Hendrix *Emily Walters* • Frank Faylen *Bill Walters* • Elizabeth Patterson *Mrs Gilley* ■ Dir Elliott Nugent • Scr Arthur Sheekman, Richard Nash [N Richard Nash], from a story by Frank Butler

Welcome to Arrow Beach ★ 18

Horror   1974 · US · Colour · 80mins

What on earth drew Laurence Harvey to such lurid material? This exploration of cannibalism was an all the more regrettable choice when it proved to be his swan song. Harvey directs and also stars as a Korean War veteran who developed a taste for human flesh when his bomber crashed on a deserted island and he was forced to live off his comrades. Now living with his sister (played by the neglected Joanna Pettet) his unusual table manners attract the attention of local cops. "He killed more than he could eat" ran the tagline. It's largely inept and distasteful, but a few touches do strike home, such as Harvey's home being decked out with the personal belongings of previous victims. 📟

Laurence Harvey *Jason Henry* • Joanna Pettet *Grace Henry* • Stuart Whitman *Deputy Rakes* • John Ireland *Sheriff H "Duke" Bingham* • Gloria LeRoy *Ginger* • David Macklin *Alex Heath* ■ Dir Laurence Harvey • Scr Wallace C Bennett, Jack Gross Jr, from a story by Wallace C Bennett

Welcome to Blood City ★★ 15

Science-fiction thriller
1977 · UK/Can · Colour · 91mins

A dull Anglo-Canadian production, listlessly directed by Peter Sasdy and owing more than just a little to *Westworld*, as Samantha Eggar monitors the progress of kidnapped Keir Dullea and his fight for survival against "immortal" sheriff Jack Palance in a Wild West town. The film is so badly constructed that caring about Dullea's plight is the last thing on an audience's mind. Talented editor Keith Palmer and composer Roy Budd have little chance to shine. For hardcore Palance fans only. 📟

Jack Palance *Frendlander* • Keir Dullea *Lewis* • Samantha Eggar *Katherine* • Barry Morse *Supervisor* • Hollis McLaren *Martine* • Chris Wiggins *Gellor* • Henry Ramer *Chumley* • Allan Royale *Peter* ■ Dir Peter Sasdy • Scr Stephen Schneck, Michael Winder

Welcome to Hard Times ★★

Western   1967 · US · Colour · 102mins

A hard-to-watch, grim and slow allegorical western, that is somewhat of a surprise coming from director Burt Kennedy, better known for his comedy westerns such as *Support Your Local Sheriff!*. Perhaps the real influence behind this bleak piece is writer EL Doctorow, of *Ragtime* fame. Aldo Ray is the vicious killer, forced into confrontation with mayor Henry Fonda, and the supporting cast is marvellous, with great performances from western regulars Warren Oates, Edgar Buchanan and Elisha Cook Jr. The women – Janice Rule, Janis Paige, Fay Spain – couldn't be bettered, but the whole leaves a very nasty taste in the mouth, and the symbolism just doesn't really come off.

Henry Fonda *Will Blue* • Janice Rule *Molly Riordan* • Keenan Wynn *Zar* • Janis Page *Adah* • Aldo Ray *Man from Bodie* • John Anderson *Ezra/Isaac Maple* • Warren Oates *Jenks* • Fay

Spain *Jessie* • Edgar Buchanan *Brown* • Denver Pyle *Alfie* ■ Dir Burt Kennedy • Scr Burt Kennedy, from the novel by EL Doctorow

Welcome to LA ★★★ 15

Drama   1976 · US · Colour · 89mins

Produced by Robert Altman, this early Alan Rudolph picture is clearly modelled after *Nashville* and centres on cynical songwriter Keith Carradine arriving in LA to work on an album and sleeping around with a number of women. Rudolph blends together sour social satire, musical numbers, improvisational scenes and jaundiced views on marriage for a compelling whole – sharply summing up Tinseltown attitudes and unhappiness. The strong ensemble cast helps to lift the bittersweet dissection to greater levels of truth. 📟

Keith Carradine *Carroll Barber* • Sally Kellerman *Ann Goode* • Geraldine Chaplin *Karen Hood* • Harvey Keitel *Ken Hood* • Lauren Hutton *Nona Bruce* • Viveca Lindfors *Susan Moore* • Sissy Spacek *Linda Murray* • Denver Pyle *Carl Barber* ■ Dir/Scr Alan Rudolph

Welcome to Paradise ★★

Romantic comedy   1995 · US · Colour

Since her heyday in *Cheers*, poor Shelley Long has generally struggled to repeat her success in films (*The Brady Bunch Movie* and its sequel being the exceptions). This TV movie does nothing for her cause as she finds unexpected romance at the holiday resort where she first discovered boys some 20 years before. Director Bill L Norton obviously set out to concoct a sexy comedy in praise of older women, but all he's come up with is a tacky, unfunny and rather squalid film that leaves Long and co-stars Mel Harris and Delane Matthews high and dry.

Shelley Long *Anne* • Mel Harris *Claire* • Delane Matthews *Denise* • Ian Ziering *Hotel desk manager* • François-Eric Gendron *Male model* • Michael McGrady *Lifeguard* ■ Dir Bill Norton [Bill L Norton] • Scr Bart Baker

Welcome to Sarajevo ★★★ 15

Drama   1997 · UK/US · Colour · 97mins

This is a vigorously unsentimental treatment of love in a time of war – the Bosnian conflict – based on a true story in which TV reporter Michael Henderson (Stephen Dillane) – Michael Nicholson of ITN – decides to smuggle a young refugee girl out to Britain. The seedy hotel-based world of foreign correspondents is expertly evoked by director Michael Winterbottom, though Woody Harrelson's tough-talking American journalist manages to upstage even the conflict itself. Contains violence and swearing. 📟

Stephen Dillane *Michael Henderson* • Woody Harrelson *Flynn* • Marisa Tomei *Nina* • Emira Nusevic *Emira* • Kerry Fox *Jane Carson* • Goran Visnjic *Risto* • James Nesbitt *Gregg* • Emily Lloyd *Annie* • Woody McGee ■ Dir Michael Winterbottom • Scr Frank Cottrell Boyce, from the book *Natasha's Story* by Michael Nicholson

Welcome to the Club ★★★

Comedy   1971 · UK · Colour · 82mins

Brian Foley, morale officer for a unit of American troops stationed in Hiroshima, is appalled by the casual racism of virtually every man in the unit. The men believe that Foley's liberal ideas, which stem from his Quaker upbringing, will lead him into clashes with his superiors and this seems likely when he questions their attitude to a group of black entertainers visiting the camp, who are to be segregated from the rest of the men. Writer Clement Biddle Wood adapted his own satirical novel but, although Walter Shenson directs sympathetically, the piece lacks punch.

Brian Foley *Andrew Oxblood* • Jack Warden *General Strapp* • Andrew Jarrell *Robert E Lee Fairfax* • Kevin O'Connor *Harrison W Morve* • Francisca Tu *Hogan* • David Toguri *Hideki Ikada* ■ Dir Walter Shenson • Scr Clement Biddle Wood, from his novel

Welcome to the Dollhouse ★★★★ 15

Comedy drama   1995 · US · Colour · 87mins

Before he made his name with the controversial *Happiness* (1998), Todd Solondz also raised a few eyebrows with this truthful look at the nightmares of growing up. Eleven-year-old New Jersey misfit Dawn Wiener (a superb performance from young Heather Matarazzo) has all the problems of an average school girl, and more: she has an unrequited crush on her brother's friend, is being threatened by the school tough guy and is overlooked by her mother in favour of her ballet-dancing younger sister. Thanks to Solondz's original ideas, no-holds-barred script and determination never to stray into sentimentality, plus an impressive young cast, this is a fascinating and ironic look at teenage life. 📟

Heather Matarazzo *Dawn Wiener* • Victoria Davis *Lolita* • Christina Brucato *Cookie* • Christina Vidal *Cynthia* • Siri Howard *Chrissy* • Brendan Sexton Jr [Brendan Sexton III] *Brandon McCarthy* • Daria Kalinina *Missy Wiener* ■ Dir/Scr Todd Solondz

Welcome II the Terrordome ★★ 18

Science-fiction thriller
1994 · UK · Colour · 89mins

A highly controversial film on its release when director Ngozi Onwurah was thought by some to be making a rallying cry for black separatism. This semi-futuristic thriller certainly has more than its fair share of heavy-handed messages to the detriment of any discernible entertainment value. Its starting point, the hounding into the sea of black slaves in 17th-century North Carolina, is powerfully drawn and provides a thumpingly dramatic opening which Onwurah utterly fails to build on. In truth, it's a bit of a yawn. Contains violence.

Suzette Llewellyn *Angela McBride/African woman #1* • Saffron Burrows *Jodie* • Felix Joseph *Black Rad/African leader* • Valentine Nonyela *Spike/African Man #1* • Ben Wynter *Hector/African boy* • Sian Martin *Chrisele/African woman #2* • Jason Traynor *Jason/Assistant overseer* ■ Dir/Scr Ngozi Onwurah

Welcome to Woop Woop ★★ 18

Black comedy
1997 · UK/Ausl · Colour · 92mins

"Crocodile" Dundee meets *The Hills Have Eyes* in this entertainingly barmy and refreshingly tasteless comedy. Jonathan Schaech plays a New York con man who falls for earthy Aussie hitchhiker Susie Porter, only to find himself abducted and taken to the freak-filled town of Woop Woop, ruled over by his psychopathic father-in-law Rod Taylor. It's not for the faint-hearted – the kangaroo abattoir scenes will upset Skippy fans – and clumsily plotted but it's certainly an original. Contains swearing, sex scenes and some violence.

Johnathon Schaech *Teddy* • Rod Taylor *Daddy O* • Susie Porter *Angie* • Dee Smart *Krystal* • Barry Humphries *Blind Wally* • Richard Moir *Reggie* • Mark Wilson *Duffy* • Paul Mercurio *Midget* ■ *Dir* Stephan Elliott • *Scr* Michael Thomas, from the novel *The Dead Heart* by Douglas Kennedy

The Well ★★★

Drama 1951 · US · BW · 85mins

The disappearance of a young black girl leads to the wrongful arrest of a white man (Harry Morgan) on a kidnapping charge. When the girl is discovered to have fallen down a deep well, the arrested man is released and eventually helps with the digging operation to rescue her, which is watched by crowds of townspeople, both black and white, several of them sensation seekers but most united in concern for the girl. Leo Popkin and Russell Rouse directed this suspenseful race relations drama from an Oscar-nominated screenplay by Rouse and Clarence Greene, drawing excellent performances from a non-star cast, and mining the rescue action for maximum tension.

Gwendolyn Laster *Carolyn Crawford* • Richard Rober *Sheriff Ben Kellogg* • Maidie Norman *Mrs Crawford* • George Hamilton *Grandfather* • Ernest Anderson *Mr Crawford* • Harry Morgan *Claude Packard* • Barry Kelley *Sam Packard* • Tom Powers *Mayor* ■ *Dir* Leo C Popkin, Russell Rouse • *Scr* Russell Rouse, Clarence Greene

We'll Meet Again ★★★ PG

Musical 1942 · UK · BW · 343mins

No prizes for guessing who's the star of this British wartime flagwaver. Based on what remains to this day her signature tune, Vera Lynn shows in this sugary confection why you can count her film appearances on the fingers of one hand. However, nostalgia nuts will not be disappointed as she keeps smiling through even though her best pal, Patricia Roc, has clouded her blue skies by eloping with her soldier boyfriend. Even though it was made by Columbia Pictures, this is a pretty amateurish affair, but tune in for a sing-song with Dame Vera, and Geraldo and his orchestra.

Vera Lynn *Peggy Brown* • Geraldo *Gerry* • Patricia Roc *Ruth* • Ronald Ward *Frank* • Donald Gray *Bruce McIntosh* • Frederick Leister *Mr Hastropp* • Betty Jardine *Miss Bohne* ■ *Dir* Phil Brandon • *Scr* James Seymour, Howard Thomas, from a story by Derek Sheils

We'll Smile Again ★★★ U

Second World War musical comedy
1942 · UK · BW · 93mins

Unlike many stage, radio or television double acts who flounder when put on the big screen, Flanagan and Allen fared rather well as movie stars, and this is a typical effort, combining bright comedy with songs and human interest. Bud Flanagan (who had a hand in the script) plays a down-and-out hired by a stage star (Chesney Allen) to be his dresser, but his actions are misunderstood when he tries to rout Nazi spies who are using Allen's act to send coded messages. Directed with no pretension by John Baxter, who made several of the duo's other popular films, it is an engaging showcase for one of Britain's best-loved song-and-comedy teams.

Bud Flanagan *Bob Parker* • Chesney Allen *Gordon Maxwell* • Meinhart Maur *Herr Steiner* • Phyllis Stanley *Gina Cavendish* • Peggy Dexter *Googie* • Horace Kenney *George* • Gordon McLeod *MacNaughton* • Alexander Kardan *Holtzman* ■ *Dir* John Baxter • *Scr* Bud Flanagan, Austin Melford, Barbara K Emary

Wells Fargo ★★★

Western 1937 · US · BW · 115mins

Director Frank Lloyd is virtually forgotten today, his epic style and passionate narrative sense well out of fashion, and yet he was responsible for such Oscar-winning movies as *The Divine Lady* (1929), *Cavalcade* (1933) and *Mutiny on the Bounty* (1935). This is the story of America's famous freight carrier, unfolding as we follow the screen marriage of leads Joel McCrea and Francis Dee (a married couple in real life). Regrettably, their tortuous relationship gets in the way of the truly epic saga of Wells Fargo itself. This was McCrea's first substantial leading role, and he stoically underplays in the style of the great silent western stars. Nevertheless, this is stirring entertainment on a grand scale.

Joel McCrea *Ramsay MacKay* • Bob Burns *Hank York* • Frances Dee *Justine* • Lloyd Nolan *Del Slade* • Porter Hall *James Oliver* • Ralph Morgan *Mr Pryor* • Mary Nash *Mrs Pryor* • Robert Cummings *Trimball* ■ *Dir* Frank Lloyd • *Scr* Paul Schofield, Gerald Geraghty, Frederick Jackson, from a story by Stuart N Lake

Went the Day Well? ★★★★★ PG

Second World War drama
1942 · UK · BW · 88mins

Without question the finest Home Front picture made during the Second World War. Adapted from Graham Greene's short story *The Lieutenant Died Last*, it depicts the seizure of a quiet English village by disguised Nazi soldiers in league with local quislings with such plausibility that it must have chilled contemporary audiences to the bone. Those watching today will be similarly struck by the steel beneath the quintessential Englishness of the villagers. What still makes this such compelling cinema is the realism and restraint with which director Alberto Cavalcanti tells his tale and the naturalistic playing of his splendid cast.

Leslie Banks *Oliver Wilsford* • Elizabeth Allan *Peggy* • Frank Lawton *Tom Sturry* • Basil Sydney *Ortler* • Valerie Taylor *Nora Ashton* • Mervyn Johns *Sims* • Edward Rigby *Poacher* • Marie Lohr *Mrs Frazer* • CV France *Vicar* • David Farrar *Jung* • Muriel George *Mrs Collins* • Thora Hird *Land Girl* • Harry Fowler *George Truscott* • Patricia Hayes *Daisy* ■ *Dir* Alberto Cavalcanti • *Scr* Angus MacPhail, Diana Morgan, John Dighton, from the short story *The Lieutenant Died Last* by Graham Greene

We're Back! A Dinosaur's Story ★★★ U

Animated fantasy 1993 · US · Colour · 67mins

Dinosaurs have represented box-office gold for Steven Spielberg over the years, but not in this case. He serves as executive producer on this animated tale that wasn't widely shown in the UK – a shame since it's a jolly enough affair, well designed and featuring a literate script from Oscar-winning writer John Patrick Shanley. The story revolves around four dinosaurs who travel through time to New York and get mixed up in a series of adventures. Children will adore the dino-antics while adults will recognise some familiar voices: John Goodman, Felicity Kendal, Rhea Perlman, Martin Short and Jay Leno.

John Goodman *Rex* • Blaze Berdahl *Buster* • Rhea Perlman *Mother Bird* • Jay Leno *Vorb* • Rene Levant *Woo* • Felicity Kendal *Elsa* • Charles Fleischer *Dweeb* • Walter Cronkite *Captain Neweyes* • Joe Shea *Louie* • Julia Child *Doctor Bleeb* • Martin Short *Stubbs, the Clown* ■ *Dir* Dick Zondag, Ralph Zondag, Phil Nibbelink, Simon Wells • *Scr* John Patrick Shanley, from the book *We're Back* by Hudson Talbott

We're Going to Be Rich ★★

Musical drama 1938 · UK · BW · 80mins

Made for 20th Century-Fox, this attempt to launch Gracie Fields as an international star was a failure outside of England. This is hardly surprising, given the feebleness of the material which finds Gracie as a 19th-century singer married to feckless Victor McLaglen. They go to South Africa where he has invested their savings in a gold mine, and find they have lost the money. She sings in a saloon, becomes romantically involved with its owner Brian Donlevy and parts from hubby, but not irrevocably...

Gracie Fields *Kit Dobson* • Victor McLaglen *Dobbie Dobson* • Brian Donlevy *Yankee Gordon* • Coral Browne *Pearl* • Ted Smith *Tim Dobson* • Gus McNaughton *Broderick* • Charles Carson *Keeler* ■ *Dir* Monty Banks • *Scr* Sam Hellman, Rohama Siegel, from a story by James Edward Grant

We're No Angels ★★ U

Comedy 1955 · US · Colour · 105mins

Humphrey Bogart, Peter Ustinov and Aldo Ray are the three cons who escape from Devil's Island and intend to rip off French shopkeeper, Leo G Carroll, and his alluring wife, Joan Bennett, in this unruly caper. Reunited with the director of *Casablanca*, Bogart isn't well matched with his co-stars or best suited to this sort of farce. And when the script turns all moralistic and gooey (with Bogart dressing up as Santa Claus and singing carols) you start looking around for Bing Crosby. A misjudgement for all concerned.

Humphrey Bogart *Joseph* • Joan Bennett *Amelie Ducotel* • Peter Ustinov *Jules* • Aldo Ray *Albert* • Leo G Carroll *Felix Ducotel* • Basil Rathbone *AndréTrochard* • Gloria Talbott *Isabelle Ducotel* • John Baer *Paul Trochard* ■ *Dir* Michael Curtiz • *Scr* Ranald MacDougall, from the play *La Cuisine des Anges* by Albert Husson

We're No Angels ★★ 15

Comedy thriller 1989 · US · Colour · 101mins

Neil Jordan's film, while not that bad, is a disappointing waste of an impressive array of talent. The script is by David Mamet, and the cast includes Robert De Niro, Sean Penn and Demi Moore. Yet the result is a leaden, only fitfully funny farce in which escaped cons De Niro (over the top) and Penn pose as priests as they attempt to cross the border to Canada. Moore's role is mainly decorative and the best performances come from a wily support cast, which includes Bruno Kirby, Wallace Shawn and, most notably, Ray McAnally in his last film role as the evil prison warden. Contains some violence, swearing and brief nudity.

Robert De Niro *Ned* • Sean Penn *Jim* • Demi Moore *Molly* • Hoyt Axton *Father Levesque* • Bruno Kirby *Deputy* • Ray McAnally *Warden* • James Russo *Bobby* • Wallace Shawn *Translator* • Jay Brazeau *Sheriff* • Elizabeth Lawrence *Mrs Blair* ■ *Dir* Neil Jordan • *Scr* David Mamet, from the play *La Cuisine des Anges* by Albert Husson

We're Not Dressing ★★★

Musical comedy 1934 · US · BW · 74mins

Culled without credit from JM Barrie's *The Admirable Crichton*, this gives the plum role to Bing Crosby and, accordingly, supplies a handful of Mack Gordon–Harry Revel songs for him to croon. Crosby is the deck hand on millionairess Carole Lombard's luxury yacht, cruising with a bunch of disparate, sometimes eccentric, friends and her pet bear in the South Seas. Shipwrecked on a desert island, none are able to cope except Crosby, who takes charge of the situation – and of spoiled heiress Lombard. An inconsequential version of the tale, but madcap and highly enjoyable.

Bing Crosby *Stephen Jones* • Carole Lombard *Doris Worthington* • George Burns *George* • Gracie Allen *Gracie* • Ethel Merman *Edith* • Leon Errol *Hubert* • Raymond Milland [Ray Milland] *Prince Michael* ■ *Dir* Norman Taurog • *Scr* Horace Jackson, Francis Martin, George Marion Jr, from a story by Benjamin Glazer • *Music/Lyrics* Mack Gordon, Harry Revel

We're Not Married ★★★

Portmanteau comedy
1952 · US · BW · 85mins

Fabulous Fox – froth a portmanteau movie about five couples who discover they're not legally married in a clever, censor-circumventing series of tales. The major attraction for today's audience, however, is not in the witty Nunnally Johnson/Dwight Taylor screenplay, but in the fourth-billed presence of Marilyn Monroe, beginning her ascendancy at 20th Century-Fox. Ginger Rogers is top-billed, but the cast also includes troupers like Victor Moore, David Wayne, Eve Arden and Mitzi Gaynor. Watch out, too, for Zsa Zsa Gabor (aptly cast!), and don't blink

1558 U = SUITABLE FOR ALL Uc = SUITABLE FOR ALL, ESPECIALLY FOR YOUNG CHILDREN (VIDEO ONLY) PG = PARENTAL GUIDANCE

or you'll miss an uncredited Lee Marvin.

Ginger Rogers *Ramona* • Fred Allen *Steve Gladwyn* • Victor Moore *Justice of the Peace* • Marilyn Monroe *Annabel Norris* • David Wayne *Jeff Norris* • Eve Arden *Katie Woodruff* • Paul Douglas *Hector Woodruff* • Eddie Bracken *Willie Fisher* • Mitzi Gaynor *Patsy Fisher* • Louis Calhern *Freddie Melrose* • Zsa Zsa Gabor *Eve Melrose* ■ *Dir* Edmund Goulding • *Scr* Nunnally Johnson, Dwight Taylor, from a story by Gina Kaus, Jay Dratler

The Werewolf ★★

Horror 1956 · US · BW · 79mins

Scientists S John Launer and George Lynn experiment on tormented family man Steven Ritch to find a cure for radiation poisoning and turn him into a werewolf in the process. A competent and timely marriage of horror with science fiction just as the latter form was going out of favour in the 1950s. Clever trick photography and Ritch's sympathetic performance take this up a few notches from a routine quickie.

Steven Ritch *Duncan Masch/The Werewolf* • Don Megowan *Jack Haines* • Joyce Holden *Amy Standish* • Eleanore Tanin *Helen Marsh* • Harry Lauter *Clovey* • Ken Christy *Dr Gilchrist* • S John Launer *Dr Emery Forrest* • George Lynn *Dr Morgan Chambers* ■ *Dir* Fred F Sears • *Scr* Robert E Kent, James B Gordon

Wes Craven's Mind Ripper ★★ 18

Horror science-fiction
1995 · US · Colour · 91mins

Everyone loves Wes Craven again following the success of *Scream* and its sequels, but this was from the period when his pictures were left on the video store shelf. He can't take all the blame here, as he only co-executive produced this mutant fifties-style B movie, which was directed with a refreshing disregard for style or cohesion by Joe Gayton. Lance Henriksen mugs valiantly as he investigates a commotion in the desert, but he's in more danger from the risible dialogue than from the brain-slurping, self-regenerating super-soldier he's been ordered to wipe out. Contains swearing and violence. [video]

Lance Henriksen *James Stockton* • Claire Stansfield *Joanne* • Natasha Gregson Wagner *Wendy* ■ *Dir* Joe Gayton • *Scr* Jonathan Craven, Phil Mittleman

Wes Craven's New Nightmare ★★★ 18

Horror 1994 · US · Colour · 107mins

Before director Wes Craven came back big time with *Scream*, he took a stab at the intellectual horror film, adding this semi-documentary style sequel to the *Nightmare on Elm Street* series. The terrorised teen from the original, Heather Langenkamp, plays herself, an actress troubled by (a real?) Freddy Krueger. There's a healthy dose of shocks, a look behind the scenes of the horror flick, and, although the project occasionally reeks of self-indulgence, you have to credit Craven (who also appears as himself) with trying something new rather than just cashing in on the franchise. Contains violence and swearing. [video]

Robert Englund *Freddy Krueger* • Heather Langenkamp • Miko Hughes *Dylan* • Jeffrey John Davis *Freddy's hand double* • Matt Winston *Chuck* • Rob Labelle *Terry* • Wes Craven • Marianne Maddalena ■ *Dir* Wes Craven • *Scr* Wes Craven, from his characters

West Beirut ★★★★ 15

Drama
1998 · Fr/Leb/Bel/Nor · Colour · 110mins

Having served as assistant cameraman on Quentin Tarantino's first three features, Ziad Doueiri makes his directorial debut with this autobiographical account of growing up in war-torn Lebanon in the seventies. Capturing the exuberance of youth and the vicarious thrill of the situation without ever losing sight of the seriousness of the conflict, Doueiri draws an outstanding performance from his younger brother, Rami, as the rebellious Muslim teenager whose passion for movies prompts him to travel across the barricaded city in search of adventure. With able support from buddy Mohammad Chamas and pretty Christian neighbour Rola Al Amin, this is a real eye-opener. In Arabic and French with English subtitles. Contains swearing.

Rami Doueiri *Tarek* • Mohammad Chamas *Omar* • Rola Al Amin *May* • Carmen Lebbos *Hala* • Joseph Bou Nassar *Riad* ■ *Dir/Scr* Ziad Doueiri

West 11 ★

Crime drama 1963 · UK · BW · 94mins

Michael Winner's skirmish with British social realism shows what life was like in the bedsits of Notting Hill, years before Julia Roberts showed up. Among the cast are Alfred Lynch as a drifter, Eric Portman as a cashiered officer and Diana Dors as a lonely heart. The script is mostly a series of loosely connected sketches, though the film's sole virtue nowadays is the location camerawork of Otto Heller that captures the then peeling and shabbily converted Regency houses that were riddled with dry rot and Rachmanism, which exchanged squalor for extortionate rents. Stanley Black and Acker Bilk's music adds a cloying note to a movie that rarely rises above basement level.

Alfred Lynch *Joe Beckett* • Kathleen Breck *Ilsa Barnes* • Eric Portman *Richard Dyce* • Diana Dors *Georgia* • Kathleen Harrison *Mrs Beckett* • Finlay Currie *Mr Cash* • Patrick Wymark *Father Hogan* • Freda Jackson *Mrs Hartley* ■ *Dir* Michael Winner • *Scr* Keith Waterhouse, Willis Hall, from the novel *The Furnished Room* by Laura del Rivo

West of the Divide ★★★ U

Western 1934 · US · BW · 52mins

John Wayne's career between Raoul Walsh's *The Big Trail* (1930) and John Ford's *Stagecoach* (1939) found him on Poverty Row in routine programme fillers like this one. Monogram studio fans insist that this is the best of Wayne's "Lone Star" series; it melds two familiar western plots, the revenge for the death of the hero's father and the cowboy masquerading as an outlaw to avenge the said death, and Wayne proves himself at ease with such material. Watch for George (later "Gabby") Hayes, and the great stuntman Yakima Canutt (the creative hand behind *Ben-Hur*'s chariot race) in an acting role. [video]

John Wayne *Ted Hayden* • Virginia Brown Faire *Fay Winters* • Lloyd Whitlock *Gentry* • George Hayes [George "Gabby" Hayes] *Dusty Rhodes* • Yakima Canutt *Hank* • Billy O'Brien *Spud* • Lafe McKee *Winters* ■ *Dir/Scr* Robert N Bradbury

West of Zanzibar ★★★

Silent melodrama 1928 · US · BW · 63mins

Lon Chaney gives his most twisted performance in silent genius Tod Browning's bitterly grim morality fable that proved to be another bizarre and amazing signpost in the evolution of modern horror. Paralysed in an altercation with his wife's lover, sadistic magician "Dead Legs" Flint (Chaney) takes their offspring to Africa, leaves her in a whorehouse and plots a terrible ritual revenge after becoming the wheelchaired god to the local natives. The ultimate Browning/Chaney freak show is an extreme depiction of parent-child alienation and as sordid a slice of atrocity exotica as twenties censors would allow. It was re-made four years later as *Kongo*.

Lon Chaney *Flint* • Lionel Barrymore *Crane* • Warner Baxter *Doc* • Mary Nolan *Maizie* ■ *Dir* Tod Browning • *Scr* Elliott Clawson, Waldemar Young, Joe Farnham [Joseph Farnham] (titles), from a story by Chester De Vonde, Kilbourne Gordon • *Set Designer* Cedric Gibbons

West of Zanzibar ★★ U

Adventure 1954 · UK · Colour · 90mins

The sequel to *Where No Vultures Fly* again features Anthony Steel as African wildlife conservationist and game warden Bob Payton. Payton's wife is now played by Sheila Sim, replacing Dinah Sheridan but perfectly transferring the social graces of Tunbridge Wells to the African bush. The emphasis is on travelogue material and shots of animals, most of which were rehashed from the earlier film. Drama is trumped up by ivory poachers and the ravages of drought and, while the film's heart is in the right place, it all seems simplistic and racist today. It was banned by the Kenyan government, then in the grip of the Mau Mau uprising, who felt the film was patronising. [video]

Anthony Steel *Bob Payton* • Sheila Sim *Mary Payton* • William Simons *Tim Payton* • Orlando Martins *M'Kwongwi* • Edric Connor *Chief Ushingo* • David Osieli *Ambrose* • Bethlehem Sketch *Bethlehem* • Martin Benson *Lawyer Dhofar* ■ *Dir* Harry Watt • *Scr* Max Catto, Jack Whittingham, from a story by Harry Watt

The West Point Story ★★ U

Musical comedy 1950 · US · BW · 106mins

James Cagney is in *Yankee Doodle Dandy* mode here, putting on a musical show for the cadets at West Point military academy. Cagney displays plenty of energy but struggles to shine, while co-stars Virginia Mayo, Doris Day and Gordon MacRae sing and strut their way through a roster of songs that badly needs a showstopper. Roy Del Ruth, a veteran of the *Broadway Melody* movies, could direct this sort of thing with his eyes closed, and probably did.

James Cagney *Elwin Bixby* • Virginia Mayo *Eve Dillon* • Doris Day *Jan Wilson* • Gordon MacRae *Tom Fletcher* • Gene Nelson *Hal Courtland* • Alan Hale Jr *Bull Gilbert* • Roland Winters *Harry Eberhart* • Raymond Roe *Bixby's "wife"* ■ *Dir* Roy Del Ruth • *Scr* John Monks Jr, Charles Hoffman, Irving Wallace, from the story *Classmates* by Irving Wallace

West Side Story ★★★★★ PG

Musical 1961 · US · Colour · 145mins

Ten well-deserved Oscars adorned this electrifying and moving epic version of the magnificent Leonard Bernstein-Stephen Sondheim update of *Romeo and Juliet*, turned into a New York gang parable set in the turbulent late fifties, with a special award for Jerome Robbins's dynamic choreography. And surely the only Oscar ever given to an actor for merely looking good went to the elegant George Chakiris, while Natalie Wood is genuinely touching as the tragic Maria. Richard Beymer, criticised at the time as Tony, now seems the very quintessence of fifties yearning. Co-director Robert Wise was no stranger to movie musicals: he had been the uncredited music editor on the Fred Astaire-Ginger Rogers series, and would later fashion *The Sound of Music* into one of the all-time box office champs. [video] DVD

Natalie Wood *Maria* • Richard Beymer *Tony* • Russ Tamblyn *Riff* • Rita Moreno *Anita* • George Chakiris *Bernardo* • Tucker Smith *Ice* • Tony Mordente *Action* • Jose De Vega *Chino* • Jay Norman *Pepe* ■ *Dir* Robert Wise, Jerome Robbins • *Scr* Ernest Lehman, from the stage play by Arthur Laurents, from an idea by Jerome Robbins, from Shakespeare's *Romeo and Juliet* • *Costume Designer* Irene Sharaff • *Cinematographer* Daniel L Fapp • *Editor* Thomas Stanford • *Art Director* Boris Leven • *Choreographer* Jerome Robbins • *Music/Lyrics* Leonard Bernstein, Stephen Sondheim

The West Side Waltz ★★★

Comedy drama 1995 · US · Colour · 90mins

A well-crafted made-for-TV comedy-drama based on the 1981 play by Ernest Thompson. Shirley MacLaine, Liza Minnelli and Jennifer Grey (*Dirty Dancing*) star as three diverse New York women – an elderly but cultured recluse, her nosy violinist neighbour and an aspiring thirtysomething actress who, through the course of their relationship, discover the true meaning of friendship. Along with Kathy Bates as a homeless woman, the actresses are topnotch and thanks to them director Ernest Thompson is saved from his own sometimes lethargic plot. A quirky character-driven film that is sure to entertain.

Shirley MacLaine *Margaret Mary Elderdice* • Liza Minnelli *Cara Varnum* • Jennifer Grey *Robin Ouiseau* • Kathy Bates *Mrs Goo* • Robert Pastorelli *Sookie Cerullo* • August Schellenberg *Serge* ■ *Dir/Scr* Ernest Thompson

Westbound ★★★ U

Western 1959 · US · Colour · 68mins

A decent Civil War western with genre stalwart Randolph Scott tearing his hair out as a Union officer transporting gold from California to finance the war effort and running into Confederate sympathisers and old flame Virginia Mayo along the way. This does not break any new ground but rather re-ploughs the old furrows with consummate professionalism, pacing and style. These westerns were a dime a dozen in the early fifties, but gradually slipped out of favour, and this is one of the last highly conventional examples to be made.

Randolph Scott *John Hayes* • Virginia Mayo *Norma Putnam* • Karen Steele *Jeannie Miller* • Michael Dante *Rod Miller* • Andrew Duggan *Clay Putnam* • Michael Pate *Mace* ■ *Dir* Budd Boetticher • *Scr* Berne Giler, from the story *The Great Divide No 2* by Berne Giler, Albert Shelby LeVino

Westbound Limited　　★★

Action melodrama　1937 · US · BW · 76mins

A hectic, low-budget Universal melodrama in which railroad agent Lyle Talbot tries to prove his innocence after he's wrongly blamed for a train crash. Director Ford Beebe, best known for such classic serials as *Flash Gordon's Trip to Mars* and *Buck Rogers*, also wrote the original story for this one, and keeps the action rattling along at a rate of knots.

Lyle Talbot *Dave Tolliver* • Polly Rowles *Janet Martin* • Henry Brandon *Joe Forbes* • Frank Reicher *Pop Martin* • Henry Hunter *Howard* ■ *Dir* Ford Beebe • *Scr* Maurice Geraghty, from a story by Ford Beebe

Western　　★★15

Romantic comedy road movie
1997 · Fr · Colour · 128mins

Quirky French road movie which won the Grand Jury Prize at Cannes in 1997. Two rootless men, Sergi Lopez and Sacha Bourdo meet, fight and become firm friends, both falling on French female hospitality in their search of hearth, love and home made bread. With its thin story line and some very questionable moral commentary this treads a fine line between good and bad taste. Perhaps because it's French it gets away with it, whereas a British or American equivalent would probably fall foul of the critics. In French with English subtitles. Contains swearing and sex scenes. ▭

Sergi Lopez *Paco Cazale* • Sacha Bourdo *Nino* • Elisabeth Vitali *Marinette* • Marie Matheron *Nathalie* • Basile Siekoua *Baptiste* ■ *Dir* Manuel Poirier • *Scr* Manuel Poirier, Jean-François Goyet, from an idea by Manuel Poirier

Western Union　　★★★U

Western　1941 · US · Colour · 94mins

German émigré director Fritz Lang seemed comfortable out west, and this movie followed quickly on the heels of his *Return of Frank James*. Today these films seem a little tame, and this tale of the building of the telegraph line between Omaha, Nebraska, and Salt Lake City, Utah, suffers from being undercast – there's a particularly uncharismatic lead in Robert Young, a phlegmatic Randolph Scott as a reforming outlaw and a notably uninteresting leading lady in Virginia Gilmore. But the set pieces are done with bravura and the cinematography is ravishing.

Robert Young *Richard Blake* • Randolph Scott *Vance Shaw* • Dean Jagger *Edward Creighton* • Virginia Gilmore *Sue Creighton* • John Carradine *Doc Murdoch* • Slim Summerville *Herman* • Chill Wills *Homer* • Barton MacLane *Jack Slade* ■ *Dir* Fritz Lang • *Scr* Robert Carson, from the novel by Zane Grey • *Cinematographer* Edward Cronjager, Allen M Davey

The Westerner　　★★★★U

Western　1940 · US · BW · 95mins

Director William Wyler cut his teeth on westerns, and here brings all his professional skills to bear in a fine example of the genre. In the lead is the star who always looked at home in the West, lanky Gary Cooper, in a tale based on the life of the notorious Judge Roy Bean, played by Walter Brennan, who won a third best supporting actor Oscar for his ferocious performance. The story itself may be fable, but Bean's celebrated obsession with Lillie Langtry was real enough, and the clever screenplay makes good use of it, particularly at the climax. It's a western for people who don't usually care for them, and the exteriors exemplary. ▭

Gary Cooper *Cole Hardin* • Walter Brennan *Judge Roy Bean* • Doris Davenport *Jane-Ellen Mathews* • Fred Stone *Caliphet Mathews* • Paul Hurst *Chickenfoot* • Chill Wills *Southeast* • Charles Halton *Mort Borrow* • Forrest Tucker *Wade Harper* ■ *Dir* William Wyler • *Scr* Jo Swerling, Niven Busch, from a story by Stuart N Lake

Westfront 1918　　★★★★

First World War drama
1930 · Ger · BW · 98mins

Released in the same year as Lewis Milestone's *All Quiet on the Western Front*, GW Pabst's film on the same subject, the Great War, caught the antiwar mood of the times. Like the American movie, the film captures the horror of trench warfare, something audiences were only then becoming familiar with 12 years after the event. The story of how it effects four soldiers is rather simple, and the plea for universal brotherhood is expressed in a naive manner, but Pabst, using sound for the first time, and low tracking shots over the battleground, gives one of the most vivid impressions of what it was actually like on the spot. A German language film.

Fritz Kampers *The Bavarian* • Gustav Diessl *Karl* • Hans Joachim Moebis *The Student* • Claus Clausen *The Lieutenant* ■ *Dir* GW Pabst • *Scr* Ladislaus Vajda, Peter Martin Lampel, from the novel *Vier von der Infanterie* by Ernst Johannsen

Westward Ho　　★★

Western　1935 · US · BW · 61mins

A far cry from the Ringo Kid, this is a B western with John Wayne before he was worth watching. It does rate a footnote in film history as the first release of Republic, a newly-formed amalgamation of several small outfits, though there is little difference between this effort and those he was making beforehand. Wayne plays the vigilante leader hunting badmen with a vengeance. However, he doesn't know that Frank McGlynn Jr, his rival for the love of the heroine and a member of an outlaw gang, is in fact his long-lost brother. Be warned that the Duke warbles a love song (dubbed, of course!) to the girl in the moonlight.

John Wayne *John Wyatt* • Sheila Mannors [Sheila Bromley] *Mary Gordon* • Frank McGlynn Jr *Jim Wyatt* • James Farley *Lafe Gordon* • Jack Curtis *Wall Ballard* • Yakima Canutt *Red* ■ *Dir* RN Bradbury [Robert N Bradbury] • *Scr* Lindsley Parsons, Robert Emmett [Robert Emmett Tansey]

Westward Ho the Wagons!　　★★U

Western　1956 · US · Colour · 90mins

After making Fess Parker a star as Davy Crockett, Walt Disney quickly came up with other westerns for him. This one's visually handsome, overly episodic, undemanding family entertainment with Parker as the wagon-train scout whose hobbies are singing ballads to his own guitar accompaniment and studying medicine – the latter comes in handy for saving the life of a Sioux chief's ailing son. Kids can identify with the boy who's captured by Indians and with the small girl they want to adopt as a princess. The lengthy battle with Pawnees, the work of the famous stunt specialist and second unit director Yakima Canutt, was weakened by Disney's original insistence that no blood should be spilt. ▭

Fess Parker *John "Doc" Grayson* • Kathleen Crowley *Laura Thompson* • Jeff York *Hank Breckenridge* • David Stollery *Dan Thompson* • Sebastian Cabot *Bissonette* • George Reeves *James Stephen* • Doreen Tracey *Bobo Stephen* • Barbara Woodell *Mrs Stephen* ■ *Dir* William Beaudine • *Scr* Tom Blackburn, from the novel by Mary Jane Carr

Westward Passage　　★★

Romantic comedy　1932 · US · BW · 72mins

A comedy of marital discord with Laurence Olivier as the vain but blocked writer who believes his wife, Ann Harding, is responsible. They bicker all day long, get divorced and she marries Irving Pichel until realising it's Olivier she loves truly, madly, deeply. The tone is decidedly Shaftesbury Avenue rather than Hollywood because Olivier, under contract to RKO, was being touted as the toast of the London stage, though he was thin, moustachioed and obviously uncertain in front of a camera. The title promised a western which is perhaps why it flopped.

Ann Harding *Olivia Van Tyne* • Laurence Olivier *Nick Allen* • ZaSu Pitts *Mrs Truedale* • Juliette Compton *Henriette* • Irving Pichel *Harry Lenman* • Irene Purcell *Diane Van Tyne* ■ *Dir* Robert Milton • *Scr* Bradley King, Humphrey Pearson, from the novel by Margaret Ayer Barnes

Westward the Women　　★★

Western　1951 · US · BW · 116mins

Frank Capra had wanted to make this western but his story was purchased by MGM and assigned to director William A Wellman. Its novelty is that Robert Taylor recruits over a hundred women in Chicago to start a new life as the wives of men out west and they make up his wagon train – learning to shoot, fight hostile tribes and endure various hardships en route to their new life. It's something of an ensemble piece but Denise Darcel is the stand-out among the women. Unfortunately, it all seems too wildly improbable and would have been better developed as an outright comedy.

Robert Taylor (1) *Buck Wyatt* • Denise Darcel *Fifi Danon* • Hope Emerson *Patience Hawley* • John McIntire *Roy Whitman* • Julie Bishop *Laurie Smith* • Beverly Dennis *Rose Meyers* • Marilyn Erskine *Jean Johnson* ■ *Dir* William A Wellman • *Scr* Charles Schnee, from a story by Frank Capra

Westworld　　★★★★15

Futuristic thriller　1973 · US · Colour · 85mins

The seeds of *Jurassic Park* and its sequel *The Lost World* can easily be recognised in writer/director Michael Crichton's futuristic suspense thriller about a holiday resort where people go to safely live out their fantasies. But Richard Benjamin and James Brolin's dream cowboy vacation turns into a nightmare when the android population malfunctions and robot gunslinger Yul Brynner pursues them relentlessly. A fun scare flick that puts its clever gimmicks to consistently imaginative and riveting use, with the inspired casting of chilling Brynner, good special effects and an incisive message about the dark side of male fantasies adding extra potent resonance. Contains violence and swearing. ▭

Yul Brynner *Gunslinger* • Richard Benjamin *Peter Martin* • James Brolin *John Blane* • Norman Bartold *Medieval Knight* • Alan Oppenheimer *Chief Supervisor* • Victoria Shaw *Medieval Queen* • Dick Van Patten *Banker* ■ *Dir/Scr* Michael Crichton

The Wet Parade　　★★

Period drama　1932 · US · BW · 118mins

This self-important MGM production is a real oddity which condemns demon drink while also criticising Prohibition. Based on the novel by Upton Sinclair which warned of the dangers of Prohibition, the film tries to be hard-hitting while not giving offence to any point of view. It takes two hours to get its muddled message across, and despite fine production and a strong cast, it is heavy going. The first half depicts Southern patriarch Lewis Stone being destroyed by alcohol addiction, while the second half focuses on the thankless work of Prohibition agents. The casting of Jimmy Durante as a government agent is just one of the film's perverse qualities, and Myrna Loy sports a blonde wig in the supporting role of a goodtime girl.

Dorothy Jordan *Maggie May Chilcote* • Lewis Stone *Roger Chilcote* • Neil Hamilton *Roger Chilcote Jr* • Emma Dunn *Mrs Sally Chilcote* • Frederick Burton *Judge Brandon* • Reginald Barlow *Major Randolph* • Robert Young *Kip Tarleton* • Walter Huston *Pow Tarleton* • Jimmy Durante *Abe Shilling* • Wallace Ford *Jerry Tyler* • Myrna Loy *Eileen Pinchon* ■ *Dir* Victor Fleming • *Scr* John Lee Mahin, from the novel by Upton Sinclair

Wetherby　　★★★★15

Drama　1985 · UK · Colour · 98mins

Written and directed by playwright David Hare, this a subtle, suddenly shocking, story set in Wetherby, a cold, bleak town in Yorkshire, where unmarried local teacher Jean Travers (Vanessa Redgrave) gives a small dinner party. The next day she is visited by one of the guests, John Morgan (Tim McInnerny), who suddenly takes out a gun and kills himself. The reasons are not at all explicable at first, but as they gradually emerge, the apparently innocuous party is seen again in a whole new light. An intriguing British movie, under-rated in its day. ▭

Vanessa Redgrave *Jean Travers* • Ian Holm *Stanley Pilborough* • Judi Dench *Marcia Pilborough* • Marjorie Yates *Verity Braithwaite*

• Tom Wilkinson *Roger Braithwaite* • Tim McInnerny *John Morgan* • Suzanna Hamilton *Karen Creasy* • Joely Richardson *Young Jean* ■ *Dir/Scr* David Hare

Whale Music ★★★
Romance 1994 · Can · Colour · 110mins

Maury Chaykin won the best actor Genie (the Canadian equivalent of an Oscar) for his performance as a washed-up rock star in this touching but rather low-key drama. The song *Claire* also took an award, but the musical centrepiece is a symphony for whales that Chaykin hopes will be his lasting memorial. However, life seems to be conspiring against his completing the piece, as his ex-wife, producer and singer brother all make demands on his time and wallet. Chaykin is highly convincing, as is Cyndy Preston as the teenage runaway who befriends him. Contains swearing, sex scenes and nudity.

Maury Chaykin *Desmond Howl* • Cyndy Preston *Claire Lowe* • Jennifer Dale *Fay Ginzburg-Howl* • Kenneth Walsh *Kenneth Sexston* • Paul Gross *Daniel Howl* • Blu Mankuma *Mookie Saunders* • Alan Jordan *Sal Goneau* ■ *Dir* Richard J Lewis • *Scr* Paul Quarrington, Richard J Lewis, from the novel by Paul Quarrington

The Whales of August
★★★★ Ⓤ
Drama 1987 · US · Colour · 90mins

While Lindsay Anderson is chiefly remembered for classic and explosive movies such as "If...", he was also in love with the theatre and with stage actors, especially illustrious names such as John Gielgud and Ralph Richardson. So Anderson naturally jumped at the chance to make this autumnal showcase for Bette Davis and Lillian Gish – and let's not overlook Vincent Price, Ann Sothern and Harry Carey either. Their combined ages makes *On Golden Pond* look like a brat pack movie and there are vague similarities between the two films: it's chiefly a battle of wits between two curmudgeonly stars. Gish, then aged 91, nurses her sister Davis who is blind. Gish – in her last film – is still the delicate actress from the silent days. Fans of Old Hollywood will adore it. 🎞

Lillian Gish *Sarah Webber* • Bette Davis *Libby Strong* • Vincent Price *Mr Nikolai Maranov* • Ann Sothern *Tisha Doughty* • Harry Carey Jr *Joshua Brackett* • Frank Grimes *Mr Beckwith* ■ *Dir* Lindsay Anderson • *Scr* David Berry, from his play

The Wharf Rat ★★★
Crime drama 1995 · US · Colour

Judge Reinhold made his name as a loveably dopey light comedian, so his casting here as a vicious corrupt policeman is a little hard to swallow. That aside, this is a satisfyingly gritty TV crime thriller in which small-time crook Lou Diamond Phillips joins forces with journalist Rachel Ticotin to find the crooked cops who murdered his brother. Writer/director Jimmy Huston handles the action and suspense with aplomb, and even finds a role for screen legend Rita Moreno. Contains violence and swearing.

Lou Diamond Phillips *Petey Martin* • Judge Reinhold *Doc* • Rachel Ticotin *Dexter Ireland* • Scott Cohen *Matt* • Rita Moreno *Petey and Matt's mother* ■ *Dir* Jimmy Huston • *Scr* Jimmy Huston, from a story by Paul Kimatian, Jimmy Huston

What? ★
Drama 1973 · It/Fr/W Ger · Colour · 112mins

Between *Macbeth* and *Chinatown* Roman Polanski made this odd little item, derived from what he called his "momentary desires". A sort of spur of the moment thing, Polanski said it showed the absurdity and extravagance of the outgoing sixties, dealing with an American flower child (Sydne Rome) who arrives at a beautiful Mediterranean villa, strips off and indulges in sex and power games with Marcello Mastroianni, Hugh Griffith and non-acting jet-set types. A crass, self-indulgent mess, it was laughed off the screen by most critics. Italian dialogue dubbed into English.

Marcello Mastroianni *Alex* • Sydne Rome *The Girl* • Romolo Valli *Administrator* • Hugh Griffith *Owner of Villa* • Guido Alberti *Priest* • Giancarlo Piacentini *Stud* • Carlo Delle Piane *The Boy* • Roman Polanski *Zanzara* ■ *Dir* Roman Polanski • *Scr* Roman Polanski, Gérard Brach

What a Carve Up! ★★★ Ⓤ
Comedy 1961 · UK · BW · 84mins

An old dark house comedy, co-written by the master of the *double entendre*, Ray Cooney. *Carry On* regulars Sid James and Kenneth Connor are among those gathering at a musty mansion in the hope of inheriting a fortune, but, as anyone who has seen *The Cat and the Canary* can tell you, the chances of a will being read without blood being shed are pretty slim. The cast works wonders with a script that too often settles for the cheap laugh, with Donald Pleasence and Michael Gough having more fun than most. 🎞

Kenneth Connor *Ernie Broughton* • Sidney James *Syd Butler* • Shirley Eaton *Linda Dickson* • Dennis Price *Guy Broughton* • Donald Pleasence *Mr Sloane, Solicitor* • Michael Gough *Fisk, The Butler* • Valerie Taylor *Janet Broughton* • Esma Cannon *Aunt Emily* ■ *Dir* Pat Jackson • *Scr* Ray Cooney, Tony Hilton, from the novel and play *The Ghoul* by Dr Frank King, Leonard J Hines

What a Crazy World ★★
Musical drama 1963 · UK · BW · 90mins

With Tommy Steele and Cliff Richard making movies, it was only a matter of time before Joe Brown would have a go. The result is an amiable but outdated musical that is still worth catching to see Brown and the Bruvvers, Freddie and the Dreamers, Susan Maughan and Marty Wilde at the height of their powers. The longueurs between the musical numbers, which the more generous might call the plot, are distinctly dodgy, however, with even Harry H Corbett struggling to raise a laugh.

Joe Brown (2) *Alf Hitchens* • Susan Maughan *Marilyn* • Marty Wilde *Herbie Shadbolt* • Harry H Corbett *Sam Hitchens* • Avis Bunnage *Mary Hitchens* • Michael Ripper *Common Man* • Grazina Frame *Doris Hitchens* ■ *Dir* Michael Carreras • *Scr* Alan Klein, Michael Carreras, from the play by Alan Klein

What a Way to Go! ★★★
Comedy 1964 · US · Colour · 110mins

A lavish, frantic comedy with Shirley MacLaine as a serial wife, marrying one of the best casts ever assembled: Dick Van Dyke's humble storekeeper turned zillionaire; Paul Newman's American artist in Paris; Robert Mitchum's Howard Hughes-type tycoon; and Gene Kelly's matinee idol. Much of the movie falls flat and it always tries too hard but Betty Comden and Adolph Green's script comes up with some clever demises for the husbands – Mitchum is kicked by the bull he is trying to milk – and mercilessly satirises the egotism of Gene Kelly. In 1964 the visual style was a knockout; today one might need to watch it through sunglasses.

Shirley MacLaine *Louisa* • Paul Newman *Larry Flint* • Robert Mitchum *Rod Anderson* • Dean Martin *Leonard Crawley* • Gene Kelly *Jerry Benson* • Bob Cummings [Robert Cummings] *Dr Stephanson* • Dick Van Dyke *Edgar Hopper* ■ *Dir* J Lee Thompson • *Scr* Betty Comden, Adolph Green, from a story by Gwen Davis • *Cinematographer* Leon Shamroy • *Music* Nelson Riddle

What a Whopper! ★★ Ⓤ
Comedy 1961 · UK · BW · 89mins

A typically lightweight comedy from former documentarist Gilbert Gunn. Adam Faith stars in this whimsical tale about a struggling writer who fakes photographs of the Loch Ness monster and then heads for the Highlands to convince the locals so that they'll back his book. Just about every comedy stalwart you can think of crops up in support, from *Carry On* regulars Sid James and Charles Hawtrey to TV favourites Wilfred Brambell and Terry Scott. Even Spike Milligan has a cameo as a tramp, but the laughs are as elusive as Nessie.

Adam Faith *Tony Blake* • Sidney James *Harry* • Charles Hawtrey *Arnold* • Freddie Frinton *Gilbert Pinner* • Terry Scott *Sergeant* • Marie France *Marie* • Carole Lesley *Charlie* • Spike Milligan *Tramp* ■ *Dir* Gilbert Gunn • *Scr* Terry Nation, from a story by Trevor Peacock, Jeremy Lloyd

What a Widow! ★★
Romantic comedy 1930 · US · BW · 90mins

Gloria Swanson lives up to the exclamation mark as the wealthy Tamarind Brooks who changes her men as often as the attractive costumes she wears. Among the many beaus to her string are a lawyer (Owen Moore, Mary Pickford's first husband), a violinist, a Spanish baritone and a nightclub dancer. Allan Dwan directs swiftly, as if unwilling to dwell on the unfunny sequences, and Miss Swanson sings a couple of songs and looks as though she was enjoying herself. Few others did, and its box-office failure caused a rift between Swanson and her patron Joseph P Kennedy, father of John F.

Gloria Swanson *Tamarind* • Owen Moore *Gerry* • Lew Cody *Victor* • Margaret Livingston *Valli* • William Holden (2) *Mr Lodge* ■ *Dir* Allan Dwan • *Scr* James Gleason, James Seymour, from a story by Josephine Lovett

What a Woman! ★★
Romantic comedy 1943 · US · BW · 93mins

Rosalind Russell stars as an all-powerful literary agent in this silly and plot-starved romantic comedy. While busily attempting to persuade author Willard Parker, whose novel she has just sold to Hollywood, that he should star in the film version, she is interviewed by journalist Brian Aherne, who gets caught up in the general mayhem while inevitably falling for her. Despite its failings, the movie is kept bubbling along by Russell, a powerhouse of comedic accomplishment; Shelley Winters makes her debut in a bit part.

Rosalind Russell *Carol Ainsley* • Brian Aherne *Henry Pepper* • Willard Parker *Professor Michael Cobb aka Anthony Street* • Alan Dinehart *Pat O'Shea* • Ann Savage *Jane Hughes* • Shelley Winter [Shelley Winters] *Actress* ■ *Dir* Irving Cummings • *Scr* Therese Lewis, Barry Trivers, from a story by Erik Charell

What about Bob? ★★★★ 🅿🅶
Comedy 1991 · US · Colour · 94mins

Richard Dreyfuss and Bill Murray make a dynamic comedy duo in this amiably manic satire on the therapy business directed by Frank Oz. Murray is especially funny as the annoying multi-phobic patient who follows psychiatrist Dreyfuss on holiday and totally ruins his control-freak life. His carefree schizo slobbishness versus Dreyfuss's Freudian posing makes for a great contrast, and the frenzied laughs come thick and fast without losing their welcome sharp edge or delightfully twisted compassion. Contains strong language. 🎞

Bill Murray *Bob Wiley* • Richard Dreyfuss *Dr Leo Marvin* • Charlie Korsmo *Siggy Marvin* • Julie Hagerty *Fay Marvin* • Kathryn Erbe *Anna Marvin* • Tom Aldredge *Mr Guttman* • Susan Willis *Mrs Guttman* ■ *Dir* Frank Oz • *Scr* Tom Schulman, from a story by Alvin Sargent, Laura Ziskin

What Becomes of the Broken Hearted? ★★
Drama 1999 · NZ/Ausl · Colour · 103mins

Once Were Warriors was a frighteningly believable account of domestic violence and did a lot to overturn the cosy picture postcard view of modern New Zealand. It was a lot to live up to and sadly this belated sequel has to go down as a disappointment despite the return of star Temuera Morrison and writer Alan Duff. Morrison is Jake the Musc, who still spends his time drinking himself – and beating other people – senseless. However, when his son (Julian Arahanga) is killed in a gang shooting, he is forced to re-evaluate his life. Director Ian Mune is fine on detailing the despair of working class Maori, but focuses too much on the gang lifestyle. Morrison is as impressive as ever, though.

Temuera Morrison *Jake Heke* • Clint Eruera *Sonny Heke* • Nancy Brunning *Tania Rogers* • Pete Smith *Apeman* • Lawrence Makoare *Grunt* • Rawiri Paratene *Mulla Rota* • Julian Arahanga *Nig Heke* • Edna Stirling *Rita* ■ *Dir* Ian Mune • *Scr* Alan Duff, from his novel

What Changed Charley Farthing? ★

Comedy adventure
1975 · UK · Colour · 100mins

Known in America as *The Bananas Boat*, this British attempt at a featherweight frolic by regular writing partners Jack Seddon and David Pursall sinks with scarcely a ripple of loss. Toothsome Doug McClure tries to escape a Cuba-style republic, while Lionel Jeffries, Warren Mitchell and Hayley Mills attempt to make some impact on the resolutely flabby plot. That they do not succeed is partly their fault: they should have read the script before they agreed to take part.

Doug McClure *Charley Farthing* • Lionel Jeffries *Henry Houlihan* • Hayley Mills *Jenny* • Warren Mitchell *MacGregor* • Alberto de Mendoza *Jumbo De Santos* ■ *Dir* Sidney Hayers • *Scr* David Pursall, Jack Seddon, from a novel by Mark Hebdon

What Did You Do in the War, Daddy? ★★

Second World War comedy
1966 · US · Colour · 115mins

You start wishing Peter Sellers had agreed to star in this silly Blake Edwards war comedy about a Sicilian village whose inhabitants will only surrender to the US Army if they can hold their annual soccer match and wine festival first. Edwards's *Pink Panther* collaborator might have breathed life into William Peter Blatty's ponderous script. As it is, James Coburn, Dick Shawn, Aldo Ray and Sergio Fantoni are just too heavy-handed for this kind of comedy.

James Coburn *Lieutenant Christian* • Dick Shawn *Captain Cash* • Sergio Fantoni *Captain Oppo* • Giovanna Ralli *Gina Romano* • Aldo Ray *Sergeant Rizzo* • Harry Morgan *Major Pott* • Carroll O'Connor *General Bolt* ■ *Dir* Blake Edwards • *Scr* William Peter Blatty, from a story by Blake Edwards, Maurice Richlin

What Dreams May Come ★★ 15

Fantasy romantic drama
1998 · US · Colour · 108mins

Ghastly love-after-death fantasy, with Annabella Sciorra as a suicide consigned to her own private hell, and Robin Williams as her dead hubby, a car-crash victim, consigned to his own painterly paradise, but forsaking it to be reunited with the love of his life – and death. Vincent Ward, director of *The Navigator – a Medieval Odyssey* (1988) and *Map Of The Human Heart*, (1992) brings his usual visual style to this tosh and as a result the film looks wonderful. But that's all that is wonderful about it as, visuals aside, this is slow and sentimental slush, with Williams at his mawkish, sincere worst. Contains some swearing, violence and semi-nudity. ▣ **DVD**

Robin Williams *Chris Nielsen* • Cuba Gooding Jr *Albert* • Annabella Sciorra *Annie Nielsen* • Max von Sydow *The Tracker* • Jessica Brooks Grant *Marie Nielsen* • Josh Paddock *Ian Nielsen* • Rosalind Chao *Leona* ■ *Dir* Vincent Ward • *Scr* Ron Bass [Ronald Bass], from the novel by Richard Matheson • *Production Designer* Eugenio Zanetti • *Set Designer* Cindy Carr • *Special Effects* Roy Arbogast, Joel Hynek, Nicholas Brooks, Stuart Robertson

What Ever Happened to Baby Jane? ★★★★★

Gothic drama
1962 · US · BW · 133mins

An innovative and much imitated chiller setting the trend for ageing Hollywood divas to revive their careers playing unhinged maniacs. But no one beats Bette Davis or Joan Crawford in the snarl-and-shriek department, here playing actress sisters divided by Tinseltown resentments. The on-screen fireworks were reportedly fuelled by off-screen hatred, but the chemistry between the stars is unquestionably hair-raising and upped the Gothic stakes to camp shock levels. On a more serious note, this *Grand Guignol*-style *Sunset Boulevard* deals with the frightening decay of illusions by cleverly incorporating both actresses' earlier work into the psychodrama.

Bette Davis *Jane Hudson* • Joan Crawford *Blanche Hudson* • Victor Buono *Edwin Flagg* • Anna Lee *Mrs Bates* • Maidie Norman *Elvira Stitt* • Marjorie Bennett *Della Flagg* ■ *Dir* Robert Aldrich • *Scr* Lukas Heller, from the novel by Henry Farrell • *Costume Designer* Norma Koch • *Cinematographer* Ernest Haller

What Ever Happened to...? ★★

Psychological thriller
1991 · US · Colour · 100mins

Robert Aldrich's son William was co-executive producer of this TV-movie remake of his father's *Grand Guignol* masterpiece *What Ever Happened to Baby Jane?* The most interesting aspect lies in the first ever screen pairing of Lynn and Vanessa Redgrave as the showbiz sisters fallen on hard times. Lynn goes right over the top in the Bette Davis role of Baby Jane, leaving Vanessa little space to improve on Joan Crawford's rendition of the wheelchair-bound Blanche. However, TV-movie specialist David Greene lacks Robert Aldrich's genius for the grotesque. Frankly, French and Saunders's *What Ever Happened to Baby Dawn?* was much better, but this remains a fascinating misfire.

Lynn Redgrave *Jane Hudson* • Vanessa Redgrave *Blanche Hudson* • John Glover *Billy Cork* • Bruce A Young *Dominick* • Amy Steel *Connie Trotter* • John Scott Clough *Frank Trotter* ■ *Dir* David Greene • *Scr* Brian Taggert, from the novel *What Ever Happened to Baby Jane?* by Henry Farrell

What Every Woman Knows ★★★

Political comedy drama
1934 · US · BW · 90mins

This charts the rise of a poverty-stricken but brilliant and ambitious young Scottish socialist (Brian Aherne) from humble beginnings to becoming a Member of Parliament. His success is made possible by financial help from the brothers of a mousy spinster (Helen Hayes) on condition that he will later marry her. Adapted from JM Barrie's sentimental play, the movie has a tedious first 25 minutes or so. It's worth persevering, though, for the poignant and charming tale that follows, for Aherne's performance, and for the rare opportunity to see the younger Hayes, Oscar-winner for the old lady in *Airport* 36 years later.

Helen Hayes *Maggie Wylie* • Brian Aherne *John Shand* • Madge Evans *Lady Sybil Tenterden* • Lucile Watson *La Comtesse* • Dudley Digges *James Wylie* • Donald Crisp *David Wylie* • David Torrence *Alick Wylie* • Henry Stephenson *Charles Venables* ■ *Dir* Gregory La Cava • *Scr* Monckton Hoffe, John Meehan, James K McGuinness, Marian Ainslee, from the play by JM Barrie

What Happened to Santiago ★★★

Romantic comedy
1989 · P Ric · Colour · 105mins

Forgetting the past and living for the present is the message of this affecting drama from director Jacobo Morales. Clinging to memories of his happy marriage, widower Tommy Muñiz has an accountant's liking for order, which is shaken both by his daughter's chaotic existence and the fact that his new lover, Gladys Rodriguez, refuses to reveal anything of her life before they met in a leafy city park. Part age-gap romance, study in dysfunction and political allegory, the action builds steadily to shocking revelations that have blighted Rodríguez's past. In Spanish with English subtitles.

Tommy Muñiz *Santiago Rodríguez* • Gladys Rodriguez *Angelina* • Jacobo Morales *Arístides Esquilín* • Johanna Rosaly *Nereida* • Roberto Vigoreaux *Geraldo* ■ *Dir/Scr* Jacobo Morales

What Happened Was... ★

Romantic comedy drama
1994 · US · Colour · 90mins

What happened was... not very much. We spend an evening with two very strange lonely hearts on their first date. Director Tom Noonan plays Michael, a paranoid, conspiracy theory-prone paralegal. Karen Sillas is Jackie, a legal assistant in the same firm who has invited him over to dinner. Together they discuss their insecurities and lack of success with the opposite sex without really getting anywhere. Depressing and difficult viewing, this is an admirable effort which, sadly, makes for a seriously dull film.

Tom Noonan *Michael* • Karen Sillas *Jackie* ■ *Dir/Scr* Tom Noonan

What Have I Done to Deserve This? ★★★ 18

Black comedy
1984 · Sp · Colour · 97mins

A typical "kitsch 'n' think" mixture of tragedy and comedy from Spanish director Pedro Almodóvar. Carmen Maura is the unhappy Madrid housewife who rebels against the pressures of modern life with drugs and manslaughter when her family's myriad problems drag her deeper into depression. Using the language of Italian neo-realism, sexual taboos, fake commercials for bogus products and his skewed sense of autobiographical social conscience, Almodóvar mines this spiky black farce for all its allegorical worth. In Spanish with English subtitles. ▣

Carmen Maura *Gloria* • Luis Hostalot *Polo* • Ángel De Andrés-López *Antonio* • Gonzalo Suarez *Lucas Villalba* • eronica Forque *Cristal* • Juan Martinez *Toni* • Chus Lampreave *Grandmother* ■ *Dir/Scr* Pedro Almodóvar

What Kind of Mother Are You? ★★★

Drama based on a true story
1996 · US · Colour

This better-than-average melodrama features one of the more disturbing tales in the true story TV-movie genre. Mel Harris gives a decent performance as a mother who decides to let her unruly daughter spend a night in jail after she commits a petty offence with her boyfriend, only to find that she's been sent to a brutal juvenile detention centre with no prospect of imminent release. This nightmare scenario is handled confidently by director Noel Nosseck. Contains some violence.

Mel Harris *Laura Hyler* • Nicholle Tom *Kelly Jameson* • Alex Carter *Rob Hyler* • Stuart Stone *Steven Hyler* • Patricia Collins *Bette* ■ *Dir* Noel Nosseck • *Scr* Kathleen Knutsen Rowell, Anne Gerard

What Love Sees ★★ PG

Drama based on a true story
1996 · US · Colour · 91mins

A fantastically syrupy true story about a romance between two blind people from different sides of the tracks in the thirties. Annabeth Gish stars as a wealthy woman who finds true love with farmer Richard Thomas, much to the distress of her city-based family who worry that he won't be able to look after her out West. The performances from the two leads are pretty good given the awesomely melodramatic material, and there are nice supporting turns from Edward Herrmann and Kathleen Noone, but director Michael Switzer lays on the treacle a little too thick. ▣

Richard Thomas *Gordon Holly* • Annabeth Gish *Jean Treadway* • Edward Herrmann *Morton Treadway* • Kathleen Noone *Sarah Treadway* • August Schellenberg *Earl* • Romy Rosemont *Lucy Treadway* ■ *Dir* Michael Switzer • *Scr* Robert L Freedman, from the book by Susan Vreeland

What – No Beer? ★★

Comedy
1933 · US · BW · 65mins

Yoked together by MGM for several comedies, Buster Keaton and Jimmy Durante here play dopey friends who put their money into a run-down brewery in the hope that Prohibition will soon be lifted. It isn't and the duo find themselves in trouble with the police and gangsters. Little of the old Keaton magic is in evidence while the rasp-voiced Durante abrades the soundtrack with unsubtle gags.

Buster Keaton *Elmer J Butts* • Jimmy Durante *Jimmy Potts* • Rosco Ates [Roscoe Ates] *Schultz* • Phyllis Barry *Hortense* • John Miljan *Butch Lorado* • Henry Armetta *Tony* • Edward Brophy *Spike Moran* • Charles Dunbar *Mulligan* ■ *Dir* Edward Sedgwick • *Scr* Carey Wilson, Jack Cluett, from a story by Robert E Hopkins

What Price Glory ★★★

Silent war drama
1926 · US · BW · 122mins

Considered very daring in its day for its mix of pathos and jokes, director Raoul Walsh's depiction of the First World War as a slapstick farrago is still a feat of arms. Rivalling US Marines Captain Flagg and Sergeant Quirk (Victor McLaglen and Edmund Lowe)

U = SUITABLE FOR ALL   Uc = SUITABLE FOR ALL, ESPECIALLY FOR YOUNG CHILDREN (VIDEO ONLY)   PG = PARENTAL GUIDANCE

squabble over women (Dolores Del Rio in particular) on the front line. Adapted from a long-running play by Laurence Stallings and Maxwell Anderson, the film juxtaposes some very realistic battle scenes with boisterous comedy. Compelling for its unusual blend of realism and farce.

Victor McLaglen *Captain Flagg* • Edmund Lowe *Sergeant Quirt* • Dolores Del Rio *Charmaine de la Cognac* • William V Mong *Cognac Pete* • Phyllis Haver *Hilda of China* ■ *Dir* Raoul Walsh • *Scr* James T O'Donohoe, Malcolm Stuart Boylan (titles), from the play by Laurence Stallings, Maxwell Anderson

What Price Glory? ★★★ U

First World War comedy
1952 · US · Colour · 109mins

A slightly misguided attempt to remake the 1926 silent hit: 20th Century-Fox's garish Technicolor and Robert Wagner's brilliantined hairstyle are quite wrong for such a tale. Even so, director John Ford seems to regard the whole enterprise as a lark, with a past-his-prime James Cagney and a likeable Dan Dailey performing as though this is a would-be musical without songs. Still enjoyable, but is there a point?

James Cagney *Captain Flagg* • Corinne Calvet *Charmaine* • Dan Dailey *Sergeant Quirt* • William Demarest *Corporal Kiper* • Craig Hill *Lieutenant Aldrich* • Robert Wagner *Lewisohn* ■ *Dir* John Ford • *Scr* Phoebe Ephron, Henry Ephron, from the play by Laurence Stallings, Maxwell Anderson

What Price Hollywood?

★★★★

Drama   1932 · US · BW · 88mins

George Cukor's sophisticated and still appealing Hollywood story with Constance Bennett as a waitress at the famous Brown Derby restaurant who becomes a star. Meanwhile, her discoverer and mentor, played by real-life director Lowell Sherman, slips into drunken obscurity. Sherman, it is said, modelled his alcoholism on observing his then brother-in-law, John Barrymore. The picture offers an atmospheric and authentic portrait of Hollywood at the time and gave producers a cast-iron storyline which they have recycled as *A Star Is Born* three times.

Constance Bennett *Mary Evans* • Lowell Sherman *Maximilian Carey* • Neil Hamilton *Lenny Borden* • Gregory Ratoff *Julius Saxe* • Brooks Benedict *Muto* • Louise Beavers *Bonita, the maid* ■ *Dir* George Cukor • *Scr* Jane Murfin, Ben Markson, Gene Fowler, Roland Brown, from a story by Adela Rogers St John • *Producer* David O Selznick

What Price Victory ★★

Drama   1988 · US · Colour · 95mins

A half-hearted morality tale set on the American football field, which examines the lengths that people will go to in order to win the game. It has an unusual choice for director, Kevin Connor, who is best known for fantasy adventure movies. Purely for fans of the game, and perhaps fans of *ER* who'd like to see Eriq La Salle in a movie made several years before he donned hospital greens.

Mac Davis *Jake Ramson* • Robert Culp *Billy Bob Claiborne* • George Kennedy *Buck Brayton* • Susan Hess *Diane* • Brian Wimmer *Denzil*

Ray* • Eriq La Salle *Trumayne* • Warren Berlinger *Pickett* • Gus Boyd *JD Decker* ■ *Dir* Kevin Connor • *Scr* DM Eyre Jr, from a story by Richard A Shepherd

What Rats Won't Do   ★★

Romantic comedy
1998 · UK · Colour · 84mins

From the producers of *Four Weddings and a Funeral*, this movie crams in elements from that hit plus a sprinkling of *A Fish Called Wanda*. It's a romantic farce about two barristers falling in love while contesting a case. Natascha McElhone is fun and Charles Dance in a leopard-skin G-string could be considered a visual bonus. Although a ghastly title, don't let that put you off as there is an oddly Swinging Sixties ambience here that is quite charming.

James Frain *Jack* • Natascha McElhone *Kate* • Parker Posey *Mirella* • Samantha Bond *Jane* • Peter Capaldi *Tony* ■ *Dir* Alastair Reid • *Scr* Steve Coombes, Dave Robinson, William Osborne

What the Butler Saw   ★ U

Comedy   1950 · UK · BW · 61mins

Elderly Edward Rigby heads a strictly B-movie cast in this impoverished (one set), stiffly directed comedy, an early product from the Hammer studio. The plot, about a Polynesian princess who follows her lover, a butler, home to England and causes consternation in a country house, has a distinctly pre-war feel. The title and one saucy scene in which the dusky maiden (played, needless to say, by a frightfully English starlet) has a bath in the sink must have given the censors palpitations.

Edward Rigby *The Earl* • Henry Mollison *Bembridge* • Mercy Haystead *Lapis* • Michael Ward *Gerald* • Eleanor Hallam *Lady Mary* • Peter Burton *Bill Fenton* • Anne Valery *Elaine* ■ *Dir* Godfrey Grayson • *Scr* AR Rawlinson, Edward J Mason, from a story by Roger Good, Donald Good

What the Deaf Man Heard

★★★

Period comedy drama   1997 · US · Colour

A sly comedy with Matthew Modine as the small-town handyman in whom everyone confides their secrets in the belief that he's a deaf mute. However, his silence is simply a ten-year-old's response to his mother's last instruction before they are accidentally parted forever at a bus depot. Wearing its charm lightly and with the excellent Modine being well supported by snooty widow Claire Bloom, kindly depot boss Tom Skerritt and junkman James Earl Jones, this TV movie is an unassuming pleasure.

Matthew Modine *Sammy Ayers* • Claire Bloom *Mrs Tynan* • Judith Ivey *Lucille* • James Earl Jones *Archibald Thacker* • Jerry O'Connell *Rev Perry Ray Pruitt* • Bernadette Peters *Helen Ayers* • Tom Skerritt *Norm Jenkins* ■ *Dir* John Kent Harrison • *Scr* Robert W Lenski, GD Gearino

What We Did That Night

★★★ 15

Thriller   1999 · US · Colour · 88mins

A nifty made-for-TV variation on *I Know What You Did Last Summer*, which makes up for what it lacks in thrills with some cunning plotting. The film

opens with four students burying a body in the deserted Devil's Glen. Fast forward eight years and one of the number (Rick Schroder) emerges from prison with some bad news for his now respectable buddies: their burial ground is about to be redeveloped and they need to move the body. The trio relives the events leading to the tragedy, unaware that Schroder still has a few more shocks up his sleeve. Director Paul Shapiro manages to keep the viewer guessing right until the end and Schroder delivers a charismatic lead turn. Contains violence and some swearing. 📺

Rick Schroder [Ricky Schroder] *Henry* • Jack Noseworthy *Oliver* • Jayce Bartok *Doc* • Michael Easton *Charlie* • Tara Reid *Girl* ■ *Dir* Paul Shapiro • *Scr* Eric Harlacher

Whatever Happened to
Aunt Alice?   ★★★★ 15

Mystery thriller 1969 · US · Colour · 101mins

And wouldn't her family like to know? Produced by Robert Aldrich, who directed Bette Davis and Joan Crawford in the classic gothic drama *What Ever Happened to Baby Jane?*, this scary story isn't quite in the same class. Ruth Gordon poses as a housekeeper to Geraldine Page, who's got into the unpleasant habit of disposing of her domestic help. Director Lee H Katzin contrives a baleful bitches' brew of women at war with each other, and he maintains the suspense with considerable skill right up to the nail-biting conclusion. 📺

Geraldine Page *Mrs Claire Marrable* • Ruth Gordon *Mrs Alice Dimmock* • Rosemary Forsyth *Harriet Vaughn* • Robert Fuller *Mike Darrah* • Mildred Dunnock *Miss Tinsley* • Joan Huntington *Julia Lawson* ■ *Dir* Lee H Katzin • *Scr* Theodore Apstein, from the novel *The Forbidden Garden* by Ursula Curtiss

Whatever Happened to
Harold Smith?   ★★★★ 15

Comedy   1999 · UK · Colour · 95mins

Veteran British star Tom Courtenay makes a magnificent comeback as Harold Smith, an old-timer in seventies Sheffield whose magical powers stop three pacemakers at an old people's home. While his son Vince (Michael Legge) dithers between punk and rock, Harold becomes a scandalous celebrity thanks to his occult powers. Peter Hewitt's comedy offers a quirky account of the times, such as Stephen Fry hailing Harold as a new messiah and Vince's randy mother (Lulu) shinning up a drainpipe. A home-grown product that, like *The Full Monty*, proves regional ideas can have a powerful metropolitan impact.

Tom Courtenay *Harold Smith* • Michael Legge *Vince Smith* • Laura Fraser *Joanna Robinson* • Stephen Fry *Doctor Peter Robinson* • Charlotte Roberts *Lucy Robinson* • Amanda Root *Margaret Robinson* • Lulu *Irene Smith* • David Thewlis *Keith Nesbitt* ■ *Dir* Peter Hewitt • *Scr* Ben Steiner

What's a Nice Girl like
You...?   ★★

Comedy drama   1971 · US · Colour · 73mins

Adapted from the EV Cunningham novel *Shirley*, this TV movie is packed with familiar faces. Yet the presence of

Jack Warden, Vincent Price, Roddy McDowall and Edmond O'Brien barely disguises the fact that this would-be comedy drama is as short on style as it is on laughs. Brenda Vaccaro has her moments as a Bronx Eliza Doolittle, kidnapped and coached to impersonate a Manhattan socialite, but she always seems to be trying a little too hard to keep pace with her distinguished co-stars. Director Jerry Paris could have done with a lighter touch, but it's worth watching for Price's deliciously camp villainy.

Brenda Vaccaro *Shirley Campbell* • Jack Warden *Lieutenant Joe Burton* • Roddy McDowall *Albert Soames* • Jo Anne Worley *Cynthia* • Edmond O'Brien *Morton Stillman* • Vincent Price *William Spevin* • Morgan Sterne *Adam Newman* • Michael Lerner *Fats Detroit* ■ *Dir* Jerry Paris • *Scr* Howard Fast, from the novel *Shirley* by EV Cunningham

What's Eating Gilbert
Grape   ★★★ 12

Comedy drama 1993 · US · Colour · 112mins

Johnny Depp has spent most of his working life trying to avoid the sort of Hollywood career his pretty boy looks would seem to demand, and this gentle oddity is a case in point. Depp takes the title role, playing the sensitive but level-headed teenager who has his hands full coping with an enormously obese mother (Darlene Cates), who won't leave the house, and a mentally disabled younger brother (Leonardo DiCaprio). The latter steals the show, but the entire cast which also includes Juliette Lewis, Mary Steenburgen and Crispin Glover turns in winning performances. Director Lasse Hallström, who made his name with *My Life as a Dog*, lets sentiment creep in, but still demonstrates a sharp outsider's eye for the quirkiness of Americana. Contains swearing and sex scenes. 📺

Johnny Depp *Gilbert Grape* • Juliette Lewis *Becky* • Mary Steenburgen *Betty Carver* • Leonardo DiCaprio *Arnie Grape* • John C Reilly *Tucker Van Dyke* • Darlene Cates *Bonnie Grape* • Laura Harrington *Amy Grape* • Mary Kate Schellhardt *Ellen Grape* • Crispin Glover *Bobby McBurney* • Kevin Tighe *Mr Carver* ■ *Dir* Lasse Hallström • *Scr* Peter Hedges, from his novel • *Cinematographer* Sven Nykvist

What's Good for the Goose

★ PG

Comedy   1969 · UK · Colour · 98mins

With a contrived title and a simply appalling script (co-written by Norman Wisdom himself), this is one of the biggest blots on the British movie copybook. Directed by Menahem Golan with no feel for Wisdom's unique brand of comedy, it is jam-packed with cringeworthy moments, which follow so hard on each other that you find yourself watching with morbid fascination to see how low it can actually stoop. It's easy to understand why Wisdom would want to escape from his usual sentimental character, but Norman the sexy banker? No wonder he didn't make another film for three years. Contains nudity. 📺

Norman Wisdom *Timothy Bartlett* • Sally Geeson *Nikki* • Sarah Atkinson *Meg* • Terence Alexander *Frisby* • Sally Bazely *Margaret Bartlett* • Derek Francis *Harrington* • David

Lodge *Hotel porter* ■ *Dir* Menahem Golan • *Scr* Norman Wisdom, Menahem Golan, Christopher Gilmore

What's New, Pussycat?   ★★★ 15
Comedy   1965 · US/Fr · Colour · 104mins

Woody Allen has never had much time for this frantic farce, which marked his debut as both writer and performer. Originally planned as a low-key black-and-white affair, it snowballed into a freewheeling star vehicle over which director Clive Donner was not always in total control. Even though the film was a box-office smash, Allen complained that unchecked ad-libbing and a disinclination to excise the mediocre had swamped his material, with Peter Sellers particularly guilty as the psychiatrist jealous of patient Peter O'Toole's success with women. Hilarious when on target, this is glossy, often exhilarating entertainment. ▭

Peter Sellers *Doctor Fritz Fassbender* • Peter O'Toole *Michael James* • Romy Schneider *Carol Werner* • Capucine *Renée Lefèbvre* • Paula Prentiss *Liz* • Woody Allen *Victor Shakapopolis* • Ursula Andress *Rita* • Richard Burton ■ *Dir* Clive Donner • *Scr* Woody Allen

What's So Bad About Feeling Good?   ★★
Comedy   1968 · US · Colour · 93mins

A quintessential sixties title about a toucan infected with a happiness virus that spreads the "disease" throughout Manhattan. Among the grouchy New Yorkers whose personalities are transformed are advertising executive turned artist George Peppard, his hippy girlfriend Mary Tyler Moore and guest star Thelma Ritter, whose acerbity is most welcome. The studio East Village backlot, period clothes and garish Universal-style Technicolor make it strangely watchable, though it's still not very good.

George Peppard *Pete* • Mary Tyler Moore *Liz* • Dom DeLuise *J Gardner Monroe* • John McMartin *The Mayor* • Nathaniel Frey *Conrad* • Charles Lane (1) *Dr Shapiro* • Jeanne Arnold *Gertrude* • George Furth *Murgatroyd* • Thelma Ritter *Mrs Schwartz* • Cleavon Little *Phil* ■ *Dir* George Seaton • *Scr* George Seaton, Robert Pirosh, from the novel *I Am Thinking of My Darling* by Vincent McHugh

What's the Matter with Helen?   ★★★
Thriller   1971 · US · Colour · 100mins

Answer: nothing a good bout of killing wouldn't cure. Strong female stars pull this number though a hedge of campy production, set in the thirties as Debbie Reynolds and Shelley Winters try to forget their sordid past by setting up a school for talented youngsters in Hollywood. Curtis Harrington directs with an acute feel for the period and personalities, which include Dennis Weaver and Agnes Moorehead.

Debbie Reynolds *Adelle Bruckner* • Shelley Winters *Helen Hill* • Dennis Weaver *Lincoln Palmer* • Agnes Moorehead *Sister Alma* • Michael MacLiammoir *Hamilton Starr* • Sammee Lee Jones *Winona Palmer* • Robbi Morgan *Rosalie Greenbaum* • Helene Winston *Mrs Greenbaum* ■ *Dir* Curtis Harrington • *Scr* Henry Farrell • *Cinematographer* Lucien Ballard

What's Up, Doc?   ★★★★★ U
Comedy   1972 · US · Colour · 90mins

This splendidly funny homage to the thirties screwball comedies of Howard Hawks and Preston Sturges has Barbra Streisand as the sexual predator with her eyes on absent-minded musicologist Ryan O'Neal. Director Peter Bogdanovich was never again to touch the heights of cartoonish wit and excitably silly pace and there's a superbly bizarre performance by Madeline Kahn, as O'Neal's fiancée, which is a thing of cutie and a joy forever. ▭

Barbra Streisand *Judy Maxwell* • Ryan O'Neal *Professor Howard Bannister* • Madeline Kahn *Eunice Burns* • Kenneth Mars *Hugh Simon* • Austin Pendleton *Frederick Larrabe* • Sorrell Booke *Harry* • Stefan Gierasch *Fritz* ■ *Dir* Peter Bogdanovich • *Scr* Buck Henry, David Newman, from a story by Peter Bogdanovich • *Editor* Verna Fields

What's Up, Tiger Lily?   ★★★ PG
Action farce   1966 · US/Jap · Colour · 79mins

A year after the sex farce *What's New, Pussycat?* which Woody Allen both appeared in and wrote came this even more questionable comedy, in which he spoofs a Japanese James Bond-style thriller by re-dubbing it with English voices at variance to the action. It's a single-track joke, which soon runs out of steam, but some of the mismatched words work wonderfully well. Contains some violence and swearing. ▭

Woody Allen *Narrator/Host/Voice* • Tatsuya Mihashi *Phil Moscowitz* • Mie Hama *Terri Yaki* • Akiko Wakabayashi *Suki Yaki* • Tadao Nakamaru *Shepherd Wong* • Susumu Kurobe *Wing Fat* • China Lee • Frank Buxton • Len Maxwell • Louise Lasser ■ *Dir* Senkichi Taniguchi • *Scr* Woody Allen, Frank Buxton, Len Maxwell, Louise Lasser, Mickey Rose, Bryna Wilson, Julie Bennett, from a film by Kazuo Yamada

The Wheeler Dealers   ★★★ U
Comedy caper   1963 · US · Colour · 104mins

James Garner goes to Wall Street. A shrewd hick from the sticks, he's in his most likeable mode as a Texas tycoon showing New York business girl Lee Remick how to make a bundle from a non-existent product. There's a whole lot of chicanery going on, but director Arthur Hiller manoeuvres his comedy options with a shrewd hand.

James Garner *Henry Tyroon* • Lee Remick *Molly Thatcher* • Phil Harris *Ray Jay* • Chill Wills *Jay Ray* • Charles Watts *JR* • Jim Backus *Bullard Bear* • Patricia Crowley [Pat Crowley] *Eloise* • John Astin *Hector Vanson* ■ *Dir* Arthur Hiller • *Scr* George JW Goodman, Ira Wallach, from the novel by George JW Goodman

Wheels of Terror   ★ 15
Action thriller   1990 · US · Colour · 100mins

This derivative thriller pits a menacing black car against a feisty school bus driver (Joanna Cassidy), who says her 12-year-old daughter has been kidnapped by the automobile. Everyone thinks she's nuts, so she has to try and rescue her daughter herself. A formulaic piece of rubbish that

blatantly attempts to cash in on the success of Steven Spielberg's excellent *Duel* and fails miserably on all fronts. ▭

Joanna Cassidy *Laura MacKenzie* • Marcie Leeds *Stephanie MacKenzie* • Arlen Dean Snyder *Detective Drummond* • Sharon Thomas Amy Donaldson ■ *Dir* Christopher Cain • *Scr* Alan B McElroy

Wheels on Meals   ★★★ 15
Martial arts comedy thriller
1984 · HK · Colour · 104mins

Swinging wildly from full-speed action to dozy interludes, this is an extremely strange mix of comedy, romance and kung fu. Jackie Chan plays one of two brothers who run a fast-food business in Spain. It reaches a witty high by spoofing *The Three Musketeers*, yet even during the longueurs there is a sense of the weird which keeps the film ticking. There's also an explosive one-on-one fight between Chan and American martial artist Benny "The Jet" Urquidez (seen to similar effect in *Grosse Pointe Blank*). Cantonese dialogue dubbed into English. Contains violence and some swearing. ▭

Jackie Chan *Thomas* • Sammo Hung *Moby* • Yuen Biao *David* • Lola Forner *Sylvia* • Susanna Sentis *Gloria* • Pepe Sancho *Mondale* ■ *Dir* Sammo Hung • *Scr* Edward Tang, Johnny Lee

When a Man Loves a Woman   ★★ 15
Drama   1994 · US · Colour · 131mins

In this sobering drama, Meg Ryan proves no more adept portraying a drunk than she was playing an action heroine in 1996's *Courage under Fire*. As a wife and mother attempting to face life without the consolation of a bottle, she's guilty of trying too hard to convince. Andy Garcia is hardly more impressive as her insensitive husband, while Ellen Burstyn is wasted in a brief appearance as Ryan's mother. There's nothing about these people to make you care what happens to them, and ultimately the film drowns in its own good intentions. Contains some swearing. ▭ *DVD*

Andy Garcia *Michael Green* • Meg Ryan *Alice Green* • Ellen Burstyn *Emily* • Tina Majorino *Jess Green* • Mae Whitman *Casey Green* • Lauren Tom *Amy* • Philip Seymour Hoffman *Gary* ■ *Dir* Luis Mandoki • *Scr* Ronald Bass, Al Franken

When a Stranger Calls   ★★ 15
Horror chiller   1979 · US · Colour · 93mins

Don't watch the opening of this suspense shocker alone. The build-up of claustrophobic tension is near-masterly, as a baby-sitter, alone in a dark house, is terrorised by a crank call from a homicidal maniac lurking in a room upstairs! But after that blistering beginning, Fred Walton's film stalls badly – with the killer escaping years later to wreak havoc upon the same woman – and only truly comes alive again in the last reel. The interesting cast features Charles Durning as the cop determined to get his man and Tony Beckley as the very British psycho, well before it became fashionable for British actors to play the Hollywood villain. ▭

Charles Durning *John Clifford* • Carol Kane *Jill Johnson* • Tony Beckley *Curt Duncan* • Colleen Dewhurst *Tracy* • Rachel Roberts *Dr Monk* • Ron O'Neal *Lt Garber* • Bill Boyett *Sgt Sacker* • Kirsten Larkin *Nancy* ■ *Dir* Fred Walton • *Scr* Steve Feke, Fred Walton

When a Stranger Calls Back   ★★★ 15
Horror thriller   1993 · US · Colour · 89mins

In *When a Stranger Calls*, Carol Kane was scared out of her wits by threatening phone calls coming from within the house in which she was baby-sitting. Now she finds herself helping one of her college students cope with the threat of a stalker. But no sooner does she take on the case than she becomes the target herself. Director Fred Walton produces a couple of chilling bookends to this patchy TV movie sequel, but wastes too much time on false shocks and red herrings to really get us hooked. Contains swearing, violence and brief nudity. ▭

Carol Kane *Jill Johnson* • Charles Durning *John Clifford* • Jill Schoelen *Julia Jenz* • Gene Lythgow *The stranger* • Karen Austin *Skid row Woman* • Babs Chula *Agent* ■ *Dir* Fred Walton • *Scr* Fred Walton, from characters created by Steve Feke, Fred Walton

When Danger Follows You Home   ★★ 12
Thriller   1997 · US · Colour · 88mins

JoBeth Williams stars as a divorced mother who juggles the demands of her job as a psychiatric social worker with family obligations. An encounter with a troubled but brilliant young patient sparks a series of mysterious events culminating in a murder. She then becomes the prime suspect, forcing her to solve the crime. Directed with skill by David Peckinpah (his debut feature), it's based on a story by popular mystery novelist Sara Paretsky. While the ending is never much in doubt, the journey there has enough twists to keep you entertained. Contains some swearing and violence.

JoBeth Williams *Anne Werden* • Michael Manasseri *Gogol* • William Russ *Detective Barnes* • Vanessa King *Julie Werden* • Bill Switzer *Andrew Werden* • Susan Hogan *Alicia* • Duncan Fraser *Dr Lensky* ■ *Dir* David Peckinpah • *Scr* Sharon Elizabeth Doyle, from a story by Sara Paretsky

When Dinosaurs Ruled the Earth   ★★★ PG
Prehistoric adventure
1969 · UK · Colour · 92mins

Hammer's sequel to *One Million Years BC* doesn't star Raquel Welch or Ray Harryhausen's marvellous special effects, but it's still pretty solid entertainment. *Playboy* playmate Victoria Vetri wears the fur bikini this time and American stop-motion animation expert Jim Danforth supplies the prehistoric monster battles. With no more than 27 words of dialogue between them, rival tribe members Vetri and Robin Hawdon fall in love, escape death and cope with the harsh elements (thanks to the formation of the Moon). They also make love in caves and ward off baby dinosaurs, pterodactyls and giant crabs. The sort of dotty, endearing and exotic fun that

only Hammer in its heyday could possibly make. ▭

Victoria Vetri *Sanna* • Robin Hawdon *Tara* • Patrick Allen *Kingsor* • Drewe Henley *Khaku* • Sean Caffrey *Kane* ■ *Dir* Val Guest • *Scr* Val Guest, from a treatment by JG Ballard

When Eight Bells Toll
★★★ 15

Adventure   1971 · UK · Colour · 90mins

Made at an early stage in Anthony Hopkins's film career, this Alistair MacLean adaptation gave him one of his rare opportunities to play an action hero. Investigating a case of piracy, he plays his naval agent as a single-minded professional, intent on doing the job without falling for the high-life distractions that other spies are prone to. Consequently, he's a rather charmless hero and, as the story (adapted by MacLean himself) simply isn't exciting enough to set pulses racing without some Bond-like fun, we find ourselves longing for more of Robert Morley's delicious comic turn as Hopkins's spymaster. Contains violence. ▭

Anthony Hopkins *Philip Calvert* • Robert Morley *Sir Arthur Arnold-Jones* • Jack Hawkins *Sir Anthony Skouras* • Nathalie Delon *Charlotte Skouras* • Corin Redgrave *Hunslett* • Derek Bond *Lord Charnley* • Ferdy Mayne *Lavorski* • Maurice Roëves *Helicopter pilot* ■ *Dir* Etienne Périer • *Scr* Alistair MacLean, from his novel

When Father Was Away on Business
★★★★ 15

Drama   1985 · Yug · Colour · 130mins

Written by Bosnian poet Abdulah Sidran, this Oscar-nominated drama was the surprise winner of the Palme d'Or at Cannes. In fifties Sarajevo, no one is safe from wagging tongues and spiteful vendettas and Miki Manojlovic is arrested by his own brother-in-law. Told from the half-comprehending perspective of his son, Moreno D'e Bartolli, this naturalistic insight into Tito's Yugoslavia in the last days of Stalinism compels thanks to Emir Kusturica's assured blend of satire, whimsy and harsh historical comment. The harrowing circumcision, whoring and rape scenes stand as startling metaphors for the corruption, brutality and treachery of the period. A Serbo-Croatian language film. ▭

Moreno D'e Bartolli *Malik* • Miki Manojlovic *Mesa* • Mirjana Karanovic *Senija* ■ *Dir* Emir Kusturica • *Scr* Abdulah Sidran

When Harry Met Sally...
★★★★★ 15

Romantic comedy
1989 · US · Colour · 91mins

This movie's fake-orgasm-in-a-deli set piece, which propelled Meg Ryan into stratospheric stardom, is so famous that it's useful to be reminded of the numerous other pleasures to be found in Nora Ephron's Oscar-nominated screenplay, Rob Reiner's astute direction, and the felicitous teaming of Ryan and Billy Crystal. Essentially concerned with the sweet meetings and partings of two college graduates over a decade or so as life and love take their toll, it wittily and romantically argues the question whether men and women can ever have friendship

without sex. In truth, the movie, with its glitzy New York locations and beguiling soundtrack of popular standards, offers a cutesy, superficial and glamorised excursion into Woody Allen territory, but triumphs as expert and irresistible escapist entertainment. Crystal is perfect, while supporting stars Carrie Fisher and Bruno Kirby are outstanding and add a welcome suggestion of edge. ▭

Billy Crystal *Harry Burns* • Meg Ryan *Sally Albright* • Carrie Fisher *Marie* • Bruno Kirby *Jess* • Steven Ford *Joe* • Lisa Jane Persky *Alice* ■ *Dir* Rob Reiner • *Scr* Nora Ephron

When He's Not a Stranger
★★★

Drama   1989 · US · Colour · 100mins

This carefully scripted and skilfully acted drama shows how to bring a controversial topic to the audience's attention without resorting to either soapbox or soap opera. Director John Gray and his co-writer Beth Sullivan expertly convey the sense of shame, anger and fear felt by a rape victim, intensifying it by the enclosed setting of a college campus and by having the assailant be the boyfriend of the victim's best friend. John Terlesky is loathsomely arrogant and unrepentant, but it's Annabeth Gish's understated performance that holds the film together.

Annabeth Gish *Lyn McKenna* • John Terlesky *Ron Cooper* • Kevin Dillon *Rick Fiorentino* • Paul Dooley *Mr McKenna* • Kim Myers *Melanie Fairchild* ■ *Dir* John Gray • *Scr* John Gray, Beth Sullivan

When Knights Were Bold
★★

Musical comedy   1936 · UK · BW · 57mins

Film version of a (then) famous West End play by Charles Marlowe with Jack Buchanan teamed with Hollywood actress Fay Wray. A satire on the British aristocracy, Buchanan plays a soldier in India who inherits a vast English estate and returns there and dreams he is the chain-mailed reincarnation of an ancestor, a medieval warlord who, being Buchanan, can also sing and tap dance. It's dated, of course.

Jack Buchanan *Sir Guy De Vere* • Fay Wray *Lady Rowena* • Garry Marsh *Brian Ballymote* • Kate Cutler *Aunt Agatha* • Martita Hunt *Aunt Esther* • Robert Horton *Cousin Bertie* • Aubrey Mather *Canon* • Aubrey Fitzgerald *Barker* ■ *Dir* Jack Raymond • *Scr* Austin Parker, Douglas Furber, from the play by Charles Marlowe

When Ladies Meet
★★★★

Comedy drama   1933 · US · BW · 73mins

Successful lady novelist Myrna Loy falls desperately in love with her publisher, Frank Morgan, and spurns her devoted suitor, newspaper reporter Robert Montgomery. However, when she meets Morgan's wife, Ann Harding, without knowing who she is, matters come to a head. Adapted from a stage play and directed by Harry Beaumont, this is an intelligent, sophisticated romantic comedy drama of the highest level, exquisitely played – especially by the sublime and undeservedly forgotten Harding – marvellously designed and dressed,

and boasting supporting performances to match the stars.

Ann Harding *Claire Woodruf* • Robert Montgomery *Jimmy Lee* • Myrna Loy *Mary Howard* • Alice Brady *Bridget Drake* • Frank Morgan *Rogers Woodruf* • Martin Burton *Walter Manning* • Sterling Holloway *Jerome* ■ *Dir* Harry Beaumont • *Scr* John Meehan, Leon Gordon, from the play by Rachel Crothers • *Art Director* Cedric Gibbons • *Costume Designer* Adrian

When Ladies Meet
★★

Comedy   1941 · US · BW · 105mins

Directed by Robert Z Leonard and sticking more or less to the original 1933 version for its dialogue and situations, this updated remake of what was a stylish look at the consequences of a lady novelist's love for her married publisher coarsens the bitingly sharp original, even vulgarising the settings. Joan Crawford makes a decent fist of the leading character (while battling an ugly lapse in Adrian's clothes sense), Greer Garson is probably the best substitute for Ann Harding, and Robert Taylor is fine as the newsman who loves Crawford. Only the usually impeccable Herbert Marshall as the publisher lover, looking anything but a womaniser and clearly and understandably embarrassed by his dialogue, fails to convince. Entertaining enough if you haven't seen the earlier film.

Joan Crawford *Mary Howard* • Robert Taylor (1) *Jimmy Lee* • Greer Garson *Claire Woodruff* • Herbert Marshall *Rogers Woodruff* • Spring Byington *Bridget Drake* • Rafael Storm *Walter Del Canto* • Max Willenz *Pierre* ■ *Dir* Robert Z Leonard • *Scr* SK Lauren, Anita Loos, from the play by Rachel Crothers • *Costume Designer* Adrian

When London Sleeps
★★

Crime drama   1932 · UK · BW · 70mins

Well, it probably didn't take the city's residents long to nod off when they were watching this creaky old British thriller. The workhorse of Twickenham Studios, Leslie Hiscott is often cited as the director who brought "quota quickies" into disrepute. The seventh of the ten films he churned out in 1932, this sounds as if it should have been a documentary about repairing the Underground. Instead, it's a trashy tale in which only gambler Harold French can save wealthy heiress René Ray from the clutches of her villainous cousin, Francis L Sullivan. In Hiscott's defence, the action rattles along, but it's poor stuff.

Harold French *Tommy Blythe* • Francis L Sullivan *Rodney Haines* • René Ray *Mary* • A Bromley Davenport *Colonel Grahame* • Alexander Field *Sam* • Diana Beaumont *Hilda* • Ben Field *Lamberti* • Barbara Everest *Mme Lamberti* • Herbert Lomas *Pollard* ■ *Dir* Leslie Hiscott • *Scr* Bernard Merivale, H Fowler Mear, from a play by Charles Darrell

When My Baby Smiles at Me
★★★★

Musical   1948 · US · Colour · 97mins

Though largely forgotten nowadays, Dan Dailey was nominated as best actor at the 1948 Academy Awards for his performance in this film, alongside Montgomery Clift for *The Search* and Laurence Olivier, the eventual winner, for *Hamlet*. Dailey is magnificent in

this remake of the hoary old Broadway play *Burlesque*, which had already been filmed twice, as *The Dance of Life* and *Swing High, Swing Low*. Top-billed Betty Grable isn't Dailey's equal in the drama stakes, though they regularly co-starred in lightweight 20th Century-Fox musicals, but she tries hard, and director Walter Lang knows well enough when to sit back and let the actors get on with it. In all, a very satisfying movie.

Betty Grable *Bonny* • Dan Dailey *Skid* • Jack Oakie *Bozo* • June Havoc *Gussie* • Richard Arlen *Harvey* • James Gleason *Lefty* • Vanita Wade *Bubbles* ■ *Dir* Walter Lang • *Scr* Elizabeth Reinhardt, Lamar Trotti, from the play *Burlesque* by George Manker Watters, Arthur Hopkins

When Night Is Falling
★★★ 18

Drama   1995 · Can · Colour · 89mins

A companion piece to *I've Heard the Mermaids Singing*, this is a less obviously comic and far more sensual study of lesbian awakening from Patricia Rozema. From its contrived beginning, the romance follows along overly familiar lines, in spite of a soaringly seductive hang-gliding sequence. But the performances of tempestuous circus artist Rachael Crawford and prissy Protestant academic Pascale Bussières give it a sensitivity and truth to match its rising passion. Henry Czerny is also impressive as Bussières's colleague and confused lover, whose response to his cuckolding provides this dreamily photographed but gushingly scripted and symbolically clumsy film's one significant surprise. ▭

Pascale Bussières *Camille* • Rachael Crawford *Petra* • Henry Czerny *Martin* • David Fox *Reverend DeBoer* • Don McKellar *Timothy* • Tracy Wright *Tory* • Clare Coulter *Tillie* ■ *Dir/Scr* Patricia Rozema

When Saturday Comes
★★★ 15

Sports drama   1995 · UK · Colour · 94mins

Football and cinema have never been the best of bedfellows. However, anyone who can look back nostalgically at *Roy of the Rovers* will lap up this unashamedly clichéd rags-to-riches tale. Sean Bean obviously relished every minute of his role here as the working-class lad who is plucked from obscurity by wise old talent scout Peter Postlethwaite to play in the big time. Along the way he wins and loses his mentor's niece (Emily Lloyd) and even gets the chance to indulge in some *Rocky*-style training. Contains swearing, and some sexual situations. ▭

Sean Bean *Jimmy Muir* • Emily Lloyd *Annie Doherty* • Pete Postlethwaite *Ken Jackson* • Craig Kelly *Russell Muir* • John McEnery *Joe Muir* ■ *Dir/Scr* Maria Giese

When the Bough Breaks
★★★

Drama   1947 · UK · BW · 80mins

Gainsborough turned from costume melodrama to contemporary problem picture with this story aimed firmly at female picturegoers. Patricia Roc is the working-class woman who allows her child to be adopted by middle-class

Rosamund John and years later wants the boy back. Should he be plucked from his comfortable existence and promising future to live with his real mother in poverty? Either way, it's a tear-jerker, made on the cheap but forcefully acted and ably directed by Lawrence Huntington.

Patricia Roc *Lily Bates* • Rosamund John *Frances Norman* • Bill Owen *Bill* • Brenda Bruce *Ruby Chapman* • Patrick Holt *Robert Norman* • Cavan Malone *George* ■ *Dir* Lawrence Huntington • *Scr* Peter Rogers, Muriel Box, Sydney Box, from a story by Moie Charles, Herbert Victor

When the Bough Breaks★★

Thriller   1986 · US · Colour · 100mins
A respectable enough adaptation of a bestselling crime novel by Jonathan Kellerman, even though it loses some of its potency in being a made-for-TV thriller. Ted Danson, who also serves as executive producer, takes the lead role of a psychologist pitting his wits against an evil paedophile ring. There is a strong supporting cast (Richard Masur, David Huddleston) and it will go down a treat with *Cracker* fans.

Ted Danson *Dr Alex Delaware* • Richard Masur *Milo Sturgis* • Rachel Ticotin *Raquel Santos* • Marcie Leeds *Melody Quinn* • James Noble *Dr Warren Towle* • Kim Miyori *Kim Hickle* • David Huddleston *Reverend McCaffrey* ■ *Dir* Waris Hussein • *Scr* Phil Penningroth, from the novel by Jonathan Kellerman

When the Boys Meet the Girls ★★ U

Comedy   1965 · US · Colour · 96mins
Escaping from a showgirl suing him for breach of promise, womanising playboy Danny Churchill (Harve Presnell) travels out of harm's way to a college in the Nevada backwoods. Once there he meets local girl Ginger (Connie Francis) and gets involved in the problems she and her father are having with the latter's gambling debts, turning their farm into a dude ranch for divorcees in order to bring in the money they need. This updated remake of the twice-filmed stage musical *Girl Crazy* is poor despite the five George and Ira Gershwin numbers that survive from the original, although guest stars Herman's Hermits, Louis Armstrong and Liberace provide some novelty value.

Connie Francis *Ginger* • Harve Presnell *Danny* • Sue Ane Langdon *Tess* • Fred Clark *Bill* • Frank Faylen *Phin* • Joby Baker *Sam* • Hortense Petra *Kate* • Stanley Adams *Lank* ■ *Dir* Alvin Ganzer • *Scr* Robert E Kent, from the musical *Girl Crazy* by Guy Bolton, John McGowan

When the Bullet Hits the Bone ★★ 18

Action thriller   1995 · Can · Colour · 88mins
This is a violent but unerringly predictable reprise of that familiar tale of one man taking a stand against the bad guys. Minor-league martial arts star Jeff Wincott is the implausible doctor who decides to launch a one-man war against dope dealers after coming to the aid of the mistress (Michelle Johnson) of the drug kingpin. There's a high body count but even that can't distract from the lazy scripting. 💬

Jeff Wincott *Jack Davies* • Michelle Johnson *Lisa* • Doug O'Keeffe *Nick Turner* • Torri Higginson *Allison* • Roy Lewis *Daemon* • Phillip Jarrett *Trevor* ■ *Dir/Scr* Damian Lee

When the Cradle Falls ★★

Thriller   1997 · US · Colour · 87mins
Director Paul Schneider is no stranger to sleazy TV-movie fare, having already made *Honor Thy Father and Mother: the Menendez Killings*. He's in slightly tamer fictional territory here, although there's still plenty of melodrama in this thriller about a young couple (Scott Reeves, Martha Byrne) who find themselves the prime suspects when their baby disappears. What part the sinister Linda Gray (of *Dallas* fame) and Cathy Lee Crosby play in the affair adds to the moderately enjoyable hokum.

Linda Gray *Helen Sawyer* • Scott Reeves *Brian McDermott* • Cathy Lee Crosby *Joan Hollins* • Martha Byrne *Donna McDermott* • Karl Makinen *Hammack* • Brigitta Dau *Rachel* • Joel De La Fuente *Bill* ■ *Dir* Paul Schneider • *Scr* Rob Hedden

When the Daltons Rode ★★★

Biographical western
1940 · US · BW · 80mins
One of the classy big-budget westerns of its time, this rousing adventure pays little heed to historic truth as it re-creates the lives and times of the notorious Dalton gang, taking its leads, Randolph Scott and Brian Donlevy, from the previous year's big hit *Jesse James*. The elegant and sophisticated Kay Francis is stunning, and Scott is sturdy as the lawyer out to give the outlaws a fair trial, but the real treats in this movie are the superb stunts, involving jumps from horseback on to moving trains, which have seldom if ever been equalled. *Destry Rides Again* director George Marshall had already proved that he was a dab hand at material like this.

Randolph Scott *Tod Jackson* • Kay Francis *Julie King* • Brian Donlevy *Grat Dalton* • George Bancroft *Caleb Winters* • Broderick Crawford *Bob Dalton* • Stuart Erwin *Ben Dalton* • Andy Devine *Ozark* • Frank Albertson *Emmett Dalton* ■ *Dir* George Marshall • *Scr* Harold Schumate, Lester Cole, Stuart Anthony, from the non-fiction book by Emmett Dalton, Jack Jungmeyer Sr

When the Dark Man Calls ★★ 15

Thriller   1995 · US · Colour · 85mins
This above-average psychological thriller depicts a nightmarish scenario in which a beautiful talk show psychologist (Joan Van Ark) is threatened by the man convicted of killing her parents. When he is murdered on being released from prison, she has to move quickly to discover the identity of the killer, and in doing so uncovers dark and deadly family secrets. The strong cast includes Geoffrey Lewis as the brooding ex-con and Chris Sarandon as Van Ark's disturbed brother, while Van Ark herself does a nice job with what could have been a routine role. This TV film never belabours its woman-in-jeopardy clichés, and achieves a frightening intensity in the stalking

scenes. It's sophisticated and compelling fare that won't leave you in the dark. 💬

Joan Van Ark *Julie Kaiser* • James Read *Detective Michael Lieberman* • Geoffrey Lewis *Parmenter* • Chris Sarandon *Lloyd Carson* • Barry Flatman *Max Kaiser* • Frances Hyland *Dr Martha Petrie* ■ *Dir* Nathaniel Gutman • *Scr* Pablo F Fenjves, from a novel by Stuart M Kaminsky

When the Legends Die ★★★★

Western drama 1972 · US · Colour · 105mins
One of those fly-blown modern westerns so full of atmosphere that you can almost smell the apple pie festering on the empty diner's counter. But this beautifully constructed piece is far more than mere effective staging and the central performances from Richard Widmark and Frederic Forrest are quite simply superb. In this complex web of conflicting desires and loyalties Widmark's dissolute drunk stands out as a man riven by emotional pain, while Forrest's talented young Indian rodeo rider is the perfect foil. Director Stuart Millar proves that you don't have to take the easiest options to produce a popular western.

Richard Widmark *Red Dillon* • Frederic Forrest *Tom Black Bull* • Luana Anders *Mary* • Vito Scotti *Meo* • Herbert Nelson *Dr Wilson* • John War Eagle *Blue Elk* • John Gruber *Tex Walker* ■ *Dir* Stuart Millar • *Scr* Robert Dozier, from the novel by Hal Borland

When the Party's Over ★★ 15

Drama   1992 · US · Colour · 110mins
There's something here, but you have to wade through an awful lot of twentysomething angst to find it. Three women and a gay man share a house in LA, and through the various flashbacks to which we are subjected, it's established that none of them are very nice people. Sandra Bullock and Rae Dawn Chong lend some limited class to this tale of desperation and manipulation, but in the end it's too confusing, petty, and exploitative to maintain interest. 💬

Elizabeth Berridge *Frankie* • Rae Dawn Chong *M J* • Sandra Bullock *Amanda* • Kris Kamm *Banks* • Brian McNamara *Taylor* • Fisher Stevens *Alexander* • Michael Landes *Willie* ■ *Dir* Matthew Irmas • *Scr* Ann Wycoff, from a story by Matthew Irmas, Ann Wycoff

When the Sky Falls ★★★ 18

Biographical drama
2000 · US · Colour · 107mins
This thinly disguised biography of Veronica Guerin, the crusading Irish journalist shot dead by the Dublin criminals she sought to expose, marks a return to form for director John Mackenzie (*The Long Good Friday*). Joan Allen stars as Sinead Hamilton, a wife and mother whose single-minded determination to bring the city's gangsters to justice becomes increasingly perilous for both herself and her family. Despite having an American lead, Mackenzie resists the temptation to Hollywood things up, while Allen brings a conviction and depth to her performance that make up for her rather shaky Oirish accent.

Joan Allen *Sinead Hamilton* • Patrick Bergin *Mackey* • Jimmy Smallhome *Mickey O'Fagan* • Liam Cunningham *The Runner* • Kevin McNally *Tom Hamilton* • Pete Postlethwaite *Martin Shaughnessy* • Jason Barry *Dempsey* ■ *Dir* John Mackenzie • *Scr* Michael Sheridan, Ronan Gallagher, Colum McCann

When the Time Comes ★★★ 15

Drama   1987 · US · Colour · 94mins
That staple of the TV movie, terminal disease, is given a respectable outing in this highly emotive drama, directed by John Erman, who seems to specialise in telling similar stories of bravery in the face of suffering. Bonnie Bedelia plays a woman who is dying slowly and painfully of cancer. Determined to die with dignity, rather than be kept alive by machines, she asks her husband (Terry O'Quinn) to help her by obtaining the necessary drugs. When her husband refuses, she turns to a friend (Brad Davis) and then her sister (Karen Austin). Pain and anguish pile up as the movie asks, with remarkable directness: "Well, what would you do?" 💬

Bonnie Bedelia *Lydie Travis* • Terry O'Quinn *Wes* • Brad Davis *Dean* • Karen Austin *Joanna* • Donald Moffat *Harold* • Wendy Schaal *Laura* • Corey Carrier *Jess* ■ *Dir* John Erman • *Scr* William Hanley

When the Whales Came ★★★ U

Drama   1989 · UK · Colour · 95mins
A modest but touching drama set in the Scilly Isles at the start of the First World War, with Paul Scofield in a rare feature film role. He plays an elderly loner, hiding away from the world on a small island, who is befriended by two curious children. The story is slight, but it is attractively directed by Clive Rees, who draws refreshingly natural performances from young leads Helen Pearce and Max Rennie. A galaxy of familiar British faces lend solid support, including Helen Mirren, John Hallam and David Suchet.

Paul Scofield *The Birdman* • Helen Mirren *Clemmie Jenkins* • Helen Pearce *Gracie Jenkins* • Max Rennie *Daniel Pender* • David Suchet *Will* • Kerra Spowart *Margaret Pender* • Barbara Ewing *Mary Pender* • John Hallam *Treve Pender* • Barbara Jefford *Auntie Mildred* • David Threlfall *Jack Jenkins* ■ *Dir* Clive Rees • *Scr* Michael Morpurgo, from his novel

When the Wind Blows ★★★★ PG

Animation   1986 · UK · Colour · 80mins
With the threat of Armageddon now, hopefully, behind us, this adaptation of Raymond Briggs's chilling cartoon book seems rather quaint. However, the fact that few of us know how to conduct ourselves should there be a nuclear winter is powerfully brought home in the superbly told story. Animator Jimmy T Murakami's decision to use flat figures against three-dimensional backgrounds hauntingly begs the question "it can't happen here, can it?", while the disarmingly charming voice-overs of John Mills and Peggy Ashcroft, recalling more innocent conflicts, add poignancy to the proceedings. Clever, credible and, ultimately, heartbreaking. 💬

Peggy Ashcroft *Hilda Bloggs* • John Mills *Jim Bloggs* • Robin Houston *Announcer* ■ *Dir* Jimmy T Murakami • *Scr* Raymond Briggs, from his comic book

When Time Expires ★★

Science-fiction drama
1997 · US · Colour · 95mins
Why has disgraced alien troubleshooter Richard Grieco been sent back in time to feed a parking meter in a small Nevada town? The answer to that question pits him and his former partner Mark Hamill against a team of sinister assassins determined to stop them fulfilling their puzzling mission. Initially intriguing before becoming increasingly daft, the ideas behind this shaky TV movie were used to far better effect in *Back to the Future* and *The Terminator*. This relies too heavily on Grieco's charisma, while the cavalier treatment of time-travel rules is annoying. However, Tim Thomerson makes a good show as the baddie. Contains violence, swearing and brief nudity.

Richard Grieco *Travis Beck* • Cynthia Geary *June Kelly* • Mark Hamill *Bill Thermot* • Tim Thomerson *Rifkin Koss* • Ron Masak *TV evangelist* • Pat Corley *TV car salesman* • Chad Everett *Walter Kelly* ■ *Dir/Scr* David Bourla

When Time Ran Out ★ PG

Adventure   1980 · US · Colour · 104mins
Irwin Allen, the producer of *The Poseidon Adventure* and *The Towering Inferno*, rehashed the disaster formula yet again with this clinker about a volcano that threatens to trash a luxury holiday resort. Paul Newman takes the Gene Hackman role, leading his co-stars and their associated subplots to possible safety, while William Holden, as per *Inferno*, is the tycoon who owns the hotel. Both stars have a certain craggy appeal and a twinkle in their eyes that betrays a lofty fee. The eruption, when it finally comes, is a wonderfully cheesy amalgam of wobbly back projection, bathtub tidal wave and scared expressions from the cast. Not as hilariously awful as *Swarm* or *Meteor*, though, which is a pity. ▨

Paul Newman *Hank Anderson* • Jacqueline Bisset *Kay Kirby* • William Holden (1) *Shelby Gilmore* • Edward Albert *Brian* • Red Buttons *Francis Fendly* • Barbara Carrera *Iolani* • Burgess Meredith *Rene Valdez* • Ernest Borgnine *Tom Conti* • James Franciscus *Bob Spangler* ■ *Dir* James Goldstone • *Scr* Carl Foreman, Stirling Silliphant, from the novel *The Day the World Ended* by Gordon Thomas, Max Morgan Witts • *Music* Lalo Schifrin

When Tomorrow Comes ★★★

Romantic melodrama
1939 · US · BW · 91mins
John M Stahl, producer, director, and specialist in romantic melodrama, hired Irene Dunne and Charles Boyer after their phenomenal success in RKO's *Love Affair* earlier in the year for this tale of a waitress and a concert pianist who meet when she serves him in a restaurant. Friendship turns to love when they're stranded in a Long Island church during a hurricane. Boyer, however, turns out to have a wife (Barbara O'Neil) who has lost her mind – a cue for Dunne to become a

noble heroine à la *Back Street* (a 1932 Stahl-Dunne smash). A clichéd weepie, but impeccably assembled and irresistible.

Irene Dunne *Helen* • Charles Boyer *Philip AndréChagal* • Barbara O'Neil *Madeleine* • Onslow Stevens *Holden* • Nydia Westman *Lulu* • Nella Walker *Madame Dumont* ■ *Dir* John M Stahl • *Scr* Dwight Taylor, from a story by James M Cain

When Trumpets Fade ★★★★ 15

Second World War drama
1998 · US · Colour · 92mins
This made-for-cable film based on a true story plays like a fine arthouse feature, with some genuinely gripping and novel situations. Not a run-of-the-mill war film, but an intimate and powerful study of the moral complexities and horrors of battle. During the winter of 1944, in western Germany, an emotionally and physically exhausted American private (Ron Eldard) is promoted against his will when he serendipitously survives as the rest of his comrades die around him. Whether or not he's a hero, coward or pure victim of circumstance is the point of this searingly affecting film, which dramatises one of the most senseless battles of the Second World War. Given both intelligence and power by the sure-handed direction of John Irvin, this is wise, affecting television that should not be missed. Contains swearing, violence and brief nudity. ▨

Ron Eldard *Private David Manning* • Frank Whaley *Medic Chamberlain* • Zak Orth *Warren Sanderson* • Dylan Bruno *Sergeant Talbot* • Martin Donovan *Captain Pritchett* • Dwight Yoakam *Lieutenant Colonel* ■ *Dir* John Irvin • *Scr* WW Vought

When We Were Kings ★★★★★ PG

Sports documentary
1996 · US · Colour · 83mins
The experts had Muhammad Ali out for the count even before he stepped into the ring against George Foreman in Zaire in 1974. But the "Rumble in the Jungle" turned out to be anything but a "Disaster in Kinshasa", as Ali fought his way to a remarkable victory. Leon Gast's Oscar-winning documentary not only focuses on Ali the athlete, but also examines his importance to the African-American community at large. With telling contributions from Norman Mailer, George Plimpton and Spike Lee, and footage from the soul concerts that accompanied the big bout, this exceptional film proves beyond any doubt that Ali was "The Greatest". ▨

Dir Leon Gast

When Willie Comes Marching Home ★★★

Comedy   1950 · US · BW · 82mins
John Ford may be remembered best for making westerns, but he also made dramas, war movies and, though it is sometimes forgotten, comedies, of which this is a prime example. It wasn't his most natural genre, but this is still a competent, likeable and even funny movie about the ups and downs of a small-town boy during the Second

World War. Dan Dailey does well in the title role, while an intelligent screenplay by Mary Loos and Richard Sale has some thoughtful things to say about wartime patriotism and the hunger for heroes.

Dan Dailey *Bill Kluggs* • Corinne Calvet *Yvonne* • Colleen Townsend *Marge Fettles* • William Demarest *Herman Kluggs* • James Lydon *Charles Fettles* • Lloyd Corrigan *Mayor Adams* • Evelyn Varden *Gertrude Kluggs* ■ *Dir* John Ford • *Scr* Mary Loos, Richard Sale, from the story *When Leo Comes Marching Home* by Sy Gomberg

When Worlds Collide ★★★ U

Science-fiction adventure
1951 · US · Colour · 78mins
From *War of the Worlds* producer George Pal, this paranoid parable about earth's imminent collision with a runaway planet – the only hope of survival being a Noah's Ark expedition to a satellite moon – is a prime example of fifties science-fiction. Compensating for the bland script and generally uninspired cast are the Oscar-winning special effects – especially the destruction of New York – and Rudolph Maté's arresting direction, which exploits the "end of the world" concept to the maximum. ▨

Richard Derr *David Randall* • Barbara Rush *Joyce Hendron* • Larry Keating *Dr Cole Hendron* • Peter Hanson *Dr Tony Drake* • John Hoyt *Sydney Stanton* • Stephen Chase *Dean Frye* • Judith Ames *Julie Cummings* ■ *Dir* Rudolph Maté • *Scr* Sydney Boehm, Philip Wylie, from the novel *When Worlds Collide* by Edwin Balmer

When You Come Home ★ U

Comedy   1947 · UK · BW · 97mins
Director John Baxter, once Britain's most uncompromising disciple of social realism, hit his cinematic nadir with this desperate flashback comedy. Rarely able to project his popular music-hall persona into movies, Frank Randle comes across as a colossal bore in this nostalgic wallow as he regales his granddaughter with tall tales from his chequered past. Adding to the torment are the songs, co-composed by Randle's co-stars, the two Leslies, Sarony and Holmes. For fans and movie masochists only.

Frank Randle • Leslie Sarony *First songwriter* • Leslie Holmes *Second songwriter* • Diana Decker *Paula Ryngelbaum* • Fred Conyngham *Mike O'Flaherty* ■ *Dir* John Baxter • *Scr* David Evans, Geoffrey Orme, Frank Randle

When You Comin' Back, Red Ryder? ★★

Drama   1979 · US · Colour · 91mins
Hopefully never, if this adaptation of Mark Medoff's Broadway play is anything to go by. Former child evangelist Marjoe Gortner plays the psychopath who, partnered by hippy girlfriend Candy Clark, menaces the patrons of a Texas diner for nearly two hours. Without giving any convincing motivation for Gortner's actions, the story's just unpleasant.

Candy Clark *Cheryl* • Marjoe Gortner *Teddy* • Stephanie Faracy *Angel Childress* • Dixie Harris *Grandma Childress* • Anne Ramsey *Rhea Childress* • Lee Grant *Clarisse Ethridge*

• Hal Linden *Richard Ethridge* • Peter Firth *Stephen Ryder* ■ *Dir* Milton Katselas • *Scr* Mark Medoff, from his play

When You Remember Me ★★ 12

Drama based on a true story
1990 · US · Colour · 90mins
Fred Savage swapped the easy-going nostalgia of the TV series *The Wonder Years* for this punchier role as a teenager suffering from muscular dystrophy who fights the medical establishment when he discovers at first hand what really goes on inside a nursing home. Director Harry Winer too often opts for easy sentimentality but does draw convincing performances from stars Savage, Ellen Burstyn and Kevin Spacey. Contains some swearing. ▨

Fred Savage *Michael Mills* • Kevin Spacey *Wade Black* • Ellen Burstyn *Nurse Cooder* • Richard Jenkins *Vaughan* • Dwier Brown *John Harlen* • Lee Garlington *Joanne Mills* • Virginia Capers *Nurse Blandings* • Ving Rhames *Leon* ■ *Dir* Harry Winer • *Scr* Jerry McNeely, Cynthia Whitcomb, from an article by Rena Dictor

When You're in Love ★★★ U

Musical romantic comedy
1937 · US · BW · 98mins
Robert Riskin was Columbia's ace screenwriter, responsible for such Frank Capra hits as *It Happened One Night* and *Mr Deeds Goes to Town*, and Columbia boss Harry Cohn rewarded him with this opera star Grace Moore vehicle to direct, believing it to be director-proof. Cohn wasn't wrong, but Riskin returned to writing such classics as *Lost Horizon* and *You Can't Take It with You*. Grace Moore was an immensely likeable soprano, sexy and talented, and an ideal partner for screen "hubby" Cary Grant. Her screen potential was never fully realised and here she's both lively and lovely, letting her hair down singing Cab Calloway's immortal *Minnie the Moocher*. The rest of the movie's fun, too, in its period sort of way. ▨

Grace Moore *Louise Fuller* • Cary Grant *Jimmy Hudson* • Aline MacMahon *Marianne Woods* • Henry Stephenson *Walter Mitchell* • Thomas Mitchell *Hank Miller* • Catherine Doucet *Jane Summers* • Luis Alberni *Luis Perugini* • Gerald Oliver Smith *Gerald Meeker* ■ *Dir* Robert Riskin • *Scr* Robert Riskin, from an idea by Ethel Hill, Cedric Worth

Where Angels Fear to Tread ★★★ PG

Drama   1991 · UK · Colour · 107mins
An adaptation of EM Forster's novel brought to the screen by the team responsible for the *Brideshead Revisited* TV drama. It's a classy story about earthy passion and xenophobia, with Helen Mirren as the strong-willed, widowed Englishwoman, Lilia Herriton, who falls in love with Tuscany and acquires a young Italian lover. Back home, her frosty family sinks in shame and sends Rupert Graves to sort things out. The inevitable lashings of dappled Tuscan sunlight and some strong performances by the cast – which also includes Helena Bonham Carter (naturally) and the excellent Judy

Davis, getting a second dose of Forster after *A Passage to India* – add up to the movie equivalent of high tea. ▣

Helena Bonham Carter *Caroline Abbott* • Judy Davis *Harriet Herriton* • Rupert Graves *Philip Herriton* • Helen Mirren *Lilia Herriton* • Giovanni Guidelli *Gino Carella* • Barbara Jefford *Mrs Herriton* • Thomas Wheatley *Mr Kingcroft* ▪ *Dir* Charles Sturridge • *Scr* Tim Sullivan, Derek Granger, Charles Sturridge, from the novel by EM Forster

Where Angels Go...Trouble Follows ★★ ▣

Comedy   1968 · US · Colour · 93mins

Although nun films are generally neither funny nor clever, this sequel to *The Trouble with Angels* (1966) is a pleasant culture clash comedy with Rosalind Russell returning to her role as the Mother Superior, this time trying to keep her young rebellious charges on the straight and narrow on a convent school trip. Look out for Susan Saint James (who later played Rock Hudson's eponymous wife in the television series *McMillan and Wife*) as one of the teenage tearaways.

Rosalind Russell *Mother Simplicia* • Stella Stevens *Sister George* • Binnie Barnes *Sister Celestine* • Mary Wickes *Sister Clarissa* • Dolores Sutton *Sister Rose Marie* • Susan Saint James *Rosabelle* • Barbara Hunter *Marvel Ann Clancy* • Milton Berle *Film director* • Van Johnson *Father Chase* • Robert Taylor (1) *Mr Farriday* ▪ *Dir* James Neilson • *Scr* Blanche Hanalis, from characters created by Jane Trahey

Where Are the Children? ★

Drama   1986 · US · Colour · 92mins

A stupid and overly manipulative whodunit, packed with daft red herrings, in which Jill Clayburgh's children are kidnapped by nasty Frederic Forrest and taken to an old dark house where he intends to kill them. Clayburgh hardly stretches herself in a banal performance that merely requires her to cry a lot. It's understandable when the inane plot takes an even more ludicrous turn – Clayburgh becomes prime suspect because years earlier she was accused of murdering her children from another marriage. Forrest enlivens the monotony by really getting under the skin of the sexually perverse abductor but he's the only plus factor in the whole turgid mess.

Jill Clayburgh *Nancy Eldridge* • Max Gail *Clay Eldridge* • Harley Cross *Michael Eldridge* • Elisabeth Harnois *Missy Eldridge* • Elizabeth Wilson *Dorothy Prentiss* • Barnard Hughes *Jonathan Knowles* • Frederic Forrest *Courtney Parrish* • James Purcell *Robin Legler* ▪ *Dir* Bruce Malmuth • *Scr* Jack Sholder, from the novel by Mary Higgins Clark

Where Danger Lives ★★★

Film noir   1950 · US · BW · 80mins

A minor-league but effective *film noir*, directed by John Farrow and featuring his wife, Maureen O'Sullivan, as well as Robert Mitchum, Claude Rains and Faith Domergue. Mitchum is a doctor, Domergue is his mentally unstable temptress and the open road to Mexico is their refuge, until she thinks maybe she should kill him; after all, she's just done the same to her husband. Slightly reminiscent of Mitchum's earlier and better *Build My Gallows High*, this doomed romance is well worth watching, not least for the way that Mitchum's physical presence is constantly undermined by the plot.

Robert Mitchum *Jeff Cameron* • Faith Domergue *Margo Lannington* • Claude Rains *Frederick Lannington* • Maureen O'Sullivan *Julie* • Charles Kemper *Police Chief* • Ralph Dumke *Klauber* • Billy House *Mr Bogardus* ▪ *Dir* John Farrow • *Scr* Charles Bennett, from a story by Leo Rosten

Where Do We Go from Here? ★★★ ▣

Musical fantasy   1945 · US · Colour · 77mins

An unfairly forgotten musical fantasy that's very much of its time, its satirical barbs numbed by the aftermath of the Second World War. Nevertheless, sympathetically viewed today, it remains a genuinely engaging period piece, and features a clever and neglected score by composing greats Kurt Weill and Ira Gershwin. The main theme involving a genie sending Fred MacMurray back through time is quite affecting, and certainly original. MacMurray and the lovely June Haver (MacMurray's future wife) play sweetly together, and there's interesting support from Anthony Quinn and Otto Preminger. The superb forties Technicolor is especially effective.

Fred MacMurray *Bill* • Joan Leslie *Sally* • June Haver *Lucilla* • Gene Sheldon *Ali* • Anthony Quinn *Indian Chief* • Carlos Ramirez *Benito* • Alan Mowbray *General George Washington* • Fortunio Bonanova *Christopher Columbus* • Otto Preminger *General Rahl* ▪ *Dir* Gregory Ratoff • *Scr* Morrie Ryskind, from a story by Morrie Ryskind, Sig Herzig

Where Does It Hurt? ★

Black comedy   1971 · US · Colour · 87mins

Crooked administrator Albert T Hopfnagel (Peter Sellers) runs his hospital stictly for profit, with the willing help of his motley, under-qualified staff. But one patient, Lester Hammond (Rick Lenz), sees through the charade and is determined to bring Hopfnagel down. A mess of a movie that, if it were a patient, would be on the critical list. Sellers (using the voice of President Nixon for his role) can do little to rescue the piece. Perhaps "everywhere" is an appropriate answer to the titular question.

Peter Sellers *Albert T Hopfnagel* • Jo Ann Pflug *Alice Gilligan* • Rick Lenz *Lester Hammond* • Eve Bruce *Nurse Lamarr* • Harold Gould *Dr Zerny* • William Elliott *Oscar* • Norman Alden *Katzen* • Keith Allison *Hinkley* ▪ *Dir* Rod Amateau • *Scr* Rod Amateau, Budd Robinson, from their novel *The Operator*

Where Eagles Dare ★★★★ ▣

Second World War adventure drama
1969 · UK · Colour · 148mins

Clint Eastwood called this wartime frolic "Where Doubles Dare", in view of the army of stuntmen who performed the acrobatics in the Austrian Alps. His co-star, Richard Burton, was paid a million dollars plus a big percentage of what turned out to be a hugely profitable picture. Made in the tradition of *The Guns of Navarone* (also based on an Alistair MacLean novel), it's the usual espionage hokum, with Burton and Eastwood infiltrating a Nazi stronghold to discover a hornet's nest of spies. There are so many double- and triple-crosses that the plot is at times incomprehensible. But this is a picture about big bangs, James Bond-like fights on cable cars and body counts. It's hilarious and exciting, often at the same time. ▣

Richard Burton *Major John Smith* • Clint Eastwood *Lieutenant Morris Schaffer* • Mary Ure *Mary Ellison* • Michael Hordern *Vice Admiral Rolland* • Patrick Wymark *Colonel Wyatt Turner* • Robert Beatty *Cartwright Jones* • Anton Diffring *Colonel Kramer* • Donald Houston *Olaf Christiansen* ▪ *Dir* Brian G Hutton • *Scr* Alistair MacLean, from his novel

Where Is My Friend's House? ★★★★

Drama   1987 · Iran · Colour · 83mins

The first part of the "friendship" trilogy (completed by *And Life Goes On...* and *Through the Olive Trees*) was made under the auspices of Iran's Institute for the Intellectual Development of Children and Young Adults and provides a deceptively simple account of conscientious schoolboy Babek Ahmed Poor's quest to the neighbouring village to spare a classmate from being expelled by returning a missing notebook. Making poetic use of the rugged landscape and highlighting the lack of communication between kids and grown-ups, Abbas Kiarostami also explores innocent notions of loyalty and everyday heroics with a mixture of realism, touching earnestness and gentle humour. In Farsi with English subtitles.

Babek Ahmed Poor *Ahmed* • Ahmed Ahmed Poor *Mahamed Reda Nematzadeh* • Kheda Barech Defai *Teacher* • Iran Outari *Mother* • Ait Ansari *Father* ▪ *Dir/Scr* Abbas Kiarostami

Where It's At ★★★

Comedy drama   1969 · US · Colour · 104mins

Belying its fashionable "sixties speak" title, this is actually a reasonably sharp portrait of a father and son in conflict. David Janssen is surprisingly convincing as a Vegas casino boss who decides it's time his laid-back offspring (played by Robert Drivas) learnt a little more about the real world. The young man gets a lesson in love courtesy of a showgirl arranged by Janssen and when it comes to the business side of things, Princeton-educated Drivas is more than a match for dad. The tale is crisply handled by writer/director Garson Kanin, who, together with his wife Ruth Gordon, wrote the classic Katharine Hepburn-Spencer Tracy vehicles *Adam's Rib* and *Pat and Mike*.

David Janssen *AC Smith* • Robert Drivas *Andy Smith* • Rosemary Forsyth *Diana Mayhew* • Brenda Vaccaro *Molly Hirsch* • Warrene Ott *Betty Avery* • Edy Williams *Phyllis Horrigan* • Vince Howard *Ralph* • Don Rickles *Willie* ▪ *Dir/Scr* Garson Kanin

Where Love Has Gone ★★★

Melodrama   1964 · US · Colour · 114mins

The pot of venomous passions boils over in this lurid melodrama as mother and daughter Bette Davis and Susan Hayward act out their mutual hatred with all stops out. The temperature rises further when Hayward's own daughter (Joey Heatherton) kills Hayward's lover. Adapted from the bestselling novel by Harold Robbins, who drew on the Lana Turner-Cheryl Crane-Johnny Stompanato scandal for his material, the film, directed by Edward Dmytryk, was slaughtered by critics while audiences flocked. Fans of the genre are guaranteed a richly entertaining wallow watching these two great stars at their committed worst.

Susan Hayward *Valerie Hayden Miller* • Bette Davis *Mrs Gerald Hayden* • Michael Connors [Mike Connors] *Gerald Hayden* • Joey Heatherton *Danielle Valerie "Dani" Miller* • Jane Greer *Marian Spicer* • DeForest Kelley *Sam Corwin* • George Macready *Gordon Harris* • Anne Seymour *Dr Sally Jennings* ▪ *Dir* Edward Dmytryk • *Scr* John Michael Hayes, from the novel by Harold Robbins

Where No Vultures Fly ★★★★ ▣

Adventure   1951 · UK · Colour · 103mins

Chosen for the Royal film performance of its year, this is a splendid semi-documentary shot on exotic African locations, with an ecological message still potently relevant today. Anthony Steel plays a game warden on the lookout for evil ivory hunters in the shadow of Mount Kilimanjaro. The suspense is exceptionally well maintained, with a stunning fight sequence between Steel and Harold Warrender, and the Technicolor matching of studio material and location footage is particularly clever. The animals themselves are enchanting, and give better performances than either Steel or Dinah Sheridan as his loyal wife, though the human roles are rather underwritten. So successful was this film that it led to a sequel, the equally popular *West of Zanzibar*. ▣

Anthony Steel *Robert Payton* • Dinah Sheridan *Mary Payton* • Harold Warrender *Mannering* • Meredith Edwards *Gwil Davies* • William Simons *Tim Payton* • Orlando Martins *M'kwongwi* ▪ *Dir* Harry Watt • *Scr* Ralph Smart, WP Lipscomb, from a story by Leslie Norman Watt • *Cinematographer* Geoffrey Unsworth

Where Pigeons Go to Die ★★

Drama   1990 · US · Colour · 96mins

Michael Landon, who gave us the delightful *Little House on the Prairie* and the mawkish *Highway to Heaven*, here directs and stars as well as producing and writing the screenplay in a sugary sweet tale of a man reminiscing about his relationship with his grandfather and a load of homing pigeons. Unashamedly sentimental, this is one of those movies which should be sponsored by Kleenex.

Michael Landon *Hugh Baudoum aged 50* • Art Carney *Da* • Robert Hy Gorman *Hugh aged ten* • Cliff De Young *Henry* • Ronne Troup *Evelyn* ▪ *Dir* Michael Landon • *Scr* Michael Landon, from the book by R Wright Campbell

Where Sleeping Dogs Lie ★ 15

Psychological thriller
1991 · US · Colour · 87mins

Dreadful thriller in which Dylan McDermott plays a struggling, self-

▣ = SUITABLE FOR ALL,   ▣c = SUITABLE FOR ALL, ESPECIALLY FOR YOUNG CHILDREN (VIDEO ONLY)   ▣ = PARENTAL GUIDANCE

absorbed author who moves into a run-down house in which an entire family was once murdered. Tom Sizemore is his twitchy tenant, taking an active interest in the author's portrait of the killer with grisly consequences. Disjointed, predictable and leaden-paced, with surprisingly unconvincing performances from the decent cast, including McDermott's superbitch-by-numbers agent Sharon Stone. At one point, the author tells his house-mate "being with you is beyond my worst nightmare", a remark which inadvertently echoes the way most people will feel about this film. ▭

Dylan McDermott *Bruce Simmons* • Tom Sizemore *Eddie Hale* • Sharon Stone *Serena Black* • Joan Chen *Sara* • Kristen Hocking *Marlee* ■ *Dir* Charles Finch • *Scr* Charles Finch, Yolande Turner

Where the Boys Are ★★★ PG

Romantic comedy
1960 · US · Colour · 95mins

The boys are at a Fort Lauderdale resort, invaded by college kids in search of romance during the Easter vacation. Against this background of youthful sun-seeking and partying, the action focuses on the contrasting relationships that develop between four girls and guys, of whom Paula Prentiss (her debut) and Jim Hutton are the most charming. Good-natured, nostalgic stuff with an interesting moral take on virginity, which was still a major issue at the time. Dolores Hart, for example, hangs on to hers and is rewarded with George Hamilton, while Yvette Mimieux learns that giving in doesn't pay! ▭

Dolores Hart *Merritt Andrews* • George Hamilton *Ryder Smith* • Yvette Mimieux *Melanie* • Jim Hutton *TV Thompson* • Barbara Nichols *Lola* • Paula Prentiss *Tuggle Carpenter* • Connie Francis *Angie* • Chill Wills *Police Captain* ■ *Dir* Henry Levin • *Scr* George Wells, from a story by Glendon Swarthout

Where the Buffalo Roam ★★★ 18

Comedy 1980 · US · Colour · 94mins

Through the eyes of the pioneer of "gonzo journalism", Hunter S Thompson, we see various facets of US political life in the late sixties and early seventies. The under-rated Bill Murray is Thompson while Peter Boyle plays his outrageous legal acquaintance, Lazlo. This movie was "based on the twisted legend of Hunter S Thompson" according to its title sequence – though its essential sources are *Fear and Loathing in Las Vegas* and *Fear and Loathing on the Campaign Trail '72*. It was panned on release in the US but it's actually an interesting and savage little piece which deserved better. ▭

Peter Boyle *Lazlo* • Bill Murray *Dr Hunter S Thompson* • Bruno Kirby *Marty Lewis* • René Auberjonois *Harris* • RG Armstrong *Judge Simpson* • Danny Goldman *Porter* • Rafael Campos *Rojas* • Leonard Frey *Desk clerk* ■ *Dir* Art Linson • *Scr* John Kaye, from writings by Hunter S Thompson • *Music* Neil Young

Where the Bullets Fly ★★★

Spy comedy 1966 · UK · Colour · 88mins

The British have the Spurium Apparatus, a small nuclear device for

powering aircraft. The Russians want it and enlist the aid of Angel (Michael Ripper) and his clandestine international crime organisation to steal it. To succeed Angel has to clash with super secret agent Charles Vine (Tom Adams), on his second outing following 1965's *Licenced to Kill*. One of a huge number of Bond spoofs about at the time, none of which seemed to realise that the 007 movies themselves were spoofs, *Where the Bullets Fly* is a jaunty enough romp, and Adams is fine as Vine.

Tom Adams *Charles Vine* • Dawn Addams *Felicity "Fiz" Moonlight* • Sidney James *Mortuary attendant* • Wilfrid Brambell *Train guard* • Joe Baker *Minister* • Tim Barrett *Seraph* • Michael Ripper *Angel* • John Arnatt *Rockwell* • Ronald Leigh-Hunt *Thursby* ■ *Dir* John Gilling • *Scr* Michael Pittock

Where the Day Takes You ★★ 18

Drama 1992 · US · Colour · 98mins

Quasi-documentary about kids living rough on the mean streets of Los Angeles. There's a feel of the real in its depiction of the seamy underside, set against the glam and glitzy City of Angels. But the characters never really engage you, and the film's so relentlessly downbeat that you're soon numb to its nastiness. Literally slumming it is a crack cast of Hollywood's younger lions, including Sean Astin, Lara Flynn Boyle, Dermot Mulroney, Balthazar Getty, Kyle MacLachan, Adam Baldwin, Alyssa Milano and Christian Slater. ▭

Dermot Mulroney *King* • Lara Flynn Boyle *Heather* • Balthazar Getty *Little J* • Sean Astin *Greg* • James LeGros *Crasher* • Ricki Lake *Brenda* • Kyle MacLachlan *Ted* • Robert Knepper *Rock Singer* • Peter Dobson *Tommy* • Will Smith *Manny* • Adam Baldwin *Officer Black* • Christian Slater *Rocky* • Alyssa Milano *Kimmy* ■ *Dir* Marc Rocco • *Scr* Michael Hitchcock, Kurt Voss, Marc Rocco

Where the Heart Is ★ 15

Comedy drama
1990 · US/Can · Colour · 102mins

Seeing that director John Boorman's prior effort was *Hope and Glory* one expected more of him than this dreadful comedy. Under the auspices of Disney, Boorman has produced an unfunny, unappealing movie about a demolition expert (Dabney Coleman) who chucks his children (Uma Thurman, David Hewlett and Suzy Amis) into squalor in downtown Brooklyn. But when Coleman is subsequently bankrupted, he and wife Joanna Cassidy are forced to join them in their hovel. Written by Boorman and his daughter Telsche, this might have worked on the page but it sure is a Bernard Matthews on screen. ▭

Dabney Coleman *Stewart McBain* • Uma Thurman *Daphne* • Christopher Plummer *Homeless gent* • Joanna Cassidy *Jean* • Suzy Amis *Chloe* • Crispin Glover *Lionel* • David Hewlett *Jimmy* • Sheila Kelley *Sheryl* ■ *Dir* John Boorman • *Scr* John Boorman, Telsche Boorman • *Cinematographer* Peter Suschitzky

Where the Hell's That Gold? ★

Comedy western 1988 · US · Colour · 91mins

Best known for the western parody *Support Your Local Sheriff!*, Burt Kennedy here directs a rather less impressive effort based on an idea from actor Gerald McRaney, who also appears in this TV movie. He and Delta Burke, along with country-and-western star Willie Nelson plus a host of revolutionaries and outlaws, are on the trail of a buried stash of gold. Because this is a comedy western, there's much ludicrous double-crossing and pratfalling as everyone tries to claim the treasure. Unoriginal, out of date and definitely missable.

Willie Nelson *Will Cross* • Jack Elam *Frank Boone* • Gerald McRaney *Jones* • Delta Burke *Germany* • Alfonso Arau *Indio* ■ *Dir* Burt Kennedy • *Scr* Burt Kennedy, from an idea by Gerald McRaney

Where the Hot Wind Blows! ★★ 12

Drama 1959 · Fr/It · BW · 111mins

Adapted from the Prix Goncourt-winning novel, *La Loi*, by Roger Vailland, this is a classic case of a film being ruined through commercial interference. Jules Dassin was about to begin shooting (from what he considered the best script he'd ever written) when the backers insisted he cast Marcello Mastroianni and Gina Lollobrigida to protect their investment. Thus, an intense study of the misuse of power in a patriarchal southern Italian community is transformed into an imbalanced star vehicle, in which "La Lollo's" feisty maid turns the tables on a coterie wrapped up in its sinisterly dictatorial parlour game. An Italian language film. ▭

Gina Lollobrigida *Marietta* • Pierre Brasseur *Don Cesare* • Marcello Mastroianni *Engineer* • Melina Mercouri *Donna Lucrezia* • Yves Montand *Matteo Brigante* ■ *Dir* Jules Dassin • *Scr* Jules Dassin, Françoise Giroud, from the novel *La Loi* by Roger Vailland

Where the Ladies Go ★★★

Comedy drama 1980 · US · Colour · 98mins

A small-town bar run by an ageing Earl Holliman is the meeting place for adventure-seeking members of the community in director Theodore J Flicker's nicely ambling TV movie. Karen Black, Candy Clark and Lisa Hartman make up a formidable trio of regulars in a pleasant film that is clearly reminiscent of *Nashville* and *Come Back to the Five and Dime, Jimmy Dean, Jimmy Dean*. Flicker's main claim to fame is the 1967 political satire *The President's Analyst*.

Earl Holliman *Buck* • Karen Black *Helen* • Candy Clark *Charlene* • Lisa Hartman *Crystal* • Lane Bradbury *Tasha* • Mary Jo Catlett *Frances* ■ *Dir* Theodore Flicker • *Scr* Carol Sobieski

Where the Lilies Bloom ★★★ U

Drama 1974 · US · Colour · 97mins

This is the old story of the loving kids who can't bear the thought of being parted and so hide the death of their parents from the authorities by putting

on a show of business as usual. But don't give up on this movie as just another chunk of family values mush. Scriptwriter Earl Hamner Jr (*The Waltons*) has not only produced a sensitive and well-observed portrait of backwoods American life, but he has also come up with flesh-and-blood children who don't seem to have been born on Walton's Mountain. It also helps having Harry Dean Stanton as the family's crotchety landlord.

Julie Gholson *Mary Call* • Jan Smithers *Devola* • Matthew Burrill *Romey* • Helen Harmon *Ima Dean* • Harry Dean Stanton *Kiser Pease* • Rance Howard *Roy Luther* ■ *Dir* William A Graham • *Scr* Earl Hamner Jr, from a novel by Vera Cleaver, Bill Cleaver

Where the Red Fern Grows ★★★ U

Adventure drama 1974 · US · Colour · 96mins

This story of a 12-year-old boy (Stewart Petersen) living in Depression-hit thirties Oklahoma is one of the most popular of all family movies. His love of and sens of responsibility for two redbone raccoon hounds helps him overcome the tribulations and trials of the times. Jack Ging and Beverly Garland are the understanding mom and dad, but for a real taste of Dust Bowl dynamics, better try *The Grapes of Wrath*.

James Whitmore *Grandpa* • Beverly Garland *Mother* • Jack Ging *Father* • Lonny Chapman *Sheriff* • Stewart Petersen *Billy* • Jill Clark *Alice* • Jeanne Wilson *Sara* ■ *Dir* Norman Tokar • *Scr* Douglas Day Stewart, Eleanor Lamb, from the novel by Wilson Rawls

Where the River Runs Black ★★ PG

Adventure 1986 · US · Colour · 92mins

A deep, meaningful, mystical experience. Well, to the writers and director maybe, but to most people this is a dumb kiddie pic about a boy in the Brazilian forest who is the result of a sudden union between a beautiful native girl and a priest who then dies for his sins. Thought to possess heavenly powers, the boy is raised with the help of river dolphins and is therefore naturally a whiz at swimming. In addition to all that, there's the ravaging of the rainforest by gold-miners and a portentous score by James Horner.

Charles Durning *Father O'Reilly* • Peter Horton *Father Mahoney* • Alessandro Rabelo *Lazaro* • Ajay Naidu *Segundo* • Conchata Ferell *Mother Marta* • Dana Delany *Sister Ana* • Chico Diaz *Raimundo* ■ *Dir* Christopher Cain • *Scr* Peter Silverman, Neal Jimenez, from the novel *Lazaro* by David Kendall

Where the Rivers Flow North ★★★ 15

Period drama 1993 · US · Colour · 106mins

In twenties Vermont, a stubborn logger and landowner (a suitably ursine Rip Torn) is refusing to sell his property to the government-backed power company about to build a dam. It's not as dull as it sounds, as director Jay Craven concentrates on the relationship between Torn and his long-suffering native American housekeeper Tantoo Cardinal. The two central performances are both excellent and moving, elevating a dreary and overused

premise so that, despite inappropriate cameos from Michael J Fox and Treat Williams, this is a very watchable film.

Rip Torn *Noel Lord* • Tantoo Cardinal *Bangor* • Bill Raymond *Wayne Quinn* • Michael J Fox *Clayton Farnsworth* • Treat Williams *Champ's Manager* • Amy Wright *Loose Woman* ■ *Dir* Jay Craven • *Scr* Jay Craven, Don Bredes, from the novel *Where the Rivers Run North* by Howard Frank Mosher

Where the Sidewalk Ends ★★★★

Film noir 1950 · US · BW · 94mins

A superb example of 20th Century-Fox *film noir* at its finest, this is a clearly plotted thriller, impeccably directed by the great Otto Preminger, which creates a nightmare world of guilt and corruption. Brutal cop Dana Andrews tries to hide the fact that, while searching for a murderer, he himself has killed Craig Stevens. The beautiful Gene Tierney is excellent in an enigmatic role as Stevens's estranged wife – a part that manages to keep her acting limitations well concealed – and watch for Neville Brand's chilling portrayal of a homosexual criminal in some censor-circumventing scenes well ahead of their time. Movie buffs and fashion aficionados should keep an eye out for a cameo from Tierney's then-husband Oleg Cassini, who designed the movie's costumes with Charles LeMaire.

Dana Andrews *Mark Dixon* • Gene Tierney *Morgan Taylor* • Gary Merrill *Tommy Scalise* • Bert Freed *Paul Klein* • Tom Tully *Jiggs Taylor* • Karl Malden *Lieutenant Bill Thomas* • Ruth Donnelly *Martha* • Oleg Cassini ■ *Dir* Otto Preminger • *Scr* Ben Hecht, Frank P Rosenberg (adaptation), Victor Trivas (adaptation), Robert E Kent (adaptation), from a novel by William L Stuart • *Cinematographer* Joseph LaShelle

Where the Spies Are ★★

Comedy adventure
1966 · UK · Colour · 112mins

One of the many dozens of Bond send-ups and rip-offs, this spoofy affair is distinguished by a typically suave and disarming performance from David Niven, who the following year played Bond himself in *Casino Royale*. Niven plays Jason Love, recruited by MI6 and sent to the Middle East to defend Britain's vital oil interests. The usual scrapes, escapes, explosions, lethal gadgets and bedroom seductions ensue, all treated in a rather obvious satirical style by co-writer/director Val Guest. John Le Mesurier, as the head of MI6, does a lovely turn at mimicking Bernard Lee.

David Niven *Dr Jason Love* • Françoise Dorléac *Vikki* • John Le Mesurier *Col Douglas MacGillivray* • Cyril Cusack *Peter Rosser* • Eric Pohlman [Eric Pohlmann] *Farouk* • Richard Marner *Josef* • Paul Stassino *Simmias* • Noel Harrison *Jackson* • Geoffrey Bayldon *Lecturer* ■ *Dir* Val Guest • *Scr* Wolf Mankowitz, Val Guest, James Leasor

Where There's a Will ★★★ PG

Comedy 1936 · UK · BW · 76mins

Will Hay created wonderful comic characters, incompetent because they were masquerading in their work or were, quite simply, not up to the job. Here the latter is true, as he plays the unsuccessful solicitor Bernard Stubbins, whose office happens to be over a bank that a gang decides to rob. Bernard is knocked out but later, as he sponges off wealthy relatives at a party, the same gang turn up for a repeat performance. Can the master of the supercilious sniff save the day? It's notable as the first collaboration between the devious Hay and his regular sidekick, Graham Moffatt, here playing an office boy.

Will Hay *Benjamin Stubbins* • Gina Malo *Goldie Kelly* • Hartley Power *Duke Wilson* • Graham Moffatt *Willie* • HF Maltby *Sir Roger Wimpleton* • Norma Varden *Lady Margaret Wimpleton* • Peggy Simpson *Barbara Stubbins* • Gibb McLaughlin *Martin* ■ *Dir* William Beaudine • *Scr* William Beaudine, Will Hay, Ralph Spence, Robert Edmunds, from a story by Leslie Arliss, Sidney Gilliat

Where There's a Will ★★ U

Comedy 1955 · UK · BW · 77mins

This sporadically charming fish-out-of-water comedy sees a family of cockneys moving to the Devon countryside when they inherit a run-down farm. Director Vernon Sewell manages a few sly touches, as local housekeeper Kathleen Harrison tries to whip the work-shy Londoners into shape. George Cole gives his rent-a-spiv character another airing, and there's a young Edward Woodward lurking among the bit players. The script is by RF Delderfield, who also wrote the novel that formed the basis of the BBC TV series *To Serve Them All My Days*.

George Cole *Fred Slater* • Kathleen Harrison *Annie Yeo* • Leslie Dwyer *Alfred Brewer* • Ann Hanslip *June Hodge* • Michael Shepley *Mr Cogent* • Dandy Nichols *Maud Hodge* • Thelma Ruby *Amy Slater* • Edward Woodward *Ralph Stokes* ■ *Dir* Vernon Sewell • *Scr* RF Delderfield, from his play

Where There's Life ★★★★

Comedy 1947 · US · BW · 75mins

Michael Valentine (Bob Hope) is a small-time New York DJ who discovers he is the heir to a mysterious European kingdom. Consequently he is chased through New York by not only those wish to take him back to the country to take up the throne but also anti-royalists who are out to kill him. This is from the golden era of Hope's work, with the fast-talking comedy actor on top wisecracking form. Satisfaction is guaranteed with this combination and at the time there was no-one better than Hope at combining thrills and comedy.

Bob Hope *Michael Valentine* • Signe Hasso *Katrina Grimovitch* • William Bendix *Victor O'Brien* • George Coulouris *Premier Krivoc* • Vera Marshe *Hazel O'Brien* • George Zucco *Paul Stertorius* • Dennis Hoey *Minister of War Grubitch* • John Alexander *Mr Herbert Jones* ■ *Dir* Sidney Lanfield • *Scr* Allen Boretz, Melville Shavelson, Barney Dean, Frank Tashlin, from a story by Melville Shavelson

Where Were You When the Lights Went Out? ★★

Comedy 1968 · US · Colour · 89mins

Doris Day's penultimate picture is notable only for the fact that she spent much of its production in traction, having pinched a nerve in her back, and for an excruciating in-joke that had her character starring in a play called *The Constant Virgin*. It's a contrived affair from start to finish, relying on blackouts, sleeping pills, embezzled funds and sexual jealousy to bring Doris and architect husband Patrick O'Neal to an inevitable happy ending. Hy Averback directs with little imagination, while only Terry-Thomas, as Day's Machiavellian agent, seems willing to play it for laughs.

Doris Day *Margaret Garrison* • Robert Morse *Waldo Zane* • Terry-Thomas *Ladislau Walichek* • Patrick O'Neal *Peter Garrison* • Lola Albright *Roberta Lane* • Steve Allen *Radio announcer* • Jim Backus *Tru-Blue Lou* ■ *Dir* Hy Averback • *Scr* Everett Freeman, Karl Tunberg, from the play *Monsieur Masure* by Claude Magnier

The Whereabouts of Jenny ★★★ PG

Thriller 1991 · US · Colour · 94mins

This above-average TV movie, written with a considerable degree of flair, deals with the controversial and dramatically fertile ground of the US Witness Relocation Program. Debrah Farentino turns in a moving performance as a woman relocated with her child and new husband, a drug dealer turned state's witness, whose first spouse decides to search for them. It is also notable for a strong performance by Ed O'Neill (*Married with Children*). The tension is maintained throughout, and all concerned treat the issues raised seriously.

Ed O'Neill *Jimmy O'Meara* • Mike Farrell *Robert Van Zandt* • Debrah Farentino *Liz Gallagher* • Cassy Friel *Jenny* • Eve Gordon *Theresa* • Michael Crabtree *Bobby Desantos* • Dan Hedaya *Vincent* • David Graf *Scranton* ■ *Dir* Gene Reynolds • *Scr* John Miglis

Where's Jack? ★★★ U

Period drama 1969 · UK · Colour · 119mins

The damaging flaw in this 18th-century account of highway skulduggery is the miscasting of pop-singer Tommy Steele as ruffian Jack Sheppard, who is pursued – and, to an extent, manipulated by – the venal Stanley Baker (who also co-produced). But director James Clavell, who would go on to write blockbuster novels such as *Shogun*, makes a brave attempt at re-creating the bawdy, squalid times.

Tommy Steele *Jack Sheppard* • Stanley Baker *Jonathan Wild* • Fiona Lewis *Edgworth Bess Lyon* • Alan Badel *The Lord Chancellor* • Dudley Foster *Blueskin* • Noel Purcell *Leatherchest* • William Marlowe *Tom Sheppard* • Sue Lloyd *Lady Darlington* ■ *Dir* James Clavell • *Scr* David Newhouse, Rafe Newhouse

Where's Poppa? ★★★★

Comedy 1970 · US · Colour · 83mins

Successful lawyer Gordon Hocheiser (George Segal) lives with his sometimes senile, widowed mother (Ruth Gordon). He is at the end of his tether due to the frustration he has trying to get a girlfriend. Whenever he brings a girl home his mother undergoes a remarkable change, springing to life and scuppering his chances. When he falls for his mother's new nurse Louise (Trish Van Devere), Gordon is driven to try and kill his mother. A fast-paced, jet black comedy with fine performances all around, this is comparable to Ruth Gordon's subsequent work, *Harold and Maude* (1971).

George Segal *Gordon Hocheiser* • Ruth Gordon *Mrs Hocheiser* • Trish Van Devere *Louise Callan* • Ron Leibman *Sidney Hocheiser* • Rae Allen *Gladys Hocheiser* • Florence Tarlow *Miss Morgiani* • Paul Sorvino *Owner of "Gus and Grace's Home"* • Rob Reiner *Roger* • Vincent Gardenia *Coach Williams* ■ *Dir* Carl Reiner • *Scr* Robert Klane, from his novel

Where's That Fire? ★★★ U

Comedy 1939 · UK · BW · 73mins

In this comic gem, Will Hay creates another variant in his gallery of incompetents – this time he's a fireman in a small village. His regular sidekicks Graham Moffatt and Moore Marriott help form what was once described as "the holy trinity of the [British] studio system". They stumble across a gang of thieves, who reassure them that they are making an historical film, when in fact they are after the crown jewels. As usual, things turn out for the best in the slightly askew world created by these three wonderful comedians create.

Will Hay *Capt Benjamin Viking* • Moore Marriott *Jerry Harbottle* • Graham Moffatt *Albert Brown* • Peter Gawthorne *Chief Officer* • Eric Clavering *Hank Sullivan* • Hugh McDermott *Jim Baker* • Charles Hawtrey *Youth* ■ *Dir* Marcel Varnel • *Scr* Marriott Edgar, Val Guest, JOC Orton, from a story by Maurice Braddell

Which Way Is Up? ★★★

Comedy 1977 · US · Colour · 94mins

Richard Pryor is a simple migrant orange picker who is manipulated into management by the boss of the large agricultural concern that employs him. But this is just the start of his seduction. This US version of Lina Wertmüller's 1972 Italian comedy *The Seduction of Mimi* doesn't match the original despite some fine work from Pryor, who not only plays Leroy but also his father and the family minister. This film reunited Pryor with his *Greased Lightning* director Michael Schultz.

Richard Pryor *Leroy Jones/Rufus Jones/Reverend Thomas* • Lonette McKee *Vanetta* • Margaret Avery *Annie Mae* • Morgan Woodward *Mr Mann* • Marilyn Coleman *Sister Sarah* ■ *Dir* Michael Schultz • *Scr* Carl Gottlieb, Cecil Brown, from the film *The Seduction of Mimi* by Lina Wertmüller

Which Way to the Front? ★ U

War comedy 1970 · US · Colour · 92mins

Few things in showbusiness are sadder to see than a comedian deserted by his muse. Jerry Lewis hits rock bottom with some untenable and tasteless material (a group of misfits deciding to wage their own war against Hitler), appallingly assembled and perfunctorily put together. Jerry himself mugs unwatchably, and John Wood and Jan Murray offer professional, but futile, support. In the UK, the title was mirthlessly preceded by "Ja, Ja, Mein General, But...". It didn't make any

difference – few people saw this stinker, and those who did were not impressed. 🖼

Jerry Lewis *Brendan Byers III* • Jan Murray *Sid Hackle* • John Wood *Finkel* • Steve Franken *Peter Bland* • Willie Davis *Lincoln* • Dack Rambo *Terry Love* • Paul Winchell *Schroeder* • Sidney Miller *Adolf Hitler* • Robert Middleton *Colonico* ■ *Dir* Jerry Lewis • *Scr* Gerald Gardner, Dee Caruso, from a story by Gerald Gardner, Dee Caruso, Richard Miller

Whiffs ★ 15

Crime comedy 1975 · US · Colour · 88mins

Soldier Elliott Gould is pensioned out of the army due to the disabling effects of the toxins he has encountered on behalf of the military. He teams up with Harry Guardino and the two form a criminal partnership, using their knowledge of chemicals to rob banks. This is a tired caper comedy, which tries to capture the style of *MASH* but fails ignominiously, despite the presence of Gould. The main problem is that the lead characters are so singularly unsympathetic, making this tall tale very hard going indeed. 🖼

Elliott Gould *Dudley Frapper* • Eddie Albert *Colonel Lockyer* • Harry Guardino *Chops* • Godfrey Cambridge *Dusty* • Jennifer O'Neill *Scottie* • Alan Manson *Sgt Poultry* ■ *Dir* Ted Post • *Scr* Malcolm Marmorstein

While I Live ★★

Drama 1947 · UK · BW · 84mins

Veteran moviegoers might just remember seeing this excitable melodrama under the title *The Dream of Olwen*, under which it was re-released to exploit the success of Charles Williams's theme tune. Sonia Dresdel dominates the proceedings with a Mrs Danvers-like display of neurotic malice, playing a Cornish spinster who becomes convinced that amnesiac Carol Raye is her reincarnated sister. Not even that arch scene-stealer Tom Walls can compete.

Sonia Dresdel *Julia Trevelyan* • Tom Walls *Nehemiah* • Clifford Evans *Peter* • Carol Raye *Sally Warwick* • Patricia Burke *Christine* • John Warwick *George Warwick* • Edward Lexy *Selby* ■ *Dir* John Harlow • *Scr* John Harlow, Doreen Montgomery, from the play *This Same Garden* by Robert Bell

While Justice Sleeps ★★ 15

Drama 1994 · US · Colour · 87mins

Histrionics badly hamper the plot of this torrid tale of small-town American life. Cybill Shepherd, never the most subtle of actresses, brings more than enough anguish to her role as a widow with a molested daughter, but the audience never properly connects with her distress. However, this low-budget effort does have the right insular feel and realistically brings the Midwest to life. If only the issues it raises could have been dealt with in a more sensitive way. 🖼

Cybill Shepherd *Jody* • Tim Matheson *Winn* • Karis Paige Bryant *Sam* • Kurtwood Smith *Leonard Rosenglass* • Dion Anderson *Spence Cunningham* • Robyn Stevan *Marlene Perkins* • Elan Ross Gibson *Doc Cunningham* ■ *Dir* Alan Smithee [Ivan Passer] • *Scr* Caliope Brattlestreet, Stephen Glantz

While My Pretty One Sleeps ★★

Thriller 1997 · Can · Colour

This appropriately glossy but sadly empty adaptation of a Mary Higgins Clark potboiler is set in the cutthroat world of high fashion. TV-movie regular Connie Sellecca is the top frock shop boss who teams up with reporter Simon MacCorkindale to investigate the disappearance of a gossip columnist who was about to blow the whistle on important figures in the fashion business. The script also stirs a Mafia subplot into the already frothy concoction, and the result is an often unintentionally funny but mildly entertaining thriller.

Connie Sellecca *Neeve Kearney* • Beau Starr *Myles Kearney* • Stewart Bick *Nicky Jr* • Richard Monette *Sal* • Vlasta Varna *Bishop* • Simon MacCorkindale *Jack Campbell* ■ *Dir* Jorge Montesi • *Scr* David Kinghorn, Marilyn Kinghorn, from the novel by Mary Higgins Clark

While the City Sleeps ★★★ PG

Thriller 1956 · US · BW · 95mins

This thriller about who gets to run a newspaper is quite intriguing, and boasts a starry cast as well as revered director Fritz Lang. With such a roster of familiar faces, it's compulsively watchable, even if Vincent Price and Ida Lupino, in particular, have little to do. Lang, making one of his final American movies, filmed this in SuperScope, which means that on TV you'll see a lot of unnecessary ceilings and floors. 🖼

Dana Andrews *Edward Mobley* • Rhonda Fleming *Dorothy Kyne* • Vincent Price *Walter Kyne Jr* • George Sanders *Mark Loving* • Thomas Mitchell *John Day Griffith* • Sally Forrest *Nancy* • Ida Lupino *Mildred* • Howard Duff *Lt Kaufman* • John Barrymore Jr [John Drew Barrymore] *Manners* ■ *Dir* Fritz Lang • *Scr* Casey Robinson, from the novel *The Bloody Spur* by Charles Einstein

While You Were Sleeping ★★★★ PG

Romantic comedy
1995 · US · Colour · 99mins

This is a warmly engaging and winning romantic comedy with plenty of novel twists and witty turns. Sandra Bullock is nothing short of sensational as the lonely Chicago subway clerk, who poswa as the fiancée of coma victim Peter Gallagher after saving his life, resulting in thrilled amazement from his family and yearning from his sceptical brother, Bill Pullman. Smartly scripted, with Jon Turteltaub's expert direction hitting all the right emotional buttons, this Cinderella love story is crammed with enough charm to qualify as the perfect dream-date diversion. Contains some swearing. 🖼 *DVD*

Sandra Bullock *Lucy Moderatz* • Bill Pullman *Jack Callaghan* • Peter Gallagher *Peter Callaghan* • Peter Boyle *Ox* • Jack Warden *Saul* • Glynis Johns *Elsie* • Michael Rispoli *Joe Jr* • Jason Bernard *Jerry* • Micole Mercurio *Midge* ■ *Dir* Jon Turteltaub • *Scr* Daniel G Sullivan, Fredric Lebow

The Whip Hand ★★★

Thriller 1951 · US · BW · 82mins

This taut thriller may lack star names, but it is masterfully directed and designed by William Cameron Menzies. Elliott Reid plays the photojournalist on vacation in Wisconsin who stumbles on a village of unfriendly inhabitants, a lake where the fish have vanished, and a mysterious, heavily guarded lodge… The original ending involved a live Adolf Hitler plotting a comeback, but RKO studio boss Howard Hughes, who was virulently anti-communist, dumped him for a bunch of Nazis who had turned into Reds.

Carla Balenda *Janet Koller* • Elliott Reid *Matt Corbin* • Edgar Barrier *Dr Edward Koller* • Raymond Burr *Steve Loomis* • Otto Waldis *Dr Willem Bucholtz* • Michael Steele *Chick* • Lurene Tuttle *Molly Loomis* ■ *Dir* William Cameron Menzies • *Scr* George Bricker, Frank L Moss, from a story by Roy Hamilton

Whipsaw ★★★

Crime drama 1935 · US · BW · 78mins

A trio of crooks, one of whom is Myrna Loy, steals some valuable jewels in Europe. Back in New York, where the booty is lifted by rival thieves, G-man Spencer Tracy is assigned to find the gems. He courts Loy, who believes he is also a thief, and they fall in love before the truth is revealed. The felicitous pairing of Loy with Tracy (replacing the intended but unavailable William Powell) and Sam Wood's direction, which has enough pace and spirit to hide the holes in a basically unconvincing script, result in an entertaining romantic crime drama, overlaid with a dash of welcome sophistication.

Myrna Loy *Vivian Palmer* • Spencer Tracy *Ross McBride* • Harvey Stephens *Ed Dexter* • William Harrigan *Doc Evans* • Clay Clement *Harry Ames* • Robert Gleckler *Steve Arnold* • Robert Warwick *Wadsworth* • Georges Renavent *Monetta* ■ *Dir* Sam Wood • *Scr* Howard Emmett Rogers, from the story by James Edward Grant

Whirlpool ★★★

Crime drama 1949 · US · BW · 97mins

This is a chunk of pure 20th Century-Fox late forties *film noir*, a highly entertaining melodrama directed by one of the past masters, Otto Preminger. He even manages to make ace ham José Ferrer credible as a dubious hypnotist treating vivacious kleptomaniac (and quintessential cool Fox goddess) Gene Tierney. The score reunites Preminger with his *Laura* composer David Raksin, and the screenplay is by a group of left-wing intellectuals, including a blacklisted Ben Hecht using the pseudonym Lester Barstow. The subtext about mind control is, therefore, by no means accidental.

Gene Tierney *Ann Sutton* • Richard Conte *Dr William Sutton* • José Ferrer *David Korvo* • Charles Bickford *Lieutenant Colton* • Barbara O'Neil *Theresa Randolph* • Eduard Franz *Martin Avery* • Constance Collier *Tina Cosgrove* • Fortunio Bonanova *Feruccio di Ravallo* • Ruth Lee *Miss Hall* ■ *Dir* Otto Preminger • *Scr* Lester Barstow [Ben Hecht], Andrew Solt, from the novel by Guy Endore • *Cinematographer* Arthur Miller

Whiskers ★★

Fantasy adventure
1997 · Can · Colour · 95mins

This bonkers but oddly appealing family feature from Canada has lonely youngster Michael Caloz being granted a secret wish that transforms his cat into a human being in the shape of Brent Carver. The largely unknown cast deliver watchable performances and the direction from Jim Kaufman is surprisingly subtle. Look out for a cameo from Suzanne Cloutier, who played Desdemona to Orson Welles's Othello in his acclaimed cinema adaptation of the Shakespeare play.

Brent Carver *Whiskers* • Michael Caloz *Jed Martin* • Steve Adams *Hal Martin* • Laurel Paetz *Jenny Martin* • Gouchy Boy *Museum guard* • Mark Bromilow *Dr Forbes* • Suzanne Cloutier *Alley lady* ■ *Dir* Jim Kaufman • *Scr* Wendy Biller, Christopher Hawthorne

Whiskey Down ★★ 15

Comedy thriller 1996 · US · Colour · 84mins

This slimly written tale begins in a café with a man dropping dead immediately after learning he's won six million dollars on the lottery. Virginia Madsen, Sean Patrick Flanery, Ernie Hudson *Ghostbusters* and Jon Favreau *Swingers*, are among the customers trying to convince the establishment's owner (Jon Polito) that they should cash in the ticket and keep the cash. Everyone in the group is so unlikeable that you won't care to sit through until the end to discover who ends up with the money. A good cast gets hemmed in by a bad, witless script and a thin plot . Contains swearing, and some violence and sexual references. 🖼

Sean Patrick Flanery *Ray* • Virginia Madsen *Kim* • Ernie Hudson *Willie* • Alanna Ubach *Angela* • Vince Vaughn *Barry* • Jon Favreau *Straker* • Jon Polito *Nick* ■ *Dir* Gary Auerbach • *Scr* Todd Alcott, Gary Auerbach, from a story by Gary Auerbach

Whisky Galore! ★★★★★ PG

Classic comedy 1949 · UK · BW · 79mins

Adapted by Compton Mackenzie and Angus Macphail from Mackenzie's own novel, Alexander Mackendrick's sublime film is one of the jewels in the Ealing crown. At the centre of this droll story of whisky smuggling in the Hebrides during the Second World War stands Basil Radford, who gives the performance of his career as the despised Sassenach commanding the local Home Guard. The Todday islanders are played to perfection by such accomplished players as Gordon Jackson, Wylie Watson and Joan Greenwood, while Catherine Lacey is a delight as Radford's wife, who greets his posturing and humiliation with equal detachment. 🖼

Basil Radford *Captain Paul Waggett* • Catherine Lacey *Mrs Waggett* • Bruce Seton *Sergeant Odd* • Joan Greenwood *Peggy Macroon* • Gordon Jackson *George Campbell* • Wylie Watson *Joseph Macroon* • Gabrielle Blunt *Catriona Macroon* • Jean Cadell *Mrs Campbell* • James Robertson-Justice *Dr MacLaren* ■ *Dir* Alexander MacKendrick • *Scr* Compton Mackenzie, Angus Macphail, from the novel by Compton Mackenzie

The Whisperers ★★★★

Drama   1967 · UK · BW · 105mins

One of writer/director Bryan Forbes's most admired films, this is essentially an effective and moving study of loneliness, which has as its subject an old lady teetering on the edge of senility. One does feel a little sidetracked by the plot development involving the poor old dear being exploited by her criminal son (Ronald Fraser) and husband (Eric Portman), but there is still the constant pleasure of Dame Edith Evans at her finest, moving us to laughter and tears. Inevitably there is a small role for Forbes's wife Nanette Newman; their daughter Sarah plays Dame Edith as a girl.

Edith Evans *Mrs Maggie Ross* • Eric Portman *Archie Ross* • Nanette Newman *Girl upstairs* • Gerald Sim *Mr Conrad* • Avis Bunnage *Mrs Noonan* • Ronald Fraser *Charlie Ross* • Leonard Rossiter *National Assistance official* • Kenneth Griffith *Mr Weaver* ■ *Dir* Bryan Forbes • *Scr* Bryan Forbes, from the novel *Mrs Ross* by Robert Nicolson

Whispering Ghosts ★

Comedy murder mystery
1942 · US · BW · 74mins

This feeble programme filler from Fox provides a showcase for the comic Milton Berle. He plays radio detective HH Van Buren, who solves crimes on the air and has to deal with the 10-year-old murder of a ship's captain. He visits the captain's old vessel in the search for clues and learns that it could be haunted. It's uninspired, with few opportunities for Berle to display his particular humorous persona, and, worst of all, plain boring.

Milton Berle *HH Van Buren* • Willie Best *Euclid White* • Brenda Joyce *Elizabeth Woods* • Abner Biberman *Mack Wolf* • John Carradine *Nobert/Long Jack* • Charles Halton *Gruber* ■ *Dir* Alfred Werker • *Scr* Lou Breslow, from a story by Philip McDonald

Whispering Smith ★★★

Western   1948 · US · Colour · 88mins

Alan Ladd hit his peak during the forties, mainly in thrillers, with his slightly glacial good looks suiting *noir* films such as *This Gun for Hire*. Towards the end of the decade he made this, his first starring western, which works more as a detective story with Ladd playing an undercover agent on the trail of train wreckers. It was his first film in colour, made just five years before he achieved immortality as Shane. The film is briskly handled by journeyman director Leslie Fenton, who brings the story to a rousing, shooting tooting climax. Ladd and co-stars Robert Preston and Frank Faylen play characters based on real western figures.

Alan Ladd *Luke "Whispering" Smith* • Robert Preston *Murray Sinclair* • Donald Crisp *Barney Rebstock* • Brenda Marshall *Marian Sinclair* • William Demarest *Bill Dansing* • Fay Holden *Emmy Dansing* • Murvyn Vye *Blake Barton* • Frank Faylen *Whitey Du Sang* ■ *Dir* Leslie Fenton • *Scr* Frank Butler, Karl Kamb, from the novel by Frank H Spearman

Whisperkill ★ 15

Thriller   1988 · US · Colour · 89mins

On the evidence of this pallid TV movie, Christian Nyby II has inherited none of the talent of his editor-turned-director father(*The Big Sleep*). This story about a small-town serial killer who dials his victims in advance is horribly contrived. There are too few suspects to keep us guessing for long and nothing about stars Loni Anderson and Joe Penny suggests they can discover whodunit before they are "done in" – yet it is told with an evident smugness at its own ingenuity. Contains violence, swearing and sex scenes.

Loni Anderson *Liz Bartlett* • Joe Penny *Dan Walker* • Jeremy Slate *Dr Oxford* • June Lockhart *Winnie* • James Sutorius *Vince* • Martin Ponch *Miller* • Bob Parnell *Chief Block* • Joe Lerer *Oz* ■ *Dir* Christian I Nyby II • *Scr* John Robert Bensink

Whispers ★★ 18

Chiller   1990 · Can · Colour · 89mins

Based on a novel by Dean R Koontz, this Canadian-made thriller puts Victoria Tennant into a real jam – she thinks she has murdered her assailant, Jean Leclerc, until he inconveniently shows up at the police station. The unfortunate cop on duty is Chris Sarandon. Tennant, the star of *War and Remembrance* who was married to Steve Martin, tends to act as if English is not her first language. Here she just needs to look scared and guilty, but it's more likely that that's how the audience will feel after watching this.

Victoria Tennant *Hilary Thomas* • Jean LeClerc *Bruno* • Chris Sarandon *Sgt Clemenza* • Linda Sorenson *Kayla* • Peter McNeil *Frank* ■ *Dir* Douglas Jackson • *Scr* Anita Doohan, from a novel by Dean R Koontz

Whispers in the Dark ★★★ 18

Erotic thriller   1992 · US · Colour · 98mins

This pacey little thriller overextends a thin plot, but still grips agreeably from the start. Annabella Sciorra is convincing as the psychiatrist who's perturbed by her response to a female patient – and gets herself and everyone else into extremely hot water by not grasping the Freudian nettle firmly enough. The high spots are Alan Alda as Sciorra's psychiatrist guru, vainly attempting to help his troubled colleague, and Anthony LaPaglia as a tough cop who will have no truck with all this "talkie feelie" stuff. Contains swearing, sex scenes and nudity.

Annabella Sciorra *Ann Hecker* • Jamey Sheridan *Doug McDowell* • Anthony LaPaglia *Morgenstern* • Jill Clayburgh *Sarah Green* • Alan Alda *Leo Green* • John Leguizamo *Johnny C* • Deborah Unger [Deborah Kara Unger] *Eve Abergray* • Anthony Heald *Paul* ■ *Dir/Scr* Christopher Crowe

The Whistle Blower ★★★★ PG

Spy thriller   1986 · UK · Colour · 99mins

In a low-key but very satisfying thriller, Michael Caine investigates the mysterious death of his son, Nigel Havers, who worked as a Russian translator at GCHQ. Caine is tremendously convincing as the former Korean war veteran (which he was in real life) who now feels betrayed by his country, as his search leads him along the corridors of power peopled by such posh types as James Fox and John Gielgud. Eschewing the usual thrills, the picture creates a totally plausible and undeniably creepy world of whispers and a seemingly impenetrable wall of class privilege and secrecy.

Michael Caine *Frank Jones* • James Fox *Lord* • Nigel Havers *Robert Jones* • John Gielgud *Sir Adrian Chapple* • Felicity Dean *Cynthia Goodburn* • Barry Foster *Charles Greig* • Gordon Jackson *Bruce* • Kenneth Colley *Bill Pickett* ■ *Dir* Simon Langton • *Scr* Julian Bond, from the novel by John Hale

Whistle down the Wind ★★★★ PG

Drama   1961 · UK · BW · 94mins

Alan Bates, a dishevelled murderer on the run, is confronted by three Lancashire children who think he is the persecuted Jesus Christ deserving of their protection. It's a daring allegory and debuting director Bryan Forbes treats it with heart-touching gravity and delicacy. The parable only starts to fall to pieces when the grown-up need for justice intrudes. Young Hayley Mills (whose mother wrote the novel on which this film is based) is wonderfully wide-eyed, while Bates, as the ambiguous stranger, gives his most involving performance. *DVD*

Hayley Mills *Kathy* • Alan Bates *The man* • Bernard Lee *Mr Bostock* • Norman Bird *Eddie* • Diane Holgate *Nan* • Alan Barnes *Charles* • Roy Holder *Jackie* • Barry Dean *Raymond* ■ *Dir* Bryan Forbes • *Scr* Keith Waterhouse, Willis Hall, from the novel by Mary Hayley Bell

Whistle Stop ★★

Crime melodrama   1946 · US · BW · 83mins

One of three American films made by the Paris-based Russian Léonide Moguy, this is a complicated crime farrago involving George Raft, Tom Conway, Victor McLaglen and – as the catalyst that sets cross and double-cross in motion – Ava Gardner. Having left gambler-lover Raft for the big city, Gardner returns and takes up with club owner Conway, whereupon McLaglen enlists the jealous Raft in a scheme to bump off Conway, whereupon Gardner… Formula crime fodder, it was a showcase for Gardner who, treading similar territory in *The Killers* later that year, became a star.

George Raft *Kenny Veech* • Ava Gardner *Mary* • Victor McLaglen *Gitlo* • Tom Conway *Lew* • Jorja Curtright *Fran* ■ *Dir* Léonide Moguy • *Scr* Philip Yordan, from the novel by Maritta Wolff • *Music* Dimitri Tiomkin [Dmitri Tiomkin]

Whistling in Brooklyn ★★

Crime comedy   1943 · US · BW · 86mins

The third and last of a set of breezy comedies starring Red Skelton (following *Whistling in the Dark* and *Whistling in Dixie*), this features more escapades of Skelton's radio sleuth. He is suspected of being a mystery killer and is chased by both cops and villain. The comic highlights include his masquerade as a bearded baseball player during a Dodgers game and a scare sequence on top of a descending freight elevator.

Red Skelton *Wally Benton* • Ann Rutherford *Carol Lambert* • Jean Rogers *Jean Pringle* • Rags Ragland *Chester* • Ray Collins *Grover Kendall* • Henry O'Neill *Inspector Holcomb* • William Frawley *Detective Ramsey* • Sam Levene *Creeper* ■ *Dir* S Sylvan Simon • *Scr* Nat Perrin, Wilkie Mahoney

Whistling in Dixie ★★★ U

Comedy   1942 · US · BW · 73mins

The sequel to MGM's surprise 1941 hit *Whistling in the Dark* has Red Skelton returning as radio detective Wally Benton, known as "The Fox". This time he's off to marry fiancée Carol Lambert (Ann Rutherford) but their sojourn in the south is interrupted by the search for some Confederate gold. While not up to the standard of the similar Bob Hope comedy thrillers, it still has some good moments.

Red Skelton *Wally Benton* • Ann Rutherford *Carol Lambert* • George Bancroft *Sheriff Claude Stagg* • Guy Kibbee *Judge George Lee* • Diana Lewis *Ellamae Downs* • Peter Whitney *Frank V Bailie* • Rags Ragland *Chester Conway/Lester Conway* ■ *Dir* S Sylvan Simon • *Scr* Nat Perrin, Wilkie Mahoney

Whistling in the Dark ★★★

Comedy mystery   1941 · US · BW · 76mins

Red Skelton gets his first starring role playing Wally Benton, the writer and star of a radio series in which his character, "The Fox", unravels seemingly unsolveable crimes. Skelton is kidnapped by an unscrupulous religious cult, headed by Conrad Veidt, and forced into concocting a perfect murder for them so they can get their hands on a million-dollar inheritance. Gripping, clever and funny, the film was a surprise success for MGM and spawned two sequels.

Red Skelton *Wally Benton* • Conrad Veidt *Joseph Jones* • Ann Rutherford *Carol Lambert* • Virginia Grey *"Fran" Post* • Rags Ragland *Sylvester* • Henry O'Neill *Philip Post* • Eve Arden *"Buzz" Baker* ■ *Dir* S Sylvan Simon • *Scr* Robert MacGonigle, Harry Clork, Albert Mannheimer, from the play by Laurence Gross, Edward Childs Carpenter

White Angel ★★ 18

Chiller   1993 · UK · Colour · 95mins

A minor addition to the serial-killer cycle made by Chris Jones and Genevieve Jolliffe, Britain's youngest film-makers in the early nineties. Reminiscent of Alfred Hitchcock's *The Lodger*, the story concerns an American crime writer and her dentist lodger who both, as it transpires, have something to hide. Shot, all too obviously, on a shoestring, in and around a house in Ruislip Manor, the thriller offers very little psychological motivation, but at least it isn't stalk-and-slash. Contains violence and some swearing.

Harriet Robinson *Ellen Carter* • Peter Firth *Leslie Steckler* • Don Henderson *Inspector Taylor* • Anne Catherine Arton *Mik* • Harry Miller *Alan Smith* • Joe Collins *Graham* • Caroline Staunton *Steckler's wife* • Mark Stevens *Carter's husband* ■ *Dir* Chris Jones • *Scr* Chris Jones, Genevieve Jolliffe

The White Balloon ★★★★ U

Drama 1995 · Iran · Colour · 80mins

Scripted by Abbas Kiarostami, who shared the Palme d'Or at Cannes for *The Taste of Cherries* in 1997, this delightful picture from director Jafar Panahi won the Camera d'Or at the same festival in 1995 for the best newcomer. Told in real time, this is a journey of discovery. As the seven-year-old experiencing the mysteries of the bazaar for the first time, Aida Mohammadkhani gives a remarkable performance, but it's Panahi's ability to convey both what she sees and what she feels that makes this deceptively simple film so miraculous. In Farsi with English subtitles.

Aida Mohammadkhani *Razieh* • Mohsen Kafili *Ali* • Fereshteh Sadr Orfani *Mother* • Anna Bourkowska *Old woman* ■ *Dir* Jafar Panahi • *Scr* Abbas Kiarostami

White Banners ★★★

Drama 1938 · US · BW · 88mins

Adapted from the book by Lloyd C Douglas, whose inspirational work included *The Robe*, this earnest morality tale seems less impressive today than it did to audiences on release, despite fine direction by Edmund Goulding and an Oscar-nominated star performance by Fay Bainter (who also won in the supporting category the same year for *Jezebel*). She plays a mystic figure who comes into the home of exploited inventor Claude Rains and his family, and has a profound effect on their lives.

Claude Rains *Paul Ward* • Fay Bainter *Hannah Parmalee* • Jackie Cooper *Peter Trimble* • Bonita Granville *Sally Ward* • Henry O'Neill *Sam Trimble* • Kay Johnson *Marcia Ward* • James Stephenson *Thomas Bradford* • J Farrell MacDonald *Dr Thompson* ■ *Dir* Edmund Goulding • *Scr* Lenore Coffee, Cameron Rogers, Abem Finkel, from the novel by Lloyd C Douglas

The White Buffalo ★

Western 1977 · US · Colour · 97mins

This attempt at an allegorical western features Charles Bronson as Wild Bill Hickok, returning to the plains in search of the white buffalo that he dreams of every night. In this quest he is joined by Crazy Horse, played by native American actor Will Sampson. Deep, deep down there is the potential for a meditative and mythical western – some critics have detected a sly transposition of *Moby Dick* – but almost everything about *The White Buffalo* doesn't work, including the buffalo itself and Bronson's self-regarding performance. Despite distracting cameos from Kim Novak, Slim Pickens and Clint Walker, this is a real clinker.

Charles Bronson *James Otis/Wild Bill Hickok* • Jack Warden *Charlie Zane* • Will Sampson *Chief Crazy Horse/"Worm"* • Kim Novak *Poker Jenny Schermerhorn* • Clint Walker *Whistling Jack Kileen* • Stuart Whitman *Winifred Coxy* • Slim Pickens *Abel Pickney* • John Carradine *Amos Briggs* ■ *Dir* J Lee Thompson • *Scr* Richard Sale, from his novel

White Cargo ★

Drama 1942 · US · BW · 87mins

Walter Pidgeon runs a British government rubber plantation in the heart of the Congo, with only a drink-sodden doctor (Frank Morgan), a disillusioned clergyman (Henry O'Neill), and his newly-arrived assistant Richard Carlson for company. Emotions boil over when Carlson falls for Tondelayo (Hedy Lamarr), a dangerously devious native sexpot who, together with the heat, damp rot and isolation, drives the white men mad. Although the atmosphere is strong and the film's early sequences are quite interesting, the descent into absurdity is total, making the result unintentionally and enjoyably hilarious.

Hedy Lamarr *Tondelayo* • Walter Pidgeon *Harry Witzel* • Frank Morgan *Doctor* • Richard Carlson *Langford* • Reginald Owen *Skipper* • Henry O'Neill *Rev Roberts* • Bramwell Fletcher *Wilbur Ashley* ■ *Dir* Richard Thorpe • *Scr* Leon Gordon, from his play, from the novel *Hell's Playground* by Ida Vera Simonton

White Cargo ★ 15

Comedy 1973 · UK · Colour · 73mins

A rare feature film appearance from *A Touch of Frost* star David Jason – and one he probably wouldn't wish to dwell on – this is a daft comedy in which a dithering civil servant becomes overinvolved in the plight of a Soho stripper. Jason's co-stars are Hugh Lloyd and Imogen Hassall. It's a lacklustre strike at "fish out of water" territory and the basic scenario fails to convince and soon descends into ludicrous farce. A non-starter from the moment it was conceived. ▭

David Jason *Albert Toddey* • Hugh Lloyd *Chumley* • Imogen Hassall *Stella* • Tim Barrett *Fosdyke* • Dave Prowse *Harry* • Raymond Cross *Dudley* • John Barber *Special agent* ■ *Dir* Ray Selfe • *Scr* Ray Selfe, David McGillivray, from a story by Ray Selfe

White Christmas ★★★★★ U

Musical 1954 · US · Colour · 115mins

A partial remake of the 1942 film *Holiday Inn*, this is the Bing Crosby movie that gave the world the bestselling Irving Berlin song. Paramount wanted an opportunity to introduce its new screen process, VistaVision – and what better way to use it than on its big holiday release of 1954? Crosby's *Holiday Inn* partner Fred Astaire wasn't available and Donald O'Connor pulled out, so Danny Kaye reluctantly agreed to second billing under Crosby, in what proved to be a fortuitous move. Kaye is superb, especially in his knockout dance routine with Vera-Ellen. Veteran director Michael Curtiz rightly embraced the sentiment. ▭

Bing Crosby *Bob Wallace* • Danny Kaye *Phil Davis* • Rosemary Clooney *Betty* • Vera-Ellen *Judy* • Dean Jagger *General Waverly* • Mary Wickes *Emma* • John Brascia *Joe* • Anne Whitfield *Susan* • Sig Rumann [Sig Ruman] *Landlord* ■ *Dir* Michael Curtiz • *Scr* Norman Krasna, Norman Panama, Melvin Frank

The White Cliffs of Dover ★★★ U

Wartime drama 1944 · US · BW · 124mins

Based on a poem by Alice Duer Miller, this is a long, lavish, starry, and tear-jerkingly sentimental account of a woman's courage through the First World War, in which her husband is killed, and the Second World War, during which her dying soldier son (Peter Lawford) is brought in to the hospital where she works as a Red Cross nurse. One of several admiring, pro-British flag-wavers from MGM, directed largely in flashback by Clarence Brown, the film stars Irene Dunne as the indestructible heroine, an American who, in 1914, comes to England and marries titled Englishman Alan Marshal. The massive cast includes Roddy McDowall, Gladys Cooper (as Dunne's mother-in-law) and a young Elizabeth Taylor.

Irene Dunne *Lady Susan Dunn Ashwood* • Alan Marshal *Sir John Ashwood* • Roddy McDowall *John Ashwood II, as a boy* • Frank Morgan *Hiram Porter Dunn* • Van Johnson *Sam Bennett* • C Aubrey Smith *Colonel Walter Forsythe* • Gladys Cooper *Lady Jean Ashwood* • Peter Lawford *John Ashwood II, as a young man* • Elizabeth Taylor *Betsy Kenney, aged 10* ■ *Dir* Clarence Brown • *Scr* Claudine West, Jan Lustig, George Froeschel, from the poem by Alice Duer Miller, with additional poetry by Robert Nathan

White Corridors ★★★ U

Medical drama 1951 · UK · BW · 101mins

This Midlands-set medical tale charts the various comings and goings of doctors and patients. The central plot involves a doctor (James Donald) who, perfecting a serum for treating a blood disease, infects himself – thus requiring the intervention of the doctor who loves him (Googie Withers). While it may sound like a hokey soap opera, it is actually a well-made British A-feature, realistically played by a large and excellent cast that includes a number of well-known faces, among them Petula Clark, Moira Lister and Jack Watling.

James Donald *Neil Marriner* • Googie Withers *Sophie Dean* • Godfrey Tearle *Groom Sr* • Jack Watling *Dick Groom* • Petula Clark *Joan Shepherd* • Moira Lister *Dolly Clark* • Barry Jones *Shoesmith* ■ *Dir* Pat Jackson • *Scr* Pat Jackson, Jan Read, from the novel *Yeoman's Hospital* by Helen Ashton

The White Dawn ★★★★

Historical drama 1974 · US · Colour and BW · 109mins

A group of whalers are shipwrecked and left stranded among an Inuit tribe in 1896. It's a study of cultural collision, done with an almost wordless script, and a paean to the beauties of the Arctic – the landscape and the animals that live there. Part Herman Melville, part Jack London and part "new-age" San Francisco, this stirring drama knocks spots off most other films of the genre. Never condescending and remarkably open-minded about the conflict between nature's and capitalism's hunters, it's superbly filmed on Frobisher Bay and well acted by a cast that must have endured a lot of discomfort. In Inuit and English with English subtitles.

Warren Oates *Billy* • Timothy Bottoms *Daggett* • Louis Gossett Jr *Portagee* • Simonie Kopapik *Sarkak* • Joanasie Salomonie *Kangiak* • Pilitak *Neevee* ■ *Dir* Philip Kaufman • *Scr* James Houston, Tom Rickman, Martin Ransohoff, from the novel by James Houston • *Cinematographer* Michael Chapman

White Dog ★★★★ 15

Drama 1981 · US · Colour · 85mins

Inside a toughie such as Sam Fuller lurks a moralist trying to get out, and this fact was never more evident than in this racist fable. His first Hollywood movie for some years, it's about actress Kristy McNichol taking on a German shepherd dog that has been trained to kill black people. Rehabilitation is slow and painful at Burl Ives's animal training centre – a canine equivalent of the apartheid condition. However, it's a story that has its source in dreadful truth. An off-the-wall idea to match Fuller's off-the-leash style. Contains violence and swearing.

Kristy McNichol *Julie Sawyer* • Paul Winfield *Keys* • Burl Ives *Carruthers* • Jameson Parker *Roland Gray* • Lynne Moody *Molly* • Marshall Thompson *Director* • Bob Minor *Joe* ■ *Dir* Samuel Fuller • *Scr* Samuel Fuller, Curtis Hanson, from the novella and *Life, magazine article* by Romain Gary • *Cinematographer* Bruce Surtees • *Music* Ennio Morricone

White Dwarf ★★

Science-fiction fantasy 1995 · US · Colour · 91mins

Executive produced by Francis Ford Coppola, this futuristic fantasy was a series pilot that failed to lead to further episodes. In the year 3040, a young New York doctor (Neal McDonough) is sent to a war-torn planet circling a white-dwarf star to complete a six-month residency. There he finds a world divided into warring hemispheres, one of perpetual darkness and the other in constant daylight, and gets caught up in quelling sinister forces. Though well acted with stylish special effects, this sci-fi TV film is marred by a murky, slow-moving style. Director Peter Markle fails to bring the complex story into emotional focus.

Paul Winfield *Dr Akada* • CCH Pounder *Nurse Shabana* • Neal McDonough *Dr Driscoll Rampart* • Ele Keats *Princess Ariel* • Joey Andrews *Never* • Tara Graham *XaXa* • Beverley Mitchell *XuXu* ■ *Dir* Peter Markle • *Scr* Bruce Wagner

White Fang ★★

Adventure 1936 · US · BW · 70mins

The novel *White Fang* was Jack London's sequel to his hugely popular *Call of the Wild*, filmed by Fox in 1935 with Clark Gable and Loretta Young. Writer Gene Fowler scripted both movies as outdoor adventures aimed at the family audience, though this second movie doesn't boast the same fine cast or the same primitive flair. Michael Whalen makes a pallid hero and Jean Muir is the love interest, her only rival the wolf of the title.

Michael Whalen *Gordon Scott/Scotty* • Jean Muir *Sylvia Burgess* • Slim Summerville *Slats Magee* • Charles Winninger *Doc McFane* • John Carradine *Beauty Smith* • Jane Darwell *Maud Mahoney* • Thomas Beck *Hal Burgess* •

Joseph Herrick *Kobi* ■ *Dir* David Butler • *Scr* Gene Fowler, Hal Long, SG Duncan, from the novel by Jack London

White Fang ★★★ PG

Adventure   1991 · US · Colour · 104mins

This is family fare for the kind of family that thinks *The Waltons* is high drama. Jack London's ferocious story about the half-wolf in the Klondike is tamed *Lassie*-style by Disney, with most of the savagery squeezed out. Ethan Hawke, with dubious partners Klaus Maria Brandauer and Seymour Cassel, is the young gold prospector who seeks to establish a prosperous claim. The film may be a bit of a letdown for previously Oscar-nominated Brandauer, but he turns a minor role into a major one. ▭ *DVD*

Klaus Maria Brandauer *Alex* • Ethan Hawke *Jack* • Seymour Cassel *Skunker* • Susan Hogan *Belinda* • James Remar *Beauty* • Bill Moseley *Luke* • Clint B Youngreen *Tinker* • Pius Savage *Grey Beaver* ■ *Dir* Randal Kleiser • *Scr* Jeanne Rosenberg, Nick Thiel, David Fallon, from the novel by Jack London

White Fang 2: Myth of the White Wolf ★★ U

Adventure   1994 · US · Colour · 101mins

Ethan Hawke puts in an uncredited appearance at the start of this handsome Disney adventure, which, unlike its predecessor, owes little or nothing to the much-loved novel by Jack London. Scott Bairstow steps into Hawke's shoes as he abandons the Alaskan gold fields and, along with his beautiful canine companion, searches for a herd of lost caribou for a tribe of starving Haida Indians. The soppy romance between Bairstow and princess Charmaine Craig won't do much for the majority of younger viewers, but they should find the tribal mythology and mysticism fascinating and the litter of puppies utterly irresistible. ▭

Scott Bairstow *Henry Casey* • Charmaine Craig *Lily Joseph* • Al Harrington *Moses Joseph* • Anthony Michael Ruivivar *Peter* • Victoria Racimo *Katrin* • Alfred Molina *Reverend Leland Drury* • Ethan Hawke *Jack* • Geoffrey Lewis *Heath* ■ *Dir* Ken Olin • *Scr* David Fallon

White Feather ★★★ U

Western   1955 · US · Colour · 102mins

One of a number of westerns made around this time that dealt sympathetically with the plight of the native American people, this has female lead Debra Paget virtually reprising her role from *Broken Arrow*. A gauche Robert Wagner is the government surveyor trying to persuade the Cheyenne that living on a reservation is their best option, but they find his resolutely fifties' cool bravado as hard to take as we do. Jeffrey Hunter looks equally uncomfortable as a brave and cavalryman John Lund acts throughout as though he'd rather be somewhere else. Yet, despite the poor casting, Lucien Ballard's handsome CinemaScope photography gives this film all the dignity it needs.

Robert Wagner *Josh Tanner* • John Lund *Colonel Lindsay* • Debra Paget *Appearing Day* • Jeffrey Hunter *Little Dog* • Eduard Franz *Chief Broken Hand* • Noah Beery Jr *Lieutenant*

Ferguson • Virginia Leith *Ann Magruder* • Emile Meyer *Magruder* ■ *Dir* Robert Webb [Robert D Webb] • *Scr* Delmer Daves, Leo Townsend, from a story by John Prebble

White Heat ★★★★★ 15

Classic crime drama
1949 · US · BW · 109mins

"Made it, Ma! Top of the world!" shrieks a demented James Cagney from the top of an oil tank before going out in a blaze of vainglory. Directed by Raoul Walsh, this is one of the greatest of all gangster pictures, a nightmarish excursion into the maladjusted mind of Arthur Cody Jarrett, a young thug who sits on his mother's knee, steals and kills for pure pleasure, and probably sucks his thumb in private. All the major gangster heroes of the thirties had their psychological problems, but here Cagney is a whole library of Freudian theory put through the blender; the poor lad suffers from epilepsy to boot. It's operatic, sinisterly funny and utterly compelling. ▭

James Cagney *Arthur Cody Jarrett* • Virginia Mayo *Verna Jarrett* • Edmond O'Brien *Hank Fallon/Vic Pardo* • Margaret Wycherly *Ma Jarrett* • Steve Cochran *"Big Ed" Somers* • John Archer *Philip Evans* • Wally Cassell *Giovanni Cotton Valetti* • Mickey Knox *Het Kohler* ■ *Dir* Raoul Walsh • *Scr* Ivan Goff, Ben Roberts, from a story by Virginia Kellogg • *Cinematographer* Sid Hickox

White Hot: the Mysterious Murder of Thelma Todd ★★

Crime drama based on a true story
1991 · US · Colour · 95mins

This TV movie attempts to re-create the raw gangsterland of the thirties and serves only to look as if a motley crew of extras are running around the studio backlot in long overcoats and big hats. This is a movie devoid of all atmosphere, featuring a wooden performance from Burt Reynolds's ex-wife Loni Anderson as the Thelma in question, a real-life Hollywood actress who died in mysterious circumstances in 1935 and whose idea of a good night out was riding romantic shotgun with Lucky Luciano.

Loni Anderson *Thelma Todd* • Robert Davi *Lucky Luciano* • Scott Paulin *Lou Marsden* • Robin Strasser *Jewel Carmen* • Paul Dooley *Hal Roach* • Lois Smith *Alice Todd* • Lawrence Pressman *Roland West* • Linda Kelsey *Ann McMahon* ■ *Dir* Paul Wendkos • *Scr* Robert E Thompson, Lindsay Harrison, from the book *Hot Toddy* by Andy Edmonds

White Hunter, Black Heart ★★★★ PG

Drama   1990 · US · Colour · 107mins

Clint Eastwood's ambitious film is a thinly veiled account of the making of John Huston's *The African Queen*, already well documented in books by Katharine Hepburn and screenwriter Peter Viertel. As "Huston", Eastwood is just marvellous – aristocratic, bombastic and so obsessed with hunting and killing an elephant that his movie-making is left on the back burner. He's a monster with enormous charm and charisma. Beautifully filmed on location in Zimbabwe, with decent representations of Bogart, Bacall, Hepburn and producer Sam Spiegel, the movie has pace, drama, a genuine

sense of adventure and an astutely critical eye for the dying vestiges of British imperialism. Contains violence and swearing. ▭

Clint Eastwood *John Wilson* • Jeff Fahey *Pete Verrill* • Charlotte Cornwell *Miss Wilding* • Norman Lumsden *Butler George* • George Dzundza *Paul Landers* • Edward Tudor-Pole *Reissar* • Roddy Maude-Roxby *Thompson* • Richard Warwick *Basil Fields* • Marisa Berenson *Kay Gibson* ■ *Dir* Clint Eastwood • *Scr* Peter Viertel, James Bridges, Burt Kennedy, from the novel by Peter Viertel

White Lie ★★ 15

Crime drama   1991 · US · Colour · 88mins

This earnestly played crime drama blows the lid off the simmering racial tensions that still exist in the American Deep South. Because it was made for television, Bill Condon's movie is less controversial than it might have been. Moreover, there's a tacky convenience about black political aide Gregory Hines's romance with white paediatrician Annette O'Toole, and it's hard not to read the revelations Hines uncovers about his past as pure melodrama. Contains some violence. ▭

Gregory Hines *Len Maddison Jr* • Annette O'Toole *Helen Lester* • Bill Nunn *Chief Adams* • Gregg Henry *David Lester* • Marc Macaulay *Donald Cambio* • John Lawhorn *Uncle Ellard* • Carole Mitchell-Leon *Martha Hoffer Jordan* ■ *Dir* Bill Condon • *Scr* Nevin Schreiner, from the novel *Louisiana Black* by Samuel Charters

White Lightning ★★★ 15

Action crime thriller
1973 · US · Colour · 97mins

One of the best of Burt Reynolds's good ol' boy movies, in which he's a moonshiner whose manufacture of illicit liquor puts him up against crooked sheriff Ned Beatty. As the corrupt lawman was responsible for the death of Burt's brother, revenge is also on the menu. Director Joseph Sargent makes good use of some interesting swampland locations, and keeps the drama from being too formulaic. A disappointing sequel, *Gator*, followed in 1976. ▭

Burt Reynolds *Gator McKlusky* • Jennifer Billingsley *Lou* • Ned Beatty *Sheriff Connors* • Bo Hopkins *Roy Boone* • Matt Clark *Dude Watson* • Louise Latham *Martha Culpepper* • Diane Ladd *Maggie* • RG Armstrong *Big Bear* ■ *Dir* Joseph Sargent • *Scr* William Norton

White Line Fever ★★★ 15

Action drama   1975 · US · Colour · 85mins

Back on civvy street after a stint in the air force, a young man (Jan-Michael Vincent) buys a truck, marries his sweetheart (Kay Lenz) and gets started in the hauling business, only to learn that it is run by racketeers and smugglers. Refusing to bow to the system, he endangers himself by fighting corruption. The movie, convincingly played by Vincent and the supporting cast, marked a step up for director Jonathan Kaplan who handles the material extremely well to make a taut action drama with a satisfying, if unrealistic, outcome. ▭

Jan-Michael Vincent *Carrol Jo Hummer* • Kay Lenz *Jerri Hummer* • Slim Pickens *Duane Haller* • LQ Jones *Buck Wessle* • Don Porter

Josh Cutler • Sam Laws *Pops* • Johnny Ray McGhee *Carnell* ■ *Dir* Jonathan Kaplan • *Scr* Ken Friedman, Jonathan Kaplan

The White Lions ★★★

Adventure   1980 · US · Colour · 96mins

Directed by Mel Stuart (*Willy Wonka and the Chocolate Factory*), this location-shot safari movie in the *Born Free* mould stars Michael York as the naturalist who takes his wife and daughter with him when he goes out to Africa to study endangered wildlife. It's too twee for comfort, but children who love natural-history TV programmes should like it.

Michael York *Chris McBride* • Glynnis O'Connor *Mrs McBride* ■ *Dir* Mel Stuart • *Scr* Corey Blechman, Peter Dixon

White Mama ★★★

Drama   1980 · US · Colour · 96mins

Bette Davis stars in this quality TV movie, which is better than it sounds. This is mainly thanks to Davis's performance as a proud but destitute widow, who hatches the scheme of taking a 16-year-old black delinquent into her home in order to qualify for foster-care payments. Ernest Harden Jr does well as the young, streetwise but illiterate half of this odd couple, while the writing diligently explores the dramatic potential of the unlikely pairing. But the film ultimately belongs to Davis.

Bette Davis *Estelle Malone* • Ernest Harden Jr *BT Williamson* • Eileen Heckart *Three bag lady* • Virginia Capers *Gorilla Sydney* • Anne Ramsey *Heavy Charm* • Lurene Tuttle *Frances McIntyre* • Peg Shirley *Judge Alice Quentin* ■ *Dir* Jackie Cooper • *Scr* Robert CS Downs

White Mane ★★★★

Adventure drama   1952 · Fr · BW · 47mins

Winner of the Prix Jean Vigo, Albert Lamorisse's third film may not be as well known as *The Red Balloon*, but it is still a charming study of the all-too-fleeting wonder of childhood. Young Alain Emery gives a spirited performance as the kid whose daily routine of fishing and poaching with his grandfather is interrupted by the appearance of a proud white stallion, which defies all attempts to capture it. With the Camargue marshlands emphasising the wildness of both the horse and his boy, this is a poetic and truly inspiring tribute to the beauty of nature. A French language film.

Alain Emery *Folco* • Pascal Lamorisse • Frank Silvera ■ *Dir/Scr* Albert Lamorisse

White Man's Burden ★★ 15

Fantasy drama   1995 · US · Colour · 85mins

This reversed-reality drama is set in an alternate Los Angeles where blacks hold all the positions of power and influence, and where whites do all the menial work. John Travolta plays a blue-collar worker who, more by default than design, winds up kidnapping black boss Harry Belafonte when he calls at his mansion to protest at being unfairly fired. During an enforced cross-town trek, Belafonte has his eyes opened to the iniquities of being white in a black man's world. It's a neat idea, less fully realised than it might

U = SUITABLE FOR ALL Uc = SUITABLE FOR ALL, ESPECIALLY FOR YOUNG CHILDREN (VIDEO ONLY) PG = PARENTAL GUIDANCE

have been. After a strong start, the film flounders, never quite knowing where it wants to wind up. There are good performances from the two stars, though. Contains swearing and some violence.

John Travolta *Louis Pinnock* • Harry Belafonte *Thaddeus Thomas* • Kelly Lynch *Marsha Pinnock* • Margaret Avery *Megan Thomas* • Tom Bower *Stanley* • Carrie Snodgress *Josine* ■ *Dir/Scr* Desmond Nakano

White Men Can't Jump ★★★★ 15

Sports comedy 1992 · US · Colour · 110mins

Writer/director Ron Shelton is that rare beast – someone who can make movies with wit, warmth and perception about American sports. This is a marvellous tale of two basketball players (Wesley Snipes and Woody Harrelson) who make their living hustling fellow street players around Los Angeles. The plot is fairly simplistic, but the pleasure comes from Shelton's fizzing, foul-mouthed dialogue, the charismatic performances of the two stars and the superbly choreographed basketball sequences. And, as an added bonus, Rosie Perez, as Harrelson's girlfriend, manages to stay the right side of irritating. Contains violence, swearing and nudity.

Wesley Snipes *Sidney Deane* • Woody Harrelson *Billy Hoyle* • Rosie Perez *Gloria Clemente* • Tyra Ferrell *Rhonda Deane* • Cylk Cozart *Robert* • Kadeem Hardison *Junior* • Ernest Harden Jr *George* • John Marshall Jones *Walter* ■ *Dir/Scr* Ron Shelton

White Mile ★★★ 15

Drama based on a true story
1994 · US · Colour · 95mins

Alan Alda has worked hard to toughen up his nice-guy liberal image and he is in convincing form in this TV movie. He plays the hard-as-nails boss of a company who refuses to accept any responsibility when a white-water rafting trip he has organised for his staff ends in tragedy. Peter Gallagher is the tormented executive wondering whether he should fall into line. Director Robert Butler's direction is unobtrusive, but he nonetheless brings considerable drama to the central action sequence, and he is well served by a better-than-average cast. Contains violence and swearing.

Alan Alda *Dan Cutler* • Peter Gallagher *Jack Robbins* • Robert Loggia *Robert Karas* ■ *Dir* Robert Butler • *Scr* Michael Butler

White Mischief ★★★ 18

Historical drama
1987 · UK · Colour · 103mins

The less-than-wholesome traits of Kenya's scandal-ridden "Happy Valley" crowd in the forties are nicely delineated, in all their dissolute, gin-swilling, servant-barking, expat glory, by director Michael Radford. Based on a true story about the murder of a promiscuous aristocrat who was servicing half of the valley's bored ladies, this rather over-egged drama has no one in which elicits any sympathy. Charles Dance makes a believable stud, however, and Greta Scacchi is gorgeous, even if Joss Ackland overacts horribly as her

cuckolded husband. There's also a truly bizarre performance from Sarah Miles. Contains swearing, sex scenes and nudity.

Charles Dance *Josslyn Hay, Earl of Erroll* • Greta Scacchi *Diana* • Joss Ackland *Sir John "Jock" Delves Broughton* • Sarah Miles *Alice de Janze* • John Hurt *Gilbert Colvile* • Geraldine Chaplin *Nina Soames* • Ray McAnally *Morris* • Trevor Howard *Jack Soames* ■ *Dir* Michael Radford • *Scr* Michael Radford, Jonathan Gems, from the book by James Fox

White Nights ★★★ U

Drama 1957 · It/Fr · BW · 98mins

Based on a Dostoyevsky story, this touching fantasy concerns a meek and lonely clerk who falls deeply in love with a girl on a bridge – she goes there every night to meet her own lover, a sailor, who has promised to return but never does. This movie marked a radical departure for the arch neorealist and communist Luchino Visconti, who treats it rather like a Fellini film. It was staged on deliberately artificial sets – supposedly the canals of Livorno – and has the ambience of a dream. Marcello Mastroianni gives one of his best performances of the fifties as the doomed clerk in a tale that was to be remade twice more – in 1959 by Soviet director Ivan Pyriev and in 1971by Robert Bresson. In Italian with English subtitles.

Maria Schell *Natalia* • Marcello Mastroianni *Mario* • Jean Marais *Lodger* • Clara Calamai *Prostitute* • Marcella Rovena *Housewife* • Maria Zanolli *Housekeeper* ■ *Dir* Luchino Visconti • *Scr* Luchino Visconti, Suso Cecchi D'Amico, from the story *Belye Nochi* by Fyodor Mikhailovich Dostoyevsky

White Nights ★★★ 15

Political thriller 1985 · US · Colour · 130mins

This entertaining blend of ballet and bullets stars dancer Mikhail Baryshnikov as a bolshy Bolshoi-er who finds himself back in the USSR when the plane he's defecting on is forced to make a (spectacular) crash-landing. Fellow hoofer Gregory Hines co-stars, as an expatriate tap-star who helps him to re-defect. As you'll have gathered, it's not the world's most credible plot. But Baryshnikov is surprisingly good and there are stunning dance and action sequences, skilfully stage-managed by director Taylor Hackford (*An Officer and a Gentleman*).

Mikhail Baryshnikov *Nikolai "Kolya" Rodchenko* • Gregory Hines *Raymond Greenwood* • Jerzy Skolimowski *Colonel Chaiko* • Helen Mirren *Galina Ivanova* • Geraldine Page *Anne Wyatt* • Isabella Rossellini *Darya Greenwood* • John Glover *Wynn Scott* ■ *Dir* Taylor Hackford • *Scr* James Goldman, Eric Hughes, from a story by James Goldman

White of the Eye ★★★ 18

Psychological thriller
1986 · UK · Colour · 106mins

Best known for *Performance* (which he co-directed with Nicolas Roeg) and the sci-fi classic *Demon Seed*, Donald Cammell ended a decade-long exile from the director's chair with this bizarre, yet decidedly disturbing thriller. The Indian mysticism is pretty half-baked, the symbolism is anything but

subtle and the Steadicam work is overly intrusive. But Cammell creates an atmosphere of real menace as he delves beneath the surface calm of a sleepy former mining town in Arizona. He's well served by a cast that never quite made the front rank, with David Keith and Alan Rosenberg the thoroughly deranged men in Cathy Moriarty's rapidly unravelling life. Contains violence and swearing.

David Keith *Paul White* • Cathy Moriarty *Joan White* • Art Evans *Detective Charles Mendoza* • Alan Rosenberg *Mike Desantos* • Alberta Watson *Ann Mason* • Michael Green *Phil Ross* • Danko Gurovich *Arnold White* • William G Schilling *Harold Gideon* • China Cammell [China Kong] *Ruby Hoy* ■ *Dir* Donald Cammell • *Scr* China Cammell [China Kong], Donald Cammell, from the novel *Mrs White* by Margaret Tracy

White Palace ★★★★ 18

Romantic drama 1990 · US · Colour · 98mins

James Spader had long been Hollywood's favourite rich-kid, but this (along with *sex, lies, and videotape*) provided him with a rare role that he could really get his teeth into. He plays a youngish middle-class ad man who falls for forty-something waitress Susan Sarandon, much to the dismay of his peers. Spader and Sarandon spark off each other superbly, making the most of a mature script that intelligently explores class and sexuality in modern America. Luis Mandoki's direction is admirably level-headed, and he successfully sidesteps the usual clichés and melodramatics. There is also a strong supporting cast, which includes Kathy Bates and Eileen Brennan. Contains swearing and sex scenes.

Susan Sarandon *Nora Baker* • James Spader *Max Baron* • Jason Alexander *Neil Horowitz* • Kathy Bates *Rosemary Powers* • Eileen Brennan *Judy* • Steven Hill *Sol Horowitz* • Corey Parker *Larry Klugman* ■ *Dir* Luis Mandoki • *Scr* Ted Tally, Alvin Sargent, from the novel by Glenn Savan

The White Parade ★★★

Medical drama 1934 · US · BW · 83mins

Set in a school for trainee nurses in the American Midwest, the focus is on Loretta Young, whose dedication to her calling is challenged by romantic involvement with wealthy Boston blueblood John Boles, who forces her to choose between him and her career. Young is excellent in a film that manages to combine an almost documentary approach with old-fashioned romantic soap opera. Directed by Irving Cummings, it's entertaining enough and was a big box-office success on release, but its Oscar nomination as best picture is something of a surprise. (The winner was *It Happened One Night*).

Loretta Young *June Arden* • John Boles *Ronald Hall III* • Dorothy Wilson *Zita Scofield* • Muriel Kirkland *Glenda Farley* • Astrid Allwyn *Gertrude Mack* • Frank Conroy *Doctor Thorne* • Jane Darwell *Sailor Roberts* • Frank Melton *Doctor Barnes* ■ *Dir* Irving Cummings • *Scr* Sonya Levien, Ernest Pascal, from the novel by Rian James, adapted by Rian James, Jesse Lasky Jr

The White Raven ★★

Thriller 1998 · US · Colour · 89mins

This melodramatic thriller, though flattered by a strong cast, is no *Maltese Falcon*. Ron Silver plays a Pulitzer Prize-winning journalist writing a story about a priceless diamond which was used to buy the freedom of a Jewish woman at the Treblinka concentration camp. The diamond has long since disappeared, but the reporter finds himself pursued by everyone from ex-Nazis to its original owner, all of whom suspect he has knowledge of its whereabouts. Daft and muddled, it's small wonder Silver, Roy Scheider and Joanna Pacula spend most of the time looking like they wished they were some place else.

Ron Silver *Tully Windsor* • Roy Scheider *Tom Heath* • Joanna Pacula *Julia Konneman* • Hannes Jaenicke *Dockmonish* • Jack Recknitz *Inspector Zielinski* ■ *Dir* Andrew Stevens • *Scr* Michael Blodgett

White Room ★★

Drama 1990 · Can · Colour · 93mins

A bizarre suburban fairy tale about a peeping tom who witnesses a singer's rape and murder, then becomes entangled with a strange woman he meets at the singer's funeral and who lives in a gingerbread house. Directed by Patricia Rozema, who had previously made the art-house hit *I've Heard the Mermaids Singing*, the film is crammed with colour codings and metaphors. The over-intellectualisation won't appeal to all tastes but is evidence of a mind at work. The cast includes Maurice Godin, and the better known Kate Nelligan and Margot Kidder.

Kate Nelligan *Jane* • Maurice Godin *Norm* • Margot Kidder *Madelaine X* • Sheila McCarthy *Zelda* • Barbara Gordon *Mrs Gentle* • Nicky Guadagni *Narrator* ■ *Dir/Scr* Patricia Rozema

White Sands ★★★ 15

Thriller 1992 · US · Colour · 97mins

Mega-black doings in New Mexico in, appropriately enough, a *film noir*, which takes to the hills when deputy sheriff Willem Dafoe finds half-a-million mysterious dollars in a suitcase belonging to a dead FBI agent. Roger Donaldson's direction loses focus when Dafoe meets up with arms dealer Mickey Rourke and his society girlfriend Mary Elizabeth Mastrantonio, while the plot's twists and turns become inextricably entangled, but it still keeps us involved in the action. Contains swearing and violence.

Willem Dafoe *Ray Dolezal* • Mary Elizabeth Mastrantonio *Lane Bodine* • Mickey Rourke *Gorman Lennox* • Sam Jackson [Samuel L Jackson] *Greg Meeker* • M Emmet Walsh *Bert Gibson* • Mimi Rogers *Molly Dolezal* ■ *Dir* Roger Donaldson • *Scr* Daniel Pyne

White Shadows in the South Seas ★★★

Drama 1928 · US · BW · 88mins

MGM sent acclaimed documentary director Robert Flaherty and rising outdoor action director WS Van Dyke to shoot a South Seas adventure on location at a time when real exotic settings had huge box-office appeal. Flaherty resigned early on and Van Dyke made his reputation with this

pictorially magnificent, sombre story of a white trader corrupting pagans, in which a small cast worked well with native performers. The studio then decided to launch the film as its first sound release, adding some crude dialogue, sound effects and music score, and these now have a quaint charm although criticised for their technical shortcomings at the time.

Monte Blue *Lloyd* • Raquel Torres *Faraway* • Robert Anderson *Sebastian* ■ *Dir* WS Van Dyke • *Scr* Jack Cunningham, John Colton, Ray Doyle, from the novel by Frederick O'Brien • *Cinematographers* Clyde De Vinna • *Cinematographer* George Nagle, Bob Roberts

The White Sheik ★★★ U

Romantic comedy drama
1951 · It · BW · 83mins

Originally devised by Michelangelo Antonioni (who retained a story credit), Federico Fellini's first solo outing not only lampoons bourgeois sensibilities, but also the photo-romance magazines that did a roaring trade in the early fifties. Arriving in Rome for her honeymoon, Brunella Bovo ditches husband Leopoldo Trieste's carefully planned itinerary in order to meet both her favourite fumetti star, Alberto Sordi, and the Pope. Vital to this sympathetic study of shattered illusions is Fellini's mischievous sense of fantasy, but Sordi's performance as the dissolute, hen-pecked idol is also top drawer. Largely overlooked on release, this is clearly a key cinematic stepping-stone. In Italian with English subtitles. ▭

Alberto Sordi *Fernando Rivoli, "The White Sheik"* • Brunella Bovo *Wanda Cavalli* • Leopoldo Trieste *Ivan Cavalli* • Giulietta Masina *Cabiria* ■ *Dir* Federico Fellini • *Scr* Federico Fellini, Tullio Pinelli, Ennio Flaiano, from a story by Federico Fellini, Tullio Pinelli, from an idea by Michelangelo Antonioni

The White Sister ★★★

Silent romantic drama
1923 · US · BW · 143mins

After the death of her father, Italian aristocrat Lillian Gish is thrown out of the ancestral home and cheated of her inheritance by her vindictive sister. Hearing that Italian army officer Ronald Colman, whom she loves, has been killed, she becomes a nun, only for Colman to reappear and attempt to prise her out of the convent. An impressive silent drama, unusual for its time in dealing with religion against a contemporary background, and well-directed by Henry King (with help from the Vatican) on location in Italy. The film brought Colman – even without the help of his exquisitely modulated voice – the stardom that would be his for three decades.

Lillian Gish *Angela Chiaromonte* • Ronald Colman *Capt Giovanni Severini* • Gail Kane *Marchesa di Mola* • J Barney Sherry *Monsignor Saracinesca* • Charles Lane (2) *Prince Chiaromonte* ■ *Dir* Henry King • *Scr* George V Hobart, Charles E Whittaker, Will M Ritchey, Don Bartlett, from the novel by F Marion Crawford

The White Sister ★★

Melodrama 1933 · US · BW · 105mins

A so-called "woman's picture", shot by Garbo's cameraman, William H Daniels, and directed by Clark Gable's

macho hunting pal, Victor Fleming. Gable and Helen Hayes play the lovelorn couple, he a soldier and she his beloved who believes he has been killed in combat. But Gable returns and is totally gutted to discover that Hayes has married someone else, a nun in fact, for she has taken her vows as a nun. Because of its profoundly religious theme, this load of tosh is wisely located in Italy. The story had been a major success as a silent film ten years earlier.

Helen Hayes *Angela Chiaromonte* • Clark Gable *Lt Giovanni Severi* • Lewis Stone *Prince Guido Chiaromonte* • Louise Closser Hale *Mina* • May Robson *Mother Superior* • Edward Arnold *Father Saracinesca* • Alan Edwards *Ernesto Traversi* ■ *Dir* Victor Fleming • *Scr* Donald Ogden Stewart, from the play *The White Sister* by F Marion Crawford, from the play *The White Sister* by Walter Hackett, from the novel *The White Sister* by F Marion Crawford

White Squall ★★★ 12

Biographical adventure
1996 · US · Colour · 123mins

Neither Jeff Bridges's quiet authority nor the "in-your-face" dramatics of a killer storm can lift director Ridley Scott's attempt to remake *Top Gun* (which was directed by brother Tony) at sea. School-ship skipper Bridges gathers a group of undisciplined students aboard the brigantine *Albatross* for a voyage of self-discovery to South America. Unfortunately, this undemanding but entertaining rites-of-passage adventure, based on a true story, takes a sudden lurch into disaster with the arrival of the storm of the title. It may be a tour de force set piece, but it represents such an abrupt change of tone that the movie's credibility is almost blown away in the process. Contains some swearing and sexual references. ▭

Jeff Bridges *"Skipper" Sheldon* • Caroline Goodall *Dr Alice Sheldon* • John Savage *McCrea* • Scott Wolf *Chuck Gieg* • Jeremy Sisto *Frank Beaumont* • Ryan Phillippe *Gil Martin* • David Lascher *Robert March* ■ *Dir* Ridley Scott • *Scr* Todd Robinson

The White Tower ★★ U

Drama 1950 · US · Colour · 97mins

A mountaineering drama with Glenn Ford joining a climb in the Swiss Alps. A lot of emotional baggage is carried along with the mountaineers: Ford falls for fellow climber Alida Valli, whose father was killed on the same peak; Lloyd Bridges is an arrogant former Nazi army officer; Cedric Hardwicke is an ageing British botanist; Claude Rains is a self-destructive French writer who is drunk most of the time; Oscar Homolka is the local Alpine guide and predictably neutral. What we have is a political digest of postwar realignment; amazingly enough, the Russians are not represented. Despite the predictability of the symbolism and some wooden performances, there is excellent location photography.

Glenn Ford *Martin Ordway* • Alida Valli *Carla Alton* • Claude Rains *Paul Delambre* • Oscar Homolka *Andreas* • Cedric Hardwicke *Nicholas Radcliffe* • Lloyd Bridges *Mr Hein* ■ *Dir* Ted Tetzlaff • *Scr* Paul Jarrico, from the novel by James Ramsay Ullman

White Water Summer ★★★ 15

Action adventure 1987 · US · Colour · 85mins

A superior coming-of-age story, with Kevin Bacon as a bullyboy wilderness guide and Sean Astin as one of four kids he hikes off into the middle of nowhere to make men of them. The plot kicks in when Bacon gets badly injured and finds his life dependent on Astin, previously the main butt of his bullying. Good plot, good performances and nice scenery. ▭

Kevin Bacon *Vic* • Sean Astin *Alan* • Jonathan Ward *Mitch* • KC Martel *George* • Matt Adler *Chris* • Caroline McWilliams *Virginia Block* • Charles Siebert *Jerry Block* ■ *Dir* Jeff Bleckner • *Scr* Manya Starr, Ernest Kinoy

White Wilderness ★★★ U

Drama documentary
1958 · US · Colour · 72mins

One of Walt Disney's *True-Life Adventure* series, this view of life in the Arctic was shot by nine photographers over a period of three years, catching many unique sights including the migration of the caribous, plus intriguing footage of such residents as the polar bear, the snowshoe rabbit, the walrus and the white whale. A highlight is an extended sequence revealing the truth about the "mass suicide" of lemmings. Winston Hibler's narration and the film's music score are both overdone, but the visual material is fascinating. Footage from the film was later cut into two smaller features titled *Large Animals of the Arctic* and *The Lemmings and Arctic Bird Life*.

Winston Hibler *Narrator* ■ *Dir/Scr* James Algar • *Cinematographer* James R Simon

White Witch Doctor ★★★ U

Romantic adventure
1953 · US · Colour · 93mins

Nurse Susan Hayward arrives in the Congo and is taken in hand by treasure hunter Robert Mitchum. Black water fever, tribal dancing, skirmishes with the Bakuba tribe and a man-eating lion persuade them to dedicate the rest of their lives to helping the Africans. Clearly influenced by the success of *The African Queen*, this blend of old-fashioned adventure and post-Imperial politics has the advantage of two appealing stars, some striking location work and an evocative score by Bernard Herrmann.

Susan Hayward *Ellen Burton* • Robert Mitchum *Lonni Douglas* • Walter Slezak *Huysman* • Mashood Ajala *Jacques* • Joseph C Narcisse *Utembo* • Elzie Emanuel *Kapuka* • Timothy Carey *Jarrett* • Otis Greene *Bakuba boy* ■ *Dir* Henry Hathaway • *Scr* Ivan Goff, Ben Roberts, from the novel by Louise A Stinetorf • *Cinematographer* Leon Shamroy

White Wolves ★★

Adventure 1993 · US · Colour · 85mins

A sequel of sorts to *A Cry in the Wild*, this teens-in-the-wilderness saga is executed with reasonable competence, but boasts no surprises whatsoever. As soon as viewers see the adult hiking leader taking five teenagers (one troubled, four snotty) into the wilderness, they will instantly know that the grown-up will be involved in

some sort of accident. Consequently the troubled teenager will go through many dangers to save the day, winning the hand of the pretty girl in the group during the process. Animal footage looks good, though we almost never see any of the actors in these shots.

Matt McCoy *Jake* • Mark-Paul Gosselaar *Scott* • Ami Dolenz *Cara* • David Moscow *Adam* • Amy O'Neill *Pandra* • Mark Riffon *Benny* ■ *Dir/Scr* Catherine Cyran

White Woman ★★★

Romantic drama 1933 · US · BW · 73mins

A torrid melodrama that plays like a combination of *Rain* (1932), *Island of Lost Souls* (1932) and *They Knew What They Wanted* (1940), this steamy vehicle can only be enjoyed if approached in the right spirit. Carole Lombard is a penniless showgirl, stranded in Malaya, who marries plantation owner Charles Laughton to get out of her predicament and is soon seeking true love in younger arms while her husband takes it out on the natives. The natives beat gongs and chant their discontent and the men all sweat a lot and grow designer stubble while Lombard somehow remains expertly gowned and coiffured in this totally artificial, but strangely irresistible, slice of hokum.

Carole Lombard *Judith Denning* • Charles Laughton *Horace H Prin* • Charles Bickford *Ballister* • Kent Taylor *David von Elst* • Percy Kilbride *Jakey* • James Bell *Hambly* • Charles B Middleton *[Charles Middleton] Fenton* ■ *Dir* Stuart Walker • *Scr* Samuel Hoffenstein, Gladys Lehman, from the play *Hangman's Whip* by Norman Reilly Raine, Frank Butler

White Zombie ★★★ PG

Horror 1932 · US · BW · 64mins

The first feature about Haiti's undead, this was a bold attempt by director Victor Halperin to break away from the endless chat of the early talkies. The long wordless passages allow an eerie atmosphere to develop as the camera glides menacingly around the jungle to the unnerving accompaniment of distant wailing. And who could be more at home in such sinister surroundings than Bela Lugosi, who gives his best performance since *Dracula* as the evil voodoo sorcerer, "Murder" Legendre. Silent star Madge Bellamy is suitably ethereal, as is the zombie make-up devised by Jack Pierce, who created Boris Karloff's *Frankenstein* look. ▭

Bela Lugosi *"Murder" Legendre* • Madge Bellamy *Madeline Short* • John Harron *Neil Parker* • Joseph Cawthorn *Dr Bruner, Missionary* • Robert Frazer *Charles Beaumont* • Clarence Muse *Coach Driver* ■ *Dir* Victor Halperin • *Scr* Garnett Weston

Whity ★★★

Melodrama 1970 · W Ger · Colour · 95mins

Shot on a spaghetti western set in Spain by Rainer Werner Fassbinder, this Deep South plantation melodrama has all the laconic intensity of Sergio Leone, the narrative rigour of classical Hollywood and the thematic resonance of Fassbinder's literary bible, Theodor Fontane's *Effi Briest*. Handsomely photographed by Michael Ballhaus and played with lowering deliberation, the story focuses on Günther Kaufmann, a slave who acquiesces in Ron Randell's

tyranny until he learns of its murderous immorality from prostitute, Hanna Schygulla. Considering patriarchy, social and sexual masochism and the misuse of status, the film was deemed so disappointing that it was denied a theatrical release. In German with English subtitles.

Günther Kaufmann *Whity* • Hanna Schygulla *Hanna* • Ulli Lommel *Frank* • Harry Baer *Davy* • Katrin Schaake *Katherine* • Ron Randell *Mr Nicholson* • Rainer Werner Fassbinder *Guest in saloon* ■ *Dir/Scr* Rainer Werner Fassbinder • *Cinematographer* Michael Ballhaus

Who? ★★

Science-fiction thriller
1974 · UK/W Ger · Colour · 93mins
An intriguing but not wholly successful sci-fi thriller that attempts to probe somewhat seriously into the nature of identity. The narrative isn't helped by being told in flashback, and Elliott Gould is perhaps a little too laid-back in the lead. There is a stunning performance, however, from third-billed actor Joseph Bova as the scientist Martino, whose face has been restructured following an alleged car crash in Russia, and he alone makes this curious mix of sci-fi and spy drama worth watching. Contains some swearing and sex scenes.

Elliott Gould *Rogers* • Trevor Howard *Azarin* • Joseph Bova *Martino* • Ed Grover *Finchley* • John Lehne *Haller* • James Noble *Deptford* • Lyndon Brook *Barrister* ■ *Dir* Jack Gold • *Scr* John Gould, from the novel by Algis Budrys

Who Am I? ★★★★ 12

Martial arts action comedy
1998 · HK · Colour · 107mins
Jackie Chan's most sensational action scenes of the nineties, impressive production values and super-slick direction (from Jackie and Bennie Chan) illuminate this little-known movie. Although the plot doesn't bear close scrutiny (something about a top secret energy source, an African tribe and amnesia) – the extraordinary set pieces – from a clog-assisted Rotterdam brawl, to a three-way rooftop battle that doesn't relent for nearly ten minutes – rival anything in a megabuck Hollywood blockbuster. Jackie's trademark use of slapstick comedy at the height of the fighting works brilliantly too. Cult status should follow. Contains violence. 📼 *DVD*

Jackie Chan *Jackie (aka Whoami)* • Michelle Ferre *Christine* • Mirai Yamamoto *Yuki* • Ron Smerczak *Morgan* • Ed Nelson *General Sherman* • Tom Pompert *CIA chairman* • Yanick Mbali *Baba* • Washington Sixolo *Village chief* ■ *Dir* Jackie Chan, Benny Chan • *Scr* Jackie Chan, Lee Reynolds, Susan Chan • *Stunt Co-ordinator* Jackie Chan

Who Dares Wins ★★ 18

Action adventure
1982 · UK · Colour · 119mins
Lewis Collins, managing to look stern-faced throughout, lives up to his tough-guy image in a British action movie inspired by the 1981 storming of the Iranian Embassy in London by the SAS. This is not much more than a glamourised episode of *The Professionals*, which at least had some wit and spark provided by Gordon Jackson. The Steven Seagals of this world would laugh at this. 📼

Lewis Collins *Captain Peter Skellen* • Judy Davis *Frankie Leith* • Richard Widmark *Secretary of State Curry* • Edward Woodward *Commander Powell* • Robert Webber *General Ira Potter* • Tony Doyle *Colonel Hadley* • John Duttine *Rod* • Kenneth Griffith *Bishop Crick* ■ *Dir* Ian Sharp • *Scr* Reginald Rose

Who Done It? ★★ U

Comedy mystery 1942 · US · BW · 78mins
Part of the abiding success of Abbott and Costello was that there were few – if any – surprises in their films. Familiarity lent contentment and Lou was always going to be put upon (but emerge triumphant) and Bud was always going to be surly. Their characters are equally familiar as two not-very-bright soda jerks with ambitions to write for radio. When they go to the station with an idea for a mystery series, the duo find themselves mixed up in a real case when the boss is killed during a live show. Cue action and some mild comedy. 📼

Bud Abbott *Chick Larkin* • Lou Costello *Mervyn Milgrim* • Patric Knowles *Jimmy Turner* • Louise Allbritton *Jane Little* • Thomas Gomez *Col JR Andrews* • Mary Wickes *Juliet Collins* ■ *Dir* Erle C Kenton • *Scr* Stanley Roberts, Edmund Joseph, John Grant, from a story by Stanley Roberts

Who Fears the Devil? ★★★

Fantasy 1972 · US · Colour · 89mins
Rare example, along with *Daniel and the Devil*, of a film about the Devil as perceived in American folklore – in this case a book of legends from the Carolinas. A young man (singer Hedges Capers in his only screen role) battles with Old Nick, who takes on various forms, all over America. There is a lot of hillbilly-cum-rock music and many familiar faces in the cast. Surprisingly, the director is John Newland, best known as the host of the TV series *One Step Beyond*. Judged too parochial for UK cinema release, this scores marks for its beautiful photography and odd charm.

Severn Darden *Mr Marduke* • Sharon Henesy *Lily* • Honor Hound *Honor Hound* • Sidney Clute *Charles* • Denver Pyle *Grandpappy John* • Hedges Capers *John* ■ *Dir* John Newland • *Scr* Melvin Levy, from the novel by Manly Wade Wellman

Who Framed Roger Rabbit ★★★★★ PG

Comedy 1988 · US · Colour · 99mins
This whiz-bang breakthrough in mixing live action with cartoon characters won a special achievement Oscar for animator Richard Williams. It follows the adventures of private eye Bob Hoskins, who ventures into Toontown – where the cartoon personalities live – to help animated superstar Roger Rabbit who suspects his wife of adultery. Guest appearances by a wealth of cartoon favourites, including Daffy Duck, Mickey Mouse and Betty Boop, adorn the tale as Hoskins's investigation leads to villain Christopher Lloyd who's planning to cleanse Toontown of its animated inhabitants. Highlights include Hoskins's encounter with Roger's wife Jessica (voiced by Kathleen Turner) and the fantastic all-action opening

sequence. A creative and box-office success for co-executive producer Steven Spielberg and director Robert Zemeckis that led the way to the likes of *Space Jam* and *Toy Story*. 📼

Bob Hoskins *Eddie Valiant* • Christopher Lloyd *Judge Doom* • Joanna Cassidy *Dolores* • Charles Fleischer *Roger Rabbit/Benny the Cab/Greasy/Psycho* • Kathleen Turner *Jessica* • Amy Irving *Jessica (singing voice)* • Stubby Kaye *Marvin Acme* • Alan Tilvern *Rk Maroon* ■ *Dir* Robert Zemeckis • *Scr* Jeffrey Price, Peter S Seaman, from the novel *Who Censored Roger Rabbit?* by Gary K Wolf • *Cinematographer* Dean Cundey • *Animator* Richard Williams

Who Gets the Friends? ★★★ PG

Romantic comedy
1988 · US · Colour · 89mins
A clumsy title for what is actually an enjoyable TV movie about a couple (Jill Clayburgh, James Farentino) who find divorce changes their relationships with friends. Clayburgh ably plays the wife, and she is well supported by Farentino, probably best known in the UK for his stint as Dr Nick Toscanni in *Dynasty*. 📼

Jill Clayburgh *Vikki Baron* • James Farentino *Buddy Baron* • Lucie Arnaz *Gloria Mcclinton* • Leigh Taylor-Young *Aggie Harden* • Robin Thomas *Paul Keaton* ■ *Dir* Lila Garrett • *Scr* Lila Garrett, Sandy Krinski

Who Has Seen the Wind ★★

Drama 1977 · Can · Colour · 100mins
Director Allan King was responsible for *Warrendale* (1967), an uncompromising portrait of life in a hostel for emotionally disturbed youngsters. This fictional tale, based on a much-loved Canadian novel about two children growing up in Depression-hit Saskatchewan, is similarly concerned with the psychology of juveniles but doesn't nearly pack the same punch and is ultimately rather dreary. However, there's a strong supporting cast, including Gordon Pinsent and José Ferrer, who gives a great performance as a silver-tongued bootlegger.

Brian Painchaud *Brian* • Douglas Junor *Young Ben* • Gordon Pinsent *Gerald O'Connal* • Chapelle Jaffe *Maggie* • José Ferrer *The Ben* • Charmion King *Mrs Abercrombie* ■ *Dir* Allan King • *Scr* Patricia Watson, from a novel by WO Mitchell

Who Is Harry Kellerman, and Why Is He Saying Those Terrible Things about Me? ★

Comedy drama 1971 · US · Colour · 107mins
This is one of those weird, vaguely experimental, sub-culture self-indulgences that got made into movies in the sixties and early seventies. Dustin Hoffman plays a pop musician driven to despair by anonymous phone calls and by sessions with his shrink, Jack Warden. Woody Allen turned this sort of material into satirical gold but here it's just a dollop of American psychobabble about life, art, ageing and all that stuff.

Dustin Hoffman *Georgie Soloway* • Jack Warden *Dr Moses* • Barbara Harris *Allison* • David Burns *Leon Soloway* • Gabriel Dell *Sid* •

Betty Walker *Margot Soloway* • Dom DeLuise *Irwin* ■ *Dir* Ulu Grosbard • *Scr* Herb Gardner, from his short story

Who Is Julia? ★★ PG

Science-fiction melodrama
1986 · US · Colour · 90mins
Mare Winningham is stuck in this implausible melodrama as a model who is fatally injured as she is rescuing a child whose mother collapses and dies at the scene. Lucky for all concerned, doctors just "happen" to be working on a remarkable new brain transplant procedure, so our plucky heroine's grey matter is put into the body of the dead mother. Both husbands must struggle with this most unexpected and confusing predicament as everyone walks around asking the burning question, "Who is Julia?" This muddled TV movie is over-plotted and far-fetched; the most you can say is it poses some provocative questions about medical experimentation. 📼

Mare Winningham *Mary Frances Beaudine/julia* • Jameson Parker *Don North* • Jeffrey DeMunn *Dr Matt Matthews* • Jonathan Banks *Jack Beaudine* • Bert Remsen *Joseph Dineen* ■ *Dir* Walter Grauman • *Scr* James S Sadwith from the novel by Barbara S Harris

Who Is Killing the Great Chefs of Europe? ★★

Murder mystery comedy
1978 · US/W Ger · Colour · 112mins
When food connoisseur Max Vandevere (Robert Morley) publishes his list of the world's greatest chefs, he inadvertently sets in motion a stream of jealousy, anger and eventually murder. Robby Ross (George Segal), ex-husband of Natasha (Jacqueline Bisset) who's on the list, finds himself in the midst of the murder spree. It's a promising premise with a soupçon of good jokes, a sprinkle of bad puns and more than a dash of bad taste. Good ingredients here but the recipe just doesn't gel resulting in a good looking dish that unfortunately leaves a bitter aftertaste and the nagging feeling that it could have been much tastier.

George Segal *Robby Ross* • Jacqueline Bisset *Natasha O'Brien* • Robert Morley *Max Vandervere* • Jean-Pierre Cassel *Louis Kohner* • Philippe Noiret *Jean-Claude Moulineau* ■ *Dir* Ted Kotcheff • *Scr* Peter Stone, from the novel *Someone Is Killing the Great Chefs of Europe* by Nan Lyons, Ivan Lyons • *Cinematographer* John Alcott • *Music* Henry Mancini

Who Killed Gail Preston? ★

Mystery 1938 · US · BW · 60mins
The spotlight is on a very young Rita Hayworth in this Columbia B-feature, but only for the first 20 minutes as her pre-Gilda nightclub singer (her voice mostly dubbed), dark-haired and voluptuously gowned, is shot dead in mid-number. It turns out she was not a nice person and there are many suspects until Don Terry's police inspector terrifies the killer into confessing. The nightclub has an amusing prison theme with the orchestra in striped outfits and cell-like cubicles for the patrons. But basically the answer to the question posed by the title has to be: who cares?

Don Terry *Inspector Kellogg* • Rita Hayworth *Gail Preston* • Robert Paige *Swing Traynor* • Wyn Cahoon *Ann Bishop* ■ *Dir* Leon Barsha • *Scr* Robert E Kent, Henry Taylor

Who Killed Mary Whats'ername? ★★★

Mystery   1971 · US · Colour · 89mins

The character set-up of this crime mystery is unusual, to say the least, with Red Buttons as the diabetic former boxer who seeks to find the killer of an anonymous prostitute about whom nobody cared. Directed by one-time animator Ernest Pintoff, it doesn't exactly carry conviction, but the idea is interesting for what amounts to a B-movie.

Red Buttons *Mickey* • Alice Playten *Della* • Sylvia Miles *Christine* • Sam Waterston *Alex* • Donald Marye *Leo* • Dick Williams [Dick Anthony Williams] *Malthus* ■ *Dir* Ernest Pintoff • *Scr* John O'Toole

Who Killed Nani? ★★

Crime thriller   1988 · Spain · Colour

One of Spain's most accomplished writer/producers, Vicente Escrivá, teamed with left-wing director Roberto Bodegas for this disappointingly routine and often heavy-handed crime thriller. Frédéric Deban stars as the criminal mastermind whose robberies are so expertly executed that rival crooks, as well as the police, are desperate to put an end to his activities. With adultery, corruption and revenge also bubbling beneath the surface, this could have been a compelling, politically-charged picture. But, once Deban has been framed for terrorist offences, the action seriously loses its way and suspense levels plummet. Spanish dialogue dubbed into English.

Frédéric Deban *Nani* • JoséPedro Carrión *Galvez* • Chemo De Miguel *Teo* • Eulalia Ramón *Lola* • Albert Vidal *Soto* • Miguel A Salomón *Molero* ■ *Dir* Roberto Bodegas • *Scr* Vincente Escriva, Gregorio Roldan

Who Killed Teddy Bear? ★★

Mystery thriller   1965 · US · BW · 0mins

A sleazy thriller, with a needlessly strong cast and ample budget, that seems to work in as many unpalatable situations as possible, including rape, stalking and pornography. A New York discotheque hostess (Juliet Prowse) becomes the victim of an obscene phone caller, suspecting an over-enthusiastic detective (Jan Murray) of being the culprit. Bizarre and exploitative, but highly enjoyable if you're in the right mood. Contains sexual situations and violence.

Sal Mineo *Lawrence* • Juliet Prowse *Norah* • Jan Murray *Bill Madden* • Elaine Stritch *Billie* • Dan Travanty [Daniel J Travanti] ■ *Dir* Joseph Cates • *Scr* Leon Tokatyan, Arnold Drake, from a story by Arnold Drake

Who Says I Can't Ride a Rainbow ★★★

Adventure   1971 · US · Colour · 85mins

This is an offbeat children's adventure about a battle to preserve an urban zoo. It stars likeable Jack Klugman as a man who believes that children hold the key to the world's future. Klugman went on to star in two long-running TV

series, *The Odd Couple* and *Quincy*, during the seventies and early eighties. This movie also marked the feature debut of talented Morgan Freeman.

Jack Klugman *Barney Marcovitz* • Norma French *Mary Lee* • Reuben Figueroa *Angel* • David Mann *David* • Kevin Riou *Kevin* • Morgan Freeman *Afro* ■ *Dir* Edward Mann • *Scr* Edward Mann, Daniel Hauer

Who Shot Patakango? ★★

Drama   1992 · US · Colour · 104mins

More serious, and thus more insightful, than the usual high-school romp, this peek at events at a Brooklyn school was a labour of love for director Robert Brooks. He not only scripted and edited the film along with his wife Halle (who produced), he even worked the camera. As the director homes in on a group of final-year pupils, he proves more skilled at documentary-style detail than at building sustained drama. Even though the film is knocked off course on more than one occasion, it does possess a convincing sense of time and place. Contains swearing and violence.

David Knight *Bic Bickham* • Sandra Bullock *Devlin Moran* • Kevin Otto *Mark Bickham* • Aaron Ingram *Cougar* • Brad Randall *Patakango* ■ *Dir* Robert Brooks • *Scr* Robert Brooks and Halle Brooks

Who Slew Auntie Roo? ★★ 15

Satirical chiller
1971 · US/UK · Colour · 87mins

An oddball update of the Hansel and Gretel fairy tale, with a frenetic Shelley Winters menacing two orphan children (Mark Lester and Chloe Franks). What begins as a well-intentioned fantasy becomes a crass nightmare of *Grand Guignol*, maybe because it's co-written by Jimmy Sangster, maestro of so many Hammer horrors. Despite its origins, this is definitely not for children. ▭

Shelley Winters *Rosie Forrest* • Mark Lester *Christopher* • Ralph Richardson *Mr Benton* • Lionel Jeffries *Inspector Willoughby* • Judy Cornwell *Clarine* • Michael Gothard *Albie* • Hugh Griffith *The Pigman/mr Harrison* • Chloe Franks *Katy* • Rosalie Crutchley *Miss Henley* ■ *Dir* Curtis Harrington • *Scr* Robert Blees, James [Jimmy] Sangster, Gavin Lambert, from a story by David Osborn

Who Was That Lady? ★★ U

Comedy   1960 · US · BW · 115mins

Adapted by Norman Krasna from his own play, *Who Was That Lady I Saw You With?*, this is a strained romantic comedy that has already outstayed its welcome before it turns into a Cold War farce. Caught in flagrante with one of his students, professor Tony Curtis persuades his TV writer buddy, Dean Martin, to concoct an excuse to assuage his jealous wife, Janet Leigh (then Mrs Curtis off screen, too). However, their story about the FBI and a nest of Russian spies is closer to the truth than they suspect. It's polished enough, but there's more to screwball than just pace.

Tony Curtis *David Wilson* • Dean Martin *Michael Haney* • Janet Leigh *Ann Wilson* • James Whitmore *Harry Powell* • John McIntire *Bob Doyle* • Barbara Nichols *Gloria Coogle* • Larry Keating *Parker* • Larry Storch *Orenov* ■

Dir George Sidney • *Scr* Norman Krasna, from his play *Who Was That Lady I Saw You With?* • *Music* André Previn

The Whole Nine Yards ★★ 15

Black comedy   2000 · US · Colour · 98mins

Friends star Matthew Perry makes another stab at big-screen stardom in this limp black comedy from British director Jonathan Lynn (*Yes, Minister*, *My Cousin Vinny*). Perry is the humble, hen-pecked dentist none too chuffed to discover that Mafia iceman Jimmy "The Tulip" Tudeski (Bruce Willis) has just bought a house in his dull Montreal neighbourhood. At the instigation of his shrewish wife (Rosanna Arquette), Perry rats on Jimmy to Chicago crime boss Kevin Pollak, only to find himself up to his eyeteeth in trouble. But the farce is too forced, the humour too broad and the end result a far cry from such superior hit-man comedies as *Prizzi's Honor* and *Grosse Pointe Blank*.

Bruce Willis *Jimmy "The Tulip" Tudeski* • Matthew Perry *"Oz" Oseransky* • Rosanna Arquette *Sophie* • Michael Clarke Duncan *Frankie Figs* • Natasha Henstridge *Cynthia* ■ *Dir* Jonathan Lynn • *Scr* Mitchell Kapner

The Whole Town's Talking ★★★★

Crime comedy   1935 · US · BW · 92mins

There's a double helping of Edward G Robinson in this crime comedy as he plays the dual role of a gangster and a meek little clerk. The clerk is the spitting image of notorious hoodlum "Killer" Mannion, and mistakenly arrested. He's eventually released and issued with an identity card, so police won't confuse the two again – that is, until the real Mannion turns up and demands a loan of the card. This is a rare pure comedy effort from John Ford, but with a script co-written by Frank Capra favourite Robert Riskin, there's also a certain Capraesque element to it. With Jean Arthur co-starring alongside the marvellous Robinson, this is a hilarious comedy of mistaken identity.

Edward G Robinson *Arthur Ferguson Jones/ "Killer"Manion* • Jean Arthur *Wilhelmina "Bill" Clark* • Arthur Hohl *Det Sgt Mike Boyle* • Wallace Ford *Healy* • Arthur Byron *Spencer* • Donald Meek *Hoyt* • Paul Harvey *JG Carpenter* ■ *Dir* John Ford • *Scr* Jo Swerling, Robert Riskin, from the story *Jail Breaker* by WR Burnett

The Whole Truth ★★★

Thriller   1958 · UK · BW · 84mins

A B-movie plot performed by an A-list cast; that is to say, stars who had had their day in Hollywood and were now looking to Britain for an honest bob. Thus, Stewart Granger plays a movie producer whose affair with an Italian starlet leads to him covering up her imagined murder and then being arrested when she's found dead for real. George Sanders makes a suitably creepy villain and Donna Reed appears as Granger's wife. The over-the-top performances and John Guillermin's overwrought direction ensure it's never boring.

Stewart Granger *Max Paulton* • Donna Reed *Carol Paulton* • George Sanders *Carliss* •

Gianna Maria Canale *Gina Bertini* • Michael Shillo *Inspector Simon* • Peter Dyneley *Willy Reichel* ■ *Dir* John Guillermin • *Scr* Jonathan Latimer, from the stage and TV play by Philip Mackie

Who'll Stop the Rain? ★★★★ 18

Crime drama   1978 · US · Colour · 121mins

Veteran marine Nick Nolte is conned by his idealist buddy Michael Moriarty into smuggling heroin from Vietnam. But when he tries to make the drop with Moriarty's wife, Tuesday Weld, all hell breaks loose and they go on the run from brutal hit men working for crooked cop Anthony Zerbe. Hard-hitting action, memorably sharp dialogue and a tour-de-force performance by Nolte makes director Karel Reisz's tension-laden foray into US drug trafficking a provocative and compelling tale of greed and cynicism. Based on Robert Stone's novel *Dog Soldiers*, this *Rambo*-for-real is an adult, gripping and witty true-to-life classic. Contains swearing and drug abuse. ▭

Nick Nolte *Ray Hicks* • Tuesday Weld *Marge Converse* • Michael Moriarty *John Converse* • Anthony Zerbe *Antheil* • Richard Masur *Danskin* • Ray Sharkey *Smitty* • Gail Strickland *Charmian* ■ *Dir* Karel Reisz • *Scr* Judith Rascoe, Robert Stone, from the novel *Dog Soldiers* by Robert Stone

Wholly Moses! ★★ 15

Comedy   1980 · US · Colour · 99mins

Everything's coming up Moses in this sub-*Monty Python* frolic in which Dudley Moore – coming from his success in *10* – tries to establish himself as an Old Testament prophet instead of the upstart Moses. Directed by Gary Weis, once of American TV's *Saturday Night Live*, it has some great guest cameos by Jack Gilford, Dom DeLuise and Richard Pryor, but comes across as fatuous rather than funny. ▭

Dudley Moore *Harvey Orkin/Herschel* • Laraine Newman *Zoey/Zerelda* • James Coco *Hyssop* • Paul Sand *Angel of the Lord* • Jack Gilford *Tailor* • Dom DeLuise *Shadrach* • John Houseman *Archangel* • Madeline Kahn *Sorceress* • Richard Pryor *Pharoah* • John Ritter *Devil* • Tom Baker *Egyptian Captain* ■ *Dir* Gary Weis • *Scr* Guy Thomas

Whoopee! ★★★

Musical comedy   1930 · US · Colour · 94mins

It may look awfully stagebound now, but this inane early Eddie Cantor vehicle was a huge hit in its day, and was cinematically important for being one of the first movies in Technicolor, albeit only two-strip. The theme of a hypochondriac at large – reused in several later films, including the remake of this one, Danny Kaye's *Up in Arms* – is enhanced here by the sumptuous early Busby Berkeley-choreographed production numbers, several of which were songs that became associated with Cantor, notably *Making Whoopee* (hence the title) and *My Baby Just Cares for Me*. Cantor himself is an acquired taste, and became slightly more palatable as he mellowed, but there was no denying the popularity of the rolling-eyed clown at the time of this movie. Watch very closely; the lead chorus girl is a ridiculously young Betty Grable.

Eddie Cantor *Henry Williams* • Eleanor Hunt *Sally Morgan* • Paul Gregory *Wanenis* • John Rutherford *Sheriff Bob Wells* • Ethel Shutta *Mary Custer* • Spencer Charters *Jerome Underwood* • Chief Caupolican *Black Eagle* ■ *Dir* Thornton Freeland • *Scr* William Conselman, from the musical by William Anthony McGuire, Gus Kahn, from the play *The Nervous Wreck* by Owen Davis, from the story *The Wreck* by EJ Rath

The Whoopee Boys ★ 15

Comedy 1986 · US · Colour · 84mins

Paul Rodriguez teams up with Michael O'Keefe as a pair of wide boys who attempt to rub shoulders with society's elite in Palm Beach. Our gauche twosome stick out like sore thumbs but prove their hearts are in the right place by coming to the aid of a school for needy children. Stand-up star Rodriguez here spectacularly fails to follow in the footsteps of other stage comedians that have made the transition to the big screen, while O'Keefe must be wondering if that Oscar nomination for *The Great Santini* in 1980 was just a dream. 🎞

Michael O'Keefe *Jake Bateman* • Paul Rodriguez *Barney* • Denholm Elliott *Colonel Hugh Phelps* • Carole Shelley *Henrietta Phelps* • Lucinda Jenney *Olivia Farragut* ■ *Dir* John Byrum • *Scr* Steve Zacharias, Jeff Buhai, David Obst

Whoops Apocalypse ★★ 15

Comedy 1986 · UK · Colour · 87mins

The four-year gap between the often hilarious TV original and this inconsistent feature seems to have sapped the inspiration from writers Andrew Marshall and David Renwick. The need to introduce a degree of narrative logic precludes much of the wackiness that made the series so biting and fresh. Even though it dissects sombre subjects like the Cold War and a Falklands-style invasion, the satire has mostly been toned down, with only the swipes at the Royals, Peter Cook's performance as a doltish prime minister and a wonderful clown funeral hitting the mark. Contains swearing and nudity. 🎞

Loretta Swit *Barbara Adams* • Peter Cook *Sir Mortimer Chris* • Michael Richards *Lacrobat* • Rik Mayall *Specialist Catering Commander* • Ian Richardson *Rear Admiral Bendish* • Alexei Sayle • Herbert Lom *General Mosquera* • Joanne Pearce *Princess Wendy* ■ *Dir* Tom Bussmann • *Scr* Andrew Marshall, David Renwick

Whore ★ 18

Drama 1991 · US · Colour · 81mins

Largely talking directly to camera, Theresa Russell is an inner city prostitute who tells of and acts out the humiliations of her job and the viciousness of her pimp, Benjamin Mouton. It's not the overt subject matter that offends but the way in which the movie seems to wallow in misogyny, exuding an excited air whenever Russell suffers abuse and giving the swaggering Mouton powerful centre stage, which at times borders on admiration. Ken Russell directs it all with a staggeringly inappropriate and jokey approach. Contains violence, swearing and nudity. 🎞

Theresa Russell *Liz* • Benjamin Mouton *Blake* • Antonio Fargas *Rasta* • Sanjay *Indian* • Elizabeth Morehead *Katie* • Michael Crabtree *Man in car* • John Diehl *Derelict* ■ *Dir* Ken Russell • *Scr* Ken Russell, Deborah Dalton, from the play *Bondage* by David Hines

Who's Afraid of Red Yellow Blue? ★★★

Drama 1990 · W Ger · Colour · 115mins

The hegemony of the West over the East in the newly unified Germany is the underlying theme of Heiko Schier's slyly satirical drama, in which a painter of broad, vulgar canvases finds fame, while a talented miniaturist is overlooked by critics and dealers alike. However, beneath the allegorical veneer, this is also a perceptive study of the art world, with its pretensions and greed, as typified by the capitalist artist who pays a seeming eccentric to damage his pictures in the hope of boosting their prices through newsworthy notoriety. Not a subtle film, but intriguing nonetheless. In German with English subtitles.

Stephanie Philipp • Max Tidof • Heino Ferch • Gunter Berger ■ *Dir/Scr* Heiko Schier

Who's Afraid of Virginia Woolf? ★★★★ 15

Drama 1966 · US · BW · 123mins

Should your front room be in need of redecoration, then Elizabeth Taylor's performance here is guaranteed to strip the paint off the walls with just one verbal volley. In tandem with her screen husband (played by then real-life husband Richard Burton), she spits malicious barbs across their comfortable abode, often hitting their dinner guests en route. The ebb and flow of the full-blown arguments are acutely judged by director Mike Nichols, who typically laces his film with juicy psychological and social pointers. He also ensures that Taylor and Burton, even after their fictional marriage has descended to an almighty roar, never reduce their characters to caricature. This five Oscar-winner (including one for Taylor) was regarded as punishingly honest in its day, though inevitably it seems a tad more muted now. Contains swearing. 🎞

Elizabeth Taylor *Martha* • Richard Burton *George* • George Segal *Nick* • Sandy Dennis *Honey* ■ *Dir* Mike Nichols • *Scr* Ernest Lehman, from the play by Edward Albee • *Costume Designer* Irene Sharaff • *Cinematographer* Haskell Wexler • *Music* Alex North

Who's Been Sleeping in My Bed? ★★

Comedy 1963 · US · Colour · 103mins

Dean Martin plays a TV matinee idol who is, you've guessed it, a smoothie male sex symbol, but not slick enough to avoid amorous shenanigans with the wives of various friends. It's up to girlfriend Elizabeth Montgomery to persuade him to abandon his loose living and settle down with her. A nudge-nudge, wink-wink bedroom farce, superficially glossy, but largely boring except for a handful of laughs and Carol Burnett in the supporting cast.

Dean Martin *Jason Steel* • Elizabeth Montgomery *Melissa Morris* • Martin Balsam *Sanford Kaufman* • Jill St John *Toby Tobler* • Richard Conte *Leonard Ashley* • Macha Meril *Jacqueline Edwards* • Louis Nye *Harry Tobler* ■ *Dir* Daniel Mann • *Scr* Jack Rose

Who's Got the Action? ★★

Comedy 1962 · US · Colour · 94mins

Dean Martin and Lana Turner are a married couple in a comedy whose humour resides in a lot of stock but nonetheless quite amusing clichés about bookies and gamblers. Martin is a lawyer who also bets compulsively on the horses, to the increasing detriment of his bank balance and the despair of his wife. She finally takes matters into her own hands, colludes with a bookie in handling his bets and turns him into a winner. The supporting cast offers a standout performance from Walter Matthau as a Mr Big on the wrong side of the law.

Dean Martin *Steve Flood* • Lana Turner *Melanie Flood* • Eddie Albert *Clint Morgan* • Nita Talbot *Saturday Knight* • Walter Matthau *Tony Gagoots* • Paul Ford *Judge Boatwright* • Margo Roza ■ *Dir* Daniel Mann • *Scr* Jack Rose, from the novel *Four Horse-Players Are Missing* by Alexander Rose

Who's Harry Crumb? ★ PG

Comedy 1989 · US · Colour · 86mins

The question on most people's lips before this lacklustre comedy is over will be, "Who cares?" The late John Candy was quite funny when he allowed a director to control his unrestrained manic mugging. Unfortunately, here Paul Flaherty (a former Candy TV associate) just lets him get away with farcical murder as a bungling private detective assigned to solve a kidnapping case. There are a few moments that raise a smile and Annie Potts is a joy as the gold-digging newlywed. But it's heavy going with very little wit and a great deal of slapstick. 🎞

John Candy *Harry Crumb* • Jeffrey Jones *Eliot Draisen* • Annie Potts *Helen Downing* • Tim Thomerson *Vince Barnes* • Barry Corbin *PJ Downing* • Shawnee Smith *Nikki Downing* ■ *Dir* Paul Flaherty • *Scr* Robert Conte, Peter Martin Wortmann

Who's Minding the Mint? ★★★ U

Comedy 1967 · US · Colour · 96mins

A comedy with a superb cast and a truly daft premise, in which a group of crooks help US mint employee Jim Hutton replace money he has accidentally disposed of, with wonderfully funny results. This is an overlooked gem, shrewdly directed by Sid Caesar associate Howard Morris with a baleful eye for the absurd. The cast is uniformly excellent, but special praise should go to the pompously demented Victor Buono as a navy veteran. Also along for the ride are the likes of Jack Gilford, Joey Bishop, Milton Berle and even Walter Brennan, and wide-eyed Dorothy Provine makes a fine foil for the gauche and confused Hutton.

Jim Hutton *Harry Lucas* • Dorothy Provine *Verna Baxter* • Milton Berle *Luther Burton* • Walter Brennan *Pop Gillis* • Joey Bishop *Ralph*

Randazzo • Bob Denver *Willie Owens* • Victor Buono *Captain* • Jamie Farr *Mario* ■ Howard Morris • *Scr* RS Allen, Harry Bullock

Who's Minding the Store? ★★★ U

Comedy 1963 · US · Colour · 89mins

Between his own triumphs behind the camera, Jerry Lewis relaxed under the direction of one of Hollywood's cleverest, wittiest craftsmen, former cartoonist Frank Tashlin, whose Lewis movies resembled a series of manic sketches strung together, and this is one of the funniest. It's wildly inventive, and peppered with a veritable gallery of fabulously eccentric character actors, used in the most simple of ideas – Lewis let loose in a department store, a ploy cinematically used to less effect by comedians as diverse as the Marx Brothers and Norman Wisdom.

Jerry Lewis *Raymond Phiffier* • Jill St John *Barbara Tuttle* • Agnes Moorehead *Phoebe Tuttle* • John McGiver *Mr Tuttle* • Ray Walston *Mr Quimby* • Francesca Bellini *Shirley* ■ *Dir* Frank Tashlin • *Scr* Frank Tashlin, Harry Tugend, from a story by Harry Tugend

Who's That Girl ★★ PG

Comedy 1987 · US · Colour · 87mins

With Griffin Dunne hot off the back of his triumph in Martin Scorsese's *After Hours* and Madonna in dire need of a hit after the *Shanghai Surprise* fiasco, you would have thought the two stars would have plumped for something more substantial than this woeful attempt at the screwball comedy flavour of *Bringing Up Baby*. Slouching, chewing gum and mistiming wisecracks with the nonchalance of a rock star convinced her presence is a favour to the producer, Madonna is a shadow of the sassy star of *Desperately Seeking Susan*. Accepting his second-fiddle status, Dunne gets on with his work quietly and efficiently. 🎞

Madonna *Nikki Finn* • Griffin Dunne *Loudon Trott* • Haviland Morris *Wendy Worthington* • John McMartin *Simon Worthington* • Bibi Besch *Mrs Worthington* • John Mills *Montgomery Bell* ■ *Dir* James Foley • *Scr* Andrew Smith, Ken Finkleman, from a story by Andrew Smith

Who's That Knocking at My Door ★★★

Drama 1968 · US · BW · 88mins

The first film not just for director Martin Scorsese, but also actor Harvey Keitel (if you overlook his uncredited appearance in *Reflections in a Golden Eye* the previous year). Displaying early indications of all Scorsese's trademark concerns, this autobiographical film is crude but compelling, with Keitel as a strict but streetwise Catholic taking a guilt trip through his relationship with a free-thinking young woman (Zina Bethune). Shot in black and white, it's essential viewing as an early example of two masters learning their respective crafts.

Harvey Keitel *JR* • Zina Bethune *The girl* • Lennard Kuras *Joey* • Ann Colette *Girl in dream* • Michael Scala *Sally* • Wendy Russell *Sally's girl friend* • Philip Carlson *Mountain guide* • Robert Uricola *Gunman at stag party* ■ *Dir/Scr* Martin Scorsese

Who's the Man? ★ 15

Comedy   1993 · US · Colour · 85mins

Ted Demme (nephew of famed director Jonathan Demme) brings his *Yo! MTV Raps* stars Ed Lover and Dr Dre to the big screen for this undistinguished hip-hop effort that makes the *Police Academy* series look like a comedy masterclass. The makers clearly wanted to say something pertinent about exploitative inner-city landlords, but a farce built around a couple of nitwit barbers who accidentally become cops is hardly the best way to go about it. The leads are amiable enough and the presence of Denis Leary and cameos by several rappers is most welcome, but they don't atone for the shortage of gags and the clumsiness of Demme's approach. Contains violence and swearing. ▣

Dr Dre • Ed Lover • Jim Moody *Nick Crawford* • Badja Djola *Lionel Douglas* • Ice-T *Nighttrain/Chauncey* ■ *Dir* Ted Demme • *Scr* Seth Greenland, from a story by Seth Greenland, Dr Dre, Ed Lover

Whose Child Is This? ★★★

Drama based on a true story
1993 · US · Colour · 120mins

Subtitled *The War for Baby Jessica*, this TV movie recounts the true story of the custody battle between a natural mother who gave up her baby for adoption and the woman who gave the child a home. After playing so many kooks, it's good to see Amanda Plummer channel her undoubted talent into a role requiring passion rather than eccentricity. The action is based on the actual court records, but there's an inescapable feeling that the film has been slanted in favour of *in situ* parents Susan Dey and Michael Ontkean, who are required to do little more than look anxious.

Susan Dey *Robby DeBoer* • Michael Ontkean *Jan DeBoer* • Amanda Plummer *Cara Clausen* • David Keith *Dan Schmidt* • Anna Ferguson *Mary* • Joy Coghill *Earlene* • Ice-T *Gina* ■ *Dir* John Kent Harrison • *Scr* Jacqueline Feather, David Seidler, from an article by Lucinda Franks

Whose Life Is it Anyway? ★★★ 15

Drama   1981 · US · Colour · 113mins

Brian Clark's award-winning play is well transposed to the screen by director John Badham and stars Richard Dreyfuss as the artist who is rendered immobile from the neck down after a terrible car accident. The crux of the narrative is his persistent demand to the hospital chief of staff (John Cassavetes) to be allowed the right to die. Meanwhile he's cared for and develops relationships with doctor Christine Lahti and nurse Kaki Hunter. Amazingly funny given the circumstances, this is both touching and relevant to ongoing issues concerning euthanasia. ▣

Richard Dreyfuss *Ken Harrison* • John Cassavetes *Dr Michael Emerson* • Christine Lahti *Dr Clare Scott* • Bob Balaban *Carter Hill* • Kenneth McMillan *Judge Wyler* • Kaki Hunter *Mary Jo Sadler* • Thomas Carter *Orderly John* ■ *Dir* John Badham • *Scr* Brian Clark, Reginald Rose, from the play by Brian Clark

Why Change Your Wife? ★★★

Silent comedy   1920 · US · BW · 100mins

The name of director Cecil B DeMille has become synonymous with the historical and Biblical epic. However, this mighty Hollywood pioneer and starmaker was responsible for dozens of sparkling and successful bedroom farces during his long and influential association with Paramount, of which this is just one. The soufflé plot, concerning the complications of extramarital flirtations, serves as an excuse to enjoy Gloria Swanson, Bebe Daniels, Thomas Meighan and Theodore Kosloff going through their risqué paces, cleverly manipulated by DeMille.

Thomas Meighan *Robert Gordon* • Gloria Swanson *Beth Gordon* • Bebe Daniels *Sally Clark* • Theodore Kosloff *Radinoff* • Clarence Geldart *The doctor* • Sylvia Ashton *Aunt Kate* ■ *Dir* Cecil B DeMille • *Scr* Olga Printzlau, Sada Cowan, from a story by William C de Mille

Why Do Fools Fall in Love? ★★★ 15

Biographical musical drama
1998 · US · Colour · 111mins

A fun, if not exactly deeply probing, look at the short life of fifties teenage singer Frankie Lymon (Larenz Tate) who left three wives (he never got around to divorcing any of them) behind when he died in 1968 at the age of 25. Because there are so many conflicting opinions about what Frankie was actually like, Tate isn't given a great deal to work with, but the wives are better drawn and well played by a cast of talented actresses – Halle Berry, Lela Rochon and Vivica A Fox. Ben Vereen and Little Richard add some history to the proceedings, which are snappily directed by Gregory Nava. Contains swearing and some violence. ▣

Ben Vereen *Richard Barrett* • Larenz Tate *Frankie Lymon* • Halle Berry *Zola Taylor* • Lela Rochon *Emira Eagle* • Vivica A Fox *Elizabeth Waters* • Little Richard • Miguel A Nunez Jr *Young Little Richard* • Paul Mazursky *Morris Levy* ■ *Dir* Gregory Nava • *Scr* Tina Andrews

Why Does Herr R Run Amok? ★★★

Drama   1970 · W Ger · Colour · 88mins

A film that is brutal in its story and in its unwillingness to come to conclusions, since the murderous Herr R of the title is not presented as a villain but as a victim of emotional exploitation, unhappy in his family and work. Director Rainer Werner Fassbinder takes no sides, but presents his central character, played by Kurt Raab, in his comfortable home, enjoying the fruits of a decent job. Why then does all this lead to shocking violence? Made as an extension of Fassbinder's "Anti-Theatre", this is a sombre work of undeniable power and pessimism. In German with English subtitles.

Kurt Raab *Kurt Raab*, "*Herr R*" • Lilith Ungerer *Frau Raab* • Amadeus Fengler *Amadeus, their son* • Franz Maron *Boss* • Hanna Schygulla *Schoolfriend* • Peter Raben *Schoolfriend* ■ *Dir/Scr* Rainer Werner Fassbinder, Michael Fengler

Why Has Bhodi-Dharma Left for the East? ★★★

Drama   1989 · S Kor · Colour · 137mins

South Korean painter Bae Yong-Kyun devoted several years of his life to making this debut feature. His genius for a telling image is readily apparent, notably in a stunning silhouetted sequence framed against some gnarled trees and a glorious sunset. But the pacing of his story is also impeccable, reflecting the contrast between life in the town and the mountain hermitage in which a Zen master imparts his wisdom to a wavering acolyte and a mischievous orphan. Concluding that there is no single path to self-knowledge or contentment, this is a moving yet intellectually and artistically rewarding experience. In Korean with English subtitles.

Yi Pan-Yong *Hyegok* • Sin Won-Sop *Kibong* • Huang Hae-Jin *Haejin* ■ *Dir* Bae Yong-Kyun • *Scr* Bae Yong-Kyun

Why Me? ★ 15

Comedy   1990 · US · Colour · 84mins

Anyone who has seen Christopher Lambert act knows that he has absolutely no flair for comedy, but that didn't stop him from being cast in this excruciatingly unfunny caper movie. Based on the novel by Donald E Westlake (who also co-scripted), Lambert's jewel thief character unknowingly steals a very valuable ruby belonging to the Turkish government, and soon finds himself pursued by not only them, but also the police, the CIA and Armenian terrorists. It's so heavy-handed in its execution that not even comic actor Christopher Lloyd, who plays Lambert's partner, can generate a single laugh. Watch *The Hot Rock* instead for a better Westlake adaptation concerning wacky jewel robberies. ▣

Christopher Lambert *Gus Cardinale* • Christopher Lloyd *Bruno* • Kim Greist *June Cardinale* • JT Walsh *Inspector Mahoney* • Michael J Pollard *Ralph* • Tony Plana *Benjy* • John Hancock *Tiny* ■ *Dir* Gene Quintano • *Scr* Donald E Westlake, Leonard Mass Jr [Leonard Mass], from the novel by Donald E Westlake

Why My Daughter? ★★ 15

Drama based on a true story
1993 · US · Colour · 90mins

Originally screened as part of an American TV-movie series *Moment of Truth*, this fact-based teleplay stars Linda Gray as a mother campaigning to find the killer of the daughter she disowned when she discovered she was working as a prostitute. While you have to admire the courage of the real-life Gayle Moffitt, who risked her own safety to bring the prime suspect to justice, there's no escaping the fact that this kind of sober melodrama has been done a dozen times before and, like many of its predecessors, is soon suffocated by its good intentions. ▣

Linda Gray *Gayle Moffitt* • Antonio Sabato Jr *AJ Treece* • James Eckhouse *Sergeant Jack Powell* • Alanna Ubach *April* • Joseph Burke *Harry Moffitt* • Louis A Lotorto *Paul Moffitt* ■ *Dir* Chuck Bowman • *Scr* Liz Coe

Why Shoot the Teacher ★★ PG

Drama   1976 · Can · Colour · 95mins

Canadian director Silvio Narizzano came to fame with *Georgy Girl*, but this altogether more attractive work found him back on home ground with an adaptation of a novel set in the mid-thirties. Bud Cort plays a young teacher whose only offer of a job is in the depressed prairie lands of Saskatchewan. He moves there but proves unpopular with the locals and his pupils because of his youth and eastern manners. Gradually matters improve, especially when he meets farmer's wife Alice (Samantha Eggar). Not a particularly original film, but the central story of his progress to manhood is nicely set against a picturesque background of an emergent nation. ▣

Bud Cort *Max Brown* • Samantha Eggar *Alice Field* • Chris Wiggins *Lyle Bishop* • Gary Reineke *Harris Montgomery* • John Friesen *Dave McDougall* • Michael J Reynolds *Bert Field* ■ *Dir* Silvio Narizzano • *Scr* James DeFelice, from the novel by Max Braithwaite

Why Would I Lie? ★ 15

Comedy drama   1980 · US · Colour · 100mins

Treat Williams uses his considerable talent to try and save this film from being entirely awful. Unfortunately, the task is too great even for him and this comic tale of a lying social worker trying to reunite a hard-bitten woman with her ex-con mother should only be viewed as an example of how not to make a movie. Miscast, unfunny and unfortunate. ▣

Treat Williams *Cletus Hayworth* • Lisa Eichhorn *Kay Lindsey* • Gabriel Swann *Jeorge* • Susan Heldfond *Amy* • Anne Byrne *Faith* ■ *Dir* Larry Peerce • *Scr* Peter Stone, from the novel *The Fabricator* by Hollis Hodges

Wichita ★★★ U

Western   1955 · US · Colour · 81mins

Excellent, intelligent and ultimately moving study of US marshal Wyatt Earp. As Earp, handsome Joel McCrea is superbly cast, his rugged middle-aged features creating instant empathy for the troubled lawman. Jacques Tourneur's direction is exemplary, as ever, and if certain incidents seem to presage later westerns like Sam Peckinpah's *The Wild Bunch*, perhaps that's because Peckinpah himself worked on this movie as dialogue director. Stuart N Lake, Earp's "official" biographer, was the film's technical adviser.

Joel McCrea *Wyatt Earp* • Vera Miles *Laurie* • Lloyd Bridges *Gyp* • Wallace Ford *Whiteside* • Edgar Buchanan *Doc Black* • Peter Graves (1) *Morgan Earp* • Keith Larsen *Bat Masterson* • Carl Benton Reid *Mayor* • John Smith *Jim Earp* ■ *Dir* Jacques Tourneur • *Scr* Daniel Ullman

Wicked City ★★★ 18

Animated science-fiction adventure
1992 · Jap · Colour · 80mins

This Japanese animated adaptation of Hideyuki Kikuchi's comic book is coherent enough to pass the typical hurdle of crunching down a *manga* story to 90 minutes. Some details remain murky, but they're almost forgotten because of the eye-catching

U = SUITABLE FOR ALL   Uc = SUITABLE FOR ALL, ESPECIALLY FOR YOUNG CHILDREN (VIDEO ONLY)   PG = PARENTAL GUIDANCE

images of the bizarre and grotesque (violent, and especially sexual) that are constantly paraded. The story concerns Earth's centuries-old relationship with alternate universe the "Black World" and the renewal of a peace treaty. Two agents (one from each world) are assigned to guard a key negotiator from warmongering Black World residents. It's never dull, though the extreme violence and sexual material may be too much for even the most jaded viewer.

Dir Yoshiaki Kawajiri, Carl Macek • *Scr* Kiseo Choo, from his story, from a comic book by Hideyuki Kikuchi

The Wicked Lady ★★★★ PG

Period drama   1945 · UK · BW · 99mins

Not a great movie, but one that struck a resounding chord with the public and gave British cinema one of its most striking images: that of highway robber Margaret Lockwood's beauty-spotted bosom heaving as she sneered at some poor male victim. Despite its popularity at the time (it was the highest earning movie in England in 1946), this is a fairly predictable costume drama, with a large selection of B-movie regulars striding about in thigh-length boots. Yet, seen from the distance of time, it is wonderful entertainment, with James Mason catching the swaggering heart of the movie, and Ms Lockwood could give Glenn Close a run for her money in the villainess stakes.

Margaret Lockwood *Barbara Worth/Lady Skelton* • James Mason *Captain Jackson* • Patricia Roc *Caroline* • Griffith Jones *Sir Ralph Skelton* • Enid Stamp-Taylor *Henrietta Kingsclere* • Michael Rennie *Kit Locksby* • Felix Aylmer *Hogarth* • David Horne *Martin Worth* • Martita Hunt *Cousin Agatha* ■ *Dir* Leslie Arliss • *Scr* Leslie Arliss, Aimee Stuart, Gordon Glennon, from the novel *The Life and Death of the Wicked Lady Skelton* by Magdalen King-Hall

The Wicked Lady ★★★ 18

Melodrama   1983 · UK · Colour · 94mins

Michael Winner's Technicolor remake of the effective 1945 hokum that made Margaret Lockwood a star fields Faye Dunaway as the amoral "lady" who takes up with a highwayman. Winner's version is in dubious taste, frankly exploitative and trashy in its unashamed injection of sex and violence, and famously caused a furore with the censors over a scene in which Dunaway takes a whip to another woman, ripping her clothes to shreds. Questionable though it may be, however, the movie is enjoyable high camp and efficiently made. Alan Bates is the highwayman, while John Gielgud is one of several other unlikely cast members. ▭

Faye Dunaway *Lady Barbara Skelton* • Alan Bates *Captain Jerry Jackson* • John Gielgud *Hogarth* • Denholm Elliott *Sir Ralph Skelton* • Prunella Scales *Lady Henrietta Kingsclere* • Glynis Barber *Caroline* • Oliver Tobias *Kit Locksby* • Joan Hickson *Aunt Agatha Trimble* ■ *Dir* Michael Winner • *Scr* Leslie Arliss, Michael Winner, from the novel *The Life and Death of the Wicked Lady Skelton* by Magdalen King-Hall

Wicked Stepmother ★ PG

Comedy horror   1989 · US · Colour · 89mins

A catastrophic climax to Bette Davis's glittering career. Shortly before her death, Davis said they should inscribe "She did it the hard way" on her tombstone, and the actress who took on the Hollywood studio system and won in the thirties was equally prepared to fight her corner in what turned out to be her last movie. Her disgust with director Larry Cohen's work led to her walking out, and her part as the stepmother who uses her paranormal powers to torment her family was drastically reduced. One hopes her atrocious performance was a poisonous act of revenge. Contains violence and swearing. ▭

Bette Davis *Miranda* • Barbara Carrera *Priscilla* • Colleen Camp *Jenny* • David Rasche *Steve* • Lionel Stander *Sam* • Tom Bosley *Lieutenant MacIntosh* • Shawn Donahue *Mike* • Richard Moll *Nat* ■ *Dir/Scr* Larry Cohen

The Wicker Man ★★★★★ 18

Horror   1973 · UK · Colour · 84mins

A devoutly Christian policeman finds his beliefs tested to the limit when he investigates the disappearance of a young girl on the pagan shores of Summerisle in one of the all-time fantasy cult classics. With a literate script by *Sleuth* playwright Anthony Shaffer and a memorable Scottish folk score, director Robin Hardy's fascinating mixture of horror, eroticism and religion is a thoughtful, challenging and highly provocative mystery thriller, which delves into strange goings-on within an island community. Christopher Lee, who plays the lord of the island, thinks it's the finest film he's ever made – and he's right. ▭

Edward Woodward *Sergeant Neil Howie* • Christopher Lee *Lord Summerisle* • Diane Cilento *Miss Rose* • Britt Ekland *Willow MacGregor* • Ingrid Pitt *Librarian/Clerk* • Lindsay Kemp *Alder MacGregor* • Russell Waters *Harbour master* • Aubrey Morris *Old gardener/Gravedigger* ■ *Dir* Robin Hardy • *Scr* Anthony Shaffer • *Cinematographer* Harry Waxman

Wide Awake ★★★

Drama   1998 · US · Colour · 90mins

Prior to writing and directing the smash hit *The Sixth Sense*, M Night Shyamalan made this film about a Catholic schoolboy who starts to question his faith after his granddad dies and devotes a whole school year to reassuring himself that gramps is spending eternity in good hands. Starring Joseph Cross, with Robert Loggia, Dana Delany, Denis Leary and Rosie O'Donnell among the supports, the film is intriguing enough, but is a little let down by a sugary script.

Denis Leary *Mr Beal* • Rosie O'Donnell *Sister Terry* • Dana Delany *Mrs Beal* • Robert Loggia *Grandpa Beal* • Joseph Cross *Joshua Beal* • Timothy Reifsnyder *Dave O'Hara* ■ *Dir/Scr* M Night Shyamalan

Wide Eyed and Legless ★★★★

Drama   1993 · UK · Colour · 87mins

Originally made for TV but given a limited theatrical release, this was the first of two films based on Deric

Longden's own life story (the other was *Lost for Words* which won a TV Bafta for Thora Hird). Julie Walters is superb as Diana, a woman suffering from a mysterious illness (now known as ME or chronic fatigue syndrome) for which the doctors have no answer. As she deteriorates, her frustration and fury are sublimated for the sake of her husband Deric (Jim Broadbent) until she can tolerate her poor quality of life no longer. Never maudlin, always convincing and with perfect performances from the two leads.

Julie Walters *Diana Longden* • Jim Broadbent *Deric Longden* • Thora Hird *Deric's mother* • Sian Thomas *Aileen Armitage* • Andrew Lancel *Nick Longden* • Anastasia Mulroney *Sally Longden* ■ *Dir* Richard Loncraine • *Scr* Jack Rosenthal, from the non-fiction books *Diana's Story* and *Lost for Words* by Deric Longden

Wide Sargasso Sea ★ 18

Period drama   1992 · Ausl · Colour · 94mins

An adaptation of the Jean Rhys novel that explores the story behind *Jane Eyre* by telling the history of the future Mrs Rochester. Set in 19th-century Jamaica, Rochester, played by Briton Nathaniel Parker, encounters the passionate and erotic Creole heiress Antoinette (Karina Lombard) and, after marrying her, discovers a family history of insanity. Unlike the novel, this is firstly pure melodrama and secondly poorly disguised erotica. What was an interesting literary tale is lost in a sea of sweaty sheets and bad acting. ▭

Karina Lombard *Antoinette Cosway* • Nathaniel Parker *Rochester* • Rachel Ward *Annette Cosway* • Michael York *Paul Mason* • Martine Beswicke [Martine Beswick] *Aunt Cora* • Claudia Robinson *Christophene* • Huw Christie Williams *Richard Mason* • Casey Berna *Young Antoinette* ■ *Dir* John Duigan • *Scr* Jan Sharp, Carole Angier, John Duigan, from the novel by Jean Rhys • *Music* Stewart Copeland

The Widow Couderc ★★★★

Romantic drama   1971 · Fr · Colour · 90mins

With such an idyllic canal-side setting and an overwhelming sense of wellbeing deriving from the fact the Popular Front is in power, Simone Signoret's rural idyll can only turn sour, as it so often does in the world of novelist Georges Simenon. Initially, the canker comes from her scheming in-laws seizing upon her relationship with fugitive Alain Delon as a pretext for reclaiming her late husband's farm. But just as sinister is the rise of fascism, which underpins the family's skulduggery. Pierre Granier-Deferre judges the tone to perfection, but it's the inspired pairing of Signoret and Delon that gives the film its heart. French dialogue dubbed into English.

Alain Delon *Jean* • Simone Signoret *Widow Couderc* • Ottavia Piccolo *Félicie* • Jean Tissier *Henri* ■ *Dir* Pierre Granier-Deferre • *Scr* Pierre Granier-Deferre, Pascal Jardin, from a story by Georges Simenon

Widow's Kiss ★★ 18

Thriller   1996 · US · Colour · 98mins

Things just aren't going well for Sean (MacKenzie Astin). His mom died, he gave up his dreams of music school to become a lawyer in order to please his father, and now dad's seeing a vampy new lady, Vivian (Beverly D'Angelo).

How could things get any worse? Well, for starters, dad could die under mysterious circumstances and Vivian could try to steal his inheritance with the help of her shifty "son". Sean has to hire a private investigator to find the truth. D'Angelo is a bit over the top, but the rest of the cast is obviously doing its best. Too bad the story is so ho-hum. Contains violence, sex scenes, nudity, swearing and drug abuse. ▭

Beverly D'Angelo *Vivian Fairchild* • MacKenzie Astin *Sean Sager* • Barbara Rush *Edith Fitzpatrick* • Dennis Haysbert *Eddie Costello* • Bruce Davison *Justin Sager* • Anna Maria Horsford *Capt Lavonda Harrison* • Michael Des Barres *Steven Rose* ■ *Dir* Peter Foldy • *Scr* Mark Donnelly, Peter Foldy

Widows' Peak ★★★ PG

Black comedy drama
1993 · UK · Colour · 97mins

The malicious, delicious old biddies of a picturesque Irish village declare war when their ranks are infiltrated by a wealthy and attractive new widow. It's tea-and-biscuits at 20 paces as hostilities prompt shameless behaviour, de-closeted skeletons and maybe even murder. Mia Farrow, Joan Plowright and Natasha Richardson play the black widows; Jim Broadbent and Adrian Dunbar are the menfolk desperate to avoid being eaten alive by them. Subtract one star if you've an allergic reaction to anything mock-Oirish. Contains violence. ▭

Mia Farrow *Catherine O'Hare* • Joan Plowright *Mrs "DC" Doyle Counihan* • Natasha Richardson *Edwina Broom* • Adrian Dunbar *Godfrey* • Jim Broadbent *Clancy* • Anne Kent *Miss Grubb* • John Kavanagh *Canon* ■ *Dir* John Irvin • *Scr* Hugh Leonard, from his story

Wife, Doctor and Nurse ★★★

Comedy   1937 · US · BW · 85mins

Loretta Young made five movies for Fox in 1937, and this was the only one in which she didn't co-star with either Tyrone Power or Don Ameche! However, she did manage to change her wardrobe for virtually every scene; even the *New York Times* commented on her changes of outfit in their normally austere review. The plot's a wisp: Young is married to doctor Warner Baxter, who is also loved by his indispensable nurse, Virginia Bruce. He sends the nurse away, his work suffers, she comes back. The ending's daring, and Walter Lang directs with skill, helped by a cast that contains many well-loved faces.

Loretta Young *Ina* • Warner Baxter *Dr Judd Lewis* • Virginia Bruce *Steve, Lewis's nurse* • Jane Darwell *Mrs Krueger, the Housekeeper* • Sidney Blackmer *Dr Therberg* • Maurice Cass *Pomout* ■ *Dir* Walter Lang • *Scr* Kathryn Scola, Darrell Ware, Lamar Trotti

Wife, Husband and Friend ★★★

Musical comedy   1939 · US · BW · 75mins

Classy comedy from 20th-Century-Fox, produced and written for the screen by that laconic southerner Nunnally Johnson, who would remake it to greater success ten years later as *Everybody Does It* with a more sophisticated cast, and Celeste Holm instead of Loretta Young. Here Young looks lovely, but never really convinces as the would-be singer whose husband really has the tuneful voice. It's entertaining, and western lovers might like to check out a film which features two notable Cisco Kids, Warner Baxter and Cesar Romero, playing alongside each other. Binnie Barnes as a prima donna and Helen Westley as Young's supportive mother get the most out of two splendidly written roles.

Loretta Young *Doris Blair Borland* • Warner Baxter *Leonard Borland* • Binnie Barnes *Cecil Carver* • Cesar Romero *Hugo* • George Barbier *Major Blair* • J Edward Bromberg *Rossi* • Eugene Pallette *Mike Craig* ■ *Dir* Gregory Ratoff • *Scr* Nunnally Johnson, from the novel *Career in C Major* by James M Cain

Wife vs Secretary ★★★★
Comedy drama   1936 · US · BW · 85mins

Clark Gable, Myrna Loy and Jean Harlow are the gold-plated trio of stars, directed by Clarence Brown, in this snappy, intelligent drama of near-fatal marital misunderstanding. Harlow is the personal secretary in a close, demanding but entirely innocent working relationship with magazine publisher Gable; Loy is the wife who almost loses Gable through jealous suspicion of Harlow, ignited by her mother (May Robson) and fuelled by coincidental circumstance. The on-screen empathy of the familiar Gable-Harlow team, devoid of the usual sexual pull, is wonderful to watch. James Stewart, pre-leading man stardom, is Harlow's boyfriend.

Clark Gable *Van "V S" Stanhope/Jake* • Jean Harlow *Helen "Whitey" Wilson* • Myrna Loy *Linda Stanhope* • May Robson *Mimi Stanhope* • George Barbier *JD Underwood* • James Stewart *Dave* • Hobart Cavanaugh *Joe* • Tom Dugan *Finney* ■ *Dir* Clarence Brown • *Scr* Norman Krasna, John Lee Mahin, Alice Duer Miller, from the short story by Faith Baldwin

Wigstock: The Movie ★★
Documentary   1995 · US · Colour · 82mins

Each year since 1985 drag queen the Lady Bunny has staged Wigstock, a mainly transvestite festival in the gay sector of New York's Greenwich Village. This documentary combines footage from the 1993 and 1994 events. However, much of the show's fun does not come across, primarily because so many of the performers display such modest talents. Exceptions are the amusing Duelling Bankheads (two men dressed as husky-voiced star Tallulah), stylish singer Crystal Waters, and the eye-popping British performance artist Leigh Bowery who died soon after.

Dir Barry Shils • *Cinematographer* Wolfgang Held

The Wilby Conspiracy
★★★ 15
Political thriller 1975 · UK · Colour · 101mins

In this drama set at the height of apartheid in South Africa, Sidney Poitier plays a political activist who drags unwilling Michael Caine on a cross-country flight from law and order, represented by the bigoted figure of Nicol Williamson. Villainous Williamson bides his time in the hope that the two fugitives will lead him to a rebel

leader. Memories of *The Defiant Ones* are strong here and, although the South African milieu is significant, Ralph Nelson's apparent return to the anti-racist controversy of *Soldier Blue* is merely a chase thriller. It's interesting, but not much more than that, although Rutger Hauer does appear in his first English language film. ▣

Sidney Poitier *Shack Twala* • Michael Caine *Keogh* • Nicol Williamson *Horn* • Prunella Gee *Rina Van Nierkirk* • Persis Khambatta *Dr Persis Ray* • Saeed Jaffrey *Dr Mukerjee* • Rutger Hauer *Blaine Van Niekirk* ■ *Dir* Ralph Nelson • *Scr* Rod Amateau, Harold Nebenzal, from the novel by Peter Driscoll

Wild America ★★ PG
Adventure 1997 · US · Colour · 101mins

A clunky eco-tale about three kids who take a walk on the wildlife side. Cameras at the ready, they embark on a trans-American trek to photo-record their country's fast-disappearing fauna. Cue lots of cute animals, and lots of none too convincingly filmed close encounters of the furred kind. A scene in which one of the kids gets caught in the antlers of an understandably enraged moose is particularly direly done. Teen heart-throbs Devon Sawa and Jonathan Taylor Thomas star in a film that has its heart in the right place, but not always its art. ▣

Jonathan Taylor Thomas *Marshall* • Devon Sawa *Mark* • Scott Bairstow *Marty* • Frances Fisher *Agnes* • Jamey Sheridan *Marty Senior* • Tracey Walter *Leon* ■ *Dir* William Dear • *Scr* David Michael Wieger

The Wild and the Innocent
★★
Comedy western 1959 · US · Colour · 84mins

Here's a suitably teamed pair of baby-faced fifties stars, as Audie Murphy and Sandra Dee play a couple of innocents from the mountains who find themselves out of their depth in an unruly town. Also on hand in this Universal co-feature are tough and sexy Joanne Dru, whose experience of character roles in John Ford and Howard Hawks westerns is put to good use here, and the always watchable Gilbert Roland. Not one of Murphy's best efforts, but not unwatchable.

Audie Murphy *Yancey* • Joanne Dru *Marcy Howard* • Gilbert Roland *Sheriff Paul Bartell* • Jim Backus *Cecil Forbes* • Sandra Dee *Rosalie Stocker* • George Mitchell *Uncle Hawkes* ■ *Dir* Jack Sher • *Scr* Sy Gomberg, Jack Sher, from a story by Jack Sher

The Wild and the Willing
★★★
Drama 1962 · UK · BW · 113mins

An unsuccessful play, *The Tinker* – written when Angry Young Men were in vogue – is the source of this exposé of British student life. Once shocking, it has aged as badly as others of its ilk, but now has considerable curiosity value, not least because of early appearances by Ian McShane, Samantha Eggar, John Hurt and others. McShane shines as the scholarship boy who vents his wrath on privileged society by having a fling with a professor's wife. The affair leads indirectly to tragedy, and then enlightenment. Relatively explicit

bedroom scenes are disconcertingly combined with student japes not far removed from those in *Doctor in the House*, which was also directed by Ralph Thomas.

Virginia Maskell *Virginia* • Paul Rogers *Professor Chown* • Ian McShane *Harry* • John Hurt *Phil* • Samantha Eggar *Josie* • Catherine Woodville *Sarah* • Johnny Sekka *Reggie* • Jeremy Brett *Gilby* ■ *Dir* Ralph Thomas • *Scr* Nicholas Phipps, Mordecai Richler, from the play *The Tinker* by Laurence Dobie, Robert Sloman

Wild and Wonderful ★★ U
Comedy 1964 · US · Colour · 87mins

Tony Curtis and his then wife Christine Kaufmann team in this romantic frippery that is more notable for the performance of a poodle called Monsieur Cognac than for the efforts of its human stars. Curtis plays yet another American in Paris, who allows his music to suffer once he hits the right note with movie star Kaufmann. But when her pooch refuses to allow them to make sweet music together, he's forced to call in reinforcements of the canine kind. The leads are clearly in love, but it gets in the way of their acting, which is as unconvincing as the fake Paris sets.

Tony Curtis *Terry Williams* • Christine Kaufmann *Giselle Ponchon* • Larry Storch *Rufus Gibbs* • Pierre Olaf *Jacquot* • Mary Ingels *Doc Bailey* • Jacques Aubuchon *Papa Ponchon* • Cliff Osmond *Hercule* ■ *Dir* Michael Anderson • *Scr* Larry Markes, Michael Morris, Waldo Salt, from a treatment by Richard M Powell, Phillip Rapp, from a short story by Dorothy Crider

The Wild Angels ★★★★ 18
Action drama 1966 · US · Colour · 82mins

The first and most controversial Hell's Angel shocker from cult director Roger Corman kick-started a whole cycle of biker movies. None were better than this brutal tale of leather-clad punks taking drugs, gang-raping women, beating up priests and having a drunken orgy at the church funeral of chapter member Bruce Dern when he's killed by "the man". Shot documentary-style for added realism, it's based on true incidents as related to Corman by Californian Angels. Super cool Peter Fonda heads a hip cast of B-movie stalwarts, anti-establishment icons and pop singers. Graphic violence and the final message "There's nowhere to go" caused Corman's counter-culture portrait to be banned in many countries. ▣

Peter Fonda *Heavenly Blues* • Nancy Sinatra *Mike* • Bruce Dern *Loser* • Lou Procopio *Joint* • Coby Denton *Bull Puckey* • Marc Cavell *Frankenstein* • Buck Taylor *Dear John* • Norman Alden *Medic* • Michael J Pollard *Pigmy* ■ *Dir* Roger Corman • *Scr* Charles Griffith

Wild at Heart ★★★★ 18
Drama 1990 · US · Colour · 119mins

Director David Lynch goes over the top, over people's heads and somewhere over the psychedelic rainbow in another ultra-violent and sleazily sexy pulp art attack. Forget the story; Lynch clearly has. Just follow convict and Elvis fan Nicolas Cage and his white trash girlfriend Laura Dern as they are pursued through the Deep South by her crazed mother's gumshoe lover.

Stuffed with the Sultan of Strange's transfixing brand of deranged visuals, haunting weirdness and exuberant camp, it's another hip and hypnotic rollercoaster ride through the twin peaks of pretentiousness and exhilaration. Contains violence, swearing, sex scenes and nudity. ▣

Nicolas Cage *Sailor Ripley* • Laura Dern *Lula Pace Fortune* • Diane Ladd *Marietta Pace* • Willem Dafoe *Bobby Peru* • Isabella Rossellini *Perdita Durango* • Harry Dean Stanton *Johnnie Farragut* • Crispin Glover *Dell* • Grace Zabriskie *Juana* ■ *Dir* David Lynch • *Scr* David Lynch, from the novel by Barry Gifford • *Music* Angelo Badalamenti

Wild Beauty ★★ U
Western 1946 · US · BW · 61mins

A desperately over-complicated Universal programme filler, ostensibly about an Indian boy and his horse called Wild Beauty, but also containing an unsavoury subplot about capturing mustangs and turning their hides into shoe leather. There are also a fair number of speeches about the rights of American Indians. Only Don Porter emerges with any credit among the grown-ups (though Jacqueline de Wit does attempt a serious portrayal), and there's no room for relief from the tedium in producer/director Wallace Fox's deathless combination of earnestness and cheapskate production values.

Don Porter *Dave Morrow* • Lois Collier *Linda Gibson* • Jacqueline de Wit *Sissy* • George Cleveland *Barney* • Robert Wilcox *Gordon Madison* ■ *Dir* Wallace W Fox [Wallace Fox] • *Scr* Adele Buffington

Wild Bill ★★★★ 15
Western 1995 · US · Colour · 93mins

Walter Hill's *Wild Bill*, like his earlier *Geronimo*, is a flawed but fascinating look at an American legend. Starring a superbly cast Jeff Bridges as William "Wild Bill" Hickok, the movie opens with the killing of a dozen or so men over the course of a decade, then focuses on the ageing gunslinger's quest for old flame Calamity Jane (Ellen Barkin) while setting up a confrontation with a vengeful youngster who may be Hickok's bastard son. Hill paints a far from pretty picture of the West in general and Hickok in particular: he's a drug addict, a killer and a monster haunted by his past. American audiences found the film easy to resist, but it oozes period atmosphere and stands with Kevin Costner's revisionist *Wyatt Earp* as an epic of disillusionment. ▣

Jeff Bridges *James Butler "Wild Bill" Hickok* • Ellen Barkin *Calamity Jane* • John Hurt *Charley Prince* • Diane Lane *Susannah Moore* • David Arquette *Jack McCall* • Keith Carradine *Buffalo Bill Cody* • Christina Applegate *Lurline* • Bruce Dern *Will Plummer* ■ *Dir* Walter Hill • *Scr* Walter Hill, from the play *Fathers and Sons* by Thomas Babe and the novel *Deadwood* by Pete Dexter

The Wild Bunch ★★★★★ 18
Classic western 1969 · US · Colour · 138mins

Arguably, one of the greatest westerns ever made. And argument is what Sam Peckinpah's masterpiece has always caused for its slow-motion spurting of blood, its surrealistically choreographed gunfights and its

portrayal of Pike Bishop's amoral Texas outlaws as heroes. Yet William Holden's laconic Bishop, however violent, is of a truly romantic breed as he leads his bunch to their deaths in a defensive revenge on revolutionary guerrilla forces. Lucien Ballard's photography gives a funereal hue to this elegy to the passing of a certain breed of chivalry. You can see why John Wayne is said to have hated the film; Peckinpah was practically reinventing a genre, with no place left for false nobility. Contains brief nudity and violence. [video] DVD

William Holden (1) *Pike Bishop* • Ernest Borgnine *Dutch Engstrom* • Robert Ryan *Deke Thornton* • Edmond O'Brien *Sykes* • Warren Oates *Lyle Gorch* • Jaime Sanchez *Angel* • Ben Johnson *Tector Gorch* • Emilio Fernandez *Mapache* ■ *Dir* Sam Peckinpah • *Scr* Walon Green, Sam Peckinpah, from a story by Walon Green, Roy N Sickner • *Cinematographer* Lucien Ballard • *Music* Jerry Fielding

Wild Card ★★ PG

Drama 1992 · US · Colour · 81mins

Powers Boothe is the ex-preacher and professional gambler who uncovers murder and corruption in a town called Farewell, New Mexico. Co-starring Cindy Pickett and René Auberjonois as Boothe's old buddy, the picture is a modern-day western that packs few surprises in its saddle-worn plot. Boothe has never fulfilled his promise, despite a fine performance in John Boorman's *The Emerald Forest* and a decent stab at Philip Marlowe in a TV series. He has physical presence, but he's a strangely inexpressive actor. [video]

Powers Boothe *Preacher* • Cindy Pickett *Dana* • Terry O'Quinn *Barlow* • René Auberjonois *Jake Spence* • John Lacy *Vollie* • M Emmet Walsh *Mose* ■ *Dir* Mel Damski • *Scr* Scobie Richardson, from the novel *Preacher* by Ted Thackrey Jr

The Wild Country ★★ U

Adventure 1971 · US · Colour · 88mins

Disney tames the wilderness yarn into suitable family fare, but in doing so creates a much dumbed-down adventure. Steve Forrest and Vera Miles take on a run-down Wyoming ranch and, incidentally, the local inhabitants, including wall-eyed Jack Elam. The characters are as two-dimensional as Disney cartoons, though Ron Howard, the *Happy Days* star and now blockbuster director, gives a creditable performance as the teenage son. [video]

Steve Forrest *Jim Tanner* • Vera Miles *Kate Tanner* • Jack Elam *Thompson* • Ronny Howard [Ron Howard] *Virgil Tanner* • Frank De Kova *Two Dog* • Morgan Woodward *Ab Cross* • Clint Howard *Andrew Tanner* • Dub Taylor *Phil* ■ *Dir* Robert Totten • *Scr* Calvin Clements Jr, Paul Savage, from the novel *Little Britches* by Ralph Moody

The Wild Duck ★★★

Drama 1983 · Ausl · Colour · 95mins

Henri Safran makes so little capital out of relocating Henrik Ibsen's play to turn-of-the-century Australia that one wonders why he bothered. Yet the structure and brooding atmosphere of this fiercely melodramatic story remain intact and, apart from name changes, so do the characters. Thus Arthur Dignam is wilfully pompous as he hauls family skeletons before the bemused Jeremy Irons, who can scarcely believe that his timid wife, Liv Ullmann, bore him another man's child. Exploring such themes as human weakness, guilt and self-sacrifice, this highly symbolic piece ends on a note of shocking tragedy, which nowadays seems strangely grotesque.

Liv Ullmann *Gina* • Jeremy Irons *Harold* • Lucinda Jones *Henrietta* • John Meillon *Major Ackland* • Arthur Dignam *Gregory* • Michael Pate *George* • Colin Croft *Mollison* ■ *Dir* Henri Safran • *Scr* Peter Smalley, John Lind, Henri Safran, from the play by Henrik Ibsen

The Wild Geese ★★★ 15

Action adventure
1978 · UK · Colour · 128mins

Richards Burton and Harris, plus Roger Moore, are evidently enjoying themselves here as mercenaries hired by Stewart Granger to rescue a deposed African president and put him back in power, all for the sake of big-business interests – a plot similar to Frederick Forsyth's *The Dogs of War*. There's hardly a moment when a hand grenade isn't in the air and, as a firework display, the movie is often exciting. Politically, it's a dog's dinner of woolly liberalism and right-wing rhetoric: it was filmed in South Africa during the height of apartheid. [video]

Richard Burton *Col Allen Faulkner* • Roger Moore *Shawn Fynn* • Richard Harris *Rafer Janders* • Hardy Kruger *Pieter Coetzee* • Stewart Granger *Sir Edward Matherson* • Jack Watson *Sandy Young* • Winston Ntshona *President Julius Limbani* ■ *Dir* Andrew V McLaglen • *Scr* Reginald Rose, from the novel by Daniel Carney

Wild Geese II ★ 18

Action adventure
1985 · UK · Colour · 119mins

This infantile follow-up to *The Wild Geese* hinges on a gang of mercenaries trying to get the ageing Rudolf Hess (Laurence Olivier in a positively embarrassing performance) out of Spandau Prison. It revamps the original – itself borrowing heavily from Aldrich's *Dirty Dozen* – in having a brutal and tedious training sequence before the actual mission. The film is cobbled together by director Peter Hunt with leaden predictability and absolutely no narrative flow whatsoever. [video]

Scott Glenn *John Haddad* • Barbara Carrera *Kathy Lukas* • Edward Fox *Alex Faulkner* • Laurence Olivier *Rudolf Hess* • Robert Webber *Robert McCann* • Robert Freitag *Stroebling* • Kenneth Haigh *Col Reed-Henry* • Stratford Johns *Mustapha El Ali* ■ *Dir* Peter Hunt • *Scr* Reginald Rose, from the novel *The Square Circle* by Daniel Carney

Wild Geese Calling ★★

Drama 1941 · US · BW · 78mins

Restless lumberjack Henry Fonda, in search of excitement, tracks down old pal and gambler Warren William in Seattle. There he meets and marries saloon dancer Joan Bennett who, unbeknown to him, is William's old flame, gets involved in William's dangerous dispute with big Barton MacLane, takes off to Alaska with friend and now pregnant wife, and... With a top-notch cast and enough plot to fill two movies, one could have expected more of this adventure drama. For all its incident, however, the script is not sharp enough, and is further flattened by John Brahm's laboured direction.

Henry Fonda *John Murdock* • Joan Bennett *Sally Murdock* • Warren William *Blackie Bedford* • Ona Munson *Clarabella* • Barton MacLane *Pirate Kelly* • Russell Simpson *Len Baker* • Iris Adrian *Mazie* • James C Morton *Mack* ■ *Dir* John Brahm • *Scr* Horace McCoy, Sam Hellman, Jack Andrews, Robert Carson, from the novel by Stewart Edward White

Wild Hearts Can't Be Broken ★★★ U

Romantic drama 1991 · US · Colour · 85mins

A lovingly re-created Depression-era America provides the setting for this beautifully mounted Disney family drama about the life of legendary stunt diver Sonora Webster, who overcame personal tragedy to become a star attraction with her horse-diving act. British-born actress Gabrielle Anwar gives a gutsy performance in the lead role, while veteran actor Cliff Robertson provides the necessary eccentricity as her cranky employer. The scenes of Anwar's horse plunging 40ft into an enormous tank of water will have dedicated equine fans reaching for the phone. [video]

Gabrielle Anwar *Sonora Webster* • Cliff Robertson *Doctor Carver* • Dylan Kussman *Clifford* • Michael Schoeffling *Al Carver* • Kathleen York *Marie* • Frank Renzulli *Mr Slater* • Nancy Moore Atchison *Arnette* • Lisa Norman *Aunt Helen* ■ *Dir* Steve Miner • *Scr* Matt Williams, Oley Sassone

Wild Heritage ★★★ U

Western 1958 · US · Colour · 78mins

An absorbing saga made on the cheap involving a brace of pioneer families and their trials and tribulations, mainly associated with their teenage offspring. Appearing among the youngsters are such icons of the era as folksie composer Rod McKuen and teen idol Troy Donahue. Newly widowed Maureen O'Sullivan presides over the gunplay, and gnarly Will Rogers Jr makes a fair bid at his real-life father's style of homespun wisdom. But the film belongs to the teenagers, as they demonstrate the solidarity rule of the Old West by ganging together and blasting the baddies to kingdom come. The colour locations are a bonus.

Will Rogers Jr *Judge Copeland* • Maureen O'Sullivan *Emma Breslin* • Rod McKuen *Dirk Breslin* • Casey Tibbs *Rusty* • Troy Donahue *Jesse Bascomb* • Judy Meredith [Judi Meredith] *Callie Bascomb* • Gigi Perreau *Missouri Breslin* • George "Foghorn" Winslow [George Winslow] *Talbot Breslin* ■ *Dir* Charles Haas • *Scr* Paul King, Joseph Stone, from a story by Steve Frazee

Wild Horses ★★★ PG

Western drama
1985 · US/New Zealand · Colour · 90mins

Country singer Kenny Rogers takes a break from warbling to star in this entertaining, contemporary cowboy flick. He plays an ex-rodeo star who finds his new blue-collar life boring, and turns his back on it to take part in a wild-horse roundup. Rogers has an easy charm, and fans will appreciate his songs that have managed to slip in. The film's feel of the real is boosted by a supporting presence from Hollywood veterans Richard Farnsworth and Ben Johnson, both of whom have ridden a few real wild horses in their time. [video]

Kenny Rogers *Matt Cooper* • Pam Dawber *Daryl Reese* • Richard Farnsworth *Chuck Reese* • Ben Johnson *Bill Ward* • David Andrews *Dean Ellis* • Richard Masur *Bob* • Jack Rader *Dick Post* ■ *Dir* Dick Lowry • *Scr* Daniel Vining, Roderick Taylor

Wild in the Country ★★★ PG

Musical drama 1961 · US · Colour · 109mins

This drama about a backwoods delinquent on parole, who ends up going to college to become a great writer, represents an attempt to unveil Elvis Presley as a straight dramatic actor. He makes a respectable attempt but is not quite good enough, and has no help from an unconvincing plot and script. In the course of the action, which goes on for too long, he is sent to psychiatrist Hope Lange, who discovers and nurtures his hidden writing talent and falls for him; meanwhile, he is two-timing ladylike Millie Perkins and earthy Tuesday Weld. Strangely, this unlikely piece is based on the true story of one Jesse Stuart, a Kentucky hillbilly who became a successful writer. [video]

Elvis Presley *Glenn Tyler* • Hope Lange *Irene Sperry* • Tuesday Weld *Noreen* • Millie Perkins *Betty Lee Parsons* • Rafer Johnson *Davis* • Christina Crawford *Monica George* • John Ireland *Phil Macy* • Gary Lockwood *Cliff Macy* • Jason Robards Jr *Judge Parker* ■ *Dir* Philip Dunne • *Scr* Clifford Odets, from the novel *The Lost Country* by JR Salamanca

Wild in the Streets ★★ 15

Drama 1968 · US · Colour · 92mins

World-famous pop megastar with a mother complex Max Frost (Christopher Jones), starts a political campaign buoyed by Barry Mann and Cynthia Weil protest songs. When several states lower the voting age, the door is open for the first teenager to win the presidency, and Frost helps the political process along by putting LSD in the Washington water supply. When this modish satire of teenage rebellion was released at the fag-end of the sixties, it must have seemed a lot more cutting then. However, the film is well-made, lively and often funny. Based on an *Esquire* feature whose title, *The Day It All Happened, Baby*, just about sums it up. [video]

Shelley Winters *Mrs Flatow* • Christopher Jones *Max Frost* • Diane Varsi *Sally LeRoy* • Ed Begley *Senator Allbright* • Millie Perkins *Mary Fergus* • Hal Holbrook *John Fergus* • Richard Pryor *Stanley X* ■ *Dir* Barry Shear • *Scr* Robert Thom, from his article *The Day It All Happened, Baby*

Wild Is the Wind ★★

Melodrama 1957 · US · BW · 114mins

This gloomy, po-faced melodrama features Anthony Quinn as a widowed Italian shepherd whose farm is in Nevada. Needing a new wife, he imports his sister-in-law (Anna Magnani) from Italy and marries her The sparks start to fly when she makes off with Quinn's adopted son, Anthony Franciosa. George Cukor came on board when John Sturges was diverted to *The Old Man and the Sea*. Vaguely reminiscent of *They Knew What They Wanted* with Charles Laughton, it was apparently a turbulent production thanks to an uncomfortable relationship with prima donna Magnani. Nevertheless she and Quinn were both nominated for Oscars.

Anna Magnani *Gioia* • Anthony Quinn *Gino* • Anthony Franciosa *Bene* • Dolores Hart *Angie* • Joseph Calleia *Alberto* • Lili Valenty *Teresa* ■ *Dir* George Cukor • *Scr* Arnold Schulman, from the novel *Furia* by Vittorio Nino Novarese

The Wild Life ★ 18

Comedy   1984 · US · Colour · 90mins

The creators behind *Fast Times at Ridgemont High* here try to repeat the formula, though the results don't come close. They even hired Sean Penn's brother Christopher to play this movie's ''Spicoli'', though he is remarkably restrained. Like the original, it's a collection of vignettes concerning eccentric teenagers as they embark on entering the adult world, as well as high school graduate Eric Stoltz struggling to make it on his own. Not only does the movie frequently forget to be funny, it is executed without any energy or passion in front of or behind the camera; aside from the golden oldie/Eddie Van Halen soundtrack, the only thing wild about it is its title. 📼

Christopher Penn *Tom Drake* • Ilan Mitchell-Smith *Jim Conrad* • Eric Stoltz *Bill Conrad* • Jenny Wright *Eileen* • Lea Thompson *Anita* • Rick Moranis *Harry* • Randy Quaid *Charlie* ■ *Dir* Art Linson • *Scr* Cameron Crowe

Wild Man Blues ★★★★ 12

Music documentary
1997 · US · Colour · 100mins

Music is low on director Barbara Kopple's list of priorities in this account of Woody Allen's 1996 European tour with his jazz band. Instead, she tags along as he's hurtled from pillar to post by civic and cultural dignitaries to receive awards and greet the great and the good (with a priceless mix of embarrassment and irritation). But it's the private moments with his then girlfriend – now his wife – Soon-Yi Previn that make this compelling portrait of a highly complex man so intriguing. Completely at home in the limelight, she comes across as the guiding light of their relationship. Yet, if you think she's overbearing, wait until you see Allen's parents in action during a hilarious coda. Contains swearing. 📼

Dir Barbara Kopple

The Wild North ★★ U

Adventure   1952 · US · Colour · 97mins

A first-rate cast figures in this below-standard adventure in which Stewart Granger kills a man in self-defence and is forced to flee into the Canadian wilderness. Hotly following is Mountie Wendell Corey, but trapper Granger knows every inch of the harsh countryside and leads him on a perilous trail. Andrew Marton directs with some pace, but with the great Cyd Charisse also featuring as Granger's gal, it's the stars who are of main interest here.

Stewart Granger *Jules Vincent* • Wendell Corey *Constable Pedley* • Cyd Charisse *Indian girl* •

Morgan Farley *Father Simon* • JM Kerrigan *Callahan* • Howard Petrie *Brody* • Houseley Stevenson *Old man* • John War Eagle *Indian chief* ■ *Dir* Andrew Marton • *Scr* Frank Fenton

Wild on the Beach ★★

Musical comedy   1965 · US · BW · 77mins

Director Maury Dexter was an expert at turning out low-budget pictures in the sixties, most of them horror movies or teen-slanted pop-music films. Sherry Jackson and singer Frankie Randall (being hailed as a new Sinatra at the time) head the cast in this tale of a group of teenagers who take over a beach house when there is a housing shortage on their campus. Their wrangling and romantic entanglements take up most of the screen time, and the film would be totally forgettable were it not for the presence of Sonny and Cher. The couple had just become pop sensations, and the film marked Cher's screen debut.

Frankie Randall *Adam* • Sherry Jackson *Lee Sullivan* • Sonny Bono • Cher ■ *Dir* Maury Dexter • *Scr* Harry Spalding, from a story by Hank Tani

The Wild One ★★★★ PG

Drama   1953 · US · BW · 75mins

''What are you rebelling against, Johnny?'' asks waitress Mary Murphy. ''What've you got?'' snarls Marlon Brando, his leather-clad biker entering the iconography of the decade. Long-banned in Britain, this is the first, the best, the quintessential motorbike movie, actually based on a 1947 incident when a cycle gang terrorised the small town of Hollister, California one desperate Fourth of July. OK, the back projection is a joke, Lee Marvin's far too old and the direction's often inadequate (as is the budget), but Brando is simply brilliant and the film still retains its unique power to astound. 📼 **DVD**

Marlon Brando *Johnny* • Mary Murphy *Kathie* • Robert Keith *Harry Bleeker* • Lee Marvin *Chino* • Jay C Flippen *Sheriff Singer* • Peggy Maley *Mildred* • Hugh Sanders *Charlie Thomas* • Ray Teal *Frank Bleeker* ■ *Dir* Laslo Benedek • *Scr* John Paxton, from a story by Frank Rooney • *Cinematographer* Hal Mohr

Wild Orchid ★ 18

Erotic drama   1990 · US · Colour · 106mins

A ghastly piece of soft-pore corn from trashmaster Zalman King. Carré Otis plays a lawyer who courts trouble when she falls for earring-wearing, super-bronzed Mickey Rourke during the carnival celebrations in Rio. Silly girl! It's the cue for much simulated sex, and precious little else.

Mickey Rourke *Wheeler* • Jacqueline Bisset *Claudia* • Carré Otis *Emily* • Assumpta Serna *Hanna* • Bruce Greenwood *Jerome* ■ *Dir* Zalman King • *Scr* Zalman King, Patricia Louisianna Knop

Wild Orchids ★★★

Silent romantic drama
1929 · US · BW · 100mins

On a boat to Java, the beautiful young wife (Greta Garbo) of a middle-aged, unemotional business tycoon (Lewis Stone), twice her age, is lusted after by a foreign prince (Nils Asther) who invites them to stay at his opulent

Javanese palace. There, the tension mounts and the situation reaches its climax during a tiger shoot. This little-known Garbo silent, lavishly mounted and directed with excellent judgement by Sidney Franklin, is out of the school of exotic, erotic, fantasy melodrama. Garbo is good, the slant-eyed Swede Asther is perfectly cast as the scheming and determined lover, and Stone's superb as the seemingly impervious husband.

Greta Garbo *Lili Sterling* • Lewis Stone *John Sterling* • Nils Asther *Prince De Gace* ■ *Dir* Sidney Franklin • *Scr* Hans Kräly, Richard Schayer, Willis Goldbeck, Marian Ainslee, Ruth Cummings, from the story *Hunt* by John Colton

The Wild Pair ★★ 18

Action crime drama
1987 · US · Colour · 91mins

This thoroughly routine action movie outing features Beau Bridges and Bubba Smith as, respectively, a yuppie FBI agent and a streetwise cop who team up to track down a bunch of drug-dealing killers. No prizes for guessing that much of the tension derives from their clash of personalities. Bridges directs, his first time for the big screen, while dad Lloyd Bridges makes it something of a family affair by taking one of the chunkier supporting roles. 📼

Beau Bridges *Joe Jennings* • Bubba Smith *Benny Avalon* • Lloyd Bridges *Colonel Hester* • Raymond St Jacques *Ivory* • Gary Lockwood *Captain Kramer* • Danny De La Paz *Tucker* • Lela Rochon *Debby* • Greg Finley *Sergeant Peterson* ■ *Dir* Beau Bridges • *Scr* Joseph Gunn, from a story by John Crowther, Joseph Gunn

The Wild Party ★★★

Comedy drama   1929 · US · BW · 77mins

Clara Bow's first talking picture has the original ''It'' girl as a larky student who develops a crush on her handsome tutor, played by Fredric March. Gossip, pranks, insubordination and twenties sophomore slang all play their part in a fascinating period piece that is hard to watch today due to its forgivable technical limitations, yet which retains enough of its original energy to be entertaining. As with many silent stars whose fame faded in the thirties, the decline of Bow's career is often attributed to her inability to handle the new technology. Yet she acquits herself well here, and it is more likely that scandal (including her elopement with screen cowboy Rex Bell) was the main reason for her subsequent obscurity.

Clara Bow *Stella Ames* • Fredric March *Gil Gilmore* • Shirley O'Hara *Helen Owens* • Marceline Day *Faith Morgan* • Joyce Compton *Eva Tutt* ■ *Dir* Dorothy Arzner • *Scr* E Lloyd Sheldon, John VA Weaver, from a story by Warner Fabian

The Wild Party ★★★

Musical drama   1975 · US · Colour · 100mins

In an impressive re-creation of silent-era Hollywood, James Coco plays a fading film funnyman whose hopes are pinned on a comeback movie hit. Raquel Welch plays the girlfriend who hosts a wild party for Tinseltown's moviebiz movers and shakers to promote it. It's a grim film that's based on the story of Fatty Arbuckle,

the silent-era comic whose fan following vanished like mist when he was charged with killing a girl during a sex romp gone wrong. Welch is actually very good and it's directed by James Ivory with scarcely a cucumber sarnie to be seen.

James Coco *Jolly Grimm* • Raquel Welch *Queenie* • Perry King *Dale Sword* • Tiffany Bolling *Kate* • Royal Dano *Tex* • David Dukes *James* • Dena Dietrich *Mrs Murchison* ■ *Dir* James Ivory • *Scr* Walter Marks, from a poem by Joseph Moncure March • *Producer* Ismail Merchant • *Cinematographer* Walter Lassally

The Wild Ride ★★

Drama   1960 · US · BW · 80mins

In one of Jack Nicholson's earliest films, the future superstar plays a homicidal hot-rodder fed up with a former pal who's given up the wild life to settle down with girlfriend Georgianna Carter. Kidnapping the girl, he takes her on a high-speed rampage pursued by the local constabulary. Like many of Nicholson's early efforts, this release came out of the Roger Corman low-budget stable and was edited by future cult director Monte Hellman (*Two-Lane Blacktop*). It's obviously a cheap quickie, but it has its own exploitative charm and young Jack looks like he's having a ball.

Jack Nicholson *Johnny Varron* • Georgianna Carter *Nancy* • Robert Bean *Dave* ■ *Dir* Harvey Berman • *Scr* Ann Porter, Marion Rothman

Wild River ★★★

Drama   1960 · US · Colour · 109mins

This was a commercial failure for Elia Kazan, one of the key directors of postwar American cinema. But today this study of an old woman's intransigence when faced by the Tennessee Valley Authority's need to sequester her property in order to build a dam proves to be an intelligent and moving film, graced by a superbly tender performance from Montgomery Clift in one of his last and most tortured roles. Lee Remick is touching as his confidante, and there's a sharply-etched portrait by Jo Van Fleet (*East of Eden*) in the role of the old woman. Watch out too for Bruce Dern in his movie debut.

Montgomery Clift *Chuck Glover* • Lee Remick *Carol Baldwin* • Jo Van Fleet *Ella Garth* • Albert Salmi *FJ Bailey* • Jay C Flippen *Hamilton Garth* • James Westerfield *Cal Garth* • Big Jeff Bess *Joe John Garth* • Bruce Dern *Jack Roper* ■ *Dir* Elia Kazan • *Scr* Paul Osborn, from the novels *Mud on the Stars* by William Bradford Huie and *Dunbar's Cove* by Borden Deal

Wild Rovers ★★★★ 15

Western   1971 · US · Colour · 125mins

Although Blake Edwards is famous for the *Pink Panther* series, he also made some fine dramas, including this western starring William Holden, Ryan O'Neal and Karl Malden. It's very much a film made in the wake of *The Wild Bunch* (in which Holden also starred), telling the story of an ageing cowboy and his adoring younger partner who dream of getting rich by robbing a bank. It's as if the boy in *Shane* grew up and fell in with bad company. Beautifully shot and with a fine Jerry Goldsmith score, this is an exciting and often touching study of honour, heroism and changing times. O'Neal is perfectly cast, for once, and Holden is as craggy and magnificent as the Rocky Mountains scenery. ▭

William Holden (1) *Ross Bodine* • Ryan O'Neal *Frank Post* • Karl Malden *Walter Buckman* • Lynn Carlin *Sada Billings* • Tom Skerritt *John Buckman* • Joe Don Baker *Paul Buckman* • James Olson *Joe Billings* • Leora Dana *Nell Buckman* • Moses Gunn *Ben* • Victor French *Sheriff* ■ *Dir/Scr* Blake Edwards

Wild Search ★★🄸

Crime thriller 1989 · UK · Colour · 94mins

One of Hong Kong star Chow Yun-Fat's more obscure films, this is nevertheless a more than able crime thriller, expertly choreographed by director Ringo Lam. While this lacks the bravura of the best Hong Kong thrillers, it still bears comparison with most Hollywood fodder. In Cantonese with English subtitles. Contains violence. ▭

Chow Yun-Fat *Mickey Lau* • Cherie Chung *Cher* • Paul Chin *Mr Hung* • Chan Cheuk-yan *Ka-ka* • Lau Kong *Leung* • Tommy Wong *Lam* • Roy Cheung *Tiger* ■ *Dir* Ringo Lam • *Scr* Nam Yin

Wild Seed ★★

Road movie 1965 · US · BW · 98mins

One of the results of a Universal Studios policy in the mid-sixties to encourage inexperienced talent – and it shows. A young woman (Celia Kaye), in search of her birth parents, crosses America bound for LA. On the way she hooks up with a young ne'er-do-well (Michael Parks). The set-up is of course a familiar one, but this highly visual film was watchable thanks to cinematographer Conrad Hall (whose first major studio film this is).

Michael Parks *Fargo* • Celia Kaye *Daphne, "Daffy"* • Ross Elliott *Mr Collinge* • Woodrow Chambliss *Mr Simms* • Rupert Crosse *Hobo* • Eva Novak *Mrs Simms* ■ *Dir* Brian G Hutton • *Scr* Les Pine, from a story by Ike Jones, Les Pine

Wild Side ★★★🄸

Erotic thriller 1996 · US · Colour · 115mins

Later released in a version closer to Donald Cammell's original vision, this early Anne Heche vehicle casts her as Alex, an investment banker who works as a prostitute in the evenings. Upon meeting infamous money launderer Bruno (Christopher Walken), Heche falls in love with his wife, played by Joan Chen. After the director's untimely death in 1996, his fourth and final film was released in a severely truncated form (he was credited as Franklin Brauner). But his widow China Kong and longtime editor Frank Mazzola have reconstructed a seemingly improvised pulp thriller that won't be to everyone's taste – there's a particularly brutal rape scene as well as a tendency for the story to ramble – yet which stands as a compelling piece of cinema from a sadly under-used talent.

Christopher Walken *Bruno Buckingham* • Joan Chen *Virginia Chow* • Steven Bauer *Tony* • Anne Heche *Alex Lee* • Allen Garfield *Dan Rackman* • Adam Novack *Lyle Litvak* • Zion Hiro Sakamoto ■ *Dir* Donald Cammell • *Scr* Donald Cammell, China Kong • *Music* Ryuichi Sakamoto

Wild Strawberries ★★★★★🄸

Drama 1957 · Swe · BW · 87mins

Contrasting the innocent expectancy of youth with the bitter regret of old age, this is Ingmar Bergman's warmest and most accessible film. Sweden's greatest silent director, Victor Sjöström, gives a magisterial performance as the frosty, vain professor who seizes the chance for redemption offered to him in the dreams and nightmares he experiences while travelling to a degree ceremony with his daughter-in-law, Ingrid Thulin. The symbolism of the nightmares (including handless clocks and runaway hearses) is occasionally overpowering, but the memories of idyllic summers spent with cousin Bibi Andersson rank among the finest moments of the director's career. In Swedish with English subtitles. ▭

Victor Sjöström *Professor Isak Borg* • Bibi Andersson *Sara* • Ingrid Thulin *Marianne Borg* • Gunnar Björnstrand *Evald Borg* ■ *Dir/Scr* Ingmar Bergman

Wild Target ★★★★🄸

Comedy thriller 1993 · Fr · Colour · 84mins

Jean Rochefort, one of the finest character actors currently working in French cinema, has rarely been better than in this scorching debut from writer/director Pierre Salvadori. Rochefort is quite superb as a meticulous hit man whose ordered existence begins to disintegrate when he takes on impetuous accomplice Guillaume Depardieu – son of Gérard – and falls in love with his next hit, glamorous art forger and petty thief Marie Trintignant (daughter of Jean-Louis and Nadine). The scenes at the hotel and Rochefort's country house are executed with great flair and a delicious black wit. There's also a fine cameo from Patachou as Rochefort's ghoulish mother. In French with English subtitles. ▭

Jean Rochefort *Victor Meynard* • Marie Trintignant *Renée* • Guillaume Depardieu *Antoine* • Patachou *Madame Meynard* • Charlie Nelson *Dremyan* • Wladimir Yordanoff *Casa Bianca* • Serge Riaboukine *Manu* • Philippe Girard *Tony* ■ *Dir/Scr* Pierre Salvadori

Wild Texas Wind ★★🄸

Drama 1991 · US · Colour · 88mins

A glossy vehicle for Dolly Parton, in which she plays an up-and-coming country singer who falls under the spell of an outwardly charming but brutish club owner. The plotting is predictable and if you don't like country music the whole affair is going to leave you pretty cold. However, there is strong support from Gary Busey and look out for a guest appearance from Willie Nelson. ▭

Dolly Parton *Thiola "T" Rayfield* • Gary Busey *Justice* • Willie Nelson • Ray Benson *Ben* • Dennis Letts *Harlan Parker* ■ *Dir* Joan Tewkesbury • *Scr* John Carlen, from a story by Mark Kiracofe, Dolly Parton

Wild Thing ★★🄸

Crime drama 1987 · US/Can · Colour · 88mins

Screenwriter John Sayles – a notable film-maker in his own right – has a

solid track record in providing decent scripts for other people's movies, such as *Piranha* and *The Howling* for Joe Dante. However, his work on *Wild Thing* is an anaemic affair concerning a boy (Robert Knepper) whose parents are murdered, forcing him to grow up wild in the city slums. Eventually he becomes a sort of feral cut-price Batman figure, vengefully protecting local inhabitants from nasty drug dealer Robert Davi. Even if Sayles's original script was any good on paper, the execution by director Max Reid does it no justice at all. ▭

Rob Knepper [Robert Knepper] *Wild Thing* • Kathleen Quinlan *Jane* • Robert Davi *Chopper* • Maury Chaykin *Trask* • Betty Buckley *Leah* • Clark Johnson *Winston* • Sean Hewitt *Father Quinn* ■ *Dir* Max Reid • *Scr* John Sayles, from a story by John Sayles, Larry Stamper

Wild Things ★★★🄸

Thriller 1998 · US · Colour · 103mins

Things are certainly steamy in Florida in this eyebrow-raising thriller. Neve Campbell and Denise Richards star as high-school students who falsely accuse teacher Matt Dillon of rape in a preposterous tale that's more notable for its X-rated scenes – a threesome among the leads, Campbell and Richards kissing, co-star Kevin Bacon's full-frontal – than for its great acting or script. There are a few nice twists, however, and the handsome cast clearly enjoys vamping it up in what is essentially a sexed-up, feature-length MTV video. Contains swearing, sex scenes and some violence. ▭ 🄳🄳🄵

Kevin Bacon *Ray Duquette* • Matt Dillon *Sam Lombardo* • Neve Campbell *Suzie Toller* • Theresa Russell *Sandra Van Ryan* • Denise Richards *Kelly Van Ryan* • Daphne Rubin-Vega *Gloria Perez* • Robert Wagner *Tom Baxter* • Bill Murray *Ken Bowden* ■ *Dir* John McNaughton • *Scr* Stephen Peters

Wild West ★★★🄸

Comedy 1992 · UK · Colour · 80mins

Rip-roaring tale of the old west (old west London, that is), with a bunch of country music-loving Pakistani "outlaws" from Southall who want to make music – but instead find themselves facing it when their band leader falls for an Asian girl who's unhappily wed to a villainous "gringo". Naveen Andrews and Sarita Choudhury star in an enjoyable romp that was one of the first films to portray multiethnic Britain accurately, and which helped pave the way for the likes of *My Son the Fanatic* and *East Is East*. ▭

Naveen Andrews *Zaf Ayub* • Sarita Choudhury *Rifat* • Ronny Jhutti *Kay Ayub* • Ravi Kapoor *Ali Ayub* • Ameet Chana *Gurdeep* • Bhasker *Jagdeep* • Lalita Ahmed *Mrs Ayub* ■ *Dir* David Attwood • *Scr* Harwant Bains

Wild Wheels ★★★

Documentary 1992 · US · Colour · 64mins

Made by the son of film-maker Les Blank, this highly engaging, witty and touching documentary is all about unconventional car owners and the way they customise their vehicles to reflect their personalities or important moments in their lives. Written and directed by Harrod Blank, whose own Volkswagen is lovingly covered in plastic globes and sunflowers with a

huge black fly on the hood, his tribute shows other cars decorated with buttons, beads, huge crucifixes, taps and even plastic flamingos. The drivers come from all walks of life and ethnic groups, and although Blank's focus is goofy eccentricity, there is frequently a meaningful motivation behind the decor. Unusual, quirky and informative.

Dir/Scr Harrod Blank • *Cinematographer* Harrod Blank, Paul Cope, Les Blank

Wild Wild West ★★🄸

Western adventure fantasy 1999 · US · Colour · 105mins

Superficial and predictable, with special effects bloated out of all proportion, director Barry Sonnenfeld's follow-up to *Men in Black* may have an invisible script, but it's still good-natured fun thanks to the winning charisma of Will Smith and some fabulous Jack-in-the-Box gadgetry. Little more than *Lethal Weapon* in the Old West, shaken and stirred with a touch of James Bond, the plot has Smith and Kevin Kline as mismatched US secret service agents using out-of-time contraptions and fancy disguises to stop mad genius Kenneth Branagh from assassinating President Grant (Kline again). The script is smut-fixated (both stars appear in drag), the one-liners are below average ("No more Mr Knife Guy") and the giant Meccano spider climax is endlessly drawn out. But the wildly inventive gizmos (the best being the metal collars that attract magnetic blades) give entertainment value and draw a shield over the flaws. Contains violence and sexual references. ▭ 🄳🄳🄵

Will Smith *James West* • Kevin Kline *Artemus Gordon/President Ulysses S Grant* • Kenneth Branagh *Dr Arliss Loveless* • Salma Hayek *Rita Escobar* • M Emmet Walsh *Coleman* • Ted Levine *General McGrath* • Frederique Van Der Wal *Amazonia* • Musetta Vander *Munitia* ■ *Dir* Barry Sonnenfeld • *Scr* SS Wilson, Brent Maddock, Jeffrey Price, Peter S Seaman, from a story by Jim Thomas, John Thomas • *Music* Elmer Bernstein

Wildcats ★★🄸

Comedy 1986 · US · Colour · 101mins

A routine Goldie Hawn comedy in which most of the interest is generated by the sight of some familiar faces in the supporting cast who were making their first steps on the way to stardom. Hawn is the fledgling American football coach who sets about transforming a terrible college side, much to the disbelief of the macho team members, who include a young Wesley Snipes and Woody Harrelson. There are some amusing moments, good supporting turns from Swoosie Kurtz and M Emmet Walsh, and, as usual, Hawn's comic timing can't be faulted. In the end, however, it remains one for die-hard fans only. Contains swearing and nudity. ▭

Goldie Hawn *Molly McGrath* • Swoosie Kurtz *Verna* • Robyn Lively *Alice McGrath* • Brandy Gold *Marian McGrath* • James Keach *Frank McGrath* • Jan Hooks *Stephanie* • Nipsey Russell *Ben Edwards* • M Emmet Walsh *Coes* ■ *Dir* Michael Ritchie • *Scr* Ezra Sacks

The Wildcats of St Trinian's ★

Comedy   1980 · UK · Colour · 91mins

In truth, there was only one genuinely funny entry (The Belles of St Trinian's) in this five-film series, with each subsequent instalment failing more dismally than the last to match the comic anarchy of the original movie. Why Frank Launder felt the need to return to the old place after a 14-year hiatus is hard to fathom, especially as he could only come up with this lame story about kidnapping and strikes, which is essentially an excuse for some scantily clad sixth-formers and lots of dodgy gags. You can only admire the cast for giving it a go.

Sheila Hancock *Olga Vandemeer* • Michael Hordern *Sir Charles Hackforth* • Joe Melia *Flash Harry* • Thorley Walters *Hugo Culpepper-Brown* • Rodney Bewes *Peregrine Butters* • Deborah Norton *Miss Brenner* • Maureen Lipman *Katy Higgs* • Julia McKenzie *Dolly Dormancott* ■ *Dir* Frank Launder • *Scr* Frank Launder, from the drawings by Ronald Searle

Wilde ★★★★ 15

Biographical drama
1997 · UK · Colour · 111mins

Once you've seen Stephen Fry in the title role of Oscar Wilde it's difficult to imagine anyone better suited. Playing to the myth of the giant of wit, restraint and wisdom, Fry conveys the strain of a public figure tied to a false marriage (with Jennifer Ehle) while besieged by his love for another man (a bitingly excellent Jude Law as the rich and spoilt Lord Alfred Douglas). Assertive in its graphic exploration of male love, this may not suit all tastes, but nevertheless it is beautifully written with spot-on attention to period detail. As a profile of one of our greatest writers this is a mildly thought-provoking and desperately sad film. Contains some swearing and sex scenes. ▦ *DVD*

Stephen Fry *Oscar Wilde* • Jude Law *Lord Alfred Douglas* • Vanessa Redgrave *Lady Speranza Wilde* • Jennifer Ehle *Constance Wilde* • Gemma Jones *Lady Queensberry* • Judy Parfitt *Lady Mount-Temple* • Michael Sheen *Robert Ross* • Zoë Wanamaker *Ada Leverson* • Tom Wilkinson *Marquess of Queensberry* • Ioan Gruffudd *John Gray* ■ *Dir* Brian Gilbert • *Scr* Julian Mitchell, from the biography *Oscar Wilde* by Richard Ellman

Wilder Napalm ★ 15

Drama   1993 · US · Colour · 104mins

Debra Winger should be one of the biggest stars in Hollywood. That she is not can be partially explained by her habit of choosing duds such as this lamentable comedy (to use the word in its loosest sense). She is caught up in the feud between brothers Dennis Quaid and Arliss Howard, who can't decide how best to exploit their fire-starting genius. With nearly every gag fizzling as soon as it's primed, it rapidly becomes almost unbearable to watch otherwise talented performers getting so badly burned. Contains violence, swearing and sex scenes. ▦ ,

Debra Winger *Vida* • Dennis Quaid *Wallace Foudroyant* • Arliss Howard *Wilder Foudroyant* • M Emmet Walsh *Fire chief* • Jim Varney *Rex*

• Mimi Lieber *Snake lady* • Marvin J McIntyre *Deputy Sheriff Spivey* ■ *Dir* Glenn Gordon Caron • *Scr* Vince Gilligan

Wilde's Domain ★★

Drama   1983 · Ausl · Colour

A sort of Down Under version of Dallas, only set in the world of entertainment rather than oil, in which Kit Taylor inherits the family business and struggles to keep hold of the reins. Fans of soapy sagas may not get a kick out of this TV movie, as both the script and the playing lack credibility. Director Charles Tingwell is a veteran actor who has appeared in TV shows such as *Emergency – Ward 10*, *Catweazle* and *Neighbours* over the years, as well as movies such as *A Cry in the Dark*, *The Castle*.

Kit Taylor *Dan Wilde* • June Salter *Hannah Wilde* • Jeanie Drynan *Liz* • Martin Vaughan *Tom Moore* • Lenore Smith *Alex Wilde* ■ *Dir* Charles Tingwell • *Scr* Ted Roberts

Wildflower ★★★★ 15

Drama   1991 · US · Colour · 90mins

Directed by actress Diane Keaton, this moving drama is set in thirties Georgia and follows the experiences of Alice (Patricia Arquette), a partially deaf epileptic imprisoned by her stepfather, who is convinced she is possessed by the Devil. Adapted by Sara Flanigan from her own book, this is subtly handled by Keaton, and her direction is complemented by involving performances from a cast that includes Beau Bridges and Reese Witherspoon. ▦

Patricia Arquette *Alice Guthrie* • Beau Bridges *Jack Perkins* • Susan Blakely *Ada Guthrie* • Reese Witherspoon *Ellie Perkins* • William McNamara *Sammy Perkins* ■ *Dir* Diane Keaton • *Scr* Sara Flanigan, from her non-fiction book *Alice*

Will Any Gentleman...? ★★ U

Comedy   1953 · UK · Colour · 84mins

Sixth-time director Michael Anderson showed he wasn't quite the finished article with this over-literal adaptation of Vernon Sylvaine's stage success. However, even laying aside the clumsiness of much of the comedy, a fair proportion of modern viewers won't be particularly well disposed towards a story in which a hypnotist turns a timid bank clerk into a swaggering lothario. As the entranced enchanter, George Cole makes the most of his awkward charm, but his enthusiasm too often gets the better of him. Worth catching, nonetheless, for a supporting cast boasting a brace of Dr Whos (Jon Pertwee and William Hartnell).

George Cole *Henry Sterling* • Veronica Hurst *Mrs Sterling* • Jon Pertwee *Charlie Sterling* • James Hayter *Dr Smith* • Heather Thatcher *Mrs Whittle* • William Hartnell *Inspector Martin* • Sidney James *Mr Hobson* • Joan Sims *Beryl* ■ *Dir* Michael Anderson • *Scr* Vernon Sylvaine, from his play

Will It Snow for Christmas? ★★★ 12

Drama   1996 · Fr · Colour · 86mins

Sandrine Veysett won a César for this, her directorial debut. It's an oblique, slow-moving tribute to farm labour and

a universal commentary on the nature of dysfunctional family. Dominique Reymond is a mother, who with her seven illegitimate children rents and works a farm. Their lives are broken up by the periodic visits of the wayward father, Daniel Duval. Married with a family elsewhere, he continues returning to bed Reymond. The film hits its crux when Duval makes advances on their eldest daughter and this forces Reymond into making a crucial decision about their lives. In French with English subtitles. ▦

Dominique Reymond *Mother* • Daniel Duval *Father* • Jessica Martinez *Jeanne* • Alexandre Roger *Bruno* • Xavier Colonna *Pierrot* • Fanny Rochetin *Marie* ■ *Dir/Scr* Sandrine Veysset

Will Penny ★★★★

Western   1967 · US · Colour · 108mins

A marvellous winter western with a fine performance by Charlton Heston as the grizzled lone rider of the title, confronting the memorable Joan Hackett and uncertain of how to break the tough habits of a lifetime: ''I'm a cowboy. I don't know nuthin' else.'' Director Tom Gries never hit these heights again: this is one of the great westerns, marred only by the florid performance of an ill-cast Donald Pleasence. The photography by Lucien Ballard, also responsible for the look of Peckinpah's *The Wild Bunch* and Henry Hathaway's *True Grit*, is particularly outstanding, as is the fine score from David Raksin.

Charlton Heston *Will Penny* • Joan Hackett *Catherine Allen* • Donald Pleasence *Preacher Quint* • Lee Majors *Blue* • Bruce Dern *Rafe Quint* • Ben Johnson *Alex* • Slim Pickens *Ike Wallerstein* ■ *Dir/Scr* Tom Gries • *Cinematographer* Lucien Ballard • *Music* David Raksin

Will Success Spoil Rock Hunter? ★★★ U

Satirical drama   1957 · US · Colour · 94mins

Fresh from her Broadway success, Jayne Mansfield reprises her role as the pouting movie star with voluptuous glee in Frank Tashlin's film version of George Axelrod's hit play. However, it's Tony Randall, as the meek advertising agent who is forced to play the fame game to keep a prestigious lipstick account, who keeps this ambitious satire on track. Swiping at everything from media hype and public gullibility to sex and the morality of advertising, Tashlin was never going to land all his punches, but this glossy, rather hollow enterprise, while very much a hit-and-miss affair, has undeniable charm.

Tony Randall *Rockwell Hunter* • Jayne Mansfield *Rita Marlow* • Betsy Drake *Jenny* • Joan Blondell *Violet* • John Williams *Le Salle Jr* • Henry Jones *Rufus* • Lili Gentle *April* • Mickey Hargitay *Bobo* • Groucho Marx *Surprise guest* ■ *Dir* Frank Tashlin • *Scr* Frank Tashlin, from the play by George Axelrod

Willard ★★★

Horror   1971 · US · Colour · 95mins

In this hugely successful story of violent vermin, oppressed office boy Bruce Davison turns the tables on his tormentors by training his two pet rats, Socrates and Ben, and their sewer pals, to attack on command. But when he neglects them after falling in love

with Sondra Locke, hell hath no fury like rodents scorned! Solid direction by Daniel Mann and Davison's creepily introverted performance turned this horror revenge tale into a huge box-office hit. Everybody cheers when bullying boss Ernest Borgnine gets it, although the movie's overall success depends on one's squeamishness towards the creatures themselves. The sequel *Ben* followed.

Bruce Davison *Willard Stiles* • Ernest Borgnine *Al Martin* • Elsa Lanchester *Henrietta Stiles* • Sondra Locke *Joan* • Michael Dante *Brandt* • Jody Gilbert *Charlotte Stassen* ■ *Dir* Daniel Mann • *Scr* Gilbert A Ralston, from the novel *Ratman's Notebooks* by Stephen Gilbert

William at the Circus ★★ U

Comedy   1948 · UK · BW · 92mins

No devotee of Richmal Crompton's delightfull creation would be satisfied by a screen version of William. However, writer/director Val Guest captures a little of the exuberant antics of the original and William Graham is nicely cast as the ever questioning boy. His parents have promised him an outing to the circus – if he's good. Not the most likely of outcomes then, especially when he is busy campaigning for shorter school hours. Still he does get his cherished visit – in a rather unconventional manner.

William Graham *William Brown* • Garry Marsh *Mr Brown* • Jane Welsh *Mrs Brown* • AE Matthews *Minister* • Muriel Aked *Emily* • Hugh Cross *Robert Brown* • Kathleen Stuart *Ethel Brown* • Brian Roper *Ginger* ■ *Dir* Val Guest • *Scr* Val Guest, from the stories by Richmal Crompton

William Faulkner's Old Man ★★★

Period drama   1997 · US · Colour · 98mins

This outstanding adaptation of a William Faulkner story was written by Academy Award winning playwright/screenwriter Horton Foote. In 1928 rural Mississippi, after a disastrous flood, a group of prisoners are sent to the area to help shore up a levee. Convict Arliss Howard, ordered to take a boat up river to save a pregnant single woman, becomes a reluctant hero while falling in love with the new mother. Howard eloquently captures the simple intelligence of his character; Jeanne Tripplehorn gives an elegant, understated performance, while director John Kent Harrison exhibits great finesse in capturing the natural essence of Faulkner's milieu. An impressive cast and evocative locations all help make this period drama a rare TV-movie treat.

Jeanne Tripplehorn *Addie Rebecca Brice* • Arliss Howard *JJ Taylor* • Leo Burmester *Plump Convict* • Daro Latiolais *Cajun Man* • Ray McKinnon *Shanty Man with Gun* ■ *Dir* John Kent Harrison • *Scr* Horton Foote, from the short story by William Faulkner

William Shakespeare's Romeo + Juliet ★★★★ 12

Romantic drama
1996 · US/Ausl/Can · Colour · 115mins

Baz Luhrmann's updated, richly visualised version of the Bard's chronicle of star-crossed young lovers made Leonardo DiCaprio an authentic teen idol. Claire Danes is the Juliet yearning for DiCaprio's Romeo on Verona Beach where family gang warfare explodes into violent attacks and biker battles. There's no doubting the quality of DiCaprio, though Claire Danes is a touch too eye-flutteringly winsome for comfort, but as a magnet to attract youngsters to Shakespeare it couldn't be bettered. Out of the classroom, the poetry has a field day. Contains some violence. 🎞

Leonardo DiCaprio *Romeo* • Claire Danes *Juliet* • Brian Dennehy *Ted Montague* • John Leguizamo *Tybalt* • Pete Postlethwaite *Father Laurence* • Paul Sorvino *Fulgencio Capulet* • Diane Venora *Gloria Capulet* • Harold Perrineau *Mercutio* • Paul Rudd *Dave Paris* • Jesse Bradford *Balthasar* • Dash Mihok *Benvolio* • Miriam Margolyes *Nurse* ■ • *Scr* Craig Pearce, Baz Luhrmann, from the play by William Shakespeare

William Shakespeare's A Midsummer Night's Dream ★★★🄿🄶

Romantic comedy
1999 · US · Colour · 120mins

Thank heavens for Kevin Kline! As Bottom he's the tops in director Michael Hoffman's stilted version of Shakespeare's ode to blighted love in that magical forest where "reason and love keep little company". Not only is Kevin Kline's Bottom a garrulous bumbler; he is also – when transformed into a donkey by Oberon (Rupert Everett) to fool Titania (Michelle Pfeiffer) – an object of abject poignancy. Updated to 19th-century Italy, the film looks most elegant: Calista Flockhart makes a beautiful Helena, and Stanley Tucci's Puck should get a prize for the best-dressed fairy. Without an animating core of real magic, however, the result is simply a pretty enchantment. Contains brief semi-nudity. 🎞 **DVD**

Kevin Kline *Nick Bottom* • Michelle Pfeiffer *Titania* • Rupert Everett *Oberon* • Stanley Tucci *Puck* • Calista Flockhart *Helena* • Anna Friel *Hermia* • Christian Bale *Demetrius* • Dominic West *Lysander* ■ • *Dir* Michael Hoffman • *Scr* Michael Hoffman, from the play by William Shakespeare

Willie and Phil ★★★

Drama
1980 · US · Colour · 116mins

Paul Mazursky was on a hiding to nothing when he embarked on this updating of François Truffaut's classic *Jules et Jim*. The *joie de vivre* that made the original so beguiling is clearly missing from this episodic drama that is more about Mazursky's perception of the seventies than it is about the relationships between teacher Michael Ontkean, photographer Ray Sharkey and the girl they both love, Margot Kidder. The performances are fine considering the shallowness of all the characters, but the lifestyle satire has dated badly and the ethnic gags at the expense of the trio's parents are pretty dubious. A curious movie time capsule. Contains swearing and nudity.

Michael Ontkean *Willie Kaufman* • Margot Kidder *Jeanette Sutherland* • Ray Sharkey *Phil D'Amico* • Jan Miner *Mrs Kaufman* • Tom Brennan *Mr Kaufman* • Julie Bovasso *Mrs D'Amico* • Louis Guss *Mr D'Amico* • *Dir/Scr* Paul Mazursky

Willow ★★🄿🄶

Fantasy adventure
1988 · US · Colour · 120mins

Despite the input of *Star Wars* guru George Lucas, this is a rare clunker from Ron Howard, the hit director of *Splash*, *Parenthood* and *Apollo 13*. It's more Wallow than Willow as the former *Happy Days* star takes too long mating the Saturday-morning-pictures wonderment of *Raiders* and *Star Wars* with the Tolkienesque elfin-twaddle of *Lord Of The Rings*. It's forced, formulaic, and sadly lacking in that sense of magic that's at the root of all successful fantasy. Val Kilmer and Joanne Whalley star in this tale of a baby whose safekeeping will overthrow an evil empire. 🎞

Val Kilmer *Madmartigan* • Joanne Whalley *Sorsha* • Warwick Davis *Willow Ufgood* • Jean Marsh *Queen Bavmorda* • Patricia Hayes *Fin Raziel* • Billy Barty *High Aldwin* • Pat Roach *General Kael* • Gavan O'Herlihy *Airk* ■ • *Dir* Ron Howard • *Scr* Bob Dolman, from a story by George Lucas

Willy/Milly ★★★🄸🄵

Comedy
1986 · US · Colour · 83mins

Years before Hilary Swank produced her Oscar-winning cross-gender performance in *Boys Don't Cry*, Pamela Segall gave an equally sterling turn in *Willy/Milly*, albeit in a comedy. Segall is Milly Niceman, a girl who longs to be a boy and gets her wish (sort of) when she takes a magic potion during an eclipse. Overnight she develops an additional set of genitals, these ones being male. Milly then has to decide whether to spend her life as a girl or as a boy (Willy). With Patty Duke Astin particularly good as Milly's mother, this winning romantic comedy deserves to be shown more often. 🎞

Pamela Segall *Milly/Willy* • Eric Gurry *Alfie* • Mary Tanner *Stephanie* • Patty Duke *Mrs Niceman* • John Glover *Mr Niceman* • Seth Green *Malcolm* • John David Cullum *Tom* • Jeb Ellis-Brown *Harry* ■ • *Dir* Paul Schneider • *Scr* Walter Carbone, Carla Reuben, from the story by Alan Friedman

Willy Wonka and the Chocolate Factory ★★★🄾

Fantasy
1971 · US · Colour · 95mins

Adults might view Roald Dahl's musical fantasy as a grim fairy tale, with wild-eyed candy-maker Gene Wilder ruthlessly sorting out the honest from the two-faced among the child winners of a tour of his sweetmeat depot. But a child's-eye view usually sees through the sadistic coating – Dahl adapted it from the even more cruel *Charlie and the Chocolate Factory* – to realise there's a happily soft centre to all this black magic. 🎞 **DVD**

Gene Wilder *Willy Wonka* • Jack Albertson *Grandpa Joe* • Peter Ostrum *Charlie Bucket* • Michael Bollner *Augustus Gloop* • Ursula Reit *Mrs Gloop* • Denise Nickerson *Violet Beauregarde* • Julie Dawn Cole *Veruca Salt* • Roy Kinnear *Mr Salt* • *Dir* Mel Stuart • *Scr* Roald Dahl, from his novel *Charlie and the Chocolate Factory* • *Music/Lyrics* Anthony Newley, Leslie Bricusse

Wilson ★★🅄

Biography
1944 · US · Colour · 153mins

This was to be 20th Century-Fox chief Darryl F Zanuck's finest hour: he personally produced this lengthy biopic about Woodrow Wilson, America's 28th president, who founded the League of Nations. Ultimately, though, despite his chronic idealism, the great man is a boring subject for a movie. Apart from winning five Oscars, the only thing really impressive about *Wilson* is that it was made at all. Alexander Knox is a resolutely uncharismatic lead, and, despite the award-winning Technicolor photography of Leon Shamroy, there's precious little to look at – it all seems like idle chat. The public stayed away in droves. Nobody ever really cared about Wilson, nor about this doorstop of a movie.

Alexander Knox *Woodrow Wilson* • Charles Coburn *Professor Henry Holmes* • Geraldine Fitzgerald *Edith Wilson* • Thomas Mitchell *Joseph Tumulty* • Ruth Nelson *Ellen Wilson* • Cedric Hardwicke *Henry Cabot Lodge* • Vincent Price *William G McAdoo* ■ • *Dir* Henry King • *Scr* Lamar Trotti

Wilt ★★🄸🄵

Comedy
1989 · UK · Colour · 88mins

Very much "alas Smith and Jones", this is a down-market version of Tom Sharpe's brilliantly comic novel about a liberal studies lecturer (Griff Rhys Jones) pursued for the murder of his wife (Alison Steadman) by police inspector Mel Smith, a copper incompetent enough to make Clouseau seem like Sherlock Holmes. The story kicks in with a hint of lesbianism, a life-sized sex doll and the kind of smut-tinged humour you might have thought British comedies had grown out of. Steadman and Rhys Jones manage to make their characters as authentic as possible with an expertise sorely missing in the rest of the film. Contains swearing and nudity. 🎞

Griff Rhys Jones *Henry Wilt* • Mel Smith *Inspector Flint* • Alison Steadman *Eva Wilt* • Diana Quick *Sally* • Jeremy Clyde *Hugh* • Roger Allam *Dave* • David Ryall *Reverend Froude* • Roger Lloyd Pack *Dr Pittman* ■ • *Dir* Michael Tuchner • *Scr* Andrew Marshall, David Renwick, from the novel by Tom Sharpe

Winchell ★★

Biographical drama
1998 · US · Colour · 110mins

Stanley Tucci gives a bold and layered performance as the lead character, radio and newspaper journalist Walter Winchell who, for several decades, was one of America's most feared and powerful gossip columnists. This made-for-TV movie dramatises the complex relationship between Winchell and his friend and ghostwriter, Herman Klurfeld, upon whose memoir the film is based. Under the skilled direction of veteran Paul Mazursky the cast and performances are uniformly strong, especially Paul Giamatti, who plays Klurfeld with great pathos and insight. Although uneven at times, humour and gravitas intersect at every turn, and the story should hold your interest.

Stanley Tucci *Walter Winchell* • Glenne Headly *Dallas Wayne* • Paul Giamatti *Herman Klurfeld* • Christopher Plummer *President Franklin D Roosevelt* • Xander Berkeley *Gavreau* • Kevin Tighe *William Randolph Hearst* ■ • *Dir* Paul Mazursky • *Scr* Scott Abbott, from the non-fiction book *Walter Winchell: His Life and Times* by Herman Klurfeld

The Winchester Conspiracy ★★

Drama based on a true story
1990 · Ausl · Colour

An unusual cop story, made for TV and based on true events, in which the police and the Mob join forces to solve a drug-related murder as marijuana worth $14 million engulfs the Australian cities of Sydney and Melbourne. Ken Cameron's direction is unspectacular, but the intriguing plot holds a fascination, and a largely unknown cast operates with quiet efficiency. Contains swearing.

Gerald Kennedy *Asst Comm Colin Winchester* • Terry Gill *Det Sgt Bill Cullen* • Frankie J Holden *Det Con Max Chapman* • Luciano Catenacci *Giuseppe Verduci* • Roderick Williams *Les Doogan* • Tim Robertson *Det Sgt Brian Lockwood* ■ • *Dir* Ken Cameron • *Scr* Ian David

Winchester '73 ★★★★🅄

Portmanteau western
1950 · US · BW · 92mins

The first of a marvellous series of movies pairing star James Stewart and director Anthony Mann, this portmanteau western doesn't really tell the tale of "the gun that won the West". Instead, it focuses on the legendary "one in a thousand" perfect Winchester, first seen here as a prize in a Dodge City shooting contest where Will Geer, as Wyatt Earp, presides over sharpshooters Stewart and a brilliantly sneering Stephen McNally. This is a fine, mature work, creating a laconic new persona for the admirable Stewart. The brilliant black-and-white camerawork is by Garbo's favourite, William Daniels, and director Mann's use of transition (dissolves, fades to black) is exemplary. Also, watch out for a pre-stardom Rock Hudson as Young Bull, and an even younger Tony Curtis as a cavalry trooper. 🎞

James Stewart *Lin McAdam* • Shelley Winters *Lola Manners* • Dan Duryea *Waco Johnny Dean* • Stephen McNally *Dutch Henry Brown* • Millard Mitchell *Johnny "High Spade" Williams* • Charles Drake *Steve Miller* • John McIntire *Joe Lamont* • Will Geer *Editor* • Jay C Flippen *Sergeant Wilkes* • Rock Hudson *Young Bull* • Steve Brodie *Wesley* • Anthony Curtis [Tony Curtis] *Doan* ■ • *Dir* Anthony Mann • *Scr* Robert L Richards, Borden Chase, from the story by Stuart N Lake • *Cinematographer* William Daniels

The Wind ★★★★★

Silent drama
1928 · US · BW · 94mins

Swedish émigré Victor Sjöström (Seastrom) made this stunning antidote to the western just prior to sound which demonstrated just how harsh life was for the pioneers in the desert. In one of the greatest screen performances in history, Lillian Gish plays the fragile Virginian girl who heads for the Texas panhandle to share a wooden shack with her cousin and his family. Not only does she cause an emotional earthquake, the weather seems to conspire against her as well, resulting in a sandstorm of Biblical proportions. Filmed under the most arduous conditions in the Mojave

Desert, the film is marred only by the unconvincing ending which was added when preview audiences found the original conclusion too bleak.

Lillian Gish *Letty* • Lars Hanson *Lige* • Montagu Love *Roddy Wirt* • Dorothy Cumming *Cora* • Edward Earle *Beverly* • William Orlamond *Sourdough* ■ *Dir* Victor Seastrom [Victor Sjöström] • *Scr* Frances Marion, from the novel by Dorothy Scarborough

Wind ★★★ PG

Sports drama   1992 · US · Colour · 120mins

Carroll Ballard brings his usual visual flair to this tale of ocean racing; it's just a shame the story is so hackneyed. Matthew Modine is the sailor, haunted by a mistake that cost his country the America's Cup, who gets another shot at wresting the trophy back from the Australians. Jennifer Grey is his old flame and the impressive support cast includes Cliff Robertson, Jack Thompson and Stellan Skarsgård. While the story remains on water, Ballard doesn't put a foot wrong and there is some breathtaking racing footage; however, on dry land the film flounders badly as trite sporting cliché. ▭

Matthew Modine *Will Parker* • Jennifer Grey *Kate Bass* • Cliff Robertson *Morgan Weld* • Jack Thompson *Jack Neville* • Stellan Skarsgård *Joe Heiser* • Rebecca Miller *Abigail Weld* • Ned Vaughn *Charley Moore* ■ *Dir* Carroll Ballard • *Scr* Rudy Wurlitzer, Mac Gudgeon, Larry Gross, from a story by Jeff Benjamin, Howard Chelsey, Kimball Livingston, Roger Vaughan

Wind across the Everglades ★★★

Drama   1958 · US · Colour · 84mins

A strange eco-melodrama, scripted by Budd Schulberg of *On the Waterfront* fame, about an alcoholic game warden intent on chasing poachers out of the swamps in turn-of-the-century Florida. Cult director Nicholas Ray fails to control his eclectic scenery-chewing cast, headed by Burl Ives and Christopher Plummer, but it's unwise to expect finesse from players such as stripper Gypsy Rose Lee, famed circus clown Emmett Kelly and author MacKinlay Kantor. Watch out, however, for a promising screen debut from a young Peter Falk. Despite its many faults, there are memorable moments in this unusual effort from Ray.

Burl Ives *Cottonmouth* • Christopher Plummer *Walt Murdock* • Gypsy Rose Lee *Mrs Bradford* • George Voskovec *Aaron Nathanson* • Tony Galento *Beef* • Howard I Smith [Howard Smith] *George* • Emmett Kelly *Bigamy Bob* • Peter Falk *Writer* ■ *Dir* Nicholas Ray • *Scr* Budd Schulberg, from his story "Across the Everglades"

The Wind and the Lion ★★★★

Period adventure
1975 · US · Colour · 118mins

A simply stunning desert adventure, with Sean Connery as the Berber chieftain who kidnaps an American woman (Candice Bergen in a role intended for Katharine Hepburn) and incurs the wrath of US President Teddy Roosevelt, who sends the "big stick" into Morocco. This brilliant satire on colonialism, written and directed by

John Milius, pays due tribute to such diverse movies as *Lawrence of Arabia* and the Samurai epics and manages to be both funny and thrilling; it's also an insightful look at America's role as world policeman. Connery gives what may be his most charismatic performance ever, Bergen is gorgeously feisty, and Brian Keith deeply in period as the one-eyed, bear-hunting, gung-ho president. Add to this a soaring Jerry Goldsmith score and some marvellous locations and you have one of the most enjoyable movies of the seventies.

Sean Connery *Mulay El Raisuli* • Candice Bergen *Eden Pedecaris* • Brian Keith *Theodore Roosevelt* • John Huston *John Hay* • Geoffrey Lewis *Gummere* • Steve Kanaly *Captain Jerome* • Roy Jenson *Admiral Chadwick* • Vladek Sheybal *Bashaw* • Darrell Fetty *Dreighton* • Nadim Sawalha *Sherif of Wazan* ■ *Dir/Scr* John Milius

The Wind Cannot Read ★★ U

Second World War romantic drama
1958 · UK · Colour · 108mins

Dirk Bogarde's fifth film in just over a year, as the Rank Organisation relentlessly paraded its biggest box-office attraction before an adoring public. But the strain shows in his tired portrayal of an RAF officer who falls for Japanese teacher Yoko Tani. Ralph Thomas, who had directed Bogarde's three previous features, certainly knew how to make the most of his looks and charm, and wrings every drop of sentiment out of this four-hankie weepie, but neither plot nor performances really convince. ▭

Dirk Bogarde *Flight Lt Michael Quinn* • Yoko Tani *"Sabby" Suzuki San* • Ronald Lewis *Squadron Leader Fenwick* • John Fraser *Flying Olfficer Peter Munroe* • Anthony Bushell *Brigadier* • Henry Okawa *Lt Nakamura* • Marne Maitland *Bahadur* ■ *Dir* Ralph Thomas • *Scr* Richard Mason, from his novel

Wind Dancer ★★

Drama based on a true story
1991 · US · Colour · 90mins

This sensitive drama delves deep into the subject of the healing forces of nature. The tale, based on a true story, has Raeanin Simpson as a young girl injured in a riding accident, coaxed back to good health with a course of equine therapy at a country ranch and an encounter there with a horse called Wind Dancer. It's sugar lumps all round for virtually the whole movie, although the adults (Mel Harris, Matt McCoy, Brian Keith and Nicholas Guest) do their best to keep their heads above the rising tide of syrup.

Brian Keith *Truman* • Raeanin Simpson *Paige* • Nicholas Guest *Raymond* • Don Shanks *Halfmoon* • Pamela Guest *Nicole* • Mel Harris *Susan* • Matt McCoy *Jim McDonald* ■ *Dir* Craig Clyde

The Wind in the Willows ★★★ U

Adventure   1996 · UK · Colour · 83mins

Alan Bennett's stage adaptation of Kenneth Grahame's timeless classic was voted a triumph by young and old alike. Unfortunately, the camera has captured little of the magic in this clumsy screen version of the book

from writer/director Terry Jones. His rendition of Toad is suitably ebullient, while fellow Python Eric Idle and Steve Coogan are pleasing enough as Rat and Mole. However, the addition of a dog-meat factory subplot to supplement Toad's brushes with the law is a major misjudgement, as is the decision to pack the supporting cast with cameoing celebrities. Nowhere near as much fun as it should be. ▭

Steve Coogan *Mole* • Eric Idle *Rat* • Terry Jones *Toad* • Anthony Sher *Chief Weasel* • Nicol Williamson *Badger* • John Cleese *Mr Toad's lawyer* • Stephen Fry *Judge* • Bernard Hill *Engine driver* • Michael Palin *The Sun* • Nigel Planer *Car salesman* • Julia Sawalha *Jailer's daughter* • Victoria Wood *Tea lady* ■ *Dir* Terry Jones • *Scr* Terry Jones, from the novel by Kenneth Grahame

The Wind of Change ★★

Crime drama   1961 · UK · BW · 63mins

Vernon Sewell's attempt at depicting gang racial hatred and its effect on a family fails mainly because of its overly simplistic approach to a complex problem. Donald Pleasence appears in an unusual role as the father of a troubled gang teenager, who is played by none other than a young Johnny Briggs, who became better known as Mike Baldwin of *Coronation Street*.

Donald Pleasence *Pop* • Johnny Briggs *Frank* • Antonita Dias *Sylvia* • Ann Lynn *Josie* • Hilda Fenemore *Gladys* • Glyn Houston *Sgt Parker* • Norman Gunn *Ron* • Bunny May *Smithy* • David Hemmings *Ginger* ■ *Dir* Vernon Sewell • *Scr* Alexander Doré, John McLaren

The Wind Will Carry Us ★★★★

Drama   1999 · Fr/Iran · Colour · 110mins

A stranger arrives in a Kurdish village on a mission he conducts with eccentric secrecy. The winner of the Golden Lion at Venice, Abbas Kiarostami's enigmatic anti-drama challenges the spectator to speculate about withheld information and, thus, play an active role in the action unfolding before a distant, largely static camera. Melding character and location, he maintains an emotional detachment in passing subtle social comment on the suppression of all things beautiful and the indolence of the intelligentsia. Celebrating the dignity of labour, the durability of woman, the energy of youth and the preciousness of life, this is a masterly film from a cinematic original. In Farsi with English subtitles.

Behzad Dourani *Engineer* ■ *Dir* Abbas Kiarostami • *Scr* Abbas Kiarostami, from a idea by Mahmoud Ayedin • *Editor* Abbas Kiarostami

Wind with the Gone ★★★★

Surreal comedy drama
1998 · Sp/Fr/Arg/Neth · Colour · 91mins

Deliciously eccentric, yet cuttingly acute in its understated socio-political criticism, this is tantamount to a Borges-scripted Ealing comedy. Set in a small village in Patagonia, Alejandro Agresti's fable is filled with lovable eccentrics, from the scientist whose inventions already have patents, to the cinema projectionist who keeps showing films in the wrong order – which goes some way to explaining

this isolated community's cockamamie worldview. However, everything changes with the arrival of two unsuspecting intruders, Buenos Aires cab-driver Vera Fogwill, and fading French movie-star, Jean Rochefort. Testament to the enduring power of cinema, this is warm and wacky. In Spanish with English subtitles.

Vera Fogwill *Soledad* • Angela Molina *Dona Maria* • Fabian Vena *Pedro* • Jean Rochefort *Edgar Wexley* • Ulises Dumont *Antonio* • Carlos Roffe *Amalfi* ■ *Dir/Scr* Alejandro Agresti

Windbag the Sailor ★★★ U

Comedy   1936 · UK · BW · 81mins

Even though he had a hand in the script, Will Hay is a shade below par in this patchy comedy that is significant only for his first teaming with those much loved stooges Moore Marriott and Graham Moffatt. After a promising start, the film is all too quickly blown off course once we're at sea, before finally running aground. Yet Hay's always watchable and still raises a few chuckles as a blustering sea dog whose bluff is called by a crooked tycoon bent on scuttling his ship for the insurance. ▭

Will Hay *Capt Ben Cutlet* • Moore Marriott *Jeremiah Harbottle* • Graham Moffatt *Albert* • Norma Varden *Olivia Potter-Porter* • Dennis Wyndham *Maryatt* ■ *Dir* William Beaudine • *Scr* Marriott Edgar, Will Hay, Stafford Dickens, Robert Edmunds, Val Guest, from a story by Robert Stevenson, Leslie Arliss

Windom's Way ★★★★ U

Drama   1957 · UK · Colour · 108mins

An undiscovered gem starring a charismatic Peter Finch at the height of his heart-throb powers as one of those doctors full of confident dedication, this time toiling away in a remote Malayan village and badgering the natives to resist a rebellious takeover. This is a very powerful, tightly directed film with some stunning supporting performances from the likes of Mary Ure and Michael Hordern. What could have been a cliché-ridden outing and a one-man demonstration of star ego emerges as a simply great movie.

Peter Finch *Dr Alec Windom* • Mary Ure *Lee Windom* • Michael Hordern *Patterson* • Natasha Parry *Anna* • John Cairney *Jan Vidal* • Robert Flemyng *George Hasbrook* ■ *Dir* Ronald Neame • *Scr* Jill Craigie, from the novel by James Ramsey Ullman

The Window ★★★★

Thriller   1949 · US · BW · 73mins

A superior B-movie, based on a Cornell Woolrich short novel about a youngster (the excellent Bobby Driscoll) who witnesses a killing, but can't get anyone to take him seriously because he has a reputation for telling tales. Despite its age-old plot, this film made a huge impression on audiences of the day, and has since been relentlessly plundered, rehashed and remade. The adults are well cast, with Arthur Kennedy and Ruth Roman especially convincing under the direction of former cameraman Ted Tetzlaff, while Driscoll was awarded a special miniature Oscar for his performance.

Barbara Hale *Mrs Woodry* • Arthur Kennedy *Mr Woodry* • Bobby Driscoll *Tommy Woodry* • Paul

U = SUITABLE FOR ALL   **Uc** = SUITABLE FOR ALL, ESPECIALLY FOR YOUNG CHILDREN (VIDEO ONLY)   **PG** = PARENTAL GUIDANCE

Stewart *Mr Kellerton* • Ruth Roman *Mrs Kellerton* • Anthony Ross *Ross* ■ *Dir* Ted Tetzlaff • *Scr* Mel Dinelli, from the novelette *The Boy Cried Murder* by Cornell Woolrich

A Window in London ★★★
Thriller   1939 · UK · BW · 77mins

From the window of a train, Michael Redgrave sees what appears to be somebody strangling a woman in a house. He goes to the police, but the couple in question (Paul Lukas, Sally Gray) turn out to be an illusionist and his wife rehearsing their act. Some weeks later, Redgrave and his wife (Patricia Roc), again from a train, witness a repeat performance of the incident. Directed by Herbert Mason, it's a short, modest but intriguing British-made thriller which offers a good cast and supplies a satisfyingly neat twist.

Michael Redgrave *Peter Thompson* • Sally Gray *Vivienne* • Paul Lukas *Louis Zoltini* • Hartley Power *Max Preston* • Patricia Roc *Pat Thompson* • Glen Alyn *Andrea* ■ *Dir* Herbert Mason • *Scr* Ian Dalrymple, Brigid Cooper, from the story *Metropolitian* by Herbert Maret

Windrider ★★★ 15
Romantic drama   1986 · Ausl · Colour · 88mins

There's a nice irony in the fact that first-time director Vincent Monton cites *Risky Business* as one of the main influences on this Australian teenage romance, as the star of that movie, Tom Cruise, would end up marrying the star of this one, Nicole Kidman. Buried beneath a mass of permed hair, Kidman is suitably perky as the pop singer pursued by beach bum Tom Burlinson, who needs her to tell his mates that she witnessed his perfect 360-degree surf turn. The usual round of squabbles and misunderstandings ensues, with former cinematographer Monton demonstrating a good grasp of soundbite storytelling. Contains swearing, sex scenes. ⬚

Tom Burlinson *PC Simpson* • Nicole Kidman *Jade* • Charles Tingwell *Simpson Sr* • Jill Perryman *Miss Dodge* ■ *Dir* Vincent Monton • *Scr* Everett de Roche, Bonnie Harris

The Winds of Jarrah ★★ PG
Romantic drama
1983 · Ausl · Colour · 77mins

Ill winds from Australia that blow few people any good, except actors needing the work. It's soap opera frothed up not at all convincingly about a lover-pursued Susan Lyons who becomes teacher to the children of a bitter recluse. Shades of *Jane Eyre*, *Rebecca* and many another romantic novel, though the authors wouldn't thank you for the connection. Two points in its favour: the lush Australian scenery and its breezy brevity. ⬚

Terence Donovan *Timber Marlow* • Susan Lyons *Diana Venness* • Emil Minty *Andy Marlow* • Nikki Gemmel *Kathy Marlow* • Mark Kounnas *Peter Marlow* • Dorothy Alison *Mrs Sullivan* • Martin Vaughan *Ben* • Harold Hopkins *Jock Farrell* ■ *Dir* Mark Egerton • *Scr* by Bob Ellis, Anne Brooksbank

Windwalker ★★★★
Western   1980 · US · Colour · 108mins

Trevor Howard is the only star in this ground-breaking independent movie by

director Kieth Merrill. He plays a Cheyenne chief recounting his life story on his deathbed, including how his wife was killed and one of his twin sons kidnapped by enemy Crow Indians. Set before the forked-tongued white man took over, this stunningly shot drama uses English subtitles for the Crow and Cheyenne dialogue spoken by the amateur cast. An English/Crow/Cheyenne language film.

Trevor Howard *Windwalker* • Nick Ramus *Narration* • James Remar *Windwalker, as a young man* • Serene Hedin *Tashina* • Dusty "Iron Wing" McCrea *Dancing Moon* • Silvana Gallardo *Little Feather* • Billy Drago *Crow Scout* • Rudy Diaz *Crow Eyes* ■ *Dir* Kieth Merrill • *Scr* Ray Goldrup, from a novel by Blaine M Yorgason

Windy City ★★★ 15
Romantic drama
1984 · US · Colour · 102mins

Yuppies caught on the downbeat in a world where heartbreak and disillusion are happy bedfellows. Danny (John Shea), Emily (Kate Capshaw) and Sol (Josh Mostel) look back in regretful nostalgia (in an *About Last Night* kind of way) as a marriage and illness threaten to alter their friendship. Director Armyan Bernstein makes it moody and melancholy and John Shea deservedly won a Best Actor award at the Montreal World Film Festival in 1884 for his moving portrayal of a man about to lose everything. ⬚

John Shea *Danny Morgan* • Kate Capshaw *Emily Ruebens* • Josh Mostel *Sol* • Jim Borrelli *Mickey* • Jeffrey DeMunn *Bobby* • Eric Pierpoint *Pete* ■ *Dir/Scr* Armyan Bernstein

Wing and a Prayer ★★★
Second World War drama
1944 · US · Colour · 97mins

Don Ameche is so familiar as the septuagenarian of *Cocoon* and *Trading Places*, it's hard to visualise his first incarnation as a versatile leading man in the thirties and forties. Here he plays the sleek hero on a Pacific-bound aircraft carrier, leading Dana Andrews and fellow pilots into battle against the Japanese just prior to the Battle of Midway. It's rousing stuff, directed with an eye for detail by Henry Hathaway, who spent a substantial amount of time on board a real carrier while preparing to shoot the film.

Don Ameche *Flight Commander Bingo Harper* • Dana Andrews *Squadron Commander Edward Moulton* • William Eythe *Oscar Scott* • Charles Bickford *Captain Waddell* • Cedric Hardwicke *Admiral* • Kevin O'Shea *Cookie Cunningham* • Richard Jaeckel *Beezy Bessemer* ■ *Dir* Henry Hathaway • *Scr* Jerome Cady, Mortimer Braus

Wing Commander ★★ PG
Science-fiction action
1999 · US · Colour · 100mins

It could be argued that 20th Century Fox released this dull space opera in the months before *Star Wars Episode I* just to make the latter film look good. Based on a popular video game, this movie plays like a pale rip-off of *Star Wars*. Most of the Gen-X actors playing pilots are atrocious and neither the game's space battles, nor its fun feline aliens – who have been drained of all their personality and now look like seals – are transposed well.

George Lucas save us! Contains some strong language and sexual references.

Freddie Prinze Jr *Christopher "Maverick" Blair* • Matthew Lillard *Todd "Maniac" Marshall* • Saffron Burrows *Jeanette "Angel" Deveraux* • Jürgen Prochnow *Commander Gerald* • Tcheky Karyo *Commander James "Paladin" Taggart* • David Warner *Admiral Geoffrey Tolwyn* • David Suchet *Captain Sansky* • Ginny Holder *Rosie Forbes* ■ *Dir* Chris Roberts • *Scr* Kevin Droney, from characters created by Chris Roberts and the video game

Winged Victory ★★ U
Second World War drama
1944 · US · BW · 130mins

George Cukor's contribution to the war effort, about the training of fighter pilots with a pathetic leading man (Lon McCallister), a pretty but vacuous heroine (Jeanne Crain) and an interesting supporting cast, including Judy Holliday in one of three tentative movie roles she played before film stardom came in 1949. With the full resources of the Army Air Force at his disposal, Cukor revelled in his power: "All I had to say was, it would be nice to have some movement in the background and next thing there were hundreds of men, planes landing and taking off. But the story was silly, full of patriotism and nothing else."

Jeanne Crain *Helen* • Judy Holliday *Ruth Miller* ■ *Dir* George Cukor • *Scr* Moss Hart, from his play

Wings ★★★
Silent war drama   1927 · US · BW · 139mins

Winner of the very first best picture Oscar, this silent epic about fighter pilots in the First World War is still exciting aloft but terribly sentimental and cliché-ridden on the ground. The director, William A "Wild Bill" Wellman, had himself been a highly decorated fighter pilot with the Lafayette Flying Corps, so he brought to the project much of his own experience, giving the thrilling action sequences their excitement and veracity. But the story – devised by former pilot John Monk Saunders – switches between a lame love affair and the friendship between two pilots who join up together. Gary Cooper makes a brief appearance and the movie is dedicated to Charles Lindbergh. On original release, the action scenes were magnified and shown on giant screens.

Clara Bow *Mary Preston* • Charles "Buddy" Rogers *Jack Powell* • Richard Arlen *David Armstrong* • Jobyna Ralston *Sylvia Lewis* • Gary Cooper *Cadet White* • Arlette Marchal *Celeste* • El Brendel *Patrick O'Brien* • Hedda Hopper *Mrs Powell* ■ *Dir* William A Wellman • *Scr* Hope Loring, Louis D Lighton, from a story by John Monk Saunders

Wings in the Dark ★★★
Romantic drama   1935 · US · BW · 68mins

The wings are those of flier Cary Grant's plane, the dark is the fact that he has been blinded in an accident but nonetheless manages to pilot his aircraft to the rescue when his stunt-flier girlfriend gets into trouble during her Moscow to New York run. She, incredibly, is Myrna Loy, who was borrowed from MGM by Paramount for what one would expect to be a romantic comedy but is in fact a

romantic drama. Bizarre casting and an unbelievable story line, but played with such conviction and polish by its two gleaming stars under the well-judged direction of James Flood that it's easy to suspend disbelief.

Myrna Loy *Sheila Mason* • Cary Grant *Ken Gordon* • Roscoe Karns *Nick Williams* • Hobart Cavanaugh *Mac* • Dean Jagger *Tops Harmon* • Russell Hopton *Jake Brashear* ■ *Dir* James Flood • *Scr* Jack Kirkland, Frank Partos, from the story *Eyes of the Eagle* by Nell Shipman, Philip D Hurn, adapted by Dale Van Every, EH Robinson

Wings of Courage ★★ U
Biographical adventure drama
1995 · US · Colour · 8mins

A 40-minute 3-D Imax movie that sets out to impress with the new process but would not stand independently of it. Explaining the origins of commercial aviation in South America, Tom Hulce plays the pioneer starting an air mail service, Craig Sheffer is the pilot who flies into dangerous territory and Elizabeth McGovern stars as his long-suffering wife. The breathtaking scenery and effects are visceral, thanks to Imax, though short. It's an entertaining and informative ride, containing the kind of material kids are forced to watch on a day trip to their local museum.

Craig Sheffer *Henri Guillaumet* • Elizabeth McGovern *Noelle Guillaumet* • Tom Hulce *Antoine de Saint-Exupéry* • Val Kilmer *Jean Mermoz* • Ken Pogue *Pierre Deley* • Ron Sauve *Jean-RenéLefèbvre* ■ *Dir* Jean-Jacques Annaud • *Scr* Alain Godard, Jean-Jacques Annaud

Wings of Danger ★ U
Crime drama   1952 · UK · BW · 74mins

Poor Zachary Scott. Dropped by Warner Bros, this forceful character actor was reduced to working for Hammer in its pre-horror days on a routine crime picture pre-sold for American release. He's miscast as the hero, a pilot who investigates the disappearance of a fellow flyer, played by Robert Beatty, and exposes a currency smuggling racket. Kay Kendall and Diane Cilento are among the supporting cast but nowhere near as interesting as they would later become, while Terence Fisher's direction is merely routine.

Zachary Scott *Van* • Robert Beatty *Nick Talbot* • Kay Kendall *Alexia* • Colin Tapley *Maxwell* • Naomi Chance *Avril* • Arthur Lane *Boyd Spencer* • Diane Cilento *Jeannette* • Harold Lang *Snell* ■ *Dir* Terence Fisher • *Scr* John Gilling, from the novel *Dead on Course* by Elleston Trevor

Wings of Desire ★★★ PG
Fantasy drama
1987 · W Ger · Colour and BW · 122mins

Mystic style matters more than emotional substance in a fable from German director Wim Wenders about two angels visiting present-day Berlin and encountering the past – and love. One angel (Bruno Ganz) decides he wants to be human because he's fallen for a circus performer (Solveig Dommartin) but passing through from the other side is more difficult than it seems. Peter Falk wanders into the action as aimlessly as the progress of the plot which, although it's magnificently photographed, never gets

airborne as an idea about ongoing reality. In German with English subtitles. 🖵

Bruno Ganz *Damiel* • Solveig Dommartin *Marion* • Otto Sander *Cassiel* • Curt Bois *Homer* • Peter Falk • Lajos Kovacs *Marion's coach* • Bruno Rosaz *Clown* ■ *Dir* Wim Wenders • *Scr* Wim Wenders, Peter Handke, Richard Reitinger

The Wings of Eagles ★★★ U

Biographical drama
1957 · US · Colour · 105mins

A ramshackle but nonetheless enjoyable biopic of tragic screenwriter/flying ace Frank "Spig" Wead, best remembered for movies like *Air Mail*, *Ceiling Zero* and *They Were Expendable*. A strangely subdued John Wayne plays Wead, actually appearing in the later scenes without his characteristic toupee. Dan Dailey is fun as Wead's buddy, but Maureen O'Hara is wasted with little more than two good scenes as the navy wife. The film's greatest delight is Ward Bond as movie director "John Dodge", in other words John Ford (Ford's study was authentically duplicated here using real props, including his Oscars). There's a smug and sentimental feel to the whole piece that makes it unworthy of its subject, who died ten years previously. 🖵

John Wayne *Frank W "Spig" Wead* • Maureen O'Hara *Minnie Wead* • Dan Dailey *"Jughead"* *Carson* • Ward Bond *John Dodge* • Ken Curtis *John Dale Price* • Edmund Lowe *Admiral Moffett* • Kenneth Tobey *Captain Herbert Allen Hazard* • James Todd *Jack Travis* ■ *Dir* John Ford • *Scr* Frank Fenton, Wiliam Wister Haines, from the life and writings of Commander Frank W Wead Usn and the biography *Wings of Men*

Wings of Fame ★★ 15

Fantasy   1990 · Neth · Colour · 109mins

A fantasy tale in which spirits of the dead end up at a huge offshore hotel, a sort of halfway house for the famous. Peter O'Toole is a movie star, murdered by a writer (Colin Firth) who himself has died in an accident. The pair meet at the hotel and talk about what happened and why. And, oh yes, Albert Einstein, the kidnapped Lindbergh child and even Lassie are there as well. It's Agatha Christie meets *Last Year in Marienbad*. The performances have some gusto, but it's weird – very weird indeed – and often just plain silly. Contains swearing and nudity.

Peter O'Toole *Valentin* • Colin Firth *Smith* • Marie Trintignant *Bianca* • Andréa Ferréol *Theresa* • Maria Becker *Dr Frisch* • Gottfried John *Zlatogorski* ■ *Dir* Otakar Votocek • *Scr* Otakar Votocek, Herman Koch

The Wings of Honneamise ★★★★ PG

Animation   1987 · Jap · Colour · 119mins

Made the year before *Akira* introduced western audiences to the *anime* movies based on Japanese *manga* comics, this was the most costly example made to date. Yet the budget has clearly been well spent, with a superb Ryuichi Sakamoto score, the feuding nations convincingly futuristic and the camera movements and lighting effects worthy of a Hollywood

blockbuster. But, although our hero is a member of the Royal Space Force, his journey is more one of self-discovery than all-conquering bravado. For all his ingenuity, 23-year-old writer/director Hiroyuki Yamaga overdoes the religious symbolism, while revealing a political naivety akin to his hero's. Nevertheless, a classic of its kind. In Japanese with English subtitles. 🖵

Dir/Scr Hiroyuki Yamaga • *Music* Ryuichi Sakamoto • *Art Director* Hiromasa Ogura

Wings of the Apache ★★ 15

Action drama   1990 · US · Colour · 82mins

A tired attempt to recapture the aerobatic excitement of *Top Gun*, with the attention this time switching to helicopters. Nicolas Cage's heart doesn't seem to be in his role of a maverick pilot, while Sean Young is even less convincing as a fellow flier/former girlfriend. In the end, it is left to the reliable Tommy Lee Jones to mop up the acting honours as the hard-nosed commander preparing his troops for the war against the drug dealers. Phil Collins is a possible attraction among those crooning away on the soundtrack, but this is really for lads who have never grown up. Contains swearing, violence. 🖵

Nicolas Cage *Jake Preston* • Tommy Lee Jones *Brad Little* • Sean Young *Billie Lee Guthrie* • Bryan Kestner *Breaker* • Dale Dye *AK McNeil* • Mary Ellen Trainor *Janet Little* • JA Preston *General Olcott* • Peter Onorati *Rice* ■ *Dir* David Green • *Scr* Nick Thiel, Paul F Edwards, from a story by Step Tyner, John K Swensson, Dale Dye

The Wings of the Dove ★★★★ 15

Period romantic drama
1997 · US · Colour · 97mins

Newcomer Hossein Amini was Oscar-nominated for his adaptation of one of Henry James's most difficult novels. And director Iain Softley also succeeds in doing James justice in this visually arresting, lyrical and dark film. Helena Bonham Carter gives her best performance to date as Kate, a modern miss who in order to elevate herself and rough lover Merton (Linus Roache), encourages him to fall for dying heiress Millie Theale (Alison Elliott). The friendship that develops between Kate and Millie and the genuine love that Millie arouses in Merton complicates the callous scheme of inheritance and threatens to destroy them all. Contains some swearing and sex scenes. 🖵 **DVD**

Helena Bonham Carter *Kate Croy* • Linus Roache *Merton Densher* • Alison Elliott *Millie Theale* • Charlotte Rampling *Aunt Maude* • Elizabeth McGovern *Susan Stringham* • Michael Gambon *Lionel Croy* • Alex Jennings *Lord Mark* ■ *Dir* Iain Softley • *Scr* Hossein Amini, from the novel by Henry James

Wings of the Morning ★★★

Sports romantic drama
1937 · UK · Colour · 87mins

Henry Fonda, imported from America, and Annabella, brought from France, co-star with beautiful soft-toned colour, lush Irish and English scenery and a racehorse in Britain's first Technicolor feature. A prologue set in the 1890s has Irish aristocrat Leslie Banks

defying convention to marry beautiful Spanish gypsy Annabella. After his death in a riding accident, she goes back to Spain, returning many years later (and played by Irene Vanbrugh) with her granddaughter (who Annabella now plays) and a horse to train for the Derby. Initially disguised as a boy, Annabella meets Canadian race trainer Fonda and both fall in love... Gentle, charming, lovely to look at, and with songs sung by John McCormack.

Annabella *Maria/Marie* • Henry Fonda *Kerry Gilfallen* • Stewart Rome *Sir Valentine MacFarland* • Irene Vanbrugh *Marie* • Harry Tate *Paddy* • Helen Haye *Jenepher* • Steve Donoghue • Leslie Banks *Lord Clontarf* ■ *Dir* Harold D Schuster [Harold Schuster] • *Scr* Tom Geraghty, from short stories by Donn Byrne • *Songs* John McCormack

The Winner ★★★ 15

Black comedy thriller
1997 · US/Ausl · Colour · 85mins

One of the more coherent films from the maverick independent director Alex Cox, of *Sid and Nancy* fame. Vincent D'Onofrio plays a Las Vegas man who can't lose. Rebecca DeMornay, Billy Bob Thornton and Michael Madsen are among the losers who latch on to him, in the hope of grabbing a share of his pot. A strange little story, nicely played and compellingly told. Contains swearing, violence. 🖵

Rebecca DeMornay *Louise* • Vincent D'Onofrio *Philip* • Richard Edson *Frankie* • Saverio Guerra *Paulie* • Delroy Lindo *Kingman* • Michael Madsen *Wolf* • Billy Bob Thornton *Jack* • Frank Whaley *Joey* • Alex Cox *Gaston* ■ *Dir* Alex Cox • *Scr* Wendy Riss, from her play *A Darker Purpose*

Winnie ★★

Drama based on a true story
1988 · US · Colour · 96mins

Meredith Baxter's poignant performance elevates this otherwise typical, sentimental TV film, based on the true story of a mildly retarded Iowa woman who longs to leave her institution home. When she and her boyfriend (David Morse) run away, they learn that the real world can be both exhilarating and frightening. Director John Korty, along with Baxter, help make what might have been a maudlin tear-jerker emerge as a touching portrayal. The treatment of mental retardation is also given a light touch, giving the story an upbeat spin. Although it rarely rises above routine, fans and viewers who like feel-good films should find something to admire.

Meredith Baxter Birney [Meredith Baxter] *Winnie* • David Morse • Jenny O'Hara ■ *Dir* John Korty • *Scr* Joyce Eliason, from the book *Winnie: My Life in the Institution* by Jamie Paster

Winning ★★★ PG

Sports drama   1969 · US · Colour · 117mins

The two biggest male stars of the sixties' Paul Newman and Steve McQueen, loved to race cars in their spare time and both men made their own motor-racing movies. Newman's was *Winning*, followed two years later by McQueen's *Le Mans*. Both were flops because no one had figured out what to do with the cast during pit stops, but *Winning* is the better movie. Newman plays a driver who values

racing more than his wife and stepson (Joanne Woodward and callow Richard Thomas), and Robert Wagner is the rival racer who steps into the romantic breach. It's all very macho stuff, with predictably exciting racing sequences. 🖵

Paul Newman *Frank Capua* • Joanne Woodward *Elora* • Richard Thomas *Charley* • Robert Wagner *Luther Erding* • David Sheiner *Crawford* • Clu Gulager *Larry* • Barry Ford *Les Bottineau* ■ *Dir* James Goldstone • *Scr* Howard Rodman

The Winning of Barbara Worth ★★★★

Silent romantic western
1926 · US · BW · 83mins

After playing extras and bit parts in two-reelers, Gary Cooper was suddenly cast as a last minute replacement for one of the supporting players. Cooper plays a local Arizona boy and rival of eastern engineer Ronald Colman for the hand of Vilma Banky (the eponymous Barbara). Shot in the Nevada desert, the film, about the harnessing of the Colorado river, offers sandstorms, floods and romance. There is some fine camerawork by George Barnes and his 22-year-old assistant Gregg Toland, who fifteen years later would shoot *Citizen Kane*.

Ronald Colman *Willard Holmes* • Vilma Banky *Barbara Worth* • Charles Lane (2) *Jefferson Worth* • Paul McAllister *The Seer* • EJ Ratcliffe *James Greenfield* • Gary Cooper *Abe Lee* ■ *Dir* Henry King • *Scr* Frances Marion, from the novel by Harold Bell Wright • *Producer* Samuel Goldwyn

Winning of the West ★★ U

Western   1953 · US · BW · 57mins

An unremarkable Gene Autry western that will appeal only to fans of the chubby-cheeked singin' cowboy, his "Wonder Horse" Champion and his oafish sidekick Smiley Burnette. He has never made a really good movie, at least not for grown-ups, and these days his clean-cut cowboy code has little relevance to youngsters. The title's a gross misnomer.

Gene Autry • Gail Davis *Ann Randolph* • Richard Crane *Jack Austin* • Robert Livingston *Art Selby* • House Peters Jr *Marshal Hackett* • Gregg Barton *Clint Raybold* ■ *Dir* George Archainbaud • *Scr* Norman S Hall

The Winslow Boy ★★★★ U

Drama   1948 · UK · BW · 113mins

An object lesson in how to transfer stage to screen, this proves it *can* be done well. Terence Rattigan's tightly wound text is left largely untouched, but the scenes are broadened out to give the original play room to breathe. Robert Donat is wonderful as the celebrated barrister defending a naval cadet charged with theft, and Rattigan's insights into class and hypocrisy are sharpened by Anthony Asquith's assured direction. Primarily a cinematic experience, but the play is left unscarred. 🖵

Robert Donat *Sir Robert Morton* • Margaret Leighton *Catherine Winslow* • Cedric Hardwicke *Arthur Winslow* • Basil Radford *Esmond Curry* • Kathleen Harrison *Violet* • Francis L Sullivan *Attorney General* • Marie Lohr *Grace Winslow* • Jack Watling *Dickie Winslow* • Frank Lawton *John Watherstone* •

U = SUITABLE FOR ALL   Uc = SUITABLE FOR ALL, ESPECIALLY FOR YOUNG CHILDREN (VIDEO ONLY)   PG = PARENTAL GUIDANCE

Neil North *Ronnie Winslow* • Wilfrid Hyde White *Wilkinson* ■ *Dir* Anthony Asquith • *Scr* Terence Rattigan, Anatole de Grunwald, from the play by Terence Rattigan

The Winslow Boy ★★★★ U

Drama   1999 · US · Colour · 100mins

An odd couple of playwrights were involved in this engrossing, fact-based story of innocence triumphant, in which David Mamet drops his fascination with scum and scams to adapt and direct Terence Rattigan's play about upper-class emotion that dare not speak its name. When his son Ronnie (Guy Edwards) is expelled from the Royal Naval Academy for theft, retired Arthur Winslow (Nigel Hawthorne) believes in the boy's virtue so much he nearly bankrupts his family trying to prove it. Suffragette daughter Rebecca Pidgeon falls for barrister Jeremy Northam, while mother Gemma Jones cannot understand her husband's obsessive pursuit of justice. Mamet usually sees the truth beneath ulterior motives; here, with the help of a remarkable cast, he brings real motives out into the light of day. ▭

DVD

Nigel Hawthorne *Arthur Winslow* • Jeremy Northam *Sir Robert Morton* • Rebecca Pidgeon *Catherine Winslow* • Gemma Jones *Grace Winslow* • Guy Edwards *Ronnie Winslow* • Matthew Pidgeon *Dickie Winslow* ■ *Dir* David Mamet • *Scr* David Mamet, from the play by Terence Rattigan

Winstanley ★★★★ PG

Historical drama   1975 · UK · BW · 91mins

Kevin Brownlow and Andrew Mollo's second film – their first was *It Happened Here* – is set in Cromwellian England and deals with a disparate group of people, united in their disillusion, poverty and landlessness who create a commune and call themselves Diggers. Their leader is Gerrard Winstanley, a man with a utopian dream of social equality. Based on David Caute's novel *Comrade Jacob*, it fits into the world of a sixties agitprop, riding the anti-everything, drop-out tide of student protest, but Brownlow and Mollo are not firebrand radicals, much less flower power hippies. They are, first and foremost, serious historians who shot the film for over a year, often in harsh conditions. As a period reconstruction it has few equals. ▭

Miles Halliwell *Gerrard Winstanley* • Jerome Willis *General Lord Fairfax* • Terry Higgins *Tom Haydon* • Phil Oliver *Will Everard* • David Bramley *Parson John Platt* • Allison Halliwell *Mrs Platt* • Dawson France *Captain Gladman* ■ *Dir* Kevin Brownlow, Andrew Mollo • *Scr* Kevin Brownlow, Andrew Mollo, from the novel *Comrade Jacob* by David Caute

The Winter Guest ★★★ 15

Drama   1997 · US/UK · Colour · 104mins

Alan Rickman's directorial debut employs Emma Thompson as a mother grieving for the death of her husband, unable to support and nurture their son and also unable to see her own mother's ill health. This family saga is interwoven with goings-on in the rest of the film's isolated Scottish village setting: two old dears get their kicks out of going to funerals and two small boys play on the ever-blustery beach.

It's a touching essay on emotions and surviving grief but overall the film never quite escapes from its original theatrical roots. ▭ DVD

Emma Thompson *Frances* • Phyllida Law *Elspeth* • Sheila Reid *Lily* • Sandra Voe *Chloe* • Arlene Cockburn *Nita* • Gary Hollywood *Alex* • Sean Biggerstaff *Tom* ■ *Dir* Alan Rickman • *Scr* Alan Rickman, Sharman MacDonald, from his play

Winter Kills ★★★ 18

Black comedy   1979 · US · Colour · 87mins

A genuine collector's item, based on the remarkable satirical novel about the Kennedys by Richard Condon, who also wrote *The Manchurian Candidate* and *Prizzi's Honor*. Jeff Bridges, playing the son of patriarch John Huston, tries to discover who was responsible for killing his brother, the US President. In the starry cast, the likes of Anthony Perkins, Sterling Hayden, Dorothy Malone and Toshiro Mifune make telling contributions, while Elizabeth Taylor appears in a cameo, and it's all held together by William Richert's assured direction. Contains swearing and nudity. ▭

Jeff Bridges *Nick Kegan* • John Huston *Pa Kegan* • Anthony Perkins *John Ceruti* • Sterling Hayden *ZK Dawson* • Eli Wallach *Joe Diamond* • Dorothy Malone *Emma Kegan* • Tomas Milian *Frank Mayo* • Belinda Bauer *Yvette Malone* • Ralph Meeker *Gameboy Baker* • Toshiro Mifune *Keith* • Richard Boone *Keifitz* • Elizabeth Taylor *Lola Comante* ■ *Dir* William Richert • *Scr* William Richert, from the novel by Richard Condon

Winter Light ★★★ PG

Drama   1962 · Swe · BW · 77mins

Anyone who thought Robert Bresson's *Diary of a Country Priest* was the most agonising portrait of clerical life should tune in for this second part of Ingmar Bergman's "religious" trilogy. Tormented by doubts about his own faith and tempted by an offer of marriage from schoolteacher Ingrid Thulin, pastor Gunnar Björnstrand is also aware of the duty he owes to parishioner Max von Sydow, who is contemplating suicide in the face of a nuclear crisis. Composed for the most part in close-ups, this is a powerful and pessimistic look at God's relationship with humanity but, in spite of exceptional performances, it won't be for all tastes. In Swedish with English subtitles. ▭

Ingrid Thulin *Marta Lundberg* • Gunnar Björnstrand *Tomas Ericsson* • Max von Sydow *Jonas Persson* • Gunnel Lindblom *Karin Persson* • Allan Edwall *Algot Frovik* ■ *Dir/Scr* Ingmar Bergman

Winter Meeting ★

Drama   1948 · US · BW · 104mins

Even Bette Davis, characteristically accomplished and uncharacteristically restrained, can't save audiences from the mind-numbing tedium of this bleak and ponderously verbose drama. Davis is a repressed spinster poetess who becomes involved with a naval officer (James Davis, no relation - and little talent) who really wants to become a Catholic priest. Directed by Bretaigne Windust, the movie is one of Bette's last duds before finally leaving Warner Bros to freelance. Who could blame her!

Bette Davis *Susan Grieve* • Janis Paige *Peggy Markham* • James [Davis Jim] Davis *Lt Slick Novak* • John Hoyt *Stacy Grant* • Florence Bates *Mrs Castle* • Walter Baldwin *Mr Castle* • Ransom Sherman *Mr Moran* • Hugh Charles *Headwaiter* ■ *Dir* Bretaigne Windust • *Scr* Catherine Turney, from the novel by Ethel Vance

The Winter of Our Discontent ★★ PG

Drama   1983 · US · Colour · 100mins

Michael DeGuzman, proving that he cannot free the complexity or even the spirit of John Steinbeck's last novel, has delivered a script so lumpy that director Waris Hussein can do little more than lurch. And yet the odd shaft of light pierces the confusion, particularly during several moral passages and when the well-chosen cast is allowed to breathe. ▭

Donald Sutherland *Ethan Hawley* • Teri Garr *Mary Hawley* • Tuesday Weld *Margie* • Richard Masur *Danny Taylor* • Michael V Gazzo *Marullo* ■ *Dir* Waris Hussein • *Scr* Michael DeGuzman, from the novel by John Steinbeck

The Winter of Our Dreams ★★ 15

Drama   1981 · Ausl · Colour · 84mins

An early film from Aussie director John Duigan. Judy Davis stars as a deeply troubled prostitute who strikes up a relationship with married bookseller Bryan Brown while he's investigating an ex-girlfriend's suicide. The soapy plot and crude direction are nothing to shout about, but Duigan has always had a reputation for extracting great performances from his actors and here Davis, in particular, is terrific. ▭

Judy Davis *Lou* • Bryan Brown *Rob* • Cathy Downes *Gretel* • Baz Luhrmann *Pete* • Peter Mochrie *Tim* ■ *Dir/Scr* John Duigan

Winter People ★★ 15

Drama   1988 · US · Colour · 105mins

It's the backwoods of North Carolina in the thirties, and Kurt Russell is deeply into his macho mode, sniffin' and snarlin' like a rampant grizzly bear and with one eye on the script and another on his personal trainer. Actually he's pretty silly here, and so's the picture, a lot of moonshine about clan rivalry that heats up when the widowed Russell comes across unmarried mother Kelly McGillis. The accents are as thick as the characters and the religious dimension to the plot may have worked in John Ehle's original novel, but it's corny and clumsy on screen. Contains some swearing. ▭

Kurt Russell *Wayland Jackson* • Kelly McGillis *Collie Wright* • Lloyd Bridges *William Wright* • Mitchell Ryan *Drury Campbell* • Amelia Burnette *Paula Jackson* • Eileen Ryan *Annie Wright* • Lanny Flaherty *Gudger Wright* ■ *Dir* Ted Kotcheff • *Scr* Carol Sobieski, from the novel by John Ehle

Winterhawk ★★★

Western   1975 · US · Colour · 86mins

A cowboys and Indians film in which the whites are the baddies. Michael Dante plays a Blackfoot brave who comes to a white settlement for a smallpox serum, only to be attacked. The Indian then takes revenge by abducting two white kids. It's good to

see genre conventions being broken down, but the film is still clichéd, even if the clichés are inverted. It's watchable, though, and notable for a panoply of familiar "cowboy" faces, including Leif Erickson, Woody Strode, Denver Pyle, Elisha Cook Jr and L Q Jones.

Leif Erickson *Guthrie* • Woody Strode *Big Rude* • Denver Pyle *Arkansas* • LQ Jones *Gates* • Michael Dante *Winterhawk* • Elisha Cook Jr *Reverend Will Finley* ■ *Dir* Charles B Pierce • *Scr* Charles B Pierce, Earl E Smith

The Winter's Tale ★★ U

Romantic comedy
1966 · UK · Colour · 150mins

Frank Dunlop's theatre production, which presumably wowed audiences at the 1966 Edinburgh Festival, transfers unconvincingly to celluloid, and the usual faults of cine-theatre, such as over-frequent close-ups, are here in all their vainglory. Nevertheless, the film has its moments. Laurence Harvey makes a competent Leontes, the king who for little apparent reason develops a jealous streak which threatens to destroy all around him. However, he's nearly upstaged by Jim Dale, who makes a fine Autolycus as well as composing the score.

Laurence Harvey *Leontes* • Jane Asher *Perdita* • Diana Churchill *Paulina* • Moira Redmond *Hermione* • Jim Dale *Autolycus* • Esmond Knight *Camillo* ■ *Dir* Frank Dunlop • *Scr* from the play by William Shakespeare

A Winter's Tale ★★★★ 15

Romantic drama   1992 · Fr · Colour · 109mins

Eric Rohmer is unique in his ability to fashion fully fleshed characters to persuade us to become utterly absorbed in the petty problems that beset lives that are every bit as ordinary as our own. This second of his *Four Seasons* series again reveals his unfailing insight into the human condition. Exploring the emotions, confusions and contradictions attendant on romance, this witty adult fairy tale, set in the heart of the callous city, is a joy to behold thanks to the naturalism of its performances and the sublime subtlety of its direction. In French with English subtitles. ▭

Charlotte Very *Félicie* • Frédéric Van Den Driessche *Charles* • Michel Voletti *Maxence* • Hervé Furic *Loïc* • Ava Loraschi *Elise* ■ *Dir/ Scr* Eric Rohmer

Winterset ★★★

Drama   1936 · US · BW · 75mins

Burgess Meredith, repeating his Broadway role, is the star of this adaptation of Maxwell Anderson's once-famous play, originally written in blank verse and inspired by the Sacco and Vanzetti case. Very much a prestige production in its day, hailed by the critics and the cognoscenti but ignored by the customers, this account of a man seeking to clear the name of his wrongfully executed, liberal father is stagey, talky, and now dated, but its passionate arguments against intolerance and mob hysteria have a powerful ring.

Burgess Meredith *Mio Romagna* • Margo Miriamne *Esdras* • Eduardo Ciannelli *Trock Estrella* • Maurice Moscovitch [Maurice

Moscovich] *Esdras* • Paul Guilfoyle *Garth Esdras* • Mischa Auer *Radical* • John Carradine *Bartolomeo Romagna* ■ *Dir* Alfred Santell • *Scr* Anthony Veiller, from the play by Maxwell Anderson • *Art Director* Van Nest Polglase

Wintersleepers ★★★ 🔟

Melodrama   1997 · Ger · Colour · 122mins

German director Tom Tykwer revives the long-dormant "mountain film" with this cool take on heroism and the formidability of nature. After a superbly controlled opening that culminates in a shocking road accident, the pace drops – a tad too deliberately – to allow the snowball of coincidence to gather momentum. Yet there's a ghoulish fascination in watching the links emerge between amnesiac projectionist Ulrich Matthes and the family of his victim. While effectively contrasting the Alpine snowscapes and the rich-hued interiors, Tykwer doesn't always keep the lid on the more extreme emotions. Lacking depth and overly melodramatic perhaps, this is still undeniably tense and beautifully filmed. In German with English subtitles. Contains sex scenes, swearing.

Ulrich Matthes *Rene* • Marie-Lou Sellem *Laura* • Floriane Daniel *Rebecca* • Heino Ferch *Marco* • Josef Bierbichler *Theo* • Laura Tonke *Nina* ■ *Dir* Tom Tykwer • *Scr* Tom Tykwer, Anne-Françoise Pyszora, from the novel *Expense of the Spirit* by Anne-Françoise Pyszora

Wintertime ★★ 🔟

Musical comedy   1943 · US · BW · 82mins

Norwegian skating star Sonja Henie, in a triumph of scriptwriting imagination, plays a Norwegian skating star in this last of her Fox musicals. She turns up at the declining Canadian resort hotel owned by her dear old uncle, SZ "Cuddles" Sakall, where her mere presence puts the place back on the tourist map. And that, as well as her romance with Cornel Wilde, is it – aside from the skating, that is. Though exhibiting an undemanding story and nondescript music, the movie at least allows former Olympic champion Henie to go through her often dazzling paces.

Sonja Henie *Nora* • Jack Oakie *Skip Hutton* • Cesar Romero *Brad Barton* • Carole Landis *Flossie Fouchere* • SZ Sakall *Hjalmar Ostgaard* • Cornel Wilde *Freddy Austin* ■ *Dir* John Brahm • *Scr* E Edwin Moran, Jack Jevne, Lynn Starling, from a story by Arthur Kober

Wired ★ 🔟

Biographical drama
1989 · US · Colour · 104mins

As if the pathetic death of comedian John Belushi wasn't tragic enough, this dreadful biopic purporting to tell the truth about his career and the drugged-out events leading up to his fatal heroin and cocaine overdose in LA's Chateau Marmont hotel in 1982 adds insult to injury. Michael Chiklis fails to convince as the doomed Blues Brother and, worse, isn't a good enough actor to give any insight into why Belushi was considered a comic genius. Told from the dead Belushi's point of view as he unzips his body bag and looks back at his past, this crude low-budget exploiter is one of the most grotesque character assassinations ever put on

film. Contains swearing, drug abuse. 🖵

Michael Chiklis *John Belushi* • Ray Sharkey *Angel Velasquez* • JT Walsh *Bob Woodward* • Patti D'Arbanville [Patti D'Arbanville-Quinn] *Cathy Smith* • Lucinda Jenney *Judy Belushi* • Gary Groomes *Dan Aykroyd* • Alex Rocco *Arnie Fromson* ■ *Dir* Larry Peerce • *Scr* Earl Mac Rauch, from the book *Wired: the short life and fast times of John Belushi* by Bob Woodward

Wisdom ★ 🔟

Crime drama   1986 · US · Colour · 104mins

If only director Emilio Estevez would demonstrate a little wisdom by quitting directing and sticking to acting, the lesser of the two evils. Here he directs himself for the first time as a high school dropout who turns into a local Robin Hood and with girlfriend Demi Moore at his side begins bombing banks to help his debt-ridden neighbours. Far from being *Bonnie and Clyde* there is nothing to recommend this except an exhilarating car chase but it's unlikely that you'll be awake long enough. 🖵

Emilio Estevez *John Wisdom* • Demi Moore *Karen Simmons* • Tom Skerritt *Lloyd Wisdom* • Veronica Cartwright *Samantha Wisdom* • William Allen Young *Williamson* • Richard Minchenberg *Cooper* • Ernie Brown *Motel manager* • Bill Henderson *Theo* ■ *Dir/Scr* Emilio Estevez

The Wisdom of Crocodiles ★★★ 🔟

Horror romance   1998 · UK · Colour · 94mins

By day a medical researcher, by night a vampire, Jude Law stars as the undead preying on women in the hope of finding the true love that will bring about his redemption. Rescuing Kerry Fox from a suicide attempt, he then beds and bloods her. However, his subsequent encounter with the beautiful Elina Löwensohn becomes a complex love affair when he can't bring himself to bite her jugular. Over-stylised by director Po Chih Leong, realism is on hand in Timothy Spall's characterisation of the downbeat detective who soon gets on Law's case. Not a bad little thriller in spite of the foregoing. Contains violence, sex scenes, swearing. 🖵

Jude Law *Steven Grlscz* • Elina Lowensohn *Anne Levels* • Timothy Spall *Inspector Healey* • Kerry Fox *Maria Vaughan* • Jack Davenport *Sergeant Roche* • Colin Salmon *Martin* ■ *Dir* Po Chih Leong • *Scr* Paul Hoffman

Wise Blood ★★★ 🔟

Gothic drama
1979 · US/W Ger · Colour · 101mins

A greatly admired and critically acclaimed film in many quarters, this blood-and-salvation southern Gothic fantasy seems to cry out for a more outré approach than that of director John Huston, who clearly relished (since he also appears in it) this virtually blasphemous and undeniably strange version of Flannery O'Connor's obsessive fable. Brad Dourif leads O'Connor's "The Church of Truth without Jesus Christ", and is mightily effective as Hazel Motes, but the character is frankly unsympathetic, despite his good intentions, and ultimately the movie's taste becomes highly questionable. But there's no

denying its powerful appeal and extremely subversive humour. 🖵

Brad Dourif *Hazel Motes* • Harry Dean Stanton *Asa Hawks* • Ned Beatty *Hoover Shoates* • Daniel Shor [Dan Shor] *Enoch Emery* • Amy Wright *Sabbath Lily Hawks* • John Huston *Hazel's grandfather* • Mary Nell Santacroce *Landlady* • William Hickey *Preacher* ■ *Dir* John Huston • *Scr* Benedict Fitzgerald, Michael Fitzgerald, from the novel by Flannery O'Connor

Wise Guys ★ 🔟

Black comedy   1986 · US · Colour · 87mins

Director Brian De Palma, whom author Martin Amis once dubbed "Brian De Plasma", is a specialist in bloody thrillers, such as *Carrie, Dressed to Kill, Scarface* and *The Untouchables*. Comedy, though, is not his forte, as most people who saw his supposed satire *The Bonfire of the Vanities* will confirm. Conclusive evidence that De Palma can't tell a joke is provided by this woeful effort in which Danny DeVito plays a Mafia messenger boy and Harvey Keitel is a hotelier. The comedy is pitched so low – words rarely having more than four letters – you need a mechanical digger to find it. 🖵

Danny DeVito *Harry Valentini* • Joe Piscopo *Moe Dickstein* • Harvey Keitel *Bobby Dilea* • Ray Sharkey *Marco* • Dan Hedaya *Anthony Castelo* • Captain Lou Albano *Frank The Fixer* • Julie Bovasso *Lil Dickstein* • Patti LuPone *Wanda Valentini* ■ *Dir* Brian De Palma • *Scr* George Gallo

Wisecracks ★★★★

Documentary   1991 · Can · Colour · 91mins

Gail Singer's impressive documentary provides a valuable insight into the careers of some of comedy's most important female stars. It combines film footage of Mae West, Gracie Allen, Lucille Ball and the like with contemporary clips from and interviews with Whoopi Goldberg, Phyllis Diller, Jenny Lecoat and others. Liberal chunks of the participants' comedy routines ensure a high level of humour throughout this excellent production. Shorter versions turn up occasionally but the original 91-minute cut is the one to see.

Dir Gail Singer • *Cinematographer* Zoe Dirse, Bob Fresco • *Editor* Gordon McClellan

Wiseguy ★★ 🔟

Action thriller   1996 · US · Colour · 95mins

It won't mean much to British viewers, but many of the original cast of the late eighties US TV series have gathered here for this one-off reunion. Ken Wahl returns as the undercover cop who has the uncanny ability to impersonate villains; Jonathan Banks and Jim Byrnes are his crusty, trusty sidekicks. All three are this time on the trail of the psychotic Ted Levine, who specialises in the very nineties crime of computer hacking. It's ably directed by James Whitmore Jr, but the plotting is predictable and the in-jokes will fly over most people's heads. Contains violence, swearing, a sex scene. 🖵

Ken Wahl *Vinnie Terranova* • Jonathan Banks *McPike* • Jim Byrnes *Lifeguard* • Debrah

Farentino *Emma* • Ted Levine *Paul Callendar* • Zachary Browne *Alex* • John Kapelos *Goss* ■ *Dir* James Whitmore Jr • *Scr* Joel Surnow

Wish You Were Here ★★★★ 🔟

Comedy drama   1987 · UK · Colour · 92mins

Emily Lloyd's startling debut as a sexually defiant seaside teenager prevents writer/director David Leland's fifties-set comedy drama from being just another rebellious youngster movie. Her vibrant performance as the 16-year-old intent on shocking everyone begs the question; why has her career since, failed to make any impact? There's also strong support from Tom Bell in a decidedly unsympathetic role as a lecherous family friend. Contains swearing, sex scenes, nudity. 🖵 **DVD**

Emily Lloyd *Lynda* • Tom Bell *Eric* • Clare Clifford *Mrs Parfitt* • Barbara Durkin *Valerie* • Geoffrey Hutchings *Hubert* • Charlotte Barker *Gillian* • Chloe Leland *Margaret* • Jesse Birdsall *Dave* • Pat Heywood *Aunt Millie* ■ *Dir/Scr* David Leland

Wishful Thinking ★★ 🔟

Fantasy comedy   1990 · US · Colour · 90mins

One of the hit acts from the twisted talent series *The Gong Show* in the seventies was a fast-talking gagster called the Unknown Comic who performed with a paper bag covering his head. The man beneath that bag was Murray Langston, the director, co-writer and star of *Wishful Thinking* which tells the tale of a frustrated screenwriter who is given a (supposedly) magic writing pad by a gnome who says that whatever he writes in the pad will come true. Langston should have written that *Wishful Thinking* will become a huge hit movie – he didn't and it didn't. 🖵

Michelle Johnson *Diane Jacobs* • Murray Langston *Michael Moore* • Ruth Buzzi *Jody Moore* • Ray "Boom Boom" Mancini [Ray Mancini] *Jake Malone* ■ *Dir* Murray Langston • *Scr* Steve Finly, Murray Langston

Wishmaster ★★★ 🔟

Horror   1997 · US · Colour · 86mins

The saying "Be careful what you wish for, it may come true" provides the basis for this oddly comforting throwback to the early eighties slasher glory days, directed by former special-effects genius Robert Kurtzman and executive produced by Wes Craven. Here, Los Angeles gem specialist Tammy Lauren must stop the evil 12th-century Persian Djinn (genie), played by Andrew Divoff, wreaking havoc after he tries to trick her into making three wishes when she discovers him trapped in an enchanted opal. The one-jolt premise does get stretched out to vanishing point, yet the stunt casting of Robert Englund, Tony Todd and Kane Hodder, plus all the exploding body parts, will be a nostalgic tonic for splatter addicts. Contains strong violence and some swearing. 🖵 **DVD**

Tammy Lauren *Alexandra Amberson* • Andrew Divoff *The Djinn/Nathaniel Demerest* • Kane Hodder *Merritt's guard* • Tony Todd *Johnny Valentine* • Robert Englund *Raymond Beaumont* • Angus Scrimm *Narrator* • Ari Barak *Zoroaster* ■ *Dir* Robert Kurtzman • *Scr* Peter Atkins • *Executive Producer* Wes Craven

🅤 = SUITABLE FOR ALL   🅤c = SUITABLE FOR ALL, ESPECIALLY FOR YOUNG CHILDREN (VIDEO ONLY)   🅟🅖 = PARENTAL GUIDANCE

Wishmaster 2: Evil Never Dies ★ 18

Horror   1999 · US · Colour · 92mins

Sporting a welcome evil smirk, Andrew Divoff returns as the Djinn (though he's off screen a lot), but this instalment completely changes his background and requirements for bringing hell to earth. This time, he must gather 1001 souls, which he does by granting people's wishes and twisting the results. Thus the bodies and his soul collection start to pile up. Except for the scene in which a convict wishes his lawyer would screw himself and the Djinn makes it literally happen, the movie completely fails to be darkly humorous, let alone scary. The low budget is painfully apparent when the movie tries to re-create the glitz and glamour of Las Vegas. ▭

Andrew Divoff *The Djinn/Nathaniel Demerest* • Holly Fields *Morgana* • Paul Johansson *Gregory* • Bokeem Woodbine *Farralon* • Carlos Leon *Webber* ■ *Dir/Scr* Jack Sholder

Witch Hunt ★★★

Supernatural detective fantasy
1994 · US · Colour · 100mins

The sequel to the TV movie *Cast a Deadly Spell* replaces Fred Ward with Dennis Hopper as LA private detective Philip Lovecraft investigating hocus pocus in fifties Hollywood. Positing the clever notion that the McCarthy hearings were all about flushing out real witches in the film business who used Communism as a cover, Hopper goes head to head with evil senator Eric Bogosian and warlock Julian Sands while falling for the actress, Penelope Ann Miller, who hired him. Mood, atmosphere and bizarre special effects make up for the faulty script and lack of action in a neat fantasy parable of alternate universes and showbiz nostalgia. ▭

Dennis Hopper *H Phillip Lovecraft* • Penelope Ann Miller *Kim Hudson* • Eric Bogosian *Senator Larson Crockett* • Sheryl Lee Ralph *Hypolita Kropotkin* • Julian Sands *Finn Macha* ■ *Dir* Paul Schrader • *Scr* Joseph Dougherty

Witchboard ★ 15

Supernatural horror
1987 · US · Colour · 93mins

On its initial release the first entry in the *Witchboard* series received a surprising amount of critical acclaim and turnout at the box office. Viewers today will wonder why, seeing that it is an incredibly slow so-called horror movie, with very little material belonging to that genre. A group of young people play around with a Ouija board at a party, indirectly leading to an evil spirit possessing Tawny Kitaen. This is bad news for those around her as they get killed off one by one. Technically poor, with cameraman shadows clearly seen and special effects of the quality and scale found in high school productions, the worst part of the entire ordeal is that hardly anything (horrible or otherwise) happens. ▭

Todd Allen *Jim Morar* • Tawny Kitaen *Linda Brewster* • Stephen Nichols *Brandon Sinclair* • Kathleen Wilhoite *Zarabeth* • Burke Byrnes *Lieutenant Dewhurst* ■ *Dir/Scr* Kevin S Tenney

Witchboard 2: The Devil's Doorway ★ 15

Horror   1993 · US · Colour · 94mins

Artist Ami Dolenz moves into a loft apartment, finds the enchanted Ouija board from the original movie, and, after conjuring up Julie Michaels, thinks she's helping a murder victim find spiritual rest. Big mistake. Instead, she's soon enveloping her friends in gory deaths and creepy nightmares. Director Kevin S Tenney clearly gears this depressing demonic dabble around too many false scares. The overall effect is one of annoyance not empathy with the supernatural mayhem. Complete with a possessed car, a Jewish occultist and a hippy landlady – and still it's boring! ▭

Ami Dolenz *Paige Benedict* • Timothy Gibbs *Mitch* • Laraine Newman *Elaine* • John Gatins *Russell* • Julie Michaels *Susan* ■ *Dir/Scr* Kevin S Tenney

Witchboard – The Possession ★ 18

Horror   1995 · US · Colour · 89mins

Compared with the first entry in this series, this third instalment is a great improvement, but still isn't worth a look. The only connection with the previous entries is the use of an Ouija board, which unemployed stockbroker David Nerman uses to try and make some quick cash. Instead, a demonic spirit traps Nerman's spirit in a mirror, then possesses his body in order to have fun with his wife. The series now has generally good production values, plus some fairly impressive special-effect sequences, but is still stuck with an extremely slow and uneventful script. ▭

David Nerman *Brian* • Locky Lambert *Julie* • Cedric Smith *Francis Redmund* • Donna Sarrasin *Lisa* ■ *Dir* Peter Svatek • *Scr* Kevin S Tenney, from a story by John Erzine

Witchcraft ★★ 18

Horror   1988 · US · Colour · 85mins

New mother Anat Topol-Barzilai reluctantly moves in with her strange mother-in-law and starts having demonic visions of witch-burnings and decapitations. Slow-moving occult nonsense grafting the *Nightmare on Elm Street* dreams-within-false-dreams concept into a basic *Rosemary's Baby* scenario. Plenty of bogus scares and very little sense keep this half-hearted horror dud grounded. ▭ *DVD*

Anat Topol-Barzilai *Grace* • Gary Sloan *John* • Mary Shelley *Elizabeth* • Alexander Kirkwood *Priest* ■ *Dir* Robert Spera • *Scr* Jody Savin

Witchcraft ★

Horror   1989 · It · Colour · 95mins

German actress Hildegarde Knef came out of retirement to play a witch holding demonic sway over a New England island in this nasty slice of Italian exploitation. Why she bothered is anyone's guess! Stranded visitors fall foul to *Omen*-style murders thanks to her black magic and suffer assorted lip-smacking fates including crucifixion, grotesque rape, mouth-stitching and being hung upside down in a fireplace. Photographer David Hasselhoff, reporter Catherine Hickland

(Hasselhoff's then wife), pregnant Linda Blair and her mother, jazz singer Annie Ross, try to fend off their destiny – and the terrible script – but fail miserably on every count. How a movie with so much graphic unpleasantness can still be boring is a question you will still be asking way after the end credits have rolled. ▭

Linda Blair *Jane Brooks* • David Hasselhoff *Gary* • Hildegarde Knef *Lady in Black* • Annie Ross *Rose Brooks* • Catherine Hickland *Linda Sullivan* • Leslie Cummings *Leslie* ■ *Dir* Fabrizio Laurenti • *Scr* Danielle Stroppa

The Witches ★★★

Horror   1966 · UK · Colour · 89mins

Hollywood stars never faded, they simply made films in Britain. That used to be the case for, among others, Joan Fontaine, who here reprises her "frightened lady" turn, first seen in *Rebecca*, as the cursed schoolmistress discovering devil worship in rural parts. It's a Hammer that never quite makes contact with your nerves, even though it's written by Nigel Kneale, who created *Quatermass*. At least director Cyril Frankel treats it as though it mattered, but for Fontaine it signalled her big screen career's end.

Joan Fontaine *Gwen Mayfield* • Kay Walsh *Stephanie Bax* • Alec McCowen *Alan Bax* • Ann Bell *Sally* • Ingrid Brett *Linda* • John Collin *Dowsett* • Michele Dotrice *Valerie* • Gwen Ffrangcon-Davies *Granny Rigg* • Duncan Lamont *Bob Curd* • Leonard Rossiter *Dr Wallis* ■ *Dir* Cyril Frankel • *Scr* Nigel Kneale, from the novel *The Devil's Own* by Peter Curtis

The Witches ★★★ PG

Fantasy adventure
1989 · UK · Colour · 87mins

Roald Dahl's ruthless story about a little boy on a seaside holiday who discovers a witches' convention plotting to annihilate children is touched with black magic by director Nicolas Roeg. As chief witch, Anjelica Huston gets a gruesome Jim Henson's Creature Shop makeover, while Mai Zetterling is transformed into lavender and old lace as the boy's granny. The film's panic-attack when the boy is turned into a mouse is as valid a piece of fairy tale as you could wish. Children should hold their parents' hands through some of it – grown-ups are notoriously nervous. ▭

Anjelica Huston *Miss Ernst/Grand High Witch* • Mai Zetterling *Helga* • Bill Paterson *Mr Jenkins* • Brenda Blethyn *Mrs Jenkins* • Rowan Atkinson *Mr Stringer* • Jasen Fisher *Luke* • Charlie Potter *Bruno Jenkins* • Jane Horrocks *Miss Irvine* ■ *Dir* Nicolas Roeg • *Scr* Allan Scott, from the novel by Roald Dah

Witches' Brew ★★ 15

Fantasy comedy   1979 · US · Colour · 93mins

File under "Bad Weird Oddity One Ought to See". Originally made in 1978 as *Which Witch is Which?*, but not released until 1985 with additional footage, this uncredited version of Fritz Leiber Jr's classic novel *Conjure Wife* (already filmed in 1944 as *Weird Woman* and in 1961 as *Night of the Eagle*) resembles a lesser episode of the TV sitcom *Bewitched*. The story concerns Professor Richard Benjamin forcing his witch wife Teri Garr to forsake her spell-casting ways, thus

allowing super-witch Lana Turner to meddle in their lives. Sadly neither the gags nor the special effects are up to much and the result is hocus-pocus with a lack of focus. ▭

Richard Benjamin *Joshua Lightman* • Teri Garr *Margaret Lightman* • Lana Turner *Vivian Cross* • Kathryn Leigh Scott *Susan Carey* • James Winker *Linus Cross* • Bill Sorrels *Nick Carey* • Kelly Jean Peters *Linda Reynolds* • Jordan Charney *Charlie Reynolds* ■ *Dir* Richard Shorr • *Scr* Syd Dutton, Richard Shorr, from the novel

The Witches of Eastwick ★★★★ 18

Comedy drama   1987 · US · Colour · 113mins

A raunchy metaphor for the battle between the sexes, *Mad Max* director George Miller's sauce-and-sorcery comedy soars with inspired lunacy as three romance-starved suburban women dabble in off-white magic for some offbeat chandelier swinging. While Jack Nicholson dominates this spellbinding adaptation of John Updike's ironic bestseller as the horny little devil, the luminous female talent (Cher, Susan Sarandon and Michelle Pfeiffer) almost matches him in a charming sensual fantasy, slightly overloaded with needless special effects. Contains swearing, sexual references, violence. ▭ *DVD*

Jack Nicholson *Daryl Van Horne* • Cher *Alexandra Medford* • Susan Sarandon *Jane Spofford* • Michelle Pfeiffer *Sukie Ridgemont* • Veronica Cartwright *Felicia Alden* • Richard Jenkins *Clyde Alden* • Keith Jochim *Walter Neff* • Carel Struycken *Fidel* • Helen Biddie *Mrs Biddie* ■ *Dir* George Miller • *Scr* Michael Cristofer, from the novel by John Updike

Witchfinder General ★★★★★ 18

Horror   1968 · UK · Colour · 82mins

Condemned on first release as extremely bloody and sadistic, Michael Reeves's penetrating chronicle of the social evils at large during the English Civil War is now an acknowledged horror classic. Vincent Price plays it straight for once as the cynical religious maniac instigating torture and degradation for pleasure and profit in an intense study of pathological cruelty. With non-gratuitous violent imagery crucial to the brutal history lesson, Reeves's final work (he died of an overdose shortly after) is a thematically fascinating and gruesomely incisive look at the lust for and abuse of power. ▭

Vincent Price *Matthew Hopkins* • Ian Ogilvy *Richard Marshall* • Rupert Davies *John Lowes* • Hilary Dwyer *Sara* • Patrick Wymark *Oliver Cromwell* • Wilfrid Brambell *Master Coach* • Nicky Henson *Trooper Swallow* ■ *Dir* Michael Reeves • *Scr* Michael Reeves, Tom Baker, Louis M Heyward, from the novel by Ronald Bassett

The Witch's Daughter ★★★

Supernatural mystery
1996 · US · Colour · 105mins

In a spooky chiller, reminiscent in tone and setting of *The Wicker Man*, a grieving widow is branded a witch for her peculiarities by the superstitious inhabitants of a small Scottish island. When the woman's suicide coincides with the mysterious disappearance of

the lobsters from which they make their living, the islanders reckon they've been cursed, and ostracise her orphan daughter. With a creepy plot, strong performances – from Patrick Bergin and Peter Firth – and vivid use of remote locations, this is an intriguing adaptation of the Nina Bawden novel.

Patrick Bergin *Mr Smith* • Peter Firth *Mr Jones* • Susan Gilmore *Annie* • Richard Claxton *Tim* • Sammy Glenn *Perdita* • Simone Lahbib *Zelda* ■ *Dir* Alan MacMillan • *Scr* Simon Booker, from the novel by Nina Bawden

With a Song in My Heart ★★★★ U

Musical biographical drama
1952 · US · Colour · 116mins

Some of the finest song standards ever written turn up in this fine Technicolor wallow, purportedly the true, tragic (but inspiring) life story of singer Jane Froman who rose from radio commercials to universal acclaim in the thirties, but was then badly injured in a wartime plane crash. It's Froman's voice on the soundtrack, and lip-synching the vocals with credible conviction is Susan Hayward, here displaying character-steel as only she can, earning a best actress Oscar nomination in the process. An Oscar did go to brilliant musical director Alfred Newman, and mention should also be made of the notable star-making performance from a very young Robert Wagner as a shell-shocked soldier. An immensely popular movie, finely performed and intelligently crafted, and typical of the 20th Century-Fox period biopic at its professional best.

Susan Hayward *Jane Froman* • Rory Calhoun *John Burns* • David Wayne *Don Ross* • Thelma Ritter *Clancy* • Robert Wagner *GI Paratrooper* • Helen Westcott *Jennifer March* • Una Merkel *Sister Marie* ■ *Dir* Walter Lang • *Scr* Lamar Trotti

With a Vengeance ★★15

Thriller 1992 · US · Colour · 93mins

Melissa Gilbert will probably never shake off the *Little House on the Prairie* tag, and using her married name in this grown-up but made-for-TV thriller does little to change things. She plays a woman stricken with amnesia who makes a new start as a nanny, but is drawn back into uncovering the truth behind her past life. The presence of other familiar TV faces such as Jack Scalia and Michael Gross hardly helps, doing little to conceal the cosy nature of the project and director Michael Switzer's routine handling.

Melissa Gilbert-Brinkman [Melissa Gilbert] *Gena King* • Jack Scalia *Mike Barcetti* • Michael Gross *Frank Tanner* • Matthew Lawrence *Phillip* • Roger Aaron Brown *Arnold* • John Cullum *Fred Mitchell* • Robert Donner *Detective Max Borovey* ■ *Dir* Michael Switzer • *Scr* Renee Schonfeld Longstreet

With Harmful Intent ★★★15

Psychological thriller
1993 · US · Colour · 92mins

Having been the perfect police captain in *Hill Street Blues*, Daniel J Travanti reveals a darker side in this hard-hitting (if unlikely) TV movie, playing a

rogue cop who helps a concerned mother protect her son from a hit-and-run stalker. While not exactly Charles Bronson, Travanti gives a good impression of a loose cannon, who seems more intent on mayhem than upholding the law. Joan Van Ark also does well as the mom resorting to desperate measures after the local force let her down. The conclusion is foregone, but director Richard Friedman keeps things pretty tense.

Joan Van Ark *Cinnie Merritt* • Daniel J Travanti *Drum* • Rick Springfield *Paul* • Christopher Noth *Dr Ferris* • Michael Patrick Carter *James* ■ *Dir* Richard Friedman • *Scr* Adam Greenman, from the novel *Someone's Watching* by Judith Kelman

With Honors ★★PG

Comedy drama 1994 · US · Colour · 96mins

You remember how, in *The Piano*, Harvey Keitel returned Holly Hunter's beloved instrument to her one key at a time? Well, the same premise kickstarts this patchy campus comedy, as homeless Joe Pesci trades the pages of student Brendan Fraser's dissertation for food. The problem here is predictability. We know Pesci can't just be any old tramp, and soon the wit and wisdom come tumbling out for the benefit of Fraser and his undeserving room-mates. It's *My Man Godfrey* all over again, with Pesci (in the David Niven role) trotting out his familiar tricks and wiping the floor with his juvenile co-stars.

Joe Pesci *Simon Wilder* • Brendan Fraser *Monty Kessler* • Moira Kelly *Courtney Blumenthal* • Patrick Dempsey *Everett Calloway* • Josh Hamilton *Jeff Hawkes* • Gore Vidal *Professor Philip Hayes* ■ *Dir* Alek Keshishian • *Scr* William Mastrosimone

With Hostile Intent ★★15

Drama 1993 · US · Colour · 88mins

Melissa Gilbert and Mel Harris team up in this TV movie based on a true story as California cops subjected to sexual harassment after their relationships with fellow officers turn sour. As verbal abuse gives way to physical danger, the pair seek the assistance of a crusading lawyer to expose the rampant sexism within the Long Beach Police Department. From start to finish, it's next to impossible to work out where truth ends and dramatic sensationalism begins. If it's subtlety and balanced argument you're looking for, this hugely manipulative movie isn't the place to find it.

Melissa Gilbert *Miranda Berkley* • Mel Harris *Kathy Arnold* • Peter Onorati *Harry McCarthy* • Cotter Smith *Rob Arnold* • Holland Taylor *Lois Baxter* • Daniel Von Bargen *Ted Campbell* • Kevin Corrigan *Arnie Dole* ■ *Dir* Paul Schneider • *Scr* Marjorie David, Alison Cross

With Intent to Kill ★★★

Thriller 1984 · US · Colour · 96mins

An exemplary made-for-television thriller notable also for providing an early film role for future Oscar-winner Holly Hunter. However, it is old hand Karl Malden who steals the show in this story of a young man, released after four years in a mental hospital for the murder of his girlfriend, who arrives home to find her father eager for

revenge. There's solid support from the likes of Shirley Knight, Paul Sorvino and William Devane and it is intelligently scripted and directed by Mike Robe.

Karl Malden *Tom Nolen* • Paul Sorvino *Doyle Reinecker* • Shirley Knight *Edna Reinecker* • Timothy Patrick Murphy *Drew Lanscott* • Catherine Mary Stewart *Lisa Nolen* • Holly Hunter *Wynn Nolen* ■ *Dir/Scr* Mike Robe

With or Without You ★★★18

Romantic comedy
1999 · UK · Colour · 87mins

Originally titled *Old New Borrowed Blue*, this low-key, Belfast-based drama from director Michael Winterbottom has Dervla Kirwan and Christopher Eccleston as a young couple desperate to start a family. When an old French pen pal of hers (Yvan Attal) turns up out of the blue, the tension that has been building between them threatens to capsize their marriage. Winterbottom's perceptive study of the power plays between husband and wife is definitely worth a watch. Writer John Forte does not shy away from Ulster's age-old sectarian divisions, but neither does he let them interfere with the refreshing seam of optimism that runs through this gentle gem. **DVD**

Christopher Eccleston *Vincent Boyd* • Dervla Kirwan *Rosie Boyd* • Yvan Attal *Benoit* • Julie Graham *Cathy* • Alun Armstrong *Sammy* • Lloyd Hutchinson *Neil* • Michael Liebman *Brian* • Doon Mackichan *Deidre* • Gordon Kennedy *Ormonde* • Fionnula Flanagan *Irene* ■ *Dir* Michael Winterbottom • *Scr* John Forte

With Savage Intent ★★★15

Drama based on a true story
1992 · US · Colour · 93mins

Also known as *With Murder in Mind*, this story stars Elizabeth Montgomery and her real-life husband Robert Foxworth. It tells the tale of a New York estate agent who is shot by a client as she shows him around a property. It could be run-of-the-mill TV fare, but the performances of the cast – the leads plus Maureen O'Sullivan and Howard E Rollins Jr – help it become an interesting and compelling drama.

Elizabeth Montgomery *Gayle Wolfer* • Robert Foxworth *Bob Sprague* • Howard E Rollins Jr *Samuel Carver/Brian Furman* • Maureen O'Sullivan *Aunt Mildred* • Lee Richardson *John Condon* ■ *Dir* Michael Tuchner • *Scr* Daniel Freudenberger

With Six You Get Eggroll ★★U

Comedy 1968 · US · Colour · 94mins

Doris Day's last movie so far is this amiable trifle, in which she plays a widow with three sons who marries convenient widower Brian Keith, father of teenage daughter Barbara Hershey, hence the arch title. The offspring object to the relationship, and mileage is gained from episodes like Doris driving off in a trailer leaving Keith in his underwear by the roadside. Presciently, Doris's best scenes are opposite a dog called Lord Nelson. There's a tired sixties gloss to the whole thing, and it's easy to see why Doris called it a Day.

Doris Day *Abby McClure* • Brian Keith *Jake Iverson* • Pat Carroll *Maxine Scott* • Barbara Hershey *Stacey Iverson* • George Carlin *Herbie Fleck* • Alice Ghostley *Housekeeper* • John Findlater *Flip McClure* • Jimmy Bracken *Mitch McClure* • Richard Steele *Jason McClure* ■ *Dir* Howard Morris • *Scr* Gwen Bagni, Paul Dubov, Harvey Bullock, RS Allen, from a story by Gwen Bagni, Paul Dubov

Within the Rock ★★★18

Science-fiction 1995 · US · Colour · 84mins

Mix *Deep Impact* with *Alien* and the result is this surprisingly effective science-fiction shocker. Xander Berkeley and Caroline Barclay head the team mounting a desperate mission to destroy a moon that's on a collision course with Earth, only to find a seemingly dead monster near its core. Naturally, before you can say "Ridley Scott", they find themselves in a life-or-death battle with the flesh-craving beast. A creature feature providing rock solid entertainment in a variety of cleverly winning ways. Contains swearing and violence.

Xander Berkeley *Ryan* • Bradford Tatum *Cody* • Brian Krause *Luke* • Caroline Barclay *Dr Dana Shaw* • Calvin Levels *Banton* • Michael Zelniker *Archer* • Duane Whitaker *Potter* • Barbara Patrick *"Nuke-em"* ■ *Dir/Scr* Gary J Tunnicliffe

Withnail & I ★★★★15

Cult black comedy
1986 · UK · Colour · 102mins

A great little film that launched the career of Richard E Grant and has since developed into a cult classic. Those born before 1950 will regard this tale of two dissolute sixties hippies, Grant and Paul McGann, with unbridled horror. There are empty bottles and dirty underwear everywhere, along with half-finished joints and fag ends stubbed out in congealing boiled eggs. But this is in fact a glorious rites of passage movie, as the lads decamp to a cottage in the Lakes where they struggle to survive the weather and a lecherous Uncle Monty. Written and directed by Bruce Robinson, based on his own Camden Town experiences. Contains swearing and drug abuse.

Richard E Grant *Withnail* • Paul McGann *...and I* • Richard Griffiths *Monty* • Ralph Brown *Danny* • Michael Elphick *Jake* • Daragh O'Malley *Irishman* • Michael Wardle *Isaac Parkin* • Una Brandon-Jones *Mrs Parkin* • Noel Johnson *General* ■ *Dir/Scr* Bruce Robinson

Without a Clue ★★★PG

Comedy mystery
1988 · UK · Colour · 101mins

The real brains behind Sherlock Holmes belonged to Dr Watson, according to this hit-and-miss, hammy Baker Street farce; in fact, the shy doctor invented the fictitious sleuth as a front for his own brilliant crime detection skills. As Holmes captured the public's imagination, Watson was forced to hire actor Reginald Kincaid to impersonate him. How they fare while investigating a plot to undermine the British Empire with forged five pound notes is the comedy basis for this mismatched buddy movie. Good fun despite the patchy laughs, with Ben Kingsley's Watson wiping the floor with Michael Caine's Holmes.

Michael Caine *Sherlock Holmes/Reginald Kincaid* • Ben Kingsley *Dr John Watson* • Jeffrey Jones *Inspector Lestrade* • Lysette Anthony *Leslie Giles* • Paul Freeman *Professor Moriarty* • Nigel Davenport *Lord Smithwick* • Pat Keen *Mrs Hudson* • Peter Cook *Greenhough* ■ *Dir* Thom Eberhardt • *Scr* Gary Murphy, Larry Strawther

Without a Trace ★★★ 15

Drama based on a true story
1983 · US · Colour · 115mins

An impressive drama, loosely based on a true event, which sadly falls down thanks to a rather ludicrous conclusion. Kate Nelligan is the mother who continues to believe her six-year-old son will return after he vanishes, though everyone around her loses faith. Nelligan is very watchable as the overwrought mother, while Judd Hirsch and stage and screen actress Stockard Channing both match her scene for scene. 🖵

Kate Nelligan *Susan Selky* • Judd Hirsch *Al Menetti* • David Dukes *Graham Selky* • Stockard Channing *Jocelyn Norris* • Jacqueline Brookes *Margaret Mayo* • Keith McDermott *Phillippe* • Kathleen Widdoes *Ms Hauser* ■ *Dir* Stanley R Jaffe • *Scr* Beth Gutcheon, from her novel *Still Missing*

Without Apparent Motive ★★★

Crime thriller 1972 · Fr · Colour · 100mins

Ed McBain's *Ten Plus One* provides the inspiration for this downbeat *film noir*, which stages its dark tale of murder in the brilliant Riviera sunshine. Combining hangdog cynicism with intuition and tenacity, Jean-Louis Trintignant's police inspector is the epitome of hard-boiled world-weariness, as he conducts an investigation into a series of seemingly motiveless killings, to which the only clue is a diary detailing the first victim's love affairs – one of which involved the cop's old flame. Reflecting Trintignant's growing dismay, director Philippe Labro reveals his hand with methodical thoroughness, but a touch of suspense might not have gone amiss. In French with English subtitles.

Jean-Louis Trintignant *Carella* • Dominique Sanda *Sandra* • Carla Gravina *Jocelyne* • Paul Crauchet *Palombo* • Sacha Distel *Julien* • Gilles Segal *Bozzo* • Laura Antonelli *Juliette* • Jean-Pierre Marielle *Perry Rupert-Foote* • Stéphane Audran *Hélène Vallee* ■ *Dir* Philippe Labro • *Scr* Philippe Labro, Jacques Lanzmann, from the novel *Ten Plus One* by Ed McBain [Evan Hunter]

Without Her Consent ★★★ 15

Drama based on a true story
1990 · US · Colour · 92mins

A superior TV movie that treats the much-debated question of date rape with complex subtlety. Based on the true story of a landmark case, and with a strong cast including Bebe Neuwirth and Melissa Gilbert, this emotionally stirring film manages to tackle the issue and give character depth without resorting to labelling people wholly good or evil. 🖵

Melissa Gilbert *Emily Briggs* • Scott Valentine *Jason Barnes* • Barry Tubb *Trey* • Bebe Neuwirth *Gloria* • Crystal Bernard ■ *Dir* Sandor Stern • *Scr* Ann Beckett

Without Limits ★★★ 15

Sports biography
1998 · US · Colour · 118mins

Co-produced by Tom Cruise, this is the tragic tale of American runner Steve Prefontaine, who came close to winning gold at the 1972 Munich Olympics, only to die in a car crash three years later. One suspects Cruise would have taken the role if he was ten years younger, but instead the honours go to the rather uninteresting Billy Crudup. It's Donald Sutherland who steals the show playing Prefontaine's coach Bill Bowerman, known for the running shoes he designed for his team and as the man who invented Nike trainers. Monica Potter gets the thankless task of playing the underwritten love interest, and she, like everyone else, is upstaged by the lovingly filmed athletic scenes, which successfully capture the unconventional qualities of Prefontaine's running. Contains some swearing. 🖵

Billy Crudup *Steve Prefontaine* • Donald Sutherland *Bill Bowerman* • Monica Potter *Mary Marckx* • Jeremy Sisto *Frank Shorter* • Matthew Lillard *Roscoe Devine* • Billy Burke *Kenny Moore* ■ *Dir* Robert Towne • *Scr* Robert Towne, Kenny Moore • *Producer* Paula Wagner, Tom Cruise

Without Love ★★★

Romantic comedy 1945 · US · BW · 110mins

Spencer Tracy and Katharine Hepburn survive the long arm of coincidence in Donald Ogden Stewart's screenplay (from a minor Philip Barry play), as well as the pedestrian direction of Harold S Bucquet, in this tale of a weary scientist who lodges himself and his work in the home of a woman who, under her cool exterior, longs for love. *Adam's Rib* it isn't, but the stars are on form, and there is added zest from Keenan Wynn and a wisecracking Lucille Ball.

Spencer Tracy *Pat Jamieson* • Katharine Hepburn *Jamie Rowan* • Lucille Ball *Kitty Trimble* • Keenan Wynn *Quentin Ladd* • Carl Esmond *Paul Carrell* • Patricia Morison *Edwina Collins* • Felix Bressart *Professor Grinza* • Emily Massey *Anna* • Gloria Grahame *Flower girl* ■ *Dir* Harold S Bucquet • *Scr* Donald Ogden Stewart, from the play by Philip Barry

Without Reservations ★★★ U

Comedy 1946 · US · BW · 102mins

A deft and under-rated Hollywood-on-Hollywood comedy, with the irresistible Claudette Colbert as a wacky author searching for a leading man to play the screen hero in the movie of her book. She settles on marine flier John Wayne and won't let him out of her sight. Director Mervyn LeRoy knows this territory well and calls on some personal friends to prop up the story: Cary Grant's surprise appearance is very funny, and keep your eyes open, too, for guest star Jack Benny. Froth, but expertly done. 🖵

Claudette Colbert *Christopher "Kit" Madden/Kit Klotch* • John Wayne *Captain Rusty Thomas* • Don DeFore *Lieut Dink Watson* • Anne Triola *Consuela "Connie" Callaghan* • Phil Brown *Soldier* • Frank Puglia *Ortega* • Thurston Hall *Baldwin* • Dona Drake *Dolores Ortega* • Charles Arnt *Salesman* • Miss Louella Parsons • Cary Grant • Jack Benny ■

Raymond Burr *Paul Gill* ■ *Dir* Mervyn LeRoy • *Scr* Andrew Solt, from the novel *Thanks, God, I'll Take It from Here* by Jane Allen, Mae Livingston

Without Warning ★★★

Thriller 1973 · Fr · Colour · 98mins

Bruno Gantillon has only made a handful of features in the last thirty years and his second is generally regarded as the most accomplished. It's certainly based on an intriguing premise, beginning with Maurice Ronet being hounded out of the police for prosecuting the drug-trafficking son of a senior officer. But Ronet is anything but an innocent victim, as Bruno Cremer is convinced he served under him as a mercenary in Indochina. Exploring the impossibility of escaping from one's past and the difficulty facing old colonialists in adapting to civilian life, this is a dark thriller full of disturbing insights into the power-broking process. French dialogue dubbed into English.

Maurice Ronet *Maury* • Mario Adorf *Capra* • Bruno Cremer *Donetti* • Anny Duperey *Cora* • Mario Pisu *Louvai* • Marina Malfatti *Isabelle* • *Dir/Scr* Bruno Gantillon

Without Warning ★

Horror 1980 · US · Colour · 96mins

An absolute turkey from the director of *Satan's Cheerleaders* is further derailed by the outrageous ham acting from two of its all-tarnished-star cast, Jack Palance and Martin Landau. An alien lands in a remote rural area and starts flinging pizza-shaped, flesh-sucking parasites around in order to decorate his spaceship with human trophies gleaned from hapless campers and redneck locals. Greydon Clark's hopeless direction wastes every opportunity for even the mildest gross-out.

Jack Palance *Taylor* • Martin Landau *Fred* • Tarah Nutter *Sandy* • Christopher S Nelson *Greg* • Cameron Mitchell *Hunter* • Neville Brand *Leo* • Sue Ann Langdon [Sue Ane Langdon] *Aggie* ■ *Dir* Greydon Clark • *Scr* Lyn Freeman, Daniel Grodnik, Ben Nett, Steve Mathis

Without Warning ★★★

Science-fiction drama 1994 · US · Colour

How would television news deal with the breaking story of huge asteroid fragments crashing into different parts of the world? This well-executed salute to Orson Welles's landmark *War of the Worlds* radio broadcast of the thirties is a fine example of TV imitating itself for potent dramatic effect. Though Brits will miss the extra *frisson* provided by using real-life US newsreader Sander Vanocur to unfold the events, this insightful survey holds the attention and transforms into a fascinating offbeat genre item with an amazing climax. The outcome was considered so real in America that thousands of panicked viewers called in for confirmation it was actually fake.

Sander Vanocur • Jane Kaczmarek *Doctor Caroline Jaffe* • Bree Walker Lampley • Ernie Anastos • Warren Olney • Sandy Hill ■ *Dir* Robert Iscove • *Scr* Peter Lance, Waon Greene, Jeremy Thorn

Without Warning: Terror in the Towers ★★ 15

Drama based on a true story
1993 · US · Colour · 92mins

This is a predictable but involving TV movie, dramatising the heroic efforts and individual crises surrounding the 1993 terrorist bombing of New York City's World Trade Center. The accounts include two grade school teachers and their class stuck in a suspended elevator, an office worker who carries a resentful paraplegic down 87 flights, and a fireman trapped in a burning basement. The large cast includes George Clooney and Fran Drescher; thanks to their solid performances, along with effective special effects, this delivers enough melodrama to be an enjoyable, reasonably absorbing entertainment. 🖵

George Clooney *Kevin Shea* • Scott Plank *Gary Geidel* • John Karlen *Jack McAllister* • James Avery *Fred Ferby* • Susan Ruttan *Anne Marie Tesoriero* • Fran Drescher *Rosemarie Russo* ■ *Dir* Alan J Levi • *Scr* Stephen Downing, Duane Poole

Without Warning: the James Brady Story ★★★★

Drama based on a true story
1991 · US · Colour

James Brady was the Presidential press secretary shot in the head during John Hinckley's assassination attempt on Ronald Reagan in 1981. The film is a deeply moving tribute to the way that Brady and his wife (Joan Allen) fought his disabilities and campaigned for tighter gun control – the so-called Brady Bill. Produced by David Puttnam for American cable TV, it is notable for a truly astonishing performance by Beau Bridges, and for its literate and insightful final script by Robert Bolt, an Oscar winner for *Doctor Zhivago* and *A Man for All Seasons* who was himself disabled by a stroke in 1979. Bolt, a staunch left-winger, never makes cheap jokes about Reagan as President; instead, Reagan is simply a caring old gentleman, concerned for his colleague. Contains swearing.

Beau Bridges *James Brady* • Joan Allen *Sarah Brady* • David Strathairn *Dr Kobrine* • Christopher Bell *Scotty* • Christine Healy *Ruth* • Timothy Landfield *Bob* • Bryan Clark *Ronald Reagan* • Susan Brown *Nancy Reagan* • Steven Flynn *John W Hinckley Jr* • Robert Strane *Baxter* ■ *Dir* Michael Toshiyuki Uno • *Scr* Robert Bolt, from the book *Thumbs Up: the Life and Courageous Comeback of White House Press Secretary Jim Brady* by Mollie Dickenson

Without *You* I'm Nothing ★★★ 15

Comedy 1990 · US · Colour · 85mins

A filmed record of bisexual comedienne Sandra Bernhard's Off-Broadway show features her on full-throttle assault. As uncomfortably mean-spirited as she is funny, Bernhard makes mincemeat of such pop icons as Diana Ross, Barbra Streisand, Andy Warhol and Prince and also explores Jewish envy, her attraction to black culture and decries the male gender. She also gives new meaning to the Laura Nyro song *I Never Meant to Hurt You* and Hank Williams's *I'm So Lonesome I Could*

Cry. Director John Boskovich cuts from Bernhard's edgy routines to shocked audience members in a successful attempt to conjure up a live atmosphere where the sense of flirtatious danger makes her brand of abrasive comedy work without the safety net of camp or kitsch. Hilarious, offensive, ugly and true. ▣

Sandra Bernhard • John Doe • Steve Antin • Lu Leonard *Sandra's manager* • Cynthia Bailey *Roxanne* • Denise Vlasis *Shoshanna* • Ken Foree *Emcee* ■ *Dir* John Boskovich • *Scr* Sandra Bernhard, John Boskovich

Witness ★★★★★15
Romantic thriller
1985 · US · Colour · 107mins

Witness begins with a murder at a city railway station. The killing is witnessed by a small boy, Lukas Haas, who is a member of the Amish community, a religious sect living in rural Pennsylvania who eschew as much of modern life – notably machinery – as they can. Pursued by the bad guys, the boy and his widowed mother (Kelly McGillis) are protected by a cop (Harrison Ford), who takes them back to their village and awaits the killers' arrival, just as Gary Cooper did in *High Noon.* Directed by Australian Peter Weir, *Witness* is partly a love story and partly a thriller, but mainly a study of cultural collision – it's as if the world of *Dirty Harry* had suddenly stumbled into a canvas by Brueghel. The performances are immaculate, with Ford shining in his first serious dramatic role after his action escapades as Han Solo and Indiana Jones. McGillis is perfectly cast, the camera adoring her Nordic beauty beneath her bonnet, and Haas looks suitably wide-eyed and innocent. Yet it's Weir's delicacy of touch that impresses the most. He juggles the various elements of the story and makes the violence seem even more shocking when played out on the fields of Amish denial. Contains swearing and brief nudity. ▣

Harrison Ford *John Book* • Kelly McGillis *Rachel Lapp* • Josef Sommer *Deputy Commissioner Schaeffer* • Lukas Haas *Samuel Lapp* • Jan Rubes *Eli Lapp* • Alexander Godunov *Daniel Hochleitner* • Danny Glover *McFee* • Brent Jennings *Carter* • Patti LuPone *Elaine* ■ *Dir* Peter Weir • *Scr* Earl W Wallace, William Kelley, from a story by Kelley, Earl W Wallace, Pamela Wallace • *Cinematographer* John Seale • *Music* Maurice Jarre

Witness for the Prosecution ★★★★★U
Courtroom drama 1957 · US · BW · 111mins

Billy Wilder's gleefully enjoyable film version of Agatha Christie's play with Tyrone Power (in his last completed role) on trial for murder and Marlene Dietrich as his wife testifying against him. The whole plot is an intricate, slightly leaky bag of tricks, with a trademark "surprise" ending. But to conceal the cracks, Wilder throws up a variety of smokescreens and provides the broadest stage imaginable for Charles Laughton's barrister – a performance of epic extravagance, invention and downright hamminess. Laughton's little foibles – the trick with the monocle, the flask of cocoa, his rudeness to his nurse (a character

invented by Wilder and his co-writers and played to perfection by Laughton's real-life wife, Elsa Lanchester) – take you away from the plot and into the mind of this wily operator. They really don't make actors like him anymore, either. The producers refused to allow Dietrich to be nominated for an Oscar because a vital plot detail would have to be betrayed in her citation. ▣

Tyrone Power *Leonard Stephen Vole* • Marlene Dietrich *Christine Vole* • Charles Laughton *Sir Wilfrid Robarts* • Elsa Lanchester *Miss Plimsoll* • John Williams *Brogan-Moore* • Henry Daniell *Mayhew* • Ian Wolfe *Carter* • Una O'Connor *Janet MacKenzie* • Torin Thatcher *Mr Meyers* • Francis Compton *Judge* ■ *Dir* Billy Wilder • *Scr* Billy Wilder, Harry Kurnitz, Larry Marcus, from the play by Agatha Christie • *Art Director* Alexandre Trauner

Witness for the Prosecution ★★★PG
Courtroom drama 1982 · US · Colour · 97mins

Although not the Billy Wilder version, this TV movie of Agatha Christie's audacious courtroom whodunit isn't bad, either. When it came to eccentric characterisations, Ralph Richardson could match Laughton twitch for twitch and he is wonderful as barrister Sir Wilfred Robarts, ably supported by Deborah Kerr (making her TV movie debut) as his fussy nurse. But it's Diana Rigg whom you'll be raving about afterwards, out-Dietriching Marlene with a wicked performance that surely ranks among her best. ▣

Ralph Richardson *Sir Wilfred Robarts* • Deborah Kerr *Miss Plimsoll* • Beau Bridges *Leonard Vole* • Donald Pleasence *Mr Myers* • Wendy Hiller *Janet MacKenzie* • Diana Rigg *Christine Vole* • David Langton *Mayhew* • Richard Vernon *Brogan Moore* • Peter Sallis *Carter* • Frank Mills *Chief Inspector Hearne* ■ *Dir* Alan Gibson • *Scr* John Gay, Lawrence B Marcus (adaptation), from the film by Billy Wilder, Harry Kurnitz, from the play by Agatha Christie

Witness in the Dark ★★U
Crime 1959 · UK · BW · 62mins

Coming between *Bachelor of Hearts* and *Village of the Damned,* this is one of Wolf Rilla's lesser efforts. However, he conjures up a pleasing sense of menace that anticipates *Wait until Dark* as he subjects blind telephonist Patricia Dainton to the murderous machinations of a prowler. As so often in thrillers of this kind, much depends on contrivance and the script might have concealed its hand with a little more artfulness. But Dainton's performance is superior to that in the majority of British Bs, even though she is never as convincingly vulnerable as Audrey Hepburn in Terence Young's film.

Patricia Dainton *Jane Pringle* • Conrad Phillips *Inspector Coates* • Madge Ryan *Mrs Finch* • Nigel Green *Intruder* • Enid Lorimer *Mrs Temple* • Richard O'Sullivan *Don Theobold* ■ *Dir* Wolf Rilla • *Scr* Leigh Vance, John Lemont

Witness in the War Zone ★★★15
Political drama
1986 · UK/W Ger/Is · Colour · 99mins

This political drama stars Christopher Walken as an American reporter

covering the war in Lebanon. The excellent Walken can play a cynical newshound as well as anyone, but those hoping for a Lebanese equivalent of Oliver Stone's *Salvador* will be disappointed. The plot starts to unravel when Walken falls for nurse Marita Marschall and finds himself making news instead of simply covering it. Tighter direction would have heightened the suspense. Contains violence, swearing and nudity.

Christopher Walken *Don Stevens* • Marita Marschall *Linda Larson* • Hywel Bennett *Mike Jessop* • Arnon Zadok *Hamdi Abu-Yussuf* • Amos Lavie *Yessin Abu-Riadd* • Etti Ankri *Samira* • Martin Umbach *Bernard* ■ *Dir* Nathanial Gutman • *Scr* Hanan Peled

Witness to Murder ★★★
Crime thriller 1954 · US · BW · 81mins

Barbara Stanwyck is the unfortunate witness who sees George Sanders murdering a girl in the apartment across the way. But, since he cannily disposes of the corpse and all the evidence, detective Gary Merrill simply doesn't believe her. A run-of-the-mill script and a plot idea as old as the hills is turned into a gripping little thriller, thanks to the all-stops-out performances and direction by Roy Rowland. He milks the material for every possible element of nail-biting tension as silky ex-Nazi Sanders closes in on a terrified Stanwyck (doing a turn similar to her performance in *Sorry, Wrong Number*).

Barbara Stanwyck *Cheryl Draper* • George Sanders *Albert Richter* • Gary Merrill *Lawrence Mathews* • Jesse White *Eddie Vincent* • Harry Shannon *Captain Donnelly* • Claire Carleton *The Blonde* • Lewis Martin *Psychiatrist* ■ *Dir* Roy Rowland • *Scr* Chester Erskine

Witness to the Execution ★★★15
Satirical drama 1994 · US · Colour · 88mins

In this tale of pay-per-view shenanigans, it's 1999 and the Tycom network has bought the rights to an execution to boost its ratings. But how long is it before executive Sean Young begins to suspect that Timothy Daly is innocent? Not long at all, actually, and from the moment of her discovery the satire is sidelined by the need for justice to be done. Rather a waste of a promising premise, though the ending is surprisingly bleak. ▣

Sean Young *Jessica Traynor* • Timothy Daly *Dennis Casterline* • Len Cariou *Jake Tyler* • George Newburn *Philip* • Alan Fudge *Wallace Sternberg* • Dee Wallace Stone *Emily Dawson* ■ *Dir* Tommy Lee Wallace • *Scr* Thomas Baum, from a story by Thomas Baum, Keith Pierce, Priscilla Prestwidge

Wittgenstein ★★15
Biographical drama
1993 · UK · Colour · 69mins

With his health and eyesight failing from Aids-related complications, avant-garde director Derek Jarman somehow managed to shoot this lucid and glowingly vibrant portrait of the tormented 20th-century gay philosopher Ludwig Wittgenstein on a minuscule budget in two weeks. Karl Johnson (Ariel in Jarman's *The Tempest*) plays the man searching for

intellectual self-development, while struggling with alienation because of his sexual preferences, in a starkly realised series of bleakly amusing and acid-coloured vignettes. One of Jarman's best, although still of a typically rarefied nature. ▣

Karl Johnson *Ludwig Wittgenstein* • Tilda Swinton *Lady Morrell* • Michael Gough *Bertrand Russell* • John Quentin *John Maynard Keynes* • Clancy Chassay *Young Ludwig* • Kevin Collins *Johnny* • Jill Balcon *Leopoldine Wittgenstein* • Sally Dexter *Hermine Wittgenstein* • Nabil Shaban *Martian* ■ *Dir* Derek Jarman • *Scr* Derek Jarman, Terry Eagleton, Ken Butler

Wives and Lovers ★★
Comedy 1963 · US · BW · 103mins

A domestic comedy-drama about the pitfalls of the American dream, directed by a graduate of the hit television comedy *The Dick Van Dyke Show.* There's also more than a touch of *The Seven Year Itch* to the tale about a struggling New York writer who suddenly hits the big time, moves to Connecticut and starts to mix with the rich and famous, leaving his marriage to crumble into pieces. As a soap opera it has the requisite gloss, emotional highs and lows and improbable Hollywood ending. It also has an anaemic performance by Van Johnson and a scene-stealing one from Shelley Winters as the sexy divorcee who becomes Johnson's neighbour.

Janet Leigh *Bertie Austin* • Van Johnson *Bill Austin* • Shelley Winters *Fran Cabrell* • Martha Hyer *Lucinda Ford* • Ray Walston *Wylie Driberg* • Jeremy Slate *Gar Aldrich* • Claire Wilcox *Julie Austin* • Lee Patrick *Mrs Swanson* ■ *Dir* John Rich • *Scr* Edward Anhalt, from the play *The First Wife* by Jay Presson Allen

Wives under Suspicion ★★
Crime drama 1938 · US · BW · 68mins

Warren William stars as a tough-minded, morally upright and obsessively dedicated district attorney. In prosecuting a man who has murdered his faithless wife in a fit of jealousy, William comes to realise that the case is a mirror of his own life in which his neglected wife (Gail Patrick) is seeking solace with William Lundigan. A modest and mildly interesting drama, directed by James Whale who made a more stylish and exciting job of *The Kiss before the Mirror* in 1933, of which this is a remake.

Warren William *District Attorney Jim Stowell* • Gail Patrick *Lucy Stowell* • Constance Moore *Elizabeth* • William Lundigan *Phil* • Ralph Morgan *Professor Shaw MacAllen* • Cecil Cunningham *"Sharpy"* • Samuel S Hinds *David Marrow* ■ *Dir* James Whale • *Scr* Myles Connolly, from the play *Der Kuss vor dem Spiegel* by Ladislaus Fodor

The Wiz ★★U
Musical fantasy 1978 · US · Colour · 128mins

A 34-year-old Diana Ross plays Dorothy in this all-black version of *The Wizard of Oz,* which casts a pall over memories of the 1939 classic. It's easy to see why director Sidney Lumet's clunker ranks as one of the most expensive movie flops of all time. While the Tony Walton sets are fabulous, the famous plot is immersed in a dark inner-city impressionism, the

quasi-rocker songs are lacklustre, and diva Ross is just ludicrous in the Judy Garland role. Michael Jackson is surprisingly good as the Scarecrow, though, and among the songs is the hit *Ease On down the Road.* 🖾

Diana Ross *Dorothy* • Michael Jackson *Scarecrow* • Nipsey Russell *Tin Man* • Ted Ross *Lion* • Mabel King *Evillene* • Theresa Merritt *Aunt Em* • Thelma Carpenter *Miss One* • Lena Horne *Glinda the Good* • Richard Pryor *The Wiz* • Stanley Greene *Uncle Henry* ■ *Dir* Sidney Lumet • *Scr* Joel Schumacher, from the musical by William F Brown, Charlie Smalls, from the novel *The Wonderful Wizard of Oz* by L Frank Baum

The Wizard of Baghdad ★★ U

Fantasy comedy 1960 · US · Colour · 92mins
After all the cardboard cutout Oriental fantasies that have masqueraded as movies over the years, at last comes a parody of the genre, though it's of little consequence. Dick Shawn, playing a lazy genie threatened with being turned human for not completing any duties, gives a performance that ensures indolence will affect the amount of laughs as well. The special effects – including a rather frayed flying carpet – are as dodgy as the plot line which, of course, involves the uniting of a prince and princess in wedded bliss.

Dick Shawn *Ali Mahmud, Genie* • Diane Baker *Princess Yasmin* • Barry Coe *Prince Husan* • John Van Dreelen *Jullnar* • Robert F Simon [Robert Simon] *Shamadin* • Vaughn Taylor *Norodeen* ■ *Dir* George Sherman • *Scr* Jesse L Lasky Jr, Pat Silver, from a story by Samuel Newman

The Wizard of Loneliness ★★★ 15

Drama 1988 · US · Colour · 106mins
Everyone knows Lukas Haas as the Amish boy in *Witness* and the geek who saves the world in *Mars Attacks!*, but he gives one of the best performances of his career to date in this rites-of-passage drama set in New England during the Second World War. This is an engaging tale in which Haas finds himself at the centre of a family crisis when the shady past of aunt Lea Thompson comes to light. Director Jenny Bowen does a good job of creating the period atmosphere, but she might have tightened up the action in places and the ending will leave many dissatisfied. Contains violence and swearing. 🖾

Lukas Haas *Wendall Olet* • Lea Thompson *Sybil* • Lance Guest *John T* • John Randolph *Doc* • Dylan Baker *Duffy* • Anne Pitoniak *Cornelia* • Jeremiah Warner *Tom* ■ *Dir* Jenny Bowen • *Scr* Nancy Larson, from the novel by John Nichols

The Wizard of Oz ★★★★★★ U

Classic musical fantasy
1939 · US · Colour and BW · 97mins
One of Hollywood's quintessential productions, the musical adaptation of L Frank Baum's classic fable is probably the most beloved fantasy film of all time and the ultimate family picture. It has something for everyone: wonderfully strange lands, fun-scary moments, a dazzling assortment of fairy-tale characters, fabulous songs to take us all somewhere over the

rainbow, a peerless Judy Garland performance, and meaningful messages in abundance. Continuously enthralling, this is one hardy perennial you can never tire of watching. Uncredited King Vidor directed some of the sequences. 🖾

Judy Garland *Dorothy* • Ray Bolger *Hunk/ Scarecrow* • Bert Lahr *Zeke/Cowardly Lion* • Jack Haley *Hickory/Tin Woodman* • Billie Burke *Glinda* • Margaret Hamilton *Miss Gulch/Wicked Witch of the West* • Frank Morgan *Prof Marvel/Wizard/Guard/Coachman* • Charley Grapewin *Uncle Henry* • Clara Blandick *Auntie Em* ■ *Dir* Victor Fleming, King Vidor • *Scr* Noel Langley, Florence Ryerson, Edgar Allen Woolf, from the novel *The Wonderful Wizard of Oz* by L Frank Baum • *Cinematographer* Harold Rosson • *Art Director* Cedric Gibbons, William A Horning • *Costume Designer* Adrian • *Music/Lyrics* Harold Arlen, EY Harburg

The Wizard of Speed and Time ★★ PG

Fantasy comedy 1988 · US · Colour · 94mins
A trippy, almost psychedelic effects extravaganza, entirely home-produced by one-man-band movie-maker Mike Jittlov. He also stars, as a freelance film effects whiz given the chance to make his own movie. Supremely self-indulgent, this labour of love nonetheless offers some interesting insights into the trials and tribulations of indie film-making. Jittlov was Hollywood flavour of the month for five minutes back in the late eighties. He's barely been heard of since. 🖾

Mike Jittlov *Mike, the Wizard/Torch carrier* • Paige Moore *Cindy Lite/Dancer/Pretty hitchhiker* • Richard Kaye *Harvey Bookman/ Voice over artist* • David Conrad *Brian Lucas/ Photographer (Wizard Film)* • John Massari *Steve Shostakovich/Photographer (Wizard Film)* • Philip Michael Thomas *Policeman Mick Polanko* • Steve Brodie *Lucky Straeker* ■ *Dir/ Scr* Mike Jittlov

Wizards ★★ PG

Animated fantasy adventure
1977 · US · Colour · 77mins
This ambitious animated sci-fi tale from the director of *Fritz the Cat*, Ralph Bakshi, is set in Earth's far-flung future where nuclear holocaust has left the world in the hands (and claws) of elves, fairies, wizards and mutants. Out of this messy miasma come twin wizards – the good Avatar and the evil Blackwolf – who of course duke it out for survival. Uncertain whether it wants to appeal to children, grown-ups or both – its anti-fascist undertones will be lost on the kids – it's ultimately something of a dull affair. 🖾

Bob Holt *Avatar* • Jesse Wells *Elinore* • Richard Romanus *Weehawk* • David Proval *Peace* • James Connell *President* • Mark Hamill *Sean* ■ *Dir/Scr* Ralph Bakshi

Wizards of the Lost Kingdom ★★★ PG

Fantasy adventure
1985 · US/Arg · Colour · 72mins
Things that go bump in the night abound in this fantasy adventure about a mercenary swordsman (Bo Svenson) helping a wizard's son (Vidal Peterson) whose father (Edward Morrow) has fallen foul of an evil magician (Thom Christopher). Ogres help out in the scuffles between good and evil, but it's

not as dependent on special effects as it would be these days. Director Hector Olivera nevertheless manages a genuinely alien atmosphere, while its sanitised events are well up to squeaky-clean Disney standards, so there's not much cause for parental alarm – which may disappoint some youngsters. 🖾

Bo Svenson *Kor* • Vidal Peterson *Simon* • Thom Christopher *Shurka* • Barbara Stock *Udea* • Maria Socas *Acrasia* • Dolores Michaels *Aura* • Edward Morrow *Wulfrick/Old Simon/Gulfax* • August Larreta *King Tylor* ■ *Dir* Hector Olivera • *Scr* Tom Edwards

Wojeck: Out of the Fire ★★

Drama 1992 · Can · Colour · 100mins
A run-of-the-mill Canadian TV movie, starring John Vernon, a veteran of over 40 features, mostly as untrustworthy friends or outright villains. With that sort of track record and those familiar shifty eyes, it's slightly difficult to accept him as a good guy, but he's solid enough as a doctor returning from a long spell in Africa to combat racial prejudice and injustice during a complex immigration case. Such important issues deserve a more intelligent discussion than they are given here, but at least the film's heart's in the right place.

John Vernon *Steve Wojeck* • Patricia Collins *Marty Wojeck* • Christianne Hirt *Anna Wojeck* • Ted Follows *Arnie Bateman* • Dominic Zamprogna *Jesus Arcadio* ■ *Dir* George Bloomfield • *Scr* Malcolm MacRury

Wolf ★★★ 15

Horror 1994 · US · Colour · 120mins
Everything is right about this film apart from the direction. Jack Nicholson and Michelle Pfeiffer are suitably stellar – he as the middle-aged book editor, she as his boss's daughter whose burgeoning romance is cursed by the fangs of a werewolf. Giuseppe Rotunno's glossy photography lends a sinister sophistication, Ennio Morricone's eerie score plays on our unease and make-up maestro Rick Baker's transformations combine ingenuity with a real sense of agony. But director Mike Nichols is so interested in the romantic entanglements that he forgets to make the horror horrific. While this is more a study in pain than a shocker, it could still do with a tad more menace and a lot less refinement. Contains violence, swearing and sex scenes. 🖾 *DVD*

Jack Nicholson *Will Randall* • Michelle Pfeiffer *Laura Alden* • James Spader *Stewart Swinton* • Kate Nelligan *Charlotte Randall* • Richard Jenkins *Detective Bridger* • Christopher Plummer *Raymond Alden* • Eileen Atkins *Mary* • David Hyde Pierce *Roy* • Om Puri *Dr Vijay Alezias* • Ron Rifkin *Doctor* • Prunella Scales *Maude* ■ *Dir* Mike Nichols • *Scr* Jim Harrison, Wesley Strick

The Wolf at the Door ★★★ 18

Biographical drama
1987 · Fr/Den · Colour · 86mins
Henning Carlsen emerged as one of the key figures in Danish cinema with *Hunger* in 1966, but it took another two decades before he found a truly international audience with this biopic of the artist Paul Gauguin. In a far cry

from Anthony Quinn's larger-than-life portrayal in *Lust for Life*, Donald Sutherland plays Gauguin as a man at the crossroads, caught between the need to support his mistresses and the desire to fulfil his artistic destiny. Intelligently scripted by Christopher Hampton and beautifully shot by Mikael Salomon, this is a laudable attempt to understand a complex personality. Contains nudity. 🖾

Donald Sutherland *Paul Gauguin* • Valerie Morea *Annah-la-Javanaise* • Max von Sydow *August Strindberg* • Sofie Gråbøl *Judith Molard* • Merete Voldstedlund *Mette Gauguin* • Jorgen Reenberg *Edward Brandes* • Yves Barsack *Edgar Degas* ■ *Dir* Henning Carlsen • *Scr* Christopher Hampton, from a story by Henning Carlsen, Jean-Claude Carriere

Wolf Lake ★★ 18

Thriller 1979 · US · Colour · 83mins
Further evidence of Rod Steiger's declining fortunes was obvious in this depressing movie (also known as *Honor Guard*), laden with Vietnam overtones. When four ex-marines meet a deserter while staying in a Canadian hunting lodge, one of them decides to avenge his son's death in Vietnam. Steiger's usual heavyweight presence only adds to the grim nature of the story. However, if writer/director Burt Kennedy was trying to get a message about Vietnam across, he fails to make it clear here. 🖾

Rod Steiger *Charlie* • David Huffman *David* • Robin Mattson *Linda* • Jerry Hardin *Wilbur* • Richard Herd *George* • Paul Mantee *Sweeney* ■ *Dir/Scr* Burt Kennedy

Wolf Larsen ★★★

Action adventure 1958 · US · BW · 83mins
Robust screen adaptation of Jack London's novel *The Sea Wolf*, starring Barry Sullivan as the eponymous sea captain and Peter Graves as the shipwreck victim with whom he spars. A rousing musical score sets the pace for this tale of cruelty, loyalty and, ultimately, mutiny.

Barry Sullivan *Wolf Larsen* • Peter Graves (1) *Van Weyden* • Gita Hall *Kristina* • Thayer David *Mugridge* • John Alderson *Johnson* • Rico Alaniz *Louis* • *Dir* Harmon Jones • *Scr* Jack DeWitt, Turnley Walker, from the novel *The Sea Wolf* by Jack London • *Music* Paul Dunlap

The Wolf Man ★★★★ PG

Horror 1941 · US · BW · 69mins
The classic Universal movie that not only established Lon Chaney Jr as a horror star but also most of the cinematic werewolf lore concerning pentagrams, the moon and the fatality of silver. As Lawrence Talbot, Chaney returns home to Wales and, after being warned of life-threatening danger by gypsy Maria Ouspenskaya, is attacked by her werewolf son Bela Lugosi and cursed to transform into a wolf man himself whenever the moon is full. An intelligent, literate script, fine direction by George Waggner, convincing make-up by Jack (*Frankenstein*) Pierce and a sympathetic performance by Chaney put this atmospheric chiller in the top ranks of the Horror Hall of Fame. 🖾

Lon Chaney Jr *Lawrence "Larry" Talbot/The Wolf Man* • Claude Rains *Sir John Talbot* • Evelyn Ankers *Gwen Conliffe* • Ralph Bellamy

Colonel Paul Montford • Warren William *Dr Lloyd* • Patric Knowles *Frank Andrews* • Maria Ouspenskaya *Maleva* • Bela Lugosi *Bela* ■ *Dir* George Waggner • *Scr* Curt Siodmak • *Makeup* Jack Pierce • *Cinematographer* Joseph Valentine

Wolfen ★★★ 18

Horror   1981 · US · Colour · 109mins

Eleven years after *Woodstock*, director Michael Wadleigh resurfaced with this classy, thoughtful, gory, but not in the least bit scary horror movie about a mutant breed of killer wolf with super-intelligent tracking abilities running wild in the Bronx. New York cop Albert Finney investigates, and, in a typical Wadleigh eco addition to Whitley Strieber's so-so supernatural novel, links the plight of the American Indian to the wolves' brutally violent acts; both were deprived of their homeland by nasty white settlers. Subjective camerawork, denoting the wolves' point of view, features extensive optical special effects so the prowling always makes for galvanising viewing, while Finney makes the most of his tart dialogue. It's a pity the pay-off is such a letdown after the initially superior suspense. Contains violence, swearing and nudity. 🖵

Albert Finney *Dewey Wilson* • Diane Venora *Rebecca Neff* • Edward James Olmos *Eddie Holt* • Gregory Hines *Whittington* • Tom Noonan *Ferguson* • Dick O'Neill *Warren* ■ *Dir* Michael Wadleigh • *Scr* David Eyre, Michael Wadleigh, from the novel by Whitley Strieber

The Wolves of Willoughby Chase ★★★ PG

Adventure   1988 · UK · Colour · 88mins

Based on Joan Aiken's children's novel, this is a fun, if slightly disappointing, romp set in a snowy Yorkshire overrun by wolves, during the Industrial Revolution. Emily Hudson and Aleks Darowska are the two girls trying to foil a plot by their evil governess, who is played with bitchy glee by Stephanie Beacham. Grown-up viewers may find parts of the film tedious, but the whole affair is brightened up by the over-the-top performances from comedian Mel Smith, Geraldine James and Richard O'Brien. 🖵

Stephanie Beacham *Letitia Slighcarp* • Mel Smith *Mr Grimshaw* • Geraldine James *Mrs Gertrude Brisket* • Richard O'Brien *James* • Emily Hudson *Bonnie Willoughby* • Aleks Darowska *Sylvia* • Jane Horrocks *Pattern* • Eleanor David *Lady Willoughby* • Jonathan Coy *Lord Willoughby* • Lynton Dearden *Simon* ■ *Dir* Stuart Orme • *Scr* William M Akers, from the novel by Joan Aiken

Woman Chases Man ★★★ U

Comedy   1937 · US · BW · 66mins

A screwball comedy about money, booze and property that is fairly typical of its genre, and is played with ineffable skill by the sparkling trio of Miriam Hopkins, Charles Winninger and a very young Joel McCrea. Unfortunately crippled by a screenplay that runs out of ideas about three-quarters of the way through its mercifully short running time, the film leaves its principal characters quite literally up a tree! Nevertheless, this is a class act from producer Samuel Goldwyn. If the title doesn't give much

idea of the plot, that's because there isn't that much plot to speak of, but this will still while away a very pleasant hour or so. 🖵

Miriam Hopkins *Virginia Travis* • Joel McCrea *Kenneth Nolan* • Charles Winninger *BJ Nolan* • Erik Rhodes *Henri Saffron* • Ella Logan *Judy Williams* • Leona Maricle *Nina Tennyson* • Broderick Crawford *Hunk Williams* • Charles Halton *Mr Judd* ■ *Dir* John Blystone [John G Blystone] • *Scr* Joseph Anthony, Mannie Seff, David Hertz, from the story *The Princess and the Pauper* by Lynn Root, Frank Fenton • *Producer* Samuel Goldwyn

A Woman Deceived ★★

Crime drama   1992 · US · Colour · 100mins

A sequel to *A Woman Scorned*, which followed the misfortunes of Betty Broderick, the tormented divorcee who murdered her ex-husband and his new wife. Here, Meredith Baxter returns as the unrepentant killer, who turns her trial into a media circus in order to increase her chances of acquittal owing to provocation. It's nonstop barnstorming, but, for once, there's no knowing how events will turn out, as this true story will be unfamiliar to British viewers. For the most part, director Dick Lowry's TV movie is routine, but the courtroom jousts between Baxter and district attorney Judith Ivey are undeniably slick.

Meredith Baxter *Elisabeth "Betty" Broderick* • Judith Ivey *Kerry Wells* • Ray Baker *Jack Earley* • Kelli Williams *Kate Broderick* • Ralph Bruneau *Larry* • Stephen Root *Kevin McDonald* ■ *Dir* Dick Lowry • *Scr* Joe Cacaci

The Woman Eater ★

Horror   1957 · UK · BW · 70mins

Fans of mad scientists and killer vegetables should on no account miss this little-known Z-grade affair, a British studio's successful attempt to match trash coming out of Hollywood in the late fifties. Boffin George Coulouris propagates a tree that eats young women in the belief that the sap excreted will make him immortal. Director Charles Saunders began his career with the charming wartime comedy *Tawny Pipit* and ended it with horror and cheap sleaze. Coulouris was in *Citizen Kane*. Their conversations in the studio canteen must have been particularly melancholic.

George Coulouris *Dr James Moran* • Vera Day *Sally* • Joy Webster *Judy Ryan* • Peter Wayn *Jack Venner* • Jimmy Vaughan *Tanga* • Sara Leighton *Susan Curtis* ■ *Dir* Charles Saunders • *Scr* Brandon Fleming

The Woman for Joe ★★ U

Drama   1955 · UK · BW · 91mins

A slow and rather disappointing Rank production. The story is the old "hunchback of Notre Dame" chestnut, about a fairground owner (George Baker) who hires a midget, only for him to turn into a Napoleon figure, lusting for power and lusting, too, for Diane Cilento, who's in love with Baker. It's pretty nasty, in fact, with none of the poetry of Victor Hugo's story, let alone Tod Browning's similarly themed masterpiece, *Freaks*, and with a cop-out ending.

Diane Cilento *Mary* • George Baker *Joe Harrap* • Jimmy Karoubi *George Wilson* • David

Kossoff *Max* • Earl Cameron *Lemmie* • Sydney Tafler *Butch* • Violet Farebrother *Ma Gollatz* ■ *Dir* George More O'Ferrall • *Scr* Neil Paterson, from his story *And Delilah*

Woman from Rose Hill ★★

Drama   1989 · Swi/Fr · Colour · 95mins

Despite employing his traditionally detached, naturalist approach, Alain Tanner is unable to prevent this treatise on Swiss isolationism from descending into barnstorming melodrama. Arriving from an island in the Indian Ocean, Marie Gaydu is soon disillusioned with her pen-pal husband and embarks on an affair with Jean-Philippe Ecoffey, despite the opposition of his industrialist father. The themes of clashing cultures, arranged marriages and abortion should have preoccupied a film-maker of Tanner's intelligence, but he seems curiously drawn to the eccentricity of Ecoffey's aunt, Denise Peron, and the soap operatic excesses (insanity, police marksmen, deportation) that he uses to resolve his tale. In French with English subtitles.

Marie Gaydu *Julie* • Jean-Philippe Ecoffey *Jean* • Denise Peron *Jeanne* • Roger Jendly *Marcel* ■ *Dir/Scr* Alain Tanner

A Woman, Her Men and Her Futon ★

Romantic drama   1992 · US · Colour · 90mins

Few things are worse than self-absorbed sex movies, but one of those things is a self-absorbed sex movie about Hollywood. Helen (Jennifer Rubin) is a sexual castaway, drifting from one man to another in hopes of finding what she wants out of life. Along the way she becomes peripherally involved in the writing and production of a film that parallels events in this movie. By the end of the journey, Helen may have discovered herself but all we've discovered is senseless avant-garde dialogue and a few cheap thrills.

Jennifer Rubin *Helen* • Lance Edwards *Donald* • Grant Show *Randy* • Michael Cerveris *Paul* • Delaune Michel *Gail* • Robert Lipton *Max* ■ *Dir/Scr* Mussef Sibay

The Woman I Love ★★★

Wartime melodrama   1937 · US · BW · 85mins

Having made a successful French film from Joseph Kessel's novel *L'Equipage*, European director Anatole Litvak was brought to RKO to make his Hollywood debut with this version of the tale, set in France during the First World War. Paul Muni stars as a fighter pilot whose safety record is questionable until he is joined by new man Louis Hayward. They form a successful partnership in the air and close friendship on the ground, until Hayward falls in love with Miriam Hopkins, unaware that she is Muni's wife. A solid romantic melodrama, with some good aerial action, but the stars are lacking in fire.

Paul Muni *Lt Claude Maury* • Miriam Hopkins *Denise LaValle/Hélène Maury* • Louis Hayward *Lt Jean Herbillion* • Colin Clive *Capt Thelis* • Minor Watson *Deschamps* • Elisabeth Risdon *Mme Herbillion* • Paul Guilfoyle *Berthier* ■ *Dir* Anatole Litvak • *Scr* Ethel Borden, from the

film *L'Equipage* by Joseph Kessel, Anatole Litvak, from the novel *L'Equipage* by Joseph Kessel

Woman in a Dressing Gown ★★★★

Drama   1957 · UK · BW · 94mins

A painfully honest drama, based on a play by Ted Willis, that was light years ahead of its time in its treatment of women and their place in marriage, starring Yvonne Mitchell in a role that should have seen her showered in awards. Mitchell's portrayal of clinical depression is stunning in its depth and understanding, and director J Lee Thompson pulls no punches in his exploration of a partnership gone sour with the intrusion of a younger woman. In many ways this movie heralded a new dawn in gritty British film-making which culminated in the "kitchen sink" social dramas of the sixties.

Yvonne Mitchell *Amy Preston* • Anthony Quayle *Jim Preston* • Sylvia Syms *Georgie Harlow* • Andrew Ray *Brian Preston* • Carole Lesley *Hilda* • Michael Ripper *Pawnbroker* • Nora Gordon *Mrs Williams* ■ *Dir* J Lee Thompson • *Scr* Ted Willis, from his play

The Woman in Green ★★★ PG

Murder mystery   1945 · US · BW · 66mins

One of the weirdest in the Sherlock Holmes series, this mystery has a psychological subtext it's best not to think about. Holmes (Basil Rathbone) is up against the evil Professor Moriarty (Henry Daniell) and a beautiful hypnotist (Hillary Brooke) as he investigates the murders of women who are found with their right forefingers severed. The grindingly eerie music used to mesmerise victims, and Holmes's own seeming submission to psychic forces, sound a note of real unease, which not even the bumbling banalities of Nigel Bruce (as Dr Watson) can dispel. Rathbone always said the restrained Daniell was his favourite Moriarty and one can see why. With his air of cerebral containment and softly-spoken precision he could so easily have made a character switch and played Holmes himself. 🖵

Basil Rathbone *Sherlock Holmes* • Nigel Bruce *Dr John H Watson* • Hillary Brooke *Lydia Marlow* • Henry Daniell *Professor Moriarty* • Paul Cavanagh *Sir George Fenwick* • Matthew Boulton *Inspector Gregson* • Eve Amber *Maude Fenwick* ■ *Dir* Roy William Neill • *Scr* Bertram Millhauser, from characters created by Sir Arthur Conan Doyle

The Woman in Question ★★★

Crime mystery   1950 · UK · BW · 99mins

One of Dirk Bogarde's earlier pictures, an inventive thriller directed by Anthony Asquith and co-starring Jean Kent as a fortune teller whose death leads to a serious case of flashback syndrome during which we try to spot her killer. Kent has a juicy role here, since all her acquaintances have a different view of her ranging from kindly neighbour to drunken bitch. As the boyfriend, Bogarde looks astonishingly young.

Jean Kent *Madame Astra* • Dirk Bogarde *Bob Baker* • John McCallum *Murray* • Susan Shaw *Catherine* • Hermione Baddeley *Mrs Finch* •

Charles Victor *Pollard* • Duncan MacRae *Superintendent Lodge* • Lana Morris *Lana* • Joe Linnane *Inspector Butler* ■ *Dir* Anthony Asquith • *Scr* John Cresswell

The Woman in Red ★★

Melodrama   1935 · US · BW · 68mins

Barbara Stanwyck struggles valiantly against an uninspired script and an irritating leading man in this thankfully short tale of a professional horsewoman who, to the ire of her mega-rich employer Genevieve Tobin, marries Gene Raymond, the man Tobin wants for herself. Trouble is, though, Raymond and his family, who cold-shoulder his bride, are upper-crust but penniless and Stanwyck's efforts to finance a business land her in some trouble. Robert Florey directs and John Eldredge is good in support, but the only honours in this dreary little film go to Tobin, who plays with relish and polish.

Barbara Stanwyck *Shelby Barrett* • Gene Raymond *Johnny Wyatt* • Genevieve Tobin *Nicko Nicholas* • John Eldredge *Eugene Fairchild* • Russell Hicks *Clayton* • Philip Reed *Dan McCall* • Nella Walker *Aunt Bettina* • Dorothy Tree *Olga* ■ *Dir* Robert Florey • *Scr* Mary McCall Jr, Peter Milne, from the novel *North Shore* by Wallace Irwin

The Woman in Red ★★★ 15

Comedy   1984 · US · Colour · 82mins

One of the enduring cinema images of the eighties is Kelly LeBrock dancing over an air vent in her flame-red dress *à la* Marilyn Monroe in *The Seven Year Itch*, hypnotising pink-cheeked Gene Wilder. The rest of this warm-hearted, bouncily amusing story of obsession and extramarital longings doesn't quite live up to this promising opening, but it's a movie that just about holds the attention. Wilder is at his frantic best, ably supported by the likes of real-life wife Gilda Radner and Charles Grodin. Stevie Wonder's hit single *I Just Called to Say I Love You* features on the soundtrack. Contains some violence, swearing and nudity. ▭

Gene Wilder *Theodore Pierce* • Kelly LeBrock *Charlotte* • Charles Grodin *Buddy* • Joseph Bologna *Joe* • Judith Ivey *Didi* • Michael Huddleston *Michael* • Gilda Radner *Ms Milner* ■ *Dir* Gene Wilder • *Scr* Gene Wilder, from the film *Pardon Mon Affaire* by Jean-Loup Dabadie, Yves Robert

Woman in the Dunes ★★★★★ 15

Drama   1963 · Jap · BW · 118mins

Adapted by Kobo Abe from his own novel, this stark human condition parable was denounced by some critics for its photographic neutrality. But director Hiroshi Teshigahara and cinematographer Hiroshi Segawa achieve a rich diversity of visual textures that adds to the sensual atmosphere of this intense drama, in which entomologist Eiji Okada finds himself trapped in the deep-dune home of social outcast, Kyoko Kishida. Even the editorial technique (shifting from languid dissolves to sharp cuts) reflects the environment and the state of the couple's relationship, which Teshigahara further explores through his use of symbolic imagery involving insects, water, skin and the

chameleon sand. In Japanese with English subtitles. ▭

Eiji Okada *Jumpei Niki* • Kyoko Kishida *Widow* ■ *Dir* Hiroshi Teshigahara • *Scr* Kobo Abe, from his novel *Suna No Onna*

The Woman in the Moon ★★★

Silent fantasy   1929 · Ger · BW · 107mins

One of the last silent films made in Germany, Fritz Lang's comic-strip fantasy concerns scientist Klaus Pohl who believes the moon is rich in gold and, with the help of rocket designer Willy Fritsch, organises the first flight there. However melodramatic and farcical the plot, the takeoff is portrayed using dramatic montage and camera angles, and there are a few sinister Langian touches. Despite the quaintness of the technology, the Nazis took the film out of distribution because they felt the rocket was too close to one they were creating on the V2 programme at the time.

Gerda Maurus *Friede Velten* • Willy Fritsch *Wolf Helius* • Fritz Rasp *Walter Turner* • Gustav von Wangenheim *Hans Windegger* • Klaus Pohl *Prof Georg Manfeldt* ■ *Dir* Fritz Lang • *Scr* Thea von Harbou, Fritz Lang, from a story by Thea von Harbou

The Woman in the Window ★★★★ PG

Film noir   1945 · US · BW · 94mins

A clever melodrama, written and produced by Nunnally Johnson and directed with just the right amount of moody atmosphere by expressionist master Fritz Lang. Edward G Robinson is marvellous as the academic who makes that fatal forties' error of falling for the subject of a portrait – see *Laura* or *Portrait of Jennie* – and then finds himself swept up in a convoluted web of murder and deception. Joan Bennett is an ideal "ideal" in one of her four fine performances for Lang, while Raymond Massey and Dan Duryea are also on hand, both with sinister and gripping information to impart. The famous ending is still controversial, but whatever conclusion you come to there's no denying the power of this particular nightmare. ▭

Edward G Robinson *Professor Richard Wanley* • Joan Bennett *Alice Reed* • Raymond Massey *Frank Lalor* • Edmond Breon *[Edmund Breon]* *Dr Michael Barkstone* • Dan Duryea *Heidt/ Doorman* • Thomas E Jackson *Inspector Jackson* • Arthur Loft *Claude Mazard* • Dorothy Peterson *Mrs Wanley* ■ *Dir* Fritz Lang • *Scr* Nunnally Johnson, from the novel *Once Off Guard* by JH Wallis

The Woman in White ★★★

Period mystery drama   1948 · US · BW · 108mins

Based on the classic Victorian gothic thriller by Wilkie Collins, the film stars an effectively histrionic Sydney Greenstreet as the evil Count Fosco, plotting to get his hands on Eleanor Parker's fortune. He has her twin sister (also Parker) committed to an insane asylum from where she escapes, returning in the guise of a ghostly apparition to foil Greenstreet's plans. The descent of Agnes Moorehead, Greenstreet's already somewhat mad wife, into murderous insanity, is one of the high points of a

film which, though atmospheric and periodically scary, is hampered by over-respectful restraint and a dull Parker.

Alex Smith *Marian Halcombe* • Eleanor Parker *Laura Fairlie/Ann Catherick* • Sydney Greenstreet *Count Alesandro Fosco* • Gig Young *Walter Hartright* • Agnes Moorehead *Countess Fosco* • John Abbott *Frederick Fairlie* • John Emery *Sir Percival Glyde* • Curt Bois *Louis* ■ *Dir* Peter Godfrey • *Scr* Stephen Morehouse Avery, from the novel by Wilkie Collins

Woman Obsessed ★★

Romantic adventure
1959 · US · Colour · 102mins

A star vehicle for tempestuous redhead Susan Hayward and, as, alas, little else. Hayward's a "widder-woman" who marries rugged Stephen Boyd, and there's plenty of cussin' and feudin', but no real dramatic force in what looks very much like a 20th Century-Fox assembly line soaper. Star Hayward and director Henry Hathaway fail to rise above the puerile material, but Hayward fans should enjoy the wallow: she's not really an actress, despite an Oscar for *I Want to Live!*, but she's undeniably a star, and unquestionably a pleasure to watch in tosh like this, making mincemeat of untrained Irish import Boyd, in a far cry from his role as Messala in *Ben-Hur*.

Susan Hayward *Mary Sharron* • Stephen Boyd *Fred Carter* • Barbara Nichols *Mayme Radzevitch* • Dennis Holmes *Robbie Sharron* • Theodore Bikel *Dr Gibbs* • Ken Scott *Sergeant Le Moyne* • Arthur Franz *Tom Sharron* ■ *Dir* Henry Hathaway • *Scr* Sydney Boehm, from the novel *The Snow Birch* by John Mantley

A Woman of Affairs ★★★

Silent melodrama   1928 · US · BW · 0mins

Prevented from marrying John Gilbert, whom she loves, rich and beautiful young English society woman Greta Garbo (with alcoholic brother Douglas Fairbanks Jr) finds her reputation tarnished by circumstance. She then goes from man to man in Europe, but meets her only love again with tragic consequences. This highly coloured, over-the-top romantic melodrama is absolute rubbish, but a characteristic silent Garbo vehicle with a starry cast, and directed and photographed by the star's favourites, Clarence Brown and William H Daniels respectively. Garbo looks wonderful and suffers nobly.

Greta Garbo *Diana* • John Gilbert *Neville* • Lewis Stone *Hugh* • John Mack Brown *[Johnny Mack Brown] David* • Douglas Fairbanks Jr *Jeffrey* ■ *Dir* Clarence Brown • *Scr* Bess Meredyth, Marian Ainslee (titles), Ruth Cummings (titles), from the novel *The Green Hat* by Michael Arlen

Woman of Desire ★★ 18

Erotic thriller   1994 · US · Colour · 98mins

Two macho men (Jeff Fahey and Steven Bauer) and one sexy woman (Bo Derek) head off in a yacht and, in a stunning turn of events, Derek takes her clothes off a lot. OK, the actual stunning turn of events is that only Derek and Fahey's characters come back. However she accuses him of murder and rape. Amazingly, Robert Mitchum does a turn here as the luckless Fahey's defence lawyer. If you've seen more than a couple of *film*

noirs, then the "shocking" twist will come as no surprise at all. ▭

Bo Derek *Christina Ford* • Robert Mitchum *Walter Hill* • Jeff Fahey *Jack Lynch* • Steven Bauer *Jonathan Ashby* ■ *Dir/Scr* Robert Ginty

A Woman of Distinction ★★ U

Romantic comedy   1950 · US · BW · 84mins

With its focus on middle-aged protagonists, this idiotic romantic comedy is part farce and occasionally embarrassing but still manages to be quite entertaining. Rosalind Russell is the uptight college dean, who has devoted her mind and her life to higher things than love and marriage. When visiting professor Ray Milland is installed, a journalist on the local paper runs a story which, to Russell's horror and Milland's bewilderment, suggests they're having an affair. No surprises here, but Edmund Gwenn is a hoot as Russell's loveable old father who thinks it's high time she descended her ivory tower.

Rosalind Russell *Susan Manning Middlecott* • Ray Milland *Alec Stevenson* • Edmund Gwenn *Mark Middlecott* • Janis Carter *Teddy Evans* • Mary Jane Saunders *Louisa Middlecott* • Francis Lederer *Paul Simone* • Jerome Courtland *Jerome* ■ *Dir* Edward Buzzell • *Scr* Charles Hoffman, Frank Tashlin, from a story by Ian McLellan Hunter, Hugo Butler

A Woman of Paris ★★★★★★

Silent drama   1923 · US · BW · 81mins

Marking a breakthrough in romantic realism, this film by Charles Chaplin is a rags-to-riches story. He makes only a brief appearance as a railway porter and devotes most of his energies to directing his favoured actress, Edna Purviance, as a country girl seduced by the big city and a suave Adolphe Menjou, yet still retaining her illusions about love. The idea may be very dated, but it's Chaplin's near-Dickensian insights that make the tale as relevant today as ever. An enchantment that can still spellbind us into belief.

Edna Purviance *Marie St Clair* • Adolphe Menjou *Pierre Revel* • Carl Miller *Jean Millet* • Lydia Knott *Jean's mother* • Charles French *[Charles K French] Jean's father* • Clarence Geldert *Marie's stepfather* • Betty Morrissey *Fifi* • Malvina Polo *Paulette* • Charles Chaplin *Station Porter* ■ *Dir/Scr* Charles Chaplin

Woman of Straw ★★

Mystery thriller   1964 · UK · Colour · 121mins

Having already made Hitchcock's *Marnie* and the Bond movie *Goldfinger*, Sean Connery seems to be taking a busman's holiday in this setbound thriller. The picture sets off at a lively pace, but gets bogged down once wheelchair-bound tyrant Ralph Richardson has been found dead and gold-digging nephew Connery finds himself among the murder suspects. Obviously revelling in Richardson's wonderfully cantankerous performance, director Basil Dearden seems to have lost interest after his demise, leaving Connery and Gina Lollobrigida, as the old devil's nurse, somewhat in the lurch.

Gina Lollobrigida *Maria* • Sean Connery *Anthony Richmond* • Ralph Richardson *Charles Richmond* • Alexander Knox *Lomer* • Johnny

Sekka *Thomas* • Laurence Hardy *Baines* • Danny Daniels *Fenton* ■ *Dir* Basil Dearden • *Scr* Robert Muller, Stanley Mann, Michael Relph, from the novel *La Femme de Paille* by Catherine Arley

Woman of the River ★★★

Drama   1955 · Fr/It · Colour · 92mins

Based on an idea by Ennio Flaiano and Alberto Moravia and boasting a debuting Pier Paolo Pasolini among its legion of screenwriters, this uncomfortable blend of rose-tinted neorealism, bawdy comedy and high melodrama owed much to Giuseppe De Santis's *Bitter Rice*. Indeed Silvana Mangano's brand of earthy sensuality clearly influenced Sophia Loren's performance as the village temptress who spurns the coy advances of policeman Gérard Oury, only to be left pregnant by cigarette smuggler Rik Battaglia. There's a distinct air of *Carmen* about the proceedings, especially when Loren performs a dance number, but it lacks class and cohesion. Italian dialogue dubbed into English.

Sophia Loren *Nives Mongolini* • Gérard Oury *Enzo Cinti* • Lise Bourdin *Tosca* • Rik Battaglia *Gino Lodi* • Enrico Olivieri *Oscar* ■ *Dir* Mario Soldati • *Scr* Basilio Franchina, Giorgio Bassani, Pier Paolo Pasolini, Florestano Vancini, Antonio Altoviti, Mario Soldati, Ben Zavin, from a idea by Ennio Flaiano, Alberto Moravia

Woman of the Year ★★★★ U

Comedy   1942 · US · BW · 114mins

The first teaming of one of Hollywood's greatest couples: the inimitable Katharine Hepburn and laconic, rugged Spencer Tracy. They're beautifully matched, she a columnist wishing to ban baseball until the end of the Second World War, he a reporter defending the sport in print. They meet, wed and generally provide a high old time for audiences everywhere. This is close to the apex of sophisticated romantic comedy, today marred slightly by its wartime conventions and a subplot involving the adoption of a young refugee. Nevertheless, adroit director George Stevens doesn't let the fun get bogged down, and just watching Tracy attempt to cut Hepburn down to size is to revel in the obvious affection these two great stars felt for one another, an affection that spilled into real life. ▭

Spencer Tracy *Sam Craig* • Katharine Hepburn *Tess Harding* • Minor Watson *William Harding* • Fay Bainter *Ellen Whitcomb* • Reginald Owen *Clayton* • William Bendix *Pinkie Peters* • Gladys Blake *Flo Peters* • Dan Tobin *Gerald* ■ *Dir* George Stevens • *Scr* Ring Lardner Jr, Michael Kanin

The Woman on Pier 13 ★★

Drama   1949 · US · BW · 72mins

When mogul Howard Hughes seized control of RKO, one of his credos was to use the studio and its product as an anti-communist tool, and this moody and suspenseful thriller was the first fruit of his labours. Originally previewed as *I Married a Communist*, the film ostensibly concerns a shipyard boss being blackmailed over past affiliations, with, interestingly, real-life liberal Robert Ryan playing the "hero".

The mercifully short movie was plagued by Hughes's predilection for constant reshoots, so don't blame director Robert Stevenson for what is, or isn't, on the screen. The film leaves a genuinely nasty taste in the mouth today, but is undeniably interesting as a social document of its time. Both Thomas Gomez and the lovely Laraine Day are extremely watchable, as is, of course, Ryan, but *On the Waterfront* would deal with similar concerns definitively.

Laraine Day *Nan Collins* • Robert Ryan *Brad Collins* • John Agar *Don Lowry* • Thomas Gomez *Vanning* • Janis Carter *Christine* • Richard Rober *Jim Travis* • William Talman *Bailey* • Paul E Burns *Arnold* • Paul Guilfoyle *Ralston* ■ *Dir* Robert Stevenson • *Scr* Charles Grayson, Robert Hardy Andrews, from a story by George W George, George F Slavin

The Woman on the Beach ★★★★

Drama   1947 · US · BW · 70mins

Jean Renoir regarded his seven-year sojourn in America as wasted time. Yet, in spite of the harmful cuts ordered by studio bosses at RKO, there is no denying the quality of his parting shot to Hollywood. Joan Bennett, in the title role, reinforced the reputation she forged in such Fritz Lang features as *The Woman in the Window* and *Scarlet Street* as one of *film noir*'s finest *femmes fatales*. By focusing on her highly charged interaction with blind husband Charles Bickford and shell-shocked lifeguard Robert Ryan, Renoir produced a smouldering melodrama that never relaxes its grip.

Joan Bennett *Peggy Butler* • Robert Ryan *Lt Scott Burnett* • Charles Bickford *Ted Butler* • Nan Leslie *Eve Geddes* • Jay Norris *Jimmy* • Walter Sande *Otto Wernecke* • Irene Ryan *Mrs Wernecke* ■ *Dir* Jean Renoir • *Scr* Frank Davis, Jean Renoir, Michael Hogan, from the novel *None So Blind* by Mitchell Wilson

Woman on the Ledge ★★

Drama   1993 · US · Colour · 100mins

An overwrought TV movie about a trio of women on the verge of a mild nervous breakdown. The three friends – Deidre Hall, Leslie Charleson and Colleen Zenk Pinter – are struggling to face up to their emotional problems, but the twist here is that one has sunk to such depths that she is contemplating suicide. The three largely unknown leads give it their best shot, but it is a curiously uninvolving drama and the direction by Chris Thomson is undistinguished.

Deidre Hall *Quinn Allen* • Leslie Charleson *Rachel Shayne* • Colleen Zenk Pinter *Steffi* • Josh Taylor *Jeff Shayne* • Peter Bergman *Bob* • Ken Kercheval *Dr Martin* ■ *Dir* Chris Thomson • *Scr* Hal Sitowitz, from a story by Louis Rudolph, Claudia Cooper

A Woman Rebels ★★

Historical drama   1936 · US · BW · 88mins

Katharine Hepburn, her popularity in decline after a series of misconceived failures, is perfectly cast as Pamela Thistlewaite, a non-conformist, asserting women's rights and her own independence in Victorian England. Pamela's fight against the rigid constraints of society, embodied by her

unbending father (Donald Crisp), makes for an interesting film, but it degenerates into soft-centred melodrama when she has an illegitimate child (by Van Heflin) and eventually allows an "old faithful" suitor (Herbert Marshall) to rescue her from misery.

Katharine Hepburn *Pamela Thistlewaite* • Herbert Marshall *Thomas Lane* • Elizabeth Allan *Flora Thistlewaite* • Donald Crisp *Judge Thistlewaite* • Doris Dudley *Young Flora* • David Manners *Alan* • Van Heflin *Gerald* ■ *Dir* Mark Sandrich • *Scr* Anthony Veiller, Ernest Vajda, from the novel *Portrait of a Rebel* by Netta Syrett

A Woman Scorned ★★ 15

Drama based on a true story
1992 · US · Colour · 89mins

Also shown as *Till Murder Do Us Part*, this "fatal attraction" story was adapted from a report in the *Los Angeles Times*. Meredith Baxter stars as Betty Broderick, the San Diego housewife who resorted to murder after the husband, for whom she had sacrificed everything in order to support him through college, left her for his young assistant. Having given a credible impression of a devoted wife, Baxter throws restraint to the wind in the second half of the film, which promptly falls apart as her jealousy turns to revenge. Contains some swearing. ▭

Meredith Baxter *Elizabeth "Betty" Broderick* • Stephen Collins *Dan Broderick* • Michelle Johnson *Linda* • Kelli Williams *Kate Broderick* • Stephen Root *Kevin McDonald* • Lori Hallier *Joan* • Christine Jansen *Susan McDonald* ■ *Dir* Dick Lowry • *Scr* Joe Cacaci, from the newspaper article *Till Murder Do Us Part* in the *LA Times* by Amy Wallace

A Woman Scorned ★★ 18

Erotic thriller   1994 · US · Colour · 102mins

An erotic thriller that sticks closely to the formula established by Shannon Tweed and Andrew Stevens in films like *Indecent Behavior*. Here, Tweed plays a woman who vows vengeance when her husband commits suicide and leaves her penniless. For some reason she decides that it's nice architect Stevens's fault, so she moves in with his family (posing as a most unlikely tutor) and sets about seducing everyone. There are shades of *The Hand That Rocks the Cradle* in the plotting, but, once again, soft-focus MTV-style sex scenes dominate and there's little logic or suspense in the storyline. ▭

Shannon Tweed *Patricia Langley/Amanda Chesfield* • Andrew Stevens *Alex Weston* • Kim Morgan Greene *Marina Weston* • Dan McVicar *Truman Langley* ■ *Dir* Andrew Stevens • *Scr* Barry Avrich

Woman Times Seven ★★★ 15

Portmanteau comedy drama
1967 · US/Fr/It · Colour · 103mins

Shirley MacLaine stars in seven vignettes, paired with or pitted against seven different men, ranging from Peter Sellers to Rossano Brazzi to Michael Caine who appears in the final episode as a mysterious stranger who never says a word. As with all portmanteau movies, some segments work better than others and much

depends on one's tolerance for MacLaine's mannerisms and trademark kookiness. Unlike MacLaine's previous episodic movie, *What a Way to Go*, in which she was a serial wife, this one isn't afraid of flirting with serious themes like suicide and what happens when women wear identical frocks. ▭

Shirley MacLaine *Paulette (Funeral Procession)/Maria Terese (Amateur Night)/Linda (Two Against One), Edith (The Super-Simone)/Eve Minou (At the Opera)/Marie (The Suicides)/Jeanne (Snow)* • Alan Arkin *Fred* • Peter Sellers *Jean* • Rossano Brazzi *Giorgio* • Vittorio Gassman *Cenci* • Lex Barker *Rik* • Robert Morley *Dr Xavier* • Michael Caine *Handsome stranger* • Anita Ekberg *Claudie* • Philippe Noiret *Victor* ■ *Dir* Vittorio De Sica • *Scr* Cesare Zavattini

A Woman under the Influence ★★★ 15

Drama   1974 · US · Colour · 140mins

The wife (Gena Rowlands) of a blue-collar worker (Peter Falk) and mother of three children falls prey to increasingly erratic behaviour, slipping in and out of reality until her devoted but distressed family are forced to institutionalise her. Discharged some months later, not much has changed. Written and directed by John Cassavetes, as a vehicle for his wife, the magnificent Rowlands, this was two years in the making, financed by friends and family. Despite a multifaceted and awesome tour de force from Rowlands (she won a best actress Oscar nomination), and sterling support from regulars of the Cassavetes stable such as Falk, the film is badly disadvantaged by a two-and-a-half hour running time that leaves an audience battered and bemused. Nonetheless, it should be seen for its undeniably brilliant elements. ▭

Peter Falk *Nick Longhetti* • Gena Rowlands *Mabel Longhetti* • Matthew Cassel *Tony Longhetti* • Matthew Laborteaux *Angelo Longhetti* • Christina Grisantii *Maria Longhetti* • Katherine Cassavetes *Mama Longhetti* • Lady Rowlands *Martha Mortensen* ■ *Dir/Scr* John Cassavetes

Woman Undone ★★★

Courtroom drama 1995 · US · Colour · 91mins

A quietly absorbing drama that manages to wring a few new twists out of a familiar story line. Mary McDonnell plays the sole survivor of a car crash that, by all accounts, has killed her husband Randy Quaid. However, she soon finds herself in court on a charge of murder when it is revealed that Quaid was in fact shot in the head. The story of her unhappy marriage unfolds in flashback, with director Evelyn Purcell effortlessly switching the action between past and present. The excellent performances from Quaid, McDonnell and Sam Elliott make this a superior made-for-TV affair. Contains sex scenes, violence and swearing.

Mary McDonnell *Terri Hansen* • Randy Quaid *Allen Hansen* • Sam Elliott *Ross Bishop* ■ *Dir* Evelyn Purcell • *Scr* William Mickelberry

The Woman Who Loved Elvis ★

Comedy 1993 · US · Colour · 104mins

In this ill-conceived TV film, sitcom diva Roseanne stars as an eccentric welfare mother who harbours an obsession for Elvis Presley, her house existing as a gaudy shrine to the singer. When a prim young social worker (Cynthia Gibb) is assigned to her case, both women come to understand that in order to find happiness, they must give up long-held resentments. While Roseanne is great with the one-liners, she is completely lost when the scene calls for empathy or sincerity. Also along for the ride are Roseanne's then-husband Tom Arnold, as well as Sally Kirkland, who does a fine job in the "best friend" role but she alone is unable to prop up this sagging effort.

Roseanne Arnold [Roseanne] *Joyce* • Tom Arnold *Jack* • Sally Kirkland *Sandee* • Cynthia Gibb *Emily* • Danielle Harris *Cilla* • Joe Guzaldo *Howard* • Kimberley Dal Santo *Lisa Marie* • Liz Muckley *Marge* ■ *Dir* Bill Bixby • *Scr* Rita Mae Brown, from the novel *Graced Land* by Laura Kalpakian

The Woman Who Sinned ★★

Thriller 1991 · US · Colour · 100mins

Yet another did-she-or-didn't-she drama, with American daytime TV star Susan Lucci playing the wife accused of murder after she has an affair. There's really nothing new here as every whodunit theme is rehashed. More time seems to have been spent on Lucci's wardrobe and hairdo than on the plot, but at least she keeps the hysterics to a minimum and valiantly battles against the constraints of the tired idea.

Susan Lucci *Victoria Robeson* • Tim Matheson *Michael Robeson* • Michael Dudikoff *Evan Ganns* • John Vernon *Lieutenant Girvetz* • Christina Belford [Christine Belford] *Randy Emerson* • Lenore Kasdorf *Jane Woodman* ■ *Dir* Michael Switzer • *Scr* Denne Peticlerc, from a story by Stu Samuels

Woman with a Past ★★★

Drama based on a true story
1991 · US · Colour · 96mins

Pamela Reed is the woman who leaves her abusive husband behind, changes her name and remarries, only to find her past catching up with her. A solid cast including Dwight Schultz and Paul LeMat and low-key direction from Mimi Leder help make this an interesting take on a familiar theme, which lacks the hysterics of the similar (but less watchable) Julia Roberts movie *Sleeping with the Enemy*. Contains violence.

Pamela Reed *Dee Johnson* • Dwight Schultz *Mike Johnson* • Paul LeMat *Merle* • Richard Lineback *Wayne* • Carrie Snodgress *Florence* • Adam Faraizl *Todd* • Nick Stahl *Brian* • James Sloyan *Dunne* ■ *Dir* Mimi Leder • *Scr* Robert L Freedman, Selma Thompson

A Woman without Love ★★

Drama 1951 · Mex · BW · 90mins

Returning to themes that he had already explored in the little-known 1932 film, *Don Quintin el Amargao* (which he co-directed, uncredited, with Luis Marquina), Luis Buñuel considered this rudimentary and overblown melodrama the worst film he ever made. Shot in just 30 days (and edited in three), it is essentially a Mexican remake of André Cayatte's 1943 adaptation of the Guy de Maupassant tale, *Pierre et Jean*. Paternal tyranny and sibling rivalry dominate the action, as inseparable half-brothers Tito Junco and Joaquin Cordero fall out over the inheritance of their respective fathers, a vulgar antique dealer and a kindly engineer. In Spanish with English subtitles.

Rosario Granados *Rosario Jiménez de Montero* • Tito Junco *Julio Mistral* • Julio Villarreal *Don Carlos Montero* • Joaquin Cordero *Carlos, hijo* • Xavier Loyà *Miguel* • Elda Peralta *Luisa Asúnsolo* • Niño Jaime Calpe *Carlitos* ■ *Dir* Luis Buñuel • *Scr* Luis Buñuel, Jaime Salvador (adaptation), Rodolfo Usigli (dialogue), from the novel *Pierre et Jean* by Guy de Maupassant

A Woman's Face ★★★★

Drama 1938 · Swe · BW · 100mins

Grotesquely disfigured in an accident during childhood, Anna Holm (Ingrid Bergman) has grown into a hard and bitter woman, but her vengeful nature is transformed, along with her face, after an operation restores her beauty. However, further distress is just around the corner when she becomes involved in a murder plot. The young Bergman gives a brilliant performance in this high-toned melodrama, adapted from a French play and made in Sweden before Hollywood adopted her. A Swedish language film.

Ingrid Bergman *Anna Holm* • Tore Svennberg *Magnus Barring* • Georg Rydeberg *Torsten Barring* • Göran Bernhard *Lars-Erik Barring* • Anders Henrikson *Dr Wegert* • Karin Kavli *Fru Vera Wegert* ■ *Dir* Gustaf Molander • *Scr* Gösta Stevens, Ragnhild Prim, Stina Bergman, from the play *Il Etait une Fois* by Francis de Croisset [François Wiener]

A Woman's Face ★★★

Melodrama 1941 · US · BW · 106mins

A major MGM vehicle for Joan Crawford, formerly a French play and previously filmed in Sweden with Ingrid Bergman, this is the melodrama about a woman whose plastic surgery changes her looks but not, it would appear, her soul. Superbly directed by the great George Cukor, and co-starring Melvyn Douglas as the surgeon and Conrad Veidt as the scheming love interest, this is Crawford's movie through and through. Her embittered and literally scarred blackmailer is thoroughly reprehensible, and therefore totally irresistible, becoming one of her all-time great creations. Sit back and wallow.

Joan Crawford *Anna Holm* • Melvyn Douglas *Dr Gustav Segert* • Conrad Veidt *Torsten Barring* • Reginald Owen *Bernard Dalvik* • Albert Basserman *Consul Barring* • Marjorie Main *Emma* • Donald Meek *Herman* • Connie Gilchrist *Christine Dalvik* ■ *Dir* George Cukor • *Scr* Donald Ogden Stewart, Elliott Paul, from the play *Il Etait une Fois* by Francis de Croisset [François Wiener]

A Woman's Secret ★★

Crime drama 1949 · US · BW · 84mins

Fans of Nicholas Ray will find little to satisfy them here. As one of the famed director's apprentice works, there's little indication of the glories to come, even for the most die-hard members of his cult following. This is daft-as-a-brush, turgid melodrama, told in flashback – a device that once worked wonderfully well for its producer/writer Herman J Mankiewicz in *Citizen Kane*, but here seems contrived and unnecessary. Gloria Grahame, Ray's wife at the time, has her moments, as does suave Victor Jory, but the whole is a very minor piece, and stars Maureen O'Hara and Melvyn Douglas both did far better work.

Maureen O'Hara *Marian Washburn* • Melvyn Douglas *Luke Jordan* • Gloria Grahame *Susan Caldwell* • Bill Williams *Lee* • Victor Jory *Brook Matthews* • Jay C Flippen *Detective Fowler* • Mary Philips *Mrs Fowler* • Robert Warwick *Roberts* ■ *Dir* Nicholas Ray • *Scr* Herman J Mankiewicz, from the novel by Vicki Baum

A Woman's Tale ★★★

Drama 1991 · Ausl · Colour · 93mins

Writer/director Paul Cox continues examining eccentric individuals with this touching tale of old age, independence and undying friendship. Sheila Florance takes centre stage as the terminally ill woman determined to die on her own terms, against the wishes of her uncomprehending son. Cox regular Norman Kaye provides admirable support as Florance's lonely neighbour, while Gosia Dobrowolska is a model of common sense as her nurse. Cox lays on the sentiment a bit thickly and offers few original insights, but it's still a pleasingly offbeat concoction. Sadly, Florance died two days after picking up the Australian equivalent of an Oscar for her performance.

Sheila Florance *Martha* • Gosia Dobrowolska *Anna* • Norman Kaye *Billy* • Chris Haywood *Johnathan* • Ernest Gray *Peter* ■ *Dir* Paul Cox • *Scr* Paul Cox, Barry Dickins

Woman's World ★★★ U

Drama 1954 · US · Colour · 94mins

A credible and often enormously entertaining look at how a giant corporation operated in the fifties, with particular reference to the treatment of its executives' wives. Clifton Webb turns in a neat portrayal as a business tycoon and has some able support from the likes of June Allyson and Van Heflin. The problem is that a great opportunity is partially thrown away to concentrate on theatrical trifles. Pretty impressive in its day, but it looks somewhat dated now.

Lauren Bacall *Elizabeth* • June Allyson *Katie* • Clifton Webb *Gifford* • Van Heflin *Jerry* • Fred MacMurray *Sid* • Arlene Dahl *Carol* • Cornel Wilde *Bill Baxter* ■ *Dir* Jean Negulesco • *Scr* Claude Binyon, Mary Loos, Howard Lindsay, Russel Crouse, Richard Sale, from a story by Mona Williams

Wombling Free ★ U

Comedy musical 1977 · UK · Colour · 92mins

The litter-gathering Wombles of Wimbledon Common turned into movie stars after first conquering television and having a number of Top 20 hits. But director Lionel Jeffries's silly and charmless musical confection came far too late to revive the careers of the adult-sized furry creations or make them as globally popular as the Muppets. Here the creatures, invisible to mankind unless they believe, lead a protest against pollution. Inoffensive child fare that will have anyone over the age of six rolling their eyes. 🖭

David Tomlinson *Roland Frogmorton* • Frances de la Tour *Julia Frogmorton* • Bonnie Langford *Kim Frogmorton* • Bernard Spear *Arnold Takahashi* • Yasuko Nagazumi *Doris Takahashi* • John Junkin *County surveyor* • Lionel Jeffries *Womble* • David Jason *Womble* • Jon Pertwee *Womble* ■ *Dir* Lionel Jeffries • *Scr* Lionel Jeffries, from characters created by Elisabeth Beresford

The Women ★★★★

Comedy 1939 · US · BW and Colour · 133mins

"There's a name for you ladies, but it's not used in high society outside of kennels." An enjoyable and witty MGM special, immaculately cast without any men, even down to the sex of the featured animals. The complicated plot, from Clare Boothe Luce's Broadway comedy, centres around divorce and infidelity, with star Norma Shearer upstaged by the magnificent Joan Crawford as queen bitch Chrystal Allen (to whom Shearer loses her off-screen hubby) and the utterly superb Rosalind Russell as a particularly venal gossip. "Woman's director" George Cukor was in his element with such material and such a cast, and there should be a famous fashion sequence in Technicolor. The 1956 musical remake entitled *The Opposite Sex* introduced men and was markedly inferior.

Norma Shearer *Mary Haines* • Joan Crawford *Chrystal Allen* • Rosalind Russell *Sylvia Fowler* • Mary Boland *Countess Delave* • Paulette Goddard *Miriam Aarons* • Joan Fontaine *Peggy Day* • Lucile Watson *Mrs Moorehead* • Phyllis Povah *Edith Potter* • Florence Nash *Nancy Blake* ■ *Dir* George Cukor • *Scr* Anita Loos, Jane Murfin, from the play by Clare Boothe Luce

Women and Men – 2 ★★★

Portmanteau drama
1991 · US · Colour · 90mins

This compilation based on three 20th-century literary classics is every bit as polished as its predecessor, *Stories of Seduction*. Walter Bernstein directs *Return to Kansas City*, Irwin Shaw's tale about an ambitious wife (Kyra Sedgwick) who pushes her boxing beau (Matt Dillon) into an ill-advised fight with a title contender. In Kristi Zea's take on Carson McCullers's *A Domestic Dilemma*, Andie MacDowell gets to play against type as a heavy drinker taken to task by her husband, Ray Liotta. But the pick of the trio is Mike Figgis's intense adaptation of Henry Miller's *Mara*, with Juliette Binoche giving a typically compelling performance as the Polish prostitute who befriends American writer in Paris Scott Glenn.

Matt Dillon *Eddie Megeffin* • Kyra Sedgwick *Arlona Megeffin* • Andie MacDowell *Emily* • Ray Liotta *Martin* • Scott Glenn *Henry* • Juliette Binoche *Mara* ■ *Dir* Walter Bernstein, Kristi Zea, Mike Figgis • *Scr* Walter Bernstein, Robert Breslo, Mike Figgis, from stories by Irwin Shaw, Carson McCullers, Henry Miller

Women and Men: Stories of Seduction ★★★ 15

Comedy drama 1990 · US · Colour · 83mins

This is a classy, starry compendium based on three short stories by Mary McCarthy, Dorothy Parker and Ernest Hemingway. The latter fares the best, with director Tony Richardson's elegiac, moving take on *Hills Like White Elephants*, boasting a typically mesmerising performance from James Woods alongside Melanie Griffith. Novelist Frederic Raphael's version of McCarthy's *The Man in the Brooks Brothers Shirt* is a witty and surprisingly accomplished piece, nicely acted by Beau Bridges and Elizabeth McGovern. Only Ken Russell lets the side down with his overblown version of Parker's story *Dusk before Fireworks*, featuring Peter Weller and Molly Ringwald.

Elizabeth McGovern *Vicki* • Beau Bridges *Gerry Breen* • Peter Weller *Hobie* • Molly Ringwald *Kit* • James Woods *Robert* • Melanie Griffith *Madley* ■ *Dir* Frederic Raphael, Ken Russell, Tony Richardson • *Scr* Frederic Raphael, Valerie Curtin, Joan Didion, John Gregory Dunne, from the short stories *The Man in the Brooks Brothers Shirt* by Mary McCarthy, *Dusk before Fireworks* by Dorothy Parker, *Hills Like White Elephants* by Ernest Hemingway

Women in Cages ★★ 18

Prison exploitation
1972 · US · Colour · 74mins

Featuring the leads from *The Big Doll House*, this Roger Corman co-produced sexploitation movie ups the sadism quotient, lowers the humour and softens the political feminist stance prevalent in other examples of the bimbos-behind-bars genre from the same era. Black icon Pam Grier is Alabama, the whip-cracking, lesbian warden of a Filipino women's prison who has it in for inmates Roberta Collins and Judy Brown and delights in making them suffer on the racks and spinning wheels in her play room torture chamber. Little gore, copious topless nudity and lip-smacking direction from Gerardo De Leon give the venerable chicks-in-chains theme a vile vitality.

Jennifer Gan *Jeff* • Judy Brown *Sandy* • Roberta Collins *Stoke* • Pam Grier *Alabama* ■ *Dir* Gerardo De Leon • *Scr* Jim Watkins

Women in Love ★★★★ 18

Drama 1969 · UK · Colour · 125mins

One of Ken Russell's most successful and, for its time, sensational forays into literature, which works so well because it is cohesively respectful of its source (D H Lawrence), besides allowing its stars acting leeway. Set in the mining community of Nottinghamshire, it stars Oliver Reed and Alan Bates who woo Glenda Jackson (an Oscar winner) and Jennie Linden, in the process bringing love and tragedy upon them all. The nude male wrestling scene makes unnecessary macho points that didn't need emphasis, but gave the film notoriety. And where would Russell be without notoriety? Contains sex scenes.

Glenda Jackson *Gudrun Brangwen* • Jennie Linden *Ursula Brangwen* • Alan Bates *Rupert Birkin* • Oliver Reed *Gerald Crich* • Eleanor

Bron *Hermione Roddice* • Alan Webb *Thomas Crich* • Vladek Sheybal *Loerke* • Catherine Willmer *Mrs Crich* • Sarah Nicholls *Winifred Crich* • Michael Gough *Tom Brangwen* ■ *Dir* Ken Russell • *Scr* Larry Kramer, from the novel by DH Lawrence

Women of the Night ★★★

Drama 1948 · Jap · BW · 75mins

War widow and mobster's mistress Kinuyo Tanaka joins her sister and sister-in-law in denouncing the evils of prostitution, only to be charged by their fellow hookers with betraying their class. This study of life in a bagnio (or legalised brothel) proved to be one of Kenji Mizoguchi's most difficult productions. Accused of being politically and cinematically obsolete, in need of funds to support his ailing sister and lambasted in the press for a phantom affair with Tanaka, it's a wonder the film is so coherent, moving and persuasive. In Japanese with English subtitles.

Kinuyo Tanaka *Fusako Owada* • Sanae Takasugi *Natsuko* • Mitsuo Nagata *Kuiyama* • Tomie Tsunoda *Kumiko* ■ *Dir* Kenji Mizoguchi • *Scr* Yoshikata Yoda, from the novel *Joseimatsuri (Girl's Holiday)* by Eijiro Hisaita

Women of Twilight ★

Drama 1952 · UK · BW · 91mins

The worst aspect of this tawdry example of tabloid film-making is that it was penned by Anatole de Grunwald, who wrote and/or produced some of the most impressive features made in postwar Britain. The twilight women are single mothers who are lured to the boarding house run by Freda Jackson as a front for her baby-farming operation. In fairness, she does give her character a John Christie-like trustworthiness, but the fallen angels and brassy madams around her are a sorry collection of clichés. Laurence Harvey wallows in a tasteless subplot about a singer caught up in murder.

Freda Jackson *Helen Allistair* • René Ray *Vivianne Bruce* • Lois Maxwell *Christine Ralston* • Joan Dowling *Rosie Gordon* • Dora Bryan *Olga Lambert* • Vida Hope *Jess Smithson* • Laurence Harvey *Jerry Nolan* ■ *Dir* Gordon Parry • *Scr* Anatole de Grunwald, from the play by Sylvia Rayman

Women of Valor ★★ 15

Second World War drama
1986 · US · Colour · 94mins

There's a patronising edge to this gung-ho Second World War drama that even acclaimed actress Susan Sarandon and her capable co-star Kristy McNichol struggle to blunt. They portray members of a group of US Army nurses held in a PoW camp on Bataan, who suffer the inevitable humiliations and hardships inflicted by the occupying Japanese. While the opening proclaims it as a tribute "to the collective courage and experiences of the American forces who served in the Philippines", it's standard fare, and not a patch on the similarly themed BBC TV series *Tenko*.

Susan Sarandon *Col Margaret Ann Jessup* • Kristy McNichol *TJ Nolan* • Alberta Watson *Lt Helen Prescott* • Valerie Mahaffey *Lt Katherine R Grace* • Suzanne Lederer *Lt Gail Polson* • Patrick Bishop *Capt Matome Nakayama* •

Terry O'Quinn *Major Tom Jessup* • Neva Patterson *Lady Judith Easton* ■ *Dir* Buzz Kulik • *Scr* Jonas McCord

Women on the Verge of a Nervous Breakdown ★★★★★ 15

Comedy 1988 · Sp · Colour · 85mins

Those unfamiliar with the work of Spanish director Pedro Almodóvar are in for a mind-boggling treat. Almodóvar's movies are full of extraordinary characters in neurotic overdrive, bursting through badly painted Art Deco doors and doing unspeakable things to each other, and this offering is no exception. Almodóvar is one of the most exciting cinema talents of the last two decades and no one remotely interested in movies should miss this film. In Spanish with English subtitles.

Carmen Maura *Pepa* • Antonio Banderas *Carlos* • Fernando Guillen [Fernando Guillen-Cuervo] *Ivan* • Julieta Serrano *Lucia* • María Barranco *Candela* • Rossy de Palma *Marisa* • Kiti Manver *Paulina* ■ *Dir/Scr* Pedro Almodóvar

Women without Men ★★

Crime drama 1956 · UK · BW · 72mins

Angela (Beverly Michaels), imprisoned for injuring a man in self-defence, escapes over Christmas in order to meet her boyfriend, who discharges himself from hospital to keep the date. Second-feature British prison drama of no particular distinction, but deploying some humour and employing some interesting names – Thora Hird, Avril Angers – which up the entertainment quotient.

Beverly Michaels *Angela Booth* • Jim Davis *Nick Randall* • Joan Rice *Cleo* • Richard Travis *Kent Foster* • Paul Cavanagh *Inspector Hedges* • Thora Hird *Granny* • Avril Angers *Bessie* • Gordon Jackson *Percy* ■ *Dir* Elmo Williams • *Scr* Richard Landau, Val Guest

Women's Prison ★★★

Drama 1955 · US · BW · 79mins

Yesterday's thick-ear melodrama becomes today's camp trash, as the enjoyable elements in this Columbia programme filler include Ida Lupino, described in the movie as a "borderline psychopath", supervisor in a jail full of fifties' blondes, including forger Jan Sterling, killer Phyllis Thaxter and a clever stripper played by the now-forgotten Vivian Marshall. The men don't get much of a look-in, and it disappoints overall because of its lack of surprises. The title says it all.

Ida Lupino *Amelia Van Zant* • Jan Sterling *Brenda Martin* • Cleo Moore *Mae* • Audrey Totter *Joan Burton* • Phyllis Thaxter *Helene Jensen* • Howard Duff *Dr Clark* • Warren Stevens *Glen Burton* ■ *Dir* Lewis Seiler • *Scr* Crane Wilbur, Jack DeWitt

Won Ton Ton, the Dog Who Saved Hollywood ★

Period parody 1976 · US · Colour · 91mins

This dismal spoof of the Golden Age of Hollywood was directed by Michael Winner while still surfing the Stateside success-wave generated by the first *Death Wish* film, which he'd made two years earlier. Mistaking fast for fun and excess for success, Winner

ploughs haphazardly through a Rin Tin Tin-type plot about a dog that becomes a movie star. He gilds his lily by raiding Tinseltown's retirement homes for cameo appearances by anyone who was still anyone in Hollywood, and a whole host who weren't. Among the 60 or so stars popping up, often pointlessly, are Johnny Weissmuller, Dorothy Lamour, and Victor Mature. Star-spotting remains the film's only abiding appeal.

Bruce Dern *Grayson Potchuck* • Madeline Kahn *Estie Del Ruth* • Art Carney *JJ Fromberg* • Ron Leibman *Rudy Montague* • Teri Garr *Fluffy Peters* • William Demarest *Studio gatekeeper* • Virginia Mayo *Miss Battley* • Henny Youngman *Manny Farber* • Ricardo Montalban *Silent film star* • Jackie Coogan *1st stagehand* • Johnny Weissmuller *2nd stagehand* • Aldo Ray *Stubby Stebbins* • Ethel Merman *Hedda Parsons* • Yvonne De Carlo *Cleaning woman* • Joan Blondell *Landlady* • Dorothy Lamour *Visiting film star* • Phil Silvers *Murray Fromberg* ■ *Dir* Michael Winner • *Scr* Arnold Schulman, Cy Howard

Wonder Bar ★★★★

Musical drama 1934 · US · BW · 84mins

From Warner Bros during their phase of musical flowering that blossomed into greats such as the *Gold Digger* movies, comes this "La Ronde" of romances that serve as an excuse for Busby Berkeley's choreography, which notably includes a production showstopper done with mirrors and the embarrassing blackface number, *Going to Heaven on a Mule*. Plotwise, nightclub owner Al Jolson and his band singer Dick Powell are both in love with dancer Dolores Del Rio, while she has her sights set on her dance partner, Ricardo Cortez, who is also the choice of wealthy socialite Kay Francis. Dirty old man comedy is provided by Guy Kibbee and Hugh Herbert, who play married men pursuing the chorus girls. Lloyd Bacon directs and, while no classic, it's terrific entertainment nonetheless.

Al Jolson *Al Wonder* • Kay Francis *Liane Renaud* • Dolores Del Rio *Ynez* • Ricardo Cortez *Harry* • Hugh Herbert *Corey* • Guy Kibbee *Simpson* ■ *Dir* Lloyd Bacon • *Scr* Earl Baldwin, from the play *Die Wunderbar,,* book by Geza Herczeg, Karl Farkas, music by Robert Katscher • *Director (Musical Numbers)* Busby Berkeley

Wonder Boys ★★★★★ 15

Comedy 2000 · US · Colour · mins

Director Curtis Hanson follows the marvellous *LA Confidential* with this quirky, dark and unforgettable little film based on the novel by Michael Chabon. Grady Tripp (Michael Douglas) is an ageing, pot-smoking college professor whose life is on shaky ground – his young third wife has left him, he's having an affair with the (married) college chancellor (Frances McDormand) and she's pregnant, he's struggling with the follow-up to his celebrated first novel, and he also has to deal with an odd, but potentially talented, student named James (Tobey Maguire). Hanson expertly weaves all of these threads (plus a dead dog, Grady's unpredictable agent and a tempting female student) into a mesmerising and often moving drama complete with fascinating characters and a wicked sense of humour. He

U = SUITABLE FOR ALL   **Uc** = SUITABLE FOR ALL, ESPECIALLY FOR YOUNG CHILDREN (VIDEO ONLY)   **PG** = PARENTAL GUIDANCE

gives Douglas one of his best roles in recent years and the film also boasts great performances from Maguire, McDormand, and Robert Downey Jr, Katie Holmes and Rip Torn.

Michael Douglas *Grady Tripp* • Tobey Maguire *James Leer* • Frances McDormand *Sara Gaskell* • Robert Downey Jr *Terry Crabtree* • Katie Holmes *Hannah Green* • Richard Thomas *Walter Gaskell* • Rip Torn *Q* • Philip Bosco *Hank Winters* ■ *Dir* Curtis Hanson • *Scr* Steve Kloves, from the novel by Michael Chabon

Wonder Man ★★★ U

Musical comedy 1945 · US · Colour · 94mins

A splendidly Technicolored fantasy in which the talented Danny Kaye plays two roles, a mild-mannered academic and his brother, a nightclub performer bumped off by gangsters, enabling his spirit to enter his brother's body. Producer Samuel Goldwyn spared no expense in surrounding Kaye with good-looking co-stars (lovely Virginia Mayo and brilliant Vera-Ellen) and a fine supporting cast (Steve Cochran is Ten-Grand Jackson, Otto Kruger's the DA), and the whole enterprise ended up taking that year's Oscar for best special effects. The opera-house climax is especially wacky, and, for those who feel resistance to Kaye's brand of clowning, this is well worth a look: his verve and genial madness keep this slightly tasteless endeavour buoyantly afloat.

Danny Kaye *Buzzy Bellew/Edwin Dingle* • Virginia Mayo *Ellen Shanley* • Vera-Ellen *Midge Mallon* • Donald Woods *Monte Rossen* • SZ Sakall *Schmidt* • Allen Jenkins *Chimp* • Steve Cochran *Ten-Grand Jackson* • Otto Kruger *DA O'Brien* ■ *Dir* Bruce Humberstone [H Bruce Humberstone] • *Scr* Don Hartman, Melville Shavelson, Philip Rapp, Jack Jevne, Eddie Moran, from a story by Arthur Sheekman

The Wonderful Country ★★★ U

Western 1959 · US · Colour · 97mins

Though director Robert Parrish's output has been continually undervalued, his movies of men in conflict with themselves, such as *The Purple Plain* and *Saddle the Wind*, are very watchable. This western benefits from a fine, brooding performance by Robert Mitchum, set against magnificent landscapes as he romances sultry Julie London. If the movie seems to ramble in its storytelling, there's never a moment when the screen isn't filled with lush visual images. Mitchum's own company produced, and the laconic star must have been proud of the result.

Robert Mitchum *Martin Brady* • Julie London *Ellen Colton* • Gary Merrill *Major Stark Colton* • Pedro Armendariz *Governor Cipriano Castro* • Jack Oakie *Travis Hight* • Albert Dekker *Captain Rucker* • Victor Mendoza [Victor Manuel Mendoza] *General Castro* • Charles McGraw *Doc Stovall* ■ *Dir* Robert Parrish • *Scr* Robert Ardrey, from the novel by Tom Lea

The Wonderful, Horrible Life of Leni Riefenstahl ★★★★

Biographical documentary 1993 · Ger · Colour and BW · 186mins

How can you possibly hope to sustain a reputation as the finest female film-

maker of all time when your sponsor was Adolf Hitler? No one can watch either *Triumph of the Will* or *Olympia* without being repulsed by their fascist overtones. But it's equally impossible to deny that Leni Riefenstahl had an unrivalled eye for a telling image and a supreme sense of visual rhythm. Celebrating her acting career and her post-Nazi achievements as a stills photographer, cultural anthropologist and underwater documentarist, Ray Muller attempts a rounded portrait that balances Riefenstahl's anti-propagandist claims with some pretty damning evidence. Riveting, revealing, but rarely irrefutable. In English and German with subtitles.

Leni Riefenstahl ■ *Dir/Scr* Ray Muller

The Wonderful Lie of Nina Petrovna ★★★★

Silent romantic melodrama 1929 · Ger · BW · 92mins

Originally screened with a lyrical orchestral score by Maurice Jaubert, Hanns Schwarz's silent melodrama was restored to something approaching its pristine glory in the late eighties. Although best known for her performance as Maria in Fritz Lang's *Metropolis*, Brigitte Helm revealed herself to be a sensitive and soulful actress with this affecting display of self-sacrificing love. Francis Lederer also impresses as the impoverished lieutenant in the Tsarist army who steals her heart, although he's made to look a little fey by Warwick Ward, as the jilted colonel, who duplicitously suggests they play poker for her affections. Pure melodrama, but tinged with art.

Brigitte Helm *Nina Petrovna* • Franz Lederer [Francis Lederer] *Lt Michael Rostoff* • Warwick Ward *Colonel Beranoff* ■ *Dir* Hanns Schwarz • *Scr* Hans Székely

Wonderful Life ★★ U

Comedy musical 1964 · UK · Colour · 108mins

The happy-clappy pop musical had been dealt a fatal blow in 1964 by the release of the Beatles' endlessly innovative and iconoclastic *A Hard Day's Night*. Yet the winsome formula continued to rear its sweetly smiling head throughout the decade. Elvis's efforts became increasingly embarrassing, but Cliff Richard and the Shadows showed enough to suggest they might have enjoyed greater success away from the cloying confines of family entertainments like this one, in which they rescue timid actress Susan Hampshire from tyrannical director Walter Slezak. The highlight, if that's the right word, is a song-and-dance history of the movies.

Cliff Richard *Johnnie* • Susan Hampshire *Jenny* • Walter Slezak *Lloyd Davis* • The Shadows *Mood musicians* • Melvyn Hayes *Jerry* • Richard O'Sullivan *Edward* • Una Stubbs *Barbara* • Derek Bond *Douglas Leslie* ■ *Dir* Sidney J Furie • *Scr* Peter Myers, Ronald Cass

The Wonderful World of the Brothers Grimm ★★ U

Musical fantasy 1962 · US · Colour · 130mins

Fantasy producer George Pal followed up his *tom thumb* with another fairy tale picture, only this time it was inflated for the giant screen Cinerama process, losing most of its potential lightness and charm. Two rather humourless actors, Laurence Harvey and Karlheinz Böhm, play the writer brothers in a framing story for three of their tales. Some excellent puppetry and animation are featured in the imaginary fables, in which Martita Hunt's witch and Jim Backus' jovial king are the most successful characters. Mary Wills won an Oscar for her costumes.

Laurence Harvey *Wilhelm Grimm* • Karl Boehm [Karlheinz Böhm] *Jacob Grimm* • Claire Bloom *Dorothea Grimm* • Walter Slezak *Stossel* • Barbara Eden *Greta Heinrich* • Oscar Homolka *The Duke* • Jim Backus *The King* • Martita Hunt *Story-teller* ■ *Dir* Henry Levin, George Pal • *Scr* David P Harmon, Charles Beaumont, William Roberts, from a story by David P Harmon, from the non-fiction book *Die Brüder Grimm* by Hermann Gerstner and from stories by Jacob Grimm, Wilhelm Grimm

Wonderland ★★★★ 18

Drama 1999 · UK · Colour · 108mins

Though the title may seem odd for a film depicting the harsh reality of London life, *Wonderland* does manage to celebrate the ordinary people who have found the capital isn't paved with the gold of opportunity. Chekhovian in form, Laurence Coriat's screenplay tells the intertwined stories of three sisters and their bickering parents (Kika Markham and Jack Shepherd). Lonely Nadia (Gina McKee) seeks love and sex via a dating agency; pregnant Molly (Molly Parker) is having trouble with her husband (John Simm); while good-time-girl Debbie (Shirley Henderson) neglects her 11-year-old son. The narrative seems to be in haphazard free fall, but the film resolves its emotional issues in satisfyingly dramatic fashion with help from Michael Nyman's music. Director Michael Winterbottom's prolific oeuvre (*Butterfly Kiss*, *Jude*, *Welcome to Sarajevo*) seems to have no theme other than stylised documentation, but he is already one of the brightest lights of British cinema. Contains swearing, sex scenes and nudity.

Gina McKee *Nadia* • Molly Parker *Molly* • Shirley Henderson *Debbie* • Ian Hart *Dan* • Stuart Townsend *Tim* • John Simm *Eddie* • Jack Shepherd *Bill* • Kika Markham *Eileen* ■ *Dir* Michael Winterbottom • *Scr* Laurence Coriat

Wonderwall ★★★ 15

Drama 1968 · UK · Colour · 74mins

One of the quintessential (and now forgotten) Swinging London films of the late sixties. Watch eccentric professor Jack MacGowran peer through his hole in the wall at disturbed model Jane Birkin amidst psychedelic butterfly effects and swirling sitars. Though Joe Massot is the movie's credited director, its real inspiration comes from its four superb collaborators: cameraman Harry Waxman, art director Assheton Gorton, editor Rusty Coppleman, and composer, Beatle

George Harrison. Contains sex scenes and drug abuse.

Jack MacGowran *Oscar Collins* • Jane Birkin *Penny* • Irene Handl *Mrs Peurofoy* • Richard Wattis *Perkins* • Iain Quarrier *Young Man* • Beatrix Lehmann *Mother* ■ *Dir* Joe Massot • *Scr* G Cain, from a story by Gérard Brach

Woo ★ 15

Romantic comedy 1998 · US · Colour · 81mins

Jada Pinkett Smith – aka Mrs Will Smith – is the stuck-up girl who proves a nightmare for date Tommy Davidson in this unfunny and hugely irritating comedy that's slightly redeemed by a decent hip-hop soundtrack. Pinkett Smith ridiculously overacts, giving a screechy, annoying performance which is only broken by numerous lingering shots of her legs in short skirts. The rest of the cast, including LL Cool J, are left to stand on the sidelines watching this disaster of a movie plod to its predictable conclusion. Contains swearing and sexual references.

Jada Pinkett Smith *Woo/Off the wall babe* • Tommy Davidson *Tim* • Duane Martin *Frankie* • Michael Ralph *Romaine* • Darrel M Heath *Hop* • Dave Chappelle *Lenny* • Paula Jai Parker *Claudette* • LL Cool J *Darryl* • Aida Turturro *Tookie* ■ *Dir* Daisy von Scherler Mayer • *Scr* David C Johnson

The Woo Woo Kid ★★ PG

Historical romantic comedy 1987 · US · Colour · 94mins

A documentary-style nostalgia film about the shenanigans of 15-year-old Ellsworth "Sonny" Wisecarver, who was put on trial in 1944 for being utterly irresistible after two affairs with older women – one of whom he married. The film is simply an excuse for a lingering look at a Waltonesque life style with Patrick Dempsey playing the seducer, Talia Balsam as his love interest and the real Wisecarver putting in a cameo amid some fake newsreel footage.

Patrick Dempsey *Ellsworth "Sonny" Wisecarver* • Talia Balsam *Judy Cusimano* • Beverly D'Angelo *Francine Glatt* • Michael Constantine *Mr Wisecarver* • Ellsworth "Sonny" Wisecarver *Mailman* ■ *Dir* Phil Alden Robinson • *Scr* Phil Alden Robinson, from a story by Bob Kosberg, David Simon, Robinson

The Wood ★★★ 15

Comedy 1999 · US · Colour · 106mins

A trio of middle-class African-Americans use one of their number's impending nuptials as an excuse to recall their early experiences in the LA suburb of Inglewood. Cue a series of extended flashbacks that show the friends dealing with school, bullies and girls. Wedding day jitters are a comedy staple, and Rick Famuyiwa's debut feature adds no new spins to the formula. What does impress is the way he steers clear of the usual gangsta/ghetto clichés while wittily revisiting the sights, sounds and outrageous fashions of the eighties.

Taye Diggs *Roland* • Omar Epps *Mike* • Richard T Jones *Slim* • Sean Nelson *Young Mike* • Trent Cameron *Young Roland* • Duane Finley *Young Slim* • Malinda Williams *Young Alicia* • De'Aundre Bonds *Stacey* ■ *Dir* Rick Famuyiwa • *Scr* Rick Famuyiwa, from a story by Rick Famuyiwa, Todd Boyd

The Wooden Horse ★★★ U

Second World War drama
1950 · UK · BW · 98mins

This is one of the most famous escape stories of the Second World War in which PoWs use a vaulting horse to hide their tunnel. What is less well known is that *Carry On* regular Peter Butterworth was one of the actual vaulters, but was refused a part in the film because he didn't look heroic enough. Scripted by Eric Williams (from his own bestseller) and directed by ex-documentary maker Jack Lee, it has a ring of authenticity that is reinforced by a splendid cast led by Leo Genn and David Tomlinson. However, the action only really becomes compelling outside Stalag Luft III as the escapees make for the coast. ▣

Leo Genn *Peter* • David Tomlinson *Phil* • Anthony Steel *John* • David Greene *Bennett* • Peter Burton *Nigel* • Patrick Waddington *Commanding Officer* • Michael Goodliffe *Robbie* • Anthony Dawson *Pomfret* ■ *Dir* Jack Lee • *Scr* Eric Williams, from his book *The Tunnel Escape*

The Woodlanders ★★ U

Drama
1997 · UK · Colour · 93mins

Director Phil Agland made his name with the Channel 4 documentary *The People of the Rainforest*. Consequently, he could not have chosen more appropriate material for his feature debut than this Thomas Hardy tale of fickle passion and betrayed devotion. Yet, while Agland admirably captures the atmosphere of the woodlands, he struggles to bring the drama to life. Much of the problem stems from the length and pacing of the scenes, although a hesitant cast, cinematographer Ashley Rowe's gloomy interiors and George Fenton's glutinous score don't help. The decision to give the ending a feminist slant is also dubious. Earnest, but undistinguished. ▣

Emily Woof *Grace Melbury* • Rufus Sewell *Giles Winterbourne* • Cal MacAninch *Dr Fitzpiers* • Tony Haygarth *Melbury* • Jodhi May *Marty South* • Polly Walker *Mrs Charmond* • Walter Sparrow *Old Creedle* • Sheila Burrell *Grandma Oliver* ■ *Dir* Phil Agland • *Scr* David Rudkin, from the novel by Thomas Hardy

Woodstock ★★★★★ 15

Music documentary
1970 · US · Colour · 177mins

Some three decades on, Woodstock the event is more ridiculed than revered. Yet, as Michael Wadleigh's vibrant documentary demonstrates, this concert in some muddy fields in upstate New York was much more than a simple moment in time – it was the end of an era. Wadleigh and assistant directors Thelma Schoonmaker and Martin Scorsese waded through untold miles of footage, using split-screen techniques to do justice to the goings-on both on stage and in the audience. Time may not have been kind to some of the views espoused here, but this is a dazzling piece of film-making and an invaluable insight into what late-sixties' youth was trying to achieve. Contains swearing and nudity. ▣

Dir Michael Wadleigh • *Scr* Country Joe and the Fish

Words and Music ★★★ U

Musical biography
1948 · US · Colour · 121mins

An engaging MGM extravaganza that purports to tell the story of brilliant songsmiths Richard Rodgers and Lorenz Hart through their music – and, to a degree, it does. Trouble is, Tom Drake is such a colourless Rodgers and Mickey Rooney such a bumptious, unsympathetic Hart that you don't give two hoots for the men behind the songs. It's a major flaw, even allowing for the fact that in 1948 Hart's homosexuality and Rodgers's ice-cold business deals couldn't really be dealt with on film at all. Still, the many pleasures include Gene Kelly and Vera-Ellen dancing a definitive *Slaughter on Tenth Avenue*, a stunning *Blue Moon* from Mel Tormé, and a touching last reunion from MGM's former child co-stars Judy Garland and Mickey Rooney, singing one of Hart's wittiest lyrics, the apt *I Wish I Were in Love Again*. Not vintage Metro, then, but today even a minor MGM musical, or a misfire like this one, is to be cherished.

Mickey Rooney *Lorenz "Larry" Hart* • Tom Drake *Richard "Dick" Rodgers* • Marshall Thompson *Herbert Fields* • Janet Leigh *Dorothy Feiner* • Betty Garrett *Peggy Lorgan McNeil* • Ann Sothern *Joyce Harmon* • Perry Como *Eddie Lorrison Anders* • Judy Garland • Mel Tormé • Gene Kelly • Vera-Ellen ■ *Dir* Norman Taurog • *Scr* Fred Finklehoffe, Ben Feiner Jr, from a story by Guy Bolton, Jean Holloway, adapted by Ben Feiner Jr, Jean Holloway, Guy Bolton, Isabel Lennart, Jack Mintz

Work ★★★★ U

Silent comedy drama
1915 · US · BW · 21mins

Charlie Chaplin's silent short is about a family that hires him to re-paper their home. Adapted from a music-hall sketch that was created during Chaplin's early days with Fred Karno, it has lost little of its slapstick hilarity and moves at a terrifically jocular pace.

Charles Chaplin *Paperhanger's assistant* • Charles Insley *Paperhanger* • Edna Purviance *Maid* • Billy Armstrong *Husband* • Marta Golden *Wife* • Leo White *Secret lover* ■ *Dir/Scr* Charles Chaplin

Work Is a Four Letter Word ★★

Comedy fantasy   1968 · UK · Colour · 93mins

In a near future dominated by automation, unemployed eccentric David Warner, under pressure from his fiancée, takes a job at the local power station. However, the hot and damp conditions of the plant are ideal for growing his hallucinogenic magic mushrooms which he proceeds to distribute as a protest against a machine-led society. This is one of those films that tells you more about its own decade than the projected futuristic era in which it is set. Nevertheless, it's interesting to see Cilla Black trying to be more than just a pop star in her role as Warner's girlfriend. A typical Swinging Sixties comedy (Peter Hall's first feature) but never as successful as the surrealistic Henry Livings stage play (*Eh?*) on which it is based.

David Warner *Val Brose* • Cilla Black *Betty Dorrick* • Elizabeth Spriggs *Mrs Murray* • Zia Mohyeddin *Dr Narayana* • Joe Gladwin *Pa Brose* • Julie May *Mrs Dorrick* • Alan Howard *The Reverend Mort* ■ *Dir* Peter Hall • *Scr* Jeremy Brooks, from the play *Eh?* by Henry Livings

Working Girl ★★★★ 15

Comedy   1988 · US · Colour · 108mins

Women, beware women! This appealing executive-suite comedy shows feminism triumphing as Melanie Griffith climbs the corporate ladder to success by stepping on Sigourney Weaver's fingers, falling for Harrison Ford in the process. Griffith is the exploited and bossed-about secretary to Weaver, taking over from her in her absence and getting Ford as the main prize. A secretary's wish-fulfiller that's an easy-going treat for all in director Mike Nichols's assured hands. Carly Simon's Oscar-winning song, *Let the River Run*, makes the soundtrack one to treasure. Contains swearing and nudity. ▣

Harrison Ford *Jack Trainer* • Sigourney Weaver *Katharine Parker* • Melanie Griffith *Tess McGill* • Alec Baldwin *Mick Dugan* • Joan Cusack *Cyn* • Oliver Platt *Lutz* • Kevin Spacey *Bob Speck* • Olympia Dukakis *Personnel Director* ■ *Dir* Mike Nichols • *Scr* Kevin Wade

Working Girls ★★★ 18

Drama   1986 · US · Colour · 89mins

Director Lizzie Borden has made a movie about prostitution that is interesting, empathic and intelligent. Set within a Manhattan brothel, the film depicts men as seeking individuality and reassurance by acting out their sexual fantasies. The women meanwhile are both support and capitalist in their satisfaction of them. Not a great film by any means, it is nevertheless a refreshing take on an industry that is usually portrayed with cliché and prejudice. Here we have the nitty gritty from birth control to bondage and Borden is frank about both. ▣

Louise Smith *Molly* • Ellen McElduff *Lucy* • Amanda Goodwin *Dawn* • Marusia Zach *Gina* • Janne Peters *April* • Helen Nicholas *Mary* ■ *Dir* Lizzie Borden • *Scr* Lizzie Borden, Sandra Kay, from a story by Borden

Working Trash ★★ U

Comedy   1990 · US · Colour · 87mins

An amusing comedy that starts off decently but winds up being spectacularly silly. Ben Stiller and comedian George Carlin star as ambitious janitors at a Wall Street brokerage house who retrieve sensitive stock data from the rubbish bins and use the insider tips to make a fortune. Don't look for in-depth character development or polished production values – this TV movie makes rather menial work of its subject. But thanks to solid performances by the cast, especially Buddy Ebsen, who plays the firm's dotty founder, this cheesy TV film delivers enough chuckles to be a reasonably pleasing entertainment. ▣

George Carlin *Ralph Sawatski* • Ben Stiller *Freddy Novak* • Michael J Pollard *Palomar* • Dan Castellaneta *George Agrande* • George Wallace [George D Wallace] *Big Dan* • Jack Blessing *R Judson Kimbrough* • Leslie Hope *Susan Fahnestock* • Buddy Ebsen *Vandevere Lodge* ■ *Dir* Alan Metter • *Scr* Jon Connolly

The World According to Garp ★★★ 15

Drama   1982 · US · Colour · 130mins

This is a magical mystery tour of a New England writer's life, which involves the mind but never engages the heart. A kind of up-market *Forrest Gump*, it's an uneasily structured exercise in pointlessness, based on John Irving's sprawling satirical novel. Robin Williams is Garp, a writer married to Mary Beth Hurt and forever at the mercy of lethal modern contraptions such as motorcars and aeroplanes. His domineering mum is played by Glenn Close in her feature debut. Director George Roy Hill contrives some felicitous moments – notably John Lithgow as a transsexual ex-footballer – and introduces topical themes such as celebrity and feminism, but felicity doesn't resolve into clarity despite good intentions. Hume Cronyn and Jessica Tandy are always a pleasure to watch, and both Close and Lithgow were nominated for Oscars. Contains violence, swearing and nudity. ▣

Robin Williams *TS Garp* • Mary Beth Hurt *Helen Holm* • Glenn Close *Jenny Fields* • John Lithgow *Roberta Muldoon* • Hume Cronyn *Mr Fields* • Jessica Tandy *Mrs Fields* • Swoosie Kurtz *Hooker* ■ *Dir* George Roy Hill • *Scr* Steve Tesich, from the novel by John Irving

A World Apart ★★★★ PG

Drama   1987 · UK · Colour · 108mins

This anti-apartheid drama is based on the true story of a white South African mother who was jailed for her support of the African National Congress. Barbara Hershey is excellent as the woman torn between the love of her family and her political beliefs, and the underused Jodhi May gives an unforgettable performance as the daughter through whose eyes the story unfolds. Stirring stuff from director Chris Menges.

Jodhi May *Molly Roth* • Barbara Hershey *Diana Roth* • Jeroen Krabbé *Gus Roth* • David Suchet *Muller* • Paul Freeman *Kruger* • Tim Roth *Harold* • Linda Mvusi *Elsie* • Carolyn Clayton-Cragg *Miriam Roth* • Yvonne Bryceland *Bertha* ■ *Dir* Chris Menges • *Scr* Shawn Slovo

The World Changes ★★★★

Drama   1933 · US · BW · 90mins

A dynastic saga that begins in uncharted 1850s Dakota and ends with the 1929 Wall Street crash, this stars Paul Muni as farm lad Orin Nordholm Jr, who becomes Chicago's leading meat industry tycoon. He is forced to watch helplessly as his wealth corrupts the values of his wife (Mary Astor) and his children and grandchildren, bringing misery and destruction in its wake. At once a hymn to the American pioneering spirit, enterprise and progress, and a pointed morality tale, the film, directed by Mervyn LeRoy, brings a striking central performance from 38-year-old Muni, who ages from early twenties to late seventies. It would be easy to pick holes in, or even deride, some of the less rigorous aspects of Edward Chodorov's solidly constructed screenplay, but this is absorbing drama.

U = SUITABLE FOR ALL   Uc = SUITABLE FOR ALL, ESPECIALLY FOR YOUNG CHILDREN (VIDEO ONLY)   PG = PARENTAL GUIDANCE

Paul Muni *Orin Nordholm Jr* • Aline MacMahon *Anna Nordholm* • Mary Astor *Virginia* • Donald Cook *Richard Nordholm* • Patricia Ellis *Natalie* • Jean Muir *Selma Peterson* • Margaret Lindsay *Jennifer* • Guy Kibbee *Claflin* ■ *Dir* Mervyn LeRoy • *Scr* Edward Chodorov, from the story *America Kneels* by Sheridan Gibney

World for Ransom ★★★

Crime drama　　1954 · US · BW · 81mins

Robert Aldrich's sophomore feature was a standard private eye outing but set in Singapore – the movie was shot in a Hollywood studio in 11 days. As with Aldrich's later masterpiece *Kiss Me Deadly*, the private eye's trail leads at first to the underworld, then to Cold War intrigue and atomic meltdown while the lady in the case proves to be the biggest mystery of all. The script is by Hugo Butler, a blacklistee, so the credit went to a "front" – someone who didn't write a word of it named Lindsay Hardy.

Dan Duryea *Mike Callahan* • Gene Lockhart *Alexis Pederas* • Patric Knowles *Julian March* • Reginald Denny *Major Bone* • Nigel Bruce *Governor Coutts* • Marian Carr *Frennessey March* • Arthur Shields *Sean O'Connor* • Douglass Dumbrille *Inspector McCollum* ■ *Dir* Robert Aldrich • *Scr* Lindsay Hardy (front for Hugo Butler)

World Gone Wild ★★ 18

Science-fiction action adventure
1988 · US · Colour · 90mins

Mad Max meets *The Magnificent Seven* in an undistinguished post-holocaust action adventure with a few imaginative riffs along the way to keep interest maintained. It's 2087, water is a precious commodity, and hippy clan leader Bruce Dern is looking for mercenaries to protect the Lost Wells oasis from an attack by power-mad Adam Ant. Unfortunately, he and his choirboy acolytes follow a "bible" based on the wit and wisdom of Charles Manson! Guru Dern acts everybody else off the screen as this lower-bracket sci-fi saga drifts into predictability and flagrant imitation. ▭

Bruce Dern *Ethan* • Adam Ant *Derek Abernathy* • Michael Paré *George Landon* • Catherine Mary Stewart *Angie* • Rick Podell *Exline* • Julius J Carry III *Nitro* • Alan Autry *Hank* • Anthony James *Ten Watt* ■ *Dir* Lee H Katzin • *Scr* Jorge Zamacona

The World in His Arms ★★ U

Romantic adventure
1952 · US · Colour · 104mins

A cornily enjoyable romantic adventure in which Gregory Peck plays an illegal sealskin trader who sails into San Francisco from Alaska, falls for a Russian countess (Ann Blyth) and has to use his fists and his sailing savvy to keep her. Directed by action expert Raoul Walsh, it's macho stuff, professionally done, with the high point an exciting race on the high seas. Amazingly, Anthony Quinn doesn't play an Eskimo or the Russian prince – he plays a Portuguese hunter. And way down the cast list is none other than British actor Bryan Forbes, with sideburns and an American accent. His bid for Hollywood stardom went nowhere; instead, Quinn commissioned Forbes's first screenplay.

Gregory Peck *Captain Jonathan Clark* • Ann Blyth *Countess Marina Selanova* • Anthony

Quinn *Portugee* • John McIntire *Deacon Greathouse* • Andrea King *Mamie* • Carl Esmond *Prince Semyon* • Eugenie Leontovich *Madame Selanova* • Sig Ruman *General Ivan Vorashilov* • Hans Conreid [Hans Conried] *Eustace* ■ *Dir* Raoul Walsh • *Scr* Borden Chase, Horris McCoy, from the novel by Rex Beach

The World Is Full of Married Men ★★ 18

Melodrama　　1979 · UK · Colour · 102mins

With a title like this, it comes as no surprise that this film is based on a sex 'n' shopping novel by Jackie Collins. Anthony Franciosa and Carroll Baker (who raised the censors' eyebrows years before in *Baby Doll*), star in this tale of a faithful wife who reassesses her life when her husband begins an affair. Made in the same year as Collins's *The Bitch* (which starred her sister Joan), this is typical British seventies titillation (lots of make-up, jewellery and low-cut tops and that's just the men), with a cast of English actors, including Gareth Hunt and Paul Nicholas, who would probably now choose to leave this opus off their CVs. Contains swearing and nudity. ▭

Anthony Franciosa *David Cooper* • Carroll Baker *Linda Cooper* • Sherrie Cronn *Claudia Parker* • Gareth Hunt *Jay Grossman* • Georgina Hale *Lori Grossman* • Paul Nicholas *Gem Gemini* • Anthony Steel *Conrad Lee* ■ *Dir* Robert William Young [Robert Young] • *Scr* Jackie Collins, from her novel

The World Is Not Enough ★★★★ 12

Spy adventure
1999 · US/UK · Colour · 127mins

A welcome return to the gritty glamour of such early outings as *From Russia with Love*, the nineteenth James Bond adventure effortlessly juggles a hard-hitting story with all the expected "super spy" embellishments and keeps it in damn-cut focus for maximum suspense and thrills. Thank director Michael Apted for the stirring, not shaky, blend of casino/ski slopes/submarine components, contained within a topical plot about the power struggle for global domination of pipelines from the oil-rich capital of Azerbaijan. Pierce Brosnan is clearly more comfortable as 007 and has more meaty drama to play besides the usual series of spectacular stunts. (The opening speedboat chase along the River Thames gets things moving in turbo drive.) Matching him every step of the way is Sophie Marceau, the best Bond Girl in ages, and Robert Carlyle, born to be a vicious Bond villain. Even Judi Dench's "M" gets out into the Middle East battlefield to show her gadget ingenuity. ▭ *DVD*

Pierce Brosnan *James Bond* • Sophie Marceau *Elektra* • Robert Carlyle *Renard* • Denise Richards *Christmas Jones* • Robbie Coltrane *Valentin Zukovsky* • Judi Dench *"M"* • Desmond Llewelyn *"Q"* • John Cleese *"R"* ■ *Dir* Michael Apted • *Scr* Neal Purvis, Robert Wade, Bruce Fierstein, from a story by Neal Purvis, Robert Wade, from characters created by Ian Fleming • *Cinematographer* Adrian Biddle

The World Moves On ★★★

Period war romance
1934 · US · BW · 104mins

The least-known of the three films John Ford directed in 1934 – the others being *Judge Priest* and *The Lost Patrol* – is a saga charting the fortunes of two New Orleans families from the 1800s to the 1920s. Along the way, it depicts the acquisition of their wealth across continents, the collapse of their commercial empires through war and the subsequent Depression, and the promise of renewal by a new generation. Ford directs this sometimes lumbering but ambitious film with impressive battlefront sequences, a strong pacifist message, and a solid cast headed by Madeleine Carroll (in a dual role) and Franchot Tone.

Madeleine Carroll *Mary Warburton* • Franchot Tone *Richard Girard* • Reginald Denny *Erik von Gerhardt* • Siegfried Rumann [Sig Ruman] *Baron von Gerhardt* • Louise Dresser *Baroness von Gerhardt* • Raul Roulien *Carlos Girard/Henri Girard* • Lumsden Hare *Sir John Warburton* • Dudley Digges *Manning* ■ *Dir* John Ford • *Scr* Reginald Berkeley, from his story

The World of Apu ★★★★★ U

Drama　　1959 · Ind · BW · 116mins

Concluding the "Apu" trilogy that began with *Pather Panchali* and *Aparajito*, this confirmed Satyajit Ray as the natural heir to both Jean Renoir and the neo-realist tradition. Adapted from Bibhutibhusan Bannerjee's semi-autobiographical novel, the unexpectedly linear narrative focuses on Soumitra Chaterjee's bid to become a writer and his struggle to accept Alok Chakravarty, the son whose birth caused the death of his beloved wife, Sharmila Tagore. Shooting on location in detail-packed long takes (pausing only for the delightfully comic father/son montage sequence), Ray coaxes heartfelt performances from his largely non-professional cast to ensure a fittingly humanist conclusion to this sublimely cinematic masterpiece. In Bengali with English subtitles.

Soumitra Chatterjee *Apurba Kumar Ray (Apu)* • Sharmila Tagore *Aparna* • Alok Chakravarty *Kajal* ■ *Dir* Satyajit Ray • *Scr* Satyajit Ray, from a novel by Bibhutibhushan Bannerjee

The World of Henry Orient ★★★★ U

Comedy　　1964 · US · Colour · 106mins

This is a charming and neglected rite-of-passage comedy, centring on the obsession of two teenage girls with a womanising concert pianist. Although Peter Sellers and his mistress Paula Prentiss turn in broadly amusing performances, it's the fantasising innocents, Tippy Walker and Merrie Spaeth, who catch the eye. Nora and Nunnally Johnson's playful script (based on the former's novel) also provides showy supporting roles for Tom Bosley and Angela Lansbury as Walker's parents. If only someone had told director George Roy Hill to stop mucking about with the film speeds, this might have garnered the attention it deserves.

Peter Sellers *Henry Orient* • Paula Prentiss *Stella* • Tippy Walker *Valerie Boyd* • Merrie

Spaeth *Marion "Gil" Gilbert* • Angela Lansbury *Isabel Boyd* • Tom Bosley *Frank Boyd* • Phyllis Thaxter *Mrs Gilbert* ■ *Dir* George Roy Hill • *Scr* Nora Johnson, Nunnally Johnson, from the novel by Nora Johnson

The World of Suzie Wong ★★

Drama　　1960 · UK · Colour · 128mins

Just about everything is wong about this drama, dealing with the life of a Hong Kong prostitute, played by Nancy Kwan, her baby son whom she hides in a slum, and the two western men in her life, American artist William Holden and playboy Michael Wilding. Both men exploit her until Holden falls in love with her. Seriously hampered by censorship restrictions, Richard Quine treats it as a comic travelogue that exploits the heroine in its own way. For Holden, the movie was part of his prolonged infatuation with the culture, food and women of the Far East and he gives the impression of an actor having a great time after the riches and fame of *The Bridge on the River Kwai*.

William Holden (1) *Robert Lomax* • Nancy Kwan *Suzie Wong* • Sylvia Syms *Kay O'Neill* • Michael Wilding *Ben* • Laurence Naismith *Mr O'Neill* • Jacqui Chan *Gwenny Lee* • Bernard Cribbins *Otis* ■ *Dir* Richard Quine • *Scr* John Patrick, from the play by Paul Osborn and the novel by Richard Mason

The World Ten Times Over ★★

Melodrama　　1963 · UK · BW · 94mins

When it appeared, this gloomy stylised melodrama struck some as a failed British attempt to emulate the French *nouvelle vague* cinema of the likes of Godard and Truffaut. Nowadays, it seems more interesting for its offbeat central situation: two over-the-hill nightclub hostesses (Sylvia Syms and June Ritchie) live together happily as long as they keep men at bay. A depressing though intelligent movie.

Sylvia Syms *Billa* • Edward Judd *Bob* • June Ritchie *Ginnie* • William Hartnell *Dad* • Sarah Lawson *Elizabeth* • Francis De Wolff *Shelbourne* • Davy Kaye *Compere* • Linda Marlowe *Penny* ■ *Dir/Scr* Wolf Rilla

The World, the Flesh and the Devil ★★

Science-fiction drama
1959 · US · BW · 94mins

A passionate, earnest and totally daft post-holocaust racial allegory. Miner Harry Belafonte lives through an atomic attack and meets two other survivors when he arrives in devastated New York City – gorgeous Inger Stevens and bigoted Mel Ferrer. Can the two men overcome their mutual hatred of each other? And who will get the girl? Aside from a few impressively mounted sequences on the deserted Manhattan streets where the two men stalk each other, this eternal triangle plea for harmony is ultimately condescending and unbelievable.

Harry Belafonte *Ralph Burton* • Inger Stevens *Sarah Crandall* • Mel Ferrer *Benson Thacker* ■ *Dir* Ranald MacDougall • *Scr* Ranald MacDougall, from the story *End of the World* by Ferdinand Reyher and the novel *The Purple Cloud* by Matthew Phipps Shiel

The World Was His Jury ★ U

Drama   1957 · US · BW · 81mins

Edmond O'Brien is the defence attorney who has never lost a case. Odd then that he takes the case of a ship's captain accused of criminal negligence resulting in numerous fatalities when there's not a shred of evidence in the man's favour. This is a drearily predictable production by Columbia's B team, producer Sam Katzman and director Fred F Sears. It's a waste of O'Brien and of Mona Freeman as his wife.

Edmond O'Brien *David Carson* • Mona Freeman *Robin Carson* • Karin Booth *Polly Barrett* • Robert McQueeney *Captain Jerry Barrett* • Paul Birch *Martin Ranker* • John Berardino [John Beradino] *Tony Armand* • Richard Cutting *DA Wendell* ■ *Dir* Fred F Sears • *Scr* Herbert Abbott Spiro

World without End ★★

Science-fiction   1955 · US · Colour · 80mins

Returning from a Mars mission, an American spaceship enters a time warp and ends up on Earth in the 26th century. Unfortunately, it's after a nuclear war has left the planet's surface inhabited by mutant cavemen, giant spiders and a superior, if listless, race forced to live underground. The shocked astronauts, led by Hugh Marlowe, finally inspire the slowly dying survivors to fight back in this colourful and very loose unofficial adaptation of HG Wells' *The Time Machine* – supporting player Rod Taylor would star in the actual adaptation five years later. Tacky and fast-paced fun, if a little moralistic, all the sets and props were recycled from other Allied Artist movies and the subterranean fairy-tale-style costumes were designed by famed pin-up artist Vargas.

Hugh Marlowe *John Borden* • Nancy Gates *Garnet* • Rod Taylor *Herbert Ellis* • Nelson Leigh *Dr Galbraithe* • Christopher Dark *Henry Jaffe* ■ *Dir/Scr* Edward Bernds

A World without Pity
★★★ 15

Romance   1989 · Fr · Colour · 84mins

Eric Rochant's directorial debut is a French equivalent of the American slacker movie. Rochant won the César (France's Oscar equivalent) for best first film, while Yvan Attal took the best newcomer prize for his performance. His co-star, Hippolyte Girardot, is the waster who comes to realise there might be more to life than scamming and partying after he falls for the ultra-respectable and brilliant Mireille Perrier. Hurrying through the action with a restless energy that reflects the pace of the young Parisians' lifestyle, the 27-year-old Rochant gives the picture a greater sense of realism by merely touching on such themes as class, social responsibility and peer pressure rather than by going into them too deeply. In French with English subtitles. Contains swearing. ▣

Hippolyte Girardot *Hippo* • Mireille Perrier *Nathalie* • Yvan Attal *Halpern* • Jean-Marie Rollin *Xavier* • Cécile Mazan *Francine* • Aline Still *Mother* ■ *Dir/Scr* Eric Rochant

World without Sun ★★★★

Documentary   1964 · Fr · Colour · 90mins

Eight years after he won the best documentary Oscar for *The Silent World*, which he co-directed with Louis Malle, Captain Jacques-Yves Cousteau landed a second statuette for this account of his mission to the bottom of the Red Sea. Living one thousand feet below the surface in a prefabricated house, Cousteau and his oceanauts conducted a thorough investigation into the region's highly diverse plant life and encountered all manner of friendly and potentially lethal creatures. In French with English commentary.

Dir Jacques-Yves Cousteau • *Scr* James Dugan, Al Ramrus, Jim Schmerer

The World's Greatest Athlete ★★★ U

Comedy   1973 · US · Colour · 88mins

Hugely enjoyable nonsense from Disney, in which beleaguered coaches John Amos and Tim Conway return from a trip to Africa with jungle dweller Jan-Michael Vincent and his pet tiger. They might just have got away with calling this *I Was a Teenage Tarzan*, as Vincent struggles to come to terms with civilisation, college campus-style. He does a nice line in bewilderment and athletic prowess, but the main fun comes when one of the coaches is shrunk by witch doctor Roscoe Lee Browne and stumbles around some giant props. The love story between Vincent and tutor Dayle Haddon slows things up, but there's enough here to keep everyone entertained. ▣

Jan-Michael Vincent *Nanu* • Tim Conway *Milo* • John Amos *Sam Archer* • Roscoe Lee Browne *Gazenga* • Dayle Haddon *Jane Douglas* • Nancy Walker *Mrs Petersen* • Danny Goldman *Leopold* ■ *Dir* Robert Scheerer • *Scr* Gerald Gardner, Dee Caruso

The World's Greatest Lover
★★ 15

Comedy   1977 · US · Colour · 89mins

In the twenties, Rudy Hickman (Gene Wilder) travels to Hollywood to enter a contest run by Rainbow Studios to find a screen lover to rival Paramount's Rudolph Valentino. His wife Annie (Carol Kane) comes along for the ride but once in town she soon falls under the spell of the real Valentino (Matt Collins). Gene Wilder's slapstick-laden romantic comedy looks handsome enough but is derailed by some lame plotting and indifferent acting. Wilder's direction is understandably similar to that of his mentor Mel Brooks, but he needed to write himself a better script. ▣

Gene Wilder *Rudy Hickman/Rudy Valentine* • Carol Kane *Annie Hickman* • Dom DeLuise *Zitz* • Fritz Feld *Hotel Manager* • Cousin Buddy • Matt Collins *Rudolph Valentino* ■ *Dir/Scr* Gene Wilder

The World's Oldest Living Bridesmaid ★★

Comedy   1990 · US · Colour · 100mins

Do not be deceived into thinking wacky title equals wacky film. This is actually a very ordinary TV movie that gives a predictable spin to a reversal-of-sex-

roles plot. Donna Mills is very funny as the high-powered lawyer who is traumatised on discovering she's fallen in love with her male secretary. But she's the only good thing in this decidedly mediocre movie, which likes to think it is keeping us guessing while all too obviously signalling each inept twist and turn.

Donna Mills *Brenda Morgan* • Brian Wimmer *Alex Dante* • Laura Press *Sheila* • Art Hindle *Roger* • Winston Reckert *Brian* ■ *Dir* Joseph L Scanlan • *Scr* Janey Kovalcik

Wounded ★★ 18

Thriller   1996 · Can · Colour · 98mins

Animal poaching isn't the theme of most thrillers but, unfortunately, that's the only original thing about this straight-to-video feature. Mädchen Amick plays a conservationist who is left for dead when an FBI raid on nasty hunter Adrian Pasdar goes horribly wrong. She is nursed back to health by sympathetic cop Graham Greene but she soon discovers that Pasdar is still intent on adding her to his trophy wall. The direction is dependable if uninspired, but the performances lift it slightly above the ordinary. Contains violence and swearing. ▣

Mädchen Amick *Julie Clayton* • Graham Greene *Rollins* • Adrian Pasdar *Hanaghan* • Richard Joseph Paul *Don Powell* • Jim Beaver *Eric Ashton* • John Paul Bivens Jr *Pearson* • Kelly Benson *Cohen's secretary* ■ *Dir* Richard Martin • *Scr* Harry Longstreet

Woyzeck ★★★★ 15

Drama   1978 · W Ger · Colour · 77mins

Filmed in 1947 by Georg Klaren and again in 1994 by the Hungarian János Szász, Georg Büchner's famous anti-militarist play has never been more perceptively staged than by Werner Herzog and his on-screen alter ego, Klaus Kinski. Revisiting the Expressionist tropes he had so recently employed on *Nosferatu, the Vampire*, Herzog conveys the mental and spiritual disintegration of Kinski's impoverished soldier, as he endures not only the dietary experiments of a local quack and the bullying of his commanding officers, but also the humiliation of being cuckolded by his wife, Eva Mattes. The heavy stylisation also reinforces the sense of socio-political and sexual suppression. A German language film. ▣

Klaus Kinski *Woyzeck* • Eva Mattes *Marie* • Wolfgang Reichmann *Captain* • Willy Semmelrogge *Doctor* ■ *Dir* Werner Herzog • *Scr* Werner Herzog, from the play *Woyzeck* by Georg Büchner

WR – Mysteries of the Organism ★★★ 18

Experimental documentary drama 1971 · Yug · Colour · 79mins

The WR of the title is Wilhelm Reich, the Austrian-born sexologist whose theories on the correlation between erogenous satisfaction and political freedom inspired this anarchic, almost stream of imagery dissertation from Dusan Makavejev. Achieving cult status on its release, the film is beginning to betray its age, although the clips of Stalin in the 1946 propaganda feature, *The Vow*, remain as amusing as the footage from the

Nazi documentary advocating euthanasia is horrifying. Makavejev provides little information about Reich or his free-loving disciples, while his allegorical fiction involving the romance between a Yugoslav girl and an inhibited Russian skater is exceedingly clumsy. In Serbian and English with subtitles. Contains strong sex scenes and swearing. ▣

Milena Dravic *Milena* • Jagoda Kaloper *Jagoda* • Zoran Radmilovic *Radmilovic* • Ivica Vidovic *Vladimir Ilyich* ■ *Dir/Scr* Dusan Makavejev

The Wraith ★ 18

Supernatural action chiller 1986 · US · Colour · 88mins

This lame-brain mix of teen comedy, stunt extravaganza and supernatural chiller plays like a modern-day *High Plains Drifter*, but with Brat Pack sensibilities. Charlie Sheen stars as a leather-clad avenging angel who returns to wreak revenge upon a gang of car thieves responsible for his death. It's a plot boring enough to make you play spot the famous sibling in the cast, which should keep you busy for most of the picture. We have Sheen, son of Martin, Nick Cassavetes, son of John, Griffin O'Neal, son of Ryan, oh and Clint Howard, brother of Ron. ▣

Charlie Sheen *Jake Kesey/The Wraith* • Nick Cassavetes *Packard Walsh* • Sherilyn Fenn *Keri Johnson* • Randy Quaid *Loomis* • Matthew Barry *Billy Hankins* • Clint Howard *Rughead* • David Sherrill *Skank* • James Bozian *Gutterboy* • Griffin O'Neal *Oggie Fisher* ■ *Dir/Scr* Mike Marvin

The Wrath of God ★★

Satirical western 1972 · US · Colour · 111mins

A certain sadness hangs over this banana republic epic since it marked the final screen appearance of Rita Hayworth, one of Hollywood's legendary sex goddesses who had developed Alzheimer's disease. She plays the mother of Frank Langella, a warlord in Central America in the twenties, while Robert Mitchum is cast as a defrocked priest who carries a gun in his Bible and ends up wired to a crucifix. It's hard to tell if the aim was to make a surrealist drama, a black comedy or merely a post-Peckinpah exercise in violence. Sadly, it succeeds only in the last category. though most will enjoy Mitchum's ironic performance.

Robert Mitchum *Father Van Horne* • Frank Langella *Tomas De La Plata* • Rita Hayworth *Senora De La Plata* • John Colicos *Colonel Santilla* • Victor Buono *Jennings* • Ken Hutchinson *Emmet* • Paula Pritchett *Chela* • Gregory Sierra *Jurado* ■ *Dir* Ralph Nelson • *Scr* Ralph Nelson, from the novel by James Graham

The Wreck of the Mary Deare ★★★ U

Adventure drama 1959 · US · Colour · 104mins

In a richly entertaining mystery adventure, Gary Cooper stars as the only man left on a freighter drifting in the English Channel when it is boarded by Charlton Heston's salvage expert. Based on the Hammond Innes novel, this MGM picture has some

spectacular scenes at sea and is lavishly staged with a strong supporting cast in the later scenes that includes Richard Harris, Michael Redgrave and Virginia McKenna. Cooper is too old to be diving underwater two years before his death but gives his co-star Heston a lesson in underplaying. Michael Anderson's unshowy direction helps make this a fine late example of a highly polished studio product.

Gary Cooper *Gideon Patch* • Charlton Heston *John Sands* • Michael Redgrave *Mr Nyland* • Emlyn Williams *Sir Wilfred Falcett* • Cecil Parker *Chairman* • Alexander Knox *Petrie* • Virginia McKenna *Janet Taggart* • Richard Harris *Higgins* ■ *Dir* Michael Anderson • *Scr* Eric Ambler, from the novel by Hammond Innes

The Wrecking Crew ★★★ PG

Action spy comedy
1969 · US · Colour · 100mins

For the fourth and last of the Matt Helm spy spoofs starring Dean Martin, Phil Karlson, director of the original movie, was dragooned back into service. The resulting romp is a send-up of *Goldfinger* – Helm has to locate tons of hijacked American bullion before its theft leads to economic meltdown. Needless to say, Helm's investigation involves the seduction of several women (including Sharon Tate), a trek across Europe and a lot of gadgets. Fans of Austin Powers will lap up its sexism, groovy styling and general lack of subtlety. ▭

Dean Martin *Matt Helm* • Elke Sommer *Linka Karensky* • Sharon Tate *Freya Carlson* • Nancy Kwan *Yu-Rang* • Nigel Green *Count Massimo Contini* • Tina Louise *Lola Medina* • John Larch *MacDonald* • Chuck Norris *Garth* ■ *Dir* Phil Karlson • *Scr* William P McGivern, from the novel by Donald Hamilton • *Karate advisor* Bruce Lee

Wrestling Ernest Hemingway ★★★ 12

Drama   1993 · US · Colour · 117mins

The most startling fact about this good-natured study of growing old in Florida is that it was actually written by a 23-year-old! Young screenwriter Steve Conrad provides meaty roles that are seized on with relish by Robert Duvall, as a lonely Cuban barber, and the sublime Richard Harris, as a flamboyant old sea dog – well, he was in *Mutiny on the Bounty*! Extra spice is provided by the excellent supporting cast, which includes a sassy, pre-*Speed* Sandra Bullock and the always welcome Piper Laurie. Only Shirley MacLaine grates, with a performance that merely goes through the motions. Overall, however, this is poignant and rather likeable, if a little theatrical. ▭

Robert Duvall *Walt* • Richard Harris *Frank* • Shirley MacLaine *Helen* • Sandra Bullock *Elaine* • Micole Mercurio *Bernice* • Marty Belafsky *Ned Ryan* • Harold Bergman *Sleeper* • Piper Laurie *Georgia* ■ *Dir* Randa Haines • *Scr* Steve Conrad

Wrestling with Alligators ★★★

Romantic drama
1998 · US/UK · Colour · 95mins

Even though rock 'n' roll was breaking down barriers, it's sometimes easy to

forget just how many taboos survived into the late fifties. Writer/director Laurie Weltz perhaps tries to tackle too many of them in this small-town melodrama, but her insights into teenage first love, abortion, matrimonial breakdown and faded glory are thoughtful and unhurried. Aleksa Palladino holds things together, as the runaway who befriends abandoned French war bride Joely Richardson, after she is impregnated by local garage owner, Jay O Sanders. However, the stand-out is Claire Bloom, as an embittered silent movie star reduced to running a boarding house for waifs and strays.

Aleksa Palladino *Maddy Hawkins* • Joely Richardson *Claire* • Claire Bloom *Lulu Fraker* • Sam Trammell *Will* • Jay O Sanders *Rick* • Adrienne Shelly *Mary* • Thomas Guiry *Pete* ■ *Dir* Laurie Weltz • *Scr* Laurie Weltz, Scott Kraft

Written on the Wind ★★★★ PG

Melodrama   1956 · US · Colour · 99mins

For all its flaunting of wealth and power, Douglas Sirk's movie is a brutal indictment of how the American dream plunges spiritual values down-market. Rock Hudson and Lauren Bacall are the "normals" sucked into the hysterical paranoia of a Texas oil millionaire's spoilt offspring – Robert Stack and Oscar-winning Dorothy Malone are outstanding in their portrayals of unleashed anger and arousal. Flashbacks, for once, explain without confusion, and watch how Sirk uses the colour red to depict Malone's sexuality. It could have been a novelette, but in Sirk's masterful hands this becomes a riveting case history.

Rock Hudson *Mitch Wayne* • Lauren Bacall *Lucy Moore* • Robert Stack *Kyle Hadley* • Dorothy Malone *Marylee Hadley* • Robert Keith *Jasper Hadley* • Grant Williams *Biff Miley* • Harry Shannon *Hoak Wayne* • Robert J Wilke *Dan Willis* ■ *Dir* Douglas Sirk • *Scr* George Zuckerman, from the novel by Robert Wilder • *Cinematographer* Russell Metty

The Wrong Arm of the Law ★★★★ U

Crime comedy   1962 · UK · BW · 90mins

Peter Sellers is at his funniest as Pearly Gates, a cockney criminal mastermind who uses a West End dress salon as a front for the illegal activities of his inept gang. He's up against Lionel Jeffries as Inspector "Nosey" Parker, whose bungling would give the future Inspector Clouseau a run for his money. Cliff Owen directs the marvellously inventive script with due care and attention as Scotland Yard and Sellers decide to co-operate to apprehend a Bill Kerr-led bunch of Australian crooks posing as policemen. There are a host of familiar faces in support, including Nanette Newman as Sellers's girl, plus a brief appearance by a pre-fame Michael Caine. ▭

Peter Sellers *Pearly Gates* • Lionel Jeffries *Inspector Parker* • Bernard Cribbins *Nervous O'Toole* • Davy Kaye *Trainer King* • Nanette Newman *Valerie* • Bill Kerr *Jack Coombes* • John Le Mesurier *Assistant Commissioner* • Michael Caine ■ *Dir* Cliff Owen • *Scr* John Warren, Len Heath, Ray Galton, Alan Simpson, John Antrobus, from a story by Ivor Jay, John Whistance Smith

The Wrong Box ★★★ U

Period comedy   1966 · UK · Colour · 101mins

Shambolic and slackly directed, Bryan Forbes's overlong period comedy was based on a Robert Louis Stevenson original about the Tontine lottery. Fortunately it managed to preserve a veritable cornucopia of British comedy talent in a film that owed more to the freewheeling Swinging Sixties than to the Victorian era in which it is set. Best of all is the redoubtable Peter Sellers, but there are also great turns from Tony Hancock and Wilfrid Lawson, as well as Peter Cook and Dudley Moore, together in their prime.The daft plot involves John Mills trying to kill Ralph Richardson over some inheritance nonsense, and among all this vintage talent, new boy Michael Caine more than holds his own. ▭

John Mills *Masterman Finsbury* • Ralph Richardson *Joseph Finsbury* • Michael Caine *Michael Finsbury* • Peter Cook *Morris Finsbury* • Dudley Moore *John Finsbury* • Nanette Newman *Julia Finsbury* • Tony Hancock *Detective* • Peter Sellers *Dr Pratt* • Wilfrid Lawson *Peacock* ■ *Dir* Bryan Forbes • *Scr* Larry Gelbart, Burt Shevelove, from the novel by Robert Louis Stevenson

The Wrong Man ★★★★ PG

Crime drama based on a true story
1956 · US · BW · 100mins

A murky and unpopular film in the Alfred Hitchcock canon, with the maestro of suspense opting for a grim and relentlessly stark style, almost documentary in nature, as he relates the true story of New York musician Manny Balestrero, arrested for a crime he did not commit. Henry Fonda is superbly believable in the title role, suggesting genuine puzzlement and dismay, and Vera Miles – Hitch cast her after being impressed by her performance in the *Revenge* episode of his TV series, *Alfred Hitchcock Presents* – is a revelation as the wife who can't handle the situation. Only distinguished English thespian Anthony Quayle seems out of place in a role that needed an American actor. Still, a fine and disturbing work that does deserve to be better known. ▭

Henry Fonda *Christopher Emmanuel "Manny" Balestrero* • Vera Miles *Rose Balestrero* • Anthony Quayle *Frank O'Connor* • Harold J Stone *Lieutenant Bowers* • Esther Minciotti *Mrs Balestrero* • Charles Cooper *Detective Matthews* • Nehemiah Persoff *Gene Conforti* • Laurinda Barrett *Constance Willis* ■ *Dir* Alfred Hitchcock • *Scr* Maxwell Anderson, Angus MacPhail, from the non-fiction book *The True Story of Christopher Emmanuel Balestrero* by Angus MacPhail • *Cinematographer* Robert Burks • *Music* Bernard Herrmann

The Wrong Man ★★★ 18

Thriller   1993 · US · Colour · 105mins

A mock *film noir* with Kevin Anderson mistakenly thought to be a murderer: well, he's found standing over a dead body with a gun in his hand. On the run in Mexico, Anderson links up with married couple Rosanna Arquette and John Lithgow. Elements of *Touch of Evil*, *Build My Gallows High* and, especially, *The Postman Always Rings Twice*, hover over the plot as Anderson and Arquette take a shine to each other. By turns funny, tense and sexy. ▭

Rosanna Arquette *Missy Mills* • Kevin Anderson *Alex Walker* • John Lithgow *Philip Mills* • Jorge Cervera Jr *Diaz* • Ernesto Laguardia *Ortega* • Robert Harper *Felix Crawley* • Dolores Heredia *Rosita* ■ *Dir* Jim McBride • *Scr* Michael Thoma, from a story by Roy Carlson

The Wrong Woman ★★ 15

Thriller   1996 · US/Can · Colour · 90mins

The story of an innocent person struggling to clear their name is one of the oldest in the book. When it's done well – *The Wrong Man*, *The Fugitive* – it makes for compelling viewing, as we suffer the innocent's growing sense of frustration and persecution. Here we simply see Nancy McKeon get framed, get arrested, go to court and then confront the real killer (who we see do the dirty deed and then bump off anyone who can expose her) without ever once feeling a pang of sympathy for her plight. Tame stuff, indeed. Contains some violence. ▭

Nancy McKeon *Melanie Brooke* • Michele Scarabelli *Christine* • Chelsea Field *Margaret* • Gary Hudson *Lt Nagel* • Stephen Shellen *Tom* • Lyman Ward *Slide* ■ *Dir* Douglas Jackson • *Scr* Douglas Soesbe

Wrongfully Accused ★★ PG

Crime spoof 1998 · US/Ger · Colour · 82mins

A non-stop assault of lame verbal and visual gags fails to elevate this second-rate spoof of *The Fugitive*, *Clear and Present Danger* and *Mission: Impossible* from director Pat Proft, co-creator of *Hot Shots* and *The Naked Gun*. Leslie Nielsen spreads himself alarmingly thin playing a superstar classical violinist accused of murder and on the run to find the real culprit, a one-armed, one-legged, one-eyed man. Even *North by Northwest* and *Chinatown* are thrown into Proft's rough and ready hodgepodge which misses practically every single target it tries so desperately to hit. Contains some sexual references. ▭

Leslie Nielsen *Ryan Harrison* • Kelly LeBrock *Lauren Goodhue* • Michael York *Hibbing Goodhue* • Richard Crenna *Marshal Fergus Falls* • Sandra Bernhard *Doctor Fridley* ■ *Dir/Scr* Pat Proft

Wuthering Heights ★★★★★ U

Classic romantic drama
1939 · US · BW · 99mins

Laurence Olivier's Heathcliff is even more handsome than the Yorkshire moors across which he howls his doomed love for Cathy (Merle Oberon) in this stirring melodrama of seething and brooding passion set in England in the 19th century. Produced by Sam Goldwyn, directed by William Wyler, and also starring David Niven, Geraldine Fitzgerald and Flora Robson, this is still the best by some way of the five big screen versions of Emily Brontë's novel (including Spanish and Egyptian productions). It garnered eight Oscar nominations, including best picture, but only won one, for Gregg Toland's black-and-white cinematography. Had there also been an Oscar for best smouldering, Olivier would have walked it. ▭

Merle Oberon *Cathy Linton* • Laurence Olivier *Heathcliff* • David Niven *Edgar Linton* • Donald

Crisp *Dr Kenneth* • Flora Robson *Ellen Dean* • Geraldine Fitzgerald *Isabella Linton* • Hugh Williams *Hindley Earnshaw* • Leo G Carroll *Joseph* ■ *Dir* William Wyler • *Scr* Ben Hecht, Charles MacArthur, from the novel by Emily Brontë • *Cinematographer* Gregg Toland

Wuthering Heights ★★★

Romantic drama 1953 · Mex · BW · 91mins

Luis Buñuel first set out to film Emily Brontë's classic novel in 1934, but lost interest in the idea. The same diminution of enthusiasm occurred in 1953, but this time he found he could not withdraw and shot the film with a script in which he had little confidence. The Mexican uplands could not be more different from the Yorkshire moors, but they still provide a suitable backdrop for this intense drama of bitterness and revenge. Notable for the ferocity of Alejandro (Jorge Mistral), Catalina's (Irasema Dilian) passion and the cruelty inflicted on animals, the film clearly captures the book's glowering mood. Buñuel disowned the use of Wagner on the soundtrack. A Spanish language film.

Irasema Dilian *Catalina* • Jorge Mistral *Alejandro* ■ *Dir* Luis Buñuel • *Scr* Luis Buñuel, Dino Maiuri [Arduino Maiuri], Julio Alejandro, from the novel *Wuthering Heights* by Emily Brontë

Wuthering Heights ★★★ 🅄

Romantic drama 1970 · UK · Colour · 80mins

In this atmospheric adaptation of Emily Brontë's famous novel Timothy Dalton's Heathcliff has clearly been modelled on Laurence Olivier's 1939 portrayal, but he still smoulders to good effect and Anna Calder-Marshall makes an appealing Cathy. Obviously aiming for a little cultural respectability, producers Samuel Z Arkoff and James H Nicholson (co-founders of B-movie factory AIP) were rewarded with some striking images from cinematographer John Coquillon and steady direction from Robert Fuest. Contains swearing. 🖭

Anna Calder-Marshall *Catherine Earnshaw* • Timothy Dalton *Heathcliff* • Harry Andrews *Mr Earnshaw* • Pamela Brown *Mrs Linton* • Judy Cornwell *Nellie* • James Cossins *Mr Linton* • Rosalie Crutchley *Mrs Earnshaw* • Hilary Dwyer *Isabella Linton* ■ *Dir* Robert Fuest • *Scr* Patrick Tilley, from the novel by Emily Brontë

Wuthering Heights ★ 🅿🅶

Romantic drama
1992 · UK · Colour · 101mins

Why there was a need to remake the superb Laurence Olivier/Merle Oberon classic adaptation of the Emily Brontë novel is one question. And then why remake it so badly is the other. Ralph Fiennes and Juliette Binoche are poorly directed by Peter Kosminsky in this tepid tale of Heathcliff, the wild child orphan, and Kathy, his lover who has ideas above her station. Binoche struggles with her English while the pair of them fail to raise even the semblance of sexual chemistry. A film that really should never have been made, it'll have you running back to the book to remember just how good it is. 🖭

Juliette Binoche *Cathy/Catherine* • Ralph Fiennes *Heathcliff* • Janet McTeer *Ellen Dean* • Sinead O'Connor *Emily Brontë* • Sophie Ward *Isabella Linton* • Simon Shepherd *Edgar*

Linton* • Jeremy Northam *Hindley Earnshaw* • Jason Riddington *Hareton* ■ *Dir* Peter Kosminsky • *Scr* Anne Devlin, from the novel by Emily Brontë

Wyatt Earp ★★★★ 🕑

Western drama 1994 · US · Colour · 182mins

Director Lawrence Kasdan's three-hour plus journey to the notorious shoot-out at the OK Corral is a monumental western that works both as a serious history lesson and as a quietly understated drama. Kasdan's beautifully filmed epic portrays the man not the legend, tracing Earp's move from boyhood innocence to knowing cynicism. It takes us from the 1860s to the turn of the century, as the Earp family move to Tombstone, Arizona, to take on the Clantons, who have been terrorising the town. On the surface, the infamous gunfight may have only been a 30-second battle, but in Kasdan's assured hands the incident is legitimately transformed into a key moment in the history of the west. Kevin Costner has seldom been better as the older Earp, and his expert range suggests all the good, bad and ugly facets of the complex character. Yet, Costner still leaves plenty of room for Dennis Quaid to steal the show as the tuberculosis-ridden dentist Doc Holliday. There's also strong support from Gene Hackman as Earp's father. Contains some violence and swearing. 🖭

Kevin Costner *Wyatt Earp* • Dennis Quaid *John "Doc" Holliday* • Gene Hackman *Nicholas Earp* • David Andrews *James Earp* • Linden Ashby *Morgan Earp* • Jeff Fahey *Ike Clanton* • Joanna Going *Josie Marcus* • Mark Harmon *Sheriff Johnny Behan* • Michael Madsen *Virgil Earp* • Catherine O'Hara *Allie Earp* • Bill Pullman *Ed Masterson* • Isabella Rossellini *Big Nose Kate* ■ *Dir* Lawrence Kasdan • *Scr* Lawrence Kasdan, Dan Gordon

Wyatt Earp: Return to Tombstone ★★

Western
1994 · US · Colour and tinted · 94mins

Not every film in the western revival of the early nineties was on a par with the Oscar-winning *Dances with Wolves* and *Unforgiven*. This TV movie is an ill-conceived attempt to wring the last drop out of *The Life and Legend of Wyatt Earp* series on American TV between 1955 and 1961, and uses colourised clips from the black-and-white original. Hugh O'Brian returns in the role that made his name, searching for a gravestone inscription and confronting a cocky young sureshot. He pluckily attempts to roll back the years, but the story would have worked better as one of the original half-hour shows.

Hugh O'Brian *Wyatt Earp* • Jay Underwood *Zack* • Harry Carey Jr *Digger Phelps* • Bruce Boxleitner *Sheriff Darling* • Alex Hyde-White *Editor Clum* • Bo Hopkins *Snake Reynolds* • Martin Kove *Bad Jack Dupree* ■ *Dir* Frank McDonald, Paul Landres • *Scr* Frederick Hazlitt Brennan, Dan Ullman

Wyoming Mail ★★ 🅄

Western 1950 · US · Colour · 86mins

This routine Universal western is made more interesting today by the fact that the supporting cast became more famous than unremarkable stars

Stephen McNally (excellent but poorly directed) and Alexis Smith (well past her glory days at Warners). Future leading man Richard Egan steals the scenes he's in, while James Arness, the bargain-basement John Wayne, makes a strong impression in his pre-Matt Dillon days. Also along for the ride are *Sweet Bird of Youth* Oscar-winner Ed Begley and Howard Da Silva as the chief villain of the piece. Despite the fact that the photography is by Russell Metty, this is really dull as ditchwater, thanks to Reginald LeBorg's turgid direction.

Stephen McNally *Steve Davis* • Alexis Smith *Mary Williams* • Howard Da Silva *Cavanaugh* • Ed Begley *Haynes* • Dan Riss *George Armstrong* • Roy Roberts *Charles DeHaven* • Whit Bissell *Sam Wallace* • James Arness *Russell* ■ *Dir* Reginald LeBorg • *Scr* Harry Essex, Leonard Lee, from a story by Robert Hardy Andrews

Wyoming Outlaw ★★ 🅄

Western 1939 · US · BW · 57mins

This is a routine *Three Mesquiteers* B-western which John Wayne made before Republic recognised that his loan-out for *Stagecoach* had turned him into a major star. He puts a professional face on having to team up with Ray Corrigan and Raymond Hatton in another trite story, about helping an outlaw expose a crooked politician. Playing the outlaw is future western lead Don Barry. Silent star Elmo Lincoln came out of retirement for the small role of a US marshal.

John Wayne *Stony Brooke* • Ray Corrigan *Tucson Smith* • Raymond Hatton *Rusty Joslin* • Don Barry [Donald Barry] *Will Parker* • Adele Pearce [Pamela Blake] *Irene Parker* • LeRoy Mason *Balsinger* • Charles Middleton *Luke Parker* • Katherine Kenworthy *Mrs Parker* • Elmo Lincoln *US marshal* • Yakima Canutt *Ed Sims* ■ *Dir* George Sherman • *Scr* Betty Burbridge, Jack Natteford, from a story by Jack Natteford, from characters created by William Colt MacDonald

X-15 ★

Drama 1961 · US · Colour · 106mins

Charles Bronson climbs into X-15, a rocket that will take man into space – just like Sputnik rival Yuri Gagarin. On the ground, meanwhile, various boffins and military types bombard us with technobabble, while the waiting women – including Mary Tyler Moore – pray the fuel doesn't run out and kill any of the three test pilots. The rich drawl of James Stewart's narration is intended to give this pseudo-documentary a much-needed gravitas. However, it nose-dived at the box office, though it did mark the debut of director Richard Donner who hit the big time with *The Omen*, *Superman* and the *Lethal Weapon* franchise.

David McLean *Matt Powell* • Charles Bronson *Lt Colonel Lee Brandon* • Ralph Taeger *Major Ernest Wilde* • Brad Dexter *Major Anthony Rinaldi* • Kenneth Tobey *Colonel Craig Brewster* • James Gregory *Tom Deparma* • Mary Tyler Moore *Pamela Stewart* • James Stewart *Narrator* ■ *Dir* Richard Donner • *Scr* Tony Lazzarino, James Warner Bellah, from a story by Tony Lazzarino

The X Files ★★★ 🕕🅕

Science-fiction conspiracy thriller
1998 · US · Colour · 117mins

The TV phenomenon of the nineties makes an effortless transition to the big screen, and, while the plot remains firmly grounded in the themes of the series, the uninitiated should not feel put off, as it plays equally well as a classy conspiracy thriller. Here, intrepid FBI duo Mulder and Scully (David Duchovny and Gillian Anderson) investigate an explosion at a federal building and stumble across the biggest alien cover-up in the world's history. Director Rob Bowman (who has also worked on the series) is faithful to the show's paranoiac roots, but gleefully opens the action out to stage some spectacular set pieces. He is well served by his leads and by the likes of Martin Landau, Armin Mueller-Stahl and John Neville. Contains violence, horror, swearing. 🖭 **DVD**

David Duchovny *Special Agent Fox Mulder* • Gillian Anderson *Special Agent Dana Scully* • John Neville *Well-Manicured Man* • William B Davis *Cigarette-Smoking Man* • Martin Landau *Dr Alvin Kurtzweil* • Mitch Pileggi *FBI Assistant Director Walter Skinner* • Armin Mueller-Stahl *Strughold* • Dean Haglund *Lone Gunman Ringo Langley* • Tom Braidwood *Lone Gunman Melvin Frohike* • Bruce Harwood *Lone Gunman John Byers* ■ *Dir* Rob Bowman • *Scr* Chris Carter, from a story by Chris Carter, Frank Spotnitz

🅄 = SUITABLE FOR ALL   🅄🅲 = SUITABLE FOR ALL, ESPECIALLY FOR YOUNG CHILDREN (VIDEO ONLY)   🅿🅶 = PARENTAL GUIDANCE

X the Unknown ★★

Science-fiction horror
1956 · UK · BW · 79mins

Cashing in on the success of the TV drama, *Quatermass*, which Hammer had already made into a feature film, this sci-fi drama deals with a series of baffling deaths at an atomic research establishment in the wilds of Scotland. It could be bog-standard radiation leaks and poisoning but maybe something else is going on, some alien slime on the loose? A typical product of the Cold War, it's all jolly polite as British boffins are led by American import Dean Jagger. His presence lends box-office appeal and also implies that British defence work has become a branch of American foreign policy.

Dean Jagger *Dr Adam Royston* • Edward Chapman *Elliott* • Leo McKern *McGill* • Marianne Brauns *Zena, nurse* • William Lucas *Peter Elliott* • John Harvey *Major Cartwright* • Peter Hammond *Lt Bannerman* ■ *Dir* Leslie Norman • *Scr* Jimmy Sangster

X, Y and Zee ★

Drama   1971 · UK · Colour · 110mins

They might have called this *Who's Afraid of Elizabeth Taylor?* Scripted by Edna O'Brien, this preposterous marital malarkey should raise a few smirks as Taylor, Michael Caine (as her husband), Susannah York (as his lover) and Margaret Leighton (as a society hostess) play it close to the edge. Taylor slashes her wrists, York's earlier affair with a nun comes to the surface and before long the pair are in bed together. Pity poor Mr Caine. But pity everyone except the costume designer who works wonders with see-through materials. So does O'Brien, for that matter. Also known as *Zee and Co.* Contains swearing, nudity.

Elizabeth Taylor *Zee Blakeley* • Michael Caine *Robert Blakeley* • Susannah York *Stella* • Margaret Leighton *Gladys* • John Standing *Gordon* • Mary Larkin *Rita* • Michael Cashman *Gavin* • Gino Melvazzi *Head Waiter* • Julian West *Oscar* ■ *Dir* Brian G Hutton • *Scr* Edna O'Brien

Xala ★★★★ 12

Satirical comedy drama
1974 · Senegal · Colour · 117mins

This savage attack on the Senegal bourgeoisie and their eagerness to indulge in the vices of their former colonial masters is couched in terms of a hilarious sex comedy, in which Thierno Leye's political promotion coincides with his third marriage and the onset of impotence. His status and dignity crumble in the face of traditional curses and cures, and Leye becomes a symbol for outdated patriarchy, with its corruption, grandiosity and superstition. His wives, on the other hand, embrace diverse historical and contemporary influences, standing for the future. Reaffirming themes explored in *Black Girl* and *The Money Order*, Ousmane Sembene confirmed his reputation as a key sub-Saharan film-maker. In Senegalese and French with English subtitles. ▣

Thierno Leye *El Hadji Aboukader Beye* • Seune Samb *Adja Assatou* • Miriam Niang *Rama* ■ *Dir* Ousmane Sembene • *Scr* Ousmane Sembene, from his novel *Xala*

Xanadu ★ PG

Musical   1980 · US · Colour · 91mins

Olivia Newton-John stars as a muse, who's descended from her heavenly seat to inspire artist Michael Beck, in a veritable cult classic of camp and glitter, roller-skating dance numbers and Gene Kelly in his final feature film role. Unfortunately, it's also an excuse for dreadful song and dance numbers, a nonexistent plot and a dose of eighties disco. Critically derided, it's no *Grease* and did nothing for Olivia's flagging career. However it is a laugh if only for its mind-boggling awfulness. ▣

Olivia Newton-John *Kira* • Gene Kelly *Danny McGuire* • Michael Beck *Sonny Malone* • James Sloyan *Simpson* • Dimitra Arliss *Helen* • Katie Hanley *Sandra* • Fred McCarren *Richie* ■ *Dir* Robert Greenwald • *Scr* Richard Christian Danus, Marc Reid Rubel, Michael Kane • *Music/Lyrics* Jeff Lynne, John Farrar

Xiao Wu ★★★

Drama   1997 · Chi/HK · Colour · 113mins

Shot on 16mm and set in the provincial town of Fenyang, Jia Zhang Ke's directorial debut is a frank portrait of a society as much in the thrall of consumerism and the black market as rigid Beijing rhetoric. Non-professional Wang Hong Wei excels as the petty thief whose world falls apart simply because he has neither the resolve nor the resources to move with the times. With its ultra-naturalistic style and theme of redemption through humiliation – recalling Robert Bresson's *Pickpocket* – this blend of uncompromising social comment and sly wit will startle those used to the lush pictorialism of such directors as Chen Kaige and Zhang Yimou. In Mandarin with English subtitles.

Wang Hong Wei *Xiao Wu* ■ *Dir* Jia Zhang Ke • *Scr* Zhang Ke Jia

Xiu Xiu: The Sent Down Girl ★★★

Political drama
1999 · US/Tai/Chi · Colour · 110mins

Actress Joan Chen makes an accomplished directorial debut with this haunting tale of unconventional love in the dying days of the Chinese Cultural Revolution. Pretty tailor's daughter Xiu Xiu (Lu Lu) is "sent down" to the countryside to share her big city smarts with the peasantry. There she is stationed with Lao Jin (Lopsang), a Tibetan herder whose simple, nomadic existence is dictated by the changing seasons. Xiu Xiu waits impatiently for orders to return home, but as months become years, she turns to prostitution in a futile attempt to end her exile. Though painfully slow in parts, Chen's powerful drama shows her to be a director of rare compassion and great promise. In Mandarin with English subtitles.

Lu Lu *Xiu Xiu* • Qian Zheng *Li Chuanbei* • Gao Jie *Mother* • Lopsang *Lao Jin* ■ *Dir* Joan Chen • *Scr* Yan Geling, Joan Chen, from the story *Tian Yu* by Yan Geling

Xtro ★ 18

Science-fiction horror
1983 · UK · Colour · 82mins

British family man Philip Sayer is abducted by a UFO. Three years later, he returns to his family, claiming to remember nothing of what happened to him in the intervening years. Soon his wife and son begin to notice some odd behavior, like his penchant for eating snake eggs, and the string of horribly mutilated bodies he leaves in his wake. Released a year after *ET* with the tagline "Not all aliens are friendly", it's only memorable now for its incredibly graphic violence and for Maryam D'Abo's first film role (and her first nude scene). ▣

Philip Sayer *Sam Phillips* • Bernice Stegers *Rachel Phillips* • Danny Brainin *Joe Daniels* • Simon Nash *Tony Phillips* • Maryam D'Abo *Analise* • David Cardy *Michael* ■ *Dir* Harry Bromley Davenport • *Scr* Robert Smith, Iain Cassie, Jo Ann Kaplan, from a screenplay by Harry Bromley Davenport, Michel Parry

Xtro 2: The Second Encounter ★ 18

Science-fiction horror
1990 · Can · Colour · 89mins

Where *Alien* inspired the first *Xtro* movie, this in-name-only sequel is a stone cold rip-off. Scientists at a secret facility discover a way to send people to an alternate dimension, and, after doing so, act really surprised when slimy killer aliens come through from the other side and infest the lab. Familiar scenes of people with guns edging down darkened corridors follow. As if it isn't hard enough to watch yet another *Alien* rip-off, *Xtro II* asks us to believe Jan-Michael Vincent is a maverick scientist. Shocking! ▣

Jan-Michael Vincent *Dr Ron Sheperd* • Paul Koslo *Dr Alex Summerfield* • Tara Buckman *Dr Julie Casserly* • Jano Frandsen *McShane* • Nicholas Lea *Baines* • WF Wadden *Jedburg* ■ *Dir* Harry Bromley Davenport • *Scr* John A Curtis, Edward Kovach, Robert Smith, Steven Lister

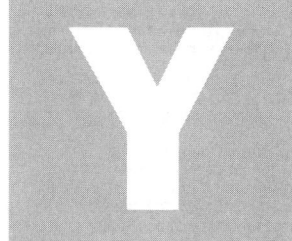

Y2K ★★ 18

Thriller   1999 · US · Colour · 99mins

It came and went so smoothly that it's hard to believe anyone believed the world's computers would crash on the stroke of the new Millennium. However, this workmanlike thriller starring Louis Gossett Jr and Malcolm McDowell is living proof of that paranoia. A secret CIA-guided missile hidden in the jungles of Colombia is about to activate itself and head off in the general direction of Moscow as the clock strikes midnight on December 31, 1999. A crack team of boffins and grunts must make sure it doesn't happen, or will the inevitable double-cross ruin the day and end existence? ▣

Louis Gossett Jr *Morgan* • Adam Harrington *Ken* • Malcolm McDowell *Seward* • Sarah Chalke *Myra* • Rick Ravanello *Thompson* • Ed O'Ross *Fairchild* ■ *Dir* Richard Pepin • *Scr* Terry Cunningham, Mick Dalrymple

Yaaba ★★★ PG

Drama tragedy
1989 · Burkina Faso · Colour · 89mins

Inspired by the folk tales he heard as a child and played with finesse by a non-professional cast, Idrissa Ouedraogo's delicately paced, neo-realist study of life in rural Burkina Faso returns to the familiar sub-Saharan themes of superstition, patriarchal arrogance and the need to strike a balance between tradition and progress. But only the landscape is barren in this unique rites-of-passage picture, in which young Noufou Ouedraogo is torn between personal feelings and communal responsibility as he tries to remain loyal to Fatima Sanga, a wizened yaaba, or grandmother, who has been ostracised by the village authorities amidst rumours of witchcraft. In Burkinabé with English subtitles.

Fatima Sanga *Yaaba* • Noufou Ouedraogo *Bila* • Roukietou Barry *Nopoko* • Adama Ouedraogo *Kougri* ■ *Dir/Scr* Idrissa Ouedraogo

Yahudi ★★★ U

Romantic melodrama
1958 · Ind · BW · 162mins

A classic Hindi film in Urdu about a Jewish woman and a Roman prince, Bimal Roy's movie is actually the fourth version of the classic story, *The Jew's Daughter*. Set in Rome at a time of Jewish persecution, it portrays the tragic love affair between a couple separated by religion. The story offers both Shakespearian echoes and universal truths, but still has room for many popular songs. In Urdu with English subtitles. ▣

Dilip Kumar *Prince Marcus* • Sohrab Modi *Ezra, the Jew* • Meena Kumari *Hannah* ■ *Dir* Bimal Roy • *Scr* Nabendu Ghosh, from the play *The Jew's Daughter* by Agha Hashar

The Yakuza ★★★★ 15

Thriller 1975 · US/Jap · Colour · 107mins

Robert Mitchum gives a brilliant performance as an ex-serviceman taking on the might of the Japanese underworld when the daughter of his best friend is kidnapped by gangsters. Writers Robert Towne (*Chinatown*) and Paul Schrader (*Taxi Driver*) working from a story by Schrader's brother Leonard, transform this simple idea into a complex and compelling thriller. Director Sydney Pollack sweeps the action along at a fast pace, allowing his cast plenty of room for manoeuvre and making the most of his Japanese locations. But this is Mitchum's film, and a must-see. Contains violence and swearing. ▭

Robert Mitchum *Harry Kilmer* • Takakura Ken *Tanaka Ken* • Brian Keith *George Tanner* • Herbert Edelman *Oliver Wheat* • Richard Jordan *Dusty* • Kishi Keiko *Tanaka Eiko* • Okada Eiji *Tono Toshiro* • James Shigeta *Goro* ■ *Dir* Sydney Pollack • *Scr* Paul Schrader, Robert Towne, from a story by Leonard Schrader

Yam Daabo ★★★

Drama 1986 · Burkina Faso · Colour · 80mins

This is a harrowing picture of the impact of drought and famine on Idrissa Ouedraogo's homeland, Burkina Faso. Just as the later *Yaaba* would rework the rites-of-passage picture, this is an sub-Saharan variation on the road movie, as a desperate family quits its parched farm and heads south in the hope of a fresh start. Some of the symbolism is heavy-handed, notably the hit-and-run death of the young son when they stop off in the city to sell their donkey, but the film concludes on a note of optimism, with the daughter and her lover expecting a child at the journey's end. In Burkinabé with English subtitles.

Auoa Guiraud *Mother* • Moussa Bologo *Bintou* • Assita Ouedraogo *Tipoko* ■ *Dir/Scr* Idrissa Ouedraogo

A Yank at Oxford ★★★

Comedy 1938 · US/UK · BW · 100mins

Designed to foster good relationships between Britain and America as Nazi stormclouds were gathering in Europe, this is the movie that marked the moment when Hollywood star factory MGM oset up production in the heart of Ye Olde England. Robert Taylor – who was mobbed throughout his stay – plays a brash American student at Oxford who shines at athletics (well, it couldn't be Latin, could it?) and gains the envy of his fellow students while Maureen O'Sullivan goes weak at the knees at the very sight of him. Vivien Leigh may have had a leading credit in the film but she misses out on a clinch with Taylor – that happened in *Waterloo Bridge*. It's still good fun, especially for the Hollywood view of the way we were then.

Robert Taylor (1) *Lee Sheridan* • Lionel Barrymore *Dan Sheridan* • Maureen O'Sullivan *Molly Beaumont* • Vivien Leigh *Elsa Craddock* • Edmund Gwenn *Dean of Cardinal College* •

Griffith Jones *Paul Beaumont* • CV France Dean Snodgrass • Edward Rigby *Scatters* ■ *Dir* Jack Conway • *Scr* Leon Gordon, Roland pertwee, Malcolm Stuart Boylan, Walter Ferris, George Oppenheimer, from a story by Sidney Gilliat, Michael Hogan, from an idea by John Monk Saunders

A Yank in Ermine ★★ U

Comedy 1955 · UK · Colour · 84mins

As there had already been a Yank at Eton, Oxford and in the RAF, it was only a matter of time before one was elevated to the peerage. Unfortunately, he came in the shape of Peter Thompson, a particularly charmless specimen of American manhood. Admittedly, he's not helped by a damp squib of a script, adapted by John Paddy Carstairs from his own novel, *Solid, Said the Earl*. What few bright moments there are come from the late Jon Pertwee, who, fittingly, made his film debut in *A Yank at Oxford*, and Harold Lloyd Jr, the son of the silent screen legend.

Peter Thompson *Joe Turner* • Jon Pertwee *"Slowburn" Jenks* • Noelle Middleton *Angela* • Harold Lloyd Jr *"Butch" Halliday* • Diana Decker *Gloria* • Reginald Beckwith *Kimp* • Edward Chapman *Duke of Fontenham* • Richard Wattis *Boone* • Guy Middleton *Bertram Maltravers* • Harry Locke *Clayton* ■ *Dir* Gordon Parry • *Scr* John Paddy Carstairs, from his novel *Solid, Said the Earl*

A Yank in the RAF ★★ U

Second World War drama
1941 · US · BW · 97mins

Many films, cynically relying on a star or single unifying idea to hook the audience in advance, tend to be woefully underscripted. Such was the fate of many a wartime flag-waver, and the need for a patriotic lift was often enough to get audiences into the threepenny fleapits. Here, aside from Betty Grable giving it her all-singing, all-dancing all in a couple of numbers, this is the very definition of a damp squib. If even the action scenes are dozing, then the characters must be fully asleep.

Tyrone Power *Tim Baker* • Betty Grable *Carol Brown* • John Sutton *Wing Commander Morley* • Reginald Gardiner *Roger Pillby* • Donald Stuart *Corporal Harry Baker* • John Wilde *Graves* • Richard Fraser *Thorndyke* • Morton Lowry *Squadron Leader* ■ *Dir* Henry King • *Scr* Darrell Ware, Karl Tunberg, from a story by Melville Crossman [Darryl F Zanuck]

Yankee Doodle Dandy ★★★★ U

Musical biography 1942 · US · BW · 120mins

As well as being responsible for *Casablanca*, Michael Curtiz was also one of the great directors of musical talent (Al Jolson, Bing Crosby, Elvis Presley), and here, under Curtiz's wing, the great James Cagney gives the performance of his life as Broadway's George M Cohan, rightly securing the best actor Oscar for the role. The film needs to be viewed in context today: it is fearsomely patriotic, overloop to a degree and extremely sentimental, but it was geared to serve a major purpose. It reminded Americans that there was a war going on in Europe and, in saluting the composer of *Over There*, Warner Bros effectively fashioned a celluloid recruiting poster.

So, if you find it heavy going, bear with it for Cagney's classic dance routines: if you only know him as a gangster, here's the reminder that he was more than a match for both Gene Kelly and Fred Astaire. ▭

James Cagney *George M Cohan* • Joan Leslie *Mary* • Walter Huston *Jerry Cohan* • Richard Whorf *Sam Harris* • George Tobias *Dietz* • Irene Manning *Fay Templeton* • Rosemary De Camp *Nellie Cohan* • Jeanne Cagney *Josie Cohan* • SZ Sakall *Schwab* ■ *Dir* Michael Curtiz • *Scr* Robert Buckner, Edmund Joseph, from a story by Buckner

Yankee Pasha ★ U

Period romantic adventure
1954 · US · Colour · 83mins

Technicolored tosh set in the early nineteenth century, it features Rhonda Fleming as the New England gal captured by Barbary pirates and sold to a Moroccan sultan for his harem. Jeff Chandler as her rough-and-ready boyfriend comes to the rescue. Mamie Van Doren, Universal's potential rival to Marilyn Monroe, is prominently featured as one of the harem slaves, while the others are Miss Universe beauty contestants. This is a good-looking, fast moving adventure that covers a lot of territory but without ever becoming the slightest bit interesting.

Jeff Chandler *Jason* • Rhonda Fleming *Roxana* • Mamie Van Doren *Lilith* • Bart Roberts [Rex Reason] *Omar-Id-Din* • Lee J Cobb *Sultan* ■ *Dir* Joseph Pevney • *Scr* Joseph Hoffman, from the novel by Edison Marshall

Yanks ★★★ 15

Second World War romantic drama
1979 · UK · Colour · 133mins

Director John Schlesinger's effort glows with a homely period charm, but never descends into sentimentality. The story is about GIs stationed in Britain during the Second World War. Richard Gere always looks good in uniform and Schlesinger gives a nice touch to the simmering juxtaposition of British working-class morality on a buzz bomb collision course with young adult hormones. The strong cast interplays superbly, and the scene where the lads march off for D-Day is particularly moving. ▭

Richard Gere *Sergeant Matt Dyson* • Vanessa Redgrave *Helen* • William Devane *John* • Lisa Eichhorn *Jean Moreton* • Chick Vennera *Sergeant Danny Ruffelo* • Rachel Roberts *Clarrie Moreton* • Tony Melody *Jim Moreton* • Wendy Morgan *Mollie* ■ *Dir* John Schlesinger • *Scr* Walter Bernstein, Colin Welland, from his story

The Yarn Princess ★★

Drama 1994 · US · Colour

There have been dozens of TV movies about custody battles before, but none quite like this one. Jean Smart gives an admirable performance as a developmentally slow but caring mother who valiantly tries to give her six sons the best of everything, even though she finds it hard to acquire the necessary skills to care for them. Naturally, this muddle-and-make-do idyll can't last for ever, and when husband Robert Pastorelli falls ill, the local welfare officers threaten to split up the family unless matters drastically improve. Shirley Knight provides some accomplished support. Keep the

tissues close at hand, just to be on the safe side.

Jean Smart *Margaret Thomas* • Robert Pastorelli *Jake Thomas* • Dennis Boutsikaris *Steven Hoffman* • Justin Burnette *Mike Thomas* • Karl David-Djerf *Jimmy Thomas* • Luke Edwards *Daniel Thomas* • Lee Garlington *Wanda* ■ *Dir* Tom McLoughlin • *Scr* Dalene Young

The Year My Voice Broke ★★★★ 15

Drama 1987 · Ausl · Colour · 100mins

One of those rare movies about teenagers which doesn't treat them as an alien species – it neither patronises nor exploits. That's because Australian writer/director John Duigan constructs his piece with understanding and insight, while the young actors in the lovesick triangle – Noah Taylor, Loene Carmen, Ben Mendelsohn – bring their characters to life with subtle authority. A success thanks to the fact that our sympathies lie with them as members of the human race, not outsiders. Contains swearing.

Noah Taylor *Danny Embling* • Loene Carmen *Freya Olson* • Ben Mendelsohn *Trevor* • Graeme Blundell *Nils Olson* • Lynette Curran *Anne Olson* • Malcolm Robertson *Bruce Embling* • Judi Farr *Sheila Embling* ■ *Dir/Scr* John Duigan

The Year of Living Dangerously ★★★★ PG

Political thriller
1982 · Ausl/US · Colour · 109mins

Atmospheric Australian-made, Hollywood-backed thriller about an Aussie radio journalist (Mel Gibson) on assignment in Indonesia in the mid-sixties, where the dictatorship is shaky and Sigourney Weaver is working as an attaché at the British embassy. Peter Weir's film wanders at times, but also offers plenty of spectacle and colour, a steamy romance between Gibson and Weaver, and its share of excitement when Gibson discovers more than it is safe for him to know. But the highlight is Linda Hunt's performance as a male Chinese-Australian photographer, for which she won an Oscar. Contains swearing. ▭

Mel Gibson *Guy Hamilton* • Sigourney Weaver *Jill Bryant* • Linda Hunt *Billy Kwan* • Bembol Roco *Kumar* • Domingo Landicho *Hortono* • Hermino De Guzman *Immigration officer* • Michael Murphy *Pete Curtis* • Noel Ferrier *Wally O'Sullivan* ■ *Dir* Peter Weir • *Scr* David Williamson, Peter Weir, CJ Koch, from the novel by CJ Koch

Year of the Comet ★★★ PG

Romantic comedy adventure
1992 · US · Colour · 86mins

Romancing the Stone meets *The 39 Steps* in a sardonic screwball adventure set around the Scottish Highlands and the French Riviera. Wine merchant Penelope Ann Miller discovers a rare bottle of 1811 Château Lafitte worth $1 million and plans to escort it to auction. But bon viveur villain Louis Jourdan wants it because written on the label is a formula for the elixir of life. Tim Daly is the suave action man hero who accidentally gets sucked into the *Boy's Own* adventure complete with off-beat action and sassy one-liners. An under-

U = SUITABLE FOR ALL   Uc = SUITABLE FOR ALL, ESPECIALLY FOR YOUNG CHILDREN (VIDEO ONLY)   PG = PARENTAL GUIDANCE

rated black comedy romp with many fun moments, it was William Goldman's first original script after *Butch Cassidy and the Sundance Kid.* 🎞

Penelope Ann Miller *Maggie Harwood* • Timothy Daly *Oliver Plexico* • Louis Jourdan *Philippe* • Art Malik *Nico* • Ian Richardson *Sir Mason Harwood* • Ian McNeice *Ian* • Timothy Bentinck *Richard Harwood* • Julia McCarthy *Landlady* ■ *Dir* Peter Yates • *Scr* William Goldman

Year of the Dragon ★★ 18

Crime drama 1985 · US · Colour · 128mins

Few directors can claim the ups and downs of Michael Cimino's career. A brilliant debut with *Thunderbolt and Lightfoot*, followed by the Oscar-winning *The Deer Hunter*, then the legendary flop *Heaven's Gate*. By comparison, this violent crime thriller is unexceptional in every respect, barring some accusations of inherent Asian racism. With a script co-written by Oliver Stone, this sour-tasting tale of highly decorated cop Mickey Rourke cleaning up corrupt Chinatown features some incredibly intense action and one of Rourke's more believable characterisations. Trouble is, there's not a likeable character in sight, the tone is absurdly melodramatic and it seems to go on forever. 🎞

Mickey Rourke *Stanley White* • John Lone *Joey Tai* • Ariane *Tracy Tzu* • Leonard Termo *Angelo Rizzo* • Raymond Barry [Raymond J Barry] *Louis Bukowski* • Caroline Kava *Connie White* • Eddie Jones *William McKenna* ■ *Dir* Michael Cimino • *Scr* Oliver Stone, Michael Cimino, from the novel by Robert Daley

Year of the Gun ★★★ 15

Political thriller 1991 · US · Colour · 107mins

A political thriller that's way below the standard of director John Frankenheimer's sixties' classics *The Manchurian Candidate* and *Seven Days in May*, but still reasonably gripping and intriguing. Set in Rome in 1978, when the Red Brigades terrorist group was active, it follows the fortunes of two journalists: Andrew McCarthy is writing a novel that features a fictitious terrorist mission; Sharon Stone is a photographer whose efforts to gatecrash McCarthy's project and his love life lead to mayhem. While Stone looks good and looks the part, too, the main problem is the bland McCarthy; the role really needs someone like James Woods or Michael Douglas to give it weight. Contains violence, swearing, nudity. 🎞

Andrew McCarthy *David Raybourne* • Sharon Stone *Alison King* • Valeria Golino *Lia Spinelli* • John Pankow *Italo Bianchi* • George Murcell *Pierre Bernier* • Mattia Sbragia *Giovanni* • Roberto Posse *Lucio Spinelli* • Thomas Elliot *Marco Spinelli* ■ *Dir* John Frankenheimer • *Scr* David Ambrose, from the novel by Michael Mewshaw

The Year of the Horse ★ 15

Musical documentary
1997 · US · BW and Colour · 107mins

Even fans of folk rocker Neil Young and his band Crazy Horse will find this arch rockumentary tedious. Filmed in Europe and America during the group's 1996 tour, cult director Jim Jarmusch combines new concert footage with archive material of Young when he was

at the height of his popularity. Slotted in between are behind-the-scenes clips of road anecdotes and to-camera interviews. Jarmusch's minimalist style and the band's boring musings (except for those of amusing guitarist Frank ''Poncho'' Sampedro) provide little insight into the Crazy Horse universe and many will be left wondering why they even bothered. Jarmusch directed this vanity production because he hooked up with Young for his *Dead Man* soundtrack and, in return, the musician asked him to shoot the video for the song *Big Time*. The rest is not very interesting history. Contains swearing, drug abuse.

Dir Jim Jarmusch • *Cinematographer* Jim Jarmusch, LA Johnson

A Year of the Quiet Sun ★★★★ 15

Romantic drama
1984 · Pol/US/W Ger · Colour · 108mins

The winner of the Golden Lion at Venice, Krzysztof Zanussi's gentle love story, involving an emotionally fractured GI and a fatalistic Polish widow is set in 1946 against a backdrop of political transformation, war-crimes trials and lingering psychological trauma. Using the devastated landscape to contrast the inhumanity of war with the indomitability of the human spirit, Zanussi similarly sets the couple's communication difficulties against their tentative passion, his largesse against her poverty and his hopes for the future against her fierce loyalty to her disabled mother. Scott Wilson and Maja Komorowska excel, while Zanussi's direction has a keen sense of place and poetry. In Polish and English with subtitles.

Maja Komorowska *Emilia* • Scott Wilson *Norman* • Hanna Skarzanka *Emilia's mother* • Ewa Dalkowska *Stella* • Vadilh Glowna *Niemiec* • Daniel Webb *David* ■ *Dir/Scr* Krzysztof Zanussi

The Yearling ★★★★ U

Drama 1946 · US · Colour · 133mins

This lovely and loving story of a boy and his pet fawn, based on Marjorie Kinnan Rawlings's Pulitzer Prize-winning novel, takes its strength from an understatement of dramatic events and the underplaying of the actors (Gregory Peck and Jane Wyman as poor crop farmers; special Oscar-winning Claude Jarman Jr as their son). Veteran director Clarence Brown shapes it into a tale that touches the heart while never patronising the mind. Sentiment without sentimentality.

Gregory Peck *Pa Baxter* • Jane Wyman *Ma Baxter* • Claude Jarman Jr *Jody Baxter* • Chill Wills *Buck Forrester* • Clem Bevans *Pa Forrester* • Margaret Wycherly *Ma Forrester* • Henry Travers *Mr Boyles* • Forrest Tucker *Lem Forrester* • Donn Gift *Fodderwing* ■ *Dir* Clarence Brown • *Scr* Paul Osborn, from the novel by Marjorie Kinnan Rawlings

The Yearling ★★★ U

Drama 1994 · US · Colour · 122mins

Claude Jarman Jr won a special Oscar for his affecting performance in the 1946 version of this tear-jerking animal tale. Wil Horneff does well enough in this TV movie remake, but his wide-

eyed innocence just doesn't have the same conviction as Jarman's. The story of a Florida kid who tries to rear a fawn while his family struggle in the Depression is still a winner, however, and Peter Strauss and Jean Smart competently handle the parental roles. 🎞

Peter Strauss *Penny Baxter* • Jean Smart *Ora Baxter* • Wil Horneff *Jody Baxter* • Jarred Blancard *Fodderwing Forrester* • Philip Seymour Hoffman *Buck Forrester* • Nancy Moore Atchison *Eulalie* • Brad Greenquist *Lem Forrester* • Richard Hamilton *Pa Forrester* ■ *Dir* Rod Hardy • *Scr* Joe Wiesenfeld, from the novel by Marjorie Kinnan Rawlings

Yeelen ★★★★ PG

Fantasy 1987 · Mali · Colour · 104mins

The timeless significance of ancient custom to the Bambara peoples of Mali is explored in this haunting political fable from Souleymane Cissé. Having been threatened with death by his shaman father, Issiaka Kane goes into exile, where he learns the power and value of the magical gifts he will need to succeed in his Oedipal struggle. Although much of the symbolism is as obscure to non-Malian viewers as the story's historical background, there's no denying the simple poetry of the landscape or Cissé's technical mastery, as he explores in minute detail the secret Komo rituals that will ensure prosperity through self-sacrifice. In Bambara with English subtitles.

Issiaka Kane *Nianankoro* • Aova Sangere *Attu* • Niamanto Sanogo *Soma* • Balla Moussa Keita *Peul King* ■ *Dir/Scr* Souleymane Cissé

The Yellow Balloon ★★

Crime drama 1952 · UK · BW · 79mins

A typical example of the many dour dramas churned out by postwar British cinema. Exploiting the period's austere atmosphere and run-down landscapes, it owes much to such Hollywood ''child in peril'' pictures as *The Window*. In his second film as writer/director, J Lee Thompson would have done better to focus on the relationship between timid pre-teen Andrew Ray and fugitive killer William Sylvester, but he can't resist throwing in a social message and a family crisis that slows the action and dilutes the suspense. Kenneth More flops as the doting dad, but Kathleen Ryan makes a monstrously shrewish mother.

Andrew Ray *Frankie* • Kathleen Ryan *Em* • Kenneth More *Ted* • Bernard Lee *Constable Chapman* • Stephen Fenemore *Ron* • William Sylvester *Len* • Marjorie Rhodes *Mrs Stokes* • Peter Jones *Spiv* • Eliot Makeham *Pawnbroker* • Sidney James *Barrow boy* ■ *Dir* J Lee Thompson • *Scr* Anne Burnaby, J Lee Thompson, from the story by Anne Burnaby

The Yellow Cab Man ★★★ U

Comedy 1950 · US · BW · 84mins

Three years after he stole the show from Cary Grant and Loretta Young in *The Bishop's Wife*, that unsung character actor James Gleason was back behind the wheel of a cab for this knockabout Red Skelton vehicle. Indeed, it's the supporting cast (which includes Edward Arnold and Gloria DeHaven) that keeps this scatterbrained comedy on the road, as

Skelton mugs along in typical fashion as an eccentric inventor who causes chaos wherever he goes. Alongside Gleason, Walter Slezak is a standout as the unscrupulous villain desperate to get his hands on the secret of unbreakable glass.

Red Skelton *Augustus ''Red'' Pirdy* • Gloria DeHaven *Ellen Goodrich* • Walter Slezak *Doctor Byron Dokstedder* • Edward Arnold *Martin Creavy* • James Gleason *Mickey Corkins* ■ *Dir* Jack Donohue • *Scr* Devery Freeman, Albert Beich, from a story by Devery Freeman

The Yellow Canary ★★

Second World War spy drama
1943 · UK · BW · 93mins

It may not sound like it, but this is a Second World War Herbert Wilcox–Anna Neagle adventure, with Anna spying for good old Blighty by pretending to be a Nazi sympathiser in Canada. Anna Neagle?? Interestingly, the screenplay of this preposterous tosh was written by actor/playwright Miles Malleson and DeWitt Bodeen, known for his RKO Val Lewton thrillers (*Cat People*) and *I Remember Mama*. Director Wilcox hasn't a clue how to build the thrills inherent in this kind of material, and as Neagle and her intelligence shadow Richard Greene sabotage the Nazi plot to blow up a Nova Scotia harbour, the whole thing becomes gently risible. Trouble is, it wasn't meant to be funny.

Anna Neagle *Sally Maitland* • Richard Greene *Jim Garrick* • Margaret Rutherford *Mrs Towcester* • Nova Pilbeam *Betty Maitland* • Albert Lieven *Jan Orlock* • Lucie Mannheim *Madame Orlock* • Marjorie Fielding *Lady Maitland* ■ *Dir* Herbert Wilcox • *Scr* Miles Malleson, DeWitt Bodeen, from a story by Pamela Bower

The Yellow Canary ★★

Thriller 1963 · US · BW · 92mins

Pop star Pat Boone and his wife Barbara Eden are experiencing marriage difficulties. But their differences are forgotten when they return home one night to find their nursemaid murdered and their baby son missing. The kidnappers have left a note citing ''canary'' as a code word in future dealings and soon a $200,000 ransom demand is made. A by-numbers thriller with sadly few twists and turns en route. Look out for Jack Klugman (later TV's *Quincy*) as a plodding police detective.

Pat Boone *Andy Paxton* • Barbara Eden *Lissa* • Steve Forrest *Hub Wiley* • Jack Klugman *Lieutenant Bonner* • Jesse White *Ed Thornburg* ■ *Dir* Buzz Kulik • *Scr* Rod Serling, from the novel *Evil Come, Evil Go* by Whit Masterson

Yellow Earth ★★★★★ U

Wartime drama 1984 · Chi · Colour · 90mins

This adaptation of Ke Lan's novel was a key film in the evolution of Fifth Generation Chinese cinema. Set in 1939, the story concerns the hopes of emancipation raised in a peasant girl by a soldier on a mission to collect folk songs. Inspired by the compositional values of traditional art, debuting director Chen Kaige and cinematographer Zhang Yimou, firmly root the characters in their desolate Shaanxi environment and use space, colour and nuance to suggest the contrast between Communist zeal and rural complacency. More philosophical than political, this is also a provocative treatise on the need for a balance between tradition and progress.

Xue Bai • Wang Xueqi • Tan Tuo • Liu Qiang ■ Dir Chen Kaige • Scr Zhang Ziliang from the novel by Ke Lan

Yellow Jack ★★★
Drama   1938 · US · BW · 83mins

In Cuba at the end of the 19th century, an American medical research team led by a lifeless Lewis Stone battles to find the cause of yellow fever – or ''yellow jack'' as the American soldiers call it – that is decimating the country. Irish sergeant Robert Montgomery and four of his men eventually answer the call for volunteers for a life-threatening experiment. Adapted from a play by Sidney Howard and Paul de Kruif, the film, based on factual events, is almost very good. Although informative, intelligent, and even at times gripping, the uneven script periodically collapses into dull repetition, a romance between Montgomery and nurse Virginia Bruce is unlikely and irritating, and George B Seitz's direction is uninspired.

Robert Montgomery John O'Hara • Virginia Bruce Frances Blake • Lewis Stone Major Walter Reed • Andy Devine Charlie Spell • Henry Hull Dr Jesse Lazear • Charles Coburn Dr Finlay • Buddy Ebsen Jellybeans ■ Dir George B Seitz • Scr Edward Chodorov, from the play by Sidney Howard, Paul de Kruif

The Yellow Mountain ★★
Western   1954 · US · Colour · 77mins

The ''yellow'' in the mountain is gold, of course, and it leads to some pretty unremarkable sparring between former Tarzan Lex Barker and former radio actor Howard Duff in a very average Universal western. Produced by Ross Hunter before he got into his stride as the purveyor of gloss 'n' froth, invariably starring Doris Day or Lana Turner.

Lex Barker Andy Martin • Mala Powers Nevada Wray • Howard Duff Pete Menlo • William Demarest Jackpot Wray • John McIntire Bannon • Leo Gordon Drake ■ Dir Jesse Hibbs • Scr George Zuckerman, Russell Hughes, Robert Blees, from a story by Harold Channing Wire

The Yellow Rolls-Royce ★★
Drama   1964 · UK · Colour · 121mins

A typically British trilogy of thin anecdotes about the owners of a Rolls-Royce Phantom II – four wheels, famous radiator, painted yellow, three careful owners. The writer and director have a similar pedigree, though Terence Rattigan and Anthony Asquith's readiness to recycle their previous excursion into jet-set gloss, The VIPs, seemed a foolish idea in the first place; all MGM wanted was a whole series of Grand Hotel remakes. The European locations match poorly with the kitsch sets and the whole thing seems all dressed up with nowhere to go. In a cast of famous names, Joyce Grenfell gets the Margaret Rutherford role and offers a pleasing diversion.

Rex Harrison Marquess of Frinton • Jeanne Moreau Marchioness of Frinton • Edmund Purdom John Fane • Michael Hordern

Harmsworth • Shirley MacLaine Mae Jenkins • George C Scott Paolo Maltese • Alain Delon Stefano • Art Carney Joey • Ingrid Bergman Gerda Millett • Omar Sharif Davich • Joyce Grenfell Hortense Astor • Wally Cox Ferguson ■ Dir Anthony Asquith • Scr Terence Rattigan

The Yellow Rose of Texas ★★ 🅄
Western   1944 · US · BW · 69mins

There's a showboat setting for this otherwise routine Roy Rogers western in which Dale Evans plays opposite him: more than two dozen further co-starring roles and off-screen marriage would follow. Here Dale runs the showboat and gives Roy a singing job on board, not knowing he's an insurance investigator after money supposedly stolen by her father. With Grant Withers in the cast, the real villain is obvious. The traditional title song, which is also the name of the showboat, is among several featured.

Roy Rogers • Dale Evans Betty Weston • Grant Withers Lukas • Harry Shannon Sam Weston • George Cleveland Captain Joe ■ Dir Joseph Kane • Scr Jack Townley

Yellow Sky ★★★
Western   1948 · US · BW · 96mins

Highly regarded in many critical quarters, this bleak western owes much to superb location photography by My Darling Clementine's Joe MacDonald, and to the confrontational leading roles played by two of 20th Century-Fox's best stars – Gregory Peck and sneering Richard Widmark – in their glorious early years. But the pace is often staggeringly slow and the story, which is clearly inspired by Shakespeare's The Tempest, sits awkwardly in its majestic Death Valley setting. It's a reasonable version of the ''outlaws ride into ghost town'' plot, but is really only a B movie dressed up in A-movie finery.

Gregory Peck Stretch • Anne Baxter Mike • Richard Widmark Dude • Robert Arthur Bull Run • John Russell Lengthy • Henry Morgan [Harry Morgan] Half Pint • James Barton Grandpa • Charles Kemper Walrus • Robert Adler Jed ■ Dir William A Wellman • Scr Lamar Trotti, from the novel by WR Burnett

Yellow Submarine ★★★★ 🅄
Animated musical fantasy
1968 · UK · Colour · 86mins

The Beatles had little to do with this amazing animated feature (although they do crop up at the end). Directed by George Dunning and boasting Love Story's Erich Segal among the screenwriters, this is an endlessly inventive picture that blends sixties psychedelia with such diverse styles as pop art and Art Deco to create the fantastical world of Pepperland and its bizarre inhabitants. The mix of new songs and old favourites works a treat, but George Martin's superb score is also well worth a listen. 📷 **DVD**

John Clive John • Geoffrey Hughes Paul • Peter Batten George • Paul Angelis Ringo/Chief Blue Meanie • Dick Emery Lord Mayor/Nowhere Man/Max • Lance Percival Old Fred ■ Dir George Dunning • Scr Lee Minoff, Al Brodax, Erich Segal, Jack Mendelsohn, from a story by Lee Minoff, from the song by John Lennon, Paul McCartney

The Yellow Tomahawk ★★
Western   1954 · US · Colour · 82mins

Feathers fly in a strongly pro-Indian western as Rory Calhoun's scout is forced to fight his good friend, Lee Van Cleef's Cheyenne warrior. The yellow tomahawk is sent as a declaration of war to Warner Anderson's arrogant army major who has massacred Native American women and children and plans to build a fort in their territory. An Indian bow of friendship figures in the ironic conclusion. Peggie Castle has the female lead while Rita Moreno plays a squaw. Veteran B-western director Lesley Selander puts pace before subtlety.

Rory Calhoun Adam • Peggie Castle Katherine • Noah Beery Jr Tonio • Warner Anderson Major Ives • Peter Graves (1) Sawyer • Lee Van Cleef Fireknife • Rita Moreno Honey Bear • Walter Reed Keats ■ Dir Lesley Selander • Scr Richard Alan Simmons, from a story by Harold Jack Bloom

Yellowbeard ★ 🄸🄵
Comedy adventure
1983 · US · Colour · 92mins

What a way to go! Surely Marty Feldman deserved a better screen swan song than this diabolical comedy. Co-stars Graham Chapman and Peter Cook should have been made to walk the plank for their contributions to a sloppy script, and they can count themselves lucky that the cast was made up of old friends, otherwise they might have had a mutiny on their hands. Awful is charitable. Contains violence, swearing and nudity. 📷

Graham Chapman Yellowbeard • Peter Boyle Moon • Richard ''Cheech'' Marin El Segundo • Tommy Chong El Nebuloso • Peter Cook Lord Lambourn • Marty Feldman Gilbert • Michael Hordern Dr Gilpin • Eric Idle Commander Clement • James Mason Captain Hughes • John Cleese Blind Pew • Spike Milligan Flunkie • Susannah York Lady Churchill • Beryl Reid Lady Lambourn ■ Dir Mel Damski • Scr Graham Chapman, Peter Cook, Bernard McKenna

Yellowstone Kelly ★★★ 🅄
Western   1959 · US · Colour · 92mins

Big Clint Walker became a major TV star as a result of playing the title role in the Warner Bros cowboy series Cheyenne, and the studio tried to capitalise on his success in three well-made western features, of which this was the second. Veteran Warners director Gordon Douglas is in charge as buckskin-clad Walker attempts to quell an ''Injun'' uprising, supported by other TV names of the time such as Edward Byrnes (77 Sunset Strip) and The Lawman's John Russell. The Technicolor exteriors are superb, but the monosyllabic Walker never cut it as a movie star, becoming a useful supporting player and occasional lead in programme fillers.

Clint Walker ''Yellowstone'' Kelly • Edward Byrnes [Edd Byrnes] Anse • John Russell Gall • Ray Danton Sayapi • Claude Akins Sergeant • Warren Oates Corporal ■ Dir Gordon Douglas • Scr Burt Kennedy, Clay Fisher

Yentl ★★ 🄿🄶
Musical drama
1983 · UK/US · Colour · 127mins

Barbra Streisand's first film as a director is based on a story by Isaac Bashevis Singer, set in 1904 in central Europe and centres on a Jewish girl who dresses as a boy to receive a religious education. Such complications suggest a kosher Victor/Victoria or Tootsie, but Streisand takes it very seriously. Despite the obvious pains taken with the period setting (British studio interiors plus Czech location work), it rather lumbers along. The film won the Oscar for best original score and two of the songs were nominated. 📷

Barbra Streisand Yentl • Mandy Patinkin Avigdor • Amy Irving Hadass • Nehemiah Persoff Reb Mendel • Steven Hill Reb Alter Vishkower ■ Dir Barbra Streisand • Scr Jack Rosenthal, Barbra Streisand, from the short story Yentl, the Yeshiva Boy by Isaac Bashevis

Yes, Giorgio ★ 🄿🄶
Romantic musical
1982 · US · Colour · 106mins

Alp-sized tenor Luciano Pavarotti's film debut ended up as a contrived star vehicle, with the singing mountain playing an opera star (surprise, surprise) who falls for the woman throat specialist called in to cure him when his voice fails during a US tour. It's just about as bad as it sounds. But add an extra star to the rating if you're potty about Pav, and have to see anything he sings in. 📷

Luciano Pavarotti Giorgio Fini • Kathryn Harrold Dr Pamela Taylor • Eddie Albert Henry Pollack • Paola Borboni Sister Teresa • James Hong Kwan • Beulah Quo Mei Ling ■ Dir Franklin J Schaffner • Scr Norman Steinberg, from the novel Yes, Giorgio by Anne Piper

Yes Virginia, There Is a Santa Claus ★★★
Drama   1991 · US · Colour

This is worth watching just to see Charles Bronson in a cuddly family drama. Mind you, he still manages to be the grumpiest person in the TV movie, playing a world-weary journalist in 1897 who has to reply to a young girl who has written to his paper asking whether there really is a Santa Claus. It's a nice twist on the familiar tale of adult cynicism versus childhood innocence, and Bronson is a joy to watch as the gruff newspaper man who doesn't believe in anything much after the death of his wife and child. Richard Thomas is the unemployed dad who can't afford to buy his daughter Virginia any Christmas presents.

Charles Bronson Francis P Church • Richard Thomas James O'Hanlon • Edward Asner [Ed Asner] Edward P Mitchell • Colleen Winton Andrea • Tamsin Kelsey Evie • Katharine Isobel [Katherine Isobel] Virginia O'Hanlon ■ Dir Charles Jarrott • Scr Val DeCrowl, Andrew J Fenady

Yesterday Girl ★★★★
Drama   1966 · W Ger · BW · 92mins

Thirty-four-year-old Alexander Kluge was already a lawyer before he made his first feature, which is based on the case of a woman he encountered during his work. Called Anita G (played

superbly by Alexandra Kluge, the director's sister), she is an anarchic East German woman who escapes to West Germany only to find herself at odds with a different but equally conservative society. Kluge, obviously influenced by the French New Wave, gives the film the feeling of a case history by using documentary-style interviews. The movie came as a breath of fresh air to the moribund German film industry, though this freshness has staled over the years. In German with English subtitles.

Alexandra Kluge *Anita G* • Günther Mack *Pichota* • Eva Maria Meinecke [Eva-Maria Meineke] *Frau Pichota* • Hans Korte *Judge* • Edith Kuntze-Pellogio *Parole board officer* • Peter Staimmer *Young man* ■ *Dir/Scr* Alexander Kluge

Yesterday, Today and Tomorrow ★★★ 15
Portmanteau comedy drama
1963 · Fr/It · Colour · 118mins

Notwithstanding its superstar backstage credentials, this Oscar-winning portmanteau only occasionally delivers on the screen. In spite of story credits for Alberto Moravia, screenwriting nods for playwright Eduardo De Filippo and neorealist guru Cesare Zavattini and the directorial elegance of Vittorio De Sica, only the first tale *Adelina*, about Neapolitan husband-and-wife smugglers who exploit a law forbidding the arrest of pregnant women, is consistently amusing. Set in Milan, *Anna* again teams Sophia Loren and Marcello Mastroianni in a parable about materialism, while in *Mara*, a Roman prostitute ends a week-long vow of chastity with a striptease that was to garner all the film's headlines. An Italian language film.

Sophia Loren *Adelina/Anna/Mara* • Marcello Mastroianni *Carmine/Renzo/Augusto Rusconi* • Tina Pica *Grandmother* ■ *Dir* Vittorio De Sica • *Scr* Eduardo DeFilippo, Isabella Quarantotti, Cesare Zavattini, Billa Billa Zanuso, from the story *Troppo Ricca* by Alberto Moravia

Yesterday's Enemy ★★★
Second World War drama
1959 · UK · BW · 95mins

Under-rated British film-maker Val Guest churned out splendid comedy scripts during the thirties, then became an energetic genre director, peaking in the fifties with science-fiction classics (*The Quatermass Experiment*), thrillers (*Hell is a City*) and this tough war movie. It was one of a group that introduced a note of cynicism and irony, replacing the slightly softer, almost nostalgic war films of the late forties. Adapted by Peter R Newman from his own television drama, it's set in 1942 and tells of the unexpected consequences when a group of British soldiers take over a Burmese village. The absence of music and the widescreen black-and-white photography lend a gritty feel to this well-acted film.

Stanley Baker *Capt Langford* • Guy Rolfe *Padre* • Leo McKern *Max* • Gordon Jackson *Sgt MacKenzie* • David Oxley *Doctor* • Richard Pasco *2nd Lt Hastings* • Russell Waters *Brigadier* ■ *Dir* Val Guest • *Scr* Peter R Newman, from a TV play by Peter R Newman

Yesterday's Hero ★
Sports drama   1979 · UK · Colour · 94mins

After *The Stud* and *The Bitch* bestselling author Jackie Collins wrote this soccer saga, only this time, sister Joan was nowhere to be seen – that says it all! Ian McShane is the George Best-inspired footballer aiming for a comeback after beating a booze problem. Will he make it to the cup final? Paul Nicholas (playing an Elton John-type rock star chairman) and Adam Faith (as McShane's manager) help him achieve his goal. But the end result is strictly fourth division in every aspect.

Ian McShane *Rod Turner* • Suzanne Somers *Cloudy Martin* • Adam Faith *Jake Marsh* • Paul Nicholas *Clint Simon* • Sandy Ratcliff *Rita* • Sam Kydd *Sam Turner* • Glynis Barber *Susan* ■ *Dir* Neil Leifer • *Scr* Jackie Collins

Yesterday's Tomorrow ★★
Drama   1978 · W Ger · Colour · 106mins

Pola Kinski – the half-sister of Nastassja – makes a rare appearance as a traumatised survivor of the Second World War who falls in love with a German-born American officer, played by Mel Ferrer. Tragedy looms all over this Occupation drama and the film doesn't surprise in this regard. In the end, the relationship isn't explored in any depth and despite the fine performances it's really just people talking in rooms while Chopin drones away on the soundtrack. German dialogue dubbed into English.

Mel Ferrer *Colonel Henry Stone* • Pola Kinski *Anna Eichmayr* • Martin Luttge *Alfons* • Hannelore Schroth *Frau Almany* ■ *Dir* Wolfgang Staudte • *Scr* Dorothee Dhan

Yield to the Night ★★★ 15
Crime drama   1956 · UK · BW · 95mins

Directed with a grim sense of purpose by J Lee Thompson, this sincere plea for the abolition of capital punishment was based on the case of Ruth Ellis, the last woman in Britain to be hanged and whose story was retold more than 30 years later with a good deal more style by Mike Newell in *Dance with a Stranger*. Diana Dors gives one of the best performances of her career as the murderess recalling the circumstances that drove her to kill while waiting to hear if she will be reprieved. Yvonne Mitchell and Athene Seyler stand out in a solid supporting cast.

Diana Dors *Mary Hilton* • Yvonne Mitchell *MacFarlane* • Michael Craig *Jim Lancaster* • Geoffrey Keen *Chaplain* • Olga Lindo *Hill* • Mary MacKenzie *Maxwell* • Joan Miller *Barker* ■ *Dir* J Lee Thompson • *Scr* Joan Henry, John Cresswell, from the novel by Joan Henry

Yojimbo ★★★★★ PG
Action   1961 · Jap · BW · 105mins

Such was the influence of the Hollywood western on Akira Kurosawa's superb samurai action adventure that it seems only fair that it, in turn, inspired Sergio Leone's *A Fistful of Dollars*, the film that launched the Italian "spaghetti" western. Combining moments of comedy, intrigue and sudden, shocking violence, Kurosawa manages to celebrate the samurai genre at the same time as he is subtly subverting

it. Toshiro Mifune is tremendous as the wandering warrior who sells his sword skills to both sides in a divided village only to dupe them into mutual slaughter. He returned in the sequel, *Sanjuro*, the following year. Japanese with English subtitles.

Toshiro Mifune *Sanjuro Kuwabatake* • Eijiro Tono *Gonji* • Seizaburo Kawazu *Seibei* • Isuzu Yamada *Orin* • Hiroshi Tachikawa *Yoichiro* • Susumu Fujita *Homma* ■ *Dir* Akira Kurosawa • *Scr* Akira Kurosawa, Ryuzo Kikushima, Hideo Oguni • *Music* Masaru Satô

Yol ★★★★★ 15
Drama   1982 · Tur · Colour · 109mins

Anger and sadness lie at the heart of this treatise on the perpetuation of the patriarchal prejudices underpinning Turkish society. The film was written by Yilmaz Güney, while in prison for so-called political offences, and directed from explicit instructions by his longtime assistant, Serif Gören. The negative was then smuggled to Switzerland, where Güney edited it following his escape. The winner of the Palme d'Or at Cannes, it testifies to the courage of Turkey's greatest-ever film-maker. But, perhaps more significantly, the story of the five parolees who must face up to personal calamity also highlights the tragedy of a nation whose future is so hidebound by its past. In Turkish with English Subtitles.

Tarik Akan *Seyit Ali* • Halil Ergün *Mehmet Salih* • Necmettin Çobanoglu *Omer* • Serif Sezer *Ziné* ■ *Dir* Serif Gören • *Scr* Yilmaz Güney

Yolande and the Thief ★★★ U
Romantic fantasy musical
1945 · US · Colour · 107mins

Fred Astaire, more balletic than usual, and Lucille Bremer, an expressionless red-haired dancer, play the title roles in an MGM musical which gave Vincente Minnelli ample scope to express his taste for decorative fantasy with some stunning dream sequences. These numbers, drenched in exotic colours, burst forth when Fred dreams himself into a surrealistic landscape and are the best parts of the film. Set in a mythical Latin American country, the mediocre yet whimsical story has Astaire as a confidence trickster, who pretends to be the guardian angel (literally) of the naive, convent-educated heroine… and her millions.

Fred Astaire *Johnny Parkson Riggs* • Lucille Bremer *Yolanda Aquaviva* • Frank Morgan *Victor Budlow Trout* • Mildred Natwick *Aunt Amarilla* • Mary Nash *Duenna* • Leon Ames *Mr Candle* ■ *Dir* Vincente Minnelli • *Scr* Ludwig Bemelmans, Irving Brecher, from a short story by Jacques Thery, Ludwig Bemelmans

Yor, the Hunter from the Future ★ 15
Science-fiction adventure
1983 · It/Tur · Colour · 84mins

An inept, cheesy muscleman epic from Italian hack director Antonio Margheriti (Anthony M Dawson) who obviously thought mixing *Conan* with *Star Wars* was a stunningly original idea. An Italian-Turkish production starring one-time Captain America Reb Brown

(which says it all really) this absolute stinker features the blond-wigged hero fighting cardboard dinosaurs and robot hordes (with a touch of the Darth Vaders), accompanied by a tacky disco theme song. Not even fun on a camp level, *Yor* is a bore and absolute hell to sit through.

Reb Brown *Yor* • Corinne Cléry *Ka-Laa* • John Steiner *Overlord* • Carole Andre *Ena* ■ *Dir* Anthony M Dawson [Antonio Margheriti] • *Scr* Robert Bailey, Anthony M Dawson [Antonio Margheriti], from the novel *Yor* by Juan Zanotto, Ray Collins

You and Me ★★★
Crime drama   1938 · US · BW · 90mins

In a department store whose humane owner employs ex-convicts on parole, a love affair blossoms, but goes horribly wrong because of a misguided deceit practised by one of the sweethearts. George Raft and the born-to-suffer Sylvia Sidney star in this very curious mixture of crime melodrama, moral message and feel-good love story, directed by Fritz Lang who injects some equally curious stylistic devices, as well as his characteristic gift for creating tension. Much reviled by serious critics at the time of its release, seen now it's actually very entertaining.

Sylvia Sidney *Helen* • George Raft *Joe Dennis* • Harry Carey *Mr Morris* • Barton MacLane *Mickey* • Warren Hymer *Gimpy* • Roscoe Karns *Cuffy* ■ *Dir* Fritz Lang • *Scr* Virginia Van Upp, from a story by Norman Krasna • *Music* Kurt Weill • *Lyrics* Sam Coslow

You Belong to Me ★★★
Romantic comedy   1941 · US · BW · 94mins

Barbara Stanwyck and Henry Fonda, the magical pairing of *The Lady Eve* were reunited in an offering which, while hardly standing comparison, is good fun. The plot has Stanwyck as a successful doctor married to wealthy Fonda. He doesn't need to work so, with time on his hands, develops an obsessive jealousy of her male patients from which springs both the humorous situations and the more sober moments. The stars are a dream, superseding the otherwise one-dimensional material.

Barbara Stanwyck *Dr Helen Hunt* • Henry Fonda *Peter Kirk* • Edgar Buchanan *Billings* • Roger Clark *"Van" Vandemer* • Ruth Donnelly *Emma* • Melville Cooper *Moody* • Ralph Peters *Joseph* • Maude Eburne *Ella* ■ *Dir* Wesley Ruggles • *Scr* Claude Binyon, from the story *You Belong to Me* by Dalton Trumbo

You Better Watch Out ★★★★ 18
Horror   1980 · US · Colour · 96mins

A taut and tense little suspense movie to put the gloom on any Christmas festival, this stars Brandon Maggart as the psycho who delivers death dressed as Santa Claus. Directed by Lewis Jackson, it was also released as *Christmas Evil* and *Terror in Toyland*. It lives up to those titles as well.

Brandon Maggart *Harry Stadling* • Dianne Hull *Jackie Stadling* • Scott McKay *Fletcher* • Joe Jamrog *Frank Stoller* • Peter Friedman *Grosch* • Ray Barry [Raymond J Barry] *Gleason* • Bobby Lesser *Gottleib* • Sam Gray *Grilla* ■ *Dir/Scr* Lewis Jackson

You Can Thank Me Later
★★

Comedy drama 1998 · Can · Colour · 110mins

As the Cooperberg family anxiously wait in a hospital ward for news of their beloved patriarch, they each flash back to black-and-white confessionals outlining some of the more unsavoury moments in their lives. Jewish director Shimon Dotan takes the dysfunctional family concept to new theatrical heights in a melodramatic comedy rich in character if not in plot. The superlative ensemble cast clearly revels in acting out the accusations, home truths and dark secrets of a family slowly losing its roots, values and morals.

Geneviève Bujold *Joelle* • Ellen Burstyn *Shirley Cooperberg* • Amanda Plummer *Susan Cooperberg* • Ted Levine *Eli Cooperberg* • Mark Blum *Edward Cooperberg* • Roc LaFortune *TV repairman* ■ *Dir* Shimon Dotan • *Scr* Oren Safdie, from his play *Hyper-Allergenic*

You Can't Cheat an Honest Man
★★

Comedy 1939 · US · BW · 76mins

Devised by WC Fields under one of his pseudonyms, this comedy had a fraught production involving two directors besides the credited George Marshall. A double had to be used in some of Fields's scenes, thanks to on-set arguments and his penchant for drinking doubles. Although not one of his classics, the film allows Fields considerable rein as Larson E Whipsnade, an impecunious circus owner whose daughter is prepared to marry a wealthy toff to help her father, even though she's in love with someone else. Some of the best moments come when Fields turns up at the proposed wedding.

WC Fields *Larson E Whipsnade* • Edgar Bergen *The Great Edgar* • Constance Moore *Victoria Whipsnade* • John Arledge *Phineas Whipsnade* • James Bush *Roger Bel-Goodie* ■ *Dir* George Marshall • *Scr* George Marion Jr, Richard Mack, Everett Freeman, Henry Johnson, Lew Lipton, from a story by Charles Bogle [WC Fields]

You Can't Escape Forever ★

Crime drama 1942 · US · BW · 77mins

Warner Bros milked its undistinguished 1934 Paul Muni picture *Hi Nellie!* for no less than three minor remakes. This is the second, with George Brent portraying the managing editor of a newspaper who's demoted to looking after the personal advice column. He stages a comeback by exposing racketeer Eduardo Ciannelli (who had temporarily renamed himself Edward). Long-time Warner Bros dialogue coach Jo Graham occupies the director's chair with lacklustre results.

George Brent *Steve "Mitch" Mitchell* • Brenda Marshall *Laurie Abbott* • Gene Lockhart *Carl Robelink* • Edward Ciannelli [Eduardo Ciannelli] *Boss Greer* ■ *Dir* Jo Graham • *Scr* Fred Niblo Jr, Hector Chevigny, from the story *Hi Nellie!* by Roy Chanslor

You Can't Get Away with Murder
★★

Prison crime drama 1939 · US · BW · 75mins

The unwieldy but graphically accurate title of this movie says it all: a formula second-rung crime tale that demands the death of both protagonists. One is Humphrey Bogart, recycling the standard gangster he played eleven times in four years; the other is Dead End Kid Billy Halop. Bogart is an irredeemable, conscience-free thug who seduces the youngster into a life of crime, with Halop's disillusion and repentance coming too late to save him. Ponderously directed by Lewis Seiler and containing not a single original idea.

Humphrey Bogart *Frank Wilson* • Gale Page *Madge Stone* • Billy Halop *Johnnie Stone* • John Litel *Attorney Carey* • Henry Travers *Pop* • Harvey Stephens *Fred Burke* ■ *Dir* Lewis Seiler • *Scr* Robert Buckner, Don Ryan, Kenneth Gamet, from the play *Chalked Out* by Lewis E Lawes, Jonathan Finn

You Can't Have Everything
★★★

Musical comedy 1937 · US · BW · 89mins

Here's a real novelty – a 20th Century-Fox musical with an original plot twist. Would you believe Alice Faye as the descendant of Edgar Allan Poe? And that she despises musical comedy? An unlikely peg on which to hang the appearance of a lot of vaudeville troupers, but this movie's got a cast-and-a-half for connoisseurs: the Ritz Brothers, Louis Prima, Tony Martin, and Tip, Tap and Toe. And watch out for featured Louise Hovick – better known as Gypsy Rose Lee. Faye is her usual self, and sings the title with style, but the plot eventually defeats her. It doesn't matter, though: it's all expertly done, and fans of Faye and Don Ameche need no recommendation.

Alice Faye *Judith Poe Wells* • Harry Ritz • Al Ritz • Jimmy Ritz • Don Ameche *George Macrea* • Charles Winninger *Sam Gordon* • Louise Hovick [Gypsy Rose Lee] *Lulu Riley* • David Rubinoff • Tony Martin *Bobby Walker* • Arthur Treacher *Bevins* ■ *Dir* Norman Taurog • *Scr* Harry Tugend, Jack Yellen, Karl Tunberg, from a story by Gregory Ratoff

You Can't Hurry Love ★★ 18

Comedy 1988 · US · Colour · 88mins

A routine if well-acted story of a hick from the sticks who comes to stay with his trendy LA cousin and hits the swinging-singles scene by signing up to a video-dating service. His ensuing love life has thoroughly predictable ups (a few) and downs (a lot). This episodic comedy has its wry and amusing moments, but is generally flattered by a cast whose best-known faces include Bridget Fonda, Kristy McNichol, Charles Grodin and Sally Kellerman. ▭

David Packer *Eddie* • Scott McGinnis *Skip* • Bridget Fonda *Peggy* • David Leisure *Newcomb* • Anthony Geary *Tony* • Frank Bonner *Chuck Hayes* • Sally Kellerman *Kelly Bones* • Charles Grodin *Mr Glerman* • Kristy McNichol *Rhonda* ■ *Dir* Richard Martini, Richard Martini • *Scr* Richard Martini

You Can't Run Away from It
★★ U

Musical 1956 · US · Colour · 94mins

A remake of the Oscar-winning classic *It Happened One Night*, with June Allyson as the runaway heiress and Jack Lemmon as the newsman she runs into on a Greyhound bus. Some sequences, including the famous "Walls of Jericho" and hitchhiking sketches are transferred from 1934 almost shot-for-shot, but there are also some musical numbers, including a cringe-making song from Stubby Kaye on the bus. And since Miss Allyson was mainly a musical star from the MGM stock company, she has a dance sequence that is a show stopper in quite the wrong way.

June Allyson *Ellie Andrews* • Jack Lemmon *Peter Warne* • Charles Bickford *AA Andrews* • Paul Gilbert *George Shapely* • Jim Backus *Danker* • Stubby Kaye *Fred Toten* ■ *Dir* Dick Powell • *Scr* Claude Binyon, from the screenplay *It Happened One Night* by Robert Riskin, from the short story *Night Bus* by Samuel Hopkins Adams

You Can't Take It with You
★★★★★ U

Comedy 1938 · US · BW · 120mins

Frank Capra won a third, well-deserved Oscar in five years for this sparkling comedy (it also won best picture). Based on the George S Kaufman and Moss Hart play and scripted by Robert Riskin – who won an Oscar for Capra's *It Happened One Night* – it's about the eccentric Vanderhof family, New Yorkers whose wealth belies a vast range of eccentricity and political opinion. It's also a fable about individualism and everyone's need to resist corporate or group control. The movie contains wonderful performances from a cast that includes bubbly Jean Arthur and James Stewart as her drawling fiancé, and, if it is a touch overlong, that is a minor fault considering the vast comic talent on display. ▭

Jean Arthur *Alice Sycamore* • Lionel Barrymore *Martin Vanderhof* • James Stewart *Tony Kirby* • Edward Arnold *Anthony P Kirby* • Mischa Auer *Kolenkhov* • Ann Miller *Essie Carmichael* • Spring Byington *Penny Sycamore* • Samuel S Hinds *Paul Sycamore* ■ *Dir* Frank Capra • *Scr* Robert Riskin, from the play by George S Kaufman, Moss Hart • *Cinematographer* Joseph Walker • *Music* Dimitri Tiomkin [Dmitri Tiomkin] • *Costume Designers* Bernard Newman • *Costume Designer* Irene

You Can't Win 'em All
★★★ PG

Adventure comedy 1970 · UK · Colour · 95mins

During the collapse of the Ottoman Empire in twenties Turkey, former American soldiers Tony Curtis and Charles Bronson are hired to protect the Sultan's three daughters and a shipment of gold. Leo V Gordon's poor script is given vitality by Peter Collinson's zippy direction and the repartee of the stars. ▭

Tony Curtis *Adam Dyer* • Charles Bronson *Josh Corey* • Michèle Mercier *Aila* • Grégoire Aslan *Osman Bey* • Fikret Hakan *Colonel Elci* • Salih Guney *Captain Enver* • Patrick Magee *General* • Tony Bonner *Reese* ■ *Dir* Peter Collinson • *Scr* Leo V Gordon

You Gotta Stay Happy ★★ U

Romantic comedy 1948 · US · BW · 100mins

Joan Fontaine – doing her best but she's no Claudette Colbert when it comes to farce – stars in this attempt at screwball romantic comedy. She plays a runaway bride who persuades a flyer (James Stewart) and his buddy (Eddie Albert) to spirit her off to California. The plane crashes in Oklahoma farmland en route, Stewart and Fontaine fall in love, and you can guess the rest. A fifth-generation carbon copy of an old idea, it's amiable enough and Stewart is a perfect fit for his role in these forgettable proceedings. ▭

Joan Fontaine *Diana "Dee Dee" Dillwood Benson aka Dottie Blucher* • James Stewart *Marvin Payne* • Eddie Albert *Bullets Baker* • Roland Young *Ralph Tutwiler* • Willard Parker *Henry Benson* ■ *Dir* HC Potter • *Scr* Karl Tunberg, from the story by Robert Carson

You Know What Sailors Are
★★ U

Comedy 1954 · UK · Colour · 89mins

Ranging from the Huggetts to Disney, all-star action pictures to cut-price comedies, what a roller-coaster career director Ken Annakin has had! This is one of his lesser outings, with too many cheap jibes, but there is some fun to be had as drunken sailor Donald Sinden plants a pawnbroker's sign and a pram on top of a ship and tries to pass it off as "Secret Weapon 998". Akim Tamiroff does what he can with one of his few leading roles, but the mediocre Cold War jokes eventually force him to surrender.

Donald Sinden *Lieutenant Sylvester Green* • Akim Tamiroff *President of Agraria* • Sarah Lawson *Betty* • Naunton Wayne *Captain Owbridge* • Bill Kerr *Lieutenant Smart* • Dora Bryan *Gladys* • Michael Hordern *Captain Hamilton* ■ *Dir* Ken Annakin • *Scr* Peter Rogers, from the novel *Sylvester* by Edward Hyams

You Light Up My Life ★★ PG

Musical 1977 · US · Colour · 86mins

Having made such a good impression as Frenchy in *Grease*, Didi Conn looked set for stardom. But this schmaltzy showbiz melodrama virtually put paid to her movie prospects. Even though the title song won an Oscar (in a very slow year), Joseph Brooks's story of the comedian's daughter with ambitions to become a singer-actress creaks under the weight of its clichés and contrivances. Heckled by her boorish father (Joe Silver), devalued by her dullard boyfriend (Stephen Nathan) and exploited by a swaggering producer (Michael Zaslow), Conn gets through more suffering than Joan Crawford managed in her entire career. For tackaholics only. ▭

Didi Conn *Laurie Robinson* • Joe Silver *Si Robinson* • Michael Zaslow *Chris Nolan* • Stephen Nathan *Ken Rothenberg* • Melanie Mayron *Annie Gerrard* • Jerry Keller *Conductor* ■ *Dir/Scr* Joseph Brooks

You Must Be Joking! ★★ U

Farce 1965 · UK · BW · 102mins

If you've ever wondered how Monty Python's "Upper-Class Twit of the Year" sketch would fare at feature

length, this scattershot comedy from Michael Winner will give you a pretty good idea. The premise – give five soldiers various unlikely tasks to assess their initiative – is basically sound. The trouble is, there are too many different tests and the slapstick solutions to them soon try the patience. Denholm Elliott and Lionel Jeffries go flat out for laughs, but with a little more gag selectivity on the part of Winner, they would not have had to work quite so hard.

Michael Callan *Lieutenant Tim Morton* • Lionel Jeffries *Sergeant Major Mcgregor* • Denholm Elliott *Captain Tabasco* • Wilfrid Hyde White *General Lockwood* • Bernard Cribbins *Sergeant Clegg* • James Robertson-Justice *Librarian* • Leslie Phillips *Young husband* • Terry-Thomas *Major Foskett* ■ *Dir* Michael Winner • *Scr* Alan Hackney, form a story by Michael Winner, Alan Hackney

You Only Live Once ★★★★★

Crime drama   1937 · US · BW · 86mins

A Depression-era ironic masterpiece, borrowing from the real-life Bonnie and Clyde saga, as Sylvia Sidney and Henry Fonda play small-timers caught up in an escalation of violence. Fonda has never been better, his punk hood Eddie a Tom Joad (*The Grapes of Wrath*) shorn of optimism. Sidney is just wonderful: tender, poignant, vulnerable, scared. Director Fritz Lang creates a bleak hard-world of sheer greyness, and, apparently, during the 46-day shoot forced his actors and production team to stay awake so they'd look and be suitably tired. It's a brilliant, stunning classic you'll remember for ever.

Henry Fonda *Eddie Taylor* • Sylvia Sidney *Joan Graham* • Barton MacLane *Stephen Whitney* • Jean Dixon *Bonnie Graham* • William Gargan *Father Dolan* • Warren Hymer *Muggsy* • Charles "Chic" Sale *Ethan* • Margaret Hamilton *Hester* ■ *Dir* Fritz Lang • *Scr* Gene Towne, Graham Baker, from a story by Gene Towne • *Cinematographer* Leon Shamroy • *Music* Alfred Newman

You Only Live Twice ★★★★★ PG

Spy adventure   1967 · UK · Colour · 111mins

One of the very best of the Bonds, boasting a jaw-dropping pace and impeccable action sequences amid stunning scenery. Sean Connery, in slyly macho mode as 007, goes on a mission to Japan to take on crime syndicate Spectre and its evil boss Blofeld (Donald Pleasence). Director Lewis Gilbert ensures no expense is spared (no wonder Blofeld's cat is a luxurious Persian) and designer Ken Adam puts that production money where his volcano is. As a bonus, one of the writers is Roald Dahl. 🎞

Sean Connery *James Bond* • Donald Pleasence *Ernst Stavro Blofeld* • Akiko Wakabayashi *Aki* • Tetsuro Tamba *Tiger Tanaka* • Mie Hama *Kissy Suzuki* • Teru Shimada *Osato* • Karin Dor *Helga Brandt* • Lois Maxwell *Miss Moneypenny* • Desmond Llewelyn "Q" • Bernard Lee "M" ■ *Dir* Lewis Gilbert • *Scr* Roald Dahl, Harry Jack Bloom, from the novel by Ian Fleming • *Cinematographer* Freddie Young • *Music* John Barry

You Pay Your Money ★ U

Crime drama   1957 · UK · BW · 66mins

The much maligned Butcher's Film Service holds an unenviable place in the history of British cinema. By sponsoring dozens of low-budget programmers, it enabled young talent on both sides of the camera to gain an industry foothold. Yet it mostly churned out dismal offerings such as this tale of kidnap and rare book smuggling, given only the merest modicum of respectability by the presence of Hugh McDermott and Honor Blackman. Although he started out in comedy, Maclean Rogers had handled several mystery movies, but here his adaptation of Michael Cronin's novel is as flat as his direction.

Hugh McDermott *Bob Westlake* • Jane Hylton *Rosemary Delgardo* • Honor Blackman *Susie Westlake* • Hugh Moxey *Tom Cookson* • Ivan Samson *Steve Mordaunt* ■ *Dir* Maclean Rogers • *Scr* Maclean Rogers, from the novel *You Pay Your Money* by Michael Cronin

You Ruined My Life ★★ U

Comedy   1987 · US · Colour · 89mins

Paul Reiser and Mimi Rogers were obviously both having off days when they agreed to star in this daft Disney comedy about a spoilt little rich girl (Soleil Moon Frye) and the professor who tries to turn her into a refined young lady. Yes, it's *My Fair Lady* with money, but without the panache or the winning performances. In fact, Frye is so irritating as the stuck-up kid that she makes Macaulay Culkin look cute and adorable. 🎞

Soleil Moon Frye *Minerva Edwards* • Paul Reiser *Dexter Bunche* • Mimi Rogers *Charlotte* • Allen Garfield *Uncle Howie* • Tony Burton *Moustache* • Lisa Raggio *Lorraine* ■ *Dir* David Ashwell • *Scr* Robin Swicord

You Talkin' to Me? ★★★

Black comedy   1987 · US · Colour · 97mins

This is the tale of an obsessed Robert De Niro fan, specifically an unemployed actor who lives and breathes the Travis Bickle character from *Taxi Driver*. When he finds work in Hollywood through a rabidly racist TV producer, it's clear that this is a two-tier film which wants to make pithy observations about the image-making process and the danger of delusion. At times, however, it's all too cumbersome, but its star Jim Youngs certainly did not deserve to be panned by New York critics for not reproducing De Niro's class act to perfection. Contains swearing.

Jim Youngs *Bronson Green* • James Noble *Peter Archer* • Mykel T Williamson [Mykel T Williamson] *Thatcher Marks* • Faith Ford *Dana Archer* • Bess Motta *Judith Margolis* • Rex Ryon *Kevin* • Brian Thompson *James* • Alan King ■ *Dir/Scr* Charles Winkler

You Were Meant for Me ★★★

Musical   1948 · US · BW · 91mins

A good example of the kind of musical made to use up contracts of personable stars. Jeanne Crain and Dan Dailey play smoothly together as the nice girl and the bandleader she marries in America during the Depression years. It's directed by Lloyd Bacon who knew the period well,

having made those great Depression-era musicals *42nd Street* and *Footlight Parade*. Also on hand are the acerbic Oscar Levant and the gracious Selena Royle. Dailey's stock was rising, and the same year he was nominated for the best actor Oscar for *When My Baby Smiles at Me*. Not bad for a song-and-dance man.

Jeanne Crain *Peggy Mayhew* • Dan Dailey *Chuck Arnold* • Oscar Levant *Oscar Hoffman* • Barbara Lawrence *Louise Crane* • Selena Royle *Mrs Cora Mayhew* • Percy Kilbride *Mr Andrew Mayhew* ■ *Dir* Lloyd Bacon • *Scr* Elick Moll, Valentine Davies

You Were Never Lovelier ★★★ U

Musical   1942 · US · BW · 93mins

The second wartime pairing (after *You'll Never Get Rich*) of the marvellous Rita Hayworth and the ineffable Fred Astaire is a delight, as they dance to a superb Jerome Kern score with Johnny Mercer lyrics, including *I'm Old Fashioned* and *Dearly Beloved*. The plot is silly and the budget skimpy, but the two stars are radiant, possibly owing to the fact that they were "an item" on this movie. They also happened to have known each other all their dancing lives, since Fred was half of Fred and Adele Astaire and the young Hayworth, as Margarita Carmen Cansino, was part of the Dancing Cansinos. Watch for a pre-*Jolson Story* Larry Parks. 🎞

Fred Astaire *Robert Davis* • Rita Hayworth *Maria Acuna* • Adolphe Menjou *Eduardo Acuno* • Leslie Brooks *Cecy Acuna* • Adele Mara *Lita Acuna* • Isobel Elsom *Mrs Maria Castro* ■ *Dir* William A Seiter • *Scr* Michael Fessier, Ernest Pagano, Delmer Daves, from a story and • *Scr* by Carlos Olivari, Sixto Pondal Rios • *Costume Designer* Irene

You'll Find Out ★★

Horror spoof   1940 · US · BW · 96mins

Murderous plotters Boris Karloff, Bela Lugosi and Peter Lorre encounter band leader Kay Kyser (with his Kollege of Musical Knowledge) in an apparently haunted house, in an odd slice of forties popular music history, which also showcased Dennis O'Keefe and musician Ish Kabibble. Who? Ask your grandparents! Advertised as "A Seance In Swing with the Ha-Ha Horror Boys", it's crammed with enough thriller devices (despite the terror trio being criminally wasted) and good clean fun to qualify as a lightweight nostalgia binge.

Kay Kyser • Peter Lorre *Professor Fenninger* • Bela Lugosi *Prince Saliano* • Boris Karloff *Judge Mainwaring* • Dennis O'Keefe *Chuck Deems* ■ *Dir* David Butler • *Scr* James V Kern, Monte Brice, Andrew Bennison, RTM Scott, from a story by James V Kern, David Butler

You'll Like My Mother ★★★

Thriller   1972 · US · Colour · 92mins

A refreshingly low-key psycho thriller eschewing all the obvious horror trappings to deliver a nail-biting climax. Pregnant widow Patty Duke stumbles on some dark family secrets when she arrives at mother-in-law Rosemary Murphy's house for the first time to grieve over her husband's death in Vietnam. For the unwelcoming Murphy

is not only keeping a mentally disabled girl locked in the attic, she's also hiding her rapist son in the cellar! Trapped in the house by a snowstorm, Duke gives birth and Murphy tells her the baby has died, which sets the scene for unnerving suspense. Despite a few lapses in logic, a certain sloppiness on director Lamont Johnson's part as the finale approaches and the miscasting of Richard Thomas as a sadistic rapist, this scare show has the finesse of a near-classic Hitchcock.

Patty Duke *Francesca Kinsolving* • Rosemary Murphy *Mrs Kinsolving* • Richard Thomas *Kenny* • Sian Barbara Allen *Kathleen Kinsolving* • Dennis Rucker *Red Cooper* • James Neumann *Joey* • James Glazman *Breadman* ■ *Dir* Lamont Johnson • *Scr* Jo Heims, from the novel by Naomi A Hintze

You'll Never Get Rich ★★★ U

Musical   1941 · US · BW · 88mins

The only co-star Fred Astaire became romantically involved with in real life was, allegedly, the lovely Rita Hayworth, herself a skilled and trained dancer. They made two movies together at Columbia (this was followed by *You Were Never Lovelier* in 1942) and their dancing together is simply exquisite: it's quite clear that there's something extra-special going on between these two extraordinary talents. Ignore the dumb wartime plot about Fred being caught in the draft, or the relentlessly pedestrian direction by Sidney Lanfield, and just revel in the Cole Porter songs, which include the sublime *So Near and Yet So Far*, and relish watching two of the most beautiful screen presences in perfect harmony. 🎞

Fred Astaire *Robert Curtis* • Rita Hayworth *Sheila Winthrop* • John Hubbard *Tom Barton* • Robert Benchley *Martin Cortland* • Osa Massen *Sonya* • Frieda Inescort *Mrs Cortland* • Guinn "Big Boy" Williams [Guinn Williams] *Kewpie Blain* ■ *Dir* Sidney Lanfield • *Scr* Michael Fessier, Ernest Pagano

Young Again ★★ U

Fantasy comedy   1986 · US · Colour · 85mins

Here's a TV movie about body-switching made when such films (*Big, 18 Again*) were in vogue and aided by the success of *Back to the Future*. Robert Urich goes back to his teens, in the form of Keanu Reeves, and turns up at his former high school where he dates the daughter of his ex-sweetheart (Lindsay Wagner). As it never tries to reach the blockbuster status which *Back to the Future* attained and has a touch of Disney fantasy polish about it, the film is a watchable diversion. 🎞

Lindsay Wagner *Laura Gordon* • Robert Urich *Michael Riley* • Keanu Reeves *Mick Riley* • Jack Gilford *Angel* • Jessica Steen *Tracy Gordon* • Jason Nicoloff *Peter Gordon* ■ *Dir* Steven Hilliard Stern • *Scr* Barbara Hall

The Young Americans ★★★ 18

Thriller   1993 · US · Colour · 98mins

Hard-bitten New York cop Harvey Keitel arrives in London to nail the drug racketeers terrorising the capital's hip night spots in this flashy movie, which landed newcomer Danny Cannon the job of directing 1995's big budget flop *Judge Dredd*. Visually impressive on all fronts, with designer violence being Cannon's forte, this glossily graphic drama at times plays as a tough documentary. Yet Keitel and barman Craig Kelly form a credible crime-busting partnership, and with hindsight the film can clearly be seen as a frontrunner in the nineties' resurgence of commercial British cinema. Contains violence, swearing and drug abuse. ▭

Harvey Keitel *John Harris* • Iain Glen *Edward Foster* • Thandie Newton *Rachel Stevens* • Viggo Mortensen *Carl Fraser* • Craig Kelly *Christian O'Neill* • Nigel Clauzel *Lionel Stevens* • James Duggan *Dermott O'Neill* • Keith Allen *Jack Doyle* ■ *Dir* Danny Cannon, David Hilton

Young and Dangerous ★★

Action 1996 · HK · Colour · 197mins

A violent Hong Kong crime thriller about a bunch of inexperienced thugs climbing the ladder of the Hung Hing Society Triads. Based on a popular series of graphic novels, this has an unusually youthful cast, who are supposed to be intimidating, although it's hard to believe that this bunch of idiotic leather-clad juveniles could provoke much fear. It certainly captures the brutality of the Triad gangs, but Cheng's no young Chow Yun-Fat and most of the major action scenes are wrecked by the misjudged use of a gimmicky blurring effect. A Cantonese/Mandarin language film. *DVD*

Cheng Yee-kin *Ho Nam* • Jordan Chan *Chicken* • Gigi Lai *Smartie* ■ *Dir* Andrew Lau • *Scr* Manfred Wong, Sharon Hui, from a story by Dickey Yau, Cow Man

Young and Innocent

★★★★ Ⓤ

Murder mystery 1937 · UK · BW · 79mins

Based on Josephine Tey's novel *A Shilling for Candles*, this may be a minor entry in the Hitchcock canon. But, as it boasts one of the most stunning sequences he ever executed – the audacious travelling shot to the murderer's twitching eye – this film still proves him to be the master of technique, as well as suspense. One of Hitch's many "wrong man" thrillers, it takes viewers on a breathless pursuit, pausing only for a nerve-jangling children's party and a mine-shaft cliffhanger, that will leave you as frayed and exhausted as the imperilled Derrick de Marney and Nova Pilbeam. Sit back and nail-bite. ▭

Derrick de Marney *Robert Tisdall* • Nova Pilbeam *Erica* • Percy Marmont *Colonel Burgoyne* • Edward Rigby *Old Will* • Mary Clare *Erica's Aunt* • John Longden *Kent* • George Curzon *Guy* • Basil Radford *Uncle Basil* ■ *Dir* Alfred Hitchcock • *Scr* Charles Bennett, Alma Reville, from the novel *A Shilling for Candles* by Josephine Tey

Young and Willing ★★ Ⓤ

Comedy drama 1942 · US · BW · 83mins

A bunch of penurious aspiring young actors share a small New York apartment, as well as their hopes, dreams, squabbles and romances, as they wait for the big break on Broadway. A forgettable, lightweight,

non-musical cousin to the once-popular "Hey kids, let's put on a show!" school of comedy, it whiles away the time pleasantly enough. Directed by Edward H Griffith, it showcases the youthful pre-stardom talents of William Holden, Susan Hayward, and Eddie Bracken, helped along by humorist, writer and actor Robert Benchley (grandfather of Peter, who wrote *Jaws*).

William Holden (1) *Norman Reese* • Eddie Bracken *George Bodell* • Robert Benchley *Arthur Kenny* • Susan Hayward *Kate Benson* • Martha O'Driscoll *Dottie Coburn* • Barbara Britton *Marge Benson* • Mabel Paige *Mrs Garnet* ■ *Dir* Edward H Griffith • *Scr* Virginia Van Upp, from the play *Out of the Frying Pan* by Francis Swann

Young at Heart ★★★ Ⓤ

Romantic musical drama 1955 · US · Colour · 112mins

A well-crafted remake from Warner Bros of *Four Daughters*, this features a surly Frank Sinatra, finely cast in the role that made John Garfield a star in the original. Playing opposite Sinatra (though they duet only sparingly) is his Columbia records cohort and Warner Bros goldmine Doris Day, who offers a performance of great warmth and sensitivity. Although not a musical (it's a drama with songs), the film still offers plenty of precious moments for the audience to savour. The supporting cast is exemplary, with Dorothy Malone and Elisabeth Fraser wholesome as the other daughters, and Gig Young, Ethel Barrymore and Robert Keith attractive as the older generation. The tacked-on ending is a spurious and unnecessary sop – Sinatra hated this particular plot resolution, and you'll almost certainly agree. ▭

Frank Sinatra *Barney Sloan* • Doris Day *Laurie Tuttle* • Gig Young *Alex Burke* • Ethel Barrymore *Aunt Jessie* • Dorothy Malone *Fran Tuttle* • Robert Keith *Gregory Tuttle* • Elisabeth Fraser *Amy Tuttle* • Alan Hale Jr *Robert Neary* ■ *Dir* Gordon Douglas • *Scr* Liam O'Brien, from the film *Four Daughters* by Julius J Epstein, Lenore Coffee, from the story *Sister Act* by Fannie Hurst

Young at Heart ★★

Drama 1995 · US · Colour

A classy music score of Frank Sinatra recordings highlights this charming, whimsical TV movie. Olympia Dukakis shines as a recently widowed matriarch of a middle-class Italian family from New Jersey who, in the middle of the night, hears a mysterious voice she swears is her idol, Frank Sinatra, telling her to get on with her life. Discovering her husband gambled away their home, she decides to open a restaurant in order to pay off the debt, but runs into trouble when a local mobster demands payment. Her family, friends and even Ol' Blue Eyes himself (in a cameo appearance) come to her rescue. Dukakis steals the show in this heart-warming drama smartly directed by Allan Arkush and executive produced by Tina Sinatra, Frank's adoring daughter.

Olympia Dukakis *Rose Garaventi* • Joe Penny *Mike Garaventi* • Yannick Bisson *Joey Garaventi* • Philip Bosco *Patsy* • Louis Zorich *Joe Garaventi* • Frank Sinatra ■ *Dir* Allan Arkush • *Scr* Judith Paige Mitchell

Young Bess ★★★ Ⓤ

Historical drama 1953 · US · Colour · 111mins

Hollywood journeyman director George Sidney did an admirable job in preventing this historical drama from toppling over into an unintentional laugh fest. With characters endlessly explaining (in a welter of thous and dosts) who they are to people they've known all their lives, the story of Elizabeth I's relationship with Thomas Seymour is told with a disregard for fact that ultimately becomes endearing. Twenty years after scooping a best actor Oscar for *The Private Life of Henry VIII*, Charles Laughton puts in an amusing cameo before leaving us in the overwrought presence of Jean Simmons as the future queen and Stewart Granger as the tragic Seymour. Bygone age, indeed.

Jean Simmons *Young Bess* • Stewart Granger *Thomas Seymour* • Deborah Kerr *Catherine Parr* • Charles Laughton *King Henry VIII* • Kay Walsh *Mrs Ashley* • Guy Rolfe *Ned Seymour* • Kathleen Byron *Anne Seymour* ■ *Dir* George Sidney • *Scr* Jan Lustig, Arthur Wimperis, from the novel by Margaret Irwin

Young Billy Young ★★★ ℙⒼ

Western adventure 1969 · US · Colour · 85mins

Not Robert Mitchum's finest hour, but a serviceable western nonetheless, *Young Billy Young* has a convoluted plot enlivened by strong performances from Mitchum, Angie Dickinson and David Carradine as a nasty villain. The Billy Young of the title (Robert Walker Jr) is a murderer on the run, picked up by lawman Mitchum during the search for the killer of his son (played by Mitchum's own son, Chris). The wicked Carradine and the honest Mitchum battle for Billy's soul; no prizes for guessing the outcome. ▭

Robert Mitchum *Ben Kane* • Angie Dickinson *Lily Beloit* • Robert Walker Jr *Billy Young* • David Carradine *Jesse Boone* • Jack Kelly *John Behan* • John Anderson *Frank Boone* ■ *Dir* Burt Kennedy • *Scr* Burt Kennedy, from the novel *Who Rides with Wyatt?* by Will Henry

The Young Captives ★★

Drama 1958 · US · BW · 86mins

Steven Marlo plays a maladjusted youth – in fact a psychopath with one corpse to his credit – who hitches a ride with an eloping couple heading for Mexico. Awash with social comment, not to mention solemnity, it's a movie that wants its kicks but doesn't want to be regarded as irresponsible. Made on a dime budget, it has a real feel for the highway and is shot in the style of a Roger Corman quickie by tyro director Irvin Kershner who went on to make *The Empire Strikes Back*, as well as Sean Connery's rogue Bond movie, *Never Say Never Again*.

Steven Marlo *Jamie Forbes* • Tom Selden *Benje Whitney* • Luana Patten *Ann Howel* • Joan Granville *Mrs Howel* • Ed Nelson *Norm Britt* • Dan Sheridan *Dave* • James Chandler *Tony* ■ *Dir* Irvin Kershner • *Scr* Andrew J Fenady, from a story by Gordon Hunt, Al Burton

Young Cassidy ★★

Biography 1965 · US/UK · Colour · 110mins

Rod Taylor plays Irish writer Sean O'Casey who for unfathomable reasons is called Johnny Cassidy in this screen treatment. John Ford directed barely 20 minutes of it before illness forced him to be replaced by Jack Cardiff. But the joins are impossible to spot since it's a standard Hollywood biopic as Taylor sees the prettified poverty and violence of Dublin and falls in and out of love – perfect preparation for his plays and poetry. The women in the cast make this just about worth watching: Julie Christie before stardom struck, Maggie Smith, Edith Evans and Sian Phillips are a formidable bunch. They all sport Oirish accents, of course, and Michael Redgrave is frankly unconvincing as WB Yeats.

Rod Taylor *John Cassidy* • Maggie Smith *Nora* • Julie Christie *Daisy Battles* • Flora Robson *Mrs Cassidy* • Sian Phillips *Ella* • Michael Redgrave *William Butler Yeats* • Edith Evans *Lady Gregory* ■ *Dir* Jack Cardiff, John Ford • *Scr* John Whiting, from the autobiography *Mirror in My House* by Sean O'Casey

Young Connecticut Yankee in King Arthur's Court ★★

Fantasy adventure 1995 · Can/Fr/UK · Colour · 95mins

Yet another in the long line of movies spun from Mark Twain's satirical fantasy, this time with a streetwise teen (Phillippe Ross) doing the time-travelling – itself a familiar device. It's the magicians who take centre stage here, with Michael York and Theresa Russell hamming it up for all they're worth as eternal adversaries Merlin and Morgan Le Fay. There's more than a touch of *Bill and Ted's Excellent Adventure* in the way it's handled, but it's all a bit out of date, too – did mid-nineties teenagers really still dream of strapping on their electric guitars and showing those creaky historical dudes how to rock?

Michael York *Merlin* • Theresa Russell *Morgan Le Fay* • Philippe Ross *Hank* • Nick Mancuso *King Arthur* • Polly Shannon *Alisande/Alexandra* • Jack Langedijk *Ulrich* • Paul Hopkins *Sir Galahad* • Ian Falconer *Sir Lancelot* ■ *Dir* Ralph L Thomas • *Scr* Frank Encarnacao, Ralph L Thomas, from the novel *A Connecticut Yankee in King Arthur's Court* by Mark Twain

Young Dillinger ★

Crime drama 1965 · US · BW · 104mins

Not simply *Dillinger*, but *Young Dillinger*, in an attempt to lure the teen audience to a dime-budget gangster picture made principally for the drive-in theatres. Nick Adams, who was in *Rebel without a Cause*, plays Dillinger, and Robert Conrad plays Pretty Boy Floyd. More of a beach party than a gangster movie, it stops short of seeing our heroes die beneath a hail of FBI bullets because that happened when they were old. The real villain of the piece is Victor Buono (the 300-pound weakling in *What Ever Happened to Baby Jane?*).

Nick Adams *John Dillinger* • Robert Conrad *Pretty Boy Floyd* • John Ashley *Baby Face Nelson* • Dan Terranova *Homer Van Meter* • Victor Buono *Professor Hoffman* ■ *Dir* Terry Morse • *Scr* Arthur Hoerl, Don Zimbalist, from a story by Don Zimbalist

Ⓤ = SUITABLE FOR ALL   ⓊⒸ = SUITABLE FOR ALL, ESPECIALLY FOR YOUNG CHILDREN (VIDEO ONLY)   ℙⒼ = PARENTAL GUIDANCE

Young Dr Kildare ★★★
Medical drama   1938 · US · BW · 81mins

After the success of the Hardy Family series, MGM was looking for another series to equal it. They developed it from the hospital stories of Max Brand, immediately establishing the magic formula and cast. Lew Ayres as the idealistic young Kildare decides to reject a country practice with his father and takes up an offer from a big city hospital. Lionel Barrymore as Dr Gillespie, his mentor, had recently found himself unable to walk because of a crippling hip disease, but continued his acting career in a wheelchair. The sparky relationship between the young medic and the old pro is one of the delights of the series.

Lew Ayres *Dr James Kildare* • Lionel Barrymore *Dr Leonard Gillespie* • Lynne Carver *Alice Raymond* • Nat Pendleton *Joe Wayman* • Jo Ann Sayers *Barbara Chanler* • Samuel S Hinds *Dr Stephen Kildare* • Emma Dunn *Mrs Martha Kildare* • Walter Kingsford *Dr Walter Carew* • Monty Woolley *Dr Lane Porteus* ■ *Dir* Harold S Bucquet • *Scr* Willis Goldbeck, Harry Ruskin, from a story by Max Brand

The Young Doctors ★★★
Drama   1961 · US · BW · 102mins

A heavyweight team of actors lend their personalities and expertise to this standard hospital soap out of the *Doctor Kildare* school of film-making. There are no surprises as new young pathologist (Ben Gazzara) clashes with venerable Dr Fredric March about correct procedure on a couple of cases; or in the romantic entanglements between medics and nurses; or in the crisis that looms with the possibility of Gazzara's nurse girlfriend Ina Balin having cancer, or... Eddie Albert is a senior doctor and George Segal makes his debut in a supporting role.

Fredric March *Dr Joseph Pearson* • Ben Gazzara *Dr David Coleman* • Dick Clark *Dr Alexander* • Ina Balin *Cathy Hunt* • Eddie Albert *Dr Charles Dornberger* ■ *Dir* Phil Karlson • *Scr* Joseph Hayes, from the novel *The Final Diagnosis* by Arthur Hailey

Young Doctors in Love
★★★ 15
Comedy   1982 · US · Colour · 91mins

The first film from *Pretty Woman* director Garry Marshall is a wacky comedy that applies the *Airplane* approach to a laugh-a-minute look at the wilder side of life in a big-city hospital. As ever with such scatter-gun tactics, some jokes stick, and some don't. But even when they don't, there's a crack cast to keep you interested, including Sean Young, Harry Dean Stanton, Patrick Macnee and a young Demi Moore, who was then appearing in *General Hospital*, the sort of telly medico-soap that this film is sending up. Stupidly watchable. ▭

Michael McKean *Dr Simon August* • Sean Young *Dr Stephanie Brody* • Harry Dean Stanton *Dr Oliver Ludwig* • Patrick Macnee *Dr Jacobs* • Hector Elizondo *Angelo/Angela Bonafetti* • Dabney Coleman *Dr Joseph Prang* ■ *Dir* Garry Marshall • *Scr* Michael Elias, Rich Eustis • *Music* Maurice Jarre

Young Einstein ★★★ PG
Comedy   1988 · Ausl · Colour · 87mins

The deliciously named Yahoo Serious, the Australian one-man band who co-wrote, directed, co-produced and stars in this oddity, has more gifts as an actor than a director. Based on the notion that Einstein not only came from Tasmania, but also invented rock 'n' roll, the film is let down by Serious's flat direction and a frantic approach to gags, which means that good, bad and indifferent are indiscriminately thrown into the mix. However, its sheer inventiveness grabs the attention, and its eccentricity and innocence are endearing. Contains swearing. ▭

Yahoo Serious *Albert Einstein* • Odile Le Clezio [Odile LeClezio] *Marie Curie* • John Howard (2) *Preston Preston* • Pee Wee Wilson *Mr Einstein* • Su Cruickshank *Mrs Einstein* • Basil Clarke *Charles Darwin* • Esben Storm *Wilbur Wright* ■ *Dir* Yahoo Serious • *Scr* David Roach, Yahoo Serious

Young Frankenstein
★★★★ 15
Horror spoof   1974 · US · BW · 105mins

One of director Mel Brooks's best comedies, this loopy send-up of classic chiller clichés from Universal's monster heyday is also one of the genre's most thorough and successful fright film parodies. Gene Wilder plays the infamous baron's grandson who copies his ancestor's experiments only to create the singularly inane Peter Boyle. Filmed in sumptuous black and white and shot on sets used in the 1931 original *Frankenstein*, Brooks's ingenious tribute is often hysterically funny and always a scream. Madeleine Kahn's "bride", Gene Hackman's blind hermit, Marty Feldman's hunchbacked Igor and the marvellous "Putting on the Ritz" musical number add to the fun and give this loving movie real staying power. ▭

Gene Wilder *Doctor Frederick Frankenstein* • Peter Boyle *Monster* • Marty Feldman *Igor* • Madeline Kahn *Elizabeth* • Cloris Leachman *Frau Blucher* • Teri Garr *Inga* • Kenneth Mars *Inspector Kemp* • Gene Hackman *Blind hermit* • Richard Haydn *Herr Falkstein* ■ *Dir* Mel Brooks • *Scr* Gene Wilder, Mel Brooks, from characters created by Mary Shelley

The Young Girls of Rochefort
★★★ U
Musical comedy 1967 · Fr · Colour · 125mins

Despite his success with *The Umbrellas of Cherbourg*, Jacques Demy failed to charm the critics with this fond tribute to the Hollywood musical. Not even Gene Kelly as an American in Rochefort could entrance this tuneful fairy tale about the caprices of love and the showbiz ambitions of twin sisters, Catherine Deneuve and Françoise Dorléac (in the last film before her car-crash death). Michel Legrand's songs ingeniously propel the narrative, the performances are spirited and the atmosphere is all pastel shades and sunshine. But, apart from the opening number, the choreography is undistinguished and the feel is considerably more Fox than MGM. In French with English subtitles.

Catherine Deneuve *Delphine Garnier* • Françoise Dorléac *Solange Garnier* • George

Chakiris *Etienne* • Gene Kelly *Andy Miller* • Danielle Darrieux *Yvonne Garnier* ■ *Dir/Scr* Jacques Demy • *Music* Michel Legrand

Young Guns ★★★ 18
Western   1988 · US · Colour · 102mins

Emilio Estevez plays Billy the Kid in this attempt to breath new life into the western. The movie's casual violence, breathless pace and relentless hard rock score offended purists who chose to ignore the fact that, at 26, Estevez was closer in age to the real Billy (who died aged 22) than any previous actor. Paul Newman had played the Kid as a Freudian case study in *The Left Handed Gun* and Kris Kristofferson as a sort of free spirited, Vietnam draft dodger in Sam Peckinpah's *Pat Garrett and Billy the Kid*; Estevez chooses to play him as a social bandit, a Robin Hood figure, in a film which also pays much attention to the look of the Old West, its broad racial mix and eccentric characters such as Terence Stamp's gang leader. It's a western that shows both box-office calculation and respect for American history. Contains swearing and violence. ▭

Emilio Estevez *"Billy the Kid"* • Kiefer Sutherland *Josiah "Doc" Scurlock* • Lou Diamond Phillips *Chavez* • Charlie Sheen *Dick Brewer* • Dermot Mulroney *"Dirty Steve"Stephens* • Casey Siemaszko *Charley Bowdre* • Terence Stamp *John Henry Tunstall* • Jack Palance *Lawrence G Murphy* ■ *Dir* Christopher Cain • *Scr* John Fusco

Young Guns II ★★ 15
Western   1990 · US · Colour · 99mins

More western romping with a modern spin in the company of Billy the Kid, who, as played by Emilio Estevez with scene-stealing shamelessness, seems to have been little more than a violent show-off. Kiefer Sutherland and Lou Diamond Phillips also return from the first film, but this time round the tone is less certain, wavering uneasily between a serious appreciation of the western (in particular the grand visual punch of John Ford) and an in-joke with the audience. There are bumps in the script that should have been flattened in pre-production, while attempts at earnest comment largely slip by unnoticed. Contains violence, swearing and brief nudity. ▭

Emilio Estevez *William H Bonney/Bushey Bill Roberts* • Kiefer Sutherland *Doc Scurlock* • Lou Diamond Phillips *Chavez Y Chavez* • Christian Slater *Arkansas Dave Rudabaugh* • William Petersen *Pat Garrett* • Alan Ruck *Hendry French* • RD Call *DA Ryerson* • James Coburn *John Chisum* • Balthazar Getty *Tom O'Folliard* ■ *Dir* Geoff Murphy • *Scr* John Fusco

Young Guns of Texas ★★ U
Western   1962 · US · Colour · 77mins

This is not to be confused with the much better *Young Guns* westerns which also recruited the offspring of talented stars. Here the main trio are James Mitchum, Alana Ladd and Jody McCrea, none of whom has the charisma of their fathers, Robert, Alan and Joel. Still it's on OK western in colour and CinemaScope and lasts under 80 minutes. It opens with a fight involving McCrea and one Gary Conway and soon has a quartet of youngsters on the run after a shooting. The film

gets bogged down with conventional action, but the director Maury Dexter, who specialised in western, horror and science fiction B-pictures, doesn't pretend it is anything more than routine.

James Mitchum *Morgan Coe* • Alana Ladd *Lily Glendenning* • Jody McCrea *Jeff Shelby* • Chill Wills *Preacher Sam Shelby* • Gary Conway *Tyler Duane* ■ *Dir* Maury Dexter • *Scr* Henry Cross [Harry Spalding]

Young Hercules ★★★
Action adventure fantasy
1998 · US · Colour · 93mins

This spin-off from the popular series *Hercules: the Legendary Journeys* probably looked like a great idea on paper, but Ian Bohen, playing the young Herc, is not nearly as charismatic as Kevin Sorbo. Still, Dean O'Gorman as Iolaus is good, and the movie as a whole is low-level fun if you're into this kind of revisionist sword and sandal epic. Series regulars Kevin Smith (Ares) and Meighan Desmond (Discord) are the villains, and the climactic fight is borrowed whole from Yuen Wo Ping's martial arts movie *Iron Monkey*.

Ian Bohen *Young Hercules* • Dean O'Gorman *Young Iolaus* • Chris Conrad *Young Jason* • Johna Stewart *Yvenna* • Kevin Smith *Ares/ Pellas* • Meighan Desmond *Discord* • Rachel Blakely *Alcmene* ■ *Dir* TJ Scott • *Scr* Andrew Dettman, Daniel Truly, from a story by Robert Tapert, Andrew Dettmann, Daniel Truly

Young Husbands ★★★
Drama   1958 · It/Fr · BW · 101mins

Having established his international reputation with *Wild Love* (1955), Mauro Bolognini (and his co-writers which included Ennio Flaiano and Pier Paolo Pasolini) won the best screenplay prize at Cannes for this amusing but somewhat superficial study of male bonding and patriarchal notions of fidelity. Faintly recalling Federico Fellini's *I Vitelloni*, the film explores how a group of married friends on a last unfettered blowout realise that their days of macho posturing and social irresponsibility are over. Played with spirit, but directed with detachment, this is entertaining, but not particularly revealing. An Italian language film.

Sylva Koscina *Mara* • Antonella Lualdi *Lucia* • Gérard Blain *Marcello* • Franco Interlenghi *Antonio* • Antonio Ciffariello *Ettore* ■ *Dir* Mauro Bolognini • *Scr* Mauro Bolognini, Ennio Flaiano, Cureli, Pier Paolo Pasolini, Martino, from a story by Pasquale Festa Campanile, Massimo Franciosa

Young Ideas ★★ U
Comedy   1943 · US · BW · 76mins

A harmless MGM comedy about a pair of student siblings (Susan Peters and Elliott Reid) trying to thwart the new relationship of their widowed mother, played by Mary Astor. Featherweight stuff, it has one or two touches of sophistication courtesy of director Jules Dassin, who would go on to make classic films such as *Naked City* and *Rififi*. Watch out for an uncredited appearance by a young Ava Gardner.

Susan Peters *Susan Evans* • Herbert Marshall *Michael Kingsley* • Elliott Reid *Jeff Evans* • Richard Carlson *Tom Farrell* • Allyn Joslyn

Adam Trent • Dorothy Morris *Co-ed* • Frances Rafferty *Co-ed* ■ *Dir* Jules Dassin • *Scr* Ian McLellan Hunter, Bill Noble

The Young in Heart ★★★★
Comedy drama 1938 · US · BW · 90mins

A family of charming and scatty con tricksters are hounded out of the Riviera where the parents (Roland Young, Billie Burke), masquerading as aristocrats, have been trying to marry their offspring (warm and loving Janet Gaynor, and devil-may-care idler Douglas Fairbanks Jr) to rich spouses. En route to England and penniless, they befriend a lonely, very rich old lady (Minnie Dupree) who takes them in. Their intentions to fleece her and become her heirs slowly disappear as their affection for her grows and brings unexpected changes to their lives. A gloriously funny, original, sentimental, and thoroughly beguiling comedy. The leads are wonderful, and the supporting cast, notably Paulette Goddard, a bonus. Richard Wallace directs with finesse.

Janet Gaynor *George-Anne* • Douglas Fairbanks Jr *Richard, her brother* • Paulette Goddard *Leslie Saunders* • Roland Young *"Sahib", their father* • Billie Burke *"Marmy", their mother* • Minnie Dupree *Miss Ellen Fortune* ■ *Dir* Richard Wallace • *Scr* Paul Osborn, Charles Bennett (adaptation), from the novel *The Gay Banditti* by IAR Wylie

Young Ivanhoe ★
Adventure 1994 · Can/Fr/UK · Colour · 95mins

There's far more talk than action in this account of Ivanhoe as a teenager, who, with a young Friar Tuck, battles not only King John but his evil henchman De Bourget in medieval England. If that sounds muddled, it's only typical of this confusing movie, which even at 95 minutes seems to be missing key scenes and lines of dialogue. The adult stars seem visibly tired. Suggestive dialogue and some surprising violence make this questionable for younger viewers, though the sterile atmosphere will probably have them asleep after the first 20 minutes.

Kris Holdenried *Young Ivanhoe* • Stacy Keach *Pembroke* • Margot Kidder *Lady Margarite* • Nick Mancuso *De Bourget* • Rachel Blanchard *Rowena* • Matthew Daniels *Tuck* ■ *Dir* Ralph L Thomas • *Scr* Frank Encarnacao, Ralph L Thomas

The Young Ladies of Wilko ★★★★
Drama 1979 · Pol/Fr · Colour · 115mins

Following the savagely political *Without Anaesthesia*, Andrzej Wajda demonstrated an elegiac side with this melancholic adaptation of a Chekhovian story by Jaroslav Iwaszkiewicz, who had also provided the inspiration for the director's 1970 feature, *The Birch Wood*. Set in the late twenties, the story follows Daniel Olbrychski on a convalescent return to the rural estate where he enjoyed an idyllic summer before the First World War, only to discover that the object of his youthful affection has died, while her five sisters (like himself disillusioned and jaded by the passage of time) had always adored him from

afar. Superbly played and exquisitely bittersweet. A Polish language film.

Daniel Olbrychski *Wiktor Ruben* • Anna Seniuk *Julia* • Christine Pascal *Tunia* • Maja Komorowska *Yola* ■ *Dir* Andrzej Wajda • *Scr* Zbigniew Kaminski, from the novella *Panny Z Wilka* by Jaroslav Iwaszkiewicz

The Young Land ★★ U
Western 1959 · US · Colour · 88mins

A rare example of a minor sub-genre, the western courtroom drama, this attempts historical accuracy in its exploration of racial tension in 1840s California. When a young Anglo murders a Mexican, sheriff Patrick Wayne and judge Dan O'Herlihy must tread carefully while the largely Hispanic population watches to see if America's justice system is as unbiased as it claims. Unfortunately this is not the best made of films, despite generous funding courtesy of Cornelius Vanderbilt Whitney, who also underwrote *The Searchers*. Its one saving grace is Dennis Hopper as the youthful villain in the dock – his charisma lights up the screen every time he appears.

Patrick Wayne *Jim Ellison* • Yvonne Craig *Elena de la Madrid* • Dennis Hopper *Hatfield Carnes* • Dan O'Herlihy *Judge Isham* • Roberto De La Madrid *Don Roberto* ■ *Dir* Ted Tetzlaff • *Scr* Norman Shannon Hall, from the story *Frontier Frenzy* by John Reese

The Young Lions ★★★★ PG
Second World War 1958 · US · BW · 160mins

A Second World War potboiler, adapted by Edward Anhalt from the doorstop novel by Irwin Shaw and oozing self-importance in every scene. The action leapfrogs from Paris to America and from North Africa to Bavaria, taking nearly three hours to unravel. But, while the script is turgid, and Edward Dmytryk's direction often slows to a crawl, the picture is an absolute corker for three reasons: Marlon Brando as a straw-blond nice guy who becomes a Nazi and ends up a martyr, Montgomery Clift as a Jewish GI and Dean Martin as a cowardly Broadway star who's Clift's fellow draftee. They fight over women (Hope Lange, May Britt), over principles, and overact only some of the time, as they stumble towards the climax when irony rules the day. 🖥

Marlon Brando *Christian Diestl* • Montgomery Clift *Noah Ackerman* • Dean Martin *Michael Whiteacre* • Hope Lange *Hope Plowman* • Barbara Rush *Margaret Freemantle* • May Britt *Gretchen Hardenberg* • Maximilian Schell *Captain Hardenberg* • Lee Van Cleef *Sergeant Rickett* ■ *Dir* Edward Dmytryk • *Scr* Edward Anhalt, from the novel by Irwin Shaw

The Young Lovers ★★ U
Drama 1954 · UK · BW · 92mins

For all his technical proficiency and fidelity to the written word, Anthony Asquith had a detached style that all too frequently diluted the dramatic impact of his pictures. With its soulless core and its slickly constructed chase finale, this Cold War tale of star-crossed lovers is a case in point, suffering as it does from that very style. The romance between an American Romeo and an Eastern European Juliet lacks both the passion

and the sense of danger that might have raised the temperature, but it's doubtful whether the mismatched David Knight and Odile Versois could have stood any greater demands being made of them. 🖥

Odile Versois *Anna Szobeck* • David Knight *Ted Hutchens* • Joseph Tomelty *Moffatt* • Paul Carpenter *Gregg Pearson* • David Kossoff *Geza Szobeck* • Theodore Bikel *Joseph* • Jill Adams *Judy* • Betty Marsden *Mrs Forrester* • Joan Sims *Operator* ■ *Dir* Anthony Asquith • *Scr* Robin Estridge, George Tabori

The Young Lovers ★★
Melodrama 1964 · US · BW · 108mins

Art student Peter Fonda and trainee teacher Sharon Hugueny are enjoying a carefree affair until she falls pregnant. Fonda, broke, feels unable to marry Hugueny, fearing it would harm his chances of getting a fellowship. She decides to forget him and have an abortion but finds she cannot go through with the treatment. A melodramatic morality tale that takes a long time to get going and then seems to take even longer to make its point.

Peter Fonda *Eddie Slocum* • Sharon Hugueny *Pam Burns* • Nick Adams *Tarragoo* • Deborah Walley *Debbie* • Beatrice Straight *Mrs Burns* • Malachi Throne *Prof Schwartz* ■ *Dir* Samuel Goldwyn Jr • *Scr* George Garrett, from the novel by Julian Halevy

Young Man with a Horn ★★★ PG
Musical drama 1950 · US · BW · 107mins

When Isodore Demsky and Betty Perske dated in New York, they little dreamed they'd one day co-star in a movie biopic of their hero, jazz cornetist Bix Biederbecke. But here they are on the Warner Bros lot, now rechristened Kirk Douglas and Lauren Bacall respectively, he dubbed by the great Harry James on trumpet, and she playing a daring-for-its-day society closet lesbian. Warners softened the source novel substantially Nevertheless, enough of the sordid drama managed to get through, and this is a finely wrought melodrama of its time, with Douglas particularly outstanding as the self-absorbed horn player, leading vocalist and good girl Doris Day on some superbly staged standards such as *The Man I Love* and *Get Happy*, and the whole tragic tale told in flashback by a warm-hearted Hoagy Carmichael. 🖥

Kirk Douglas *Rick Martin* • Lauren Bacall *Amy North* • Doris Day *Jo Jordan* • Hoagy Carmichael *Smoke Willoughby* • Juano Hernandez *Art Hazzard* • Jerome Cowan *Phil Morrison* • Mary Beth Hughes *Margo Martin* ■ *Dir* Michael Curtiz • *Scr* Carl Foreman, Edmund H North, from the novel by Dorothy Baker

Young Man with Ideas ★★★ U
Comedy 1952 · US · BW · 84mins

Glenn Ford is the eponymous hero – a small time lawyer of a small town, trying to break into the Los Angeles legal circuit, at the insistence of wife Ruth Roman, in this MGM production. Director Mitchell Leisen approaches what could be called camp in the treatment, but pulls it back securely to make it a likeable, if modest, comedy.

Glenn Ford *Maxwell Webster* • Ruth Roman *Julie Webster* • Denise Darcel *Dorianne Gray* • Nina Foch *Joyce Laramie* • Donna Corcoran *Caroline Webster* • Ray Collins *Edmund Jethrow* • Mary Wickes *Mrs Gilpin* • Bobby Diamond *Willis Gilpin* ■ *Dir* Mitchell Leisen • *Scr* Arthur Sheekman

The Young Master ★★ 15
Martial arts comedy adventure 1979 · HK · Colour · 86mins

Jackie Chan embarked on his first film for the famous Golden Harvest studio without a completed script and there's an inescapable sense of muddle and make-do throughout this comedy/action tale set in the Chinese city of Kwangchow in the early twenties. Chan (who also co-wrote and directed the picture) plays a raw martial arts student who's forced to fight for the honour of his school after the defection of its most accomplished champion. It's pretty standard stuff, but the lively mix of slapstick, criminality and sentimentality ensures entertainment aplenty. Cantonese dialogue dubbed into English. 🖥

Jackie Chan *Ching Loong "Dragon"* • Wei Pai *Cheng Keung* • Lily Li ■ *Dir* Jackie Chan • *Scr* Jackie Chan, Lau Tin-Chee, Tun Lu, Tank Kin-Sang

Young Maverick ★★★
Western 1979 · US · Colour · 100mins

This sequel to *The New Maverick* misses the presence of James Garner and Jack Kelly, but it's still worthy of the original TV series. Charles Frank returns as the Maverick's nephew Ben, who inherits a winning hand from a gambler rewarding a good turn. However, determined to prevent him from cashing in are cardsharp James Woods, trigger happy Harry Dean Stanton and Susan Blanchard as a conwoman posing as the dead gambler's long-lost niece. The final twist is hardly a surprise and the humour is rather self-satisfied, but the polished cast keep this brisk comedy well above the TV-movie average.

Charles Frank *Ben Maverick* • Susan Blanchard *Nell* • John Dehner *Sheriff Troy* • Donna Mills *Lila Gates* • James Woods *Len Fraker* • George Dzundza *Cal Spahn* • Harry Dean Stanton *Pokey Tindle* ■ *Dir* Hy Averback

Young Mr Lincoln ★★★★
Biographical drama 1939 · US · BW · 100mins

If ever a movie could be said to encapsulate the attitudes and ideals of its director, it is this study by John Ford of the early life of Abraham Lincoln, when the future president was a lawyer in Springfield, Illinois. A statesmanlike Henry Fonda is perfectly cast as Lincoln, portraying the man as a truly romantic and heroic figure despite being lumbered with a quite unnecessary false nose. Some may find this pure hagiography, but it is, nevertheless, a mighty fine slice of Americana, and Ford keeps up the tension in the courtroom scenes.

Henry Fonda *Abraham Lincoln* • Alice Brady *Abigail Clay* • Marjorie Weaver *Mary Todd* • Arleen Whelan *Hannah Clay* • Eddie Collins *Efe Turner* • Pauline Moore *Ann Rutledge* ■ *Dir* John Ford • *Scr* Lamar Trotti • *Cinematographer* Bert Glennon

U = SUITABLE FOR ALL   Uc = SUITABLE FOR ALL, ESPECIALLY FOR YOUNG CHILDREN (VIDEO ONLY)   PG = PARENTAL GUIDANCE

The Young Mr Pitt ★★★★ U
Biographical drama 1942 · UK · BW · 118mins
This under-rated film was designed to show how Britain would always triumph over tyranny providing there was a born war leader at the helm. Yet director Carol Reed's account of how Pitt the Younger simultaneously resisted domestic disquiet and tamed Napoleon rises far above its flag-waving objectives. Reed handles the passing parade of political luminaries with an assurance that has rarely been surpassed. The period detail is nearly perfect and the parliamentary sequences are highly impressive. Leading a fine cast, Robert Donat is a model of embattled dignity, while Robert Morley is suitably flamboyant as Charles James Fox.
Robert Morley *Charles James Fox* • Robert Donat *William Pitt/Earl of Chatham* • Phyllis Calvert *Eleanor Eden* • Raymond Lovell *George III* • Max Adrian *Richard Brinsley Sheridan* ■ *Dir* Carol Reed • *Scr* Frank Launder, Sidney Gilliat

The Young One ★★★
Drama 1960 · US/Mex · BW · 95mins
"This film was made with love, but American morality just couldn't accept it," said Luis Buñuel about this tale of racial hatred, corruption and seduction. The controversial subject concerns the rape of a 14-year-old orphan girl on an isolated island by her guardian. The Lolita-like girl is played rather amateurishly by Key Meersman, while Zachary Scott does his usual nasty bit. But this rather turgid film does have a rough poetry, and even a gleam of hope at the end.
Zachary Scott *Miller* • Key Meersman *Evalyn* • Bernie Hamilton *Traver* • Crahan Denton *Jackson* • Claudio Brook *Reverend Fleetwood* ■ *Dir* Luis Buñuel • *Scr* Luis Buñuel, HB Addis [Hugo Butler], from the story *Travellin' Man* by Peter Matthiessen

The Young Ones ★★★ U
Comedy musical
1961 · UK · Colour · 103mins
This is the epitome of the "it's trad, dad" musical. The "putting on a show" format was as old as the talkies, but Sidney J Furie spruces it up with the help of a sprightly Cliff Richard, the Shadows and Robert Morley, on top form as the millionaire father who refuses to cough up the dough needed to save a youth club. The songs are a hit-and-miss bunch, but it all makes for amiable entertainment. ▭
Cliff Richard *Nicky Black* • Robert Morley *Hamilton Black* • Carole Gray *Toni* • Richard O'Sullivan *Ernest* • Melvyn Hayes *Jimmy* • Teddy Green *Chris* • Bruce Welch • Jet Harris • Tony Meehan ■ *Dir* Sidney J Furie • *Scr* Ronald Cass, Peter Myers

The Young Philadelphians
★★★ PG
Melodrama 1959 · US · BW · 136mins
A polished example of the "poor boy who'll stop at nothing to succeed" melodrama – much in vogue in the late fifties – gets a charisma boost from a devastatingly handsome Paul Newman. He plays a hungry young lawyer conniving his way to success. Barbara

Rush is fine too, but it was Robert Vaughn who won an Oscar nomination (and a role as one of *The Magnificent Seven*) on the strength of his performance as the army buddy on trial for murder for whom Newman risks everything to defend. ▭
Paul Newman *Tony Lawrence* • Barbara Rush *Joan Dickinson* • Alexis Smith *Carol Wharton* • Brian Keith *Mike Flanagan* • Diane Brewster *Kate Judson* • Billie Burke *Mrs J Arthur Allen* ■ *Dir* Vincent Sherman • *Scr* James Gunn, from the novel *The Philadelphian* by Richard Powell

The Young Poisoner's Handbook ★★★★ 15
Black comedy
1994 · UK/Ger · Colour · 95mins
A witty, first-class effort in the grim but stylish *Shallow Grave* tradition. Hugh O'Conor – the young Christy Brown in *My Left Foot* – is frightfully wonderful in this controversial, fact-based crime drama (the 1961 Graham Young case provided much of the inspiration) as the teen chemist who poisons his family and co-workers as part of a warped series of experiments to satisfy his deviant curiosity. Director Benjamin Ross expertly balances black humour, morbidity and heightened reality, and along the creepy way perfectly captures the atmosphere of sixties' London suburbia. Written by Ross, with Jeff Rawle of *Drop the Dead Donkey* fame, this toxic delight is extraordinary if disturbing entertainment. Contains swearing. ▭
Hugh O'Conor *Graham* • Antony Sher *Dr Zeigler* • Ruth Sheen *Molly* • Roger Lloyd Pack *Fred* • Charlotte Coleman *Winnie* • Paul Stacey *Dennis* • Samantha Edmonds *Sue* • Vilma Hollingbery *Aunt Panty* ■ *Dir* Benjamin Ross • *Scr* Jeff Rawle, Benjamin Ross

The Young Savages ★★★
Crime crime 1961 · US · BW · 103mins
A typical slice of New York liberal drama stars Burt Lancaster as the DA who prosecutes three delinquents accused of murdering a blind Puerto Rican youth. The story is spiced up by Lancaster's love life as well as his own background in the city slums – he sees in the three kids a mirror image of himself. It's taut, literate and forcefully directed by John Frankenheimer – his second feature. The eagle-eyed may spot Lee Grant in long shots – she walked off the picture and was replaced by Shelley Winters.
Burt Lancaster *Hank Bell* • Dina Merrill *Karin Bell* • Shelley Winters *Mary Di Pace* • Edward Andrews *Dan Cole* • Vivian Nathan *Mrs Escalante* • Larry Gates *Randolph* • Telly Savalas *Lt Gunnison* • Pilar Seurat *Louisa Escalante* ■ *Dir* John Frankenheimer • *Scr* Edward Anhalt, JP Miller, from the novel *A Matter of Conviction* by Evan Hunter

Young Sherlock Holmes
★★★ PG
Mystery adventure
1985 · US · Colour · 104mins
Director Barry Levinson, working for Steven Spielberg's production company Amblin, has tended to the sensational, even the supernatural, in this supposed biography of the young sleuth, hardly surprising considering

the film's pedigree. As an account of the detective team's first meeting at school, it's commendable – Nicholas Rowe a dashing Holmes, Alan Cox a solid Watson – but it's rather deficient in the proper atmosphere of hansom cabs and ugly deeds. ▭
Nicholas Rowe *Sherlock Holmes* • Alan Cox *John Watson* • Anthony Higgins *Rathe* • Freddie Jones *Chester Cragwitch* • Sophie Ward *Elizabeth* • Susan Fleetwood *Mrs Dribb* • Nigel Stock *Waxflatter* ■ *Dir* Barry Levinson • *Scr* Chris Columbus, from the characters created by Sir Arthur Conan Doyle

Young Soul Rebels ★ 18
Drama 1991 · UK · Colour · 100mins
There's no soul whatsoever in Isaac Julien's inept social drama set during the Queen's Silver Jubilee year of 1977. Heavily promoted as the first movie from a British-born gay black director, Julien throws everything (and the kitchen sink) into his unsubtle appraisal of how both minority groups blossomed during the punk era. It could have worked if he'd used proper actors to play the two pirate radio disc jockeys out to solve the violent death of a gay friend. Valentine Nonyela and Mo Sesay just don't have the presence to focus attention away from the embarrassment of glitches they're surrounded by. Contains swearing and drug abuse. ▭
Valentine Nonyela *Chris* • Mo Sesay *Caz* • Dorian Healy *Ken* • Frances Barber *Ann* • Sophie Okonedo *Tracy* • Jason Durr *Billibud* ■ *Dir* Isaac Julien • *Scr* Isaac Julien, Paul Hallam, Derrick Saldaan McClintock

The Young Stranger ★★★ U
Drama 1957 · US · BW · 84mins
It's one of the cinema's current clichés that parents are mostly to blame for juvenile hostility. This film is one of the first to establish the stereotype a year after James Dean's *Rebel without a Cause* with James MacArthur as the young son, whose film-executive father James Daly and mother Kim Hunter are too busy with their lives to support his. Resentful of this neglect, he eventually bursts out and assaults a cinema manager and a cop. Self-therapy of the worst kind. This was director John Frankenheimer's first movie after working in TV, a fact betrayed by the small-screen style of the segmented narrative, but the acting is true and touching, with MacArthur's performance – unlike his role marvellously mature. ▭
James MacArthur *Hal Ditmar* • Kim Hunter *Helen Ditmar* • James Daly *Tom Ditmar* • James Gregory *Sgt Shipley* • Whit Bissell *Grubbs, theatre manager* • Jeff Silver *Jerry* • Jack Mullaney *Confused boy* ■ *Dir* John Frankenheimer • *Scr* Robert Dozier, from his TV play *Deal a Blow*

Young Tom Edison ★★★★ U
Biographical drama 1940 · US · BW · 85mins
MGM's attempt to make a genius seem like the kid next door, though Mickey Rooney acquits himself more than adequately as the American inventor in his early days as a small-town lad with brilliant thoughts. This was the first of a two-parter for MGM's best-known redheads, with Spencer

Tracy following hot on Rooney's heels in the follow-on film *Edison, the Man*.
Mickey Rooney *Tom Edison* • Fay Bainter *Mrs Samuel Nancy Edison* • George Bancroft *Samuel Edison* • Virginia Weidler *Tannie Edison* • Eugene Pallette *Mr Nelson* • Victor Killian [Victor Kilian] *Mr Dingle* • Bobbie Jordan [Bobby Jordan] *Joe Dingle* • JM Kerrigan *Mr McCarney* ■ *Dir* Norman Taurog • *Scr* Bradbury Foote, Dore Schary, Jack Mintz, from material assembled by H Alan Dunn

Young Toscanini ★★
Biographical drama
1988 · Fr/It/Tur · Colour · 120mins
Coming between *Otello* and *Hamlet*, this is an all-too-easily overlooked period biopic from director Franco Zeffirelli. Facts are at a premium and soap operatic excess is very much to the fore in this handsome, sincere, but painfully overwrought melodrama, in which acting styles clash more loudly than the cymbals. C Thomas Howell is hopelessly miscast as the 18-year-old Arturo Toscanini, touring Latin America under the baton of John Rhys-Davies. But his over-exuberance pales beside the grande dame antics of Elizabeth Taylor, as the mistress of Brazilian emperor Philippe Noiret, whose sudden championing of the abolition of slavery beggars belief.
C Thomas Howell *Arturo Toscanini* • Elizabeth Taylor *Nadina Bulichoff* • Sophie Ward *Margherita* • John Rhys-Davies *Claudio Rossi* • Pat Heywood *Mother Allegri* • Philippe Noiret *Dom Pedro II* ■ *Dir* Franco Zeffirelli • *Scr* William Stadiem, Meno Menjes, from a story by Franco Zeffirelli, Ennio De Concini

The Young Warriors ★★
Second World War drama
1967 · US · Colour · 93mins
A standard Universal programme filler, made to break in a string of contract players. It's a war tale – shot entirely on the back lot – that looks like one of those "you carry on with the TV series and we promise we'll put you in a feature" jobbies. The star is James Drury – who, at the time, was appearing in a popular television series called *The Virginian*. Nobody in the supporting cast is worthy of note, but what is somewhat surprising is that this compendium of clichés is scripted by the estimable Richard Matheson, author of Steven Spielberg's *Duel*. Director John Peyser eventually fetched up in Spain making cut-price melodramas with ageing US stars – no surprises there.
James Drury *Sergeant Cooley* • Steve Carlson *Hacker* • Jonathan Daly *Guthrie* • Robert Pine *Foley* • Jeff Scott *Lippincott* • Michael Stanwood *Riley* ■ *Dir* John Peyser • *Scr* Richard Matheson, from his novel *The Beardless Warriors*

Young Warriors ★★ 18
Crime 1983 · US · Colour · 102mins
When his sister is raped and murdered, student James Van Patten won't wait for justice to take its course like his cop father, Ernest Borgnine, and rounds up some college friends to get revenge on the gang responsible. As the vigilante group roam the neighbourhood looking for the culprits, they viciously punish any other criminals they come across. The rule-of-law message of this brutal

exploitation movie is swamped by the one-man-above-all action, making it all the more unpleasant.

Ernest Borgnine *Lieutenant Bob Carrigan* • Richard Roundtree *Sergeant John Austin* • Lynda Day George *Beverly Carrigan* • James Van Patten *Kevin Carrigan* • Anne Lockhart *Lucy* ■ *Dir* Lawrence D Foldes • *Scr* Lawrence D Foldes, Russell W Colgin

Young Winston ★★★ PG
Biographical drama
1972 · UK · Colour · 119mins

Richard Attenborough's account of Winston Churchill's early years, from school at Harrow to the Boer War to his first major parliamentary speech as MP for Oldham. It's *Tom Brown's Schooldays* meets *The Four Feathers*, lavishly mounted but often lifeless, and stodgily scripted by producer Carl Foreman. Robert Shaw and Anne Bancroft are excellent as Churchill's parents, and there's an impressive array of British talent in supporting roles, including Anthony Hopkins as Lloyd George, while in the title role, young Simon Ward makes a fair stab at playing the budding British bulldog. Morocco stands in for all places exotic, while Blenheim plays itself. ▭

Simon Ward *Young Winston Churchill/Sir Winston Churchill's voice* • Robert Shaw *Lord Randolph Churchill* • Anne Bancroft *Lady Jennie Churchill* • John Mills *General Herbert Kitchener* • Ian Holm *George Buckle* • Anthony Hopkins *Lloyd George* ■ *Dir* Richard Attenborough • *Scr* Carl Foreman, from the autobiography *My Early Life: A Roving Commission* by Sir Winston Churchill

Young Wives' Tale ★★
Comedy 1951 · UK · BW · 78mins

A comedy of domestic chaos that suffers from the problem that blights so many theatrical transfers – the inability to re-create the breathlessly contrived precision of a stage farce on the screen. To his credit, director Henry Cass keeps the action brisk, but the story of two respectable couples who share their house with a man-mad minx lacks the frantic danger that clearly made the live renditions so appealing. A young and flirtatious Audrey Hepburn steals every scene, but there's also much to admire in the polished playing of Joan Greenwood, Nigel Patrick and everyone's favourite pre-Terry-Thomas cad, Guy Middleton.

Joan Greenwood *Sabina Pennant* • Nigel Patrick *Rodney Pennant* • Derek Farr *Bruce Banning* • Guy Middleton *Victor Manifold* • Athene Seyler *Nanny Gallop* • Helen Cherry *Mary Banning* • Audrey Hepburn *Eve Lester* ■ *Dir* Henry Cass • *Scr* Ann Burnaby, from the play by Ronald Jeans

Youngblood ★★ 15
Sports drama 1986 · US · Colour · 105mins

A routine sports drama which features Rob Lowe as an up-and-coming hockey player who joins a smalltown team, and falls for the daughter of its stereotypically tough-nut coach. The film toddles along, but never really gets its skates on. If you've seen any *Rocky* or *Karate Kid* films, then the "plot" will have a familiar ring, so to stay awake, try to spot Keanu Reeves. It's his feature debut. ▭

Rob Lowe *Dean Youngblood* • Cynthia Gibb *Jessie Chadwick* • Patrick Swayze *Derek Sutton* • Ed Lauter *Coach Murray Chadwick* • Keanu Reeves *Heaver* ■ *Dir* Peter Markle • *Scr* Peter Markle, from a story by John Whitmore, Peter Markle

Youngblood Hawke ★★
Drama 1964 · US · BW · 136mins

Absurdity is piled upon absurdity in this adaptation of a Herman Wouk bestseller about a Kentucky truck driver who becomes a novelist and is corrupted by the excesses of success. James Franciscus is the driver/writer while Genevieve Page and Suzanne Pleshette are two of his lay-by temptations. Glossy gush that filled a gap at the time.

James Franciscus *Youngblood Hawke* • Suzanne Pleshette *Jeanne Greene* • Genevieve Page *Frieda Winter* • Eva Gabor *Fannie Prince* • Mary Astor *Irene Perry* • Lee Bowman *Jason Prince* • Edward Andrews *Quentin Judd* • Don Porter *Ferdie Lax* ■ *Dir* Delmer Daves • *Scr* Delmer Daves, from the novel by Herman Wouk

Younger and Younger ★★ 15
Comedy 1993 · Ger/Fr/Can · Colour · 93mins

Another quirky story from German director Percy Adlon, of *Bagdad Café* and *Rosalie Goes Shopping* fame. A wife drops dead when she overhears her husband having his latest fling. But her image returns to haunt him and grows younger with every visit, ultimately resulting in him being aptly punished for his misdeeds. The film strives for an offbeat charm, but there's an air of desperation about its attempts. Its main interest resides in a cast which includes Donald Sutherland, Lolita Davidovich, Brendan Fraser and Julie Delpy. ▭

Donald Sutherland *Jonathan Younger* • Lolita Davidovich *Penelope Younger* • Brendan Fraser *Winston Younger* • Sally Kellerman *Zig Zag Lilian* • Julie Delpy *Melodie* • Linda Hunt *Frances* • Nicholas Gunn *Benjamin* ■ *Dir* Percy Adlon • *Scr* Percy Adlon, Felix O Adlon

The Younger Generation ★★
Drama 1929 · US · BW · 75mins

An early sound entry, directed by Frank Capra, and adapted from a story by novelist Fanny Hurst, whose prolific output provided material for dozens of successful melodramas of which this is not one. The film concerns the emotional upheavals and moral conflicts that beset a poor New York Jewish family when their son makes a mint of money and leaves tradition behind for a Park Avenue life. Not without interest, and fielding a good cast headed by Jewish actors Jean Hersholt and the now-forgotten Rosa Rosanova, but it's woolly-minded, contrived, and over-sentimental.

Jean Hersholt *Julius Goldfish* • Lina Basquette *Birdie Goldfish* • Rosa Rosanova *Tildie Goldfish* • Ricardo Cortez *Morris* • Rex Lease *Eddie Lesser* • Martha Franklin *Mrs Lesser* ■ *Dir* Frank R Capra [Frank Capra] • *Scr* Sonya Levien, Howard J Green, from a story by Fannie Hurst

Your Beating Heart ★★★ 15
Romantic drama 1991 · Fr · Colour · 99mins

Making stylishly symbolic use of his Parisian locations, director François

Dupeyron has succeeded in fashioning a Rohmeresque romance for fortysomethings. Unwilling to risk her marriage to an antique dealer, Dominique Faysse, nevertheless, can't resist Thierry Fortineau, the stranger who seduced her in a trance and now offers her a passion that is absent from her ordered houseboat existence. As talkative and indecisive as a teenager experiencing first love, Faysse gives a marvellous display of disarranged dignity, which is given space to develop by Dupeyron's use of leisurely takes and gentle humour. A French language film.

Dominique Faysse *Mado* • Thierry Fortineau *Yves* • Jean-Marie Winling *Jean* • Christophe Pichon *Stéphane* • Steve Kalfa *Luc* • Coralie Seyrig *Jeanne* ■ *Dir/Scr* François Dupeyron

Your Cheatin' Heart ★★★ U
Musical biography 1964 · US · BW · 98mins

George Hamilton turns in one of his most memorable performances as country singer Hank Williams, whose work is probably more famous in the hands of artists as diverse as The Carpenters (*Jambalaya*) and Ray Charles (*Your Cheatin' Heart*). Williams died young in 1953, after alcoholism put paid to a swift and packed career. Curiously his son, Hank Jr, who's a respected country star in his own right, provides the vocals, and there's sterling support from Red Buttons and Arthur O'Connell.

George Hamilton *Hank Williams* • Susan Oliver *Audrey Williams* • Red Buttons *Shorty Younger* • Arthur O'Connell *Fred Rose* • Shary Marshall *Ann Younger* • Rex Ingram *Teetot* • Chris Crosby *Sam Priddy* ■ *Dir* Gene Nelson • *Scr* Stanford Whitmore

Your Friends & Neighbours ★★★ 18
Comedy drama 1998 · US · Colour · 95mins

Writer/director Neil LaBute's follow-up to his stirring, nasty debut, *In The Company of Men*, is a slightly tamer affair which suffers somewhat from an imbalance of unlikeable characters. Jason Patric has finally found his niche in the role of an insensitive macho who has no problem bedding the wives and girlfriends of the men he hangs out with. Ben Stiller – unhappy in his domesticated relationship with Catherine Keener – lusts after pal Aaron Eckhart's missus, while she (*NYPD Blue*'s Amy Brenneman) has given up on having a fulfilling sex life with anyone. Sometimes depressing and always bitter, this is definitely not a date movie as it will put all viewers off entering any type of relationship ever again. Troubling, twisted stuff. ▭

Amy Brenneman *Mary* • Aaron Eckhart *Barry* • Catherine Keener *Terri* • Nastassja Kinski *Cheri* • Jason Patric *Cary* • Ben Stiller *Jerry* ■ *Dir/Scr* Neil LaBute

Your Money or Your Wife ★
Comedy 1960 · UK · BW · 90mins

Nice title, shame about the movie. This is a farce in every sense of the word, as blissfully married Peggy Cummins and Donald Sinden have to divorce in order to come into an inheritance. Naturally, their plans to remarry come unstuck and Sinden is forced to check in as one of his ex's

many lodgers. Both screenwriter Ronald Jeans and director Anthony Simmons seemed to think that an abundance of slapstick, a little innuendo and bags of mugging would be enough to have the audience in convulsions. How wrong they were.

Donald Sinden *Pelham Butterworth* • Peggy Cummins *Gay Butterworth* • Richard Wattis *Hubert Fry* • Peter Reynolds *Theodore Malek* • Georgina Cookson *Thelma Cressingdon* ■ *Dir* Anthony Simmons • *Scr* Ronald Jeans

Your Three Minutes Are Up ★★
Comedy drama 1973 · US · Colour · 93mins

Beau Bridges and Ron Leibman star in this comedy about two wildly different friends and their relationship, Bridges being the straight arrow trying to come to terms with his wayward pal. Not as funny as you'd hope, this is still an interesting film thanks to the characterisations and the observations about America in the seventies.

Beau Bridges *Charlie Reed* • Ron Leibman *Mike Robinson* • Janet Margolin *Betty* • Kathleen Freeman *Mrs Wilk* • David Ketchum *Mr Kellogg* • Stu Nisbet *Dr Claymore* • Read Morgan *Eddie Abruzzi* ■ *Dir* Douglas N Schwartz [Douglas Schwartz] • *Scr* James Dixon

You're a Big Boy Now ★★★
Comedy drama 1966 · US · Colour · 97mins

This laid-back coming-of-age tale is probably most important nowadays as an example of the early work of director Francis Ford Coppola. As such, it is easy enough to overlook the quality cast, as teenager Peter Kastner, the pampered son of parents Geraldine Page and Rip Torn, discovers sex and drugs in the big wide world of New York when he falls for disco-dancer Elizabeth Hartman. For his second movie writer/director Coppola transferred the action from the London of David Benedictus's source novel to America, at a time when coming-of-age movies – *The Graduate* was made the following year – were all the rage. Coppola's style and insight are already apparent in the range of characters and situations offered by this entertaining movie. And, as a bonus, there's music by the Lovin' Spoonful.

Elizabeth Hartman *Barbara Darling* • Geraldine Page *Margery Chanticleer* • Julie Harris *Miss Thing* • Rip Torn *IH Chanticleer* • Michael Dunn *Richard Mudd* • Karen Black *Amy* ■ *Dir* Francis Ford Coppola • *Scr* Francis Ford Coppola, from the novel by David Benedictus

You're Dead ★ 15
Crime comedy
1999 · US/Ger · Colour · 92mins

Vaguely inspired by JG Ballard's novel *High Rise*, this is supposed to be a darkly surreal exploration of how civilised people can descend into savagery under pressure. Yet what emerges is a crass crime caper, in which a bungled bank raid goes nowhere near as badly wrong as the film itself. Demonstrating a gleeful disregard for nuance and timing, director Andy Hurst hurls the action at the audience, turning the likes of John Hurt and Rhys Ifans into boorish hams in the process. However, nothing can

prepare you for the awfulness of the "clever" twist. 📺

John Hurt *Michael Maitland* • Rhys Ifans *Eddie Hayderhall* • Claire Skinner *Jo Simpson* • Barbara Flynn *Professor Corner* • John Benfield *Inspector Dick Badger* • David Schneider *Ian Jeffries* ■ *Dir/Scr* Andy Hurst

You're In the Army Now ★ 🔞

Comedy   1936 · UK · BW · 79mins

Surprisingly enough, this turgid slab of British melodrama was directed by the great Raoul Walsh. But this picture predates his glory years at Warner Bros and so it can be explained away as the kind of assignment a journeyman director was forced to accept in order to eat. Wallace Ford also made the trip across the Atlantic to give a dreadful performance as a New York gangster lying low in Blighty to avoid a murder rap. The British stars are no better, with a very young John Mills snarling with hammy jealousy as Ford moves in on Anna Lee, the girl they're both after.

Wallace Ford *Jim Tracey* • John Mills *Corporal Bert Dawson* • Anna Lee *Sally Bridges* • Grace Bradley *Jean Burdett* • Frank Cellier *Sergeant Major Briggs* ■ *Dir* Raoul Walsh • *Scr* Bryan Edgar Wallace, Austin Melford, AR Rawlinson, from a story by Lesser Samuels, Ralph Gilbert Bettinson

You're in the Navy Now ★★ 🔞

Comedy   1951 · US · BW · 92mins

A misadventure for star Gary Cooper and veteran director Henry Hathaway, following their successful collaborations in the thirties on films such as *The Lives of a Bengal Lancer* and *The Real Glory*. The gag in this weary comedy is that the ship's running on steam (hence the original title *USS Teakettle*), but the tone is extremely uncertain, and the comedic intentions misfire as often as the ship's engine. Cooper has the good grace to look uncomfortable, but always in character. Watch very closely for a couple of major movie debuts: Lee Marvin and Charles Bronson (then known as Buchinsky) made their official screen bows in this film.

Gary Cooper *Lieutenant John Harkness* • Jane Greer *Ellie* • Millard Mitchell *Larrabee* • Eddie Albert *Lieutenant Bill Barron* • John McIntire *Commander Reynolds* • Ray Collins *Admiral Tennant* ■ *Dir* Henry Hathaway • *Scr* Richard Murphy, from a magazine article in the *New Yorker* by John W Hazard

You're My Everything ★★ 🔞

Musical   1949 · US · Colour · 94mins

A rose-tinted slice of 20th Century-Fox nostalgia, set at the beginning of the talkie era, a time that producer George Jessel (who also wrote the original story) had more than a passing interest in since he was once a star of early sound films. But this is no *Singin' in the Rain*, despite the rich use of Technicolor and a hard-working Dan Dailey in the lead. The pace is leaden, the plotline cliché ridden, and leading lady Anne Baxter, quite frankly, inadequate – this lightweight fare would have been better served Betty Grable. The unexpected bonus is the great Buster Keaton, in the re-creation

of a silent movie, his stone face alone making this worth a look.

Dan Dailey *Timothy O'Connor* • Anne Baxter *Hannah Adams* • Anne Revere *Aunt Jane* • Stanley Ridges *Mr Mercer, producer* • Shari Robinson *Jane O'Connor* • Buster Keaton ■ *Dir* Walter Lang • *Scr* Lamar Trotti, Will H Hays Jr, from a story by George Jessel

You're Never Too Young ★★★ 🔞

Comedy   1955 · US · Colour · 102mins

Dean Martin and Jerry Lewis were in their prime for this funny movie, though the personal cracks were starting to appear in their relationship after six years on screen together. If the plot seems a mite familiar, that's because it's a Sidney Sheldon reworking of Billy Wilder's directing debut *The Major and the Minor*, only this time with the great Lewis masquerading as the 12-year-old Ginger Rogers – don't ask! The film looks stunning in rich Technicolor and trivia buffs might care to note that Diana Lynn appeared in both film versions of this plot.

Dean Martin *Bob Miles* • Jerry Lewis *Wilbur Hoolick* • Diana Lynn *Nancy Collins* • Nina Foch *Gretchen Brendan* • Raymond Burr *Noonan* • Mitzi McCall *Skeets* • Veda Ann Borg *Mrs Noonan* ■ *Dir* Norman Taurog • *Scr* Sidney Sheldon, from the play *Sunny Goes Home* by Edward Childs Carpenter, from the story *Connie Goes Home* by Fannie Kilbourne • *Cinematographer* Daniel L Fapp

You're Only Young Once ★★

Comedy drama   1938 · US · BW · 77mins

The second of the Andy Hardy films, with Lewis Stone taking over the role of Mickey Rooney's dad from Lionel Barrymore who played him in the first film, *A Family Affair*. Adored by studio boss Louis B Mayer, a Jewish émigré who wished to extol the virtues of small-town American life and childhood, the films struck a chord with American audiences on the brink of war. If *A Family Affair* was a try-out, this was the full dress rehearsal for a series that spawned 14 more movies between 1938 and 1958.

Lewis Stone *Judge James K Hardy* • Cecilia Parker *Marian Hardy* • Mickey Rooney *Andy Hardy* • Fay Holden *Mrs Emily Hardy* • Frank Craven *Frank Redman* • Ann Rutherford *Polly Benedict* • Eleanor Lynn *"Jerry" Lane* ■ *Dir* George B Seitz • *Scr* Kay Van Riper, from characters created by Aurania Rouverol

You're Only Young Twice ★★ 🔞

Comedy   1952 · UK · BW · 84mins

This theatrical comedy was shakily brought to the screen by an unlikely alliance of producers, including documentary pioneer John Grierson, then involved in a publicly funded outfit called Group 3, based at studios in Southall. Dealing with various shenanigans at a Scottish university, the story involves mistaken identity, Celtic poetry, horse racing and the rigging of Rectorial elections. Blink and you'll miss Ronnie Corbett in what, of course, can only be described as a small role.

Duncan Macrae *Professor Hayman* • Joseph Tomelty *Dan McEntee* • Patrick Barr *Sir Archibald Asher* • Diane Hart *Ada Shore* • Charles Hawtrey *Adolphus Hayman* • Robert Urquhart *Sheltie* ■ *Dir* Terry Bishop • *Scr* Terry Bishop, Reginald Beckwith, Lindsay Galloway, from the play *What Say They* by James Bridie

You're Telling Me! ★★★

Comedy   1934 · US · BW · 67mins

This sound remake of his silent vehicle, *So's Your Old Man*, gave WC Fields the chance to trot out his legendary golf course sketch one last time. But there's plenty to enjoy before this classic finale, as Fields's failed small-town inventor receives some unexpected support from a holidaying royal (Adrienne Ames). The highlights are the demonstration of his puncture-proof car tyre and the merciless repartee he shares with his shrewish wife, Louise Carter, and snobbish daughter, Joan Marsh, whose boyfriend is played by a pre-*Flash Gordon* Larry "Buster" Crabbe.

WC Fields *Sam Bisbee* • Larry "Buster" Crabbe *Bob Murchison* • Joan Marsh *Pauline Bisbee* • Adrienne Ames *Princess Marie Lescaboura* • Louise Carter *Mrs Bessie Bisbee* • Kathleen Howard *Mrs Edward Quimby Murchison* ■ *Dir* Erle C Kenton • *Scr* Walter DeLeon, Paul M Jones, JP Mcevoy, from the short story *Mr Bisbee's Princess* by Julian Leonard Street

Yours, Mine and Ours ★★★

Comedy drama   1968 · US · Colour · 111mins

Widower Henry Fonda has ten children. When he starts dating nurse Lucille Ball he neglects to tell her or his huge family just as she doesn't tell him about her own eight children. Eventually they come clean, marry and amalgamate their offspring – but its then their troubles really start. Based on the story of a real-life household, this is a slick and professional bit of fluff. Some of Ball's wilder antics seem out of step with the rest of the film but it certainly works as an undemanding family comedy.

Lucille Ball *Helen North* • Henry Fonda *Frank Beardsley* • Van Johnson *Darrel Harrison* • Tom Bosley *Doctor* • Louise Troy *Frank's Date* • Ben Murphy *Larry* • Jennifer Leak *Colleen* ■ *Dir* Melville Shavelson • *Scr* Melville Shavelson, Mort Lachman, from the story *Who Gets the Drumstick?* by Madelyn Davis, Bob Carroll Jr

Youth Runs Wild ★

Second World War drama
1944 · US · BW · 66mins

The working class community of a town is changed by war. With parents working in the local munitions factory, kids are neglected, family misunderstandings arise, and teenagers get into various kinds of trouble. A misjudged programmer produced by RKO's horror specialist, Val Lewton, was intended a "social conscience" drama but ended up with an earnest, preachy, unfocused mess. Mark Robson directs a largely mediocre and uninteresting cast (Bonita Granville is the one exception) who, like him, are hamstrung by a simplistic, cliché-ridden and heavy-handed script.

Bonita Granville *Toddy* • Kent Smith *Danny* • Jean Brooks *Mary* • Glenn Vernon *Frank* • Tessa Brind *Sarah Taylor* • Ben Bard *Mr Taylor* • Mary Servoss *Mrs Hauser* • Arthur Shields *Mr Dunlop* • Lawrence Tierney *Duncan* ■ *Dir* Mark Robson • *Scr* John Fante, Ardel Wray, from a story by John Fante, Herbert Klein

You've Got Mail ★★★ 🅿🅖

Romantic comedy
1998 · US · Colour · 114mins

Reworking director Ernst Lubitsch's classic *The Shop around the Corner*, and billed as the screen's first internet love story, this frail but winsome comedy reunited Tom Hanks with both his *Sleepless in Seattle* co-star Meg Ryan and its director, Nora Ephron. Rarely as amusing as it should be, this is, for the most part, frustratingly unromantic, with the stars coming together more like merged files than infatuated lovers. What's more, Ephron's Capraesque combination of battle-of-the-sexes comedy and the struggle between community and capitalism lacks social resonance. However, this latter-day screwball tale is certainly slickly staged and played with consummate ease, and Ryan and her bookshop staff exude a pleasant feeling of cosiness. Contains some sexual references and strong language. 📺 *DVD*

Meg Ryan *Kathleen Kelly* • Tom Hanks *Joe Fox* • Greg Kinnear *Frank Navasky* • Parker Posey *Patricia Eden* • Steve Zahn *George Pappas* • Dave Chappelle *Kevin Scanlon* • Dabney Coleman *Nelson Fox* ■ *Dir* Nora Ephron • *Scr* Nora Ephron, Delia Ephron, from the film *The Shop around the Corner* by Samson Raphaelson, from the play *Parfumerie* by Miklos Laszlo

You've Got to Live Dangerously ★★

Thriller   1975 · Fr · Colour

Claude Makovski had clearly been boning up on his Georges Lautner before embarking on this comedy thriller, in which sibling rivalry, an errant daughter, a diamond and a serial killer in golf shoes all play prominent parts. However, he lacks Lautner's lightness of touch, with the result that the humour is too broad and the mystery short on surprises. Even so, there's a tangible rapport between shamus Claude Brasseur and his feisty mistress, Annie Girardot, who knows more about the case than she lets on. A serviceable time-passer, but it's odd to find a film-maker of Nelly Kaplan's calibre among the scriptwriters. French dialogue dubbed into English.

Claude Brasseur *Diquet* • Annie Girardot *Leone* • Sydne Rome *Lorraine* • Roger Blein *Murdoc* ■ *Dir* Claude Makovski • *Scr* Claude Makovski, Nelly Kaplan, Claude Veillot

You've Got to Walk It Like You Talk It or You'll Lose That Beat ★★

Comedy drama   1971 · US · Colour · 85mins

This picaresque, would-be hip saga charts one man's odyssey through the absurdities of modern life. The young man in question is played by Zalman King, who is cast adrift in a New York populated by an endless stream of self-consciously off-the-wall stereotypes. The film is meant to be a sharp, satirical reflection on various big questions of the time, but succeeds only in being daft and pretentious. It's made notable by the budding talents cutting their teeth here – the score, for instance, is co-composed by the pre-Steely Dan pairing of Walter Becker and Donald Fagen, while one of the editors is none other than horrormeister Wes Craven.

Zalman King *Carter Fields* • Allen Garfield *Herby Moss* • Suzette Green *Susan* • Richard Pryor *Wino* • Robert Downey Sr *Ad Agency Head* • Liz Torres *Singer in Men's Room* ■ *Dir/Scr* Peter Locke

Yoyo ★★★★
Silent comedy   1964 · Fr · BW · 92mins

Pierre Etaix assisted Jacques Tati on *Mon Oncle*, and, while it is not exactly true to say that if you love Tati you'll like Etaix, in his second feature film, the similarities are never more apparent. The picture is as much a tribute to the much-mourned visual delights of the silent cinema as it is a homage to mime and clowning. As director, Etaix makes superb use of the camera, and some of the sound gags are inspired, while in the dual role of a millionaire and a circus clown he gives a performance worthy of Chaplin, but, mercifully, without all of the pathos.

Pierre Etaix *Millionaire/Yoyo* • Philippe Dionnet *Yoyo, as a child* • Luce Klein *Equestrienne* • Claudine Auger *Isolina* ■ *Dir* Pierre Etaix • *Scr* Pierre Etaix, Jean-Claude Carrière

Z ★★★★ 15
Political drama
1968 · Fr/Alg · Colour · 121mins

Two of Europe's finest actors – Yves Montand and Jean-Louis Trintignant – star in this Oscar-winning political thriller about corruption in high places. Though shot in Algeria and serving as a universal condemnation of totalitarianism, Costa-Gavras's film is in fact based on the murder of a prominent liberal opponent of the military regime in Greece in 1963. As the investigating magistrate, Trintignant uncovers a vicious betrayal surrounding the death of Montand and, as his inquiry progresses and links to the government are established, he is increasingly under pressure to discontinue his probe. This is a landmark, eye-opening movie for its depiction of government depravity, winning an Academy Award for best foreign film and the Jury Prize at Cannes. Unsurprisingly, it was banned in Greece until the military government was overthrown in 1974. In French with English subtitles. 🎬

Yves Montand *The Deputy* • Jean-Louis Trintignant *Examining Magistrate* • Irene Papas *Helene* • Charles Denner *Manuel* • Georges Géret *Nick* • Jacques Perrin *Journalist* • François Périer *Attorney* • Pierre Dux *General* ■ *Dir* Costa-Gavras • *Scr* Costa-Gavras, Jorge Semprun, from the novel by Vassilis Vassilikos • *Cinematographer* Raoul Coutard • *Music* Mikis Theodorakis

ZPG: Zero Population Growth ★★
Science-fiction   1971 · US · Colour · 96mins

With thought outlawed in *Nineteen Eighty-Four* and age prohibited in *Logan's Run*, it was only a matter of time before reproduction would find itself outside the law. In a smog-bound, overpopulated future a tyrannical regime has launched a line of robot-children and made birth a death penalty offence. Oliver Reed and Geraldine Chaplin play the parents in peril in this dreary hide-and-seek saga. Contains violence.

Oliver Reed *Russ McNeil* • Geraldine Chaplin *Carole McNeil* • Don Gordon *George Borden* • Diane Cilento *Edna Borden* • David Markham *Dr Herrick* • Sheila Reed *Dr Mary Herrick* • Aubrey Woods *Dr Mallory* ■ *Dir* Michael Campus • *Scr* Max Ehrlich, Frank De Felitta

Zabriskie Point ★★★ 15
Drama   1970 · US · Colour · 106mins

Michelangelo Antonioni's US debut is a sprawling and often unconvincing examination of American decadence. Made when the radical activism of the sixties had begun to wane, it has an unmistakeable "turn on, tune in and drop out" feel to it, as student Mark Frechette and pot-smoking secretary Daria Halprin throw themselves into a Death Valley love affair. The endless billboards, the carefree frolics in the sand and the psychedelic painting of Frechette's stolen plane all drip with significance, but you can't help feeling that Antonioni hadn't really got to grips with the States or modern youth. Cracking last shot, though. Contains swearing, drug abuse and some nudity. 🎬

Mark Frechette *Mark* • Daria Halprin *Daria* • Rod Taylor *Lee Allen* • Paul Fix *Caféowner* • Bill Garaway *Morty* • Kathleen Cleaver *Kathleen* ■ *Dir* Michelangelo Antonioni • *Scr* Michelangelo Antonioni, Fred Gardner, Sam Shepard, Tonino Guerra, Clare Peploe, from a story by Michelangelo Antonioni • *Music* Pink Floyd

Zachariah ★★ 15
Musical western   1970 · US · Colour · 92mins

An offbeat and satirical rock western about two young men embarking on a life of violent crime features Don Johnson in an early role. Co-written by members of the US's ever-so-hip Firesign Theatre, *Zachariah* boasts appearances by a whole host of contemporary musicians, including Country Joe and The Fish (of *Woodstock* fame), The James Gang, Elvin Jones and the New York Rock Ensemble. It's the sort of film that the phrase "you'll either love it or loathe it" might have been specially coined for. 🎬

John Rubinstein *Zachariah* • Pat Quinn *Belle Starr* • Don Johnson *Matthew* • Elvin Jones *Job Cain* • Doug Kershaw *Fiddler* • Dick Van Patten *The Dude* ■ *Dir* George Englund • *Scr* Joe Massot, Philip Austin, Peter Bergman, David Ossman, Philip Proctor

Zandalee ★★ 18
Romantic thriller   1991 · US · Colour · 99mins

In sultry New Orleans, feisty Erika Anderson (the Zandalee of the title) tires of her pre-occupied poet husband, Judge Reinhold, and starts an affair with his best friend, painter Nicolas Cage. Standard love-tangle stuff, which is notable mainly for its steamy sex scenes (one involving virgin olive oil!) and daft dialogue ("I want to shake you naked and eat you alive"). This is mumbo-gumbo that Nic Cage would probably like to forget. 🎬

Nicolas Cage *Johnny Collins* • Judge Reinhold *Thierry Martin* • Erika Anderson *Zandalee Martin* • Joe Pantoliano *Gerri* • Viveca Lindfors *Tatta* • Aaron Neville *Jack* • Steve Buscemi *OPP Man* • Marisa Tomei *Remy* ■ *Dir* Sam Pillsbury • *Scr* Mari Kornhauser

Zandy's Bride ★★★
Western   1974 · US · Colour · 115mins

Even though it's set in the Old West, don't expect stampedes and shoot-outs, for the only showdowns at high noon in what is actually a domestic drama are between a coarse rancher and his feisty mail-order bride. Swedish director Jan Troell was no stranger to the American wilderness after the Oscar-nominated *The Emigrants* and its sequel *The New Land*, but here he has become so preoccupied with scenery, mood and period detail that he has left his cast with precious little to do. In the circumstances, Gene Hackman and Liv Ullmann's over-the-top performances are excusable.

Gene Hackman *Zandy Allan* • Liv Ullmann *Hannah Lund* • Eileen Heckart *Ma Allan* • Harry Dean Stanton *Songer* • Joe Santos *Frank Gallo* • Frank Cady *Pa Allan* • Sam Bottoms *Mel Allan* ■ *Dir* Jan Troell • *Scr* Marc Norman, from the novel *The Stranger* by Lillian Bos Ross

Zapped! ★★★ 15
Comedy   1982 · US · Colour · 93mins

An entertaining cross between *Porky's* and *Carrie* which stars Scott Baio as a nerdy high-school kid who gets zapped in a chem-lab explosion, and finds he has the power to move objects by thought alone. Cue lots of teen hi-jinks, such as telekinetically divesting the busty local girls of their blouses, and taking control of the ball during a school baseball game. There are further tips of the hat to De Palma's seminal shocker, only this is much more madcap, and surprisingly amusing. 🎬

Scott Baio *Barney Springboro* • Willie Aames *Peyton Nichols* • Robert Mandan *Walter Johnson* • Felice Schachter *Bernadette* • Scatman Crothers *Dexter Jones* ■ *Dir* Robert J Rosenthal • *Scr* Bruce Rubin, Robert J Rosenthal

Zar Gul ★★★
Action adventure
1997 · Pak/UK · Colour · 140mins

Achieving notoriety through its use of live ammunition in the action sequences, Salmaan Peerzada's controversial blockbuster is both a politically inspired adventure and a passionate love story. Imraan Peerzada stars as the philanthropic businessman who becomes a latterday Robin Hood, seeking to fight the injustices that oppress the masses. However, he is also bent on revenge against Jamil Malik, the gangster who enslaved him as a boy and is now seeking election to the National Assembly. Thrillingly exploiting the rugged Pakistani scenery, this is both epic and angry. In Pushtu, Urdu, Punjabi and English with subtitles.

Imraan Peerzada *Zar Gul* • Talat Hussain *Zahid* • Steve Masty *Jack* • Salmaan Alik *Salmaan* • Faryal Gohar *Yasmin* • Jamil Malik *Yar Badshah* ■ *Dir/Scr* Salmaan Peerzada

Zarak ★★
Adventure   1956 · UK · Colour · 88mins

Victor Mature, in full Afghan mode, leads his gang of cutthroats against the might of the British army, headed by Michael Wilding, in a trashy adventure yarn set in the halcyon days of Empire. Apart from a belly dance by Anita Ekberg – which should have earned the movie an X rating – it's notable only as one of producer Cubby Broccoli's pre-Bond collaborations with director Terence Young, writer Richard Maibaum and cameraman Ted Moore, all of whom went on to make *Dr No*.

Victor Mature *Zarak Khan* • Anita Ekberg *Salma* • Michael Wilding *Major Ingram* • Bonar Colleano *Biri* • Finlay Currie *The Mullah* • Bernard Miles *Hassu* • Frederick Valk *Haji Khan* • Eunice Gayson *Cathy Ingram* • Patrick McGoohan *Moor Larkin* ■ *Dir* Terence Young • *Scr* Richard Maibaum, from the novel *The Story Of Zarak Khan* by AJ Bevan

Zardoz ★★ 15
Science-fiction adventure
1973 · UK · Colour · 101mins

A naive piece of futuristic hokum from director John Boorman. Poor Sean Connery – Burt Reynolds obviously knew what he was doing when he said no to this film. Yet, thanks to Geoffrey Unsworth's stunning photography, this patently silly story, set in 2293 and telling of a rebellion against sexless intellectualism and soulless technology, has become one of those "risible but unmissable" cult movies, whose main attraction now is the unintentional comedy. The title is a contraction of "Wizard of Oz". Contains swearing and nudity. 🖷

Sean Connery *Zed* • Charlotte Rampling *Consuella* • Sara Kestelman *May* • Sally Anne Newton *Avalow* • John Alderton *Friend* • Niall Buggy *Zardoz/Arthur Frayn* • Bosco Hogan *George Saden* • Jessica Swift *Apathetic* • Bairbre Dowling *Star* • Christopher Casson *Old scientist* • Reginald Jarman *Death* ■ *Dir/Scr* John Boorman

Zaza ★
Drama 1939 · US · BW · 83mins

Claudette Colbert stars as a touring vaudeville singer in the French provinces who falls desperately in love with a classy, middle-aged Parisian businessman Herbert Marshall and temporarily abandons her career until she discovers that he is married. A thin period romance with music, in which Marshall looks uncomfortable and Colbert substitutes stridency for vivacity.

Claudette Colbert *Zaza* • Herbert Marshall *Dufresne* • Bert Lahr *Cascart* • Helen Westley *Anais* • Constance Collier *Nathalie* • Genevieve Tobin *Florianne* • Walter Catlett *Malaidot* • Ann E Todd *Toto* ■ *Dir* George Cukor • *Scr* Zoë Akins, from the play *Zaza* by Pierre Berton, Charles Simon, adapted by David Belasco

Zazie dans le Métro ★★★ 15
Surreal comedy 1960 · Fr · Colour · 88mins

Although he is often spoken of in the same breath as Jean-Luc Godard and François Truffaut, Louis Malle was always on the periphery of the French New Wave rather than an integral part of it. Here, however, he employs all the paraphernalia of his more iconoclastic contemporaries – jump cuts, games with film speed, rapid editing and movie in-jokes – to fashion an exhilarating comic fantasy, which follows the adventures of a young girl and her female impersonator uncle. Demonstrating ridiculous precocity, Catherine Demongeot almost blows the brilliant Philippe Noiret and the whole city of Paris off the screen. In French with English subtitles. 🖷

Catherine Demongeot *Zazie* • Philippe Noiret *Uncle Gabriel* • Hubert Deschamps *Turnadot* • Antoine Roblot *Charles* • Annie Fratellini *Mado* • Carla Marlier *Albertine* ■ *Dir* Louis Malle • *Scr* Louis Malle, Jean-Paul Rappeneau, from the novel *Zazie* by Raymond Queneau

Zebrahead ★★ 15
Romantic drama
1992 · US · Colour · 102mins

Made with the backing of Robert Redford's Sundance Institute and executive produced by Oliver Stone, this interracial romance boldly attempts to tackle a number of controversial themes. But such is the uncertainty of debutant Anthony Drazan's direction that the action all-too-rapidly becomes entangled in the knot of loose ends. Somewhere in the middle of the protests against their relationship, Michael Rapaport and N'Bushe Wright turn in touchingly honest performances.

Michael Rapaport *Zack Glass* • Kevin Corrigan *Dominic* • Lois Bendler *Dominic's mother* • Dan Ziskie *Mr Cimino* • Deshonn Castle *Dee Wimms* • N'Bushe Wright *Nikki* • Marsha Florence *Mrs Wilson* • Shula Van Buren *Michelle* • Ron Johnson *Nut* • Ray Sharkey *Richard Glass* ■ *Dir/Scr* Anthony Drazan

A Zed & Two Noughts ★★ 15
Surreal drama
1985 · UK/Neth · Colour · 111mins

British director Peter Greenaway is one of those cinematic luminaries who provoke extreme reactions in people. Some fervently regard his highly stylised, elliptical films as works of deep and majestic genius while others think Greenaway is a classic case of the Emperor's New Celluloid Clothes. A Zed and Two Noughts is a perfect example of the latter. Concerned with the behaviour of two zoologist brothers after the bizarre demise of their wives, it looks wonderful, hints at hidden, even subterranean depths, but is so painfully slow and visually driven that this is merely a painting on a cinema screen. Contains nudity. 🖷

Andrea Ferreol *Alba Bewick* • Brian Deacon *Oswald Deuce* • Eric Deacon *Oliver Deuce* • Frances Barber *Venus de Milo* • Joss Ackland *Van Hoyten* • Jim Davidson *Joshua Plate* • Agnes Brulet *Beta Bewick* • David Attenborough *Narrator of wild-life footage* ■ *Dir/Scr* Peter Greenaway • *Cinematographer* Sacha Vierny • *Music* Michael Nyman

Zelda ★★
Biographical drama
1993 · US · Colour · 100mins

This uneven TV movie chronicles the wild relationship of literary lion F Scott Fitzgerald and his unstable Southern wife, Zelda. From their first meeting at an Alabama cotillion in 1918, the picture depicts their often scandalous, wanton and decadent lifestyle which ended in 1930 when Zelda had her first mental breakdown. More hysterical then historical, this superficial biography is clumsily written and mechanically directed. Actor Timothy Hutton and actress Natasha Richardson are rather mediocre, failing to capture the charm and torment of their respective characters.

Natasha Richardson *Zelda Sayre Fitzgerald* • Timothy Hutton *F Scott Fitzgerald* • Jon DeVries *Gerald Murphy* • Daniel Gerroll *Maxwell Perkins* • Spalding Gray *Judge Sayre* ■ *Dir* Pat O'Connor • *Scr* Anthony Ivor, Benedict Fitzgerald

Zelig ★★★★★ PG
Comedy 1983 · US · BW and Colour · 75mins

A simply brilliant Woody Allen picture that has Allen playing Leonard Zelig, the human chameleon who is always in the right place at the right time. Thus, via some pioneering special effects that were later used in *Forrest Gump*, he gets to meet the likes of Hitler and Babe Ruth, Eugene O'Neill and other cultural figures: Zelig's always in the group picture but seems somehow nebulous. Mia Farrow is the psychiatrist who studies the bizarre marvel and eventually falls for him. Witty, compressed and a technical marvel, this little parable about conformity is just about perfect. 🖷

Woody Allen *Leonard Zelig* • Mia Farrow *Dr Eudora Fletcher* • John Buckwalter *Dr Sindell* • Garrett Brown [Garrett M Brown] *Actor Zelig* • Stephanie Farrow *Sister Meryl* • Will Holt *Rally Chancellor* • Sol Lomita *Martin Geist* • Deborah Rush *Lita Fox* ■ *Dir/Scr* Woody Allen • *Cinematographer* Gordon Willis • *Editor* Susan E Morse • *Production Designer* Mel Bourne

Zelly and Me ★★★ 15
Drama 1988 · US · Colour · 88mins

A graceful film that deals with an ungraceful subject: psychological violence visited on the young. Alexandra Johnes is an orphaned eight-year-old who goes to live with her grandmother Glynis Johns, a lonely woman who jealously tries to keep Johnes for herself. The young girl is attached to her nanny Isabella Rossellini, whom she calls Zelly (a childish corruption of mademoiselle) but her grandmother tries to separate the two by banishing Rossellini for a jumped-up violation of trust. Johns is excellent at evincing selfish cruelty just as Tina Rathbone's fine direction adds that extra dimension to the turn of the screw. Watch out for Rossellini's then partner, film director David Lynch, in a supporting role. 🖷

Isabella Rossellini *Zelly* • Glynis Johns *Co-Co* • Alexandra Johnes *Phoebe* • Kaiulani Lee *Nora* • David Lynch *Willie* • Joe Morton *Earl* ■ *Dir/Scr* Tina Rathbone

Zenobia ★★★ U
Comedy 1939 · US · BW · 69mins

Known in Britain as *Elephants Never Forget*, this gentle comedy would be forgettable except for the fact that Oliver Hardy starred without Stan Laurel (who was having contract difficulties with the Hal Roach Studios). So Ollie has it all his own way as a doctor in a small town who is given an elephant (the title character) to look after by showman Harry Langdon. The pesky pachyderm then follows Ollie everywhere, even into court when his benefactor is put on trial. Amiable stuff. 🖷

Oliver Hardy *Dr Henry Tibbett* • Harry Langdon *Prof McCrackle* • Billie Burke *Mrs Bessie Tibbett* • Alice Brady *Mrs Carter* • James Ellison *Jeff Carter* • Jean Parker *Mary Tibbett* • Step'n Fetchit [Stepin Fetchit] *Zero* • Hattie McDaniel *Dehlia* ■ *Dir* Gordon Douglas • *Scr* Corey Ford, from a story by Walter De Leon, Harold Belgard, from the short story *Zenobia's Infidelity* by Henry C Bunner

Zeppelin ★★ PG
First World War drama
1971 · UK · Colour · 97mins

Warners threw a fair bit of money at this First World War drama, but in spite of some well-staged flight sequences it simply failed to take off with audiences. Michael York admirably conveys the dilemma facing a Scottish-German soldier unsure where his true loyalties lie, but his spying mission for the Admiralty is hamstrung by an over-abundance of civilised chat and a distinct lack of tension. There's no bite in York's jousts with alluring agent Alexandra Stewart or Elke Sommer, the suspicious wife of airship designer Marius Goring. However, the finale is breathtaking. Contains some swearing. 🖷

Michael York *Geoffrey Richter-Douglas* • Elke Sommer *Erika Altschul* • Marius Goring *Professor Christian Altschul* • Peter Carsten *Major Alfred Tauntler* • Anton Diffring *Colonel Johann Hirsch* • Andrew Keir *Lt Cmdr Horst Von Gorian* • Rupert Davies *Captain Whitney* • Alexandra Stewart *Stephanie Ross* ■ *Dir* Etienne Périer • *Scr* Arthur Rowe, Donald Churchill, from a story by Owen Crump

Zéro de conduite ★★★★★ PG
Classic comedy drama
1933 · Fr · BW · 41mins

Comical, lyrical, surreal and packed with references to animator Emile Cohl, Abel Gance and Charlie Chaplin, this savage satire on public school life was considered so inflammatory by the French authorities that it was banned until 1945. Reflecting the militancy of his anarchist father and a loathing of the institutions that blighted his sickly childhood, Jean Vigo abandoned traditional narrative and formal principles and experimented with angles, perspectives and space to convey the pschological state of the rebellious students. However, the film's elliptical poetry was something of an accident, as Vigo was forced to abbreviate the action to fit the agreed running time. In French with English subtitles.

Jean Dasté *Superintendent Huguet* • Robert Le Flon *Superintendent Parrain aka "Pète-Sec"* • Delphin *Principal* • Blanchar *Superintendent Général aka "Bec de gaz"* • Larive [Léon Larive] *Chemistry professor* • Mme Emile *Madame Colin aka "Mère Haricot"* • Louis de Gonzague-Frick *Le Préfet* ■ *Dir/Scr* Jean Vigo • *Cinematographer* Boris Kaufman

Zero Effect ★★★★ 15
Detective comedy thriller
1997 · US · Colour · 111mins

Bill Pullman is the world's greatest private detective, but he's also a recluse who only ventures out when on a case, relying the rest of the time on front man Ben Stiller. The pair are hired by tycoon Ryan O'Neal to solve a quirky mystery, and we're taken on a *Moonlighting*-style ride of comedy, romance and sleuthing as the reclusive Pullman tangles with paramedic Kim Dickens, who seems to have found a way through his defences. Packed with wickedly wacky moments and a terrific performance from Pullman, this is decidedly offbeat, but also smart, witty and thoroughly entertaining. Contains swearing and some violence. 🖷

Bill Pullman *Daryl Zero* • Ben Stiller *Steve Arlo* • Ryan O'Neal *Gregory Stark* • Kim Dickens *Gloria Sullivan* • Angela Featherstone *Jess* • Hugh Ross *Bill* • Sara Devincentis *Daisy* ■ *Dir/Scr* Jake Kasdan

Zero Hour ★★★ U
Drama thriller 1957 · US · BW · 81mins

Watching this fifties airborne drama now, you can see what a wonderful template it was for the spoof *Airplane!*

Passengers and crew on a jetplane suffer from food poisoning leaving stressed-out former pilot Dana Andrews as the man of the hour. He's forced to take over the controls – more than director Hall Bartlet does – much to the joy of wife Linda Darnell and the sneers of ground controller Sterling Hayden. It's solid entertainment and is adapted from a story by Arthur Hailey, whose later novel *Airport* would successfully kick off the trend for disaster movies in the seventies.

Dana Andrews *Ted Stryker* • Linda Darnell *Ellen Stryker* • Sterling Hayden *Treleaven* • Elroy ''Crazylegs'' Hirsch *Captain Wilson* • Geoffrey Toone *Dr Baird* • Jerry Paris *Tony Decker* ■ *Dir* Hall Bartlett • *Scr* Arthur Hailey, Hall Bartlett, John C Champion, from a story and TV drama by Arthur Hailey

Zero Kelvin ★★★
Period adventure drama
1995 · Nor · Colour · 113mins

Set in 1925, this titanic battle of wills shuns an easy reliance on blockbuster-style heroics to concentrate on the complex interaction between the members of an expedition stranded in the frozen Arctic. Recalling the wilderness tales of Jack London with its blend of physical endurance and psychological strain, Hans Petter Moland's intense adventure contains striking photography by Philip Øgaard. It's also simmeringly played by Gard B Eidsvold as the poet seeking inspiration for a book, Stellan Skarsgård as the trapper who incurs his ire and Bjorn Sundquist, as the scientist whose disappearance forces the rivals to reassess their relationship. In Norwegian with English subtitles.

Gard B Eidsvold *Larsen* • Stellan Skarsgård *Randbaek* • Bjorn Sundquist *Holm* • Camilla Martens *Gertrude* ■ *Dir* Hans Petter Moland • *Scr* Hans Petter Moland, Lars Bill Lundheim, from the novel *Larsen* by Peter Tutein

Zero Patience ★★18
Musical   1993 · Can · Colour · 96mins

Out of the glut of Aids awareness movies, this stands alone for treating the subject in a light-hearted and irreverent manner. In a sort of HIV-positive *The Rocky Horror Picture Show*, Zero is the promiscuous airline steward supposedly responsible for introducing the virus into the Northern Hemisphere. Through his ghostly visitations to Victorian anthropologist Richard Burton (don't ask!), we're taken on an outrageous musical odyssey through all aspects of gay life, featuring Esther Williams-inspired rock videos and a surreal sphincter duet. Tasteless, trivial, moving and angry, your reactions will depend on whether you have been touched in any way by the issue. Contains swearing and nudity. ▭

John Robinson *Sir Richard Francis Burton* • Normand Fauteux *Patient Zero* • Dianne Heatherington *Mary* • Richardo Keens-Douglas *George* • Bernard Behrens *Doctor Placebo* ■ *Dir/Scr* John Greyson

Zero to Sixty ★★15
Comedy   1978 · Can · Colour · 97mins

This lively if raucous car-chase comedy involves a middle-aged man (Darren McGavin) and a teenage girl (Denise Nickerson) who fall foul of the Mafia when they repossess a car with a body in the boot. This is watchable enough, though it somewhat lacks depth. Veteran vamps Sylvia Miles and Joan Collins turn up for the ride, and Dick Martin, in his post-*Rowan and Martin's Laugh-In* days, plays an attorney. ▭

Darren McGavin *Mike* • Denise Nickerson *Larry* • Joan Collins *Gloria* • Dick Martin *Attorney* • Sylvia Miles *Flo* ■ *Dir* Don Weis • *Scr* W Lyle Richardson, from a story by Peg Shirley, Judith Bustany

Zeus and Roxanne ★★U
Comedy   1997 · US · Colour · 94mins

An adequate family film, in which neighbouring kids play Cupid in a bid to bring their respective single parents together – the mother's a marine biologist, the father's a rock composer. Meanwhile, his pet dog strikes up a special relationship with her research dolphin, leading to much talk about inter-species communication, and even more about inter-human communication. Steve Guttenberg and Kathleen Quinlan star in a film directed by the George Miller who made *The Man from Snowy River* and *Les Patterson Saves the World*. ▭

Steve Guttenberg *Terry* • Kathleen Quinlan *Mary Beth* • Arnold Vosloo *Claude Carver* • Dawn McMillan *Becky* ■ *Dir* George Miller (1) • *Scr* Tom Benedek

Ziegfeld Follies ★★★★★U
Musical   1944 · US · Colour · 104mins

A completely plotless musical, with William Powell in heaven reprising his Great Ziegfeld persona from 1936's *The Great Ziegfeld*, unsurprisingly, and dreaming of the kind of show he could produce in the gloriously Technicolored forties. This potpourri of a music fest, started in 1944 but not properly released until 1946, contains brilliant examples of MGM's finest: here's *This Heart of Mine* with the inimitable Fred Astaire as the amorous jewel thief, Vincente Minnelli's camera and design dazzlingly framing Astaire and Lucille Bremer in their heart-stopping pas de deux; here's the witty Judy Garland mercilessly imitating Greer Garson in a devastating lavender-hued parody; and here's a rarity: Astaire and Gene Kelly stepping out with each other for the first time on screen. Who could ask for more? But there is much, much more before the somewhat glutinous finale is reached. A one-off to treasure. ▭

Fred Astaire • Lucille Ball • Lena Home • Judy Garland • Fanny Brice • Cyd Charisse • Kathryn Grayson • Virginia O'Brien • Gene Kelly • Esther Williams • William Powell *Florenz Ziegfeld* ■ *Dir* Vincente Minnelli, George Sidney, Robert Lewis, Charles Walters, Roy Del Ruth, Lemuel Ayres, Norman Taurog • *Scr* Peter Barry, Harry Tugend, George White, Al Lewis, Robert Alton, David Freedman, Irving Brecher

Ziegfeld Girl ★★★
Musical   1941 · US · BW · 132mins

It looks lavish, it's fabulously cast, and it wears all the production hallmarks of an MGM classic, but closer inspection reveals that this high-octane melodrama is really an excuse to utilise those leftover stock shots from 1936's *The Great Ziegfeld*, and to skimp on sets in wartime – James Stewart describes his new truck to his girl, but there's no cut to the truck! But this is MGM, and the three Ziegfeld recruits couldn't be more glam: Hedy Lamarr and the young Lana Turner emote to the manner born, but it's Judy Garland, on the cusp of adulthood, who steals the show, while lovers of high camp will relish Turner toppling down those stairs to the strains of *You Stepped Out of a Dream*. Not vintage Metro, but you'll forgive its overlength and sheer preposterousness for a timeless glimpse of Garland performing, with all her heart, *I'm Always Chasing Rainbows*.

James Stewart *Gilbert Young* • Judy Garland *Susan Gallagher* • Hedy Lamarr *Sandra Kolter* • Lana Turner *Sheila Regan* • Tony Martin *Frank Merton* • Jackie Cooper *Jerry Regan* • Ian Hunter *Geoffrey Collis* • Charles Winninger *Pop Gallagher* • Edward Everett Horton *Noble Sage* ■ *Dir* Robert Z Leonard • *Scr* Marguerite Roberts, Sonya Levien, from a story by William Anthony McGuire

Ziggy Stardust and the Spiders from Mars ★★★PG
Concert   1982 · UK · Colour · 85mins

As the director of the Bob Dylan documentary *Don't Look Back* and the concert film *Monterey Pop*, DA Pennebaker was the ideal person to capture the Hammersmith Odeon gig that saw David Bowie bid farewell to his most famous alter ego. Released nearly a decade after the event, the sight of Bowie and his band in full glam regalia is likely to induce more chuckles than nostalgic longing, and Pennebaker's *cinéma-vérité* style is often too intrusive. But there are some cracking songs on offer, notably the glorious *All the Young Dudes*, the Bowie-penned anthem made famous by Mott the Hoople. ▭

Dir DA Pennebaker

Zigzag ★★★
Thriller   1970 · US · Colour · 105mins

Though he usually plays the heavy, George Kennedy here has a sympathetic starring role as a dying insurance investigator who confesses to a murder he didn't commit in order to ensure a hefty pay-off for his family. This intriguingly complex drama may seem far-fetched, but Kennedy makes it work by the sheer weight of his personality.

George Kennedy *Paul R Cameron* • Anne Jackson *Jean Cameron* • Eli Wallach *Mario Gambretti* • Steve Ihnat *Assistant District Attorney Gates* • William Marshall *Morrie Bronson* • Joe Maross *Lt Max Hines* • Dana Elcar *Harold Tracey* • Walter Brooke *Adam Mercer* ■ *Dir* Richard A Colla • *Scr* John T Kelley, from a story by Robert Enders

Zina ★★★15
Biographical drama
1985 · UK · BW and Colour · 94mins

Skipping around from Berlin to Blackpool to Lanzarote, this intellectually static but emotionally volatile drama draws an analogy between the disturbed mind of Zina (Domiziana Giordano) and the gathering forces of Nazism and communism in the thirties. It's a connection made more relevant because she's the daughter of Leon Trotsky, arch rival to Stalin. Psychiatrist Ian McKellen sees Zina's divided nature as a symbol of a divided Europe, a conclusion which is difficult for us to understand because her imaginings are more codified than comprehensible. Fatiguing, but intriguing, director Ken McMullen's movie seems to be following guidelines the audience is neither aware of, nor cares about.

Domiziana Giordano *Zina Bronstein* • Ian McKellen *Professor Kronfeld* • Philip Madoc *Trotsky* • Rom Anderson *Maria* • Micha Bergese *Molanov* • Gabrielle Dellal *Stenographer* • Paul Geoffrey *Lyova* • William Hootkins *Walter Adams* ■ *Dir* Ken McMullen • *Scr* Ken McMullen, Terry James

Zoltan... Hound of Dracula ★18
Horror   1977 · US · Colour · 83mins

Russian soldiers discover Dracula's crypt and unwittingly resurrect the Count's undead pet dog in this barking mad horror howler. It gets even worse when the fanged fido travels to the USA and finds his master's descendant on a lakeside holiday. José Ferrer slums it as the bargain basement Van Helsing-style investigator on the scent of zombie Zoltan, who is about as scary as Lassie! Any initial outrageous canine humour soon evaporates in this mongrel monster mash that sends all its Bram Stoker plagiarism straight to the dogs. ▭

Michael Pataki *Michael Drake/Count Dracula* • Jan Shutan *Marla Drake* • Libbie Chase *Linda Drake* • John Levin *Steve Drake* • Reggie Nalder *Veidt Smit* • José Ferrer *Inspector Branco* ■ *Dir* Albert Band • *Scr* Frank Ray Perilli, from characters created by Bram Stoker

Zombie Flesh Eaters ★★★★18
Horror   1979 · It · Colour · 87mins

Voodoo causes an army of cannibal zombies to leave its tropical island paradise and head for New York in this ultra-gory rip-off of *Dawn of the Dead*, which put Italian director Lucio Fulci on the cult map. Although the movie is extremely silly (a crusty underwater zombie battling a shark) and extremely violent, with several watershed special effects, Fulci often creates a chilling atmosphere amid the hard-core splatter. Tisa Farrow (Mia's sister) had a mini career as a starlet in Italy and heads the cast here, but many will be surprised to see staunch British actor Richard Johnson up to his neck in exploding heads and entrail eating in this landmark fright flick. Contains strong violence and nudity. ▭ **DVD**

Tisa Farrow *Anne* • Ian McCulloch *Peter* • Richard Johnson *Dr Menard* • Al Cliver *Brian* • Arnetta Gay *Susan* • Olga Karlatos *Mrs Menard* • Stefania D'Amario *Nurse* ■ *Dir* Lucio Fulci • *Scr* Elsia Briganti

Zombie High ★★15
Horror thriller   1987 · US · Colour · 86mins

When female students are admitted to a formerly all-male prep school for the first time, they discover their new

classmates are walking zombies, the results of experiments carried out by teachers who crave immortal life. The title suggests a kind of camp teen horror flick, but what you get plays more like a masculine version of *The Stepford Wives* – albeit one that's alternately tedious and unintentionally hilarious. It's a pity as Virginia Madsen's committed central performance deserved a better vehicle than this lacklustre attempt at social satire. ▣

Virginia Madsen *Andrea* • Richard Cox *Philo* • James Wilder *Barry* • Sherilyn Fenn *Suzi* • Paul Feig *Emerson* • Kay E Kuter *Dean Eisner* ▣ *Dir* Ron Link • *Scr* Elizabeth Passerelli, Tim Doyle, Aziz Ghazal

Zoo ★★★★
Documentary   1993 · US · Colour · 93 mins
The fact that there are some 2,000 crosscuts in this epic portrait of the Miami Metro Zoo emphasises the importance Frederick Wiseman places on the editorial process in the creation of his impressionistic documentaries. Shooting some 80 hours of footage during his six-week sojourn, Wiseman took a year to fashion scenes of fabulous creatures, diligent keepers, dedicated veterinarians and curious visitors into a compelling whole that is all the better for its lack of linear structure and intrusive narration. He also takes time to balance ethical and scientific concerns, as he explores every aspect of this institution's meticulous daily routine.

Dir Frederick Wiseman

Zoo in Budapest ★★★
Romantic drama   1933 · US · BW · 85 mins
This must rank as one of the cinema's most romantic movies, thanks to the sublime technique of cinematographer Lee Garmes. Framed by the highly stylised zoo sets, his subtle, misty compositions enhance the natural beauty of lovely Loretta Young, creating a look unique to this over-whimsical film and making it a rare collector's item. Sadly, director Rowland V Lee fails to extract an acceptable performance from fey leading man Gene Raymond or convey the Hungarian atmosphere. Nevertheless, this is a real one-off, and demands to be seen and savoured.

Loretta Young *Eve* • Gene Raymond *Zani* • OP Heggie *Dr Grunbaum* • Wally Albright *Paul Vandor* • Paul Fix *Heine* • Murray Kinnell *Garbosh* • Ruth Warren *Katrina* • Roy Stewart *Karl* ▣ *Dir* Rowland V Lee • *Scr* Dan Totheroh, Louise Long, Rowland V Lee, from a story by Melville Baker, John Kirkland • *Cinematographer* Lee Garmes

Zooman ★★★
Drama   1995 · US · Colour · 100 mins
Sometimes it hurts to be entertained as this socially conscious TV movie proves. Louis Gossett Jr plays the distraught father of a little girl who is killed by a stray bullet when an inner-city gang member (Khalil Kain) starts firing at a rival gang. Seeking justice, he and his estranged wife (Cynthia Martells) must cope with the apathy of scared neighbours, who witnessed the shooting but refuse to identify the killer. They use the media to fuel their

fight while their teenage son seeks revenge. This is a riveting, powerful drama with built-in emotional appeal that is only strengthened by its fine cast. Director Leon Ichaso pulls no punches as his raw honesty and layered nuances permeate the entire production. Violence and strong language shouldn't discourage viewers from watching this potent drama.

Louis Gossett Jr *Rueben Tate* • Charles S Dutton *Emmett* • Cynthia Martells *Rachel* • Khalil Kain *Zooman* • Hill Harper *Victor* • CCH Pounder *Ash* • Vondie Curtis-Hall *Davis* ▣ *Dir* Leon Ichaso • *Scr* Charles Fuller, from his play *Zooman and the Sign*

Zoot Suit ★★
Musical drama   1981 · US · Colour · 103 mins
Luis Valdez directed this film adaptation of his hit stage musical, which is loosely based on the 1940s Sleepy Lagoon murder trial that unfairly convicted several Mexican-American zoot suit gang members. Except for the spirited musical numbers and an arresting performance by Edward James Olmos as the cynical conscience of gang member Daniel Valdez, the movie largely fails to bring the impact it had on stage. It's shot on a sound stage with a visible audience watching, which creates a barrier that makes it hard for the viewer to feel the anguish the characters go through. The exaggerated, theatrical acting style also doesn't help.

Daniel Valdez *Henry Reyna* • Edward James Olmos *El Pachuco* • Charles Aidman *George* • Tyne Daly *Alice* • John Anderson *Judge* • Abel Franco *Enrique* • Mike Gomez *Joey* ▣ *Dir* Luis Valdez • *Scr* Luis Valdez, from his stage musical

Zorba the Greek ★★★★▣
Drama   1964 · US/Gr · BW · 135 mins
Marvellously emotive and perfectly cast film version of Nikos Kazantzakis's novel about the salt-of-the-earth peasant who teaches an uptight Englishman the secret of life. As Zorba, Anthony Quinn plays the part of a lifetime, so much so that the role greatly impinged on the actor both in real life and in all his movies ever since. Also adding to the film's particular and unusual grace are wonderful Oscar-winning black-and-white photography by Walter Lassally, a haunting Mikis Theodorakis score and a glowingly warm portrayal (also Oscar-rewarded) by Lila Kedrova as an aged prostitute. It's a shade too long for its own good, though. ▣

Anthony Quinn *Alexis Zorba* • Alan Bates *Basil* • Irene Papas *Widow* • Lila Kedrova *Madame Hortense* • George Foundas *Mavrandoni* • Eleni Anousaki *Lola* • Sotiris Moustakas *Mimithos* • Takis Emmanuel *Manolakas* ▣ *Dir* Michael Cacoyannis • *Scr* Michael Cacoyannis, from the novel by Nikos Kazantzakis

Zorro ★★
Action adventure
1975 · Fr/It · Colour · 120 mins
Dashing French star Alain Delon takes on the black cape and rapier of the legendary swordsman, although the province governed by Spanish hardman, Stanley Baker, is more banana republic than old California. Unfortunately, that isn't the only liberty

taken with Johnston McCulley's immortal man in black. Pitched as a children's film, it's probably a bit too long and might well test youthful patience before the climactic duel. French and Italian dialogue dubbed into English.

Alain Delon *Diego/Zorro* • Stanley Baker *Colonel Huerta* • Ottavia Piccolo *Hortensia* • Giampiero Albertini *Brother Francisco* ▣ *Dir* Duccio Tessari • *Scr* Giorgio Alorio, from characters created by Johnston McCulley

Zorro, the Gay Blade ★▣
Swashbuckling spoof
1981 · US · Colour · 89 mins
George Hamilton hams it up shamelessly playing the legendary Zorro's twin sons – one a dashing, macho sword-fighter, the other a limp-wristed queen – in a witless swashbuckling parody. When villainous Ron Liebman threatens the peace of a Mexican village, both brothers swish into action and the cheap laughs come thin and slow. Even the set piece of everyone turning up at a masked ball disguised as Zorro is off-handedly thrown away by director Peter Medak who clearly doesn't have a clue when it comes to comedy. ▣

George Hamilton *Don Diego Vega/Bunny Wigglesworth* • Lauren Hutton *Charlotte Taylor Wilson* • Brenda Vaccaro *Florinda* • Ron Leibman *Esteban* • Donovan Scott *Paco* • James Booth *Velasquez* • Helen Burns *Consuela* • Clive Revill *Garcia* ▣ *Dir* Peter Medak • *Scr* Hal Dresner

Zotz ★★▣
Comedy   1962 · US · BW · 86 mins
Professor Tom Poston discovers that an ancient coin found on an archaeological dig has magical powers that allow the owner to inflict pain from a distance, make things move in slow motion and even kill. Poston offers the coin to the Pentagon as a weapon, but it's Nikita Khrushchev and his Russian spies who are more interested. This fantasy comedy from schlock horror maestro William Castle isn't a classic but it's pleasingly weird and does have its moments.

Tom Poston *Prof Jonathan Jones* • Julia Meade *Prof Virginia Fenster* • Jim Backus *Horatio Kellgore* • Fred Clark *General Bulliver* • Cecil Kellaway *Dean Updike* • Zeme North *Cynthia Jones* • Margaret Dumont *Persephone Updike* ▣ *Dir* William Castle • *Scr* Ray Russell, from a novel by Walter Karig

Zu Warriors ★★★★▣
Fantasy   1983 · HK · Colour · 93 mins
In the distant past all humanity is at war with itself. Evil beings from the netherworld see their opportunity to take over the Earth while its inhabitants are divided. A young warrior hiding out on a magical mountain embarks on a quest through a mythological realm to find the two swords that, when brought together, form the only weapon powerful enough to repel the evil hordes. A truly mind-blowing Hong Kong action fantasy with director Tsui Hark using special effects wizards from *Star Wars* (Robert Blalack), *Star Trek* (Peter Kuran) and *Tron* (Arnie Wong, John Scheele) to create a state-of-the-art adventure. Look out for action star Samo Hung (now known as Sammo Hung) among

the cast. In Cantonese with English subtitles. Contains some violence. ▣

Adam Cheng *Ting Ying* • Chung Yan Lau *Spellbinder* • Yuen Biao *Ti Ming-chi (virgin boy)* • Meng Hai *I-chen* • Brigitte Lin *Ice Countess* • Tsui Siu Keung *Heaven's Blade* • Judy Ongg *Lil-chi* • Samo Hung [Sammo Hung] *Long Brows* ▣ *Dir* Tsui Hark • *Scr* Hong Sze To Chuck

Zulu ★★★★▣
War drama   1964 · UK · Colour · 138 mins
A superb re-creation of the 1879 battle of Rorke's Drift, a personal triumph for producer/director Cy Endfield and Welsh producer/star Stanley Baker. Baker heads a remarkable cast, including Michael Caine in a star-making performance, playing against type as a toffee-nosed lieutenant. Technically the movie is a revelation, with stunning Technirama photography (by Stephen Dade), brilliant picture editing (John Jympson) and a wonderfully evocative soundtrack – who could ever forget the approaching sound of the 4,000 Zulu warriors before we see them, while Richard Burton's narration is genuinely moving. ▣

Stanley Baker *Lieutenant John Chard* • Michael Caine *Lieutenant Gonville Bromhead* • Jack Hawkins *Reverend Otto Witt* • Ulla Jacobsson *Margareta Witt* • James Booth *Private Henry Hook* • Nigel Green *Colour-Sergeant Bourne* • Ivor Emmanuel *Private Owen* • Paul Daneman *Sergeant Maxfield* • Glynn Edwards *Corporal Allen* • Neil McCarthy *Private Thomas* • David Kernan *Private Hitch* ▣ *Dir* Cy Endfield • *Scr* John Prebble, Cy Endfield • *Music* John Barry

Zulu Dawn ★★▣
Historical drama
1979 · UK · Colour · 112 mins
Zulu plonked us down in the heat of battle and didn't have the time to tell us why Britain and the Zulus were arguing so violently. But because the 1964 epic was such a big hit, star Stanley Baker and writer/director Cy Endfield conceived this prequel, although by 1979 Baker had died and Endfield was sidelined. There's spectacle in abundance here but little of the characterisation that made *Zulu* so memorable. American Burt Lancaster doesn't quite fit his uniform or have the required stiff-upper lip, but the assemblage of British stalwarts certainly do as they blunder on towards the massacre of Isandhlwana, the bloody aftermath of which opened this film's predecessor. Contains some violence. ▣

Burt Lancaster *Colonel Anthony Durnford* • Peter O'Toole *Lord Chelmsford* • Simon Ward *William Vereker* • John Mills *Sir Henry Bartle Frere* • Nigel Davenport *Colonel Hamilton-Brown* • Denholm Elliott *Lt Col Pulleine* • Freddie Jones *Bishop Colenso* • Bob Hoskins *Sgt Major Williams* ▣ *Dir* Douglas Hickox • *Scr* Cy Endfield, Anthony Storey, from a story by Cy Endfield

Directors' index

RadioTimes DIRECTORS' INDEX

The Man from Bitter Ridge 1955; *Red Sundown* 1956; *The Incredible Shrinking Man* 1957; *Man in the Shadow* 1957; *High School Confidential* 1958; *Monster on the Campus* 1958; *The Lady Takes a Flyer* 1958; *The Mouse That Roared* 1959; *No Name on the Bullet* 1959; *Bachelor in Paradise* 1961; *A Global Affair* 1964; *Hello Down There* 1969; *The Swiss Conspiracy* 1975; *Sex and the Married Woman* 1977; *Marilyn – The Untold Story* 1980
Arthur, Karen *The Rape of Richard Beck* 1985; *Lady Beware* 1987; *Evil in Clear River* 1988; *Bridge to Silence* 1989; *Blue Bayou* 1990; *Fall from Grace* 1990; *Bump in the Night* 1991; *Shadow of a Doubt* 1991; *The Secret* 1992; *Journey of the Heart* 1997
Arzner, Dorothy *The Wild Party* 1929; *Anybody's Woman* 1930; *Paramount on Parade* 1930; *Sarah and Son* 1930; *Honor among Lovers* 1931; *Merrily We Go to Hell* 1932; *Christopher Strong* 1933; *Nana* 1934; *Craig's Wife* 1936; *The Bride Wore Red* 1937; *Dance, Girl, Dance* 1940
Ashby, Hal *The Landlord* 1970; *Harold and Maude* 1972; *The Last Detail* 1973; *Shampoo* 1975; *Bound for Glory* 1976; *Coming Home* 1978; *Being There* 1979; *Let's Spend the Night Together* 1982; *Lookin' to Get Out* 1982; *The Slugger's Wife* 1985; *8 Million Ways to Die* 1986
Asher, Robert *Follow a Star* 1959; *The Bulldog Breed* 1960; *Make Mine Mink* 1960; *She'll Have to Go* 1961; *On the Beat* 1962; *A Stitch in Time* 1963; *The Early Bird* 1965; *The Intelligence Men* 1965; *Press for Time* 1966
Asher, William *The 27th Day* 1957; *Beach Party* 1963; *Johnny Cool* 1963; *Muscle Beach Party* 1964; *Beach Blanket Bingo* 1965; *How to Fill a Wild Bikini* 1965; *Fireball 500* 1966; *Night Warning* 1982; *I Dream of Jeannie... 15 Years Later* 1985; *Movers and Shakers* 1985; *Return to Green Acres* 1990
Ashida, Toyoo *Vampire Hunter D* 1985; *Fist of the North Star* 1986
Asquith, Anthony *The Unfinished Symphony* 1934; *Moscow Nights* 1935; *Pygmalion* 1938; *Cottage to Let* 1941; *Freedom Radio* 1941; *Uncensored* 1942; *The Demi-Paradise* 1943; *We Dive at Dawn* 1943; *Fanny by Gaslight* 1944; *The Way to the Stars* 1945; *The Winslow Boy* 1948; *The Woman in Question* 1950; *The Browning Version* 1951; *The Importance of Being Earnest* 1952; *The Final Test* 1953; *The Net* 1953; *Carrington VC* 1954; *The Young Lovers* 1954; *The Doctor's Dilemma* 1958; *Orders to Kill* 1958; *Libel* 1959; *The Millionairess* 1960; *Guns of Darkness* 1962; *The VIPs* 1963; *The Yellow Rolls-Royce* 1964
Assayas, Olivier *L'Eau Froide* 1994; *Late August, Early September* 1998
Astruc, Alexandre *The Crimson Curtain* 1952; *The Bad Liaisons* 1955
Attenborough, Richard *Oh! What a Lovely War* 1969; *Young Winston* 1972; *A Bridge Too Far* 1977; *Magic* 1978; *Gandhi* 1982; *A Chorus Line* 1985; *Cry Freedom* 1987; *Chaplin* 1992; *Shadowlands* 1993; *In Love and War* 1996
Audiard, Jacques *See How They Fall* 1993; *A Self-Made Hero* 1995
Audry, Jacqueline *No Exit* 1954; *Mitsou* 1957
Auer, John H *A Man Betrayed* 1941; *Music in Manhattan* 1944; *Pan-Americana* 1945; *Thunderbirds* 1952; *City That Never Sleeps* 1953; *Hell's Half Acre* 1954; *Johnny Trouble* 1957
August, Bille *Buster's World* 1984; *Twist and Shout* 1985; *Pelle the Conqueror* 1987; *Best Intentions* 1992; *The House of the Spirits* 1993; *Smilla's Feeling for Snow* 1996; *Jerusalem* 1996; *Les Misérables* 1997
Auster, Paul *Blue in the Face* 1995; *Lulu on the Bridge* 1998
Austin, Michael *Killing Dad* 1989; *Princess Caraboo* 1994
Autant-Lara, Claude *Devil in the Flesh* 1946; *The Seven Deadly Sins* 1952; *The Ripening Seed* 1953; *Le Rouge et le Noir* 1954; *Marguerite de la Nuit* 1955; *Thou Shalt Not Kill* 1961; *The Oldest Profession* 1967
Auzins, Igor *We of the Never Never* 1982; *The Gold and Glory* 1984
Avakian, Aram *End of the Road* 1970; *Cops and Robbers* 1973; *11 Harrowhouse* 1974
Avati, Pupi *Noi Tre* 1984; *Christmas Present* 1986; *Fratelli e Sorelle* 1992
Avedis, Howard *Scorchy* 1976; *The Fifth Floor* 1980; *Separate Ways* 1981; *They're Playing With Fire* 1984
Averback, Hy *Chamber of Horrors* 1966; *I Love You, Alice B Toklas* 1968; *Where Were You When the Lights Went Out?* 1968; *The Great Bank Robbery* 1969; *Suppose They Gave a War and Nobody Came?* 1970; *Young Maverick* 1979
Avery, Rick *The Expert* 1994; *Deadly Takeover* 1996
Avildsen, John G *Joe* 1970; *Save the Tiger* 1973; *WW and the Dixie Dancekings* 1975; *Rocky* 1976; *Slow Dancing in the Big City* 1978; *The Formula* 1980; *Neighbors* 1981; *A Night in Heaven* 1983; *The Karate Kid* 1984; *The Karate Kid Part II* 1986; *Happy New Year* 1987; *For Keeps* 1987; *The Karate Kid III* 1989; *Lean on Me* 1989; *Rocky V* 1990; *The Power of One* 1991; *8 Seconds* 1994
Avnet, Jon *Fried Green Tomatoes at the Whistle Stop Cafe* 1991; *The War* 1994; *Up Close & Personal* 1996; *Red Corner* 1997
Axel, Gabriel *Babette's Feast* 1987; *Prince of Jutland* 1994
Axelrod, George *Lord Love a Duck* 1966; *The Secret Life of an American Wife* 1968
Azzopardi, Mario *Nowhere to Hide* 1987; *Bone Daddy* 1998

B

Babenco, Hector *Pixote* 1981; *Kiss of the Spider Woman* 1985; *Ironweed* 1987; *At Play in the Fields of the Lord* 1991; *Foolish Heart* 1998
Bacon, Lloyd *The Singing Fool* 1928; *Say It With Songs* 1929; *Moby Dick* 1930; *Kept Husbands* 1931; *Fireman Save My Child* 1932; *Footlight Parade* 1933; *42nd Street* 1933; *Picture Snatcher* 1933; *He Was Her Man* 1934; *Here Comes the Navy* 1934; *Wonder Bar* 1934; *Frisco Kid* 1935; *In Caliente* 1935; *Devil Dogs of the Air* 1935; *Cain and Mabel* 1936; *Gold Diggers of 1937* 1936; *Marked Woman* 1937; *San Quentin* 1937; *Boy Meets Girl* 1938; *A Slight Case of Murder* 1938; *The Oklahoma Kid* 1939; *Indianapolis Speedway* 1939; *Brother Orchid* 1940; *Invisible Stripes* 1940; *Knute Rockne – All American* 1940; *Footsteps in the Dark* 1941; *Affectionately Yours* 1941; *Larceny, Inc* 1942; *Action in the North Atlantic* 1943; *The Fighting Sullivans* 1944; *Sunday Dinner for a Soldier* 1944; *Captain Eddie* 1945; *I Wonder Who's Kissing Her Now* 1947; *Give My Regards to Broadway* 1948; *You Were Meant for Me* 1948; *It Happens Every Spring* 1949; *Mother Is a Freshman* 1949; *Miss Grant Takes Richmond* 1949; *Call Me Mister* 1951; *The Frogmen* 1951; *Golden Girl* 1951; *The I Don't Care Girl* 1952; *The Great Sioux Uprising* 1953; *Beautiful but Dangerous* 1954; *The French Line* 1954
Badger, Clarence *Hands Up!* 1926; *It* 1927
Badham, John *Isn't It Shocking?* 1973; *The Bingo Long Travelling All-Stars and Motor Kings* 1976; *Saturday Night Fever* 1977; *Dracula* 1979; *Whose Life Is it Anyway?* 1981; *Blue Thunder* 1983; *WarGames* 1983; *American Flyers* 1985; *Short Circuit* 1986; *Stakeout* 1987; *Bird on a Wire* 1990; *The Hard Way* 1991; *Another Stakeout* 1993; *The Assassin* 1993; *Point of No Return* 1993; *Drop Zone* 1994; *Nick of Time* 1995; *Incognito* 1997; *Floating Away* 1998; *The Jack Bull* 1999
Badiyi, Reza *aka* **Badiyi, Reza S** *The Eyes of Charles Sand* 1972; *Joe Dancer: the Big Black Pill* 1981; *Cagney & Lacey: Together Again* 1994; *Criminal Passion* 1995; *Eye of the Stalker* 1995
Baer Jr, Max *Ode to Billy Joe* 1976; *Hometown USA* 1979
Bagdadi, Maroun *Hors la Vie* 1991; *La Fille de l'Air* 1992
Bail, Chuck *Cleopatra Jones and the Casino of Gold* 1975; *The Gumball Rally* 1976; *On Dangerous Ground* 1986
Bailey, John *The Search for Signs of Intelligent Life in the Universe* 1991; *China Moon* 1994
Bailey, Norma *Martha, Ruth and Edie* 1988; *Bordertown Cafe* 1991
Baird, Stuart *Executive Decision* 1996; *US Marshals* 1998
Baker, Graham *The Final Conflict* 1980; *Impulse* 1984; *Alien Nation* 1988; *Born to Ride* 1991
Baker, Robert S *Blackout* 1950; *13 East Street* 1952; *The Steel Key* 1953; *Passport to Treason* 1956; *Jack the Ripper* 1958; *The Siege of Sidney Street* 1960; *The Treasure of Monte Cristo* 1960; *The Hellfire Club* 1961
Baker, Roy Ward *aka* **Baker, Roy** *The October Man* 1947; *The Weaker Sex* 1948; *Highly Dangerous* 1950; *Morning Departure* 1950; *Don't Bother to Knock* 1952; *Inferno* 1953; *Passage Home* 1955; *Jacqueline* 1956; *Tiger in the Smoke* 1956; *The One That Got Away* 1957; *A Night to Remember* 1958; *The Singer Not the Song* 1960; *Flame in the Streets* 1961; *Two Left Feet* 1963; *Quatermass and the Pit* 1967; *The Anniversary* 1968; *Moon Zero Two* 1969; *The Scars of Dracula* 1970; *The Vampire Lovers* 1970; *Dr Jekyll and Sister Hyde* 1971; *Asylum* 1972; *And Now the Screaming Starts!* 1973; *Vault of Horror* 1973; *The Legend of the Seven Golden Vampires* 1974; *The Monster Club* 1980
Bakshi, Ralph *Fritz the Cat* 1972; *Wizards* 1977; *The Lord of the Rings* 1978; *Fire and Ice* 1983; *Cool World* 1992; *The Cool and the Crazy* 1994
Balaban, Bob *Parents* 1988; *My Boyfriend's Back* 1993; *The Last Good Time* 1994
Balaban, Burt *Stranger from Venus* 1954; *High Hell* 1957; *Murder, Inc* 1960; *The Gentle Rain* 1966
Balabanov, Alexei *Brother* 1997; *Of Freaks and Men* 1998
Baldi, Ferdinando *Duel of Champions* 1961; *Texas Adios* 1966
Baldwin, Peter *A Very Brady Christmas* 1988; *Meet Wally Sparks* 1997
Ballard, Carroll *The Black Stallion* 1979; *Never Cry Wolf* 1983; *Nutcracker* 1986; *Wind* 1992; *Fly Away Home* 1996
Band, Albert *Face of Fire* 1959; *Zoltan... Hound of Dracula* 1977; *Ghoulies II* 1987; *Robot Wars* 1993; *Prehysteria!* 1993
Band, Charles *Crash!* 1977; *The Alchemist* 1981; *Parasite* 1982; *Trancers* 1985; *Trancers II: The Return of Jack Deth* 1991; *Prehysteria!* 1993
Banks, Monty *No Limit* 1935; *We're Going to Be Rich* 1938; *Great Guns* 1941
Barba, Norberto *Blue Tiger* 1994; *Solo* 1996; *Terror in the Mall* 1998
Barbash, Uri *Beyond the Walls* 1984; *One of Us* 1989
Barbera, Joseph *The Man Called Flintstone* 1966; *Jetsons: the Movie* 1990
Barclay, Paris *Don't Be a Menace to South Central while Drinking Your Juice in the Hood* 1996; *The Cherokee Kid* 1996
Bare, Richard L *aka* **Bare, Richard** *Prisoners of the Casbah* 1953; *Shoot-Out at Medicine Bend* 1957; *Girl on the Run* 1958; *This Rebel Breed* 1960
Barker, Clive *Hellraiser* 1987; *Nightbreed* 1990; *Lord of Illusions* 1995
Barker, Mike *aka* **Barker, Michael** *The James Gang* 1997; *Best Laid Plans* 1999
Barnett, Steve *Mindwarp* 1992; *Mission of Justice* 1992
Barnette, Neema *Scattered Dreams* 1993; *Better Off Dead* 1993; *Run for the Dream: the Gail Devers Story* 1996
Barr, Douglas *Conundrum* 1995; *Dead Badge* 1995; *Ed McBain's 87th Precinct: Heatwave* 1997; *Cloned* 1997
Barreto, Bruno *Dona Flor and Her Two Husbands* 1977; *A Show of Force* 1990; *The Heart of Justice* 1992; *Acts of Love* 1995; *Four Days in September* 1997; *One Tough Cop* 1998
Barron, Arthur *Jeremy* 1973; *Brothers* 1977
Barron, Steve *Electric Dreams* 1984; *Teenage Mutant Ninja Turtles* 1990; *Coneheads* 1993; *The Adventures of Pinocchio* 1996
Barron, Zelda *Secret Places* 1984; *Shag* 1988
Barry, Ian *The Chain Reaction* 1980; *Crime Broker* 1993; *Blackwater Trail* 1995; *Seventh Floor* 1995; *Robo Warriors* 1996
Barrymore, Lionel *Madame X* 1929; *The Rogue Song* 1930
Bartel, Paul *Death Race 2000* 1975; *Cannonball* 1976; *Eating Raoul* 1982; *Lust in the Dust* 1984; *Not for Publication* 1984; *The Longshot* 1986; *Scenes from the Class Struggle In Beverly Hills* 1989; *Shelf Life* 1993
Bartlett, Hall *Unchained* 1955; *Zero Hour* 1957; *Drango* 1957; *All the Young Men* 1960; *The Caretakers* 1963; *The Defiant* 1972; *Jonathan Livingston Seagull* 1973; *The Children of Sanchez* 1978; *Comeback* 1983
Bartlett, Richard *Rock, Pretty Baby* 1956; *Money, Women and Guns* 1958
Barton, Charles *aka* **Barton, Charles T** *The Last Outpost* 1935; *Reveille with Beverly* 1943; *The Time of Their Lives* 1946; *Buck Privates Come Home* 1947; *Abbott and Costello Meet Frankenstein* 1948; *The Noose Hangs High* 1948; *Abbott and Costello Meet the Killer, Boris Karloff* 1949; *Africa Screams* 1949; *Double Crossbones* 1951; *Dance with Me Henry* 1956; *The Shaggy Dog* 1959; *Toby Tyler, or Ten Weeks with a Circus* 1960
Bass, Jules *Mad Monster Party* 1967; *The Last Unicorn* 1980
Bassoff, Lawrence *Weekend Pass* 1984; *Hunk* 1987
Baumbach, Noah *Kicking and Screaming* 1995; *Mr Jealousy* 1997
Bava, Mario *aka* **Lion, Mickey** *Caltiki, the Immortal Monster* 1959; *The Mask of Satan* 1960; *Black Sabbath* 1963; *Dr Goldfoot and the Girl Bombs* 1966; *Danger: Diabolik* 1967; *Four Times That Night* 1972; *Lisa and the Devil* 1976
Baxley, Craig R *aka* **Baxley, Craig** *Action Jackson* 1988; *Dark Angel* 1989; *Stone Cold* 1991; *Silent Thunder* 1992; *Sudden Fury* 1993; *Deep Red* 1994; *The Avenging Angel* 1995; *Under Pressure* 1997; *Silencing Mary* 1998
Baxter, John *Song of the Road* 1937; *Crooks' Tour* 1940; *Love on the Dole* 1941; *We'll Smile Again* 1942; *Dreaming* 1944; *Here Comes the Sun* 1945; *When You Come Home* 1947; *Judgment Deferred* 1951
Bay, Michael *Bad Boys* 1995; *The Rock* 1996; *Armageddon* 1998
Beaird, David *My Chauffeur* 1986; *Pass the Ammo* 1988; *Scorchers* 1991
Beatty, Warren *Heaven Can Wait* 1978; *Reds* 1981; *Dick Tracy* 1990; *Bulworth* 1998
Beaudine, William *Little Annie Rooney* 1925; *Sparrows* 1926; *Three Wise Girls* 1932; *The Old-Fashioned Way* 1934; *Boys Will Be Boys* 1935; *Where There's a Will* 1936; *Windbag the Sailor* 1936; *Clancy Street Boys* 1943; *Ghosts in the Night* 1943; *Bowery Champs* 1944; *Follow the Leader* 1944; *Voodoo Man* 1944; *Come Out Fighting* 1945; *Kidnapped* 1948; *Jalopy* 1953; *Pride of the Blue Grass* 1954; *Jail Busters* 1955; *Westward Ho the Wagons!* 1956; *Ten Who Dared* 1960; *Lassie's Great Adventure* 1963
Beaumont, Gabrielle *The Godsend* 1980; *He's My Girl* 1987; *Cradle of Conspiracy* 1994; *The Other Woman* 1994; *Beastmaster III: the Eye of Braxus* 1995
Beaumont, Harry *Our Dancing Daughters* 1928; *The Broadway Melody* 1929; *Dance, Fools, Dance* 1931; *Laughing Sinners* 1931; *When Ladies Meet* 1933;

Up Goes Maisie 1946; *Undercover Maisie* 1947

Becker, Harold *The Ragman's Daughter* 1972; *The Onion Field* 1979; *The Black Marble* 1980; *Taps* 1981; *Vision Quest* 1985; *The Boost* 1988; *Sea of Love* 1989; *Malice* 1993; *City Hall* 1996; *Mercury Rising* 1998

Becker, Jacques *La Vie Est à Nous* 1936; *Casque d'Or* 1952; *Casque d'Or* 1952; *Honour among Thieves* 1954; *Montparnasses 19* 1958; *Le Trou* 1959

Becker, Jean *One Deadly Summer* 1983; *Elisa* 1994; *The Children of the Marshland* 1998

Beebe, Ford *Trouble at Midnight* 1937; *Westbound Limited* 1937; *Fantasia* 1940; *The Reluctant Dragon* 1941; *Frontier Badmen* 1943; *Enter Arsene Lupin* 1944; *Challenge to Be Free* 1972

Beeman, Greg *aka* **Beeman, Gregg** *Little Spies* 1986; *The Richest Cat in the World* 1986; *License to Drive* 1988; *Mom and Dad Save the World* 1992; *Bushwhacked* 1995; *Problem Child 3* 1995

Beineix, Jean-Jacques *Diva* 1981; *The Moon in the Gutter* 1983; *Betty Blue* 1986; *Roselyne and the Lions* 1989; *IP5* 1992

Bell, Martin *Streetwise* 1985; *American Heart* 1992; *Hidden in America* 1996

Bellamy, Earl *Stagecoach to Dancer's Rock* 1962; *Fluffy* 1965; *Incident at Phantom Hill* 1966; *Gunpoint* 1966; *Munster, Go Home!* 1966; *Seven Alone* 1974; *Against a Crooked Sky* 1975; *Part 2 Walking Tall* 1975; *Flood!* 1976; *Fire!* 1977; *Sidewinder One* 1977

Bellocchio, Marco *Fists in the Pocket* 1965; *The Prince of Homburg* 1997

Belmont, Véra *Rouge Baiser* 1985; *Milena* 1990; *Marquise* 1997

Belson, Jerry *Jekyll and Hyde... Together Again* 1982; *Surrender* 1987

Bemberg, Maria Luisa *Camila* 1984; *Miss Mary* 1986; *I, the Worst of All* 1990; *We Don't Want to Talk about It* 1993

Bender, Jack *Deadly Messages* 1985; *Letting Go* 1985; *Side by Side* 1988; *Tricks of the Trade* 1988; *My Brother's Wife* 1989; *Child's Play 3* 1991; *Armed and Innocent* 1994; *The Face* 1996; *Sweet Dreams* 1996

Benedek, Laslo *aka* **Benedek, László**, *aka* **Benedek, Laszlo** *Port of New York* 1949; *The Kissing Bandit* 1949; *Death of a Salesman* 1951; *The Wild One* 1953; *Bengal Brigade* 1954; *Affair in Havana* 1957; *Moment of Danger* 1960; *Namu, the Killer Whale* 1966; *Daring Game* 1968; *The Night Visitor* 1970

Benigni, Roberto *Johnny Stecchino* 1991; *Life Is Beautiful* 1997

Benjamin, Richard *My Favorite Year* 1982; *City Heat* 1984; *Racing with the Moon* 1984; *The Money Pit* 1985; *My Stepmother Is an Alien* 1988; *The Sleepers* 1988; *Downtown* 1990; *Mermaids* 1990; *Made in America* 1993; *Milk Money* 1994; *Mrs Winterbourne* 1995; *The Pentagon Wars* 1998; *Tourist Trap* 1998

Benner, Richard *Outrageous!* 1977; *Happy Birthday, Gemini* 1980; *Too Outrageous!* 1987

Bennet, Spencer Gordon *aka* **Bennet, Spencer G** *Submarine Seahawk* 1959; *The Atomic Submarine* 1960; *The Bounty Killer* 1965

Bennett, Bill *A Street to Die* 1985; *Backlash* 1986; *Malpractice* 1989; *Mortgage* 1989; *Spider and Rose* 1994; *Stolen Hearts* 1996; *Kiss or Kill* 1997

Bennett, Compton *The Seventh Veil* 1945; *Daybreak* 1946; *The Forsyte Saga* 1949; *King Solomon's Mines* 1950; *The Gift Horse* 1952; *Desperate Moment* 1953; *The Flying Scot* 1957; *That Woman Opposite* 1957; *Beyond the Curtain* 1960

Bentley, Thomas *The Old Curiosity Shop* 1934; *Those Were the Days* 1934; *Music Hath Charms* 1935

Benton, Robert *Bad Company* 1972; *The Late Show* 1977; *Kramer vs Kramer* 1979; *Still of the Night* 1982; *Places in the Heart* 1984; *Nadine* 1987; *Billy Bathgate* 1991; *Nobody's Fool* 1994; *Twilight* 1998

Bercovici, Luca *Ghoulies* 1985; *Dark Tide* 1993; *Convict 762* 1997

Beresford, Bruce *The Adventures of Barry McKenzie* 1972; *Barry McKenzie Holds His Own* 1974; *Side by Side* 1975; *Don's Party* 1976; *The Getting of Wisdom* 1977; *Money Movers* 1978; *Breaker Morant* 1979; *The Club* 1980; *Puberty Blues* 1981; *Tender Mercies* 1982; *The Fringe Dwellers* 1985; *King David* 1985; *Crimes of the Heart* 1986; *Aria* 1987; *Driving Miss Daisy* 1989; *Her Alibi* 1989; *Black Robe* 1991; *Mister Johnson* 1991; *Rich in Love* 1992; *A Good Man in Africa* 1993; *Silent Fall* 1994; *Last Dance* 1995; *Paradise Road* 1997; *Double Jeopardy* 1999

Bergman, Andrew *So Fine* 1981; *The Freshman* 1990; *Honeymoon in Vegas* 1992; *It Could Happen to You* 1994; *Striptease* 1996; *Isn't She Great* 1999

Bergman, Ingmar *It Rains on Our Love* 1946; *A Ship to India* 1947; *Port of Call* 1948; *Night Is My Future* 1948; *Thirst* 1949; *To Joy* 1949; *The Devil's Wanton* 1949; *Summer Interlude* 1950; *Summer with Monika* 1952; *Waiting Women* 1952; *Sawdust and Tinsel* 1953; *Lesson in Love* 1954; *Smiles of a Summer Night* 1955; *Dreams* 1955; *The Seventh Seal* 1957; *So Close to Life* 1957; *Wild Strawberries* 1957; *The Face* 1958; *The Devil's Eye* 1960; *The Virgin Spring* 1960; *Through a Glass Darkly* 1961; *Winter Light* 1962; *The Silence* 1963; *Now about These Women* 1964; *Persona* 1966; *The Hour of the Wolf* 1967; *Shame* 1968; *The Rite* 1969; *A Passion* 1969; *The Touch* 1971; *Cries and Whispers* 1972; *Scenes from a Marriage* 1973; *The Magic Flute* 1974; *Face to Face* 1976; *The Serpent's Egg* 1977; *Autumn Sonata* 1978; *From the Life of the Marionettes* 1980; *Fanny and Alexander* 1982; *After the Rehearsal* 1984

Berke, William *The Falcon in Mexico* 1944; *Betrayal from the East* 1945; *Dick Tracy* 1945; *The Falcon's Adventure* 1946

Berkeley, Busby *Footlight Parade* 1933; *Gold Diggers of 1935* 1935; *Stage Struck* 1936; *Hollywood Hotel* 1937; *Garden of the Moon* 1938; *Babes in Arms* 1939; *Fast and Furious* 1939; *They Made Me a Criminal* 1939; *Strike Up the Band* 1940; *Babes on Broadway* 1941; *For Me and My Gal* 1942; *The Gang's All Here* 1943; *Cinderella Jones* 1946; *Take Me Out to the Ball Game* 1949

Berman, Monty *Jack the Ripper* 1958; *The Siege of Sidney Street* 1960; *The Treasure of Monte Cristo* 1960; *The Hellfire Club* 1961

Berman, Ted *The Fox and the Hound* 1981; *The Black Cauldron* 1985

Bernard, Raymond *The Chess Player* 1927; *Les Misérables* 1934

Bernds, Edward *The Bowery Boys Meet the Monsters* 1954; *Jungle Gents* 1954; *World without End* 1955; *Reform School Girl* 1957; *Quantrill's Raiders* 1958; *Queen of Outer Space* 1958; *Space Master X 7* 1958; *Return of the Fly* 1959; *The Three Stooges in Orbit* 1962; *The Three Stooges Meet Hercules* 1962

Bernhardt, Curtis *aka* **Bernhardt, Kurt** *Three Loves* 1929; *Million Dollar Baby* 1941; *Happy Go Lucky* 1943; *Conflict* 1945; *Devotion* 1946; *My Reputation* 1946; *A Stolen Life* 1946; *High Wall* 1947; *Possessed* 1947; *The Doctor and the Girl* 1949; *The Blue Veil* 1951; *Sirocco* 1951; *Payment on Demand* 1951; *Miss Sadie Thompson* 1953; *Beau Brummell* 1954; *Interrupted Melody* 1955; *Gaby* 1956; *Kisses for My President* 1964

Bernstein, Armyan *Windy City* 1984; *Cross My Heart* 1987

Bernstein, Walter *Little Miss Marker* 1980; *Women and Men – 2* 1991

Berri, Claude *The Two of Us* 1967; *Marry Me! Marry Me!* 1968; *Je Vous Aime* 1980; *Le Maître d'école* 1981; *Jean de Florette* 1986; *Manon des Sources* 1986; *Uranus* 1990; *Germinal* 1993; *Lucie Aubrac* 1997

Berry, John *Miss Susie Slagle's* 1945; *From This Day Forward* 1946; *Casbah* 1948; *Tension* 1949; *He Ran All the Way* 1951; *Claudine* 1974; *Thieves* 1977; *The Bad News Bears Go to Japan* 1978; *A Captive in the Land* 1991

Berry, Tom *Something about Love* 1987; *Twin Sisters* 1992

Bertolucci, Bernardo *La Commare Secca* 1962; *Before the Revolution* 1964; *Partner* 1968; *The Conformist* 1969; *The Spider's Stratagem* 1970; *Last Tango in Paris* 1972; *1900* 1976; *La Luna* 1979; *The Tragedy of a Ridiculous Man* 1981; *The Last Emperor* 1987; *The Sheltering Sky* 1990; *Little Buddha* 1993; *Stealing Beauty* 1995; *Besieged* 1998

Bertucelli, Jean-Louis *Ramparts of Clay* 1969; *Doctor Françoise Gailland* 1975

Besson, Luc *The Last Battle* 1983; *Subway* 1985; *The Big Blue* 1988; *Nikita* 1990; *Atlantis* 1991; *Leon* 1994; *The Fifth Element* 1997; *Joan of Arc* 1999

Betancor, Antonio Jose *aka* **Betancor, Antonio J** *Valentina* 1982; *1919* 1983

Betuel, Jonathan *My Science Project* 1985; *Theodore Rex* 1995

Bianchi, Edward *The Fan* 1981; *Off and Running* 1991

Biberman, Abner *The Looters* 1955; *Running Wild* 1955; *Gun for a Coward* 1957; *The Night Runner* 1957

Biberman, Herbert J *aka* **Biberman, Herbert** *Meet Nero Wolfe* 1936; *The Master Race* 1944; *Salt of the Earth* 1954; *Slaves* 1969

Bierman, Robert *Apology* 1986; *Vampire's Kiss* 1988; *Keep the Aspidistra Flying* 1997

Bigelow, Kathryn *The Loveless* 1981; *Near Dark* 1987; *Blue Steel* 1990; *Point Break* 1991; *Strange Days* 1995

Bill, Tony *My Bodyguard* 1980; *Six Weeks* 1982; *2 ½ Dads* 1986; *Five Corners* 1987; *Crazy People* 1990; *A Home of Our Own* 1993; *Untamed Heart* 1993; *Next Door* 1994; *One Christmas* 1994; *Beyond the Call* 1996

Billington, Kevin *Interlude* 1968; *The Rise and Rise of Michael Rimmer* 1970; *The Light at the Edge of the World* 1971

Bilson, Bruce *Hill's Angels* 1979; *Chattanooga Choo Choo* 1984

Binder, Mike *Crossing the Bridge* 1992; *Indian Summer* 1993; *Blankman* 1994; *Blankman* 1994; *The Sex Monster* 1998

Binder, Steve *The TAMI Show* 1964; *Give 'Em Hell, Harry!* 1975

Bindley, William *Freeze Frame* 1989; *Judicial Consent* 1995; *The Eighteenth Angel* 1997

Binyon, Claude *The Saxon Charm* 1948; *Stella* 1950; *Dreamboat* 1952; *Here Come the Girls* 1953

Bird, Antonia *Priest* 1994; *Mad Love* 1995; *Face* 1997; *Ravenous* 1999

Birkin, Andrew *Burning Secret* 1988; *The Cement Garden* 1992; *Salt on Our Skin* 1992

Birt, Daniel *The Interrupted Journey* 1949; *Background* 1953

Bishop, Terry *You're Only Young Twice* 1952; *Cover Girl Killer* 1959; *Life in Danger* 1959

Bixby, Bill *The Trial of the Incredible Hulk* 1989; *The Death of the Incredible Hulk* 1990; *Another Pair of Aces: Three of a Kind* 1991; *The Woman Who Loved Elvis* 1993

Black, Noel *Pretty Poison* 1968; *Jennifer on My Mind* 1971; *A Man, a Woman and a Bank* 1979; *The Other Victim* 1981; *Private School* 1983; *My Two Loves* 1986; *A Time to Triumph* 1986; *Conspiracy of Love* 1987; *The Town Bully* 1988

Blair, Les *Number One* 1984; *Bad Behaviour* 1992; *Jump the Gun* 1996

Blakeley, John E *Somewhere on Leave* 1942; *Demobbed* 1944; *Home Sweet Home* 1945; *It's a Grand Life* 1953

Blakemore, Michael *Privates on Parade* 1982; *Country Life* 1994

Blasetti, Alessandro *1860* 1933; *Too Bad She's Bad* 1955; *Lucky to Be a Woman* 1955

Blatt, Edward A *Between Two Worlds* 1944; *Smart Woman* 1948

Blatty, William Peter *The Ninth Configuration* 1979; *The Exorcist III* 1990

Bleckner, Jeff *Do You Remember Love* 1985; *Hostile Witness* 1987; *White Water Summer* 1987; *My Father, My Son* 1988; *Hearts on Fire* 1992; *Serving in Silence* 1995; *Rear Window* 1998

Blier, Bertrand *Les Valseuses* 1974; *Get out Your Handkerchiefs* 1977; *Buffet Froid* 1979; *Tenue de Soirée* 1986; *Trop Belle pour Toi* 1989; *Merci la Vie* 1991; *Mon Homme* 1996

Bloom, Jason *Bio-Dome* 1996; *Overnight Delivery* 1997

Bloom, Jeffrey *Dogpound Shuffle* 1974; *Blood Beach* 1981; *Flowers in the Attic* 1987

Bloomfield, George *Jenny* 1969; *To Kill a Clown* 1972; *Nothing Personal* 1980; *Wojeck: Out of the Fire* 1992; *The Awakening* 1995

Blumenberg, Hans-Christoph *Thousand Eyes* 1984; *Operation Madonna* 1987

Bluth, Don *The Secret of NIMH* 1982; *An American Tail* 1986; *The Land before Time* 1988; *All Dogs Go to Heaven* 1989; *Rock-a-Doodle* 1990; *Thumbelina* 1994; *Stanley's Magic Garden* 1994; *The Pebble and the Penguin* 1995; *Anastasia* 1997; *Titan AE* 2000

Blystone, John G *aka* **Blystone, John** *Our Hospitality* 1923; *Tol'able David* 1930; *Great Guy* 1936; *Woman Chases Man* 1937; *Blockheads* 1938; *Swiss Miss* 1938

Bochner, Hart *Politically Correct Party Animals* 1994; *High School High* 1996

Bodrov, Sergei *I Wanted to See Angels* 1992; *Prisoner of the Mountains* 1996

Boetticher, Budd *The Bullfighter and the Lady* 1951; *Bronco Buster* 1952; *Horizons West* 1952; *Red Ball Express* 1952; *City beneath the Sea* 1953; *East of Sumatra* 1953; *The Man from the Alamo* 1953; *Seminole* 1953; *The Magnificent Matador* 1955; *Seven Men from Now* 1956; *Decision at Sundown* 1957; *The Tall T* 1957; *Buchanan Rides Alone* 1958; *Ride Lonesome* 1959; *Westbound* 1959; *Comanche Station* 1960; *The Rise and Fall of Legs Diamond* 1960; *A Time for Dying* 1971

Bogart, Paul *The Three Sisters* 1966; *Marlowe* 1969; *Halls of Anger* 1970; *Skin Game* 1971; *Cancel My Reservation* 1972; *Class of '44* 1973; *Oh, God! You Devil* 1984; *Torch Song Trilogy* 1988; *Broadway Bound* 1991; *The Gift of Love* 1994; *The Heidi Chronicles* 1995

Bogayevicz, Yurek *Anna* 1987; *Three of Hearts* 1992; *Exit in Red* 1996

Bogdanovich, Peter *aka* **Thomas, Derek** *Voyage to the Planet of Prehistoric Women* 1966; *Targets* 1968; *The Last Picture Show* 1971; *What's Up, Doc?* 1972; *Paper Moon* 1973; *Daisy Miller* 1974; *At Long Last Love* 1975; *Nickelodeon* 1976; *Saint Jack* 1979; *They All Laughed* 1981; *Mask* 1985; *Illegally Yours* 1988; *Texasville* 1990; *Noises Off* 1992; *The Thing Called Love* 1993; *To Sir with Love 2* 1996; *The Price of Heaven* 1997; *Rescuers: Stories of Courage – Two Women* 1997; *Naked City: a Killer Christmas* 1998; *A Saintly Switch* 1999

Boisset, Yves *The Evil Trap* 1975; *The Purple Taxi* 1977; *The Lady Cop* 1979

Boleslawski, Richard *Rasputin and the Empress* 1932; *Hollywood Party* 1934; *Men in White* 1934; *The Painted Veil* 1934; *Clive of India* 1935; *Les Misérables* 1935; *The Garden of Allah* 1936; *Theodora Goes Wild* 1936; *The Last of Mrs Cheyney* 1937

Bolognini, Mauro *Young Husbands* 1958; *Arabella* 1967; *The Oldest Profession* 1967; *The Inheritance* 1976

Bond, Timothy *aka* **Bond, Tim** *The Night of the Twisters* 1996; *The Shadow Men* 1997

Bondarchuk, Sergei *Destiny of a Man* 1959; *War and Peace* 1966; *Waterloo* 1970

Bonerz, Peter *Sharing Richard* 1988; *Police Academy 6: City under Siege* 1989

Again 1993; *Slam Dunk Ernest* 1995; *Ernest Goes to Africa* 1997; *Ernest in the Army* 1998
Chetwynd, Lionel *Hanoi Hilton* 1987; *So Proudly We Hail* 1990
Ching Siu-Tung *A Chinese Ghost Story* 1987; *A Chinese Ghost Story II* 1990
Chomsky, Marvin J *Evel Knievel* 1971; *Family Flight* 1972; *The Magician* 1973; *Live a Little, Steal a Lot* 1974; *A Matter of Wife...and Death* 1976; *Victory at Entebbe* 1976; *Good Luck, Miss Wyckoff* 1979; *My Body, My Child* 1982; *Nairobi Affair* 1984; *Tank* 1984; *Anastasia: the Mystery of Anna* 1986; *Triumph over Disaster: the Hurricane Andrew Story* 1993
Chong, Tommy *aka* **Chong, Thomas** *Cheech & Chong's Next Movie* 1980; *Cheech & Chong's Nice Dreams* 1981; *Cheech & Chong's Still Smokin'* 1983; *Cheech & Chong's The Corsican Brothers* 1984
Chopra, B R *Ek Hi Rasta* 1956; *Naya Daur* 1957; *Sadhna* 1958; *Kanoon* 1960
Chopra, Joyce *Smooth Talk* 1985; *The Lemon Sisters* 1989; *Murder in New Hampshire* 1991; *Baby Snatcher* 1992; *The Danger of Love* 1992; *My Very Best Friend* 1996; *Replacing Dad* 1999
Chopra, Yash *Waqt* 1965; *Kabhi Kabhie* 1976
Chouikh, Mohamed *The Citadel* 1989; *L'Arche du Désert* 1997
Chouraqui, Elie *Love Songs* 1984; *Man on Fire* 1987
Christian, Roger *The Sender* 1982; *Nostradamus* 1993; *The Final Cut* 1995; *Underworld* 1996; *Masterminds* 1997; *Battlefield Earth* 2000
Christian-Jaque *Fanfan la Tulipe* 1951; *Madame du Barry* 1954; *Nana* 1955; *Madame* 1961; *The Black Tulip* 1963; *The Dirty Game* 1965; *Dead Run* 1967
Chudnow, Byron Ross *The Doberman Gang* 1972; *The Daring Dobermans* 1973; *The Amazing Dobermans* 1976
Chukhrai, Grigori *aka* **Ciukhrai, Grigorij** *Ballad of a Soldier* 1959; *They Made Him a Criminal* 1980
Chukhrai, Pavel *Remember Me This Way* 1988; *The Thief* 1997
Ciccoritti, Gérard *aka* **Ciccoritti, Gerard** *Graveyard Shift* 1986; *Paris France* 1993
Cimino, Michael *Thunderbolt and Lightfoot* 1974; *The Deer Hunter* 1978; *Heaven's Gate* 1980; *Year of the Dragon* 1985; *The Sicilian* 1987; *Desperate Hours* 1990; *Sunchaser* 1996
Cissé, Souleymane *Yeelen* 1987; *Waati* 1995
Clair, René *Paris Qui Dort* 1923; *An Italian Straw Hat* 1927; *Sous les Toits de Paris* 1930; *A Nous la Liberté* 1931; *Le Million* 1931; *The Ghost Goes West* 1935; *The Flame of New Orleans* 1941; *I Married a Witch* 1942; *Forever and a Day* 1943; *It Happened Tomorrow* 1944; *And Then There Were None* 1945; *Man about Town* 1947; *La Beauté du Diable* 1949; *Les Belles de Nuit* 1952; *Les Grandes Manoeuvres* 1955; *Gates of Paris* 1957
Clark, Bob *Black Christmas* 1974; *Breaking Point* 1976; *Murder by Decree* 1978; *Tribute* 1980; *Porky's* 1981; *A Christmas Story* 1983; *Porky's II: The Next Day* 1983; *Rhinestone* 1984; *Turk 182!* 1985; *From the Hip* 1987; *Loose Cannons* 1990; *Arthur Miller's The American Clock* 1993; *My Summer Story* 1994; *Derby* 1995; *Fudge-a-Mania* 1995; *Baby Geniuses* 1999
Clark, Duane *Shaking the Tree* 1990; *Bitter Harvest* 1993; *Valentine's Day* 1998
Clark, Greydon *Satan's Cheerleaders* 1977; *Without Warning* 1980; *Wacko* 1981; *Lambada! The Forbidden Dance* 1990
Clark, James B *Villa!* 1958; *Sierra Baron* 1958; *The Sad Horse* 1959; *A Dog of Flanders* 1959; *One Foot in Hell* 1960; *The Big Show* 1961; *Flipper* 1963; *Island of the Blue Dolphins* 1964; *And Now Miguel* 1966; *My Side of the Mountain* 1969; *The Little Ark* 1972
Clark, Jim *Every Home Should Have One* 1970; *Rentadick* 1972; *Madhouse* 1974
Clark, Larry *kids* 1995; *Another Day in Paradise* 1998
Clarke, Alan *Scum* 1979; *Rita, Sue and Bob Too* 1987
Clarke, James Kenelm *Let's Get Laid* 1977; *Going Undercover* 1984
Clarke, Shirley *The Connection* 1961; *The Cool World* 1963
Clavell, James *Five Gates to Hell* 1959; *Walk like a Dragon* 1960; *To Sir, with Love* 1967; *Where's Jack?* 1969; *The Last Valley* 1971
Claxton, William F *Desire in the Dust* 1960; *Bonanza: the Next Generation* 1988
Clayton, Jack *Room at the Top* 1958; *The Innocents* 1961; *The Pumpkin Eater* 1964; *Our Mother's House* 1967; *The Great Gatsby* 1974; *Something Wicked This Way Comes* 1983; *The Lonely Passion of Judith Hearne* 1987
Clegg, Tom *Sweeney 2* 1978; *McVicar* 1980; *The Inside Man* 1984; *Any Man's Death* 1990
Clemens, William *The Case of the Velvet Claws* 1936; *The Case of the Stuttering Bishop* 1937; *Devil's Island* 1940; *The Falcon and the Co-Eds* 1943; *The Falcon in Danger* 1943; *The Falcon Out West* 1944
Clement, Dick *Otley* 1968; *A Severed Head* 1970; *Catch Me a Spy* 1971; *Porridge* 1979; *Bullshot* 1983; *Water* 1985
Clément, René *La Bataille du Rail* 1946; *La Belle et la Bête* 1946; *Les Jeux Interdits* 1953; *Knave of Hearts* 1954; *Gervaise* 1956; *This Angry Age* 1957; *Plein Soleil* 1960; *The Love Cage* 1964; *Is Paris Burning?* 1966; *Rider on the Rain* 1970; *The Deadly Trap* 1971; *And Hope to Die* 1972
Clements, Ron *Basil the Great Mouse Detective* 1986; *The Little Mermaid* 1989; *Aladdin* 1992; *Hercules* 1997
Clifford, Graeme *Frances* 1982; *Burke and Wills* 1985; *Gleaming the Cube* 1988; *Ruby Cairo* 1992; *Past Tense* 1994; *A Loss of Innocence* 1996; *My Husband's Secret Life* 1998
Cline, Edward *aka* **Cline, Eddie,** *aka* **Cline, Edward F** *One Week* 1920; *The Paleface* 1921; *Three Ages* 1923; *Million Dollar Legs* 1932; *Go Chase Yourself* 1938; *The Bank Dick* 1940; *My Little Chickadee* 1940; *The Villain Still Pursued Her* 1940; *Never Give a Sucker an Even Break* 1941; *Ghost Catchers* 1944
Clouse, Robert *Darker than Amber* 1970; *Enter the Dragon* 1973; *Black Belt Jones* 1974; *Golden Needles* 1974; *The Ultimate Warrior* 1975; *The Pack* 1977; *The Amsterdam Kill* 1978; *Game of Death* 1978; *The Big Brawl* 1980; *Gymkata* 1985; *China O'Brien* 1988
Clouzot, Henri-Georges *The Raven* 1943; *Quai des Orfèvres* 1947; *The Wages of Fear* 1953; *Les Diaboliques* 1954; *La Vérité* 1960
Clyde, Craig *Wind Dancer* 1991; *Little Heroes* 1992
Cochran, Stacy *My New Gun* 1992; *Boys* 1995
Cocteau, Jean *The Blood of a Poet* 1930; *La Belle et la Bête* 1946; *Eagle with Two Heads* 1948; *Les Parents Terribles* 1948; *Orphée* 1950; *Le Testament d'Orphée* 1960
Coen, Joel *Blood Simple* 1983; *Raising Arizona* 1987; *Miller's Crossing* 1990; *Barton Fink* 1991; *The Hudsucker Proxy* 1994; *Fargo* 1995; *The Big Lebowski* 1997; *O Brother, Where Art Thou?* 2000
Cohen, Howard R *Saturday the 14th* 1981; *Space Raiders* 1983; *Saturday the 14th Strikes Back* 1988; *Time Trackers* 1989
Cohen, Larry *Housewife* 1972; *Black Caesar* 1973; *Hell Up in Harlem* 1973; *It's Alive* 1974; *God Told Me to* 1976; *The Private Files of J Edgar Hoover* 1977; *It Lives Again* 1978; *Full Moon High* 1982; *Q – the Winged Serpent* 1982; *Blind Alley* 1984; *The Stuff* 1985; *Deadly Illusion* 1987; *It's Alive III: Island of the Alive* 1987; *Wicked Stepmother* 1989; *The Ambulance* 1990; *As Good as Dead* 1995; *Original Gangstas* 1996
Cohen, Norman *Till Death Us Do Part* 1968; *Dad's Army* 1971; *Adolf Hitler – My Part in His Downfall* 1972; *Confessions of a Pop Performer* 1975; *Confessions of a Driving Instructor* 1976; *Confessions from a Holiday Camp* 1977; *Stand Up Virgin Soldiers* 1977
Cohen, Rob *A Small Circle of Friends* 1980; *Scandalous* 1983; *Dragon: the Bruce Lee Story* 1993; *Daylight* 1996; *DragonHeart* 1996; *The Rat Pack* 1998; *The Skulls* 2000
Cohn, Michael *Interceptor* 1992; *Snow White: a Tale of Terror* 1996
Cokliss, Harley *Battletruck* 1982; *Black Moon Rising* 1985; *Malone* 1987; *Dream Demon* 1988
Cole, Marcus *The Christmas Box* 1995; *From the Mixed-Up Files of Mrs Basil E Frankweiler* 1995; *Childhood Sweetheart?* 1997; *Three Secrets* 1999
Coles, John David *Rising Son* 1990; *Against Her Will: the Carrie Buck Story* 1994; *Friends at Last* 1995
Colla, Richard A *aka* **Colla, Richard** *Zigzag* 1970; *Fuzz* 1972; *Battlestar Galactica* 1978; *The Great Balloon Adventure* 1978; *That Secret Sunday* 1986; *Something Is Out There* 1988; *Blind Witness* 1989; *Naked Lie* 1989; *Roxanne: the Prize Pulitzer* 1989; *Sparks: the Price of Passion* 1990; *Storm and Sorrow* 1990; *Desperate Rescue* 1993; *Roseanne and Tom: Behind the Scenes* 1994; *Her Last Chance* 1996
Collector, Robert *aka* **Blake, T C** *Red Heat* 1985; *Nightflyers* 1987
Collier, James F *The Hiding Place* 1975; *The Prodigal* 1983; *China Cry* 1990
Collins, Robert *Walk Proud* 1979; *Gideon's Trumpet* 1980; *Savage Harvest* 1981; *Mafia Princess* 1986; *J Edgar Hoover* 1987; *Prime Target* 1989; *In the Arms of a Killer* 1992
Collinson, Peter *Up the Junction* 1967; *The Penthouse* 1967; *The Long Day's Dying* 1968; *The Italian Job* 1969; *You Can't Win 'em All* 1970; *Fright* 1971; *Innocent Bystanders* 1972; *And Then There Were None* 1974; *Open Season* 1974; *The Sellout* 1975; *Tomorrow Never Comes* 1977; *The Earthling* 1980
Columbus, Chris *A Night on the Town* 1987; *Heartbreak Hotel* 1988; *Home Alone* 1990; *Only the Lonely* 1991; *Home Alone 2: Lost in New York* 1992; *Mrs Doubtfire* 1993; *Nine Months* 1995; *Stepmom* 1998; *Bicentennial Man* 1999
Comencini, Luigi *Bread, Love and Dreams* 1953; *Somewhere beyond Love* 1974
Comerford, Joe *Reefer and the Model* 1988; *High Boot Benny* 1993
Comfort, Lance *Hatter's Castle* 1941; *Great Day* 1944; *Hotel Reserve* 1944; *Bedelia* 1946; *Daughter of Darkness* 1948; *Silent Dust* 1948; *Portrait of Clare* 1950; *Eight O'Clock Walk* 1953; *Bang! You're Dead* 1954; *Man from Tangier* 1957; *The Man in the Road* 1957; *Make Mine a Million* 1959; *Rag Doll* 1960; *The Breaking Point* 1961; *The Painted Smile* 1961; *Pit of Darkness* 1961; *The Break* 1962; *Tomorrow at Ten* 1962; *Live It Up* 1963; *Devils of Darkness* 1964
Compton, Richard *Welcome Home, Soldier Boys* 1971; *Macon County Line* 1973; *Return to Macon County* 1975; *Maniac* 1977; *Baywatch: Panic at Malibu Pier* 1989; *The Keys* 1992
Condon, Bill *Dead in the Water* 1991; *Murder 101* 1991; *White Lie* 1991; *Deadly Relations* 1993; *Candyman II: Farewell to the Flesh* 1995; *The Man Who Wouldn't Die* 1995; *Gods and Monsters* 1998
Connor, Kevin *From beyond the Grave* 1973; *The Land That Time Forgot* 1974; *At the Earth's Core* 1976; *Trial by Combat* 1976; *The People That Time Forgot* 1977; *Warlords of Atlantis* 1978; *Arabian Adventure* 1979; *The House Where Evil Dwells* 1982; *The Lion of Africa* 1987; *The Return of Sherlock Holmes* 1987; *What Price Victory* 1988; *The Hollywood Detective* 1989; *Sunset Grill* 1992; *Jack Reed: Badge of Honor* 1993; *Shadow of Obsession* 1994; *The Little Riders* 1996
Conrad, William *The Man from Galveston* 1964; *Two on a Guillotine* 1965
Contner, James A *aka* **Contner, James** *The Return of Eliot Ness* 1991; *The 10 Million Dollar Getaway* 1991; *The Cover Girl Murders* 1993; *Abduction of Innocence* 1996; *Crimes of Silence* 1996; *A Secret between Friends* 1996; *Crimes of Passion: One Hot Summer Night* 1998; *A Champion's Fight* 1998
Conway, Jack *Our Modern Maidens* 1929; *The Unholy Three* 1930; *Arsene Lupin* 1932; *Red-Headed Woman* 1932; *Viva Villa!* 1934; *The Girl from Missouri* 1934; *The Gay Bride* 1934; *A Tale of Two Cities* 1935; *Libeled Lady* 1936; *Saratoga* 1937; *Too Hot to Handle* 1938; *A Yank at Oxford* 1938; *Lady of the Tropics* 1939; *Boom Town* 1940; *Honky Tonk* 1941; *Love Crazy* 1941; *Crossroads* 1942; *Dragon Seed* 1944; *High Barbaree* 1947; *The Hucksters* 1947; *Julia Misbehaves* 1948
Conway, James L *Hangar 18* 1980; *Earthbound* 1981
Conyers, Darcy *The Night We Dropped a Clanger* 1959; *The Night We Got the Bird* 1960; *In the Doghouse* 1961
Cook, Fielder *Patterns* 1956; *Big Deal at Dodge City* 1966; *How to Save a Marriage and Ruin Your Life* 1968; *Prudence and the Pill* 1968; *The Homecoming: a Christmas Story* 1971; *Eagle in a Cage* 1971; *The Hideaways* 1973; *Beauty and the Beast* 1976; *Family Reunion* 1981; *Seize the Day* 1986; *The Member of the Wedding* 1997
Coolidge, Martha *Valley Girl* 1983; *The City Girl* 1984; *Joy of Sex* 1984; *Real Genius* 1985; *Plain Clothes* 1988; *Trenchcoat in Paradise* 1989; *Bare Essentials* 1991; *Rambling Rose* 1991; *Crazy in Love* 1992; *Lost in Yonkers* 1993; *Angie* 1994; *Three Wishes* 1995; *Out to Sea* 1997; *If These Walls Could Talk 2* 2000
Cooney, Ray *Not Now Darling* 1972; *Not Now, Comrade* 1976
Cooper, George A *The Black Abbot* 1934; *The Shadow* 1936
Cooper, Jackie *aka* **Smithee, Allan** *Perfect Gentlemen* 1978; *White Mama* 1980; *Leave 'Em Laughing* 1981; *Moonlight* 1982; *Rosie: the Rosemary Clooney Story* 1982; *The Night They Saved Christmas* 1984; *Izzy and Moe* 1985
Cooper, Merian C *aka* **Cooper, Merian** *Grass: a Nation's Battle for Life* 1925; *Chang* 1927; *Four Feathers* 1929; *King Kong* 1933
Cooper, Stuart *Little Malcolm and His Struggle Against the Eunuchs* 1974; *Overlord* 1975; *The Disappearance* 1977; *Payoff* 1991; *Rubdown* 1993; *Bitter Vengeance* 1994; *Dancing with Danger* 1994; *Out of Annie's Past* 1995; *Dead Ahead* 1996; *The Ticket* 1997; *The Hunted* 1998
Coppola, Christopher *Dracula's Widow* 1988; *Deadfall* 1993; *Palmer's Pick-Up* 1999
Coppola, Francis Ford *aka* **Coppola, Francis** *Tonight for Sure* 1961; *Dementia 13* 1963; *You're a Big Boy Now* 1966; *Finian's Rainbow* 1968; *The Rain People* 1969; *The Godfather* 1972; *The Conversation* 1974; *The Godfather, Part II* 1974; *Apocalypse Now* 1979; *One from the Heart* 1982; *The Outsiders* 1983; *Rumble Fish* 1983; *The Cotton Club* 1984; *Peggy Sue Got Married* 1986; *Gardens of Stone* 1987; *Tucker: the Man and His Dream* 1988; *New York Stories* 1989; *The Godfather Part III* 1990; *Bram Stoker's Dracula* 1992; *Jack* 1996; *The Rainmaker* 1997
Coraci, Frank *The Waterboy* 1998; *The Wedding Singer* 1998
Corbiau, Gérard *The Music Teacher* 1988; *Farinelli il Castrato* 1994
Corbucci, Sergio *Duel of the Titans* 1961; *Django* 1966; *Ringo and His Golden Pistol* 1966; *Navajo Joe* 1966; *The Big Silence* 1967; *A Professional Gun* 1968; *The Con Artists* 1976
Corcoran, Bill *Shattered Trust* 1993; *Trust in Me* 1994; *Web of Deceit* 1994; *Dancing in the Dark* 1995; *A Walton Easter* 1997; *Mary Higgins Clark's Moonlight Becomes You* 1998; *Outlaw Justice* 1999
Corman, Roger *aka* **Neill, Harry** *Apache Woman* 1955; *Five Guns West* 1955; *The Day the World*

Ended 1956; *It Conquered the World* 1956; *The Oklahoma Woman* 1956; *Not of This Earth* 1956; *The Gunslinger* 1956; *Rock All Night* 1957; *Sorority Girl* 1957; *The Undead* 1957; *Viking Women and the Sea Serpent* 1957; *Attack of the Crab Monsters* 1957; *Machine Gun Kelly* 1958; *The Mobster* 1958; *Teenage Caveman* 1958; *War of the Satellites* 1958; *A Bucket of Blood* 1959; *The Wasp Woman* 1959; *The Fall of the House of Usher* 1960; *Little Shop of Horrors* 1960; *The Last Woman on Earth* 1960; *Atlas* 1960; *The Intruder* 1961; *The Pit and the Pendulum* 1961; *The Premature Burial* 1962; *Tales of Terror* 1962; *Tower of London* 1962; *The Haunted Palace* 1963; *The Man with the X-Ray Eyes* 1963; *The Raven* 1963; *The Terror* 1963; *The Masque of the Red Death* 1964; *The Tomb of Ligeia* 1964; *The Secret Invasion* 1964; *The Wild Angels* 1966; *The St Valentine's Day Massacre* 1967; *The Trip* 1967; *Target: Harry* 1968; *Bloody Mama* 1970; *Gas-s-s-s, or It Became Necessary to Destroy the World in Order to Save It* 1970; *Von Richthofen and Brown* 1971; *Frankenstein Unbound* 1990

Corneau, Alain *Choice of Arms* 1981; *Fort Saganne* 1984; *Tous les Matins du Monde* 1992; *Les Enfants de Lumière* 1995

Cornelius, Henry *Passport to Pimlico* 1949; *Genevieve* 1953; *I Am a Camera* 1955; *Next to No Time* 1958

Cornell, John *"Crocodile" Dundee II* 1988; *Almost an Angel* 1990

Cornfield, Hubert *Plunder Road* 1957; *The Third Voice* 1960; *Pressure Point* 1962; *The Night of the Following Day* 1968

Cornwell, Stephen *The Philadelphia Experiment 2* 1993; *Marshal Law* 1996

Correll, Charles *Gunsmoke: the Last Apache* 1990; *Cry in the Wild: the Taking of Peggy Ann* 1991; *In the Deep Woods* 1992; *Dead before Dawn* 1993; *Mother of the Bride* 1993; *Hijacked: Flight 285* 1996; *The Stepsister* 1997

Corrente, Michael *Federal Hill* 1994; *American Buffalo* 1995; *Outside Providence* 1999

Corrigan, Lloyd *No One Man* 1932; *Murder on a Honeymoon* 1935

Coscarelli, Don *Phantasm* 1978; *The Beastmaster* 1982; *Phantasm II* 1988; *Phantasm III – Lord Of The Dead* 1994

Cosmatos, George Pan *Sin* 1972; *Massacre in Rome* 1973; *The Cassandra Crossing* 1976; *Escape to Athena* 1979; *Of Unknown Origin* 1983; *Rambo: First Blood, Part II* 1985; *Cobra* 1986; *Leviathan* 1989; *Tombstone* 1993; *Shadow Conspiracy* 1996

Costa, Mario *The Barber of Seville* 1946; *Pagliacci* 1948; *Queen of the Pirates* 1960; *Gordon the Black Pirate* 1961

Costa-Gavras *aka* **Costa-Gavras, Constantin** *The Sleeping Car Murders* 1965; *Z* 1968; *The Confession* 1970; *State of Siege* 1972; *Missing* 1981; *Betrayed* 1988; *Music Box* 1989; *Mad City* 1997

Costner, Kevin *Dances with Wolves* 1990; *The Postman* 1997

Coto, Manny *Cover-Up* 1991; *Dr Giggles* 1992; *Star Kid* 1997

Couffer, Jack *Ring of Bright Water* 1969; *Living Free* 1972; *The Darwin Adventure* 1972

Cousteau, Jacques-Yves *Le Monde du Silence* 1956; *World without Sun* 1964

Couturie, Bill *Dear America: Letters Home from Vietnam* 1987; *Ed* 1996

Cox, Alex *Repo Man* 1984; *Sid and Nancy* 1986; *Walker* 1987; *Straight to Hell* 1987; *Highway Patrolman* 1991; *The Winner* 1997

Cox, Paul *Lonely Hearts* 1981; *Man of Flowers* 1984; *My First Wife* 1984; *Cactus* 1986; *Vincent: the Life and Death of Vincent Van Gogh* 1987; *Island* 1989; *Golden Braid* 1991; *A Woman's Tale* 1991; *The Nun and the Bandit* 1992; *Erotic Tales* 1994

Cozzi, Luigi *aka* **Coates, Lewis** *Hercules* 1983; *Hercules II* 1983

Crabtree, Arthur *Madonna of the Seven Moons* 1944; *They Were Sisters* 1945; *Caravan* 1946; *Dear Murderer* 1947; *The Calendar* 1948; *Quartet* 1948; *Don't Ever Leave Me* 1949; *Hindle Wakes* 1952; *Fiend without a Face* 1957

Crane, Peter *Assassin* 1973; *Coopersmith: Sweet Scent of Murder* 1992

Craven, Wes *Last House on the Left* 1972; *The Hills Have Eyes* 1978; *Deadly Blessing* 1981; *Swamp Thing* 1982; *A Nightmare on Elm Street* 1984; *Chiller* 1985; *The Hills Have Eyes Part II* 1985; *Deadly Friend* 1986; *The Serpent and the Rainbow* 1987; *Shocker* 1989; *Night Visions* 1990; *The People under the Stairs* 1991; *Wes Craven's New Nightmare* 1994; *Vampire in Brooklyn* 1995; *Scream* 1996; *Scream 2* 1997; *Music of the Heart* 1999; *Scream 3* 1999

Crawford, Wayne *Crime Lords* 1991; *Americanski Blues* 1993

Crichton, Charles *For Those in Peril* 1943; *Dead of Night* 1945; *Against the Wind* 1947; *Hue and Cry* 1947; *Another Shore* 1948; *Train of Events* 1949; *Dance Hall* 1950; *The Lavender Hill Mob* 1951; *Hunted* 1952; *The Titfield Thunderbolt* 1952; *The Love Lottery* 1953; *The Divided Heart* 1954; *Floods of Fear* 1958; *Law and Disorder* 1958; *The Battle of the Sexes* 1960; *The Boy Who Stole a Million* 1960; *The Third Secret* 1964; *He Who Rides a Tiger* 1965; *A Fish Called Wanda* 1988

Crichton, Michael *Westworld* 1973; *Coma* 1977; *The First Great Train Robbery* 1978; *Looker* 1981; *Runaway* 1984; *Physical Evidence* 1989

Crisp, Donald *The Navigator* 1924; *Don Q, Son of Zorro* 1925

Cristofer, Michael *Gia* 1998; *Body Shots* 1999

Croghan, Emma-Kate *Love and Other Catastrophes* 1996; *Strange Planet* 1999

Crombie, Donald *Caddie* 1976; *The Irishman* 1978; *Cathy's Child* 1979; *The Killing of Angel Street* 1981; *Kitty and the Bagman* 1982; *Robbery under Arms* 1985; *Rough Diamonds* 1994

Cromwell, John *The Texan* 1930; *Tom Sawyer* 1930; *Ann Vickers* 1933; *The Silver Cord* 1933; *The Fountain* 1934; *Spitfire* 1934; *Of Human Bondage* 1934; *This Man Is Mine* 1934; *I Dream Too Much* 1935; *Banjo on My Knee* 1936; *Little Lord Fauntleroy* 1936; *The Prisoner of Zenda* 1937; *Algiers* 1938; *In Name Only* 1939; *Made for Each Other* 1939; *Abe Lincoln in Illinois* 1940; *Victory* 1940; *So Ends Our Night* 1941; *Son of Fury* 1942; *Since You Went Away* 1944; *The Enchanted Cottage* 1945; *Anna and the King of Siam* 1946; *Dead Reckoning* 1947; *Night Song* 1947; *Caged* 1950; *The Company She Keeps* 1950; *The Racket* 1951; *The Goddess* 1958

Cronenberg, David *Stereo* 1969; *Crimes of the Future* 1970; *Shivers* 1975; *Rabid* 1976; *The Brood* 1979; *Scanners* 1981; *Videodrome* 1982; *The Dead Zone* 1983; *The Fly* 1986; *Dead Ringers* 1988; *Naked Lunch* 1991; *M Butterfly* 1993; *Crash* 1996; *eXistenZ* 1999

Crosland, Alan *Don Juan* 1926; *The Jazz Singer* 1927; *The Case of the Howling Dog* 1934

Crowe, Cameron *Say Anything* 1989; *Singles* 1992; *Jerry Maguire* 1996

Crowe, Christopher *Saigon* 1988; *Steel Justice* 1992; *Whispers in the Dark* 1992

Cruze, James *The Covered Wagon* 1923; *Hollywood* 1923; *Ruggles of Red Gap* 1923; *The Pony Express* 1925; *The Great Gabbo* 1929; *If I Had a Million* 1932; *Washington Merry-Go-Round* 1932; *I Cover the Waterfront* 1933

Crystal, Billy *Mr Saturday Night* 1992; *Forget Paris* 1995

Cuarón, Alfonso *A Little Princess* 1995; *Great Expectations* 1997

Cukor, George *The Royal Family of Broadway* 1930; *The Virtuous Sin* 1930; *Girls about Town* 1931; *Tarnished Lady* 1931; *A Bill of Divorcement* 1932; *What Price Hollywood?* 1932; *Rockabye* 1932; *One Hour with You* 1932; *Dinner at Eight* 1933; *Little Women* 1933; *Our Betters* 1933; *David Copperfield* 1935; *Romeo and Juliet* 1936; *Sylvia Scarlett* 1936; *Camille* 1937; *The Prisoner of Zenda* 1937; *Holiday* 1938; *The Women* 1939; *Zaza* 1939; *The Philadelphia Story* 1940; *Susan and God* 1940; *Two-Faced Woman* 1941; *A Woman's Face* 1941; *Keeper of the Flame* 1942; *Her Cardboard Lover* 1942; *Gaslight* 1944; *Winged Victory* 1944; *A Double Life* 1947; *Adam's Rib* 1949; *Edward, My Son* 1949; *Born Yesterday* 1950; *A Life of Her Own* 1950; *The Model and the Marriage Broker* 1951; *The Marrying Kind* 1952; *Pat and Mike* 1952; *The Actress* 1953; *It Should Happen to You* 1954; *A Star Is Born* 1954; *Bhowani Junction* 1956; *Les Girls* 1957; *Wild Is the Wind* 1957; *Heller in Pink Tights* 1960; *Let's Make Love* 1960; *Song without End* 1960; *The Chapman Report* 1962; *My Fair Lady* 1964; *Justine* 1969; *Travels with My Aunt* 1972; *Love among the Ruins* 1975; *The Blue Bird* 1976; *The Corn Is Green* 1979; *Rich and Famous* 1981

Cullingham, Mark *Sunday Drive* 1986; *Dead on the Money* 1991

Cummings, Irving *In Old Arizona* 1929; *The Mad Game* 1933; *The White Parade* 1934; *Curly Top* 1935; *Poor Little Rich Girl* 1936; *Vogues* 1937; *Little Miss Broadway* 1938; *Just around the Corner* 1938; *Hollywood Cavalcade* 1939; *The Story of Alexander Graham Bell* 1939; *Down Argentine Way* 1940; *Lillian Russell* 1940; *Louisiana Purchase* 1941; *That Night in Rio* 1941; *Belle Starr* 1941; *My Gal Sal* 1942; *Springtime in the Rockies* 1942; *Sweet Rosie O'Grady* 1943; *What a Woman!* 1943; *The Dolly Sisters* 1945; *Double Dynamite* 1951

Cundieff, Rusty *Fear of a Black Hat* 1992; *Tales from the Hood* 1995; *Sprung* 1997

Cunningham, Sean S *Kick!* 1979; *Friday the 13th* 1980; *DeepStar Six* 1989

Curtis, Dan *House of Dark Shadows* 1970; *Night of Dark Shadows* 1971; *The Night Strangler* 1973; *Dracula* 1974; *Burnt Offerings* 1976; *The Last Ride of the Dalton Gang* 1979; *Mrs R's Daughter* 1979; *The Long Days of Summer* 1980; *Me and the Kid* 1993; *Trilogy of Terror II* 1996; *The Love Letter* 1998

Curtiz, Michael *Noah's Ark* 1928; *Mammy* 1930; *The Mad Genius* 1931; *Cabin in the Cotton* 1932; *Doctor X* 1932; *The Strange Love of Molly Louvain* 1932; *The Kennel Murder Case* 1933; *Mystery of the Wax Museum* 1933; *20,000 Years in Sing Sing* 1933; *Female* 1933; *British Agent* 1934; *Jimmy the Gent* 1934; *The Key* 1934; *Mandalay* 1934; *Black Fury* 1935; *Captain Blood* 1935; *Front Page Woman* 1935; *The Charge of the Light Brigade* 1936; *The Walking Dead* 1936; *Kid Galahad* 1937; *The Perfect Specimen* 1937; *The Adventures of Robin Hood* 1938; *Angels with Dirty Faces* 1938; *Four Daughters* 1938; *Four's a Crowd* 1938; *Gold Is Where You Find It* 1938; *Daughters Courageous* 1939; *Dodge City* 1939; *The Private Lives of Elizabeth and Essex* 1939; *Four Wives* 1939; *Santa Fe Trail* 1940; *The Sea Hawk* 1940; *Virginia City* 1940; *Dive Bomber* 1941; *The Sea Wolf* 1941; *Captains of the Clouds* 1942; *Casablanca* 1942; *Yankee Doodle Dandy* 1942; *Mission to Moscow* 1943; *This Is the Army* 1943; *Passage to Marseille* 1944; *Mildred Pierce* 1945; *Roughly Speaking* 1945; *Night and Day* 1946; *Life with Father* 1947; *The Unsuspected* 1947; *It's Magic* 1948; *Romance on the High Seas* 1948; *Flamingo Road* 1949; *My Dream Is Yours* 1949; *The Breaking Point* 1950; *Bright Leaf* 1950; *Young Man with a Horn* 1950; *Force of Arms* 1951; *I'll See You in My Dreams* 1951; *The Jazz Singer* 1952; *Trouble along the Way* 1953; *The Boy from Oklahoma* 1954; *The Egyptian* 1954; *White Christmas* 1954; *We're No Angels* 1955; *The Best Things in Life Are Free* 1956; *The Vagabond King* 1956; *The Helen Morgan Story* 1957; *King Creole* 1958; *The Proud Rebel* 1958; *The Man in the Net* 1959; *The Hangman* 1959; *The Adventures of Huckleberry Finn* 1960; *A Breath of Scandal* 1960; *The Comancheros* 1961; *Francis of Assisi* 1961

Cutts, Graham *Looking on the Bright Side* 1931; *Car of Dreams* 1935; *Oh Daddy!* 1935; *Over She Goes* 1937; *Just William* 1939

Cyran, Catherine *White Wolves* 1993; *Behind Closed Doors* 1994; *Hostile Intentions* 1995; *Dangerous Waters* 1999

Czinner, Paul *Ariane* 1931; *Catherine the Great* 1934; *Escape Me Never* 1935; *As You Like It* 1936; *Romeo and Juliet* 1966

D

Da Costa, Morton *Auntie Mame* 1958; *The Music Man* 1962; *Island of Love* 1963

Dahl, John *Kill Me Again* 1989; *Red Rock West* 1992; *The Last Seduction* 1993; *Unforgettable* 1996; *Rounders* 1998

Dalen, Zale *Skip Tracer* 1977; *Expect No Mercy* 1995

Dalrymple, Ian *Storm in a Teacup* 1937; *Esther Waters* 1948

Damiani, Damiano *The Empty Canvas* 1963; *A Bullet for the General* 1966; *Amityville II: the Possession* 1982

Damski, Mel *The Legend of Walks Far Woman* 1982; *Yellowbeard* 1983; *Badge of the Assassin* 1985; *Mischief* 1985; *Murder by the Book* 1986; *A Connecticut Yankee in King Arthur's Court* 1989; *Everybody's Baby: the Rescue of Jessica McClure* 1989; *Happy Together* 1989; *Victim of Innocence* 1990; *Blood River* 1991; *Vigilante Cop* 1991; *Shoot First: a Cop's Vengeance* 1991; *Wild Card* 1992

Daniel, Rod *Teen Wolf* 1985; *Like Father, Like Son* 1987; *K-9* 1989; *The Super* 1991; *Beethoven's 2nd* 1993

Daniels, Marc *Planet Earth* 1974; *Vengeance: the Story of Tony Cimo* 1986

Dante, Joe *Hollywood Boulevard* 1976; *Piranha* 1978; *The Howling* 1981; *Twilight Zone: the Movie* 1983; *Gremlins* 1984; *Explorers* 1985; *Amazon Women on the Moon* 1987; *Innerspace* 1987; *The 'Burbs* 1989; *Gremlins 2: the New Batch* 1990; *Matinee* 1993; *Runaway Daughters* 1994; *The Second Civil War* 1997; *Small Soldiers* 1998

Darabont, Frank *Buried Alive* 1990; *The Shawshank Redemption* 1994; *The Green Mile* 1999

Darby, Jonathan *The Enemy Within* 1994; *Hush* 1998

Dardenne, Jean-Pierre *La Promesse* 1996; *Rosetta* 1999

Dardenne, Luc *La Promesse* 1996; *Rosetta* 1999

Darling, Joan *First Love* 1977; *The Check Is in the Mail* 1986

D'Arrast, Harry d'Abbadie *Laughter* 1930; *Raffles* 1930; *Topaze* 1933

Dassin, Jules *Reunion in France* 1942; *Young Ideas* 1943; *The Canterville Ghost* 1944; *Brute Force* 1947; *The Naked City* 1948; *Thieves' Highway* 1949; *Night and the City* 1950; *Rififi* 1955; *Where the Hot Wind Blows!* 1959; *Never on Sunday* 1960; *Phaedra* 1962; *Topkapi* 1964; *10:30 PM Summer* 1966; *A Dream of Passion* 1978; *Circle of Two* 1980

Davenport, Harry Bromley *Xtro* 1983; *Xtro 2: The Second Encounter* 1990

Daves, Delmer *Destination Tokyo* 1943; *Hollywood Canteen* 1944; *The Very Thought of You* 1944; *Pride of the Marines* 1945; *Dark Passage* 1947; *The Red House* 1947; *Task Force* 1949; *A Kiss in the Dark* 1949; *Broken Arrow* 1950; *Bird of Paradise* 1951; *Treasure of the Golden Condor* 1953; *Never Let Me Go* 1953; *Demetrius and the Gladiators* 1954; *Drum Beat* 1954; *Jubal* 1956; *3:10 to Yuma* 1957; *The Badlanders* 1958; *Cowboy* 1958; *Kings Go Forth* 1958; *The Hanging*

Tree 1959; *A Summer Place* 1959; *Susan Slade* 1961; *Parrish* 1961; *Lovers Must Learn* 1962; *Spencer's Mountain* 1963; *The Battle of the Villa Fiorita* 1964; *Youngblood Hawke* 1964

David, Pierre *Scanner Cop* 1994; *Serial Killer* 1996

Davidson, Boaz *Lemon Popsicle* 1978; *Salsa* 1988

Davidson, Martin *The Lords of Flatbush* 1974; *Almost Summer* 1977; *Hero at Large* 1980; *Eddie and the Cruisers* 1983; *Long Gone* 1987; *Heart of Dixie* 1989; *Hard Promises* 1991; *A Murderous Affair* 1992; *Follow the River* 1995

Davies, Terence *Distant Voices, Still Lives* 1988; *The Long Day Closes* 1992; *The Neon Bible* 1995; *The House of Mirth* 2000

Davis, Andrew *Code of Silence* 1985; *Nico* 1988; *The Package* 1989; *Under Siege* 1992; *The Fugitive* 1993; *Steal Big, Steal Little* 1995; *Chain Reaction* 1996; *A Perfect Murder* 1998

Davis, Desmond *Girl with Green Eyes* 1963; *The Uncle* 1964; *I Was Happy Here* 1966; *Smashing Time* 1967; *A Nice Girl Like Me* 1969; *Clash of the Titans* 1981; *The Country Girls* 1983; *The Sign of Four* 1983; *Ordeal by Innocence* 1984

Davis, Eddie *Panic in the City* 1968; *Color Me Dead* 1969

Davis, Michael *aka* **Davis, Michael Paul** *Beanstalk* 1994; *Eight Days a Week* 1996

Davis, Ossie *Cotton Comes to Harlem* 1970; *Black Girl* 1972; *Gordon's War* 1973

Davis, Phil *aka* **Davis, Philip** *i.d.* 1994; *Hold Back the Night* 1999

Davis, Robin *The Police War* 1979; *Shock* 1982; *I Married a Dead Man* 1983

Davis, Tamra *Guncrazy* 1992; *CB4* 1993; *Billy Madison* 1995; *Best Men* 1997; *Half-Baked* 1998

Day, Ernest *Green Ice* 1981; *Waltz across Texas* 1982

Day, Robert *The Green Man* 1956; *Stranger's Meeting* 1957; *First Man into Space* 1958; *Grip of the Strangler* 1958; *Bobbikins* 1959; *Life in Emergency Ward 10* 1959; *The Rebel* 1960; *Tarzan the Magnificent* 1960; *Two Way Stretch* 1960; *Corridors of Blood* 1962; *Tarzan's Three Challenges* 1963; *She* 1965; *Tarzan and the Valley of Gold* 1966; *Tarzan and the Great River* 1967; *Twin Detectives* 1976; *Black Market Baby* 1977; *The Man with Bogart's Face* 1980; *The Lady from Yesterday* 1985; *The Quick and the Dead* 1987; *Fire! Trapped on the 37th Floor* 1991

Dayton, Lyman *aka* **Dayton, Lyman D** *Baker's Hawk* 1976; *The Dream Machine* 1990; *Second Chance* 1995

De Bont, Jan *Speed* 1994; *Twister* 1996; *Speed 2: Cruise Control* 1997; *The Haunting* 1999

de Broca, Philippe *Cartouche* 1961; *The Seven Deadly Sins* 1961; *That Man from Rio* 1964; *Up to His Ears* 1965; *King of Hearts* 1966; *The Oldest Profession* 1967; *Le Bossu* 1997

De Cordova, Frederick *The Countess of Monte Cristo* 1948; *For the Love of Mary* 1948; *Bedtime for Bonzo* 1951; *Column South* 1953; *I'll Take Sweden* 1965; *Frankie & Johnny* 1966

De Felitta, Frank *Trapped* 1973; *Scissors* 1991

De Filippo, Eduardo *The Seven Deadly Sins* 1952; *Shout Loud, Louder… I Don't Understand* 1966

De Heer, Rolf *Tail of a Tiger* 1984; *Encounter at Raven's Gate* 1988; *Dingo* 1991; *Bad Boy Bubby* 1993

De Jong, Ate *Drop Dead Fred* 1991; *Highway to Hell* 1992; *All Men Are Mortal* 1995

de la Iglesia, Alex *Acción Mutante* 1993; *The Day of the Beast* 1995; *Perdita Durango* 1997; *Dying of Laughter* 1999

de Lautour, Charles *The Limping Man* 1953; *Impulse* 1955

de Oliveira, Manoel *The Divine Comedy* 1992; *Abraham Valley* 1993; *The Convent* 1995; *Journey to the Beginning of the World* 1997

De Palma, Brian *The Wedding Party* 1966; *Greetings* 1968; *Hi, Mom!* 1970; *Get to Know Your Rabbit* 1972; *Sisters* 1973; *Phantom of the Paradise* 1974; *Carrie* 1976; *Obsession* 1976; *The Fury* 1978; *Home Movies* 1979; *Dressed to Kill* 1980; *Blow Out* 1981; *Scarface* 1983; *Body Double* 1984; *Wise Guys* 1986; *The Untouchables* 1987; *Casualties of War* 1989; *The Bonfire of the Vanities* 1990; *Raising Cain* 1992; *Carlito's Way* 1993; *Mission: Impossible* 1996; *Snake Eyes* 1998; *Mission to Mars* 1999

De Sica, Vittorio *Shoeshine* 1946; *Bicycle Thieves* 1948; *Miracle in Milan* 1950; *Umberto D* 1952; *Gold of Naples* 1954; *Indiscretion of an American Wife* 1954; *Two Women* 1960; *Boccaccio '70* 1961; *The Condemned of Altona* 1962; *Yesterday, Today and Tomorrow* 1963; *Marriage – Italian Style* 1964; *After the Fox* 1966; *Woman Times Seven* 1967; *Sunflower* 1969; *A Place for Lovers* 1969; *The Garden of the Finzi-Continis* 1971; *The Voyage* 1974

De Toth, Andre *Passport to Suez* 1943; *Dark Waters* 1944; *None Shall Escape* 1944; *The Other Love* 1947; *Ramrod* 1947; *Pitfall* 1948; *Slattery's Hurricane* 1949; *Man in the Saddle* 1951; *Carson City* 1952; *Springfield Rifle* 1952; *Last of the Comanches* 1952; *House of Wax* 1953; *Thunder over the Plains* 1953; *The Stranger Wore a Gun* 1953; *The Bounty Hunter* 1954; *Riding Shotgun* 1954; *Tanganyika* 1954; *The City Is Dark* 1954; *The Indian Fighter* 1955; *Hidden Fear* 1957; *The Two-Headed Spy* 1958; *Day of the Outlaw* 1959; *Morgan the Pirate* 1960; *The Mongols* 1961; *Gold for the Caesars* 1964; *Play Dirty* 1969

Dean, Basil *Escape* 1930; *Looking on the Bright Side* 1931; *The Constant Nymph* 1933; *Lorna Doone* 1934; *The Show Goes On* 1937; *21 Days* 1937

Dear, William *Bigfoot and the Hendersons* 1987; *Teen Agent* 1991; *Journey to the Center of the Earth* 1993; *Angels* 1994; *Wild America* 1997; *Balloon Farm* 1999

Dearden, Basil *The Black Sheep of Whitehall* 1941; *The Goose Steps Out* 1942; *The Bells Go Down* 1943; *The Halfway House* 1943; *My Learned Friend* 1943; *Dead of Night* 1945; *The Captive Heart* 1946; *Frieda* 1947; *Saraband for Dead Lovers* 1948; *The Blue Lamp* 1949; *Train of Events* 1949; *Cage of Gold* 1950; *Pool of London* 1950; *The Gentle Gunman* 1952; *I Believe in You* 1952; *The Square Ring* 1953; *Out of the Clouds* 1954; *The Ship That Died of Shame* 1955; *The Smallest Show on Earth* 1957; *The Rainbow Jacket* 1958; *Violent Playground* 1958; *Sapphire* 1959; *The League of Gentlemen* 1960; *Man in the Moon* 1960; *The Secret Partner* 1961; *Victim* 1961; *All Night Long* 1961; *Life for Ruth* 1962; *The Mind Benders* 1963; *A Place to Go* 1963; *Woman of Straw* 1964; *Masquerade* 1965; *Khartoum* 1966; *Only When I Larf* 1968; *The Assassination Bureau* 1969; *The Man Who Haunted Himself* 1970

Dearden, James *The Cold Room* 1984; *Pascali's Island* 1988; *A Kiss before Dying* 1991; *Rogue Trader* 1998

DeBello, John *Attack of the Killer Tomatoes* 1978; *Return of the Killer Tomatoes* 1988

Decoin, Henri *Secrets d'Alcove* 1954; *Razzia sur la Chnouf* 1955; *One Night at the Music Hall* 1956; *Too Many Lovers* 1957; *Le Masque de Fer* 1962

DeCoteau, David *Prey of the Jaguar* 1996; *Skeletons* 1996

Dehlavi, Jamil *Born of Fire* 1987; *Immaculate Conception* 1991

Dein, Edward *Shack Out on 101* 1955; *Calypso Joe* 1957; *The Leech Woman* 1960

Deitch, Donna *Desert Hearts* 1985; *Prison Stories: Women on the Inside* 1991; *Sexual Advances* 1992; *Angel of Desire* 1993; *A Change of Place* 1994; *The Devil's Arithmetic* 1999

Dekker, Fred *The Monster Squad* 1987; *RoboCop 3* 1993

Del Ruth, Roy *The Desert Song* 1929; *Gold Diggers of Broadway* 1929; *Blonde Crazy* 1931; *Dangerous Female* 1931; *Taxi!* 1932; *Bureau of Missing Persons* 1933; *Lady Killer* 1933; *The Little Giant* 1933; *Bulldog Drummond Strikes Back* 1934; *Kid Millions* 1934; *Upper World* 1934; *Broadway Melody of 1936* 1935; *Folies Bergère* 1935; *Thanks a Million* 1935; *Born to Dance* 1936; *Broadway Melody of 1938* 1937; *On the Avenue* 1937; *Happy Landing* 1938; *My Lucky Star* 1938; *The Star Maker* 1939; *Topper Returns* 1941; *DuBarry Was a Lady* 1943; *Barbary Coast Gent* 1944; *Broadway Rhythm* 1944; *Ziegfeld Follies* 1944; *It Happened on Fifth Avenue* 1947; *Always Leave Them Laughing* 1949; *Red Light* 1949; *The West Point Story* 1950; *On Moonlight Bay* 1951; *Stop, You're Killing Me* 1952; *Three Sailors and a Girl* 1953; *Phantom of the Rue Morgue* 1954; *The Alligator People* 1959

Del Toro, Guillermo *Cronos* 1992; *Mimic* 1997

Delannoy, Jean *Eternal Love* 1943; *La Symphonie Pastorale* 1946; *Secrets d'Alcove* 1954; *Obsession* 1954; *Marie Antoinette* 1956; *The Hunchback of Notre Dame* 1956; *Imperial Venus* 1963

D'Elia, Bill *The Feud* 1989; *Big Dreams & Broken Hearts: the Dottie West Story* 1995; *The Tomorrow Man* 1995

Dell, Jeffrey *Don't Take It to Heart* 1944; *It's Hard to Be Good* 1948; *Carlton-Browne of the FO* 1958

DeMille, Cecil B *aka* **De Mille, Cecil B** *Carmen* 1915; *The Cheat* 1915; *A Romance of the Redwoods* 1917; *Male and Female* 1919; *Why Change Your Wife?* 1920; *The Ten Commandments* 1923; *The Road to Yesterday* 1925; *The King of Kings* 1927; *Dynamite* 1929; *Madam Satan* 1930; *The Squaw Man* 1931; *The Sign of the Cross* 1932; *This Day and Age* 1933; *Cleopatra* 1934; *Four Frightened People* 1934; *The Crusades* 1935; *The Plainsman* 1936; *The Buccaneer* 1938; *Union Pacific* 1939; *Northwest Mounted Police* 1940; *Reap the Wild Wind* 1942; *The Story of Dr Wassell* 1944; *Unconquered* 1947; *Samson and Delilah* 1949; *The Greatest Show on Earth* 1952; *The Ten Commandments* 1956

Demme, Jonathan *Caged Heat* 1974; *Crazy Mama* 1975; *Fighting Mad* 1976; *Citizens Band* 1977; *Last Embrace* 1979; *Melvin and Howard* 1980; *Stop Making Sense* 1984; *Swing Shift* 1984; *Something Wild* 1986; *Swimming to Cambodia* 1987; *Married to the Mob* 1988; *The Silence of the Lambs* 1991; *Cousin Bobby* 1992; *Philadelphia* 1993; *Beloved* 1998; *Storefront Hitchcock* 1998

Demme, Ted *Who's the Man?* 1993; *Hostile Hostages* 1994; *Beautiful Girls* 1996; *Noose* 1997; *Life* 1999

Demy, Jacques *Lola* 1960; *The Seven Deadly Sins* 1961; *The Umbrellas of Cherbourg* 1964; *The Young Girls of Rochefort* 1967; *Model Shop* 1969; *The Magic Donkey* 1970; *The Pied Piper* 1971

Denis, Claire *Chocolat* 1988; *Beau Travail* 1999

Dennehy, Brian *Jack Reed: a Search for Justice* 1994; *Deadly Justice* 1995; *Shadow of a Doubt* 1995; *Jack Reed: Death and Vengeance* 1996; *A Father's Betrayal* 1997

Densham, Pen *The Kiss* 1988; *Moll Flanders* 1995; *Houdini* 1998

Deray, Jacques *That Man George* 1965; *The Swimming Pool* 1968; *Borsalino* 1970; *Take It Easy* 1971; *Borsalino and Co* 1974; *Police Story* 1975; *Three Men to Destroy* 1980

Derek, John *Once Before I Die* 1965; *Tarzan, the Ape Man* 1981; *Bolero* 1984; *Ghosts Can't Do It* 1990

Deruddere, Dominique *Wait until Spring, Bandini* 1989; *Suite 16* 1994

Deschanel, Caleb *The Escape Artist* 1982; *Crusoe* 1988

DeSimone, Tom *The Concrete Jungle* 1982; *Reform School Girls* 1986

Detiege, David *The Man from Button Willow* 1965; *Bugs Bunny 1001 Rabbit Tales* 1982

Deutch, Howard *Pretty in Pink* 1986; *Some Kind of Wonderful* 1987; *The Great Outdoors* 1988; *Article 99* 1992; *Getting Even with Dad* 1994; *Grumpier Old Men* 1996; *The Odd Couple II* 1998

Deville, Michel *The Theft of the Mona Lisa* 1965; *Death in a French Garden* 1985; *La Lectrice* 1988

DeVito, Danny *The Ratings Game* 1984; *Throw Momma from the Train* 1987; *The War of the Roses* 1989; *Hoffa* 1992; *Matilda* 1996

Dewolf, Patrick *Lapse of Memory* 1992; *Innocent Lies* 1995

Dexter, John *The Virgin Soldiers* 1969; *The Sidelong Glances of a Pigeon Kicker* 1970; *I Want What I Want* 1971

Dexter, Maury *Young Guns of Texas* 1962; *Wild on the Beach* 1965

DiCillo, Tom *Johnny Suede* 1991; *Living in Oblivion* 1995; *Box of Moon Light* 1996; *The Real Blonde* 1997

Dick, Nigel *Private Investigations* 1987; *Final Combination* 1993

Dickerson, Ernest R *Juice* 1992; *Surviving the Game* 1994; *Tales from the Crypt: Demon Knight* 1995; *Bulletproof* 1996; *Ambushed* 1998; *Blind Faith* 1998; *Futuresport* 1998

Dickinson, Thorold *The Arsenal Stadium Mystery* 1939; *Gaslight* 1940; *The Prime Minister* 1940; *Men of Two Worlds* 1946; *The Queen of Spades* 1948; *The Secret People* 1951

Diegues, Carlos *Bye Bye Brazil* 1979; *Quilombo* 1984

Dieterle, William *aka* **Dieterle, Wilhelm**, *aka* **Dieterle, William S** *Her Majesty Love* 1931; *The Last Flight* 1931; *Jewel Robbery* 1932; *Lawyer Man* 1932; *Scarlet Dawn* 1932; *The Devil's in Love* 1933; *Fashions of 1934* 1934; *Madame Du Barry* 1934; *Fog over Frisco* 1934; *The Secret Bride* 1934; *Dr Socrates* 1935; *A Midsummer Night's Dream* 1935; *The Story of Louis Pasteur* 1936; *Satan Met a Lady* 1936; *Another Dawn* 1937; *The Great O'Malley* 1937; *The Life of Emile Zola* 1937; *Blockade* 1938; *The Hunchback of Notre Dame* 1939; *Juarez* 1939; *Dr Ehrlich's Magic Bullet* 1940; *A Dispatch from Reuters* 1940; *Daniel and the Devil* 1941; *Syncopation* 1942; *I'll Be Seeing You* 1944; *Kismet* 1944; *Love Letters* 1945; *This Love of Ours* 1945; *The Searching Wind* 1946; *Portrait of Jennie* 1948; *The Accused* 1949; *Rope of Sand* 1949; *Dark City* 1950; *September Affair* 1950; *Volcano* 1950; *Boots Malone* 1951; *Red Mountain* 1951; *Peking Express* 1951; *The Turning Point* 1952; *Salome* 1953; *Elephant Walk* 1954; *Magic Fire* 1956; *Omar Khayyam* 1957; *Quick, Let's Get Married* 1964

Dignam, Erin *Denial* 1991; *Loved* 1996

Dinner, Michael *Catholic Boys* 1985; *Off Beat* 1986; *Hot to Trot* 1988; *Thicker than Blood* 1993; *Rise and Walk: the Dennis Byrd Story* 1994

DiSalle, Mark *Kickboxer* 1989; *The Perfect Weapon* 1991

Dixon, Ivan *Trouble Man* 1972; *Percy and Thunder* 1993

Dmytryk, Edward *The Devil Commands* 1941; *Sweetheart of the Campus* 1941; *Behind the Rising Sun* 1943; *The Falcon Strikes Back* 1943; *Hitler's Children* 1943; *Tender Comrade* 1943; *Back to Bataan* 1945; *Cornered* 1945; *Farewell My Lovely* 1945; *Till the End of Time* 1946; *Crossfire* 1947; *Obsession* 1948; *Give Us This Day* 1949; *The Sniper* 1952; *The Juggler* 1953; *Broken Lance* 1954; *The Caine Mutiny* 1954; *The Left Hand of God* 1955; *Soldier of Fortune* 1955; *The End of the Affair* 1955; *The Mountain* 1956; *Raintree County* 1957; *The Young Lions* 1958; *The Blue Angel* 1959; *Warlock* 1959; *Walk on the Wild Side* 1962; *The Carpetbaggers* 1964; *Where Love Has Gone* 1964; *Mirage* 1965; *Alvarez Kelly* 1966; *Anzio* 1968; *Shalako* 1968; *Bluebeard* 1972; *He Is My Brother* 1974; *The Human Factor* 1975

Dobson, Kevin James *The Mango Tree* 1977; *For Love of a Child* 1990; *Miracle in the Wilderness* 1991; *Shades of Gray* 1992; *Survive the Savage Sea* 1992;

1950; *The Quiet Man* 1952; *What Price Glory?* 1952; *Mogambo* 1953; *The Sun Shines Bright* 1953; *The Long Gray Line* 1955; *Mister Roberts* 1955; *The Searchers* 1956; *The Wings of Eagles* 1957; *The Last Hurrah* 1958; *Gideon's Day* 1959; *The Horse Soldiers* 1959; *Sergeant Rutledge* 1960; *Two Rode Together* 1961; *How the West Was Won* 1962; *The Man Who Shot Liberty Valance* 1962; *Donovan's Reef* 1963; *Cheyenne Autumn* 1964; *Young Cassidy* 1965; *7 Women* 1966

Forde, Eugene aka **Forde, Eugene J** *Charlie Chan in London* 1934; *Charlie Chan on Broadway* 1937; *Step Lively, Jeeves* 1937; *International Settlement* 1938; *Michael Shayne, Private Detective* 1940; *Berlin Correspondent* 1942; *Shadows in the Night* 1944

Forde, Walter *The Ghost Train* 1931; *Rome Express* 1932; *Bulldog Jack* 1934; *Chu Chin Chow* 1934; *Jack Ahoy!* 1934; *Forever England* 1935; *King of the Damned* 1935; *Land without Music* 1936; *Cheer Boys Cheer* 1939; *The Four Just Men* 1939; *Let's Be Famous* 1939; *Sailors Three* 1940; *Saloon Bar* 1940; *The Ghost Train* 1941; *It's That Man Again* 1942; *Time Flies* 1944; *The Master of Bankdam* 1947; *Cardboard Cavalier* 1949

Forman, Milos *Peter and Pavla* 1964; *A Blonde in Love* 1965; *The Fireman's Ball* 1967; *Taking Off* 1971; *Visions of Eight* 1973; *One Flew over the Cuckoo's Nest* 1975; *Hair* 1979; *Ragtime* 1981; *Amadeus* 1984; *Valmont* 1989; *The People vs Larry Flynt* 1996; *Man on the Moon* 1999

Forsyth, Bill *That Sinking Feeling* 1979; *Gregory's Girl* 1980; *Local Hero* 1983; *Comfort and Joy* 1984; *Housekeeping* 1987; *Breaking In* 1989; *Being Human* 1994; *Gregory's Two Girls* 1999

Fortenberry, John *Jury Duty* 1995; *A Night at the Roxbury* 1998

Fosse, Bob *Sweet Charity* 1968; *Cabaret* 1972; *Lenny* 1974; *All That Jazz* 1979; *Star 80* 1983

Foster, Giles *Tree of Hands* 1988; *Consuming Passions* 1988

Foster, Jodie *Little Man Tate* 1991; *Home for the Holidays* 1995

Foster, Lewis R *Men o' War* 1929; *The Man Who Cried Wolf* 1937; *The Lucky Stiff* 1949; *Jamaica Run* 1953; *Crashout* 1955; *The Bold and the Brave* 1956; *Dakota Incident* 1956; *Tonka* 1958

Foster, Norman *Fair Warning* 1937; *Thank You, Mr Moto* 1937; *Think Fast, Mr Moto* 1937; *Mr Moto Takes a Chance* 1938; *Mysterious Mr Moto* 1938; *Charlie Chan at Treasure Island* 1939; *Charlie Chan in Reno* 1939; *Mr Moto Takes a Vacation* 1939; *Mr Moto's Last Warning* 1939; *Journey into Fear* 1942; *Blood on My Hands* 1948; *Rachel and the Stranger* 1948; *Tell It to the Judge* 1949; *Davy Crockett, King of the Wild Frontier* 1955; *Davy Crockett and the River Pirates* 1956; *Brighty of the Grand Canyon* 1966

Fowler Jr, Gene *I Was a Teenage Werewolf* 1957; *I Married a Monster from Outer Space* 1958; *Showdown at Boot Hill* 1958; *Gang War* 1958; *The Oregon Trail* 1959; *The Rebel Set* 1959

Fox, Wallace aka **Fox, Wallace W** *Block Busters* 1944; *Docks of*

New York 1945; *Mr Muggs Rides Again* 1945; *Wild Beauty* 1946

Fraker, William A *Monte Walsh* 1970; *A Reflection of Fear* 1973; *The Legend of the Lone Ranger* 1981

Frakes, Jonathan *Star Trek: First Contact* 1996; *Star Trek: Insurrection* 1998

Francis, Freddie *Two and Two Make Six* 1961; *The Brain* 1962; *Paranoiac* 1963; *Dr Terror's House of Horrors* 1964; *Evil of Frankenstein* 1964; *Nightmare* 1964; *The Skull* 1965; *The Psychopath* 1966; *The Deadly Bees* 1967; *They Came from beyond Space* 1967; *Torture Garden* 1967; *Dracula Has Risen from the Grave* 1968; *Mumsy, Nanny, Sonny & Girly* 1970; *Trog* 1970; *The Creeping Flesh* 1972; *Tales from the Crypt* 1972; *Craze* 1973; *Tales That Witness Madness* 1973; *Legend of the Werewolf* 1974; *The Ghoul* 1975; *The Doctor and the Devils* 1985; *Dark Tower* 1989

Francis, Karl *Giro City* 1982; *Rebecca's Daughters* 1991

Francisci, Pietro *Hercules* 1957; *Hercules Unchained* 1959; *The Siege of Syracuse* 1959

Franco, Jesus aka **Moutier, Norbert,** aka **Franco, Jess** *The Awful Dr Orloff* 1962; *The Blood of Fu Manchu* 1968; *The Castle of Fu Manchu* 1968; *Count Dracula* 1970; *Dracula, Prisoner of Frankenstein* 1972; *The Female Vampire* 1973

Franju, Georges *Eyes without a Face* 1959; *Thérèse Desqueyroux* 1962; *Judex* 1963; *Thomas the Imposter* 1964

Frank, Melvin *Callaway Went Thataway* 1951; *Above and Beyond* 1952; *Knock on Wood* 1954; *The Court Jester* 1956; *That Certain Feeling* 1956; *Li'l Abner* 1959; *The Jayhawkers* 1959; *The Facts of Life* 1960; *Strange Bedfellows* 1965; *Buona Sera, Mrs Campbell* 1968; *A Touch of Class* 1973; *The Prisoner of Second Avenue* 1974; *The Duchess and the Dirtwater Fox* 1976; *Lost and Found* 1979; *Walk like a Man* 1987

Frank, Robert *Pull My Daisy* 1959; *Candy Mountain* 1987

Frankel, Cyril *Devil on Horseback* 1954; *Man of Africa* 1954; *It's Great to Be Young* 1956; *No Time for Tears* 1957; *Alive and Kicking* 1958; *Never Take Sweets from a Stranger* 1960; *Don't Bother to Knock* 1961; *On the Fiddle* 1961; *The Very Edge* 1962; *The Witches* 1966; *The Trygon Factor* 1967

Frankenheimer, John aka **Smithee, Alan** *The Young Stranger* 1957; *The Young Savages* 1961; *Birdman of Alcatraz* 1962; *The Manchurian Candidate* 1962; *Seven Days in May* 1964; *The Train* 1964; *Grand Prix* 1966; *Seconds* 1966; *The Fixer* 1968; *The Extraordinary Seaman* 1969; *The Gypsy Moths* 1969; *I Walk the Line* 1970; *The Horsemen* 1971; *The Iceman Cometh* 1973; *Story of a Love Story* 1973; *99 and 44/100% Dead* 1974; *French Connection II* 1975; *Black Sunday* 1976; *Prophecy* 1979; *The Challenge* 1982; *The Holcroft Covenant* 1985; *52 Pick-Up* 1986; *Riviera* 1987; *Dead-Bang* 1989; *The Fourth War* 1990; *Year of the Gun* 1991; *Against the Wall* 1994; *The Burning Season* 1994; *The Island of Dr Moreau* 1996; *Ronin* 1998; *Deception* 2000

Franklin, Carl *Full Fathom Five* 1990; *One False Move* 1992; *Devil in a Blue Dress* 1995; *One True Thing* 1998

Franklin, Howard *Quick Change* 1990; *The Public Eye* 1992; *Larger than Life* 1996

Franklin, Richard *Patrick* 1978; *Road Games* 1981; *Psycho II* 1983; *Cloak and Dagger* 1984; *Link* 1986; *F/X2: the Deadly Art of Illusion* 1991; *Running Delilah* 1992; *Hotel Sorrento* 1994; *Brilliant Lies* 1996

Franklin, Sidney *The Last of Mrs Cheyney* 1929; *Wild Orchids* 1929; *A Lady's Morals* 1930; *The Guardsman* 1931; *Private Lives* 1931; *Smilin' Through* 1932; *Reunion in Vienna* 1933; *The Barretts of Wimpole Street* 1934; *The Dark Angel* 1935; *The Good Earth* 1937; *The Barretts of Wimpole Street* 1957

Fraser, Harry *'Neath the Arizona Skies* 1934; *Randy Rides Alone* 1934

Frawley, James *Kid Blue* 1971; *The Christian Licorice Store* 1971; *The Big Bus* 1976; *The Muppet Movie* 1979; *Fraternity Vacation* 1985; *Spies, Lies and Naked Thighs* 1988; *Runaway Heart* 1990; *Cagney & Lacey: the Return* 1994; *Sins of the Mind* 1997; *On the 2nd Day of Christmas* 1997

Frears, Stephen *Gumshoe* 1971; *The Hit* 1984; *My Beautiful Laundrette* 1985; *Prick Up Your Ears* 1987; *Sammy and Rosie Get Laid* 1987; *Dangerous Liaisons* 1988; *The Grifters* 1990; *Accidental Hero* 1992; *The Snapper* 1993; *Mary Reilly* 1995; *The Van* 1996; *The Hi-Lo Country* 1998; *High Fidelity* 2000

Freda, Riccardo aka **Hampton, Robert** *Les Misérables* 1946; *Lust of the Vampire* 1956; *Caltiki, the Immortal Monster* 1959; *The Horrible Dr Hichcock* 1962; *The Spectre* 1963; *Gold for the Caesars* 1964

Freedman, Jerrold aka **Smithee, Alan** *Kansas City Bomber* 1972; *This Man Stands Alone* 1979; *Borderline* 1980; *The Boy Who Drank Too Much* 1980; *Legs* 1983; *Seduced* 1985; *Thompson's Last Run* 1986; *Native Son* 1986; *Family Sins* 1987; *Night Walk* 1989; *The OJ Simpson Story* 1995

Freeland, Thornton *Whoopee!* 1930; *Love Affair* 1932; *Flying down to Rio* 1933; *George White's Scandals* 1934; *Accused* 1936; *Over the Moon* 1937; *Hold My Hand* 1938; *The Gang's All Here* 1939; *Meet Me at Dawn* 1946; *The Brass Monkey* 1948

Freeman, Morgan J *Hurricane Streets* 1997; *Desert Blue* 1998

Fregonese, Hugo *Saddle Tramp* 1950; *One Way Street* 1950; *Apache Drums* 1951; *My Six Convicts* 1952; *Untamed Frontier* 1952; *Blowing Wild* 1953; *Decameron Nights* 1953; *Man in the Attic* 1953; *The Raid* 1954; *Seven Thunders* 1957

Freleng, Friz *Looney Looney Looney Bugs Bunny Movie* 1981; *Bugs Bunny 1001 Rabbit Tales* 1982; *Daffy Duck's Movie: Fantastic Island* 1983

French, Harold *Jeannie* 1941; *Major Barbara* 1941; *The Day Will Dawn* 1942; *Secret Mission* 1942; *English without Tears* 1944; *Quiet Weekend* 1946; *The Blind Goddess* 1947; *My Brother Jonathan* 1947; *Quartet* 1948; *Adam and Evelyne* 1949; *The Dancing Years* 1949; *Trio* 1950;

Encore 1951; *Isn't Life Wonderful!* 1952; *The Man Who Watched Trains Go By* 1952; *Rob Roy, the Highland Rogue* 1953; *Forbidden Cargo* 1954; *The Man Who Loved Redheads* 1954

Frend, Charles *The Foreman Went to France* 1941; *San Demetrio London* 1943; *Johnny Frenchman* 1945; *The Loves of Joanna Godden* 1947; *Scott of the Antarctic* 1948; *A Run for Your Money* 1949; *The Magnet* 1950; *The Cruel Sea* 1953; *Lease of Life* 1954; *The Long Arm* 1956; *Barnacle Bill* 1957; *Cone of Silence* 1960; *Girl on Approval* 1962

Fresco, Rob *Evil Has a Face* 1996; *Dirty Little Secret* 1998

Freund, Karl *The Mummy* 1932; *Mad Love* 1935

Fridriksson, Fridrik Thor *Cold Fever* 1994; *Devil's Island* 1996

Friedenberg, Richard *The Life and Times of Grizzly Adams* 1974; *Mr and Mrs Loving* 1993; *The Education of Little Tree* 1997

Friedkin, David *Hot Summer Night* 1957; *Handle with Care* 1958

Friedkin, William *Good Times* 1967; *The Birthday Party* 1968; *The Night They Raided Minsky's* 1968; *The Boys in the Band* 1970; *The French Connection* 1971; *The Exorcist* 1973; *Sorcerer* 1977; *The Brink's Job* 1978; *Cruising* 1980; *Deal of the Century* 1983; *To Live and Die in LA* 1985; *Rampage* 1987; *The Guardian* 1990; *Blue Chips* 1994; *Jailbreakers* 1994; *Jade* 1995; *Twelve Angry Men* 1997; *Rules of Engagement* 2000

Friedman, Jeffrey *Common Threads: Stories from the Quilt* 1989; *The Celluloid Closet* 1995

Friedman, Richard *Deathmask* 1984; *Doom Asylum* 1987; *Shadow of a Stranger* 1992; *With Harmful Intent* 1993

Friedman, Seymour *Escape Route* 1952; *Khyber Patrol* 1954; *Secret of Treasure Mountain* 1956

Frost, Harvey aka **Frost, F Harvey** *Midnight Heat* 1994; *National Lampoon's Golf Punks* 1998

Frost, Lee aka **Frost, R L** *House on Bare Mountain* 1962; *The Thing with Two Heads* 1972; *Dixie Dynamite* 1976

Fruet, William *Wedding in White* 1972; *Search and Destroy* 1978; *Bedroom Eyes* 1984; *Killer Party* 1986; *Blue Monkey* 1987

Fuest, Robert *Just like a Woman* 1966; *And Soon the Darkness* 1970; *Wuthering Heights* 1970; *The Abominable Dr Phibes* 1971; *Dr Phibes Rises Again* 1972; *The Final Programme* 1973; *The Devil's Rain* 1975; *Revenge of the Stepford Wives* 1980

Fukasaku, Kinji *Tora! Tora! Tora!* 1970; *Virus* 1980

Fukuda, Jun *Ebirah, Horror of the Deep* 1966; *Son of Godzilla* 1967; *Godzilla vs Gigan* 1972; *Godzilla vs Megalon* 1973; *Godzilla vs the Cosmic Monster* 1974

Fulci, Lucio *Beatrice Cenci* 1969; *Zombie Flesh Eaters* 1979

Fuller, Samuel *I Shot Jesse James* 1949; *The Baron of Arizona* 1950; *Fixed Bayonets* 1951; *The Steel Helmet* 1951; *Park Row* 1952; *Pickup on South Street* 1953; *Hell and High Water* 1954; *House of Bamboo* 1955; *China Gate* 1957; *Forty Guns* 1957; *Run of the Arrow* 1957; *The Crimson Kimono* 1959; *Verboten!* 1959; *Underworld USA* 1961; *Merrill's Marauders* 1962; *Shock Corridor* 1963; *The Naked*

Kiss 1964; *Shark!* 1969; *Dead Pigeon on Beethoven Street* 1972; *The Big Red One* 1980; *White Dog* 1981

Fuller, Tex *Stranded* 1987; *Prey of the Chameleon* 1991

Furie, Sidney J *Doctor Blood's Coffin* 1960; *The Young Ones* 1961; *The Boys* 1961; *The Leather Boys* 1963; *Wonderful Life* 1964; *The Ipcress File* 1965; *The Appaloosa* 1966; *The Naked Runner* 1967; *The Lawyer* 1969; *Little Fauss and Big Halsy* 1970; *Lady Sings the Blues* 1972; *Hit!* 1973; *Sheila Levine Is Dead and Living in New York* 1975; *Gable and Lombard* 1976; *The Boys in Company C* 1978; *The Entity* 1981; *Purple Hearts* 1984; *Iron Eagle* 1985; *Superman IV: the Quest for Peace* 1987; *Iron Eagle II* 1988; *The Taking of Beverly Hills* 1991; *Ladybugs* 1992; *Iron Eagle IV* 1995; *Hollow Point* 1996; *Top of the World* 1997; *Married to a Stranger* 1997

G

Gabor, Pal *Angi Vera* 1980; *The Long Ride* 1984

Gabriel, Mike *The Rescuers Down Under* 1990; *Pocahontas* 1995

Gallo, Fred *The Finishing Touch* 1992; *Hollywood Madam* 1994; *Mind Breakers* 1996

Gallo, George *29th Street* 1991; *Trapped in Paradise* 1994

Gallone, Carmine *Rigoletto* 1946; *La Forza del Destino* 1949; *Carthage in Flames* 1960

Gance, Abel *La Roue* 1923; *Napoléon* 1927; *Abel Gance's Beethoven* 1936; *J'Accuse* 1938; *The Battle of Austerlitz* 1960

Gans, Christophe *Necronomicon* 1993; *Crying Freeman* 1995

Ganzer, Alvin *When the Boys Meet the Girls* 1965; *Three Bites of the Apple* 1967

Gardner, Herb *The Goodbye People* 1984; *I'm Not Rappaport* 1996

Garnett, Tay *Her Man* 1930; *One Way Passage* 1932; *SOS Iceberg* 1933; *China Seas* 1935; *Slave Ship* 1937; *Stand-In* 1937; *Joy of Living* 1938; *Trade Winds* 1938; *Eternally Yours* 1939; *Slightly Honorable* 1939; *Seven Sinners* 1940; *Cheers for Miss Bishop* 1941; *My Favorite Spy* 1942; *Bataan* 1943; *The Cross of Lorraine* 1943; *Mrs Parkington* 1944; *The Valley of Decision* 1945; *The Postman Always Rings Twice* 1946; *A Connecticut Yankee in King Arthur's Court* 1949; *The Fireball* 1950; *Cause for Alarm* 1951; *Soldiers Three* 1951; *One Minute to Zero* 1952; *Main Street to Broadway* 1953; *The Black Knight* 1954; *A Terrible Beauty* 1960; *Cattle King* 1963; *The Delta Factor* 1970; *Challenge to Be Free* 1972

Garris, Mick *Critters 2: the Main Course* 1988; *Psycho IV: the Beginning* 1990; *Sleepwalkers* 1992; *Quicksilver Highway* 1997

Gasnier, Louis *The Virtuous Sin* 1930; *The Last Outpost* 1935; *Reefer Madness* 1936

Gatlif, Tony *Les Princes* 1982; *Latcho Drom* 1993; *Gadjo Dilo* 1997

Gaup, Nils *Pathfinder* 1987; *Shipwrecked* 1990; *North Star* 1996

Gerber, Fred *Rent-a-Kid* 1992; *Closer and Closer* 1996; *Race against Time: the Search for*

Hare, David *Wetherby* 1985; *Paris by Night* 1988; *Strapless* 1988; *The Designated Mourner* 1997
Harlin, Renny *Prison* 1987; *A Nightmare on Elm Street 4: The Dream Master* 1988; *The Adventures of Ford Fairlane* 1990; *Die Hard 2: Die Harder* 1990; *Cliffhanger* 1993; *CutThroat Island* 1995; *The Long Kiss Goodnight* 1996; *Deep Blue Sea* 1999
Harlow, John *While I Live* 1947; *The Blue Parrot* 1953; *Delayed Action* 1954
Harmon, Robert *The Hitcher* 1986; *Eyes of an Angel* 1991; *Nowhere to Run* 1992; *Gotti* 1996
Harrington, Curtis aka **Sebastian, John** *Night Tide* 1961; *Voyage to the Prehistoric Planet* 1965; *Planet of Blood* 1966; *Games* 1967; *How Awful about Allan* 1970; *What's the Matter with Helen?* 1971; *Who Slew Auntie Roo?* 1971; *The Killing Kind* 1973; *The Dead Don't Die* 1975; *Ruby* 1977; *Mata Hari* 1985
Harris, Damian *The Rachel Papers* 1989; *Deceived* 1991; *Bad Company* 1995
Harris, Harry *A Day for Thanks on Waltons Mountain* 1982; *Eight Is Enough: a Family Reunion* 1987; *A Walton Thanksgiving Reunion* 1993
Harris, James B *The Bedford Incident* 1965; *Fast-Walking* 1982; *Cop* 1988; *Boiling Point* 1993
Harris, Trent *Rubin & Ed* 1991; *Plan 10 from Outer Space* 1995
Harrison, John Kent *Beautiful Dreamers* 1990; *For the Love of Aaron* 1993; *Whose Child Is This?* 1993; *City Boy* 1994; *The Ranger, the Cook and a Hole in the Sky* 1995; *Johnny's Girl* 1995; *William Faulkner's Old Man* 1997; *What the Deaf Man Heard* 1997
Harrison, Matthew *Rhythm Thief* 1994; *Kicked in the Head* 1997
Harron, Mary *I Shot Andy Warhol* 1995; *American Psycho* 2000
Hart, Harvey *Bus Riley's Back in Town* 1965; *Dark Intruder* 1965; *The Sweet Ride* 1967; *Fortune and Men's Eyes* 1971; *Shoot* 1976; *The High Country* 1981; *Utilities* 1981; *Beverly Hills Madam* 1986
Hartford-Davis, Robert aka **Burrowes, Michael** *Saturday Night Out* 1963; *The Black Torment* 1964; *The Sandwich Man* 1966; *The Smashing Bird I Used to Know* 1969; *Bloodsuckers* 1970; *Incense for the Damned* 1970; *The Take* 1974
Hartley, Hal *Surviving Desire* 1989; *The Unbelievable Truth* 1989; *Trust* 1990; *Simple Men* 1992; *Amateur* 1994; *Flirt* 1995; *Henry Fool* 1997; *The Book of Life* 1998
Hartman, Don *Every Girl Should Be Married* 1948; *Holiday Affair* 1949; *Mr Imperium* 1951; *It's a Big Country* 1951
Harvey, Anthony *Dutchman* 1966; *The Lion in Winter* 1968; *They Might Be Giants* 1971; *The Abdication* 1974; *The Disappearance of Aimee* 1976; *Eagle's Wing* 1978; *Players* 1979; *The Patricia Neal Story: an Act of Love* 1981; *Svengali* 1983; *Grace Quigley* 1984; *This Can't Be Love* 1994
Harvey, Laurence *The Ceremony* 1963; *A Dandy in Aspic* 1968; *Welcome to Arrow Beach* 1974
Haskin, Byron *I Walk Alone* 1947; *Treasure Island* 1950; *Tarzan's Peril* 1951; *Warpath* 1951; *His Majesty O'Keefe* 1953; *The Naked Jungle* 1953; *The War of the Worlds* 1953; *Conquest of Space* 1955; *From the Earth to the Moon* 1958; *Jet over the Atlantic* 1960; *Armored Command* 1961; *The Power* 1968
Hathaway, Henry *Now and Forever* 1934; *The Lives of a Bengal Lancer* 1935; *Peter Ibbetson* 1935; *Go West, Young Man* 1936; *The Trail of the Lonesome Pine* 1936; *Souls at Sea* 1937; *Spawn of the North* 1938; *The Real Glory* 1939; *Brigham Young* 1940; *Johnny Apollo* 1940; *The Shepherd of the Hills* 1941; *Sundown* 1941; *China Girl* 1942; *Ten Gentlemen from West Point* 1942; *Home in Indiana* 1944; *Wing and a Prayer* 1944; *The House on 92nd Street* 1945; *Nob Hill* 1945; *The Dark Corner* 1946; *13 Rue Madeleine* 1946; *Kiss of Death* 1947; *Call Northside 777* 1948; *Down to the Sea in Ships* 1949; *The Black Rose* 1950; *The Desert Fox* 1951; *Fourteen Hours* 1951; *Rawhide* 1951; *You're in the Navy Now* 1951; *Diplomatic Courier* 1952; *O Henry's Full House* 1952; *Niagara* 1953; *White Witch Doctor* 1953; *Garden of Evil* 1954; *Prince Valiant* 1954; *The Racers* 1955; *Beyond the River* 1956; *23 Paces to Baker Street* 1956; *Legend of the Lost* 1957; *From Hell to Texas* 1958; *Woman Obsessed* 1959; *North to Alaska* 1960; *Seven Thieves* 1960; *How the West Was Won* 1962; *The Magnificent Showman* 1964; *Of Human Bondage* 1964; *The Sons of Katie Elder* 1965; *Nevada Smith* 1966; *The Last Safari* 1967; *5 Card Stud* 1968; *True Grit* 1969; *Airport* 1970; *Raid on Rommel* 1971; *Shoot Out* 1971; *Hangup* 1973
Hatton, Maurice *Praise Marx and Pass the Ammunition* 1968; *Long Shot* 1978; *American Roulette* 1988
Hawks, Howard *A Girl in Every Port* 1928; *Fazil* 1928; *The Criminal Code* 1930; *The Dawn Patrol* 1930; *The Crowd Roars* 1932; *Tiger Shark* 1932; *Scarface* 1932; *Today We Live* 1933; *Twentieth Century* 1934; *Barbary Coast* 1935; *Ceiling Zero* 1935; *Come and Get It* 1936; *The Road to Glory* 1936; *Bringing Up Baby* 1938; *His Girl Friday* 1939; *Only Angels Have Wings* 1939; *Ball of Fire* 1941; *Sergeant York* 1941; *Air Force* 1943; *To Have and Have Not* 1944; *The Big Sleep* 1946; *Red River* 1948; *A Song Is Born* 1948; *I Was a Male War Bride* 1949; *The Big Sky* 1952; *Monkey Business* 1952; *O Henry's Full House* 1952; *Gentlemen Prefer Blondes* 1953; *Land of the Pharaohs* 1955; *Rio Bravo* 1959; *Hatari!* 1962; *Man's Favorite Sport?* 1964; *Red Line 7000* 1965; *El Dorado* 1967; *Rio Lobo* 1970
Hay, Will *The Black Sheep of Whitehall* 1941; *The Goose Steps Out* 1942; *My Learned Friend* 1943
Hayashi, Kaizo *Circus Boys* 1989; *The Most Terrible Time in My Life* 1993
Haydn, Richard *Miss Tatlock's Millions* 1948; *Dear Wife* 1949; *Mr Music* 1950
Hayers, Sidney *Circus of Horrors* 1960; *Night of the Eagle* 1961; *Payroll* 1961; *This Is My Street* 1963; *Three Hats for Lisa* 1965; *Finders Keepers* 1966; *The Trap* 1966; *Mister Jerico* 1969; *The Southern Star* 1969; *Assault* 1970; *The Firechasers* 1970; *Revenge* 1971; *All Coppers Are…* 1972; *Diagnosis: Murder* 1974; *What Changed Charley Farthing?* 1975
Hayes, John *Mama's Dirty Girls* 1974; *End of the World* 1977
Hayman, David *Silent Scream* 1989; *The Hawk* 1992; *The Near Room* 1995
Haynes, Todd *Superstar: the Karen Carpenter Story* 1987; *Safe* 1995; *Velvet Goldmine* 1998
Haywood-Carter, Annette *Foxfire* 1996; *Love Is Strange* 1998
Hazan, Jack *A Bigger Splash* 1974; *Rude Boy* 1980
Heap, Jonathan *Benefit of the Doubt* 1993; *Hostile Intent* 1997
Heavener, David *Outlaw Force* 1988; *Prime Target* 1991; *Eye of the Stranger* 1993
Hecht, Ben *Crime without Passion* 1934; *The Scoundrel* 1935; *Angels over Broadway* 1940; *Specter of the Rose* 1946; *Actors and Sin* 1952
Heckerling, Amy *Fast Times at Ridgemont High* 1982; *Johnny Dangerously* 1984; *National Lampoon's European Vacation* 1985; *Look Who's Talking* 1989; *Look Who's Talking Too* 1990; *Clueless* 1995
Hedden, Rob *Friday the 13th Part VIII: Jason Takes Manhattan* 1989; *The Colony* 1995; *Dying to Live* 1999
Heerman, Victor *Animal Crackers* 1930; *Paramount on Parade* 1930
Heffron, Richard T aka **Heffron, Richard** *The California Kid* 1974; *Newman's Law* 1974; *Futureworld* 1976; *Trackdown* 1976; *Outlaw Blues* 1977; *Foolin' Around* 1980; *I, the Jury* 1982; *Anatomy of an Illness* 1984; *Tagget* 1991; *Deadly Family Secrets* 1995; *Danielle Steel's No Greater Love* 1996
Heisler, Stuart *Among the Living* 1941; *The Glass Key* 1942; *Along Came Jones* 1945; *Blue Skies* 1946; *Smash-Up, the Story of a Woman* 1947; *Tokyo Joe* 1949; *Tulsa* 1949; *Chain Lightning* 1950; *Dallas* 1950; *Storm Warning* 1950; *The Star* 1953; *Beachhead* 1954; *I Died a Thousand Times* 1955; *The Burning Hills* 1956; *The Lone Ranger* 1956; *Hitler* 1962
Hellman, Monte *Beast from Haunted Cave* 1959; *Back Door to Hell* 1964; *Ride in the Whirlwind* 1966; *Flight to Fury* 1966; *The Shooting* 1967; *Two-Lane Blacktop* 1971; *Shatter* 1974; *China 9, Liberty 37* 1978; *Silent Night, Deadly Night 3: Better Watch Out!* 1989
Hemmings, David *Just a Gigolo* 1978; *The Survivor* 1981; *Treasure of the Yankee Zephyr* 1981; *Dark Horse* 1992; *Passport to Murder* 1993
Henderson, John *Loch Ness* 1994; *Bring Me the Head of Mavis Davis* 1997
Henenlotter, Frank *Basket Case* 1982; *Brain Damage* 1988; *Basket Case 2* 1990; *Frankenhooker* 1990; *Basket Case 3: the Progeny* 1992
Henley, Hobart *The Big Pond* 1930; *Bad Sister* 1931
Henreid, Paul *Battle Shock* 1956; *Live Fast, Die Young* 1958; *Dead Ringer* 1964; *Ballad in Blue* 1966
Henry, Buck *Heaven Can Wait* 1978; *First Family* 1980
Henson, Brian *The Muppet Christmas Carol* 1992; *Muppet Treasure Island* 1996
Henson, Jim *The Great Muppet Caper* 1981; *The Dark Crystal* 1982; *Labyrinth* 1986
Herek, Stephen *Critters* 1986; *Bill & Ted's Excellent Adventure* 1988; *Don't Tell Mom the Babysitter's Dead* 1991; *The Mighty Ducks* 1992; *The Three Musketeers* 1993; *Mr Holland's Opus* 1995; *101 Dalmatians* 1996; *Holy Man* 1998
Herman, Mark *Blame It on the Bellboy* 1992; *Brassed Off* 1996; *Little Voice* 1998
Herrington, Rowdy *Jack's Back* 1988; *Road House* 1989; *Gladiator* 1992; *Striking Distance* 1993; *A Murder of Crows* 1998
Herskovitz, Marshall *Jack the Bear* 1993; *The Honest Courtesan* 1998
Herz, Michael *The Toxic Avenger* 1985; *The Toxic Avenger, Part II* 1988; *Sgt Kabukiman NYPD* 1991
Herzfeld, John *Two of a Kind* 1983; *Daddy* 1987; *A Father's Revenge* 1987; *The Ryan White Story* 1989; *Casualties of Love: the Long Island Lolita Story* 1993; *2 Days in the Valley* 1996
Herzog, Werner *Aguirre, Wrath of God* 1972; *The Enigma of Kaspar Hauser* 1974; *Woyzeck* 1978; *Nosferatu, the Vampire* 1979; *Fitzcarraldo* 1982; *Cobra Verde* 1988; *Scream of Stone* 1991; *My Best Fiend* 1999
Hess, Jon *Watchers* 1988; *Alligator II: the Mutation* 1991; *Excessive Force* 1993; *Mars* 1996; *Legion* 1998
Hessler, Gordon *The Oblong Box* 1969; *Scream and Scream Again* 1969; *Cry of the Banshee* 1970; *Murders in the Rue Morgue* 1971; *Embassy* 1972; *The Golden Voyage of Sinbad* 1973; *Puzzle* 1978; *The Secret War of Jackie's Girls* 1980; *The Girl in a Swing* 1988; *Shogun Warrior* 1991
Heston, Charlton *Antony and Cleopatra* 1972; *Mother Lode* 1982; *A Man for All Seasons* 1988
Heston, Fraser C *Treasure Island* 1990; *The Crucifer of Blood* 1991; *Needful Things* 1993; *Alaska* 1996
Hewitt, Peter *Bill & Ted's Bogus Journey* 1991; *Tom and Huck* 1995; *The Borrowers* 1997; *Whatever Happened to Harold Smith?* 1999
Heyes, Douglas *Kitten with a Whip* 1964; *Beau Geste* 1966
Hibbs, Jesse *The All American* 1953; *Rails into Laramie* 1954; *Ride Clear of Diablo* 1954; *Black Horse Canyon* 1954; *The Yellow Mountain* 1954; *To Hell and Back* 1955; *The Spoilers* 1955; *Walk the Proud Land* 1956; *Joe Butterfly* 1957; *Ride a Crooked Trail* 1958
Hickenlooper, George *Hearts of Darkness: a Film-Maker's Apocalypse* 1991; *Killing Box* 1993; *The Low Life* 1995; *Persons Unknown* 1996
Hickox, Anthony *Waxwork* 1988; *Hellraiser III: Hell on Earth* 1992; *Waxwork II: Lost in Time* 1992; *Full Eclipse* 1993; *Warlock: the Armageddon* 1993; *Invasion of Privacy* 1996; *Prince Valiant* 1997
Hickox, Douglas *The Giant Behemoth* 1959; *Entertaining Mr Sloane* 1969; *Sitting Target* 1972; *Theatre of Blood* 1973; *Brannigan* 1975; *Sky Riders* 1976; *Zulu Dawn* 1979; *The Hound of the Baskervilles* 1983; *Blackout* 1985
Hicks, Scott *Shine* 1996; *Snow Falling on Cedars* 1999
Higgin, Howard *The Leatherneck* 1929; *The Painted Desert* 1931; *Hell's House* 1932
Higgins, Colin *Foul Play* 1978; *Nine to Five* 1980; *The Best Little Whorehouse in Texas* 1982
Hill, George aka **Hill, George W** *The Big House* 1930; *Min and Bill* 1930; *The Secret Six* 1931; *Hell Divers* 1932
Hill, George Roy *Period of Adjustment* 1962; *Toys in the Attic* 1963; *The World of Henry Orient* 1964; *Hawaii* 1966; *Thoroughly Modern Millie* 1967; *Butch Cassidy and the Sundance Kid* 1969; *Slaughterhouse-Five* 1972; *The Sting* 1973; *The Great Waldo Pepper* 1975; *Slap Shot* 1977; *A Little Romance* 1979; *The World According to Garp* 1982; *The Little Drummer Girl* 1984; *Funny Farm* 1988
Hill, Jack *House of Evil* 1968; *Alien Terror* 1969; *The Big Doll House* 1971; *The Big Bird Cage* 1972; *Coffy* 1973; *Foxy Brown* 1974; *Switchblade Sisters* 1975
Hill, James *Lunch Hour* 1962; *Trial and Error* 1962; *Every Day's a Holiday* 1964; *A Study in Terror* 1965; *Born Free* 1966; *Captain Nemo and the Underwater City* 1969; *An Elephant Called Slowly* 1969; *Black Beauty* 1971; *The Belstone Fox* 1973
Hill, Walter aka **Lee, Thomas** *The Streetfighter* 1975; *The Driver* 1978; *The Warriors* 1979; *The Long Riders* 1980; *Southern Comfort* 1981; *48 HRS* 1982; *Streets of Fire* 1984; *Brewster's Millions* 1985; *Crossroads* 1986; *Extreme Prejudice* 1987; *Red Heat* 1988; *Johnny Handsome* 1989; *Another 48 HRS* 1990; *Trespass* 1992; *Geronimo* 1993; *Wild Bill* 1995; *Last Man Standing* 1996; *Supernova* 2000
Hillcoat, John *Ghosts…of the Civil Dead* 1988; *To Have & to Hold* 1996
Hiller, Arthur aka **Smithee, Alan** *Miracle of the White Stallions* 1963; *The Wheeler Dealers* 1963; *The Americanization of Emily* 1964; *Promise Her Anything* 1966; *Tobruk* 1966; *Penelope* 1966; *The Tiger Makes Out* 1967; *Popi* 1969; *Love Story* 1970; *The Out of Towners* 1970; *The Hospital* 1971; *Plaza Suite* 1971; *Man of La Mancha* 1972; *The Man in the Glass Booth* 1975; *Silver Streak* 1976; *WC Fields and Me* 1976; *The In-Laws* 1979; *Nightwing* 1979; *Author! Author!* 1982; *Making Love* 1982; *Romantic Comedy* 1983; *The Lonely Guy* 1984; *Teachers* 1984; *Outrageous Fortune* 1987; *See No Evil, Hear No Evil* 1989; *Taking Care of Business* 1990; *Married to It* 1991; *The Babe* 1992; *Carpool* 1996; *Burn Hollywood Burn* 1997
Hillyer, Lambert *Dracula's Daughter* 1936; *The Invisible Ray* 1936; *Girls Can Play* 1937
Hippolyte, Gregory aka **Hippolyte, A Gregory** *Mirror Images* 1991; *Animal Instincts* 1992; *Secret Games* 1992; *Sins of the Night* 1993; *Body of Influence* 1993; *Mirror Images II* 1994; *Object of Obsession* 1995
Hiscott, Leslie aka **Hiscott, Leslie S** *When London Sleeps* 1932; *Death on the Set* 1935; *A Fire Has Been Arranged* 1935; *The Time of His Life* 1955
Hitchcock, Alfred aka **Hitchcock, Alfred J** *The Pleasure Garden* 1925; *The Lodger* 1926; *The Ring* 1927; *Easy Virtue* 1927;

Blackmail 1929; The Manxman 1929; Juno and the Paycock 1930; Murder 1930; The Skin Game 1931; Rich and Strange 1932; Number Seventeen 1932; The Man Who Knew Too Much 1934; The 39 Steps 1935; Secret Agent 1936; Sabotage 1936; Young and Innocent 1937; The Lady Vanishes 1938; Jamaica Inn 1939; Foreign Correspondent 1940; Rebecca 1940; Mr and Mrs Smith 1941; Suspicion 1941; Saboteur 1942; Shadow of a Doubt 1943; Aventure Malgache 1944; Bon Voyage 1944; Lifeboat 1944; Spellbound 1945; Notorious 1946; The Paradine Case 1947; Rope 1948; Under Capricorn 1949; Stage Fright 1950; Strangers on a Train 1951; I Confess 1953; Dial M for Murder 1954; Rear Window 1954; To Catch a Thief 1955; The Trouble with Harry 1955; The Man Who Knew Too Much 1956; The Wrong Man 1956; Vertigo 1958; North by Northwest 1959; Psycho 1960; The Birds 1963; Marnie 1964; Torn Curtain 1966; Topaz 1969; Frenzy 1972; Family Plot 1976

Hitzig, Rupert Night Visitor 1989; Backstreet Dreams 1990

Hively, Jack The Spellbinder 1939; Anne of Windy Poplars 1940; The Saint Takes Over 1940; The Saint's Double Trouble 1940; The Saint in Palm Springs 1941

Hoblit, Gregory Roe vs Wade 1989; Primal Fear 1996; Fallen 1998; Frequency 2000

Hodges, Mike aka **Hodges, Michael** Get Carter 1971; Pulp 1972; The Terminal Man 1974; Flash Gordon 1980; And the Ship Sails On 1983; Missing Pieces 1983; Morons from Outer Space 1985; Florida Straits 1986; A Prayer for the Dying 1988; Black Rainbow 1989; Croupier 1998

Hoffman, Michael Restless Natives 1985; Promised Land 1988; Sisters 1988; Soapdish 1991; Restoration 1995; One Fine Day 1996; William Shakespeare's A Midsummer Night's Dream 1999

Hofmeyr, Gray aka **Hofmyer, Gray** Jock of the Bushveld 1988; Out of Darkness 1990

Hogan, David aka **Hogan, David Glenn** Barb Wire 1995; Most Wanted 1997

Hogan, James The Last Train from Madrid 1937; The Texans 1938; Texas Rangers Ride Again 1940

Hogan, P J Muriel's Wedding 1994; My Best Friend's Wedding 1997

Holcomb, Rod aka **Smithee, Allan** Captain America 1979; Moonlight 1982; The Cartier Affair 1984; The Red-Light Sting 1984; Two Fathers' Justice 1985; The Long Journey Home 1987; Stillwatch 1987; Chains of Gold 1989; Finding the Way Home 1991; A Message from Holly 1992; Donato and Daughter 1993; Royce 1994; Convict Cowboy 1995; The Underworld 1997

Holland, Agnieszka To Kill a Priest 1988; Europa, Europa 1991; Olivier Olivier 1991; The Secret Garden 1993; Total Eclipse 1995; Washington Square 1997

Holland, Savage Steve Better Off Dead 1985; One Crazy Summer 1986; How I Got Into College 1989

Holland, Tom aka **Smithee, Allan** Fright Night 1985; Fatal Beauty 1987; Child's Play 1988; The Stranger Within 1990; The Owl 1991; The Temp 1993; Stephen King's Thinner 1996

Holmes, Ben The Plot Thickens 1936; The Saint in New York 1938; Maid's Night Out 1938

Holt, Seth Nowhere to Go 1958; Scream of Fear 1961; Station Six-Sahara 1962; The Nanny 1965; Danger Route 1967; Blood from the Mummy's Tomb 1971

Honda, Inoshiro aka **Honda, Ishiro** Godzilla 1954; The H-Man 1954; Rodan 1956; Mothra 1962; Frankenstein Meets the Devil Fish 1964; Invasion of the Astro-Monster 1965; Ghidrah, the Three-Headed Monster 1965; Destroy All Monsters 1968; Godzilla's Revenge 1969; War of the Gargantuas 1970; Terror of Mechagodzilla 1975

Hondo, Med Sarraouina 1986; Lumière Noire 1994

Hook, Harry The Kitchen Toto 1987; Lord of the Flies 1990

Hooks, Kevin Heat Wave 1990; Strictly Business 1991; Murder without Motive 1992; Passenger 57 1992; Irresistible Force 1993; To My Daughter with Love 1994; Fled 1996; Black Dog 1998; Glory & Honor 1998; Mutiny 1999

Hooper, Tobe The Texas Chain Saw Massacre 1974; Eaten Alive 1976; Salem's Lot 1979; The Funhouse 1981; Poltergeist 1982; Lifeforce 1985; Invaders from Mars 1986; The Texas Chainsaw Massacre Part 2 1986; I'm Dangerous Tonight 1990; Body Bags 1993; The Mangler 1994; Tobe Hooper's Night Terrors 1994

Hopkins, Stephen A Nightmare on Elm Street 5: The Dream Child 1989; Predator 2 1990; Judgment Night 1993; Blown Away 1994; The Ghost and the Darkness 1996; Lost in Space 1997

Hopper, Dennis aka **Smithee, Alan** Easy Rider 1969; The Last Movie 1971; Out of the Blue 1980; Colors 1988; Catchfire 1990; The Hot Spot 1990; Chasers 1994

Hopper, Jerry Pony Express 1953; Secret of the Incas 1954; Naked Alibi 1954; Alaska Seas 1954; Smoke Signal 1955; The Private War of Major Benson 1955; Never Say Goodbye 1955; The Square Jungle 1955; One Desire 1955; The Missouri Traveler 1958; Madron 1970

Horne, James W aka **Horne, James** College 1927; Big Business 1929; Bonnie Scotland 1935; Thicker than Water 1935; The Bohemian Girl 1936; All over Town 1937; Way Out West 1937

Horner, Harry Beware, My Lovely 1952; Red Planet Mars 1952; New Faces 1954; A Life in the Balance 1955

Horton, Peter Amazon Women on the Moon 1987; Extreme Close-Up 1990; The Cure 1995

Hoskins, Bob The Raggedy Rawney 1987; Rainbow 1995

Hou Hsiao-Hsien aka **Hou Xiaoxian** A Summer at Grandpa's 1984; The Time to Live and the Time to Die 1985; Daughter of the Nile 1987; Dust in the Wind 1987; A City of Sadness 1989; The Puppetmaster 1993; Flowers of Shanghai 1998

Hough, John Eyewitness 1970; Treasure Island 1972; The Legend of Hell House 1973; Dirty Mary Crazy Larry 1974; Escape to Witch Mountain 1975; Brass Target 1978; Return from Witch Mountain 1978; The Watcher in the Woods 1982; Triumphs of a Man Called Horse 1983; Biggles 1986; A Hazard of Hearts 1987; American Gothic 1987; Duel of Hearts 1990; A Ghost in Monte Carlo 1990; Something to Believe In 1997

Hovde, Ellen Grey Gardens 1975; Enormous Changes at the Last Minute 1983

Howard, Cy Lovers and Other Strangers 1970; Every Little Crook and Nanny 1972

Howard, David Painted Desert 1938; Arizona Legion 1939

Howard, Leslie Pygmalion 1938; Pimpernel Smith 1941; The First of the Few 1942; The Gentle Sex 1943

Howard, Ron Grand Theft Auto 1977; Night Shift 1982; Splash 1984; Cocoon 1985; Gung Ho 1986; Willow 1988; Parenthood 1989; Backdraft 1991; Far and Away 1992; The Paper 1994; Apollo 13 1995; Ransom 1996; EDtv 1999

Howard, William K The First Year 1932; Sherlock Holmes 1932; The Power and the Glory 1933; The Cat and the Fiddle 1934; Evelyn Prentice 1934; Vanessa, Her Love Story 1935; Rendezvous 1935; The Princess Comes Across 1936; Fire over England 1937; The Squeaker 1937; Back Door to Heaven 1939; Johnny Come Lately 1943

Howson, Frank Hunting 1992; Flynn 1995

Hudlin, Reginald House Party 1990; Boomerang 1992; The Great White Hype 1996

Hudson, Hugh Chariots of Fire 1981; Greystoke: the Legend of Tarzan, Lord of the Apes 1984; Revolution 1985; The Road Home 1989; My Life So Far 1999

Hughes, Albert Menace II Society 1993; Dead Presidents 1995

Hughes, Allen Menace II Society 1993; Dead Presidents 1995

Hughes, Bronwen Harriet the Spy 1996; Forces of Nature 1998

Hughes, Howard Hell's Angels 1930; The Outlaw 1943

Hughes, John Sixteen Candles 1984; The Breakfast Club 1985; Weird Science 1985; Ferris Bueller's Day Off 1986; Planes, Trains and Automobiles 1987; She's Having a Baby 1988; Uncle Buck 1989; Curly Sue 1991

Hughes, Ken The Brain Machine 1954; Confession 1955; Joe Macbeth 1955; Little Red Monkey 1955; Timeslip 1955; The Trials of Oscar Wilde 1960; The Small World of Sammy Lee 1963; Of Human Bondage 1964; Drop Dead Darling 1966; Casino Royale 1967; Chitty Chitty Bang Bang 1968; Cromwell 1970; The Internecine Project 1974; Alfie Darling 1975; Sextette 1978

Hughes, Terry aka **Hughes, Terry W** Monty Python Live at the Hollywood Bowl 1982; For Love or Money 1984; The Butcher's Wife 1991

Humberstone, H Bruce aka **Humberstone, Bruce** If I Had a Million 1932; Charlie Chan at the Opera 1936; Charlie Chan at the Olympics 1937; Pack Up Your Troubles 1939; I Wake Up Screaming 1941; Sun Valley Serenade 1941; To the Shores of Tripoli 1942; Hello, Frisco, Hello 1943; Pin Up Girl 1944; Wonder Man 1945; Three Little Girls in Blue 1946; Fury at Furnace Creek 1948; Happy Go Lovely 1950; She's Working Her Way through College 1952; The Desert Song 1953; The Purple Mask 1955; Tarzan and the Lost Safari 1956; Tarzan's Fight for Life 1958; Madison Avenue 1962

Hunebelle, André Le Bossu 1959; The Captain 1960; The Mysteries of Paris 1962; Shadow of Evil 1964

Hung, Sammo The Prodigal Son 1983; Wheels on Meals 1984; Mr Nice Guy 1996

Hunt, Peter On Her Majesty's Secret Service 1969; Gold 1974; Shout at the Devil 1976; Gulliver's Travels 1977; Death Hunt 1981; Wild Geese II 1985; Assassination 1986; Danielle Steel's Secrets 1992; Dead Man's Island 1996

Hunt, Peter H The Parade 1984; Sworn to Vengeance 1993

Hunter, Tim Tex 1982; Sylvester 1985; River's Edge 1987; Paint It Black 1989; Beverly Hills 90210 1990; Lies of the Twins 1991; The Saint of Fort Washington 1993; The People Next Door 1996; The Maker 1997; Rescuers: Stories of Courage – Two Couples 1998

Huntington, Lawrence Night Boat to Dublin 1946; Wanted for Murder 1946; When the Bough Breaks 1947; The Upturned Glass 1947; Mr Perrin and Mr Traill 1948; The Franchise Affair 1950; Contraband Spain 1955; Death Drums along the River 1963

Hurran, Nick Remember Me? 1996; Girls' Night 1997; Virtual Sexuality 1999

Hurst, Brian Desmond The Lion Has Wings 1939; Dangerous Moonlight 1941; Hungry Hill 1947; Trottie True 1949; Scrooge 1951; The Malta Story 1953; Simba 1955; The Black Tent 1956; Dangerous Exile 1957; Behind the Mask 1958

Hurwitz, Harry The Projectionist 1970; The Comeback Trail 1972; Fleshtone 1994

Hussein, Waris A Touch of Love 1969; Quackser Fortune Has a Cousin in the Bronx 1970; Melody 1971; Henry VIII and His Six Wives 1972; The Possession of Joel Delaney 1972; And Baby Makes Six 1979; The Winter of Our Discontent 1983; Copacabana 1985; Surviving 1985; When the Bough Breaks 1986; Downpayment on Murder 1987; Killer Instinct 1988; Those She Left Behind 1989; Forbidden Nights 1990; She Woke Up 1992; Murder between Friends 1994; Face on the Milk Carton 1995; Sixth Happiness 1997; Life of the Party: the Pamela Harriman Story 1998

Huston, Anjelica Bastard out of Carolina 1996; Agnes Browne 1999

Huston, Danny Mr Corbett's Ghost 1986; Bigfoot 1987; Mr North 1988; Becoming Colette 1991; The Maddening 1995

Huston, John The Maltese Falcon 1941; Across the Pacific 1942; In This Our Life 1942; Key Largo 1948; The Treasure of the Sierra Madre 1948; We Were Strangers 1949; The Asphalt Jungle 1950; The African Queen 1951; The Red Badge of Courage 1951; Moulin Rouge 1952; Beat the Devil 1953; Moby Dick 1956; Heaven Knows, Mr Allison 1957; The Barbarian and the Geisha 1958; The Roots of Heaven 1958; The Unforgiven 1960; The Misfits 1961; Freud 1962; The List of Adrian Messenger 1963; The Night of the Iguana 1964; The Bible...in the Beginning 1966; Casino Royale 1967; Reflections in a Golden Eye 1967; Sinful Davey 1969; A Walk with Love and Death 1969; The Kremlin Letter 1970; Fat City 1972; The Life and Times of Judge Roy Bean 1972; The Mackintosh Man 1973; The Man Who Would Be King 1975; Wise Blood 1979; Phobia 1980; Escape to Victory 1981; Annie 1982; Under the Volcano 1984; Prizzi's Honor 1985; The Dead 1987

Huth, Harold East of Piccadilly 1940; Night Beat 1948

Hutton, Brian G Wild Seed 1965; The Pad (and How to Use It) 1966; Sol Madrid 1968; Where Eagles Dare 1969; Kelly's Heroes 1970; X, Y and Zee 1971; Night Watch 1973; The First Deadly Sin 1980; High Road to China 1983

Huyck, Willard Best Defense 1984; Howard, a New Breed of Hero 1986

Hyams, Peter Busting 1974; Peeper 1975; Capricorn One 1978; Hanover Street 1979; Outland 1981; The Star Chamber 1983; 2010 1984; Running Scared 1986; The Presidio 1988; Narrow Margin 1990; Stay Tuned 1992; Timecop 1994; Sudden Death 1995; The Relic 1997; End of Days 1999

Hytner, Nicholas The Madness of King George 1995; The Crucible 1996; The Object of My Affection 1998

I

Ichaso, Leon Crossover Dreams 1985; The Take 1990; Sugar Hill 1993; Those Bedroom Eyes 1993; Zooman 1995; Free of Eden 1999

Ichikawa, Kon The Burmese Harp 1956; Conflagration 1958; Fires on the Plain 1959; The Key 1959; An Actor's Revenge 1963; Alone on the Pacific 1963; Tokyo Olympiad 1965; Visions of Eight 1973; The Makioka Sisters 1983; The Burmese Harp 1985

Imamura, Shohei Vengeance Is Mine 1979; The Ballad of Narayama 1983; Black Rain 1988; The Eel 1997

Ingram, Rex The Four Horsemen of the Apocalypse 1921; The Prisoner of Zenda 1922; The Arab 1924; Mare Nostrum 1926; The Garden of Allah 1927

Irmas, Matthew When the Party's Over 1992; Edie & Pen 1996

Irvin, John The Dogs of War 1980; Ghost Story 1981; Champions 1983; Turtle Diary 1985; Raw Deal 1986; Hamburger Hill 1987; Next of Kin 1989; Robin Hood 1990; Eminent Domain 1991; Widows' Peak 1993; Freefall 1994; A Month by the Lake 1994; City of Industry 1996; When Trumpets Fade 1998

Irvin, Sam Guilty as Charged 1991; Oblivion 1993; Magic Island 1995; Out There 1995; Kiss of a Stranger 1997

Irving, David Rumpelstiltskin 1986; The Emperor's New Clothes 1987; Perfume of the Cyclone 1989; CHUD II: Bud the Chud 1989

Iscove, Robert The Flash 1990; Murder in Black & White 1990; Shattered Dreams 1990; Mission of the Shark 1991; Breaking the Silence 1992; Terror on Track 9 1992; Dying to Love You 1993; Murder on the Rio Grande 1993; Janek: a Silent Betrayal 1994; Trapped and Deceived 1994; Without Warning 1994; It Was Him or Us 1995; Dark Angel

1996; *Murder in My Mind* 1997; *Rodgers & Hammerstein's Cinderella* 1997; *She's All That* 1999

Israel, Neal *Tunnelvision* 1976; *Americathon* 1979; *Bachelor Party* 1984; *Moving Violations* 1985; *Combat Academy* 1986; *Beauty and Denise* 1989; *Breaking the Rules* 1992; *Surf Ninjas* 1993; *Kidz in the Wood* 1996; *National Lampoon's Dad's Week Off* 1997

Itami, Juzo *Death Japanese Style* 1984; *Tampopo* 1986; *A Taxing Woman* 1987; *Minbo – or the Gentle Art of Japanese Extortion* 1992

Ivory, James *The Householder* 1963; *Shakespeare Wallah* 1965; *The Guru* 1969; *Bombay Talkie* 1970; *The Wild Party* 1975; *Autobiography of a Princess* 1975; *Roseland* 1977; *The Europeans* 1979; *Hullabaloo over Georgie and Bonnie's Pictures* 1979; *Jane Austen in Manhattan* 1980; *Quartet* 1981; *Heat and Dust* 1982; *The Bostonians* 1984; *A Room with a View* 1985; *Maurice* 1987; *Slaves of New York* 1989; *Mr and Mrs Bridge* 1990; *Howards End* 1992; *The Remains of the Day* 1993; *Jefferson in Paris* 1995; *Surviving Picasso* 1996; *A Soldier's Daughter Never Cries* 1998

Izzard, Bryan *Holiday on the Buses* 1973; *Julie and the Cadillacs* 1997

J

Jackson, David *aka* **Jackson, David S** *Death Train* 1993; *Night Watch* 1995; *Code Name: Wolverine* 1996

Jackson, Doug *Midnight in St Petersburg* 1995; *Random Encounter* 1998

Jackson, Douglas *aka* **Jackson, Doug** *Whispers* 1990; *Deadbolt* 1992; *The Paperboy* 1994; *Natural Enemy* 1996; *The Wrong Woman* 1996; *False Pretense* 1997

Jackson, Mick *Chattahoochee* 1989; *LA Story* 1991; *The Bodyguard* 1992; *Clean Slate* 1994; *Indictment: the McMartin Trial* 1995; *Volcano* 1997

Jackson, Pat *Encore* 1951; *White Corridors* 1951; *The Feminine Touch* 1956; *The Birthday Present* 1957; *Virgin Island* 1958; *What a Carve Up!* 1961; *Don't Talk to Strange Men* 1962

Jackson, Peter *Bad Taste* 1987; *Meet the Feebles* 1989; *Braindead* 1992; *Heavenly Creatures* 1994; *The Frighteners* 1996

Jackson, Wilfred *Fantasia* 1940; *Saludos Amigos* 1943; *Song of the South* 1946; *Melody Time* 1948; *Cinderella* 1950; *Alice in Wonderland* 1951; *Peter Pan* 1953; *Lady and the Tramp* 1955

Jacobs, Alan *Nina Takes a Lover* 1993; *Diary of a Serial Killer* 1997

Jacobson, Rick *Terminal Voyage* 1994; *Night Hunter* 1995; *Suspect Device* 1995; *Reasons of the Heart* 1996

Jacoby, Joseph *Hurry Up, or I'll Be 30* 1973; *The Great Georgia Bank Hoax* 1977

Jaeckin, Just *Emmanuelle* 1974; *The Story of O* 1975; *Lady Chatterley's Lover* 1981

Jaglom, Henry *A Safe Place* 1971; *Tracks* 1977; *Sitting Ducks* 1979; *National Lampoon's Movie Madness* 1981; *Can She Bake a Cherry Pie?* 1983; *Always* 1985; *Someone to Love* 1987; *Eating* 1990; *Venice/Venice* 1992; *Babyfever* 1994; *Last Summer in the Hamptons* 1995; *Déjà Vu* 1997

James, Steve *Hoop Dreams* 1994; *Prefontaine* 1997

Jameson, Jerry *Airport '77* 1977; *A Fire in the Sky* 1978; *Raise the Titanic* 1980; *Stand by Your Man* 1981; *Starflight One* 1983; *The Red Spider* 1988; *Terror on Highway 91* 1989; *Fire and Rain* 1989; *Gunsmoke: To the Last Man* 1992; *Bonanza – the Return* 1993; *Taken Away* 1996

Jancsó, Miklós *The Round-Up* 1966; *The Red and the White* 1967

Jankel, Annabel *DOA* 1988; *Super Mario Bros* 1993

Jarman, Derek *Sebastiane* 1976; *Jubilee* 1978; *The Tempest* 1979; *The Angelic Conversation* 1985; *Caravaggio* 1986; *Aria* 1987; *The Last of England* 1987; *War Requiem* 1988; *The Garden* 1990; *Edward II* 1991; *Blue* 1993; *Wittgenstein* 1993

Jarmusch, Jim *Stranger than Paradise* 1984; *Down by Law* 1986; *Mystery Train* 1989; *Night on Earth* 1992; *Dead Man* 1995; *The Year of the Horse* 1997; *Ghost Dog: the Way of the Samurai* 1999

Jarrott, Charles *Anne of the Thousand Days* 1969; *Mary, Queen of Scots* 1971; *Lost Horizon* 1973; *The Dove* 1974; *Escape from the Dark* 1976; *The Other Side of Midnight* 1977; *The Last Flight of Noah's Ark* 1980; *The Amateur* 1981; *Condorman* 1981; *The Boy in Blue* 1986; *Changes* 1991; *Lucy and Desi: before the Laughter* 1991; *Yes Virginia, There Is a Santa Claus* 1991; *A Stranger in the Mirror* 1993; *Treacherous Beauties* 1994; *At the Midnight Hour* 1995

Jarvilaturi, Ilkka *Darkness in Tallinn* 1993; *History Is Made at Night* 1999

Jasny, Vojtech *All My Good Countrymen* 1968; *Great Land of the Small* 1987

Jason, Leigh *The Bride Walks Out* 1936; *New Faces of 1937* 1937; *The Mad Miss Manton* 1938; *Lady for a Night* 1942; *Out of the Blue* 1947

Jean, Vadim *Leon the Pig Farmer* 1992; *Beyond Bedlam* 1993; *Clockwork Mice* 1994; *The Real Howard Spitz* 1998; *One More Kiss* 1999

Jeffrey, Tom *Weekend of Shadows* 1978; *The Odd Angry Shot* 1979

Jeffries, Lionel *The Railway Children* 1971; *The Amazing Mr Blunden* 1972; *Baxter* 1973; *Wombling Free* 1977; *The Water Babies* 1978

Jenkins, Michael *Rebel* 1985; *The Heartbreak Kid* 1993

Jeunet, Jean-Pierre *Delicatessen* 1990; *The City of Lost Children* 1995; *Alien: Resurrection* 1997

Jewison, Norman *Forty Pounds of Trouble* 1962; *The Thrill of It All* 1963; *Send Me No Flowers* 1964; *Art of Love* 1965; *The Cincinnati Kid* 1965; *The Russians Are Coming, the Russians Are Coming* 1966; *In the Heat of the Night* 1967; *The Thomas Crown Affair* 1968; *Gaily, Gaily* 1969; *Fiddler on the Roof* 1971; *Jesus Christ Superstar* 1973; *Rollerball* 1975; *F.I.S.T.* 1978; *...And Justice for All* 1979; *Best Friends* 1982; *A Soldier's Story* 1984; *Agnes of God* 1985; *Moonstruck* 1987; *In Country* 1989; *Other People's Money* 1991; *Only You* 1994; *Bogus* 1996; *The Hurricane* 1999

Jires, Jaromil *The Joke* 1968; *Labyrinth* 1991

Joanou, Phil *Three O'Clock High* 1987; *U2 Rattle and Hum* 1988; *State of Grace* 1990; *Final Analysis* 1992; *Heaven's Prisoners* 1996

Jodorowsky, Alexandro *El Topo* 1971; *Santa Sangre* 1989; *The Rainbow Thief* 1990

Jodrell, Steve *Shame* 1987; *Tudawali* 1987

Joffe, Mark *Skin Deep* 1985; *Grievous Bodily Harm* 1987; *Spotswood* 1991; *Cosi* 1996; *The Matchmaker* 1997

Joffé, Roland *The Killing Fields* 1984; *The Mission* 1986; *Shadow Makers* 1989; *City of Joy* 1992; *The Scarlet Letter* 1995; *Goodbye Lover* 1997; *Vatel* 2000

Johnson, Alan *To Be or Not to Be* 1983; *Solarwarriors* 1986

Johnson, Kenneth *The Liberators* 1987; *Short Circuit 2* 1988; *Alien Nation: Dark Horizon* 1994; *Steel* 1997

Johnson, Lamont *A Covenant with Death* 1967; *Kona Coast* 1968; *The McKenzie Break* 1970; *A Gunfight* 1971; *The Groundstar Conspiracy* 1972; *You'll Like My Mother* 1972; *The Last American Hero* 1973; *Fear on Trial* 1975; *Lipstick* 1976; *One on One* 1977; *Somebody Killed Her Husband* 1978; *Off the Minnesota Strip* 1980; *Cattle Annie and Little Britches* 1981; *Spacehunter: Adventures in the Forbidden Zone* 1983; *Unnatural Causes: the Agent Orange Story* 1986; *A Thousand Heroes* 1992; *The Broken Chain* 1993; *The Man Next Door* 1996

Johnson, Nunnally *Black Widow* 1954; *Night People* 1954; *How to Be Very, Very Popular* 1955; *The Man in the Gray Flannel Suit* 1956; *Oh, Men! Oh, Women!* 1957; *The Three Faces of Eve* 1957; *The Man Who Understood Women* 1959; *The Angel Wore Red* 1960

Johnson, Patrick Read *Baby's Day Out* 1994; *Angus* 1995

Johnston, Joe *Honey, I Shrunk the Kids* 1989; *The Rocketeer* 1991; *The Pagemaster* 1994; *Jumanji* 1995; *October Sky* 1999

Jolivet, Pierre *Force Majeure* 1989; *In All Innocence* 1998

Jones, Amy Holden *aka* **Jones, Amy** *The Slumber Party Massacre* 1982; *Love Letters* 1983; *Maid to Order* 1987; *The Rich Man's Wife* 1996

Jones, Chuck *The Phantom Tollbooth* 1970; *The Bugs Bunny/Road Runner Movie* 1979

Jones, David *Betrayal* 1982; *84 Charing Cross Road* 1986; *Jacknife* 1988; *Fire in the Dark* 1991; *The Trial* 1993; *And Then There Was One* 1994; *For the Future: the Irvine Fertility Scandal* 1996; *An Unexpected Life* 1998; *The Confession* 1999

Jones, F Richard *The Gaucho* 1927; *Bulldog Drummond* 1929

Jones, Harmon *As Young as You Feel* 1951; *Bloodhounds of Broadway* 1952; *The Pride of St Louis* 1952; *The Kid from Left Field* 1953; *Princess of the Nile* 1954; *Gorilla at Large* 1954; *A Day of Fury* 1956; *Bullwhip* 1958; *Wolf Larsen* 1958

Jones, Terry *Monty Python and the Holy Grail* 1975; *Monty Python's Life of Brian* 1979; *Monty Python's The Meaning of Life* 1983; *Personal Services* 1987; *Erik the Viking* 1989; *The Wind in the Willows* 1996

Jordan, Glenn *Frankenstein* 1973; *Les Misérables* 1978; *Only When I Laugh* 1981; *Mass Appeal* 1984; *The Buddy System* 1984; *Promise* 1986; *Something in Common* 1986; *Jesse* 1988; *Home Fires Burning* 1989; *The Boys* 1991; *The Other Side of Murder* 1991; *Sarah, Plain and Tall* 1991; *O Pioneers!* 1992; *Barbarians at the Gate* 1993; *To Dance with the White Dog* 1993; *Jane's House* 1994; *Neil Simon's Jake's Women* 1996; *Legalese* 1998; *Night Ride Home* 1999

Jordan, Neil *Angel* 1982; *The Company of Wolves* 1984; *Mona Lisa* 1986; *High Spirits* 1988; *We're No Angels* 1989; *The Miracle* 1990; *The Crying Game* 1992; *Interview with the Vampire: the Vampire Chronicles* 1994; *Michael Collins* 1996; *The Butcher Boy* 1997; *In Dreams* 1998; *The End of the Affair* 1999

Jost, Jon *All the Vermeers in New York* 1990; *Sure Fire* 1990; *Frameup* 1993

Judge, Mike *Beavis and Butt-head Do America* 1996; *Office Space* 1999

Julien, Isaac *Young Soul Rebels* 1991; *Frantz Fanon: Black Skin White Mask* 1996

Juran, Nathan *aka* **Hertz, Nathan,** *aka* **Juran, Nathan H** *Law and Order* 1953; *The Golden Blade* 1953; *Gunsmoke* 1953; *Tumbleweed* 1953; *Drums across the River* 1954; *Hellcats of the Navy* 1957; *20 Million Miles to Earth* 1957; *The Deadly Mantis* 1957; *The Brain from Planet Arous* 1958; *The 7th Voyage of Sinbad* 1958; *Good Day for a Hanging* 1958; *Jack the Giant Killer* 1962; *The Siege of the Saxons* 1963; *First Men in the Moon* 1964; *Land Raiders* 1969

K

Kachyna, Karel *The Ear* 1969; *The Last Butterfly* 1990

Kaczender, George *Agency* 1981; *Chanel Solitaire* 1981; *PrettyKill* 1987; *Blind Judgement: Seduction in Travis County* 1991; *Christmas on Division Street* 1991; *Jonathan: the Boy Nobody Wanted* 1992; *Betrayal of Trust* 1994; *Ebbie* 1995; *Danielle Steel's Vanished* 1995; *Devil's Food* 1996; *Maternal Instincts* 1996; *Indiscretion of an American Wife* 1998

Kadar, Jan *The Shop on the High Street* 1965; *The Angel Levine* 1970; *Lies My Father Told Me* 1975; *Freedom Road* 1979

Kagan, Jeremy Paul *aka* **Kagan, Jeremy** *Katherine* 1975; *Heroes* 1977; *Scott Joplin* 1977; *The Big Fix* 1978; *The Chosen* 1981; *The Sting II* 1983; *The Journey of Natty Gann* 1985; *Courage* 1986; *Big Man on Campus* 1989; *Descending Angel* 1990; *By the Sword* 1992; *Roswell* 1994; *Color of Justice* 1997; *The Hired Heart* 1997

Kalatozov, Mikhail *aka* **Kalatozov, Mikhail K** *The Cranes Are Flying* 1957; *The Red Tent* 1969

Kane, Joseph *aka* **Kane, Joe** *Billy the Kid Returns* 1938; *Shine On, Harvest Moon* 1938; *The Arizona Kid* 1939; *Rough Riders' Roundup* 1939; *Song of Texas* 1943; *The Yellow Rose of Texas* 1944; *The Cheaters* 1945; *Dakota* 1945; *Flame of the Barbary Coast* 1945; *Hoodlum Empire* 1952; *Ride the Man Down* 1952; *Fair Wind to Java* 1953; *The Maverick Queen* 1955; *The Road to Denver* 1955; *Timberjack* 1955; *Thunder over Arizona* 1956

Kaneko, Shusuke *aka* **Kaneko, Shu** *Summer Vacation: 1999* 1988; *Necronomicon* 1993

Kanew, Jeff *Eddie Macon's Run* 1983; *Revenge of the Nerds* 1984; *Gotcha!* 1985; *Tough Guys* 1986; *Troop Beverly Hills* 1989; *VI Warshawski* 1991

Kanganis, Charles T *Chance* 1990; *A Time to Die* 1991; *Intent to Kill* 1992; *No Escape, No Return* 1994; *3 Ninjas Kick Back* 1994; *Race the Sun* 1996; *Dennis Strikes Again* 1998

Kanievska, Marek *Another Country* 1984; *Less than Zero* 1987

Kanin, Garson *Bachelor Mother* 1939; *The Great Man Votes* 1939; *My Favorite Wife* 1940; *They Knew What They Wanted* 1940; *Tom, Dick and Harry* 1941; *Where It's At* 1969

Kanter, Hal *Loving You* 1957; *I Married a Woman* 1958

Kaplan, Ed *For Their Own Good* 1993; *Primal Secrets* 1994

Kaplan, Jonathan *The Slams* 1973; *Truck Turner* 1974; *White Line Fever* 1975; *Mr Billion* 1977; *Over the Edge* 1979; *Death Ride to Osaka* 1983; *Heart like a Wheel* 1983; *Project X* 1987; *The Accused* 1988; *Immediate Family* 1989; *Love Field* 1992; *Unlawful Entry* 1992; *Bad Girls* 1994; *Reform School Girl* 1994; *Brokedown Palace* 1999

Kapur, Shekhar *Mr India* 1986; *Bandit Queen* 1994; *Elizabeth* 1998

Karbelnikoff, Michael *Mobsters* 1991; *FTW* 1994

Karlson, Phil *Dark Alibi* 1946; *Ladies of the Chorus* 1948; *Lorna Doone* 1951; *Kansas City Confidential* 1952; *They Rode West* 1954; *Five against the House* 1955; *Hell's Island* 1955; *The Phenix City Story* 1955; *Tight Spot* 1955; *The Brothers Rico* 1957; *Key Witness* 1960; *Hell to Eternity* 1960; *The Young Doctors* 1961; *The Secret Ways* 1961; *Kid Galahad* 1962; *Rampage* 1963; *The Silencers* 1966; *The Long Ride Home* 1967; *The Wrecking Crew* 1969; *Hornet's Nest* 1970; *Ben* 1972; *Walking Tall* 1973; *Framed* 1975

Karn, Bill *Gang Busters* 1955; *Door-to-Door Maniac* 1961

Karson, Eric *The Octagon* 1980; *Opposing Force* 1986; *Hell Camp* 1987; *Black Eagle* 1988

Kasdan, Lawrence *Body Heat* 1981; *The Big Chill* 1983; *Silverado* 1985; *The Accidental Tourist* 1988; *I Love You to Death* 1990; *Grand Canyon* 1991; *Wyatt Earp* 1994; *French Kiss* 1995; *Mumford* 1999

Katselas, Milton *Butterflies Are Free* 1972; *40 Carats* 1973; *Report to the Commissioner* 1975; *When You Comin' Back, Red Ryder?* 1979

Katzin, Lee H *Whatever Happened to Aunt Alice?* 1969; *Le Mans* 1971; *The Salzburg Connection* 1972; *Sky Heist* 1975; *The Dirty Dozen: the Deadly Mission* 1987; *Confessions of a Lady Cop* 1988; *The Dirty Dozen: the Fatal Mission* 1988; *World Gone Wild* 1988; *Jake Spanner, Private Eye* 1989

Kaufman, Jim *Back Stab* 1990; *Whiskers* 1997
Kaufman, Lloyd *aka* **Weil, Samuel** *Class of Nuke 'Em High* 1986; *The Toxic Avenger, Part II* 1988; *Sgt Kabukiman NYPD* 1991; *Tromeo & Juliet* 1996
Kaufman, Philip *Goldstein* 1964; *Frank's Greatest Adventure* 1967; *The Great Northfield Minnesota Raid* 1972; *The White Dawn* 1974; *Invasion of the Body Snatchers* 1978; *The Wanderers* 1979; *The Right Stuff* 1983; *The Unbearable Lightness of Being* 1988; *Henry & June* 1990; *Rising Sun* 1993
Kaurismäki, Aki *Crime and Punishment* 1983; *Hamlet Goes Business* 1987; *Ariel* 1988; *Leningrad Cowboys Go America* 1989; *I Hired a Contract Killer* 1990; *The Match Factory Girl* 1990; *Leningrad Cowboys Meet Moses* 1993; *Take Care of Your Scarf, Tatjana* 1994; *The Total Balalaika Show* 1994; *Drifting Clouds* 1996; *Juha* 1999
Kaurismäki, Mika *Tigrero: a Film That Was Never Made* 1994; *LA without a Map* 1998
Käutner, Helmut *The Devil's General* 1955; *A Stranger in My Arms* 1959
Kautner, Helmut *The Last Bridge* 1954; *The Restless Years* 1958
Kawajiri, Yoshiaki *Lensman* 1984; *Wicked City* 1992
Kawalerowicz, Jerzy *The Devil and the Nun* 1960; *Pharaoh* 1966
Kazan, Elia *A Tree Grows in Brooklyn* 1945; *Boomerang!* 1947; *Gentleman's Agreement* 1947; *The Sea of Grass* 1947; *Pinky* 1949; *Panic in the Streets* 1950; *A Streetcar Named Desire* 1951; *Viva Zapata!* 1952; *Man on a Tightrope* 1953; *On the Waterfront* 1954; *East of Eden* 1955; *Baby Doll* 1956; *A Face in the Crowd* 1957; *Wild River* 1960; *Splendor in the Grass* 1961; *America, America* 1963; *The Arrangement* 1969; *The Visitors* 1972; *The Last Tycoon* 1976
Keach, James *False Identity* 1990; *Sunstroke* 1992; *Praying Mantis* 1993; *Quest for Justice* 1993; *The Stars Fell on Henrietta* 1995; *The Absolute Truth* 1997
Keaton, Buster *One Week* 1920; *Scarecrow* 1920; *The Paleface* 1921; *Daydreams* 1922; *Our Hospitality* 1923; *Three Ages* 1923; *The Navigator* 1924; *Sherlock Junior* 1924; *Go West* 1925; *Seven Chances* 1925; *Battling Butler* 1926; *The General* 1927
Keaton, Diane *Heaven* 1987; *Wildflower* 1991; *Unstrung Heroes* 1995; *Hanging Up* 1999
Keen, Bob *To Catch a Yeti* 1993; *Proteus* 1995
Keeter, Worth *Snapdragon* 1993; *Last Lives* 1997
Keighley, William *Ladies They Talk About* 1933; *Easy to Love* 1934; ''G'' *Men* 1935; *Special Agent* 1935; *Bullets or Ballots* 1936; *The Green Pastures* 1936; *The Singing Kid* 1936; *God's Country and the Woman* 1937; *The Prince and the Pauper* 1937; *The Adventures of Robin Hood* 1938; *Each Dawn I Die* 1939; *The Fighting 69th* 1940; *Torrid Zone* 1940; *No Time for Comedy* 1940; *The Bride Came C.O.D.* 1941; *The Man Who Came to Dinner* 1941; *George Washington Slept Here* 1942; *The Street with No Name* 1948; *Rocky Mountain* 1950; *Close to My Heart* 1951; *The Master of Ballantrae* 1953

Keiller, Patrick *London* 1994; *Robinson in Space* 1997
Keller, Harry *Rose of Cimarron* 1952; *Quantez* 1957; *Voice in the Mirror* 1958; *The Female Animal* 1958; *Day of the Bad Man* 1958; *Seven Ways from Sundown* 1960; *Six Black Horses* 1962; *Tammy and the Doctor* 1963; *The Brass Bottle* 1964; *In Enemy Country* 1968
Kellett, Bob *Up Pompeii* 1971; *Up the Chastity Belt* 1971; *Our Miss Fred* 1972; *Up the Front* 1972; *Don't Just Lie There, Say Something!* 1973; *Are You Being Served?* 1977
Kellino, Roy *The Last Adventurers* 1937; *The Silken Affair* 1957
Kelljan, Bob *aka* **Kelljchian, Robert** *Count Yorga, Vampire* 1970; *The Return of Count Yorga* 1971; *Scream Blacula Scream* 1973; *Act of Vengeance* 1974
Kellman, Barnet *Key Exchange* 1985; *Straight Talk* 1992
Kellogg, David *Cool as Ice* 1991; *Inspector Gadget* 1999
Kellogg, Ray *The Killer Shrews* 1959; *The Giant Gila Monster* 1959; *The Green Berets* 1968
Kelly, Gene *On the Town* 1949; *Singin' in the Rain* 1952; *It's Always Fair Weather* 1955; *Invitation to the Dance* 1956; *The Happy Road* 1956; *The Tunnel of Love* 1958; *Gigot* 1962; *A Guide for the Married Man* 1967; *Hello, Dolly!* 1969; *The Cheyenne Social Club* 1970; *That's Entertainment, Part II* 1976
Kelly, Rory *Sleep with Me* 1994; *Some Girls* 1998
Kennedy, Burt *The Canadians* 1961; *Mail Order Bride* 1964; *The Rounders* 1965; *The Money Trap* 1966; *Return of the Seven* 1966; *The War Wagon* 1967; *Welcome to Hard Times* 1967; *The Good Guys and the Bad Guys* 1969; *Support Your Local Sheriff!* 1969; *Young Billy Young* 1969; *Dirty Dingus Magee* 1970; *The Deserter* 1971; *Hannie Caulder* 1971; *Support Your Local Gunfighter* 1971; *The Train Robbers* 1973; *The Killer inside Me* 1975; *Wolf Lake* 1979; *Down the Long Hills* 1987; *The Trouble with Spies* 1987; *Once upon a Texas Train* 1988; *Where the Hell's That Gold?* 1988; *Suburban Commando* 1991
Kennedy, Michael *Hard Evidence* 1994; *Legacy of Evil* 1995; *Hostile Force* 1996; *Robin of Locksley* 1996
Kenton, Erle C *Island of Lost Souls* 1932; *You're Telling Me!* 1934; *Pardon My Sarong* 1942; *Who Done It?* 1942; *The Ghost of Frankenstein* 1942; *It Ain't Hay* 1943; *House of Frankenstein* 1944; *House of Dracula* 1945
Kern, James V *The Doughgirls* 1944; *Never Say Goodbye* 1946; *The Second Woman* 1951; *Two Tickets to Broadway* 1951
Kershner, Irvin *The Young Captives* 1958; *The Hoodlum Priest* 1961; *A Face in the Rain* 1963; *The Luck of Ginger Coffey* 1964; *A Fine Madness* 1966; *One Born Every Minute* 1967; *Loving* 1970; *Up the Sandbox* 1972; *S*P*Y*S* 1974; *The Return of a Man Called Horse* 1976; *Eyes of Laura Mars* 1978; *The Empire Strikes Back* 1980; *Never Say Never Again* 1983; *Traveling Man* 1989; *RoboCop 2* 1990
Keusch, Michael *Lena's Holiday* 1990; *Huck and the King of Hearts* 1993; *Just One of the Girls* 1993; *Samurai Cowboy* 1993; *Double Cross* 1994
Khan, Mehboob *Andaz* 1949; *Mother India* 1957
Khleifi, Michel *Wedding in Galilee* 1987; *Canticle of the Stones* 1990
Kiarostami, Abbas *The Traveller* 1974; *Where Is My Friend's House?* 1987; *Close-Up* 1989; *And Life Goes On...* 1991; *Through the Olive Trees* 1994; *A Taste of Cherry* 1997; *The Wind Will Carry Us* 1999
Kidron, Beeban *Vroom* 1988; *Antonia & Jane* 1990; *Used People* 1992; *Shades of Fear* 1993; *To Wong Foo, Thanks for Everything, Julie Newmar* 1995; *Amy Foster* 1997
Kiersch, Fritz *Children of the Corn* 1984; *Tuff Turf* 1984; *Gor* 1987; *Under the Boardwalk* 1988; *Into the Sun* 1992
Kieslowski, Krzysztof *No End* 1984; *A Short Film about Killing* 1988; *A Short Film about Love* 1988; *The Double Life of Véronique* 1991; *Three Colours Blue* 1993; *Three Colours White* 1993; *Three Colours Red* 1994
Kikoine, Gérard *Dragonard* 1987; *Edge of Sanity* 1989; *Buried Alive* 1990
Killy, Edward *Seven Keys to Baldpate* 1935; *Murder on a Bridle Path* 1936; *Along the Rio Grande* 1941
Kimmins, Anthony *Keep Fit* 1937; *I See Ice* 1938; *It's in the Air* 1938; *Come On George* 1939; *Trouble Brewing* 1939; *Mine Own Executioner* 1947; *Bonnie Prince Charlie* 1948; *Mr Denning Drives North* 1951; *The Captain's Paradise* 1953; *Smiley* 1956; *Smiley Gets a Gun* 1959; *The Amorous Prawn* 1962
King, Allan *Warrendale* 1967; *Who Has Seen the Wind* 1977; *Silence of the North* 1981
King, George *The Crimes of Stephen Hawke* 1936; *Sweeney Todd, the Demon Barber of Fleet Street* 1936; *The Ticket of Leave Man* 1937; *Sexton Blake and the Hooded Terror* 1938; *Crimes at the Dark House* 1939; *The Face at the Window* 1939; *Tomorrow We Live* 1942; *Tomorrow We Live* 1942; *Candlelight in Algeria* 1943; *Gaiety George* 1946; *The Shop at Sly Corner* 1948
King, Henry *Tol'able David* 1921; *Fury* 1923; *The White Sister* 1923; *Stella Dallas* 1925; *The Winning of Barbara Worth* 1926; *State Fair* 1933; *Way Down East* 1935; *The Country Doctor* 1936; *Lloyd's of London* 1936; *In Old Chicago* 1937; *Alexander's Ragtime Band* 1938; *Jesse James* 1939; *Stanley and Livingstone* 1939; *Chad Hanna* 1940; *Little Old New York* 1940; *Maryland* 1940; *Remember the Day* 1941; *A Yank in the RAF* 1941; *The Black Swan* 1942; *The Song of Bernadette* 1943; *Wilson* 1944; *A Bell for Adano* 1945; *Margie* 1946; *Captain from Castile* 1947; *Prince of Foxes* 1949; *Twelve O'Clock High* 1949; *The Gunfighter* 1950; *David and Bathsheba* 1951; *I'd Climb the Highest Mountain* 1951; *The Snows of Kilimanjaro* 1952; *Wait 'til the Sun Shines, Nellie* 1952; *O Henry's Full House* 1952; *King of the Khyber Rifles* 1953; *Love Is a Many-Splendored Thing* 1955; *Untamed* 1955; *Carousel* 1956; *The Sun Also Rises* 1957; *The Bravados* 1958; *Beloved Infidel*

1959; This Earth Is Mine 1959; *Tender Is the Night* 1961
King, Louis *Charlie Chan in Egypt* 1935; *Typhoon* 1940; *The Way of All Flesh* 1940; *Thunderhead – Son of Flicka* 1945; *Smoky* 1946; *Bob, Son of Battle* 1947; *Green Grass of Wyoming* 1948; *Mrs Mike* 1949; *Powder River* 1953; *Dangerous Mission* 1954
King, Rick *Hard Choices* 1984; *Hot Shot* 1986; *The Killing Time* 1987; *Forced March* 1989; *Prayer of the Rollerboys* 1990; *Kickboxer III: the Art of War* 1992; *Quick* 1993; *A Passion to Kill* 1994; *Terminal Justice* 1996; *Road Ends* 1999
King, Zalman *Two Moon Junction* 1988; *Wild Orchid* 1990; *The Red Shoe Diaries* 1992; *Delta of Venus* 1995; *In God's Hands* 1998
Kinney, Jack *Saludos Amigos* 1943; *Victory through Air Power* 1943; *The Three Caballeros* 1944; *Make Mine Music* 1946; *Fun and Fancy Free* 1947; *Melody Time* 1948; *The Adventures of Ichabod and Mr Toad* 1949
Kinugasa, Teinosuke *A Page of Madness* 1926; *Gate of Hell* 1953
Kitano, Takeshi *Violent Cop* 1989; *Boiling Point* 1990; *A Scene at the Sea* 1991; *Sonatine* 1993; *Kids Return* 1996; *Hana-Bi* 1997; *Kikujiro* 1999
Kizer, R J *Godzilla* 1984; *Hell Comes to Frogtown* 1988
Kjellin, Alf *Midas Run* 1969; *The McMasters* 1970
Klane, Robert *Thank God It's Friday* 1978; *Weekend at Bernie's II* 1992; *The Odd Couple: Together Again* 1993
Klapisch, Cédric *Un Air de Famille* 1996; *Chacun Cherche Son Chat* 1996
Kleiser, Randal *Dawn: Portrait of a Teenage Runaway* 1976; *Grease* 1978; *The Blue Lagoon* 1980; *Summer Lovers* 1982; *Grandview, USA* 1984; *Flight of the Navigator* 1986; *Big Top Pee-wee* 1988; *Getting It Right* 1989; *White Fang* 1991; *Honey I Blew Up the Kid* 1992; *It's My Party* 1996; *Shadow of Doubt* 1998
Klenhard, Walter *The Haunting of Seacliff Inn* 1994; *Baby Monitor: Sound of Fear* 1998
Kletter, Richard *The Tower* 1992; *Dangerous Indiscretion* 1994; *The Android Affair* 1995
Kleven, Max *The Night Stalker* 1985; *WB, Blue and the Bean* 1988
Klimov, Elem *Agony* 1975; *Come and See* 1985
Kloves, Steve *The Fabulous Baker Boys* 1989; *Flesh and Bone* 1993
Kluge, Alexander *Yesterday Girl* 1966; *Germany in Autumn* 1978
Knowles, Bernard *A Place of One's Own* 1944; *The Magic Bow* 1946; *Jassy* 1947; *The Man Within* 1947; *Easy Money* 1948; *The Perfect Woman* 1949; *Park Plaza 605* 1953
Kobayashi, Masaki *Somewhere under the Broad Sky* 1954; *The Human Condition* 1958; *Harakiri* 1962; *Kwaidan* 1964; *Rebellion* 1967; *The Empty Table* 1985
Koch, Howard W *Shield for Murder* 1954; *Big House, USA* 1955; *The Girl in Black Stockings* 1957; *Andy Hardy Comes Home* 1958; *Violent Road* 1958; *Frankenstein – 1970* 1958; *The Last Mile* 1959; *Born Reckless* 1959; *Badge 373* 1973
Koepp, David *The Trigger Effect* 1996; *Stir of Echoes* 1999

Kokkinos, Ana *Only the Brave* 1994; *Head On* 1997
Kollek, Amos *Goodbye New York* 1984; *Forever Lulu* 1987; *High Stakes* 1989; *Double Edge* 1992
Koller, Xavier *Journey of Hope* 1990; *The Last Great Warrior* 1994
Konchalovsky, Andrei *aka* **Mikhalkov-Konchalovsky, Andrei** *Asya's Happiness* 1967; *Maria's Lovers* 1984; *Runaway Train* 1985; *Duet for One* 1986; *Shy People* 1987; *Homer and Eddie* 1989; *Tango and Cash* 1989; *The Inner Circle* 1991; *The Odyssey* 1997
Kopple, Barbara *Harlan County, USA* 1976; *Wild Man Blues* 1997
Korda, Alexander *The Private Life of Helen of Troy* 1927; *Marius* 1931; *Wedding Rehearsal* 1932; *The Private Life of Henry VIII* 1933; *The Private Life of Don Juan* 1934; *Rembrandt* 1936; *The Thief of Bagdad* 1940; *That Hamilton Woman* 1941; *Perfect Strangers* 1945; *An Ideal Husband* 1947
Korda, Zoltan *Sanders of the River* 1935; *Conquest of the Air* 1936; *Forget-Me-Not* 1936; *Elephant Boy* 1937; *The Drum* 1938; *The Four Feathers* 1939; *The Thief of Bagdad* 1940; *Jungle Book* 1942; *Sahara* 1943; *The Macomber Affair* 1947; *Cry, the Beloved Country* 1951; *Storm over the Nile* 1955
Korine, Harmony *Gummo* 1997; *julien donkey-boy* 1999
Korty, John *The Autobiography of Miss Jane Pittman* 1974; *Alex and the Gypsy* 1976; *Oliver's Story* 1978; *The Haunting Passion* 1983; *Twice upon a Time* 1983; *A Deadly Business* 1986; *Resting Place* 1986; *Eye on the Sparrow* 1987; *Winnie* 1988; *Cast the First Stone* 1989; *A Son's Promise* 1990; *Blind Hate* 1991; *Keeping Secrets* 1991; *Long Road Home* 1991; *Getting Out* 1993; *They Watch* 1993; *Redwood Curtain* 1995; *Ms Scrooge* 1997
Koster, Henry *Three Smart Girls* 1937; *One Hundred Men and a Girl* 1937; *The Rage of Paris* 1938; *First Love* 1939; *It Started with Eve* 1941; *Music for Millions* 1945; *Two Sisters from Boston* 1946; *The Bishop's Wife* 1947; *Come to the Stable* 1949; *The Inspector General* 1949; *Harvey* 1950; *My Blue Heaven* 1950; *Wabash Avenue* 1950; *Mr Belvedere Rings the Bell* 1951; *No Highway* 1951; *My Cousin Rachel* 1952; *Stars and Stripes Forever* 1952; *O Henry's Full House* 1952; *The Robe* 1953; *Desiree* 1954; *Good Morning, Miss Dove* 1955; *A Man Called Peter* 1955; *The Virgin Queen* 1955; *D-Day the Sixth of June* 1956; *The Power and the Prize* 1956; *My Man Godfrey* 1957; *The Naked Maja* 1959; *The Story of Ruth* 1960; *Flower Drum Song* 1961; *Mr Hobbs Takes a Vacation* 1962; *Take Her, She's Mine* 1963; *Dear Brigitte* 1966; *The Singing Nun* 1966
Kotcheff, Ted *aka* **Kotcheff, William T** *Tiara Tahiti* 1962; *Life at the Top* 1965; *Two Gentlemen Sharing* 1969; *Billy Two Hats* 1973; *The Apprenticeship of Duddy Kravitz* 1974; *Fun with Dick and Jane* 1977; *Who Is Killing the Great Chefs of Europe?* 1978; *North Dallas Forty* 1979; *First Blood* 1982; *Split Image* 1982; *Uncommon Valor* 1983; *Joshua Then and Now* 1985; *Switching*

L

Lee, Damian *Ski School* 1991; *Abraxas* 1991; *The Donor* 1994; *When the Bullet Hits the Bone* 1995
Lee, Jack *Once a Jolly Swagman* 1948; *The Wooden Horse* 1950; *South of Algiers* 1952; *Turn the Key Softly* 1953; *A Town like Alice* 1956; *Robbery under Arms* 1957; *The Captain's Table* 1958; *Circle of Deception* 1960
Lee, Rowland V *Paramount on Parade* 1930; *The Return of Dr Fu Manchu* 1930; *Zoo in Budapest* 1933; *The Count of Monte Cristo* 1934; *Cardinal Richelieu* 1935; *The Three Musketeers* 1935; *Love from a Stranger* 1936; *One Rainy Afternoon* 1936; *The Toast of New York* 1937; *Son of Frankenstein* 1939; *Tower of London* 1939; *Son of Monte Cristo* 1940; *Captain Kidd* 1945
Lee, Spike *She's Gotta Have It* 1986; *School Daze* 1988; *Do the Right Thing* 1989; *Mo' Better Blues* 1990; *Jungle Fever* 1991; *Malcolm X* 1992; *Crooklyn* 1994; *Clockers* 1995; *Get on the Bus* 1996; *Girl 6* 1996; *4 Little Girls* 1997; *He Got Game* 1998; *Summer of Sam* 1999
Lee Thompson, J *Murder without Crime* 1950; *The Yellow Balloon* 1952; *The Weak and the Wicked* 1953; *For Better, for Worse* 1954; *An Alligator Named Daisy* 1955; *As Long as They're Happy* 1955; *The Good Companions* 1956; *Yield to the Night* 1956; *Woman in a Dressing Gown* 1957; *Ice Cold in Alex* 1958; *No Trees in the Street* 1958; *North West Frontier* 1959; *Tiger Bay* 1959; *I Aim at the Stars* 1960; *The Guns of Navarone* 1961; *Cape Fear* 1962; *Taras Bulba* 1962; *Kings of the Sun* 1963; *What a Way to Go!* 1964; *John Goldfarb, Please Come Home* 1964; *Return from the Ashes* 1965; *Before Winter Comes* 1968; *Eye of the Devil* 1968; *The Chairman* 1969; *Mackenna's Gold* 1969; *Country Dance* 1970; *Conquest of the Planet of the Apes* 1972; *Battle for the Planet of the Apes* 1973; *Huckleberry Finn* 1974; *The Reincarnation of Peter Proud* 1975; *St Ives* 1976; *The White Buffalo* 1977; *The Greek Tycoon* 1978; *The Passage* 1978; *Caboblanco* 1980; *10 to Midnight* 1983; *The Ambassador* 1984; *The Evil That Men Do* 1984; *King Solomon's Mines* 1985; *Firewalker* 1986; *Murphy's Law* 1986; *Death Wish 4: the Crackdown* 1987; *Messenger of Death* 1988; *Kinjite: Forbidden Subjects* 1989
Leeds, Herbert I *The Cisco Kid and the Lady* 1939; *Mr Moto in Danger Island* 1939; *The Return of the Cisco Kid* 1939; *It Shouldn't Happen to a Dog* 1946; *Bunco Squad* 1950
Lehmann, Michael *Heathers* 1989; *Hudson Hawk* 1991; *Meet the Applegates* 1991; *Airheads* 1994; *The Truth about Cats and Dogs* 1996; *My Giant* 1998
Leifer, Neil *Yesterday's Hero* 1979; *Trading Hearts* 1988
Leigh, Mike *Bleak Moments* 1971; *Abigail's Party* 1977; *High Hopes* 1988; *Life Is Sweet* 1990; *Naked* 1993; *Secrets & Lies* 1995; *Career Girls* 1997; *Topsy-Turvy* 1999
Leisen, Mitchell *The Eagle and the Hawk* 1933; *Death Takes a Holiday* 1934; *Murder at the Vanities* 1934; *Hands across the Table* 1935; *The Big Broadcast of 1937* 1936; *The Big Broadcast of 1938* 1937; *Easy Living* 1937; *Swing High, Swing Low* 1937; *Artists and Models Abroad* 1938; *Midnight* 1939; *Arise, My Love* 1940; *Remember the Night* 1940; *Hold Back the Dawn* 1941; *I Wanted Wings* 1941; *The Lady Is Willing* 1942; *Take a Letter, Darling* 1942; *No Time for Love* 1943; *Frenchman's Creek* 1944; *Lady in the Dark* 1944; *Kitty* 1945; *To Each His Own* 1946; *Golden Earrings* 1947; *Suddenly It's Spring* 1947; *Dream Girl* 1948; *Bride of Vengeance* 1949; *Captain Carey, USA* 1950; *No Man of Her Own* 1950; *The Mating Season* 1951; *Darling, How Could You!* 1951; *Young Man with Ideas* 1952; *Tonight We Sing* 1953; *Bedevilled* 1955; *The Girl Most Likely* 1957
Leitch, Christopher *Courage Mountain* 1989; *Murder or Memory?* 1994; *She Fought Alone* 1995; *Nightmare Come True* 1996; *Crowned and Dangerous* 1997
Leland, David *Wish You Were Here* 1987; *Checking Out* 1988; *The Big Man* 1990; *The Land Girls* 1997
Lelouch, Claude *A Man and a Woman* 1966; *Vivre pour Vivre* 1967; *Far from Vietnam* 1967; *Visions of Eight* 1973; *Happy New Year* 1974; *And Now My Love* 1974; *Second Chance* 1976; *Another Man, Another Chance* 1977; *Robert et Robert* 1978; *An Adventure for Two* 1979; *Les Uns et les Autres* 1981; *Edith and Marcel* 1983; *Long Live Life* 1984; *A Man and a Woman: 20 Years Later* 1986; *Les Misérables* 1995; *Men, Women: a User's Manual* 1996; *Chance or Coincidence* 1999
Lemmo, James *Heart* 1987; *Bodily Harm* 1995
Lemont, John *The Shakedown* 1959; *And Women Shall Weep* 1960; *Konga* 1960; *The Frightened City* 1961
Lemorande, Rusty *Journey to the Center of the Earth* 1986; *The Turn of the Screw* 1992
Leni, Paul *Waxworks* 1924; *The Cat and the Canary* 1927; *The Man Who Laughs* 1928
Lenzi, Umberto aka **Milestone, Hank** *Sandokan the Great* 1963; *The Pirates of Malaysia* 1964; *From Hell to Victory* 1979
Leonard, Brett *The Lawnmower Man* 1992; *Hideaway* 1995; *Virtuosity* 1995
Leonard, Herbert B *The Perils of Pauline* 1967; *Going Home* 1971
Leonard, Robert Z *The Divorcee* 1930; *The Bachelor Father* 1931; *Susan Lenox: Her Fall and Rise* 1931; *Strange Interlude* 1932; *Dancing Lady* 1933; *Peg o' My Heart* 1933; *Escapade* 1935; *After Office Hours* 1935; *The Great Ziegfeld* 1936; *Piccadilly Jim* 1936; *The Firefly* 1937; *Maytime* 1937; *The Girl of the Golden West* 1938; *Broadway Serenade* 1939; *New Moon* 1940; *Pride and Prejudice* 1940; *Third Finger, Left Hand* 1940; *When Ladies Meet* 1941; *Ziegfeld Girl* 1941; *Stand by for Action* 1942; *The Man from Down Under* 1943; *Marriage Is a Private Affair* 1944; *Week-End at the Waldorf* 1945; *The Secret Heart* 1946; *Cynthia* 1947; *BF's Daughter* 1948; *The Bribe* 1949; *In the Good Old Summertime* 1949; *Nancy Goes to Rio* 1950; *Everything I Have Is Yours* 1952; *The Clown* 1952; *The Great Diamond Robbery* 1953; *Her Twelve Men* 1954; *Beautiful but Dangerous* 1955; *The King's Thief* 1955
Leone, Sergio *The Colossus of Rhodes* 1961; *Sodom and Gomorrah* 1962; *A Fistful of Dollars* 1964; *For a Few Dollars More* 1965; *The Good, the Bad and the Ugly* 1967; *Once upon a Time in the West* 1968; *A Fistful of Dynamite* 1971; *Once upon a Time in America* 1984
Lepage, Robert *The Confessional* 1995; *Le Polygraphe* 1996; *Nô* 1998
Lerner, Dan *Shame* 1992; *Hit and Run* 1999
Lerner, Irving *Murder by Contract* 1958; *City of Fear* 1959; *Studs Lonigan* 1960; *The Royal Hunt of the Sun* 1969
LeRoy, Mervyn *Five Star Final* 1931; *Little Caesar* 1931; *High Pressure* 1932; *I Am a Fugitive from a Chain Gang* 1932; *Three on a Match* 1932; *Gold Diggers of 1933* 1933; *Hard to Handle* 1933; *Tugboat Annie* 1933; *The World Changes* 1933; *Hi, Nellie!* 1934; *I Found Stella Parish* 1935; *Oil for the Lamps of China* 1935; *Page Miss Glory* 1935; *Sweet Adeline* 1935; *Anthony Adverse* 1936; *Three Men on a Horse* 1936; *The King and the Chorus Girl* 1937; *They Won't Forget* 1937; *Fools for Scandal* 1938; *Escape* 1940; *Waterloo Bridge* 1940; *Blossoms in the Dust* 1941; *Johnny Eager* 1941; *Unholy Partners* 1941; *Random Harvest* 1942; *Madame Curie* 1943; *Thirty Seconds over Tokyo* 1944; *Without Reservations* 1946; *Homecoming* 1948; *Any Number Can Play* 1949; *East Side, West Side* 1949; *Little Women* 1949; *Quo Vadis* 1951; *Lovely to Look At* 1952; *Million Dollar Mermaid* 1952; *Latin Lovers* 1953; *Rose Marie* 1954; *Mister Roberts* 1955; *Strange Lady in Town* 1955; *The Bad Seed* 1956; *Toward the Unknown* 1956; *Home before Dark* 1958; *No Time for Sergeants* 1958; *The FBI Story* 1959; *Wake Me when It's Over* 1960; *The Devil at Four o'Clock* 1961; *A Majority of One* 1961; *Gypsy* 1962; *Mary, Mary* 1963; *Moment to Moment* 1966
Lester, Mark L *Truck Stop Women* 1974; *Stunts* 1977; *Roller Boogie* 1979; *Class of 1984* 1982; *Firestarter* 1984; *Commando* 1985; *Armed and Dangerous* 1986; *Class of 1999* 1990; *Showdown in Little Tokyo* 1991; *SIS Extreme Justice* 1993; *Night of the Running Man* 1994; *The Public Enemy #1* 1995; *The Ex* 1996; *Double Take* 1997; *The Base* 1999
Lester, Richard aka **Lester, Dick** *The Running, Jumping and Standing Still Film* 1959; *It's Trad, Dad* 1961; *The Mouse on the Moon* 1963; *A Hard Day's Night* 1964; *Help!* 1965; *The Knack... and How to Get It* 1965; *A Funny Thing Happened on the Way to the Forum* 1966; *How I Won the War* 1967; *Petulia* 1968; *The Bed Sitting Room* 1969; *The Three Musketeers* 1973; *The Four Musketeers* 1974; *Juggernaut* 1974; *Royal Flash* 1975; *Robin and Marian* 1976; *The Ritz* 1976; *Butch and Sundance: the Early Days* 1979; *Cuba* 1979; *Superman II* 1980; *Superman III* 1983; *Finders Keepers* 1984; *The Return of the Musketeers* 1989; *Get Back* 1991
Lettich, Sheldon *AWOL* 1990; *Double Impact* 1991; *Only the Strong* 1993
Letts, Don *The Punk Rock Movie* 1978; *Dancehall Queen* 1996
Levant, Brian *Problem Child 2* 1991; *Beethoven* 1992; *The Flintstones* 1994; *Little Giants* 1994; *Jingle All the Way* 1996; *The Flintstones in Viva Rock Vegas* 2000
Levey, William A *The Happy Hooker Goes to Washington* 1977; *Skatetown, USA* 1979; *Lightning the White Stallion* 1986
Levi, Alan J *The Stepford Children* 1987; *Bionic Showdown: the Six Million Dollar Man and the Bionic Woman* 1989; *The Return of Sam McCloud* 1989; *Without Warning: Terror in the Towers* 1993
Levin, Henry *The Bandit of Sherwood Forest* 1946; *The Guilt of Janet Ames* 1947; *The Man from Colorado* 1948; *And Baby Makes Three* 1949; *Jolson Sings Again* 1949; *Convicted* 1950; *The Petty Girl* 1950; *Belles on Their Toes* 1952; *The Farmer Takes a Wife* 1953; *The President's Lady* 1953; *The Dark Avenger* 1955; *April Love* 1957; *The Lonely Man* 1957; *A Nice Little Bank That Should Be Robbed* 1958; *Holiday for Lovers* 1959; *Journey to the Center of the Earth* 1959; *The Remarkable Mr Pennypacker* 1959; *Where the Boys Are* 1960; *Come Fly with Me* 1962; *The Wonderful World of the Brothers Grimm* 1962; *If a Man Answers* 1962; *Genghis Khan* 1964; *Honeymoon Hotel* 1964; *Murderers' Row* 1966; *The Ambushers* 1967; *The Desperados* 1969; *That Man Bolt* 1973; *The Treasure Seekers* 1977; *Run for the Roses* 1978
Levin, Marc *The Last Party* 1993; *Slam* 1998; *Slam* 1998
Levin, Peter *Sworn to Silence* 1987; *Hostage* 1988; *A Killer among Us* 1990; *My Son Johnny* 1991; *Deliver Them from Evil: the Taking of Alta View* 1992; *Overkill: the Aileen Wuornos Story* 1992; *Precious Victims* 1993; *Fighting for My Daughter* 1995; *A Stranger in Town* 1995; *A Stranger to Love* 1996; *Death in the Shadows* 1998
Levinson, Barry *Diner* 1982; *The Natural* 1984; *Young Sherlock Holmes* 1985; *Good Morning, Vietnam* 1987; *Tin Men* 1987; *Rain Man* 1988; *Avalon* 1990; *Bugsy* 1991; *Toys* 1992; *Disclosure* 1994; *Jimmy Hollywood* 1994; *Sleepers* 1996; *Wag the Dog* 1997; *Sphere* 1998
Levitow, Abe *Gay Purr-ee* 1962; *The Phantom Tollbooth* 1970
Levitt, Gene *The Phantom of Hollywood* 1974; *Magee and the Lady* 1978
Levy, Eugene *Once upon a Crime* 1992; *Partners in Love* 1992; *Sodbusters* 1994
Levy, Jefery *Inside Monkey Zetterland* 1992; *SFW* 1994
Levy, Ralph *Bedtime Story* 1964; *Do Not Disturb* 1965
Levy, Scott aka **Levy, Scott P** *Midnight Tease* 1994; *The Alien Within* 1995; *Escape to Nowhere* 1996; *Piranha* 1996; *National Lampoon's Men in White* 1998
Levy, Shuki *Blind Vision* 1992; *Power Rangers 2* 1997
Lewin, Albert *The Moon and Sixpence* 1942; *The Picture of Dorian Gray* 1945; *The Private Affairs of Bel Ami* 1947; *Pandora and the Flying Dutchman* 1951; *Saadia* 1953
Lewin, Ben *Georgia* 1988; *The Favour, the Watch and the Very Big Fish* 1991; *Paperback Romance* 1994
Lewis, Jay *The Baby and the Battleship* 1956; *Invasion Quartet* 1961; *Live Now – Pay Later* 1962
Lewis, Jerry *The Bellboy* 1960; *The Errand Boy* 1961; *The Ladies' Man* 1961; *The Nutty Professor* 1963; *The Patsy* 1964; *The Family Jewels* 1965; *Three on a Couch* 1966; *The Big Mouth* 1967; *Which Way to the Front?* 1970; *One More Time* 1970; *Hardly Working* 1981; *Smorgasbord* 1983
Lewis, Joseph H aka **Lewis, Joseph** *Boys of the City* 1940; *That Gang of Mine* 1940; *Pride of the Bowery* 1941; *Invisible Ghost* 1941; *The Mad Doctor of Market Street* 1942; *The Falcon in San Francisco* 1945; *My Name Is Julia Ross* 1945; *So Dark the Night* 1946; *The Return of October* 1948; *Gun Crazy* 1949; *The Undercover Man* 1949; *A Lady without Passport* 1950; *Desperate Search* 1952; *Retreat, Hell!* 1952; *Cry of the Hunted* 1953; *The Big Combo* 1955; *A Lawless Street* 1955; *Seventh Cavalry* 1956; *The Halliday Brand* 1957; *Terror in a Texas Town* 1958
Lewis, Mark *Cane Toads – an Unnatural History* 1987; *Gordy* 1994
Lewis, Robert aka **Lewis, Robert Michael** *Ziegfeld Follies* 1944; *Anything Goes* 1956; *The Invisible Man* 1975; *The Night They Took Miss Beautiful* 1977; *No Room to Run* 1978; *Escape* 1980; *Fallen Angel* 1981; *Agatha Christie's A Caribbean Mystery* 1983; *Agatha Christie's Sparkling Cyanide* 1983; *Flight 90: Disaster on the Potomac* 1984; *Embassy* 1985; *A Stranger Waits* 1987; *Ladykillers* 1988; *The Secret Life of Kathy McCormick* 1988; *Dead Reckoning* 1990; *Memories of Murder* 1990; *Don't Talk to Strangers* 1994; *Circumstances Unknown* 1995
L'Herbier, Marcel *L'Inhumaine* 1923; *La Nuit Fantastique* 1942
Lieberman, Jeff *Squirm* 1976; *Just before Dawn* 1980; *Remote Control* 1988
Lieberman, Robert *Fighting Back* 1980; *Table for Five* 1983; *All I Want for Christmas* 1991; *A Child for Satan* 1991; *Fire in the Sky* 1993; *D3: the Mighty Ducks* 1996
Lima, Kevin *A Goofy Movie* 1995; *Tarzan* 1999
Liman, Doug *Getting In* 1994; *Swingers* 1996; *Go* 1999
Lindsay-Hogg, Michael *Let It Be* 1970; *Nasty Habits* 1976; *Nazi Hunter: the Beate Klarsfeld Story* 1986; *The Object of Beauty* 1991; *Running Mates* 1992; *Frankie Starlight* 1995; *The Rolling Stones Rock and Roll Circus* 1995; *Guy* 1996; *Ivana Trump's For Love Alone* 1996; *Horton Foote's Alone* 1997
Linklater, Richard *Slacker* 1989; *Dazed and Confused* 1993; *Before Sunrise* 1995; *subUrbia* 1996; *The Newton Boys* 1998
Linson, Art *Where the Buffalo Roam* 1980; *The Wild Life* 1984
Lipstadt, Aaron *Android* 1982; *City Limits* 1985; *Pair of Aces* 1990
Lisberger, Steven *Animalympics* 1979; *Tron* 1982; *Hot Pursuit* 1987; *Slipstream* 1989
Little, Dwight H aka **Little, Dwight** *Getting Even* 1986; *The Phantom of the Opera* 1989; *Marked for Death* 1990; *Rapid*

DIRECTORS' INDEX RadioTimes

Mackenzie, John *Act of Vengeance* 1986; *The Fourth Protocol* 1987; *Blue Heat* 1990; *Ruby* 1992; *Voyage* 1993; *The Infiltrator* 1995; *Aldrich Ames: Traitor Within* 1998; *When the Sky Falls* 2000

Mackenzie, Will *A Hobo's Christmas* 1987; *Stormy Weathers* 1992

MacKinnon, Gillies *Conquest of the South Pole* 1989; *The Playboys* 1992; *A Simple Twist of Fate* 1994; *Small Faces* 1995; *Trojan Eddie* 1996; *Regeneration* 1997; *Hideous Kinky* 1998

McLachlan, Duncan *The Double O Kid* 1992; *The Second Jungle Book* 1997

McLaglen, Andrew V *McLintock!* 1963; *Shenandoah* 1965; *The Rare Breed* 1966; *Monkeys, Go Home!* 1967; *The Way West* 1967; *The Ballad of Josie* 1968; *Bandolero!* 1968; *The Devil's Brigade* 1968; *Hellfighters* 1969; *The Undefeated* 1969; *Chisum* 1970; *One More Train to Rob* 1971; *something big* 1971; *Fools' Parade* 1971; *Cahill, United States Marshal* 1973; *Mitchell* 1975; *The Last Hard Men* 1976; *Murder at the World Series* 1977; *Breakthrough* 1978; *The Wild Geese* 1978; *North Sea Hijack* 1979; *The Sea Wolves* 1980; *Sahara* 1983; *The Dirty Dozen: the Next Mission* 1985; *Return from the River Kwai* 1988

Maclean, Alison *Crush* 1992; *Jesus' Son* 1999

McLennan, Don *Hard Knocks* 1980; *Slate, Wyn & Me* 1987

McLeod, Norman Z *Monkey Business* 1931; *Horse Feathers* 1932; *If I Had a Million* 1932; *Alice in Wonderland* 1933; *It's a Gift* 1934; *Pennies from Heaven* 1936; *Topper* 1937; *Merrily We Live* 1938; *There Goes My Heart* 1938; *Remember?* 1939; *Topper Takes a Trip* 1939; *Lady Be Good* 1941; *The Trial of Mary Dugan* 1941; *Swing Shift Maisie* 1943; *The Kid from Brooklyn* 1946; *Road to Rio* 1947; *The Secret Life of Walter Mitty* 1947; *The Paleface* 1948; *Isn't It Romantic* 1948; *Let's Dance* 1950; *My Favorite Spy* 1951; *Never Wave at a WAC* 1952; *Casanova's Big Night* 1954; *Alias Jesse James* 1959

McLoughlin, Tom *One Dark Night* 1982; *Friday the 13th Part VI: Jason Lives* 1986; *Date with an Angel* 1987; *Sometimes They Come Back* 1991; *Fatal Love* 1992; *Murder of Innocence* 1993; *Leave of Absence* 1994; *Take Me Home Again* 1994; *The Yarn Princess* 1994; *The Haunting of Helen Walker* 1995; *Journey* 1995; *A Different Kind of Christmas* 1996; *Behind the Mask* 1999

McMullen, Ken *Zina* 1985; *1871* 1989

McNamara, Sean *Casper: a Spirited Beginning* 1997; *Casper Meets Wendy* 1998

MacNaughton, Ian *And Now for Something Completely Different* 1971; *Monty Python Live at the Hollywood Bowl* 1982

McNaughton, John *Henry: Portrait of a Serial Killer* 1986; *The Borrower* 1989; *Sex, Drugs, Rock & Roll* 1991; *Mad Dog and Glory* 1992; *Girls in Prison* 1994; *Normal Life* 1995; *Wild Things* 1998; *Lansky* 1999

McPherson, John *Strays* 1991; *Fade to Black* 1993; *Terror at Deception Ridge* 1994

McTiernan, John *Nomads* 1985; *Predator* 1987; *Die Hard* 1988; *The Hunt for Red October* 1990; *Medicine Man* 1992; *Last Action Hero* 1993; *Die Hard with a Vengeance* 1995; *The 13th Warrior* 1999; *The Thomas Crown Affair* 1999

Madden, John *Ethan Frome* 1993; *Golden Gate* 1994; *Mrs Brown* 1997; *Shakespeare in Love* 1998

Maddin, Guy *Careful* 1992; *The Twilight of the Ice Nymphs* 1997

Magnoli, Albert *Purple Rain* 1984; *Born to Run* 1993; *Dark Planet* 1997

Mailer, Norman *Beyond the Law* 1968; *Tough Guys Don't Dance* 1987

Makavejev, Dusan *Innocence Unprotected* 1968; *WR – Mysteries of the Organism* 1971; *Montenegro* 1981; *The Coca-Cola Kid* 1985

Makin, Kelly *National Lampoon's Senior Trip* 1995; *Kids in the Hall: Brain Candy* 1996; *Mickey Blue Eyes* 1999

Makk, Karoly *Love* 1971; *Deadly Game* 1982; *Lily in Love* 1985; *The Gambler* 1997

Malick, Terrence *Badlands* 1973; *Days of Heaven* 1978; *The Thin Red Line* 1998

Malle, Louis *Le Monde du Silence* 1956; *Lift to the Scaffold* 1957; *The Lovers* 1958; *Zazie dans le Métro* 1960; *A Very Private Affair* 1962; *Le Feu Follet* 1963; *Viva Maria!* 1965; *The Thief of Paris* 1967; *Histoires Extraordinaires* 1967; *Phantom India* 1968; *Le Souffle au Coeur* 1971; *Lacombe Lucien* 1974; *Black Moon* 1974; *Pretty Baby* 1978; *Atlantic City USA* 1980; *My Dinner with Andre* 1981; *Crackers* 1984; *Alamo Bay* 1985; *God's Country* 1985; *Au Revoir les Enfants* 1987; *Milou en Mai* 1989; *Damage* 1992; *Vanya on 42nd Street* 1994

Malmuth, Bruce *Nighthawks* 1981; *Where Are the Children?* 1986; *Hard to Kill* 1989; *Pentathlon* 1994

Malone, Mark *Killer* 1994; *Hoods* 1998

Mamet, David *House of Games* 1987; *Things Change* 1988; *Homicide* 1991; *Oleanna* 1994; *The Spanish Prisoner* 1997; *The Winslow Boy* 1999

Mamoulian, Rouben *Applause* 1929; *City Streets* 1931; *Dr Jekyll and Mr Hyde* 1932; *Love Me Tonight* 1932; *Queen Christina* 1933; *The Song of Songs* 1933; *We Live Again* 1934; *Becky Sharp* 1935; *The Gay Desperado* 1936; *High, Wide and Handsome* 1937; *Golden Boy* 1939; *The Mark of Zorro* 1940; *Blood and Sand* 1941; *Rings on Her Fingers* 1942; *Summer Holiday* 1948; *Silk Stockings* 1957

Mandel, Robert *Independence Day* 1983; *F/X* 1985; *Touch and Go* 1986; *Perfect Witness* 1989; *The Haunted* 1991; *School Ties* 1992; *The Substitute* 1996; *Special Report: Journey to Mars* 1996

Mandoki, Luis *White Palace* 1990; *Born Yesterday* 1993; *When a Man Loves a Woman* 1994; *Message in a Bottle* 1998

Manduke, Joseph *Kid Vengeance* 1977; *The Gumshoe Kid* 1990

Mangold, James *Heavy* 1995; *Cop Land* 1997; *Girl, Interrupted* 1999

Mankiewicz, Joseph L *Dragonwyck* 1946; *The Ghost and Mrs Muir* 1947; *The Late George Apley* 1947; *House of Strangers* 1949; *A Letter to Three Wives* 1949; *All about Eve* 1950; *No Way Out* 1950; *People Will Talk* 1951; *5 Fingers* 1952; *Julius Caesar* 1953; *The Barefoot Contessa* 1954; *Guys and Dolls* 1955; *The Quiet American* 1958; *Suddenly, Last Summer* 1959; *Cleopatra* 1963; *The Honey Pot* 1967; *There Was a Crooked Man...* 1970; *King: a Filmed Record... Montgomery to Memphis* 1970; *Sleuth* 1972

Mankiewicz, Tom *Dragnet* 1987; *Delirious* 1991

Mann, Anthony *Dr Broadway* 1942; *The Great Flamarion* 1945; *Two O'Clock Courage* 1945; *Strange Impersonation* 1946; *Desperate* 1947; *T-Men* 1947; *Railroaded* 1947; *Raw Deal* 1948; *Border Incident* 1949; *Reign of Terror* 1949; *Devil's Doorway* 1950; *The Furies* 1950; *Side Street* 1950; *Winchester '73* 1950; *The Tall Target* 1951; *Bend of the River* 1952; *The Glenn Miller Story* 1953; *The Naked Spur* 1953; *Thunder Bay* 1953; *The Far Country* 1955; *The Last Frontier* 1955; *The Man from Laramie* 1955; *Strategic Air Command* 1955; *Serenade* 1956; *Men in War* 1957; *The Tin Star* 1957; *God's Little Acre* 1958; *Man of the West* 1958; *Cimarron* 1960; *El Cid* 1961; *The Fall of the Roman Empire* 1964; *The Heroes of Telemark* 1965; *A Dandy in Aspic* 1968

Mann, Daniel *Come Back, Little Sheba* 1952; *About Mrs Leslie* 1954; *I'll Cry Tomorrow* 1955; *The Rose Tattoo* 1955; *The Teahouse of the August Moon* 1956; *Hot Spell* 1958; *The Last Angry Man* 1959; *Butterfield 8* 1960; *The Mountain Road* 1960; *Ada* 1961; *Five Finger Exercise* 1962; *Who's Got the Action?* 1962; *Who's Been Sleeping in My Bed?* 1963; *Judith* 1966; *Our Man Flint* 1966; *For Love of Ivy* 1968; *A Dream of Kings* 1969; *Willard* 1971; *The Revengers* 1972; *Interval* 1973; *Lost in the Stars* 1974; *Matilda* 1978; *Playing for Time* 1980; *The Day the Loving Stopped* 1981; *The Man Who Broke 1,000 Chains* 1987

Mann, Delbert *Marty* 1955; *The Bachelor Party* 1957; *Desire under the Elms* 1958; *Separate Tables* 1958; *Middle of the Night* 1959; *The Dark at the Top of the Stairs* 1960; *Lover Come Back* 1961; *The Outsider* 1961; *That Touch of Mink* 1962; *A Gathering of Eagles* 1963; *Dear Heart* 1964; *Mister Buddwing* 1966; *Fitzwilly* 1967; *The Pink Jungle* 1968; *David Copperfield* 1969; *Jane Eyre* 1970; *Kidnapped* 1971; *Francis Gary Powers: the True Story of the U-2* 1976; *Birch Interval* 1976; *All Quiet on the Western Front* 1979; *Torn between Two Lovers* 1979; *Night Crossing* 1981; *Love Leads the Way* 1984; *Last Days of Patton* 1986; *The Ted Kennedy Jr Story* 1986; *Against Her Will* 1991; *Incident in a Small Town* 1993

Mann, Farhad *Nick Knight* 1989; *The Face of Fear* 1990; *Return to Two Moon Junction* 1994; *Lawnmower Man 2: Beyond Cyberspace* 1995; *Stranger in My Home* 1997

Mann, Michael *Thief* 1981; *The Keep* 1983; *Manhunter* 1986; *LA Takedown* 1989; *The Last of the Mohicans* 1992; *Heat* 1995; *The Insider* 1999

Mann, Ron *Comic Book Confidential* 1988; *Twist* 1992

Manners, Kim *Broken Badges* 1990; *Greyhounds* 1994

Marcel, Terry *aka* **Marcel, Terence** *There Goes the Bride* 1979; *Hawk the Slayer* 1980; *Jane and the Lost City* 1987; *Bejewelled* 1990; *The Last Seduction 2* 1998

Marcellini, Siro *The Secret Mark of D'Artagnan* 1962; *Hero of Babylon* 1963

March, Alex *Paper Lion* 1968; *The Big Bounce* 1969; *Mastermind* 1976; *The Amazing Captain Nemo* 1978

Margheriti, Antonio *aka* **Dawson, Anthony,** *aka* **Dawson, Anthony M** *The Long Hair of Death* 1964; *Blood Money* 1974; *Take a Hard Ride* 1975; *Killer Fish* 1978; *Yor, the Hunter from the Future* 1983; *Codename Wildgeese* 1984

Margolin, Stuart *A Shining Season* 1979; *The Room Upstairs* 1987; *Medicine River* 1992; *Double, Double Toil and Trouble* 1993; *Salt Water Moose* 1996

Marin, Edwin L *The Death Kiss* 1933; *The Casino Murder Case* 1935; *Speed* 1936; *A Christmas Carol* 1938; *Everybody Sing* 1938; *Listen, Darling* 1938; *Fast and Loose* 1939; *Maisie* 1939; *Florian* 1940; *Gold Rush Maisie* 1940; *Maisie Was a Lady* 1941; *Ringside Maisie* 1941; *Paris Calling* 1941; *A Gentleman after Dark* 1942; *Miss Annie Rooney* 1942; *Show Business* 1944; *Tall in the Saddle* 1944; *Abilene Town* 1945; *Johnny Angel* 1945; *Lady Luck* 1946; *Nocturne* 1946; *Intrigue* 1947; *Canadian Pacific* 1949; *Fighting Man of the Plains* 1949; *The Cariboo Trail* 1950; *Colt .45* 1950; *Fort Worth* 1951; *Sugarfoot* 1951

Marinos, Lex *Remember Me* 1985; *Boundaries of the Heart* 1988

Maris, Peter *Diplomatic Immunity* 1991; *Hangfire* 1991

Marker, Chris *La Jetée* 1962; *Le Joli Mai* 1962; *Sans Soleil* 1983

Markle, Fletcher *Jigsaw* 1949; *The Man with a Cloak* 1951; *The Incredible Journey* 1963

Markle, Peter *The Personals* 1982; *Hot Dog – The Movie* 1984; *Youngblood* 1986; *BAT-21* 1988; *Breaking Point* 1989; *Nightbreaker* 1989; *El Diablo* 1990; *In the Line of Duty: Mob Justice* 1991; *Through the Eyes of a Killer* 1992; *Wagons East!* 1994; *Jake Lassiter: Justice on the Bayou* 1995; *White Dwarf* 1995; *The Last Days of Frankie the Fly* 1996; *Target Earth* 1998

Markowitz, Robert *Voices* 1979; *The Belarus File* 1985; *Adam: His Song Continues* 1986; *A Cry for Help: the Tracey Thurman Story* 1989; *Decoration Day* 1990; *Too Young to Die?* 1990; *Afterburn* 1992; *Overexposed* 1992; *Because Mommy Works* 1994; *Twilight Zone: Rod Serling's Lost Classics* 1994; *The Tuskegee Airmen* 1995; *Into Thin Air: Death on Everest* 1997; *Nicholas' Gift* 1998

Marks, Arthur *Detroit 9000* 1973; *Friday Foster* 1975; *JD's Revenge* 1976

Marks, Ross Kagan *Homage* 1995; *The Twilight of the Golds* 1996

Marquand, Richard *The Legacy* 1978; *Birth of the Beatles* 1979; *Eye of the Needle* 1981; *Return of the Jedi* 1983; *Until September* 1984; *Jagged Edge* 1985; *Hearts of Fire* 1987

Marshall, Frank *Arachnophobia* 1990; *Alive* 1992; *Congo* 1995

Marshall, Garry *Young Doctors in Love* 1982; *The Flamingo Kid* 1984; *Nothing in Common* 1986; *Overboard* 1987; *Beaches* 1988; *Pretty Woman* 1990; *Frankie & Johnny* 1991; *Exit to Eden* 1994; *Dear God* 1996; *The Other Sister* 1999; *Runaway Bride* 1999

Marshall, George *Pack Up Your Troubles* 1932; *Their First Mistake* 1932; *Towed in a Hole* 1932; *In Old Kentucky* 1935; *Life Begins at 40* 1935; *A Message to Garcia* 1936; *Nancy Steele Is Missing* 1937; *The Goldwyn Follies* 1938; *Hold That Co-Ed* 1938; *Destry Rides Again* 1939; *You Can't Cheat an Honest Man* 1939; *The Ghost Breakers* 1940; *When the Daltons Rode* 1940; *The Golden Hour* 1941; *Texas* 1941; *Valley of the Sun* 1942; *Star Spangled Rhythm* 1942; *Riding High* 1943; *True to Life* 1943; *Hold That Blonde* 1945; *Incendiary Blonde* 1945; *Murder, He Says* 1945; *The Blue Dahlia* 1946; *Monsieur Beaucaire* 1946; *Variety Girl* 1947; *The Perils of Pauline* 1947; *My Friend Irma* 1949; *Fancy Pants* 1950; *Never a Dull Moment* 1950; *A Millionaire for Christy* 1951; *Houdini* 1953; *Military Policeman* 1953; *Money from Home* 1953; *Scared Stiff* 1953; *Off Limits* 1953; *The Savage* 1953; *Destry* 1954; *Duel in the Jungle* 1954; *Red Garters* 1954; *Pillars of the Sky* 1956; *The Sad Sack* 1957; *Beyond Mombasa* 1957; *The Sheepman* 1958; *Imitation General* 1958; *The Gazebo* 1959; *It Started with a Kiss* 1959; *The Mating Game* 1959; *Cry for Happy* 1961; *The Happy Thieves* 1962; *Papa's Delicate Condition* 1963; *Advance to the Rear* 1964; *Boy, Did I Get a Wrong Number* 1966; *Eight on the Lam* 1967; *Hook, Line and Sinker* 1969

Marshall, Penny *Jumpin' Jack Flash* 1986; *Big* 1988; *Awakenings* 1990; *A League of Their Own* 1992; *Renaissance Man* 1994; *The Preacher's Wife* 1996

Martin, Charles *My Dear Secretary* 1948; *Death of a Scoundrel* 1956; *One Man Jury* 1978

Martin, Eugenio *aka* **Martin, Gene** *Bad Man's River* 1971; *Horror Express* 1972

Martin, Richard *Wounded* 1996; *Air Bud: Golden Receiver* 1998

Martini, Richard *You Can't Hurry Love* 1988; *You Can't Hurry Love* 1988; *Limit Up* 1989

Martinson, Leslie H *aka* **Martinson, Leslie** *The Atomic Kid* 1954; *PT 109* 1963; *Batman* 1966; *Fathom* 1967; *Mrs Pollifax – Spy* 1970; *And Millions Will Die!* 1973; *Cruise Missile* 1978

Marton, Andrew *King Solomon's Mines* 1950; *The Devil Makes Three* 1952; *The Wild North* 1952; *Green Fire* 1954; *Gypsy Colt* 1954; *Men of the Fighting Lady* 1954; *Prisoner of War* 1954; *The Longest Day* 1962; *55 Days at Peking* 1963; *The Thin Red Line* 1964; *Clarence, the Cross-Eyed Lion* 1965; *Crack in the World* 1965; *Around the World under the Sea* 1966; *Africa – Texas Style* 1967

Maselli, Francesco *Love in the City* 1953; *A Fine Pair* 1969

Mason, Herbert *His Lordship* 1936; *Strange Boarders* 1938; *A Window in London* 1939; *Back Room Boy* 1942

Massot, Joe *Wonderwall* 1968; *The Song Remains the Same* 1976
Masters, Quentin *Thumb Tripping* 1972; *The Stud* 1978; *A Dangerous Summer* 1981
Masterson, Peter *The Trip to Bountiful* 1985; *Blood Red* 1988; *Full Moon in Blue Water* 1988; *Night Game* 1989; *Convicts* 1991; *Arctic Blue* 1993; *Lily Dale* 1996
Mastorakis, Nico *Next One* 1984; *Blind Date* 1984; *Hired to Kill* 1990
Mastroianni, Armand *He Knows You're Alone* 1981; *Distortions* 1987; *Cameron's Closet* 1988; *Desperate Justice* 1993; *Come Die with Me* 1994; *One of Her Own* 1994; *Victim of Rage* 1994; *Robin Cook's Formula for Death* 1995; *Sleep, Baby, Sleep* 1995; *Dare to Love* 1995
Maté, Rudolph *The Dark Past* 1948; *DOA* 1949; *Branded* 1950; *No Sad Songs for Me* 1950; *Union Station* 1950; *When Worlds Collide* 1951; *The Prince Who Was a Thief* 1951; *The Mississippi Gambler* 1953; *Second Chance* 1953; *Forbidden* 1953; *The Black Shield of Falworth* 1954; *The Siege at Red River* 1954; *The Violent Men* 1955; *The Far Horizons* 1955; *Miracle in the Rain* 1956; *The Rawhide Years* 1956; *Three Violent People* 1956; *The Deep Six* 1958; *For the First Time* 1959; *Seven Seas to Calais* 1962; *The 300 Spartans* 1962
Matheson, Tim *Breach of Conduct* 1994; *Tails You Live, Heads You're Dead* 1995
Matthau, Charles *Doin' Time on Planet Earth* 1988; *Mrs Lambert Remembers Love* 1991; *The Grass Harp* 1995; *The Marriage Fool* 1998
Maurer, Norman *The Three Stooges Go around the World in a Daze* 1963; *The Outlaws Is Coming* 1965
Maxwell, Peter *Dilemma* 1962; *Serena* 1962; *Impact* 1963; *Run, Rebecca, Run* 1981
Maxwell, Ronald F *Little Darlings* 1980; *The Night the Lights Went Out in Georgia* 1981; *Parent Trap II* 1986; *Gettysburg* 1993
May, Bradford *Legacy of Lies* 1992; *Mortal Sins* 1992; *Marilyn and Bobby: Her Final Affair* 1993; *Trouble Shooters: Trapped beneath the Earth* 1993; *Madonna: Innocence Lost* 1994; *Darkman II – the Return of Durant* 1995; *Lethal Intent* 1995; *The Return of Hunter: Everyone Walks in LA* 1995; *Ed McBain's 87th Precinct: Ice* 1996
May, Elaine *A New Leaf* 1971; *The Heartbreak Kid* 1972; *Mikey and Nicky* 1976; *Ishtar* 1987
May, Joe *Heimkehr* 1928; *Asphalt* 1928; *Confession* 1937; *The Invisible Man Returns* 1940; *And So They Were Married* 1944
Mayberry, Russ *The Spaceman and King Arthur* 1979; *Side by Side* 1982
Mayer, Gerald *The Sellout* 1951; *Bright Road* 1953; *The Marauders* 1955
Mayfield, Les *California Man* 1992; *Miracle on 34th Street* 1994; *Flubber* 1997; *Blue Streak* 1999
Maylam, Tony *The Riddle of the Sands* 1978; *The Burning* 1981; *Hero* 1987; *Split Second* 1991
Mayo, Archie *Doorway to Hell* 1931; *Illicit* 1931; *Svengali* 1931; *Night after Night* 1932; *The Mayor of Hell* 1933; *Ever in My Heart* 1933; *Gambling Lady* 1934; *Bordertown* 1935; *The Case of the Lucky Legs* 1935; *Go into Your Dance* 1935; *The Petrified Forest* 1936; *The Black Legion* 1937; *It's Love I'm After* 1937; *The Adventures of Marco Polo* 1938; *They Shall Have Music* 1939; *Four Sons* 1940; *Charley's Aunt* 1941; *Confirm or Deny* 1941; *The Great American Broadcast* 1941; *Moontide* 1942; *Orchestra Wives* 1942; *Crash Dive* 1943; *Sweet and Lowdown* 1944; *Angel on My Shoulder* 1946; *A Night in Casablanca* 1946
Mayron, Melanie *The Baby-Sitter's Club* 1995; *Freaky Friday* 1995; *Toothless* 1997
Mazo, Michael *Time Runner* 1993; *Crackerjack* 1994
Mazursky, Paul *Bob & Carol & Ted & Alice* 1969; *Alex in Wonderland* 1970; *Blume in Love* 1973; *Harry and Tonto* 1974; *Next Stop, Greenwich Village* 1976; *An Unmarried Woman* 1978; *Willie and Phil* 1980; *Tempest* 1982; *Moscow on the Hudson* 1984; *Down and Out in Beverly Hills* 1986; *Moon over Parador* 1988; *Enemies, a Love Story* 1989; *Scenes from a Mall* 1991; *The Pickle* 1993; *Faithful* 1996; *Winchell* 1998
Mead, Nick *Bank Robber* 1993; *Swing* 1998
Meadows, Shane *Smalltime* 1996; *TwentyFourSeven* 1997; *A Room for Romeo Brass* 1999
Meckler, Nancy *Sister My Sister* 1994; *Alive and Kicking* 1996
Medak, Peter *A Day in the Death of Joe Egg* 1971; *The Ruling Class* 1972; *Ghost in the Noonday Sun* 1973; *The Odd Job* 1978; *The Changeling* 1980; *Zorro, the Gay Blade* 1981; *The Men's Club* 1986; *The Krays* 1990; *Let Him Have It* 1991; *Romeo Is Bleeding* 1992; *Pontiac Moon* 1994; *The Hunchback* 1997; *Species II* 1998
Medem, Julio *Vacas* 1992; *The Red Squirrel* 1993; *Tierra* 1995; *The Lovers of the Arctic Circle* 1998
Medford, Don *To Trap a Spy* 1966; *The Hunting Party* 1971; *The Organization* 1971
Megahy, Francis *Taffin* 1988; *Red Sun Rising* 1994; *The Disappearance of Kevin Johnson* 1995
Mehta, Deepa aka **Mehta Saltzman, Deepa** *Martha, Ruth and Edie* 1988; *Sam and Me* 1991; *Camilla* 1993; *Fire* 1996; *Earth* 1998
Mehta, Ketan *Mirch Masala* 1987; *Maya* 1992; *Sardar* 1993
Melançon, André *The Dog Who Stopped the War* 1984; *Bach and Broccoli* 1986; *Summer of the Colt* 1989
Melendez, Bill *A Boy Named Charlie Brown* 1969; *Snoopy, Come Home* 1972; *Race for Your Life, Charlie Brown* 1977; *The Lion, the Witch and the Wardrobe* 1978; *Bon Voyage, Charlie Brown* 1980
Melford, Austin *Car of Dreams* 1935; *Oh Daddy!* 1935
Melville, Jean-Pierre *Le Silence de la Mer* 1947; *Les Enfants Terribles* 1949; *Bob Le Flambeur* 1955; *Two Men in Manhattan* 1959; *Léon Morin, Priest* 1961; *Le Doulos* 1962; *Le Deuxième Souffle* 1966; *Le Samouraï* 1967; *L'Armée des Ombres* 1969; *The Red Circle* 1970; *Dirty Money* 1972
Menaul, Christopher *Fatherland* 1994; *Feast of July* 1995
Mendeluk, George *The Kidnapping of the President* 1980; *Stone Cold Dead* 1980; *Meatballs III: Summer Job* 1987
Mendes, Lothar *Four Feathers* 1929; *The Marriage Playground* 1929; *Paramount on Parade* 1930; *Ladies' Man* 1931; *If I Had a Million* 1932; *Payment Deferred* 1932; *Jew Süss* 1934; *The Man Who Could Work Miracles* 1936; *Moonlight Sonata* 1937; *Flight for Freedom* 1943
Menendez, Ramon *Stand and Deliver* 1988; *Money for Nothing* 1993
Menges, Chris *A World Apart* 1987; *CrissCross* 1992; *Second Best* 1994; *The Lost Son* 1998
Menzel, Jirí *Closely Observed Trains* 1966; *Capricious Summer* 1968; *Larks on a String* 1969; *Cutting It Short* 1980; *My Sweet Little Village* 1986; *The Last of the Good Old Days* 1989; *The Life and Extraordinary Adventures of Private Ivan Chonkin* 1994
Menzies, William Cameron *Things to Come* 1936; *The Green Cockatoo* 1937; *The Thief of Bagdad* 1940; *Address Unknown* 1944; *The Whip Hand* 1951; *Invaders from Mars* 1953
Merchant, Ismail *In Custody* 1993; *The Proprietor* 1996; *Cotton Mary* 1999
Merendino, James *Hard Drive* 1994; *SLC Punk!* 1999
Merhi, Joseph *CIA – Codename Alexa* 1992; *Inflammable* 1994; *Rage* 1995; *Executive Target* 1997
Merrill, Kieth *The Great American Cowboy* 1973; *Take Down* 1978; *Windwalker* 1980; *Harry's War* 1981
Mészáros, Marta *Diary for My Children* 1982; *Diary for My Loves* 1987; *Diary for My Father and Mother* 1990
Metter, Alan *Girls Just Want to Have Fun* 1985; *Back to School* 1986; *Moving* 1988; *Cold Dog Soup* 1989; *Working Trash* 1990; *Police Academy: Mission to Moscow* 1994
Metzger, Alan *The China Lake Murders* 1990; *Murder COD* 1990; *Exclusive* 1992; *From the Files of Joseph Wambaugh: a Jury of One* 1992; *In the Shadow of a Killer* 1992; *Black Widow Murders* 1993; *Deadly Vows* 1994; *New Eden* 1994; *Roommates* 1994; *Dangerous Affair* 1995; *Trial by Fire* 1995; *Indecent Seduction* 1996; *Frequent Flyer* 1996; *Nightmare in Big Sky Country* 1998
Meyer, Kevin *Under Investigation* 1993; *Perfect Alibi* 1995
Meyer, Muffie *Grey Gardens* 1975; *Enormous Changes at the Last Minute* 1983
Meyer, Nicholas *Time after Time* 1979; *Star Trek II: the Wrath of Khan* 1982; *The Day After* 1983; *Volunteers* 1985; *The Deceivers* 1988; *Company Business* 1991; *Star Trek VI: the Undiscovered Country* 1991; *Vendetta* 1999
Meyer, Russ *Immoral Mr Teas* 1959; *Lorna* 1964; *Fanny Hill: Memoirs of a Woman of Pleasure* 1964; *Faster, Pussycat! Kill! Kill!* 1965; *Motor Psycho* 1965; *Mudhoney* 1965; *Common Law Cabin* 1967; *Good Morning… and Goodbye* 1967; *Finders Keepers, Lovers Weepers* 1968; *Vixen* 1968; *Cherry, Harry & Raquel* 1969; *Beyond the Valley of the Dolls* 1970; *The Seven Minutes* 1971; *Supervixens* 1975; *Up* 1976; *Beneath the Valley of the Ultra Vixens* 1979
Meyers, Janet *Letter to My Killer* 1995; *The Ripper* 1997
Michaels, Richard *Once upon a Family* 1980; *Heart of a Champion: the Ray Mancini Story* 1985; *Rockabye* 1986; *Indiscreet* 1988; *Red River* 1988; *The Queen of Mean* 1990; *Backfield in Motion* 1991; *Lethal Charm* 1991; *Triumph of the Heart* 1991; *Father and Scout* 1994
Michell, Roger *Persuasion* 1995; *Titanic Town* 1998; *Notting Hill* 1999
Mihalka, George *The Final Heist* 1991; *Edge of Deception* 1994; *Bullet to Beijing* 1995; *Relative Fear* 1995
Mikhalkov, Nikita *An Unfinished Piece for Mechanical Piano* 1976; *Oblomov* 1980; *A Private Conversation* 1983; *Dark Eyes* 1987; *Urga* 1990; *Burnt by the Sun* 1994; *The Barber of Siberia* 1999
Miles, Bernard *Tawny Pipit* 1944; *Chance of a Lifetime* 1950
Miles, Christopher *The Virgin and the Gypsy* 1970; *A Time for Loving* 1971; *The Maids* 1974; *That Lucky Touch* 1975; *Priest of Love* 1981; *The Clandestine Marriage* 1999
Milestone, Lewis *The Kid Brother* 1927; *Two Arabian Knights* 1927; *The Racket* 1928; *All Quiet on the Western Front* 1930; *The Front Page* 1931; *Rain* 1932; *Hallelujah, I'm a Bum* 1933; *The Captain Hates the Sea* 1934; *Anything Goes* 1936; *The General Died at Dawn* 1936; *Of Mice and Men* 1939; *Lucky Partners* 1940; *My Life with Caroline* 1941; *Edge of Darkness* 1943; *The North Star* 1943; *The Purple Heart* 1944; *A Walk in the Sun* 1945; *The Strange Love of Martha Ivers* 1946; *Arch of Triumph* 1948; *No Minor Vices* 1948; *The Red Pony* 1949; *Halls of Montezuma* 1950; *Les Misérables* 1952; *Kangaroo* 1952; *They Who Dare* 1953; *Pork Chop Hill* 1959; *Ocean's Eleven* 1960; *Mutiny on the Bounty* 1962
Milius, John *Dillinger* 1973; *The Wind and the Lion* 1975; *Big Wednesday* 1978; *Conan the Barbarian* 1982; *Red Dawn* 1984; *Farewell to the King* 1988; *Flight of the Intruder* 1991; *Motorcycle Gang* 1994
Milland, Ray aka **Milland, R** *A Man Alone* 1955; *Lisbon* 1956; *The Safecracker* 1958; *Panic in Year Zero* 1962; *Hostile Witness* 1968
Millar, Gavin *Dreamchild* 1985; *Danny, the Champion of the World* 1989; *Complicity* 1999
Millar, Stuart *When the Legends Die* 1972; *Rooster Cogburn* 1975
Miller (1), George *The Man from Snowy River* 1982; *The Aviator* 1985; *Les Patterson Saves the World* 1987; *Farewell Miss Freedom* 1988; *A Mom for Christmas* 1990; *The NeverEnding Story II: the Next Chapter* 1991; *Frozen Assets* 1992; *Over the Hill* 1992; *Andre* 1994; *The Great Elephant Escape* 1995; *Silver Strand* 1995; *Zeus and Roxanne* 1997; *Tidal Wave: No Escape* 1997; *In the Doghouse* 1998
Miller (2), George *Mad Max* 1979; *Mad Max 2* 1981; *Twilight Zone: the Movie* 1983; *Mad Max beyond Thunderdome* 1985; *Lorenzo's Oil* 1992; *Babe: Pig in the City* 1998
Miller, Claude *Garde à Vue* 1981; *An Impudent Girl* 1985; *La Petite Voleuse* 1988; *L'Accompagnatrice* 1992; *Les Enfants de Lumière* 1995; *Class Trip* 1998; *Class Trip* 1998
Miller, David *Billy the Kid* 1941; *Flying Tigers* 1942; *Love Happy* 1949; *Our Very Own* 1950; *Sudden Fear* 1952; *Beautiful Stranger* 1954; *Diane* 1955; *The Opposite Sex* 1956; *The Story of Esther Costello* 1957; *Happy Anniversary* 1959; *Midnight Lace* 1960; *Back Street* 1961; *Lonely Are the Brave* 1962; *Captain Newman, MD* 1963; *Hail, Hero!* 1969; *Executive Action* 1973; *Bittersweet Love* 1976
Miller, Harvey *Bad Medicine* 1985; *Getting Away with Murder* 1996
Miller, Michael aka **Miller, Michael L** *Jackson County Jail* 1976; *National Lampoon's Class Reunion* 1982; *Silent Rage* 1982; *Silent Witness* 1985; *Can You Feel Me Dancing?* 1986; *Necessity* 1988; *Always Remember I Love You* 1990; *Dangerous Passion* 1990; *Daddy* 1991; *Palomino* 1991; *Criminal Behaviour* 1992; *Heartbeat* 1992; *Danielle Steel's Star* 1993; *Judith Krantz's Torch Song* 1993; *Danielle Steel's Once in a Lifetime* 1994; *Barbara Taylor Bradford's Everything to Gain* 1996
Miller, Mollie *The BRAT Patrol* 1986; *Student Exchange* 1987; *Parent Trap Hawaiian Honeymoon* 1989
Miller, Randall *Class Act* 1992; *Houseguest* 1995; *The Sixth Man* 1997
Miller, Robert Ellis *Any Wednesday* 1966; *The Heart Is a Lonely Hunter* 1968; *Sweet November* 1968; *The Buttercup Chain* 1970; *The Girl from Petrovka* 1974; *The Baltimore Bullet* 1980; *Reuben, Reuben* 1983; *Her Life as a Man* 1984; *Hawks* 1988; *Brenda Starr* 1989; *Bed & Breakfast* 1992; *Killer Rules* 1993; *A Walton Wedding* 1995
Miller, Sam *Among Giants* 1998; *Elephant Juice* 1999
Miller, Troy *Beverly Hills Family Robinson* 1997; *Jack Frost* 1998
Milton, Robert *Outward Bound* 1930; *Westward Passage* 1932
Miner, Steve *Friday the 13th Part 2* 1981; *Friday the 13th Part III* 1982; *House* 1986; *Soul Man* 1986; *Warlock* 1989; *Wild Hearts Can't Be Broken* 1991; *Forever Young* 1992; *My Father, the Hero* 1994; *Big Bully* 1996; *Halloween H20: 20 Years Later* 1998; *Lake Placid* 1999
Minghella, Anthony *Truly Madly Deeply* 1990; *Mr Wonderful* 1992; *The English Patient* 1996; *The Talented Mr Ripley* 1999
Minkoff, Rob *The Lion King* 1994; *Stuart Little* 1999
Minnelli, Vincente *Cabin in the Sky* 1943; *I Dood It* 1943; *Meet Me in St Louis* 1944; *Ziegfeld Follies* 1944; *The Clock* 1945; *Yolande and the Thief* 1945; *Undercurrent* 1946; *The Pirate* 1948; *Madame Bovary* 1949; *Father of the Bride* 1950; *An American in Paris* 1951; *Father's Little Dividend* 1951; *The Bad and the Beautiful* 1952; *The Band Wagon* 1953; *The Story of Three Loves* 1953; *Brigadoon* 1954; *The Long, Long Trailer* 1954; *The Cobweb* 1955; *Kismet* 1955; *Lust for Life* 1956; *Tea and Sympathy* 1956; *Designing Woman* 1957;

RadioTimes DIRECTORS' INDEX

1954; *This Island Earth* 1955; *Kiss of Fire* 1955; *The Big Circus* 1959; *Tarzan, the Ape Man* 1959; *The George Raft Story* 1961; *King of the Roaring 20s – the Story of Arnold Rothstein* 1961; *A Thunder of Drums* 1961
Newman, Paul *Rachel, Rachel* 1968; *Never Give an Inch* 1971; *The Effect of Gamma Rays on Man-in-the-Moon Marigolds* 1972; *The Shadow Box* 1980; *Harry and Son* 1984; *The Glass Menagerie* 1987
Newmeyer, Fred C *A Sailor-Made Man* 1921; *Safety Last* 1923; *Girl Shy* 1924; *Hot Water* 1924; *The Freshman* 1925; *Fast and Loose* 1930
Newton, Joel *Main Street to Broadway* 1953; *Jennifer* 1953
Nibbelink, Phil *An American Tail: Fievel Goes West* 1991; *We're Back! A Dinosaur's Story* 1993
Niblo, Fred *The Mark of Zorro* 1920; *The Three Musketeers* 1921; *Blood and Sand* 1922; *Ben-Hur: a Tale of Christ* 1925; *The Temptress* 1926; *Camille* 1927; *The Mysterious Lady* 1928
Nichetti, Maurizio *The Icicle Thief* 1989; *Volere, Volare* 1991
Nichols, Dudley *Sister Kenny* 1946; *Mourning Becomes Electra* 1947
Nichols Jr, George *Anne of Green Gables* 1934; *Finishing School* 1934; *The Return of Peter Grimm* 1935; *Chatterbox* 1936; *The Adventures of Michael Strogoff* 1937; *Man of Conquest* 1939
Nichols, Mike *Who's Afraid of Virginia Woolf?* 1966; *The Graduate* 1967; *Catch-22* 1970; *Carnal Knowledge* 1971; *The Day of the Dolphin* 1973; *The Fortune* 1975; *Silkwood* 1983; *Heartburn* 1986; *Biloxi Blues* 1988; *Working Girl* 1988; *Postcards from the Edge* 1990; *Regarding Henry* 1991; *Wolf* 1994; *The Birdcage* 1996; *Primary Colors* 1998
Nicholson, Jack *Drive, He Said* 1971; *Goin' South* 1978; *The Two Jakes* 1990
Nicolaou, Ted *TerrorVision* 1986; *Dragonworld* 1994; *Dragonworld: the Legend Continues* 1997
Nicolella, John *Mickey Spillane's Mike Hammer: Murder Takes All* 1989; *Rock Hudson* 1990; *Kull the Conqueror* 1997
Nilsson, Rob *Signal 7* 1983; *On the Edge* 1985; *Heat and Sunlight* 1988; *Chalk* 1996; *A Town Has Turned to Dust* 1998
Nimoy, Leonard *Star Trek III: the Search for Spock* 1984; *Star Trek IV: the Voyage Home* 1986; *Three Men and a Baby* 1987; *The Good Mother* 1988; *Funny about Love* 1990; *Holy Matrimony* 1994
Nolbandov, Sergei *Ships with Wings* 1942; *Undercover* 1943
Norman, Leslie *The Night My Number Came Up* 1955; *X the Unknown* 1956; *The Shiralee* 1957; *Dunkirk* 1958; *The Long and the Short and the Tall* 1960; *Season of Passion* 1960; *Spare the Rod* 1961
Norrington, Stephen *Death Machine* 1994; *Blade* 1998
Norris, Aaron *Platoon Leader* 1988; *Delta Force 2* 1990; *The Hitman* 1991; *Hellbound* 1993; *Sidekicks* 1993; *Top Dog* 1995; *Walker: Texas Ranger* 1997
Norton, Bill L *aka* **Norton, B W L**, *aka* **Norton, Bill** *Cisco Pike* 1971; *More American Graffiti* 1979; *Baby: Secret of the Lost Legend* 1985; *Three for the Road* 1987; *Grand Slam* 1990; *Deadly Whispers* 1995; *Welcome to Paradise* 1995; *Them* 1996; *Bad to the Bone* 1997; *Thirst* 1998
Nosseck, Max *The Brighton Strangler* 1945; *Dillinger* 1945; *Black Beauty* 1946
Nosseck, Noel *Dreamer* 1979; *King of the Mountain* 1981; *Full Exposure: the Sex Tapes Scandal* 1989; *Opposites Attract* 1990; *Born Too Soon* 1993; *Falsely Accused* 1993; *French Silk* 1993; *No One Would Tell* 1996; *Search for Justice* 1996; *Tornado!* 1996; *What Kind of Mother Are You?* 1996; *Nightscream* 1997; *The Killing Secret* 1997
Nossiter, Jonathan *Resident Alien* 1990; *Sunday* 1997
Nostro, Nick *aka* **Howard, Nick** *Spartacus and the Ten Gladiators* 1964; *One after the Other* 1968
Noyce, Phillip *Newsfront* 1978; *Heatwave* 1983; *Shadows of the Peacock* 1987; *Dead Calm* 1988; *Blind Fury* 1990; *Patriot Games* 1992; *Sliver* 1993; *Clear and Present Danger* 1994; *The Saint* 1997; *The Bone Collector* 1999
Nugent, Elliott *Life Begins* 1932; *Enter Madame!* 1933; *If I Were Free* 1933; *She Loves Me Not* 1934; *Splendor* 1935; *And So They Were Married* 1936; *The Cat and the Canary* 1939; *Never Say Die* 1939; *Nothing but the Truth* 1941; *The Male Animal* 1942; *The Crystal Ball* 1943; *Up in Arms* 1944; *My Favorite Brunette* 1947; *Welcome Stranger* 1947; *My Girl Tisa* 1948; *The Great Gatsby* 1949; *Mr Belvedere Goes to College* 1949; *Just for You* 1952
Nunez, Victor *Gal Young Un* 1979; *A Flash of Green* 1984; *Ruby in Paradise* 1993; *Ulee's Gold* 1997
Nunn, Trevor *Lady Jane* 1985; *Twelfth Night* 1996
Nutley, Colin *House of Angels* 1992; *House of Angels II: The Second Summer* 1994
Nyby, Christian *The Thing from Another World* 1951; *Operation CIA* 1965; *First to Fight* 1967
Nyby II, Christian I *Too Good to Be True* 1988; *Whisperkill* 1988

O

O'Bannon, Dan *Return of the Living Dead* 1985; *The Resurrected* 1992
O'Bannon, Rockne S *Fear* 1990; *Deadly Invasion* 1995
Oboler, Arch *Strange Holiday* 1942; *Bewitched* 1945; *The Arnelo Affair* 1947; *Five* 1951; *Bwana Devil* 1952
O'Brien, Edmond *Shield for Murder* 1954; *Man-Trap* 1961
O'Brien, Jim *The Dressmaker* 1988; *Foreign Affairs* 1993
Obrow, Jeffrey *The Kindred* 1986; *The Servants of Twilight* 1991; *Bram Stoker's Legend of the Mummy* 1998
O'Connolly, Jim *aka* **O'Connolly, James** *The Hi-Jackers* 1963; *Smokescreen* 1964; *Crooks and Coronets* 1969; *The Valley of Gwangi* 1969; *Tower of Evil* 1972
O'Connor, Pat *Cal* 1984; *A Month in the Country* 1987; *Stars and Bars* 1988; *The January Man* 1989; *Fools of Fortune* 1990; *Zelda* 1993; *Circle of Friends* 1995; *Inventing the Abbotts* 1997; *Dancing at Lughnasa* 1998
Oedekerk, Steve *Ace Ventura: When Nature Calls* 1995; *Nothing to Lose* 1997
O'Fallon, Peter *Dead Silence* 1991; *Suicide Kings* 1997
O'Ferrall, George More *Angels One Five* 1952; *The Holly and the Ivy* 1952; *Three Cases of Murder* 1954; *The Woman for Joe* 1955
Ogilvie, George *Mad Max beyond Thunderdome* 1985; *The Shiralee* 1986
O'Hara, Gerry *The Pleasure Girls* 1965; *Maroc 7* 1967; *The Bitch* 1979
O'Herlihy, Michael *The Fighting Prince of Donegal* 1966; *The One and Only, Genuine, Original Family Band* 1968; *Smith!* 1969; *Deadly Harvest* 1972; *Cry of the Innocent* 1980
Olin, Ken *The Broken Cord* 1992; *White Fang 2: Myth of the White Wolf* 1994; *In Pursuit of Honor* 1995
Olivier, Laurence *Henry V* 1944; *Hamlet* 1948; *Richard III* 1955; *The Prince and the Showgirl* 1957; *Three Sisters* 1970
Olmi, Ermanno *Il Posto* 1961; *The Tree of Wooden Clogs* 1978; *Long Live the Lady!* 1987; *The Legend of the Holy Drinker* 1988
O'Neil, Robert Vincent *Paco* 1975; *Angel* 1984; *Avenging Angel* 1985
Ophüls, Marcel *Love at Twenty* 1962; *The Sorrow and the Pity* 1970; *A Sense of Loss* 1972; *Hotel Terminus: the Life and Times of Klaus Barbie* 1987
Ophüls, Max *Liebelei* 1932; *La Signora di Tutti* 1934; *The Exile* 1947; *Letter from an Unknown Woman* 1948; *Caught* 1949; *The Reckless Moment* 1949; *La Ronde* 1950; *Le Plaisir* 1951; *Madame de...* 1953; *Lola Montès* 1955
Orme, Stuart *The Wolves of Willoughby Chase* 1988; *The Heist* 1989; *The Puppet Masters* 1994
Orr, James *Mr Destiny* 1990; *Man of the House* 1994
Ortega, Kenny *The News Boys* 1992; *Hocus Pocus* 1993
Oshii, Mamoru *Patlabor: the Mobile Police* 1989; *Ghost in the Shell* 1995
Oshima, Nagisa *Death by Hanging* 1968; *In the Realm of the Senses* 1976; *Merry Christmas Mr Lawrence* 1982; *Max Mon Amour* 1986
O'Sullivan, Thaddeus *December Bride* 1990; *Nothing Personal* 1995; *Ordinary Decent Criminal* 1999
Oswald, Gerd *A Kiss before Dying* 1956; *The Brass Legend* 1956; *Fury at Showdown* 1957; *Valerie* 1957; *Crime of Passion* 1957; *Screaming Mimi* 1958; *Paris Holiday* 1958; *Eighty Steps to Jonah* 1969; *Bunny O'Hare* 1971
Oswald, Richard *aka* **Ornstein, Richard** *The Living Dead* 1932; *The Lovable Cheat* 1949
Othenin-Girard, Dominique *After Darkness* 1985; *Halloween 5* 1989; *Omen IV: the Awakening* 1991
Otto, Linda *Unspeakable Acts* 1990; *Shattered Silence* 1992; *Shattering the Silence* 1992; *Switching Parents* 1992
Ouedraogo, Idrissa *Yam Daabo* 1986; *Yaaba* 1989; *Tilaï* 1990; *Samba Traore* 1992; *Le Cri du Coeur* 1994; *Kini and Adams* 1997
Ouellette, Jean-Paul *The Unnamable* 1988; *The Unnamable Returns* 1992
Oury, Gérard *Don't Look Now... We're Being Shot At* 1966; *The Brain* 1969; *Delusions of Grandeur* 1971
Owen, Cliff *Offbeat* 1960; *A Prize of Arms* 1961; *The Wrong Arm of the Law* 1962; *A Man Could Get Killed* 1966; *That Riviera Touch* 1966; *The Magnificent Two* 1967; *The Vengeance of She* 1968; *Ooh... You Are Awful* 1972; *Steptoe and Son* 1972; *No Sex Please, We're British* 1973
Owen, Don *Nobody Waved Goodbye* 1964; *Partners* 1976; *Unfinished Business* 1983
Oz, Frank *The Dark Crystal* 1982; *The Muppets Take Manhattan* 1984; *Little Shop of Horrors* 1986; *Dirty Rotten Scoundrels* 1988; *What about Bob?* 1991; *HouseSitter* 1992; *The Indian in the Cupboard* 1995; *In & Out* 1997; *Bowfinger* 1999
Ozpetek, Ferzan *The Turkish Bath* 1996; *Harem Suare* 1999
Ozu, Yasujiro *I Was Born, but...* 1932; *The Only Son* 1936; *Record of a Tenement Gentleman* 1947; *Hen in the Wind* 1948; *Late Spring* 1949; *Early Summer* 1951; *The Flavour of Green Tea over Rice* 1952; *Tokyo Story* 1953; *Early Spring* 1956; *Equinox Flower* 1958; *Good Morning* 1959; *Floating Weeds* 1959; *Late Autumn* 1960; *Early Autumn* 1961; *An Autumn Afternoon* 1962

P

Pabst, G W *The Joyless Street* 1925; *The Love of Jeanne Ney* 1927; *Diary of a Lost Girl* 1929; *Pandora's Box* 1929; *Westfront 1918* 1930; *Kameradschaft* 1931; *The Threepenny Opera* 1931; *Don Quixote* 1933; *Mademoiselle Docteur* 1936; *Paracelsus* 1943
Page, Anthony *Inadmissible Evidence* 1968; *Alpha Beta* 1973; *I Never Promised You a Rose Garden* 1977; *Absolution* 1978; *The Lady Vanishes* 1979; *FDR: the Last Year* 1980; *The Patricia Neal Story: an Act of Love* 1981; *Bill* 1981; *Forbidden* 1985; *Second Serve* 1986; *Pack of Lies* 1987; *Scandal in a Small Town* 1988; *Chernobyl: the Final Warning* 1991
Pagnol, Marcel *Jofroi* 1933; *César* 1936; *The Baker's Wife* 1938; *Topaze* 1951; *Manon des Sources* 1952
Pakula, Alan J *The Sterile Cuckoo* 1969; *Klute* 1971; *Love and Pain and the Whole Damn Thing* 1973; *The Parallax View* 1974; *All the President's Men* 1976; *Comes a Horseman* 1978; *Starting Over* 1979; *Rollover* 1981; *Sophie's Choice* 1982; *Dream Lover* 1986; *Orphans* 1987; *See You in the Morning* 1989; *Presumed Innocent* 1990; *Consenting Adults* 1992; *The Pelican Brief* 1993; *The Devil's Own* 1997
Pal, George *tom thumb* 1958; *The Time Machine* 1960; *Atlantis, the Lost Continent* 1961; *The Wonderful World of the Brothers Grimm* 1962; *7 Faces of Dr Lao* 1963
Palcy, Euzhan *Rue Cases Nègres* 1983; *A Dry White Season* 1989
Palmer, Tony *200 Motels* 1971; *Wagner* 1983; *Testimony* 1987; *The Children* 1990
Paltenghi, David *Orders Are Orders* 1954; *The Love Match* 1955; *Dick Turpin – Highwayman* 1956
Paltrow, Bruce *A Little Sex* 1981; *Ed McBain's 87th Precinct* 1995
Panama, Norman *Callaway Went Thataway* 1951; *Above and Beyond* 1952; *Knock on Wood* 1954; *The Court Jester* 1956; *That Certain Feeling* 1956; *The Baited Trap* 1959; *The Road to Hong Kong* 1962; *Not with My Wife, You Don't!* 1966; *How to Commit Marriage* 1969; *The Maltese Bippy* 1969; *I Will... I Will... for Now* 1976
Panfilov, Gleb *The Theme* 1979; *Vassa* 1983
Paradjanov, Sergei *Shadows of Our Forgotten Ancestors* 1964; *The Colour of Pomegranates* 1969; *The Legend of the Suram Fortress* 1984; *Ashik Kerib* 1988
Paragon, John *Double Trouble* 1992; *The Babysitters* 1994; *Ring of the Musketeers* 1994
Paris, Jerry *Don't Raise the Bridge, Lower the River* 1968; *How Sweet It Is!* 1968; *Never a Dull Moment* 1968; *Viva Max!* 1969; *The Grasshopper* 1970; *What's a Nice Girl like You...?* 1971; *How to Break Up a Happy Divorce* 1976; *Police Academy 2: Their First Assignment* 1985; *Police Academy 3: Back in Training* 1986
Parisot, Dean *Framed* 1990; *Home Fries* 1998; *Galaxy Quest* 1999
Parker, Alan *Bugsy Malone* 1976; *Midnight Express* 1978; *Fame* 1980; *Pink Floyd – The Wall* 1982; *Shoot the Moon* 1982; *Birdy* 1984; *Angel Heart* 1987; *Mississippi Burning* 1988; *Come See the Paradise* 1990; *The Commitments* 1991; *The Road to Wellville* 1994; *Evita* 1996; *Angela's Ashes* 1999
Parker, David *Hercules Returns* 1993; *Diana & Me* 1997
Parker, Oliver *Othello* 1995; *An Ideal Husband* 1999
Parker, Trey *Cannibal! the Musical* 1993; *Orgazmo* 1997; *South Park: Bigger, Longer & Uncut* 1999
Parks, Gordon *The Learning Tree* 1969; *Shaft* 1971; *Shaft's Big Score!* 1972; *The Super Cops* 1973; *Leadbelly* 1976
Parks Jr, Gordon *Superfly* 1972; *Three the Hard Way* 1974; *Aaron Loves Angela* 1975
Parolini, Gianfranco *aka* **Kramer, Frank** *Sartana* 1968; *God's Gun* 1977
Parrish, Robert *Cry Danger* 1951; *The Mob* 1951; *Assignment – Paris* 1952; *My Pal Gus* 1952; *Rough Shoot* 1952; *The San Francisco Story* 1952; *The Purple Plain* 1954; *Lucy Gallant* 1955; *Fire Down Below* 1957; *Saddle the Wind* 1958; *The Wonderful Country* 1959; *In the French Style* 1963; *Up from the Beach* 1965; *The Bobo* 1967; *Casino Royale* 1967; *Duffy* 1968; *Journey to the Far Side of the Sun* 1969; *A Town Called Hell* 1971; *The Marseilles Contract* 1974
Parrott, James *The Two Tars* 1928; *Perfect Day* 1929; *Pardon Us* 1931; *County Hospital* 1932; *The Music Box* 1932; *Twice Two* 1933
Parry, Gordon *Bond Street* 1948; *Third Time Lucky* 1949; *The Gay Adventure* 1949; *Now Barabbas Was a Robber* 1949; *Tom Brown's Schooldays* 1951; *Women of Twilight* 1952; *Front Page Story* 1953; *Innocents in Paris* 1953; *A Yank in Ermine* 1955; *Sailor Beware!* 1956; *Tread Softly Stranger* 1958; *The Navy Lark* 1959
Pascal, Christine *La Garce* 1984; *Le Petit Prince A Dit* 1992
Pascal, Gabriel *Major Barbara* 1941; *Caesar and Cleopatra* 1945

1965; *Hurry Sundown* 1967; *Skidoo* 1968; *Tell Me That You Love Me, Junie Moon* 1970; *Such Good Friends* 1971; *Rosebud* 1975; *The Human Factor* 1979

Pressburger, Emeric *One of Our Aircraft Is Missing* 1942; *The Life and Death of Colonel Blimp* 1943; *A Canterbury Tale* 1944; *I Know Where I'm Going* 1945; *Black Narcissus* 1946; *A Matter of Life and Death* 1946; *The Red Shoes* 1948; *The Small Back Room* 1949; *The Elusive Pimpernel* 1950; *Gone to Earth* 1950; *The Tales of Hoffmann* 1951; *Oh, Rosalinda!!* 1955; *The Battle of the River Plate* 1956; *Ill Met by Moonlight* 1956

Pressman, Michael *The Great Texas Dynamite Chase* 1976; *Boulevard Nights* 1979; *Those Lips, Those Eyes* 1980; *Some Kind of Hero* 1982; *Doctor Detroit* 1983; *Private Sessions* 1985; *Shootdown* 1988; *To Heal a Nation* 1988; *Man against the Mob: the Chinatown Murders* 1989; *The Revenge of Al Capone* 1989; *Joshua's Heart* 1990; *Teenage Mutant Ninja Turtles II: the Secret of the Ooze* 1991; *Quicksand: No Escape* 1992; *To Gillian on Her 37th Birthday* 1996; *To Gillian on Her 37th Birthday* 1996; *Anne Tyler's Saint Maybe* 1998

Preston, Gaylene *Mr Wrong* 1985; *Ruby and Rata* 1990

Preuss, Ruben *Deceptions* 1990; *Dead on Sight* 1994

Price, David F *Children of the Corn II: the Final Sacrifice* 1993; *Dr Jekyll and Ms Hyde* 1995

Prince *Under the Cherry Moon* 1986; *Sign o' the Times* 1987; *Graffiti Bridge* 1990

Prior, David A *Raw Nerve* 1991; *Double Threat* 1992; *Raw Justice* 1993

Prowse, Andrew *Driving Force* 1988; *Demonstone* 1989

Proyas, Alex *The Crow* 1994; *Dark City* 1998

Pudovkin, Vsevolod I *Chess Fever* 1925; *Mother* 1926; *The End of St Petersburg* 1927; *Storm over Asia* 1928

Puenzo, Luis *The Official Version* 1985; *Old Gringo* 1989; *The Plague* 1992

Purcell, Evelyn *Nobody's Fool* 1986; *Woman Undone* 1995

Purdy, Jon *Reflections on a Crime* 1994; *Dillinger and Capone* 1995; *Unabomber* 1996

Pytka, Joe *Let It Ride* 1989; *Space Jam* 1997

Pyun, Albert *The Sword and the Sorcerer* 1982; *Radioactive Dreams* 1986; *Dangerously Close* 1986; *Down Twisted* 1987; *Cyborg* 1989; *Captain America* 1990; *Kickboxer 2: the Road Back* 1990; *Arcade* 1993; *Brain Smasher... a Love Story* 1993; *Knights* 1993; *Nemesis* 1993; *Hong Kong '97* 1994; *Adrenalin: Fear the Rush* 1995; *Heatseeker* 1995; *Nemesis 2 – Nebula* 1995; *Blast* 1996; *Mean Guns* 1996; *Nemesis 3 – Time Lapse* 1996; *Omega Doom* 1996; *Raven Hawk* 1996; *Postmortem* 1999

Q

Quay, Stephen *Street of Crocodiles* 1986; *Institute Benjamenta, or This Dream People Call Human Life* 1995

Quay, Timothy *Street of Crocodiles* 1986; *Institute Benjamenta, or This Dream People Call Human Life* 1995

Quested, John *Philadelphia, Here I Come* 1975; *Loophole* 1980

Quine, Richard *All Ashore* 1953; *Drive a Crooked Road* 1954; *Pushover* 1954; *So This Is Paris* 1954; *My Sister Eileen* 1955; *Full of Life* 1956; *The Solid Gold Cadillac* 1956; *Operation Mad Ball* 1957; *Bell, Book and Candle* 1958; *It Happened to Jane* 1959; *Strangers When We Meet* 1960; *The World of Suzie Wong* 1960; *The Notorious Landlady* 1962; *Paris When It Sizzles* 1964; *Sex and the Single Girl* 1964; *Get off My Back* 1965; *How to Murder Your Wife* 1965; *Hotel* 1967; *Oh Dad, Poor Dad, Mama's Hung You in the Closet and I'm Feelin' So Sad* 1967; *W* 1974; *The Prisoner of Zenda* 1979

Quintano, Gene *Honeymoon Academy* 1990; *Why Me?* 1990; *National Lampoon's Loaded Weapon 1* 1993; *Dollar for the Dead* 1998

R

Rademakers, Fons *The Assault* 1986; *The Rose Garden* 1989

Rader, Peter *Hired to Kill* 1990; *Escape to Witch Mountain* 1995

Radford, Michael *Another Time, Another Place* 1983; *Nineteen Eighty-Four* 1984; *White Mischief* 1987; *Il Postino* 1994; *B Monkey* 1996

Radler, Robert *Best of the Best* 1989; *Best of the Best II* 1992

Rafelson, Bob *Head* 1968; *Five Easy Pieces* 1970; *The King of Marvin Gardens* 1972; *Stay Hungry* 1976; *The Postman Always Rings Twice* 1981; *Black Widow* 1987; *Mountains of the Moon* 1989; *Man Trouble* 1992; *Erotic Tales* 1994; *Blood and Wine* 1996; *Poodle Springs* 1998

Raffill, Stewart *The Adventures of the Wilderness Family* 1975; *Across the Great Divide* 1977; *The Sea Gypsies* 1978; *High Risk* 1981; *The Ice Pirates* 1984; *The Philadelphia Experiment* 1984; *Mac and Me* 1988; *Mannequin on the Move* 1991; *The New Swiss Family Robinson* 1999

Rafkin, Alan *Ski Party* 1965; *The Ghost and Mr Chicken* 1966; *The Ride to Hangman's Tree* 1967; *The Shakiest Gun in the West* 1967; *Angel in My Pocket* 1968; *Nobody's Perfect* 1968; *How to Frame a Figg* 1971

Raimi, Sam *The Evil Dead* 1983; *Crimewave* 1985; *Evil Dead II* 1987; *Darkman* 1990; *Army of Darkness* 1993; *The Quick and the Dead* 1995; *A Simple Plan* 1998; *For Love of the Game* 1999

Rainone, Frank *Me and the Mob* 1992; *A Brooklyn State of Mind* 1997

Rakoff, Alvin *Passport to Shame* 1958; *The Treasure of San Teresa* 1959; *The Comedy Man* 1964; *Crossplot* 1969; *Hoffman* 1970; *Say Hello to Yesterday* 1971; *King Solomon's Treasure* 1977; *City on Fire* 1979

Ramis, Harold *Caddyshack* 1980; *National Lampoon's Vacation* 1983; *Club Paradise* 1986; *Groundhog Day* 1993; *Stuart Saves His Family* 1995; *Multiplicity* 1996; *Analyze This* 1999

Randall, Addison *East LA* 1989; *Chance* 1990

Randel, Tony *Hellbound: Hellraiser II* 1988; *Amityville 1992: It's About Time* 1992; *Ticks* 1993; *Fist of the North Star* 1995; *One Good Turn* 1996; *Rattled* 1996

Rappeneau, Jean-Paul *La Vie de Château* 1965; *Sink or Swim* 1971; *Call Him Savage* 1975; *Cyrano de Bergerac* 1990; *The Horseman on the Roof* 1995

Rapper, Irving *One Foot in Heaven* 1941; *Shining Victory* 1941; *The Gay Sisters* 1942; *Now, Voyager* 1942; *The Adventures of Mark Twain* 1944; *The Corn Is Green* 1945; *Rhapsody in Blue* 1945; *Deception* 1946; *Anna Lucasta* 1949; *The Glass Menagerie* 1950; *Another Man's Poison* 1951; *Forever Female* 1953; *Bad for Each Other* 1954; *The Brave One* 1956; *Marjorie Morningstar* 1958; *The Miracle* 1959; *Pontius Pilate* 1961; *Born Again* 1978

Rash, Steve *The Buddy Holly Story* 1978; *Under the Rainbow* 1981; *Can't Buy Me Love* 1987; *Queens Logic* 1991; *Son in Law* 1993; *Eddie* 1996

Rathnam, Mani *Roja* 1992; *Bombay* 1995; *Dil Se...* 1998

Ratner, Brett *Money Talks* 1997; *Rush Hour* 1998

Ratoff, Gregory *Lancer Spy* 1937; *Intermezzo* 1939; *Rose of Washington Square* 1939; *Wife, Husband and Friend* 1939; *I Was an Adventuress* 1940; *Adam Had Four Sons* 1941; *The Corsican Brothers* 1941; *The Men in Her Life* 1941; *Footlight Serenade* 1942; *The Heat's On* 1943; *Irish Eyes Are Smiling* 1944; *Where Do We Go from Here?* 1945; *Do You Love Me?* 1946; *Moss Rose* 1947; *Black Magic* 1949; *Taxi* 1953; *Oscar Wilde* 1959

Rawlins, John *Arabian Nights* 1942; *Sherlock Holmes and the Voice of Terror* 1942; *Dick Tracy Meets Gruesome* 1947; *Dick Tracy's Dilemma* 1947; *The Arizona Ranger* 1948

Ray, Fred Olen *The Alien Dead* 1980; *Armed Response* 1986; *Terminal Force* 1987; *Haunting Fear* 1990

Ray, Nicholas *Knock on Any Door* 1949; *They Live by Night* 1949; *A Woman's Secret* 1949; *Born to Be Bad* 1950; *In a Lonely Place* 1950; *Flying Leathernecks* 1951; *On Dangerous Ground* 1951; *The Racket* 1951; *The Lusty Men* 1952; *Macao* 1952; *Johnny Guitar* 1954; *Rebel without a Cause* 1955; *Run for Cover* 1955; *Bigger than Life* 1956; *Hot Blood* 1956; *Bitter Victory* 1957; *The True Story of Jesse James* 1957; *Party Girl* 1958; *Wind across the Everglades* 1958; *The Savage Innocents* 1960; *King of Kings* 1961; *55 Days at Peking* 1963

Ray, Satyajit *Pather Panchali* 1955; *Aparajito* 1956; *The Music Room* 1958; *The World of Apu* 1959; *Devi* 1960; *Teen Kanya* 1961; *Kangchenjunga* 1962; *The Big City* 1963; *Charulata* 1964; *Days and Nights in the Forest* 1969; *The Adversary* 1970; *Company Limited* 1971; *Distant Thunder* 1973; *The Middleman* 1975; *The Chess Players* 1977; *Sadgati* 1981; *The Home and the World* 1984; *An Enemy of the People* 1989; *Branches of the Tree* 1990; *The Stranger* 1991

Razatos, Spiro *Fast Getaway* 1991; *Class of 1999 II: The Substitute* 1993

Rebane, Bill *The Giant Spider Invasion* 1975; *The Alpha Incident* 1977

Red, Eric *Cohen and Tate* 1988; *Body Parts* 1991; *Bad Moon* 1996; *Undertow* 1996

Redford, Robert *Ordinary People* 1980; *The Milagro Beanfield War* 1988; *A River Runs through It* 1992; *Quiz Show* 1994; *The Horse Whisperer* 1998

Reed, Carol *Bank Holiday* 1938; *Climbing High* 1938; *Penny Paradise* 1938; *The Stars Look Down* 1939; *The Girl in the News* 1940; *Night Train to Munich* 1940; *Kipps* 1941; *The Young Mr Pitt* 1942; *The Way Ahead* 1944; *Odd Man Out* 1946; *The Fallen Idol* 1948; *The Third Man* 1949; *Outcast of the Islands* 1951; *The Man between* 1953; *A Kid for Two Farthings* 1955; *Trapeze* 1956; *The Key* 1958; *Our Man in Havana* 1959; *The Running Man* 1963; *The Agony and the Ecstasy* 1965; *Oliver!* 1968; *Flap* 1970; *Follow Me* 1971

Reed, Luther *Rio Rita* 1929; *Hell's Angels* 1930

Reed, Peyton *The Computer Wore Tennis Shoes* 1995; *The Love Bug* 1997

Rees, Clive *The Blockhouse* 1973; *When the Whales Came* 1989

Rees, Jerry *The Brave Little Toaster* 1987; *Too Hot to Handle* 1991

Reeve, Geoffrey *Puppet on a Chain* 1970; *Caravan to Vaccares* 1974; *Souvenir* 1987

Reeves, Michael *The She Beast* 1965; *The Sorcerers* 1967; *Witchfinder General* 1968

Refn, Nicolas Winding *Pusher* 1996; *Bleeder* 1999

Reggio, Godfrey *Koyaanisqatsi* 1982; *Powaqqatsi* 1988

Reid, Alastair *Something to Hide* 1971; *Teamster Boss: the Jackie Presser Story* 1992; *What Rats Won't Do* 1998

Reiner, Carl *Enter Laughing* 1967; *The Comic* 1969; *Where's Poppa?* 1970; *Oh, God!* 1977; *The One and Only* 1978; *The Jerk* 1979; *Dead Men Don't Wear Plaid* 1982; *The Man with Two Brains* 1983; *All of Me* 1984; *Summer Rental* 1985; *Summer School* 1987; *Bert Rigby, You're a Fool* 1989; *Sibling Rivalry* 1990; *Fatal Instinct* 1993; *That Old Feeling* 1997

Reiner, Jeffrey *Trouble Bound* 1993; *Serpent's Lair* 1995

Reiner, Rob *This Is Spinal Tap* 1984; *The Sure Thing* 1985; *Stand by Me* 1986; *The Princess Bride* 1987; *When Harry Met Sally...* 1989; *Misery* 1990; *A Few Good Men* 1992; *North* 1994; *The American President* 1995; *Ghosts from the Past* 1996; *The Story of Us* 1999

Reinhardt, Gottfried *The Story of Three Loves* 1953; *Betrayed* 1954; *Town without Pity* 1961; *Situation Hopeless – but Not Serious* 1965

Reinisch, Deborah *Caught in the Act* 1993; *A Step toward Tomorrow* 1996

Reis, Irving *A Date with the Falcon* 1941; *The Gay Falcon* 1941; *The Big Street* 1942; *The Falcon Takes Over* 1942; *Crack-Up* 1946; *Bachelor Knight* 1947; *All My Sons* 1948; *Enchantment* 1948; *Dancing in the Dark* 1949; *Roseanna McCoy* 1949; *The Four Poster* 1953

Reisch, Walter *Men Are Not Gods* 1936; *Song of Scheherazade* 1947

Reisner, Allen *The Day They Gave Babies Away* 1957; *St Louis Blues* 1958

Reisner, Charles *Steamboat Bill, Jr* 1928; *Hollywood Revue* 1929; *Meet the People* 1944

Reisz, Karel *Saturday Night and Sunday Morning* 1960; *Night Must Fall* 1964; *Morgan – a Suitable Case for Treatment* 1966; *Isadora* 1968; *The Gambler* 1974; *Who'll Stop the Rain?* 1978; *The French Lieutenant's Woman* 1981; *Sweet Dreams* 1985; *Everybody Wins* 1990

Reitherman, Wolfgang *Sleeping Beauty* 1959; *One Hundred and One Dalmatians* 1960; *The Sword in the Stone* 1963; *The Jungle Book* 1967; *The Aristocats* 1970; *Robin Hood* 1973; *The Rescuers* 1977

Reitman, Ivan *Meatballs* 1979; *Stripes* 1981; *Ghostbusters* 1984; *Legal Eagles* 1986; *Twins* 1988; *Ghostbusters II* 1989; *Kindergarten Cop* 1990; *Dave* 1993; *Junior* 1994; *Fathers' Day* 1997; *Six Days Seven Nights* 1998

Reitz, Edgar *Germany in Autumn* 1978; *Heimat* 1984

Relph, Michael *Saraband for Dead Lovers* 1948; *The Gentle Gunman* 1952; *I Believe in You* 1952; *The Square Ring* 1953; *The Ship That Died of Shame* 1955; *Rockets Galore* 1958; *Desert Mice* 1959

René, Norman *Longtime Companion* 1990; *Prelude to a Kiss* 1992; *Reckless* 1995

Renoir, Jean *La Chienne* 1931; *Boudu, Saved from Drowning* 1932; *Madame Bovary* 1933; *Le Crime de Monsieur Lange* 1935; *Toni* 1935; *Une Partie de Campagne* 1936; *The Lower Depths* 1936; *La Vie Est à Nous* 1936; *La Grande Illusion* 1937; *La Bête Humaine* 1938; *La Marseillaise* 1938; *La Règle du Jeu* 1939; *Swamp Water* 1941; *This Land Is Mine* 1943; *The Southerner* 1945; *Diary of a Chambermaid* 1946; *The Woman on the Beach* 1947; *The River* 1951; *The Golden Coach* 1953; *French Cancan* 1955; *Elena et les Hommes* 1956; *Lunch on the Grass* 1959; *The Testament of Dr Cordelier* 1959; *The Vanishing Corporal* 1962; *The Little Theatre of Jean Renoir* 1969

Resnais, Alain *Nuit et Brouillard* 1955; *Hiroshima, Mon Amour* 1959; *Last Year at Marienbad* 1961; *Muriel* 1963; *La Guerre Est Finie* 1966; *Far from Vietnam* 1967; *Je T'Aime, Je T'Aime* 1968; *Stavisky* 1974; *Providence* 1977; *Mon Oncle d'Amérique* 1980; *Life Is a Bed of Roses* 1983; *Mélo* 1986; *I Want to Go Home* 1989; *Smoking/No Smoking* 1993; *On Connaît la Chanson* 1997

Reynolds, Burt *Gator* 1976; *The End* 1978; *Sharky's Machine* 1981; *Stick* 1985; *The Man from Left Field* 1993; *Hard Time* 1998

Reynolds, Kevin *Fandango* 1985; *The Beast* 1988; *Robin Hood: Prince of Thieves* 1991; *Rapa Nui* 1994; *Waterworld* 1995; *One Eight Seven* 1997

Reynolds, Sheldon *Foreign Intrigue* 1956; *Assignment to Kill* 1968

Rhee, Phillip *Best of the Best 3: No Turning Back* 1995; *Best of the Best: Without Warning* 1998

Rhodes, Michael Ray *Babies* 1990; *Matters of the Heart* 1990; *The Killing Mind* 1991; *Reason for Living: the Jill Ireland Story* 1991; *In the Best Interest of the Children* 1992; *Seduction: Three Tales from the Inner Sanctum* 1992; *Not Our Son* 1995; *Co-ed*

RadioTimes DIRECTORS' INDEX

Rouse, Russell *The Well* 1951; *The Thief* 1952; *New York Confidential* 1955; *The Fastest Gun Alive* 1956; *House of Numbers* 1957; *Thunder in the Sun* 1959; *The Oscar* 1966
Rowland, Roy *Hollywood Party* 1934; *Lost Angel* 1943; *Our Vines Have Tender Grapes* 1945; *Killer McCoy* 1947; *Scene of the Crime* 1949; *The Outriders* 1950; *Bugles in the Afternoon* 1952; *Affair with a Stranger* 1953; *The 5,000 Fingers of Dr T* 1953; *The Moonlighter* 1953; *Rogue Cop* 1954; *Witness to Murder* 1954; *Hit the Deck* 1955; *Many Rivers to Cross* 1955; *Meet Me in Las Vegas* 1956; *These Wilder Years* 1956; *Seven Hills of Rome* 1957; *Gun Glory* 1957; *The Girl Hunters* 1963
Rozema, Patricia *I've Heard the Mermaids Singing* 1987; *White Room* 1990; *When Night Is Falling* 1995; *Mansfield Park* 1999
Ruane, John *Death in Brunswick* 1990; *That Eye, the Sky* 1994; *Dead Letter Office* 1998
Rubbo, Michael *The Peanut Butter Solution* 1985; *Tommy Tricker and the Stamp Traveller* 1988; *Vincent and Me* 1990
Ruben, J Walter *The Roadhouse Murder* 1932; *Ace of Aces* 1933; *Java Head* 1935; *Public Hero No 1* 1935; *Riffraff* 1936; *Trouble for Two* 1936
Ruben, Joseph *Joyride* 1977; *G.O.R.P.* 1980; *Dreamscape* 1984; *The Stepfather* 1986; *Fighting Justice* 1989; *Sleeping with the Enemy* 1991; *The Good Son* 1993; *Money Train* 1995; *Return to Paradise* 1998
Ruben, Katt Shea *aka* **Shea, Katt** *Streets* 1990; *Poison Ivy* 1992; *The Rage: Carrie 2* 1999
Rubie, Howard *The Settlement* 1982; *Mission Top Secret* 1990; *The Phantom Horsemen* 1990
Rudolph, Alan *Welcome to LA* 1976; *Remember My Name* 1978; *Roadie* 1980; *Endangered Species* 1982; *Choose Me* 1984; *Songwriter* 1984; *Trouble in Mind* 1985; *Made in Heaven* 1987; *The Moderns* 1988; *Love at Large* 1990; *Mortal Thoughts* 1991; *Equinox* 1992; *Mrs Parker and the Vicious Circle* 1994; *Afterglow* 1997; *Breakfast of Champions* 1999
Ruggles, Wesley *Condemned* 1929; *Cimarron* 1931; *No Man of Her Own* 1932; *I'm No Angel* 1933; *Bolero* 1934; *The Bride Comes Home* 1935; *The Gilded Lily* 1935; *Accent on Youth* 1935; *Valiant Is the Word for Carrie* 1936; *I Met Him in Paris* 1937; *True Confession* 1937; *Too Many Husbands* 1940; *Arizona* 1940; *You Belong to Me* 1941; *Somewhere I'll Find You* 1942; *Slightly Dangerous* 1943; *See Here, Private Hargrove* 1944; *London Town* 1946
Ruiz, Raúl *Treasure Island* 1991; *Three Lives and Only One Death* 1996; *Shattered Image* 1998
Rush, Richard *Too Soon to Love* 1960; *Of Love and Desire* 1963; *Hell's Angels on Wheels* 1967; *Thunder Alley* 1967; *Psych-Out* 1968; *Getting Straight* 1970; *Freebie and the Bean* 1974; *The Stunt Man* 1980; *Color of Night* 1994
Russell, Chuck *aka* **Russell, Charles** *A Nightmare on Elm Street 3: Dream Warriors* 1987; *The Blob* 1988; *The Mask* 1994; *Eraser* 1996
Russell, David O *Spanking the Monkey* 1994; *Flirting with Disaster* 1996; *Three Kings* 1999
Russell, Ken *French Dressing* 1964; *Billion Dollar Brain* 1967; *Women in Love* 1969; *The Music Lovers* 1970; *The Boy Friend* 1971; *The Devils* 1971; *Savage Messiah* 1972; *Mahler* 1974; *Lisztomania* 1975; *Tommy* 1975; *Valentino* 1977; *Altered States* 1980; *Crimes of Passion* 1984; *Gothic* 1986; *Aria* 1987; *The Lair of the White Worm* 1988; *The Rainbow* 1988; *Salome's Last Dance* 1988; *Women and Men: Stories of Seduction* 1990; *Prisoner of Honor* 1991; *Whore* 1991; *Erotic Tales* 1994; *Dogboys* 1998
Russell, William D *Dear Ruth* 1947; *The Sainted Sisters* 1948; *Bride for Sale* 1949; *Best of the Badmen* 1951
Ryan, Frank *Call Out the Marines* 1942; *Hers to Hold* 1943; *Can't Help Singing* 1944; *Patrick the Great* 1944; *So Goes My Love* 1946
Rydell, Mark *The Fox* 1967; *The Reivers* 1969; *The Cowboys* 1972; *Cinderella Liberty* 1973; *Harry and Walter Go to New York* 1976; *The Rose* 1979; *On Golden Pond* 1981; *The River* 1984; *For the Boys* 1991; *Intersection* 1994; *Crime of the Century* 1996
Rymer, Michael *Angel Baby* 1995; *In Too Deep* 1999

S

Sachs, William *The Incredible Melting Man* 1977; *Van Nuys Blvd* 1979; *Exterminator 2* 1980; *Galaxina* 1980
Sadwith, James Steven *Deadly Intentions... Again?* 1991; *In Broad Daylight* 1991
Safran, Henri *Storm Boy* 1976; *Norman Loves Rose* 1982; *Bush Christmas* 1983; *The Wild Duck* 1983; *The Rogue Stallion* 1990
Sagal, Boris *Twilight of Honor* 1963; *Girl Happy* 1965; *Made in Paris* 1966; *The Helicopter Spies* 1968; *Mosquito Squadron* 1968; *Night Gallery* 1969; *The Harness* 1971; *The Omega Man* 1971; *Deliver Us from Evil* 1973; *Hitched* 1973; *The Greatest Gift* 1974; *Three for the Road* 1975; *The Oregon Trail* 1976; *Sherlock Holmes in New York* 1976; *The Diary of Anne Frank* 1980
Sagan, Leontine *Girls in Uniform* 1931; *Gaiety George* 1946
St Clair, Malcolm *Canary Murder Case* 1929; *Crack-Up* 1936; *Born Reckless* 1937; *The Man in the Trunk* 1942; *The Dancing Masters* 1943; *Jitterbugs* 1943; *The Big Noise* 1944; *The Bullfighters* 1945
Saks, Gene *Barefoot in the Park* 1967; *The Odd Couple* 1968; *Cactus Flower* 1969; *The Last of the Red Hot Lovers* 1972; *Mame* 1974; *Brighton Beach Memoirs* 1986; *A Touch of Adultery* 1992
Sale, Richard *A Ticket to Tomahawk* 1950; *Half Angel* 1951; *Let's Make It Legal* 1951; *Meet Me after the Show* 1951; *The Girl Next Door* 1953; *Malaga* 1954; *Gentlemen Marry Brunettes* 1955; *Abandon Ship!* 1957
Salkow, Sidney *The Lone Wolf Strikes* 1940; *The Lone Wolf Keeps a Date* 1941; *Shadow of the Eagle* 1950; *Prince of Pirates* 1953; *Raiders of the Seven Seas* 1953; *Sitting Bull* 1954; *Las Vegas Shakedown* 1955; *Chicago Confidential* 1957; *Gun Duel in Durango* 1957; *The Iron Sheriff* 1957; *Twice Told Tales* 1963; *The Great Sioux Massacre* 1965
Salles, Walter *Central Station* 1998; *Midnight* 1998
Salomon, Mikael *A Far Off Place* 1993; *Hard Rain* 1997
Salva, Victor *Clownhouse* 1988; *Hatchet Man* 1994; *Powder* 1995
Salvadori, Pierre *Wild Target* 1993; *Les Apprentis* 1995
Salvatores, Gabriele *Mediterraneo* 1991; *Puerto Escondido* 1992; *Nirvana* 1996
Sanders, Denis *Crime and Punishment, USA* 1959; *War Hunt* 1962; *One Man's Way* 1964; *Shock Treatment* 1964; *Elvis: That's the Way It Is* 1970
Sandler, Allan *The Killings at Outpost Zeta* 1980; *Laboratory* 1980
Sandrich, Jay *Seems like Old Times* 1980; *Father, Son and the Mistress* 1992; *Neil Simon's London Suite* 1996
Sandrich, Mark *Melody Cruise* 1933; *The Gay Divorcee* 1934; *Top Hat* 1935; *Follow the Fleet* 1936; *A Woman Rebels* 1936; *Shall We Dance* 1937; *Carefree* 1938; *Skylark* 1941; *Holiday Inn* 1942; *So Proudly We Hail* 1943; *Here Come the Waves* 1944; *I Love a Soldier* 1944
Sanford, Arlene *Seeds of Deception* 1993; *A Very Brady Sequel* 1996; *I'll Be Home for Christmas* 1998
Sanger, Jonathan *Code Name: Emerald* 1985; *Children of the Bride* 1990; *Chance of a Lifetime* 1991; *Obsessed* 1992; *Down Came a Blackbird* 1995
Sangster, Jimmy *The Horror of Frankenstein* 1970; *Lust for a Vampire* 1970; *Fear in the Night* 1972
Santell, Alfred *Daddy Long Legs* 1931; *Body and Soul* 1931; *Polly of the Circus* 1932; *Winterset* 1936; *Breakfast for Two* 1937; *Internes Can't Take Money* 1937; *Having Wonderful Time* 1938; *Beyond the Blue Horizon* 1942; *The Hairy Ape* 1944; *Jack London* 1944
Santley, Joseph *The Cocoanuts* 1929; *There Goes the Groom* 1937; *Blond Cheat* 1938; *Music in My Heart* 1940; *Down Mexico Way* 1941; *Chatterbox* 1943; *Brazil* 1944; *Rosie the Riveter* 1944; *Earl Carroll Vanities* 1945
Saperstein, David *A Killing Affair* 1985; *Beyond the Stars* 1988
Sarafian, Deran *Death Warrant* 1990; *Back in the USSR* 1992; *Gunmen* 1994; *Terminal Velocity* 1994; *Roadflower* 1994
Sarafian, Richard C *aka* **Smithee, Alan** *Run Wild, Run Free* 1969; *Fragment of Fear* 1970; *Man in the Wilderness* 1971; *Vanishing Point* 1971; *The Lolly-Madonna War* 1973; *The Man Who Loved Cat Dancing* 1973; *One of Our Own* 1975; *The Next Man* 1976; *Disaster on the Coastliner* 1979; *Sunburn* 1979; *Eye of the Tiger* 1986; *Solar Crisis* 1990
Sargent, Joseph *One Spy Too Many* 1966; *The Spy in the Green Hat* 1966; *The Hell with Heroes* 1968; *Colossus: the Forbin Project* 1969; *The Man* 1972; *White Lightning* 1973; *The Taking of Pelham One Two Three* 1974; *Hustling* 1975; *The Night that Panicked America* 1975; *MacArthur* 1977; *Goldengirl* 1979; *Nightmares* 1983; *Of Pure Blood* 1986; *Passion Flower* 1986; *There Must Be a Pony* 1986; *Jaws the Revenge* 1987; *The Karen Carpenter Story* 1989; *Day One* 1989; *Caroline?* 1990; *A Green Journey* 1990; *The Incident* 1990; *Ivory Hunters* 1990; *Never Forget* 1991; *Miss Rose White* 1992; *Skylark* 1993; *My Antonia* 1995; *Mandela and de Klerk* 1997; *Miss Evers' Boys* 1997; *A Lesson Before Dying* 1999
Sarin, Vic *aka* **Sarin, Victor** *Cold Comfort* 1989; *The Legend of Gator Face* 1996
Sarne, Michael *aka* **Sarne, Mike** *Joanna* 1969; *Myra Breckinridge* 1970; *The Punk* 1993; *Glastonbury the Movie* 1995
Sasdy, Peter *Taste the Blood of Dracula* 1969; *Countess Dracula* 1970; *Hands of the Ripper* 1971; *Doomwatch* 1972; *Nothing but the Night* 1972; *I Don't Want to Be Born* 1975; *Welcome to Blood City* 1977; *The Lonely Lady* 1983
Saunders, Charles *Tawny Pipit* 1944; *Death of an Angel* 1951; *Love in Pawn* 1953; *The Hornet's Nest* 1955; *Behind the Headlines* 1956; *Find the Lady* 1956; *The Woman Eater* 1957; *The Man without a Body* 1957; *Naked Fury* 1959; *The Gentle Trap* 1960; *Dangerous Afternoon* 1961; *Danger by My Side* 1962
Saura, Carlos *The Hunt* 1966; *Peppermint Frappé* 1967; *Cria Cuervos* 1975; *Mamá Cumple 100 Años* 1979; *Blood Wedding* 1981; *Carmen* 1983; *El Amor Brujo* 1986; *El Dorado* 1988; *Ay, Carmela!* 1990; *Outrage* 1993; *Tango* 1998; *Goya in Bordeaux* 1999
Sautet, Claude *The Big Risk* 1960; *The Things of Life* 1969; *César and Rosalie* 1972; *Vincent, François, Paul and the Others* 1974; *Mado* 1976; *Une Histoire Simple* 1978; *Un Coeur en Hiver* 1992; *Les Enfants de Lumière* 1995; *Nelly & Monsieur Arnaud* 1995
Saville, Philip *Stop the World, I Want to Get Off* 1966; *Oedipus the King* 1968; *Those Glory, Glory Days* 1983; *Shadey* 1985; *Fellow Traveller* 1989; *Crash: the Mystery of Flight 1501* 1990; *Max and Helen* 1990; *Metroland* 1997
Saville, Victor *Friday the Thirteenth* 1933; *The Good Companions* 1933; *Evensong* 1934; *Evergreen* 1934; *I Was a Spy* 1934; *The Dictator* 1935; *First a Girl* 1935; *It's Love Again* 1936; *Dark Journey* 1937; *Storm in a Teacup* 1937; *South Riding* 1938; *Forever and a Day* 1943; *Tonight and Every Night* 1945; *The Green Years* 1946; *Green Dolphin Street* 1947; *If Winter Comes* 1947; *Conspirator* 1949; *Kim* 1950; *Calling Bulldog Drummond* 1951; *The Silver Chalice* 1954; *The Long Wait* 1954
Savoca, Nancy *True Love* 1989; *Dogfight* 1991; *Household Saints* 1993; *If These Walls Could Talk* 1996; *The 24 Hour Woman* 1999
Sax, Geoffrey *Broken Trust* 1995; *Ruby Jean and Joe* 1996
Sayadian, Stephen *aka* **Dream, Rinse** *Cafe Flesh* 1982; *Dr Caligari* 1989
Sayles, John *Return of the Secaucus Seven* 1980; *Baby It's You* 1983; *Lianna* 1983; *The Brother from Another Planet* 1984; *Matewan* 1987; *Eight Men Out* 1988; *City of Hope* 1991; *Passion Fish* 1992; *The Secret of Roan Inish* 1993; *Lone Star* 1995; *Men with Guns* 1997; *Limbo* 1999
Scanlan, Joseph L *aka* **Scanlan, Joseph** *The World's Oldest Living Bridesmaid* 1990; *I Still Dream of Jeannie* 1991; *Unlikely Suspects* 1996; *Stand against Fear* 1996; *Race against Fear* 1998
Schachter, Steven *Getting Up and Going Home* 1992; *The Water Engine* 1992; *The Legacy of Sin: the William Coit Jr Story* 1995; *Lady Killer* 1995; *Above Suspicion* 1995; *Every Woman's Dream* 1996; *To Face Her Past* 1996
Schaefer, Armand *The Hurricane Express* 1932; *Sagebrush Trail* 1934
Schaefer, George *Pendulum* 1969; *Generation* 1969; *Doctors' Wives* 1970; *Once Upon a Scoundrel* 1973; *An Enemy of the People* 1977; *Right of Way* 1983; *Stone Pillow* 1985; *Mrs Delafield Wants to Marry* 1986; *Laura Lansing Slept Here* 1988; *Harvey* 1996
Schaeffer, Eric *If Lucy Fell* 1996; *Fall* 1997
Schaffner, Franklin J *aka* **Schaffner, Franklin** *The Stripper* 1963; *The Best Man* 1964; *The War Lord* 1965; *The Double Man* 1967; *Planet of the Apes* 1968; *Patton: Lust for Glory* 1970; *Nicholas and Alexandra* 1971; *Papillon* 1973; *Islands in the Stream* 1977; *The Boys from Brazil* 1978; *Sphinx* 1980; *Yes, Giorgio* 1982; *Lionheart* 1986; *Welcome Home* 1989
Schatzberg, Jerry *Puzzle of a Downfall Child* 1970; *The Panic in Needle Park* 1971; *Scarecrow* 1973; *The Seduction of Joe Tynan* 1979; *Honeysuckle Rose* 1980; *Misunderstood* 1984; *No Small Affair* 1984; *Street Smart* 1987; *Blood Money* 1988; *Reunion* 1989
Scheerer, Robert *Adam at 6 AM* 1970; *The World's Greatest Athlete* 1973; *How to Beat the High Cost of Living* 1980
Schell, Maximilian *First Love* 1970; *The Pedestrian* 1974; *End of the Game* 1976; *Marlene* 1984
Schenkel, Carl *Out of Order* 1984; *Bay Cove* 1987; *The Mighty Quinn* 1989; *Silence like Glass* 1989; *Silhouette* 1990; *Knight Moves* 1992; *Exquisite Tenderness* 1995; *In the Lake of the Woods* 1996; *Tarzan and the Lost City* 1998
Schepisi, Fred *The Devil's Playground* 1976; *The Chant of Jimmie Blacksmith* 1978; *Barbarosa* 1982; *Iceman* 1984; *Plenty* 1985; *Roxanne* 1987; *A Cry in the Dark* 1988; *The Russia House* 1990; *Mr Baseball* 1992; *Six Degrees of Separation* 1993; *IQ* 1995; *Fierce Creatures* 1997
Schertzinger, Victor *Paramount on Parade* 1930; *Friends and Lovers* 1931; *One Night of Love* 1934; *Something to Sing About* 1937; *The Mikado* 1939; *Road to Singapore* 1940; *Rhythm on the River* 1940; *The Birth of the Blues* 1941; *Kiss the Boys Goodbye* 1941; *Road to Zanzibar* 1941; *The Fleet's In* 1942
Schiller, Lawrence *Marilyn – The Untold Story* 1980; *Margaret Bourke-White* 1989; *The Plot to Kill Hitler* 1990; *Double Jeopardy* 1992
Schlamme, Thomas *Miss Firecracker* 1989; *Crazy from the Heart* 1991; *So I Married an Axe Murderer* 1993; *Kingfish: a Story of Huey P Long* 1995
Schlesinger, John *A Kind of Loving* 1962; *Billy Liar* 1963; *Darling* 1965; *Far from the Madding Crowd* 1967; *Midnight Cowboy*

Radio Times DIRECTORS' INDEX

Shelton, Ron *Bull Durham* 1988; *Blaze* 1989; *White Men Can't Jump* 1992; *Cobb* 1994; *Tin Cup* 1996; *Play It to the Bone* 2000
Shepard, Richard *Cool Blue* 1988; *The Linguini Incident* 1991; *Oxygen* 1999
Shepard, Sam *Far North* 1988; *Silent Tongue* 1993
Sher, Jack *The Three Worlds of Gulliver* 1959; *The Wild and the Innocent* 1959; *Love in a Goldfish Bowl* 1961
Sheridan, Jim *My Left Foot* 1989; *The Field* 1990; *In the Name of the Father* 1993; *The Boxer* 1997
Sherin, Edwin *aka* **Sherin, Ed** *Valdez Is Coming* 1971; *Glory Boy* 1971; *The Father Clements Story* 1987; *Lena: My 100 Children* 1987; *Settle the Score* 1989
Sherman, Gary *aka* **Sherman, Gary A** *Death Line* 1972; *Vice Squad* 1982; *Wanted Dead or Alive* 1986; *Poltergeist III* 1988
Sherman, George *Overland Stage Raiders* 1938; *Red River Range* 1938; *Santa Fe Stampede* 1938; *Frontier Horizon* 1939; *Three Texas Steers* 1939; *Wyoming Outlaw* 1939; *The Bandit of Sherwood Forest* 1946; *Calamity Jane and Sam Bass* 1949; *Red Canyon* 1949; *Comanche Territory* 1950; *The Sleeping City* 1950; *Against All Flags* 1952; *The Battle at Apache Pass* 1952; *The Lone Hand* 1953; *War Arrow* 1953; *Dawn at Socorro* 1954; *Johnny Dark* 1954; *Chief Crazy Horse* 1955; *Count Three and Pray* 1955; *The Treasure of Pancho Villa* 1955; *Comanche* 1956; *Son of Robin Hood* 1958; *For the Love of Mike* 1960; *Hell Bent for Leather* 1960; *The Wizard of Baghdad* 1960; *The Fiercest Heart* 1961; *Panic Button* 1964; *Big Jake* 1971
Sherman, Lowell *Bachelor Apartment* 1931; *Broadway through a Keyhole* 1933; *Morning Glory* 1933; *She Done Him Wrong* 1933
Sherman, Vincent *The Return of Dr X* 1939; *Saturday's Children* 1940; *Underground* 1941; *Across the Pacific* 1942; *All through the Night* 1942; *The Hard Way* 1942; *Old Acquaintance* 1943; *Mr Skeffington* 1944; *Nora Prentiss* 1947; *The Unfaithful* 1947; *Adventures of Don Juan* 1948; *The Hasty Heart* 1949; *The Damned Don't Cry* 1950; *Harriet Craig* 1950; *Backfire* 1950; *Goodbye, My Fancy* 1951; *Affair in Trinidad* 1952; *Lone Star* 1952; *The Garment Jungle* 1957; *The Naked Earth* 1958; *The Young Philadelphians* 1959; *Ice Palace* 1960; *The Second Time Around* 1961; *A Fever in the Blood* 1961; *Cervantes* 1968
Sherwood, John *Raw Edge* 1956; *The Monolith Monsters* 1957
Shields, Frank *Hostage: the Christine Maresch Story* 1982; *Project: Alien* 1990
Shindo, Kaneto *The Island* 1961; *Onibaba* 1964
Shire, Talia *One Night Stand* 1994; *Before the Night* 1995
Sholder, Jack *Alone in the Dark* 1982; *A Nightmare on Elm Street 2: Freddy's Revenge* 1985; *The Hidden* 1987; *Renegades* 1989; *By Dawn's Early Light* 1990; *12:01* 1993; *Natural Selection* 1994; *A Feel for Murder* 1995; *Generation X* 1996; *Runaway Car* 1997; *Wishmaster 2: Evil Never Dies* 1999
Sholem, Lee *Tarzan's Magic Fountain* 1949; *Tarzan and the Slave Girl* 1950; *The Redhead from Wyoming* 1953; *The Stand at Apache River* 1953; *Hell Ship Mutiny* 1957
Shonteff, Lindsay *Devil Doll* 1964; *Licensed to Kill* 1965
Shumlin, Herman *Watch on the Rhine* 1943; *Confidential Agent* 1945
Shyamalan, M Night *Wide Awake* 1998; *The Sixth Sense* 1999
Shyer, Charles *Irreconcilable Differences* 1984; *Baby Boom* 1987; *Father of the Bride* 1991; *I Love Trouble* 1994; *Father of the Bride Part II* 1995
Sidney, George *Pilot #5* 1943; *Thousands Cheer* 1943; *Bathing Beauty* 1944; *Ziegfeld Follies* 1944; *Anchors Aweigh* 1945; *The Harvey Girls* 1946; *Holiday in Mexico* 1946; *Cass Timberlane* 1947; *The Three Musketeers* 1948; *The Red Danube* 1949; *Annie Get Your Gun* 1950; *Key to the City* 1950; *Show Boat* 1951; *Scaramouche* 1952; *Kiss Me Kate* 1953; *Young Bess* 1953; *Jupiter's Darling* 1955; *The Eddy Duchin Story* 1956; *Pal Joey* 1957; *Jeanne Eagels* 1957; *Who Was That Lady?* 1960; *Pepe* 1960; *Bye Bye Birdie* 1963; *A Ticklish Affair* 1963; *Viva Las Vegas* 1964; *The Swinger* 1966; *Half a Sixpence* 1967
Siegel, Don *aka* **Siegel, Donald,** *aka* **Smithee, Allen** *The Verdict* 1946; *The Big Steal* 1949; *Night unto Night* 1949; *The Duel at Silver Creek* 1952; *Count the Hours* 1953; *Riot in Cell Block 11* 1954; *Private Hell 36* 1954; *An Annapolis Story* 1955; *Crime in the Streets* 1956; *Invasion of the Body Snatchers* 1956; *Baby Face Nelson* 1957; *The Lineup* 1958; *The Gun Runners* 1958; *Edge of Eternity* 1959; *Hound Dog Man* 1959; *Flaming Star* 1960; *Hell Is for Heroes* 1962; *The Killers* 1964; *Stranger on the Run* 1967; *Coogan's Bluff* 1968; *Madigan* 1968; *Death of a Gunfighter* 1969; *Two Mules for Sister Sara* 1970; *The Beguiled* 1971; *Dirty Harry* 1971; *Charley Varrick* 1973; *The Black Windmill* 1974; *The Shootist* 1976; *Telefon* 1977; *Escape from Alcatraz* 1979; *Rough Cut* 1980; *Jinxed!* 1982
Signorelli, James *Easy Money* 1983; *Elvira, Mistress of the Dark* 1988
Silberg, Joel *Breakdance* 1984; *Rappin'* 1985; *Bad Guys* 1986; *Lambada* 1990
Silberling, Brad *Casper* 1995; *City of Angels* 1998
Silver, Joan Micklin *Hester Street* 1975; *Between the Lines* 1977; *Chilly Scenes of Winter* 1979; *Crossing Delancey* 1988; *Loverboy* 1989; *Prison Stories: Women on the Inside* 1991; *Big Girls Don't Cry... They Get Even* 1992; *In the Presence of Mine Enemies* 1996; *Invisible Child* 1999
Silver, Marisa *Old Enough* 1984; *Permanent Record* 1988; *Vital Signs* 1990; *He Said, She Said* 1991
Silver, Scott *Johns* 1995; *The Mod Squad* 1999
Silverstein, Elliot *Cat Ballou* 1965; *The Happening* 1967; *A Man Called Horse* 1970; *The Car* 1977; *Night of Courage* 1987; *Rich Men, Single Women* 1990; *Flashfire* 1993
Simmons, Anthony *Your Money or Your Wife* 1960; *Four in the Morning* 1965; *The Optimists of Nine Elms* 1973; *Black Joy* 1977
Simon, Adam *Brain Dead* 1990; *Body Chemistry 2: Voice of a Stranger* 1992; *Carnosaur* 1993
Simon, S Sylvan *aka* **Simon, Sylvan** *Dancing Co-Ed* 1939; *Four Girls in White* 1939; *Whistling in the Dark* 1941; *Grand Central Murder* 1942; *Rio Rita* 1942; *Whistling in Dixie* 1942; *Salute to the Marines* 1943; *Whistling in Brooklyn* 1943; *Song of the Open Road* 1944; *Abbott and Costello in Hollywood* 1945; *Son of Lassie* 1945; *Bad Bascomb* 1946; *Her Husband's Affairs* 1947; *The Fuller Brush Man* 1948
Simoneau, Yves *Perfectly Normal* 1990; *Married for Murder* 1992; *Memphis* 1992; *Mother's Boys* 1993; *Amelia Earhart: the Final Flight* 1994; *Free Money* 1998; *36 Hours to Die* 1999
Simpson, Jane *Number One Fan* 1994; *Little Witches* 1996
Sinclair, Andrew *Under Milk Wood* 1971; *Blue Blood* 1973
Sinclair, Robert B *Dramatic School* 1938; *Mr and Mrs North* 1941; *That Wonderful Urge* 1948
Singer, Alexander *A Cold Wind in August* 1961; *Psyche '59* 1964; *Love Has Many Faces* 1965; *Captain Apache* 1971; *Glass Houses* 1972; *The Million Dollar Rip-off* 1976
Singer, Bryan *Public Access* 1993; *The Usual Suspects* 1995; *Apt Pupil* 1997
Singer, Gail *True Confections* 1990; *Wisecracks* 1991
Singleton, John *Boyz N the Hood* 1991; *Poetic Justice* 1993; *Higher Learning* 1995; *Rosewood* 1997
Sinise, Gary *Miles from Home* 1988; *Of Mice and Men* 1992
Sinyor, Gary *Leon the Pig Farmer* 1992; *Solitaire for 2* 1994; *Stiff Upper Lips* 1997; *The Bachelor* 1999
Siodmak, Robert *aka* **Siodmark, Robert** *People on Sunday* 1929; *Pièges* 1939; *Fly by Night* 1942; *Son of Dracula* 1943; *Christmas Holiday* 1944; *Cobra Woman* 1944; *Phantom Lady* 1944; *The Suspect* 1944; *The Strange Affair of Uncle Harry* 1945; *The Dark Mirror* 1946; *The Killers* 1946; *The Spiral Staircase* 1946; *Cry of the City* 1948; *Criss Cross* 1949; *The File on Thelma Jordon* 1949; *The Great Sinner* 1949; *The Crimson Pirate* 1952; *The Rats* 1955; *The Rough and the Smooth* 1959; *Custer of the West* 1968
Sippy, Ramesh *Sholay* 1975; *Shaan* 1980; *Saagar* 1985
Sirk, Douglas *aka* **Sierck, Detlef** *Pillars of Society* 1935; *Hitler's Madman* 1943; *Summer Storm* 1944; *Thieves' Holiday* 1946; *Lured* 1947; *Sleep, My Love* 1948; *Shockproof* 1949; *Slightly French* 1949; *Mystery Submarine* 1950; *The First Legion* 1951; *Thunder on the Hill* 1951; *The Lady Pays Off* 1951; *Weekend with Father* 1951; *Has Anybody Seen My Gal?* 1952; *Meet Me at the Fair* 1952; *No Room for the Groom* 1952; *All I Desire* 1953; *Take Me to Town* 1953; *Magnificent Obsession* 1954; *Sign of the Pagan* 1954; *Taza, Son of Cochise* 1954; *All That Heaven Allows* 1955; *Never Say Goodbye* 1955; *Captain Lightfoot* 1955; *There's Always Tomorrow* 1956; *Written on the Wind* 1956; *Battle Hymn* 1957; *Interlude* 1957; *The Tarnished Angels* 1957; *A Time to Love and a Time to Die* 1958; *Imitation of Life* 1959
Sjöberg, Alf *Torment* 1944; *Miss Julie* 1951
Sjöström, Victor *aka* **Seastrom, Victor** *He Who Gets Slapped* 1924; *The Tower of Lies* 1925; *The Scarlet Letter* 1926; *The Divine Woman* 1928; *The Wind* 1928; *Under the Red Robe* 1937
Skolimowski, Jerzy *The Adventures of Gerard* 1970; *Deep End* 1970; *King, Queen, Knave* 1972; *The Shout* 1978; *Moonlighting* 1982; *Success Is the Best Revenge* 1984; *The Lightship* 1985; *Torrents of Spring* 1989
Sloane, Paul H *aka* **Sloane, Paul** *Half Shot at Sunrise* 1930; *Consolation Marriage* 1931; *Geronimo* 1939
Sloman, Edward *Gun Smoke* 1931; *His Woman* 1931
Sluizer, George *The Vanishing* 1988; *Utz* 1992; *The Vanishing* 1993; *Crimetime* 1996
Smart, Ralph *Bush Christmas* 1947; *Quartet* 1948; *A Boy, a Girl and a Bike* 1949; *Bitter Springs* 1950; *Never Take No for an Answer* 1951; *Curtain Up* 1952
Smight, Jack *I'd Rather Be Rich* 1964; *The Third Day* 1965; *Kaleidoscope* 1966; *The Moving Target* 1966; *The Secret War of Harry Frigg* 1967; *No Way to Treat a Lady* 1968; *The Illustrated Man* 1969; *The Traveling Executioner* 1970; *Frankenstein: the True Story* 1973; *Airport 1975* 1974; *Battle of Midway* 1976; *Damnation Alley* 1977; *Fast Break* 1979; *Loving Couples* 1980; *Remembrance of Love* 1982; *Number One with a Bullet* 1986
Smith, Charles Martin *Trick or Treat* 1986; *Fifty/Fifty* 1991; *Air Bud* 1997
Smith, John N *The Masculine Mystique* 1984; *Sitting in Limbo* 1986; *Train of Dreams* 1987; *Dangerous Minds* 1995; *Sugartime* 1995; *A Cool, Dry Place* 1998
Smith, Kevin *Clerks* 1994; *Mallrats* 1995; *Chasing Amy* 1996; *Dogma* 1999
Smith, Mel *The Tall Guy* 1989; *Radioland Murders* 1994; *Bean* 1997
Smolan, Sandy *Rachel River* 1987; *Shattered Family* 1993
Soavi, Michele *Stage Fright – Aquarius* 1987; *The Church* 1988; *The Sect* 1991; *Cemetery Man* 1994
Sobel, Mark *Trial & Error* 1992; *Ordeal in the Arctic* 1993; *Fall into Darkness* 1996
Soderbergh, Steven *sex, lies, and videotape* 1989; *Kafka* 1991; *King of the Hill* 1993; *The Underneath* 1995; *Gray's Anatomy* 1996; *Schizopolis* 1996; *Out of Sight* 1998; *The Limey* 1999; *Erin Brockovich* 2000
Softley, Iain *BackBeat* 1993; *Hackers* 1995; *The Wings of the Dove* 1997
Sokurov, Alexander *Mother and Son* 1997; *Moloch* 1999
Solanas, Fernando E *Tangos, Exilo de Gardel* 1985; *Sur* 1987; *The Voyage* 1991
Soldati, Mario *The Stranger's Hand* 1953; *Woman of the River* 1955
Sollima, Sergio *Face to Face* 1967; *Violent City* 1970
Solondz, Todd *Fear, Anxiety, and Depression* 1989; *Welcome to the Dollhouse* 1995; *Happiness* 1998
Solt, Andrew *This Is Elvis* 1981; *Imagine: John Lennon* 1988
Sommers, Stephen *The Adventures of Huck Finn* 1993; *Rudyard Kipling's The Jungle Book* 1994; *Deep Rising* 1997
Sonnenfeld, Barry *The Addams Family* 1991; *The Concierge* 1993; *Get Shorty* 1995; *Men in Black* 1997; *Wild Wild West* 1999
Sparr, Robert *More Dead than Alive* 1969; *Once You Kiss a Stranger* 1969
Spence, Greg *Children of the Corn IV: the Gathering* 1996; *The Prophecy II* 1997
Spence, Richard *Blind Justice* 1994; *Different for Girls* 1996
Spheeris, Penelope *The Decline of Western Civilization* 1980; *The Boys Next Door* 1985; *Hollywood Vice Squad* 1986; *Dudes* 1987; *The Decline of Western Civilization Part II: the Metal Years* 1988; *Prison Stories: Women on the Inside* 1991; *Wayne's World* 1992; *The Beverly Hillbillies* 1993; *The Little Rascals* 1994; *Black Sheep* 1996; *The Decline of Western Civilization Part III* 1997; *Senseless* 1998
Spicer, Bryan *Mighty Morphin Power Rangers: the Movie* 1995; *For Richer or Poorer* 1997; *McHale's Navy* 1997
Spielberg, Steven *Night Gallery* 1969; *Duel* 1971; *The Sugarland Express* 1974; *Jaws* 1975; *Close Encounters of the Third Kind* 1977; *1941* 1979; *Raiders of the Lost Ark* 1981; *ET the Extra-Terrestrial* 1982; *Twilight Zone: the Movie* 1983; *Indiana Jones and the Temple of Doom* 1984; *The Color Purple* 1985; *Empire of the Sun* 1987; *Always* 1989; *Indiana Jones and the Last Crusade* 1989; *Hook* 1991; *Jurassic Park* 1993; *Schindler's List* 1993; *Amistad* 1997; *The Lost World: Jurassic Park* 1997; *Saving Private Ryan* 1998
Spiers, Bob *Spice World* 1997; *That Darn Cat* 1997
Spottiswoode, Roger *Terror Train* 1980; *The Pursuit of DB Cooper* 1981; *The Best of Times* 1986; *The Last Innocent Man* 1987; *Deadly Pursuit* 1988; *Turner & Hooch* 1989; *Air America* 1990; *Stop! or My Mom Will Shoot* 1992; *And the Band Played On* 1993; *Mesmer* 1994; *Tomorrow Never Dies* 1997
Springsteen, R G *Come Next Spring* 1956; *Showdown* 1963; *Bullet for a Badman* 1964; *He Rides Tall* 1964; *Apache Uprising* 1965; *Black Spurs* 1965; *Waco* 1966; *Johnny Reno* 1966; *Hostile Guns* 1967; *Tiger by the Tail* 1970
Spry, Robin *Keeping Track* 1986; *Obsessed* 1989
Stafford, Stephen *Double Edge* 1992; *Bionic Ever After?* 1994
Stahl, Eric Steven *Final Approach* 1991; *Safe House* 1997
Stahl, John M *Back Street* 1932; *Only Yesterday* 1933; *Imitation of Life* 1934; *Magnificent Obsession* 1935; *Parnell* 1937; *Letter of Introduction* 1938; *When Tomorrow Comes* 1939; *Our Wife* 1941; *Holy Matrimony* 1943; *The Immortal Sergeant* 1943; *The Eve of St Mark* 1944; *The Keys of the Kingdom* 1944; *Leave Her to Heaven* 1945; *The Foxes of Harrow* 1947; *Father Was a Fullback* 1949; *Oh, You Beautiful Doll* 1949
Stallone, Sylvester *Paradise Alley* 1978; *Rocky II* 1979; *Rocky III* 1982; *Staying Alive* 1983; *Rocky IV* 1985
Stanley, Richard *Hardware* 1990; *Dust Devil* 1992
Starewicz, Ladislaw *Town Rat, Country Rat* 1923; *The Tale of the Fox* 1931

Starrett, Jack Run, Angel, Run 1969; Slaughter 1972; The Strange Vengeance of Rosalie 1972; Cleopatra Jones 1973; The Gravy Train 1974; Race with the Devil 1975; A Small Town in Texas 1976; Final Chapter – Walking Tall 1977
Staudte, Wolfgang The Murderers Are amongst Us 1946; Yesterday's Tomorrow 1978
Stein, Jeff The Kids Are Alright 1978; Mother Goose Rock 'n' Rhyme 1990
Stein, Paul L aka **Stein, Paul** One Romantic Night 1930; Heart's Desire 1935; Poison Pen 1939; The Saint Meets the Tiger 1943
Steinberg, David Paternity 1981; Going Berserk 1983
Steinberg, Michael The Waterdance 1991; Bodies, Rest and Motion 1993
Steinmann, Danny Savage Streets 1984; Friday the 13th: a New Beginning 1985
Sterling, Joseph The Case of the Mukkinese Battle Horn 1955; Cloak without Dagger 1955
Stern, Leonard B aka **Stern, Leonard** The Snoop Sisters 1972; Just You and Me, Kid 1979; Missing Pieces 1991
Stern, Sandor Passions 1984; John and Yoko: a Love Story 1985; Assassin 1986; Easy Prey 1986; Glitz 1988; Shattered Innocence 1988; Pin 1988; Amityville: the Evil Escapes 1989; Without Her Consent 1990; Tell Me No Lies 1991; Jericho Fever 1993; A Child's Cry for Help 1994; Heart of a Child 1994; Gridlock 1995; The Stranger beside Me 1995; Badge of Betrayal 1996; In My Sister's Shadow 1999
Stern, Steven Hilliard The Harrad Summer 1974; I Wonder Who's Killing Her Now? 1975; Escape from Bogen County 1977; Running 1979; The Devil and Max Devlin 1981; A Small Killing 1981; Draw! 1984; Young Again 1986; Not Quite Human 1987; Murder in the City of Angels 1988; Morning Glory 1993; To Save the Children 1994; Black Fox 1995; Silence of Adultery 1995
Stevens, Andrew Illicit Dreams 1994; A Woman Scorned 1994; The Skateboard Kid II 1995; Crash Dive 1996; Grid Runners 1996; The White Raven 1998
Stevens, Art The Rescuers 1977; The Fox and the Hound 1981
Stevens, David Undercover 1983; Kansas 1988
Stevens, George Bachelor Bait 1934; Alice Adams 1935; Annie Oakley 1935; Swing Time 1936; A Damsel in Distress 1937; Quality Street 1937; Vivacious Lady 1938; Gunga Din 1939; Vigil in the Night 1940; Penny Serenade 1941; Woman of the Year 1942; The Talk of the Town 1942; The More the Merrier 1943; I Remember Mama 1948; A Place in the Sun 1951; Something to Live For 1952; Shane 1953; Giant 1956; The Diary of Anne Frank 1959; The Greatest Story Ever Told 1965; The Only Game in Town 1970
Stevens, Leslie Hero's Island 1962; Incubus 1965
Stevens, Mark Cry Vengeance 1954; Timetable 1956
Stevens, Robert The Big Caper 1957; Never Love a Stranger 1958; I Thank a Fool 1962; In the Cool of the Day 1963
Stevenson, Robert The Man Who Changed His Mind 1936; Tudor Rose 1936; King Solomon's Mines 1937; Owd Bob 1938; Return to Yesterday 1940; Tom Brown's Schooldays 1940; Back Street 1941; Joan of Paris 1942; Forever and a Day 1943; Jane Eyre 1943; Dishonored Lady 1947; The Woman on Pier 13 1949; The Las Vegas Story 1951; My Forbidden Past 1951; Johnny Tremain 1957; Old Yeller 1957; Darby O'Gill and the Little People 1959; Kidnapped 1960; The Absent-Minded Professor 1961; In Search of the Castaways 1961; Son of Flubber 1962; Mary Poppins 1964; The Misadventures of Merlin Jones 1964; The Monkey's Uncle 1965; That Darn Cat! 1965; Blackbeard's Ghost 1967; The Gnome-Mobile 1967; The Love Bug 1969; Bedknobs and Broomsticks 1971; Herbie Rides Again 1974; The Island at the Top of the World 1974; One of Our Dinosaurs Is Missing 1975; The Shaggy DA 1976
Stewart, Douglas Day Thief of Hearts 1984; Listen to Me 1989
Stiller, Ben Reality Bites 1994; The Cable Guy 1996
Stiller, Mauritz Gunnar Hede's Saga 1922; Hotel Imperial 1927
Stillman, Whit Metropolitan 1990; Barcelona 1994; The Last Days of Disco 1998
Stoloff, Benjamin aka **Stoloff, Ben** Palooka 1934; Sea Devils 1937; Super-Sleuth 1937; The Affairs of Annabel 1938; Radio City Revels 1938; The Bermuda Mystery 1944
Stone, Andrew L aka **Stone, Andrew** Bedside Manner 1945; Stormy Weather 1943; Sensations 1944; The Steel Trap 1952; The Night Holds Terror 1955; Julie 1956; Cry Terror 1958; The Decks Ran Red 1958; The Last Voyage 1960; Ring of Fire 1961; The Password Is Courage 1962; The Secret of My Success 1965; Song of Norway 1970; The Great Waltz 1972
Stone, Oliver Seizure 1974; The Hand 1981; Platoon 1986; Salvador 1986; Wall Street 1987; Talk Radio 1988; Born on the Fourth of July 1989; The Doors 1991; JFK 1991; Heaven and Earth 1993; Natural Born Killers 1994; Nixon 1995; U Turn 1997; Any Given Sunday 1999
Stones, Tad The Return of Jafar 1994; Aladdin and the King of Thieves 1996
Straub, Jean-Marie Not Reconciled, or Only Violence Helps Where Violence Rules 1965; Chronicle of Anna Magdalena Bach 1968
Strayer, Frank R The Vampire Bat 1933; Blondie 1938; Blondie Meets the Boss 1939; Blondie Takes a Vacation 1939; Footlight Glamour 1943
Streisand, Barbra Yentl 1983; The Prince of Tides 1991; The Mirror Has Two Faces 1996
Strick, Joseph The Savage Eye 1959; The Balcony 1963; Ulysses 1967; A Portrait of the Artist as a Young Man 1977
Strock, Herbert L Gog 1954; Battle Taxi 1955; Blood of Dracula 1957; I Was a Teenage Frankenstein 1957; How to Make a Monster 1958
Stuart, Mel If It's Tuesday, This Must Be Belgium 1969; I Love My... Wife 1970; Willy Wonka and the Chocolate Factory 1971; One Is a Lonely Number 1972; Wattstax 1972; Mean Dog Blues 1978; The White Lions 1980
Sturges, John The Walking Hills 1949; The Capture 1950; The Magnificent Yankee 1950; Mystery Street 1950; Right Cross 1950; The People against O'Hara 1951; It's a Big Country 1951; Escape from Fort Bravo 1953; Jeopardy 1953; Bad Day at Black Rock 1955; Underwater! 1955; The Scarlet Coat 1955; Backlash 1956; Gunfight at the OK Corral 1957; The Law and Jake Wade 1958; The Old Man and the Sea 1958; Last Train from Gun Hill 1959; Never So Few 1959; The Magnificent Seven 1960; By Love Possessed 1961; A Girl Named Tamiko 1962; Sergeants 3 1962; The Great Escape 1963; The Hallelujah Trail 1965; The Satan Bug 1965; Hour of the Gun 1967; Ice Station Zebra 1968; Marooned 1969; Joe Kidd 1972; The Valdez Horses 1973; McQ 1974; The Eagle Has Landed 1976
Sturges, Preston Christmas in July 1940; The Great McGinty 1940; The Lady Eve 1941; Sullivan's Travels 1941; The Palm Beach Story 1942; The Great Moment 1944; Hail the Conquering Hero 1944; The Miracle of Morgan's Creek 1944; Unfaithfully Yours 1948; The Beautiful Blonde from Bashful Bend 1949; Mad Wednesday 1950; The Diary of Major Thompson 1955
Sturridge, Charles Runners 1983; Aria 1987; A Handful of Dust 1987; Where Angels Fear to Tread 1991; FairyTale: a True Story 1997
Styles, Eric Dreaming of Joseph Lees 1998; Relative Values 2000
Subiela, Eliseo Hombre Mirando al Sudeste 1986; Last Images of the Shipwreck 1989; The Dark Side of the Heart 1992
Suissa, Danièle J Martha, Ruth and Edie 1988; Pocahontas: the Legend 1995
Sullivan, Kevin aka **Sullivan, Kevin Rodney** Soul of the Game 1996; How Stella Got Her Groove Back 1998
Summers, Jeremy The Punch and Judy Man 1962; Crooks in Cloisters 1963; The Vengeance of Fu Manchu 1967; Five Golden Dragons 1967
Summers, Walter The Return of Bulldog Drummond 1934; Music Hath Charms 1935; Dark Eyes of London 1939
Sundstrom, Cedric Captive Rage 1988; American Ninja 3: Blood Hunt 1989
Surjik, Stephen Wayne's World 2 1993; Little Criminals 1995; Weapons of Mass Distraction 1997
Sutherland, A Edward aka **Sutherland, Edward** It's the Old Army Game 1926; The Saturday Night Kid 1929; Paramount on Parade 1930; Palmy Days 1931; International House 1933; Murders in the Zoo 1933; Mississippi 1935; Poppy 1936; Every Day's a Holiday 1937; The Flying Deuces 1939; The Boys from Syracuse 1940; The Navy Comes Through 1942; Dixie 1943; Follow the Boys 1944; Secret Command 1944; Abie's Irish Rose 1946
Sutherland, Kiefer Last Light 1993; Truth or Consequences, NM 1997
Suzuki, Seijun Tokyo Drifter 1966; Branded to Kill 1967
Svankmajer, Jan Alice 1988; Faust 1994; Conspirators of Pleasure 1996
Svatek, Peter Witchboard – The Possession 1995; Sci-Fighters 1996; Jack London's The Call of the Wild 1996; Hemoglobin 1997
Sverak, Jan Elementary School 1991; Kolya 1996
Swackhamer, E W Man and Boy 1971; Death at Love House 1976; Spider-Man 1977; Are You Lonesome Tonight 1992
Swaim, Bob La Balance 1982; Half Moon Street 1986; Masquerade 1988; Target of Suspicion 1994
Swenson, Charles aka **Swenson, Chuck** The Mouse and His Child 1977; Twice upon a Time 1983
Swift, David Pollyanna 1960; The Parent Trap 1961; The Interns 1962; Love Is a Ball 1963; Under the Yum Yum Tree 1963; Good Neighbor Sam 1964; How to Succeed in Business without Really Trying 1967
Switzer, Michael Nitti: the Enforcer 1988; Revealing Evidence 1990; The Story of the Beach Boys: Summer Dreams 1990; The Woman Who Sinned 1991; With a Vengeance 1992; Stalking Laura 1993; Children of the Dark 1994; Touch of Truth 1994; Nothing but the Truth 1995; Remember Me 1995; What Love Sees 1996; Best Friends for Life 1998
Sykes, Peter Demons of the Mind 1971; The House in Nightmare Park 1973; Steptoe and Son Ride Again 1973; To the Devil a Daughter 1976; Jesus 1979
Szabó, István Apa 1966; Confidence 1979; Mephisto 1981; Colonel Redl 1984; Hanussen 1988; Meeting Venus 1990; Sweet Emma Dear Böbe 1992
Szwarc, Jeannot Extreme Close-Up 1973; Bug 1975; Jaws 2 1978; Somewhere in Time 1980; Enigma 1982; Supergirl 1984; Santa Claus 1985; The Murders in the Rue Morgue 1986

T

Tabio, Juan Carlos Strawberry and Chocolate 1993; The Elephant and the Bicycle 1995; Guantanamera 1995
Tacchella, Jean-Charles Cousin, Cousine 1975; L'Homme de Ma Vie 1992
Takacs, Tibor The Gate 1987; Deadly Past 1995; Sabotage 1996; Redline 1997; Sanctuary 1998
Talalay, Rachel Freddy's Dead: the Final Nightmare 1991; Ghost in the Machine 1993; Tank Girl 1995
Tamahori, Lee Once Were Warriors 1994; Mulholland Falls 1996; The Edge 1997
Tannen, William Flashpoint 1984; Deadly Illusion 1987; Hero and the Terror 1988
Tanner, Alain Jonah Who Will Be 25 in the Year 2000 1976; Messidor 1978; In the White City 1983; Woman from Rose Hill 1989; The Diary of Lady M 1992; Requiem 1998
Taplitz, Daniel Nightlife 1989; Black Magic 1992; Commandments 1996
Tarantino, Quentin Reservoir Dogs 1991; Pulp Fiction 1994; Four Rooms 1995; Jackie Brown 1997
Tarkovsky, Andrei Katok i Skrypka 1961; Ivan's Childhood 1962; Andrei Rublev 1966; Solaris 1972; Mirror 1974; Stalker 1979; Nostalgia 1983; The Sacrifice 1986
Tashlin, Frank Son of Paleface 1952; Marry Me Again 1953; Susan Slept Here 1954; Artists and Models 1955; The Girl Can't Help It 1956; Hollywood or Bust 1956; The Lieutenant Wore Skirts 1956; Will Success Spoil Rock Hunter? 1957; The Geisha Boy 1958; Rock-a-Bye Baby 1958; Say One for Me 1959; Cinderfella 1960; Bachelor Flat 1961; It'$ Only Money 1962; Who's Minding the Store? 1963; The Man from the Diner's Club 1963; The Disorderly Orderly 1964; The Alphabet Murders 1966; The Glass Bottom Boat 1966; Caprice 1967; The Private Navy of Sgt O'Farrell 1968
Tass, Nadia Malcolm 1986; Rikky and Pete 1988; The Big Steal 1990; Pure Luck 1991; Mr Reliable 1996
Tati, Jacques Jour de Fête 1947; School for Postmen 1947; Monsieur Hulot's Holiday 1953; Mon Oncle 1958; Playtime 1967; Traffic 1972; Parade 1974
Tatoulis, John In Too Deep 1990; The Silver Brumby 1992
Taurog, Norman Huckleberry Finn 1931; Skippy 1931; If I Had a Million 1932; The Phantom President 1932; We're Not Dressing 1934; Mrs Wiggs of the Cabbage Patch 1934; The Big Broadcast of 1936 1935; Strike Me Pink 1936; Rhythm on the Range 1936; You Can't Have Everything 1937; The Adventures of Tom Sawyer 1938; Boys Town 1938; Mad about Music 1938; Broadway Melody of 1940 1940; Little Nellie Kelly 1940; Young Tom Edison 1940; Design for Scandal 1941; Men of Boys Town 1941; Girl Crazy 1943; Presenting Lily Mars 1943; Ziegfeld Follies 1944; The Hoodlum Saint 1946; The Beginning or the End 1947; Words and Music 1948; That Midnight Kiss 1949; The Toast of New Orleans 1950; The Stooge 1951; Room for One More 1952; Jumping Jacks 1952; The Caddy 1953; Living It Up 1954; You're Never Too Young 1955; Bundle of Joy 1956; Pardners 1956; The Birds and the Bees 1956; The Fuzzy Pink Nightgown 1957; Onionhead 1958; Don't Give Up the Ship 1959; GI Blues 1960; Visit to a Small Planet 1960; All Hands on Deck 1961; Blue Hawaii 1961; Girls! Girls! Girls! 1962; It Happened at the World's Fair 1962; Palm Springs Weekend 1963; Sergeant Deadhead 1965; Tickle Me 1965; Dr Goldfoot and the Bikini Machine 1965; Double Trouble 1967; Live a Little, Love a Little 1968; Speedway 1968
Tavernier, Bertrand The Watchmaker of St Paul 1973; Deathwatch 1980; Clean Slate 1981; Sunday in the Country 1984; 'Round Midnight 1986; Life and Nothing But 1989; These Foolish Things 1990; L.627 1992; The Undeclared War 1992; D'Artagnan's Daughter 1994; The Bait 1995; It All Starts Today 1999
Taviani, Paolo Padre Padrone 1977; The Night of San Lorenzo 1981; Kaos 1984; Good Morning, Babylon 1987; Night Sun 1990; Fiorile 1993
Taviani, Vittorio Padre Padrone 1977; The Night of San Lorenzo 1981; Kaos 1984; Good Morning, Babylon 1987; Night Sun 1990; Fiorile 1993

RadioTimes DIRECTORS' INDEX

Taylor, Don *Ride the Wild Surf* 1964; *Jack of Diamonds* 1967; *The Manhunter* 1968; *Escape from the Planet of the Apes* 1971; *Tom Sawyer* 1973; *The Great Scout & Cathouse Thursday* 1976; *Echoes of a Summer* 1976; *The Island of Dr Moreau* 1977; *Damien – Omen II* 1978; *The Final Countdown* 1980; *Broken Promise* 1981; *September Gun* 1983; *Sexpionage* 1985
Taylor, Jud *Future Cop* 1976; *Packin' It In* 1983; *Out of the Darkness* 1985; *Broken Vows* 1987; *Foxfire* 1987; *Kaleidoscope* 1990; *Murder Times Seven* 1990; *The Old Man and the Sea* 1990; *In My Daughter's Name* 1992; *Prophet of Evil* 1993; *Secrets* 1995
Taylor, Ray *The Daltons Ride Again* 1945; *The Vigilantes Return* 1947
Taylor, Robert *The Nine Lives of Fritz the Cat* 1974; *Heidi's Song* 1982
Taylor, Sam *Safety Last* 1923; *Girl Shy* 1924; *Hot Water* 1924; *The Freshman* 1925; *For Heaven's Sake* 1926; *My Best Girl* 1927; *Coquette* 1929; *The Taming of the Shrew* 1929; *The Cat's Paw* 1934; *Nothing but Trouble* 1944; *The Monte Carlo Story* 1957
Teague, Lewis *The Lady in Red* 1979; *Alligator* 1980; *Death Vengeance* 1982; *Cujo* 1983; *Cat's Eye* 1984; *The Jewel of the Nile* 1985; *Collision Course* 1987; *Shannon's Deal* 1989; *Navy SEALS* 1990; *Wedlock* 1991; *Op Center* 1995; *Saved By the Light* 1995; *Dukes of Hazzard Reunion* 1997
Téchiné, André *The Brontë Sisters* 1979; *Rendez-vous* 1985; *The Scene of the Crime* 1986; *J'Embrasse Pas* 1991; *Ma Saison Préférée* 1993; *Les Roseaux Sauvages* 1994; *Les Voleurs* 1996; *Alice et Martin* 1998
Temple, Julien *The Great Rock 'n' Roll Swindle* 1979; *Running Out of Luck* 1985; *Absolute Beginners* 1986; *Aria* 1987; *Earth Girls Are Easy* 1988; *Bullet* 1995; *Vigo: Passion for Life* 1997; *The Filth and the Fury* 2000
Templeton, George *The Sundowners* 1950; *A Gift for Heidi* 1958
Tennant, Andy *Solomon's Choice* 1992; *Keep the Change* 1992; *The Amy Fisher Story* 1993; *It Takes Two* 1995; *Fools Rush In* 1997; *Ever After* 1998; *Anna and the King* 1999
Tenney, Kevin S *aka* **Tenney, Kevin** *Witchboard* 1987; *Night of the Demons* 1988; *Peacemaker* 1990; *Witchboard 2: The Devil's Doorway* 1993; *Pinocchio's Revenge* 1996
Tennyson, Pen *aka* **Tennyson, Penrose** *Convoy* 1940; *The Proud Valley* 1940
Teshigahara, Hiroshi *Woman in the Dunes* 1963; *The Face of Another* 1966; *Rikyu* 1989
Tessari, Duccio *The Heroes* 1972; *Three Tough Guys* 1974; *Zorro* 1975; *Tex and the Lord of the Deep* 1985; *Please Let the Flowers Live* 1986
Tetzlaff, Ted *Fighting Father Dunne* 1948; *A Dangerous Profession* 1949; *Johnny Allegro* 1949; *The Window* 1949; *The White Tower* 1950; *Treasure of Lost Canyon* 1952; *Son of Sinbad* 1955; *The Young Land* 1959
Tewkesbury, Joan *Old Boyfriends* 1979; *Cold Sassy Tree* 1989; *Sudie and Simpson* 1990; *Wild Texas Wind* 1991
Tewksbury, Peter *Sunday in New York* 1963; *Emil and the Detectives* 1964; *The Trouble with Girls* 1969
Thiele, William *aka* **Thiele, Wilhelm** *The Love Waltz* 1930; *London by Night* 1937; *Tarzan Triumphs* 1943; *Tarzan's Desert Mystery* 1943
Thomas (1), Dave *Strange Brew* 1983; *The Experts* 1989; *Bury Me in Niagara* 1993
Thomas, Betty *Only You* 1992; *My Breast* 1994; *The Brady Bunch Movie* 1995; *The Late Shift* 1996; *Private Parts* 1997; *Doctor Dolittle* 1998; *28 Days* 2000
Thomas, Gerald *Circus Friends* 1956; *Time Lock* 1957; *The Vicious Circle* 1957; *Carry On Sergeant* 1958; *The Duke Wore Jeans* 1958; *Carry On Nurse* 1959; *Carry On Teacher* 1959; *Carry On Constable* 1960; *Carry On Regardless* 1960; *Please Turn Over* 1960; *Watch Your Stern* 1960; *No Kidding* 1960; *Raising the Wind* 1961; *Carry On Cruising* 1962; *The Iron Maiden* 1962; *Twice round the Daffodils* 1962; *Carry On Cabby* 1963; *Carry On Jack* 1963; *Nurse on Wheels* 1963; *Carry On Cleo* 1964; *Carry On Spying* 1964; *The Big Job* 1965; *Carry On Cowboy* 1965; *Carry On – Don't Lose Your Head* 1966; *Carry On Screaming* 1966; *Carry On Follow That Camel* 1967; *Carry On Doctor* 1968; *Carry On Up the Khyber* 1968; *Carry On Again Doctor* 1969; *Carry On Camping* 1969; *Carry On Loving* 1970; *Carry On Up the Jungle* 1970; *Carry On at Your Convenience* 1971; *Carry On Henry* 1971; *Bless This House* 1972; *Carry On Abroad* 1972; *Carry On Matron* 1972; *Carry On Girls* 1973; *Carry On Dick* 1974; *Carry On Behind* 1975; *Carry On England* 1976; *That's Carry On* 1977; *Carry On Emmannuelle* 1978; *The Second Victory* 1986; *Carry On Columbus* 1992
Thomas, Ralph *The Clouded Yellow* 1950; *Appointment with Venus* 1951; *Venetian Bird* 1952; *A Day to Remember* 1953; *The Dog and the Diamonds* 1953; *Doctor in the House* 1954; *Mad about Men* 1954; *Above Us the Waves* 1955; *Doctor at Sea* 1955; *Checkpoint* 1956; *The Iron Petticoat* 1956; *Campbell's Kingdom* 1957; *Doctor at Large* 1957; *A Tale of Two Cities* 1957; *The Wind Cannot Read* 1958; *The Thirty-Nine Steps* 1959; *Upstairs and Downstairs* 1959; *Conspiracy of Hearts* 1960; *Doctor in Love* 1960; *No Love for Johnnie* 1960; *No My Darling Daughter* 1961; *A Pair of Briefs* 1961; *The Wild and the Willing* 1962; *Doctor in Distress* 1963; *Hot Enough for June* 1963; *Hot Enough for June* 1963; *The High Bright Sun* 1965; *Deadlier than the Male* 1966; *Doctor in Clover* 1966; *Nobody Runs Forever* 1968; *Some Girls Do* 1969; *Doctor in Trouble* 1970; *Percy* 1971; *Quest for Love* 1971; *Percy's Progress* 1974; *A Nightingale Sang in Berkeley Square* 1979
Thomas, Ralph L *aka* **Thomas, R L** *Ticket to Heaven* 1981; *Apprentice to Murder* 1988; *Young Ivanhoe* 1994; *Young Connecticut Yankee in King Arthur's Court* 1995
Thompson, Caroline *Black Beauty* 1994; *Buddy* 1997
Thompson, Ernest *1969* 1988; *The West Side Waltz* 1995
Thomson, Chris *The Empty Beach* 1985; *Moving Target* 1988; *She Was Marked for Murder* 1988; *The Delinquents* 1989; *Swimsuit* 1989; *Stop at Nothing* 1991; *Woman on the Ledge* 1993; *The Morrison Murders* 1997; *Meteorites!* 1998
Thorpe, Jerry *The Venetian Affair* 1966; *Day of the Evil Gun* 1968; *Company of Killers* 1970; *Kung Fu* 1972; *Smile, Jenny, You're Dead* 1974
Thorpe, Richard *Tarzan Escapes* 1936; *Double Wedding* 1937; *Man-Proof* 1937; *Night Must Fall* 1937; *The Crowd Roars* 1938; *Three Loves Has Nancy* 1938; *The Toy Wife* 1938; *The Adventures of Huckleberry Finn* 1939; *Tarzan Finds a Son!* 1939; *The Earl of Chicago* 1940; *Tarzan's Secret Treasure* 1941; *Joe Smith, American* 1942; *Tarzan's New York Adventure* 1942; *White Cargo* 1942; *Apache Trail* 1942; *Above Suspicion* 1943; *Cry Havoc* 1943; *Two Girls and a Sailor* 1944; *The Thin Man Goes Home* 1944; *Thrill of a Romance* 1945; *Fiesta* 1947; *A Date with Judy* 1948; *On an Island with You* 1948; *Challenge to Lassie* 1949; *Malaya* 1949; *Big Jack* 1949; *The Black Hand* 1950; *Three Little Words* 1950; *The Great Caruso* 1951; *Vengeance Valley* 1951; *It's a Big Country* 1951; *Ivanhoe* 1952; *The Prisoner of Zenda* 1952; *Carbine Williams* 1952; *All the Brothers Were Valiant* 1953; *Knights of the Round Table* 1953; *The Girl Who Had Everything* 1953; *The Student Prince* 1954; *Athena* 1954; *The Adventures of Quentin Durward* 1955; *The Prodigal* 1955; *Jailhouse Rock* 1957; *Tip on a Dead Jockey* 1957; *Ten Thousand Bedrooms* 1957; *The House of the Seven Hawks* 1959; *Killers of Kilimanjaro* 1960; *The Honeymoon Machine* 1961; *How the West Was Won* 1962; *Follow the Boys* 1963; *Fun in Acapulco* 1963; *The Truth about Spring* 1964; *That Funny Feeling* 1965; *The Last Challenge* 1967
Tian Zhuangzhuang *Horse Thief* 1986; *The Blue Kite* 1992
Till, Eric *Hot Millions* 1968; *The Walking Stick* 1970; *It Shouldn't Happen to a Vet* 1979; *Improper Channels* 1981; *Oh, What a Night* 1992; *Final Appeal* 1993; *Lifeline to Victory* 1993; *Silhouette* 1994; *Falling for You* 1995; *Murder at My Door* 1996
Tinling, James *Mr Moto's Gamble* 1938; *Riders of the Purple Sage* 1941
Tinto Brass, Giovanni *aka* **Brass, Tinto** *Salon Kitty* 1976; *Caligula* 1979
Toback, James *Fingers* 1978; *Love and Money* 1982; *Exposed* 1983; *The Pick-Up Artist* 1987; *The Big Bang* 1989; *Two Girls and a Guy* 1997; *Black and White* 1999
Tokar, Norman *Big Red* 1962; *Sammy, the Way Out Seal* 1962; *Savage Sam* 1963; *A Tiger Walks* 1964; *Those Calloways* 1964; *Follow Me, Boys!* 1966; *The Ugly Dachshund* 1966; *The Happiest Millionaire* 1967; *The Horse in the Gray Flannel Suit* 1968; *The Boatniks* 1970; *Snowball Express* 1972; *The Apple Dumpling Gang* 1974; *Where the Red Fern Grows* 1974; *No Deposit No Return* 1976; *Candleshoe* 1977; *The Cat from Outer Space* 1978
Tolkin, Michael *The Rapture* 1991; *The New Age* 1994
Tong, Stanley *Police Story III: Supercop* 1992; *Project S* 1993; *Jackie Chan's First Strike* 1996; *Rumble in the Bronx* 1996; *Mr Magoo* 1997
Topper, Burt *The Strangler* 1964; *The Hard Ride* 1971
Tornatore, Giuseppe *Cinema Paradiso* 1988; *Everybody's Fine* 1990; *The Starmaker* 1994; *A Pure Formality* 1994; *The Legend of 1900* 1999
Totten, Robert *aka* **Smithee, Allen** *Death of a Gunfighter* 1969; *The Wild Country* 1971; *Pony Express Rider* 1976
Tourneur, Jacques *Nick Carter, Master Detective* 1939; *Phantom Raiders* 1940; *Cat People* 1942; *I Walked with a Zombie* 1943; *The Leopard Man* 1943; *Days of Glory* 1944; *Experiment Perilous* 1944; *Canyon Passage* 1946; *Build My Gallows High* 1947; *Berlin Express* 1948; *Easy Living* 1949; *Circle of Danger* 1950; *The Flame and the Arrow* 1950; *Stars in My Crown* 1950; *Anne of the Indies* 1951; *Way of a Gaucho* 1952; *Appointment in Honduras* 1953; *Wichita* 1955; *Stranger on Horseback* 1955; *Great Day in the Morning* 1956; *Nightfall* 1956; *Night of the Demon* 1957; *The Fearmakers* 1958; *Timbuktu* 1959; *The Giant of Marathon* 1960; *The Comedy of Terrors* 1964; *City under the Sea* 1965
Tourneur, Maurice *The Pride of the Clan* 1917; *The Last of the Mohicans* 1920; *The Ship of Lost Men* 1929; *Königsmark* 1935; *Volpone* 1940
Towne, Robert *Personal Best* 1982; *Tequila Sunrise* 1988; *Without Limits* 1998
Townsend, Robert *Hollywood Shuffle* 1987; *Eddie Murphy Raw* 1987; *The Five Heartbeats* 1991; *The Meteor Man* 1993; *B.A.P.S.* 1997; *Jackie's Back!* 1999
Toye, Wendy *The Teckman Mystery* 1954; *Three Cases of Murder* 1954; *All for Mary* 1955; *Raising a Riot* 1955; *True as a Turtle* 1956; *We Joined the Navy* 1962
Toynton, Ian *The Maid* 1991; *Annie: a Royal Adventure* 1995
Tramont, Jean-Claude *All Night Long* 1981; *As Summers Die* 1986
Tran Anh Hung *The Scent of Green Papaya* 1993; *Cyclo* 1995
Trenchard-Smith, Brian *The Man from Hong Kong* 1975; *Turkey Shoot* 1981; *BMX Bandits* 1983; *Jenny Kissed Me* 1984; *Frog Dreaming* 1985; *Out of the Body* 1988; *Official Denial* 1993; *Night of the Demons 2* 1994; *Sahara* 1995; *Escape Clause* 1996; *Doomsday Rock* 1997; *Voyage of Terror* 1998
Trent, John *Homer* 1970; *The Only Way Out Is Dead* 1970; *Sunday in the Country* 1975; *Find the Lady* 1976; *Middle Age Crazy* 1980; *Best Revenge* 1983
Treut, Monika *Seduction: the Cruel Woman* 1985; *Virgin Machine* 1988; *My Father Is Coming* 1991; *Erotique* 1994
Trikonis, Gus *Moonshine County Express* 1977; *The Evil* 1978; *The Darker Side of Terror* 1979; *Touched by Love* 1979; *Take This Job and Shove It* 1981; *Malice in Wonderland* 1985; *The Great Pretender* 1991
Troche, Rose *Go Fish* 1994; *Bedrooms and Hallways* 1998
Troell, Jan *The Emigrants* 1971; *The New Land* 1972; *Zandy's Bride* 1974; *Hurricane* 1979; *Hamsun* 1996
Trousdale, Gary *Beauty and the Beast* 1991; *The Hunchback of Notre Dame* 1996
Trueba, Fernando *Belle Epoque* 1992; *Two Much* 1995
Truffaut, François *The 400 Blows* 1959; *Shoot the Pianist* 1960; *Jules et Jim* 1961; *Love at Twenty* 1962; *La Peau Douce* 1964; *Fahrenheit 451* 1966; *The Bride Wore Black* 1967; *Stolen Kisses* 1968; *Mississippi Mermaid* 1969; *Bed and Board* 1970; *L'Enfant Sauvage* 1970; *Anne and Muriel* 1971; *Day for Night* 1973; *Une Belle Fille Comme Moi* 1973; *L'Histoire d'Adèle H* 1975; *Small Change* 1976; *The Man Who Loved Women* 1977; *The Green Room* 1978; *Love on the Run* 1979; *The Last Metro* 1980; *Confidentially Yours* 1983
Truman, Michael *Touch and Go* 1955; *Go to Blazes* 1961; *Girl in the Headlines* 1963; *Daylight Robbery* 1964
Trumbull, Douglas *Silent Running* 1971; *Brainstorm* 1983
Tryon, Glenn *The Law West of Tombstone* 1938; *Beauty for the Asking* 1939
Tsai Ming-Liang *The River* 1997; *The Hole* 1998
Tsui Hark *The Butterfly Murders* 1979; *Zu Warriors* 1983; *Peking Opera Blues* 1986; *A Better Tomorrow III* 1989; *Once upon a Time in China* 1991; *The Master* 1992; *Twin Dragons* 1992; *Once upon a Time in China II* 1992; *Double Team* 1997; *Knock Off* 1998
Tsukamoto, Shinya *Tetsuo* 1989; *Tetsuo II: Body Hammer* 1991; *Tokyo Fist* 1995
Tucci, Stanley *Big Night* 1996; *The Impostors* 1998
Tuchner, Michael *Villain* 1971; *Fear Is the Key* 1972; *Mister Quilp* 1975; *The Likely Lads* 1976; *The Hunchback of Notre Dame* 1982; *Adam* 1983; *Trenchcoat* 1983; *Amos* 1985; *Not My Kid* 1985; *Trapped in Silence* 1986; *Mistress* 1987; *Desperate for Love* 1989; *Wilt* 1989; *Captive* 1991; *The Summer My Father Grew Up* 1991; *With Savage Intent* 1992; *Rainbow Warrior* 1992; *The Conviction of Kitty Dodds* 1993; *Good King Wenceslas* 1994; *Awake to Danger* 1995
Tully, Montgomery *Boys in Brown* 1949; *The Glass Cage* 1955; *The Hypnotist* 1957; *No Road Back* 1957; *Escapement* 1958; *Clash by Night* 1963; *Master Spy* 1964; *Battle beneath the Earth* 1968
Turman, Lawrence *The Marriage of a Young Stockbroker* 1971; *Second Thoughts* 1982
Turner, Ann *Celia* 1988; *Dallas Doll* 1994
Turner, Brad *Paris or Somewhere* 1995; *The Inspectors* 1998
Turteltaub, Jon *Think Big* 1990; *3 Ninja Kids* 1992; *Cool Runnings* 1993; *While You Were Sleeping* 1995; *Phenomenon* 1996; *Instinct* 1999
Tuttle, Frank *Canary Murder Case* 1929; *Her Wedding Night* 1930; *Paramount on Parade* 1930; *The Big Broadcast* 1932; *This Reckless Age* 1932; *This Is the Night* 1932; *Roman Scandals* 1933; *Ladies Should Listen* 1934; *All the King's Horses* 1935; *The Glass Key* 1935; *Waikiki Wedding* 1937; *Doctor Rhythm* 1938; *Paris Honeymoon* 1939; *This Gun for*

Hire 1942; *Hostages* 1943; *The Hour before the Dawn* 1944; *The Great John L* 1945; *Swell Guy* 1946; *Hell on Frisco Bay* 1955; *A Cry in the Night* 1956
Twist, Derek *The End of the River* 1947; *Green Grow the Rushes* 1951; *Police Dog* 1955
Twohy, David N *aka* **Twohy, David** *Timescape* 1991; *The Arrival* 1996; *Pitch Black* 2000
Tykwer, Tom *Wintersleepers* 1997; *Run Lola Run* 1998

U

Uderzo, Albert *Asterix the Gaul* 1967; *The 12 Tasks of Asterix* 1975
Ullmann, Liv *Sofie* 1992; *Kristin Lavransdatter* 1995; *Private Confessions* 1996
Ulmer, Edgar G *People on Sunday* 1929; *The Black Cat* 1934; *Bluebeard* 1944; *Detour* 1945; *The Strange Woman* 1946; *Carnegie Hall* 1947; *Ruthless* 1948; *The Man from Planet X* 1951; *The Loves of Three Queens* 1954; *The Naked Dawn* 1955; *Daughter of Dr Jekyll* 1957; *Hannibal* 1959
Underwood, Ron *Tremors* 1989; *City Slickers* 1991; *Heart and Souls* 1993; *Speechless* 1994; *Mighty Joe Young* 1998
Uno, Michael Toshiyuki *aka* **Smithee, Alan** *Without Warning: the James Brady Story* 1991; *Blind Spot* 1993; *Call of the Wild* 1993; *Dangerous Intentions* 1995; *The Road to Galveston* 1996
Ustinov, Peter *School for Secrets* 1946; *Vice Versa* 1947; *Romanoff and Juliet* 1961; *Lady L* 1965; *Hammersmith Is Out* 1972
Uys, Jamie *The Gods Must Be Crazy* 1980; *The Gods Must Be Crazy II* 1989

V

Vadim, Roger *And God Created Woman* 1956; *Les Liaisons Dangereuses* 1959; *The Seven Deadly Sins* 1961; *La Ronde* 1964; *The Game Is Over* 1966; *Barbarella* 1967; *Histoires Extraordinaires* 1967; *Pretty Maids All in a Row* 1971; *Don Juan 73, or If Don Juan Were a Woman* 1973; *Night Games* 1979; *The Hot Touch* 1982; *And God Created Woman* 1988
Valdez, Luis *Zoot Suit* 1981; *La Bamba* 1986; *The Cisco Kid* 1994
Vallelonga, Nick *A Brilliant Disguise* 1993; *In the Kingdom of the Blind* 1994
Van Dormael, Jaco *Toto Le Héros* 1991; *The Eighth Day* 1996
Van Dyke, W S *aka* **Van Dyke II, Major W S** *White Shadows in the South Seas* 1928; *Trader Horn* 1931; *Guilty Hands* 1931; *Tarzan, the Ape Man* 1932; *Penthouse* 1933; *The Prizefighter and the Lady* 1933; *Forsaking All Others* 1934; *Manhattan Melodrama* 1934; *The Thin Man* 1934; *I Live My Life* 1935; *Naughty Marietta* 1935; *After the Thin Man* 1936; *The Devil Is a Sissy* 1936; *His Brother's Wife* 1936; *Love on the Run* 1936; *Rose Marie* 1936; *San Francisco* 1936; *Personal Property* 1937; *The Prisoner of Zenda* 1937; *They Gave Him a Gun* 1937; *Rosalie* 1937; *Marie Antoinette* 1938; *Sweethearts* 1938; *Andy Hardy Gets Spring Fever* 1939; *Another Thin Man* 1939; *It's a Wonderful World* 1939; *Bitter Sweet* 1940; *I Love You Again* 1940; *I Take This Woman* 1940; *Dr Kildare's Victory* 1941; *The Feminine Touch* 1941; *Rage in Heaven* 1941; *Shadow of the Thin Man* 1941; *I Married an Angel* 1942; *Journey for Margaret* 1942
Van Horn, Buddy *Any Which Way You Can* 1980; *The Dead Pool* 1988; *Pink Cadillac* 1989
Van Peebles, Mario *New Jack City* 1991; *Posse* 1993; *Panther* 1995; *Gang in Blue* 1996; *Love Kills* 1998
Van Peebles, Melvin *Watermelon Man* 1970; *Sweet Sweetback's Baad Asssss Song* 1971; *Erotic Tales* 1994; *Gang in Blue* 1996
Van Sant, Gus *Drugstore Cowboy* 1989; *My Own Private Idaho* 1991; *Even Cowgirls Get the Blues* 1993; *To Die For* 1995; *Good Will Hunting* 1997; *Psycho* 1998
van Warmerdam, Alex *Abel* 1986; *The Northerners* 1992
Vane, Norman Thaddeus *Frightmare* 1981; *The Black Room* 1983; *Midnight* 1989
Vanzina, Carlo *The Gamble* 1988; *Millions* 1991
Varda, Agnès *Cleo from 5 to 7* 1961; *Le Bonheur* 1965; *Far from Vietnam* 1967; *Lions Love* 1969; *One Sings, the Other Doesn't* 1976; *Vagabond* 1985; *Jacquot de Nantes* 1991
Varnel, Marcel *Good Morning, Boys* 1937; *O-Kay for Sound* 1937; *Oh, Mr Porter!* 1937; *Alf's Button Afloat* 1938; *Ask a Policeman* 1938; *Convict 99* 1938; *Hey! Hey! USA* 1938; *Old Bones of the River* 1938; *Band Waggon* 1939; *Where's That Fire?* 1939; *Gasbags* 1940; *Let George Do It* 1940; *Neutral Port* 1940; *The Ghost of St Michael's* 1941; *Hi, Gang!* 1941; *I Thank You* 1941; *South American George* 1941; *It's Turned Out Nice Again* 1941; *King Arthur Was a Gentleman* 1942; *Much Too Shy* 1942; *Bell-Bottom George* 1943; *Get Cracking* 1943; *I Didn't Do It* 1945; *George in Civvy Street* 1946
Veber, Francis *Les Compères* 1983; *Three Fugitives* 1989; *Out on a Limb* 1992; *Le Dîner de Cons* 1998
Verhoeven, Michael *Killing Cars* 1986; *The Nasty Girl* 1990; *My Mother's Courage* 1995
Verhoeven, Paul *Turkish Delight* 1973; *Keetje Tippel* 1975; *Soldier of Orange* 1977; *Spetters* 1980; *The Fourth Man* 1983; *Flesh + Blood* 1985; *RoboCop* 1987; *Total Recall* 1990; *Basic Instinct* 1992; *Showgirls* 1995; *Starship Troopers* 1997
Verneuil, Henri *The Sheep Has Five Legs* 1954; *Any Number Can Win* 1963; *The 25th Hour* 1967; *Guns for San Sebastian* 1968; *The Sicilian Clan* 1969; *The Burglars* 1971; *The Serpent* 1972
Verona, Stephen *The Lords of Flatbush* 1974; *Pipe Dreams* 1976; *Boardwalk* 1979
VeSota, Bruno *The Female Jungle* 1955; *The Brain Eaters* 1958
Vicas, Victor *Count Five and Die* 1957; *The Wayward Bus* 1957
Vidor, Charles *The Arizonian* 1935; *Strangers All* 1935; *Blind Alley* 1939; *My Son, My Son* 1940; *The Lady in Question* 1940; *Ladies in Retirement* 1941; *The Tuttles of Tahiti* 1942; *The Desperadoes* 1943; *Cover Girl* 1944; *Together Again* 1944; *A Song to Remember* 1945; *Over 21* 1945; *Gilda* 1946; *The Loves of Carmen* 1948; *It's a Big Country* 1951; *Hans Christian Andersen* 1952; *Rhapsody* 1954; *Love Me or Leave Me* 1955; *The Swan* 1956; *A Farewell to Arms* 1957; *The Joker Is Wild* 1957; *Song without End* 1960
Vidor, King *The Big Parade* 1925; *La Bohème* 1926; *The Crowd* 1928; *The Patsy* 1928; *Show People* 1928; *Hallelujah* 1929; *Billy the Kid* 1930; *The Champ* 1931; *Street Scene* 1931; *Bird of Paradise* 1932; *Cynara* 1932; *The Mask of Fu Manchu* 1932; *The Stranger's Return* 1933; *Our Daily Bread* 1934; *So Red the Rose* 1935; *The Wedding Night* 1935; *The Texas Rangers* 1936; *Stella Dallas* 1937; *The Citadel* 1938; *The Wizard of Oz* 1939; *Comrade X* 1940; *Northwest Passage* 1940; *HM Pulham Esq* 1941; *An American Romance* 1944; *Duel in the Sun* 1946; *On Our Merry Way* 1948; *Beyond the Forest* 1949; *The Fountainhead* 1949; *Lightning Strikes Twice* 1951; *Japanese War Bride* 1952; *Ruby Gentry* 1952; *Man without a Star* 1955; *War and Peace* 1956; *Solomon and Sheba* 1959
Viertel, Berthold *The Man from Yesterday* 1932; *The Passing of the Third Floor Back* 1935
Vigo, Jean *A Propos de Nice* 1930; *Zéro de conduite* 1933; *L'Atalante* 1934
Vila, Camilo *The Unholy* 1988; *Unlawful Passage* 1994
Villalobos, Reynaldo *Conagher* 1991; *Hollywood Confidential* 1997
Vincent, Chuck *Hollywood Hot Tubs* 1984; *Preppies* 1984; *Warrior Queen* 1986; *Sensations* 1987
Virgo, Clément *Rude* 1995; *The Planet of Junior Brown* 1999
Visconti, Luchino *Ossessione* 1942; *La Terra Trema* 1947; *Bellissima* 1951; *Senso* 1954; *White Nights* 1957; *Rocco and His Brothers* 1960; *Boccaccio '70* 1961; *The Leopard* 1962; *Of a Thousand Delights* 1965; *The Stranger* 1967; *The Damned* 1969; *Death in Venice* 1971; *Ludwig* 1973; *Conversation Piece* 1974; *L'Innocente* 1976
Vogel, Virgil W *aka* **Vogel, Virgil** *The Land Unknown* 1957; *No Margin for Error* 1978; *Desperado* 1987; *Longarm* 1988; *Mario and the Mob* 1992
Voizard, Marc F *Hawk's Vengeance* 1996; *Marked Man* 1996
von Scherler Mayer, Daisy *Party Girl* 1994; *Madeline* 1998; *Woo* 1998
von Sternberg, Josef *The Salvation Hunters* 1925; *Underworld* 1927; *The Docks of New York* 1928; *The Dragnet* 1928; *The Last Command* 1928; *Thunderbolt* 1929; *The Blue Angel* 1930; *Morocco* 1930; *An American Tragedy* 1931; *Dishonored* 1931; *Blonde Venus* 1932; *Shanghai Express* 1932; *The Scarlet Empress* 1934; *Crime and Punishment* 1935; *The Devil Is a Woman* 1935; *The King Steps Out* 1936; *Sergeant Madden* 1939; *The Shanghai Gesture* 1941; *Duel in the Sun* 1946; *Macao* 1952; *The Saga of Anatahan* 1953; *Jet Pilot* 1957
von Stroheim, Erich *Blind Husbands* 1919; *Foolish Wives* 1920; *Greed* 1925; *The Merry Widow* 1925; *Queen Kelly* 1928; *The Wedding March* 1928; *Hello Sister!* 1933
von Trier, Lars *The Element of Crime* 1984; *Europa* 1991; *The Kingdom* 1994; *Breaking the Waves* 1996; *The Idiots* 1998
von Trotta, Margarethe *The Lost Honour of Katharina Blum* 1975; *Sisters, or the Balance of Happiness* 1979; *The German Sisters* 1981; *Rosa Luxemburg* 1986; *Three Sisters* 1988; *The Promise* 1994
Vorhaus, Bernard *Crime on the Hill* 1933; *The Ghost Camera* 1933; *Street Song* 1935; *Dusty Ermine* 1936; *The Last Journey* 1936; *Cotton Queen* 1937; *Three Faces West* 1940; *Lady from Louisiana* 1941
Voss, Kurt *Border Radio* 1987; *Knife Edge* 1990; *Genuine Risk* 1990; *Amnesia* 1996

W

Wachowski, Andy *Bound* 1996; *The Matrix* 1999
Wachowski, Larry *Bound* 1996; *The Matrix* 1999
Wacks, Jonathan *Powwow Highway* 1988; *Mystery Date* 1991; *Motherhood* 1993
Wadleigh, Michael *Woodstock* 1970; *Wolfen* 1981
Waggner, George *Man Made Monster* 1941; *The Wolf Man* 1941; *The Fighting Kentuckian* 1949; *Operation Pacific* 1951
Wagner, Bruce *I'm Losing You* 1998; *I'm Losing You* 1998
Wainwright, Rupert *Dillinger* 1991; *Blank Cheque* 1994; *Stigmata* 1999
Wajda, Andrzej *A Generation* 1954; *Kanal* 1957; *Ashes and Diamonds* 1958; *Love at Twenty* 1962; *Landscape after Battle* 1970; *Man of Marble* 1977; *The Young Ladies of Wilko* 1979; *The Conductor* 1980; *Man of Iron* 1981; *Danton* 1982; *Korczak* 1990; *Miss Nobody* 1997
Walas, Chris *The Fly II* 1989; *The Vagrant* 1992
Walker, Giles *The Masculine Mystique* 1984; *90 Days* 1986; *Princes in Exile* 1990; *Ordinary Magic* 1993
Walker, Hal *Duffy's Tavern* 1945; *Road to Utopia* 1945; *The Stork Club* 1945; *Out of This World* 1945; *At War with the Army* 1950; *My Friend Irma Goes West* 1950; *Sailor Beware* 1951; *That's My Boy* 1951; *Road to Bali* 1952
Walker, Peter *Die Screaming Marianne* 1970; *Tiffany Jones* 1973; *House of Whipcord* 1974; *House of Mortal Sin* 1975; *The Comeback* 1977; *House of the Long Shadows* 1983
Walker, Stuart *The Eagle and the Hawk* 1933; *White Woman* 1933; *The Mystery of Edwin Drood* 1935
Wallace, Richard *The Shopworn Angel* 1928; *Man of the World* 1931; *The Masquerader* 1933; *The Little Minister* 1934; *The Young in Heart* 1938; *The Navy Steps Out* 1941; *A Night to Remember* 1942; *Bombardier* 1943; *The Fallen Sparrow* 1943; *Bride by Mistake* 1944; *It's in the Bag* 1945; *Kiss and Tell* 1945; *Because of Him* 1946; *Framed* 1947; *Sinbad the Sailor* 1947; *Tycoon* 1947; *Let's Live a Little* 1948; *Adventure in Baltimore* 1949; *A Kiss for Corliss* 1949
Wallace, Rick *A Time to Live* 1985; *Acceptable Risks* 1986
Wallace, Stephen *The Boy Who Had Everything* 1984; *Blood Oath* 1990; *Turtle Beach* 1992
Wallace, Tommy Lee *Halloween III: Season of the Witch* 1982; *Aloha Summer* 1988; *Fright Night Part 2* 1988; *The Comrades of Summer* 1992; *Danger Island* 1992; *Witness to the Execution* 1994; *Once You Meet a Stranger* 1996; *Born Free: A New Adventure* 1996; *Final Justice* 1998
Waller, Anthony *Mute Witness* 1995; *An American Werewolf in Paris* 1997
Walls, Tom *A Cuckoo in the Nest* 1933; *Fighting Stock* 1935; *Foreign Affaires* 1935; *For Valour* 1937
Walsh, Raoul *The Thief of Bagdad* 1924; *What Price Glory* 1926; *The Lucky Lady* 1926; *Sadie Thompson* 1928; *The Red Dance* 1928; *The Cock-Eyed World* 1929; *In Old Arizona* 1929; *The Big Trail* 1930; *Me and My Gal* 1932; *The Bowery* 1933; *Going Hollywood* 1933; *Klondike Annie* 1936; *You're in the Army Now* 1936; *Spendthrift* 1936; *Big Brown Eyes* 1936; *Artists and Models* 1937; *College Swing* 1938; *The Roaring Twenties* 1939; *Dark Command* 1940; *They Drive by Night* 1940; *High Sierra* 1941; *Manpower* 1941; *The Strawberry Blonde* 1941; *They Died with Their Boots On* 1941; *Desperate Journey* 1942; *Gentleman Jim* 1942; *Background to Danger* 1943; *Northern Pursuit* 1943; *Uncertain Glory* 1944; *The Horn Blows at Midnight* 1945; *Objective, Burma!* 1945; *Salty O'Rourke* 1945; *The Man I Love* 1946; *Pursued* 1947; *Fighter Squadron* 1948; *Silver River* 1948; *Colorado Territory* 1949; *White Heat* 1949; *Along the Great Divide* 1951; *Captain Horatio Hornblower* 1951; *Distant Drums* 1951; *Murder, Inc* 1951; *Blackbeard the Pirate* 1952; *Glory Alley* 1952; *The Lawless Breed* 1952; *Sea Devils* 1952; *The World in His Arms* 1952; *Gun Fury* 1953; *A Lion Is in the Streets* 1953; *Saskatchewan* 1954; *Battle Cry* 1955; *The Tall Men* 1955; *The King and Four Queens* 1956; *The Revolt of Mamie Stover* 1956; *Band of Angels* 1957; *The Naked and the Dead* 1958; *The Sheriff of Fractured Jaw* 1958; *A Private's Affair* 1959; *Esther and the King* 1960; *A Distant Trumpet* 1964
Walters, Charles *Ziegfeld Follies* 1944; *Good News* 1947; *Easter Parade* 1948; *The Barkleys of Broadway* 1949; *Summer Stock* 1950; *The Belle of New York* 1952; *Dangerous When Wet* 1953; *Easy to Love* 1953; *Lili* 1953; *Torch Song* 1953; *The Glass Slipper* 1955; *The Tender Trap* 1955; *High Society* 1956; *Don't Go Near the Water* 1957; *Ask Any Girl* 1959; *Please Don't Eat the Daisies* 1960; *Two Loves* 1961; *Billy Rose's Jumbo* 1962; *The Unsinkable Molly Brown* 1964; *Walk, Don't Run* 1966
Walton, Fred *When a Stranger Calls* 1979; *Hadley's Rebellion* 1984; *April Fool's Day* 1986; *The Rosary Murders* 1987; *Trapped* 1989; *Murder in Paradise* 1990; *Plan of Attack* 1992; *When a Stranger Calls Back* 1993; *Dead Air* 1994; *The Courtyard* 1995; *The Stepford Husbands* 1996
Wanamaker, Sam *The File of the Golden Goose* 1969; *The Executioner* 1970; *Catlow* 1971;

DIRECTORS' INDEX
RadioTimes

1967; *The Jokers* 1967; *Hannibal Brooks* 1968; *The Games* 1970; *Lawman* 1971; *Chato's Land* 1972; *The Mechanic* 1972; *The Nightcomers* 1972; *Scorpio* 1973; *The Stone Killer* 1973; *Death Wish* 1974; *Won Ton Ton, the Dog Who Saved Hollywood* 1976; *The Sentinel* 1977; *The Big Sleep* 1978; *Firepower* 1979; *Death Wish II* 1981; *The Wicked Lady* 1983; *Death Wish 3* 1985; *Appointment with Death* 1988; *A Chorus of Disapproval* 1988; *Bullseye!* 1990; *Dirty Weekend* 1992; *Parting Shots* 1998

Winning, David *Profile for Murder* 1996; *Exception to the Rule* 1996; *Power Rangers 2* 1997

Winsor, Terry *aka* **Smithee, Alan** *Party, Party* 1983; *Home Front* 1987; *Essex Boys* 1999

Winston, Ron *Ambush Bay* 1966; *Don't Just Stand There* 1968; *The Gamblers* 1969

Winston, Stan *Vengeance: the Demon* 1988; *Upworld* 1993

Winterbottom, Michael *Butterfly Kiss* 1994; *Go Now* 1995; *Jude* 1996; *Welcome to Sarajevo* 1997; *I Want You* 1998; *Wonderland* 1999; *With or Without You* 1999

Winters, David *Thrashin'* 1986; *Rage to Kill* 1988

Wise, Herbert *The Lovers* 1972; *Skokie* 1981; *Welcome Home, Bobby* 1986

Wise, Kirk *Beauty and the Beast* 1991; *The Hunchback of Notre Dame* 1996

Wise, Robert *The Curse of the Cat People* 1944; *The Silent Bell* 1944; *The Body Snatcher* 1945; *A Game of Death* 1945; *Criminal Court* 1946; *Lady of Deceit* 1947; *Blood on the Moon* 1948; *Mystery in Mexico* 1948; *The Set-Up* 1949; *Three Secrets* 1950; *Two Flags West* 1950; *The Day the Earth Stood Still* 1951; *The House on Telegraph Hill* 1951; *The Captive City* 1952; *The Desert Rats* 1953; *Destination Gobi* 1953; *So Big* 1953; *Executive Suite* 1954; *Helen of Troy* 1955; *Somebody Up There Likes Me* 1956; *Tribute to a Bad Man* 1956; *Until They Sail* 1957; *This Could Be the Night* 1957; *I Want to Live!* 1958; *Run Silent, Run Deep* 1958; *Odds against Tomorrow* 1959; *West Side Story* 1961; *Two for the Seesaw* 1962; *The Haunting* 1963; *The Sound of Music* 1965; *The Sand Pebbles* 1966; *Star!* 1968; *The Andromeda Strain* 1970; *Two People* 1973; *The Hindenburg* 1975; *Audrey Rose* 1977; *Star Trek: the Motion Picture* 1979; *Rooftops* 1989

Wiseman, Carol *May Wine* 1990; *Face the Music* 1992

Wiseman, Frederick *High School* 1968; *Zoo* 1993

Witney, William *Bells of San Angelo* 1947; *Springtime in the Sierras* 1947; *Under California Stars* 1948; *The Far Frontier* 1949; *The Outcast* 1954; *Santa Fe Passage* 1955; *Stranger at My Door* 1956; *The Bonnie Parker Story* 1958; *The Cool and the Crazy* 1958; *The Secret of the Purple Reef* 1960; *Master of the World* 1961; *Apache Rifles* 1964; *Arizona Raiders* 1965; *I Escaped from Devil's Island* 1973

Wittman, Peter *Play Dead* 1981; *Ellie* 1984

Wohl, Ira *Best Boy* 1979; *Best Man* 1997

Wolk, Andy *Criminal Justice* 1990; *Traces of Red* 1992; *Kiss and Tell* 1996; *All Lies End in Murder* 1997

Wong Kar-Wai *aka* **Wang Jiawei** *Days of Being Wild* 1990; *Chung King Express* 1994; *Fallen Angels* 1995; *Happy Together* 1997

Wong, Kirk *aka* **Wong, Che Kirk,** *aka* **Wong, Che-Kirk** *Crime Story* 1993; *Rock'n'Roll Cop* 1994; *The Big Hit* 1998

Woo, John *A Better Tomorrow* 1986; *A Better Tomorrow II* 1987; *The Killer* 1989; *Bullet in the Head* 1990; *Once a Thief* 1991; *Hard-Boiled* 1992; *Hard Target* 1993; *Broken Arrow* 1996; *Once a Thief* 1996; *Face/Off* 1997; *Blackjack* 1998; *Mission: Impossible 2* 1999

Wood, Duncan *The Bargee* 1964; *Some Will, Some Won't* 1969

Wood Jr, Edward D *Glen or Glenda* 1953; *Jail Bait* 1954; *Bride of the Monster* 1955; *Plan 9 from Outer Space* 1959; *Night of the Ghouls* 1960; *Hellborn* 1961

Wood, Sam *Hold Your Man* 1933; *The Barbarian* 1933; *Stamboul Quest* 1934; *Let 'em Have It* 1935; *A Night at the Opera* 1935; *Whipsaw* 1935; *A Day at the Races* 1937; *Madame X* 1937; *Navy Blue and Gold* 1937; *Goodbye, Mr Chips* 1939; *Raffles* 1939; *Kitty Foyle* 1940; *Our Town* 1940; *The Devil and Miss Jones* 1941; *Kings Row* 1942; *The Pride of the Yankees* 1942; *For Whom the Bell Tolls* 1943; *Casanova Brown* 1944; *Guest Wife* 1945; *Saratoga Trunk* 1945; *Heartbeat* 1946; *Ivy* 1947; *Command Decision* 1948; *The Stratton Story* 1949; *Ambush* 1949

Woodhead, Leslie *The Tragedy of Flight 103: the Inside Story* 1990; *Endurance* 1998

Woods, Arthur B *aka* **Woods, Arthur** *Music Hath Charms* 1935; *Busman's Honeymoon* 1940

Workman, Chuck *Cuba Crossing* 1980; *Superstar: the Life and Times of Andy Warhol* 1991

Wrede, Casper *aka* **Wrede, Caspar** *Private Potter* 1963; *One Day in the Life of Ivan Denisovich* 1971; *Ransom* 1975

Wright, Basil *Song of Ceylon* 1934; *Night Mail* 1936

Wright, Mack V *Somewhere in Sonora* 1933; *Hit the Saddle* 1937

Wright, Tenny *The Big Stampede* 1932; *The Telegraph Trail* 1933

Wright, Thomas J *No Holds Barred* 1989; *The Operation* 1990; *Hell Hath No Fury* 1991

Wrye, Donald *The Entertainer* 1975; *Ice Castles* 1978; *Divorce Wars* 1982; *83 Hours till Dawn* 1990; *Lucky Day* 1991; *Stranger in the Family* 1991; *Separated by Murder* 1994; *Ultimate Betrayal* 1994; *A Family Divided* 1995; *Trail of Tears* 1995; *Not in This Town* 1997

Wyler, William *aka* **Wyler, Lt Col William** *Counsellor-at-Law* 1933; *The Gay Deception* 1935; *The Good Fairy* 1935; *Come and Get It* 1936; *Dodsworth* 1936; *These Three* 1936; *Dead End* 1937; *Jezebel* 1938; *Raffles* 1939; *Wuthering Heights* 1939; *The Letter* 1940; *The Westerner* 1940; *The Little Foxes* 1941; *Mrs Miniver* 1942; *Memphis Belle* 1943; *The Best Years of Our Lives* 1946; *The Heiress* 1949; *Detective Story* 1951; *Carrie* 1952; *Roman Holiday* 1953; *The Desperate Hours* 1955; *Friendly Persuasion* 1956; *The Big Country* 1958; *Ben-Hur* 1959; *The Children's Hour* 1961; *The Collector* 1965; *How to Steal a Million* 1966; *Funny Girl* 1968; *The Liberation of LB Jones* 1970

Wynorski, Jim *Big Bad Mama II* 1987; *Not of This Earth* 1988; *The Return of Swamp Thing* 1989; *Transylvania Twist* 1989; *The Haunting of Morella* 1990; *976-EVIL 2* 1992; *Munchie* 1992; *Little Miss Millions* 1993; *Sins of Desire* 1993; *Implicated* 1994; *Ghoulies IV* 1994; *Vampirella* 1996; *The Pandora Project* 1998

Y

Yaitanes, Greg *Hard Justice* 1995; *Double Tap* 1997

Yakin, Boaz *Fresh* 1994; *A Price above Rubies* 1997

Yang, Edward *Taipei Story* 1984; *A Brighter Summer Day* 1991

Yarbrough, Jean *Devil Bat* 1940; *Abbott and Costello in Society* 1944; *Twilight on the Prairie* 1944; *Here Come the Co-Eds* 1945; *Under Western Skies* 1945

Yates, Peter *Summer Holiday* 1962; *One Way Pendulum* 1965; *Robbery* 1967; *Bullitt* 1968; *John and Mary* 1969; *Murphy's War* 1971; *The Hot Rock* 1972; *The Friends of Eddie Coyle* 1973; *For Pete's Sake* 1974; *Mother, Jugs & Speed* 1976; *The Deep* 1977; *Breaking Away* 1979; *Eyewitness* 1981; *The Dresser* 1983; *Krull* 1983; *Eleni* 1985; *The House on Carroll Street* 1987; *Suspect* 1987; *An Innocent Man* 1989; *Year of the Comet* 1992; *The Run of the Country* 1995; *Roommates* 1995; *Curtain Call* 1998

Yeaworth Jr, Irvin S *The Blob* 1958; *Dinosaurus!* 1960

Yellen, Linda *Parallel Lives* 1994; *Northern Lights* 1997

Yorkin, Bud *Come Blow Your Horn* 1963; *Never Too Late* 1965; *Divorce American Style* 1967; *Inspector Clouseau* 1968; *Start the Revolution without Me* 1970; *The Thief Who Came to Dinner* 1973; *Twice in a Lifetime* 1985; *Arthur 2: On the Rocks* 1988; *Love Hurts* 1990

Young, Harold *The Scarlet Pimpernel* 1934; *The Storm* 1938; *There's One Born Every Minute* 1942; *The Three Caballeros* 1944

Young, Robert *aka* **Young, Robert William** *Vampire Circus* 1971; *The World Is Full of Married Men* 1979; *Hostage* 1992; *Doomsday Gun* 1994; *Fierce Creatures* 1997; *Captain Jack* 1998

Young, Robert M *aka* **Young, Robert Malcolm** *Trauma* 1962; *Keep It Up Downstairs* 1976; *Rich Kids* 1979; *One-Trick Pony* 1980; *The Ballad of Gregorio Cortez* 1983; *Saving Grace* 1985; *Extremities* 1986; *Dominick and Eugene* 1988; *Triumph of the Spirit* 1989; *Talent for the Game* 1991; *Splitting Heirs* 1993; *Roosters* 1993; *Caught* 1996

Young, Roger *Lassiter* 1984; *Into Thin Air* 1985; *Under Siege* 1986; *Love among Thieves* 1987; *The Squeeze* 1987; *Murder in Mississippi* 1990; *True Betrayal* 1990; *Victim of Beauty* 1991; *Double Crossed* 1991; *Geronimo* 1993; *Mercy Mission: the Rescue of Flight 771* 1993; *Getting Gotti* 1994; *Joseph in Egypt* 1995; *Heart Full of Rain* 1997; *A Knight in Camelot* 1998

Young, Terence *They Were Not Divided* 1950; *Valley of Eagles* 1951; *The Red Beret* 1953; *Storm over the Nile* 1955; *That Lady* 1955; *Safari* 1956; *Zarak* 1956; *Action of the Tiger* 1957; *No Time to Die* 1958; *Serious Charge* 1959; *Duel of Champions* 1961; *Dr No* 1962; *From Russia with Love* 1963; *The Amorous Adventures of Moll Flanders* 1965; *Thunderball* 1965; *The Dirty Game* 1965; *Triple Cross* 1966; *The Poppy Is Also a Flower* 1966; *Wait until Dark* 1967; *The Rover* 1967; *Mayerling* 1968; *The Christmas Tree* 1969; *Cold Sweat* 1971; *Red Sun* 1971; *The Valachi Papers* 1972; *The Klansman* 1974; *Bloodline* 1979; *Inchon* 1981; *The Jigsaw Man* 1984

Youngson, Robert *Days of Thrills and Laughter* 1961; *The Big Parade of Comedy* 1964; *Laurel and Hardy's Laughing 20s* 1965; *4 Clowns* 1970

Yu, Ronny *Warriors of Virtue* 1997; *Bride of Chucky* 1998

Yuen Kwai *aka* **Yuen, Corey** *The Legend of Fong Sai-Yuk I* 1993; *The Legend of Fong Sai-Yuk II* 1993

Yuzna, Brian *Society* 1989; *Bugs* 1990; *Bride of Re-Animator* 1991; *Necronomicon* 1993; *Return of the Living Dead III* 1993; *The Dentist* 1996; *Progeny* 1998; *The Dentist II* 1998

Z

Zaillian, Steven *Innocent Moves* 1993; *A Civil Action* 1998

Zamm, Alex *My Date with the President's Daughter* 1998; *Chairman of the Board* 1998

Zampa, Luigi *Children of Chance* 1949; *The Masters* 1975; *Tigers in Lipstick* 1979

Zampi, Mario *Laughter in Paradise* 1951; *Happy Ever After* 1954; *The Naked Truth* 1957; *Too Many Crooks* 1958; *Bottoms Up* 1959

Zanussi, Krzysztof *Illumination* 1972; *The Catamount Killing* 1974; *Camouflage* 1977; *The Contract* 1980; *Imperative* 1982; *A Year of the Quiet Sun* 1984; *The Silent Touch* 1992

Zaslove, Alan *GoBots: Battle of the Rocklords* 1986; *The Return of Jafar* 1994

Zeffirelli, Franco *The Taming of the Shrew* 1967; *Romeo and Juliet* 1968; *Brother Sun, Sister Moon* 1972; *The Champ* 1979; *Endless Love* 1981; *La Traviata* 1982; *Otello* 1986; *Young Toscanini* 1988; *Hamlet* 1990; *Sparrow* 1993; *Jane Eyre* 1996; *Tea with Mussolini* 1998

Zeglio, Primo *Morgan the Pirate* 1960; *Seven Seas to Calais* 1962

Zelnik, Fred *aka* **Zelnik, Frederick** *Happy* 1933; *Southern Roses* 1936

Zeltser, Yuri *Eye of the Storm* 1991; *Playmaker* 1994

Zeman, Karel *Invention of Destruction* 1958; *Baron Munchhausen* 1961

Zemeckis, Robert *I Wanna Hold Your Hand* 1978; *Used Cars* 1980; *Romancing the Stone* 1984; *Back to the Future* 1985; *Who Framed Roger Rabbit* 1988; *Back to the Future Part II* 1989; *Back to the Future Part III* 1990; *Death Becomes Her* 1992; *Forrest Gump* 1994; *Contact* 1997

Zetterling, Mai *Visions of Eight* 1973; *Scrubbers* 1982

Zhang Yimou *Red Sorghum* 1987; *Ju Dou* 1990; *Raise the Red Lantern* 1991; *The Story of Qiu Ju* 1992; *To Live* 1994; *Shanghai Triad* 1995; *Keep Cool* 1997; *Not One Less* 1999; *The Road Home* 2000

Zhang Yuan *Beijing Bastards* 1993; *Behind the Forbidden City* 1996

Zheng Junli *Spring River Flows East* 1947; *Crows and Sparrows* 1949

Zhou Xiaowen *Ermo* 1994; *The Emperor's Shadow* 1996

Zidi, Claude *Le Cop* 1985; *Le Cop II* 1989; *Asterix and Obelix Take on Caesar* 1999

Zieff, Howard *Slither* 1973; *Hearts of the West* 1975; *House Calls* 1978; *The Main Event* 1979; *Private Benjamin* 1980; *Unfaithfully Yours* 1983; *The Dream Team* 1989; *My Girl* 1991; *My Girl 2* 1994

Zielinski, Rafal *Screwballs* 1983; *Fun* 1994; *National Lampoon's Last Resort* 1994

Ziller, Paul *Pledge Night* 1990; *Deadly Surveillance* 1991; *Double Suspicion* 1993; *Beyond Suspicion* 1994; *Addicted to Love* 1995; *Panic in the Skies!* 1996

Zimmerman, Vernon *The Unholy Rollers* 1972; *Deadhead Miles* 1972; *Fade to Black* 1980

Zinnemann, Fred *Eyes in the Night* 1942; *Kid Glove Killer* 1942; *The Seventh Cross* 1944; *My Brother Talks to Horses* 1946; *The Search* 1948; *Act of Violence* 1949; *The Men* 1950; *Teresa* 1951; *High Noon* 1952; *The Member of the Wedding* 1952; *From Here to Eternity* 1953; *Oklahoma!* 1955; *A Hatful of Rain* 1957; *The Nun's Story* 1959; *The Sundowners* 1960; *Behold a Pale Horse* 1964; *A Man for All Seasons* 1966; *The Day of the Jackal* 1973; *Julia* 1977; *Five Days One Summer* 1982

Zito, Joseph *Abduction* 1975; *Friday the 13th: the Final Chapter* 1984; *Missing in Action* 1984; *Invasion USA* 1985; *Red Scorpion* 1989

Zlotoff, Lee David *Plymouth* 1991; *The Spitfire Grill* 1996

Zondag, Ralph *We're Back! A Dinosaur's Story* 1993; *Dinosaur* 2000

Zucker, David *Airplane!* 1980; *Top Secret!* 1984; *Ruthless People* 1986; *The Naked Gun* 1988; *The Naked Gun 2½: the Smell of Fear* 1991; *BASEketball* 1998

Zucker, Jerry *Airplane!* 1980; *Top Secret!* 1984; *Ruthless People* 1986; *Ghost* 1990; *First Knight* 1995

Zulawski, Andrzej *Possession* 1981; *La Femme Publique* 1984

Zurinaga, Marcos *Tango Bar* 1988; *The Disappearance of Garcia Lorca* 1997

Zwerin, Charlotte *Gimme Shelter* 1970; *Thelonious Monk: Straight No Chaser* 1988

Zwick, Edward *About Last Night...* 1986; *Glory* 1989; *Leaving Normal* 1992; *Legends of the Fall* 1994; *Courage under Fire* 1996; *The Siege* 1998

Actors' index

A

Aaker, Lee *Desperate Search* 1952; *Hondo* 1953; *Jeopardy* 1953
Aames, Willie *Zapped!* 1982; *Paradise* 1982; *Eight Is Enough: a Family Reunion* 1987
Aaron, Caroline *Big Night* 1996; *Deconstructing Harry* 1997
Abatantuono, Diego *Christmas Present* 1986; *Mediterraneo* 1991; *Puerto Escondido* 1992; *Nirvana* 1996; *Children of Hannibal* 1998
Abbott, Bruce *Re-Animator* 1985; *Trapped* 1989; *Bride of Re-Animator* 1991; *The Demolitionist* 1995; *Black Scorpion* 1995
Abbott, Bud *Buck Privates* 1941; *Hold That Ghost* 1941; *In the Navy* 1941; *Keep 'em Flying* 1941; *Pardon My Sarong* 1942; *Ride 'em Cowboy* 1942; *Rio Rita* 1942; *Who Done It?* 1942; *Hit the Ice* 1943; *It Ain't Hay* 1943; *Abbott and Costello in Society* 1944; *Lost in a Harem* 1944; *Abbott and Costello in Hollywood* 1945; *Here Come the Co-Eds* 1945; *The Time of Their Lives* 1946; *Little Giant* 1946; *Buck Privates Come Home* 1947; *Abbott and Costello Meet Frankenstein* 1948; *The Noose Hangs High* 1948; *Abbott and Costello Meet the Killer, Boris Karloff* 1949; *Africa Screams* 1949; *Abbott and Costello in the Foreign Legion* 1950; *Abbott and Costello Meet the Invisible Man* 1951; *Abbott and Costello Meet Captain Kidd* 1952; *Abbott and Costello Go to Mars* 1953; *Abbott and Costello Meet Dr Jekyll and Mr Hyde* 1953; *Abbott and Costello Meet the Keystone Cops* 1955; *Abbott and Costello Meet the Mummy* 1955; *Dance with Me Henry* 1956
Abbott, Diahnne *The King of Comedy* 1983; *Love Streams* 1984
Abbott, John *Conquest of the Air* 1936; *The Falcon in Hollywood* 1944; *Pursuit to Algiers* 1945; *The Bandit of Sherwood Forest* 1946; *Deception* 1946; *The Web* 1947; *The Woman in White* 1948; *Gigi* 1958; *Gambit* 1966; *The Jungle Book* 1967; *Slapstick of Another Kind* 1982
Abbott, Philip *The Bachelor Party* 1957; *Sweet Bird of Youth* 1962; *The Spiral Road* 1962; *Those Calloways* 1964; *Nightmare in Chicago* 1968; *Escape from Bogen County* 1977; *Prophet of Evil* 1993
Abdul-Jabbar, Kareem *Game of Death* 1978; *The Fish That Saved Pittsburgh* 1979; *Airplane!* 1980; *Slam Dunk Ernest* 1995; *Rebound* 1996
Abel, Alfred *Dr Mabuse, the Gambler* 1922; *Metropolis* 1926
Abel, Walter *The Three Musketeers* 1935; *Fury* 1936; *Green Light* 1937; *Law of the Underworld* 1938; *Men with Wings* 1938; *King of the Turf* 1939; *Arise, My Love* 1940; *Michael Shayne, Private Detective* 1940; *Miracle on Main Street* 1940; *Hold Back the Dawn* 1941; *Skylark* 1941; *Beyond the Blue Horizon* 1942; *Holiday Inn* 1942; *Wake Island* 1942; *Star Spangled Rhythm* 1942; *So Proudly We Hail* 1943; *An American Romance* 1944; *Mr Skeffington* 1944; *The Affairs of Susan* 1945; *Kiss and Tell* 1945; *The Kid from Brooklyn* 1946; *13 Rue Madeleine* 1946; *Dream Girl* 1948; *That Lady in Ermine* 1948; *Island in the Sky* 1953; *So This Is Love* 1953; *Night People* 1954; *The Indian Fighter* 1955; *Handle with Care* 1958; *Quick, Let's Get Married* 1964; *Mirage* 1965; *Silent Night, Bloody Night* 1972
Abelanski, Lionel *Didier* 1997; *Train of Life* 1999
Abercrombie, Ian *Army of Darkness* 1993; *Curse IV: The Ultimate Sacrifice* 1993; *Johnny Mysto* 1996
Abineri, John *The McKenzie Break* 1970; *Death Train* 1993
Abraham, F Murray *The Prisoner of Second Avenue* 1974; *The Sunshine Boys* 1975; *The Ritz* 1976; *Sex and the Married Woman* 1977; *The Big Fix* 1978; *Scarface* 1983; *Amadeus* 1984; *The Name of the Rose* 1986; *Beyond the Stars* 1988; *An Innocent Man* 1989; *Slipstream* 1989; *The Bonfire of the Vanities* 1990; *Mobsters* 1991; *Stockade* 1991; *By the Sword* 1992; *Journey to the Center of the Earth* 1993; *Last Action Hero* 1993; *National Lampoon's Loaded Weapon 1* 1993; *Nostradamus* 1993; *Surviving the Game* 1994; *Mighty Aphrodite* 1995; *Dillinger and Capone* 1995; *Children of the Revolution* 1996; *Color of Justice* 1997; *Mimic* 1997; *Eruption* 1997; *Star Trek: Insurrection* 1998; *Muppets from Space* 1999
Abrams, Michele *Victim of Beauty* 1991; *Buffy the Vampire Slayer* 1992; *Cool World* 1992
Abril, Victoria *The Moon in the Gutter* 1983; *Padre Nuestro* 1985; *After Darkness* 1985; *Max Mon Amour* 1986; *Tie Me Up! Tie Me Down!* 1990; *High Heels* 1991; *Lovers* 1991; *Kika* 1993; *Jimmy Hollywood* 1994; *French Twist* 1995
Abu Warda, Yussef *Cup Final* 1991; *Kadosh* 1999
Acheson, James *Body Language* 1992; *Kazaam* 1996
Acker, Sharon *Lucky Jim* 1957; *Point Blank* 1967; *The First Time* 1969; *Threshold* 1981
Ackerman, Bettye *Face of Fire* 1959; *Confessions of a Married Man* 1983
Ackerman, Leslie *Law and Disorder* 1974; *Blame It on the Night* 1984
Ackland, Joss *A Midsummer Night's Dream* 1961; *Rasputin, the Mad Monk* 1965; *Crescendo* 1970; *The House That Dripped Blood* 1971; *Villain* 1971; *The Happiness Cage* 1972; *England Made Me* 1973; *Hitler: the Last Ten Days* 1973; *Penny Gold* 1973; *The Black Windmill* 1974; *Great Expectations* 1974; *The Little Prince* 1974; *S*P*Y*S* 1974; *One of Our Dinosaurs Is Missing* 1975; *Operation Daybreak* 1975; *Royal Flash* 1975; *Silver Bears* 1978; *A Nightingale Sang in Berkeley Square* 1979; *Saint Jack* 1979; *Rough Cut* 1980; *The Apple* 1980; *Lady Jane* 1985; *A Zed & Two Noughts* 1985; *The Sicilian* 1987; *White Mischief* 1987; *To Kill a Priest* 1988; *Jekyll and Hyde* 1989; *Lethal Weapon 2* 1989; *The Bridge* 1990; *The Hunt for Red October* 1990; *Spymaker: the Secret Life of Ian Fleming* 1990; *Bill & Ted's Bogus Journey* 1991; *The Object of Beauty* 1991; *The Mighty Ducks* 1992; *Nowhere to Run* 1992; *Once upon a Crime* 1992; *The Princess and the Goblin* 1992; *Project: Shadowchaser* 1992; *Mother's Boys* 1993; *Jacob* 1994; *Mad Dogs and Englishmen* 1994; *A Kid in King Arthur's Court* 1995; *D3: the Mighty Ducks* 1996; *Surviving Picasso* 1996; *Amy Foster* 1997; *Firelight* 1997
Ackroyd, David *Mind over Murder* 1979; *The Mountain Men* 1980; *Memories of Me* 1988; *Dark Angel* 1989; *Hell Hath No Fury* 1991; *Breaking the Silence* 1992; *Dead On* 1993; *Love, Cheat & Steal* 1994
Acosta, Rodolfo *aka* **Acosta, Rudolph,** *aka* **Acosta, Rudy** *Appointment in Honduras* 1953; *Hondo* 1953; *Drum Beat* 1954; *Passion* 1954; *A Life in the Balance* 1955; *Bandido* 1956; *Flaming Star* 1960; *Let No Man Write My Epitaph* 1960; *Posse from Hell* 1961; *Return of the Seven* 1966; *Impasse* 1969; *Run, Simon, Run* 1970
Acovone, Jay *Cold Steel* 1987; *Born to Run* 1993; *Lookin' Italian* 1994; *Crash Dive* 1996; *On the Line* 1998
Acquanetta *Tarzan and the Leopard Woman* 1946; *The Legend of Grizzly Adams* 1990
Acuff, Eddie *The Case of the Velvet Claws* 1936; *Vengeance* 1937; *Law of the Underworld* 1938; *Rough Riders' Roundup* 1939
Adair, Jean *Advice to the Lovelorn* 1933; *Arsenic and Old Lace* 1944
Adair, Robert *The Ticket of Leave Man* 1937; *There Is Another Sun* 1951; *Park Plaza 605* 1953
Adalist, Jack *Chain of Command* 1993; *Hellbound* 1993
Adam, Ronald *Strange Boarders* 1938; *Obsession* 1948; *The Lavender Hill Mob* 1951; *Hindle Wakes* 1952; *Assignment Redhead* 1956; *Kill Me Tomorrow* 1957; *The Golden Disc* 1958; *Postman's Knock* 1961
Adams, Beverly *How to Fill a Wild Bikini* 1965; *Murderers' Row* 1966; *The Ambushers* 1967; *Torture Garden* 1967
Adams, Brandon *aka* **Adams, Brandon Quintin** *Moonwalker* 1988; *The People under the Stairs* 1991; *Ghost in the Machine* 1993; *The Sandlot* 1993
Adams, Brooke *Shock Waves* 1975; *Days of Heaven* 1978; *Invasion of the Body Snatchers* 1978; *Cuba* 1979; *A Man, a Woman and a Bank* 1979; *Tell Me a Riddle* 1980; *Utilities* 1981; *The Dead Zone* 1983; *Almost You* 1984; *Key Exchange* 1985; *The Lion of Africa* 1987; *Man on Fire* 1987; *Sometimes They Come Back* 1991; *The Unborn* 1991; *Gas, Food, Lodging* 1992
Adams, Catlin *The Jerk* 1979; *The Jazz Singer* 1980; *Freaky Friday* 1995
Adams, Don *The Nude Bomb* 1980; *Jimmy the Kid* 1982; *Get Smart, Again!* 1989
Adams, Dorothy *The Devil Commands* 1941; *Laura* 1944; *Johnny Concho* 1956; *Peeper* 1975
Adams, Edie *The Apartment* 1960; *Lover Come Back* 1961; *Call Me Bwana* 1963; *Love with the Proper Stranger* 1963; *Under the Yum Yum Tree* 1963; *The Best Man* 1964; *Made in Paris* 1966; *The Oscar* 1966; *The Honey Pot* 1967; *The Happy Hooker Goes to Hollywood* 1980
Adams, Jane *House of Dracula* 1945; *Rising Son* 1990; *Vital Signs* 1990; *Light Sleeper* 1991; *Kansas City* 1995; *Happiness* 1998
Adams, Jill *The Young Lovers* 1954; *One Way Out* 1955; *Value for Money* 1955; *Brothers in Law* 1956; *The Green Man* 1956; *The Scamp* 1957
Adams, Joe *Carmen Jones* 1954; *Ballad in Blue* 1966
Adams, Joey Lauren *aka* **Adams, Joey** *SFW* 1994; *Mallrats* 1995; *Bio-Dome* 1996; *Chasing Amy* 1996; *A Cool, Dry Place* 1998; *Big Daddy* 1999
Adams, Julie *aka* **Adams, Julia** *Bright Victory* 1951; *Bend of the River* 1952; *Horizons West* 1952; *The Lawless Breed* 1952; *Treasure of Lost Canyon* 1952; *The Man from the Alamo* 1953; *The Mississippi Gambler* 1953; *The Stand at Apache River* 1953; *Creature from the Black Lagoon* 1954; *The Looters* 1955; *The Private War of Major Benson* 1955; *Six Bridges to Cross* 1955; *One Desire* 1955; *Away All Boats* 1956; *Slaughter on Tenth Avenue* 1957; *Tickle Me* 1965; *Valley of Mystery* 1967; *The Last Movie* 1971; *Psychic Killer* 1975
Adams, Kathryn *Fifth Avenue Girl* 1939; *Argentine Nights* 1940
Adams, Kim *Ted & Venus* 1991; *Leaving Las Vegas* 1995
Adams, Lynne *Silent Hunter* 1995; *False Pretense* 1997
Adams, Mary *Blood of Dracula* 1957; *Diary of a Madman* 1963
Adams, Mason *The Final Conflict* 1980; *Revenge of the Stepford Wives* 1980; *Adam* 1983; *The Night They Saved Christmas* 1984; *Passions* 1984; *F/X* 1985; *Under Siege* 1986; *Toy Soldiers* 1991; *Son in Law* 1993; *Assault at West Point: the Court Martial of John Whittaker* 1994
Adams, Maud *The Christian Licorice Store* 1971; *The Man with the Golden Gun* 1974; *Killer Force* 1975; *Rollerball* 1975; *Playing for Time* 1980; *Tattoo* 1980; *Target Eagle* 1982; *Octopussy* 1983; *Nairobi Affair* 1984; *Jane and the Lost City* 1987; *Bugs* 1990
Adams, Nick *The Last Wagon* 1956; *Fury at Showdown* 1957; *Teacher's Pet* 1958; *Sing, Boy, Sing* 1958; *No Time for Sergeants* 1958; *The FBI Story* 1959; *Pillow Talk* 1959; *The Interns* 1962; *Twilight of Honor* 1963; *The Hook* 1963; *Frankenstein Meets the Devil Fish* 1964; *The Young Lovers* 1964; *Invasion of the Astro-Monster* 1965; *Young Dillinger* 1965; *Die, Monster, Die!* 1965
Adams, Peter *Bullwhip* 1958; *The Territorians* 1996
Adams, Robert *Song of Freedom* 1936; *Old Bones of the River* 1938; *Men of Two Worlds* 1946; *Sapphire* 1959
Adams, Stanley *Hell on Frisco Bay* 1955; *Lilies of the Field* 1963; *When the Boys Meet the Girls* 1965; *Thunder Alley* 1967; *The Grasshopper* 1970
Adams, Steve *Whiskers* 1997; *For Hire* 1997
Adams, Tom *A Prize of Arms* 1961; *Licensed to Kill* 1965; *The Fighting Prince of Donegal* 1966; *Where the Bullets Fly* 1966
Adamson, Christopher *Dirty Weekend* 1992; *Razor Blade Smile* 1998
Addams, Dawn *Plymouth Adventure* 1952; *The Moon Is Blue* 1953; *Khyber Patrol* 1954; *Secrets d'Alcove* 1954; *Return to Treasure Island* 1954; *A King in New York* 1957; *The Silent Enemy* 1958; *The Treasure of San Teresa* 1959; *The Two Faces of Dr Jekyll* 1960; *The Thousand Eyes of Dr Mabuse* 1960; *Come Fly with Me* 1962; *The Black Tulip* 1963; *Ballad in Blue* 1966; *Where the Bullets Fly* 1966; *The Vampire Lovers* 1970; *Vault of Horror* 1973
Addie, Robert *Excalibur* 1981; *Another Country* 1984; *A Knight in Camelot* 1998
Addison, Bernard *Brother Future* 1991; *The Farm: Angola, USA* 1996
Addy, Mark *The Full Monty* 1997; *Jack Frost* 1998; *The Last Yellow* 1999; *The Flintstones in Viva Rock Vegas* 2000
Addy, Wesley *Kiss Me Deadly* 1955; *Timetable* 1956; *Ten Seconds to Hell* 1959; *Hush... Hush, Sweet Charlotte* 1964; *Network* 1976; *The Europeans* 1979; *The Bostonians* 1984
Adelin, Jean-Claude *Chocolat* 1988; *Annabelle Partagée* 1990
Ades, Daniel *The Last Movie* 1971; *Aguirre, Wrath of God* 1972
Adiarte, Patrick *The King and I* 1956; *High Time* 1960
Adjani, Isabelle *L'Histoire d'Adèle H* 1975; *The Tenant* 1976; *The Driver* 1978; *Nosferatu, the Vampire* 1979; *The Brontë Sisters* 1979; *Possession* 1981; *Quartet* 1981; *One Deadly Summer* 1983; *Subway* 1985; *Ishtar* 1987; *Camille Claudel* 1988; *La Reine Margot* 1994; *Diabolique* 1996
Adler, Bill *Love and the Midnight Auto Supply* 1977; *Van Nuys Blvd* 1979
Adler, Jay *Cry Danger* 1951; *My Six Convicts* 1952; *The Family Jewels* 1965
Adler, Jerry *Exclusive* 1992; *The Public Eye* 1992; *Manhattan Murder Mystery* 1993; *The Odd Couple: Together Again* 1993; *Getting Away with Murder* 1996; *Six Ways to Sunday* 1997
Adler, Luther *The Loves of Carmen* 1948; *Saigon* 1948; *DOA* 1949; *House of Strangers* 1949; *Wake of the Red Witch* 1949; *Kiss Tomorrow Goodbye* 1950; *The Desert Fox* 1951; *M* 1951; *Hoodlum Empire* 1952; *Crashout* 1955; *The Girl in the Red Velvet Swing* 1955; *Hot Blood* 1956; *The Last Angry Man* 1959; *The Three Sisters* 1966; *The Brotherhood* 1968; *Live a Little, Steal a Lot* 1974; *The Man in the Glass Booth* 1975; *Absence of Malice* 1981
Adler, Matt *Teen Wolf* 1985; *Amazon Women on the Moon* 1987; *North Shore* 1987; *White Water Summer* 1987; *Doin' Time on Planet Earth* 1988
Adler, Robert *Green Grass of Wyoming* 1948; *Yellow Sky* 1948
Adolphson, Edvin *Dollar* 1938; *One Single Night* 1939; *Paw* 1959
Adonis, Frank *Eyes of Laura Mars* 1978; *Ace Ventura: Pet Detective* 1993
Adorée, Renée *Daydreams* 1922; *The Big Parade* 1925; *The Black Bird* 1926; *La Bohème* 1926
Adorf, Mario *Station Six-Sahara* 1962; *Major Dundee* 1965; *Ghosts – Italian Style* 1967; *The Bird with the Crystal Plumage* 1969; *The Red Tent* 1969; *King, Queen, Knave* 1972; *Without Warning* 1973; *The Italian Connection* 1973; *The Lost Honour of Katharina Blum* 1975; *The Tin Drum* 1979; *Lola* 1982; *The Holcroft Covenant* 1985; *The Second Victory* 1986

1990; *Pretty Woman* 1990; *White Palace* 1990; *I Don't Buy Kisses Anymore* 1992; *Coneheads* 1993; *Blankman* 1994; *North* 1994; *The Paper* 1994; *The Return of Jafar* 1994; *The Last Supper* 1995; *For Better or Worse* 1995; *Dunston Checks In* 1996; *The Hunchback of Notre Dame* 1996; *Love! Valour! Compassion!* 1997; *Rodgers & Hammerstein's Cinderella* 1997
Alexander, John *Arsenic and Old Lace* 1944; *The Horn Blows at Midnight* 1945; *The Jolson Story* 1946; *Where There's Life* 1947; *The Sleeping City* 1950; *The Marrying Kind* 1952
Alexander, Katherine *aka* **Alexander, Katharine** *The Barretts of Wimpole Street* 1934; *Death Takes a Holiday* 1934; *The Painted Veil* 1934; *She Married Her Boss* 1935; *After Office Hours* 1935; *The Devil Is a Sissy* 1936; *That Certain Woman* 1937; *The Great Man Votes* 1939; *In Name Only* 1939; *Dance, Girl, Dance* 1940; *Kiss and Tell* 1945
Alexander, Khandi *Poetic Justice* 1993; *Tina: What's Love Got to Do with It* 1993
Alexander, Richard *Law and Order* 1932; *Flash Gordon* 1936
Alexander, Ross *Flirtation Walk* 1934; *Captain Blood* 1935; *A Midsummer Night's Dream* 1935; *China Clipper* 1936
Alexander, Tad *Rasputin and the Empress* 1932; *Broadway to Hollywood* 1933
Alexander, Terence *The One That Got Away* 1957; *The Square Peg* 1958; *The League of Gentlemen* 1960; *Bitter Harvest* 1963; *Judith* 1966; *Only When I Larf* 1968; *What's Good for the Goose* 1969; *Waterloo* 1970
Alexander, Terry *Day of the Dead* 1985; *Conspiracy Theory* 1997
Alexandra, Charlotte *Contes Immoraux* 1974; *Goodbye Emmanuelle* 1977
Alfonsi, Lydia *Morgan the Pirate* 1960; *The Trojan War* 1961; *Black Sabbath* 1963
Alfonso, Kristian *Army of One* 1993; *Blindfold: Acts of Obsession* 1994; *Murder in a College Town* 1997
Alfonso, Yves *Made in USA* 1966; *Vladimir et Rosa* 1970
Alford, Phillip *To Kill a Mockingbird* 1962; *Shenandoah* 1965
Alfredson, Hans *Pippi Longstocking* 1968; *The Emigrants* 1971; *The New Land* 1972; *The Simple-Minded Murderer* 1982
Ali, Muhammad *aka* **Clay, Cassius** *Requiem for a Heavyweight* 1962; *The Greatest* 1977; *Freedom Road* 1979; *Body and Soul* 1981
Ali, Tatyana *aka* **Ali, Tatyana M** *Eddie Murphy Raw* 1987; *Fall into Darkness* 1996; *Kidz in the Wood* 1996; *Clown at Midnight* 1998
Alice, Mary *This Man Stands Alone* 1979; *Beat Street* 1984; *To Sleep with Anger* 1990; *Freedom Road: the Vernon Johns Story* 1994; *Down in the Delta* 1997
Alicia, Ana *aka* **Ana-Alicia** *The Ordeal of Bill Carney* 1981; *Romero* 1989; *Miracle Landing* 1990
Alison, Dorothy *The Maggie* 1953; *Turn the Key Softly* 1953; *Child's Play* 1954; *The Long Arm* 1956; *Reach for the Sky* 1956; *The Scamp* 1957; *The Silken Affair* 1957; *The Man Upstairs* 1958; *Life in Emergency Ward 10* 1959; *Blind Terror* 1971; *Dr Jekyll and Sister Hyde* 1971; *The Amazing Mr Blunden* 1972; *The Winds of Jarrah* 1983; *Rikky and Pete* 1988; *Malpractice* 1989
Allan, Elizabeth *Ace of Aces* 1933; *Men in White* 1934; *David Copperfield* 1935; *Java Head* 1935; *Mark of the Vampire* 1935; *A Tale of Two Cities* 1935; *The Shadow* 1936; *A Woman Rebels* 1936; *The Adventures of Michael Strogoff* 1937; *Camille* 1937; *Slave Ship* 1937; *Saloon Bar* 1940; *Went the Day Well?* 1942; *Folly to Be Wise* 1952; *Front Page Story* 1953; *The Heart of the Matter* 1953; *The Brain Machine* 1954; *Grip of the Strangler* 1958
Allbritton, Louise *Who Done It?* 1942; *Pittsburgh* 1942; *Son of Dracula* 1943; *The Egg and I* 1947; *Sitting Pretty* 1948; *Walk a Crooked Mile* 1948; *The Doolins of Oklahoma* 1949
Alldredge, Michael *The Incredible Melting Man* 1977; *Just Me and You* 1978; *About Last Night...* 1986; *Promise* 1986; *Night Walk* 1989; *Robot Jox* 1989
Allégret, Catherine *The Sleeping Car Murders* 1965; *Last Tango in Paris* 1972; *Burnt Barns* 1973; *Paul and Michelle* 1974; *Chanel Solitaire* 1981; *Nazi Hunter: the Beate Klarsfeld Story* 1986
Allen, Adrianne *Merrily We Go to Hell* 1932; *The Final Test* 1953
Allen, Barbara Jo *aka* **Vague, Vera** *Kiss the Boys Goodbye* 1941; *Girl Rush* 1944; *Rosie the Riveter* 1944; *Mohawk* 1956; *Sleeping Beauty* 1959
Allen, Chad *TerrorVision* 1986; *Murder in New Hampshire* 1991; *Praying Mantis* 1993
Allen, Chesney *A Fire Has Been Arranged* 1935; *O-Kay for Sound* 1937; *Alf's Button Afloat* 1938; *Gasbags* 1940; *We'll Smile Again* 1942; *Dreaming* 1944; *Here Comes the Sun* 1945; *Life Is a Circus* 1958
Allen, Corey *Rebel without a Cause* 1955; *The Big Caper* 1957; *Party Girl* 1958; *Key Witness* 1960
Allen, Debbie *Fame* 1980; *Jo Jo Dancer, Your Life Is Calling* 1986; *Out of Sync* 1995
Allen, Elizabeth *From the Terrace* 1960; *Donovan's Reef* 1963; *The Carey Treatment* 1972
Allen, Fred *Thanks a Million* 1935; *Sally, Irene and Mary* 1938; *It's in the Bag* 1945; *We're Not Married* 1952; *O Henry's Full House* 1952
Allen, Ginger Lynn *Buried Alive* 1990; *Leather Jackets* 1991; *Bound and Gagged: a Love Story* 1992
Allen, Gracie *The Big Broadcast* 1932; *International House* 1933; *We're Not Dressing* 1934; *Six of a Kind* 1934; *The Big Broadcast of 1936* 1935; *The Big Broadcast of 1937* 1936; *A Damsel in Distress* 1937; *College Swing* 1938; *Honolulu* 1939; *Mr and Mrs North* 1941
Allen, Jack *The Four Feathers* 1939; *The Sound Barrier* 1952; *Impulse* 1955; *Man from Tangier* 1957; *Life in Danger* 1959; *The Breaking Point* 1961
Allen, Jed *Lethal Charm* 1991; *Suspect Device* 1995
Allen, Jo Harvey *Checking Out* 1988; *Cold Sassy Tree* 1989
Allen, Joan *All My Sons* 1986; *Manhunter* 1986; *Peggy Sue Got Married* 1986; *The Room Upstairs* 1987; *Tucker: the Man and His Dream* 1988; *In Country* 1989; *Without Warning: the James Brady Story* 1991; *Ethan Frome* 1993; *Innocent Moves* 1993; *Josh and S.A.M.* 1993; *Mad Love* 1995; *Nixon* 1995; *The Crucible* 1996; *Face/Off* 1997; *The Ice Storm* 1997; *Pleasantville* 1998; *When the Sky Falls* 2000
Allen, Jonelle *Foster and Laurie* 1975; *The River Niger* 1976; *Grave Secrets: the Legacy of Hilltop Drive* 1992
Allen, Judith *This Day and Age* 1933; *The Old-Fashioned Way* 1934; *Bright Eyes* 1934
Allen, Karen *The Wanderers* 1979; *Cruising* 1980; *A Small Circle of Friends* 1980; *Raiders of the Lost Ark* 1981; *Shoot the Moon* 1982; *Split Image* 1982; *Starman* 1984; *Until September* 1984; *The Glass Menagerie* 1987; *Backfire* 1987; *Scrooged* 1988; *Animal Behavior* 1989; *Secret Weapon* 1990; *The Turning* 1992; *Ghost in the Machine* 1993; *King of the Hill* 1993; *The Sandlot* 1993; *Voyage* 1993; *The Perfect Storm* 2000
Allen, Keith *Loose Connections* 1983; *The Supergrass* 1985; *Comrades: a Lanternist's Account of the Tolpuddle Martyrs and What Became of Them* 1986; *Chicago Joe and the Showgirl* 1989; *Kafka* 1991; *Rebecca's Daughters* 1991; *Carry On Columbus* 1992; *Beyond Bedlam* 1993; *The Young Americans* 1993; *Captives* 1994; *Loch Ness* 1994; *Second Best* 1994; *Shallow Grave* 1994; *Blue Juice* 1995; *Rancid Aluminium* 1999
Allen, Lester *The Heat's On* 1943; *The Great Flamarion* 1945
Allen, Marty *The Last of the Secret Agents* 1966; *Mister Jerico* 1969
Allen, Nancy *Carrie* 1976; *I Wanna Hold Your Hand* 1978; *Home Movies* 1979; *1941* 1979; *Dressed to Kill* 1980; *Blow Out* 1981; *Strange Invaders* 1983; *The Philadelphia Experiment* 1984; *Not for Publication* 1984; *The Buddy System* 1984; *RoboCop* 1987; *Poltergeist III* 1988; *Limit Up* 1989; *Memories of Murder* 1990; *RoboCop 2* 1990; *RoboCop 3* 1993; *Patriots* 1994; *The Man Who Wouldn't Die* 1995
Allen, Patrick *Dial M for Murder* 1954; *Confession* 1955; *The Man Who Wouldn't Talk* 1957; *High Hell* 1957; *I Was Monty's Double* 1958; *Tread Softly Stranger* 1958; *Never Take Sweets from a Stranger* 1960; *Night of the Big Heat* 1967; *The Body Stealers* 1969; *When Dinosaurs Ruled the Earth* 1969; *Puppet on a Chain* 1970; *The Sea Wolves* 1980; *Agatha Christie's Murder Is Easy* 1982
Allen, Penelope *aka* **Allen, Penny** *Scarecrow* 1973; *Dog Day Afternoon* 1975; *On the Nickel* 1979
Allen, Rae *Damn Yankees* 1958; *Where's Poppa?* 1970; *Face of a Stranger* 1991
Allen, Rex *For the Love of Mike* 1960; *The Incredible Journey* 1963; *Charlotte's Web* 1973
Allen, Robert *The Black Room* 1935; *Crime and Punishment* 1935; *Terror in the City* 1963
Allen, Ronald *A Night to Remember* 1958; *The Projected Man* 1966; *Hell Boats* 1970; *Eat the Rich* 1987
Allen, Rosalind *Children of the Corn II: the Final Sacrifice* 1993; *Ticks* 1993; *Pinocchio's Revenge* 1996
Allen, Sage *Puppet Master II* 1990; *Ed* 1996
Allen, Sheila *Children of the Damned* 1964; *The Alphabet Murders* 1966; *Viva Knievel!* 1977; *Pascali's Island* 1988
Allen, Sian Barbara *You'll Like My Mother* 1972; *Billy Two Hats* 1973; *Eric* 1975
Allen, Steve *The Benny Goodman Story* 1955; *Warning Shot* 1967; *Where Were You When the Lights Went Out?* 1968; *The Comic* 1969; *The Ratings Game* 1984
Allen, Tanya *Lyddie* 1995; *The Morrison Murders* 1997; *Regeneration* 1997; *Tail Lights Fade* 1999
Allen, Tim *The Santa Clause* 1994; *Toy Story* 1995; *For Richer or Poorer* 1997; *Jungle 2 Jungle* 1997; *Toy Story 2* 1999; *Galaxy Quest* 1999
Allen, Todd *High Mountain Rangers* 1987; *Witchboard* 1987; *Brothers in Arms* 1988; *Storm and Sorrow* 1990; *Tall, Dark and Deadly* 1995; *Pinocchio's Revenge* 1996; *Night Visitors* 1996; *The Apostle* 1997
Allen, Woody *What's New, Pussycat?* 1965; *What's Up, Tiger Lily?* 1966; *Casino Royale* 1967; *Take the Money and Run* 1969; *Bananas* 1971; *Everything You Always Wanted to Know about Sex (But Were Afraid to Ask)* 1972; *Play It Again, Sam* 1972; *Sleeper* 1973; *Love and Death* 1975; *The Front* 1976; *Annie Hall* 1977; *Manhattan* 1979; *Stardust Memories* 1980; *A Midsummer Night's Sex Comedy* 1982; *Zelig* 1983; *Broadway Danny Rose* 1984; *Hannah and Her Sisters* 1986; *King Lear – Fear and Loathing* 1987; *Radio Days* 1987; *Crimes and Misdemeanors* 1989; *New York Stories* 1989; *Scenes from a Mall* 1991; *Shadows and Fog* 1991; *Husbands and Wives* 1992; *Manhattan Murder Mystery* 1993; *Don't Drink the Water* 1994; *Mighty Aphrodite* 1995; *Everyone Says I Love You* 1996; *Deconstructing Harry* 1997; *The Sunshine Boys* 1997; *Antz* 1998; *The Impostors* 1998; *Sweet and Lowdown* 1999
Allenby, Frank *The Black Sheep of Whitehall* 1941; *Madame Bovary* 1949; *Soldiers Three* 1951
Allende, Fernando *Agatha Christie's Murder in Three Acts* 1986; *Naked Lies* 1997
Allerson, Alexander *The McKenzie Break* 1970; *I Only Want You to Love Me* 1976; *Chinese Roulette* 1976; *Despair* 1978
Alley, Kirstie *Star Trek II: the Wrath of Khan* 1982; *Champions* 1983; *Runaway* 1984; *Blind Date* 1984; *Prince of Bel Air* 1986; *Summer School* 1987; *Deadly Pursuit* 1988; *Look Who's Talking* 1989; *Loverboy* 1989; *Look Who's Talking Too* 1990; *Madhouse* 1990; *Sibling Rivalry* 1990; *Look Who's Talking Now!* 1993; *David's Mother* 1994; *It Takes Two* 1995; *Village of the Damned* 1995; *Radiant City* 1996; *Suddenly* 1996; *Deconstructing Harry* 1997; *For Richer or Poorer* 1997; *Toothless* 1997; *Drop Dead Gorgeous* 1999
Allgood, Sara *Blackmail* 1929; *Juno and the Paycock* 1930; *Lazybones* 1935; *It's Love Again* 1936; *Southern Roses* 1936; *Storm in a Teacup* 1937; *How Green Was My Valley* 1941; *Lydia* 1941; *That Hamilton Woman* 1941; *Life Begins at 8.30* 1942; *Roxie Hart* 1942; *The War against Mrs Hadley* 1942; *Jane Eyre* 1943; *The Lodger* 1944; *Kitty* 1945; *The Strange Affair of Uncle Harry* 1945; *The Spiral Staircase* 1946; *The Fabulous Dorseys* 1947; *Mother Wore Tights* 1947; *My Wild Irish Rose* 1947; *The Accused* 1949; *Cheaper by the Dozen* 1950
Allison, Patricia *Out on the Edge* 1989; *Orpheus Descending* 1990
Allister, Claud *aka* **Allister, Claude** *Bulldog Drummond* 1929; *Monte Carlo* 1930; *Those Were the Days* 1934; *The Return of Bulldog Drummond* 1934; *Confirm or Deny* 1941
Allnutt, Wendy *Oh! What a Lovely War* 1969; *All Coppers Are...* 1972; *From beyond the Grave* 1973
Allport, Christopher *News at Eleven* 1986; *David: the David Rothenberg Story* 1988
Allred, Corbin *Quest of the Delta Knights* 1993; *Blue Rodeo* 1996; *Diamonds* 1999
Allwyn, Astrid *Love Affair* 1932; *The White Parade* 1934; *Hands across the Table* 1935; *Accent on Youth* 1935; *Dimples* 1936; *Follow the Fleet* 1936; *Love Affair* 1939; *Miracles for Sale* 1939; *The Lone Wolf Strikes* 1940
Allyson, June *Best Foot Forward* 1943; *Girl Crazy* 1943; *Meet the People* 1944; *Two Girls and a Sailor* 1944; *Music for Millions* 1945; *The Sailor Takes a Wife* 1945; *Two Sisters from Boston* 1946; *The Secret Heart* 1946; *Good News* 1947; *High Barbaree* 1947; *The Three Musketeers* 1948; *Little Women* 1949; *The Stratton Story* 1949; *Right Cross* 1950; *The Glenn Miller Story* 1953; *Battle Circus* 1953; *Executive Suite* 1954; *Woman's World* 1954; *The McConnell Story* 1955; *Strategic Air Command* 1955; *The Shrike* 1955; *The Opposite Sex* 1956; *You Can't Run Away from It* 1956; *Interlude* 1957; *My Man Godfrey* 1957; *A Stranger in My Arms* 1959; *They Only Kill Their Masters* 1972
Almagor, Gila *Sallah* 1964; *Every Time We Say Goodbye* 1986; *The Summer of Aviya* 1988
Almgren, Susan *aka* **Almgren, Suzie** *Separate Vacations* 1986; *Deadly Surveillance* 1991; *Twin Sisters* 1992
Alonso, Chelo *The Sign of the Gladiator* 1958; *Goliath and the Barbarians* 1959; *Morgan the Pirate* 1960
Alonso, Maria Conchita *Moscow on the Hudson* 1984; *A Fine Mess* 1986; *Touch and Go* 1986; *Extreme Prejudice* 1987; *The Running Man* 1987; *Colors* 1988; *Vampire's Kiss* 1988; *Predator 2* 1990; *McBain* 1991; *Teamster Boss: the Jackie Presser Story* 1992; *The House of the Spirits* 1993; *Roosters* 1993; *Caught* 1996; *My Husband's Secret Life* 1998
Alper, Murray *Down Mexico Way* 1941; *Security Risk* 1954
Alt, Carol *Millions* 1991; *Thunder in Paradise* 1993; *Ring of Steel* 1994; *Deadly Past* 1995; *Body Armor* 1996; *Private Parts* 1997
Alterio, Hector *Camila* 1984; *The Official Version* 1985; *Summer of the Colt* 1989; *I, the Worst of All* 1990
Altman, Bruce *Regarding Henry* 1991; *My New Gun* 1992; *Rookie of the Year* 1993; *To Gillian on Her 37th Birthday* 1996
Altman, John *Birth of the Beatles* 1979; *To Die For* 1994

Arcand, Denys *Jesus of Montreal* 1989; *Léolo* 1992

Arcand, Gabriel *Agnes of God* 1985; *The Decline of the American Empire* 1986; *The Revolving Doors* 1988

Archard, Bernard *The List of Adrian Messenger* 1963; *Play Dirty* 1969; *The Horror of Frankenstein* 1970; *Dad's Army* 1971; *Separate Tables* 1983

Archer, Anne *The Honkers* 1971; *Cancel My Reservation* 1972; *The Blue Knight* 1973; *The All-American Boy* 1973; *The Mark of Zorro* 1974; *Lifeguard* 1976; *A Matter of Wife...and Death* 1976; *Trackdown* 1976; *Good Guys Wear Black* 1977; *Paradise Alley* 1978; *Hero at Large* 1980; *Raise the Titanic* 1980; *Green Ice* 1981; *Waltz across Texas* 1982; *Too Scared to Scream* 1982; *The Naked Face* 1984; *The Check Is in the Mail* 1986; *Fatal Attraction* 1987; *Leap of Faith* 1988; *Love at Large* 1990; *Narrow Margin* 1990; *Eminent Domain* 1991; *Family Prayers* 1991; *Body of Evidence* 1992; *Patriot Games* 1992; *Nails* 1992; *Short Cuts* 1993; *Because Mommy Works* 1994; *Clear and Present Danger* 1994; *Jane's House* 1994; *The Man in the Attic* 1995; *Mojave Moon* 1996; *Neil Simon's Jake's Women* 1996; *Nico the Unicorn* 1998; *Indiscretion of an American Wife* 1998; *My Husband's Secret Life* 1998; *Nightmare in Big Sky Country* 1998; *Rules of Engagement* 2000

Archer, Barbara *The Feminine Touch* 1956; *Stranger's Meeting* 1957

Archer, John *Sherlock Holmes in Washington* 1943; *The Lost Moment* 1947; *Colorado Territory* 1949; *White Heat* 1949; *Destination Moon* 1950; *The Great Jewel Robber* 1950; *High Lonesome* 1950; *Best of the Badmen* 1951; *My Favorite Spy* 1951; *Santa Fe* 1951; *The Big Trees* 1952; *Rock around the Clock* 1956; *Decision at Sundown* 1957; *City of Fear* 1959; *Blue Hawaii* 1961; *Apache Rifles* 1964

Archer, Karen *Giro City* 1982; *Forever Young* 1984

Archibald, Stephen *My Childhood* 1972; *My Ain Folk* 1973; *My Way Home* 1978

Ardant, Fanny *Life Is a Bed of Roses* 1983; *Confidentially Yours* 1983; *Swann in Love* 1984; *Mélo* 1986; *The Family* 1987; *Three Sisters* 1988; *Australia* 1989; *Afraid of the Dark* 1991; *Le Colonel Chabert* 1994; *Beyond the Clouds* 1995; *Ridicule* 1996; *Elizabeth* 1998

Arden, Eve *Stage Door* 1937; *Having Wonderful Time* 1938; *Letter of Introduction* 1938; *At the Circus* 1939; *Eternally Yours* 1939; *Comrade X* 1940; *No, No, Nanette* 1940; *Manpower* 1941; *That Uncertain Feeling* 1941; *Whistling in the Dark* 1941; *Bedtime Story* 1942; *Change of Heart* 1943; *Let's Face It* 1943; *Cover Girl* 1944; *The Doughgirls* 1944; *Patrick the Great* 1944; *Earl Carroll Vanities* 1945; *Mildred Pierce* 1945; *Pan-Americana* 1945; *The Kid from Brooklyn* 1946; *My Reputation* 1946; *Night and Day* 1946; *The Arnelo Affair* 1947; *The Unfaithful* 1947; *Song of Scheherazade* 1947; *One Touch of Venus* 1948; *My Dream Is Yours* 1949; *Tea for Two* 1950; *Goodbye, My Fancy* 1951; *We're Not Married* 1952; *The Lady*

Wants Mink 1953; *Anatomy of a Murder* 1959; *The Dark at the Top of the Stairs* 1960; *The Strongest Man in the World* 1975; *Under the Rainbow* 1981; *Grease 2* 1982

Arden, Robert *Confidential Report* 1955; *Joe Macbeth* 1955; *The Final Conflict* 1980

Ardisson, George aka **Ardisson, Giorgio** *The Long Hair of Death* 1964; *Django against Sartana* 1970

Arditi, Pierre *Mélo* 1986; *Smoking/No Smoking* 1993; *Men, Women: a User's Manual* 1996; *On Connaît la Chanson* 1997; *Chance or Coincidence* 1999

Arenas, Reynaldo aka **Arenas, Reinaldo** *Hour of the Assassin* 1987; *Sniper* 1992

Arestrup, Niels *Je, Tu, Il, Elle* 1974; *Second Chance* 1976; *Meeting Venus* 1990

Argento, Asia *The Church* 1988; *Trauma* 1993; *Bits and Pieces* 1995; *B Monkey* 1996; *New Rose Hotel* 1998

Argenziano, Carmen *Punishment Park* 1971; *The Accused* 1988; *Stand and Deliver* 1988; *Red Scorpion* 1989; *Unlawful Entry* 1992; *Final Combination* 1993; *The Burning Season* 1994; *Cradle of Conspiracy* 1994; *To Walk Again* 1994; *Co-ed Call Girl* 1996; *A Murder of Crows* 1998

Argo, Victor aka **Argo, Vic** *Boxcar Bertha* 1972; *Mean Streets* 1973; *Florida Straits* 1986; *King of New York* 1989; *Bad Lieutenant* 1992; *Dangerous Game* 1993; *Household Saints* 1993; *Sins of Silence* 1995; *Lulu on the Bridge* 1998; *Next Stop Wonderland* 1998

Argue, David *Gallipoli* 1981; *BMX Bandits* 1983; *Backlash* 1986; *Hercules Returns* 1993; *Angel Baby* 1995

Arias, Imanol *Labyrinth of Passion* 1982; *Camila* 1984; *The Flower of My Secret* 1995

Arima, Ineko *The Human Condition* 1958; *Equinox Flower* 1958

Arizmendi, Yareli *Like Water for Chocolate* 1993; *The Big Green* 1995

Arkin, Adam *Chu Chu and the Philly Flash* 1981; *Full Moon High* 1982; *Personal Foul* 1987; *Babies* 1990; *The Doctor* 1991; *In the Line of Duty: Hunt for Justice* 1995; *Not in This Town* 1997; *Halloween H20: 20 Years Later* 1998; *Thirst* 1998; *Hanging Up* 1999

Arkin, Alan *The Russians Are Coming, the Russians Are Coming* 1966; *Wait until Dark* 1967; *Woman Times Seven* 1967; *The Heart Is a Lonely Hunter* 1968; *Inspector Clouseau* 1968; *Popi* 1969; *Catch-22* 1970; *Little Murders* 1971; *The Last of the Red Hot Lovers* 1972; *Deadhead Miles* 1972; *Freebie and the Bean* 1974; *Rafferty and the Gold Dust Twins* 1974; *Hearts of the West* 1975; *The Seven-Per-Cent Solution* 1976; *Fire Sale* 1977; *The In-Laws* 1979; *The Magician of Lublin* 1979; *The Last Unicorn* 1980; *Simon* 1980; *Improper Channels* 1981; *Chu Chu and the Philly Flash* 1981; *The Return of Captain Invincible* 1983; *Joshua Then and Now* 1985; *Bad Medicine* 1985; *Big Trouble* 1986; *A Deadly Business* 1986; *Coupe de Ville* 1990; *Edward Scissorhands* 1990; *Havana* 1990; *The Rocketeer* 1991; *Glengarry Glen Ross* 1992; *Indian Summer* 1993; *Cooperstown*

1993; *Doomsday Gun* 1994; *North* 1994; *Heck's Way Home* 1995; *The Jerky Boys* 1995; *Steal Big, Steal Little* 1995; *Mother Night* 1996; *Four Days in September* 1997; *Gattaca* 1997; *Grosse Pointe Blank* 1997; *Slums of Beverly Hills* 1998; *Jakob the Liar* 1999

Arkin, David *I Love You, Alice B Toklas* 1968; *Up in the Cellar* 1970; *The Long Goodbye* 1973; *Nashville* 1975

Arledge, John *Daddy Long Legs* 1931; *Flirtation Walk* 1934; *Murder on a Bridle Path* 1936; *You Can't Cheat an Honest Man* 1939

Arlen, Richard *Wings* 1927; *Beggars of Life* 1928; *Four Feathers* 1929; *The Virginian* 1929; *Thunderbolt* 1929; *Gun Smoke* 1931; *Island of Lost Souls* 1932; *Tiger Shark* 1932; *Alice in Wonderland* 1933; *Let 'em Have It* 1935; *Artists and Models* 1937; *When My Baby Smiles at Me* 1948; *The Mountain* 1956; *Warlock* 1959; *The Last Time I Saw Archie* 1961; *The Bounty Killer* 1965; *Apache Uprising* 1965; *Black Spurs* 1965

Arletty *Hôtel du Nord* 1938; *Le Jour se Lève* 1939; *Les Visiteurs du Soir* 1942; *Les Enfants du Paradis* 1945; *No Exit* 1954

Arliss, Dimitra *A Perfect Couple* 1979; *Xanadu* 1980

Arliss, George *Disraeli* 1929; *The Green Goddess* 1930; *The Man Who Played God* 1932; *A Successful Calamity* 1932; *The House of Rothschild* 1934; *The Last Gentleman* 1934; *Cardinal Richelieu* 1935; *The Tunnel* 1935; *His Lordship* 1936; *Dr Syn* 1937

Armendariz, Pedro *Portrait of Maria* 1943; *The Fugitive* 1947; *Fort Apache* 1948; *Three Godfathers* 1948; *We Were Strangers* 1949; *Tulsa* 1949; *El Bruto* 1952; *Diane* 1955; *The Conqueror* 1956; *Manuela* 1957; *The Wonderful Country* 1959; *Francis of Assisi* 1961; *From Russia with Love* 1963; *Agatha Christie's Murder in Three Acts* 1986

Armendariz Jr, Pedro *Macho Callahan* 1970; *The Magnificent Seven Ride!* 1972; *The Deadly Trackers* 1973; *Survival Run* 1979; *Old Gringo* 1989; *Highway Patrolman* 1991

Armetta, Henry *The Unholy Garden* 1931; *A Farewell to Arms* 1932; *Bogus Bandits* 1933; *What – No Beer?* 1933; *The Black Cat* 1934; *Magnificent Obsession* 1935; *Dust Be My Destiny* 1939

Armitage, George *Gas-s-s-s, or It Became Necessary to Destroy the World in Order to Save It* 1970; *Von Richthofen and Brown* 1971

Armstrong, Alun *Get Carter* 1971; *Krull* 1983; *That Summer of White Roses* 1989; *American Friends* 1991; *London Kills Me* 1991; *Split Second* 1991; *Blue Ice* 1992; *An Awfully Big Adventure* 1994; *Black Beauty* 1994; *The Saint* 1997; *Onegin* 1999; *With or Without You* 1999

Armstrong, Bess *The Four Seasons* 1981; *Jekyll and Hyde... Together Again* 1982; *High Road to China* 1983; *Jaws III* 1983; *Nothing in Common* 1986; *Second Sight* 1989; *Dream Lover* 1993; *The Skateboard Kid* 1993; *Take Me Home Again* 1994; *Danielle Steel's Mixed Blessings* 1995; *She Stood Alone: the Tailhook Scandal* 1995; *Forgotten Sins*

1996; *Christmas Every Day* 1996; *That Darn Cat* 1997; *Pecker* 1998

Armstrong, Bridget *The Amorous Prawn* 1962; *For the Love of Benji* 1977

Armstrong, Curtis *Risky Business* 1983; *Revenge of the Nerds* 1984; *Bad Medicine* 1985; *The Clan of the Cave Bear* 1986; *One Crazy Summer* 1986; *Hi Honey, I'm Dead* 1991; *Big Bully* 1996

Armstrong, Katherine *Ambition* 1991; *Blood Money* 1996

Armstrong, Kerry *The Getting of Wisdom* 1977; *Hunting* 1992

Armstrong, Louis *Pennies from Heaven* 1936; *Artists and Models* 1937; *Every Day's a Holiday* 1937; *Going Places* 1938; *Cabin in the Sky* 1943; *Atlantic City* 1944; *Here Comes the Groom* 1951; *Glory Alley* 1952; *High Society* 1956; *The Five Pennies* 1959; *The Beat Generation* 1959; *Paris Blues* 1961; *A Man Called Adam* 1966; *Hello, Dolly!* 1969

Armstrong, R G *From Hell to Texas* 1958; *No Name on the Bullet* 1959; *Ten Who Dared* 1960; *Ride the High Country* 1962; *He Rides Tall* 1964; *El Dorado* 1967; *Eighty Steps to Jonah* 1969; *The Great White Hope* 1970; *JW Coop* 1971; *The Great Northfield Minnesota Raid* 1972; *My Name Is Nobody* 1973; *Running Wild* 1973; *White Lightning* 1973; *Race with the Devil* 1975; *Stay Hungry* 1976; *The Car* 1977; *Mr Billion* 1977; *The Pack* 1977; *Fast Charlie: the Moonbeam Rider* 1978; *Where the Buffalo Roam* 1980; *The Pursuit of DB Cooper* 1981; *Raggedy Man* 1981; *Hammett* 1982; *Children of the Corn* 1984; *Jocks* 1986; *Warlock: the Armageddon* 1993; *Invasion of Privacy* 1996

Armstrong, Robert *A Girl in Every Port* 1928; *The Leatherneck* 1929; *Big News* 1929; *Danger Lights* 1930; *The Iron Man* 1931; *The Hounds of Zaroff* 1932; *The Lost Squadron* 1932; *The Penguin Pool Murder* 1932; *Blind Adventure* 1933; *King Kong* 1933; *Son of Kong* 1933; *Palooka* 1934; *"G" Men* 1935; *Remember Last Night?* 1935; *The Ex-Mrs Bradford* 1936; *Dive Bomber* 1941; *Baby Face Morgan* 1942; *My Favorite Spy* 1942; *Blood on the Sun* 1945; *Criminal Court* 1946; *The Paleface* 1948; *Return of the Bad Men* 1948; *The Lucky Stiff* 1949; *Mighty Joe Young* 1949

Armstrong, Todd *Jason and the Argonauts* 1963; *King Rat* 1965; *Dead Heat on a Merry-Go-Round* 1966; *The Long Ride Home* 1967

Armstrong, Vaughn *Triumphs of a Man Called Horse* 1983; *High Desert Kill* 1989

Armstrong, William *Riders of the Storm* 1986; *Danny, the Champion of the World* 1989

Arnall, Julia *Lost* 1955; *House of Secrets* 1956; *Mark of the Phoenix* 1957; *The Man without a Body* 1957

Arnatt, John *House of Blackmail* 1953; *Only Two Can Play* 1962; *Shadow of Fear* 1963; *Licensed to Kill* 1965; *Where the Bullets Fly* 1966; *A Challenge for Robin Hood* 1967; *Crucible of Terror* 1971

Arnaud, Yvonne *A Cuckoo in the Nest* 1933; *Neutral Port* 1940; *Tomorrow We Live* 1942; *The Ghosts of Berkeley Square* 1947

Arnaz, Desi *Too Many Girls* 1940; *The Navy Comes Through* 1942; *The Long, Long Trailer* 1954; *Forever, Darling* 1956; *The Escape Artist* 1982

Arnaz Jr, Desi *Billy Two Hats* 1973; *Marco* 1973; *Black Market Baby* 1977; *Joyride* 1977; *A Wedding* 1978; *House of the Long Shadows* 1983

Arnaz, Lucie *Billy Jack Goes to Washington* 1977; *The Jazz Singer* 1980; *Second Thoughts* 1982; *Who Gets the Friends?* 1988; *Abduction of Innocence* 1996

Arndt, Adelheid *Chinese Boxes* 1984; *Rosa Luxemburg* 1986

Arndt, Denis *Distant Thunder* 1988; *Basic Instinct* 1992; *Amelia Earhart: the Final Flight* 1994; *Nightscream* 1997

Arne, Peter *For Those in Peril* 1943; *The Cockleshell Heroes* 1955; *Timeslip* 1955; *The Moonraker* 1957; *Stranger's Meeting* 1957; *Intent to Kill* 1958; *Sands of the Desert* 1960; *The Treasure of Monte Cristo* 1960; *The Hellfire Club* 1961; *Girl in the Headlines* 1963; *The Black Torment* 1964; *Battle beneath the Earth* 1968; *The Oblong Box* 1969; *The Return of the Pink Panther* 1974

Arness, James aka **Arness, Jim** *Stars in My Crown* 1950; *Wyoming Mail* 1950; *Sierra* 1950; *Wagonmaster* 1950; *Cavalry Scout* 1951; *The People against O'Hara* 1951; *The Thing from Another World* 1951; *Big Jim McLain* 1952; *Hellgate* 1952; *Horizons West* 1952; *Hondo* 1953; *Island in the Sky* 1953; *The Lone Hand* 1953; *Them!* 1954; *Her Twelve Men* 1954; *The Sea Chase* 1955; *Many Rivers to Cross* 1955; *The First Travelling Saleslady* 1956; *Alias Jesse James* 1959; *Red River* 1988; *Gunsmoke: the Last Apache* 1990; *Gunsmoke: To the Last Man* 1992

Arnette, Jeanetta aka **Arnette, Jeannetta** *Flight 90: Disaster on the Potomac* 1984; *Ladybugs* 1992; *Boys Don't Cry* 1999

Arngrim, Stefan *Fear No Evil* 1980; *Misbegotten* 1998

Arnold, Edward *I'm No Angel* 1933; *Roman Scandals* 1933; *The White Sister* 1933; *The Barbarian* 1933; *Jennie Gerhardt* 1933; *Sadie McKee* 1934; *Thirty-Day Princess* 1934; *Cardinal Richelieu* 1935; *Crime and Punishment* 1935; *The Glass Key* 1935; *Remember Last Night?* 1935; *Come and Get It* 1936; *Meet Nero Wolfe* 1936; *Easy Living* 1937; *The Toast of New York* 1937; *The Crowd Roars* 1938; *You Can't Take It with You* 1938; *Idiot's Delight* 1939; *Mr Smith Goes to Washington* 1939; *Slightly Honorable* 1939; *The Earl of Chicago* 1940; *Johnny Apollo* 1940; *Lillian Russell* 1940; *Daniel and the Devil* 1941; *Design for Scandal* 1941; *Johnny Eager* 1941; *Meet John Doe* 1941; *The Penalty* 1941; *Unholy Partners* 1941; *Nothing but the Truth* 1941; *Eyes in the Night* 1942; *The War against Mrs Hadley* 1942; *Kismet* 1944; *Mrs Parkington* 1944; *Standing Room Only* 1944; *The Hidden Eye* 1945; *Week-End at the Waldorf* 1945; *My Brother Talks to Horses* 1946; *Dear Ruth* 1947; *The Hucksters* 1947; *Command Decision* 1948; *Take Me Out to the Ball Game* 1949; *Dear Wife* 1949; *Big Jack* 1949; *Annie Get Your Gun* 1950; *The Yellow Cab Man* 1950; *Belles on Their Toes* 1952; *City That Never Sleeps* 1953; *Living It Up* 1954; *The Ambassador's Daughter* 1956

Prisoner of Zenda 1937; Listen, Darling 1938; Paradise for Three 1938; There's Always a Woman 1938; Midnight 1939; Brigham Young 1940; Turnabout 1940; The Great Lie 1941; The Maltese Falcon 1941; Across the Pacific 1942; The Palm Beach Story 1942; Thousands Cheer 1943; Meet Me in St Louis 1944; Blonde Fever 1944; Claudia and David 1946; Cass Timberlane 1947; Cynthia 1947; Desert Fury 1947; Fiesta 1947; Act of Violence 1949; Any Number Can Play 1949; Little Women 1949; A Kiss before Dying 1956; The Power and the Prize 1956; The Devil's Hairpin 1957; This Happy Feeling 1958; A Stranger in My Arms 1959; Return to Peyton Place 1961; Hush... Hush, Sweet Charlotte 1964; Youngblood Hawke 1964

Atchison, Nancy Moore Wild Hearts Can't Be Broken 1991; They Watch 1993; The Yearling 1994

Ates, Roscoe aka **Ates, Rosco** The Champ 1931; Freaks 1932; Alice in Wonderland 1933; What – No Beer? 1933; Three Texas Steers 1939

Atherton, William Class of '44 1973; The Sugarland Express 1974; The Day of the Locust 1975; The Hindenburg 1975; Looking for Mr Goodbar 1977; Ghostbusters 1984; Real Genius 1985; A Fight for Jenny 1986; No Mercy 1986; Die Hard 1988; Buried Alive 1990; Die Hard 2: Die Harder 1990; Grim Prairie Tales 1990; The Pelican Brief 1993; Broken Trust 1995; Frank and Jesse 1995; Robin Cook's Formula for Death 1995; Saints and Sinners 1995; Bio-Dome 1996; Raven Hawk 1996; Mad City 1997; Executive Power 1998

Atkin, Harvey Meatballs 1979; Visiting Hours 1982; Love and Death on Long Island 1998

Atkine, Feodor Love and Death 1975; Le Beau Mariage 1982; Pauline at the Beach 1983; Leave All Fair 1985; Lola 1986; Nazi Hunter: the Beate Klarsfeld Story 1986; Sarraouina 1986; El Dorado 1988; High Heels 1991; Three Lives and Only One Death 1996

Atkins, Christopher The Blue Lagoon 1980; The Pirate Movie 1982; A Night in Heaven 1983; Sexpionage 1985; Listen to Me 1989; Die Watching 1993; Dead Man's Island 1996

Atkins, Eileen Inadmissible Evidence 1968; I Don't Want to Be Born 1975; Equus 1977; Oliver Twist 1982; The Dresser 1983; Let Him Have It 1991; Wolf 1994; Cold Comfort Farm 1995; Jack & Sarah 1995; The Avengers 1998

Atkins, Tom Special Delivery 1976; The Fog 1980; Halloween III: Season of the Witch 1982; Lethal Weapon 1987; A Stranger Waits 1987; Maniac Cop 1988; The Heist 1989; Cry in the Wild: the Taking of Peggy Ann 1991

Atkinson, Frank Ladies' Man 1931; The Green Cockatoo 1937

Atkinson, Jayne The Revenge of Al Capone 1989; Free Willy 1993; Blank Cheque 1994

Atkinson, Rowan The Tall Guy 1989; The Witches 1989; Hot Shots! Part Deux 1993; Four Weddings and a Funeral 1994; The Lion King 1994; Bean 1997; Maybe Baby 1999

Attal, Henri Les Biches 1968; Juste avant la Nuit 1971

Attal, Yvan A World without Pity 1989; Autobus 1991; Après l'Amour 1992; Patriots 1994; Portraits Chinois 1996; Love etc 1997; With or Without You 1999; The Criminal 1999

Attaway, Ruth Porgy and Bess 1959; Conrack 1974; Being There 1979

Attenborough, Richard In Which We Serve 1942; Journey Together 1944; Dancing with Crime 1946; A Matter of Life and Death 1946; School for Secrets 1946; Brighton Rock 1947; The Man Within 1947; The Guinea Pig 1948; London Belongs to Me 1948; Boys in Brown 1949; Morning Departure 1950; The Magic Box 1951; Father's Doing Fine 1952; The Gift Horse 1952; Eight O'Clock Walk 1953; The Ship That Died of Shame 1955; The Baby and the Battleship 1956; Brothers in Law 1956; Private's Progress 1956; The Scamp 1957; Danger Within 1958; Dunkirk 1958; Sea of Sand 1958; The Man Upstairs 1958; I'm All Right Jack 1959; Jet Storm 1959; SOS Pacific 1959; The Angry Silence 1960; The League of Gentlemen 1960; All Night Long 1961; Only Two Can Play 1962; Trial and Error 1962; The Great Escape 1963; Guns at Batasi 1964; Seance on a Wet Afternoon 1964; The Third Secret 1964; The Flight of the Phoenix 1966; The Sand Pebbles 1966; Doctor Dolittle 1967; The Bliss of Mrs Blossom 1968; Only When I Larf 1968; David Copperfield 1969; The Magic Christian 1969; Loot 1970; A Severed Head 1970; 10 Rillington Place 1970; The Last Grenade 1970; And Then There Were None 1974; Brannigan 1975; Conduct Unbecoming 1975; Rosebud 1975; The Chess Players 1977; The Human Factor 1979; Jurassic Park 1993; Miracle on 34th Street 1994; Hamlet 1996; The Lost World: Jurassic Park 1997; Elizabeth 1998

Atterbury, Malcolm Crime in the Streets 1956; Blood of Dracula 1957; How to Make a Monster 1958; Cattle King 1963; The Learning Tree 1969; Emperor of the North 1973

Atterton, Edward The Hunchback 1997; Relative Values 2000

Atwater, Barry The True Story of Lynn Stuart 1957; Pork Chop Hill 1959; The Night Stalker 1971

Atwill, Lionel Doctor X 1932; Murders in the Zoo 1933; Mystery of the Wax Museum 1933; The Vampire Bat 1933; The Song of Songs 1933; The Sphinx 1933; The Secret of Madame Blanche 1933; Nana 1934; One More River 1934; Stamboul Quest 1934; The Age of Innocence 1934; Captain Blood 1935; The Devil Is a Woman 1935; Mark of the Vampire 1935; Murder Man 1935; Rendezvous 1935; Till We Meet Again 1936; The Great Garrick 1937; Lancer Spy 1937; The Last Train from Madrid 1937; The Great Waltz 1938; Three Comrades 1938; The Hound of the Baskervilles 1939; Mr Moto Takes a Vacation 1939; The Secret of Dr Kildare 1939; Son of Frankenstein 1939; The Three Musketeers 1939; Balalaika 1939; Boom Town 1940; Johnny Apollo 1940; Man Made Monster 1941; Pardon My Sarong 1942; Sherlock Holmes and the Secret

Weapon 1942; To Be or Not to Be 1942; The Ghost of Frankenstein 1942; The Mad Doctor of Market Street 1942; Frankenstein Meets the Wolf Man 1943; House of Frankenstein 1944; House of Dracula 1945; Fog Island 1945

Atzmon, Anat Lemon Popsicle 1978; Every Time We Say Goodbye 1986; Double Edge 1992

Atzorn, Robert From the Life of the Marionettes 1980; The Beautiful End of This World 1983

Auberjonois, René Lilith 1964; MASH 1969; Brewster McCloud 1970; McCabe and Mrs Miller 1971; Images 1972; Pete 'n' Tillie 1972; The Big Bus 1976; King Kong 1976; Eyes of Laura Mars 1978; Where the Buffalo Roam 1980; The Christmas Star 1986; Walker 1987; Longarm 1988; Police Academy 5: Assignment Miami Beach 1988; Gore Vidal's Billy the Kid 1989; The Little Mermaid 1989; The Feud 1989; Little Nemo: Adventures in Slumberland 1992; Wild Card 1992; The Ballad of Little Jo 1993; Lone Justice 1994; Los Locos 1997; Cats Don't Dance 1998

Aubert, Lenore They Got Me Covered 1943; I Wonder Who's Kissing Her Now 1947; Abbott and Costello Meet Frankenstein 1948; Abbott and Costello Meet the Killer, Boris Karloff 1949

Aubrey, Anne No Time to Die 1958; The Bandit of Zhobe 1959; Killers of Kilimanjaro 1960; Let's Get Married 1960

Aubrey, James Lord of the Flies 1963; Forever Young 1984; Riders of the Storm 1986

Aubrey, Juliet Jacob 1994; Go Now 1995; Food of Love 1997; Still Crazy 1998

Aubrey, Skye The Carey Treatment 1972; The Phantom of Hollywood 1974

Aubuchon, Jacques Short Cut to Hell 1957; The Way to the Gold 1957; Gun Glory 1957; Wild and Wonderful 1964; September Gun 1983

Auclair, Michel aka **Auclair, Michael** La Belle et la Bête 1946; Funny Face 1957; Sink or Swim 1971; Story of a Love Story 1973; Three Men to Destroy 1980

Audley, Eleanor Cinderella 1950; Sleeping Beauty 1959

Audley, Maxine The Sleeping Tiger 1954; A King in New York 1957; Hell Is a City 1959; Peeping Tom 1960; The Trials of Oscar Wilde 1960; Petticoat Pirates 1961; The Brain 1962; The Battle of the Villa Fiorita 1964; A Jolly Bad Fellow 1964; House of Cards 1968; Sinful Davey 1969

Audran, Stéphane The Sign of Leo 1959; Les Bonnes Femmes 1960; Bluebeard 1962; Paris Vu Par... 1965; The Champagne Murders 1966; Les Biches 1968; La Femme Infidèle 1968; Le Boucher 1969; The Lady in the Car with Glasses and a Gun 1970; La Rupture 1970; Juste avant la Nuit 1971; The Discreet Charm of the Bourgeoisie 1972; Without Apparent Motive 1972; Les Noces Rouges 1973; And Then There Were None 1974; Vincent, François, Paul and the Others 1974; The Black Bird 1975; The Twist 1976; Blood Relatives 1977; The Devil's Advocate 1977; To Kill a Rat 1977; Violette Nozière 1977; Eagle's Wing 1978; Silver Bears 1978; The Big Red

One 1980; Clean Slate 1981; Shock 1982; Cop au Vin 1984; The Blood of Others 1984; Bay Boy 1984; La Cage aux Folles III: ''Elles'' se Marient 1985; Babette's Feast 1987; Sons 1989; The Turn of the Screw 1992; Maximum Risk 1996; Madeline 1998

Auer, Mischa Paramount on Parade 1930; Tarzan the Fearless 1933; Bulldog Drummond Strikes Back 1934; Stamboul Quest 1934; My Man Godfrey 1936; Winterset 1936; Vogues 1937; Three Smart Girls 1937; One Hundred Men and a Girl 1937; Sweethearts 1938; You Can't Take It with You 1938; The Rage of Paris 1938; Destry Rides Again 1939; East Side of Heaven 1939; Trail of the Vigilantes 1940; Seven Sinners 1940; The Flame of New Orleans 1941; Hellzapoppin' 1941; Twin Beds 1942; Lady in the Dark 1944; Up in Mabel's Room 1944; And Then There Were None 1945; Brewster's Millions 1945; A Royal Scandal 1945; Sentimental Journey 1946; Confidential Report 1955; The Monte Carlo Story 1957; We Joined the Navy 1962; Drop Dead Darling 1966

Auger, Claudine Le Masque de Fer 1962; Yoyo 1964; That Man George 1965; Thunderball 1965; Triple Cross 1966; Travels with Anita 1978; Secret Places 1984; Salt on Our Skin 1992

August, Pernilla aka **Wallgren, Pernilla** Fanny and Alexander 1982; Best Intentions 1992; Jerusalem 1996; Private Confessions 1996; The Last Contract 1998; Star Wars Episode I: the Phantom Menace 1999

Augustus, Sherman Digital Man 1994; Virus 1998

Aumont, Jean-Pierre Drôle de Drame 1937; Hôtel du Nord 1938; The Cross of Lorraine 1943; Heartbeat 1946; Song of Scheherazade 1947; The Gay Adventure 1949; Lili 1953; Royal Affairs in Versailles 1953; Charge of the Lancers 1954; Napoléon 1955; Hilda Crane 1956; The Devil at Four o'Clock 1961; Five Miles to Midnight 1963; Cauldron of Blood 1967; Castle Keep 1969; Day for Night 1973; The Happy Hooker 1975; Mahogany 1975; Something Short of Paradise 1979; The Memory of Eva Ryker 1980; The Blood of Others 1984; Becoming Colette 1991; Jefferson in Paris 1995; The Proprietor 1996

Aumont, Michel Nada 1974; To Kill a Rat 1977; Pourquoi Pas! 1977; Les Compères 1983; Dangerous Moves 1984; Sunday in the Country 1984; Angel Dust 1987; Le Cop II 1989; A Shadow of Doubt 1992; The King of Paris 1995; Man Is a Woman 1998

Aumont, Tina aka **Marquand, Tina** The Game Is Over 1966; Partner 1968; Lifespan 1975; Casanova 1976; Illustrious Corpses 1976; A Matter of Time 1976

Aureli, Andrea Duel of Champions 1961; Tiger of the Seven Seas 1962

Aussey, Germaine A Nous la Liberté 1931; The Golem 1936

Austin, Albert Behind the Screen 1916; The Pawnshop 1916; The Immigrant 1917; The Cure 1917

Austin, Charlotte The Farmer Takes a Wife 1953; Desiree 1954; Gorilla at Large 1954; How to Be Very, Very Popular 1955; The Bride and the Beast 1958

Austin, Jerry Saratoga Trunk 1945; Adventures of Don Juan 1948

Austin, Karen Summer Rental 1985; Assassin 1986; The Ladies Club 1986; When the Time Comes 1987; Laura Lansing Slept Here 1988; Far from Home 1989; For Love of a Child 1990; When a Stranger Calls Back 1993

Austin, Pamela aka **Austin, Pam** Kissin' Cousins 1964; The Perils of Pauline 1967

Austin, William It 1927; County Hospital 1932; Alice in Wonderland 1933

Auteuil, Daniel Jean de Florette 1986; Manon des Sources 1986; Romuald et Juliette 1989; Un Coeur en Hiver 1992; Ma Saison Préférée 1993; Une Femme Française 1994; La Reine Margot 1994; La Séparation 1994; The Eighth Day 1996; Les Voleurs 1996; Le Bossu 1997; Lucie Aubrac 1997; The Lost Son 1998; The Girl on the Bridge 1999; La Veuve de Saint-Pierre 2000

Autry, Alan Roadhouse 66 1984; Destination: America 1987; Street of Dreams 1988; World Gone Wild 1988

Autry, Gene Down Mexico Way 1941; Riders in the Sky 1949; Mule Train 1950; Valley of Fire 1951; Blue Canadian Rockies 1952; On Top of Old Smoky 1953; Winning of the West 1953; Last of the Pony Riders 1953; Alias Jesse James 1959

Avalon, Frankie The Alamo 1960; Guns of the Timberland 1960; Voyage to the Bottom of the Sea 1961; Sail a Crooked Ship 1961; Panic in Year Zero 1962; Beach Party 1963; The Castilian 1963; Muscle Beach Party 1964; Pajama Party 1964; Beach Blanket Bingo 1965; How to Fill a Wild Bikini 1965; Sergeant Deadhead 1965; Ski Party 1965; Dr Goldfoot and the Bikini Machine 1965; I'll Take Sweden 1965; Fireball 500 1966; Skidoo 1968; The Haunted House of Horror 1969; The Take 1974

Avalos, Luis Hot Stuff 1979; Fires Within 1991; Lone Justice 1994

Avari, Erick The Beast 1988; Scam 1993

Avery, Brian The Graduate 1967; Under the Boardwalk 1988

Avery, James Timestalkers 1987; Beastmaster 2: through the Portal of Time 1991; Without Warning: Terror in the Towers 1993; Death of a Cheerleader 1994

Avery, Margaret Curtain Up 1952; Hell Up in Harlem 1973; Louis Armstrong: Chicago Style 1976; Scott Joplin 1977; Which Way Is Up? 1977; The Lathe of Heaven 1979; The Color Purple 1985; Blueberry Hill 1988; Heat Wave 1990; Lightning in a Bottle 1992; The Set Up 1995; White Man's Burden 1995

Avery, Val Hud 1963; Faces 1968; A Dream of Kings 1969; The Anderson Tapes 1971; Minnie and Moskowitz 1971; The Laughing Policeman 1973; Black Caesar 1973; Heroes 1977; Touchdown 1981; Continental Divide 1981; Jinxed! 1982; Easy Money 1983; Courage 1986; Teamster Boss: the Jackie Presser Story 1992; Assault at West Point: the Court Martial of John Whittaker 1994

Aviles, Angel Mi Vida Loca 1993; Scorpion Spring 1995

Aviles, Rick Ghost 1990; The Saint of Fort Washington 1993

Avital, Mili Stargate 1994; Dead Man 1995; Invasion of Privacy

ACTORS' INDEX RadioTimes

1996; *Kissing a Fool* 1998; *Polish Wedding* 1998
Avonde, Richard *Captain Carey, USA* 1950; *The 49th Man* 1953
Awaji, Keiko *Stray Dog* 1949; *The Bridges at Toko-Ri* 1954
Awashima, Chikage *Early Summer* 1951; *The Flavour of Green Tea over Rice* 1952; *Early Spring* 1956
Axberg, Eddie *The Emigrants* 1971; *The New Land* 1972
Axton, Hoyt *The Black Stallion* 1979; *Endangered Species* 1982; *Liar's Moon* 1982; *The Black Stallion Returns* 1983; *Heart like a Wheel* 1983; *Gremlins* 1984; *Act of Vengeance* 1986; *Disorganized Crime* 1989; *We're No Angels* 1989; *Buried Alive* 1990; *Number One Fan* 1994
Ayars, Ann *Dr Kildare's Victory* 1941; *Apache Trail* 1942; *The Tales of Hoffmann* 1951
Aykroyd, Dan *1941* 1979; *The Blues Brothers* 1980; *Neighbors* 1981; *Trading Places* 1983; *Twilight Zone: the Movie* 1983; *Doctor Detroit* 1983; *Ghostbusters* 1984; *Nothing Lasts Forever* 1984; *Into the Night* 1985; *Spies like Us* 1985; *Dragnet* 1987; *Caddyshack II* 1988; *The Couch Trip* 1988; *The Great Outdoors* 1988; *My Stepmother Is an Alien* 1988; *Driving Miss Daisy* 1989; *Ghostbusters II* 1989; *Loose Cannons* 1990; *My Girl* 1991; *Nothing but Trouble* 1991; *Chaplin* 1992; *Sneakers* 1992; *This Is My Life* 1992; *Coneheads* 1993; *Exit to Eden* 1994; *My Girl 2* 1994; *North* 1994; *Rainbow* 1995; *Tommy Boy* 1995; *Celtic Pride* 1996; *Feeling Minnesota* 1996; *Getting Away with Murder* 1996; *My Fellow Americans* 1996; *Sgt Bilko* 1996; *Grosse Pointe Blank* 1997; *Antz* 1998; *Blues Brothers 2000* 1998; *Susan's Plan* 1998; *Diamonds* 1999; *The House of Mirth* 2000
Aylesworth, Arthur *The Plot Thickens* 1936; *Test Pilot* 1938
Aylmer, Felix *The Ghost Camera* 1933; *The Clairvoyant* 1934; *Doctor's Orders* 1934; *Dusty Ermine* 1936; *The Shadow* 1936; *Tudor Rose* 1936; *As You Like It* 1936; *The Vicar of Bray* 1937; *Victoria the Great* 1937; *The Mill on the Floss* 1937; *Sixty Glorious Years* 1938; *The Black Sheep of Whitehall* 1941; *The Ghost of St Michael's* 1941; *Hi, Gang!* 1941; *I Thank You* 1941; *The Saint's Vacation* 1941; *South American George* 1941; *The Demi-Paradise* 1943; *Time Flies* 1944; *The Way to the Stars* 1945; *The Wicked Lady* 1945; *The Magic Bow* 1946; *The Ghosts of Berkeley Square* 1947; *A Man about the House* 1947; *The Man Within* 1947; *The October Man* 1947; *The Calendar* 1948; *Hamlet* 1948; *Edward, My Son* 1949; *Trio* 1950; *The Lady with the Lamp* 1951; *The Man Who Watched Trains Go By* 1952; *Knights of the Round Table* 1953; *The Master of Ballantrae* 1953; *The Angel Who Pawned Her Harp* 1954; *Anastasia* 1956; *Saint Joan* 1957; *The Doctor's Dilemma* 1958; *The Two-Headed Spy* 1958; *The Mummy* 1959; *The Hands of Orlac* 1960; *Never Take Sweets from a Stranger* 1960; *The Boys* 1961; *The Road to Hong Kong* 1962; *The Running Man* 1963; *The Chalk Garden* 1964; *Hostile Witness* 1968
Aylward, John *Buddy* 1997; *The Escape* 1997
Ayres, Agnes *The Sheik* 1921; *Hollywood* 1923; *The Son of the Sheik* 1926
Ayres, Leah *The Burning* 1981; *Eddie Macon's Run* 1983; *Bloodsport* 1988
Ayres, Lew *aka* **Ayres, Lewis** *The Kiss* 1929; *Big News* 1929; *All Quiet on the Western Front* 1930; *Doorway to Hell* 1931; *The Iron Man* 1931; *State Fair* 1933; *The Last Train from Madrid* 1937; *Holiday* 1938; *Young Dr Kildare* 1938; *Broadway Serenade* 1939; *Calling Dr Kildare* 1939; *The Ice Follies of 1939* 1939; *Remember?* 1939; *The Secret of Dr Kildare* 1939; *Dr Kildare Goes Home* 1940; *Dr Kildare's Crisis* 1940; *Dr Kildare's Strange Case* 1940; *Dr Kildare's Victory* 1941; *Dr Kildare's Wedding Day* 1941; *Maisie Was a Lady* 1941; *The People vs Dr Kildare* 1941; *Fingers at the Window* 1942; *The Dark Mirror* 1946; *The Unfaithful* 1947; *Johnny Belinda* 1948; *The Capture* 1950; *Donovan's Brain* 1953; *Advise and Consent* 1962; *The Carpetbaggers* 1964; *The Biscuit Eater* 1972; *The Man* 1972; *Battle for the Planet of the Apes* 1973; *End of the World* 1977; *Damien – Omen II* 1978; *Salem's Lot* 1979; *Under Siege* 1986; *Cast the First Stone* 1989
Ayres, Robert *Night without Stars* 1951; *To Have and to Hold* 1951; *Cosh Boy* 1952; *13 East Street* 1952; *Delayed Action* 1954; *River Beat* 1954; *Time Lock* 1957; *First Man into Space* 1958; *A Night to Remember* 1958; *The Sicilians* 1964; *Battle beneath the Earth* 1968
Ayres, Rosalind *That'll Be the Day* 1973; *Little Malcolm and His Struggle Against the Eunuchs* 1974; *Stardust* 1974; *Emily's Ghost* 1992; *Beautiful People* 1999
Azaria, Hank *Cool Blue* 1988; *Quiz Show* 1994; *The Birdcage* 1996; *Anastasia* 1997; *Godzilla* 1997; *Great Expectations* 1997; *Grosse Pointe Blank* 1997; *Celebrity* 1998; *Homegrown* 1998; *Cradle Will Rock* 1999; *Mystery Men* 1999; *Mystery, Alaska* 1999
Azéma, Sabine *Life Is a Bed of Roses* 1983; *Sunday in the Country* 1984; *Mélo* 1986; *Life and Nothing But* 1989; *Smoking/No Smoking* 1993; *Le Bonheur Est dans le Pré* 1995; *Mon Homme* 1996; *On Connaît la Chanson* 1997
Azito, Tony *The Pirates of Penzance* 1983; *Bloodhounds of Broadway* 1989; *Necronomicon* 1993
Azmi, Shabana *The Chess Players* 1977; *Junoon* 1978; *Madame Sousatzka* 1988; *Disha* 1990; *Immaculate Conception* 1991; *City of Joy* 1992; *Son of the Pink Panther* 1993; *Fire* 1996; *Side Streets* 1998
Aznavour, Charles *Le Testament d'Orphée* 1960; *Shoot the Pianist* 1960; *Candy* 1968; *The Last Shot* 1969; *The Adventurers* 1970; *The Games* 1970; *The Blockhouse* 1973; *And Then There Were None* 1974; *The Twist* 1976; *Sky Riders* 1976; *The Tin Drum* 1979; *Edith and Marcel* 1983; *Long Live Life* 1984; *Il Maestro* 1989
Azzara, Candy *aka* **Azzara, Candice** *House Calls* 1978; *Fatso* 1979; *Divorce Wars* 1982; *Easy Money* 1983; *Doin' Time on Planet Earth* 1988

B

Baal, Karin *Hannibal Brooks* 1968; *Berlin Alexanderplatz* 1980; *Deadly Game* 1982; *Lola* 1982; *Thousand Eyes* 1984
Baas, Balduin *Orchestra Rehearsal* 1978; *Mischief* 1983
Babatunde, Obba *aka* **Babatundé, Obba** *God Bless the Child* 1988; *The Importance of Being Earnest* 1992; *Life* 1999
Babcock, Barbara *The Black Marble* 1980; *The Lords of Discipline* 1983; *That Was Then... This Is Now* 1985; *News at Eleven* 1986; *Happy Together* 1989; *Far and Away* 1992; *Fugitive Nights: Danger in the Desert* 1993; *Childhood Sweetheart?* 1997
Babe, Fabienne *Fatherland* 1986; *Les Voleurs* 1996
Bacall, Lauren *To Have and Have Not* 1944; *Confidential Agent* 1945; *The Big Sleep* 1946; *Two Guys from Milwaukee* 1946; *Dark Passage* 1947; *Key Largo* 1948; *Bright Leaf* 1950; *Young Man with a Horn* 1950; *How to Marry a Millionaire* 1953; *Woman's World* 1954; *Blood Alley* 1955; *The Cobweb* 1955; *Written on the Wind* 1956; *Designing Woman* 1957; *The Gift of Love* 1958; *North West Frontier* 1959; *Sex and the Single Girl* 1964; *Shock Treatment* 1964; *The Moving Target* 1966; *Murder on the Orient Express* 1974; *The Shootist* 1976; *Perfect Gentlemen* 1978; *H.E.A.L.T.H.* 1980; *The Fan* 1981; *Appointment with Death* 1988; *Mr North* 1988; *Tree of Hands* 1988; *Dinner at Eight* 1989; *Misery* 1990; *All I Want for Christmas* 1991; *The Portrait* 1993; *Prêt-à-Porter* 1994; *From the Mixed-Up Files of Mrs Basil E Frankweiler* 1995; *The Mirror Has Two Faces* 1996; *My Fellow Americans* 1996; *Diamonds* 1999
Baccaloni, Salvatore *aka* **Baccaloni** *Full of Life* 1956; *Merry Andrew* 1958; *Rock-a-Bye Baby* 1958; *Fanny* 1961; *The Pigeon That Took Rome* 1962
Bach, Barbara *The Spy Who Loved Me* 1977; *Force 10 from Navarone* 1978; *Jaguar Lives!* 1979; *Caveman* 1981; *Give My Regards to Broad Street* 1984
Bach, Catherine *Thunderbolt and Lightfoot* 1974; *Driving Force* 1988; *Masters of Menace* 1990; *Rage and Honor* 1992; *Dukes of Hazzard Reunion* 1997
Bach, John *Battletruck* 1982; *Georgia* 1988; *Blood Oath* 1990; *Crime Broker* 1993
Bachar, Dian *Orgazmo* 1997; *BASEketball* 1998
Bacharach, Burt *Austin Powers: International Man of Mystery* 1997; *Austin Powers: The Spy Who Shagged Me* 1999
Bachchan, Amitabh *Sholay* 1975; *Kabhi Kabhie* 1976; *Shaan* 1980; *Hindustan Ki Kasam* 1999
Bachelor, Stephanie *Earl Carroll Vanities* 1945; *Springtime in the Sierras* 1947
Backer, Brian *The Burning* 1981; *Fast Times at Ridgemont High* 1982; *Moving Violations* 1985
Backus, Georgia *Apache Drums* 1951; *Cause for Alarm* 1951
Backus, Jim *A Dangerous Profession* 1949; *The Great Lover* 1949; *Bright Victory* 1951; *Half Angel* 1951; *I'll See You in My Dreams* 1951; *M* 1951; *The Man with a Cloak* 1951; *Don't Bother to Knock* 1952; *Angel Face* 1953; *Rebel without a Cause* 1955; *The Square Jungle* 1955; *The Girl He Left Behind* 1956; *The Great Man* 1956; *Meet Me in Las Vegas* 1956; *You Can't Run Away from It* 1956; *Man of a Thousand Faces* 1957; *Top Secret Affair* 1957; *Macabre* 1958; *The High Cost of Loving* 1958; *Ask Any Girl* 1959; *A Private's Affair* 1959; *The Wild and the Innocent* 1959; *The Big Operator* 1959; *Ice Palace* 1960; *My Six Loves* 1962; *The Wonderful World of the Brothers Grimm* 1962; *Zotz* 1962; *Johnny Cool* 1963; *Sunday in New York* 1963; *The Wheeler Dealers* 1963; *Advance to the Rear* 1964; *John Goldfarb, Please Come Home* 1964; *Billie* 1965; *Fluffy* 1965; *Where Were You When the Lights Went Out?* 1968; *Hello Down There* 1969; *Myra Breckinridge* 1970; *The Cockeyed Cowboys of Calico County* 1970; *Now You See Him, Now You Don't* 1972; *Crazy Mama* 1975; *Friday Foster* 1975; *Good Guys Wear Black* 1977; *Pete's Dragon* 1977; *Slapstick of Another Kind* 1982
Baclanova, Olga *The Docks of New York* 1928; *Freaks* 1932; *Claudia* 1943
Bacon, Irving *Internes Can't Take Money* 1937; *Blondie* 1938; *Blondie Takes a Vacation* 1939; *The Howards of Virginia* 1940; *A Guy Named Joe* 1944; *Under Western Skies* 1945; *Cause for Alarm* 1951; *Room for One More* 1952; *The Glenn Miller Story* 1953; *A Star Is Born* 1954; *Black Horse Canyon* 1954; *At Gunpoint* 1955
Bacon, Kevin *National Lampoon's Animal House* 1978; *Friday the 13th* 1980; *Hero at Large* 1980; *Diner* 1982; *Enormous Changes at the Last Minute* 1983; *Footloose* 1984; *Quicksilver* 1986; *Planes, Trains and Automobiles* 1987; *White Water Summer* 1987; *End of the Line* 1987; *Criminal Law* 1988; *She's Having a Baby* 1988; *The Big Picture* 1989; *Tremors* 1989; *Flatliners* 1990; *He Said, She Said* 1991; *JFK* 1991; *Pyrates* 1991; *Queens Logic* 1991; *A Few Good Men* 1992; *The Air up There* 1993; *Murder in the First* 1994; *The River Wild* 1994; *Apollo 13* 1995; *Balto* 1995; *Sleepers* 1996; *Picture Perfect* 1997; *Telling Lies in America* 1997; *Wild Things* 1998; *Digging to China* 1998; *Stir of Echoes* 1999
Bacon, Lloyd *The Tramp* 1915; *Behind the Screen* 1916
Bacon, Max *King Arthur Was a Gentleman* 1942; *Bees in Paradise* 1943; *Miss London Ltd* 1943; *Give Us the Moon* 1944; *Privilege* 1967
Bacri, Jean-Pierre *Entre Nous* 1983; *Subway* 1985; *C'est la Vie* 1990; *L'Homme de Ma Vie* 1992; *Un Air de Famille* 1996; *Didier* 1997; *On Connaît la Chanson* 1997; *Place Vendôme* 1998
Badalucco, Michael *Mac* 1992; *Leon* 1994; *Stolen Hearts* 1996; *The Search for One-Eye Jimmy* 1996; *Love Walked In* 1997; *O Brother, Where Art Thou?* 2000
Baddeley, Angela *The Ghost Train* 1931; *Those Were the Days* 1934
Baddeley, Hermione *Brighton Rock* 1947; *Quartet* 1948; *Passport to Pimlico* 1949; *The Woman in Question* 1950; *Scrooge* 1951; *Tom Brown's Schooldays* 1951; *There Is Another Sun* 1951; *Cosh Boy* 1952; *The Pickwick Papers* 1952; *Time Gentlemen Please!* 1952; *Counterspy* 1953; *The Belles of St Trinian's* 1954; *Jet Storm* 1959; *Midnight Lace* 1960; *Rag Doll* 1960; *Let's Get Married* 1960; *Information Received* 1962; *Mary Poppins* 1964; *The Unsinkable Molly Brown* 1964; *Do Not Disturb* 1965; *Marriage on the Rocks* 1965; *Harlow* 1965; *The Adventures of Bullwhip Griffin* 1967; *The Happiest Millionaire* 1967; *The Aristocats* 1970; *Up the Front* 1972; *The Secret of NIMH* 1982
Badel, Alan *Salome* 1953; *Three Cases of Murder* 1954; *Three Cases of Murder* 1954; *Magic Fire* 1956; *Bitter Harvest* 1963; *This Sporting Life* 1963; *Children of the Damned* 1964; *Arabesque* 1966; *Otley* 1968; *Where's Jack?* 1969; *The Adventurers* 1970; *The Day of the Jackal* 1973; *Luther* 1974; *Telefon* 1977; *Agatha* 1978; *The Riddle of the Sands* 1978; *Shogun* 1980; *Nijinsky* 1980
Badel, Sarah *Not without My Daughter* 1990; *Mrs Dalloway* 1997; *Cotton Mary* 1999
Bader, Diedrich *The Beverly Hillbillies* 1993; *Office Space* 1999
Badham, Mary *To Kill a Mockingbird* 1962; *This Property Is Condemned* 1966
Badie, Laurence *Les Jeux Interdits* 1953; *Muriel* 1963
Badland, Annette *Jabberwocky* 1977; *Anchoress* 1993; *Captives* 1994; *Angels and Insects* 1995; *Caught in the Act* 1996; *Little Voice* 1998
Baer, Buddy *Africa Screams* 1949; *The Big Sky* 1952; *Dream Wife* 1953; *Fair Wind to Java* 1953; *Slightly Scarlet* 1956
Baer, Harry *Gods of the Plague* 1969; *Whity* 1970; *Jail Bait* 1972; *Ludwig – Requiem for a Virgin King* 1972; *Fox and His Friends* 1975; *The Third Generation* 1979; *La Amiga* 1988
Baer, John *The Mississippi Gambler* 1953; *We're No Angels* 1955
Baer, Max *The Prizefighter and the Lady* 1933; *Over She Goes* 1937; *The Navy Comes Through* 1942; *Ladies' Day* 1943; *Africa Screams* 1949; *Bride for Sale* 1949; *The Harder They Fall* 1956
Baer Jr, Max *The Long Ride Home* 1967; *Macon County Line* 1973
Baer, Parley *Comanche Territory* 1950; *Gypsy* 1962; *Bedtime Story* 1964; *Two on a Guillotine* 1965; *The Ugly Dachshund* 1966
Baeyens, Dominique *Karnaval* 1998; *Les Convoyeurs Attendent* 1999
Bagdasarian, Carol *The Octagon* 1980; *The Aurora Encounter* 1985
Bagdasarian, Ross *aka* **Seville, David** *Rear Window* 1954; *Alaska Seas* 1954; *The Proud and Profane* 1956
Bahns, Maxine *The Brothers McMullen* 1995; *She's the One* 1996
Bai Ling *Red Corner* 1997; *Anna and the King* 1999
Bailey, Bill *On the Edge* 1985; *Saving Grace* 2000
Bailey, Blake *Lurking Fear* 1994; *Head of the Family* 1996
Bailey, G W *Police Academy* 1984; *Runaway* 1984; *North Beach and Rawhide* 1985; *Rustler's Rhapsody* 1985; *Warning Sign* 1985; *Short Circuit* 1986; *Burglar* 1987; *Downpayment on Murder* 1987; *Mannequin* 1987; *Police Academy*

Radio Times ACTORS' INDEX

5: Assignment Miami Beach 1988; *True Betrayal* 1990; *Double Crossed* 1991; *After the Glory* 1992; *Dead before Dawn* 1993; *Police Academy: Mission to Moscow* 1994; *Seduction in a Small Town* 1996
Bailey, Janet *Race to Freedom: the Underground Railroad* 1994; *Black Fox* 1995
Bailey, John *Celia* 1949; *Meet Simon Cherry* 1949
Bailey, Pearl *Variety Girl* 1947; *Carmen Jones* 1954; *That Certain Feeling* 1956; *St Louis Blues* 1958; *Porgy and Bess* 1959; *All the Fine Young Cannibals* 1960; *The Landlord* 1970; *Norman... Is That You?* 1976; *The Fox and the Hound* 1981; *Peter Gunn* 1989
Bailey, Raymond *Tarantula* 1955; *Congo Crossing* 1956; *The Incredible Shrinking Man* 1957; *The Lineup* 1958; *Vertigo* 1958; *The Gallant Hours* 1960
Bailey, Robin *Portrait of Clare* 1950; *Catch Us If You Can* 1965; *Blind Terror* 1971; *Jane and the Lost City* 1987
Bailey-Gates, Charles *Knight Moves* 1992; *Exquisite Tenderness* 1995
Bain, Conrad *C.H.O.M.P.S.* 1979; *Postcards from the Edge* 1990
Bain, Cynthia *Vengeance: the Demon* 1988; *Hometown Boy Makes Good* 1990
Bainter, Fay *Make Way for Tomorrow* 1937; *Quality Street* 1937; *Jezebel* 1938; *The Shining Hour* 1938; *White Banners* 1938; *Daughters Courageous* 1939; *A Bill of Divorcement* 1940; *Maryland* 1940; *Our Town* 1940; *Young Tom Edison* 1940; *Babes on Broadway* 1941; *Journey for Margaret* 1942; *The War against Mrs Hadley* 1942; *Woman of the Year* 1942; *Cry Havoc* 1943; *The Heavenly Body* 1943; *The Human Comedy* 1943; *Presenting Lily Mars* 1943; *Salute to the Marines* 1943; *Dark Waters* 1944; *State Fair* 1945; *The Kid from Brooklyn* 1946; *The Virginian* 1946; *Deep Valley* 1947; *The Secret Life of Walter Mitty* 1947; *Give My Regards to Broadway* 1948; *June Bride* 1948; *Close to My Heart* 1951; *The President's Lady* 1953; *The Children's Hour* 1961
Baio, Scott *Bugsy Malone* 1976; *Skatetown, USA* 1979; *The Boy Who Drank Too Much* 1980; *Foxes* 1980; *Zapped!* 1982; *Danielle Steel's Mixed Blessings* 1995
Baird, Anthony *Dead of Night* 1945; *Night Comes Too Soon* 1949
Baird, Harry *Sapphire* 1959; *Offbeat* 1960; *Station Six-Sahara* 1962; *The Oblong Box* 1969
Baird, Jimmy *The Return of Dracula* 1958; *The Black Orchid* 1959
Bairstow, Scott *There Was a Little Boy* 1993; *White Fang 2: Myth of the White Wolf* 1994; *Wild America* 1997; *Two for Texas* 1998
Baisho, Mitsuko *Vengeance Is Mine* 1979; *Akira Kurosawa's Dreams* 1990; *The Eel* 1997
Baitz, Jon Robin *Last Summer in the Hamptons* 1995; *One Fine Day* 1996
Bajema, Don *Signal 7* 1983; *Heat and Sunlight* 1988; *Chalk* 1996
Bakalyan, Richard *aka* **Bakalyan, Dick** *The Delicate Delinquent* 1957; *Dino* 1957; *The Delinquents* 1957; *The Bonnie Parker Story* 1958; *The Cool and the Crazy* 1958; *The Computer Wore Tennis Shoes* 1970; *Return from Witch Mountain* 1978; *Blame It on the Night* 1984
Baker, Art *Abie's Irish Rose* 1946; *The Beginning or the End* 1947; *Homecoming* 1948; *Walk a Crooked Mile* 1948
Baker, Becky Ann *She Said No* 1990; *A Simple Plan* 1998
Baker, Benny *Thanks a Million* 1935; *Up in Arms* 1944; *Boy, Did I Get a Wrong Number* 1966; *Jory* 1972
Baker, Blanche *Embassy* 1985; *Nobody's Child* 1986; *The Handmaid's Tale* 1990; *Dead Funny* 1995
Baker, Carroll *Easy to Love* 1953; *Baby Doll* 1956; *Giant* 1956; *The Big Country* 1958; *The Miracle* 1959; *But Not for Me* 1959; *How the West Was Won* 1962; *Station Six-Sahara* 1962; *The Carpetbaggers* 1964; *Cheyenne Autumn* 1964; *Sylvia* 1964; *The Greatest Story Ever Told* 1965; *Harlow* 1965; *Mister Moses* 1965; *Jack of Diamonds* 1967; *Captain Apache* 1971; *Rich and Respectable* 1975; *Bad* 1976; *The World Is Full of Married Men* 1979; *The Watcher in the Woods* 1982; *Star 80* 1983; *The Secret Diary of Sigmund Freud* 1984; *Native Son* 1986; *Ironweed* 1987; *On Fire* 1987; *Kindergarten Cop* 1990; *Blonde Fist* 1991; *Those Bedroom Eyes* 1993; *Judgment Day: the John List Story* 1993; *Desperate Measures* 1995; *The Game* 1997; *North Shore Fish* 1997; *Heart Full of Rain* 1997
Baker, Diane *The Best of Everything* 1959; *The Diary of Anne Frank* 1959; *Journey to the Center of the Earth* 1959; *Tess of the Storm Country* 1960; *The Wizard of Baghdad* 1960; *Hemingway's Adventures of a Young Man* 1962; *The 300 Spartans* 1962; *Nine Hours to Rama* 1963; *The Prize* 1963; *Stolen Hours* 1963; *Strait-Jacket* 1963; *Marnie* 1964; *Della* 1965; *Mirage* 1965; *The Horse in the Gray Flannel Suit* 1968; *Krakatoa, East of Java* 1969; *A Tree Grows in Brooklyn* 1974; *Baker's Hawk* 1976; *The Pilot* 1979; *The Closer* 1990; *The Haunted* 1991; *Imaginary Crimes* 1994; *The Net* 1995; *The Cable Guy* 1996; *Murder at 1600* 1997; *About Sarah* 1998
Baker, Dylan *Planes, Trains and Automobiles* 1987; *The Wizard of Loneliness* 1988; *The Long Walk Home* 1990; *Delirious* 1991; *Love Potion No 9* 1992; *Disclosure* 1994; *True Blue* 1996; *Happiness* 1998; *Simply Irresistible* 1999; *Oxygen* 1999
Baker, Fay *Tell It to the Judge* 1949; *The Company She Keeps* 1950; *The House on Telegraph Hill* 1951; *Don't Knock the Rock* 1956; *Sorority Girl* 1957
Baker, Frank *The New Adventures of Tarzan* 1935; *Tarzan and the Green Goddess* 1938
Baker, George *The Intruder* 1953; *The Dam Busters* 1954; *The Ship That Died of Shame* 1955; *The Woman for Joe* 1955; *The Extra Day* 1956; *The Feminine Touch* 1956; *A Hill in Korea* 1956; *The Moonraker* 1957; *No Time for Tears* 1957; *Tread Softly Stranger* 1958; *Lancelot and Guinevere* 1963; *Curse of the Fly* 1965; *Goodbye, Mr Chips* 1969; *Justine* 1969; *On Her Majesty's Secret Service* 1969; *The Executioner* 1970; *A Warm December* 1973; *The Thirty-Nine Steps* 1978; *For Queen and Country* 1988
Baker, Hylda *Saturday Night and Sunday Morning* 1960; *Up the Junction* 1967; *Oliver!* 1968; *Nearest and Dearest* 1972
Baker, Joby *Gidget* 1959; *The Last Angry Man* 1959; *Key Witness* 1960; *The Wackiest Ship in the Army* 1961; *Gidget Goes to Rome* 1963; *When the Boys Meet the Girls* 1965; *Girl Happy* 1965; *Blackbeard's Ghost* 1967; *Valley of Mystery* 1967; *Superdad* 1974
Baker, Joe *Where the Bullets Fly* 1966; *Pocahontas* 1995
Baker, Joe Don *Guns of the Magnificent Seven* 1969; *Adam at 6 AM* 1970; *Wild Rovers* 1971; *Welcome Home, Soldier Boys* 1971; *Junior Bonner* 1972; *Charley Varrick* 1973; *The Outfit* 1973; *Walking Tall* 1973; *Golden Needles* 1974; *Mitchell* 1975; *Framed* 1975; *The Pack* 1977; *Wacko* 1981; *The Natural* 1984; *Fletch* 1985; *Getting Even* 1986; *The Killing Time* 1987; *The Living Daylights* 1987; *Leonard, Part 6* 1987; *Criminal Law* 1988; *The Children* 1990; *Cape Fear* 1991; *The Distinguished Gentleman* 1992; *Citizen Cohn* 1992; *Complex of Fear* 1993; *Reality Bites* 1994; *Ring of Steel* 1994; *Congo* 1995; *GoldenEye* 1995; *Panther* 1995; *The Underneath* 1995; *Tomorrow Never Dies* 1997
Baker, Kathy *A Killing Affair* 1985; *Nobody's Child* 1986; *Street Smart* 1987; *Clean and Sober* 1988; *Jacknife* 1988; *Dad* 1989; *Edward Scissorhands* 1990; *The Image* 1990; *Mister Frost* 1990; *Article 99* 1992; *Jennifer Eight* 1992; *Mad Dog and Glory* 1992; *Lush Life* 1993; *To Gillian on Her 37th Birthday* 1996; *Inventing the Abbotts* 1997; *Weapons of Mass Distraction* 1997; *Not in This Town* 1997; *The Cider House Rules* 1999
Baker (1), Kenny *Star Wars Episode IV: A New Hope* 1977; *The Empire Strikes Back* 1980; *Return of the Jedi* 1983; *Star Wars Episode I: the Phantom Menace* 1999
Baker (2), Kenny *The Goldwyn Follies* 1938; *Radio City Revels* 1938; *At the Circus* 1939; *The Mikado* 1939; *The Harvey Girls* 1946
Baker, Mark *The Flying Scot* 1957; *Raggedy Ann and Andy* 1977
Baker, Phil *The Goldwyn Follies* 1938; *The Gang's All Here* 1943
Baker, Ray *aka* **Baker, Raymond** *Nobody's Child* 1986; *Rockabye* 1986; *The Long Journey Home* 1987; *Everybody's All-American* 1988; *Heart Condition* 1990; *Masters of Menace* 1990; *She Said No* 1990; *Total Recall* 1990; *Hearts on Fire* 1992; *A Woman Deceived* 1992; *Hexed* 1993; *Camp Nowhere* 1994; *The Hard Truth* 1994; *Anywhere but Here* 1999
Baker, Rick *aka* **Baker, Richard A** *King Kong* 1976; *The Kentucky Fried Movie* 1977
Baker, Simon *Smoke Signals* 1998; *Ride with the Devil* 1999
Baker, Stanley *Captain Horatio Hornblower* 1951; *Home to Danger* 1951; *The Cruel Sea* 1953; *Knights of the Round Table* 1953; *The Red Beret* 1953; *The Good Die Young* 1954; *Hell below Zero* 1954; *Beautiful Stranger* 1954; *Helen of Troy* 1955; *Richard III* 1955; *Alexander the Great* 1956; *Checkpoint* 1956; *Child in the House* 1956; *A Hill in Korea* 1956; *Campbell's Kingdom* 1957; *Hell Drivers* 1957; *Sea Fury* 1958; *Violent Playground* 1958; *The Angry Hills* 1959; *Blind Date* 1959; *Hell Is a City* 1959; *Jet Storm* 1959; *Yesterday's Enemy* 1959; *The Criminal* 1960; *The Guns of Navarone* 1961; *A Prize of Arms* 1961; *Eva* 1962; *Sodom and Gomorrah* 1962; *The Man Who Finally Died* 1962; *In the French Style* 1963; *Zulu* 1964; *Sands of the Kalahari* 1965; *Accident* 1967; *Robbery* 1967; *Where's Jack?* 1969; *The Games* 1970; *Perfect Friday* 1970; *Popsy-Pop* 1970; *The Last Grenade* 1970; *Innocent Bystanders* 1972; *Zorro* 1975
Baker, Tom *Nicholas and Alexandra* 1971; *The Canterbury Tales* 1971; *Frankenstein: the True Story* 1973; *The Golden Voyage of Sinbad* 1973; *Vault of Horror* 1973; *The Mutations* 1973; *Wholly Moses!* 1980
Bakewell, William *Gold Diggers of Broadway* 1929; *All Quiet on the Western Front* 1930; *Dance, Fools, Dance* 1931; *Guilty Hands* 1931; *Lucky Devils* 1933; *Strangers All* 1935; *The Capture* 1950; *Davy Crockett, King of the Wild Frontier* 1955
Bakke, Brenda *Gunhed* 1989; *I Want Him Back* 1990; *Solar Crisis* 1990; *Hot Shots! Part Deux* 1993; *Terminal Voyage* 1994; *Twogether* 1994; *Tales from the Crypt: Demon Knight* 1995; *The Fixer* 1997; *Criminal Intent* 1998
Bako, Brigitte *The Red Shoe Diaries* 1992; *Dark Tide* 1993; *I Love a Man in Uniform* 1993; *Replikator* 1994; *Double Take* 1997; *The Escape* 1997
Bakri, Muhamad *aka* **Bacri, Muhamad** *Beyond the Walls* 1984; *Cup Final* 1991; *Double Edge* 1992
Bakula, Scott *The Last Fling* 1987; *Sibling Rivalry* 1990; *Necessary Roughness* 1991; *In the Shadow of a Killer* 1992; *Mercy Mission: the Rescue of Flight 771* 1993; *Color of Night* 1994; *A Passion to Kill* 1994; *Nowhere to Hide* 1994; *Lord of Illusions* 1995; *Cats Don't Dance* 1998; *Major League: Back to the Minors* 1998; *American Beauty* 1999
Balaban, Bob *aka* **Balaban, Robert** *Bank Shot* 1974; *Report to the Commissioner* 1975; *Close Encounters of the Third Kind* 1977; *Girlfriends* 1978; *Altered States* 1980; *Absence of Malice* 1981; *Whose Life Is it Anyway?* 1981; *2010* 1984; *End of the Line* 1987; *Dead-Bang* 1989; *The Face of Fear* 1990; *The Concierge* 1993; *Pie in the Sky* 1995; *Waiting for Guffman* 1996; *The Late Shift* 1996; *Deconstructing Harry* 1997; *Jakob the Liar* 1999; *Three to Tango* 1999
Balaski, Belinda *The Food of the Gods* 1975; *Cannonball* 1976; *The Howling* 1981; *Deadly Care* 1987
Balasko, Josiane *Le Maître d'école* 1981; *Trop Belle pour Toi* 1989; *A Shadow of Doubt* 1992; *French Twist* 1995
Baldwin, A Michael *Phantasm* 1978; *Phantasm III – Lord Of The Dead* 1994
Baldwin, Adam *My Bodyguard* 1980; *DC Cab* 1983; *Hadley's Rebellion* 1984; *Poison Ivy* 1985; *Bad Guys* 1986; *Welcome Home, Bobby* 1986; *Full Metal Jacket* 1987; *The Chocolate War* 1988; *Cohen and Tate* 1988; *Next of Kin* 1989; *Murder in High Places* 1991; *Deadbolt* 1992; *Radio Flyer* 1992; *Where the Day Takes You* 1992; *800 Leagues down the Amazon* 1993; *Cold Sweat* 1993; *Bitter Harvest* 1993; *Blind Justice* 1994; *Digital Man* 1994; *How to Make an American Quilt* 1995; *Trade-Off* 1995; *Lover's Knot* 1995; *Independence Day* 1996; *In the Line of Duty: Smoke Jumpers* 1996; *Mind Breakers* 1996; *Indiscreet* 1998
Baldwin, Alec *Forever Lulu* 1987; *Beetle Juice* 1988; *Married to the Mob* 1988; *She's Having a Baby* 1988; *Talk Radio* 1988; *Working Girl* 1988; *Great Balls of Fire!* 1989; *Alice* 1990; *The Hunt for Red October* 1990; *Miami Blues* 1990; *Too Hot to Handle* 1991; *Glengarry Glen Ross* 1992; *Prelude to a Kiss* 1992; *Malice* 1993; *The Getaway* 1994; *The Shadow* 1994; *Ghosts from the Past* 1996; *Heaven's Prisoners* 1996; *The Juror* 1996; *Looking for Richard* 1996; *The Edge* 1997; *Mercury Rising* 1998; *Outside Providence* 1999; *The Confession* 1999
Baldwin, Daniel *LA Takedown* 1989; *Car 54 Where Are You?* 1991; *Harley Davidson and the Marlboro Man* 1991; *Knight Moves* 1992; *Attack of the 50 Ft Woman* 1993; *Dead on Sight* 1994; *Lone Justice* 1994; *Bodily Harm* 1995; *Family of Cops* 1995; *The Invader* 1997; *John Carpenter's Vampires* 1998; *The Pandora Project* 1998; *Phoenix* 1998; *Love Kills* 1998
Baldwin, Dick *Life Begins in College* 1937; *International Settlement* 1938; *Mr Moto's Gamble* 1938
Baldwin, Janit *The California Kid* 1974; *Ruby* 1977
Baldwin, Peter *Short Cut to Hell* 1957; *I Married a Monster from Outer Space* 1958; *Teacher's Pet* 1958; *The Spectre* 1963
Baldwin, Roy *Georgia* 1988; *Stan and George's New Life* 1990
Baldwin, Stephen *The Beast* 1988; *Last Exit to Brooklyn* 1989; *Crossing the Bridge* 1992; *Posse* 1993; *Bitter Harvest* 1993; *8 Seconds* 1994; *Fall Time* 1994; *New Eden* 1994; *A Simple Twist of Fate* 1994; *Threesome* 1994; *The Usual Suspects* 1995; *Under the Hula Moon* 1995; *Bio-Dome* 1996; *Crimetime* 1996; *Fled* 1996; *Sub Down* 1997; *One Tough Cop* 1998; *Scarred City* 1998; *Mr Murder* 1998; *The Flintstones in Viva Rock Vegas* 2000
Baldwin, Walter *Together Again* 1944; *Winter Meeting* 1948
Baldwin, William *Flatliners* 1990; *Internal Affairs* 1990; *Backdraft* 1991; *Three of Hearts* 1992; *Sliver* 1993; *Curdled* 1995; *Fair Game* 1995; *A Pyromaniac's Love Story* 1995; *Virus* 1998; *Shattered Image* 1998; *Relative Values* 2000
Bale, Christian *Anastasia: the Mystery of Anna* 1986; *Empire of the Sun* 1987; *Treasure Island* 1990; *The News Boys* 1992; *Swing Kids* 1993; *Prince of Jutland* 1994; *Little Women* 1995; *Pocahontas* 1995; *The Secret Agent* 1996; *The Portrait of a Lady* 1996; *Metroland* 1997; *All the Little Animals* 1998; *Velvet Goldmine* 1998; *William Shakespeare's A Midsummer Night's Dream* 1999; *American Psycho* 2000

RadioTimes ACTORS' INDEX

Sister Hyde 1971; Fear in the Night 1972; Persecution 1974; I Don't Want to Be Born 1975; Letters to an Unknown Lover 1985; King of the Wind 1989
Bateson, Timothy The Mouse That Roared 1959; There Was a Crooked Man 1960; It's Trad, Dad 1961; The Anniversary 1968; Autobiography of a Princess 1975
Batinkoff, Randall The Stepford Children 1987; For Keeps 1987; School Ties 1992; Walking and Talking 1996; The Peacemaker 1997; Dead Man's Curve 1997
Battaglia, Matt Army of One 1993; Kiss of a Stranger 1997
Battaglia, Rik aka **Battaglia, Rick** Woman of the River 1955; Hannibal 1959; Esther and the King 1960; Don't Bother to Knock 1961; Sandokan the Great 1963; This Man Can't Die 1970; A Fistful of Dynamite 1971
Batten, John The Love Waltz 1930; For Those in Peril 1943
Battista, Lloyd Last Plane Out 1983; Round Trip to Heaven 1992
Battley, David That's Your Funeral 1972; Krull 1983
Bauchau, Patrick La Collectionneuse 1967; The State of Things 1982; Entre Nous 1983; Choose Me 1984; Lola 1986; Love among Thieves 1987; Riviera 1987; The Music Teacher 1988; Australia 1989; Erreur de jeunesse 1989; Blood Ties 1991; The Rapture 1991; Every Breath 1993; The New Age 1994; Serpent's Lair 1995; Twin Falls Idaho 1999
Bauer, Belinda The American Success Company 1979; Winter Kills 1979; Samson and Delilah 1984; The Game of Love 1987; The Rosary Murders 1987; Act of Piracy 1990; RoboCop 2 1990; The Servants of Twilight 1991; A Case for Murder 1993; Poison Ivy II: Lily 1995
Bauer, David The Double Man 1967; Embassy 1972
Bauer, Michelle aka **Snow, Pia** Cafe Flesh 1982; Terminal Force 1987
Bauer, Richard Good to Go 1986; The Sicilian 1987
Bauer, Steven aka **Bauer, Steve** Scarface 1983; Thief of Hearts 1984; Running Scared 1986; Sword of Gideon 1986; The Beast 1988; Gleaming the Cube 1988; A Row of Crows 1991; Sweet Poison 1991; Raising Cain 1992; Snapdragon 1993; Improper Conduct 1994; Terminal Voyage 1994; Woman of Desire 1994; Plato's Run 1996; Wild Side 1996; The Blackout 1997; Naked Lies 1997
Baumann, Katherine aka **Baumann, Kathy** The Thing with Two Heads 1972; 99 and 44/100% Dead 1974
Baur, Harry Les Misérables 1934; Crime and Punishment 1935; Moscow Nights 1935; The Golem 1936; Abel Gance's Beethoven 1936; Volpone 1940
Bavier, Frances The Day the Earth Stood Still 1951; Man in the Attic 1953
Baxendale, Helen Macbeth 1997; Ordinary Decent Criminal 1999
Baxley, Barbara The Savage Eye 1959; All Fall Down 1962; Countdown 1968; Nashville 1975; Norma Rae 1979
Baxter, Alan Big Brown Eyes 1936; Boy Slaves 1938; I Met My Love Again 1938; Each Dawn I Die 1939; Abe Lincoln in Illinois 1940; The Lone Wolf Strikes 1940; Shadow of the Thin Man 1941; China Girl 1942; Saboteur 1942; Pilot #5 1943; The Set-Up 1949; The True Story of Jesse James 1957; The Restless Years 1958; Face of a Fugitive 1959; This Property Is Condemned 1966
Baxter, Anne Charley's Aunt 1941; Swamp Water 1941; The Magnificent Ambersons 1942; The Pied Piper 1942; Crash Dive 1943; Five Graves to Cairo 1943; The North Star 1943; The Eve of St Mark 1944; The Fighting Sullivans 1944; Guest in the House 1944; Sunday Dinner for a Soldier 1944; A Royal Scandal 1945; Angel on My Shoulder 1946; The Razor's Edge 1946; Smoky 1946; Mother Wore Tights 1947; Blaze of Noon 1947; Homecoming 1948; Yellow Sky 1948; You're My Everything 1949; All about Eve 1950; A Ticket to Tomahawk 1950; O Henry's Full House 1952; The Blue Gardenia 1953; I Confess 1953; Carnival Story 1954; The Spoilers 1955; One Desire 1955; Bedevilled 1955; The Ten Commandments 1956; Three Violent People 1956; The Come On 1956; Chase a Crooked Shadow 1957; Cimarron 1960; Season of Passion 1960; Walk on the Wild Side 1962; The Busy Body 1967; Stranger on the Run 1967; The Late Liz 1971; Fools' Parade 1971; Jane Austen in Manhattan 1980
Baxter, Jane The Constant Nymph 1933; The Clairvoyant 1934; Night of the Party 1934; We Live Again 1934; Dusty Ermine 1936; Ships with Wings 1942; Death of an Angel 1951
Baxter, Keith Chimes at Midnight 1966; Ash Wednesday 1973
Baxter, Lynsey The French Lieutenant's Woman 1981; The Pleasure Principle 1991; The Cold Light of Day 1995
Baxter, Meredith aka **Baxter Birney, Meredith** Ben 1972; The Night that Panicked America 1975; All the President's Men 1976; Bittersweet Love 1976; The Two Lives of Carol Letner 1981; Take Your Best Shot 1982; The Rape of Richard Beck 1985; The Long Journey Home 1987; Winnie 1988; She Knows Too Much 1989; Bump in the Night 1991; Darkness before Dawn 1992; A Woman Deceived 1992; A Woman Scorned 1992; For the Love of Aaron 1993; My Breast 1994; Betrayed: a Story of Three Women 1995
Baxter, Stanley Very Important Person 1961; Crooks Anonymous 1962; The Fast Lady 1963; Father Came Too 1963; Joey Boy 1965
Baxter, Warner West of Zanzibar 1928; In Old Arizona 1929; Renegades 1930; Daddy Long Legs 1931; The Squaw Man 1931; 42nd Street 1933; Penthouse 1933; Broadway Bill 1934; Stand up and Cheer! 1934; King of Burlesque 1936; The Prisoner of Shark Island 1936; The Road to Glory 1936; The Robin Hood of El Dorado 1936; Slave Ship 1937; Vogues 1937; Wife, Doctor and Nurse 1937; Kidnapped 1938; The Return of the Cisco Kid 1939; Wife, Husband and Friend 1939; Adam Had Four Sons 1941; Lady in the Dark 1944; Shadows in the Night 1944
Bay, Frances The Pit and the Pendulum 1991; Single White Female 1992; The Paperboy 1994; Happy Gilmore 1996
Baye, Nathalie Day for Night 1973; The Mouth Agape 1974; The Man Who Loved Women 1977; The Green Room 1978; Slow Motion 1980; A Strange Affair 1981; La Balance 1982; The Return of Martin Guerre 1982; I Married a Dead Man 1983; Right Bank, Left Bank 1984; Detective 1985; C'est la Vie 1990; The Man Inside 1990; The Lie 1992; The Machine 1994; Food of Love 1997; Venus Beauty 1998; Une Liaison Pornographique 1999
Bayer, Gary Not My Kid 1985; Sworn to Vengeance 1993
Bayldon, Geoffrey Sky West and Crooked 1965; Where the Spies Are 1966; Casino Royale 1967; To Sir, with Love 1967; Tales from the Crypt 1972; The Monster Club 1980; Madame Sousatzka 1988; Asterix Conquers America 1994
Bayley, Hilda Much Too Shy 1942; Home Sweet Home 1945
Bayliss, Peter House of Cards 1968; Vampira 1975; Emily's Ghost 1992
Baylor, Hal Big Jim McLain 1952; Lord Love a Duck 1966; A Boy and His Dog 1975
Bayly, Lorraine Ride a Wild Pony 1976; The Man from Snowy River 1982
Baynaud, Erwan The Machine 1994; Est-Ouest 1999
Bazinet, Brenda Dancing in the Dark 1986; Thicker than Blood 1993
Bazlen, Brigid King of Kings 1961; The Honeymoon Machine 1961
Beach, Adam Dance Me Outside 1994; The Last Great Warrior 1994; A Boy Called Hate 1995; Smoke Signals 1998
Beach, Michael Vengeance: the Story of Tony Cimo 1986; In a Shallow Grave 1988; Dangerous Passion 1990; Fire! Trapped on the 37th Floor 1991; Late for Dinner 1991; Stockade 1991; One False Move 1992; The Hit List 1993; Bad Company 1995; A Feel for Murder 1995; Waiting to Exhale 1995; A Family Thing 1996; Rebound 1996; Casualties 1997; Soul Food 1997; Ms Scrooge 1997
Beacham, Stephanie Dracula AD 1972 1972; The Nightcomers 1972; And Now the Screaming Starts! 1973; House of Mortal Sin 1975; The Wolves of Willoughby Chase 1988; Troop Beverly Hills 1989; Danielle Steel's Secrets 1992; Foreign Affairs 1993; A Change of Place 1994; Wedding Bell Blues 1996
Beal, John The Little Minister 1934; Break of Hearts 1935; Les Misérables 1935; Danger Patrol 1937; Double Wedding 1937; Madame X 1937; I Am the Law 1938; The Cat and the Canary 1939; Edge of Darkness 1943; My Six Convicts 1952; Ten Who Dared 1960; Amityville III: the Demon 1983
Beale, Simon Russell Orlando 1992; Persuasion 1995
Beals, Jennifer Flashdance 1983; The Bride 1985; Vampire's Kiss 1988; The Gamble 1988; Dr M 1989; Sons 1989; In the Soup 1992; Day of Atonement 1993; Night Owl 1993; Dear Diary 1994; Dead on Sight 1994; Arabian Knight 1995; Devil in a Blue Dress 1995; The Search for One-Eye Jimmy 1996; The Twilight of the Golds 1996; The Prophecy II 1997; The Last Days of Disco 1998; Let It Be Me 1998
Bean, Orson How to Be Very, Very Popular 1955; Twinky 1969; Chance of a Lifetime 1991; Being John Malkovich 1999
Bean, Sean Caravaggio 1986; Stormy Monday 1987; War Requiem 1988; The Field 1990; Patriot Games 1992; Shopping 1993; Black Beauty 1994; Jacob 1994; GoldenEye 1995; When Saturday Comes 1995; Anna Karenina 1997; Airborne 1997; Ronin 1998; Essex Boys 1999
Bearse, Amanda Fright Night 1985; Here Come the Munsters 1995
Béart, Emmanuelle Manon des Sources 1986; Date with an Angel 1987; La Belle Noiseuse 1991; J'Embrasse Pas 1991; Un Coeur en Hiver 1992; L'Enfer 1994; Une Femme Française 1994; Nelly & Monsieur Arnaud 1995; Mission: Impossible 1996; Class Trip 1998; Elephant Juice 1999; Time Regained 1999
Beasley, John Lucky Day 1991; The Apostle 1997
Beaton, Norman Black Joy 1977; Playing Away 1986
Beatty, May Mad Love 1935; The Adventures of Sherlock Holmes 1939
Beatty, Nancy The Michelle Apartments 1995; Dead Innocent 1996
Beatty, Ned Deliverance 1972; The Life and Times of Judge Roy Bean 1972; The Last American Hero 1973; The Thief Who Came to Dinner 1973; White Lightning 1973; Nashville 1975; WW and the Dixie Dancekings 1975; All the President's Men 1976; The Big Bus 1976; Mikey and Nicky 1976; Network 1976; Silver Streak 1976; Exorcist II: The Heretic 1977; The Great Georgia Bank Hoax 1977; Gray Lady Down 1978; Superman 1978; The American Success Company 1979; Friendly Fire 1979; 1941 1979; Wise Blood 1979; Promises in the Dark 1979; Hopscotch 1980; Superman II 1980; The Incredible Shrinking Woman 1981; The Toy 1982; Stroker Ace 1983; Restless Natives 1985; The Big Easy 1986; The Fourth Protocol 1987; Switching Channels 1987; The Trouble with Spies 1987; Go toward the Light 1988; Midnight Crossing 1988; The Purple People Eater 1988; The Unholy 1988; Chattahoochee 1989; Physical Evidence 1989; Time Trackers 1989; Angel Square 1990; Captain America 1990; Repossessed 1990; Back to Hannibal: the Return of Tom Sawyer and Huckleberry Finn 1990; The Tragedy of Flight 103: the Inside Story 1990; A Cry in the Wild 1990; Hear My Song 1991; Blind Vision 1992; Prelude to a Kiss 1992; Illusions 1992; Motherhood 1993; Rudy 1993; Radioland Murders 1994; Replikator 1994; Just Cause 1995; The Affair 1995; He Got Game 1998; Cookie's Fortune 1999; Life 1999
Beatty, Robert San Demetrio London 1943; Odd Man Out 1946; Against the Wind 1947; Another Shore 1948; Portrait from Life 1948; Calling Bulldog Drummond 1951; Captain Horatio Hornblower 1951; The Magic Box 1951; The Gentle Gunman 1952; The Oracle 1952; Wings of Danger 1952; Albert, RN 1953; Man on a Tightrope 1953; The Net 1953; The Square Ring 1953; Out of the Clouds 1954; The Loves of Three Queens 1954; Postmark for Danger 1955; Tarzan and the Lost Safari 1956; Time Lock 1957; Something of Value 1957; The Shakedown 1959; The Amorous Prawn 1962; 2001: a Space Odyssey 1968; Where Eagles Dare 1969; The Spaceman and King Arthur 1979
Beatty, Warren The Roman Spring of Mrs Stone 1961; Splendor in the Grass 1961; All Fall Down 1962; Lilith 1964; Mickey One 1965; Kaleidoscope 1966; Promise Her Anything 1966; Bonnie and Clyde 1967; The Only Game in Town 1970; The Heist 1971; McCabe and Mrs Miller 1971; The Parallax View 1974; The Fortune 1975; Shampoo 1975; Heaven Can Wait 1978; Reds 1981; Ishtar 1987; Dick Tracy 1990; Bugsy 1991; Love Affair 1994; Bulworth 1998
Beaumont, Diana When London Sleeps 1932; Let George Do It 1940; Home at Seven 1952
Beaumont, Hugh The Seventh Victim 1943; The Blue Dahlia 1946; Railroaded 1947; The Counterfeiters 1948
Beaumont, Kathryn On an Island with You 1948; Alice in Wonderland 1951; Peter Pan 1953
Beaumont, Lucy A Free Soul 1931; His Double Life 1933; The Devil-Doll 1936
Beaumont, Susan Eyewitness 1956; The Spaniard's Curse 1958; The Man Who Liked Funerals 1959
Beauvallet, Céline Mignon Has Left 1988; A Private Affair 1992
Beauvois, Xavier Don't Forget You're Going to Die 1995; Le Vent de la Nuit 1999
Beauvy, Nicolas Rage 1972; Take Down 1978
Beaver, Jim Twogether 1994; Wounded 1996; Divided by Hate 1997
Beavers, Louise What Price Hollywood? 1932; Imitation of Life 1934; Rainbow on the River 1936; Belle Starr 1941; Holiday Inn 1942; Barbary Coast Gent 1944; Good Sam 1948; Mr Blandings Builds His Dream House 1948; My Blue Heaven 1950; Good-bye, My Lady 1956
Beck, Billy The Blob 1988; The Killing Mind 1991
Beck, Jennifer Tightrope 1984; Troll 1986; Gypsy 1993
Beck, John Mrs Pollifax – Spy 1970; Paperback Hero 1972; Pat Garrett and Billy the Kid 1973; Sleeper 1973; Rollerball 1975; The Big Bus 1976; Audrey Rose 1977; The Other Side of Midnight 1977; Deadly Illusion 1987; A Row of Crows 1991; Suspect Device 1995; Black Day Blue Night 1995
Beck, Julian Oedipus Rex 1967; Poltergeist II: the Other Side 1986
Beck, Kimberly Roller Boogie 1979; Friday the 13th: the Final Chapter 1984
Beck, Michael The Warriors 1979; Xanadu 1980; Battletruck 1982; The Last Ninja 1983; Triumphs of a Man Called Horse 1983; Blackout 1985; Chiller 1985; Dead Run 1991; Fade to Black 1993
Beck, Stanley John and Mary 1969; Lenny 1974
Beck, Thomas Charlie Chan in Egypt 1935; Charlie Chan in Paris 1935; Charlie Chan at the Opera

Radio Times ACTORS' INDEX

or Leave Me 1955; *Serenade* 1956; *The Birds and the Bees* 1956; *The Brothers Rico* 1957; *The Old Man and the Sea* 1958; *One Potato, Two Potato* 1964; *Blue Collar* 1978; *Hero at Large* 1980

Belle, Camilla *Annie: a Royal Adventure* 1995; *Marshal Law* 1996; *Replacing Dad* 1999

Beller, Kathleen *Something for Joey* 1977; *The Betsy* 1978; *Promises in the Dark* 1979; *Fort Apache, the Bronx* 1981; *The Sword and the Sorcerer* 1982; *Deadly Messages* 1985; *Time Trackers* 1989

Belli, Agostina *Bluebeard* 1972; *The Seduction of Mimi* 1972; *Scent of a Woman* 1974; *Holocaust 2000* 1977; *The Purple Taxi* 1977

Bellingham, Lynda *Sweeney!* 1976; *Stand Up Virgin Soldiers* 1977

Bellini, Francesca *Bachelor Flat* 1961; *Who's Minding the Store?* 1963

Bellis, Scott *Timecop* 1994; *The Man Who Wouldn't Die* 1995

Bellman, Gina *Secret Friends* 1991; *Leon the Pig Farmer* 1992; *Silent Trigger* 1996

Bello, Maria *Permanent Midnight* 1998; *Payback* 1999

Bellows, Gil *Love and a .45* 1994; *The Shawshank Redemption* 1994; *Miami Rhapsody* 1995; *Silver Strand* 1995; *Black Day Blue Night* 1995; *Radiant City* 1996; *Snow White: a Tale of Terror* 1996; *Judas Kiss* 1998

Bellucci, Monica *L'Appartement* 1996; *Dobermann* 1997

Bellwood, Pamela *Hangar 18* 1980; *Serial* 1980; *Agatha Christie's Sparkling Cyanide* 1983

Belmondo, Jean-Paul *A Bout de Souffle* 1959; *Web of Passion* 1959; *Two Women* 1960; *The Big Risk* 1960; *Cartouche* 1961; *Une Femme Est une Femme* 1961; *Léon Morin, Priest* 1961; *Le Doulos* 1962; *That Man from Rio* 1964; *Male Hunt* 1964; *Pierrot le Fou* 1965; *Up to His Ears* 1965; *Is Paris Burning?* 1966; *Casino Royale* 1967; *The Thief of Paris* 1967; *Ho!* 1968; *The Brain* 1969; *Mississippi Mermaid* 1969; *Borsalino* 1970; *The Burglars* 1971; *Sink or Swim* 1971; *The Inheritor* 1973; *Stavisky* 1974; *The Professional* 1981; *Hold-Up* 1985; *Les Misérables* 1995

Belmore, Bertha *Broken Blossoms* 1936; *In the Soup* 1936; *Please Teacher* 1937; *Hold My Hand* 1938

Belmore, Lionel *Oliver Twist* 1922; *The Matinee Idol* 1928; *Monte Carlo* 1930; *The Rogue Song* 1930; *Frankenstein* 1931; *One Heavenly Night* 1931; *Berkeley Square* 1933

Beltran, Robert *Eating Raoul* 1982; *Lone Wolf McQuade* 1983; *Calendar Girl Murders* 1984; *Night of the Comet* 1984; *Latino* 1985; *Slam Dance* 1987; *Scenes from the Class Struggle In Beverly Hills* 1989; *The Chase* 1991; *Stormy Weathers* 1992; *Rio Shannon* 1993; *State of Emergency* 1994

Belushi, James aka **Belushi, Jim** *Thief* 1981; *Trading Places* 1983; *The Man with One Red Shoe* 1985; *About Last Night…* 1986; *Jumpin' Jack Flash* 1986; *Little Shop of Horrors* 1986; *Salvador* 1986; *Real Men* 1987; *The Principal* 1987; *Red Heat* 1988; *Homer and Eddie* 1989; *K-9* 1989; *Mr Destiny* 1990; *Taking Care of Business* 1990; *Curly Sue* 1991; *Only the Lonely* 1991; *Diary of a Hit Man* 1992; *Once upon a Crime* 1992; *Traces of Red* 1992; *Parallel Lives* 1994; *Royce* 1994; *Canadian Bacon* 1995; *Destiny Turns on the Radio* 1995; *The Pebble and the Penguin* 1995; *Separate Lives* 1995; *Sahara* 1995; *Gold in the Streets* 1996; *Jingle All the Way* 1996; *Race the Sun* 1996; *Gang Related* 1997; *Retroactive* 1997; *Wag the Dog* 1997; *Living in Peril* 1997; *Return to Me* 2000

Belushi, John *Goin' South* 1978; *National Lampoon's Animal House* 1978; *1941* 1979; *Old Boyfriends* 1979; *The Blues Brothers* 1980; *Continental Divide* 1981; *Neighbors* 1981

Belvaux, Lucas *Cop au Vin* 1984; *Madame Bovary* 1991

Belzer, Richard *The Groove Tube* 1974; *America* 1986; *Freeway* 1988; *Missing Pieces* 1991; *Off and Running* 1991; *The Puppet Masters* 1994; *Deadly Pursuits* 1996; *Get on the Bus* 1996

Benben, Brian *Dark Angel* 1989; *Mortal Sins* 1989; *Radioland Murders* 1994

Benchley, Robert *Dancing Lady* 1933; *China Seas* 1935; *Piccadilly Jim* 1936; *Live, Love and Learn* 1937; *Foreign Correspondent* 1940; *Hired Wife* 1940; *Nice Girl?* 1941; *You'll Never Get Rich* 1941; *Bedtime Story* 1942; *I Married a Witch* 1942; *The Major and the Minor* 1942; *Young and Willing* 1942; *Take a Letter, Darling* 1942; *Flesh and Fantasy* 1943; *The Sky's the Limit* 1943; *See Here, Private Hargrove* 1944; *It's in the Bag* 1945; *Pan-Americana* 1945; *Road to Utopia* 1945; *Week-End at the Waldorf* 1945; *The Stork Club* 1945; *Kiss and Tell* 1945; *Blue Skies* 1946; *The Bride Wore Boots* 1946

Bender, Russ *The Amazing Colossal Man* 1957; *Motorcycle Gang* 1957; *Suicide Battalion* 1958; *War of the Colossal Beast* 1958

Bendix, William *The Glass Key* 1942; *Two Mugs from Brooklyn* 1942; *Wake Island* 1942; *Woman of the Year* 1942; *Star Spangled Rhythm* 1942; *China* 1943; *The Crystal Ball* 1943; *Guadalcanal Diary* 1943; *Hostages* 1943; *Abroad with Two Yanks* 1944; *Greenwich Village* 1944; *The Hairy Ape* 1944; *Lifeboat* 1944; *A Bell for Adano* 1945; *It's in the Bag* 1945; *The Blue Dahlia* 1946; *The Dark Corner* 1946; *Sentimental Journey* 1946; *Two Years before the Mast* 1946; *Calcutta* 1947; *The Web* 1947; *I'll Be Yours* 1947; *Where There's Life* 1947; *Blaze of Noon* 1947; *The Time of Your Life* 1948; *The Big Steal* 1949; *A Connecticut Yankee in King Arthur's Court* 1949; *Streets of Laredo* 1949; *Detective Story* 1951; *Blackbeard the Pirate* 1952; *A Girl in Every Port* 1952; *Macao* 1952; *Dangerous Mission* 1954; *Crashout* 1955; *The Deep Six* 1958; *The Rough and the Smooth* 1959; *For Love or Money* 1963

Benedetti, Pierre *The Beast* 1975; *Heroines of Evil* 1979

Benedict, Billy *Ghosts in the Night* 1943; *Block Busters* 1944; *Bowery Champs* 1944; *Come Out Fighting* 1945; *Docks of New York* 1945; *Mr Muggs Rides Again* 1945

Benedict, Brooks *The Freshman* 1925; *Speedy* 1928; *Gun Smoke* 1931; *What Price Hollywood?* 1932

Benedict, Dirk *Georgia, Georgia* 1972; *Ssssss* 1973; *W* 1974; *Battlestar Galactica* 1978; *Scavenger Hunt* 1979; *Trenchcoat in Paradise* 1989; *Bejewelled* 1990; *Official Denial* 1993; *The November Conspiracy* 1995; *Abduction of Innocence* 1996; *Alaska* 1996

Benedict, Paul *Taking Off* 1971; *Jeremiah Johnson* 1972; *Deadhead Miles* 1972; *The Goodbye Girl* 1977; *The Man with Two Brains* 1983; *Arthur 2: On the Rocks* 1988; *The Freshman* 1990; *The Addams Family* 1991; *Attack of the 50 Ft Woman* 1993

Benedict, Richard *OSS* 1946; *Ace in the Hole* 1951; *Jalopy* 1953; *Beginning of the End* 1957

Benet, Marianne *Shake Hands with the Devil* 1959; *The Boy Who Stole a Million* 1960; *A Terrible Beauty* 1960

Beneyton, Yves *Weekend* 1967; *The Lacemaker* 1977; *Letters to an Unknown Lover* 1985; *Eminent Domain* 1991; *Rogue Trader* 1998

Benfield, John *Hidden Agenda* 1990; *You're Dead* 1999

Benge, Wilson *Bulldog Drummond* 1929; *The Bat Whispers* 1930

Bengell, Norma *The Given Word* 1962; *The Color of Destiny* 1986

Benguigui, Jean *La Garce* 1984; *Salut Cousin!* 1996

Benham, Joan *King's Rhapsody* 1955; *Murder Ahoy* 1964

Benigni, Roberto *La Luna* 1979; *Tigers in Lipstick* 1979; *Down by Law* 1986; *Johnny Stecchino* 1991; *Night on Earth* 1992; *Son of the Pink Panther* 1993; *Life Is Beautiful* 1997; *Asterix and Obelix Take on Caesar* 1999

Bening, Annette *Manhunt for Claude Dallas* 1986; *The Great Outdoors* 1988; *Hostage* 1988; *Valmont* 1989; *The Grifters* 1990; *Guilty by Suspicion* 1990; *Postcards from the Edge* 1990; *Bugsy* 1991; *Regarding Henry* 1991; *Love Affair* 1994; *The American President* 1995; *Richard III* 1995; *Mars Attacks!* 1996; *In Dreams* 1998; *The Siege* 1998; *American Beauty* 1999

Benjamin, Paul *Across 110th Street* 1972; *Mr Inside/Mr Outside* 1973; *The Deadly Trackers* 1973; *Distance* 1975; *Leadbelly* 1976; *Escape from Alcatraz* 1979; *Some Kind of Hero* 1982; *Last Rites* 1998

Benjamin, Richard *Goodbye, Columbus* 1969; *Catch-22* 1970; *Diary of a Mad Housewife* 1970; *The Marriage of a Young Stockbroker* 1971; *Portnoy's Complaint* 1972; *The Last of Sheila* 1973; *Westworld* 1973; *The Sunshine Boys* 1975; *House Calls* 1978; *No Room to Run* 1978; *Love at First Bite* 1979; *Witches' Brew* 1979; *Scavenger Hunt* 1979; *The Last Married Couple in America* 1980; *How to Beat the High Cost of Living* 1980; *First Family* 1980; *Saturday the 14th* 1981; *Packin' It In* 1983; *Deconstructing Harry* 1997; *The Pentagon Wars* 1998

Bennent, David *The Tin Drum* 1979; *Legend* 1985

Bennent, Heinz *The Lost Honour of Katharina Blum* 1975; *The Serpent's Egg* 1977; *The Last Metro* 1980; *Possession* 1981; *The Death of Mario Ricci* 1983; *Une Femme Française* 1994

Bennes, John *Black Rainbow* 1989; *Stephen King's The Night Flier* 1997

Bennett, Alan *Long Shot* 1978; *In Love and War* 1996

Bennett, Belle *Stella Dallas* 1925; *The Way of All Flesh* 1927; *The Iron Mask* 1929

Bennett, Bruce aka **Brix, Herman** *The New Adventures of Tarzan* 1935; *A Million to One* 1937; *Tarzan and the Green Goddess* 1938; *Before I Hang* 1940; *The Lone Wolf Keeps a Date* 1941; *The More the Merrier* 1943; *Mildred Pierce* 1945; *The Man I Love* 1946; *A Stolen Life* 1946; *Dark Passage* 1947; *Nora Prentiss* 1947; *Silver River* 1948; *The Treasure of the Sierra Madre* 1948; *Task Force* 1949; *The Doctor and the Girl* 1949; *Mystery Street* 1950; *Angels in the Outfield* 1951; *Sudden Fear* 1952; *The Big Tip Off* 1955; *Strategic Air Command* 1955; *Beyond the River* 1956; *Three Violent People* 1956; *Daniel Boone, Trail Blazer* 1957; *The Cosmic Man* 1959; *The Alligator People* 1959; *The Outsider* 1961

Bennett, Charles *Tillie's Punctured Romance* 1914; *America* 1924

Bennett, Constance *Sally, Irene and Mary* 1925; *What Price Hollywood?* 1932; *Rockabye* 1932; *Lady with a Past* 1932; *Our Betters* 1933; *The Affairs of Cellini* 1934; *After Office Hours* 1935; *Ladies in Love* 1936; *Topper* 1937; *Merrily We Live* 1938; *Topper Takes a Trip* 1939; *Two-Faced Woman* 1941; *Sin Town* 1942; *Centennial Summer* 1946; *The Unsuspected* 1947; *Smart Woman* 1948; *As Young as You Feel* 1951; *Madame X* 1966

Bennett, Enid *Robin Hood* 1922; *The Sea Hawk* 1924; *Skippy* 1931; *Intermezzo* 1939

Bennett, Hywel *The Family Way* 1966; *Twisted Nerve* 1968; *The Virgin Soldiers* 1969; *The Buttercup Chain* 1970; *Loot* 1970; *Endless Night* 1971; *Percy* 1971; *Witness in the War Zone* 1986; *Deadly Advice* 1993

Bennett, Jill *Hell below Zero* 1954; *Lust for Life* 1956; *The Criminal* 1960; *The Nanny* 1965; *The Skull* 1965; *The Charge of the Light Brigade* 1968; *Inadmissible Evidence* 1968; *Julius Caesar* 1970; *I Want What I Want* 1971; *Mister Quilp* 1975; *Full Circle* 1977; *For Your Eyes Only* 1981; *Britannia Hospital* 1982; *Lady Jane* 1985; *Hawks* 1988; *The Sheltering Sky* 1990

Bennett, Joan *Bulldog Drummond* 1929; *Disraeli* 1929; *Moby Dick* 1930; *Me and My Gal* 1932; *Little Women* 1933; *The Man Who Broke the Bank at Monte Carlo* 1935; *Mississippi* 1935; *Private Worlds* 1935; *Big Brown Eyes* 1936; *Vogues* 1937; *Trade Winds* 1938; *The Texans* 1938; *I Met My Love Again* 1938; *Artists and Models Abroad* 1938; *The Housekeeper's Daughter* 1939; *The Man in the Iron Mask* 1939; *The Man I Married* 1940; *Son of Monte Cristo* 1940; *Confirm or Deny* 1941; *Man Hunt* 1941; *Wild Geese Calling* 1941; *Twin Beds* 1942; *Margin for Error* 1943; *Colonel Effingham's Raid* 1945; *Nob Hill* 1945; *Scarlet Street* 1945; *The Woman in the Window* 1945; *The Macomber Affair* 1947; *The Woman on the Beach* 1947; *Hollow Triumph* 1948; *Secret beyond the Door* 1948; *The Reckless Moment* 1949; *Father of the Bride* 1950; *For Heaven's Sake* 1950; *Father's Little Dividend* 1951; *We're No Angels* 1955; *There's Always Tomorrow* 1956; *Desire in the Dust* 1960; *House of Dark Shadows* 1970; *The Eyes of Charles Sand* 1972; *Suspiria* 1976; *Divorce Wars* 1982

Bennett, John *The House That Dripped Blood* 1971; *The House in Nightmare Park* 1973; *Watership Down* 1978; *Antonia & Jane* 1990

Bennett, Leila *The First Year* 1932; *Taxi!* 1932; *Tiger Shark* 1932

Bennett, Marjorie *Limelight* 1952; *What Ever Happened to Baby Jane?* 1962; *Games* 1967

Bennett, Nigel *Sanctuary* 1998; *Naked City: a Killer Christmas* 1998

Bennett, Richard *Arrowsmith* 1931; *If I Had a Million* 1932; *This Reckless Age* 1932; *Nana* 1934; *The Magnificent Ambersons* 1942

Bennett, Rosalind *Dealers* 1989; *Smack and Thistle* 1989

Bennett, Zachary *Back to Hannibal: the Return of Tom Sawyer and Huckleberry Finn* 1990; *Bury Me in Niagara* 1993

Benny, Jack *Hollywood Revue* 1929; *Broadway Melody of 1936* 1935; *The Big Broadcast of 1937* 1936; *Artists and Models* 1937; *Artists and Models Abroad* 1938; *Charley's Aunt* 1941; *George Washington Slept Here* 1942; *To Be or Not to Be* 1942; *The Meanest Man in the World* 1943; *Hollywood Canteen* 1944; *The Horn Blows at Midnight* 1945; *It's in the Bag* 1945; *Without Reservations* 1946; *Somebody Loves Me* 1952; *The Man* 1972

Benrath, Martin *The Saboteur, Code Name Morituri* 1965; *From the Life of the Marionettes* 1980; *Stalingrad* 1992

Benskin, Tyrone *Marked Man* 1996; *Sci-Fighters* 1996

Benson, Chris *The Cutting Edge* 1992; *Black Fox* 1995

Benson, Deborah *9/30/55* 1977; *Just before Dawn* 1980; *The Danger of Love* 1992

Benson, George *Keep Fit* 1937; *The Creeping Flesh* 1972

Benson, Jodi *The Little Mermaid* 1989; *Thumbelina* 1994

Benson, Lucille *Little Fauss and Big Halsy* 1970; *Duel* 1971; *Tom Sawyer* 1973; *Huckleberry Finn* 1974; *Black Market Baby* 1977

Benson, Martin *I'll Get You for This* 1950; *Assassin for Hire* 1951; *The Dark Light* 1951; *West of Zanzibar* 1954; *The King and I* 1956; *The Flesh Is Weak* 1957; *Man from Tangier* 1957; *The Strange World of Planet X* 1957; *Oscar Wilde* 1959; *The Gentle Trap* 1960; *Gorgo* 1960; *Satan Never Sleeps* 1962; *Goldfinger* 1964; *The Magnificent Two* 1967; *Battle beneath the Earth* 1968; *The Omen* 1976

Benson, Perry *Annie: a Royal Adventure* 1995; *Final Cut* 1998

Benson, Robby *Jory* 1972; *Jeremy* 1973; *Lucky Lady* 1975; *Ode to Billy Joe* 1976; *One on One* 1977; *Ice Castles* 1978; *Walk Proud* 1979; *Tribute* 1980; *The Chosen* 1981; *National Lampoon's Movie Madness* 1981; *Running Brave* 1983; *Harry and Son* 1984; *Rent-a-Cop* 1988; *Modern Love* 1990; *Beauty and the Beast* 1991; *Precious Victims* 1993; *Beauty* and the Beast: the Enchanted Christmas 1997

Benson, Roy Sweet and Lowdown 1944; Billy Rose's Diamond Horseshoe 1945

Bentine, Michael Down among the Z-Men 1952; Forces' Sweetheart 1953; Raising a Riot 1955; We Joined the Navy 1962; The Sandwich Man 1966; Rentadick 1972

Bentivoglio, Fabrizio Apartment Zero 1988; Eternity and a Day 1998

Bentley, Beverly Scent of Mystery 1960; Beyond the Law 1968

Bentley, Dick Desert Mice 1959; And the Same to You 1960; In the Doghouse 1961; Tamahine 1963; The Adventures of Barry McKenzie 1972; Barry McKenzie Holds His Own 1974

Bentley, John The Happiest Days of Your Life 1950; The Lost Hours 1952; Tread Softly 1952; Double Exposure 1954; The Flaw 1954; River Beat 1954; Profile 1954; Confession 1955; Istanbul 1957; Submarine Seahawk 1959; The Singer Not the Song 1960

Benton, Jerome Purple Rain 1984; Under the Cherry Moon 1986; Graffiti Bridge 1990

Benton, Susanne That Cold Day in the Park 1969; A Boy and His Dog 1975

Bentzen, Jayne A Breed Apart 1984; A Breed Apart 1984

Ben-Victor, Paul Body Parts 1991; Trouble Bound 1993; Ed McBain's 87th Precinct: Heatwave 1997; The Corruptor 1999

Benzali, Daniel Last Days of Patton 1986; Pack of Lies 1987; Messenger of Death 1988; A Day in October 1991; A Child's Cry for Help 1994; Murder at 1600 1997; All the Little Animals 1998

Beradino, John aka **Berardino, John** The World Was His Jury 1957; Do Not Fold, Spindle or Mutilate 1971

Beranger, George Broken Blossoms 1919; Road House 1948

Bercovici, Luca Frightmare 1981; Parasite 1982; American Flyers 1985; Clean and Sober 1988; Mortal Passions 1989; Pacific Heights 1990; K2 1991; Mission of Justice 1992; Drop Zone 1994; Mirror Images II 1994; The Big Squeeze 1996

Beregi, Oscar Anything Can Happen 1952; Desert Legion 1953

Berenger, Tom Looking for Mr Goodbar 1977; The Sentinel 1977; Butch and Sundance: the Early Days 1979; The Dogs of War 1980; The Big Chill 1983; Eddie and the Cruisers 1983; Fear City 1984; Rustler's Rhapsody 1985; Platoon 1986; Someone to Watch over Me 1987; Betrayed 1988; Deadly Pursuit 1988; Last Rites 1988; Born on the Fourth of July 1989; Major League 1989; The Field 1990; Love at Large 1990; At Play in the Fields of the Lord 1991; Shattered 1991; Sniper 1992; Gettysburg 1993; Sliver 1993; Chasers 1994; Major League II 1994; The Avenging Angel 1995; Last of the Dogmen 1995; Body Language 1995; An Occasional Hell 1996; The Substitute 1996; The Gingerbread Man 1997; A Murder of Crows 1998; Shadow of Doubt 1998

Berens, Harold Live Now – Pay Later 1962; Hear My Song 1991

Berenson, Marisa Death in Venice 1971; Cabaret 1972; Barry Lyndon 1975; Casanova & Co 1976; Killer Fish 1978; Playing for Time 1980; SOB 1981; The Secret Diary of Sigmund Freud 1984; Perfume of the Cyclone 1989; White Hunter, Black Heart 1990; Notorious 1992

Beresford, Harry Doctor X 1932; High Pressure 1932; The Sign of the Cross 1932; I Cover the Waterfront 1933; Murders in the Zoo 1933; Follow the Fleet 1936; Klondike Annie 1936

Berg, Peter Quiet Victory: the Charlie Wedemeyer Story 1988; Never on Tuesday 1988; Race for Glory 1989; Shocker 1989; Genuine Risk 1990; Crooked Hearts 1991; Late for Dinner 1991; A Midnight Clear 1991; Aspen Extreme 1993; A Case for Murder 1993; Fire in the Sky 1993; The Last Seduction 1993; FTW 1994; Rise and Walk: the Dennis Byrd Story 1994; Girl 6 1996; The Great White Hype 1996; Cop Land 1997

Bergan, Judith-Marie Abduction 1975; The Secret Life of Kathy McCormick 1988

Bergé, Francine Judex 1963; La Ronde 1964; La Religieuse 1965; Une Histoire Simple 1978

Bergen, Candice The Group 1966; The Sand Pebbles 1966; Vivre pour Vivre 1967; The Day the Fish Came Out 1967; The Magus 1968; The Adventurers 1970; Getting Straight 1970; Soldier Blue 1970; Carnal Knowledge 1971; A Date with a Lonely Girl 1971; The Hunting Party 1971; 11 Harrowhouse 1974; Bite the Bullet 1975; The Wind and the Lion 1975; The Domino Principle 1977; Oliver's Story 1978; A Night Full of Rain 1978; Starting Over 1979; Rich and Famous 1981; Gandhi 1982; Merlin and the Sword 1982; Stick 1985; Mayflower Madam 1987

Bergen, Edgar The Goldwyn Follies 1938; You Can't Cheat an Honest Man 1939; Look Who's Laughing 1941; Here We Go Again 1942; Song of the Open Road 1944; Fun and Fancy Free 1947; I Remember Mama 1948; Don't Make Waves 1967; The Homecoming: a Christmas Story 1971

Bergen, Polly At War with the Army 1950; The Stooge 1951; That's My Boy 1951; Warpath 1951; Escape from Fort Bravo 1953; Cry of the Hunted 1953; Arena 1953; Cape Fear 1962; Move Over, Darling 1963; The Caretakers 1963; Kisses for My President 1964; Making Mr Right 1987; Addicted to His Love 1988; She Was Marked for Murder 1988; Cry-Baby 1989; My Brother's Wife 1989; Leave of Absence 1994; Dr Jekyll and Ms Hyde 1995; In the Blink of an Eye 1996

Bergen, Tushka Swing Kids 1993; Barcelona 1994; Murderous Intent 1995

Berger, Helmut The Damned 1969; The Garden of the Finzi-Continis 1971; Ash Wednesday 1973; Ludwig 1973; Conversation Piece 1974; The Romantic Englishwoman 1975; Salon Kitty 1976; Victory at Entebbe 1976; Deadly Game 1982; Code Name: Emerald 1985

Berger, Nicole The Ripening Seed 1953; The Siege of Sidney Street 1960; Shoot the Pianist 1960

Berger, Senta The Secret Ways 1961; The Victors 1963; The Glory Guys 1965; Major Dundee 1965; Cast a Giant Shadow 1966; Our Man in Marrakesh 1966; The Quiller Memorandum 1966; The Spy with My Face 1966; The Ambushers 1967; Diabolically Yours 1967; Istanbul Express 1968; De Sade 1969; The Swiss Conspiracy 1975; Killing Cars 1986

Berger, Toni The Serpent's Egg 1977; Sugarbaby 1985

Berger, William Face to Face 1967; Sartana 1968; Today It's Me... Tomorrow You! 1968; On the Third Day Arrived the Crow 1973; Situation 1973; Three Tough Guys 1974; Keoma 1976; Hercules 1983; Hercules II 1983; Tex and the Lord of the Deep 1985; Dr M 1989

Bergerac, Jacques Beautiful Stranger 1954; Les Girls 1957; Gigi 1958; Thunder in the Sun 1959; Achilles 1962; The Unkissed Bride 1966

Bergere, Lee Bob & Carol & Ted & Alice 1969; Time Trackers 1989

Berggren, Thommy The Pram 1963; Raven's End 1963; Elvira Madigan 1967; Joe Hill 1971; Sunday's Children 1992

Berghof, Herbert Assignment – Paris 1952; 5 Fingers 1952; Red Planet Mars 1952; Times Square 1980; Those Lips, Those Eyes 1980; The Belarus File 1985; Target 1985

Bergin, Patrick The Courier 1987; Taffin 1988; Mountains of the Moon 1989; Robin Hood 1990; Love Crimes 1991; Sleeping with the Enemy 1991; Frankenstein 1992; Map of the Human Heart 1992; Patriot Games 1992; Highway to Hell 1992; They Watch 1993; Double Cross 1994; Soft Deceit 1994; Twilight Zone: Rod Serling's Lost Classics 1994; Lawnmower Man 2: Beyond Cyberspace 1995; Triplecross 1995; The Proposition 1996; The Witch's Daughter 1996; Suspicious Minds 1997; The Ripper 1997; When the Sky Falls 2000

Berglund, Erik Walpurgis Night 1935; One Single Night 1939

Bergman, Henry Behind the Screen 1916; The Rink 1916; The Pawnshop 1916; Sunnyside 1919; The Idle Class 1921; The Circus 1928; Modern Times 1936

Bergman, Ingrid The Count of the Old Town 1935; Swedenhielms 1935; Walpurgis Night 1935; Intermezzo 1936; Dollar 1938; A Woman's Face 1938; Intermezzo 1939; One Single Night 1939; June Night 1940; Adam Had Four Sons 1941; Dr Jekyll and Mr Hyde 1941; Rage in Heaven 1941; Casablanca 1942; For Whom the Bell Tolls 1943; Gaslight 1944; The Bells of St Mary's 1945; Saratoga Trunk 1945; Spellbound 1945; Notorious 1946; Arch of Triumph 1948; Joan of Arc 1948; Under Capricorn 1949; Stromboli 1950; Europa '51 1952; Journey to Italy 1953; Fear 1954; Anastasia 1956; Elena et les Hommes 1956; Indiscreet 1958; The Inn of the Sixth Happiness 1958; Goodbye Again 1961; The Yellow Rolls-Royce 1964; The Visit 1964; Cactus Flower 1969; A Walk in the Spring Rain 1970; The Hideaways 1973; Murder on the Orient Express 1974; A Matter of Time 1976; Autumn Sonata 1978

Bergman, Mary Kay The Hunchback of Notre Dame 1996; South Park: Bigger, Longer & Uncut 1999

Bergman, Peter Phantom of the Ritz 1988; Palomino 1991; Woman on the Ledge 1993

Bergman, Sandahl All That Jazz 1979; Conan the Barbarian 1982; Red Sonja 1985; Hell Comes to Frogtown 1988; Raw Nerve 1991; In the Arms of a Killer 1992; Silent Thunder 1992; Body of Influence 1993

Bergner, Elisabeth aka **Bergner, Elizabeth** Ariane 1931; Catherine the Great 1934; Escape Me Never 1935; As You Like It 1936; Paris Calling 1941; Cry of the Banshee 1970; The Pedestrian 1974

Bergström, Helena House of Angels 1992; House of Angels II: The Second Summer 1994

Beristain, Luis El 1952; The Exterminating Angel 1962

Berkeley, Ballard The Last Adventurers 1937; The Blue Parrot 1953; Child's Play 1954; Impact 1963; The BFG 1989

Berkeley, Xander The Fabulous Baker Boys 1989; Short Time 1990; Candyman 1992; Donato and Daughter 1993; Roswell 1994; Apollo 13 1995; Barb Wire 1995; Safe 1995; Within the Rock 1995; Poison Ivy II: Lily 1995; If These Walls Could Talk 1996; Persons Unknown 1996; The Killing Jar 1996; Air Force One 1997; Gattaca 1997; Winchell 1998; Universal Soldier – the Return 1999; Shanghai Noon 2000

Berkes, John Branded 1950; Ace in the Hole 1951

Berkley, Elizabeth Showgirls 1995; The First Wives Club 1996; The Real Blonde 1997; Random Encounter 1998; Tail Lights Fade 1999

Berkoff, Steven A Clockwork Orange 1971; Barry Lyndon 1975; The Passenger 1975; McVicar 1980; Outland 1981; Octopussy 1983; Beverly Hills Cop 1984; Rambo: First Blood, Part II 1985; Revolution 1985; Absolute Beginners 1986; Under the Cherry Moon 1986; Prisoner of Rio 1988; The Krays 1990; Decadence 1993; Fair Game 1995; Flynn 1995; Another Nine ½ Weeks 1997; Rancid Aluminium 1999

Berle, Milton New Faces of 1937 1937; Radio City Revels 1938; Sun Valley Serenade 1941; A Gentleman at Heart 1942; Whispering Ghosts 1942; Margin for Error 1943; Always Leave Them Laughing 1949; Let's Make Love 1960; It's a Mad Mad Mad Mad World 1963; Journey back to Oz 1964; The Loved One 1965; The Oscar 1966; The Happening 1967; Who's Minding the Mint? 1967; Where Angels Go...Trouble Follows 1968; Can Heironymus Merkin Ever Forget Mercy Humppe and Find True Happiness? 1969; Lepke 1975; Smorgasbord 1983; Side by Side 1988; Storybook 1995

Berléand, François Au Revoir les Enfants 1987; Milou en Mai 1989; Place Vendôme 1998

Berleand, François The School of Flesh 1998; Romance 1998

Berlin, Jeannie The Baby Maker 1970; The Heartbreak Kid 1972; Housewife 1972; Portnoy's Complaint 1972; Sheila Levine Is Dead and Living in New York 1975; In the Spirit 1990

Berling, Charles Salt on Our Skin 1992; Ridicule 1996; Dry Cleaning 1997; Love etc 1997; Those Who Love Me Can Take the Train 1998; L'Ennui 1998; The Bridge 1999

Berling, Peter Aguirre, Wrath of God 1972; Haunted Summer 1988

Berlinger, Warren Teenage Rebel 1956; Blue Denim 1959; Because They're Young 1960; All Hands on Deck 1961; The Wackiest Ship in the Army 1961; Billie 1965; Thunder Alley 1967; Lepke 1975; The Four Deuces 1976; What Price Victory 1988; Outlaw Force 1988; Accidental Hero 1992

Berman, Marc Noir et Blanc 1986; The Last Island 1990; Autobus 1991; The Voyage 1991

Berman, Shelley The Best Man 1964; Divorce American Style 1967; Every Home Should Have One 1970; Beware! The Blob 1971; Teen Witch 1989

Berman, Susan Smithereens 1982; Making Mr Right 1987

Bernard, Carl The Silver Darlings 1947; The Hour of Decision 1957

Bernard, Crystal Without Her Consent 1990; As Good as Dead 1995

Bernard, Ed Across 110th Street 1972; Blue Thunder 1983

Bernard, Jason Going Home 1971; All of Me 1984; No Way Out 1986; Paint It Black 1989; The Computer Wore Tennis Shoes 1995; While You Were Sleeping 1995; Suddenly 1996; Liar Liar 1997

Bernard, Sue aka **Bernard, Susan** Faster, Pussycat! Kill! Kill! 1965; Teenager 1974

Bernardi, Herschel Murder by Contract 1958; The Savage Eye 1959; A Cold Wind in August 1961; Irma la Douce 1963; Love with the Proper Stranger 1963; The Front 1976; No Deposit No Return 1976

Bernhard, Sandra Cheech & Chong's Nice Dreams 1981; The King of Comedy 1983; Follow That Bird 1985; Track 29 1988; Without You I'm Nothing 1990; Hudson Hawk 1991; Inside Monkey Zetterland 1992; Dallas Doll 1994; Freaky Friday 1995; Burn Hollywood Burn 1997; Wrongfully Accused 1998

Bernhardsson, Lena-Pia Elvis! Elvis! 1977; The Simple-Minded Murderer 1982

Bernhardt, Kevin Counterforce 1987; Hellraiser III: Hell on Earth 1992; The Immortals 1995

Bernsen, Collin Puppet Master II 1990; Double Trouble 1992; Midnight Blue 1996

Bernsen, Corbin Hello Again 1987; Bert Rigby, You're a Fool 1989; Breaking Point 1989; Disorganized Crime 1989; Major League 1989; Blind Hate 1991; Dead on the Money 1991; Shattered 1991; Frozen Assets 1992; Appointment for a Killing 1993; A Brilliant Disguise 1993; Final Mission 1993; Killing Box 1993; Major League II 1994; Silhouette 1994; Web of Deceit 1994; Ring of the Musketeers 1994; Dangerous Intentions 1995; Murderous Intent 1995; Someone to Die For 1995; Temptress 1995; Murder on the Iditarod Trail 1995; Tails You Live, Heads You're Dead 1995; Circuit Breaker 1996; The Dentist 1996; The Great White Hype 1996; Tidal Wave: No Escape 1997; Kiss of a Stranger 1997; The Misadventures of Margaret 1998; Major League: Back to the Minors 1998; The Dentist II 1998

Berrell, George Straight Shooting 1917; Pollyanna 1920

Berri, Claude *Les Bonnes Femmes* 1960; *Marry Me! Marry Me!* 1968
Berridge, Elizabeth *The Funhouse* 1981; *Amadeus* 1984; *Five Corners* 1987; *Home Fires Burning* 1989; *Montana* 1990; *When the Party's Over* 1992
Berroyer, Jackie *L'Eau Froide* 1994; *Rien Ne Va Plus* 1997
Berry, Halle *Jungle Fever* 1991; *The Last Boy Scout* 1991; *Strictly Business* 1991; *Boomerang* 1992; *Father Hood* 1993; *The Program* 1993; *The Flintstones* 1994; *Losing Isaiah* 1995; *Executive Decision* 1996; *Race the Sun* 1996; *The Rich Man's Wife* 1996; *B.A.P.S.* 1997; *Bulworth* 1998; *Why Do Fools Fall in Love?* 1998
Berry, John *Golden Eighties* 1986; *A Man in Love* 1987
Berry, Jules *Le Crime de Monsieur Lange* 1935; *Le Jour se Lève* 1939; *Les Visiteurs du Soir* 1942
Berry, Ken *Hello Down There* 1969; *Herbie Rides Again* 1974; *The Cat from Outer Space* 1978
Berry, Richard *La Balance* 1982; *La Garce* 1984; *Brothers in Arms* 1990; *C'est la Vie* 1990; *Shadows of the Past* 1991; *Le Petit Prince A Dit* 1992; *Day of Atonement* 1993; *The Bait* 1995
Berry, Vincent *Amnesia* 1996; *Free Willy 3: the Rescue* 1997; *Hoods* 1998
Berryman, Dorothée *The Decline of the American Empire* 1986; *A Paper Wedding* 1989; *Back Stab* 1990
Berryman, Michael *The Hills Have Eyes* 1978; *The Hills Have Eyes Part II* 1985; *Armed Response* 1986; *Haunting Fear* 1990; *Evil Spirits* 1991; *Auntie Lee's Meat Pies* 1991; *The Guyver* 1992
Bertheau, Julien *La Vie Est à Nous* 1936; *Celà s'Appelle l'Aurore* 1956; *Madame* 1961; *The Discreet Charm of the Bourgeoisie* 1972; *The Phantom of Liberty* 1974; *Verdict* 1974; *That Obscure Object of Desire* 1977
Berti, Dehl *Seven Alone* 1974; *Sweet Hostage* 1975
Berti, Marina *Prince of Foxes* 1949; *Marie Antoinette* 1956; *Madame* 1961; *A Face in the Rain* 1963
Bertie, Diego *Full Fathom Five* 1990; *No Mercy* 1994
Bertin, Pierre *Orphée* 1950; *Elena et les Hommes* 1956; *The Stranger* 1967
Bertin, Roland *The Brontë Sisters* 1979; *Cyrano de Bergerac* 1990; *The Hairdresser's Husband* 1990; *La Fille de l'Air* 1992; *Lumière Noire* 1994
Bertinelli, Valerie *C.H.O.M.P.S.* 1979; *Silent Witness* 1985; *Rockabye* 1986; *Number One with a Bullet* 1986; *Shades of Gray* 1992; *Murder of Innocence* 1993; *The Haunting of Helen Walker* 1995; *Two Mothers for Zachary* 1996
Bertish, Suzanne *Hearts of Fire* 1987; *Venice/Venice* 1992
Berto, Juliet *La Chinoise* 1967; *Le Gai Savoir* 1968; *Vladimir et Rosa* 1970; *Out 1: Spectre* 1973; *Celine and Julie Go Boating* 1974; *Mr Klein* 1976
Bertorelli, Toni *Strong Hands* 1997; *The Prince of Homburg* 1997; *Elvjs & Merilijn* 1998
Bervoets, Gene *aka* **Bervoets, Eugene** *The Vanishing* 1988; *Anchoress* 1993
Besch, Bibi *Distance* 1975; *The Pack* 1977; *Star Trek II: the Wrath of Khan* 1982; *The Day After* 1983; *The Lonely Lady* 1983; *Who's That Girl* 1987; *Rattled* 1996
Besnéhard, Dominique *To Our Loves* 1984; *The Lie* 1992
Bessell, Ted *Billie* 1965; *Don't Drink the Water* 1969
Besserer, Eugenie *The Jazz Singer* 1927; *Madame X* 1929; *Thunderbolt* 1929
Bessho, Tetsuya *Solar Crisis* 1990; *Godzilla vs Mothra* 1992
Best, Alyson *Man of Flowers* 1984; *Relatives* 1985
Best, Edna *Escape* 1930; *The Key* 1934; *The Man Who Knew Too Much* 1934; *South Riding* 1938; *Intermezzo* 1939; *A Dispatch from Reuters* 1940; *Swiss Family Robinson* 1940; *The Ghost and Mrs Muir* 1947; *The Iron Curtain* 1948
Best, James *Kansas Raiders* 1950; *Seven Angry Men* 1955; *Last of the Badmen* 1957; *Hot Summer Night* 1957; *The Left Handed Gun* 1958; *The Naked and the Dead* 1958; *Ride Lonesome* 1959; *Verboten!* 1959; *Cast a Long Shadow* 1959; *The Killer Shrews* 1959; *The Mountain Road* 1960; *Shock Corridor* 1963; *Black Spurs* 1965; *Three on a Couch* 1966; *Run, Simon, Run* 1970; *Sounder* 1972; *Ode to Billy Joe* 1976; *Rolling Thunder* 1977; *Hooper* 1978; *Dukes of Hazzard Reunion* 1997
Best, Willie *The Littlest Rebel* 1935; *The Bride Walks Out* 1936; *The Ghost Breakers* 1940; *Nothing but the Truth* 1941; *Whispering Ghosts* 1942; *The Red Dragon* 1945; *The Bride Wore Boots* 1946; *Dangerous Money* 1946
Beswick, Martine *aka* **Beswicke, Martine** *Thunderball* 1965; *One Million Years BC* 1966; *The Penthouse* 1967; *Dr Jekyll and Sister Hyde* 1971; *Seizure* 1974; *The Happy Hooker Goes to Hollywood* 1980; *Trancers II: The Return of Jack Deth* 1991; *Evil Spirits* 1991; *Wide Sargasso Sea* 1992
Bethmann, Sabine *The Tiger of Eschnapur* 1959; *The Indian Tomb* 1959
Bettger, Lyle *No Man of Her Own* 1950; *Union Station* 1950; *The First Legion* 1951; *The Greatest Show on Earth* 1952; *All I Desire* 1953; *The Great Sioux Uprising* 1953; *Forbidden* 1953; *Carnival Story* 1954; *Destry* 1954; *Drums across the River* 1954; *The Sea Chase* 1955; *The Lone Ranger* 1956; *Guns of the Timberland* 1960; *Johnny Reno* 1966; *Impasse* 1969; *The Seven Minutes* 1971
Betti, Laura *RoGoPaG* 1962; *Theorem* 1968; *The Canterbury Tales* 1971; *1900* 1976; *La Luna* 1979; *Courage Mountain* 1989; *Marianna Ucria* 1997
Bettin, Val *Basil the Great Mouse Detective* 1986; *Aladdin and the King of Thieves* 1996
Bettis, Valerie *Affair in Trinidad* 1952; *Let's Do It Again* 1953
Bettles, Robert *The Fourth Wish* 1976; *Ride a Wild Pony* 1976
Betz, Carl *Inferno* 1953; *Powder River* 1953; *Killdozer* 1974
Betz, Matthew *The Unholy Three* 1925; *The Wedding March* 1928
Betzler, Geri *Fear* 1988; *Amityville: the Evil Escapes* 1989
Bevan, Billy *Journey's End* 1930; *Payment Deferred* 1932; *The Lost Patrol* 1934; *Another Dawn* 1937
Bevans, Clem *Thunder Afloat* 1939; *Saboteur* 1942; *The Yearling* 1946; *Big Jack* 1949; *The Boy from Oklahoma* 1954
Bevis, Leslie *The Squeeze* 1987; *Alien Nation* 1988; *The November Men* 1993
Bewes, Rodney *A Prize of Arms* 1961; *Billy Liar* 1963; *Decline and Fall... of a Birdwatcher* 1968; *Spring and Port Wine* 1969; *The Likely Lads* 1976; *Jabberwocky* 1977; *The Spaceman and King Arthur* 1979; *Saint Jack* 1979; *The Wildcats of St Trinian's* 1980
Bexton, Nathan *Nowhere* 1997; *Go* 1999
Bey, Marki *The Landlord* 1970; *Hangup* 1973
Bey, Turhan *Shadows on the Stairs* 1941; *Arabian Nights* 1942; *Background to Danger* 1943; *Ali Baba and the Forty Thieves* 1944; *Dragon Seed* 1944; *Out of the Blue* 1947; *Prisoners of the Casbah* 1953
Beyer, Troy *Uncle Tom's Cabin* 1987; *Disorderlies* 1987; *Rooftops* 1989; *Weekend at Bernie's II* 1992; *Eddie* 1996; *B.A.P.S.* 1997; *Let's Talk about Sex* 1998
Beymer, Richard *aka* **Beymer, Dick** *Indiscretion of an American Wife* 1954; *Johnny Tremain* 1957; *The Diary of Anne Frank* 1959; *High Time* 1960; *Bachelor Flat* 1961; *West Side Story* 1961; *Five Finger Exercise* 1962; *Hemingway's Adventures of a Young Man* 1962; *The Longest Day* 1962; *The Stripper* 1963; *Silent Night, Deadly Night 3: Better Watch Out!* 1989; *Blackbelt* 1992; *Danger Island* 1992; *Under Investigation* 1993; *State of Emergency* 1994
Bezace, Didier *La Petite Voleuse* 1988; *L.627* 1992; *Les Voleurs* 1996; *The Chambermaid on the Titanic* 1997
Bhasker *aka* **Patel, Bhasker** *Wild West* 1992; *Brothers in Trouble* 1995; *My Son the Fanatic* 1997
Bhatti, Ahsen *Brothers in Trouble* 1995; *Sixth Happiness* 1997
Bibb, Leon *For Love of Ivy* 1968; *The Lost Man* 1969; *Dead Wrong* 1983
Biberman, Abner *Whispering Ghosts* 1942; *The Leopard Man* 1943; *Betrayal from the East* 1945; *Elephant Walk* 1954; *Knock on Wood* 1954
Bice, Robert *Invasion USA* 1952; *Three for the Show* 1955
Bichir, Bruno *Highway Patrolman* 1991; *Midaq Alley* 1995
Bichir, Demian *'Til Death* 1993; *Sex, Shame and Tears* 1999
Bick, Stewart *While My Pretty One Sleeps* 1997; *A Walk on the Moon* 1999
Bickford, Charles *Dynamite* 1929; *Anna Christie* 1930; *The Squaw Man* 1931; *This Day and Age* 1933; *White Woman* 1933; *Little Miss Marker* 1934; *The Farmer Takes a Wife* 1935; *The Plainsman* 1936; *High, Wide and Handsome* 1937; *The Storm* 1938; *Of Mice and Men* 1939; *Tarzan's New York Adventure* 1942; *Mr Lucky* 1943; *The Song of Bernadette* 1943; *Wing and a Prayer* 1944; *Captain Eddie* 1945; *Fallen Angel* 1945; *Duel in the Sun* 1946; *The Farmer's Daughter* 1946; *Brute Force* 1947; *The Woman on the Beach* 1947; *Command Decision* 1948; *Johnny Belinda* 1948; *They Passed This Way* 1948; *Roseanna McCoy* 1949; *Whirlpool* 1949; *Branded* 1950; *Riding High* 1950; *Jim Thorpe – All-American* 1951; *The Last Posse* 1953; *A Star Is Born* 1954; *The Court-Martial of Billy Mitchell* 1955; *Not as a Stranger* 1955; *Prince of Players* 1955; *You Can't Run Away from It* 1956; *Mister Cory* 1957; *The Big Country* 1958; *The Unforgiven* 1960; *Days of Wine and Roses* 1962; *Della* 1965; *Big Deal at Dodge City* 1966
Bideau, Jean-Luc *State of Siege* 1972; *The Invitation* 1973; *Jonah Who Will Be 25 in the Year 2000* 1976; *D'Artagnan's Daughter* 1994
Biehn, Michael *The Fan* 1981; *The Lords of Discipline* 1983; *The Terminator* 1984; *Aliens* 1986; *Rampage* 1987; *The Seventh Sign* 1988; *In a Shallow Grave* 1988; *The Abyss* 1989; *Navy SEALS* 1990; *K2* 1991; *Terminator 2: Judgment Day* 1991; *Time Bomb* 1991; *A Taste for Killing* 1992; *Deadfall* 1993; *Tombstone* 1993; *Deep Red* 1994; *In the Kingdom of the Blind* 1994; *Conundrum* 1995; *Jade* 1995; *Mojave Moon* 1996; *The Rock* 1996; *Dead Men Can't Dance* 1997; *Susan's Plan* 1998
Biel, Jessica *Ulee's Gold* 1997; *I'll Be Home for Christmas* 1998
Bieri, Ramon *The Andromeda Strain* 1970; *The Grasshopper* 1970; *Brother John* 1970; *The Honkers* 1971; *Badlands* 1973; *Sorcerer* 1977; *The Frisco Kid* 1979; *Vibes* 1988
Bierko, Craig *Danielle Steel's Star* 1993; *The Long Kiss Goodnight* 1996; *'Til There Was You* 1997; *Sour Grapes* 1998; *The Thirteenth Floor* 1999
Biesk, Adam *Meet the Applegates* 1991; *Gas, Food, Lodging* 1992; *Leprechaun 2* 1994
Bigagli, Claudio *The Night of San Lorenzo* 1981; *Kaos* 1984; *Mediterraneo* 1991; *Fiorile* 1993
Biggins, Christopher *The Tempest* 1979; *Decadence* 1993; *Asterix Conquers America* 1994
Biggs, Julie *Nobody Waved Goodbye* 1964; *Unfinished Business* 1983
Biggs, Roxann *New York Mounted* 1991; *Mortal Sins* 1992; *Greyhounds* 1994
Bigham, Lexie *aka* **Bigham, Lexie D** *South Central* 1992; *High School High* 1996
Bikel, Theodore *The African Queen* 1951; *A Day to Remember* 1953; *The Kidnappers* 1953; *Never Let Me Go* 1953; *Forbidden Cargo* 1954; *The Young Lovers* 1954; *Above Us the Waves* 1955; *The Enemy Below* 1957; *The Pride and the Passion* 1957; *The Defiant Ones* 1958; *I Want to Live!* 1958; *The Angry Hills* 1959; *The Blue Angel* 1959; *Woman Obsessed* 1959; *A Dog of Flanders* 1959; *My Fair Lady* 1964; *Sands of the Kalahari* 1965; *The Russians Are Coming, the Russians Are Coming* 1966; *Sweet November* 1968; *My Side of the Mountain* 1969; *Darker than Amber* 1970; *200 Motels* 1971; *The Little Ark* 1972; *Victory at Entebbe* 1976; *Prince Jack* 1984; *The Final Days* 1989; *Dark Tower* 1989; *Benefit of the Doubt* 1993; *Shadow Conspiracy* 1996
Bill, Tony *Come Blow Your Horn* 1963; *Soldier in the Rain* 1963; *Marriage on the Rocks* 1965; *None but the Brave* 1965; *Ice Station Zebra* 1968; *Never a Dull Moment* 1968; *Flap* 1970; *Shampoo* 1975; *Heart Beat* 1979; *Less than Zero* 1987; *The Killing Mind* 1991
Billerey, Raoul *L'Enfance Nue* 1968; *An Impudent Girl* 1985; *Le Grand Chemin* 1987; *La Petite Voleuse* 1988; *D'Artagnan's Daughter* 1994
Billett, Don *Prince of the City* 1981; *Gloria* 1998
Billing, Roy *Dallas Doll* 1994; *Siam Sunset* 1999
Billings, Earl *Stakeout* 1987; *One False Move* 1992
Billingsley, Barbara *Bay Cove* 1987; *Leave It to Beaver* 1997
Billingsley, Jennifer *Lady in a Cage* 1964; *Welcome Home, Soldier Boys* 1971; *White Lightning* 1973
Billingsley, Peter *Paternity* 1981; *Death Valley* 1982; *A Christmas Story* 1983; *The Dirt Bike Kid* 1986; *Beverly Hills Brats* 1989; *Arcade* 1993
Binder, Sybilla *The Man from Morocco* 1944; *Blanche Fury* 1948
Bindon, John *Poor Cow* 1967; *Performance* 1970
Bing, Herman *The Guardsman* 1931; *The King Steps Out* 1936; *Every Day's a Holiday* 1937; *Maytime* 1937; *Bluebeard's Eighth Wife* 1938; *Dumbo* 1941
Bingham, Barbara *Deathmask* 1984; *Friday the 13th Part VIII: Jason Takes Manhattan* 1989
Binns, Edward *Vice Squad* 1953; *Beyond a Reasonable Doubt* 1956; *12 Angry Men* 1957; *Desire in the Dust* 1960; *The Americanization of Emily* 1964; *Fail-Safe* 1964; *Lovin' Molly* 1974; *Night Moves* 1975; *Oliver's Story* 1978; *FDR: the Last Year* 1980; *The Verdict* 1982
Binoche, Juliette *Je Vous Salue, Marie* 1984; *Rendez-vous* 1985; *The Night Is Young* 1986; *The Unbearable Lightness of Being* 1988; *Les Amants du Pont-Neuf* 1990; *Women and Men – 2* 1991; *Damage* 1992; *Wuthering Heights* 1992; *Three Colours Blue* 1993; *The Horseman on the Roof* 1995; *The English Patient* 1996; *Alice et Martin* 1998; *La Veuve de Saint-Pierre* 2000
Biraud, Maurice *Any Number Can Win* 1963; *The Last Train* 1972
Birch, Paul *The War of the Worlds* 1953; *Ride Clear of Diablo* 1954; *Apache Woman* 1955; *Five Guns West* 1955; *The Day the World Ended* 1956; *Not of This Earth* 1956; *The 27th Day* 1957; *The World Was His Jury* 1957; *Queen of Outer Space* 1958; *Two Rode Together* 1961
Birch, Thora *The Purple People Eater* 1988; *All I Want for Christmas* 1991; *Paradise* 1991; *Patriot Games* 1992; *Hocus Pocus* 1993; *Monkey Trouble* 1994; *Now and Then* 1995; *Alaska* 1996; *Night Ride Home* 1999; *American Beauty* 1999
Bird, Billie *Somebody Loves Me* 1952; *Too Soon to Love* 1960
Bird, John *30 Is a Dangerous Age, Cynthia* 1967; *Take a Girl Like You* 1970; *Bejewelled* 1990
Bird, Norman *Man in the Moon* 1960; *The Secret Partner* 1961; *Victim* 1961; *Whistle down the Wind* 1961; *Bitter Harvest* 1963; *80,000 Suspects* 1963; *The Bargee* 1964; *The Beauty Jungle* 1964; *The Black Torment* 1964; *Sky West and Crooked* 1965; *Hands of the Ripper* 1971; *Ooh... You Are Awful* 1972; *The Lord of the Rings* 1978

Blanc, Mel *Neptune's Daughter* 1949; *The Man Called Flintstone* 1966; *The Phantom Tollbooth* 1970; *Scalawag* 1973; *Buck Rogers in the 25th Century* 1979; *The Bugs Bunny/Road Runner Movie* 1979; *Looney Looney Looney Bugs Bunny Movie* 1981; *Bugs Bunny 1001 Rabbit Tales* 1982; *Daffy Duck's Movie: Fantastic Island* 1983; *Daffy Duck's Quackbusters* 1988; *Jetsons: the Movie* 1990
Blanc, Michel *Tenue de Soirée* 1986; *Monsieur Hire* 1989; *Uranus* 1990; *The Favour, the Watch and the Very Big Fish* 1991; *Merci la Vie* 1991; *Prospero's Books* 1991
Blancard, Jarred *The Yearling* 1994; *The Boys Club* 1996
Blancard, René *A Cage of Nightingales* 1947; *Quai des Orfèvres* 1947
Blanchar, Dominique *Decision before Dawn* 1951; *L'Avventura* 1959
Blanchar, Pierre *The Chess Player* 1927; *Crime and Punishment* 1935; *Mademoiselle Docteur* 1936; *La Symphonie Pastorale* 1946
Blanchard, Mari *Abbott and Costello Go to Mars* 1953; *Destry* 1954; *Rails into Laramie* 1954; *Black Horse Canyon* 1954; *Son of Sinbad* 1955; *Twice Told Tales* 1963
Blanchard, Rachel *Young Ivanhoe* 1994; *Road Trip* 2000
Blanchard, Ron *Caddie* 1976; *Warming Up* 1983
Blanchard, Susan *Young Maverick* 1979; *Prince of Darkness* 1987
Blanche, Roland *Les Compères* 1983; *Trop Belle pour Toi* 1989
Blanchett, Cate *Oscar and Lucinda* 1997; *Paradise Road* 1997; *Thank God He Met Lizzie* 1997; *Elizabeth* 1998; *An Ideal Husband* 1999; *The Talented Mr Ripley* 1999; *Pushing Tin* 1999
Blancke, Sandrine *Toto Le Héros* 1991; *A Shadow of Doubt* 1992
Blandick, Clara *Romance* 1930; *Tom Sawyer* 1930; *Huckleberry Finn* 1931; *Rockabye* 1932; *The Bitter Tea of General Yen* 1933; *Turn Back the Clock* 1933; *Ever in My Heart* 1933; *The Girl from Missouri* 1934; *The Adventures of Huckleberry Finn* 1939; *The Wizard of Oz* 1939
Blane, Sally *Advice to the Lovelorn* 1933; *Crime on the Hill* 1933
Blankfield, Mark *Jekyll and Hyde... Together Again* 1982; *The Road Raiders* 1989; *Robin Hood: Men in Tights* 1993; *Dracula: Dead and Loving It* 1995
Blanks, Billy *Bloodfist* 1989; *Time Bomb* 1991; *Back in Action* 1993; *TC 2000* 1993; *Expect No Mercy* 1995
Blasco, Txema *Vacas* 1992; *Tierra* 1995
Blaser, Brandon *The Butter Cream Gang* 1991; *Secret of Treasure Mountain* 1993
Blatchford, Edward *Nowhere to Run* 1992; *All Tied Up* 1994
Blatchley, Joseph *L'Histoire d'Adèle H* 1975; *Merlin and the Sword* 1982
Blavette, Charles *Jofroi* 1933; *Toni* 1935; *Stormy Waters* 1941
Blech, Hans Christian *Decision before Dawn* 1951; *The Visit* 1964; *The Saboteur, Code Name Morituri* 1965; *Dirty Hands* 1976; *Knife in the Head* 1978; *Colonel Redl* 1984; *Please Let the Flowers Live* 1986
Blechman, Jonah *Empty Cradle* 1993; *This Boy's Life* 1993
Bleeth, Yasmine *Baywatch the Movie: Forbidden Paradise* 1995; *The Face* 1996; *Crowned and Dangerous* 1997; *BASEketball* 1998
Blendick, James *Shoot* 1976; *The Other Victim* 1981; *Utilities* 1981
Blessed, Brian *Till Death Us Do Part* 1968; *Country Dance* 1970; *The Trojan Women* 1971; *Henry VIII and His Six Wives* 1972; *Man of La Mancha* 1972; *High Road to China* 1983; *Asterix and the Big Fight* 1989; *Henry V* 1989; *Prisoner of Honor* 1991; *Robin Hood: Prince of Thieves* 1991; *Back in the USSR* 1992; *Freddie as FRO7* 1992; *Chasing the Deer* 1994; *The Bruce* 1996; *Hamlet* 1996; *Macbeth* 1997; *Star Wars Episode I: the Phantom Menace* 1999; *Tarzan* 1999
Blessing, Jack *Joshua's Heart* 1990; *Working Trash* 1990; *Face Value* 1991
Blethyn, Brenda *The Witches* 1989; *A River Runs through It* 1992; *Secrets & Lies* 1995; *Remember Me?* 1996; *Girls' Night* 1997; *Little Voice* 1998; *Night Train* 1998; *RKO 281* 1999; *Saving Grace* 2000
Blick, Newton *The Long Arm* 1956; *The Gypsy and the Gentleman* 1958; *Morgan – a Suitable Case for Treatment* 1966
Blicker, Jason *American Boyfriends* 1989; *Baby on Board* 1993; *Superstar* 1999
Blier, Bernard *Hôtel du Nord* 1938; *Le Jour se Lève* 1939; *La Nuit Fantastique* 1942; *Quai des Orfèvres* 1947; *Secrets d'Alcove* 1954; *Les Misérables* 1957; *The Great War* 1959; *The Organizer* 1963; *Male Hunt* 1964; *Uncle Benjamin* 1969; *Catch Me a Spy* 1971; *The Tall Blond Man with One Black Shoe* 1972; *Buffet Froid* 1979
Bliss, Caroline *The Living Daylights* 1987; *Licence to Kill* 1989
Block, Hunt *Sexpionage* 1985; *The Dirty Dozen: the Fatal Mission* 1988; *She Was Marked for Murder* 1988
Block, Larry *Shamus* 1973; *Big Night* 1996
Blocker, Dan *Come Blow Your Horn* 1963; *Lady in Cement* 1968; *The Cockeyed Cowboys of Calico County* 1970
Blocker, Dirk *My Father, My Son* 1988; *Bonanza – the Return* 1993
Blodgett, Michael *Beyond the Valley of the Dolls* 1970; *The Velvet Vampire* 1971
Blondell, Joan *Blonde Crazy* 1931; *Night Nurse* 1931; *The Public Enemy* 1931; *Illicit* 1931; *Other Men's Women* 1931; *The Crowd Roars* 1932; *Lawyer Man* 1932; *Three on a Match* 1932; *Union Depot* 1932; *Footlight Parade* 1933; *Gold Diggers of 1933* 1933; *Havana Widows* 1933; *Dames* 1934; *He Was Her Man* 1934; *Bullets or Ballots* 1936; *Colleen* 1936; *Gold Diggers of 1937* 1936; *Three Men on a Horse* 1936; *Stage Struck* 1936; *The King and the Chorus Girl* 1937; *The Perfect Specimen* 1937; *Stand-In* 1937; *There's Always a Woman* 1938; *The Amazing Mr Williams* 1939; *East Side of Heaven* 1939; *Topper Returns* 1941; *Lady for a Night* 1942; *Cry Havoc* 1943; *Adventure* 1945; *A Tree Grows in Brooklyn* 1945; *Nightmare Alley* 1947; *For Heaven's Sake* 1950; *The Blue Veil* 1951; *Desk Set* 1957; *Lizzie* 1957; *Will Success Spoil Rock Hunter?* 1957; *This Could Be the Night* 1957; *Angel Baby* 1961; *Advance to the Rear* 1964; *The Cincinnati Kid* 1965; *The Spy in the Green Hat* 1966; *Ride beyond Vengeance* 1966; *Waterhole #3* 1967; *Kona Coast* 1968; *Support Your Local Gunfighter* 1971; *The Dead Don't Die* 1975; *Death at Love House* 1976; *Won Ton Ton, the Dog Who Saved Hollywood* 1976; *Opening Night* 1977; *The Glove* 1978; *The Champ* 1979
Bloom, Brian *Walls of Glass* 1985; *Desperate for Love* 1989; *Brotherhood of the Gun* 1992; *The Keys* 1992; *The Sender* 1997
Bloom, Claire *The Blind Goddess* 1947; *Limelight* 1952; *Innocents in Paris* 1953; *The Man between* 1953; *Richard III* 1955; *Alexander the Great* 1956; *The Brothers Karamazov* 1958; *The Buccaneer* 1958; *Look Back in Anger* 1959; *The Chapman Report* 1962; *The Wonderful World of the Brothers Grimm* 1962; *80,000 Suspects* 1963; *The Haunting* 1963; *The Outrage* 1964; *The Spy Who Came in from the Cold* 1965; *Charly* 1968; *The Illustrated Man* 1969; *Three into Two Won't Go* 1969; *A Severed Head* 1970; *A Doll's House* 1973; *Islands in the Stream* 1977; *Clash of the Titans* 1981; *Separate Tables* 1983; *Déjà Vu* 1984; *Anastasia: the Mystery of Anna* 1986; *Sammy and Rosie Get Laid* 1987; *Crimes and Misdemeanors* 1989; *The Princess and the Goblin* 1992; *Mad Dogs and Englishmen* 1994; *Mighty Aphrodite* 1995; *Daylight* 1996; *What the Deaf Man Heard* 1997; *Wrestling with Alligators* 1998
Bloom, John *Dracula vs Frankenstein* 1970; *The Incredible Two-Headed Transplant* 1971
Bloom, Lindsay *Mickey Spillane's Mike Hammer: Murder Takes All* 1989; *Grizzly Adams: the Treasure of the Bear* 1995
Bloom, Verna *Medium Cool* 1969; *The Hired Hand* 1971; *High Plains Drifter* 1973; *Badge 373* 1973; *Sarah T: Portrait of a Teenage Alcoholic* 1975; *National Lampoon's Animal House* 1978; *Playing for Time* 1980; *Honkytonk Man* 1982; *After Hours* 1985; *The Journey of Natty Gann* 1985; *The Last Temptation of Christ* 1988
Blore, Eric *Tarnished Lady* 1931; *The Gay Divorcee* 1934; *Folies Bergère* 1935; *The Good Fairy* 1935; *I Dream Too Much* 1935; *I Live My Life* 1935; *Old Man Rhythm* 1935; *Seven Keys to Baldpate* 1935; *Top Hat* 1935; *The Ex-Mrs Bradford* 1936; *Piccadilly Jim* 1936; *Swing Time* 1936; *The Adventures of Michael Strogoff* 1937; *Breakfast for Two* 1937; *It's Love I'm After* 1937; *Quality Street* 1937; *Shall We Dance* 1937; *Joy of Living* 1938; *Swiss Miss* 1938; *The Boys from Syracuse* 1940; *The Lone Wolf Strikes* 1940; *The Man Who Wouldn't Talk* 1940; *'Til We Meet Again* 1940; *Music in My Heart* 1940; *Confirm or Deny* 1941; *The Lady Eve* 1941; *The Lone Wolf Keeps a Date* 1941; *Road to Zanzibar* 1941; *The Shanghai Gesture* 1941; *Sullivan's Travels* 1941; *The Moon and Sixpence* 1942; *One Dangerous Night* 1943; *Passport to Suez* 1943; *The Sky's the Limit* 1943; *Abie's Irish Rose* 1946; *The Lone Wolf in London* 1947; *It's Magic* 1948; *Romance on the High Seas* 1948; *The Adventures of Ichabod and Mr Toad* 1949
Blossom, Roberts *Slaughterhouse-Five* 1972; *Deranged* 1974; *Citizens Band* 1977; *Close Encounters of the Third Kind* 1977; *Escape from Alcatraz* 1979; *Resurrection* 1980; *Reuben, Reuben* 1983; *Candy Mountain* 1987; *The Last Temptation of Christ* 1988; *Always* 1989; *Home Alone* 1990; *Balloon Farm* 1999
Blount, Lisa *9/30/55* 1977; *An Officer and a Gentleman* 1982; *Secrets of the Phantom Caverns* 1984; *The Annihilator* 1986; *Radioactive Dreams* 1986; *Prince of Darkness* 1987; *Nightflyers* 1987; *Out Cold* 1989; *Blind Fury* 1990; *Femme Fatale* 1991; *After the Glory* 1992; *Hearts on Fire* 1992; *Murder between Friends* 1994; *Judicial Consent* 1995; *Box of Moon Light* 1996
Blue, Ben *Artists and Models* 1937; *College Swing* 1938; *Paris Honeymoon* 1939; *For Me and My Gal* 1942; *Broadway Rhythm* 1944; *Two Girls and a Sailor* 1944; *Two Sisters from Boston* 1946
Blue, Jean *The Overlanders* 1946; *Bitter Springs* 1950
Blue, Monte *Orphans of the Storm* 1921; *The Marriage Circle* 1924; *Kiss Me Again* 1925; *So This Is Paris* 1926; *White Shadows in the South Seas* 1928; *The Lives of a Bengal Lancer* 1935; *A Million to One* 1937; *Silver River* 1948; *Apache* 1954
Blum, Mark *Desperately Seeking Susan* 1985; *"Crocodile" Dundee* 1986; *Blind Date* 1987; *The Presidio* 1988; *Indictment: the McMartin Trial* 1995; *You Can Thank Me Later* 1998
Blumenfeld, Alan *Shakedown on the Sunset Strip* 1988; *Out Cold* 1989; *Blackbelt* 1992; *Dying to Love You* 1993; *Ed McBain's 87th Precinct* 1995
Blundell, Graeme *Alvin Purple* 1973; *Don's Party* 1976; *Weekend of Shadows* 1978; *The Odd Angry Shot* 1979; *The Year My Voice Broke* 1987; *Idiot Box* 1996
Bluteau, Lothaire *Jesus of Montreal* 1989; *Black Robe* 1991; *Mrs 'arris Goes to Paris* 1992; *Orlando* 1992; *The Silent Touch* 1992; *The Confessional* 1995; *I Shot Andy Warhol* 1995; *Other Voices, Other Rooms* 1995; *Bent* 1996
Bluthal, John *The Knack... and How to Get It* 1965; *Carry On Follow That Camel* 1967; *The Bliss of Mrs Blossom* 1968; *Digby, the Biggest Dog in the World* 1973; *Stan and George's New Life* 1990
Blyden, Larry *The Bachelor Party* 1957; *Kiss Them for Me* 1957; *On a Clear Day You Can See Forever* 1970
Blye, Maggie aka **Blye, Margaret** *Waterhole #3* 1967; *Diamonds for Breakfast* 1968; *The Italian Job* 1969; *Every Little Crook and Nanny* 1972; *The Streetfighter* 1975; *Final Chapter – Walking Tall* 1977; *The Entity* 1981; *Liar's Moon* 1982; *Mischief* 1985
Blyth, Ann *Mildred Pierce* 1945; *Swell Guy* 1946; *Brute Force* 1947; *Killer McCoy* 1947; *Another Part of the Forest* 1948; *Mr Peabody and the Mermaid* 1948; *Once More, My Darling* 1949; *Red Canyon* 1949; *Our Very Own* 1950; *The Great Caruso* 1951; *Thunder on the Hill* 1951; *One Minute to Zero* 1952; *The World in His Arms* 1952; *All the Brothers Were Valiant* 1953; *Rose Marie* 1954; *The Student Prince* 1954; *The King's Thief* 1955; *Kismet* 1955; *The Helen Morgan Story* 1957; *The Buster Keaton Story* 1957
Blythe, Benedick *The Little Riders* 1996; *The Hunchback* 1997
Blythe, Janus *The Hills Have Eyes* 1978; *The Hills Have Eyes Part II* 1985
Blythe, John *Bon Voyage* 1944; *The Frightened Man* 1952; *Gaolbreak* 1962
Blythe, Peter *Frankenstein Created Woman* 1966; *A Challenge for Robin Hood* 1967; *Carrington* 1995
Boa, Bruce *Stopover Forever* 1964; *Journey into Darkness: the Bruce Curtis Story* 1991
Boardman, Eleanor *The Crowd* 1928; *The Squaw Man* 1931
Boatman, Michael aka **Boatman, Michael Patrick** *Hamburger Hill* 1987; *Deadly Identity* 1991; *Street War* 1992; *House of Secrets* 1993; *The Glass Shield* 1995
Boatman, Ross *Hard Men* 1996; *Bring Me the Head of Mavis Davis* 1997
Bobby, Anne *Nightbreed* 1990; *Mother of the Bride* 1993; *Finding North* 1997
Boccardo, Delia *Inspector Clouseau* 1968; *Panhandle Calibre 38* 1972; *Snow Job* 1972; *Massacre in Rome* 1973; *Tentacles* 1977
Bochner, Hart *Breaking Away* 1979; *Terror Train* 1980; *Rich and Famous* 1981; *Apartment Zero* 1988; *Die Hard* 1988; *Fellow Traveller* 1989; *Mr Destiny* 1990; *Mad at the Moon* 1992; *Batman: Mask of the Phantasm* 1993; *Complex of Fear* 1993; *The Innocent* 1993
Bochner, Lloyd *The Night Walker* 1964; *Harlow* 1965; *Point Blank* 1967; *Tony Rome* 1967; *Stranger on the Run* 1967; *The Detective* 1968; *The Horse in the Gray Flannel Suit* 1968; *Tiger by the Tail* 1970; *Ulzana's Raid* 1972; *A Fire in the Sky* 1978; *The Hot Touch* 1982; *The Lonely Lady* 1983; *Crystal Heart* 1987; *Millennium* 1989; *The Naked Gun 2½: the Smell of Fear* 1991; *Morning Glory* 1993; *Bram Stoker's Legend of the Mummy* 1998
Bodison, Wolfgang *Angel of Desire* 1993; *The Expert* 1994; *Rise and Walk: the Dennis Byrd Story* 1994; *Freeway* 1996
Bodnia, Kim *Nightwatch* 1994; *Pusher* 1996; *Bleeder* 1999
Bodrov Jr, Sergei *Prisoner of the Mountains* 1996; *Brother* 1997; *Est-Ouest* 1999
Boen, Earl *The Terminator* 1984; *The Annihilator* 1986; *Terminator 2: Judgment Day* 1991; *The Dentist* 1996
Boes, Richard *Permanent Vacation* 1982; *Johnny Suede* 1991; *Dead Man* 1995
Bogarde, Dirk *Dancing with Crime* 1946; *Esther Waters* 1948; *Once a Jolly Swagman* 1948; *Quartet* 1948; *The Blue Lamp* 1949; *Boys in Brown* 1949; *So Long at the Fair* 1950; *The Woman in Question* 1950; *Appointment in London* 1952; *The Gentle Gunman* 1952; *Hunted* 1952; *Penny Princess* 1952; *Desperate Moment* 1953; *They Who Dare* 1953; *Doctor in the House* 1954; *For Better, for Worse* 1954; *The*

Mutiny on the Bounty 1962; *The Ugly American* 1963; *Bedtime Story* 1964; *The Saboteur, Code Name Morituri* 1965; *The Chase* 1966; *The Appaloosa* 1966; *A Countess from Hong Kong* 1967; *Reflections in a Golden Eye* 1967; *Candy* 1968; *The Night of the Following Day* 1968; *Burn!* 1969; *The Godfather* 1972; *Last Tango in Paris* 1972; *The Nightcomers* 1972; *The Missouri Breaks* 1976; *Superman* 1978; *Apocalypse Now* 1979; *The Formula* 1980; *A Dry White Season* 1989; *The Freshman* 1990; *Christopher Columbus: the Discovery* 1992; *Don Juan DeMarco* 1995; *The Island of Dr Moreau* 1996; *The Brave* 1997; *Free Money* 1998

Brandon, David *All Hands on Deck* 1961; *State Fair* 1962; *Stage Fright – Aquarius* 1987

Brandon, Henry *aka* **Kleinbach, Henry** *Babes in Toyland* 1934; *Westbound Limited* 1937; *Cattle Drive* 1951; *Tarzan and the She-Devil* 1953; *War Arrow* 1953; *Vera Cruz* 1954; *Bandido* 1956; *Comanche* 1956; *The Searchers* 1956; *The Land Unknown* 1957

Brandon, Michael *Lovers and Other Strangers* 1970; *Jennifer on My Mind* 1971; *FM* 1977; *Promises in the Dark* 1979; *A Change of Seasons* 1980; *Deadly Messages* 1985; *Rock 'n' Roll Mom* 1988; *Shattering the Silence* 1992; *Murder or Memory?* 1994; *Déjà Vu* 1997

Brandt, Janet *A Cold Wind in August* 1961; *Hit!* 1973; *Sheila Levine Is Dead and Living in New York* 1975

Brandy *aka* **Norwood, Brandy** *Rodgers & Hammerstein's Cinderella* 1997; *I Still Know What You Did Last Summer* 1998; *Double Platinum* 1999

Bransfield, Marjorie *Easy Wheels* 1989; *Abraxas* 1991

Brantford, Mickey *The Phantom Light* 1934; *The Last Journey* 1936

Brantley, Betsy *Five Days One Summer* 1982; *Another Country* 1984; *Dark Angel* 1989; *Havana* 1990; *Schizopolis* 1996; *Washington Square* 1997; *Rogue Trader* 1998

Braschi, Nicoletta *Down by Law* 1986; *Mystery Train* 1989; *Johnny Stecchino* 1991; *Life Is Beautiful* 1997

Brascia, John *White Christmas* 1954; *Walking Tall* 1973

Brassard, Marie *Le Polygraphe* 1996; *Nô* 1998

Brasselle, Keefe *A Place in the Sun* 1951; *It's a Big Country* 1951; *Skirts Ahoy!* 1952; *The Eddie Cantor Story* 1953; *Bring Your Smile Along* 1955

Brasseur, Claude *The Vanishing Corporal* 1962; *Bande à Part* 1964; *The Loser* 1971; *The Heroes* 1972; *Une Belle Fille Comme Moi* 1973; *Someone Is Bleeding* 1974; *You've Got to Live Dangerously* 1975; *Pardon Mon Affaire* 1976; *Une Histoire Simple* 1978; *The Police War* 1979; *Detective* 1985; *Descent into Hell* 1986; *Dandin* 1988; *The Edge of the Horizon* 1993

Brasseur, Pierre *Le Quai des Brumes* 1938; *Les Enfants du Paradis* 1945; *Les Portes de la Nuit* 1946; *Napoléon* 1955; *Gates of Paris* 1957; *Eyes without a Face* 1959; *Where the Hot Wind Blows!* 1959; *Carthage in Flames* 1960; *La Vie de Château* 1965; *King of Hearts* 1966; *Goto, l'Ile d'Amour* 1968; *Sink or Swim* 1971

Bratt, Benjamin *Bright Angel* 1990; *One Good Cop* 1991; *Blood In Blood Out* 1992; *Demolition Man* 1993; *The River Wild* 1994; *The Next Best Thing* 2000

Braugher, André *Glory* 1989; *The Court-Martial of Jackie Robinson* 1990; *Somebody Has to Shoot the Picture* 1990; *The Tuskegee Airmen* 1995; *Get on the Bus* 1996; *Primal Fear* 1996; *City of Angels* 1998; *Frequency* 2000

Braun, Judith *Horizons West* 1952; *Red Ball Express* 1952

Braun, Pinkas *City of Fear* 1965; *The Last Escape* 1970

Brauss, Arthur *The Goalkeeper's Fear of the Penalty Kick* 1971; *The Heist* 1971; *Montana Trap* 1976; *Knight Moves* 1992

Bray, Robert *Return of the Bad Men* 1948; *Stagecoach Kid* 1949; *Bus Stop* 1956; *The Traitor* 1957; *Never Love a Stranger* 1958

Bray, Thom *House III: The Horror Show* 1989; *Child in the Night* 1990

Brazeau, Jay *We're No Angels* 1989; *Slam Dunk Ernest* 1995; *Kissed* 1996; *Air Bud* 1997

Brazzi, Rossano *We the Living* 1942; *Little Women* 1949; *Volcano* 1950; *The Barefoot Contessa* 1954; *Three Coins in the Fountain* 1954; *Angela* 1955; *Summertime* 1955; *Interlude* 1957; *Legend of the Lost* 1957; *The Story of Esther Costello* 1957; *A Certain Smile* 1958; *South Pacific* 1958; *Count Your Blessings* 1959; *The Siege of Syracuse* 1959; *Light in the Piazza* 1962; *Lovers Must Learn* 1962; *The Battle of the Villa Fiorita* 1964; *The Bobo* 1967; *Woman Times Seven* 1967; *The Italian Job* 1969; *Krakatoa, East of Java* 1969; *The Adventurers* 1970; *Mr Kingstreet's War* 1970; *The Great Waltz* 1972; *The Final Conflict* 1980; *Fear City* 1984

Breakston, George *No Greater Glory* 1934; *The Return of Peter Grimm* 1935

Brecher, Egon *The Black Cat* 1934; *So Dark the Night* 1946

Breck, Peter *Shock Corridor* 1963; *The Glory Guys* 1965; *Benji* 1974; *Highway 61* 1992; *Decoy* 1995

Bredin, Patricia *Left, Right and Centre* 1959; *The Treasure of Monte Cristo* 1960

Breen, Patrick *The Concierge* 1993; *Sweet Nothing* 1995; *One True Thing* 1998; *Galaxy Quest* 1999

Breese, Edmund *The Hatchet Man* 1932; *Madame Butterfly* 1932

Brel, Jacques *Uncle Benjamin* 1969; *A Pain in the A...!* 1973

Bremer, Lucille *Meet Me in St Louis* 1944; *Yolande and the Thief* 1945; *Till the Clouds Roll By* 1946; *Ruthless* 1948

Bremner, Ewen *Heavenly Pursuits* 1986; *Conquest of the South Pole* 1989; *As You Like It* 1992; *Naked* 1993; *Trainspotting* 1995; *The Life of Stuff* 1997; *Mojo* 1998; *The Acid House* 1998; *julien donkey-boy* 1999

Brendel, El *Wings* 1927; *Sunny Side Up* 1929; *The Big Trail* 1930; *The Beautiful Blonde from Bashful Bend* 1949

Brennan, Brid *Anne Devlin* 1984; *Trojan Eddie* 1996; *Dancing at Lughnasa* 1998; *Felicia's Journey* 1999

Brennan, Eileen *The Last Picture Show* 1971; *The Blue Knight* 1973; *The Sting* 1973; *Scarecrow* 1973; *Daisy Miller* 1974; *At Long Last Love* 1975; *Hustle* 1975; *The Night that Panicked America* 1975; *Murder by Death* 1976; *The Great Smokey Roadblock* 1977; *FM* 1977; *The Cheap Detective* 1978; *Private Benjamin* 1980; *Clue* 1985; *Babes in Toyland* 1986; *The New Adventures of Pippi Longstocking* 1988; *Sticky Fingers* 1988; *Stella* 1990; *Texasville* 1990; *White Palace* 1990; *Deadly Intentions... Again?* 1991; *I Don't Buy Kisses Anymore* 1992; *Taking Back My Life* 1992; *Take Me Home Again* 1994; *My Name Is Kate* 1994; *Freaky Friday* 1995; *Reckless* 1995; *If These Walls Could Talk* 1996; *Changing Habits* 1997; *Toothless* 1997

Brennan, Michael *Blackout* 1950; *Morning Departure* 1950; *They Were Not Divided* 1950; *13 East Street* 1952; *It's a Grand Life* 1953; *Not Wanted on Voyage* 1957

Brennan, Walter *The King of Jazz* 1930; *Law and Order* 1932; *Barbary Coast* 1935; *The Man on the Flying Trapeze* 1935; *Seven Keys to Baldpate* 1935; *Public Hero No 1* 1935; *Banjo on My Knee* 1936; *Come and Get It* 1936; *Fury* 1936; *The Adventures of Tom Sawyer* 1938; *The Buccaneer* 1938; *The Cowboy and the Lady* 1938; *Kentucky* 1938; *The Texans* 1938; *Stanley and Livingstone* 1939; *The Story of Vernon and Irene Castle* 1939; *They Shall Have Music* 1939; *Maryland* 1940; *Northwest Passage* 1940; *The Westerner* 1940; *Meet John Doe* 1941; *Nice Girl?* 1941; *Sergeant York* 1941; *Swamp Water* 1941; *The Pride of the Yankees* 1942; *Stand by for Action* 1942; *Hangmen Also Die* 1943; *The North Star* 1943; *Slightly Dangerous* 1943; *Home in Indiana* 1944; *The Princess and the Pirate* 1944; *To Have and Have Not* 1944; *Dakota* 1945; *Centennial Summer* 1946; *Driftwood* 1946; *My Darling Clementine* 1946; *Nobody Lives Forever* 1946; *A Stolen Life* 1946; *Blood on the Moon* 1948; *Red River* 1948; *Task Force* 1949; *A Ticket to Tomahawk* 1950; *Along the Great Divide* 1951; *Best of the Badmen* 1951; *Drums across the River* 1954; *Four Guns to the Border* 1954; *At Gunpoint* 1955; *Bad Day at Black Rock* 1955; *The Far Country* 1955; *Come Next Spring* 1956; *Good-bye, My Lady* 1956; *The Proud Ones* 1956; *Tammy and the Bachelor* 1957; *The Way to the Gold* 1957; *Rio Bravo* 1959; *How the West Was Won* 1962; *Those Calloways* 1964; *The Oscar* 1966; *The Gnome-Mobile* 1967; *Who's Minding the Mint?* 1967; *The One and Only, Genuine, Original Family Band* 1968; *Support Your Local Sheriff!* 1969

Brenneman, Amy *Bye Bye Love* 1995; *Heat* 1995; *Daylight* 1996; *Fear* 1996; *Your Friends & Neighbours* 1998

Brenner, Dori *Summer Wishes, Winter Dreams* 1973; *Next Stop, Greenwich Village* 1976; *Altered States* 1980; *Opposites Attract* 1990; *Infinity* 1996

Brent, Eve *Tarzan's Fight for Life* 1958; *Tarzan and the Trappers* 1958

Brent, Evelyn *Underworld* 1927; *The Dragnet* 1928; *The Last Command* 1928; *Beau Sabreur* 1928; *Broadway* 1929; *High Pressure* 1932; *The Law West of Tombstone* 1938; *The Seventh Victim* 1943

Brent, George *The Rich Are Always with Us* 1932; *The Purchase Price* 1932; *Baby Face* 1933; *42nd Street* 1933; *Female* 1933; *Stamboul Quest* 1934; *The Painted Veil* 1934; *Front Page Woman* 1935; *In Person* 1935; *Special Agent* 1935; *God's Country and the Woman* 1937; *Gold Is Where You Find It* 1938; *Jezebel* 1938; *Dark Victory* 1939; *The Old Maid* 1939; *The Rains Came* 1939; *The Fighting 69th* 1940; *'Til We Meet Again* 1940; *The Great Lie* 1941; *International Lady* 1941; *The Gay Sisters* 1942; *In This Our Life* 1942; *Twin Beds* 1942; *You Can't Escape Forever* 1942; *Experiment Perilous* 1944; *The Affairs of Susan* 1945; *Tomorrow Is Forever* 1945; *My Reputation* 1946; *The Spiral Staircase* 1946; *Temptation* 1946; *Out of the Blue* 1947; *Bride for Sale* 1949; *Red Canyon* 1949; *The Last Page* 1952; *Born Again* 1978

Brent, Romney *Dinner at the Ritz* 1937; *Head over Heels in Love* 1937; *Under the Red Robe* 1937; *Let George Do It* 1940; *Adventures of Don Juan* 1948; *Screaming Mimi* 1958

Breon, Edmund *aka* **Breon, Edmond** *Keep Fit* 1937; *Crackerjack* 1938; *Casanova Brown* 1944; *The Woman in the Window* 1945; *Dressed to Kill* 1946

Breslin, Patricia *aka* **Breslin, Pat** *Go, Man, Go!* 1953; *Andy Hardy Comes Home* 1958; *Homicidal* 1961; *I Saw What You Did* 1965

Bressart, Felix *Ninotchka* 1939; *Swanee River* 1939; *Bitter Sweet* 1940; *Comrade X* 1940; *Edison, the Man* 1940; *Escape* 1940; *The Shop around the Corner* 1940; *Third Finger, Left Hand* 1940; *Blossoms in the Dust* 1941; *Crossroads* 1942; *To Be or Not to Be* 1942; *Greenwich Village* 1944; *Blonde Fever* 1944; *Without Love* 1945; *I've Always Loved You* 1946

Bresslaw, Bernard *Blood of the Vampire* 1958; *Too Many Crooks* 1958; *It's All Happening* 1963; *Carry On Cowboy* 1965; *Morgan – a Suitable Case for Treatment* 1966; *Carry On Follow That Camel* 1967; *Carry On Doctor* 1968; *Carry On Up the Khyber* 1968; *Carry On Camping* 1969; *Moon Zero Two* 1969; *Carry On Loving* 1970; *Carry On Up the Jungle* 1970; *Carry On at Your Convenience* 1971; *Up Pompeii* 1971; *Carry On Abroad* 1972; *Carry On Matron* 1972; *Carry On Girls* 1973; *Carry On Dick* 1974; *Carry On Behind* 1975; *One of Our Dinosaurs Is Missing* 1975; *Jabberwocky* 1977; *Hawk the Slayer* 1980; *Krull* 1983; *Asterix and the Big Fight* 1989

Brestoff, Richard *Car Wash* 1976; *The Entity* 1981; *The Man with Two Brains* 1983

Brett, Jeremy *The Very Edge* 1962; *The Wild and the Willing* 1962; *Girl in the Headlines* 1963; *Mad Dogs and Englishmen* 1994

Brewster, Diane *Courage of Black Beauty* 1957; *Quantrill's Raiders* 1958; *Torpedo Run* 1958; *The Man in the Net* 1959; *The Young Philadelphians* 1959

Breznahan, Tom *Twice Dead* 1988; *Diplomatic Immunity* 1991; *Ski School* 1991

Brialy, Jean-Claude *Le Beau Serge* 1958; *Les Cousins* 1959; *Paris Nous Appartient* 1960; *Cleo from 5 to 7* 1961; *Une Femme Est une Femme* 1961; *La Ronde* 1964; *Male Hunt* 1964; *King of Hearts* 1966; *The Bride Wore Black* 1967; *The Oldest Profession* 1967; *Claire's Knee* 1970; *The Phantom of Liberty* 1974; *Robert et Robert* 1978; *Edith and Marcel* 1983; *La Nuit de Varennes* 1983; *An Impudent Girl* 1985; *Inspecteur Lavardin* 1986; *Le Cop II* 1989; *Une Femme Française* 1994; *Portraits Chinois* 1996

Brian, David *Beyond the Forest* 1949; *Flamingo Road* 1949; *Intruder in the Dust* 1949; *The Damned Don't Cry* 1950; *The Great Jewel Robber* 1950; *Fort Worth* 1951; *Million Dollar Mermaid* 1952; *Springfield Rifle* 1952; *This Woman Is Dangerous* 1952; *Ambush at Tomahawk Gap* 1953; *Dawn at Socorro* 1954; *The High and the Mighty* 1954; *Timberjack* 1955; *The First Travelling Saleslady* 1956; *Pocketful of Miracles* 1961; *The Rare Breed* 1966; *Castle of Evil* 1966; *The Manhunter* 1968; *The Girl Who Knew Too Much* 1969

Brian, Mary *Beau Geste* 1926; *Running Wild* 1927; *The Virginian* 1929; *The Marriage Playground* 1929; *The Royal Family of Broadway* 1930; *The Front Page* 1931; *Gun Smoke* 1931; *Hard to Handle* 1933; *Charlie Chan in Paris* 1935; *The Man on the Flying Trapeze* 1935; *Spendthrift* 1936; *Amazing Adventure* 1936

Briant, Shane *Captain Kronos: Vampire Hunter* 1972; *Frankenstein and the Monster from Hell* 1973; *Lady Chatterley's Lover* 1981; *Agatha Christie's Murder Is Easy* 1982; *Constance* 1984; *Shaker Run* 1985; *Cassandra* 1987; *Grievous Bodily Harm* 1987; *Mission Top Secret* 1990; *Till There Was You* 1990; *Tunnel Vision* 1994

Brice, Fanny *Everybody Sing* 1938; *Ziegfeld Follies* 1944

Brice, Pierre *The Cossacks* 1959; *The Bacchantes* 1960

Brice, Ron *Fresh* 1994; *The Keeper* 1995; *Ripe* 1996

Bridges, Beau *The Red Pony* 1949; *The Explosive Generation* 1961; *Village of the Giants* 1965; *The Incident* 1967; *For Love of Ivy* 1968; *Gaily, Gaily* 1969; *Adam's Woman* 1970; *The Landlord* 1970; *The Christian Licorice Store* 1971; *Child's Play* 1972; *Hammersmith Is Out* 1972; *Your Three Minutes Are Up* 1973; *Lovin' Molly* 1974; *The Other Side of the Mountain* 1975; *One Summer Love* 1975; *Swashbuckler* 1976; *Two-Minute Warning* 1976; *Greased Lightning* 1977; *The Four Feathers* 1978; *Shimmering Light* 1978; *The Fifth Musketeer* 1979; *Norma Rae* 1979; *The Runner Stumbles* 1979; *Silver Dream Racer* 1980; *Honky Tonk Freeway* 1981; *Night Crossing* 1981; *Love Child* 1982; *Witness for the Prosecution* 1982; *Heart like a Wheel* 1983; *The Hotel New Hampshire* 1984; *The Red-Light Sting* 1984; *A Fighting Choice* 1986; *Outrage!* 1986; *The Thanksgiving Promise* 1986; *The Killing Time* 1987; *The Wild Pair* 1987; *Seven Hours to Judgment* 1988; *The Iron Triangle* 1988; *Everybody's Baby: the Rescue of Jessica McClure* 1989; *The Fabulous Baker Boys* 1989; *Daddy's Dyin'... Who's Got the Will?* 1990; *Women and Men: Stories of Seduction* 1990; *Married to It* 1991; *Wildflower*

1991; Without Warning: the James Brady Story 1991; Elvis and the Colonel: the Untold Story 1993; The Positively True Adventures of the Alleged Texas Cheerleader-Murdering Mom 1993; Sidekicks 1993; Secret Sins of the Father 1994; Kissinger and Nixon 1995; Losing Chase 1996; A Stranger to Love 1996; Hidden in America 1996; Victim of the Haunt 1996; Rocketman 1997; The Second Civil War 1997; Inherit the Wind 1999

Bridges, Dorothy Dean The Thanksgiving Promise 1986; Secret Sins of the Father 1994

Bridges, Jeff Silent Night, Lonely Night 1969; Halls of Anger 1970; The Last Picture Show 1971; Bad Company 1972; Fat City 1972; The Iceman Cometh 1973; The Last American Hero 1973; The Lolly-Madonna War 1973; Thunderbolt and Lightfoot 1974; Hearts of the West 1975; Rancho Deluxe 1975; King Kong 1976; Stay Hungry 1976; Somebody Killed Her Husband 1978; The American Success Company 1979; Winter Kills 1979; Heaven's Gate 1980; The Last Unicorn 1980; Cutter's Way 1981; Kiss Me Goodbye 1982; Tron 1982; Against All Odds 1984; Starman 1984; Jagged Edge 1985; 8 Million Ways to Die 1986; The Morning After 1986; Nadine 1987; Tucker: the Man and His Dream 1988; Cold Feet 1989; The Fabulous Baker Boys 1989; See You in the Morning 1989; Texasville 1990; The Fisher King 1991; American Heart 1992; Fearless 1993; The Vanishing 1993; Blown Away 1994; Wild Bill 1995; The Mirror Has Two Faces 1996; White Squall 1996; Hidden in America 1996; The Big Lebowski 1997; Arlington Road 1998; The Muse 1999; Simpatico 1999

Bridges, Jordan The Thanksgiving Promise 1986; Secret Sins of the Father 1994

Bridges, Lloyd The Heat's On 1943; Passport to Suez 1943; Sahara 1943; The Master Race 1944; Abilene Town 1945; A Walk in the Sun 1945; Miss Susie Slagle's 1945; Ramrod 1947; Calamity Jane and Sam Bass 1949; Home of the Brave 1949; Red Canyon 1949; Colt .45 1950; The White Tower 1950; The Sound of Fury 1950; High Noon 1952; Plymouth Adventure 1952; Last of the Comanches 1952; The Limping Man 1953; The Kid from Left Field 1953; Pride of the Blue Grass 1954; Apache Woman 1955; Wichita 1955; The Rainmaker 1956; Around the World under the Sea 1966; Attack on the Iron Coast 1968; Daring Game 1968; The Happy Ending 1969; Silent Night, Lonely Night 1969; Death Race 1973; Running Wild 1973; Shimmering Light 1978; Bear Island 1979; Disaster on the Coastliner 1979; The Fifth Musketeer 1979; Airplane! 1980; Airplane II: the Sequel 1982; The Thanksgiving Promise 1986; Weekend Warriors 1986; The Wild Pair 1987; She Was Marked for Murder 1988; Winter People 1988; Tucker: the Man and His Dream 1988; Cousins 1989; Joe versus the Volcano 1990; The Queen of Mean 1990; Hot Shots! 1991; Honey I Blew Up the Kid 1992; Devlin 1992; Hot Shots! Part Deux 1993; Blown Away 1994; The Other Woman 1994; Secret Sins of the Father 1994; Jane Austen's Mafia 1998

Bridges, Todd High School USA 1983; Twice Dead 1988; Homeboyz 1992

Briers, Richard Bottoms Up 1959; The Girl on the Boat 1962; The Bargee 1964; Fathom 1967; Rentadick 1972; Watership Down 1978; A Chorus of Disapproval 1988; Henry V 1989; Much Ado about Nothing 1993; Mary Shelley's Frankenstein 1994; In the Bleak Midwinter 1995; Hamlet 1996; Love's Labour's Lost 1999

Brieux, Bernard Hit List 1984; Petit Con 1984

Briggs, Johnny Light Up the Sky 1960; The Wind of Change 1961; The Last Escape 1970

Briggs, Matt Advice to the Lovelorn 1933; The Dancing Masters 1943; The Meanest Man in the World 1943; The Ox-Bow Incident 1943

Bright, Richard Lions Love 1969; The Panic in Needle Park 1971; The Getaway 1972; Marathon Man 1976; On the Yard 1978; Two of a Kind 1983; The Ambulance 1990; Sweet Nothing 1995

Brightwell, Paul The Innocent Sleep 1995; Sliding Doors 1997

Brill, Patti Girl Rush 1944; Music in Manhattan 1944

Brill, Steven sex, lies, and videotape 1989; Dead Silence 1991

Brimble, Nick Frankenstein Unbound 1990; Robin Hood: Prince of Thieves 1991; Loch Ness 1994; Gone Fishin' 1997

Brimley, Wilford The China Syndrome 1979; The Electric Horseman 1979; Death Valley 1982; Tender Mercies 1982; The Thing 1982; Tough Enough 1982; High Road to China 1983; 10 to Midnight 1983; Country 1984; Harry and Son 1984; The Hotel New Hampshire 1984; The Natural 1984; The Stone Boy 1984; Cocoon 1985; Remo – Unarmed and Dangerous 1985; Act of Vengeance 1986; Thompson's Last Run 1986; End of the Line 1987; Cocoon: the Return 1988; Gore Vidal's Billy the Kid 1989; Eternity 1990; Blood River 1991; The Firm 1993; Hard Target 1993; Last of the Dogmen 1995; Op Center 1995; The Good Old Boys 1995; My Fellow Americans 1996

Brin, Michelle Secret Games 1992; Sins of the Night 1993

Brine, Adrian The Girl with Red Hair 1981; Vincent and Theo 1990; Between the Devil and the Deep Blue Sea 1995

Brinegar, Paul Cattle Empire 1958; How to Make a Monster 1958

Brinkley, John The Mobster 1958; A Bucket of Blood 1959

Brinkley, Ritch Cabin Boy 1994; Breakdown 1997

Brisbane, Syd Bad Boy Bubby 1993; Dead Letter Office 1998

Brisbane, William There Goes the Groom 1937; Maid's Night Out 1938

Brisbin, David Dead End Kids 1986; Kiss Daddy Good Night 1987

Briscoe, Brent Another Day in Paradise 1998; A Simple Plan 1998

Brissac, Virginia Dark Victory 1939; About Mrs Leslie 1954

Brisson, Carl The Ring 1927; The Manxman 1929; Murder at the Vanities 1934; All the King's Horses 1935

Britt, May The Hunters 1958; The Young Lions 1958; The Blue Angel 1959; Murder, Inc 1960

Brittany, Morgan The Prodigal 1983; Body Armor 1996

Britton, Barbara Young and Willing 1942; So Proudly We Hail 1943; Till We Meet Again 1944; Captain Kidd 1945; The Great John L 1945; The Virginian 1946; I Shot Jesse James 1949; Champagne for Caesar 1950; Bwana Devil 1952; Ride the Man Down 1952; The Spoilers 1955; Ain't Misbehavin' 1955

Britton, Connie The Brothers McMullen 1995; Escape Clause 1996; No Looking Back 1998

Britton, Pamela aka **Britton, Pam** Anchors Aweigh 1945; DOA 1949; Watch the Birdie 1950

Britton, Tony The Birthday Present 1957; Behind the Mask 1958; Operation Amsterdam 1958; The Rough and the Smooth 1959; Suspect 1960; The Break 1962; Dr Syn, Alias the Scarecrow 1963; There's a Girl in My Soup 1970; Sunday, Bloody Sunday 1971; The Day of the Jackal 1973; Night Watch 1973; The People That Time Forgot 1977; Agatha 1978

Broadbent, Jim Brazil 1985; Running Out of Luck 1985; The Good Father 1986; Vroom 1988; Life Is Sweet 1990; Enchanted April 1991; The Crying Game 1992; Widows' Peak 1993; Wide Eyed and Legless 1993; Bullets over Broadway 1994; Princess Caraboo 1994; Richard III 1995; Rough Magic 1995; The Secret Agent 1996; Smilla's Feeling for Snow 1996; The Borrowers 1997; The Avengers 1998; Little Voice 1998; Topsy-Turvy 1999

Broadhurst, Kent Stars and Bars 1988; In the Line of Duty: Ambush in Waco 1993

Brochet, Anne Masques 1987; Cyrano de Bergerac 1990; Tous les Matins du Monde 1992; Driftwood 1996

Brock, Phil POW the Escape 1986; The Allnighter 1987; Date with an Angel 1987

Brock, Stanley Tin Men 1987; UHF 1989

Brocksmith, Roy Killer Fish 1978; Tales of Ordinary Madness 1981; Total Recall 1990; Nickel & Dime 1991; Kull the Conqueror 1997

Brockwell, Gladys Oliver Twist 1922; Long Pants 1927; Lights of New York 1928

Broderick, Beth Are You Lonesome Tonight 1992; Hard Evidence 1994; Maternal Instincts 1996; A Champion's Fight 1998

Broderick, Helen Top Hat 1935; The Bride Walks Out 1936; Murder on a Bridle Path 1936; Swing Time 1936; Radio City Revels 1938; The Rage of Paris 1938; Naughty but Nice 1939; No, No, Nanette 1940; Nice Girl? 1941; Because of Him 1946

Broderick, James Girl of the Night 1960; Alice's Restaurant 1969; The Todd Killings 1971; The Taking of Pelham One Two Three 1974; Dog Day Afternoon 1975; The Shadow Box 1980

Broderick, Matthew Max Dugan Returns 1983; WarGames 1983; Ladyhawke 1985; 1918 1985; Ferris Bueller's Day Off 1986; Project X 1987; Biloxi Blues 1988; Torch Song Trilogy 1988; Family Business 1989; Glory 1989; The Freshman 1990; Out on a Limb 1992; A Life in the Theater 1993; The Night We Never Met 1993; The Lion King 1994; Mrs Parker and the Vicious Circle 1994; The Road to Wellville 1994; Arabian Knight 1995; The Cable Guy 1996; Infinity 1996; Addicted to Love 1997; Godzilla 1997; Election 1999; Inspector Gadget 1999

Broderick, Shirley Andre 1994; Beauty 1998

Brodie, Kevin The Night of the Grizzly 1966; The Giant Spider Invasion 1975

Brodie, Steve A Walk in the Sun 1945; Badman's Territory 1946; Criminal Court 1946; The Falcon's Adventure 1946; Build My Gallows High 1947; Desperate 1947; Trail Street 1947; Crossfire 1947; The Arizona Ranger 1948; Guns of Hate 1948; Return of the Bad Men 1948; Station West 1948; The Big Wheel 1949; Home of the Brave 1949; The Admiral Was a Lady 1950; Armored Car Robbery 1950; Winchester '73 1950; M 1951; The Sword of Monte Cristo 1951; The Steel Helmet 1951; The Beast from 20,000 Fathoms 1953; Donovan's Brain 1953; Gun Duel in Durango 1957; Sierra Baron 1958; A Girl Named Tamiko 1962; Of Love and Desire 1963; The Giant Spider Invasion 1975; Delta Pi 1985; The Wizard of Speed and Time 1988

Brodsky, Vlastimil All My Good Countrymen 1968; Capricious Summer 1968

Brody, Adrien The Boy Who Cried Bitch 1991; Bullet 1995; Six Ways to Sunday 1997; Summer of Sam 1999; Oxygen 1999

Brolin, James Von Ryan's Express 1965; Skyjacked 1972; Trapped 1973; Westworld 1973; Gable and Lombard 1976; The Car 1977; Capricorn One 1978; The Amityville Horror 1979; Night of the Juggler 1980; High Risk 1981; Hotel 1983; Beverly Hills Connection 1985; Bad Jim 1989; Back Stab 1990; Ted & Venus 1991; Gas, Food, Lodging 1992; Twin Sisters 1992; Paper Hearts 1993; City Boy 1994; The Expert 1994; Indecent Behavior 2 1994; Terminal Virus 1995; Relative Fear 1995; Hijacked: Flight 285 1996; To Face Her Past 1996; Blood Money 1996

Brolin, Josh The Goonies 1985; Thrashin' 1986; Roadflower 1994; Bed of Roses 1995; Flirting with Disaster 1996; Gang in Blue 1996; Mimic 1997; Nightwatch 1997; Best Laid Plans 1999; The Mod Squad 1999

Bromberg, J Edward Stowaway 1936; Under Two Flags 1936; Charlie Chan on Broadway 1937; Fair Warning 1937; Seventh Heaven 1937; Mr Moto Takes a Chance 1938; Suez 1938; Hollywood Cavalcade 1939; Wife, Husband and Friend 1939; The Mark of Zorro 1940; The Return of Frank James 1940; Strange Cargo 1940; Life Begins at 8.30 1942; Son of Dracula 1943; Lady of Burlesque 1943; Cloak and Dagger 1946; I Shot Jesse James 1949; Guilty Bystander 1950

Bromfield, John Rope of Sand 1949; Easy to Love 1953; Revenge of the Creature 1955

Bron, Eleanor Help! 1965; Alfie 1966; Bedazzled 1967; Two for the Road 1967; Women in Love 1969; A Touch of Love 1969; The National Health 1973; Pleasure at Her Majesty's 1976; The Hound of the Baskervilles 1983; Turtle Diary 1985; The Attic: the Hiding of Anne Frank 1988; Deadly Advice 1993; Black Beauty 1994; A Little Princess 1995; The House of Mirth 2000

Bronson, Betty Ben-Hur: a Tale of Christ 1925; The Singing Fool 1928; The Naked Kiss 1964

Bronson, Charles aka **Buchinski, Charles,** aka **Buchinsky, Charles** The Mob 1951; The People against O'Hara 1951; My Six Convicts 1952; Pat and Mike 1952; Red Skies of Montana 1952; House of Wax 1953; Miss Sadie Thompson 1953; Apache 1954; Drum Beat 1954; Riding Shotgun 1954; Vera Cruz 1954; Tennessee Champ 1954; The City Is Dark 1954; Big House, USA 1955; Jubal 1956; Run of the Arrow 1957; Machine Gun Kelly 1958; Showdown at Boot Hill 1958; Gang War 1958; Never So Few 1959; The Magnificent Seven 1960; Master of the World 1961; A Thunder of Drums 1961; X-15 1961; Kid Galahad 1962; 4 for Texas 1963; The Great Escape 1963; Battle of the Bulge 1965; The Sandpiper 1965; This Property Is Condemned 1966; The Dirty Dozen 1967; Guns for San Sebastian 1968; Once upon a Time in the West 1968; Villa Rides 1968; Twinky 1969; Rider on the Rain 1970; Violent City 1970; You Can't Win 'em All 1970; Cold Sweat 1971; Red Sun 1971; Someone behind the Door 1971; Chato's Land 1972; The Mechanic 1972; The Valachi Papers 1972; The Stone Killer 1973; The Valdez Horses 1973; Death Wish 1974; Mr Majestyk 1974; Breakout 1975; The Streetfighter 1975; Breakheart Pass 1976; From Noon till Three 1976; St Ives 1976; Telefon 1977; The White Buffalo 1977; Love and Bullets 1978; Borderline 1980; Caboblanco 1980; Death Hunt 1981; Death Wish II 1981; 10 to Midnight 1983; The Evil That Men Do 1984; Death Wish 3 1985; Act of Vengeance 1986; Assassination 1986; Murphy's Law 1986; Death Wish 4: the Crackdown 1987; Messenger of Death 1988; Kinjite: Forbidden Subjects 1989; The Indian Runner 1991; Yes Virginia, There Is a Santa Claus 1991; Donato and Daughter 1993; The Sea Wolf 1993; Death Wish V: the Face of Death 1994; Family of Cops 1995; Breach of Faith: Family of Cops II 1996

Brook, Claudio The Young One 1960; The Exterminating Angel 1962; Simon of the Desert 1965; Don't Look Now... We're Being Shot At 1966; Jory 1972; Interval 1973; The Return of a Man Called Horse 1976; Cronos 1992

Brook, Clive Underworld 1927; Four Feathers 1929; Anybody's Woman 1930; Paramount on Parade 1930; East Lynne 1931; Tarnished Lady 1931; Shanghai Express 1932; Sherlock Holmes 1932; The Man from Yesterday 1932; Cavalcade 1933; If I Were Free 1933; Gallant Lady 1934; The Dictator 1935; Convoy 1940; Return to Yesterday 1940; Freedom Radio 1941; The List of Adrian Messenger 1963

Brook, Faith Jungle Book 1942; The Intimate Stranger 1956; Chase a Crooked Shadow 1957; The Thirty-Nine Steps 1959; To Sir, with Love 1967; The Smashing Bird I Used to Know 1969; Walk a Crooked Path 1969; North Sea Hijack 1979; Eye of the Needle 1981

Brook, Irina *The Girl in the Picture* 1985; *Captive* 1986; *The Fool* 1990

Brook, Jayne *Clean Slate* 1994; *Last Dance* 1995; *The Four Diamonds* 1995; *Ed* 1996

Brook, Lyndon *The Purple Plain* 1954; *One Way Out* 1955; *Reach for the Sky* 1956; *The Spanish Gardener* 1956; *The Gypsy and the Gentleman* 1958; *Invasion* 1965; *Who?* 1974

Brooke, Hillary *Sherlock Holmes Faces Death* 1943; *Standing Room Only* 1944; *The Enchanted Cottage* 1945; *Ministry of Fear* 1945; *Road to Utopia* 1945; *The Woman in Green* 1945; *Up Goes Maisie* 1946; *The Strange Woman* 1946; *Strange Impersonation* 1946; *The Fuller Brush Man* 1948; *Africa Screams* 1949; *The Admiral Was a Lady* 1950; *Abbott and Costello Meet Captain Kidd* 1952; *Invaders from Mars* 1953; *Bengazi* 1955; *The Man Who Knew Too Much* 1956

Brooke Jr, Michael *The Magnet* 1950; *The Long Arm* 1956

Brooke, Paul *The Lair of the White Worm* 1988; *The Fool* 1990

Brooke, Tyler *Fazil* 1928; *Dynamite* 1929; *Monte Carlo* 1930; *Hallelujah, I'm a Bum* 1933

Brooke, Walter *Conquest of Space* 1955; *The Graduate* 1967; *Sergeant Ryker* 1968; *Zigzag* 1970

Brookes, Jacqueline *The Gambler* 1974; *Last Embrace* 1979; *The Entity* 1981; *Without a Trace* 1983; *Silent Witness* 1985; *The Good Son* 1993

Brooke-Taylor, Tim *Twelve plus One* 1969; *Pleasure at Her Majesty's* 1976

Brook-Jones, Elwyn *Bonnie Prince Charlie* 1948; *It's Hard to Be Good* 1948; *The Gilded Cage* 1954; *Rogue's Yarn* 1956; *Passport to Shame* 1958

Brooks, Albert *Taxi Driver* 1976; *Real Life* 1979; *Private Benjamin* 1980; *Modern Romance* 1981; *Twilight Zone: the Movie* 1983; *Unfaithfully Yours* 1983; *Lost in America* 1985; *Broadcast News* 1987; *Defending Your Life* 1991; *I'll Do Anything* 1994; *The Scout* 1994; *Mother* 1996; *Critical Care* 1997; *Out of Sight* 1998; *The Muse* 1999

Brooks, Avery *Uncle Tom's Cabin* 1987; *American History X* 1998; *The Big Hit* 1998

Brooks, Claude *Solarwarriors* 1986; *Hiding Out* 1987

Brooks, Foster *Cactus Jack* 1979; *Smorgasbord* 1983

Brooks, Geraldine *Cry Wolf* 1947; *Possessed* 1947; *Challenge to Lassie* 1949; *The Reckless Moment* 1949; *Volcano* 1950; *Johnny Tiger* 1966

Brooks, Hazel *Body and Soul* 1947; *Sleep, My Love* 1948

Brooks, Jean *The Falcon and the Co-Eds* 1943; *The Falcon in Danger* 1943; *The Leopard Man* 1943; *The Seventh Victim* 1943; *The Falcon in Hollywood* 1944; *Youth Runs Wild* 1944

Brooks, Joel *Skin Deep* 1989; *Are You Lonesome Tonight* 1992; *Indecent Proposal* 1993

Brooks, Leslie *You Were Never Lovelier* 1942; *Cover Girl* 1944; *Tonight and Every Night* 1945; *Hollow Triumph* 1948

Brooks, Louise *It's the Old Army Game* 1926; *A Girl in Every Port* 1928; *Beggars of Life* 1928; *Canary Murder Case* 1929; *Diary of a Lost Girl* 1929; *Pandora's Box* 1929; *Prix de Beauté* 1930; *Overland Stage Raiders* 1938

Brooks, Martin E *The Execution* 1985; *Bionic Showdown: the Six Million Dollar Man and the Bionic Woman* 1989; *Bionic Ever After?* 1994

Brooks, Mel *Putney Swope* 1969; *The Twelve Chairs* 1970; *Blazing Saddles* 1974; *Silent Movie* 1976; *High Anxiety* 1977; *History of the World Part 1* 1981; *To Be or Not to Be* 1983; *Spaceballs* 1987; *Look Who's Talking Too* 1990; *Life Stinks* 1991; *Robin Hood: Men in Tights* 1993; *The Little Rascals* 1994; *Dracula: Dead and Loving It* 1995

Brooks, Phyllis *Little Miss Broadway* 1938; *Rebecca of Sunnybrook Farm* 1938; *Charlie Chan in Reno* 1939; *The Shanghai Gesture* 1941; *The Unseen* 1945

Brooks, Rand *The Devil's Playground* 1946; *Fool's Gold* 1946; *The Dead Don't Dream* 1947; *The Marauders* 1947; *False Paradise* 1948; *Ladies of the Chorus* 1948; *Silent Conflict* 1948; *Comanche Station* 1960

Brooks, Randy *Assassination* 1986; *8 Million Ways to Die* 1986; *Colors* 1988; *Reservoir Dogs* 1991

Brooks, Ray *Some People* 1962; *The Knack... and How to Get It* 1965; *Daleks – Invasion Earth 2150 AD* 1966; *The Last Grenade* 1970; *Assassin* 1973; *Tiffany Jones* 1973; *House of Whipcord* 1974

Brooks, Richard *Good to Go* 1986; *The Hidden* 1987; *Blue Jean Cop* 1988; *84 Charlie Mopic* 1989; *Shocker* 1989; *To Sleep with Anger* 1990; *Memphis* 1992; *The Crow: City of Angels* 1996; *Code Name: Wolverine* 1996

Brooks, Victor *Cover Girl Killer* 1959; *Life in Danger* 1959; *Give Us Tomorrow* 1978

Brophy, Anthony *The Run of the Country* 1995; *Snow White: a Tale of Terror* 1996; *The Last Bus Home* 1997

Brophy, Brian *Brain Dead* 1990; *Love to Kill* 1997

Brophy, Edward *aka* **Brophy, Edward S** *Doughboys* 1930; *The Champ* 1931; *What – No Beer?* 1933; *Evelyn Prentice* 1934; *Mad Love* 1935; *Strike Me Pink* 1936; *Spendthrift* 1936; *Great Guy* 1936; *The Adventures of Michael Strogoff* 1937; *The Last Gangster* 1937; *The Amazing Mr Williams* 1939; *Golden Boy* 1939; *Dance, Girl, Dance* 1940; *Dumbo* 1941; *The Gay Falcon* 1941; *Broadway* 1942; *Larceny, Inc* 1942; *It Happened Tomorrow* 1944; *The Falcon in San Francisco* 1945; *The Falcon's Adventure* 1946; *The Last Hurrah* 1958

Brosnan, Pierce *The Long Good Friday* 1979; *Nomads* 1985; *The Fourth Protocol* 1987; *The Deceivers* 1988; *Taffin* 1988; *The Heist* 1989; *Mister Johnson* 1991; *Murder 101* 1991; *Victim of Love* 1991; *The Lawnmower Man* 1992; *Live Wire* 1992; *The Broken Chain* 1993; *Death Train* 1993; *Mrs Doubtfire* 1993; *Don't Talk to Strangers* 1994; *Love Affair* 1994; *The Disappearance of Kevin Johnson* 1995; *GoldenEye* 1995; *Night Watch* 1995; *Mars Attacks!* 1996; *The Mirror Has Two Faces* 1996; *Dante's Peak* 1997; *The Nephew* 1997; *Tomorrow Never Dies* 1997; *The Magic Sword: Quest for Camelot* 1997; *The Match* 1999; *The World Is Not Enough* 1999; *The Thomas Crown Affair* 1999

Brothers, Dr Joyce *Oh God! Book II* 1980; *The Lonely Guy* 1984; *Age Isn't Everything* 1991

Brousse, Liliane *Paranoiac* 1963; *Maniac* 1963

Browder, Ben *A Kiss before Dying* 1991; *Danielle Steel's Secrets* 1992; *Big Dreams & Broken Hearts: the Dottie West Story* 1995; *Bad to the Bone* 1997

Brown, Barbara *Hollywood Canteen* 1944; *Born Yesterday* 1950; *An Annapolis Story* 1955

Brown, Barry *Flesh* 1968; *Bad Company* 1972; *Daisy Miller* 1974; *This Man Stands Alone* 1979

Brown, Blair *The Oregon Trail* 1976; *Altered States* 1980; *One-Trick Pony* 1980; *Continental Divide* 1981; *A Flash of Green* 1984; *Stealing Home* 1988; *Strapless* 1988; *Extreme Close-Up* 1990; *Lethal Innocence* 1991; *Those Secrets* 1991; *Majority Rule* 1992; *Passed Away* 1992; *Rio Shannon* 1993; *The Gift of Love* 1994; *The Good Policeman* 1994; *To Walk Again* 1994; *Ultimate Lie* 1996

Brown, Bryan *The Irishman* 1978; *Money Movers* 1978; *Newsfront* 1978; *Breaker Morant* 1979; *Cathy's Child* 1979; *The Odd Angry Shot* 1979; *Blood Money* 1980; *The Winter of Our Dreams* 1981; *Far East* 1982; *Give My Regards to Broad Street* 1984; *Kim* 1984; *Parker* 1984; *The Empty Beach* 1985; *F/X* 1985; *Rebel* 1985; *The Good Wife* 1986; *The Shiralee* 1986; *Tai-Pan* 1986; *Cocktail* 1988; *Gorillas in the Mist* 1988; *Blood Oath* 1990; *Dead in the Water* 1991; *F/X2: the Deadly Art of Illusion* 1991; *Blame It on the Bellboy* 1992; *Devlin* 1992; *Full Body Massage* 1995; *Dead Heart* 1996; *Dogboys* 1998

Brown, Charles D *Gold Diggers of 1937* 1936; *The Duke of West Point* 1938; *The Shopworn Angel* 1938; *Brother Orchid* 1940; *The Senator Was Indiscreet* 1947; *Smash-Up, the Story of a Woman* 1947; *Undercover Maisie* 1947

Brown, Clancy *The Bride* 1985; *Highlander* 1986; *Extreme Prejudice* 1987; *The Room Upstairs* 1987; *Deadly Pursuit* 1988; *Season of Fear* 1989; *Waiting for the Light* 1989; *Blue Steel* 1990; *Ambition* 1991; *Cast a Deadly Spell* 1991; *Pet Sematary II* 1992; *Past Midnight* 1992; *Desperate Rescue* 1993; *Last Light* 1993; *The Shawshank Redemption* 1994; *Radiant City* 1996; *Flubber* 1997; *Starship Troopers* 1997; *The Hurricane* 1999; *Vendetta* 1999

Brown, D W *Weekend Pass* 1984; *Mischief* 1985

Brown, Dwier *House II: the Second Story* 1987; *The Guardian* 1990; *When You Remember Me* 1990; *The Cutting Edge* 1992; *Mom and Dad Save the World* 1992; *Dennis Strikes Again* 1998

Brown, Eric *Private Lessons* 1981; *They're Playing With Fire* 1984

Brown, Garrett M *aka* **Brown, Garrett** *Zelig* 1983; *Uncle Buck* 1989

Brown, Georg Stanford *The Comedians* 1967; *Bullitt* 1968; *Dayton's Devils* 1968; *Colossus: the Forbin Project* 1969; *The Man* 1972; *Black Jack* 1972; *Stir Crazy* 1980

Brown, Georgia *The Fixer* 1968; *Lock Up Your Daughters!* 1969; *The Raging Moon* 1970; *Nothing but the Night* 1972; *Galileo* 1974; *Victim of Love* 1991

Brown, Henry *The Man in the Glass Booth* 1975; *Stepfather II* 1989

Brown (1), James *The Blues Brothers* 1980; *Rocky IV* 1985; *Blues Brothers 2000* 1998; *Holy Man* 1998

Brown (2), James *Corvette K-225* 1943; *Going My Way* 1944; *Objective, Burma!* 1945; *Sands of Iwo Jima* 1949; *Chain Lightning* 1950; *The Fireball* 1950; *Montana* 1950; *The Pride of St Louis* 1952; *A Star Is Born* 1954; *Targets* 1968; *Adios Amigo* 1975

Brown, Jim *Rio Conchos* 1964; *Dark of the Sun* 1967; *The Dirty Dozen* 1967; *Ice Station Zebra* 1968; *The Split* 1968; *100 Rifles* 1969; *Riot* 1969; *El Condor* 1970; *The Grasshopper* 1970; *Slaughter* 1972; *The Slams* 1973; *Slaughter's Big Rip-Off* 1973; *I Escaped from Devil's Island* 1973; *Three the Hard Way* 1974; *Take a Hard Ride* 1975; *Kid Vengeance* 1977; *Fingers* 1978; *Pacific Inferno* 1979; *The Running Man* 1987; *Crack House* 1989; *Original Gangstas* 1996; *He Got Game* 1998; *Any Given Sunday* 1999

Brown, Joe E *Sunny Side Up* 1929; *Fireman Save My Child* 1932; *A Midsummer Night's Dream* 1935; *Chatterbox* 1943; *Pin Up Girl* 1944; *The Tender Years* 1947; *Show Boat* 1951; *Some Like It Hot* 1959; *The Comedy of Terrors* 1964

Brown, John *Hans Christian Andersen* 1952; *Master Spy* 1964

Brown, Johnny Mack *aka* **Brown, John Mack** *The Divine Woman* 1928; *Our Dancing Daughters* 1928; *A Woman of Affairs* 1928; *Coquette* 1929; *The Single Standard* 1929; *Billy the Kid* 1930; *The Last Flight* 1931; *The Secret Six* 1931; *Vanishing Frontier* 1932; *Female* 1933; *Belle of the Nineties* 1934; *The Bounty Killer* 1965; *Apache Uprising* 1965

Brown, Jophery *The Bingo Long Travelling All-Stars and Motor Kings* 1976; *Sudden Death* 1995

Brown, Juanita *Caged Heat* 1974; *Foxy Brown* 1974

Brown, Judy *The Big Doll House* 1971; *Women in Cages* 1972

Brown, Julie *Earth Girls Are Easy* 1988; *Shakes the Clown* 1991; *The Opposite Sex and How to Live with Them* 1993; *Raining Stones* 1993

Brown, Kenneth *Never Give a Sucker an Even Break* 1941; *Bomber's Moon* 1943

Brown, Kimberly J *aka* **Brown, Kimberly** *Ellen Foster* 1997; *Tumbleweeds* 1999

Brown, Lew *Crime and Punishment, USA* 1959; *Grand Theft Auto* 1977

Brown, Lou *The Irishman* 1978; *Alison's Birthday* 1979

Brown, Pamela *One of Our Aircraft Is Missing* 1942; *I Know Where I'm Going* 1945; *The Tales of Hoffmann* 1951; *Richard III* 1955; *Lust for Life* 1956; *The Scapegoat* 1959; *Cleopatra* 1963; *Becket* 1964; *Secret Ceremony* 1969; *Figures in a Landscape* 1970; *On a Clear Day You Can See Forever* 1970; *Wuthering Heights* 1970; *Lady Caroline Lamb* 1972; *Dracula* 1974

Brown, Pat Crawford *Elvira, Mistress of the Dark* 1988; *Johnny Mysto* 1996

Brown, Peter *Darby's Rangers* 1958; *Merrill's Marauders* 1962; *Kitten with a Whip* 1964; *A Tiger Walks* 1964; *Ride the Wild Surf* 1964; *Act of Vengeance* 1974; *Foxy Brown* 1974; *The Concrete Jungle* 1982; *The Aurora Encounter* 1985; *Demonstone* 1989

Brown, Phil *Calling Dr Gillespie* 1942; *The Killers* 1946; *Without Reservations* 1946; *If You Knew Susie* 1948; *Obsession* 1948; *A King in New York* 1957; *The Adding Machine* 1969; *Valdez Is Coming* 1971; *A Special Kind of Love* 1978

Brown, Ralph *Withnail & I* 1986; *Buster* 1988; *Diamond Skulls* 1989; *Impromptu* 1991; *Alien^3* 1992; *Wayne's World 2* 1993; *Don't Get Me Started* 1994; *Up 'n' Under* 1997

Brown, Reb *Captain America* 1979; *Fast Break* 1979; *Uncommon Valor* 1983; *Yor, the Hunter from the Future* 1983; *Howling II: Your Sister Is a Werewolf* 1984; *Death of a Soldier* 1985; *Distant Thunder* 1988; *Cage* 1989; *Cage 2: the Arena of Death* 1994

Brown, Robert *Time Gentlemen Please!* 1952; *The Abominable Snowman* 1957; *The Steel Bayonet* 1957; *Passport to Shame* 1958; *Tower of London* 1962; *One Million Years BC* 1966; *Octopussy* 1983; *A View to a Kill* 1985; *The Living Daylights* 1987; *Licence to Kill* 1989

Brown, Roger Aaron *Foster and Laurie* 1975; *With a Vengeance* 1992; *Tall Tale: the Unbelievable Adventures of Pecos Bill* 1994; *DNA* 1996

Brown, Russ *Damn Yankees* 1958; *South Pacific* 1958; *It Happened to Jane* 1959

Brown, Ruth *Hairspray* 1988; *Shake, Rattle and Rock* 1994

Brown, Samantha *New Jersey Drive* 1995; *Double Platinum* 1999

Brown, Sharon *A Chorus Line* 1985; *For Keeps* 1987

Brown, Stanley *aka* **Taylor, Brad** *The Face behind the Mask* 1941; *Atlantic City* 1944

Brown, Susan *Without Warning: the James Brady Story* 1991; *To Face Her Past* 1996

Brown, Thomas Wilson *aka* **Brown, Thomas** *Down the Long Hills* 1987; *Evil in Clear River* 1988; *Honey, I Shrunk the Kids* 1989; *Welcome Home* 1989; *Welcome Home, Roxy Carmichael* 1990; *Midnight Sting* 1992; *Silent Thunder* 1992

Brown, Timothy *aka* **Brown, Tim** *Nashville* 1975; *Pacific Inferno* 1979

Brown, Tom *Hell's Highway* 1932; *Central Airport* 1933; *Anne of Green Gables* 1934; *Judge Priest* 1934; *The Man Who Cried Wolf* 1937; *Maytime* 1937; *Navy Blue and Gold* 1937; *The Duke of West Point* 1938; *Merrily We Live* 1938; *The Storm* 1938; *Sergeant Madden* 1939; *There's One Born Every Minute* 1942; *Buck Privates Come Home* 1947; *Fireman Save My Child* 1954

Brown, Vanessa *The Foxes of Harrow* 1947; *The Ghost and Mrs Muir* 1947; *The Late George Apley* 1947; *Mother Wore Tights* 1947; *The Heiress* 1949; *Big Jack* 1949; *Tarzan and the Slave Girl* 1950; *The Bad and the Beautiful* 1952; *The Fighter* 1952; *Rosie!* 1967

Brown, Wally *Girl Rush* 1944; *Step Lively* 1944; *From This Day*

Forward 1946; *Holiday for Lovers* 1959; *The Absent-Minded Professor* 1961
Browne, Coral *We're Going to Be Rich* 1938; *Let George Do It* 1940; *The Courtneys of Curzon Street* 1947; *Beautiful Stranger* 1954; *Auntie Mame* 1958; *Go to Blazes* 1961; *The Roman Spring of Mrs Stone* 1961; *Dr Crippen* 1962; *Tamahine* 1963; *The Night of the Generals* 1966; *The Killing of Sister George* 1968; *The Ruling Class* 1972; *Theatre of Blood* 1973; *American Dreamer* 1984; *Dreamchild* 1985
Browne, Irene *The Letter* 1929; *Berkeley Square* 1933; *Peg o' My Heart* 1933; *Meet Me at Dawn* 1946; *Barnacle Bill* 1957; *Serious Charge* 1959
Browne, Leslie *The Turning Point* 1977; *Nijinsky* 1980; *Dancers* 1987
Browne, Roscoe Lee *Black Like Me* 1964; *Topaz* 1969; *The Liberation of LB Jones* 1970; *Cisco Pike* 1971; *The Cowboys* 1972; *The World's Greatest Athlete* 1973; *Uptown Saturday Night* 1974; *Logan's Run* 1976; *Nothing Personal* 1980; *Oliver & Company* 1988; *Stuck with Each Other* 1989; *Babe* 1995; *Last Summer in the Hamptons* 1995; *The Pompatus of Love* 1995; *Dear God* 1996
Browning, Ricou *Creature from the Black Lagoon* 1954; *Revenge of the Creature* 1955
Brubaker, Tony *Buck and the Preacher* 1972; *WB, Blue and the Bean* 1988
Bruce, Betty *Gypsy* 1962; *Island of Love* 1963
Bruce, Brenda *When the Bough Breaks* 1947; *The Final Test* 1953; *Behind the Mask* 1958; *Law and Disorder* 1958; *Peeping Tom* 1960; *The Uncle* 1964; *Nightmare* 1964; *All Creatures Great and Small* 1974; *Swallows and Amazons* 1974; *The Man in the Iron Mask* 1977; *Steaming* 1985; *The Tenth Man* 1988; *December Bride* 1990; *Antonia & Jane* 1990; *Splitting Heirs* 1993
Bruce, Carol *Keep 'em Flying* 1941; *Planes, Trains and Automobiles* 1987
Bruce, Cheryl Lynn *Music Box* 1989; *Daughters of the Dust* 1991
Bruce, Colin *Crusoe* 1988; *The Dead Can't Lie* 1988
Bruce, David *Gung Ho!* 1943; *Can't Help Singing* 1944; *Christmas Holiday* 1944
Bruce, Ed *Down the Long Hills* 1987; *Separated by Murder* 1994
Bruce, Nigel *I Was a Spy* 1934; *The Scarlet Pimpernel* 1934; *Treasure Island* 1934; *Stand up and Cheer!* 1934; *Becky Sharp* 1935; *The Man Who Broke the Bank at Monte Carlo* 1935; *She* 1935; *The Charge of the Light Brigade* 1936; *The Trail of the Lonesome Pine* 1936; *Under Two Flags* 1936; *The Last of Mrs Cheyney* 1937; *Thunder in the City* 1937; *Kidnapped* 1938; *The Adventures of Sherlock Holmes* 1939; *The Hound of the Baskervilles* 1939; *The Rains Came* 1939; *Rebecca* 1940; *Susan and God* 1940; *The Blue Bird* 1940; *A Dispatch from Reuters* 1940; *Suspicion* 1941; *Journey for Margaret* 1942; *Roxie Hart* 1942; *Sherlock Holmes and the Secret Weapon* 1942; *Sherlock Holmes and the Voice of Terror* 1942; *This above All* 1942; *Lassie Come Home* 1943; *Sherlock Holmes Faces Death* 1943; *Sherlock Holmes in Washington* 1943; *Frenchman's Creek* 1944; *The House of Fear* 1944; *The Pearl of Death* 1944; *The Scarlet Claw* 1944; *Sherlock Holmes and the Spider Woman* 1944; *The Corn Is Green* 1945; *Pursuit to Algiers* 1945; *Son of Lassie* 1945; *The Two Mrs Carrolls* 1945; *The Woman in Green* 1945; *Dressed to Kill* 1946; *Terror by Night* 1946; *The Exile* 1947; *Julia Misbehaves* 1948; *Bwana Devil* 1952; *Limelight* 1952; *World for Ransom* 1954
Bruce, Virginia *Dangerous Corner* 1934; *The Mighty Barnum* 1934; *Escapade* 1935; *Let 'em Have It* 1935; *Murder Man* 1935; *Born to Dance* 1936; *The Great Ziegfeld* 1936; *Wife, Doctor and Nurse* 1937; *Arsene Lupin Returns* 1938; *Bad Man of Brimstone* 1938; *Yellow Jack* 1938; *There Goes My Heart* 1938; *Hired Wife* 1940; *Careful, Soft Shoulder* 1942; *Pardon My Sarong* 1942; *Brazil* 1944; *Night Has a Thousand Eyes* 1948; *Strangers When We Meet* 1960
Bruel, Patrick *Force Majeure* 1989; *Brothers in Arms* 1990; *Lost & Found* 1999
Bruhanski, Alex *The Penthouse* 1989; *Bird on a Wire* 1990; *Beyond Obsession* 1994
Brundin, Bo *The Great Waldo Pepper* 1975; *Late for Dinner* 1991
Brunetti, Argentina *The Brothers Rico* 1957; *The Midnight Story* 1957
Brunius, Jacques aka **Borel, Jacques** *Une Partie de Campagne* 1936; *Sea Devils* 1952; *South of Algiers* 1952
Bruno, Dylan *When Trumpets Fade* 1998; *The Rage: Carrie 2* 1999
Brunot, André *Hôtel du Nord* 1938; *Pièges* 1939; *Le Rouge et le Noir* 1954
Bruns, Philip *Mr Inside/Mr Outside* 1973; *Corvette Summer* 1978; *The Christmas Star* 1986; *Return of the Living Dead Part II* 1988
Bryan, Dora *Adam and Evelyne* 1949; *The Interrupted Journey* 1949; *Now Barabbas Was a Robber* 1949; *Circle of Danger* 1950; *No Trace* 1950; *The Quiet Woman* 1950; *Something in the City* 1950; *Lady Godiva Rides Again* 1951; *The Gift Horse* 1952; *Miss Robin Hood* 1952; *13 East Street* 1952; *Time Gentlemen Please!* 1952; *Women of Twilight* 1952; *The Intruder* 1953; *Mad about Men* 1954; *You Know What Sailors Are* 1954; *As Long as They're Happy* 1955; *Child in the House* 1956; *The Man Who Wouldn't Talk* 1957; *Carry On Sergeant* 1958; *Desert Mice* 1959; *Operation Bullshine* 1959; *The Night We Got the Bird* 1960; *A Taste of Honey* 1961; *The Great St Trinian's Train Robbery* 1966; *The Sandwich Man* 1966; *Hands of the Ripper* 1971; *Up the Front* 1972; *Apartment Zero* 1988
Bryan, Jane *The Case of the Black Cat* 1936; *Confession* 1937; *Kid Galahad* 1937; *Marked Woman* 1937; *The Sisters* 1938; *A Slight Case of Murder* 1938; *Each Dawn I Die* 1939; *The Old Maid* 1939; *We Are Not Alone* 1939; *Invisible Stripes* 1940
Bryant, Karis Paige aka **Bryant, Karis** *The Substitute Wife* 1994; *While Justice Sleeps* 1994; *The Unspoken Truth* 1995
Bryant, Michael *The Mind Benders* 1963; *Torture Garden* 1967; *Goodbye, Mr Chips* 1969; *Mumsy, Nanny, Sonny & Girly* 1970; *The Ruling Class* 1972; *Caravan to Vaccares* 1974; *The Miracle Maker* 1999
Bryant, Nana *Atlantic Adventure* 1935; *The Man Who Lived Twice* 1936; *Pennies from Heaven* 1936; *Meet Nero Wolfe* 1936; *Man-Proof* 1937; *The League of Frightened Men* 1937; *The Adventures of Tom Sawyer* 1938; *Her Husband's Affairs* 1947; *Possessed* 1947; *Ladies of the Chorus* 1948; *The Outcast* 1954
Bryant, Peter *It's a Great Day* 1955; *The Hunted* 1998
Bryant, William *The Other Side of the Mountain* 1975; *The Other Side of the Mountain – Part 2* 1978; *Corvette Summer* 1978
Bryar, Paul *Easy to Love* 1953; *The Bob Mathias Story* 1954; *Vertigo* 1958
Bryce, Scott *Exclusive* 1992; *Stalking Laura* 1993; *Up Close & Personal* 1996
Brynner, Yul *Port of New York* 1949; *Anastasia* 1956; *The King and I* 1956; *The Ten Commandments* 1956; *The Brothers Karamazov* 1958; *The Buccaneer* 1958; *The Journey* 1959; *Solomon and Sheba* 1959; *The Sound and the Fury* 1959; *Once More, with Feeling* 1959; *The Magnificent Seven* 1960; *Le Testament d'Orphée* 1960; *Escape from Zahrain* 1962; *Taras Bulba* 1962; *Kings of the Sun* 1963; *Flight from Ashiya* 1964; *Invitation to a Gunfighter* 1964; *The Saboteur, Code Name Morituri* 1965; *Cast a Giant Shadow* 1966; *The Long Duel* 1966; *Return of the Seven* 1966; *Triple Cross* 1966; *The Poppy Is Also a Flower* 1966; *The Double Man* 1967; *Villa Rides* 1968; *The Battle of Neretva* 1969; *The File of the Golden Goose* 1969; *The Magic Christian* 1969; *The Bounty Hunters* 1970; *Catlow* 1971; *The Light at the Edge of the World* 1971; *Romance of a Horse Thief* 1971; *Fuzz* 1972; *The Serpent* 1972; *Westworld* 1973; *The Ultimate Warrior* 1975; *Futureworld* 1976
Brynolfsson, Reine *House of Angels* 1992; *House of Angels II: The Second Summer* 1994; *Jerusalem* 1996; *Les Misérables* 1997; *The Last Contract* 1998
Buccella, Maria Grazia *The Dirty Game* 1965; *Dead Run* 1967
Bucci, Flavio *Suspiria* 1976; *Tex and the Lord of the Deep* 1985
Buchanan, Beth *Mission Top Secret* 1990; *The Phantom Horsemen* 1990; *Pirates' Island* 1990; *The Rogue Stallion* 1990
Buchanan, Edgar *Too Many Husbands* 1940; *Penny Serenade* 1941; *Texas* 1941; *You Belong to Me* 1941; *The Talk of the Town* 1942; *The Desperadoes* 1943; *Bride by Mistake* 1944; *Buffalo Bill* 1944; *Abilene Town* 1945; *The Bandit of Sherwood Forest* 1946; *Framed* 1947; *The Sea of Grass* 1947; *The Black Arrow* 1948; *The Man from Colorado* 1948; *The Walking Hills* 1949; *Red Canyon* 1949; *The Big Hangover* 1950; *Cheaper by the Dozen* 1950; *Devil's Doorway* 1950; *Cave of Outlaws* 1951; *Rawhide* 1951; *The Big Trees* 1952; *Shane* 1953; *Beautiful but Dangerous* 1954; *Dawn at Socorro* 1954; *Destry* 1954; *Human Desire* 1954; *Make Haste to Live* 1954; *Wichita* 1955; *Rage at Dawn* 1955; *Come Next Spring* 1956; *The Sheepman* 1958; *Day of the Bad Man* 1958; *Edge of Eternity* 1959; *Ride the High Country* 1962; *A Ticklish Affair* 1963; *The Man from Button Willow* 1965; *The Rounders* 1965; *Gunpoint* 1966; *Welcome to Hard Times* 1967; *Angel in My Pocket* 1968; *Benji* 1974
Buchanan, Ian *The Cool Surface* 1993; *Double Exposure* 1993
Buchanan, Jack *Monte Carlo* 1930; *When Knights Were Bold* 1936; *The Gang's All Here* 1939; *The Band Wagon* 1953; *As Long as They're Happy* 1955; *The Diary of Major Thompson* 1955; *Josephine and Men* 1955
Buchanan, Robert *That Sinking Feeling* 1979; *Gregory's Girl* 1980
Buchanan, Simone *Run, Rebecca, Run* 1981; *Shame* 1987
Buchholz, Horst *Tiger Bay* 1959; *The Magnificent Seven* 1960; *Fanny* 1961; *One, Two, Three* 1961; *Nine Hours to Rama* 1963; *The Empty Canvas* 1963; *Cervantes* 1968; *The Great Waltz* 1972; *The Catamount Killing* 1974; *The Amazing Captain Nemo* 1978; *Avalanche Express* 1979; *From Hell to Victory* 1979; *Sahara* 1983; *Code Name: Emerald* 1985; *Aces: Iron Eagle III* 1992; *Faraway, So Close* 1993; *Life Is Beautiful* 1997
Buck, David *The Mummy's Shroud* 1966; *Deadfall* 1968; *Mosquito Squadron* 1968
Buckler, John *The Black Room* 1935; *Tarzan Escapes* 1936
Buckley, Betty *Carrie* 1976; *The Ordeal of Bill Carney* 1981; *Tender Mercies* 1982; *Wild Thing* 1987; *Another Woman* 1988; *Frantic* 1988; *Babycakes* 1989; *Bonnie and Clyde: the True Story* 1992; *Betrayal of Trust* 1994; *Critical Choices* 1996; *Simply Irresistible* 1999
Buckley, Keith *Spring and Port Wine* 1969; *Dr Phibes Rises Again* 1972; *Hanover Street* 1979; *Half Moon Street* 1986; *Gunbus* 1986
Buetel, Jack *The Outlaw* 1943; *Best of the Badmen* 1951; *The Half-Breed* 1952; *Rose of Cimarron* 1952
Buferd, Marilyn *Les Belles de Nuit* 1952; *The Unearthly* 1957
Buffalo Bill Jr aka **Wilsey, Jay** *'Neath the Arizona Skies* 1934; *Texas Terror* 1935
Buggy, Niall *Zardoz* 1973; *King David* 1985
Buhagiar, Valerie *Roadkill* 1989; *Highway 61* 1992; *Romantic Undertaking* 1995
Buhr, Gérard *Bob Le Flambeur* 1955; *Five Days One Summer* 1982
Bujold, Geneviève *La Guerre Est Finie* 1966; *King of Hearts* 1966; *The Thief of Paris* 1967; *Anne of the Thousand Days* 1969; *Act of the Heart* 1970; *The Trojan Women* 1971; *Earthquake* 1974; *Alex and the Gypsy* 1976; *Obsession* 1976; *Swashbuckler* 1976; *Another Man, Another Chance* 1977; *Coma* 1977; *Murder by Decree* 1978; *The Last Flight of Noah's Ark* 1980; *Monsignor* 1982; *Choose Me* 1984; *Tightrope* 1984; *Trouble in Mind* 1985; *Dead Ringers* 1988; *The Moderns* 1988; *A Paper Wedding* 1989; *Snake Treaty* 1989; *The Dance Goes On* 1990; *False Identity* 1990; *Oh, What a Night* 1992; *The Adventures of Pinocchio* 1996; *Dead Innocent* 1996; *The House of Yes* 1997; *Last Night* 1998; *You Can Thank Me Later* 1998
Buktenica, Ray *The Jayne Mansfield Story* 1980; *Wait till Your Mother Gets Home!* 1983; *Heart of a Champion: the Ray Mancini Story* 1985
Bull, Peter *Saraband for Dead Lovers* 1948; *The African Queen* 1951; *Dr Strangelove, or How I Learned to Stop Worrying and Love the Bomb* 1963; *Licensed to Kill* 1965; *Doctor Dolittle* 1967; *The Tempest* 1979
Bull, Richard *The Secret Life of an American Wife* 1968; *A Different Story* 1978
Bulloch, Jeremy aka **Bullock, Jeremy** *The Cat Gang* 1959; *Summer Holiday* 1962; *Hoffman* 1970; *Can You Keep It Up for a Week?* 1974
Bullock, Sandra *Bionic Showdown: the Six Million Dollar Man and the Bionic Woman* 1989; *Love Potion No 9* 1992; *Who Shot Patakango?* 1992; *When the Party's Over* 1992; *Me and the Mob* 1992; *Demolition Man* 1993; *The Thing Called Love* 1993; *The Vanishing* 1993; *Wrestling Ernest Hemingway* 1993; *Speed* 1994; *The Net* 1995; *While You Were Sleeping* 1995; *In Love and War* 1996; *Stolen Hearts* 1996; *A Time to Kill* 1996; *Speed 2: Cruise Control* 1997; *Forces of Nature* 1998; *Hope Floats* 1998; *Practical Magic* 1998; *The Prince of Egypt* 1998; *28 Days* 2000
Buloff, Joseph *Let's Make Music* 1940; *Carnegie Hall* 1947; *The Loves of Carmen* 1948; *A Kiss in the Dark* 1949; *Silk Stockings* 1957
Bunce, Alan *The Last Mile* 1959; *Sunrise at Campobello* 1960; *Homicidal* 1961
Bunce, Stuart *Bring Me the Head of Mavis Davis* 1997; *Regeneration* 1997
Bundy, Brooke *Francis Gary Powers: the True Story of the U-2* 1976; *Two Fathers' Justice* 1985; *Twice Dead* 1988
Bunnage, Avis *The L-Shaped Room* 1962; *The Loneliness of the Long Distance Runner* 1962; *Sparrows Can't Sing* 1962; *What a Crazy World* 1963; *Rotten to the Core* 1965; *The Whisperers* 1967; *No Surrender* 1986; *The Krays* 1990
Bunston, Herbert *The Last of Mrs Cheyney* 1929; *Dracula* 1931; *The Moonstone* 1934
Buono, Cara *The Cowboy Way* 1994; *Kicking and Screaming* 1995; *Killer: a Journal of Murder* 1995; *Next Stop Wonderland* 1998
Buono, Victor *What Ever Happened to Baby Jane?* 1962; *4 for Texas* 1963; *Hush... Hush, Sweet Charlotte* 1964; *Robin and the 7 Hoods* 1964; *The Strangler* 1964; *Young Dillinger* 1965; *The Silencers* 1966; *Who's Minding the Mint?* 1967; *Target: Harry* 1968; *Beneath the Planet of the Apes* 1969; *The Wrath of God* 1972; *Arnold* 1973; *The Evil* 1978; *The Man with Bogart's Face* 1980
Burden, Hugh *One of Our Aircraft Is Missing* 1942; *The Way Ahead* 1944; *Fame Is the Spur* 1947; *Ghost Ship* 1952; *No Love for Johnnie* 1960; *The Secret Partner* 1961; *Blood from the Mummy's Tomb* 1971; *The Ruling Class* 1972; *The House in Nightmare Park* 1973

Burfield, Kim *Bloomfield* 1969; *Treasure Island* 1972
Burgard, Christopher *Twice Dead* 1988; *84 Charlie Mopic* 1989; *Full Body Massage* 1995
Burgers, Michele *Friends* 1993; *Jump the Gun* 1996
Burgess, Dorothy *In Old Arizona* 1929; *Taxi!* 1932; *Hold Your Man* 1933; *Ladies They Talk About* 1933
Buric, Zlatko *Pusher* 1996; *Bleeder* 1999
Burke, Alfred *Bitter Victory* 1957; *The Angry Silence* 1960; *Children of the Damned* 1964; *The Nanny* 1965; *The Night Caller* 1965; *Guns in the Heather* 1969; *One Day in the Life of Ivan Denisovich* 1971; *Kim* 1984
Burke, Billie *A Bill of Divorcement* 1932; *Christopher Strong* 1933; *Dinner at Eight* 1933; *Only Yesterday* 1933; *Forsaking All Others* 1934; *Finishing School* 1934; *Becky Sharp* 1935; *After Office Hours* 1935; *Craig's Wife* 1936; *Piccadilly Jim* 1936; *The Bride Wore Red* 1937; *Parnell* 1937; *Topper* 1937; *Navy Blue and Gold* 1937; *Everybody Sing* 1938; *Merrily We Live* 1938; *The Young in Heart* 1938; *Eternally Yours* 1939; *Remember?* 1939; *Topper Takes a Trip* 1939; *The Wizard of Oz* 1939; *Zenobia* 1939; *Irene* 1940; *The Man Who Came to Dinner* 1941; *Topper Returns* 1941; *They All Kissed the Bride* 1942; *The Cheaters* 1945; *And Baby Makes Three* 1949; *The Barkleys of Broadway* 1949; *Father of the Bride* 1950; *Father's Little Dividend* 1951; *The Young Philadelphians* 1959; *Sergeant Rutledge* 1960
Burke, Billy *Jane Austen's Mafia* 1998; *Without Limits* 1998; *Don't Look Down* 1998
Burke, Brandon *The Odd Angry Shot* 1979; *Mushrooms* 1995
Burke, Delta *Where the Hell's That Gold?* 1988; *Maternal Instincts* 1996; *A Promise to Carolyn* 1996
Burke, Georgia *Anna Lucasta* 1958; *The Cool World* 1963
Burke, James *Lady by Choice* 1934; *Great Guy* 1936; *The Dawn Patrol* 1938; *Ellery Queen Master Detective* 1940; *Little Nellie Kelly* 1940; *The Saint Takes Over* 1940
Burke, Kathleen *Island of Lost Souls* 1932; *Murders in the Zoo* 1933; *The Lives of a Bengal Lancer* 1935
Burke, Kathy *Scrubbers* 1982; *Eat the Rich* 1987; *Nil by Mouth* 1997; *Dancing at Lughnasa* 1998; *Elizabeth* 1998; *This Year's Love* 1999; *Love, Honour and Obey* 2000; *Kevin & Perry Go Large* 2000
Burke, Marie *Odette* 1950; *Miracle in Soho* 1957
Burke, Michelle aka **Thomas, Michelle Rene** *Coneheads* 1993; *Dazed and Confused* 1993; *Cosa Nostra: the Last Word* 1995; *Midnight in St Petersburg* 1995
Burke, Patricia *While I Live* 1947; *Dilemma* 1962; *The Impersonator* 1962
Burke, Paul *Della* 1965; *Valley of the Dolls* 1967; *The Thomas Crown Affair* 1968; *Daddy's Gone A-Hunting* 1969; *Once You Kiss a Stranger* 1969; *Psychic Killer* 1975; *The Red-Light Sting* 1984
Burke, Robert aka **Burke, Robert John** *The Unbelievable Truth* 1989; *Dust Devil* 1992; *Simple Men* 1992; *A Far Off Place* 1993; *RoboCop 3* 1993; *Killer: a Journal of Murder* 1995; *Fled* 1996; *If Lucy Fell* 1996; *Stephen King's Thinner* 1996
Burke, Simon *The Devil's Playground* 1976; *The Irishman* 1978; *Slate, Wyn & Me* 1987
Burke, Walter *Jack the Giant Killer* 1962; *The Three Stooges Go around the World in a Daze* 1963; *Support Your Local Sheriff!* 1969; *The Stone Killer* 1973
Burkholder, Scott *Cobb* 1994; *A Feel for Murder* 1995
Burkley, Dennis *Heroes* 1977; *Mask* 1985; *Murphy's Romance* 1985; *Pass the Ammo* 1988; *Lambada* 1990; *The Doors* 1991; *Son in Law* 1993; *Criminal Passion* 1995; *Eye of the Stalker* 1995; *Tin Cup* 1996; *Possums* 1998
Burlinson, Tom *The Man from Snowy River* 1982; *Phar Lap* 1983; *Flesh + Blood* 1985; *Windrider* 1986; *The Time Guardian* 1987; *Return to Snowy River* 1988
Burmester, Leo *Odd Jobs* 1986; *The Abyss* 1989; *A Perfect World* 1993; *The Great Elephant Escape* 1995; *The Neon Bible* 1995; *William Faulkner's Old Man* 1997
Burnaby, Davy *A Shot in the Dark* 1933; *Boys Will Be Boys* 1935; *Song of the Road* 1937
Burnett, Carol *Pete 'n' Tillie* 1972; *The Front Page* 1974; *A Wedding* 1978; *Friendly Fire* 1979; *H.E.A.L.T.H.* 1980; *The Four Seasons* 1981; *Chu Chu and the Philly Flash* 1981; *Annie* 1982; *Between Friends* 1983; *Hostage* 1988; *Noises Off* 1992; *The Marriage Fool* 1998
Burnette, Olivia *Planes, Trains and Automobiles* 1987; *A Stoning in Fulham County* 1988; *For Love of a Child* 1990; *Final Verdict* 1991; *Hard Promises* 1991; *A Murderous Affair* 1992; *The Gift of Love* 1994; *Eye for an Eye* 1995
Burnette, Smiley *Billy the Kid Returns* 1938; *Down Mexico Way* 1941; *On Top of Old Smoky* 1953; *Last of the Pony Riders* 1953
Burnham, Edward *To Sir, with Love* 1967; *The Abominable Dr Phibes* 1971
Burnham, Jeremy *Bachelor of Hearts* 1958; *Law and Disorder* 1958
Burns, Bob *The Big Broadcast of 1937* 1936; *Rhythm on the Range* 1936; *Waikiki Wedding* 1937; *Wells Fargo* 1937; *Radio City Revels* 1938; *Belle of the Yukon* 1944
Burns, Carol *The Mango Tree* 1977; *Bad Blood* 1982; *Dusty* 1982
Burns, David *Hey! Hey! USA* 1938; *The Gang's All Here* 1939; *The Saint in London* 1939; *Knock on Wood* 1954; *It's Always Fair Weather* 1955; *Let's Make Love* 1960; *Who Is Harry Kellerman, and Why Is He Saying Those Terrible Things about Me?* 1971
Burns, Edward *The Brothers McMullen* 1995; *She's the One* 1996; *No Looking Back* 1998; *Saving Private Ryan* 1998
Burns, George *The Big Broadcast* 1932; *International House* 1933; *We're Not Dressing* 1934; *Six of a Kind* 1934; *The Big Broadcast of 1936* 1935; *The Big Broadcast of 1937* 1936; *A Damsel in Distress* 1937; *College Swing* 1938; *Honolulu* 1939; *The Sunshine Boys* 1975; *Oh, God!* 1977; *Sgt Pepper's Lonely Hearts Club Band* 1978; *Going in Style* 1979; *Just You and Me, Kid* 1979; *Oh God! Book II* 1980; *Oh, God! You Devil* 1984; *18 Again!* 1988; *Radioland Murders* 1994
Burns, Jere *Hit List* 1988; *Turn Back the Clock* 1989; *Greedy* 1994; *Criminal Passion* 1995; *Eye of the Stalker* 1995; *My Giant* 1998
Burns, Larry *The Hornet's Nest* 1955; *Count Five and Die* 1957
Burns, Marilyn *The Texas Chain Saw Massacre* 1974; *Eaten Alive* 1976
Burns, Marion *Me and My Gal* 1932; *The Dawn Rider* 1935; *Paradise Canyon* 1935
Burns, Mark *The Adventures of Gerard* 1970; *The Virgin and the Gypsy* 1970; *Death in Venice* 1971; *A Time for Loving* 1971; *The Maids* 1974; *The Bitch* 1979; *Bullseye!* 1990
Burns, Martha *Never Talk to Strangers* 1995; *Long Day's Journey into Night* 1996
Burns, Michael *Stranger on the Run* 1967; *Journey to Shiloh* 1968; *That Cold Day in the Park* 1969; *Thumb Tripping* 1972; *Santee* 1973
Burns, Paul E *The Woman on Pier 13* 1949; *Montana* 1950
Burr, Raymond *Without Reservations* 1946; *Desperate* 1947; *Pitfall* 1948; *Raw Deal* 1948; *Ruthless* 1948; *Station West* 1948; *Walk a Crooked Mile* 1948; *Black Magic* 1949; *Bride of Vengeance* 1949; *Love Happy* 1949; *Red Light* 1949; *Key to the City* 1950; *His Kind of Woman* 1951; *M* 1951; *A Place in the Sun* 1951; *The Whip Hand* 1951; *Horizons West* 1952; *Meet Danny Wilson* 1952; *The Bandits of Corsica* 1953; *The Blue Gardenia* 1953; *Fort Algiers* 1953; *Tarzan and the She-Devil* 1953; *Serpent of the Nile* 1953; *Casanova's Big Night* 1954; *Khyber Patrol* 1954; *Passion* 1954; *Rear Window* 1954; *Thunder Pass* 1954; *Godzilla* 1954; *Gorilla at Large* 1954; *Count Three and Pray* 1955; *A Man Alone* 1955; *You're Never Too Young* 1955; *Great Day in the Morning* 1956; *Secret of Treasure Mountain* 1956; *A Cry in the Night* 1956; *The Brass Legend* 1956; *Crime of Passion* 1957; *Affair in Havana* 1957; *Desire in the Dust* 1960; *New Face in Hell* 1968; *Tomorrow Never Comes* 1977; *Disaster on the Coastliner* 1979; *Out of the Blue* 1980; *Airplane II: the Sequel* 1982; *Godzilla* 1984; *Delirious* 1991
Burrell, Sheila *Cloudburst* 1951; *Colonel March Investigates* 1953; *Paranoiac* 1963; *Cold Comfort Farm* 1995; *The Woodlanders* 1997
Burress, Hedy *If These Walls Could Talk* 1996; *Foxfire* 1996
Burroughs, Jackie *Heavy Metal* 1981; *The Grey Fox* 1982; *The Care Bears Movie* 1985; *Night Owl* 1993; *Hemoglobin* 1997; *Evidence of Blood* 1998
Burroughs, William S *Chappaqua* 1966; *Drugstore Cowboy* 1989
Burrows, Saffron *Welcome II the Terrordome* 1994; *Circle of Friends* 1995; *Hotel de Love* 1996; *Wing Commander* 1999; *The Loss of Sexual Innocence* 1999; *Deep Blue Sea* 1999; *Miss Julie* 1999; *Gangster No 1* 2000
Burstyn, Ellen aka **McRae, Ellen** *Goodbye Charlie* 1964; *Alex in Wonderland* 1970; *The Last Picture Show* 1971; *Thursday's Game* 1971; *The King of Marvin Gardens* 1972; *The Exorcist* 1973; *Alice Doesn't Live Here Anymore* 1974; *Harry and Tonto* 1974; *Providence* 1977; *A Dream of Passion* 1978; *Same Time, Next Year* 1978; *Resurrection* 1980; *Silence of the North* 1981; *The Ambassador* 1984; *Into Thin Air* 1985; *Surviving* 1985; *Twice in a Lifetime* 1985; *Act of Vengeance* 1986; *Something in Common* 1986; *Pack of Lies* 1987; *Hanna's War* 1988; *When You Remember Me* 1990; *Dying Young* 1991; *Mrs Lambert Remembers Love* 1991; *Taking Back My Life* 1992; *The Cemetery Club* 1993; *Getting Out* 1993; *Shattered Trust* 1993; *Getting Gotti* 1994; *When a Man Loves a Woman* 1994; *Primal Secrets* 1994; *The Baby-Sitter's Club* 1995; *Follow the River* 1995; *How to Make an American Quilt* 1995; *Roommates* 1995; *The Spitfire Grill* 1996; *Liar* 1997; *Flash* 1997; *Playing by Heart* 1998; *You Can Thank Me Later* 1998; *Night Ride Home* 1999
Burton, Frederick *The Big Trail* 1930; *An American Tragedy* 1931; *One Way Passage* 1932; *The Wet Parade* 1932; *The Man from Dakota* 1940
Burton, Kate *Big Trouble in Little China* 1986; *Love Matters* 1993; *August* 1995; *Ellen Foster* 1997
Burton, LeVar *Star Trek: First Contact* 1996; *Star Trek: Insurrection* 1998
Burton, Martin *Ladies' Man* 1931; *When Ladies Meet* 1933
Burton, Norman aka **Burton, Normann** *Diamonds Are Forever* 1971; *Save the Tiger* 1973; *The Terminal Man* 1974; *The Reincarnation of Peter Proud* 1975; *The Gumball Rally* 1976; *Scorchy* 1976; *Mausoleum* 1983; *Crimes of Passion* 1984; *Bloodsport* 1988
Burton, Peter *What the Butler Saw* 1950; *The Wooden Horse* 1950; *Dr No* 1962
Burton, Richard *The Last Days of Dolwyn* 1949; *Now Barabbas Was a Robber* 1949; *Waterfront* 1950; *Green Grow the Rushes* 1951; *My Cousin Rachel* 1952; *The Desert Rats* 1953; *The Robe* 1953; *The Rains of Ranchipur* 1955; *Prince of Players* 1955; *Alexander the Great* 1956; *Bitter Victory* 1957; *Sea Wife* 1957; *Look Back in Anger* 1959; *The Bramble Bush* 1960; *Ice Palace* 1960; *A Midsummer Night's Dream* 1961; *The Longest Day* 1962; *Cleopatra* 1963; *The VIPs* 1963; *Becket* 1964; *The Night of the Iguana* 1964; *The Sandpiper* 1965; *The Spy Who Came in from the Cold* 1965; *What's New, Pussycat?* 1965; *Who's Afraid of Virginia Woolf?* 1966; *The Comedians* 1967; *Doctor Faustus* 1967; *The Taming of the Shrew* 1967; *Boom* 1968; *Candy* 1968; *Anne of the Thousand Days* 1969; *Staircase* 1969; *Where Eagles Dare* 1969; *Raid on Rommel* 1971; *Villain* 1971; *Under Milk Wood* 1971; *The Assassination of Trotsky* 1972; *Bluebeard* 1972; *Hammersmith Is Out* 1972; *Massacre in Rome* 1973; *Brief Encounter* 1974; *The Klansman* 1974; *The Voyage* 1974; *Equus* 1977; *Exorcist II: The Heretic* 1977; *Absolution* 1978; *Breakthrough* 1978; *The Medusa Touch* 1978; *The Wild Geese* 1978; *Lovespell* 1979; *Circle of Two* 1980; *Wagner* 1983; *Nineteen Eighty-Four* 1984
Burton, Robert *Above and Beyond* 1952; *Desperate Search* 1952; *Confidentially Connie* 1953; *The Girl Who Had Everything* 1953; *Cry of the Hunted* 1953; *Taza, Son of Cochise* 1954; *A Man Called Peter* 1955; *The Brass Legend* 1956; *I Was a Teenage Frankenstein* 1957; *The Hired Gun* 1957; *The Gallant Hours* 1960
Burton, Tony *Assault on Precinct 13* 1976; *The Bingo Long Travelling All-Stars and Motor Kings* 1976; *Heroes* 1977; *Rocky II* 1979; *Inside Moves: the Guys from Max's Bar* 1980; *Heart of a Champion: the Ray Mancini Story* 1985; *Rocky IV* 1985; *Oceans of Fire* 1986; *You Ruined My Life* 1987; *Rocky V* 1990; *Mission of Justice* 1992
Burton, Wendell *The Sterile Cuckoo* 1969; *Fortune and Men's Eyes* 1971
Burtwell, Frederick *Dr Syn* 1937; *The Silver Fleet* 1943; *I'll Be Your Sweetheart* 1945
Bury, Sean *Friends* 1971; *Paul and Michelle* 1974
Buryak, Zoya *The Cold Summer of 1953* 1987; *The Life and Extraordinary Adventures of Private Ivan Chonkin* 1994; *Checkpoint* 1998
Buscemi, Steve *Parting Glances* 1985; *Heart* 1987; *Kiss Daddy Good Night* 1987; *Heart of Midnight* 1988; *Call Me* 1988; *Bloodhounds of Broadway* 1989; *King of New York* 1989; *Mystery Train* 1989; *New York Stories* 1989; *Slaves of New York* 1989; *Miller's Crossing* 1990; *Barton Fink* 1991; *Billy Bathgate* 1991; *Reservoir Dogs* 1991; *Tales from the Darkside: the Movie* 1991; *Zandalee* 1991; *CrissCross* 1992; *In the Soup* 1992; *Me and the Mob* 1992; *Motherhood* 1993; *Rising Sun* 1993; *The Last Outlaw* 1993; *Twenty Bucks* 1993; *Airheads* 1994; *Floundering* 1994; *Pulp Fiction* 1994; *Somebody to Love* 1994; *Desperado* 1995; *Fargo* 1995; *Kansas City* 1995; *Living in Oblivion* 1995; *Things to Do in Denver When You're Dead* 1995; *Escape from LA* 1996; *Trees Lounge* 1996; *The Search for One-Eye Jimmy* 1996; *The Big Lebowski* 1997; *Con Air* 1997; *The Real Blonde* 1997; *Armageddon* 1998; *The Impostors* 1998; *Big Daddy* 1999; *28 Days* 2000
Busch, Ernst *Kameradschaft* 1931; *Kühle Wampe* 1931
Busch, Mae *Foolish Wives* 1920; *The Unholy Three* 1925; *Fazil* 1928; *Alibi* 1929; *Their First Mistake* 1932; *Sons of the Desert* 1933; *Oliver the Eighth* 1934; *Them Thar Hills!* 1934; *Tit for Tat* 1934; *The Bohemian Girl* 1936
Busey, Gary *The Last American Hero* 1973; *The Lolly-Madonna War* 1973; *Thunderbolt and Lightfoot* 1974; *The Gumball Rally* 1976; *A Star Is Born* 1976; *Big Wednesday* 1978; *The Buddy Holly Story* 1978; *Straight Time* 1978; *Carny* 1980; *Foolin' Around* 1980; *Barbarosa* 1982; *DC Cab* 1983; *Insignificance* 1985; *Silver Bullet* 1985; *Eye of the Tiger* 1986; *Let's Get Harry* 1986; *Lethal Weapon* 1987; *Bulletproof* 1987; *Hider in the House* 1989; *The Neon Empire* 1989; *Act of Piracy* 1990; *Predator 2* 1990; *My Heroes Have Always Been Cowboys* 1991; *Point Break* 1991; *Wild Texas Wind* 1991; *Under Siege* 1992; *Double Suspicion* 1993; *Rookie of the Year* 1993; *Chasers* 1994; *Drop Zone* 1994; *Surviving the Game* 1994; *Acts of Love* 1995; *Man with a Gun*

Off 1997; *City of Angels* 1998; *Snake Eyes* 1998; *8mm* 1999; *Bringing out the Dead* 1999; *Gone in 60 Seconds* 2000

Cagney, James *Blonde Crazy* 1931; *Doorway to Hell* 1931; *The Public Enemy* 1931; *Smart Money* 1931; *Other Men's Women* 1931; *The Crowd Roars* 1932; *Taxi!* 1932; *Footlight Parade* 1933; *Hard to Handle* 1933; *Lady Killer* 1933; *The Mayor of Hell* 1933; *Picture Snatcher* 1933; *He Was Her Man* 1934; *Here Comes the Navy* 1934; *Jimmy the Gent* 1934; *Ceiling Zero* 1935; *Frisco Kid* 1935; *"G" Men* 1935; *A Midsummer Night's Dream* 1935; *Mutiny on the Bounty* 1935; *Devil Dogs of the Air* 1935; *Great Guy* 1936; *Something to Sing About* 1937; *Angels with Dirty Faces* 1938; *Boy Meets Girl* 1938; *Each Dawn I Die* 1939; *The Oklahoma Kid* 1939; *The Roaring Twenties* 1939; *City for Conquest* 1940; *The Fighting 69th* 1940; *Torrid Zone* 1940; *The Bride Came C.O.D.* 1941; *The Strawberry Blonde* 1941; *Captains of the Clouds* 1942; *Yankee Doodle Dandy* 1942; *Johnny Come Lately* 1943; *Blood on the Sun* 1945; *13 Rue Madeleine* 1946; *The Time of Your Life* 1948; *White Heat* 1949; *Kiss Tomorrow Goodbye* 1950; *The West Point Story* 1950; *Come Fill the Cup* 1951; *What Price Glory?* 1952; *A Lion Is in the Streets* 1953; *Love Me or Leave Me* 1955; *Mister Roberts* 1955; *Run for Cover* 1955; *Seven Little Foys* 1955; *Tribute to a Bad Man* 1956; *These Wilder Years* 1956; *Man of a Thousand Faces* 1957; *Never Steal Anything Small* 1959; *Shake Hands with the Devil* 1959; *The Gallant Hours* 1960; *One, Two, Three* 1961; *Arizona Bushwhackers* 1968; *Ragtime* 1981

Cagney, Jeanne *Yankee Doodle Dandy* 1942; *The Time of Your Life* 1948; *Don't Bother to Knock* 1952; *A Lion Is in the Streets* 1953; *Man of a Thousand Faces* 1957; *Quicksand* 1959

Cagney, William aka **Cagney, Bill** *Ace of Aces* 1933; *Palooka* 1934; *Kiss Tomorrow Goodbye* 1950

Cahill, Barry *Daddy's Gone A-Hunting* 1969; *Coffy* 1973; *Grand Theft Auto* 1977

Caicedo, Franklin *The Color of Destiny* 1986; *The Voyage* 1991

Cain, Dean *The Stone Boy* 1984; *Best Men* 1997; *Dogboys* 1998; *Futuresport* 1998

Caine, Henry *The Ghost Train* 1931; *Number Seventeen* 1932

Caine, Howard *The Man from the Diner's Club* 1963; *Watermelon Man* 1970

Caine, Michael *A Hill in Korea* 1956; *Sailor Beware!* 1956; *How to Murder a Rich Uncle* 1957; *The Steel Bayonet* 1957; *The Key* 1958; *Passport to Shame* 1958; *Carve Her Name with Pride* 1958; *Danger Within* 1958; *The Two-Headed Spy* 1958; *Foxhole in Cairo* 1960; *The Bulldog Breed* 1960; *The Day the Earth Caught Fire* 1961; *The Wrong Arm of the Law* 1962; *Solo for Sparrow* 1962; *Zulu* 1964; *The Ipcress File* 1965; *Alfie* 1966; *Funeral in Berlin* 1966; *Gambit* 1966; *The Wrong Box* 1966; *Billion Dollar Brain* 1967; *Hurry Sundown* 1967; *Woman Times Seven* 1967; *Deadfall* 1968; *The Magus* 1968; *Battle of Britain* 1969; *The Italian Job* 1969; *Play Dirty* 1969; *Simon, Simon* 1970; *Too Late the Hero* 1970; *Get Carter* 1971; *Kidnapped* 1971; *The Last Valley* 1971; *X, Y and Zee* 1971; *Pulp* 1972; *Sleuth* 1972; *The Black Windmill* 1974; *The Marseilles Contract* 1974; *The Man Who Would Be King* 1975; *The Romantic Englishwoman* 1975; *Peeper* 1975; *The Wilby Conspiracy* 1975; *The Eagle Has Landed* 1976; *Harry and Walter Go to New York* 1976; *A Bridge Too Far* 1977; *California Suite* 1978; *Silver Bears* 1978; *The Swarm* 1978; *Ashanti* 1979; *Beyond the Poseidon Adventure* 1979; *Dressed to Kill* 1980; *The Island* 1980; *Escape to Victory* 1981; *The Hand* 1981; *Deathtrap* 1982; *Educating Rita* 1983; *The Honorary Consul* 1983; *Blame It on Rio* 1984; *The Jigsaw Man* 1984; *The Holcroft Covenant* 1985; *Water* 1985; *Half Moon Street* 1986; *Hannah and Her Sisters* 1986; *Mona Lisa* 1986; *Sweet Liberty* 1986; *The Whistle Blower* 1986; *The Fourth Protocol* 1987; *Hero* 1987; *Jaws the Revenge* 1987; *Surrender* 1987; *Dirty Rotten Scoundrels* 1988; *Jack the Ripper* 1988; *Without a Clue* 1988; *Jekyll and Hyde* 1989; *Bullseye!* 1990; *Mr Destiny* 1990; *A Shock to the System* 1990; *Blue Ice* 1992; *The Muppet Christmas Carol* 1992; *Noises Off* 1992; *On Deadly Ground* 1994; *Bullet to Beijing* 1995; *Midnight in St Petersburg* 1995; *Blood and Wine* 1996; *Mandela and de Klerk* 1997; *Little Voice* 1998; *Curtain Call* 1998; *The Cider House Rules* 1999

Cairney, John *Windom's Way* 1957; *A Night to Remember* 1958; *Operation Bullshine* 1959; *The Devil-Ship Pirates* 1964

Calamai, Clara *Ossessione* 1942; *White Nights* 1957

Calder, David *Defence of the Realm* 1985; *American Friends* 1991

Calderon, Paul aka **Calderone, Paul** *King of New York* 1989; *Sea of Love* 1989; *Bad Lieutenant* 1992; *CrissCross* 1992; *The Addiction* 1994; *Sweet Nothing* 1995; *Dark Angel* 1996; *Oxygen* 1999

Caldicot, Richard *One Good Turn* 1954; *The Fool* 1990

Caldwell, L Scott *God Bless the Child* 1988; *Dangerous Passion* 1990

Calfa, Don *Return of the Living Dead* 1985; *Weekend at Bernie's* 1989; *Chopper Chicks in Zombietown* 1990; *Me, Myself and I* 1992

Calfan, Nicole *The Burglars* 1971; *Max Mon Amour* 1986

Calhern, Louis *Blonde Crazy* 1931; *Duck Soup* 1933; *20,000 Years in Sing Sing* 1933; *The Affairs of Cellini* 1934; *The Count of Monte Cristo* 1934; *The Arizonian* 1935; *The Last Days of Pompeii* 1935; *The Gorgeous Hussy* 1936; *Fast Company* 1938; *Up in Arms* 1944; *Notorious* 1946; *Arch of Triumph* 1948; *The Red Pony* 1949; *The Red Danube* 1949; *Annie Get Your Gun* 1950; *The Asphalt Jungle* 1950; *Devil's Doorway* 1950; *A Life of Her Own* 1950; *The Magnificent Yankee* 1950; *Nancy Goes to Rio* 1950; *The Man with a Cloak* 1951; *The Prisoner of Zenda* 1952; *We're Not Married* 1952; *Julius Caesar* 1953; *Latin Lovers* 1953; *Confidentially Connie* 1953; *Executive Suite* 1954; *The Student Prince* 1954; *Men of the Fighting Lady* 1954; *Rhapsody* 1954; *Betrayed* 1954; *Athena* 1954; *The Blackboard Jungle* 1955; *The Prodigal* 1955; *High Society* 1956; *Forever, Darling* 1956

Calhoun, Monica *Bagdad Café* 1987; *The Players Club* 1998; *The Best Man* 1999

Calhoun, Rory *The Red House* 1947; *A Ticket to Tomahawk* 1950; *I'd Climb the Highest Mountain* 1951; *Meet Me after the Show* 1951; *Way of a Gaucho* 1952; *With a Song in My Heart* 1952; *How to Marry a Millionaire* 1953; *Powder River* 1953; *Dawn at Socorro* 1954; *River of No Return* 1954; *The Yellow Tomahawk* 1954; *A Bullet Is Waiting* 1954; *Four Guns to the Border* 1954; *The Looters* 1955; *The Treasure of Pancho Villa* 1955; *The Spoilers* 1955; *Ain't Misbehavin'* 1955; *Raw Edge* 1956; *Red Sundown* 1956; *The Hired Gun* 1957; *The Big Caper* 1957; *The Saga of Hemp Brown* 1958; *The Treasure of Monte Cristo* 1960; *The Colossus of Rhodes* 1961; *A Face in the Rain* 1963; *Apache Uprising* 1965; *Black Spurs* 1965; *Dayton's Devils* 1968; *Love and the Midnight Auto Supply* 1977; *Angel* 1984; *Avenging Angel* 1985; *Hell Comes to Frogtown* 1988; *Bad Jim* 1989; *Pure Country* 1992

Cali, Joseph *Saturday Night Fever* 1977; *The Competition* 1980; *The Lonely Lady* 1983

Call, Brandon *The Richest Cat in the World* 1986; *Blind Fury* 1990

Call, R D *Unconquered* 1989; *Young Guns II* 1990; *Other People's Money* 1991; *Jack Reed: Badge of Honor* 1993; *Waterworld* 1995

Callahan, James *Lady Sings the Blues* 1972; *Outlaw Blues* 1977; *The Burning Bed* 1984; *Copacabana* 1985; *Heart of a Champion: the Ray Mancini Story* 1985

Callan, K *A Touch of Class* 1973; *The Unborn* 1991

Callan, Michael *They Came to Cordura* 1959; *Because They're Young* 1960; *Gidget Goes Hawaiian* 1961; *Mysterious Island* 1961; *Bon Voyage!* 1962; *The Interns* 1962; *The New Interns* 1964; *Cat Ballou* 1965; *You Must Be Joking!* 1965; *The Magnificent Seven Ride!* 1972; *Frasier, the Sensuous Lion* 1973; *Lepke* 1975; *The Cat and the Canary* 1979; *Freeway* 1988

Callard, Kay *They Who Dare* 1953; *Find the Lady* 1956; *The Flying Scot* 1957; *The Hypnotist* 1957; *Escapement* 1958; *Undercover Girl* 1958

Calleia, Joseph *Public Hero No 1* 1935; *After the Thin Man* 1936; *His Brother's Wife* 1936; *Riffraff* 1936; *Algiers* 1938; *Bad Man of Brimstone* 1938; *Full Confession* 1939; *Golden Boy* 1939; *My Little Chickadee* 1940; *Sundown* 1941; *The Glass Key* 1942; *Jungle Book* 1942; *The Cross of Lorraine* 1943; *The Conspirators* 1944; *Deadline at Dawn* 1946; *Gilda* 1946; *Noose* 1948; *They Passed This Way* 1948; *The Noose Hangs High* 1948; *Branded* 1950; *Captain Carey, USA* 1950; *Valentino* 1951; *The Iron Mistress* 1952; *The Caddy* 1953; *The Treasure of Pancho Villa* 1955; *Underwater!* 1955; *Serenade* 1956; *Hot Blood* 1956; *Wild Is the Wind* 1957; *The Light in the Forest* 1958; *Touch of Evil* 1958; *The Alamo* 1960

Callie, Dayton *The Last Days of Frankie the Fly* 1996; *Executive Target* 1997

Callow, Simon *Amadeus* 1984; *A Room with a View* 1985; *The Good Father* 1986; *Maurice* 1987; *Mr and Mrs Bridge* 1990; *Postcards from the Edge* 1990; *The Crucifer of Blood* 1991; *Soft Top, Hard Shoulder* 1992; *Four Weddings and a Funeral* 1994; *Street Fighter* 1994; *Ace Ventura: When Nature Calls* 1995; *Jefferson in Paris* 1995; *James and the Giant Peach* 1996; *The Scarlet Tunic* 1997; *Bedrooms and Hallways* 1998; *Shakespeare in Love* 1998

Calloway, Cab *International House* 1933; *Stormy Weather* 1943; *St Louis Blues* 1958; *The Blues Brothers* 1980

Caloz, Michael *Whiskers* 1997; *Little Men* 1998

Calthrop, Donald *Blackmail* 1929; *The Ghost Train* 1931; *FP1* 1932; *Rome Express* 1932; *The Clairvoyant* 1934; *The Phantom Light* 1934; *Scrooge* 1935; *Broken Blossoms* 1936; *The Man Who Changed His Mind* 1936

Calvé, Jean-François *Marguerite de la Nuit* 1955; *The Bride Is Much Too Beautiful* 1956; *Shock Treatment* 1973

Calvert, Bill *Six Weeks* 1982; *CHUD II: Bud the Chud* 1989; *Heart and Souls* 1993

Calvert, Phyllis *Let George Do It* 1940; *Neutral Port* 1940; *Kipps* 1941; *The Young Mr Pitt* 1942; *Uncensored* 1942; *The Man in Grey* 1943; *Fanny by Gaslight* 1944; *Madonna of the Seven Moons* 1944; *Two Thousand Women* 1944; *They Were Sisters* 1945; *The Magic Bow* 1946; *Men of Two Worlds* 1946; *The Root of All Evil* 1946; *Broken Journey* 1948; *Appointment with Danger* 1950; *Mr Denning Drives North* 1951; *Mandy* 1952; *The Net* 1953; *Child in the House* 1956; *It's Never Too Late* 1956; *Indiscreet* 1958; *A Lady Mislaid* 1958; *Oscar Wilde* 1959; *The Battle of the Villa Fiorita* 1964; *Twisted Nerve* 1968; *Oh! What a Lovely War* 1969; *The Walking Stick* 1970

Calvet, Corinne *Rope of Sand* 1949; *When Willie Comes Marching Home* 1950; *My Friend Irma Goes West* 1950; *On the Riviera* 1951; *Sailor Beware* 1951; *Peking Express* 1951; *What Price Glory?* 1952; *Powder River* 1953; *Flight to Tangier* 1953; *So This Is Paris* 1954; *The Far Country* 1955; *Hemingway's Adventures of a Young Man* 1962; *Apache Uprising* 1965

Calvin, Henry *Toby Tyler, or Ten Weeks with a Circus* 1960; *Babes in Toyland* 1961

Calvin, John *Foolin' Around* 1980; *Critters 3* 1991; *Unbecoming Age* 1992; *Dragonworld* 1994

Camacho, Mark *The Myth of the Male Orgasm* 1993; *Fatal Affair* 1998

Camardiel, Roberto *Adios Gringo* 1965; *Django Kill* 1967

Cambridge, Godfrey *Gone Are the Days* 1963; *The President's Analyst* 1967; *The Biggest Bundle of Them All* 1968; *Bye Bye Braverman* 1968; *Cotton Comes to Harlem* 1970; *Watermelon Man* 1970; *Beware! The Blob* 1971; *The Biscuit Eater* 1972; *Friday Foster* 1975; *Whiffs* 1975; *Scott Joplin* 1977

Cameron, Candace *Little Spies* 1986; *Bigfoot* 1987; *Sharon's Secret* 1995; *Visitors of the Night* 1995; *No One Would Tell* 1996; *Kidz in the Wood* 1996

Cameron, Dean *Summer School* 1987; *Men at Work* 1990; *Ski School* 1991; *Sleep with Me* 1994

Cameron, Earl *Pool of London* 1950; *Emergency Call* 1952; *The Woman for Joe* 1955; *Sapphire* 1959; *Flame in the Streets* 1961; *Tarzan's Three Challenges* 1963; *Guns at Batasi* 1964; *A Warm December* 1973

Cameron, Kirk *Like Father, Like Son* 1987; *Listen to Me* 1989; *The Computer Wore Tennis Shoes* 1995

Cameron, Rod *Riding High* 1943; *Frontier Gal* 1945; *Belle Starr's Daughter* 1948; *Cavalry Scout* 1951; *Ride the Man Down* 1952; *Santa Fe Passage* 1955; *Passport to Treason* 1956; *Escapement* 1958; *The Bounty Killer* 1965; *Evel Knievel* 1971

Camilleri, Terry *The Cars That Ate Paris* 1974; *Bill & Ted's Excellent Adventure* 1988; *Encounter at Raven's Gate* 1988

Camp, Colleen *Smile* 1975; *Death Game* 1976; *Love and the Midnight Auto Supply* 1977; *Game of Death* 1978; *They All Laughed* 1981; *Smokey and the Bandit III* 1983; *Joy of Sex* 1984; *DARYL* 1985; *Police Academy 2: Their First Assignment* 1985; *Walk like a Man* 1987; *Addicted to His Love* 1988; *Illegally Yours* 1988; *Track 29* 1988; *Wicked Stepmother* 1989; *Backfield in Motion* 1991; *The Vagrant* 1992; *Unbecoming Age* 1992; *Sliver* 1993; *Die Hard with a Vengeance* 1995; *Suddenly* 1996

Camp, Hamilton *The Perils of Pauline* 1967; *All Night Long* 1981; *Twice upon a Time* 1983; *Meatballs 2* 1984

Campanella, Joseph *The St Valentine's Day Massacre* 1967; *Ben* 1972; *Sky Heist* 1975; *Hangar 18* 1980; *Earthbound* 1981; *My Body, My Child* 1982; *Body Chemistry* 1990; *Terror on Track 9* 1992; *Grizzly Adams: the Treasure of the Bear* 1995; *The Glass Cage* 1996

Campbell, Beatrice *Meet Me at Dawn* 1946; *Silent Dust* 1948; *No Place for Jennifer* 1949; *Now Barabbas Was a Robber* 1949; *Last Holiday* 1950; *The Mudlark* 1950; *Laughter in Paradise* 1951; *The Master of Ballantrae* 1953

Campbell, Bill aka **Campbell, William** *Checkered Flag* 1990; *The Rocketeer* 1991; *Bram Stoker's Dracula* 1992; *Out There* 1995; *Lover's Knot* 1995; *The Brylcreem Boys* 1996; *The Second Jungle Book* 1997

Campbell, Bruce *The Evil Dead* 1983; *Crimewave* 1985; *Evil Dead II* 1987; *Maniac Cop* 1988; *Maniac Cop 2* 1990; *Lunatics: a Love Story* 1991; *Mindwarp* 1992; *Waxwork II: Lost in Time* 1992; *Army of Darkness* 1993; *The Hudsucker Proxy* 1994; *Chase Morran* 1996; *Tornado!* 1996; *The Love Bug* 1997; *Blaze of Glory* 1997

Campbell, Cheryl *Hawk the Slayer* 1980; *McVicar* 1980; *Chariots of Fire* 1981; *Greystoke: the Legend of Tarzan, Lord of the Apes* 1984; *The Shooting Party* 1984

Campbell, Christian *Born to Run* 1993; *City Boy* 1994; *Trick* 1999

Campbell, Colin *The Leather Boys* 1963; *Saturday Night Out* 1963; *The High Bright Sun* 1965

Carey, Ron *The Out of Towners* 1970; *Dynamite Chicken* 1971; *Silent Movie* 1976; *High Anxiety* 1977; *Fatso* 1979; *History of the World Part 1* 1981
Carey, Timothy *aka* **Carey, Timothy Agoglia** *White Witch Doctor* 1953; *Paths of Glory* 1957; *Waterhole #3* 1967; *The Long Ride Home* 1967; *Head* 1968; *Minnie and Moskowitz* 1971; *The Outfit* 1973; *The Killing of a Chinese Bookie* 1976
Cargill, Patrick *The Hi-Jackers* 1963; *A Countess from Hong Kong* 1967; *Inspector Clouseau* 1968; *Every Home Should Have One* 1970; *Up Pompeii* 1971; *Father Dear Father* 1972; *The Picture Show Man* 1977
Carhart, Timothy *Pink Cadillac* 1989; *Thelma & Louise* 1991; *Quicksand: No Escape* 1992; *Beverly Hills Cop III* 1994; *Candyman II: Farewell to the Flesh* 1995; *Black Sheep* 1996; *In the Line of Duty: Smoke Jumpers* 1996; *Before He Wakes* 1998
Carides, Gia *Bliss* 1985; *Backlash* 1986; *Daydream Believer* 1991; *Strictly Ballroom* 1992; *Paperback Romance* 1994; *Bad Company* 1995; *Brilliant Lies* 1996; *Lifebreath* 1997; *Austin Powers: The Spy Who Shagged Me* 1999
Carides, Zoe *Death in Brunswick* 1990; *Brilliant Lies* 1996
Caridi, Carmine *The Gambler* 1974; *Prince of the City* 1981; *Life Stinks* 1991; *Top Dog* 1995
Cariou, Len *A Little Night Music* 1977; *The Four Seasons* 1981; *Surviving* 1985; *Lady in White* 1988; *The Sea Wolf* 1993; *Witness to the Execution* 1994; *Derby* 1995; *The Man in the Attic* 1995; *Never Talk to Strangers* 1995; *The Summer of Ben Tyler* 1996
Carle, Richard *Fireman Save My Child* 1932; *The Bride Comes Home* 1935; *Anything Goes* 1936; *Spendthrift* 1936; *I'll Take Romance* 1937; *Remember?* 1939
Carleton, Claire *Witness to Murder* 1954; *The Buster Keaton Story* 1957
Carlin, George *With Six You Get Eggroll* 1968; *Car Wash* 1976; *Outrageous Fortune* 1987; *Bill & Ted's Excellent Adventure* 1988; *Justin Case* 1988; *Working Trash* 1990; *Bill & Ted's Bogus Journey* 1991; *The Prince of Tides* 1991; *Dogma* 1999
Carlin, Gloria *The Hot Touch* 1982; *So Proudly We Hail* 1990
Carlin, Lynn *Faces* 1968; *Silent Night, Lonely Night* 1969; *Taking Off* 1971; *Wild Rovers* 1971; *Baxter* 1973; *Dawn: Portrait of a Teenage Runaway* 1976
Carlini, Paolo *Roman Holiday* 1953; *It Started in Naples* 1960; *Chronicle of Anna Magdalena Bach* 1968
Carlisi, Olimpia *Casanova* 1976; *The Tragedy of a Ridiculous Man* 1981
Carlisle, Anne *Liquid Sky* 1982; *Blind Alley* 1984
Carlisle, Kitty *Murder at the Vanities* 1934; *She Loves Me Not* 1934; *A Night at the Opera* 1935
Carlisle, Mary *Palooka* 1934; *Kind Lady* 1935; *Doctor Rhythm* 1938; *Dance, Girl, Dance* 1940; *Baby Face Morgan* 1942
Carlson, Karen *The Candidate* 1972; *Matilda* 1978; *The Octagon* 1980
Carlson, Les *Shoot* 1976; *Videodrome* 1982; *The Fly* 1986
Carlson, Richard *The Duke of West Point* 1938; *Dancing Co-Ed* 1939; *The Ghost Breakers* 1940; *Too Many Girls* 1940; *No, No, Nanette* 1940; *The Howards of Virginia* 1940; *Back Street* 1941; *Hold That Ghost* 1941; *The Little Foxes* 1941; *Fly by Night* 1942; *White Cargo* 1942; *The Man from Down Under* 1943; *Presenting Lily Mars* 1943; *Young Ideas* 1943; *King Solomon's Mines* 1950; *The Sound of Fury* 1950; *The Blue Veil* 1951; *A Millionaire for Christy* 1951; *Valentino* 1951; *Retreat, Hell!* 1952; *All I Desire* 1953; *It Came from Outer Space* 1953; *Seminole* 1953; *The Magnetic Monster* 1953; *Creature from the Black Lagoon* 1954; *Bengazi* 1955; *The Last Command* 1955; *The Helen Morgan Story* 1957; *Della* 1965; *Kid Rodelo* 1966; *The Power* 1968; *The Valley of Gwangi* 1969
Carlson, Veronica *Dracula Has Risen from the Grave* 1968; *Frankenstein Must Be Destroyed* 1969; *The Horror of Frankenstein* 1970; *The Ghoul* 1975
Carlyle, Robert *Silent Scream* 1989; *Riff-Raff* 1991; *Priest* 1994; *Trainspotting* 1995; *Go Now* 1995; *Carla's Song* 1996; *Face* 1997; *The Full Monty* 1997; *Plunkett & Macleane* 1999; *Ravenous* 1999; *Angela's Ashes* 1999; *The World Is Not Enough* 1999; *The Beach* 2000
Carmel, Roger C *Goodbye Charlie* 1964; *Alvarez Kelly* 1966; *Gambit* 1966; *The Venetian Affair* 1966; *Skullduggery* 1969; *Myra Breckinridge* 1970; *Breezy* 1973; *Thunder and Lightning* 1977; *Hardly Working* 1981
Carmen, Julie *Gloria* 1980; *Night of the Juggler* 1980; *Last Plane Out* 1983; *Blue City* 1986; *Fright Night Part 2* 1988; *The Milagro Beanfield War* 1988; *The Penitent* 1988; *Gore Vidal's Billy the Kid* 1989; *Manhunt: Search for the Night Stalker* 1989; *The Neon Empire* 1989; *Paint It Black* 1989; *Finding the Way Home* 1991; *Cold Heaven* 1992; *In the Mouth of Madness* 1994; *Seduced by Evil* 1994
Carmet, Jean *The Vanishing Corporal* 1962; *The Little Theatre of Jean Renoir* 1969; *The Tall Blond Man with One Black Shoe* 1972; *Black and White in Color* 1976; *Violette Nozière* 1977; *Buffet Froid* 1979; *Circle of Deceit* 1981; *Les Misérables* 1982; *Merci la Vie* 1991; *Germinal* 1993
Carmichael, Hoagy *To Have and Have Not* 1944; *Johnny Angel* 1945; *The Best Years of Our Lives* 1946; *Night Song* 1947; *Young Man with a Horn* 1950; *The Las Vegas Story* 1951; *Belles on Their Toes* 1952; *Timberjack* 1955
Carmichael, Ian *The Colditz Story* 1954; *Betrayed* 1954; *Simon and Laura* 1955; *Storm over the Nile* 1955; *The Big Money* 1956; *Brothers in Law* 1956; *Private's Progress* 1956; *Lucky Jim* 1957; *Happy Is the Bride* 1958; *I'm All Right Jack* 1959; *Left, Right and Centre* 1959; *Light Up the Sky* 1960; *School for Scoundrels* 1960; *Double Bunk* 1961; *The Amorous Prawn* 1962; *Heavens Above!* 1963; *Hide and Seek* 1963; *Smashing Time* 1967; *From beyond the Grave* 1973; *The Lady Vanishes* 1979; *Diamond Skulls* 1989
Carminati, Tullio *One Night of Love* 1934; *Gallant Lady* 1934; *London Melody* 1937; *Roman Holiday* 1953; *A Breath of Scandal* 1960; *The Swordsman of Siena* 1962
Carmine, Michael **batteries not included* 1987; *Leviathan* 1989
Carnera, Primo *The Prizefighter and the Lady* 1933; *A Kid for Two Farthings* 1955; *Hercules Unchained* 1959
Carney, Alan *Mr Lucky* 1943; *Girl Rush* 1944; *Step Lively* 1944; *Li'l Abner* 1959
Carney, Art *The Yellow Rolls-Royce* 1964; *The Snoop Sisters* 1972; *Harry and Tonto* 1974; *Katherine* 1975; *WW and the Dixie Dancekings* 1975; *Won Ton Ton, the Dog Who Saved Hollywood* 1976; *The Late Show* 1977; *House Calls* 1978; *Defiance* 1979; *Going in Style* 1979; *Sunburn* 1979; *Fighting Back* 1980; *Roadie* 1980; *Steel* 1980; *Take This Job and Shove It* 1981; *Better Late Than Never* 1983; *Firestarter* 1984; *The Naked Face* 1984; *The Night They Saved Christmas* 1984; *Izzy and Moe* 1985; *The Blue Yonder* 1985; *Where Pigeons Go to Die* 1990; *Last Action Hero* 1993
Carney, George *Love on the Dole* 1941; *In Which We Serve* 1942; *I Know Where I'm Going* 1945; *Good Time Girl* 1948
Carnovsky, Morris *The City* 1939; *Edge of Darkness* 1943; *Address Unknown* 1944; *The Master Race* 1944; *Cornered* 1945; *Rhapsody in Blue* 1945; *Our Vines Have Tender Grapes* 1945; *Dead Reckoning* 1947; *Dishonored Lady* 1947; *Gun Crazy* 1949; *Thieves' Highway* 1949; *Cyrano de Bergerac* 1950; *The Second Woman* 1951; *The Gambler* 1974
Carol, Cindy *Gidget Goes to Rome* 1963; *Dear Brigitte* 1966
Carol, Joan *Mr Moto's Last Warning* 1939; *Ghost Ship* 1952
Carol, Martine *Les Belles de Nuit* 1952; *Secrets d'Alcove* 1954; *Madame du Barry* 1954; *The Diary of Major Thompson* 1955; *Lola Montès* 1955; *Nana* 1955; *Action of the Tiger* 1957; *Ten Seconds to Hell* 1959; *The Battle of Austerlitz* 1960; *Violent Summer* 1961
Caron, Leslie *An American in Paris* 1951; *The Man with a Cloak* 1951; *Glory Alley* 1952; *Lili* 1953; *The Story of Three Loves* 1953; *Daddy Long Legs* 1955; *The Glass Slipper* 1955; *Gaby* 1956; *The Doctor's Dilemma* 1958; *Gigi* 1958; *The Man Who Understood Women* 1959; *The Battle of Austerlitz* 1960; *The Subterraneans* 1960; *Fanny* 1961; *Guns of Darkness* 1962; *The L-Shaped Room* 1962; *Father Goose* 1964; *A Very Special Favor* 1965; *Is Paris Burning?* 1966; *Promise Her Anything* 1966; *Madron* 1970; *The Man Who Loved Women* 1977; *Valentino* 1977; *Goldengirl* 1979; *The Contract* 1980; *Imperative* 1982; *Dangerous Moves* 1984; *Courage Mountain* 1989; *Damage* 1992; *Funny Bones* 1994; *The Reef* 1996; *Let It Be Me* 1998
Carotenuto, Memmo *Umberto D* 1952; *Bread, Love and Dreams* 1953; *Big Deal on Madonna Street* 1958
Carpenter, David *Crimes of the Heart* 1986; *Amelia Earhart: the Final Flight* 1994
Carpenter, Ken *Spirit of the Eagle* 1991; *Hellraiser III: Hell on Earth* 1992
Carpenter, Paul *Face the Music* 1954; *The Young Lovers* 1954; *A Stranger Came Home* 1954; *The Hornet's Nest* 1955; *Stock Car* 1955; *Behind the Headlines* 1956; *Fire Maidens from Outer Space* 1956; *The Hypnotist* 1957; *No Road Back* 1957; *Undercover Girl* 1958; *Intent to Kill* 1958
Carpentieri, Renato *Open Doors* 1990; *Puerto Escondido* 1992; *The Stolen Children* 1992
Carr, Alexander *The Death Kiss* 1933; *Christmas in July* 1940
Carr, Darleen *The Jungle Book* 1967; *The Beguiled* 1971; *Runaway!* 1973; *Piranha* 1996
Carr (1), Jane *Lord Edgware Dies* 1934; *Those Were the Days* 1934; *The Lad* 1935
Carr (2), Jane *The Prime of Miss Jean Brodie* 1969; *Neil Simon's London Suite* 1996
Carr, Marian *San Quentin* 1946; *The Devil Thumbs a Ride* 1947; *World for Ransom* 1954
Carr, Mary *Lights of New York* 1928; *Kept Husbands* 1931; *Pack Up Your Troubles* 1932
Carr, Paul *Posse from Hell* 1961; *Ben* 1972; *Executive Action* 1973
Carradine, David *The Violent Ones* 1967; *The Good Guys and the Bad Guys* 1969; *Young Billy Young* 1969; *Macho Callahan* 1970; *The McMasters* 1970; *Boxcar Bertha* 1972; *Kung Fu* 1972; *Death Race 2000* 1975; *Bound for Glory* 1976; *Cannonball* 1976; *The Serpent's Egg* 1977; *Thunder and Lightning* 1977; *Deathsport* 1978; *Fast Charlie: the Moonbeam Rider* 1978; *Gray Lady Down* 1978; *Cloud Dancer* 1980; *The Long Riders* 1980; *Americana* 1981; *Q – the Winged Serpent* 1982; *Trick or Treats* 1982; *Lone Wolf McQuade* 1983; *The Warrior and the Sorceress* 1983; *Oceans of Fire* 1986; *POW the Escape* 1986; *Armed Response* 1986; *Beauty and Denise* 1989; *Bird on a Wire* 1990; *Midnight Fear* 1990; *Think Big* 1990; *Deadly Surveillance* 1991; *Animal Instincts* 1992; *Brotherhood of the Gun* 1992; *Roadside Prophets* 1992; *Waxwork II: Lost in Time* 1992; *Double Trouble* 1992; *Distant Justice* 1992; *Lost Treasure of Dos Santos* 1997; *Last Stand at Saber River* 1997; *Jailbreak* 1997; *The New Swiss Family Robinson* 1999
Carradine, John *Mary of Scotland* 1936; *The Prisoner of Shark Island* 1936; *White Fang* 1936; *Winterset* 1936; *Captains Courageous* 1937; *The Hurricane* 1937; *The Last Gangster* 1937; *Nancy Steele Is Missing* 1937; *Thank You, Mr Moto* 1937; *This Is My Affair* 1937; *Danger – Love at Work* 1937; *Alexander's Ragtime Band* 1938; *Four Men and a Prayer* 1938; *International Settlement* 1938; *Kentucky Moonshine* 1938; *Kidnapped* 1938; *Of Human Hearts* 1938; *Submarine Patrol* 1938; *Drums along the Mohawk* 1939; *Five Came Back* 1939; *Frontier Marshal* 1939; *The Hound of the Baskervilles* 1939; *Jesse James* 1939; *Mr Moto's Last Warning* 1939; *Stagecoach* 1939; *The Three Musketeers* 1939; *Brigham Young* 1940; *Chad Hanna* 1940; *The Grapes of Wrath* 1940; *The Return of Frank James* 1940; *Blood and Sand* 1941; *Man Hunt* 1941; *Swamp Water* 1941; *Western Union* 1941; *Son of Fury* 1942; *Whispering Ghosts* 1942; *Reunion in France* 1942; *Hitler's Madman* 1943; *The Adventures of Mark Twain* 1944; *Barbary Coast Gent* 1944; *Bluebeard* 1944; *House of Frankenstein* 1944; *Voodoo Man* 1944; *Captain Kidd* 1945; *Fallen Angel* 1945; *House of Dracula* 1945; *The Private Affairs of Bel Ami* 1947; *Casanova's Big Night* 1954; *Johnny Guitar* 1954; *Thunder Pass* 1954; *The Female Jungle* 1955; *The Kentuckian* 1955; *Stranger on Horseback* 1955; *The Ten Commandments* 1956; *The Black Sleep* 1956; *The True Story of Jesse James* 1957; *The Unearthly* 1957; *Hell Ship Mutiny* 1957; *Showdown at Boot Hill* 1958; *The Cosmic Man* 1959; *The Oregon Trail* 1959; *Tarzan the Magnificent* 1960; *Sex Kittens Go to College* 1960; *The Man Who Shot Liberty Valance* 1962; *The Patsy* 1964; *The Hostage* 1966; *Munster, Go Home!* 1966; *Blood of Dracula's Castle* 1967; *The Good Guys and the Bad Guys* 1969; *The Trouble with Girls* 1969; *The McMasters* 1970; *Myra Breckinridge* 1970; *The Seven Minutes* 1971; *Shinbone Alley* 1971; *Boxcar Bertha* 1972; *Everything You Always Wanted to Know about Sex (But Were Afraid to Ask)* 1972; *Silent Night, Bloody Night* 1972; *The House of Seven Corpses* 1973; *The Night Strangler* 1973; *Terror in the Wax Museum* 1973; *The Killer inside Me* 1975; *Shock Waves* 1975; *Death at Love House* 1976; *The Last Tycoon* 1976; *Crash!* 1977; *Golden Rendezvous* 1977; *The Sentinel* 1977; *Satan's Cheerleaders* 1977; *The White Buffalo* 1977; *Cruise Missile* 1978; *The Monster Club* 1980; *The Howling* 1981; *The Nesting* 1981; *The Secret of NIMH* 1982; *The Scarecrow* 1982; *House of the Long Shadows* 1983; *Monster in the Closet* 1983; *The Ice Pirates* 1984; *Peggy Sue Got Married* 1986; *Buried Alive* 1990
Carradine, Keith *McCabe and Mrs Miller* 1971; *Kung Fu* 1972; *Emperor of the North* 1973; *Idaho Transfer* 1973; *Thieves like Us* 1974; *Nashville* 1975; *Welcome to LA* 1976; *The Duellists* 1977; *Pretty Baby* 1978; *An Almost Perfect Affair* 1979; *Old Boyfriends* 1979; *The Long Riders* 1980; *Southern Comfort* 1981; *Choose Me* 1984; *Maria's Lovers* 1984; *Scorned and Swindled* 1984; *Blackout* 1985; *Trouble in Mind* 1985; *Eye on the Sparrow* 1987; *Backfire* 1987; *The Moderns* 1988; *My Father, My Son* 1988; *Stones for Ibarra* 1988; *Cold Feet* 1989; *The Revenge of Al Capone* 1989; *Daddy's Dyin'... Who's Got the Will?* 1990; *The Bachelor* 1990; *The Ballad of the Sad Café* 1991; *Payoff* 1991; *CrissCross* 1992; *Andre* 1994; *The Tie That Binds* 1995; *Trial by Fire* 1995; *Wild Bill* 1995; *Special Report: Journey to Mars* 1996; *A Thousand Acres* 1997; *Keeping the Promise* 1997; *Last Stand at Saber River* 1997; *Night Ride Home* 1999
Carradine, Robert *Mean Streets* 1973; *Aloha, Bobby and Rose* 1975; *Cannonball* 1976; *Jackson County Jail* 1976; *Joyride* 1977; *Orca* 1977; *Coming Home* 1978; *The Big Red One* 1980; *The Long Riders* 1980; *Heartaches* 1981; *Wavelength* 1983; *Just the Way You Are* 1984; *Revenge of the Nerds* 1984; *Number One with a Bullet* 1986; *The Liberators* 1987; *Buy & Cell* 1988; *All's Fair* 1989;

1972; *Uptown Saturday Night* 1974; *The Class of Miss MacMichael* 1978; *Go Tell It on the Mountain* 1984; *Dangerous Affair* 1995
Cashman, Michael *I've Gotta Horse* 1965; *X, Y and Zee* 1971; *Unman, Wittering and Zigo* 1971
Casini, Stefania *Blood for Dracula* 1974; *Bad* 1976; *Suspiria* 1976; *The Belly of an Architect* 1987
Casnoff, Philip *G.O.R.P.* 1980; *The Red Spider* 1988; *Special Report: Journey to Mars* 1996
Caso, Mark *Teenage Mutant Ninja Turtles II: the Secret of the Ooze* 1991; *Teenage Mutant Ninja Turtles III* 1992
Caspary, Tina aka **Caspary, Katrina** *Can't Buy Me Love* 1987; *Mac and Me* 1988
Cass, Peggy *The Marrying Kind* 1952; *Auntie Mame* 1958; *Gidget Goes Hawaiian* 1961
Cassavetes, John *Taxi* 1953; *The Night Holds Terror* 1955; *Crime in the Streets* 1956; *Edge of the City* 1957; *Affair in Havana* 1957; *Saddle the Wind* 1958; *Virgin Island* 1958; *The Killers* 1964; *The Dirty Dozen* 1967; *Rosemary's Baby* 1968; *If It's Tuesday, This Must Be Belgium* 1969; *Husbands* 1970; *Capone* 1975; *Mikey and Nicky* 1976; *Two-Minute Warning* 1976; *Opening Night* 1977; *Brass Target* 1978; *The Fury* 1978; *Whose Life Is it Anyway?* 1981; *Tempest* 1982; *Marvin and Tige* 1983; *Love Streams* 1984
Cassavetes, Katherine *Minnie and Moskowitz* 1971; *A Woman under the Influence* 1974
Cassavetes, Nick *Black Moon Rising* 1985; *The Wraith* 1986; *Quiet Cool* 1986; *Class of 1999 II: The Substitute* 1993; *Sins of the Night* 1993; *Sins of Desire* 1993; *Body of Influence* 1993; *Mrs Parker and the Vicious Circle* 1994; *Twogether* 1994; *Just like Dad* 1996; *Face/Off* 1997; *The Astronaut's Wife* 1999
Cassel, Jean-Pierre *The Vanishing Corporal* 1962; *Those Magnificent Men in Their Flying Machines* 1965; *Is Paris Burning?* 1966; *L'Armée des Ombres* 1969; *Oh! What a Lovely War* 1969; *La Rupture* 1970; *The Discreet Charm of the Bourgeoisie* 1972; *Baxter* 1973; *Murder on the Orient Express* 1974; *Doctor Françoise Gailland* 1975; *That Lucky Touch* 1975; *The Twist* 1976; *Who Is Killing the Great Chefs of Europe?* 1978; *From Hell to Victory* 1979; *Mister Frost* 1990; *The Favour, the Watch and the Very Big Fish* 1991; *The Maid* 1991; *Notorious* 1992; *Pétain* 1992; *La Cérémonie* 1995
Cassel, Seymour *Too Late Blues* 1962; *Faces* 1968; *The Revolutionary* 1970; *Minnie and Moskowitz* 1971; *Death Game* 1976; *The Killing of a Chinese Bookie* 1976; *Valentino* 1977; *Scott Joplin* 1977; *The Mountain Men* 1980; *Love Streams* 1984; *Eye of the Tiger* 1986; *Tin Men* 1987; *Plain Clothes* 1988; *Track 29* 1988; *Johnny Be Good* 1988; *Cold Dog Soup* 1989; *Sweet Bird of Youth* 1989; *Dead in the Water* 1991; *Face of a Stranger* 1991; *White Fang* 1991; *Chain of Desire* 1992; *Diary of a Hit Man* 1992; *In the Soup* 1992; *Boiling Point* 1993; *Indecent Proposal* 1993; *Trouble Bound* 1993; *Chasers* 1994; *Hand Gun* 1994; *Tollbooth* 1994; *Dream for an Insomniac* 1996; *This World, Then the Fireworks* 1996; *Rushmore* 1998; *Hoods* 1998
Cassel, Vincent *La Haine* 1995; *L'Appartement* 1996; *Dobermann* 1997; *Guest House Paradiso* 1999
Cassell, Alan *Cathy's Child* 1979; *Harlequin* 1980; *The Settlement* 1982
Cassell, Wally *The Story of GI Joe* 1945; *Saigon* 1948; *Sands of Iwo Jima* 1949; *White Heat* 1949; *We Were Strangers* 1949; *Princess of the Nile* 1954; *The Come On* 1956; *Until They Sail* 1957
Casseus, Gabriel *New Jersey Drive* 1995; *Get on the Bus* 1996; *Fallen* 1998; *Black Dog* 1998
Cassidy, Elaine *The Sun, the Moon and the Stars* 1995; *Felicia's Journey* 1999
Cassidy, Jack *Look in Any Window* 1961; *Bunny O'Hare* 1971; *The Phantom of Hollywood* 1974; *The Eiger Sanction* 1975; *WC Fields and Me* 1976
Cassidy, Joanna *The Outfit* 1973; *Bank Shot* 1974; *The Late Show* 1977; *Stunts* 1977; *The Glove* 1978; *Night Games* 1979; *Under Fire* 1983; *Club Paradise* 1986; *A Father's Revenge* 1987; *The Fourth Protocol* 1987; *Nightmare at Bitter Creek* 1988; *1969* 1988; *Who Framed Roger Rabbit* 1988; *The Package* 1989; *May Wine* 1990; *Where the Heart Is* 1990; *Wheels of Terror* 1990; *Don't Tell Mom the Babysitter's Dead* 1991; *Live! From Death Row* 1992; *Taking Back My Life* 1992; *Barbarians at the Gate* 1993; *Criminal Passion* 1995; *Sleep, Baby, Sleep* 1995; *Vampire in Brooklyn* 1995; *Eye of the Stalker* 1995; *Chain Reaction* 1996; *Loved* 1996; *The Second Civil War* 1997; *Executive Power* 1998
Cassidy, Patrick *Something in Common* 1986; *Love at Stake* 1987; *Longtime Companion* 1990
Cassidy, Ted *Genesis II* 1973; *The Slams* 1973; *Planet Earth* 1974; *Goin' Coconuts* 1978
Casson, Lewis *Escape* 1930; *Crime on the Hill* 1933
Castaldi, Jean-Pierre *French Connection II* 1975; *Le Cop II* 1989; *A Touch of Adultery* 1992
Castel, Lou *Fists in the Pocket* 1965; *A Bullet for the General* 1966; *Kill and Pray* 1968; *Beware of a Holy Whore* 1970; *Nada* 1974; *Killer Nun* 1978; *Trauma* 1983; *Treasure Island* 1991
Castellaneta, Dan *Working Trash* 1990; *The Return of Jafar* 1994; *My Giant* 1998
Castellano, Richard *Lovers and Other Strangers* 1970; *The Godfather* 1972; *Night of the Juggler* 1980
Castellanos, Vincent *The Crow: City of Angels* 1996; *Anaconda* 1997
Castellitto, Sergio *The Big Blue* 1988; *Three Sisters* 1988; *The Starmaker* 1994; *Portraits Chinois* 1996
Castello, Don *The New Adventures of Tarzan* 1935; *Tarzan and the Green Goddess* 1938
Castelnuovo, Nino *The Umbrellas of Cherbourg* 1964; *A Pain in the A...!* 1973; *Loving in the Rain* 1974
Castelot, Jacques *Nana* 1955; *One Night at the Music Hall* 1956
Castile, Christopher *Beethoven* 1992; *Beethoven's 2nd* 1993
Castillo, Enrique aka **Castillo, Enrique J** *Borderline* 1980; *Blood In Blood Out* 1992; *The Hi-Lo Country* 1998
Castillo, Gloria *Invasion of the Saucer Men* 1957; *Reform School Girl* 1957; *Teenage Monster* 1958
Castle, Don *Out West with the Hardys* 1938; *Wake Island* 1942; *The Big Land* 1957
Castle, John *Blow Up* 1966; *The Lion in Winter* 1968; *Antony and Cleopatra* 1972; *Man of La Mancha* 1972; *Eagle's Wing* 1978; *Dealers* 1989; *The Crucifer of Blood* 1991; *RoboCop 3* 1993; *Sparrow* 1993
Castle, Mary *The Lawless Breed* 1952; *Gunsmoke* 1953; *The Jailbreakers* 1960
Castle, Peggie *Payment on Demand* 1951; *The Prince Who Was a Thief* 1951; *Invasion USA* 1952; *I, the Jury* 1953; *The Yellow Tomahawk* 1954; *The Long Wait* 1954; *Tall Man Riding* 1955; *Miracle in the Rain* 1956; *The Oklahoma Woman* 1956; *Seven Hills of Rome* 1957; *Beginning of the End* 1957
Castle, Roy *Dr Terror's House of Horrors* 1964; *Dr Who and the Daleks* 1965; *The Plank* 1967; *Carry On Up the Khyber* 1968; *Legend of the Werewolf* 1974
Cater, John *Loot* 1970; *Captain Kronos: Vampire Hunter* 1972; *Rising Damp* 1980
Cates, Georgina *An Awfully Big Adventure* 1994; *Frankie Starlight* 1995; *Stiff Upper Lips* 1997; *Clay Pigeons* 1998; *A Soldier's Sweetheart* 1998
Cates, Phoebe *Fast Times at Ridgemont High* 1982; *Paradise* 1982; *Private School* 1983; *Gremlins* 1984; *Date with an Angel* 1987; *Bright Lights, Big City* 1988; *Shag* 1988; *Heart of Dixie* 1989; *Gremlins 2: the New Batch* 1990; *Drop Dead Fred* 1991; *Bodies, Rest and Motion* 1993; *Princess Caraboo* 1994
Catillon, Brigitte *La Lectrice* 1988; *Un Coeur en Hiver* 1992; *Artemisia* 1997
Catlett, Mary Jo *Where the Ladies Go* 1980; *Battling for Baby* 1992; *Bram Stoker's Legend of the Mummy* 1998
Catlett, Walter *The Front Page* 1931; *Rain* 1932; *Rockabye* 1932; *Banjo on My Knee* 1936; *Cain and Mabel* 1936; *Every Day's a Holiday* 1937; *On the Avenue* 1937; *Danger – Love at Work* 1937; *Bringing Up Baby* 1938; *Going Places* 1938; *Zaza* 1939; *Change of Heart* 1943; *His Butler's Sister* 1943; *I'll Be Yours* 1947; *The Boy with Green Hair* 1948
Caton, Juliette *The Last Temptation of Christ* 1988; *Courage Mountain* 1989
Caton, Michael *Monkey Grip* 1983; *The Castle* 1997; *The Echo of Thunder* 1998
Cattrall, Kim *Tribute* 1980; *Porky's* 1981; *Ticket to Heaven* 1981; *Police Academy* 1984; *City Limits* 1985; *Hold-Up* 1985; *Turk 182!* 1985; *Big Trouble in Little China* 1986; *Mannequin* 1987; *Masquerade* 1988; *Midnight Crossing* 1988; *Palais Royale* 1988; *The Return of the Musketeers* 1989; *The Bonfire of the Vanities* 1990; *Honeymoon Academy* 1990; *Miracle in the Wilderness* 1991; *Split Second* 1991; *Star Trek VI: the Undiscovered Country* 1991; *Running Delilah* 1992; *Double Suspicion* 1993; *The Heidi Chronicles* 1995; *Live Nude Girls* 1995; *Op Center* 1995; *Above Suspicion* 1995; *Every Woman's Dream* 1996; *Exception to the Rule* 1996; *Baby Geniuses* 1999; *36 Hours to Die* 1999
Caubère, Philippe *Le Château de Ma Mère* 1990; *La Gloire de Mon Père* 1990
Cauchy, Daniel *Bob Le Flambeur* 1955; *The Gendarme of St Tropez* 1964
Caulfield, Joan *Miss Susie Slagle's* 1945; *Blue Skies* 1946; *Monsieur Beaucaire* 1946; *Dear Ruth* 1947; *The Unsuspected* 1947; *Welcome Stranger* 1947; *The Sainted Sisters* 1948; *Dear Wife* 1949; *The Petty Girl* 1950; *The Rains of Ranchipur* 1955; *Cattle King* 1963; *The Daring Dobermans* 1973; *The Magician* 1973; *Pony Express Rider* 1976
Caulfield, Maxwell *Grease 2* 1982; *The Parade* 1984; *Electric Dreams* 1984; *The Boys Next Door* 1985; *Blue Bayou* 1990; *Project: Alien* 1990; *Animal Instincts* 1992; *Gettysburg* 1993; *Midnight Witness* 1993; *No Escape, No Return* 1994; *Inevitable Grace* 1994; *Empire Records* 1995; *Prey of the Jaguar* 1996; *The Real Blonde* 1997
Caussimon, Jean-Roger *French Cancan* 1955; *The House on the Waterfront* 1955
Cavalli, Valeria *Everybody's Fine* 1990; *Double Team* 1997
Cavanagh, Megan *A League of Their Own* 1992; *Robin Hood: Men in Tights* 1993
Cavanagh, Paul aka **Cavanaugh, Paul** *The Devil to Pay* 1930; *The Squaw Man* 1931; *A Bill of Divorcement* 1932; *The Kennel Murder Case* 1933; *Tarzan and His Mate* 1934; *Splendor* 1935; *Goin' to Town* 1935; *I Take This Woman* 1940; *The Case of the Black Parrot* 1941; *Shadows on the Stairs* 1941; *The Hard Way* 1942; *The House of Fear* 1944; *The Scarlet Claw* 1944; *The Woman in Green* 1945; *The Verdict* 1946; *Dishonored Lady* 1947; *Secret beyond the Door* 1948; *Rogues of Sherwood Forest* 1950; *The Strange Door* 1951; *The Mississippi Gambler* 1953; *The All American* 1953; *Khyber Patrol* 1954; *Women without Men* 1956
Cavanaugh, Christine *Babe* 1995; *The Rugrats Movie* 1998
Cavanaugh, Hobart *I Cover the Waterfront* 1933; *Hi, Nellie!* 1934; *The Key* 1934; *Wings in the Dark* 1935; *Cain and Mabel* 1936; *Wife vs Secretary* 1936; *Stage Struck* 1936; *The Great O'Malley* 1937; *Rose of Washington Square* 1939; *Black Angel* 1946; *Up in Central Park* 1948; *A Letter to Three Wives* 1949
Cavanaugh, Michael *The Gauntlet* 1977; *Any Which Way You Can* 1980; *Forced Vengeance* 1982; *Street of Dreams* 1988; *Crash Dive* 1996
Cavazos, Lumi *Like Water for Chocolate* 1993; *Bottle Rocket* 1996
Cave, Nick *Ghosts...of the Civil Dead* 1988; *Johnny Suede* 1991
Caven, Ingrid *Gods of the Plague* 1969; *The American Soldier* 1970; *Mother Küsters Goes to Heaven* 1975; *Satan's Brew* 1976; *Fear of Fear* 1976; *In a Year of 13 Moons* 1978
Cavendish, Nicola *Angel Square* 1990; *The Diviners* 1992; *Air Bud* 1997
Caviezel, James aka **Caviezel, Jim** *The Thin Red Line* 1998; *Ride with the Devil* 1999; *Frequency* 2000
Cavina, Gianni *Noi Tre* 1984; *Christmas Present* 1986
Cawdron, Robert *Street of Shadows* 1953; *Saturday Night and Sunday Morning* 1960
Cawthorn, Joseph *The Taming of the Shrew* 1929; *Love Me Tonight* 1932; *White Zombie* 1932; *Sweet Adeline* 1935; *One Rainy Afternoon* 1936
Cazale, John *The Conversation* 1974; *The Godfather, Part II* 1974; *Dog Day Afternoon* 1975; *The Deer Hunter* 1978
Cazenove, Christopher *Royal Flash* 1975; *East of Elephant Rock* 1976; *Eye of the Needle* 1981; *Heat and Dust* 1982; *Until September* 1984; *Mata Hari* 1985; *Souvenir* 1987; *Three Men and a Little Lady* 1990; *Aces: Iron Eagle III* 1992; *The Proprietor* 1996
Ceccaldi, Daniel *Bed and Board* 1970; *Love in the Afternoon* 1972; *The Pink Telephone* 1975; *The Secret Steak* 1992
Cecchi, Carlo *La Scorta* 1993; *The Turkish Bath* 1996
Cecchini, Mimi *Eat and Run* 1986; *Cadillac Man* 1990
Cecil, Jonathan *Under the Doctor* 1976; *Thirteen at Dinner* 1985; *Dead Man's Folly* 1986; *Agatha Christie's Murder in Three Acts* 1986
Cecil, Nora *The Old-Fashioned Way* 1934; *The Unknown Guest* 1943
Cedar, Jon *The Manitou* 1978; *Death Hunt* 1981; *Interceptor* 1992; *Murder in Mind* 1996
Cederlund, Gosta *Torment* 1944; *It Rains on Our Love* 1946
Cei, Pina *Dark Eyes* 1987; *A Private Affair* 1992
Celano, Guido *Never Take No for an Answer* 1951; *The Man from Cairo* 1953; *The Loves of Three Queens* 1954; *Seven Hills of Rome* 1957
Celarié, Clementine *Betty Blue* 1986; *Le Cri du Coeur* 1994
Cele, Henry *Out of Darkness* 1990; *Curse III: Blood Sacrifice* 1991
Celedonio, Maria *Danger Island* 1992; *Confessions of a Trick Baby* 1999
Celi, Adolfo *That Man from Rio* 1964; *The Agony and the Ecstasy* 1965; *Thunderball* 1965; *The Bobo* 1967; *The Honey Pot* 1967; *Danger: Diabolik* 1967; *Midas Run* 1969; *Fragment of Fear* 1970; *In Search of Gregory* 1970; *Murders in the Rue Morgue* 1971; *Hitler: the Last Ten Days* 1973; *The Italian Connection* 1973; *And Then There Were None* 1974; *The Phantom of Liberty* 1974; *The Next Man* 1976; *Monsignor* 1982
Celinska, Stanislawa *Landscape after Battle* 1970; *Miss Nobody* 1997
Celio, Teco *Three Colours Red* 1994; *The Truce* 1997
Celli, Teresa *Border Incident* 1949; *The Black Hand* 1950; *Right Cross* 1950
Cellier, Antoinette *Music Hath Charms* 1935; *Bees in Paradise* 1943; *The End of the River* 1947
Cellier, Caroline *Killer!* 1969; *Sweet Torture* 1971; *A Pain in the A...!* 1973; *Petit Con* 1984; *Farinelli il Castrato* 1994; *Didier* 1997
Cellier, Frank *The Passing of the Third Floor Back* 1935; *The Man Who Changed His Mind* 1936; *You're In the Army Now* 1936; *Tudor Rose* 1936; *The Black Sheep of Whitehall* 1941; *Love on the Dole* 1941; *Give Us the Moon*

Clarke, Caitlin *Dragonslayer* 1981; *Mayflower Madam* 1987; *Penn & Teller Get Killed* 1989; *Blown Away* 1994; *Kiss and Tell* 1996; *The Stepford Husbands* 1996

Clarke, David *The Narrow Margin* 1952; *The Great St Louis Bank Robbery* 1959

Clarke, Gage *aka* **Clark, Gage** *Nightmare* 1956; *Fury at Showdown* 1957; *The Return of Dracula* 1958

Clarke, Hope *Book of Numbers* 1972; *A Piece of the Action* 1977

Clarke, Jean *There Was a Crooked Man* 1960; *Goodbye Again* 1961

Clarke, John *Footrot Flats: the Dog's Tale* 1986; *Blood Oath* 1990; *Death in Brunswick* 1990

Clarke, Mae *Frankenstein* 1931; *The Public Enemy* 1931; *The Penguin Pool Murder* 1932; *Three Wise Girls* 1932; *Turn Back the Clock* 1933; *Penthouse* 1933; *Nana* 1934; *Great Guy* 1936; *Flying Tigers* 1942

Clarke, Margi *Letter to Brezhnev* 1985; *I Hired a Contract Killer* 1990; *Loser Takes All* 1990; *Strike It Rich* 1990; *Blonde Fist* 1991

Clarke, Melinda *Killer Tongue* 1996; *Spawn* 1997

Clarke, Mindy *Return of the Living Dead III* 1993; *Return to Two Moon Junction* 1994

Clarke, Richard *The Man Who Wouldn't Talk* 1940; *The Siege of the Saxons* 1963

Clarke, Robert *A Game of Death* 1945; *Outrage* 1950; *Hard, Fast and Beautiful* 1951; *The Man from Planet X* 1951; *Hideous Sun Demon* 1955; *The Astounding She-Monster* 1958; *Midnight Movie Massacre* 1987

Clarke, Warren *A Clockwork Orange* 1971; *Hawk the Slayer* 1980; *Firefox* 1982; *The Cold Room* 1984; *Lassiter* 1984; *Top Secret!* 1984; *Crusoe* 1988; *i.d.* 1994

Clarke-Smith, D A *The Ghoul* 1933; *Murder by Rope* 1936; *Southern Roses* 1936; *Flying 55* 1939

Clarkson, Lana *Blind Date* 1984; *The Haunting of Morella* 1990

Clarkson, Patricia *The Dead Pool* 1988; *Everybody's All-American* 1988; *Rocket Gibraltar* 1988; *Aunt Julia and the Scriptwriter* 1990; *The Old Man and the Sea* 1990; *After the Glory* 1992; *Four Eyes and Six-Guns* 1992; *Legacy of Lies* 1992; *Caught in the Act* 1993; *Jumanji* 1995; *Neil Simon's London Suite* 1996; *High Art* 1998; *Simply Irresistible* 1999

Clary, Robert *Thief of Damascus* 1952; *New Faces* 1954; *Remembrance of Love* 1982

Clash, Kevin *Teenage Mutant Ninja Turtles II: the Secret of the Ooze* 1991; *The Adventures of Elmo in Grouchland* 1999

Clausen, Claus *Westfront 1918* 1930; *The Devil Makes Three* 1952

Clavering, Eric *Where's That Fire?* 1939; *To Kill a Clown* 1972

Clavier, Christian *Les Visiteurs* 1993; *Guardian Angels* 1995; *Les Visiteurs 2: Les Couloirs du Temps* 1998; *Asterix and Obelix Take on Caesar* 1999

Claxton, Richard *The Witch's Daughter* 1996; *The Girl with Brains in Her Feet* 1997

Clay, Andrew Dice *aka* **Clay, Andrew** *Wacko* 1981; *Casual Sex?* 1988; *The Adventures of Ford Fairlane* 1990; *Brain Smasher... a Love Story* 1993; *No Contest* 1995

Clay, Juanin *The Legend of the Lone Ranger* 1981; *WarGames* 1983

Clay, Nicholas *The Darwin Adventure* 1972; *Victor Frankenstein* 1977; *Lovespell* 1979; *Excalibur* 1981; *Lady Chatterley's Lover* 1981; *Evil under the Sun* 1982; *The Hound of the Baskervilles* 1983; *Lionheart* 1986

Clay, Philippe *French Cancan* 1955; *The Hunchback of Notre Dame* 1956; *Shanks* 1974; *The Music Freelancers* 1998

Clayburgh, Jill *The Wedding Party* 1966; *The Snoop Sisters* 1972; *The Thief Who Came to Dinner* 1973; *The Terminal Man* 1974; *Hustling* 1975; *Gable and Lombard* 1976; *Silver Streak* 1976; *Semi-Tough* 1977; *An Unmarried Woman* 1978; *La Luna* 1979; *Starting Over* 1979; *It's My Turn* 1980; *First Monday in October* 1981; *I'm Dancing as Fast as I Can* 1982; *Miles to Go* 1986; *Where Are the Children?* 1986; *Shy People* 1987; *Who Gets the Friends?* 1988; *Fear Stalk* 1989; *Unspeakable Acts* 1990; *Reason for Living: the Jill Ireland Story* 1991; *Rich in Love* 1992; *Whispers in the Dark* 1992; *Day of Atonement* 1993; *Honor Thy Father and Mother: the Menendez Killings* 1994; *Naked in New York* 1994; *Face on the Milk Carton* 1995; *Going All the Way* 1997; *Sins of the Mind* 1997; *Crowned and Dangerous* 1997

Clayton, Jan *The Llano Kid* 1939; *This Man's Navy* 1945

Clayton, John *Unfinished Business* 1985; *High Tide* 1987; *Warm Nights on a Slow Moving Train* 1987; *Boundaries of the Heart* 1988; *Out of the Body* 1988; *Cappuccino* 1989

Clayton, Merry *Blame It on the Night* 1984; *Maid to Order* 1987

Clayworth, June *Criminal Court* 1946; *Dick Tracy Meets Gruesome* 1947; *Sons of the Musketeers* 1951; *The Marriage-Go-Round* 1960

Cleese, John *The Bliss of Mrs Blossom* 1968; *The Rise and Rise of Michael Rimmer* 1970; *And Now for Something Completely Different* 1971; *Monty Python and the Holy Grail* 1975; *Monty Python's Life of Brian* 1979; *The Great Muppet Caper* 1981; *Time Bandits* 1981; *Monty Python Live at the Hollywood Bowl* 1982; *Privates on Parade* 1982; *Monty Python's The Meaning of Life* 1983; *Yellowbeard* 1983; *Silverado* 1985; *Clockwise* 1986; *A Fish Called Wanda* 1988; *Erik the Viking* 1989; *The Big Picture* 1989; *An American Tail: Fievel Goes West* 1991; *Splitting Heirs* 1993; *Mary Shelley's Frankenstein* 1994; *Rudyard Kipling's The Jungle Book* 1994; *The Swan Princess* 1994; *The Wind in the Willows* 1996; *Fierce Creatures* 1997; *George of the Jungle* 1997; *Parting Shots* 1998; *The Out-of-Towners* 1999; *The World Is Not Enough* 1999; *Isn't She Great* 1999

Clem, Jimmy *Grayeagle* 1977; *The Evictors* 1979

Clemens, Paul *Promises in the Dark* 1979; *They're Playing With Fire* 1984

Clemenson, Christian *Broadcast News* 1987; *Bad Influence* 1990; *Accidental Hero* 1992

Clément, Aurore *Lacombe Lucien* 1974; *Travels with Anita* 1978; *Les Rendez-vous d'Anna* 1978; *Paris, Texas* 1984

Clément, Coralie *Diabolo Menthe* 1977; *The Aviator's Wife* 1980

Clementi, Margareth *Medea* 1970; *Casanova* 1976

Clémenti, Pierre *Belle de Jour* 1967; *The Milky Way* 1968; *Partner* 1968; *The Conformist* 1969; *Steppenwolf* 1974; *Quartet* 1981; *Exposed* 1983; *The Silent Woman* 1989; *Hideous Kinky* 1998

Clemento, Steve *The Hounds of Zaroff* 1932; *King Kong* 1933

Clements, John *Knight without Armour* 1937; *South Riding* 1938; *The Four Feathers* 1939; *Convoy* 1940; *Ships with Wings* 1942; *Tomorrow We Live* 1942; *Undercover* 1943; *The Silent Enemy* 1958; *The Mind Benders* 1963; *Oh! What a Lovely War* 1969

Clements, Stanley *aka* **Clements, Stanley "Stash"** *Ghosts in the Night* 1943; *Salty O'Rourke* 1945; *Destination Murder* 1950; *Boots Malone* 1951; *Military Policeman* 1953; *Off Limits* 1953

Clennon, David *aka* **Clennon, Dave** *Go Tell the Spartans* 1977; *Being There* 1979; *Missing* 1981; *The Thing* 1982; *Ladies and Gentlemen, the Fabulous Stains* 1982; *Star 80* 1983; *Falling in Love* 1984; *Sweet Dreams* 1985; *Legal Eagles* 1986; *He's My Girl* 1987; *Betrayed* 1988; *Downtown* 1990; *Light Sleeper* 1991; *Black Widow Murders* 1993; *Nurses on the Line* 1993; *Original Sins* 1995; *Tecumseh: the Last Warrior* 1995

Cléry, Corinne *The Story of O* 1975; *The Con Artists* 1976; *Moonraker* 1979; *Yor, the Hunter from the Future* 1983; *The Gamble* 1988

Cleveland, Carol *Moon Zero Two* 1969; *The Adding Machine* 1969; *And Now for Something Completely Different* 1971; *Pleasure at Her Majesty's* 1976; *Monty Python Live at the Hollywood Bowl* 1982

Cleveland, George *Blue Steel* 1934; *The Man from Utah* 1934; *The Star Packer* 1934; *The Navy Steps Out* 1941; *Two-Faced Woman* 1941; *Abroad with Two Yanks* 1944; *The Yellow Rose of Texas* 1944; *Angel on My Shoulder* 1946; *Courage of Lassie* 1946; *Wild Beauty* 1946; *Little Giant* 1946; *Carson City* 1952

Clevenot, Philippe *Celine and Julie Go Boating* 1974; *Roselyne and the Lions* 1989; *The Hairdresser's Husband* 1990

Cliff, Jimmy *The Harder They Come* 1972; *Club Paradise* 1986

Cliff, John *Back to God's Country* 1953; *I Was a Teenage Frankenstein* 1957

Cliff, Laddie *Happy* 1933; *Over She Goes* 1937

Clifford, Colleen *Careful, He Might Hear You* 1983; *Frauds* 1992

Clifford, Jefferson *Confession* 1955; *The Bridal Path* 1959

Clift, Montgomery *Red River* 1948; *The Search* 1948; *The Heiress* 1949; *The Big Lift* 1950; *A Place in the Sun* 1951; *From Here to Eternity* 1953; *I Confess* 1953; *Indiscretion of an American Wife* 1954; *Raintree County* 1957; *The Young Lions* 1958; *Lonelyhearts* 1958; *Suddenly, Last Summer* 1959; *Wild River* 1960; *Judgment at Nuremberg* 1961; *The Misfits* 1961; *Freud* 1962; *The Defector* 1966

Climo, Brett *Relatives* 1985; *Blackwater Trail* 1995

Cline, Edward *aka* **Cline, Eddie,** *aka* **Cline, Edward F** *The Paleface* 1921; *Daydreams* 1922

Clinton, Roger *The Revenge of Pumpkinhead – Blood Wings* 1994; *Bio-Dome* 1996

Clitheroe, Jimmy *Rhythm Serenade* 1943; *Jules Verne's Rocket to the Moon* 1967

Clive, Colin *Journey's End* 1930; *Frankenstein* 1931; *Christopher Strong* 1933; *The Key* 1934; *One More River* 1934; *Bride of Frankenstein* 1935; *Clive of India* 1935; *The Girl from 10th Avenue* 1935; *Mad Love* 1935; *The Man Who Broke the Bank at Monte Carlo* 1935; *History Is Made at Night* 1937; *The Woman I Love* 1937

Clive, E E *Charlie Chan in London* 1934; *Long Lost Father* 1934; *Atlantic Adventure* 1935; *The Mystery of Edwin Drood* 1935; *Libeled Lady* 1936; *Tarzan Escapes* 1936; *Trouble for Two* 1936; *Isle of Fury* 1936; *Personal Property* 1937; *Live, Love and Learn* 1937; *Arsene Lupin Returns* 1938; *The Adventures of Sherlock Holmes* 1939; *Bachelor Mother* 1939; *Congo Maisie* 1940; *The Earl of Chicago* 1940

Clive, John *Yellow Submarine* 1968; *A Clockwork Orange* 1971; *Never Too Young to Rock* 1975

Clooney, George *Combat Academy* 1986; *Return of the Killer Tomatoes* 1988; *Sunset Beat* 1990; *Red Surf* 1990; *Unbecoming Age* 1992; *Without Warning: Terror in the Towers* 1993; *From Dusk till Dawn* 1995; *One Fine Day* 1996; *Batman and Robin* 1997; *The Peacemaker* 1997; *Out of Sight* 1998; *The Thin Red Line* 1998; *Three Kings* 1999; *South Park: Bigger, Longer & Uncut* 1999; *The Perfect Storm* 2000; *O Brother, Where Art Thou?* 2000

Clooney, Rosemary *Here Come the Girls* 1953; *Deep in My Heart* 1954; *White Christmas* 1954; *Red Garters* 1954

Close, Glenn *Orphan Train* 1979; *The World According to Garp* 1982; *The Big Chill* 1983; *The Natural* 1984; *The Stone Boy* 1984; *Jagged Edge* 1985; *Maxie* 1985; *Fatal Attraction* 1987; *Dangerous Liaisons* 1988; *Stones for Ibarra* 1988; *Light Years* 1988; *Immediate Family* 1989; *Hamlet* 1990; *Meeting Venus* 1990; *Reversal of Fortune* 1990; *Sarah, Plain and Tall* 1991; *The House of the Spirits* 1993; *Skylark* 1993; *The Paper* 1994; *Mary Reilly* 1995; *Serving in Silence* 1995; *Mars Attacks!* 1996; *101 Dalmatians* 1996; *Air Force One* 1997; *In & Out* 1997; *In the Gloaming* 1997; *Paradise Road* 1997; *Cookie's Fortune* 1999; *Tarzan* 1999

Clough, John Scott *A Cut Above* 1989; *What Ever Happened to...?* 1991

Cloutier, Suzanne *Derby Day* 1952; *Othello* 1952; *Doctor in the House* 1954; *Whiskers* 1997

Clouzot, Vera *The Wages of Fear* 1953; *Les Diaboliques* 1954

Clunes, Alec *Saloon Bar* 1940; *The Adventures of Quentin Durward* 1955; *Richard III* 1955; *Tiger in the Smoke* 1956; *Tomorrow at Ten* 1962

Clunes, Martin *The Russia House* 1990; *Carry On Columbus* 1992; *Staggered* 1993; *The Revengers' Comedies* 1997; *Shakespeare in Love* 1998; *The Acid House* 1998; *Saving Grace* 2000

Clutesi, George *I Heard the Owl Call My Name* 1973; *Prophecy* 1979; *Kelly* 1981; *The Legend of Walks Far Woman* 1982

Cluzet, François *L'Enfer* 1994; *Le Cheval d'Orgeuil* 1980; *One Deadly Summer* 1983; *'Round Midnight* 1986; *Chocolat* 1988; *Story of Women* 1988; *Force Majeure* 1989; *Trop Belle pour Toi* 1989; *Olivier Olivier* 1991; *Les Apprentis* 1995; *French Kiss* 1995; *Rien Ne Va Plus* 1997; *Late August, Early September* 1998

Clyde, Andy *MIllion Dollar Legs* 1932; *The Little Minister* 1934; *Annie Oakley* 1935; *Bad Lands* 1939; *Cherokee Strip* 1940; *The Devil's Playground* 1946; *Fool's Gold* 1946; *The Dead Don't Dream* 1947; *The Marauders* 1947; *False Paradise* 1948; *Silent Conflict* 1948; *The Road to Denver* 1955

Clyde, Jeremy *Wilt* 1989; *Kaspar Hauser* 1993

Clyde, June *Back Street* 1932; *Only Yesterday* 1933; *Land without Music* 1936; *Night without Stars* 1951; *Treasure Hunt* 1952

Coates, Kim *Palais Royale* 1988; *Cold Front* 1989; *Dead before Dawn* 1993; *Black Fox* 1995; *Dead Silence* 1996; *Deadly Current* 1996; *Carpool* 1996; *Married to a Stranger* 1997; *Airborne* 1997; *Battlefield Earth* 2000

Coates, Phyllis *I Was a Teenage Frankenstein* 1957; *Cattle Empire* 1958

Çobanoglu, Necmettin *Yol* 1982; *Journey of Hope* 1990

Cobb, Lee J *Golden Boy* 1939; *This Thing Called Love* 1940; *Men of Boys Town* 1941; *Paris Calling* 1941; *The Moon Is Down* 1943; *The Song of Bernadette* 1943; *Anna and the King of Siam* 1946; *Boomerang!* 1947; *Captain from Castile* 1947; *Johnny O'Clock* 1947; *Call Northside 777* 1948; *The Dark Past* 1948; *The Miracle of the Bells* 1948; *Thieves' Highway* 1949; *Sirocco* 1951; *The Fighter* 1952; *On the Waterfront* 1954; *Yankee Pasha* 1954; *Gorilla at Large* 1954; *The Left Hand of God* 1955; *The Road to Denver* 1955; *The Racers* 1955; *The Man in the Gray Flannel Suit* 1956; *The Three Faces of Eve* 1957; *12 Angry Men* 1957; *The Garment Jungle* 1957; *The Brothers Karamazov* 1958; *Man of the West* 1958; *Party Girl* 1958; *The Baited Trap* 1959; *Green Mansions* 1959; *But Not for Me* 1959; *Exodus* 1960; *The Four Horsemen of the Apocalypse* 1962; *How the West Was Won* 1962; *Come Blow Your Horn* 1963; *Our Man Flint* 1966; *In like Flint* 1967; *Coogan's Bluff* 1968; *They Came to Rob Las Vegas* 1968; *Mackenna's Gold* 1969; *The Liberation of LB Jones* 1970; *Macho Callahan* 1970; *Lawman* 1971; *The Exorcist* 1973; *The Man Who Loved Cat Dancing* 1973; *That Lucky Touch* 1975

Cobb, Randall "Tex" *Uncommon Valor* 1983; *The Golden Child* 1986; *Critical Condition* 1987; *The Dirty Dozen: the Deadly Mission* 1987; *Buy & Cell* 1988; *Fletch Lives* 1989; *Blind Fury* 1990; *Ernest Goes to Jail* 1990; *Raw Nerve* 1991; *Midnight Sting* 1992

Cobbs, Bill *aka* **Cobbs, William** *The Brother from Another Planet* 1984; *Dominick and Eugene* 1988; *Decoration Day* 1990; *Carolina Skeletons* 1991; *The People under the Stairs* 1991; *The Bodyguard* 1992; *The Hudsucker Proxy* 1994; *Man with a Gun* 1995; *Out There* 1995; *Air Bud* 1997; *Always Outnumbered* 1998; *Hope Floats* 1998; *I Still Know What You Did Last Summer* 1998

Cobo, Eva *aka* **Cobo de Garcia, Eva** *Matador* 1986; *Operation Condor: the Armour of God II* 1990

Cobo, Roberto *Los Olvidados* 1950; *Mexican Bus Ride* 1951

Coburn, Charles *Of Human Hearts* 1938; *Vivacious Lady* 1938; *Yellow Jack* 1938; *Bachelor Mother* 1939; *Idiot's Delight* 1939; *In Name Only* 1939; *Made for Each Other* 1939; *Stanley and Livingstone* 1939; *The Story of Alexander Graham Bell* 1939; *Edison, the Man* 1940; *Florian* 1940; *Road to Singapore* 1940; *Three Faces West* 1940; *The Devil and Miss Jones* 1941; *HM Pulham Esq* 1941; *The Lady Eve* 1941; *Our Wife* 1941; *George Washington Slept Here* 1942; *In This Our Life* 1942; *Kings Row* 1942; *The Constant Nymph* 1943; *Forever and a Day* 1943; *Heaven Can Wait* 1943; *The More the Merrier* 1943; *Princess O'Rourke* 1943; *Knickerbocker Holiday* 1944; *Wilson* 1944; *Together Again* 1944; *Colonel Effingham's Raid* 1945; *Rhapsody in Blue* 1945; *A Royal Scandal* 1945; *Over 21* 1945; *The Green Years* 1946; *Lured* 1947; *The Paradine Case* 1947; *BF's Daughter* 1948; *Green Grass of Wyoming* 1948; *Everybody Does It* 1949; *Impact* 1949; *The Doctor and the Girl* 1949; *Mr Music* 1950; *Has Anybody Seen My Gal?* 1952; *Monkey Business* 1952; *Gentlemen Prefer Blondes* 1953; *Trouble along the Way* 1953; *The Long Wait* 1954; *How to Be Very, Very Popular* 1955; *Town on Trial* 1956; *The Power and the Prize* 1956; *How to Murder a Rich Uncle* 1957; *John Paul Jones* 1959; *The Remarkable Mr Pennypacker* 1959; *A Stranger in My Arms* 1959; *Pepe* 1960

Coburn, James *Ride Lonesome* 1959; *Face of a Fugitive* 1959; *The Magnificent Seven* 1960; *Hell Is for Heroes* 1962; *Charade* 1963; *The Great Escape* 1963; *The Americanization of Emily* 1964; *The Man from Galveston* 1964; *A High Wind in Jamaica* 1965; *The Loved One* 1965; *Major Dundee* 1965; *Dead Heat on a Merry-Go-Round* 1966; *Our Man Flint* 1966; *What Did You Do in the War, Daddy?* 1966; *In like Flint* 1967; *The President's Analyst* 1967; *Waterhole #3* 1967; *Candy* 1968; *Duffy* 1968; *Hard Contract* 1969; *Last of the Mobile Hot-Shots* 1970; *A Fistful of Dynamite* 1971; *The Honkers* 1971; *The Carey Treatment* 1972; *Harry in Your Pocket* 1973; *The Last of Sheila* 1973; *Pat Garrett and Billy the Kid* 1973; *The Internecine Project* 1974; *Bite the Bullet* 1975; *The Streetfighter* 1975; *Battle of Midway* 1976; *The Last Hard Men* 1976; *Sky Riders* 1976; *Cross of Iron* 1977; *Firepower* 1979; *Goldengirl* 1979; *The Baltimore Bullet* 1980; *Loving Couples* 1980; *High Risk* 1981; *Looker* 1981; *Draw!* 1984; *Martin's Day* 1984; *Death of a Soldier* 1985; *Young Guns II* 1990; *Hudson Hawk* 1991; *A Thousand Heroes* 1992; *Deadfall* 1993; *The Hit List* 1993; *Sister Act 2: Back in the Habit* 1993; *Greyhounds* 1994; *Maverick* 1994; *The Avenging Angel* 1995; *The Disappearance of Kevin Johnson* 1995; *The Set Up* 1995; *Eraser* 1996; *Keys to Tulsa* 1996; *The Nutty Professor* 1996; *The Cherokee Kid* 1996; *Skeletons* 1996; *Affliction* 1997; *The Second Civil War* 1997; *Mr Murder* 1998; *Payback* 1999

Coca, Imogene *Under the Yum Yum Tree* 1963; *National Lampoon's Vacation* 1983; *Nothing Lasts Forever* 1984

Coca, Richard *Little White Lies* 1989; *The Truth about Cats and Dogs* 1996

Cochran, Robert *Moscow Nights* 1935; *Sanders of the River* 1935; *Scrooge* 1935; *The Man Who Could Work Miracles* 1936

Cochran, Steve *Wonder Man* 1945; *The Chase* 1946; *The Kid from Brooklyn* 1946; *Copacabana* 1947; *A Song Is Born* 1948; *White Heat* 1949; *Dallas* 1950; *The Damned Don't Cry* 1950; *Storm Warning* 1950; *Jim Thorpe – All-American* 1951; *Back to God's Country* 1953; *The Desert Song* 1953; *Carnival Story* 1954; *Private Hell 36* 1954; *Come Next Spring* 1956; *Il Grido* 1957; *The Mobster* 1958; *Quantrill's Raiders* 1958; *The Beat Generation* 1959; *The Big Operator* 1959; *The Deadly Companions* 1961; *Of Love and Desire* 1963

Cochrane, Rory *Fathers and Sons* 1992; *Dazed and Confused* 1993; *Love and a .45* 1994; *Empire Records* 1995; *The Low Life* 1995

Cockburn, Arlene *The Governess* 1997; *The Winter Guest* 1997

Cockrell, Gary *Lolita* 1961; *The War Lover* 1962

Coco, James *Generation* 1969; *Tell Me That You Love Me, Junie Moon* 1970; *End of the Road* 1970; *A New Leaf* 1971; *Such Good Friends* 1971; *Man of La Mancha* 1972; *The Wild Party* 1975; *Murder by Death* 1976; *The Cheap Detective* 1978; *Bye Bye Monkey* 1978; *Scavenger Hunt* 1979; *The Diary of Anne Frank* 1980; *Wholly Moses!* 1980; *Only When I Laugh* 1981; *There Must Be a Pony* 1986; *Hunk* 1987

Cocteau, Jean *The Blood of a Poet* 1930; *Les Parents Terribles* 1948; *Les Enfants Terribles* 1949; *Orphée* 1950; *Le Testament d'Orphée* 1960

Coduri, Camille *Hawks* 1988; *Nuns on the Run* 1990; *King Ralph* 1991

Cody, Iron Eyes *Sitting Bull* 1954; *Gun for a Coward* 1957; *The Great Sioux Massacre* 1965; *El Condor* 1970; *Grayeagle* 1977; *Ernest Goes to Camp* 1987

Cody, Kathleen *Charley and the Angel* 1973; *Superdad* 1974

Cody, Lew *What a Widow!* 1930; *Dishonored* 1931; *Sporting Blood* 1931; *Sitting Pretty* 1933

Coe, Barry *The Bravados* 1958; *A Private's Affair* 1959; *But Not for Me* 1959; *One Foot in Hell* 1960; *The Wizard of Baghdad* 1960; *The 300 Spartans* 1962; *Jaws 2* 1978

Coe, David Allan *Take This Job and Shove It* 1981; *The Last Days of Frank and Jesse James* 1986

Coe, George *Kramer vs Kramer* 1979; *The First Deadly Sin* 1980; *The Amateur* 1981; *Broken Promise* 1981; *The Entity* 1981; *A Flash of Green* 1984; *Remo – Unarmed and Dangerous* 1985; *Best Seller* 1987; *Blind Date* 1987; *Uncle Tom's Cabin* 1987; *Shootdown* 1988; *The Hollywood Detective* 1989; *My Name Is Bill W* 1989; *The End of Innocence* 1990; *To My Daughter* 1990; *Cagney & Lacey: the View through the Glass Ceiling* 1995; *Nick and Jane* 1996

Coe, Peter *House of Frankenstein* 1944; *Hellgate* 1952; *Road to Bali* 1952

Coffey, Colleen *Coopersmith: Sweet Scent of Murder* 1992; *The Lawnmower Man* 1992

Coffey, Denise *Waltz of the Toreadors* 1962; *Georgy Girl* 1966; *Sir Henry at Rawlinson End* 1980; *Another Time, Another Place* 1983

Coffey, Scott *Satisfaction* 1988; *Shag* 1988; *Shout* 1991

Coffin, Frederick *Manhunt for Claude Dallas* 1986; *Under Siege* 1986; *Hard to Kill* 1989; *Settle the Score* 1989; *Crash: the Mystery of Flight 1501* 1990; *VI Warshawski* 1991; *Dragstrip Girl* 1994; *Secret Sins of the Father* 1994

Coghill, Joy *Omen IV: the Awakening* 1991; *Whose Child Is This?* 1993; *The Other Mother* 1995

Cohen, J J *aka* **Cohen, Jeffrey Jay** *Fire with Fire* 1986; *Daddy* 1987; *The Principal* 1987

Cohen, Lynn *Manhattan Murder Mystery* 1993; *Vanya on 42nd Street* 1994; *Hurricane Streets* 1997

Cohen, Scott *The Mambo Kings* 1992; *The Wharf Rat* 1995

Colantoni, Enrico *The Member of the Wedding* 1997; *Cloned* 1997; *Stigmata* 1999; *Galaxy Quest* 1999

Colasanto, Nicholas *Fat City* 1972; *Raging Bull* 1980

Colbert, Claudette *The Big Pond* 1930; *Manslaughter* 1930; *Honor among Lovers* 1931; *The Smiling Lieutenant* 1931; *His Woman* 1931; *The Phantom President* 1932; *The Sign of the Cross* 1932; *The Man from Yesterday* 1932; *I Cover the Waterfront* 1933; *Cleopatra* 1934; *Four Frightened People* 1934; *Imitation of Life* 1934; *It Happened One Night* 1934; *The Bride Comes Home* 1935; *The Gilded Lily* 1935; *She Married Her Boss* 1935; *Private Worlds* 1935; *Under Two Flags* 1936; *I Met Him in Paris* 1937; *Tovarich* 1937; *Bluebeard's Eighth Wife* 1938; *Drums along the Mohawk* 1939; *It's a Wonderful World* 1939; *Midnight* 1939; *Zaza* 1939; *Arise, My Love* 1940; *Boom Town* 1940; *Remember the Day* 1941; *Skylark* 1941; *The Palm Beach Story* 1942; *So Proudly We Hail* 1943; *No Time for Love* 1943; *Since You Went Away* 1944; *Guest Wife* 1945; *Tomorrow Is Forever* 1945; *Without Reservations* 1946; *The Secret Heart* 1946; *The Egg and I* 1947; *Sleep, My Love* 1948; *Bride for Sale* 1949; *Three Came Home* 1950; *Let's Make It Legal* 1951; *Thunder on the Hill* 1951; *The Planter's Wife* 1952; *Royal Affairs in Versailles* 1953; *Texas Lady* 1955; *Parrish* 1961

Colbert, Robert *aka* **Colbert, Bob** *Have Rocket, Will Travel* 1959; *The Lawyer* 1969; *City beneath the Sea* 1971

Colby, Anita *Cover Girl* 1944; *Brute Force* 1947

Cole, Carol *The Mad Room* 1969; *Model Shop* 1969

Cole, Gary *Those She Left Behind* 1989; *The Old Man and the Sea* 1990; *In the Line of Fire* 1993; *The Switch* 1993; *Twilight Zone: Rod Serling's Lost Classics* 1994; *The Brady Bunch Movie* 1995; *Indecent Seduction* 1996; *A Very Brady Sequel* 1996; *Gang Related* 1997; *I'll Be Home for Christmas* 1998; *A Simple Plan* 1998; *Office Space* 1999

Cole, George *Cottage to Let* 1941; *My Brother's Keeper* 1948; *Quartet* 1948; *The Spider and the Fly* 1949; *Gone to Earth* 1950; *Lady Godiva Rides Again* 1951; *Laughter in Paradise* 1951; *Scrooge* 1951; *The Happy Family* 1952; *The Intruder* 1953; *Our Girl Friday* 1953; *Will Any Gentleman...?* 1953; *The Belles of St Trinian's* 1954; *Happy Ever After* 1954; *The Adventures of Quentin Durward* 1955; *The Constant Husband* 1955; *Where There's a Will* 1955; *A Prize of Gold* 1955; *The Green Man* 1956; *It's a Wonderful World* 1956; *Blue Murder at St Trinian's* 1957; *Too Many Crooks* 1958; *The Bridal Path* 1959; *The Pure Hell of St Trinian's* 1960; *Cleopatra* 1963; *Dr Syn, Alias the Scarecrow* 1963; *The Legend of Young Dick Turpin* 1965; *One Way Pendulum* 1965; *The Great St Trinian's Train Robbery* 1966; *The Vampire Lovers* 1970; *Fright* 1971; *Take Me High* 1973; *Gone in 60 Seconds* 1974; *The Blue Bird* 1976; *Double Nickels* 1977; *Mary Reilly* 1995

Cole, Nat King *China Gate* 1957; *Istanbul* 1957; *St Louis Blues* 1958

Cole, Natalie *Fugitive from Justice* 1996; *Always Outnumbered* 1998; *Cats Don't Dance* 1998

Cole, Olivia *Heroes* 1977; *Some Kind of Hero* 1982; *Go Tell It on the Mountain* 1984

Coleby, Robert *The Plumber* 1979; *Now and Forever* 1983; *The Blue Lightning* 1986

Coleman, Charles *That Certain Age* 1938; *The Rage of Paris* 1938

Coleman, Charlotte *Four Weddings and a Funeral* 1994; *The Young Poisoner's Handbook* 1994; *Different for Girls* 1996; *If Only* 1998; *Beautiful People* 1999

Coleman, Dabney *The Slender Thread* 1965; *This Property Is Condemned* 1966; *The Scalphunters* 1968; *Downhill Racer* 1969; *I Love My... Wife* 1970; *Cinderella Liberty* 1973; *The Dove* 1974; *The Other Side of the Mountain* 1975; *Rolling Thunder* 1977; *North Dallas Forty* 1979; *Nine to Five* 1980; *Nothing Personal* 1980; *How to Beat the High Cost of Living* 1980; *On Golden Pond* 1981; *Modern Problems* 1981; *Tootsie* 1982; *Young Doctors in Love* 1982; *WarGames* 1983; *Cloak and Dagger* 1984; *The Man with One Red Shoe* 1985; *Murrow* 1986; *Dragnet* 1987; *Sworn to Silence* 1987; *Baby Makes Three* 1988; *Hot to Trot* 1988; *Short Time* 1990; *Where the Heart Is* 1990; *Meet the Applegates* 1991; *Never Forget* 1991; *Paydirt* 1992; *Amos & Andrew* 1993; *The Beverly Hillbillies* 1993; *Clifford* 1994; *In the Line of Duty: Kidnapped* 1995; *Judicial Consent* 1995; *Devil's Food* 1996; *You've Got Mail* 1998; *My Date with the President's Daughter* 1998

Coleman, Frank J *Behind the Screen* 1916; *The Cure* 1917

Coleman, Gary *On the Right Track* 1981; *Jimmy the Kid* 1982

Coleman, Jack *Children of the Bride* 1990; *Daughter of Darkness* 1990; *The Return of Eliot Ness* 1991; *Rubdown* 1993; *Trapped in Space* 1994; *Last Rites* 1998; *Replacing Dad* 1999

Coleman, Marilyn *Which Way Is Up?* 1977; *Remember My Name* 1978; *Better Off Dead* 1993

Coleman, Nancy *Dangerously They Live* 1942; *Desperate Journey* 1942; *The Gay Sisters* 1942; *Kings Row* 1942; *Edge of Darkness* 1943; *Devotion* 1946; *Mourning Becomes Electra* 1947

Coles, Michael *Solo for Sparrow* 1962; *Dr Who and the Daleks* 1965; *A Touch of Love* 1969; *I Want What I Want* 1971; *Dracula AD 1972* 1972; *The Satanic Rites of Dracula* 1973

Colgan, Eileen *Quackser Fortune Has a Cousin in the Bronx* 1970; *The Secret of Roan Inish* 1993

Colicos, John *Anne of the Thousand Days* 1969; *Raid on Rommel* 1971; *The Wrath of God* 1972; *Scorpio* 1973; *Breaking Point* 1976; *Drum* 1976; *A Matter of Wife...and Death* 1976; *King Solomon's Treasure* 1977; *Phobia* 1980; *The Postman Always Rings Twice* 1981; *Nowhere to Hide* 1987

Colin, Grégoire *Olivier Olivier* 1991; *Before the Rain* 1994; *Secret Defense* 1997; *The Dream Life of Angels* 1998; *Beau Travail* 1999

Colin, Ian *It's Never Too Late to Mend* 1937; *The Big Chance* 1957

Colin, Margaret *Something Wild* 1986; *Like Father, Like Son* 1987; *The Return of Sherlock Holmes* 1987; *Three Men and a Baby* 1987; *Fighting Justice* 1989; *Traveling Man* 1989; *The Butcher's Wife* 1991; *Amos & Andrew* 1993; *In the Shadow of Evil* 1995; *Independence Day* 1996; *The Devil's Own* 1997; *Hit and Run* 1999

Colleano, Bonar *A Matter of Life and Death* 1946; *Wanted for Murder* 1946; *Good Time Girl* 1948; *Once a Jolly Swagman* 1948; *Give Us This Day* 1949; *Dance Hall* 1950; *Pool of London* 1950; *Escape by Night* 1953; *The Sea Shall Not Have Them* 1954; *Joe Macbeth* 1955; *Zarak* 1956; *Fire Down Below* 1957; *Interpol* 1957; *No Time to Die* 1958; *The Man Inside* 1958

Collet, Christopher *Firstborn* 1984; *Right to Kill?* 1985; *The Deadly Game* 1986; *Prayer of the Rollerboys* 1990

Collet, Pierre *The Invitation* 1973; *French Connection II* 1975

Collette, Toni *Spotswood* 1991; *Muriel's Wedding* 1994; *Arabian Knight* 1995; *Emma* 1996; *The Pallbearer* 1996; *Cosi* 1996; *Clockwatchers* 1997; *The James Gang* 1997; *Diana & Me* 1997; *The Boys* 1998; *Velvet Goldmine* 1998; *8½ Women* 1999; *The Sixth Sense* 1999

Colley, Kenneth *aka* **Colley, Ken** *The Music Lovers* 1970; *The Triple Echo* 1972; *Giro City* 1982; *The Scarlet and the Black* 1983; *The Whistle Blower* 1986; *A Summer Story* 1987; *I Hired a Contract Killer* 1990; *The Last Island* 1990; *Prisoner of Honor* 1991; *Brassed Off* 1996; *Hold Back the Night* 1999

Collier, Constance *A Damsel in Distress* 1937; *Stage Door* 1937; *Thunder in the City* 1937; *Zaza* 1939; *Kitty* 1945; *The Dark Corner* 1946; *Monsieur Beaucaire* 1946; *An Ideal Husband* 1947; *The Perils of Pauline* 1947; *Rope* 1948; *Whirlpool* 1949

Collier, Don *Safe at Home* 1962; *Flap* 1970

Collier, Lois *Cobra Woman* 1944; *A Night in Casablanca* 1946; *Wild Beauty* 1946

Collier, Patience *Countess Dracula* 1970; *Perfect Friday* 1970; *Every Home Should Have One* 1970

Collier Sr, William *Up the River* 1930; *The Bride Comes Home* 1935; *Murder Man* 1935; *Miracle on Main Street* 1940

Collier Jr, William *aka* **Collier, William** *The Lucky Lady* 1926; *Rain or Shine* 1930; *Cimarron* 1931; *Little Caesar* 1931; *Street Scene* 1931

Collin, John *The Witches* 1966; *Before Winter Comes* 1968; *The Last Escape* 1970; *All Creatures Great and Small* 1974; *Tess* 1979

Collinge, Patricia *The Little Foxes* 1941; *Shadow of a Doubt* 1943; *Tender Comrade* 1943; *Casanova Brown* 1944; *Teresa* 1951

Collings, Anne *The Mask* 1961; *Seven Alone* 1974

Collins, Eddie *Drums along the Mohawk* 1939; *Young Mr Lincoln* 1939; *The Blue Bird* 1940

Collins, Elaine *Up* 1976; *Soft Top, Hard Shoulder* 1992

Collins, Gary *Angel in My Pocket* 1968; *The Night They Took Miss Beautiful* 1977; *Killer Fish* 1978; *Hangar 18* 1980; *Danielle Steel's Secrets* 1992

Collins, Jackie *Barnacle Bill* 1957; *Undercover Girl* 1958

Collins, Joan *Judgment Deferred* 1951; *Lady Godiva Rides Again* 1951; *Cosh Boy* 1952; *I Believe in You* 1952; *Decameron Nights* 1953; *Our Girl Friday* 1953; *The Square Ring* 1953; *Turn the Key Softly* 1953; *The Good Die Young* 1954; *Land of the Pharaohs* 1955; *The Virgin Queen* 1955; *The Girl in the Red Velvet Swing* 1955; *The Opposite Sex* 1956; *Island in the Sun* 1957; *Sea Wife* 1957; *Stopover Tokyo* 1957; *The Wayward Bus* 1957; *The Bravados* 1958; *Rally 'round the Flag, Boys!* 1958; *Esther and the King* 1960; *Seven Thieves* 1960; *The Road to Hong Kong* 1962; *Warning Shot* 1967; *Can Heironymus Merkin Ever Forget Mercy Humppe and Find True Happiness?* 1969; *If It's Tuesday, This Must Be Belgium* 1969; *The Executioner* 1970; *Up in the Cellar* 1970; *Quest for Love* 1971; *Revenge* 1971; *Fear in the Night* 1972; *Tales from the Crypt* 1972; *Tales That Witness Madness* 1973; *Dark Places* 1973; *Alfie Darling* 1975; *I Don't Want to Be Born* 1975; *Empire of the Ants* 1977; *The Big Sleep* 1978; *The Stud* 1978; *Zero to Sixty* 1978; *The Bitch* 1979; *Sunburn* 1979; *A Game for Vultures* 1979; *Nutcracker* 1982; *The Cartier Affair* 1984; *Her Life as a Man* 1984; *Decadence* 1993; *Annie: a Royal Adventure* 1995; *In the Bleak Midwinter* 1995; *The Clandestine Marriage* 1999; *The Flintstones in Viva Rock Vegas* 2000

Collins, Judy *Junior* 1994; *A Town Has Turned to Dust* 1998

Collins, Kevin *The Garden* 1990; *Edward II* 1991; *Wittgenstein* 1993

Collins, Lewis *Who Dares Wins* 1982; *Codename Wildgeese* 1984; *Jack the Ripper* 1988; *A Ghost in Monte Carlo* 1990

Collins, Lisa *Deep Red* 1994; *Danger Zone* 1996

Collins, Patricia *Bear Island* 1979; *Circle of Two* 1980; *Speaking Parts* 1989; *Deep Sleep* 1990; *Wojeck: Out of the Fire* 1992; *What Kind of Mother Are You?* 1996

Collins, Paul *Peter Pan* 1953; *Mother* 1996

Collins, Pauline *Shirley Valentine* 1989; *City of Joy* 1992; *My Mother's Courage* 1995; *Paradise Road* 1997

Collins, Phil *Buster* 1988; *Hook* 1991; *Frauds* 1992; *And the Band Played On* 1993; *Balto* 1995

Collins, Ray *Citizen Kane* 1941; *The Big Street* 1942; *The Commandos Strike at Dawn* 1942; *The Magnificent Ambersons* 1942; *The Human Comedy* 1943; *Salute to the Marines* 1943; *Whistling in Brooklyn* 1943; *Can't Help Singing* 1944; *The Eve of St Mark* 1944; *See Here, Private Hargrove* 1944; *The Hidden Eye* 1945; *Leave Her to Heaven* 1945; *Miss Susie Slagle's* 1945; *Badman's Territory* 1946; *Crack-Up* 1946; *Up Goes Maisie* 1946; *Bachelor Knight* 1947; *A Double Life* 1947; *The Senator Was Indiscreet* 1947; *Good Sam* 1948; *Homecoming* 1948; *The Man from Colorado* 1948; *For the Love of Mary* 1948; *The Fountainhead* 1949; *Francis* 1949; *The Heiress* 1949; *Summer Stock* 1950; *The Racket* 1951; *Vengeance Valley* 1951; *You're in the Navy Now* 1951; *Young Man with Ideas* 1952; *Column South* 1953; *The Desert Song* 1953; *The Kid from Left Field* 1953; *Rose Marie* 1954; *Bad for Each Other* 1954; *Texas Lady* 1955; *Never Say Goodbye* 1955; *The Solid Gold Cadillac* 1956; *Touch of Evil* 1958

Collins, Roberta *The Big Doll House* 1971; *The Unholy Rollers* 1972; *Women in Cages* 1972; *Caged Heat* 1974; *Death Race 2000* 1975; *School Spirit* 1985

Collins, Russell *Shockproof* 1949; *Miss Sadie Thompson* 1953; *Bad Day at Black Rock* 1955; *The Last Frontier* 1955; *The Enemy Below* 1957

Collins, Stephen *All the President's Men* 1976; *Between the Lines* 1977; *Face of a Stranger* 1978; *Star Trek: the Motion Picture* 1979; *The Promise* 1979; *Loving Couples* 1980; *Threesome* 1984; *Brewster's Millions* 1985; *Jumpin' Jack Flash* 1986; *On Dangerous Ground* 1986; *Stella* 1990; *My New Gun* 1992; *A Woman Scorned* 1992; *A Family Divided* 1995; *The Babysitter's Seduction* 1996; *Ivana Trump's For Love Alone* 1996; *An Unexpected Family* 1996; *An Unexpected Life* 1998; *Drive Me Crazy* 1999

Collura, Steve Allie *Trackdown: Finding the Goodbar Killer* 1983; *Between Love and Honor* 1995

Colman, Ronald *The White Sister* 1923; *Lady Windermere's Fan* 1925; *Stella Dallas* 1925; *Beau Geste* 1926; *The Winning of Barbara Worth* 1926; *Bulldog Drummond* 1929; *Condemned* 1929; *The Devil to Pay* 1930; *Raffles* 1930; *Arrowsmith* 1931; *The Unholy Garden* 1931; *Cynara* 1932; *The Masquerader* 1933; *Bulldog Drummond Strikes Back* 1934; *Clive of India* 1935; *The Man Who Broke the Bank at Monte Carlo* 1935; *A Tale of Two Cities* 1935; *Under Two Flags* 1936; *Lost Horizon* 1937; *The Prisoner of Zenda* 1937; *If I Were King* 1938; *The Light That Failed* 1939; *Lucky Partners* 1940; *My Life with Caroline* 1941; *Random Harvest* 1942; *The Talk of the Town* 1942; *Kismet* 1944; *A Double Life* 1947; *The Late George Apley* 1947; *Champagne for Caesar* 1950; *The Story of Mankind* 1957

Colmans, Edward *Thief of Damascus* 1952; *Diary of a Madman* 1963

Colomby, Scott *Caddyshack* 1980; *Porky's II: The Next Day* 1983; *Porky's Revenge* 1985

Colon, Alex *Death of an Angel* 1985; *Invasion USA* 1985; *Red Scorpion* 1989

Colon, Miriam *Thunder Island* 1963; *Back Roads* 1981; *Scarface* 1983

Colonna, Jerry *Road to Singapore* 1940; *Atlantic City* 1944; *Make Mine Music* 1946; *Alice in Wonderland* 1951; *Andy Hardy Comes Home* 1958

Colosimo, Clara *Alfredo Alfredo* 1971; *Orchestra Rehearsal* 1978; *Vampire in Venice* 1987

Colpeyn, Louisa *aka* **Colpeyn, Luisa** *Bande à Part* 1964; *Marry Me! Marry Me!* 1968

Colt, Marshall *Jagged Edge* 1985; *Beverly Hills Madam* 1986; *To Heal a Nation* 1988; *Deceptions* 1990

Colton, Jacque Lynn *Uphill All the Way* 1985; *Heartbreak Hotel* 1988

Coltrane, Robbie *Scrubbers* 1982; *Krull* 1983; *Loose Connections* 1983; *Chinese Boxes* 1984; *Defence of the Realm* 1985; *National Lampoon's European Vacation* 1985; *The Supergrass* 1985; *Caravaggio* 1986; *Mona Lisa* 1986; *Eat the Rich* 1987; *Bert Rigby, You're a Fool* 1989; *Danny, the Champion of the World* 1989; *Henry V* 1989; *Let It Ride* 1989; *Nuns on the Run* 1990; *Perfectly Normal* 1990; *The Pope Must Die* 1991; *Triple Bogey on a Par Five Hole* 1991; *Oh, What a Night* 1992; *The Adventures of Huck Finn* 1993; *GoldenEye* 1995; *Buddy* 1997; *Montana* 1997; *Message in a Bottle* 1998; *The World Is Not Enough* 1999

Combeau, Muriel *Romuald et Juliette* 1989; *Near Mrs* 1990

Combs, Holly Marie *Sweet Hearts Dance* 1988; *Dr Giggles* 1992; *Danielle Steel's A Perfect Stranger* 1994; *Sins of Silence* 1995

Combs, Jeffrey *Re-Animator* 1985; *From Beyond* 1986; *Bride of Re-Animator* 1991; *The Pit and the Pendulum* 1991; *Trancers II: The Return of Jack Deth* 1991; *Necronomicon* 1993; *Love and a .45* 1994; *Lurking Fear* 1994; *Castle Freak* 1995; *The Frighteners* 1996; *Spoiler* 1998

Comer, Anjanette *The Loved One* 1965; *The Appaloosa* 1966; *Guns for San Sebastian* 1968; *In Enemy Country* 1968; *The Firechasers* 1970; *The Baby* 1973; *The Manchu Eagle Murder Caper Mystery* 1973; *Lepke* 1975; *Fire Sale* 1977; *Deadly Family Secrets* 1995

Comer, John *The Family Way* 1966; *There's a Girl in My Soup* 1970; *The Lovers* 1972

Comerate, Sheridan *Crash Landing* 1958; *Live Fast, Die Young* 1958

Comingore, Dorothy *Blondie Meets the Boss* 1939; *Citizen Kane* 1941; *The Hairy Ape* 1944; *The Big Night* 1951

Como, Perry *Something for the Boys* 1944; *Words and Music* 1948

Compson, Betty *Hollywood* 1923; *The Pony Express* 1925; *The Barker* 1928; *The Docks of New York* 1928; *The Great Gabbo* 1929

Compton, Fay *The Mill on the Floss* 1937; *The Prime Minister* 1940; *Odd Man Out* 1946; *Esther Waters* 1948; *London Belongs to Me* 1948; *Britannia Mews* 1949; *Laughter in Paradise* 1951; *Othello* 1952; *The Vanquished* 1953; *Double Cross* 1955; *The Story of Esther Costello* 1957; *The Haunting* 1963; *The Virgin and the Gypsy* 1970

Compton, Joyce *The Wild Party* 1929; *The Awful Truth* 1937; *Artists and Models Abroad* 1938; *Rose of Washington Square* 1939; *Let's Make Music* 1940; *Sky Murder* 1940; *The Villain Still Pursued Her* 1940; *Bedtime Story* 1942; *Christmas in Connecticut* 1945

Compton, Juliette *Anybody's Woman* 1930; *Ladies of Leisure* 1930; *Morocco* 1930; *Westward Passage* 1932; *No One Man* 1932; *Devil and the Deep* 1932; *The Masquerader* 1933; *Peg o' My Heart* 1933

Compton, O'Neal *Attack of the 50 Ft Woman* 1993; *Murder between Friends* 1994; *Roadracers* 1994

Conant, Oliver *Summer of '42* 1971; *Class of '44* 1973

Conaway, Jeff *Grease* 1978; *The Patriot* 1986; *Bay Cove* 1987; *The Dirty Dozen: the Fatal Mission* 1988; *Elvira, Mistress of the Dark* 1988; *Ghost Writer* 1989; *A Time to Die* 1991; *Mirror Images* 1991

Condra, Julie *Crying Freeman* 1995; *Danielle Steel's Mixed Blessings* 1995

Congdon, James *The Left Handed Gun* 1958; *The Gardener* 1972

Conklin, Chester *Tillie's Punctured Romance* 1914; *Greed* 1925; *The Big Noise* 1928; *The Virginian* 1929; *Her Majesty Love* 1931; *Hallelujah, I'm a Bum* 1933; *Modern Times* 1936; *The Perils of Pauline* 1947

Conklin, Peggy *The Devil Is a Sissy* 1936; *Having Wonderful Time* 1938

Conley, Corinne *Butterbox Babies* 1995; *Salt Water Moose* 1996

Conlin, Jimmy *aka* **Conlin, James** *Rose Marie* 1936; *Seven Keys to Baldpate* 1947; *Knock on Any Door* 1949; *Tulsa* 1949; *Mad Wednesday* 1950

Conn, Didi *Raggedy Ann and Andy* 1977; *You Light Up My Life* 1977; *Almost Summer* 1977; *Murder at the Mardi Gras* 1978; *Grease 2* 1982

Connell, Maureen *The Abominable Snowman* 1957; *Lucky Jim* 1957; *Next to No Time* 1958; *Danger by My Side* 1962

Connelly, Christopher *aka* **Connelly, Chris** *They Only Kill Their Masters* 1972; *Corky* 1972; *Hawmps* 1976; *No Margin for Error* 1978; *The Norseman* 1978; *Earthbound* 1981; *Liar's Moon* 1982

Connelly, Edward *Camille* 1921; *The Saphead* 1921; *The Torrent* 1926

Connelly, Jennifer *Labyrinth* 1986; *Sisters* 1988; *The Hot Spot* 1990; *Career Opportunities* 1991; *The Rocketeer* 1991; *The Heart of Justice* 1992; *Of Love and Shadows* 1994; *Higher Learning* 1995; *Mulholland Falls* 1996; *Inventing the Abbotts* 1997; *Dark City* 1998

Connery, Jason *The Lords of Discipline* 1983; *The Boy Who Had Everything* 1984; *Spymaker: the Secret Life of Ian Fleming* 1990; *Bullet to Beijing* 1995; *Midnight in St Petersburg* 1995; *Macbeth* 1997; *Shanghai Noon* 2000

Connery, Sean *Lilacs in the Spring* 1955; *Hell Drivers* 1957; *No Road Back* 1957; *Action of the Tiger* 1957; *Time Lock* 1957; *Another Time, Another Place* 1958; *A Night to Remember* 1958; *Darby O'Gill and the Little People* 1959; *Tarzan's Greatest Adventure* 1959; *The Frightened City* 1961; *On the Fiddle* 1961; *Dr No* 1962; *The Longest Day* 1962; *From Russia with Love* 1963; *Goldfinger* 1964; *Marnie* 1964; *Woman of Straw* 1964; *The Hill* 1965; *Thunderball* 1965; *A Fine Madness* 1966; *You Only Live Twice* 1967; *Shalako* 1968; *The Red Tent* 1969; *The Molly Maguires* 1970; *The Anderson Tapes* 1971; *Diamonds Are Forever* 1971; *The Offence* 1972; *Zardoz* 1973; *Murder on the Orient Express* 1974; *The Man Who Would Be King* 1975; *The Wind and the Lion* 1975; *Ransom* 1975; *The Next Man* 1976; *Robin and Marian* 1976; *A Bridge Too Far* 1977; *The First Great Train Robbery* 1978; *Cuba* 1979; *Meteor* 1979; *Outland* 1981; *Time Bandits* 1981; *Five Days One Summer* 1982; *The Man with the Deadly Lens* 1982; *Never Say Never Again* 1983; *Sword of the Valiant* 1984; *Highlander* 1986; *The Name of the Rose* 1986; *The Untouchables* 1987; *Memories of Me* 1988; *The Presidio* 1988; *Family Business* 1989; *Indiana Jones and the Last Crusade* 1989; *Highlander II: the Quickening* 1990; *The Hunt for Red October* 1990; *The Russia House* 1990; *Robin Hood: Prince of Thieves* 1991; *Medicine Man* 1992; *A Good Man in Africa* 1993; *Rising Sun* 1993; *First Knight* 1995; *Just Cause* 1995; *DragonHeart* 1996; *The Rock* 1996; *The Avengers* 1998; *Playing by Heart* 1998; *Entrapment* 1999

Connick Jr, Harry *Memphis Belle* 1990; *Little Man Tate* 1991; *Copycat* 1995; *Excess Baggage* 1997; *Hope Floats* 1998; *The Iron Giant* 1999

Connolly, Andrew *Joyriders* 1988; *Mad Dogs and Englishmen* 1994; *Vendetta* 1999

Connolly, Billy *Absolution* 1978; *Bullshot* 1983; *Water* 1985; *The Big Man* 1990; *Indecent Proposal* 1993; *Pocahontas* 1995; *Muppet Treasure Island* 1996; *Middleton's Changeling* 1997; *Mrs Brown* 1997; *Paws* 1997; *The Impostors* 1998; *Still Crazy* 1998; *The Debt Collector* 1999

Connolly, Kevin *Alan & Naomi* 1992; *Sub Down* 1997

Connolly, Walter *Washington Merry-Go-Round* 1932; *The Bitter Tea of General Yen* 1933; *Lady for a Day* 1933; *Man's Castle* 1933; *Broadway Bill* 1934; *The Captain Hates the Sea* 1934; *It Happened One Night* 1934; *Lady by Choice* 1934; *Twentieth Century* 1934; *So Red the Rose* 1935; *The King Steps Out* 1936; *Libeled Lady* 1936; *First Lady* 1937; *The Good Earth* 1937; *Nancy Steele Is Missing* 1937; *Nothing Sacred* 1937; *The League of Frightened*

Cooney, Ray *Not Now Darling* 1972; *Not Now, Comrade* 1976
Cooper, Alice *Sextette* 1978; *Sgt Pepper's Lonely Hearts Club Band* 1978; *Prince of Darkness* 1987
Cooper, Ben *Johnny Guitar* 1954; *The Outcast* 1954; *The Rose Tattoo* 1955; *Rebel in Town* 1956; *Gunfight at Comanche Creek* 1964; *Arizona Raiders* 1965
Cooper, Camille *aka* **Cooper, Cami** *Like Father, Like Son* 1987; *Shocker* 1989; *Meet the Applegates* 1991; *Lawnmower Man 2: Beyond Cyberspace* 1995
Cooper, Charles *The Wrong Man* 1956; *A Dog's Best Friend* 1960
Cooper, Chris *Matewan* 1987; *Guilty by Suspicion* 1990; *Thousand Pieces of Gold* 1990; *Bed of Lies* 1991; *City of Hope* 1991; *In Broad Daylight* 1991; *This Boy's Life* 1993; *Lone Justice* 1994; *Boys* 1995; *Lone Star* 1995; *Money Train* 1995; *Breast Men* 1997; *Great Expectations* 1997; *Horton Foote's Alone* 1997; *The Horse Whisperer* 1998; *October Sky* 1999; *American Beauty* 1999; *The Patriot* 2000
Cooper, Clancy *Distant Drums* 1951; *A Gift for Heidi* 1958
Cooper, Garry *Quadrophenia* 1979; *Caravaggio* 1986
Cooper, Gary *The Winning of Barbara Worth* 1926; *It* 1927; *Wings* 1927; *Lilac Time* 1928; *The Shopworn Angel* 1928; *Beau Sabreur* 1928; *The Virginian* 1929; *Morocco* 1930; *Paramount on Parade* 1930; *The Texan* 1930; *City Streets* 1931; *Fighting Caravans* 1931; *His Woman* 1931; *A Farewell to Arms* 1932; *If I Had a Million* 1932; *Devil and the Deep* 1932; *Design for Living* 1933; *Today We Live* 1933; *Alice in Wonderland* 1933; *Now and Forever* 1934; *The Lives of a Bengal Lancer* 1935; *Peter Ibbetson* 1935; *The Wedding Night* 1935; *Desire* 1936; *The General Died at Dawn* 1936; *Mr Deeds Goes to Town* 1936; *The Plainsman* 1936; *Souls at Sea* 1937; *The Adventures of Marco Polo* 1938; *Bluebeard's Eighth Wife* 1938; *The Cowboy and the Lady* 1938; *Beau Geste* 1939; *The Real Glory* 1939; *Northwest Mounted Police* 1940; *The Westerner* 1940; *Ball of Fire* 1941; *Meet John Doe* 1941; *Sergeant York* 1941; *The Pride of the Yankees* 1942; *For Whom the Bell Tolls* 1943; *Casanova Brown* 1944; *The Story of Dr Wassell* 1944; *Along Came Jones* 1945; *Saratoga Trunk* 1945; *Cloak and Dagger* 1946; *Unconquered* 1947; *Variety Girl* 1947; *Good Sam* 1948; *The Fountainhead* 1949; *It's a Great Feeling* 1949; *Task Force* 1949; *Bright Leaf* 1950; *Dallas* 1950; *Distant Drums* 1951; *You're in the Navy Now* 1951; *High Noon* 1952; *Springfield Rifle* 1952; *Blowing Wild* 1953; *Return to Paradise* 1953; *Garden of Evil* 1954; *Vera Cruz* 1954; *The Court-Martial of Billy Mitchell* 1955; *Friendly Persuasion* 1956; *Love in the Afternoon* 1957; *Man of the West* 1958; *Ten North Frederick* 1958; *The Hanging Tree* 1959; *The Wreck of the Mary Deare* 1959; *They Came to Cordura* 1959; *Alias Jesse James* 1959; *The Naked Edge* 1961
Cooper, George *The Barker* 1928; *Lilac Time* 1928; *Renegades* 1930; *Think Fast, Mr Moto* 1937; *Crossfire* 1947; *Roughshod* 1949
Cooper, George A *Violent Playground* 1958; *Hell Is a City* 1959; *Nightmare* 1964; *The Strange Affair* 1968; *The Rise and Rise of Michael Rimmer* 1970
Cooper, Gladys *Kitty Foyle* 1940; *Rebecca* 1940; *The Gay Falcon* 1941; *That Hamilton Woman* 1941; *Now, Voyager* 1942; *This above All* 1942; *Mr Lucky* 1943; *The Song of Bernadette* 1943; *Mrs Parkington* 1944; *The White Cliffs of Dover* 1944; *Love Letters* 1945; *The Valley of Decision* 1945; *Beware of Pity* 1946; *The Green Years* 1946; *The Bishop's Wife* 1947; *Homecoming* 1948; *The Pirate* 1948; *Madame Bovary* 1949; *The Secret Garden* 1949; *Sons of the Musketeers* 1951; *Thunder on the Hill* 1951; *The Man Who Loved Redheads* 1954; *Separate Tables* 1958; *The List of Adrian Messenger* 1963; *My Fair Lady* 1964; *The Happiest Millionaire* 1967; *A Nice Girl Like Me* 1969
Cooper, Jackie *The Champ* 1931; *Skippy* 1931; *The Bowery* 1933; *Broadway to Hollywood* 1933; *Treasure Island* 1934; *The Devil Is a Sissy* 1936; *That Certain Age* 1938; *White Banners* 1938; *The Return of Frank James* 1940; *Ziegfeld Girl* 1941; *Men of Texas* 1942; *The Navy Comes Through* 1942; *Syncopation* 1942; *The Love Machine* 1971; *The Invisible Man* 1975; *Superman* 1978; *Superman II* 1980; *Superman III* 1983; *Superman IV: the Quest for Peace* 1987; *Surrender* 1987
Cooper, Jeanne *The Man from the Alamo* 1953; *The Redhead from Wyoming* 1953; *Five Steps to Danger* 1957; *Plunder Road* 1957; *The Intruder* 1961; *Kansas City Bomber* 1972; *Sweet Hostage* 1975
Cooper, Jeff *Born Losers* 1967; *Sharaz* 1968
Cooper, Justin *Liar Liar* 1997; *Dennis Strikes Again* 1998
Cooper, Maggie *And Baby Makes Six* 1979; *An Eye for an Eye* 1981; *Divorce Wars* 1982
Cooper, Maxine *Kiss Me Deadly* 1955; *Autumn Leaves* 1956
Cooper, Melville *The Great Garrick* 1937; *Tovarich* 1937; *The Adventures of Robin Hood* 1938; *The Dawn Patrol* 1938; *Garden of the Moon* 1938; *Gold Diggers in Paris* 1938; *Blind Alley* 1939; *Too Many Husbands* 1940; *The Lady Eve* 1941; *You Belong to Me* 1941; *Life Begins at 8.30* 1942; *Change of Heart* 1943; *Holy Matrimony* 1943; *The Immortal Sergeant* 1943; *Heartbeat* 1946; *13 Rue Madeleine* 1946; *Love Happy* 1949; *Father of the Bride* 1950; *Let's Dance* 1950; *The Petty Girl* 1950; *The Underworld Story* 1950; *The King's Thief* 1955; *Bundle of Joy* 1956
Cooper, Richard *The Black Abbot* 1934; *Lord Edgware Dies* 1934
Cooper, Terence *Calculated Risk* 1963; *Sylvia* 1984; *The Shrimp on the Barbie* 1990
Cooper, Tommy *And the Same to You* 1960; *The Plank* 1967
Coote, Robert *Blond Cheat* 1938; *Bad Lands* 1939; *Mr Moto's Last Warning* 1939; *Vigil in the Night* 1940; *The Commandos Strike at Dawn* 1942; *A Matter of Life and Death* 1946; *The Exile* 1947; *The Ghost and Mrs Muir* 1947; *Berlin Express* 1948; *The Elusive Pimpernel* 1950; *Soldiers Three* 1951; *Othello* 1952; *Scaramouche* 1952; *The Horse's Mouth* 1958; *Merry Andrew* 1958; *The League of Gentlemen* 1960; *A Man Could Get Killed* 1966; *The Swinger* 1966; *Prudence and the Pill* 1968; *Theatre of Blood* 1973
Cope, Kenneth *Naked Fury* 1959; *The Damned* 1961; *Tomorrow at Ten* 1962; *Night of the Big Heat* 1967; *Carry On Matron* 1972; *Rentadick* 1972; *George and Mildred* 1980; *Captives* 1994
Copeland, James *aka* **Copeland, Jimmy** *Innocents in Paris* 1953; *The Maggie* 1953; *Mask of Dust* 1954
Copeland, Joan *The Goddess* 1958; *Cagney & Lacey* 1981; *A Little Sex* 1981; *Happy New Year* 1987; *The Laserman* 1988
Copley, Peter *Golden Salamander* 1949; *The Sword and the Rose* 1952; *Victim* 1961; *King and Country* 1964; *The Knack... and How to Get It* 1965
Copley, Teri *Transylvania Twist* 1989; *Masters of Menace* 1990; *Brain Donors* 1992
Coppola, Marc *Dracula's Widow* 1988; *Deadfall* 1993
Coppola, Sofia *Peggy Sue Got Married* 1986; *The Godfather Part III* 1990; *Inside Monkey Zetterland* 1992; *Star Wars Episode I: the Phantom Menace* 1999
Corbett, Glenn *The Crimson Kimono* 1959; *All the Young Men* 1960; *The Mountain Road* 1960; *Homicidal* 1961; *The Pirates of Blood River* 1961; *Shenandoah* 1965; *Guns in the Heather* 1969; *Chisum* 1970; *Dead Pigeon on Beethoven Street* 1972
Corbett, Gretchen *Let's Scare Jessica to Death* 1971; *The Other Side of the Mountain – Part 2* 1978; *Jaws of Satan* 1979; *Final Verdict* 1991
Corbett, Harry H *Floods of Fear* 1958; *Cover Girl Killer* 1959; *The Shakedown* 1959; *Ladies Who Do* 1963; *Sammy Going South* 1963; *What a Crazy World* 1963; *The Bargee* 1964; *Rattle of a Simple Man* 1964; *Joey Boy* 1965; *Carry On Screaming* 1966; *The Sandwich Man* 1966; *Crooks and Coronets* 1969; *Steptoe and Son* 1972; *Steptoe and Son Ride Again* 1973; *Percy's Progress* 1974; *Jabberwocky* 1977; *Adventures of a Private Eye* 1977; *Silver Dream Racer* 1980
Corbett, John *Don't Look Back* 1995; *Wedding Bell Blues* 1996; *The Morrison Murders* 1997; *Volcano* 1997
Corbett, Leonora *The Constant Nymph* 1933; *Heart's Desire* 1935; *Under Your Hat* 1940
Corbett, Ronnie *Rockets Galore* 1958; *Casino Royale* 1967; *Some Will, Some Won't* 1969; *The Rise and Rise of Michael Rimmer* 1970; *No Sex Please, We're British* 1973; *Fierce Creatures* 1997
Corbin, Barry *Stir Crazy* 1980; *Urban Cowboy* 1980; *Honkytonk Man* 1982; *Six Pack* 1982; *WarGames* 1983; *Flight 90: Disaster on the Potomac* 1984; *The Ratings Game* 1984; *Hard Traveling* 1985; *My Science Project* 1985; *The Defiant Ones* 1986; *Nothing in Common* 1986; *Critters 2: the Main Course* 1988; *Murder in the City of Angels* 1988; *The People across the Lake* 1988; *Who's Harry Crumb?* 1989; *Ghost Dad* 1990; *The Hot Spot* 1990; *Short Time* 1990; *Career Opportunities* 1991; *The Chase* 1991; *Conagher* 1991; *Curdled* 1995; *Robin Cook's Formula for Death* 1995; *Deadly Family Secrets* 1995; *Solo* 1996; *The Hired Heart* 1997
Corby, Ellen *Caged* 1950; *Harriet Craig* 1950; *On Moonlight Bay* 1951; *Shane* 1953; *The Bowery Boys Meet the Monsters* 1954; *Illegal* 1955; *Vertigo* 1958; *Macabre* 1958; *Visit to a Small Planet* 1960; *The Strangler* 1964; *The Night of the Grizzly* 1966; *The Homecoming: a Christmas Story* 1971; *A Day for Thanks on Waltons Mountain* 1982; *A Walton Thanksgiving Reunion* 1993; *A Walton Wedding* 1995
Corcoran, Donna *Angels in the Outfield* 1951; *Don't Bother to Knock* 1952; *Million Dollar Mermaid* 1952; *Young Man with Ideas* 1952; *Dangerous When Wet* 1953; *Scandal at Scourie* 1953; *Gypsy Colt* 1954
Corcoran, Kevin *Old Yeller* 1957; *The Shaggy Dog* 1959; *Swiss Family Robinson* 1960; *Toby Tyler, or Ten Weeks with a Circus* 1960; *Babes in Toyland* 1961; *Bon Voyage!* 1962; *Savage Sam* 1963; *A Tiger Walks* 1964
Corcoran, Noreen *I Love Melvin* 1953; *Tanganyika* 1954
Cord, Alex *Get off My Back* 1965; *Stagecoach* 1966; *The Brotherhood* 1968; *The Last Grenade* 1970; *Genesis II* 1973; *Fire!* 1977; *Grayeagle* 1977; *Sidewinder One* 1977; *The Dirty Dozen: the Fatal Mission* 1988; *CIA – Codename Alexa* 1992
Corday, Mara *Drums across the River* 1954; *So This Is Paris* 1954; *Man without a Star* 1955; *Tarantula* 1955; *Foxfire* 1955; *The Man from Bitter Ridge* 1955; *A Day of Fury* 1956; *Raw Edge* 1956; *The Black Scorpion* 1957
Corday, Marcelle *The Scarlet Letter* 1926; *Peter Ibbetson* 1935
Corday, Rita *aka* **Croset, Paula,** *aka* **Corday, Paula** *The Falcon and the Co-Eds* 1943; *The Falcon Strikes Back* 1943; *The Falcon in Hollywood* 1944; *The Body Snatcher* 1945; *The Falcon in San Francisco* 1945; *Dick Tracy vs Cueball* 1946; *The Falcon's Alibi* 1946; *The Exile* 1947; *The Sword of Monte Cristo* 1951; *Because You're Mine* 1952
Cordero, Joaquin *A Woman without Love* 1951; *The River and Death* 1954
Cording, Harry *The Patriot* 1928; *Arizona Legion* 1939
Cording, John *One Day in the Life of Ivan Denisovich* 1971; *Ransom* 1975
Cordy, Annie *Rider on the Rain* 1970; *La Rupture* 1970
Cordy, Raymond *A Nous la Liberté* 1931; *La Belle Équipe* 1936; *Les Belles de Nuit* 1952
Corey, Isabelle *Bob Le Flambeur* 1955; *It Happened in Rome* 1956; *Aphrodite Goddess of Love* 1957
Corey, Jeff *My Friend Flicka* 1943; *Kidnapped* 1948; *City across the River* 1949; *Home of the Brave* 1949; *Roughshod* 1949; *The Next Voice You Hear* 1950; *Only the Valiant* 1950; *The Outriders* 1950; *Red Mountain* 1951; *The Prince Who Was a Thief* 1951; *The Balcony* 1963; *Lady in a Cage* 1964; *Mickey One* 1965; *Once a Thief* 1965; *Seconds* 1966; *In Cold Blood* 1967; *The Boston Strangler* 1968; *Butch Cassidy and the Sundance Kid* 1969; *Impasse* 1969; *True Grit* 1969; *Getting Straight* 1970; *Little Big Man* 1970; *They Call Me Mister Tibbs!* 1970; *Catlow* 1971; *Shoot Out* 1971; *The Premonition* 1975; *Moonshine County Express* 1977; *Butch and Sundance: the Early Days* 1979; *Bird on a Wire* 1990; *Surviving the Game* 1994
Corey, Wendell *Desert Fury* 1947; *I Walk Alone* 1947; *The Search* 1948; *Sorry, Wrong Number* 1948; *The Accused* 1949; *Any Number Can Play* 1949; *The File on Thelma Jordon* 1949; *Holiday Affair* 1949; *The Furies* 1950; *Harriet Craig* 1950; *No Sad Songs for Me* 1950; *The Wild North* 1952; *Carbine Williams* 1952; *Jamaica Run* 1953; *Hell's Half Acre* 1954; *Rear Window* 1954; *The Big Knife* 1955; *The Bold and the Brave* 1956; *The Rainmaker* 1956; *The Rack* 1956; *Loving You* 1957; *The Light in the Forest* 1958; *Alias Jesse James* 1959; *Picture Mommy Dead* 1966; *Waco* 1966
Corlan, Anthony *Taste the Blood of Dracula* 1969; *A Walk with Love and Death* 1969
Corley, Al *And Baby Makes Six* 1979; *Torchlight* 1984
Corley, Annie *The Bridges of Madison County* 1995; *Box of Moon Light* 1996; *Free Willy 3: the Rescue* 1997; *Here on Earth* 2000
Corley, Pat *The Black Marble* 1980; *Night Shift* 1982; *Against All Odds* 1984; *Calendar Girl Murders* 1984; *When Time Expires* 1997
Cormack, Lynne *Too Outrageous!* 1987; *Dead Ringers* 1988
Corman, Maddie *The Adventures of Ford Fairlane* 1990; *My New Gun* 1992; *Mickey Blue Eyes* 1999
Corman, Roger *War of the Satellites* 1958; *Cannonball* 1976; *The State of Things* 1982; *Body Bags* 1993; *Runaway Daughters* 1994; *Scream 3* 1999
Cornell, Ellie *Halloween 4: the Return of Michael Myers* 1988; *Halloween 5* 1989
Cornthwaite, Robert *The Thing from Another World* 1951; *The War of the Worlds* 1953; *The Spirit of St Louis* 1957; *Ten Seconds to Hell* 1959; *Waterhole #3* 1967
Cornwell, Charlotte *The Krays* 1990; *White Hunter, Black Heart* 1990
Cornwell, Judy *Country Dance* 1970; *Wuthering Heights* 1970; *Every Home Should Have One* 1970; *Who Slew Auntie Roo?* 1971; *Santa Claus* 1985; *Persuasion* 1995
Corone, Antoni *Murder 101* 1991; *Staying Afloat* 1993
Corr, Andrea *Evita* 1996; *The Magic Sword: Quest for Camelot* 1997
Corradi, Nelly *La Signora di Tutti* 1934; *The Barber of Seville* 1946; *La Forza del Destino* 1949
Corraface, Georges *aka* **Corraface, George** *Not without My Daughter* 1990; *Impromptu* 1991; *Christopher Columbus: the Discovery* 1992; *Escape from LA* 1996
Corri, Adrienne *The Romantic Age* 1949; *The River* 1951; *The Kidnappers* 1953; *Lease of Life* 1954; *Behind the Headlines* 1956; *The Feminine Touch* 1956; *The Big Chance* 1957; *The Rough and the Smooth* 1959; *The Hellfire Club* 1961; *Corridors of Blood* 1962; *A Study in Terror* 1965; *Africa – Texas Style* 1967; *The Viking Queen* 1967; *Moon Zero Two* 1969; *A Clockwork Orange* 1971; *Vampire Circus*

1983; *Legend* 1985; *The Color of Money* 1986; *Top Gun* 1986; *Cocktail* 1988; *Rain Man* 1988; *Born on the Fourth of July* 1989; *Days of Thunder* 1990; *Far and Away* 1992; *A Few Good Men* 1992; *The Firm* 1993; *Interview with the Vampire: the Vampire Chronicles* 1994; *Jerry Maguire* 1996; *Mission: Impossible* 1996; *Eyes Wide Shut* 1999; *Mission: Impossible 2* 1999; *Magnolia* 1999

Crutchley, Jeremy *A Good Man in Africa* 1993; *The Mangler* 1994

Crutchley, Rosalie *Take My Life* 1947; *Prelude to Fame* 1950; *The Sword and the Rose* 1952; *Miracle in Soho* 1957; *Seven Thunders* 1957; *A Tale of Two Cities* 1957; *Beyond This Place* 1959; *The Nun's Story* 1959; *No Love for Johnnie* 1960; *Girl in the Headlines* 1963; *The Haunting* 1963; *Wuthering Heights* 1970; *Blood from the Mummy's Tomb* 1971; *Creatures the World Forgot* 1971; *Who Slew Auntie Roo?* 1971; *And Now the Screaming Starts!* 1973; *The House in Nightmare Park* 1973; *Mahler* 1974; *The Fool* 1990; *Four Weddings and a Funeral* 1994

Cruttenden, Abigail *P'Tang, Yang, Kipperbang* 1982; *Hideous Kinky* 1998

Cruttwell, Greg *Naked* 1993; *2 Days in the Valley* 1996; *George of the Jungle* 1997

Cruz, Alexis *Rooftops* 1989; *Stargate* 1994

Cruz, Ernesto Gomez *Reed: Insurgent Mexico* 1971; *El Norte* 1983; *Midaq Alley* 1995

Cruz, Lito *Sur* 1987; *La Amiga* 1988

Cruz, Penelope *Belle Epoque* 1992; *Jamon Jamon* 1992; *Open Your Eyes* 1997; *The Hi-Lo Country* 1998; *Talk of Angels* 1998; *If Only* 1998; *All about My Mother* 1999

Cruz, Raymond *Dragstrip Girl* 1994; *The Substitute* 1996

Cruz, Wilson *All over Me* 1996; *Supernova* 2000

Cryer, Jon *No Small Affair* 1984; *Pretty in Pink* 1986; *Dudes* 1987; *Hiding Out* 1987; *Home Front* 1987; *OC and Stiggs* 1987; *Superman IV: the Quest for Peace* 1987; *Penn & Teller Get Killed* 1989; *Hot Shots!* 1991; *Heads* 1994; *The Pompatus of Love* 1995; *Holy Man* 1998

Crystal, Billy *Human Feelings* 1978; *This Is Spinal Tap* 1984; *Running Scared* 1986; *The Princess Bride* 1987; *Throw Momma from the Train* 1987; *Memories of Me* 1988; *When Harry Met Sally...* 1989; *City Slickers* 1991; *Mr Saturday Night* 1992; *City Slickers II: the Legend of Curly's Gold* 1994; *Forget Paris* 1995; *Deconstructing Harry* 1997; *Fathers' Day* 1997; *My Giant* 1998; *Analyze This* 1999

Cucciolla, Riccardo *Sacco and Vanzetti* 1971; *Borsalino and Co* 1974

Cucinotta, Maria Grazia *Il Postino* 1994; *The Day of the Beast* 1995; *A Brooklyn State of Mind* 1997

Cudlitz, Michael *The Liar's Club* 1992; *Thirst* 1998

Cugat, Xavier *Holiday in Mexico* 1946; *A Date with Judy* 1948; *Neptune's Daughter* 1949

Cuka, Frances *Henry VIII and His Six Wives* 1972; *The Watcher in the Woods* 1982; *The Attic: the Hiding of Anne Frank* 1988

Culkin, Kieran *Father of the Bride* 1991; *Nowhere to Run* 1992; *My Summer Story* 1994; *Father of the Bride Part II* 1995; *The Mighty* 1998; *She's All That* 1999

Culkin, Macaulay *Rocket Gibraltar* 1988; *Uncle Buck* 1989; *Home Alone* 1990; *Jacob's Ladder* 1990; *My Girl* 1991; *Only the Lonely* 1991; *Home Alone 2: Lost in New York* 1992; *George Balanchine's The Nutcracker* 1993; *The Good Son* 1993; *Getting Even with Dad* 1994; *The Pagemaster* 1994; *Richie Rich* 1994

Cullen, Brett *Dead Solid Perfect* 1988; *In a Stranger's Hand* 1991; *By the Sword* 1992; *Leaving Normal* 1992; *Complex of Fear* 1993; *Prehysteria!* 1993; *Keys* 1994; *Something to Talk About* 1995; *The Terror Inside* 1996; *The Killing Jar* 1996; *The Hired Heart* 1997

Cullen, Max *Sunday Too Far Away* 1974; *Summerfield* 1977; *My Brilliant Career* 1979; *Hard Knocks* 1980; *Boundaries of the Heart* 1988; *Rough Diamonds* 1994; *Kiss or Kill* 1997

Cullen, Peter *Heidi's Song* 1982; *The Tigger Movie* 2000

Culley, Frederick *Conquest of the Air* 1936; *The Four Feathers* 1939; *Uncensored* 1942

Cullum, John *All the Way Home* 1963; *The Day After* 1983; *The Prodigal* 1983; *Money, Power, Murder* 1989; *With a Vengeance* 1992

Cullum, John David *aka* **Cullum, J D** *Willy/Milly* 1986; *Ambition* 1991

Culp, Robert *Sammy, the Way Out Seal* 1962; *PT 109* 1963; *Sunday in New York* 1963; *Rhino!* 1964; *Bob & Carol & Ted & Alice* 1969; *Hannie Caulder* 1971; *Hickey and Boggs* 1972; *The Castaway Cowboy* 1974; *Inside Out* 1975; *Breaking Point* 1976; *Flood!* 1976; *The Great Scout & Cathouse Thursday* 1976; *Sky Riders* 1976; *Goldengirl* 1979; *National Lampoon's Movie Madness* 1981; *Calendar Girl Murders* 1984; *Her Life as a Man* 1984; *Turk 182!* 1985; *The Blue Lightning* 1986; *Combat Academy* 1986; *Big Bad Mama II* 1987; *What Price Victory* 1988; *Silent Night, Deadly Night 3: Better Watch Out!* 1989; *Pucker Up and Bark Like a Dog* 1989; *Voyage of Terror: the Achille Lauro Affair* 1990; *The Pelican Brief* 1993; *I Spy Returns* 1994; *Mercenary* 1997; *Most Wanted* 1997

Culver, Roland *The Day Will Dawn* 1942; *The First of the Few* 1942; *Secret Mission* 1942; *The Life and Death of Colonel Blimp* 1943; *English without Tears* 1944; *Give Us the Moon* 1944; *Dead of Night* 1945; *Perfect Strangers* 1945; *Wanted for Murder* 1946; *To Each His Own* 1946; *Down to Earth* 1947; *Singapore* 1947; *The Emperor Waltz* 1948; *Isn't It Romantic* 1948; *The Great Lover* 1949; *Trio* 1950; *Encore* 1951; *Hotel Sahara* 1951; *The Late Edwina Black* 1951; *Folly to Be Wise* 1952; *Rough Shoot* 1952; *The Man Who Loved Redheads* 1954; *The Teckman Mystery* 1954; *Betrayed* 1954; *An Alligator Named Daisy* 1955; *The Ship That Died of Shame* 1955; *Touch and Go* 1955; *Safari* 1956; *The Hypnotist* 1957; *The Vicious Circle* 1957; *Next to No Time* 1958; *Rockets Galore* 1958; *A Pair of Briefs* 1961; *Term of Trial* 1962; *A Man Could Get Killed* 1966; *In Search of Gregory* 1970; *The Legend of Hell House* 1973

Cumming, Alan *Black Beauty* 1994; *Circle of Friends* 1995; *Emma* 1996; *Buddy* 1997; *Romy and Michele's High School Reunion* 1997; *Spice World* 1997; *Eyes Wide Shut* 1999; *Plunkett & Macleane* 1999; *Titus* 1999; *Annie* 1999; *The Flintstones in Viva Rock Vegas* 2000

Cumming, Dorothy *The King of Kings* 1927; *The Divine Woman* 1928; *The Wind* 1928; *Our Dancing Daughters* 1928

Cummings, Constance *The Criminal Code* 1930; *American Madness* 1932; *Movie Crazy* 1932; *Washington Merry-Go-Round* 1932; *Night after Night* 1932; *Broadway through a Keyhole* 1933; *This Man Is Mine* 1934; *Remember Last Night?* 1935; *Busman's Honeymoon* 1940; *The Foreman Went to France* 1941; *Blithe Spirit* 1945; *The Intimate Stranger* 1956; *The Battle of the Sexes* 1960; *In the Cool of the Day* 1963; *Sammy Going South* 1963; *Dead Man's Folly* 1986

Cummings, Jim *The Lion King* 1994; *Balto* 1995; *A Goofy Movie* 1995; *The Tigger Movie* 2000; *The Road to El Dorado* 2000

Cummings, Robert *aka* **Cummings, Bob** *So Red the Rose* 1935; *The Last Train from Madrid* 1937; *Souls at Sea* 1937; *Wells Fargo* 1937; *The Texans* 1938; *The Devil and Miss Jones* 1941; *It Started with Eve* 1941; *Moon over Miami* 1941; *Kings Row* 1942; *Saboteur* 1942; *Flesh and Fantasy* 1943; *Princess O'Rourke* 1943; *The Bride Wore Boots* 1946; *The Chase* 1946; *Heaven Only Knows* 1947; *The Lost Moment* 1947; *Let's Live a Little* 1948; *Sleep, My Love* 1948; *The Accused* 1949; *Reign of Terror* 1949; *Tell It to the Judge* 1949; *For Heaven's Sake* 1950; *The Petty Girl* 1950; *Marry Me Again* 1953; *Dial M for Murder* 1954; *Lucky Me* 1954; *How to Be Very, Very Popular* 1955; *My Geisha* 1962; *Beach Party* 1963; *The Carpetbaggers* 1964; *What a Way to Go!* 1964; *Promise Her Anything* 1966; *Stagecoach* 1966; *Five Golden Dragons* 1967

Cummings, Susan *Secret of Treasure Mountain* 1956; *Verboten!* 1959

Cummins, Martin *Born to Run* 1993; *Search for Justice* 1996

Cummins, Peggy *English without Tears* 1944; *The Late George Apley* 1947; *Moss Rose* 1947; *Green Grass of Wyoming* 1948; *Gun Crazy* 1949; *The Love Lottery* 1953; *Meet Mr Lucifer* 1953; *To Dorothy, a Son* 1954; *The March Hare* 1956; *Carry On Admiral* 1957; *Hell Drivers* 1957; *Night of the Demon* 1957; *The Captain's Table* 1958; *Dentist in the Chair* 1960; *Your Money or Your Wife* 1960; *In the Doghouse* 1961

Cummins, Peter *Sunday Too Far Away* 1974; *Storm Boy* 1976; *Blue Fire Lady* 1977; *Double Deal* 1981; *Kangaroo* 1986; *Ground Zero* 1987

Cundieff, Rusty *Fear of a Black Hat* 1992; *Sprung* 1997

Cunningham, Anne *Bitter Harvest* 1963; *This Sporting Life* 1963

Cunningham, Cecil *Anybody's Woman* 1930; *Artists and Models* 1937; *The Awful Truth* 1937; *Blond Cheat* 1938; *Wives under Suspicion* 1938; *Above Suspicion* 1943

Cunningham, Colin *Robin of Locksley* 1996; *Volcano: Fire on the Mountain* 1997

Cunningham, Jack *Dublin Nightmare* 1958; *The Quare Fellow* 1962

Cunningham, Liam *First Knight* 1995; *A Little Princess* 1995; *Jude* 1996; *The Life of Stuff* 1997; *When the Sky Falls* 2000

Cunningham, Neil *The Tempest* 1979; *The Draughtsman's Contract* 1982

Cuny, Alain *Les Visiteurs du Soir* 1942; *La Signora senza Camelie* 1953; *The Hunchback of Notre Dame* 1956; *The Lovers* 1958; *La Dolce Vita* 1960; *Satyricon* 1969; *Emmanuelle* 1974; *Illustrious Corpses* 1976; *Christ Stopped at Eboli* 1979; *Detective* 1985; *Camille Claudel* 1988

Cupisti, Barbara *Stage Fright – Aquarius* 1987; *The Church* 1988

Curram, Roland *Darling* 1965; *Ooh... You Are Awful* 1972

Curran, Lynette *Bliss* 1985; *The Year My Voice Broke* 1987; *The Delinquents* 1989; *Mushrooms* 1995; *Road to Nhill* 1997; *The Boys* 1998

Curreri, Lee *Fame* 1980; *Crystal Heart* 1987

Currie, Cherie *Foxes* 1980; *Parasite* 1982; *Wavelength* 1983

Currie, Finlay *Command Performance* 1937; *The Edge of the World* 1937; *The Day Will Dawn* 1942; *Thunder Rock* 1942; *The Bells Go Down* 1943; *Great Expectations* 1946; *School for Secrets* 1946; *The Brothers* 1947; *My Brother Jonathan* 1947; *Bonnie Prince Charlie* 1948; *The History of Mr Polly* 1948; *Mr Perrin and Mr Traill* 1948; *Sleeping Car to Trieste* 1948; *The Black Rose* 1950; *The Mudlark* 1950; *Treasure Island* 1950; *People Will Talk* 1951; *Stars and Stripes Forever* 1952; *Walk East on Beacon* 1952; *Kangaroo* 1952; *Rob Roy, the Highland Rogue* 1953; *Treasure of the Golden Condor* 1953; *Footsteps in the Fog* 1955; *King's Rhapsody* 1955; *Captain Lightfoot* 1955; *Zarak* 1956; *Dangerous Exile* 1957; *The Little Hut* 1957; *Saint Joan* 1957; *The Naked Earth* 1958; *Tempest* 1959; *The Angel Wore Red* 1960; *Kidnapped* 1960; *Go to Blazes* 1961; *Corridors of Blood* 1962; *The Inspector* 1962; *Billy Liar* 1963; *The Cracksman* 1963; *The Three Lives of Thomasina* 1963; *West 11* 1963; *Bunny Lake Is Missing* 1965

Currie, Gordon *The Killing Mind* 1991; *Janek: a Silent Betrayal* 1994; *Listen* 1996; *Ripe* 1996; *Dog Park* 1998

Currie, Sandee *Terror Train* 1980; *Gas* 1981

Currie, Sondra *Mama's Dirty Girls* 1974; *The Concrete Jungle* 1982

Currier, Mary *The Falcon in Mexico* 1944; *Stars on Parade* 1944

Curry, Christopher *CHUD* 1984; *Betrayed by Love* 1994

Curry, Tim *The Rocky Horror Picture Show* 1975; *The Shout* 1978; *Times Square* 1980; *Annie* 1982; *Oliver Twist* 1982; *The Ploughman's Lunch* 1983; *Clue* 1985; *Legend* 1985; *Pass the Ammo* 1988; *The Hunt for Red October* 1990; *Oscar* 1991; *FernGully: the Last Rainforest* 1992; *Passed Away* 1992; *National Lampoon's Loaded Weapon 1* 1993; *The Three Musketeers* 1993; *The Shadow* 1994; *Congo* 1995; *The Pebble and the Penguin* 1995; *Lover's Knot* 1995; *Muppet Treasure Island* 1996; *Beauty and the Beast: the Enchanted Christmas* 1997; *McHale's Navy* 1997; *The Rugrats Movie* 1998; *Addams Family Reunion* 1998; *Jackie's Back!* 1999

Curtin, Jane *How to Beat the High Cost of Living* 1980; *Divorce Wars* 1982; *OC and Stiggs* 1987; *Baby Makes Three* 1988; *Coneheads* 1993; *Antz* 1998

Curtin, Valerie *A Different Story* 1978; *Maxie* 1985; *Big Trouble* 1986

Curtis, Alan *Mannequin* 1937; *The Duke of West Point* 1938; *Hollywood Cavalcade* 1939; *Sergeant Madden* 1939; *Four Sons* 1940; *Buck Privates* 1941; *High Sierra* 1941; *Gung Ho!* 1943; *Hitler's Madman* 1943; *Phantom Lady* 1944; *The Daltons Ride Again* 1945

Curtis, Cliff *Desperate Remedies* 1993; *Deep Rising* 1997; *Virus* 1998; *Three Kings* 1999

Curtis, Donald *Phffft!* 1954; *It Came from beneath the Sea* 1955; *Earth vs the Flying Saucers* 1956

Curtis, Jamie Lee *Halloween* 1978; *The Fog* 1980; *Terror Train* 1980; *Prom Night* 1980; *Halloween II* 1981; *Road Games* 1981; *Love Letters* 1983; *Trading Places* 1983; *Grandview, USA* 1984; *Perfect* 1985; *As Summers Die* 1986; *Amazing Grace and Chuck* 1987; *A Man in Love* 1987; *Dominick and Eugene* 1988; *A Fish Called Wanda* 1988; *Blue Steel* 1990; *My Girl* 1991; *Queens Logic* 1991; *Forever Young* 1992; *Mother's Boys* 1993; *My Girl 2* 1994; *True Lies* 1994; *The Heidi Chronicles* 1995; *House Arrest* 1996; *Fierce Creatures* 1997; *Halloween H20: 20 Years Later* 1998; *Homegrown* 1998; *Virus* 1998; *Nicholas' Gift* 1998; *Drowning Mona* 2000

Curtis, Keene *Macbeth* 1948; *The Magician* 1973; *The Buddy System* 1984; *Lambada* 1990

Curtis, Kelly *aka* **Curtis, Kelly Leigh** *The Good Family* 1990; *The Sect* 1991

Curtis, Ken *The Searchers* 1956; *The Wings of Eagles* 1957; *The Missouri Traveler* 1958; *The Killer Shrews* 1959; *Pony Express Rider* 1976; *Once upon a Texas Train* 1988; *Conagher* 1991

Curtis, Mickey *Fires on the Plain* 1959; *Gunhed* 1989

Curtis, Robin *Star Trek III: the Search for Spock* 1984; *Star Trek IV: the Voyage Home* 1986; *Darkbreed* 1996; *Santa with Muscles* 1996

Curtis, Tony *aka* **Curtis, Anthony,** *aka* **Curtis, James** *City across the River* 1949; *Criss Cross* 1949; *Francis* 1949; *The Lady Gambles* 1949; *Johnny Stool Pigeon* 1949; *Sierra* 1950; *Winchester '73* 1950; *Kansas Raiders* 1950; *I Was a Shoplifter* 1950; *The Prince Who Was a Thief* 1951; *No Room for the Groom* 1952; *Son of Ali Baba* 1952; *Meet Danny Wilson* 1952; *Houdini* 1953; *Forbidden* 1953; *The All American* 1953; *Beachhead* 1954; *The Black Shield of Falworth* 1954; *So This Is Paris* 1954; *Johnny Dark* 1954; *Six Bridges to Cross* 1955; *The Square Jungle* 1955; *The Purple Mask* 1955; *The Rawhide Years* 1956; *Trapeze* 1956; *Sweet Smell of Success* 1957; *Mister Cory* 1957; *The Midnight Story* 1957; *The Defiant Ones* 1958; *Kings Go*

Getting Up and Going Home 1992; Husbands and Wives 1992; Leave of Absence 1994; Homage 1995; To Wong Foo, Thanks for Everything, Julie Newmar 1995; The Myth of Fingerprints 1996; Mad City 1997; Forces of Nature 1998; No Looking Back 1998; The Proposition 1998; Anne Tyler's Saint Maybe 1998; The Love Letter 1999

Danning, Sybil Death in the Sun 1975; God's Gun 1977; Battle beyond the Stars 1980; Cuba Crossing 1980; The Salamander 1981; Chained Heat 1983; Hercules 1983; Howling II: Your Sister Is a Werewolf 1984; They're Playing With Fire 1984; Reform School Girls 1986; Warrior Queen 1986; Amazon Women on the Moon 1987

Dano, Royal Undercover Girl 1950; The Red Badge of Courage 1951; The Trouble with Harry 1955; Tension at Table Rock 1956; Man in the Shadow 1957; Trooper Hook 1957; Crime of Passion 1957; Man of the West 1958; Saddle the Wind 1958; Never Steal Anything Small 1959; Face of Fire 1959; Posse from Hell 1961; Gunpoint 1966; The Manhunter 1968; Run, Simon, Run 1970; Cahill, United States Marshal 1973; Electra Glide in Blue 1973; Big Bad Mama 1974; The Wild Party 1975; Joe Dancer: the Big Trade 1983; Something Wicked This Way Comes 1983; Teachers 1984; House II: the Second Story 1987; Ghoulies II 1987; Once upon a Texas Train 1988; Killer Klowns from Outer Space 1988

Danon, Géraldine Erreur de jeunesse 1989; The Old Lady Who Walked in the Sea 1991

Danova, Cesare Crossed Swords 1954; The Man Who Understood Women 1959; Tarzan, the Ape Man 1959; Tender Is the Night 1961; Cleopatra 1963; Gidget Goes to Rome 1963; Viva Las Vegas 1964; Boy, Did I Get a Wrong Number 1966; Chamber of Horrors 1966; Che! 1969; Mean Streets 1973; Scorchy 1976; Tentacles 1977

Danson, Ted The Onion Field 1979; Once upon a Spy 1980; Body Heat 1981; Creepshow 1982; Little Treasure 1985; A Fine Mess 1986; Just between Friends 1986; When the Bough Breaks 1986; Three Men and a Baby 1987; Cousins 1989; Dad 1989; Three Men and a Little Lady 1990; Made in America 1993; Getting Even with Dad 1994; Loch Ness 1994; Pontiac Moon 1994; Homegrown 1998; Saving Private Ryan 1998; Jerry and Tom 1998; Mumford 1999

Dante, Joe Cannonball 1976; Sleepwalkers 1992

Dante, Michael Westbound 1959; Seven Thieves 1960; The Naked Kiss 1964; Apache Rifles 1964; Arizona Raiders 1965; Willard 1971; Winterhawk 1975; Cruise Missile 1978; Cage 1989

Dantine, Helmut Edge of Darkness 1943; Northern Pursuit 1943; Passage to Marseille 1944; Hotel Berlin 1945; Stranger from Venus 1954; War and Peace 1956; Tempest 1959; Bring Me the Head of Alfredo Garcia 1974

Danton, Ray Chief Crazy Horse 1955; I'll Cry Tomorrow 1955; The Looters 1955; The Spoilers 1955; The Night Runner 1957; Onionhead 1958; Too Much, Too Soon 1958; Yellowstone Kelly 1959; The Beat Generation 1959; The Big Operator 1959; Ice Palace 1960; The Rise and Fall of Legs Diamond 1960; The George Raft Story 1961; A Majority of One 1961; A Fever in the Blood 1961; Sandokan against the Leopard of Sarawak 1964; Sandokan Fights Back 1964

Danza, Tony Going Ape! 1981; Single Bars, Single Women 1984; She's Out of Control 1989; In the Line of Duty: Mob Justice 1991; Angels 1994; Deadly Whispers 1995; illtown 1996; Love to Kill 1997; Twelve Angry Men 1997; North Shore Fish 1997; Noah 1998

Danziger, Maia The Kirlian Witness 1978; The Magician of Lublin 1979; Dr Heckyl & Mr Hype 1980

Dapkunaite, Ingeborga Burnt by the Sun 1994; Katia Ismailova 1994; Letters from the East 1995

D'Arbanville-Quinn, Patti aka **D'Arbanville, Patti** Flesh 1968; Big Wednesday 1978; The Main Event 1979; Time after Time 1979; The Fifth Floor 1980; Modern Problems 1981; The Boys Next Door 1985; Real Genius 1985; Call Me 1988; Fresh Horses 1988; Wired 1989; Blind Spot 1993; The Fan 1996; Bad to the Bone 1997

Darbo, Patrika Daddy's Dyin'... Who's Got the Will? 1990; Leaving Normal 1992; The Vagrant 1992; Roseanne and Tom: Behind the Scenes 1994; Secret Sins of the Father 1994; Fast Money 1995

Darby, Kim True Grit 1969; Generation 1969; The Strawberry Statement 1970; The Grissom Gang 1971; The One and Only 1978; Better Off Dead 1985; Embassy 1985; Halloween 6: the Curse of Michael Myers 1995

Darc, Mireille Weekend 1967; There Was Once a Cop 1969; The Tall Blond Man with One Black Shoe 1972; Man in the Trunk 1973; Someone Is Bleeding 1974; The Pink Telephone 1975; The Hurried Man 1977; To Kill a Rat 1977

Darcel, Denise Tarzan and the Slave Girl 1950; Westward the Women 1951; Young Man with Ideas 1952; Dangerous When Wet 1953; Vera Cruz 1954

D'Arcy, Alex aka **D'Arcy, Alexandre,** aka **D'Arcy, Alexander** A Nous la Liberté 1931; The Awful Truth 1937; Topper Takes a Trip 1939; How to Marry a Millionaire 1953; Man on a Tightrope 1953; Fanny Hill: Memoirs of a Woman of Pleasure 1964; Blood of Dracula's Castle 1967; Dead Pigeon on Beethoven Street 1972

D'Arcy, Roy The Merry Widow 1925; La Bohème 1926; The Temptress 1926; The Black Watch 1929

Darden, Severn Goldstein 1964; Frank's Greatest Adventure 1967; The President's Analyst 1967; The Mad Room 1969; Model Shop 1969; The Hired Hand 1971; Conquest of the Planet of the Apes 1972; The War between Men and Women 1972; Who Fears the Devil? 1972; Battle for the Planet of the Apes 1973; Jackson County Jail 1976; Wanda Nevada 1979; In God We Trust 1980; Saturday the 14th 1981; The Telephone 1988

DaRe, Eric Silent Night, Deadly Night 3: Better Watch Out! 1989; Final Combination 1993; The Takeover 1995

Dare, John Girl on Approval 1962; The Impersonator 1962

Darel, Dominique The Big Showdown 1972; Blood for Dracula 1974

Darel, Florence A Tale of Springtime 1989; Fausto 1992; The Secret Steak 1992

Darien, Frank Bad Girl 1931; The Outlaw 1943

Darin, Bobby Pepe 1960; Come September 1961; Hell Is for Heroes 1962; Pressure Point 1962; Too Late Blues 1962; If a Man Answers 1962; State Fair 1962; Captain Newman, MD 1963; That Funny Feeling 1965; Gunfight in Abilene 1967; Stranger in the House 1967; Happy Mother's Day... Love, George 1973

Dark, Christopher Suddenly 1954; World without End 1955; The Halliday Brand 1957; Scandalous John 1971

Darling, Candy Flesh 1968; Silent Night, Bloody Night 1972

Darling, Joan The Troublemaker 1964; Frank's Greatest Adventure 1967

Darlow, Linda Dead Reckoning 1990; The Amy Fisher Story 1993; Beyond Obsession 1994; My Name Is Kate 1994

Darmon, Gérard Les Princes 1982; Betty Blue 1986; Day of Atonement 1993; The Tit and the Moon 1994

Darnell, Linda Brigham Young 1940; Chad Hanna 1940; The Mark of Zorro 1940; Star Dust 1940; Blood and Sand 1941; The Song of Bernadette 1943; Buffalo Bill 1944; It Happened Tomorrow 1944; Summer Storm 1944; Sweet and Lowdown 1944; Fallen Angel 1945; The Great John L 1945; Hangover Square 1945; Anna and the King of Siam 1946; Centennial Summer 1946; My Darling Clementine 1946; Forever Amber 1947; Unfaithfully Yours 1948; Everybody Does It 1949; A Letter to Three Wives 1949; Slattery's Hurricane 1949; No Way Out 1950; Two Flags West 1950; The 13th Letter 1951; The Lady Pays Off 1951; Blackbeard the Pirate 1952; Second Chance 1953; Dakota Incident 1956; Zero Hour 1957; Black Spurs 1965

Darren, James The Brothers Rico 1957; Operation Mad Ball 1957; Gidget 1959; The Gene Krupa Story 1959; All the Young Men 1960; Let No Man Write My Epitaph 1960; Gidget Goes Hawaiian 1961; The Guns of Navarone 1961; Diamond Head 1962; Gidget Goes to Rome 1963

Darrieux, Danielle Mayerling 1936; The Rage of Paris 1938; La Ronde 1950; Le Plaisir 1951; 5 Fingers 1952; Madame de... 1953; Le Rouge et le Noir 1954; Napoléon 1955; Alexander the Great 1956; The Greengage Summer 1961; Bluebeard 1962; The Young Girls of Rochefort 1967; The Scene of the Crime 1986

Darro, Frankie The Mad Genius 1931; The Mayor of Hell 1933; No Greater Glory 1934

Darroussin, Jean-Pierre L'Eau Froide 1994; Un Air de Famille 1996

Darrow, Barbara The Mountain 1956; Queen of Outer Space 1958

Darrow, Henry Badge 373 1973; The Invisible Man 1975; Walk Proud 1979; Losin' It 1983; Blue Heat 1990

Darrow, John The Racket 1928; Hell's Angels 1930

Darrow, Tony GoodFellas 1990; Me and the Mob 1992

Darvas, Lili Meet Me in Las Vegas 1956; Love 1971

Darvi, Bella Hell and High Water 1954; The Racers 1955

Darwell, Jane Tom Sawyer 1930; The White Parade 1934; Bright Eyes 1934; Curly Top 1935; Life Begins at 40 1935; The Country Doctor 1936; Craig's Wife 1936; Poor Little Rich Girl 1936; White Fang 1936; Captain January 1936; Slave Ship 1937; Wife, Doctor and Nurse 1937; Little Miss Broadway 1938; Brigham Young 1940; Chad Hanna 1940; The Grapes of Wrath 1940; Miracle on Main Street 1940; Daniel and the Devil 1941; All through the Night 1942; The Battle of Midway 1942; The Ox-Bow Incident 1943; Tender Comrade 1943; Music in Manhattan 1944; I Live in Grosvenor Square 1945; Three Godfathers 1948; Red Canyon 1949; Caged 1950; Wagonmaster 1950; The Lemon Drop Kid 1951; Affair with a Stranger 1953; The Bigamist 1953

Dary, René Honour among Thieves 1954; Goto, l'Ile d'Amour 1968

Das, Nandita Fire 1996; Earth 1998

Dash, Stacey Enemy Territory 1987; Moving 1988; Mo' Money 1992; Renaissance Man 1994; Clueless 1995; Illegal in Blue 1995; Cold Heart 1997

Dassin, Jules aka **Vita, Perlo** Rififi 1955; Never on Sunday 1960

Dasté, Jean Boudu, Saved from Drowning 1932; Zéro de conduite 1933; L'Atalante 1934; La Vie Est à Nous 1936; La Grande Illusion 1937; La Guerre Est Finie 1966; The Green Room 1978; Noce Blanche 1989

Datcher, Alex Passenger 57 1992; The Expert 1994

Dau, Brigitta The Substitute 1993; Face of Evil 1996; Stand against Fear 1996; When the Cradle Falls 1997

Dauphin, Claude English without Tears 1944; Le Plaisir 1951; April in Paris 1952; Casque d'Or 1952; Innocents in Paris 1953; Little Boy Lost 1953; Phantom of the Rue Morgue 1954; The Bad Liaisons 1955; The Quiet American 1958; The Full Treatment 1961; Tiara Tahiti 1962; Lady L 1965; Barbarella 1967; Two for the Road 1967; Hard Contract 1969; The Madwoman of Chaillot 1969; Rosebud 1975; Madame Rosa 1977; Les Misérables 1978

Davalos, Dominique Howard, a New Breed of Hero 1986; Salvation! Have You Said Your Prayers Today? 1987

Davalos, Elyssa The Apple Dumpling Gang Rides Again 1979; Herbie Goes Bananas 1980; Riviera 1987; A House in the Hills 1993; Jericho Fever 1993

Davalos, Richard East of Eden 1955; The Sea Chase 1955; The Cabinet of Caligari 1962; Hot Stuff 1979

Davenport, A Bromley When London Sleeps 1932; A Shot in the Dark 1933

Davenport, Harry The Cowboy and the Lady 1938; Made for Each Other 1939; All This, and Heaven Too 1940; Lucky Partners 1940; Too Many Husbands 1940; The Bride Came C.O.D. 1941; One Foot in Heaven 1941; That Uncertain Feeling 1941; Ten Gentlemen from West Point 1942; Government Girl 1943; Princess O'Rourke 1943; The Amazing Mrs Holliday 1943; Jack London 1944; Kismet 1944; Meet Me in St Louis 1944; The Thin Man Goes Home 1944; Pardon My Past 1945; This Love of Ours 1945; Claudia and David 1946; Courage of Lassie 1946; Lady Luck 1946; Bachelor Knight 1947; That Lady in Ermine 1948; For the Love of Mary 1948; Down to the Sea in Ships 1949; The Forsyte Saga 1949; Tell It to the Judge 1949

Davenport, Jack Talos the Mummy 1997; The Wisdom of Crocodiles 1998; The Talented Mr Ripley 1999

Davenport, Nigel Lunch Hour 1962; In the Cool of the Day 1963; Ladies Who Do 1963; Sands of the Kalahari 1965; A Man for All Seasons 1966; Sebastian 1968; Play Dirty 1969; Sinful Davey 1969; The Virgin Soldiers 1969; The Royal Hunt of the Sun 1969; The Last Valley 1971; Mary, Queen of Scots 1971; Villain 1971; Living Free 1972; Phase IV 1973; Dracula 1974; The Island of Dr Moreau 1977; Stand Up Virgin Soldiers 1977; Zulu Dawn 1979; Cry of the Innocent 1980; Chariots of Fire 1981; Nighthawks 1981; A Christmas Carol 1984; Greystoke: the Legend of Tarzan, Lord of the Apes 1984; Caravaggio 1986; Without a Clue 1988

Davey, Belinda Death of a Soldier 1985; Proof 1991

Davi, Robert The Goonies 1985; Raw Deal 1986; Hostile Witness 1987; Wild Thing 1987; Action Jackson 1988; Licence to Kill 1989; Deceptions 1990; Maniac Cop 2 1990; Peacemaker 1990; White Hot: the Mysterious Murder of Thelma Todd 1991; The Taking of Beverly Hills 1991; Christopher Columbus: the Discovery 1992; Son of the Pink Panther 1993; Quick 1993; Blind Justice 1994; Cops and Robbersons 1994; No Contest 1995; Showgirls 1995; An Occasional Hell 1996

David, Angel Mixed Blood 1984; The Crow 1994; Two Girls and a Guy 1997; The Substitute 2: School's Out 1997

David, Clifford The Last Mile 1959; The Party's Over 1965; Resurrection 1980

David, Eleanor Pink Floyd – The Wall 1982; The Scarlet Pimpernel 1982; Comfort and Joy 1984; Sylvia 1984; 84 Charing Cross Road 1986; Ladder of Swords 1988; The Wolves of Willoughby Chase 1988; London Kills Me 1991

David, Joanna Anna Karenina 1985; Secret Friends 1991; Cotton Mary 1999

David, Keith The Thing 1982; Platoon 1986; Bird 1988; They Live 1988; Saigon 1988; Always 1989; Marked for Death 1990; Men at Work 1990; Murder in Black & White 1990; Article 99 1992; Final Analysis 1992; Nails 1992; There Are No Children Here 1993; The Last Outlaw 1993; The Puppet Masters 1994; Clockers 1995; Dead Presidents 1995; Johns 1995; Flipping 1996; Executive Target 1997; Volcano 1997; Vanishing Point 1997; Armageddon 1998; The Tiger Woods Story 1998; Pitch Black 2000

David, Mario Les Bonnes Femmes 1960; L'Enfer 1994

David, Michael Let's Make Love 1960; The Fiercest Heart 1961
David, Thayer Wolf Larsen 1958; A Time to Love and a Time to Die 1958; Journey to the Center of the Earth 1959; The Story of Ruth 1960; Save the Tiger 1973; The Eiger Sanction 1975; Peeper 1975; The Duchess and the Dirtwater Fox 1976; Rocky 1976; Spider-Man 1977
David-Djerf, Karl Murder or Memory? 1994; The Yarn Princess 1994
Davidovich, Lolita Blaze 1989; The Inner Circle 1991; The Object of Beauty 1991; Prison Stories: Women on the Inside 1991; Leap of Faith 1992; Raising Cain 1992; Keep the Change 1992; Boiling Point 1993; Younger and Younger 1993; Cobb 1994; Intersection 1994; Indictment: the McMartin Trial 1995; For Better or Worse 1995; Dead Silence 1996; Harvest of Fire 1996; Neil Simon's Jake's Women 1996; Salt Water Moose 1996; Jungle 2 Jungle 1997; Gods and Monsters 1998; Mystery, Alaska 1999; Play It to the Bone 2000
Davidson, Eileen House of Evil 1983; Sharing Richard 1988; Easy Wheels 1989; Broken Badges 1990; Eternity 1990
Davidson, Holly Food of Love 1997; Final Cut 1998
Davidson, Jack Shock Waves 1975; Baby It's You 1983; The Autumn Heart 1998
Davidson, Jaye The Crying Game 1992; Stargate 1994
Davidson, Jim A Zed & Two Noughts 1985; Reasons of the Heart 1996
Davidson, John The Happiest Millionaire 1967; The One and Only, Genuine, Original Family Band 1968; The Squeeze 1987
Davidson, Tommy Strictly Business 1991; Ace Ventura: When Nature Calls 1995; Booty Call 1997; Woo 1998
Davidson, William The Singing Kid 1936; Man Made Monster 1941
Davidtz, Embeth Married for Murder 1992; Army of Darkness 1993; Schindler's List 1993; Murder in the First 1994; Feast of July 1995; Matilda 1996; The Gingerbread Man 1997; Fallen 1998; Last Rites 1998; Simon Magus 1998; Mansfield Park 1999; Bicentennial Man 1999
Davies, Betty Ann The History of Mr Polly 1948; The Passionate Friends 1948; Outcast of the Islands 1951; Cosh Boy 1952; Meet Me Tonight 1952; The Belles of St Trinian's 1954
Davies, Brian American Gigolo 1980; Masquerade 1988
Davies, Jeremy Nell 1994; Spanking the Monkey 1994; Going All the Way 1997; The Locusts 1997; Saving Private Ryan 1998; Up at the Villa 1998; Ravenous 1999; The Million Dollar Hotel 1999
Davies, John Howard Oliver Twist 1948; The Rocking Horse Winner 1949; Tom Brown's Schooldays 1951
Davies, Marion The Patsy 1928; Show People 1928; Hollywood Revue 1929; The Bachelor Father 1931; Blondie of the Follies 1932; Polly of the Circus 1932; Going Hollywood 1933; Peg o' My Heart 1933; Page Miss Glory 1935; Cain and Mabel 1936
Davies, Richard The Falcon in Danger 1943; Please Sir! 1971; Blue Blood 1973

Davies, Rudi The Lonely Passion of Judith Hearne 1987; Resurrected 1989; Frankie Starlight 1995
Davies, Rupert The Traitor 1957; Bobbikins 1959; Devil's Bait 1959; Sapphire 1959; The Criminal 1960; The Uncle 1964; The Spy Who Came in from the Cold 1965; Submarine X-1 1967; Five Golden Dragons 1967; Curse of the Crimson Altar 1968; Dracula Has Risen from the Grave 1968; Witchfinder General 1968; The Firechasers 1970; The Night Visitor 1970; Zeppelin 1971
Davies, Stephen Inserts 1975; The Boy Who Drank Too Much 1980; Desperado 1987; Hanoi Hilton 1987; Dillinger and Capone 1995
Davies, Windsor Adolf Hitler – My Part in His Downfall 1972; Carry On Behind 1975; Carry On England 1976; Confessions of a Driving Instructor 1976; Not Now, Comrade 1976; Old Scores 1991
Davion, Alex The Plague of the Zombies 1965; Bloodsuckers 1970; Incense for the Damned 1970
Davion, Alexander Paranoiac 1963; Valley of the Dolls 1967
Davis, Altovise Pipe Dreams 1976; Kingdom of the Spiders 1977
Davis, Bette Bad Sister 1931; Cabin in the Cotton 1932; The Man Who Played God 1932; The Rich Are Always with Us 1932; Three on a Match 1932; Hell's House 1932; Bureau of Missing Persons 1933; 20,000 Years in Sing Sing 1933; Ex-Lady 1933; Fashions of 1934 1934; Jimmy the Gent 1934; Fog over Frisco 1934; Of Human Bondage 1934; Bordertown 1935; Dangerous 1935; Front Page Woman 1935; The Girl from 10th Avenue 1935; Special Agent 1935; The Petrified Forest 1936; Satan Met a Lady 1936; It's Love I'm After 1937; Kid Galahad 1937; Marked Woman 1937; That Certain Woman 1937; Jezebel 1938; The Sisters 1938; Dark Victory 1939; Juarez 1939; The Old Maid 1939; The Private Lives of Elizabeth and Essex 1939; All This, and Heaven Too 1940; The Letter 1940; The Bride Came C.O.D. 1941; The Great Lie 1941; The Little Foxes 1941; The Man Who Came to Dinner 1941; In This Our Life 1942; Now, Voyager 1942; Old Acquaintance 1943; Watch on the Rhine 1943; Hollywood Canteen 1944; Mr Skeffington 1944; The Corn Is Green 1945; Deception 1946; A Stolen Life 1946; June Bride 1948; Winter Meeting 1948; Beyond the Forest 1949; All about Eve 1950; Payment on Demand 1951; Another Man's Poison 1951; Phone Call from a Stranger 1952; The Star 1953; The Virgin Queen 1955; The Catered Affair 1956; Storm Center 1956; John Paul Jones 1959; The Scapegoat 1959; Pocketful of Miracles 1961; What Ever Happened to Baby Jane? 1962; The Empty Canvas 1963; Dead Ringer 1964; Hush... Hush, Sweet Charlotte 1964; Where Love Has Gone 1964; The Nanny 1965; The Anniversary 1968; Connecting Rooms 1969; Bunny O'Hare 1971; The Judge and Jake Wyler 1972; Madame Sin 1972; Burnt Offerings 1976; The Disappearance of Aimee 1976; Death on the Nile 1978; Return from Witch Mountain 1978; White Mama 1980; Family

Reunion 1981; The Watcher in the Woods 1982; Hotel 1983; Right of Way 1983; Agatha Christie's Murder with Mirrors 1985; As Summers Die 1986; The Whales of August 1987; Wicked Stepmother 1989
Davis, Brad Midnight Express 1978; A Small Circle of Friends 1980; Chariots of Fire 1981; Querelle 1982; Vengeance: the Story of Tony Cimo 1986; Heart 1987; When the Time Comes 1987; Cold Steel 1987; Rosalie Goes Shopping 1989; The Plot to Kill Hitler 1990; Unspeakable Acts 1990; Hangfire 1991
Davis, Carole Mannequin 1987; The Princess Academy 1987; The Shrimp on the Barbie 1990
Davis, Charles The Man from Planet X 1951; The Desert Rats 1953; Five Steps to Danger 1957
Davis, Clifton Lost in the Stars 1974; Scott Joplin 1977; Dream Date 1989
Davis, Daniel K-9 1989; Havana 1990; Palomino 1991
Davis, Don S aka Davis, Don Memories of Murder 1990; Omen IV: the Awakening 1991; Avalanche 1994; Max 1994; The Ranger, the Cook and a Hole in the Sky 1995; The Limbic Region 1996; Volcano: Fire on the Mountain 1997
Davis, Duane Midnight Sting 1992; Mind Breakers 1996; Rocky Marciano 1999
Davis, Essie The Custodian 1993; River Street 1996
Davis, Gail The Far Frontier 1949; Valley of Fire 1951; Blue Canadian Rockies 1952; On Top of Old Smoky 1953; Winning of the West 1953; Alias Jesse James 1959
Davis, Geena Tootsie 1982; Fletch 1985; Sexpionage 1985; Transylvania 6-5000 1985; The Fly 1986; The Accidental Tourist 1988; Beetle Juice 1988; Earth Girls Are Easy 1988; Quick Change 1990; Thelma & Louise 1991; Accidental Hero 1992; A League of Their Own 1992; Angie 1994; Speechless 1994; CutThroat Island 1995; The Long Kiss Goodnight 1996; Stuart Little 1999
Davis, Gene Night Games 1979; 10 to Midnight 1983
Davis, George The Circus 1928; The Kiss 1929; I Met Him in Paris 1937
Davis, Harry America, America 1963; One of Our Spies Is Missing 1966; Rollercoaster 1977
Davis, Hope Guy 1996; Mr Wrong 1996; The Myth of Fingerprints 1996; Arlington Road 1998; The Daytrippers 1998; The Impostors 1998; Next Stop Wonderland 1998; Mumford 1999
Davis, Jim The Cariboo Trail 1950; Cavalry Scout 1951; The Big Sky 1952; Rose of Cimarron 1952; Ride the Man Down 1952; The Outcast 1954; Timberjack 1955; Women without Men 1956; The Restless Breed 1957; Monster from Green Hell 1958; Alias Jesse James 1959; Monte Walsh 1970; Dracula vs Frankenstein 1970; Bad Company 1972; Comes a Horseman 1978; The Day Time Ended 1980
Davis, Joan Life Begins in College 1937; On the Avenue 1937; Thin Ice 1937; Hold That Co-Ed 1938; Josette 1938; My Lucky Star 1938; Sally, Irene and Mary 1938; Just around the Corner 1938; Hold That Ghost 1941; Sun Valley Serenade 1941; Show

Business 1944; George White's Scandals 1945; If You Knew Susie 1948; Love That Brute 1950
Davis, Johnnie Hollywood Hotel 1937; Garden of the Moon 1938
Davis, Judy My Brilliant Career 1979; The Winter of Our Dreams 1981; Who Dares Wins 1982; Heatwave 1983; A Passage to India 1984; Kangaroo 1986; High Tide 1987; Georgia 1988; Barton Fink 1991; Impromptu 1991; Naked Lunch 1991; One against the Wind 1991; Where Angels Fear to Tread 1991; Husbands and Wives 1992; On My Own 1992; Hostile Hostages 1994; The New Age 1994; Serving in Silence 1995; Absolute Power 1996; Blood and Wine 1996; Children of the Revolution 1996; Deconstructing Harry 1997; Celebrity 1998; The Echo of Thunder 1998
Davis, Kristin Doom Asylum 1987; Ultimate Lie 1996
Davis, Mac North Dallas Forty 1979; The Sting II 1983; What Price Victory 1988; Possums 1998
Davis, Mildred A Sailor-Made Man 1921; Safety Last 1923
Davis, Nancy aka Reagan, Nancy East Side, West Side 1949; The Doctor and the Girl 1949; The Next Voice You Hear 1950; It's a Big Country 1951; Donovan's Brain 1953; Hellcats of the Navy 1957; Crash Landing 1958
Davis, Nathan Code of Silence 1985; Flowers in the Attic 1987; Dunston Checks In 1996
Davis, Ossie The Cardinal 1963; Gone Are the Days 1963; Shock Treatment 1964; The Hill 1965; A Man Called Adam 1966; The Scalphunters 1968; Sam Whiskey 1969; Slaves 1969; Night Gallery 1969; Hot Stuff 1979; Harry and Son 1984; Avenging Angel 1985; School Daze 1988; Do the Right Thing 1989; Joe versus the Volcano 1990; Jungle Fever 1991; Gladiator 1992; Grumpy Old Men 1993; The Android Affair 1995; I'm Not Rappaport 1996; Twelve Angry Men 1997; Miss Evers' Boys 1997; Doctor Dolittle 1998; Dinosaur 2000
Davis Jr, Owen They Had to See Paris 1929; Murder on a Bridle Path 1936; The Plot Thickens 1936
Davis, Philip aka Davis, Phil Quadrophenia 1979; The Bounty 1984; Comrades: a Lanternist's Account of the Tolpuddle Martyrs and What Became of Them 1986; High Hopes 1988; Blue Ice 1992; Crimetime 1996; Face 1997; Photographing Fairies 1997; Still Crazy 1998
Davis, Roger House of Dark Shadows 1970; Ruby 1977
Davis, Sammi Mona Lisa 1986; Hope and Glory 1987; Pack of Lies 1987; The Lair of the White Worm 1988; The Rainbow 1988; A Prayer for the Dying 1988; Consuming Passions 1988; Knife Edge 1990; Chernobyl: the Final Warning 1991
Davis Jr, Sammy Anna Lucasta 1958; Porgy and Bess 1959; Ocean's Eleven 1960; Pepe 1960; Convicts Four 1962; Sergeants 3 1962; Johnny Cool 1963; Robin and the 7 Hoods 1964; Nightmare in the Sun 1964; A Man Called Adam 1966; Sweet Charity 1968; Salt and Pepper 1968; One More Time 1970; Sammy Stops the World 1978; Little Moon & Jud McGraw

1978; The Cannonball Run 1981; Heidi's Song 1982; Cannonball Run II 1983; Smorgasbord 1983; Moon over Parador 1988; Tap 1989
Davis, Sonny Carl Thelma & Louise 1991; Blood Money 1996
Davis, Stringer Murder at the Gallop 1963; Murder Ahoy 1964; Murder Most Foul 1964
Davis, Ursula Brennus – Enemy of Rome 1963; Spartacus and the Ten Gladiators 1964
Davis, Viveka Shoot the Moon 1982; Not My Kid 1985; Home Front 1987; Student Exchange 1987; Stalking Laura 1993
Davis, Warwick Willow 1988; Leprechaun 1992; Leprechaun 2 1994; Prince Valiant 1997
Davis, William B Heart of a Child 1994; Circumstances Unknown 1995; The X Files 1998
Davison, Bruce Last Summer 1969; The Strawberry Statement 1970; Willard 1971; The Jerusalem File 1972; Ulzana's Raid 1972; The Affair 1973; Mame 1974; Grand Jury 1976; Mother, Jugs & Speed 1976; Brass Target 1978; Mind over Murder 1979; The Lathe of Heaven 1979; High Risk 1981; Crimes of Passion 1984; Spies like Us 1985; The Ladies Club 1986; I Want Him Back 1990; Longtime Companion 1990; Live! From Death Row 1992; Solomon's Choice 1992; Desperate Justice 1993; Short Cuts 1993; Six Degrees of Separation 1993; Far from Home: the Adventures of Yellow Dog 1994; Someone Else's Child 1994; The Baby-Sitter's Club 1995; The Cure 1995; Homage 1995; The Skateboard Kid II 1995; The Crucible 1996; Grace of My Heart 1996; Widow's Kiss 1996; Hidden in America 1996; Apt Pupil 1997; Color of Justice 1997; At First Sight 1998; Paulie 1998; Vendetta 1999
Davison, Davey The Strangler 1964; Angel, Angel Down We Go 1969; No Drums, No Bugles 1971
Davison, Peter Black Beauty 1994; Parting Shots 1998
Davoli, Ninetto Hawks and Sparrows 1966; Oedipus Rex 1967; The Decameron 1970; The Arabian Nights 1974
Dawber, Pam Remembrance of Love 1982; This Wife for Hire 1985; Wild Horses 1985; Quiet Victory: the Charlie Wedemeyer Story 1988; The Face of Fear 1990; Stay Tuned 1992; A Child's Cry for Help 1994; Trail of Tears 1995; A Stranger to Love 1996
Dawson, Anthony aka Dawson, Tony The Queen of Spades 1948; The Wooden Horse 1950; The Long Dark Hall 1951; Valley of Eagles 1951; Dial M for Murder 1954; The Hour of Decision 1957; Action of the Tiger 1957; Grip of the Strangler 1958; Libel 1959; Tiger Bay 1959; Offbeat 1960; The Curse of the Werewolf 1961; Dr No 1962; Seven Seas to Calais 1962; Pirates 1986
Dawson, Hal K Dr Socrates 1935; Billy Rose's Diamond Horseshoe 1945; Cattle Empire 1958
Dawson, Kamala The Burning Season 1994; Lightning Jack 1994
Dawson, Rosario kids 1995; He Got Game 1998; Down to You 2000
Day, Dennis Music in Manhattan 1944; Golden Girl 1951; The Girl Next Door 1953

Day, Doris *It's Magic* 1948; *Romance on the High Seas* 1948; *It's a Great Feeling* 1949; *My Dream Is Yours* 1949; *Tea for Two* 1950; *The West Point Story* 1950; *Young Man with a Horn* 1950; *Storm Warning* 1950; *I'll See You in My Dreams* 1951; *Lullaby of Broadway* 1951; *On Moonlight Bay* 1951; *April in Paris* 1952; *By the Light of the Silvery Moon* 1953; *Calamity Jane* 1953; *Lucky Me* 1954; *Love Me or Leave Me* 1955; *Young at Heart* 1955; *Julie* 1956; *The Man Who Knew Too Much* 1956; *The Pajama Game* 1957; *Teacher's Pet* 1958; *The Tunnel of Love* 1958; *It Happened to Jane* 1959; *Pillow Talk* 1959; *Midnight Lace* 1960; *Please Don't Eat the Daisies* 1960; *Lover Come Back* 1961; *Billy Rose's Jumbo* 1962; *That Touch of Mink* 1962; *Move Over, Darling* 1963; *The Thrill of It All* 1963; *Send Me No Flowers* 1964; *Do Not Disturb* 1965; *The Glass Bottom Boat* 1966; *Caprice* 1967; *The Ballad of Josie* 1968; *Where Were You When the Lights Went Out?* 1968; *With Six You Get Eggroll* 1968

Day, Frances *Oh Daddy!* 1935; *Fiddlers Three* 1944; *Tread Softly* 1952

Day, Gary *Harbour Beat* 1990; *Tunnel Vision* 1994

Day George, Lynda *aka* **Day, Lynda** *The Gentle Rain* 1966; *Day of the Animals* 1977; *Murder at the World Series* 1977; *The Amazing Captain Nemo* 1978; *Pieces* 1982; *Young Warriors* 1983

Day, Josette *La Belle et la Bête* 1946; *Les Parents Terribles* 1948

Day, Laraine *aka* **Johnson, Laraine** *Painted Desert* 1938; *Arizona Legion* 1939; *Calling Dr Kildare* 1939; *The Secret of Dr Kildare* 1939; *Tarzan Finds a Son!* 1939; *Sergeant Madden* 1939; *Dr Kildare Goes Home* 1940; *Dr Kildare's Crisis* 1940; *Dr Kildare's Strange Case* 1940; *Foreign Correspondent* 1940; *My Son, My Son* 1940; *Dr Kildare's Wedding Day* 1941; *The People vs Dr Kildare* 1941; *The Trial of Mary Dugan* 1941; *Unholy Partners* 1941; *Fingers at the Window* 1942; *Journey for Margaret* 1942; *Mr Lucky* 1943; *Bride by Mistake* 1944; *The Story of Dr Wassell* 1944; *Keep Your Powder Dry* 1945; *Those Endearing Young Charms* 1945; *The Locket* 1946; *Tycoon* 1947; *My Dear Secretary* 1948; *The Woman on Pier 13* 1949; *The High and the Mighty* 1954; *The Third Voice* 1960

Day, Marceline *London after Midnight* 1927; *The Cameraman* 1928; *The Wild Party* 1929; *The Telegraph Trail* 1933

Day, Matt *Muriel's Wedding* 1994; *Love and Other Catastrophes* 1996; *Kiss or Kill* 1997; *Doing Time for Patsy Cline* 1997

Day, Morris *Purple Rain* 1984; *The Adventures of Ford Fairlane* 1990; *Graffiti Bridge* 1990

Day, Vera *It's a Great Day* 1955; *A Kid for Two Farthings* 1955; *Quatermass II* 1957; *The Woman Eater* 1957; *Grip of the Strangler* 1958; *Too Many Crooks* 1958; *Up the Creek* 1958; *Trouble with Eve* 1959; *And the Same to You* 1960; *Watch It, Sailor!* 1961; *Saturday Night Out* 1963

Dayan, Assaf *A Walk with Love and Death* 1969; *The Sellout* 1975

Day-Lewis, Daniel *The Bounty* 1984; *My Beautiful Laundrette* 1985; *A Room with a View* 1985; *Nanou* 1986; *Stars and Bars* 1988; *The Unbearable Lightness of Being* 1988; *Eversmile, New Jersey* 1989; *My Left Foot* 1989; *The Last of the Mohicans* 1992; *The Age of Innocence* 1993; *In the Name of the Father* 1993; *The Crucible* 1996; *The Boxer* 1997

Dayton, Dan *At War with the Army* 1950; *The Turning Point* 1952

De Acutis, William *Nine ½ Weeks* 1985; *Chattahoochee* 1989

de Almeida, Joaquim *The Honorary Consul* 1983; *Good Morning, Babylon* 1987; *Clear and Present Danger* 1994; *Only You* 1994; *Desperado* 1995

De Baer, Jean *A Flash of Green* 1984; *84 Charing Cross Road* 1986

de Bankole, Isaach *Chocolat* 1988; *Night on Earth* 1992; *Heart of Darkness* 1993; *The Keeper* 1995; *Ghost Dog: the Way of the Samurai* 1999

de Banzie, Brenda *Hobson's Choice* 1953; *The Purple Plain* 1954; *As Long as They're Happy* 1955; *Doctor at Sea* 1955; *A Kid for Two Farthings* 1955; *House of Secrets* 1956; *The Man Who Knew Too Much* 1956; *Passport to Shame* 1958; *Too Many Crooks* 1958; *The Thirty-Nine Steps* 1959; *The Entertainer* 1960; *Flame in the Streets* 1961; *The Mark* 1961; *A Pair of Briefs* 1961; *The Pink Panther* 1964; *Pretty Polly* 1967

de Bray, Yvonne *Eternal Love* 1943; *Les Parents Terribles* 1948

De Brulier, Nigel *The Three Musketeers* 1921; *Salome* 1922; *The Hunchback of Notre Dame* 1923; *Moby Dick* 1930; *The Three Musketeers* 1935

De Burgh, Celia *The Getting of Wisdom* 1977; *Sound of Love* 1977; *Phar Lap* 1983

De Cadenet, Amanda *The Rachel Papers* 1989; *Four Rooms* 1995; *Fall* 1997

De Camp, Rosemary *aka* **DeCamp, Rosemary** *Hold Back the Dawn* 1941; *Jungle Book* 1942; *Yankee Doodle Dandy* 1942; *This Is the Army* 1943; *Blood on the Sun* 1945; *Pride of the Marines* 1945; *Rhapsody in Blue* 1945; *From This Day Forward* 1946; *Two Guys from Milwaukee* 1946; *Nora Prentiss* 1947; *Look for the Silver Lining* 1949; *The Story of Seabiscuit* 1949; *On Moonlight Bay* 1951; *Treasure of Lost Canyon* 1952; *By the Light of the Silvery Moon* 1953; *Main Street to Broadway* 1953; *Night unto Night* 1949; *So This Is Love* 1953; *Saturday the 14th* 1981

De Capitani, Grace *Le Cop* 1985; *Le Cop II* 1989

De Carlo, Yvonne *True to Life* 1943; *Frontier Gal* 1945; *Brute Force* 1947; *Song of Scheherazade* 1947; *Casbah* 1948; *Calamity Jane and Sam Bass* 1949; *Criss Cross* 1949; *Hotel Sahara* 1951; *The San Francisco Story* 1952; *Sea Devils* 1952; *The Captain's Paradise* 1953; *Fort Algiers* 1953; *Happy Ever After* 1954; *Passion* 1954; *Shotgun* 1955; *Death of a Scoundrel* 1956; *Raw Edge* 1956; *The Ten Commandments* 1956; *Magic Fire* 1956; *Band of Angels* 1957; *The Sword and the Cross* 1958; *Timbuktu* 1959; *McLintock!* 1963; *A Global Affair* 1964; *Munster, Go Home!* 1966; *Hostile Guns* 1967; *The Power* 1968; *Arizona Bushwhackers* 1968; *The Delta Factor* 1970; *The Seven Minutes* 1971; *The Mark of Zorro* 1974; *Won Ton Ton, the Dog Who Saved Hollywood* 1976; *Satan's Cheerleaders* 1977; *Play Dead* 1981; *Liar's Moon* 1982; *The Masterpiece of Murder* 1986; *American Gothic* 1987

de Casalis, Jeanne *Nell Gwyn* 1934; *Sailors Three* 1940; *Cottage to Let* 1941

De Castro, Isabel *Tall Stories* 1990; *Here on Earth* 1993

De Cordoba, Pedro *Girl Loves Boy* 1937; *Devil's Island* 1940; *The Ghost Breakers* 1940; *Tarzan Triumphs* 1943; *Comanche Territory* 1950

De Cordova, Arturo *For Whom the Bell Tolls* 1943; *Hostages* 1943; *Frenchman's Creek* 1944; *Incendiary Blonde* 1945; *A Medal for Benny* 1945; *El* 1952

De Corsia, Ted *The Lady from Shanghai* 1948; *The Naked City* 1948; *It Happens Every Spring* 1949; *Three Secrets* 1950; *Murder, Inc* 1951; *Ride, Vaquero!* 1953; *Man in the Dark* 1953; *20,000 Leagues under the Sea* 1954; *The City Is Dark* 1954; *The Big Combo* 1955; *The Killing* 1956; *Slightly Scarlet* 1956; *The Midnight Story* 1957

De, Dipankar *Branches of the Tree* 1990; *The Stranger* 1991

De Filippo, Eduardo *The Seven Deadly Sins* 1952; *Shout Loud, Louder… I Don't Understand* 1966

De Filippo, Peppino *Lights of Variety* 1950; *Boccaccio '70* 1961

De Funès, Louis *The Sheep Has Five Legs* 1954; *The Gendarme of St Tropez* 1964; *The Gendarme in New York* 1965; *Don't Look Now… We're Being Shot At* 1966; *Delusions of Grandeur* 1971; *The Spacemen of St Tropez* 1978; *The Gendarme Wore Skirts* 1982

De Grasse, Sam *Blind Husbands* 1919; *Robin Hood* 1922; *The Black Pirate* 1926

de Havilland, Olivia *Captain Blood* 1935; *A Midsummer Night's Dream* 1935; *Anthony Adverse* 1936; *The Charge of the Light Brigade* 1936; *The Great Garrick* 1937; *It's Love I'm After* 1937; *The Adventures of Robin Hood* 1938; *Four's a Crowd* 1938; *Gold Is Where You Find It* 1938; *Hard to Get* 1938; *Dodge City* 1939; *Gone with the Wind* 1939; *The Private Lives of Elizabeth and Essex* 1939; *Raffles* 1939; *Santa Fe Trail* 1940; *Hold Back the Dawn* 1941; *The Strawberry Blonde* 1941; *They Died with Their Boots On* 1941; *In This Our Life* 1942; *The Male Animal* 1942; *Government Girl* 1943; *Princess O'Rourke* 1943; *The Dark Mirror* 1946; *Devotion* 1946; *To Each His Own* 1946; *The Snake Pit* 1948; *The Heiress* 1949; *My Cousin Rachel* 1952; *Not as a Stranger* 1955; *That Lady* 1955; *The Ambassador's Daughter* 1956; *The Proud Rebel* 1958; *Libel* 1959; *Light in the Piazza* 1962; *Hush… Hush, Sweet Charlotte* 1964; *Lady in a Cage* 1964; *The Adventurers* 1970; *Pope Joan* 1972; *Airport '77* 1977; *The Swarm* 1978; *The Fifth Musketeer* 1979; *Agatha Christie's Murder Is Easy* 1982; *Anastasia: the Mystery of Anna* 1986

De Keyser, David *Leo the Last* 1970; *The Ploughman's Lunch* 1983; *Leon the Pig Farmer* 1992; *The Designated Mourner* 1997; *Sunshine* 1999

De Kova, Frank *Shack Out on 101* 1955; *Teenage Caveman* 1958; *The Wild Country* 1971; *The Mechanic* 1972; *The Slams* 1973

de la Brosse, Simon *Pauline at the Beach* 1983; *La Petite Voleuse* 1988; *Loser Takes All* 1990; *Strike It Rich* 1990

de la Fontaine, Agathe *Another Nine ½ Weeks* 1997; *Train of Life* 1999

De La Fuente, Joel *When the Cradle Falls* 1997; *Return to Paradise* 1998

De La Motte, Marguerite *The Mark of Zorro* 1920; *The Iron Mask* 1929

De La Paz, Danny *Boulevard Nights* 1979; *Barbarosa* 1982; *City Limits* 1985; *The Wild Pair* 1987; *American Me* 1992

De La Pena, George *Nijinsky* 1980; *Kuffs* 1991; *Brain Donors* 1992

de la Tour, Frances *Our Miss Fred* 1972; *Wombling Free* 1977; *Rising Damp* 1980; *Agatha Christie's Murder with Mirrors* 1985; *Bejewelled* 1990; *Loser Takes All* 1990; *Strike It Rich* 1990; *The Cherry Orchard* 1998

De Lacy, Philippe *The Student Prince in Old Heidelberg* 1927; *Sarah and Son* 1930

de Lancie, John *The Hand That Rocks the Cradle* 1992; *Fearless* 1993; *Deep Red* 1994; *Final Descent* 1997

De Lint, Derek *Soldier of Orange* 1977; *The Assault* 1986; *Mascara* 1987; *The Unbearable Lightness of Being* 1988; *Stealing Heaven* 1988

De Luca, Lorella *The Swindle* 1955; *The Sign of the Gladiator* 1958

de Marney, Derrick *Land without Music* 1936; *Things to Come* 1936; *Young and Innocent* 1937; *Flying 55* 1939; *Dangerous Moonlight* 1941; *Uncle Silas* 1947; *Sleeping Car to Trieste* 1948

de Medeiros, Maria *1871* 1989; *Henry & June* 1990; *L'Homme de Ma Vie* 1992; *The Divine Comedy* 1992; *Golden Balls* 1993; *Pulp Fiction* 1994; *Le Polygraphe* 1996; *News from the Good Lord* 1996

de Mendoza, Alberto *aka* **Mendoza, Albert** *That Man George* 1965; *A Bullet for Sandoval* 1970; *Delusions of Grandeur* 1971; *Horror Express* 1972; *Open Season* 1974; *What Changed Charley Farthing?* 1975

de Metz, Danielle *Return of the Fly* 1959; *Gidget Goes to Rome* 1963; *Raid on Rommel* 1971

De Monaghan, Laurence *Claire's Knee* 1970; *Story of a Love Story* 1973

De Mornay, Rebecca *Risky Business* 1983; *Testament* 1983; *Runaway Train* 1985; *The Trip to Bountiful* 1985; *The Slugger's Wife* 1985; *The Murders in the Rue Morgue* 1986; *Beauty and the Beast* 1987; *And God Created Woman* 1988; *Feds* 1988; *Dealers* 1989; *By Dawn's Early Light* 1990; *Backdraft* 1991; *The Hand That Rocks the Cradle* 1992; *Blind Side* 1993; *Getting Out* 1993; *Guilty as Sin* 1993; *The Three Musketeers* 1993; *Never Talk to Strangers* 1995; *Night Ride Home* 1999

De Niro, Robert *aka* **DeNero, Robert** *The Wedding Party* 1966; *Greetings* 1968; *Sam's Song* 1969; *Bloody Mama* 1970; *Hi, Mom!* 1970; *Jennifer on My Mind* 1971; *Born to Win* 1971; *The Gang That Couldn't Shoot Straight* 1971; *Bang the Drum Slowly* 1973; *Mean Streets* 1973; *The Godfather, Part II* 1974; *The Last Tycoon* 1976; *1900* 1976; *Taxi Driver* 1976; *New York, New York* 1977; *The Deer Hunter* 1978; *Raging Bull* 1980; *True Confessions* 1981; *The King of Comedy* 1983; *Falling in Love* 1984; *Once upon a Time in America* 1984; *Brazil* 1985; *The Mission* 1986; *Angel Heart* 1987; *The Untouchables* 1987; *Jacknife* 1988; *Midnight Run* 1988; *Stanley & Iris* 1989; *We're No Angels* 1989; *Awakenings* 1990; *GoodFellas* 1990; *Guilty by Suspicion* 1990; *Backdraft* 1991; *Cape Fear* 1991; *Mad Dog and Glory* 1992; *Mistress* 1992; *Night and the City* 1992; *A Bronx Tale* 1993; *This Boy's Life* 1993; *Mary Shelley's Frankenstein* 1994; *Casino* 1995; *Heat* 1995; *The Fan* 1996; *Marvin's Room* 1996; *Sleepers* 1996; *Cop Land* 1997; *Great Expectations* 1997; *Jackie Brown* 1997; *Wag the Dog* 1997; *Ronin* 1998; *Analyze This* 1999; *Flawless* 1999

de Palma, Rossy *Women on the Verge of a Nervous Breakdown* 1988; *Kika* 1993; *The Flower of My Secret* 1995

de Pencier, Miranda *The Myth of the Male Orgasm* 1993; *Harrison Bergeron* 1995

De Rita, Joe *Have Rocket, Will Travel* 1959; *The Three Stooges in Orbit* 1962; *The Three Stooges Meet Hercules* 1962; *The Three Stooges Go around the World in a Daze* 1963; *The Outlaws Is Coming* 1965

De Rossi, Barbara *Quo Vadis?* 1985; *Vampire in Venice* 1987

De Sade, Ana *The Return of a Man Called Horse* 1976; *Triumphs of a Man Called Horse* 1983

De Santis, Joe *aka* **De Santis, Joseph** *The Man with a Cloak* 1951; *Deadline – USA* 1952; *Full of Life* 1956; *Tension at Table Rock* 1956; *The Unholy Wife* 1957; *Dino* 1957; *Jeanne Eagels* 1957; *Al Capone* 1959; *A Cold Wind in August* 1961; *The Professionals* 1966; *And Now Miguel* 1966; *Blue* 1968

De Sapio, Francesca *Blood Red* 1988; *Torrents of Spring* 1989

De Sica, Vittorio *Bread, Love and Dreams* 1953; *Madame de…* 1953; *Gold of Naples* 1954; *Secrets d'Alcove* 1954; *Too Bad She's Bad* 1955; *The Miller's Wife* 1955; *It Happened in Rome* 1956; *A Farewell to Arms* 1957; *The Monte Carlo Story* 1957; *General Della Rovere* 1959; *The Angel Wore Red* 1960; *It Started in Naples* 1960; *The Millionairess* 1960; *The Amorous Adventures of Moll Flanders* 1965; *The Biggest Bundle of Them All* 1968; *The Shoes of the Fisherman* 1968; *Snow Job* 1972; *Blood for Dracula* 1974; *We All Loved Each Other So Much* 1974; *Blood for Dracula* 1974

De Soto, Rosana *La Bamba* 1986; *Stand and Deliver* 1988

De Souza, Edward *The Phantom of the Opera* 1962; *The Return of the Soldier* 1982

De Turckheim, Charlotte *Le Maître d'école* 1981; *Right Bank, Left Bank* 1984; *Mon Père Ce Héros* 1991

De Villalonga, José-Luis *Cleo from 5 to 7* 1961; *Darling* 1965; *The Burglars* 1971

de Vries, Dolf *Turkish Delight* 1973; *The Fourth Man* 1983
de Wilde, Brandon *The Member of the Wedding* 1952; *Shane* 1953; *Good-bye, My Lady* 1956; *Night Passage* 1957; *The Missouri Traveler* 1958; *Blue Denim* 1959; *All Fall Down* 1962; *Hud* 1963; *Those Calloways* 1964; *The Deserter* 1971; *Black Jack* 1972
de Wit, Jacqueline *Wild Beauty* 1946; *Little Giant* 1946; *The Great Jewel Robber* 1950; *All That Heaven Allows* 1955; *Tea and Sympathy* 1956; *Twice Told Tales* 1963
De Wolfe, Billy *Miss Susie Slagle's* 1945; *Blue Skies* 1946; *Dear Ruth* 1947; *The Perils of Pauline* 1947; *Isn't It Romantic* 1948; *Dear Wife* 1949; *Tea for Two* 1950; *Lullaby of Broadway* 1951; *Call Me Madam* 1953; *Billie* 1965
De Wolff, Francis *The Kidnappers* 1953; *Geordie* 1955; *King's Rhapsody* 1955; *The Hound of the Baskervilles* 1959; *The Man Who Could Cheat Death* 1959; *The Two Faces of Dr Jekyll* 1960; *From Russia with Love* 1963; *The World Ten Times Over* 1963; *Devil Doll* 1964; *Licensed to Kill* 1965
De Young, Cliff *The Night that Panicked America* 1975; *Shock Treatment* 1981; *The Hunger* 1983; *Independence Day* 1983; *Protocol* 1984; *F/X* 1985; *Secret Admirer* 1985; *Flight of the Navigator* 1986; *Code Name: Dancer* 1987; *Pulse* 1988; *Fear* 1988; *Rude Awakening* 1989; *Flashback* 1990; *Where Pigeons Go to Die* 1990; *Deadly Identity* 1991; *New York Mounted* 1991; *Criminal Behaviour* 1992; *Dr Giggles* 1992; *An Element of Truth* 1995; *The Craft* 1996
Déa, Marie *Pièges* 1939; *Orphée* 1950
Deacon, Brian *The Triple Echo* 1972; *Jesus* 1979; *Separate Tables* 1983; *A Zed & Two Noughts* 1985
Deacon, Kim *The Getting of Wisdom* 1977; *Rebel* 1985
Deacon, Richard *Abbott and Costello Meet the Mummy* 1955; *Blackbeard's Ghost* 1967; *The Gnome-Mobile* 1967; *The Happy Hooker Goes to Hollywood* 1980
Deakin, Julia *Mr Love* 1985; *Dancin' thru the Dark* 1989
Deakins, Lucy *The Boy Who Could Fly* 1986; *Cheetah* 1989; *There Goes My Baby* 1994
Dean, Allison *Coming to America* 1988; *Ruby in Paradise* 1993
Dean, Bill *Family Life* 1971; *Night Watch* 1973
Dean, Felicity *Steaming* 1985; *The Whistle Blower* 1986
Dean, Isabel *The Passionate Friends* 1948; *The Story of Gilbert and Sullivan* 1953; *Out of the Clouds* 1954; *Virgin Island* 1958; *Light in the Piazza* 1962; *Ransom* 1975; *Rough Cut* 1980; *Five Days One Summer* 1982
Dean, James *Sailor Beware* 1951; *Has Anybody Seen My Gal?* 1952; *East of Eden* 1955; *Rebel without a Cause* 1955; *Giant* 1956
Dean, Julia *The Curse of the Cat People* 1944; *Nightmare Alley* 1947
Dean, Laura *Fame* 1980; *Almost You* 1984
Dean, Loren *Say Anything* 1989; *Billy Bathgate* 1991; *1492: Conquest of Paradise* 1992; *Mrs Winterbourne* 1995; *The Passion of Darkly Noon* 1995; *The End of Violence* 1997; *Gattaca* 1997; *Rosewood* 1997; *Mumford* 1999

Dean, Margia *The Quatermass Experiment* 1955; *Villa!* 1958; *The Secret of the Purple Reef* 1960; *The Big Show* 1961
Dean, Rick *aka* **Dean, Richard** *Heroes Stand Alone* 1989; *Quake!* 1992; *Cheyenne Warrior* 1994
Dean, Ron *Cocktail* 1988; *Cold Justice* 1991
Deane, Lezlie *976-EVIL* 1988; *Freddy's Dead: the Final Nightmare* 1991; *To Protect and Serve* 1992
Dear, Elizabeth *The Greengage Summer* 1961; *The Battle of the Villa Fiorita* 1964
Dearing, Edgar *Free and Easy* 1930; *They Gave Him a Gun* 1937
Deas, Justin *Dream Lover* 1986; *A Stranger Waits* 1987; *Montana* 1990
Deayton, Angus *Savage Hearts* 1995; *Elizabeth* 1998
Debar, Andrée *The House on the Waterfront* 1955; *Guilty?* 1956
DeBell, Kristine *Meatballs* 1979; *The Big Brawl* 1980
DeBenning, Burr *Beach Red* 1967; *Sweet November* 1968; *City beneath the Sea* 1971; *The Face of Fear* 1971; *The Incredible Melting Man* 1977; *The Amazing Captain Nemo* 1978
deBoer, Nicole *aka* **DeBoer, Nikki** *The Counterfeit Contessa* 1994; *Cube* 1997
DeBroux, Lee *Run, Angel, Run* 1969; *Sweet Hostage* 1975; *Louis Armstrong: Chicago Style* 1976; *MADD: Mothers against Drunk Drivers* 1983; *Longarm* 1988; *Hangfire* 1991; *Open Fire* 1995
Debucourt, Jean *Mayerling* 1936; *Abel Gance's Beethoven* 1936; *Devil in the Flesh* 1946; *Eagle with Two Heads* 1948; *Madame de...* 1953; *Nana* 1955
Decker, Diana *Fiddlers Three* 1944; *When You Come Home* 1947; *Murder at the Windmill* 1949; *Knave of Hearts* 1954; *A Yank in Ermine* 1955; *Lolita* 1961; *Devils of Darkness* 1964
Deckers, Eugene *Highly Dangerous* 1950; *Hotel Sahara* 1951; *Foreign Intrigue* 1956; *Seven Thunders* 1957; *North West Frontier* 1959
Deckert, Blue *The Lady from Yesterday* 1985; *Getting Even* 1986; *A Taste for Killing* 1992
Decleir, Jan *Daens* 1992; *Antonia's Line* 1995; *Character* 1997
Declie, Xavier *Adrenalin: Fear the Rush* 1995; *Nemesis 3 – Time Lapse* 1996
Decomble, Guy *Jour de Fête* 1947; *Bob Le Flambeur* 1955; *Les Cousins* 1959; *The 400 Blows* 1959
Dee, Frances *An American Tragedy* 1931; *If I Had a Million* 1932; *Love Is a Racket* 1932; *This Reckless Age* 1932; *Little Women* 1933; *The Silver Cord* 1933; *Of Human Bondage* 1934; *Finishing School* 1934; *Becky Sharp* 1935; *The Gay Deception* 1935; *Souls at Sea* 1937; *Wells Fargo* 1937; *If I Were King* 1938; *A Man Betrayed* 1941; *So Ends Our Night* 1941; *Happy Land* 1943; *I Walked with a Zombie* 1943; *Patrick the Great* 1944; *The Private Affairs of Bel Ami* 1947; *They Passed This Way* 1948; *Payment on Demand* 1951; *Gypsy Colt* 1954
Dee, Ruby *The Tall Target* 1951; *Go, Man, Go!* 1953; *Edge of the City* 1957; *St Louis Blues* 1958; *Take a Giant Step* 1959; *A Raisin in the Sun* 1961; *The Balcony*

1963; *Gone Are the Days* 1963; *The Incident* 1967; *King: a Filmed Record... Montgomery to Memphis* 1970; *Buck and the Preacher* 1972; *Do the Right Thing* 1989; *The Court-Martial of Jackie Robinson* 1990; *Decoration Day* 1990; *Jungle Fever* 1991; *Cop and a Half* 1993; *Mr and Mrs Loving* 1993; *Captive Heart: the James Mink Story* 1996; *A Simple Wish* 1997; *Baby Geniuses* 1999; *Having Our Say: the Delany Sisters' First 100 Years* 1999
Dee, Sandra *Until They Sail* 1957; *The Reluctant Debutante* 1958; *The Restless Years* 1958; *Gidget* 1959; *Imitation of Life* 1959; *The Snow Queen* 1959; *The Wild and the Innocent* 1959; *A Summer Place* 1959; *A Stranger in My Arms* 1959; *Portrait in Black* 1960; *Come September* 1961; *Romanoff and Juliet* 1961; *If a Man Answers* 1962; *Tammy and the Doctor* 1963; *Take Her, She's Mine* 1963; *I'd Rather Be Rich* 1964; *That Funny Feeling* 1965; *A Man Could Get Killed* 1966; *Rosie!* 1967; *The Manhunter* 1968; *The Dunwich Horror* 1970
Deering, Olive *Samson and Delilah* 1949; *Shock Treatment* 1964
Dees, Stephanie *Evil in Clear River* 1988; *The Butter Cream Gang* 1991
Deezen, Eddie *Delta Pi* 1985; *Money Mania* 1987; *Rock-a-Doodle* 1990
DeFore, Don *The Affairs of Susan* 1945; *The Stork Club* 1945; *Without Reservations* 1946; *It Happened on Fifth Avenue* 1947; *It's Magic* 1948; *My Friend Irma* 1949; *Dark City* 1950; *A Girl in Every Port* 1952; *She's Working Her Way through College* 1952; *No Room for the Groom* 1952; *Battle Hymn* 1957; *A Time to Love and a Time to Die* 1958; *The Facts of Life* 1960
DeGeneres, Ellen *Coneheads* 1993; *Mr Wrong* 1996; *Goodbye Lover* 1997; *EDtv* 1999; *The Love Letter* 1999; *If These Walls Could Talk 2* 2000
Degermark, Pia *Elvira Madigan* 1967; *The Looking Glass War* 1969
DeHaven, Gloria *aka* **De Haven, Gloria** *Best Foot Forward* 1943; *Broadway Rhythm* 1944; *Step Lively* 1944; *Two Girls and a Sailor* 1944; *The Thin Man Goes Home* 1944; *Summer Holiday* 1948; *Scene of the Crime* 1949; *The Doctor and the Girl* 1949; *Summer Stock* 1950; *Three Little Words* 1950; *The Yellow Cab Man* 1950; *Two Tickets to Broadway* 1951; *So This Is Paris* 1954; *The Girl Rush* 1955; *Out to Sea* 1997
Dehner, John *Ten Tall Men* 1951; *China Corsair* 1951; *Desert Passage* 1952; *Fort Algiers* 1953; *Powder River* 1953; *Apache* 1954; *The Bowery Boys Meet the Monsters* 1954; *The King's Thief* 1955; *Tall Man Riding* 1955; *The Scarlet Coat* 1955; *The Man from Bitter Ridge* 1955; *Trooper Hook* 1957; *The Girl in Black Stockings* 1957; *The Iron Sheriff* 1957; *The Left Handed Gun* 1958; *Man of the West* 1958; *Timbuktu* 1959; *Cast a Long Shadow* 1959; *The Canadians* 1961; *Critic's Choice* 1963; *The Helicopter Spies* 1968; *Dirty Dingus Magee* 1970; *Tiger by the Tail* 1970; *Support Your Local Gunfighter* 1971; *The Killer inside Me* 1975; *Young Maverick* 1979; *Jagged Edge* 1985; *Creator* 1985

Dekker, Albert *Beau Geste* 1939; *Paris Honeymoon* 1939; *Dr Cyclops* 1940; *Strange Cargo* 1940; *Seven Sinners* 1940; *Among the Living* 1941; *Honky Tonk* 1941; *In Old California* 1942; *Once upon a Honeymoon* 1942; *Wake Island* 1942; *War of the Wildcats* 1943; *Experiment Perilous* 1944; *Hold That Blonde* 1945; *Incendiary Blonde* 1945; *California* 1946; *The Killers* 1946; *Two Years before the Mast* 1946; *Cass Timberlane* 1947; *Gentleman's Agreement* 1947; *Fury at Furnace Creek* 1948; *Lulu Belle* 1948; *Bride of Vengeance* 1949; *Tarzan's Magic Fountain* 1949; *Destination Murder* 1950; *Wait 'til the Sun Shines, Nellie* 1952; *East of Eden* 1955; *Illegal* 1955; *Kiss Me Deadly* 1955; *Middle of the Night* 1959; *Suddenly, Last Summer* 1959; *These Thousand Hills* 1959; *The Wonderful Country* 1959; *Gamera* 1965
DeKova, Frank *Atlantis, the Lost Continent* 1961; *Frasier, the Sensuous Lion* 1973
Del Grande, Louis *Sugartime* 1995; *Hostile Intent* 1997
Del Mar, Maria *Cold Sweat* 1993; *Tails You Live, Heads You're Dead* 1995
Del Prete, Duilio *The Assassination of Trotsky* 1972; *Daisy Miller* 1974; *At Long Last Love* 1975
D'el Rey, Geraldo *The Given Word* 1962; *Black God, White Devil* 1964
Del Rey, Pilar *Black Horse Canyon* 1954; *And Now Miguel* 1966
Del Rio, Delores *Bird of Paradise* 1932; *Madame Du Barry* 1934
Del Rio, Dolores *What Price Glory* 1926; *The Red Dance* 1928; *Flying down to Rio* 1933; *Wonder Bar* 1934; *In Caliente* 1935; *Accused* 1936; *Lancer Spy* 1937; *International Settlement* 1938; *The Man from Dakota* 1940; *Journey into Fear* 1942; *Portrait of Maria* 1943; *The Fugitive* 1947; *Flaming Star* 1960; *Cheyenne Autumn* 1964; *More than a Miracle* 1967; *The Children of Sanchez* 1978
Del Sol, Laura *The Hit* 1984; *El Amor Brujo* 1986; *Killing Dad* 1989
Del Toro, Benicio *Christopher Columbus: the Discovery* 1992; *Fearless* 1993; *Golden Balls* 1993; *Money for Nothing* 1993; *China Moon* 1994; *Swimming with Sharks* 1994; *The Usual Suspects* 1995; *Basquiat* 1996; *The Fan* 1996; *The Funeral* 1996; *Excess Baggage* 1997; *Fear and Loathing in Las Vegas* 1998
Delahaye, Michel *Alphaville* 1965; *Shiver of the Vampires* 1970; *Une Belle Fille Comme Moi* 1973
Delair, Suzy *Quai des Orfèvres* 1947; *Gervaise* 1956
Delamare, Lise *La Marseillaise* 1938; *Lola Montès* 1955; *Les Grandes Manoeuvres* 1955
Delamere, Matthew *Under the Skin* 1997; *8½ Women* 1999
Delamere, Victorien *Le Château de Ma Mère* 1990; *La Gloire de Mon Père* 1990
DeLancie, John *Arcade* 1993; *Evolver* 1994
Delaney, Joan *The President's Analyst* 1967; *Don't Drink the Water* 1969; *Bunny O'Hare* 1971
Delaney, Kim *That Was Then... This Is Now* 1985; *Take My Daughters, Please* 1988; *Something Is Out There* 1988; *The Drifter* 1988; *Body Parts*

1991; *Hangfire* 1991; *The Broken Cord* 1992; *Darkman II – the Return of Durant* 1995; *Metal Beast* 1995; *Temptress* 1995; *Tall, Dark and Deadly* 1995; *Closer and Closer* 1996; *Serial Killer* 1996; *All Lies End in Murder* 1997; *Devil's Child* 1997
Delaney, Maureen *Another Shore* 1948; *Jacqueline* 1956; *The Scamp* 1957
Delano, Michael *Catlow* 1971; *Not of This Earth* 1988
Delany, Dana *Almost You* 1984; *Threesome* 1984; *Where the River Runs Black* 1986; *Masquerade* 1988; *Patty Hearst* 1988; *Light Sleeper* 1991; *HouseSitter* 1992; *Batman: Mask of the Phantasm* 1993; *Donato and Daughter* 1993; *The Enemy Within* 1994; *Exit to Eden* 1994; *Choices of the Heart: the Margaret Sanger Story* 1995; *Live Nude Girls* 1995; *Fly Away Home* 1996; *Wide Awake* 1998; *Rescuers: Stories of Courage – Two Couples* 1998
Delevanti, Cyril *The Night of the Iguana* 1964; *The Killing of Sister George* 1968
Delfosse, Raoul *The Burglars* 1971; *The Frog Prince* 1984
Delgado, Roger *The Road to Hong Kong* 1962; *Hot Enough for June* 1963; *The Mummy's Shroud* 1966
Dell, Gabriel *Dead End* 1937; *Angels with Dirty Faces* 1938; *Angels Wash Their Faces* 1939; *Block Busters* 1944; *Bowery Champs* 1944; *Follow the Leader* 1944; *Come Out Fighting* 1945; *300 Year Weekend* 1971; *Who Is Harry Kellerman, and Why Is He Saying Those Terrible Things about Me?* 1971; *The Manchu Eagle Murder Caper Mystery* 1973; *Framed* 1975; *The Escape Artist* 1982
Dell, Myrna *The Falcon's Adventure* 1946; *Nocturne* 1946; *Guns of Hate* 1948; *The Judge Steps Out* 1949; *Roughshod* 1949; *Destination Murder* 1950
Delle Piane, Carlo *What?* 1973; *Noi Tre* 1984; *Christmas Present* 1986
Delon, Alain *Plein Soleil* 1960; *Rocco and His Brothers* 1960; *Eclipse* 1962; *The Leopard* 1962; *The Black Tulip* 1963; *Any Number Can Win* 1963; *The Love Cage* 1964; *The Yellow Rolls-Royce* 1964; *Once a Thief* 1965; *Is Paris Burning?* 1966; *The Lost Command* 1966; *Texas across the River* 1966; *Diabolically Yours* 1967; *Le Samouraï* 1967; *Histoires Extraordinaires* 1967; *The Adventurers* 1968; *The Girl on a Motorcycle* 1968; *The Swimming Pool* 1968; *The Sicilian Clan* 1969; *Borsalino* 1970; *The Red Circle* 1970; *Red Sun* 1971; *Take It Easy* 1971; *The Widow Couderc* 1971; *The Assassination of Trotsky* 1972; *Dirty Money* 1972; *Burnt Barns* 1973; *Scorpio* 1973; *Shock Treatment* 1973; *Two against the Law* 1973; *Borsalino and Co* 1974; *Someone Is Bleeding* 1974; *Police Story* 1975; *Zorro* 1975; *Boomerang* 1976; *Mr Klein* 1976; *The Hurried Man* 1977; *To Kill a Rat* 1977; *Airport: the Concorde* 1979; *Three Men to Destroy* 1980; *Shock* 1982; *Swann in Love* 1984; *The Passage* 1986; *Nouvelle Vague* 1990
Delon, Nathalie *Le Samouraï* 1967; *Take It Easy* 1971; *When Eight Bells Toll* 1971; *Bluebeard* 1972; *The Romantic Englishwoman* 1975

Mask 1997; *Asterix and Obelix Take on Caesar* 1999; *The Bridge* 1999; *Vatel* 2000

Depardieu, Guillaume *Tous les Matins du Monde* 1992; *Wild Target* 1993; *Les Apprentis* 1995; *Pola X* 1999

Depp, Johnny *A Nightmare on Elm Street* 1984; *Private Resort* 1985; *Platoon* 1986; *Cry-Baby* 1989; *Edward Scissorhands* 1990; *Arizona Dream* 1991; *Benny and Joon* 1993; *What's Eating Gilbert Grape* 1993; *Ed Wood* 1994; *Dead Man* 1995; *Don Juan DeMarco* 1995; *Nick of Time* 1995; *Donnie Brasco* 1997; *The Brave* 1997; *Fear and Loathing in Las Vegas* 1998; *LA without a Map* 1998; *The Astronaut's Wife* 1999; *Sleepy Hollow* 1999; *The Ninth Gate* 2000

Derek, Bo *Orca* 1977; *10* 1979; *A Change of Seasons* 1980; *Tarzan, the Ape Man* 1981; *Bolero* 1984; *Ghosts Can't Do It* 1990; *Woman of Desire* 1994; *Tommy Boy* 1995

Derek, John *All the King's Men* 1949; *Knock on Any Door* 1949; *Rogues of Sherwood Forest* 1950; *Thunderbirds* 1952; *Ambush at Tomahawk Gap* 1953; *Prince of Pirates* 1953; *The Last Posse* 1953; *The Adventures of Hajji Baba* 1954; *The Outcast* 1954; *Run for Cover* 1955; *Prince of Players* 1955; *An Annapolis Story* 1955; *The Ten Commandments* 1956; *The Flesh Is Weak* 1957; *Fury at Showdown* 1957; *Omar Khayyam* 1957; *High Hell* 1957; *Exodus* 1960; *Nightmare in the Sun* 1964; *Once Before I Die* 1965

Dermit, Edouard *Les Enfants Terribles* 1949; *Orphée* 1950; *Le Testament d'Orphée* 1960

Dern, Bruce *Wild River* 1960; *The Wild Angels* 1966; *Rebel Rousers* 1967; *The War Wagon* 1967; *Waterhole #3* 1967; *Will Penny* 1967; *The St Valentine's Day Massacre* 1967; *The Trip* 1967; *Hang 'em High* 1968; *Psych-Out* 1968; *Castle Keep* 1969; *Number One* 1969; *Support Your Local Sheriff!* 1969; *They Shoot Horses, Don't They?* 1969; *Bloody Mama* 1970; *Drive, He Said* 1971; *Silent Running* 1971; *The Incredible Two-Headed Transplant* 1971; *The Cowboys* 1972; *The King of Marvin Gardens* 1972; *Thumb Tripping* 1972; *The Laughing Policeman* 1973; *The Great Gatsby* 1974; *Posse* 1975; *Smile* 1975; *Black Sunday* 1976; *Family Plot* 1976; *The Twist* 1976; *Won Ton Ton, the Dog Who Saved Hollywood* 1976; *Coming Home* 1978; *The Driver* 1978; *Middle Age Crazy* 1980; *Tattoo* 1980; *That Championship Season* 1982; *On the Edge* 1985; *The Big Town* 1987; *Uncle Tom's Cabin* 1987; *1969* 1988; *World Gone Wild* 1988; *The 'Burbs* 1989; *Trenchcoat in Paradise* 1989; *After Dark, My Sweet* 1990; *The Court-Martial of Jackie Robinson* 1990; *Carolina Skeletons* 1991; *Into the Badlands* 1991; *Midnight Sting* 1992; *Amelia Earhart: the Final Flight* 1994; *Mrs Munck* 1995; *Wild Bill* 1995; *Down Periscope* 1996; *Mulholland Falls* 1996; *Small Soldiers* 1998; *Perfect Prey* 1998; *The Haunting* 1999

Dern, Laura *Ladies and Gentlemen, the Fabulous Stains* 1982; *Teachers* 1984; *Mask* 1985; *Smooth Talk* 1985; *Blue Velvet* 1986; *Haunted Summer* 1988; *Shadow Makers* 1989; *Wild at Heart* 1990; *Rambling Rose* 1991; *Afterburn* 1992; *Jurassic Park* 1993; *A Perfect World* 1993; *Down Came a Blackbird* 1995; *Bastard out of Carolina* 1996; *Citizen Ruth* 1996; *The Baby Dance* 1998; *October Sky* 1999

Derr, Richard *A Gentleman at Heart* 1942; *The Secret Heart* 1946; *When Worlds Collide* 1951; *Something to Live For* 1952; *Terror Is a Man* 1959

Derricks, Cleavant *Moscow on the Hudson* 1984; *The Slugger's Wife* 1985; *Off Beat* 1986

Des Barres, Michael *Ghoulies* 1985; *Nightflyers* 1987; *Pink Cadillac* 1989; *The High Crusade* 1994; *Widow's Kiss* 1996

Desailly, Jean *La Symphonie Pastorale* 1946; *Les Grandes Manoeuvres* 1955; *Violent Summer* 1961; *Le Doulos* 1962; *La Peau Douce* 1964

DeSalvo, Anne *My Favorite Year* 1982; *Burglar* 1987; *Spike of Bensonhurst* 1988; *Taking Care of Business* 1990; *Dead in the Water* 1991

DeSando, Anthony *Federal Hill* 1994; *Party Girl* 1994; *Kiss Me, Guido* 1997

DeSantis, Stanley *Broken Trust* 1995; *The Truth about Cats and Dogs* 1996; *Clockwatchers* 1997

Desarthe, Gérard *The Police War* 1979; *Uranus* 1990; *Daens* 1992

Descas, Alex *Le Cri du Coeur* 1994; *Harem Suare* 1999

Deschamps, Hubert *Zazie dans le Métro* 1960; *Le Feu Follet* 1963; *The Mouth Agape* 1974

Descher, Sandy *It Grows on Trees* 1952; *A Gift for Heidi* 1958

Desert, Alex *The Flash* 1990; *Swingers* 1996

Desiderio, Robert *Moonlight* 1982; *Oh, God! You Devil* 1984; *Original Sin* 1989; *Stop at Nothing* 1991; *Silence of Adultery* 1995; *Once You Meet a Stranger* 1996; *No Laughing Matter* 1998

Desmond, Florence *Sally in Our Alley* 1931; *No Limit* 1935; *Accused* 1936; *Three Came Home* 1950; *Charley Moon* 1956

Desmonde, Jerry *London Town* 1946; *Cardboard Cavalier* 1949; *Trouble in Store* 1953; *The Angel Who Pawned Her Harp* 1954; *Man of the Moment* 1955; *Up in the World* 1956; *Follow a Star* 1959; *A Stitch in Time* 1963; *The Early Bird* 1965

Desni, Tamara *Jack Ahoy!* 1934; *The Squeaker* 1937

Desny, Ivan *aka* Desny, Yvan *Madeleine* 1949; *La Signora senza Camelie* 1953; *Lola Montès* 1955; *Anastasia* 1956; *Song without End* 1960; *The Magnificent Rebel* 1961; *Kidnapped to Mystery Island* 1964; *Paper Tiger* 1974; *The Marriage of Maria Braun* 1978; *Lola* 1982; *J'Embrasse Pas* 1991

Despotovich, Nada *Smithereens* 1982; *Babycakes* 1989

Desselle, Natalie *B.A.P.S.* 1997; *Def Jam's How to Be a Player* 1997; *Rodgers & Hammerstein's Cinderella* 1997

Deste, Luli *Thunder in the City* 1937; *The Case of the Black Parrot* 1941

Detmers, Maruschka *First Name: Carmen* 1983; *Hanna's War* 1988; *The Mambo Kings* 1992; *Love in the Strangest Way* 1994; *The Shooter* 1994

Deutsch, Ernst *The Golem* 1920; *The Third Man* 1949

Devane, William *McCabe and Mrs Miller* 1971; *300 Year Weekend* 1971; *The Pursuit of Happiness* 1971; *Glory Boy* 1971; *Lady Liberty* 1971; *Fear on Trial* 1975; *Report to the Commissioner* 1975; *Family Plot* 1976; *Marathon Man* 1976; *Rolling Thunder* 1977; *The Dark* 1979; *Yanks* 1979; *Honky Tonk Freeway* 1981; *The Other Victim* 1981; *Testament* 1983; *Hadley's Rebellion* 1984; *Timestalkers* 1987; *Murder COD* 1990; *Victim of Beauty* 1991; *Obsessed* 1992; *The President's Child* 1992; *Prophet of Evil* 1993; *Rubdown* 1993; *Freefall: Flight 174* 1995; *Night Watch* 1995; *Robin Cook's Formula for Death* 1995; *Forgotten Sins* 1996; *Exception to the Rule* 1996; *The Absolute Truth* 1997; *Doomsday Rock* 1997; *Payback* 1999

Devereaux, Ed *Watch Your Stern* 1960; *The Password Is Courage* 1962; *Live It Up* 1963; *They're a Weird Mob* 1966; *Money Movers* 1978; *Robbery under Arms* 1985

Devi, Kamala *Geronimo* 1962; *The Brass Bottle* 1964

Devillers, Renée *J'Accuse* 1938; *Thérèse Desqueyroux* 1962

Devine, Andy *Three Wise Girls* 1932; *The Man from Yesterday* 1932; *Dr Bull* 1933; *Upper World* 1934; *The Farmer Takes a Wife* 1935; *Way Down East* 1935; *In Old Chicago* 1937; *A Star Is Born* 1937; *Doctor Rhythm* 1938; *Men with Wings* 1938; *Yellow Jack* 1938; *The Storm* 1938; *Geronimo* 1939; *Stagecoach* 1939; *Never Say Die* 1939; *Little Old New York* 1940; *Torrid Zone* 1940; *Trail of the Vigilantes* 1940; *When the Daltons Rode* 1940; *The Flame of New Orleans* 1941; *Road Agent* 1941; *Sin Town* 1942; *Corvette K-225* 1943; *Frontier Badmen* 1943; *Ali Baba and the Forty Thieves* 1944; *Ghost Catchers* 1944; *Frontier Gal* 1945; *Canyon Passage* 1946; *Bells of San Angelo* 1947; *Springtime in the Sierras* 1947; *The Vigilantes Return* 1947; *Under California Stars* 1948; *The Far Frontier* 1949; *Never a Dull Moment* 1950; *Slaughter Trail* 1951; *Thunder Pass* 1954; *Pete Kelly's Blues* 1955; *The Adventures of Huckleberry Finn* 1960; *Two Rode Together* 1961; *The Man Who Shot Liberty Valance* 1962; *The Ballad of Josie* 1968; *Myra Breckinridge* 1970; *Robin Hood* 1973; *The Mouse and His Child* 1977

Devine, George *The Beggar's Opera* 1953; *Tom Jones* 1963

Devine, Loretta *Sticky Fingers* 1988; *Waiting to Exhale* 1995; *The Preacher's Wife* 1996; *Rebound* 1996; *Down in the Delta* 1997; *Urban Legend* 1998; *Love Kills* 1998; *Jackie's Back!* 1999

DeVito, Danny *Lady Liberty* 1971; *Hurry Up, or I'll Be 30* 1973; *Scalawag* 1973; *One Flew over the Cuckoo's Nest* 1975; *Goin' South* 1978; *Going Ape!* 1981; *Terms of Endearment* 1983; *Johnny Dangerously* 1984; *The Ratings Game* 1984; *Romancing the Stone* 1984; *The Jewel of the Nile* 1985; *Ruthless People* 1986; *Wise Guys* 1986; *My Little Pony* 1986; *Head Office* 1986; *Throw Momma from the Train* 1987; *Tin Men* 1987; *Twins* 1988; *The War of the Roses* 1989; *Other People's Money* 1991; *Batman Returns* 1992; *Hoffa* 1992; *Jack the Bear* 1993; *Look Who's Talking Now!* 1993; *Junior* 1994; *Renaissance Man* 1994; *Get Shorty* 1995; *Mars Attacks!* 1996; *Matilda* 1996; *Hercules* 1997; *LA Confidential* 1997; *The Rainmaker* 1997; *Space Jam* 1997; *Living Out Loud* 1998; *The Virgin Suicides* 1999; *Man on the Moon* 1999; *Drowning Mona* 2000

Devlin, Alan *Angel* 1982; *The Lonely Passion of Judith Hearne* 1987; *The Playboys* 1992; *High Boot Benny* 1993

Devlin, J G *Sir Henry at Rawlinson End* 1980; *No Surrender* 1986; *The Miracle* 1990

Devlin, William *Blood of the Vampire* 1958; *The Shuttered Room* 1967

Devon, Laura *Goodbye Charlie* 1964; *Red Line 7000* 1965; *Chamber of Horrors* 1966; *Gunn* 1967; *A Covenant with Death* 1967

Devon, Richard *Viking Women and the Sea Serpent* 1957; *War of the Satellites* 1958

DeVries, Jon *aka* De Vries, Jon *Lianna* 1983; *Rachel River* 1987; *Too Young the Hero* 1988; *Sarah, Plain and Tall* 1991; *Skylark* 1993; *Zelda* 1993

Devry, Elaine *Man-Trap* 1961; *Diary of a Madman* 1963; *A Guide for the Married Man* 1967; *The Cheyenne Social Club* 1970; *Bless the Beasts and Children* 1971

Dewaere, Patrick *Les Valseuses* 1974; *Get out Your Handkerchiefs* 1977

Dewhurst, Colleen *A Fine Madness* 1966; *The Last Run* 1971; *The Cowboys* 1972; *McQ* 1974; *Annie Hall* 1977; *Ice Castles* 1978; *And Baby Makes Six* 1979; *When a Stranger Calls* 1979; *Escape* 1980; *Tribute* 1980; *The Dead Zone* 1983; *The Boy Who Could Fly* 1986; *Johnny Bull* 1986; *Sword of Gideon* 1986; *Bigfoot* 1987; *Those She Left Behind* 1989; *Kaleidoscope* 1990; *Dying Young* 1991; *Bed & Breakfast* 1992

Dexter, Alan *Forbidden* 1953; *Time Limit* 1957; *Paint Your Wagon* 1969

Dexter, Anthony *Valentino* 1951; *Fire Maidens from Outer Space* 1956; *He Laughed Last* 1956; *The Parson and the Outlaw* 1957

Dexter, Aubrey *The Love Test* 1935; *Please Teacher* 1937

Dexter, Brad *The Las Vegas Story* 1951; *Macao* 1952; *House of Bamboo* 1955; *Between Heaven and Hell* 1956; *Beyond the River* 1956; *The Oklahoman* 1957; *Run Silent, Run Deep* 1958; *Last Train from Gun Hill* 1959; *The Magnificent Seven* 1960; *The George Raft Story* 1961; *X-15* 1961; *Taras Bulba* 1962; *Johnny Cool* 1963; *Kings of the Sun* 1963; *Invitation to a Gunfighter* 1964; *Bus Riley's Back in Town* 1965; *None but the Brave* 1965; *Von Ryan's Express* 1965; *Blindfold* 1966; *Jory* 1972; *Vigilante Force* 1975

Dexter, William *The Knack... and How to Get It* 1965; *The Hand of Night* 1966

Dey, Dipankar *The Middleman* 1975; *In Search of Famine* 1980; *An Enemy of the People* 1989

Dey, Susan *Skyjacked* 1972; *First Love* 1977; *Looker* 1981; *Love Leads the Way* 1984; *Echo Park* 1985; *Bed of Lies* 1991; *Love, Lies and Lullabies* 1993; *Whose Child Is This?* 1993; *Bridge of Time* 1997

Diamond, Arnold *The Breaking Point* 1961; *The Anniversary* 1968

Diamond, Reed *O Pioneers!* 1992; *Blind Spot* 1993; *Awake to Danger* 1995; *Her Hidden Truth* 1995; *A Father's Betrayal* 1997

Diamond, Selma *Bang the Drum Slowly* 1973; *All of Me* 1984

Diaz, Cameron *The Mask* 1994; *The Last Supper* 1995; *Feeling Minnesota* 1996; *Keys to Tulsa* 1996; *She's the One* 1996; *Head above Water* 1996; *A Life Less Ordinary* 1997; *My Best Friend's Wedding* 1997; *Fear and Loathing in Las Vegas* 1998; *There's Something about Mary* 1998; *Very Bad Things* 1998; *Being John Malkovich* 1999; *Any Given Sunday* 1999

Diaz, Guillermo *Party Girl* 1994; *Stonewall* 1995; *High School High* 1996; *I'm Not Rappaport* 1996; *Half-Baked* 1998

Diaz, Vic *Operation CIA* 1965; *Bloodfist* 1989

Dibbs, Kem *The Twinkle in God's Eye* 1955; *Daniel Boone, Trail Blazer* 1957

Diberti, Luigi *The Seduction of Mimi* 1972; *The Oberwald Mystery* 1980

DiCaprio, Leonardo *Critters 3* 1991; *Poison Ivy* 1992; *This Boy's Life* 1993; *What's Eating Gilbert Grape* 1993; *The Basketball Diaries* 1995; *The Quick and the Dead* 1995; *Total Eclipse* 1995; *Marvin's Room* 1996; *William Shakespeare's Romeo + Juliet* 1996; *The Man in the Iron Mask* 1997; *Titanic* 1997; *Celebrity* 1998; *The Beach* 2000

DiCenzo, George *Going Home* 1971; *The Frisco Kid* 1979; *Starflight One* 1983; *About Last Night...* 1986; *Walk like a Man* 1987; *18 Again!* 1988; *Sing* 1989

DiCicco, Bobby *I Wanna Hold Your Hand* 1978; *The Big Red One* 1980; *The Philadelphia Experiment* 1984; *Tiger Warsaw* 1988

Dick, Andy *...And God Spoke* 1993; *In the Army Now* 1994; *Best Men* 1997

Dick, Douglas *The Searching Wind* 1946; *Casbah* 1948; *Saigon* 1948; *The Accused* 1949; *Home of the Brave* 1949; *The Red Badge of Courage* 1951; *Something to Live For* 1952; *The Oklahoman* 1957

Dickens, Kim *Great Expectations* 1997; *Truth or Consequences, NM* 1997; *Zero Effect* 1997; *Mercury Rising* 1998

Dickerson, George *Space Raiders* 1983; *Blue Velvet* 1986; *Death Wish 4: the Crackdown* 1987; *After Dark, My Sweet* 1990; *Death Warrant* 1990; *Death Dreams* 1991; *As Good as Dead* 1995

Dickey, Lucinda *Breakdance* 1984; *Breakdance 2 – Electric Boogaloo* 1984

Dickinson, Angie *Lucky Me* 1954; *Man with the Gun* 1955; *Tension at Table Rock* 1956; *China Gate* 1957; *Shoot-Out at Medicine Bend* 1957; *Calypso Joe* 1957; *Cry Terror* 1958; *I Married a Woman* 1958; *Rio Bravo* 1959; *The Bramble Bush* 1960; *Ocean's Eleven* 1960; *The Sins of Rachel Cade* 1960; *A Fever in the Blood* 1961; *Jessica* 1962; *Lovers Must Learn* 1962; *Captain Newman, MD* 1963; *The Killers* 1964; *Art of Love* 1965; *Cast a Giant Shadow* 1966; *The Chase* 1966; *The Poppy Is Also a Flower* 1966; *Point Blank* 1967; *The Last Challenge* 1967; *Sam Whiskey* 1969; *Young Billy Young* 1969; *Pretty Maids all in a Row* 1971; *The Resurrection of Zachary Wheeler* 1971; *Big Bad Mama*

1974; *Dressed to Kill* 1980; *Charlie Chan and the Curse of the Dragon Queen* 1981; *Death Hunt* 1981; *A Touch of Scandal* 1984; *Big Bad Mama II* 1987; *The Freeway Killings* 1987; *Stillwatch* 1987; *Once upon a Texas Train* 1988; *Prime Target* 1989; *Fire and Rain* 1989; *Even Cowgirls Get the Blues* 1993; *The Maddening* 1995; *Sabrina* 1995; *The Sun, the Moon and the Stars* 1995; *Danielle Steel's Remembrance* 1996; *National Lampoon's The Don's Analyst* 1997; *Deep Family Secrets* 1997
Dickson, Gloria *They Won't Forget* 1937; *Gold Diggers in Paris* 1938; *They Made Me a Criminal* 1939; *This Thing Called Love* 1940; *Lady of Burlesque* 1943
Dickson, Neil *Biggles* 1986; *Lionheart* 1986; *The Murders in the Rue Morgue* 1986; *A Hazard of Hearts* 1987; *King of the Wind* 1989
Diddley, Bo *Trading Places* 1983; *Eddie and the Cruisers II: Eddie Lives!* 1989
Diefenthal, Frédéric *Taxi* 1998; *Taxi 2* 2000
Diego, Gabino *Ay, Carmela!* 1990; *Belle Epoque* 1992; *Two Much* 1995
Diego, Juan *Jarrapellejos* 1987; *Cabeza de Vaca* 1990; *Jamon Jamon* 1992
Diehl, John *Angel* 1984; *City Limits* 1985; *Glitz* 1988; *Kickboxer 2: the Road Back* 1990; *Madhouse* 1990; *A Row of Crows* 1991; *Whore* 1991; *Mo' Money* 1992; *Stargate* 1994; *Three Wishes* 1995; *Ruby Jean and Joe* 1996; *Anywhere but Here* 1999
Dierkes, John *Macbeth* 1948; *The Red Badge of Courage* 1951; *The Naked Jungle* 1953; *Shane* 1953; *The Moonlighter* 1953; *Daughter of Dr Jekyll* 1957; *The Hanging Tree* 1959
Dierkop, Charles *The Face of Fear* 1971; *Messenger of Death* 1988
Diesel, Vin *Saving Private Ryan* 1998; *The Iron Giant* 1999; *Pitch Black* 2000; *Boiler Room* 2000
Diessl, Gustav *Westfront 1918* 1930; *The Testament of Dr Mabuse* 1932
Dietrich, Dena *The Strange and Deadly Occurrence* 1974; *The Wild Party* 1975; *On the Air Live with Captain Midnight* 1979
Dietrich, Marlene *The Joyless Street* 1925; *The Ship of Lost Men* 1929; *Three Loves* 1929; *The Blue Angel* 1930; *Morocco* 1930; *Dishonored* 1931; *Blonde Venus* 1932; *Shanghai Express* 1932; *The Song of Songs* 1933; *The Scarlet Empress* 1934; *The Devil Is a Woman* 1935; *Desire* 1936; *The Garden of Allah* 1936; *Angel* 1937; *Knight without Armour* 1937; *Destry Rides Again* 1939; *Seven Sinners* 1940; *The Flame of New Orleans* 1941; *Manpower* 1941; *The Lady Is Willing* 1942; *The Spoilers* 1942; *Pittsburgh* 1942; *Follow the Boys* 1944; *Kismet* 1944; *Martin Roumagnac* 1946; *Golden Earrings* 1947; *A Foreign Affair* 1948; *Jigsaw* 1949; *Stage Fright* 1950; *No Highway* 1951; *Rancho Notorious* 1952; *Around the World in 80 Days* 1956; *Witness for the Prosecution* 1957; *The Monte Carlo Story* 1957; *Touch of Evil* 1958; *Judgment at Nuremberg* 1961; *The Black Fox* 1962; *Paris When It Sizzles* 1964; *Just a Gigolo* 1978; *Marlene* 1984
Diffring, Anton *Albert, RN* 1953; *Park Plaza 605* 1953; *Double Cross* 1955; *I Am a Camera* 1955; *The Black Tent* 1956; *House of Secrets* 1956; *The Crooked Sky* 1957; *Mark of the Phoenix* 1957; *The Traitor* 1957; *The Man Who Could Cheat Death* 1959; *Circus of Horrors* 1960; *The Heroes of Telemark* 1965; *The Blue Max* 1966; *Fahrenheit 451* 1966; *Counterpoint* 1967; *The Double Man* 1967; *Where Eagles Dare* 1969; *Zeppelin* 1971; *Dead Pigeon on Beethoven Street* 1972; *The Beast Must Die* 1974; *Shatter* 1974; *Operation Daybreak* 1975; *The Swiss Conspiracy* 1975; *Montana Trap* 1976; *Operation Dead End* 1986
Digard, Uschi *aka* **Lillimor, Astrid** *Cherry, Harry & Raquel* 1969; *Supervixens* 1975; *Beneath the Valley of the Ultra Vixens* 1979
Digges, Dudley *Condemned* 1929; *Outward Bound* 1930; *Dangerous Female* 1931; *The First Year* 1932; *The Hatchet Man* 1932; *The Emperor Jones* 1933; *The Mayor of Hell* 1933; *What Every Woman Knows* 1934; *The World Moves On* 1934; *China Seas* 1935; *Kind Lady* 1935; *Mutiny on the Bounty* 1935; *The General Died at Dawn* 1936; *Valiant Is the Word for Carrie* 1936; *The Light That Failed* 1939; *Raffles* 1939; *The Searching Wind* 1946
Diggs, Taye *How Stella Got Her Groove Back* 1998; *The Best Man* 1999; *The Wood* 1999; *House on Haunted Hill* 1999
Dignam, Arthur *Petersen* 1974; *The Devil's Playground* 1976; *Cathy's Child* 1979; *Grendel, Grendel, Grendel* 1981; *We of the Never Never* 1982; *The Wild Duck* 1983; *The Right Hand Man* 1986
Dignam, Basil *Seven Seas to Calais* 1962; *80,000 Suspects* 1963
Dignam, Mark *The Siege of the Saxons* 1963; *Hamlet* 1969; *Dead Cert* 1974
Dillane, Stephen *Hamlet* 1990; *Stolen Hearts* 1996; *Déjà Vu* 1997; *Firelight* 1997; *Welcome to Sarajevo* 1997; *Ordinary Decent Criminal* 1999; *The Darkest Light* 1999
Dillard, Victoria *Ricochet* 1991; *Deep Cover* 1992; *Out of Sync* 1995; *The Best Man* 1999
Dillaway, Donald *Min and Bill* 1930; *Platinum Blonde* 1931; *Body and Soul* 1931; *The Animal Kingdom* 1932; *Pack Up Your Troubles* 1932; *The Little Giant* 1933
Diller, Phyllis *Boy, Did I Get a Wrong Number* 1966; *Mad Monster Party* 1967; *Eight on the Lam* 1967; *The Private Navy of Sgt O'Farrell* 1968; *Did You Hear the One about the Traveling Saleslady?* 1968; *The Adding Machine* 1969; *Pucker Up and Bark Like a Dog* 1989; *Happily Ever After* 1990; *The Silence of the Hams* 1993; *A Bug's Life* 1998
Dillman, Bradford *aka* **Dillman, Brad** *A Certain Smile* 1958; *In Love and War* 1958; *Compulsion* 1959; *Circle of Deception* 1960; *Crack in the Mirror* 1960; *Francis of Assisi* 1961; *Sanctuary* 1961; *A Rage to Live* 1965; *The Helicopter Spies* 1968; *Sergeant Ryker* 1968; *Jigsaw* 1968; *The Bridge at Remagen* 1969; *Suppose They Gave a War and Nobody Came?* 1970; *Brother John* 1970; *Escape from the Planet of the Apes* 1971; *The Mephisto Waltz* 1971; *The Resurrection of Zachary Wheeler* 1971; *The Eyes of Charles Sand* 1972; *Deliver Us from Evil* 1973; *The Iceman Cometh* 1973; *The Way We Were* 1973; *Gold* 1974; *99 and 44/100% Dead* 1974; *Bug* 1975; *The Enforcer* 1976; *Mastermind* 1976; *The Amsterdam Kill* 1978; *Love and Bullets* 1978; *Piranha* 1978; *The Memory of Eva Ryker* 1980; *The Legend of Walks Far Woman* 1982; *Sudden Impact* 1983; *Heroes Stand Alone* 1989; *The Heart of Justice* 1992
Dillon, Edward *aka* **Dillon, Eddie** *The Broadway Melody* 1929; *The Iron Man* 1931
Dillon, Kevin *No Big Deal* 1983; *Catholic Boys* 1985; *Platoon* 1986; *The Blob* 1988; *The Rescue* 1988; *War Party* 1988; *Remote Control* 1988; *Immediate Family* 1989; *When He's Not a Stranger* 1989; *The Doors* 1991; *A Midnight Clear* 1991; *No Escape* 1994; *Criminal Hearts* 1995; *Stag* 1996; *Misbegotten* 1998
Dillon, Matt *Over the Edge* 1979; *Little Darlings* 1980; *My Bodyguard* 1980; *Liar's Moon* 1982; *Tex* 1982; *The Outsiders* 1983; *Rumble Fish* 1983; *The Flamingo Kid* 1984; *Rebel* 1985; *Target* 1985; *Native Son* 1986; *The Big Town* 1987; *Kansas* 1988; *Bloodhounds of Broadway* 1989; *Drugstore Cowboy* 1989; *A Kiss before Dying* 1991; *Women and Men – 2* 1991; *Mr Wonderful* 1992; *Singles* 1992; *The Saint of Fort Washington* 1993; *Golden Gate* 1994; *Frankie Starlight* 1995; *To Die For* 1995; *Albino Alligator* 1996; *Beautiful Girls* 1996; *Grace of My Heart* 1996; *In & Out* 1997; *There's Something about Mary* 1998; *Wild Things* 1998
Dillon, Melinda *The April Fools* 1969; *Bound for Glory* 1976; *Close Encounters of the Third Kind* 1977; *F.I.S.T.* 1978; *The Shadow Box* 1980; *Absence of Malice* 1981; *Fallen Angel* 1981; *A Christmas Story* 1983; *Right of Way* 1983; *Songwriter* 1984; *Shattered Spirits* 1986; *Bigfoot and the Hendersons* 1987; *Shattered Innocence* 1988; *Nightbreaker* 1989; *Staying Together* 1989; *Captain America* 1990; *The Prince of Tides* 1991; *Judgment Day: the John List Story* 1993; *Confessions: Two Faces of Evil* 1994; *State of Emergency* 1994; *To Wong Foo, Thanks for Everything, Julie Newmar* 1995; *Magnolia* 1999
Dillon, Paul *Kiss Daddy Good Night* 1987; *Blink* 1994; *CutThroat Island* 1995
Dimitri, Richard *Human Feelings* 1978; *Johnny Dangerously* 1984
Dimitriades, Alex *The Heartbreak Kid* 1993; *Head On* 1997
Dinehart, Alan *Girls about Town* 1931; *Lawyer Man* 1932; *Washington Merry-Go-Round* 1932; *Bureau of Missing Persons* 1933; *Supernatural* 1933; *The Cat's Paw* 1934; *Jimmy the Gent* 1934; *Baby, Take a Bow* 1934; *Dante's Inferno* 1935; *Born to Dance* 1936; *Human Cargo* 1936; *Step Lively, Jeeves* 1937; *This Is My Affair* 1937; *Fast and Loose* 1939; *Second Fiddle* 1939; *The Heat's On* 1943; *Sweet Rosie O'Grady* 1943; *What a Woman!* 1943
Dingle, Charles *The Little Foxes* 1941; *Unholy Partners* 1941; *The Talk of the Town* 1942; *Somewhere I'll Find You* 1942; *Lady of Burlesque* 1943; *Home in Indiana* 1944; *Together Again* 1944; *Guest Wife* 1945; *A Medal for Benny* 1945; *The Beast with Five Fingers* 1946; *Cinderella Jones* 1946; *Sister Kenny* 1946; *My Favorite Brunette* 1947; *If You Knew Susie* 1948; *Big Jack* 1949; *Never Wave at a WAC* 1952
Dingo, Ernie *Tudawali* 1987; *"Crocodile" Dundee II* 1988; *Until the End of the World* 1991; *Dead Heart* 1996; *The Echo of Thunder* 1998
Dinome, Jerry *Tomboy* 1985; *Dangerously Close* 1986
Dinsdale, Reece *A Private Function* 1984; *i.d.* 1994; *Hamlet* 1996; *So This Is Romance?* 1997
Dione, Rose *Salome* 1922; *Freaks* 1932
Dionisi, Stefano *Farinelli il Castrato* 1994; *The Truce* 1997; *Shooting the Moon* 1998; *The Loss of Sexual Innocence* 1999
Dionisotti, Paola *The Sailor's Return* 1978; *Vigo: Passion for Life* 1997; *The Tichborne Claimant* 1998
Dishy, Bob *aka* **Dishy, Robert** *The Tiger Makes Out* 1967; *Lovers and Other Strangers* 1970; *I Wonder Who's Killing Her Now?* 1975; *The Big Bus* 1976; *First Family* 1980; *Author! Author!* 1982; *Brighton Beach Memoirs* 1986; *Critical Condition* 1987; *Used People* 1992; *Thicker than Blood* 1993; *Don Juan DeMarco* 1995
Dispina, Teresa *Reform School Girl* 1994; *The Big Squeeze* 1996
Ditson, Harry *The Sender* 1982; *The Tragedy of Flight 103: the Inside Story* 1990; *Back in the USSR* 1992
Divine *Multiple Maniacs* 1970; *Mondo Trasho* 1970; *Pink Flamingos* 1972; *Female Trouble* 1974; *Polyester* 1981; *Lust in the Dust* 1984; *Trouble in Mind* 1985; *Hairspray* 1988; *Out of the Dark* 1988
Divoff, Andrew *Another 48 HRS* 1990; *Toy Soldiers* 1991; *Back in the USSR* 1992; *Interceptor* 1992; *Running Cool* 1993; *SIS Extreme Justice* 1993; *Oblivion* 1993; *Adrenalin: Fear the Rush* 1995; *A Low Down Dirty Shame* 1995; *Magic Island* 1995; *Blast* 1996; *Wishmaster* 1997; *Wishmaster 2: Evil Never Dies* 1999
Dix, Richard *The Ten Commandments* 1923; *Cimarron* 1931; *Hell's Highway* 1932; *The Lost Squadron* 1932; *Ace of Aces* 1933; *The Arizonian* 1935; *The Tunnel* 1935; *Man of Conquest* 1939; *Cherokee Strip* 1940; *The Roundup* 1941; *The Ghost Ship* 1943
Dix, William *The Nanny* 1965; *Doctor Dolittle* 1967
Dixon, Donna *Doctor Detroit* 1983; *Spies like Us* 1985; *Beverly Hills Madam* 1986; *The Couch Trip* 1988; *Cannonball Fever* 1989
Dixon, Ivan *A Raisin in the Sun* 1961; *Nothing but a Man* 1964; *A Patch of Blue* 1965; *Suppose They Gave a War and Nobody Came?* 1970
Dixon, James *It's Alive* 1974; *It Lives Again* 1978; *Q – the Winged Serpent* 1982; *The Stuff* 1985; *It's Alive III: Island of the Alive* 1987
Dixon, Jean *She Married Her Boss* 1935; *My Man Godfrey* 1936; *You Only Live Once* 1937; *Swing High, Swing Low* 1937; *Joy of Living* 1938
Dixon, Jill *Just My Luck* 1957; *A Night to Remember* 1958
Dixon, Joan *Bunco Squad* 1950; *Roadblock* 1951; *Desert Passage* 1952
Dixon, Lee *Gold Diggers of 1937* 1936; *Angel and the Badman* 1947
Dixon, MacIntyre *Starting Over* 1979; *Funny Farm* 1988
Dixon, Reg *Love in Pawn* 1953; *No Smoking* 1954
Djola, Badja *The Lightship* 1985; *The Serpent and the Rainbow* 1987; *An Innocent Man* 1989; *Christmas on Division Street* 1991; *A Rage in Harlem* 1991; *Who's the Man?* 1993; *Heaven's Prisoners* 1996
D'Lyn, Shae *Bury Me in Niagara* 1993; *Awake to Danger* 1995; *Secrets* 1995; *Convict 762* 1997
Dobie, Alan *The Long Day's Dying* 1968; *Alfred the Great* 1969; *The Chairman* 1969
Dobkin, Lawrence *aka* **Dobkin, Larry** *The Gene Krupa Story* 1959; *Geronimo* 1962; *The Cabinet of Caligari* 1962; *Curiosity Kills* 1990
Dobrowolska, Gosia *Silver City* 1984; *A Woman's Tale* 1991; *Careful* 1992; *The Nun and the Bandit* 1992; *Erotic Tales* 1994
Dobson, Anita *Beyond Bedlam* 1993; *Darkness Falls* 1998
Dobson, James *The Tall Stranger* 1957; *Jet Attack* 1958; *Impulse* 1975
Dobson, Kevin *Orphan Train* 1979; *All Night Long* 1981; *Money, Power, Murder* 1989; *For Love of a Child* 1990; *A House of Secrets and Lies* 1992; *The Conviction of Kitty Dodds* 1993; *Criminal Intent* 1998
Dobson, Peter *LA Takedown* 1989; *Last Exit to Brooklyn* 1989; *Sing* 1989; *So Proudly We Hail* 1990; *Too Hot to Handle* 1991; *Shades of Gray* 1992; *Where the Day Takes You* 1992; *Killer Rules* 1993; *The Big Squeeze* 1996; *Dead Cold* 1996; *The Frighteners* 1996; *Norma Jean & Marilyn* 1996; *All Lies End in Murder* 1997
Dobson, Tamara *Cleopatra Jones* 1973; *Cleopatra Jones and the Casino of Gold* 1975; *Norman... Is That You?* 1976; *Chained Heat* 1983
Dobtcheff, Vernon *Condorman* 1981; *Berlin Jerusalem* 1989; *Venice/Venice* 1992; *M Butterfly* 1993; *Déjà Vu* 1997
Dodd, Claire *Lawyer Man* 1932; *Hard to Handle* 1933; *Ex-Lady* 1933; *Gambling Lady* 1934; *The Glass Key* 1935; *Roberta* 1935; *The Case of the Velvet Claws* 1936; *Fast Company* 1938; *Three Loves Has Nancy* 1938; *Slightly Honorable* 1939; *In the Navy* 1941; *The Mad Doctor of Market Street* 1942
Doe, John *Border Radio* 1987; *Slam Dance* 1987; *Great Balls of Fire!* 1989; *Without You I'm Nothing* 1990; *Pure Country* 1992; *Roadside Prophets* 1992; *Georgia* 1995
Doermer, Christian *Love at Twenty* 1962; *Joanna* 1969
Doherty, Shannen *Night Shift* 1982; *The Secret of NIMH* 1982; *Girls Just Want to Have Fun* 1985; *Freeze Frame* 1989; *Heathers* 1989; *Beverly Hills 90210* 1990; *Obsessed* 1992; *Blindfold: Acts of Obsession* 1994; *Jailbreakers* 1994; *A Burning Passion: the Margaret Mitchell Story* 1994; *Mallrats* 1995; *The Ticket* 1997; *Sleeping with the Devil* 1997
Dolan, Michael *Hamburger Hill* 1987; *Light of Day* 1987; *Biloxi Blues* 1988; *The Turning* 1992

Soup 1970; Hannie Caulder 1971; The Pied Piper 1971; The Amazing Mr Blunden 1972; Nothing but the Night 1972; Craze 1973; From beyond the Grave 1973; Steptoe and Son Ride Again 1973; The Amorous Milkman 1974; Adventures of a Taxi Driver 1975; Keep It Up Downstairs 1976; Adventures of a Private Eye 1977; Steaming 1985
D'Orsay, Fifi They Had to See Paris 1929; Going Hollywood 1933; The Gangster 1947
Dorsey, Joe Brainstorm 1983; WarGames 1983; The Philadelphia Experiment 1984; Deadly Care 1987
Dorsey, Tommy Presenting Lily Mars 1943; The Fabulous Dorseys 1947
Dorziat, Gabrielle Mayerling 1936; The End of the Day 1939; Les Parents Terribles 1948; Act of Love 1953; Little Boy Lost 1953; Gigot 1962
Dossett, John Longtime Companion 1990; That Night 1992
Dotrice, Karen The Three Lives of Thomasina 1963; Mary Poppins 1964; The Gnome-Mobile 1967; The Thirty-Nine Steps 1978
Dotrice, Michele The Witches 1966; And Soon the Darkness 1970; Blood on Satan's Claw 1970; Not Now, Comrade 1976
Dotrice, Roy Lock Up Your Daughters! 1969; The Buttercup Chain 1970; One of Those Things 1970; Tales from the Crypt 1972; Family Reunion 1981; Amadeus 1984; Cheech & Chong's The Corsican Brothers 1984; The Cutting Edge 1992; Children of the Dark 1994; The Good Policeman 1994; Swimming with Sharks 1994; The Scarlet Letter 1995
Doucet, Catherine aka **Doucet, Catharine** Little Man, What Now? 1934; Accent on Youth 1935; These Three 1936; Poppy 1936; When You're in Love 1937; There's One Born Every Minute 1942
Doucette, John Cavalry Scout 1951; Beachhead 1954; Gang War 1958; One Little Indian 1973; Fighting Mad 1976
Doug, Doug E Hangin' with the Homeboys 1991; Cool Runnings 1993; Operation Dumbo Drop 1995; That Darn Cat 1997
Douglas, Angela Some People 1962; It's All Happening 1963; The Comedy Man 1964; Carry On Cowboy 1965; Carry On Follow That Camel 1967; Digby, the Biggest Dog in the World 1973
Douglas, Burt The Law and Jake Wade 1958; Handle with Care 1958
Douglas, Craig The Painted Smile 1961; It's Trad, Dad 1961
Douglas, Don aka **Douglas, Donald** The Great Gabbo 1929; Smashing the Rackets 1938; I Love You Again 1940; Behind the Rising Sun 1943; The Falcon Out West 1944; Show Business 1944; Tall in the Saddle 1944
Douglas, Donna Career 1959; Frankie & Johnny 1966
Douglas, Eric A Gunfight 1971; Remembrance of Love 1982; Tomboy 1985
Douglas, Howard No Limit 1935; Night Comes Too Soon 1949
Douglas, Illeana Cape Fear 1991; Alive 1992; Grief 1993; To Die For 1995; Search and Destroy 1995; Grace of My Heart 1996; Wedding Bell Blues 1996; Picture Perfect 1997; Weapons of Mass

Distraction 1997; Message in a Bottle 1998; Happy, Texas 1999; Lansky 1999; Stir of Echoes 1999; The Next Best Thing 2000
Douglas, Jack Carry On Abroad 1972; Carry On Girls 1973; Carry On Dick 1974; Carry On Behind 1975; Carry On England 1976; Carry On Emmannuelle 1978; The Boys in Blue 1983
Douglas, James GI Blues 1960; A Thunder of Drums 1961
Douglas, Kirk The Strange Love of Martha Ivers 1946; Build My Gallows High 1947; I Walk Alone 1947; Mourning Becomes Electra 1947; My Dear Secretary 1948; Champion 1949; A Letter to Three Wives 1949; The Glass Menagerie 1950; Young Man with a Horn 1950; Ace in the Hole 1951; Along the Great Divide 1951; Detective Story 1951; The Bad and the Beautiful 1952; The Big Sky 1952; The Big Trees 1952; Act of Love 1953; The Juggler 1953; The Story of Three Loves 1953; 20,000 Leagues under the Sea 1954; Ulysses 1954; The Indian Fighter 1955; Man without a Star 1955; The Racers 1955; Lust for Life 1956; Gunfight at the OK Corral 1957; Paths of Glory 1957; Top Secret Affair 1957; The Vikings 1958; The Devil's Disciple 1959; Last Train from Gun Hill 1959; Spartacus 1960; Strangers When We Meet 1960; The Last Sunset 1961; Town without Pity 1961; Lonely Are the Brave 1962; Two Weeks in Another Town 1962; For Love or Money 1963; The Hook 1963; Seven Days in May 1964; The Heroes of Telemark 1965; In Harm's Way 1965; Cast a Giant Shadow 1966; Is Paris Burning? 1966; The War Wagon 1967; The Way West 1967; The Brotherhood 1968; A Lovely Way to Go 1968; The Arrangement 1969; There Was a Crooked Man... 1970; Catch Me a Spy 1971; A Gunfight 1971; The Light at the Edge of the World 1971; Scalawag 1973; Once Is Not Enough 1975; Posse 1975; Victory at Entebbe 1976; Holocaust 2000 1977; The Fury 1978; Cactus Jack 1979; Home Movies 1979; The Final Countdown 1980; Saturn 3 1980; The Man from Snowy River 1982; Remembrance of Love 1982; Eddie Macon's Run 1983; Draw! 1984; Amos 1985; Tough Guys 1986; Inherit the Wind 1988; Oscar 1991; The Secret 1992; Greedy 1994; Take Me Home Again 1994; Diamonds 1999
Douglas, Melvyn As You Desire Me 1932; The Old Dark House 1932; Counsellor-at-Law 1933; The Vampire Bat 1933; Dangerous Corner 1934; Annie Oakley 1935; She Married Her Boss 1935; The Gorgeous Hussy 1936; Theodora Goes Wild 1936; And So They Were Married 1936; Angel 1937; Captains Courageous 1937; I Met Him in Paris 1937; I'll Take Romance 1937; Arsene Lupin Returns 1938; Fast Company 1938; The Shining Hour 1938; That Certain Age 1938; The Toy Wife 1938; There's Always a Woman 1938; The Amazing Mr Williams 1939; Ninotchka 1939; Third Finger, Left Hand 1940; This Thing Called Love 1940; Too Many Husbands 1940; Two-Faced Woman 1941; A Woman's Face 1941; Our Wife 1941; That Uncertain Feeling 1941; They All Kissed the Bride 1942; The Sea of Grass 1947; The Guilt of Janet

Ames 1947; Mr Blandings Builds His Dream House 1948; The Great Sinner 1949; A Woman's Secret 1949; My Forbidden Past 1951; Billy Budd 1962; Hud 1963; Advance to the Rear 1964; The Americanization of Emily 1964; Hotel 1967; I Never Sang for My Father 1969; The Candidate 1972; One Is a Lonely Number 1972; The Death Squad 1974; The Tenant 1976; Twilight's Last Gleaming 1977; Being There 1979; The Seduction of Joe Tynan 1979; The Changeling 1980; Tell Me a Riddle 1980; Ghost Story 1981; The Hot Touch 1982
Douglas, Michael Hail, Hero! 1969; Adam at 6 AM 1970; Napoleon and Samantha 1972; Coma 1977; The China Syndrome 1979; Running 1979; It's My Turn 1980; The Star Chamber 1983; Romancing the Stone 1984; A Chorus Line 1985; The Jewel of the Nile 1985; Fatal Attraction 1987; Wall Street 1987; Black Rain 1989; The War of the Roses 1989; Basic Instinct 1992; Falling Down 1992; Shining Through 1992; Disclosure 1994; The American President 1995; The Ghost and the Darkness 1996; The Game 1997; A Perfect Murder 1998; One Day in September 1999; Wonder Boys 2000
Douglas, Paul Everybody Does It 1949; It Happens Every Spring 1949; A Letter to Three Wives 1949; The Big Lift 1950; Love That Brute 1950; Panic in the Streets 1950; Angels in the Outfield 1951; Fourteen Hours 1951; Clash by Night 1952; We're Not Married 1952; Never Wave at a WAC 1952; The Maggie 1953; Forever Female 1953; Executive Suite 1954; Green Fire 1954; Joe Macbeth 1955; The Solid Gold Cadillac 1956; Beau James 1957; This Could Be the Night 1957; The Mating Game 1959
Douglas, Robert London Melody 1937; Over the Moon 1937; The Challenge 1938; The Lion Has Wings 1939; The End of the River 1947; Adventures of Don Juan 1948; The Fountainhead 1949; Barricade 1950; The Flame and the Arrow 1950; Kim 1950; Mystery Submarine 1950; Sons of the Musketeers 1951; Thunder on the Hill 1951; Ivanhoe 1952; The Desert Rats 1953; Fair Wind to Java 1953; Flight to Tangier 1953; King Richard and the Crusaders 1954; Saskatchewan 1954; Good Morning, Miss Dove 1955; The Virgin Queen 1955; The Scarlet Coat 1955; Tarzan, the Ape Man 1959; Secret Ceremony 1969
Douglas, Sarah The People That Time Forgot 1977; Superman II 1980; Conan the Destroyer 1984; The Return of Swamp Thing 1989; Beastmaster 2: through the Portal of Time 1991; Tagget 1991; Voodoo 1995; The Stepford Husbands 1996
Douglas, Shirley Dead Ringers 1988; Barney's Great Adventure 1998
Douglas, Suzzanne Tap 1989; Jason's Lyric 1994; No Ordinary Summer 1994; Search for Grace 1994; How Stella Got Her Groove Back 1998
Douglass, Judie Constance 1984; Absent without Leave 1993
Douglass, Robyn Breaking Away 1979; Partners 1982; Romantic Comedy 1983; Her Life as a Man

1984; The Lonely Guy 1984; Freeze Frame 1989
Dourdan, Gary Keys 1994; Alien: Resurrection 1997; Scarred City 1998
Dourif, Brad One Flew over the Cuckoo's Nest 1975; Eyes of Laura Mars 1978; Wise Blood 1979; Heaven's Gate 1980; Ragtime 1981; Dune 1984; Blue Velvet 1986; Vengeance: the Story of Tony Cimo 1986; Fatal Beauty 1987; Child's Play 1988; Mississippi Burning 1988; Terror on Highway 91 1989; Child's Play 2 1990; The Exorcist III 1990; Grim Prairie Tales 1990; Hidden Agenda 1990; Knife Edge 1990; Body Parts 1991; Chaindance 1991; Child's Play 3 1991; Jungle Fever 1991; London Kills Me 1991; Scream of Stone 1991; Critters 4 1992; Amos & Andrew 1993; Trauma 1993; Color of Night 1994; Death Machine 1994; Murder in the First 1994; Escape from Terror 1995; Escape to Witch Mountain 1995; A Step toward Tomorrow 1996; Nightwatch 1997; Bride of Chucky 1998; Senseless 1998; Urban Legend 1998; Brown's Requiem 1998; Progeny 1998
Dove, Billie The Black Pirate 1926; Blondie of the Follies 1932
Dow, Peggy Harvey 1950; The Sleeping City 1950; Bright Victory 1951; I Want You 1951
Dowd, Ann Bushwhacked 1995; Kingfish: a Story of Huey P Long 1995; Shiloh 1996; Apt Pupil 1997
Dowie, Freda Distant Voices, Still Lives 1988; The Monk 1990; Butterfly Kiss 1994
Dowling, Constance Knickerbocker Holiday 1944; Up in Arms 1944; Black Angel 1946; Gog 1954
Dowling, Doris The Lost Weekend 1945; The Blue Dahlia 1946; Bitter Rice 1949
Dowling, Joan Murder without Crime 1950; Pool of London 1950; Women of Twilight 1952
Dowling, Kathryn Diner 1982; Stranger in the Family 1991; Ultimate Betrayal 1994
Dowling, Rachael aka **Dowling, Rachel** The Dead 1987; Bogwoman 1997; The Tichborne Claimant 1998
Down, Lesley-Anne Assault 1970; Countess Dracula 1970; Pope Joan 1972; From beyond the Grave 1973; Scalawag 1973; Brannigan 1975; The Pink Panther Strikes Again 1976; A Little Night Music 1977; The Betsy 1978; The First Great Train Robbery 1978; Hanover Street 1979; Rough Cut 1980; Sphinx 1980; Agatha Christie's Murder Is Easy 1982; The Hunchback of Notre Dame 1982; Nomads 1985; Indiscreet 1988; Ladykillers 1988; Night Walk 1989; Behind Closed Doors 1994; Death Wish V: the Face of Death 1994; Beastmaster III: the Eye of Braxus 1995; Family of Cops 1995; The Secret Agent Club 1995
Downer, David The Killing of Angel Street 1981; Norman Loves Rose 1982
Downey Jr, Robert Baby It's You 1983; Tuff Turf 1984; Weird Science 1985; Back to School 1986; America 1986; Less than Zero 1987; The Pick-Up Artist 1987; 1969 1988; Johnny Be Good 1988; Chances Are 1989; Fighting Justice 1989; Air America 1990; Too Much Sun 1990; Soapdish 1991; Chaplin 1992;

Heart and Souls 1993; Short Cuts 1993; Natural Born Killers 1994; Only You 1994; Hail Caesar 1994; Home for the Holidays 1995; Restoration 1995; Richard III 1995; Danger Zone 1996; The Gingerbread Man 1997; One Night Stand 1997; Two Girls and a Guy 1997; Hugo Pool 1997; In Dreams 1998; US Marshals 1998; Bowfinger 1999; Black and White 1999; Wonder Boys 2000
Downey, Roma Getting Up and Going Home 1992; Devlin 1992; Cosa Nostra: the Last Word 1995; A Child Is Missing 1995
Downey Sr, Robert You've Got to Walk It Like You Talk It or You'll Lose That Beat 1971; Is There Sex after Death? 1971; To Live and Die in LA 1985; Johnny Be Good 1988
Downing, Vernon Clive of India 1935; Sherlock Holmes and the Spider Woman 1944
Downs, Cathy The Dark Corner 1946; My Darling Clementine 1946; The Noose Hangs High 1948; The Sundowners 1950; The Big Tip Off 1955; The Oklahoma Woman 1956; The She-Creature 1956; The Amazing Colossal Man 1957
Downs, Johnny So Red the Rose 1935; Pigskin Parade 1936; Adam Had Four Sons 1941; Twilight on the Prairie 1944
Doyen, Jacqueline Entre Nous 1983; The Frog Prince 1984
Doyle, David Paper Lion 1968; The April Fools 1969; Loving 1970; Black Market Baby 1977; The Comeback 1977; Wait till Your Mother Gets Home! 1983; Ghost Writer 1989; Weekend Reunion 1990; Love or Money 1990
Doyle Kennedy, Maria aka **Doyle, Maria** The Commitments 1991; The General 1998; Gregory's Two Girls 1999; Miss Julie 1999; I Could Read the Sky 2000
Doyle, Kevin The Courier 1987; A Midsummer Night's Dream 1996
Doyle, Tony Loophole 1980; Who Dares Wins 1982; Eat the Peach 1986; Secret Friends 1991
Doyle-Murray, Brian Caddyshack 1980; Modern Problems 1981; JFK 1991; Wayne's World 1992; Groundhog Day 1993; Cabin Boy 1994; Jury Duty 1995; Dennis Strikes Again 1998; Legalese 1998; The Jungle Book: Mowgli's Story 1998
Dr Dre Who's the Man? 1993; Set It Off 1996; Ride 1998
Drache, Heinz The Brides of Fu Manchu 1966; Circus of Fear 1967
Drago, Billy Windwalker 1980; Hollow Point 1987; The Untouchables 1987; Freeway 1988; Delta Force 2 1990; Diplomatic Immunity 1991; Guncrazy 1992; Secret Games 1992; Cyborg 2: Glass Shadow 1993; The Outfit 1993; The Takeover 1995; Sci-Fighters 1996; Blood Money 1996; Assault on Devil's Island 1997; Convict 762 1997
Drake, Betsy Every Girl Should Be Married 1948; Dancing in the Dark 1949; Pretty Baby 1950; The Second Woman 1951; Room for One More 1952; Will Success Spoil Rock Hunter? 1957; Next to No Time 1958; Intent to Kill 1958; Clarence, the Cross-Eyed Lion 1965
Drake, Charles Air Force 1943; Conflict 1945; A Night in Casablanca 1946; The Tender Years 1947; Tarzan's Magic

Fountain 1949; *Comanche Territory* 1950; *Harvey* 1950; *Winchester '73* 1950; *I Was a Shoplifter* 1950; *Red Ball Express* 1952; *Treasure of Lost Canyon* 1952; *The Glenn Miller Story* 1953; *It Came from Outer Space* 1953; *The Lone Hand* 1953; *War Arrow* 1953; *Gunsmoke* 1953; *All That Heaven Allows* 1955; *To Hell and Back* 1955; *Walk the Proud Land* 1956; *Until They Sail* 1957; *Jeanne Eagels* 1957; *No Name on the Bullet* 1959; *Back Street* 1961; *Showdown* 1963; *Dear Heart* 1964; *Valley of the Dolls* 1967; *The Smugglers* 1968; *Hail, Hero!* 1969; *The Seven Minutes* 1971

Drake, Charlie *Sands of the Desert* 1960; *Petticoat Pirates* 1961; *The Cracksman* 1963; *Mister Ten Per Cent* 1967

Drake, Claudia *Bedside Manner* 1945; *Detour* 1945; *Calypso Joe* 1957

Drake, Dona *Louisiana Purchase* 1941; *Road to Morocco* 1942; *Without Reservations* 1946; *Another Part of the Forest* 1948; *So This Is New York* 1948; *Beyond the Forest* 1949; *The Doolins of Oklahoma* 1949; *Valentino* 1951; *Kansas City Confidential* 1952; *The Bandits of Corsica* 1953; *Princess of the Nile* 1954

Drake, Fabia *Not Wanted on Voyage* 1957; *Girls at Sea* 1958; *Operation Bullshine* 1959; *Valmont* 1989

Drake, Frances *Forsaking All Others* 1934; *Bolero* 1934; *Ladies Should Listen* 1934; *Mad Love* 1935; *Les Misérables* 1935; *The Invisible Ray* 1936; *There's Always a Woman* 1938; *It's a Wonderful World* 1939

Drake, Gabrielle *Connecting Rooms* 1969; *There's a Girl in My Soup* 1970

Drake, Larry *Darkman* 1990; *Murder in New Hampshire* 1991; *Dr Giggles* 1992; *Darkman II – the Return of Durant* 1995; *The Journey of August King* 1995; *Power 98* 1996; *Bean* 1997; *Overnight Delivery* 1997

Drake, Tom *Meet Me in St Louis* 1944; *Two Girls and a Sailor* 1944; *This Man's Navy* 1945; *Courage of Lassie* 1946; *The Green Years* 1946; *The Beginning or the End* 1947; *Cass Timberlane* 1947; *I'll Be Yours* 1947; *Hills of Home* 1948; *Words and Music* 1948; *Mr Belvedere Goes to College* 1949; *Scene of the Crime* 1949; *The Cyclops* 1957; *Money, Women and Guns* 1958; *Warlock* 1959; *The Bramble Bush* 1960; *Johnny Reno* 1966

Draper, David *Lord Love a Duck* 1966; *Don't Make Waves* 1967

Draper, Paul *Colleen* 1936; *The Time of Your Life* 1948

Draper, Polly *Heartbeat* 1992; *The Innocent* 1993; *A Million to Juan* 1994; *Schemes* 1994; *Gold Diggers: the Secret of Bear Mountain* 1995; *LaVyrle Spencer's Home Song* 1996

Dravic, Milena *The Battle of Neretva* 1969; *WR – Mysteries of the Organism* 1971

Drayton, Alfred *It's a Boy* 1933; *Jack Ahoy!* 1934; *The Dictator* 1935; *First a Girl* 1935; *Oh Daddy!* 1935; *Banana Ridge* 1941; *The Halfway House* 1943; *Don't Take It to Heart* 1944; *Nicholas Nickleby* 1947

Dremann, Beau *The Heavenly Kid* 1985; *The Thanksgiving Promise* 1986

Drescher, Fran *American Hot Wax* 1977; *G.O.R.P.* 1980; *Doctor Detroit* 1983; *Cadillac Man* 1990; *Car 54 Where Are You?* 1991; *Without Warning: Terror in the Towers* 1993; *Jack* 1996; *The Beautician and the Beast* 1997

Dresdel, Sonia *While I Live* 1947; *The Fallen Idol* 1948; *The Clouded Yellow* 1950; *The Break* 1962

Dresser, Louise *Ruggles of Red Gap* 1923; *The Eagle* 1925; *Mammy* 1930; *Dr Bull* 1933; *State Fair* 1933; *The Scarlet Empress* 1934; *The World Moves On* 1934

Dressler, Lieux *Truck Stop Women* 1974; *Kingdom of the Spiders* 1977

Dressler, Marie *Tillie's Punctured Romance* 1914; *The Patsy* 1928; *The Divine Lady* 1928; *Hollywood Revue* 1929; *Anna Christie* 1930; *Min and Bill* 1930; *One Romantic Night* 1930; *Emma* 1932; *Dinner at Eight* 1933; *Tugboat Annie* 1933

Drew, Ellen *If I Were King* 1938; *Geronimo* 1939; *Christmas in July* 1940; *Texas Rangers Ride Again* 1940; *Our Wife* 1941; *My Favorite Spy* 1942; *The Impostor* 1944; *China Sky* 1945; *Isle of the Dead* 1945; *Johnny O'Clock* 1947; *The Man from Colorado* 1948; *Stars in My Crown* 1950; *The Baron of Arizona* 1950; *Man in the Saddle* 1951

Drew, Roland *The Bermuda Mystery* 1944; *Two O'Clock Courage* 1945

Drexel, Ruth *Jail Bait* 1972; *The Marquise of O* 1976

Dreyfus, James *Thin Ice* 1994; *Boyfriends* 1996; *Notting Hill* 1999

Dreyfus, Jean-Claude *Heroines of Evil* 1979; *Delicatessen* 1990; *La Fille de l'Air* 1992; *Pétain* 1992; *The City of Lost Children* 1995

Dreyfuss, Richard *Hello Down There* 1969; *American Graffiti* 1973; *Dillinger* 1973; *The Apprenticeship of Duddy Kravitz* 1974; *The Second Coming of Suzanne* 1974; *Inserts* 1975; *Jaws* 1975; *Victory at Entebbe* 1976; *Close Encounters of the Third Kind* 1977; *The Goodbye Girl* 1977; *The Big Fix* 1978; *The Competition* 1980; *Whose Life Is it Anyway?* 1981; *The Buddy System* 1984; *Down and Out in Beverly Hills* 1986; *Stand by Me* 1986; *Nuts* 1987; *Stakeout* 1987; *Tin Men* 1987; *Moon over Parador* 1988; *Always* 1989; *Let It Ride* 1989; *Postcards from the Edge* 1990; *Rosencrantz and Guildenstern Are Dead* 1990; *Once Around* 1991; *Prisoner of Honor* 1991; *What about Bob?* 1991; *Another Stakeout* 1993; *Lost in Yonkers* 1993; *Silent Fall* 1994; *The American President* 1995; *Cosa Nostra: the Last Word* 1995; *Mr Holland's Opus* 1995; *James and the Giant Peach* 1996; *Trigger Happy* 1996; *Jack London's The Call of the Wild* 1996; *Night Falls on Manhattan* 1997; *Krippendorf's Tribe* 1998; *Lansky* 1999

Drier, Moosie *The War between Men and Women* 1972; *American Hot Wax* 1977

Drinkwater, Carol *The Shout* 1978; *Father* 1990

Driscoll, Bobby *From This Day Forward* 1946; *So Goes My Love* 1946; *Song of the South* 1946; *So Dear to My Heart* 1949; *The Window* 1949; *Treasure Island* 1950; *Peter Pan* 1953

Driscoll, Patricia *Charley Moon* 1956; *The Wackiest Ship in the Army* 1961

Drivas, Robert *Cool Hand Luke* 1967; *The Illustrated Man* 1969; *Where It's At* 1969; *God Told Me to* 1976

Driver, Betty *Boots! Boots!* 1934; *Penny Paradise* 1938; *Let's Be Famous* 1939

Driver, Minnie *Circle of Friends* 1995; *Big Night* 1996; *Sleepers* 1996; *Good Will Hunting* 1997; *The Governess* 1997; *Grosse Pointe Blank* 1997; *Hard Rain* 1997; *Princess Mononoke* 1997; *An Ideal Husband* 1999; *Tarzan* 1999; *South Park: Bigger, Longer & Uncut* 1999; *Return to Me* 2000

Drouot, Jean-Claude *Le Bonheur* 1965; *Laughter in the Dark* 1969; *The Light at the Edge of the World* 1971; *The Confessions of Pastor Burg* 1992

Dru, Joanne *Abie's Irish Rose* 1946; *Red River* 1948; *All the King's Men* 1949; *She Wore a Yellow Ribbon* 1949; *711 Ocean Drive* 1950; *Wagonmaster* 1950; *Mr Belvedere Rings the Bell* 1951; *Vengeance Valley* 1951; *My Pal Gus* 1952; *The Pride of St Louis* 1952; *Thunder Bay* 1953; *Forbidden* 1953; *The Siege at Red River* 1954; *Three Ring Circus* 1954; *The Dark Avenger* 1955; *Hell on Frisco Bay* 1955; *Sincerely Yours* 1955; *Drango* 1957; *The Light in the Forest* 1958; *The Wild and the Innocent* 1959; *Sylvia* 1964

Drukarova, Dinara *Don't Move, Die and Rise Again* 1989; *Of Freaks and Men* 1998

Drury, James *Good Day for a Hanging* 1958; *Toby Tyler, or Ten Weeks with a Circus* 1960; *Ten Who Dared* 1960; *Ride the High Country* 1962; *The Young Warriors* 1967

Drury, Patrick *The Awakening* 1980; *Laughterhouse* 1984

Dryer, Fred *Something So Right* 1982; *Death before Dishonor* 1987; *The Return of Hunter: Everyone Walks in LA* 1995

Drynan, Jeanie *Wilde's Domain* 1983; *Cappuccino* 1989; *Muriel's Wedding* 1994; *Paperback Hero* 1998; *Soft Fruit* 1999

Du Maurier, Gerald *Escape* 1930; *Catherine the Great* 1934; *I Was a Spy* 1934; *Jew Süss* 1934

Dubbins, Don *Tribute to a Bad Man* 1956; *These Wilder Years* 1956; *From the Earth to the Moon* 1958; *The Illustrated Man* 1969; *Run, Simon, Run* 1970

Duberg, Axel *The Devil's Eye* 1960; *The Virgin Spring* 1960

DuBois, Ja'net *Heart Condition* 1990; *Other Women's Children* 1993

Dubois, Marie *Shoot the Pianist* 1960; *Une Femme Est une Femme* 1961; *Jules et Jim* 1961; *La Ronde* 1964; *Don't Look Now... We're Being Shot At* 1966; *The Thief of Paris* 1967; *Vincent, François, Paul and the Others* 1974; *L'Innocente* 1976; *Mon Oncle d'Amérique* 1980; *Descent into Hell* 1986

Dubost, Paulette *La Règle du Jeu* 1939; *Lola Montès* 1955; *Le Bossu* 1959; *The Last Metro* 1980

Dubov, Paul *China Gate* 1957; *Voodoo Woman* 1957; *Verboten!* 1959; *The Atomic Submarine* 1960; *Underworld USA* 1961

Duby, Jacques *Thérèse Raquin* 1953; *Piaf: the Early Years* 1974

Duchaussoy, Michel *La Femme Infidèle* 1968; *Killer!* 1969; *Shock Treatment* 1973; *Nada* 1974; *The Hurried Man* 1977; *Fort Saganne* 1984; *Milou en Mai* 1989; *Road to Ruin* 1992; *La Veuve de Saint-Pierre* 2000

Duchene, Deborah *Perfectly Normal* 1990; *The Broken Cord* 1992; *Sugartime* 1995

Duchesne, Roger *The Golem* 1936; *Bob Le Flambeur* 1955

Duchovny, David *Bad Influence* 1990; *Julia Has Two Lovers* 1990; *Don't Tell Mom the Babysitter's Dead* 1991; *The Rapture* 1991; *Baby Snatcher* 1992; *Beethoven* 1992; *Chaplin* 1992; *Ruby* 1992; *Venice/Venice* 1992; *The Red Shoe Diaries* 1992; *Kalifornia* 1993; *Playing God* 1997; *The X Files* 1998; *Return to Me* 2000

Ducommun, Rick *The 'Burbs* 1989; *Ghost in the Machine* 1993; *Groundhog Day* 1993

Dudgeon, Neil *Red King, White Knight* 1989; *Revolver* 1992; *Different for Girls* 1996

Dudikoff, Michael *American Ninja* 1985; *Radioactive Dreams* 1986; *Avenging Force* 1986; *American Ninja 2: The Confrontation* 1987; *Platoon Leader* 1988; *River of Death* 1989; *The Woman Who Sinned* 1991; *Rescue Me* 1991; *Chain of Command* 1993; *Bounty Hunters* 1996; *Crash Dive* 1996

Dudley, Doris *A Woman Rebels* 1936; *The Moon and Sixpence* 1942

Dudley-Ward, Penelope *Escape Me Never* 1935; *Moscow Nights* 1935; *Convoy* 1940; *The Demi-Paradise* 1943

Duel, Peter *The Hell with Heroes* 1968; *Generation* 1969; *Cannon for Cordoba* 1970

Duell, William *Deadhead Miles* 1972; *Grace Quigley* 1984

Duering, Carl *Arabesque* 1966; *Duffy* 1968; *A Clockwork Orange* 1971

Duff, Amanda *Just around the Corner* 1938; *Mr Moto in Danger Island* 1939; *The Devil Commands* 1941

Duff, Howard *All My Sons* 1948; *The Naked City* 1948; *Calamity Jane and Sam Bass* 1949; *Red Canyon* 1949; *Johnny Stool Pigeon* 1949; *Spaceways* 1953; *Jennifer* 1953; *Private Hell 36* 1954; *Tanganyika* 1954; *The Yellow Mountain* 1954; *Women's Prison* 1955; *While the City Sleeps* 1956; *Boys' Night Out* 1962; *Panic in the City* 1968; *Kramer vs Kramer* 1979; *Monster in the Closet* 1983; *No Way Out* 1986; *Settle the Score* 1989; *Too Much Sun* 1990

Duffy, Julia *Wacko* 1981; *Baby Makes Three* 1988; *Beauty and Denise* 1989; *Menu for Murder* 1990; *Kidz in the Wood* 1996

Duffy, Karen *Blank Cheque* 1994; *Dumb and Dumber* 1994; *Memory Run* 1995

Duffy, Patrick *Too Good to Be True* 1988; *Children of the Bride* 1990; *Murder COD* 1990; *Daddy* 1991; *Dallas: JR Returns* 1996; *Dallas: War of the Ewings* 1998

Dufilho, Jacques *War of the Buttons* 1962; *A Full Day's Work* 1973; *Black and White in Color* 1976; *Le Cheval d'Orgueil* 1980; *Pétain* 1992; *The Children of the Marshland* 1998

Dugan, Dennis *Death Race* 1973; *Norman... Is That You?* 1976; *The Spaceman and King Arthur* 1979; *The Howling* 1981; *The Toughest Man in the World* 1984; *Can't Buy Me Love* 1987; *The New Adventures of Pippi Longstocking* 1988; *Happy Gilmore* 1996

Dugan, Tom *Lights of New York* 1928; *Drag* 1929; *Pennies from Heaven* 1936; *Wife vs Secretary* 1936; *The Lone Wolf Spy Hunt* 1939; *To Be or Not to Be* 1942; *Take Me Out to the Ball Game* 1949

Duggan, Andrew *Decision at Sundown* 1957; *Westbound* 1959; *The Chapman Report* 1962; *Merrill's Marauders* 1962; *House of Women* 1962; *Palm Springs Weekend* 1963; *The Incredible Mr Limpet* 1964; *The Glory Guys* 1965; *In like Flint* 1967; *The Secret War of Harry Frigg* 1967; *The Homecoming: a Christmas Story* 1971; *Skin Game* 1971; *Housewife* 1972; *Jigsaw* 1972; *The Bears and I* 1974; *It's Alive* 1974; *It Lives Again* 1978; *The Long Days of Summer* 1980; *A Return to Salem's Lot* 1987

Duggan, Gerry *The Siege of Pinchgut* 1959; *The Devil's Playground* 1976

Duggan, Tom *Frankenstein – 1970* 1958; *Born Reckless* 1959

Dukakis, Olympia *John and Mary* 1969; *National Lampoon's Movie Madness* 1981; *Walls of Glass* 1985; *Moonstruck* 1987; *Working Girl* 1988; *Dad* 1989; *Look Who's Talking* 1989; *Steel Magnolias* 1989; *In the Spirit* 1990; *Look Who's Talking Too* 1990; *Fire in the Dark* 1991; *Lucky Day* 1991; *Over the Hill* 1992; *The Cemetery Club* 1993; *Look Who's Talking Now!* 1993; *I Love Trouble* 1994; *Jeffrey* 1995; *Mighty Aphrodite* 1995; *Mr Holland's Opus* 1995; *Mother* 1995; *Young at Heart* 1995; *Dead Badge* 1995; *Jerusalem* 1996; *Picture Perfect* 1997; *Jane Austen's Mafia* 1998

Duke, Bill *Car Wash* 1976; *American Gigolo* 1980; *Commando* 1985; *No Man's Land* 1987; *Predator* 1987; *Action Jackson* 1988; *Bird on a Wire* 1990; *Menace II Society* 1993; *Payback* 1999

Duke, Patty *aka* **Duke Astin, Patty** *Happy Anniversary* 1959; *The Miracle Worker* 1962; *Billie* 1965; *Valley of the Dolls* 1967; *Deadly Harvest* 1972; *You'll Like My Mother* 1972; *Fire!* 1977; *The Swarm* 1978; *Something So Right* 1982; *September Gun* 1983; *A Time to Triumph* 1986; *Willy/Milly* 1986; *Amityville: the Evil Escapes* 1989; *Everybody's Baby: the Rescue of Jessica McClure* 1989; *Always Remember I Love You* 1990; *Call Me Anna* 1990; *Absolute Strangers* 1991; *Grave Secrets: the Legacy of Hilltop Drive* 1992; *A Killer among Friends* 1992; *Prelude to a Kiss* 1992; *A Family of Strangers* 1993; *One Woman's Courage* 1994; *Touch of Truth* 1994; *Harvest of Fire* 1996; *Race against Time: the Search for Sarah* 1996; *To Face Her Past* 1996

Duke, Robin *Blue Monkey* 1987; *Hostage for a Day* 1994

Dukes, David *The Wild Party* 1975; *A Fire in the Sky* 1978; *A Little Romance* 1979; *The First Deadly Sin* 1980; *Only When I Laugh* 1981; *Without a Trace* 1983; *Sentimental Journey* 1984; *The Men's Club* 1986; *Rawhead Rex* 1986; *Date with an Angel* 1987; *See You in the Morning* 1989; *Turn Back the Clock* 1989; *The Josephine Baker Story* 1991; *She Woke Up* 1992; *Me and the Kid* 1993; *The Surrogate* 1995;

Norma Jean & Marilyn 1996; Gods and Monsters 1998; Life of the Party: the Pamela Harriman Story 1998

Dulany, Caitlin Class of 1999 II: The Substitute 1993; Trouble Shooters: Trapped beneath the Earth 1993

Dullaghan, John Sweet Sweetback's Baad Asssss Song 1971; The Thing with Two Heads 1972

Dullea, Keir The Hoodlum Priest 1961; David and Lisa 1962; The Thin Red Line 1964; Mail Order Bride 1964; Bunny Lake Is Missing 1965; Madame X 1966; The Fox 1967; 2001: a Space Odyssey 1968; De Sade 1969; Pope Joan 1972; Paperback Hero 1972; Black Christmas 1974; Paul and Michelle 1974; Full Circle 1977; Welcome to Blood City 1977; Because He's My Friend 1978; Brainwaves 1982; Next One 1984; 2010 1984; Blind Date 1984; Oh, What a Night 1992

Dullin, Charles The Chess Player 1927; Mademoiselle Docteur 1936; Quai des Orfèvres 1947

Dumas, Roger The Bride Is Much Too Beautiful 1956; La Femme Publique 1984; Masques 1987

Dumas, Sandrine Hit List 1984; Beyond Therapy 1987; The Legend of the Holy Drinker 1988

Dumbrille, Douglass aka

Dumbrille, Douglas Blondie of the Follies 1932; Broadway Bill 1934; Hi, Nellie! 1934; Stamboul Quest 1934; Fog over Frisco 1934; The Secret Bride 1934; Cardinal Richelieu 1935; Crime and Punishment 1935; The Lives of a Bengal Lancer 1935; Naughty Marietta 1935; Peter Ibbetson 1935; Mr Deeds Goes to Town 1936; The Princess Comes Across 1936; The Emperor's Candlesticks 1937; The Firefly 1937; The Buccaneer 1938; Fast Company 1938; Kentucky 1938; Charlie Chan at Treasure Island 1939; Mr Moto in Danger Island 1939; Thunder Afloat 1939; The Three Musketeers 1939; Michael Shayne, Private Detective 1940; South of Pago Pago 1940; The Roundup 1941; Ten Gentlemen from West Point 1942; DuBarry Was a Lady 1943; Lost in a Harem 1944; Uncertain Glory 1944; A Medal for Benny 1945; Road to Utopia 1945; Pardon My Past 1945; Dishonored Lady 1947; Tell It to the Judge 1949; Abbott and Costello in the Foreign Legion 1950; A Millionaire for Christy 1951; Son of Paleface 1952; Apache War Smoke 1952; World for Ransom 1954; Shake, Rattle and Rock! 1957; Shock Treatment 1964

Dumke, Ralph All the King's Men 1949; The Breaking Point 1950; The Fireball 1950; Where Danger Lives 1950; Boots Malone 1951; Alaska Seas 1954; Invasion of the Body Snatchers 1956; The Solid Gold Cadillac 1956

Dumont, Margaret The Cocoanuts 1929; Animal Crackers 1930; Duck Soup 1933; A Night at the Opera 1935; A Day at the Races 1937; Dramatic School 1938; At the Circus 1939; The Big Store 1941; Never Give a Sucker an Even Break 1941; The Dancing Masters 1943; Billy Rose's Diamond Horseshoe 1945; The Horn Blows at Midnight 1945; Little Giant 1946; Stop, You're Killing Me 1952; Shake, Rattle and Rock! 1957; Zotz 1962

Dumont, Ulises Sur 1987; Wind with the Gone 1998

Dun, Dennis Big Trouble in Little China 1986; The Last Emperor 1987; Prince of Darkness 1987; Thousand Pieces of Gold 1990; Warriors of Virtue 1997

Duna, Steffi Anthony Adverse 1936; Pagliacci 1936; Waterloo Bridge 1940; Phantom Raiders 1940

Dunaway, Faye Bonnie and Clyde 1967; The Happening 1967; Hurry Sundown 1967; The Thomas Crown Affair 1968; The Arrangement 1969; The Extraordinary Seaman 1969; A Place for Lovers 1969; Little Big Man 1970; Puzzle of a Downfall Child 1970; Doc 1971; The Deadly Trap 1971; Oklahoma Crude 1973; The Three Musketeers 1973; Chinatown 1974; The Four Musketeers 1974; The Towering Inferno 1974; Three Days of the Condor 1975; Network 1976; Voyage of the Damned 1976; The Disappearance of Aimee 1976; Eyes of Laura Mars 1978; The Champ 1979; The First Deadly Sin 1980; Mommie Dearest 1981; The Wicked Lady 1983; Ordeal by Innocence 1984; Supergirl 1984; Thirteen at Dinner 1985; Beverly Hills Madam 1986; Barfly 1987; Burning Secret 1988; Midnight Crossing 1988; The Gamble 1988; Cold Sassy Tree 1989; Wait until Spring, Bandini 1989; The Handmaid's Tale 1990; Silhouette 1990; Arizona Dream 1991; Scorchers 1991; Double Edge 1992; The Temp 1993; Don Juan DeMarco 1995; Drunks 1995; A Family Divided 1995; Albino Alligator 1996; The Chamber 1996; Dunston Checks In 1996; The People Next Door 1996; The Twilight of the Golds 1996; Gia 1998; Joan of Arc 1999; The Thomas Crown Affair 1999

Dunbar, Adrian Dealers 1989; Hear My Song 1991; The Crying Game 1992; Widows' Peak 1993; Innocent Lies 1995; The Near Room 1995; The General 1998; The Wedding Tackle 2000

Dunbar, Dixie One in a Million 1936; Pigskin Parade 1936

Duncan, Andrew Loving 1970; The Hospital 1971; Slap Shot 1977; An Unmarried Woman 1978; A Little Romance 1979; The Gig 1985; Home Front 1987

Duncan, Archie The Gorbals Story 1949; Counterspy 1953; Rob Roy, the Highland Rogue 1953; Trouble in the Glen 1954; Tess of the Storm Country 1960; Postman's Knock 1961; Lancelot and Guinevere 1963

Duncan, Carmen Harlequin 1980; Turkey Shoot 1981; Now and Forever 1983; Skin Deep 1985

Duncan, Kenne My Pal Trigger 1946; On Top of Old Smoky 1953; The Astounding She-Monster 1958; Night of the Ghouls 1960; Hellborn 1961

Duncan, Lindsay Loose Connections 1983; Prick Up Your Ears 1987; The Reflecting Skin 1990; Body Parts 1991; City Hall 1996; A Midsummer Night's Dream 1996; An Ideal Husband 1999; Star Wars Episode I: the Phantom Menace 1999; Mansfield Park 1999

Duncan, Michael Clarke The Green Mile 1999; The Whole Nine Yards 2000

Duncan, Pamela The Undead 1957; Attack of the Crab Monsters 1957

Duncan, Rachel Two Much Trouble 1995; Amityville Dollhouse 1996; One Man's Justice 1996; Last Stand at Saber River 1997

Duncan, Sandy The Million Dollar Duck 1971; The Cat from Outer Space 1978; The Fox and the Hound 1981; My Boyfriend's Back 1989; Rock-a-Doodle 1990

Duncan, Todd Syncopation 1942; Unchained 1955

Dundas, David Mosquito Squadron 1968; Avalanche 1975

Dundas, Jennie The Hotel New Hampshire 1984; Mrs Soffel 1984

Dunford, Christine Reversal of Fortune 1990; Ulee's Gold 1997

Dunham, Joanna The Breaking Point 1961; Dangerous Afternoon 1961; The House That Dripped Blood 1971

Dunham, Katherine Stormy Weather 1943; Mambo 1954

Dunn, Clive She'll Have to Go 1961; Just like a Woman 1966; The Bliss of Mrs Blossom 1968; Dad's Army 1971

Dunn, Emma Manslaughter 1930; The Texan 1930; Bad Sister 1931; Hell's House 1932; The Wet Parade 1932; George White's 1935 Scandals 1935; The Cowboy and the Lady 1938; Young Dr Kildare 1938; The Llano Kid 1939; Dr Kildare's Crisis 1940; Dr Kildare's Strange Case 1940; The Penalty 1941; The Talk of the Town 1942; Life with Father 1947

Dunn, James Bad Girl 1931; Hello Sister! 1933; Baby, Take a Bow 1934; Bright Eyes 1934; George White's 1935 Scandals 1935; Government Girl 1943; A Tree Grows in Brooklyn 1945; Killer McCoy 1947; The Bramble Bush 1960; Hemingway's Adventures of a Young Man 1962

Dunn, Josephine The Singing Fool 1928; Our Modern Maidens 1929

Dunn, Kevin Blue Steel 1990; The Bonfire of the Vanities 1990; Hot Shots! 1991; Only the Lonely 1991; Chaplin 1992; 1492: Conquest of Paradise 1992; Dave 1993; Little Big League 1994; Shadow of a Doubt 1995; Unforgivable 1995; The Four Diamonds 1995; Chain Reaction 1996; The Terror Inside 1996; Godzilla 1997; Picture Perfect 1997; The Sixth Man 1997; The Second Civil War 1997; Almost Heroes 1998; Snake Eyes 1998; Stir of Echoes 1999

Dunn, Liam Blazing Saddles 1974; Peeper 1975

Dunn, Michael You're a Big Boy Now 1966; Boom 1968; No Way to Treat a Lady 1968; The Mutations 1973; The Abdication 1974

Dunn, Nora The Last Supper 1995; Air Bud: Golden Receiver 1998; Three Kings 1999

Dunne, Dominique The Day the Loving Stopped 1981; Poltergeist 1982

Dunne, Elizabeth Blondie Takes a Vacation 1939; Cat People 1942

Dunne, Griffin Chilly Scenes of Winter 1979; An American Werewolf in London 1981; Almost You 1984; Johnny Dangerously 1984; After Hours 1985; Who's That Girl 1987; The Big Blue 1988; Lip Service 1988; Secret Weapon 1990; My Girl 1991; Big Girls Don't Cry... They Get Even 1992; Straight Talk 1992; Love Matters 1993; The Pickle 1993; I

Like It like That 1994; The Android Affair 1995; Search and Destroy 1995

Dunne, Irene Cimarron 1931; Bachelor Apartment 1931; Consolation Marriage 1931; Back Street 1932; Symphony of Six Million 1932; Ann Vickers 1933; The Silver Cord 1933; The Secret of Madame Blanche 1933; If I Were Free 1933; This Man Is Mine 1934; The Age of Innocence 1934; Magnificent Obsession 1935; Roberta 1935; Sweet Adeline 1935; Show Boat 1936; Theodora Goes Wild 1936; The Awful Truth 1937; High, Wide and Handsome 1937; Joy of Living 1938; Love Affair 1939; When Tomorrow Comes 1939; My Favorite Wife 1940; Penny Serenade 1941; Lady in a Jam 1942; A Guy Named Joe 1944; The White Cliffs of Dover 1944; Together Again 1944; Over 21 1945; Anna and the King of Siam 1946; Life with Father 1947; I Remember Mama 1948; The Mudlark 1950; Never a Dull Moment 1950; It Grows on Trees 1952

Dunne, Stephen The Dark Past 1948; Above and Beyond 1952

Dunne, Steve Home before Dark 1958; I Married a Woman 1958; The Explosive Generation 1961

Dunning, Ruth It's a Great Day 1955; And Women Shall Weep 1960; Dangerous Afternoon 1961; Hoffman 1970; The House in Nightmare Park 1973

Dunnock, Mildred The Corn Is Green 1945; Death of a Salesman 1951; I Want You 1951; The Jazz Singer 1952; Bad for Each Other 1954; The Trouble with Harry 1955; Baby Doll 1956; Love Me Tender 1956; The Nun's Story 1959; Butterfield 8 1960; Sweet Bird of Youth 1962; Behold a Pale Horse 1964; 7 Women 1966; Whatever Happened to Aunt Alice? 1969; One Summer Love 1975; The Pick-Up Artist 1987

Dunsmore, Rosemary Dancing in the Dark 1986; Miles to Go 1986; After the Promise 1987; The Boys 1991

Dunst, Kirsten Interview with the Vampire: the Vampire Chronicles 1994; Jumanji 1995; Little Women 1995; Mother Night 1996; Anastasia 1997; Wag the Dog 1997; Small Soldiers 1998; Strike! 1998; The Virgin Suicides 1999; Dick 1999; Drop Dead Gorgeous 1999; The Devil's Arithmetic 1999

Duperey, Anny Two or Three Things I Know about Her 1966; Without Warning 1973; Stavisky 1974; No Problem! 1975; Pardon Mon Affaire 1976; Bobby Deerfield 1977; Les Compères 1983

DuPois, Starletta Hollywood Shuffle 1987; Convicts 1991; The Road to Galveston 1996

Duprez, June The Four Feathers 1939; The Lion Has Wings 1939; The Spy in Black 1939; The Thief of Bagdad 1940; None but the Lonely Heart 1944; And Then There Were None 1945; The Brighton Strangler 1945; Calcutta 1947

Dupuis, Paul Johnny Frenchman 1945; Against the Wind 1947; Sleeping Car to Trieste 1948; Madness of the Heart 1949; The Romantic Age 1949

Dupuis, Roy Being at Home with Claude 1991; Screamers 1995; Waiting for Michelangelo 1995; Hemoglobin 1997

Durang, Christopher Penn & Teller Get Killed 1989; Simply Irresistible 1999

Durante, Jimmy Blondie of the Follies 1932; The Passionate Plumber 1932; The Phantom President 1932; Speak Easily 1932; The Wet Parade 1932; Broadway to Hollywood 1933; What – No Beer? 1933; George White's Scandals 1934; Hollywood Party 1934; Palooka 1934; Land without Music 1936; Little Miss Broadway 1938; Start Cheering 1938; Sally, Irene and Mary 1938; The Man Who Came to Dinner 1941; Two Girls and a Sailor 1944; Music for Millions 1945; Two Sisters from Boston 1946; It Happened in Brooklyn 1947; On an Island with You 1948; Pepe 1960; Billy Rose's Jumbo 1962

Durbin, Deanna Every Sunday 1936; Three Smart Girls 1937; One Hundred Men and a Girl 1937; Mad about Music 1938; That Certain Age 1938; First Love 1939; It's a Date 1940; It Started with Eve 1941; Nice Girl? 1941; Hers to Hold 1943; His Butler's Sister 1943; The Amazing Mrs Holliday 1943; Can't Help Singing 1944; Christmas Holiday 1944; Lady on a Train 1945; Because of Him 1946; I'll Be Yours 1947; Up in Central Park 1948; For the Love of Mary 1948

Duret, Marc The Big Blue 1988; Nikita 1990; La Haine 1995

Düringer, Annemarie aka

Düringer, Anne-Marie Count Five and Die 1957; The Lacemaker 1977; Veronika Voss 1982

Durkin, Junior Tom Sawyer 1930; Huckleberry Finn 1931; Hell's House 1932

Durning, Charles aka Durnham, Charles Harvey Middleman, Fireman 1965; Hi, Mom! 1970; I Walk the Line 1970; Dealing: or the Berkeley-to-Boston Forty-Brick Lost-Bag Blues 1971; Deadhead Miles 1972; The Sting 1973; Sisters 1973; Dog Day Afternoon 1975; Breakheart Pass 1976; Harry and Walter Go to New York 1976; The Choirboys 1977; An Enemy of the People 1977; Twilight's Last Gleaming 1977; The Fury 1978; The Greek Tycoon 1978; A Special Kind of Love 1978; Tilt 1978; North Dallas Forty 1979; Starting Over 1979; When a Stranger Calls 1979; The Final Countdown 1980; Sharky's Machine 1981; True Confessions 1981; The Best Little Whorehouse in Texas 1982; Tootsie 1982; To Be or Not to Be 1983; Two of a Kind 1983; Mass Appeal 1984; Death of a Salesman 1985; The Man with One Red Shoe 1985; Stand Alone 1985; Stick 1985; Big Trouble 1986; Solarwarriors 1986; Tough Guys 1986; Where the River Runs Black 1986; Happy New Year 1987; The Man Who Broke 1,000 Chains 1987; The Rosary Murders 1987; A Tiger's Tale 1987; Cop 1988; Far North 1988; Brenda Starr 1989; Cat Chaser 1989; Dinner at Eight 1989; Prime Target 1989; Dick Tracy 1990; Project: Alien 1990; The Return of Eliot Ness 1991; The Story Lady 1991; VI Warshawski 1991; The Water Engine 1992; The Music of Chance 1993; When a Stranger Calls Back 1993; The Hudsucker Proxy 1994; Roommates 1994; Home for the Holidays 1995; The Last Supper 1995; One Fine Day 1996; Spy Hard 1996; Hi-Life

1998; *Hard Time* 1998; *Jerry and Tom* 1998; *O Brother, Where Art Thou?* 2000
Durock, Dick *Swamp Thing* 1982; *The Return of Swamp Thing* 1989
Durr, Jason *Young Soul Rebels* 1991; *Killer Tongue* 1996
Durrell, Michael *The American Success Company* 1979; *Family Sins* 1987; *Illegal in Blue* 1995
Dury, Ian *Number One* 1984; *Rocinante* 1986; *Hearts of Fire* 1987; *The Raggedy Rawney* 1987; *The Cook, the Thief, His Wife and Her Lover* 1989; *After Midnight* 1990; *Split Second* 1991; *The Crow: City of Angels* 1996; *Middleton's Changeling* 1997; *Underground* 1998
Duryea, Dan *The Little Foxes* 1941; *Sahara* 1943; *Mrs Parkington* 1944; *None but the Lonely Heart* 1944; *Along Came Jones* 1945; *The Great Flamarion* 1945; *Lady on a Train* 1945; *Ministry of Fear* 1945; *Scarlet Street* 1945; *The Woman in the Window* 1945; *Black Angel* 1946; *Another Part of the Forest* 1948; *Criss Cross* 1949; *Johnny Stool Pigeon* 1949; *The Underworld Story* 1950; *Winchester '73* 1950; *One Way Street* 1950; *Thunder Bay* 1953; *Rails into Laramie* 1954; *Ride Clear of Diablo* 1954; *Silver Lode* 1954; *World for Ransom* 1954; *The Marauders* 1955; *Foxfire* 1955; *The Burglar* 1956; *Battle Hymn* 1957; *Night Passage* 1957; *Slaughter on Tenth Avenue* 1957; *Platinum High School* 1960; *Six Black Horses* 1962; *He Rides Tall* 1964; *The Bounty Killer* 1965; *Incident at Phantom Hill* 1966; *Five Golden Dragons* 1967; *Stranger on the Run* 1967
Dusay, Marj *Sweet November* 1968; *Breezy* 1973; *MacArthur* 1977; *Love Walked In* 1997
Duse, Vittorio *Ossessione* 1942; *Queen of Hearts* 1989
Dusenberry, Ann *Jaws 2* 1978; *Heart Beat* 1979; *The Secret War of Jackie's Girls* 1980; *Cutter's Way* 1981; *Confessions of a Married Man* 1983
Dushku, Eliza *That Night* 1992; *This Boy's Life* 1993; *True Lies* 1994; *Bye Bye Love* 1995; *Journey* 1995; *Race the Sun* 1996
Dussollier, André *Une Belle Fille Comme Moi* 1973; *And Now My Love* 1974; *Perceval le Gallois* 1978; *Le Beau Mariage* 1982; *Just the Way You Are* 1984; *L'Amour par Terre* 1984; *3 Men and a Cradle* 1985; *Mélo* 1986; *Un Coeur en Hiver* 1992; *Le Colonel Chabert* 1994; *On Connaît la Chanson* 1997; *The Children of the Marshland* 1999
Dutronc, Jacques *Mado* 1976; *An Adventure for Two* 1979; *Slow Motion* 1980; *Les Tricheurs* 1984; *Van Gogh* 1991; *Place Vendôme* 1998
Dutt, Guru *Mr and Mrs '55* 1955; *Kaagaz Ke Phool* 1959
Dutt, Sunil *Ek Hi Rasta* 1956; *Mother India* 1957; *Waqt* 1965
Dutt, Utpal *Shakespeare Wallah* 1965; *The Guru* 1969; *Bombay Talkie* 1970; *The Middleman* 1975; *The Stranger* 1991
Duttine, John *Who Dares Wins* 1982; *The Hawk* 1992
Dutton, Charles S *Apology* 1986; *Jacknife* 1988; *Q & A* 1990; *Mississippi Masala* 1991; *Alien³* 1992; *The Distinguished Gentleman* 1992; *Menace II Society* 1993; *Rudy* 1993; *Jack Reed: a Search for Justice* 1994; *Surviving the Game* 1994; *Cry, the Beloved Country* 1995; *Deadly Justice* 1995; *A Low Down Dirty Shame* 1995; *Nick of Time* 1995; *Zooman* 1995; *Jack Reed: Death and Vengeance* 1996; *A Time to Kill* 1996; *Night Visitors* 1996; *Mimic* 1997; *Black Dog* 1998; *Blind Faith* 1998; *Cookie's Fortune* 1999; *Random Hearts* 1999
Dutton, Tim *Tom & Viv* 1994; *Into Thin Air: Death on Everest* 1997; *Darkness Falls* 1998
Duval, Daniel *Will It Snow for Christmas?* 1996; *Le Vent de la Nuit* 1999
Duval, James *Totally F***ed Up* 1993; *The Doom Generation* 1995; *Nowhere* 1997; *Clown at Midnight* 1998
DuVall, Clea *The Faculty* 1998; *The Astronaut's Wife* 1999; *Girl, Interrupted* 1999; *But I'm a Cheerleader* 1999
Duvall, Robert *To Kill a Mockingbird* 1962; *Captain Newman, MD* 1963; *Nightmare in the Sun* 1964; *The Chase* 1966; *Bullitt* 1968; *Countdown* 1968; *The Detective* 1968; *MASH* 1969; *The Rain People* 1969; *True Grit* 1969; *The Revolutionary* 1970; *Lawman* 1971; *THX 1138* 1971; *The Godfather* 1972; *The Great Northfield Minnesota Raid* 1972; *Joe Kidd* 1972; *Tomorrow* 1972; *Lady Ice* 1973; *The Outfit* 1973; *Badge 373* 1973; *The Godfather, Part II* 1974; *Breakout* 1975; *The Killer Elite* 1975; *The Eagle Has Landed* 1976; *Network* 1976; *The Seven-Per-Cent Solution* 1976; *The Greatest* 1977; *The Betsy* 1978; *Invasion of the Body Snatchers* 1978; *Apocalypse Now* 1979; *The Great Santini* 1979; *The Pursuit of DB Cooper* 1981; *True Confessions* 1981; *Tender Mercies* 1982; *The Natural* 1984; *The Stone Boy* 1984; *The Lightship* 1985; *Belizaire the Cajun* 1985; *Let's Get Harry* 1986; *Hotel Colonial* 1987; *Colors* 1988; *Days of Thunder* 1990; *The Handmaid's Tale* 1990; *A Show of Force* 1990; *Rambling Rose* 1991; *Convicts* 1991; *Falling Down* 1992; *The News Boys* 1992; *Stalin* 1992; *The Plague* 1992; *Geronimo* 1993; *Wrestling Ernest Hemingway* 1993; *The Paper* 1994; *The Scarlet Letter* 1995; *Something to Talk About* 1995; *The Stars Fell on Henrietta* 1995; *A Family Thing* 1996; *Phenomenon* 1996; *The Man Who Captured Eichmann* 1996; *The Apostle* 1997; *The Gingerbread Man* 1997; *A Civil Action* 1998; *Deep Impact* 1998; *Gone in 60 Seconds* 2000
Duvall, Shelley *Brewster McCloud* 1970; *McCabe and Mrs Miller* 1971; *Thieves like Us* 1974; *Nashville* 1975; *Annie Hall* 1977; *3 Women* 1977; *Popeye* 1980; *The Shining* 1980; *Time Bandits* 1981; *Roxanne* 1987; *Mother Goose Rock 'n' Rhyme* 1990; *Suburban Commando* 1991; *The Portrait of a Lady* 1996; *Talos the Mummy* 1997; *The Twilight of the Ice Nymphs* 1997; *Rocketman* 1997; *Horton Foote's Alone* 1997; *Changing Habits* 1997; *Casper Meets Wendy* 1998; *Home Fries* 1998
Duvitski, Janine *Abigail's Party* 1977; *Dracula* 1979
Dux, Pierre *Les Grandes Manoeuvres* 1955; *Goodbye Again* 1961; *Z* 1968; *Three Men to Destroy* 1980
Dvorak, Ann *Hollywood Revue* 1929; *The Crowd Roars* 1932; *Love Is a Racket* 1932; *Three on a Match* 1932; *Scarface* 1932; *The Strange Love of Molly Louvain* 1932; *Dr Socrates* 1935; *"G" Men* 1935; *Thanks a Million* 1935; *The Case of the Stuttering Bishop* 1937; *Merrily We Live* 1938; *Blind Alley* 1939; *Abilene Town* 1945; *Flame of the Barbary Coast* 1945; *The Long Night* 1947; *The Private Affairs of Bel Ami* 1947; *Out of the Blue* 1947; *A Life of Her Own* 1950; *Our Very Own* 1950; *The Secret of Convict Lake* 1951
Dvorsky, Peter *Videodrome* 1982; *Miles to Go* 1986
Dwire, Earl *Randy Rides Alone* 1934; *The Star Packer* 1934; *The Trail Beyond* 1934; *The Lawless Frontier* 1935; *Trouble in Texas* 1937; *The Arizona Kid* 1939
Dwyer, Hilary *Witchfinder General* 1968; *The Body Stealers* 1969; *The Oblong Box* 1969; *Two Gentlemen Sharing* 1969; *Cry of the Banshee* 1970; *Wuthering Heights* 1970
Dwyer, Leslie *The Way Ahead* 1944; *When the Bough Breaks* 1947; *The Calendar* 1948; *The Bad Lord Byron* 1949; *A Boy, a Girl and a Bike* 1949; *Judgment Deferred* 1951; *There Is Another Sun* 1951; *Hindle Wakes* 1952; *The Black Rider* 1954; *Cloak without Dagger* 1955; *Where There's a Will* 1955; *Left, Right and Centre* 1959; *A Hole Lot of Trouble* 1969
Dyall, Franklin *Easy Virtue* 1927; *Conquest of the Air* 1936
Dyall, Valentine *Dr Morelle – the Case of the Missing Heiress* 1949; *Night Comes Too Soon* 1949; *Room to Let* 1949; *Suspended Alibi* 1956; *The City of the Dead* 1960; *The Haunting* 1963
Dye, Cameron *Valley Girl* 1983; *Joy of Sex* 1984; *Fraternity Vacation* 1985; *Stranded* 1987; *Out of the Dark* 1988; *Natural Selection* 1994
Dye, Dale *Wings of the Apache* 1990; *Kid* 1990; *Blue Sky* 1991; *Mission: Impossible* 1996
Dyer, Danny *Human Traffic* 1999; *The Trench* 1999
Dylan, Bob *Pat Garrett and Billy the Kid* 1973; *Hearts of Fire* 1987
Dymon Jr, Frankie *Some People* 1962; *One Plus One* 1968
Dyne, Aminta *Molly and Me* 1945; *Blood on My Hands* 1948
Dyneley, Peter *Hell below Zero* 1954; *The Golden Disc* 1958; *The Whole Truth* 1958; *House of Mystery* 1961
Dysart, Richard aka **Dysart, Richard A** *The Lost Man* 1969; *The Autobiography of Miss Jane Pittman* 1974; *The Terminal Man* 1974; *An Enemy of the People* 1977; *Being There* 1979; *Meteor* 1979; *Prophecy* 1979; *The Thing* 1982; *The Falcon and the Snowman* 1985; *Malice in Wonderland* 1985; *Mask* 1985; *Pale Rider* 1985; *Warning Sign* 1985; *Last Days of Patton* 1986; *Moving Target* 1988; *Day One* 1989; *Back to the Future Part III* 1990; *Marilyn and Bobby: Her Final Affair* 1993; *A Child Is Missing* 1995; *Truman* 1995; *Hard Rain* 1997
Dyson, Noel *Mister Ten Per Cent* 1967; *Father Dear Father* 1972
Dzundza, George *The Deer Hunter* 1978; *Young Maverick* 1979; *Skokie* 1981; *Streamers* 1983; *Best Defense* 1984; *The Execution of Raymond Graham* 1985; *The Rape of Richard Beck* 1985; *No Mercy* 1986; *No Way Out* 1986; *2 ½ Dads* 1986; *The Beast* 1988; *Something Is Out There* 1988; *The Ryan White Story* 1989; *Terror on Highway 91* 1989; *Impulse* 1990; *White Hunter, Black Heart* 1990; *The Butcher's Wife* 1991; *Basic Instinct* 1992; *Shades of Gray* 1992; *Seeds of Deception* 1993; *The Enemy Within* 1994; *Crimson Tide* 1995; *Dangerous Minds* 1995; *The Limbic Region* 1996; *That Darn Cat* 1997; *Species II* 1998; *Subzero* 1998; *Instinct* 1999

E

Eagan, Daisy *Losing Isaiah* 1995; *Ripe* 1996
Eagger, Victoria *The Nun and the Bandit* 1992; *Diana & Me* 1997
Earl, Elizabeth *The Letter* 1940; *FairyTale: a True Story* 1997
Earle, Edward *The Wind* 1928; *Spite Marriage* 1929
Earles, Harry *The Unholy Three* 1925; *The Unholy Three* 1930; *Freaks* 1932
East, Jeff *Tom Sawyer* 1973; *Huckleberry Finn* 1974; *The Hazing* 1977; *Deadly Blessing* 1981; *Vengeance: the Demon* 1988
Easterbrook, Leslie *Police Academy* 1984; *Police Academy 3: Back in Training* 1986; *Police Academy 4: Citizens on Patrol* 1987; *Police Academy 5: Assignment Miami Beach* 1988; *The Taking of Flight 847* 1988; *Police Academy 6: City under Siege* 1989; *Police Academy: Mission to Moscow* 1994
Eastham, Richard *There's No Business like Show Business* 1954; *Toby Tyler, or Ten Weeks with a Circus* 1960; *Not with My Wife, You Don't!* 1966
Eastman, George *Tiger from the River Kwai* 1975; *Christmas Present* 1986
Easton, Michael *Shadow of a Stranger* 1992; *What We Did That Night* 1999
Easton, Robert *The War Lover* 1962; *Mr Sycamore* 1974; *The Giant Spider Invasion* 1975; *Long Gone* 1987
Easton, Sheena *Body Bags* 1993; *David Copperfield* 1993; *Indecent Proposal* 1993; *All Dogs Go to Heaven 2* 1996
Eastwood, Alison *Tightrope* 1984; *Absolute Power* 1996; *Midnight in the Garden of Good and Evil* 1997
Eastwood, Clint *Revenge of the Creature* 1955; *Tarantula* 1955; *Lady Godiva* 1955; *The First Travelling Saleslady* 1956; *Star in the Dust* 1956; *Away All Boats* 1956; *Escapade in Japan* 1957; *Hell Bent for Glory* 1957; *A Fistful of Dollars* 1964; *For a Few Dollars More* 1965; *The Good, the Bad and the Ugly* 1967; *Coogan's Bluff* 1968; *Hang 'em High* 1968; *Paint Your Wagon* 1969; *Where Eagles Dare* 1969; *Kelly's Heroes* 1970; *Two Mules for Sister Sara* 1970; *The Beguiled* 1971; *Dirty Harry* 1971; *Play Misty for Me* 1971; *Joe Kidd* 1972; *High Plains Drifter* 1973; *Magnum Force* 1973; *Thunderbolt and Lightfoot* 1974; *The Eiger Sanction* 1975; *The Enforcer* 1976; *The Outlaw Josey Wales* 1976; *The Gauntlet* 1977; *Every Which Way but Loose* 1978; *Escape from Alcatraz* 1979; *Any Which Way You Can* 1980; *Bronco Billy* 1980; *Firefox* 1982; *Honkytonk Man* 1982; *Sudden Impact* 1983; *City Heat* 1984; *Tightrope* 1984; *Pale Rider* 1985; *Heartbreak Ridge* 1986; *The Dead Pool* 1988; *Pink Cadillac* 1989; *The Rookie* 1990; *White Hunter, Black Heart* 1990; *Unforgiven* 1992; *In the Line of Fire* 1993; *A Perfect World* 1993; *The Bridges of Madison County* 1995; *Casper* 1995; *Absolute Power* 1996; *True Crime* 1999
Eastwood, Jayne *My Pleasure Is My Business* 1974; *Partners in Love* 1992; *Bury Me in Niagara* 1993
Eaton, Shirley *The Love Match* 1955; *Charley Moon* 1956; *Sailor Beware!* 1956; *Three Men in a Boat* 1956; *Doctor at Large* 1957; *The Naked Truth* 1957; *Carry On Sergeant* 1958; *Further up the Creek* 1958; *Life Is a Circus* 1958; *Carry On Nurse* 1959; *Dentist on the Job* 1961; *Nearly a Nasty Accident* 1961; *What a Carve Up!* 1961; *The Girl Hunters* 1963; *Goldfinger* 1964; *Rhino!* 1964; *Ten Little Indians* 1965; *Around the World under the Sea* 1966; *Eight on the Lam* 1967; *The Blood of Fu Manchu* 1968
Eaton, Wallas *Adventure in the Hopfields* 1954; *Mad Dog* 1976
Eberhardt, Norma *The Return of Dracula* 1958; *Live Fast, Die Young* 1958
Ebersole, Christine *Amadeus* 1984; *Thief of Hearts* 1984; *Acceptable Risks* 1986; *Mac and Me* 1988; *Ghost Dad* 1990; *Folks!* 1992; *Dying to Love You* 1993; *Richie Rich* 1994; *Pie in the Sky* 1995; *Black Sheep* 1996; *An Unexpected Family* 1996; *An Unexpected Life* 1998; *My Favorite Martian* 1999; *Double Platinum* 1999
Ebsen, Buddy *Broadway Melody of 1936* 1935; *Banjo on My Knee* 1936; *Captain January* 1936; *Broadway Melody of 1938* 1937; *The Girl of the Golden West* 1938; *My Lucky Star* 1938; *Yellow Jack* 1938; *Night People* 1954; *Davy Crockett, King of the Wild Frontier* 1955; *Attack!* 1956; *Between Heaven and Hell* 1956; *Davy Crockett and the River Pirates* 1956; *Breakfast at Tiffany's* 1961; *The Interns* 1962; *Mail Order Bride* 1964; *The One and Only, Genuine, Original Family Band* 1968; *Smash-Up on Interstate 5* 1976; *Working Trash* 1990; *The Beverly Hillbillies* 1993
Eburne, Maude *The Bat Whispers* 1930; *The Guardsman* 1931; *Her Majesty Love* 1931; *Indiscreet* 1931; *Polly of the Circus* 1932; *The Vampire Bat* 1933; *Ladies They Talk About* 1933; *Ruggles of Red Gap* 1935; *Among the Living* 1941; *You Belong to Me* 1941; *The Boogie Man Will Get You* 1942; *Rosie the Riveter* 1944
Eccles, Aimee aka **Eccles, Amy** *Little Big Man* 1970; *Marco* 1973; *The Concrete Jungle* 1982
Eccleston, Christopher aka **Eccleston, Chris** *Let Him Have It* 1991; *Anchoress* 1993; *Shallow Grave* 1994; *Jude* 1996; *Heart* 1997; *A Price above Rubies* 1997; *Elizabeth* 1998; *eXistenZ* 1999; *With or Without You* 1999; *Gone in 60 Seconds* 2000
Eckhart, Aaron *In the Company of Men* 1997; *Thursday* 1998; *Your Friends & Neighbours* 1998; *Molly* 1999; *Any Given Sunday* 1999; *Erin Brockovich* 2000

Malachi's Cove 1973; *Are You Being Served?* 1977; *The Boys in Blue* 1983

English, Marla *Shield for Murder* 1954; *The She-Creature* 1956; *Voodoo Woman* 1957

Englund, Robert *Buster and Billie* 1974; *St Ives* 1976; *Stay Hungry* 1976; *Eaten Alive* 1976; *The Great Smokey Roadblock* 1977; *Mind over Murder* 1979; *The Fifth Floor* 1980; *Don't Cry, It's Only Thunder* 1982; *Starflight One* 1983; *A Nightmare on Elm Street* 1984; *A Nightmare on Elm Street 2: Freddy's Revenge* 1985; *A Nightmare on Elm Street 3: Dream Warriors* 1987; *A Nightmare on Elm Street 4: The Dream Master* 1988; *A Nightmare on Elm Street 5: The Dream Child* 1989; *The Phantom of the Opera* 1989; *The Adventures of Ford Fairlane* 1990; *Freddy's Dead: the Final Nightmare* 1991; *The Mangler* 1994; *Mortal Fear* 1994; *Wes Craven's New Nightmare* 1994; *Tobe Hooper's Night Terrors* 1994; *Killer Tongue* 1996; *Mind Breakers* 1996; *Wishmaster* 1997; *Dee Snider's Strangeland* 1998; *Urban Legend* 1998; *Meet the Deedles* 1998

Enos, John *aka* **Enos III, John** *Bullet* 1995; *Raven Hawk* 1996

Enriquez, Rene *The Evil That Men Do* 1984; *Bulletproof* 1987

Ensign, Michael *Buddy Buddy* 1981; *House* 1986; *Inherit the Wind* 1988; *Rock Hudson* 1990; *Life Stinks* 1991; *Born Yesterday* 1993; *Children of the Corn III: Urban Harvest* 1995; *The Christmas Box* 1995

Epps, Omar *Juice* 1992; *Daybreak* 1993; *The Program* 1993; *Major League II* 1994; *Higher Learning* 1995; *First Time Felon* 1997; *Scream 2* 1997; *Breakfast of Champions* 1999; *The Wood* 1999; *The Mod Squad* 1999; *In Too Deep* 1999; *Love & Basketball* 2000

Epstein, Pierre *Indecent Proposal* 1993; *Mind of a Killer* 1993

Erbe, Kathryn *What about Bob?* 1991; *Rich in Love* 1992; *Breathing Lessons* 1994; *D2: the Mighty Ducks* 1994; *Kiss of Death* 1994; *Dream with the Fishes* 1996; *Stir of Echoes* 1999

Ercy, Elizabeth *Phaedra* 1962; *The Sorcerers* 1967

Erdman, Richard *The Admiral Was a Lady* 1950; *The Men* 1950; *Cry Danger* 1951; *The Stooge* 1951; *The San Francisco Story* 1952; *The Blue Gardenia* 1953; *Stalag 17* 1953; *Bengazi* 1955; *Face of Fire* 1959; *Namu, the Killer Whale* 1966; *Heidi's Song* 1982; *Tomboy* 1985; *Jesse* 1988

Erhard, Bernard *GoBots: Battle of the Rocklords* 1986; *Little Nemo: Adventures in Slumberland* 1992

Erickson, Leif *Waikiki Wedding* 1937; *HM Pulham Esq* 1941; *Nothing but the Truth* 1941; *Arabian Nights* 1942; *Pardon My Sarong* 1942; *Joan of Arc* 1948; *The Snake Pit* 1948; *Sorry, Wrong Number* 1948; *Johnny Stool Pigeon* 1949; *Dallas* 1950; *Three Secrets* 1950; *Stella* 1950; *Sailor Beware* 1951; *Abbott and Costello Meet Captain Kidd* 1952; *Never Wave at a WAC* 1952; *Fort Algiers* 1953; *Invaders from Mars* 1953; *On the Waterfront* 1954; *The Fastest Gun Alive* 1956; *Tea and Sympathy* 1956; *Star in the Dust* 1956; *Kiss Them for Me* 1957; *Istanbul* 1957; *Twilight for the Gods* 1958; *Strait-Jacket* 1963; *Roustabout* 1964; *Mirage* 1965; *I*

Saw What You Did 1965; *Terror in the Sky* 1971; *Man and Boy* 1971; *The Family Rico* 1972; *Winterhawk* 1975; *Abduction* 1975

Ericson, John *Teresa* 1951; *Green Fire* 1954; *The Student Prince* 1954; *Rhapsody* 1954; *Bad Day at Black Rock* 1955; *Forty Guns* 1957; *Day of the Bad Man* 1958; *Under Ten Flags* 1960; *Pretty Boy Floyd* 1960; *7 Faces of Dr Lao* 1963; *Bedknobs and Broomsticks* 1971; *Crash!* 1977

Ermey, R Lee *aka* **Ermey, Lee,** *aka* **Ermey, Ronald Lee** *The Boys in Company C* 1978; *Purple Hearts* 1984; *Full Metal Jacket* 1987; *Mississippi Burning* 1988; *Fletch Lives* 1989; *Demonstone* 1989; *I'm Dangerous Tonight* 1990; *The Take* 1990; *Kid* 1990; *Toy Soldiers* 1991; *Body Snatchers* 1993; *Chain of Command* 1993; *Hexed* 1993; *Sommersby* 1993; *Love Is a Gun* 1994; *Murder in the First* 1994; *On Deadly Ground* 1994; *Rise and Walk: the Dennis Byrd Story* 1994; *Dead Man Walking* 1995; *Se7en* 1995; *Soul of the Game* 1996; *Switchback* 1997; *Prefontaine* 1997; *The Sender* 1997; *Dead Men Can't Dance* 1997

Errickson, Krista *Little Darlings* 1980; *Jekyll and Hyde... Together Again* 1982; *Mortal Passions* 1989; *Martial Outlaw* 1993; *The Paperboy* 1994

Errol, Leon *Her Majesty Love* 1931; *One Heavenly Night* 1931; *Alice in Wonderland* 1933; *We're Not Dressing* 1934; *Dancing Co-Ed* 1939; *The Girl from Mexico* 1939; *Mexican Spitfire* 1940; *Never Give a Sucker an Even Break* 1941; *Higher and Higher* 1943; *Twilight on the Prairie* 1944; *Under Western Skies* 1945; *The Noose Hangs High* 1948

Erskine, Marilyn *Westward the Women* 1951; *Above and Beyond* 1952; *The Eddie Cantor Story* 1953

Ertmanis, Victor *Paris France* 1993; *Brainscan* 1994

Erwin, Bill *How Awful about Allan* 1970; *Somewhere in Time* 1980; *The Land before Time* 1988; *Silent Assassins* 1988

Erwin, Stuart *The Big Broadcast* 1932; *Going Hollywood* 1933; *International House* 1933; *Hold Your Man* 1933; *The Stranger's Return* 1933; *Bachelor Bait* 1934; *Chained* 1934; *Palooka* 1934; *Viva Villa!* 1934; *Ceiling Zero* 1935; *After Office Hours* 1935; *Pigskin Parade* 1936; *I'll Take Romance* 1937; *Slim* 1937; *Hollywood Cavalcade* 1939; *When the Daltons Rode* 1940; *The Bride Came C.O.D.* 1941; *Heaven Only Knows* 1947; *For the Love of Mike* 1960; *The Misadventures of Merlin Jones* 1964

Esformes, Nate *Black Belt Jones* 1974; *Gore Vidal's Billy the Kid* 1989

Eshley, Norman *The Immortal Story* 1968; *Blind Terror* 1971; *House of Mortal Sin* 1975; *George and Mildred* 1980

Eskelson, Dana *Past Midnight* 1992; *To Sir with Love 2* 1996

Esmond, Annie *Thunder in the City* 1937; *Gert and Daisy's Weekend* 1941

Esmond, Carl *Evensong* 1934; *The Dawn Patrol* 1938; *Thunder Afloat* 1939; *The Navy Comes Through* 1942; *Margin for Error* 1943; *Address Unknown* 1944; *Experiment Perilous* 1944; *The Master Race* 1944; *The Story of*

Dr Wassell 1944; *Ministry of Fear* 1945; *Without Love* 1945; *This Love of Ours* 1945; *Smash-Up, the Story of a Woman* 1947; *Walk a Crooked Mile* 1948; *Mystery Submarine* 1950; *The World in His Arms* 1952; *Thunder in the Sun* 1959

Esmond, Jill *The Skin Game* 1931; *FP1* 1932; *The Pied Piper* 1942; *Casanova Brown* 1944; *The Bandit of Sherwood Forest* 1946; *Bedelia* 1946; *A Man Called Peter* 1955

Esposito, Giancarlo *School Daze* 1988; *Do the Right Thing* 1989; *King of New York* 1989; *Harley Davidson and the Marlboro Man* 1991; *Bob Roberts* 1992; *Night on Earth* 1992; *Mind of a Killer* 1993; *Fresh* 1994; *Smoke* 1995; *The Tomorrow Man* 1995; *The Usual Suspects* 1995; *Reckless* 1995; *The Keeper* 1995; *Nothing to Lose* 1997; *Twilight* 1998; *Thirst* 1998

Esposito, Gianni *French Cancan* 1955; *Celà s'Appelle l'Aurore* 1956; *Les Misérables* 1957; *Paris Nous Appartient* 1960

Essex, David *All Coppers Are...* 1972; *That'll Be the Day* 1973; *Stardust* 1974; *Silver Dream Racer* 1980; *Shogun Warrior* 1991

Estes, Rob *aka* **Estes, Robert** *Perfect People* 1988; *Checkered Flag* 1990; *Come Die with Me* 1994; *A Loss of Innocence* 1996; *Sweet Temptation* 1996; *Terror in the Mall* 1998

Estevez, Emilio *In the Custody of Strangers* 1982; *Tex* 1982; *Nightmares* 1983; *The Outsiders* 1983; *Repo Man* 1984; *The Breakfast Club* 1985; *St Elmo's Fire* 1985; *That Was Then... This Is Now* 1985; *Maximum Overdrive* 1986; *Wisdom* 1986; *Stakeout* 1987; *Young Guns* 1988; *Never on Tuesday* 1988; *Nightbreaker* 1989; *Men at Work* 1990; *Young Guns II* 1990; *Freejack* 1992; *The Mighty Ducks* 1992; *Another Stakeout* 1993; *Judgment Night* 1993; *National Lampoon's Loaded Weapon 1* 1993; *D2: the Mighty Ducks* 1994; *D3: the Mighty Ducks* 1996; *The War at Home* 1996; *Dollar for the Dead* 1998

Estevez, Joe *The California Kid* 1974; *Soultaker* 1991; *Eye of the Stranger* 1993; *Double Blast* 1994; *Orbit* 1996

Estevez, Renée *Dead Silence* 1991; *Paper Hearts* 1993

Estrada, Erik *Precinct 45: Los Angeles Police* 1972; *Trackdown* 1976; *Hour of the Assassin* 1987; *The Dirty Dozen: the Fatal Mission* 1988; *She Knows Too Much* 1989; *A Show of Force* 1990; *Earth Angel* 1991; *Panic in the Skies!* 1996

Etaix, Pierre *Pickpocket* 1959; *Yoyo* 1964

Evans, Art *Leadbelly* 1976; *A Soldier's Story* 1984; *Ruthless People* 1986; *White of the Eye* 1986; *Native Son* 1986; *Jo Jo Dancer, Your Life Is Calling* 1986; *School Daze* 1988; *The Mighty Quinn* 1989; *Die Hard 2: Die Harder* 1990; *Downtown* 1990; *Trespass* 1992; *The Finishing Touch* 1992; *Metro* 1997

Evans, Barry *Here We Go round the Mulberry Bush* 1967; *Die Screaming Marianne* 1970; *Adventures of a Taxi Driver* 1975; *Under the Doctor* 1976

Evans, Charles *Black Beauty* 1946; *The Dark Mirror* 1946

Evans, Clifford *The Foreman Went to France* 1941; *Love on the Dole* 1941; *The Saint Meets the Tiger*

1943; *The Silver Darlings* 1947; *While I Live* 1947; *Escape Route* 1952; *Valley of Song* 1953; *The Gilded Cage* 1954; *Passport to Treason* 1956; *Violent Playground* 1958; *The Curse of the Werewolf* 1961; *The Long Ships* 1963

Evans, Dale *War of the Wildcats* 1943; *The Yellow Rose of Texas* 1944; *Bells of Rosarita* 1945; *My Pal Trigger* 1946; *Bells of San Angelo* 1947

Evans, Edith *The Queen of Spades* 1948; *The Importance of Being Earnest* 1952; *Look Back in Anger* 1959; *The Nun's Story* 1959; *Tom Jones* 1963; *The Chalk Garden* 1964; *Young Cassidy* 1965; *Fitzwilly* 1967; *The Whisperers* 1967; *Prudence and the Pill* 1968; *Crooks and Coronets* 1969; *David Copperfield* 1969; *The Madwoman of Chaillot* 1969; *Scrooge* 1970; *Craze* 1973; *A Doll's House* 1973; *The Slipper and the Rose* 1976

Evans, Edward *Valley of Song* 1953; *It's a Great Day* 1955; *One More Time* 1970

Evans, Estelle *To Kill a Mockingbird* 1962; *The Learning Tree* 1969

Evans, Evans *All Fall Down* 1962; *Bonnie and Clyde* 1967; *Story of a Love Story* 1973

Evans, Gene *Fixed Bayonets* 1951; *Force of Arms* 1951; *The Steel Helmet* 1951; *Park Row* 1952; *Thunderbirds* 1952; *Donovan's Brain* 1953; *The Golden Blade* 1953; *Cattle Queen of Montana* 1954; *Hell and High Water* 1954; *The Long Wait* 1954; *Crashout* 1955; *The Helen Morgan Story* 1957; *The Sad Sack* 1957; *Money, Women and Guns* 1958; *Damn Citizen* 1958; *Operation Petticoat* 1959; *The Giant Behemoth* 1959; *The Hangman* 1959; *Gold of the Seven Saints* 1961; *Shock Corridor* 1963; *Apache Uprising* 1965; *Waco* 1966; *Walking Tall* 1973

Evans, Joan *Roseanna McCoy* 1949; *Edge of Doom* 1950; *Our Very Own* 1950; *Skirts Ahoy!* 1952; *It Grows on Trees* 1952; *Column South* 1953; *The Outcast* 1954; *No Name on the Bullet* 1959

Evans, John *I've Heard the Mermaids Singing* 1987; *Lena: My 100 Children* 1987

Evans, Josh *Born on the Fourth of July* 1989; *The Doors* 1991

Evans, Lee *Funny Bones* 1994; *The Fifth Element* 1997; *Mousehunt* 1997; *There's Something about Mary* 1998

Evans, Linda *Those Calloways* 1964; *Beach Blanket Bingo* 1965; *The Klansman* 1974; *Mitchell* 1975; *Avalanche Express* 1979; *Tom Horn* 1980; *She'll Take Romance* 1990; *The Stepsister* 1997

Evans, Madge *Sporting Blood* 1931; *Guilty Hands* 1931; *Broadway to Hollywood* 1933; *Dinner at Eight* 1933; *Hallelujah, I'm a Bum* 1933; *The Mayor of Hell* 1933; *What Every Woman Knows* 1934; *Stand up and Cheer!* 1934; *David Copperfield* 1935; *The Tunnel* 1935; *Pennies from Heaven* 1936; *Piccadilly Jim* 1936; *Espionage* 1937; *Sinners in Paradise* 1938

Evans, Maurice *Wedding Rehearsal* 1932; *Androcles and the Lion* 1952; *The Story of Gilbert and Sullivan* 1953; *The War Lord* 1965; *One of Our Spies Is Missing* 1966; *Jack of Diamonds* 1967; *Planet of the*

Apes 1968; *Rosemary's Baby* 1968; *Beneath the Planet of the Apes* 1969; *The Body Stealers* 1969; *Terror in the Wax Museum* 1973

Evans, Monica *The Odd Couple* 1968; *Robin Hood* 1973

Evans, Peggy *The Blue Lamp* 1949; *Calling Bulldog Drummond* 1951

Evans, Reg *Kitty and the Bagman* 1982; *Mesmerized* 1984

Evans, Rex *The Brighton Strangler* 1945; *Merry Andrew* 1958

Evans, Richard *Too Soon to Love* 1960; *Dirty Little Billy* 1972; *Islands in the Stream* 1977; *Deadly Care* 1987

Evans, Robert *Man of a Thousand Faces* 1957; *The Sun Also Rises* 1957; *The Best of Everything* 1959; *Burn Hollywood Burn* 1997

Evans, Troy *Kuffs* 1991; *Under Siege* 1992; *Ace Ventura: Pet Detective* 1993; *My Summer Story* 1994; *Father and Scout* 1994; *Bodily Harm* 1995; *Crowned and Dangerous* 1997

Evanson, Edith *Rope* 1948; *The Magnificent Yankee* 1950

Eve, Trevor *Dracula* 1979; *Aspen Extreme* 1993; *Don't Get Me Started* 1994; *Ivana Trump's For Love Alone* 1996

Evelyn, Judith *The 13th Letter* 1951; *Rear Window* 1954; *Female on the Beach* 1955; *Hilda Crane* 1956; *The Brothers Karamazov* 1958; *Twilight for the Gods* 1958; *The Tingler* 1959

Everest, Barbara *When London Sleeps* 1932; *The Lad* 1935; *The Passing of the Third Floor Back* 1935; *Gaslight* 1944; *The Uninvited* 1944; *Wanted for Murder* 1946; *Children of Chance* 1949; *Madeleine* 1949; *Tony Draws a Horse* 1950; *The Safecracker* 1958; *The Man Who Finally Died* 1962; *Nurse on Wheels* 1963

Everett, Chad *Claudelle Inglish* 1961; *Lovers Must Learn* 1962; *Get Yourself a College Girl* 1964; *Johnny Tiger* 1966; *Made in Paris* 1966; *The Singing Nun* 1966; *First to Fight* 1967; *The Last Challenge* 1967; *The Firechasers* 1970; *Airplane II: the Sequel* 1982; *Fever Pitch* 1985; *Heroes Stand Alone* 1989; *Official Denial* 1993; *When Time Expires* 1997; *Psycho* 1998

Everett, Rupert *Merlin and the Sword* 1982; *Another Country* 1984; *Dance with a Stranger* 1984; *Duet for One* 1986; *The Right Hand Man* 1986; *Chronicle of a Death Foretold* 1987; *Hearts of Fire* 1987; *The Comfort of Strangers* 1991; *Inside Monkey Zetterland* 1992; *Cemetery Man* 1994; *Prêt-à-Porter* 1994; *The Madness of King George* 1995; *B Monkey* 1996; *Dunston Checks In* 1996; *My Best Friend's Wedding* 1997; *Shakespeare in Love* 1998; *An Ideal Husband* 1999; *William Shakespeare's A Midsummer Night's Dream* 1999; *Inspector Gadget* 1999; *The Next Best Thing* 2000

Everett, Tom *Leatherface: the Texas Chainsaw Massacre III* 1990; *A Thousand Heroes* 1992

Everhard, Nancy *DeepStar Six* 1989; *The Trial of the Incredible Hulk* 1989; *Demonstone* 1989; *The China Lake Murders* 1990; *This Gun for Hire* 1991

Everhart, Angie *Tales from the Crypt Presents: Bordello of Blood* 1996; *Another Nine ½ Weeks* 1997; *Executive Target* 1997

Sonata 1937; *Just around the Corner* 1938; *Bell-Bottom George* 1943; *The Hornet's Nest* 1955; *Hidden Homicide* 1958
Farrell, Colin J *Drinking Crude* 1997; *The War Zone* 1999
Farrell, Glenda *Little Caesar* 1931; *I Am a Fugitive from a Chain Gang* 1932; *Life Begins* 1932; *Bureau of Missing Persons* 1933; *Havana Widows* 1933; *Lady for a Day* 1933; *Man's Castle* 1933; *Mystery of the Wax Museum* 1933; *Hi, Nellie!* 1934; *The Secret Bride* 1934; *Go into Your Dance* 1935; *Gold Diggers of 1935* 1935; *In Caliente* 1935; *Gold Diggers of 1937* 1936; *Breakfast for Two* 1937; *Hollywood Hotel* 1937; *Johnny Eager* 1941; *Twin Beds* 1942; *The Talk of the Town* 1942; *Lulu Belle* 1948; *Apache War Smoke* 1952; *Secret of the Incas* 1954; *Susan Slept Here* 1954; *The Girl in the Red Velvet Swing* 1955; *Middle of the Night* 1959; *The Disorderly Orderly* 1964; *Kissin' Cousins* 1964; *Tiger by the Tail* 1970
Farrell, Mike *Private Sessions* 1985; *Vanishing Act* 1986; *A Deadly Silence* 1989; *Silent Motive* 1991; *The Whereabouts of Jenny* 1991; *Sins of the Mind* 1997
Farrell, Nicholas *Chariots of Fire* 1981; *Playing Away* 1986; *In the Bleak Midwinter* 1995; *Othello* 1995; *Hamlet* 1996; *Twelfth Night* 1996; *Beautiful People* 1999
Farrell, Paul *The Rising of the Moon* 1957; *A Clockwork Orange* 1971
Farrell, Sharon *The Spy with My Face* 1966; *A Lovely Way to Go* 1968; *Marlowe* 1969; *The Reivers* 1969; *The Eyes of Charles Sand* 1972; *It's Alive* 1974; *The Premonition* 1975; *The Last Ride of the Dalton Gang* 1979; *The Stunt Man* 1980; *Out of the Blue* 1980; *The Fifth Floor* 1980; *Separate Ways* 1981; *One Man Force* 1989; *Arcade* 1993; *Sworn to Vengeance* 1993
Farrell, Terry *Back to School* 1986; *Beverly Hills Madam* 1986; *Hellraiser III: Hell on Earth* 1992; *Danielle Steel's Star* 1993; *Red Sun Rising* 1994; *Reasons of the Heart* 1996; *Legion* 1998
Farrell, Timothy *Glen or Glenda* 1953; *Jail Bait* 1954
Farrell, Tommy *At War with the Army* 1950; *Meet Danny Wilson* 1952
Farrow, Mia *Guns at Batasi* 1964; *A Dandy in Aspic* 1968; *Rosemary's Baby* 1968; *John and Mary* 1969; *Secret Ceremony* 1969; *Blind Terror* 1971; *Follow Me* 1971; *The Great Gatsby* 1974; *Full Circle* 1977; *Avalanche* 1978; *Death on the Nile* 1978; *A Wedding* 1978; *Hurricane* 1979; *The Last Unicorn* 1980; *A Midsummer Night's Sex Comedy* 1982; *Zelig* 1983; *Broadway Danny Rose* 1984; *Supergirl* 1984; *The Purple Rose of Cairo* 1985; *Hannah and Her Sisters* 1986; *Radio Days* 1987; *September* 1987; *Another Woman* 1988; *Crimes and Misdemeanors* 1989; *New York Stories* 1989; *Alice* 1990; *Shadows and Fog* 1991; *Husbands and Wives* 1992; *Widows' Peak* 1993; *Miami Rhapsody* 1995; *Reckless* 1995; *Private Parts* 1997; *Miracle at Midnight* 1998
Farrow, Tisa *Homer* 1970; *And Hope to Die* 1972; *Fingers* 1978; *Search and Destroy* 1978; *Zombie Flesh Eaters* 1979
Fassbinder, Rainer Werner *Love Is Colder than Death* 1969; *Gods of the Plague* 1969; *The American Soldier* 1970; *Beware of a Holy Whore* 1970; *Whity* 1970; *Fear Eats the Soul* 1973; *Fox and His Friends* 1975; *Kamikaze 1989* 1983
Faulds, Andrew *The One That Got Away* 1957; *Blood of the Vampire* 1958
Faulkner, Edward *Tickle Me* 1965; *Hellfighters* 1969
Faulkner, James *The Great Waltz* 1972; *The Abdication* 1974; *Death in the Sun* 1975; *The Maid* 1991; *Crimetime* 1996; *Vigo: Passion for Life* 1997; *All the Little Animals* 1998; *A Kid in Aladdin's Palace* 1998
Faulkner, Keith *The Man in the Back Seat* 1961; *Strongroom* 1961
Faulkner, Lisa *The Lover* 1992; *A Feast at Midnight* 1995
Favreau, Jon *Rudy* 1993; *Politically Correct Party Animals* 1994; *Persons Unknown* 1996; *Swingers* 1996; *Whiskey Down* 1996; *Very Bad Things* 1998; *Rocky Marciano* 1999; *Love and Sex* 2000
Fawcett, Alan *Conspiracy of Love* 1987; *Afterglow* 1997
Fawcett, Farrah *aka* **Fawcett-Majors, Farrah** *Three's a Crowd* 1969; *Myra Breckinridge* 1970; *Logan's Run* 1976; *Somebody Killed Her Husband* 1978; *Sunburn* 1979; *Saturn 3* 1980; *The Cannonball Run* 1981; *The Burning Bed* 1984; *The Red-Light Sting* 1984; *Extremities* 1986; *Nazi Hunter: the Beate Klarsfeld Story* 1986; *Margaret Bourke-White* 1989; *See You in the Morning* 1989; *Criminal Behaviour* 1992; *Man of the House* 1994; *The Substitute Wife* 1994; *Dalva* 1996; *The Apostle* 1997
Fawcett, George *Flesh and the Devil* 1926; *The Son of the Sheik* 1926; *Love* 1927; *The Private Life of Helen of Troy* 1927; *The Wedding March* 1928; *Ladies of Leisure* 1930
Fawcett, William *Gun Glory* 1957; *King Rat* 1965
Fawdon, Michele *Cathy's Child* 1979; *Unfinished Business* 1985; *Travelling North* 1986
Fay, Frank *The Show of Shows* 1929; *Nothing Sacred* 1937; *They Knew What They Wanted* 1940; *Love Nest* 1951
Faye, Alice *George White's Scandals* 1934; *George White's 1935 Scandals* 1935; *King of Burlesque* 1936; *Poor Little Rich Girl* 1936; *Sing, Baby, Sing* 1936; *Stowaway* 1936; *In Old Chicago* 1937; *On the Avenue* 1937; *Wake Up and Live* 1937; *You Can't Have Everything* 1937; *Alexander's Ragtime Band* 1938; *Sally, Irene and Mary* 1938; *Hollywood Cavalcade* 1939; *Rose of Washington Square* 1939; *Lillian Russell* 1940; *Little Old New York* 1940; *Tin Pan Alley* 1940; *The Great American Broadcast* 1941; *That Night in Rio* 1941; *Weekend in Havana* 1941; *The Gang's All Here* 1943; *Hello, Frisco, Hello* 1943; *Fallen Angel* 1945; *State Fair* 1962; *The Magic of Lassie* 1978
Faye, Herbie *Top Banana* 1953; *Requiem for a Heavyweight* 1962
Faye, Janina *The Adventures of Hal 5* 1958; *Don't Talk to Strange Men* 1962; *The Beauty Jungle* 1964; *The Dance of Death* 1969
Faye, Julia *The Ten Commandments* 1923; *Dynamite* 1929; *Samson and Delilah* 1949
Faylen, Frank *It's a Wonderful Life* 1946; *Road to Rio* 1947; *Welcome Stranger* 1947; *Suddenly It's Spring* 1947; *The Perils of Pauline* 1947; *Blood on the Moon* 1948; *Whispering Smith* 1948; *Convicted* 1950; *Copper Canyon* 1950; *Detective Story* 1951; *The Lusty Men* 1952; *The Sniper* 1952; *Riot in Cell Block 11* 1954; *The Looters* 1955; *The McConnell Story* 1955; *Seventh Cavalry* 1956; *Gunfight at the OK Corral* 1957; *Dino* 1957; *The Monkey's Uncle* 1965; *When the Boys Meet the Girls* 1965; *Fluffy* 1965
Faysse, Dominique *Your Beating Heart* 1991; *L'Eau Froide* 1994
Fazenda, Louise *Noah's Ark* 1928; *The Desert Song* 1929; *Rain or Shine* 1930; *Gun Smoke* 1931; *Alice in Wonderland* 1933; *Colleen* 1936
Fearn, Sheila *The Likely Lads* 1976; *George and Mildred* 1980
Featherstone, Angela *Family of Cops* 1995; *Breach of Faith: Family of Cops II* 1996; *Zero Effect* 1997; *The Wedding Singer* 1998; *200 Cigarettes* 1999
Feeney, Caroleen *Denise Calls Up* 1995; *Cadillac Ranch* 1996; *Bad Manners* 1998
Fehmiu, Bekim *I Even Met Happy Gypsies* 1967; *The Adventurers* 1970; *The Deserter* 1971; *Black Sunday* 1976; *Salon Kitty* 1976
Feig, Paul *Zombie High* 1987; *Ski Patrol* 1989; *Heavyweights* 1995
Feinberg, Ron *Brian's Song* 1971; *A Boy and His Dog* 1975; *Thunder and Lightning* 1977
Feinstein, Alan *Joe Panther* 1976; *Looking for Mr Goodbar* 1977
Feld, Fritz *The Affairs of Annabel* 1938; *Bringing Up Baby* 1938; *Go Chase Yourself* 1938; *Gold Diggers in Paris* 1938; *I Was an Adventuress* 1940; *The World's Greatest Lover* 1977; *Heidi's Song* 1982
Felder, Clarence *Slayground* 1983; *The Killing Floor* 1984; *Ruthless People* 1986; *The Hidden* 1987
Feldman, Andrea *Trash* 1970; *Heat* 1972
Feldman, Corey *Friday the 13th: the Final Chapter* 1984; *The Goonies* 1985; *Stand by Me* 1986; *The Lost Boys* 1987; *License to Drive* 1988; *The 'Burbs* 1989; *Dream a Little Dream* 1989; *The Magic Voyage* 1992; *Round Trip to Heaven* 1992; *Blown Away* 1992; *National Lampoon's Last Resort* 1994; *Voodoo* 1995; *Born Bad* 1996; *Tales from the Crypt Presents: Bordello of Blood* 1996; *Legion* 1998
Feldman, Marty *The Bed Sitting Room* 1969; *Every Home Should Have One* 1970; *Young Frankenstein* 1974; *The Adventure of Sherlock Holmes' Smarter Brother* 1975; *Silent Movie* 1976; *The Last Remake of Beau Geste* 1977; *In God We Trust* 1980; *Slapstick of Another Kind* 1982; *Yellowbeard* 1983
Feldon, Barbara *Fitzwilly* 1967; *Smile* 1975; *No Deposit No Return* 1976; *Get Smart, Again!* 1989
Feldshuh, Tovah *The Idolmaker* 1980; *Daniel* 1983; *Brewster's Millions* 1985; *A Day in October* 1991; *A Walk on the Moon* 1999
Fell, Norman *Pork Chop Hill* 1959; *The Killers* 1964; *Bullitt* 1968; *Sergeant Ryker* 1968; *If It's Tuesday, This Must Be Belgium* 1969; *Three's a Crowd* 1969; *The Boatniks* 1970; *Thursday's Game* 1971; *The Stone Killer* 1973; *Cleopatra Jones and the Casino of Gold* 1975; *The End* 1978; *Paternity* 1981; *On the Right Track* 1981; *For the Boys* 1991
Fellini, Federico *L'Amore* 1948; *Alex in Wonderland* 1970; *Fellini's Roma* 1972; *We All Loved Each Other So Much* 1974; *Intervista* 1987
Fellowes, Julian *The Scarlet Pimpernel* 1982; *Baby: Secret of the Lost Legend* 1985; *Fellow Traveller* 1989; *Damage* 1992; *Shadowlands* 1993; *Savage Hearts* 1995
Fellows, Edith *She Married Her Boss* 1935; *Pennies from Heaven* 1936; *And So They Were Married* 1936; *Music in My Heart* 1940
Felmy, Hansjörg *Station Six-Sahara* 1962; *Torn Curtain* 1966
Felton, Felix *Night Was Our Friend* 1951; *It's Trad, Dad* 1961
Felton, Verna *Dumbo* 1941; *Cinderella* 1950; *The Gunfighter* 1950; *Alice in Wonderland* 1951; *Lady and the Tramp* 1955; *The Oklahoman* 1957; *Sleeping Beauty* 1959; *Guns of the Timberland* 1960; *The Jungle Book* 1967
Fenemore, Hilda *Adventure in the Hopfields* 1954; *The Tommy Steele Story* 1957; *The Wind of Change* 1961
Fenn, Sherilyn *Just One of the Guys* 1985; *Thrashin'* 1986; *The Wraith* 1986; *Zombie High* 1987; *Two Moon Junction* 1988; *Backstreet Dreams* 1990; *Desire & Hell at Sunset Motel* 1991; *Dillinger* 1991; *Diary of a Hit Man* 1992; *Of Mice and Men* 1992; *Ruby* 1992; *Three of Hearts* 1992; *Boxing Helena* 1993; *Fatal Instinct* 1993; *National Lampoon's The Don's Analyst* 1997; *The Shadow Men* 1997; *Darkness Falls* 1998; *Nightmare Street* 1998
Fennell, Willie *Little Jungle Boy* 1969; *The Earthling* 1980
Fennelly, Parker *The Trouble with Harry* 1955; *Angel in My Pocket* 1968
Fenton, Frank *Buffalo Bill* 1944; *Hold That Blonde* 1945
Fenton, Lance *Night of the Demons* 1988; *Heathers* 1989
Fenton, Leslie *The Dragnet* 1928; *The Public Enemy* 1931; *FP1* 1932; *The Hatchet Man* 1932; *The Strange Love of Molly Louvain* 1932; *Lady Killer* 1933; *Star of Midnight* 1935; *Boys Town* 1938
Fenton, Sarah-Jane *The Bachelor* 1990; *A Good Man in Africa* 1993
Fenwick, Perry *Party, Party* 1983; *i.d.* 1994
Feore, Colm *Beautiful Dreamers* 1990; *Bethune: the Making of a Hero* 1990; *Thirty Two Short Films about Glenn Gould* 1993; *Friends at Last* 1995; *Truman* 1995; *The Escape* 1997; *City of Angels* 1998; *The Red Violin* 1998; *Titus* 1999
Ferch, Heino *Who's Afraid of Red Yellow Blue?* 1990; *Lucie Aubrac* 1997; *Wintersleepers* 1997; *Run Lola Run* 1998
Ferdin, Pamelyn *A Boy Named Charlie Brown* 1969; *The Beguiled* 1971; *Happy Birthday, Wanda June* 1971; *The Mephisto Waltz* 1971; *A Tree Grows in Brooklyn* 1974
Ferguson, Anna *Mark Twain & Me* 1991; *Whose Child Is This?* 1993; *Tokyo Cowboy* 1994; *Dangerous Intentions* 1995
Ferguson, Craig *The Big Tease* 1999; *Saving Grace* 2000
Ferguson, Frank *Abbott and Costello Meet Frankenstein* 1948; *Caught* 1949; *Gun Duel in Durango* 1957; *Andy Hardy Comes Home* 1958
Ferguson, Jessie Lawrence *Darkman* 1990; *To Protect and Serve* 1992
Ferguson, Matthew *On My Own* 1992; *Love and Human Remains* 1993; *Lilies* 1996
Ferguson, Myles *Avalanche* 1994; *Little Criminals* 1995
Ferjac, Anouk *Vivre pour Vivre* 1967; *Je T'Aime, Je T'Aime* 1968; *Killer!* 1969; *Piaf: the Early Years* 1974; *Diabolo Menthe* 1977
Fernandel *Topaze* 1951; *The Sheep Has Five Legs* 1954; *Paris Holiday* 1958
Fernandes, Miguel *The Kidnapping of the President* 1980; *Gridlock* 1995
Fernandez, Emilio *The Reward* 1965; *Return of the Seven* 1966; *The Appaloosa* 1966; *The Smugglers* 1968; *The Wild Bunch* 1969; *Bring Me the Head of Alfredo Garcia* 1974
Fernandez, Jaime *The Adventures of Robinson Crusoe* 1952; *The River and Death* 1954; *A Bullet for the General* 1966; *Guns for San Sebastian* 1968
Fernandez, Jesus *Nazarín* 1958; *Simon of the Desert* 1965
Fernandez, Juan *Kinjite: Forbidden Subjects* 1989; *Grand Slam* 1990; *Extralarge: Moving Target* 1990; *A Show of Force* 1990
Fernside, John *The Overlanders* 1946; *Bush Christmas* 1947; *Eureka Stockade* 1949
Ferraday, Lisa *China Corsair* 1951; *The Belle of New York* 1952; *Last Train from Bombay* 1952; *Death of a Scoundrel* 1956
Ferrara, Abel *aka* **Laine, Jimmy** *The Driller Killer* 1979; *Ms 45* 1981
Ferratti, Rebecca *Gor* 1987; *Cyborg 3: The Recycler* 1994; *Vegas Vice* 1994
Ferrell, Conchata *Heartland* 1979; *The Seduction of Miss Leona* 1980; *North Beach and Rawhide* 1985; *Eye on the Sparrow* 1987; *For Keeps* 1987; *Mystic Pizza* 1988; *Mom's Army* 1989; *Deadly Intentions... Again?* 1991; *Samurai Cowboy* 1993; *Sweet Dreams* 1996
Ferrell, Tyra *Lady Beware* 1987; *Boyz N the Hood* 1991; *Equinox* 1992; *White Men Can't Jump* 1992; *Poetic Justice* 1993; *Better Off Dead* 1993
Ferrell, Will *A Night at the Roxbury* 1998; *Dick* 1999; *Superstar* 1999
Ferreol, Andrea *La Grande Bouffe* 1973; *Despair* 1978; *The Last Metro* 1980; *Three Brothers* 1980; *A Zed & Two Noughts* 1985; *Letters to an Unknown Lover* 1985; *Il Maestro* 1989; *Wings of Fame* 1990; *The Edge of the Horizon* 1993
Ferrer, José *Joan of Arc* 1948; *Whirlpool* 1949; *Crisis* 1950; *Cyrano de Bergerac* 1950; *Anything Can Happen* 1952; *Moulin Rouge* 1952; *Miss Sadie Thompson* 1953; *The Caine Mutiny* 1954; *Deep in My Heart* 1954; *The Cockleshell Heroes* 1955; *The Shrike* 1955; *The Great Man* 1956; *I Accuse!* 1958; *The High Cost of Loving* 1958; *Lawrence of Arabia* 1962; *Nine Hours to Rama* 1963; *The Greatest Story Ever Told* 1965; *Ship of Fools* 1965; *Enter Laughing* 1967; *Cervantes* 1968;

RadioTimes ACTORS' INDEX

Flippen, Jay C *Oh, You Beautiful Doll* 1949; *They Live by Night* 1949; *A Woman's Secret* 1949; *Love That Brute* 1950; *Winchester '73* 1950; *Two Flags West* 1950; *Flying Leathernecks* 1951; *The Las Vegas Story* 1951; *The People against O'Hara* 1951; *The Lemon Drop Kid* 1951; *Bend of the River* 1952; *Devil's Canyon* 1953; *East of Sumatra* 1953; *Thunder Bay* 1953; *The Wild One* 1953; *Carnival Story* 1954; *The Far Country* 1955; *Kismet* 1955; *Man without a Star* 1955; *Oklahoma!* 1955; *Strategic Air Command* 1955; *Six Bridges to Cross* 1955; *The Killing* 1956; *Seventh Cavalry* 1956; *The Halliday Brand* 1957; *Jet Pilot* 1957; *The Restless Breed* 1957; *Run of the Arrow* 1957; *The Midnight Story* 1957; *The Deerslayer* 1957; *Hot Summer Night* 1957; *From Hell to Texas* 1958; *Wild River* 1960; *Hellfighters* 1969; *The Seven Minutes* 1971

Floberg, Bjørn *Insomnia* 1997; *The Last Contract* 1998

Flockhart, Calista *Getting In* 1994; *Drunks* 1995; *The Birdcage* 1996; *Telling Lies in America* 1997; *William Shakespeare's A Midsummer Night's Dream* 1999

Flon, Suzanne *Moulin Rouge* 1952; *Thou Shalt Not Kill* 1961; *The Trial* 1962; *The Train* 1964; *The Silent One* 1973; *Loving in the Rain* 1974; *Boomerang* 1976; *Mr Klein* 1976; *One Deadly Summer* 1983; *The Children of the Marshland* 1998

Florance, Sheila *Cactus* 1986; *Nirvana Street Murder* 1990; *A Woman's Tale* 1991

Florelle aka **Florelle, Odette** *Les Misérables* 1934; *Le Crime de Monsieur Lange* 1935

Flores, Von *The Assignment* 1997; *Johnny 2.0* 1998

Flower, George "Buck" *Across the Great Divide* 1977; *They Live* 1988; *Masters of Menace* 1990

Fluegel, Darlanne *Battle beyond the Stars* 1980; *To Live and Die in LA* 1985; *Running Scared* 1986; *Tough Guys* 1986; *Bulletproof* 1987; *Freeway* 1988; *Lock Up* 1989; *Project: Alien* 1990; *Double Suspicion* 1993; *Slaughter of the Innocents* 1993; *Come Die with Me* 1994; *Scanner Cop* 1994; *Relative Fear* 1995

Fluellen, Joel *Monster from Green Hell* 1958; *The Learning Tree* 1969; *The Great White Hope* 1970

Flynn, Bill *Kill and Kill Again* 1981; *Saturday Night at the Palace* 1987

Flynn, Colleen *Late for Dinner* 1991; *The Temp* 1993; *Terror at Deception Ridge* 1994; *Two Mothers for Zachary* 1996; *Devil's Child* 1997

Flynn, Errol *Captain Blood* 1935; *The Charge of the Light Brigade* 1936; *Another Dawn* 1937; *Green Light* 1937; *The Perfect Specimen* 1937; *The Prince and the Pauper* 1937; *The Adventures of Robin Hood* 1938; *The Dawn Patrol* 1938; *Four's a Crowd* 1938; *The Sisters* 1938; *Dodge City* 1939; *The Private Lives of Elizabeth and Essex* 1939; *Santa Fe Trail* 1940; *The Sea Hawk* 1940; *Virginia City* 1940; *Dive Bomber* 1941; *Footsteps in the Dark* 1941; *They Died with Their Boots On* 1941; *Desperate Journey* 1942; *Gentleman Jim* 1942; *Edge of Darkness* 1943; *Northern Pursuit* 1943; *Uncertain Glory* 1944; *Objective, Burma!* 1945; *San Antonio* 1945; *Never Say Goodbye* 1946; *Cry Wolf* 1947; *Escape Me Never* 1947; *Adventures of Don Juan* 1948; *Silver River* 1948; *It's a Great Feeling* 1949; *The Forsyte Saga* 1949; *Kim* 1950; *Montana* 1950; *Rocky Mountain* 1950; *Against All Flags* 1952; *The Master of Ballantrae* 1953; *Crossed Swords* 1954; *The Dark Avenger* 1955; *King's Rhapsody* 1955; *Lilacs in the Spring* 1955; *The Sun Also Rises* 1957; *Istanbul* 1957; *Too Much, Too Soon* 1958; *The Roots of Heaven* 1958

Flynn, Jerome *A Summer Story* 1987; *Edward II* 1991; *Best* 1999

Flynn, Joe *The Last Time I Saw Archie* 1961; *McHale's Navy* 1964; *Divorce American Style* 1967; *Did You Hear the One about the Traveling Saleslady?* 1968; *The Love Bug* 1969; *The Computer Wore Tennis Shoes* 1970; *The Barefoot Executive* 1971; *The Million Dollar Duck* 1971; *How to Frame a Figg* 1971; *Now You See Him, Now You Don't* 1972; *Superdad* 1974; *The Strongest Man in the World* 1975; *The Rescuers* 1977

Flynn, Michael *Evil in Clear River* 1988; *Before He Wakes* 1998

Flynn, Miriam *National Lampoon's Class Reunion* 1982; *Her Life as a Man* 1984; *For Keeps* 1987; *18 Again!* 1988; *National Lampoon's Christmas Vacation* 1989; *Babe* 1995; *From the Mixed-Up Files of Mrs Basil E Frankweiler* 1995

Flynn, Steven *Without Warning: the James Brady Story* 1991; *And Then There Was One* 1994; *Ulee's Gold* 1997

Foà, Arnoldo *Angela* 1955; *The Angel Wore Red* 1960; *The Trial* 1962

Focas, Spiros *Shaft in Africa* 1973; *The Jewel of the Nile* 1985; *Rambo III* 1988

Foch, Nina *The Return of the Vampire* 1943; *Shadows in the Night* 1944; *My Name is Julia Ross* 1945; *A Song to Remember* 1945; *Johnny O'Clock* 1947; *The Guilt of Janet Ames* 1947; *The Dark Past* 1948; *Johnny Allegro* 1949; *The Undercover Man* 1949; *An American in Paris* 1951; *Scaramouche* 1952; *Young Man with Ideas* 1952; *Executive Suite* 1954; *Four Guns to the Border* 1954; *Illegal* 1955; *You're Never Too Young* 1955; *The Ten Commandments* 1956; *Three Brave Men* 1956; *Cash McCall* 1960; *Spartacus* 1960; *Such Good Friends* 1971; *Mahogany* 1975; *Jennifer* 1978; *Morning Glory* 1993; *Hush* 1998; *Shadow of Doubt* 1998

Fogel, Vladimir *Chess Fever* 1925; *By the Law* 1926; *The House on Trubnaya Square* 1928

Foley, Dave *Kids in the Hall: Brain Candy* 1996; *Blast from the Past* 1998; *A Bug's Life* 1998; *Dick* 1999

Foley, Jeremy *Casper: a Spirited Beginning* 1997; *Dante's Peak* 1997; *Casper Meets Wendy* 1998; *Legion of Fire: Killer Ants!* 1998

Foley, Scott *Someone to Love Me* 1998; *Scream 3* 1999

Folland, Alison *To Die For* 1995; *All over Me* 1996; *Boys Don't Cry* 1999

Follows, Megan *Hockey Night* 1984; *Silver Bullet* 1985; *Season of Dreams* 1987; *Inherit the Wind* 1988; *Deep Sleep* 1990; *The Nutcracker Prince* 1990; *Back to Hannibal: the Return of Tom Sawyer and Huckleberry Finn* 1990; *The Chase* 1991; *Cry in the Wild: the Taking of Peggy Ann* 1991; *Under the Piano* 1995

Fonda, Bridget *Aria* 1987; *Scandal* 1988; *Shag* 1988; *Strapless* 1988; *You Can't Hurry Love* 1988; *Light Years* 1988; *Frankenstein Unbound* 1990; *The Godfather Part III* 1990; *Doc Hollywood* 1991; *Drop Dead Fred* 1991; *Iron Maze* 1991; *Out of the Rain* 1991; *Leather Jackets* 1991; *Single White Female* 1992; *Singles* 1992; *Army of Darkness* 1993; *The Assassin* 1993; *Bodies, Rest and Motion* 1993; *Camilla* 1993; *Little Buddha* 1993; *Point of No Return* 1993; *It Could Happen to You* 1994; *The Road to Wellville* 1994; *Balto* 1995; *Rough Magic* 1995; *City Hall* 1996; *Grace of My Heart* 1996; *Touch* 1996; *In the Gloaming* 1997; *Jackie Brown* 1997; *Mr Jealousy* 1997; *A Simple Plan* 1998; *Lake Placid* 1999; *Finding Graceland* 1999

Fonda, Henry *The Farmer Takes a Wife* 1935; *I Dream Too Much* 1935; *Way Down East* 1935; *The Trail of the Lonesome Pine* 1936; *The Moon's Our Home* 1936; *Spendthrift* 1936; *That Certain Woman* 1937; *Wings of the Morning* 1937; *You Only Live Once* 1937; *Slim* 1937; *Blockade* 1938; *Jezebel* 1938; *The Mad Miss Manton* 1938; *Spawn of the North* 1938; *I Met My Love Again* 1938; *Drums along the Mohawk* 1939; *Jesse James* 1939; *The Story of Alexander Graham Bell* 1939; *Young Mr Lincoln* 1939; *Chad Hanna* 1940; *The Grapes of Wrath* 1940; *Lillian Russell* 1940; *The Return of Frank James* 1940; *The Lady Eve* 1941; *You Belong to Me* 1941; *Wild Geese Calling* 1941; *The Battle of Midway* 1942; *The Big Street* 1942; *The Magnificent Dope* 1942; *The Male Animal* 1942; *Rings on Her Fingers* 1942; *Tales of Manhattan* 1942; *The Immortal Sergeant* 1943; *The Ox-Bow Incident* 1943; *My Darling Clementine* 1946; *Daisy Kenyon* 1947; *The Fugitive* 1947; *The Long Night* 1947; *Fort Apache* 1948; *On Our Merry Way* 1948; *Jigsaw* 1949; *Mister Roberts* 1955; *War and Peace* 1956; *The Wrong Man* 1956; *The Tin Star* 1957; *12 Angry Men* 1957; *Stage Struck* 1958; *The Man Who Understood Women* 1959; *Warlock* 1959; *Advise and Consent* 1962; *How the West Was Won* 1962; *The Longest Day* 1962; *Spencer's Mountain* 1963; *The Best Man* 1964; *Fail-Safe* 1964; *Sex and the Single Girl* 1964; *Battle of the Bulge* 1965; *In Harm's Way* 1965; *The Rounders* 1965; *The Dirty Game* 1965; *Big Deal at Dodge City* 1966; *Welcome to Hard Times* 1967; *Stranger on the Run* 1967; *The Boston Strangler* 1968; *Firecreek* 1968; *Madigan* 1968; *Once upon a Time in the West* 1968; *Yours, Mine and Ours* 1968; *The Cheyenne Social Club* 1970; *Too Late the Hero* 1970; *There Was a Crooked Man...* 1970; *Never Give an Inch* 1971; *The Serpent* 1972; *Ash Wednesday* 1973; *My Name Is Nobody* 1973; *The Last Days of Mussolini* 1974; *Battle of Midway* 1976; *The Great Smokey Roadblock* 1977; *Rollercoaster* 1977; *Tentacles* 1977; *Fedora* 1978; *City on Fire* 1979; *Meteor* 1979; *Wanda Nevada* 1979; *Gideon's Trumpet* 1980; *On Golden Pond* 1981

Fonda, Jane *The Chapman Report* 1962; *Period of Adjustment* 1962; *Walk on the Wild Side* 1962; *In the Cool of the Day* 1963; *Sunday in New York* 1963; *The Love Cage* 1964; *La Ronde* 1964; *Cat Ballou* 1965; *Any Wednesday* 1966; *The Chase* 1966; *The Game Is Over* 1966; *Barbarella* 1967; *Barefoot in the Park* 1967; *Hurry Sundown* 1967; *Histoires Extraordinaires* 1967; *They Shoot Horses, Don't They?* 1969; *Klute* 1971; *Tout Va Bien* 1972; *FTA* 1972; *A Doll's House* 1973; *Steelyard Blues* 1973; *The Blue Bird* 1976; *Fun with Dick and Jane* 1977; *Julia* 1977; *California Suite* 1978; *Comes a Horseman* 1978; *Coming Home* 1978; *The China Syndrome* 1979; *The Electric Horseman* 1979; *Nine to Five* 1980; *On Golden Pond* 1981; *Rollover* 1981; *The Dollmaker* 1984; *Agnes of God* 1985; *The Morning After* 1986; *Leonard, Part 6* 1987; *Old Gringo* 1989; *Stanley & Iris* 1989

Fonda, Peter *Tammy and the Doctor* 1963; *The Victors* 1963; *Lilith* 1964; *The Young Lovers* 1964; *The Wild Angels* 1966; *The Trip* 1967; *Histoires Extraordinaires* 1967; *Easy Rider* 1969; *The Hired Hand* 1971; *The Last Movie* 1971; *Two People* 1973; *Dirty Mary Crazy Larry* 1974; *Open Season* 1974; *Killer Force* 1975; *92 in the Shade* 1975; *Race with the Devil* 1975; *Futureworld* 1976; *Fighting Mad* 1976; *Outlaw Blues* 1977; *High-ballin'* 1978; *Wanda Nevada* 1979; *The Cannonball Run* 1981; *Split Image* 1982; *Certain Fury* 1985; *The Rose Garden* 1989; *Hawken's Breed* 1989; *Fatal Mission* 1990; *Deadfall* 1993; *Love and a .45* 1994; *Nadja* 1995; *Shadow of the Past* 1995; *Escape from LA* 1996; *Ulee's Gold* 1997; *The Limey* 1999

Fondacaro, Phil *Troll* 1986; *The Garbage Pail Kids Movie* 1987; *Ghoulies II* 1987; *Double, Double Toil and Trouble* 1993

Fong, Benson *The Red Dragon* 1945; *Dark Alibi* 1946; *Deception* 1946; *Peking Express* 1951; *His Majesty O'Keefe* 1953; *Conquest of Space* 1955; *Flower Drum Song* 1961; *Girls! Girls! Girls!* 1962; *Our Man Flint* 1966; *The Love Bug* 1969; *Kung Fu* 1972; *He Is My Brother* 1974; *Oliver's Story* 1978

Fontaine, Frank *Stella* 1950; *The Model and the Marriage Broker* 1951

Fontaine, Joan *A Damsel in Distress* 1937; *A Million to One* 1937; *Quality Street* 1937; *Blond Cheat* 1938; *The Duke of West Point* 1938; *Maid's Night Out* 1938; *Gunga Din* 1939; *Man of Conquest* 1939; *The Women* 1939; *Rebecca* 1940; *Suspicion* 1941; *This above All* 1942; *The Constant Nymph* 1943; *Jane Eyre* 1943; *Frenchman's Creek* 1944; *The Affairs of Susan* 1945; *From This Day Forward* 1946; *Ivy* 1947; *Blood on My Hands* 1948; *The Emperor Waltz* 1948; *Letter from an Unknown Woman* 1948; *You Gotta Stay Happy* 1948; *Born to Be Bad* 1950; *September Affair* 1950; *Darling, How Could You!* 1951; *Ivanhoe* 1952; *Something to Live For* 1952; *The Bigamist* 1953; *Decameron Nights* 1953; *Flight to Tangier* 1953; *Casanova's Big Night* 1954; *Beyond a Reasonable Doubt* 1956; *Serenade* 1956; *Island in the Sun* 1957; *Until They Sail* 1957; *A Certain Smile* 1958; *South Pacific* 1958; *Tender Is the Night* 1961; *Voyage to the Bottom of the Sea* 1961; *The Witches* 1966; *Good King Wenceslas* 1994

Foody, Ralph *Code of Silence* 1985; *Cold Justice* 1991

Foote, Hallie *1918* 1985; *Horton Foote's Alone* 1997

Foran, Dick *Dangerous* 1935; *The Petrified Forest* 1936; *The Black Legion* 1937; *The Perfect Specimen* 1937; *Boy Meets Girl* 1938; *Four Daughters* 1938; *Daughters Courageous* 1939; *My Little Chickadee* 1940; *Keep 'em Flying* 1941; *Road Agent* 1941; *Ride 'em Cowboy* 1942; *Chicago Confidential* 1957; *Violent Road* 1958; *The Fearmakers* 1958; *The Atomic Submarine* 1960; *Studs Lonigan* 1960; *Brighty of the Grand Canyon* 1966

Foray, June *Daffy Duck's Movie: Fantastic Island* 1983; *Duck Tales: the Movie – Treasure of the Lost Lamp* 1990; *Thumbelina* 1994

Forbes, Brenda *Mrs Delafield Wants to Marry* 1986; *The Man Upstairs* 1992

Forbes, Bryan *Appointment in London* 1952; *Sea Devils* 1952; *The Colditz Story* 1954; *An Inspector Calls* 1954; *Passage Home* 1955; *The Baby and the Battleship* 1956; *Quatermass II* 1957; *The Key* 1958; *The League of Gentlemen* 1960; *Restless Natives* 1985

Forbes, Mary *Sunny Side Up* 1929; *The Devil to Pay* 1930; *Blonde Bombshell* 1933; *We Live Again* 1934; *Tender Comrade* 1943

Forbes, Meriel *Come On George* 1939; *The Bells Go Down* 1943; *Home at Seven* 1952

Forbes, Michelle *Kalifornia* 1993; *Swimming with Sharks* 1994; *Roadflower* 1994; *Black Day Blue Night* 1995; *Escape from LA* 1996

Forbes, Ralph *Beau Geste* 1926; *The Green Goddess* 1930; *Her Wedding Night* 1930; *The Bachelor Father* 1931; *Beau Ideal* 1931; *Smilin' Through* 1932; *The Fountain* 1934; *Riptide* 1934; *Piccadilly Jim* 1936; *The Last of Mrs Cheyney* 1937; *Annabel Takes a Tour* 1938; *Kidnapped* 1938; *Frenchman's Creek* 1944

Forbes, Scott *Rocky Mountain* 1950; *Operation Pacific* 1951

Ford, Bette *Marked for Death* 1990; *Lucy and Desi: before the Laughter* 1991

Ford, Constance *The Last Hunt* 1956; *The Iron Sheriff* 1957; *A Summer Place* 1959; *Claudelle Inglish* 1961; *All Fall Down* 1962; *Lovers Must Learn* 1962; *The Cabinet of Caligari* 1962; *House of Women* 1962; *99 and 44/100% Dead* 1974

Ford Davies, Oliver *Titanic Town* 1998; *Star Wars Episode I: the Phantom Menace* 1999

Ford, Faith *You Talkin' to Me?* 1987; *A Weekend in the Country* 1996; *Night Visitors* 1996

Ford, Francis *Bad Lands* 1939; *South of Pago Pago* 1940; *The Ox-Bow Incident* 1943; *The Far Frontier* 1949; *The Sun Shines Bright* 1953

Ford, Fritz *The Bridge at Remagen* 1969; *Challenge to Be Free* 1972

Ford, Glenn *The Lady in Question* 1940; *So Ends Our Night* 1941; *Texas* 1941; *The Desperadoes* 1943; *Gilda* 1946; *A Stolen Life*

Foster, Susanna *Phantom of the Opera* 1943; *Detour* 1992
Foulger, Byron *Arizona* 1940; *Circumstantial Evidence* 1945; *The Magnetic Monster* 1953; *The River's Edge* 1957
Foulk, Robert *The 49th Man* 1953; *Last of the Badmen* 1957
Foundas, George *Stella* 1955; *Never on Sunday* 1960; *Zorba the Greek* 1964
Fowlds, Derek *aka* **Fowldes, Derek** *We Joined the Navy* 1962; *Frankenstein Created Woman* 1966; *Hotel Paradiso* 1966; *The Smashing Bird I Used to Know* 1969; *Tower of Evil* 1972; *The Copter Kids* 1976; *Over the Hill* 1992
Fowler, Harry *Went the Day Well?* 1942; *Hue and Cry* 1947; *I Believe in You* 1952; *Conflict of Wings* 1953; *A Day to Remember* 1953; *The Blue Peter* 1955; *Stock Car* 1955; *Behind the Headlines* 1956; *Fire Maidens from Outer Space* 1956; *Booby Trap* 1957; *Clash by Night* 1963; *Sir Henry at Rawlinson End* 1980
Fowley, Douglas *aka* **Fowley, Douglas V** *Big Brown Eyes* 1936; *Charlie Chan on Broadway* 1937; *On the Avenue* 1937; *Mr Moto's Gamble* 1938; *Charlie Chan at Treasure Island* 1939; *Jitterbugs* 1943; *Desperate* 1947; *Mighty Joe Young* 1949; *Armored Car Robbery* 1950; *Bunco Squad* 1950; *Rider from Tucson* 1950; *Tarzan's Peril* 1951; *Singin' in the Rain* 1952; *The Naked Jungle* 1953; *Bandido* 1956; *A Gift for Heidi* 1958; *From Noon till Three* 1976; *The Oregon Trail* 1976
Fox, Bernard *One of Our Spies Is Missing* 1966; *The Hound of the Baskervilles* 1972; *The Private Eyes* 1980
Fox, Colin *My Pleasure Is My Business* 1974; *Beautiful Dreamers* 1990
Fox, David *The Top of His Head* 1988; *Ordinary Magic* 1993; *When Night Is Falling* 1995
Fox, Edward *The Mind Benders* 1963; *I'll Never Forget What's 'Is Name* 1967; *The Jokers* 1967; *The Naked Runner* 1967; *Skullduggery* 1969; *The Go-Between* 1971; *The Day of the Jackal* 1973; *A Doll's House* 1973; *Galileo* 1974; *A Bridge Too Far* 1977; *The Duellists* 1977; *The Squeeze* 1977; *Soldier of Orange* 1977; *The Big Sleep* 1978; *Force 10 from Navarone* 1978; *The Cat and the Canary* 1979; *The Mirror Crack'd* 1980; *Gandhi* 1982; *The Dresser* 1983; *Never Say Never Again* 1983; *The Bounty* 1984; *The Shooting Party* 1984; *Wild Geese II* 1985; *Anastasia: the Mystery of Anna* 1986; *A Hazard of Hearts* 1987; *Return from the River Kwai* 1988; *Robin Hood* 1990; *A Month by the Lake* 1994; *A Feast at Midnight* 1995; *Prince Valiant* 1997; *Forbidden Territory* 1997
Fox, Huckleberry *Terms of Endearment* 1983; *American Dreamer* 1984; *Misunderstood* 1984; *The Blue Yonder* 1985
Fox, James *aka* **Fox, William** *The Magnet* 1950; *The Servant* 1963; *Tamahine* 1963; *King Rat* 1965; *Those Magnificent Men in Their Flying Machines* 1965; *The Chase* 1966; *Arabella* 1967; *Thoroughly Modern Millie* 1967; *Duffy* 1968; *Isadora* 1968; *Performance* 1970; *Runners* 1983; *Greystoke: the Legend of Tarzan, Lord of the Apes* 1984; *A Passage to India* 1984; *Absolute Beginners* 1986; *Comrades: a Lanternist's Account of the Tolpuddle Martyrs and What Became of Them* 1986; *The Whistle Blower* 1986; *High Season* 1987; *Farewell to the King* 1988; *The Mighty Quinn* 1989; *The Russia House* 1990; *Afraid of the Dark* 1991; *As You Like It* 1992; *Patriot Games* 1992; *Hostage* 1992; *Heart of Darkness* 1993; *The Remains of the Day* 1993; *Doomsday Gun* 1994; *Circle of Passion* 1996; *Anna Karenina* 1997; *Up at the Villa* 1998; *Mickey Blue Eyes* 1999
Fox, Kerry *An Angel at My Table* 1990; *The Last Days of Chez Nous* 1992; *Rainbow Warrior* 1992; *Friends* 1993; *Country Life* 1994; *Shallow Grave* 1994; *The Affair* 1995; *The Hanging Garden* 1997; *Welcome to Sarajevo* 1997; *The Wisdom of Crocodiles* 1998; *Fanny & Elvis* 1999; *The Darkest Light* 1999; *To Walk with Lions* 1999
Fox, Matthew *My Boyfriend's Back* 1993; *Behind the Mask* 1999
Fox, Michael *Last Train from Bombay* 1952; *The Magnetic Monster* 1953; *Top Secret Affair* 1957; *War of the Satellites* 1958
Fox, Michael J *Class of 1984* 1982; *High School USA* 1983; *Back to the Future* 1985; *Poison Ivy* 1985; *Teen Wolf* 1985; *Light of Day* 1987; *The Secret of My Success* 1987; *Bright Lights, Big City* 1988; *Back to the Future Part II* 1989; *Casualties of War* 1989; *Back to the Future Part III* 1990; *Doc Hollywood* 1991; *The Hard Way* 1991; *The Concierge* 1993; *Homeward Bound: the Incredible Journey* 1993; *Life with Mikey* 1993; *Where the Rivers Flow North* 1993; *Greedy* 1994; *Don't Drink the Water* 1994; *The American President* 1995; *Blue in the Face* 1995; *Coldblooded* 1995; *The Frighteners* 1996; *Homeward Bound II: Lost in San Francisco* 1996; *Mars Attacks!* 1996; *Stuart Little* 1999
Fox, Sidney *Bad Sister* 1931; *Murders in the Rue Morgue* 1932; *Don Quixote* 1933; *Midnight* 1934
Fox, Vivica A *Independence Day* 1996; *Set It Off* 1996; *Booty Call* 1997; *Soul Food* 1997; *Why Do Fools Fall in Love?* 1998; *Idle Hands* 1999; *A Saintly Switch* 1999
Foxe, Earle *Four Sons* 1928; *Hangman's House* 1928; *Dance, Fools, Dance* 1931
Foxworth, Robert *Frankenstein* 1973; *Treasure of Matecumbe* 1976; *Invisible Strangler* 1976; *Airport '77* 1977; *Damien – Omen II* 1978; *Prophecy* 1979; *The Black Marble* 1980; *The Memory of Eva Ryker* 1980; *Beyond the Stars* 1988; *Face to Face* 1990; *With Savage Intent* 1992
Foxx, Jamie *The Truth about Cats and Dogs* 1996; *Booty Call* 1997; *The Players Club* 1998; *Any Given Sunday* 1999
Foxx, Redd *Cotton Comes to Harlem* 1970; *Norman... Is That You?* 1976; *Harlem Nights* 1989
Foy Jr, Eddie *The Case of the Black Parrot* 1941; *Dixie* 1943; *The Farmer Takes a Wife* 1953; *Lucky Me* 1954; *Seven Little Foys* 1955; *The Pajama Game* 1957; *Bells Are Ringing* 1960; *Gidget Goes Hawaiian* 1961; *30 Is a Dangerous Age, Cynthia* 1967
Foyt, Victoria *Babyfever* 1994; *Last Summer in the Hamptons* 1995; *Déjà Vu* 1997
Frain, James *Loch Ness* 1994; *Nothing Personal* 1995; *Vigo: Passion for Life* 1997; *Hilary and Jackie* 1998; *What Rats Won't Do* 1998; *Sunshine* 1999; *Deception* 2000
Frakes, Jonathan *Beauty and Denise* 1989; *Star Trek: Generations* 1994; *Star Trek: First Contact* 1996; *Star Trek: Insurrection* 1998; *Dying to Live* 1999
Frame, Grazina *What a Crazy World* 1963; *Every Day's a Holiday* 1964
France, C V *The Skin Game* 1931; *Scrooge* 1935; *Victoria the Great* 1937; *If I Were King* 1938; *Strange Boarders* 1938; *A Yank at Oxford* 1938; *Cheer Boys Cheer* 1939; *Ten Days in Paris* 1939; *Went the Day Well?* 1942
Francen, Victor *J'Accuse* 1938; *The End of the Day* 1939; *Hold Back the Dawn* 1941; *Ten Gentlemen from West Point* 1942; *The Tuttles of Tahiti* 1942; *Madame Curie* 1943; *The Conspirators* 1944; *The Desert Song* 1944; *Passage to Marseille* 1944; *Confidential Agent* 1945; *San Antonio* 1945; *The Beast with Five Fingers* 1946; *Night and Day* 1946; *Hell and High Water* 1954; *Bedevilled* 1955; *Fanny* 1961
Francey, Micheline *The Raven* 1943; *A Cage of Nightingales* 1947
Franchi, Franco *War Italian Style* 1966; *Dr Goldfoot and the Girl Bombs* 1966; *Kaos* 1984
Francine, Francis *Flaming Creatures* 1962; *Lonesome Cowboys* 1968
Franciosa, Anthony *aka* **Franciosa, Tony** *A Face in the Crowd* 1957; *A Hatful of Rain* 1957; *Wild Is the Wind* 1957; *This Could Be the Night* 1957; *The Long Hot Summer* 1958; *Career* 1959; *The Naked Maja* 1959; *Go Naked in the World* 1961; *Period of Adjustment* 1962; *The Pleasure Seekers* 1964; *Rio Conchos* 1964; *Assault on a Queen* 1966; *A Man Could Get Killed* 1966; *The Swinger* 1966; *Fathom* 1967; *The Sweet Ride* 1967; *In Enemy Country* 1968; *A Man Called Gannon* 1969; *Earth II* 1971; *Across 110th Street* 1972; *Ghost in the Noonday Sun* 1973; *The Drowning Pool* 1975; *Firepower* 1979; *The World Is Full of Married Men* 1979; *Death Wish II* 1981; *Tenebrae* 1982; *Ghost Writer* 1989; *Backstreet Dreams* 1990; *Double Threat* 1992; *City Hall* 1996
Francis, Alec B *aka* **Francis, Alec** *Camille* 1927; *Feet First* 1930; *Outward Bound* 1930; *Mata Hari* 1931
Francis, Anne *aka* **Francis, Anne Lloyd** *Dreamboat* 1952; *Lydia Bailey* 1952; *A Lion Is in the Streets* 1953; *Rogue Cop* 1954; *Susan Slept Here* 1954; *Bad Day at Black Rock* 1955; *The Blackboard Jungle* 1955; *The Scarlet Coat* 1955; *Forbidden Planet* 1956; *Don't Go Near the Water* 1957; *The Hired Gun* 1957; *The Crowded Sky* 1960; *Girl of the Night* 1960; *The Satan Bug* 1965; *Funny Girl* 1968; *Impasse* 1969; *More Dead than Alive* 1969; *The Love God?* 1969; *Hook, Line and Sinker* 1969; *Pancho Villa* 1971; *Born Again* 1978; *Return* 1985; *The Masterpiece of Murder* 1986; *Laguna Heat* 1987; *Little Vegas* 1990
Francis, Arlene *All My Sons* 1948; *One, Two, Three* 1961; *The Thrill of It All* 1963
Francis, Connie *Where the Boys Are* 1960; *Follow the Boys* 1963; *When the Boys Meet the Girls* 1965
Francis, Derek *The Hi-Jackers* 1963; *The Tomb of Ligeia* 1964; *What's Good for the Goose* 1969
Francis, Dick *Dreaming* 1944; *Here Comes the Sun* 1945
Francis, Jan *Dracula* 1979; *Champions* 1983
Francis, Kay *The Marriage Playground* 1929; *Raffles* 1930; *The Virtuous Sin* 1930; *Girls about Town* 1931; *Ladies' Man* 1931; *Guilty Hands* 1931; *Cynara* 1932; *Jewel Robbery* 1932; *One Way Passage* 1932; *Trouble in Paradise* 1932; *British Agent* 1934; *Mandalay* 1934; *Wonder Bar* 1934; *I Found Stella Parish* 1935; *Another Dawn* 1937; *Confession* 1937; *First Lady* 1937; *In Name Only* 1939; *King of the Underworld* 1939; *It's a Date* 1940; *When the Daltons Rode* 1940; *Charley's Aunt* 1941; *The Feminine Touch* 1941
Francis, Noel *Blonde Crazy* 1931; *Smart Money* 1931; *Bachelor Apartment* 1931; *I Am a Fugitive from a Chain Gang* 1932
Francis, Robert *They Rode West* 1954; *The Long Gray Line* 1955
Franciscus, James *The Outsider* 1961; *Miracle of the White Stallions* 1963; *Youngblood Hawke* 1964; *Beneath the Planet of the Apes* 1969; *Marooned* 1969; *The Valley of Gwangi* 1969; *Hell Boats* 1970; *Cat o'Nine Tails* 1971; *Jonathan Livingston Seagull* 1973; *The Amazing Dobermans* 1976; *Good Guys Wear Black* 1977; *The Greek Tycoon* 1978; *Killer Fish* 1978; *Puzzle* 1978; *City on Fire* 1979; *When Time Ran Out* 1980; *Butterfly* 1982; *Sexpionage* 1985
Francks, Don *Finian's Rainbow* 1968; *Terminal Choice* 1983; *The Diviners* 1992; *Heck's Way Home* 1995
François, Jacques *South of Algiers* 1952; *To Paris with Love* 1954; *Les Grandes Manoeuvres* 1955; *The Gendarme Wore Skirts* 1982; *North Star* 1996
Frandsen, Jano *Dead Reckoning* 1990; *Xtro 2: The Second Encounter* 1990
Frank, Ben *Death Wish II* 1981; *Assassin* 1986; *Hollywood Vice Squad* 1986
Frank, Charles *Young Maverick* 1979; *Take My Daughters, Please* 1988
Frank, Gary *The New Love Boat* 1977; *Enemy Territory* 1987; *Deliver Them from Evil: the Taking of Alta View* 1992; *Getting Up and Going Home* 1992; *Nurses on the Line* 1993; *Untamed Love* 1994; *Death in Small Doses* 1995; *Prison of Secrets* 1997
Frank, Horst *Thou Shalt Not Kill* 1961; *Dead Run* 1967; *The Big Showdown* 1972; *Cold Blood* 1975; *Death in the Sun* 1975
Frank, Jason David *Mighty Morphin Power Rangers: the Movie* 1995; *Power Rangers 2* 1997
Frankel, Mark *Leon the Pig Farmer* 1992; *Solitaire for 2* 1994; *Roseanna's Grave* 1996
Franken, Steve *The Party* 1968; *Which Way to the Front?* 1970; *Avalanche* 1978
Frankeur, Paul *Jour de Fête* 1947; *Honour among Thieves* 1954; *Nana* 1955; *The Theft of the Mona Lisa* 1965; *The Milky Way* 1968; *The Discreet Charm of the Bourgeoisie* 1972
Frankfather, William *Alamo Bay* 1985; *Cool World* 1992
Frankham, David *aka* **Frankham, Dave** *Return of the Fly* 1959; *One Hundred and One Dalmatians* 1960; *Master of the World* 1961
Franklin, Aretha *The Blues Brothers* 1980; *Blues Brothers 2000* 1998
Franklin, Diane *Amityville II: the Possession* 1982; *Better Off Dead* 1985; *TerrorVision* 1986
Franklin, Pamela *The Innocents* 1961; *The Lion* 1962; *Flipper and the Pirates* 1964; *The Third Secret* 1964; *A Tiger Walks* 1964; *The Nanny* 1965; *Our Mother's House* 1967; *The Night of the Following Day* 1968; *David Copperfield* 1969; *The Prime of Miss Jean Brodie* 1969; *Sinful Davey* 1969; *And Soon the Darkness* 1970; *The Legend of Hell House* 1973; *Ace Eli and Rodger of the Skies* 1973; *The Food of the Gods* 1975
Franklyn, Leo *The Night We Dropped a Clanger* 1959; *And the Same to You* 1960; *The Night We Got the Bird* 1960
Franklyn, William *The Flesh Is Weak* 1957; *Quatermass II* 1957; *That Woman Opposite* 1957; *Pit of Darkness* 1961; *The Intelligence Men* 1965; *Cul-de-Sac* 1966; *Ooh... You Are Awful* 1972; *The Satanic Rites of Dracula* 1973; *Nutcracker* 1982
Franks, Chloe *Who Slew Auntie Roo?* 1971; *A Little Night Music* 1977
Frann, Mary *Eight Is Enough: a Family Reunion* 1987; *Single Women, Married Men* 1989; *I'm Dangerous Tonight* 1990
Franz, Arthur *Abbott and Costello Meet the Invisible Man* 1951; *Flight to Mars* 1951; *The Member of the Wedding* 1952; *The Sniper* 1952; *The Eddie Cantor Story* 1953; *Invaders from Mars* 1953; *Bad for Each Other* 1954; *Battle Taxi* 1955; *Beyond a Reasonable Doubt* 1956; *Hellcats of the Navy* 1957; *The Unholy Wife* 1957; *The Devil's Hairpin* 1957; *Monster on the Campus* 1958; *Woman Obsessed* 1959; *The Atomic Submarine* 1960; *The Human Factor* 1975; *That Championship Season* 1982
Franz, Dennis *Dressed to Kill* 1980; *Blow Out* 1981; *Psycho II* 1983; *Body Double* 1984; *Deadly Messages* 1985; *A Fine Mess* 1986; *Kiss Shot* 1989; *The Package* 1989; *Die Hard 2: Die Harder* 1990; *New York Mounted* 1991; *In the Line of Duty: Siege at Marion* 1992; *Caught in the Crossfire* 1994; *American Buffalo* 1995; *City of Angels* 1998
Franz, Eduard *Hollow Triumph* 1948; *Wake of the Red Witch* 1949; *Whirlpool* 1949; *The Magnificent Yankee* 1950; *Everything I Have Is Yours* 1952; *The Jazz Singer* 1952; *Dream Wife* 1953; *Latin Lovers* 1953; *Beachhead* 1954; *Broken Lance* 1954; *Sign of the Pagan* 1954; *White Feather* 1955; *Lady Godiva* 1955; *The Burning Hills* 1956; *A Certain Smile* 1958
Franz, Elizabeth *Jacknife* 1988; *Face of a Stranger* 1991
Frappat, Francis *Noir et Blanc* 1986; *Erreur de jeunesse* 1989; *Requiem* 1998
Fraser, Bill *The Captain's Paradise* 1953; *Orders Are Orders* 1954; *The Man Who Liked*

Funerals 1959; Joey Boy 1965; Masquerade 1965; I've Gotta Horse 1965; Captain Nemo and the Underwater City 1969; Up Pompeii 1971; Up the Chastity Belt 1971; That's Your Funeral 1972; Up the Front 1972; The Amorous Milkman 1974; The Corn Is Green 1979

Fraser, Brendan Presumed Guilty 1991; California Man 1992; School Ties 1992; Younger and Younger 1993; Twenty Bucks 1993; Airheads 1994; With Honors 1994; The Scout 1994; Mrs Winterbourne 1995; The Passion of Darkly Noon 1995; The Twilight of the Golds 1996; George of the Jungle 1997; Blast from the Past 1998; Gods and Monsters 1998; The Mummy 1999; Dudley Do-Right 1999

Fraser, David Teenage Mutant Ninja Turtles III 1992; Airborne 1997

Fraser, Duncan Watchers 1988; The Reflecting Skin 1990; Call of the Wild 1993; Needful Things 1993; Alaska 1996; Unforgettable 1996; To Brave Alaska 1996; When Danger Follows You Home 1997

Fraser, Elisabeth One Foot in Heaven 1941; So Big 1953; Young at Heart 1955; The Tunnel of Love 1958; Ask Any Girl 1959; Sammy, the Way Out Seal 1962; Two for the Seesaw 1962; A Patch of Blue 1965

Fraser, Helen Billy Liar 1963; The Uncle 1964; Repulsion 1965; Something to Hide 1971

Fraser, Hugh The Draughtsman's Contract 1982; 101 Dalmatians 1996

Fraser, John Valley of Song 1953; The Dam Busters 1954; Touch and Go 1955; The Good Companions 1956; The Wind Cannot Read 1958; The Trials of Oscar Wilde 1960; Tunes of Glory 1960; El Cid 1961; Fury at Smugglers Bay 1961; Waltz of the Toreadors 1962; Tamahine 1963; Repulsion 1965; A Study in Terror 1965; Doctor in Clover 1966; Isadora 1968

Fraser, Laura Small Faces 1995; Cousin Bette 1997; Left Luggage 1997; Divorcing Jack 1998; The Match 1999; Virtual Sexuality 1999; Whatever Happened to Harold Smith? 1999; Titus 1999; Kevin & Perry Go Large 2000

Fraser, Liz Desert Mice 1959; I'm All Right Jack 1959; The Night We Dropped a Clanger 1959; Carry On Regardless 1960; Doctor in Love 1960; The Night We Got the Bird 1960; The Rebel 1960; Two Way Stretch 1960; Double Bunk 1961; The Painted Smile 1961; A Pair of Briefs 1961; Raising the Wind 1961; Watch It, Sailor! 1961; The Amorous Prawn 1962; Carry On Cruising 1962; Live Now – Pay Later 1962; Carry On Cabby 1963; The Americanization of Emily 1964; Every Day's a Holiday 1964; Up the Junction 1967; Dad's Army 1971; Carry On Behind 1975; Adventures of a Taxi Driver 1975; Confessions of a Driving Instructor 1976; Under the Doctor 1976; Adventures of a Private Eye 1977; Chicago Joe and the Showgirl 1989

Fraser, Richard A Yank in the RAF 1941; The Picture of Dorian Gray 1945; Bedlam 1946; The Lone Wolf in London 1947

Fraser, Ronald The Long and the Short and the Tall 1960; The Best of Enemies 1962; The Punch and Judy Man 1962; The Pot Carriers 1962; Crooks in Cloisters 1963; Girl in the Headlines 1963; Private Potter 1963; The Beauty Jungle 1964; Daylight Robbery 1964; The Flight of the Phoenix 1966; Fathom 1967; The Whisperers 1967; The Killing of Sister George 1968; Sebastian 1968; Sinful Davey 1969; Too Late the Hero 1970; The Rise and Rise of Michael Rimmer 1970; Ooh... You Are Awful 1972; Rentadick 1972; Paper Tiger 1974; Swallows and Amazons 1974; Tangier 1982; Let Him Have It 1991; The Mystery of Edwin Drood 1993

Fraser, Sally It Conquered the World 1956; War of the Colossal Beast 1958

Fraser, Shelagh The History of Mr Polly 1948; Raising a Riot 1955

Fratkin, Stuart Ski School 1991; Prehysteria! 1993

Frawley, James Ladybug, Ladybug 1963; The Troublemaker 1964

Frawley, John The Devil's Playground 1976; Dallas Doll 1994

Frawley, William The Lemon Drop Kid 1934; Bolero 1934; Desire 1936; The General Died at Dawn 1936; Strike Me Pink 1936; The Princess Comes Across 1936; Something to Sing About 1937; Mad about Music 1938; The Adventures of Huckleberry Finn 1939; Rose of Washington Square 1939; Rhythm on the River 1940; The Bride Came C.O.D. 1941; Footsteps in the Dark 1941; Gentleman Jim 1942; Roxie Hart 1942; Whistling in Brooklyn 1943; The Fighting Seabees 1944; Flame of the Barbary Coast 1945; I Wonder Who's Kissing Her Now 1947; Miracle on 34th Street 1947; Mother Wore Tights 1947; Abbott and Costello Meet the Invisible Man 1951; Rhubarb 1951; The Lemon Drop Kid 1951; Rancho Notorious 1952; Safe at Home 1962

Frazee, Jane Buck Privates 1941; Hellzapoppin' 1941; Rosie the Riveter 1944; Springtime in the Sierras 1947; Under California Stars 1948

Frazer, Dan Lilies of the Field 1963; Cleopatra Jones 1973; The Super Cops 1973; The Belarus File 1985

Frazer, Robert White Zombie 1932; The Trail Beyond 1934

Frazer, Rupert The Shooting Party 1984; The Girl in a Swing 1988; Back Home 1990

Frazier, Ron Rollover 1981; The Road Home 1989; Shadow Makers 1989; Disaster at Valdez 1992; In My Daughter's Name 1992; She Woke Up 1992

Frazier, Sheila Superfly 1972; The Super Cops 1973; Three the Hard Way 1974

Frechette, Peter Grease 2 1982; No Small Affair 1984; The Unholy 1988; Empire City 1991; Against Her Will: the Carrie Buck Story 1994

Fréchette, Richard The Confessional 1995; Nô 1998

Frederici, Blanche Sadie Thompson 1928; The Trespasser 1929; Billy the Kid 1930; Mata Hari 1931; Night Nurse 1931; A Farewell to Arms 1932; If I Had a Million 1932; Secrets 1933; The Barbarian 1933

Frederick, Lynne Nicholas and Alexandra 1971; Vampire Circus 1971; The Amazing Mr Blunden 1972; Henry VIII and His Six Wives 1972; Phase IV 1973; Voyage of the Damned 1976; The Prisoner of Zenda 1979

Frederick, Vicki The California Dolls 1981; A Chorus Line 1985; Scissors 1991

Freed, Alan Don't Knock the Rock 1956; Rock around the Clock 1956; Go, Johnny, Go! 1959

Freed, Bert The Company She Keeps 1950; Halls of Montezuma 1950; Where the Sidewalk Ends 1950; Detective Story 1951; Red Mountain 1951; Men of the Fighting Lady 1954; The Gazebo 1959; Billy Jack 1971; Evel Knievel 1971

Freeman Jr, Al Dutchman 1966; The Lost Man 1969; Seven Hours to Judgment 1988; Malcolm X 1992; Down in the Delta 1997

Freeman, Alan Dr Terror's House of Horrors 1964; Sebastian 1968

Freeman, Arny Popi 1969; The Super Cops 1973

Freeman, Howard Hitler's Madman 1943; Slightly Dangerous 1943; Margin for Error 1943; Once upon a Time 1944; Secret Command 1944; Abilene Town 1945; The Blue Dahlia 1946; The Long Night 1947; Letter from an Unknown Woman 1948; Perfect Strangers 1950; Double Dynamite 1951; Million Dollar Mermaid 1952

Freeman, J E Hard Traveling 1985; Miller's Crossing 1990; Married for Murder 1992; Memphis 1992; Casualties of Love: the Long Island Lolita Story 1993; Dream with the Fishes 1996

Freeman, Joan Panic in Year Zero 1962; Tower of London 1962; The Three Stooges Go around the World in a Daze 1963; Roustabout 1964; The Rounders 1965; The Reluctant Astronaut 1967

Freeman, Jonathan Aladdin 1992; The Return of Jafar 1994

Freeman, K Todd The End of Violence 1997; Grosse Pointe Blank 1997

Freeman, Kathleen Love Is Better Than Ever 1951; The Fly 1958; The Ladies' Man 1961; Madison Avenue 1962; The Nutty Professor 1963; The Disorderly Orderly 1964; The Rounders 1965; Three on a Couch 1966; Your Three Minutes Are Up 1973; The Blues Brothers 1980; Nickel & Dime 1991; Reckless Kelly 1993; Naked Gun $33\frac{1}{3}$: the Final Insult 1994; ...At First Sight 1995

Freeman, Mona Till We Meet Again 1944; Together Again 1944; Junior Miss 1945; Black Beauty 1946; Dear Ruth 1947; Mother Wore Tights 1947; Isn't It Romantic 1948; The Heiress 1949; Streets of Laredo 1949; Dear Wife 1949; Branded 1950; I Was a Shoplifter 1950; Copper Canyon 1950; Darling, How Could You! 1951; Jumping Jacks 1952; Thunderbirds 1952; Angel Face 1953; Battle Cry 1955; The Road to Denver 1955; Dragoon Wells Massacre 1957; The World Was His Jury 1957

Freeman, Morgan Who Says I Can't Ride a Rainbow 1971; Brubaker 1980; Eyewitness 1981; Harry and Son 1984; Teachers 1984; The Execution of Raymond Graham 1985; Marie: a True Story 1985; That Was Then... This Is Now 1985; Resting Place 1986; Street Smart 1987; Blood Money 1988; Clean and Sober 1988; Driving Miss Daisy 1989; Glory 1989; Johnny Handsome 1989; Lean on Me 1989; The Bonfire of the Vanities 1990; The Power of One 1991; Robin Hood: Prince of Thieves 1991; Unforgiven 1992; The Shawshank Redemption 1994; Moll Flanders 1995; Outbreak 1995; Se7en 1995; Chain Reaction 1996; The Long Way Home 1996; Amistad 1997; Hard Rain 1997; Kiss the Girls 1997; Deep Impact 1998

Freeman, Paul The Dogs of War 1980; Raiders of the Lost Ark 1981; An Unsuitable Job for a Woman 1981; The Sender 1982; Shanghai Surprise 1986; A World Apart 1987; Without a Clue 1988; Prisoner of Rio 1988; The Last Island 1990; May Wine 1990; Eminent Domain 1991; Aces: Iron Eagle III 1992; Double Edge 1992; Just like a Woman 1992; Mighty Morphin Power Rangers: the Movie 1995; Double Team 1997; The Devil's Arithmetic 1999

Frees, Paul Riot in Cell Block 11 1954; Suddenly 1954; Space Master X 7 1958; The Snow Queen 1959; Gay Purr-ee 1962

Freindlikh, Alisa Agony 1975; Stalker 1979; Katia Ismailova 1994

French, Bruce Pipe Dreams 1976; Black Eagle 1988

French, Dawn The Supergrass 1985; Eat the Rich 1987; The Adventures of Pinocchio 1996; Maybe Baby 1999

French, Harold When London Sleeps 1932; A Fire Has Been Arranged 1935

French, Leslie Orders to Kill 1958; The Singer Not the Song 1960; The Leopard 1962; More than a Miracle 1967

French, Valerie Jubal 1956; Secret of Treasure Mountain 1956; Decision at Sundown 1957; The 27th Day 1957; The Garment Jungle 1957; Shalako 1968

French, Victor Charro! 1969; Rio Lobo 1970; Wild Rovers 1971; Chato's Land 1972; The Other 1972; Touchdown 1981

Fresnay, Pierre Marius 1931; Fanny 1932; The Man Who Knew Too Much 1934; Königsmark 1935; César 1936; Mademoiselle Docteur 1936; La Grande Illusion 1937; The Raven 1943

Fresson, Bernard Hiroshima, Mon Amour 1959; The Lady in the Car with Glasses and a Gun 1970; French Connection II 1975; The Tenant 1976; To Each His Own Hell 1977; Right Bank, Left Bank 1984; Voyage of Terror: the Achille Lauro Affair 1990; Place Vendôme 1998

Frewer, Matt Cannonball Fever 1989; Far from Home 1989; Honey, I Shrunk the Kids 1989; Short Time 1990; The Taking of Beverly Hills 1991; The Positively True Adventures of the Alleged Texas Cheerleader-Murdering Mom 1993; Lawnmower Man 2: Beyond Cyberspace 1995; National Lampoon's Senior Trip 1995; Kissinger and Nixon 1995; Generation X 1996; Breast Men 1997; Quicksilver Highway 1997; In the Doghouse 1998

Frey, Barbara Love at Twenty 1962; Kill and Pray 1968

Frey, Leonard The Boys in the Band 1970; Fiddler on the Roof 1971; Tattoo 1980; Where the Buffalo Roam 1980

Frey, Nathaniel Kiss Them for Me 1957; Damn Yankees 1958; What's So Bad About Feeling Good? 1968

Frey, Sami La Vérité 1960; Cleo from 5 to 7 1961; Thérèse Desqueyroux 1962; Bande à Part 1964; Sink or Swim 1971; César and Rosalie 1972; Pourquoi Pas! 1977; Ecoute Voir... 1978; The Little Drummer Girl 1984; Black Widow 1987; D'Artagnan's Daughter 1994; Traps 1994

Fricker, Brenda My Left Foot 1989; The Field 1990; Utz 1992; Deadly Advice 1993; So I Married an Axe Murderer 1993; Angels 1994; A Man of No Importance 1994; Moll Flanders 1995; Journey 1995; Swann 1996; A Time to Kill 1996; Masterminds 1997; Resurrection Man 1997; Painted Angels 1997

Frid, Jonathan House of Dark Shadows 1970; Seizure 1974

Fridh, Gertrud A Ship to India 1947; The Face 1958; The Devil's Eye 1960

Fridley, Tom Friday the 13th Part VI: Jason Lives 1986; Vegas Vice 1994

Friedle, Will The Gift of Love 1994; Trojan War 1997; My Date with the President's Daughter 1998

Friedman, Peter You Better Watch Out 1980; The Seventh Sign 1988; Single White Female 1992; Blink 1994; The Heidi Chronicles 1995; Safe 1995

Friedman, Shraga Sallah 1964; Bloomfield 1969

Friedrich, John Almost Summer 1977; The Wanderers 1979; A Small Circle of Friends 1980

Friel, Anna The Land Girls 1997; Rogue Trader 1998; William Shakespeare's A Midsummer Night's Dream 1999; Mad Cows 1999

Friel, Cassy Absolute Strangers 1991; The Whereabouts of Jenny 1991

Friels, Colin Monkey Grip 1983; The Gold and Glory 1984; Kangaroo 1986; Malcolm 1986; Grievous Bodily Harm 1987; Ground Zero 1987; High Tide 1987; Warm Nights on a Slow Moving Train 1987; Darkman 1990; Class Action 1991; Dingo 1991; A Good Man in Africa 1993; Back of Beyond 1995; Angel Baby 1995; Mr Reliable 1996; Cosi 1996; Dark City 1998

Friend, Philip The Bells Go Down 1943; Great Day 1944; Enchantment 1948; Thunder on the Hill 1951; Background 1953; Desperate Moment 1953; Cloak without Dagger 1955; Dick Turpin – Highwayman 1956; Son of Robin Hood 1958

Friend, Rachel Frog Dreaming 1985; Mission Top Secret 1990

Frinton, Freddie Forces' Sweetheart 1953; What a Whopper! 1961

Frith, Rebecca Love Serenade 1996; Strange Planet 1999; Me Myself I 1999

Fritsch, Willy Spies 1928; The Woman in the Moon 1929; Congress Dances 1931

Frizzell, Lou The Stalking Moon 1968; Duel 1971; Summer of '42 1971; Hickey and Boggs 1972; The Other 1972

Frobe, Gert aka **Fröbe, Gert** The Thousand Eyes of Dr Mabuse 1960; Goldfinger 1964; A High Wind in Jamaica 1965; Those Magnificent Men in Their Flying Machines 1965; Triple Cross 1966; Jules Verne's Rocket to the Moon 1967; Chitty Chitty Bang Bang 1968; The Heist 1971; Ludwig 1973; And Then There Were None 1974; The Serpent's Egg 1977

Fröhlich, Gustav Heimkehr 1928; Asphalt 1928

Froler, Samuel Best Intentions 1992; Private Confessions 1996

Fröling, Ewa *Fanny and Alexander* 1982; *Letters from the East* 1995

Frome, Milton *Go, Johnny, Go!* 1959; *The Swinger* 1966

Frost, Lindsay *Dead Heat* 1988; *Palomino* 1991; *Stop at Nothing* 1991; *In the Shadow of a Killer* 1992; *Monolith* 1993; *Op Center* 1995; *In the Line of Duty: Smoke Jumpers* 1996; *Death in the Shadows* 1998

Frost, Sadie *Diamond Skulls* 1989; *Bram Stoker's Dracula* 1992; *Shopping* 1993; *Splitting Heirs* 1993; *The Cisco Kid* 1994; *Magic Hunter* 1994; *A Pyromaniac's Love Story* 1995; *Crimetime* 1996; *Captain Jack* 1998; *Final Cut* 1998; *Rancid Aluminium* 1999; *Love, Honour and Obey* 2000

Frost, Terry *The Monster Maker* 1944; *Valley of Fire* 1951

Frost, Warren *Psycho IV: the Beginning* 1990; *Fugitive Nights: Danger in the Desert* 1993

Frot, Catherine *Un Air de Famille* 1996; *Le Dîner de Cons* 1998; *La Nouvelle Eve* 1999

Fry, Stephen *The Good Father* 1986; *Peter's Friends* 1992; *The Steal* 1994; *Cold Comfort Farm* 1995; *IQ* 1995; *The Wind in the Willows* 1996; *Wilde* 1997; *A Civil Action* 1998; *The Tichborne Claimant* 1998; *Whatever Happened to Harold Smith?* 1999; *Relative Values* 2000

Fry, Taylor *Cry in the Wild: the Taking of Peggy Ann* 1991; *Death Dreams* 1991; *Lone Justice* 1994

Frye, Dwight *Dracula* 1931; *Frankenstein* 1931; *The Vampire Bat* 1933; *Atlantic Adventure* 1935

Frye, Soleil Moon *You Ruined My Life* 1987; *The Liar's Club* 1992; *The Revenge of Pumpkinhead – Blood Wings* 1994; *The Killing Secret* 1997

Frye, Virgil *Dr Heckyl & Mr Hype* 1980; *Revenge of the Ninja* 1983; *Running Hot* 1983

Fuchs, Leo *The Frisco Kid* 1979; *Avalon* 1990

Fudge, Alan *Two People* 1973; *Bug* 1975; *Chapter Two* 1979; *The Children of An Lac* 1980; *MADD: Mothers against Drunk Drivers* 1983; *My Demon Lover* 1987; *Witness to the Execution* 1994

Fugard, Athol *Meetings with Remarkable Men* 1979; *The Killing Fields* 1984

Fujioka, John *The Last Flight of Noah's Ark* 1980; *They Call Me Bruce* 1982; *Conspiracy of Love* 1987

Fujita, Susumu *Sanshiro Sugata* 1943; *No Regrets for Our Youth* 1946; *Escapade in Japan* 1957; *The Hidden Fortress* 1958; *Yojimbo* 1961

Fujiwara, Kamatari *Seven Samurai* 1954; *The Hidden Fortress* 1958; *Mickey One* 1965

Fujiwara, Toshizo *A Scene at the Sea* 1991; *Mr Baseball* 1992

Fulford, Christopher *Resurrected* 1989; *Bedrooms and Hallways* 1998

Fulger, Holly *Night of Courage* 1987; *God's Will* 1989; *Lover's Knot* 1995

Fuller, Dale *The Wedding March* 1928; *Twentieth Century* 1934

Fuller, Dolores *Glen or Glenda* 1953; *Jail Bait* 1954

Fuller, Jonathan *The Pit and the Pendulum* 1991; *Arcade* 1993; *Castle Freak* 1995

Fuller, Kurt *Elvira, Mistress of the Dark* 1988; *No Holds Barred* 1989; *Bingo* 1991; *Eve of Destruction* 1991; *Stormy Weathers* 1992; *Calendar Girl* 1993; *Harmful Intent* 1993; *Mind of a Killer* 1993; *Reflections on a Crime* 1994; *Pushing Tin* 1999; *Diamonds* 1999

Fuller, Lance *Cattle Queen of Montana* 1954; *Apache Woman* 1955; *Pearl of the South Pacific* 1955; *This Island Earth* 1955; *Secret of Treasure Mountain* 1956; *The She-Creature* 1956; *Slightly Scarlet* 1956; *Voodoo Woman* 1957; *The Bride and the Beast* 1958

Fuller, Penny *Miss Rose White* 1992; *Rio Shannon* 1993; *The Gift of Love* 1994

Fuller, Robert *The Brain from Planet Arous* 1958; *Incident at Phantom Hill* 1966; *Return of the Seven* 1966; *Whatever Happened to Aunt Alice?* 1969; *Emergency!* 1971; *The Hard Ride* 1971; *Mustang Country* 1976; *Disaster on the Coastliner* 1979; *Separate Ways* 1981; *Bonanza: the Next Generation* 1988

Fuller, Samuel *aka* **Fuller, Sam** *Pierrot le Fou* 1965; *The Last Movie* 1971; *The American Friend* 1977; *1941* 1979; *The State of Things* 1982; *Slapstick of Another Kind* 1982; *A Return to Salem's Lot* 1987; *Sons* 1989; *Somebody to Love* 1994

Fullerton, Fiona *Run Wild, Run Free* 1969; *Nicholas and Alexandra* 1971; *Alice's Adventures in Wonderland* 1972; *A View to a Kill* 1985; *A Hazard of Hearts* 1987; *A Ghost in Monte Carlo* 1990

Fulton, Christina *Dangerous Game* 1993; *Hard Drive* 1994

Fulton, Rad *Hell Bent for Leather* 1960; *The Last Sunset* 1961; *No My Darling Daughter* 1961

Fulton, Rikki *Gorky Park* 1983; *Local Hero* 1983; *Comfort and Joy* 1984; *The Girl in the Picture* 1985

Funicello, Annette *aka* **Annette** *The Shaggy Dog* 1959; *Babes in Toyland* 1961; *Beach Party* 1963; *Muscle Beach Party* 1964; *Pajama Party* 1964; *The Misadventures of Merlin Jones* 1964; *Beach Blanket Bingo* 1965; *How to Fill a Wild Bikini* 1965; *The Monkey's Uncle* 1965; *Ski Party* 1965; *Fireball 500* 1966; *Thunder Alley* 1967; *Head* 1968

Funk, Terry *Paradise Alley* 1978; *Over the Top* 1987

Furia, Giacomo *Gold of Naples* 1954; *Boccaccio '70* 1961

Furlong, Edward *Terminator 2: Judgment Day* 1991; *American Heart* 1992; *Pet Sematary II* 1992; *A Home of Our Own* 1993; *Brainscan* 1994; *Little Odessa* 1994; *The Grass Harp* 1995; *Before and After* 1996; *American History X* 1998; *Pecker* 1998; *Detroit Rock City* 1999

Furlong, John *Mudhoney* 1965; *The Desperate Trail* 1995

Furman, Rosa *Guns for San Sebastian* 1968; *Deep Crimson* 1996

Furneaux, Yvonne *The Master of Ballantrae* 1953; *The Dark Avenger* 1955; *Le Amiche* 1955; *Lisbon* 1956; *The Mummy* 1959; *La Dolce Vita* 1960; *Repulsion* 1965; *The Champagne Murders* 1966

Furness, Betty *Dangerous Corner* 1934; *Magnificent Obsession* 1935; *Swing Time* 1936; *Fair Warning* 1937

Furness, Deborra-Lee *Jenny Kissed Me* 1984; *The Bit Part* 1987; *Shame* 1987; *Blue Heat* 1990; *Waiting* 1990; *Voyager* 1991; *Angel Baby* 1995

Furst, Joseph *The High Bright Sun* 1965; *The Brides of Fu Manchu* 1966; *Diamonds Are Forever* 1971

Furst, Stephen *National Lampoon's Animal House* 1978; *Take Down* 1978; *National Lampoon's Class Reunion* 1982; *Silent Rage* 1982; *The Dream Team* 1989; *Shake, Rattle and Rock* 1994; *American Yakuza 2: Back to Back* 1996

Furtado, Ruy *Recollections of the Yellow House* 1989; *The Divine Comedy* 1992

Furth, George *What's So Bad About Feeling Good?* 1968; *Butch Cassidy and the Sundance Kid* 1969; *The Man with Two Brains* 1983

Fury, Billy *Play It Cool* 1963; *I've Gotta Horse* 1965; *That'll Be the Day* 1973

Futterman, Dan *Keys to the Kingdom* 1991; *Big Girls Don't Cry... They Get Even* 1992; *The Birdcage* 1996; *Shooting Fish* 1997; *Thicker than Blood* 1998

Fyffe, Will *Happy* 1933; *Cotton Queen* 1937; *Owd Bob* 1938; *Rulers of the Sea* 1939; *Neutral Port* 1940; *The Prime Minister* 1940; *The Brothers* 1947

G

Gaal, Franciska *The Buccaneer* 1938; *Paris Honeymoon* 1939

Gabel, Martin *M* 1951; *Deadline – USA* 1952; *The Thief* 1952; *Tip on a Dead Jockey* 1957; *The James Dean Story* 1957; *Goodbye Charlie* 1964; *Marnie* 1964; *Lord Love a Duck* 1966; *Lady in Cement* 1968; *Smile, Jenny, You're Dead* 1974; *The First Deadly Sin* 1980

Gabel, Scilla *Tarzan's Greatest Adventure* 1959; *Queen of the Pirates* 1960; *Modesty Blaise* 1966

Gabin, Jean *La Belle Équipe* 1936; *The Lower Depths* 1936; *La Grande Illusion* 1937; *Pépé le Moko* 1937; *La Bête Humaine* 1938; *Le Quai des Brumes* 1938; *Le Jour se Lève* 1939; *Stormy Waters* 1941; *Moontide* 1942; *The Impostor* 1944; *Martin Roumagnac* 1946; *Le Plaisir* 1951; *Honour among Thieves* 1954; *French Cancan* 1955; *The House on the Waterfront* 1955; *Razzia sur la Chnouf* 1955; *Napoléon* 1955; *Les Misérables* 1957; *The Case of Dr Laurent* 1957; *Any Number Can Win* 1963; *The Sicilian Clan* 1969; *Two against the Law* 1973; *Verdict* 1974

Gable, Christopher *The Music Lovers* 1970; *The Boy Friend* 1971; *The Slipper and the Rose* 1976; *The Rainbow* 1988

Gable, Clark *A Free Soul* 1931; *Susan Lenox: Her Fall and Rise* 1931; *Dance, Fools, Dance* 1931; *Laughing Sinners* 1931; *Possessed* 1931; *Sporting Blood* 1931; *The Secret Six* 1931; *The Finger Points* 1931; *The Painted Desert* 1931; *Hell Divers* 1932; *Red Dust* 1932; *No Man of Her Own* 1932; *Polly of the Circus* 1932; *Strange Interlude* 1932; *Dancing Lady* 1933; *The White Sister* 1933; *Night Flight* 1933; *Hold Your Man* 1933; *Chained* 1934; *Forsaking All Others* 1934; *It Happened One Night* 1934; *Manhattan Melodrama* 1934; *Men in White* 1934; *The Call of the Wild* 1935; *China Seas* 1935; *Mutiny on the Bounty* 1935; *After Office Hours* 1935; *Cain and Mabel* 1936; *Love on the Run* 1936; *San Francisco* 1936; *Wife vs Secretary* 1936; *Parnell* 1937; *Saratoga* 1937; *Test Pilot* 1938; *Too Hot to Handle* 1938; *Gone with the Wind* 1939; *Idiot's Delight* 1939; *Boom Town* 1940; *Comrade X* 1940; *Strange Cargo* 1940; *Honky Tonk* 1941; *They Met in Bombay* 1941; *Somewhere I'll Find You* 1942; *Adventure* 1945; *The Hucksters* 1947; *Command Decision* 1948; *Homecoming* 1948; *Any Number Can Play* 1949; *Key to the City* 1950; *To Please a Lady* 1950; *Across the Wide Missouri* 1951; *Callaway Went Thataway* 1951; *Lone Star* 1952; *Mogambo* 1953; *Never Let Me Go* 1953; *Betrayed* 1954; *Soldier of Fortune* 1955; *The Tall Men* 1955; *The King and Four Queens* 1956; *Band of Angels* 1957; *Run Silent, Run Deep* 1958; *Teacher's Pet* 1958; *But Not for Me* 1959; *It Started in Naples* 1960; *The Misfits* 1961

Gable, John Clark *Bad Jim* 1989; *A Burning Passion: the Margaret Mitchell Story* 1994

Gabor, Eva *The Last Time I Saw Paris* 1954; *The Mad Magician* 1954; *Artists and Models* 1955; *My Man Godfrey* 1957; *Gigi* 1958; *The Truth about Women* 1958; *It Started with a Kiss* 1959; *A New Kind of Love* 1963; *Youngblood Hawke* 1964; *The Aristocats* 1970; *The Rescuers* 1977; *The Princess Academy* 1987; *The Rescuers Down Under* 1990; *Return to Green Acres* 1990

Gabor, Miklos *Somewhere in Europe* 1947; *Apa* 1966

Gabor, Zsa Zsa *Lovely to Look At* 1952; *Moulin Rouge* 1952; *We're Not Married* 1952; *Lili* 1953; *Three Ring Circus* 1954; *Death of a Scoundrel* 1956; *The Man Who Wouldn't Talk* 1957; *Queen of Outer Space* 1958; *Touch of Evil* 1958; *For the First Time* 1959; *Pepe* 1960; *The Road to Hong Kong* 1962; *Drop Dead Darling* 1966; *Picture Mommy Dead* 1966; *Jack of Diamonds* 1967; *Up the Front* 1972; *Happily Ever After* 1990; *The Beverly Hillbillies* 1993

Gabriel, John *The Hunters* 1958; *The Cat Gang* 1959

Gabriello, André *aka* **Gabriello** *Une Partie de Campagne* 1936; *The Lower Depths* 1936

Gadd, Renee *aka* **Gadd, Renée** *Happy* 1933; *The Man in the Mirror* 1936

Gaden, John *Children of the Revolution* 1996; *Thank God He Met Lizzie* 1997

Gades, Antonio *Blood Wedding* 1981; *Carmen* 1983; *El Amor Brujo* 1986

Gaffney, Liam *Curtain Up* 1952; *Street of Shadows* 1953

Gaffney, Mo *Other People's Money* 1991; *The Shot* 1996

Gage, Erford *The Falcon Strikes Back* 1943; *The Seventh Victim* 1943; *The Curse of the Cat People* 1944

Gage, Kevin *Double Tap* 1997; *GI Jane* 1997; *Point Blank* 1997; *Dee Snider's Strangeland* 1998

Gage, Patricia *Rabid* 1976; *The Little Kidnappers* 1990; *Perfectly Normal* 1990; *The Morrison Murders* 1997

Gago, Jenny *Old Gringo* 1989; *Unspeakable Acts* 1990; *My Family* 1994

Gail, Jane *Traffic in Souls* 1913; *20,000 Leagues under the Sea* 1916

Gail, Max *aka* **Gail Jr, Max** *DC Cab* 1983; *Heartbreakers* 1984; *Can You Feel Me Dancing?* 1986; *Where Are the Children?* 1986; *The Game of Love* 1987; *Judgment in Berlin* 1988; *Murder in the City of Angels* 1988; *The Outside Woman* 1989; *The Switch* 1993; *Dangerous Touch* 1994; *Mortal Fear* 1994; *Pontiac Moon* 1994; *Ride with the Wind* 1994; *Sodbusters* 1994; *Good Luck* 1996; *Not in This Town* 1997

Gaines, Boyd *Fame* 1980; *The Sure Thing* 1985; *Heartbreak Ridge* 1986; *Call Me* 1988; *A Son's Promise* 1990; *I'm Not Rappaport* 1996; *The Confession* 1999

Gaines, Lynn *Quest for Love* 1988; *Jobman* 1990

Gaines, Richard *The More the Merrier* 1943; *Double Indemnity* 1944; *The Enchanted Cottage* 1945; *Do You Love Me?* 1946; *So Goes My Love* 1946; *Dangerous Years* 1947; *Flight to Mars* 1951; *Marry Me Again* 1953; *Love Me or Leave Me* 1955; *Five Steps to Danger* 1957

Gainey, M C *Leap of Faith* 1992; *Blind Justice* 1994; *New Eden* 1994; *Citizen Ruth* 1996; *Breakdown* 1997; *Happy, Texas* 1999

Gains, Courtney *Children of the Corn* 1984; *Can't Buy Me Love* 1987; *The 'Burbs* 1989

Gainsbourg, Charlotte *Love Songs* 1984; *An Impudent Girl* 1985; *La Petite Voleuse* 1988; *Night Sun* 1990; *Autobus* 1991; *Merci la Vie* 1991; *The Cement Garden* 1992; *Jane Eyre* 1996; *Love etc* 1997

Gainsbourg, Serge *The Looters* 1966; *Romance of a Horse Thief* 1971; *Je Vous Aime* 1980

Gajos, Janusz *The Contract* 1980; *Interrogation* 1982; *Three Colours White* 1993

Galabru, Michel *The Gendarme of St Tropez* 1964; *The Gendarme in New York* 1965; *La Cage aux Folles* 1978; *The Spacemen of St Tropez* 1978; *La Cage aux Folles II* 1980; *Choice of Arms* 1981; *Double Dare* 1981; *The Gendarme Wore Skirts* 1982; *One Deadly Summer* 1983; *La Cage aux Folles III: "Elles" se Marient* 1985; *Subway* 1985; *Kamikaze* 1986; *Soigne Ta Droite* 1986; *Uranus* 1990; *Asterix and Obelix Take on Caesar* 1999

Galbraith, Alastair *Conquest of the South Pole* 1989; *The Debt Collector* 1999

Gale, David *Gold Diggers* 1983; *Re-Animator* 1985; *Bride of Re-Animator* 1991; *The Guyver* 1992

Gale, Lorena *Barnum* 1986; *Ebbie* 1995; *Behind the Mask* 1999

Galecki, Johnny *National Lampoon's Christmas Vacation* 1989; *Sudden Fury* 1993; *Murder at My Door* 1996; *Bean* 1997; *Suicide Kings* 1997; *The Opposite of Sex* 1998

Galiena, Anna *The Hairdresser's Husband* 1990; *Jamon Jamon* 1992; *Being Human* 1994; *The Leading Man* 1996; *Three Lives and Only One Death* 1996

Galik, Denise *Monster* 1980; *Melvin and Howard* 1980; *Eye of the Tiger* 1986

Galindo, Nacho *Gypsy Colt* 1954; *Thunder over Arizona* 1956; *Born Reckless* 1959

Gallacher, Frank *Deadly* 1991; *Dallas Doll* 1994; *Dark City* 1998

Dying to Love You 1993; My Life 1993; Reflections on a Crime 1994; The Yarn Princess 1994; The Babysitter 1995; See Jane Run 1995

Garner, Alice Monkey Grip 1983; Love and Other Catastrophes 1996; Strange Planet 1999

Garner, James The Girl He Left Behind 1956; Toward the Unknown 1956; Sayonara 1957; Shoot-Out at Medicine Bend 1957; Darby's Rangers 1958; Up Periscope 1959; Alias Jesse James 1959; Cash McCall 1960; The Children's Hour 1961; Boys' Night Out 1962; The Great Escape 1963; Move Over, Darling 1963; The Thrill of It All 1963; The Wheeler Dealers 1963; The Americanization of Emily 1964; 36 Hours 1964; Art of Love 1965; Duel at Diablo 1966; Grand Prix 1966; A Man Could Get Killed 1966; Mister Buddwing 1966; Hour of the Gun 1967; How Sweet It Is! 1968; The Pink Jungle 1968; Marlowe 1969; Support Your Local Sheriff! 1969; Skin Game 1971; Support Your Local Gunfighter 1971; They Only Kill Their Masters 1972; One Little Indian 1973; The Castaway Cowboy 1974; H.E.A.L.T.H. 1980; The Fan 1981; Victor/Victoria 1982; Tank 1984; Murphy's Romance 1985; Promise 1986; Sunset 1988; My Name Is Bill W 1989; Decoration Day 1990; The Distinguished Gentleman 1992; Barbarians at the Gate 1993; Fire in the Sky 1993; Breathing Lessons 1994; Maverick 1994; Dead Silence 1996; My Fellow Americans 1996; Twilight 1998; Legalese 1998

Garner, Jennifer Mr Magoo 1997; Washington Square 1997

Garner, Peggy Ann Jane Eyre 1943; Junior Miss 1945; Nob Hill 1945; A Tree Grows in Brooklyn 1945; Bob, Son of Battle 1947; Daisy Kenyon 1947; The Lovable Cheat 1949; Teresa 1951; Black Widow 1954

Garofalo, Janeane Reality Bites 1994; Bye Bye Love 1995; Coldblooded 1995; The Cable Guy 1996; Larger than Life 1996; Touch 1996; The Truth about Cats and Dogs 1996; Cop Land 1997; The Matchmaker 1997; Romy and Michele's High School Reunion 1997; Clay Pigeons 1998; Permanent Midnight 1998; Dog Park 1998; The Minus Man 1999; 200 Cigarettes 1999; Dogma 1999; Mystery Men 1999; Titan AE 2000

Garr, Teri Head 1968; The Conversation 1974; Young Frankenstein 1974; Won Ton Ton, the Dog Who Saved Hollywood 1976; Close Encounters of the Third Kind 1977; Oh, God! 1977; The Black Stallion 1979; Witches' Brew 1979; Honky Tonk Freeway 1981; The Escape Artist 1982; One from the Heart 1982; Tootsie 1982; The Black Stallion Returns 1983; Mr Mom 1983; The Sting II 1983; The Winter of Our Discontent 1983; Firstborn 1984; To Catch a King 1984; After Hours 1985; Miracles 1985; Pack of Lies 1987; Full Moon in Blue Water 1988; Let It Ride 1989; Waiting for the Light 1989; Out Cold 1989; A Perfect Little Murder 1990; Short Time 1990; Mother Goose Rock 'n' Rhyme 1990; Stranger in the Family 1991; Deliver Them from Evil: the Taking of Alta View 1992; Mom and Dad Save the World 1992; Fugitive Nights: Danger in the Desert 1993; Dumb and Dumber 1994; Perfect Alibi 1995; Michael 1996; Nightscream 1997; A Simple Wish 1997; Changing Habits 1997; Casper Meets Wendy 1998; Dick 1999

Garralaga, Martin A Message to Garcia 1936; They Passed This Way 1948; The Bribe 1949; The Ring 1952

Garrani, Ivo Aphrodite Goddess of Love 1957; Hercules 1957; General Della Rovere 1959; The Mask of Satan 1960; The Giant of Marathon 1960; Morgan the Pirate 1960; The Leopard 1962; The Rover 1967; The Sicilian Cross 1976

Garrett, Betty Words and Music 1948; Neptune's Daughter 1949; On the Town 1949; Take Me Out to the Ball Game 1949; My Sister Eileen 1955; The Long Way Home 1998

Garrett, Eliza Schlock 1971; Love Is a Gun 1994

Garrett, Leif Three for the Road 1975; Part 2 Walking Tall 1975; God's Gun 1977; Final Chapter – Walking Tall 1977; Kid Vengeance 1977; Skateboard 1978; The Outsiders 1983; Shaker Run 1985; Delta Fever 1988; Party Line 1988

Garrett, Patsy Benji 1974; For the Love of Benji 1977

Garrick, Barbara Miami Rhapsody 1995; Ellen Foster 1997

Garrick, John Song O' My Heart 1930; Chu Chin Chow 1934; D'Ye Ken John Peel? 1934; Street Song 1935

Garrison, Miranda Salsa 1988; Mack the Knife 1989

Garrison, Sean Violent Road 1958; Moment to Moment 1966

Garrone, Riccardo Pontius Pilate 1961; Eva 1962; The Swordsman of Siena 1962; Killer Rules 1993

Garson, Greer Goodbye, Mr Chips 1939; Remember? 1939; Pride and Prejudice 1940; Blossoms in the Dust 1941; When Ladies Meet 1941; Mrs Miniver 1942; Random Harvest 1942; Madame Curie 1943; Mrs Parkington 1944; Adventure 1945; The Valley of Decision 1945; Desire Me 1947; Julia Misbehaves 1948; The Forsyte Saga 1949; The Miniver Story 1950; Julius Caesar 1953; Scandal at Scourie 1953; Her Twelve Men 1954; Strange Lady in Town 1955; Sunrise at Campobello 1960; Pepe 1960; The Singing Nun 1966; The Happiest Millionaire 1967

Garson, Willie Every Breath 1993; Untamed Heart 1993

Garth, David John of the Fair 1952; Neither the Sea nor the Sand 1972

Garth, Jennie Beverly Hills 90210 1990; Danielle Steel's Star 1993; Trapped and Deceived 1994; Falling for You 1995; A Loss of Innocence 1996; An Unfinished Affair 1996; Power 98 1996

Gartin, Christopher No Big Deal 1983; Matters of the Heart 1990; Changes 1991; The Story Lady 1991; Johns 1995; Tremors 2: Aftershocks 1995

Garwood, John Hell's Angels on Wheels 1967; The Stunt Man 1980

Gary, Lorraine Jaws 1975; I Never Promised You a Rose Garden 1977; Jaws 2 1978; 1941 1979; Just You and Me, Kid 1979; Jaws the Revenge 1987

Gascoine, Jill Confessions of a Pop Performer 1975; King of the Wind 1989

Gaspar, Dominique Virgin Machine 1988; My Father Is Coming 1991

Gassman, Alessandro Snow White 1989; Golden Balls 1993; A Month by the Lake 1994; The Turkish Bath 1996

Gassman, Vittorio Bitter Rice 1949; The Glass Wall 1953; Cry of the Hunted 1953; Mambo 1954; Rhapsody 1954; Beautiful but Dangerous 1955; War and Peace 1956; Big Deal on Madonna Street 1958; The Great War 1959; The Miracle 1959; Tempest 1959; Barabbas 1961; The Easy Life 1962; Let's Talk About Women 1964; The Dirty Game 1965; Woman Times Seven 1967; The Tiger and the Pussycat 1967; Ghosts – Italian Style 1967; Twelve plus One 1969; Scent of a Woman 1974; We All Loved Each Other So Much 1974; A Wedding 1978; Viva Italia! 1978; Quintet 1979; Immortal Bachelor 1980; The Nude Bomb 1980; Sharky's Machine 1981; Tempest 1982; Life Is a Bed of Roses 1983; The Family 1987; Sleepers 1996

Gastoni, Lisa The Baby and the Battleship 1956; Three Men in a Boat 1956; Man from Tangier 1957; Intent to Kill 1958; The Breaking Point 1961; Eva 1962; RoGoPaG 1962; The Last Days of Mussolini 1974

Gates, Larry Above and Beyond 1952; Glory Alley 1952; Has Anybody Seen My Gal? 1952; Take Me to Town 1953; Invasion of the Body Snatchers 1956; The Brothers Rico 1957; The Strange One 1957; Jeanne Eagels 1957; Cat on a Hot Tin Roof 1958; One Foot in Hell 1960; Ada 1961; The Hoodlum Priest 1961; Underworld USA 1961; The Young Savages 1961; Toys in the Attic 1963; The Sand Pebbles 1966; FDR: the Last Year 1980

Gates, Nancy The Master Race 1944; Sons of the Musketeers 1951; The Member of the Wedding 1952; Hell's Half Acre 1954; Suddenly 1954; Stranger on Horseback 1955; World without End 1955; Death of a Scoundrel 1956; The Brass Legend 1956; Some Came Running 1958; Comanche Station 1960

Gateson, Marjorie Chained 1934; Goin' to Town 1935; Big Brown Eyes 1936; Vogues 1937; Geronimo 1939; Rings on Her Fingers 1942; The Sky's the Limit 1943; No Time for Love 1943

Gatliff, Frank The Ipcress File 1965; Déjà Vu 1984

Gatlin, Jerry An Eye for an Eye 1966; The Train Robbers 1973

Gauge, Alexander Murder in the Cathedral 1952; The Pickwick Papers 1952; Counterspy 1953; House of Blackmail 1953; Double Exposure 1954

Gaup, Mikkel Pathfinder 1987; Breaking the Waves 1996

Gauthier, Dan Teen Witch 1989; New York Mounted 1991; Shame 1992; Illegal in Blue 1995

Gauthier, Vincent Nazi Hunter: the Beate Klarsfeld Story 1986; The Green Ray 1986

Gautier, Dick Black Jack 1972; Billy Jack Goes to Washington 1977; Fun with Dick and Jane 1977; This Wife for Hire 1985; Get Smart, Again! 1989

Gautier, Jean-Yves The Promise 1994; Three Lives and Only One Death 1996; Journey to the Beginning of the World 1997

Gaven, Jean Obsession 1954; Rider on the Rain 1970; And Hope to Die 1972; The Story of O 1975

Gavin, Erica Vixen 1968; Beyond the Valley of the Dolls 1970; Caged Heat 1974

Gavin, John Quantez 1957; A Time to Love and a Time to Die 1958; Imitation of Life 1959; A Breath of Scandal 1960; Midnight Lace 1960; Psycho 1960; Spartacus 1960; Romanoff and Juliet 1961; Back Street 1961; Thoroughly Modern Millie 1967; The Madwoman of Chaillot 1969

Gaviola, Cassandra Conan the Barbarian 1982; The Black Room 1983

Gawthorne, Peter The Camels Are Coming 1934; No Limit 1935; Amazing Adventure 1936; Good Morning, Boys 1937; The Last Adventurers 1937; The Ticket of Leave Man 1937; Alf's Button Afloat 1938; Ask a Policeman 1938; Convict 99 1938; Band Waggon 1939; Flying 55 1939; Where's That Fire? 1939; I Thank You 1941; Pimpernel Smith 1941

Gaxton, William It's the Old Army Game 1926; Best Foot Forward 1943; The Heat's On 1943; Billy Rose's Diamond Horseshoe 1945

Gaye, Gregory Renegades 1930; Charlie Chan at the Opera 1936; Dodsworth 1936; Ninotchka 1939; Creature with the Atom Brain 1955; The Eddy Duchin Story 1956

Gaye, Lisa Drums across the River 1954; Rock around the Clock 1956; Shake, Rattle and Rock! 1957; Ten Thousand Bedrooms 1957; Castle of Evil 1966; The Violent Ones 1967

Gayheart, Rebecca Urban Legend 1998; Jawbreaker 1999

Gayle, Jackie Tin Men 1987; Plain Clothes 1988; Bert Rigby, You're a Fool 1989

Gayle, Monica Switchblade Sisters 1975; Love and the Midnight Auto Supply 1977

Gaylor, Anna Seven Thunders 1957; Nor the Moon by Night 1958

Gaylord, Mitch Animal Instincts 1992; Sexual Outlaws 1994

Gaynes, George Dead Men Don't Wear Plaid 1982; Tootsie 1982; Micki & Maude 1984; Police Academy 1984; Police Academy 4: Citizens on Patrol 1987; Police Academy 5: Assignment Miami Beach 1988; Police Academy: Mission to Moscow 1994; Vanya on 42nd Street 1994

Gaynor, Janet Sunrise 1927; 7th Heaven 1927; Street Angel 1928; Sunny Side Up 1929; Daddy Long Legs 1931; The First Year 1932; State Fair 1933; The Farmer Takes a Wife 1935; Ladies in Love 1936; Small Town Girl 1936; A Star Is Born 1937; Three Loves Has Nancy 1938; The Young in Heart 1938

Gaynor, Mitzi My Blue Heaven 1950; Golden Girl 1951; Bloodhounds of Broadway 1952; The I Don't Care Girl 1952; We're Not Married 1952; There's No Business like Show Business 1954; Anything Goes 1956; The Birds and the Bees 1956; Les Girls 1957; The Joker Is Wild 1957; South Pacific 1958; Happy Anniversary 1959; For Love or Money 1963

Gayson, Eunice Dance Hall 1950; To Have and to Hold 1951; Dance Little Lady 1954; Out of the Clouds 1954; Zarak 1956; Carry On Admiral 1957; The Revenge of Frankenstein 1958; Dr No 1962; From Russia with Love 1963

Gazelle, Wendy Hot Pursuit 1987; Sammy and Rosie Get Laid 1987; The In Crowd 1988; Triumph of the Spirit 1989; The Net 1995

Gazzara, Ben The Strange One 1957; Anatomy of a Murder 1959; The Young Doctors 1961; Convicts Four 1962; A Rage to Live 1965; The Bridge at Remagen 1969; If It's Tuesday, This Must Be Belgium 1969; Husbands 1970; King: a Filmed Record... Montgomery to Memphis 1970; The Family Rico 1972; The Neptune Factor 1973; Capone 1975; The Killing of a Chinese Bookie 1976; Voyage of the Damned 1976; Opening Night 1977; High Velocity 1977; Bloodline 1979; Saint Jack 1979; Inchon 1981; They All Laughed 1981; Tales of Ordinary Madness 1981; An Early Frost 1985; Downpayment on Murder 1987; The Freeway Killings 1987; Quicker than the Eye 1989; Road House 1989; Lies before Kisses 1991; Blindsided 1993; Fatal Vows 1994; Parallel Lives 1994; Convict Cowboy 1995; Shadow Conspiracy 1996; Stag 1996; Scene of the Crime 1996; Buffalo '66 1997; The Spanish Prisoner 1997; Happiness 1998; Valentine's Day 1998; The Thomas Crown Affair 1999

Gazzo, Michael V aka **Gazzo, Michael** The Godfather, Part II 1974; Black Sunday 1976; Fingers 1978; Alligator 1980; Back Roads 1981; Body and Soul 1981; The Winter of Our Discontent 1983; Fear City 1984; Cookie 1989

Ge You Farewell My Concubine 1993; To Live 1994; The Emperor's Shadow 1996; Keep Cool 1997

Ge Zhijun The Story of Qiu Ju 1992; Ermo 1994

Gear, Luella Carefree 1938; Phffft! 1954

Gearon, Valerie Nine Hours to Rama 1963; Invasion 1965; Anne of the Thousand Days 1969

Geary, Anthony Disorderlies 1987; You Can't Hurry Love 1988; High Desert Kill 1989; UHF 1989; Crack House 1989; Scorchers 1991

Geary, Cynthia 8 Seconds 1994; The Awakening 1995; Hostile Force 1996; When Time Expires 1997

Geary, Karl Nadja 1995; Gold in the Streets 1996

Gebert, Gordon Holiday Affair 1949; The House on Telegraph Hill 1951; The Narrow Margin 1952

Geddes, Barbara Bel The Long Night 1947; Blood on the Moon 1948; I Remember Mama 1948; Caught 1949; Panic in the Streets 1950; Fourteen Hours 1951; Vertigo 1958; The Five Pennies 1959; Five Branded Women 1960; By Love Possessed 1961; The Todd Killings 1971

Gedrick, Jason Iron Eagle 1985; The Heavenly Kid 1985; Season of Dreams 1987; Promised Land 1988; Rooftops 1989; Backdraft 1991; Crossing the Bridge 1992; Dare to Love 1995; Power 98 1996

Geer, Ellen Kotch 1971; Harold and Maude 1972; Over the Edge 1979; Hard Traveling 1985

Geer, Will Anna Lucasta 1949; Intruder in the Dust 1949; Johnny Allegro 1949; Broken Arrow 1950; Comanche Territory 1950;

Rich 1990; *The Power of One* 1991; *Prospero's Books* 1991; *Shining Through* 1992; *Haunted* 1995; *DragonHeart* 1996; *Hamlet* 1996; *The Portrait of a Lady* 1996; *Shine* 1996; *The Magic Sword: Quest for Camelot* 1997; *Elizabeth* 1998; *The Tichborne Claimant* 1998
Gierasch, Stefan *Jeremiah Johnson* 1972; *What's Up, Doc?* 1972; *High Plains Drifter* 1973; *Blood Beach* 1981; *Perfect* 1985; *Shannon's Deal* 1989; *Jack the Bear* 1993
Gifford, Alan *Across the Bridge* 1957; *The Flying Scot* 1957; *Time Lock* 1957; *Screaming Mimi* 1958; *Phase IV* 1973
Gifford, Frances *Beyond the Blue Horizon* 1942; *Cry Havoc* 1943; *Tarzan Triumphs* 1943; *Marriage Is a Private Affair* 1944; *Thrill of a Romance* 1945; *The Arnelo Affair* 1947; *Riding High* 1950
Gifford, Frank *Up Periscope* 1959; *Viva Knievel!* 1977
Gifford, Gloria *DC Cab* 1983; *Vice Versa* 1988
Gift, Roland *Sammy and Rosie Get Laid* 1987; *Scandal* 1988
Giglio, Sandro *Assignment – Paris* 1952; *The War of the Worlds* 1953
Gil, Ariadna *Belle Epoque* 1992; *Revolver* 1992
Gil, Vincent *Ghosts...of the Civil Dead* 1988; *Encounter at Raven's Gate* 1988; *Body Melt* 1993
Gilbert, Andrew S *aka* **Gilbert, Andrew** *Mortgage* 1989; *Kiss or Kill* 1997; *Paperback Hero* 1998
Gilbert, Billy *County Hospital* 1932; *The Music Box* 1932; *Pack Up Your Troubles* 1932; *Their First Mistake* 1932; *Towed in a Hole* 1932; *Them Thar Hills!* 1934; *The Bride Walks Out* 1936; *Poor Little Rich Girl* 1936; *Espionage* 1937; *Snow White and the Seven Dwarfs* 1937; *Rosalie* 1937; *One Hundred Men and a Girl* 1937; *Blockheads* 1938; *Happy Landing* 1938; *My Lucky Star* 1938; *Maid's Night Out* 1938; *Destry Rides Again* 1939; *The Great Dictator* 1940; *Lucky Partners* 1940; *No, No, Nanette* 1940; *Seven Sinners* 1940; *The Villain Still Pursued Her* 1940; *Anchors Aweigh* 1945; *Fun and Fancy Free* 1947; *Bride of Vengeance* 1949
Gilbert, Helen *Andy Hardy Gets Spring Fever* 1939; *The Secret of Dr Kildare* 1939; *Florian* 1940; *Beyond the Blue Horizon* 1942; *The Falcon Takes Over* 1942
Gilbert, Joanne *Red Garters* 1954; *The Great Man* 1956; *The High Cost of Loving* 1958
Gilbert, Jody *House by the River* 1950; *Willard* 1971
Gilbert, John *He Who Gets Slapped* 1924; *The Big Parade* 1925; *The Merry Widow* 1925; *La Bohème* 1926; *Flesh and the Devil* 1926; *Love* 1927; *Show People* 1928; *A Woman of Affairs* 1928; *Hollywood Revue* 1929; *Queen Christina* 1933; *The Captain Hates the Sea* 1934
Gilbert, Lou *Goldstein* 1964; *Frank's Greatest Adventure* 1967; *The Great White Hope* 1970; *Jennifer on My Mind* 1971
Gilbert, Marcus *Biggles* 1986; *A Hazard of Hearts* 1987; *A Ghost in Monte Carlo* 1990; *Army of Darkness* 1993
Gilbert, Melissa *aka* **Gilbert-Brinkman, Melissa** *The Diary of Anne Frank* 1980; *Sylvester* 1985; *Choices* 1986; *Killer Instinct* 1988; *Donor* 1990; *Forbidden Nights* 1990; *Joshua's Heart* 1990; *The Lookalike* 1990; *Without Her Consent* 1990; *With a Vengeance* 1992; *A Family of Strangers* 1993; *House of Secrets* 1993; *Seeds of Deception* 1993; *Shattered Trust* 1993; *With Hostile Intent* 1993; *Touch of Truth* 1994; *Against Her Will: the Carrie Buck Story* 1994; *Seduction in a Small Town* 1996; *Childhood Sweetheart?* 1997; *Barbara Taylor Bradford's Her Own Rules* 1998
Gilbert, Paul *So This Is Paris* 1954; *You Can't Run Away from It* 1956
Gilbert, Sara *Sudie and Simpson* 1990; *Poison Ivy* 1992; *Dead Beat* 1994; *Desert Blue* 1998
Gilborn, Steven *Safe* 1995; *Her Costly Affair* 1996; *About Sarah* 1998
Gilchrist, Connie *A Woman's Face* 1941; *Apache Trail* 1942; *Swing Shift Maisie* 1943; *Act of Violence* 1949; *A Letter to Three Wives* 1949; *A Ticket to Tomahawk* 1950; *The Half-Breed* 1952; *Houdini* 1953; *It Should Happen to You* 1954; *Say One for Me* 1959; *The Misadventures of Merlin Jones* 1964; *Two on a Guillotine* 1965; *Tickle Me* 1965
Giles, Sandra *Daddy-O* 1959; *Crazy Times* 1981
Gilford, Jack *A Funny Thing Happened on the Way to the Forum* 1966; *Mister Buddwing* 1966; *Enter Laughing* 1967; *The Incident* 1967; *They Might Be Giants* 1971; *Save the Tiger* 1973; *Wholly Moses!* 1980; *Caveman* 1981; *Cocoon* 1985; *Young Again* 1986; *Cocoon: the Return* 1988
Gill, John *After Pilkington* 1986; *That Summer of White Roses* 1989
Gill, Tom *Something in the City* 1950; *Behind the Headlines* 1956; *Up the Creek* 1958
Gillain, Marie *Mon Père Ce Héros* 1991; *The Bait* 1995; *Le Bossu* 1997; *Harem Suare* 1999
Gillen, Aidan *Circle of Friends* 1995; *Gold in the Streets* 1996; *Some Mother's Son* 1996; *Mojo* 1998
Gillespie, Dana *The People That Time Forgot* 1977; *Bad Timing* 1980; *Scrubbers* 1982
Gillette, Anita *Boys on the Side* 1995; *Larger than Life* 1996
Gilliam, Burton *Thunderbolt and Lightfoot* 1974; *Quake!* 1992
Gilliam, Seth *Assault at West Point: the Court Martial of John Whittaker* 1994; *Jefferson in Paris* 1995; *Courage under Fire* 1996
Gilliam, Stu *Three's a Crowd* 1969; *Brothers* 1977; *Return from Witch Mountain* 1978
Gilliam, Terry *And Now for Something Completely Different* 1971; *Monty Python and the Holy Grail* 1975; *Monty Python's Life of Brian* 1979; *Monty Python Live at the Hollywood Bowl* 1982; *Monty Python's The Meaning of Life* 1983
Gilliard Jr, Larry *aka* **Gilliard Jr, Lawrence** *Straight out of Brooklyn* 1991; *The Substitute 2: School's Out* 1997; *Next Stop Wonderland* 1998; *The Waterboy* 1998; *Simply Irresistible* 1999
Gillie, Jean *The Gentle Sex* 1943; *The Saint Meets the Tiger* 1943; *Tawny Pipit* 1944
Gillies, Carol *Rocinante* 1986; *Back Home* 1990
Gillies, Max *The Cars That Ate Paris* 1974; *As Time Goes By* 1987
Gilliland, Richard *Bug* 1975; *Embassy* 1985; *Happy Hour* 1987; *Evidence of Love* 1990; *Bad Attitudes* 1991; *Take Me Home Again* 1994; *The Man Next Door* 1996; *Star Kid* 1997; *Dogwatch* 1997
Gillin, Hugh *Psycho II* 1983; *Psycho III* 1986; *Doin' Time on Planet Earth* 1988
Gilling, Rebecca *The Naked Country* 1985; *The Blue Lightning* 1986; *Heaven Tonight* 1990
Gillingwater, Claude *aka* **Gillingwater Sr, Claude** *Little Lord Fauntleroy* 1921; *Daddy Long Legs* 1931; *The Prisoner of Shark Island* 1936; *Just around the Corner* 1938
Gillis, Ann *aka* **Gillis, Anne** *The Adventures of Tom Sawyer* 1938; *Nice Girl?* 1941; *Abbott and Costello in Society* 1944; *The Cheaters* 1945
Gillmer, Caroline *Hotel Sorrento* 1994; *Paws* 1997
Gillmore, Margalo *Perfect Strangers* 1950; *Cause for Alarm* 1951; *Scandal at Scourie* 1953; *Gaby* 1956
Gilman, Sam *Macon County Line* 1973; *Every Which Way but Loose* 1978
Gilmore, Craig *The Living End* 1992; *Totally F***ed Up* 1993
Gilmore, Lowell *Days of Glory* 1944; *Johnny Angel* 1945; *The Picture of Dorian Gray* 1945; *Calcutta* 1947; *The Black Arrow* 1948; *Dream Girl* 1948; *King Solomon's Mines* 1950; *Rogues of Sherwood Forest* 1950; *Roadblock* 1951; *Lone Star* 1952; *Comanche* 1956
Gilmore, Peter *I've Gotta Horse* 1965; *The Abominable Dr Phibes* 1971; *Warlords of Atlantis* 1978
Gilmore, Virginia *Swamp Water* 1941; *Western Union* 1941; *Berlin Correspondent* 1942; *Orchestra Wives* 1942; *Walk East on Beacon* 1952
Gilmour, Ian *The Odd Angry Shot* 1979; *A Dangerous Summer* 1981; *The Boy Who Had Everything* 1984; *Malpractice* 1989
Gilpin, Jack *Something Wild* 1986; *Funny Farm* 1988; *Reversal of Fortune* 1990; *Kiss and Tell* 1996
Gilroy, Tom *Land and Freedom* 1995; *Ratchet* 1996
Gimenez Cacho, Daniel *Cabeza de Vaca* 1990; *Deep Crimson* 1996
Ging, Jack *Tess of the Storm Country* 1960; *High Plains Drifter* 1973; *Sssssss* 1973; *Where the Red Fern Grows* 1974
Gingold, Hermione *Someone at the Door* 1936; *Cosh Boy* 1952; *The Pickwick Papers* 1952; *Our Girl Friday* 1953; *Around the World in 80 Days* 1956; *Bell, Book and Candle* 1958; *Gigi* 1958; *The Naked Edge* 1961; *Gay Purr-ee* 1962; *The Music Man* 1962; *I'd Rather Be Rich* 1964; *Harvey Middleman, Fireman* 1965; *Promise Her Anything* 1966; *Munster, Go Home!* 1966; *Jules Verne's Rocket to the Moon* 1967; *A Little Night Music* 1977
Ginsberg, Allen *Pull My Daisy* 1959; *Chappaqua* 1966
Ginty, Robert *Coming Home* 1978; *The Exterminator* 1980; *Exterminator 2* 1980; *The Alchemist* 1981; *Loverboy* 1989; *Madhouse* 1990; *Harley Davidson and the Marlboro Man* 1991
Giordani, Rocky *After Dark, My Sweet* 1990; *Cop and a Half* 1993
Giordano, Domiziana *Nostalgia* 1983; *Zina* 1985; *Nouvelle Vague* 1990; *Interview with the Vampire: the Vampire Chronicles* 1994
Giorgetti, Florence *La Grande Bouffe* 1973; *The Lacemaker* 1977
Girard, Philippe *Wild Target* 1993; *Les Apprentis* 1995
Girard, Rémy *The Decline of the American Empire* 1986; *Jesus of Montreal* 1989
Girardon, Michèle *Death in the Garden* 1956; *The Sign of Leo* 1959; *The Seven Deadly Sins* 1961; *Hatari!* 1962
Girardot, Annie *Rocco and His Brothers* 1960; *The Organizer* 1963; *The Dirty Game* 1965; *Vivre pour Vivre* 1967; *Shock Treatment* 1973; *Doctor Françoise Gailland* 1975; *You've Got to Live Dangerously* 1975; *To Each His Own Hell* 1977; *Hit List* 1984
Girardot, Etienne *Twentieth Century* 1934; *Fast and Loose* 1939; *The Story of Vernon and Irene Castle* 1939
Girardot, Hippolyte *First Name: Carmen* 1983; *Manon des Sources* 1986; *A World without Pity* 1989; *Hors la Vie* 1991; *Après l'Amour* 1992; *La Fille de l'Air* 1992; *Le Parfum d'Yvonne* 1994
Giraud, Roland *3 Men and a Cradle* 1985; *Mister Frost* 1990
Giraudeau, Bernard *Angel Dust* 1987; *Après l'Amour* 1992; *Ridicule* 1996; *Marquise* 1997
Girling, Cindy *The Kidnapping of the President* 1980; *Heart of a Child* 1994
Girotti, Massimo *Ossessione* 1942; *Chronicle of a Love* 1950; *Senso* 1954; *Marguerite de la Nuit* 1955; *It Happened in Rome* 1956; *Duel of the Titans* 1961; *Imperial Venus* 1963; *Gold for the Caesars* 1964; *Theorem* 1968; *The Red Tent* 1969; *Medea* 1970; *L'Innocente* 1976
Gish, Annabeth *Desert Bloom* 1985; *Hiding Out* 1987; *Mystic Pizza* 1988; *Shag* 1988; *When He's Not a Stranger* 1989; *Coupe de Ville* 1990; *The Last to Go* 1991; *Don't Look Back* 1995; *The Last Supper* 1995; *Beautiful Girls* 1996; *What Love Sees* 1996; *Steel* 1997; *Double Jeopardy* 1999; *SLC Punk!* 1999
Gish, Dorothy *Home, Sweet Home* 1914; *Hearts of the World* 1918; *Orphans of the Storm* 1921; *Fury* 1923; *Centennial Summer* 1946; *The Cardinal* 1963
Gish, Lillian *The Musketeers of Pig Alley* 1912; *The Battle of the Sexes* 1914; *Home, Sweet Home* 1914; *The Battle of Elderbush* 1914; *The Birth of a Nation* 1915; *Intolerance* 1916; *Hearts of the World* 1918; *Broken Blossoms* 1919; *Way Down East* 1920; *Orphans of the Storm* 1921; *The White Sister* 1923; *La Bohème* 1926; *The Scarlet Letter* 1926; *Annie Laurie* 1927; *The Wind* 1928; *One Romantic Night* 1930; *His Double Life* 1933; *The Commandos Strike at Dawn* 1942; *Miss Susie Slagle's* 1945; *Duel in the Sun* 1946; *Portrait of Jennie* 1948; *The Cobweb* 1955; *The Night of the Hunter* 1955; *Orders to Kill* 1958; *The Unforgiven* 1960; *Follow Me, Boys!* 1966; *The Comedians* 1967; *Warning Shot* 1967; *Twin Detectives* 1976; *A Wedding* 1978; *Hambone and Hillie* 1984; *Sweet Liberty* 1986; *The Whales of August* 1987
Gish, Sheila *A Day in the Death of Joe Egg* 1971; *Highlander* 1986; *Mansfield Park* 1999
Gist, Robert *The Band Wagon* 1953; *D-Day the Sixth of June* 1956
Gittins, Paul *Other Halves* 1984; *The End of the Golden Weather* 1992
Giuffre, Carlo *Madame* 1961; *La Pelle* 1981
Giuntoli, Neil *Child's Play* 1988; *The Borrower* 1989; *Henry: Portrait of a Serial Killer, Part II* 1996; *Palmer's Pick-Up* 1999
Giustini, Carlo *The Passionate Stranger* 1957; *The Savage Innocents* 1960
Givens, Robin *Beverly Hills Madam* 1986; *The Penthouse* 1989; *A Rage in Harlem* 1991; *Boomerang* 1992; *Blankman* 1994; *Foreign Student* 1994; *Dangerous Intentions* 1995; *The Face* 1996
Givney, Kathryn *My Friend Irma* 1949; *Lightning Strikes Twice* 1951; *Operation Pacific* 1951; *Three Coins in the Fountain* 1954; *Congo Crossing* 1956
Givot, George *Step Lively, Jeeves* 1937; *Behind the Rising Sun* 1943; *DuBarry Was a Lady* 1943; *The Falcon and the Co-Eds* 1943; *April in Paris* 1952; *Three Sailors and a Girl* 1953; *China Gate* 1957
Gladwin, Joe *Night Must Fall* 1964; *Work Is a Four Letter Word* 1968; *Nearest and Dearest* 1972
Glaser, Paul Michael *Fiddler on the Roof* 1971; *Phobia* 1980; *Wait till Your Mother Gets Home!* 1983; *Single Bars, Single Women* 1984
Glass, Ned *Jennifer* 1953; *The Rebel Set* 1959; *Experiment in Terror* 1962; *Kid Galahad* 1962; *Charade* 1963; *The All-American Boy* 1973
Glasser, Isabel *Forever Young* 1992; *Pure Country* 1992; *Circumstances Unknown* 1995; *Exquisite Tenderness* 1995
Glasser, Phillip *An American Tail* 1986; *An American Tail: Fievel Goes West* 1991; *Stanley's Magic Garden* 1994
Glatzeder, Winfried *Forget Mozart* 1985; *Point of No Return* 1986
Glaubrecht, Frank *The Bridge* 1959; *Codename Wildgeese* 1984
Glaudini, Robert *The Alchemist* 1981; *Parasite* 1982
Glave, Matthew *The Wedding Singer* 1998; *Mutiny* 1999
Glazer, Eugene Robert *Bounty Tracker* 1993; *The Substitute* 1993
Gleason, Jackie *All through the Night* 1942; *Larceny, Inc* 1942; *Orchestra Wives* 1942; *Springtime in the Rockies* 1942; *The Hustler* 1961; *Gigot* 1962; *Requiem for a Heavyweight* 1962; *Papa's Delicate Condition* 1963; *Soldier in the Rain* 1963; *Skidoo* 1968; *Don't Drink the Water* 1969; *How to Commit Marriage* 1969; *How Do I Love Thee?* 1970; *Mr Billion* 1977; *Smokey and the Bandit* 1977; *Smokey and the Bandit II* 1980; *The Toy* 1982; *Smokey and the Bandit III* 1983; *The Sting II* 1983; *Izzy and Moe* 1985; *Nothing in Common* 1986
Gleason, James *Her Man* 1930; *A Free Soul* 1931; *Blondie of the Follies* 1932; *The Penguin Pool Murder* 1932; *Murder on the Blackboard* 1934; *Murder on a Honeymoon* 1935; *The Ex-Mrs Bradford* 1936; *Murder on a Bridle Path* 1936; *The Plot Thickens* 1936; *On Your Toes* 1939; *A Date with the Falcon* 1941; *Here Comes Mr Jordan* 1941; *Meet John Doe* 1941; *Affectionately Yours* 1941; *The Falcon Takes*

RadioTimes ACTORS' INDEX

Golino, Valeria *Big Top Pee-wee* 1988; *Rain Man* 1988; *Three Sisters* 1988; *Torrents of Spring* 1989; *The King's Whore* 1990; *Hot Shots!* 1991; *The Indian Runner* 1991; *Year of the Gun* 1991; *Puerto Escondido* 1992; *Hot Shots! Part Deux* 1993; *Clean Slate* 1994; *Immortal Beloved* 1994; *Leaving Las Vegas* 1995; *Escape from LA* 1996; *An Occasional Hell* 1996; *Shooting the Moon* 1998; *Side Streets* 1998; *Harem Suare* 1999
Golonka, Arlene *Harvey Middleman, Fireman* 1965; *The Busy Body* 1967; *Hang 'em High* 1968; *The In-Laws* 1979; *The Last Married Couple in America* 1980; *Separate Ways* 1981; *The Gumshoe Kid* 1990; *Skeletons* 1996
Gombell, Minna *Bad Girl* 1931; *The First Year* 1932; *Hello Sister!* 1933; *The Lemon Drop Kid* 1934; *The Merry Widow* 1934; *The Thin Man* 1934; *Banjo on My Knee* 1936; *Blockheads* 1938; *And So They Were Married* 1944
Gomez, Carlos *Silhouette* 1990; *Those Bedroom Eyes* 1993; *Hostile Intentions* 1995; *Out of Annie's Past* 1995; *In the Blink of an Eye* 1996; *Fools Rush In* 1997
Gomez, Carmelo *Vacas* 1992; *The Red Squirrel* 1993; *Tierra* 1995; *Secrets of the Heart* 1997
Gomez, Fernando Fernan *The Spirit of the Beehive* 1973; *Mamá Cumple 100 Años* 1979; *Belle Epoque* 1992
Gomez, Jaime *aka* **Gomez, Jaime P** *Untamed Love* 1994; *Solo* 1996
Gómez, José Luis *Roads to the South* 1978; *Prince of Shadows* 1991
Gomez, Panchito *Run for the Roses* 1978; *Max Dugan Returns* 1983
Gomez, Thomas *Sherlock Holmes and the Voice of Terror* 1942; *Who Done It?* 1942; *Abbott and Costello in Society* 1944; *Phantom Lady* 1944; *The Daltons Ride Again* 1945; *Swell Guy* 1946; *Johnny O'Clock* 1947; *Singapore* 1947; *Angel in Exile* 1948; *Casbah* 1948; *Force of Evil* 1948; *Key Largo* 1948; *Come to the Stable* 1949; *Sorrowful Jones* 1949; *That Midnight Kiss* 1949; *The Woman on Pier 13* 1949; *The Furies* 1950; *Kim* 1950; *Anne of the Indies* 1951; *The Sellout* 1951; *Macao* 1952; *Pony Soldier* 1952; *The Adventures of Hajji Baba* 1954; *Las Vegas Shakedown* 1955; *The Looters* 1955; *The Magnificent Matador* 1955; *The Conqueror* 1956; *Trapeze* 1956; *But Not for Me* 1959
Gonzalez-Gonzales, Pedro *aka* **Gonzalez, Pedro** *I Died a Thousand Times* 1955; *Hostile Guns* 1967; *Hook, Line and Sinker* 1969
Goodall, Caroline *The Silver Brumby* 1992; *Cliffhanger* 1993; *Schindler's List* 1993; *Disclosure* 1994; *Hotel Sorrento* 1994; *White Squall* 1996; *Casualties* 1997
Goodall, Louise *Carla's Song* 1996; *My Name Is Joe* 1998
Goodfellow, Joan *Buster and Billie* 1974; *A Flash of Green* 1984
Gooding Jr, Cuba *Boyz N the Hood* 1991; *Gladiator* 1992; *Murder without Motive* 1992; *Daybreak* 1993; *Judgment Night* 1993; *Lightning Jack* 1994; *Losing Isaiah* 1995; *Outbreak* 1995; *The Tuskegee Airmen* 1995; *Jerry Maguire* 1996; *As Good As It Gets* 1997; *What Dreams May Come* 1998; *A Murder of Crows* 1998; *Instinct* 1999; *Chill Factor* 1999
Goodliffe, Michael *The Wooden Horse* 1950; *Sea Devils* 1952; *Front Page Story* 1953; *The End of the Affair* 1955; *The Battle of the River Plate* 1956; *The One That Got Away* 1957; *Up the Creek* 1958; *The Thirty-Nine Steps* 1959; *Peeping Tom* 1960; *The Day the Earth Caught Fire* 1961; *Jigsaw* 1962; *80,000 Suspects* 1963; *The Gorgon* 1964; *The 7th Dawn* 1964; *633 Squadron* 1964; *Henry VIII and His Six Wives* 1972; *To the Devil a Daughter* 1976
Goodman, Benny *The Big Broadcast of 1937* 1936; *Hollywood Hotel* 1937; *Sweet and Lowdown* 1944; *A Song Is Born* 1948
Goodman, Dody *Bedtime Story* 1964; *Max Dugan Returns* 1983; *Splash* 1984; *I Dream of Jeannie… 15 Years Later* 1985; *Private Resort* 1985; *Cool as Ice* 1991; *Frozen Assets* 1992
Goodman, John *Eddie Macon's Run* 1983; *Maria's Lovers* 1984; *Sweet Dreams* 1985; *The Big Easy* 1986; *True Stories* 1986; *Burglar* 1987; *Raising Arizona* 1987; *Everybody's All-American* 1988; *Punchline* 1988; *Always* 1989; *Sea of Love* 1989; *Arachnophobia* 1990; *Stella* 1990; *Barton Fink* 1991; *King Ralph* 1991; *The Babe* 1992; *Born Yesterday* 1993; *Matinee* 1993; *We're Back! A Dinosaur's Story* 1993; *The Flintstones* 1994; *Pie in the Sky* 1995; *Kingfish: a Story of Huey P Long* 1995; *Mother Night* 1996; *The Big Lebowski* 1997; *The Borrowers* 1997; *Blues Brothers 2000* 1998; *Fallen* 1998; *Bringing out the Dead* 1999; *The Jack Bull* 1999; *The Runner* 1999; *O Brother, Where Art Thou?* 2000
Goodrich, Deborah *Just One of the Guys* 1985; *April Fool's Day* 1986; *Remote Control* 1988
Goodrow, Garry *The Connection* 1961; *Steelyard Blues* 1973
Goodwin, Alexander *Box of Moon Light* 1996; *Mimic* 1997
Goodwin, Bill *Riding High* 1943; *Bathing Beauty* 1944; *The Stork Club* 1945; *The Jolson Story* 1946; *To Each His Own* 1946; *Heaven Only Knows* 1947; *So This Is New York* 1948; *It's a Great Feeling* 1949; *Jolson Sings Again* 1949; *Tea for Two* 1950; *Lucky Me* 1954; *The Atomic Kid* 1954; *Bundle of Joy* 1956
Goodwin, Harold *College* 1927; *The Cameraman* 1928; *Flight* 1929; *Dirigible* 1931; *Angels One Five* 1952; *Barnacle Bill* 1957; *Sea Wife* 1957; *The Hi-Jackers* 1963
Goodwin, Laurel *Girls! Girls! Girls!* 1962; *Papa's Delicate Condition* 1963
Goodwin, Michael *Remembrance of Love* 1982; *Murderous Intent* 1995
Goorjian, Michael *David's Mother* 1994; *Hard Rain* 1997; *SLC Punk!* 1999
Gopal, Ram *The Planter's Wife* 1952; *The Purple Plain* 1954; *The Blue Peter* 1955
Gorcey, Bernard *Abie's Irish Rose* 1928; *No Minor Vices* 1948; *Jalopy* 1953; *The Bowery Boys Meet the Monsters* 1954; *Jungle Gents* 1954; *Jail Busters* 1955
Gorcey, David *aka* **Condon, David** *Sergeant Madden* 1939; *That Gang of Mine* 1940; *Pride of the Bowery* 1941; *Spooks Run Wild* 1941; *Jungle Gents* 1954
Gorcey, Leo *Dead End* 1937; *Mannequin* 1937; *Angels with Dirty Faces* 1938; *Angels Wash Their Faces* 1939; *They Made Me a Criminal* 1939; *Boys of the City* 1940; *That Gang of Mine* 1940; *Pride of the Bowery* 1941; *Spooks Run Wild* 1941; *Clancy Street Boys* 1943; *Ghosts in the Night* 1943; *Block Busters* 1944; *Bowery Champs* 1944; *Follow the Leader* 1944; *Come Out Fighting* 1945; *Docks of New York* 1945; *Mr Muggs Rides Again* 1945; *So This Is New York* 1948; *Jalopy* 1953; *The Bowery Boys Meet the Monsters* 1954; *Jungle Gents* 1954; *Jail Busters* 1955
Gordon, Barbara *Dead Ringers* 1988; *White Room* 1990
Gordon, C Henry *Renegades* 1930; *Mata Hari* 1931; *Hell's Highway* 1932; *Rasputin and the Empress* 1932; *Scarface* 1932; *Gabriel over the White House* 1933; *Turn Back the Clock* 1933; *Penthouse* 1933; *The Devil's in Love* 1933; *Stamboul Quest* 1934; *Charlie Chan at the Olympics* 1937; *Conquest* 1937; *Stand-In* 1937; *Tarzan's Revenge* 1938; *The Return of the Cisco Kid* 1939
Gordon, Claire *And Women Shall Weep* 1960; *Beat Girl* 1960; *Konga* 1960
Gordon, Clarke *Impasse* 1969; *Glass Houses* 1972
Gordon, Colin *Green Grow the Rushes* 1951; *Folly to Be Wise* 1952; *Little Red Monkey* 1955; *The Extra Day* 1956; *Up in the World* 1956; *The One That Got Away* 1957; *Virgin Island* 1958; *Bobbikins* 1959; *House of Mystery* 1961; *In the Doghouse* 1961; *Night of the Eagle* 1961; *Strongroom* 1961; *Don't Raise the Bridge, Lower the River* 1968
Gordon, Don *Bullitt* 1968; *The Gamblers* 1969; *Cannon for Cordoba* 1970; *WUSA* 1970; *The Last Movie* 1971; *ZPG: Zero Population Growth* 1971; *Slaughter* 1972; *Papillon* 1973; *The Mack* 1973; *The Final Conflict* 1980; *Skin Deep* 1989; *The Borrower* 1989
Gordon, Dorothy *The Silver Fleet* 1943; *House of Whipcord* 1974
Gordon, Eve *Avalon* 1990; *The Boys* 1991; *Paradise* 1991; *The Whereabouts of Jenny* 1991; *Leaving Normal* 1992; *Honey, We Shrunk Ourselves* 1997; *I'll Be Home for Christmas* 1998
Gordon, Gale *Here We Go Again* 1942; *Don't Give Up the Ship* 1959; *All in a Night's Work* 1960; *Visit to a Small Planet* 1960; *All Hands on Deck* 1961; *Sergeant Deadhead* 1965; *Speedway* 1968
Gordon, Gavin *Romance* 1930; *American Madness* 1932; *The Bitter Tea of General Yen* 1933; *Black Beauty* 1933; *Hard to Handle* 1933; *Mystery of the Wax Museum* 1933; *The Scarlet Empress* 1934; *Bordertown* 1935; *Bride of Frankenstein* 1935; *The Bat* 1959
Gordon, Hannah *Spring and Port Wine* 1969; *Alfie Darling* 1975; *Watership Down* 1978; *The Elephant Man* 1980
Gordon, Harold *The Jazz Singer* 1952; *Viva Zapata!* 1952; *East of Eden* 1955
Gordon, Hilary *The Mosquito Coast* 1986; *The Great Outdoors* 1988
Gordon, Huntley *The Marriage Playground* 1929; *Anybody's Woman* 1930
Gordon, Keith *Home Movies* 1979; *Dressed to Kill* 1980; *Christine* 1983; *Single Bars, Single Women* 1984; *The Legend of Billie Jean* 1985; *Static* 1985; *Back to School* 1986; *Combat Academy* 1986
Gordon, Leo *Gun Fury* 1953; *Hondo* 1953; *Riot in Cell Block 11* 1954; *The Yellow Mountain* 1954; *Tennessee's Partner* 1955; *Seven Angry Men* 1955; *Great Day in the Morning* 1956; *Seventh Cavalry* 1956; *Baby Face Nelson* 1957; *The Restless Breed* 1957; *Quantrill's Raiders* 1958; *Ride a Crooked Trail* 1958; *Escort West* 1959; *The Jayhawkers* 1959; *Tarzan Goes to India* 1962; *The Haunted Palace* 1963; *Kings of the Sun* 1963; *Beau Geste* 1966; *Hostile Guns* 1967; *My Name Is Nobody* 1973; *Savage Dawn* 1985
Gordon, Mary *The Great O'Malley* 1937; *The Golden Hour* 1941; *Little Giant* 1946
Gordon, Nora *Night Was Our Friend* 1951; *Police Dog* 1955; *Woman in a Dressing Gown* 1957
Gordon, Rebecca *The Mosquito Coast* 1986; *The Great Outdoors* 1988
Gordon, Ruth *Abe Lincoln in Illinois* 1940; *Dr Ehrlich's Magic Bullet* 1940; *Two-Faced Woman* 1941; *Action in the North Atlantic* 1943; *Edge of Darkness* 1943; *Inside Daisy Clover* 1965; *Lord Love a Duck* 1966; *Rosemary's Baby* 1968; *Whatever Happened to Aunt Alice?* 1969; *Where's Poppa?* 1970; *Harold and Maude* 1972; *Isn't It Shocking?* 1973; *The Big Bus* 1976; *Every Which Way but Loose* 1978; *Perfect Gentlemen* 1978; *Boardwalk* 1979; *Any Which Way You Can* 1980; *My Bodyguard* 1980; *Jimmy the Kid* 1982; *Maxie* 1985; *Delta Pi* 1985; *The Trouble with Spies* 1987
Gordon, Susan *The Five Pennies* 1959; *Picture Mommy Dead* 1966
Gordon-Levitt, Joseph *Changes* 1991; *Hi Honey, I'm Dead* 1991; *Switching Parents* 1992; *Angels* 1994; *Holy Matrimony* 1994; *Roadflower* 1994; *The Great Elephant Escape* 1995; *The Juror* 1996; *Halloween H20: 20 Years Later* 1998; *10 Things I Hate about You* 1999
Gordon-Sinclair, John *aka* **Sinclair, Gordon John** *That Sinking Feeling* 1979; *Gregory's Girl* 1980; *The Girl in the Picture* 1985; *Erik the Viking* 1989; *The Brylcreem Boys* 1996; *Gregory's Two Girls* 1999
Gore, Sandy *Undercover* 1983; *Remember Me* 1985
Gorg, Galyn *America 3000* 1986; *Dance Academy* 1988
Gorham, Mel *Blue in the Face* 1995; *Curdled* 1995
Goring, Marius *Flying 55* 1939; *The Spy in Black* 1939; *Pastor Hall* 1940; *A Matter of Life and Death* 1946; *Night Boat to Dublin* 1946; *Take My Life* 1947; *Mr Perrin and Mr Traill* 1948; *The Red Shoes* 1948; *Circle of Danger* 1950; *Highly Dangerous* 1950; *Odette* 1950; *The Man Who Watched Trains Go By* 1952; *Rough Shoot* 1952; *The Barefoot Contessa* 1954; *The Adventures of Quentin Durward* 1955; *Break in the Circle* 1955; *Ill Met by Moonlight* 1956; *The Moonraker* 1957; *I Was Monty's Double* 1958; *Son of Robin Hood* 1958; *The Treasure of San Teresa* 1959; *Beyond the Curtain* 1960; *The Inspector* 1962; *The Crooked Road* 1964; *Up from the Beach* 1965; *The 25th Hour* 1967; *The Girl on a Motorcycle* 1968; *First Love* 1970; *Zeppelin* 1971
Gorman, Bud *Bowery Champs* 1944; *Follow the Leader* 1944; *Docks of New York* 1945; *Mr Muggs Rides Again* 1945
Gorman, Cliff *The Boys in the Band* 1970; *Cops and Robbers* 1973; *Strike Force* 1975; *Rosebud* 1975; *An Unmarried Woman* 1978; *All That Jazz* 1979; *Night of the Juggler* 1980; *Angel* 1984; *Making the Case for Murder: the Howard Beach Story* 1989; *Murder in Black & White* 1990; *Murder Times Seven* 1990; *Vestige of Honor* 1990; *Night and the City* 1992; *Terror on Track 9* 1992; *Janek: a Silent Betrayal* 1994; *Down Came a Blackbird* 1995; *Ghost Dog: the Way of the Samurai* 1999
Gorman, Robert Hy *aka* **Gorman, Robert** *The Accidental Tourist* 1988; *Where Pigeons Go to Die* 1990; *Sometimes They Come Back* 1991; *Tell Me No Lies* 1991; *Mr Nanny* 1992; *Leprechaun* 1992
Gorney, Karen Lynn *Saturday Night Fever* 1977; *Ripe* 1996
Gorshin, Frank *Dragstrip Girl* 1957; *Invasion of the Saucer Men* 1957; *Bells Are Ringing* 1960; *Studs Lonigan* 1960; *The George Raft Story* 1961; *Ring of Fire* 1961; *Sail a Crooked Ship* 1961; *Batman* 1966; *Skidoo* 1968; *Sky Heist* 1975; *Uphill All the Way* 1985; *Hot Resort* 1985; *The Masterpiece of Murder* 1986; *Hollywood Vice Squad* 1986; *Midnight* 1989; *Sweet Justice* 1992; *Hail Caesar* 1994; *Twelve Monkeys* 1995; *The Twilight of the Ice Nymphs* 1997
Gortner, Marjoe *Earthquake* 1974; *The Food of the Gods* 1975; *Acapulco Gold* 1976; *Sidewinder One* 1977; *When You Comin' Back, Red Ryder?* 1979; *Mausoleum* 1983; *American Ninja 3: Blood Hunt* 1989
Gosselaar, Mark-Paul *White Wolves* 1993; *Dying to Belong* 1997; *Dead Man on Campus* 1998
Gossett Jr, Louis *aka* **Gossett, Louis** *A Raisin in the Sun* 1961; *The Landlord* 1970; *Skin Game* 1971; *Travels with My Aunt* 1972; *The Laughing Policeman* 1973; *The White Dawn* 1974; *The River Niger* 1976; *JD's Revenge* 1976; *The Choirboys* 1977; *The Deep* 1977; *This Man Stands Alone* 1979; *An Officer and a Gentleman* 1982; *Jaws III* 1983; *Finders Keepers* 1984; *The Guardian* 1984; *Enemy Mine* 1985; *Iron Eagle* 1985; *Firewalker* 1986; *The Father Clements Story* 1987; *A Gathering of Old Men* 1987; *The Principal* 1987; *Farewell Miss Freedom* 1988; *Iron Eagle II* 1988; *The Punisher* 1989; *El Diablo* 1990; *Sudie and Simpson* 1990; *Carolina Skeletons* 1991; *The Josephine Baker Story* 1991; *On the Streets of LA* 1991; *Toy Soldiers* 1991; *Cover-Up* 1991; *Aces: Iron Eagle III* 1992; *Keeper of the City* 1992; *Midnight Sting* 1992; *Flashfire* 1993; *A Good Man in Africa* 1993; *Monolith* 1993; *Blue Chips* 1994; *Curse of the Starving Class* 1994; *Iron Eagle IV* 1995; *Zooman* 1995; *Captive Heart: the James Mink Story* 1996; *Inside* 1996; *Run for the Dream: the Gail Devers Story*

RadioTimes ACTORS' INDEX

Grant, David Marshall *aka* **Grant, David** *Happy Birthday, Gemini* 1980; *Legs* 1983; *American Flyers* 1985; *The Big Town* 1987; *BAT-21* 1988; *Breaking Point* 1989; *Air America* 1990; *Strictly Business* 1991; *Shades of Gray* 1992; *Through the Eyes of a Killer* 1992; *Three Wishes* 1995
Grant, Faye *The January Man* 1989; *Omen IV: the Awakening* 1991; *Traces of Red* 1992; *Drive Me Crazy* 1999
Grant, Hugh *Maurice* 1987; *Rowing with the Wind* 1987; *The Dawning* 1988; *The Lair of the White Worm* 1988; *The Big Man* 1990; *Impromptu* 1991; *Our Sons* 1991; *Bitter Moon* 1992; *The Remains of the Day* 1993; *Night Train to Venice* 1993; *An Awfully Big Adventure* 1994; *Four Weddings and a Funeral* 1994; *Sirens* 1994; *The Englishman Who Went up a Hill, but Came down a Mountain* 1995; *Nine Months* 1995; *Restoration* 1995; *Sense and Sensibility* 1995; *Extreme Measures* 1996; *Mickey Blue Eyes* 1999; *Notting Hill* 1999
Grant, Kathryn *The Phenix City Story* 1955; *The Brothers Rico* 1957; *Operation Mad Ball* 1957; *Mister Cory* 1957; *The 7th Voyage of Sinbad* 1958; *Anatomy of a Murder* 1959; *The Big Circus* 1959
Grant, Kirby *Red River Range* 1938; *Abbott and Costello in Society* 1944; *Ghost Catchers* 1944
Grant, Lawrence *Bulldog Drummond* 1929; *The Unholy Garden* 1931; *The Mask of Fu Manchu* 1932; *Shanghai Express* 1932; *Speak Easily* 1932; *By Candlelight* 1934; *Under the Red Robe* 1937
Grant, Lee *Detective Story* 1951; *Middle of the Night* 1959; *The Balcony* 1963; *Terror in the City* 1963; *In the Heat of the Night* 1967; *Valley of the Dolls* 1967; *Buona Sera, Mrs Campbell* 1968; *Marooned* 1969; *The Big Bounce* 1969; *The Landlord* 1970; *Plaza Suite* 1971; *Portnoy's Complaint* 1972; *The Internecine Project* 1974; *Shampoo* 1975; *Voyage of the Damned* 1976; *Airport '77* 1977; *Damien – Omen II* 1978; *The Swarm* 1978; *When You Comin' Back, Red Ryder?* 1979; *Little Miss Marker* 1980; *Charlie Chan and the Curse of the Dragon Queen* 1981; *Visiting Hours* 1982; *A Billion for Boris* 1984; *Teachers* 1984; *The Big Town* 1987; *She Said No* 1990; *Defending Your Life* 1991; *Fatal Love* 1992; *In My Daughter's Name* 1992; *Citizen Cohn* 1992; *It's My Party* 1996
Grant, Leon W *Beat Street* 1984; *Playing for Keeps* 1986
Grant, Micah *Like Father, Like Son* 1987; *High Desert Kill* 1989; *Terminal Bliss* 1990
Grant, Richard E *Withnail & I* 1986; *Hidden City* 1987; *How to Get Ahead in Advertising* 1989; *Killing Dad* 1989; *Mountains of the Moon* 1989; *Warlock* 1989; *Henry & June* 1990; *Hudson Hawk* 1991; *LA Story* 1991; *Bram Stoker's Dracula* 1992; *The Player* 1992; *The Age of Innocence* 1993; *Prêt-à-Porter* 1994; *The Cold Light of Day* 1995; *Jack & Sarah* 1995; *The Portrait of a Lady* 1996; *Twelfth Night* 1996; *Keep the Aspidistra Flying* 1997; *Spice World* 1997; *The Serpent's Kiss* 1997; *Food of Love* 1997; *The Match* 1999; *The Miracle Maker* 1999
Grant, Rodney A *Dances with Wolves* 1990; *Geronimo* 1993; *Wagons East!* 1994; *The Killing Grounds* 1997; *Vanishing Point* 1997; *Two for Texas* 1998; *The Jack Bull* 1999
Grant, Salim *Ghost Dad* 1990; *The Hitman* 1991
Granville, Bonita *These Three* 1936; *Hard to Get* 1938; *Merrily We Live* 1938; *White Banners* 1938; *Angels Wash Their Faces* 1939; *The Mortal Storm* 1940; *Third Finger, Left Hand* 1940; *The People vs Dr Kildare* 1941; *The Glass Key* 1942; *Now, Voyager* 1942; *Syncopation* 1942; *Hitler's Children* 1943; *Andy Hardy's Blonde Trouble* 1944; *Youth Runs Wild* 1944; *Song of the Open Road* 1944; *Love Laughs at Andy Hardy* 1946; *The Lone Ranger* 1956
Grapewin, Charley *aka* **Grapewin, Charles** *Hell's House* 1932; *Pilgrimage* 1933; *Anne of Green Gables* 1934; *Ah, Wilderness* 1935; *Alice Adams* 1935; *Libeled Lady* 1936; *The Petrified Forest* 1936; *Big City* 1937; *Captains Courageous* 1937; *A Family Affair* 1937; *The Good Earth* 1937; *Listen, Darling* 1938; *Of Human Hearts* 1938; *The Shopworn Angel* 1938; *Artists and Models Abroad* 1938; *Dust Be My Destiny* 1939; *The Wizard of Oz* 1939; *Ellery Queen Master Detective* 1940; *The Grapes of Wrath* 1940; *Johnny Apollo* 1940; *Texas Rangers Ride Again* 1940; *Rhythm on the River* 1940; *They Died with Their Boots On* 1941; *Tobacco Road* 1941; *Atlantic City* 1944; *Follow the Boys* 1944
Graves, George *Those Were the Days* 1934; *Heart's Desire* 1935
Graves (1), Peter *Red Planet Mars* 1952; *Beneath the 12-Mile Reef* 1953; *Stalag 17* 1953; *The Raid* 1954; *The Yellow Tomahawk* 1954; *The Court-Martial of Billy Mitchell* 1955; *Lilacs in the Spring* 1955; *The Night of the Hunter* 1955; *Wichita* 1955; *The Naked Street* 1955; *It Conquered the World* 1956; *Beginning of the End* 1957; *Wolf Larsen* 1958; *A Stranger in My Arms* 1959; *A Rage to Live* 1965; *Texas across the River* 1966; *Valley of Mystery* 1967; *The Ballad of Josie* 1968; *Sergeant Ryker* 1968; *The Adventurers* 1970; *Cruise Missile* 1978; *Survival Run* 1979; *Airplane!* 1980; *The Memory of Eva Ryker* 1980; *Airplane II: the Sequel* 1982; *Savannah Smiles* 1982; *Number One with a Bullet* 1986
Graves (2), Peter *King Arthur Was a Gentleman* 1942; *Bees in Paradise* 1943; *Miss London Ltd* 1943; *Give Us the Moon* 1944; *I'll Be Your Sweetheart* 1945; *Gaiety George* 1946; *Spring in Park Lane* 1948; *Maytime in Mayfair* 1949; *Derby Day* 1952; *The Admirable Crichton* 1957
Graves, Ralph *Dream Street* 1921; *Flight* 1929; *Ladies of Leisure* 1930; *Dirigible* 1931; *Three Texas Steers* 1939
Graves, Rupert *A Room with a View* 1985; *A Handful of Dust* 1987; *Maurice* 1987; *The Children* 1990; *Where Angels Fear to Tread* 1991; *Damage* 1992; *A Private Affair* 1992; *The Innocent Sleep* 1995; *Intimate Relations* 1995; *The Madness of King George* 1995; *Different for Girls* 1996; *Mrs Dalloway* 1997; *The Revengers' Comedies* 1997; *Dreaming of Joseph Lees* 1998
Graves, Teresa *That Man Bolt* 1973; *Vampira* 1975
Gravet, Fernand *aka* **Graavey, Fernand,** *aka* **Gravey, Fernand** *Bitter Sweet* 1933; *The King and the Chorus Girl* 1937; *The Great Waltz* 1938; *Fools for Scandal* 1938; *La Nuit Fantastique* 1942; *La Ronde* 1950; *Mitsou* 1957; *How to Steal a Million* 1966
Gravina, Carla *Big Deal on Madonna Street* 1958; *Five Branded Women* 1960; *Alfredo Alfredo* 1971; *Without Apparent Motive* 1972; *The Bit Player* 1973; *The Inheritor* 1973; *And Now My Love* 1974; *Boomerang* 1976
Gravina, Cesare *The Divine Woman* 1928; *The Wedding March* 1928
Gray, Billy *The Day the Earth Stood Still* 1951; *On Moonlight Bay* 1951; *All I Desire* 1953; *By the Light of the Silvery Moon* 1953; *The Girl Next Door* 1953; *Some Like It Hot* 1959; *The Explosive Generation* 1961; *Two for the Seesaw* 1962; *The Navy vs the Night Monsters* 1966
Gray, Bruce *Between Friends* 1983; *Odd Birds* 1985; *Dragnet* 1987
Gray, Carole *The Young Ones* 1961; *Devils of Darkness* 1964; *Curse of the Fly* 1965; *The Brides of Fu Manchu* 1966; *Island of Terror* 1966
Gray, Charles *Tommy the Toreador* 1959; *Man in the Moon* 1960; *Masquerade* 1965; *The Night of the Generals* 1966; *The Secret War of Harry Frigg* 1967; *The Devil Rides Out* 1968; *Mosquito Squadron* 1968; *The File of the Golden Goose* 1969; *The Executioner* 1970; *Diamonds Are Forever* 1971; *The Beast Must Die* 1974; *The Rocky Horror Picture Show* 1975; *Seven Nights in Japan* 1976; *The Legacy* 1978; *Shock Treatment* 1981; *The Jigsaw Man* 1984; *The Tichborne Claimant* 1998
Gray, Coleen *Kiss of Death* 1947; *Nightmare Alley* 1947; *Fury at Furnace Creek* 1948; *Red River* 1948; *I'll Get You for This* 1950; *Riding High* 1950; *The Sleeping City* 1950; *Apache Drums* 1951; *Kansas City Confidential* 1952; *Arrow in the Dust* 1954; *Las Vegas Shakedown* 1955; *Tennessee's Partner* 1955; *The Twinkle in God's Eye* 1955; *Death of a Scoundrel* 1956; *The Killing* 1956; *Star in the Dust* 1956; *The Leech Woman* 1960; *New Face in Hell* 1968; *The Late Liz* 1971
Gray, David Barry *Mr Wonderful* 1992; *Cops and Robbersons* 1994; *Lawn Dogs* 1997
Gray, Dolores *It's Always Fair Weather* 1955; *Kismet* 1955; *The Opposite Sex* 1956; *Designing Woman* 1957
Gray, Donald *The Four Feathers* 1939; *We'll Meet Again* 1942; *Timeslip* 1955
Gray, Dulcie *A Place of One's Own* 1944; *They Were Sisters* 1945; *Wanted for Murder* 1946; *A Man about the House* 1947; *Mine Own Executioner* 1947; *My Brother Jonathan* 1947; *The Glass Mountain* 1949; *The Franchise Affair* 1950; *Angels One Five* 1952; *A Man Could Get Killed* 1966
Gray, Erin *Buck Rogers in the 25th Century* 1979; *Six Pack* 1982; *Norman Rockwell's Breaking Home Ties* 1987; *Addicted to His Love* 1988; *Jason Goes to Hell: the Final Friday* 1993; *Official Denial* 1993; *Honor Thy Father and Mother: the Menendez Killings* 1994; *T-Force* 1995
Gray, Eve *Death on the Set* 1935; *The Vicar of Bray* 1937
Gray, Gary *Rachel and the Stranger* 1948; *The Next Voice You Hear* 1950
Gray, Lawrence *Stage Struck* 1925; *The Patsy* 1928; *Man of the World* 1931
Gray, Linda *The Golden Disc* 1958; *Bonanza – the Return* 1993; *Why My Daughter?* 1993; *Accidental Meeting* 1994; *Broken Pledges* 1994; *To My Daughter with Love* 1994; *Dallas: JR Returns* 1996; *When the Cradle Falls* 1997; *Dallas: War of the Ewings* 1998
Gray, Nadia *The Spider and the Fly* 1949; *Night without Stars* 1951; *Valley of Eagles* 1951; *Crossed Swords* 1954; *One Night at the Music Hall* 1956; *The Captain's Table* 1958; *La Dolce Vita* 1960; *Mr Topaze* 1961; *Maniac* 1963; *The Crooked Road* 1964; *The Naked Runner* 1967; *Two for the Road* 1967; *The Oldest Profession* 1967
Gray, Robert *Elvis – the Movie* 1979; *UFOria* 1980
Gray, Sally *Cheer Up!* 1936; *Over She Goes* 1937; *Hold My Hand* 1938; *The Saint in London* 1939; *A Window in London* 1939; *Dangerous Moonlight* 1941; *The Saint's Vacation* 1941; *Green for Danger* 1946; *They Made Me a Fugitive* 1947; *Obsession* 1948; *Silent Dust* 1948; *Escape Route* 1952; *The Keeper* 1976
Gray, Spalding *The Killing Fields* 1984; *Hard Choices* 1984; *True Stories* 1986; *Swimming to Cambodia* 1987; *Beaches* 1988; *Clara's Heart* 1988; *The Image* 1990; *A Child for Satan* 1991; *Straight Talk* 1992; *King of the Hill* 1993; *Zelda* 1993; *The Paper* 1994; *Bad Company* 1995; *Beyond Rangoon* 1995; *Drunks* 1995; *Diabolique* 1996; *Gray's Anatomy* 1996; *Bliss* 1997
Gray, Vernon *A Day to Remember* 1953; *To Paris with Love* 1954; *The Gold Express* 1955
Gray, Vivean *Picnic at Hanging Rock* 1975; *The Last Wave* 1977
Gray, Willoughby *Stranger from Venus* 1954; *Absolution* 1978; *A View to a Kill* 1985
Grayson, Diane *The Prime of Miss Jean Brodie* 1969; *Blind Terror* 1971
Grayson, Kathryn *Andy Hardy's Private Secretary* 1941; *Rio Rita* 1942; *Thousands Cheer* 1943; *Ziegfeld Follies* 1944; *Anchors Aweigh* 1945; *Two Sisters from Boston* 1946; *It Happened in Brooklyn* 1947; *That Midnight Kiss* 1949; *The Kissing Bandit* 1949; *The Toast of New Orleans* 1950; *Show Boat* 1951; *Lovely to Look At* 1952; *The Desert Song* 1953; *Kiss Me Kate* 1953; *So This Is Love* 1953; *The Vagabond King* 1956
Greco, Joe *The Toughest Man in the World* 1984; *The Package* 1989
Greco, José *Ship of Fools* 1965; *The Proud and the Damned* 1972
Greco, Juliette *Orphée* 1950; *Elena et les Hommes* 1956; *The Sun Also Rises* 1957; *Bonjour Tristesse* 1958; *The Naked Earth* 1958; *The Roots of Heaven* 1958; *Crack in the Mirror* 1960; *The Big Gamble* 1961
Green, Adolph *Simon* 1980; *Lily in Love* 1985; *I Want to Go Home* 1989
Green, Brian Austin *Beverly Hills 90210* 1990; *Kid* 1990; *She Fought Alone* 1995; *Her Costly Affair* 1996
Green, Danny *Someone at the Door* 1950; *The Ladykillers* 1955; *Assignment Redhead* 1956; *The 7th Voyage of Sinbad* 1958
Green, Garard *Profile* 1954; *Emergency* 1962
Green, Gilbert *Dark Intruder* 1965; *Executive Action* 1973
Green, Harry *This Day and Age* 1933; *A King in New York* 1957; *Next to No Time* 1958
Green, Johnny *Face on the Milk Carton* 1995; *Eight Days a Week* 1996
Green, Kerri *The Goonies* 1985; *Summer Rental* 1985; *Lucas* 1986; *Three for the Road* 1987; *Tainted Blood* 1993; *Blue Flame* 1995
Green, Marika *Pickpocket* 1959; *Emmanuelle* 1974
Green, Martyn *The Mikado* 1939; *The Story of Gilbert and Sullivan* 1953; *A Lovely Way to Go* 1968
Green, Michele *To My Daughter* 1990; *Heart of a Child* 1994
Green, Mitzi *Paramount on Parade* 1930; *Tom Sawyer* 1930; *Huckleberry Finn* 1931; *Skippy* 1931; *Bloodhounds of Broadway* 1952
Green, Nigel *Witness in the Dark* 1959; *Sword of Sherwood Forest* 1960; *Pit of Darkness* 1961; *The Man Who Finally Died* 1962; *Saturday Night Out* 1963; *The Masque of the Red Death* 1964; *Zulu* 1964; *The Face of Fu Manchu* 1965; *The Ipcress File* 1965; *The Skull* 1965; *Deadlier than the Male* 1966; *Khartoum* 1966; *Tobruk* 1966; *Africa – Texas Style* 1967; *The Pink Jungle* 1968; *Play Dirty* 1969; *The Wrecking Crew* 1969; *Countess Dracula* 1970; *The Ruling Class* 1972; *Gawain and the Green Knight* 1973
Green, Seth *A Billion for Boris* 1984; *The Hotel New Hampshire* 1984; *Willy/Milly* 1986; *Can't Buy Me Love* 1987; *Radio Days* 1987; *My Stepmother Is an Alien* 1988; *Airborne* 1993; *Arcade* 1993; *Ticks* 1993; *Austin Powers: International Man of Mystery* 1997; *Austin Powers: The Spy Who Shagged Me* 1999; *Idle Hands* 1999
Green, Teddy *The Young Ones* 1961; *Summer Holiday* 1962
Greene, Angela *Shotgun* 1955; *The Cosmic Man* 1959
Greene, Daniel *Weekend Warriors* 1986; *Elvira, Mistress of the Dark* 1988
Greene, David *The Wooden Horse* 1950; *The Dark Light* 1951
Greene, Ellen *Next Stop, Greenwich Village* 1976; *Little Shop of Horrors* 1986; *Talk Radio* 1988; *Dinner at Eight* 1989; *Pump Up the Volume* 1990; *Rock-a-Doodle* 1990; *Stepping Out* 1991; *Fathers and Sons* 1992; *Leon* 1994; *Naked Gun $33\frac{1}{3}$: the Final Insult* 1994; *Wagons East!* 1994; *Killer: a Journal of Murder* 1995; *One Fine Day* 1996
Greene, Graham *Looks and Smiles* 1981; *Running Brave* 1983; *Dances with Wolves* 1990; *Clearcut* 1992; *Medicine River* 1992; *Thunderheart* 1992; *Benefit of the Doubt* 1993; *Camilla* 1993; *Huck and the King of Hearts* 1993; *Cooperstown* 1993; *Maverick* 1994; *Die Hard with a*

Vengeance 1995; *Sabotage* 1996; *Wounded* 1996; *Dead Innocent* 1996; *The Education of Little Tree* 1997; *Shattered Image* 1998; *The Green Mile* 1999
Greene, Kim Morgan *A Woman Scorned* 1994; *Grizzly Mountain* 1997
Greene, Leon *A Challenge for Robin Hood* 1967; *The Devil Rides Out* 1968
Greene, Lorne *The Silver Chalice* 1954; *Tight Spot* 1955; *Autumn Leaves* 1956; *The Buccaneer* 1958; *The Gift of Love* 1958; *The Baited Trap* 1959; *The Harness* 1971; *Earthquake* 1974; *Battlestar Galactica* 1978; *Heidi's Song* 1982
Greene, Michael *Americana* 1981; *Lost in America* 1985; *To Live and Die in LA* 1985; *Stranded* 1987; *Moon over Parador* 1988; *Palomino* 1991; *Rubin & Ed* 1991; *Eve of Destruction* 1991
Greene, Michele *In the Best Interest of the Child* 1990; *A Child Too Many* 1993; *Badge of Betrayal* 1996; *Crimes of Silence* 1996; *Lost Treasure of Dos Santos* 1997
Greene, Peter *Laws of Gravity* 1992; *Clean, Shaven* 1993; *Judgment Night* 1993; *The Mask* 1994; *Pulp Fiction* 1994; *Bang* 1995; *The Rich Man's Wife* 1996; *Double Tap* 1997; *Blue Streak* 1999
Greene, Richard *Four Men and a Prayer* 1938; *Kentucky* 1938; *My Lucky Star* 1938; *Submarine Patrol* 1938; *The Hound of the Baskervilles* 1939; *The Little Princess* 1939; *Stanley and Livingstone* 1939; *Little Old New York* 1940; *I Was an Adventuress* 1940; *The Yellow Canary* 1943; *Don't Take It to Heart* 1944; *Gaiety George* 1946; *Forever Amber* 1947; *The Fan* 1949; *Now Barabbas Was a Robber* 1949; *Shadow of the Eagle* 1950; *Lorna Doone* 1951; *The Bandits of Corsica* 1953; *Captain Scarlett* 1953; *Contraband Spain* 1955; *Beyond the Curtain* 1960; *Sword of Sherwood Forest* 1960; *The Blood of Fu Manchu* 1968; *The Castle of Fu Manchu* 1968; *Tales from the Crypt* 1972
Greenleaf, Raymond *All the King's Men* 1949; *Slattery's Hurricane* 1949; *Harriet Craig* 1950; *Storm Warning* 1950; *A Millionaire for Christy* 1951; *Angel Face* 1953; *The Bandits of Corsica* 1953; *Three Sailors and a Girl* 1953
Greenquist, Brad *Pet Sematary* 1989; *The Yearling* 1994; *In the Shadow of Evil* 1995
Greenstreet, Sydney *The Maltese Falcon* 1941; *Across the Pacific* 1942; *Casablanca* 1942; *Background to Danger* 1943; *Between Two Worlds* 1944; *The Conspirators* 1944; *Hollywood Canteen* 1944; *The Mask of Dimitrios* 1944; *Passage to Marseille* 1944; *Christmas in Connecticut* 1945; *Conflict* 1945; *Devotion* 1946; *Three Strangers* 1946; *The Verdict* 1946; *The Hucksters* 1947; *Ruthless* 1948; *The Velvet Touch* 1948; *The Woman in White* 1948; *Flamingo Road* 1949; *It's a Great Feeling* 1949; *Malaya* 1949
Greenwood, Bruce *Destination: America* 1987; *The Little Kidnappers* 1990; *The Story of the Beach Boys: Summer Dreams* 1990; *Wild Orchid* 1990; *The Great Pretender* 1991; *The Servants of Twilight* 1991; *Passenger 57* 1992; *Rio Diablo* 1993; *Bitter Vengeance* 1994; *Exotica* 1994; *Heart of a Child* 1994; *Treacherous Beauties* 1994; *Danielle Steel's Mixed Blessings* 1995; *Dream Man* 1995; *Tell Me No Secrets* 1996; *The Sweet Hereafter* 1997; *The Absolute Truth* 1997; *Disturbing Behaviour* 1998; *The Lost Son* 1998; *Double Jeopardy* 1999; *Rules of Engagement* 2000; *Here on Earth* 2000
Greenwood, Charlotte *Palmy Days* 1931; *Parlor, Bedroom and Bath* 1931; *Down Argentine Way* 1940; *Star Dust* 1940; *Moon over Miami* 1941; *Springtime in the Rockies* 1942; *The Gang's All Here* 1943; *Home in Indiana* 1944; *Up in Mabel's Room* 1944; *Driftwood* 1946; *Oh, You Beautiful Doll* 1949; *Dangerous When Wet* 1953
Greenwood, Joan *The Gentle Sex* 1943; *The Man Within* 1947; *The October Man* 1947; *Saraband for Dead Lovers* 1948; *The Bad Lord Byron* 1949; *Kind Hearts and Coronets* 1949; *Whisky Galore!* 1949; *The Man in the White Suit* 1951; *Young Wives' Tale* 1951; *The Importance of Being Earnest* 1952; *Father Brown* 1954; *Knave of Hearts* 1954; *Moonfleet* 1955; *Stage Struck* 1958; *Mysterious Island* 1961; *The Amorous Prawn* 1962; *The Moon-Spinners* 1964; *The Hound of the Baskervilles* 1977; *The Uncanny* 1977; *The Water Babies* 1978; *Little Dorrit* 1987
Greer, Dabbs *Affair with a Stranger* 1953; *Riot in Cell Block 11* 1954; *It! The Terror from beyond Space* 1958; *The Cheyenne Social Club* 1970; *The Greatest Gift* 1974
Greer, Jane *aka* **Greer, Bettejane** *Dick Tracy* 1945; *Two O'Clock Courage* 1945; *The Falcon's Alibi* 1946; *Build My Gallows High* 1947; *Sinbad the Sailor* 1947; *They Won't Believe Me* 1947; *Station West* 1948; *The Big Steal* 1949; *The Company She Keeps* 1950; *You're in the Navy Now* 1951; *Desperate Search* 1952; *The Clown* 1952; *Run for the Sun* 1956; *Man of a Thousand Faces* 1957; *Where Love Has Gone* 1964; *Billie* 1965; *The Outfit* 1973; *Against All Odds* 1984; *Immediate Family* 1989
Gregg, Bradley *Stand by Me* 1986; *Class of 1999* 1990; *Madhouse* 1990; *Eye of the Storm* 1991; *Fire in the Sky* 1993
Gregg, Christina *Cover Girl Killer* 1959; *Rag Doll* 1960; *Don't Talk to Strange Men* 1962
Gregg, Clark *Lana in Love* 1991; *Tyson* 1995
Gregg, Everley *The Private Life of Henry VIII* 1933; *The Ghost Goes West* 1935; *Pygmalion* 1938; *Brief Encounter* 1945
Gregg, Hubert *29 Acacia Avenue* 1945; *The Root of All Evil* 1946; *The Story of Robin Hood and His Merrie Men* 1952; *The Maggie* 1953; *Doctor at Sea* 1955; *Simon and Laura* 1955
Gregg, John *Heatwave* 1983; *Ebbtide* 1994
Gregg, Virginia *Dragnet* 1954; *Love Is a Many-Splendored Thing* 1955; *Crime in the Streets* 1956; *The Hanging Tree* 1959; *Spencer's Mountain* 1963; *Two on a Guillotine* 1965; *A Walk in the Spring Rain* 1970
Greggory, Pascal *The Brontë Sisters* 1979; *Pauline at the Beach* 1983; *Lucie Aubrac* 1997; *Those Who Love Me Can Take the Train* 1998; *Time Regained* 1999
Gregorio, Rose *Five Corners* 1987; *The Last Innocent Man* 1987
Gregory, Andre *My Dinner with Andre* 1981; *Protocol* 1984; *Street Smart* 1987; *The Last Temptation of Christ* 1988; *Sisters* 1988; *The Linguini Incident* 1991; *Vanya on 42nd Street* 1994; *Last Summer in the Hamptons* 1995
Gregory, Benjamin *aka* **Gregory, Ben** *Thompson's Last Run* 1986; *Once upon a Forest* 1992
Gregory, Celia *Agatha* 1978; *The Inside Man* 1984; *The Baby of Macon* 1993
Gregory, David *Gaolbreak* 1962; *The Hi-Jackers* 1963; *The Marked One* 1963
Gregory, James *Nightfall* 1956; *The Young Stranger* 1957; *Gun Glory* 1957; *The Big Caper* 1957; *Onionhead* 1958; *Al Capone* 1959; *Hey Boy! Hey Girl!* 1959; *X-15* 1961; *The Manchurian Candidate* 1962; *Two Weeks in Another Town* 1962; *PT 109* 1963; *Twilight of Honor* 1963; *A Distant Trumpet* 1964; *Murderers' Row* 1966; *The Silencers* 1966; *The Ambushers* 1967; *Clambake* 1967; *Beneath the Planet of the Apes* 1969; *The Love God?* 1969; *The Million Dollar Duck* 1971; *Shoot Out* 1971; *The Late Liz* 1971
Gregson, John *The Lavender Hill Mob* 1951; *Angels One Five* 1952; *The Brave Don't Cry* 1952; *The Holly and the Ivy* 1952; *The Titfield Thunderbolt* 1952; *Venetian Bird* 1952; *Conflict of Wings* 1953; *Genevieve* 1953; *The Weak and the Wicked* 1953; *Three Cases of Murder* 1954; *To Dorothy, a Son* 1954; *Above Us the Waves* 1955; *Value for Money* 1955; *The Battle of the River Plate* 1956; *Jacqueline* 1956; *True as a Turtle* 1956; *Miracle in Soho* 1957; *The Captain's Table* 1958; *Rooney* 1958; *Sea of Sand* 1958; *SOS Pacific* 1959; *Faces in the Dark* 1960; *The Treasure of Monte Cristo* 1960; *The Frightened City* 1961; *Live Now – Pay Later* 1962; *Tomorrow at Ten* 1962; *Fright* 1971
Gregson Wagner, Natasha *Fathers and Sons* 1992; *The Substitute* 1993; *Tainted Blood* 1993; *Dragstrip Girl* 1994; *The Shaggy Dog* 1994; *Dead Beat* 1994; *Wes Craven's Mind Ripper* 1995; *Lost Highway* 1996; *Two Girls and a Guy* 1997; *Another Day in Paradise* 1998; *Play It to the Bone* 2000; *High Fidelity* 2000
Greig, Robert *Love Me Tonight* 1932; *Trouble in Paradise* 1932; *The Devil-Doll* 1936; *Rose Marie* 1936; *Sullivan's Travels* 1941
Greist, Kim *CHUD* 1984; *Brazil* 1985; *Manhunter* 1986; *Throw Momma from the Train* 1987; *Punchline* 1988; *Why Me?* 1990; *Payoff* 1991; *Homeward Bound: the Incredible Journey* 1993; *Roswell* 1994; *Houseguest* 1995
Grenfell, Joyce *The Demi-Paradise* 1943; *The Lamp Still Burns* 1943; *A Run for Your Money* 1949; *The Happiest Days of Your Life* 1950; *Stage Fright* 1950; *Laughter in Paradise* 1951; *The Pickwick Papers* 1952; *Genevieve* 1953; *The Million Pound Note* 1953; *The Belles of St Trinian's* 1954; *Forbidden Cargo* 1954; *The Good Companions* 1956; *Blue Murder at St Trinian's* 1957; *Happy Is the Bride* 1958; *The Pure Hell of St Trinian's* 1960; *The Americanization of Emily* 1964; *The Yellow Rolls-Royce* 1964
Grenier, Zach *Liebestraum* 1991; *Gang in Blue* 1996; *Maximum Risk* 1996
Gress, Googy *Maxie* 1985; *Promised Land* 1988; *Vibes* 1988
Grey, Anne *Number Seventeen* 1932; *Bonnie Scotland* 1935
Grey, Denise *Devil in the Flesh* 1946; *Carve Her Name with Pride* 1958
Grey, Jennifer *Red Dawn* 1984; *American Flyers* 1985; *Ferris Bueller's Day Off* 1986; *Dirty Dancing* 1987; *Light Years* 1988; *Bloodhounds of Broadway* 1989; *Criminal Justice* 1990; *Murder in Mississippi* 1990; *Wind* 1992; *A Case for Murder* 1993; *The West Side Waltz* 1995; *Lover's Knot* 1995; *Outrage* 1998
Grey, Joel *Cabaret* 1972; *Buffalo Bill and the Indians, or Sitting Bull's History Lesson* 1976; *The Seven-Per-Cent Solution* 1976; *Remo – Unarmed and Dangerous* 1985; *Kafka* 1991; *Marilyn and Me* 1991; *The Music of Chance* 1993
Grey, Nan *Dracula's Daughter* 1936; *Three Smart Girls* 1937; *The Storm* 1938; *Tower of London* 1939; *The Invisible Man Returns* 1940
Grey, Shirley *Back Street* 1932; *The Hurricane Express* 1932; *The Little Giant* 1933
Grey, Virginia *Another Thin Man* 1939; *Broadway Serenade* 1939; *Thunder Afloat* 1939; *The Big Store* 1941; *Mr and Mrs North* 1941; *Whistling in the Dark* 1941; *Grand Central Murder* 1942; *Tarzan's New York Adventure* 1942; *Sweet Rosie O'Grady* 1943; *Flame of the Barbary Coast* 1945; *So This Is New York* 1948; *The Bullfighter and the Lady* 1951; *Slaughter Trail* 1951; *All That Heaven Allows* 1955; *The Rose Tattoo* 1955; *Crime of Passion* 1957; *Jeanne Eagels* 1957; *The Restless Years* 1958; *No Name on the Bullet* 1959; *Portrait in Black* 1960; *Bachelor in Paradise* 1961; *Back Street* 1961; *The Naked Kiss* 1964; *Love Has Many Faces* 1965
Greyeyes, Michael *Geronimo* 1993; *Dance Me Outside* 1994
Grieco, Richard *Mobsters* 1991; *Teen Agent* 1991; *Born to Run* 1993; *Dangerous Desire* 1993; *Suspicious Agenda* 1994; *The Demolitionist* 1995; *It Was Him or Us* 1995; *A Vow to Kill* 1995; *Circuit Breaker* 1996; *When Time Expires* 1997; *A Night at the Roxbury* 1998
Griem, Helmut *The Damned* 1969; *The McKenzie Break* 1970; *Cabaret* 1972; *Ludwig* 1973; *Breakthrough* 1978; *Germany in Autumn* 1978; *Les Rendez-vous d'Anna* 1978; *The Second Victory* 1986
Grier, David Alan *Streamers* 1983; *A Soldier's Story* 1984; *Beer* 1985; *Amazon Women on the Moon* 1987; *Boomerang* 1992; *Blankman* 1994; *In the Army Now* 1994; *Jumanji* 1995; *Top of the World* 1997; *McHale's Navy* 1997; *A Saintly Switch* 1999; *Return to Me* 2000
Grier, Pam *The Big Doll House* 1971; *Women in Cages* 1972; *Black Mama, White Mama* 1972; *The Big Bird Cage* 1972; *Coffy* 1973; *Twilight People* 1973; *Scream Blacula Scream* 1973; *Foxy Brown* 1974; *Friday Foster* 1975; *Drum* 1976; *Greased Lightning* 1977; *Fort Apache, the Bronx* 1981; *Tough Enough* 1982; *Something Wicked This Way Comes* 1983; *Badge of the Assassin* 1985; *Stand Alone* 1985; *On the Edge* 1985; *The Allnighter* 1987; *Nico* 1988; *The Package* 1989; *Class of 1999* 1990; *Shattered Silence* 1992; *Escape from LA* 1996; *Original Gangstas* 1996; *Serial Killer* 1996; *Jackie Brown* 1997; *Jawbreaker* 1999; *Holy Smoke* 1999; *In Too Deep* 1999; *Snow Day* 2000
Grier, Rosey *aka* **Grier, Roosevelt** *The Thing with Two Heads* 1972; *Skyjacked* 1972; *The Glove* 1978
Gries, Jonathan *aka* **Gries, Jon** *TerrorVision* 1986; *Fright Night Part 2* 1988; *Kill Me Again* 1989; *Pucker Up and Bark Like a Dog* 1989; *Get Shorty* 1995; *Casualties* 1997
Grieve, Helen *The Overlanders* 1946; *Bush Christmas* 1947
Grifasi, Joe *On the Yard* 1978; *Something Short of Paradise* 1979; *Hide in Plain Sight* 1980; *Still of the Night* 1982; *F/X* 1985; *The Feud* 1989; *Primary Motive* 1992; *Benny and Joon* 1993; *Heavy* 1995; *Shadow of a Doubt* 1995; *One Fine Day* 1996; *Sunday* 1997
Griffeth, Simone *Death Race 2000* 1975; *Hot Target* 1985; *The Patriot* 1986
Griffies, Ethel *We Live Again* 1934; *Crackerjack* 1938; *Stranger on the Third Floor* 1940; *Billy Liar* 1963; *The Birds* 1963
Griffin, David *The Blood Beast Terror* 1967; *Trog* 1970
Griffin, Eddie *The Meteor Man* 1993; *The Walking Dead* 1995; *Deuce Bigalow: Male Gigolo* 1999
Griffin, Josephine *The Man Who Never Was* 1955; *Postmark for Danger* 1955; *The Extra Day* 1956; *The Spanish Gardener* 1956
Griffin, Lynne *Black Christmas* 1974; *Strange Brew* 1983
Griffin, Merv *So This Is Love* 1953; *The Boy from Oklahoma* 1954; *Phantom of the Rue Morgue* 1954; *Hello Down There* 1969; *Slapstick of Another Kind* 1982; *The Lonely Guy* 1984
Griffin, Robert *aka* **Griffin, Robert E** *Barricade* 1950; *Gunsight Ridge* 1957; *Monster from Green Hell* 1958
Griffith, Andy *A Face in the Crowd* 1957; *Onionhead* 1958; *No Time for Sergeants* 1958; *The Second Time Around* 1961; *Angel in My Pocket* 1968; *Hearts of the West* 1975; *Salvage* 1979; *Rustler's Rhapsody* 1985; *Under the Influence* 1986; *The Gift of Love* 1994; *Lethal Intent* 1995; *Spy Hard* 1996
Griffith, Anthony *Panther* 1995; *Tales from the Hood* 1995; *Dead Man's Curve* 1997
Griffith, Gordon *Tarzan of the Apes* 1918; *Little Annie Rooney* 1925
Griffith, Hugh *Neutral Port* 1940; *Kind Hearts and Coronets* 1949; *The Last Days of Dolwyn* 1949; *A Run for Your Money* 1949; *Gone to Earth* 1950; *The Titfield Thunderbolt* 1952; *The Beggar's Opera* 1953; *The Sleeping Tiger* 1954; *Passage Home* 1955; *The Good Companions* 1956; *Lucky Jim* 1957; *Ben-Hur* 1959; *Exodus* 1960; *The Day They Robbed the Bank of England* 1960; *The Counterfeit Traitor* 1962; *Mutiny on the Bounty* 1962; *Term of Trial* 1962; *The Inspector* 1962; *Hide and Seek* 1963; *Tom Jones* 1963;

Radio Times ACTORS' INDEX

The Bargee 1964; *The Amorous Adventures of Moll Flanders* 1965; *How to Steal a Million* 1966; *Oh Dad, Poor Dad, Mama's Hung You in the Closet and I'm Feelin' So Sad* 1967; *On My Way to the Crusades, I Met a Girl Who...* 1967; *The Sailor from Gibraltar* 1967; *The Fixer* 1968; *Oliver!* 1968; *Cry of the Banshee* 1970; *Start the Revolution without Me* 1970; *The Abominable Dr Phibes* 1971; *Who Slew Auntie Roo?* 1971; *Dr Phibes Rises Again* 1972; *Craze* 1973; *The Final Programme* 1973; *Take Me High* 1973; *What?* 1973; *Luther* 1974; *Legend of the Werewolf* 1974; *The Passover Plot* 1976; *Casanova & Co* 1976
Griffith, James *Apache Drums* 1951; *Red Skies of Montana* 1952; *Tribute to a Bad Man* 1956; *Bullwhip* 1958; *Lorna* 1964; *Seven Alone* 1974; *The Legend of Sleepy Hollow* 1980
Griffith, Kenneth *Blue Scar* 1947; *The Shop at Sly Corner* 1948; *Waterfront* 1950; *The Prisoner* 1955; *The Two-Headed Spy* 1958; *Circus of Horrors* 1960; *A French Mistress* 1960; *Rag Doll* 1960; *The Painted Smile* 1961; *Payroll* 1961; *Only Two Can Play* 1962; *Rotten to the Core* 1965; *The Bobo* 1967; *The Whisperers* 1967; *Great Catherine* 1968; *The Gamblers* 1969; *Revenge* 1971; *The House in Nightmare Park* 1973; *Callan* 1974; *S*P*Y*S* 1974; *Sky Riders* 1976; *Who Dares Wins* 1982; *The Englishman Who Went up a Hill, but Came down a Mountain* 1995
Griffith, Kristin *Interiors* 1978; *The Europeans* 1979
Griffith, Melanie *The Harrad Experiment* 1973; *The Drowning Pool* 1975; *Night Moves* 1975; *Smile* 1975; *Joyride* 1977; *One on One* 1977; *Roar* 1981; *Body Double* 1984; *Fear City* 1984; *Something Wild* 1986; *Stormy Monday* 1987; *Cherry 2000* 1988; *The Milagro Beanfield War* 1988; *Working Girl* 1988; *The Bonfire of the Vanities* 1990; *In the Spirit* 1990; *Pacific Heights* 1990; *Women and Men: Stories of Seduction* 1990; *Paradise* 1991; *Shining Through* 1992; *A Stranger among Us* 1992; *Born Yesterday* 1993; *Milk Money* 1994; *Nobody's Fool* 1994; *Now and Then* 1995; *Two Much* 1995; *Mulholland Falls* 1996; *Lolita* 1997; *Another Day in Paradise* 1998; *Celebrity* 1998; *Shadow of Doubt* 1998; *Crazy in Alabama* 1999; *RKO 281* 1999
Griffith, Raymond *Hands Up!* 1926; *All Quiet on the Western Front* 1930
Griffith, Thomas Ian *The Karate Kid III* 1989; *Rock Hudson* 1990; *Excessive Force* 1993; *Beyond Forgiveness* 1994; *Crackerjack* 1994; *Hollow Point* 1996; *Kull the Conqueror* 1997; *John Carpenter's Vampires* 1998; *The Unexpected Mrs Pollifax* 1999
Griffith, Tom *The Alien Factor* 1977; *The Alien Factor* 1977
Griffith, Tracy *Fast Food* 1989; *The First Power* 1990; *The Finest Hour* 1991; *Skeeter* 1993; *All Tied Up* 1994
Griffiths, Derek *Rentadick* 1972; *Rising Damp* 1980
Griffiths, Jane *The Million Pound Note* 1953; *The Green Scarf* 1954; *The Traitor* 1957; *Tread Softly Stranger* 1958; *The Impersonator* 1962; *Dead Man's Evidence* 1962
Griffiths, Linda *Lianna* 1983; *Mama's Going to Buy You a Mockingbird* 1988; *A Town Torn Apart* 1992
Griffiths, Rachel *Muriel's Wedding* 1994; *Jude* 1996; *To Have & to Hold* 1996; *Cosi* 1996; *Children of the Revolution* 1996; *My Best Friend's Wedding* 1997; *My Son the Fanatic* 1997; *Divorcing Jack* 1998; *Hilary and Jackie* 1998; *Among Giants* 1998; *Since You've Been Gone* 1998; *Me Myself I* 1999
Griffiths, Richard *Chariots of Fire* 1981; *Gorky Park* 1983; *Greystoke: the Legend of Tarzan, Lord of the Apes* 1984; *A Private Function* 1984; *Shanghai Surprise* 1986; *Withnail & I* 1986; *King Ralph* 1991; *The Naked Gun 2 ½: the Smell of Fear* 1991; *Blame It on the Bellboy* 1992; *Funny Bones* 1994; *Guarding Tess* 1994; *Sleepy Hollow* 1999
Griggs, Camila *Forced Vengeance* 1982; *Bar Girls* 1994
Griggs, Jeff *Hit the Dutchman* 1992; *Double Suspicion* 1993
Grimaldi, Dan *Don't Go in the House* 1979; *Joey* 1985
Grimes, Frank *The Outsider* 1979; *Britannia Hospital* 1982; *The Whales of August* 1987; *Crystalstone* 1988; *The Dive* 1989
Grimes, Gary *Summer of '42* 1971; *The Culpepper Cattle Co* 1972; *Cahill, United States Marshal* 1973; *Class of '44* 1973; *The Spikes Gang* 1974; *Gus* 1976
Grimes, Scott *The Night They Saved Christmas* 1984; *Critters* 1986; *Bring Me the Head of Dobie Gillis* 1988; *Critters 2: the Main Course* 1988
Grimes, Tammy *Three Bites of the Apple* 1967; *Somebody Killed Her Husband* 1978; *The Runner Stumbles* 1979; *Can't Stop the Music* 1980; *The Last Unicorn* 1980; *America* 1986; *High Art* 1998
Grimm, Oliver *The Magnificent Rebel* 1961; *Reach for Glory* 1962
Grimm, Tim *Overkill: the Aileen Wuornos Story* 1992; *Precious Victims* 1993
Grinberg, Anouk *Merci la Vie* 1991; *A Self-Made Hero* 1995; *Mon Homme* 1996
Grinko, Nikolai *Andrei Rublev* 1966; *Stalker* 1979
Grizzard, George *Advise and Consent* 1962; *Warning Shot* 1967; *Happy Birthday, Wanda June* 1971; *Comes a Horseman* 1978; *Seems like Old Times* 1980; *The Man with the Deadly Lens* 1982; *Bachelor Party* 1984; *Embassy* 1985; *David: the David Rothenberg Story* 1988; *False Witness* 1989; *Caroline?* 1990; *Shattering the Silence* 1992; *Triumph over Disaster: the Hurricane Andrew Story* 1993
Grodin, Charles *The Heartbreak Kid* 1972; *11 Harrowhouse* 1974; *King Kong* 1976; *Thieves* 1977; *Heaven Can Wait* 1978; *Just Me and You* 1978; *Sunburn* 1979; *It's My Turn* 1980; *Seems like Old Times* 1980; *The Great Muppet Caper* 1981; *The Incredible Shrinking Woman* 1981; *The Lonely Guy* 1984; *The Woman in Red* 1984; *Movers and Shakers* 1985; *Ishtar* 1987; *The Couch Trip* 1988; *Midnight Run* 1988; *You Can't Hurry Love* 1988; *Taking Care of Business* 1990; *Beethoven* 1992; *Beethoven's 2nd* 1993; *Dave* 1993; *Heart and Souls* 1993; *So I Married an Axe Murderer* 1993; *Clifford* 1994; *My Summer Story* 1994
Grody, Kathryn *Parents* 1988; *The Lemon Sisters* 1989
Grogan, Clare *aka* **Grogan, C P** *Gregory's Girl* 1980; *Comfort and Joy* 1984
Groh, David *Smash-Up on Interstate 5* 1976; *Murder at the Mardi Gras* 1978; *A Hero Ain't Nothin' but a Sandwich* 1978; *Hot Shot* 1986; *Broken Vows* 1987; *Illegal in Blue* 1995
Groom, Sam *The Baby Maker* 1970; *Run for the Roses* 1978; *The Day the Loving Stopped* 1981
Gross, Arye *Just One of the Guys* 1985; *Soul Man* 1986; *House II: the Second Story* 1987; *Into the Homeland* 1987; *The Experts* 1989; *Coupe de Ville* 1990; *Shaking the Tree* 1990; *For the Boys* 1991; *A Midnight Clear* 1991; *Hexed* 1993; *The Opposite Sex and How to Live with Them* 1993; *Confessions: Two Faces of Evil* 1994; *Mother Night* 1996
Gross, Edan *And You Thought Your Parents Were Weird* 1991; *Best of the Best II* 1992
Gross, Mary *Casual Sex?* 1988; *The Couch Trip* 1988; *Feds* 1988; *Troop Beverly Hills* 1989
Gross, Michael *FDR: the Last Year* 1980; *Right to Die* 1987; *Big Business* 1988; *In the Line of Duty: the FBI Murders* 1988; *A Connecticut Yankee in King Arthur's Court* 1989; *Tremors* 1989; *Vestige of Honor* 1990; *Cool as Ice* 1991; *In the Line of Duty: the Twilight Murders* 1991; *With a Vengeance* 1992; *Alan & Naomi* 1992; *Snowbound* 1993; *Behind Closed Doors* 1994; *In the Line of Duty: the Price of Vengeance* 1994; *Awake to Danger* 1995; *Deceived by Trust* 1995; *Tremors 2: Aftershocks* 1995; *Ed McBain's 87th Precinct: Ice* 1996; *Hijacked: Flight 285* 1996; *Sometimes They Come Back... Again* 1996; *Ed McBain's 87th Precinct: Heatwave* 1997
Gross, Paul *Cold Comfort* 1989; *Aspen Extreme* 1993; *Whale Music* 1994
Grossmann, Mechthild *Berlin Alexanderplatz* 1980; *Seduction: the Cruel Woman* 1985
Grove, Richard *Army of Darkness* 1993; *Scanner Cop* 1994
Grover, Edward *Report to the Commissioner* 1975; *Strike Force* 1975
Groves, Fred *Sally in Our Alley* 1931; *The Ghost Camera* 1933; *The Challenge* 1938; *An Ideal Husband* 1947
Groves, Marianne *Fausto* 1992; *The Chambermaid on the Titanic* 1997
Grubb, Robert *My Brilliant Career* 1979; *Gallipoli* 1981; *Remember Me* 1985
Grubbs, Gary *The Burning Bed* 1984; *Convicted* 1986; *Foxfire* 1987; *JFK* 1991; *Murder on the Rio Grande* 1993; *Gone Fishin'* 1997; *The Astronaut's Wife* 1999
Gruffudd, Ioan *Wilde* 1997; *Solomon and Gaenor* 1998
Gruner, Mark *Fantastic Planet* 1973; *Jaws 2* 1978
Gruner, Olivier *Nemesis* 1993; *Automatic* 1994; *Savage* 1995; *Mars* 1996; *Mercenary* 1997
Guadagni, Nicky *White Room* 1990; *We the Jury* 1996; *Cube* 1997; *Rescuers: Stories of Courage – Two Women* 1997
Guard, Christopher *A Little Night Music* 1977; *The Lord of the Rings* 1978; *Dead Man's Folly* 1986; *The Haunting of Helen Walker* 1995
Guard, Dominic *The Go-Between* 1971; *Bequest to the Nation* 1972; *Picnic at Hanging Rock* 1975; *Absolution* 1978; *The Lord of the Rings* 1978; *An Unsuitable Job for a Woman* 1981
Guardino, Harry *Houseboat* 1958; *The Five Pennies* 1959; *Pork Chop Hill* 1959; *Five Branded Women* 1960; *King of Kings* 1961; *Hell Is for Heroes* 1962; *The Pigeon That Took Rome* 1962; *Rhino!* 1964; *The Adventures of Bullwhip Griffin* 1967; *Valley of Mystery* 1967; *Madigan* 1968; *Jigsaw* 1968; *The Hell with Heroes* 1968; *Lovers and Other Strangers* 1970; *Dirty Harry* 1971; *They Only Kill Their Masters* 1972; *Capone* 1975; *Whiffs* 1975; *The Enforcer* 1976; *St Ives* 1976; *Rollercoaster* 1977; *No Margin for Error* 1978; *Matilda* 1978; *Goldengirl* 1979; *Any Which Way You Can* 1980; *The Neon Empire* 1989
Guastaferro, Vincent *Nitti: the Enforcer* 1988; *LA Takedown* 1989; *Homicide* 1991; *Tagget* 1991; *Eyes of an Angel* 1991; *Sweet and Lowdown* 1999
Guérin, François *Mitsou* 1957; *Eyes without a Face* 1959
Guerra, Blanca *Separate Vacations* 1986; *Santa Sangre* 1989; *Danzón* 1991
Guerra, Castulo *Stick* 1985; *Terminator 2: Judgment Day* 1991; *For the Future: the Irvine Fertility Scandal* 1996
Guerra, Saverio *The Winner* 1997; *Summer of Sam* 1999
Guerrero, Evelyn *Cheech & Chong's Next Movie* 1980; *Cheech & Chong's Nice Dreams* 1981; *Things Are Tough All Over* 1982
Guest, Christopher *Girlfriends* 1978; *The Long Riders* 1980; *Heartbeeps* 1981; *This Is Spinal Tap* 1984; *Little Shop of Horrors* 1986; *The Princess Bride* 1987; *Beyond Therapy* 1987; *Sticky Fingers* 1988; *Waiting for Guffman* 1996
Guest, Lance *Halloween II* 1981; *I Ought to Be in Pictures* 1982; *Confessions of a Married Man* 1983; *The Last Starfighter* 1984; *The Roommate* 1984; *Jaws the Revenge* 1987; *The Wizard of Loneliness* 1988
Guest, Nicholas *The Long Riders* 1980; *The Return of Sherlock Holmes* 1987; *Timescape* 1991; *Wind Dancer* 1991; *Knights* 1993; *Forever* 1993; *Adrenalin: Fear the Rush* 1995; *Night Hunter* 1995
Guevara, Nacha *Miss Mary* 1986; *The Dark Side of the Heart* 1992
Gugino, Carla *Murder without Motive* 1992; *Son in Law* 1993; *This Boy's Life* 1993; *Motorcycle Gang* 1994; *The War at Home* 1996; *Snake Eyes* 1998; *Judas Kiss* 1998
Guidall, George *Golden Gate* 1994; *The Impostors* 1998
Guilbert, Jean-Claude *Au Hasard, Balthazar* 1966; *Mouchette* 1966
Guild, Nancy *Give My Regards to Broadway* 1948; *Black Magic* 1949; *Abbott and Costello Meet the Invisible Man* 1951
Guilfoyle, Paul *Winterset* 1936; *The Adventures of Michael Strogoff* 1937; *Behind the Headlines* 1937; *Super-Sleuth* 1937; *The Woman I Love* 1937; *Flight from Glory* 1937; *Law of the Underworld* 1938; *The Saint in New York* 1938; *The Saint Takes Over* 1940; *Remember the Night* 1940; *The Saint in Palm Springs* 1941; *The Woman on Pier 13* 1949; *Apache* 1954; *Chief Crazy Horse* 1955; *Billy Galvin* 1986; *Howard, a New Breed of Hero* 1986; *Dealers* 1989; *Cadillac Man* 1990; *The Great Pretender* 1991; *Those Secrets* 1991; *True Colors* 1991; *Disaster at Valdez* 1992; *Final Analysis* 1992; *Notorious* 1992; *Mother's Boys* 1993; *Amelia Earhart: the Final Flight* 1994; *Little Odessa* 1994; *Celtic Pride* 1996; *Extreme Measures* 1996; *Striptease* 1996; *Air Force One* 1997; *LA Confidential* 1997; *Primary Colors* 1998
Guillaume, Robert *Seems like Old Times* 1980; *Prince Jack* 1984; *Wanted Dead or Alive* 1986; *Lean on Me* 1989; *The Penthouse* 1989; *Death Warrant* 1990; *The Meteor Man* 1993; *Greyhounds* 1994; *The Lion King* 1994; *Panic in the Skies!* 1996; *Run for the Dream: the Gail Devers Story* 1996; *His Bodyguard* 1998
Guillen-Cuervo, Fernando *aka* **Guillen, Fernando** *La Señora* 1987; *Women on the Verge of a Nervous Breakdown* 1988; *The Ages of Lulu* 1990; *A Business Affair* 1993; *Mouth to Mouth* 1995
Guinan, Francis *Mortal Sins* 1992; *Shining Through* 1992; *Guinevere* 1999
Guinee, Tim *Tai-Pan* 1986; *American Blue Note* 1989; *Once Around* 1991; *Follow the River* 1995; *Black Day Blue Night* 1995; *The Pompatus of Love* 1995; *Lily Dale* 1996; *The Three Lives of Karen* 1997; *John Carpenter's Vampires* 1998
Guinness, Alec *Evensong* 1934; *Great Expectations* 1946; *Oliver Twist* 1948; *Kind Hearts and Coronets* 1949; *A Run for Your Money* 1949; *Last Holiday* 1950; *The Mudlark* 1950; *The Lavender Hill Mob* 1951; *The Man in the White Suit* 1951; *The Card* 1952; *The Captain's Paradise* 1953; *The Malta Story* 1953; *Father Brown* 1954; *To Paris with Love* 1954; *The Ladykillers* 1955; *The Prisoner* 1955; *The Swan* 1956; *Barnacle Bill* 1957; *The Bridge on the River Kwai* 1957; *The Horse's Mouth* 1958; *Our Man in Havana* 1959; *The Scapegoat* 1959; *Tunes of Glory* 1960; *A Majority of One* 1961; *Damn the Defiant!* 1962; *Lawrence of Arabia* 1962; *The Fall of the Roman Empire* 1964; *Doctor Zhivago* 1965; *Situation Hopeless – but Not Serious* 1965; *Hotel Paradiso* 1966; *The Quiller Memorandum* 1966; *The Comedians* 1967; *Cromwell* 1970; *Scrooge* 1970; *Brother Sun, Sister Moon* 1972; *Hitler: the Last Ten Days* 1973; *Murder by Death* 1976; *Star Wars Episode IV: A New Hope* 1977; *The Empire Strikes Back* 1980; *Raise the Titanic* 1980; *Little Lord Fauntleroy* 1980; *Lovesick* 1983; *Return of the Jedi* 1983; *A Passage to India* 1984; *A Handful of Dust* 1987; *Little Dorrit* 1987; *Kafka* 1991; *Mute Witness* 1995
Guiomar, Julien *King of Hearts* 1966; *The Thief of Paris* 1967; *Take It Easy* 1971; *Mado* 1976; *Double Dare* 1981; *Le Cop* 1985; *Léolo* 1992
Guiry, Thomas *Lassie* 1994; *Lassie* 1994; *The Four Diamonds* 1995; *Wrestling with Alligators* 1998; *Strike!* 1998; *Ride with the Devil* 1999
Guiry, Tom *The Sandlot* 1993; *Shattered Family* 1993

Colors 1998; Dallas: War of the Ewings 1998

Hagon, Garrick The Message 1976; Revolver 1992

Hahn, Archie Meatballs 2 1984; Amazon Women on the Moon 1987

Hahn, Jess The Sign of Leo 1959; Cartouche 1961; The Trial 1962; Topkapi 1964; The Night of the Following Day 1968

Haid, Charles Oliver's Story 1978; Altered States 1980; Divorce Wars 1982; Cop 1988; The Great Escape II: the Untold Story 1988; The Rescue 1988; A Deadly Silence 1989; Freeze Frame 1989; Man against the Mob: the Chinatown Murders 1989; The Revenge of Al Capone 1989; Fire and Rain 1989; A Cop for the Killing 1990; Nightbreed 1990; Storyville 1992; For Their Own Good 1993; Cooperstown 1993; Broken Trust 1995

Haig, Sid THX 1138 1971; The Big Doll House 1971; Black Mama, White Mama 1972; The Big Bird Cage 1972; Coffy 1973; Chu Chu and the Philly Flash 1981; Lambada! The Forbidden Dance 1990; Genuine Risk 1990

Haigh, Kenneth My Teenage Daughter 1956; High Flight 1957; Cleopatra 1963; A Hard Day's Night 1964; The Deadly Affair 1966; A Lovely Way to Go 1968; Eagle in a Cage 1971; Robin and Marian 1976; The Bitch 1979; Wild Geese II 1985; Shuttlecock 1991

Haim, Corey Firstborn 1984; Murphy's Romance 1985; A Time to Live 1985; Silver Bullet 1985; Lucas 1986; The Lost Boys 1987; License to Drive 1988; Watchers 1988; Dream a Little Dream 1989; The Dream Machine 1990; Prayer of the Rollerboys 1990; Fast Getaway 1991; The Double O Kid 1992; Oh, What a Night 1992; Blown Away 1992; Just One of the Girls 1993; National Lampoon's Last Resort 1994

Haines, Donald No Greater Glory 1934; That Gang of Mine 1940; Pride of the Bowery 1941; Spooks Run Wild 1941

Haines, Larry The Odd Couple 1968; The Seven-Ups 1973

Haines, Patricia The Night Caller 1965; Walk a Crooked Path 1969

Haines, William Little Annie Rooney 1925; Sally, Irene and Mary 1925; The Tower of Lies 1925; Show People 1928

Haji Faster, Pussycat! Kill! Kill! 1965; Motor Psycho 1965; Good Morning... and Goodbye 1967

Hale, Alan The Four Horsemen of the Apocalypse 1921; Robin Hood 1922; The Covered Wagon 1923; The Leatherneck 1929; Susan Lenox: Her Fall and Rise 1931; Union Depot 1932; It Happened One Night 1934; The Little Minister 1934; The Lost Patrol 1934; Little Man, What Now? 1934; Of Human Bondage 1934; The Good Fairy 1935; The Last Days of Pompeii 1935; A Message to Garcia 1936; Our Relations 1936; God's Country and the Woman 1937; Stella Dallas 1937; The Adventures of Marco Polo 1938; The Adventures of Robin Hood 1938; Algiers 1938; Four Men and a Prayer 1938; Listen, Darling 1938; Dodge City 1939; Dust Be My Destiny 1939; The Man in the Iron Mask 1939; On Your Toes 1939; The Private Lives of Elizabeth and Essex 1939; The Fighting 69th 1940; Santa Fe Trail 1940; The

Sea Hawk 1940; They Drive by Night 1940; Virginia City 1940; Footsteps in the Dark 1941; Manpower 1941; The Strawberry Blonde 1941; Captains of the Clouds 1942; Desperate Journey 1942; Gentleman Jim 1942; Action in the North Atlantic 1943; Destination Tokyo 1943; This Is the Army 1943; The Adventures of Mark Twain 1944; Make Your Own Bed 1944; God Is My Co-Pilot 1945; Hotel Berlin 1945; Roughly Speaking 1945; The Man I Love 1946; Night and Day 1946; My Wild Irish Rose 1947; Pursued 1947; Adventures of Don Juan 1948; My Girl Tisa 1948; Always Leave Them Laughing 1949; The Inspector General 1949; South of St Louis 1949; Colt .45 1950; Rogues of Sherwood Forest 1950; Stars in My Crown 1950; Battle Hymn 1957

Hale Jr, Alan aka Hale, Alan Sweetheart of the Campus 1941; Riders in the Sky 1949; The West Point Story 1950; Sons of the Musketeers 1951; The Big Trees 1952; Wait 'til the Sun Shines, Nellie 1952; The Iron Glove 1954; A Man Alone 1955; Young at Heart 1955; Many Rivers to Cross 1955; The True Story of Jesse James 1957; Up Periscope 1959; The Iron Maiden 1962; Bullet for a Badman 1964; Hang 'em High 1968; Tiger by the Tail 1970; The Giant Spider Invasion 1975; The Fifth Musketeer 1979; Hambone and Hillie 1984

Hale, Barbara Higher and Higher 1943; The Falcon in Hollywood 1944; The Falcon Out West 1944; First Yank into Tokyo 1945; Lady Luck 1946; The Boy with Green Hair 1948; And Baby Makes Three 1949; Jolson Sings Again 1949; The Window 1949; The Jackpot 1950; Lorna Doone 1951; Last of the Comanches 1952; A Lion Is in the Streets 1953; Seminole 1953; The Lone Hand 1953; Unchained 1955; The Far Horizons 1955; Seventh Cavalry 1956; The Oklahoman 1957; The Giant Spider Invasion 1975; Big Wednesday 1978

Hale, Binnie The Phantom Light 1934; Love from a Stranger 1936

Hale, Creighton The Marriage Circle 1924; The Cat and the Canary 1927; Annie Laurie 1927; The Masquerader 1933; The Perils of Pauline 1947

Hale, Diana My Friend Flicka 1943; Thunderhead – Son of Flicka 1945

Hale, Elvi True as a Turtle 1956; Happy Is the Bride 1958; The Navy Lark 1959

Hale, Georgia The Gold Rush 1925; The Salvation Hunters 1925

Hale, Georgina The Devils 1971; Eagle in a Cage 1971; Butley 1973; Mahler 1974; The World Is Full of Married Men 1979; McVicar 1980; Castaway 1986; Beyond Bedlam 1993; Preaching to the Perverted 1997

Hale, Jean Psychomania 1964; In like Flint 1967; The St Valentine's Day Massacre 1967

Hale, Jonathan Charlie Chan at the Olympics 1937; Madame X 1937; Blondie 1938; The Saint in New York 1938; The Amazing Mr Williams 1939; Blondie Meets the Boss 1939; In Name Only 1939; The Saint Strikes Back 1939; The Saint Takes Over 1940; The Saint's Double Trouble 1940; The Saint in Palm Springs 1941; Strange Alibi 1941; Joe Smith,

American 1942; Miss Annie Rooney 1942; Footlight Glamour 1943; Hollywood Canteen 1944; Her Husband's Affairs 1947; The Vigilantes Return 1947; Silver River 1948; Strangers on a Train 1951

Hale, Louise Closser Platinum Blonde 1931; The Man Who Played God 1932; Shanghai Express 1932; The White Sister 1933; Today We Live 1933

Hale, Richard Knickerbocker Holiday 1944; None Shall Escape 1944; Abilene Town 1945; The Other Love 1947; The Man with a Cloak 1951; The Miracle of Fatima 1952; The Diamond Queen 1953; Julius Caesar 1953

Hale, Sonnie Friday the Thirteenth 1933; Evergreen 1934; First a Girl 1935; It's Love Again 1936; Let's Be Famous 1939; Fiddlers Three 1944; London Town 1946

Haley, Brian Into the Sun 1992; Baby's Day Out 1994

Haley, Jack Sitting Pretty 1933; Pigskin Parade 1936; Poor Little Rich Girl 1936; Wake Up and Live 1937; Danger – Love at Work 1937; Alexander's Ragtime Band 1938; Hold That Co-Ed 1938; Thanks for Everything 1938; Rebecca of Sunnybrook Farm 1938; The Wizard of Oz 1939; Moon over Miami 1941; Beyond the Blue Horizon 1942; Higher and Higher 1943; George White's Scandals 1945

Haley, Jackie Earle The Bad News Bears 1976; Damnation Alley 1977; The Bad News Bears Go to Japan 1978; Breaking Away 1979; Losin' It 1983

Hall, Albert aka Hall, Albert P Leadbelly 1976; Apocalypse Now 1979; Betrayed 1988; Malcolm X 1992; Rookie of the Year 1993; Devil in a Blue Dress 1995; Get on the Bus 1996; Beloved 1998

Hall, Anthony Michael National Lampoon's Vacation 1983; Sixteen Candles 1984; The Breakfast Club 1985; Weird Science 1985; Johnny Be Good 1988; Edward Scissorhands 1990; Into the Sun 1992; Six Degrees of Separation 1993; Upworld 1993; Hail Caesar 1994; Dark Secrets 1995; Hijacked: Flight 285 1996; Exit in Red 1996; The Killing Grounds 1997

Hall, Arsenio Coming to America 1988; Harlem Nights 1989; Blankman 1994

Hall, Brad Limit Up 1989; The Guardian 1990

Hall, Bug The Little Rascals 1994; The Stupids 1995; Honey, We Shrunk Ourselves 1997

Hall, Charlie The Music Box 1932; Twice Two 1933; Them Thar Hills! 1934; Tit for Tat 1934; Thicker than Water 1935

Hall, Daisy I'm Dangerous Tonight 1990; Triple Bogey on a Par Five Hole 1991

Hall, Deidre Take My Daughters, Please 1988; Woman on the Ledge 1993; Op Center 1995

Hall, Grayson Satan in High Heels 1962; The Night of the Iguana 1964; Adam at 6 AM 1970; End of the Road 1970; House of Dark Shadows 1970; Night of Dark Shadows 1971

Hall, Hanna Homecoming 1996; The Virgin Suicides 1999

Hall, Harriet Foxfire 1987; Relentless 1989

Hall, Huntz Dead End 1937; Angels with Dirty Faces 1938; Angels Wash Their Faces 1939; They Made Me a Criminal 1939; The Return of Dr X 1939; Spooks

Run Wild 1941; Clancy Street Boys 1943; Ghosts in the Night 1943; Block Busters 1944; Bowery Champs 1944; Follow the Leader 1944; Come Out Fighting 1945; Docks of New York 1945; Mr Muggs Rides Again 1945; A Walk in the Sun 1945; Jalopy 1953; The Bowery Boys Meet the Monsters 1954; Jungle Gents 1954; Jail Busters 1955; Gentle Giant 1967; Herbie Rides Again 1974; Valentino 1977; Auntie Lee's Meat Pies 1991

Hall, Irma P A Family Thing 1996; Buddy 1997; Midnight in the Garden of Good and Evil 1997; Steel 1997; Beloved 1998; Patch Adams 1998; A Lesson Before Dying 1999

Hall, James Hotel Imperial 1927; Four Sons 1928; Canary Murder Case 1929; The Saturday Night Kid 1929; Hell's Angels 1930

Hall, Jerry Running Out of Luck 1985; Batman 1989; Bejewelled 1990; Savage Hearts 1995; Diana & Me 1997

Hall, Jon aka Locher, Charles Charlie Chan in Shanghai 1935; The Hurricane 1937; Kit Carson 1940; South of Pago Pago 1940; Arabian Nights 1942; The Tuttles of Tahiti 1942; Ali Baba and the Forty Thieves 1944; Cobra Woman 1944; Lady in the Dark 1944; The Vigilantes Return 1947; China Corsair 1951; Last Train from Bombay 1952; Hell Ship Mutiny 1957; Forbidden Island 1959

Hall, Juanita South Pacific 1958; Flower Drum Song 1961

Hall, Kevin Peter One Dark Night 1982; Monster in the Closet 1983; Bigfoot and the Hendersons 1987; Predator 1987; Predator 2 1990

Hall, Philip Baker Secret Honor 1984; Three O'Clock High 1987; How I Got Into College 1989; Live Wire 1992; A Thousand Heroes 1992; Kiss of Death 1994; Hard Eight 1996; Rush Hour 1998; Psycho 1998; The Talented Mr Ripley 1999; Cradle Will Rock 1999; Magnolia 1999; The Insider 1999; Rules of Engagement 2000

Hall, Porter The Thin Man 1934; The General Died at Dawn 1936; The Petrified Forest 1936; The Plainsman 1936; Satan Met a Lady 1936; Make Way for Tomorrow 1937; True Confession 1937; Wells Fargo 1937; Men with Wings 1938; His Girl Friday 1939; Dark Command 1940; Trail of the Vigilantes 1940; Arizona 1940; Sullivan's Travels 1941; The Desperadoes 1943; Double Indemnity 1944; Going My Way 1944; The Great Moment 1944; The Miracle of Morgan's Creek 1944; Standing Room Only 1944; Murder, He Says 1945; Kiss and Tell 1945; Miracle on 34th Street 1947; Singapore 1947; That Wonderful Urge 1948; The Beautiful Blonde from Bashful Bend 1949; Intruder in the Dust 1949; Ace in the Hole 1951; Pony Express 1953; Vice Squad 1953; Return to Treasure Island 1954

Hall, Ron Double Blast 1994; Bloodsport II: The Next Kumite 1996

Hall, Ruth Monkey Business 1931; The Kid from Spain 1932; Ride Him, Cowboy 1932

Hall, Thurston The Black Room 1935; Hooray for Love 1935; The Man Who Lived Twice 1936; Theodora Goes Wild 1936; The Affairs of Annabel 1938; The Amazing Dr Clitterhouse 1938; Dancing Co-Ed 1939; The Star

Maker 1939; The Blue Bird 1940; The Lone Wolf Keeps a Date 1941; The Great Man's Lady 1942; Footlight Glamour 1943; I Dood It 1943; Without Reservations 1946; The Secret Life of Walter Mitty 1947; Up in Central Park 1948; Stagecoach Kid 1949

Hallahan, Charles Going in Style 1979; The Other Victim 1981; PK and the Kid 1982; The Thing 1982; Twilight Zone: the Movie 1983; Vision Quest 1985; J Edgar Hoover 1987; Warlock: the Armageddon 1993; Jack Reed: a Search for Justice 1994; The Rich Man's Wife 1996; Ambushed 1998

Hallam, John A Walk with Love and Death 1969; Murphy's War 1971; The Offence 1972; Dragonslayer 1981; When the Whales Came 1989; Good King Wenceslas 1994

Hallaren, Jane Hero at Large 1980; Body Heat 1981; Modern Romance 1981; Lianna 1983; A Night in the Life of Jimmy Reardon 1988

Hallatt, May The Gold Express 1955; Dangerous Afternoon 1961

Hallett, Neil The Brain Machine 1954; Can You Keep It Up for a Week? 1974

Hallick, Tom The Amazing Captain Nemo 1978; A Rare Breed 1981

Halliday, Bryant Devil Doll 1964; The Projected Man 1966; Tower of Evil 1972

Halliday, John Consolation Marriage 1931; Age of Consent 1932; Bird of Paradise 1932; Finishing School 1934; The Dark Angel 1935; Peter Ibbetson 1935; Desire 1936; Fatal Lady 1936; Arsene Lupin Returns 1938; Blockade 1938; That Certain Age 1938; Intermezzo 1939; Lydia 1941

Hallier, Lori A Woman Scorned 1992; Incident in a Small Town 1993; The Night of the Twisters 1996

Halloran, John Blood on the Sun 1945; The Deerslayer 1957

Hallyday, Johnny Detective 1985; The Iron Triangle 1988

Halop, Billy Dead End 1937; Angels with Dirty Faces 1938; Angels Wash Their Faces 1939; Dust Be My Destiny 1939; They Made Me a Criminal 1939; You Can't Get Away with Murder 1939; Tom Brown's Schooldays 1940; Dangerous Years 1947

Halpin, Luke Flipper 1963; Flipper and the Pirates 1964; Shock Waves 1975; Flipper 1996

Halprin, Daria Zabriskie Point 1970; The Jerusalem File 1972

Halsey, Brett aka Ford, Montgomery The Cry Baby Killer 1958; Return of the Fly 1959; Submarine Seahawk 1959; The Atomic Submarine 1960; Desire in the Dust 1960; Return to Peyton Place 1961; Twice Told Tales 1963; Today It's Me... Tomorrow You! 1968; Four Times That Night 1972; Back Stab 1990; Expect No Mercy 1995

Halsey, Michael Mean Guns 1996; Postmortem 1999

Halton, Charles Woman Chases Man 1937; Bluebeard's Eighth Wife 1938; Dr Cyclops 1940; Stranger on the Third Floor 1940; The Westerner 1940; Mr and Mrs Smith 1941; Across the Pacific 1942; Whispering Ghosts 1942; Because of Him 1946; Three Little Girls in Blue 1946

Hama, Mie What's Up, Tiger Lily? 1966; You Only Live Twice 1967

ACTORS' INDEX
RadioTimes

Hamel, Veronica *Cannonball* 1976; *Beyond the Poseidon Adventure* 1979; *A New Life* 1988; *She Said No* 1990; *Taking Care of Business* 1990; *Stop at Nothing* 1991; *Baby Snatcher* 1992; *The Conviction of Kitty Dodds* 1993; *A Child's Cry for Help* 1994; *Shadow of Obsession* 1994; *Here Come the Munsters* 1995; *Secrets* 1995; *In the Blink of an Eye* 1996; *Stranger in My Home* 1997
Hamill, John *The Beast in the Cellar* 1970; *Trog* 1970
Hamill, Mark *Eric* 1975; *Sarah T: Portrait of a Teenage Alcoholic* 1975; *Star Wars Episode IV: A New Hope* 1977; *Wizards* 1977; *Corvette Summer* 1978; *The Big Red One* 1980; *The Empire Strikes Back* 1980; *The Night the Lights Went Out in Georgia* 1981; *Return of the Jedi* 1983; *Slipstream* 1989; *Earth Angel* 1991; *The Guyver* 1992; *Body Bags* 1993; *Time Runner* 1993; *The Raffle* 1994; *Village of the Damned* 1995; *When Time Expires* 1997; *Hamilton* 1998
Hamilton, Alexa *Beverly Hills Connection* 1985; *Three for the Road* 1987
Hamilton, Allen *Code of Silence* 1985; *Lucky Day* 1991
Hamilton, Antony *Samson and Delilah* 1984; *Mirrors* 1985
Hamilton, Bernie *The Young One* 1960; *One Potato, Two Potato* 1964; *The Organization* 1971
Hamilton, Carrie *Hostage* 1988; *Tokyo Pop* 1988; *Single Women, Married Men* 1989; *Checkered Flag* 1990; *Cool World* 1992
Hamilton, Gay *A Challenge for Robin Hood* 1967; *Barry Lyndon* 1975
Hamilton, George *The Well* 1951; *Crime and Punishment, USA* 1959; *All the Fine Young Cannibals* 1960; *Home from the Hill* 1960; *Where the Boys Are* 1960; *Angel Baby* 1961; *By Love Possessed* 1961; *A Thunder of Drums* 1961; *Light in the Piazza* 1962; *Two Weeks in Another Town* 1962; *The Victors* 1963; *Act One* 1963; *Your Cheatin' Heart* 1964; *That Man George* 1965; *Viva Maria!* 1965; *The Long Ride Home* 1967; *Jack of Diamonds* 1967; *The Power* 1968; *Evel Knievel* 1971; *The Man Who Loved Cat Dancing* 1973; *The Dead Don't Die* 1975; *Once Is Not Enough* 1975; *The Happy Hooker Goes to Washington* 1977; *Sextette* 1978; *From Hell to Victory* 1979; *Love at First Bite* 1979; *Zorro, the Gay Blade* 1981; *Two Fathers' Justice* 1985; *Poker Alice* 1987; *The Godfather Part III* 1990; *Doc Hollywood* 1991; *Once upon a Crime* 1992; *Amore!* 1993; *Two Fathers: Justice for the Innocent* 1993; *Danielle Steel's Vanished* 1995; *Playback* 1995; *8 Heads in a Duffel Bag* 1997; *Casper Meets Wendy* 1998
Hamilton, Hale *The Champ* 1931; *Susan Lenox: Her Fall and Rise* 1931; *Strangers May Kiss* 1931; *A Successful Calamity* 1932; *Black Beauty* 1933; *After Office Hours* 1935
Hamilton, Josh *Alive* 1992; *O Pioneers!* 1992; *With Honors* 1994; *Don't Look Back* 1995; *Kicking and Screaming* 1995; *The Proprietor* 1996; *The House of Yes* 1997
Hamilton, Julie *The Fourth Wish* 1976; *Holy Smoke* 1999
Hamilton, Kipp *Good Morning, Miss Dove* 1955; *War of the Gargantuas* 1970
Hamilton, Leigh *A Man, a Woman and a Bank* 1979; *PK and the Kid* 1982
Hamilton, Linda *Children of the Corn* 1984; *The Terminator* 1984; *Black Moon Rising* 1985; *Sexpionage* 1985; *King Kong Lives* 1986; *Go toward the Light* 1988; *Mr Destiny* 1990; *Terminator 2: Judgment Day* 1991; *Silent Fall* 1994; *Separate Lives* 1995; *Shadow Conspiracy* 1996; *Dante's Peak* 1997; *On the Line* 1998; *Rescuers: Stories of Courage – Two Couples* 1998
Hamilton, Lisa Gay *Drunks* 1995; *Jackie Brown* 1997; *Beloved* 1998; *True Crime* 1999
Hamilton, Margaret *Way Down East* 1935; *Chatterbox* 1936; *The Moon's Our Home* 1936; *I'll Take Romance* 1937; *You Only Live Once* 1937; *A Slight Case of Murder* 1938; *The Wizard of Oz* 1939; *My Little Chickadee* 1940; *The Villain Still Pursued Her* 1940; *Twin Beds* 1942; *George White's Scandals* 1945; *Driftwood* 1946; *The Red Pony* 1949; *Mad Wednesday* 1950; *Wabash Avenue* 1950; *People Will Talk* 1951; *Rosie!* 1967; *The Anderson Tapes* 1971; *The Night Strangler* 1973
Hamilton, Murray *The Girl He Left Behind* 1956; *Toward the Unknown* 1956; *The Spirit of St Louis* 1957; *Houseboat* 1958; *Too Much, Too Soon* 1958; *No Time for Sergeants* 1958; *The FBI Story* 1959; *The Hustler* 1961; *An American Dream* 1966; *The Graduate* 1967; *The Boston Strangler* 1968; *The Brotherhood* 1968; *No Way to Treat a Lady* 1968; *If It's Tuesday, This Must Be Belgium* 1969; *The Harness* 1971; *Deadly Harvest* 1972; *The Way We Were* 1973; *The Drowning Pool* 1975; *Jaws* 1975; *Murder at the World Series* 1977; *Casey's Shadow* 1978; *Jaws 2* 1978; *1941* 1979; *Brubaker* 1980; *Last Days of Patton* 1986
Hamilton, Neil *Isn't Life Wonderful* 1924; *America* 1924; *Beau Geste* 1926; *The Patriot* 1928; *The Dawn Patrol* 1930; *The Return of Dr Fu Manchu* 1930; *Laughing Sinners* 1931; *The Sin of Madelon Claudet* 1931; *Strangers May Kiss* 1931; *The Animal Kingdom* 1932; *Payment Deferred* 1932; *Tarzan, the Ape Man* 1932; *What Price Hollywood?* 1932; *The Wet Parade* 1932; *Tarzan and His Mate* 1934; *Southern Roses* 1936; *The Saint Strikes Back* 1939; *Betrayed* 1944
Hamilton, Richard *Ladybug, Ladybug* 1963; *Greetings* 1968; *Pals* 1986; *Riviera* 1987; *In Country* 1989; *Plymouth* 1991; *On Deadly Ground* 1994; *The Yearling* 1994
Hamilton, Suzanna *Brimstone and Treacle* 1982; *Nineteen Eighty-Four* 1984; *Out of Africa* 1985; *Wetherby* 1985; *Johnny Bull* 1986; *Duel of Hearts* 1990; *Tale of a Vampire* 1992
Hamlett, Dilys *Assault* 1970; *Diagnosis: Murder* 1974
Hamlin, Harry *Clash of the Titans* 1981; *King of the Mountain* 1981; *Making Love* 1982; *Laguna Heat* 1987; *Dinner at Eight* 1989; *Deceptions* 1990; *Deadly Intentions... Again?* 1991; *Deliver Them from Evil: the Taking of Alta View* 1992; *Murder So Sweet* 1993; *Under Investigation* 1993; *Ebbtide* 1994; *Save Me* 1994; *Op Center* 1995; *Her Deadly Rival* 1995; *Badge of Betrayal* 1996; *The Hunted* 1998
Hammond, Earl *Satan in High Heels* 1962; *Light Years* 1988
Hammond, Kay *The Trespasser* 1929; *Abraham Lincoln* 1930; *Blithe Spirit* 1945
Hammond, Nicholas *The Sound of Music* 1965; *Spider-Man* 1977; *Trouble in Paradise* 1989
Hammond, Peter *Holiday Camp* 1947; *Vote for Huggett* 1948; *The Adventurers* 1950; *Confession* 1955; *X the Unknown* 1956
Hammond, Virginia *Anybody's Woman* 1930; *No One Man* 1932
Hamnett, Olivia *The Last Wave* 1977; *The Earthling* 1980
Hamon, Lucienne *Force Majeure* 1989; *Becoming Colette* 1991
Hampden, Walter *The Hunchback of Notre Dame* 1939; *All This, and Heaven Too* 1940; *5 Fingers* 1952; *Treasure of the Golden Condor* 1953; *Sabrina Fair* 1954; *The Silver Chalice* 1954; *The Prodigal* 1955; *Strange Lady in Town* 1955; *The Vagabond King* 1956
Hampshire, Susan *The Three Lives of Thomasina* 1963; *Night Must Fall* 1964; *Wonderful Life* 1964; *The Fighting Prince of Donegal* 1966; *The Trygon Factor* 1967; *David Copperfield* 1969; *Monte Carlo or Bust* 1969; *The Violent Enemy* 1969; *A Time for Loving* 1971; *Living Free* 1972; *Neither the Sea nor the Sand* 1972
Hampton, James *aka* **Hampton, Jim** *The Mean Machine* 1974; *WW and the Dixie Dancekings* 1975; *Hawmps* 1976; *The China Syndrome* 1979; *Condorman* 1981; *Stand by Your Man* 1981; *Teen Wolf* 1985; *Sling Blade* 1996
Hampton, Paul *Senior Prom* 1958; *More Dead than Alive* 1969; *Lady Sings the Blues* 1972; *Hit!* 1973; *Shivers* 1975; *Never Forget* 1991
Han, Maggie *The Last Emperor* 1987; *Murder in Paradise* 1990; *Open Season* 1995
Hanauer, Terri *Communion* 1989; *A Cry for Help: the Tracey Thurman Story* 1989; *The Rapture* 1991
Hanayagi, Shotaro *Story of the Late Chrysanthemums* 1939; *The Famous Sword* 1945
Hancock, Herbie *'Round Midnight* 1986; *Indecent Proposal* 1993
Hancock, John *The Black Marble* 1980; *Collision Course* 1987; *The Bonfire of the Vanities* 1990; *Why Me?* 1990; *Criminal Behaviour* 1992
Hancock, Sheila *Light Up the Sky* 1960; *The Girl on the Boat* 1962; *Carry On Cleo* 1964; *The Moon-Spinners* 1964; *Night Must Fall* 1964; *The Anniversary* 1968; *Take a Girl Like You* 1970; *The Wildcats of St Trinian's* 1980; *Buster* 1988; *Hawks* 1988; *Asterix and the Big Fight* 1989; *Three Men and a Little Lady* 1990; *A Business Affair* 1993; *Love and Death on Long Island* 1998; *Hold Back the Night* 1999
Hancock, Tony *Orders Are Orders* 1954; *The Rebel* 1960; *The Punch and Judy Man* 1962; *Those Magnificent Men in Their Flying Machines* 1965; *The Wrong Box* 1966
Hand, Mat *Smalltime* 1996; *TwentyFourSeven* 1997
Handl, Irene *Strange Boarders* 1938; *The Girl in the News* 1940; *Uncensored* 1942; *Rhythm Serenade* 1943; *Give Us the Moon* 1944; *Brief Encounter* 1945; *Adam and Evelyne* 1949; *Cardboard Cavalier* 1949; *The Perfect Woman* 1949; *Mad about Men* 1954; *A Kid for Two Farthings* 1955; *Brothers in Law* 1956; *It's Never Too Late* 1956; *Small Hotel* 1957; *Desert Mice* 1959; *I'm All Right Jack* 1959; *Doctor in Love* 1960; *A French Mistress* 1960; *Make Mine Mink* 1960; *The Night We Got the Bird* 1960; *The Pure Hell of St Trinian's* 1960; *The Rebel* 1960; *School for Scoundrels* 1960; *Two Way Stretch* 1960; *No Kidding* 1960; *Double Bunk* 1961; *Watch It, Sailor!* 1961; *Heavens Above!* 1963; *Morgan – a Suitable Case for Treatment* 1966; *Smashing Time* 1967; *Wonderwall* 1968; *The Italian Job* 1969; *Doctor in Trouble* 1970; *On a Clear Day You Can See Forever* 1970; *The Private Life of Sherlock Holmes* 1970; *For the Love of Ada* 1972; *Confessions of a Driving Instructor* 1976; *The Hound of the Baskervilles* 1977; *The Last Remake of Beau Geste* 1977; *Stand Up Virgin Soldiers* 1977; *Adventures of a Private Eye* 1977
Handley, Tommy *It's That Man Again* 1942; *Time Flies* 1944
Handy, James *Burglar* 1987; *Bird* 1988; *K-9* 1989; *Unspeakable Acts* 1990; *The Rocketeer* 1991; *Obsessed* 1992; *The OJ Simpson Story* 1995
Haney, Anne *The Thanksgiving Promise* 1986; *Liar Liar* 1997; *Psycho* 1998
Haney, Carol *Invitation to the Dance* 1956; *The Pajama Game* 1957
Hanft, Helen *Stardust Memories* 1980; *License to Drive* 1988
Hanin, Roger *A Bout de Souffle* 1959; *Rocco and His Brothers* 1960; *They Came to Rob Las Vegas* 1968; *Sweet Torture* 1971; *The Revengers* 1972; *Day of Atonement* 1993
Hankin, Larry *Thumb Tripping* 1972; *Escape from Alcatraz* 1979; *Ratboy* 1986; *Out on a Limb* 1992; *Billy Madison* 1995
Hanks, Tom *He Knows You're Alone* 1981; *Bachelor Party* 1984; *Splash* 1984; *The Man with One Red Shoe* 1985; *The Money Pit* 1985; *Volunteers* 1985; *Every Time We Say Goodbye* 1986; *Nothing in Common* 1986; *Dragnet* 1987; *Big* 1988; *Punchline* 1988; *The 'Burbs* 1989; *Turner & Hooch* 1989; *The Bonfire of the Vanities* 1990; *Joe versus the Volcano* 1990; *A League of Their Own* 1992; *Radio Flyer* 1992; *Philadelphia* 1993; *Sleepless in Seattle* 1993; *Forrest Gump* 1994; *Apollo 13* 1995; *Toy Story* 1995; *That Thing You Do!* 1996; *Saving Private Ryan* 1998; *You've Got Mail* 1998; *Toy Story 2* 1999; *The Green Mile* 1999
Hanley, Jimmy *Boys Will Be Boys* 1935; *Forever England* 1935; *Cotton Queen* 1937; *Housemaster* 1938; *Gaslight* 1940; *The Way Ahead* 1944; *29 Acacia Avenue* 1945; *Holiday Camp* 1947; *The Master of Bankdam* 1947; *Here Come the Huggetts* 1948; *It's Hard to Be Good* 1948; *The Blue Lamp* 1949; *Don't Ever Leave Me* 1949; *The Huggetts Abroad* 1949; *Room to Let* 1949; *Boys in Brown* 1949; *The Black Rider* 1954
Hanley, Katie *Godspell* 1973; *Xanadu* 1980
Hannah, Daryl *Hard Country* 1981; *Blade Runner* 1982; *Summer Lovers* 1982; *The Pope of Greenwich Village* 1984; *Splash* 1984; *The Clan of the Cave Bear* 1986; *Legal Eagles* 1986; *Roxanne* 1987; *Wall Street* 1987; *High Spirits* 1988; *Steel Magnolias* 1989; *Crazy People* 1990; *At Play in the Fields of the Lord* 1991; *Memoirs of an Invisible Man* 1992; *Attack of the 50 Ft Woman* 1993; *Grumpy Old Men* 1993; *The Little Rascals* 1994; *The Tie That Binds* 1995; *Two Much* 1995; *Grumpier Old Men* 1996; *The Last Days of Frankie the Fly* 1996; *The Gingerbread Man* 1997; *The Real Blonde* 1997; *Hi-Life* 1998; *Rear Window* 1998; *Addams Family Reunion* 1998; *My Favorite Martian* 1999
Hannah, John *Harbour Beat* 1990; *Four Weddings and a Funeral* 1994; *The Innocent Sleep* 1995; *Madagascar Skin* 1995; *The Final Cut* 1995; *The James Gang* 1997; *Resurrection Man* 1997; *Sliding Doors* 1997; *So This Is Romance?* 1997; *The Love Bug* 1997; *The Mummy* 1999; *Circus* 1999; *The Hurricane* 1999
Hannah, Page *My Man Adam* 1985; *Shag* 1988
Hann-Byrd, Adam *Little Man Tate* 1991; *Diabolique* 1996; *The Ice Storm* 1997; *Halloween H20: 20 Years Later* 1998
Hannen, Nicholas *FP1* 1932; *The Dictator* 1935
Hannigan, Alyson *My Stepmother Is an Alien* 1988; *Indecent Seduction* 1996; *Dead Man on Campus* 1998
Hanray, Lawrence *Street Song* 1935; *The Man Who Could Work Miracles* 1936; *It's Never Too Late to Mend* 1937; *Moonlight Sonata* 1937; *Mine Own Executioner* 1947
Hansen, Gale *Dead Poets Society* 1989; *Shaking the Tree* 1990; *The Finest Hour* 1991
Hansen, Gunnar *The Texas Chain Saw Massacre* 1974; *Mosquito* 1995
Hansen, Myrna *Man without a Star* 1955; *The Purple Mask* 1955; *Cult of the Cobra* 1955
Hansen, Patti *They All Laughed* 1981; *Hard to Hold* 1984
Hansen, William *The Member of the Wedding* 1952; *Fail-Safe* 1964; *Save the Tiger* 1973; *The Terminal Man* 1974
Hanson, Lars *Flesh and the Devil* 1926; *The Scarlet Letter* 1926; *The Divine Woman* 1928; *The Wind* 1928; *Heimkehr* 1928; *Walpurgis Night* 1935
Hanson, Peter *When Worlds Collide* 1951; *Darling, How Could You!* 1951; *The Savage* 1953; *A Bullet for Joey* 1955
Hanzlik, Jaromir *Cutting It Short* 1980; *The Last of the Good Old Days* 1989
Hara, Setsuko *No Regrets for Our Youth* 1946; *Late Spring* 1949; *Early Summer* 1951; *The Idiot* 1951; *Tokyo Story* 1953; *Late Autumn* 1960; *Early Autumn* 1961
Harada, Mieko *Ran* 1985; *Akira Kurosawa's Dreams* 1990
Harareet, Haya *Ben-Hur* 1959; *The Secret Partner* 1961; *The Interns* 1962
Harari, Clément *Monkeys, Go Home!* 1967; *Once in Paris* 1978; *Train of Life* 1999
Harben, Hubert *For Valour* 1937; *Victoria the Great* 1937
Harbord, Carl *Heart's Desire* 1935; *Dressed to Kill* 1946; *The Macomber Affair* 1947

RadioTimes ACTORS' INDEX

1962; *Walk on the Wild Side* 1962; *The Wonderful World of the Brothers Grimm* 1962; *The Ceremony* 1963; *The Running Man* 1963; *Of Human Bondage* 1964; *The Outrage* 1964; *Darling* 1965; *Life at the Top* 1965; *The Spy with a Cold Nose* 1966; *The Winter's Tale* 1966; *A Dandy in Aspic* 1968; *The Magic Christian* 1969; *WUSA* 1970; *Night Watch* 1973; *Welcome to Arrow Beach* 1974
Harvey, Lilian *aka* **Harvey, Lillian** *The Love Waltz* 1930; *Congress Dances* 1931
Harvey, Morris *The Love Test* 1935; *Squibs* 1935
Harvey, Paul *Advice to the Lovelorn* 1933; *The Whole Town's Talking* 1935; *The Walking Dead* 1936; *Never Say Die* 1939; *Arizona* 1940; *Side Street* 1950; *April in Paris* 1952; *Dreamboat* 1952; *Calamity Jane* 1953; *Three for the Show* 1955
Harvey, Phil *The Land Unknown* 1957; *The Monolith Monsters* 1957; *Monster on the Campus* 1958
Harvey, Rodney *Initiation* 1987; *Salsa* 1988; *My Own Private Idaho* 1991
Harvey, Terence *Gunbus* 1986; *The Phantom of the Opera* 1989
Harvey, Tom *The Luck of Ginger Coffey* 1964; *The Only Way Out Is Dead* 1970; *Strange Brew* 1983
Harvey, Verna *The Nightcomers* 1972; *Assassin* 1973
Hasegawa, Kazuo *Gate of Hell* 1953; *The Crucified Lovers* 1954; *An Actor's Revenge* 1963
Haskell, David *Godspell* 1973; *Broken Promise* 1981; *Missing Pieces* 1983; *Body Double* 1984
Haskell, Peter *The Eyes of Charles Sand* 1972; *The Phantom of Hollywood* 1974; *The Night They Took Miss Beautiful* 1977; *The Cracker Factory* 1979; *Child's Play 3* 1991
Hassall, Imogen *The Long Duel* 1966; *Bloodsuckers* 1970; *El Condor* 1970; *White Cargo* 1973
Hasse, O E *The Big Lift* 1950; *Decision before Dawn* 1951; *I Confess* 1953; *Betrayed* 1954; *Above Us the Waves* 1955; *The Vanishing Corporal* 1962; *State of Siege* 1972
Hassel, Danny *A Nightmare on Elm Street 4: The Dream Master* 1988; *A Nightmare on Elm Street 5: The Dream Child* 1989
Hasselhoff, David *Knight Rider – the Movie* 1982; *The Cartier Affair* 1984; *WB, Blue and the Bean* 1988; *Witchcraft* 1989; *Baywatch: Panic at Malibu Pier* 1989; *Fire and Rain* 1989; *Avalanche* 1994; *Ring of the Musketeers* 1994; *Gridlock* 1995; *Baywatch the Movie: Forbidden Paradise* 1995; *The Big Tease* 1999
Hassett, Marilyn *The Other Side of the Mountain* 1975; *Two-Minute Warning* 1976; *The Other Side of the Mountain – Part 2* 1978; *The Bell Jar* 1979; *Messenger of Death* 1988
Hasso, Signe *Journey for Margaret* 1942; *The Story of Dr Wassell* 1944; *The Seventh Cross* 1944; *The House on 92nd Street* 1945; *Johnny Angel* 1945; *Thieves' Holiday* 1946; *A Double Life* 1947; *Where There's Life* 1947; *Crisis* 1950; *Picture Mommy Dead* 1966; *The Magician* 1973; *A Reflection of Fear* 1973; *The Black Bird* 1975; *Sherlock Holmes in New York* 1976; *Mirrors* 1985
Hastings, Bob *Did You Hear the One about the Traveling Saleslady?* 1968; *Trapped* 1973; *The All-American Boy* 1973
Hatch, Richard *aka* **Hatch, Richard L** *Battlestar Galactica* 1978; *Charlie Chan and the Curse of the Dragon Queen* 1981; *Party Line* 1988; *Second Chance* 1995
Hatcher, Mary *Variety Girl* 1947; *Isn't It Romantic* 1948; *The Big Wheel* 1949
Hatcher, Teri *The Big Picture* 1989; *Tango and Cash* 1989; *Dead in the Water* 1991; *Soapdish* 1991; *Straight Talk* 1992; *Brain Smasher... a Love Story* 1993; *The Cool Surface* 1993; *All Tied Up* 1994; *Heaven's Prisoners* 1996; *2 Days in the Valley* 1996; *Tomorrow Never Dies* 1997; *Since You've Been Gone* 1998
Hatfield, Hurd *Dragon Seed* 1944; *The Picture of Dorian Gray* 1945; *Diary of a Chambermaid* 1946; *The Beginning or the End* 1947; *The Unsuspected* 1947; *Destination Murder* 1950; *Tarzan and the Slave Girl* 1950; *The Left Handed Gun* 1958; *El Cid* 1961; *King of Kings* 1961; *Mickey One* 1965; *Harlow* 1965; *The Boston Strangler* 1968; *Von Richthofen and Brown* 1971; *King David* 1985; *Crimes of the Heart* 1986; *Her Alibi* 1989; *Lies of the Twins* 1991
Hathaway, Noah *Battlestar Galactica* 1978; *The NeverEnding Story* 1984; *Troll* 1986
Hatosy, Shawn *The Faculty* 1998; *Outside Providence* 1999; *Anywhere but Here* 1999; *Down to You* 2000
Hatton, Raymond *A Romance of the Redwoods* 1917; *Male and Female* 1919; *The Hunchback of Notre Dame* 1923; *The Squaw Man* 1931; *Law and Order* 1932; *Vanishing Frontier* 1932; *Polly of the Circus* 1932; *Lady Killer* 1933; *The Texans* 1938; *Rough Riders' Roundup* 1939; *Frontier Horizon* 1939; *Wyoming Outlaw* 1939; *Thunder Pass* 1954; *Invasion of the Saucer Men* 1957; *Motorcycle Gang* 1957
Haudepin, Didier *L'Innocente* 1976; *Ecoute Voir...* 1978
Haudepin, Sabine *Jules et Jim* 1961; *The Last Metro* 1980; *Force Majeure* 1989
Hauer, Rutger *Turkish Delight* 1973; *Cold Blood* 1975; *Keetje Tippel* 1975; *The Wilby Conspiracy* 1975; *Soldier of Orange* 1977; *Spetters* 1980; *Nighthawks* 1981; *Chanel Solitaire* 1981; *Blade Runner* 1982; *Eureka* 1982; *The Osterman Weekend* 1983; *A Breed Apart* 1984; *Flesh + Blood* 1985; *Ladyhawke* 1985; *The Hitcher* 1986; *Wanted Dead or Alive* 1986; *The Legend of the Holy Drinker* 1988; *Bloodhounds of Broadway* 1989; *The Salute of the Jugger* 1989; *Blind Fury* 1990; *Split Second* 1991; *Wedlock* 1991; *Buffy the Vampire Slayer* 1992; *Past Midnight* 1992; *Arctic Blue* 1993; *Blind Side* 1993; *Nostradamus* 1993; *Voyage* 1993; *Amelia Earhart: the Final Flight* 1994; *The Beans of Egypt, Maine* 1994; *Beyond Forgiveness* 1994; *Fatherland* 1994; *Surviving the Game* 1994; *Blast* 1996; *Crossworlds* 1996; *Omega Doom* 1996; *Jack London's The Call of the Wild* 1996; *Hostile Waters* 1996; *Redline* 1997; *Hemoglobin* 1997; *Bone Daddy* 1998; *Simon Magus* 1998
Haun, Lindsey *Desperate Rescue* 1993; *Deep Red* 1994
Haupt, Ullrich *aka* **Haupt, Ulrich** *Morocco* 1930; *The Unholy Garden* 1931
Hauser, Cole *School Ties* 1992; *Higher Learning* 1995; *All over Me* 1996; *The Hi-Lo Country* 1998; *Pitch Black* 2000
Hauser, Fay *Marvin and Tige* 1983; *Jo Jo Dancer, Your Life Is Calling* 1986; *Candyman II: Farewell to the Flesh* 1995
Hauser, Wings *Vice Squad* 1982; *Deadly Force* 1983; *Mutant* 1984; *Tough Guys Don't Dance* 1987; *Beastmaster 2: through the Portal of Time* 1991; *Bump in the Night* 1991; *Implicated* 1994; *Tales from the Hood* 1995
Havens, Richie *Catch My Soul* 1973; *Greased Lightning* 1977; *Hearts of Fire* 1987
Haver, June *Home in Indiana* 1944; *Irish Eyes Are Smiling* 1944; *The Dolly Sisters* 1945; *Where Do We Go from Here?* 1945; *Three Little Girls in Blue* 1946; *I Wonder Who's Kissing Her Now* 1947; *Look for the Silver Lining* 1949; *Oh, You Beautiful Doll* 1949; *The Daughter of Rosie O'Grady* 1950; *Love Nest* 1951; *The Girl Next Door* 1953
Haver, Phyllis *What Price Glory* 1926; *The Way of All Flesh* 1927
Havers, Nigel *Chariots of Fire* 1981; *A Passage to India* 1984; *Burke and Wills* 1985; *The Whistle Blower* 1986; *Empire of the Sun* 1987; *Farewell to the King* 1988; *Bridge of Time* 1997
Havoc, June *Hello, Frisco, Hello* 1943; *No Time for Love* 1943; *Brewster's Millions* 1945; *Gentleman's Agreement* 1947; *Intrigue* 1947; *The Iron Curtain* 1948; *When My Baby Smiles at Me* 1948; *Can't Stop the Music* 1980; *A Return to Salem's Lot* 1987
Hawes, Keeley *The Last September* 1999; *Complicity* 1999
Hawke, Ethan *Explorers* 1985; *Dad* 1989; *Dead Poets Society* 1989; *A Midnight Clear* 1991; *Mystery Date* 1991; *White Fang* 1991; *Alive* 1992; *Rich in Love* 1992; *Waterland* 1992; *Floundering* 1994; *Reality Bites* 1994; *White Fang 2: Myth of the White Wolf* 1994; *Before Sunrise* 1995; *Search and Destroy* 1995; *Gattaca* 1997; *Great Expectations* 1997; *The Newton Boys* 1998; *Snow Falling on Cedars* 1999; *Joe the King* 1999
Hawkes, John *Rosalie Goes Shopping* 1989; *Sweet Poison* 1991; *Dead Air* 1994; *Roadracers* 1994; *Night of the Scarecrow* 1995
Hawkins, Frank *The Crooked Sky* 1957; *Information Received* 1962
Hawkins, Jack *A Shot in the Dark* 1933; *Bonnie Prince Charlie* 1948; *The Fallen Idol* 1948; *The Small Back Room* 1949; *The Adventurers* 1950; *The Black Rose* 1950; *The Elusive Pimpernel* 1950; *State Secret* 1950; *No Highway* 1951; *Angels One Five* 1952; *Home at Seven* 1952; *Mandy* 1952; *The Planter's Wife* 1952; *The Cruel Sea* 1953; *Front Page Story* 1953; *The Intruder* 1953; *The Malta Story* 1953; *The Seekers* 1954; *Land of the Pharaohs* 1955; *The Prisoner* 1955; *Touch and Go* 1955; *Fortune Is a Woman* 1956; *The Long Arm* 1956; *The Bridge on the River Kwai* 1957; *The Two-Headed Spy* 1958; *Ben-Hur* 1959; *Gideon's Day* 1959; *The League of Gentlemen* 1960; *Two Loves* 1961; *Five Finger Exercise* 1962; *Lawrence of Arabia* 1962; *Rampage* 1963; *Guns at Batasi* 1964; *The Third Secret* 1964; *Zulu* 1964; *Lord Jim* 1965; *Masquerade* 1965; *Judith* 1966; *Great Catherine* 1968; *Shalako* 1968; *Monte Carlo or Bust* 1969; *Oh! What a Lovely War* 1969; *Twinky* 1969; *The Adventures of Gerard* 1970; *Jane Eyre* 1970; *Waterloo* 1970; *Kidnapped* 1971; *When Eight Bells Toll* 1971; *Sin* 1972; *Tales That Witness Madness* 1973; *Theatre of Blood* 1973
Hawkins, Screamin' Jay *Mystery Train* 1989; *Perdita Durango* 1997
Hawley, Richard *Paper Marriage* 1991; *Captives* 1994
Hawn, Goldie *aka* **Hawn, Goldie Jeanne** *The One and Only, Genuine, Original Family Band* 1968; *Cactus Flower* 1969; *There's a Girl in My Soup* 1970; *The Heist* 1971; *Butterflies Are Free* 1972; *The Girl from Petrovka* 1974; *The Sugarland Express* 1974; *Shampoo* 1975; *The Duchess and the Dirtwater Fox* 1976; *Foul Play* 1978; *Travels with Anita* 1978; *Private Benjamin* 1980; *Seems like Old Times* 1980; *Best Friends* 1982; *Protocol* 1984; *Swing Shift* 1984; *Wildcats* 1986; *Overboard* 1987; *Bird on a Wire* 1990; *Deceived* 1991; *CrissCross* 1992; *Death Becomes Her* 1992; *HouseSitter* 1992; *Everyone Says I Love You* 1996; *The First Wives Club* 1996; *The Out-of-Towners* 1999
Haworth, Jill *The Mysteries of Paris* 1962; *It!* 1966; *The Haunted House of Horror* 1969; *Tower of Evil* 1972; *The Mutations* 1973
Hawthorne, Denys *The Chinese Connection* 1988; *Emma* 1996
Hawthorne, Nigel *Sweeney 2* 1978; *The Plague Dogs* 1982; *The Hunchback of Notre Dame* 1982; *The Chain* 1984; *The Black Cauldron* 1985; *Turtle Diary* 1985; *King of the Wind* 1989; *Freddie as FRO7* 1992; *Demolition Man* 1993; *The Madness of King George* 1995; *Richard III* 1995; *Inside* 1996; *Murder in Mind* 1996; *Twelfth Night* 1996; *Amistad* 1997; *Forbidden Territory* 1997; *Madeline* 1998; *The Object of My Affection* 1998; *The Clandestine Marriage* 1999; *The Winslow Boy* 1999; *Tarzan* 1999
Hawtrey, Charles *Where's That Fire?* 1939; *The Ghost of St Michael's* 1941; *The Goose Steps Out* 1942; *A Canterbury Tale* 1944; *Room to Let* 1949; *Brandy for the Parson* 1951; *You're Only Young Twice* 1952; *Timeslip* 1955; *The March Hare* 1956; *Carry On Sergeant* 1958; *Carry On Nurse* 1959; *Carry On Teacher* 1959; *Carry On Constable* 1960; *Carry On Regardless* 1960; *Inn for Trouble* 1960; *Please Turn Over* 1960; *Dentist on the Job* 1961; *What a Whopper!* 1961; *Carry On Cabby* 1963; *Carry On Jack* 1963; *Carry On Cleo* 1964; *Carry On Spying* 1964; *Carry On Cowboy* 1965; *Carry On – Don't Lose Your Head* 1966; *Carry On Screaming* 1966; *Carry On Follow That Camel* 1967; *Carry On Doctor* 1968; *Carry On Up the Khyber* 1968; *Carry On Again Doctor* 1969; *Carry On Camping* 1969; *Carry On Loving* 1970; *Carry On Up the Jungle* 1970; *Carry On at Your Convenience* 1971; *Carry On Henry* 1971; *Carry On Abroad* 1972; *Carry On Matron* 1972
Hay, Alexandra *Model Shop* 1969; *One Man Jury* 1978
Hay, Will *Those Were the Days* 1934; *Boys Will Be Boys* 1935; *Where There's a Will* 1936; *Windbag the Sailor* 1936; *Good Morning, Boys* 1937; *Oh, Mr Porter!* 1937; *Ask a Policeman* 1938; *Convict 99* 1938; *Hey! Hey! USA* 1938; *Old Bones of the River* 1938; *Where's That Fire?* 1939; *The Black Sheep of Whitehall* 1941; *The Ghost of St Michael's* 1941; *The Goose Steps Out* 1942; *My Learned Friend* 1943
Hayakawa, Sessue *The Cheat* 1915; *Tokyo Joe* 1949; *Three Came Home* 1950; *House of Bamboo* 1955; *The Bridge on the River Kwai* 1957; *The Geisha Boy* 1958; *Green Mansions* 1959; *Swiss Family Robinson* 1960; *Hell to Eternity* 1960
Hayashi, Marc *Chan Is Missing* 1982; *The Laserman* 1988
Hayden, Harry *The Meanest Man in the World* 1943; *The Unknown Guest* 1943; *Two Sisters from Boston* 1946; *Double Dynamite* 1951
Hayden, Linda *Taste the Blood of Dracula* 1969; *Blood on Satan's Claw* 1970; *Something to Hide* 1971; *Confessions of a Window Cleaner* 1974; *Madhouse* 1974; *Vampira* 1975; *Confessions from a Holiday Camp* 1977; *Let's Get Laid* 1977
Hayden, Nora *Plunder Road* 1957; *The Angry Red Planet* 1959
Hayden, Peter *Shaker Run* 1985; *Footrot Flats: the Dog's Tale* 1986
Hayden, Sterling *Blaze of Noon* 1947; *The Asphalt Jungle* 1950; *Hellgate* 1952; *The Star* 1953; *So Big* 1953; *Take Me to Town* 1953; *Arrow in the Dust* 1954; *Johnny Guitar* 1954; *Prince Valiant* 1954; *Suddenly* 1954; *Naked Alibi* 1954; *The City Is Dark* 1954; *The Last Command* 1955; *Timberjack* 1955; *Shotgun* 1955; *Battle Taxi* 1955; *The Killing* 1956; *The Come On* 1956; *Five Steps to Danger* 1957; *Valerie* 1957; *Zero Hour* 1957; *Crime of Passion* 1957; *The Iron Sheriff* 1957; *Terror in a Texas Town* 1958; *Dr Strangelove, or How I Learned to Stop Worrying and Love the Bomb* 1963; *Hard Contract* 1969; *Sweet Hunters* 1969; *Loving* 1970; *The Godfather* 1972; *The Final Programme* 1973; *The Long Goodbye* 1973; *1900* 1976; *King of the Gypsies* 1978; *Winter Kills* 1979; *The Outsider* 1979; *Nine to Five* 1980; *Gas* 1981; *Venom* 1982
Haydn, Richard *aka* **Rancyd, Richard** *No Time for Love* 1943; *Adventure* 1945; *Forever Amber* 1947; *The Foxes of Harrow* 1947; *The Late George Apley* 1947; *Singapore* 1947; *The Emperor Waltz* 1948; *Miss Tatlock's Millions* 1948; *Sitting Pretty* 1948; *Alice in Wonderland* 1951; *Money from Home* 1953; *Never Let Me Go* 1953; *Her Twelve Men* 1954; *Jupiter's Darling* 1955; *Twilight for the Gods* 1958; *The Lost World* 1960; *Please Don't Eat the Daisies* 1960; *Five Weeks in a Balloon* 1962; *Mutiny on the Bounty* 1962; *Clarence, the Cross-Eyed Lion* 1965; *The Sound of Music* 1965; *The Adventures of Bullwhip Griffin* 1967; *Young Frankenstein* 1974
Haydon, Julie *The Age of Innocence* 1934; *The Scoundrel* 1935; *A Family Affair* 1937
Haye, Helen *The Skin Game* 1931; *The Dictator* 1935; *The 39*

Hebert, Chris *The Last Starfighter* 1984; *The Check Is in the Mail* 1986
Heche, Anne *O Pioneers!* 1992; *The Adventures of Huck Finn* 1993; *Against the Wall* 1994; *Girls in Prison* 1994; *Milk Money* 1994; *Pie in the Sky* 1995; *Kingfish: a Story of Huey P Long* 1995; *If These Walls Could Talk* 1996; *The Juror* 1996; *Walking and Talking* 1996; *Wild Side* 1996; *Donnie Brasco* 1997; *I Know What You Did Last Summer* 1997; *Volcano* 1997; *Wag the Dog* 1997; *Return to Paradise* 1998; *Six Days Seven Nights* 1998; *Psycho* 1998
Hecht, Ben *The Scoundrel* 1935; *Specter of the Rose* 1946
Hecht, Gina *Night Shift* 1982; *Unfinished Business...* 1987; *Taking Back My Life* 1992; *One Night Stand* 1994
Heckart, Eileen *The Bad Seed* 1956; *Bus Stop* 1956; *Miracle in the Rain* 1956; *Somebody Up There Likes Me* 1956; *Hot Spell* 1958; *Heller in Pink Tights* 1960; *My Six Loves* 1962; *Up the Down Staircase* 1967; *No Way to Treat a Lady* 1968; *Butterflies Are Free* 1972; *Zandy's Bride* 1974; *The Hiding Place* 1975; *Burnt Offerings* 1976; *FDR: the Last Year* 1980; *White Mama* 1980; *Heartbreak Ridge* 1986; *Stuck with Each Other* 1989; *Triumph over Disaster: the Hurricane Andrew Story* 1993; *Breathing Lessons* 1994; *Ultimate Betrayal* 1994
Hedaya, Dan *Night of the Juggler* 1980; *Endangered Species* 1982; *Blood Simple* 1983; *The Hunger* 1983; *Tightrope* 1984; *Commando* 1985; *Courage* 1986; *Running Scared* 1986; *Wise Guys* 1986; *The Reluctant Agent* 1989; *Aunt Julia and the Scriptwriter* 1990; *Joe versus the Volcano* 1990; *The Addams Family* 1991; *The Whereabouts of Jenny* 1991; *Mr Wonderful* 1992; *Benny and Joon* 1993; *Rookie of the Year* 1993; *Based on an Untrue Story* 1993; *Clueless* 1995; *The Usual Suspects* 1995; *Daylight* 1996; *The First Wives Club* 1996; *Marvin's Room* 1996; *Freeway* 1996; *Alien: Resurrection* 1997; *A Life Less Ordinary* 1997; *The Second Civil War* 1997; *A Civil Action* 1998; *A Night at the Roxbury* 1998; *Dick* 1999; *The Hurricane* 1999
Hedin, Serene *Windwalker* 1980; *Sacred Ground* 1983; *Hawken's Breed* 1989
Hedison, David aka **Hedison, Al** *The Enemy Below* 1957; *The Fly* 1958; *Son of Robin Hood* 1958; *The Lost World* 1960; *Live and Let Die* 1973; *North Sea Hijack* 1979; *The Naked Face* 1984; *Licence to Kill* 1989
Hedley, Jack *Left, Right and Centre* 1959; *Make Mine Mink* 1960; *The Very Edge* 1962; *In the French Style* 1963; *The Scarlet Blade* 1963; *Of Human Bondage* 1964; *The Secret of Blood Island* 1964; *How I Won the War* 1967; *The Anniversary* 1968; *Goodbye, Mr Chips* 1969; *Brief Encounter* 1974
Hedren, Tippi *The Petty Girl* 1950; *The Birds* 1963; *Marnie* 1964; *Satan's Harvest* 1965; *A Countess from Hong Kong* 1967; *Mr Kingstreet's War* 1970; *Tiger by the Tail* 1970; *The Harrad Experiment* 1973; *Roar* 1981; *Deadly Spygames* 1989; *Pacific Heights* 1990; *Shadow of a Doubt*

1991; *Through the Eyes of a Killer* 1992; *The Birds II: Land's End* 1994; *Treacherous Beauties* 1994; *Inevitable Grace* 1994; *Citizen Ruth* 1996; *I Woke Up Early the Day I Died* 1998; *Replacing Dad* 1999
Heffernan, John *Puzzle of a Downfall Child* 1970; *The Sting* 1973
Heffley, Wayne *Submarine Seahawk* 1959; *Crime and Punishment, USA* 1959
Heffner, Kyle T *Flashdance* 1983; *Runaway Train* 1985
Heflin, Marta *A Star Is Born* 1976; *A Perfect Couple* 1979; *Come Back to the Five and Dime, Jimmy Dean, Jimmy Dean* 1982
Heflin, Nora *Fantastic Planet* 1973; *Chilly Scenes of Winter* 1979
Heflin, Van *A Woman Rebels* 1936; *Flight from Glory* 1937; *Back Door to Heaven* 1939; *Santa Fe Trail* 1940; *The Feminine Touch* 1941; *HM Pulham Esq* 1941; *Johnny Eager* 1941; *Grand Central Murder* 1942; *Kid Glove Killer* 1942; *Presenting Lily Mars* 1943; *The Strange Love of Martha Ivers* 1946; *Till the Clouds Roll By* 1946; *Green Dolphin Street* 1947; *Possessed* 1947; *BF's Daughter* 1948; *The Three Musketeers* 1948; *Act of Violence* 1949; *East Side, West Side* 1949; *Madame Bovary* 1949; *The Prowler* 1951; *Weekend with Father* 1951; *My Son John* 1952; *South of Algiers* 1952; *Shane* 1953; *Black Widow* 1954; *The Raid* 1954; *Woman's World* 1954; *Tanganyika* 1954; *Battle Cry* 1955; *Count Three and Pray* 1955; *Patterns* 1956; *3:10 to Yuma* 1957; *Tempest* 1959; *They Came to Cordura* 1959; *Five Branded Women* 1960; *Under Ten Flags* 1960; *Once a Thief* 1965; *Stagecoach* 1966; *The Big Bounce* 1969; *Airport* 1970
Heggie, O P *The Letter* 1929; *One Romantic Night* 1930; *East Lynne* 1931; *Smilin' Through* 1932; *Zoo in Budapest* 1933; *Anne of Green Gables* 1934; *The Count of Monte Cristo* 1934; *Midnight* 1934
Hehir, Peter *A Street to Die* 1985; *Kangaroo* 1986; *Two Friends* 1986
Heigl, Katherine *That Night* 1992; *My Father, the Hero* 1994; *Under Siege 2* 1995; *Prince Valiant* 1997; *Bride of Chucky* 1998
Heilbron, Lorna *The Creeping Flesh* 1972; *The Girl in a Swing* 1988
Heineman, Laurie *Save the Tiger* 1973; *The Lady in Red* 1979
Heinz, Gerard *Caravan* 1946; *Desperate Moment* 1953
Heitmeyer, Jayne *Hawk's Vengeance* 1996; *Sci-Fighters* 1996; *Suspicious Minds* 1997
Held, Ingrid *Gunbus* 1986; *The Last Butterfly* 1990; *Après l'Amour* 1992
Heldfond, Susan *Why Would I Lie?* 1980; *Love and Money* 1982
Helgenberger, Marg *After Midnight* 1989; *Blind Vengeance* 1990; *Death Dreams* 1991; *Hearts on Fire* 1992; *Through the Eyes of a Killer* 1992; *The Cowboy Way* 1994; *Keys* 1994; *Bad Boys* 1995; *Conundrum* 1995; *Inflammable* 1995; *Species* 1995; *Elmore Leonard's Gold Coast* 1997; *Fire Down Below* 1997; *Species II* 1998; *Erin Brockovich* 2000
Helia, Jenny *Toni* 1935; *La Bête Humaine* 1938
Hell, Erik *Port of Call* 1948; *The Rite* 1969

Heller, Ariane *Up the Sandbox* 1972; *Mixed Company* 1974
Heller, Barbara *Hey Boy! Hey Girl!* 1959; *The Comic* 1969
Heller, Randee *The Karate Kid* 1984; *The Last Fling* 1987
Hellman, Jaclyn aka **Hellman, Jacqueline** *Flight to Fury* 1966; *Two-Lane Blacktop* 1971
Helm, Anne *Follow That Dream* 1962; *The Interns* 1962; *The Iron Maiden* 1962; *The Magic Sword* 1962; *The Unkissed Bride* 1966
Helm, Brigitte *Metropolis* 1926; *The Love of Jeanne Ney* 1927; *The Wonderful Lie of Nina Petrovna* 1929
Helm, Fay *Phantom Lady* 1944; *The Falcon in San Francisco* 1945
Helm, Levon *Coal Miner's Daughter* 1980; *Best Revenge* 1983; *The Right Stuff* 1983; *The Dollmaker* 1984; *Smooth Talk* 1985; *End of the Line* 1987; *Staying Together* 1989; *Feeling Minnesota* 1996
Helmond, Katherine *Larry* 1974; *Family Plot* 1976; *Time Bandits* 1981; *Rosie: the Rosemary Clooney Story* 1982; *Brazil* 1985; *Shadey* 1985; *Overboard* 1987; *Lady in White* 1988; *Save the Dog!* 1988; *Tell Me No Lies* 1991; *Inside Monkey Zetterland* 1992; *Amore!* 1993; *Flight of the Dove* 1995; *Ms Scrooge* 1997
Helmore, Tom *Trouble along the Way* 1953; *Lucy Gallant* 1955; *Designing Woman* 1957; *Vertigo* 1958; *Count Your Blessings* 1959; *The Time Machine* 1960; *Flipper and the Pirates* 1964
Helpmann, Robert *Caravan* 1946; *The Red Shoes* 1948; *The Tales of Hoffmann* 1951; *The Big Money* 1956; *The Iron Petticoat* 1956; *The Quiller Memorandum* 1966; *Alice's Adventures in Wonderland* 1972; *Don Quixote* 1973; *The Mango Tree* 1977; *Patrick* 1978; *Puzzle* 1978
Helton, Percy *The Set-Up* 1949; *Jail Busters* 1955
Hemblen, David *Family Viewing* 1987; *Short Circuit 2* 1988; *Speaking Parts* 1989; *The Adjuster* 1991; *I Love a Man in Uniform* 1993; *Lifeline to Victory* 1993; *Brainscan* 1994; *Exotica* 1994; *Mesmer* 1994; *Hollow Point* 1996
Hembrow, Mark *High Tide* 1987; *Return to Snowy River* 1988; *Out of the Body* 1988; *The Last Island* 1990; *Redheads* 1992
Hemingway, Margaux *Lipstick* 1976; *Killer Fish* 1978; *They Call Me Bruce* 1982; *Over the Brooklyn Bridge* 1983; *Deadly Rivals* 1992
Hemingway, Mariel *Lipstick* 1976; *Manhattan* 1979; *Personal Best* 1982; *Star 80* 1983; *The Mean Season* 1985; *Creator* 1985; *Superman IV: the Quest for Peace* 1987; *Sunset* 1988; *Delirious* 1991; *Into the Badlands* 1991; *Falling from Grace* 1992; *Desperate Rescue* 1993; *Edge of Deception* 1994; *Bad Moon* 1996; *Deconstructing Harry* 1997; *Kiss of a Stranger* 1997; *Little Men* 1998; *The Sex Monster* 1998; *Road Ends* 1999
Hemmings, David *The Painted Smile* 1961; *The Wind of Change* 1961; *Some People* 1962; *Live It Up* 1963; *Two Left Feet* 1963; *The System* 1964; *Blow Up* 1966; *Barbarella* 1967; *Camelot* 1967; *The Charge of the Light Brigade* 1968; *Eye of the Devil* 1968; *The Long Day's Dying* 1968; *Only When I Larf* 1968; *Alfred the Great* 1969; *Fragment of Fear* 1970; *The Walking Stick* 1970;

The Love Machine 1971; *Unman, Wittering and Zigo* 1971; *Juggernaut* 1974; *Mister Quilp* 1975; *Blood Relatives* 1977; *The Disappearance* 1977; *Islands in the Stream* 1977; *The Prince and the Pauper* 1977; *The Squeeze* 1977; *Just a Gigolo* 1978; *Murder by Decree* 1978; *Power Play* 1978; *Thirst* 1979; *Beyond Reasonable Doubt* 1980; *Harlequin* 1980; *Man, Woman and Child* 1983; *Beverly Hills Connection* 1985; *The Rainbow* 1988
Hempel, Anouska *The Scars of Dracula* 1970; *Tiffany Jones* 1973
Hemsley, Estelle *Take a Giant Step* 1959; *America, America* 1963; *Baby the Rain Must Fall* 1965
Hemsley, Sherman *Love at First Bite* 1979; *Mr Nanny* 1992
Henderson, Albert *Greaser's Palace* 1972; *Big Top Pee-wee* 1988
Henderson, Bill *Trouble Man* 1972; *Inside Moves: the Guys from Max's Bar* 1980; *Continental Divide* 1981; *Murphy's Law* 1986; *Wisdom* 1986; *Trippin'* 1999
Henderson, Dell *The Crowd* 1928; *The Patsy* 1928; *Show People* 1928
Henderson, Don *Callan* 1974; *The Ghoul* 1975; *The Island* 1980; *The Chinese Connection* 1988; *The BFG* 1989; *As You Like It* 1992; *The Baby of Macon* 1993; *White Angel* 1993; *No Escape* 1994
Henderson, Florence *Song of Norway* 1970; *A Very Brady Christmas* 1988; *Shakes the Clown* 1991; *Fudge-a-Mania* 1995
Henderson, Jo *Lianna* 1983; *Hostile Witness* 1987; *Rachel River* 1987
Henderson, Marcia *All I Desire* 1953; *Back to God's Country* 1953; *The Glass Web* 1953; *Thunder Bay* 1953; *Naked Alibi* 1954; *Timbuktu* 1959; *A Dog's Best Friend* 1960
Henderson, Shirley *Salt on Our Skin* 1992; *Wonderland* 1999; *Topsy-Turvy* 1999
Henderson, Ty *The Competition* 1980; *Happy Hour* 1987
Hendrickson, Benjamin *Manhunter* 1986; *Spanking the Monkey* 1994
Hendrix, Elaine *Romy and Michele's High School Reunion* 1997; *The Parent Trap* 1998; *Superstar* 1999
Hendrix, Wanda *Confidential Agent* 1945; *Welcome Stranger* 1947; *Miss Tatlock's Millions* 1948; *Prince of Foxes* 1949; *The Admiral Was a Lady* 1950; *Captain Carey, USA* 1950; *Saddle Tramp* 1950; *Sierra* 1950; *South of Algiers* 1952; *The Last Posse* 1953; *The Boy Who Caught a Crook* 1961
Hendry, Gloria *Live and Let Die* 1973; *Slaughter's Big Rip-Off* 1973; *Black Caesar* 1973; *Hell Up in Harlem* 1973; *Black Belt Jones* 1974; *The Revenge of Pumpkinhead – Blood Wings* 1994
Hendry, Ian *Live Now – Pay Later* 1962; *Girl in the Headlines* 1963; *This Is My Street* 1963; *The Beauty Jungle* 1964; *Children of the Damned* 1964; *The Hill* 1965; *Repulsion* 1965; *The Sandwich Man* 1966; *Journey to the Far Side of the Sun* 1969; *The Southern Star* 1969; *The McKenzie Break* 1970; *Get Carter* 1971; *All Coppers Are...* 1972; *Captain Kronos: Vampire Hunter* 1972; *The Jerusalem File* 1972; *Tales from the Crypt* 1972;

Assassin 1973; *Theatre of Blood* 1973; *The Internecine Project* 1974; *The Passenger* 1975; *The Bitch* 1979; *McVicar* 1980
Henie, Sonja *One in a Million* 1936; *Thin Ice* 1937; *Happy Landing* 1938; *My Lucky Star* 1938; *Second Fiddle* 1939; *Sun Valley Serenade* 1941; *Wintertime* 1943; *The Countess of Monte Cristo* 1948
Henner, Marilu *Between the Lines* 1977; *Bloodbrothers* 1978; *Hammett* 1982; *The Man Who Loved Women* 1983; *Johnny Dangerously* 1984; *Perfect* 1985; *Rustler's Rhapsody* 1985; *Ladykillers* 1988; *Chains of Gold* 1989; *LA Story* 1991; *Noises Off* 1992; *For the Future: the Irvine Fertility Scandal* 1996; *My Son Is Innocent* 1996
Hennessey, Dan *The Care Bears Movie II: a New Generation* 1986; *The Care Bears Adventure in Wonderland* 1987
Hennessy, Jill *RoboCop 3* 1993; *Most Wanted* 1997; *A Smile like Yours* 1997; *Molly* 1999
Henney, Del *Straw Dogs* 1971; *Brannigan* 1975
Henning, Eva *Thirst* 1949; *The Devil's Wanton* 1949
Henning, Uno *The Love of Jeanne Ney* 1927; *Three Loves* 1929
Henreid, Paul *Goodbye, Mr Chips* 1939; *Night Train to Munich* 1940; *Casablanca* 1942; *Joan of Paris* 1942; *Now, Voyager* 1942; *Between Two Worlds* 1944; *The Conspirators* 1944; *The Spanish Main* 1945; *Deception* 1946; *Devotion* 1946; *Of Human Bondage* 1946; *Song of Love* 1947; *Hollow Triumph* 1948; *Rope of Sand* 1949; *Mantrap* 1952; *Stolen Face* 1952; *Thief of Damascus* 1952; *Deep in My Heart* 1954; *Battle Shock* 1956; *Ten Thousand Bedrooms* 1957; *Holiday for Lovers* 1959; *Never So Few* 1959; *The Four Horsemen of the Apocalypse* 1962; *Operation Crossbow* 1965; *The Madwoman of Chaillot* 1969; *Exorcist II: the Heretic* 1977
Henriksen, Lance *Mansion of the Doomed* 1975; *Damien – Omen II* 1978; *The Visitor* 1980; *Piranha II: The Spawning* 1983; *The Terminator* 1984; *Jagged Edge* 1985; *Savage Dawn* 1985; *Aliens* 1986; *On Dangerous Ground* 1986; *Near Dark* 1987; *Vengeance: the Demon* 1988; *Hit List* 1988; *Johnny Handsome* 1989; *House III: The Horror Show* 1989; *Stone Cold* 1991; *The Pit and the Pendulum* 1991; *Reason for Living: the Jill Ireland Story* 1991; *Alien³* 1992; *Jennifer Eight* 1992; *Excessive Force* 1993; *Hard Target* 1993; *Knights* 1993; *Man's Best Friend* 1993; *The Outfit* 1993; *Boulevard* 1994; *Color of Night* 1994; *No Escape* 1994; *Hatchet Man* 1994; *Dead Man* 1995; *Powder* 1995; *The Quick and the Dead* 1995; *Wes Craven's Mind Ripper* 1995; *The Criminal Mind* 1995; *Profile for Murder* 1996; *The Day Lincoln Was Shot* 1998; *Tarzan* 1999; *Scream 3* 1999
Henrikson, Anders *A Woman's Face* 1938; *The Devil's Wanton* 1949
Henry, Buck *The Troublemaker* 1964; *Taking Off* 1971; *Is There Sex after Death?* 1971; *The Man Who Fell to Earth* 1976; *Heaven Can Wait* 1978; *Old Boyfriends* 1979; *Gloria* 1980; *First Family* 1980; *Eating Raoul* 1982; *Aria* 1987; *Rude Awakening* 1989;

1970; *The Barefoot Executive* 1971

Hewitt, Henry *Sailors Three* 1940; *The Black Sheep of Whitehall* 1941

Hewitt, Jennifer Love aka **Hewitt, Love** *Munchie* 1992; *Little Miss Millions* 1993; *Sister Act 2: Back in the Habit* 1993; *House Arrest* 1996; *I Know What You Did Last Summer* 1997; *Trojan War* 1997; *Can't Hardly Wait* 1998; *I Still Know What You Did Last Summer* 1998

Hewitt, Martin *Endless Love* 1981; *Killer Party* 1986; *Two Moon Junction* 1988; *Crime Lords* 1991; *Secret Games* 1992; *Night Fire* 1994; *Bombshell* 1997

Hewitt, Paul *A Perfect World* 1993; *Ed* 1996

Hewitt, Sean *The Sender* 1982; *Wild Thing* 1987; *Swann* 1996

Hewlett, David *Pin* 1988; *The Penthouse* 1989; *Deep Sleep* 1990; *Where the Heart Is* 1990; *Desire & Hell at Sunset Motel* 1991; *Scanners II: The New Order* 1991; *Black Death* 1992; *Cube* 1997; *On the 2nd Day of Christmas* 1997

Heyden, Yvette *A Cry for Help: the Tracey Thurman Story* 1989; *Too Young to Die?* 1990

Heydt, Louis Jean *The Great McGinty* 1940; *Let's Make Music* 1940; *The Great Moment* 1944; *The Big Sleep* 1946; *Roadblock* 1951; *The Boy from Oklahoma* 1954; *Stranger at My Door* 1956

Heyerdahl, Christopher *Silent Trigger* 1996; *The Peacekeeper* 1997

Heyes, Herbert *Union Station* 1950; *Bedtime for Bonzo* 1951; *A Place in the Sun* 1951; *Park Row* 1952; *Carbine Williams* 1952; *Something to Live For* 1952; *Seven Little Foys* 1955

Heyman, Barton *Valdez Is Coming* 1971; *Let's Scare Jessica to Death* 1971; *This Man Stands Alone* 1979; *Trackdown: Finding the Goodbar Killer* 1983; *Static* 1985; *Billy Galvin* 1986; *Against Her Will* 1991; *Final Verdict* 1991

Heywood, Anne *Dangerous Exile* 1957; *Floods of Fear* 1958; *Violent Playground* 1958; *Upstairs and Downstairs* 1959; *Carthage in Flames* 1960; *A Terrible Beauty* 1960; *Petticoat Pirates* 1961; *The Brain* 1962; *The Very Edge* 1962; *The Fox* 1967; *The Chairman* 1969; *Midas Run* 1969; *I Want What I Want* 1971; *Good Luck, Miss Wyckoff* 1979; *Secrets of the Phantom Caverns* 1984

Heywood, John *Dead Man's Float* 1980; *Survive the Savage Sea* 1992

Heywood, Pat *Romeo and Juliet* 1968; *Mumsy, Nanny, Sonny & Girly* 1970; *10 Rillington Place* 1970; *Wish You Were Here* 1987; *Young Toscanini* 1988

Hiatt, Philippa *The Bells Go Down* 1943; *The Halfway House* 1943; *George in Civvy Street* 1946

Hibbert, Geoffrey *Love on the Dole* 1941; *In Which We Serve* 1942; *Gaolbreak* 1962

Hibler, Winston *White Wilderness* 1958; *Jungle Cat* 1959; *King of the Grizzlies* 1970

Hickey, John Benjamin *Only You* 1994; *Eddie* 1996; *Love! Valour! Compassion!* 1997; *Finding North* 1997; *The Bone Collector* 1999

Hickey, Tom *Fools of Fortune* 1990; *Raining Stones* 1993; *Gold in the Streets* 1996

Hickey, William *A Hatful of Rain* 1957; *The Producers* 1968; *Happy Birthday, Wanda June*

1971; *92 in the Shade* 1975; *Mikey and Nicky* 1976; *Wise Blood* 1979; *Prizzi's Honor* 1985; *Walls of Glass* 1985; *The Name of the Rose* 1986; *Seize the Day* 1986; *One Crazy Summer* 1986; *A Hobo's Christmas* 1987; *Da* 1988; *Pink Cadillac* 1989; *Sea of Love* 1989; *Sons* 1989; *Starlight* 1989; *Puppet Master* 1989; *My Blue Heaven* 1990; *Any Man's Death* 1990; *The Runestone* 1991; *Tales from the Darkside: the Movie* 1991; *Tim Burton's The Nightmare before Christmas* 1993; *The Jerky Boys* 1995; *The Maddening* 1995; *Love Is All There Is* 1996; *Mousehunt* 1997

Hickland, Catherine *Ghost Town* 1988; *Witchcraft* 1989; *Millions* 1991

Hickman, Bill *The French Connection* 1971; *The Seven-Ups* 1973

Hickman, Darryl *Men of Boys Town* 1941; *Joe Smith, American* 1942; *Salty O'Rourke* 1945; *Kiss and Tell* 1945; *Fighting Father Dunne* 1948; *A Kiss for Corliss* 1949; *Lightning Strikes Twice* 1951; *Destination Gobi* 1953; *Tea and Sympathy* 1956; *The Iron Sheriff* 1957; *The Tingler* 1959

Hickman, Dwayne *Cat Ballou* 1965; *How to Fill a Wild Bikini* 1965; *Ski Party* 1965; *Dr Goldfoot and the Bikini Machine* 1965; *High School USA* 1983; *Bring Me the Head of Dobie Gillis* 1988

Hicks, Catherine *Marilyn – The Untold Story* 1980; *Death Valley* 1982; *Better Late Than Never* 1983; *Garbo Talks* 1984; *The Razor's Edge* 1984; *Fever Pitch* 1985; *Peggy Sue Got Married* 1986; *Star Trek IV: the Voyage Home* 1986; *Laguna Heat* 1987; *Like Father, Like Son* 1987; *Souvenir* 1987; *Child's Play* 1988; *She's Out of Control* 1989; *Running against Time* 1990; *Hi Honey, I'm Dead* 1991; *Redwood Curtain* 1995; *Dillinger and Capone* 1995; *Eight Days a Week* 1996

Hicks, Danny aka **Hicks, Dan** *Evil Dead II* 1987; *Darkman* 1990

Hicks, Russell *Charlie Chan in Shanghai* 1935; *The Woman in Red* 1935; *Follow the Fleet* 1936; *The Big Broadcast of 1938* 1937; *Kentucky* 1938; *Swanee River* 1939; *Flame of the Barbary Coast* 1945; *A Game of Death* 1945; *The Bandit of Sherwood Forest* 1946; *The Black Arrow* 1948

Hicks, Seymour *Scrooge* 1935; *Vintage Wine* 1935; *Busman's Honeymoon* 1940; *Pastor Hall* 1940

Hicks, Taral *A Bronx Tale* 1993; *Belly* 1998

Hickson, Joan *Love from a Stranger* 1936; *Don't Take It to Heart* 1944; *The Guinea Pig* 1948; *Seven Days to Noon* 1950; *The Card* 1952; *Hindle Wakes* 1952; *Deadly Nightshade* 1953; *Jumping for Joy* 1955; *Child in the House* 1956; *The Extra Day* 1956; *Sea Wife* 1957; *Law and Disorder* 1958; *Upstairs and Downstairs* 1959; *Carry On Regardless* 1960; *Please Turn Over* 1960; *No Kidding* 1960; *Murder She Said* 1961; *I Thank a Fool* 1962; *Nurse on Wheels* 1963; *Carry On Loving* 1970; *A Day in the Death of Joe Egg* 1971; *Carry On Girls* 1973; *Confessions of a Window Cleaner* 1974; *The Wicked Lady* 1983; *Clockwise* 1986; *King of the Wind* 1989; *Century* 1993

Higashiyama, Chieko *Early Summer* 1951; *Tokyo Story* 1953

Higgins, Anthony *Raiders of the Lost Ark* 1981; *Quartet* 1981; *The Draughtsman's Contract* 1982; *The Cold Room* 1984; *She'll Be Wearing Pink Pyjamas* 1984; *The Bride* 1985; *Young Sherlock Holmes* 1985; *Max Mon Amour* 1986; *The Bridge* 1990; *One against the Wind* 1991; *The Concierge* 1993; *Nostradamus* 1993; *Alive and Kicking* 1996

Higgins, Clare *Nineteen Nineteen* 1985; *Hellraiser* 1987; *Hellbound: Hellraiser II* 1988; *Bad Behaviour* 1992; *Thin Ice* 1994; *Small Faces* 1995

Higgins, Joel *Salvage* 1979; *Threesome* 1984; *Laura Lansing Slept Here* 1988; *Rich Men, Single Women* 1990

Higgins, John Michael *The Late Shift* 1996; *GI Jane* 1997

Higgins, Michael *Terror in the City* 1963; *The Arrangement* 1969; *Wanda* 1971; *The Conversation* 1974; *An Enemy of the People* 1977; *The Black Stallion* 1979; *A Midsummer Night's Sex Comedy* 1982; *Angel Heart* 1987

Higginson, Torri *When the Bullet Hits the Bone* 1995; *Airborne* 1997

Hiken, Gerald *The Goddess* 1958; *The Three Sisters* 1966; *Street of Dreams* 1988

Hilary, Jennifer *The Idol* 1966; *Five Days One Summer* 1982

Hilboldt, Lise *Noon Wine* 1985; *Sweet Liberty* 1986; *The Karen Carpenter Story* 1989

Hill, Arthur *The Deep Blue Sea* 1955; *In the Cool of the Day* 1963; *The Ugly American* 1963; *Moment to Moment* 1966; *The Moving Target* 1966; *Petulia* 1968; *The Chairman* 1969; *The Andromeda Strain* 1970; *The Pursuit of Happiness* 1971; *The Killer Elite* 1975; *Futureworld* 1976; *The Champ* 1979; *A Little Romance* 1979; *Revenge of the Stepford Wives* 1980; *The Amateur* 1981; *Making Love* 1982; *Something Wicked This Way Comes* 1983; *The Guardian* 1984; *Love Leads the Way* 1984; *One Magic Christmas* 1985

Hill, Benny *Light Up the Sky* 1960; *Those Magnificent Men in Their Flying Machines* 1965; *Chitty Chitty Bang Bang* 1968; *The Italian Job* 1969

Hill, Bernard *The Sailor's Return* 1978; *The Bounty* 1984; *The Chain* 1984; *Restless Natives* 1985; *No Surrender* 1986; *Bellman & True* 1987; *Drowning by Numbers* 1988; *Mountains of the Moon* 1989; *Shirley Valentine* 1989; *Double X: the Name of the Game* 1991; *Madagascar Skin* 1995; *The Ghost and the Darkness* 1996; *The Wind in the Willows* 1996; *Titanic* 1997; *True Crime* 1999; *The Loss of Sexual Innocence* 1999; *The Criminal* 1999

Hill, Craig *Detective Story* 1951; *Fixed Bayonets* 1951; *The I Don't Care Girl* 1952; *What Price Glory?* 1952; *The Siege at Red River* 1954; *The Swinger* 1966; *Scapegoat* 1982

Hill, Dana *Fallen Angel* 1981; *Shoot the Moon* 1982; *Cross Creek* 1983; *National Lampoon's European Vacation* 1985; *Rover Dangerfield* 1991; *Tom and Jerry: the Movie* 1992

Hill, Dave *The Draughtsman's Contract* 1982; *The Raggedy Rawney* 1987

Hill, Harry *Crazy Moon* 1986; *Shadow of the Wolf* 1992

Hill, Marianna aka **Hill, Mariana** *Red Line 7000* 1965; *Paradise, Hawaiian Style* 1966; *Medium Cool* 1969; *El Condor* 1970; *The Traveling Executioner* 1970; *Thumb Tripping* 1972; *The Baby* 1973; *High Plains Drifter* 1973; *Death at Love House* 1976; *Blood Beach* 1981

Hill, Matt *Teenage Mutant Ninja Turtles III* 1992; *A Monkey's Tale* 2000

Hill, Melanie *The Hawk* 1992; *Brassed Off* 1996

Hill, Steven *The Goddess* 1958; *A Child Is Waiting* 1962; *The Slender Thread* 1965; *It's My Turn* 1980; *Rich and Famous* 1981; *Yentl* 1983; *Garbo Talks* 1984; *Heartburn* 1986; *Legal Eagles* 1986; *The Boost* 1988; *White Palace* 1990; *Billy Bathgate* 1991

Hill, Terence aka **Girotti, Mario** *The Sword and the Cross* 1958; *Hannibal* 1959; *The Leopard* 1962; *Seven Seas to Calais* 1962; *Boot Hill* 1969; *My Name Is Nobody* 1973; *March or Die* 1977; *Mr Billion* 1977; *Renegade* 1987

Hill, Teresa *Behind Closed Doors* 1994; *Twin Falls Idaho* 1999

Hill, Thelma *The Two Tars* 1928; *The Miracle Woman* 1931

Hill, Thomas *Revenge of the Stepford Wives* 1980; *The NeverEnding Story* 1984

Hillaire, Marcel *Sabrina Fair* 1954; *Take the Money and Run* 1969

Hiller, Wendy *Pygmalion* 1938; *Major Barbara* 1941; *I Know Where I'm Going* 1945; *Outcast of the Islands* 1951; *Sailor of the King* 1953; *Something of Value* 1957; *How to Murder a Rich Uncle* 1957; *Separate Tables* 1958; *Sons and Lovers* 1960; *Toys in the Attic* 1963; *A Man for All Seasons* 1966; *David Copperfield* 1969; *Murder on the Orient Express* 1974; *The Cat and the Canary* 1979; *The Elephant Man* 1980; *Making Love* 1982; *Witness for the Prosecution* 1982; *The Lonely Passion of Judith Hearne* 1987

Hillerman, John *Paper Moon* 1973; *Chinatown* 1974; *At Long Last Love* 1975; *Lucky Lady* 1975; *Kill Me If You Can* 1977; *Sunburn* 1979

Hilliard, Harriet *New Faces of 1937* 1937; *Sweetheart of the Campus* 1941; *The Falcon Strikes Back* 1943

Hillie, Verna *Duck Soup* 1933; *The Star Packer* 1934; *The Trail Beyond* 1934

Hills, Beverley *The Comedy of Terrors* 1964; *Knights and Emeralds* 1986

Hills, Gillian *Beat Girl* 1960; *Blow Up* 1966; *Demons of the Mind* 1971

Hilton, George *The Battle of El Alamein* 1968; *A Bullet for Sandoval* 1970

Hilton-Jacobs, Lawrence *Claudine* 1974; *East LA* 1989; *Indecent Behavior* 1993; *Tidal Wave: No Escape* 1997

Hinchley, Pippa *Secret Places* 1984; *The Dressmaker* 1988

Hinde, Madeline *The Smashing Bird I Used to Know* 1969; *Bloodsuckers* 1970; *Incense for the Damned* 1970; *The Last Valley* 1971; *Brief Encounter* 1974

Hindle, Art *Black Christmas* 1974; *A Small Town in Texas* 1976; *The Brood* 1979; *The Octagon* 1980; *Raw Courage* 1984; *J Edgar Hoover* 1987; *The World's Oldest*

Living Bridesmaid 1990; *Liar Liar* 1992; *Silence of Adultery* 1995

Hindman, Earl *The Parallax View* 1974; *The Taking of Pelham One Two Three* 1974; *Greased Lightning* 1977; *Rising Son* 1990

Hinds, Ciaran *December Bride* 1990; *Hostages* 1993; *Circle of Friends* 1995; *Persuasion* 1995; *The Affair* 1995; *Some Mother's Son* 1996; *The Life of Stuff* 1997; *Oscar and Lucinda* 1997; *The Lost Son* 1998; *Titanic Town* 1998

Hinds, Samuel S aka **Hinds, Samuel** *Gabriel over the White House* 1933; *She* 1935; *Strangers All* 1935; *Private Worlds* 1935; *The Raven* 1935; *Rendezvous* 1935; *His Brother's Wife* 1936; *Rhythm on the Range* 1936; *Stage Door* 1937; *Navy Blue and Gold* 1937; *Forbidden Valley* 1938; *Test Pilot* 1938; *You Can't Take It with You* 1938; *Young Dr Kildare* 1938; *The Storm* 1938; *Wives under Suspicion* 1938; *Calling Dr Kildare* 1939; *The Secret of Dr Kildare* 1939; *The Boys from Syracuse* 1940; *Dr Kildare Goes Home* 1940; *Dr Kildare's Strange Case* 1940; *It's a Date* 1940; *Seven Sinners* 1940; *Back Street* 1941; *Blossoms in the Dust* 1941; *Dr Kildare's Wedding Day* 1941; *Man Made Monster* 1941; *Road Agent* 1941; *The Shepherd of the Hills* 1941; *Grand Central Murder* 1942; *Kid Glove Killer* 1942; *Ride 'em Cowboy* 1942; *Lady in a Jam* 1942; *Hers to Hold* 1943; *Son of Dracula* 1943; *Cobra Woman* 1944; *The Singing Sheriff* 1944; *The Strange Affair of Uncle Harry* 1945; *The Boy with Green Hair* 1948; *The Bribe* 1949

Hines, Damon *Lethal Weapon* 1987; *Lethal Weapon 3* 1992

Hines, Gregory *History of the World Part 1* 1981; *Wolfen* 1981; *Deal of the Century* 1983; *The Cotton Club* 1984; *White Nights* 1985; *Running Scared* 1986; *Saigon* 1988; *Tap* 1989; *A Rage in Harlem* 1991; *White Lie* 1991; *Eve of Destruction* 1991; *Dead Air* 1994; *Renaissance Man* 1994; *A Stranger in Town* 1995; *Waiting to Exhale* 1995; *The Preacher's Wife* 1996; *Trigger Happy* 1996; *The Cherokee Kid* 1996; *Good Luck* 1996; *Color of Justice* 1997

Hingle, Pat *The Strange One* 1957; *No Down Payment* 1957; *Splendor in the Grass* 1961; *All the Way Home* 1963; *The Ugly American* 1963; *Nevada Smith* 1966; *Hang 'em High* 1968; *Jigsaw* 1968; *Sol Madrid* 1968; *Bloody Mama* 1970; *WUSA* 1970; *The Carey Treatment* 1972; *One Little Indian* 1973; *Running Wild* 1973; *The Super Cops* 1973; *Escape from Bogen County* 1977; *The Gauntlet* 1977; *Disaster on the Coastliner* 1979; *Elvis – the Movie* 1979; *Norma Rae* 1979; *Running Brave* 1983; *Going Berserk* 1983; *Sudden Impact* 1983; *Brewster's Millions* 1985; *The Falcon and the Snowman* 1985; *The Lady from Yesterday* 1985; *Noon Wine* 1985; *The Rape of Richard Beck* 1985; *Manhunt for Claude Dallas* 1986; *Maximum Overdrive* 1986; *Baby Boom* 1987; *The Land before Time* 1988; *Stranger on My Land* 1988; *The Town Bully* 1988; *Batman* 1989; *Everybody's Baby: the Rescue of Jessica McClure* 1989; *The Grifters* 1990; *Gunsmoke: To the Last Man* 1992; *Citizen Cohn* 1992; *Lightning Jack* 1994;*

RadioTimes ACTORS' INDEX

Holder, Roy *Whistle down the Wind* 1961; *Loot* 1970; *Psychomania* 1972

Holding, Thomas *The Three Musketeers* 1921; *Ruggles of Red Gap* 1923

Holgado, Ticky *Delicatessen* 1990; *French Twist* 1995

Holland, Anthony *Frank's Greatest Adventure* 1967; *Popi* 1969; *Lucky Lady* 1975; *The Lonely Lady* 1983

Holland, John *Ladies' Man* 1931; *The Girl in Black Stockings* 1957

Hollander, Tom *Some Mother's Son* 1996; *Martha – Meet Frank, Daniel and Laurence* 1997; *Bedrooms and Hallways* 1998; *The Clandestine Marriage* 1999; *Maybe Baby* 1999

Holles, Antony *Limelight* 1936; *Ten Days in Paris* 1939

Holliday, Judy *Winged Victory* 1944; *Adam's Rib* 1949; *Born Yesterday* 1950; *The Marrying Kind* 1952; *It Should Happen to You* 1954; *Phffft!* 1954; *Full of Life* 1956; *The Solid Gold Cadillac* 1956; *Bells Are Ringing* 1960

Holliday, Kene *The Philadelphia Experiment* 1984; *The Josephine Baker Story* 1991

Holliday, Polly *The One and Only* 1978; *Gremlins* 1984; *Triumph of the Heart* 1991; *Mrs Doubtfire* 1993; *A Loss of Innocence* 1996

Holliman, Earl *The Bridges at Toko-Ri* 1954; *Broken Lance* 1954; *Tennessee Champ* 1954; *I Died a Thousand Times* 1955; *The Burning Hills* 1956; *Forbidden Planet* 1956; *The Rainmaker* 1956; *Don't Go Near the Water* 1957; *Gunfight at the OK Corral* 1957; *Trooper Hook* 1957; *Hot Spell* 1958; *The Baited Trap* 1959; *Last Train from Gun Hill* 1959; *Visit to a Small Planet* 1960; *Armored Command* 1961; *The Sons of Katie Elder* 1965; *A Covenant with Death* 1967; *Anzio* 1968; *The Biscuit Eater* 1972; *Trapped* 1973; *Where the Ladies Go* 1980; *Sharky's Machine* 1981

Hollis, Tommy *Malcolm X* 1992; *Freedom Road: the Vernon Johns Story* 1994

Holloman, Laurel *The Incredibly True Adventures of Two Girls in Love* 1995; *The Myth of Fingerprints* 1996; *Dying to Belong* 1997; *Tumbleweeds* 1999

Holloway, Stanley *D'Ye Ken John Peel?* 1934; *Squibs* 1935; *Cotton Queen* 1937; *The Vicar of Bray* 1937; *Champagne Charlie* 1944; *This Happy Breed* 1944; *The Way Ahead* 1944; *Brief Encounter* 1945; *The Way to the Stars* 1945; *Meet Me at Dawn* 1946; *Wanted for Murder* 1946; *Carnival* 1946; *Nicholas Nickleby* 1947; *Another Shore* 1948; *Hamlet* 1948; *Noose* 1948; *Snowbound* 1948; *Passport to Pimlico* 1949; *The Perfect Woman* 1949; *Lady Godiva Rides Again* 1951; *The Lavender Hill Mob* 1951; *The Magic Box* 1951; *The Happy Family* 1952; *Meet Me Tonight* 1952; *The Titfield Thunderbolt* 1952; *The Beggar's Opera* 1953; *A Day to Remember* 1953; *Meet Mr Lucifer* 1953; *An Alligator Named Daisy* 1955; *Jumping for Joy* 1955; *Alive and Kicking* 1958; *No Trees in the Street* 1958; *No Love for Johnnie* 1960; *On the Fiddle* 1961; *My Fair Lady* 1964; *Ten Little Indians* 1965; *The Sandwich Man* 1966; *Target: Harry* 1968; *The Private Life of Sherlock Holmes* 1970; *Flight of the Doves* 1971; *Up the Front* 1972

Holloway, Sterling *Advice to the Lovelorn* 1933; *When Ladies Meet* 1933; *The Merry Widow* 1934; *Life Begins at 40* 1935; *Remember the Night* 1940; *Cheers for Miss Bishop* 1941; *Dumbo* 1941; *A Walk in the Sun* 1945; *Make Mine Music* 1946; *The Beautiful Blonde from Bashful Bend* 1949; *Alice in Wonderland* 1951; *Shake, Rattle and Rock!* 1957; *The Jungle Book* 1967; *Live a Little, Love a Little* 1968; *The Aristocats* 1970; *Thunder and Lightning* 1977

Holly, Ellen *Take a Giant Step* 1959; *Cops and Robbers* 1973; *School Daze* 1988

Holly, Lauren *The Adventures of Ford Fairlane* 1990; *Weekend Reunion* 1990; *Dragon: the Bruce Lee Story* 1993; *Dangerous Heart* 1994; *Dumb and Dumber* 1994; *Sabrina* 1995; *Beautiful Girls* 1996; *Down Periscope* 1996; *A Smile like Yours* 1997; *Turbulence* 1997; *No Looking Back* 1998

Holm, Celeste *Three Little Girls in Blue* 1946; *Gentleman's Agreement* 1947; *Chicken Every Sunday* 1948; *Road House* 1948; *The Snake Pit* 1948; *Come to the Stable* 1949; *Everybody Does It* 1949; *A Letter to Three Wives* 1949; *All about Eve* 1950; *Champagne for Caesar* 1950; *The Tender Trap* 1955; *High Society* 1956; *Bachelor Flat* 1961; *Tom Sawyer* 1973; *Bittersweet Love* 1976; *The Private Files of J Edgar Hoover* 1977; *Murder by the Book* 1986; *Three Men and a Baby* 1987; *Once You Meet a Stranger* 1996

Holm, Claus *The Tiger of Eschnapur* 1959; *The Indian Tomb* 1959

Holm, Ian *The Bofors Gun* 1968; *The Fixer* 1968; *Oh! What a Lovely War* 1969; *A Midsummer Night's Dream* 1969; *A Severed Head* 1970; *Mary, Queen of Scots* 1971; *Young Winston* 1972; *The Homecoming* 1973; *Juggernaut* 1974; *Robin and Marian* 1976; *Shout at the Devil* 1976; *The Man in the Iron Mask* 1977; *March or Die* 1977; *Les Misérables* 1978; *The Thief of Baghdad* 1978; *Alien* 1979; *All Quiet on the Western Front* 1979; *SOS Titanic* 1979; *Chariots of Fire* 1981; *Time Bandits* 1981; *The Return of the Soldier* 1982; *Dance with a Stranger* 1984; *Greystoke: the Legend of Tarzan, Lord of the Apes* 1984; *Laughterhouse* 1984; *Brazil* 1985; *Dreamchild* 1985; *Wetherby* 1985; *Another Woman* 1988; *Henry V* 1989; *Hamlet* 1990; *Kafka* 1991; *Naked Lunch* 1991; *Blue Ice* 1992; *The Hour of the Pig* 1993; *Loch Ness* 1994; *Mary Shelley's Frankenstein* 1994; *The Madness of King George* 1995; *Big Night* 1996; *The Fifth Element* 1997; *Night Falls on Manhattan* 1997; *The Sweet Hereafter* 1997; *eXistenZ* 1999; *The Match* 1999; *The Miracle Maker* 1999

Holm, Sonia *Miranda* 1947; *Broken Journey* 1948; *The Calendar* 1948; *The Bad Lord Byron* 1949; *13 East Street* 1952

Holman, Clare *Afraid of the Dark* 1991; *Let Him Have It* 1991; *Tom & Viv* 1994

Holman, Vincent *Love Story* 1944; *The Sound Barrier* 1952

Holmen, Kjersti *Orion's Belt* 1985; *Bloody Angels* 1998

Holmes, Katie *The Ice Storm* 1997; *Disturbing Behaviour* 1998; *Go* 1999; *Teaching Mrs Tingle* 1999; *Wonder Boys* 2000

Holmes, Phillips *The Criminal Code* 1930; *The Devil's Holiday* 1930; *Her Man* 1930; *An American Tragedy* 1931; *The Man I Killed* 1932; *Penthouse* 1933; *The Secret of Madame Blanche* 1933; *Nana* 1934; *Chatterbox* 1936; *Housemaster* 1938

Holmes, Stuart *The Prisoner of Zenda* 1922; *Belle of the Nineties* 1934

Holmes, Taylor *Boomerang!* 1947; *Kiss of Death* 1947; *Nightmare Alley* 1947; *Act of Violence* 1949; *Rhubarb* 1951; *Beware, My Lovely* 1952; *Gentlemen Prefer Blondes* 1953; *The Outcast* 1954; *Sleeping Beauty* 1959

Holmes, Wendell *Good Day for a Hanging* 1958; *But Not for Me* 1959

Holt, Charlene *Man's Favorite Sport?* 1964; *Red Line 7000* 1965; *El Dorado* 1967

Holt, Jack *Flight* 1929; *Dirigible* 1931; *The Littlest Rebel* 1935; *San Francisco* 1936; *Cat People* 1942; *They Were Expendable* 1945; *The Chase* 1946; *My Pal Trigger* 1946; *The Arizona Ranger* 1948; *Task Force* 1949; *Across the Wide Missouri* 1951

Holt, Jany *The Lower Depths* 1936; *The Golem* 1936; *Abel Gance's Beethoven* 1936; *Les Anges du Péché* 1943

Holt, Jim *"Crocodile" Dundee II* 1988; *Fever* 1988; *Backsliding* 1991

Holt, Patrick *When the Bough Breaks* 1947; *Portrait from Life* 1948; *A Boy, a Girl and a Bike* 1949; *Marry Me!* 1949; *Boys in Brown* 1949; *13 East Street* 1952; *Men of Sherwood Forest* 1954; *A Stranger Came Home* 1954; *The Dark Avenger* 1955; *The Girl in the Picture* 1956; *Suspended Alibi* 1956; *I Was Monty's Double* 1958; *The Night of the Prowler* 1962; *Serena* 1962; *Psychomania* 1972; *Legend of the Werewolf* 1974

Holt, Sandrine *Black Robe* 1991; *Rapa Nui* 1994; *Pocahontas: the Legend* 1995; *Once a Thief* 1996

Holt, Tim *Stella Dallas* 1937; *Gold Is Where You Find It* 1938; *The Law West of Tombstone* 1938; *Fifth Avenue Girl* 1939; *Stagecoach* 1939; *Swiss Family Robinson* 1940; *Along the Rio Grande* 1941; *Back Street* 1941; *The Magnificent Ambersons* 1942; *Hitler's Children* 1943; *My Darling Clementine* 1946; *The Arizona Ranger* 1948; *Guns of Hate* 1948; *The Treasure of the Sierra Madre* 1948; *Stagecoach Kid* 1949; *Rider from Tucson* 1950; *Storm over Wyoming* 1950; *His Kind of Woman* 1951; *Desert Passage* 1952; *The Monster That Challenged the World* 1957

Holt, Ula *The New Adventures of Tarzan* 1935; *Tarzan and the Green Goddess* 1938

Holton, Mark *Pee-wee's Big Adventure* 1985; *Leprechaun* 1992

Holub, Miroslav aka **Holub, Miloslav** *Invention of Destruction* 1958; *The Ear* 1969

Holzboer, Max aka **Holzboer, Dr Max** *The Blue Light* 1932; *SOS Iceberg* 1933

Homeier, Skip aka **Homeier, Skippy** *Tomorrow the World!* 1944; *The Gunfighter* 1950; *Halls of Montezuma* 1950; *Fixed Bayonets* 1951; *Sealed Cargo* 1951; *Has Anybody Seen My Gal?* 1952; *Beachhead* 1954; *Cry Vengeance* 1954; *At Gunpoint* 1955; *The Road to Denver* 1955; *The Burning Hills* 1956; *Stranger at My Door* 1956; *Thunder over Arizona* 1956; *No Road Back* 1957; *The Tall T* 1957; *Day of the Bad Man* 1958; *Comanche Station* 1960; *Showdown* 1963; *Bullet for a Badman* 1964; *The Ghost and Mr Chicken* 1966

Homolka, Oscar aka **Homolka, Oskar** *Sabotage* 1936; *Comrade X* 1940; *Seven Sinners* 1940; *Ball of Fire* 1941; *Hostages* 1943; *Mission to Moscow* 1943; *I Remember Mama* 1948; *The Shop at Sly Corner* 1948; *Anna Lucasta* 1949; *The White Tower* 1950; *Prisoner of War* 1954; *The Seven Year Itch* 1955; *War and Peace* 1956; *A Farewell to Arms* 1957; *The Key* 1958; *Tempest* 1959; *Mr Sardonicus* 1961; *Boys' Night Out* 1962; *The Wonderful World of the Brothers Grimm* 1962; *The Long Ships* 1963; *Joy in the Morning* 1965; *Funeral in Berlin* 1966; *Billion Dollar Brain* 1967; *The Happening* 1967; *Assignment to Kill* 1968; *The Madwoman of Chaillot* 1969; *The Executioner* 1970; *Song of Norway* 1970; *The Tamarind Seed* 1974

Hong, James *Yes, Giorgio* 1982; *Missing in Action* 1984; *Big Trouble in Little China* 1986; *The Golden Child* 1986; *Black Widow* 1987; *Leap of Faith* 1988; *Vice Versa* 1988; *Tango and Cash* 1989; *Framed* 1990; *Shadowzone* 1990; *The Perfect Weapon* 1991; *Crime Lords* 1991; *Wayne's World 2* 1993; *Come Die with Me* 1994; *Operation Golden Phoenix* 1994; *Bloodsport II: The Next Kumite* 1996; *Broken Vessels* 1998

Hood, Don *Blackout* 1985; *Marie: a True Story* 1985; *Inherit the Wind* 1988; *Blind Vengeance* 1990; *Blind Judgement: Seduction in Travis County* 1991

Hood, Ed *My Hustler* 1965; *The Chelsea Girls* 1967

Hood, Noel *The Curse of Frankenstein* 1957; *How to Murder a Rich Uncle* 1957; *The Inn of the Sixth Happiness* 1958

Hooks, Kevin *Sounder* 1972; *Aaron Loves Angela* 1975; *Take Down* 1978; *A Hero Ain't Nothin' but a Sandwich* 1978

Hooks, Robert *Hurry Sundown* 1967; *Last of the Mobile Hot-Shots* 1970; *Trouble Man* 1972; *Trapped* 1973; *Aaron Loves Angela* 1975; *Fast-Walking* 1982; *Passenger 57* 1992; *Fled* 1996; *Free of Eden* 1999

Hooper, Tobe *Sleepwalkers* 1992; *Body Bags* 1993

Hoosier, Trula *Sidewalk Stories* 1989; *Daughters of the Dust* 1991

Hootkins, William *Zina* 1985; *Biggles* 1986; *The Return of Sherlock Holmes* 1987; *American Gothic* 1987; *Hardware* 1990; *Hear My Song* 1991; *The Pope Must Die* 1991; *Dust Devil* 1992; *Death Machine* 1994; *This World, Then the Fireworks* 1996

Hope, Bob *The Big Broadcast of 1938* 1937; *College Swing* 1938; *The Cat and the Canary* 1939; *Never Say Die* 1939; *The Ghost Breakers* 1940; *Road to Singapore* 1940; *Louisiana Purchase* 1941; *Road to Zanzibar* 1941; *Nothing but the Truth* 1941; *My Favorite Blonde* 1942; *Road to Morocco* 1942; *Star Spangled Rhythm* 1942; *Let's Face It* 1943; *They Got Me Covered* 1943; *The Princess and the Pirate* 1944; *Road to Utopia* 1945; *Monsieur Beaucaire* 1946; *My Favorite Brunette* 1947; *Road to Rio* 1947; *Variety Girl* 1947; *Where There's Life* 1947; *The Paleface* 1948; *The Great Lover* 1949; *Sorrowful Jones* 1949; *Fancy Pants* 1950; *My Favorite Spy* 1951; *The Lemon Drop Kid* 1951; *The Greatest Show on Earth* 1952; *Road to Bali* 1952; *Son of Paleface* 1952; *Here Come the Girls* 1953; *Military Policeman* 1953; *Scared Stiff* 1953; *Off Limits* 1953; *Casanova's Big Night* 1954; *Seven Little Foys* 1955; *The Iron Petticoat* 1956; *That Certain Feeling* 1956; *Beau James* 1957; *Paris Holiday* 1958; *The Five Pennies* 1959; *Alias Jesse James* 1959; *The Facts of Life* 1960; *Bachelor in Paradise* 1961; *The Road to Hong Kong* 1962; *Call Me Bwana* 1963; *Critic's Choice* 1963; *A Global Affair* 1964; *I'll Take Sweden* 1965; *Boy, Did I Get a Wrong Number* 1966; *The Oscar* 1966; *Eight on the Lam* 1967; *The Private Navy of Sgt O'Farrell* 1968; *How to Commit Marriage* 1969; *Cancel My Reservation* 1972; *Spies like Us* 1985; *The Masterpiece of Murder* 1986

Hope, Leslie *Sword of Gideon* 1986; *Kansas* 1988; *Talk Radio* 1988; *Men at Work* 1990; *True Confections* 1990; *Working Trash* 1990; *Paris France* 1993; *Doppelganger* 1993; *Caught in the Act* 1993; *Fun* 1994; *Schemes* 1994; *First Degree* 1995; *The Conspiracy of Fear* 1996

Hope, Nicholas *Bad Boy Bubby* 1993; *The Darkest Light* 1999

Hope, Richard *Laughterhouse* 1984; *Bellman & True* 1987

Hope, Vida *They Made Me a Fugitive* 1947; *Green Grow the Rushes* 1951; *The Man in the White Suit* 1951; *Women of Twilight* 1952

Hope, William *Aliens* 1986; *Hellbound: Hellraiser II* 1988

Hopkins, Anthony *The Lion in Winter* 1968; *Hamlet* 1969; *The Looking Glass War* 1969; *When Eight Bells Toll* 1971; *Young Winston* 1972; *A Doll's House* 1973; *All Creatures Great and Small* 1974; *The Girl from Petrovka* 1974; *Juggernaut* 1974; *Victory at Entebbe* 1976; *Audrey Rose* 1977; *A Bridge Too Far* 1977; *International Velvet* 1978; *Magic* 1978; *A Change of Seasons* 1980; *The Elephant Man* 1980; *The Hunchback of Notre Dame* 1982; *The Bounty* 1984; *Guilty Conscience* 1985; *84 Charing Cross Road* 1986; *The Good Father* 1986; *A Chorus of Disapproval* 1988; *The Dawning* 1988; *The Tenth Man* 1988; *Desperate Hours* 1990; *The Silence of the Lambs* 1991; *Spotswood* 1991; *Bram Stoker's Dracula* 1992; *Chaplin* 1992; *Freejack* 1992; *Howards End* 1992; *The Innocent* 1993; *The Remains of the Day* 1993; *Shadowlands* 1993; *The Trial* 1993; *Legends of the Fall* 1994; *The Road to Wellville* 1994; *August* 1995; *Nixon* 1995; *Surviving Picasso* 1996; *Amistad* 1997; *The Edge* 1997; *The Mask of Zorro* 1998; *Meet Joe Black* 1998; *Instinct* 1999; *Mission: Impossible 2* 1999; *Titus* 1999

Hopkins, Bo *The Culpepper Cattle Co* 1972; *American Graffiti* 1973; *The Man Who Loved Cat Dancing* 1973; *White Lightning* 1973; *The Killer Elite* 1975; *Posse* 1975; *A Small Town in Texas* 1976;

Tentacles 1977; *Midnight Express* 1978; *More American Graffiti* 1979; *The Fifth Floor* 1980; *Mutant* 1984; *Down the Long Hills* 1987; *Blood Ties* 1991; *Inside Monkey Zetterland* 1992; *The Ballad of Little Jo* 1993; *Cheyenne Warrior* 1994; *Wyatt Earp: Return to Tombstone* 1994; *Op Center* 1995; *Shadow of the Past* 1995; *The November Conspiracy* 1995; *U Turn* 1997; *Uncle Sam* 1997; *The Newton Boys* 1998

Hopkins, Harold *Age of Consent* 1969; *Don's Party* 1976; *The Picture Show Man* 1977; *The Club* 1980; *Monkey Grip* 1983; *The Winds of Jarrah* 1983; *No Worries* 1993

Hopkins, Jermaine aka **Hopkins, Jermaine "Big Hugg"** *Lean on Me* 1989; *Juice* 1992; *Def Jam's How to Be a Player* 1997

Hopkins, Joan *We Dive at Dawn* 1943; *The Weaker Sex* 1948

Hopkins, Josh *Silencing Mary* 1998; *Love and Sex* 2000

Hopkins, Miriam *Fast and Loose* 1930; *The Smiling Lieutenant* 1931; *Dr Jekyll and Mr Hyde* 1932; *Trouble in Paradise* 1932; *Design for Living* 1933; *The Stranger's Return* 1933; *The Richest Girl in the World* 1934; *She Loves Me Not* 1934; *Barbary Coast* 1935; *Becky Sharp* 1935; *Splendor* 1935; *Men Are Not Gods* 1936; *These Three* 1936; *The Woman I Love* 1937; *Woman Chases Man* 1937; *The Old Maid* 1939; *Virginia City* 1940; *A Gentleman after Dark* 1942; *Old Acquaintance* 1943; *The Heiress* 1949; *The Mating Season* 1951; *Carrie* 1952; *The Children's Hour* 1961; *Fanny Hill: Memoirs of a Woman of Pleasure* 1964; *The Chase* 1966

Hopkins, Telma *Trancers* 1985; *Rock 'n' Roll Mom* 1988; *How to Murder a Millionaire* 1990; *Trancers II: The Return of Jack Deth* 1991

Hoppe, Rolf *Mephisto* 1981; *Schtonk!* 1992; *Palmetto* 1998

Hopper, Dennis *I Died a Thousand Times* 1955; *Rebel without a Cause* 1955; *Giant* 1956; *Gunfight at the OK Corral* 1957; *From Hell to Texas* 1958; *The Young Land* 1959; *Key Witness* 1960; *Night Tide* 1961; *The Sons of Katie Elder* 1965; *Planet of Blood* 1966; *Cool Hand Luke* 1967; *The Trip* 1967; *The Glory Stompers* 1967; *Hang 'em High* 1968; *Panic in the City* 1968; *Easy Rider* 1969; *True Grit* 1969; *Kid Blue* 1971; *The Last Movie* 1971; *Mad Dog* 1976; *Tracks* 1977; *The American Friend* 1977; *Apocalypse Now* 1979; *Out of the Blue* 1980; *King of the Mountain* 1981; *Human Highway* 1982; *The Osterman Weekend* 1983; *Rumble Fish* 1983; *The Inside Man* 1984; *My Science Project* 1985; *Running Out of Luck* 1985; *Blue Velvet* 1986; *Best Shot* 1986; *The Texas Chainsaw Massacre Part 2* 1986; *Riders of the Storm* 1986; *Black Widow* 1987; *OC and Stiggs* 1987; *The Pick-Up Artist* 1987; *River's Edge* 1987; *Straight to Hell* 1987; *Blood Red* 1988; *Chattahoochee* 1989; *Catchfire* 1990; *Flashback* 1990; *The Indian Runner* 1991; *Paris Trout* 1991; *Double Crossed* 1991; *Eye of the Storm* 1991; *The Heart of Justice* 1992; *Red Rock West* 1992; *Nails* 1992; *Boiling Point* 1993; *Super Mario Bros* 1993; *True Romance* 1993; *Speed* 1994; *Witch Hunt* 1994; *Acts of Love* 1995; *Waterworld* 1995; *Search and Destroy* 1995; *Basquiat* 1996; *Space Truckers* 1996; *The Last Days of Frankie the Fly* 1996; *The Blackout* 1997; *Top of the World* 1997; *Meet the Deedles* 1998; *EDtv* 1999; *Road Ends* 1999; *Jesus' Son* 1999

Hopper, Hal *Lorna* 1964; *Mudhoney* 1965

Hopper, Hedda *Wings* 1927; *The Last of Mrs Cheyney* 1929; *Holiday* 1930; *As You Desire Me* 1932; *Speak Easily* 1932; *Pilgrimage* 1933; *Alice Adams* 1935; *Dracula's Daughter* 1936; *Nothing Sacred* 1937; *Topper* 1937; *Vogues* 1937; *Tarzan's Revenge* 1938; *Maid's Night Out* 1938; *Midnight* 1939; *The Oscar* 1966

Hopper, Victoria *The Constant Nymph* 1933; *Lorna Doone* 1934; *The Mill on the Floss* 1937

Hopper, William *Track of the Cat* 1954; *Conquest of Space* 1955; *Rebel without a Cause* 1955; *The Bad Seed* 1956; *Good-bye, My Lady* 1956; *20 Million Miles to Earth* 1957; *The Deadly Mantis* 1957

Hopton, Russell *Arrowsmith* 1931; *The Miracle Woman* 1931; *Air Mail* 1932; *Law and Order* 1932; *Lady Killer* 1933; *The Little Giant* 1933; *He Was Her Man* 1934; *Star of Midnight* 1935; *Wings in the Dark* 1935

Hordern, Michael *School for Secrets* 1946; *The Astonished Heart* 1949; *Highly Dangerous* 1950; *Trio* 1950; *Scrooge* 1951; *Tom Brown's Schooldays* 1951; *The Card* 1952; *The Beachcomber* 1954; *You Know What Sailors Are* 1954; *The Dark Avenger* 1955; *The Man Who Never Was* 1955; *The Night My Number Came Up* 1955; *Storm over the Nile* 1955; *Alexander the Great* 1956; *The Baby and the Battleship* 1956; *The Spanish Gardener* 1956; *Windom's Way* 1957; *Girls at Sea* 1958; *I Was Monty's Double* 1958; *The Spaniard's Curse* 1958; *Man in the Moon* 1960; *Sink the Bismarck!* 1960; *Moment of Danger* 1960; *El Cid* 1961; *Dr Syn, Alias the Scarecrow* 1963; *The Yellow Rolls-Royce* 1964; *A Funny Thing Happened on the Way to the Forum* 1966; *Khartoum* 1966; *How I Won the War* 1967; *I'll Never Forget What's 'Is Name* 1967; *The Jokers* 1967; *The Taming of the Shrew* 1967; *Anne of the Thousand Days* 1969; *The Bed Sitting Room* 1969; *Some Will, Some Won't* 1969; *Where Eagles Dare* 1969; *Demons of the Mind* 1971; *The Pied Piper* 1971; *Up Pompeii* 1971; *Alice's Adventures in Wonderland* 1972; *The Possession of Joel Delaney* 1972; *England Made Me* 1973; *Theatre of Blood* 1973; *Lucky Lady* 1975; *Mister Quilp* 1975; *Royal Flash* 1975; *The Slipper and the Rose* 1976; *Joseph Andrews* 1977; *The Medusa Touch* 1978; *Watership Down* 1978; *Shogun* 1980; *The Wildcats of St Trinian's* 1980; *The Missionary* 1982; *Oliver Twist* 1982; *Yellowbeard* 1983; *Lady Jane* 1985; *Comrades: a Lanternist's Account of the Tolpuddle Martyrs and What Became of Them* 1986; *Labyrinth* 1986; *The Secret Garden* 1987; *The Trouble with Spies* 1987; *Danny, the Champion of the World* 1989; *Diamond Skulls* 1989; *Freddie as FRO7* 1992

Horino, Tad *Pacific Inferno* 1979; *Galaxina* 1980

Horne, David *Crimes at the Dark House* 1939; *The First of the Few* 1942; *Don't Take It to Heart* 1944; *The Man from Morocco* 1944; *The Seventh Veil* 1945; *The Wicked Lady* 1945; *It's Hard to Be Good* 1948; *The Sheriff of Fractured Jaw* 1958

Horne, Geoffrey *The Bridge on the River Kwai* 1957; *Bonjour Tristesse* 1958; *Tempest* 1959

Horne, Lena *Cabin in the Sky* 1943; *Stormy Weather* 1943; *Swing Fever* 1943; *Broadway Rhythm* 1944; *Ziegfeld Follies* 1944; *Death of a Gunfighter* 1969; *The Wiz* 1978

Horneff, Wil *Ghost in the Machine* 1993; *The Yearling* 1994; *Born to Be Wild* 1995

Horner, Penelope *Half a Sixpence* 1967; *The Man Who Had Power over Women* 1970; *Dracula* 1974

Horney, Brigitte *Baron Münchhausen* 1943; *The Trygon Factor* 1967

Horovitch, David *An Unsuitable Job for a Woman* 1981; *Solomon and Gaenor* 1998

Horovitz, Adam *The Road Home* 1989; *Roadside Prophets* 1992

Horrocks, Jane *The Dressmaker* 1988; *The Wolves of Willoughby Chase* 1988; *Getting It Right* 1989; *The Witches* 1989; *Life Is Sweet* 1990; *Memphis Belle* 1990; *Deadly Advice* 1993; *Second Best* 1994; *Bring Me the Head of Mavis Davis* 1997; *Little Voice* 1998; *Chicken Run* 2000

Horsfall, Bernard *On Her Majesty's Secret Service* 1969; *Gold* 1974

Horsford, Anna Maria *An Almost Perfect Affair* 1979; *Times Square* 1980; *The Fan* 1981; *Bill* 1981; *Stone Pillow* 1985; *A Killer among Us* 1990; *Murder without Motive* 1992; *Baby Brokers* 1994; *Friday* 1995; *Dear God* 1996; *Widow's Kiss* 1996

Horsley, John *Deadly Nightshade* 1953; *Double Exposure* 1954; *Circus Friends* 1956; *Operation Amsterdam* 1958; *The Night of the Prowler* 1962; *Serena* 1962

Horsley, Lee *The Sword and the Sorcerer* 1982; *Single Women, Married Men* 1989; *The Face of Fear* 1990; *Palomino* 1991; *French Silk* 1993; *Unlawful Passage* 1994; *LaVyrle Spencer's Home Song* 1996

Horton, Edward Everett aka **Horton, Edward** *Ruggles of Red Gap* 1923; *La Bohème* 1926; *Holiday* 1930; *The Front Page* 1931; *Trouble in Paradise* 1932; *Design for Living* 1933; *It's a Boy* 1933; *Alice in Wonderland* 1933; *The Gay Divorcee* 1934; *The Merry Widow* 1934; *Ladies Should Listen* 1934; *Easy to Love* 1934; *All the King's Horses* 1935; *The Devil Is a Woman* 1935; *In Caliente* 1935; *The Private Secretary* 1935; *Top Hat* 1935; *The Man in the Mirror* 1936; *The Singing Kid* 1936; *Angel* 1937; *The Great Garrick* 1937; *The King and the Chorus Girl* 1937; *Lost Horizon* 1937; *The Perfect Specimen* 1937; *Shall We Dance* 1937; *Danger – Love at Work* 1937; *Bluebeard's Eighth Wife* 1938; *Holiday* 1938; *College Swing* 1938; *The Gang's All Here* 1939; *Paris Honeymoon* 1939; *Here Comes Mr Jordan* 1941; *Ziegfeld Girl* 1941; *Sunny* 1941; *I Married an Angel* 1942; *The Magnificent Dope* 1942; *Springtime in the Rockies* 1942; *The Gang's All Here* 1943; *Thank Your Lucky Stars* 1943; *Arsenic and Old Lace* 1944; *Brazil* 1944; *Summer Storm* 1944; *Lady on a Train* 1945; *Cinderella Jones* 1946; *Down to Earth* 1947; *Her Husband's Affairs* 1947; *Pocketful of Miracles* 1961; *Sex and the Single Girl* 1964; *The Perils of Pauline* 1967; *Cold Turkey* 1969

Horton, Helen *The Mark of the Hawk* 1957; *Phase IV* 1973; *Alien* 1979

Horton, Louisa *All My Sons* 1948; *Walk East on Beacon* 1952

Horton, Michael *My Father, My Son* 1988; *Happily Ever After* 1990

Horton, Peter *Children of the Corn* 1984; *Where the River Runs Black* 1986; *Side Out* 1990; *Children of the Dark* 1994; *Death Benefit* 1996; *Into Thin Air: Death on Everest* 1997

Horton, Robert *When Knights Were Bold* 1936; *Pony Soldier* 1952; *Apache War Smoke* 1952; *Bright Road* 1953; *Arena* 1953; *Men of the Fighting Lady* 1954; *Red River* 1988

Hosea, Bobby *The OJ Simpson Story* 1995; *Nightscream* 1997

Hoskins, Bob *Up the Front* 1972; *The National Health* 1973; *Inserts* 1975; *The Long Good Friday* 1979; *Zulu Dawn* 1979; *Pink Floyd – The Wall* 1982; *The Honorary Consul* 1983; *The Cotton Club* 1984; *Lassiter* 1984; *Brazil* 1985; *Mona Lisa* 1986; *Sweet Liberty* 1986; *The Lonely Passion of Judith Hearne* 1987; *The Raggedy Rawney* 1987; *Who Framed Roger Rabbit* 1988; *A Prayer for the Dying* 1988; *Heart Condition* 1990; *Mermaids* 1990; *The Favour, the Watch and the Very Big Fish* 1991; *Hook* 1991; *The Inner Circle* 1991; *Shattered* 1991; *Passed Away* 1992; *Super Mario Bros* 1993; *Balto* 1995; *Nixon* 1995; *Rainbow* 1995; *The Secret Agent* 1996; *Michael* 1996; *Cousin Bette* 1997; *TwentyFourSeven* 1997; *Captain Jack* 1998; *Parting Shots* 1998; *Felicia's Journey* 1999; *A Room for Romeo Brass* 1999

Hossack, Allison *Night Owl* 1993; *Dangerous Intentions* 1995; *The Hired Heart* 1997; *In the Doghouse* 1998

Hossein, Robert *Madame* 1961; *Shadow of Evil* 1964; *The Dirty Game* 1965; *The Battle of El Alamein* 1968; *The Last Shot* 1969; *The Burglars* 1971; *Don Juan 73, or If Don Juan Were a Woman* 1973; *Les Uns et les Autres* 1981; *The Professional* 1981; *Wax Mask* 1997

Hotchkis, Joan *The Late Liz* 1971; *Breezy* 1973; *Ode to Billy Joe* 1976; *Old Boyfriends* 1979

Hotton, Donald *The Hearse* 1980; *One Dark Night* 1982; *Brainstorm* 1983

Houghton, Katharine *Guess Who's Coming to Dinner* 1967; *The Gardener* 1972; *Ethan Frome* 1993

Hounsou, Djimon *Amistad* 1997; *Gladiator* 2000

House, Billy *The Stranger* 1946; *Bedlam* 1946; *The Egg and I* 1947; *Trail Street* 1947; *Rogues of Sherwood Forest* 1950; *Where Danger Lives* 1950

Houseman, John *The Paper Chase* 1973; *Rollerball* 1975; *Three Days of the Condor* 1975; *St Ives* 1976; *The Cheap Detective* 1978; *Old Boyfriends* 1979; *The Fog* 1980; *Gideon's Trumpet* 1980; *My Bodyguard* 1980; *Wholly Moses!* 1980; *Ghost Story* 1981; *Murder by Phone* 1982; *Another Woman* 1988; *Bright Lights, Big City* 1988

Houser, Jerry *Summer of '42* 1971; *Bad Company* 1972; *Class of '44* 1973; *Slap Shot* 1977; *Magic* 1978; *Another You* 1991

Housman, Arthur *The Singing Fool* 1928; *Feet First* 1930; *Scram!* 1932

Houston, Donald *The Blue Lagoon* 1949; *A Run for Your Money* 1949; *Dance Hall* 1950; *The Red Beret* 1953; *Doctor in the House* 1954; *The Flaw* 1954; *Double Cross* 1955; *Escape of the Amethyst* 1956; *Find the Lady* 1956; *The Girl in the Picture* 1956; *Danger Within* 1958; *Room at the Top* 1958; *The Man Upstairs* 1958; *The Mark* 1961; *The Prince and the Pauper* 1962; *The 300 Spartans* 1962; *Twice round the Daffodils* 1962; *Carry On Jack* 1963; *Doctor in Distress* 1963; *Maniac* 1963; *633 Squadron* 1964; *A Study in Terror* 1965; *The Viking Queen* 1967; *Where Eagles Dare* 1969; *Sunstruck* 1972

Houston, Glyn *The Cruel Sea* 1953; *Turn the Key Softly* 1953; *River Beat* 1954; *The Sleeping Tiger* 1954; *The Wind of Change* 1961; *Emergency* 1962; *Solo for Sparrow* 1962; *A Stitch in Time* 1963; *Conspiracy* 1989; *Old Scores* 1991; *The Mystery of Edwin Drood* 1993

Houston, Renee *Two Thousand Women* 1944; *Lady Godiva Rides Again* 1951; *The Big Money* 1956; *A Town like Alice* 1956; *Time without Pity* 1957; *The Horse's Mouth* 1958; *The Flesh and the Fiends* 1959; *And the Same to You* 1960; *No My Darling Daughter* 1961; *Repulsion* 1965; *Cul-de-Sac* 1966; *Legend of the Werewolf* 1974

Houston, Whitney *The Bodyguard* 1992; *Waiting to Exhale* 1995; *The Preacher's Wife* 1996; *Rodgers & Hammerstein's Cinderella* 1997

Hoven, Adrian *Foxhole in Cairo* 1960; *I Aim at the Stars* 1960; *Inside Out* 1975; *Fox and His Friends* 1975; *Fear of Fear* 1976

Howard, Adam Coleman *Quiet Cool* 1986; *Slaves of New York* 1989

Howard, Alan *Work Is a Four Letter Word* 1968; *Oxford Blues* 1984; *Strapless* 1988; *The Cook, the Thief, His Wife and Her Lover* 1989; *The Secret Rapture* 1993

Howard, Arliss *The Prodigal* 1983; *The Lightship* 1985; *Full Metal Jacket* 1987; *Plain Clothes* 1988; *Tequila Sunrise* 1988; *Men Don't Leave* 1990; *Somebody Has to Shoot the Picture* 1990; *Those Secrets* 1991; *CrissCross* 1992; *Married for Murder* 1992; *Ruby* 1992; *Wilder Napalm* 1993; *Erotic Tales* 1994; *The Infiltrator* 1995; *Johns* 1995; *To Wong Foo, Thanks for Everything, Julie Newmar* 1995; *Beyond the Call* 1996; *The Man Who Captured Eichmann* 1996; *The Lost World: Jurassic Park* 1997; *William Faulkner's Old Man* 1997; *A Map of the World* 1999

Howard, Arthur *Broken Blossoms* 1919; *Bottoms Up* 1959; *Paradisio* 1962; *The Love Cage* 1964; *Steptoe and Son* 1972

Howard, Clint *An Eye for an Eye* 1966; *The Jungle Book* 1967; *Gentle Giant* 1967; *The Wild Country* 1971; *Eat My Dust!* 1976; *Rock 'n' Roll High School* 1979; *Night Shift* 1982; *The Wraith* 1986; *Bugs* 1990;

RadioTimes ACTORS' INDEX

Disturbed 1990; *Body Chemistry 2: Voice of a Stranger* 1992; *Carnosaur* 1993; *Cheyenne Warrior* 1994; *Dillinger and Capone* 1995; *Santa with Muscles* 1996; *The Dentist II* 1998; *EDtv* 1999
Howard, Dennis *Go Tell the Spartans* 1977; *Shattered Innocence* 1988
Howard, Esther *Detour* 1945; *Dick Tracy vs Cueball* 1946; *The Falcon's Alibi* 1946; *Lady of Deceit* 1947
Howard, Jean *Claudia* 1943; *The Bermuda Mystery* 1944
Howard, Jean Speegle *Los Locos* 1997; *Spoiler* 1998
Howard (1), John *Valiant Is the Word for Carrie* 1936; *Lost Horizon* 1937; *The Man from Dakota* 1940; *The Philadelphia Story* 1940; *Texas Rangers Ride Again* 1940; *The Undying Monster* 1942; *The Fighting Kentuckian* 1949; *Make Haste to Live* 1954
Howard (2), John *The Club* 1980; *Bush Christmas* 1983; *Young Einstein* 1988
Howard, Joyce *Freedom Radio* 1941; *Love on the Dole* 1941; *Back Room Boy* 1942; *The Night Has Eyes* 1942; *The Gentle Sex* 1943; *They Met in the Dark* 1943
Howard, Kathleen *Death Takes a Holiday* 1934; *It's a Gift* 1934; *You're Telling Me!* 1934; *The Man on the Flying Trapeze* 1935; *Blossoms in the Dust* 1941; *The Navy Steps Out* 1941; *Sweetheart of the Campus* 1941; *Take a Letter, Darling* 1942
Howard, Ken *Tell Me That You Love Me, Junie Moon* 1970; *Such Good Friends* 1971; *The Strange Vengeance of Rosalie* 1972; *The Manhunter* 1974; *A Real American Hero* 1978; *Second Thoughts* 1982; *The Man in the Brown Suit* 1989; *Murder in New Hampshire* 1991; *Oscar* 1991; *To Walk Again* 1994; *Her Hidden Truth* 1995; *The Net* 1995; *Op Center* 1995; *Something Borrowed, Something Blue* 1997; *At First Sight* 1998
Howard, Kevyn Major *Alien Nation* 1988; *War Party* 1988
Howard, Kyle *House Arrest* 1996; *Robo Warriors* 1996; *Skeletons* 1996; *Baby Geniuses* 1999
Howard, Leslie *Outward Bound* 1930; *A Free Soul* 1931; *The Animal Kingdom* 1932; *Smilin' Through* 1932; *Berkeley Square* 1933; *Secrets* 1933; *British Agent* 1934; *The Scarlet Pimpernel* 1934; *Of Human Bondage* 1934; *The Petrified Forest* 1936; *Romeo and Juliet* 1936; *It's Love I'm After* 1937; *Stand-In* 1937; *Pygmalion* 1938; *Gone with the Wind* 1939; *Intermezzo* 1939; *49th Parallel* 1941; *Pimpernel Smith* 1941; *The First of the Few* 1942
Howard, Mary *All over Town* 1937; *Four Girls in White* 1939; *Abe Lincoln in Illinois* 1940; *Billy the Kid* 1941; *Riders of the Purple Sage* 1941; *Swamp Water* 1941
Howard, Michael *Out of the Clouds* 1954; *The Baby and the Battleship* 1956
Howard, Moe *Hollywood Party* 1934; *Have Rocket, Will Travel* 1959; *The Three Stooges in Orbit* 1962; *The Three Stooges Meet Hercules* 1962; *The Three Stooges Go around the World in a Daze* 1963; *The Outlaws Is Coming* 1965
Howard, Norah *Car of Dreams* 1935; *The Last Adventurers* 1937; *Two Loves* 1961
Howard, Rance *Gentle Giant* 1967; *Where the Lilies Bloom* 1974; *Eat My Dust!* 1976; *Limit Up* 1989
Howard, Ron *aka* **Howard, Ronnie,** *aka* **Howard, Ronny** *Door-to-Door Maniac* 1961; *The Courtship of Eddie's Father* 1963; *Village of the Giants* 1965; *The Wild Country* 1971; *American Graffiti* 1973; *Happy Mother's Day... Love, George* 1973; *The Spikes Gang* 1974; *Eat My Dust!* 1976; *The Shootist* 1976; *Grand Theft Auto* 1977; *More American Graffiti* 1979
Howard, Ronald *My Brother Jonathan* 1947; *Bond Street* 1948; *Night Beat* 1948; *Now Barabbas Was a Robber* 1949; *Portrait of Clare* 1950; *Assassin for Hire* 1951; *The Browning Version* 1951; *Night Was Our Friend* 1951; *House in the Woods* 1957; *Drango* 1957; *No Trees in the Street* 1958; *Gideon's Day* 1959; *The Monster of Highgate Ponds* 1961; *Live Now – Pay Later* 1962; *The Bay of Saint Michel* 1963; *Nurse on Wheels* 1963; *The Siege of the Saxons* 1963; *The Curse of the Mummy's Tomb* 1964; *Africa – Texas Style* 1967; *The Hunting Party* 1971
Howard, Shemp *The Bank Dick* 1940; *Arabian Nights* 1942
Howard, Sherman *The Hit List* 1993; *The Jungle Book: Mowgli's Story* 1998
Howard, Susan *Moonshine County Express* 1977; *Sidewinder One* 1977
Howard, Terrence *aka* **Howard, Terrence Dashon** *Mr Holland's Opus* 1995; *Sunset Park* 1996; *Best Laid Plans* 1999; *The Best Man* 1999
Howard, Trevor *Brief Encounter* 1945; *The Way to the Stars* 1945; *Green for Danger* 1946; *I See a Dark Stranger* 1946; *They Made Me a Fugitive* 1947; *The Passionate Friends* 1948; *Golden Salamander* 1949; *The Third Man* 1949; *The Clouded Yellow* 1950; *Odette* 1950; *Outcast of the Islands* 1951; *The Gift Horse* 1952; *The Heart of the Matter* 1953; *The Stranger's Hand* 1953; *The Cockleshell Heroes* 1955; *Around the World in 80 Days* 1956; *Run for the Sun* 1956; *Manuela* 1957; *Interpol* 1957; *The Key* 1958; *The Roots of Heaven* 1958; *Sons and Lovers* 1960; *Moment of Danger* 1960; *The Lion* 1962; *Mutiny on the Bounty* 1962; *Father Goose* 1964; *The Man in the Middle* 1964; *Operation Crossbow* 1965; *The Saboteur, Code Name Morituri* 1965; *Von Ryan's Express* 1965; *The Liquidator* 1966; *The Long Duel* 1966; *Triple Cross* 1966; *The Poppy Is Also a Flower* 1966; *Pretty Polly* 1967; *The Charge of the Light Brigade* 1968; *Battle of Britain* 1969; *Twinky* 1969; *The Night Visitor* 1970; *Ryan's Daughter* 1970; *Catch Me a Spy* 1971; *Kidnapped* 1971; *Mary, Queen of Scots* 1971; *The Offence* 1972; *Pope Joan* 1972; *Catholics* 1973; *Craze* 1973; *A Doll's House* 1973; *Ludwig* 1973; *The Count of Monte Cristo* 1974; *11 Harrowhouse* 1974; *Persecution* 1974; *Who?* 1974; *Conduct Unbecoming* 1975; *Hennessy* 1975; *Death in the Sun* 1975; *Aces High* 1976; *The Last Remake of Beau Geste* 1977; *Slavers* 1977; *Superman* 1978; *Stevie* 1978; *Hurricane* 1979; *Meteor* 1979; *The Sea Wolves* 1980; *Sir Henry at Rawlinson End* 1980; *Windwalker* 1980; *Gandhi* 1982; *The Missionary* 1982; *Sword of the Valiant* 1984; *Dust* 1985; *Foreign Body* 1986; *White Mischief* 1987; *The Dawning* 1988; *The Unholy* 1988
Howard, Vanessa *The Blood Beast Terror* 1967; *Here We Go round the Mulberry Bush* 1967; *Mumsy, Nanny, Sonny & Girly* 1970; *The Rise and Rise of Michael Rimmer* 1970
Howarth, Kevin *The Big Swap* 1997; *Razor Blade Smile* 1998
Howat, Clark *The Glass Web* 1953; *Billy Jack* 1971
Howell, C Thomas *The Outsiders* 1983; *Grandview, USA* 1984; *Red Dawn* 1984; *Tank* 1984; *Secret Admirer* 1985; *The Hitcher* 1986; *Soul Man* 1986; *Into the Homeland* 1987; *A Tiger's Tale* 1987; *Young Toscanini* 1988; *The Return of the Musketeers* 1989; *Curiosity Kills* 1990; *Side Out* 1990; *Kid* 1990; *Nickel & Dime* 1991; *That Night* 1992; *To Protect and Serve* 1992; *Breaking the Rules* 1992; *Gettysburg* 1993; *Dangerous Indiscretion* 1994; *Mad Dogs and Englishmen* 1994; *Natural Selection* 1994; *Suspect Device* 1995; *Hourglass* 1996; *Last Lives* 1997; *Fatal Affair* 1998
Howell, Hoke *Grand Theft Auto* 1977; *The Alarmist* 1997
Howell, Kenneth *The Eagle and the Hawk* 1933; *Pride of the Bowery* 1941
Howells, Ursula *The Oracle* 1952; *The Gilded Cage* 1954; *They Can't Hang Me* 1954; *Account Rendered* 1957; *The Sicilians* 1964; *Mumsy, Nanny, Sonny & Girly* 1970
Howerd, Frankie *The Runaway Bus* 1954; *Jumping for Joy* 1955; *The Ladykillers* 1955; *Further up the Creek* 1958; *Watch It, Sailor!* 1961; *The Great St Trinian's Train Robbery* 1966; *Carry On Doctor* 1968; *Carry On Up the Jungle* 1970; *Up Pompeii* 1971; *Up the Chastity Belt* 1971; *Up the Front* 1972; *The House in Nightmare Park* 1973; *Sgt Pepper's Lonely Hearts Club Band* 1978
Howes, Bobby *Please Teacher* 1937; *Happy Go Lovely* 1950
Howes, Hans *aka* **Howes, Hans R** *Fire and Ice* 1983; *Terminal Velocity* 1994
Howes, Reed *The Singing Fool* 1928; *The Dawn Rider* 1935; *Paradise Canyon* 1935; *A Million to One* 1937; *The Lone Rider in Ghost Town* 1941
Howes, Sally Ann *The Halfway House* 1943; *Dead of Night* 1945; *Pink String and Sealing Wax* 1945; *Anna Karenina* 1947; *Nicholas Nickleby* 1947; *The History of Mr Polly* 1948; *The Admirable Crichton* 1957; *Chitty Chitty Bang Bang* 1968; *The Hound of the Baskervilles* 1972
Howland, Jobyna *Rockabye* 1932; *Topaze* 1933
Howlett, Noel *Serious Charge* 1959; *Please Sir!* 1971
Howlin, Olin *Belle Starr* 1941; *The Blob* 1958
Howman, Karl *Babylon* 1980; *Party, Party* 1983
Hoyos, Cristina *Blood Wedding* 1981; *Carmen* 1983; *El Amor Brujo* 1986
Hoyos, Rodolfo *aka* **Hoyos Jr, Rodolfo** *Gypsy Colt* 1954; *The Americano* 1955; *The Brave One* 1956; *Villa!* 1958
Hoyt, Arthur *Camille* 1921; *The Lost World* 1925; *The Great McGinty* 1940; *Sullivan's Travels* 1941
Hoyt, John *OSS* 1946; *Brute Force* 1947; *My Favorite Brunette* 1947; *The Unfaithful* 1947; *Winter Meeting* 1948; *The Bribe* 1949; *Everybody Does It* 1949; *The Lady Gambles* 1949; *The Company She Keeps* 1950; *The Lawless* 1950; *When Worlds Collide* 1951; *The Blackboard Jungle* 1955; *The Purple Mask* 1955; *The Conqueror* 1956; *Death of a Scoundrel* 1956; *Mohawk* 1956; *Forever, Darling* 1956; *The Come On* 1956; *Merrill's Marauders* 1962; *The Man with the X-Ray Eyes* 1963; *Operation CIA* 1965; *Duel at Diablo* 1966; *Flesh Gordon* 1974
Hrusinsky, Rudolf *Baron Munchhausen* 1961; *Capricious Summer* 1968; *Cutting It Short* 1980; *My Sweet Little Village* 1986; *The Last of the Good Old Days* 1989; *Elementary School* 1991
Hubbard, John *aka* **Allan, Anthony** *Dramatic School* 1938; *The Housekeeper's Daughter* 1939; *Maisie* 1939; *Man and His Mate* 1940; *Turnabout* 1940; *Road Show* 1941; *You'll Never Get Rich* 1941; *Our Wife* 1941; *Chatterbox* 1943; *Up in Mabel's Room* 1944; *The Bullfighter and the Lady* 1951; *Escort West* 1959; *Gunfight at Comanche Creek* 1964
Hubbert, Cork *Under the Rainbow* 1981; *Caveman* 1981; *Not for Publication* 1984; *Legend* 1985; *The Ballad of the Sad Café* 1991
Huber, Harold *He Was Her Man* 1934; *The Gay Desperado* 1936; *Klondike Annie* 1936; *Charlie Chan on Broadway* 1937; *Mysterious Mr Moto* 1938; *Going Places* 1938; *Kit Carson* 1940; *Charlie Chan in Rio* 1941; *Down Mexico Way* 1941; *A Gentleman after Dark* 1942
Huber, Rhys *Circumstances Unknown* 1995; *National Lampoon's Golf Punks* 1998
Hubley, Season *The Lolly-Madonna War* 1973; *Catch My Soul* 1973; *Elvis – the Movie* 1979; *Hardcore* 1979; *Mrs R's Daughter* 1979; *Vice Squad* 1982; *Agatha Christie's A Caribbean Mystery* 1983; *Under the Influence* 1986; *PrettyKill* 1987; *Shakedown on the Sunset Strip* 1988; *Child in the Night* 1990; *Vestige of Honor* 1990; *Steel Justice* 1992; *No One Would Tell* 1996
Hubley, Whip *A Connecticut Yankee in King Arthur's Court* 1989; *Desire & Hell at Sunset Motel* 1991; *Lake Consequence* 1992; *Devlin* 1992; *Black Scorpion: Ground Zero* 1996
Hubschmid, Paul *The Tiger of Eschnapur* 1959; *The Indian Tomb* 1959; *Funeral in Berlin* 1966; *In Enemy Country* 1968; *Skullduggery* 1969
Huckabee, Cooper *Urban Cowboy* 1980; *The Funhouse* 1981; *Stand by Your Man* 1981; *The Curse* 1987; *Cohen and Tate* 1988; *Night Eyes* 1990
Hudd, Roy *The Blood Beast Terror* 1967; *Up Pompeii* 1971; *Up the Chastity Belt* 1971; *A Kind of Hush* 1998
Hudd, Walter *Rembrandt* 1936; *Elephant Boy* 1937; *I Know Where I'm Going* 1945; *The Two-Headed Spy* 1958
Huddleston, David *Brian's Song* 1971; *Bad Company* 1972; *Billy Two Hats* 1973; *Blazing Saddles* 1974; *The Klansman* 1974; *McQ* 1974; *Breakheart Pass* 1976; *The Oregon Trail* 1976; *Sherlock Holmes in New York* 1976; *Smokey and the Bandit II* 1980; *G.O.R.P.* 1980; *Family Reunion* 1981; *Santa Claus* 1985; *When the Bough Breaks* 1986; *Frantic* 1988; *Margaret Bourke-White* 1989; *The Big Lebowski* 1997
Hudson, Ernie *Crazy Times* 1981; *Spacehunter: Adventures in the Forbidden Zone* 1983; *Ghostbusters* 1984; *Collision Course* 1987; *Weeds* 1987; *The Dirty Dozen: the Fatal Mission* 1988; *Ghostbusters II* 1989; *Leviathan* 1989; *Broken Badges* 1990; *The Hand That Rocks the Cradle* 1992; *Sugar Hill* 1993; *Airheads* 1994; *The Cowboy Way* 1994; *The Crow* 1994; *Speechless* 1994; *The Basketball Diaries* 1995; *Congo* 1995; *The Substitute* 1996; *Tornado!* 1996; *Whiskey Down* 1996; *Operation Delta Force* 1996; *Mr Magoo* 1997; *Best of the Best: Without Warning* 1998
Hudson, Gary *Indecent Behavior* 1993; *Martial Outlaw* 1993; *The Wrong Woman* 1996; *Serial Killer* 1996
Hudson, John *The Battle at Apache Pass* 1952; *Return to Paradise* 1953; *Silver Lode* 1954; *The Marauders* 1955; *A Man for All Seasons* 1988
Hudson, Kate *Desert Blue* 1998; *200 Cigarettes* 1999; *Gossip* 1999
Hudson, Rochelle *Hell's Highway* 1932; *Dr Bull* 1933; *Bachelor Bait* 1934; *The Mighty Barnum* 1934; *Curly Top* 1935; *Life Begins at 40* 1935; *Les Misérables* 1935; *Way Down East* 1935; *Poppy* 1936; *Born Reckless* 1937; *Mr Moto Takes a Chance* 1938; *Rebel without a Cause* 1955; *Strait-Jacket* 1963; *The Night Walker* 1964
Hudson, Rock *Fighter Squadron* 1948; *Winchester '73* 1950; *I Was a Shoplifter* 1950; *One Way Street* 1950; *Bright Victory* 1951; *Bend of the River* 1952; *Has Anybody Seen My Gal?* 1952; *Horizons West* 1952; *The Lawless Breed* 1952; *Sea Devils* 1952; *Back to God's Country* 1953; *Gun Fury* 1953; *Seminole* 1953; *The Golden Blade* 1953; *Bengal Brigade* 1954; *Magnificent Obsession* 1954; *Taza, Son of Cochise* 1954; *All That Heaven Allows* 1955; *Never Say Goodbye* 1955; *One Desire* 1955; *Captain Lightfoot* 1955; *Giant* 1956; *Written on the Wind* 1956; *Battle Hymn* 1957; *A Farewell to Arms* 1957; *The Tarnished Angels* 1957; *Something of Value* 1957; *Twilight for the Gods* 1958; *Pillow Talk* 1959; *This Earth Is Mine* 1959; *Come September* 1961; *The Last Sunset* 1961; *Lover Come Back* 1961; *The Spiral Road* 1962; *A Gathering of Eagles* 1963; *Man's Favorite Sport?* 1964; *Send Me No Flowers* 1964; *Strange Bedfellows* 1965; *A Very Special Favor* 1965; *Blindfold* 1966; *Seconds* 1966; *Tobruk* 1966; *Ice Station Zebra* 1968; *A Fine Pair* 1969; *The Undefeated* 1969; *Darling Lili* 1970; *Hornet's Nest* 1970; *Pretty Maids All in a Row* 1971; *Showdown* 1973; *Avalanche* 1978; *The Mirror Crack'd* 1980; *The Ambassador* 1984
Hudson, Toni *Just One of the Guys* 1985; *Prime Risk* 1985; *Leatherface: the Texas Chainsaw Massacre III* 1990

Radio Times ACTORS' INDEX

Hunter, Tab *Track of the Cat* 1954; *Return to Treasure Island* 1954; *Battle Cry* 1955; *The Sea Chase* 1955; *The Burning Hills* 1956; *The Girl He Left Behind* 1956; *Hell Bent for Glory* 1957; *Damn Yankees* 1958; *They Came to Cordura* 1959; *That Kind of Woman* 1959; *The Pleasure of His Company* 1961; *Ride the Wild Surf* 1964; *City under the Sea* 1965; *The Loved One* 1965; *Hostile Guns* 1967; *The Arousers* 1970; *The Life and Times of Judge Roy Bean* 1972; *Katie: Portrait of a Centerfold* 1978; *Polyester* 1981; *Lust in the Dust* 1984; *Out of the Dark* 1988; *Cameron's Closet* 1988; *Dark Horse* 1992
Huntington, Sam *Jungle 2 Jungle* 1997; *Detroit Rock City* 1999
Huntley Jr, G P aka **Huntley Jr, George P** *The Charge of the Light Brigade* 1936; *Two-Faced Woman* 1941
Huntley, Raymond *Freedom Radio* 1941; *The Ghost of St Michael's* 1941; *The Ghost Train* 1941; *Pimpernel Smith* 1941; *The Way Ahead* 1944; *I See a Dark Stranger* 1946; *School for Secrets* 1946; *Broken Journey* 1948; *It's Hard to Be Good* 1948; *Mr Perrin and Mr Traill* 1948; *The Long Dark Hall* 1951; *Mr Denning Drives North* 1951; *The Last Page* 1952; *Laxdale Hall* 1953; *Orders Are Orders* 1954; *The Teckman Mystery* 1954; *The Constant Husband* 1955; *Brothers in Law* 1956; *The Green Man* 1956; *Room at the Top* 1958; *Bottoms Up* 1959; *The Mummy* 1959; *A French Mistress* 1960; *Sands of the Desert* 1960; *Suspect* 1960; *On the Beat* 1962; *The Black Torment* 1964; *Hostile Witness* 1968; *The Adding Machine* 1969; *That's Your Funeral* 1972
Huppert, Isabelle *Les Valseuses* 1974; *Doctor Françoise Gailland* 1975; *The Lacemaker* 1977; *Violette Nozière* 1977; *The Brontë Sisters* 1979; *Heaven's Gate* 1980; *Loulou* 1980; *Slow Motion* 1980; *Clean Slate* 1981; *Passion* 1982; *Entre Nous* 1983; *La Garce* 1984; *Cactus* 1986; *The Bedroom Window* 1987; *Story of Women* 1988; *Madame Bovary* 1991; *Après l'Amour* 1992; *The Flood* 1993; *Amateur* 1994; *La Séparation* 1994; *La Cérémonie* 1995; *Rien Ne Va Plus* 1997; *The School of Flesh* 1998
Hurlbut, Gladys *The Long, Long Trailer* 1954; *A Man Called Peter* 1955
Hurley, Elizabeth *Aria* 1987; *Rowing with the Wind* 1987; *Passenger 57* 1992; *Beyond Bedlam* 1993; *Mad Dogs and Englishmen* 1994; *Dangerous Ground* 1996; *Austin Powers: International Man of Mystery* 1997; *Permanent Midnight* 1998; *My Favorite Martian* 1999; *Austin Powers: The Spy Who Shagged Me* 1999; *EDtv* 1999
Hursey, Sherry *Friendly Fire* 1979; *Mrs Lambert Remembers Love* 1991
Hurst, Brandon *Dr Jekyll and Mr Hyde* 1920; *The Hunchback of Notre Dame* 1923; *The Thief of Bagdad* 1924; *Love* 1927; *Annie Laurie* 1927; *Murders in the Rue Morgue* 1932
Hurst, Paul *The Secret Six* 1931; *The Big Stampede* 1932; *The Sphinx* 1933; *Hold Your Man* 1933; *Josette* 1938; *Bad Lands* 1939; *The Westerner* 1940; *Girl Rush* 1944
Hurst, Rick *Tunnelvision* 1976; *Going Ape!* 1981
Hurst, Veronica *Laughter in Paradise* 1951; *Angels One Five* 1952; *Will Any Gentleman...?* 1953; *Bang! You're Dead* 1954; *The Gilded Cage* 1954; *Dead Man's Evidence* 1962; *Licensed to Kill* 1965
Hurt, John *The Wild and the Willing* 1962; *This Is My Street* 1963; *A Man for All Seasons* 1966; *Before Winter Comes* 1968; *Sinful Davey* 1969; *In Search of Gregory* 1970; *10 Rillington Place* 1970; *The Pied Piper* 1971; *Little Malcolm and His Struggle Against the Eunuchs* 1974; *The Ghoul* 1975; *East of Elephant Rock* 1976; *The Disappearance* 1977; *The Lord of the Rings* 1978; *Midnight Express* 1978; *The Shout* 1978; *Watership Down* 1978; *Alien* 1979; *The Elephant Man* 1980; *Heaven's Gate* 1980; *Night Crossing* 1981; *Partners* 1982; *The Plague Dogs* 1982; *Champions* 1983; *The Osterman Weekend* 1983; *The Hit* 1984; *Nineteen Eighty-Four* 1984; *Success Is the Best Revenge* 1984; *The Black Cauldron* 1985; *After Darkness* 1985; *Jake Speed* 1986; *Rocinante* 1986; *Aria* 1987; *From the Hip* 1987; *Spaceballs* 1987; *Vincent: the Life and Death of Vincent Van Gogh* 1987; *White Mischief* 1987; *Scandal* 1988; *The Field* 1990; *Frankenstein Unbound* 1990; *King Ralph* 1991; *Lapse of Memory* 1992; *Even Cowgirls Get the Blues* 1993; *Monolith* 1993; *Shades of Fear* 1993; *Second Best* 1994; *Dead Man* 1995; *Rob Roy* 1995; *Wild Bill* 1995; *Contact* 1997; *All the Little Animals* 1998; *Love and Death on Long Island* 1998; *Night Train* 1998; *You're Dead* 1999; *The Tigger Movie* 2000; *A Monkey's Tale* 2000
Hurt, Mary Beth *Interiors* 1978; *Chilly Scenes of Winter* 1979; *A Change of Seasons* 1980; *The World According to Garp* 1982; *Compromising Positions* 1985; *DARYL* 1985; *Parents* 1988; *Slaves of New York* 1989; *Defenseless* 1991; *Light Sleeper* 1991; *The Age of Innocence* 1993; *My Boyfriend's Back* 1993; *Six Degrees of Separation* 1993; *Affliction* 1997; *Bringing out the Dead* 1999
Hurt, William *Altered States* 1980; *Body Heat* 1981; *Eyewitness* 1981; *The Big Chill* 1983; *Gorky Park* 1983; *Kiss of the Spider Woman* 1985; *Children of a Lesser God* 1986; *Broadcast News* 1987; *The Accidental Tourist* 1988; *A Time of Destiny* 1988; *Alice* 1990; *I Love You to Death* 1990; *The Doctor* 1991; *Until the End of the World* 1991; *Mr Wonderful* 1992; *The Plague* 1992; *Second Best* 1994; *Trial by Jury* 1994; *Smoke* 1995; *Jane Eyre* 1996; *Loved* 1996; *Michael* 1996; *Lost in Space* 1997; *Dark City* 1998; *One True Thing* 1998; *The Proposition* 1998; *The Miracle Maker* 1999; *Sunshine* 1999
Hussey, Olivia *The Battle of the Villa Fiorita* 1964; *Romeo and Juliet* 1968; *Lost Horizon* 1973; *Black Christmas* 1974; *Death on the Nile* 1978; *The Cat and the Canary* 1979; *The Man with Bogart's Face* 1980; *Virus* 1980; *Turkey Shoot* 1981; *Distortions* 1987; *Psycho IV: the Beginning* 1990; *Quest of the Delta Knights* 1993; *Save Me* 1994
Hussey, Ruth *Man-Proof* 1937; *Another Thin Man* 1939; *Blackmail* 1939; *Fast and Furious* 1939; *Maisie* 1939; *Flight Command* 1940; *Northwest Passage* 1940; *The Philadelphia Story* 1940; *Susan and God* 1940; *HM Pulham Esq* 1941; *Our Wife* 1941; *Tender Comrade* 1943; *Marine Raiders* 1944; *The Uninvited* 1944; *Bedside Manner* 1945; *The Great Gatsby* 1949; *Mr Music* 1950; *That's My Boy* 1951; *Stars and Stripes Forever* 1952; *The Lady Wants Mink* 1953; *The Facts of Life* 1960
Huster, Francis *Second Chance* 1976; *Another Man, Another Chance* 1977; *Edith and Marcel* 1983; *I Married a Dead Man* 1983; *La Femme Publique* 1984; *Le Dîner de Cons* 1998
Huston, Anjelica *Hamlet* 1969; *Sinful Davey* 1969; *A Walk with Love and Death* 1969; *The Last Tycoon* 1976; *Swashbuckler* 1976; *The Postman Always Rings Twice* 1981; *The Ice Pirates* 1984; *This Is Spinal Tap* 1984; *Prizzi's Honor* 1985; *The Dead* 1987; *Gardens of Stone* 1987; *A Handful of Dust* 1987; *Mr North* 1988; *Crimes and Misdemeanors* 1989; *Enemies, a Love Story* 1989; *The Witches* 1989; *The Grifters* 1990; *The Addams Family* 1991; *Addams Family Values* 1993; *And the Band Played On* 1993; *Manhattan Murder Mystery* 1993; *The Crossing Guard* 1995; *The Perez Family* 1995; *Buffalo '66* 1997; *Ever After* 1998; *Phoenix* 1998; *Agnes Browne* 1999
Huston, John *The Treasure of the Sierra Madre* 1948; *The Cardinal* 1963; *The Bible...in the Beginning* 1966; *Casino Royale* 1967; *Candy* 1968; *De Sade* 1969; *Myra Breckinridge* 1970; *The Deserter* 1971; *Man in the Wilderness* 1971; *The Life and Times of Judge Roy Bean* 1972; *Battle for the Planet of the Apes* 1973; *Chinatown* 1974; *Breakout* 1975; *The Wind and the Lion* 1975; *Sherlock Holmes in New York* 1976; *Tentacles* 1977; *Winter Kills* 1979; *Wise Blood* 1979; *Head On* 1980; *The Visitor* 1980; *Cannery Row* 1982; *The Black Cauldron* 1985; *Mr Corbett's Ghost* 1986
Huston, Virginia *Nocturne* 1946; *Build My Gallows High* 1947; *The Doolins of Oklahoma* 1949; *Flamingo Road* 1949; *Flight to Mars* 1951; *Tarzan's Peril* 1951
Huston, Walter *The Virginian* 1929; *Abraham Lincoln* 1930; *The Criminal Code* 1930; *The Virtuous Sin* 1930; *American Madness* 1932; *Law and Order* 1932; *Rain* 1932; *The Beast of the City* 1932; *The Wet Parade* 1932; *Ann Vickers* 1933; *Gabriel over the White House* 1933; *The Prizefighter and the Lady* 1933; *The Tunnel* 1935; *Dodsworth* 1936; *Of Human Hearts* 1938; *The Light That Failed* 1939; *Daniel and the Devil* 1941; *The Shanghai Gesture* 1941; *Swamp Water* 1941; *Yankee Doodle Dandy* 1942; *The Battle of Russia* 1943; *Edge of Darkness* 1943; *Mission to Moscow* 1943; *The North Star* 1943; *The Outlaw* 1943; *Prelude to War* 1943; *Dragon Seed* 1944; *And Then There Were None* 1945; *Dragonwyck* 1946; *Duel in the Sun* 1946; *Summer Holiday* 1948; *The Treasure of the Sierra Madre* 1948; *The Great Sinner* 1949; *The Furies* 1950
Hutchence, Michael *Dogs in Space* 1986; *Frankenstein Unbound* 1990
Hutcheson, David *The Love Test* 1935; *The Life and Death of Colonel Blimp* 1943; *Vice Versa* 1947
Hutchings, Geoffrey *Clockwise* 1986; *Wish You Were Here* 1987; *Heart of Darkness* 1993
Hutchins, Will *Hell Bent for Glory* 1957; *No Time for Sergeants* 1958; *Claudelle Inglish* 1961; *Merrill's Marauders* 1962; *Clambake* 1967; *The Shooting* 1967
Hutchinson, Harry *Dublin Nightmare* 1958; *Blow Up* 1966
Hutchinson, Josephine *Oil for the Lamps of China* 1935; *The Story of Louis Pasteur* 1936; *Son of Frankenstein* 1939; *My Son, My Son* 1940; *Tom Brown's Schooldays* 1940; *The Tender Years* 1947; *Adventure in Baltimore* 1949; *Love Is Better Than Ever* 1951; *Ruby Gentry* 1952; *Miracle in the Rain* 1956; *Gun for a Coward* 1957; *Sing, Boy, Sing* 1958; *Walk like a Dragon* 1960; *Baby the Rain Must Fall* 1965
Hutchinson, Ken *The Wrath of God* 1972; *Blonde Fist* 1991
Hutchison, Doug *The Chocolate War* 1988; *The Green Mile* 1999
Hutchison, Fiona *Biggles* 1986; *American Gothic* 1987; *Rage* 1995
Hutchison, Ken *Straw Dogs* 1971; *Sweeney 2* 1978; *Ladyhawke* 1985
Huth, Harold *Rome Express* 1932; *The Ghoul* 1933; *The Camels Are Coming* 1934
Hutson, Candace aka **Hutson, Candy** *Hider in the House* 1989; *The Land before Time II: the Great Valley Adventure* 1994
Hutton, Betty *The Fleet's In* 1942; *Star Spangled Rhythm* 1942; *Happy Go Lucky* 1943; *Let's Face It* 1943; *Here Come the Waves* 1944; *The Miracle of Morgan's Creek* 1944; *Duffy's Tavern* 1945; *Incendiary Blonde* 1945; *The Stork Club* 1945; *The Perils of Pauline* 1947; *Dream Girl* 1948; *Annie Get Your Gun* 1950; *Let's Dance* 1950; *Sailor Beware* 1951; *The Greatest Show on Earth* 1952; *Somebody Loves Me* 1952
Hutton, Jim *The Subterraneans* 1960; *Where the Boys Are* 1960; *Bachelor in Paradise* 1961; *The Honeymoon Machine* 1961; *Period of Adjustment* 1962; *The Hallelujah Trail* 1965; *Major Dundee* 1965; *Never Too Late* 1965; *Walk, Don't Run* 1966; *Who's Minding the Mint?* 1967; *The Green Berets* 1968; *Hellfighters* 1969; *Psychic Killer* 1975
Hutton, Lauren *Paper Lion* 1968; *Little Fauss and Big Halsy* 1970; *The Gambler* 1974; *Gator* 1976; *Welcome to LA* 1976; *Viva Knievel!* 1977; *Someone's Watching Me!* 1978; *American Gigolo* 1980; *Paternity* 1981; *Zorro, the Gay Blade* 1981; *Starflight One* 1983; *Lassiter* 1984; *Scandal Sheet* 1985; *Once Bitten* 1985; *Malone* 1987; *Timestalkers* 1987; *Perfect People* 1988; *Fear* 1990; *Millions* 1991; *Missing Pieces* 1991; *Guilty as Charged* 1991; *My Father, the Hero* 1994; *We the Jury* 1996
Hutton, Marion *Orchestra Wives* 1942; *Abbott and Costello in Society* 1944; *Love Happy* 1949
Hutton, Robert *Destination Tokyo* 1943; *Hollywood Canteen* 1944; *Roughly Speaking* 1945; *And Baby Makes Three* 1949; *The Man on the Eiffel Tower* 1949; *Slaughter Trail* 1951; *The Steel Helmet* 1951; *Man from Tangier* 1957; *The Man without a Body* 1957; *The Colossus of New York* 1958; *Showdown at Boot Hill* 1958; *Cinderfella* 1960; *The Jailbreakers* 1960; *The Sicilians* 1964; *They Came from beyond Space* 1967; *Torture Garden* 1967
Hutton, Timothy *And Baby Makes Six* 1979; *Friendly Fire* 1979; *Ordinary People* 1980; *Taps* 1981; *Daniel* 1983; *Iceman* 1984; *The Falcon and the Snowman* 1985; *Turk 182!* 1985; *Made in Heaven* 1987; *Everybody's All-American* 1988; *A Time of Destiny* 1988; *Torrents of Spring* 1989; *Q & A* 1990; *The Dark Half* 1991; *Mr and Mrs Loving* 1993; *The Temp* 1993; *Zelda* 1993; *Cosa Nostra: the Last Word* 1995; *French Kiss* 1995; *Beautiful Girls* 1996; *City of Industry* 1996; *Playing God* 1997; *Aldrich Ames: Traitor Within* 1998; *The General's Daughter* 1999
Huxtable, Judy *The Psychopath* 1966; *Scream and Scream Again* 1969; *Die Screaming Marianne* 1970
Hyams, Leila *The Big House* 1930; *The Big Broadcast* 1932; *Freaks* 1932; *Island of Lost Souls* 1932; *Red-Headed Woman* 1932; *Ruggles of Red Gap* 1935
Hyatt, Bobby *He Ran All the Way* 1951; *Gypsy Colt* 1954
Hyatt, Pam *The Care Bears Movie II: a New Generation* 1986; *Visitors of the Night* 1995
Hyde, Jonathan *Deadly Advice* 1993; *Being Human* 1994; *I Spy Returns* 1994; *Richie Rich* 1994; *Jumanji* 1995; *Anaconda* 1997; *The Mummy* 1999
Hyde White, Wilfrid *Murder by Rope* 1936; *Elephant Boy* 1937; *Poison Pen* 1939; *It's Turned Out Nice Again* 1941; *The Demi-Paradise* 1943; *The Winslow Boy* 1948; *Adam and Evelyne* 1949; *Conspirator* 1949; *Britannia Mews* 1949; *Golden Salamander* 1949; *The Man on the Eiffel Tower* 1949; *The Third Man* 1949; *Highly Dangerous* 1950; *Last Holiday* 1950; *Mr Drake's Duck* 1950; *Trio* 1950; *The Browning Version* 1951; *Mr Denning Drives North* 1951; *The Million Pound Note* 1953; *The Story of Gilbert and Sullivan* 1953; *Duel in the Jungle* 1954; *To Dorothy, a Son* 1954; *Betrayed* 1954; *The Adventures of Quentin Durward* 1955; *John and Julie* 1955; *The March Hare* 1956; *My Teenage Daughter* 1956; *Tarzan and the Lost Safari* 1956; *That Woman Opposite* 1957; *The Vicious Circle* 1957; *The Silken Affair* 1957; *The Rainbow Jacket* 1958; *Up the Creek* 1958; *Carry On Nurse* 1959; *Libel* 1959; *Life in Emergency Ward 10* 1959; *North West Frontier* 1959; *Let's Make Love* 1960; *Two Way Stretch* 1960; *Ada* 1961; *In Search of the Castaways* 1961; *On the Double* 1961; *On the Fiddle* 1961; *Crooks Anonymous* 1962; *My Fair Lady* 1964; *John Goldfarb, Please Come Home* 1964; *Ten Little Indians* 1965; *You Must Be Joking!* 1965; *Chamber of Horrors* 1966; *The Liquidator* 1966; *Our Man in Marrakesh* 1966; *The Sandwich Man* 1966; *New Face in*

Ivernel, Daniel *Ulysses* 1954; *Madame du Barry* 1954; *Sundays and Cybèle* 1962; *The Diary of a Chambermaid* 1964; *That Man George* 1965; *Borsalino and Co* 1974

Ivers, Robert *The Delicate Delinquent* 1957; *Short Cut to Hell* 1957; *I Married a Monster from Outer Space* 1958; *GI Blues* 1960

Ives, Burl *Smoky* 1946; *Green Grass of Wyoming* 1948; *Station West* 1948; *So Dear to My Heart* 1949; *Sierra* 1950; *East of Eden* 1955; *The Power and the Prize* 1956; *The Big Country* 1958; *Cat on a Hot Tin Roof* 1958; *Desire under the Elms* 1958; *Wind across the Everglades* 1958; *Day of the Outlaw* 1959; *Our Man in Havana* 1959; *Let No Man Write My Epitaph* 1960; *The Spiral Road* 1962; *Summer Magic* 1963; *Ensign Pulver* 1964; *The Brass Bottle* 1964; *Jules Verne's Rocket to the Moon* 1967; *The McMasters* 1970; *The Only Way Out Is Dead* 1970; *Baker's Hawk* 1976; *Just You and Me, Kid* 1979; *Earthbound* 1981; *White Dog* 1981; *Uphill All the Way* 1985; *Two Moon Junction* 1988

Ivey, Dana *Explorers* 1985; *Dirty Rotten Scoundrels* 1988; *The Addams Family* 1991; *A Child Lost Forever* 1992; *The Adventures of Huck Finn* 1993; *Guilty as Sin* 1993; *Simon Birch* 1998

Ivey, Judith *Harry and Son* 1984; *The Lonely Guy* 1984; *The Woman in Red* 1984; *Compromising Positions* 1985; *Brighton Beach Memoirs* 1986; *Hello Again* 1987; *In Country* 1989; *Decoration Day* 1990; *Everybody Wins* 1990; *Love Hurts* 1990; *A Woman Deceived* 1992; *Almost Golden: the Jessica Savitch Story* 1995; *The Devil's Advocate* 1997; *Washington Square* 1997; *What the Deaf Man Heard* 1997

Ivo, Tommy *Treasure of Lost Canyon* 1952; *Dragstrip Girl* 1957

Iwashita, Shima *An Autumn Afternoon* 1962; *Harakiri* 1962; *Twin Sisters of Kyoto* 1963; *The Empty Table* 1985

Izay, Victor *Billy Jack* 1971; *The Trial of Billy Jack* 1974

Izzard, Eddie *The Secret Agent* 1996; *The Avengers* 1998; *Velvet Goldmine* 1998; *Circus* 1999; *The Criminal* 1999

J

Jack, Wolfman *American Graffiti* 1973; *Murder at the Mardi Gras* 1978

Jackée *Driving Academy* 1988; *The Reluctant Agent* 1989; *Ladybugs* 1992

Jacklin, Ian *Kickboxer III: the Art of War* 1992; *Death Match* 1994

Jackson, Anne *The Tiger Makes Out* 1967; *How to Save a Marriage and Ruin Your Life* 1968; *The Secret Life of an American Wife* 1968; *Dirty Dingus Magee* 1970; *Zigzag* 1970; *Nasty Habits* 1976; *The Bell Jar* 1979; *The Shining* 1980; *Leave 'Em Laughing* 1981; *Sam's Son* 1984; *Folks!* 1992; *Rescuers: Stories of Courage – Two Women* 1997

Jackson, Barry *The Bofors Gun* 1968; *Alfred the Great* 1969; *Diamonds on Wheels* 1973; *Mr Love* 1985

Jackson, Brad *April Love* 1957; *Viking Women and the Sea Serpent* 1957

Jackson, Freda *Beware of Pity* 1946; *Women of Twilight* 1952; *The Flesh Is Weak* 1957; *The Brides of Dracula* 1960; *The Shadow of the Cat* 1961; *West 11* 1963; *Die, Monster, Die!* 1965; *The Valley of Gwangi* 1969

Jackson, Glenda *Marat/Sade* 1966; *Tell Me Lies* 1967; *Women in Love* 1969; *The Music Lovers* 1970; *Mary, Queen of Scots* 1971; *Sunday, Bloody Sunday* 1971; *Bequest to the Nation* 1972; *The Triple Echo* 1972; *A Touch of Class* 1973; *The Maids* 1974; *Hedda* 1975; *The Romantic Englishwoman* 1975; *The Incredible Sarah* 1976; *Nasty Habits* 1976; *The Class of Miss MacMichael* 1978; *House Calls* 1978; *Stevie* 1978; *Lost and Found* 1979; *H.E.A.L.T.H.* 1980; *Hopscotch* 1980; *The Patricia Neal Story: an Act of Love* 1981; *Giro City* 1982; *The Return of the Soldier* 1982; *Turtle Diary* 1985; *Beyond Therapy* 1987; *Business as Usual* 1987; *The Rainbow* 1988; *Salome's Last Dance* 1988; *King of the Wind* 1989

Jackson, Gordon *The Foreman Went to France* 1941; *Millions like Us* 1943; *San Demetrio London* 1943; *Pink String and Sealing Wax* 1945; *The Captive Heart* 1946; *Against the Wind* 1947; *Eureka Stockade* 1949; *Whisky Galore!* 1949; *Bitter Springs* 1950; *Happy Go Lovely* 1950; *The Love Lottery* 1953; *Meet Mr Lucifer* 1953; *Passage Home* 1955; *The Quatermass Experiment* 1955; *The Baby and the Battleship* 1956; *Sailor Beware!* 1956; *Women without Men* 1956; *Hell Drivers* 1957; *Abandon Ship!* 1957; *Rockets Galore* 1958; *Blind Date* 1959; *The Bridal Path* 1959; *Devil's Bait* 1959; *The Navy Lark* 1959; *Yesterday's Enemy* 1959; *Cone of Silence* 1960; *Greyfriars Bobby* 1960; *Tunes of Glory* 1960; *Mutiny on the Bounty* 1962; *The Great Escape* 1963; *The Long Ships* 1963; *Daylight Robbery* 1964; *The Ipcress File* 1965; *The Fighting Prince of Donegal* 1966; *Danger Route* 1967; *Hamlet* 1969; *The Prime of Miss Jean Brodie* 1969; *Run Wild, Run Free* 1969; *Scrooge* 1970; *Kidnapped* 1971; *Madame Sin* 1972; *Golden Rendezvous* 1977; *The Medusa Touch* 1978; *The Shooting Party* 1984; *Gunpowder* 1985; *The Whistle Blower* 1986

Jackson, Harry *The True Story of Lynn Stuart* 1957; *The Night Runner* 1957

Jackson, Jay *Days of Thrills and Laughter* 1961; *Laurel and Hardy's Laughing 20s* 1965

Jackson, John M *aka* **Jackson, John** *Baja Oklahoma* 1988; *Cold Sassy Tree* 1989; *Sudie and Simpson* 1990; *Blind Hate* 1991; *Career Opportunities* 1991; *Eve of Destruction* 1991; *A Thousand Heroes* 1992; *Black Widow Murders* 1993; *Sudden Fury* 1993; *The Glimmer Man* 1996

Jackson, Jonathan *Camp Nowhere* 1994; *The Deep End of the Ocean* 1999

Jackson, Joshua *aka* **Jackson, Josh** *The Mighty Ducks* 1992; *Andre* 1994; *Magic in the Water* 1995; *D3: the Mighty Ducks* 1996; *Robin of Locksley* 1996; *Apt Pupil* 1997; *Urban Legend* 1998; *Cruel Intentions* 1999; *Gossip* 1999; *The Skulls* 2000

Jackson, Kate *Night of Dark Shadows* 1971; *Limbo* 1972; *Death at Love House* 1976; *Thunder and Lightning* 1977; *Making Love* 1982; *Loverboy* 1989; *The Stranger Within* 1990; *Black Death* 1992; *Empty Cradle* 1993; *Armed and Innocent* 1994; *Hard Evidence* 1994; *Silence of Adultery* 1995; *Murder on the Iditarod Trail* 1995; *Panic in the Skies!* 1996; *A Kidnapping in the Family* 1996; *Murder in a College Town* 1997

Jackson, Leonard *Ganja and Hess* 1973; *The Brother from Another Planet* 1984

Jackson, Mary *Targets* 1968; *A Small Killing* 1981; *A Family Thing* 1996

Jackson, Michael *The Wiz* 1978; *Moonwalker* 1988

Jackson, Peter *Bad Taste* 1987; *Braindead* 1992

Jackson, Philip *High Hopes* 1988; *Bad Behaviour* 1992; *Little Voice* 1998

Jackson, Ray *The Final Test* 1953; *Dunkirk* 1958

Jackson, Rose *aka* **Jackson, Rosemarie** *Hangin' with the Homeboys* 1991; *Dead Presidents* 1995

Jackson, Samuel L *aka* **Jackson, Samuel** *Uncle Tom's Cabin* 1987; *Eddie Murphy Raw* 1987; *School Daze* 1988; *Do the Right Thing* 1989; *Betsy's Wedding* 1990; *Def by Temptation* 1990; *The Exorcist III* 1990; *A Shock to the System* 1990; *In the Line of Duty: Mob Justice* 1991; *Johnny Suede* 1991; *Jungle Fever* 1991; *Jumpin' at the Boneyard* 1991; *Strictly Business* 1991; *Fathers and Sons* 1992; *Juice* 1992; *Patriot Games* 1992; *White Sands* 1992; *Amos & Andrew* 1993; *Jurassic Park* 1993; *Menace II Society* 1993; *National Lampoon's Loaded Weapon 1* 1993; *Against the Wall* 1994; *Assault at West Point: the Court Martial of John Whittaker* 1994; *Fresh* 1994; *Kiss of Death* 1994; *Pulp Fiction* 1994; *Hail Caesar* 1994; *Die Hard with a Vengeance* 1995; *Fluke* 1995; *Losing Isaiah* 1995; *The Great White Hype* 1996; *Hard Eight* 1996; *The Long Kiss Goodnight* 1996; *A Time to Kill* 1996; *The Search for One-Eye Jimmy* 1996; *Eve's Bayou* 1997; *Jackie Brown* 1997; *One Eight Seven* 1997; *The Negotiator* 1998; *Out of Sight* 1998; *Sphere* 1998; *The Red Violin* 1998; *Star Wars Episode I: the Phantom Menace* 1999; *Deep Blue Sea* 1999; *Rules of Engagement* 2000

Jackson, Selmer *Stars on Parade* 1944; *Autumn Leaves* 1956

Jackson, Sherry *The Miracle of Fatima* 1952; *Trouble along the Way* 1953; *Come Next Spring* 1956; *Wild on the Beach* 1965; *Gunn* 1967

Jackson, Stoney *Blind Vision* 1992; *By the Sword* 1992; *Trespass* 1992; *Black Scorpion: Ground Zero* 1996

Jackson, Thomas E *aka* **Jackson, Thomas** *Broadway* 1929; *Little Caesar* 1931; *The Woman in the Window* 1945

Jackson, Tom *The Diviners* 1992; *Medicine River* 1992

Jackson, Victoria *Casual Sex?* 1988; *Family Business* 1989; *UHF* 1989; *Based on an Untrue Story* 1993; *Bombshell* 1997

Jacob, Catherine *Tatie Danielle* 1990; *Merci la Vie* 1991; *Mon Père Ce Héros* 1991; *Nine Months* 1994

Jacob, Irène *Erreur de jeunesse* 1989; *The Double Life of Véronique* 1991; *The Secret Garden* 1993; *Three Colours Red* 1994; *All Men Are Mortal* 1995; *Beyond the Clouds* 1995; *Othello* 1995; *Victory* 1995; *Incognito* 1997; *US Marshals* 1998; *My Life So Far* 1999; *History Is Made at Night* 1999

Jacobi, Derek *Othello* 1965; *Three Sisters* 1970; *Blue Blood* 1973; *The Day of the Jackal* 1973; *The Odessa File* 1974; *The Medusa Touch* 1978; *The Human Factor* 1979; *Enigma* 1982; *The Secret of NIMH* 1982; *The Hunchback of Notre Dame* 1982; *Little Dorrit* 1987; *The Secret Garden* 1987; *The Tenth Man* 1988; *Henry V* 1989; *The Fool* 1990; *Dead Again* 1991; *Hamlet* 1996; *Love Is the Devil: Study for a Portrait of Francis Bacon* 1998; *Up at the Villa* 1998; *Basil* 1998; *Gladiator* 2000

Jacobi, Lou *The Diary of Anne Frank* 1959; *Irma la Douce* 1963; *The Last of the Secret Agents* 1966; *Everything You Always Wanted to Know about Sex (But Were Afraid to Ask)* 1972; *The Judge and Jake Wyler* 1972; *Roseland* 1977; *The Magician of Lublin* 1979; *The Lucky Star* 1980; *My Favorite Year* 1982; *Isaac Littlefeathers* 1984; *Avalon* 1990; *I Don't Buy Kisses Anymore* 1992; *IQ* 1995

Jacobs, Martin *Over the Hill* 1992; *Turtle Beach* 1992

Jacobs, Paula *She'll Be Wearing Pink Pyjamas* 1984; *The Remains of the Day* 1993

Jacobs, Steve *aka* **Jacobs, Steven** *Shadows of the Peacock* 1987; *Kokoda Crescent* 1989; *Father* 1990; *To Have & to Hold* 1996

Jacobson, Dean *Lobster Man from Mars* 1989; *Child's Play 3* 1991

Jacobsson, Ulla *Smiles of a Summer Night* 1955; *Zulu* 1964; *The Heroes of Telemark* 1965; *Fox and His Friends* 1975

Jacoby, Billy *The Beastmaster* 1982; *Just One of the Guys* 1985

Jacoby, Bobby *Tremors* 1989; *Meet the Applegates* 1991; *Night of the Demons 2* 1994

Jacoby, Scott *Baxter* 1973; *The Little Girl Who Lives Down the Lane* 1976; *Love and the Midnight Auto Supply* 1977; *The Diary of Anne Frank* 1980

Jacott, Carlos *Kicking and Screaming* 1995; *Mr Jealousy* 1997; *Being John Malkovich* 1999

Jacques, Hattie *Trottie True* 1949; *Chance of a Lifetime* 1950; *Scrooge* 1951; *The Pickwick Papers* 1952; *Our Girl Friday* 1953; *Carry On Sergeant* 1958; *The Square Peg* 1958; *Carry On Nurse* 1959; *Carry On Teacher* 1959; *Follow a Star* 1959; *The Navy Lark* 1959; *Carry On Constable* 1960; *Carry On Regardless* 1960; *Make Mine Mink* 1960; *School for Scoundrels* 1960; *Watch Your Stern* 1960; *In the Doghouse* 1961; *She'll Have to Go* 1961; *Carry On Cabby* 1963; *The Bobo* 1967; *The Plank* 1967; *Carry On Doctor* 1968; *Carry On Again Doctor* 1969; *Carry On Camping* 1969; *Crooks and Coronets* 1969; *Monte Carlo or Bust* 1969; *Carry On Loving* 1970; *Carry On at Your Convenience* 1971; *Carry On Abroad* 1972; *Carry On Matron* 1972; *Carry On Dick* 1974

Jacques, Yves *The Decline of the American Empire* 1986; *Jesus of Montreal* 1989; *Class Trip* 1998

Jade, Claude *Stolen Kisses* 1968; *Topaz* 1969; *Uncle Benjamin* 1969; *Bed and Board* 1970; *Love on the Run* 1979

Jaeckel, Richard *Guadalcanal Diary* 1943; *Wing and a Prayer* 1944; *Come Back, Little Sheba* 1952; *My Son John* 1952; *Big Leaguer* 1953; *The Shanghai Story* 1954; *Attack!* 1956; *3:10 to Yuma* 1957; *Cowboy* 1958; *The Lineup* 1958; *The Naked and the Dead* 1958; *The Gun Runners* 1958; *The Gallant Hours* 1960; *Platinum High School* 1960; *Town without Pity* 1961; *Nightmare in the Sun* 1964; *Once Before I Die* 1965; *The Dirty Dozen* 1967; *The Devil's Brigade* 1968; *Chisum* 1970; *Never Give an Inch* 1971; *Ulzana's Raid* 1972; *The Outfit* 1973; *Pat Garrett and Billy the Kid* 1973; *The Drowning Pool* 1975; *Part 2 Walking Tall* 1975; *Grizzly* 1976; *Day of the Animals* 1977; *The Dark* 1979; *Salvage* 1979; *Pacific Inferno* 1979; *Herbie Goes Bananas* 1980; *The California Dolls* 1981; *Cold River* 1982; *Starman* 1984; *Black Moon Rising* 1985; *The Dirty Dozen: the Next Mission* 1985; *Baywatch: Panic at Malibu Pier* 1989; *Delta Force 2* 1990; *Martial Outlaw* 1993

Jaeger, Frederick *One of Those Things* 1970; *Situation* 1973

Jaenicke, Hannes *Out of Order* 1984; *Operation Dead End* 1986; *Hostile Force* 1996; *Midnight Man* 1998; *The Hunted* 1998; *The White Raven* 1998

Jaffe, Carl *I Didn't Do It* 1945; *State Secret* 1950; *Desperate Moment* 1953; *Park Plaza 605* 1953; *Child's Play* 1954; *The Traitor* 1957; *Escapement* 1958; *First Man into Space* 1958; *Subway in the Sky* 1958

Jaffe, Chapelle *Who Has Seen the Wind* 1977; *Confidential* 1986

Jaffe, Sam *The Scarlet Empress* 1934; *We Live Again* 1934; *Lost Horizon* 1937; *Gunga Din* 1939; *Stage Door Canteen* 1943; *The Accused* 1949; *Rope of Sand* 1949; *The Asphalt Jungle* 1950; *The Day the Earth Stood Still* 1951; *I Can Get It for You Wholesale* 1951; *The Barbarian and the Geisha* 1958; *Ben-Hur* 1959; *Guns for San Sebastian* 1968; *The Great Bank Robbery* 1969; *Night Gallery* 1969; *The Dunwich Horror* 1970; *Bedknobs and Broomsticks* 1971; *Battle beyond the Stars* 1980; *Gideon's Trumpet* 1980

Jaffer, Melissa *Caddie* 1976; *Ride a Wild Pony* 1976; *Weekend of Shadows* 1978; *The Gold and Glory* 1984

Jaffrey, Madhur *Shakespeare Wallah* 1965; *The Guru* 1969; *Autobiography of a Princess* 1975; *Heat and Dust* 1982; *The Assam Garden* 1985; *Saagar* 1985; *The Perfect Murder* 1988; *Vanya on 42nd Street* 1994; *Cotton Mary* 1999

Jaffrey, Saeed *The Horsemen* 1971; *The Man Who Would Be King* 1975; *The Wilby Conspiracy* 1975; *The Chess Players* 1977; *Hullabaloo over Georgie and Bonnie's Pictures* 1979; *Sphinx* 1980; *A Passage to India* 1984; *The Razor's Edge* 1984; *My Beautiful Laundrette* 1985; *The Deceivers* 1988; *After Midnight* 1990; *Henna* 1990; *Masala* 1991; *Balmaa* 1993; *Guru in Seven* 1997; *The Journey* 1997

Jagger, Bianca *The American Success Company* 1979; *The Cannonball Run* 1981

Jagger, Dean *Wings in the Dark* 1935; *Having Wonderful Time*

Johnson, Dots aka **Johnson, Dotts** Paisà 1946; The Joe Louis Story 1953
Johnson, Dyke Ride Lonesome 1959; Comanche Station 1960
Johnson, Fred Break in the Circle 1955; Doctor Blood's Coffin 1960
Johnson, Geordie The Diviners 1992; A Stranger in the Mirror 1993; Bionic Ever After? 1994
Johnson, Georgann Short Cut to Hell 1957; The Hideaways 1973; Murphy's Romance 1985; David: the David Rothenberg Story 1988; Side by Side 1988; Shattered Dreams 1990; A House of Secrets and Lies 1992
Johnson, Jason The Butter Cream Gang 1991; Secret of Treasure Mountain 1993
Johnson, Karl Jubilee 1978; The Tempest 1979; Avenging Force 1986; Close My Eyes 1991; Wittgenstein 1993; Love Is the Devil: Study for a Portrait of Francis Bacon 1998
Johnson, Katie The Last Adventurers 1937; Death of an Angel 1951; The Ladykillers 1955; How to Murder a Rich Uncle 1957
Johnson, Kay Dynamite 1929; Billy the Kid 1930; Madam Satan 1930; American Madness 1932; Of Human Bondage 1934; This Man Is Mine 1934; White Banners 1938; The Real Glory 1939
Johnson, Kurt Jane Austen in Manhattan 1980; The Fan 1981
Johnson, Lamont The Human Jungle 1954; The Brothers Rico 1957
Johnson, Laura Chiller 1985; Nick Knight 1989; Paper Hearts 1993; Trauma 1993; Awake to Danger 1995; Judge & Jury 1995; And the Beat Goes On: the Sonny and Cher Story 1999
Johnson, Lynn-Holly Ice Castles 1978; For Your Eyes Only 1981; The Watcher in the Woods 1982
Johnson, Melodie The Ride to Hangman's Tree 1967; Coogan's Bluff 1968
Johnson, Michelle Blame It on Rio 1984; Waxwork 1988; Wishful Thinking 1990; Genuine Risk 1990; Blood Ties 1991; Dr Giggles 1992; Far and Away 1992; A Woman Scorned 1992; Body Shot 1994; The Donor 1994; Terror at Deception Ridge 1994; When the Bullet Hits the Bone 1995; The Glimmer Man 1996; Dallas: War of the Ewings 1998
Johnson, Mike Get Cracking 1943; George in Civvy Street 1946
Johnson, Noble The Navigator 1924; Hands Up! 1926; Four Feathers 1929; The Hounds of Zaroff 1932; Murders in the Rue Morgue 1932; She 1935; A Game of Death 1945
Johnson, Penny Automatic 1994; The Road to Galveston 1996; Death Benefit 1996
Johnson, Rafer The Fiercest Heart 1961; Wild in the Country 1961; Tarzan and the Jungle Boy 1968; The Last Grenade 1970
Johnson, Reggie Platoon 1986; Seven Hours to Judgment 1988
Johnson, Richard Never So Few 1959; Cairo 1962; 80,000 Suspects 1963; The Haunting 1963; The Pumpkin Eater 1964; The Amorous Adventures of Moll Flanders 1965; Operation Crossbow 1965; Deadlier than the Male 1966; Khartoum 1966; Danger Route 1967; The Rover 1967; Oedipus the King 1968; Some Girls Do 1969; Julius Caesar 1970; Sin 1972;

Hennessy 1975; Aces High 1976; The Four Feathers 1978; A Nightingale Sang in Berkeley Square 1979; Zombie Flesh Eaters 1979; The Monster Club 1980; Secrets of the Phantom Caverns 1984; Turtle Diary 1985; A Man for All Seasons 1988; Spymaker: the Secret Life of Ian Fleming 1990; Treasure Island 1990; The Crucifer of Blood 1991
Johnson, Rick Thundercrack! 1975; Foreign Student 1994
Johnson, Rita London by Night 1937; Man-Proof 1937; Smashing the Rackets 1938; Letter of Introduction 1938; Broadway Serenade 1939; Nick Carter, Master Detective 1939; Congo Maisie 1940; Edison, the Man 1940; Appointment for Love 1941; Here Comes Mr Jordan 1941; The Major and the Minor 1942; My Friend Flicka 1943; The Affairs of Susan 1945; Thunderhead – Son of Flicka 1945; Pardon My Past 1945; They Won't Believe Me 1947; The Big Clock 1948; Sleep, My Love 1948
Johnson, Robin Times Square 1980; DOA 1988
Johnson, Russell It Came from Outer Space 1953; Law and Order 1953; Seminole 1953; The Stand at Apache River 1953; Tumbleweed 1953; Ride Clear of Diablo 1954; This Island Earth 1955; Courage of Black Beauty 1957; Attack of the Crab Monsters 1957; The Saga of Hemp Brown 1958; Beg, Borrow or Steal 1973
Johnson, Sunny Dr Heckyl & Mr Hype 1980; Flashdance 1983; The Red-Light Sting 1984
Johnson, Tor Bride of the Monster 1955; The Black Sleep 1956; The Unearthly 1957; Night of the Ghouls 1960
Johnson, Van Too Many Girls 1940; Dr Gillespie's New Assistant 1942; The War against Mrs Hadley 1942; Somewhere I'll Find You 1942; Dr Gillespie's Criminal Case 1943; The Human Comedy 1943; Pilot #5 1943; A Guy Named Joe 1944; Three Men in White 1944; Two Girls and a Sailor 1944; The White Cliffs of Dover 1944; Thirty Seconds over Tokyo 1944; Thrill of a Romance 1945; Week-End at the Waldorf 1945; Easy to Wed 1946; High Barbaree 1947; Command Decision 1948; State of the Union 1948; Battleground 1949; In the Good Old Summertime 1949; Mother Is a Freshman 1949; Scene of the Crime 1949; The Big Hangover 1950; Go for Broke! 1951; It's a Big Country 1951; Plymouth Adventure 1952; Easy to Love 1953; Confidentially Connie 1953; Brigadoon 1954; The Caine Mutiny 1954; The Last Time I Saw Paris 1954; The Siege at Red River 1954; Men of the Fighting Lady 1954; The End of the Affair 1955; Beyond the River 1956; Miracle in the Rain 1956; 23 Paces to Baker Street 1956; Action of the Tiger 1957; Subway in the Sky 1958; The Last Blitzkrieg 1958; Beyond This Place 1959; Wives and Lovers 1963; The Doomsday Flight 1966; Divorce American Style 1967; Yours, Mine and Ours 1968; Where Angels Go...Trouble Follows 1968; Company of Killers 1970; The Kidnapping of the President 1980; The Purple Rose of Cairo 1985
Johnston, Amy The Buddy Holly Story 1978; Jennifer 1978

Johnston, Grace Beaches 1988; God Bless the Child 1988
Johnston, J J Things Change 1988; The Fixer 1997
Johnston, John Dennis A Breed Apart 1984; Communion 1989; Pink Cadillac 1989; Miracle in the Wilderness 1991; Art Deco Detective 1994
Johnston, Johnny Unchained 1955; Rock around the Clock 1956
Johnston, Kristen Austin Powers: The Spy Who Shagged Me 1999; The Flintstones in Viva Rock Vegas 2000
Johnston, Margaret A Man about the House 1947; Portrait of Clare 1950; The Magic Box 1951; Knave of Hearts 1954; Touch and Go 1955; Night of the Eagle 1961; Girl in the Headlines 1963; The Psychopath 1966; Sebastian 1968
Johnston, Oliver The Hypnotist 1957; A King in New York 1957; A Touch of Larceny 1959; Dr Crippen 1962; The Tomb of Ligeia 1964; It! 1966; A Countess from Hong Kong 1967
Johnston, Sue Brassed Off 1996; Face 1997
Jokovic, Mirjana Eversmile, New Jersey 1989; Underground 1995; Side Streets 1998
Jolie, Angelina Cyborg 2: Glass Shadow 1993; Hackers 1995; Mojave Moon 1996; Foxfire 1996; Love Is All There Is 1996; Playing God 1997; Playing by Heart 1998; Gia 1998; Pushing Tin 1999; Girl, Interrupted 1999; The Bone Collector 1999; Gone in 60 Seconds 2000
Jolson, Al The Jazz Singer 1927; The Singing Fool 1928; Say It With Songs 1929; Mammy 1930; Hallelujah, I'm a Bum 1933; Wonder Bar 1934; Go into Your Dance 1935; The Singing Kid 1936; Rose of Washington Square 1939; Swanee River 1939
Jones, Allan A Night at the Opera 1935; Show Boat 1936; A Day at the Races 1937; The Firefly 1937; Everybody Sing 1938; The Boys from Syracuse 1940
Jones, Barry Dancing with Crime 1946; Madeleine 1949; The Clouded Yellow 1950; Seven Days to Noon 1950; Appointment with Venus 1951; White Corridors 1951; Plymouth Adventure 1952; Return to Paradise 1953; Brigadoon 1954; Demetrius and the Gladiators 1954; The Glass Slipper 1955; Alexander the Great 1956; Saint Joan 1957; The Safecracker 1958; The Thirty-Nine Steps 1959
Jones, Bruce Raining Stones 1993; The Full Monty 1997; TwentyFourSeven 1997
Jones, Carolyn House of Wax 1953; Shield for Murder 1954; The Tender Trap 1955; Invasion of the Body Snatchers 1956; Baby Face Nelson 1957; The Bachelor Party 1957; Johnny Trouble 1957; King Creole 1958; Marjorie Morningstar 1958; Career 1959; A Hole in the Head 1959; Last Train from Gun Hill 1959; The Man in the Net 1959; Ice Palace 1960; Sail a Crooked Ship 1961; How the West Was Won 1962; A Ticklish Affair 1963; Color Me Dead 1969; The Dance of Death 1969; Eaten Alive 1976; Good Luck, Miss Wyckoff 1979
Jones, Cherry Light of Day 1987; Julian Po 1997; Cradle Will Rock 1999; Erin Brockovich 2000
Jones, Christopher Chubasco 1968; Wild in the Streets 1968;

Three in the Attic 1968; The Looking Glass War 1969; Ryan's Daughter 1970
Jones, Claude Earl Impulse 1984; Bride of Re-Animator 1991
Jones, Clifford The Power and the Glory 1933; Tillie and Gus 1933; Strangers All 1935
Jones, Clifton Only When I Larf 1968; Sheena, Queen of the Jungle 1984
Jones, Dean Tea and Sympathy 1956; These Wilder Years 1956; Jailhouse Rock 1957; Until They Sail 1957; Torpedo Run 1958; Handle with Care 1958; Imitation General 1958; Never So Few 1959; Under the Yum Yum Tree 1963; The New Interns 1964; That Darn Cat! 1965; Two on a Guillotine 1965; Any Wednesday 1966; The Ugly Dachshund 1966; Blackbeard's Ghost 1967; Monkeys, Go Home! 1967; The Horse in the Gray Flannel Suit 1968; The Love Bug 1969; The Million Dollar Duck 1971; Snowball Express 1972; The Shaggy DA 1976; Herbie Goes to Monte Carlo 1977; Born Again 1978; The Long Days of Summer 1980; Fire and Rain 1989; Other People's Money 1991; Beethoven 1992; The Computer Wore Tennis Shoes 1995; Special Report: Journey to Mars 1996; That Darn Cat 1997; The Love Bug 1997
Jones, Dickie aka **Jones, Dick** Pinocchio 1940; Rocky Mountain 1950; Fort Worth 1951; Last of the Pony Riders 1953; The Cool and the Crazy 1958
Jones, Duane Night of the Living Dead 1968; Ganja and Hess 1973
Jones, Eddie Year of the Dragon 1985; Apprentice to Murder 1988; Cadillac Man 1990; Final Appeal 1993; Ed McBain's 87th Precinct 1995; Letter to My Killer 1995; Return to Me 2000
Jones, Emrys One of Our Aircraft Is Missing 1942; Blue Scar 1947; The Small Back Room 1949; Deadly Nightshade 1953; Three Cases of Murder 1954; Serena 1962
Jones, Freddie The Bliss of Mrs Blossom 1968; Otley 1968; Frankenstein Must Be Destroyed 1969; Assault 1970; Doctor in Trouble 1970; Antony and Cleopatra 1972; Sitting Target 1972; The Satanic Rites of Dracula 1973; All Creatures Great and Small 1974; Never Too Young to Rock 1975; Zulu Dawn 1979; The Elephant Man 1980; Agatha Christie's Murder Is Easy 1982; Firefox 1982; And the Ship Sails On 1983; Krull 1983; Dune 1984; Firestarter 1984; The Black Cauldron 1985; Young Sherlock Holmes 1985; Consuming Passions 1988; The Last Butterfly 1990; The NeverEnding Story III 1994; Cold Comfort Farm 1995; House! 2000
Jones, Gemma The Devils 1971; On the Black Hill 1987; Paperhouse 1988; Feast of July 1995; Wilde 1997; Captain Jack 1998; The Theory of Flight 1998; The Winslow Boy 1999
Jones, Gordon Red Salute 1935; Strike Me Pink 1936; Sea Devils 1937; Among the Living 1941; The Feminine Touch 1941; The Secret Life of Walter Mitty 1947; Tokyo Joe 1949; Smoke Signal 1955
Jones, Grace Gordon's War 1973; Conan the Destroyer 1984; A View to a Kill 1985; Vamp 1986; Siesta 1987; Straight to Hell

1987; Boomerang 1992; Palmer's Pick-Up 1999
Jones, Griffith Catherine the Great 1934; Escape Me Never 1935; First a Girl 1935; Return of a Stranger 1937; The Mill on the Floss 1937; A Yank at Oxford 1938; The Four Just Men 1939; Uncensored 1942; The Rake's Progress 1945; The Wicked Lady 1945; Miranda 1947; They Made Me a Fugitive 1947; Account Rendered 1957; Not Wanted on Voyage 1957; Hidden Homicide 1958
Jones, Hannah Blackmail 1929; Piccadilly 1929
Jones, Helen Bliss 1985; Waiting 1990
Jones, Henry The Bad Seed 1956; The Girl Can't Help It 1956; The Girl He Left Behind 1956; 3:10 to Yuma 1957; Will Success Spoil Rock Hunter? 1957; Vertigo 1958; The Bramble Bush 1960; Cash McCall 1960; Angel Baby 1961; Never Too Late 1965; Angel in My Pocket 1968; Project X 1968; Butch Cassidy and the Sundance Kid 1969; Support Your Local Sheriff! 1969; The Cockeyed Cowboys of Calico County 1970; Skin Game 1971; Support Your Local Gunfighter 1971; Napoleon and Samantha 1972; The Outfit 1973; Tom Sawyer 1973; Nine to Five 1980; Deathtrap 1982; Arachnophobia 1990; The Grifters 1990; Over Her Dead Body 1990; Breathing Lessons 1994
Jones, Jack The Dawn Rider 1935; Juke Box Rhythm 1959; The Comeback 1977; Airplane II: the Sequel 1982
Jones, James Earl Dr Strangelove, or How I Learned to Stop Worrying and Love the Bomb 1963; The Comedians 1967; The Great White Hope 1970; End of the Road 1970; King: a Filmed Record... Montgomery to Memphis 1970; The Man 1972; Claudine 1974; The Bingo Long Travelling All-Stars and Motor Kings 1976; Deadly Hero 1976; Swashbuckler 1976; The River Niger 1976; Exorcist II: The Heretic 1977; The Greatest 1977; The Last Remake of Beau Geste 1977; A Piece of the Action 1977; Star Wars Episode IV: A New Hope 1977; The Bushido Blade 1981; Conan the Barbarian 1982; Return of the Jedi 1983; City Limits 1985; My Little Girl 1986; Soul Man 1986; Allan Quatermain and the Lost City of Gold 1987; Gardens of Stone 1987; Matewan 1987; Coming to America 1988; Field of Dreams 1989; Three Fugitives 1989; Best of the Best 1989; By Dawn's Early Light 1990; Grim Prairie Tales 1990; Heat Wave 1990; The Hunt for Red October 1990; Ivory Hunters 1990; The Ambulance 1990; Scorchers 1991; Convicts 1991; Patriot Games 1992; Sneakers 1992; Excessive Force 1993; The Meteor Man 1993; The Sandlot 1993; Sommersby 1993; Percy and Thunder 1993; Clean Slate 1994; Confessions: Two Faces of Evil 1994; Freedom Road: the Vernon Johns Story 1994; The Lion King 1994; Cry, the Beloved Country 1995; Jefferson in Paris 1995; A Family Thing 1996; Rebound 1996; Good Luck 1996; Casper: a Spirited Beginning 1997; Gang Related 1997; The Second Civil War 1997; What the Deaf Man Heard 1997; Horton Foote's Alone 1997

RadioTimes ACTORS' INDEX

Jones, Jeffrey *Easy Money* 1983; *Amadeus* 1984; *Transylvania 6-5000* 1985; *Ferris Bueller's Day Off* 1986; *Howard, a New Breed of Hero* 1986; *Beetle Juice* 1988; *Without a Clue* 1988; *Valmont* 1989; *Who's Harry Crumb?* 1989; *Over Her Dead Body* 1990; *Mom and Dad Save the World* 1992; *Out on a Limb* 1992; *Stay Tuned* 1992; *Ed Wood* 1994; *The Crucible* 1996; *The Devil's Advocate* 1997; *The Pest* 1997; *Ravenous* 1999; *Sleepy Hollow* 1999; *Stuart Little* 1999
Jones, Jennifer *aka* **Isley, Phyllis** *Frontier Horizon* 1939; *The Song of Bernadette* 1943; *Since You Went Away* 1944; *Love Letters* 1945; *Cluny Brown* 1946; *Duel in the Sun* 1946; *Portrait of Jennie* 1948; *Madame Bovary* 1949; *We Were Strangers* 1949; *Gone to Earth* 1950; *Carrie* 1952; *Ruby Gentry* 1952; *Beat the Devil* 1953; *Indiscretion of an American Wife* 1954; *Good Morning, Miss Dove* 1955; *Love Is a Many-Splendored Thing* 1955; *The Man in the Gray Flannel Suit* 1956; *The Barretts of Wimpole Street* 1957; *A Farewell to Arms* 1957; *Tender Is the Night* 1961; *The Idol* 1966; *Angel, Angel Down We Go* 1969; *The Towering Inferno* 1974
Jones, Jocelyn *The Great Texas Dynamite Chase* 1976; *Tourist Trap* 1979
Jones, John Marshall *White Men Can't Jump* 1992; *Noah* 1998
Jones, L Q *aka* **McQueen, Justus E** *Battle Cry* 1955; *An Annapolis Story* 1955; *Santiago* 1956; *Toward the Unknown* 1956; *Men in War* 1957; *Buchanan Rides Alone* 1958; *Torpedo Run* 1958; *Ten Who Dared* 1960; *Hell Is for Heroes* 1962; *Ride the High Country* 1962; *Showdown* 1963; *Apache Rifles* 1964; *The Ballad of Cable Hogue* 1970; *The McMasters* 1970; *Brotherhood of Satan* 1970; *The Hunting Party* 1971; *Smash-Up Alley* 1972; *The Manhunter* 1974; *The Strange and Deadly Occurrence* 1974; *White Line Fever* 1975; *Winterhawk* 1975; *Mother, Jugs & Speed* 1976; *Fast Charlie: the Moonbeam Rider* 1978; *Lone Wolf McQuade* 1983; *Sacred Ground* 1983; *Bulletproof* 1987; *River of Death* 1989; *The Legend of Grizzly Adams* 1990; *Lightning Jack* 1994; *The Edge* 1997; *The Mask of Zorro* 1998; *The Patriot* 1998; *The Jack Bull* 1999
Jones, Mickey *Dead-Bang* 1989; *It Came from Outer Space II* 1996
Jones, Morgan *Apache Woman* 1955; *Not of This Earth* 1956
Jones, Nicholas *The Blockhouse* 1973; *Daisy Miller* 1974
Jones, Paul *Privilege* 1967; *Demons of the Mind* 1971
Jones, Peter *The Blue Lagoon* 1949; *Miss Robin Hood* 1952; *The Yellow Balloon* 1952; *A Day to Remember* 1953; *Private's Progress* 1956; *Never Let Go* 1960; *School for Scoundrels* 1960; *Nearly a Nasty Accident* 1961; *Just like a Woman* 1966; *Press for Time* 1966; *The Sandwich Man* 1966; *Carry On England* 1976
Jones, Renee *Friday the 13th Part VI: Jason Lives* 1986; *The Liberators* 1987; *Talkin' Dirty after Dark* 1991
Jones, Richard T *Renaissance Man* 1994; *The Trigger Effect* 1996; *Event Horizon* 1997; *Hollywood Confidential* 1997; *The Wood* 1999
Jones, Robert Earl *Cold River* 1982; *Starlight* 1989
Jones, Sam *aka* **Jones, Sam J** *10* 1979; *Flash Gordon* 1980; *This Wife for Hire* 1985; *My Chauffeur* 1986; *Jane and the Lost City* 1987; *Driving Force* 1988; *Silent Assassins* 1988; *Vegas Vice* 1994; *American Strays* 1996
Jones, Samantha *Wait until Dark* 1967; *Get to Know Your Rabbit* 1972
Jones, Shirley *Oklahoma!* 1955; *Carousel* 1956; *April Love* 1957; *Bobbikins* 1959; *Never Steal Anything Small* 1959; *Elmer Gantry* 1960; *Pepe* 1960; *Two Rode Together* 1961; *The Music Man* 1962; *The Courtship of Eddie's Father* 1963; *A Ticklish Affair* 1963; *Bedtime Story* 1964; *The Secret of My Success* 1965; *Fluffy* 1965; *The Happy Ending* 1969; *Silent Night, Lonely Night* 1969; *The Cheyenne Social Club* 1970; *Beyond the Poseidon Adventure* 1979; *The Children of An Lac* 1980; *Tank* 1984
Jones, Simon *Giro City* 1982; *American Friends* 1991; *Miracle on 34th Street* 1994
Jones, Steve *The Great Rock 'n' Roll Swindle* 1979; *Ladies and Gentlemen, the Fabulous Stains* 1982
Jones, Sue *Dead Man's Float* 1980; *Blood Money* 1980
Jones, Terry *And Now for Something Completely Different* 1971; *Monty Python and the Holy Grail* 1975; *Monty Python's Life of Brian* 1979; *Monty Python Live at the Hollywood Bowl* 1982; *Monty Python's The Meaning of Life* 1983; *Erik the Viking* 1989; *The Wind in the Willows* 1996
Jones, Tom *Mars Attacks!* 1996; *Agnes Browne* 1999
Jones, Tommy Lee *aka* **Jones, Tom Lee** *Love Story* 1970; *Jackson County Jail* 1976; *Smash-Up on Interstate 5* 1976; *Rolling Thunder* 1977; *The Betsy* 1978; *Eyes of Laura Mars* 1978; *Coal Miner's Daughter* 1980; *Back Roads* 1981; *Savage Islands* 1983; *The River Rat* 1984; *Black Moon Rising* 1985; *The Big Town* 1987; *Broken Vows* 1987; *Stormy Monday* 1987; *The Dead Can't Lie* 1988; *Stranger on My Land* 1988; *The Package* 1989; *Wings of the Apache* 1990; *Blue Sky* 1991; *JFK* 1991; *Under Siege* 1992; *The Fugitive* 1993; *Heaven and Earth* 1993; *House of Cards* 1993; *Blown Away* 1994; *The Client* 1994; *Cobb* 1994; *Natural Born Killers* 1994; *Batman Forever* 1995; *The Good Old Boys* 1995; *Men in Black* 1997; *Volcano* 1997; *Small Soldiers* 1998; *US Marshals* 1998; *Double Jeopardy* 1999; *Rules of Engagement* 2000
Jones-Davies, Sue *Radio On* 1979; *Elenya* 1992
Jordan, Alan *Whale Music* 1994; *The Conspiracy of Fear* 1996
Jordan, Bobby *aka* **Jordan, Bobbie** *Dead End* 1937; *Angels with Dirty Faces* 1938; *Angels Wash Their Faces* 1939; *Dust Be My Destiny* 1939; *They Made Me a Criminal* 1939; *Young Tom Edison* 1940; *Boys of the City* 1940; *That Gang of Mine* 1940; *Pride of the Bowery* 1941; *Spooks Run Wild* 1941; *Clancy Street Boys* 1943; *Ghosts in the Night* 1943; *Bowery Champs* 1944
Jordan, Dorothy *Min and Bill* 1930; *Cabin in the Cotton* 1932; *Hell Divers* 1932; *The Lost Squadron* 1932; *The Roadhouse Murder* 1932; *The Wet Parade* 1932
Jordan, Jim *Look Who's Laughing* 1941; *Here We Go Again* 1942
Jordan, Joanne Moore *Faces* 1968; *The Dunwich Horror* 1970; *Bury Me an Angel* 1972
Jordan, Marian *Look Who's Laughing* 1941; *Here We Go Again* 1942
Jordan, Patrick *Rag Doll* 1960; *Dilemma* 1962; *The Marked One* 1963; *The Last Escape* 1970
Jordan, Richard *Valdez Is Coming* 1971; *The Friends of Eddie Coyle* 1973; *Rooster Cogburn* 1975; *The Yakuza* 1975; *Logan's Run* 1976; *Interiors* 1978; *Les Misérables* 1978; *A Nightingale Sang in Berkeley Square* 1979; *Old Boyfriends* 1979; *Raise the Titanic* 1980; *Dune* 1984; *A Flash of Green* 1984; *The Mean Season* 1985; *The Men's Club* 1986; *Solarwarriors* 1986; *The Secret of My Success* 1987; *Manhunt: Search for the Night Stalker* 1989; *Romero* 1989; *The Hunt for Red October* 1990; *Shout* 1991; *Time Bomb* 1991; *Heaven Is a Playground* 1991; *Gettysburg* 1993
Jordan, William *A Man Called Horse* 1970; *The Buddy Holly Story* 1978; *Mission of the Shark* 1991; *Kingpin* 1996
Jordano, Daniel *Alphabet City* 1984; *Playing for Keeps* 1986
Jory, Victor *Renegades* 1930; *The Devil's in Love* 1933; *He Was Her Man* 1934; *Madame Du Barry* 1934; *A Midsummer Night's Dream* 1935; *The King Steps Out* 1936; *Meet Nero Wolfe* 1936; *First Lady* 1937; *The Adventures of Tom Sawyer* 1938; *Man of Conquest* 1939; *Susannah of the Mounties* 1939; *Cherokee Strip* 1940; *Charlie Chan in Rio* 1941; *The Unknown Guest* 1943; *The Loves of Carmen* 1948; *Canadian Pacific* 1949; *Fighting Man of the Plains* 1949; *South of St Louis* 1949; *A Woman's Secret* 1949; *The Capture* 1950; *The Cariboo Trail* 1950; *Cave of Outlaws* 1951; *Son of Ali Baba* 1952; *The Man from the Alamo* 1953; *Valley of the Kings* 1954; *Death of a Scoundrel* 1956; *The Fugitive Kind* 1960; *The Miracle Worker* 1962; *Jigsaw* 1968; *Flap* 1970; *A Time for Dying* 1971; *Papillon* 1973; *Frasier, the Sensuous Lion* 1973
Joseph, Allen *Eraserhead* 1976; *Marathon Man* 1976
Josephson, Erland *So Close to Life* 1957; *The Face* 1958; *The Hour of the Wolf* 1967; *A Passion* 1969; *Cries and Whispers* 1972; *Scenes from a Marriage* 1973; *Face to Face* 1976; *Autumn Sonata* 1978; *Montenegro* 1981; *Nostalgia* 1983; *After the Rehearsal* 1984; *Saving Grace* 1985; *The Sacrifice* 1986; *Hanussen* 1988; *The Unbearable Lightness of Being* 1988; *The Ox* 1991; *Prospero's Books* 1991; *Sofie* 1992; *Ulysses' Gaze* 1995; *Kristin Lavransdatter* 1995
Joshua, Larry *The Burning* 1981; *Svengali* 1983; *A Midnight Clear* 1991; *Sugar Hill* 1993
Joslyn, Allyn *They Won't Forget* 1937; *The Shining Hour* 1938; *Fast and Furious* 1939; *The Great McGinty* 1940; *No Time for Comedy* 1940; *This Thing Called Love* 1940; *Bedtime Story* 1942; *My Sister Eileen* 1942; *Heaven Can Wait* 1943; *The Immortal Sergeant* 1943; *Young Ideas* 1943; *Bride by Mistake* 1944; *The Impostor* 1944; *Sweet and Lowdown* 1944; *Colonel Effingham's Raid* 1945; *The Horn Blows at Midnight* 1945; *Junior Miss* 1945; *It Shouldn't Happen to a Dog* 1946; *The Shocking Miss Pilgrim* 1947; *If You Knew Susie* 1948; *Moonrise* 1948; *Harriet Craig* 1950; *The Jazz Singer* 1952; *I Love Melvin* 1953; *The Fastest Gun Alive* 1956; *Nightmare in the Sun* 1964
Jostyn, Jennifer *The Brothers McMullen* 1995; *Midnight Blue* 1996
Jourdan, Louis *The Paradine Case* 1947; *Letter from an Unknown Woman* 1948; *No Minor Vices* 1948; *Madame Bovary* 1949; *Anne of the Indies* 1951; *Bird of Paradise* 1951; *Decameron Nights* 1953; *Three Coins in the Fountain* 1954; *The Bride Is Much Too Beautiful* 1956; *Julie* 1956; *The Swan* 1956; *Dangerous Exile* 1957; *Gigi* 1958; *The Best of Everything* 1959; *Can-Can* 1960; *The VIPs* 1963; *Made in Paris* 1966; *Cervantes* 1968; *A Flea in Her Ear* 1968; *The Count of Monte Cristo* 1974; *The Man in the Iron Mask* 1977; *Silver Bears* 1978; *Double Deal* 1981; *Swamp Thing* 1982; *Octopussy* 1983; *Beverly Hills Madam* 1986; *Counterforce* 1987; *The Return of Swamp Thing* 1989; *Year of the Comet* 1992
Jouvet, Louis *Carnival in Flanders* 1935; *The Lower Depths* 1936; *Mademoiselle Docteur* 1936; *Drôle de Drame* 1937; *Hôtel du Nord* 1938; *La Marseillaise* 1938; *The End of the Day* 1939; *Volpone* 1940; *Quai des Orfèvres* 1947
Jovovich, Milla *Kuffs* 1991; *Return to the Blue Lagoon* 1991; *Chaplin* 1992; *Dazed and Confused* 1993; *The Fifth Element* 1997; *He Got Game* 1998; *Joan of Arc* 1999; *The Million Dollar Hotel* 1999
Joy, Leatrice *The Ten Commandments* 1923; *First Love* 1939; *Love Nest* 1951
Joy, Mark *Black Rainbow* 1989; *Night Walk* 1989; *Lovestruck* 1997; *Pecker* 1998
Joy, Nicholas *The Iron Curtain* 1948; *And Baby Makes Three* 1949; *Native Son* 1951; *Affair with a Stranger* 1953
Joy, Robert *Atlantic City USA* 1980; *Ragtime* 1981; *Amityville III: the Demon* 1983; *Terminal Choice* 1983; *Desperately Seeking Susan* 1985; *Sword of Gideon* 1986; *Millennium* 1989; *The Dark Half* 1991; *Switching Parents* 1992; *Harriet the Spy* 1996
Joyce, Alice *Stella Dallas* 1925; *Beau Geste* 1926; *The Green Goddess* 1930
Joyce, Brenda *The Rains Came* 1939; *Little Old New York* 1940; *Maryland* 1940; *Whispering Ghosts* 1942; *Tarzan and the Amazons* 1945; *Tarzan and the Leopard Woman* 1946; *Little Giant* 1946; *Tarzan and the Huntress* 1947; *Tarzan and the Mermaids* 1948; *Tarzan's Magic Fountain* 1949
Joyce, Elaine *How to Frame a Figg* 1971; *Uphill All the Way* 1985; *Trick or Treat* 1986
Joyce, Paddy *The Girl in the Picture* 1956; *The Cat Gang* 1959
Joyce, Patricia *The Visitors* 1972; *The Catamount Killing* 1974
Joyce, Yootha *Die! Die! My Darling* 1964; *Stranger in the House* 1967; *Nearest and Dearest* 1972; *Man about the House* 1974; *George and Mildred* 1980
Joyner, Michelle *Grim Prairie Tales* 1990; *Bonnie and Clyde: the True Story* 1992; *Traces of Red* 1992; *Shadow of the Past* 1995
Judd, Ashley *Kuffs* 1991; *Ruby in Paradise* 1993; *Heat* 1995; *Normal Life* 1995; *The Passion of Darkly Noon* 1995; *Smoke* 1995; *Norma Jean & Marilyn* 1996; *Kiss the Girls* 1997; *The Locusts* 1997; *Simon Birch* 1998; *Double Jeopardy* 1999; *Eye of the Beholder* 1999
Judd, Edward *The Day the Earth Caught Fire* 1961; *The Long Ships* 1963; *Stolen Hours* 1963; *The World Ten Times Over* 1963; *First Men in the Moon* 1964; *Invasion* 1965; *Strange Bedfellows* 1965; *Island of Terror* 1966; *The Vengeance of She* 1968; *Living Free* 1972; *Assassin* 1973; *Vault of Horror* 1973; *The Boys in Blue* 1983; *The Hound of the Baskervilles* 1983; *The Kitchen Toto* 1987
Judels, Charles *Sweetheart of the Campus* 1941; *Baby Face Morgan* 1942
Judge, Arline *Age of Consent* 1932; *George White's 1935 Scandals* 1935; *King of Burlesque* 1936; *One in a Million* 1936; *Pigskin Parade* 1936; *Valiant Is the Word for Carrie* 1936; *The Lady Is Willing* 1942; *Song of Texas* 1943; *Mad Wednesday* 1950
Juerging, Arno *Blood for Dracula* 1974; *Flesh for Frankenstein* 1974
Julia, Raul *The Organization* 1971; *The Panic in Needle Park* 1971; *The Gumball Rally* 1976; *Eyes of Laura Mars* 1978; *The Escape Artist* 1982; *One from the Heart* 1982; *Tempest* 1982; *Compromising Positions* 1985; *Kiss of the Spider Woman* 1985; *Florida Straits* 1986; *The Morning After* 1986; *Moon over Parador* 1988; *Tequila Sunrise* 1988; *Trading Hearts* 1988; *Tango Bar* 1988; *The Penitent* 1988; *Romero* 1989; *Mack the Knife* 1989; *Frankenstein Unbound* 1990; *Havana* 1990; *Presumed Innocent* 1990; *The Rookie* 1990; *The Addams Family* 1991; *The Plague* 1992; *Addams Family Values* 1993; *The Burning Season* 1994; *Street Fighter* 1994; *Down Came a Blackbird* 1995
Julian, Janet *On Dangerous Ground* 1986; *King of New York* 1989; *Heaven Is a Playground* 1991
Julien, Max *Psych-Out* 1968; *Getting Straight* 1970; *The Mack* 1973
Julien, Sandra *aka* **Jullien, Sandra** *Shiver of the Vampires* 1970; *I Am Frigid... Why?* 1972; *Ladies' House of Pleasure* 1973
Jump, Gordon *On Fire* 1987; *Justin Case* 1988
Junco, Victor *Bandido* 1956; *La Fièvre Monte à el Pao* 1959
Junkin, John *A Hard Day's Night* 1964; *Simon, Simon* 1970; *Wombling Free* 1977
Jurado, Katy *The Bullfighter and the Lady* 1951; *El Bruto* 1952; *High Noon* 1952; *Arrowhead* 1953; *Broken Lance* 1954; *Trial* 1955; *Trapeze* 1956; *Dragoon Wells Massacre* 1957; *The Badlanders* 1958; *Barabbas* 1961; *One-Eyed Jacks* 1961; *A Covenant with Death* 1967; *Pat Garrett and Billy the Kid* 1973; *Once Upon a Scoundrel* 1973; *The Children of Sanchez* 1978; *Under the Volcano* 1984

Radio Times ACTORS' INDEX

Pirate 1967; The Perils of Pauline 1967; The Smugglers 1968
Katarina, Anna The Salute of the Jugger 1989; Omega Doom 1996; The Game 1997
Katch, Kurt Berlin Correspondent 1942; Ali Baba and the Forty Thieves 1944; Abbott and Costello Meet the Mummy 1955
Kath, Katherine Moulin Rouge 1952; The Man Who Wouldn't Talk 1957; Seven Thunders 1957; Subway in the Sky 1958; Gigot 1962; The High Bright Sun 1965
Kato, Masaya Crime Broker 1993; Seventh Floor 1995; Drive 1997
Katsaros, Andonia Age of Consent 1969; Time after Time 1979
Katsulas, Andreas Someone to Watch over Me 1987; Communion 1989; The Neon Empire 1989; Next of Kin 1989; True Identity 1991; Blame It on the Bellboy 1992; Seduction: Three Tales from the Inner Sanctum 1992; New York Cop 1995
Katt, Nicky The Babysitter 1995; subUrbia 1996; One True Thing 1998; Phantoms 1998; The Limey 1999; Boiler Room 2000
Katt, William Carrie 1976; First Love 1977; Big Wednesday 1978; Butch and Sundance: the Early Days 1979; Baby: Secret of the Lost Legend 1985; House 1986; Swimsuit 1989; Double X: the Name of the Game 1991; Americanski Blues 1993; The Paperboy 1994; Tollbooth 1994; Romantic Undertaking 1995; Problem Child 3 1995; Devil's Food 1996; Piranha 1996; Rattled 1996
Kattan, Chris A Night at the Roxbury 1998; House on Haunted Hill 1999
Katz, Allan Hard Feelings 1981; Big Man on Campus 1989
Katz, Omri Hocus Pocus 1993; Matinee 1993; Dallas: JR Returns 1996
Kaufman, Andy In God We Trust 1980; Heartbeeps 1981
Kaufman, David Mom's Army 1989; The Last Prostitute 1991
Kaufman, Maurice Die! Die! My Darling 1964; The Abominable Dr Phibes 1971
Kaufmann, Christine The Last Days of Pompeii 1960; Town without Pity 1961; Taras Bulba 1962; Wild and Wonderful 1964; Murders in the Rue Morgue 1971; Rich and Respectable 1975; Swing 1983
Kaufmann, Günther Gods of the Plague 1969; Whity 1970; The Third Generation 1979; Querelle 1982; Kamikaze 1989 1983
Kaufmann, Maurice Find the Lady 1956; The Girl in the Picture 1956; The Giant Behemoth 1959; House of Mystery 1961; Bloomfield 1969
Kaushal, Kamini Shaheed 1948; Upkaar 1967
Kava, Caroline Year of the Dragon 1985; Nobody's Child 1986; Body of Evidence 1988; The Sleepers 1988; Born on the Fourth of July 1989; Murder Times Seven 1990; The Terror Inside 1996
Kavanagh, John The Country Girls 1983; Cal 1984; Bellman & True 1987; Joyriders 1988; Fools of Fortune 1990; Widows' Peak 1993; The Tale of Sweeney Todd 1998
Kavli, Karin Walpurgis Night 1935; A Woman's Face 1938
Kavner, Julie Katherine 1975; Revenge of the Stepford Wives 1980; National Lampoon's Movie Madness 1981; Hannah and Her Sisters 1986; Radio Days 1987; Surrender 1987; New York Stories 1989; Awakenings 1990; Shadows and Fog 1991; This Is My Life 1992; I'll Do Anything 1994; Don't Drink the Water 1994; Forget Paris 1995; Neil Simon's Jake's Women 1996; Deconstructing Harry 1997
Kawahara, Takashi Eat the Peach 1986; Road to Ruin 1992
Kawarazaki, Chojuro The Loyal 47 Ronin 1941; Musashi Miyamoto 1944
Kawazu, Seizaburo The Straits of Love and Hate 1937; Yojimbo 1961
Kay, Beatrice Billy Rose's Diamond Horseshoe 1945; Underworld USA 1961; A Time for Dying 1971
Kay, Bernard Doctor Zhivago 1965; The Shuttered Room 1967; They Came from beyond Space 1967; Interlude 1968; Darling Lili 1970; Trog 1970
Kay, Charles Bachelor of Hearts 1958; Amadeus 1984
Kay, Hadley Head On 1980; The Care Bears Movie II: a New Generation 1986
Kay, Mary Ellen Thunder Pass 1954; The Long Wait 1954
Kay, Melody Camp Nowhere 1994; The NeverEnding Story III 1994
Kaye, Caren Cuba Crossing 1980; Poison Ivy 1985
Kaye, Celia Island of the Blue Dolphins 1964; Wild Seed 1965; The Final Comedown 1972
Kaye, Clarissa aka **Kaye-Mason, Clarissa** Age of Consent 1969; The Good Wife 1986
Kaye, Danny Up in Arms 1944; Wonder Man 1945; The Kid from Brooklyn 1946; The Secret Life of Walter Mitty 1947; A Song Is Born 1948; The Inspector General 1949; It's a Great Feeling 1949; On the Riviera 1951; Hans Christian Andersen 1952; Knock on Wood 1954; White Christmas 1954; The Court Jester 1956; Merry Andrew 1958; Me and the Colonel 1958; The Five Pennies 1959; On the Double 1961; The Man from the Diner's Club 1963; Skokie 1981
Kaye, Davy Crooks in Cloisters 1963; The World Ten Times Over 1963; Satan's Harvest 1965; The Biggest Bundle of Them All 1968
Kaye, Lila An American Werewolf in London 1981; The Return of Sherlock Holmes 1987; Nuns on the Run 1990; Reason for Living: the Jill Ireland Story 1991; Mrs 'arris Goes to Paris 1992; Dragonworld 1994
Kaye, Norman Lonely Hearts 1981; Man of Flowers 1984; Relatives 1985; Unfinished Business 1985; Cactus 1986; Warm Nights on a Slow Moving Train 1987; Boundaries of the Heart 1988; Island 1989; Golden Braid 1991; A Woman's Tale 1991; Turtle Beach 1992; The Nun and the Bandit 1992; Bad Boy Bubby 1993
Kaye, Stubby Guys and Dolls 1955; You Can't Run Away from It 1956; Li'l Abner 1959; The Way West 1967; Sweet Charity 1968; Can Heironymus Merkin Ever Forget Mercy Humppe and Find True Happiness? 1969; The Cockeyed Cowboys of Calico County 1970; Who Framed Roger Rabbit 1988
Kazan, Elia City for Conquest 1940; Blues in the Night 1941
Kazan, Lainie Lady in Cement 1968; Dayton's Devils 1968; Romance of a Horse Thief 1971; My Favorite Year 1982; One from the Heart 1982; Lust in the Dust 1984; The Journey of Natty Gann 1985; The Delta Force 1986; Bigfoot and the Hendersons 1987; Beaches 1988; Out of the Dark 1988; Eternity 1990; 29th Street 1991; I Don't Buy Kisses Anymore 1992; The Associate 1996; Love Is All There Is 1996; The Big Hit 1998
Kazann, Zitto Ghost Town 1988; Slaughter of the Innocents 1993
Ke Huy Quan Indiana Jones and the Temple of Doom 1984; The Goonies 1985
Keach, James FM 1977; Lacy and the Mississippi Queen 1978; Hurricane 1979; The Long Riders 1980; Love Letters 1983; National Lampoon's Vacation 1983; The Razor's Edge 1984; Moving Violations 1985; Stand Alone 1985; Wildcats 1986; The Experts 1989; The Cops Are Robbers 1990; The Dance Goes On 1990; Murder in High Places 1991; The New Swiss Family Robinson 1999
Keach, Stacy The Heart Is a Lonely Hunter 1968; Brewster McCloud 1970; The Traveling Executioner 1970; End of the Road 1970; Doc 1971; Fat City 1972; The Life and Times of Judge Roy Bean 1972; Precinct 45: Los Angeles Police 1972; The Gravy Train 1974; Luther 1974; Watched 1974; Conduct Unbecoming 1975; James Dean – the First American Teenager 1975; The Killer inside Me 1975; The Sicilian Cross 1976; The Squeeze 1977; Gray Lady Down 1978; Cheech & Chong's Up in Smoke 1978; The Ninth Configuration 1979; The Long Riders 1980; Road Games 1981; Cheech & Chong's Nice Dreams 1981; Butterfly 1982; That Championship Season 1982; Mickey Spillane's Mike Hammer: Murder Takes All 1989; Class of 1999 1990; False Identity 1990; Milena 1990; Mission of the Shark 1991; Silent Thunder 1992; Sunset Grill 1992; Batman: Mask of the Phantasm 1993; Body Bags 1993; Irresistible Force 1993; Rio Diablo 1993; Raw Justice 1993; Trust in Me 1994; Young Ivanhoe 1994; Escape from LA 1996; Prey of the Jaguar 1996; Murder in My Mind 1997
Kean, Marie Rooney 1958; The Big Gamble 1961; Girl with Green Eyes 1963; I Was Happy Here 1966; Ryan's Daughter 1970; Barry Lyndon 1975; The Lonely Passion of Judith Hearne 1987
Keane, Edward The Singing Kid 1936; Devil's Island 1940
Keane, Kerrie Second Serve 1986; Bates Motel 1987; Mistress 1987; Distant Thunder 1988; Malarek 1989; Obsessed 1989
Keane, Robert Emmett Laugh and Get Rich 1931; The Spellbinder 1939; The Saint Takes Over 1940; Fool's Gold 1946; Fear in the Night 1947
Kearns, Billy aka **Kearns, Bill** Plein Soleil 1960; Playtime 1967; Asterix in Britain 1986
Keating, Larry Three Secrets 1950; The Mating Season 1951; When Worlds Collide 1951; Above and Beyond 1952; Carson City 1952; Inferno 1953; Gypsy Colt 1954; Stopover Tokyo 1957; The Wayward Bus 1957; The Buster Keaton Story 1957; Who Was That Lady? 1960
Keaton, Buster The Butcher Boy 1917; One Week 1920; Scarecrow 1920; The Paleface 1921; The Saphead 1921; Daydreams 1922; Our Hospitality 1923; Three Ages 1923; The Navigator 1924; Sherlock Junior 1924; Go West 1925; Seven Chances 1925; Battling Butler 1926; College 1927; The General 1927; The Cameraman 1928; Steamboat Bill, Jr 1928; Hollywood Revue 1929; Spite Marriage 1929; Doughboys 1930; Free and Easy 1930; Parlor, Bedroom and Bath 1931; The Passionate Plumber 1932; Speak Easily 1932; What – No Beer? 1933; An Old Spanish Custom 1935; The Villain Still Pursued Her 1940; Forever and a Day 1943; In the Good Old Summertime 1949; The Lovable Cheat 1949; You're My Everything 1949; Limelight 1952; Around the World in 80 Days 1956; The Adventures of Huckleberry Finn 1960; Pajama Party 1964; Beach Blanket Bingo 1965; How to Fill a Wild Bikini 1965; The Railrodder 1965; Sergeant Deadhead 1965; Film 1965; A Funny Thing Happened on the Way to the Forum 1966; War Italian Style 1966; 4 Clowns 1970; The Golden Age of Buster Keaton 1975
Keaton, Diane Lovers and Other Strangers 1970; The Godfather 1972; Play It Again, Sam 1972; Sleeper 1973; The Godfather, Part II 1974; Love and Death 1975; Harry and Walter Go to New York 1976; I Will... I Will... for Now 1976; Annie Hall 1977; Looking for Mr Goodbar 1977; Interiors 1978; Manhattan 1979; Reds 1981; Shoot the Moon 1982; The Little Drummer Girl 1984; Mrs Soffel 1984; Crimes of the Heart 1986; Baby Boom 1987; Radio Days 1987; The Good Mother 1988; The Lemon Sisters 1989; The Godfather Part III 1990; Father of the Bride 1991; Running Mates 1992; Look Who's Talking Now! 1993; Manhattan Murder Mystery 1993; Amelia Earhart: the Final Flight 1994; Father of the Bride Part II 1995; The First Wives Club 1996; Marvin's Room 1996; Northern Lights 1997; The Other Sister 1999; Hanging Up 1999
Keaton, Joe aka **Keaton, Joseph** Daydreams 1922; Our Hospitality 1923; Sherlock Junior 1924; Steamboat Bill, Jr 1928
Keaton, Michael Night Shift 1982; Mr Mom 1983; Johnny Dangerously 1984; Gung Ho 1986; Touch and Go 1986; The Squeeze 1987; Beetle Juice 1988; Clean and Sober 1988; Batman 1989; The Dream Team 1989; Pacific Heights 1990; One Good Cop 1991; Batman Returns 1992; Much Ado about Nothing 1993; My Life 1993; The Paper 1994; Speechless 1994; Multiplicity 1996; Jackie Brown 1997; Desperate Measures 1998; Out of Sight 1998; Jack Frost 1998
Keats, Ele Mother 1995; White Dwarf 1995; Race against Time: the Search for Sarah 1996
Keats, Steven The Friends of Eddie Coyle 1973; Death Wish 1974; The Gambler 1974; Hester Street 1975; Black Sunday 1976; The American Success Company 1979; Silent Rage 1982; Badge of the Assassin 1985; Turk 182! 1985; Eternity 1990; The Spring 1990
Keays-Byrne, Hugh The Man from Hong Kong 1975; Mad Max 1979; The Chain Reaction 1980; Kangaroo 1986; Les Patterson Saves the World 1987; The Salute of the Jugger 1989
Kedrova, Lila Razzia sur la Chnouf 1955; Calle Mayor 1956; Zorba the Greek 1964; A High Wind in Jamaica 1965; Torn Curtain 1966; A Time for Loving 1971; Soft Beds, Hard Battles 1973; The Tenant 1976; Tell Me a Riddle 1980; Sword of the Valiant 1984
Keefer, Don Riot in Cell Block 11 1954; Ace Eli and Rodger of the Skies 1973; Amos 1985
Keegan, Andrew Camp Nowhere 1994; 10 Things I Hate about You 1999
Keehne, Virginya Ticks 1993; The Dentist 1996
Keel, Howard Annie Get Your Gun 1950; Across the Wide Missouri 1951; Show Boat 1951; Callaway Went Thataway 1951; Desperate Search 1952; Lovely to Look At 1952; Calamity Jane 1953; Kiss Me Kate 1953; Ride, Vaquero! 1953; Deep in My Heart 1954; Rose Marie 1954; Seven Brides for Seven Brothers 1954; Jupiter's Darling 1955; Kismet 1955; Floods of Fear 1958; The Big Fisherman 1959; Armored Command 1961; The Day of the Triffids 1962; The Man from Button Willow 1965; Waco 1966; The War Wagon 1967; Arizona Bushwhackers 1968
Keeler, Ruby Footlight Parade 1933; 42nd Street 1933; Gold Diggers of 1933 1933; Dames 1934; Flirtation Walk 1934; Go into Your Dance 1935; Colleen 1936; Sweetheart of the Campus 1941
Keen, Diane Here We Go round the Mulberry Bush 1967; Sweeney! 1976; Silver Dream Racer 1980; Thirteen at Dinner 1985; Jekyll and Hyde 1989
Keen, Geoffrey It's Hard to Be Good 1948; The Third Man 1949; Cry, the Beloved Country 1951; Green Grow the Rushes 1951; Hunted 1952; The Long Memory 1952; Genevieve 1953; The Maggie 1953; Rob Roy, the Highland Rogue 1953; Turn the Key Softly 1953; The Divided Heart 1954; Face the Music 1954; The Glass Cage 1955; Passage Home 1955; Postmark for Danger 1955; Storm over the Nile 1955; House of Secrets 1956; The Long Arm 1956; Sailor Beware! 1956; Yield to the Night 1956; The Birthday Present 1957; Nowhere to Go 1958; Devil's Bait 1959; The Scapegoat 1959; The Angry Silence 1960; Sink the Bismarck! 1960; Spare the Rod 1961; Live Now – Pay Later 1962; The Spiral Road 1962; Dr Syn, Alias the Scarecrow 1963; The Mind Benders 1963; Born Free 1966; Berserk 1967; Taste the Blood of Dracula 1969; Sacco and Vanzetti 1971; Doomwatch 1972; Living Free 1972; The Spy Who Loved Me 1977; Octopussy 1983
Keen, Malcolm The Lodger 1926; The Manxman 1929; Operation Amsterdam 1958; Two and Two Make Six 1961; Life for Ruth 1962
Keen, Noah Battle for the Planet of the Apes 1973; Gable and Lombard 1976
Keen, Pat A Kind of Loving 1962; Clockwise 1986; Without a Clue 1988; Lyddie 1995
Keena, Monica Snow White: a Tale of Terror 1996; Ripe 1996

RadioTimes ACTORS' INDEX

Kinnear, Greg *Blankman* 1994; *Sabrina* 1995; *Dear God* 1996; *As Good As It Gets* 1997; *A Smile like Yours* 1997; *You've Got Mail* 1998; *Mystery Men* 1999
Kinnear, Roy *Sparrows Can't Sing* 1962; *Tiara Tahiti* 1962; *A Place to Go* 1963; *The Small World of Sammy Lee* 1963; *French Dressing* 1964; *Help!* 1965; *The Hill* 1965; *The Deadly Affair* 1966; *How I Won the War* 1967; *The Bed Sitting Room* 1969; *Lock Up Your Daughters!* 1969; *Taste the Blood of Dracula* 1969; *Egghead's Robot* 1970; *The Firechasers* 1970; *On a Clear Day You Can See Forever* 1970; *Scrooge* 1970; *The Pied Piper* 1971; *Willy Wonka and the Chocolate Factory* 1971; *Madame Sin* 1972; *That's Your Funeral* 1972; *The Three Musketeers* 1973; *Barry McKenzie Holds His Own* 1974; *The Amorous Milkman* 1974; *The Adventure of Sherlock Holmes' Smarter Brother* 1975; *One of Our Dinosaurs Is Missing* 1975; *Royal Flash* 1975; *Not Now, Comrade* 1976; *Herbie Goes to Monte Carlo* 1977; *The Hound of the Baskervilles* 1977; *The Last Remake of Beau Geste* 1977; *Watership Down* 1978; *Hawk the Slayer* 1980; *Hammett* 1982; *The Boys in Blue* 1983; *Pirates* 1986; *Just Ask for Diamond* 1988; *A Man for All Seasons* 1988; *The Return of the Musketeers* 1989; *The Princess and the Goblin* 1992
Kinnell, Murray *The Purchase Price* 1932; *Zoo in Budapest* 1933; *Anne of Green Gables* 1934; *Think Fast, Mr Moto* 1937
Kinney, Terry *No Mercy* 1986; *Talent for the Game* 1991; *Body Snatchers* 1993; *The Firm* 1993; *Devil in a Blue Dress* 1995; *The Good Old Boys* 1995; *Fly Away Home* 1996; *Don't Look Down* 1998; *Oxygen* 1999; *That Championship Season* 1999; *The House of Mirth* 2000
Kinsey, Lance *Police Academy 6: City under Siege* 1989; *Masters of Menace* 1990; *Dollar for the Dead* 1998
Kinskey, Leonid *Duck Soup* 1933; *The Great Waltz* 1938; *Broadway Limited* 1941; *That Night in Rio* 1941; *Weekend in Havana* 1941; *Lady for a Night* 1942; *Can't Help Singing* 1944; *The Fighting Seabees* 1944
Kinski, Klaus *A Time to Love and a Time to Die* 1958; *Doctor Zhivago* 1965; *For a Few Dollars More* 1965; *The Pleasure Girls* 1965; *A Bullet for the General* 1966; *Our Man in Marrakesh* 1966; *The Big Silence* 1967; *Circus of Fear* 1967; *Five Golden Dragons* 1967; *Sartana, Angel of Death* 1969; *Count Dracula* 1970; *Aguirre, Wrath of God* 1972; *Shanghai Joe* 1974; *Lifespan* 1975; *To Kill a Rat* 1977; *Woyzeck* 1978; *Nosferatu, the Vampire* 1979; *Buddy Buddy* 1981; *Android* 1982; *Fitzcarraldo* 1982; *Love and Money* 1982; *Venom* 1982; *Codename Wildgeese* 1984; *The Little Drummer Girl* 1984; *The Secret Diary of Sigmund Freud* 1984; *Timestalkers* 1987; *Vampire in Venice* 1987; *Cobra Verde* 1988
Kinski, Nastassja aka **Kinski, Nastassia** *To the Devil a Daughter* 1976; *Tess* 1979; *Cat People* 1982; *One from the Heart* 1982; *Exposed* 1983; *The Moon in the Gutter* 1983; *Unfaithfully Yours* 1983; *The Hotel New Hampshire* 1984; *Maria's Lovers* 1984; *Paris, Texas* 1984; *Harem* 1985; *Revolution* 1985; *Torrents of Spring* 1989; *Night Sun* 1990; *Faraway, So Close* 1993; *Crackerjack* 1994; *Terminal Velocity* 1994; *Fathers' Day* 1997; *One Night Stand* 1997; *Savior* 1997; *The Lost Son* 1998; *Playing by Heart* 1998; *Susan's Plan* 1998; *Your Friends & Neighbours* 1998
Kinsky, Leonid *On Your Toes* 1939; *Ball of Fire* 1941
Kinsolving, Lee *The Dark at the Top of the Stairs* 1960; *The Explosive Generation* 1961
Kirby, Bruce *Throw Momma from the Train* 1987; *Getting Up and Going Home* 1992; *All She Ever Wanted* 1996; *A Different Kind of Christmas* 1996
Kirby, Bruno aka **Kirby Jr, Bruno** *Cinderella Liberty* 1973; *The Harrad Experiment* 1973; *Superdad* 1974; *Between the Lines* 1977; *Almost Summer* 1977; *Borderline* 1980; *Where the Buffalo Roam* 1980; *Modern Romance* 1981; *Birdy* 1984; *This Is Spinal Tap* 1984; *Good Morning, Vietnam* 1987; *Tin Men* 1987; *The In Crowd* 1988; *Bert Rigby, You're a Fool* 1989; *We're No Angels* 1989; *When Harry Met Sally...* 1989; *The Freshman* 1990; *City Slickers* 1991; *Golden Gate* 1994; *The Basketball Diaries* 1995; *Donnie Brasco* 1997; *History Is Made at Night* 1999
Kirby, Michael *The Countess of Monte Cristo* 1948; *The Silent Partner* 1978; *Swoon* 1992
Kirchenbauer, Bill *They Call Me Bruce* 1982; *The Great American Sex Scandal* 1990
Kirk, Phyllis *Our Very Own* 1950; *The Iron Mistress* 1952; *House of Wax* 1953; *Thunder over the Plains* 1953; *River Beat* 1954; *The City Is Dark* 1954; *Back from Eternity* 1956; *Johnny Concho* 1956; *The Sad Sack* 1957; *That Woman Opposite* 1957
Kirk, Tommy aka **Kirk, Tom** *Old Yeller* 1957; *The Shaggy Dog* 1959; *The Snow Queen* 1959; *Swiss Family Robinson* 1960; *The Absent-Minded Professor* 1961; *Babes in Toyland* 1961; *Bon Voyage!* 1962; *Son of Flubber* 1962; *Savage Sam* 1963; *Pajama Party* 1964; *The Misadventures of Merlin Jones* 1964; *The Monkey's Uncle* 1965; *Village of the Giants* 1965; *The Unkissed Bride* 1966; *The Ghost in the Invisible Bikini* 1966
Kirkland, Alexander *Tarnished Lady* 1931; *Strange Interlude* 1932; *Black Beauty* 1933
Kirkland, Muriel *Hold Your Man* 1933; *Nana* 1934; *The White Parade* 1934; *Little Man, What Now?* 1934
Kirkland, Sally *Going Home* 1971; *A Star Is Born* 1976; *Human Highway* 1982; *Anna* 1987; *Cold Feet* 1989; *Paint It Black* 1989; *High Stakes* 1989; *Best of the Best* 1989; *Bullseye!* 1990; *Heat Wave* 1990; *Revenge* 1990; *Two Evil Eyes* 1990; *The Haunted* 1991; *Double Jeopardy* 1992; *Double Threat* 1992; *Hit the Dutchman* 1992; *Primary Motive* 1992; *Double Deception* 1993; *Paper Hearts* 1993; *The Woman Who Loved Elvis* 1993; *Eye of the Stranger* 1993; *Forever* 1993; *Gunmen* 1994; *Amnesia* 1996; *EDtv* 1999
Kirkwood, Jack *Fancy Pants* 1950; *Never a Dull Moment* 1950
Kirkwood, Pat *Band Waggon* 1939; *Come On George* 1939
Kirshner, Mia *Love and Human Remains* 1993; *Exotica* 1994; *Johnny's Girl* 1995; *The Crow: City of Angels* 1996; *Anna Karenina* 1997; *Mad City* 1997
Kirwan, Dervla *December Bride* 1990; *With or Without You* 1999
Kirwan, Kitty *The Vicar of Bray* 1937; *Odd Man Out* 1946
Kiser, Terry *Rachel, Rachel* 1968; *Fast Charlie: the Moonbeam Rider* 1978; *Rich Kids* 1979; *Six Pack* 1982; *Friday the 13th Part VII: the New Blood* 1988; *Weekend at Bernie's* 1989; *Mannequin on the Move* 1991; *Into the Sun* 1992; *Weekend at Bernie's II* 1992; *Pet Shop* 1995; *Hourglass* 1996
Kiser, Virginia *Kill Me If You Can* 1977; *Katie: Portrait of a Centerfold* 1978; *Poltergeist* 1982
Kishi, Keiko *Early Spring* 1956; *Kwaidan* 1964; *Mastermind* 1976; *The Makioka Sisters* 1983
Kishimoto, Kayoko *Hana-Bi* 1997; *Kikujiro* 1999
Kitabayashi, Tanie *The Burmese Harp* 1956; *The Key* 1959; *The Burmese Harp* 1985
Kitaen, Tawny *Bachelor Party* 1984; *Crystal Heart* 1987; *Witchboard* 1987; *Happy Hour* 1987; *Playback* 1995
Kitano, Takeshi aka **Takeshi,** aka **"Beat" Takeshi** *Merry Christmas Mr Lawrence* 1982; *Violent Cop* 1989; *Sonatine* 1993; *Johnny Mnemonic* 1995; *Hana-Bi* 1997; *Kikujiro* 1999
Kitchen, Michael *Out of Africa* 1985; *The Dive* 1989; *Fools of Fortune* 1990; *The Russia House* 1990; *Enchanted April* 1991; *Hostage* 1992; *Doomsday Gun* 1994; *Fatherland* 1994; *Mrs Dalloway* 1997; *The Last Contract* 1998
Kitosch, Cole *Texas Adios* 1966; *Killer Calibre 32* 1967
Kitt, Eartha *Casbah* 1948; *New Faces* 1954; *The Mark of the Hawk* 1957; *St Louis Blues* 1958; *Anna Lucasta* 1958; *Get off My Back* 1965; *Up the Chastity Belt* 1971; *Friday Foster* 1975; *Dragonard* 1987; *Erik the Viking* 1989; *Ernest Scared Stupid* 1991; *Boomerang* 1992; *Harriet the Spy* 1996; *The Jungle Book: Mowgli's Story* 1998
Kitzmiller, John *The Naked Earth* 1958; *Dr No* 1962
Kjellin, Alf aka **Kent, Christopher** *Torment* 1944; *Madame Bovary* 1949; *Summer Interlude* 1950; *My Six Convicts* 1952; *The Juggler* 1953; *Assault on a Queen* 1966; *Ice Station Zebra* 1968
Kjellman, Björn *Best Intentions* 1992; *The Premonition* 1992; *All Things Fair* 1995
Klein, Chris *American Pie* 1999; *Election* 1999; *Here on Earth* 2000
Klein, Nita *Muriel* 1963; *Total Eclipse* 1995
Klein, Robert *The Thirteenth Guest* 1932; *The Landlord* 1970; *The Owl and the Pussycat* 1970; *The Pursuit of Happiness* 1971; *Hooper* 1978; *The Bell Jar* 1979; *The Last Unicorn* 1980; *Poison Ivy* 1985; *This Wife for Hire* 1985; *Jeffrey* 1995; *Mixed Nuts* 1995
Klein-Rogge, Rudolf *Destiny* 1921; *Dr Mabuse, the Gambler* 1922; *Metropolis* 1926; *Spies* 1928; *The Testament of Dr Mabuse* 1932
Klemperer, Werner *Five Steps to Danger* 1957; *Kiss Them for Me* 1957; *Ship of Fools* 1965; *Dark Intruder* 1965
Kline, Kevin *Sophie's Choice* 1982; *The Big Chill* 1983; *The Pirates of Penzance* 1983; *Silverado* 1985; *Violets Are Blue* 1986; *Cry Freedom* 1987; *A Fish Called Wanda* 1988; *The January Man* 1989; *I Love You to Death* 1990; *Grand Canyon* 1991; *Soapdish* 1991; *Chaplin* 1992; *Consenting Adults* 1992; *Dave* 1993; *George Balanchine's The Nutcracker* 1993; *Princess Caraboo* 1994; *French Kiss* 1995; *The Hunchback of Notre Dame* 1996; *Fierce Creatures* 1997; *The Ice Storm* 1997; *In & Out* 1997; *Wild Wild West* 1999; *William Shakespeare's A Midsummer Night's Dream* 1999; *The Road to El Dorado* 2000
Kline, Richard *Side by Side* 1988; *Hell Hath No Fury* 1991
Kling, Heidi *The Mighty Ducks* 1992; *Out on a Limb* 1992; *D3: the Mighty Ducks* 1996
Klugman, Jack *Timetable* 1956; *12 Angry Men* 1957; *Cry Terror* 1958; *Days of Wine and Roses* 1962; *I Could Go On Singing* 1963; *The Yellow Canary* 1963; *Act One* 1963; *The Detective* 1968; *The Split* 1968; *Goodbye, Columbus* 1969; *Who Says I Can't Ride a Rainbow* 1971; *Two-Minute Warning* 1976; *The Odd Couple: Together Again* 1993
Knaggs, Skelton *The Ghost Ship* 1943; *Terror by Night* 1946; *Dick Tracy Meets Gruesome* 1947
Knapp, Evalyn *Smart Money* 1931; *High Pressure* 1932; *Vanishing Frontier* 1932; *A Successful Calamity* 1932; *Fireman Save My Child* 1932; *Confidential* 1935
Knaup, Herbert *Waller's Last Walk* 1989; *Run Lola Run* 1998
Knell, David *The Devil and Max Devlin* 1981; *September Gun* 1983; *Turner & Hooch* 1989; *Jailbirds* 1991
Knepper, Robert aka **Knepper, Rob** *Wild Thing* 1987; *DOA* 1988; *Renegades* 1989; *Gas, Food, Lodging* 1992; *Where the Day Takes You* 1992; *Getting Out* 1993
Knight (2), Christopher *A Very Brady Christmas* 1988; *The Doom Generation* 1995
Knight, David *Out of the Clouds* 1954; *The Young Lovers* 1954; *Lost* 1955; *Eyewitness* 1956; *Across the Bridge* 1957; *Nightmare* 1964; *Who Shot Patakango?* 1992
Knight, Don *The Hell with Heroes* 1968; *Master of the Islands* 1970; *something big* 1971; *Swamp Thing* 1982
Knight, Esmond *Pagliacci* 1936; *The Vicar of Bray* 1937; *The Arsenal Stadium Mystery* 1939; *Contraband* 1940; *The Halfway House* 1943; *The Silver Fleet* 1943; *Henry V* 1944; *Black Narcissus* 1946; *The End of the River* 1947; *Uncle Silas* 1947; *The Red Shoes* 1948; *Gone to Earth* 1950; *The River* 1951; *Peeping Tom* 1960; *The Winter's Tale* 1966; *The Boy Who Turned Yellow* 1972; *Robin and Marian* 1976; *The Element of Crime* 1984
Knight, Fuzzy *The Cowboy and the Lady* 1938; *Spawn of the North* 1938; *The Singing Sheriff* 1944; *Frontier Gal* 1945; *The Bounty Killer* 1965
Knight, Gladys *Pipe Dreams* 1976; *Desperado* 1987; *Twenty Bucks* 1993
Knight, Keith *Meatballs* 1979; *Gas* 1981
Knight, Lily *Static* 1985; *Crowned and Dangerous* 1997
Knight, Michael E *Date with an Angel* 1987; *Hexed* 1993; *A Different Kind of Christmas* 1996
Knight, Shirley *The Dark at the Top of the Stairs* 1960; *Sweet Bird of Youth* 1962; *House of Women* 1962; *Flight from Ashiya* 1964; *Dutchman* 1966; *The Group* 1966; *Petulia* 1968; *The Rain People* 1969; *Juggernaut* 1974; *Beyond the Poseidon Adventure* 1979; *Endless Love* 1981; *The Sender* 1982; *With Intent to Kill* 1984; *Bump in the Night* 1991; *A Child for Satan* 1991; *Shadow of a Doubt* 1991; *Desperate Justice* 1993; *Baby Brokers* 1994; *Indictment: the McMartin Trial* 1995; *Stuart Saves His Family* 1995; *Diabolique* 1996; *If These Walls Could Talk* 1996; *A Promise to Carolyn* 1996; *As Good As It Gets* 1997
Knight, Ted *Nightmare in Chicago* 1968; *Caddyshack* 1980
Knight, Trenton *Charlie's Ghost Story* 1994; *The Tin Soldier* 1995; *The Skateboard Kid II* 1995
Knight, Wayne *Dead Again* 1991; *Jurassic Park* 1993; *Chameleon* 1995; *For Richer or Poorer* 1997; *Space Jam* 1997
Knight, Wyatt *Porky's* 1981; *Porky's II: The Next Day* 1983; *Porky's Revenge* 1985
Knott, Andrew *The Secret Garden* 1993; *Black Beauty* 1994
Knotts, Don *No Time for Sergeants* 1958; *Wake Me when It's Over* 1960; *The Last Time I Saw Archie* 1961; *Move Over, Darling* 1963; *The Incredible Mr Limpet* 1964; *The Ghost and Mr Chicken* 1966; *The Shakiest Gun in the West* 1967; *The Reluctant Astronaut* 1967; *The Love God?* 1969; *How to Frame a Figg* 1971; *The Apple Dumpling Gang* 1974; *No Deposit No Return* 1976; *Gus* 1976; *Herbie Goes to Monte Carlo* 1977; *Hot Lead and Cold Feet* 1978; *The Apple Dumpling Gang Rides Again* 1979; *The Prize Fighter* 1979; *The Private Eyes* 1980; *Pleasantville* 1998
Knowlden, Marilyn *Les Misérables* 1935; *The Way of All Flesh* 1940
Knowles, Patric *The Charge of the Light Brigade* 1936; *It's Love I'm After* 1937; *The Adventures of Robin Hood* 1938; *Four's a Crowd* 1938; *Another Thin Man* 1939; *Beauty for the Asking* 1939; *The Spellbinder* 1939; *Anne of Windy Poplars* 1940; *A Bill of Divorcement* 1940; *The Wolf Man* 1941; *Sin Town* 1942; *Who Done It?* 1942; *Lady in a Jam* 1942; *Frankenstein Meets the Wolf Man* 1943; *Hit the Ice* 1943; *Kitty* 1945; *The Bride Wore Boots* 1946; *Monsieur Beaucaire* 1946; *OSS* 1946; *Of Human Bondage* 1946; *Ivy* 1947; *Dream Girl* 1948; *Isn't It Romantic* 1948; *The Big Steal* 1949; *Three Came Home* 1950; *Tarzan's Savage Fury* 1952; *Jamaica Run* 1953; *Khyber Patrol* 1954; *World for Ransom* 1954; *Band of Angels* 1957; *Auntie Mame* 1958
Knox, Alexander *Cheer Boys Cheer* 1939; *The Sea Wolf* 1941; *This above All* 1942; *None Shall Escape* 1944; *Wilson* 1944; *Over 21* 1945; *Sister Kenny* 1946; *The Judge Steps Out* 1949; *Tokyo Joe* 1949; *I'd Climb the Highest Mountain* 1951; *Man in the Saddle* 1951; *Europa '51* 1952; *The Divided Heart* 1954; *The Sleeping Tiger* 1954; *The Night My Number Came Up* 1955; *Reach for the Sky* 1956; *Chase a Crooked Shadow* 1957; *High Tide*

Lagerwall, Sture *Walpurgis Night* 1935; *The Devil's Eye* 1960
Lagrange, Valérie *Morgan the Pirate* 1960; *La Ronde* 1964; *Up to His Ears* 1965; *A Man and a Woman* 1966; *Weekend* 1967; *The Valley* 1972
Laguna, Sylvie *Delicatessen* 1990; *Road to Ruin* 1992
Lahr, Bert *Josette* 1938; *Just around the Corner* 1938; *The Wizard of Oz* 1939; *Zaza* 1939; *Ship Ahoy* 1942; *Meet the People* 1944; *Always Leave Them Laughing* 1949; *Rose Marie* 1954
Lahti, Christine *...And Justice for All* 1979; *Whose Life Is it Anyway?* 1981; *Ladies and Gentlemen, the Fabulous Stains* 1982; *Single Bars, Single Women* 1984; *Swing Shift* 1984; *Just between Friends* 1986; *Housekeeping* 1987; *Season of Dreams* 1987; *Running on Empty* 1988; *A Cut Above* 1989; *No Place like Home* 1989; *Funny about Love* 1990; *Crazy from the Heart* 1991; *The Doctor* 1991; *Leaving Normal* 1992; *Hideaway* 1995; *Pie in the Sky* 1995; *The Four Diamonds* 1995; *A Weekend in the Country* 1996; *Hope* 1997
Laine, Frankie *Bring Your Smile Along* 1955; *He Laughed Last* 1956
Laird, Jenny *Just William* 1939; *Black Narcissus* 1946; *Village of the Damned* 1960
Lake, Arthur *Indiscreet* 1931; *Topper* 1937; *Blondie* 1938; *Blondie Meets the Boss* 1939; *Blondie Takes a Vacation* 1939; *Footlight Glamour* 1943
Lake, Don *Blue Monkey* 1987; *Short Circuit 2* 1988
Lake, Florence *The Rogue Song* 1930; *Romance* 1930
Lake, Ricki *Hairspray* 1988; *Babycakes* 1989; *Cry-Baby* 1989; *Last Exit to Brooklyn* 1989; *The Chase* 1991; *Inside Monkey Zetterland* 1992; *Where the Day Takes You* 1992; *Based on an Untrue Story* 1993; *Serial Mom* 1994; *Mrs Winterbourne* 1995
Lake, Veronica *I Wanted Wings* 1941; *Sullivan's Travels* 1941; *The Glass Key* 1942; *I Married a Witch* 1942; *This Gun for Hire* 1942; *Star Spangled Rhythm* 1942; *So Proudly We Hail* 1943; *The Hour before the Dawn* 1944; *Bring on the Girls* 1945; *Duffy's Tavern* 1945; *Hold That Blonde* 1945; *Miss Susie Slagle's* 1945; *Out of This World* 1945; *The Blue Dahlia* 1946; *Ramrod* 1947; *Variety Girl* 1947; *Saigon* 1948; *Isn't It Romantic* 1948; *The Sainted Sisters* 1948; *Slattery's Hurricane* 1949; *Flesh Feast* 1970
Lally, Mick *Fools of Fortune* 1990; *The Secret of Roan Inish* 1993; *Circle of Friends* 1995
Lam Ching Ying *The Prodigal Son* 1983; *Mr Vampire* 1986
Lamarr, Hedy aka **Kiesler, Hedy** *Ecstasy* 1933; *Algiers* 1938; *Lady of the Tropics* 1939; *Boom Town* 1940; *Comrade X* 1940; *I Take This Woman* 1940; *Come Live with Me* 1941; *HM Pulham Esq* 1941; *Ziegfeld Girl* 1941; *Crossroads* 1942; *Tortilla Flat* 1942; *White Cargo* 1942; *The Heavenly Body* 1943; *The Conspirators* 1944; *Experiment Perilous* 1944; *The Strange Woman* 1946; *Dishonored Lady* 1947; *Let's Live a Little* 1948; *Samson and Delilah* 1949; *A Lady without Passport* 1950; *Copper Canyon* 1950; *My Favorite Spy* 1951; *The Loves of Three Queens* 1954; *The Story of Mankind* 1957; *The Female Animal* 1958
Lamas, Fernando *Dangerous When Wet* 1953; *The Diamond Queen* 1953; *The Girl Who Had Everything* 1953; *Rose Marie* 1954; *Jivaro* 1954; *The Girl Rush* 1955; *The Lost World* 1960; *Valley of Mystery* 1967; *The Violent Ones* 1967; *Kill a Dragon* 1967; *100 Rifles* 1969
Lamas, Lorenzo *Take Down* 1978; *CIA – Codename Alexa* 1992; *Bounty Tracker* 1993; *Final Round* 1993; *Terminal Justice* 1996
Lamb, Gil *The Fleet's In* 1942; *Riding High* 1943
Lamb, Larry *Shadey* 1985; *Buster* 1988; *Essex Boys* 1999
Lambert, Anne Louise aka **Lambert, Anne** *Picnic at Hanging Rock* 1975; *The Draughtsman's Contract* 1982; *To the Four Winds* 1987
Lambert, Christopher aka **Lambert, Christophe** *Greystoke: the Legend of Tarzan, Lord of the Apes* 1984; *Love Songs* 1984; *Subway* 1985; *Highlander* 1986; *The Sicilian* 1987; *To Kill a Priest* 1988; *Highlander II: the Quickening* 1990; *Why Me?* 1990; *Fortress* 1992; *Knight Moves* 1992; *Gunmen* 1994; *Roadflower* 1994; *Adrenalin: Fear the Rush* 1995; *Highlander III: the Sorcerer* 1995; *The Hunted* 1995; *Mortal Kombat* 1995; *Mean Guns* 1996; *North Star* 1996; *Nirvana* 1996
Lambert, Jack *Abilene Town* 1945; *Dick Tracy's Dilemma* 1947; *The Unsuspected* 1947; *Belle Starr's Daughter* 1948; *Eureka Stockade* 1949; *The Lost Hours* 1952; *Scared Stiff* 1953; *At Gunpoint* 1955; *Run for Cover* 1955; *Storm over the Nile* 1955; *Machine Gun Kelly* 1958; *The Bridal Path* 1959; *Neither the Sea nor the Sand* 1972
Lambert, Paul *The Big Mouth* 1967; *Mama's Dirty Girls* 1974
Lamberts, Heath *To Kill a Clown* 1972; *Sam and Me* 1991; *Change of Heart* 1993; *Ordinary Magic* 1993
Lambie, Joe aka **Lambie, Joseph** *Nightmares* 1983; *Seduction: Three Tales from the Inner Sanctum* 1992
Lamble, Lloyd *Suspended Alibi* 1956; *Blue Murder at St Trinian's* 1957; *The Bank Raiders* 1958
Lamm, Karen *Trackdown* 1976; *The Night They Took Miss Beautiful* 1977
Lamont, Duncan *The Man in the White Suit* 1951; *The Golden Coach* 1953; *The Teckman Mystery* 1954; *Passage Home* 1955; *Murder at the Gallop* 1963; *The Devil-Ship Pirates* 1964; *Evil of Frankenstein* 1964; *Arabesque* 1966; *The Witches* 1966; *Quatermass and the Pit* 1967; *The Creeping Flesh* 1972
Lamont, Molly *The Awful Truth* 1937; *The Moon and Sixpence* 1942; *The Suspect* 1944; *So Goes My Love* 1946
Lamorisse, Pascal *White Mane* 1952; *Red Balloon* 1956
LaMotta, John *American Ninja* 1985; *Lookin' Italian* 1994
Lamour, Dorothy *The Big Broadcast of 1938* 1937; *High, Wide and Handsome* 1937; *The Hurricane* 1937; *The Last Train from Madrid* 1937; *Swing High, Swing Low* 1937; *Spawn of the North* 1938; *Chad Hanna* 1940; *Johnny Apollo* 1940; *Road to Singapore* 1940; *Typhoon* 1940; *Road to Zanzibar* 1941; *Beyond the Blue Horizon* 1942; *The Fleet's In* 1942; *Road to Morocco* 1942; *Star Spangled Rhythm* 1942; *Dixie* 1943; *Riding High* 1943; *They Got Me Covered* 1943; *Duffy's Tavern* 1945; *A Medal for Benny* 1945; *Road to Utopia* 1945; *My Favorite Brunette* 1947; *Road to Rio* 1947; *Lulu Belle* 1948; *On Our Merry Way* 1948; *The Lucky Stiff* 1949; *Slightly French* 1949; *Here Comes the Groom* 1951; *The Greatest Show on Earth* 1952; *Road to Bali* 1952; *The Road to Hong Kong* 1962; *Donovan's Reef* 1963; *Pajama Party* 1964; *Death at Love House* 1976; *Won Ton Ton, the Dog Who Saved Hollywood* 1976; *Creepshow 2* 1987
Lampe, Jutta *Sisters, or the Balance of Happiness* 1979; *The German Sisters* 1981
Lampert, Zohra *Pay or Die* 1960; *Posse from Hell* 1961; *Splendor in the Grass* 1961; *Hey, Let's Twist!* 1961; *Let's Scare Jessica to Death* 1971; *Opening Night* 1977; *Alphabet City* 1984; *Izzy and Moe* 1985; *American Blue Note* 1989; *Stanley & Iris* 1989; *The Last Good Time* 1994
Lampley, Oni Faida *Lone Star* 1995; *First Do No Harm* 1997
Lampreave, Chus *What Have I Done to Deserve This?* 1984; *Matador* 1986; *The Flower of My Secret* 1995
Lamprecht, Günter aka **Lamprecht, Günther** *Berlin Alexanderplatz* 1980; *Rouge Baiser* 1985
Lancaster, Burt *The Killers* 1946; *Brute Force* 1947; *Desert Fury* 1947; *I Walk Alone* 1947; *Variety Girl* 1947; *All My Sons* 1948; *Blood on My Hands* 1948; *Sorry, Wrong Number* 1948; *Criss Cross* 1949; *Rope of Sand* 1949; *The Flame and the Arrow* 1950; *Mister 880* 1950; *Jim Thorpe – All-American* 1951; *Ten Tall Men* 1951; *Vengeance Valley* 1951; *Come Back, Little Sheba* 1952; *The Crimson Pirate* 1952; *From Here to Eternity* 1953; *His Majesty O'Keefe* 1953; *South Sea Woman* 1953; *Apache* 1954; *Vera Cruz* 1954; *The Kentuckian* 1955; *The Rose Tattoo* 1955; *The Rainmaker* 1956; *Trapeze* 1956; *Gunfight at the OK Corral* 1957; *Sweet Smell of Success* 1957; *Run Silent, Run Deep* 1958; *Separate Tables* 1958; *The Devil's Disciple* 1959; *Elmer Gantry* 1960; *The Unforgiven* 1960; *Judgment at Nuremberg* 1961; *The Young Savages* 1961; *Birdman of Alcatraz* 1962; *A Child Is Waiting* 1962; *The Leopard* 1962; *Seven Days in May* 1964; *The Train* 1964; *The Hallelujah Trail* 1965; *The Professionals* 1966; *The Scalphunters* 1968; *The Swimmer* 1968; *Castle Keep* 1969; *The Gypsy Moths* 1969; *Airport* 1970; *King: a Filmed Record... Montgomery to Memphis* 1970; *Lawman* 1971; *Valdez Is Coming* 1971; *Ulzana's Raid* 1972; *Executive Action* 1973; *Scorpio* 1973; *Conversation Piece* 1974; *The Midnight Man* 1974; *Moses* 1975; *Buffalo Bill and the Indians, or Sitting Bull's History Lesson* 1976; *The Cassandra Crossing* 1976; *1900* 1976; *Victory at Entebbe* 1976; *Go Tell the Spartans* 1977; *The Island of Dr Moreau* 1977; *Twilight's Last Gleaming* 1977; *Zulu Dawn* 1979; *Atlantic City USA* 1980; *Cattle Annie and Little Britches* 1981; *La Pelle* 1981; *Local Hero* 1983; *The Osterman Weekend* 1983; *Scandal Sheet* 1985; *Little Treasure* 1985; *Tough Guys* 1986; *Barnum* 1986; *Rocket Gibraltar* 1988; *Field of Dreams* 1989; *Voyage of Terror: the Achille Lauro Affair* 1990
Lancaster, James *Leprechaun 2* 1994; *Entertaining Angels: the Dorothy Day Story* 1996; *Hijacked: Flight 285* 1996
Lancaster, Stuart *Faster, Pussycat! Kill! Kill!* 1965; *Mudhoney* 1965; *Good Morning... and Goodbye* 1967
Lanchester, Elsa *The Private Life of Henry VIII* 1933; *Bride of Frankenstein* 1935; *David Copperfield* 1935; *The Ghost Goes West* 1935; *Naughty Marietta* 1935; *Rembrandt* 1936; *Vessel of Wrath* 1938; *Ladies in Retirement* 1941; *Son of Fury* 1942; *Tales of Manhattan* 1942; *Lassie Come Home* 1943; *The Razor's Edge* 1946; *The Spiral Staircase* 1946; *The Bishop's Wife* 1947; *Northwest Outpost* 1947; *The Big Clock* 1948; *Come to the Stable* 1949; *The Inspector General* 1949; *The Secret Garden* 1949; *Mystery Street* 1950; *The Petty Girl* 1950; *Androcles and the Lion* 1952; *Dreamboat* 1952; *Les Misérables* 1952; *Hell's Half Acre* 1954; *Three Ring Circus* 1954; *The Glass Slipper* 1955; *Witness for the Prosecution* 1957; *Bell, Book and Candle* 1958; *Pajama Party* 1964; *Honeymoon Hotel* 1964; *That Darn Cat!* 1965; *Blackbeard's Ghost* 1967; *Easy Come, Easy Go* 1967; *Willard* 1971; *Terror in the Wax Museum* 1973; *Arnold* 1973; *Murder by Death* 1976
Land, Geoffrey *The Female Bunch* 1969; *Against a Crooked Sky* 1975
Landau, David *Street Scene* 1931; *Horse Feathers* 1932; *I Am a Fugitive from a Chain Gang* 1932; *Lawyer Man* 1932; *Taxi!* 1932; *The Purchase Price* 1932; *Polly of the Circus* 1932; *Gabriel over the White House* 1933; *She Done Him Wrong* 1933; *Judge Priest* 1934
Landau, Juliet *Theodore Rex* 1995; *Ravager* 1997
Landau, Martin *The Gazebo* 1959; *North by Northwest* 1959; *Pork Chop Hill* 1959; *Stagecoach to Dancer's Rock* 1962; *Cleopatra* 1963; *The Greatest Story Ever Told* 1965; *The Hallelujah Trail* 1965; *Nevada Smith* 1966; *They Call Me Mister Tibbs!* 1970; *A Town Called Hell* 1971; *Meteor* 1979; *Without Warning* 1980; *Alone in the Dark* 1982; *Delta Fever* 1988; *Tucker: the Man and His Dream* 1988; *Crimes and Misdemeanors* 1989; *The Neon Empire* 1989; *Paint It Black* 1989; *By Dawn's Early Light* 1990; *Max and Helen* 1990; *Treasure Island* 1991; *Firehead* 1991; *Fatal Love* 1992; *Legacy of Lies* 1992; *Mistress* 1992; *No Place to Hide* 1992; *Sliver* 1993; *12:01* 1993; *Eye of the Stranger* 1993; *Ed Wood* 1994; *Intersection* 1994; *Joseph in Egypt* 1995; *The Adventures of Pinocchio* 1996; *City Hall* 1996; *B.A.P.S.* 1997; *Rounders* 1998; *The X Files* 1998; *EDtv* 1999
Landen, Dinsdale *We Joined the Navy* 1962; *Mosquito Squadron* 1968; *Every Home Should Have One* 1970; *Digby, the Biggest Dog in the World* 1973; *International Velvet* 1978; *Morons from Outer Space* 1985; *The Steal* 1994
Lander, David L *Used Cars* 1980; *Betrayal of the Dove* 1993
Landers, Audrey *A Chorus Line* 1985; *Getting Even* 1986; *Ghost Writer* 1989
Landers, Harry *Guilty Bystander* 1950; *Drive a Crooked Road* 1954
Landers, Judy *The Black Marble* 1980; *Ghost Writer* 1989
Landes, Michael *When the Party's Over* 1992; *Danielle Steel's No Greater Love* 1996; *Dream for an Insomniac* 1996
Landesberg, Steve *Little Miss Millions* 1993; *Sodbusters* 1994
Landfield, Timothy *Cheetah* 1989; *Without Warning: the James Brady Story* 1991
Landgard, Janet *The Swimmer* 1968; *Land Raiders* 1969
Landgrebe, Gudrun *Colonel Redl* 1984; *Snow White* 1989; *Milena* 1990
Landham, Sonny *The Dirty Dozen: the Next Mission* 1985; *Firewalker* 1986; *Lock Up* 1989; *Best of the Best II* 1992
Landi, Elissa *Body and Soul* 1931; *The Sign of the Cross* 1932; *The Masquerader* 1933; *Enter Madame!* 1933; *The Count of Monte Cristo* 1934; *By Candlelight* 1934; *Königsmark* 1935; *After the Thin Man* 1936
Landi, Marla *The Hornet's Nest* 1955; *Across the Bridge* 1957; *Dublin Nightmare* 1958; *First Man into Space* 1958; *The Hound of the Baskervilles* 1959; *The Pirates of Blood River* 1961
Landi, Sal *Savage Streets* 1984; *Rover Dangerfield* 1991
Landis, Carole *Hollywood Hotel* 1937; *Three Texas Steers* 1939; *Man and His Mate* 1940; *Turnabout* 1940; *I Wake Up Screaming* 1941; *Moon over Miami* 1941; *Road Show* 1941; *Topper Returns* 1941; *A Gentleman at Heart* 1942; *My Gal Sal* 1942; *Orchestra Wives* 1942; *Wintertime* 1943; *Secret Command* 1944; *It Shouldn't Happen to a Dog* 1946; *Thieves' Holiday* 1946; *Out of the Blue* 1947; *The Brass Monkey* 1948; *Noose* 1948
Landis, Jessie Royce *Mr Belvedere Goes to College* 1949; *My Foolish Heart* 1949; *To Catch a Thief* 1955; *The Girl He Left Behind* 1956; *The Swan* 1956; *My Man Godfrey* 1957; *I Married a Woman* 1958; *North by Northwest* 1959; *A Private's Affair* 1959; *Goodbye Again* 1961; *Bon Voyage!* 1962; *Boys' Night Out* 1962; *Critic's Choice* 1963; *Gidget Goes to Rome* 1963
Landis, John *Schlock* 1971; *1941* 1979; *Into the Night* 1985; *Sleepwalkers* 1992; *Venice/Venice* 1992; *Body Chemistry 2: Voice of a Stranger* 1992; *Diamonds* 1999
Landis, Monte aka **Landis, Monty** *Targets* 1968; *Pee-wee's Big Adventure* 1985
Lando, Joe *The Devil's Bed* 1994; *No Code of Conduct* 1998
Landon, Laurene *The California Dolls* 1981; *I, the Jury* 1982; *America 3000* 1986; *Armed Response* 1986; *It's Alive III: Island of the Alive* 1987; *Maniac Cop* 1988; *Maniac Cop 2* 1990
Landon, Michael *I Was a Teenage Werewolf* 1957; *Maracaibo* 1958; *The Legend of Tom Dooley* 1959; *Comeback* 1983; *Sam's Son* 1984; *Where Pigeons Go to Die* 1990

Landon Jr, Michael *Bonanza: the Next Generation* 1988; *Bonanza – the Return* 1993
Landone, Avice *True as a Turtle* 1956; *Gaolbreak* 1962; *The Leather Boys* 1963; *This Is My Street* 1963; *The Adventures of Barry McKenzie* 1972
Landor, Rosalyn *The Amazing Mr Blunden* 1972; *Merlin and the Sword* 1982
Landry, Gerard *La Bête Humaine* 1938; *Night without Stars* 1951
Landry, Karen *The Personals* 1982; *The Christmas Star* 1986; *Patti Rocks* 1987
Landsburg, Valerie *Thank God It's Friday* 1978; *Babies* 1990; *One of Her Own* 1994
Lane, Abbe *Ride Clear of Diablo* 1954; *The Americano* 1955; *Maracaibo* 1958
Lane, Allan *Charlie Chan at the Olympics* 1937; *The Law West of Tombstone* 1938; *Maid's Night Out* 1938; *The Spellbinder* 1939; *Bells of Rosarita* 1945; *The Saga of Hemp Brown* 1958
Lane (1), Charles *aka* **Levison, Charles** *Blonde Crazy* 1931; *Advice to the Lovelorn* 1933; *Twentieth Century* 1934; *The Juggler* 1953; *The Affairs of Dobie Gillis* 1953; *Teacher's Pet* 1958; *But Not for Me* 1959; *Good Neighbor Sam* 1964; *Billie* 1965; *The Ugly Dachshund* 1966; *What's So Bad About Feeling Good?* 1968; *The Little Dragons* 1980
Lane (2), Charles *Dr Jekyll and Mr Hyde* 1920; *The White Sister* 1923; *The Winning of Barbara Worth* 1926; *Sadie Thompson* 1928; *Canary Murder Case* 1929
Lane (3), Charles *Sidewalk Stories* 1989; *True Identity* 1991; *Posse* 1993
Lane, Colin *Broken Harvest* 1994; *The Blood Oranges* 1997
Lane, Diane *A Little Romance* 1979; *Touched by Love* 1979; *Cattle Annie and Little Britches* 1981; *National Lampoon's Movie Madness* 1981; *Six Pack* 1982; *Ladies and Gentlemen, the Fabulous Stains* 1982; *The Outsiders* 1983; *Rumble Fish* 1983; *The Cotton Club* 1984; *Streets of Fire* 1984; *The Big Town* 1987; *Lady Beware* 1987; *Descending Angel* 1990; *Vital Signs* 1990; *Chaplin* 1992; *Knight Moves* 1992; *My New Gun* 1992; *Indian Summer* 1993; *Judge Dredd* 1995; *Wild Bill* 1995; *Jack* 1996; *Trigger Happy* 1996; *Murder at 1600* 1997; *Grace & Glorie* 1998; *A Walk on the Moon* 1999; *The Perfect Storm* 2000
Lane, Jackie *Goodbye Again* 1961; *Two and Two Make Six* 1961
Lane, Jocelyn *Tickle Me* 1965; *Incident at Phantom Hill* 1966; *Land Raiders* 1969
Lane, Lenita *The Mad Magician* 1954; *The Bat* 1959
Lane, Lola *Fox Movietone Follies of 1929* 1929; *Murder on a Honeymoon* 1935; *Hollywood Hotel* 1937; *Marked Woman* 1937; *Four Daughters* 1938; *Daughters Courageous* 1939; *Four Wives* 1939; *Deadline at Dawn* 1946
Lane, Mara *Decameron Nights* 1953; *Angela* 1955
Lane, Mark *Rush to Judgment* 1967; *There Are No Children Here* 1993
Lane, Mike *aka* **Lane, Michael** *The Harder They Fall* 1956; *Hero of Babylon* 1963; *Stryker* 1983; *Code Name: Zebra* 1986
Lane, Nathan *Frankie & Johnny* 1991; *He Said, She Said* 1991; *Life with Mikey* 1993; *The Lion King* 1994; *Jeffrey* 1995; *The Birdcage* 1996; *The Boys Next Door* 1996; *Mousehunt* 1997; *At First Sight* 1998; *Love's Labour's Lost* 1999; *Stuart Little* 1999; *Isn't She Great* 1999; *Titan AE* 2000
Lane, Priscilla *Four Daughters* 1938; *Daughters Courageous* 1939; *Dust Be My Destiny* 1939; *The Roaring Twenties* 1939; *Four Wives* 1939; *Blues in the Night* 1941; *Million Dollar Baby* 1941; *Saboteur* 1942; *The Meanest Man in the World* 1943; *Arsenic and Old Lace* 1944
Lane, Richard *Flight from Glory* 1937; *Go Chase Yourself* 1938; *Mr Moto in Danger Island* 1939; *Hellzapoppin'* 1941; *Riders of the Purple Sage* 1941; *Arabian Nights* 1942; *Ride 'em Cowboy* 1942; *Dr Broadway* 1942; *Corvette K-225* 1943; *The Bermuda Mystery* 1944; *Brazil* 1944; *Mr Winkle Goes to War* 1944; *The Bullfighters* 1945; *Two O'Clock Courage* 1945; *Take Me Out to the Ball Game* 1949
Lane, Rosemary *Hollywood Hotel* 1937; *Four Daughters* 1938; *Gold Diggers in Paris* 1938; *Daughters Courageous* 1939; *The Oklahoma Kid* 1939; *The Return of Dr X* 1939; *Four Wives* 1939; *The Boys from Syracuse* 1940; *Chatterbox* 1943
Lane, Rusty *Bigger than Life* 1956; *Johnny Tremain* 1957
Laneuville, Eric *The Omega Man* 1971; *Black Belt Jones* 1974; *A Force of One* 1979
Lang, Doreen *The House That Would Not Die* 1970; *Almost an Angel* 1990
Lang, Harold *Cairo Road* 1950; *Cloudburst* 1951; *Wings of Danger* 1952; *Adventure in the Hopfields* 1954; *Dance Little Lady* 1954; *It's a Wonderful World* 1956
Lang, June *Bonnie Scotland* 1935; *The Country Doctor* 1936; *The Road to Glory* 1936; *Captain January* 1936; *Nancy Steele Is Missing* 1937; *Wee Willie Winkie* 1937; *International Settlement* 1938; *Footlight Serenade* 1942
Lang, Katherine Kelly *The Night Stalker* 1985; *Delta Fever* 1988
lang, kd *Salmonberries* 1991; *Eye of the Beholder* 1999
Lang, Perry *Alligator* 1980; *Body and Soul* 1981; *O'Hara's Wife* 1982; *Sahara* 1983; *Jocks* 1986; *Little Vegas* 1990; *Jennifer Eight* 1992; *Betrayed by Love* 1994
Lang, Robert *Othello* 1965; *The Dance of Death* 1969; *Night Watch* 1973; *Hawks* 1988
Lang, Stephen *Death of a Salesman* 1985; *Stone Pillow* 1985; *Twice in a Lifetime* 1985; *Manhunter* 1986; *Project X* 1987; *Last Exit to Brooklyn* 1989; *Another You* 1991; *The Hard Way* 1991; *Darkness before Dawn* 1992; *Taking Back My Life* 1992; *Gettysburg* 1993; *Guilty as Sin* 1993; *Murder between Friends* 1994; *Tall Tale: the Unbelievable Adventures of Pecos Bill* 1994; *The Amazing Panda Adventure* 1995; *Legacy of Evil* 1995; *Lone Star* 1995; *Gang in Blue* 1996; *An Occasional Hell* 1996; *Shadow Conspiracy* 1996; *Fire Down Below* 1997; *Niagara Niagara* 1997; *Journey of the Heart* 1997; *Escape: Human Cargo* 1998; *A Town Has Turned to Dust* 1998
Langan, Glenn *Something for the Boys* 1944; *A Bell for Adano* 1945; *Hangover Square* 1945; *Dragonwyck* 1946; *Margie* 1946; *Sentimental Journey* 1946; *Fury at Furnace Creek* 1948; *The Snake Pit* 1948
Langdon, Harry *The Strong Man* 1926; *Tramp, Tramp, Tramp* 1926; *Long Pants* 1927; *Hallelujah, I'm a Bum* 1933; *Atlantic Adventure* 1935; *Zenobia* 1939; *Block Busters* 1944
Langdon, Sue Ane *aka* **Langdon, Sue Ann,** *aka* **Langdon, Sue Anne** *Roustabout* 1964; *The Rounders* 1965; *When the Boys Meet the Girls* 1965; *Frankie & Johnny* 1966; *A Guide for the Married Man* 1967; *The Cheyenne Social Club* 1970; *The Evictors* 1979; *Without Warning* 1980; *Hawken's Breed* 1989
Lange, Artie *Dirty Work* 1998; *Lost & Found* 1999; *The Bachelor* 1999
Lange, Hope *Bus Stop* 1956; *Peyton Place* 1957; *The True Story of Jesse James* 1957; *In Love and War* 1958; *The Young Lions* 1958; *The Best of Everything* 1959; *Pocketful of Miracles* 1961; *Wild in the Country* 1961; *Love Is a Ball* 1963; *Jigsaw* 1968; *Death Wish* 1974; *The Prodigal* 1983; *I Am the Cheese* 1983; *A Nightmare on Elm Street 2: Freddy's Revenge* 1985; *Blue Velvet* 1986; *Aunt Julia and the Scriptwriter* 1990; *Dead before Dawn* 1993; *Before He Wakes* 1998
Lange, Jessica *King Kong* 1976; *All That Jazz* 1979; *How to Beat the High Cost of Living* 1980; *The Postman Always Rings Twice* 1981; *Frances* 1982; *Tootsie* 1982; *Country* 1984; *Sweet Dreams* 1985; *Crimes of the Heart* 1986; *Everybody's All-American* 1988; *Far North* 1988; *Music Box* 1989; *Men Don't Leave* 1990; *Blue Sky* 1991; *Cape Fear* 1991; *Night and the City* 1992; *O Pioneers!* 1992; *Losing Isaiah* 1995; *Rob Roy* 1995; *Cousin Bette* 1997; *A Thousand Acres* 1997; *Hush* 1998; *Titus* 1999
Langella, Frank *Diary of a Mad Housewife* 1970; *The Twelve Chairs* 1970; *The Deadly Trap* 1971; *The Wrath of God* 1972; *The Mark of Zorro* 1974; *Dracula* 1979; *Sphinx* 1980; *Those Lips, Those Eyes* 1980; *The Men's Club* 1986; *Masters of the Universe* 1987; *And God Created Woman* 1988; *True Identity* 1991; *Dave* 1993; *Brainscan* 1994; *Doomsday Gun* 1994; *Junior* 1994; *Bad Company* 1995; *CutThroat Island* 1995; *Eddie* 1996; *Lolita* 1997; *Small Soldiers* 1998; *I'm Losing You* 1998; *The Ninth Gate* 2000
Langenkamp, Heather *A Nightmare on Elm Street* 1984; *Passions* 1984; *A Nightmare on Elm Street 3: Dream Warriors* 1987; *Shocker* 1989; *Wes Craven's New Nightmare* 1994
Langer, A J *The People under the Stairs* 1991; *Escape from LA* 1996; *Meet the Deedles* 1998
Langford, Frances *Born to Dance* 1936; *Too Many Girls* 1940; *Girl Rush* 1944
Langham, Wallace *aka* **Ward, Wally** *The Chocolate War* 1988; *The Invisible Kid* 1988; *Michael* 1996
Langlet, Amanda *Pauline at the Beach* 1983; *A Summer's Tale* 1996
Langlois, Lisa *Blood Relatives* 1977; *Phobia* 1980; *Hard Feelings* 1981; *Class of 1984* 1982; *Joy of Sex* 1984; *The Slugger's Wife* 1985
Langrick, Margaret *My American Cousin* 1985; *Bigfoot and the Hendersons* 1987; *American Boyfriends* 1989; *Cold Comfort* 1989; *Death of a Cheerleader* 1994; *Sweet Angel Mine* 1996
Langrishe, Caroline *Eagle's Wing* 1978; *Hawks* 1988; *Rogue Trader* 1998
Langton, Brooke *Criminal Passion* 1995; *Eye of the Stalker* 1995; *Listen* 1996
Langton, David *The Incredible Sarah* 1976; *Witness for the Prosecution* 1982
Langton, Paul *The Hidden Eye* 1945; *They Were Expendable* 1945; *Till the Clouds Roll By* 1946; *Big Leaguer* 1953; *The Incredible Shrinking Man* 1957; *Chicago Confidential* 1957; *The Cosmic Man* 1959
Lankford, Kim *Missing Pieces* 1991; *Night of the Running Man* 1994
Lanning, Frank *The Kid Brother* 1927; *The Unknown* 1927
Lannom, Les *Lacy and the Mississippi Queen* 1978; *Southern Comfort* 1981
Lanoux, Victor *Two against the Law* 1973; *Cousin, Cousine* 1975; *Pardon Mon Affaire* 1976; *The Scene of the Crime* 1986
Lansbury, Angela *Gaslight* 1944; *National Velvet* 1944; *The Picture of Dorian Gray* 1945; *The Harvey Girls* 1946; *The Hoodlum Saint* 1946; *If Winter Comes* 1947; *The Private Affairs of Bel Ami* 1947; *The Three Musketeers* 1948; *State of the Union* 1948; *Samson and Delilah* 1949; *The Red Danube* 1949; *A Lawless Street* 1955; *The Purple Mask* 1955; *The Court Jester* 1956; *The Reluctant Debutante* 1958; *A Breath of Scandal* 1960; *The Dark at the Top of the Stairs* 1960; *Season of Passion* 1960; *Blue Hawaii* 1961; *All Fall Down* 1962; *The Manchurian Candidate* 1962; *In the Cool of the Day* 1963; *Dear Heart* 1964; *The World of Henry Orient* 1964; *The Amorous Adventures of Moll Flanders* 1965; *The Greatest Story Ever Told* 1965; *Harlow* 1965; *Mister Buddwing* 1966; *Bedknobs and Broomsticks* 1971; *Death on the Nile* 1978; *The Lady Vanishes* 1979; *The Last Unicorn* 1980; *The Mirror Crack'd* 1980; *The Pirates of Penzance* 1983; *The Company of Wolves* 1984; *Shootdown* 1988; *A Green Journey* 1990; *Beauty and the Beast* 1991; *Mrs 'arris Goes to Paris* 1992; *Anastasia* 1997; *Beauty and the Beast: the Enchanted Christmas* 1997; *The Unexpected Mrs Pollifax* 1999
Lansbury, David *Gorillas in the Mist* 1988; *Empty Cradle* 1993
Lansing, Joi *The Brave One* 1956; *The Atomic Submarine* 1960
Lansing, Robert *A Gathering of Eagles* 1963; *Under the Yum Yum Tree* 1963; *An Eye for an Eye* 1966; *Namu, the Killer Whale* 1966; *The Grissom Gang* 1971; *Black Jack* 1972; *Acapulco Gold* 1976; *Bittersweet Love* 1976; *Empire of the Ants* 1977; *Bionic Showdown: the Six Million Dollar Man and the Bionic Woman* 1989
Lanteau, William *On Golden Pond* 1981; *Shadow of a Doubt* 1991
Lanvin, Gérard *Choice of Arms* 1981; *Double Dare* 1981; *A Strange Affair* 1981; *Mon Homme* 1996; *In All Innocence* 1998
Lanza, Mario *That Midnight Kiss* 1949; *The Toast of New Orleans* 1950; *The Great Caruso* 1951; *Because You're Mine* 1952; *The Student Prince* 1954; *Serenade* 1956; *Seven Hills of Rome* 1957; *For the First Time* 1959
LaPaglia, Anthony *Nitti: the Enforcer* 1988; *Mortal Sins* 1989; *Betsy's Wedding* 1990; *Criminal Justice* 1990; *He Said, She Said* 1991; *One Good Cop* 1991; *29th Street* 1991; *Innocent Blood* 1992; *Keeper of the City* 1992; *Whispers in the Dark* 1992; *Black Magic* 1992; *The Custodian* 1993; *So I Married an Axe Murderer* 1993; *The Client* 1994; *Killer* 1994; *Past Tense* 1994; *Paperback Romance* 1994; *Chameleon* 1995; *Empire Records* 1995; *Mixed Nuts* 1995; *Commandments* 1996; *Trees Lounge* 1996; *Brilliant Lies* 1996; *Phoenix* 1998; *Sweet and Lowdown* 1999; *Lansky* 1999; *The House of Mirth* 2000
LaPaine, Daniel *Elephant Juice* 1999; *Brokedown Palace* 1999
Lapotaire, Jane *Crescendo* 1970; *Antony and Cleopatra* 1972; *The Asphyx* 1972; *Eureka* 1982; *To Catch a King* 1984; *Lady Jane* 1985; *Surviving Picasso* 1996
Lara, Joe *Tarzan in Manhattan* 1989; *Operation Delta Force* 1996
Larbi, Doghmi *The Man Who Would Be King* 1975; *The Black Stallion* 1979
Larch, John *Seven Men from Now* 1956; *Man in the Shadow* 1957; *Quantez* 1957; *The Saga of Hemp Brown* 1958; *Miracle of the White Stallions* 1963; *The Wrecking Crew* 1969; *Hail, Hero!* 1969; *Dirty Harry* 1971; *Play Misty for Me* 1971; *Santee* 1973; *Future Cop* 1976
Laresca, Vincent *Juice* 1992; *Ripe* 1996
Larive, Léon *aka* **Larive** *Zéro de conduite* 1933; *La Marseillaise* 1938
Larken, Sheila *Dangerous Intentions* 1995; *Behind the Mask* 1999
Larkin, John *Those Calloways* 1964; *The Satan Bug* 1965
Larkin, Linda *Aladdin* 1992; *The Return of Jafar* 1994; *Aladdin and the King of Thieves* 1996
Larkin, Mary *X, Y and Zee* 1971; *Psychomania* 1972
LaRoche, Mary *The Lineup* 1958; *Gidget* 1959; *The Swinger* 1966
Laroque, Michèle *Tango* 1993; *Ma Vie en Rose* 1997
Larquey, Pierre *Madame Bovary* 1933; *Les Diaboliques* 1954
Larroquette, John *Green Ice* 1981; *Stripes* 1981; *Choose Me* 1984; *Meatballs 2* 1984; *Summer Rental* 1985; *Convicted* 1986; *Blind Date* 1987; *Second Sight* 1989; *Madhouse* 1990; *Richie Rich* 1994
Larsen, Ham *The Adventures of the Wilderness Family* 1975; *Mountain Family Robinson* 1979
Larsen, Keith *Arrow in the Dust* 1954; *Security Risk* 1954; *Chief Crazy Horse* 1955; *Wichita* 1955; *Last of the Badmen* 1957
Larson, Christine *Valley of Fire* 1951; *Last Train from Bombay* 1952
Larson, Darrell *Kotch* 1971; *UFOria* 1980; *Brainstorm* 1983; *Mike's Murder* 1984; *City Limits* 1985; *Twice in a Lifetime* 1985; *The Last Innocent Man* 1987; *Eye for an Eye* 1995
Larson, Wolf *Expect No Mercy* 1995; *Hostile Force* 1996

Larter, Ali *House on Haunted Hill* 1999; *Final Destination* 2000

LaRue, Jack *aka* **La Rue, Jack** *A Farewell to Arms* 1932; *The Kennel Murder Case* 1933; *The Gang's All Here* 1939; *Follow the Leader* 1944; *Cornered* 1945; *Road to Utopia* 1945; *My Favorite Brunette* 1947; *For Heaven's Sake* 1950; *Robin and the 7 Hoods* 1964; *The Spy in the Green Hat* 1966

Lascher, David *Victim of Rage* 1994; *White Squall* 1996; *Kidz in the Wood* 1996

Laser, Dieter *The Lost Honour of Katharina Blum* 1975; *Germany in Autumn* 1978; *The Man Inside* 1990

Lasser, Louise *What's Up, Tiger Lily?* 1966; *Bananas* 1971; *Such Good Friends* 1971; *Everything You Always Wanted to Know about Sex (But Were Afraid to Ask)* 1972; *Isn't It Shocking?* 1973; *Slither* 1973; *Just Me and You* 1978; *In God We Trust* 1980; *Crimewave* 1985; *Surrender* 1987; *Rude Awakening* 1989; *Sing* 1989; *Frankenhooker* 1990; *Happiness* 1998

Lassez, Sarah *Roosters* 1993; *The Shaggy Dog* 1994; *Malicious* 1995; *The Blackout* 1997; *Clown at Midnight* 1998

Lassick, Sydney *aka* **Lassick, Sidney** *One Flew over the Cuckoo's Nest* 1975; *The Billion Dollar Hobo* 1978; *Alligator* 1980; *Ratboy* 1986; *Cool as Ice* 1991; *Shakes the Clown* 1991; *Deep Cover* 1992

Latell, Lyle *Dick Tracy* 1945; *Dick Tracy vs Cueball* 1946; *Dick Tracy Meets Gruesome* 1947; *Dick Tracy's Dilemma* 1947

Latessa, Dick *Izzy and Moe* 1985; *Stigmata* 1999

Latham, Louise *Marnie* 1964; *Adam at 6 AM* 1970; *The Harness* 1971; *White Lightning* 1973; *The Sugarland Express* 1974; *Mass Appeal* 1984; *Stillwatch* 1987; *Settle the Score* 1989; *Crazy from the Heart* 1991; *The Haunted* 1991; *Paradise* 1991; *Love Field* 1992

Lathan, Sanaa *The Best Man* 1999; *Love & Basketball* 2000

Lathouris, Nico *Death in Brunswick* 1990; *The Heartbreak Kid* 1993

Latimer, Hugh *Someone at the Door* 1950; *Ghost Ship* 1952; *Counterspy* 1953; *Rogue's Yarn* 1956; *The Strange World of Planet X* 1957; *The Gentle Trap* 1960

Latimer, Louise *Murder on a Bridle Path* 1936; *The Plot Thickens* 1936; *California Straight Ahead* 1937

Latimore, Frank *In the Meantime, Darling* 1944; *The Dolly Sisters* 1945; *13 Rue Madeleine* 1946; *Three Little Girls in Blue* 1946; *Black Magic* 1949; *Plein Soleil* 1960; *The Sergeant* 1968; *Patton: Lust for Glory* 1970

Lattanzi, Matt *Rich and Famous* 1981; *Blueberry Hill* 1988

Lau, Carina *Days of Being Wild* 1990; *Flowers of Shanghai* 1998

Lau Siu-Ming *Eat a Bowl of Tea* 1989; *Kitchen* 1997

Lauchlan, Agnes *Oh, Mr Porter!* 1937; *The Spy in Black* 1939

Laudenbach, Philippe *Confidentially Yours* 1983; *Four Adventures of Reinette and Mirabelle* 1986

Lauer, Andrew *aka* **Lauer, Andy** *Never on Tuesday* 1988; *Screamers* 1995

Laughlin, John *Crimes of Passion* 1984; *Footloose* 1984; *Midnight Crossing* 1988; *Fire! Trapped on the 37th Floor* 1991; *Memphis* 1992; *Improper Conduct* 1994; *Night Fire* 1994; *Sexual Malice* 1994; *American Yakuza 2: Back to Back* 1996

Laughlin, Teresa *The Trial of Billy Jack* 1974; *Billy Jack Goes to Washington* 1977

Laughlin, Tom *These Wilder Years* 1956; *The Delinquents* 1957; *Senior Prom* 1958; *Gidget* 1959; *Born Losers* 1967; *Billy Jack* 1971; *The Trial of Billy Jack* 1974; *The Master Gunfighter* 1975; *Billy Jack Goes to Washington* 1977

Laughton, Charles *Piccadilly* 1929; *If I Had a Million* 1932; *Island of Lost Souls* 1932; *The Old Dark House* 1932; *Payment Deferred* 1932; *The Sign of the Cross* 1932; *Devil and the Deep* 1932; *The Private Life of Henry VIII* 1933; *White Woman* 1933; *The Barretts of Wimpole Street* 1934; *Les Misérables* 1935; *Mutiny on the Bounty* 1935; *Ruggles of Red Gap* 1935; *Rembrandt* 1936; *St Martin's Lane* 1938; *Vessel of Wrath* 1938; *The Hunchback of Notre Dame* 1939; *Jamaica Inn* 1939; *They Knew What They Wanted* 1940; *It Started with Eve* 1941; *Tales of Manhattan* 1942; *The Tuttles of Tahiti* 1942; *Stand by for Action* 1942; *Forever and a Day* 1943; *The Man from Down Under* 1943; *This Land Is Mine* 1943; *The Canterville Ghost* 1944; *The Suspect* 1944; *Captain Kidd* 1945; *Because of Him* 1946; *The Paradine Case* 1947; *Arch of Triumph* 1948; *The Big Clock* 1948; *The Bribe* 1949; *The Man on the Eiffel Tower* 1949; *The Blue Veil* 1951; *The Strange Door* 1951; *Abbott and Costello Meet Captain Kidd* 1952; *O Henry's Full House* 1952; *Hobson's Choice* 1953; *Salome* 1953; *Young Bess* 1953; *Witness for the Prosecution* 1957; *Spartacus* 1960; *Under Ten Flags* 1960; *Advise and Consent* 1962

Launer, S John *Creature with the Atom Brain* 1955; *The Werewolf* 1956; *Marnie* 1964

Lauper, Cyndi *Vibes* 1988; *Mother Goose Rock 'n' Rhyme* 1990; *Off and Running* 1991; *Life with Mikey* 1993

Laurance, Matthew *Eddie and the Cruisers* 1983; *Eddie and the Cruisers II: Eddie Lives!* 1989

Laurance, Mitchell *Conspiracy of Love* 1987; *Stepfather II* 1989; *The Runestone* 1991; *The Hand That Rocks the Cradle* 1992

Laure, Carole *Get out Your Handkerchiefs* 1977; *Maria Chapdelaine* 1982; *Heartbreakers* 1984; *Flight from Justice* 1993

Laure, Odette *Mitsou* 1957; *These Foolish Things* 1990

Laurel, Stan *aka* **Laurel, Stanley** *The Two Tars* 1928; *Hollywood Revue* 1929; *Men o' War* 1929; *Perfect Day* 1929; *Big Business* 1929; *The Rogue Song* 1930; *Pardon Us* 1931; *County Hospital* 1932; *The Music Box* 1932; *Pack Up Your Troubles* 1932; *Scram!* 1932; *Their First Mistake* 1932; *Towed in a Hole* 1932; *Bogus Bandits* 1933; *Sons of the Desert* 1933; *Twice Two* 1933; *Babes in Toyland* 1934; *Hollywood Party* 1934; *Oliver the Eighth* 1934; *Them Thar Hills!* 1934; *Tit for Tat* 1934; *Bonnie Scotland* 1935; *Thicker than Water* 1935; *The Bohemian Girl* 1936; *Our Relations* 1936; *Way Out West* 1937; *Blockheads* 1938; *Swiss Miss* 1938; *The Flying Deuces* 1939; *A Chump at Oxford* 1940; *Saps at Sea* 1940; *Great Guns* 1941; *A-Haunting We Will Go* 1942; *The Dancing Masters* 1943; *Jitterbugs* 1943; *The Big Noise* 1944; *Nothing but Trouble* 1944; *The Bullfighters* 1945; *The Crazy World of Laurel and Hardy* 1964; *4 Clowns* 1970

Lauren, Tammy *The Last Flight of Noah's Ark* 1980; *The Stepford Children* 1987; *The People across the Lake* 1988; *Desperate for Love* 1989; *Wishmaster* 1997

Lauren, Veronica *Homeward Bound: the Incredible Journey* 1993; *Homeward Bound II: Lost in San Francisco* 1996

Laurence, Ashley *aka* **Lauren, Ashley** *Hellraiser* 1987; *Hellbound: Hellraiser II* 1988; *Americanski Blues* 1993; *Lurking Fear* 1994; *Triplecross* 1995; *Cupid* 1997; *A Murder of Crows* 1998

Laurence, Michael *The Kentucky Fried Movie* 1977; *Someone's Watching Me!* 1978

Laurence, Rachel *Gunpowder* 1985; *John and Yoko: a Love Story* 1985

Laurenson, James *Assault* 1970; *The Monster Club* 1980; *Pink Floyd – The Wall* 1982; *Heartbreakers* 1984; *The Man Who Fell to Earth* 1986; *A House in the Hills* 1993

Lauria, Dan *Stakeout* 1987; *David: the David Rothenberg Story* 1988; *Making the Case for Murder: the Howard Beach Story* 1989; *A Cop for the Killing* 1990; *In the Line of Duty: Mob Justice* 1991; *Overexposed* 1992; *In the Line of Duty: Ambush in Waco* 1993; *In the Line of Duty: Hunt for Justice* 1995; *No One Could Protect Her* 1996; *Terror in the Family* 1996; *Prison of Secrets* 1997; *Dogwatch* 1997

Laurie, Hugh *Strapless* 1988; *Peter's Friends* 1992; *A Pin for the Butterfly* 1994; *101 Dalmatians* 1996; *The Borrowers* 1997; *Cousin Bette* 1997; *The Man in the Iron Mask* 1997; *Stuart Little* 1999; *Maybe Baby* 1999

Laurie, John *Juno and the Paycock* 1930; *The 39 Steps* 1935; *As You Like It* 1936; *The Edge of the World* 1937; *Convoy* 1940; *The Ghost of St Michael's* 1941; *The Lamp Still Burns* 1943; *The Way Ahead* 1944; *I Know Where I'm Going* 1945; *School for Secrets* 1946; *The Brothers* 1947; *Jassy* 1947; *Mine Own Executioner* 1947; *Bonnie Prince Charlie* 1948; *No Trace* 1950; *Treasure Island* 1950; *Happy Go Lovely* 1950; *Laughter in Paradise* 1951; *Pandora and the Flying Dutchman* 1951; *Tread Softly* 1952; *Campbell's Kingdom* 1957; *Kidnapped* 1960; *The Siege of the Saxons* 1963; *The Reptile* 1966; *Dad's Army* 1971

Laurie, Piper *The Prince Who Was a Thief* 1951; *Has Anybody Seen My Gal?* 1952; *No Room for the Groom* 1952; *Son of Ali Baba* 1952; *The Mississippi Gambler* 1953; *The Golden Blade* 1953; *Dangerous Mission* 1954; *Dawn at Socorro* 1954; *Johnny Dark* 1954; *Smoke Signal* 1955; *Ain't Misbehavin'* 1955; *Until They Sail* 1957; *The Hustler* 1961; *Carrie* 1976; *Ruby* 1977; *Tim* 1979; *Return to Oz* 1985; *Children of a Lesser God* 1986; *Promise* 1986; *Distortions* 1987; *Appointment with Death* 1988; *Go toward the Light* 1988; *Tiger Warsaw* 1988; *Dream a Little Dream* 1989; *Rising Son* 1990; *Other People's Money* 1991; *Rich in Love* 1992; *Love, Lies and Lullabies* 1993; *Wrestling Ernest Hemingway* 1993; *Trauma* 1993; *The Devil's Bed* 1994; *The Crossing Guard* 1995; *Fighting for My Daughter* 1995; *The Grass Harp* 1995; *In the Blink of an Eye* 1996; *The Road to Galveston* 1996; *Horton Foote's Alone* 1997; *The Faculty* 1998; *Inherit the Wind* 1999; *Palmer's Pick-Up* 1999

Lauter, Ed *Executive Action* 1973; *The Last American Hero* 1973; *The Mean Machine* 1974; *Breakheart Pass* 1976; *Family Plot* 1976; *The Chicken Chronicles* 1977; *Magic* 1978; *The Boy Who Drank Too Much* 1980; *The Amateur* 1981; *Eureka* 1982; *In the Custody of Strangers* 1982; *Cujo* 1983; *Finders Keepers* 1984; *Lassiter* 1984; *Death Wish 3* 1985; *The Defiant Ones* 1986; *Last Days of Patton* 1986; *The Thanksgiving Promise* 1986; *Youngblood* 1986; *Gleaming the Cube* 1988; *The Rocketeer* 1991; *School Ties* 1992; *Murder So Sweet* 1993; *Under Investigation* 1993; *SIS Extreme Justice* 1993; *Digital Man* 1994; *Secret Sins of the Father* 1994; *Trial by Jury* 1994; *Wagons East!* 1994; *Rattled* 1996; *Raven Hawk* 1996; *Childhood Sweetheart?* 1997; *Mercenary* 1997; *Married to a Stranger* 1997; *Dollar for the Dead* 1998

Lauter, Harry *Valley of Fire* 1951; *Return to Treasure Island* 1954; *The Werewolf* 1956; *Hellcats of the Navy* 1957; *The Cry Baby Killer* 1958; *Ambush Bay* 1966

Lauterbach, Heiner *Men…* 1985; *A Girl Called Rosemarie* 1996

Lavanant, Dominique *Love Songs* 1984; *3 Men and a Cradle* 1985; *Rendez-vous* 1985; *Kamikaze* 1986; *Soigne Ta Droite* 1986

Lavant, Denis *The Night Is Young* 1986; *Les Amants du Pont-Neuf* 1990; *Beau Travail* 1999

Lavender, Ian *Dad's Army* 1971; *Adventures of a Taxi Driver* 1975; *Adventures of a Private Eye* 1977

Laverick, June *It Happened in Rome* 1956; *The Duke Wore Jeans* 1958; *The Gypsy and the Gentleman* 1958; *Son of Robin Hood* 1958; *The Flesh and the Fiends* 1959; *Follow a Star* 1959

Lavi, Daliah *Violent Summer* 1961; *Lord Jim* 1965; *Ten Little Indians* 1965; *The Silencers* 1966; *The Spy with a Cold Nose* 1966; *Nobody Runs Forever* 1968; *Some Girls Do* 1969; *Catlow* 1971

Lavin, Linda *Lena: My 100 Children* 1987; *I Want to Go Home* 1989; *For the Future: the Irvine Fertility Scandal* 1996; *Best Friends for Life* 1998

LaVorgna, Adam *The Beautician and the Beast* 1997; *I'll Be Home for Christmas* 1998

Law, John Phillip *Barbarella* 1967; *Hurry Sundown* 1967; *Danger: Diabolik* 1967; *The Sergeant* 1968; *Skidoo* 1968; *Death Rides a Horse* 1969; *Master of the Islands* 1970; *The Love Machine* 1971; *Von Richthofen and Brown* 1971; *The Golden Voyage of Sinbad* 1973; *Open Season* 1974; *The Cassandra Crossing* 1976; *Attack Force Z* 1981; *Tarzan, the Ape Man* 1981

Law, Jude *Shopping* 1993; *Bent* 1996; *Gattaca* 1997; *Midnight in the Garden of Good and Evil* 1997; *Wilde* 1997; *I Love You, I Love You Not* 1997; *The Wisdom of Crocodiles* 1998; *Final Cut* 1998; *eXistenZ* 1999; *The Talented Mr Ripley* 1999; *Love, Honour and Obey* 2000

Law, Phyllida *Tree of Hands* 1988; *Peter's Friends* 1992; *Much Ado about Nothing* 1993; *Before the Rain* 1994; *Emma* 1996; *Anna Karenina* 1997; *The Winter Guest* 1997; *Mad Cows* 1999

Lawford, Betty *Love before Breakfast* 1936; *Criminal Lawyer* 1937; *The Devil Thumbs a Ride* 1947

Lawford, Christopher *Blankman* 1994; *Kiss Me, Guido* 1997

Lawford, Peter *Paris after Dark* 1943; *Pilot #5* 1943; *The Sky's the Limit* 1943; *The Canterville Ghost* 1944; *The White Cliffs of Dover* 1944; *The Picture of Dorian Gray* 1945; *Son of Lassie* 1945; *Cluny Brown* 1946; *My Brother Talks to Horses* 1946; *Two Sisters from Boston* 1946; *Good News* 1947; *It Happened in Brooklyn* 1947; *Easter Parade* 1948; *Julia Misbehaves* 1948; *On an Island with You* 1948; *Little Women* 1949; *The Red Danube* 1949; *Royal Wedding* 1951; *Kangaroo* 1952; *It Should Happen to You* 1954; *Never So Few* 1959; *Exodus* 1960; *Ocean's Eleven* 1960; *Pepe* 1960; *Advise and Consent* 1962; *The Longest Day* 1962; *Sergeants 3* 1962; *Dead Ringer* 1964; *Sylvia* 1964; *Harlow* 1965; *The Oscar* 1966; *A Man Called Adam* 1966; *Dead Run* 1967; *How I Spent My Summer Vacation* 1967; *Buona Sera, Mrs Campbell* 1968; *Skidoo* 1968; *Salt and Pepper* 1968; *The April Fools* 1969; *Hook, Line and Sinker* 1969; *One More Time* 1970; *They Only Kill Their Masters* 1972; *The Phantom of Hollywood* 1974; *Rosebud* 1975; *Body and Soul* 1981

Lawley, Yvonne *Death in Brunswick* 1990; *Ruby and Rata* 1990

Lawlor, Sean *Reefer and the Model* 1988; *The Disappearance of Finbar* 1996

Lawrance, Jody *aka* **Lawrence, Jody** *Ten Tall Men* 1951; *All Ashore* 1953; *Hot Spell* 1958; *Stagecoach to Dancer's Rock* 1962

Lawrence, Andre *The Pleasure Seekers* 1964; *And Hope to Die* 1972

Lawrence, Barbara *Margie* 1946; *Give My Regards to Broadway* 1948; *The Street with No Name* 1948; *Unfaithfully Yours* 1948; *You Were Meant for Me* 1948; *A Letter to Three Wives* 1949; *Mother Is a Freshman* 1949; *Thieves' Highway* 1949; *Two Tickets to Broadway* 1951; *Arena* 1953; *Her Twelve Men* 1954; *Man with the Gun* 1955; *Oklahoma!* 1955; *Kronos* 1957; *Man in the Shadow* 1957

Lawrence, Bruno *Smash Palace* 1981; *Treasure of the Yankee Zephyr* 1981; *Battletruck* 1982; *Utu* 1983; *The Quiet Earth* 1985; *As Time Goes By* 1987; *Grievous Bodily Harm* 1987; *Initiation* 1987; *Rikky and Pete* 1988; *Spotswood* 1991; *Jack Be Nimble* 1992

Lawrence, Burke *The Myth of the Male Orgasm* 1993; *Jack*

London's The Call of the Wild 1996
Lawrence, Delphi *Blood Orange* 1953; *Double Cross* 1955; *The Gold Express* 1955; *The Feminine Touch* 1956; *Just My Luck* 1957; *Stranger's Meeting* 1957; *Son of Robin Hood* 1958; *Too Many Crooks* 1958; *The Man Who Could Cheat Death* 1959; *The Last Challenge* 1967
Lawrence, Elizabeth *We're No Angels* 1989; *Sleeping with the Enemy* 1991
Lawrence, Gertrude *Men Are Not Gods* 1936; *Rembrandt* 1936; *Stage Door Canteen* 1943; *The Glass Menagerie* 1950
Lawrence, Joey *Summer Rental* 1985; *Pulse* 1988; *Oliver & Company* 1988; *Chains of Gold* 1989
Lawrence, Josie *Riders of the Storm* 1986; *Enchanted April* 1991
Lawrence, Marc *Vengeance* 1937; *Blind Alley* 1939; *The Housekeeper's Daughter* 1939; *Sergeant Madden* 1939; *Johnny Apollo* 1940; *Hold That Ghost* 1941; *Hit the Ice* 1943; *Dillinger* 1945; *Key Largo* 1948; *Jigsaw* 1949; *The Asphalt Jungle* 1950; *The Black Hand* 1950; *Johnny Tiger* 1966; *The Man with the Golden Gun* 1974; *Marathon Man* 1976; *Goin' Coconuts* 1978; *Hot Stuff* 1979; *Donor* 1990; *Ruby* 1992; *From Dusk till Dawn* 1995; *Gotti* 1996
Lawrence, Martin *House Party* 1990; *Talkin' Dirty after Dark* 1991; *House Party 2* 1991; *Boomerang* 1992; *Bad Boys* 1995; *A Thin Line between Love and Hate* 1996; *Nothing to Lose* 1997; *Life* 1999; *Blue Streak* 1999
Lawrence, Matthew *David: the David Rothenberg Story* 1988; *Pulse* 1988; *Joshua's Heart* 1990; *The Summer My Father Grew Up* 1991; *Tales from the Darkside: the Movie* 1991; *With a Vengeance* 1992; *Mrs Doubtfire* 1993
Lawrence, Michael *Return to Glennascaul* 1951; *Othello* 1952
Lawrence, Peter Lee *Killer Calibre 32* 1967; *Black Beauty* 1971
Lawrence, Sharon *The Shaggy Dog* 1994; *Someone She Knows* 1994; *Face on the Milk Carton* 1995; *Victim of the Haunt* 1996; *Gossip* 1999
Lawrence, Sheldon *The Crooked Sky* 1957; *Mark of the Phoenix* 1957; *The Man without a Body* 1957; *The Pursuers* 1961
Lawrence, Stephanie *Buster* 1988; *The Phantom of the Opera* 1989
Laws, Sam *Truck Turner* 1974; *White Line Fever* 1975
Lawson, Denis *Providence* 1977; *Local Hero* 1983; *The Chain* 1984; *Bejewelled* 1990
Lawson, Leigh *Brother Sun, Sister Moon* 1972; *Ghost Story* 1974; *Percy's Progress* 1974; *Love among the Ruins* 1975; *The Devil's Advocate* 1977; *Tess* 1979; *Agatha Christie's Murder Is Easy* 1982; *Sword of the Valiant* 1984; *Madame Sousatzka* 1988; *Battling for Baby* 1992; *O Pioneers!* 1992
Lawson, Linda *Night Tide* 1961; *Apache Rifles* 1964; *Never Give an Inch* 1971
Lawson, Mary *D'Ye Ken John Peel?* 1934; *A Fire Has Been Arranged* 1935; *Cotton Queen* 1937
Lawson, Priscilla *Flash Gordon* 1936; *The Girl of the Golden West* 1938
Lawson, Richard *Scream Blacula Scream* 1973; *The Main Event* 1979; *Stick* 1985; *Johnnie Mae Gibson: FBI* 1986; *The Reluctant Agent* 1989; *How Stella Got Her Groove Back* 1998
Lawson, Sarah *You Know What Sailors Are* 1954; *The Blue Peter* 1955; *It's Never Too Late* 1956; *The World Ten Times Over* 1963; *Night of the Big Heat* 1967; *The Devil Rides Out* 1968
Lawson, Shannon *April One* 1993; *Butterbox Babies* 1995; *Heck's Way Home* 1995; *The War between Us* 1995; *Devil's Food* 1996
Lawson, Wilfrid *Pygmalion* 1938; *The First Rebel* 1939; *The Long Voyage Home* 1940; *Pastor Hall* 1940; *Danny Boy* 1941; *Jeannie* 1941; *The Night Has Eyes* 1942; *Fanny by Gaslight* 1944; *The Prisoner* 1955; *Hell Drivers* 1957; *Postman's Knock* 1961; *The Wrong Box* 1966; *The Viking Queen* 1967
Lawton, Frank *The Skin Game* 1931; *One More River* 1934; *David Copperfield* 1935; *The Devil-Doll* 1936; *The Invisible Ray* 1936; *The Mill on the Floss* 1937; *The Four Just Men* 1939; *Went the Day Well?* 1942; *The Winslow Boy* 1948; *Rough Shoot* 1952; *Double Cross* 1955
Laye, Dilys *Please Turn Over* 1960; *Carry On Cruising* 1962; *Carry On Spying* 1964
Laye, Evelyn *One Heavenly Night* 1931; *Evensong* 1934; *Theatre of Death* 1966; *Say Hello to Yesterday* 1971
Layton, George *Confessions of a Driving Instructor* 1976; *Stand Up Virgin Soldiers* 1977
Lazar, Veronica aka **Lazare, Veronica** *La Luna* 1979; *Identification of a Woman* 1982; *Berlin Jerusalem* 1989
Lazard, Justin *Born to Ride* 1991; *Universal Soldier – the Return* 1999
Lazenby, George *On Her Majesty's Secret Service* 1969; *The Man from Hong Kong* 1975; *The Kentucky Fried Movie* 1977; *Saint Jack* 1979; *The Return of the Man from UNCLE* 1983; *Gettysburg* 1993; *The Babysitters* 1994
Lazure, Gabrielle *Joshua Then and Now* 1985; *The Final Heist* 1991
Le Coq, Bernard *Burnt Barns* 1973; *Van Gogh* 1991; *The School of Flesh* 1998
Le Mesurier, John *The Blue Parrot* 1953; *Police Dog* 1955; *Brothers in Law* 1956; *The Moonraker* 1957; *High Flight* 1957; *Blood of the Vampire* 1958; *Carlton-Browne of the FO* 1958; *Happy Is the Bride* 1958; *Jack the Ripper* 1958; *Law and Disorder* 1958; *Too Many Crooks* 1958; *Follow a Star* 1959; *The Hound of the Baskervilles* 1959; *I'm All Right Jack* 1959; *The Bulldog Breed* 1960; *Never Let Go* 1960; *The Night We Got the Bird* 1960; *The Rebel* 1960; *School for Scoundrels* 1960; *Let's Get Married* 1960; *The Day They Robbed the Bank of England* 1960; *Don't Bother to Knock* 1961; *Invasion Quartet* 1961; *Jigsaw* 1962; *Only Two Can Play* 1962; *The Punch and Judy Man* 1962; *Waltz of the Toreadors* 1962; *The Wrong Arm of the Law* 1962; *We Joined the Navy* 1962; *Hot Enough for June* 1963; *In the Cool of the Day* 1963; *The Mouse on the Moon* 1963; *The Moon-Spinners* 1964; *The Pink Panther* 1964; *City under the Sea* 1965; *The Early Bird* 1965; *Masquerade* 1965; *Finders Keepers* 1966; *Our Man in Marrakesh* 1966; *The Sandwich Man* 1966; *Where the Spies Are* 1966; *Mister Ten Per Cent* 1967; *The 25th Hour* 1967; *Eye of the Devil* 1968; *Salt and Pepper* 1968; *The Italian Job* 1969; *Midas Run* 1969; *Doctor in Trouble* 1970; *On a Clear Day You Can See Forever* 1970; *Dad's Army* 1971; *Brief Encounter* 1974; *Confessions of a Window Cleaner* 1974; *Barry McKenzie Holds His Own* 1974; *The Adventure of Sherlock Holmes' Smarter Brother* 1975; *Jabberwocky* 1977; *Stand Up Virgin Soldiers* 1977; *The Spaceman and King Arthur* 1979; *The Fiendish Plot of Dr Fu Manchu* 1980
Le Noire, Rosetta *Anna Lucasta* 1958; *The Father Clements Story* 1987
Le Poulain, Jean *Le Bossu* 1959; *The Sign of Leo* 1959
Le Prevost, Nicholas *The Girl in a Swing* 1988; *Letters from the East* 1995
Le Saché, Bernadette *Le Cheval d'Orgeuil* 1980; *The Vanishing* 1988
Le Vaillant, Nigel *Seven Minutes* 1989; *Tom's Midnight Garden* 1998
Lea, Nicholas *Xtro 2: The Second Encounter* 1990; *The Raffle* 1994; *Once a Thief* 1996
Lea, Ron *Criminal Law* 1988; *The Return of Eliot Ness* 1991; *Clearcut* 1992; *Ebbie* 1995
Leach, Britt *Silent Night, Deadly Night* 1984; *Baby Boom* 1987
Leach, Rosemary *That'll Be the Day* 1973; *Brief Encounter* 1974; *A Room with a View* 1985; *Turtle Diary* 1985; *The Children* 1990; *The Hawk* 1992; *The Mystery of Edwin Drood* 1993
Leachman, Cloris *Kiss Me Deadly* 1955; *The Rack* 1956; *Butch Cassidy and the Sundance Kid* 1969; *Silent Night, Lonely Night* 1969; *WUSA* 1970; *The People Next Door* 1970; *The Last Picture Show* 1971; *Thursday's Game* 1971; *Charley and the Angel* 1973; *Dillinger* 1973; *Happy Mother's Day... Love, George* 1973; *Daisy Miller* 1974; *Young Frankenstein* 1974; *Crazy Mama* 1975; *High Anxiety* 1977; *The Mouse and His Child* 1977; *Hill's Angels* 1979; *Mrs R's Daughter* 1979; *SOS Titanic* 1979; *Scavenger Hunt* 1979; *Foolin' Around* 1980; *Herbie Goes Bananas* 1980; *History of the World Part 1* 1981; *Shadow Play* 1986; *My Little Pony* 1986; *Walk like a Man* 1987; *Prancer* 1989; *Fine Things* 1990; *Love Hurts* 1990; *Texasville* 1990; *In Broad Daylight* 1991; *The Beverly Hillbillies* 1993; *Double, Double Toil and Trouble* 1993; *Falsely Accused* 1993; *Fade to Black* 1993; *Stanley's Magic Garden* 1994; *Between Love and Honor* 1995; *Beavis and Butt-head Do America* 1996; *The Iron Giant* 1999; *Music of the Heart* 1999
Leadbitter, Bill *Knights and Emeralds* 1986; *Tai-Pan* 1986
Leak, Jennifer *Yours, Mine and Ours* 1968; *Eye of the Cat* 1969
Learned, Michael *Touched by Love* 1979; *Off the Minnesota Strip* 1980; *Mother's Day on Waltons Mountain* 1982; *The Parade* 1984; *All My Sons* 1986; *A Deadly Business* 1986; *Power* 1986; *Mercy or Murder?* 1987; *Gunsmoke: the Last Apache* 1990; *Keeping Secrets* 1991; *Murder in New Hampshire* 1991; *The Other Side of Murder* 1991; *Dragon: the Bruce Lee Story* 1993; *A Walton Thanksgiving Reunion* 1993; *A Walton Wedding* 1995; *A Walton Easter* 1997
Leary, Denis *Demolition Man* 1993; *Judgment Night* 1993; *The Sandlot* 1993; *Gunmen* 1994; *Hostile Hostages* 1994; *The Neon Bible* 1995; *Operation Dumbo Drop* 1995; *Stolen Hearts* 1996; *Underworld* 1996; *The Matchmaker* 1997; *The Real Blonde* 1997; *Noose* 1997; *Suicide Kings* 1997; *Wag the Dog* 1997; *Love Walked In* 1997; *A Bug's Life* 1998; *Small Soldiers* 1998; *Wide Awake* 1998; *True Crime* 1999; *The Thomas Crown Affair* 1999; *Jesus' Son* 1999
Leary, Timothy *Ted & Venus* 1991; *Roadside Prophets* 1992
Lease, Rex *The Younger Generation* 1929; *Aces and Eights* 1936
Léaud, Jean-Pierre *The 400 Blows* 1959; *Le Testament d'Orphée* 1960; *Love at Twenty* 1962; *Masculine Feminine* 1966; *Made in USA* 1966; *Weekend* 1967; *La Chinoise* 1967; *The Oldest Profession* 1967; *Le Gai Savoir* 1968; *Stolen Kisses* 1968; *Bed and Board* 1970; *Anne and Muriel* 1971; *Last Tango in Paris* 1972; *Day for Night* 1973; *La Maman et la Putain* 1973; *Out 1: Spectre* 1973; *Love on the Run* 1979; *Detective* 1985; *Grandeur et Décadence d'un Petit Commerce de Cinéma* 1986; *I Hired a Contract Killer* 1990; *Mon Homme* 1996; *Pour Rire!* 1996
Leaver, Philip *Dr Morelle – the Case of the Missing Heiress* 1949; *Spaceways* 1953
Lebeau, Madeleine *Casablanca* 1942; *Paris after Dark* 1943; *Cage of Gold* 1950
Lebedeff, Ivan *Bachelor Apartment* 1931; *Blonde Bombshell* 1933; *Goin' to Town* 1935; *Love on the Run* 1936; *Angel* 1937; *History Is Made at Night* 1937
Lebihan, Samuel aka **LeBihan, Samuel** *Three Colours Red* 1994; *Venus Beauty* 1998
LeBlanc, Matt *Killing Box* 1993; *Lookin' Italian* 1994; *Reform School Girl* 1994; *Ed* 1996; *Lost in Space* 1997
LeBrock, Kelly *The Woman in Red* 1984; *Weird Science* 1985; *Hard to Kill* 1989; *Betrayal of the Dove* 1993; *David Copperfield* 1993; *Wrongfully Accused* 1998
Leclerc, Ginette *The Baker's Wife* 1938; *The Raven* 1943; *Goto, l'Ile d'Amour* 1968; *Popsy-Pop* 1970
LeClerc, Jean *Whispers* 1990; *Blown Away* 1992
LeClezio, Odile aka **Le Clezio, Odile** *Young Einstein* 1988; *Backsliding* 1991
Ledebur, Friedrich *Moby Dick* 1956; *The 27th Day* 1957; *The Christmas Tree* 1969
Lederer, Francis aka **Lederer, Franz** *Pandora's Box* 1929; *The Wonderful Lie of Nina Petrovna* 1929; *Romance in Manhattan* 1934; *The Gay Deception* 1935; *One Rainy Afternoon* 1936; *Confessions of a Nazi Spy* 1939; *Midnight* 1939; *The Man I Married* 1940; *Diary of a Chambermaid* 1946; *A Woman of Distinction* 1950; *The Ambassador's Daughter* 1956; *Lisbon* 1956; *The Return of Dracula* 1958; *Maracaibo* 1958; *Terror Is a Man* 1959
Lederman, Caz *Tail of a Tiger* 1984; *Malpractice* 1989; *Deadly* 1991; *Fatal Bond* 1991
Ledger, Heath *10 Things I Hate about You* 1999; *The Patriot* 2000
Ledoux, Fernand *La Bête Humaine* 1938; *Volpone* 1940; *Les Visiteurs du Soir* 1942; *Les Misérables* 1957; *The Magic Donkey* 1970; *To Each His Own Hell* 1977
Ledoyen, Virginie *L'Eau Froide* 1994; *La Cérémonie* 1995; *Late August, Early September* 1998; *In All Innocence* 1998; *The Beach* 2000
Lee, Anna *The Camels Are Coming* 1934; *First a Girl* 1935; *The Passing of the Third Floor Back* 1935; *The Man Who Changed His Mind* 1936; *You're In the Army Now* 1936; *King Solomon's Mines* 1937; *The Four Just Men* 1939; *Return to Yesterday* 1940; *Seven Sinners* 1940; *How Green Was My Valley* 1941; *My Life with Caroline* 1941; *The Commandos Strike at Dawn* 1942; *Flying Tigers* 1942; *Hangmen Also Die* 1943; *Summer Storm* 1944; *Bedlam* 1946; *The Ghost and Mrs Muir* 1947; *The Crimson Kimono* 1959; *Gideon's Day* 1959; *The Horse Soldiers* 1959; *Jet over the Atlantic* 1960; *What Ever Happened to Baby Jane?* 1962; *7 Women* 1966; *In like Flint* 1967
Lee, Belinda *No Smoking* 1954; *The Runaway Bus* 1954; *Footsteps in the Fog* 1955; *Man of the Moment* 1955; *The Big Money* 1956; *Eyewitness* 1956; *The Feminine Touch* 1956; *Dangerous Exile* 1957; *Miracle in Soho* 1957; *Nor the Moon by Night* 1958
Lee, Bernard *Let George Do It* 1940; *Spare a Copper* 1940; *The Fallen Idol* 1948; *The Blue Lamp* 1949; *The Third Man* 1949; *The Adventurers* 1950; *Cage of Gold* 1950; *Last Holiday* 1950; *Odette* 1950; *Appointment with Venus* 1951; *Calling Bulldog Drummond* 1951; *Mr Denning Drives North* 1951; *The Gift Horse* 1952; *The Yellow Balloon* 1952; *Beat the Devil* 1953; *Sailor of the King* 1953; *Seagulls over Sorrento* 1954; *Father Brown* 1954; *The Purple Plain* 1954; *The Ship That Died of Shame* 1955; *The Battle of the River Plate* 1956; *The Spanish Gardener* 1956; *Across the Bridge* 1957; *High Flight* 1957; *Danger Within* 1958; *Dunkirk* 1958; *The Key* 1958; *Nowhere to Go* 1958; *The Man Upstairs* 1958; *Beyond This Place* 1959; *The Angry Silence* 1960; *Cone of Silence* 1960; *Kidnapped* 1960; *Fury at Smugglers Bay* 1961; *The Secret Partner* 1961; *Whistle down the Wind* 1961; *The Brain* 1962; *Dr No* 1962; *The L-Shaped Room* 1962; *From Russia with Love* 1963; *A Place to Go* 1963; *Ring of Spies* 1963; *Saturday Night Out* 1963; *Two Left Feet* 1963; *Goldfinger* 1964; *The Legend of Young Dick Turpin* 1965; *Thunderball* 1965; *You Only Live Twice* 1967; *Crossplot* 1969; *On Her Majesty's Secret Service* 1969; *The Raging Moon* 1970; *Diamonds Are Forever* 1971; *Dulcima* 1971; *Frankenstein and the Monster from Hell* 1973; *Live and Let Die* 1973; *The Man with the Golden Gun* 1974; *Beauty and the Beast* 1976; *The Spy Who Loved Me* 1977; *Moonraker* 1979

LeMat, Paul *American Graffiti* 1973; *Aloha, Bobby and Rose* 1975; *Citizens Band* 1977; *More American Graffiti* 1979; *Melvin and Howard* 1980; *Death Valley* 1982; *Jimmy the Kid* 1982; *PK and the Kid* 1982; *Strange Invaders* 1983; *The Burning Bed* 1984; *The Night They Saved Christmas* 1984; *Hanoi Hilton* 1987; *Into the Homeland* 1987; *Private Investigations* 1987; *Blind Witness* 1989; *Puppet Master* 1989; *Easy Wheels* 1989; *Woman with a Past* 1991; *In the Line of Duty: Siege at Marion* 1992; *Someone's Watching* 1993

Lembeck, Harvey *Stalag 17* 1953; *The Command* 1954; *Beach Party* 1963; *Love with the Proper Stranger* 1963; *Pajama Party* 1964; *The Unsinkable Molly Brown* 1964; *Beach Blanket Bingo* 1965; *How to Fill a Wild Bikini* 1965; *Sergeant Deadhead* 1965; *Fireball 500* 1966; *The Ghost in the Invisible Bikini* 1966; *Hello Down There* 1969

Lembeck, Michael *The Boys in Company C* 1978; *G.O.R.P.* 1980; *On the Right Track* 1981

Lemkow, Tutte *The Captain's Paradise* 1953; *The Boy Who Stole a Million* 1960

Lemmeke, Ole *A Day in October* 1991; *The Magnetist's Fifth Winter* 1999

Lemmon, Chris *aka* **Lemmon, Christopher** *Just before Dawn* 1980; *Going Undercover* 1984; *That's Life* 1986; *Weekend Warriors* 1986; *Lena's Holiday* 1990; *Firehead* 1991; *Thunder In Paradise* 1993; *Best of the Best: Without Warning* 1998

Lemmon, Jack *It Should Happen to You* 1954; *Phffft!* 1954; *Mister Roberts* 1955; *My Sister Eileen* 1955; *Three for the Show* 1955; *You Can't Run Away from It* 1956; *Fire Down Below* 1957; *Operation Mad Ball* 1957; *Bell, Book and Candle* 1958; *Cowboy* 1958; *It Happened to Jane* 1959; *Some Like It Hot* 1959; *The Apartment* 1960; *Pepe* 1960; *The Wackiest Ship in the Army* 1961; *Days of Wine and Roses* 1962; *The Notorious Landlady* 1962; *Irma la Douce* 1963; *Under the Yum Yum Tree* 1963; *Good Neighbor Sam* 1964; *The Great Race* 1965; *How to Murder Your Wife* 1965; *The Fortune Cookie* 1966; *Luv* 1967; *The Odd Couple* 1968; *The April Fools* 1969; *The Out of Towners* 1970; *Avanti!* 1972; *The War between Men and Women* 1972; *Save the Tiger* 1973; *The Front Page* 1974; *The Prisoner of Second Avenue* 1974; *The Entertainer* 1975; *Alex and the Gypsy* 1976; *Airport '77* 1977; *The China Syndrome* 1979; *Tribute* 1980; *Buddy Buddy* 1981; *Missing* 1981; *Mass Appeal* 1984; *Macaroni* 1985; *That's Life* 1986; *Dad* 1989; *JFK* 1991; *Father, Son and the Mistress* 1992; *Glengarry Glen Ross* 1992; *Grumpy Old Men* 1993; *A Life in the Theater* 1993; *Short Cuts* 1993; *The Grass Harp* 1995; *Getting Away with Murder* 1996; *Grumpier Old Men* 1996; *Hamlet* 1996; *My Fellow Americans* 1996; *A Weekend in the Country* 1996; *Out to Sea* 1997; *Twelve Angry Men* 1997; *The Odd Couple II* 1998; *The Long Way Home* 1998; *Inherit the Wind* 1999

Lemmons, Kasi *Vampire's Kiss* 1988; *The Court-Martial of Jackie Robinson* 1990; *The Silence of the Lambs* 1991; *Candyman*

1992; *Fear of a Black Hat* 1992; *Hard Target* 1993

Lemon, Genevieve *Sweetie* 1989; *The Piano* 1993; *Soft Fruit* 1999

Lenard, Mark *Star Trek III: the Search for Spock* 1984; *Star Trek IV: the Voyage Home* 1986; *Star Trek VI: the Undiscovered Country* 1991

Lenehan, Nancy *Assassin* 1986; *Rock 'n' Roll Mom* 1988

Lennix, Harry J *aka* **Lennix, Harry** *The Five Heartbeats* 1991; *Bob Roberts* 1992; *Mo' Money* 1992; *Get on the Bus* 1996; *Titus* 1999

Lennon, Jarrett *The Servants of Twilight* 1991; *Highway to Hell* 1992; *Just like Dad* 1996

Lennon, John *A Hard Day's Night* 1964; *Help!* 1965; *How I Won the War* 1967; *Dynamite Chicken* 1971; *Imagine: John Lennon* 1988

Lennon, Julian *David Copperfield* 1993; *Leaving Las Vegas* 1995

Leno, Jay *American Hot Wax* 1977; *Silver Bears* 1978; *Americathon* 1979; *Collision Course* 1987; *We're Back! A Dinosaur's Story* 1993; *In & Out* 1997

Lenya, Lotte *The Threepenny Opera* 1931; *The Roman Spring of Mrs Stone* 1961; *From Russia with Love* 1963; *The Appointment* 1968; *Semi-Tough* 1977

Lenz, Kay *Breezy* 1973; *White Line Fever* 1975; *The Great Scout & Cathouse Thursday* 1976; *The Passage* 1978; *Mean Dog Blues* 1978; *Escape* 1980; *Fast-Walking* 1982; *House* 1986; *Death Wish 4: the Crackdown* 1987; *Fear* 1988; *Murder by Night* 1989; *Physical Evidence* 1989; *Falling from Grace* 1992; *Trapped in Space* 1994

Lenz, Rick *Cactus Flower* 1969; *Where Does It Hurt?* 1971; *Scandalous John* 1971; *The Little Dragons* 1980; *Hollow Point* 1987; *Shadow of a Doubt* 1991

Leo, Melissa *aka* **Leo, Melissa Chessington** *Always* 1985; *Silent Witness* 1985; *A Time of Destiny* 1988; *The Bride in Black* 1990; *Carolina Skeletons* 1991; *Immaculate Conception* 1991; *In the Line of Duty: Hunt for Justice* 1995; *Last Summer in the Hamptons* 1995

Leon *aka* **Robinson, Leon** *The Father Clements Story* 1987; *The Five Heartbeats* 1991; *Cliffhanger* 1993; *Cool Runnings* 1993; *Above the Rim* 1994; *Runaway Car* 1997; *Side Streets* 1998; *Bats* 1999

Leon, Joseph *Sweet Smell of Success* 1957; *Act One* 1963; *Daniel* 1983

Leon, Valerie *Blood from the Mummy's Tomb* 1971; *Ups and Downs of a Handyman* 1975

Leonard, Lu *The Princess Academy* 1987; *Circuitry Man* 1990; *Without You I'm Nothing* 1990; *Shadowzone* 1990

Leonard, Queenie *Moonlight Sonata* 1937; *The Lodger* 1944; *Molly and Me* 1945; *The Lone Wolf in London* 1947; *The Narrow Margin* 1952

Leonard, Robert Sean *Dead Poets Society* 1989; *Mr and Mrs Bridge* 1990; *Married to It* 1991; *The Age of Innocence* 1993; *Much Ado about Nothing* 1993; *Swing Kids* 1993; *Safe Passage* 1994; *Killer: a Journal of Murder* 1995; *The Boys Next Door* 1996; *In the Gloaming* 1997; *The Last Days of Disco* 1998

Leonard, Sheldon *Weekend in Havana* 1941; *Tortilla Flat* 1942; *Hit the Ice* 1943; *Passport to*

Suez 1943; *The Falcon in Hollywood* 1944; *To Have and Have Not* 1944; *Frontier Gal* 1945; *Abbott and Costello Meet the Invisible Man* 1951; *The Diamond Queen* 1953; *Guys and Dolls* 1955; *The Brink's Job* 1978

Leonardi, Marco *Like Water for Chocolate* 1993; *Desperate Measures* 1995; *The Five Senses* 1999

Leong, Al *Bill & Ted's Excellent Adventure* 1988; *Cage* 1989

Leoni, Téa *The Counterfeit Contessa* 1994; *Bad Boys* 1995; *Flirting with Disaster* 1996; *Deep Impact* 1998

Leontovich, Eugenie *Four Sons* 1940; *The Men in Her Life* 1941; *Anything Can Happen* 1952; *The World in His Arms* 1952; *The Rains of Ranchipur* 1955; *Homicidal* 1961

Leopardi, Chauncey *Huck and the King of Hearts* 1993; *The Sandlot* 1993; *The Big Green* 1995; *Houseguest* 1995

Léotard, Philippe *Anne and Muriel* 1971; *Une Belle Fille Comme Moi* 1973; *The Mouth Agape* 1974; *La Balance* 1982; *Shock* 1982; *Tangos, Exilo de Gardel* 1985; *Sur* 1987; *Death of a Schoolboy* 1990; *Elisa* 1994

Lerner, Ken *Relentless* 1989; *Fast Getaway* 1991; *Unlawful Entry* 1992; *Trial by Fire* 1995

Lerner, Michael *What's a Nice Girl like You...?* 1971; *The Candidate* 1972; *Hangup* 1973; *Newman's Law* 1974; *Sarah T: Portrait of a Teenage Alcoholic* 1975; *The Other Side of Midnight* 1977; *Outlaw Blues* 1977; *The Baltimore Bullet* 1980; *Borderline* 1980; *The Postman Always Rings Twice* 1981; *Threshold* 1981; *National Lampoon's Class Reunion* 1982; *Strange Invaders* 1983; *This Child Is Mine* 1985; *That Secret Sunday* 1986; *The King of Love* 1987; *Vibes* 1988; *Harlem Nights* 1989; *Framed* 1990; *Maniac Cop 2* 1990; *Any Man's Death* 1990; *Barton Fink* 1991; *Omen IV: the Awakening* 1991; *The Comrades of Summer* 1992; *Amos & Andrew* 1993; *Blank Cheque* 1994; *No Escape* 1994; *The Road to Wellville* 1994; *A Pyromaniac's Love Story* 1995; *No Way Back* 1996; *The Beautician and the Beast* 1997; *For Richer or Poorer* 1997; *Godzilla* 1997; *Talos the Mummy* 1997; *My Favorite Martian* 1999

Leroux, Maxime *Romuald et Juliette* 1989; *Tango* 1993

LeRoy, Baby *Tillie and Gus* 1933; *It's a Gift* 1934; *The Lemon Drop Kid* 1934; *The Old-Fashioned Way* 1934

LeRoy, Gloria *Welcome to Arrow Beach* 1974; *Barfly* 1987; *Cool Blue* 1988

Leroy, Philippe *Le Trou* 1959; *The Married Woman* 1964; *The Night Porter* 1973

Leroy-Beaulieu, Philippine *3 Men and a Cradle* 1985; *Nine Months* 1994

Lesley, Carole *Woman in a Dressing Gown* 1957; *Operation Bullshine* 1959; *Doctor in Love* 1960; *What a Whopper!* 1961; *The Pot Carriers* 1962

Lesley, Lorna *The Settlement* 1982; *The Shiralee* 1986

Leslie, Bethel *A Rage to Live* 1965; *The Molly Maguires* 1970; *Old Boyfriends* 1979

Leslie, Joan *Love Affair* 1939; *High Sierra* 1941; *Sergeant York* 1941; *The Wagons Roll at Night* 1941; *The Hard Way* 1942; *The*

Male Animal 1942; *Yankee Doodle Dandy* 1942; *The Sky's the Limit* 1943; *Thank Your Lucky Stars* 1943; *This Is the Army* 1943; *Hollywood Canteen* 1944; *Rhapsody in Blue* 1945; *Where Do We Go from Here?* 1945; *Cinderella Jones* 1946; *Two Guys from Milwaukee* 1946; *Northwest Stampede* 1948; *Born to Be Bad* 1950; *Man in the Saddle* 1951; *Hellgate* 1952; *The Revolt of Mamie Stover* 1956

Leslie, Nan *The Devil Thumbs a Ride* 1947; *The Woman on the Beach* 1947; *The Arizona Ranger* 1948; *Guns of Hate* 1948

Leslie, William *The Long Gray Line* 1955; *Bring Your Smile Along* 1955; *Hellcats of the Navy* 1957; *The Lineup* 1958; *Up Periscope* 1959

Lessey, George *Sky Murder* 1940; *Strike Up the Band* 1940; *Blossoms in the Dust* 1941

Lester, Adrian *The Affair* 1995; *Primary Colors* 1998; *Love's Labour's Lost* 1999; *Maybe Baby* 1999

Lester, Bruce *Boy Meets Girl* 1938; *The Letter* 1940; *My Son, My Son* 1940; *Shadows on the Stairs* 1941; *Golden Earrings* 1947

Lester, Buddy *Three on a Couch* 1966; *The Big Mouth* 1967; *Smorgasbord* 1983

Lester, Eleese *The Devil's Bed* 1994; *Lone Star* 1995

Lester (1), Mark *Our Mother's House* 1967; *Oliver!* 1968; *Run Wild, Run Free* 1969; *Eyewitness* 1970; *Black Beauty* 1971; *Melody* 1971; *Scalawag* 1973; *The Prince and the Pauper* 1977

Lester, Ron *Good Burger* 1997; *Varsity Blues* 1999

Lester, Tom *Return to Green Acres* 1990; *Gordy* 1994

Lester, Vicki *The Mad Miss Manton* 1938; *Tom, Dick and Harry* 1941

Letch, David *Sylvia* 1984; *Mr Wrong* 1985

Lether, Shelli *Born to Run* 1993; *The Sender* 1997

Leto, Jared *The Cool and the Crazy* 1994; *Last of the High Kings* 1996; *Switchback* 1997; *Prefontaine* 1997; *Urban Legend* 1998; *Basil* 1998; *Fight Club* 1999; *Girl, Interrupted* 1999; *Black and White* 1999; *American Psycho* 2000

Letondal, Henri *On the Riviera* 1951; *Monkey Business* 1952

Lett, Dan *Paris France* 1993; *Conundrum* 1995; *Under the Piano* 1995; *No One Could Protect Her* 1996; *The Secret Laughter of Women* 1998

Lettieri, Al *aka* **Lettieri, Alfredo** *The Bobo* 1967; *The Getaway* 1972; *Pulp* 1972; *The Don Is Dead* 1973; *The Deadly Trackers* 1973; *Mr Majestyk* 1974

Lettinger, Rudolf *aka* **Lettinger, Rudolph** *The Cabinet of Dr Caligari* 1919; *The Spiders* 1919

Leung (1), Tony *aka* **Leung, Tony Chiu-Wai** *A City of Sadness* 1989; *Bullet in the Head* 1990; *Days of Being Wild* 1990; *Hard-Boiled* 1992; *Chung King Express* 1994; *Cyclo* 1995; *Happy Together* 1997; *Flowers of Shanghai* 1998

Leung (2), Tony *aka* **Leung, Tony Kar-Fai** *The Laserman* 1988; *A Better Tomorrow III* 1989; *The Lover* 1992; *Love Will Tear Us Apart* 1999

Levant, Oscar *Rhythm on the River* 1940; *Kiss the Boys Goodbye* 1941; *Humoresque* 1946; *It's Magic* 1948; *Romance*

on the High Seas 1948; *You Were Meant for Me* 1948; *The Barkleys of Broadway* 1949; *An American in Paris* 1951; *The I Don't Care Girl* 1952; *O Henry's Full House* 1952; *The Band Wagon* 1953

Levels, Calvin *A Night on the Town* 1987; *Johnny Suede* 1991; *Hellbound* 1993; *Within the Rock* 1995

Levene, Sam *Three Men on a Horse* 1936; *The Mad Miss Manton* 1938; *Golden Boy* 1939; *Shadow of the Thin Man* 1941; *The Big Street* 1942; *Grand Central Murder* 1942; *Action in the North Atlantic* 1943; *I Dood It* 1943; *Whistling in Brooklyn* 1943; *The Killers* 1946; *Boomerang!* 1947; *Brute Force* 1947; *Killer McCoy* 1947; *Crossfire* 1947; *Guilty Bystander* 1950; *Three Sailors and a Girl* 1953; *Designing Woman* 1957; *Sweet Smell of Success* 1957; *Act One* 1963; *A Dream of Kings* 1969; *God Told Me to* 1976; *...And Justice for All* 1979; *Last Embrace* 1979

Levesque, Marcel *Judex* 1916; *Le Crime de Monsieur Lange* 1935

Levine, Anna *aka* **Thomson, Anna** *Dead in the Water* 1991; *Unforgiven* 1992; *Hand Gun* 1994; *Angus* 1995; *Other Voices, Other Rooms* 1995

Levine, Floyd *Bloodbrothers* 1978; *Ice* 1994

Levine, James *Fantasia 2000* 1999; *Fantasia 2000* 1999

Levine, Jerry *Teen Wolf* 1985; *Casual Sex?* 1988

Levine, Ted *Betrayed* 1988; *In the Line of Duty: Mob Justice* 1991; *Murder in High Places* 1991; *The Silence of the Lambs* 1991; *Nowhere to Run* 1992; *Death Train* 1993; *The Last Outlaw* 1993; *The Mangler* 1994; *Bullet* 1995; *Georgia* 1995; *Wiseguy* 1996; *Mad City* 1997; *Switchback* 1997; *Ellen Foster* 1997; *You Can Thank Me Later* 1998; *Wild Wild West* 1999

Levisetti, Emile *Sexual Response* 1992; *The Alien Within* 1995

Levy, Eugene *Running* 1979; *Going Berserk* 1983; *Splash* 1984; *Armed and Dangerous* 1986; *Club Paradise* 1986; *Partners in Love* 1992; *Stay Tuned* 1992; *Harrison Bergeron* 1995; *Multiplicity* 1996; *Waiting for Guffman* 1996; *Almost Heroes* 1998; *American Pie* 1999

Levy, Ori *Before Winter Comes* 1968; *The Chairman* 1969; *Moon Zero Two* 1969; *The Sellout* 1975; *Hellbound* 1993

Lewgoy, Jose *Fitzcarraldo* 1982; *Blame It on Rio* 1984; *Kiss of the Spider Woman* 1985; *The Lady from the Shanghai Cinema* 1987; *Cobra Verde* 1988

Lewis, Al *Munster, Go Home!* 1966; *They Shoot Horses, Don't They?* 1969; *The Night Strangler* 1973; *Car 54 Where Are You?* 1991

Lewis, Charlotte *The Golden Child* 1986; *Pirates* 1986; *Bare Essentials* 1991; *Storyville* 1992; *Excessive Force* 1993; *Embrace of the Vampire* 1994; *Decoy* 1995; *Men of War* 1995; *The Glass Cage* 1996

Lewis, David *That Certain Feeling* 1956; *The Apartment* 1960; *Generation* 1969

Lewis, Dawnn *Race to Freedom: the Underground Railroad* 1994; *Under Pressure* 1997

Lewis, Diana *Bitter Sweet* 1940; *Marx Brothers Go West* 1940; *The People vs Dr Kildare* 1941;

Longden, Terence aka **Longdon, Terence** Carry On Nurse 1959; Carry On Regardless 1960; Clash by Night 1963

Longley, Victoria The More Things Change 1985; Celia 1988; Turtle Beach 1992; Dallas Doll 1994

Longo, Tony Bloodhounds of Broadway 1989; Prehysteria! 1993

Longstreth, Emily Private Resort 1985; The Game of Love 1987; The Big Picture 1989; Rising Son 1990; Confessions of a Hit Man 1994

Lonsdale, Michel aka **Lonsdale, Michael** The Trial 1962; The Bride Wore Black 1967; Stolen Kisses 1968; There Was Once a Cop 1969; Le Souffle au Coeur 1971; The Day of the Jackal 1973; Out 1: Spectre 1973; Caravan to Vaccares 1974; The Phantom of Liberty 1974; Galileo 1974; Stavisky 1974; The Evil Trap 1975; The Pink Telephone 1975; The Romantic Englishwoman 1975; Mr Klein 1976; The Passage 1978; Moonraker 1979; Enigma 1982; Erendira 1982; The Holcroft Covenant 1985; The Name of the Rose 1986; Operation Madonna 1987; Riviera 1987; Souvenir 1987; The Remains of the Day 1993; Jefferson in Paris 1995; Ronin 1998

Loo, Richard The Bitter Tea of General Yen 1933; Back to Bataan 1945; Betrayal from the East 1945; China Sky 1945; First Yank into Tokyo 1945; The Steel Helmet 1951; Love Is a Many-Splendored Thing 1955; The Man with the Golden Gun 1974

Loomis, Rod The Beastmaster 1982; Bill & Ted's Excellent Adventure 1988; Jack's Back 1988

Loos, Theodor aka **Loos, Theodore** The Nibelungen 1924; Metropolis 1926; M 1931; Ariane 1931

Lopert, Tanya Navajo Joe 1966; Once in Paris 1978; Tales of Ordinary Madness 1981

Lopez, Fernando Defiance 1979; Killer Instinct 1988; To Sir with Love 2 1996

Lopez, Gerry Conan the Barbarian 1982; North Shore 1987

Lopez, Jennifer Nurses on the Line 1993; Money Train 1995; Blood and Wine 1996; Jack 1996; Anaconda 1997; Selena 1997; U Turn 1997; Antz 1998; Out of Sight 1998

Lopez, Kamala Born in East LA 1987; Break of Dawn 1988

Lopez, Perry Hell on Frisco Bay 1955; I Died a Thousand Times 1955; The Lone Ranger 1956; Violent Road 1958; Taras Bulba 1962; Chinatown 1974; Death Wish 4: the Crackdown 1987; Kinjite: Forbidden Subjects 1989

Lopez, Sal Pucker Up and Bark Like a Dog 1989; From the Files of Joseph Wambaugh: a Jury of One 1992; Blue Tiger 1994; Journey 1995

Lopez, Sergi Western 1997; La Nouvelle Eve 1999; Une Liaison Pornographique 1999

Lopez, Trini Marriage on the Rocks 1965; The Dirty Dozen 1967

Lorca, Isabel Lightning the White Stallion 1986; She's Having a Baby 1988

Lord, Jack The Court-Martial of Billy Mitchell 1955; The Vagabond King 1956; Tip on a Dead Jockey 1957; The True Story of Lynn Stuart 1957; God's Little Acre

1958; Man of the West 1958; The Hangman 1959; Walk like a Dragon 1960; Dr No 1962; The Doomsday Flight 1966; The Ride to Hangman's Tree 1967

Lord, Marion aka **Lord, Marian** Broadway 1929; One Heavenly Night 1931

Lord, Marjorie Johnny Come Lately 1943; Sherlock Holmes in Washington 1943; Boy, Did I Get a Wrong Number 1966; Side by Side 1988

Lords, Traci Not of This Earth 1988; Cry-Baby 1989; Fast Food 1989; Murder in High Places 1991; Raw Nerve 1991; A Time to Die 1991; Intent to Kill 1992; Dragstrip Girl 1994; Plughead Rewired: Circuitry Man II 1994; Ice 1994; As Good as Dead 1995; Dead Man's Island 1996; Underworld 1996; Blood Money 1996; Blade 1998

Loren, Sophia Gold of Naples 1954; Too Bad She's Bad 1955; The Miller's Wife 1955; Lucky to Be a Woman 1955; Woman of the River 1955; Boy on a Dolphin 1957; Legend of the Lost 1957; The Pride and the Passion 1957; Desire under the Elms 1958; Houseboat 1958; The Key 1958; The Black Orchid 1959; That Kind of Woman 1959; A Breath of Scandal 1960; Heller in Pink Tights 1960; It Started in Naples 1960; The Millionairess 1960; Two Women 1960; Boccaccio '70 1961; El Cid 1961; Madame 1961; The Condemned of Altona 1962; Yesterday, Today and Tomorrow 1963; Five Miles to Midnight 1963; The Fall of the Roman Empire 1964; Marriage – Italian Style 1964; Lady L 1965; Operation Crossbow 1965; Arabesque 1966; Judith 1966; A Countess from Hong Kong 1967; More than a Miracle 1967; Ghosts – Italian Style 1967; Sunflower 1969; The Priest's Wife 1970; Lady Liberty 1971; Man of La Mancha 1972; Brief Encounter 1974; Verdict 1974; The Voyage 1974; The Cassandra Crossing 1976; A Special Day 1977; Brass Target 1978; Firepower 1979; Blood Feud 1979; Aurora 1984; Courage 1986; Prêt-à-Porter 1994; Grumpier Old Men 1996

Lorenzon, Livio Goliath and the Barbarians 1959; Pontius Pilate 1961

Lorimer, Glennis Alf's Button Afloat 1938; Ask a Policeman 1938

Lorimer, Louise Japanese War Bride 1952; –30– 1959

Loring, Teala Bluebeard 1944; Dark Alibi 1946

Lorinz, James Frankenhooker 1990; Me and the Mob 1992; The Jerky Boys 1995

Lorit, Jean-Pierre Jeanne la Pucelle 1994; Three Colours Red 1994; Alice et Martin 1998

Lorne, Marion Strangers on a Train 1951; The Girl Rush 1955

Loros, George Apology 1986; Blue Jean Cop 1988

Lorre, Peter M 1931; The Man Who Knew Too Much 1934; Crime and Punishment 1935; Mad Love 1935; Crack-Up 1936; Secret Agent 1936; Lancer Spy 1937; Nancy Steele Is Missing 1937; Thank You, Mr Moto 1937; Think Fast, Mr Moto 1937; Mr Moto Takes a Chance 1938; Mr Moto's Gamble 1938; Mysterious Mr Moto 1938; Mr Moto in Danger Island 1939; Mr Moto Takes a Vacation 1939; Mr Moto's Last Warning 1939; Strange Cargo

1940; Stranger on the Third Floor 1940; You'll Find Out 1940; I Was an Adventuress 1940; The Face behind the Mask 1941; The Maltese Falcon 1941; They Met in Bombay 1941; All through the Night 1942; The Boogie Man Will Get You 1942; Casablanca 1942; Background to Danger 1943; The Constant Nymph 1943; The Cross of Lorraine 1943; Arsenic and Old Lace 1944; The Conspirators 1944; Hollywood Canteen 1944; The Mask of Dimitrios 1944; Passage to Marseille 1944; Confidential Agent 1945; Hotel Berlin 1945; The Beast with Five Fingers 1946; Black Angel 1946; The Chase 1946; Three Strangers 1946; The Verdict 1946; My Favorite Brunette 1947; Casbah 1948; Rope of Sand 1949; Beat the Devil 1953; 20,000 Leagues under the Sea 1954; Around the World in 80 Days 1956; Congo Crossing 1956; The Sad Sack 1957; Silk Stockings 1957; The Buster Keaton Story 1957; Hell Ship Mutiny 1957; The Big Circus 1959; Quicksand 1959; Scent of Mystery 1960; Voyage to the Bottom of the Sea 1961; Five Weeks in a Balloon 1962; Tales of Terror 1962; The Raven 1963; The Comedy of Terrors 1964; Muscle Beach Party 1964; The Patsy 1964

Lorring, Joan The Corn Is Green 1945; Three Strangers 1946; The Verdict 1946; The Gangster 1947; The Lost Moment 1947; The Other Love 1947; Good Sam 1948; The Big Night 1951; The Midnight Man 1974

Lorys, Diana The Awful Dr Orloff 1962; Bad Man's River 1971

Losch, Tilly The Garden of Allah 1936; The Good Earth 1937

Lotis, Dennis The City of the Dead 1960; She'll Have to Go 1961

Lottimer, Eb Streets 1990; The Finest Hour 1991; Quake! 1992

Louanne The Long Days of Summer 1980; Oh God! Book II 1980; Missing Pieces 1983; A Night in the Life of Jimmy Reardon 1988

Loughlin, Lori Amityville III: the Demon 1983; North Beach and Rawhide 1985; Secret Admirer 1985; Brotherhood of Justice 1986; The Night Before 1988; Empty Cradle 1993; A Stranger in the Mirror 1993; One of Her Own 1994; Tell Me No Secrets 1996; The Price of Heaven 1997; Blaze of Glory 1997

Louie, "Ducky" Back to Bataan 1945; China Sky 1945

Louie, John Oh God! Book II 1980; Gremlins 1984

Louis, Joe This Is the Army 1943; The Square Jungle 1955

Louis, Justin Night Owl 1993; Deadly Justice 1995; National Lampoon's Dad's Week Off 1997

Louis, Willard Robin Hood 1922; Kiss Me Again 1925; Don Juan 1926

Louis-Dreyfus, Julia Troll 1986; North 1994; Neil Simon's London Suite 1996; Deconstructing Harry 1997; Fathers' Day 1997; A Bug's Life 1998

Louise, Anita Our Betters 1933; Madame Du Barry 1934; Judge Priest 1934; A Midsummer Night's Dream 1935; Anthony Adverse 1936; The Story of Louis Pasteur 1936; First Lady 1937; Green Light 1937; That Certain Woman 1937; Tovarich 1937; Marie Antoinette 1938; The Sisters 1938; Going Places 1938; The Little Princess 1939; The Villain

Still Pursued Her 1940; Casanova Brown 1944; Love Letters 1945; The Bandit of Sherwood Forest 1946; Retreat, Hell! 1952

Louise, Tina God's Little Acre 1958; The Baited Trap 1959; Day of the Outlaw 1959; The Siege of Syracuse 1959; The Hangman 1959; Armored Command 1961; The Good Guys and the Bad Guys 1969; The Happy Ending 1969; The Wrecking Crew 1969; The Stepford Wives 1975; Mean Dog Blues 1978

Louiso, Todd Jerry Maguire 1996; 8 Heads in a Duffel Bag 1997; High Fidelity 2000

Love, Alan That Sinking Feeling 1979; The Apple 1980

Love, Bessie The Lost World 1925; The Matinee Idol 1928; The Broadway Melody 1929; Hollywood Revue 1929; Next to No Time 1958; Nowhere to Go 1958; Isadora 1968; Catlow 1971; Lady Chatterley's Lover 1981; Reds 1981

Love, Courtney Sid and Nancy 1986; Straight to Hell 1987; Basquiat 1996; Feeling Minnesota 1996; The People vs Larry Flynt 1996; 200 Cigarettes 1999; Man on the Moon 1999

Love, Darlene Lethal Weapon 1987; Lethal Weapon 2 1989; Lethal Weapon 3 1992; Lethal Weapon 4 1998

Love, Montagu aka **Love, Montague** The Son of the Sheik 1926; Hands Up! 1926; The Wind 1928; Bulldog Drummond 1929; Outward Bound 1930; The Man Who Broke the Bank at Monte Carlo 1935; Lloyd's of London 1936; One in a Million 1936; Sing, Baby, Sing 1936; A Damsel in Distress 1937; London by Night 1937; Parnell 1937; Gunga Din 1939; Rulers of the Sea 1939; We Are Not Alone 1939; Dr Ehrlich's Magic Bullet 1940; The Lone Wolf Strikes 1940; The Mark of Zorro 1940; Son of Monte Cristo 1940; The Devil and Miss Jones 1941; Shining Victory 1941; Lady for a Night 1942; Sherlock Holmes and the Voice of Terror 1942; Forever and a Day 1943

Love, Pee Wee Radio Inside 1994; Clockers 1995

Love, Victor Native Son 1986; Heaven Is a Playground 1991

Lovegrove, Arthur The Steel Key 1953; Naked Fury 1959

Lovejoy, Frank Home of the Brave 1949; In a Lonely Place 1950; Three Secrets 1950; The Sound of Fury 1950; Force of Arms 1951; Goodbye, My Fancy 1951; I Was a Communist for the FBI 1951; I'll See You in My Dreams 1951; Retreat, Hell! 1952; The Charge at Feather River 1953; House of Wax 1953; The Hitch-Hiker 1953; Beachhead 1954; Men of the Fighting Lady 1954; The Americano 1955; Strategic Air Command 1955; Shack Out on 101 1955; Julie 1956; Three Brave Men 1956

Lovelace, Linda Deep Throat 1972; Linda Lovelace for President 1975

Lovell, Raymond Contraband 1940; The Young Mr Pitt 1942; Uncensored 1942; Candlelight in Algeria 1943; The Man in Grey 1943; Hotel Reserve 1944; Caesar and Cleopatra 1945; Night Boat to Dublin 1946; The Blind Goddess 1947; The End of the River 1947; The Calendar 1948; My Brother's Keeper 1948; The Bad Lord Byron 1949; Madness of

the Heart 1949; The Romantic Age 1949; The Mudlark 1950; Time Gentlemen Please! 1952; The Steel Key 1953

Lovelock, Raymond Django Kill 1967; Fiddler on the Roof 1971

Lovett, Dorothy Look Who's Laughing 1941; Call Out the Marines 1942

Lovett, Lyle Bastard out of Carolina 1996; Breast Men 1997; Fear and Loathing in Las Vegas 1998; The Opposite of Sex 1998

Lovgren, David Live Bait 1995; Rollercoaster 1999

Lovitz, Jon The Brave Little Toaster 1987; Big 1988; My Stepmother Is an Alien 1988; Mr Destiny 1990; An American Tail: Fievel Goes West 1991; Mom and Dad Save the World 1992; Coneheads 1993; National Lampoon's Loaded Weapon 1 1993; City Slickers II: the Legend of Curly's Gold 1994; North 1994; Trapped in Paradise 1994; The Great White Hype 1996; High School High 1996; Happiness 1998; Lost & Found 1999

Lovsky, Celia Captain Carey, USA 1950; Man of a Thousand Faces 1957; The Mobster 1958; The Gene Krupa Story 1959

Lowe, Alex Peter's Friends 1992; Haunted 1995

Lowe, Arthur One Way Out 1955; This Sporting Life 1963; if... 1968; The Bed Sitting Room 1969; A Hole Lot of Trouble 1969; The Rise and Rise of Michael Rimmer 1970; Dad's Army 1971; Adolf Hitler – My Part in His Downfall 1972; The Ruling Class 1972; No Sex Please, We're British 1973; O Lucky Man! 1973; Theatre of Blood 1973; Man about the House 1974; The Lady Vanishes 1979

Lowe, Chad There Must Be a Pony 1986; Apprentice to Murder 1988; So Proudly We Hail 1990; Captive 1991; Highway to Hell 1992; Fighting for My Daughter 1995; Dare to Love 1995

Lowe, Edmund What Price Glory 1926; The Cock-Eyed World 1929; In Old Arizona 1929; Born Reckless 1930; Dinner at Eight 1933; Espionage 1937; Every Day's a Holiday 1937; The Squeaker 1937; I Love You Again 1940; Call Out the Marines 1942; Dillinger 1945; Good Sam 1948; The Wings of Eagles 1957; Heller in Pink Tights 1960

Lowe, Rob Class 1983; The Outsiders 1983; The Hotel New Hampshire 1984; Oxford Blues 1984; St Elmo's Fire 1985; About Last Night... 1986; Youngblood 1986; Square Dance 1987; Illegally Yours 1988; Masquerade 1988; Bad Influence 1990; The Finest Hour 1991; The Dark Backward 1991; Wayne's World 1992; First Degree 1995; Frank and Jesse 1995; Tommy Boy 1995; Contact 1997; Hostile Intent 1997; Living in Peril 1997; For Hire 1997; Midnight Man 1998; Outrage 1998; Austin Powers: The Spy Who Shagged Me 1999

Lowell, Carey Dangerously Close 1986; Down Twisted 1987; Licence to Kill 1989; The Guardian 1990; Road to Ruin 1992; Fierce Creatures 1997

Lowell, Helen Isn't Life Wonderful 1924; Devil Dogs of the Air 1935; Strike Me Pink 1936

Lowensohn, Elina Simple Men 1992; Amateur 1994; My Antonia 1995; Nadja 1995; In the Presence of Mine Enemies 1996;

I'm Not Rappaport 1996; Six Ways to Sunday 1997; The Wisdom of Crocodiles 1998
Lowery, Andrew A Son's Promise 1990; School Ties 1992; My Boyfriend's Back 1993; Color of Night 1994; The Conspiracy of Fear 1996
Lowery, Robert Four Sons 1940; Jalopy 1953; The Parson and the Outlaw 1957; The Rise and Fall of Legs Diamond 1960
Löwitsch, Klaus aka **Lowitsch, Klaus,** aka **Loewitsch, Klaus** The Odessa File 1974; Cross of Iron 1977; Breakthrough 1978; Despair 1978; The Marriage of Maria Braun 1978; Gotcha! 1985
Lowry, Lynn The Crazies 1973; Shivers 1975; Fighting Mad 1976
Lowry, Morton A Yank in the RAF 1941; Pursuit to Algiers 1945; The Verdict 1946
Lowther, T J A Home of Our Own 1993; A Perfect World 1993; One Christmas 1994
Loy, Myrna Don Juan 1926; So This Is Paris 1926; The Jazz Singer 1927; Noah's Ark 1928; The Black Watch 1929; The Desert Song 1929; The Show of Shows 1929; The Devil to Pay 1930; Renegades 1930; Arrowsmith 1931; A Connecticut Yankee 1931; Body and Soul 1931; Consolation Marriage 1931; The Animal Kingdom 1932; Emma 1932; Love Me Tonight 1932; The Mask of Fu Manchu 1932; The Wet Parade 1932; Night Flight 1933; Penthouse 1933; The Prizefighter and the Lady 1933; When Ladies Meet 1933; The Barbarian 1933; Topaze 1933; Broadway Bill 1934; Manhattan Melodrama 1934; Men in White 1934; Stamboul Quest 1934; The Thin Man 1934; Evelyn Prentice 1934; Whipsaw 1935; Wings in the Dark 1935; After the Thin Man 1936; The Great Ziegfeld 1936; Libeled Lady 1936; Wife vs Secretary 1936; Double Wedding 1937; Man-Proof 1937; Parnell 1937; Test Pilot 1938; Too Hot to Handle 1938; Another Thin Man 1939; The Rains Came 1939; I Love You Again 1940; Third Finger, Left Hand 1940; Love Crazy 1941; Shadow of the Thin Man 1941; The Thin Man Goes Home 1944; The Best Years of Our Lives 1946; So Goes My Love 1946; Bachelor Knight 1947; The Senator Was Indiscreet 1947; Mr Blandings Builds His Dream House 1948; The Red Pony 1949; Cheaper by the Dozen 1950; Belles on Their Toes 1952; The Ambassador's Daughter 1956; Lonelyhearts 1958; From the Terrace 1960; Midnight Lace 1960; The April Fools 1969; Do Not Fold, Spindle or Mutilate 1971; Airport 1975 1974; The End 1978; Just Tell Me What You Want 1980
Lozano, Margarita Viridiana 1961; A Fistful of Dollars 1964; The Night of San Lorenzo 1981; Kaos 1984; Manon des Sources 1986; Night Sun 1990
Lu Liping The Blue Kite 1992; Love Will Tear Us Apart 1999
Lu, Lisa The Mountain Road 1960; Demon Seed 1977; Don't Cry, It's Only Thunder 1982; The Joy Luck Club 1993
Lualdi, Antonella Le Rouge et le Noir 1954; Young Husbands 1958; Web of Passion 1959; The Mongols 1961; Let's Talk About Women 1964; Ragan 1967; Vincent, François, Paul and the Others 1974
Luca, Loos The Girl with Red Hair 1981; Abel 1986
Lucas, Josh True Blue 1996; American Psycho 2000
Lucas, Laurent Rien sur Robert 1998; La Nouvelle Eve 1999; Pola X 1999
Lucas, Lisa An Unmarried Woman 1978; Hadley's Rebellion 1984; Heart and Souls 1993
Lucas, Wilfred Pardon Us 1931; Criminal Lawyer 1937
Lucas, William X the Unknown 1956; Crack in the Mirror 1960; Sons and Lovers 1960; Payroll 1961; The Shadow of the Cat 1961; The Break 1962; Calculated Risk 1963; The Marked One 1963; Night of the Big Heat 1967
Lucci, Susan Mafia Princess 1986; The Bride in Black 1990; The Woman Who Sinned 1991; Double Edge 1992; French Silk 1993; Ebbie 1995; Seduced and Betrayed 1995
Luce, Angela The Decameron 1970; L'Amore Molesto 1995
Luce, Claire Up the River 1930; Lazybones 1935; Vintage Wine 1935; Over She Goes 1937
Lucero, Enrique Villa! 1958; Macario 1960; Tarzan and the Valley of Gold 1966; Shark! 1969; Two Mules for Sister Sara 1970; The Return of a Man Called Horse 1976; Green Ice 1981
Luchini, Fabrice Contes Immoraux 1974; Perceval le Gallois 1978; Full Moon in Paris 1984; Hôtel du Paradis 1986; Uranus 1990; Le Colonel Chabert 1994; Beaumarchais l'Insolent 1996; Men, Women: a User's Manual 1996; Le Bossu 1997; Rien sur Robert 1998
Luckham, Cyril Stranger from Venus 1954; The Naked Runner 1967; Providence 1977
Luckinbill, Laurence The Boys in the Band 1970; Such Good Friends 1971; Corky 1972; Face of a Stranger 1978; The Promise 1979; Not for Publication 1984; Cocktail 1988; To Heal a Nation 1988; Messenger of Death 1988; Star Trek V: the Final Frontier 1989
Lucking, William aka **Lucking, Bill** The Magnificent Seven Ride! 1972; Oklahoma Crude 1973; Doc Savage: the Man of Bronze 1975; The Return of a Man Called Horse 1976; Birch Interval 1976; That Secret Sunday 1986; Ladykillers 1988; Naked Lie 1989; Sparks: the Price of Passion 1990; Rescue Me 1991; The River Wild 1994
Luddy, Barbara Lady and the Tramp 1955; Sleeping Beauty 1959
Ludlow, Patrick Evergreen 1934; Gangway 1937
Ludwig, Pamela Over the Edge 1979; Death of an Angel 1985; Race for Glory 1989
Ludwig, Salem Never Love a Stranger 1958; America, America 1963
Luft, Lorna Grease 2 1982; Fear Stalk 1989; 54 1998
Lugosi, Bela Renegades 1930; Dracula 1931; Island of Lost Souls 1932; Murders in the Rue Morgue 1932; White Zombie 1932; The Death Kiss 1933; International House 1933; The Devil's in Love 1933; The Black Cat 1934; Mark of the Vampire 1935; The Raven 1935; The Invisible Ray 1936; Dark Eyes of London 1939; Ninotchka 1939; Son of Frankenstein 1939; The Saint's Double Trouble 1940; You'll Find Out 1940; Devil Bat 1940; Spooks Run Wild 1941; The Wolf Man 1941; Invisible Ghost 1941; The Ghost of Frankenstein 1942; Frankenstein Meets the Wolf Man 1943; Ghosts in the Night 1943; The Return of the Vampire 1943; Voodoo Man 1944; The Body Snatcher 1945; Abbott and Costello Meet Frankenstein 1948; Glen or Glenda 1953; Bride of the Monster 1955; The Black Sleep 1956; Plan 9 from Outer Space 1959
Luguet, Andre The Mad Genius 1931; Jewel Robbery 1932; The Man Who Played God 1932; Madame du Barry 1954
Luisi, James Stunts 1977; Feds 1988
Lukas, Paul The Shopworn Angel 1928; Anybody's Woman 1930; The Devil's Holiday 1930; City Streets 1931; Rockabye 1932; No One Man 1932; Little Women 1933; The Fountain 1934; By Candlelight 1934; The Casino Murder Case 1935; I Found Stella Parish 1935; The Three Musketeers 1935; Dodsworth 1936; Ladies in Love 1936; Dinner at the Ritz 1937; Espionage 1937; The Lady Vanishes 1938; Confessions of a Nazi Spy 1939; A Window in London 1939; The Ghost Breakers 1940; Strange Cargo 1940; Hostages 1943; Watch on the Rhine 1943; Address Unknown 1944; Experiment Perilous 1944; Uncertain Glory 1944; Deadline at Dawn 1946; Temptation 1946; Berlin Express 1948; Kim 1950; 20,000 Leagues under the Sea 1954; The Roots of Heaven 1958; Scent of Mystery 1960; Tender Is the Night 1961; Fun in Acapulco 1963; Lord Jim 1965; Sol Madrid 1968
Luke, Benny La Cage aux Folles 1978; La Cage aux Folles II 1980; La Cage aux Folles III: "Elles" se Marient 1985
Luke, Jorge The Revengers 1972; Ulzana's Raid 1972; The Return of a Man Called Horse 1976; Eagle's Wing 1978
Luke, Keye Charlie Chan in Paris 1935; Charlie Chan in Shanghai 1935; Charlie Chan at the Opera 1936; Charlie Chan at the Olympics 1937; Charlie Chan on Broadway 1937; The Good Earth 1937; International Settlement 1938; Mr Moto's Gamble 1938; Dr Gillespie's New Assistant 1942; Dr Gillespie's Criminal Case 1943; Salute to the Marines 1943; Andy Hardy's Blonde Trouble 1944; Three Men in White 1944; First Yank into Tokyo 1945; Sleep, My Love 1948; Hell's Half Acre 1954; Escape of the Amethyst 1956; Kung Fu 1972; The Amsterdam Kill 1978; Just You and Me, Kid 1979; Gremlins 1984; Dead Heat 1988
Lukschy, Wolfgang A Fistful of Dollars 1964; Inside Out 1975
Lulli, Folco Lights of Variety 1950; The Wages of Fear 1953; The Sign of the Gladiator 1958; The Great War 1959
Lulli, Piero Hero of Babylon 1963; Revolt of the Preatorians 1965; Django Kill 1967; My Name Is Nobody 1973
Lulu To Sir, with Love 1967; Whatever Happened to Harold Smith? 1999
Lumbly, Carl The Bedroom Window 1987; Everybody's All-American 1988; Judgment in Berlin 1988; Pacific Heights 1990; To Sleep with Anger 1990; Brother Future 1991; South Central 1992; Cagney & Lacey: the Return 1994; Out of Darkness 1994; Buffalo Soldiers 1997
Lumet, Baruch The Killer Shrews 1959; The Pawnbroker 1965
Lumley, Joanna Don't Just Lie There, Say Something! 1973; The Satanic Rites of Dracula 1973; Trail of the Pink Panther 1982; The Curse of the Pink Panther 1983; Shirley Valentine 1989; A Ghost in Monte Carlo 1990; Cold Comfort Farm 1995; Innocent Lies 1995; James and the Giant Peach 1996; Prince Valiant 1997; Parting Shots 1998; The Tale of Sweeney Todd 1998; Mad Cows 1999; Maybe Baby 1999
Luna, Barbara The Devil at Four o'Clock 1961; Mail Order Bride 1964; Get off My Back 1965; Che! 1969; The Concrete Jungle 1982
Lund, Art The Molly Maguires 1970; The Last American Hero 1973; Black Caesar 1973
Lund, Deanna Hardly Working 1981; Elves 1989
Lund, Jana Don't Knock the Rock 1956; Frankenstein – 1970 1958
Lund, John To Each His Own 1946; The Perils of Pauline 1947; A Foreign Affair 1948; Miss Tatlock's Millions 1948; Night Has a Thousand Eyes 1948; Bride of Vengeance 1949; My Friend Irma 1949; No Man of Her Own 1950; My Friend Irma Goes West 1950; The Mating Season 1951; Darling, How Could You! 1951; The Battle at Apache Pass 1952; Bronco Buster 1952; Latin Lovers 1953; Chief Crazy Horse 1955; White Feather 1955; Five Guns West 1955; Dakota Incident 1956; High Society 1956; The Wackiest Ship in the Army 1961; If a Man Answers 1962
Lund, Lucille The Black Cat 1934; Vengeance 1937
Lundgren, Dolph Rocky IV 1985; Masters of the Universe 1987; Dark Angel 1989; The Punisher 1989; Red Scorpion 1989; Showdown in Little Tokyo 1991; Cover-Up 1991; Universal Soldier 1992; Army of One 1993; The Shooter 1994; Pentathlon 1994; Johnny Mnemonic 1995; Men of War 1995; Silent Trigger 1996; The Peacekeeper 1997; Blackjack 1998; The Minion 1998; Sweepers 1999; Bridge of Dragons 1999
Lundigan, William Wives under Suspicion 1938; The Case of the Black Parrot 1941; Andy Hardy's Double Life 1942; The Courtship of Andy Hardy 1942; Apache Trail 1942; Dishonored Lady 1947; The Fabulous Dorseys 1947; Mystery in Mexico 1948; Pinky 1949; The House on Telegraph Hill 1951; I'd Climb the Highest Mountain 1951; Love Nest 1951; Inferno 1953; Serpent of the Nile 1953
Lundy, Jessica Vampire's Kiss 1988; Madhouse 1990; The Stupids 1995; Rocketman 1997
Lung Sihung Pushing Hands 1991; The Wedding Banquet 1993; Eat Drink Man Woman 1994
Lunge, Romilly Königsmark 1935; His Lordship 1936
Lunghi, Cherie Excalibur 1981; Oliver Twist 1982; The Sign of Four 1983; Parker 1984; King David 1985; Letters to an Unknown Lover 1985; The Mission 1986; To Kill a Priest 1988; Jack & Sarah 1995; The Canterville Ghost 1996; Burn Hollywood Burn 1997
Lunt, Alfred Sally of the Sawdust 1925; The Guardsman 1931
Lupi, Roldano Crossed Swords 1954; The Mongols 1961
Lupien, Tabitha Rent-a-Kid 1992; Look Who's Talking Now! 1993
Lupino, Ida The Ghost Camera 1933; Peter Ibbetson 1935; Anything Goes 1936; The Gay Desperado 1936; One Rainy Afternoon 1936; Artists and Models 1937; Sea Devils 1937; The Adventures of Sherlock Holmes 1939; The Light That Failed 1939; The Lone Wolf Spy Hunt 1939; They Drive by Night 1940; High Sierra 1941; Ladies in Retirement 1941; Out of the Fog 1941; The Sea Wolf 1941; The Hard Way 1942; Life Begins at 8.30 1942; Moontide 1942; Forever and a Day 1943; Devotion 1946; The Man I Love 1946; Deep Valley 1947; Escape Me Never 1947; Road House 1948; On Dangerous Ground 1951; Beware, My Lovely 1952; The Bigamist 1953; Jennifer 1953; Private Hell 36 1954; The Big Knife 1955; Women's Prison 1955; While the City Sleeps 1956; Junior Bonner 1972; Deadhead Miles 1972; The Devil's Rain 1975; The Food of the Gods 1975
Lupino, Stanley Happy 1933; Cheer Up! 1936; Over She Goes 1937; Hold My Hand 1938
Lupo, Alberto The Bacchantes 1960; The Giant of Marathon 1960; The Agony and the Ecstasy 1965
LuPone, Patti Death Vengeance 1982; Witness 1985; Wise Guys 1986; Driving Miss Daisy 1989; Family Prayers 1991; The Water Engine 1992; Her Last Chance 1996; The 24 Hour Woman 1999
Luppi, Federico La Amiga 1988; Cronos 1992; A Place in the World 1992; Men with Guns 1997
Lupton, John Man with the Gun 1955; Drango 1957; The Man in the Net 1959; The Rebel Set 1959; Red River 1988
Lurie, John Permanent Vacation 1982; Stranger than Paradise 1984; Down by Law 1986
Lutes, Eric Distant Justice 1992; Bram Stoker's Legend of the Mummy 1998; Legion of Fire: Killer Ants! 1998
Luttazzi, Lelio L'Avventura 1959; Snow Job 1972
Lutter, Alfred aka **Lutter, Alfred W** Alice Doesn't Live Here Anymore 1974; The Bad News Bears 1976
Lutz, Adelle Beyond Rangoon 1995; Dead Funny 1995
Lycan, Georges Gold for the Caesars 1964; Triple Cross 1966
Lydon, Gary Ailsa 1994; Nothing Personal 1995
Lydon, James aka **Lydon, Jimmy** Back Door to Heaven 1939; Tom Brown's Schooldays 1940; Cynthia 1947; Life with Father 1947; September Affair 1950; When Willie Comes Marching Home 1950; The Last Time I Saw Archie 1961
Lydon, John aka **Rotten, Johnny** The Great Rock 'n' Roll Swindle 1979; Order of Death 1983
Lye, Reg Smiley Gets a Gun 1959; The Amorous Prawn 1962; Sunday Too Far Away 1974; Tarka the Otter 1978; The Killing of Angel Street 1981
Lyman, Dorothy 300 Year Weekend 1971; Ruby in Paradise 1993

McCarthy, Neil *Offbeat* 1960; *Sands of the Desert* 1960; *Zulu* 1964; *Steptoe and Son Ride Again* 1973
McCarthy, Nobu aka **McCarthy, Nobu Atsumi** *The Geisha Boy* 1958; *Five Gates to Hell* 1959; *Walk like a Dragon* 1960; *Wake Me when It's Over* 1960; *Two Loves* 1961; *The Karate Kid Part II* 1986; *Pacific Heights* 1990
McCarthy, Sheila *I've Heard the Mermaids Singing* 1987; *Beautiful Dreamers* 1990; *White Room* 1990; *Paradise* 1991; *Stepping Out* 1991; *George's Island* 1991; *The Awakening* 1995; *Legacy of Evil* 1995
McCarthy, Thomas *Anne Tyler's Saint Maybe* 1998; *In My Sister's Shadow* 1999
McCartney, Paul *A Hard Day's Night* 1964; *Help!* 1965; *Breaking Glass* 1980; *Give My Regards to Broad Street* 1984; *Eat the Rich* 1987
McCarty, Chris *Over the Top* 1987; *The Shadow Men* 1997
McCarty, Mary *The French Line* 1954; *Somebody Killed Her Husband* 1978
McCary, Rod *No Drums, No Bugles* 1971; *Night of the Demons 2* 1994
McCay, Peggy *Second Thoughts* 1982; *Wait till Your Mother Gets Home!* 1983
Macchio, Ralph *Up the Academy* 1980; *The Outsiders* 1983; *The Karate Kid* 1984; *Teachers* 1984; *Crossroads* 1986; *The Karate Kid Part II* 1986; *Distant Thunder* 1988; *The Karate Kid III* 1989; *Prisoner of War* 1990; *Too Much Sun* 1990; *My Cousin Vinny* 1992; *Naked in New York* 1994; *The Secret of NIMH II: Timmy to the Rescue* 1998
Maccione, Aldo *The Loves and Times of Scaramouche* 1976; *The Chambermaid on the Titanic* 1997
McClain, Saundra *Criminal Justice* 1990; *Free of Eden* 1999
McClanahan, Rue *The People Next Door* 1970; *They Might Be Giants* 1971; *Take My Daughters, Please* 1988; *The Man in the Brown Suit* 1989; *Children of the Bride* 1990; *Modern Love* 1990; *To My Daughter* 1990; *Mother of the Bride* 1993; *A Burning Passion: the Margaret Mitchell Story* 1994; *Dear God* 1996; *This World, Then the Fireworks* 1996; *A Saintly Switch* 1999
McCleery, Gary *Hard Choices* 1984; *Matewan* 1987
McClements, Catherine *Just Us* 1986; *The Right Hand Man* 1986; *Struck by Lightning* 1990; *Redheads* 1992
McClory, Sean *The Daughter of Rosie O'Grady* 1950; *Anne of the Indies* 1951; *Lorna Doone* 1951
McClory, Sean *The Gnome-Mobile* 1967; *My Chauffeur* 1986
McCloskey, Leigh aka **McCloskey, Leigh J** *Dawn: Portrait of a Teenage Runaway* 1976; *Inferno* 1980; *Fraternity Vacation* 1985; *Cameron's Closet* 1988; *Trouble Shooters: Trapped beneath the Earth* 1993; *Accidental Meeting* 1994
McClure, Doug *Because They're Young* 1960; *Shenandoah* 1965; *Beau Geste* 1966; *The King's Pirate* 1967; *Nobody's Perfect* 1968; *Terror in the Sky* 1971; *The Judge and Jake Wyler* 1972; *Death Race* 1973; *The Land That Time Forgot* 1974; *What Changed Charley Farthing?* 1975; *At the Earth's Core* 1976; *The People That Time Forgot* 1977; *Warlords of Atlantis* 1978; *Firebird 2015 AD* 1980; *Monster* 1980; *The House Where Evil Dwells* 1982; *52 Pick-Up* 1986; *Tapeheads* 1988; *Battling for Baby* 1992
McClure, Greg *The Great John L* 1945; *Lulu Belle* 1948
McClure, Marc *I Wanna Hold Your Hand* 1978; *Back to the Future* 1985; *Perfect Match* 1987; *Superman IV: the Quest for Peace* 1987; *After Midnight* 1989; *Little White Lies* 1989; *Grim Prairie Tales* 1990; *The Vagrant* 1992
McClure, Molly *Daddy's Dyin'... Who's Got the Will?* 1990; *Pure Country* 1992; *The Patriot* 1998
McClurg, Edie *Ferris Bueller's Day Off* 1986; *Driving Academy* 1988; *Elvira, Mistress of the Dark* 1988; *The Little Mermaid* 1989; *Menu for Murder* 1990; *A River Runs through It* 1992; *Airborne* 1993; *Circuit Breaker* 1996
McCole, Stephen *Orphans* 1998; *The Acid House* 1998; *Postmortem* 1999
McComb, Heather *New York Stories* 1989; *Stay Tuned* 1992; *Generation X* 1996; *No One Would Tell* 1996
McConaughey, Matthew *Dazed and Confused* 1993; *Angels* 1994; *Boys on the Side* 1995; *Lone Star* 1995; *The Return of the Texas Chainsaw Massacre* 1995; *Scorpion Spring* 1995; *Glory Daze* 1995; *Larger than Life* 1996; *A Time to Kill* 1996; *Amistad* 1997; *Contact* 1997; *The Newton Boys* 1998; *EDtv* 1999; *U-571* 2000
McCord, Kent *Beg, Borrow or Steal* 1973; *Return of the Living Dead III* 1993; *Accidental Meeting* 1994
MacCorkindale, Simon *Death on the Nile* 1978; *The Riddle of the Sands* 1978; *The Quatermass Conclusion* 1979; *Caboblanco* 1980; *The Sword and the Sorcerer* 1982; *Jaws III* 1983; *Robbers of the Sacred Mountain* 1983; *At the Midnight Hour* 1995; *Family of Cops* 1995; *Danielle Steel's No Greater Love* 1996; *While My Pretty One Sleeps* 1997
McCormack, Catherine *Loaded* 1994; *Braveheart* 1995; *North Star* 1996; *The Land Girls* 1997; *Dancing at Lughnasa* 1998; *The Honest Courtesan* 1998; *This Year's Love* 1999
McCormack, Eric *Double, Double Toil and Trouble* 1993; *The Man Who Wouldn't Die* 1995; *Night Visitors* 1996; *Exception to the Rule* 1996; *Holy Man* 1998
McCormack, Mary *The Alarmist* 1997; *Private Parts* 1997; *The Big Tease* 1999; *Mystery, Alaska* 1999
McCormack, Patty *The Bad Seed* 1956; *The Day They Gave Babies Away* 1957; *The Snow Queen* 1959; *The Adventures of Huckleberry Finn* 1960; *The Explosive Generation* 1961; *Saturday the 14th Strikes Back* 1988
McCormick, F J *The Plough and the Stars* 1936; *Odd Man Out* 1946; *Hungry Hill* 1947
McCormick, Gilmer *Godspell* 1973; *Silent Night, Deadly Night* 1984
McCormick, Maureen *Pony Express Rider* 1976; *Moonshine County Express* 1977; *Take Down* 1978; *The Idolmaker* 1980; *A Very Brady Christmas* 1988; *Panic in the Skies!* 1996
McCormick, Myron *China Girl* 1942; *Jigsaw* 1949; *Jolson Sings Again* 1949; *Not as a Stranger* 1955; *Three for the Show* 1955; *No Time for Sergeants* 1958; *The Man Who Understood Women* 1959; *The Hustler* 1961
McCormick, Pat *Smokey and the Bandit* 1977; *Smokey and the Bandit III* 1983; *Broadway Bound* 1991
McCourt, Emer *London Kills Me* 1991; *Riff-Raff* 1991; *Boston Kickout* 1995
McCourt, Malachy *Kick!* 1979; *Q – the Winged Serpent* 1982; *She's the One* 1996
McCowen, Alec *The Cruel Sea* 1953; *The Deep Blue Sea* 1955; *The Long Arm* 1956; *Town on Trial* 1956; *The Good Companions* 1956; *The One That Got Away* 1957; *Time without Pity* 1957; *The Silent Enemy* 1958; *A Midsummer Night's Dream* 1961; *The Witches* 1966; *Master of the Islands* 1970; *Frenzy* 1972; *Travels with My Aunt* 1972; *Stevie* 1978; *Hanover Street* 1979; *Never Say Never Again* 1983; *Forever Young* 1984; *The Assam Garden* 1985; *Cry Freedom* 1987; *Personal Services* 1987; *Henry V* 1989; *The Age of Innocence* 1993
McCoy, Matt *Police Academy 5: Assignment Miami Beach* 1988; *DeepStar Six* 1989; *Police Academy 6: City under Siege* 1989; *Wind Dancer* 1991; *The Hand That Rocks the Cradle* 1992; *Rent-a-Kid* 1992; *Lightning in a Bottle* 1992; *The Cool Surface* 1993; *Dead On* 1993; *Samurai Cowboy* 1993; *Snapdragon* 1993; *White Wolves* 1993; *Hard Drive* 1994; *Memory Run* 1995; *Fast Money* 1995; *Desperate Measures* 1995; *LA Confidential* 1997; *Nightmare in Big Sky Country* 1998; *Dangerous Waters* 1999
McCracken, Jeff *One Man Jury* 1978; *Running Brave* 1983; *Waiting for the Light* 1989
McCrane, Paul *The Hotel New Hampshire* 1984; *Purple Hearts* 1984; *Money, Power, Murder* 1989; *The Portrait* 1993
McCrea, Jody *Young Guns of Texas* 1962; *The Broken Land* 1962; *Beach Party* 1963; *Muscle Beach Party* 1964; *Beach Blanket Bingo* 1965; *The Glory Stompers* 1967
McCrea, Joel *Dynamite* 1929; *Girls about Town* 1931; *Kept Husbands* 1931; *Bird of Paradise* 1932; *The Hounds of Zaroff* 1932; *The Lost Squadron* 1932; *Rockabye* 1932; *The Silver Cord* 1933; *Gambling Lady* 1934; *The Richest Girl in the World* 1934; *Barbary Coast* 1935; *Our Little Girl* 1935; *Splendor* 1935; *Private Worlds* 1935; *Banjo on My Knee* 1936; *Come and Get It* 1936; *These Three* 1936; *Dead End* 1937; *Internes Can't Take Money* 1937; *Woman Chases Man* 1937; *Wells Fargo* 1937; *They Shall Have Music* 1939; *Union Pacific* 1939; *Foreign Correspondent* 1940; *Primrose Path* 1940; *Sullivan's Travels* 1941; *The Great Man's Lady* 1942; *The Palm Beach Story* 1942; *The More the Merrier* 1943; *Buffalo Bill* 1944; *The Great Moment* 1944; *The Unseen* 1945; *The Virginian* 1946; *Ramrod* 1947; *They Passed This Way* 1948; *Colorado Territory* 1949; *South of St Louis* 1949; *The Outriders* 1950; *Saddle Tramp* 1950; *Cattle Drive* 1951; *Rough Shoot* 1952; *The San Francisco Story* 1952; *The Lone Hand* 1953; *Black Horse Canyon* 1954; *Wichita* 1955; *Stranger on Horseback* 1955; *The Oklahoman* 1957; *The Tall Stranger* 1957; *Trooper Hook* 1957; *Gunsight Ridge* 1957; *Cattle Empire* 1958; *Ride the High Country* 1962; *The Great American Cowboy* 1973; *Mustang Country* 1976
McCrory, Helen *Dad Savage* 1997; *The James Gang* 1997
McCulloch, Bruce *Kids in the Hall: Brain Candy* 1996; *Dog Park* 1998; *Dick* 1999
McCulloch, Ian *The Ghoul* 1975; *Zombie Flesh Eaters* 1979
McCulloch, Kyle *True Confections* 1990; *Careful* 1992
McCullough, Julie *Big Bad Mama II* 1987; *Round Trip to Heaven* 1992
McCullough, Rohan *Strapless* 1988; *War Requiem* 1988
McCullough, Suli *Terminal Velocity* 1994; *Don't Be a Menace to South Central while Drinking Your Juice in the Hood* 1996
McCurley, Mathew *North* 1994; *The Computer Wore Tennis Shoes* 1995; *The Secret Agent Club* 1995
McCurry, John *The Last Mile* 1959; *Fritz the Cat* 1972; *Deathmask* 1984
McCutcheon, Bill *Family Business* 1989; *Aunt Julia and the Scriptwriter* 1990; *Mr Destiny* 1990
McDaniel, Hattie aka **McDaniels, Hattie** *Hello Sister!* 1933; *Judge Priest* 1934; *Alice Adams* 1935; *The Little Colonel* 1935; *The Bride Walks Out* 1936; *Nothing Sacred* 1937; *True Confession* 1937; *The Shining Hour* 1938; *The Shopworn Angel* 1938; *Gone with the Wind* 1939; *Zenobia* 1939; *Maryland* 1940; *The Great Lie* 1941; *Affectionately Yours* 1941; *George Washington Slept Here* 1942; *In This Our Life* 1942; *The Male Animal* 1942; *Johnny Come Lately* 1943; *Since You Went Away* 1944; *Margie* 1946; *Song of the South* 1946; *Never Say Goodbye* 1946
McDaniel, James *Murder Times Seven* 1990; *Strictly Business* 1991; *Scam* 1993; *The Road to Galveston* 1996; *Silencing Mary* 1998
McDermott, Dylan *Hamburger Hill* 1987; *The Blue Iguana* 1988; *The Neon Empire* 1989; *Steel Magnolias* 1989; *Twister* 1989; *Hardware* 1990; *Into the Badlands* 1991; *Where Sleeping Dogs Lie* 1991; *Jersey Girl* 1992; *In the Line of Fire* 1993; *The Cowboy Way* 1994; *Miracle on 34th Street* 1994; *Destiny Turns on the Radio* 1995; *Home for the Holidays* 1995; *'Til There Was You* 1997; *Three to Tango* 1999
McDermott, Hugh *Where's That Fire?* 1939; *Neutral Port* 1940; *Pimpernel Smith* 1941; *The Seventh Veil* 1945; *The Huggetts Abroad* 1949; *Trent's Last Case* 1952; *Malaga* 1954; *The Man Who Wouldn't Talk* 1957; *You Pay Your Money* 1957; *Guns in the Heather* 1969; *The Adding Machine* 1969
MacDermott, John *My Hustler* 1965; *Vinyl* 1965
McDermott, Keith *Tourist Trap* 1979; *Without a Trace* 1983
MacDermott, Marc *The Sea Hawk* 1924; *He Who Gets Slapped* 1924; *The Temptress* 1926; *The Lucky Lady* 1926
McDevitt, Ruth *The Birds* 1963; *Love Is a Ball* 1963; *The Shakiest Gun in the West* 1967
McDiarmid, Ian *Return of the Jedi* 1983; *Dirty Rotten Scoundrels* 1988; *Chernobyl: the Final Warning* 1991; *Annie: a Royal Adventure* 1995; *Restoration* 1995; *Star Wars Episode I: the Phantom Menace* 1999
MacDonald, Aimi *Take a Girl Like You* 1970; *Keep It Up Downstairs* 1976
MacDonald, Bill *Closer and Closer* 1996; *Dead Husbands* 1998
McDonald, Christopher *Grease 2* 1982; *The Black Room* 1983; *Breakdance* 1984; *Chattanooga Choo Choo* 1984; *The Boys Next Door* 1985; *Chances Are* 1989; *Driving Me Crazy* 1991; *Thelma & Louise* 1991; *Conflict of Interest* 1992; *Benefit of the Doubt* 1993; *Fatal Instinct* 1993; *Monkey Trouble* 1994; *Terminal Velocity* 1994; *Roadflower* 1994; *Best of the Best 3: No Turning Back* 1995; *Fair Game* 1995; *Happy Gilmore* 1996; *Unforgettable* 1996; *The Rich Man's Wife* 1996; *The Eighteenth Angel* 1997; *Flubber* 1997; *Lawn Dogs* 1997; *A Smile like Yours* 1997; *Leave It to Beaver* 1997; *Into Thin Air: Death on Everest* 1997; *Dirty Work* 1998; *The Iron Giant* 1999; *SLC Punk!* 1999; *The Skulls* 2000
MacDonald, Donald *The Kentuckian* 1955; *The Brass Legend* 1956; *Constance* 1984
MacDonald, Edmund *The Gay Caballero* 1940; *Great Guns* 1941; *Flying Tigers* 1942; *Detour* 1945
McDonald, Francis *Battling Butler* 1926; *The Dragnet* 1928; *A Girl in Every Port* 1928; *Morocco* 1930
McDonald, Garry *The Pirate Movie* 1982; *Struck by Lightning* 1990
McDonald, Grace *Gung Ho!* 1943; *It Ain't Hay* 1943; *Follow the Boys* 1944
MacDonald, Ian *Ramrod* 1947; *Colt .45* 1950; *Comanche Territory* 1950; *Montana* 1950; *This Woman Is Dangerous* 1952; *Blowing Wild* 1953; *Apache* 1954
MacDonald, J Farrell *3 Bad Men* 1926; *Sunrise* 1927; *Abie's Irish Rose* 1928; *In Old Arizona* 1929; *Dangerous Female* 1931; *Sporting Blood* 1931; *The Painted Desert* 1931; *Other Men's Women* 1931; *Me and My Gal* 1932; *Vanishing Frontier* 1932; *The Thirteenth Guest* 1932; *Peg o' My Heart* 1933; *Stormy* 1935; *Star of Midnight* 1935; *Riffraff* 1936; *Slim* 1937; *White Banners* 1938; *Susannah of the Mounties* 1939; *Clancy Street Boys* 1943
MacDonald, Jeanette *The Love Parade* 1929; *Monte Carlo* 1930; *Love Me Tonight* 1932; *One Hour with You* 1932; *The Cat and the Fiddle* 1934; *The Merry Widow* 1934; *Naughty Marietta* 1935; *Rose Marie* 1936; *San Francisco* 1936; *The Firefly* 1937; *Maytime* 1937; *The Girl of the Golden West* 1938; *Sweethearts* 1938; *Broadway Serenade* 1939; *Bitter Sweet* 1940; *New Moon* 1940; *Smilin' Through* 1941; *I Married an Angel* 1942; *Follow the Boys* 1944
Macdonald, Kelly *Trainspotting* 1995; *Cousin Bette* 1997; *Stella Does Tricks* 1997
MacDonald, Kelly *The Loss of Sexual Innocence* 1999; *My Life So Far* 1999
McDonald, Mac *Back Home* 1990; *The Russia House* 1990
McDonald, Marie *Guest in the House* 1944; *Getting Gertie's Garter* 1945; *Living in a Big Way* 1947; *Tell It to the Judge* 1949; *The Geisha Boy* 1958

MacDonald, Norm *Billy Madison* 1995; *Dirty Work* 1998
McDonald, Peter *I Went Down* 1997; *Captain Jack* 1998; *Felicia's Journey* 1999; *Nora* 1999
McDonald, Ray *Babes on Broadway* 1941; *Life Begins for Andy Hardy* 1941; *Good News* 1947; *All Ashore* 1953
McDonnell, Mary *Courage* 1986; *Tiger Warsaw* 1988; *Dances with Wolves* 1990; *Grand Canyon* 1991; *Passion Fish* 1992; *Sneakers* 1992; *Arthur Miller's The American Clock* 1993; *Blue Chips* 1994; *Woman Undone* 1995; *Independence Day* 1996; *Evidence of Blood* 1998; *Behind the Mask* 1999; *Replacing Dad* 1999; *Mumford* 1999
McDonough, Mary Beth *Mother's Day on Waltons Mountain* 1982; *A Walton Thanksgiving Reunion* 1993; *A Walton Wedding* 1995; *A Walton Easter* 1997
McDonough, Neal *In the Line of Duty: Ambush in Waco* 1993; *White Dwarf* 1995; *One Man's Justice* 1996; *Grace & Glorie* 1998
McDormand, Frances *Blood Simple* 1983; *Vengeance: the Story of Tony Cimo* 1986; *Raising Arizona* 1987; *Mississippi Burning* 1988; *Chattahoochee* 1989; *Darkman* 1990; *Hidden Agenda* 1990; *The Butcher's Wife* 1991; *Crazy in Love* 1992; *Passed Away* 1992; *Short Cuts* 1993; *Beyond Rangoon* 1995; *Fargo* 1995; *Lone Star* 1995; *Palookaville* 1995; *The Good Old Boys* 1995; *Primal Fear* 1996; *Hidden in America* 1996; *Paradise Road* 1997; *Madeline* 1998; *Talk of Angels* 1998; *Johnny Skidmarks* 1998; *Wonder Boys* 2000
McDowall, Betty *Time Lock* 1957; *Jack the Ripper* 1958; *Spare the Rod* 1961; *Echo of Diana* 1963; *First Men in the Moon* 1964; *Ballad in Blue* 1966
McDowall, Roddy *Just William* 1939; *Confirm or Deny* 1941; *How Green Was My Valley* 1941; *Man Hunt* 1941; *The Pied Piper* 1942; *Son of Fury* 1942; *Lassie Come Home* 1943; *My Friend Flicka* 1943; *The Keys of the Kingdom* 1944; *The White Cliffs of Dover* 1944; *Molly and Me* 1945; *Thunderhead – Son of Flicka* 1945; *Holiday in Mexico* 1946; *Kidnapped* 1948; *Macbeth* 1948; *Midnight Lace* 1960; *The Subterraneans* 1960; *The Longest Day* 1962; *Cleopatra* 1963; *Shock Treatment* 1964; *The Greatest Story Ever Told* 1965; *Inside Daisy Clover* 1965; *That Darn Cat!* 1965; *The Third Day* 1965; *The Defector* 1966; *Lord Love a Duck* 1966; *It!* 1966; *The Adventures of Bullwhip Griffin* 1967; *5 Card Stud* 1968; *Planet of the Apes* 1968; *Hello Down There* 1969; *Angel, Angel Down We Go* 1969; *Night Gallery* 1969; *Midas Run* 1969; *Bedknobs and Broomsticks* 1971; *Escape from the Planet of the Apes* 1971; *A Taste of Evil* 1971; *Terror in the Sky* 1971; *What's a Nice Girl like You...?* 1971; *Pretty Maids All in a Row* 1971; *Conquest of the Planet of the Apes* 1972; *The Life and Times of Judge Roy Bean* 1972; *The Poseidon Adventure* 1972; *Battle for the Planet of the Apes* 1973; *The Legend of Hell House* 1973; *Arnold* 1973; *Dirty Mary Crazy Larry* 1974; *Funny Lady* 1975; *Flood!* 1976; *Sixth and Main* 1977; *The Cat from Outer Space* 1978; *The Thief of Baghdad* 1978; *Laserblast* 1978; *Scavenger Hunt* 1979; *The Memory of Eva Ryker* 1980; *Charlie Chan and the Curse of the Dragon Queen* 1981; *Class of 1984* 1982; *Evil under the Sun* 1982; *Fright Night* 1985; *GoBots: Battle of the Rocklords* 1986; *Dead of Winter* 1987; *Overboard* 1987; *Fright Night Part 2* 1988; *Cutting Class* 1989; *Earth Angel* 1991; *Double Trouble* 1992; *Heads* 1994; *The Alien Within* 1995; *Last Summer in the Hamptons* 1995; *Dead Man's Island* 1996; *It's My Party* 1996; *Something to Believe In* 1997; *The Second Jungle Book* 1997; *A Bug's Life* 1998
MacDowell, Andie *Greystoke: the Legend of Tarzan, Lord of the Apes* 1984; *St Elmo's Fire* 1985; *sex, lies, and videotape* 1989; *Green Card* 1990; *Hudson Hawk* 1991; *The Object of Beauty* 1991; *Women and Men – 2* 1991; *Ruby Cairo* 1992; *Groundhog Day* 1993; *Short Cuts* 1993; *Bad Girls* 1994; *Four Weddings and a Funeral* 1994; *Unstrung Heroes* 1995; *Michael* 1996; *Multiplicity* 1996; *The End of Violence* 1997; *Just the Ticket* 1998; *Muppets from Space* 1999; *The Muse* 1999
McDowell, Claire *The Mark of Zorro* 1920; *Ben-Hur: a Tale of Christ* 1925; *The Big Parade* 1925; *The Tower of Lies* 1925; *An American Tragedy* 1931; *It Happened One Night* 1934
McDowell, Malcolm *Poor Cow* 1967; *if....* 1968; *Figures in a Landscape* 1970; *The Raging Moon* 1970; *A Clockwork Orange* 1971; *O Lucky Man!* 1973; *Royal Flash* 1975; *Aces High* 1976; *Voyage of the Damned* 1976; *The Passage* 1978; *Caligula* 1979; *Time after Time* 1979; *Britannia Hospital* 1982; *Cat People* 1982; *Merlin and the Sword* 1982; *The Compleat Beatles* 1982; *Blue Thunder* 1983; *Cross Creek* 1983; *Get Crazy* 1983; *The Caller* 1987; *Buy & Cell* 1988; *Sunset* 1988; *Il Maestro* 1989; *Class of 1999* 1990; *Happily Ever After* 1990; *Out of Darkness* 1990; *Moon 44* 1990; *Disturbed* 1990; *Assassin of the Tsar* 1991; *Chain of Desire* 1992; *Bopha!* 1993; *Night Train to Venice* 1993; *Cyborg 3: The Recycler* 1994; *Dangerous Indiscretion* 1994; *Milk Money* 1994; *Star Trek: Generations* 1994; *Exquisite Tenderness* 1995; *The Man Who Wouldn't Die* 1995; *Tank Girl* 1995; *Fist of the North Star* 1995; *The Little Riders* 1996; *Mr Magoo* 1997; *Hugo Pool* 1997; *My Life So Far* 1999; *Y2K* 1999; *Gangster No 1* 2000
McEachin, James *Play Misty for Me* 1971; *Buck and the Preacher* 1972; *Fuzz* 1972; *The Groundstar Conspiracy* 1972; *The Dead Don't Die* 1975
Macedo, Rita *The Criminal Life of Archibaldo de la Cruz* 1955; *Nazarín* 1958
McElduff, Ellen *Maximum Overdrive* 1986; *Working Girls* 1986; *Dead End Kids* 1986
McElhatton, Michael *I Went Down* 1997; *Crush Proof* 1998
McElhinney, Ian *Reefer and the Model* 1988; *Blind Justice* 1994
McElhone, Natascha *Surviving Picasso* 1996; *The Devil's Own* 1997; *Mrs Dalloway* 1997; *Ronin* 1998; *The Truman Show* 1998; *What Rats Won't Do* 1998; *Love's Labour's Lost* 1999
McEnery, John *Romeo and Juliet* 1968; *The Lady in the Car with Glasses and a Gun* 1970; *Nicholas and Alexandra* 1971; *Bartleby* 1971; *The Land That Time Forgot* 1974; *Little Malcolm and His Struggle Against the Eunuchs* 1974; *Hamlet* 1990; *Prince of Shadows* 1991; *Black Beauty* 1994; *When Saturday Comes* 1995
McEnery, Peter *Beat Girl* 1960; *Victim* 1961; *The Moon-Spinners* 1964; *The Fighting Prince of Donegal* 1966; *The Game Is Over* 1966; *Entertaining Mr Sloane* 1969; *The Adventures of Gerard* 1970; *Tales That Witness Madness* 1973; *The Cat and the Canary* 1979
McEnnan, Jaime *And God Created Woman* 1988; *Munchie* 1992
McEnroe, Annie *The Hand* 1981; *Battletruck* 1982; *The Survivors* 1983; *Howling II: Your Sister Is a Werewolf* 1984; *Purple Hearts* 1984; *True Stories* 1986
McEntire, Reba *Tremors* 1989; *The Man from Left Field* 1993
McEwan, Geraldine *No Kidding* 1960; *The Dance of Death* 1969; *Escape from the Dark* 1976; *Foreign Body* 1986; *Robin Hood: Prince of Thieves* 1991; *Love's Labour's Lost* 1999; *The Love Letter* 1999
McFadden, Gates *Star Trek: Generations* 1994; *Star Trek: First Contact* 1996; *Crowned and Dangerous* 1997; *Star Trek: Insurrection* 1998
McFadden, Joseph *Small Faces* 1995; *Dad Savage* 1997
McFadden, Tom *Black Sunday* 1976; *Breach of Conduct* 1994
MacFadyen, Angus *Braveheart* 1995; *The Brylcreem Boys* 1996; *Warriors of Virtue* 1997; *The Rat Pack* 1998; *Cradle Will Rock* 1999; *Titus* 1999
MacFadyen, Christie *The Top of His Head* 1988; *Risk* 1993
McFarlane, Andrew *Break of Day* 1977; *Boulevard of Broken Dreams* 1988
McFee, Dwight *Blood River* 1991; *Profile for Murder* 1996
McGann, Joe *The Brylcreem Boys* 1996; *Food of Love* 1997
McGann, Mark *John and Yoko: a Love Story* 1985; *Business as Usual* 1987; *Let Him Have It* 1991
McGann, Paul *Withnail & I* 1986; *Empire of the Sun* 1987; *The Rainbow* 1988; *Tree of Hands* 1988; *Dealers* 1989; *The Monk* 1990; *Paper Mask* 1990; *Afraid of the Dark* 1991; *Alien³* 1992; *The Three Musketeers* 1993; *Downtime* 1997; *FairyTale: a True Story* 1997
McGavin, Darren *The Court-Martial of Billy Mitchell* 1955; *The Man with the Golden Arm* 1955; *Summertime* 1955; *Beau James* 1957; *The Delicate Delinquent* 1957; *Bullet for a Badman* 1964; *The Great Sioux Massacre* 1965; *Mrs Pollifax – Spy* 1970; *The Night Stalker* 1971; *Smash-Up Alley* 1972; *The Night Strangler* 1973; *No Deposit No Return* 1976; *Airport '77* 1977; *Zero to Sixty* 1978; *Hot Lead and Cold Feet* 1978; *Firebird 2015 AD* 1980; *Hangar 18* 1980; *A Christmas Story* 1983; *The Baron and the Kid* 1984; *Turk 182!* 1985; *From the Hip* 1987; *Inherit the Wind* 1988; *Dead Heat* 1988; *By Dawn's Early Light* 1990; *Captain America* 1990; *Child in the Night* 1990; *Arthur Miller's The American Clock* 1993; *Danielle Steel's A Perfect Stranger* 1994; *Billy Madison* 1995; *Derby* 1995; *Fudge-a-Mania* 1995
McGaw, Patrick *Amongst Friends* 1993; *The Beans of Egypt, Maine* 1994; *The Basketball Diaries* 1995; *Malicious* 1995; *Scorpion Spring* 1995; *Dream with the Fishes* 1996
McGee, Henry *Adventures of a Taxi Driver* 1975; *Carry On Emmannuelle* 1978; *Asterix Conquers America* 1994
McGee, Jack *Across the Tracks* 1990; *Star Kid* 1997
McGee, Vonetta *The Big Silence* 1967; *Blacula* 1972; *Detroit 9000* 1973; *Shaft in Africa* 1973; *The Eiger Sanction* 1975; *Brothers* 1977; *To Sleep with Anger* 1990; *Cagney & Lacey: the Return* 1994; *The Man Next Door* 1996
McGhee, Johnny Ray *White Line Fever* 1975; *Project X* 1987
McGill, Bruce *Citizens Band* 1977; *The Hand* 1981; *Tough Enough* 1982; *The Ballad of Gregorio Cortez* 1983; *Into the Night* 1985; *The Man Who Fell to Earth* 1986; *The Last Innocent Man* 1987; *Waiting for the Moon* 1987; *Out Cold* 1989; *Little Vegas* 1990; *The Last Boy Scout* 1991; *My Cousin Vinny* 1992; *Black Widow Murders* 1993; *Timecop* 1994; *Black Sheep* 1996; *Lawn Dogs* 1997; *Rosewood* 1997; *Everything That Rises* 1998
McGill, Everett *Union City* 1980; *Quest for Fire* 1981; *Silver Bullet* 1985; *Heartbreak Ridge* 1986; *Licence to Kill* 1989; *The People under the Stairs* 1991; *Under Siege 2* 1995; *The Straight Story* 1999
MacGill, Moyna *The Strange Affair of Uncle Harry* 1945; *Black Beauty* 1946
McGillis, Kelly *Reuben, Reuben* 1983; *Private Sessions* 1985; *Witness* 1985; *Top Gun* 1986; *The House on Carroll Street* 1987; *Made in Heaven* 1987; *The Accused* 1988; *Winter People* 1988; *Cat Chaser* 1989; *The Babe* 1992; *Bonds of Love* 1993; *Remember Me* 1995; *We the Jury* 1996; *Painted Angels* 1997; *At First Sight* 1998; *Perfect Prey* 1998
McGinley, John C *Platoon* 1986; *Blood Money* 1988; *Talk Radio* 1988; *Shadow Makers* 1989; *Suffering Bastards* 1989; *Highlander II: the Quickening* 1990; *Car 54 Where Are You?* 1991; *A Midnight Clear* 1991; *Point Break* 1991; *Article 99* 1992; *Watch It* 1992; *Little Noises* 1992; *Hear No Evil* 1993; *The Last Outlaw* 1993; *On Deadly Ground* 1994; *Wagons East!* 1994; *Surviving the Game* 1994; *Born to Be Wild* 1995; *The Return of Hunter: Everyone Walks in LA* 1995; *Se7en* 1995; *Mother* 1996; *The Rock* 1996; *Set It Off* 1996; *Nothing to Lose* 1997; *The Pentagon Wars* 1998; *Target Earth* 1998; *The Jack Bull* 1999; *Three to Tango* 1999
McGinley, Sean *Trojan Eddie* 1996; *The Disappearance of Finbar* 1996; *Resurrection Man* 1997; *Bogwoman* 1997; *The General* 1998; *Simon Magus* 1998; *The Closer You Get* 2000
McGinley, Ted *Revenge of the Nerds* 1984; *Physical Evidence* 1989; *Lust for Murder* 1993; *Deadly Web* 1995; *Tails You Live, Heads You're Dead* 1995; *Major League: Back to the Minors* 1998
McGinn, Walter *The Parallax View* 1974; *The Night that Panicked America* 1975; *Three Days of the Condor* 1975; *Bobby Deerfield* 1977
MacGinnis, Niall *The Last Adventurers* 1937; *The Edge of the World* 1937; *East of Piccadilly* 1940; *49th Parallel* 1941; *The Day Will Dawn* 1942; *Undercover* 1943; *We Dive at Dawn* 1943; *Tawny Pipit* 1944; *Anna Karenina* 1947; *Captain Boycott* 1947; *Chance of a Lifetime* 1950; *Conflict of Wings* 1953; *Hell below Zero* 1954; *Betrayed* 1954; *Helen of Troy* 1955; *Special Delivery* 1955; *Lust for Life* 1956; *Night of the Demon* 1957; *Behind the Mask* 1958; *Tarzan's Greatest Adventure* 1959; *This Other Eden* 1959; *Foxhole in Cairo* 1960; *Kidnapped* 1960; *Sword of Sherwood Forest* 1960; *Never Take Sweets from a Stranger* 1960; *A Terrible Beauty* 1960; *The Man Who Finally Died* 1962; *The Prince and the Pauper* 1962; *Jason and the Argonauts* 1963; *A Face in the Rain* 1963; *The Truth about Spring* 1964; *The War Lord* 1965; *The Viking Queen* 1967
McGinnis, Scott *Wacko* 1981; *Odd Jobs* 1986; *Gunbus* 1986; *You Can't Hurry Love* 1988
McGiver, John *Love in the Afternoon* 1957; *I Married a Woman* 1958; *The Gazebo* 1959; *Breakfast at Tiffany's* 1961; *Love in a Goldfish Bowl* 1961; *The Manchurian Candidate* 1962; *Mr Hobbs Takes a Vacation* 1962; *Period of Adjustment* 1962; *Who's Minding the Store?* 1963; *Take Her, She's Mine* 1963; *Man's Favorite Sport?* 1964; *Marriage on the Rocks* 1965; *The Glass Bottom Boat* 1966; *Made in Paris* 1966; *Fitzwilly* 1967; *Midnight Cowboy* 1969; *Arnold* 1973; *The Apple Dumpling Gang* 1974
McGlone, Mike *The Brothers McMullen* 1995; *She's the One* 1996; *One Tough Cop* 1998; *The Bone Collector* 1999
McGlynn Sr, Frank *Riders of the Purple Sage* 1931; *The Littlest Rebel* 1935; *The Plainsman* 1936
McGlynn Jr, Frank *Hopalong Cassidy* 1935; *Westward Ho* 1935
McGoohan, Patrick *Passage Home* 1955; *Zarak* 1956; *Hell Drivers* 1957; *High Tide at Noon* 1957; *The Gypsy and the Gentleman* 1958; *Nor the Moon by Night* 1958; *All Night Long* 1961; *Life for Ruth* 1962; *The Quare Fellow* 1962; *Dr Syn, Alias the Scarecrow* 1963; *The Three Lives of Thomasina* 1963; *Ice Station Zebra* 1968; *Mary, Queen of Scots* 1971; *Silver Streak* 1976; *The Man in the Iron Mask* 1977; *Brass Target* 1978; *Escape from Alcatraz* 1979; *The Hard Way* 1980; *Kings and Desperate Men* 1981; *Scanners* 1981; *Baby: Secret of the Lost Legend* 1985; *Of Pure Blood* 1986; *Braveheart* 1995
McGovern, Barry *Dear Sarah* 1990; *Driftwood* 1996
McGovern, Elizabeth *Ordinary People* 1980; *Ragtime* 1981; *Lovesick* 1983; *Once upon a Time in America* 1984; *Racing with the Moon* 1984; *Native Son* 1986; *The Bedroom Window* 1987; *She's Having a Baby* 1988; *Johnny Handsome* 1989; *Aunt Julia and the Scriptwriter* 1990; *The Handmaid's Tale* 1990; *A Shock to the System* 1990; *Women and Men: Stories of Seduction* 1990; *King of the Hill*

1993; *The Favor* 1994; *Broken Trust* 1995; *Wings of Courage* 1995; *The Summer of Ben Tyler* 1996; *The Wings of the Dove* 1997; *The Misadventures of Margaret* 1998; *If Only* 1998; *The House of Mirth* 2000
McGowan, J P *Somewhere in Sonora* 1933; *Hit the Saddle* 1937
McGowan, Rose *California Man* 1992; *The Doom Generation* 1995; *Lewis & Clark & George* 1996; *Scream* 1996; *Going All the Way* 1997; *Dearly Devoted* 1998; *Phantoms* 1998; *Jawbreaker* 1999
McGowan, Tom *Mrs Parker and the Vicious Circle* 1994; *Heavyweights* 1995
MacGowran, Jack *Sailor Beware!* 1956; *Manuela* 1957; *The Rising of the Moon* 1957; *Rooney* 1958; *Blind Date* 1959; *The Giant Behemoth* 1959; *Cul-de-Sac* 1966; *The Fearless Vampire Killers* 1967; *How I Won the War* 1967; *Wonderwall* 1968; *Age of Consent* 1969; *Start the Revolution without Me* 1970; *King Lear* 1971; *The Exorcist* 1973
MacGowran, Tara *Secret Places* 1984; *The Dawning* 1988
McGrail, Walter *Men without Women* 1930; *In Old Montana* 1939
McGrath, Doug *Twilight Zone: the Movie* 1983; *Pale Rider* 1985
McGrath, Frank *Riders of the Purple Sage* 1941; *The Shakiest Gun in the West* 1967
MacGrath, Leueen *The Saint's Vacation* 1941; *Edward, My Son* 1949
McGrath, Matt *The Member of the Wedding* 1997; *Boys Don't Cry* 1999
McGrath, Pat *Somewhere on Leave* 1942; *Confession* 1955
MacGraw, Ali *A Lovely Way to Go* 1968; *Goodbye, Columbus* 1969; *Love Story* 1970; *The Getaway* 1972; *Convoy* 1978; *Players* 1979; *Just Tell Me What You Want* 1980; *Survive the Savage Sea* 1992
McGraw, Charles *The Killers* 1946; *T-Men* 1947; *Blood on the Moon* 1948; *Reign of Terror* 1949; *Armored Car Robbery* 1950; *Side Street* 1950; *Double Crossbones* 1951; *His Kind of Woman* 1951; *Roadblock* 1951; *The Narrow Margin* 1952; *One Minute to Zero* 1952; *Thunder over the Plains* 1953; *The Bridges at Toko-Ri* 1954; *Toward the Unknown* 1956; *Slaughter on Tenth Avenue* 1957; *The Defiant Ones* 1958; *Saddle the Wind* 1958; *Twilight for the Gods* 1958; *The Man in the Net* 1959; *The Wonderful Country* 1959; *The Birds* 1963; *Nightmare in Chicago* 1968; *Tell Them Willie Boy Is Here* 1969; *Pendulum* 1969; *Johnny Got His Gun* 1971; *A Boy and His Dog* 1975; *The Killer inside Me* 1975
McGreevey, Michael *Sammy, the Way Out Seal* 1962; *The Way West* 1967; *Now You See Him, Now You Don't* 1972; *Snowball Express* 1972
McGregor, Charles *Superfly* 1972; *Three the Hard Way* 1974
McGregor, Ewan *Being Human* 1994; *Shallow Grave* 1994; *Blue Juice* 1995; *The Pillow Book* 1995; *Trainspotting* 1995; *Brassed Off* 1996; *Emma* 1996; *A Life Less Ordinary* 1997; *The Serpent's Kiss* 1997; *Nightwatch* 1997; *Little Voice* 1998; *Rogue Trader* 1998; *Velvet Goldmine* 1998; *Star Wars Episode I: the Phantom Menace* 1999; *Eye of the Beholder* 1999; *Nora* 1999
McGregor-Stewart, Kate *Safe* 1995; *The Maker* 1997
McGuire, Biff *The Phenix City Story* 1955; *Station Six-Sahara* 1962; *The Heart Is a Lonely Hunter* 1968; *The Thomas Crown Affair* 1968; *Serpico* 1973
McGuire, Don *The Fuller Brush Man* 1948; *Armored Car Robbery* 1950; *Double Dynamite* 1951
McGuire, Dorothy *Claudia* 1943; *The Enchanted Cottage* 1945; *A Tree Grows in Brooklyn* 1945; *Claudia and David* 1946; *The Spiral Staircase* 1946; *Till the End of Time* 1946; *Gentleman's Agreement* 1947; *Mister 880* 1950; *I Want You* 1951; *Callaway Went Thataway* 1951; *Make Haste to Live* 1954; *Three Coins in the Fountain* 1954; *Trial* 1955; *Friendly Persuasion* 1956; *Old Yeller* 1957; *The Remarkable Mr Pennypacker* 1959; *This Earth Is Mine* 1959; *A Summer Place* 1959; *The Dark at the Top of the Stairs* 1960; *Swiss Family Robinson* 1960; *Susan Slade* 1961; *Summer Magic* 1963; *The Greatest Story Ever Told* 1965; *Flight of the Doves* 1971; *Amos* 1985; *The Last Best Year* 1990
McGuire, John *Steamboat round the Bend* 1935; *Stranger on the Third Floor* 1940; *Invisible Ghost* 1941; *Bells of San Angelo* 1947
McGuire, Kathryn *The Navigator* 1924; *Sherlock Junior* 1924
McGuire, Marcy *Seven Days' Leave* 1942; *Higher and Higher* 1943
McGuire, Michael *The Dog and the Diamonds* 1953; *Larry* 1974; *Report to the Commissioner* 1975; *The Streetfighter* 1975; *Jekyll and Hyde... Together Again* 1982; *Bird* 1988; *The Karen Carpenter Story* 1989
McHattie, Stephen *The People Next Door* 1970; *The Ultimate Warrior* 1975
McHattie, Stephen *Gray Lady Down* 1978; *Death Valley* 1982; *Best Revenge* 1983; *Belizaire the Cajun* 1985; *Salvation! Have You Said Your Prayers Today?* 1987; *Sticky Fingers* 1988; *Call Me* 1988; *Bloodhounds of Broadway* 1989; *Art Deco Detective* 1994; *Beverly Hills Cop III* 1994; *The Dark* 1994; *Convict Cowboy* 1995; *Theodore Rex* 1995; *Visitors of the Night* 1995
Machiavelli, Nicoletta *Navajo Joe* 1966; *Someone Is Bleeding* 1974
Macht, Stephen *The Choirboys* 1977; *Nightwing* 1979; *Galaxina* 1980; *The Mountain Men* 1980; *Agatha Christie's A Caribbean Mystery* 1983; *Flight 90: Disaster on the Potomac* 1984; *Samson and Delilah* 1984; *The Monster Squad* 1987; *Strange Voices* 1987; *Blind Witness* 1989; *Fear Stalk* 1989; *My Boyfriend's Back* 1989; *Amityville 1992: It's About Time* 1992; *A Child Too Many* 1993; *Cult Rescue* 1994
McHugh, Frank *The Crowd Roars* 1932; *High Pressure* 1932; *Union Depot* 1932; *One Way Passage* 1932; *The Strange Love of Molly Louvain* 1932; *Mystery of the Wax Museum* 1933; *Ex-Lady* 1933; *The Telegraph Trail* 1933; *Fashions of 1934* 1934; *Here Comes the Navy* 1934; *A Midsummer Night's Dream* 1935; *Page Miss Glory* 1935; *Devil Dogs of the Air* 1935; *Bullets or Ballots* 1936; *Three Men on a Horse* 1936; *Stage Struck* 1936; *Boy Meets Girl* 1938; *Daughters Courageous* 1939; *Dodge City* 1939; *Dust Be My Destiny* 1939; *On Your Toes* 1939; *The Roaring Twenties* 1939; *Indianapolis Speedway* 1939; *The Fighting 69th* 1940; *I Love You Again* 1940; *'Til We Meet Again* 1940; *Virginia City* 1940; *Back Street* 1941; *Manpower* 1941; *All through the Night* 1942; *Her Cardboard Lover* 1942; *Going My Way* 1944; *Marine Raiders* 1944; *A Medal for Benny* 1945; *State Fair* 1945; *Carnegie Hall* 1947; *The Velvet Touch* 1948; *Mighty Joe Young* 1949; *Miss Grant Takes Richmond* 1949; *My Son John* 1952; *A Lion Is in the Streets* 1953; *Career* 1959; *Say One for Me* 1959; *Easy Come, Easy Go* 1967
McHugh, Matt *Street Scene* 1931; *Taxi!* 1932
McIlwraith, David *Outrageous!* 1977; *Too Outrageous!* 1987; *Millennium* 1989; *On My Own* 1992
McInnerny, Lizzy *Rowing with the Wind* 1987; *Being Human* 1994
McInnerny, Tim *Wetherby* 1985; *Anastasia: the Mystery of Anna* 1986; *Erik the Viking* 1989; *101 Dalmatians* 1996; *Rogue Trader* 1998; *Notting Hill* 1999
MacInnes, Angus *aka* **McInnes, Angus** *Force 10 from Navarone* 1978; *Strange Brew* 1983; *A Father's Revenge* 1987
McIntire, John *The Street with No Name* 1948; *Down to the Sea in Ships* 1949; *Francis* 1949; *Scene of the Crime* 1949; *Ambush* 1949; *Red Canyon* 1949; *Johnny Stool Pigeon* 1949; *The Asphalt Jungle* 1950; *No Sad Songs for Me* 1950; *Saddle Tramp* 1950; *Winchester '73* 1950; *That's My Boy* 1951; *You're in the Navy Now* 1951; *Westward the Women* 1951; *Glory Alley* 1952; *Horizons West* 1952; *The Lawless Breed* 1952; *The World in His Arms* 1952; *A Lion Is in the Streets* 1953; *The Mississippi Gambler* 1953; *The President's Lady* 1953; *War Arrow* 1953; *Apache* 1954; *Four Guns to the Border* 1954; *The Yellow Mountain* 1954; *The Far Country* 1955; *The Kentuckian* 1955; *The Phenix City Story* 1955; *Stranger on Horseback* 1955; *The Spoilers* 1955; *The Scarlet Coat* 1955; *Backlash* 1956; *The Tin Star* 1957; *The Mark of the Hawk* 1957; *The Light in the Forest* 1958; *Sing, Boy, Sing* 1958; *Flaming Star* 1960; *Psycho* 1960; *Seven Ways from Sundown* 1960; *Who Was That Lady?* 1960; *Two Rode Together* 1961; *Rough Night in Jericho* 1967; *Challenge to Be Free* 1972; *Herbie Rides Again* 1974; *Rooster Cogburn* 1975; *Mrs R's Daughter* 1979; *Honkytonk Man* 1982; *Cloak and Dagger* 1984; *Dream Breakers* 1989; *Turner & Hooch* 1989
McIntire, Tim *The Sterile Cuckoo* 1969; *Smile, Jenny, You're Dead* 1974; *Aloha, Bobby and Rose* 1975; *The Gumball Rally* 1976; *American Hot Wax* 1977; *The Choirboys* 1977; *Brubaker* 1980; *Stand by Your Man* 1981; *Fast-Walking* 1982; *Sacred Ground* 1983
McIntosh, Burr *Way Down East* 1920; *Lilac Time* 1928
McIntosh, Judy *Ngati* 1987; *Ebbtide* 1994
Macintosh, Keegan *For the Love of Aaron* 1993; *Don't Talk to Strangers* 1994; *At the Midnight Hour* 1995; *A Child Is Missing* 1995; *The Road Home* 1995
McIntyre, John *Elmer Gantry* 1960; *Summer and Smoke* 1961
McIntyre, Marvin J *The Running Man* 1987; *Wilder Napalm* 1993; *Born to Be Wild* 1995
MacIvor, Daniel *Justice Denied* 1989; *I Love a Man in Uniform* 1993
Mack, Allison *Desperate Justice* 1993; *Honey, We Shrunk Ourselves* 1997
Mack, Charles Emmett *Dream Street* 1921; *America* 1924
Mack, Helen *Blind Adventure* 1933; *Melody Cruise* 1933; *Son of Kong* 1933; *The Lemon Drop Kid* 1934; *Captain Hurricane* 1935; *The Return of Peter Grimm* 1935; *She* 1935; *The Milky Way* 1936; *The Last Train from Madrid* 1937; *His Girl Friday* 1939
Mack, James *aka* **Mack, James T** *Anna Christie* 1930; *Bonnie Scotland* 1935
Mackaill, Dorothy *No Man of Her Own* 1932; *Love Affair* 1932
MacKay, Barry *Evergreen* 1934; *Forever England* 1935; *Oh Daddy!* 1935; *The Private Secretary* 1935; *Gangway* 1937; *A Christmas Carol* 1938; *Sailing Along* 1938
McKay, David *The Girl in the Picture* 1985; *My Name Is Joe* 1998
Mackay, Fulton *The Brave Don't Cry* 1952; *Laxdale Hall* 1953; *Gumshoe* 1971; *Nothing but the Night* 1972; *Porridge* 1979; *Britannia Hospital* 1982; *Local Hero* 1983; *Defence of the Realm* 1985; *Water* 1985
McKay, George *Girls Can Play* 1937; *The Boogie Man Will Get You* 1942
MacKay, John *Trust* 1990; *Niagara Niagara* 1997
Mackay, Mathew *The Peanut Butter Solution* 1985; *Lapse of Memory* 1992
McKay, Scott *Guest in the House* 1944; *Thirty Seconds over Tokyo* 1944; *You Better Watch Out* 1980
McKay, Wanda *The Monster Maker* 1944; *Voodoo Man* 1944
McKean, Michael *Used Cars* 1980; *Young Doctors in Love* 1982; *This Is Spinal Tap* 1984; *Clue* 1985; *DARYL* 1985; *Light of Day* 1987; *Planes, Trains and Automobiles* 1987; *Earth Girls Are Easy* 1988; *Short Circuit 2* 1988; *The Big Picture* 1989; *Hider in the House* 1989; *Flashback* 1990; *True Identity* 1991; *Man Trouble* 1992; *Memoirs of an Invisible Man* 1992; *Coneheads* 1993; *Airheads* 1994; *Radioland Murders* 1994; *The Brady Bunch Movie* 1995; *Jack* 1996; *Casper: a Spirited Beginning* 1997; *Nothing to Lose* 1997; *That Darn Cat* 1997; *Final Justice* 1998; *Teaching Mrs Tingle* 1999
McKechnie, James *The Life and Death of Colonel Blimp* 1943; *Two Thousand Women* 1944
McKee, Gina *The Lair of the White Worm* 1988; *Croupier* 1998; *Notting Hill* 1999; *Wonderland* 1999; *The Loss of Sexual Innocence* 1999; *Joan of Arc* 1999
McKee, John *That Touch of Mink* 1962; *Monte Walsh* 1970
McKee, Lafe *Riders of Destiny* 1933; *The Man from Utah* 1934; *West of the Divide* 1934; *The Desert Trail* 1935
McKee, Lonette *Which Way Is Up?* 1977; *The Cotton Club* 1984; *Brewster's Millions* 1985; *'Round Midnight* 1986; *Gardens of Stone* 1987; *Dangerous Passion* 1990; *Jungle Fever* 1991; *Malcolm X* 1992; *He Got Game* 1998; *Blind Faith* 1998; *Having Our Say: the Delany Sisters' First 100 Years* 1999
McKellar, Danica *Sidekicks* 1993; *Cradle of Conspiracy* 1994; *Search for Justice* 1996
McKellar, Don *Roadkill* 1989; *Highway 61* 1992; *Exotica* 1994; *When Night Is Falling* 1995; *Last Night* 1998; *eXistenZ* 1999
McKellen, Ian *Alfred the Great* 1969; *A Touch of Love* 1969; *Priest of Love* 1981; *The Scarlet Pimpernel* 1982; *The Keep* 1983; *Plenty* 1985; *Zina* 1985; *Scandal* 1988; *And the Band Played On* 1993; *The Ballad of Little Jo* 1993; *Last Action Hero* 1993; *Six Degrees of Separation* 1993; *I'll Do Anything* 1994; *The Shadow* 1994; *Thin Ice* 1994; *To Die For* 1994; *Cold Comfort Farm* 1995; *Jack & Sarah* 1995; *Restoration* 1995; *Richard III* 1995; *Bent* 1996; *A Bit of Scarlet* 1996; *Rasputin* 1996; *Amy Foster* 1997; *Apt Pupil* 1997; *Gods and Monsters* 1998
McKenna, Bernard *My Childhood* 1972; *My Ain Folk* 1973
MacKenna, Kenneth *Men without Women* 1930; *The Virtuous Sin* 1930
McKenna, Siobhan *Daughter of Darkness* 1948; *The Adventurers* 1950; *King of Kings* 1961; *Of Human Bondage* 1964; *Doctor Zhivago* 1965; *Philadelphia, Here I Come* 1975
McKenna, T P *The Siege of Sidney Street* 1960; *Girl with Green Eyes* 1963; *Ulysses* 1967; *The Beast in the Cellar* 1970; *Perfect Friday* 1970; *Straw Dogs* 1971; *Villain* 1971; *All Creatures Great and Small* 1974; *A Portrait of the Artist as a Young Man* 1977; *The Outsider* 1979; *Pascali's Island* 1988; *Valmont* 1989; *Red Scorpion* 1989
McKenna, Virginia *Father's Doing Fine* 1952; *The Oracle* 1952; *The Cruel Sea* 1953; *The Ship That Died of Shame* 1955; *Simba* 1955; *A Town like Alice* 1956; *The Barretts of Wimpole Street* 1957; *The Smallest Show on Earth* 1957; *Carve Her Name with Pride* 1958; *Passionate Summer* 1958; *The Wreck of the Mary Deare* 1959; *Born Free* 1966; *An Elephant Called Slowly* 1969; *Ring of Bright Water* 1969; *Waterloo* 1970; *Swallows and Amazons* 1974; *Beauty and the Beast* 1976; *The Disappearance* 1977; *Holocaust 2000* 1977
Mackenzie, Alex *The Maggie* 1953; *The Bridal Path* 1959; *The Battle of the Sexes* 1960; *Greyfriars Bobby* 1960
McKenzie, Fay *Down Mexico Way* 1941; *The Singing Sheriff* 1944; *The Party* 1968
McKenzie, Jacqueline *Romper Stomper* 1992; *Traps* 1994; *Angel Baby* 1995; *Mr Reliable* 1996; *Deep Blue Sea* 1999
MacKenzie, Joyce *Broken Arrow* 1950; *Destination Murder* 1950
MacKenzie, Joyce *The French Line* 1954; *Rails into Laramie* 1954
McKenzie, Julia *The Wildcats of St Trinian's* 1980; *Those Glory, Glory Days* 1983; *Shirley Valentine* 1989
Mackenzie, Mary *Stolen Face* 1952; *The Master Plan* 1954; *Cloak without Dagger* 1955
MacKenzie, Phillip *Circumstances Unknown* 1995; *Blackjack* 1998
McKenzie, Tim *Gallipoli* 1981; *The Lighthorsemen* 1987

Radio Times ACTORS' INDEX

McKeon, Doug *On Golden Pond* 1981; *Night Crossing* 1981; *Heart of a Champion: the Ray Mancini Story* 1985; *Mischief* 1985; *Norman Rockwell's Breaking Home Ties* 1987
McKeon, Nancy *High School USA* 1983; *Poison Ivy* 1985; *This Child Is Mine* 1985; *Strange Voices* 1987; *A Cry for Help: the Tracey Thurman Story* 1989; *Baby Snatcher* 1992; *The Wrong Woman* 1996; *In My Sister's Shadow* 1999
McKern, Leo *Murder in the Cathedral* 1952; *All for Mary* 1955; *X the Unknown* 1956; *Time without Pity* 1957; *Beyond This Place* 1959; *The Mouse That Roared* 1959; *The Running, Jumping and Standing Still Film* 1959; *Yesterday's Enemy* 1959; *The Day the Earth Caught Fire* 1961; *Mr Topaze* 1961; *The Inspector* 1962; *Doctor in Distress* 1963; *Hot Enough for June* 1963; *A Jolly Bad Fellow* 1964; *King and Country* 1964; *The Amorous Adventures of Moll Flanders* 1965; *Help!* 1965; *A Man for All Seasons* 1966; *Decline and Fall... of a Birdwatcher* 1968; *The Shoes of the Fisherman* 1968; *Assignment K* 1968; *Ryan's Daughter* 1970; *Massacre in Rome* 1973; *The Adventure of Sherlock Holmes' Smarter Brother* 1975; *The Omen* 1976; *Candleshoe* 1977; *The Blue Lagoon* 1980; *The French Lieutenant's Woman* 1981; *The Chain* 1984; *Agatha Christie's Murder with Mirrors* 1985; *Ladyhawke* 1985; *Travelling North* 1986; *Good King Wenceslas* 1994
McKidd, Kevin *Small Faces* 1995; *Trainspotting* 1995; *Dad Savage* 1997; *Bedrooms and Hallways* 1998; *The Acid House* 1998; *Topsy-Turvy* 1999
McKim, Robert *The Mark of Zorro* 1920; *The Strong Man* 1926
McKinney, Bill *She Freak* 1967; *Deliverance* 1972; *Junior Bonner* 1972; *Cleopatra Jones* 1973; *The Strange and Deadly Occurrence* 1974; *Cannonball* 1976; *The Outlaw Josey Wales* 1976; *The Shootist* 1976; *The Gauntlet* 1977; *Bronco Billy* 1980; *Tex* 1982; *Heart like a Wheel* 1983; *Kinjite: Forbidden Subjects* 1989; *The China Lake Murders* 1990; *City Slickers II: the Legend of Curly's Gold* 1994; *It Came from Outer Space II* 1996
McKinney, Florine *Cynara* 1932; *Strangers All* 1935
McKinney, Mark *Kids in the Hall: Brain Candy* 1996; *The Out-of-Towners* 1999; *Superstar* 1999
McKinney, Nina Mae *Hallelujah* 1929; *Sanders of the River* 1935
McKinnon, Ray *Paris Trout* 1991; *The Gun in Betty Lou's Handbag* 1992; *Needful Things* 1993; *Caught in the Crossfire* 1994; *The Net* 1995; *Goodbye Lover* 1997; *William Faulkner's Old Man* 1997
Mackintosh, Kenneth *Othello* 1965; *Three Sisters* 1970
Mackintosh, Louise *The Phantom President* 1932; *The Little Giant* 1933
Mackintosh, Steven *London Kills Me* 1991; *The Return of the Native* 1994; *Blue Juice* 1995; *The Grotesque* 1995; *Different for Girls* 1996; *House of America* 1996; *Twelfth Night* 1996; *The Land Girls* 1997; *Lock, Stock and Two Smoking Barrels* 1998; *The Criminal* 1999
McKnight, David *Pizza Man* 1991; *Under Siege* 1992
MacKrell, James *aka* **MacKrell, Jim** *Teen Wolf* 1985; *The Dream Machine* 1990
McKuen, Rod *Rock, Pretty Baby* 1956; *Wild Heritage* 1958
MacLachlan, Janet *Halls of Anger* 1970; *The Man* 1972; *Louis Armstrong: Chicago Style* 1976; *The Boy Who Could Fly* 1986
MacLachlan, Kyle *Dune* 1984; *Blue Velvet* 1986; *The Hidden* 1987; *Dream Breakers* 1989; *Don't Tell Her It's Me* 1990; *The Doors* 1991; *Rich in Love* 1992; *Twin Peaks: Fire Walk with Me* 1992; *Where the Day Takes You* 1992; *The Trial* 1993; *Against the Wall* 1994; *The Flintstones* 1994; *Roswell* 1994; *Showgirls* 1995; *The Trigger Effect* 1996; *Trigger Happy* 1996; *One Night Stand* 1997; *Route 9* 1998
McLaglen, Victor *The Unholy Three* 1925; *Beau Geste* 1926; *What Price Glory* 1926; *A Girl in Every Port* 1928; *Hangman's House* 1928; *The Black Watch* 1929; *The Cock-Eyed World* 1929; *Dishonored* 1931; *The Captain Hates the Sea* 1934; *The Lost Patrol* 1934; *Murder at the Vanities* 1934; *The Informer* 1935; *Klondike Annie* 1936; *Under Two Flags* 1936; *Nancy Steele Is Missing* 1937; *Sea Devils* 1937; *This Is My Affair* 1937; *Wee Willie Winkie* 1937; *We're Going to Be Rich* 1938; *Full Confession* 1939; *Gunga Din* 1939; *South of Pago Pago* 1940; *Broadway Limited* 1941; *Call Out the Marines* 1942; *China Girl* 1942; *The Princess and the Pirate* 1944; *Whistle Stop* 1946; *The Foxes of Harrow* 1947; *Fort Apache* 1948; *She Wore a Yellow Ribbon* 1949; *Rio Grande* 1950; *The Quiet Man* 1952; *Fair Wind to Java* 1953; *Prince Valiant* 1954; *Trouble in the Glen* 1954; *Bengazi* 1955; *Many Rivers to Cross* 1955; *Lady Godiva* 1955; *Sea Fury* 1958
MacLaine, Shirley *Artists and Models* 1955; *The Trouble with Harry* 1955; *Around the World in 80 Days* 1956; *The Matchmaker* 1958; *The Sheepman* 1958; *Some Came Running* 1958; *Hot Spell* 1958; *Ask Any Girl* 1959; *Career* 1959; *All in a Night's Work* 1960; *The Apartment* 1960; *Can-Can* 1960; *The Children's Hour* 1961; *Two Loves* 1961; *My Geisha* 1962; *Two for the Seesaw* 1962; *Irma la Douce* 1963; *What a Way to Go!* 1964; *The Yellow Rolls-Royce* 1964; *John Goldfarb, Please Come Home* 1964; *Gambit* 1966; *Woman Times Seven* 1967; *The Bliss of Mrs Blossom* 1968; *Sweet Charity* 1968; *Two Mules for Sister Sara* 1970; *Desperate Characters* 1971; *The Possession of Joel Delaney* 1972; *The Turning Point* 1977; *Being There* 1979; *A Change of Seasons* 1980; *Loving Couples* 1980; *Cannonball Run II* 1983; *Terms of Endearment* 1983; *Madame Sousatzka* 1988; *Steel Magnolias* 1989; *Waiting for the Light* 1989; *Postcards from the Edge* 1990; *Used People* 1992; *Wrestling Ernest Hemingway* 1993; *Guarding Tess* 1994; *Mrs Winterbourne* 1995; *The West Side Waltz* 1995; *The Evening Star* 1996; *A Smile like Yours* 1997
MacLane, Barton *Tillie and Gus* 1933; *Black Fury* 1935; *The Case of the Lucky Legs* 1935; *Ceiling Zero* 1935; *Dr Socrates* 1935; *Frisco Kid* 1935; *"G" Men* 1935; *Go into Your Dance* 1935; *Bullets or Ballots* 1936; *The Walking Dead* 1936; *God's Country and the Woman* 1937; *The Prince and the Pauper* 1937; *San Quentin* 1937; *You Only Live Once* 1937; *Born Reckless* 1937; *Gold Is Where You Find It* 1938; *You and Me* 1938; *The Storm* 1938; *Come Live with Me* 1941; *Dr Jekyll and Mr Hyde* 1941; *High Sierra* 1941; *The Maltese Falcon* 1941; *Manpower* 1941; *Western Union* 1941; *Wild Geese Calling* 1941; *All through the Night* 1942; *The Big Street* 1942; *Bombardier* 1943; *Song of Texas* 1943; *Marine Raiders* 1944; *Secret Command* 1944; *The Spanish Main* 1945; *Tarzan and the Amazons* 1945; *San Quentin* 1946; *Tarzan and the Huntress* 1947; *Angel in Exile* 1948; *Silver River* 1948; *The Treasure of the Sierra Madre* 1948; *Red Light* 1949; *Let's Dance* 1950; *Best of the Badmen* 1951; *Bugles in the Afternoon* 1952; *The Half-Breed* 1952; *Thunderbirds* 1952; *Rails into Laramie* 1954; *Foxfire* 1955; *Jail Busters* 1955; *Backlash* 1956; *Three Violent People* 1956; *The Geisha Boy* 1958; *Girl on the Run* 1958; *The Rounders* 1965; *Arizona Bushwhackers* 1968
McLaren, Hollis *Sunday in the Country* 1975; *Partners* 1976; *Welcome to Blood City* 1977; *Outrageous!* 1977; *Lost and Found* 1979; *Atlantic City USA* 1980; *Too Outrageous!* 1987
MacLaren, Ian *Journey's End* 1930; *Body and Soul* 1931
McLarty, Ron *Tiger Town* 1983; *The Feud* 1989
McLaughlin, Gibb *Congress Dances* 1931; *Bulldog Jack* 1934; *The Old Curiosity Shop* 1934; *Broken Blossoms* 1936; *Where There's a Will* 1936; *The Lavender Hill Mob* 1951; *The Man Who Watched Trains Go By* 1952; *The Brain Machine* 1954
McLean, David *X-15* 1961; *The Strangler* 1964; *Kingdom of the Spiders* 1977; *Deathsport* 1978
McLeod, Catherine *I've Always Loved You* 1946; *The Outcast* 1954
MacLeod, Gavin *War Hunt* 1962; *The Party* 1968
McLeod, Gordon *The Saint in London* 1939; *Crooks' Tour* 1940; *The Saint's Vacation* 1941; *We'll Smile Again* 1942; *The Saint Meets the Tiger* 1943; *A Case for PC 49* 1950
McLerie, Allyn Ann *aka* **McLerie, Allyn** *Calamity Jane* 1953; *The Desert Song* 1953; *Phantom of the Rue Morgue* 1954; *Jeremiah Johnson* 1972; *Cinderella Liberty* 1973; *The Way We Were* 1973; *A Shining Season* 1979
MacLiam, Eanna *My Left Foot* 1989; *The Snapper* 1993; *The General* 1998; *Angela's Ashes* 1999
McLiam, John *Showdown* 1973; *The Dove* 1974; *The Food of the Gods* 1975; *The Missouri Breaks* 1976; *Walk like a Man* 1987
MacLiammoir, Michael *Othello* 1952; *What's the Matter with Helen?* 1971
McLish, Rachel *Aces: Iron Eagle III* 1992; *Raven Hawk* 1996
MacMahon, Aline *Life Begins* 1932; *One Way Passage* 1932; *Gold Diggers of 1933* 1933; *The World Changes* 1933; *Ah, Wilderness* 1935; *I Live My Life* 1935; *Kind Lady* 1935; *When You're in Love* 1937; *Back Door to Heaven* 1939; *Out of the Fog* 1941; *The Lady Is Willing* 1942; *Dragon Seed* 1944; *Guest in the House* 1944; *The Search* 1948; *The Flame and the Arrow* 1950; *The Eddie Cantor Story* 1953; *The Man from Laramie* 1955; *Diamond Head* 1962; *All the Way Home* 1963; *I Could Go On Singing* 1963
McMahon, Ed *Slaughter's Big Rip-Off* 1973; *Fun with Dick and Jane* 1977; *Butterfly* 1982; *Full Moon High* 1982
McMahon, Horace *Detective Story* 1951; *Abbott and Costello Go to Mars* 1953; *Man in the Dark* 1953; *Susan Slept Here* 1954; *Beau James* 1957; *The Delicate Delinquent* 1957; *Never Steal Anything Small* 1959; *The Detective* 1968
McManus, Michael *Poltergeist* 1982; *Speaking Parts* 1989; *Secret Sins of the Father* 1994
McMartin, John *Sweet Charity* 1968; *What's So Bad About Feeling Good?* 1968; *Thieves* 1977; *Blow Out* 1981; *Pennies from Heaven* 1981; *The Last Ninja* 1983; *Dream Lover* 1986; *Legal Eagles* 1986; *Murrow* 1986; *Native Son* 1986; *Who's That Girl* 1987; *Day One* 1989
McMillan, Kenneth *Bloodbrothers* 1978; *Oliver's Story* 1978; *Chilly Scenes of Winter* 1979; *Salem's Lot* 1979; *Borderline* 1980; *Carny* 1980; *Hide in Plain Sight* 1980; *Little Miss Marker* 1980; *Eyewitness* 1981; *Ragtime* 1981; *True Confessions* 1981; *Whose Life Is it Anyway?* 1981; *Heartbeeps* 1981; *In the Custody of Strangers* 1982; *Partners* 1982; *Joe Dancer: the Big Trade* 1983; *Cat's Eye* 1984; *Dune* 1984; *The Pope of Greenwich Village* 1984; *Runaway Train* 1985; *Acceptable Risks* 1986; *Armed and Dangerous* 1986; *Malone* 1987; *Three Fugitives* 1989
McMillan, Roddy *The Gorbals Story* 1949; *The Bridal Path* 1959; *The Battle of the Sexes* 1960; *Ring of Bright Water* 1969
McMullan, Jim *aka* **McMullan, James** *Downhill Racer* 1969; *Extreme Close-Up* 1973
MacMurray, Fred *Alice Adams* 1935; *The Bride Comes Home* 1935; *The Gilded Lily* 1935; *Hands across the Table* 1935; *The Texas Rangers* 1936; *The Trail of the Lonesome Pine* 1936; *The Princess Comes Across* 1936; *True Confession* 1937; *Swing High, Swing Low* 1937; *Men with Wings* 1938; *Little Old New York* 1940; *Remember the Night* 1940; *Too Many Husbands* 1940; *Dive Bomber* 1941; *The Lady Is Willing* 1942; *Star Spangled Rhythm* 1942; *Take a Letter, Darling* 1942; *Above Suspicion* 1943; *Flight for Freedom* 1943; *No Time for Love* 1943; *Double Indemnity* 1944; *Standing Room Only* 1944; *Captain Eddie* 1945; *Murder, He Says* 1945; *Where Do We Go from Here?* 1945; *Pardon My Past* 1945; *Smoky* 1946; *The Egg and I* 1947; *Suddenly It's Spring* 1947; *Singapore* 1947; *The Miracle of the Bells* 1948; *On Our Merry Way* 1948; *Father Was a Fullback* 1949; *Never a Dull Moment* 1950; *A Millionaire for Christy* 1951; *Callaway Went Thataway* 1951; *Fair Wind to Java* 1953; *The Moonlighter* 1953; *The Caine Mutiny* 1954; *Pushover* 1954; *Woman's World* 1954; *At Gunpoint* 1955; *The Rains of Ranchipur* 1955; *The Far Horizons* 1955; *There's Always Tomorrow* 1956; *Gun for a Coward* 1957; *Quantez* 1957; *Good Day for a Hanging* 1958; *Day of the Bad Man* 1958; *The Oregon Trail* 1959; *The Shaggy Dog* 1959; *Face of a Fugitive* 1959; *The Apartment* 1960; *The Absent-Minded Professor* 1961; *Bon Voyage!* 1962; *Son of Flubber* 1962; *Kisses for My President* 1964; *Follow Me, Boys!* 1966; *The Happiest Millionaire* 1967; *Charley and the Angel* 1973; *The Swarm* 1978
McMurray, Sam *Union City* 1980; *LA Story* 1991; *Stone Cold* 1991; *Getting Even with Dad* 1994; *Savage* 1995; *Drop Dead Gorgeous* 1999
McMurtrey, Joan *The Betty Ford Story* 1987; *Welcome Home, Roxy Carmichael* 1990
McNair, Barbara *Change of Habit* 1969; *They Call Me Mister Tibbs!* 1970; *The Organization* 1971
McNally, Kevin *Enigma* 1982; *Not Quite Jerusalem* 1985; *Cry Freedom* 1987; *All Things Bright and Beautiful* 1994; *Entrapment* 1999; *When the Sky Falls* 2000
McNally, Stephen *aka* **McNally, Horace** *Dr Gillespie's New Assistant* 1942; *Eyes in the Night* 1942; *For Me and My Gal* 1942; *Keeper of the Flame* 1942; *The Man from Down Under* 1943; *Magnificent Doll* 1946; *Up Goes Maisie* 1946; *Johnny Belinda* 1948; *City across the River* 1949; *Criss Cross* 1949; *The Lady Gambles* 1949; *No Way Out* 1950; *Winchester '73* 1950; *Wyoming Mail* 1950; *Apache Drums* 1951; *The Lady Pays Off* 1951; *Diplomatic Courier* 1952; *The Duel at Silver Creek* 1952; *Devil's Canyon* 1953; *Split Second* 1953; *The Stand at Apache River* 1953; *Make Haste to Live* 1954; *A Bullet Is Waiting* 1954; *Violent Saturday* 1955; *The Man from Bitter Ridge* 1955; *Tribute to a Bad Man* 1956; *Hell Bent for Leather* 1960; *Panic in the City* 1968; *Once You Kiss a Stranger* 1969
McNamara, Brian *The Flamingo Kid* 1984; *Short Circuit* 1986; *Detective Sadie and Son* 1987; *On Fire* 1987; *Arachnophobia* 1990; *Mystery Date* 1991; *When the Party's Over* 1992; *Triumph over Disaster: the Hurricane Andrew Story* 1993; *Seduction in a Small Town* 1996
McNamara, J Patrick *Obsession* 1976; *Close Encounters of the Third Kind* 1977
McNamara, John *From Hell It Came* 1957; *The Return of Dracula* 1958; *War of the Colossal Beast* 1958
McNamara, Maggie *The Moon Is Blue* 1953; *Three Coins in the Fountain* 1954; *Prince of Players* 1955
McNamara, Pat *The Last Time I Committed Suicide* 1996; *The Daytrippers* 1998
McNamara, William *Stealing Home* 1988; *Wildflower* 1991; *Honor Thy Mother* 1992; *Sworn to Vengeance* 1993; *Chasers* 1994; *Surviving the Game* 1994; *Radio Inside* 1994; *Copycat* 1995; *Storybook* 1995; *The Brylcreem Boys* 1996; *Natural Enemy* 1996; *Stag* 1996; *Something to Believe In* 1997
MacNaughtan, Alan *Frankenstein Created Woman* 1966; *Family Life* 1971

Maguire, Tobey *This Boy's Life* 1993; *Spoils of War* 1994; *The Ice Storm* 1997; *Fear and Loathing in Las Vegas* 1998; *Pleasantville* 1998; *Ride with the Devil* 1999; *The Cider House Rules* 1999; *Wonder Boys* 2000

Mahaffey, Valerie *Women of Valor* 1986; *Code Name: Dancer* 1987; *Married for Murder* 1992; *They Watch* 1993; *National Lampoon's Senior Trip* 1995; *Jungle 2 Jungle* 1997

Mahal, Taj *Sounder* 1972; *Part 2, Sounder* 1976

Maharis, George *Sylvia* 1964; *The Satan Bug* 1965; *The Happening* 1967; *A Covenant with Death* 1967; *The Desperados* 1969; *Land Raiders* 1969; *The Sword and the Sorcerer* 1982; *Doppelganger* 1993

Maher, Bill *House II: the Second Story* 1987; *Cannibal Women in the Avocado Jungle of Death* 1989; *Pizza Man* 1991

Maher, Joseph *Under the Rainbow* 1981; *The Evil That Men Do* 1984; *Bigfoot* 1987; *Funny Farm* 1988; *My Stepmother Is an Alien* 1988; *Baby Brokers* 1994; *Killer* 1994; *IQ* 1995; *Surviving Picasso* 1996; *Hoods* 1998

Mahler, Bruce *Police Academy 2: Their First Assignment* 1985; *Police Academy 6: City under Siege* 1989

Mahoney, Jock *A Day of Fury* 1956; *Battle Hymn* 1957; *The Land Unknown* 1957; *Money, Women and Guns* 1958; *A Time to Love and a Time to Die* 1958; *Tarzan the Magnificent* 1960; *Tarzan Goes to India* 1962; *Tarzan's Three Challenges* 1963; *The Glory Stompers* 1967; *Tarzan's Deadly Silence* 1970

Mahoney, John *The Deadly Game* 1986; *Trapped in Silence* 1986; *Moonstruck* 1987; *Suspect* 1987; *Tin Men* 1987; *Betrayed* 1988; *Eight Men Out* 1988; *Frantic* 1988; *Dinner at Eight* 1989; *Say Anything* 1989; *The Image* 1990; *Love Hurts* 1990; *The Russia House* 1990; *Barton Fink* 1991; *The 10 Million Dollar Getaway* 1991; *Article 99* 1992; *The Water Engine* 1992; *In the Line of Fire* 1993; *Striking Distance* 1993; *The Hudsucker Proxy* 1994; *The American President* 1995; *Primal Fear* 1996; *She's the One* 1996; *Antz* 1998; *The Iron Giant* 1999

Mailer, Norman *Beyond the Law* 1968; *Ragtime* 1981; *King Lear – Fear and Loathing* 1987

Mailer, Stephen *Reversal of Fortune* 1990; *Getting In* 1994

Mailes, Charles Hill *aka* **Mailes, Charles H** *The Battle of Elderbush* 1914; *The Mark of Zorro* 1920

Main, Laurie *The Master Plan* 1954; *Time after Time* 1979

Main, Marjorie *Dead End* 1937; *The Man Who Cried Wolf* 1937; *Stella Dallas* 1937; *Too Hot to Handle* 1938; *Honky Tonk* 1941; *The Shepherd of the Hills* 1941; *A Woman's Face* 1941; *Heaven Can Wait* 1943; *Johnny Come Lately* 1943; *Meet Me in St Louis* 1944; *Murder, He Says* 1945; *The Harvey Girls* 1946; *Bad Bascomb* 1946; *The Egg and I* 1947; *Ma and Pa Kettle* 1949; *Big Jack* 1949; *Summer Stock* 1950; *Mr Imperium* 1951; *The Belle of New York* 1952; *The Long, Long Trailer* 1954; *Rose Marie* 1954; *Friendly Persuasion* 1956

Maistre, François *Paris Nous Appartient* 1960; *Dirty Hands* 1976

Maitland, Lorna *Lorna* 1964; *Mudhoney* 1965

Maitland, Marne *Bhowani Junction* 1956; *The Mark of the Hawk* 1957; *The Wind Cannot Read* 1958; *Sands of the Desert* 1960; *The Reptile* 1966; *The Bobo* 1967

Majorino, Tina *Andre* 1994; *Corrina, Corrina* 1994; *When a Man Loves a Woman* 1994; *Waterworld* 1995; *Before Women Had Wings* 1997

Majors, Lee *Will Penny* 1967; *The Liberation of LB Jones* 1970; *Francis Gary Powers: the True Story of the U-2* 1976; *Killer Fish* 1978; *The Norseman* 1978; *Steel* 1980; *Agency* 1981; *The Last Chase* 1981; *Starflight One* 1983; *Bionic Showdown: the Six Million Dollar Man and the Bionic Woman* 1989; *Keaton's Cop* 1990; *Fire! Trapped on the 37th Floor* 1991; *The Cover Girl Murders* 1993; *Bionic Ever After?* 1994; *Lost Treasure of Dos Santos* 1997

Majumdar, Sreela *And Quiet Rolls the Dawn* 1979; *In Search of Famine* 1980

Makeham, Eliot *Rome Express* 1932; *Friday the Thirteenth* 1933; *Dark Journey* 1937; *Head over Heels in Love* 1937; *Bell-Bottom George* 1943; *Daybreak* 1946; *Children of Chance* 1949; *Murder at the Windmill* 1949; *Green Grow the Rushes* 1951; *The Yellow Balloon* 1952

Makepeace, Chris *My Bodyguard* 1980; *The Last Chase* 1981; *Vamp* 1986; *Aloha Summer* 1988; *Captive Hearts* 1988; *Memory Run* 1995

Makhmalbaf, Mohsen *Close-Up* 1989; *A Moment of Innocence* 1996

Makkena, Wendy *Sister Act* 1992; *Black Magic* 1992; *Sister Act 2: Back in the Habit* 1993; *Serving in Silence* 1995; *Death Benefit* 1996; *Air Bud* 1997; *Finding North* 1997

Mako *The Sand Pebbles* 1966; *The Ugly Dachshund* 1966; *The Private Navy of Sgt O'Farrell* 1968; *Master of the Islands* 1970; *The Island at the Top of the World* 1974; *The Killer Elite* 1975; *The Big Brawl* 1980; *The Bushido Blade* 1981; *An Eye for an Eye* 1981; *Under the Rainbow* 1981; *Conan the Barbarian* 1982; *Death Ride to Osaka* 1983; *The Last Ninja* 1983; *Conan the Destroyer* 1984; *POW the Escape* 1986; *Armed Response* 1986; *Silent Assassins* 1988; *Tucker: the Man and His Dream* 1988; *An Unremarkable Life* 1989; *Hiroshima: Out of the Ashes* 1990; *Murder in Paradise* 1990; *Pacific Heights* 1990; *Fatal Mission* 1990; *The Perfect Weapon* 1991; *Rising Sun* 1993; *RoboCop 3* 1993; *Sidekicks* 1993; *Red Sun Rising* 1994; *Crying Freeman* 1995; *Highlander III: the Sorcerer* 1995; *Seven Years in Tibet* 1997

Makovetsky, Sergei *Rothschild's Violin* 1996; *Of Freaks and Men* 1998

Maksimovic, Dragan *Meetings with Remarkable Men* 1979; *Time of Miracles* 1990; *Pretty Village Pretty Flame* 1996

Malahide, Patrick *Comfort and Joy* 1984; *A Month in the Country* 1987; *Smack and Thistle* 1989; *December Bride* 1990; *A Man of No Importance* 1994; *Two Deaths* 1994; *CutThroat Island* 1995; *The Long Kiss Goodnight* 1996; *The Beautician and the Beast* 1997; *Captain Jack* 1998; *Miracle at Midnight* 1998; *Ordinary Decent Criminal* 1999

Malavoy, Christophe *La Balance* 1982; *Death in a French Garden* 1985; *Madame Bovary* 1991

Malcolm, Christopher *Figures in a Landscape* 1970; *Labyrinth* 1986

Malden, Karl *They Knew What They Wanted* 1940; *Kiss of Death* 1947; *The Gunfighter* 1950; *Halls of Montezuma* 1950; *Where the Sidewalk Ends* 1950; *The Sellout* 1951; *A Streetcar Named Desire* 1951; *Diplomatic Courier* 1952; *Ruby Gentry* 1952; *I Confess* 1953; *On the Waterfront* 1954; *Phantom of the Rue Morgue* 1954; *Baby Doll* 1956; *Bombers B-52* 1957; *Fear Strikes Out* 1957; *The Hanging Tree* 1959; *Pollyanna* 1960; *One-Eyed Jacks* 1961; *Parrish* 1961; *All Fall Down* 1962; *Birdman of Alcatraz* 1962; *Come Fly with Me* 1962; *Gypsy* 1962; *How the West Was Won* 1962; *Cheyenne Autumn* 1964; *Dead Ringer* 1964; *The Cincinnati Kid* 1965; *Murderers' Row* 1966; *Nevada Smith* 1966; *The Adventures of Bullwhip Griffin* 1967; *Billion Dollar Brain* 1967; *Hotel* 1967; *Blue* 1968; *Hot Millions* 1968; *Patton: Lust for Glory* 1970; *Cat o'Nine Tails* 1971; *Wild Rovers* 1971; *Beyond the Poseidon Adventure* 1979; *Meteor* 1979; *The Sting II* 1983; *With Intent to Kill* 1984; *Billy Galvin* 1986; *Nuts* 1987; *My Father, My Son* 1988; *Absolute Strangers* 1991; *Vanished without a Trace* 1993

Malet, Arthur *Lt Robin Crusoe, USN* 1966; *Halloween* 1978; *Savage Harvest* 1981; *The Secret of NIMH* 1982; *The Black Cauldron* 1985; *Toys* 1992; *A Little Princess* 1995

Malet, Laurent *Blood Relatives* 1977; *Roads to the South* 1978; *Querelle* 1982

Maley, Peggy *The Wild One* 1953; *Human Desire* 1954; *Live Fast, Die Young* 1958

Malfatti, Marina *More than a Miracle* 1967; *Without Warning* 1973

Malherbe, Annet *Abel* 1986; *The Northerners* 1992

Malhotra, Pavan *Bagh Bahadur* 1989; *Brothers in Trouble* 1995

Malick, Wendie *Madonna: Innocence Lost* 1994; *North Shore Fish* 1997

Malik, Art *aka* **Malik, Athar** *Arabian Adventure* 1979; *A Passage to India* 1984; *The Living Daylights* 1987; *City of Joy* 1992; *Turtle Beach* 1992; *Year of the Comet* 1992; *Hostage* 1992; *Clockwork Mice* 1994; *True Lies* 1994; *A Kid in King Arthur's Court* 1995; *Booty Call* 1997; *Side Streets* 1998

Malin, Eddie *A Hard Day's Night* 1964; *Nearest and Dearest* 1972

Malina, Judith *Enemies, a Love Story* 1989; *Awakenings* 1990; *The Addams Family* 1991; *Household Saints* 1993

Malinger, Ross *Sleepless in Seattle* 1993; *Sudden Death* 1995; *Toothless* 1997

Malkovich, John *The Killing Fields* 1984; *Places in the Heart* 1984; *Death of a Salesman* 1985; *Eleni* 1985; *Empire of the Sun* 1987; *The Glass Menagerie* 1987; *Making Mr Right* 1987; *Dangerous Liaisons* 1988; *Miles from Home* 1988; *The Sheltering Sky* 1990; *The Object of Beauty* 1991; *Shadows and Fog* 1991; *Queens Logic* 1991; *Jennifer Eight* 1992; *Of Mice and Men* 1992; *Heart of Darkness* 1993; *In the Line of Fire* 1993; *Beyond the Clouds* 1995; *Mary Reilly* 1995; *The Convent* 1995; *Mulholland Falls* 1996; *The Portrait of a Lady* 1996; *Con Air* 1997; *The Man in the Iron Mask* 1997; *Rounders* 1998; *Being John Malkovich* 1999; *Joan of Arc* 1999; *RKO 281* 1999; *Time Regained* 1999

Mallalieu, Aubrey *Music Hath Charms* 1935; *The Face at the Window* 1939; *Gert and Daisy's Weekend* 1941; *My Learned Friend* 1943

Malle, Louis *Phantom India* 1968; *God's Country* 1985

Malleson, Miles *Nell Gwyn* 1934; *Vintage Wine* 1935; *The Thief of Bagdad* 1940; *Golden Salamander* 1949; *Kind Hearts and Coronets* 1949; *The Perfect Woman* 1949; *Stage Fright* 1950; *Folly to Be Wise* 1952; *Treasure Hunt* 1952; *Trent's Last Case* 1952; *The Captain's Paradise* 1953; *Brothers in Law* 1956; *The Silken Affair* 1957; *Dracula* 1958; *The Hound of the Baskervilles* 1959; *And the Same to You* 1960; *The Brides of Dracula* 1960; *Kidnapped* 1960; *Double Bunk* 1961; *Fury at Smugglers Bay* 1961; *Go to Blazes* 1961; *The Hellfire Club* 1961; *Postman's Knock* 1961; *A Jolly Bad Fellow* 1964

Mallinson, Rory *Deep Valley* 1947; *Cavalry Scout* 1951

Malloy, Matt *Surviving Desire* 1989; *Boys* 1995; *In the Company of Men* 1997

Malm, Mona *Fanny and Alexander* 1982; *Best Intentions* 1992

Malmsten, Birger *It Rains on Our Love* 1946; *A Ship to India* 1947; *Night Is My Future* 1948; *Thirst* 1949; *The Devil's Wanton* 1949; *Summer Interlude* 1950; *Waiting Women* 1952

Malo, Gina *Southern Roses* 1936; *Where There's a Will* 1936; *Over She Goes* 1937

Malone, Dorothy *The Big Sleep* 1946; *Night and Day* 1946; *Colorado Territory* 1949; *South of St Louis* 1949; *Convicted* 1950; *Law and Order* 1953; *Scared Stiff* 1953; *Pushover* 1954; *Private Hell 36* 1954; *Security Risk* 1954; *Artists and Models* 1955; *At Gunpoint* 1955; *Young at Heart* 1955; *Tall Man Riding* 1955; *Sincerely Yours* 1955; *Five Guns West* 1955; *Pillars of the Sky* 1956; *Tension at Table Rock* 1956; *Written on the Wind* 1956; *Man of a Thousand Faces* 1957; *The Tarnished Angels* 1957; *Tip on a Dead Jockey* 1957; *Quantez* 1957; *Too Much, Too Soon* 1958; *Warlock* 1959; *The Last Voyage* 1960; *The Last Sunset* 1961; *Beach Party* 1963; *The Man Who Would Not Die* 1975; *Abduction* 1975; *Golden Rendezvous* 1977; *Katie: Portrait of a Centerfold* 1978; *Winter Kills* 1979; *Good Luck, Miss Wyckoff* 1979; *The Day Time Ended* 1980

Malone, Jena *Bastard out of Carolina* 1996; *Hidden in America* 1996; *Hope* 1997; *Ellen Foster* 1997; *Stepmom* 1998; *For Love of the Game* 1999

Malone, Mark *Dead of Winter* 1987; *Straight out of Brooklyn* 1991

Maloney, Michael *La Maschera* 1988; *Henry V* 1989; *Hamlet* 1990; *Truly Madly Deeply* 1990; *In the Bleak Midwinter* 1995; *Othello* 1995; *Hamlet* 1996

Maloney, Peter *The Thing* 1982; *Washington Square* 1997; *Thicker than Blood* 1998

Maltby, H F *Where There's a Will* 1936; *Under Your Hat* 1940; *Home Sweet Home* 1945

Manahan, Anna *A Business Affair* 1993; *A Man of No Importance* 1994

Manahan, Sheila *Another Shore* 1948; *Seven Days to Noon* 1950; *Only Two Can Play* 1962

Mancini, Al *Miller's Crossing* 1990; *My Summer Story* 1994

Mancini, Ray *aka* **Mancini, Ray "Boom Boom"** *Oceans of Fire* 1986; *The Dirty Dozen: the Fatal Mission* 1988; *Wishful Thinking* 1990; *Time Bomb* 1991; *Aces: Iron Eagle III* 1992; *The Search for One-Eye Jimmy* 1996

Mancuso, Nick *Nightwing* 1979; *Ticket to Heaven* 1981; *The Legend of Walks Far Woman* 1982; *Mother Lode* 1982; *Maria Chapdelaine* 1982; *Heartbreakers* 1984; *Love Songs* 1984; *Blame It on the Night* 1984; *Death of an Angel* 1985; *Embassy* 1985; *The King of Love* 1987; *Lena's Holiday* 1990; *Milena* 1990; *Lies before Kisses* 1991; *Rapid Fire* 1992; *For the Love of Aaron* 1993; *Flinch* 1994; *Suspicious Agenda* 1994; *Young Ivanhoe* 1994; *Under Siege 2* 1995; *Young Connecticut Yankee in King Arthur's Court* 1995; *The Takeover* 1995; *The Ex* 1996; *Once You Meet a Stranger* 1996; *The Invader* 1997; *Misbegotten* 1998

Mandalis, Elena *Only the Brave* 1994; *Head On* 1997

Mandan, Robert *The Best Little Whorehouse in Texas* 1982; *Zapped!* 1982; *National Lampoon's Last Resort* 1994

Mandel, Howie *Gas* 1981; *A Fine Mess* 1986; *Walk like a Man* 1987; *Little Monsters* 1989; *Gremlins 2: the New Batch* 1990; *David Copperfield* 1993; *Shake, Rattle and Rock* 1994; *Harrison Bergeron* 1995

Mander, Miles *The Pleasure Garden* 1925; *Murder* 1930; *Bitter Sweet* 1933; *Don Quixote* 1933; *Kidnapped* 1938; *The Man in the Iron Mask* 1939; *The Three Musketeers* 1939; *Primrose Path* 1940; *Shadows on the Stairs* 1941; *Fingers at the Window* 1942; *Apache Trail* 1942; *Five Graves to Cairo* 1943; *The Return of the Vampire* 1943; *Enter Arsene Lupin* 1944; *The Pearl of Death* 1944; *The Brighton Strangler* 1945; *Farewell My Lovely* 1945

Mandylor, Costas *Triumph of the Spirit* 1989; *Mobsters* 1991; *Crosscut* 1995; *Delta of Venus* 1995; *Falling for You* 1995; *Fist of the North Star* 1995; *Double Take* 1997; *Lovestruck* 1997

Mandylor, Louis *The Heartbreak Kid* 1993; *The Set Up* 1995

Maneri, Luisa *La Cage aux Folles* 1978; *Renegade* 1987

Manfredi, Nino *We All Loved Each Other So Much* 1974; *Down and Dirty* 1976; *In the Name of the Pope King* 1977

Mangano, Silvana *Bitter Rice* 1949; *Gold of Naples* 1954; *Mambo* 1954; *Ulysses* 1954; *This Angry Age* 1957; *The Great War* 1959; *Tempest* 1959; *Five Branded Women* 1960; *Barabbas* 1961; *Oedipus Rex* 1967; *Theorem* 1968; *Death in Venice* 1971; *Ludwig* 1973; *Conversation Piece* 1974; *Dune* 1984; *Dark Eyes* 1987

Mango, Alec *They Who Dare* 1953; *Mask of Dust* 1954; *The Strange World of Planet X* 1957; *Interpol* 1957; *The 7th Voyage of Sinbad* 1958; *Gothic* 1986
Mangold, Erni *I Only Want You to Love Me* 1976; *Before Sunrise* 1995
Manion, Cindy *Preppies* 1984; *The Toxic Avenger* 1985
Mankuma, Blu *Stockade* 1991; *Double Suspicion* 1993; *Whale Music* 1994; *Bliss* 1997; *Bone Daddy* 1998
Mann, Byron *Crying Freeman* 1995; *Red Corner* 1997; *The Corruptor* 1999
Mann, Collette *Kitty and the Bagman* 1982; *Outback Bound* 1988
Mann, Danny *Little Nemo: Adventures in Slumberland* 1992; *Babe* 1995
Mann, Gabriel *High Art* 1998; *Dying to Live* 1999
Mann, Leslie *The Cable Guy* 1996; *George of the Jungle* 1997; *Big Daddy* 1999
Mann, Terrence *A Chorus Line* 1985; *Critters* 1986; *Critters 2: the Main Course* 1988; *Critters 4* 1992
Mann, Tracy *Hard Knocks* 1980; *The Scarecrow* 1982
Manners, David *Journey's End* 1930; *Dracula* 1931; *The Last Flight* 1931; *The Miracle Woman* 1931; *A Bill of Divorcement* 1932; *The Mummy* 1932; *Lady with a Past* 1932; *The Death Kiss* 1933; *Roman Scandals* 1933; *The Devil's in love* 1933; *The Black Cat* 1934; *The Moonstone* 1934; *The Mystery of Edwin Drood* 1935; *A Woman Rebels* 1936
Mannheim, Lucie *The 39 Steps* 1935; *The Yellow Canary* 1943; *Hotel Reserve* 1944; *Tawny Pipit* 1944; *Beyond the Curtain* 1960
Manni, Ettore *Le Amiche* 1955; *Gold for the Caesars* 1964; *Mademoiselle* 1966; *Ringo and His Golden Pistol* 1966; *City of Women* 1980
Manning, Irene *The Big Shot* 1942; *Yankee Doodle Dandy* 1942; *The Desert Song* 1944; *Make Your Own Bed* 1944; *Shine On, Harvest Moon* 1944
Manoff, Dinah *Ordinary People* 1980; *I Ought to Be in Pictures* 1982; *Flight 90: Disaster on the Potomac* 1984; *Child's Play* 1988; *Beauty and Denise* 1989; *Staying Together* 1989; *Babies* 1990; *Maid for Each Other* 1992
Manojlovic, Miki *aka* **Manojlovic, Predrag Miki,** *aka* **Manojlovic, Pedrag** *When Father Was Away on Business* 1985; *Time of Miracles* 1990; *Tito and Me* 1992; *Someone Else's America* 1995; *Underground* 1995; *Artemisia* 1997
Mansfield, Jayne *The Female Jungle* 1955; *Hell on Frisco Bay* 1955; *Illegal* 1955; *The Burglar* 1956; *The Girl Can't Help It* 1956; *Kiss Them for Me* 1957; *Will Success Spoil Rock Hunter?* 1957; *The Wayward Bus* 1957; *The Sheriff of Fractured Jaw* 1958; *The Challenge* 1960; *The George Raft Story* 1961; *Panic Button* 1964
Manson, Alan *Let's Scare Jessica to Death* 1971; *Whiffs* 1975; *Leadbelly* 1976
Mantee, Paul *Breakout* 1975; *Wolf Lake* 1979; *Lurking Fear* 1994
Mantegna, Joe *Second Thoughts* 1982; *Compromising Positions* 1985; *The Money Pit* 1985; *Off Beat* 1986; *Critical Condition*

1987; *House of Games* 1987; *Suspect* 1987; *Weeds* 1987; *Things Change* 1988; *Wait until Spring, Bandini* 1989; *Alice* 1990; *The Godfather Part III* 1990; *Bugsy* 1991; *Family Prayers* 1991; *Homicide* 1991; *Queens Logic* 1991; *Body of Evidence* 1992; *The Comrades of Summer* 1992; *The Water Engine* 1992; *Innocent Moves* 1993; *Airheads* 1994; *Baby's Day Out* 1994; *State of Emergency* 1994; *Eye for an Eye* 1995; *Forget Paris* 1995; *Above Suspicion* 1995; *For Better or Worse* 1995; *Captain Nuke and the Bomber Boys* 1995; *Albino Alligator* 1996; *Face Down* 1996; *Persons Unknown* 1996; *Stephen King's Thinner* 1996; *Up Close & Personal* 1996; *Underworld* 1996; *For Hire* 1997; *Celebrity* 1998; *The Rat Pack* 1998; *Hoods* 1998; *Jerry and Tom* 1998; *The Runner* 1999
Mantel, Bronwen *Barnum* 1986; *Pin* 1988
Mantell, Joe *Marty* 1955; *Storm Center* 1956; *Beau James* 1957; *The Sad Sack* 1957; *Onionhead* 1958
Manuel, Robert *Rififi* 1955; *The Black Tulip* 1963
Manville, Lesley *Dance with a Stranger* 1984; *High Season* 1987; *High Hopes* 1988; *Secrets & Lies* 1995; *Topsy-Turvy* 1999
Manz, Linda *Days of Heaven* 1978; *Orphan Train* 1979; *The Wanderers* 1979; *Out of the Blue* 1980
Manza, Ralph *Gang War* 1958; *Too Soon to Love* 1960; *Lookin' Italian* 1994
Maples, Marla *Happiness* 1998; *Black and White* 1999
Mara, Adele *You Were Never Lovelier* 1942; *Reveille with Beverly* 1943; *Atlantic City* 1944; *Bells of Rosarita* 1945; *Angel in Exile* 1948; *Sands of Iwo Jima* 1949; *Wake of the Red Witch* 1949
Mara, Mary *Empire City* 1991; *The Hard Way* 1991; *Love Potion No 9* 1992; *Mr Saturday Night* 1992; *Bound* 1996
Marachuk, Steve *Piranha II: The Spawning* 1983; *Hot Target* 1985
Marais, Jean *Eternal Love* 1943; *La Belle et la Bête* 1946; *Eagle with Two Heads* 1948; *Les Parents Terribles* 1948; *Orphée* 1950; *Royal Affairs in Versailles* 1953; *Napoléon* 1955; *Elena et les Hommes* 1956; *White Nights* 1957; *Le Bossu* 1959; *The Battle of Austerlitz* 1960; *The Captain* 1960; *Le Testament d'Orphée* 1960; *Pontius Pilate* 1961; *The Mysteries of Paris* 1962; *Le Masque de Fer* 1962; *The Magic Donkey* 1970; *Stealing Beauty* 1995
Marangosoff, Janna *Trauma* 1983; *In the Belly of the Whale* 1984; *Men...* 1985
Maranne, André *Darling Lili* 1970; *The Return of the Pink Panther* 1974; *The Pink Panther Strikes Again* 1976; *Revenge of the Pink Panther* 1978; *Plenty* 1985
Marceau, Marcel *Barbarella* 1967; *Shanks* 1974
Marceau, Sophie *Fort Saganne* 1984; *Police* 1985; *Descent into Hell* 1986; *D'Artagnan's Daughter* 1994; *Beyond the Clouds* 1995; *Braveheart* 1995; *Anna Karenina* 1997; *Firelight* 1997; *Marquise* 1997; *Lost & Found* 1999; *The World Is Not Enough* 1999
March, Eve *The Curse of the Cat People* 1944; *Adam's Rib* 1949

March, Fredric *The Wild Party* 1929; *The Marriage Playground* 1929; *Laughter* 1930; *Manslaughter* 1930; *Paramount on Parade* 1930; *The Royal Family of Broadway* 1930; *Sarah and Son* 1930; *Honor among Lovers* 1931; *Dr Jekyll and Mr Hyde* 1932; *The Sign of the Cross* 1932; *Smilin' Through* 1932; *Merrily We Go to Hell* 1932; *Design for Living* 1933; *The Eagle and the Hawk* 1933; *The Affairs of Cellini* 1934; *The Barretts of Wimpole Street* 1934; *Death Takes a Holiday* 1934; *We Live Again* 1934; *Anna Karenina* 1935; *The Dark Angel* 1935; *Les Misérables* 1935; *Anthony Adverse* 1936; *Mary of Scotland* 1936; *The Road to Glory* 1936; *Nothing Sacred* 1937; *A Star Is Born* 1937; *The Buccaneer* 1938; *Trade Winds* 1938; *There Goes My Heart* 1938; *Susan and God* 1940; *Victory* 1940; *One Foot in Heaven* 1941; *So Ends Our Night* 1941; *Bedtime Story* 1942; *I Married a Witch* 1942; *The Adventures of Mark Twain* 1944; *Tomorrow the World!* 1944; *The Best Years of Our Lives* 1946; *Another Part of the Forest* 1948; *Christopher Columbus* 1949; *Death of a Salesman* 1951; *It's a Big Country* 1951; *Man on a Tightrope* 1953; *The Bridges at Toko-Ri* 1954; *Executive Suite* 1954; *The Desperate Hours* 1955; *Alexander the Great* 1956; *The Man in the Gray Flannel Suit* 1956; *Middle of the Night* 1959; *Inherit the Wind* 1960; *The Young Doctors* 1961; *The Condemned of Altona* 1962; *Seven Days in May* 1964; *Hombre* 1967; *The Iceman Cometh* 1973
March, Jane *The Lover* 1992; *Color of Night* 1994; *Circle of Passion* 1996; *Tarzan and the Lost City* 1998
March, Philippe *Two People* 1973; *Once in Paris* 1978
Marchal, Georges *Death in the Garden* 1956; *Celà s'Appelle l'Aurore* 1956; *The Sign of the Gladiator* 1958; *The Colossus of Rhodes* 1961; *The Secret Mark of D'Artagnan* 1962; *The Milky Way* 1968
Marchand, Corinne *Cleo from 5 to 7* 1961; *Borsalino* 1970; *Rider on the Rain* 1970; *Le Parfum d'Yvonne* 1994
Marchand, Guy *Une Belle Fille Comme Moi* 1973; *Cousin, Cousine* 1975; *Loulou* 1980; *Clean Slate* 1981; *Garde à Vue* 1981; *Entre Nous* 1983; *Petit Con* 1984; *Hold-Up* 1985; *Le Cop II* 1989; *May Wine* 1990
Marchand, Nancy *The Bachelor Party* 1957; *The Hospital* 1971; *Once upon a Family* 1980; *Agatha Christie's Sparkling Cyanide* 1983; *The Bostonians* 1984; *The Naked Gun* 1988; *Brain Donors* 1992; *Sabrina* 1995
Marcon, André *Jeanne la Pucelle* 1994; *Requiem* 1998
Marcoux, Ted *The Nightman* 1992; *Ghost in the Machine* 1993; *Visions of Terror* 1994; *Thrill* 1996
Marcovicci, Andrea *Smile, Jenny, You're Dead* 1974; *The Front* 1976; *The Hand* 1981; *Kings and Desperate Men* 1981; *Packin' It In* 1983; *Spacehunter: Adventures in the Forbidden Zone* 1983; *The Stuff* 1985; *Someone to Love* 1987
Marcus, James *Little Lord Fauntleroy* 1921; *The Iron Horse* 1924; *The Eagle* 1925; *The Texan* 1930

Marcus, Richard *Enemy Mine* 1985; *Deadly Friend* 1986; *Jesse* 1988; *Tremors* 1989
Marcus, Stephen *Savage Hearts* 1995; *Lock, Stock and Two Smoking Barrels* 1998
Marcuse, Theo *aka* **Marcuse, Theodore** *A Tiger Walks* 1964; *Harem Holiday* 1965; *The Picasso Summer* 1969
Marescotti, Ivano *Johnny Stecchino* 1991; *Bits and Pieces* 1995
Margetson, Arthur *Music Hath Charms* 1935; *Broken Blossoms* 1936; *Pagliacci* 1936; *Sherlock Holmes Faces Death* 1943
Margo *Crime without Passion* 1934; *Rumba* 1935; *The Robin Hood of El Dorado* 1936; *Winterset* 1936; *Lost Horizon* 1937; *Miracle on Main Street* 1940; *Behind the Rising Sun* 1943; *The Leopard Man* 1943; *Viva Zapata!* 1952; *I'll Cry Tomorrow* 1955; *Who's Got the Action?* 1962
Margolin, Janet *David and Lisa* 1962; *Bus Riley's Back in Town* 1965; *The Saboteur, Code Name Morituri* 1965; *Nevada Smith* 1966; *Enter Laughing* 1967; *Buona Sera, Mrs Campbell* 1968; *Take the Money and Run* 1969; *Family Flight* 1972; *Your Three Minutes Are Up* 1973; *Planet Earth* 1974; *Annie Hall* 1977; *Last Embrace* 1979; *The Game of Love* 1987; *Distant Thunder* 1988
Margolin, Stuart *The Gamblers* 1969; *Kelly's Heroes* 1970; *Limbo* 1972; *The California Kid* 1974; *Death Wish* 1974; *Futureworld* 1976; *Days of Heaven* 1978; *SOB* 1981; *Class* 1983; *Running Hot* 1983; *A Fine Mess* 1986; *Iron Eagle II* 1988; *Bye Bye Blues* 1989; *Deep Sleep* 1990
Margolis, Mark *Delta Force 2* 1990; *Descending Angel* 1990; *Pi* 1997
Margolyes, Miriam *The Awakening* 1980; *The Apple* 1980; *Electric Dreams* 1984; *The Good Father* 1986; *Little Dorrit* 1987; *I Love You to Death* 1990; *Orpheus Descending* 1990; *The Butcher's Wife* 1991; *As You Like It* 1992; *The Age of Innocence* 1993; *Motherhood* 1993; *Immortal Beloved* 1994; *Babe* 1995; *Cold Comfort Farm* 1995; *Different for Girls* 1996; *James and the Giant Peach* 1996; *William Shakespeare's Romeo + Juliet* 1996; *Babe: Pig in the City* 1998; *Dreaming of Joseph Lees* 1998; *Mulan* 1998; *End of Days* 1999; *House!* 2000
Margotta, Michael *Drive, He Said* 1971; *Partners* 1976; *Can She Bake a Cherry Pie?* 1983
Margulies, David *Dressed to Kill* 1980; *Times Square* 1980; *Nine ½ Weeks* 1985; *Out on a Limb* 1992
Margulies, Julianna *Paradise Road* 1997; *A Price above Rubies* 1997; *Traveller* 1997; *The Newton Boys* 1998; *Dinosaur* 2000
Maricle, Leona *Woman Chases Man* 1937; *Beauty for the Asking* 1939
Marielle, Jean-Pierre *Without Apparent Motive* 1972; *Man in the Trunk* 1973; *Clean Slate* 1981; *Hold-Up* 1985; *Tenue de Soirée* 1986; *Uranus* 1990; *Tous les Matins du Monde* 1992; *Le Parfum d'Yvonne* 1994
Marienthal, Eli *Slums of Beverly Hills* 1998; *The Iron Giant* 1999
Marietto *It Started in Naples* 1960; *The Pigeon That Took Rome* 1962

Marihugh, Tammy *The Last Voyage* 1960; *Back Street* 1961
Marin, Jacques *Les Jeux Interdits* 1953; *Gigot* 1962; *Tiara Tahiti* 1962; *Charade* 1963; *How to Steal a Million* 1966; *Darling Lili* 1970; *The Island at the Top of the World* 1974; *Herbie Goes to Monte Carlo* 1977
Marin, Richard "Cheech" *aka* **Marin, Cheech** *Cheech & Chong's Up in Smoke* 1978; *Cheech & Chong's Next Movie* 1980; *Cheech & Chong's Nice Dreams* 1981; *Things Are Tough All Over* 1982; *Yellowbeard* 1983; *Cheech & Chong's Still Smokin'* 1983; *Cheech & Chong's The Corsican Brothers* 1984; *After Hours* 1985; *Echo Park* 1985; *Born in East LA* 1987; *Fatal Beauty* 1987; *Oliver & Company* 1988; *Rude Awakening* 1989; *The Shrimp on the Barbie* 1990; *The Cisco Kid* 1994; *The Lion King* 1994; *Ring of the Musketeers* 1994; *Charlie's Ghost Story* 1994; *The Courtyard* 1995; *Desperado* 1995; *From Dusk till Dawn* 1995; *The Great White Hype* 1996; *Tin Cup* 1996; *Paulie* 1998
Marin, Rikki *Cheech & Chong's Next Movie* 1980; *Things Are Tough All Over* 1982; *Cheech & Chong's The Corsican Brothers* 1984
Marinaro, Ed *The Game of Love* 1987; *Sharing Richard* 1988; *Menu for Murder* 1990; *Passport to Murder* 1993; *Dancing with Danger* 1994; *Deadly Web* 1995; *Panic in the Skies!* 1996; *Doomsday Rock* 1997
Marion, George F *Anna Christie* 1930; *The Big House* 1930
Marion, Joan *For Valour* 1937; *Ten Days in Paris* 1939
Marion, Paul *Scared Stiff* 1953; *Shotgun* 1955
Marion-Crawford, Howard *Forever England* 1935; *Freedom Radio* 1941; *The Hasty Heart* 1949; *Mr Drake's Duck* 1950; *The Man in the White Suit* 1951; *The Birthday Present* 1957; *The Silken Affair* 1957; *Nowhere to Go* 1958; *Virgin Island* 1958; *Life in Danger* 1959; *The Face of Fu Manchu* 1965; *The Brides of Fu Manchu* 1966; *The Vengeance of Fu Manchu* 1967; *The Blood of Fu Manchu* 1968; *The Castle of Fu Manchu* 1968
Maris, Mona *A Date with the Falcon* 1941; *Underground* 1941; *Berlin Correspondent* 1942; *The Falcon in Mexico* 1944
Marken, Jane *Abel Gance's Beethoven* 1936; *Eternal Love* 1943
Marken, Jeanne *Une Partie de Campagne* 1936; *Hôtel du Nord* 1938; *And God Created Woman* 1956
Markham, David *Blood from the Mummy's Tomb* 1971; *ZPG: Zero Population Growth* 1971; *Tess* 1979
Markham, Kika *Anne and Muriel* 1971; *Outland* 1981; *The Innocent* 1984; *Wonderland* 1999
Markham, Monte *Project X* 1968; *Guns of the Magnificent Seven* 1969; *One Is a Lonely Number* 1972; *Ginger in the Morning* 1973; *Hot Pursuit* 1987; *Baywatch: Panic at Malibu Pier* 1989; *...At First Sight* 1995; *Piranha* 1996
Markinson, Brian *Forgotten Sins* 1996; *Sweet and Lowdown* 1999
Markland, Ted *The Hired Hand* 1971; *Wanda Nevada* 1979; *Fatal Mission* 1990
Marks, Alfred *Desert Mice* 1959; *There Was a Crooked Man* 1960;

The Frightened City 1961; *She'll Have to Go* 1961; *Scream and Scream Again* 1969; *Our Miss Fred* 1972; *Antonia & Jane* 1990

Marle, Arnold *Men of Two Worlds* 1946; *Portrait from Life* 1948; *Break in the Circle* 1955; *Little Red Monkey* 1955

Marleau, Louise *Anne Trister* 1986; *Une Histoire Inventée* 1990

Marley, John *The Joe Louis Story* 1953; *Cat Ballou* 1965; *Faces* 1968; *Love Story* 1970; *The Family Rico* 1972; *The Godfather* 1972; *Jory* 1972; *Framed* 1975; *WC Fields and Me* 1976; *The Car* 1977; *The Greatest* 1977; *Kid Vengeance* 1977; *Hooper* 1978; *It Lives Again* 1978; *Tribute* 1980; *The Amateur* 1981; *Threshold* 1981; *Utilities* 1981; *Mother Lode* 1982; *Robbers of the Sacred Mountain* 1983; *On the Edge* 1985

Marlier, Carla *Zazie dans le Métro* 1960; *Any Number Can Win* 1963

Marlow, Lucy *A Star Is Born* 1954; *My Sister Eileen* 1955; *Bring Your Smile Along* 1955; *He Laughed Last* 1956

Marlowe, Faye *Junior Miss* 1945; *Rendezvous with Annie* 1946

Marlowe, Hugh *Marriage Is a Private Affair* 1944; *Come to the Stable* 1949; *Twelve O'Clock High* 1949; *All about Eve* 1950; *Night and the City* 1950; *The Day the Earth Stood Still* 1951; *Mr Belvedere Rings the Bell* 1951; *Rawhide* 1951; *Bugles in the Afternoon* 1952; *Monkey Business* 1952; *Wait 'til the Sun Shines, Nellie* 1952; *Way of a Gaucho* 1952; *The Stand at Apache River* 1953; *Garden of Evil* 1954; *Illegal* 1955; *World without End* 1955; *Earth vs the Flying Saucers* 1956; *Birdman of Alcatraz* 1962; *Seven Days in May* 1964; *Castle of Evil* 1966

Marlowe, Linda *Impact* 1963; *The World Ten Times Over* 1963; *Mr Love* 1985

Marlowe, Scott *Gaby* 1956; *The Restless Breed* 1957; *The Cool and the Crazy* 1958; *The Subterraneans* 1960; *A Cold Wind in August* 1961; *No Place like Home* 1989

Marlowe, William *The Uncle* 1964; *Where's Jack?* 1969

Marly, Florence *Tokyo Joe* 1949; *Planet of Blood* 1966

Marmont, Percy *Mantrap* 1926; *Rich and Strange* 1932; *Secret Agent* 1936; *Young and Innocent* 1937; *Knave of Hearts* 1954; *Lisbon* 1956

Marner, Richard *The Password Is Courage* 1962; *Where the Spies Are* 1966; *Tiffany Jones* 1973

Maro, Akaji *The Most Terrible Time in My Life* 1993; *Kikujiro* 1999

Maroney, Kelli *Night of the Comet* 1984; *Face Down* 1996

Maross, Joe *Elmer Gantry* 1960; *Zigzag* 1970; *The Salzburg Connection* 1972; *Sixth and Main* 1977

Marquand, Christian *And God Created Woman* 1956; *Behold a Pale Horse* 1964; *The Other Side of Midnight* 1977; *Je Vous Aime* 1980; *Choice of Arms* 1981

Marquand, Serge *The Last Train* 1972; *The Big Red One* 1980

Marques, Maria Elena *Across the Wide Missouri* 1951; *Ambush at Tomahawk Gap* 1953

Marquet, Mary *Bluebeard* 1962; *La Vie de Château* 1965

Marquette, Ron *Public Access* 1993; *Deadly Past* 1995

Marr, Eddie *aka* **Marr, Edward** *The Steel Trap* 1952; *The Night Holds Terror* 1955

Marriott, Moore *Windbag the Sailor* 1936; *Oh, Mr Porter!* 1937; *Ask a Policeman* 1938; *Convict 99* 1938; *Old Bones of the River* 1938; *Owd Bob* 1938; *Band Waggon* 1939; *Cheer Boys Cheer* 1939; *Where's That Fire?* 1939; *Gasbags* 1940; *Hi, Gang!* 1941; *I Thank You* 1941; *Back Room Boy* 1942; *Time Flies* 1944; *I'll Be Your Sweetheart* 1945; *Green for Danger* 1946; *The History of Mr Polly* 1948

Marriott, Sylvia *Return of a Stranger* 1937; *Crimes at the Dark House* 1939; *Anne and Muriel* 1971; *L'Histoire d'Adèle H* 1975

Mars, Kenneth *The Producers* 1968; *The April Fools* 1969; *Viva Max!* 1969; *Desperate Characters* 1971; *What's Up, Doc?* 1972; *Young Frankenstein* 1974; *Night Moves* 1975; *Goin' Coconuts* 1978; *The Apple Dumpling Gang Rides Again* 1979; *Full Moon High* 1982; *Prince Jack* 1984; *Beer* 1985; *For Keeps* 1987; *Illegally Yours* 1988; *The Little Mermaid* 1989; *Thumbelina* 1994; *Rough Magic* 1995; *Citizen Ruth* 1996

Marsalis, Branford *Throw Momma from the Train* 1987; *School Daze* 1988; *Eve's Bayou* 1997

Marsden, Betty *The Young Lovers* 1954; *Let's Get Married* 1960; *The Leather Boys* 1963; *Eyewitness* 1970; *The Dresser* 1983

Marsden, James *The Public Enemy #1* 1995; *Taken Away* 1996; *Disturbing Behaviour* 1998; *Gossip* 1999

Marsden, Jason *A Goofy Movie* 1995; *Trojan War* 1997

Marsh, Carol *Brighton Rock* 1947; *Marry Me!* 1949; *The Romantic Age* 1949; *Scrooge* 1951; *Dracula* 1958

Marsh, Garry *Dreyfus* 1931; *Number Seventeen* 1932; *Death on the Set* 1935; *Scrooge* 1935; *The Man in the Mirror* 1936; *When Knights Were Bold* 1936; *The Vicar of Bray* 1937; *Bank Holiday* 1938; *Convict 99* 1938; *I See Ice* 1938; *It's in the Air* 1938; *Trouble Brewing* 1939; *Let George Do It* 1940; *Return to Yesterday* 1940; *Pink String and Sealing Wax* 1945; *Dancing with Crime* 1946; *Just William's Luck* 1947; *The Shop at Sly Corner* 1948; *William at the Circus* 1948; *Murder at the Windmill* 1949; *Someone at the Door* 1950; *Something in the City* 1950; *The Lost Hours* 1952; *Double Exposure* 1954; *Man of the Moment* 1955; *Trouble with Eve* 1959

Marsh, Jamie *Montenegro* 1981; *Brainscan* 1994; *Best Laid Plans* 1999

Marsh, Jean *Frenzy* 1972; *The Eagle Has Landed* 1976; *The Changeling* 1980; *Return to Oz* 1985; *Willow* 1988; *A Connecticut Yankee in King Arthur's Court* 1989; *Danny, the Champion of the World* 1989; *Bejewelled* 1990; *Fatherland* 1994

Marsh, Joan *You're Telling Me!* 1934; *Charlie Chan on Broadway* 1937; *Follow the Leader* 1944

Marsh, Mae *The Escape* 1914; *The Battle of Elderbush* 1914; *The Birth of a Nation* 1915; *Intolerance* 1916; *Three Godfathers* 1948; *Impact* 1949

Marsh, Marian *Five Star Final* 1931; *The Mad Genius* 1931; *Svengali* 1931; *The Black Room* 1935; *Crime and Punishment* 1935; *The Man Who Lived Twice* 1936

Marsh, Matthew *John and Yoko: a Love Story* 1985; *Diamond Skulls* 1989

Marsh, Reginald *Shadow of Fear* 1963; *The Sicilians* 1964

Marsh, Sally Ann *The Princess and the Goblin* 1992; *A Monkey's Tale* 2000

Marshal, Alan *After the Thin Man* 1936; *Conquest* 1937; *Night Must Fall* 1937; *Parnell* 1937; *Dramatic School* 1938; *I Met My Love Again* 1938; *The Adventures of Sherlock Holmes* 1939; *Four Girls in White* 1939; *The Hunchback of Notre Dame* 1939; *Irene* 1940; *The Howards of Virginia* 1940; *Lydia* 1941; *Tom, Dick and Harry* 1941; *Bride by Mistake* 1944; *The White Cliffs of Dover* 1944; *House on Haunted Hill* 1958; *Day of the Outlaw* 1959

Marshall, Brenda *The Sea Hawk* 1940; *Footsteps in the Dark* 1941; *Captains of the Clouds* 1942; *You Can't Escape Forever* 1942; *Background to Danger* 1943; *The Constant Nymph* 1943; *Paris after Dark* 1943; *Strange Impersonation* 1946; *Whispering Smith* 1948

Marshall, Bryan *I Start Counting* 1970; *The Tamarind Seed* 1974; *The Spy Who Loved Me* 1977; *The Long Good Friday* 1979; *BMX Bandits* 1983; *Bliss* 1985; *Hot Target* 1985; *Return to Snowy River* 1988; *The Punisher* 1989; *The Phantom Horsemen* 1990

Marshall, Connie *Sunday Dinner for a Soldier* 1944; *Mother Wore Tights* 1947; *Mr Blandings Builds His Dream House* 1948

Marshall, David Anthony *Another 48 HRS* 1990; *Across the Tracks* 1990; *The Owl* 1991; *Roadside Prophets* 1992

Marshall, Don *The Thing with Two Heads* 1972; *Terminal Island* 1973

Marshall, E G *Broken Lance* 1954; *The Caine Mutiny* 1954; *Pushover* 1954; *The Left Hand of God* 1955; *The Mountain* 1956; *The Bachelor Party* 1957; *12 Angry Men* 1957; *The Buccaneer* 1958; *Compulsion* 1959; *The Journey* 1959; *Cash McCall* 1960; *Town without Pity* 1961; *The Chase* 1966; *The Poppy Is Also a Flower* 1966; *The Bridge at Remagen* 1969; *Tora! Tora! Tora!* 1970; *The Pursuit of Happiness* 1971; *Billy Jack Goes to Washington* 1977; *Interiors* 1978; *Disaster on the Coastliner* 1979; *Creepshow* 1982; *My Chauffeur* 1986; *Under Siege* 1986; *National Lampoon's Christmas Vacation* 1989; *Two Evil Eyes* 1990; *Consenting Adults* 1992; *Nixon* 1995; *Absolute Power* 1996; *Miss Evers' Boys* 1997

Marshall, Garry *The Twilight of the Golds* 1996; *Never Been Kissed* 1999

Marshall, Herbert *The Letter* 1929; *Murder* 1930; *Blonde Venus* 1932; *Trouble in Paradise* 1932; *Four Frightened People* 1934; *I Was a Spy* 1934; *Riptide* 1934; *The Painted Veil* 1934; *The Dark Angel* 1935; *The Good Fairy* 1935; *If You Could Only Cook* 1935; *Accent on Youth* 1935; *Till We Meet Again* 1936; *A Woman Rebels* 1936; *Angel* 1937; *Breakfast for Two* 1937; *Mad about Music* 1938; *Always Goodbye* 1938; *Zaza* 1939; *A Bill of Divorcement* 1940; *Foreign Correspondent* 1940; *The Letter* 1940; *The Little Foxes* 1941; *When Ladies Meet* 1941; *The Moon and Sixpence* 1942; *Flight for Freedom* 1943; *Young Ideas* 1943; *Andy Hardy's Blonde Trouble* 1944; *The Enchanted Cottage* 1945; *The Unseen* 1945; *Crack-Up* 1946; *Duel in the Sun* 1946; *The Razor's Edge* 1946; *High Wall* 1947; *Ivy* 1947; *The Secret Garden* 1949; *The Underworld Story* 1950; *Anne of the Indies* 1951; *Black Jack* 1952; *Angel Face* 1953; *The Black Shield of Falworth* 1954; *Gog* 1954; *The Virgin Queen* 1955; *The Fly* 1958; *Stage Struck* 1958; *Midnight Lace* 1960; *A Fever in the Blood* 1961; *The List of Adrian Messenger* 1963; *The Caretakers* 1963; *The Third Day* 1965

Marshall, James *Stockade* 1991; *A Few Good Men* 1992; *Gladiator* 1992; *The Unspoken Truth* 1995; *All She Ever Wanted* 1996; *The Ticket* 1997

Marshall, Ken *Tilt* 1978; *La Pelle* 1981; *Krull* 1983; *Feds* 1988

Marshall, Marion *aka* **Marshall, M T** *I Was a Male War Bride* 1949; *Stella* 1950; *Sailor Beware* 1951; *The Stooge* 1951; *That's My Boy* 1951; *Gunn* 1967

Marshall, Paula *Hellraiser III: Hell on Earth* 1992; *Warlock: the Armageddon* 1993; *The New Age* 1994; *That Old Feeling* 1997; *Thursday* 1998

Marshall, Penny *The Hard Way* 1991; *The Odd Couple: Together Again* 1993

Marshall, Ruth *Love and Human Remains* 1993; *The Myth of the Male Orgasm* 1993; *Waiting for Michelangelo* 1995

Marshall, Sarah *Lord Love a Duck* 1966; *French Silk* 1993

Marshall, Trudy *The Dancing Masters* 1943; *The Fighting Sullivans* 1944; *The Purple Heart* 1944; *Circumstantial Evidence* 1945; *The Fuller Brush Man* 1948

Marshall, Tully *A Romance of the Redwoods* 1917; *The Fall of Babylon* 1919; *The Covered Wagon* 1923; *The Hunchback of Notre Dame* 1923; *He Who Gets Slapped* 1924; *The Merry Widow* 1925; *The Cat and the Canary* 1927; *Thunderbolt* 1929; *The Big Trail* 1930; *Mammy* 1930; *Tom Sawyer* 1930; *The Unholy Garden* 1931; *Fighting Caravans* 1931; *Arsene Lupin* 1932; *The Hatchet Man* 1932; *Red Dust* 1932; *The Beast of the City* 1932; *The Hurricane Express* 1932; *Murder on the Blackboard* 1934; *California Straight Ahead* 1937; *Ball of Fire* 1941; *This Gun for Hire* 1942

Marshall, William *Belle of the Yukon* 1944; *Murder in the Music Hall* 1946; *Lydia Bailey* 1952; *Something of Value* 1957; *To Trap a Spy* 1966; *The Hell with Heroes* 1968; *Zigzag* 1970; *Blacula* 1972; *Scream Blacula Scream* 1973; *Abby* 1974

Marshall, Zena *Marry Me!* 1949; *Meet Simon Cherry* 1949; *Deadly Nightshade* 1953; *Dr No* 1962; *The Marked One* 1963

Marshe, Vera *Getting Gertie's Garter* 1945; *Where There's Life* 1947

Marsillach, Cristina *1919* 1983; *Every Time We Say Goodbye* 1986; *Opera* 1987

Marson, Ania *Puppet on a Chain* 1970; *Nicholas and Alexandra* 1971; *The Abdication* 1974

Marstini, Rosita *Blood and Sand* 1922; *The Big Parade* 1925

Marston, Nathaniel *The Craft* 1996; *Love Is All There Is* 1996

Marta, Lynne *Smash-Up Alley* 1972; *Genesis II* 1973

Martel, K C *The Amityville Horror* 1979; *ET the Extra-Terrestrial* 1982; *White Water Summer* 1987

Martell, Donna *Last Train from Bombay* 1952; *Project Moonbase* 1953

Martell, Gregg *I Was a Shoplifter* 1950; *Dinosaurus!* 1960

Martelli, Norma *The Night of San Lorenzo* 1981; *Everybody's Fine* 1990

Martells, Cynthia *Blind Spot* 1993; *Zooman* 1995

Marthouret, François *Hit List* 1984; *Marquis* 1989; *Annabelle Partagée* 1990; *Sitcom* 1997

Martial, Jacques *Broken English* 1981; *Noir et Blanc* 1986

Martin, Andra *The Lady Takes a Flyer* 1958; *Up Periscope* 1959

Martin, Andrea *Black Christmas* 1974; *Martha, Ruth and Edie* 1988; *Rude Awakening* 1989; *Too Much Sun* 1990; *Harrison Bergeron* 1995; *Bogus* 1996; *Wag the Dog* 1997

Martin, Chris-Pin *The Cisco Kid and the Lady* 1939; *Stagecoach* 1939; *The Gay Caballero* 1940

Martin, Christopher *House Party* 1990; *House Party 2* 1991; *Class Act* 1992; *House Party 3* 1994

Martin, Damon *Pee-wee's Big Adventure* 1985; *Ghoulies II* 1987; *Kid* 1990; *Amityville 1992: It's About Time* 1992

Martin, Daniel *A Fistful of Dollars* 1964; *The Devil's Kiss* 1971

Martin, Dean *My Friend Irma* 1949; *At War with the Army* 1950; *My Friend Irma Goes West* 1950; *Sailor Beware* 1951; *The Stooge* 1951; *That's My Boy* 1951; *Jumping Jacks* 1952; *The Caddy* 1953; *Money from Home* 1953; *Scared Stiff* 1953; *Living It Up* 1954; *Three Ring Circus* 1954; *Artists and Models* 1955; *You're Never Too Young* 1955; *Hollywood or Bust* 1956; *Pardners* 1956; *Ten Thousand Bedrooms* 1957; *Some Came Running* 1958; *The Young Lions* 1958; *Career* 1959; *Rio Bravo* 1959; *All in a Night's Work* 1960; *Bells Are Ringing* 1960; *Ocean's Eleven* 1960; *Who Was That Lady?* 1960; *Pepe* 1960; *Ada* 1961; *The Road to Hong Kong* 1962; *Sergeants 3* 1962; *Who's Got the Action?* 1962; *4 for Texas* 1963; *Who's Been Sleeping in My Bed?* 1963; *Toys in the Attic* 1963; *Kiss Me, Stupid* 1964; *Robin and the 7 Hoods* 1964; *What a Way to Go!* 1964; *Marriage on the Rocks* 1965; *The Sons of Katie Elder* 1965; *Murderers' Row* 1966; *The Silencers* 1966; *Texas across the River* 1966; *The Ambushers* 1967; *Rough Night in Jericho* 1967; *Bandolero!* 1968; *5 Card Stud* 1968; *How to Save a Marriage and Ruin Your Life* 1968; *The Wrecking Crew* 1969; *Airport* 1970; *something big* 1971; *Showdown* 1973; *The Cannonball Run* 1981; *Cannonball Run II* 1983

Martin, Dean Paul *Players* 1979; *Heart like a Wheel* 1983; *Backfire* 1987

Martin, Dewey *Kansas Raiders* 1950; *The Thing from Another World* 1951; *The Big Sky* 1952; *Tennessee Champ* 1954; *Men of the Fighting Lady* 1954; *Prisoner of War* 1954; *The Desperate Hours* 1955; *Land of the*

Pharaohs 1955; *The Proud and Profane* 1956; *Ten Thousand Bedrooms* 1957; *Savage Sam* 1963; *Flight to Fury* 1966; *Seven Alone* 1974

Martin, Dick *The Maltese Bippy* 1969; *Zero to Sixty* 1978; *Carbon Copy* 1981

Martin, Duane *Above the Rim* 1994; *Woo* 1998; *Mutiny* 1999

Martin, D'Urville *Watermelon Man* 1970; *The Final Comedown* 1972; *Black Caesar* 1973; *Hell Up in Harlem* 1973

Martin, Edie *The Demi-Paradise* 1943; *The Lavender Hill Mob* 1951; *The Ladykillers* 1955

Martin, Eugene *Terror in a Texas Town* 1958; *This Rebel Breed* 1960; *Tower of London* 1962

Martin, George *Falling in Love* 1984; *Give My Regards to Broad Street* 1984; *CHUD* 1984; *The Associate* 1996

Martin, Helen *A Hero Ain't Nothin' but a Sandwich* 1978; *Hollywood Shuffle* 1987; *Don't Be a Menace to South Central while Drinking Your Juice in the Hood* 1996

Martin, Jared *The Second Coming of Suzanne* 1974; *The Lonely Lady* 1983; *Quiet Cool* 1986

Martin, Jean *The Battle of Algiers* 1965; *My Name Is Nobody* 1973; *Lucie Aubrac* 1997

Martin, Jose Manuel *A Bullet for the General* 1966; *A Bullet for Sandoval* 1970

Martin, Kellie *The Richest Cat in the World* 1986; *Matinee* 1993; *Death of a Cheerleader* 1994; *Face on the Milk Carton* 1995; *A Goofy Movie* 1995; *Her Hidden Truth* 1995; *Her Last Chance* 1996; *About Sarah* 1998

Martin, Lewis *Ace in the Hole* 1951; *Arrowhead* 1953; *The War of the Worlds* 1953; *Witness to Murder* 1954; *Diary of a Madman* 1963

Martin, Marion *Sinners in Paradise* 1938; *Sergeant Madden* 1939; *The Big Street* 1942; *They Got Me Covered* 1943

Martin, Mary *Rhythm on the River* 1940; *The Birth of the Blues* 1941; *Kiss the Boys Goodbye* 1941; *Star Spangled Rhythm* 1942; *Happy Go Lucky* 1943; *True to Life* 1943

Martin, Millicent *Libel* 1959; *Invasion Quartet* 1961; *The Girl on the Boat* 1962; *Nothing but the Best* 1964; *Alfie* 1966; *Stop the World, I Want to Get Off* 1966

Martin, Nan *Toys in the Attic* 1963; *For Love of Ivy* 1968; *Three in the Attic* 1968; *Goodbye, Columbus* 1969; *The Other Side of the Mountain* 1975; *Jackson County Jail* 1976; *Katie: Portrait of a Centerfold* 1978; *The Other Side of the Mountain – Part 2* 1978; *Loving Couples* 1980; *A Small Circle of Friends* 1980; *Animal Behavior* 1989

Martin, Pamela Sue *The Poseidon Adventure* 1972; *Buster and Billie* 1974; *Human Feelings* 1978; *The Lady in Red* 1979; *Torchlight* 1984; *Bay Cove* 1987; *A Cry in the Wild* 1990

Martin, Richard *Marine Raiders* 1944; *The Arizona Ranger* 1948; *Guns of Hate* 1948; *Stagecoach Kid* 1949; *Rider from Tucson* 1950; *Storm over Wyoming* 1950; *Desert Passage* 1952

Martin, Rosemary *Tess* 1979; *Laughterhouse* 1984; *The Dressmaker* 1988; *The Object of Beauty* 1991

Martin, Ross *Conquest of Space* 1955; *The Colossus of New York*

1958; *Experiment in Terror* 1962; *Geronimo* 1962

Martin, Sandy *Extremities* 1986; *Barfly* 1987

Martin, Skip *The Masque of the Red Death* 1964; *Horror Hospital* 1973

Martin, Steve *Sgt Pepper's Lonely Hearts Club Band* 1978; *The Jerk* 1979; *Pennies from Heaven* 1981; *Dead Men Don't Wear Plaid* 1982; *The Man with Two Brains* 1983; *All of Me* 1984; *The Lonely Guy* 1984; *Movers and Shakers* 1985; *Little Shop of Horrors* 1986; *¡hree Amigos!* 1986; *Planes, Trains and Automobiles* 1987; *Roxanne* 1987; *Dirty Rotten Scoundrels* 1988; *Parenthood* 1989; *My Blue Heaven* 1990; *Father of the Bride* 1991; *Grand Canyon* 1991; *LA Story* 1991; *HouseSitter* 1992; *Leap of Faith* 1992; *And the Band Played On* 1993; *A Simple Twist of Fate* 1994; *Father of the Bride Part II* 1995; *Mixed Nuts* 1995; *Sgt Bilko* 1996; *The Spanish Prisoner* 1997; *The Prince of Egypt* 1998; *The Out-of-Towners* 1999; *Bowfinger* 1999; *Fantasia 2000* 1999

Martin, Strother *The Deadly Companions* 1961; *Showdown* 1963; *An Eye for an Eye* 1966; *Cool Hand Luke* 1967; *Butch Cassidy and the Sundance Kid* 1969; *The Ballad of Cable Hogue* 1970; *Brotherhood of Satan* 1970; *Hannie Caulder* 1971; *Fools' Parade* 1971; *Pocket Money* 1972; *Sssssss* 1973; *One of Our Own* 1975; *Rooster Cogburn* 1975; *The Streetfighter* 1975; *The Great Scout & Cathouse Thursday* 1976; *Slap Shot* 1977; *The End* 1978; *Love and Bullets* 1978; *Cheech & Chong's Up in Smoke* 1978; *Cactus Jack* 1979; *The Champ* 1979; *Nightwing* 1979

Martin, Todd *The Thomas Crown Affair* 1968; *Jory* 1972; *Alex and the Gypsy* 1976

Martin, Tony aka **Martin, Anthony** *Banjo on My Knee* 1936; *Pigskin Parade* 1936; *Life Begins in College* 1937; *You Can't Have Everything* 1937; *Kentucky Moonshine* 1938; *Sally, Irene and Mary* 1938; *Music in My Heart* 1940; *The Big Store* 1941; *Ziegfeld Girl* 1941; *Casbah* 1948; *Two Tickets to Broadway* 1951; *Easy to Love* 1953; *Here Come the Girls* 1953; *Deep in My Heart* 1954; *Hit the Deck* 1955

Martindale, Margo *Lorenzo's Oil* 1992; *Eye of God* 1997; *First Do No Harm* 1997; *Critical Care* 1997

Martindel, Edward *Lady Windermere's Fan* 1925; *The Phantom of the Opera* 1925; *The Singing Fool* 1928; *The Desert Song* 1929

Martinelli, Elsa *The Indian Fighter* 1955; *Manuela* 1957; *The Captain* 1960; *Hatari!* 1962; *The Trial* 1962; *The Pigeon That Took Rome* 1962; *Rampage* 1963; *The VIPs* 1963; *The Tenth Victim* 1965; *Maroc 7* 1967; *Madigan's Millions* 1967; *The Oldest Profession* 1967

Martinelli, Jean *Le Rouge et le Noir* 1954; *To Catch a Thief* 1955; *Heroines of Evil* 1979

Martines, Alessandra *Les Misérables* 1995; *Men, Women: a User's Manual* 1996; *Chance or Coincidence* 1999

Martinez, A *Once Upon a Scoundrel* 1973; *The Take* 1974; *The Honorary Consul* 1983; *Confessions of a Lady Cop* 1988;

Powwow Highway 1988; *Manhunt: Search for the Night Stalker* 1989; *Criminal Behaviour* 1992; *One Night Stand* 1994; *Before the Night* 1995; *Sweet Dreams* 1996; *The Cherokee Kid* 1996; *Last Rites* 1998

Martinez, Alma *Barbarosa* 1982; *Under Fire* 1983

Martinez, Fele *Open Your Eyes* 1997; *The Lovers of the Arctic Circle* 1998

Martinez, Joaquin *Jeremiah Johnson* 1972; *Ulzana's Raid* 1972; *He Is My Brother* 1974; *Flashpoint* 1984; *Revenge* 1990

Martinez, Olivier *IP5* 1992; *The Horseman on the Roof* 1995; *Mon Homme* 1996; *The Chambermaid on the Titanic* 1997

Martini, Nino *Paramount on Parade* 1930; *The Gay Desperado* 1936

Martins, Orlando *Men of Two Worlds* 1946; *The End of the River* 1947; *Where No Vultures Fly* 1951; *West of Zanzibar* 1954; *Safari* 1956; *Sapphire* 1959; *Mister Moses* 1965

Martyn, Peter *Child's Play* 1954; *Mad about Men* 1954; *No Smoking* 1954

Marvin, Lee *The Duel at Silver Creek* 1952; *The Big Heat* 1953; *The Glory Brigade* 1953; *Gun Fury* 1953; *Seminole* 1953; *The Wild One* 1953; *The Stranger Wore a Gun* 1953; *The Caine Mutiny* 1954; *The Raid* 1954; *Gorilla at Large* 1954; *Bad Day at Black Rock* 1955; *I Died a Thousand Times* 1955; *Not as a Stranger* 1955; *Pete Kelly's Blues* 1955; *Violent Saturday* 1955; *A Life in the Balance* 1955; *Shack Out on 101* 1955; *Attack!* 1956; *Pillars of the Sky* 1956; *Seven Men from Now* 1956; *The Rack* 1956; *Raintree County* 1957; *The Missouri Traveler* 1958; *The Comancheros* 1961; *The Man Who Shot Liberty Valance* 1962; *Donovan's Reef* 1963; *The Killers* 1964; *Cat Ballou* 1965; *Ship of Fools* 1965; *The Professionals* 1966; *The Dirty Dozen* 1967; *Point Blank* 1967; *Hell in the Pacific* 1968; *Sergeant Ryker* 1968; *Paint Your Wagon* 1969; *Monte Walsh* 1970; *Pocket Money* 1972; *Prime Cut* 1972; *Emperor of the North* 1973; *The Iceman Cometh* 1973; *The Klansman* 1974; *The Spikes Gang* 1974; *The Great Scout & Cathouse Thursday* 1976; *Shout at the Devil* 1976; *Avalanche Express* 1979; *The Big Red One* 1980; *Death Hunt* 1981; *Gorky Park* 1983; *The Dirty Dozen: the Next Mission* 1985; *The Delta Force* 1986

Marx, Brett *The Bad News Bears Go to Japan* 1978; *The Lucky Star* 1980; *Thrashin'* 1986

Marx, Chico *The Cocoanuts* 1929; *Animal Crackers* 1930; *Monkey Business* 1931; *Horse Feathers* 1932; *Duck Soup* 1933; *A Night at the Opera* 1935; *A Day at the Races* 1937; *Room Service* 1938; *At the Circus* 1939; *Marx Brothers Go West* 1940; *The Big Store* 1941; *A Night in Casablanca* 1946; *Love Happy* 1949; *The Story of Mankind* 1957

Marx, Groucho *The Cocoanuts* 1929; *Animal Crackers* 1930; *Monkey Business* 1931; *Horse Feathers* 1932; *Duck Soup* 1933; *A Night at the Opera* 1935; *A Day at the Races* 1937; *Room Service* 1938; *At the Circus* 1939; *Marx Brothers Go West* 1940; *The Big Store* 1941; *A Night in Casablanca* 1946; *Copacabana*

1947; *Love Happy* 1949; *Double Dynamite* 1951; *A Girl in Every Port* 1952; *Will Success Spoil Rock Hunter?* 1957; *The Story of Mankind* 1957; *Skidoo* 1968

Marx, Harpo *The Cocoanuts* 1929; *Animal Crackers* 1930; *Monkey Business* 1931; *Horse Feathers* 1932; *Duck Soup* 1933; *A Night at the Opera* 1935; *A Day at the Races* 1937; *Room Service* 1938; *At the Circus* 1939; *Marx Brothers Go West* 1940; *The Big Store* 1941; *Stage Door Canteen* 1943; *A Night in Casablanca* 1946; *Love Happy* 1949; *The Story of Mankind* 1957

Marx, Zeppo *The Cocoanuts* 1929; *Animal Crackers* 1930; *Monkey Business* 1931; *Horse Feathers* 1932; *Duck Soup* 1933

Masak, Ron *Laserblast* 1978; *Listen to Me* 1989; *When Time Expires* 1997

Mascia, Tony *The Man Who Fell to Earth* 1976; *Silver Bears* 1978

Mascolo, Joseph *Shaft's Big Score!* 1972; *Happy Mother's Day... Love, George* 1973; *Jaws 2* 1978; *Heat* 1987; *The Trial of the Incredible Hulk* 1989

Mase, Marino *Les Carabiniers* 1963; *Fists in the Pocket* 1965

Mashkov, Vladimir *Katia Ismailova* 1994; *The Thief* 1997

Masina, Giulietta *Lights of Variety* 1950; *The White Sheik* 1951; *Europa '51* 1952; *La Strada* 1954; *The Swindle* 1955; *Nights of Cabiria* 1957; *Juliet of the Spirits* 1965; *The Madwoman of Chaillot* 1969; *Ginger & Fred* 1986

Masini, Galliano *Pagliacci* 1948; *La Forza del Destino* 1949

Mask, Ace *Not of This Earth* 1988; *The Return of Swamp Thing* 1989; *Transylvania Twist* 1989

Maskell, Virginia *Virgin Island* 1958; *The Man Upstairs* 1958; *Jet Storm* 1959; *Doctor in Love* 1960; *Suspect* 1960; *Only Two Can Play* 1962; *The Wild and the Willing* 1962; *Interlude* 1968

Maslow, Walter *The Cosmic Man* 1959; *Atlas* 1960

Mason, Brewster *Private Potter* 1963; *The Quatermass Conclusion* 1979

Mason, Elliot *The Ghost of St Michael's* 1941; *It's Turned Out Nice Again* 1941

Mason, Hilary *Don't Look Now* 1973; *I Don't Want to Be Born* 1975; *Dolls* 1987; *Robot Jox* 1989

Mason, James *Fire over England* 1937; *The Return of the Scarlet Pimpernel* 1937; *The Mill on the Floss* 1937; *Hatter's Castle* 1941; *The Night Has Eyes* 1942; *Secret Mission* 1942; *Thunder Rock* 1942; *The Bells Go Down* 1943; *Candlelight in Algeria* 1943; *The Man in Grey* 1943; *They Met in the Dark* 1943; *Fanny by Gaslight* 1944; *Hotel Reserve* 1944; *A Place of One's Own* 1944; *The Seventh Veil* 1945; *They Were Sisters* 1945; *The Wicked Lady* 1945; *Odd Man Out* 1946; *The Upturned Glass* 1947; *Caught* 1949; *East Side, West Side* 1949; *Madame Bovary* 1949; *The Reckless Moment* 1949; *One Way Street* 1950; *The Desert Fox* 1951; *Pandora and the Flying Dutchman* 1951; *Botany Bay* 1952; *Face to Face* 1952; *5 Fingers* 1952; *The Prisoner of Zenda* 1952; *The Desert Rats* 1953; *Julius Caesar* 1953; *The Man between* 1953; *The Story of Three Loves* 1953; *Prince Valiant* 1954; *A Star Is Born* 1954;

20,000 Leagues under the Sea 1954; *Bigger than Life* 1956; *Forever, Darling* 1956; *Island in the Sun* 1957; *Cry Terror* 1958; *The Decks Ran Red* 1958; *Journey to the Center of the Earth* 1959; *North by Northwest* 1959; *A Touch of Larceny* 1959; *The Marriage-Go-Round* 1960; *The Trials of Oscar Wilde* 1960; *Lolita* 1961; *Escape from Zahrain* 1962; *Tiara Tahiti* 1962; *Hero's Island* 1962; *The Fall of the Roman Empire* 1964; *Genghis Khan* 1964; *The Pumpkin Eater* 1964; *Lord Jim* 1965; *The Blue Max* 1966; *The Deadly Affair* 1966; *Georgy Girl* 1966; *Stranger in the House* 1967; *Duffy* 1968; *Mayerling* 1968; *The Sea Gull* 1968; *Age of Consent* 1969; *Spring and Port Wine* 1969; *Bad Man's River* 1971; *Cold Sweat* 1971; *Child's Play* 1972; *Kill!* 1972; *Frankenstein: the True Story* 1973; *The Last of Sheila* 1973; *The Mackintosh Man* 1973; *11 Harrowhouse* 1974; *Great Expectations* 1974; *The Marseilles Contract* 1974; *Inside Out* 1975; *Mandingo* 1975; *The Masters* 1975; *Autobiography of a Princess* 1975; *Voyage of the Damned* 1976; *Cross of Iron* 1977; *The Boys from Brazil* 1978; *Heaven Can Wait* 1978; *Murder by Decree* 1978; *The Passage* 1978; *The Water Babies* 1978; *Bloodline* 1979; *North Sea Hijack* 1979; *Salem's Lot* 1979; *A Dangerous Summer* 1981; *Evil under the Sun* 1982; *The Verdict* 1982; *Yellowbeard* 1983; *The Shooting Party* 1984; *The Assisi Underground* 1985

Mason, Laura *Khyber Patrol* 1954; *The Bowery Boys Meet the Monsters* 1954

Mason, LeRoy *Santa Fe Stampede* 1938; *Wyoming Outlaw* 1939; *Riders of the Purple Sage* 1941; *My Pal Trigger* 1946

Mason, Lola *The Brain That Wouldn't Die* 1959; *The End of Innocence* 1990

Mason, Madison *Dangerously Close* 1986; *Glitz* 1988; *Omen IV: the Awakening* 1991

Mason, Marsha *Blume in Love* 1973; *Cinderella Liberty* 1973; *Audrey Rose* 1977; *The Goodbye Girl* 1977; *The Cheap Detective* 1978; *Chapter Two* 1979; *Promises in the Dark* 1979; *Only When I Laugh* 1981; *Max Dugan Returns* 1983; *Surviving* 1985; *Heartbreak Ridge* 1986; *Trapped in Silence* 1986; *Dinner at Eight* 1989; *The Image* 1990; *Stella* 1990; *Drop Dead Fred* 1991; *I Love Trouble* 1994; *Broken Trust* 1995; *Nick of Time* 1995; *2 Days in the Valley* 1996

Mason, Pamela *Sex Kittens Go to College* 1960; *Door-to-Door Maniac* 1961; *The Navy vs the Night Monsters* 1966

Mason, Tom *The Return of the Man from UNCLE* 1983; *Men Don't Leave* 1990; *Jonathan: the Boy Nobody Wanted* 1992; *A Murderous Affair* 1992; *A Nightmare in the Daylight* 1992; *Final Appeal* 1993; *Flashfire* 1993; *The Puppet Masters* 1994; *My Very Best Friend* 1996

Massari, Lea *L'Avventura* 1959; *The Colossus of Rhodes* 1961; *The Four Days of Naples* 1962; *The Things of Life* 1969; *Le Souffle au Coeur* 1971; *And Hope to Die* 1972; *The Silent One* 1973; *Story of a Love Story* 1973; *Les Rendez-vous d'Anna* 1978; *Christ Stopped at Eboli* 1979

ACTORS' INDEX
RadioTimes

Mattson, Robin *Namu, the Killer Whale* 1966; *Return to Macon County* 1975; *Captain America* 1979; *Wolf Lake* 1979; *False Witness* 1989
Mature, Victor *The Housekeeper's Daughter* 1939; *Man and His Mate* 1940; *No, No, Nanette* 1940; *I Wake Up Screaming* 1941; *The Shanghai Gesture* 1941; *Footlight Serenade* 1942; *My Gal Sal* 1942; *Seven Days' Leave* 1942; *Song of the Islands* 1942; *My Darling Clementine* 1946; *Kiss of Death* 1947; *Moss Rose* 1947; *Cry of the City* 1948; *Fury at Furnace Creek* 1948; *Easy Living* 1949; *Samson and Delilah* 1949; *Wabash Avenue* 1950; *Stella* 1950; *The Las Vegas Story* 1951; *Androcles and the Lion* 1952; *Million Dollar Mermaid* 1952; *Affair with a Stranger* 1953; *The Glory Brigade* 1953; *The Robe* 1953; *Dangerous Mission* 1954; *Demetrius and the Gladiators* 1954; *The Egyptian* 1954; *Betrayed* 1954; *Chief Crazy Horse* 1955; *The Last Frontier* 1955; *Violent Saturday* 1955; *Safari* 1956; *Zarak* 1956; *Interpol* 1957; *China Doll* 1958; *No Time to Die* 1958; *The Big Circus* 1959; *Escort West* 1959; *Hannibal* 1959; *Timbuktu* 1959; *The Bandit of Zhobe* 1959; *After the Fox* 1966; *Head* 1968; *Every Little Crook and Nanny* 1972; *Firepower* 1979; *Samson and Delilah* 1984
Matuszak, John *Caveman* 1981; *The Ice Pirates* 1984; *The Goonies* 1985; *The Dirty Dozen: the Fatal Mission* 1988; *One Man Force* 1989
Mauban, Maria *Cage of Gold* 1950; *Cairo Road* 1950; *Journey to Italy* 1953; *The Spacemen of St Tropez* 1978
Mauch, Billy *Anthony Adverse* 1936; *The Prince and the Pauper* 1937
Maude-Roxby, Roddy *The Aristocats* 1970; *White Hunter, Black Heart* 1990; *Shadowlands* 1993
Maughan, Monica *Annie's Coming Out* 1984; *Cactus* 1986; *Golden Braid* 1991; *Road to Nhill* 1997
Maunder, Wayne *The Seven Minutes* 1971; *Kung Fu* 1972
Maura, Carmen *Pepi, Luci, Bom...* 1980; *What Have I Done to Deserve This?* 1984; *Matador* 1986; *The Law of Desire* 1987; *Women on the Verge of a Nervous Breakdown* 1988; *Ay, Carmela!* 1990; *How to Be a Woman and Not Die in the Attempt* 1991; *Le Bonheur Est dans le Pré* 1995; *Alice et Martin* 1998
Maurey, Nicole *Diary of a Country Priest* 1950; *Little Boy Lost* 1953; *Secret of the Incas* 1954; *The Constant Husband* 1955; *The Bold and the Brave* 1956; *Rogue's Yarn* 1956; *Me and the Colonel* 1958; *The House of the Seven Hawks* 1959; *The Scapegoat* 1959; *The Jayhawkers* 1959; *High Time* 1960; *Don't Bother to Knock* 1961; *The Day of the Triffids* 1962; *The Very Edge* 1962
Maurier, Claire *The 400 Blows* 1959; *La Cage aux Folles* 1978; *Un Air de Famille* 1996
Maur-Thorp, Sarah *River of Death* 1989; *Edge of Sanity* 1989
Maurus, Gerda *Spies* 1928; *The Woman in the Moon* 1929
Maury, Jean-Louis *Ophélia* 1962; *Madame Bovary* 1991
Maximova, Antonina *Othello* 1955; *Ballad of a Soldier* 1959
Maxwell Conover, Theresa *Chained* 1934; *The Age of Innocence* 1934
Maxwell, Edwin *The Taming of the Shrew* 1929; *Inspiration* 1931; *Tiger Shark* 1932; *Mystery of the Wax Museum* 1933; *The Blue Bird* 1940; *The Great Moment* 1944
Maxwell, Frank *Lonelyhearts* 1958; *Ada* 1961; *The Intruder* 1961; *The Haunted Palace* 1963; *Mr Majestyk* 1974
Maxwell, James *Girl on Approval* 1962; *Private Potter* 1963; *One Day in the Life of Ivan Denisovich* 1971
Maxwell, John *The Prowler* 1951; *The Bigamist* 1953
Maxwell, Lois *The Dark Past* 1948; *Mantrap* 1952; *Women of Twilight* 1952; *Passport to Treason* 1956; *Kill Me Tomorrow* 1957; *Time without Pity* 1957; *Come Fly with Me* 1962; *Dr No* 1962; *From Russia with Love* 1963; *The Haunting* 1963; *Goldfinger* 1964; *Thunderball* 1965; *You Only Live Twice* 1967; *On Her Majesty's Secret Service* 1969; *The Adventurers* 1970; *Diamonds Are Forever* 1971; *Endless Night* 1971; *Live and Let Die* 1973; *The Man with the Golden Gun* 1974; *The Spy Who Loved Me* 1977; *Moonraker* 1979; *For Your Eyes Only* 1981; *Octopussy* 1983; *A View to a Kill* 1985; *Martha, Ruth and Edie* 1988
Maxwell, Marilyn *Salute to the Marines* 1943; *Swing Fever* 1943; *Lost in a Harem* 1944; *Three Men in White* 1944; *High Barbaree* 1947; *Summer Holiday* 1948; *Champion* 1949; *Key to the City* 1950; *The Lemon Drop Kid* 1951; *East of Sumatra* 1953; *Military Policeman* 1953; *Off Limits* 1953; *New York Confidential* 1955; *Rock-a-Bye Baby* 1958; *Critic's Choice* 1963; *Arizona Bushwhackers* 1968
Maxwell, Paul *Submarine Seahawk* 1959; *Shadow of Fear* 1963; *City of Fear* 1965; *It!* 1966; *Madame Sin* 1972; *Baxter* 1973; *The Return of Sherlock Holmes* 1987
Maxwell, Roberta *Rich Kids* 1979; *Popeye* 1980; *Psycho III* 1986; *Last Night* 1998
May, Deborah *Two Friends* 1986; *Sexual Advances* 1992; *The Other Mother* 1995
May, Donald *Kisses for My President* 1964; *Confessions of a Lady Cop* 1988
May, Elaine *Enter Laughing* 1967; *Luv* 1967; *A New Leaf* 1971; *California Suite* 1978; *In the Spirit* 1990
May, Jack *Trog* 1970; *The Man Who Would Be King* 1975
May, Jodhi *A World Apart* 1987; *Max and Helen* 1990; *Eminent Domain* 1991; *The Last of the Mohicans* 1992; *Sister My Sister* 1994; *The Scarlet Letter* 1995; *The Gambler* 1997; *The Woodlanders* 1997; *The House of Mirth* 2000
May, Mathilda *Lifeforce* 1985; *Letters to an Unknown Lover* 1985; *Naked Tango* 1990; *Becoming Colette* 1991; *Scream of Stone* 1991; *The Tit and the Moon* 1994; *The Jackal* 1997
Mayall, Rik *An American Werewolf in London* 1981; *Shock Treatment* 1981; *Whoops Apocalypse* 1986; *Eat the Rich* 1987; *Drop Dead Fred* 1991; *Carry On Columbus* 1992; *The Princess and the Goblin* 1992; *Little Noises* 1992; *Remember Me?* 1996; *Bring Me the Head of Mavis Davis* 1997; *Guest House Paradiso* 1999; *A Monkey's Tale* 2000
Mayama, Miko *Impasse* 1969; *That Man Bolt* 1973
Mayehoff, Eddie *The Stooge* 1951; *That's My Boy* 1951; *Military Policeman* 1953; *Off Limits* 1953; *Artists and Models* 1955; *How to Murder Your Wife* 1965; *Luv* 1967
Mayhew, Peter *Star Wars Episode IV: A New Hope* 1977; *The Empire Strikes Back* 1980; *Return of the Jedi* 1983
Maynard, Bill *Till Death Us Do Part* 1968; *A Hole Lot of Trouble* 1969; *Carry On Loving* 1970; *Carry On at Your Convenience* 1971; *Carry On Henry* 1971; *Adolf Hitler – My Part in His Downfall* 1972; *Bless This House* 1972; *Carry On Matron* 1972; *Steptoe and Son Ride Again* 1973; *Confessions of a Window Cleaner* 1974; *Confessions of a Pop Performer* 1975; *Confessions of a Driving Instructor* 1976; *Robin and Marian* 1976; *Confessions from a Holiday Camp* 1977; *It Shouldn't Happen to a Vet* 1979; *Oddball Hall* 1990
Maynard, Mimi *Hawmps* 1976; *False Identity* 1990
Mayne, Ferdy aka **Mayne, Ferdinand** *The Blue Parrot* 1953; *Beautiful Stranger* 1954; *Gentlemen Marry Brunettes* 1955; *The Big Chance* 1957; *The Fearless Vampire Killers* 1967; *The Vampire Lovers* 1970; *The Walking Stick* 1970; *When Eight Bells Toll* 1971; *Eagle in a Cage* 1971; *Frightmare* 1981; *The Black Stallion Returns* 1983; *The Secret Diary of Sigmund Freud* 1984; *Pirates* 1986; *Knight Moves* 1992; *Benefit of the Doubt* 1993
Mayniel, Juliette *Les Cousins* 1959; *Eyes without a Face* 1959; *The Trojan War* 1961; *Bluebeard* 1962; *Ophélia* 1962
Mayo, Alfredo *The Hunt* 1966; *Peppermint Frappé* 1967
Mayo, Virginia *Jack London* 1944; *The Princess and the Pirate* 1944; *Wonder Man* 1945; *The Best Years of Our Lives* 1946; *The Kid from Brooklyn* 1946; *The Secret Life of Walter Mitty* 1947; *Out of the Blue* 1947; *A Song Is Born* 1948; *Always Leave Them Laughing* 1949; *Colorado Territory* 1949; *Red Light* 1949; *White Heat* 1949; *The Flame and the Arrow* 1950; *The West Point Story* 1950; *Backfire* 1950; *Along the Great Divide* 1951; *Captain Horatio Hornblower* 1951; *Painting the Clouds with Sunshine* 1951; *The Iron Mistress* 1952; *She's Working Her Way through College* 1952; *Devil's Canyon* 1953; *South Sea Woman* 1953; *King Richard and the Crusaders* 1954; *The Silver Chalice* 1954; *Pearl of the South Pacific* 1955; *Congo Crossing* 1956; *Great Day in the Morning* 1956; *The Proud Ones* 1956; *The Big Land* 1957; *The Tall Stranger* 1957; *The Story of Mankind* 1957; *Westbound* 1959; *Jet over the Atlantic* 1960; *Castle of Evil* 1966; *Haunted* 1976; *Won Ton Ton, the Dog Who Saved Hollywood* 1976; *Evil Spirits* 1991
Mayron, Gale *Heart of Midnight* 1988; *The Feud* 1989; *Donor* 1990
Mayron, Melanie *Harry and Tonto* 1974; *Hustling* 1975; *Gable and Lombard* 1976; *The Great Smokey Roadblock* 1977; *You Light Up My Life* 1977; *Girlfriends* 1978; *Missing* 1981; *Heartbeeps* 1981; *Checking Out* 1988; *Sticky Fingers* 1988; *My Blue Heaven* 1990; *Ordeal in the Arctic* 1993; *Other Women's Children* 1993; *Toothless* 1997
Maza, Bob *The Fringe Dwellers* 1985; *Ground Zero* 1987; *Reckless Kelly* 1993; *Back of Beyond* 1995
Mazar, Debi *Little Man Tate* 1991; *Inside Monkey Zetterland* 1992; *Beethoven's 2nd* 1993; *Money for Nothing* 1993; *So I Married an Axe Murderer* 1993; *Empire Records* 1995; *Girl 6* 1996; *Space Truckers* 1996; *Meet Wally Sparks* 1997; *Nowhere* 1997; *She's So Lovely* 1997; *Hush* 1998; *David and Lisa* 1998; *The Insider* 1999
Mazurki, Mike *Abbott and Costello in Hollywood* 1945; *Dick Tracy* 1945; *Farewell My Lovely* 1945; *Nightmare Alley* 1947; *Sinbad the Sailor* 1947; *The Noose Hangs High* 1948; *Neptune's Daughter* 1949; *Night and the City* 1950; *Ten Tall Men* 1951; *Blood Alley* 1955; *Kismet* 1955; *Hell Ship Mutiny* 1957; *Pocketful of Miracles* 1961; *Donovan's Reef* 1963; *7 Women* 1966; *Challenge to Be Free* 1972
Mazurowna, Ernestine *Jean de Florette* 1986; *Manon des Sources* 1986
Mazursky, Paul *Fear and Desire* 1953; *Blume in Love* 1973; *A Star Is Born* 1976; *A Man, a Woman and a Bank* 1979; *Punchline* 1988; *Scenes from the Class Struggle In Beverly Hills* 1989; *Scenes from a Mall* 1991; *Love Affair* 1994; *Miami Rhapsody* 1995; *Faithful* 1996; *Touch* 1996; *Weapons of Mass Distraction* 1997; *Antz* 1998; *Why Do Fools Fall in Love?* 1998
Mazzello, Joseph aka **Mazzello, Joe** *Jersey Girl* 1992; *Radio Flyer* 1992; *Solomon's Choice* 1992; *Jurassic Park* 1993; *Shadowlands* 1993; *The River Wild* 1994; *The Cure* 1995; *Three Wishes* 1995; *Star Kid* 1997; *Simon Birch* 1998
Meacham, Anne *Lilith* 1964; *Seizure* 1974
Meadows, Audrey *That Touch of Mink* 1962; *Take Her, She's Mine* 1963; *Rosie!* 1967
Meadows, Jayne *Lady in the Lake* 1947; *Enchantment* 1948; *David and Bathsheba* 1951; *The Masterpiece of Murder* 1986
Meadows, Shane *Smalltime* 1996; *A Room for Romeo Brass* 1999
Meadows, Stephen *The End of Innocence* 1990; *Night Eyes* 1990; *Revealing Evidence* 1990; *A Cry in the Wild* 1990; *Plan of Attack* 1992; *Sunstroke* 1992; *Overdrive* 1997
Meaney, Colm *Far and Away* 1992; *Under Siege* 1992; *War of the Buttons* 1993; *The Snapper* 1993; *The Road to Wellville* 1994; *The Englishman Who Went up a Hill, but Came down a Mountain* 1995; *Last of the High Kings* 1996; *The Van* 1996; *Con Air* 1997; *Noose* 1997; *This Is My Father* 1998; *Mystery, Alaska* 1999
Means, Russell *The Last of the Mohicans* 1992; *Pocahontas II: Journey to a New World* 1998
Meara, Anne *The Out of Towners* 1970; *Nasty Habits* 1976; *The Longshot* 1986; *My Little Girl* 1986; *The Search for One-Eye Jimmy* 1996; *The Daytrippers* 1998
Meat Loaf aka **Aday, Meat Loaf** *The Rocky Horror Picture Show* 1975; *Americathon* 1979; *Roadie* 1980; *Leap of Faith* 1992; *To Catch a Yeti* 1993; *The Mighty* 1998; *Black Dog* 1998; *Everything That Rises* 1998; *Crazy in Alabama* 1999; *Fight Club* 1999
Mechoso, Julio Oscar *A Pyromaniac's Love Story* 1995; *Virus* 1998
Medford, Kay *Guilty Bystander* 1950; *The Rat Race* 1960; *Girl of the Night* 1960; *Ensign Pulver* 1964; *The Busy Body* 1967; *Angel in My Pocket* 1968; *Funny Girl* 1968
Medina, Ofelia *The Big Fix* 1978; *Wall of Silence* 1993
Medina, Patricia *Don't Take It to Heart* 1944; *The Foxes of Harrow* 1947; *Moss Rose* 1947; *Children of Chance* 1949; *Francis* 1949; *Abbott and Costello in the Foreign Legion* 1950; *The Jackpot* 1950; *Valentino* 1951; *Botany Bay* 1952; *Desperate Search* 1952; *The Black Knight* 1954; *Phantom of the Rue Morgue* 1954; *Confidential Report* 1955; *The Beast of Hollow Mountain* 1956; *Stranger at My Door* 1956; *The Killing of Sister George* 1968
Medvedev, Vadim *Hamlet* 1964; *Vassa* 1983
Medway, Heather *The Fear* 1995; *Serpent's Lair* 1995
Medwin, Michael *The Courtneys of Curzon Street* 1947; *Another Shore* 1948; *Night Beat* 1948; *Trottie True* 1949; *Someone at the Door* 1950; *Miss Robin Hood* 1952; *The Oracle* 1952; *The Intruder* 1953; *Spaceways* 1953; *Bang! You're Dead* 1954; *The Teckman Mystery* 1954; *Above Us the Waves* 1955; *Doctor at Sea* 1955; *A Man on the Beach* 1955; *Charley Moon* 1956; *Checkpoint* 1956; *A Hill in Korea* 1956; *Doctor at Large* 1957; *The Steel Bayonet* 1957; *The Duke Wore Jeans* 1958; *Crooks Anonymous* 1962; *It's All Happening* 1963; *Night Must Fall* 1964; *Rattle of a Simple Man* 1964; *I've Gotta Horse* 1965; *The Sandwich Man* 1966; *A Countess from Hong Kong* 1967; *Scrooge* 1970; *The Jigsaw Man* 1984; *Hôtel du Paradis* 1986
Meek, Donald *Mrs Wiggs of the Cabbage Patch* 1934; *The Bride Comes Home* 1935; *The Gilded Lily* 1935; *Mark of the Vampire* 1935; *The Return of Peter Grimm* 1935; *The Whole Town's Talking* 1935; *Accent on Youth* 1935; *One Rainy Afternoon* 1936; *Pennies from Heaven* 1936; *And So They Were Married* 1936; *Artists and Models* 1937; *Behind the Headlines* 1937; *Breakfast for Two* 1937; *Parnell* 1937; *The Toast of New York* 1937; *The Adventures of Tom Sawyer* 1938; *Hold That Co-Ed* 1938; *Blondie Takes a Vacation* 1939; *The Housekeeper's Daughter* 1939; *Stagecoach* 1939; *Nick Carter, Master Detective* 1939; *The Man from Dakota* 1940; *My Little Chickadee* 1940; *The Return of Frank James* 1940; *Sky Murder* 1940; *Star Dust* 1940; *Phantom Raiders* 1940; *Babes on Broadway* 1941; *Come Live with Me* 1941; *Design for Scandal* 1941; *The Feminine Touch* 1941; *A Woman's Face* 1941; *Keeper of the Flame* 1942; *Tortilla Flat* 1942; *DuBarry Was a Lady* 1943; *They Got Me Covered* 1943; *Bathing Beauty* 1944; *State Fair*

1945; *Because of Him* 1946; *Magic Town* 1947

Meek, Jeffrey aka **Meek, Jeff** *Perfume of the Cyclone* 1989; *Heart Condition* 1990

Meeker, George *Four Sons* 1928; *Back Street* 1932; *The First Year* 1932; *Only Yesterday* 1933; *The Richest Girl in the World* 1934; *Murder on a Honeymoon* 1935; *Remember Last Night?* 1935; *History Is Made at Night* 1937; *Tarzan's Revenge* 1938; *Rough Riders' Roundup* 1939; *Come Out Fighting* 1945; *Docks of New York* 1945; *Mr Muggs Rides Again* 1945

Meeker, Ralph *Teresa* 1951; *Glory Alley* 1952; *Somebody Loves Me* 1952; *Jeopardy* 1953; *The Naked Spur* 1953; *Kiss Me Deadly* 1955; *Big House, USA* 1955; *Battle Shock* 1956; *The Fuzzy Pink Nightgown* 1957; *Paths of Glory* 1957; *Run of the Arrow* 1957; *Ada* 1961; *The Dirty Dozen* 1967; *The St Valentine's Day Massacre* 1967; *Gentle Giant* 1967; *The Detective* 1968; *I Walk the Line* 1970; *The Anderson Tapes* 1971; *The Night Stalker* 1971; *The Happiness Cage* 1972; *The Dead Don't Die* 1975; *The Food of the Gods* 1975; *The Alpha Incident* 1977; *Winter Kills* 1979

Megowan, Don *The Werewolf* 1956; *Tarzan and the Valley of Gold* 1966

Mehler, Tobias *Disturbing Behaviour* 1998; *The Inspectors* 1998

Meier, Armin *Mother Küsters Goes to Heaven* 1975; *Fear of Fear* 1976

Meier, Shane *Andre* 1994; *Taken Away* 1996

Meighan, Thomas *Male and Female* 1919; *Why Change Your Wife?* 1920; *The Racket* 1928

Meillon, John *The Long and the Short and the Tall* 1960; *Offbeat* 1960; *Watch It, Sailor!* 1961; *Cairo* 1962; *Walkabout* 1970; *Sunstruck* 1972; *The Cars That Ate Paris* 1974; *The Fourth Wish* 1976; *The Picture Show Man* 1977; *Shimmering Light* 1978; *Heatwave* 1983; *The Wild Duck* 1983; *The Blue Lightning* 1986; *"Crocodile" Dundee* 1986; *"Crocodile" Dundee II* 1988; *Outback Bound* 1988

Meintjes, Tertius *Jobman* 1990; *Friends* 1993

Meisel, Kurt *The Odessa File* 1974; *Please Let the Flowers Live* 1986

Meiser, Edith *It Grows on Trees* 1952; *Middle of the Night* 1959

Meisner, Gunter *Inside Out* 1975; *Roselyne and the Lions* 1989

Mejias, Isabelle *Unfinished Business* 1983; *Bay Boy* 1984; *Meatballs III: Summer Job* 1987; *Scanners II: The New Order* 1991

Melato, Mariangela *The Seduction of Mimi* 1972; *Swept Away... by an Unusual Destiny in the Blue Sea of August* 1974; *Moses* 1975; *So Fine* 1981

Melchior, Lauritz *Thrill of a Romance* 1945; *Two Sisters from Boston* 1946

Meldrum, Wendel *Beautiful Dreamers* 1990; *Hush Little Baby* 1993; *City Boy* 1994; *Sodbusters* 1994

Melendez, Ron *Children of the Corn III: Urban Harvest* 1995; *Voodoo* 1995

Melford, Jack *Command Performance* 1937; *Hold My Hand* 1938

Melford, Jill *A Stitch in Time* 1963; *The Vengeance of She* 1968

Melia, Joe *Too Many Crooks* 1958; *Four in the Morning* 1965; *Modesty Blaise* 1966; *Oh! What a Lovely War* 1969; *The Wildcats of St Trinian's* 1980; *The Sign of Four* 1983

Mell, Marisa *French Dressing* 1964; *Casanova '70* 1965; *City of Fear* 1965; *Masquerade* 1965; *Danger: Diabolik* 1967; *Mahogany* 1975; *Casanova & Co* 1976

Mell, Randle *Stranger in the Family* 1991; *Sex, Love and Cold Hard Cash* 1993; *For the Future: the Irvine Fertility Scandal* 1996

Mellish Jr, Fuller *Applause* 1929; *Sarah and Son* 1930

Melly, Andrée *Nowhere to Go* 1958; *Beyond the Curtain* 1960

Meloni, Christopher *Falsely Accused* 1993; *Dangerous Affair* 1995; *Bound* 1996; *Target Earth* 1998; *Runaway Bride* 1999

Melton, Frank *The White Parade* 1934; *Stand up and Cheer!* 1934; *Second Chorus* 1940; *The Golden Hour* 1941

Melton, Sid *The Steel Helmet* 1951; *Lady Sings the Blues* 1972; *Sheila Levine Is Dead and Living in New York* 1975

Melville, Jean-Pierre *A Bout de Souffle* 1959; *Two Men in Manhattan* 1959

Melville, Sam *The Thomas Crown Affair* 1968; *Big Wednesday* 1978; *Twice Dead* 1988

Melvin, Murray *A Taste of Honey* 1961; *Damn the Defiant!* 1962; *Kaleidoscope* 1966; *A Day in the Death of Joe Egg* 1971; *The Devils* 1971; *Gawain and the Green Knight* 1973; *Ghost Story* 1974

Memmoli, George *Phantom of the Paradise* 1974; *New York, New York* 1977; *Blue Collar* 1978

Mendel, Stephen *Fire and Ice* 1983; *Midnight Heat* 1994; *Exception to the Rule* 1996

Mendelsohn, Ben *The Year My Voice Broke* 1987; *Return Home* 1989; *The Big Steal* 1990; *Nirvana Street Murder* 1990; *Spotswood* 1991; *Idiot Box* 1996; *Cosi* 1996

Mendenhall, David *Space Raiders* 1983; *Over the Top* 1987; *Streets* 1990

Mendillo, Stephen *Lianna* 1983; *City of Hope* 1991; *Ethan Frome* 1993; *Lone Star* 1995

Mendoza, Victor Manuel aka **Mendoza, Victor** *Susana* 1951; *The Proud Ones* 1953; *Garden of Evil* 1954; *Cowboy* 1958; *The Wonderful Country* 1959

Menez, Bernard *Day for Night* 1973; *Day for Night* 1973; *No Problem!* 1975

Menglet, Alex *Georgia* 1988; *Holidays on the River Yarra* 1991

Menjou, Adolphe *The Sheik* 1921; *The Three Musketeers* 1921; *A Woman of Paris* 1923; *The Marriage Circle* 1924; *Morocco* 1930; *The Front Page* 1931; *Friends and Lovers* 1931; *A Farewell to Arms* 1932; *Forbidden* 1932; *Morning Glory* 1933; *Little Miss Marker* 1934; *The Mighty Barnum* 1934; *Easy to Love* 1934; *Gold Diggers of 1935* 1935; *One in a Million* 1936; *Sing, Baby, Sing* 1936; *The Milky Way* 1936; *Stage Door* 1937; *A Star Is Born* 1937; *One Hundred Men and a Girl* 1937; *The Goldwyn Follies* 1938; *Thanks for Everything* 1938; *Letter of Introduction* 1938; *Golden Boy* 1939; *The Housekeeper's*

Daughter 1939; *King of the Turf* 1939; *That's Right – You're Wrong* 1939; *A Bill of Divorcement* 1940; *Turnabout* 1940; *Road Show* 1941; *Roxie Hart* 1942; *Syncopation* 1942; *You Were Never Lovelier* 1942; *Sweet Rosie O'Grady* 1943; *Step Lively* 1944; *Heartbeat* 1946; *The Hucksters* 1947; *I'll Be Yours* 1947; *State of the Union* 1948; *Dancing in the Dark* 1949; *My Dream Is Yours* 1949; *To Please a Lady* 1950; *Across the Wide Missouri* 1951; *The Tall Target* 1951; *The Sniper* 1952; *Man on a Tightrope* 1953; *Timberjack* 1955; *The Ambassador's Daughter* 1956; *Bundle of Joy* 1956; *The Fuzzy Pink Nightgown* 1957; *Paths of Glory* 1957; *I Married a Woman* 1958; *Pollyanna* 1960

Menshikov, Oleg *Dream Flights* 1983; *Burnt by the Sun* 1994; *Prisoner of the Mountains* 1996; *The Barber of Siberia* 1999; *Est-Ouest* 1999

Mensik, Vladimir *A Blonde in Love* 1965; *All My Good Countrymen* 1968

Menzer, Ernest *Bande à Part* 1964; *Made in USA* 1966

Menzies, Heather *The Sound of Music* 1965; *Hawaii* 1966; *Sssssss* 1973; *Piranha* 1978; *Captain America* 1979

Menzies, Robert *Cactus* 1986; *Tender Hooks* 1988; *Golden Braid* 1991

Merande, Doro *Mr Belvedere Rings the Bell* 1951; *The Gazebo* 1959

Merasty, Billy *Justice Denied* 1989; *Snake Treaty* 1989; *The Broken Cord* 1992; *Pocahontas: the Legend* 1995

Mercadier, Marthe *Act of Love* 1953; *Obsession* 1954

Mercado, Hector *Nomads* 1985; *Delta Force 2* 1990

Mercer, Beryl *All Quiet on the Western Front* 1930; *Outward Bound* 1930; *East Lynne* 1931; *Inspiration* 1931; *The Miracle Woman* 1931; *The Public Enemy* 1931; *Smilin' Through* 1932; *Berkeley Square* 1933; *Cavalcade* 1933; *Supernatural* 1933; *The Little Minister* 1934; *The Richest Girl in the World* 1934; *The Hound of the Baskervilles* 1939

Mercer, Frances *Annabel Takes a Tour* 1938; *The Mad Miss Manton* 1938; *Smashing the Rackets* 1938; *Vivacious Lady* 1938; *Beauty for the Asking* 1939

Mercer, Mae *The Beguiled* 1971; *Dirty Harry* 1971

Mercer, Marian *Sammy Stops the World* 1978; *The Cracker Factory* 1979; *Out on a Limb* 1992

Merchant, Veronica *'Til Death* 1993; *Deep Crimson* 1996

Merchant, Vivien *Alfie* 1966; *Accident* 1967; *Alfred the Great* 1969; *Under Milk Wood* 1971; *Frenzy* 1972; *The Offence* 1972; *The Homecoming* 1973; *The Maids* 1974; *The Man in the Iron Mask* 1977

Mercier, Michèle *Shoot the Pianist* 1960; *Fury at Smugglers Bay* 1961; *Goodbye Again* 1961; *Black Sabbath* 1963; *A Global Affair* 1964; *Casanova '70* 1965; *The Oldest Profession* 1967; *You Can't Win 'em All* 1970; *The Call of the Wild* 1972

Mercouri, Melina *Stella* 1955; *The Gypsy and the Gentleman* 1958; *Where the Hot Wind Blows!* 1959; *Never on Sunday* 1960; *Phaedra* 1962; *The Victors* 1963; *Topkapi* 1964; *A Man Could Get Killed* 1966; *10:30 PM Summer*

1966; *Gaily, Gaily* 1969; *Once Is Not Enough* 1975; *Nasty Habits* 1976; *A Dream of Passion* 1978

Mercure, Jean *Le Rouge et le Noir* 1954; *The Battle of Austerlitz* 1960

Mercure, Monique *My Uncle Antoine* 1971; *Naked Lunch* 1991

Mercurio, Gus *The Blue Lagoon* 1980; *Harlequin* 1980; *Dead Man's Float* 1980; *Turkey Shoot* 1981; *The Man from Snowy River* 1982; *"Crocodile" Dundee II* 1988; *Survive the Savage Sea* 1992; *Doing Time for Patsy Cline* 1997

Mercurio, Micole *Mask* 1985; *Gleaming the Cube* 1988; *Roe vs Wade* 1989; *Shades of Gray* 1992; *Elvis and the Colonel: the Untold Story* 1993; *Wrestling Ernest Hemingway* 1993; *While You Were Sleeping* 1995

Mercurio, Paul *Strictly Ballroom* 1992; *Exit to Eden* 1994; *Back of Beyond* 1995; *Joseph in Egypt* 1995; *Welcome to Woop Woop* 1997; *Dark Planet* 1997

Meredith, Burgess *The Scoundrel* 1935; *Winterset* 1936; *There Goes the Groom* 1937; *Idiot's Delight* 1939; *Of Mice and Men* 1939; *Castle on the Hudson* 1940; *Second Chorus* 1940; *Tom, Dick and Harry* 1941; *That Uncertain Feeling* 1941; *The Story of GI Joe* 1945; *Diary of a Chambermaid* 1946; *Magnificent Doll* 1946; *Mine Own Executioner* 1947; *On Our Merry Way* 1948; *The Man on the Eiffel Tower* 1949; *The Gay Adventure* 1949; *Joe Butterfly* 1957; *Advise and Consent* 1962; *The Cardinal* 1963; *Batman* 1966; *Big Deal at Dodge City* 1966; *Madame X* 1966; *Hurry Sundown* 1967; *Torture Garden* 1967; *Skidoo* 1968; *Hard Contract* 1969; *Mackenna's Gold* 1969; *The Reivers* 1969; *There Was a Crooked Man...* 1970; *Such Good Friends* 1971; *The Man* 1972; *Golden Needles* 1974; *The Day of the Locust* 1975; *The Hindenburg* 1975; *92 in the Shade* 1975; *Burnt Offerings* 1976; *Rocky* 1976; *Golden Rendezvous* 1977; *The Great Georgia Bank Hoax* 1977; *The Sentinel* 1977; *The Amazing Captain Nemo* 1978; *Foul Play* 1978; *Magic* 1978; *Rocky II* 1979; *When Time Ran Out* 1980; *Clash of the Titans* 1981; *True Confessions* 1981; *The Last Chase* 1981; *Rocky III* 1982; *Twilight Zone: the Movie* 1983; *Santa Claus* 1985; *Outrage!* 1986; *Mr Corbett's Ghost* 1986; *King Lear – Fear and Loathing* 1987; *Full Moon in Blue Water* 1988; *Oddball Hall* 1990; *Rocky V* 1990; *State of Grace* 1990; *Night of the Hunter* 1991; *Grumpy Old Men* 1993; *Camp Nowhere* 1994; *Grumpier Old Men* 1996

Meredith, Don *Sky Heist* 1975; *The Freeway Killings* 1987

Meredith, Judi aka **Meredith, Judy**, aka **Meredith, Judith** *Wild Heritage* 1958; *Jack the Giant Killer* 1962; *The Night Walker* 1964; *Dark Intruder* 1965; *Planet of Blood* 1966

Meredith, Lee *The Producers* 1968; *The Sunshine Boys* 1975

Meredith, Madge *Child of Divorce* 1946; *The Falcon's Adventure* 1946; *Trail Street* 1947; *Tumbleweed* 1953

Merhi, Jalal *TC 2000* 1993; *Operation Golden Phoenix* 1994; *Expect No Mercy* 1995

Méril, Macha *The Married Woman* 1964; *Vagabond* 1985

Meril, Macha *Who's Been Sleeping in My Bed?* 1963; *The Defector* 1966; *Belle de Jour* 1967; *Chinese Roulette* 1976; *Robert et Robert* 1978

Meritz, Michèle *Le Beau Serge* 1958; *Les Cousins* 1959

Merivale, John *Caltiki, the Immortal Monster* 1959; *The List of Adrian Messenger* 1963; *Arabesque* 1966

Merivale, Philip *Mr and Mrs Smith* 1941; *Lady for a Night* 1942; *This above All* 1942; *Lost Angel* 1943; *Nothing but Trouble* 1944; *The Hour before the Dawn* 1944; *Sister Kenny* 1946; *The Stranger* 1946

Meriwether, Lee *Batman* 1966; *Namu, the Killer Whale* 1966; *Angel in My Pocket* 1968

Merkel, Una *Abraham Lincoln* 1930; *Daddy Long Legs* 1931; *Dangerous Female* 1931; *Private Lives* 1931; *Red-Headed Woman* 1932; *Blonde Bombshell* 1933; *42nd Street* 1933; *Reunion in Vienna* 1933; *The Secret of Madame Blanche* 1933; *Bulldog Drummond Strikes Back* 1934; *The Cat's Paw* 1934; *The Merry Widow* 1934; *Evelyn Prentice* 1934; *Broadway Melody of 1936* 1935; *Born to Dance* 1936; *Riffraff* 1936; *Speed* 1936; *Saratoga* 1937; *True Confession* 1937; *Destry Rides Again* 1939; *Four Girls in White* 1939; *The Bank Dick* 1940; *Road to Zanzibar* 1941; *Twin Beds* 1942; *The Mad Doctor of Market Street* 1942; *My Blue Heaven* 1950; *Golden Girl* 1951; *A Millionaire for Christy* 1951; *With a Song in My Heart* 1952; *I Love Melvin* 1953; *The Kentuckian* 1955; *Bundle of Joy* 1956; *The Girl Most Likely* 1957; *The Mating Game* 1959; *The Parent Trap* 1961; *Summer and Smoke* 1961; *Summer Magic* 1963

Merkerson, S Epatha aka **Merkinson, Epatha** *She's Gotta Have It* 1986; *Terminator 2: Judgment Day* 1991; *A Place for Annie* 1994

Merlin, Jan *Running Wild* 1955; *Hell Bent for Leather* 1960; *Gunfight at Comanche Creek* 1964; *Take the Money and Run* 1969

Merlin, Joanna *Love Child* 1982; *Baby It's You* 1983; *Class Action* 1991

Merlini, Marisa *Bread, Love and Dreams* 1953; *Jealousy, Italian Style* 1970; *Aurora* 1984

Merman, Ethel *Kid Millions* 1934; *We're Not Dressing* 1934; *The Big Broadcast of 1936* 1935; *Anything Goes* 1936; *Strike Me Pink* 1936; *Alexander's Ragtime Band* 1938; *Happy Landing* 1938; *Stage Door Canteen* 1943; *Call Me Madam* 1953; *There's No Business like Show Business* 1954; *It's a Mad Mad Mad Mad World* 1963; *Journey back to Oz* 1964; *Art of Love* 1965; *Won Ton Ton, the Dog Who Saved Hollywood* 1976

Merrall, Mary *Love on the Dole* 1941; *Dead of Night* 1945; *Pink String and Sealing Wax* 1945; *Nicholas Nickleby* 1947; *They Made Me a Fugitive* 1947; *The Late Edwina Black* 1951; *Duel in the Jungle* 1954; *It's Great to Be Young* 1956

Merrick, Doris *The Big Noise* 1944; *Child of Divorce* 1946; *The Counterfeiters* 1948

Merrill, Dina *Desk Set* 1957; *A Nice Little Bank That Should Be Robbed* 1958; *Don't Give Up the Ship* 1959; *Operation Petticoat* 1959; *Butterfield 8* 1960; *The Sundowners* 1960; *The Young Savages* 1961; *The Courtship of Eddie's Father* 1963; *I'll Take Sweden* 1965; *Family Flight* 1972; *Running Wild* 1973; *Caddyshack II* 1988; *Turn Back the Clock* 1989; *Fear* 1990; *True Colors* 1991; *Shattering the Silence* 1992; *Suture* 1993; *Open Season* 1995; *Something Borrowed, Something Blue* 1997

Merrill, Gary *Twelve O'Clock High* 1949; *Slattery's Hurricane* 1949; *All about Eve* 1950; *Where the Sidewalk Ends* 1950; *Decision before Dawn* 1951; *The Frogmen* 1951; *Another Man's Poison* 1951; *Phone Call from a Stranger* 1952; *The Human Jungle* 1954; *Witness to Murder* 1954; *The Missouri Traveler* 1958; *Crash Landing* 1958; *The Wonderful Country* 1959; *The Savage Eye* 1959; *The Great Impostor* 1960; *Mysterious Island* 1961; *The Pleasure of His Company* 1961; *A Girl Named Tamiko* 1962; *Cast a Giant Shadow* 1966; *Ride beyond Vengeance* 1966; *Clambake* 1967; *The Last Challenge* 1967; *Earth II* 1971; *Huckleberry Finn* 1974; *Thieves* 1977

Merriman, Ryan *Everything That Rises* 1998; *The Deep End of the Ocean* 1999; *Night Ride Home* 1999

Merrison, Clive *Rebecca's Daughters* 1991; *Heavenly Creatures* 1994

Merritt, George *Dreyfus* 1931; *FP1* 1932; *The Ghost Camera* 1933; *Dr Syn* 1937; *Q Planes* 1939; *Spare a Copper* 1940; *I, Monster* 1971

Merritt, Theresa *The Goodbye Girl* 1977; *The Wiz* 1978; *The Great Santini* 1979; *The Serpent and the Rainbow* 1987

Merrow, Jane *The System* 1964; *Night of the Big Heat* 1967; *The Lion in Winter* 1968; *Assignment K* 1968; *Adam's Woman* 1970; *Hands of the Ripper* 1971; *Diagnosis: Murder* 1974; *The Appointment* 1981; *The Patricia Neal Story: an Act of Love* 1981

Merton, John *In Old Montana* 1939; *Knight of the Plains* 1939

Mervyn, William *Murder Ahoy* 1964; *Bloodsuckers* 1970; *The Railway Children* 1971; *The Ruling Class* 1972; *Up the Front* 1972

Messemer, Hannes *General Della Rovere* 1959; *The Defector* 1966

Messick, Don *Charlotte's Web* 1973; *Jetsons: the Movie* 1990

Messier, Marc *Portion d'Eternité* 1989; *Une Histoire Inventée* 1990

Messing, Debra *A Walk in the Clouds* 1995; *McHale's Navy* 1997

Messinger, Jack *Stereo* 1969; *Crimes of the Future* 1970

Mestral, Armand *Gervaise* 1956; *Morgan the Pirate* 1960; *That Riviera Touch* 1966; *Uncle Benjamin* 1969

Metcalf, Laurie *Desperately Seeking Susan* 1985; *The Execution of Raymond Graham* 1985; *Candy Mountain* 1987; *Making Mr Right* 1987; *Miles from Home* 1988; *Stars and Bars* 1988; *Uncle Buck* 1989; *Internal Affairs* 1990; *Pacific Heights* 1990; *JFK* 1991; *Mistress* 1992; *Blink* 1994; *Leaving Las Vegas* 1995; *Dear God* 1996; *Scream 2* 1997; *Always Outnumbered* 1998;

Bulworth 1998; *Runaway Bride* 1999; *Balloon Farm* 1999

Metcalf, Mark *The Heavenly Kid* 1985; *One Crazy Summer* 1986; *Presumed Guilty* 1991; *Disaster at Valdez* 1992; *Hijacking Hollywood* 1997; *Drive Me Crazy* 1999

Metrano, Art *The All-American Boy* 1973; *Seven* 1979; *Going Ape!* 1981; *Breathless* 1983; *Police Academy 2: Their First Assignment* 1985; *Police Academy 3: Back in Training* 1986

Metzler, Jim *Tex* 1982; *Do You Remember Love* 1985; *The Christmas Star* 1986; *976-EVIL* 1988; *Hot to Trot* 1988; *Murder by Night* 1989; *Old Gringo* 1989; *Circuitry Man* 1990; *Crash: the Mystery of Flight 1501* 1990; *Delusion* 1991; *One False Move* 1992; *French Silk* 1993; *Plughead Rewired: Circuitry Man II* 1994; *Children of the Corn III: Urban Harvest* 1995; *Cadillac Ranch* 1996

Metzman, Irving *Still of the Night* 1982; *WarGames* 1983

Meurisse, Paul *Les Diaboliques* 1954; *Lunch on the Grass* 1959; *La Vérité* 1960; *Le Deuxième Souffle* 1966; *L'Armée des Ombres* 1969; *Take It Easy* 1971

Meury, Anne-Laure *The Aviator's Wife* 1980; *My Girlfriend's Boyfriend* 1987

Mewes, Jason *Clerks* 1994; *Mallrats* 1995; *Chasing Amy* 1996; *Dogma* 1999

Meyer, Bess *Quiet Victory: the Charlie Wedemeyer Story* 1988; *Unspeakable Acts* 1990

Meyer, Breckin *Freddy's Dead: the Final Nightmare* 1991; *Betrayed: a Story of Three Women* 1995; *The Craft* 1996; *Prefontaine* 1997; *Tail Lights Fade* 1999; *Road Trip* 2000

Meyer, David *The Tempest* 1979; *Octopussy* 1983

Meyer, Dina *Johnny Mnemonic* 1995; *DragonHeart* 1996; *Starship Troopers* 1997; *Poodle Springs* 1998; *Bats* 1999

Meyer, Emile aka **Meyer, Emil** *The Big Night* 1951; *Shane* 1953; *The Human Jungle* 1954; *Riot in Cell Block 11* 1954; *Silver Lode* 1954; *Shield for Murder* 1954; *The Blackboard Jungle* 1955; *Man with the Gun* 1955; *The Tall Men* 1955; *White Feather* 1955; *Stranger on Horseback* 1955; *Baby Face Nelson* 1957; *The Lineup* 1958; *The Blue Knight* 1973

Meyer, Russ *Cherry, Harry & Raquel* 1969; *Amazon Women on the Moon* 1987

Meyers, Ari *Call Me Anna* 1990; *Driving Me Crazy* 1991; *Dark Horse* 1992; *Murder on the Rio Grande* 1993; *Not Our Son* 1995; *The Killing Secret* 1997

Meylan, Gérard *Marius et Jeannette* 1997; *A la Place du Coeur* 1998

Meyrink, Michelle *Valley Girl* 1983; *Revenge of the Nerds* 1984; *Joy of Sex* 1984; *Real Genius* 1985; *Nice Girls Don't Explode* 1987; *Permanent Record* 1988

Mézières, Myriam *Jonah Who Will Be 25 in the Year 2000* 1976; *The Diary of Lady M* 1992

Mezzogiorno, Vittorio *Three Brothers* 1980; *The Moon in the Gutter* 1983; *La Garce* 1984; *Scream of Stone* 1991; *Golem, the Spirit of Exile* 1992

Miao, Cora *Dim Sum: a Little Bit of Heart* 1985; *The Terroriser* 1986; *Eat a Bowl of Tea* 1989;

Life Is Cheap... but Toilet Paper Is Expensive 1990

Miao, Nora *The Big Boss* 1971; *Fist of Fury* 1972; *The Way of the Dragon* 1973; *Return of the Dragon* 1973

Miao Tien *The River* 1997; *The Hole* 1998

Michael, Gertrude *Ann Vickers* 1933; *I'm No Angel* 1933; *Cleopatra* 1934; *Murder at the Vanities* 1934; *Murder on the Blackboard* 1934; *Bolero* 1934; *The Last Outpost* 1935; *Till We Meet Again* 1936; *Bugles in the Afternoon* 1952

Michael, Ralph *For Those in Peril* 1943; *San Demetrio London* 1943; *Dead of Night* 1945; *Johnny Frenchman* 1945; *The Astonished Heart* 1949; *The Hasty Heart* 1949; *The Sound Barrier* 1952; *Private Potter* 1963; *Murder Most Foul* 1964; *House of Cards* 1968; *Romance on the Orient Express* 1985

Michael, Ryan *Birth of the Beatles* 1979; *Stranded* 1989; *Malicious* 1995; *Profile for Murder* 1996

Michaels, Beverly *Crashout* 1955; *Women without Men* 1956

Michaels, Dolores *April Love* 1957; *The Wayward Bus* 1957; *Time Limit* 1957; *Warlock* 1959; *Five Gates to Hell* 1959; *One Foot in Hell* 1960; *Wizards of the Lost Kingdom* 1985

Michaels, Julie *Road House* 1989; *Witchboard 2: The Devil's Doorway* 1993

Michaelsen, Melissa *Orphan Train* 1979; *Broken Promise* 1981

Michas, Jason *Draw!* 1984; *Ernest Goes to School* 1994

Michel, Marc *Le Trou* 1959; *Lola* 1960; *The Umbrellas of Cherbourg* 1964

Michele, Michael *New Jack City* 1991; *The Sixth Man* 1997; *The Substitute 2: School's Out* 1997

Michell, Keith *True as a Turtle* 1956; *Dangerous Exile* 1957; *The Gypsy and the Gentleman* 1958; *The Hellfire Club* 1961; *All Night Long* 1961; *Seven Seas to Calais* 1962; *House of Cards* 1968; *Prudence and the Pill* 1968; *Henry VIII and His Six Wives* 1972; *Grendel, Grendel, Grendel* 1981; *The Deceivers* 1988

Michelle, Ann *House of Whipcord* 1974; *Haunted* 1976

Michie, John *Monk Dawson* 1997; *To Walk with Lions* 1999

Micklewood, Eric *The Lamp Still Burns* 1943; *Death Race* 1973

Middleton, Charles aka **Middleton, Charles B** *The Miracle Woman* 1931; *White Woman* 1933; *Murder at the Vanities* 1934; *Mrs Wiggs of the Cabbage Patch* 1934; *Hopalong Cassidy* 1935; *Flash Gordon* 1936; *The Flying Deuces* 1939; *The Oklahoma Kid* 1939; *Wyoming Outlaw* 1939

Middleton, Guy *Keep Fit* 1937; *Night Boat to Dublin* 1946; *A Man about the House* 1947; *Snowbound* 1948; *Marry Me!* 1949; *No Place for Jennifer* 1949; *The Happiest Days of Your Life* 1950; *Laughter in Paradise* 1951; *Young Wives' Tale* 1951; *Albert, RN* 1953; *Conflict of Wings* 1953; *Malaga* 1954; *Break in the Circle* 1955; *A Yank in Ermine* 1955; *Gentlemen Marry Brunettes* 1955; *Passionate Summer* 1958

Middleton, Noelle *Carrington VC* 1954; *Happy Ever After* 1954; *John and Julie* 1955; *A Yank in Ermine* 1955; *The Vicious Circle* 1957

Middleton, Ray *Lady from Louisiana* 1941; *Lady for a Night* 1942; *I Dream of Jeanie* 1952; *The Road to Denver* 1955

Middleton, Robert *The Big Combo* 1955; *Trial* 1955; *The Court Jester* 1956; *Friendly Persuasion* 1956; *Love Me Tender* 1956; *The Proud Ones* 1956; *Red Sundown* 1956; *The Tarnished Angels* 1957; *The Lonely Man* 1957; *The Law and Jake Wade* 1958; *Day of the Bad Man* 1958; *Career* 1959; *Don't Give Up the Ship* 1959; *Hell Bent for Leather* 1960; *The Great Impostor* 1960; *Gold of the Seven Saints* 1961; *Cattle King* 1963; *Big Deal at Dodge City* 1966; *The Cheyenne Social Club* 1970; *Which Way to the Front?* 1970; *The Mark of Zorro* 1974

Midkiff, Dale *A Cry for Help: the Tracey Thurman Story* 1989; *Pet Sematary* 1989; *Face Value* 1991; *Plymouth* 1991; *Sins of the Mother* 1991; *Vigilante Cop* 1991; *Shoot First: a Cop's Vengeance* 1991; *Love Potion No 9* 1992; *A Burning Passion: the Margaret Mitchell Story* 1994; *A Child Is Missing* 1995; *Visitors of the Night* 1995; *Ed McBain's 87th Precinct: Ice* 1996; *Ed McBain's 87th Precinct: Heatwave* 1997; *Toothless* 1997

Midler, Bette *The Rose* 1979; *Jinxed!* 1982; *Down and Out in Beverly Hills* 1986; *Ruthless People* 1986; *Outrageous Fortune* 1987; *Beaches* 1988; *Big Business* 1988; *Oliver & Company* 1988; *Stella* 1990; *For the Boys* 1991; *Scenes from a Mall* 1991; *Gypsy* 1993; *Hocus Pocus* 1993; *The First Wives Club* 1996; *That Old Feeling* 1997; *Isn't She Great* 1999; *Drowning Mona* 2000

Mifune, Toshiro *Drunken Angel* 1948; *Stray Dog* 1949; *Rashomon* 1950; *The Idiot* 1951; *The Life of Oharu* 1952; *Seven Samurai* 1954; *Samurai* 1954; *I Live in Fear* 1955; *Throne of Blood* 1957; *The Hidden Fortress* 1958; *The Bad Sleep Well* 1960; *The Important Man* 1961; *Yojimbo* 1961; *Sanjuro* 1962; *High and Low* 1963; *Red Beard* 1965; *Grand Prix* 1966; *Rebellion* 1967; *Hell in the Pacific* 1968; *Red Sun* 1971; *Paper Tiger* 1974; *Battle of Midway* 1976; *1941* 1979; *Winter Kills* 1979; *Shogun* 1980; *The Bushido Blade* 1981; *The Challenge* 1982; *Shogun Warrior* 1991; *Shadow of the Wolf* 1992; *Picture Bride* 1994

Migenes-Johnson, Julia *Carmen* 1984; *Mack the Knife* 1989

Mihashi, Tatsuya *The Burmese Harp* 1956; *High and Low* 1963; *None but the Brave* 1965; *What's Up, Tiger Lily?* 1966; *Tora! Tora! Tora!* 1970

Mihok, Dash *Murderous Intent* 1995; *William Shakespeare's Romeo + Juliet* 1996

Mikael, Ludmila *The Sergeant* 1968; *Noce Blanche* 1989

Mikami, Hiroshi *Tokyo Pop* 1988; *Circus Boys* 1989

Mikell, George *Beyond the Curtain* 1960; *The Primitives* 1962

Mikhalkov, Nikita *A Station for Two* 1983; *Burnt by the Sun* 1994

Mikhelson, Andre *Desperate Moment* 1953; *The Intimate Stranger* 1956

Mikuni, Rentaro *Samurai* 1954; *The Burmese Harp* 1956; *Harakiri* 1962; *Kwaidan* 1964; *Kwaidan* 1964; *Vengeance Is Mine* 1979; *Rikyu* 1989

Milan, Lita *The Left Handed Gun* 1958; *The Mobster* 1958; *Never Love a Stranger* 1958

Milano, Alyssa *Commando* 1985; *Conflict of Interest* 1992; *Where the Day Takes You* 1992; *Casualties of Love: the Long Island Lolita Story* 1993; *Double Dragon* 1994; *Embrace of the Vampire* 1994; *The Public Enemy #1* 1995; *The Surrogate* 1995; *Poison Ivy II: Lily* 1995; *Glory Daze* 1995; *Deadly Sins* 1996; *Fear* 1996; *To Brave Alaska* 1996; *Hugo Pool* 1997

Milburn, Oliver *Good King Wenceslas* 1994; *Loaded* 1994; *Sweet Angel Mine* 1996

Miles, Bernard *The Love Test* 1935; *Midnight at Madame Tussaud's* 1936; *In Which We Serve* 1942; *One of Our Aircraft Is Missing* 1942; *Tawny Pipit* 1944; *Great Expectations* 1946; *Carnival* 1946; *Fame Is the Spur* 1947; *Nicholas Nickleby* 1947; *The Guinea Pig* 1948; *Chance of a Lifetime* 1950; *Never Let Me Go* 1953; *The Man Who Knew Too Much* 1956; *Moby Dick* 1956; *Tiger in the Smoke* 1956; *Zarak* 1956; *Saint Joan* 1957; *The Smallest Show on Earth* 1957; *tom thumb* 1958; *Sapphire* 1959; *Heavens Above!* 1963; *Run Wild, Run Free* 1969

Miles, Joanna *Bug* 1975; *The Ultimate Warrior* 1975; *A Fire in the Sky* 1978; *All My Sons* 1986; *Right to Die* 1987; *Rosencrantz and Guildenstern Are Dead* 1990; *The Heart of Justice* 1992; *The Water Engine* 1992; *Natural Selection* 1994; *Barbara Taylor Bradford's Everything to Gain* 1996

Miles, Kevin *The Cars That Ate Paris* 1974; *Boulevard of Broken Dreams* 1988

Miles, Peter *Heaven Only Knows* 1947; *The Red Pony* 1949

Miles, Sarah *Term of Trial* 1962; *The Ceremony* 1963; *The Servant* 1963; *Those Magnificent Men in Their Flying Machines* 1965; *Blow Up* 1966; *I Was Happy Here* 1966; *Ryan's Daughter* 1970; *Lady Caroline Lamb* 1972; *The Hireling* 1973; *The Man Who Loved Cat Dancing* 1973; *Great Expectations* 1974; *The Sailor Who Fell from Grace with the Sea* 1976; *The Big Sleep* 1978; *Priest of Love* 1981; *Venom* 1982; *Ordeal by Innocence* 1984; *Steaming* 1985; *Hope and Glory* 1987; *White Mischief* 1987; *A Ghost in Monte Carlo* 1990; *The Silent Touch* 1992

Miles, Sherry *The Velvet Vampire* 1971; *The Todd Killings* 1971

Miles, Sylvia *Psychomania* 1964; *Midnight Cowboy* 1969; *Who Killed Mary Whats'ername?* 1971; *Heat* 1972; *Farewell, My Lovely* 1975; *92 in the Shade* 1975; *The Great Scout & Cathouse Thursday* 1976; *Zero to Sixty* 1978; *Evil under the Sun* 1982; *No Big Deal* 1983; *Critical Condition* 1987; *Wall Street* 1987; *Crossing Delancey* 1988; *Spike of Bensonhurst* 1988; *She-Devil* 1989

Miles, Vera *The Charge at Feather River* 1953; *Pride of the Blue Grass* 1954; *Tarzan's Hidden Jungle* 1955; *Wichita* 1955; *Autumn Leaves* 1956; *The Searchers* 1956; *23 Paces to Baker Street* 1956; *The Wrong Man* 1956; *Beau James* 1957; *Beyond This Place* 1959; *The FBI Story* 1959; *A Touch of Larceny* 1959; *Five Branded Women* 1960;

Psycho 1960; Back Street 1961; The Man Who Shot Liberty Valance 1962; A Tiger Walks 1964; Those Calloways 1964; Follow Me, Boys! 1966; One of Our Spies Is Missing 1966; Gentle Giant 1967; Sergeant Ryker 1968; Kona Coast 1968; Hellfighters 1969; The Wild Country 1971; Jigsaw 1972; Molly and Lawless John 1972; One Little Indian 1973; Runaway! 1973; The Castaway Cowboy 1974; The Strange and Deadly Occurrence 1974; Smash-Up on Interstate 5 1976; Fire! 1977; Run for the Roses 1978; Brainwaves 1982; Psycho II 1983; The Initiation 1984; Separate Lives 1995

Milford, Kim Laserblast 1978; Corvette Summer 1978

Milford, Penelope Coming Home 1978; Take This Job and Shove It 1981; Rosie: the Rosemary Clooney Story 1982; The Burning Bed 1984; Heathers 1989; Cold Justice 1991; Henry: Portrait of a Serial Killer, Part II 1996

Milian, Tomas Boccaccio '70 1961; Django Kill 1967; Face to Face 1967; Beatrice Cenci 1969; A Fine Pair 1969; The Last Movie 1971; The Evil Trap 1975; La Luna 1979; Winter Kills 1979; Identification of a Woman 1982; Cat Chaser 1989; Havana 1990; Revenge 1990; Nails 1992; The Burning Season 1994; The Cowboy Way 1994; Fools Rush In 1997

Military, Frank Dead-Bang 1989; Everybody Wins 1990

Miljan, John The Unholy Three 1930; Free and Easy 1930; Inspiration 1931; Susan Lenox: Her Fall and Rise 1931; The Iron Man 1931; Arsene Lupin 1932; Emma 1932; Flesh 1932; The Kid from Spain 1932; The Rich Are Always with Us 1932; The Beast of the City 1932; The Mad Game 1933; What – No Beer? 1933; Belle of the Nineties 1934; The Plainsman 1936; Fast and Furious 1939; Mrs Mike 1949

Millais, Hugh Images 1972; The Dogs of War 1980

Millan, Victor Terror in a Texas Town 1958; Boulevard Nights 1979

Milland, Ray aka **Milland, Raymond** Piccadilly 1929; The Bachelor Father 1931; Blonde Crazy 1931; Payment Deferred 1932; Polly of the Circus 1932; Charlie Chan in London 1934; We're Not Dressing 1934; Bolero 1934; The Gilded Lily 1935; The Glass Key 1935; The Big Broadcast of 1937 1936; Next Time We Love 1936; Easy Living 1937; Three Smart Girls 1937; Men with Wings 1938; Beau Geste 1939; Arise, My Love 1940; Irene 1940; I Wanted Wings 1941; Skylark 1941; The Major and the Minor 1942; Reap the Wild Wind 1942; Star Spangled Rhythm 1942; The Crystal Ball 1943; Forever and a Day 1943; Lady in the Dark 1944; Till We Meet Again 1944; The Uninvited 1944; Kitty 1945; The Lost Weekend 1945; Ministry of Fear 1945; California 1946; The Imperfect Lady 1947; Variety Girl 1947; Golden Earrings 1947; The Big Clock 1948; Miss Tatlock's Millions 1948; It Happens Every Spring 1949; Circle of Danger 1950; A Life of Her Own 1950; A Woman of Distinction 1950; Copper Canyon 1950; Rhubarb 1951; Close to My Heart 1951;

Bugles in the Afternoon 1952; The Thief 1952; Something to Live For 1952; Let's Do It Again 1953; Jamaica Run 1953; Dial M for Murder 1954; A Man Alone 1955; The Girl in the Red Velvet Swing 1955; Lisbon 1956; Three Brave Men 1956; The River's Edge 1957; High Flight 1957; The Safecracker 1958; The Premature Burial 1962; Panic in Year Zero 1962; The Man with the X-Ray Eyes 1963; Quick, Let's Get Married 1964; Hostile Witness 1968; Love Story 1970; Company of Killers 1970; Embassy 1972; Frogs 1972; The Thing with Two Heads 1972; The House in Nightmare Park 1973; Terror in the Wax Museum 1973; Gold 1974; The Dead Don't Die 1975; Escape to Witch Mountain 1975; The Swiss Conspiracy 1975; Aces High 1976; The Last Tycoon 1976; The Uncanny 1977; Slavers 1977; Oliver's Story 1978; The Darker Side of Terror 1979; Survival Run 1979; A Game for Vultures 1979; Starflight One 1983

Millar, Marjie Money from Home 1953; About Mrs Leslie 1954

Millard, Helene The Divorcee 1930; Break of Hearts 1935

Miller, Allan Fun with Dick and Jane 1977; Murder COD 1990; Lethal Charm 1991

Miller, Andrew Last of the Dogmen 1995; Cube 1997

Miller, Ann New Faces of 1937 1937; Stage Door 1937; Radio City Revels 1938; Room Service 1938; You Can't Take It with You 1938; Too Many Girls 1940; Reveille with Beverly 1943; Easter Parade 1948; On the Town 1949; The Kissing Bandit 1949; Watch the Birdie 1950; Two Tickets to Broadway 1951; Lovely to Look At 1952; Kiss Me Kate 1953; Deep in My Heart 1954; Hit the Deck 1955; The Opposite Sex 1956

Miller, Barry Saturday Night Fever 1977; Voices 1979; The Chosen 1981; The Roommate 1984; The Journey of Natty Gann 1985; Peggy Sue Got Married 1986; The Pickle 1993; Flawless 1999

Miller, Carl The Kid 1921; A Woman of Paris 1923

Miller, Colleen Playgirl 1954; Four Guns to the Border 1954; The Purple Mask 1955; The Rawhide Years 1956; Man in the Shadow 1957; The Night Runner 1957; Hot Summer Night 1957; Gunfight at Comanche Creek 1964

Miller, David Attack of the Killer Tomatoes 1978; Gunpowder 1985

Miller, Dean Because You're Mine 1952; Everything I Have Is Yours 1952; Skirts Ahoy! 1952

Miller, Dennis Heatwave 1983; Frog Dreaming 1985; Madhouse 1990; Disclosure 1994; The Net 1995; Never Talk to Strangers 1995; Tales from the Crypt Presents: Bordello of Blood 1996; Murder at 1600 1997

Miller, Denny Tarzan, the Ape Man 1959; Buck and the Preacher 1972; The Gravy Train 1974

Miller, Dick aka **Miller, Richard** Not of This Earth 1956; The Gunslinger 1956; Rock All Night 1957; Sorority Girl 1957; War of the Satellites 1958; A Bucket of Blood 1959; The Terror 1963; The Trip 1967; Big Bad Mama 1974; Hollywood Boulevard 1976; Mr Billion 1977; Piranha 1978; Rock 'n' Roll High School 1979; The Howling 1981; Heartbeeps 1981; Get Crazy 1983; Gremlins 1984; The Terminator 1984; Explorers

1985; Armed Response 1986; Gremlins 2: the New Batch 1990; Amityville 1992: It's About Time 1992; Batman: Mask of the Phantasm 1993; Runaway Daughters 1994; Shake, Rattle and Rock 1994; Tales from the Crypt: Demon Knight 1995

Miller, Eve April in Paris 1952; The Big Trees 1952

Miller, Glenn Sun Valley Serenade 1941; Orchestra Wives 1942

Miller, Jason The Exorcist 1973; The Devil's Advocate 1977; The Ninth Configuration 1979; Marilyn – The Untold Story 1980; Monsignor 1982; A Touch of Scandal 1984; Deadly Care 1987; Light of Day 1987; The Exorcist III 1990

Miller, Joan Yield to the Night 1956; No Trees in the Street 1958

Miller, John The Girl in the Picture 1956; Ratcatcher 1999

Miller, Jonny Lee Hackers 1995; Trainspotting 1995; Afterglow 1997; Regeneration 1997; Plunkett & Macleane 1999; Mansfield Park 1999; Complicity 1999; Love, Honour and Obey 2000

Miller, Joshua Near Dark 1987; River's Edge 1987; Teen Witch 1989; And You Thought Your Parents Were Weird 1991

Miller, Kristine Desert Fury 1947; I Walk Alone 1947; High Lonesome 1950; Thunder over Arizona 1956

Miller, Larry Frankenstein: the College Years 1991; Necessary Roughness 1991; Suburban Commando 1991; Frozen Assets 1992; Dream Lover 1993; Undercover Blues 1993; Corrina, Corrina 1994; The Favor 1994; The Computer Wore Tennis Shoes 1995; The Nutty Professor 1996; Chairman of the Board 1998; The Big Tease 1999; Carnival of Souls 1999

Miller, Linda One Summer Love 1975; An Unmarried Woman 1978

Miller, Lydia Backlash 1986; Deadly 1991

Miller, Mandy Mandy 1952; Background 1953; Adventure in the Hopfields 1954; Dance Little Lady 1954; Raising a Riot 1955; Child in the House 1956

Miller, Mark Ginger in the Morning 1973; Savannah Smiles 1982

Miller, Martin Hotel Reserve 1944; Night Boat to Dublin 1946; Mark of the Phoenix 1957; Libel 1959; The Phantom of the Opera 1962

Miller, Marvin Johnny Angel 1945; Deadline at Dawn 1946; Dead Reckoning 1947; Intrigue 1947; Peking Express 1951; Red Planet Mars 1952; Forbidden 1953; The Shanghai Story 1954; Forbidden Planet 1956; Senior Prom 1958; Fantastic Planet 1973

Miller, Maxine The Care Bears Movie II: a New Generation 1986; This Can't Be Love 1994

Miller, Michael Doc Savage: the Man of Bronze 1975; Knock Off 1998

Miller, Patsy Ruth The Hunchback of Notre Dame 1923; So This Is Paris 1926

Miller, Penelope Ann A Night on the Town 1987; Big Top Pee-wee 1988; Biloxi Blues 1988; Dead-Bang 1989; Awakenings 1990; Downtown 1990; The Freshman 1990; Kindergarten Cop 1990; Other People's Money 1991; Chaplin 1992; The Gun in Betty Lou's Handbag 1992; Year of the Comet 1992; Carlito's Way 1993;

The Shadow 1994; Witch Hunt 1994; The Relic 1997; The Hired Heart 1997; Rocky Marciano 1999

Miller, Rebecca Seven Minutes 1989; Regarding Henry 1991; Consenting Adults 1992; Wind 1992

Miller, Sherry Rent-a-Kid 1992; Dead Husbands 1998

Miller, Stephen E Home Is Where the Hart Is 1987; The Baby Dance 1998

Miller, Walter aka **Miller, W Chrystie** The Musketeers of Pig Alley 1912; The Battle of Elderbush 1914; Stormy 1935

Millican, James The Tender Years 1947; The Man from Colorado 1948; Mister 880 1950; Cavalry Scout 1951; I Was a Communist for the FBI 1951; Warpath 1951; Bugles in the Afternoon 1952; Diplomatic Courier 1952; Springfield Rifle 1952; Riding Shotgun 1954; The Big Tip Off 1955; Red Sundown 1956

Milligan, Deanna Avalanche 1994; My Name Is Kate 1994

Milligan, Spike Down among the Z-Men 1952; The Case of the Mukkinese Battle Horn 1955; The Running, Jumping and Standing Still Film 1959; Suspect 1960; Watch Your Stern 1960; Invasion Quartet 1961; Postman's Knock 1961; What a Whopper! 1961; The Bed Sitting Room 1969; The Magic Christian 1969; Adolf Hitler – My Part in His Downfall 1972; The Adventures of Barry McKenzie 1972; Alice's Adventures in Wonderland 1972; Rentadick 1972; Digby, the Biggest Dog in the World 1973; The Three Musketeers 1973; Ghost in the Noonday Sun 1973; The Great McGonagall 1974; The Hound of the Baskervilles 1977; The Last Remake of Beau Geste 1977; Yellowbeard 1983

Milliken, Angie Harbour Beat 1990; Act of Necessity 1991; Rough Diamonds 1994; Dead Heart 1996; Paperback Hero 1998

Mills, Alley Going Berserk 1983; Jonathan: the Boy Nobody Wanted 1992; Tainted Blood 1993; Caught in the Crossfire 1994

Mills, Brooke The Big Doll House 1971; The Million Dollar Rip-off 1976

Mills, Donna The Incident 1967; Play Misty for Me 1971; Live a Little, Steal a Lot 1974; Smash-Up on Interstate 5 1976; Fire! 1977; Young Maverick 1979; Outback Bound 1988; The World's Oldest Living Bridesmaid 1990; In My Daughter's Name 1992; The President's Child 1992; My Name Is Kate 1994; Dangerous Intentions 1995; An Element of Truth 1995; The Stepford Husbands 1996; Mary Higgins Clark's Moonlight Becomes You 1998

Mills, Freddie Emergency Call 1952; Kill Me Tomorrow 1957; Saturday Night Out 1963

Mills, Hayley Tiger Bay 1959; Pollyanna 1960; In Search of the Castaways 1961; The Parent Trap 1961; Whistle down the Wind 1961; Summer Magic 1963; The Chalk Garden 1964; The Moon-Spinners 1964; The Truth about Spring 1964; Sky West and Crooked 1965; That Darn Cat! 1965; The Family Way 1966; The Trouble with Angels 1966; Africa – Texas Style 1967; Pretty Polly 1967; Twisted Nerve 1968; Take a Girl Like You 1970; Endless

Night 1971; What Changed Charley Farthing? 1975; Parent Trap II 1986; Appointment with Death 1988; Parent Trap Hawaiian Honeymoon 1989; After Midnight 1990; Back Home 1990; Stanley's Magic Garden 1994

Mills, John The Ghost Camera 1933; Doctor's Orders 1934; Those Were the Days 1934; Car of Dreams 1935; Forever England 1935; You're in the Army Now 1936; Tudor Rose 1936; The Green Cockatoo 1937; Goodbye, Mr Chips 1939; The Black Sheep of Whitehall 1941; Cottage to Let 1941; In Which We Serve 1942; We Dive at Dawn 1943; This Happy Breed 1944; Waterloo Road 1944; The Way to the Stars 1945; Great Expectations 1946; The October Man 1947; The History of Mr Polly 1948; Scott of the Antarctic 1948; The Rocking Horse Winner 1949; Morning Departure 1950; Mr Denning Drives North 1951; The Gentle Gunman 1952; The Long Memory 1952; Hobson's Choice 1953; The Colditz Story 1954; Above Us the Waves 1955; The End of the Affair 1955; Around the World in 80 Days 1956; The Baby and the Battleship 1956; It's Great to Be Young 1956; Town on Trial 1956; War and Peace 1956; The Vicious Circle 1957; Dunkirk 1958; I Was Monty's Double 1958; Ice Cold in Alex 1958; Tiger Bay 1959; Season of Passion 1960; The Singer Not the Song 1960; Swiss Family Robinson 1960; Tunes of Glory 1960; Flame in the Streets 1961; Tiara Tahiti 1962; The Chalk Garden 1964; The Truth about Spring 1964; Operation Crossbow 1965; The Family Way 1966; The Wrong Box 1966; Africa – Texas Style 1967; Chuka 1967; A Black Veil for Lisa 1969; Oh! What a Lovely War 1969; Run Wild, Run Free 1969; Adam's Woman 1970; Ryan's Daughter 1970; Dulcima 1971; Lady Caroline Lamb 1972; Young Winston 1972; Oklahoma Crude 1973; The Human Factor 1975; Trial by Combat 1976; The Devil's Advocate 1977; The Big Sleep 1978; The Thirty-Nine Steps 1978; Zulu Dawn 1979; The Quatermass Conclusion 1979; Gandhi 1982; Sahara 1983; Agatha Christie's Murder with Mirrors 1985; When the Wind Blows 1986; Who's That Girl 1987; Frankenstein 1992; Deadly Advice 1993

Mills, Juliet No My Darling Daughter 1961; Twice round the Daffodils 1962; Carry On Jack 1963; Nurse on Wheels 1963; The Rare Breed 1966; Avanti! 1972; Jonathan Livingston Seagull 1973; The Cracker Factory 1979; A Stranger in the Mirror 1993; The Other Sister 1999

Mills, Mort Davy Crockett and the River Pirates 1956; Ride a Crooked Trail 1958; The Outlaws Is Coming 1965

Milner, Martin aka **Milner, Marty** Life with Father 1947; Operation Pacific 1951; Springfield Rifle 1952; Destination Gobi 1953; Sweet Smell of Success 1957; Too Much, Too Soon 1958; Compulsion 1959; Sex Kittens Go to College 1960; Valley of the Dolls 1967; Emergency! 1971; Runaway! 1973; Flood! 1976

Milo, Jean-Roger Sarraouina 1986; L.627 1992; Germinal 1993; Lucie Aubrac 1997

1989; *Cape Fear* 1991; *Tombstone* 1993; *Woman of Desire* 1994; *Dead Man* 1995
Mitevska, Labina *Before the Rain* 1994; *I Want You* 1998
Mito, Mitsuko *My Love Has Been Burning* 1949; *Ugetsu Monogatari* 1953
Miyaguchi, Seiji *Seven Samurai* 1954; *The Ballad of Narayama* 1958; *Twin Sisters of Kyoto* 1963
Miyake, Kuniko *Poppy* 1935; *Hen in the Wind* 1948; *My Love Has Been Burning* 1949; *Early Summer* 1951; *The Flavour of Green Tea over Rice* 1952; *Early Spring* 1956; *Escapade in Japan* 1957; *Good Morning* 1959
Miyamoto, Nobuko *Death Japanese Style* 1984; *Tampopo* 1986; *A Taxing Woman* 1987; *Minbo – or the Gentle Art of Japanese Extortion* 1992
Miyori, Kim *John and Yoko: a Love Story* 1985; *When the Bough Breaks* 1986; *The Big Picture* 1989; *The Punisher* 1989; *Fire! Trapped on the 37th Floor* 1991; *Journey to the Center of the Earth* 1993; *Body Shot* 1994; *Shadow of Obsession* 1994; *Metro* 1997
Miyoshi, Eiko *No Regrets for Our Youth* 1946; *I Live in Fear* 1955
Mizuno, Kumi *Frankenstein Meets the Devil Fish* 1964; *Invasion of the Astro-Monster* 1965; *Ebirah, Horror of the Deep* 1966; *War of the Gargantuas* 1970
Mlodzik, Ronald *Stereo* 1969; *Crimes of the Future* 1970
Mobley, Mary Ann *Get Yourself a College Girl* 1964; *Harem Holiday* 1965; *Girl Happy* 1965; *Three on a Couch* 1966; *The King's Pirate* 1967; *Istanbul Express* 1968
Mobley, Roger *A Dog's Best Friend* 1960; *The Boy Who Caught a Crook* 1961; *Jack the Giant Killer* 1962; *Emil and the Detectives* 1964
Mochrie, Peter *The Winter of Our Dreams* 1981; *Frauds* 1992
Mocky, Jean-Pierre *The Vanquished* 1953; *Grandeur et Décadence d'un Petit Commerce de Cinéma* 1986
Modine, Matthew *Streamers* 1983; *Private School* 1983; *Birdy* 1984; *The Hotel New Hampshire* 1984; *Mrs Soffel* 1984; *Vision Quest* 1985; *Full Metal Jacket* 1987; *Orphans* 1987; *Married to the Mob* 1988; *The Gamble* 1988; *A Cut Above* 1989; *Memphis Belle* 1990; *Pacific Heights* 1990; *Equinox* 1992; *Wind* 1992; *And the Band Played On* 1993; *Short Cuts* 1993; *The Browning Version* 1994; *Jacob* 1994; *Bye Bye Love* 1995; *CutThroat Island* 1995; *Fluke* 1995; *The Blackout* 1997; *The Maker* 1997; *The Real Blonde* 1997; *What the Deaf Man Heard* 1997; *Any Given Sunday* 1999
Modot, Gaston *The Ship of Lost Men* 1929; *L'Age d'Or* 1930; *Sous les Toits de Paris* 1930; *La Grande Illusion* 1937; *La Règle du Jeu* 1939; *Casque d'Or* 1952
Moeller, Ralph *Best of the Best II* 1992; *Universal Soldier* 1992; *The Viking Sagas* 1995
Moffat, Donald *The Great Northfield Minnesota Raid* 1972; *Showdown* 1973; *The Terminal Man* 1974; *Mrs R's Daughter* 1979; *Promises in the Dark* 1979; *On the Nickel* 1979; *The Long Days of Summer* 1980; *Popeye* 1980; *The Right Stuff* 1983; *Monster in the Closet* 1983; *Alamo Bay* 1985; *The Best of Times* 1986; *When the Time Comes* 1987; *Far North* 1988; *The Unbearable Lightness of Being* 1988; *Music Box* 1989; *Kaleidoscope* 1990; *A Son's Promise* 1990; *Class Action* 1991; *The Great Pretender* 1991; *Regarding Henry* 1991; *HouseSitter* 1992; *Majority Rule* 1992; *Clear and Present Danger* 1994; *Love, Cheat & Steal* 1994; *Trapped in Paradise* 1994
Moffatt, Graham *Where There's a Will* 1936; *Windbag the Sailor* 1936; *Dr Syn* 1937; *Good Morning, Boys* 1937; *Oh, Mr Porter!* 1937; *Ask a Policeman* 1938; *Convict 99* 1938; *Old Bones of the River* 1938; *Owd Bob* 1938; *Cheer Boys Cheer* 1939; *Where's That Fire?* 1939; *Hi, Gang!* 1941; *I Thank You* 1941; *Back Room Boy* 1942; *Time Flies* 1944
Moffett, D W *An Early Frost* 1985; *Dream Breakers* 1989; *Fine Things* 1990; *In the Deep Woods* 1992; *Love, Lies and Lullabies* 1993; *Quest for Justice* 1993; *The Counterfeit Contessa* 1994; *Rough Magic* 1995; *Stealing Beauty* 1995; *Perfect Prey* 1998; *Molly* 1999
Moffett, Gregory *Let's Dance* 1950; *Robot Monster* 1953
Moffett, Michelle *Hired to Kill* 1990; *Indecent Behavior* 1993
Moffett, Sharyn *The Body Snatcher* 1945; *The Falcon in San Francisco* 1945; *Child of Divorce* 1946; *The Locket* 1946; *Mr Blandings Builds His Dream House* 1948; *The Judge Steps Out* 1949
Mohner, Carl *The Last Bridge* 1954; *Rififi* 1955; *Behind the Mask* 1958; *The Camp on Blood Island* 1958; *Passionate Summer* 1958; *The Challenge* 1960; *Sink the Bismarck!* 1960; *Callan* 1974
Mohr, Gerald *One Dangerous Night* 1943; *Gilda* 1946; *The Lone Wolf in London* 1947; *Undercover Girl* 1950; *Sirocco* 1951; *The Duel at Silver Creek* 1952; *Invasion USA* 1952; *The Sniper* 1952; *The Ring* 1952; *The Eddie Cantor Story* 1953; *Raiders of the Seven Seas* 1953; *The Angry Red Planet* 1959; *This Rebel Breed* 1960
Mohr, Jay *The Barefoot Executive* 1995; *For Better or Worse* 1995; *Jerry Maguire* 1996; *Picture Perfect* 1997; *Suicide Kings* 1997; *Jane Austen's Mafia* 1998; *Paulie* 1998; *Go* 1999; *200 Cigarettes* 1999
Mohyeddin, Zia *Sammy Going South* 1963; *Khartoum* 1966; *They Came from beyond Space* 1967; *The Sailor from Gibraltar* 1967; *Work Is a Four Letter Word* 1968; *Bombay Talkie* 1970; *The Assam Garden* 1985; *Doomsday Gun* 1994
Moir, Richard *The Odd Angry Shot* 1979; *Heatwave* 1983; *Remember Me* 1985; *Welcome to Woop Woop* 1997
Mok, Karen *aka* **Mo Wenwei** *Fallen Angels* 1995; *Black Mask* 1996; *Kitchen* 1997
Mokae, Zakes *Agatha Christie's A Caribbean Mystery* 1983; *Cry Freedom* 1987; *The Serpent and the Rainbow* 1987; *A Cut Above* 1989; *Dad* 1989; *A Dry White Season* 1989; *Body Parts* 1991; *A Rage in Harlem* 1991; *Dust Devil* 1992; *Percy and Thunder* 1993; *Vampire in Brooklyn* 1995
Mol, Gretchen *The Funeral* 1996; *Girl 6* 1996; *The Last Time I Committed Suicide* 1996; *Rounders* 1998; *The Thirteenth Floor* 1999; *Sweet and Lowdown* 1999; *Finding Graceland* 1999
Molina, Alfred *Raiders of the Lost Ark* 1981; *Number One* 1984; *Eleni* 1985; *Ladyhawke* 1985; *Letter to Brezhnev* 1985; *Prick Up Your Ears* 1987; *Not without My Daughter* 1990; *American Friends* 1991; *Enchanted April* 1991; *The Trial* 1993; *Maverick* 1994; *The Steal* 1994; *White Fang 2: Myth of the White Wolf* 1994; *Hideaway* 1995; *The Perez Family* 1995; *Species* 1995; *Scorpion Spring* 1995; *Before and After* 1996; *A Further Gesture* 1996; *Mojave Moon* 1996; *Anna Karenina* 1997; *The Man Who Knew Too Little* 1997; *The Impostors* 1998; *Rescuers: Stories of Courage – Two Couples* 1998; *Dudley Do-Right* 1999
Molina, Angela *Lola* 1986; *Streets of Gold* 1986; *1492: Conquest of Paradise* 1992; *Live Flesh* 1997; *Wind with the Gone* 1998
Molina, Miguel *1919* 1983; *The Law of Desire* 1987
Moll, Giorgia *aka* **Moll, Georgia** *The Quiet American* 1958; *The Cossacks* 1959; *Island of Love* 1963; *Le Mépris* 1963
Moll, Richard *The Sword and the Sorcerer* 1982; *House* 1986; *Wicked Stepmother* 1989; *Beanstalk* 1994; *No Dessert Dad, Till You Mow the Lawn* 1994; *The Secret Agent Club* 1995; *Storybook* 1995; *The Glass Cage* 1996; *Living in Peril* 1997
Mollà, Jordi *Jamon Jamon* 1992; *Revolver* 1992; *Dollar for the Dead* 1998
Mollison, Henry *The Loves of Joanna Godden* 1947; *What the Butler Saw* 1950; *The Man in the White Suit* 1951
Molloy, Dearbhla *Taffin* 1988; *The Run of the Country* 1995; *This Is the Sea* 1996
Molnár, Tibor *The Round-Up* 1966; *The Red and the White* 1967
Monahan, Dan *Porky's* 1981; *Porky's II: The Next Day* 1983; *Porky's Revenge* 1985; *Stephen King's The Night Flier* 1997
Mondy, Pierre *The Battle of Austerlitz* 1960; *The Mysteries of Paris* 1962; *The Sleeping Car Murders* 1965; *The Pink Telephone* 1975
Monette, Richard *Dancing in the Dark* 1986; *I've Heard the Mermaids Singing* 1987; *While My Pretty One Sleeps* 1997
Monfort, Sylvia *Eagle with Two Heads* 1948; *The Case of Dr Laurent* 1957
Mong, William V *The Strong Man* 1926; *What Price Glory* 1926; *Treasure Island* 1934
Monk, Debra *Redwood Curtain* 1995; *Ellen Foster* 1997
Monkhouse, Bob *The Secret People* 1951; *Carry On Sergeant* 1958; *Dentist in the Chair* 1960; *Dentist on the Job* 1961; *She'll Have to Go* 1961; *The Bliss of Mrs Blossom* 1968; *Simon, Simon* 1970
Monlaur, Yvonne *The Brides of Dracula* 1960; *Circus of Horrors* 1960; *Inn for Trouble* 1960
Monroe, Marilyn *Dangerous Years* 1947; *Ladies of the Chorus* 1948; *Love Happy* 1949; *All about Eve* 1950; *The Asphalt Jungle* 1950; *The Fireball* 1950; *Right Cross* 1950; *As Young as You Feel* 1951; *Let's Make It Legal* 1951; *Love Nest* 1951; *Clash by Night* 1952; *Don't Bother to Knock* 1952; *Monkey Business* 1952; *We're Not Married* 1952; *O Henry's Full House* 1952; *Gentlemen Prefer Blondes* 1953; *How to Marry a Millionaire* 1953; *Niagara* 1953; *River of No Return* 1954; *There's No Business like Show Business* 1954; *The Seven Year Itch* 1955; *Bus Stop* 1956; *The Prince and the Showgirl* 1957; *Some Like It Hot* 1959; *Let's Make Love* 1960; *The Misfits* 1961
Montague, Lee *Blind Date* 1959; *The Secret Partner* 1961; *The Secret of Blood Island* 1964; *How I Won the War* 1967; *Eagle in a Cage* 1971; *The Best Pair of Legs in the Business* 1972; *Brother Sun, Sister Moon* 1972; *Mahler* 1974; *The Legacy* 1978; *Silver Dream Racer* 1980; *Kim* 1984; *Madame Sousatzka* 1988
Montaigu, Sandra *Polar* 1984; *L'Amour par Terre* 1984
Montalban, Carlos *The Harder They Fall* 1956; *Pepe* 1960; *Bananas* 1971
Montalban, Ricardo *Fiesta* 1947; *On an Island with You* 1948; *Battleground* 1949; *Border Incident* 1949; *Neptune's Daughter* 1949; *The Kissing Bandit* 1949; *Mystery Street* 1950; *Right Cross* 1950; *Across the Wide Missouri* 1951; *Latin Lovers* 1953; *A Life in the Balance* 1955; *Sayonara* 1957; *Let No Man Write My Epitaph* 1960; *Gordon the Black Pirate* 1961; *Hemingway's Adventures of a Young Man* 1962; *Love Is a Ball* 1963; *Cheyenne Autumn* 1964; *Madame X* 1966; *The Money Trap* 1966; *The Singing Nun* 1966; *Blue* 1968; *Sweet Charity* 1968; *Sol Madrid* 1968; *The Deserter* 1971; *The Face of Fear* 1971; *Conquest of the Planet of the Apes* 1972; *The Train Robbers* 1973; *The Mark of Zorro* 1974; *Joe Panther* 1976; *Won Ton Ton, the Dog Who Saved Hollywood* 1976; *Star Trek II: the Wrath of Khan* 1982; *The Naked Gun* 1988
Montand, Yves *Les Portes de la Nuit* 1946; *The Wages of Fear* 1953; *Marguerite de la Nuit* 1955; *Napoléon* 1955; *Where the Hot Wind Blows!* 1959; *Let's Make Love* 1960; *Goodbye Again* 1961; *Sanctuary* 1961; *Le Joli Mai* 1962; *My Geisha* 1962; *The Sleeping Car Murders* 1965; *Grand Prix* 1966; *La Guerre Est Finie* 1966; *Is Paris Burning?* 1966; *Vivre pour Vivre* 1967; *Z* 1968; *The Confession* 1970; *On a Clear Day You Can See Forever* 1970; *The Red Circle* 1970; *Delusions of Grandeur* 1971; *César and Rosalie* 1972; *State of Siege* 1972; *Tout Va Bien* 1972; *Vincent, François, Paul and the Others* 1974; *Call Him Savage* 1975; *Roads to the South* 1978; *Choice of Arms* 1981; *Jean de Florette* 1986; *Manon des Sources* 1986; *IP5* 1992
Montell, Lisa *Escape to Burma* 1955; *Ten Thousand Bedrooms* 1957; *The Lone Ranger and the Lost City of Gold* 1958
Montenegro, Fernanda *Hour of the Star* 1985; *Central Station* 1998
Montero, Germaine *Knave of Hearts* 1954; *Le Masque de Fer* 1962; *Any Number Can Win* 1963; *Robert et Robert* 1978
Monteros, Rosenda *Battle Shock* 1956; *Villa!* 1958; *The Magnificent Seven* 1960; *Tiara Tahiti* 1962; *She* 1965; *Cauldron of Blood* 1967
Montes, Elisa *As If It Were Raining* 1963; *Return of the Seven* 1966; *Texas Adios* 1966; *Captain Apache* 1971
Montevecchi, Liliane *Moonfleet* 1955; *Meet Me in Las Vegas* 1956; *King Creole* 1958
Montez, Maria *That Night in Rio* 1941; *Arabian Nights* 1942; *Ali Baba and the Forty Thieves* 1944; *Cobra Woman* 1944; *Follow the Boys* 1944; *The Exile* 1947
Montgomery, Belinda J *aka* **Montgomery, Belinda** *The Todd Killings* 1971; *The Other Side of the Mountain* 1975; *Breaking Point* 1976; *The Other Side of the Mountain – Part 2* 1978; *Stone Cold Dead* 1980; *For Love of a Child* 1990
Montgomery, Douglass *Little Women* 1933; *Little Man, What Now?* 1934; *The Mystery of Edwin Drood* 1935; *The Cat and the Canary* 1939; *The Way to the Stars* 1945
Montgomery, Elizabeth *The Court-Martial of Billy Mitchell* 1955; *Johnny Cool* 1963; *Who's Been Sleeping in My Bed?* 1963; *How to Fill a Wild Bikini* 1965; *Missing Pieces* 1983; *Amos* 1985; *Face to Face* 1990; *Sins of the Mother* 1991; *With Savage Intent* 1992; *Black Widow Murders* 1993
Montgomery, George *The Cisco Kid and the Lady* 1939; *Riders of the Purple Sage* 1941; *China Girl* 1942; *Orchestra Wives* 1942; *Roxie Hart* 1942; *Ten Gentlemen from West Point* 1942; *Bomber's Moon* 1943; *Coney Island* 1943; *Three Little Girls in Blue* 1946; *Belle Starr's Daughter* 1948; *Lulu Belle* 1948; *The Sword of Monte Cristo* 1951; *Indian Uprising* 1951; *Last of the Badmen* 1957; *Gun Duel in Durango* 1957; *Samar* 1962; *Battle of the Bulge* 1965; *Satan's Harvest* 1965; *Hostile Guns* 1967
Montgomery, Lee *aka* **Montgomery, Lee H,** *aka* **Montgomery, Lee Harcourt** *The Harness* 1971; *The Million Dollar Duck* 1971; *Ben* 1972; *Pete 'n' Tillie* 1972; *Runaway!* 1973; *The Savage Is Loose* 1974; *Baker's Hawk* 1976; *Burnt Offerings* 1976; *Mutant* 1984; *Girls Just Want to Have Fun* 1985; *Prime Risk* 1985
Montgomery, Poppy *Dead Man on Campus* 1998; *The Other Sister* 1999
Montgomery, Robert *The Big House* 1930; *The Divorcee* 1930; *Free and Easy* 1930; *Inspiration* 1931; *Private Lives* 1931; *Strangers May Kiss* 1931; *Blondie of the Follies* 1932; *Night Flight* 1933; *When Ladies Meet* 1933; *Forsaking All Others* 1934; *Riptide* 1934; *Vanessa, Her Love Story* 1935; *Piccadilly Jim* 1936; *Trouble for Two* 1936; *The Last of Mrs Cheyney* 1937; *Night Must Fall* 1937; *Live, Love and Learn* 1937; *Three Loves Has Nancy* 1938; *Yellow Jack* 1938; *Fast and Loose* 1939; *Busman's Honeymoon* 1940; *The Earl of Chicago* 1940; *Here Comes Mr Jordan* 1941; *Mr and Mrs Smith* 1941; *Rage in Heaven* 1941; *They Were Expendable* 1945; *Lady in the Lake* 1947; *June Bride* 1948; *The Saxon Charm* 1948; *Once More, My Darling* 1949
Montiel, Sarita *Vera Cruz* 1954; *Serenade* 1956; *Run of the Arrow* 1957
Montoute, Edouard *La Haine* 1995; *Port Djema* 1997
Montoya, Alex *The Appaloosa* 1966; *Daring Game* 1968

ACTORS' INDEX
RadioTimes

Moody, Jim *Personal Best* 1982; *Bad Boys* 1983; *Who's the Man?* 1993
Moody, Lynne *Scream Blacula Scream* 1973; *The Evil* 1978; *White Dog* 1981; *Some Kind of Hero* 1982; *Wait till Your Mother Gets Home!* 1983; *The Toughest Man in the World* 1984; *Last Light* 1993; *Escape to Witch Mountain* 1995
Moody, Ralph *Road to Bali* 1952; *The Lone Ranger and the Lost City of Gold* 1958; *The Legend of Tom Dooley* 1959
Moody, Ron *A Pair of Briefs* 1961; *Ladies Who Do* 1963; *The Mouse on the Moon* 1963; *Every Day's a Holiday* 1964; *Murder Most Foul* 1964; *The Sandwich Man* 1966; *Oliver!* 1968; *David Copperfield* 1969; *The Twelve Chairs* 1970; *Flight of the Doves* 1971; *Dogpound Shuffle* 1974; *Legend of the Werewolf* 1974; *Dominique* 1978; *The Spaceman and King Arthur* 1979; *Asterix and the Big Fight* 1989; *Emily's Ghost* 1992; *A Kid in King Arthur's Court* 1995
Moog, Heinz *Senso* 1954; *The Secret Ways* 1961
Moon, Keith *200 Motels* 1971; *That'll Be the Day* 1973; *Stardust* 1974; *Tommy* 1975; *Sextette* 1978
Mooney, Debra *Too Young the Hero* 1988; *Joshua's Heart* 1990
Mooney, Laura *She's Out of Control* 1989; *Little Nemo: Adventures in Slumberland* 1992
Moore, Alvy *The Glory Brigade* 1953; *Riot in Cell Block 11* 1954; *Susan Slept Here* 1954; *Five against the House* 1955; *An Annapolis Story* 1955; *Brotherhood of Satan* 1970; *A Boy and His Dog* 1975
Moore Jr, Carlyle *The Case of the Black Cat* 1936; *Arizona Legion* 1939
Moore, Clayton *The Far Frontier* 1949; *The Lone Ranger* 1956; *The Lone Ranger and the Lost City of Gold* 1958
Moore, Colleen *Lilac Time* 1928; *The Power and the Glory* 1933
Moore, Constance *Wives under Suspicion* 1938; *You Can't Cheat an Honest Man* 1939; *Argentine Nights* 1940; *I Wanted Wings* 1941; *Take a Letter, Darling* 1942; *Atlantic City* 1944; *Show Business* 1944; *Earl Carroll Vanities* 1945
Moore, Deborah aka **Moore, Deborah Maria** *Into the Sun* 1992; *Midnight Man* 1998
Moore, Del *The Last Time I Saw Archie* 1961; *Stagecoach to Dancer's Rock* 1962; *The Nutty Professor* 1963; *The Disorderly Orderly* 1964; *The Big Mouth* 1967
Moore, Demi *Touchdown* 1981; *Parasite* 1982; *Blame It on Rio* 1984; *No Small Affair* 1984; *St Elmo's Fire* 1985; *About Last Night...* 1986; *One Crazy Summer* 1986; *Wisdom* 1986; *The Seventh Sign* 1988; *We're No Angels* 1989; *Ghost* 1990; *The Butcher's Wife* 1991; *Mortal Thoughts* 1991; *Nothing but Trouble* 1991; *A Few Good Men* 1992; *Indecent Proposal* 1993; *Disclosure* 1994; *Now and Then* 1995; *The Scarlet Letter* 1995; *Beavis and Butt-head Do America* 1996; *The Hunchback of Notre Dame* 1996; *If These Walls Could Talk* 1996; *The Juror* 1996; *Striptease* 1996; *Deconstructing Harry* 1997; *GI Jane* 1997
Moore, Dennie *Sylvia Scarlett* 1936; *Meet Nero Wolfe* 1936; *Saturday's Children* 1940
Moore, Dickie *Blonde Venus* 1932; *Union Depot* 1932; *Gabriel over the White House* 1933; *Man's Castle* 1933; *Upper World* 1934; *Gallant Lady* 1934; *Peter Ibbetson* 1935; *Miss Annie Rooney* 1942; *Sweet and Lowdown* 1944
Moore, Dudley *The Wrong Box* 1966; *Bedazzled* 1967; *30 Is a Dangerous Age, Cynthia* 1967; *The Bed Sitting Room* 1969; *Monte Carlo or Bust* 1969; *Alice's Adventures in Wonderland* 1972; *The Hound of the Baskervilles* 1977; *Foul Play* 1978; *10* 1979; *Wholly Moses!* 1980; *Arthur* 1981; *Six Weeks* 1982; *Lovesick* 1983; *Romantic Comedy* 1983; *Unfaithfully Yours* 1983; *Best Defense* 1984; *Micki & Maude* 1984; *Santa Claus* 1985; *The Adventures of Milo and Otis* 1986; *Like Father, Like Son* 1987; *Arthur 2: On the Rocks* 1988; *Crazy People* 1990; *Blame It on the Bellboy* 1992; *The Pickle* 1993; *Parallel Lives* 1994; *The Disappearance of Kevin Johnson* 1995; *A Weekend in the Country* 1996
Moore, Eileen *Mr Denning Drives North* 1951; *The Happy Family* 1952; *An Inspector Calls* 1954; *Men of Sherwood Forest* 1954; *Devil's Bait* 1959
Moore, Eva *The Old Dark House* 1932; *Vintage Wine* 1935
Moore, Gar *Abbott and Costello Meet the Killer, Boris Karloff* 1949; *Johnny Stool Pigeon* 1949; *The Underworld Story* 1950
Moore, Grace *A Lady's Morals* 1930; *One Night of Love* 1934; *The King Steps Out* 1936; *I'll Take Romance* 1937; *When You're in Love* 1937
Moore, Ida *Mr Music* 1950; *Rock-a-Bye Baby* 1958
Moore, Joanna *Ride a Crooked Trail* 1958; *Touch of Evil* 1958; *Monster on the Campus* 1958; *The Last Angry Man* 1959; *Follow That Dream* 1962; *Son of Flubber* 1962; *Walk on the Wild Side* 1962; *The Man from Galveston* 1964; *Countdown* 1968; *Never a Dull Moment* 1968
Moore, Juanita *The Girl Can't Help It* 1956; *Imitation of Life* 1959; *Abby* 1974; *Paternity* 1981
Moore, Julianne *Money, Power, Murder* 1989; *Cast a Deadly Spell* 1991; *Tales from the Darkside: the Movie* 1991; *Body of Evidence* 1992; *The Gun in Betty Lou's Handbag* 1992; *The Hand That Rocks the Cradle* 1992; *Benny and Joon* 1993; *The Fugitive* 1993; *Short Cuts* 1993; *Vanya on 42nd Street* 1994; *Assassins* 1995; *Nine Months* 1995; *Safe* 1995; *Roommates* 1995; *The Myth of Fingerprints* 1996; *Surviving Picasso* 1996; *The Big Lebowski* 1997; *Boogie Nights* 1997; *The Lost World: Jurassic Park* 1997; *Psycho* 1998; *An Ideal Husband* 1999; *Cookie's Fortune* 1999; *The End of the Affair* 1999; *Magnolia* 1999; *A Map of the World* 1999
Moore, Kieron *Anna Karenina* 1947; *A Man about the House* 1947; *Mine Own Executioner* 1947; *David and Bathsheba* 1951; *Ten Tall Men* 1951; *Mantrap* 1952; *Conflict of Wings* 1953; *The Green Scarf* 1954; *The Blue Peter* 1955; *The Steel Bayonet* 1957; *The Key* 1958; *Darby O'Gill and the Little People* 1959; *Doctor Blood's Coffin* 1960; *The League of Gentlemen* 1960; *The Siege of Sidney Street* 1960; *The Day They Robbed the Bank of England* 1960; *The Day of the Triffids* 1962; *The 300 Spartans* 1962; *I Thank a Fool* 1962; *Girl in the Headlines* 1963; *Hide and Seek* 1963; *Crack in the World* 1965; *Arabesque* 1966
Moore, Margo *Wake Me when It's Over* 1960; *The George Raft Story* 1961
Moore, Mary Tyler *X-15* 1961; *Thoroughly Modern Millie* 1967; *Don't Just Stand There* 1968; *What's So Bad About Feeling Good?* 1968; *Change of Habit* 1969; *Ordinary People* 1980; *Six Weeks* 1982; *Just between Friends* 1986; *The Good Family* 1990; *Stolen Babies* 1993; *Flirting with Disaster* 1996; *Keys to Tulsa* 1996; *Payback* 1997
Moore, Matt *Traffic in Souls* 1913; *20,000 Leagues under the Sea* 1916; *The Pride of the Clan* 1917; *The Unholy Three* 1925; *Coquette* 1929; *Consolation Marriage* 1931
Moore, Melba *Lost in the Stars* 1974; *All Dogs Go to Heaven* 1989; *Def by Temptation* 1990
Moore (2), Michael *EDtv* 1999; *The Insider* 1999
Moore, Owen *The Battle of the Sexes* 1914; *The Escape* 1914; *The Black Bird* 1926; *The Road to Mandalay* 1926; *What a Widow!* 1930; *As You Desire Me* 1932; *She Done Him Wrong* 1933; *A Star Is Born* 1937
Moore, Pauline *Charlie Chan at the Olympics* 1937; *Heidi* 1937; *Born Reckless* 1937; *Charlie Chan at Treasure Island* 1939; *Charlie Chan in Reno* 1939; *Young Mr Lincoln* 1939; *The Three Musketeers* 1939
Moore, Robyn *Dot and the Kangaroo* 1976; *Dot and the Bunny* 1983; *Dot and the Koala* 1985; *Dot and the Whale* 1985; *Dot and Keeto* 1986; *Dot and the Smugglers* 1987
Moore, Roger *The Last Time I Saw Paris* 1954; *Diane* 1955; *Interrupted Melody* 1955; *The King's Thief* 1955; *The Miracle* 1959; *The Sins of Rachel Cade* 1960; *Gold of the Seven Saints* 1961; *Crossplot* 1969; *The Man Who Haunted Himself* 1970; *Live and Let Die* 1973; *Gold* 1974; *The Man with the Golden Gun* 1974; *That Lucky Touch* 1975; *Sherlock Holmes in New York* 1976; *Shout at the Devil* 1976; *The Sicilian Cross* 1976; *The Spy Who Loved Me* 1977; *The Wild Geese* 1978; *Escape to Athena* 1979; *Moonraker* 1979; *North Sea Hijack* 1979; *The Sea Wolves* 1980; *The Cannonball Run* 1981; *For Your Eyes Only* 1981; *The Curse of the Pink Panther* 1983; *Octopussy* 1983; *The Naked Face* 1984; *A View to a Kill* 1985; *Bullseye!* 1990; *Fire, Ice and Dynamite* 1990; *Bed & Breakfast* 1992; *The Man Who Wouldn't Die* 1995; *The Quest* 1996
Moore, Sheila *Bye Bye Blues* 1989; *The Reflecting Skin* 1990
Moore, Stephen *A Midsummer Night's Dream* 1961; *Laughterhouse* 1984; *Clockwise* 1986
Moore, Terry *The Return of October* 1948; *Mighty Joe Young* 1949; *Come Back, Little Sheba* 1952; *Beneath the 12-Mile Reef* 1953; *King of the Khyber Rifles* 1953; *Man on a Tightrope* 1953; *Daddy Long Legs* 1955; *Postmark for Danger* 1955; *Shack Out on 101* 1955; *Between Heaven and Hell* 1956; *A Private's Affair* 1959; *Cast a Long Shadow* 1959; *Platinum High School* 1960; *City of Fear* 1965; *Black Spurs* 1965; *Waco* 1966; *Beverly Hills Brats* 1989
Moore, Victor *Gold Diggers of 1937* 1936; *Swing Time* 1936; *Make Way for Tomorrow* 1937; *Radio City Revels* 1938; *Louisiana Purchase* 1941; *Star Spangled Rhythm* 1942; *The Heat's On* 1943; *Riding High* 1943; *True to Life* 1943; *Duffy's Tavern* 1945; *It Happened on Fifth Avenue* 1947; *On Our Merry Way* 1948; *A Kiss in the Dark* 1949; *We're Not Married* 1952; *The Seven Year Itch* 1955
Moorehead, Agnes *Citizen Kane* 1941; *The Big Street* 1942; *Journey into Fear* 1942; *The Magnificent Ambersons* 1942; *Government Girl* 1943; *Jane Eyre* 1943; *Dragon Seed* 1944; *Mrs Parkington* 1944; *Since You Went Away* 1944; *The Seventh Cross* 1944; *Tomorrow the World!* 1944; *Keep Your Powder Dry* 1945; *Our Vines Have Tender Grapes* 1945; *Dark Passage* 1947; *The Lost Moment* 1947; *Johnny Belinda* 1948; *Station West* 1948; *Summer Holiday* 1948; *The Woman in White* 1948; *The Great Sinner* 1949; *The Stratton Story* 1949; *Caged* 1950; *The Blue Veil* 1951; *Fourteen Hours* 1951; *Show Boat* 1951; *Black Jack* 1952; *The Story of Three Loves* 1953; *Scandal at Scourie* 1953; *Main Street to Broadway* 1953; *Magnificent Obsession* 1954; *All That Heaven Allows* 1955; *The Left Hand of God* 1955; *Untamed* 1955; *The Conqueror* 1956; *Meet Me in Las Vegas* 1956; *The Opposite Sex* 1956; *Pardners* 1956; *The Revolt of Mamie Stover* 1956; *The Swan* 1956; *Raintree County* 1957; *The True Story of Jesse James* 1957; *Jeanne Eagels* 1957; *The Story of Mankind* 1957; *Tempest* 1959; *The Bat* 1959; *Pollyanna* 1960; *How the West Was Won* 1962; *Jessica* 1962; *Who's Minding the Store?* 1963; *Hush... Hush, Sweet Charlotte* 1964; *The Singing Nun* 1966; *What's the Matter with Helen?* 1971; *Charlotte's Web* 1973
Moorhead, Natalie *Manslaughter* 1930; *Illicit* 1931; *Three Wise Girls* 1932; *Lady of the Tropics* 1939
Morales, Esai *Bad Boys* 1983; *La Bamba* 1986; *The Principal* 1987; *Naked Tango* 1990; *The Burning Season* 1994; *In the Army Now* 1994; *My Family* 1994; *Rapa Nui* 1994; *Scorpion Spring* 1995; *Dogwatch* 1997; *The Disappearance of Garcia Lorca* 1997
Morales, Hector *From Noon till Three* 1976; *One on One* 1977
Morales, Jacobo *Bananas* 1971; *Up the Sandbox* 1972; *What Happened to Santiago* 1989
Moran, Dolores *Old Acquaintance* 1943; *To Have and Have Not* 1944; *The Horn Blows at Midnight* 1945; *The Man I Love* 1946; *Count the Hours* 1953; *Silver Lode* 1954
Moran, Erin *Eighty Steps to Jonah* 1969; *Watermelon Man* 1970
Moran, Jackie *And So They Were Married* 1936; *The Adventures of Tom Sawyer* 1938; *Mad about Music* 1938; *Song of the Open Road* 1944
Moran, Lois *Stella Dallas* 1925; *The Road to Mandalay* 1926; *Mammy* 1930; *Alice in the Cities* 1974
Moran, Nick *Buddy's Song* 1990; *Lock, Stock and Two Smoking Barrels* 1998
Moran, Peggy *Argentine Nights* 1940; *Trail of the Vigilantes* 1940; *There's One Born Every Minute* 1942
Moran, Polly *The Divine Woman* 1928; *Guilty Hands* 1931; *The Passionate Plumber* 1932; *Red River Range* 1938; *Adam's Rib* 1949
Moranis, Rick *Strange Brew* 1983; *Ghostbusters* 1984; *Hockey Night* 1984; *Streets of Fire* 1984; *The Wild Life* 1984; *Brewster's Millions* 1985; *Club Paradise* 1986; *Little Shop of Horrors* 1986; *Head Office* 1986; *Spaceballs* 1987; *Ghostbusters II* 1989; *Honey, I Shrunk the Kids* 1989; *Parenthood* 1989; *My Blue Heaven* 1990; *Honey I Blew Up the Kid* 1992; *Splitting Heirs* 1993; *The Flintstones* 1994; *Little Giants* 1994; *Big Bully* 1996; *Honey, We Shrunk Ourselves* 1997
Morant, Richard *Mahler* 1974; *John and Yoko: a Love Story* 1985
Morante, Laura *The Tragedy of a Ridiculous Man* 1981; *Man on Fire* 1987; *Marianna Ucria* 1997
Mordyukova, Nonna *The Commissar* 1967; *A Station for Two* 1983
More, Kenneth *Scott of the Antarctic* 1948; *Now Barabbas Was a Robber* 1949; *Chance of a Lifetime* 1950; *The Clouded Yellow* 1950; *Appointment with Venus* 1951; *Brandy for the Parson* 1951; *The Yellow Balloon* 1952; *Genevieve* 1953; *Our Girl Friday* 1953; *Never Let Me Go* 1953; *Doctor in the House* 1954; *Raising a Riot* 1955; *The Deep Blue Sea* 1955; *Reach for the Sky* 1956; *The Admirable Crichton* 1957; *Next to No Time* 1958; *A Night to Remember* 1958; *The Sheriff of Fractured Jaw* 1958; *North West Frontier* 1959; *The Thirty-Nine Steps* 1959; *Man in the Moon* 1960; *Sink the Bismarck!* 1960; *The Greengage Summer* 1961; *The Longest Day* 1962; *We Joined the Navy* 1962; *Some People* 1962; *The Comedy Man* 1964; *Dark of the Sun* 1967; *Fraulein Doktor* 1968; *Battle of Britain* 1969; *Oh! What a Lovely War* 1969; *Scrooge* 1970; *The Slipper and the Rose* 1976; *The Spaceman and King Arthur* 1979
Moreau, Jeanne *La Reine Margot* 1954; *Honour among Thieves* 1954; *Secrets d'Alcove* 1954; *Lift to the Scaffold* 1957; *The Lovers* 1958; *Les Liaisons Dangereuses* 1959; *Five Branded Women* 1960; *Une Femme Est une Femme* 1961; *Jules et Jim* 1961; *La Notte* 1961; *Eva* 1962; *The Trial* 1962; *Le Feu Follet* 1963; *The Victors* 1963; *The Diary of a Chambermaid* 1964; *The Train* 1964; *The Yellow Rolls-Royce* 1964; *Viva Maria!* 1965; *Chimes at Midnight* 1966; *Mademoiselle* 1966; *The Sailor from Gibraltar* 1967; *The Bride Wore Black* 1967; *The Oldest Profession* 1967; *Great Catherine* 1968; *The Immortal Story* 1968; *The Little Theatre of Jean Renoir* 1969; *Alex in Wonderland* 1970; *Monte Walsh* 1970; *Les Valseuses* 1974; *The Last Tycoon* 1976; *Mr Klein* 1976; *Querelle* 1982; *Hotel Terminus: the Life and Times of*

RadioTimes ACTORS' INDEX

Klaus Barbie 1987; *Nikita* 1990; *The Old Lady Who Walked in the Sea* 1991; *Until the End of the World* 1991; *Map of the Human Heart* 1992; *Beyond the Clouds* 1995; *The Proprietor* 1996; *I Love You, I Love You Not* 1997
Moreau, Marsha *Mama's Going to Buy You a Mockingbird* 1988; *The Last Winter* 1989
Morecambe, Eric *The Intelligence Men* 1965; *That Riviera Touch* 1966; *The Magnificent Two* 1967; *Simon, Simon* 1970
Morehead, Elizabeth *Whore* 1991; *Interceptor* 1992
Morel, Jacques *Topaze* 1951; *One Night at the Music Hall* 1956; *Marie Antoinette* 1956
Moreland, Mantan *Footlight Serenade* 1942; *Dark Alibi* 1946; *The Trap* 1947; *Watermelon Man* 1970
Morell, André *Madeleine* 1949; *The Clouded Yellow* 1950; *Seven Days to Noon* 1950; *Stolen Face* 1952; *His Majesty O'Keefe* 1953; *The Black Knight* 1954; *They Can't Hang Me* 1954; *The Man Who Never Was* 1955; *The Black Tent* 1956; *The Bridge on the River Kwai* 1957; *The Camp on Blood Island* 1958; *Paris Holiday* 1958; *The Hound of the Baskervilles* 1959; *The Giant Behemoth* 1959; *The Shadow of the Cat* 1961; *The Plague of the Zombies* 1965; *The Mummy's Shroud* 1966
Morelli, Rina *Senso* 1954; *The Leopard* 1962; *L'Innocente* 1976
Morelli, Robert *Back Stab* 1990; *Twin Sisters* 1992
Moreno, Antonio *Mare Nostrum* 1926; *The Temptress* 1926; *It* 1927; *The Bohemian Girl* 1936; *Valley of the Sun* 1942; *Captain from Castile* 1947; *Dallas* 1950; *Creature from the Black Lagoon* 1954
Moreno, Rita *Singin' in the Rain* 1952; *The Ring* 1952; *Garden of Evil* 1954; *The Yellow Tomahawk* 1954; *Jivaro* 1954; *Seven Cities of Gold* 1955; *Untamed* 1955; *The King and I* 1956; *The Lieutenant Wore Skirts* 1956; *The Vagabond King* 1956; *The Deerslayer* 1957; *This Rebel Breed* 1960; *Summer and Smoke* 1961; *West Side Story* 1961; *The Night of the Following Day* 1968; *Marlowe* 1969; *Popi* 1969; *Carnal Knowledge* 1971; *The Ritz* 1976; *Happy Birthday, Gemini* 1980; *The Four Seasons* 1981; *Age Isn't Everything* 1991; *Angus* 1995; *The Wharf Rat* 1995; *Slums of Beverly Hills* 1998
Moreno, Rosita *Her Wedding Night* 1930; *The Scoundrel* 1935
Moretti, Nanni *Dear Diary* 1994; *Aprile* 1998
Morfogen, George *The Thief Who Came to Dinner* 1973; *Those Lips, Those Eyes* 1980; *Rescuers: Stories of Courage – Two Women* 1997
Morgan, Cindy *Caddyshack* 1980; *Tron* 1982
Morgan, Debbi *Eve's Bayou* 1997; *The Hurricane* 1999; *Love & Basketball* 2000
Morgan, Dennis *The Return of Dr X* 1939; *Kitty Foyle* 1940; *Affectionately Yours* 1941; *Captains of the Clouds* 1942; *The Hard Way* 1942; *In This Our Life* 1942; *Thank Your Lucky Stars* 1943; *The Desert Song* 1944; *Shine On, Harvest Moon* 1944; *The Very Thought of You* 1944; *Christmas in Connecticut* 1945; *God Is My Co-Pilot* 1945; *Two Guys from Milwaukee* 1946; *My Wild Irish Rose* 1947; *It's a Great Feeling* 1949; *Pretty Baby* 1950; *Perfect Strangers* 1950; *Painting the Clouds with Sunshine* 1951; *This Woman Is Dangerous* 1952; *Pearl of the South Pacific* 1955
Morgan, Frank *Fast and Loose* 1930; *Laughter* 1930; *The Half Naked Truth* 1932; *Blonde Bombshell* 1933; *Broadway to Hollywood* 1933; *Hallelujah, I'm a Bum* 1933; *Reunion in Vienna* 1933; *When Ladies Meet* 1933; *The Affairs of Cellini* 1934; *The Cat and the Fiddle* 1934; *Escapade* 1935; *The Good Fairy* 1935; *I Live My Life* 1935; *Naughty Marietta* 1935; *Dimples* 1936; *The Great Ziegfeld* 1936; *Piccadilly Jim* 1936; *Trouble for Two* 1936; *The Emperor's Candlesticks* 1937; *The Last of Mrs Cheyney* 1937; *Saratoga* 1937; *Rosalie* 1937; *The Crowd Roars* 1938; *Sweethearts* 1938; *Paradise for Three* 1938; *Broadway Serenade* 1939; *The Wizard of Oz* 1939; *Balalaika* 1939; *Boom Town* 1940; *Broadway Melody of 1940* 1940; *The Mortal Storm* 1940; *The Shop around the Corner* 1940; *Honky Tonk* 1941; *Tortilla Flat* 1942; *White Cargo* 1942; *The Human Comedy* 1943; *Casanova Brown* 1944; *The White Cliffs of Dover* 1944; *Yolande and the Thief* 1945; *Courage of Lassie* 1946; *Lady Luck* 1946; *Green Dolphin Street* 1947; *Summer Holiday* 1948; *The Three Musketeers* 1948; *Any Number Can Play* 1949; *The Great Sinner* 1949; *The Stratton Story* 1949; *Key to the City* 1950
Morgan, Gary *The California Kid* 1974; *Logan's Run* 1976; *Matilda* 1978; *Storybook* 1995
Morgan, Gene *Blonde Venus* 1932; *If You Could Only Cook* 1935
Morgan, Harry *aka* **Morgan, Henry** *To the Shores of Tripoli* 1942; *Happy Land* 1943; *The Ox-Bow Incident* 1943; *A Bell for Adano* 1945; *From This Day Forward* 1946; *It Shouldn't Happen to a Dog* 1946; *The Gangster* 1947; *Moonrise* 1948; *Yellow Sky* 1948; *The Saxon Charm* 1948; *Down to the Sea in Ships* 1949; *Holiday Affair* 1949; *Appointment with Danger* 1950; *Dark City* 1950; *The Well* 1951; *High Noon* 1952; *My Six Convicts* 1952; *Apache War Smoke* 1952; *The Glenn Miller Story* 1953; *Torch Song* 1953; *Arena* 1953; *The Far Country* 1955; *The Teahouse of the August Moon* 1956; *Inherit the Wind* 1960; *The Mountain Road* 1960; *Frankie & Johnny* 1966; *What Did You Do in the War, Daddy?* 1966; *One Born Every Minute* 1967; *Support Your Local Sheriff!* 1969; *Viva Max!* 1969; *The Barefoot Executive* 1971; *Support Your Local Gunfighter* 1971; *Scandalous John* 1971; *Snowball Express* 1972; *Charley and the Angel* 1973; *The Apple Dumpling Gang* 1974; *The Shootist* 1976; *The Cat from Outer Space* 1978; *Murder at the Mardi Gras* 1978; *The Apple Dumpling Gang Rides Again* 1979; *Dragnet* 1987; *The Incident* 1990; *Against Her Will* 1991; *Incident in a Small Town* 1993
Morgan, Helen *Applause* 1929; *Go into Your Dance* 1935; *Show Boat* 1936; *Slavers* 1977
Morgan, Henry *The Eve of St Mark* 1944; *So This Is New York* 1948; *Murder, Inc* 1960
Morgan, Horace *aka* **Morgan, H A** *Three Ages* 1923; *Beggars of Life* 1928
Morgan, Michèle *Gribouille* 1937; *Le Quai des Brumes* 1938; *Stormy Waters* 1941; *Joan of Paris* 1942; *Higher and Higher* 1943; *Passage to Marseille* 1944; *The Chase* 1946; *La Symphonie Pastorale* 1946; *The Fallen Idol* 1948; *The Seven Deadly Sins* 1952; *The Proud Ones* 1953; *Obsession* 1954; *Les Grandes Manoeuvres* 1955; *Marguerite de la Nuit* 1955; *Napoléon* 1955; *Marie Antoinette* 1956; *Bluebeard* 1962; *The Lost Command* 1966; *Everybody's Fine* 1990
Morgan, Nancy *Fraternity Row* 1977; *Grand Theft Auto* 1977; *Americathon* 1979; *Heartbeat* 1992
Morgan, Ralph *Rasputin and the Empress* 1932; *Strange Interlude* 1932; *The Kennel Murder Case* 1933; *The Mad Game* 1933; *The Power and the Glory* 1933; *The Last Gentleman* 1934; *Stand up and Cheer!* 1934; *Magnificent Obsession* 1935; *Star of Midnight* 1935; *Crack-Up* 1936; *Human Cargo* 1936; *Speed* 1936; *Mannequin* 1937; *Wells Fargo* 1937; *Wives under Suspicion* 1938; *Fast and Loose* 1939; *Geronimo* 1939; *The Lone Wolf Spy Hunt* 1939; *Hitler's Madman* 1943; *The Impostor* 1944; *Jack London* 1944; *The Monster Maker* 1944
Morgan, Read *Your Three Minutes Are Up* 1973; *Hollywood Harry* 1985
Morgan, Robbi *What's the Matter with Helen?* 1971; *Friday the 13th* 1980
Morgan, Russ *The Great Man* 1956; *Mister Cory* 1957
Morgan, Stafford *Cleopatra Jones* 1973; *The Alpha Incident* 1977
Morgan, Terence *Hamlet* 1948; *Captain Horatio Hornblower* 1951; *Encore* 1951; *Mandy* 1952; *The Steel Key* 1953; *Turn the Key Softly* 1953; *Dance Little Lady* 1954; *Forbidden Cargo* 1954; *Svengali* 1954; *They Can't Hang Me* 1954; *It's a Wonderful World* 1956; *The March Hare* 1956; *The Scamp* 1957; *Tread Softly Stranger* 1958; *The Shakedown* 1959; *Piccadilly Third Stop* 1960; *The Curse of the Mummy's Tomb* 1964; *The Penthouse* 1967
Morgan, Trevor *Barney's Great Adventure* 1998; *In the Doghouse* 1998; *The Sixth Sense* 1999
Morgan, Wendy *Birth of the Beatles* 1979; *Yanks* 1979; *84 Charing Cross Road* 1986
Mori, Masayuki *Rashomon* 1950; *The Idiot* 1951; *Ugetsu Monogatari* 1953; *The Princess Yang Kwei Fei* 1955; *The Bad Sleep Well* 1960; *Alone on the Pacific* 1963
Mori, Paola *Crossed Swords* 1954; *Confidential Report* 1955
Moriarty, Cathy *Raging Bull* 1980; *Neighbors* 1981; *White of the Eye* 1986; *Kindergarten Cop* 1990; *Soapdish* 1991; *The Gun in Betty Lou's Handbag* 1992; *The Mambo Kings* 1992; *Another Stakeout* 1993; *Matinee* 1993; *Me and the Kid* 1993; *Pontiac Moon* 1994; *Casper* 1995; *Dream with the Fishes* 1996; *Cop Land* 1997; *Hugo Pool* 1997; *Casper Meets Wendy* 1998; *Gloria* 1998; *Digging to China* 1998; *Crazy in Alabama* 1999; *But I'm a Cheerleader* 1999
Moriarty, Michael *Glory Boy* 1971; *The Last Detail* 1973; *Report to the Commissioner* 1975; *Who'll Stop the Rain?* 1978; *Q – the Winged Serpent* 1982; *Pale Rider* 1985; *The Stuff* 1985; *Odd Birds* 1985; *Troll* 1986; *Hanoi Hilton* 1987; *A Return to Salem's Lot* 1987; *It's Alive III: Island of the Alive* 1987; *Nitti: the Enforcer* 1988; *Dark Tower* 1989; *Full Fathom Five* 1990; *Born Too Soon* 1993; *Courage under Fire* 1996; *Crime of the Century* 1996; *Shiloh* 1996; *Cagney & Lacey: True Convictions* 1996
Moriarty, P H *Jaws III* 1983; *Number One* 1984; *Lock, Stock and Two Smoking Barrels* 1998
Morice, Tara *Strictly Ballroom* 1992; *Hotel Sorrento* 1994
Morier-Genoud, Philippe *Au Revoir les Enfants* 1987; *Cyrano de Bergerac* 1990
Morison, Patricia *The Roundup* 1941; *Beyond the Blue Horizon* 1942; *The Fallen Sparrow* 1943; *Hitler's Madman* 1943; *Without Love* 1945; *Dressed to Kill* 1946; *Tarzan and the Huntress* 1947; *Song without End* 1960; *Mirrors* 1985
Morita, Pat *aka* **Morita, Noriyuki "Pat"** *Full Moon High* 1982; *Slapstick of Another Kind* 1982; *The Karate Kid* 1984; *Amos* 1985; *Babes in Toyland* 1986; *The Karate Kid Part II* 1986; *Collision Course* 1987; *Captive Hearts* 1988; *The Karate Kid III* 1989; *Hiroshima: Out of the Ashes* 1990; *Lena's Holiday* 1990; *Auntie Lee's Meat Pies* 1991; *Honeymoon in Vegas* 1992; *Even Cowgirls Get the Blues* 1993; *Greyhounds* 1994; *The Next Karate Kid* 1994; *Bloodsport II: The Next Kumite* 1996; *Mulan* 1998
Moritzen, Henning *Cries and Whispers* 1972; *Waltzing Regitze* 1989
Morley, Karen *Mata Hari* 1931; *Arsene Lupin* 1932; *Flesh* 1932; *The Mask of Fu Manchu* 1932; *Scarface* 1932; *Gabriel over the White House* 1933; *Our Daily Bread* 1934; *Black Fury* 1935; *The Littlest Rebel* 1935; *Beloved Enemy* 1936; *The Last Train from Madrid* 1937; *Kentucky* 1938; *Framed* 1947; *M* 1951
Morley, Robert *Marie Antoinette* 1938; *The Foreman Went to France* 1941; *Major Barbara* 1941; *The Young Mr Pitt* 1942; *I Live in Grosvenor Square* 1945; *The Ghosts of Berkeley Square* 1947; *The Small Back Room* 1949; *The African Queen* 1951; *Outcast of the Islands* 1951; *Curtain Up* 1952; *Beat the Devil* 1953; *The Final Test* 1953; *The Story of Gilbert and Sullivan* 1953; *Beau Brummell* 1954; *The Good Die Young* 1954; *The Adventures of Quentin Durward* 1955; *Around the World in 80 Days* 1956; *The Doctor's Dilemma* 1958; *Law and Disorder* 1958; *The Rainbow Jacket* 1958; *The Sheriff of Fractured Jaw* 1958; *The Journey* 1959; *Libel* 1959; *Oscar Wilde* 1959; *The Battle of the Sexes* 1960; *Go to Blazes* 1961; *The Young Ones* 1961; *The Boys* 1961; *The Road to Hong Kong* 1962; *Hot Enough for June* 1963; *Ladies Who Do* 1963; *Murder at the Gallop* 1963; *Nine Hours to Rama* 1963; *Take Her, She's Mine* 1963; *Genghis Khan* 1964; *Of Human Bondage* 1964; *Topkapi* 1964; *Life at the Top* 1965; *A Study in Terror* 1965; *Those Magnificent Men in Their Flying Machines* 1965; *The Alphabet Murders* 1966; *Finders Keepers* 1966; *Hotel Paradiso* 1966; *Way... Way Out* 1966; *Woman Times Seven* 1967; *The Trygon Factor* 1967; *Hot Millions* 1968; *Sinful Davey* 1969; *Some Girls Do* 1969; *Twinky* 1969; *Cromwell* 1970; *Doctor in Trouble* 1970; *Song of Norway* 1970; *When Eight Bells Toll* 1971; *Theatre of Blood* 1973; *Great Expectations* 1974; *The Blue Bird* 1976; *Who Is Killing the Great Chefs of Europe?* 1978; *The Human Factor* 1979; *Scavenger Hunt* 1979; *Loophole* 1980; *Oh, Heavenly Dog!* 1980; *The Great Muppet Caper* 1981; *High Road to China* 1983; *The Trouble with Spies* 1987
Morris, Anita *Maria's Lovers* 1984; *Blue City* 1986; *Ruthless People* 1986; *Aria* 1987; *18 Again!* 1988; *A Sinful Life* 1989; *Little Miss Millions* 1993; *Me and the Kid* 1993
Morris, Aubrey *Blood from the Mummy's Tomb* 1971; *A Clockwork Orange* 1971; *The Wicker Man* 1973; *Oxford Blues* 1984; *The Rachel Papers* 1989; *A Mom for Christmas* 1990; *Tales from the Crypt Presents: Bordello of Blood* 1996; *Bram Stoker's Legend of the Mummy* 1998
Morris, Barboura *A Bucket of Blood* 1959; *The Wasp Woman* 1959; *Atlas* 1960; *The Trip* 1967
Morris, Beth *Crucible of Terror* 1971; *Old Scores* 1991
Morris, Chester *Alibi* 1929; *The Bat Whispers* 1930; *The Big House* 1930; *The Divorcee* 1930; *Red-Headed Woman* 1932; *Sinners in the Sun* 1932; *The Gay Bride* 1934; *Public Hero No 1* 1935; *Flight from Glory* 1937; *Law of the Underworld* 1938; *Smashing the Rackets* 1938; *Blind Alley* 1939; *Five Came Back* 1939; *Thunder Afloat* 1939; *Secret Command* 1944; *Unchained* 1955; *The She-Creature* 1956; *The Great White Hope* 1970
Morris, Dorothy *Young Ideas* 1943; *None Shall Escape* 1944
Morris, Garrett *The Stuff* 1985; *Maid for Each Other* 1992; *Black Scorpion* 1995; *Black Scorpion: Ground Zero* 1996; *Santa with Muscles* 1996
Morris, Haviland *Sixteen Candles* 1984; *Who's That Girl* 1987; *Love or Money* 1990; *Home Alone 3* 1997
Morris, Howard *Forty Pounds of Trouble* 1962; *Fluffy* 1965; *Way... Way Out* 1966; *High Anxiety* 1977; *Life Stinks* 1991; *It Came from Outer Space II* 1996
Morris, Jeff *Goin' South* 1978; *The Border* 1981
Morris, Judy *The Plumber* 1979; *Phar Lap* 1983; *The More Things Change* 1985
Morris, Lana *The Weaker Sex* 1948; *The Chiltern Hundreds* 1949; *Trottie True* 1949; *Morning Departure* 1950; *The Woman in Question* 1950; *Trouble in Store* 1953; *Man of the Moment* 1955; *Home and Away* 1956; *I Start Counting* 1970
Morris, Libby *Tiara Tahiti* 1962; *The Adding Machine* 1969
Morris, Mary *Victoria the Great* 1937; *The Thief of Bagdad* 1940; *Pimpernel Smith* 1941; *Undercover* 1943; *The Man from Morocco* 1944
Morris, Phil *Private Investigations* 1987; *Dearly Devoted* 1998

ACTORS' INDEX
RadioTimes

Morris, Phyllis *The Adventures of Tartu* 1943; *The Silver Darlings* 1947; *Three Came Home* 1950
Morris, Wayne *Kid Galahad* 1937; *The Return of Dr X* 1939; *I Wanted Wings* 1941; *Deep Valley* 1947; *The Time of Your Life* 1948; *Task Force* 1949; *A Kiss in the Dark* 1949; *The Master Plan* 1954; *Port of Hell* 1954; *Riding Shotgun* 1954; *The Crooked Sky* 1957; *Paths of Glory* 1957; *Plunder Road* 1957
Morrison, Jenny *Intersection* 1994; *Stir of Echoes* 1999
Morrison, Kenny *The Quick and the Dead* 1987; *The NeverEnding Story II: the Next Chapter* 1991
Morrison, Shelley *Castle of Evil* 1966; *Man and Boy* 1971
Morrison, "Sunshine Sammy" *Boys of the City* 1940; *That Gang of Mine* 1940; *Pride of the Bowery* 1941; *Spooks Run Wild* 1941; *Ghosts in the Night* 1943
Morrison, Temuera *Once Were Warriors* 1994; *Barb Wire* 1995; *The Island of Dr Moreau* 1996; *Speed 2: Cruise Control* 1997; *Six Days Seven Nights* 1998; *What Becomes of the Broken Hearted?* 1999
Morrissey, Betty *A Woman of Paris* 1923; *The Gold Rush* 1925
Morrissey, David *Drowning by Numbers* 1988; *Robin Hood* 1990; *Waterland* 1992; *Hilary and Jackie* 1998; *Fanny & Elvis* 1999
Morrissey, Neil *I Bought a Vampire Motorcycle* 1989; *Up 'n' Under* 1997
Morrow, Jeff *The Siege at Red River* 1954; *Sign of the Pagan* 1954; *Tanganyika* 1954; *This Island Earth* 1955; *Captain Lightfoot* 1955; *Pardners* 1956; *The Hour of Decision* 1957; *Kronos* 1957; *The Story of Ruth* 1960
Morrow, Jo *Our Man in Havana* 1959; *The Three Worlds of Gulliver* 1959; *Juke Box Rhythm* 1959; *The Legend of Tom Dooley* 1959; *Sunday in New York* 1963; *He Rides Tall* 1964
Morrow, Rob *Private Resort* 1985; *Quiz Show* 1994; *Last Dance* 1995; *Mother* 1996; *The Day Lincoln Was Shot* 1998
Morrow, Susan *The Savage* 1953; *Macabre* 1958
Morrow, Vic *Tribute to a Bad Man* 1956; *Men in War* 1957; *God's Little Acre* 1958; *King Creole* 1958; *Posse from Hell* 1961; *Target: Harry* 1968; *The California Kid* 1974; *Dirty Mary Crazy Larry* 1974; *The Take* 1974; *The Night that Panicked America* 1975; *The Bad News Bears* 1976; *Treasure of Matecumbe* 1976; *The Man with the Power* 1977; *The Evictors* 1979; *Monster* 1980; *Twilight Zone: the Movie* 1983
Morse, Barry *Daughter of Darkness* 1948; *No Trace* 1950; *Kings of the Sun* 1963; *Puzzle of a Downfall Child* 1970; *Asylum* 1972; *Welcome to Blood City* 1977; *Power Play* 1978; *The Changeling* 1980; *Murder by Phone* 1982; *The Return of Sherlock Holmes* 1987
Morse, David *Inside Moves: the Guys from Max's Bar* 1980; *Downpayment on Murder* 1987; *Personal Foul* 1987; *Winnie* 1988; *Desperate Hours* 1990; *Cry in the Wild: the Taking of Peggy Ann* 1991; *The Indian Runner* 1991; *The Good Son* 1993; *The Getaway* 1994; *The Crossing Guard* 1995; *Twelve Monkeys* 1995; *Tecumseh: the Last Warrior* 1995; *Extreme Measures* 1996; *The Long Kiss Goodnight* 1996; *The Rock* 1996; *Contact* 1997; *The Negotiator* 1998; *The Green Mile* 1999; *Crazy in Alabama* 1999
Morse, Helen *Petersen* 1974; *Picnic at Hanging Rock* 1975; *Caddie* 1976; *Agatha* 1978; *Far East* 1982
Morse, Natalie *Anchoress* 1993; *My Mother's Courage* 1995
Morse, Robert *The Matchmaker* 1958; *Honeymoon Hotel* 1964; *The Loved One* 1965; *A Guide for the Married Man* 1967; *How to Succeed in Business without Really Trying* 1967; *Oh Dad, Poor Dad, Mama's Hung You in the Closet and I'm Feelin' So Sad* 1967; *Where Were You When the Lights Went Out?* 1968; *The Boatniks* 1970; *Calendar Girl Murders* 1984; *Hunk* 1987; *The Emperor's New Clothes* 1987; *Here Come the Munsters* 1995
Morse, Robin *Rock All Night* 1957; *Strange Voices* 1987
Mortensen, Viggo *Prison* 1987; *Salvation! Have You Said Your Prayers Today?* 1987; *The Reflecting Skin* 1990; *Leatherface: the Texas Chainsaw Massacre III* 1990; *The Indian Runner* 1991; *Ruby Cairo* 1992; *Boiling Point* 1993; *Carlito's Way* 1993; *The Young Americans* 1993; *American Yakuza* 1994; *The Prophecy* 1994; *Crimson Tide* 1995; *The Passion of Darkly Noon* 1995; *Albino Alligator* 1996; *Daylight* 1996; *The Portrait of a Lady* 1996; *GI Jane* 1997; *Vanishing Point* 1997; *A Perfect Murder* 1998; *Psycho* 1998; *A Walk on the Moon* 1999; *28 Days* 2000
Mortimer, Caroline *A Place for Lovers* 1969; *The Hireling* 1973
Mortimer, Charles *The Return of Bulldog Drummond* 1934; *Someone at the Door* 1936
Mortimer, Emily *The Ghost and the Darkness* 1996; *Last of the High Kings* 1996; *Love's Labour's Lost* 1999
Morton, Amy *Mrs Cage* 1992; *Rookie of the Year* 1993
Morton, Clive *Kind Hearts and Coronets* 1949; *A Run for Your Money* 1949; *The Lavender Hill Mob* 1951; *Carrington VC* 1954; *Orders Are Orders* 1954; *Lucky Jim* 1957; *The Moonraker* 1957; *Abandon Ship!* 1957; *The Duke Wore Jeans* 1958; *Stranger in the House* 1967
Morton, James C *Tit for Tat* 1934; *Wild Geese Calling* 1941
Morton, Joe *The Brother from Another Planet* 1984; *Trouble in Mind* 1985; *Crossroads* 1986; *Hostile Witness* 1987; *Stranded* 1987; *Command in Hell* 1988; *The Good Mother* 1988; *Zelly and Me* 1988; *Making the Case for Murder: the Howard Beach Story* 1989; *Tap* 1989; *City of Hope* 1991; *Terminator 2: Judgment Day* 1991; *Forever Young* 1992; *Legacy of Lies* 1992; *Of Mice and Men* 1992; *The Good Policeman* 1994; *No Ordinary Summer* 1994; *Speed* 1994; *In the Shadow of Evil* 1995; *The Walking Dead* 1995; *Executive Decision* 1996; *The Pest* 1997; *Miss Evers' Boys* 1997; *Blues Brothers 2000* 1998; *The Astronaut's Wife* 1999; *Mutiny* 1999
Morton, Samantha *This Is the Sea* 1996; *Under the Skin* 1997; *Dreaming of Joseph Lees* 1998; *The Last Yellow* 1999; *Sweet and Lowdown* 1999; *Jesus' Son* 1999
Morton, Tom aka **Morton, Tommy** *Wait 'til the Sun Shines, Nellie* 1952; *Main Street to Broadway* 1953
Moschin, Gastone *The Birds, the Bees, and the Italians* 1965; *The Conformist* 1969
Moscovich, Maurice aka **Moscovitch, Maurice** *Winterset* 1936; *Lancer Spy* 1937; *Suez* 1938; *In Name Only* 1939; *Love Affair* 1939; *Susannah of the Mounties* 1939
Moscow, David *Big* 1988; *White Wolves* 1993
Moseley, Bill aka **Mosley, Bill** *The Texas Chainsaw Massacre Part 2* 1986; *Silent Night, Deadly Night 3: Better Watch Out!* 1989; *Night of the Living Dead* 1990; *White Fang* 1991
Moseley, Page *Seeds of Tragedy* 1991; *Shadow of Obsession* 1994
Moses, William R *Mystic Pizza* 1988; *Rock Hudson* 1990; *Double Exposure* 1993; *Fun* 1994; *The Haunting of Seacliff Inn* 1994; *Circumstances Unknown* 1995; *Crimes of Silence* 1996; *Evil Has a Face* 1996
Mosley, Roger E *The Mack* 1973; *Leadbelly* 1976; *Stay Hungry* 1976; *The River Niger* 1976; *Semi-Tough* 1977; *Steel* 1980; *Heart Condition* 1990; *Unlawful Entry* 1992; *A Thin Line between Love and Hate* 1996
Moss, Arnold *Temptation* 1946; *The Loves of Carmen* 1948; *Border Incident* 1949; *Reign of Terror* 1949; *Kim* 1950; *My Favorite Spy* 1951; *Viva Zapata!* 1952; *Bengal Brigade* 1954; *Hell's Island* 1955; *The 27th Day* 1957; *The Fool Killer* 1965; *Gambit* 1966
Moss, Carrie-Anne *Deadly Current* 1996; *Sabotage* 1996; *The Matrix* 1999
Moss, Elisabeth *Once upon a Forest* 1992; *Escape to Witch Mountain* 1995; *Separate Lives* 1995; *Earthly Possessions* 1999
Mostel, Josh *Going Home* 1971; *Sophie's Choice* 1982; *Star 80* 1983; *Almost You* 1984; *Windy City* 1984; *The Money Pit* 1985; *Radio Days* 1987; *Animal Behavior* 1989; *Naked Tango* 1990; *The Chase* 1994; *Billy Madison* 1995; *The Maddening* 1995; *Great Expectations* 1997; *Rounders* 1998; *Thicker than Blood* 1998; *Big Daddy* 1999
Mostel, Zero *DuBarry Was a Lady* 1943; *Panic in the Streets* 1950; *Mr Belvedere Rings the Bell* 1951; *The Model and the Marriage Broker* 1951; *Murder, Inc* 1951; *Sirocco* 1951; *A Funny Thing Happened on the Way to the Forum* 1966; *Great Catherine* 1968; *The Producers* 1968; *The Great Bank Robbery* 1969; *The Angel Levine* 1970; *The Hot Rock* 1972; *Once Upon a Scoundrel* 1973; *Marco* 1973; *Rhinoceros* 1974; *The Front* 1976; *Mastermind* 1976; *Watership Down* 1978
Motta, Bess *The Terminator* 1984; *You Talkin' to Me?* 1987
Mottet, Alain *Ho!* 1968; *The Last Known Address* 1969
Moulder-Brown, John *Deep End* 1970; *First Love* 1970; *Vampire Circus* 1971; *King, Queen, Knave* 1972; *Rumpelstiltskin* 1986
Mount, Peggy *Dry Rot* 1956; *Sailor Beware!* 1956; *The Naked Truth* 1957; *Inn for Trouble* 1960; *Ladies Who Do* 1963; *One Way Pendulum* 1965; *Hotel Paradiso* 1966; *Oliver!* 1968; *The Princess and the Goblin* 1992
Mouton, Benjamin *And God Created Woman* 1988; *Whore* 1991
Mowbray, Alan *Guilty Hands* 1931; *Sherlock Holmes* 1932; *The Man from Yesterday* 1932; *Berkeley Square* 1933; *Our Betters* 1933; *Roman Scandals* 1933; *Peg o' My Heart* 1933; *Charlie Chan in London* 1934; *One More River* 1934; *The Girl from Missouri* 1934; *Long Lost Father* 1934; *The Gay Deception* 1935; *In Person* 1935; *Desire* 1936; *My Man Godfrey* 1936; *Rainbow on the River* 1936; *The King and the Chorus Girl* 1937; *On the Avenue* 1937; *Stand-In* 1937; *Topper* 1937; *Vogues* 1937; *Merrily We Live* 1938; *There Goes My Heart* 1938; *The Llano Kid* 1939; *Topper Takes a Trip* 1939; *Never Say Die* 1939; *The Boys from Syracuse* 1940; *Music in My Heart* 1940; *The Villain Still Pursued Her* 1940; *I Wake Up Screaming* 1941; *That Hamilton Woman* 1941; *That Uncertain Feeling* 1941; *Holy Matrimony* 1943; *Slightly Dangerous* 1943; *Earl Carroll Vanities* 1945; *Where Do We Go from Here?* 1945; *Terror by Night* 1946; *Lured* 1947; *Every Girl Should Be Married* 1948; *The Lovable Cheat* 1949; *The Jackpot* 1950; *Wagonmaster* 1950; *Androcles and the Lion* 1952; *Blackbeard the Pirate* 1952; *The King and I* 1956; *The Man Who Knew Too Much* 1956
Mower, Patrick *The Devil Rides Out* 1968; *The Smashing Bird I Used to Know* 1969; *Bloodsuckers* 1970; *Cry of the Banshee* 1970; *Incense for the Damned* 1970; *Black Beauty* 1971; *Catch Me a Spy* 1971; *Carry On England* 1976; *The Devil's Advocate* 1977
Moxey, Hugh *Meet Simon Cherry* 1949; *Assignment Redhead* 1956; *You Pay Your Money* 1957
Mudie, Leonard *The Magnetic Monster* 1953; *Timbuktu* 1959
Mueller, Cookie *Multiple Maniacs* 1970; *Pink Flamingos* 1972; *Female Trouble* 1974; *Desperate Living* 1977
Mueller, Elisabeth *The Power and the Prize* 1956; *The Angry Hills* 1959
Mueller, Maureen *A Stoning in Fulham County* 1988; *In a Shallow Grave* 1988; *Over Her Dead Body* 1990; *She Woke Up* 1992
Mueller-Stahl, Armin *Lola* 1982; *Trauma* 1983; *Colonel Redl* 1984; *Thousand Eyes* 1984; *Forget Mozart* 1985; *Midnight Cop* 1988; *Music Box* 1989; *Avalon* 1990; *Kafka* 1991; *The Power of One* 1991; *Night on Earth* 1992; *Utz* 1992; *The House of the Spirits* 1993; *Holy Matrimony* 1994; *The Last Good Time* 1994; *A Pyromaniac's Love Story* 1995; *Theodore Rex* 1995; *In the Presence of Mine Enemies* 1996; *Shine* 1996; *The Game* 1997; *Twelve Angry Men* 1997; *The Peacemaker* 1997; *The X Files* 1998; *The Thirteenth Floor* 1999; *Jakob the Liar* 1999; *Mission to Mars* 1999
Muhich, Donald F *Bob & Carol & Ted & Alice* 1969; *Blume in Love* 1973; *Down and Out in Beverly Hills* 1986
Mui, Anita *Rouge* 1987; *A Better Tomorrow III* 1989; *Drunken Master II* 1994; *Rumble in the Bronx* 1996
Muir, Gavin *Mary of Scotland* 1936; *Fair Warning* 1937; *Sherlock Holmes in Washington* 1943; *Calcutta* 1947; *Abbott and Costello Meet the Invisible Man* 1951; *Night Tide* 1961
Muir, Jean *The World Changes* 1933; *A Midsummer Night's Dream* 1935; *Oil for the Lamps of China* 1935; *White Fang* 1936
Mukherjee, Arun *Kangchenjunga* 1962; *And Quiet Rolls the Dawn* 1979
Mukherjee, Madhabi *The Big City* 1963; *Charulata* 1964
Muldaur, Diana *The Lawyer* 1969; *Number One* 1969; *One More Train to Rob* 1971; *The Other* 1972; *McQ* 1974; *Planet Earth* 1974; *The Return of Frank Cannon* 1980; *The Return of Sam McCloud* 1989; *Locked Up: a Mother's Rage* 1991
Mulgrew, Kate *Lovespell* 1979; *Remo – Unarmed and Dangerous* 1985; *Throw Momma from the Train* 1987; *Daddy* 1991; *Camp Nowhere* 1994; *Captain Nuke and the Bomber Boys* 1995
Mulhare, Edward *Signpost to Murder* 1964; *Von Ryan's Express* 1965; *Our Man Flint* 1966; *Caprice* 1967; *Eye of the Devil* 1968; *Knight Rider – the Movie* 1982
Mulhern, Matt *Extreme Prejudice* 1987; *Biloxi Blues* 1988; *Gunsmoke: To the Last Man* 1992; *A Burning Passion: the Margaret Mitchell Story* 1994; *Sunchaser* 1996
Mulkey, Chris *Runaway* 1984; *Patti Rocks* 1987; *Heartbreak Hotel* 1988; *Tricks of the Trade* 1988; *From Hollywood to Deadwood* 1989; *Roe vs Wade* 1989; *Rainbow Drive* 1990; *Hometown Boy Makes Good* 1990; *Bound and Gagged: a Love Story* 1992; *Deadbolt* 1992; *Gas, Food, Lodging* 1992; *Ghost in the Machine* 1993; *The Switch* 1993; *Dead Cold* 1996; *Behind Enemy Lines* 1996; *Weapons of Mass Distraction* 1997; *Sub Down* 1997
Mull, Martin *FM* 1977; *Serial* 1980; *Take This Job and Shove It* 1981; *Mr Mom* 1983; *Clue* 1985; *Home Is Where the Hart Is* 1987; *Ski Patrol* 1989; *Cutting Class* 1989; *Think Big* 1990; *Jingle All the Way* 1996; *Edie & Pen* 1996; *Beverly Hills Family Robinson* 1997
Mullan, Peter *Trainspotting* 1995; *Bogwoman* 1997; *My Name Is Joe* 1998; *Ordinary Decent Criminal* 1999; *Miss Julie* 1999
Mullaney, Jack *The Young Stranger* 1957; *All the Fine Young Cannibals* 1960; *Tickle Me* 1965; *Dr Goldfoot and the Bikini Machine* 1965
Mullard, Arthur *The Bank Raiders* 1958; *Postman's Knock* 1961; *It's Trad, Dad* 1961; *Smashing Time* 1967; *Crooks and Coronets* 1969; *Holiday on the Buses* 1973; *Adventures of a Plumber's Mate* 1978
Mullavey, Greg *The Hollywood Detective* 1989; *Not Quite Human II* 1989
Mullen, Barbara *Jeannie* 1941; *Thunder Rock* 1942; *A Place of One's Own* 1944; *The Gentle Gunman* 1952; *The Siege of Pinchgut* 1959; *The Very Edge* 1962
Mullen, Patty *Doom Asylum* 1987; *Frankenhooker* 1990
Muller, Paul *Journey to Italy* 1953; *Checkpoint* 1956; *Queen of the Pirates* 1960; *Count Dracula* 1970; *Treasure Island* 1972

Müller-Westernhagen, Marius *The Snowman* 1985; *Operation Madonna* 1987

Mulligan, Richard *One Potato, Two Potato* 1964; *Little Big Man* 1970; *The Hideaways* 1973; *Scavenger Hunt* 1979; *SOB* 1981; *Trail of the Pink Panther* 1982; *Meatballs 2* 1984; *Micki & Maude* 1984; *Teachers* 1984; *The Heavenly Kid* 1985; *Babes in Toyland* 1986; *A Fine Mess* 1986; *Poker Alice* 1987; *Oliver & Company* 1988; *Neil Simon's London Suite* 1996

Mulligan, Terry David *Deadly Sins* 1996; *Search for Justice* 1996

Mullinar, Rod *Magee and the Lady* 1978; *Patrick* 1978; *Thirst* 1979; *Shadows of the Peacock* 1987; *Dead Calm* 1988

Mulock, Al *High Hell* 1957; *Tarzan's Greatest Adventure* 1959; *Battle beneath the Earth* 1968

Mulroney, Dermot *Daddy* 1987; *Long Gone* 1987; *Young Guns* 1988; *Unconquered* 1989; *Staying Together* 1989; *Bright Angel* 1990; *Career Opportunities* 1991; *The Heart of Justice* 1992; *Where the Day Takes You* 1992; *The Assassin* 1993; *Silent Tongue* 1993; *The Thing Called Love* 1993; *Point of No Return* 1993; *The Last Outlaw* 1993; *Angels* 1994; *Bad Girls* 1994; *There Goes My Baby* 1994; *Copycat* 1995; *How to Make an American Quilt* 1995; *Kansas City* 1995; *Living in Oblivion* 1995; *Bastard out of Carolina* 1996; *Box of Moon Light* 1996; *The Trigger Effect* 1996; *Goodbye Lover* 1997; *My Best Friend's Wedding* 1997

Mulroney, Kieran *Career Opportunities* 1991; *The Immortals* 1995; *The Spitfire Grill* 1996

Mummert, Danny *Blondie Meets the Boss* 1939; *Blondie Takes a Vacation* 1939

Mumy, Bill *aka* **Mumy, Billy** *Sammy, the Way Out Seal* 1962; *Palm Springs Weekend* 1963; *A Ticklish Affair* 1963; *Dear Brigitte* 1966; *Bless the Beasts and Children* 1971; *Papillon* 1973; *Double Trouble* 1992

Munch, Richard *The Train* 1964; *Of Pure Blood* 1986

Mundin, Herbert *Cavalcade* 1933; *The Devil's in Love* 1933; *Mutiny on the Bounty* 1935; *A Message to Garcia* 1936; *Tarzan Escapes* 1936; *Under Two Flags* 1936; *Angel* 1937; *Another Dawn* 1937

Muni, Paul *I Am a Fugitive from a Chain Gang* 1932; *Scarface* 1932; *The World Changes* 1933; *Hi, Nellie!* 1934; *Black Fury* 1935; *Bordertown* 1935; *Dr Socrates* 1935; *The Story of Louis Pasteur* 1936; *The Good Earth* 1937; *The Life of Emile Zola* 1937; *The Woman I Love* 1937; *Juarez* 1939; *We Are Not Alone* 1939; *Hudson's Bay* 1940; *The Commandos Strike at Dawn* 1942; *Stage Door Canteen* 1943; *A Song to Remember* 1945; *Angel on My Shoulder* 1946; *The Last Angry Man* 1959

Munks, Sheryl *The Big Steal* 1990; *Holidays on the River Yarra* 1991

Munro, Caroline *Captain Kronos: Vampire Hunter* 1972; *Dracula AD 1972* 1972; *The Golden Voyage of Sinbad* 1973; *I Don't Want to Be Born* 1975; *At the Earth's Core* 1976; *The Spy Who Loved Me* 1977; *To Die For* 1994

Munro, Janet *Small Hotel* 1957; *The Trollenberg Terror* 1958; *Darby O'Gill and the Little People* 1959; *Third Man on the Mountain* 1959; *Tommy the Toreador* 1959; *Swiss Family Robinson* 1960; *The Day the Earth Caught Fire* 1961; *Life for Ruth* 1962; *Bitter Harvest* 1963; *Hide and Seek* 1963; *A Jolly Bad Fellow* 1964; *Sebastian* 1968

Munro, Lochlyn *Abduction of Innocence* 1996; *Unlikely Suspects* 1996; *Stand against Fear* 1996; *Dead Man on Campus* 1998; *Silencing Mary* 1998

Munro, Neil *Confidential* 1986; *Dancing in the Dark* 1986

Munshin, Jules *Easter Parade* 1948; *On the Town* 1949; *Take Me Out to the Ball Game* 1949; *That Midnight Kiss* 1949; *Silk Stockings* 1957; *Mastermind* 1976

Munson, Ona *Five Star Final* 1931; *Lady from Louisiana* 1941; *The Shanghai Gesture* 1941; *Wild Geese Calling* 1941; *The Cheaters* 1945; *Dakota* 1945

Murat, Jean *Carnival in Flanders* 1935; *Eternal Love* 1943; *On the Riviera* 1951

Murata, Takehiro *Godzilla vs Mothra* 1992; *Okoge* 1992

Murcell, George *The Pursuers* 1961; *Pascali's Island* 1988; *Year of the Gun* 1991

Murcelo, Karmin *Borderline* 1980; *Right to Kill?* 1985; *Seduced* 1985; *Empty Cradle* 1993

Murdoch, Richard *Over She Goes* 1937; *Band Waggon* 1939; *The Ghost Train* 1941; *I Thank You* 1941; *The Gay Adventure* 1949

Murdock, George *The Death Squad* 1974; *Thunder and Lightning* 1977; *Certain Fury* 1985; *Firepower* 1993

Murdock, Jack *Big Top Pee-wee* 1988; *Rain Man* 1988

Murgia, Tiberio *Big Deal on Madonna Street* 1958; *That Man George* 1965

Murney, Christopher *The Last Dragon* 1985; *The Secret of My Success* 1987

Murnik, Peter *Body Parts* 1991; *Pastime* 1991; *Golden Gate* 1994

Murphy, Audie *Sierra* 1950; *Kansas Raiders* 1950; *The Red Badge of Courage* 1951; *The Duel at Silver Creek* 1952; *Column South* 1953; *Gunsmoke* 1953; *Tumbleweed* 1953; *Destry* 1954; *Drums across the River* 1954; *Ride Clear of Diablo* 1954; *To Hell and Back* 1955; *Walk the Proud Land* 1956; *Night Passage* 1957; *Joe Butterfly* 1957; *The Quiet American* 1958; *Ride a Crooked Trail* 1958; *The Gun Runners* 1958; *No Name on the Bullet* 1959; *The Wild and the Innocent* 1959; *Cast a Long Shadow* 1959; *Hell Bent for Leather* 1960; *Seven Ways from Sundown* 1960; *The Unforgiven* 1960; *Posse from Hell* 1961; *Six Black Horses* 1962; *Showdown* 1963; *Bullet for a Badman* 1964; *Gunfight at Comanche Creek* 1964; *Apache Rifles* 1964; *Arizona Raiders* 1965; *Gunpoint* 1966; *A Time for Dying* 1971

Murphy, Ben *Yours, Mine and Ours* 1968; *Runaway!* 1973; *The Secret War of Jackie's Girls* 1980

Murphy, Bill *The Story of GI Joe* 1945; *A Foreign Affair* 1948

Murphy, Brian *Sparrows Can't Sing* 1962; *The Ragman's Daughter* 1972; *Man about the House* 1974; *George and Mildred* 1980

Murphy, Brittany *Clueless* 1995; *Drive* 1997; *The Prophecy II* 1997; *David and Lisa* 1998; *The Devil's Arithmetic* 1999; *Girl, Interrupted* 1999

Murphy, Donna *Jade* 1995; *Passion* 1996; *The Day Lincoln Was Shot* 1998; *Star Trek: Insurrection* 1998; *The Astronaut's Wife* 1999

Murphy, Eddie *48 HRS* 1982; *Trading Places* 1983; *Best Defense* 1984; *Beverly Hills Cop* 1984; *The Golden Child* 1986; *Beverly Hills Cop II* 1987; *Eddie Murphy Raw* 1987; *Coming to America* 1988; *Harlem Nights* 1989; *Another 48 HRS* 1990; *Boomerang* 1992; *The Distinguished Gentleman* 1992; *Beverly Hills Cop III* 1994; *Vampire in Brooklyn* 1995; *The Nutty Professor* 1996; *Metro* 1997; *Doctor Dolittle* 1998; *Holy Man* 1998; *Mulan* 1998; *Life* 1999; *Bowfinger* 1999

Murphy, George *Kid Millions* 1934; *Broadway Melody of 1938* 1937; *London by Night* 1937; *Hold That Co-Ed* 1938; *Little Miss Broadway* 1938; *Letter of Introduction* 1938; *Broadway Melody of 1940* 1940; *Little Nellie Kelly* 1940; *The Navy Steps Out* 1941; *Ringside Maisie* 1941; *Tom, Dick and Harry* 1941; *For Me and My Gal* 1942; *The Navy Comes Through* 1942; *Bataan* 1943; *This Is the Army* 1943; *Broadway Rhythm* 1944; *Show Business* 1944; *Step Lively* 1944; *Up Goes Maisie* 1946; *The Arnelo Affair* 1947; *Cynthia* 1947; *Battleground* 1949; *Border Incident* 1949; *Walk East on Beacon* 1952

Murphy, Gerard *The Brink's Job* 1978; *Waterworld* 1995

Murphy, Johnny *The Commitments* 1991; *Into the West* 1992

Murphy, Mary *The Wild One* 1953; *Main Street to Broadway* 1953; *Beachhead* 1954; *The Mad Magician* 1954; *Make Haste to Live* 1954; *Sitting Bull* 1954; *The Desperate Hours* 1955; *Hell's Island* 1955; *A Man Alone* 1955; *The Maverick Queen* 1955; *The Intimate Stranger* 1956; *Escapement* 1958; *Live Fast, Die Young* 1958; *Crime and Punishment, USA* 1959; *Junior Bonner* 1972

Murphy, Maurice *Pilgrimage* 1933; *Curly Top* 1935; *Tovarich* 1937

Murphy, Michael *Countdown* 1968; *Brewster McCloud* 1970; *Count Yorga, Vampire* 1970; *Phase IV* 1973; *The Thief Who Came to Dinner* 1973; *The Autobiography of Miss Jane Pittman* 1974; *The Front* 1976; *The Great Georgia Bank Hoax* 1977; *The Class of Miss MacMichael* 1978; *An Unmarried Woman* 1978; *Hot Money* 1979; *Manhattan* 1979; *The Year of Living Dangerously* 1982; *Mesmerized* 1984; *Cloak and Dagger* 1984; *Salvador* 1986; *Shocker* 1989; *Batman Returns* 1992; *Disaster at Valdez* 1992; *Clean Slate* 1994; *Kansas City* 1995; *Ultimate Lie* 1996; *Special Report: Journey to Mars* 1996; *Indiscretion of an American Wife* 1998

Murphy, Reilly *Body Snatchers* 1993; *Dangerous Game* 1993

Murphy, Rosemary *To Kill a Mockingbird* 1962; *Any Wednesday* 1966; *Ben* 1972; *You'll Like My Mother* 1972; *Ace Eli and Rodger of the Skies* 1973; *Julia* 1977; *The Hand* 1981; *For the Boys* 1991

Murphy, Timothy Patrick *With Intent to Kill* 1984; *Sam's Son* 1984; *Doin' Time on Planet Earth* 1988

Murray, Barbara *Boys in Brown* 1949; *Tony Draws a Horse* 1950; *Another Man's Poison* 1951; *The Frightened Man* 1952; *Meet Mr Lucifer* 1953; *Campbell's Kingdom* 1957; *A Cry from the Streets* 1957; *Operation Bullshine* 1959; *The Punch and Judy Man* 1962; *Doctor in Distress* 1963; *A Dandy in Aspic* 1968; *Some Will, Some Won't* 1969; *Up Pompeii* 1971

Murray, Bill *Meatballs* 1979; *Caddyshack* 1980; *Where the Buffalo Roam* 1980; *Stripes* 1981; *Tootsie* 1982; *Ghostbusters* 1984; *The Razor's Edge* 1984; *Nothing Lasts Forever* 1984; *Little Shop of Horrors* 1986; *Scrooged* 1988; *Ghostbusters II* 1989; *Quick Change* 1990; *What about Bob?* 1991; *Mad Dog and Glory* 1992; *Groundhog Day* 1993; *Ed Wood* 1994; *Kingpin* 1996; *Larger than Life* 1996; *The Man Who Knew Too Little* 1997; *Space Jam* 1997; *Rushmore* 1998; *Wild Things* 1998; *Cradle Will Rock* 1999

Murray, Billy *McVicar* 1980; *Essex Boys* 1999

Murray, Chic *Ups and Downs of a Handyman* 1975; *Gregory's Girl* 1980

Murray, Don *Bus Stop* 1956; *The Bachelor Party* 1957; *A Hatful of Rain* 1957; *From Hell to Texas* 1958; *These Thousand Hills* 1959; *Shake Hands with the Devil* 1959; *One Foot in Hell* 1960; *The Hoodlum Priest* 1961; *Advise and Consent* 1962; *One Man's Way* 1964; *Baby the Rain Must Fall* 1965; *Kid Rodelo* 1966; *The Viking Queen* 1967; *Happy Birthday, Wanda June* 1971; *Conquest of the Planet of the Apes* 1972; *Deadly Hero* 1976; *The Boy Who Drank Too Much* 1980; *Endless Love* 1981; *I Am the Cheese* 1983; *A Touch of Scandal* 1984; *Peggy Sue Got Married* 1986; *Something in Common* 1986; *Radioactive Dreams* 1986; *Made in Heaven* 1987; *Mistress* 1987; *The Stepford Children* 1987; *Stillwatch* 1987; *Confessions of a Lady Cop* 1988; *Ghosts Can't Do It* 1990

Murray Hill, Peter *The Ghost Train* 1941; *Bell-Bottom George* 1943; *Rhythm Serenade* 1943; *Madonna of the Seven Moons* 1944; *They Were Sisters* 1945

Murray, James *The Crowd* 1928; *Central Airport* 1933; *Teenage Mutant Ninja Turtles III* 1992

Murray, Jan *Who Killed Teddy Bear?* 1965; *Tarzan and the Great River* 1967; *Thunder Alley* 1967; *The Busy Body* 1967; *Which Way to the Front?* 1970; *Day of the Wolves* 1973

Murray, Ken *The Man Who Shot Liberty Valance* 1962; *Son of Flubber* 1962

Murray, Mae *The Merry Widow* 1925; *Bachelor Apartment* 1931

Murray, Sean *Hamlet* 1990; *Murder on the Rio Grande* 1993; *Fall into Darkness* 1996

Murray, Stephen *The Prime Minister* 1940; *The Master of Bankdam* 1947; *My Brother Jonathan* 1947; *London Belongs to Me* 1948; *Silent Dust* 1948; *Now Barabbas Was a Robber* 1949; *The Magnet* 1950; *The End of the Affair* 1955; *Guilty?* 1956; *A Tale of Two Cities* 1957; *Master Spy* 1964

Murray, Tom *The Pilgrim* 1923; *The Gold Rush* 1925

Murtaugh, James *The Rosary Murders* 1987; *Letter to My Killer* 1995

Murton, Lionel *The Pickwick Papers* 1952; *Our Girl Friday* 1953; *The Battle of the River Plate* 1956; *The Truth about Spring* 1964; *The Revolutionary* 1970

Murua, Lautaro *Triumphs of a Man Called Horse* 1983; *I, the Worst of All* 1990; *The Plague* 1992

Musante, Tony *Once a Thief* 1965; *The Incident* 1967; *A Professional Gun* 1968; *The Bird with the Crystal Plumage* 1969; *The Grissom Gang* 1971; *The Last Run* 1971; *The Pope of Greenwich Village* 1984

Muse, Clarence *Dirigible* 1931; *Huckleberry Finn* 1931; *Washington Merry-Go-Round* 1932; *White Zombie* 1932; *Broadway Bill* 1934; *That Gang of Mine* 1940; *Invisible Ghost* 1941; *Riding High* 1950; *Apache Drums* 1951; *The Black Stallion* 1979

Muti, Ornella *To Kill a Rat* 1977; *Viva Italia!* 1978; *Flash Gordon* 1980; *They Made Him a Criminal* 1980; *Tales of Ordinary Madness* 1981; *Love and Money* 1982; *Swann in Love* 1984; *Chronicle of a Death Foretold* 1987; *Wait until Spring, Bandini* 1989; *Oscar* 1991; *Once upon a Crime* 1992; *Pour Rire!* 1996

Muzquiz, Carlos *Captain Scarlett* 1953; *The Black Scorpion* 1957; *Villa!* 1958

Myers, Bruce *Henry & June* 1990; *Fausto* 1992

Myers, Carmel *Ben-Hur: a Tale of Christ* 1925; *The Mad Genius* 1931

Myers, Cynthia *Beyond the Valley of the Dolls* 1970; *Molly and Lawless John* 1972

Myers, Kim *A Nightmare on Elm Street 2: Freddy's Revenge* 1985; *When He's Not a Stranger* 1989; *Fatal Love* 1992

Myers, Mike *Wayne's World* 1992; *So I Married an Axe Murderer* 1993; *Wayne's World 2* 1993; *Austin Powers: International Man of Mystery* 1997; *54* 1998; *Austin Powers: The Spy Who Shagged Me* 1999; *Mystery, Alaska* 1999

Myers, Peter *Bachelor of Hearts* 1958; *The Reluctant Debutante* 1958; *Hello – Goodbye* 1970

Myhers, John *The Private Navy of Sgt O'Farrell* 1968; *The Billion Dollar Hobo* 1978

N

N !xau *The Gods Must Be Crazy* 1980; *The Gods Must Be Crazy II* 1989

Nabors, Jim *The Best Little Whorehouse in Texas* 1982; *Stroker Ace* 1983

Naceri, Samy *Taxi* 1998; *Taxi 2* 2000

Nader, George *Robot Monster* 1953; *Carnival Story* 1954; *Four Guns to the Border* 1954; *Six Bridges to Cross* 1955; *Lady Godiva* 1955; *Away All Boats* 1956; *Congo Crossing* 1956; *Joe Butterfly* 1957; *Nowhere to Go* 1958; *The Female Animal* 1958; *The Secret Mark of D'Artagnan* 1962

Nader, Michael *Nick Knight* 1989; *The Flash* 1990; *The Finishing Touch* 1992

ACTORS' INDEX
RadioTimes

Nadir, Robert *Better Off Dead* 1993; *Mad Love* 1995
Nagase, Masatoshi *Mystery Train* 1989; *Autumn Moon* 1992; *The Most Terrible Time in My Life* 1993; *Cold Fever* 1994
Nagel, Anne *The Case of the Stuttering Bishop* 1937; *Argentine Nights* 1940; *Man Made Monster* 1941; *Never Give a Sucker an Even Break* 1941; *Road Agent* 1941
Nagel, Conrad *London after Midnight* 1927; *The Mysterious Lady* 1928; *Dynamite* 1929; *Hollywood Revue* 1929; *The Kiss* 1929; *The Divorcee* 1930; *One Romantic Night* 1930; *East Lynne* 1931; *Bad Sister* 1931; *Hell Divers* 1932; *Ann Vickers* 1933; *Dangerous Corner* 1934; *Man and His Mate* 1940; *All That Heaven Allows* 1955; *Hidden Fear* 1957; *The Man Who Understood Women* 1959; *A Stranger in My Arms* 1959
Nagy, Bill *The Brain Machine* 1954; *Across the Bridge* 1957; *First Man into Space* 1958; *The Boy Who Stole a Million* 1960; *Never Take Sweets from a Stranger* 1960; *Danger by My Side* 1962; *The Night of the Prowler* 1962
Naidu, Ajay *Where the River Runs Black* 1986; *Touch and Go* 1986; *subUrbia* 1996; *Office Space* 1999
Naidu, Leela *The Householder* 1963; *Electric Moon* 1992
Nail, Jimmy *Morons from Outer Space* 1985; *Crusoe* 1988; *Dream Demon* 1988; *Just Ask for Diamond* 1988; *Danny, the Champion of the World* 1989; *Evita* 1996; *Still Crazy* 1998
Nail, Joanne *Switchblade Sisters* 1975; *The Visitor* 1980; *Full Moon High* 1982
Naish, J Carrol *The Hatchet Man* 1932; *The Kid from Spain* 1932; *Tiger Shark* 1932; *The Mad Game* 1933; *The Devil's in Love* 1933; *British Agent* 1934; *Upper World* 1934; *Black Fury* 1935; *Confidential* 1935; *The Lives of a Bengal Lancer* 1935; *The Robin Hood of El Dorado* 1936; *King of Alcatraz* 1938; *Beau Geste* 1939; *Down Argentine Way* 1940; *Typhoon* 1940; *The Birth of the Blues* 1941; *Blood and Sand* 1941; *The Corsican Brothers* 1941; *That Night in Rio* 1941; *A Gentleman at Heart* 1942; *The Man in the Trunk* 1942; *The Pied Piper* 1942; *Dr Broadway* 1942; *Behind the Rising Sun* 1943; *Gung Ho!* 1943; *Sahara* 1943; *Enter Arsene Lupin* 1944; *House of Frankenstein* 1944; *The Monster Maker* 1944; *Getting Gertie's Garter* 1945; *A Medal for Benny* 1945; *The Southerner* 1945; *The Beast with Five Fingers* 1946; *Humoresque* 1946; *Bad Bascomb* 1946; *The Fugitive* 1947; *Joan of Arc* 1948; *Canadian Pacific* 1949; *That Midnight Kiss* 1949; *The Kissing Bandit* 1949; *Annie Get Your Gun* 1950; *The Black Hand* 1950; *Rio Grande* 1950; *The Toast of New Orleans* 1950; *Across the Wide Missouri* 1951; *Clash by Night* 1952; *Ride the Man Down* 1952; *Beneath the 12-Mile Reef* 1953; *Saskatchewan* 1954; *Sitting Bull* 1954; *The Last Command* 1955; *Violent Saturday* 1955; *New York Confidential* 1955; *Rage at Dawn* 1955; *Rebel in Town* 1956; *Dracula vs Frankenstein* 1970
Naismith, Laurence *Mogambo* 1953; *The Black Knight* 1954; *Carrington VC* 1954; *The Man Who Never Was* 1955; *The Extra Day* 1956; *Tiger in the Smoke* 1956; *Boy on a Dolphin* 1957; *Robbery under Arms* 1957; *Abandon Ship!* 1957; *The Naked Earth* 1958; *Solomon and Sheba* 1959; *Third Man on the Mountain* 1959; *The Angry Silence* 1960; *Greyfriars Bobby* 1960; *The Singer Not the Song* 1960; *Sink the Bismarck!* 1960; *Village of the Damned* 1960; *The World of Suzie Wong* 1960; *The Prince and the Pauper* 1962; *We Joined the Navy* 1962; *Jason and the Argonauts* 1963; *The Three Lives of Thomasina* 1963; *Sky West and Crooked* 1965; *The Long Duel* 1966; *Camelot* 1967; *Eye of the Cat* 1969; *The Valley of Gwangi* 1969; *Scrooge* 1970; *Quest for Love* 1971; *The Amazing Mr Blunden* 1972
Najimy, Kathy *Soapdish* 1991; *Sister Act* 1992; *Hocus Pocus* 1993; *Sister Act 2: Back in the Habit* 1993; *Cats Don't Dance* 1998; *Hope Floats* 1998; *The Jungle Book: Mowgli's Story* 1998
Nakadai, Tatsuya *The Human Condition* 1958; *Conflagration* 1958; *The Key* 1959; *Harakiri* 1962; *Sanjuro* 1962; *High and Low* 1963; *Kwaidan* 1964; *The Face of Another* 1966; *Today It's Me... Tomorrow You!* 1968; *Kagemusha* 1980; *The Empty Table* 1985; *Ran* 1985
Nakai, Kiichi *The Empty Table* 1985; *The Burmese Harp* 1985
Nakamura, Ganjiro *Conflagration* 1958; *The Key* 1959; *Floating Weeds* 1959; *Early Autumn* 1961; *An Actor's Revenge* 1963
Nakamura, Toru *Blue Tiger* 1994; *New York Cop* 1995
Nalder, Reggie *The Man Who Knew Too Much* 1956; *The Dead Don't Die* 1975; *Zoltan... Hound of Dracula* 1977
Naldi, Nita *Dr Jekyll and Mr Hyde* 1920; *Blood and Sand* 1922; *The Pleasure Garden* 1925
Namath, Joe *The Last Rebel* 1971; *Avalanche Express* 1979; *Chattanooga Choo Choo* 1984
Nance, Jack *aka* **Nance, John** *Eraserhead* 1976; *Ghoulies* 1985; *Blue Velvet* 1986; *Barfly* 1987; *The Secret Agent Club* 1995; *Voodoo* 1995; *Chase Morran* 1996; *Little Witches* 1996; *Lost Highway* 1996
Napier, Alan *The Four Just Men* 1939; *We Are Not Alone* 1939; *Cat People* 1942; *Lost Angel* 1943; *The Uninvited* 1944; *The Silent Bell* 1944; *Ministry of Fear* 1945; *The Lone Wolf in London* 1947; *Macbeth* 1948; *Tarzan's Magic Fountain* 1949; *Across the Wide Missouri* 1951; *Double Crossbones* 1951; *Big Jim McLain* 1952; *Julius Caesar* 1953; *Until They Sail* 1957; *The Premature Burial* 1962; *The Sword in the Stone* 1963; *Marnie* 1964; *Batman* 1966
Napier, Charles *Cherry, Harry & Raquel* 1969; *Beyond the Valley of the Dolls* 1970; *Supervixens* 1975; *Citizens Band* 1977; *Last Embrace* 1979; *Rambo: First Blood, Part II* 1985; *The Night Stalker* 1985; *Hit List* 1988; *One Man Force* 1989; *Ernest Goes to Jail* 1990; *Philadelphia* 1993; *Skeeter* 1993; *Raw Justice* 1993; *Hard Justice* 1995; *Jury Duty* 1995; *3 Ninjas Knuckle Up* 1995; *Steel* 1997; *Jailbreak* 1997; *The Big Tease* 1999
Napier, Diana *Heart's Desire* 1935; *Land without Music* 1936; *Pagliacci* 1936
Napier, Marshall *Bad Blood* 1982; *Starlight Hotel* 1987; *Georgia* 1988; *The Navigator – a Medieval Odyssey* 1988; *The Big Steal* 1990; *Paperback Romance* 1994
Napier, Russell *Death of an Angel* 1951; *The Brain Machine* 1954; *A Stranger Came Home* 1954; *The Blue Peter* 1955; *Little Red Monkey* 1955
Nardini, Tom *Cat Ballou* 1965; *Africa – Texas Style* 1967
Nares, Owen *The Show Goes On* 1937; *The Prime Minister* 1940
Nargis *Andaz* 1949; *Babul* 1950; *Anhonee* 1951; *Chori Chori* 1956; *Mother India* 1957
Nash, Chris *Mischief* 1985; *Silent Witness* 1985
Nash, Johnny *Take a Giant Step* 1959; *Key Witness* 1960
Nash, Mary *Easy Living* 1937; *Heidi* 1937; *The King and the Chorus Girl* 1937; *Wells Fargo* 1937; *The Little Princess* 1939; *Cobra Woman* 1944; *In the Meantime, Darling* 1944; *Yolande and the Thief* 1945; *Till the Clouds Roll By* 1946; *Swell Guy* 1946
Nash, Noreen *The Tender Years* 1947; *Storm over Wyoming* 1950; *The Lone Ranger and the Lost City of Gold* 1958
Nat, Marie-José *La Vérité* 1960; *The Seven Deadly Sins* 1961; *Embassy* 1972
Nathan, Vivian *The Young Savages* 1961; *The Outsider* 1961; *Klute* 1971
Nathenson, Zoe *Those Glory, Glory Days* 1983; *Mona Lisa* 1986
Natsukawa, Daijiro *Poppy* 1935; *The Downfall of Osen* 1935
Natwick, Mildred *The Long Voyage Home* 1940; *The Enchanted Cottage* 1945; *Yolande and the Thief* 1945; *The Late George Apley* 1947; *Three Godfathers* 1948; *She Wore a Yellow Ribbon* 1949; *The Kissing Bandit* 1949; *Cheaper by the Dozen* 1950; *Against All Flags* 1952; *The Trouble with Harry* 1955; *The Court Jester* 1956; *Teenage Rebel* 1956; *Tammy and the Bachelor* 1957; *Barefoot in the Park* 1967; *If It's Tuesday, This Must Be Belgium* 1969; *The Maltese Bippy* 1969; *Do Not Fold, Spindle or Mutilate* 1971; *The Snoop Sisters* 1972; *At Long Last Love* 1975; *Kiss Me Goodbye* 1982; *Dangerous Liaisons* 1988
Naughton, Charlie *O-Kay for Sound* 1937; *Alf's Button Afloat* 1938; *Gasbags* 1940; *Life Is a Circus* 1958
Naughton, David *An American Werewolf in London* 1981; *Separate Ways* 1981; *Not for Publication* 1984; *Hot Dog – The Movie* 1984; *The Boy in Blue* 1986; *Separate Vacations* 1986
Naughton, James *My Body, My Child* 1982; *Cat's Eye* 1984; *The Glass Menagerie* 1987; *The Good Mother* 1988; *Necessity* 1988; *The Birds II: Land's End* 1994; *Cagney & Lacey: the Return* 1994; *Cagney & Lacey: Together Again* 1994; *Danielle Steel's Mixed Blessings* 1995; *First Kid* 1996; *Oxygen* 1999
Navin Jr, John P *Taps* 1981; *Losin' It* 1983; *The Toughest Man in the World* 1984
Nayar, Nisha K *aka* **Nayar, Nisha** *Bhaji on the Beach* 1993; *The Darkest Light* 1999
Nayyar, Harsh *Making Mr Right* 1987; *Vestige of Honor* 1990
Nazimova, Alla *aka* **Nazimova** *Camille* 1921; *Salome* 1922; *Escape* 1940; *Blood and Sand* 1941
Nazzari, Amedeo *Nights of Cabiria* 1957; *The Naked Maja* 1959; *Nefertite, Queen of the Nile* 1961; *The Sicilian Clan* 1969; *The Valachi Papers* 1972
Neagle, Anna *Bitter Sweet* 1933; *Nell Gwyn* 1934; *Limelight* 1936; *London Melody* 1937; *Victoria the Great* 1937; *Sixty Glorious Years* 1938; *Nurse Edith Cavell* 1939; *Irene* 1940; *No, No, Nanette* 1940; *They Flew Alone* 1941; *Sunny* 1941; *Forever and a Day* 1943; *The Yellow Canary* 1943; *I Live in Grosvenor Square* 1945; *The Courtneys of Curzon Street* 1947; *Spring in Park Lane* 1948; *Maytime in Mayfair* 1949; *Odette* 1950; *The Lady with the Lamp* 1951; *Derby Day* 1952; *King's Rhapsody* 1955; *Lilacs in the Spring* 1955; *My Teenage Daughter* 1956; *The Man Who Wouldn't Talk* 1957; *No Time for Tears* 1957
Neal, Billie *Down by Law* 1986; *Mortal Thoughts* 1991; *Sweet Nothing* 1995
Neal, Elise *Rosewood* 1997; *Scream 2* 1997
Neal, Patricia *The Fountainhead* 1949; *The Hasty Heart* 1949; *It's a Great Feeling* 1949; *The Breaking Point* 1950; *Bright Leaf* 1950; *Three Secrets* 1950; *The Day the Earth Stood Still* 1951; *Operation Pacific* 1951; *Weekend with Father* 1951; *Diplomatic Courier* 1952; *Stranger from Venus* 1954; *A Face in the Crowd* 1957; *Breakfast at Tiffany's* 1961; *Hud* 1963; *Psyche '59* 1964; *In Harm's Way* 1965; *The Subject Was Roses* 1968; *The Homecoming: a Christmas Story* 1971; *Baxter* 1973; *Happy Mother's Day... Love, George* 1973; *Eric* 1975; *The Passage* 1978; *All Quiet on the Western Front* 1979; *Ghost Story* 1981; *Love Leads the Way* 1984; *An Unremarkable Life* 1989; *Caroline?* 1990; *Shattered Silence* 1992; *Cookie's Fortune* 1999
Neal, Tom *Andy Hardy Meets Debutante* 1940; *Behind the Rising Sun* 1943; *Detour* 1945; *First Yank into Tokyo* 1945
Neame, Christopher *Dracula AD 1972* 1972; *Love among Thieves* 1987; *DOA* 1988; *Diplomatic Immunity* 1991; *Still Not Quite Human* 1992; *Hellbound* 1993
Near, Holly *Angel, Angel Down We Go* 1969; *The Todd Killings* 1971; *FTA* 1972; *Dogfight* 1991
Neckar, Vaclav *Closely Observed Trains* 1966; *Larks on a String* 1969
Nedjari, Al *Frantz Fanon: Black Skin White Mask* 1996; *Strong Language* 1998
Needham, Tracey *Bonnie and Clyde: the True Story* 1992; *Lush Life* 1993; *Prophet of Evil* 1993; *Last Stand at Saber River* 1997
Needles, Nique *The Boy Who Had Everything* 1984; *Dogs in Space* 1986; *As Time Goes By* 1987; *Afraid to Dance* 1988; *Tender Hooks* 1988
Neeson, Liam *Excalibur* 1981; *Merlin and the Sword* 1982; *Krull* 1983; *The Bounty* 1984; *The Innocent* 1984; *Lamb* 1985; *The Mission* 1986; *Suspect* 1987; *Sworn to Silence* 1987; *The Dead Pool* 1988; *The Good Mother* 1988; *High Spirits* 1988; *Satisfaction* 1988; *A Prayer for the Dying* 1988; *Next of Kin* 1989; *The Big Man* 1990; *Darkman* 1990; *Under Suspicion* 1991; *Husbands and Wives* 1992; *Leap of Faith* 1992; *Ruby Cairo* 1992; *Shining Through* 1992; *Ethan Frome* 1993; *Schindler's List* 1993; *Rob Roy* 1995; *Before and After* 1996; *Michael Collins* 1996; *Les Misérables* 1997; *Star Wars Episode I: the Phantom Menace* 1999; *The Haunting* 1999
Neff, Hildegarde *aka* **Knef, Hildegarde** *The Murderers Are amongst Us* 1946; *Decision before Dawn* 1951; *Diplomatic Courier* 1952; *The Snows of Kilimanjaro* 1952; *The Man between* 1953; *Svengali* 1954; *Subway in the Sky* 1958; *Bluebeard* 1962; *The Lost Continent* 1968; *Fedora* 1978
Negishi, Toshie *Akira Kurosawa's Dreams* 1990; *Rhapsody in August* 1990
Negoda, Natalya *Little Vera* 1988; *Back in the USSR* 1992; *The Comrades of Summer* 1992
Négret, François *Mister Frost* 1990; *Night and Day* 1991
Negri, Pola *Hotel Imperial* 1927; *The Moon-Spinners* 1964
Negron, Taylor *Easy Money* 1983; *The Last Boy Scout* 1991; *Nothing but Trouble* 1991; *A Kid in Aladdin's Palace* 1998
Neil, Christopher *Adventures of a Private Eye* 1977; *Adventures of a Plumber's Mate* 1978; *Train of Dreams* 1987
Neil, Hildegard *The Man Who Haunted Himself* 1970; *Antony and Cleopatra* 1972; *England Made Me* 1973; *A Touch of Class* 1973; *The Legacy* 1978
Neill, James *The Cheat* 1915; *The Ten Commandments* 1923; *The King of Kings* 1927
Neill, Sam *My Brilliant Career* 1979; *The Final Conflict* 1980; *Attack Force Z* 1981; *Possession* 1981; *Enigma* 1982; *The Country Girls* 1983; *The Blood of Others* 1984; *Plenty* 1985; *Robbery under Arms* 1985; *The Good Wife* 1986; *A Cry in the Dark* 1988; *Dead Calm* 1988; *Leap of Faith* 1988; *Death in Brunswick* 1990; *The Hunt for Red October* 1990; *One against the Wind* 1991; *Until the End of the World* 1991; *Memoirs of an Invisible Man* 1992; *Rainbow Warrior* 1992; *Hostage* 1992; *Jurassic Park* 1993; *The Piano* 1993; *Country Life* 1994; *In the Mouth of Madness* 1994; *Rudyard Kipling's The Jungle Book* 1994; *Sirens* 1994; *Restoration* 1995; *Victory* 1995; *Snow White: a Tale of Terror* 1996; *Children of the Revolution* 1996; *Event Horizon* 1997; *The Revengers' Comedies* 1997; *The Horse Whisperer* 1998; *Bicentennial Man* 1999
Neise, George N *aka* **Neise, George** *The Tall Stranger* 1957; *The Three Stooges in Orbit* 1962; *The Three Stooges Meet Hercules* 1962
Nell, Nathalie *Man, Woman and Child* 1983; *Echoes* 1983
Nelligan, Kate *The Count of Monte Cristo* 1974; *The Romantic Englishwoman* 1975; *Dracula* 1979; *Eye of the Needle* 1981; *Without a Trace* 1983; *Eleni* 1985; *White Room* 1990; *Frankie & Johnny* 1991; *The Prince of Tides* 1991; *Liar Liar* 1992; *Fatal Instinct* 1993; *Shattered Trust* 1993; *Spoils of War* 1994; *Wolf* 1994; *How to Make an American Quilt* 1995; *Margaret's Museum* 1995; *Captive Heart: the James*

RadioTimes ACTORS' INDEX

Mink Story 1996; *Up Close & Personal* 1996; *US Marshals* 1998; *Love Is Strange* 1998; *The Cider House Rules* 1999
Nelson, Barry *Shadow of the Thin Man* 1941; *A Guy Named Joe* 1944; *Undercover Maisie* 1947; *The First Travelling Saleslady* 1956; *Mary, Mary* 1963; *Pete 'n' Tillie* 1972; *The Shining* 1980
Nelson, Bob *Brain Donors* 1992; *This Is My Life* 1992
Nelson, Craig T *Stir Crazy* 1980; *Poltergeist* 1982; *All the Right Moves* 1983; *Call to Glory* 1983; *Man, Woman and Child* 1983; *The Osterman Weekend* 1983; *Silkwood* 1983; *The Killing Fields* 1984; *Poltergeist II: the Other Side* 1986; *The Ted Kennedy Jr Story* 1986; *Rachel River* 1987; *Red Riding Hood* 1987; *Action Jackson* 1988; *Turner & Hooch* 1989; *Troop Beverly Hills* 1989; *Extreme Close-Up* 1990; *The Josephine Baker Story* 1991; *The Switch* 1993; *Take Me Home Again* 1994; *Ride with the Wind* 1994; *Ghosts from the Past* 1996; *I'm Not Rappaport* 1996; *The Devil's Advocate* 1997; *Wag the Dog* 1997; *The Skulls* 2000
Nelson, David *The Big Circus* 1959; *The Remarkable Mr Pennypacker* 1959; *-30-* 1959; *The Big Show* 1961
Nelson, Ed *The Young Captives* 1958; *A Bucket of Blood* 1959; *Runaway!* 1973; *Acapulco Gold* 1976; *Battle of Midway* 1976; *For the Love of Benji* 1977; *The Return of Frank Cannon* 1980; *Who Am I?* 1998
Nelson, Gene *I Wonder Who's Kissing Her Now* 1947; *The Daughter of Rosie O'Grady* 1950; *Tea for Two* 1950; *The West Point Story* 1950; *Lullaby of Broadway* 1951; *Painting the Clouds with Sunshine* 1951; *She's Working Her Way through College* 1952; *Three Sailors and a Girl* 1953; *So This Is Paris* 1954; *The City Is Dark* 1954; *Oklahoma!* 1955; *Timeslip* 1955; *Thunder Island* 1963; *Family Flight* 1972
Nelson, Gwen *Don't Talk to Strange Men* 1962; *A Kind of Loving* 1962; *Say Hello to Yesterday* 1971
Nelson, Herbert *When the Legends Die* 1972; *Future Cop* 1976
Nelson, Jerry *The Muppet Movie* 1979; *The Muppet Christmas Carol* 1992
Nelson, John Allen *Hunk* 1987; *Killer Klowns from Outer Space* 1988; *Rich Men, Single Women* 1990; *Angel of Desire* 1993
Nelson, Judd *The Breakfast Club* 1985; *Fandango* 1985; *St Elmo's Fire* 1985; *Blue City* 1986; *Transformers – The Movie* 1986; *From the Hip* 1987; *Never on Tuesday* 1988; *Relentless* 1989; *Hiroshima: Out of the Ashes* 1990; *New Jack City* 1991; *The Dark Backward* 1991; *Conflict of Interest* 1992; *Primary Motive* 1992; *Every Breath* 1993; *Someone's Watching* 1993; *Airheads* 1994; *Blindfold: Acts of Obsession* 1994; *Flinch* 1994; *Hail Caesar* 1994; *Blackwater Trail* 1995; *Circumstances Unknown* 1995; *Steel* 1997
Nelson, Lori *Bend of the River* 1952; *All I Desire* 1953; *The All American* 1953; *Tumbleweed* 1953; *Destry* 1954; *I Died a Thousand Times* 1955; *Underwater!* 1955; *Revenge of the Creature* 1955; *Sincerely Yours* 1955; *The Day the World Ended* 1956; *Mohawk* 1956; *Pardners* 1956
Nelson, Mimi *Port of Call* 1948; *Thirst* 1949
Nelson, Ricky *The Story of Three Loves* 1953; *Rio Bravo* 1959; *The Wackiest Ship in the Army* 1961
Nelson, Ruth *The Eve of St Mark* 1944; *Wilson* 1944; *A Tree Grows in Brooklyn* 1945; *Humoresque* 1946; *Mother Wore Tights* 1947; *The Sea of Grass* 1947; *Arch of Triumph* 1948; *3 Women* 1977; *The Haunting Passion* 1983; *Awakenings* 1990
Nelson, Sandra *Trust in Me* 1994; *Captains Courageous* 1995; *Maternal Instincts* 1996
Nelson, Sean *Fresh* 1994; *American Buffalo* 1995; *The Wood* 1999
Nelson, Tracy *Down and Out in Beverly Hills* 1986; *The Game of Love* 1987; *The Night Caller* 1998
Nelson, Willie *The Electric Horseman* 1979; *Honeysuckle Rose* 1980; *Thief* 1981; *Barbarosa* 1982; *Songwriter* 1984; *The Last Days of Frank and Jesse James* 1986; *Once upon a Texas Train* 1988; *Where the Hell's That Gold?* 1988; *Pair of Aces* 1990; *Another Pair of Aces: Three of a Kind* 1991; *Wild Texas Wind* 1991; *Big Dreams & Broken Hearts: the Dottie West Story* 1995; *Gone Fishin'* 1997; *Wag the Dog* 1997; *Half-Baked* 1998; *Outlaw Justice* 1999
Nemec, Corin aka **Nemec, Corin "Corky"** *Solar Crisis* 1990; *My Son Johnny* 1991; *Drop Zone* 1994; *Operation Dumbo Drop* 1995; *The War at Home* 1996; *Silencing Mary* 1998
Neri, Francesca *The Ages of Lulu* 1990; *Flight of the Innocent* 1993; *Outrage* 1993; *Live Flesh* 1997; *Strong Hands* 1997
Nerman, David *Incident in a Small Town* 1993; *Witchboard – The Possession* 1995; *The Conspiracy of Fear* 1996
Nero, Franco *The Bible...in the Beginning* 1966; *Django* 1966; *Texas Adios* 1966; *Camelot* 1967; *A Professional Gun* 1968; *The Battle of Neretva* 1969; *Tristana* 1970; *The Virgin and the Gypsy* 1970; *The Last Days of Mussolini* 1974; *The Masters* 1975; *Keoma* 1976; *Force 10 from Navarone* 1978; *The Man with Bogart's Face* 1980; *Enter the Ninja* 1981; *The Salamander* 1981; *Querelle* 1982; *Kamikaze 1989* 1983; *The Girl* 1986; *Die Hard 2: Die Harder* 1990; *Fratelli e Sorelle* 1992; *The Innocent Sleep* 1995; *Talk of Angels* 1998
Nervo, Jimmy *O-Kay for Sound* 1937; *Alf's Button Afloat* 1938; *Gasbags* 1940; *Life Is a Circus* 1958
Nesbitt, Cathleen *The Passing of the Third Floor Back* 1935; *The Lamp Still Burns* 1943; *Fanny by Gaslight* 1944; *Men of Two Worlds* 1946; *So Long at the Fair* 1950; *Desiree* 1954; *Three Coins in the Fountain* 1954; *An Affair to Remember* 1957; *Separate Tables* 1958; *The Parent Trap* 1961; *The Trygon Factor* 1967; *Staircase* 1969; *Villain* 1971; *Family Plot* 1976; *Full Circle* 1977
Nesbitt, Derren *Life in Danger* 1959; *The Man in the Back Seat* 1961; *Strongroom* 1961; *The Informers* 1963; *The Naked Runner* 1967; *Innocent Bystanders* 1972; *Not Now Darling* 1972; *Ooh... You Are Awful* 1972; *Give Us Tomorrow* 1978; *Double X: the Name of the Game* 1991
Nesbitt, James *Hear My Song* 1991; *Go Now* 1995; *Resurrection Man* 1997; *Welcome to Sarajevo* 1997; *Waking Ned* 1998
Nettleton, John *And Soon the Darkness* 1970; *Black Beauty* 1971; *Burning Secret* 1988
Nettleton, Lois *Come Fly with Me* 1962; *Period of Adjustment* 1962; *Mail Order Bride* 1964; *Valley of Mystery* 1967; *The Good Guys and the Bad Guys* 1969; *Dirty Dingus Magee* 1970; *The Sidelong Glances of a Pigeon Kicker* 1970; *The Honkers* 1971; *Terror in the Sky* 1971; *The Man in the Glass Booth* 1975; *Echoes of a Summer* 1976; *Deadly Blessing* 1981; *The Best Little Whorehouse in Texas* 1982; *Butterfly* 1982; *Manhunt for Claude Dallas* 1986
Neufeld, Martin *Highlander III: the Sorcerer* 1995; *Relative Fear* 1995
Neuwirth, Bebe *Say Anything* 1989; *Green Card* 1990; *Without Her Consent* 1990; *Bugsy* 1991; *Painted Heart* 1992; *Malice* 1993; *Jumanji* 1995; *The Adventures of Pinocchio* 1996; *The Associate* 1996; *All Dogs Go to Heaven 2* 1996; *Celebrity* 1998
Neve, Suzanne *Mosquito Squadron* 1968; *Scrooge* 1970
Neville, John *Oscar Wilde* 1959; *Mr Topaze* 1961; *Billy Budd* 1962; *A Study in Terror* 1965; *The Adventures of Gerard* 1970; *The Adventures of Baron Munchausen* 1988; *Journey to the Center of the Earth* 1993; *The Road to Wellville* 1994; *Swann* 1996; *Sabotage* 1996; *Regeneration* 1997; *The X Files* 1998; *Johnny 2.0* 1998
Neville, Sophie *Swallows and Amazons* 1974; *The Copter Kids* 1976
Nevin, Robyn *The Fourth Wish* 1976; *The Irishman* 1978; *Careful, He Might Hear You* 1983; *The Gold and Glory* 1984; *Paperback Romance* 1994
Nevins, Claudette *The Mask* 1961; *Tuff Turf* 1984; *Dead Silence* 1991; *Sleeping with the Enemy* 1991
Newark, Derek *City under the Sea* 1965; *Dad's Army* 1971; *The Offence* 1972; *Diamonds on Wheels* 1973; *Bellman & True* 1987
Newbern, George *Switching Channels* 1987; *Father of the Bride* 1991; *Doppelganger* 1993; *Judith Krantz's Torch Song* 1993; *I Spy Returns* 1994; *Father of the Bride Part II* 1995; *Theodore Rex* 1995; *The Evening Star* 1996; *Twice Upon a Time* 1998; *The Simple Life of Noah Dearborn* 1999
Newell, Patrick *Go for a Take* 1972; *Man about the House* 1974
Newhart, Bob *Hell Is for Heroes* 1962; *Hot Millions* 1968; *Cold Turkey* 1969; *Catch-22* 1970; *On a Clear Day You Can See Forever* 1970; *Thursday's Game* 1971; *The Rescuers* 1977; *Little Miss Marker* 1980; *First Family* 1980; *The Rescuers Down Under* 1990
Newlands, Anthony *Solo for Sparrow* 1962; *Kaleidoscope* 1966; *Circus of Fear* 1967; *Scream and Scream Again* 1969
Newley, Anthony *Vice Versa* 1947; *Oliver Twist* 1948; *A Boy, a Girl and a Bike* 1949; *Don't Ever Leave Me* 1949; *Above Us the Waves* 1955; *The Blue Peter* 1955; *The Cockleshell Heroes* 1955; *The Good Companions* 1956; *Fire Down Below* 1957; *High Flight* 1957; *How to Murder a Rich Uncle* 1957; *No Time to Die* 1958; *The Man Inside* 1958; *The Bandit of Zhobe* 1959; *Killers of Kilimanjaro* 1960; *Let's Get Married* 1960; *The Small World of Sammy Lee* 1963; *Doctor Dolittle* 1967; *Sweet November* 1968; *Can Heironymus Merkin Ever Forget Mercy Humppe and Find True Happiness?* 1969; *Mister Quilp* 1975; *Outrage!* 1986; *The Garbage Pail Kids Movie* 1987; *Coins in the Fountain* 1990
Newman, Barry *Pretty Boy Floyd* 1960; *The Lawyer* 1969; *Vanishing Point* 1971; *Fear Is the Key* 1972; *The Salzburg Connection* 1972; *Sex and the Married Woman* 1977; *City on Fire* 1979; *Amy* 1981; *My Two Loves* 1986; *The Limey* 1999; *Bowfinger* 1999
Newman, Laraine *Tunnelvision* 1976; *American Hot Wax* 1977; *Wholly Moses!* 1980; *Her Life as a Man* 1984; *Perfect* 1985; *This Wife for Hire* 1985; *Invaders from Mars* 1986; *Problem Child 2* 1991; *Coneheads* 1993; *Witchboard 2: The Devil's Doorway* 1993; *Radiant City* 1996
Newman, Nanette *Faces in the Dark* 1960; *House of Mystery* 1961; *The Painted Smile* 1961; *Pit of Darkness* 1961; *The Wrong Arm of the Law* 1962; *Of Human Bondage* 1964; *Seance on a Wet Afternoon* 1964; *The Wrong Box* 1966; *The Whisperers* 1967; *Deadfall* 1968; *Captain Nemo and the Underwater City* 1969; *The Raging Moon* 1970; *The Stepford Wives* 1975; *International Velvet* 1978; *Restless Natives* 1985; *The Mystery of Edwin Drood* 1993
Newman, Paul *The Silver Chalice* 1954; *Somebody Up There Likes Me* 1956; *The Rack* 1956; *The Helen Morgan Story* 1957; *Until They Sail* 1957; *Cat on a Hot Tin Roof* 1958; *The Left Handed Gun* 1958; *The Long Hot Summer* 1958; *Rally 'round the Flag, Boys!* 1958; *The Young Philadelphians* 1959; *Exodus* 1960; *From the Terrace* 1960; *The Hustler* 1961; *Paris Blues* 1961; *Hemingway's Adventures of a Young Man* 1962; *Sweet Bird of Youth* 1962; *Hud* 1963; *A New Kind of Love* 1963; *The Prize* 1963; *The Outrage* 1964; *What a Way to Go!* 1964; *Lady L* 1965; *The Moving Target* 1966; *Torn Curtain* 1966; *Cool Hand Luke* 1967; *Hombre* 1967; *The Secret War of Harry Frigg* 1967; *Butch Cassidy and the Sundance Kid* 1969; *Winning* 1969; *WUSA* 1970; *King: a Filmed Record... Montgomery to Memphis* 1970; *Never Give an Inch* 1971; *The Life and Times of Judge Roy Bean* 1972; *Pocket Money* 1972; *The Mackintosh Man* 1973; *The Sting* 1973; *The Towering Inferno* 1974; *The Drowning Pool* 1975; *Buffalo Bill and the Indians, or Sitting Bull's History Lesson* 1976; *Slap Shot* 1977; *Quintet* 1979; *When Time Ran Out* 1980; *Absence of Malice* 1981; *Fort Apache, the Bronx* 1981; *The Verdict* 1982; *Harry and Son* 1984; *The Color of Money* 1986; *Blaze* 1989; *Shadow Makers* 1989; *Mr and Mrs Bridge* 1990; *The Hudsucker Proxy* 1994; *Nobody's Fool* 1994; *Message in a Bottle* 1998; *Twilight* 1998
Newman, Phyllis *Bye Bye Braverman* 1968; *The Beautician and the Beast* 1997
Newmar, Julie *Li'l Abner* 1959; *The Marriage-Go-Round* 1960; *For Love or Money* 1963; *The Maltese Bippy* 1969; *Dance Academy* 1988; *Ghosts Can't Do It* 1990; *Oblivion* 1993
Newmarch, Johannah *Miles from Nowhere* 1992; *Just One of the Girls* 1993
Newsom, David *Trouble Shooters: Trapped beneath the Earth* 1993; *Sweet Dreams* 1996
Newton, Robert *The Green Cockatoo* 1937; *The Squeaker* 1937; *21 Days* 1937; *Vessel of Wrath* 1938; *Jamaica Inn* 1939; *Poison Pen* 1939; *Busman's Honeymoon* 1940; *Gaslight* 1940; *Hatter's Castle* 1941; *Major Barbara* 1941; *They Flew Alone* 1941; *Henry V* 1944; *This Happy Breed* 1944; *Night Boat to Dublin* 1946; *Odd Man Out* 1946; *Blood on My Hands* 1948; *Obsession* 1948; *Oliver Twist* 1948; *Snowbound* 1948; *Waterfront* 1950; *Treasure Island* 1950; *Soldiers Three* 1951; *Tom Brown's Schooldays* 1951; *Androcles and the Lion* 1952; *Blackbeard the Pirate* 1952; *Les Misérables* 1952; *The Desert Rats* 1953; *The Beachcomber* 1954; *The High and the Mighty* 1954; *Around the World in 80 Days* 1956
Newton, Thandie *Flirting* 1989; *The Young Americans* 1993; *Loaded* 1994; *Jefferson in Paris* 1995; *The Journey of August King* 1995; *Gridlock'd* 1996; *The Leading Man* 1996; *Beloved* 1998; *Besieged* 1998; *Mission: Impossible 2* 1999
Newton, Theodore *Ace of Aces* 1933; *The Sphinx* 1933; *Upper World* 1934; *The Come On* 1956
Newton, Wayne *Eighty Steps to Jonah* 1969; *Licence to Kill* 1989; *The Adventures of Ford Fairlane* 1990; *The Dark Backward* 1991; *Best of the Best II* 1992; *Vegas Vacation* 1997
Newton-John, Olivia *Grease* 1978; *Xanadu* 1980; *Two of a Kind* 1983; *A Mom for Christmas* 1990; *A Christmas Romance* 1994; *It's My Party* 1996
Ney, Marie *Scrooge* 1935; *Night Was Our Friend* 1951; *Simba* 1955
Ney, Richard *Mrs Miniver* 1942; *The War against Mrs Hadley* 1942; *Ivy* 1947; *The Late George Apley* 1947; *The Lovable Cheat* 1949; *The Premature Burial* 1962
Neyland, Anne *Jailhouse Rock* 1957; *Motorcycle Gang* 1957; *Hidden Fear* 1957
Ng, Carrie *City on Fire* 1987; *Rock'n'Roll Cop* 1994
Ng, Irene *Night Watch* 1995; *Hard Men* 1996; *Rogue Trader* 1998
Ngor, Haing S aka **Ngor, Dr Haing S** *The Killing Fields* 1984; *In Love and War* 1987; *The Iron Triangle* 1988; *Ambition* 1991; *Heaven and Earth* 1993; *My Life* 1993
Nguyen, Dustin *No Escape, No Return* 1994; *3 Ninjas Kick Back* 1994; *The Doom Generation* 1995
Niblo, Fred *Free and Easy* 1930; *Ellery Queen Master Detective* 1940
Nicastro, Michelle *Bad Guys* 1986; *The Swan Princess* 1994; *The Swan Princess: The Secret of the Castle* 1997
Nichetti, Maurizio *The Icicle Thief* 1989; *Volere, Volare* 1991
Nicholas, Denise aka **Nicholas-Hill, Denise** *Blacula* 1972; *Let's Do It Again* 1975; *A Piece of the Action* 1977; *Marvin and Tige* 1983; *Ghost Dad* 1990
Nicholas, Paul *Blind Terror* 1971; *Stardust* 1974; *Lisztomania* 1975;

RadioTimes ACTORS' INDEX

Nono, Clare *Fire and Ice* 1983; *Nightmares* 1983
Nonyela, Valentine *Young Soul Rebels* 1991; *Welcome II the Terrordome* 1994
Noonan, Tom *Gloria* 1980; *Wolfen* 1981; *Eddie Macon's Run* 1983; *Manhunter* 1986; *Collision Course* 1987; *The Monster Squad* 1987; *RoboCop 2* 1990; *The 10 Million Dollar Getaway* 1991; *Last Action Hero* 1993; *What Happened Was...* 1994; *Phoenix* 1998
Noonan, Tommy *Gentlemen Prefer Blondes* 1953; *A Star Is Born* 1954; *How to Be Very, Very Popular* 1955; *Violent Saturday* 1955; *The Ambassador's Daughter* 1956; *The Best Things in Life Are Free* 1956; *Bundle of Joy* 1956; *The Girl Most Likely* 1957
Noone, Kathleen *Serpent's Lair* 1995; *What Love Sees* 1996
Norby, Ghita *Waltzing Regitze* 1989; *Best Intentions* 1992; *Sofie* 1992; *The Kingdom* 1994; *Hamsun* 1996
Norden, Christine *An Ideal Husband* 1947; *Mine Own Executioner* 1947; *Night Beat* 1948; *The Interrupted Journey* 1949; *A Case for PC 49* 1950
Nordling, Jeffrey *Black Death* 1992; *Ruby* 1992; *Journey to the Center of the Earth* 1993; *Baby Brokers* 1994; *Dangerous Heart* 1994; *Someone She Knows* 1994; *A Stranger in Town* 1995; *D3: the Mighty Ducks* 1996; *Danielle Steel's Remembrance* 1996; *Anne Tyler's Saint Maybe* 1998
Norgaard, Carsten *D2: the Mighty Ducks* 1994; *Out of Annie's Past* 1995
Noriega, Eduardo *Captain Scarlett* 1953; *Hell's Island* 1955; *Seven Cities of Gold* 1955; *The Magnificent Matador* 1955; *The Far Horizons* 1955; *The Beast of Hollow Mountain* 1956; *Daniel Boone, Trail Blazer* 1957; *Of Love and Desire* 1963; *Tarzan and the Valley of Gold* 1966; *Open Your Eyes* 1997; *Cha-Cha-Cha* 1998
Norman, Lucille *Painting the Clouds with Sunshine* 1951; *Carson City* 1952
Norman, Maidie *The Well* 1951; *Bright Road* 1953; *What Ever Happened to Baby Jane?* 1962
Norman, Susan *The Tower* 1992; *Safe* 1995
Norman, Zack *Sitting Ducks* 1979; *Romancing the Stone* 1984; *America* 1986; *Cadillac Man* 1990; *Babyfever* 1994
Noro, Line *Pépé le Moko* 1937; *J'Accuse* 1938; *La Symphonie Pastorale* 1946
Norris, Chuck *The Wrecking Crew* 1969; *The Way of the Dragon* 1973; *Return of the Dragon* 1973; *Good Guys Wear Black* 1977; *A Force of One* 1979; *The Octagon* 1980; *An Eye for an Eye* 1981; *Forced Vengeance* 1982; *Silent Rage* 1982; *Lone Wolf McQuade* 1983; *Missing in Action* 1984; *Code of Silence* 1985; *Invasion USA* 1985; *Missing in Action 2: the Beginning* 1985; *The Delta Force* 1986; *Firewalker* 1986; *Hero and the Terror* 1988; *Delta Force 2* 1990; *The Hitman* 1991; *Hellbound* 1993; *Sidekicks* 1993; *Deadly Reunion* 1994; *Top Dog* 1995; *Walker: Texas Ranger* 1997
Norris, Dean *Hard to Kill* 1989; *The Lawnmower Man* 1992; *The Last Seduction* 1993; *Forgotten Sins* 1996
Norris, Edward *They Won't Forget* 1937; *Boys Town* 1938; *Frontier Marshal* 1939; *The Singing Sheriff* 1944
North, Alan *Trackdown: Finding the Goodbar Killer* 1983; *Billy Galvin* 1986; *The Christmas Star* 1986; *Highlander* 1986; *Rachel River* 1987; *Blood Money* 1988; *Lean on Me* 1989; *See No Evil, Hear No Evil* 1989; *Crazy People* 1990; *The Jerky Boys* 1995
North, Sheree *Living It Up* 1954; *How to Be Very, Very Popular* 1955; *The Best Things in Life Are Free* 1956; *The Lieutenant Wore Skirts* 1956; *The Way to the Gold* 1957; *No Down Payment* 1957; *In Love and War* 1958; *Mardi Gras* 1958; *Madigan* 1968; *The Gypsy Moths* 1969; *The Trouble with Girls* 1969; *Lawman* 1971; *The Organization* 1971; *Charley Varrick* 1973; *The Outfit* 1973; *Breakout* 1975; *The Night They Took Miss Beautiful* 1977; *Telefon* 1977; *Legs* 1983; *Scorned and Swindled* 1984; *Cold Dog Soup* 1989; *Dead on the Money* 1991
North, Ted *Chad Hanna* 1940; *Charlie Chan in Rio* 1941; *Syncopation* 1942; *The Devil Thumbs a Ride* 1947
North, Virginia *The Long Duel* 1966; *The Abominable Dr Phibes* 1971
Northam, Jeremy *Soft Top, Hard Shoulder* 1992; *Wuthering Heights* 1992; *Carrington* 1995; *The Net* 1995; *Emma* 1996; *Amistad* 1997; *Mimic* 1997; *Gloria* 1998; *The Misadventures of Margaret* 1998; *An Ideal Husband* 1999; *Happy, Texas* 1999; *The Winslow Boy* 1999
Northup, Harry *Over the Edge* 1979; *Kansas* 1988
Norton, Alex *Gregory's Girl* 1980; *Comfort and Joy* 1984; *Every Picture Tells a Story* 1984; *Comrades: a Lanternist's Account of the Tolpuddle Martyrs and What Became of Them* 1986; *Hidden City* 1987; *Robin Hood* 1990; *Orphans* 1998
Norton, Barry *Dishonored* 1931; *Lady for a Day* 1933
Norton, Dee Dee *Dakota* 1987; *Confessions of a Serial Killer* 1987
Norton, Edgar *The Love Parade* 1929; *One Romantic Night* 1930; *Dr Jekyll and Mr Hyde* 1932
Norton, Edward *Everyone Says I Love You* 1996; *The People vs Larry Flynt* 1996; *Primal Fear* 1996; *American History X* 1998; *Rounders* 1998; *Fight Club* 1999; *Keeping the Faith* 2000
Norton, Jim *Straw Dogs* 1971; *Adolf Hitler – My Part in His Downfall* 1972; *Cry of the Innocent* 1980; *Hidden Agenda* 1990; *Memoirs of an Invisible Man* 1992; *Sunset Heights* 1996
Norton, Ken *Mandingo* 1975; *Drum* 1976; *Oceans of Fire* 1986
Norton, Richard *Gymkata* 1985; *China O'Brien* 1988; *Rage and Honor* 1992; *Mr Nice Guy* 1996
Norton-Taylor, Judy *aka* **Norton, Judy** *A Day for Thanks on Waltons Mountain* 1982; *Mother's Day on Waltons Mountain* 1982; *A Walton Thanksgiving Reunion* 1993; *A Walton Wedding* 1995; *A Walton Easter* 1997
Noseworthy, Jack *A Place for Annie* 1994; *Barb Wire* 1995; *Mojave Moon* 1996; *Breakdown* 1997; *Idle Hands* 1999; *What We Did That Night* 1999
Noth, Christopher *aka* **Noth, Chris** *With Harmful Intent* 1993; *Fugitive from Justice* 1996; *Born Free: A New Adventure* 1996; *Cold Heart* 1997
Nouri, Michael *Flashdance* 1983; *The Imagemaker* 1986; *GoBots: Battle of the Rocklords* 1986; *The Hidden* 1987; *Quiet Victory: the Charlie Wedemeyer Story* 1988; *Shattered Dreams* 1990; *Project: Alien* 1990; *Little Vegas* 1990; *Changes* 1991; *Exclusive* 1992; *In the Arms of a Killer* 1992; *A Passion for Murder* 1992; *American Yakuza* 1994; *The Hidden II* 1994; *Hollywood Madam* 1994; *No Escape, No Return* 1994; *Visions of Terror* 1994; *Between Love and Honor* 1995
Nourse, Allen *Pushover* 1954; *Tight Spot* 1955
Novak, Kim *Phffft!* 1954; *Pushover* 1954; *Five against the House* 1955; *The Man with the Golden Arm* 1955; *Picnic* 1955; *Son of Sinbad* 1955; *The Eddy Duchin Story* 1956; *Pal Joey* 1957; *Jeanne Eagels* 1957; *Bell, Book and Candle* 1958; *Vertigo* 1958; *Middle of the Night* 1959; *Strangers When We Meet* 1960; *Pepe* 1960; *Boys' Night Out* 1962; *The Notorious Landlady* 1962; *Kiss Me, Stupid* 1964; *Of Human Bondage* 1964; *The Amorous Adventures of Moll Flanders* 1965; *The Legend of Lylah Clare* 1968; *The Great Bank Robbery* 1969; *Tales That Witness Madness* 1973; *The White Buffalo* 1977; *Just a Gigolo* 1978; *The Mirror Crack'd* 1980; *The Children* 1990; *Liebestraum* 1991
Novarro, Ramon *aka* **Samaniegos, Ramon** *The Prisoner of Zenda* 1922; *The Arab* 1924; *Ben-Hur: a Tale of Christ* 1925; *The Student Prince in Old Heidelberg* 1927; *Daybreak* 1931; *Mata Hari* 1931; *The Barbarian* 1933; *The Cat and the Fiddle* 1934; *The Big Steal* 1949; *We Were Strangers* 1949; *Crisis* 1950; *The Outriders* 1950; *Heller in Pink Tights* 1960
Novello, Don *Head Office* 1986; *One Night Stand* 1994; *Before the Night* 1995
Novello, Ivor *The Lodger* 1926; *The Constant Nymph* 1928
Novello, Jay *Blood on My Hands* 1948; *The Miracle of Fatima* 1952; *The Diamond Queen* 1953; *The City Is Dark* 1954; *Bengazi* 1955; *Son of Sinbad* 1955; *Lisbon* 1956; *The Pride and the Passion* 1957; *The Perfect Furlough* 1958; *The Lost World* 1960; *This Rebel Breed* 1960; *Harem Holiday* 1965
Novo, Nancho *The Red Squirrel* 1993; *Tierra* 1995; *The Lovers of the Arctic Circle* 1998
Novotna, Jarmila *The Search* 1948; *The Great Caruso* 1951
Nowicki, Jan *Diary for My Children* 1982; *Diary for My Loves* 1987; *Diary for My Father and Mother* 1990
Nowicki, Tom *Somebody Has to Shoot the Picture* 1990; *Stolen Babies* 1993
Noy, Zachi *Lemon Popsicle* 1978; *Enter the Ninja* 1981
Nozick, Bruce *Hit the Dutchman* 1992; *And the Beat Goes On: the Sonny and Cher Story* 1999
Ntshona, Winston *The Wild Geese* 1978; *A Dry White Season* 1989; *The Air up There* 1993; *Tarzan and the Lost City* 1998
Nucci, Danny *Rescue Me* 1991; *Roosters* 1993; *Blind Justice* 1994; *Homage* 1995; *The Big Squeeze* 1996; *Eraser* 1996; *That Old Feeling* 1997
Nugent, Edward *aka* **Nugent, Eddie** *Our Dancing Daughters* 1928; *Our Modern Maidens* 1929; *Night Nurse* 1931; *This Day and Age* 1933; *She Loves Me Not* 1934
Nugent, Elliott *Romance* 1930; *The Unholy Three* 1930; *The Last Flight* 1931
Nunez Jr, Miguel A *aka* **Nunez, Miguel A** *Return of the Living Dead* 1985; *Shadowzone* 1990; *Vegas Vice* 1994; *Why Do Fools Fall in Love?* 1998
Nunn, Bill *School Daze* 1988; *Do the Right Thing* 1989; *Def by Temptation* 1990; *New Jack City* 1991; *Regarding Henry* 1991; *White Lie* 1991; *Sister Act* 1992; *The Last Seduction* 1993; *Mr and Mrs Loving* 1993; *Blood Brothers* 1994; *Save Me* 1994; *Canadian Bacon* 1995; *Candyman II: Farewell to the Flesh* 1995; *Things to Do in Denver When You're Dead* 1995; *The Affair* 1995; *Extreme Measures* 1996; *Kiss the Girls* 1997; *Quicksilver Highway* 1997; *Always Outnumbered* 1998; *Ambushed* 1998; *He Got Game* 1998; *The Legend of 1900* 1999
Nunn, Larry *Strike Up the Band* 1940; *Men of Boys Town* 1941
Nureyev, Rudolf *Romeo and Juliet* 1966; *Don Quixote* 1973; *Valentino* 1977; *Exposed* 1983
Nurmi, Maila *aka* **Vampira** *The Beat Generation* 1959; *Night of the Ghouls* 1960; *Sex Kittens Go to College* 1960
Nussbaum, Danny *TwentyFourSeven* 1997; *One More Kiss* 1999
Nussbaum, Mike *House of Games* 1987; *Things Change* 1988; *Desperate Hours* 1990; *Overexposed* 1992; *The Water Engine* 1992; *Shadow of a Doubt* 1995
Nuttall, Jeff *Robin Hood* 1990; *The Baby of Macon* 1993; *Captives* 1994
Nutter, Tarah *Chilly Scenes of Winter* 1979; *Without Warning* 1980
Nuyen, France *In Love and War* 1958; *South Pacific* 1958; *The Last Time I Saw Archie* 1961; *Diamond Head* 1962; *A Girl Named Tamiko* 1962; *Satan Never Sleeps* 1962; *The Man in the Middle* 1964; *One More Train to Rob* 1971; *China Cry* 1990; *The Joy Luck Club* 1993
Nye, Carrie *The Seduction of Joe Tynan* 1979; *Too Scared to Scream* 1982
Nye, Louis *The Facts of Life* 1960; *Sex Kittens Go to College* 1960; *The Last Time I Saw Archie* 1961; *The Stripper* 1963; *Who's Been Sleeping in My Bed?* 1963; *Harper Valley P.T.A.* 1978; *Full Moon High* 1982
Nyman, Lena *I Am Curious – Yellow* 1967; *Autumn Sonata* 1978

O

Oakie, Jack *Paramount on Parade* 1930; *If I Had a Million* 1932; *Million Dollar Legs* 1932; *The Eagle and the Hawk* 1933; *Sitting Pretty* 1933; *Murder at the Vanities* 1934; *The Big Broadcast of 1936* 1935; *The Call of the Wild* 1935; *Colleen* 1936; *King of Burlesque* 1936; *The Texas Rangers* 1936; *Super-Sleuth* 1937; *The Toast of New York* 1937; *The Affairs of Annabel* 1938; *Annabel Takes a Tour* 1938; *Radio City Revels* 1938; *Thanks for Everything* 1938; *The Great Dictator* 1940; *Tin Pan Alley* 1940; *The Great American Broadcast* 1941; *Song of the Islands* 1942; *Hello, Frisco, Hello* 1943; *Wintertime* 1943; *It Happened Tomorrow* 1944; *Sweet and Lowdown* 1944; *Northwest Stampede* 1948; *When My Baby Smiles at Me* 1948; *Thieves' Highway* 1949; *The Wonderful Country* 1959; *The Rat Race* 1960; *Lover Come Back* 1961
Oakland, Simon *I Want to Live!* 1958; *Murder, Inc* 1960; *Psycho* 1960; *The Rise and Fall of Legs Diamond* 1960; *Tony Rome* 1967; *Bullitt* 1968; *Chubasco* 1968; *On a Clear Day You Can See Forever* 1970; *The Hunting Party* 1971; *The Night Stalker* 1971; *Scandalous John* 1971; *Chato's Land* 1972; *Emperor of the North* 1973; *The Night Strangler* 1973; *Happy Mother's Day... Love, George* 1973
Oakman, Wheeler *Lights of New York* 1928; *Aces and Eights* 1936
Oates, Warren *Yellowstone Kelly* 1959; *The Rise and Fall of Legs Diamond* 1960; *Ride the High Country* 1962; *Hero's Island* 1962; *Mail Order Bride* 1964; *Return of the Seven* 1966; *In the Heat of the Night* 1967; *The Shooting* 1967; *Welcome to Hard Times* 1967; *The Split* 1968; *Crooks and Coronets* 1969; *The Wild Bunch* 1969; *Smith!* 1969; *Barquero* 1970; *There Was a Crooked Man...* 1970; *The Hired Hand* 1971; *Kid Blue* 1971; *Two-Lane Blacktop* 1971; *Badlands* 1973; *Dillinger* 1973; *The Thief Who Came to Dinner* 1973; *Tom Sawyer* 1973; *Bring Me the Head of Alfredo Garcia* 1974; *The White Dawn* 1974; *92 in the Shade* 1975; *Race with the Devil* 1975; *Drum* 1976; *Dixie Dynamite* 1976; *The Brink's Job* 1978; *China 9, Liberty 37* 1978; *And Baby Makes Six* 1979; *1941* 1979; *The Border* 1981; *Stripes* 1981; *Tough Enough* 1982; *Blue Thunder* 1983
Obata, Toshishiro *Teenage Mutant Ninja Turtles II: the Secret of the Ooze* 1991; *Showdown in Little Tokyo* 1991
Ober, Philip *The Magnificent Yankee* 1950; *Never a Dull Moment* 1950; *Come Back, Little Sheba* 1952; *The Clown* 1952; *From Here to Eternity* 1953; *Scandal at Scourie* 1953; *Ten North Frederick* 1958; *Torpedo Run* 1958; *The High Cost of Loving* 1958; *Beloved Infidel* 1959; *North by Northwest* 1959; *The Facts of Life* 1960; *Go Naked in the World* 1961; *The Brass Bottle* 1964; *The Ghost and Mr Chicken* 1966
Oberman, Claire *Goodbye Pork Pie* 1981; *The Beautiful End of This World* 1983

Celine and Julie Go Boating 1974; *Maîtresse* 1976; *The Third Generation* 1979; *Les Tricheurs* 1984; *Candy Mountain* 1987; *See How They Fall* 1993; *Don't Forget You're Going to Die* 1995; *Venus Beauty* 1998; *Shattered Image* 1998

Ogilvy, Ian *The She Beast* 1965; *The Sorcerers* 1967; *Stranger in the House* 1967; *The Day the Fish Came Out* 1967; *Witchfinder General* 1968; *The Heroes* 1968; *And Now the Screaming Starts!* 1973; *From beyond the Grave* 1973; *No Sex Please, We're British* 1973; *Anna Karenina* 1985; *Death Becomes Her* 1992; *The Disappearance of Kevin Johnson* 1995

Ogle, Charles *Rebecca of Sunnybrook Farm* 1917; *A Romance of the Redwoods* 1917; *The Covered Wagon* 1923; *Ruggles of Red Gap* 1923

O'Gorman, Dean *The Rogue Stallion* 1990; *Young Hercules* 1998

O'Grady, Gail *She Stood Alone: the Tailhook Scandal* 1995; *Trial by Fire* 1995; *Celtic Pride* 1996; *That Old Feeling* 1997; *The Three Lives of Karen* 1997; *Deuce Bigalow: Male Gigolo* 1999

Oh, Soon-Teck aka **Oh, Soon Taik**, aka **Oh, Soon-Tek** *One More Train to Rob* 1971; *The Man with the Golden Gun* 1974; *Death Ride to Osaka* 1983; *Missing in Action 2: the Beginning* 1985; *Death Wish 4: the Crackdown* 1987; *The Red Spider* 1988; *Soursweet* 1988; *A Home of Our Own* 1993; *Beverly Hills Ninja* 1997

O'Halloran, Jack *Farewell, My Lovely* 1975; *March or Die* 1977; *The Baltimore Bullet* 1980; *Superman II* 1980; *Dragnet* 1987; *Hero and the Terror* 1988

Ohana, Claudia *Erendira* 1982; *Opera do Malandro* 1986

O'Hanlon, George *The Counterfeiters* 1948; *Park Row* 1952; *Kronos* 1957; *Jetsons: the Movie* 1990

O'Hara, Catherine *Heartburn* 1986; *Beetle Juice* 1988; *Betsy's Wedding* 1990; *Home Alone* 1990; *Little Vegas* 1990; *Home Alone 2: Lost in New York* 1992; *Paydirt* 1992; *Tim Burton's The Nightmare before Christmas* 1993; *The Paper* 1994; *A Simple Twist of Fate* 1994; *Tall Tale: the Unbelievable Adventures of Pecos Bill* 1994; *Wyatt Earp* 1994; *Last of the High Kings* 1996; *Waiting for Guffman* 1996; *Pippi Longstocking* 1997; *Hope* 1997; *Home Fries* 1998

O'Hara, David *Link* 1986; *The Bridge* 1990; *Braveheart* 1995; *The Near Room* 1995; *Some Mother's Son* 1996; *The Devil's Own* 1997; *Janice Beard 45 WPM* 1999

O'Hara, Jenny *The Secret Life of Kathy McCormick* 1988; *Winnie* 1988; *Career Opportunities* 1991; *Angie* 1994

O'Hara, Maureen *The Hunchback of Notre Dame* 1939; *Jamaica Inn* 1939; *A Bill of Divorcement* 1940; *Dance, Girl, Dance* 1940; *How Green Was My Valley* 1941; *The Black Swan* 1942; *Ten Gentlemen from West Point* 1942; *To the Shores of Tripoli* 1942; *The Fallen Sparrow* 1943; *The Immortal Sergeant* 1943; *This Land Is Mine* 1943; *Buffalo Bill* 1944; *The Spanish Main* 1945; *Do You Love Me?* 1946; *Sentimental Journey* 1946; *The Foxes of Harrow* 1947; *Miracle on 34th Street* 1947; *Sinbad the Sailor* 1947; *Sitting Pretty* 1948; *Father Was a Fullback* 1949; *Britannia Mews* 1949; *A Woman's Secret* 1949; *Comanche Territory* 1950; *Rio Grande* 1950; *Sons of the Musketeers* 1951; *Against All Flags* 1952; *The Quiet Man* 1952; *Kangaroo* 1952; *The Redhead from Wyoming* 1953; *War Arrow* 1953; *Malaga* 1954; *The Long Gray Line* 1955; *The Magnificent Matador* 1955; *Lady Godiva* 1955; *Lisbon* 1956; *The Wings of Eagles* 1957; *Our Man in Havana* 1959; *The Deadly Companions* 1961; *The Parent Trap* 1961; *Mr Hobbs Takes a Vacation* 1962; *McLintock!* 1963; *Spencer's Mountain* 1963; *The Battle of the Villa Fiorita* 1964; *The Rare Breed* 1966; *How Do I Love Thee?* 1970; *Big Jake* 1971; *Only the Lonely* 1991; *The Christmas Box* 1995

O'Hara, Paige *Beauty and the Beast* 1991; *Beauty and the Beast: the Enchanted Christmas* 1997

O'Herlihy, Dan aka **O'Herlihy, Daniel** *Kidnapped* 1948; *Macbeth* 1948; *Soldiers Three* 1951; *Sons of the Musketeers* 1951; *Actors and Sin* 1952; *The Adventures of Robinson Crusoe* 1952; *Invasion USA* 1952; *Bengal Brigade* 1954; *The Black Shield of Falworth* 1954; *The Virgin Queen* 1955; *The Purple Mask* 1955; *That Woman Opposite* 1957; *Home before Dark* 1958; *Imitation of Life* 1959; *The Young Land* 1959; *One Foot in Hell* 1960; *A Terrible Beauty* 1960; *King of the Roaring 20s – the Story of Arnold Rothstein* 1961; *The Cabinet of Caligari* 1962; *Fail-Safe* 1964; *100 Rifles* 1969; *The Big Cube* 1969; *Waterloo* 1970; *The Carey Treatment* 1972; *The Tamarind Seed* 1974; *MacArthur* 1977; *Halloween III: Season of the Witch* 1982; *The Last Starfighter* 1984; *The Dead* 1987; *RoboCop* 1987; *RoboCop 2* 1990; *Love, Cheat & Steal* 1994

O'Herlihy, Gavan *Death Wish 3* 1985; *Willow* 1988; *Red King, White Knight* 1989; *Conagher* 1991; *The Shooter* 1994

Ohmart, Carol *House on Haunted Hill* 1958; *Born Reckless* 1959; *One Man's Way* 1964

Ojeda, Manuel *Eagle's Wing* 1978; *Romancing the Stone* 1984

Okada, Eiji *Hiroshima, Mon Amour* 1959; *Woman in the Dunes* 1963; *The Ugly American* 1963

Okada, Mariko *Late Autumn* 1960; *An Autumn Afternoon* 1962

Okawa, Henry *The Wind Cannot Read* 1958; *One of Those Things* 1970

O'Keefe, Dennis aka **Flanagan, Bud** *A Fire Has Been Arranged* 1935; *O-Kay for Sound* 1937; *Alf's Button Afloat* 1938; *Bad Man of Brimstone* 1938; *That's Right – You're Wrong* 1939; *Arise, My Love* 1940; *Gasbags* 1940; *You'll Find Out* 1940; *Broadway Limited* 1941; *Topper Returns* 1941; *Hangmen Also Die* 1943; *The Leopard Man* 1943; *Abroad with Two Yanks* 1944; *Dreaming* 1944; *The Fighting Seabees* 1944; *Sensations* 1944; *The Story of Dr Wassell* 1944; *Up in Mabel's Room* 1944; *The Affairs of Susan* 1945; *Brewster's Millions* 1945; *Earl Carroll Vanities* 1945; *Getting Gertie's Garter* 1945; *Here Comes the Sun* 1945; *Dishonored Lady* 1947; *T-Men* 1947; *Raw Deal* 1948; *Walk a Crooked Mile* 1948; *The Company She Keeps* 1950; *Everything I Have Is Yours* 1952; *The Lady Wants Mink* 1953; *Angela* 1955; *Las Vegas Shakedown* 1955; *Dragoon Wells Massacre* 1957; *Life Is a Circus* 1958; *All Hands on Deck* 1961

O'Keefe, Jodi Lyn *Halloween H20: 20 Years Later* 1998; *She's All That* 1999

O'Keefe, Michael *The Great Santini* 1979; *Caddyshack* 1980; *Split Image* 1982; *Savage Islands* 1983; *Finders Keepers* 1984; *The Slugger's Wife* 1985; *The Whoopee Boys* 1986; *Ironweed* 1987; *Disaster at Silo 7* 1988; *Bridge to Silence* 1989; *Fear* 1990; *Too Young to Die?* 1990; *Out of the Rain* 1991; *Nina Takes a Lover* 1993; *Terror at Deception Ridge* 1994; *Three Wishes* 1995; *The People Next Door* 1996

O'Keeffe, Miles aka **O'Keefe, Miles** *Tarzan, the Ape Man* 1981; *Sword of the Valiant* 1984; *Waxwork* 1988; *The Drifter* 1988; *Relentless 2: Dead On* 1991; *Sins of the Night* 1993; *Inflammable* 1994; *Silent Hunter* 1995; *Pocahontas: the Legend* 1995; *Marked Man* 1996

O'Kelly, Donal *The Van* 1996; *The Last Bus Home* 1997

Okhlopkov, Nikolai P aka **Okhlopkov, N P** *Lenin in October* 1937; *Alexander Nevsky* 1938

Okking, Jens *The Kingdom* 1994; *The Beast Within* 1995

Okochi, Denjiro *Sanshiro Sugata* 1943; *No Regrets for Our Youth* 1946

Okonedo, Sophie *Young Soul Rebels* 1991; *Ace Ventura: When Nature Calls* 1995; *Go Now* 1995; *This Year's Love* 1999

Okumoto, Yuji *The Karate Kid Part II* 1986; *Aloha Summer* 1988; *Fighting Justice* 1989; *Murder in Paradise* 1990; *Blue Tiger* 1994; *Hard Justice* 1995; *Mean Guns* 1996

Olaf, Pierre *Wild and Wonderful* 1964; *Art of Love* 1965; *Camelot* 1967; *The Gamblers* 1969

Oland, Warner *Don Q, Son of Zorro* 1925; *Riders of the Purple Sage* 1925; *Don Juan* 1926; *The Jazz Singer* 1927; *The Return of Dr Fu Manchu* 1930; *Dishonored* 1931; *Shanghai Express* 1932; *Bulldog Drummond Strikes Back* 1934; *Charlie Chan in London* 1934; *Mandalay* 1934; *The Painted Veil* 1934; *Charlie Chan in Egypt* 1935; *Charlie Chan in Paris* 1935; *Charlie Chan in Shanghai* 1935; *Charlie Chan at the Opera* 1936; *Charlie Chan at the Olympics* 1937; *Charlie Chan on Broadway* 1937

Olandt, Ken *April Fool's Day* 1986; *Leprechaun* 1992; *Digital Man* 1994

Olbrychski, Daniel *Landscape after Battle* 1970; *The Young Ladies of Wilko* 1979; *Les Uns et les Autres* 1981; *Dangerous Moves* 1984; *Rosa Luxemburg* 1986; *The Barber of Siberia* 1999

Oldham, Will *Matewan* 1987; *Everybody's Baby: the Rescue of Jessica McClure* 1989

Oldman, Gary *Sid and Nancy* 1986; *Prick Up Your Ears* 1987; *Criminal Law* 1988; *Track 29* 1988; *We Think the World of You* 1988; *Chattahoochee* 1989; *Rosencrantz and Guildenstern Are Dead* 1990; *State of Grace* 1990; *JFK* 1991; *Bram Stoker's Dracula* 1992; *Romeo Is Bleeding* 1992; *True Romance* 1993; *Immortal Beloved* 1994; *Leon* 1994; *Murder in the First* 1994; *The Scarlet Letter* 1995; *Basquiat* 1996; *Air Force One* 1997; *The Fifth Element* 1997; *Lost in Space* 1997; *The Magic Sword: Quest for Camelot* 1997

Olds, Gabriel *Calendar Girl* 1993; *A Town Has Turned to Dust* 1998

O'Leary, Jack *Inside Moves: the Guys from Max's Bar* 1980; *Death Valley* 1982

O'Leary, William *Nice Girls Don't Explode* 1987; *Bull Durham* 1988; *Hot Shots!* 1991; *In the Line of Duty: Ambush in Waco* 1993; *Candyman II: Farewell to the Flesh* 1995; *Project Alf* 1996

Oleynik, Larisa *The Baby-Sitter's Club* 1995; *10 Things I Hate about You* 1999

Olin, Ken *There Must Be a Pony* 1986; *The Game of Love* 1987; *A Stoning in Fulham County* 1988; *Queens Logic* 1991; *Nothing but the Truth* 1995

Olin, Lena *Fanny and Alexander* 1982; *After the Rehearsal* 1984; *The Unbearable Lightness of Being* 1988; *Enemies, a Love Story* 1989; *Havana* 1990; *Romeo Is Bleeding* 1992; *Mr Jones* 1993; *Night Falls on Manhattan* 1997; *Polish Wedding* 1998; *Hamilton* 1998; *The Ninth Gate* 2000

Olin, Stig *To Joy* 1949; *The Devil's Wanton* 1949

Oliver, Anthony *They Can't Hang Me* 1954; *Lost* 1955; *Danger by My Side* 1962

Oliver, Barret *The NeverEnding Story* 1984; *Cocoon* 1985; *DARYL* 1985; *The Secret Garden* 1987

Oliver, Charles *The Avenging Hand* 1936; *Midnight at Madame Tussaud's* 1936; *The Green Cockatoo* 1937; *Ask a Policeman* 1938; *Sexton Blake and the Hooded Terror* 1938; *Crooks' Tour* 1940; *Under Your Hat* 1940

Oliver, Edna May *The Saturday Night Kid* 1929; *Laugh and Get Rich* 1931; *The Penguin Pool Murder* 1932; *Ann Vickers* 1933; *Little Women* 1933; *Only Yesterday* 1933; *Alice in Wonderland* 1933; *The Last Gentleman* 1934; *Murder on the Blackboard* 1934; *David Copperfield* 1935; *Murder on a Honeymoon* 1935; *A Tale of Two Cities* 1935; *Romeo and Juliet* 1936; *Parnell* 1937; *Rosalie* 1937; *Little Miss Broadway* 1938; *Paradise for Three* 1938; *Drums along the Mohawk* 1939; *Nurse Edith Cavell* 1939; *Second Fiddle* 1939; *The Story of Vernon and Irene Castle* 1939; *Pride and Prejudice* 1940; *Lydia* 1941

Oliver, Gordon *Sweetheart of the Campus* 1941; *The Spiral Staircase* 1946; *Station West* 1948; *The Las Vegas Story* 1951; *My Forbidden Past* 1951

Oliver, Guy *The Covered Wagon* 1923; *The Docks of New York* 1928

Oliver, Michael *Problem Child* 1990; *Problem Child 2* 1991; *Dillinger and Capone* 1995

Oliver, Stephen *Motor Psycho* 1965; *The Naked Zoo* 1970

Oliver, Susan *The Gene Krupa Story* 1959; *The Disorderly Orderly* 1964; *Your Cheatin' Heart* 1964; *A Man Called Gannon* 1969; *Ginger in the Morning* 1973; *Hardly Working* 1981

Oliver, Tom *ABBA The Movie* 1977; *Because He's My Friend* 1978

Oliver, Vic *Hi, Gang!* 1941; *Give Us the Moon* 1944; *I'll Be Your Sweetheart* 1945

Olivier, Laurence *Friends and Lovers* 1931; *Westward Passage* 1932; *Moscow Nights* 1935; *Conquest of the Air* 1936; *As You Like It* 1936; *Fire over England* 1937; *21 Days* 1937; *The Divorce of Lady X* 1938; *Q Planes* 1939; *Wuthering Heights* 1939; *Pride and Prejudice* 1940; *Rebecca* 1940; *49th Parallel* 1941; *That Hamilton Woman* 1941; *The Demi-Paradise* 1943; *Henry V* 1944; *This Happy Breed* 1944; *Hamlet* 1948; *The Magic Box* 1951; *Carrie* 1952; *The Beggar's Opera* 1953; *Richard III* 1955; *The Prince and the Showgirl* 1957; *The Devil's Disciple* 1959; *The Entertainer* 1960; *Spartacus* 1960; *Term of Trial* 1962; *Bunny Lake Is Missing* 1965; *Othello* 1965; *Khartoum* 1966; *Romeo and Juliet* 1968; *The Shoes of the Fisherman* 1968; *Battle of Britain* 1969; *David Copperfield* 1969; *Oh! What a Lovely War* 1969; *The Dance of Death* 1969; *Three Sisters* 1970; *Lady Caroline Lamb* 1972; *Sleuth* 1972; *Love among the Ruins* 1975; *Marathon Man* 1976; *The Seven-Per-Cent Solution* 1976; *A Bridge Too Far* 1977; *The Betsy* 1978; *The Boys from Brazil* 1978; *Dracula* 1979; *A Little Romance* 1979; *The Jazz Singer* 1980; *Clash of the Titans* 1981; *Inchon* 1981; *Wagner* 1983; *The Bounty* 1984; *The Jigsaw Man* 1984; *Wild Geese II* 1985; *War Requiem* 1988

Olivier, Paul *A Nous la Liberté* 1931; *Le Million* 1931

Olivieri, Enrico *Woman of the River* 1955; *The Mask of Satan* 1960

Olmos, Edward James aka **Olmos, Eddie** *Aloha, Bobby and Rose* 1975; *Virus* 1980; *Wolfen* 1981; *Zoot Suit* 1981; *Blade Runner* 1982; *The Ballad of Gregorio Cortez* 1983; *Saving Grace* 1985; *Stand and Deliver* 1988; *Triumph of the Spirit* 1989; *Talent for the Game* 1991; *American Me* 1992; *Roosters* 1993; *The Burning Season* 1994; *A Million to Juan* 1994; *My Family* 1994; *Mirage* 1995; *The Limbic Region* 1996; *Caught* 1996; *Hollywood Confidential* 1997; *Selena* 1997; *Twelve Angry Men* 1997; *The Disappearance of Garcia Lorca* 1997; *Gossip* 1999; *The Road to El Dorado* 2000

Olmsted, Gertrude *The Monster* 1925; *The Torrent* 1926

O'Loughlin, Gerald S aka **O'Loughlin, Gerald** *A Hatful of Rain* 1957; *Ensign Pulver* 1964; *In Cold Blood* 1967; *Riot* 1969; *Desperate Characters* 1971; *The Organization* 1971; *The Valachi Papers* 1972; *Murder at the World Series* 1977; *Something for Joey* 1977; *Frances* 1982

Olsen, Ashley *Double, Double Toil and Trouble* 1993; *It Takes Two* 1995

Olsen, Gary *Party, Party* 1983; *The Cook, the Thief, His Wife and Her Lover* 1989; *Up 'n' Under* 1997

Olsen, Mary-Kate *Double, Double Toil and Trouble* 1993; *It Takes Two* 1995

Olsen, Moroni *Annie Oakley* 1935; *Seven Keys to Baldpate* 1935; *The Three Musketeers* 1935; *Snow White and the Seven Dwarfs* 1937; *Kentucky* 1938; *Rose of Washington Square* 1939; *One Foot in Heaven* 1941; *Dangerously They Live* 1942; *Ali Baba and the Forty Thieves* 1944; *Buffalo Bill* 1944; *Cobra Woman* 1944; *Mildred Pierce* 1945; *High Wall* 1947; *The Long Night* 1947;

ACTORS' INDEX

Radio Times

Valiant 1954; Princess of the Nile 1954; White Feather 1955; Seven Angry Men 1955; The Last Hunt 1956; Love Me Tender 1956; The Ten Commandments 1956; Omar Khayyam 1957; The River's Edge 1957; From the Earth to the Moon 1958; The Tiger of Eschnapur 1959; The Indian Tomb 1959; The Most Dangerous Man Alive 1961; Tales of Terror 1962; The Haunted Palace 1963

Pagett, Nicola The Viking Queen 1967; There's a Girl in My Soup 1970; Frankenstein: the True Story 1973; Operation Daybreak 1975; Oliver's Story 1978; Privates on Parade 1982; An Awfully Big Adventure 1994

Paglia, Camille The Watermelon Woman 1996; Henry Fool 1997

Pagnol, Jacqueline Topaze 1951; Manon des Sources 1952

Paige, Janis Hollywood Canteen 1944; Of Human Bondage 1946; Two Guys from Milwaukee 1946; It's Magic 1948; Romance on the High Seas 1948; Winter Meeting 1948; Silk Stockings 1957; Please Don't Eat the Daisies 1960; Bachelor in Paradise 1961; Follow the Boys 1963; The Caretakers 1963

Paige, Mabel Young and Willing 1942; Happy Go Lucky 1943; True to Life 1943

Paige, Robert Who Killed Gail Preston? 1938; Hellzapoppin' 1941; Pardon My Sarong 1942; Frontier Badmen 1943; Son of Dracula 1943; Can't Help Singing 1944; Abbott and Costello Go to Mars 1953; Split Second 1953; The Marriage-Go-Round 1960

Pailhas, Geraldine IP5 1992; Suite 16 1994; Don Juan DeMarco 1995

Pain, Didier Le Château de Ma Mère 1990; La Gloire de Mon Père 1990; Le Bossu 1997

Pais, Josh Teenage Mutant Ninja Turtles 1990; Safe Men 1998

Paiva, Nestor Fly by Night 1942; The Falcon in Mexico 1944; The Southerner 1945; Badman's Territory 1946; Road to Rio 1947; Double Dynamite 1951; A Millionaire for Christy 1951; Prisoners of the Casbah 1953; Creature from the Black Lagoon 1954; Hell on Frisco Bay 1955; Revenge of the Creature 1955; Tarantula 1955; Comanche 1956

Pajala, Turo Hamlet Goes Business 1987; Ariel 1988

Palance, Holly The Comeback 1977; Under Fire 1983; The Best of Times 1986

Palance, Jack aka **Palance, Walter**, aka **Palance, Walter Jack** Halls of Montezuma 1950; Panic in the Streets 1950; Sudden Fear 1952; Arrowhead 1953; Man in the Attic 1953; Second Chance 1953; Shane 1953; Flight to Tangier 1953; Sign of the Pagan 1954; The Silver Chalice 1954; The Big Knife 1955; I Died a Thousand Times 1955; Kiss of Fire 1955; Attack! 1956; The Lonely Man 1957; House of Numbers 1957; The Man Inside 1958; Ten Seconds to Hell 1959; The Battle of Austerlitz 1960; Barabbas 1961; The Mongols 1961; Le Mépris 1963; Once a Thief 1965; The Professionals 1966; The Spy in the Green Hat 1966; Torture Garden 1967; Kill a Dragon 1967; A Professional Gun 1968; They Came to Rob Las Vegas 1968; Che! 1969; The Desperados 1969; The McMasters 1970; Monte Walsh 1970; The Horsemen 1971; Chato's Land 1972; Craze 1973; Oklahoma Crude 1973; Dracula 1974; The Four Deuces 1976; God's Gun 1977; Portrait of a Hitman 1977; Welcome to Blood City 1977; One Man Jury 1978; The Last Ride of the Dalton Gang 1979; Hawk the Slayer 1980; Without Warning 1980; Alone in the Dark 1982; Bagdad Café 1987; Gor 1987; Young Guns 1988; Batman 1989; Tango and Cash 1989; Solar Crisis 1990; City Slickers 1991; Keep the Change 1992; Cyborg 2: Glass Shadow 1993; City Slickers II: the Legend of Curly's Gold 1994; Cops and Robbersons 1994; The Swan Princess 1994; Twilight Zone: Rod Serling's Lost Classics 1994; Ebenezer 1998

Palau aka **Palau, Pierre** Devil in the Flesh 1946; Marguerite de la Nuit 1955

Palin, Michael And Now for Something Completely Different 1971; Monty Python and the Holy Grail 1975; Jabberwocky 1977; Monty Python's Life of Brian 1979; Time Bandits 1981; The Missionary 1982; Monty Python Live at the Hollywood Bowl 1982; Monty Python's The Meaning of Life 1983; A Private Function 1984; Brazil 1985; A Fish Called Wanda 1988; American Friends 1991; The Wind in the Willows 1996; Fierce Creatures 1997

Palk, Anna Play It Cool 1963; Tower of Evil 1972

Pallenberg, Anita Barbarella 1967; Candy 1968; Performance 1970

Pallette, Eugene The Three Musketeers 1921; Mantrap 1926; Lights of New York 1928; The Virginian 1929; Paramount on Parade 1930; Girls about Town 1931; Gun Smoke 1931; Shanghai Express 1932; The Half Naked Truth 1932; The Kennel Murder Case 1933; All the King's Horses 1935; Bordertown 1935; The Ghost Goes West 1935; Steamboat round the Bend 1935; My Man Godfrey 1936; Stowaway 1936; Topper 1937; One Hundred Men and a Girl 1937; The Adventures of Robin Hood 1938; First Love 1939; Wife, Husband and Friend 1939; The Mark of Zorro 1940; Young Tom Edison 1940; Appointment for Love 1941; The Bride Came C.O.D. 1941; The Lady Eve 1941; Swamp Water 1941; The Big Street 1942; The Male Animal 1942; Lady in a Jam 1942; The Gang's All Here 1943; It Ain't Hay 1943; Slightly Dangerous 1943; In the Meantime, Darling 1944; Pin Up Girl 1944; Sensations 1944; Step Lively 1944; The Cheaters 1945

Palma, Andrea Tarzan and the Mermaids 1948; The Criminal Life of Archibaldo de la Cruz 1955

Palme, Ulf Miss Julie 1951; Dreams 1955; The Counterfeit Traitor 1962

Palmer, Betsy The Long Gray Line 1955; Mister Roberts 1955; Queen Bee 1955; The Tin Star 1957; The True Story of Lynn Stuart 1957; The Last Angry Man 1959; Friday the 13th 1980; Still Not Quite Human 1992

Palmer, Geoffrey A Fish Called Wanda 1988; Smack and Thistle 1989; The Madness of King George 1995; Mrs Brown 1997; Tomorrow Never Dies 1997

Palmer, Gregg The All American 1953; Magnificent Obsession 1954; Taza, Son of Cochise 1954; Playgirl 1954; To Hell and Back 1955; Hilda Crane 1956; From Hell It Came 1957; The Sad Horse 1959; The Rebel Set 1959; The Most Dangerous Man Alive 1961

Palmer, Joel Far from Home: the Adventures of Yellow Dog 1994; Seduction in a Small Town 1996

Palmer, Lilli Secret Agent 1936; Command Performance 1937; Good Morning, Boys 1937; Crackerjack 1938; Thunder Rock 1942; The Gentle Sex 1943; English without Tears 1944; The Rake's Progress 1945; Beware of Pity 1946; Cloak and Dagger 1946; Body and Soul 1947; My Girl Tisa 1948; No Minor Vices 1948; The Long Dark Hall 1951; The Four Poster 1953; Montparnasses 19 1958; But Not for Me 1959; Conspiracy of Hearts 1960; The Pleasure of His Company 1961; The Counterfeit Traitor 1962; Miracle of the White Stallions 1963; The Amorous Adventures of Moll Flanders 1965; Operation Crossbow 1965; Jack of Diamonds 1967; Nobody Runs Forever 1968; Sebastian 1968; Oedipus the King 1968; De Sade 1969; Hard Contract 1969; Murders in the Rue Morgue 1971; The Boys from Brazil 1978; The Holcroft Covenant 1985

Palmer, Maria Days of Glory 1944; The Web 1947; By the Light of the Silvery Moon 1953

Palminteri, Chazz Home Free All 1983; Oscar 1991; Innocent Blood 1992; A Bronx Tale 1993; Bullets over Broadway 1994; Cosa Nostra: the Last Word 1995; Jade 1995; The Perez Family 1995; The Usual Suspects 1995; Diabolique 1996; Faithful 1996; Mulholland Falls 1996; Hurlyburly 1998; Scarred City 1998; Analyze This 1999; Stuart Little 1999

Palomino, Carlos Strangers Kiss 1983; Die Watching 1993

Paltrow, Gwyneth Flesh and Bone 1993; Malice 1993; Deadly Relations 1993; Jefferson in Paris 1995; Moonlight and Valentino 1995; Se7en 1995; Emma 1996; Hard Eight 1996; The Pallbearer 1996; Great Expectations 1997; Sliding Doors 1997; Hush 1998; A Perfect Murder 1998; Shakespeare in Love 1998; The Talented Mr Ripley 1999

Paluzzi, Luciana Carlton-Browne of the FO 1958; Sea Fury 1958; No Time to Die 1958; Return to Peyton Place 1961; Muscle Beach Party 1964; Thunderball 1965; To Trap a Spy 1966; The Venetian Affair 1966; Chuka 1967; Sharaz 1968; A Black Veil for Lisa 1969; Captain Nemo and the Underwater City 1969; The Italian Connection 1973; The Klansman 1974

Panaro, Alessandra aka **Panaro, Sandra** The Bacchantes 1960; The Secret Mark of D'Artagnan 1962; The Executioner of Venice 1963

Pandey, Nirmal Bandit Queen 1994; The Square Circle 1996; Train to Pakistan 1997

Panebianco, Richard China Girl 1987; Dogfight 1991

Pangborn, Franklin Her Man 1930; The Half Naked Truth 1932; Design for Living 1933; All over Town 1937; Easy Living 1937; Three Smart Girls 1937; Bluebeard's Eighth Wife 1938; Vivacious Lady 1938; Just around the Corner 1938; Topper Takes a Trip 1939; The Bank Dick 1940; Christmas in July 1940; The Navy Steps Out 1941; Sullivan's Travels 1941; Call Out the Marines 1942; Reveille with Beverly 1943; The Horn Blows at Midnight 1945; I'll Be Yours 1947; Mad Wednesday 1950

Pankin, Stuart The Dirt Bike Kid 1986; Fatal Attraction 1987; Love at Stake 1987; Second Sight 1989; Arachnophobia 1990; Life Stinks 1991; Mannequin on the Move 1991; Betrayal of the Dove 1993; Father and Scout 1994; Congo 1995

Pankow, John To Live and Die in LA 1985; The Secret of My Success 1987; Monkey Shines 1988; Talk Radio 1988; Mortal Thoughts 1991; Year of the Gun 1991; A Stranger among Us 1992; The Object of My Affection 1998

Pantoliano, Joe The Idolmaker 1980; Eddie and the Cruisers 1983; Risky Business 1983; The Goonies 1985; The Mean Season 1985; La Bamba 1986; Running Scared 1986; Destination: America 1987; Empire of the Sun 1987; Midnight Run 1988; Rock 'n' Roll Mom 1988; The In Crowd 1988; Nightbreaker 1989; Blue Heat 1990; Downtown 1990; Short Time 1990; Zandalee 1991; Three of Hearts 1992; Through the Eyes of a Killer 1992; Calendar Girl 1993; The Fugitive 1993; A Robot Called Golddigger 1993; Me and the Kid 1993; Baby's Day Out 1994; Dangerous Heart 1994; Cosa Nostra: the Last Word 1995; Flight of the Dove 1995; The Immortals 1995; Steal Big, Steal Little 1995; Bound 1996; Ed McBain's 87th Precinct: Ice 1996; Natural Enemy 1996; Top of the World 1997; US Marshals 1998; The Matrix 1999

Paoli, Cecile Near Mrs 1990; Kaspar Hauser 1993

Papas, Irene The Man from Cairo 1953; Tribute to a Bad Man 1956; The Guns of Navarone 1961; Elektra 1962; The Moon-Spinners 1964; Zorba the Greek 1964; We Still Kill the Old Way 1967; The Brotherhood 1968; Z 1968; Anne of the Thousand Days 1969; A Dream of Kings 1969; The Trojan Women 1971; Moses 1975; Iphigenia 1976; The Message 1976; Bloodline 1979; Christ Stopped at Eboli 1979; Lion of the Desert 1981; Erendira 1982; The Assisi Underground 1985; Chronicle of a Death Foretold 1987; High Season 1987; Island 1989; Jacob 1994; The Odyssey 1997

Pape, Lionel The Big Broadcast of 1938 1937; Raffles 1939

Paquin, Anna The Piano 1993; Fly Away Home 1996; Jane Eyre 1996; Amistad 1997; The Member of the Wedding 1997; Hurlyburly 1998; She's All That 1999; A Walk on the Moon 1999

Paradis, Vanessa Noce Blanche 1989; Elisa 1994; The Girl on the Bridge 1999

Paramore, Kiri The Last Days of Chez Nous 1992; Doing Time for Patsy Cline 1997

Paratene, Rawiri Footrot Flats: the Dog's Tale 1986; The Rogue Stallion 1990; What Becomes of the Broken Hearted? 1999

Paré, Michael Crazy Times 1981; Eddie and the Cruisers 1983; Undercover 1983; The Philadelphia Experiment 1984; Streets of Fire 1984; World Gone Wild 1988; Eddie and the Cruisers II: Eddie Lives! 1989; Moon 44 1990; The Closer 1990; Empire City 1991; Into the Sun 1992; Triplecross 1995; Village of the Damned 1995; Bad Moon 1996; Hope Floats 1998

Paredes, Jean La Nuit Fantastique 1942; Fanfan la Tulipe 1951

Paredes, Marisa High Heels 1991; The Flower of My Secret 1995; Deep Crimson 1996; Three Lives and Only One Death 1996; Life Is Beautiful 1997; Talk of Angels 1998; All about My Mother 1999; No One Writes to the Colonel 1999

Parely, Mila La Règle du Jeu 1939; Les Anges du Péché 1943; La Belle et la Bête 1946; Blood Orange 1953

Parfitt, Judy Hide and Seek 1963; Hamlet 1969; Champions 1983; The Chain 1984; Maurice 1987; Diamond Skulls 1989; Dolores Claiborne 1995; Wilde 1997; Ever After 1998

Parillaud, Anne Ecoute Voir... 1978; Nikita 1990; Innocent Blood 1992; Map of the Human Heart 1992; Six Days, Six Nights 1994; Frankie Starlight 1995; The Man in the Iron Mask 1997; Shattered Image 1998

Paris, Cheryl Sweet Bird of Youth 1989; From the Files of Joseph Wambaugh: a Jury of One 1992

Paris, Jerry The Glass Wall 1953; Drive a Crooked Road 1954; Good Morning, Miss Dove 1955; Marty 1955; Unchained 1955; The Naked Street 1955; D-Day the Sixth of June 1956; Zero Hour 1957; Sing, Boy, Sing 1958

Parke, Macdonald Summertime 1955; Beyond Mombasa 1957; The Mouse That Roared 1959

Parker, Cecil The Man Who Changed His Mind 1936; Storm in a Teacup 1937; The Citadel 1938; Housemaster 1938; The Lady Vanishes 1938; Under Your Hat 1940; The Saint's Vacation 1941; Caesar and Cleopatra 1945; The Magic Bow 1946; Captain Boycott 1947; Hungry Hill 1947; Quartet 1948; The Weaker Sex 1948; The Chiltern Hundreds 1949; Under Capricorn 1949; Tony Draws a Horse 1950; The Man in the White Suit 1951; I Believe in You 1952; Isn't Life Wonderful! 1952; Father Brown 1954; For Better, for Worse 1954; The Constant Husband 1955; The Ladykillers 1955; The Court Jester 1956; It's Great to Be Young 1956; True as a Turtle 1956; 23 Paces to Baker Street 1956; The Admirable Crichton 1957; A Tale of Two Cities 1957; Happy Is the Bride 1958; I Was Monty's Double 1958; Indiscreet 1958; The Navy Lark 1959; The Night We Dropped a Clanger 1959; The Wreck of the Mary Deare 1959; A French Mistress 1960; The Pure Hell of St Trinian's 1960; Swiss Family Robinson 1960; Under Ten Flags 1960; On the Fiddle 1961; Petticoat Pirates 1961; The Amorous Prawn 1962; The Brain 1962; Heavens Above! 1963; The Comedy Man 1964; Lady L 1965; A Man Could Get Killed 1966; The Magnificent Two 1967

Parker, Cecilia Riders of Destiny 1933; Enter Madame! 1933; The Painted Veil 1934; Ah, Wilderness 1935; A Family Affair 1937; Girl Loves Boy 1937; Judge Hardy's Children 1938; Love Finds Andy Hardy 1938; Out West with the Hardys 1938; You're Only Young Once 1938; Andy Hardy Gets Spring Fever 1939; The Hardys Ride High 1939; Judge Hardy and Son 1939; Andy Hardy Meets Debutante 1940; Andy Hardy's

Alley 1939; *The Lone Wolf Strikes* 1940; *Maisie Was a Lady* 1941; *Strange Alibi* 1941
Perry, John Bennett *Lipstick* 1976; *I Dream of Jeannie... 15 Years Later* 1985; *The Last Fling* 1987; *She Knows Too Much* 1989; *Danielle Steel's Secrets* 1992; *Fools Rush In* 1997
Perry, Linda *The Case of the Stuttering Bishop* 1937; *They Won't Forget* 1937
Perry, Luke *Terminal Bliss* 1990; *Scorchers* 1991; *Buffy the Vampire Slayer* 1992; *8 Seconds* 1994; *Normal Life* 1995; *American Strays* 1996; *The Fifth Element* 1997; *Lifebreath* 1997; *Indiscreet* 1998
Perry, Matthew *aka* **Perry, Matthew L** *A Night in the Life of Jimmy Reardon* 1988; *Deadly Relations* 1993; *Getting In* 1994; *Fools Rush In* 1997; *Almost Heroes* 1998; *Three to Tango* 1999; *The Whole Nine Yards* 2000
Perry, Roger *Count Yorga, Vampire* 1970; *The Return of Count Yorga* 1971; *The Thing with Two Heads* 1972; *The Man with the Power* 1977; *Roller Boogie* 1979
Perschy, Maria *The Password Is Courage* 1962; *Man's Favorite Sport?* 1964; *633 Squadron* 1964; *Murders in the Rue Morgue* 1971
Persky, Lisa Jane *aka* **Persky, Lisa** *The Great Santini* 1979; *Breathless* 1983; *The Sure Thing* 1985; *The Big Easy* 1986; *Sharing Richard* 1988; *When Harry Met Sally...* 1989; *Pontiac Moon* 1994; *Dead Funny* 1995
Persoff, Nehemiah *The Wrong Man* 1956; *Men in War* 1957; *This Angry Age* 1957; *The Badlanders* 1958; *Al Capone* 1959; *Day of the Outlaw* 1959; *Green Mansions* 1959; *Never Steal Anything Small* 1959; *Some Like It Hot* 1959; *The Comancheros* 1961; *The Big Show* 1961; *The Hook* 1963; *A Global Affair* 1964; *Panic in the City* 1968; *The Girl Who Knew Too Much* 1969; *Mrs Pollifax – Spy* 1970; *Eric* 1975; *Psychic Killer* 1975; *Francis Gary Powers: the True Story of the U-2* 1976; *FDR: the Last Year* 1980; *Yentl* 1983; *An American Tail* 1986; *An American Tail: Fievel Goes West* 1991
Pertwee, Jon *Murder at the Windmill* 1949; *Mr Drake's Duck* 1950; *Will Any Gentleman...?* 1953; *A Yank in Ermine* 1955; *Nearly a Nasty Accident* 1961; *Ladies Who Do* 1963; *Carry On Cowboy* 1965; *I've Gotta Horse* 1965; *The House That Dripped Blood* 1971; *Wombling Free* 1977; *Adventures of a Private Eye* 1977; *The Boys in Blue* 1983; *Carry On Columbus* 1992
Pertwee, Sean *Dirty Weekend* 1992; *Leon the Pig Farmer* 1992; *Shopping* 1993; *i.d.* 1994; *Blue Juice* 1995; *Event Horizon* 1997; *Stiff Upper Lips* 1997; *Talos the Mummy* 1997; *Soldier* 1998; *Love, Honour and Obey* 2000
Perugorria, Jorge *Strawberry and Chocolate* 1993; *Guantanamera* 1995
Pesci, Joe *Death Collector* 1976; *Raging Bull* 1980; *Eureka* 1982; *I'm Dancing as Fast as I Can* 1982; *Easy Money* 1983; *Once upon a Time in America* 1984; *Man on Fire* 1987; *Moonwalker* 1988; *Lethal Weapon 2* 1989; *Betsy's Wedding* 1990; *Catchfire* 1990; *GoodFellas* 1990; *Home Alone* 1990; *JFK* 1991; *The Super* 1991; *Home Alone 2: Lost in New York* 1992; *Lethal Weapon 3* 1992; *My Cousin Vinny* 1992; *The Public Eye* 1992; *A Bronx Tale* 1993; *Jimmy Hollywood* 1994; *With Honors* 1994; *Casino* 1995; *8 Heads in a Duffel Bag* 1997; *Gone Fishin'* 1997; *Lethal Weapon 4* 1998
Pescia, Lisa *Body Chemistry* 1990; *Body Chemistry 2: Voice of a Stranger* 1992
Pescow, Donna *Saturday Night Fever* 1977; *Human Feelings* 1978
Petelius, Pirkka-Pekka *The Unknown Soldier* 1983; *Hamlet Goes Business* 1987
Peters, Bernadette *Ace Eli and Rodger of the Skies* 1973; *Vigilante Force* 1975; *Silent Movie* 1976; *WC Fields and Me* 1976; *The Jerk* 1979; *Pennies from Heaven* 1981; *Heartbeeps* 1981; *Annie* 1982; *David: the David Rothenberg Story* 1988; *Pink Cadillac* 1989; *Slaves of New York* 1989; *Alice* 1990; *Fall from Grace* 1990; *The Last Best Year* 1990; *Impromptu* 1991; *Anastasia* 1997; *Beauty and the Beast: the Enchanted Christmas* 1997; *Rodgers & Hammerstein's Cinderella* 1997; *What the Deaf Man Heard* 1997; *The Odyssey* 1997
Peters, Brock *Carmen Jones* 1954; *Porgy and Bess* 1959; *The L-Shaped Room* 1962; *To Kill a Mockingbird* 1962; *Heavens Above!* 1963; *Major Dundee* 1965; *The Pawnbroker* 1965; *The Incident* 1967; *New Face in Hell* 1968; *The McMasters* 1970; *Black Girl* 1972; *Soylent Green* 1973; *Slaughter's Big Rip-Off* 1973; *Lost in the Stars* 1974; *Alligator II: the Mutation* 1991; *The Secret* 1992; *The Importance of Being Earnest* 1992; *An Element of Truth* 1995
Peters, Clarke *Silver Dream Racer* 1980; *Outland* 1981; *Mona Lisa* 1986; *Death Train* 1993
Peters Jr, House *Under California Stars* 1948; *Winning of the West* 1953
Peters, Jean *Captain from Castile* 1947; *It Happens Every Spring* 1949; *Love That Brute* 1950; *Anne of the Indies* 1951; *As Young as You Feel* 1951; *Viva Zapata!* 1952; *Wait 'til the Sun Shines, Nellie* 1952; *O Henry's Full House* 1952; *Niagara* 1953; *Pickup on South Street* 1953; *Apache* 1954; *Broken Lance* 1954; *Three Coins in the Fountain* 1954; *A Man Called Peter* 1955
Peters, Kelly Jean *Any Wednesday* 1966; *Little Big Man* 1970; *Pocket Money* 1972; *Ace Eli and Rodger of the Skies* 1973; *Witches' Brew* 1979
Peters, Lauri *Mr Hobbs Takes a Vacation* 1962; *Summer Holiday* 1962; *For Love of Ivy* 1968
Peters, Scott *Suicide Battalion* 1958; *The Girl Hunters* 1963
Peters, Susan *The Big Shot* 1942; *Dr Gillespie's New Assistant* 1942; *Random Harvest* 1942; *Young Ideas* 1943; *Keep Your Powder Dry* 1945
Peters, Werner *The Thousand Eyes of Dr Mabuse* 1960; *36 Hours* 1964; *Dead Run* 1967
Petersen, Colin *Smiley* 1956; *A Cry from the Streets* 1957; *The Scamp* 1957
Petersen, Pat *The Little Dragons* 1980; *Cold River* 1982
Petersen, Stewart *Where the Red Fern Grows* 1974; *Seven Alone* 1974; *Against a Crooked Sky* 1975; *Pony Express Rider* 1976
Petersen, William *aka* **Petersen, William L** *To Live and Die in LA* 1985; *Manhunter* 1986; *Amazing Grace and Chuck* 1987; *Long Gone* 1987; *Cousins* 1989; *Young Guns II* 1990; *Hard Promises* 1991; *Passed Away* 1992; *Keep the Change* 1992; *Curacao* 1993; *In the Kingdom of the Blind* 1994; *Fear* 1996; *Mulholland Falls* 1996; *Twelve Angry Men* 1997; *The Rat Pack* 1998; *The Skulls* 2000
Peterson, Amanda *Explorers* 1985; *Can't Buy Me Love* 1987; *Listen to Me* 1989; *Hell Hath No Fury* 1991
Peterson, Cassandra *Allan Quatermain and the Lost City of Gold* 1987; *Elvira, Mistress of the Dark* 1988
Peterson, Dorothy *Forbidden* 1932; *Payment Deferred* 1932; *The Beast of the City* 1932; *The Mayor of Hell* 1933; *The Country Doctor* 1936; *Confession* 1937; *Girl Loves Boy* 1937; *Lillian Russell* 1940; *Too Many Husbands* 1940; *The Man in the Trunk* 1942; *The Woman in the Window* 1945
Peterson, Lenka *The Phenix City Story* 1955; *Black Like Me* 1964; *Homer* 1970; *Pals* 1986
Peterson, Marion *Lapse of Memory* 1992; *For Better and for Worse* 1993
Peterson, Paul *The Happiest Millionaire* 1967; *Journey to Shiloh* 1968
Peterson, Vidal *Something Wicked This Way Comes* 1983; *Wizards of the Lost Kingdom* 1985
Petrenko, Alexei *Agony* 1975; *The Barber of Siberia* 1999
Petri, Mario *Achilles* 1962; *The Secret Mark of D'Artagnan* 1962; *The Executioner of Venice* 1963; *Sandokan against the Leopard of Sarawak* 1964
Petrie, Doris *Wedding in White* 1972; *Confidential* 1986
Petrie, Hay *The Old Curiosity Shop* 1934; *Conquest of the Air* 1936; *21 Days* 1937; *Crimes at the Dark House* 1939; *Contraband* 1940; *Pastor Hall* 1940; *The Thief of Bagdad* 1940; *The Ghost of St Michael's* 1941; *A Canterbury Tale* 1944
Petrie, Howard *Rocky Mountain* 1950; *Cattle Drive* 1951; *Pony Soldier* 1952; *The Wild North* 1952; *The Bounty Hunter* 1954; *Seven Brides for Seven Brothers* 1954; *The Bob Mathias Story* 1954; *The Maverick Queen* 1955
Petrovitch, Michael *Neither the Sea nor the Sand* 1972; *Tales That Witness Madness* 1973; *Turkey Shoot* 1981
Petruzzi, Joe *Secret Weapon* 1990; *Dingo* 1991; *Paws* 1997
Pettet, Joanna *The Group* 1966; *The Night of the Generals* 1966; *Robbery* 1967; *Blue* 1968; *Welcome to Arrow Beach* 1974; *Sex and the Married Woman* 1977; *The Evil* 1978; *Cry of the Innocent* 1980; *The Return of Frank Cannon* 1980
Pettiet, Christopher *Danger Island* 1992; *Acts of Love* 1995
Pettingell, Frank *Sailing Along* 1938; *Busman's Honeymoon* 1940; *Gaslight* 1940; *The Goose Steps Out* 1942; *Get Cracking* 1943; *Gaiety George* 1946; *Value for Money* 1955; *Trial and Error* 1962
Petty, Lori *Bates Motel* 1987; *Cadillac Man* 1990; *Point Break* 1991; *A League of Their Own* 1992; *Free Willy* 1993; *Poetic Justice* 1993; *In the Army Now* 1994; *The Glass Shield* 1995; *Tank Girl* 1995; *Countdown* 1996
Petty, Tom *FM* 1977; *The Postman* 1997
Pevney, Joseph *Nocturne* 1946; *Body and Soul* 1947; *The Street with No Name* 1948; *Thieves' Highway* 1949
Peyser, Penny *The Frisco Kid* 1979; *The In-Laws* 1979
Pfeiffer, Dedee *Vamp* 1986; *Dangerously Close* 1986; *The Allnighter* 1987; *Brothers in Arms* 1988; *House III: The Horror Show* 1989; *Red Surf* 1990; *A Row of Crows* 1991; *Double Exposure* 1993; *Running Cool* 1993; *Deadly Past* 1995; *Up Close & Personal* 1996
Pfeiffer, Michelle *Falling in Love Again* 1980; *Charlie Chan and the Curse of the Dragon Queen* 1981; *Grease 2* 1982; *Scarface* 1983; *Into the Night* 1985; *Ladyhawke* 1985; *Sweet Liberty* 1986; *Amazon Women on the Moon* 1987; *The Witches of Eastwick* 1987; *Dangerous Liaisons* 1988; *Married to the Mob* 1988; *Tequila Sunrise* 1988; *The Fabulous Baker Boys* 1989; *The Russia House* 1990; *Frankie & Johnny* 1991; *Batman Returns* 1992; *Love Field* 1992; *The Age of Innocence* 1993; *Wolf* 1994; *Dangerous Minds* 1995; *One Fine Day* 1996; *To Gillian on Her 37th Birthday* 1996; *Up Close & Personal* 1996; *A Thousand Acres* 1997; *The Prince of Egypt* 1998; *The Deep End of the Ocean* 1999; *William Shakespeare's A Midsummer Night's Dream* 1999; *The Story of Us* 1999
Pflug, Jo Ann *MASH* 1969; *Catlow* 1971; *Where Does It Hurt?* 1971; *The Night Strangler* 1973
Phelan, Brian *Four in the Morning* 1965; *Accident* 1967
Phelan, Shawn *Caroline?* 1990; *Miles from Nowhere* 1992; *Breaking the Rules* 1992
Phelps, Lee *Anna Christie* 1930; *Chained* 1934
Phelps, Peter *Undercover* 1983; *The Lighthorsemen* 1987; *Starlight Hotel* 1987; *Rough Diamonds* 1994; *Blackwater Trail* 1995
Phifer, Mekhi *Clockers* 1995; *High School High* 1996; *Soul Food* 1997; *I Still Know What You Did Last Summer* 1998; *A Lesson Before Dying* 1999
Philbin, John *Children of the Corn* 1984; *Return of the Living Dead* 1985; *Resting Place* 1986; *North Shore* 1987; *Shy People* 1987; *The Killing Jar* 1996
Philbin, Mary *The Phantom of the Opera* 1925; *The Man Who Laughs* 1928
Philipe, Gérard *Devil in the Flesh* 1946; *La Beauté du Diable* 1949; *Fanfan la Tulipe* 1951; *Les Belles de Nuit* 1952; *The Seven Deadly Sins* 1952; *The Proud Ones* 1953; *Royal Affairs in Versailles* 1953; *Le Rouge et le Noir* 1954; *Knave of Hearts* 1954; *Les Grandes Manoeuvres* 1955; *Montparnasses 19* 1958; *Les Liaisons Dangereuses* 1959; *La Fièvre Monte à el Pao* 1959
Philippe, Andre *Alex in Wonderland* 1970; *Black Belt Jones* 1974; *Goodbye, Norma Jean* 1976
Philips, Gina *aka* **Phillips, Gina** *Deadly Invasion* 1995; *Unforgivable* 1995; *Danielle Steel's No Greater Love* 1996; *Her Costly Affair* 1996
Philips, Lee *Peyton Place* 1957; *The Hunters* 1958; *Middle of the Night* 1959; *Tess of the Storm Country* 1960; *Psychomania* 1964
Philips, Mary *aka* **Phillips, Mary** *A Farewell to Arms* 1932; *The Bride Wore Red* 1937; *Mannequin* 1937; *Leave Her to Heaven* 1945; *Dear Ruth* 1947; *A Woman's Secret* 1949
Philliber, John *It Happened Tomorrow* 1944; *Summer Storm* 1944
Phillippe, Ryan *Deadly Invasion* 1995; *White Squall* 1996; *Lifeform* 1996; *I Know What You Did Last Summer* 1997; *54* 1998; *Homegrown* 1998; *Playing by Heart* 1998; *Cruel Intentions* 1999
Phillips, Barney *I Was a Teenage Werewolf* 1957; *Gang War* 1958
Phillips, Bobbie *The Cover Girl Murders* 1993; *TC 2000* 1993; *Carnival of Souls* 1999
Phillips, Chris *Felix the Cat: the Movie* 1989; *Doug's 1st Movie* 1999
Phillips, Chynna *Some Kind of Wonderful* 1987; *Farewell Miss Freedom* 1988; *Moving Target* 1988; *The Invisible Kid* 1988; *Roxanne: the Prize Pulitzer* 1989; *Traveling Man* 1989
Phillips, Conrad *The Last Page* 1952; *Stranger's Meeting* 1957; *Witness in the Dark* 1959; *Circus of Horrors* 1960; *Sons and Lovers* 1960; *The Shadow of the Cat* 1961; *Don't Talk to Strange Men* 1962; *Dead Man's Evidence* 1962; *Impact* 1963; *Stopover Forever* 1964
Phillips, Eddie *The Thirteenth Guest* 1932; *Champagne Charlie* 1944
Phillips, Ethan *Lean on Me* 1989; *Green Card* 1990; *Natural Selection* 1994
Phillips, Grace *All the Vermeers in New York* 1990; *Truth or Consequences, NM* 1997
Phillips, Gregory *I Could Go On Singing* 1963; *I Start Counting* 1970
Phillips, Greigh *The Brain Eaters* 1958; *Forbidden Island* 1959
Phillips, Jean *Among the Living* 1941; *Dr Broadway* 1942
Phillips, John *Floods of Fear* 1958; *Man in the Moon* 1960; *Offbeat* 1960; *Romanoff and Juliet* 1961; *The Mummy's Shroud* 1966
Phillips, Jonathan *Killing Dad* 1989; *Max and Helen* 1990
Phillips, Joseph C *Strictly Business* 1991; *Let's Talk about Sex* 1998
Phillips, Julianne *Odd Jobs* 1986; *Seven Hours to Judgment* 1988; *Fletch Lives* 1989; *Skin Deep* 1989; *Getting Up and Going Home* 1992; *The Only Way Out* 1993; *A Vow to Kill* 1995; *Original Sins* 1995; *Big Bully* 1996; *Tidal Wave: No Escape* 1997
Phillips, Leslie *The Sound Barrier* 1952; *The Limping Man* 1953; *The Big Money* 1956; *Les Girls* 1957; *Just My Luck* 1957; *The Smallest Show on Earth* 1957; *High Flight* 1957; *I Was Monty's Double* 1958; *The Angry Hills* 1959; *Carry On Nurse* 1959; *Carry On Teacher* 1959; *The Man Who Liked Funerals* 1959; *The Navy Lark* 1959; *The Night We Dropped a Clanger* 1959; *This Other Eden* 1959; *Carry On Constable* 1960; *Doctor in Love* 1960; *Inn for Trouble* 1960; *Please Turn Over*

While the City Sleeps 1956; *The Story of Mankind* 1957; *The Fly* 1958; *House on Haunted Hill* 1958; *The Big Circus* 1959; *Return of the Fly* 1959; *The Tingler* 1959; *The Bat* 1959; *The Fall of the House of Usher* 1960; *Gordon the Black Pirate* 1961; *Master of the World* 1961; *Nefertite, Queen of the Nile* 1961; *The Pit and the Pendulum* 1961; *Convicts Four* 1962; *Tales of Terror* 1962; *Tower of London* 1962; *Diary of a Madman* 1963; *The Haunted Palace* 1963; *The Raven* 1963; *Twice Told Tales* 1963; *The Comedy of Terrors* 1964; *The Masque of the Red Death* 1964; *The Tomb of Ligeia* 1964; *City under the Sea* 1965; *Dr Goldfoot and the Bikini Machine* 1965; *Dr Goldfoot and the Girl Bombs* 1966; *Histoires Extraordinaires* 1967; *Witchfinder General* 1968; *The Oblong Box* 1969; *Scream and Scream Again* 1969; *The Trouble with Girls* 1969; *More Dead than Alive* 1969; *Cry of the Banshee* 1970; *The Abominable Dr Phibes* 1971; *What's a Nice Girl like You...?* 1971; *Dr Phibes Rises Again* 1972; *Theatre of Blood* 1973; *Madhouse* 1974; *Percy's Progress* 1974; *Scavenger Hunt* 1979; *The Monster Club* 1980; *House of the Long Shadows* 1983; *Bloodbath at the House of Death* 1983; *Basil the Great Mouse Detective* 1986; *The Whales of August* 1987; *Dead Heat* 1988; *Catchfire* 1990; *Edward Scissorhands* 1990; *The Heart of Justice* 1992; *Arabian Knight* 1995
Prichard, Robert *The Toxic Avenger* 1985; *Class of Nuke 'Em High* 1986; *Alien Space Avenger* 1989
Priest, Pat *Easy Come, Easy Go* 1967; *The Incredible Two-Headed Transplant* 1971
Priestley, Jason *Beverly Hills 90210* 1990; *Calendar Girl* 1993; *Tombstone* 1993; *Choices of the Heart: the Margaret Sanger Story* 1995; *Coldblooded* 1995; *Vanishing Point* 1997; *Love and Death on Long Island* 1998; *Eye of the Beholder* 1999
Prieto, Aurore *Thérèse* 1986; *Docteur Petiot* 1990
Prim, Suzy *Mayerling* 1936; *The Lower Depths* 1936
Prima, Louis *Senior Prom* 1958; *Hey Boy! Hey Girl!* 1959; *The Jungle Book* 1967
Primus, Barry *Puzzle of a Downfall Child* 1970; *Von Richthofen and Brown* 1971; *Boxcar Bertha* 1972; *The Gravy Train* 1974; *New York, New York* 1977; *Avalanche* 1978; *Heartland* 1979; *The Rose* 1979; *Night Games* 1979; *Absence of Malice* 1981; *The River* 1984; *SpaceCamp* 1986; *Stillwatch* 1987; *The Stranger* 1987; *Big Business* 1988; *Torn Apart* 1990; *Denial* 1991; *Night and the City* 1992; *Trade-Off* 1995; *Flipping* 1996; *Elmore Leonard's Gold Coast* 1997
Prince *Purple Rain* 1984; *Under the Cherry Moon* 1986; *Graffiti Bridge* 1990
Prince, Faith *The Last Dragon* 1985; *Dave* 1993; *My Father, the Hero* 1994; *Friends at Last* 1995; *Big Bully* 1996; *Picture Perfect* 1997
Prince, William *Destination Tokyo* 1943; *Objective, Burma!* 1945; *Cinderella Jones* 1946; *Carnegie Hall* 1947; *Dead Reckoning* 1947; *Cyrano de Bergerac* 1950; *Secret of Treasure Mountain* 1956; *The Vagabond King* 1956; *Macabre* 1958; *The Heartbreak Kid* 1972; *The Gauntlet* 1977; *Face of a Stranger* 1978; *The Promise* 1979; *Gideon's Trumpet* 1980; *Kiss Me Goodbye* 1982; *Moonlight* 1982; *Joe Dancer: the Big Trade* 1983; *Spies like Us* 1985; *Vice Versa* 1988
Principal, Victoria *The Life and Times of Judge Roy Bean* 1972; *Earthquake* 1974; *Vigilante Force* 1975; *I Will... I Will... for Now* 1976; *The Night They Took Miss Beautiful* 1977; *Mistress* 1987; *Blind Witness* 1989; *Naked Lie* 1989; *Sparks: the Price of Passion* 1990; *Nightmare* 1991; *Don't Touch My Daughter* 1991; *Seduction: Three Tales from the Inner Sanctum* 1992; *Murder on the Rio Grande* 1993; *Beyond Obsession* 1994; *Dancing in the Dark* 1995; *Barbara Taylor Bradford's Love in Another Town* 1997
Prine, Andrew *The Miracle Worker* 1962; *Bandolero!* 1968; *The Devil's Brigade* 1968; *Generation* 1969; *Grizzly* 1976; *The Evil* 1978; *Mind over Murder* 1979; *A Small Killing* 1981; *Amityville II: the Possession* 1982; *They're Playing With Fire* 1984; *Scattered Dreams* 1993; *Serial Killer* 1996; *The Shadow Men* 1997; *Possums* 1998
Pringle, Bryan *Saturday Night and Sunday Morning* 1960; *French Dressing* 1964; *The Early Bird* 1965; *The Boy Friend* 1971; *Haunted Honeymoon* 1986; *Drowning by Numbers* 1988; *The Steal* 1994; *Darkness Falls* 1998
Pringle, Joan *JD's Revenge* 1976; *Greyhounds* 1994; *Visions of Terror* 1994
Prinsloo, Sandra *The Gods Must Be Crazy* 1980; *Quest for Love* 1988
Prinze Jr, Freddie *I Know What You Did Last Summer* 1997; *The House of Yes* 1997; *I Still Know What You Did Last Summer* 1998; *Wing Commander* 1999; *She's All That* 1999; *Down to You* 2000
Pritchard, Hilary *Under the Doctor* 1976; *No Secrets* 1982
Pritchett, Paula *Chappaqua* 1966; *The Wrath of God* 1972
Prival, Lucien *Hell's Angels* 1930; *Party Girl* 1930
Privat, Gilles *Romuald et Juliette* 1989; *La Crise* 1992
Prochnow, Jürgen *The Lost Honour of Katharina Blum* 1975; *Das Boot* 1981; *The Keep* 1983; *Comeback* 1983; *Forbidden* 1985; *Killing Cars* 1986; *Beverly Hills Cop II* 1987; *The Seventh Sign* 1988; *A Dry White Season* 1989; *The Fourth War* 1990; *Robin Hood* 1990; *The Man Inside* 1990; *Body of Evidence* 1992; *Interceptor* 1992; *In the Mouth of Madness* 1994; *Judge Dredd* 1995; *DNA* 1996; *Air Force One* 1997; *The Replacement Killers* 1998; *Wing Commander* 1999
Procter, Emily *Breast Men* 1997; *Family Plan* 1997; *Body Shots* 1999
Proctor, Phil *aka* **Proctor, Philip** *A Safe Place* 1971; *Tunnelvision* 1976; *The Rugrats Movie* 1998
Proietti, Luigi *Lady Liberty* 1971; *The Inheritance* 1976
Prophet, Melissa *Van Nuys Blvd* 1979; *Players* 1979; *Better Late Than Never* 1983; *Invasion USA* 1985
Prosky, Robert *aka* **Prosky, Robert J** *Thief* 1981; *Hanky Panky* 1982; *Christine* 1983; *The Keep* 1983; *The Lords of Discipline* 1983; *The Natural* 1984; *Into Thin Air* 1985; *Outrageous Fortune* 1987; *Things Change* 1988; *Home Fires Burning* 1989; *The Heist* 1989; *Funny about Love* 1990; *Green Card* 1990; *A Green Journey* 1990; *Gremlins 2: the New Batch* 1990; *Loose Cannons* 1990; *Age Isn't Everything* 1991; *Double Edge* 1992; *Far and Away* 1992; *Teamster Boss: the Jackie Presser Story* 1992; *Last Action Hero* 1993; *Dead Man Walking* 1995; *The Scarlet Letter* 1995; *The Chamber* 1996; *Mad City* 1997; *Dudley Do-Right* 1999
Prouty, Jed *The Broadway Melody* 1929; *The Devil's Holiday* 1930; *The Duke of West Point* 1938; *Hollywood Cavalcade* 1939; *The Golden Hour* 1941; *The Lone Wolf Keeps a Date* 1941; *Guilty Bystander* 1950
Proval, David *Mean Streets* 1973; *Wizards* 1977; *Vice Versa* 1988; *Innocent Blood* 1992; *Romeo Is Bleeding* 1992; *Flipping* 1996
Provenza, Paul *Odd Jobs* 1986; *Under the Influence* 1986
Provine, Dorothy *The Bonnie Parker Story* 1958; *Good Neighbor Sam* 1964; *The Great Race* 1965; *That Darn Cat!* 1965; *One Spy Too Many* 1966; *Who's Minding the Mint?* 1967; *Never a Dull Moment* 1968
Provost, Jon *Escapade in Japan* 1957; *Lassie's Great Adventure* 1963
Prowse, Dave *aka* **Prowse, David** *The Horror of Frankenstein* 1970; *A Clockwork Orange* 1971; *Frankenstein and the Monster from Hell* 1973; *White Cargo* 1973; *Callan* 1974; *The People That Time Forgot* 1977; *Star Wars Episode IV: A New Hope* 1977; *The Empire Strikes Back* 1980; *Return of the Jedi* 1983
Prowse, Juliet *Can-Can* 1960; *GI Blues* 1960; *The Fiercest Heart* 1961; *The Second Time Around* 1961; *Who Killed Teddy Bear?* 1965
Pryce, Jonathan *Breaking Glass* 1980; *Loophole* 1980; *Agatha Christie's Murder Is Easy* 1982; *Something Wicked This Way Comes* 1983; *The Ploughman's Lunch* 1983; *Brazil* 1985; *The Doctor and the Devils* 1985; *Haunted Honeymoon* 1986; *Man on Fire* 1987; *The Adventures of Baron Munchausen* 1988; *Consuming Passions* 1988; *The Rachel Papers* 1989; *Freddie as FRO7* 1992; *Glengarry Glen Ross* 1992; *Barbarians at the Gate* 1993; *A Business Affair* 1993; *Deadly Advice* 1993; *Shopping* 1993; *Shades of Fear* 1993; *Stanley's Magic Garden* 1994; *Carrington* 1995; *Evita* 1996; *Regeneration* 1997; *Tomorrow Never Dies* 1997; *Ronin* 1998; *Stigmata* 1999
Pryor, Nicholas *The Happy Hooker* 1975; *Smile* 1975; *Damien – Omen II* 1978; *Gideon's Trumpet* 1980; *Risky Business* 1983; *Into Thin Air* 1985; *On Dangerous Ground* 1986; *Home Front* 1987; *Less than Zero* 1987; *Nightbreaker* 1989; *Brain Dead* 1990; *Hail Caesar* 1994
Pryor, Richard *The Busy Body* 1967; *Wild in the Streets* 1968; *You've Got to Walk It Like You Talk It or You'll Lose That Beat* 1971; *Dynamite Chicken* 1971; *Lady Sings the Blues* 1972; *Hit!* 1973; *The Mack* 1973; *Uptown Saturday Night* 1974; *Adios Amigo* 1975; *The Bingo Long Travelling All-Stars and Motor Kings* 1976; *Car Wash* 1976; *Silver Streak* 1976; *Greased Lightning* 1977; *Which Way Is Up?* 1977; *Blue Collar* 1978; *California Suite* 1978; *The Wiz* 1978; *In God We Trust* 1980; *Stir Crazy* 1980; *Wholly Moses!* 1980; *Bustin' Loose* 1981; *Some Kind of Hero* 1982; *Richard Pryor: Live on the Sunset Strip* 1982; *The Toy* 1982; *Superman III* 1983; *Brewster's Millions* 1985; *Jo Jo Dancer, Your Life Is Calling* 1986; *Critical Condition* 1987; *Moving* 1988; *Harlem Nights* 1989; *See No Evil, Hear No Evil* 1989; *Another You* 1991; *Lost Highway* 1996
Pryor, Roger *Belle of the Nineties* 1934; *Lady by Choice* 1934; *The Man They Could Not Hang* 1939
Pryse, Hugh *Valley of Song* 1953; *Three Cases of Murder* 1954
Pszoniak, Wojciech *aka* **Pszoniak, Wojtek** *Danton* 1982; *Korczak* 1990
Pugh, Robert *Old Scores* 1991; *Priest* 1994; *The Englishman Who Went up a Hill, but Came down a Mountain* 1995; *The Tichborne Claimant* 1998
Pugh, Willard *The Color Purple* 1985; *RoboCop 2* 1990; *Ambition* 1991
Puglia, Frank *Isn't Life Wonderful* 1924; *Arise, My Love* 1940; *That Night in Rio* 1941; *The Boogie Man Will Get You* 1942; *Jungle Book* 1942; *Ali Baba and the Forty Thieves* 1944; *Blood on the Sun* 1945; *Without Reservations* 1946; *Road to Rio* 1947; *Colorado Territory* 1949; *The Black Hand* 1950; *The Bandits of Corsica* 1953; *20 Million Miles to Earth* 1957; *The Black Orchid* 1959; *Girls! Girls! Girls!* 1962
Puglisi, Aldo *Marriage – Italian Style* 1964; *Seduced and Abandoned* 1964
Pulliam, Keshia Knight *aka* **Pulliam, Keshia** *The Last Dragon* 1985; *A Connecticut Yankee in King Arthur's Court* 1989; *Polly* 1989
Pullman, Bill *Ruthless People* 1986; *The Serpent and the Rainbow* 1987; *Spaceballs* 1987; *The Accidental Tourist* 1988; *Rocket Gibraltar* 1988; *Cold Feet* 1989; *Home Fires Burning* 1989; *Bright Angel* 1990; *Sibling Rivalry* 1990; *Brain Dead* 1990; *Liebestraum* 1991; *Crazy in Love* 1992; *The News Boys* 1992; *Singles* 1992; *The Last Seduction* 1993; *Malice* 1993; *Mr Jones* 1993; *Sleepless in Seattle* 1993; *Sommersby* 1993; *The Favor* 1994; *Wyatt Earp* 1994; *Casper* 1995; *While You Were Sleeping* 1995; *Independence Day* 1996; *Lost Highway* 1996; *Mr Wrong* 1996; *Mistrial* 1996; *The End of Violence* 1997; *Zero Effect* 1997; *Lake Placid* 1999; *Brokedown Palace* 1999; *History Is Made at Night* 1999; *Titan AE* 2000
Pully, B S *Greenwich Village* 1944; *Nob Hill* 1945; *Do You Love Me?* 1946; *Guys and Dolls* 1955
Pulver, Liselotte *aka* **Pulver, Lilo** *Arms and the Man* 1958; *A Time to Love and a Time to Die* 1958; *One, Two, Three* 1961; *A Global Affair* 1964; *La Religieuse* 1965
Punch McGregor, Angela *aka* **Punch, Angela** *The Chant of Jimmie Blacksmith* 1978; *Newsfront* 1978; *The Island* 1980; *The Survivor* 1981; *Double Deal* 1981; *We of the Never Never* 1982; *Annie's Coming Out* 1984; *The Delinquents* 1989
Punsley, Bernard *Dead End* 1937; *Angels Wash Their Faces* 1939
Purcell, Dick *aka* **Purcell, Richard** *Bullets or Ballots* 1936; *Arise, My Love* 1940; *New Moon* 1940; *Reveille with Beverly* 1943
Purcell, Irene *Westward Passage* 1932; *The Passionate Plumber* 1932
Purcell, James *Where Are the Children?* 1986; *Glitz* 1988; *On the 2nd Day of Christmas* 1997
Purcell, Lee *Adam at 6 AM* 1970; *Kid Blue* 1971; *Dirty Little Billy* 1972; *Mr Majestyk* 1974; *Almost Summer* 1977; *Big Wednesday* 1978; *The Secret War of Jackie's Girls* 1980; *Eddie Macon's Run* 1983; *The Incredible Hulk Returns* 1988; *Secret Sins of the Father* 1994
Purcell, Noel *The Blue Lagoon* 1949; *Appointment with Venus* 1951; *Encore* 1951; *Father's Doing Fine* 1952; *The Seekers* 1954; *Jacqueline* 1956; *Lust for Life* 1956; *The Rising of the Moon* 1957; *Ferry to Hong Kong* 1958; *The Key* 1958; *Merry Andrew* 1958; *Rockets Galore* 1958; *Rooney* 1958; *No Kidding* 1960; *Double Bunk* 1961; *The Iron Maiden* 1962; *The Violent Enemy* 1969; *Where's Jack?* 1969
Purdell, Reginald *The Old Curiosity Shop* 1934; *Variety Jubilee* 1942; *Bell-Bottom George* 1943; *We Dive at Dawn* 1943; *Love Story* 1944; *Two Thousand Women* 1944
Purdom, Edmund *The Egyptian* 1954; *The Student Prince* 1954; *Athena* 1954; *The King's Thief* 1955; *The Prodigal* 1955; *The Cossacks* 1959; *Moment of Danger* 1960; *Nefertite, Queen of the Nile* 1961; *The Beauty Jungle* 1964; *The Comedy Man* 1964; *The Yellow Rolls-Royce* 1964; *Pieces* 1982
Purefoy, James *Feast of July* 1995; *Bedrooms and Hallways* 1998; *Mansfield Park* 1999; *Maybe Baby* 1999; *The Wedding Tackle* 2000
Puri, Amrish *Indiana Jones and the Temple of Doom* 1984; *Mr India* 1986; *Taal* 1999
Puri, Om *Sadgati* 1981; *Mirch Masala* 1987; *Disha* 1990; *Sam and Me* 1991; *City of Joy* 1992; *In Custody* 1993; *Wolf* 1994; *Brothers in Trouble* 1995; *The Ghost and the Darkness* 1996; *Maachis* 1996; *My Son the Fanatic* 1997; *Such a Long Journey* 1998; *East Is East* 1999
Purl, Linda *Crazy Mama* 1975; *Black Market Baby* 1977; *The High Country* 1981; *Visiting Hours* 1982; *Outrage!* 1986; *Hollow Point* 1987; *Addicted to His Love* 1988; *Spies, Lies and Naked Thighs* 1988; *Body Language* 1992; *Danielle Steel's Secrets* 1992; *Accidental Meeting* 1994; *Terror at Deception Ridge* 1994; *Born Free: A New Adventure* 1996; *The Absolute Truth* 1997
Purviance, Edna *The Tramp* 1915; *Work* 1915; *The Vagabond* 1916; *Behind the Screen* 1916; *The Floorwalker* 1916; *The Rink* 1916; *The Pawnshop* 1916; *The Immigrant* 1917; *The Cure* 1917; *Shoulder Arms* 1918; *A Day's Pleasure* 1919; *Sunnyside* 1919; *The Idle Class* 1921; *The Kid* 1921; *Pay Day* 1922; *The Pilgrim* 1923; *A Woman of Paris* 1923
Pustil, Jeff *Def-Con 4* 1984; *Tails You Live, Heads You're Dead* 1995

Rae, Charlotte *Jenny* 1969; *Sidewinder One* 1977; *Tom and Jerry: the Movie* 1992
Rae, John *The Brave Don't Cry* 1952; *The Kidnappers* 1953; *The Big Chance* 1957; *The Bridal Path* 1959
Rafferty, Chips *Forty Thousand Horsemen* 1941; *The Overlanders* 1946; *The Loves of Joanna Godden* 1947; *Bush Christmas* 1947; *Eureka Stockade* 1949; *Bitter Springs* 1950; *Kangaroo* 1952; *The Desert Rats* 1953; *Smiley* 1956; *Smiley Gets a Gun* 1959; *The Sundowners* 1960; *The Wackiest Ship in the Army* 1961; *They're a Weird Mob* 1966; *Double Trouble* 1967; *Kona Coast* 1968; *Skullduggery* 1969
Rafferty, Frances *Young Ideas* 1943; *Barbary Coast Gent* 1944; *Dragon Seed* 1944; *Mrs Parkington* 1944; *Abbott and Costello in Hollywood* 1945; *The Hidden Eye* 1945; *Bad Bascomb* 1946
Raffin, Deborah *40 Carats* 1973; *The Dove* 1974; *Once Is Not Enough* 1975; *God Told Me to* 1976; *Maniac* 1977; *Mind over Murder* 1979; *Touched by Love* 1979; *Agatha Christie's Sparkling Cyanide* 1983; *Threesome* 1984; *Death Wish 3* 1985; *Scanners II: The New Order* 1991; *Morning Glory* 1993; *LaVyrle Spencer's Home Song* 1996
Raft, George *Palmy Days* 1931; *Quick Millions* 1931; *If I Had a Million* 1932; *Taxi!* 1932; *Scarface* 1932; *Night after Night* 1932; *The Bowery* 1933; *Bolero* 1934; *The Glass Key* 1935; *Rumba* 1935; *Souls at Sea* 1937; *Spawn of the North* 1938; *You and Me* 1938; *Each Dawn I Die* 1939; *Invisible Stripes* 1940; *They Drive by Night* 1940; *Manpower* 1941; *Broadway* 1942; *Background to Danger* 1943; *Stage Door Canteen* 1943; *Follow the Boys* 1944; *Johnny Angel* 1945; *Nob Hill* 1945; *Nocturne* 1946; *Whistle Stop* 1946; *Intrigue* 1947; *A Dangerous Profession* 1949; *Johnny Allegro* 1949; *Red Light* 1949; *I'll Get You for This* 1950; *Escape Route* 1952; *The Man from Cairo* 1953; *Black Widow* 1954; *Rogue Cop* 1954; *A Bullet for Joey* 1955; *Around the World in 80 Days* 1956; *Some Like It Hot* 1959; *Jet over the Atlantic* 1960; *The Ladies' Man* 1961; *Casino Royale* 1967; *Five Golden Dragons* 1967; *Skidoo* 1968; *Hammersmith Is Out* 1972; *Deadhead Miles* 1972; *Sextette* 1978; *The Man with Bogart's Face* 1980
Raglan, Robert *Man from Tangier* 1957; *Hidden Homicide* 1958; *Information Received* 1962
Ragland, Rags *Whistling in the Dark* 1941; *Whistling in Dixie* 1942; *DuBarry Was a Lady* 1943; *Girl Crazy* 1943; *Whistling in Brooklyn* 1943; *Meet the People* 1944; *Anchors Aweigh* 1945
Ragsdale, William *Fright Night* 1985; *Fright Night Part 2* 1988; *Frankenstein: the College Years* 1991; *Mannequin on the Move* 1991
Raho, Umberto *aka* **Newman, Raoul H** *The Spectre* 1963; *Aladdin* 1986
Railsback, Steve *The Visitors* 1972; *The Stunt Man* 1980; *Turkey Shoot* 1981; *Torchlight* 1984; *Lifeforce* 1985; *Distortions* 1987; *Blue Monkey* 1987; *The Cops Are Robbers* 1990; *Scissors* 1991; *Alligator II: the Mutation* 1991; *Nukie* 1992; *Sunstroke* 1992; *Quake!* 1992; *Bonds of Love* 1993; *Final Mission* 1993; *Separated by Murder* 1994; *Save Me* 1994; *Barb Wire* 1995; *Vanishing Point* 1997; *Disturbing Behaviour* 1998
Raimi, Sam *Body Bags* 1993; *Indian Summer* 1993
Raimi, Ted *Easy Wheels* 1989; *Lunatics: a Love Story* 1991; *Candyman* 1992; *The Finishing Touch* 1992; *The Shot* 1996
Raimi, Theodore *Evil Dead II* 1987; *Darkman* 1990
Raimondi, Ruggero *Don Giovanni* 1979; *Life Is a Bed of Roses* 1983; *Carmen* 1984
Raimu *Marius* 1931; *Fanny* 1932; *César* 1936; *Gribouille* 1937; *The Baker's Wife* 1938
Raine, Patricia *Vice Versa* 1947; *Pandora and the Flying Dutchman* 1951
Rainer, Luise *Escapade* 1935; *The Great Ziegfeld* 1936; *Big City* 1937; *The Emperor's Candlesticks* 1937; *The Good Earth* 1937; *Dramatic School* 1938; *The Great Waltz* 1938; *The Toy Wife* 1938; *Hostages* 1943; *The Gambler* 1997
Raines, Cristina *The Duellists* 1977; *The Sentinel* 1977; *Touched by Love* 1979; *Silver Dream Racer* 1980; *Nightmares* 1983
Raines, Ella *Corvette K-225* 1943; *Cry Havoc* 1943; *Enter Arsene Lupin* 1944; *Hail the Conquering Hero* 1944; *Phantom Lady* 1944; *Tall in the Saddle* 1944; *The Suspect* 1944; *The Strange Affair of Uncle Harry* 1945; *Brute Force* 1947; *The Senator Was Indiscreet* 1947; *The Web* 1947; *A Dangerous Profession* 1949; *Impact* 1949; *The Walking Hills* 1949; *Ride the Man Down* 1952; *The Man in the Road* 1957
Rainey, Ford *The Last Mile* 1959; *Ada* 1961; *The Naked Zoo* 1970; *Glory Boy* 1971; *Bed & Breakfast* 1992
Rains, Claude *The Invisible Man* 1933; *The Clairvoyant* 1934; *Crime without Passion* 1934; *The Mystery of Edwin Drood* 1935; *The Last Outpost* 1935; *Anthony Adverse* 1936; *The Prince and the Pauper* 1937; *They Won't Forget* 1937; *The Adventures of Robin Hood* 1938; *Four Daughters* 1938; *Gold Is Where You Find It* 1938; *White Banners* 1938; *Daughters Courageous* 1939; *Juarez* 1939; *Mr Smith Goes to Washington* 1939; *They Made Me a Criminal* 1939; *Four Wives* 1939; *Saturday's Children* 1940; *The Sea Hawk* 1940; *Here Comes Mr Jordan* 1941; *The Wolf Man* 1941; *Casablanca* 1942; *Kings Row* 1942; *Moontide* 1942; *Now, Voyager* 1942; *Strange Holiday* 1942; *Forever and a Day* 1943; *Phantom of the Opera* 1943; *Mr Skeffington* 1944; *Passage to Marseille* 1944; *Caesar and Cleopatra* 1945; *This Love of Ours* 1945; *Angel on My Shoulder* 1946; *Deception* 1946; *Notorious* 1946; *The Unsuspected* 1947; *The Passionate Friends* 1948; *Rope of Sand* 1949; *Where Danger Lives* 1950; *The White Tower* 1950; *Sealed Cargo* 1951; *The Man Who Watched Trains Go By* 1952; *Lisbon* 1956; *This Earth Is Mine* 1959; *The Lost World* 1960; *Lawrence of Arabia* 1962; *Twilight of Honor* 1963; *The Greatest Story Ever Told* 1965
Rajot, Pierre-Loup *Aduefue, the Lords of the Street* 1988; *La Nouvelle Eve* 1999
Rall, Tommy *aka* **Rall, Thomas** *Kiss Me Kate* 1953; *Seven Brides for Seven Brothers* 1954; *My Sister Eileen* 1955; *Invitation to the Dance* 1956; *Walk the Proud Land* 1956; *Merry Andrew* 1958; *Dancers* 1987
Ralli, Giovanna *General Della Rovere* 1959; *What Did You Do in the War, Daddy?* 1966; *Deadfall* 1968; *A Professional Gun* 1968; *Cannon for Cordoba* 1970; *We All Loved Each Other So Much* 1974
Ralph, Hanna *The Nibelungen* 1924; *Faust* 1926
Ralph, Jessie *The Affairs of Cellini* 1934; *Murder at the Vanities* 1934; *One Night of Love* 1934; *David Copperfield* 1935; *I Found Stella Parish* 1935; *Les Misérables* 1935; *After the Thin Man* 1936; *San Francisco* 1936; *Camille* 1937; *Double Wedding* 1937; *The Good Earth* 1937; *The Last of Mrs Cheyney* 1937; *Drums along the Mohawk* 1939; *The Bank Dick* 1940; *They Met in Bombay* 1941
Ralph, Michael *DROP Squad* 1994; *Woo* 1998
Ralph, Sheryl Lee *Oliver & Company* 1988; *The Mighty Quinn* 1989; *The Distinguished Gentleman* 1992; *Witch Hunt* 1994; *Bogus* 1996
Ralston, Esther *Rome Express* 1932; *Black Beauty* 1933; *Sadie McKee* 1934; *By Candlelight* 1934; *Tin Pan Alley* 1940
Ralston, Jobyna *Girl Shy* 1924; *Hot Water* 1924; *The Freshman* 1925; *For Heaven's Sake* 1926; *The Kid Brother* 1927; *Wings* 1927
Ralston, Vera *aka* **Ralston, Vera Hruba** *Dakota* 1945; *The Fighting Kentuckian* 1949; *Hoodlum Empire* 1952; *Fair Wind to Java* 1953; *Timberjack* 1955
Ramage, Cecil *King of the Damned* 1935; *Return of a Stranger* 1937; *Kind Hearts and Coronets* 1949
Rambeau, Marjorie *Her Man* 1930; *Min and Bill* 1930; *Inspiration* 1931; *Laughing Sinners* 1931; *The Secret Six* 1931; *Strangers May Kiss* 1931; *Hell Divers* 1932; *Man's Castle* 1933; *Palooka* 1934; *Primrose Path* 1940; *Tobacco Road* 1941; *Broadway* 1942; *War of the Wildcats* 1943; *The Lucky Stiff* 1949; *Torch Song* 1953; *Forever Female* 1953; *A Man Called Peter* 1955; *The View from Pompey's Head* 1955; *Man of a Thousand Faces* 1957
Rambo, Dack *Which Way to the Front?* 1970; *The Spring* 1990
Ramer, Henry *The Apprenticeship of Duddy Kravitz* 1974; *My Pleasure Is My Business* 1974; *Welcome to Blood City* 1977; *Between Friends* 1983; *Hockey Night* 1984
Ramírez, Carlos *Bathing Beauty* 1944; *Two Girls and a Sailor* 1944; *Where Do We Go from Here?* 1945
Ramis, Harold *Heavy Metal* 1981; *Stripes* 1981; *Ghostbusters* 1984; *Baby Boom* 1987; *Stealing Home* 1988; *Ghostbusters II* 1989
Ramón, Eulalia *Who Killed Nani?* 1988; *Outrage* 1993; *Goya in Bordeaux* 1999
Ramos, Rudy *The Driver* 1978; *Defiance* 1979; *Quicksilver* 1986; *Blindsided* 1993
Rampling, Charlotte *Rotten to the Core* 1965; *Georgy Girl* 1966; *The Long Duel* 1966; *Target: Harry* 1968; *The Damned* 1969; *Three* 1969; *Asylum* 1972; *Henry VIII and His Six Wives* 1972; *Corky* 1972; *The Night Porter* 1973; *Zardoz* 1973; *Caravan to Vaccares* 1974; *The Flesh of the Orchid* 1974; *Farewell, My Lovely* 1975; *Sherlock Holmes in New York* 1976; *Orca* 1977; *The Purple Taxi* 1977; *Stardust Memories* 1980; *The Verdict* 1982; *Long Live Life* 1984; *Max Mon Amour* 1986; *Angel Heart* 1987; *Mascara* 1987; *DOA* 1988; *Paris by Night* 1988; *Invasion of Privacy* 1996; *The Wings of the Dove* 1997; *The Cherry Orchard* 1998
Ramsay, Bruce *Alive* 1992; *Dead Beat* 1994; *Curdled* 1995; *Hellraiser: Bloodline* 1996
Ramsay, Remak *The House on Carroll Street* 1987; *Addicted to Love* 1997
Ramsey, Anne *When You Comin' Back, Red Ryder?* 1979; *White Mama* 1980; *The Goonies* 1985; *Deadly Friend* 1986; *Throw Momma from the Train* 1987; *Homer and Eddie* 1989
Ramsey, Logan *The Hoodlum Priest* 1961; *Head* 1968; *Beg, Borrow or Steal* 1973; *Busting* 1974
Ramsey, Marion *Police Academy 2: Their First Assignment* 1985; *Police Academy 3: Back in Training* 1986; *Police Academy 6: City under Siege* 1989
Ramsey, Ward *Dinosaurus!* 1960; *Posse from Hell* 1961
Ramus, Nick *Windwalker* 1980; *The Legend of Walks Far Woman* 1982; *Geronimo* 1993
Rand, Edwin *The Capture* 1950; *Tarantula* 1955
Rand, John *The Pawnshop* 1916; *The Cure* 1917; *The Idle Class* 1921
Randall, Anne *A Time for Dying* 1971; *The Christian Licorice Store* 1971
Randall, Lexi *Sarah, Plain and Tall* 1991; *Skylark* 1993; *The War* 1994; *The Stars Fell on Henrietta* 1995
Randall, Meg *Ma and Pa Kettle* 1949; *Last of the Badmen* 1957
Randall, Tony *Oh, Men! Oh, Women!* 1957; *Will Success Spoil Rock Hunter?* 1957; *No Down Payment* 1957; *The Mating Game* 1959; *Pillow Talk* 1959; *The Adventures of Huckleberry Finn* 1960; *Let's Make Love* 1960; *Lover Come Back* 1961; *Boys' Night Out* 1962; *Island of Love* 1963; *7 Faces of Dr Lao* 1963; *Send Me No Flowers* 1964; *The Brass Bottle* 1964; *Fluffy* 1965; *The Alphabet Murders* 1966; *Our Man in Marrakesh* 1966; *Hello Down There* 1969; *Everything You Always Wanted to Know about Sex (But Were Afraid to Ask)* 1972; *Scavenger Hunt* 1979; *Foolin' Around* 1980; *The King of Comedy* 1983; *Sunday Drive* 1986; *Save the Dog!* 1988; *The Man in the Brown Suit* 1989; *Gremlins 2: the New Batch* 1990; *The Odd Couple: Together Again* 1993
Randell, Ron *Bulldog Drummond Strikes Back* 1947; *The Loves of Carmen* 1948; *Lorna Doone* 1951; *China Corsair* 1951; *Kiss Me Kate* 1953; *I Am a Camera* 1955; *The Story of Esther Costello* 1957; *Beyond Mombasa* 1957; *The Girl in Black Stockings* 1957; *The Most Dangerous Man Alive* 1961; *Follow the Boys* 1963; *Gold for the Caesars* 1964; *Whity* 1970; *Exposed* 1983
Randle, Frank *Somewhere on Leave* 1942; *Home Sweet Home* 1945; *When You Come Home* 1947; *It's a Grand Life* 1953
Randle, Theresa *Malcolm X* 1992; *Sugar Hill* 1993; *Beverly Hills Cop III* 1994; *Bad Boys* 1995; *Girl 6* 1996; *Space Jam* 1997; *Spawn* 1997
Randolf, Anders *The Black Pirate* 1926; *The Kiss* 1929
Randolph, Donald *Bride of Vengeance* 1949; *Assignment – Paris* 1952; *Khyber Patrol* 1954; *The Mad Magician* 1954; *Phffft!* 1954; *The Deadly Mantis* 1957
Randolph, Jane *Cat People* 1942; *The Falcon's Brother* 1942; *The Falcon Strikes Back* 1943; *The Curse of the Cat People* 1944; *Fool's Gold* 1946; *T-Men* 1947; *Railroaded* 1947; *Abbott and Costello Meet Frankenstein* 1948
Randolph, John *Seconds* 1966; *Number One* 1969; *Smith!* 1969; *There Was a Crooked Man...* 1970; *Escape from the Planet of the Apes* 1971; *Little Murders* 1971; *Conquest of the Planet of the Apes* 1972; *Serpico* 1973; *King Kong* 1976; *Prizzi's Honor* 1985; *As Summers Die* 1986; *The Wizard of Loneliness* 1988; *National Lampoon's Christmas Vacation* 1989; *Iron Maze* 1991; *A Price above Rubies* 1997
Randolph, Lillian *Bachelor Knight* 1947; *Once More, My Darling* 1949
Randone, Salvo *Salvatore Giuliano* 1961; *Hands over the City* 1963; *The Tenth Victim* 1965; *We Still Kill the Old Way* 1967; *Satyricon* 1969; *Investigation of a Citizen above Suspicion* 1970
Ransom, Tim *The Dressmaker* 1988; *Vital Signs* 1990; *The Last to Go* 1991; *Vanished without a Trace* 1993
Ransome, Prunella *Far from the Madding Crowd* 1967; *Alfred the Great* 1969; *Man in the Wilderness* 1971
Rapaport, Michael *Zebrahead* 1992; *Money for Nothing* 1993; *Hand Gun* 1994; *Kiss of Death* 1994; *The Scout* 1994; *Higher Learning* 1995; *Mighty Aphrodite* 1995; *Beautiful Girls* 1996; *The Pallbearer* 1996; *illtown* 1996; *Cop Land* 1997; *Metro* 1997; *Kicked in the Head* 1997; *Palmetto* 1998; *Some Girls* 1998; *Deep Blue Sea* 1999
Rapp, Anthony *A Night on the Town* 1987; *Far from Home* 1989; *School Ties* 1992; *Dazed and Confused* 1993
Rappaport, David *The Bride* 1985; *Peter Gunn* 1989
Rasche, David *Death Vengeance* 1982; *An Innocent Man* 1989; *Wicked Stepmother* 1989; *Masters of Menace* 1990; *Silhouette* 1990; *Bingo* 1991; *Delirious* 1991; *That Old Feeling* 1997; *Tourist Trap* 1998
Rashad, Phylicia *Uncle Tom's Cabin* 1987; *False Witness* 1989; *Polly* 1989; *Jailbirds* 1991; *David's Mother* 1994; *Legacy of Evil* 1995; *The Babysitter's Seduction* 1996; *Free of Eden* 1999
Rasp, Fritz *Metropolis* 1926; *The Love of Jeanne Ney* 1927; *Diary of a Lost Girl* 1929; *The Woman in the Moon* 1929; *The Threepenny Opera* 1931; *Paracelsus* 1943; *The Red Circle* 1960
Rasulala, Thalmus *Blacula* 1972; *The Autobiography of Miss Jane Pittman* 1974; *Adios Amigo* 1975;

Friday Foster 1975; Bulletproof 1987; Blind Vengeance 1990; Mom and Dad Save the World 1992

Rasumny, Mikhail Road to Morocco 1942; Wake Island 1942; For Whom the Bell Tolls 1943; A Medal for Benny 1945; The Stork Club 1945; Anna and the King of Siam 1946; Heartbeat 1946; Her Husband's Affairs 1947; Anything Can Happen 1952; Hot Blood 1956

Ratchford, Jeremy Change of Heart 1993; Getting Gotti 1994; Generation X 1996

Ratcliff, Sandy Family Life 1971; Radio On 1979; Yesterday's Hero 1979

Rathbone, Basil The Last of Mrs Cheyney 1929; Anna Karenina 1935; Captain Blood 1935; David Copperfield 1935; Kind Lady 1935; The Last Days of Pompeii 1935; A Tale of Two Cities 1935; The Garden of Allah 1936; Love from a Stranger 1936; Romeo and Juliet 1936; Confession 1937; Tovarich 1937; The Adventures of Marco Polo 1938; The Adventures of Robin Hood 1938; The Dawn Patrol 1938; If I Were King 1938; The Adventures of Sherlock Holmes 1939; The Hound of the Baskervilles 1939; Son of Frankenstein 1939; Tower of London 1939; The Mark of Zorro 1940; Rhythm on the River 1940; International Lady 1941; Paris Calling 1941; Crossroads 1942; Fingers at the Window 1942; Sherlock Holmes and the Secret Weapon 1942; Sherlock Holmes and the Voice of Terror 1942; Above Suspicion 1943; Sherlock Holmes Faces Death 1943; Sherlock Holmes in Washington 1943; Bathing Beauty 1944; Frenchman's Creek 1944; The House of Fear 1944; The Pearl of Death 1944; The Scarlet Claw 1944; Sherlock Holmes and the Spider Woman 1944; Pursuit to Algiers 1945; The Woman in Green 1945; Dressed to Kill 1946; Heartbeat 1946; Terror by Night 1946; The Adventures of Ichabod and Mr Toad 1949; Casanova's Big Night 1954; We're No Angels 1955; The Court Jester 1956; The Black Sleep 1956; The Last Hurrah 1958; Pontius Pilate 1961; Tales of Terror 1962; The Magic Sword 1962; The Comedy of Terrors 1964; Voyage to the Prehistoric Planet 1965; The Ghost in the Invisible Bikini 1966; Planet of Blood 1966

Rathebe, Dolly Mapantsula 1988; Friends 1993

Ratner, Benjamin aka **Ratner, Ben** Dangerous Desire 1993; Profile for Murder 1996

Ratoff, Gregory What Price Hollywood? 1932; Symphony of Six Million 1932; Broadway through a Keyhole 1933; I'm No Angel 1933; Sitting Pretty 1933; George White's Scandals 1934; Remember Last Night? 1935; The Road to Glory 1936; Sing, Baby, Sing 1936; Under Two Flags 1936; Seventh Heaven 1937; Sally, Irene and Mary 1938; All about Eve 1950; O Henry's Full House 1952; The Sun Also Rises 1957; Once More, with Feeling 1959; Exodus 1960; The Big Gamble 1961

Rattray, Heather Across the Great Divide 1977; The Sea Gypsies 1978; Mountain Family Robinson 1979; Basket Case 2 1990

Ratzenberger, John Warlords of Atlantis 1978; Arabian Adventure

1979; The Bitch 1979; Hanover Street 1979; Outland 1981; Battletruck 1982; Combat Academy 1986; House II: the Second Story 1987; Timestalkers 1987; Toy Story 1995; Under Pressure 1997; That Darn Cat 1997; Toy Story 2 1999

Rauch, Siegfried Le Mans 1971; Battleflag 1977; The Big Red One 1980

Raven, Elsa The Moderns 1988; Descending Angel 1990

Raven, Mike Crucible of Terror 1971; I, Monster 1971

Ravenscroft, Thurl The Aristocats 1970; The Brave Little Toaster 1987

Rawlings, Margaret Roman Holiday 1953; Beautiful Stranger 1954; No Road Back 1957; Follow Me 1971; Hands of the Ripper 1971

Rawlins, Adrian Mountains of the Moon 1989; Breaking the Waves 1996

Rawlinson, Herbert Confidential 1935; The Counterfeiters 1948; Jail Bait 1954

Rawls, Lou Angel, Angel Down We Go 1969; Lookin' Italian 1994

Ray, Aldo The Marrying Kind 1952; Pat and Mike 1952; Let's Do It Again 1953; Miss Sadie Thompson 1953; Battle Cry 1955; We're No Angels 1955; Nightfall 1956; Men in War 1957; God's Little Acre 1958; The Naked and the Dead 1958; The Siege of Pinchgut 1959; The Day They Robbed the Bank of England 1960; Sylvia 1964; Nightmare in the Sun 1964; Dead Heat on a Merry-Go-Round 1966; What Did You Do in the War, Daddy? 1966; Welcome to Hard Times 1967; The Violent Ones 1967; Kill a Dragon 1967; The Green Berets 1968; And Hope to Die 1972; Seven Alone 1974; Inside Out 1975; The Man Who Would Not Die 1975; Psychic Killer 1975; Haunted 1976; Won Ton Ton, the Dog Who Saved Hollywood 1976; The Glove 1978; Little Moon & Jud McGraw 1978

Ray, Andrew The Mudlark 1950; The Yellow Balloon 1952; Escape by Night 1953; Woman in a Dressing Gown 1957; Gideon's Day 1959; Serious Charge 1959; Twice round the Daffodils 1962; Paris by Night 1988

Ray, Michel The Divided Heart 1954; The Brave One 1956; The Tin Star 1957

Ray, Nicholas The American Friend 1977; Hair 1979

Ray, René When London Sleeps 1932; The Passing of the Third Floor Back 1935; Street Song 1935; His Lordship 1936; The Green Cockatoo 1937; Please Teacher 1937; Bank Holiday 1938; Housemaster 1938; They Made Me a Fugitive 1947; Women of Twilight 1952; The Good Die Young 1954; The Vicious Circle 1957

Ray, Ted Meet Me Tonight 1952; Escape by Night 1953; Carry On Teacher 1959; Please Turn Over 1960

Raye, Carol While I Live 1947; Remember Me 1985

Raye, Martha The Big Broadcast of 1937 1936; Rhythm on the Range 1936; Artists and Models 1937; The Big Broadcast of 1938 1937; Waikiki Wedding 1937; College Swing 1938; Never Say Die 1939; The Boys from Syracuse 1940; Hellzapoppin' 1941; Keep 'em Flying 1941; Pin Up Girl 1944; Monsieur Verdoux

1947; Billy Rose's Jumbo 1962; Pufnstuf 1970

Raymond, Bill My New Gun 1992; Where the Rivers Flow North 1993

Raymond, Candy The Plumber 1979; Monkey Grip 1983

Raymond, Cyril The Ghost Train 1931; Accused 1936; The Shadow 1936; Come On George 1939; Saloon Bar 1940; Brief Encounter 1945; Angels One Five 1952; Lease of Life 1954; The Safecracker 1958; Don't Talk to Strange Men 1962

Raymond, Gary The Moonraker 1957; Look Back in Anger 1959; Suddenly, Last Summer 1959; The Millionairess 1960; El Cid 1961; Jason and the Argonauts 1963

Raymond, Gene If I Had a Million 1932; Red Dust 1932; Flying down to Rio 1933; Zoo in Budapest 1933; Ex-Lady 1933; Sadie McKee 1934; Hooray for Love 1935; Seven Keys to Baldpate 1935; The Woman in Red 1935; The Bride Walks Out 1936; Mr and Mrs Smith 1941; Smilin' Through 1941; The Locket 1946; Hit the Deck 1955; Plunder Road 1957; The Best Man 1964; I'd Rather Be Rich 1964

Raymond, Paula Crisis 1950; Devil's Doorway 1950; The Sellout 1951; The Tall Target 1951; The Bandits of Corsica 1953; The Beast from 20,000 Fathoms 1953; City That Never Sleeps 1953; The Human Jungle 1954; Blood of Dracula's Castle 1967

Rea, Peggy Love Field 1992; Made in America 1993

Rea, Stephen Angel 1982; Loose Connections 1983; The Company of Wolves 1984; The Doctor and the Devils 1985; Life Is Sweet 1990; Bad Behaviour 1992; The Crying Game 1992; Angie 1994; Interview with the Vampire: the Vampire Chronicles 1994; Prêt-à-Porter 1994; Princess Caraboo 1994; All Men Are Mortal 1995; Between the Devil and the Deep Blue Sea 1995; Citizen X 1995; Crime of the Century 1996; Fever Pitch 1996; A Further Gesture 1996; Last of the High Kings 1996; Michael Collins 1996; Trojan Eddie 1996; The Butcher Boy 1997; Double Tap 1997; In Dreams 1998; Still Crazy 1998; This Is My Father 1998; Guinevere 1999; The End of the Affair 1999; I Could Read the Sky 2000

Read, Barbara Make Way for Tomorrow 1937; The Man Who Cried Wolf 1937; Three Smart Girls 1937; The Spellbinder 1939

Read, James The Initiation 1984; Beaches 1988; Love Crimes 1991; The President's Child 1992; The Other Woman 1994; When the Dark Man Calls 1995

Reagan, Ronald Hollywood Hotel 1937; Boy Meets Girl 1938; Going Places 1938; Angels Wash Their Faces 1939; Dark Victory 1939; Naughty but Nice 1939; Knute Rockne – All American 1940; Santa Fe Trail 1940; Million Dollar Baby 1941; Desperate Journey 1942; Kings Row 1942; This Is the Army 1943; The Hasty Heart 1949; It's a Great Feeling 1949; Night unto Night 1949; Storm Warning 1950; Bedtime for Bonzo 1951; She's Working Her Way through College 1952; Law and Order 1953; Cattle Queen of Montana 1954; Prisoner of War 1954; Tennessee's Partner 1955; Hellcats of the Navy 1957; The Killers 1964

Reason, Rex aka **Roberts, Bart** Taza, Son of Cochise 1954; Yankee Pasha 1954; Smoke Signal 1955; This Island Earth 1955; Kiss of Fire 1955; Raw Edge 1956; Band of Angels 1957; The Sad Horse 1959

Rebhorn, James He Knows You're Alone 1981; Scent of a Woman 1992; Carlito's Way 1993; Blank Cheque 1994; 8 Seconds 1994; Guarding Tess 1994; I Love Trouble 1994; If Lucy Fell 1996; Mistrial 1996; Up Close & Personal 1996; The Game 1997; The Talented Mr Ripley 1999; Snow Falling on Cedars 1999

Reddin, Keith The Heart of Justice 1992; Lolita 1997

Reddy, Helen Airport 1975 1974; Pete's Dragon 1977

Redeker, Quinn The Three Stooges Meet Hercules 1962; The Candidate 1972; At Long Last Love 1975

Redfield, William Conquest of Space 1955; The Proud and Profane 1956; I Married a Woman 1958; The Connection 1961; Duel at Diablo 1966; Fantastic Voyage 1966; The Sidelong Glances of a Pigeon Kicker 1970; A New Leaf 1971; Death Wish 1974; For Pete's Sake 1974; Fear on Trial 1975; One Flew over the Cuckoo's Nest 1975; Mr Billion 1977

Redford, Robert War Hunt 1962; Inside Daisy Clover 1965; Situation Hopeless – but Not Serious 1965; The Chase 1966; This Property Is Condemned 1966; Barefoot in the Park 1967; Butch Cassidy and the Sundance Kid 1969; Downhill Racer 1969; Tell Them Willie Boy Is Here 1969; Little Fauss and Big Halsy 1970; The Candidate 1972; The Hot Rock 1972; Jeremiah Johnson 1972; The Sting 1973; The Way We Were 1973; The Great Gatsby 1974; The Great Waldo Pepper 1975; Three Days of the Condor 1975; All the President's Men 1976; A Bridge Too Far 1977; The Electric Horseman 1979; Brubaker 1980; The Natural 1984; Out of Africa 1985; Legal Eagles 1986; Havana 1990; Sneakers 1992; Indecent Proposal 1993; Up Close & Personal 1996; The Horse Whisperer 1998

Redgrave, Corin Crooks in Cloisters 1963; A Man for All Seasons 1966; The Charge of the Light Brigade 1968; David Copperfield 1969; Oh! What a Lovely War 1969; When Eight Bells Toll 1971; Von Richthofen and Brown 1971; Excalibur 1981; Eureka 1982; In the Name of the Father 1993; Four Weddings and a Funeral 1994; Persuasion 1995; Honest 2000

Redgrave, Jemma Dream Demon 1988; Howards End 1992

Redgrave, Lynn Girl with Green Eyes 1963; Tom Jones 1963; The Deadly Affair 1966; Georgy Girl 1966; Smashing Time 1967; The Virgin Soldiers 1969; Last of the Mobile Hot-Shots 1970; Every Little Crook and Nanny 1972; Everything You Always Wanted to Know about Sex (But Were Afraid to Ask) 1972; The National Health 1973; The Happy Hooker 1975; The Seduction of Miss Leona 1980; Rehearsal for Murder 1982; My Two Loves 1986; Home Front 1987; Getting It Right 1989; Midnight 1989; The Great American Sex Scandal 1990; What Ever Happened to...? 1991; Shine 1996; A Father's Betrayal 1997; Toothless 1997; Gods and

Monsters 1998; Strike! 1998; The Next Best Thing 2000

Redgrave, Michael Climbing High 1938; The Lady Vanishes 1938; The Stars Look Down 1939; A Window in London 1939; Jeannie 1941; Kipps 1941; Thunder Rock 1942; Dead of Night 1945; The Way to the Stars 1945; The Captive Heart 1946; Fame Is the Spur 1947; The Man Within 1947; Mourning Becomes Electra 1947; Secret beyond the Door 1948; The Browning Version 1951; The Magic Box 1951; The Importance of Being Earnest 1952; The Dam Busters 1954; The Sea Shall Not Have Them 1954; The Green Scarf 1954; Confidential Report 1955; The Night My Number Came Up 1955; Oh, Rosalinda!! 1955; 1984 1955; The Happy Road 1956; Time without Pity 1957; Behind the Mask 1958; Law and Disorder 1958; The Quiet American 1958; Shake Hands with the Devil 1959; The Wreck of the Mary Deare 1959; The Innocents 1961; No My Darling Daughter 1961; The Loneliness of the Long Distance Runner 1962; The Heroes of Telemark 1965; The Hill 1965; Young Cassidy 1965; The 25th Hour 1967; Assignment K 1968; Battle of Britain 1969; Connecting Rooms 1969; David Copperfield 1969; Goodbye, Mr Chips 1969; Oh! What a Lovely War 1969; The Go-Between 1971

Redgrave, Vanessa Behind the Mask 1958; Blow Up 1966; A Man for All Seasons 1966; Morgan – a Suitable Case for Treatment 1966; Camelot 1967; The Sailor from Gibraltar 1967; The Charge of the Light Brigade 1968; Isadora 1968; The Sea Gull 1968; Oh! What a Lovely War 1969; The Devils 1971; Mary, Queen of Scots 1971; The Trojan Women 1971; Murder on the Orient Express 1974; Out of Season 1975; The Seven-Per-Cent Solution 1976; Julia 1977; Agatha 1978; Bear Island 1979; Yanks 1979; Playing for Time 1980; My Body, My Child 1982; Wagner 1983; The Bostonians 1984; Steaming 1985; Wetherby 1985; Comrades: a Lanternist's Account of the Tolpuddle Martyrs and What Became of Them 1986; Second Serve 1986; Prick Up Your Ears 1987; A Man for All Seasons 1988; Consuming Passions 1988; Orpheus Descending 1990; The Ballad of the Sad Café 1991; What Ever Happened to...? 1991; Howards End 1992; Wall of Silence 1993; The House of the Spirits 1993; Mother's Boys 1993; Sparrow 1993; They Watch 1993; Shades of Fear 1993; Little Odessa 1994; A Month by the Lake 1994; Down Came a Blackbird 1995; Mission: Impossible 1996; Smilla's Feeling for Snow 1996; Two Mothers for Zachary 1996; Déjà Vu 1997; Mrs Dalloway 1997; Wilde 1997; Deep Impact 1998; Lulu on the Bridge 1998; Cradle Will Rock 1999; Girl, Interrupted 1999; If These Walls Could Talk 2 2000

Reding, Nick Captive 1986; Mister Johnson 1991

Redman, Amanda For Queen and Country 1988; The Wedding Tackle 2000

Redman, Joyce Othello 1965; Prudence and the Pill 1968

Redmond, Liam I See a Dark Stranger 1946; Daughter of Darkness 1948; Devil on

Horseback 1954; *The Divided Heart* 1954; *The Glass Cage* 1955; *Jacqueline* 1956; *23 Paces to Baker Street* 1956; *Night of the Demon* 1957; *Alive and Kicking* 1958; *Rooney* 1958; *Under Ten Flags* 1960; *Scent of Mystery* 1960; *The Luck of Ginger Coffey* 1964; *The Ghost and Mr Chicken* 1966; *The Adventures of Bullwhip Griffin* 1967; *The Last Safari* 1967; *Till Death Us Do Part* 1968; *Philadelphia, Here I Come* 1975

Redmond, Moira *Pit of Darkness* 1961; *Jigsaw* 1962; *Kill or Cure* 1962; *Nightmare* 1964; *The Winter's Tale* 1966

Redmond, Siobhan *Captives* 1994; *Beautiful People* 1999

Reece, Brian *A Case for PC 49* 1950; *Orders Are Orders* 1954; *Carry On Admiral* 1957

Reed, Alan *aka* **Openshaw, Falstaff,** *aka* **Reed Sr, Alan** *Days of Glory* 1944; *Nob Hill* 1945; *Perfect Strangers* 1950; *Viva Zapata!* 1952; *I, the Jury* 1953; *Lady and the Tramp* 1955; *The Far Horizons* 1955; *Kiss of Fire* 1955; *Timetable* 1956; *He Laughed Last* 1956; *The Tarnished Angels* 1957; *The Man Called Flintstone* 1966; *A Dream of Kings* 1969; *Shinbone Alley* 1971; *The Seniors* 1978

Reed, Alyson *A Chorus Line* 1985; *Skin Deep* 1989

Reed, Donna *Shadow of the Thin Man* 1941; *Calling Dr Gillespie* 1942; *The Courtship of Andy Hardy* 1942; *Eyes in the Night* 1942; *Apache Trail* 1942; *Dr Gillespie's Criminal Case* 1943; *The Human Comedy* 1943; *The Man from Down Under* 1943; *See Here, Private Hargrove* 1944; *The Picture of Dorian Gray* 1945; *They Were Expendable* 1945; *It's a Wonderful Life* 1946; *Green Dolphin Street* 1947; *The Caddy* 1953; *From Here to Eternity* 1953; *Gun Fury* 1953; *Raiders of the Seven Seas* 1953; *Trouble along the Way* 1953; *The Last Time I Saw Paris* 1954; *They Rode West* 1954; *Three Hours to Kill* 1954; *The Benny Goodman Story* 1955; *The Far Horizons* 1955; *Backlash* 1956; *Ransom!* 1956; *Beyond Mombasa* 1957; *The Whole Truth* 1958

Reed, George *The Green Pastures* 1936; *Swanee River* 1939

Reed, Jerry *WW and the Dixie Dancekings* 1975; *Gator* 1976; *Smokey and the Bandit* 1977; *High-ballin'* 1978; *Hot Stuff* 1979; *Smokey and the Bandit II* 1980; *Smokey and the Bandit III* 1983; *The Survivors* 1983; *BAT-21* 1988; *The Waterboy* 1998

Reed, Lou *One-Trick Pony* 1980; *Get Crazy* 1983; *Faraway, So Close* 1993; *Blue in the Face* 1995

Reed, Marshall *The Lineup* 1958; *The Hard Ride* 1971

Reed, Maxwell *Daybreak* 1946; *The Brothers* 1947; *Dear Murderer* 1947; *Daughter of Darkness* 1948; *Night Beat* 1948; *Madness of the Heart* 1949; *Blackout* 1950; *The Clouded Yellow* 1950; *There Is Another Sun* 1951; *Sea Devils* 1952; *The Square Ring* 1953; *The Brain Machine* 1954; *The Notorious Landlady* 1962; *Picture Mommy Dead* 1966

Reed, Oliver *The Angry Silence* 1960; *Beat Girl* 1960; *The Two Faces of Dr Jekyll* 1960; *The Bulldog Breed* 1960; *The Curse of the Werewolf* 1961; *The Damned* 1961; *The Pirates of Blood River* 1961; *The Scarlet Blade* 1963; *Paranoiac* 1963; *The System* 1964; *The Party's Over* 1965; *The Trap* 1966; *I'll Never Forget What's 'Is Name* 1967; *The Jokers* 1967; *The Shuttered Room* 1967; *Hannibal Brooks* 1968; *Oliver!* 1968; *The Assassination Bureau* 1969; *Women in Love* 1969; *Take a Girl Like You* 1970; *The Lady in the Car with Glasses and a Gun* 1970; *The Devils* 1971; *The Hunting Party* 1971; *ZPG: Zero Population Growth* 1971; *The Triple Echo* 1972; *Sitting Target* 1972; *Blue Blood* 1973; *The Three Musketeers* 1973; *And Then There Were None* 1974; *The Four Musketeers* 1974; *Royal Flash* 1975; *The Sellout* 1975; *Tommy* 1975; *Burnt Offerings* 1976; *The Great Scout & Cathouse Thursday* 1976; *The Prince and the Pauper* 1977; *Tomorrow Never Comes* 1977; *Maniac* 1977; *The Big Sleep* 1978; *The Class of Miss MacMichael* 1978; *The Brood* 1979; *Dr Heckyl & Mr Hype* 1980; *Condorman* 1981; *Lion of the Desert* 1981; *No Secrets* 1982; *Venom* 1982; *The Sting II* 1983; *Two of a Kind* 1983; *Captive* 1986; *Castaway* 1986; *Dragonard* 1987; *Gor* 1987; *The Adventures of Baron Munchausen* 1988; *The House of Usher* 1988; *Rage to Kill* 1988; *Captive Rage* 1988; *The Return of the Musketeers* 1989; *A Ghost in Monte Carlo* 1990; *Treasure Island* 1990; *Hired to Kill* 1990; *Prisoner of Honor* 1991; *The Pit and the Pendulum* 1991; *Funny Bones* 1994; *The Bruce* 1996; *Parting Shots* 1998; *Gladiator* 2000

Reed, Pamela *Eyewitness* 1981; *The Right Stuff* 1983; *The Goodbye People* 1984; *Scandal Sheet* 1985; *The Best of Times* 1986; *The Clan of the Cave Bear* 1986; *Rachel River* 1987; *Chattahoochee* 1989; *Cadillac Man* 1990; *Caroline?* 1990; *Kindergarten Cop* 1990; *Woman with a Past* 1991; *Passed Away* 1992; *Born Too Soon* 1993; *Junior* 1994; *Deadly Whispers* 1995; *The Man Next Door* 1996; *Critical Choices* 1996; *Bean* 1997

Reed, Paul *The Ride to Hangman's Tree* 1967; *Did You Hear the One about the Traveling Saleslady?* 1968

Reed, Philip *aka* **Reed, Phillip** *British Agent* 1934; *Fashions of 1934* 1934; *Gambling Lady* 1934; *The Girl from 10th Avenue* 1935; *Accent on Youth* 1935; *The Woman in Red* 1935; *Klondike Annie* 1936; *A Gentleman after Dark* 1942; *Old Acquaintance* 1943; *Rendezvous with Annie* 1946; *Song of Scheherazade* 1947; *Take Me to Town* 1953; *Harem Holiday* 1965

Reed, Ralph *Reform School Girl* 1957; *The Cry Baby Killer* 1958

Reed, Robert *Star!* 1968; *The Maltese Bippy* 1969; *A Very Brady Christmas* 1988; *Prime Target* 1991

Reed, Shanna *Mirrors* 1985; *Coins in the Fountain* 1990; *Stalking Back* 1993; *Seeds of Deception* 1993; *Don't Talk to Strangers* 1994; *Remember Me* 1995; *Unlikely Suspects* 1996; *Rattled* 1996; *Stand against Fear* 1996; *The Night Caller* 1998

Reed, Tracy *Dr Strangelove, or How I Learned to Stop Worrying and Love the Bomb* 1963; *Devils of Darkness* 1964; *A Shot in the Dark* 1964; *Adam's Woman* 1970; *The Take* 1974; *A Piece of the Action* 1977; *The California Dolls* 1981

Reed, Walter *Seven Days' Leave* 1942; *Bombardier* 1943; *Child of Divorce* 1946; *Mystery in Mexico* 1948; *Return of the Bad Men* 1948; *Desert Passage* 1952; *The Clown* 1952; *The Yellow Tomahawk* 1954; *Hell's Island* 1955; *Seven Men from Now* 1956; *Moment to Moment* 1966

Reedus, Norman *Six Ways to Sunday* 1997; *Dark Harbor* 1998; *Gossip* 1999

Reenberg, Jorgen *The Wolf at the Door* 1987; *Europa* 1991

Rees, Donogh *Constance* 1984; *Crush* 1992

Rees, John *The Long and the Short and the Tall* 1960; *Passenger* 1963

Rees, Roger *Star 80* 1983; *A Christmas Carol* 1984; *The Return of Sam McCloud* 1989; *Teen Agent* 1991; *Stop! or My Mom Will Shoot* 1992; *The Tower* 1992; *Charles & Diana: Unhappily Ever After* 1992; *Robin Hood: Men in Tights* 1993; *Legacy of Evil* 1995; *Double Platinum* 1999

Reese, Della *Psychic Killer* 1975; *Harlem Nights* 1989; *A Thin Line between Love and Hate* 1996; *Dinosaur* 2000

Reese, Tom *The Money Trap* 1966; *Stranger on the Run* 1967; *The Hollywood Detective* 1989

Reeve, Christopher *Superman* 1978; *Somewhere in Time* 1980; *Superman II* 1980; *Deathtrap* 1982; *Monsignor* 1982; *Superman III* 1983; *The Bostonians* 1984; *Anna Karenina* 1985; *The Aviator* 1985; *Superman IV: the Quest for Peace* 1987; *Switching Channels* 1987; *Street Smart* 1987; *The Great Escape II: the Untold Story* 1988; *The Rose and the Jackal* 1990; *Bump in the Night* 1991; *Death Dreams* 1991; *Mortal Sins* 1992; *A Nightmare in the Daylight* 1992; *Noises Off* 1992; *Morning Glory* 1993; *The Remains of the Day* 1993; *The Sea Wolf* 1993; *Speechless* 1994; *Black Fox* 1995; *Village of the Damned* 1995; *Above Suspicion* 1995; *A Step toward Tomorrow* 1996; *Rear Window* 1998

Reeves, George *Argentine Nights* 1940; *Lydia* 1941; *So Proudly We Hail* 1943; *The Sainted Sisters* 1948; *Bugles in the Afternoon* 1952; *The Blue Gardenia* 1953; *Westward Ho the Wagons!* 1956

Reeves, Keanu *Act of Vengeance* 1986; *Babes in Toyland* 1986; *Brotherhood of Justice* 1986; *Under the Influence* 1986; *Young Again* 1986; *Youngblood* 1986; *River's Edge* 1987; *Bill & Ted's Excellent Adventure* 1988; *Dangerous Liaisons* 1988; *Permanent Record* 1988; *The Night Before* 1988; *The Prince of Pennsylvania* 1988; *Parenthood* 1989; *Aunt Julia and the Scriptwriter* 1990; *I Love You to Death* 1990; *Bill & Ted's Bogus Journey* 1991; *My Own Private Idaho* 1991; *Point Break* 1991; *Bram Stoker's Dracula* 1992; *Even Cowgirls Get the Blues* 1993; *Freaked* 1993; *Little Buddha* 1993; *Much Ado about Nothing* 1993; *Speed* 1994; *Johnny Mnemonic* 1995; *A Walk in the Clouds* 1995; *Chain Reaction* 1996; *Feeling Minnesota* 1996; *The Last Time I Committed Suicide* 1996; *The Devil's Advocate* 1997; *The Matrix* 1999

Reeves, Kynaston *Vintage Wine* 1935; *Penny Princess* 1952; *Eight O'Clock Walk* 1953; *Fiend without a Face* 1957

Reeves, Perrey *Child's Play 3* 1991; *An Element of Truth* 1995; *Escape to Witch Mountain* 1995

Reeves, Saskia *The Bridge* 1990; *December Bride* 1990; *Antonia & Jane* 1990; *Close My Eyes* 1991; *Butterfly Kiss* 1994; *i.d.* 1994; *Traps* 1994; *Different for Girls* 1996; *Heart* 1997; *LA without a Map* 1998

Reeves, Scott *Friday the 13th Part VIII: Jason Takes Manhattan* 1989; *When the Cradle Falls* 1997

Reeves, Steve *Athena* 1954; *Jail Bait* 1954; *Hercules* 1957; *Goliath and the Barbarians* 1959; *Hercules Unchained* 1959; *The Giant of Marathon* 1960; *Morgan the Pirate* 1960; *The Last Days of Pompeii* 1960; *Duel of the Titans* 1961; *The Trojan War* 1961; *Sandokan the Great* 1963; *The Pirates of Malaysia* 1964

Reevis, Steve *Miracle in the Wilderness* 1991; *Geronimo* 1993; *Last of the Dogmen* 1995

Regalbuto, Joe *Six Weeks* 1982; *The Star Chamber* 1983; *Lassiter* 1984; *Prime Target* 1989; *The Queen of Mean* 1990; *Beyond Obsession* 1994; *Bodily Harm* 1995

Regan, Jayne *Thank You, Mr Moto* 1937; *Mr Moto's Gamble* 1938

Regan, Mary *Sylvia* 1984; *Fever* 1988

Regan, Phil *Dames* 1934; *In Caliente* 1935; *Sweet Rosie O'Grady* 1943

Regas, George *Bulldog Drummond Strikes Back* 1934; *Rose Marie* 1936; *Mr Moto Takes a Chance* 1938

Regehr, Duncan *The Monster Squad* 1987; *Gore Vidal's Billy the Kid* 1989; *Danielle Steel's Once in a Lifetime* 1994; *The Haunting of Lisa* 1996

Régent, Benoît *Dr M* 1989; *Three Colours Blue* 1993

Reggiani, Serge *Les Portes de la Nuit* 1946; *La Ronde* 1950; *The Secret People* 1951; *Casque d'Or* 1952; *Napoléon* 1955; *Paris Blues* 1961; *Le Doulos* 1962; *The Leopard* 1962; *The 25th Hour* 1967; *L'Armée des Ombres* 1969; *Vincent, François, Paul and the Others* 1974; *The Bee Keeper* 1986; *The Night Is Young* 1986

Regin, Nadja *The Man without a Body* 1957; *Solo for Sparrow* 1962

Regina, Paul *A Change of Seasons* 1980; *Adam* 1983; *Adam: His Song Continues* 1986; *Bounty Tracker* 1993; *Sharon's Secret* 1995

Regine *Marry Me! Marry Me!* 1968; *The Last Train* 1972; *Robert et Robert* 1978

Regnier, Carola *Seduction: the Cruel Woman* 1985; *Hôtel du Paradis* 1986

Rehak, Frantisek *Capricious Summer* 1968; *Cutting It Short* 1980

Rehman, Waheeda *Kaagaz Ke Phool* 1959; *Teesri Kasam* 1966; *Kabhi Kabhie* 1976

Reicher, Frank *Beau Sabreur* 1928; *King Kong* 1933; *Son of Kong* 1933; *Topaze* 1933; *Espionage* 1937; *Westbound Limited* 1937; *Dr Cyclops* 1940

Reichmann, Wolfgang *Woyzeck* 1978; *The Second Victory* 1986

Reid, Audrey *Dancehall Queen* 1996; *Third World Cop* 1999

Reid, Beryl *Two Way Stretch* 1960; *Trial and Error* 1962; *Inspector Clouseau* 1968; *The Killing of Sister George* 1968; *Star!* 1968; *The Assassination Bureau* 1969; *Entertaining Mr Sloane* 1969; *The Beast in the Cellar* 1970; *Father Dear Father* 1972; *Psychomania* 1972; *No Sex Please, We're British* 1973; *Joseph Andrews* 1977; *Carry On Emmannuelle* 1978; *Yellowbeard* 1983

Reid, Carl Benton *The Little Foxes* 1941; *Convicted* 1950; *In a Lonely Place* 1950; *Boots Malone* 1951; *The Great Caruso* 1951; *Lorna Doone* 1951; *Indian Uprising* 1951; *Carbine Williams* 1952; *Escape from Fort Bravo* 1953; *The Command* 1954; *Wichita* 1955; *The Spoilers* 1955; *One Desire* 1955; *A Day of Fury* 1956; *The Last Wagon* 1956; *Time Limit* 1957; *Tarzan's Fight for Life* 1958; *The Baited Trap* 1959; *The Bramble Bush* 1960; *Pressure Point* 1962

Reid, Christopher *House Party* 1990; *House Party 2* 1991; *Class Act* 1992; *House Party 3* 1994

Reid, Elliott *Young Ideas* 1943; *The Whip Hand* 1951; *Gentlemen Prefer Blondes* 1953; *Inherit the Wind* 1960; *The Absent-Minded Professor* 1961; *Son of Flubber* 1962; *The Thrill of It All* 1963; *Follow Me, Boys!* 1966; *Blackbeard's Ghost* 1967

Reid, Kate *This Property Is Condemned* 1966; *The Andromeda Strain* 1970; *The Sidelong Glances of a Pigeon Kicker* 1970; *A Delicate Balance* 1973; *Equus* 1977; *Highpoint* 1979; *Atlantic City USA* 1980; *Circle of Two* 1980; *Catholic Boys* 1985; *Death of a Salesman* 1985; *The Execution of Raymond Graham* 1985; *Fire with Fire* 1986; *Sweet Hearts Dance* 1988; *Deceived* 1991

Reid, Sheila *Othello* 1965; *Three Sisters* 1970; *The Touch* 1971; *Sir Henry at Rawlinson End* 1980; *The Dresser* 1983; *American Friends* 1991; *The Winter Guest* 1997

Reid, Tara *The Big Lebowski* 1997; *Girl* 1998; *American Pie* 1999; *Body Shots* 1999; *What We Did That Night* 1999

Reid, Tim *The Fourth War* 1990; *Race to Freedom: the Underground Railroad* 1994

Reidy, Gabrielle *Robin Hood* 1990; *All Things Bright and Beautiful* 1994

Reilly, Charles Nelson *All Dogs Go to Heaven* 1989; *Rock-a-Doodle* 1990

Reilly, John *The Secret War of Jackie's Girls* 1980; *The Patricia Neal Story: an Act of Love* 1981; *Missing Pieces* 1983; *Touch and Go* 1986

Reilly, John C *Casualties of War* 1989; *Days of Thunder* 1990; *State of Grace* 1990; *Hoffa* 1992; *Out on a Limb* 1992; *What's Eating Gilbert Grape* 1993; *The River Wild* 1994; *Boys* 1995; *Dolores Claiborne* 1995; *Georgia* 1995; *Hard Eight* 1996; *Boogie Nights* 1997; *Never Been Kissed* 1999; *For Love of the Game* 1999; *Magnolia* 1999; *The Perfect Storm* 2000

Reilly, Tom *Animal Instincts* 1992; *Mirror Images II* 1994

Reina, Lucy *The Penitent* 1988; *Romero* 1989

Reineke, Gary *Why Shoot the Teacher* 1976; *The Grey Fox*

1982; *Murder by Phone* 1982; *The Top of His Head* 1988
Reiner, Carl *The Gazebo* 1959; *Happy Anniversary* 1959; *Gidget Goes Hawaiian* 1961; *The Thrill of It All* 1963; *Art of Love* 1965; *The Russians Are Coming, the Russians Are Coming* 1966; *Generation* 1969; *The Jerk* 1979; *Skokie* 1981; *Dead Men Don't Wear Plaid* 1982; *Slums of Beverly Hills* 1998
Reiner, Rob *Where's Poppa?* 1970; *Halls of Anger* 1970; *Thursday's Game* 1971; *Fire Sale* 1977; *This Is Spinal Tap* 1984; *Throw Momma from the Train* 1987; *Postcards from the Edge* 1990; *Sleepless in Seattle* 1993; *Bullets over Broadway* 1994; *Bye Bye Love* 1995; *Mixed Nuts* 1995; *For Better or Worse* 1995; *Primary Colors* 1998; *EDtv* 1999
Reinheart, Alice *The Lieutenant Wore Skirts* 1956; *Grand Jury* 1976
Reinhold, Judge *Stripes* 1981; *Fast Times at Ridgemont High* 1982; *The Lords of Discipline* 1983; *Beverly Hills Cop* 1984; *Roadhouse 66* 1984; *Off Beat* 1986; *Ruthless People* 1986; *Head Office* 1986; *Beverly Hills Cop II* 1987; *Promised a Miracle* 1988; *A Soldier's Tale* 1988; *Vice Versa* 1988; *Rosalie Goes Shopping* 1989; *Daddy's Dyin'... Who's Got the Will?* 1990; *Near Mrs* 1990; *Over Her Dead Body* 1990; *Zandalee* 1991; *Four Eyes and Six-Guns* 1992; *Black Magic* 1992; *Baby on Board* 1993; *Bank Robber* 1993; *Beverly Hills Cop III* 1994; *The Santa Clause* 1994; *As Good as Dead* 1995; *The Wharf Rat* 1995; *Special Report: Journey to Mars* 1996; *Family Plan* 1997; *Last Lives* 1997; *Runaway Car* 1997; *Homegrown* 1998; *Floating Away* 1998
Reinking, Ann *All That Jazz* 1979; *Annie* 1982; *Micki & Maude* 1984
Reis, Diana *Thrillkill* 1984; *Something about Love* 1987
Reis, Michelle aka **Li Jiaxin** *A Chinese Ghost Story II* 1990; *Fallen Angels* 1995; *Flowers of Shanghai* 1998
Reiser, Paul *Diner* 1982; *Aliens* 1986; *Odd Jobs* 1986; *Cross My Heart* 1987; *You Ruined My Life* 1987; *Crazy People* 1990; *Family Prayers* 1991; *Too Hot to Handle* 1991; *The Tower* 1992; *Bye Bye Love* 1995; *The Story of Us* 1999
Rekert, Winston *Heartaches* 1981; *Dead Wrong* 1983; *Walls* 1984; *Agnes of God* 1985; *Silhouette* 1994; *Captive Heart: the James Mink Story* 1996; *To Brave Alaska* 1996
Relin, Marie-Theres *Secret Places* 1984; *Quo Vadis?* 1985
Relph, George *I Believe in You* 1952; *The Titfield Thunderbolt* 1952; *The Final Test* 1953
Remar, James *The Warriors* 1979; *Windwalker* 1980; *48 HRS* 1982; *The Cotton Club* 1984; *The Clan of the Cave Bear* 1986; *Quiet Cool* 1986; *Rent-a-Cop* 1988; *Drugstore Cowboy* 1989; *Night Visions* 1990; *Tales from the Darkside: the Movie* 1991; *White Fang* 1991; *Wedlock* 1991; *Brotherhood of the Gun* 1992; *Fatal Instinct* 1993; *Blink* 1994; *Miracle on 34th Street* 1994; *Renaissance Man* 1994; *Confessions of a Hit Man* 1994; *Boys on the Side* 1995; *Exquisite Tenderness* 1995; *Born Bad* 1996; *The Phantom* 1996; *The Quest* 1996; *Robo Warriors* 1996; *One Good Turn* 1996; *Mortal Kombat: Annihilation* 1997
Remberg, Erika *Circus of Horrors* 1960; *Saturday Night Out* 1963
Remick, Lee *A Face in the Crowd* 1957; *The Long Hot Summer* 1958; *Anatomy of a Murder* 1959; *These Thousand Hills* 1959; *Wild River* 1960; *Sanctuary* 1961; *Days of Wine and Roses* 1962; *Experiment in Terror* 1962; *The Running Man* 1963; *The Wheeler Dealers* 1963; *Baby the Rain Must Fall* 1965; *The Hallelujah Trail* 1965; *The Detective* 1968; *No Way to Treat a Lady* 1968; *Hard Contract* 1969; *Loot* 1970; *A Severed Head* 1970; *Never Give an Inch* 1971; *The Blue Knight* 1973; *A Delicate Balance* 1973; *Hennessy* 1975; *Hustling* 1975; *The Omen* 1976; *Telefon* 1977; *The Medusa Touch* 1978; *The Europeans* 1979; *Torn between Two Lovers* 1979; *The Competition* 1980; *Tribute* 1980; *Emma's War* 1985; *Of Pure Blood* 1986; *Jesse* 1988; *Bridge to Silence* 1989
Remsen, Bert *Tess of the Storm Country* 1960; *McCabe and Mrs Miller* 1971; *Thieves like Us* 1974; *Sweet Hostage* 1975; *Fast Break* 1979; *Borderline* 1980; *Lookin' to Get Out* 1982; *Code of Silence* 1985; *Stand Alone* 1985; *Eye of the Tiger* 1986; *Who Is Julia?* 1986; *TerrorVision* 1986; *Three for the Road* 1987; *Remote Control* 1988; *Daddy's Dyin'... Who's Got the Will?* 1990; *Peacemaker* 1990; *Only the Lonely* 1991; *Evil Spirits* 1991; *Ladykiller* 1992
Remsen, Kerry *Dreams of Gold: the Mel Fisher Story* 1986; *Ghoulies II* 1987; *Vengeance: the Demon* 1988
Rémy, Albert *Razzia sur la Chnouf* 1955; *The 400 Blows* 1959; *Shoot the Pianist* 1960; *Gigot* 1962; *The Train* 1964
Renaldo, Duncan *Trader Horn* 1931; *Down Mexico Way* 1941; *The Capture* 1950
Renaldo, Tito *Anna and the King of Siam* 1946; *The Bribe* 1949; *Tension* 1949; *One Way Street* 1950
Renant, Simone *Quai des Orfèvres* 1947; *Bedevilled* 1955; *Les Liaisons Dangereuses* 1959; *That Man from Rio* 1964
Renaud, Madeleine *Stormy Waters* 1941; *Le Plaisir* 1951
Renavent, Georges *Rio Rita* 1929; *Whipsaw* 1935
Renfro, Brad *The Client* 1994; *The Cure* 1995; *Tom and Huck* 1995; *Apt Pupil* 1997; *Telling Lies in America* 1997
Renna, Patrick *The Sandlot* 1993; *Son in Law* 1993; *Beanstalk* 1994; *The Big Green* 1995; *Johnny Mysto* 1996
Rennie, Callum Keith *Paris or Somewhere* 1995; *Tricks* 1997; *Last Night* 1998; *eXistenZ* 1999
Rennie, Michael *Pimpernel Smith* 1941; *I'll Be Your Sweetheart* 1945; *The Wicked Lady* 1945; *The Root of All Evil* 1946; *The Black Rose* 1950; *Trio* 1950; *The Day the Earth Stood Still* 1951; *The 13th Letter* 1951; *5 Fingers* 1952; *Les Misérables* 1952; *Phone Call from a Stranger* 1952; *King of the Khyber Rifles* 1953; *The Robe* 1953; *Sailor of the King* 1953; *Demetrius and the Gladiators* 1954; *Desiree* 1954; *Mambo* 1954; *Princess of the Nile* 1954; *The Rains of Ranchipur* 1955; *Seven Cities of Gold* 1955; *Soldier of Fortune* 1955; *Teenage Rebel* 1956; *Omar Khayyam* 1957; *Third Man on the Mountain* 1959; *The Lost World* 1960; *Mary, Mary* 1963; *Ride beyond Vengeance* 1966; *Hotel* 1967; *The Battle of El Alamein* 1968; *The Devil's Brigade* 1968; *The Power* 1968
Reno, Jean *The Last Battle* 1983; *Subway* 1985; *The Big Blue* 1988; *Nikita* 1990; *Flight from Justice* 1993; *Les Visiteurs* 1993; *Leon* 1994; *Beyond the Clouds* 1995; *French Kiss* 1995; *Mission: Impossible* 1996; *Roseanna's Grave* 1996; *Godzilla* 1997; *Ronin* 1998; *Les Visiteurs 2: Les Couloirs du Temps* 1998
Reno, Kelly *The Black Stallion* 1979; *The Black Stallion Returns* 1983; *The Long Ride* 1984
Renoir, Jean *Une Partie de Campagne* 1936; *La Vie Est à Nous* 1936; *La Bête Humaine* 1938; *La Règle du Jeu* 1939; *The Testament of Dr Cordelier* 1959; *The Little Theatre of Jean Renoir* 1969; *The Christian Licorice Store* 1971
Renoir, Pierre *Madame Bovary* 1933; *La Marseillaise* 1938; *Pièges* 1939; *Les Enfants du Paradis* 1945
Renoir, Sophie *Le Beau Mariage* 1982; *My Girlfriend's Boyfriend* 1987
Renucci, Robin *Entre Nous* 1983; *Masques* 1987; *The Chinese Connection* 1988; *The King's Whore* 1990
Renzi, Eva *Funeral in Berlin* 1966; *The Pink Jungle* 1968; *The Bird with the Crystal Plumage* 1969
Renzulli, Frank *Broadway Danny Rose* 1984; *Wild Hearts Can't Be Broken* 1991
Rescher, Dee Dee *Communion* 1989; *The Tower* 1992
Resines, Antonio *How to Be a Woman and Not Die in the Attempt* 1991; *Acción Mutante* 1993
Restorick, Hughie *My Childhood* 1972; *My Ain Folk* 1973
Rettig, Tommy *For Heaven's Sake* 1950; *The Jackpot* 1950; *Weekend with Father* 1951; *The 5,000 Fingers of Dr T* 1953; *The Raid* 1954; *River of No Return* 1954; *At Gunpoint* 1955; *The Last Wagon* 1956
Reuben, Gloria *Percy and Thunder* 1993; *Dead Air* 1994; *Timecop* 1994; *Nick of Time* 1995; *Johnny's Girl* 1995; *Indiscreet* 1998
Reubens, Paul aka **Herman, Pee-wee** *Cheech & Chong's Next Movie* 1980; *Cheech & Chong's Nice Dreams* 1981; *Meatballs 2* 1984; *Pee-wee's Big Adventure* 1985; *Big Top Pee-wee* 1988; *Buffy the Vampire Slayer* 1992; *Tim Burton's The Nightmare before Christmas* 1993; *Dunston Checks In* 1996; *Matilda* 1996; *Beauty and the Beast: the Enchanted Christmas* 1997; *Buddy* 1997; *Mystery Men* 1999
Revere, Anne *The Devil Commands* 1941; *Star Spangled Rhythm* 1942; *The Meanest Man in the World* 1943; *The Song of Bernadette* 1943; *National Velvet* 1944; *Sunday Dinner for a Soldier* 1944; *The Thin Man Goes Home* 1944; *Fallen Angel* 1945; *Dragonwyck* 1946; *Body and Soul* 1947; *Forever Amber* 1947; *Gentleman's Agreement* 1947; *The Shocking Miss Pilgrim* 1947; *Secret beyond the Door* 1948; *You're My Everything* 1949; *A Place in the Sun* 1951; *Macho Callahan* 1970; *Birch Interval* 1976
Revier, Dorothy *The Red Dance* 1928; *The Iron Mask* 1929; *By Candlelight* 1934
Revill, Clive *Bunny Lake Is Missing* 1965; *A Fine Madness* 1966; *Kaleidoscope* 1966; *Modesty Blaise* 1966; *The Double Man* 1967; *Nobody Runs Forever* 1968; *The Assassination Bureau* 1969; *The Buttercup Chain* 1970; *The Private Life of Sherlock Holmes* 1970; *A Severed Head* 1970; *Avanti!* 1972; *The Legend of Hell House* 1973; *Ghost in the Noonday Sun* 1973; *The Black Windmill* 1974; *The Little Prince* 1974; *Galileo* 1974; *One of Our Dinosaurs Is Missing* 1975; *Matilda* 1978; *The Diary of Anne Frank* 1980; *Joe Dancer: the Monkey Mission* 1981; *Zorro, the Gay Blade* 1981; *Samson and Delilah* 1984; *Rumpelstiltskin* 1986; *The Emperor's New Clothes* 1987; *Mack the Knife* 1989; *The Sea Wolf* 1993; *Arabian Knight* 1995
Rey, Alejandro *Solomon and Sheba* 1959; *Get off My Back* 1965; *Blindfold* 1966; *The Defiant* 1972; *Mr Majestyk* 1974; *Breakout* 1975; *High Velocity* 1977; *Moscow on the Hudson* 1984; *TerrorVision* 1986
Rey, Fernando *The Last Days of Pompeii* 1960; *Viridiana* 1961; *The Castilian* 1963; *Chimes at Midnight* 1966; *Return of the Seven* 1966; *Navajo Joe* 1966; *Cervantes* 1968; *The Immortal Story* 1968; *Villa Rides* 1968; *Guns of the Magnificent Seven* 1969; *The Adventurers* 1970; *Tristana* 1970; *The French Connection* 1971; *The Light at the Edge of the World* 1971; *A Town Called Hell* 1971; *Antony and Cleopatra* 1972; *The Discreet Charm of the Bourgeoisie* 1972; *The Lady with Red Boots* 1974; *French Connection II* 1975; *Illustrious Corpses* 1976; *Seven Beauties* 1976; *That Obscure Object of Desire* 1977; *Quintet* 1979; *Caboblanco* 1980; *Monsignor* 1982; *The Hit* 1984; *Rustler's Rhapsody* 1985; *Saving Grace* 1985; *Padre Nuestro* 1985; *Hôtel du Paradis* 1986; *Moon over Parador* 1988; *Naked Tango* 1990; *1492: Conquest of Paradise* 1992
Reyer, Walter *The Tiger of Eschnapur* 1959; *The Indian Tomb* 1959
Reyes Jr, Ernie *Red Sonja* 1985; *Teenage Mutant Ninja Turtles II: the Secret of the Ooze* 1991; *Surf Ninjas* 1993
Reymond, Dominique *Will It Snow for Christmas?* 1996; *The Bridge* 1999
Reynolds, Adeline De Walt *The Tuttles of Tahiti* 1942; *Behind the Rising Sun* 1943; *Lydia Bailey* 1952; *Pony Soldier* 1952
Reynolds, Burt *Angel Baby* 1961; *Armored Command* 1961; *Operation CIA* 1965; *Navajo Joe* 1966; *Impasse* 1969; *100 Rifles* 1969; *Sam Whiskey* 1969; *Skullduggery* 1969; *Shark!* 1969; *Run, Simon, Run* 1970; *Deliverance* 1972; *Everything You Always Wanted to Know about Sex (But Were Afraid to Ask)* 1972; *Fuzz* 1972; *The Man Who Loved Cat Dancing* 1973; *Shamus* 1973; *White Lightning* 1973; *The Mean Machine* 1974; *At Long Last Love* 1975; *Hustle* 1975; *Lucky Lady* 1975; *WW and the Dixie Dancekings* 1975; *Gator* 1976; *Nickelodeon* 1976; *Semi-Tough* 1977; *Smokey and the Bandit* 1977; *The End* 1978; *Hooper* 1978; *Starting Over* 1979; *Rough Cut* 1980; *Smokey and the Bandit II* 1980; *The Cannonball Run* 1981; *Paternity* 1981; *Sharky's Machine* 1981; *Best Friends* 1982; *The Best Little Whorehouse in Texas* 1982; *Cannonball Run II* 1983; *The Man Who Loved Women* 1983; *Smokey and the Bandit III* 1983; *Stroker Ace* 1983; *City Heat* 1984; *Stick* 1985; *Uphill All the Way* 1985; *Malone* 1987; *Switching Channels* 1987; *Heat* 1987; *Rent-a-Cop* 1988; *All Dogs Go to Heaven* 1989; *Breaking In* 1989; *Physical Evidence* 1989; *Modern Love* 1990; *Cop and a Half* 1993; *The Man from Left Field* 1993; *The Maddening* 1995; *Striptease* 1996; *Trigger Happy* 1996; *The Cherokee Kid* 1996; *Citizen Ruth* 1996; *Bean* 1997; *Boogie Nights* 1997; *Meet Wally Sparks* 1997; *Hard Time* 1998; *Mystery, Alaska* 1999
Reynolds, Craig *The Case of the Black Cat* 1936; *The Case of the Stuttering Bishop* 1937
Reynolds, Debbie *June Bride* 1948; *The Daughter of Rosie O'Grady* 1950; *Three Little Words* 1950; *Mr Imperium* 1951; *Singin' in the Rain* 1952; *Skirts Ahoy!* 1952; *Give a Girl a Break* 1953; *I Love Melvin* 1953; *The Affairs of Dobie Gillis* 1953; *Susan Slept Here* 1954; *Athena* 1954; *Hit the Deck* 1955; *The Tender Trap* 1955; *Bundle of Joy* 1956; *The Catered Affair* 1956; *Tammy and the Bachelor* 1957; *This Happy Feeling* 1958; *The Gazebo* 1959; *It Started with a Kiss* 1959; *The Mating Game* 1959; *Say One for Me* 1959; *The Rat Race* 1960; *Pepe* 1960; *The Pleasure of His Company* 1961; *The Second Time Around* 1961; *How the West Was Won* 1962; *My Six Loves* 1962; *Mary, Mary* 1963; *Goodbye Charlie* 1964; *The Unsinkable Molly Brown* 1964; *The Singing Nun* 1966; *Divorce American Style* 1967; *How Sweet It Is!* 1968; *What's the Matter with Helen?* 1971; *Charlotte's Web* 1973; *Detective Sadie and Son* 1987; *Battling for Baby* 1992; *Heaven and Earth* 1993; *Mother* 1996; *Wedding Bell Blues* 1996; *In & Out* 1997
Reynolds, Gene *Boys Town* 1938; *They Shall Have Music* 1939; *The Penalty* 1941; *The Tuttles of Tahiti* 1942; *The Country Girl* 1954; *Down Three Dark Streets* 1954
Reynolds, Helene *Confirm or Deny* 1941; *Moontide* 1942; *The Bermuda Mystery* 1944
Reynolds, Joyce *George Washington Slept Here* 1942; *The Constant Nymph* 1943
Reynolds, Marjorie *Holiday Inn* 1942; *Dixie* 1943; *Up in Mabel's Room* 1944; *Bring on the Girls* 1945; *Duffy's Tavern* 1945; *Ministry of Fear* 1945; *Monsieur Beaucaire* 1946; *The Time of Their Lives* 1946; *Heaven Only Knows* 1947; *The Great Jewel Robber* 1950
Reynolds, Michael J *Why Shoot the Teacher* 1976; *Too Outrageous!* 1987; *Trial & Error* 1992
Reynolds, Peter *The Guinea Pig* 1948; *The Last Page* 1952; *The Vanquished* 1953; *The Bank Raiders* 1958; *The Challenge* 1960; *Your Money or Your Wife* 1960; *The Breaking Point* 1961;

The Painted Smile 1961; *Spare the Rod* 1961; *Gaolbreak* 1962

Reynolds, Robert *Daughter of Darkness* 1990; *Tunnel Vision* 1994; *Traps* 1994

Reynolds, Ryan *Ordinary Magic* 1993; *My Name Is Kate* 1994; *The Alarmist* 1997; *Tourist Trap* 1998

Reynolds, Simon *The Guardian* 1984; *Journey into Darkness: the Bruce Curtis Story* 1991; *Lifeline to Victory* 1993

Reynolds, William *Has Anybody Seen My Gal?* 1952; *Son of Ali Baba* 1952; *The Mississippi Gambler* 1953; *Gunsmoke* 1953; *All That Heaven Allows* 1955; *Away All Boats* 1956; *There's Always Tomorrow* 1956; *The Land Unknown* 1957; *Mister Cory* 1957; *A Distant Trumpet* 1964

Rhames, Ving *Go Tell It on the Mountain* 1984; *Patty Hearst* 1988; *Casualties of War* 1989; *The Long Walk Home* 1990; *Rising Son* 1990; *When You Remember Me* 1990; *Homicide* 1991; *The People under the Stairs* 1991; *Dave* 1993; *The Saint of Fort Washington* 1993; *DROP Squad* 1994; *Kiss of Death* 1994; *Pulp Fiction* 1994; *Deadly Whispers* 1995; *Ed McBain's 87th Precinct* 1995; *Dangerous Ground* 1996; *Mission: Impossible* 1996; *Striptease* 1996; *Body Count* 1997; *Con Air* 1997; *Rosewood* 1997; *Out of Sight* 1998; *Entrapment* 1999; *Bringing out the Dead* 1999; *Mission: Impossible 2* 1999

Rhee, Phillip *Silent Assassins* 1988; *Best of the Best* 1989; *Best of the Best II* 1992; *Best of the Best 3: No Turning Back* 1995; *Best of the Best: Without Warning* 1998

Rhind-Tutt, Julian *The Madness of King George* 1995; *The Trench* 1999

Rhoades, Barbara *The Shakiest Gun in the West* 1967; *Don't Just Stand There* 1968; *The Goodbye Girl* 1977

Rhoades, Michael *Eddie and the Cruisers II: Eddie Lives!* 1989; *Johnny 2.0* 1998

Rhodes, Christopher *The Colditz Story* 1954; *Tiger in the Smoke* 1956; *Operation Amsterdam* 1958; *Gorgo* 1960

Rhodes, Cynthia *Staying Alive* 1983; *Runaway* 1984; *Dirty Dancing* 1987

Rhodes, Donnelly *Gunfight in Abilene* 1967; *Oh, Heavenly Dog!* 1980; *After the Promise* 1987; *The Penthouse* 1989; *Beyond Obsession* 1994

Rhodes, Erik *The Gay Divorcee* 1934; *Charlie Chan in Paris* 1935; *Top Hat* 1935; *Chatterbox* 1936; *One Rainy Afternoon* 1936; *Criminal Lawyer* 1937; *Woman Chases Man* 1937; *Mysterious Mr Moto* 1938; *On Your Toes* 1939

Rhodes, Grandon *Magnificent Doll* 1946; *Born Yesterday* 1950; *On Top of Old Smoky* 1953; *Revenge of the Creature* 1955; *Earth vs the Flying Saucers* 1956

Rhodes, Hari *Blindfold* 1966; *Earth II* 1971; *Conquest of the Planet of the Apes* 1972; *Detroit 9000* 1973

Rhodes, Harry *aka* **Rhodes, Hari** *Shock Corridor* 1963; *Coma* 1977

Rhodes, Marjorie *Great Day* 1944; *The Yellow Balloon* 1952; *Children Galore* 1954; *Just My Luck* 1957; *Alive and Kicking* 1958; *Watch It, Sailor!* 1961; *I've Gotta Horse* 1965; *The Family Way* 1966; *Hands of the Ripper* 1971

Rhue, Madlyn *A Majority of One* 1961; *Escape from Zahrain* 1962; *He Rides Tall* 1964

Rhys Jones, Griff *Morons from Outer Space* 1985; *Wilt* 1989; *As You Like It* 1992; *Staggered* 1993; *The Adventures of Pinocchio* 1996; *Up 'n' Under* 1997

Rhys, Matthew *House of America* 1996; *Heart* 1997; *Titus* 1999

Rhys, Paul *Vincent and Theo* 1990; *Becoming Colette* 1991; *Rebecca's Daughters* 1991; *Chaplin* 1992; *Nina Takes a Lover* 1993; *The Haunting of Helen Walker* 1995

Rhys-Davies, John *Raiders of the Lost Ark* 1981; *Victor/Victoria* 1982; *Best Revenge* 1983; *Sahara* 1983; *Kim* 1984; *Nairobi Affair* 1984; *King Solomon's Mines* 1985; *Firewalker* 1986; *The Living Daylights* 1987; *Waxwork* 1988; *Young Toscanini* 1988; *Indiana Jones and the Last Crusade* 1989; *The Trial of the Incredible Hulk* 1989; *Secret Weapon* 1990; *Shogun Warrior* 1991; *The Double O Kid* 1992; *Sunset Grill* 1992; *The Unnamable Returns* 1992; *A Robot Called Golddigger* 1993; *The Seventh Coin* 1993; *Cyborg Cop* 1993; *Beyond Forgiveness* 1994; *The High Crusade* 1994; *Ring of the Musketeers* 1994; *Aladdin and the King of Thieves* 1996; *Body Armor* 1996; *Cats Don't Dance* 1998

Rhys-Meyers, Jonathan *B Monkey* 1996; *The Disappearance of Finbar* 1996; *The Governess* 1997; *Velvet Goldmine* 1998; *The Loss of Sexual Innocence* 1999; *Ride with the Devil* 1999; *Titus* 1999

Rialson, Candice *Mama's Dirty Girls* 1974; *Hollywood Boulevard* 1976

Ribisi, Giovanni *aka* **Ribisi, Vonni** *Promised a Miracle* 1988; *subUrbia* 1996; *Saving Private Ryan* 1998; *Some Girls* 1998; *The Other Sister* 1999; *The Mod Squad* 1999; *Boiler Room* 2000; *Gone in 60 Seconds* 2000

Ricci, Christina *Mermaids* 1990; *The Addams Family* 1991; *The Hard Way* 1991; *Addams Family Values* 1993; *The Cemetery Club* 1993; *Casper* 1995; *Now and Then* 1995; *Gold Diggers: the Secret of Bear Mountain* 1995; *Bastard out of Carolina* 1996; *Last of the High Kings* 1996; *Buffalo '66* 1997; *The Ice Storm* 1997; *That Darn Cat* 1997; *Fear and Loathing in Las Vegas* 1998; *The Opposite of Sex* 1998; *Pecker* 1998; *Desert Blue* 1998; *200 Cigarettes* 1999; *Sleepy Hollow* 1999

Ricci, Renzo *L'Avventura* 1959; *Of a Thousand Delights* 1965

Rice, Florence *Double Wedding* 1937; *Navy Blue and Gold* 1937; *Fast Company* 1938; *Sweethearts* 1938; *Paradise for Three* 1938; *At the Circus* 1939; *Four Girls in White* 1939; *Miracles for Sale* 1939; *Broadway Melody of 1940* 1940; *Cherokee Strip* 1940; *Phantom Raiders* 1940

Rice, Gigi *Deadly Web* 1995; *Deadly Family Secrets* 1995

Rice, Joan *Curtain Up* 1952; *The Gift Horse* 1952; *The Story of Robin Hood and His Merrie Men* 1952; *A Day to Remember* 1953; *His Majesty O'Keefe* 1953; *The Steel Key* 1953; *One Good Turn* 1954; *Police Dog* 1955; *Women without Men* 1956; *Operation Bullshine* 1959; *The Horror of Frankenstein* 1970

Rich, Adam *The Devil and Max Devlin* 1981; *Eight Is Enough: a Family Reunion* 1987

Rich, Allan *Highlander II: the Quickening* 1990; *Dead on the Money* 1991

Rich, Christopher *Weekend Reunion* 1990; *In the Line of Duty: the Twilight Murders* 1991

Rich, Claude *Mitsou* 1957; *The Vanishing Corporal* 1962; *Male Hunt* 1964; *The Bride Wore Black* 1967; *Je T'Aime, Je T'Aime* 1968; *Stavisky* 1974; *The Police War* 1979; *Maria Chapdelaine* 1982; *L'Accompagnatrice* 1992; *D'Artagnan's Daughter* 1994; *Lautrec* 1998

Rich, Irene *Rosita* 1923; *Lady Windermere's Fan* 1925; *They Had to See Paris* 1929; *Beau Ideal* 1931; *The Champ* 1931; *Strangers May Kiss* 1931; *That Certain Age* 1938; *The Mortal Storm* 1940; *The Lady in Question* 1940; *Angel and the Badman* 1947

Richard, Cliff *Expresso Bongo* 1959; *Serious Charge* 1959; *The Young Ones* 1961; *Summer Holiday* 1962; *Wonderful Life* 1964; *Finders Keepers* 1966; *Take Me High* 1973

Richard, Frida *Faust* 1926; *Three Loves* 1929

Richard, Jean-Louis *The Last Metro* 1980; *Jeanne la Pucelle* 1994; *The Bait* 1995; *Don't Forget You're Going to Die* 1995

Richard, Little *Down and Out in Beverly Hills* 1986; *The Purple People Eater* 1988; *The Pickle* 1993

Richard, Pierre *The Tall Blond Man with One Black Shoe* 1972; *Les Compères* 1983

Richard, Wendy *Gumshoe* 1971; *Bless This House* 1972; *Carry On Girls* 1973; *Are You Being Served?* 1977

Richards, Addison *Our Daily Bread* 1934; *The Black Legion* 1937; *Boys Town* 1938; *Bad Lands* 1939; *The Man from Dakota* 1940; *Betrayal from the East* 1945; *Bewitched* 1945; *Come Out Fighting* 1945; *Criminal Court* 1946; *Gunsight Ridge* 1957

Richards, Ann *An American Romance* 1944; *Love Letters* 1945; *Badman's Territory* 1946; *The Searching Wind* 1946; *Sorry, Wrong Number* 1948

Richards, Ariana *Tremors* 1989; *Against Her Will* 1991; *Timescape* 1991; *Jurassic Park* 1993; *Angus* 1995; *Born Free: A New Adventure* 1996; *Race against Fear* 1998

Richards, Aubrey *The Ipcress File* 1965; *It!* 1966; *Endless Night* 1971

Richards, Beah *The Miracle Worker* 1962; *Gone Are the Days* 1963; *Guess Who's Coming to Dinner* 1967; *Hurry Sundown* 1967; *The Biscuit Eater* 1972; *Mahogany* 1975; *As Summers Die* 1986; *Drugstore Cowboy* 1989; *Homer and Eddie* 1989; *Out of Darkness* 1994; *Beloved* 1998

Richards, Denise *Starship Troopers* 1997; *Wild Things* 1998; *Drop Dead Gorgeous* 1999; *The World Is Not Enough* 1999; *Tail Lights Fade* 1999

Richards, Evan *Down and Out in Beverly Hills* 1986; *Society* 1989; *The Dream Machine* 1990; *Midnight Fear* 1990; *Mute Witness* 1995

Richards, Jeff *Big Leaguer* 1953; *Seagulls over Sorrento* 1954; *Seven Brides for Seven Brothers* 1954; *The Marauders* 1955; *Many Rivers to Cross* 1955; *The Opposite Sex* 1956; *Born Reckless* 1959; *The Secret of the Purple Reef* 1960

Richards, Kim *Escape to Witch Mountain* 1975; *Assault on Precinct 13* 1976; *No Deposit No Return* 1976; *Return from Witch Mountain* 1978; *Meatballs 2* 1984; *Tuff Turf* 1984

Richards, Kyle *Halloween* 1978; *The Watcher in the Woods* 1982

Richards, Lisa *Rolling Thunder* 1977; *Return* 1985; *Eating* 1990

Richards, Michael *Transylvania 6-5000* 1985; *Whoops Apocalypse* 1986; *UHF* 1989; *Unstrung Heroes* 1995; *Neil Simon's London Suite* 1996; *Trial and Error* 1997

Richards, Michele Lamar *The Bodyguard* 1992; *Top Dog* 1995

Richards (1), Paul *Tall Man Riding* 1955; *The Strange One* 1957; *Hot Summer Night* 1957; *Beneath the Planet of the Apes* 1969

Richards, Tom *Dawn!* 1979; *Afraid to Dance* 1988

Richardson, Ian *Marat/Sade* 1966; *A Midsummer Night's Dream* 1969; *The Darwin Adventure* 1972; *The Hound of the Baskervilles* 1983; *The Sign of Four* 1983; *Brazil* 1985; *Whoops Apocalypse* 1986; *Cry Freedom* 1987; *Burning Secret* 1988; *King of the Wind* 1989; *The Plot to Kill Hitler* 1990; *Rosencrantz and Guildenstern Are Dead* 1990; *Dirty Weekend* 1992; *Year of the Comet* 1992; *Foreign Affairs* 1993; *M Butterfly* 1993; *A Change of Place* 1994; *B.A.P.S.* 1997; *Incognito* 1997; *Dark City* 1998; *A Knight in Camelot* 1998; *The King and I* 1999

Richardson, Jake *Fudge-a-Mania* 1995; *Honey, We Shrunk Ourselves* 1997

Richardson, Jay *Terminal Force* 1987; *Haunting Fear* 1990; *Sins of Desire* 1993

Richardson, Joely *The Hotel New Hampshire* 1984; *Wetherby* 1985; *Drowning by Numbers* 1988; *King Ralph* 1991; *Rebecca's Daughters* 1991; *Shining Through* 1992; *I'll Do Anything* 1994; *Loch Ness* 1994; *Sister My Sister* 1994; *Hollow Reed* 1995; *101 Dalmatians* 1996; *Event Horizon* 1997; *Wrestling with Alligators* 1998; *Maybe Baby* 1999; *Return to Me* 2000; *The Patriot* 2000

Richardson, John *The Mask of Satan* 1960; *She* 1965; *One Million Years BC* 1966; *On My Way to the Crusades, I Met a Girl Who…* 1967; *The Vengeance of She* 1968; *On a Clear Day You Can See Forever* 1970

Richardson, Lee *Prizzi's Honor* 1985; *Amazing Grace and Chuck* 1987; *The Believers* 1987; *Tiger Warsaw* 1988; *The Fly II* 1989; *Q & A* 1990; *A Stranger among Us* 1992; *With Savage Intent* 1992

Richardson, Miranda *Dance with a Stranger* 1984; *The Innocent* 1984; *After Pilkington* 1986; *Empire of the Sun* 1987; *Eat the Rich* 1987; *The Bachelor* 1990; *Enchanted April* 1991; *The Crying Game* 1992; *Damage* 1992; *Century* 1993; *Fatherland* 1994; *Tom & Viv* 1994; *Kansas City* 1995; *The Evening Star* 1996; *Swann* 1996; *The Apostle* 1997; *The Designated Mourner* 1997; *The King and I* 1999; *Sleepy Hollow* 1999; *The Miracle Maker* 1999; *Chicken Run* 2000

Richardson, Natasha *Every Picture Tells a Story* 1984; *Gothic* 1986; *A Month in the Country* 1987; *Patty Hearst* 1988; *Shadow Makers* 1989; *The Handmaid's Tale* 1990; *The Comfort of Strangers* 1991; *The Favour, the Watch and the Very Big Fish* 1991; *Past Midnight* 1992; *Widows' Peak* 1993; *Zelda* 1993; *Hostages* 1993; *Nell* 1994; *The Parent Trap* 1998

Richardson, Patricia *The Road Home* 1989; *Ulee's Gold* 1997

Richardson, Peter *The Supergrass* 1985; *Carry On Columbus* 1992

Richardson, Ralph *The Ghoul* 1933; *Bulldog Jack* 1934; *The Return of Bulldog Drummond* 1934; *Java Head* 1935; *The Man Who Could Work Miracles* 1936; *Things to Come* 1936; *Thunder in the City* 1937; *The Citadel* 1938; *The Divorce of Lady X* 1938; *South Riding* 1938; *The Four Feathers* 1939; *The Lion Has Wings* 1939; *Q Planes* 1939; *The Day Will Dawn* 1942; *The Silver Fleet* 1943; *School for Secrets* 1946; *Anna Karenina* 1947; *The Fallen Idol* 1948; *The Heiress* 1949; *Outcast of the Islands* 1951; *The Holly and the Ivy* 1952; *Home at Seven* 1952; *The Sound Barrier* 1952; *Richard III* 1955; *Smiley* 1956; *The Passionate Stranger* 1957; *Oscar Wilde* 1959; *Our Man in Havana* 1959; *Exodus* 1960; *Long Day's Journey into Night* 1962; *The 300 Spartans* 1962; *Woman of Straw* 1964; *Doctor Zhivago* 1965; *Chimes at Midnight* 1966; *Khartoum* 1966; *The Wrong Box* 1966; *Battle of Britain* 1969; *The Bed Sitting Room* 1969; *David Copperfield* 1969; *The Looking Glass War* 1969; *Oh! What a Lovely War* 1969; *Midas Run* 1969; *Who Slew Auntie Roo?* 1971; *Eagle in a Cage* 1971; *Alice's Adventures in Wonderland* 1972; *Lady Caroline Lamb* 1972; *Tales from the Crypt* 1972; *A Doll's House* 1973; *Frankenstein: the True Story* 1973; *O Lucky Man!* 1973; *Rollerball* 1975; *The Man in the Iron Mask* 1977; *Watership Down* 1978; *Dragonslayer* 1981; *Time Bandits* 1981; *Witness for the Prosecution* 1982; *Invitation to the Wedding* 1983; *Wagner* 1983; *Give My Regards to Broad Street* 1984; *Greystoke: the Legend of Tarzan, Lord of the Apes* 1984

Richardson, Salli *How U Like Me Now* 1992; *I Spy Returns* 1994; *A Low Down Dirty Shame* 1995

Richardson, Sy *Repo Man* 1984; *Walker* 1987; *Straight to Hell* 1987; *Cold Steel* 1987; *Kinjite: Forbidden Subjects* 1989; *Eye of the Stranger* 1993

Richert, William *My Own Private Idaho* 1991; *The Man in the Iron Mask* 1997

Richfield, Edwin *The Brain Machine* 1954; *The Adventures of Hal 5* 1958; *The Break* 1962

Richman, Charles *His Double Life* 1933; *The Adventures of Tom Sawyer* 1938

Richman, Josh *Thrashin'* 1986; *River's Edge* 1987

Richman, Peter Mark *aka* **Richman, Mark** *The Strange One* 1957; *The Black Orchid* 1959; *Dark Intruder* 1965; *Bonanza: the Next Generation* 1988; *Friday the 13th Part VIII: Jason Takes Manhattan* 1989

Richmond, Branscombe *The Chicken Chronicles* 1977; *Cage* 1989; *The Taking of Beverly Hills* 1991; *Jericho Fever* 1993

Richmond, Deon *Enemy Territory* 1987; *Trippin'* 1999

Black Rainbow 1989; *Parenthood* 1989; *Reunion* 1989; *Dream a Little Dream* 1989; *Quick Change* 1990; *Chernobyl: the Final Warning* 1991; *Mark Twain & Me* 1991; *Storyville* 1992; *The Adventures of Huck Finn* 1993; *Philadelphia* 1993; *The Trial* 1993; *The Enemy Within* 1994; *Little Big League* 1994; *The Paper* 1994; *My Antonia* 1995; *Journey* 1995; *A Thousand Acres* 1997; *Enemy of the State* 1998; *Magnolia* 1999

Robards, Sam *Tempest* 1982; *Fandango* 1985; *Into Thin Air* 1985; *Not Quite Jerusalem* 1985; *The Ballad of Little Jo* 1993; *American Beauty* 1999

Robb, R D *A Christmas Story* 1983; *Eight Days a Week* 1996

Robbins, Gale *My Girl Tisa* 1948; *Oh, You Beautiful Doll* 1949; *Three Little Words* 1950; *The Belle of New York* 1952; *Calamity Jane* 1953; *Quantrill's Raiders* 1958

Robbins, James *San Quentin* 1937; *The Barbarian and the Geisha* 1958

Robbins, Michael *Lunch Hour* 1962; *On the Buses* 1971; *Mutiny on the Buses* 1972; *Holiday on the Buses* 1973; *Just Ask for Diamond* 1988

Robbins, Peter *A Ticklish Affair* 1963; *Moment to Moment* 1966; *And Now Miguel* 1966; *A Boy Named Charlie Brown* 1969

Robbins, Tim *No Small Affair* 1984; *The Sure Thing* 1985; *Fraternity Vacation* 1985; *Howard, a New Breed of Hero* 1986; *Top Gun* 1986; *Five Corners* 1987; *Bull Durham* 1988; *Tapeheads* 1988; *Erik the Viking* 1989; *Miss Firecracker* 1989; *Cadillac Man* 1990; *Jacob's Ladder* 1990; *Jungle Fever* 1991; *Bob Roberts* 1992; *The Player* 1992; *Short Cuts* 1993; *The Hudsucker Proxy* 1994; *Prêt-à-Porter* 1994; *The Shawshank Redemption* 1994; *IQ* 1995; *Nothing to Lose* 1997; *Arlington Road* 1998; *Mission to Mars* 1999; *High Fidelity* 2000

Rober, Richard *The File on Thelma Jordon* 1949; *Port of New York* 1949; *The Woman on Pier 13* 1949; *Sierra* 1950; *Watch the Birdie* 1950; *Man in the Saddle* 1951; *The Tall Target* 1951; *The Well* 1951; *The Devil Makes Three* 1952; *The Savage* 1953; *Jet Pilot* 1957

Robert, Yves *The Bad Liaisons* 1955; *Les Grandes Manoeuvres* 1955; *One Night at the Music Hall* 1956; *Cleo from 5 to 7* 1961; *La Crise* 1992

Roberti, Lyda *The Kid from Spain* 1932; *Million Dollar Legs* 1932; *George White's 1935 Scandals* 1935

Roberts, Aled *A Feast at Midnight* 1995; *The Haunting of Helen Walker* 1995

Roberts, Allene *The Red House* 1947; *Knock on Any Door* 1949; *Union Station* 1950

Roberts, Arthur *Revenge of the Ninja* 1983; *Not of This Earth* 1988; *Illegal Entry: Formula for Fear* 1993

Roberts, Beverly *China Clipper* 1936; *God's Country and the Woman* 1937; *The Perfect Specimen* 1937

Roberts, Christian *To Sir, with Love* 1967; *The Anniversary* 1968; *The Desperados* 1969; *The Last Valley* 1971

Roberts, Doris *A Lovely Way to Go* 1968; *The Honeymoon Killers* 1969; *Little Murders* 1971;

Hester Street 1975; *Good Luck, Miss Wyckoff* 1979; *The Diary of Anne Frank* 1980; *Number One with a Bullet* 1986; *A Mom for Christmas* 1990

Roberts, Eric *The North Star* 1943; *King of the Gypsies* 1978; *Raggedy Man* 1981; *Star 80* 1983; *The Pope of Greenwich Village* 1984; *The Coca-Cola Kid* 1985; *Runaway Train* 1985; *Nobody's Fool* 1986; *Blood Red* 1988; *To Heal a Nation* 1988; *Rude Awakening* 1989; *Best of the Best* 1989; *Descending Angel* 1990; *The Lost Capone* 1990; *The Ambulance* 1990; *Best of the Best II* 1992; *By the Sword* 1992; *Final Analysis* 1992; *Voyage* 1993; *Babyfever* 1994; *Freefall* 1994; *The Hard Truth* 1994; *Love, Cheat & Steal* 1994; *Love Is a Gun* 1994; *The Specialist* 1994; *Hatchet Man* 1994; *The Immortals* 1995; *The Public Enemy #1* 1995; *Saved By the Light* 1995; *The Cable Guy* 1996; *Dark Angel* 1996; *The Glass Cage* 1996; *Heaven's Prisoners* 1996; *It's My Party* 1996; *Power 98* 1996; *American Strays* 1996; *The Shadow Men* 1997; *The Prophecy II* 1997; *False Pretense* 1997; *The Odyssey* 1997; *Purgatory* 1999; *Lansky* 1999

Roberts, Evelyn *Keep Fit* 1937; *Man of the Moment* 1955

Roberts, Ewan *Colonel March Investigates* 1953; *River Beat* 1954; *Night of the Demon* 1957

Roberts, Florence *Kept Husbands* 1931; *Babes in Toyland* 1934

Roberts, Ian *Jane and the Lost City* 1987; *Cry, the Beloved Country* 1995; *Inside* 1996; *Tarzan and the Lost City* 1998; *Sweepers* 1999

Roberts, Ivor *The Sailor's Return* 1978; *We Think the World of You* 1988

Roberts, Joe *Scarecrow* 1920; *The Paleface* 1921; *Three Ages* 1923

Roberts, Julia *Baja Oklahoma* 1988; *Blood Red* 1988; *Mystic Pizza* 1988; *Satisfaction* 1988; *Steel Magnolias* 1989; *Flatliners* 1990; *Pretty Woman* 1990; *Dying Young* 1991; *Hook* 1991; *Sleeping with the Enemy* 1991; *The Pelican Brief* 1993; *I Love Trouble* 1994; *Prêt-à-Porter* 1994; *Mary Reilly* 1995; *Something to Talk About* 1995; *Everyone Says I Love You* 1996; *Michael Collins* 1996; *Conspiracy Theory* 1997; *My Best Friend's Wedding* 1997; *Stepmom* 1998; *Notting Hill* 1999; *Runaway Bride* 1999; *Erin Brockovich* 2000

Roberts, Ken *Great Land of the Small* 1987; *Edge of Deception* 1994

Roberts, Lynne *aka* **Hart, Mary** *Billy the Kid Returns* 1938; *Shine On, Harvest Moon* 1938; *Rough Riders' Roundup* 1939; *Riders of the Purple Sage* 1941; *The Man in the Trunk* 1942; *Quiet Please, Murder* 1942

Roberts, Michael D *The Ice Pirates* 1984; *Rain Man* 1988; *Live! From Death Row* 1992

Roberts, Nancy *Cosh Boy* 1952; *It's a Great Day* 1955

Roberts, Pascale *The Sleeping Car Murders* 1965; *Three* 1969; *Le Grand Chemin* 1987; *Marius et Jeannette* 1997

Roberts, Pernell *Desire under the Elms* 1958; *The Sheepman* 1958; *Ride Lonesome* 1959; *The Magic of Lassie* 1978; *Desperado* 1987

Roberts, Rachel *Valley of Song* 1953; *The Good Companions*

1956; *Saturday Night and Sunday Morning* 1960; *Girl on Approval* 1962; *This Sporting Life* 1963; *A Flea in Her Ear* 1968; *Doctors' Wives* 1970; *The Belstone Fox* 1973; *O Lucky Man!* 1973; *Alpha Beta* 1973; *Murder on the Orient Express* 1974; *Picnic at Hanging Rock* 1975; *Foul Play* 1978; *When a Stranger Calls* 1979; *Yanks* 1979; *Charlie Chan and the Curse of the Dragon Queen* 1981

Roberts, Rick *Love and Human Remains* 1993; *The Man in the Attic* 1995; *Waiting for Michelangelo* 1995

Roberts, Roy *Guadalcanal Diary* 1943; *Circumstantial Evidence* 1945; *Smoky* 1946; *Force of Evil* 1948; *He Walked by Night* 1948; *Wyoming Mail* 1950; *Murder, Inc* 1951; *The Glory Brigade* 1953; *House of Wax* 1953; *Tumbleweed* 1953

Roberts, Stephen *Gog* 1954; *Diary of a Madman* 1963

Roberts, Tanya *Tourist Trap* 1979; *The Beastmaster* 1982; *Sheena, Queen of the Jungle* 1984; *A View to a Kill* 1985; *Purgatory* 1988; *Night Eyes* 1990; *Sins of Desire* 1993

Roberts, Theodore *Male and Female* 1919; *The Ten Commandments* 1923

Roberts, Tony *The Million Dollar Duck* 1971; *Play It Again, Sam* 1972; *Serpico* 1973; *Call Him Savage* 1975; *Annie Hall* 1977; *Stardust Memories* 1980; *Just Tell Me What You Want* 1980; *A Midsummer Night's Sex Comedy* 1982; *Amityville III: the Demon* 1983; *Packin' It In* 1983; *Key Exchange* 1985; *Hannah and Her Sisters* 1986; *Seize the Day* 1986; *18 Again!* 1988; *Switch* 1991; *Shattering the Silence* 1992; *Arthur Miller's The American Clock* 1993

Robertson, Cliff *Picnic* 1955; *Autumn Leaves* 1956; *The Girl Most Likely* 1957; *The Naked and the Dead* 1958; *Gidget* 1959; *All in a Night's Work* 1960; *Underworld USA* 1961; *The Big Show* 1961; *The Interns* 1962; *My Six Loves* 1962; *PT 109* 1963; *Sunday in New York* 1963; *The Best Man* 1964; *633 Squadron* 1964; *Love Has Many Faces* 1965; *Masquerade* 1965; *Up from the Beach* 1965; *The Honey Pot* 1967; *Charly* 1968; *The Devil's Brigade* 1968; *Too Late the Hero* 1970; *JW Coop* 1971; *The Great Northfield Minnesota Raid* 1972; *Ace Eli and Rodger of the Skies* 1973; *A Tree Grows in Brooklyn* 1974; *Three Days of the Condor* 1975; *Out of Season* 1975; *Battle of Midway* 1976; *Obsession* 1976; *Shoot* 1976; *Fraternity Row* 1977; *Dominique* 1978; *The Pilot* 1979; *Brainstorm* 1983; *Class* 1983; *Star 80* 1983; *Shaker Run* 1985; *Dreams of Gold: the Mel Fisher Story* 1986; *Malone* 1987; *Dead Reckoning* 1990; *Wild Hearts Can't Be Broken* 1991; *Wind* 1992; *Renaissance Man* 1994; *Escape from LA* 1996

Robertson, Dale *Fighting Man of the Plains* 1949; *The Cariboo Trail* 1950; *Two Flags West* 1950; *Call Me Mister* 1951; *Golden Girl* 1951; *Lydia Bailey* 1952; *O Henry's Full House* 1952; *Devil's Canyon* 1953; *The Farmer Takes a Wife* 1953; *Sitting Bull* 1954; *Son of Sinbad* 1955; *Dakota Incident* 1956; *A Day of Fury* 1956; *The Man from Button Willow* 1965; *The Last Ride of the Dalton Gang* 1979

Robertson, Iain *Small Faces* 1995; *The Debt Collector* 1999

Robertson, Jenny *Unconquered* 1989; *Call Me Anna* 1990; *The Danger of Love* 1992; *The Nightman* 1992; *Notorious* 1992

Robertson, Kathleen *Lapse of Memory* 1992; *Blown Away* 1992; *Nowhere* 1997; *Dog Park* 1998

Robertson, Robbie *Carny* 1980; *The Crossing Guard* 1995

Robertson, Tim *Bliss* 1985; *The Time Guardian* 1987; *The Big Steal* 1990; *The Winchester Conspiracy* 1990; *Holy Smoke* 1999

Robertson, Willard *Skippy* 1931; *Lady Killer* 1933; *Tugboat Annie* 1933; *Kentucky* 1938; *Background to Danger* 1943; *Deep Valley* 1947

Robertson-Justice, James *For Those in Peril* 1943; *Against the Wind* 1947; *My Brother Jonathan* 1947; *Vice Versa* 1947; *Scott of the Antarctic* 1948; *Whisky Galore!* 1949; *Pool of London* 1950; *Anne of the Indies* 1951; *Captain Horatio Hornblower* 1951; *David and Bathsheba* 1951; *Les Misérables* 1952; *Miss Robin Hood* 1952; *The Story of Robin Hood and His Merrie Men* 1952; *The Sword and the Rose* 1952; *Voice of Merrill* 1952; *Rob Roy, the Highland Rogue* 1953; *Doctor in the House* 1954; *Out of the Clouds* 1954; *Above Us the Waves* 1955; *An Alligator Named Daisy* 1955; *Doctor at Sea* 1955; *Land of the Pharaohs* 1955; *Storm over the Nile* 1955; *Checkpoint* 1956; *The Iron Petticoat* 1956; *Moby Dick* 1956; *Campbell's Kingdom* 1957; *Doctor at Large* 1957; *Seven Thunders* 1957; *Orders to Kill* 1958; *Upstairs and Downstairs* 1959; *Doctor in Love* 1960; *Foxhole in Cairo* 1960; *A French Mistress* 1960; *Murder She Said* 1961; *A Pair of Briefs* 1961; *Raising the Wind* 1961; *Very Important Person* 1961; *Crooks Anonymous* 1962; *Dr Crippen* 1962; *Guns of Darkness* 1962; *Doctor in Distress* 1963; *The Fast Lady* 1963; *Father Came Too* 1963; *The Face of Fu Manchu* 1965; *You Must Be Joking!* 1965; *Up from the Beach* 1965; *Doctor in Clover* 1966; *The Trygon Factor* 1967; *Chitty Chitty Bang Bang* 1968; *Mayerling* 1968; *Some Will, Some Won't* 1969; *Doctor in Trouble* 1970

Robeson, Paul *The Emperor Jones* 1933; *Sanders of the River* 1935; *Show Boat* 1936; *Song of Freedom* 1936; *King Solomon's Mines* 1937; *The Proud Valley* 1940; *Tales of Manhattan* 1942

Robey, George *Don Quixote* 1933; *Chu Chin Chow* 1934; *Southern Roses* 1936

Robie, Wendy *The People under the Stairs* 1991; *The Dentist II* 1998

Robin, Dany *Man about Town* 1947; *Act of Love* 1953; *The Mysteries of Paris* 1962; *Waltz of the Toreadors* 1962; *Follow the Boys* 1963; *Topaz* 1969

Robin, Michel *Harem* 1985; *Marquis* 1989

Robins, Laila *Dream Breakers* 1989; *An Innocent Man* 1989; *Welcome Home, Roxy Carmichael* 1990; *Live Nude Girls* 1995; *Female Perversions* 1996; *The Blood Oranges* 1997

Robinson, Andrew *Dirty Harry* 1971; *Charley Varrick* 1973; *Not My Kid* 1985; *Cobra* 1986; *Hellraiser* 1987; *Rock Hudson*

1990; *Prime Target* 1991; *The Revenge of Pumpkinhead – Blood Wings* 1994; *My Son Is Innocent* 1996

Robinson, Ann *The War of the Worlds* 1953; *The Glass Wall* 1953; *Dragnet* 1954; *Gun Duel in Durango* 1957; *Damn Citizen* 1958; *Midnight Movie Massacre* 1987

Robinson, Bartlett *The Spirit of St Louis* 1957; *All Hands on Deck* 1961; *Sleeper* 1973

Robinson, Bill *The Big Broadcast of 1936* 1935; *Hooray for Love* 1935; *In Old Kentucky* 1935; *The Littlest Rebel* 1935; *Rebecca of Sunnybrook Farm* 1938; *Just around the Corner* 1938; *Stormy Weather* 1943

Robinson, Bruce *L'Histoire d'Adèle H* 1975; *Still Crazy* 1998

Robinson, Bumper *Enemy Mine* 1985; *The Liberators* 1987

Robinson, Cardew *The Navy Lark* 1959; *Light Up the Sky* 1960; *Let's Get Married* 1960; *I Was Happy Here* 1966

Robinson, Charles *Shenandoah* 1965; *The Sand Pebbles* 1966; *Brotherhood of Satan* 1970; *Driving Academy* 1988; *Murder COD* 1990

Robinson, Chris *Amy* 1981; *Savannah Smiles* 1982

Robinson, Edward G *Five Star Final* 1931; *Little Caesar* 1931; *Smart Money* 1931; *The Hatchet Man* 1932; *Tiger Shark* 1932; *The Little Giant* 1933; *Barbary Coast* 1935; *The Whole Town's Talking* 1935; *Bullets or Ballots* 1936; *Kid Galahad* 1937; *The Last Gangster* 1937; *Thunder in the City* 1937; *The Amazing Dr Clitterhouse* 1938; *I Am the Law* 1938; *A Slight Case of Murder* 1938; *Blackmail* 1939; *Confessions of a Nazi Spy* 1939; *Brother Orchid* 1940; *Dr Ehrlich's Magic Bullet* 1940; *A Dispatch from Reuters* 1940; *Manpower* 1941; *The Sea Wolf* 1941; *Unholy Partners* 1941; *Larceny, Inc* 1942; *Tales of Manhattan* 1942; *Flesh and Fantasy* 1943; *Double Indemnity* 1944; *Journey Together* 1944; *Mr Winkle Goes to War* 1944; *Scarlet Street* 1945; *The Woman in the Window* 1945; *Our Vines Have Tender Grapes* 1945; *The Stranger* 1946; *The Red House* 1947; *All My Sons* 1948; *Key Largo* 1948; *Night Has a Thousand Eyes* 1948; *House of Strangers* 1949; *It's a Great Feeling* 1949; *Actors and Sin* 1952; *The Glass Web* 1953; *Vice Squad* 1953; *Big Leaguer* 1953; *Hell on Frisco Bay* 1955; *Illegal* 1955; *The Violent Men* 1955; *Tight Spot* 1955; *A Bullet for Joey* 1955; *The Ten Commandments* 1956; *Nightmare* 1956; *A Hole in the Head* 1959; *Seven Thieves* 1960; *Pepe* 1960; *My Geisha* 1962; *Two Weeks in Another Town* 1962; *The Prize* 1963; *Sammy Going South* 1963; *Cheyenne Autumn* 1964; *Good Neighbor Sam* 1964; *The Outrage* 1964; *Robin and the 7 Hoods* 1964; *The Cincinnati Kid* 1965; *The Biggest Bundle of Them All* 1968; *Never a Dull Moment* 1968; *Mackenna's Gold* 1969; *Song of Norway* 1970; *Soylent Green* 1973

Robinson, Forrest *Tol'able David* 1921; *Tess of the Storm Country* 1922

Robinson, Frances *Forbidden Valley* 1938; *The Lone Wolf Keeps a Date* 1941; *Smilin' Through* 1941

ACTORS' INDEX
RadioTimes

Robinson, Jay *The Robe* 1953; *Demetrius and the Gladiators* 1954; *The Virgin Queen* 1955; *My Man Godfrey* 1957; *Bunny O'Hare* 1971; *Three the Hard Way* 1974; *Shampoo* 1975; *Born Again* 1978; *Partners* 1982; *Skeeter* 1993
Robinson, John *Emergency Call* 1952; *Ghost Ship* 1952; *The Doctor's Dilemma* 1958; *Nothing but the Night* 1972; *Zero Patience* 1993; *And Then There Was One* 1994
Robinson, Madeleine *Passionate Summer* 1955; *Web of Passion* 1959; *Une Histoire Simple* 1978; *I Married a Dead Man* 1983; *Camille Claudel* 1988
Robinson, Roger *Believe in Me* 1971; *Newman's Law* 1974
Robson, Flora *Catherine the Great* 1934; *Fire over England* 1937; *Poison Pen* 1939; *We Are Not Alone* 1939; *Wuthering Heights* 1939; *Invisible Stripes* 1940; *The Sea Hawk* 1940; *Great Day* 1944; *Two Thousand Women* 1944; *Caesar and Cleopatra* 1945; *Saratoga Trunk* 1945; *Black Narcissus* 1946; *Frieda* 1947; *Holiday Camp* 1947; *Good Time Girl* 1948; *Saraband for Dead Lovers* 1948; *The Malta Story* 1953; *Romeo and Juliet* 1954; *High Tide at Noon* 1957; *No Time for Tears* 1957; *The Gypsy and the Gentleman* 1958; *55 Days at Peking* 1963; *Murder at the Gallop* 1963; *Guns at Batasi* 1964; *Those Magnificent Men in Their Flying Machines* 1965; *Young Cassidy* 1965; *7 Women* 1966; *The Shuttered Room* 1967; *Eye of the Devil* 1968; *The Beast in the Cellar* 1970; *Fragment of Fear* 1970; *Alice's Adventures in Wonderland* 1972; *Sin* 1972; *Dominique* 1978; *Les Misérables* 1978
Robson, Greer *Smash Palace* 1981; *Starlight Hotel* 1987
Robson, May *If I Had a Million* 1932; *Red-Headed Woman* 1932; *Strange Interlude* 1932; *Dancing Lady* 1933; *Lady for a Day* 1933; *Reunion in Vienna* 1933; *The White Sister* 1933; *Lady by Choice* 1934; *Anna Karenina* 1935; *Reckless* 1935; *Strangers All* 1935; *Vanessa, Her Love Story* 1935; *Rainbow on the River* 1936; *Wife vs Secretary* 1936; *The Perfect Specimen* 1937; *A Star Is Born* 1937; *The Adventures of Tom Sawyer* 1938; *Bringing Up Baby* 1938; *Four Daughters* 1938; *The Texans* 1938; *Daughters Courageous* 1939; *Nurse Edith Cavell* 1939; *That's Right – You're Wrong* 1939; *They Made Me a Criminal* 1939; *Texas Rangers Ride Again* 1940; *Playmates* 1941; *Million Dollar Baby* 1941; *Joan of Paris* 1942
Robson, Wayne *The Grey Fox* 1982; *One Magic Christmas* 1985; *Housekeeping* 1987; *Bye Bye Blues* 1989; *Justice Denied* 1989; *The Diviners* 1992; *Double, Double Toil and Trouble* 1993; *Stolen Hearts* 1996; *Cube* 1997; *Pippi Longstocking* 1997
Roc, Patricia *A Window in London* 1939; *We'll Meet Again* 1942; *Millions like Us* 1943; *Love Story* 1944; *Madonna of the Seven Moons* 1944; *Two Thousand Women* 1944; *Johnny Frenchman* 1945; *The Wicked Lady* 1945; *Canyon Passage* 1946; *The Brothers* 1947; *Jassy* 1947; *When the Bough Breaks* 1947; *The Man on the Eiffel Tower* 1949; *The Perfect Woman* 1949; *Circle of Danger* 1950; *Black Jack* 1952; *Cartouche* 1954; *House in the Woods* 1957; *The Hypnotist* 1957
Rocca, Daniela *Caltiki, the Immortal Monster* 1959; *The Giant of Marathon* 1960; *Divorce – Italian Style* 1961; *The Empty Canvas* 1963; *Behold a Pale Horse* 1964
Rocco, Alex *Motor Psycho* 1965; *Detroit 9000* 1973; *The Friends of Eddie Coyle* 1973; *Rafferty and the Gold Dust Twins* 1974; *Hearts of the West* 1975; *Hustling* 1975; *Three for the Road* 1975; *Voices* 1979; *The Stunt Man* 1980; *PK and the Kid* 1982; *Badge of the Assassin* 1985; *Gotcha!* 1985; *Lady in White* 1988; *Rock 'n' Roll Mom* 1988; *Wired* 1989; *How to Murder a Millionaire* 1990; *The Pope Must Die* 1991; *Harmful Intent* 1993; *Goodbye Lover* 1997; *Dudley Do-Right* 1999
Roche, Eugene *Slaughterhouse-Five* 1972; *W* 1974; *Newman's Law* 1974; *The Late Show* 1977; *Corvette Summer* 1978; *Oh, God! You Devil* 1984; *A Case for Murder* 1993
Roche, John *Kiss Me Again* 1925; *Don Juan* 1926
Rochefort, Jean *Le Masque de Fer* 1962; *Up to His Ears* 1965; *The Tall Blond Man with One Black Shoe* 1972; *The Bit Player* 1973; *The Inheritor* 1973; *The Watchmaker of St Paul* 1973; *Pardon Mon Affaire* 1976; *Dirty Hands* 1976; *The Hairdresser's Husband* 1990; *Wild Target* 1993; *Tango* 1993; *Ridicule* 1996; *Circle of Passion* 1996; *Wind with the Gone* 1998
Rochon, Lela *The Wild Pair* 1987; *Boomerang* 1992; *Mr and Mrs Loving* 1993; *Waiting to Exhale* 1995; *The Chamber* 1996; *Gang Related* 1997; *Knock Off* 1998; *Why Do Fools Fall in Love?* 1998
Rock, Chris *New Jack City* 1991; *Boomerang* 1992; *CB4* 1993; *Beverly Hills Ninja* 1997; *Lethal Weapon 4* 1998; *Dogma* 1999
Rocket, Charles *Down Twisted* 1987; *Earth Girls Are Easy* 1988; *How I Got Into College* 1989; *Dances with Wolves* 1990; *Delirious* 1991; *Brain Smasher... a Love Story* 1993; *Dumb and Dumber* 1994; *Charlie's Ghost Story* 1994; *Tom and Huck* 1995; *The Killing Grounds* 1997
Rockwell, Sam *Clownhouse* 1988; *Strictly Business* 1991; *Glory Daze* 1995; *Box of Moon Light* 1996; *Lawn Dogs* 1997; *Safe Men* 1998; *Jerry and Tom* 1998; *The Green Mile* 1999; *Galaxy Quest* 1999
Rodann, Ziva *Last Train from Gun Hill* 1959; *Samar* 1962
Rodd, Marcia *A Date with a Lonely Girl* 1971; *Little Murders* 1971; *How to Break Up a Happy Divorce* 1976; *Citizens Band* 1977
Roderick, Sue *Rebecca's Daughters* 1991; *Hedd Wyn* 1992
Rodgers, Anton *Part-Time Wife* 1961; *Rotten to the Core* 1965; *The Man Who Haunted Himself* 1970; *Scrooge* 1970; *East of Elephant Rock* 1976; *Agatha Christie's Murder with Mirrors* 1985; *Dirty Rotten Scoundrels* 1988; *Impromptu* 1991
Rodgers, Ilona *Salt and Pepper* 1968; *Utu* 1983
Rodman, Dennis *Double Team* 1997; *Simon Sez* 1999
Rodney, John *Pursued* 1947; *Fighter Squadron* 1948; *Key Largo* 1948
Rodrigues, Percy *Genesis II* 1973; *Brainwaves* 1982
Rodriguez, Freddy *Dead Presidents* 1995; *A Walk in the Clouds* 1995; *The Pest* 1997
Rodriguez, José Antonio *The Last Supper* 1976; *Knocks at My Door* 1991
Rodriguez, Marco *Disorderlies* 1987; *Serial Killer* 1996
Rodriguez, Paul *Miracles* 1985; *Quicksilver* 1986; *The Whoopee Boys* 1986; *Born in East LA* 1987; *Grand Slam* 1990; *Hi Honey, I'm Dead* 1991; *Made in America* 1993; *A Million to Juan* 1994; *Rough Magic* 1995
Rodriguez, Valente *Roosters* 1993; *The Big Squeeze* 1996; *Guy* 1996
Rodway, Norman *This Other Eden* 1959; *Four in the Morning* 1965; *Chimes at Midnight* 1966; *The Penthouse* 1967
Roe, Matt *Puppet Master* 1989; *Sins of the Night* 1993
Roe, Raymond *The Major and the Minor* 1942; *The West Point Story* 1950
Roebling, Paul *Blue Thunder* 1983; *Carolina Skeletons* 1991
Roebuck, Daniel *Dudes* 1987; *River's Edge* 1987; *Caught in the Crossfire* 1994; *The Late Shift* 1996; *US Marshals* 1998
Roel, Gabriela *El Dorado* 1988; *Old Gringo* 1989
Roerick, William *Not of This Earth* 1956; *The Wasp Woman* 1959
Roëves, Maurice *Ulysses* 1967; *Oh! What a Lovely War* 1969; *When Eight Bells Toll* 1971; *The Big Man* 1990; *The Last of the Mohicans* 1992; *The Acid House* 1998
Rogers, Charles "Buddy" *My Best Girl* 1927; *Wings* 1927; *This Reckless Age* 1932; *Old Man Rhythm* 1935; *The Parson and the Outlaw* 1957
Rogers, Ginger *Honor among Lovers* 1931; *The Thirteenth Guest* 1932; *Flying down to Rio* 1933; *42nd Street* 1933; *Gold Diggers of 1933* 1933; *Sitting Pretty* 1933; *The Gay Divorcee* 1934; *Romance in Manhattan* 1934; *Upper World* 1934; *Finishing School* 1934; *In Person* 1935; *Roberta* 1935; *Top Hat* 1935; *Star of Midnight* 1935; *Follow the Fleet* 1936; *Swing Time* 1936; *Shall We Dance* 1937; *Stage Door* 1937; *Carefree* 1938; *Having Wonderful Time* 1938; *Vivacious Lady* 1938; *Bachelor Mother* 1939; *Fifth Avenue Girl* 1939; *The Story of Vernon and Irene Castle* 1939; *Kitty Foyle* 1940; *Lucky Partners* 1940; *Primrose Path* 1940; *Tom, Dick and Harry* 1941; *The Major and the Minor* 1942; *Once upon a Honeymoon* 1942; *Roxie Hart* 1942; *Tales of Manhattan* 1942; *Tender Comrade* 1943; *I'll Be Seeing You* 1944; *Lady in the Dark* 1944; *Week-End at the Waldorf* 1945; *Heartbeat* 1946; *Magnificent Doll* 1946; *The Barkleys of Broadway* 1949; *Perfect Strangers* 1950; *Storm Warning* 1950; *Dreamboat* 1952; *Monkey Business* 1952; *We're Not Married* 1952; *Forever Female* 1953; *Black Widow* 1954; *Beautiful Stranger* 1954; *Tight Spot* 1955; *The First Travelling Saleslady* 1956; *Teenage Rebel* 1956; *Oh, Men! Oh, Women!* 1957; *Quick, Let's Get Married* 1964; *Harlow* 1965
Rogers, Jean *Stormy* 1935; *Flash Gordon* 1936; *Brigham Young* 1940; *Let's Make Music* 1940; *The Man Who Wouldn't Talk* 1940; *Design for Scandal* 1941; *Dr Kildare's Victory* 1941; *The War against Mrs Hadley* 1942; *Swing Shift Maisie* 1943; *Whistling in Brooklyn* 1943
Rogers, John *Think Fast, Mr Moto* 1937; *Bob, Son of Battle* 1947
Rogers, Kenny *Six Pack* 1982; *Wild Horses* 1985; *Rio Diablo* 1993; *Big Dreams & Broken Hearts: the Dottie West Story* 1995
Rogers, Mimi *Embassy* 1985; *Gung Ho* 1986; *Someone to Watch over Me* 1987; *You Ruined My Life* 1987; *Street Smart* 1987; *Hider in the House* 1989; *The Mighty Quinn* 1989; *Desperate Hours* 1990; *Deadly Identity* 1991; *The Rapture* 1991; *Wedlock* 1991; *Ladykiller* 1992; *White Sands* 1992; *Dark Horse* 1992; *Those Bedroom Eyes* 1993; *Far from Home: the Adventures of Yellow Dog* 1994; *Killer* 1994; *Monkey Trouble* 1994; *Reflections on a Crime* 1994; *Full Body Massage* 1995; *In the Blink of an Eye* 1996; *The Mirror Has Two Faces* 1996; *Austin Powers: International Man of Mystery* 1997; *Lost in Space* 1997; *Tricks* 1997; *Weapons of Mass Distraction* 1997; *The Devil's Arithmetic* 1999
Rogers, Paul *The Beachcomber* 1954; *Beau Brummell* 1954; *Svengali* 1954; *Circle of Deception* 1960; *Life for Ruth* 1962; *The Pot Carriers* 1962; *The Wild and the Willing* 1962; *Stolen Hours* 1963; *The Third Secret* 1964; *He Who Rides a Tiger* 1965; *The Looking Glass War* 1969; *Three into Two Won't Go* 1969; *I Want What I Want* 1971; *The Homecoming* 1973; *Lost in the Stars* 1974; *Mister Quilp* 1975; *The Tenth Man* 1988; *The Return of the Native* 1994
Rogers, Roy *Billy the Kid Returns* 1938; *Shine On, Harvest Moon* 1938; *The Arizona Kid* 1939; *Rough Riders' Roundup* 1939; *Dark Command* 1940; *Song of Texas* 1943; *Brazil* 1944; *Hollywood Canteen* 1944; *The Yellow Rose of Texas* 1944; *Bells of Rosarita* 1945; *My Pal Trigger* 1946; *Bells of San Angelo* 1947; *Springtime in the Sierras* 1947; *Under California Stars* 1948; *The Far Frontier* 1949; *Son of Paleface* 1952; *Alias Jesse James* 1959
Rogers, Wayne *Pocket Money* 1972; *Once in Paris* 1978; *The Hot Touch* 1982; *The Gig* 1985; *I Dream of Jeannie... 15 Years Later* 1985; *The Lady from Yesterday* 1985; *The Girl Who Spelled Freedom* 1986; *The Killing Time* 1987; *Miracle Landing* 1990
Rogers, Will *Hollywood* 1923; *They Had to See Paris* 1929; *A Connecticut Yankee* 1931; *Dr Bull* 1933; *State Fair* 1933; *Judge Priest* 1934; *In Old Kentucky* 1935; *Life Begins at 40* 1935; *Steamboat round the Bend* 1935
Rogers Jr, Will *Look for the Silver Lining* 1949; *The Boy from Oklahoma* 1954; *Wild Heritage* 1958
Rohde, Armin *Life Is All You Get* 1998; *Run Lola Run* 1998
Rohm, Maria *The Blood of Fu Manchu* 1968; *Count Dracula* 1970; *Black Beauty* 1971; *Treasure Island* 1972
Rohner, Clayton *Just One of the Guys* 1985; *April Fool's Day* 1986; *Private Investigations* 1987; *BAT-21* 1988; *Destroyer* 1988; *Someone's Watching* 1993; *The Relic* 1997
Rojas, Eduardo Lopez *Reed: Insurgent Mexico* 1971; *My Family* 1994
Rojas, Manuel *The Magnificent Matador* 1955; *Buchanan Rides Alone* 1958
Rojo, Gustavo *Action of the Tiger* 1957; *It Started with a Kiss* 1959; *The Miracle* 1959; *The Valley of Gwangi* 1969; *El Condor* 1970
Rojo, Maria *Break of Dawn* 1988; *Danzón* 1991; *Midaq Alley* 1995
Roland, Gilbert *Camille* 1927; *Life Begins* 1932; *The Passionate Plumber* 1932; *Our Betters* 1933; *She Done Him Wrong* 1933; *The Last Train from Madrid* 1937; *My Life with Caroline* 1941; *Captain Kidd* 1945; *The Other Love* 1947; *Malaya* 1949; *We Were Strangers* 1949; *Crisis* 1950; *The Furies* 1950; *The Bullfighter and the Lady* 1951; *Ten Tall Men* 1951; *Glory Alley* 1952; *The Miracle of Fatima* 1952; *My Six Convicts* 1952; *Apache War Smoke* 1952; *Beneath the 12-Mile Reef* 1953; *The Diamond Queen* 1953; *Thunder Bay* 1953; *The French Line* 1954; *That Lady* 1955; *The Treasure of Pancho Villa* 1955; *Underwater!* 1955; *The Racers* 1955; *Bandido* 1956; *Three Violent People* 1956; *The Midnight Story* 1957; *The Big Circus* 1959; *The Wild and the Innocent* 1959; *Guns of the Timberland* 1960; *Samar* 1962; *The Reward* 1965; *The Poppy Is Also a Flower* 1966; *The Christian Licorice Store* 1971; *Running Wild* 1973; *The Mark of Zorro* 1974; *Islands in the Stream* 1977; *Caboblanco* 1980; *Barbarosa* 1982
Roland, Jeanne *The Curse of the Mummy's Tomb* 1964; *Salt and Pepper* 1968
Rolf, Tutta *Swedenhielms* 1935; *Dollar* 1938
Rolfe, Guy *Broken Journey* 1948; *Portrait from Life* 1948; *The Spider and the Fly* 1949; *Prelude to Fame* 1950; *Home to Danger* 1951; *King of the Khyber Rifles* 1953; *Young Bess* 1953; *Dance Little Lady* 1954; *It's Never Too Late* 1956; *Girls at Sea* 1958; *Yesterday's Enemy* 1959; *Mr Sardonicus* 1961; *Taras Bulba* 1962; *The Alphabet Murders* 1966; *And Now the Screaming Starts!* 1973; *Dolls* 1987
Rolffes, Kirsten *Buster's World* 1984; *The Kingdom* 1994
Rolle, Esther *PK and the Kid* 1982; *Driving Miss Daisy* 1989; *The Mighty Quinn* 1989; *House of Cards* 1993; *To Dance with the White Dog* 1993; *Down in the Delta* 1997; *Rosewood* 1997
Rollett, Raymond *Dick Turpin – Highwayman* 1956; *Blue Murder at St Trinian's* 1957
Rollins, David *The Black Watch* 1929; *The Big Trail* 1930
Rollins, Henry *The Chase* 1994; *Johnny Mnemonic* 1995; *Lost Highway* 1996; *Jack Frost* 1998
Rollins Jr, Howard E *A Soldier's Story* 1984; *Johnnie Mae Gibson: FBI* 1986; *With Savage Intent* 1992; *Drunks* 1995
Rolston, Mark *Lethal Weapon 2* 1989; *A Sinful Life* 1989; *The Comrades of Summer* 1992; *Black Widow Murders* 1993; *The Conviction of Kitty Dodds* 1993; *The Shawshank Redemption* 1994; *Best of the Best 3: No Turning Back* 1995; *The Set Up* 1995
Romain, Yvonne aka **Warren, Yvonne** *Action of the Tiger* 1957; *The Curse of the Werewolf* 1961;

Devil Doll 1964; *Smokescreen* 1964; *The Swinger* 1966; *Double Trouble* 1967
Roman, Candice *The Unholy Rollers* 1972; *The Big Bird Cage* 1972
Roman, Leticia *GI Blues* 1960; *Gold of the Seven Saints* 1961; *Pontius Pilate* 1961; *Fanny Hill: Memoirs of a Woman of Pleasure* 1964
Roman, Ric *Appointment in Honduras* 1953; *Lizzie* 1957
Roman, Ruth *Belle Starr's Daughter* 1948; *Always Leave Them Laughing* 1949; *Beyond the Forest* 1949; *Champion* 1949; *The Window* 1949; *Barricade* 1950; *Colt .45* 1950; *Dallas* 1950; *Three Secrets* 1950; *Lightning Strikes Twice* 1951; *Strangers on a Train* 1951; *Young Man with Ideas* 1952; *Blowing Wild* 1953; *Tanganyika* 1954; *The Shanghai Story* 1954; *Down Three Dark Streets* 1954; *The Far Country* 1955; *Joe Macbeth* 1955; *Beyond the River* 1956; *Great Day in the Morning* 1956; *Rebel in Town* 1956; *Bitter Victory* 1957; *Five Steps to Danger* 1957; *Look in Any Window* 1961; *Love Has Many Faces* 1965; *The Baby* 1973; *The Killing Kind* 1973; *Impulse* 1975; *Echoes* 1983
Roman, Susan *Rabid* 1976; *Heavy Metal* 1981
Romance, Viviane *La Belle Équipe* 1936; *Mademoiselle Docteur* 1936; *Any Number Can Win* 1963
Romand, Béatrice *Claire's Knee* 1970; *Soft Beds, Hard Battles* 1973; *The Romantic Englishwoman* 1975; *Le Beau Mariage* 1982; *Four Adventures of Reinette and Mirabelle* 1986; *The Green Ray* 1986; *An Autumn Tale* 1998
Romano, Andy *Over the Edge* 1979; *Pump Up the Volume* 1990; *Pizza Man* 1991; *The Gun in Betty Lou's Handbag* 1992; *Victim of Love: the Shannon Mohr Story* 1993; *Death of a Cheerleader* 1994; *Ring of the Musketeers* 1994; *Under Siege 2* 1995; *Two Bits* 1995; *Eraser* 1996; *Getting Away with Murder* 1996; *Listen* 1996
Romano, Larry *Lock Up* 1989; *No Way Home* 1996
Romano, Renato *The Bird with the Crystal Plumage* 1969; *The Last Rebel* 1971
Romanus, Richard *Mean Streets* 1973; *The Gravy Train* 1974; *Wizards* 1977; *Sitting Ducks* 1979; *Heavy Metal* 1981; *Strangers Kiss* 1983; *Protocol* 1984; *Murphy's Law* 1986; *The Couch Trip* 1988; *To Protect and Serve* 1992; *The Resurrected* 1992; *The Assassin* 1993; *Point of No Return* 1993
Romay, Lina *The Big Wheel* 1949; *The Female Vampire* 1973
Rome, Stewart *Dinner at the Ritz* 1937; *Wings of the Morning* 1937
Rome, Sydne *Some Girls Do* 1969; *What?* 1973; *That Lucky Touch* 1975; *You've Got to Live Dangerously* 1975; *The Twist* 1976; *Just a Gigolo* 1978
Rome, Tina *The Baron of Arizona* 1950; *Park Row* 1952
Romero, Cesar *British Agent* 1934; *Cardinal Richelieu* 1935; *The Devil Is a Woman* 1935; *The Good Fairy* 1935; *Rendezvous* 1935; *Love before Breakfast* 1936; *Wee Willie Winkie* 1937; *Happy Landing* 1938; *My Lucky Star* 1938; *Always Goodbye* 1938; *Charlie Chan at Treasure Island* 1939; *The Cisco Kid and the Lady*

1939; *Frontier Marshal* 1939; *The Little Princess* 1939; *The Return of the Cisco Kid* 1939; *Wife, Husband and Friend* 1939; *The Gay Caballero* 1940; *The Great American Broadcast* 1941; *Weekend in Havana* 1941; *A Gentleman at Heart* 1942; *Orchestra Wives* 1942; *Springtime in the Rockies* 1942; *Tales of Manhattan* 1942; *Coney Island* 1943; *Wintertime* 1943; *Captain from Castile* 1947; *Julia Misbehaves* 1948; *That Lady in Ermine* 1948; *The Beautiful Blonde from Bashful Bend* 1949; *Happy Go Lovely* 1950; *Love That Brute* 1950; *Street of Shadows* 1953; *Prisoners of the Casbah* 1953; *Vera Cruz* 1954; *The Americano* 1955; *Villa!* 1958; *Ocean's Eleven* 1960; *Pepe* 1960; *If a Man Answers* 1962; *Donovan's Reef* 1963; *The Castilian* 1963; *Marriage on the Rocks* 1965; *Two on a Guillotine* 1965; *Sergeant Deadhead* 1965; *Batman* 1966; *Madigan's Millions* 1967; *Hot Millions* 1968; *Target: Harry* 1968; *Crooks and Coronets* 1969; *Midas Run* 1969; *The Computer Wore Tennis Shoes* 1970; *Now You See Him, Now You Don't* 1972; *The Proud and the Damned* 1972; *The Strongest Man in the World* 1975; *Lust in the Dust* 1984
Romero, George A *Martin* 1978; *Dawn of the Dead* 1979
Ron, Tiny *aka* **Taylor, Tiny Ron** *Seven Hours to Judgment* 1988; *The Rocketeer* 1991; *Ace Ventura: Pet Detective* 1993
Ronane, John *Doctor Blood's Coffin* 1960; *That's Your Funeral* 1972
Ronay, Edina *The Black Torment* 1964; *The Big Job* 1965; *Praise Marx and Pass the Ammunition* 1968; *Three* 1969
Ronet, Maurice *Lift to the Scaffold* 1957; *Carve Her Name with Pride* 1958; *Plein Soleil* 1960; *Le Feu Follet* 1963; *The Victors* 1963; *La Ronde* 1964; *The Lost Command* 1966; *The Champagne Murders* 1966; *La Femme Infidèle* 1968; *How Sweet It Is!* 1968; *The Swimming Pool* 1968; *Without Warning* 1973; *Don Juan 73, or If Don Juan Were a Woman* 1973; *The Marseilles Contract* 1974; *To Kill a Rat* 1977; *Bloodline* 1979; *Sphinx* 1980; *La Balance* 1982
Ronstadt, Linda *FM* 1977; *The Pirates of Penzance* 1983
Rooker, Michael *Henry: Portrait of a Serial Killer* 1986; *Mississippi Burning* 1988; *Sea of Love* 1989; *Days of Thunder* 1990; *The Dark Half* 1991; *JFK* 1991; *Afterburn* 1992; *Cliffhanger* 1993; *The Hard Truth* 1994; *American Yakuza 2: Back to Back* 1996; *The Trigger Effect* 1996; *Bram Stoker's Shadowbuilder* 1997; *Liar* 1997; *The Replacement Killers* 1998; *Brown's Requiem* 1998; *The Bone Collector* 1999; *Here on Earth* 2000
Rooney, Brian *Mission Top Secret* 1990; *The Phantom Horsemen* 1990; *The Rogue Stallion* 1990
Rooney, Mickey *The Beast of the City* 1932; *Broadway to Hollywood* 1933; *Manhattan Melodrama* 1934; *Upper World* 1934; *Ah, Wilderness* 1935; *A Midsummer Night's Dream* 1935; *The Devil Is a Sissy* 1936; *Little Lord Fauntleroy* 1936; *Riffraff* 1936; *Captains Courageous* 1937; *A Family Affair* 1937; *Slave Ship* 1937; *Thoroughbreds Don't Cry*

1937; *Live, Love and Learn* 1937; *Boys Town* 1938; *Judge Hardy's Children* 1938; *Love Finds Andy Hardy* 1938; *Out West with the Hardys* 1938; *You're Only Young Once* 1938; *The Adventures of Huckleberry Finn* 1939; *Andy Hardy Gets Spring Fever* 1939; *Babes in Arms* 1939; *The Hardys Ride High* 1939; *Judge Hardy and Son* 1939; *Andy Hardy Meets Debutante* 1940; *Strike Up the Band* 1940; *Young Tom Edison* 1940; *Andy Hardy's Private Secretary* 1941; *Babes on Broadway* 1941; *Life Begins for Andy Hardy* 1941; *Men of Boys Town* 1941; *Andy Hardy's Double Life* 1942; *The Courtship of Andy Hardy* 1942; *Girl Crazy* 1943; *The Human Comedy* 1943; *Andy Hardy's Blonde Trouble* 1944; *National Velvet* 1944; *Love Laughs at Andy Hardy* 1946; *Killer McCoy* 1947; *Summer Holiday* 1948; *Words and Music* 1948; *The Big Wheel* 1949; *The Fireball* 1950; *Military Policeman* 1953; *Off Limits* 1953; *All Ashore* 1953; *The Bridges at Toko-Ri* 1954; *Drive a Crooked Road* 1954; *The Atomic Kid* 1954; *The Twinkle in God's Eye* 1955; *The Bold and the Brave* 1956; *Baby Face Nelson* 1957; *Operation Mad Ball* 1957; *Andy Hardy Comes Home* 1958; *A Nice Little Bank That Should Be Robbed* 1958; *Quicksand* 1959; *The Last Mile* 1959; *The Big Operator* 1959; *Platinum High School* 1960; *Breakfast at Tiffany's* 1961; *King of the Roaring 20s – the Story of Arnold Rothstein* 1961; *Requiem for a Heavyweight* 1962; *It's a Mad Mad Mad Mad World* 1963; *Journey back to Oz* 1964; *The Secret Invasion* 1964; *How to Fill a Wild Bikini* 1965; *Ambush Bay* 1966; *Skidoo* 1968; *The Comic* 1969; *The Extraordinary Seaman* 1969; *Eighty Steps to Jonah* 1969; *The Cockeyed Cowboys of Calico County* 1970; *Pulp* 1972; *Rachel's Man* 1975; *Find the Lady* 1976; *The Domino Principle* 1977; *Pete's Dragon* 1977; *The Magic of Lassie* 1978; *Arabian Adventure* 1979; *The Black Stallion* 1979; *The Fox and the Hound* 1981; *Leave 'Em Laughing* 1981; *Bill* 1981; *The Care Bears Movie* 1985; *Lightning the White Stallion* 1986; *Little Spies* 1986; *There Must Be a Pony* 1986; *Erik the Viking* 1989; *Home for Christmas* 1990; *My Heroes Have Always Been Cowboys* 1991; *Little Nemo: Adventures in Slumberland* 1992; *The Magic Voyage* 1992; *Sweet Justice* 1992; *The Road Home* 1995; *Babe: Pig in the City* 1998
Rooney, Teddy *Andy Hardy Comes Home* 1958; *It Happened to Jane* 1959
Roope, Fay *Callaway Went Thataway* 1951; *The Clown* 1952; *All Ashore* 1953
Roos, Joanna *Patterns* 1956; *Two Weeks in Another Town* 1962
Root, Amanda *The BFG* 1989; *Persuasion* 1995; *Whatever Happened to Harold Smith?* 1999
Root, Stephen *Monkey Shines* 1988; *Bed & Breakfast* 1992; *A Woman Deceived* 1992; *A Woman Scorned* 1992; *Night of the Scarecrow* 1995; *Office Space* 1999; *Bicentennial Man* 1999
Roper, Brian *Just William's Luck* 1947; *William at the Circus* 1948; *The Secret Garden* 1949
Roquevert, Noël *Fanfan la Tulipe* 1951; *Cartouche* 1961

Rorke, Hayden *Room for One More* 1952; *The Girl Next Door* 1953; *South Sea Woman* 1953; *Project Moonbase* 1953; *Confidentially Connie* 1953; *Lucky Me* 1954; *A Stranger in My Arms* 1959; *The Night Walker* 1964; *I Dream of Jeannie… 15 Years Later* 1985
Rory, Rossana *The Angel Wore Red* 1960; *Come September* 1961; *Eclipse* 1962
Rosanova, Rosa *Blood and Sand* 1922; *The Younger Generation* 1929
Rosario, Bert *Cold Justice* 1991; *A Million to Juan* 1994
Rosato, Tony *Mystery Date* 1991; *Rent-a-Kid* 1992; *Kissinger and Nixon* 1995
Rosay, Françoise *Le Grand Jeu* 1933; *Carnival in Flanders* 1935; *Drôle de Drame* 1937; *The Halfway House* 1943; *Johnny Frenchman* 1945; *Saraband for Dead Lovers* 1948; *September Affair* 1950; *The 13th Letter* 1951; *La Reine Margot* 1954; *That Lady* 1955; *Interlude* 1957; *Me and the Colonel* 1958; *The Sound and the Fury* 1959; *The Full Treatment* 1961; *Up from the Beach* 1965; *The Pedestrian* 1974
Roscoe, Alan *Long Pants* 1927; *Flight* 1929
Rose, Clifford *Marat/Sade* 1966; *The Girl* 1986
Rose, Gabrielle *Family Viewing* 1987; *Speaking Parts* 1989; *The Adjuster* 1991; *The Sweet Hereafter* 1997
Rose, George *The Square Ring* 1953; *Barnacle Bill* 1957; *The Shiralee* 1957; *Cat and Mouse* 1958; *Jack the Ripper* 1958; *The Flesh and the Fiends* 1959; *A New Leaf* 1971; *The Hideaways* 1973; *The Pirates of Penzance* 1983; *Pound Puppies and the Legend of Big Paw* 1988
Rose, Jamie *Heartbreakers* 1984; *Chopper Chicks in Zombietown* 1990; *Brotherhood of the Gun* 1992
Rose, Jane *Summertime* 1955; *The Monte Carlo Story* 1957; *Flipper* 1963
Rose Marie *Top Banana* 1953; *Dead Heat on a Merry-Go-Round* 1966
Rose, Reva *Bunny O'Hare* 1971; *The Nine Lives of Fritz the Cat* 1974
Rose, Robin Pearson *Promised a Miracle* 1988; *Lucy and Desi: before the Laughter* 1991
Rose, Sherrie *Double Threat* 1992; *Black Scorpion: Ground Zero* 1996
Rose, Veronica *A Cuckoo in the Nest* 1933; *Fighting Stock* 1935; *For Valour* 1937
Roseanne *aka* **Barr, Roseanne,** *aka* **Arnold, Roseanne** *She-Devil* 1989; *Look Who's Talking Too* 1990; *Backfield in Motion* 1991; *Even Cowgirls Get the Blues* 1993; *The Woman Who Loved Elvis* 1993; *Blue in the Face* 1995
Rosenberg, Alan *The Wanderers* 1979; *Happy Birthday, Gemini* 1980; *The Belarus File* 1985; *Promise* 1986; *White of the Eye* 1986; *Impulse* 1990; *The Boys* 1991; *Freaky Friday* 1995; *Cloned* 1997
Rosenberg, Arthur *Cutter's Way* 1981; *Second Thoughts* 1982; *Desperate for Love* 1989
Rosenbloom, Maxie *Nothing Sacred* 1937; *Louisiana Purchase* 1941; *Ringside Maisie* 1941; *The Boogie Man Will Get You* 1942; *To the Shores of Tripoli* 1942;

Abbott and Costello Meet the Keystone Cops 1955; *Hollywood or Bust* 1956
Rosing, Bodil *Sunrise* 1927; *The Big Noise* 1928
Rosmer, Milton *The Phantom Light* 1934; *South Riding* 1938; *Goodbye, Mr Chips* 1939; *Return to Yesterday* 1940
Ross, Annie *Alfie Darling* 1975; *Superman III* 1983; *Witchcraft* 1989; *Basket Case 2* 1990; *Basket Case 3: the Progeny* 1992; *Short Cuts* 1993
Ross, Anthony *Kiss of Death* 1947; *The Window* 1949; *The Gunfighter* 1950; *Perfect Strangers* 1950; *On Dangerous Ground* 1951; *The Country Girl* 1954
Ross, Beverly *SOS Titanic* 1979; *Broken English* 1981
Ross, Charlotte *Foreign Student* 1994; *Fall into Darkness* 1996
Ross, Chelcie *The Package* 1989; *The Last Boy Scout* 1991; *Amos & Andrew* 1993; *Chain Reaction* 1996; *Evil Has a Face* 1996; *A Simple Plan* 1998
Ross, Diana *Lady Sings the Blues* 1972; *Mahogany* 1975; *The Wiz* 1978; *Out of Darkness* 1994; *Double Platinum* 1999
Ross, Hector *Deadly Nightshade* 1953; *The Steel Key* 1953
Ross, Joe E *Teaserama* 1955; *Maracaibo* 1958; *All Hands on Deck* 1961
Ross, Katharine *Shenandoah* 1965; *The Singing Nun* 1966; *Mister Buddwing* 1966; *Games* 1967; *The Graduate* 1967; *Butch Cassidy and the Sundance Kid* 1969; *Hellfighters* 1969; *Tell Them Willie Boy Is Here* 1969; *Fools* 1970; *They Only Kill Their Masters* 1972; *Get to Know Your Rabbit* 1972; *The Stepford Wives* 1975; *Voyage of the Damned* 1976; *The Betsy* 1978; *The Legacy* 1978; *The Swarm* 1978; *The Final Countdown* 1980; *The Man with the Deadly Lens* 1982; *A Row of Crows* 1991; *Conagher* 1991
Ross, Lee *Buddy's Song* 1990; *Secrets & Lies* 1995; *Hard Men* 1996; *Metroland* 1997; *Vigo: Passion for Life* 1997; *Dreaming of Joseph Lees* 1998
Ross, Marion *The Glenn Miller Story* 1953; *The Proud and Profane* 1956; *Lizzie* 1957; *Grand Theft Auto* 1977; *Danielle Steel's A Perfect Stranger* 1994; *About Sarah* 1998
Ross, Matt *Ed's Next Move* 1996; *Pushing Tin* 1999
Ross, Shirley *The Big Broadcast of 1937* 1936; *San Francisco* 1936; *The Big Broadcast of 1938* 1937; *Waikiki Wedding* 1937; *Paris Honeymoon* 1939
Ross, Ted *The Wiz* 1978; *Arthur* 1981
Ross, Terry Ann *The Three Faces of Eve* 1957; *Cry Terror* 1958
Rossellini, Isabella *A Matter of Time* 1976; *White Nights* 1985; *Blue Velvet* 1986; *Siesta* 1987; *Tough Guys Don't Dance* 1987; *Red Riding Hood* 1987; *Zelly and Me* 1988; *Cousins* 1989; *Ivory Hunters* 1990; *Wild at Heart* 1990; *Lies of the Twins* 1991; *Death Becomes Her* 1992; *Fearless* 1993; *The Innocent* 1993; *Immortal Beloved* 1994; *Wyatt Earp* 1994; *Big Night* 1996; *Crime of the Century* 1996; *The Funeral* 1996; *Left Luggage* 1997; *The Odyssey* 1997; *The Impostors* 1998

1942; *Desperate Journey* 1942; *To Be or Not to Be* 1942; *Sweet Rosie O'Grady* 1943; *Tarzan Triumphs* 1943; *Summer Storm* 1944; *A Royal Scandal* 1945; *A Night in Casablanca* 1946; *The Emperor Waltz* 1948; *Give My Regards to Broadway* 1948; *On the Riviera* 1951; *The World in His Arms* 1952; *O Henry's Full House* 1952; *Houdini* 1953; *Stalag 17* 1953; *Three Ring Circus* 1954; *White Christmas* 1954; *The Errand Boy* 1961

Runacre, Jenny *Husbands* 1970; *The Final Programme* 1973; *The Passenger* 1975; *Jubilee* 1978; *Hussy* 1979

Runningfox, Joseph *Porky's II: The Next Day* 1983; *A Child for Satan* 1991; *Geronimo* 1993

Runyon, Jennifer *Dreams of Gold: the Mel Fisher Story* 1986; *18 Again!* 1988; *A Very Brady Christmas* 1988; *The In Crowd* 1988; *Carnosaur* 1993

Rupp, Sieghardt *A Fistful of Dollars* 1964; *Dead Pigeon on Beethoven Street* 1972

Ruscio, Elizabeth *Born Too Soon* 1993; *Frequent Flyer* 1996; *Death Benefit* 1996

Rush, Barbara *When Worlds Collide* 1951; *The First Legion* 1951; *It Came from Outer Space* 1953; *Prince of Pirates* 1953; *The Black Shield of Falworth* 1954; *Magnificent Obsession* 1954; *Taza, Son of Cochise* 1954; *Captain Lightfoot* 1955; *Kiss of Fire* 1955; *Bigger than Life* 1956; *Oh, Men! Oh, Women!* 1957; *No Down Payment* 1957; *The Young Lions* 1958; *The Young Philadelphians* 1959; *The Bramble Bush* 1960; *Strangers When We Meet* 1960; *Come Blow Your Horn* 1963; *Robin and the 7 Hoods* 1964; *Hombre* 1967; *The Eyes of Charles Sand* 1972; *The Man* 1972; *Superdad* 1974; *Can't Stop the Music* 1980; *Summer Lovers* 1982; *Widow's Kiss* 1996

Rush, Deborah *A Night in Heaven* 1983; *Zelig* 1983; *Big Business* 1988; *Parents* 1988; *Family Business* 1989; *My Blue Heaven* 1990; *Three to Tango* 1999

Rush, Geoffrey *Shine* 1996; *Children of the Revolution* 1996; *Les Misérables* 1997; *Elizabeth* 1998; *Shakespeare in Love* 1998; *House on Haunted Hill* 1999

Rushbrook, Claire *Secrets & Lies* 1995; *Under the Skin* 1997

Rushton, Jared *Overboard* 1987; *Big* 1988; *Lady in White* 1988; *Honey, I Shrunk the Kids* 1989; *A Cry in the Wild* 1990; *Pet Sematary II* 1992

Rushton, William *The Bliss of Mrs Blossom* 1968; *Flight of the Doves* 1971; *Keep It Up Downstairs* 1976; *Adventures of a Private Eye* 1977; *Consuming Passions* 1988

Ruskin, Joseph *Firepower* 1993; *Cyber-Tracker* 1994

Rusler, Robert *Weird Science* 1985; *A Nightmare on Elm Street 2: Freddy's Revenge* 1985; *Thrashin'* 1986; *Vamp* 1986; *The Game of Love* 1987; *Shag* 1988; *Sometimes They Come Back* 1991; *The Underworld* 1997

Russ, Tim *Dead Silence* 1991; *Final Combination* 1993; *Journey to the Center of the Earth* 1993

Russ, William *Rehearsal for Murder* 1982; *Beer* 1985; *Second Serve* 1986; *Wanted Dead or Alive* 1986; *Dead of Winter* 1987; *The Unholy* 1988; *Crazy from the Heart* 1991; *Pastime* 1991; *Sexual Advances* 1992; *Traces of Red* 1992; *Aspen Extreme* 1993; *Big Dreams & Broken Hearts: the Dottie West Story* 1995; *A Strange Affair* 1995; *When Danger Follows You Home* 1997; *Replacing Dad* 1999

Russek, Jorge *The Return of a Man Called Horse* 1976; *Miracles* 1985; *Pure Luck* 1991

Russell, Andy *Make Mine Music* 1946; *Copacabana* 1947

Russell, Betsy *Private School* 1983; *Avenging Angel* 1985; *Tomboy* 1985; *Roxanne: the Prize Pulitzer* 1989

Russell, Bing *Cattle Empire* 1958; *Suicide Battalion* 1958; *Last Train from Gun Hill* 1959; *A Taste of Evil* 1971; *Elvis – the Movie* 1979

Russell, Bryan *Safe at Home* 1962; *A Ticklish Affair* 1963; *Emil and the Detectives* 1964; *The Adventures of Bullwhip Griffin* 1967

Russell, Catherine *Soft Top, Hard Shoulder* 1992; *Clockwork Mice* 1994

Russell, Charles *The Late George Apley* 1947; *Give My Regards to Broadway* 1948

Russell, Clive *The Hawk* 1992; *Margaret's Museum* 1995; *Oscar and Lucinda* 1997

Russell, Craig *Outrageous!* 1977; *Too Outrageous!* 1987

Russell, Gail *The Uninvited* 1944; *The Unseen* 1945; *Salty O'Rourke* 1945; *Angel and the Badman* 1947; *Calcutta* 1947; *Moonrise* 1948; *Night Has a Thousand Eyes* 1948; *Wake of the Red Witch* 1949; *The Lawless* 1950; *Seven Men from Now* 1956

Russell, Jane *The Outlaw* 1943; *The Paleface* 1948; *Double Dynamite* 1951; *His Kind of Woman* 1951; *The Las Vegas Story* 1951; *Macao* 1952; *Son of Paleface* 1952; *Gentlemen Prefer Blondes* 1953; *The French Line* 1954; *The Tall Men* 1955; *Underwater!* 1955; *Foxfire* 1955; *Gentlemen Marry Brunettes* 1955; *The Revolt of Mamie Stover* 1956; *Hot Blood* 1956; *The Fuzzy Pink Nightgown* 1957; *Fate Is the Hunter* 1964; *Waco* 1966; *Johnny Reno* 1966; *Born Losers* 1967; *Darker than Amber* 1970

Russell, John *Yellow Sky* 1948; *Slattery's Hurricane* 1949; *Saddle Tramp* 1950; *Man in the Saddle* 1951; *Hoodlum Empire* 1952; *Fair Wind to Java* 1953; *The Sun Shines Bright* 1953; *Rio Bravo* 1959; *Yellowstone Kelly* 1959; *Apache Uprising* 1965; *Hostile Guns* 1967

Russell, Ken *Valentino* 1977; *Salome's Last Dance* 1988; *The Russia House* 1990

Russell, Keri *Honey I Blew Up the Kid* 1992; *The Babysitter's Seduction* 1996; *Eight Days a Week* 1996; *Dead Man's Curve* 1997

Russell, Kimberly *Ghost Dad* 1990; *Hangin' with the Homeboys* 1991; *The OJ Simpson Story* 1995

Russell, Kurt *It Happened at the World's Fair* 1962; *Follow Me, Boys!* 1966; *The Horse in the Gray Flannel Suit* 1968; *The One and Only, Genuine, Original Family Band* 1968; *Guns in the Heather* 1969; *The Computer Wore Tennis Shoes* 1970; *The Barefoot Executive* 1971; *Fools' Parade* 1971; *Now You See Him, Now You Don't* 1972; *Charley and the Angel* 1973; *Superdad* 1974; *The Strongest Man in the World* 1975; *Elvis – the Movie* 1979; *Used Cars* 1980; *Escape from New York* 1981; *The Fox and the Hound* 1981; *The Thing* 1982; *Silkwood* 1983; *Swing Shift* 1984; *The Mean Season* 1985; *The Best of Times* 1986; *Big Trouble in Little China* 1986; *Overboard* 1987; *Tequila Sunrise* 1988; *Winter People* 1988; *Tango and Cash* 1989; *Backdraft* 1991; *Captain Ron* 1992; *Unlawful Entry* 1992; *Tombstone* 1993; *Stargate* 1994; *Executive Decision* 1996; *Escape from LA* 1996; *Breakdown* 1997; *Soldier* 1998

Russell, Nipsey *The Wiz* 1978; *Wildcats* 1986; *Car 54 Where Are You?* 1991

Russell, Rebel *Emma's War* 1985; *Frauds* 1992

Russell, Rosalind *Forsaking All Others* 1934; *Evelyn Prentice* 1934; *The Casino Murder Case* 1935; *China Seas* 1935; *Reckless* 1935; *Rendezvous* 1935; *Craig's Wife* 1936; *Trouble for Two* 1936; *Under Two Flags* 1936; *Man-Proof* 1937; *Night Must Fall* 1937; *Live, Love and Learn* 1937; *The Citadel* 1938; *Four's a Crowd* 1938; *Fast and Loose* 1939; *His Girl Friday* 1939; *The Women* 1939; *No Time for Comedy* 1940; *This Thing Called Love* 1940; *Hired Wife* 1940; *Design for Scandal* 1941; *The Feminine Touch* 1941; *They Met in Bombay* 1941; *My Sister Eileen* 1942; *Take a Letter, Darling* 1942; *Flight for Freedom* 1943; *What a Woman!* 1943; *Roughly Speaking* 1945; *Sister Kenny* 1946; *Mourning Becomes Electra* 1947; *The Guilt of Janet Ames* 1947; *The Velvet Touch* 1948; *Tell It to the Judge* 1949; *A Woman of Distinction* 1950; *Never Wave at a WAC* 1952; *Picnic* 1955; *The Girl Rush* 1955; *Auntie Mame* 1958; *A Majority of One* 1961; *Five Finger Exercise* 1962; *Gypsy* 1962; *The Trouble with Angels* 1966; *Rosie!* 1967; *Oh Dad, Poor Dad, Mama's Hung You in the Closet and I'm Feelin' So Sad* 1967; *Where Angels Go...Trouble Follows* 1968; *Mrs Pollifax – Spy* 1970

Russell, T E *Trespass* 1992; *Lust for Murder* 1993; *Swimming with Sharks* 1994

Russell, Theresa *The Last Tycoon* 1976; *Straight Time* 1978; *Bad Timing* 1980; *Eureka* 1982; *The Razor's Edge* 1984; *Insignificance* 1985; *Aria* 1987; *Black Widow* 1987; *Track 29* 1988; *Physical Evidence* 1989; *Impulse* 1990; *Kafka* 1991; *Whore* 1991; *Cold Heaven* 1992; *Being Human* 1994; *Flight of the Dove* 1995; *The Grotesque* 1995; *The Public Enemy #1* 1995; *Trade-Off* 1995; *Young Connecticut Yankee in King Arthur's Court* 1995; *Once You Meet a Stranger* 1996; *The Proposition* 1996; *Wild Things* 1998

Russell, William *One Good Turn* 1954; *Above Us the Waves* 1955; *The Big Chance* 1957; *The Adventures of Hal 5* 1958

Russo, Chelsea *Under Pressure* 1997; *An Unexpected Life* 1998

Russo, Gianni *Lepke* 1975; *Laserblast* 1978

Russo, James *Exposed* 1983; *Beverly Hills Cop* 1984; *Extremities* 1986; *China Girl* 1987; *The Blue Iguana* 1988; *Freeway* 1988; *We're No Angels* 1989; *A Kiss before Dying* 1991; *My Own Private Idaho* 1991; *Cold Heaven* 1992; *Dangerous Game* 1993; *Desperate Rescue* 1993; *Double Deception* 1993; *Trauma* 1993; *Bad Girls* 1994; *The Set Up* 1995; *No Way Home* 1996; *Under Oath* 1996; *American Strays* 1996; *Donnie Brasco* 1997; *Love to Kill* 1997; *The Postman* 1997; *My Husband's Secret Life* 1998; *The Ninth Gate* 2000

Russo, Rene *Major League* 1989; *Mr Destiny* 1990; *One Good Cop* 1991; *Freejack* 1992; *Lethal Weapon 3* 1992; *In the Line of Fire* 1993; *Get Shorty* 1995; *Outbreak* 1995; *Ransom* 1996; *Tin Cup* 1996; *Buddy* 1997; *Lethal Weapon 4* 1998; *The Thomas Crown Affair* 1999

Russom, Leon *A Thousand Heroes* 1992; *Broken Pledges* 1994; *Reasons of the Heart* 1996; *Childhood Sweetheart?* 1997

Rust, Richard *The Legend of Tom Dooley* 1959; *Comanche Station* 1960; *This Rebel Breed* 1960; *Homicidal* 1961; *Underworld USA* 1961; *Walk on the Wild Side* 1962; *I Escaped from Devil's Island* 1973

Ruth, Babe *aka* **Ruth, George Herman "Babe"** *Speedy* 1928; *The Pride of the Yankees* 1942

Rutherford, Ann *Dramatic School* 1938; *Judge Hardy's Children* 1938; *Love Finds Andy Hardy* 1938; *Of Human Hearts* 1938; *Out West with the Hardys* 1938; *You're Only Young Once* 1938; *Andy Hardy Gets Spring Fever* 1939; *Dancing Co-Ed* 1939; *Four Girls in White* 1939; *The Hardys Ride High* 1939; *Judge Hardy and Son* 1939; *Andy Hardy Meets Debutante* 1940; *Pride and Prejudice* 1940; *Andy Hardy's Private Secretary* 1941; *Life Begins for Andy Hardy* 1941; *Whistling in the Dark* 1941; *Andy Hardy's Double Life* 1942; *The Courtship of Andy Hardy* 1942; *Orchestra Wives* 1942; *Whistling in Dixie* 1942; *Happy Land* 1943; *Whistling in Brooklyn* 1943; *The Bermuda Mystery* 1944; *Bedside Manner* 1945; *Two O'Clock Courage* 1945; *Murder in the Music Hall* 1946; *The Secret Life of Walter Mitty* 1947; *Adventures of Don Juan* 1948; *They Only Kill Their Masters* 1972

Rutherford, John *Half Shot at Sunrise* 1930; *Whoopee!* 1930

Rutherford, Kelly *Breaking the Silence* 1992; *I Love Trouble* 1994; *Danielle Steel's No Greater Love* 1996

Rutherford, Margaret *Dusty Ermine* 1936; *The Demi-Paradise* 1943; *The Yellow Canary* 1943; *English without Tears* 1944; *Blithe Spirit* 1945; *Meet Me at Dawn* 1946; *Miranda* 1947; *Passport to Pimlico* 1949; *The Happiest Days of Your Life* 1950; *The Magic Box* 1951; *Curtain Up* 1952; *The Importance of Being Earnest* 1952; *Miss Robin Hood* 1952; *Innocents in Paris* 1953; *Trouble in Store* 1953; *Mad about Men* 1954; *The Runaway Bus* 1954; *An Alligator Named Daisy* 1955; *Just My Luck* 1957; *The Smallest Show on Earth* 1957; *I'm All Right Jack* 1959; *Murder She Said* 1961; *On the Double* 1961; *The Mouse on the Moon* 1963; *Murder at the Gallop* 1963; *The VIPs* 1963; *Murder Ahoy* 1964; *Murder Most Foul* 1964; *The Alphabet Murders* 1966; *Chimes at Midnight* 1966; *Arabella* 1967; *A Countess from Hong Kong* 1967

Ruttan, Susan *Do You Remember Love* 1985; *Bay Cove* 1987; *Take My Daughters, Please* 1988; *Fire and Rain* 1989; *A Perfect Little Murder* 1990; *Triumph of the Heart* 1991; *Jack Reed: Badge of Honor* 1993; *Without Warning: Terror in the Towers* 1993; *Jack Reed: a Search for Justice* 1994; *Deadly Justice* 1995; *Jack Reed: Death and Vengeance* 1996; *Search for Justice* 1996

Ruud, Michael *The Legend of Sleepy Hollow* 1980; *Divided by Hate* 1997

Ruysdael, Basil *Colorado Territory* 1949; *Come to the Stable* 1949; *Pinky* 1949; *Broken Arrow* 1950; *High Lonesome* 1950; *Boots Malone* 1951; *Half Angel* 1951; *Carrie* 1952; *The Shanghai Story* 1954; *Davy Crockett, King of the Wild Frontier* 1955; *Jubal* 1956; *These Wilder Years* 1956

Ryall, David *Wilt* 1989; *Truly Madly Deeply* 1990; *Revolver* 1992

Ryan, Edmon *aka* **Ryan, Edmond** *Dark Eyes of London* 1939; *The Breaking Point* 1950; *Side Street* 1950; *Undercover Girl* 1950; *Go, Man, Go!* 1953; *Good Day for a Hanging* 1958; *Two for the Seesaw* 1962

Ryan, Eileen *At Close Range* 1985; *Winter People* 1988; *Anywhere but Here* 1999

Ryan, Irene *Diary of a Chambermaid* 1946; *The Woman on the Beach* 1947; *Half Angel* 1951; *Blackbeard the Pirate* 1952

Ryan, James *Kill and Kill Again* 1981; *Rage to Kill* 1988; *Any Man's Death* 1990

Ryan, Jeri *aka* **Ryan, Jeri Lynn** *Victim of Beauty* 1991; *Overexposed* 1992; *Co-ed Call Girl* 1996

Ryan, John *aka* **Ryan, John** *Cops and Robbers* 1973; *Shamus* 1973

Ryan, John P *aka* **Ryan, John** *Dillinger* 1973; *It's Alive* 1974; *Futureworld* 1976; *It Lives Again* 1978; *The Last Flight of Noah's Ark* 1980; *The Postman Always Rings Twice* 1981; *The Escape Artist* 1982; *Breathless* 1983; *Runaway Train* 1985; *Avenging Force* 1986; *Death Wish 4: the Crackdown* 1987; *Three O'Clock High* 1987; *Class of 1999* 1990; *Delta Force 2* 1990; *Blood River* 1991; *Bound* 1996

Ryan, Kathleen *Odd Man Out* 1946; *Captain Boycott* 1947; *Esther Waters* 1948; *Christopher Columbus* 1949; *Give Us This Day* 1949; *Prelude to Fame* 1950; *The Sound of Fury* 1950; *The Yellow Balloon* 1952; *Laxdale Hall* 1953; *Captain Lightfoot* 1955; *Jacqueline* 1956

Ryan, Lisa Dean *Hostile Intentions* 1995; *Silencing Mary* 1998

Ryan, Madge *Witness in the Dark* 1959; *Tiara Tahiti* 1962; *This Is My Street* 1963; *Kokoda Crescent* 1989

Ryan, Meg *Rich and Famous* 1981; *Amityville III: the Demon* 1983; *Armed and Dangerous* 1986; *Innerspace* 1987; *DOA* 1988; *The Presidio* 1988; *Promised Land* 1988; *When Harry Met Sally...* 1989; *Joe versus the Volcano* 1990; *The Doors* 1991; *Prelude to a Kiss* 1992; *Flesh and Bone* 1993; *Sleepless in Seattle* 1993; *When a Man Loves a Woman* 1994; *French Kiss* 1995; *IQ* 1995; *Restoration* 1995; *Courage under Fire* 1996; *Addicted to Love* 1997; *Anastasia* 1997; *City of Angels* 1998; *Hurlyburly* 1998; *You've Got Mail* 1998; *Hanging Up* 1999

Ryan, Mitchell *aka* **Ryan, Mitch** *Monte Walsh* 1970; *The Hunting Party* 1971; *Glory Boy* 1971;

RadioTimes ACTORS' INDEX

1971; *something big* 1971; *Kung Fu* 1972; *The Take* 1974; *Empire of the Ants* 1977; *Cloud Dancer* 1980; *Steel* 1980; *Dragonslayer* 1981; *Love Child* 1982; *Hard to Hold* 1984; *Jesse* 1988; *Breaking In* 1989

Salminen, Esko *Flame Top* 1980; *Hamlet Goes Business* 1987

Salmon, Colin *Captives* 1994; *All Men Are Mortal* 1995; *Frantz Fanon: Black Skin White Mask* 1996; *Tomorrow Never Dies* 1997; *The Wisdom of Crocodiles* 1998; *Fanny & Elvis* 1999

Salo, Elina *Hamlet Goes Business* 1987; *The Match Factory Girl* 1990; *Take Care of Your Scarf, Tatjana* 1994; *Drifting Clouds* 1996

Salonga, Lea *Aladdin* 1992; *Redwood Curtain* 1995; *Mulan* 1998

Salsedo, Frank *aka* **Salsedo, Frank S,** *aka* **Salsedo, Frank Sotonoma** *Creepshow 2* 1987; *Magic in the Water* 1995

Salt, Jennifer *The Wedding Party* 1966; *Midnight Cowboy* 1969; *Hi, Mom!* 1970; *The Revolutionary* 1970; *Play It Again, Sam* 1972; *Sisters* 1973; *Out of the Darkness* 1985; *Deadly Care* 1987

Salvatori, Renato *Big Deal on Madonna Street* 1958; *Rocco and His Brothers* 1960; *Two Women* 1960; *The Organizer* 1963; *Burn!* 1969; *The Burglars* 1971; *The Light at the Edge of the World* 1971; *State of Siege* 1972; *Burnt Barns* 1973; *Police Story* 1975; *La Luna* 1979

Salviat, Catherine *Just the Way You Are* 1984; *Romuald et Juliette* 1989

Sambrell, Aldo *Navajo Joe* 1966; *Sea Devils* 1982

Samel, Udo *Knife in the Head* 1978; *Kaspar Hauser* 1993

Samms, Emma *Arabian Adventure* 1979; *Agatha Christie's Murder in Three Acts* 1986; *Driving Force* 1988; *A Connecticut Yankee in King Arthur's Court* 1989; *Bejewelled* 1990; *The Shrimp on the Barbie* 1990; *Delirious* 1991; *Shadow of a Stranger* 1992; *Illusions* 1992; *Harmful Intent* 1993; *Terminal Voyage* 1994; *Treacherous Beauties* 1994

Sampson, Robert *Look in Any Window* 1961; *Hero's Island* 1962; *The Broken Land* 1962; *Re-Animator* 1985; *Robot Jox* 1989

Sampson, Will *One Flew over the Cuckoo's Nest* 1975; *Orca* 1977; *The White Buffalo* 1977; *Insignificance* 1985; *Firewalker* 1986; *Poltergeist II: the Other Side* 1986

Sams, Jeffrey D *Run for the Dream: the Gail Devers Story* 1996; *Soul Food* 1997; *Hope* 1997

Samuel, Joanne *Alison's Birthday* 1979; *Mad Max* 1979

San Giacomo, Laura *sex, lies, and videotape* 1989; *Pretty Woman* 1990; *Quigley Down Under* 1990; *Vital Signs* 1990; *Once Around* 1991; *Under Suspicion* 1991; *For Their Own Good* 1993; *Nina Takes a Lover* 1993; *Stuart Saves His Family* 1995

San Juan, Olga *Blue Skies* 1946; *Variety Girl* 1947; *The Countess of Monte Cristo* 1948; *One Touch of Venus* 1948; *The Beautiful Blonde from Bashful Bend* 1949

Sanchez, Jaime *The Pawnbroker* 1965; *The Wild Bunch* 1969; *Bobby Deerfield* 1977; *Florida Straits* 1986

Sanchez, Pedro *The Bounty Hunters* 1970; *Night and the City* 1992

Sanchez-Gijon, Aitana *Jarrapellejos* 1987; *The Monk* 1990; *A Walk in the Clouds* 1995; *Mouth to Mouth* 1995; *The Chambermaid on the Titanic* 1997; *Love Walked In* 1997

Sancho, Jose *El Dorado* 1988; *Ay, Carmela!* 1990; *Live Flesh* 1997

Sand, Paul *Every Little Crook and Nanny* 1972; *The Hot Rock* 1972; *The Second Coming of Suzanne* 1974; *The Great Georgia Bank Hoax* 1977; *The Main Event* 1979; *Can't Stop the Music* 1980; *The Legend of Sleepy Hollow* 1980; *Wholly Moses!* 1980; *The Last Fling* 1987

Sanda, Dominique *The Conformist* 1969; *A Gentle Creature* 1969; *First Love* 1970; *The Garden of the Finzi-Continis* 1971; *Without Apparent Motive* 1972; *The Mackintosh Man* 1973; *Story of a Love Story* 1973; *Steppenwolf* 1974; *The Inheritance* 1976; *1900* 1976; *Damnation Alley* 1977; *Caboblanco* 1980; *I, the Worst of All* 1990; *Voyage of Terror: the Achille Lauro Affair* 1990; *Nobody's Children* 1994; *Joseph in Egypt* 1995

Sande, Walter *Corvette K-225* 1943; *I Love a Soldier* 1944; *Killer McCoy* 1947; *The Woman on the Beach* 1947; *The Duel at Silver Creek* 1952; *Red Planet Mars* 1952; *Apache* 1954; *Texas Lady* 1955; *Johnny Tremain* 1957

Sander, Casey *The Story of the Beach Boys: Summer Dreams* 1990; *Crosscut* 1995

Sander, Otto *The Marquise of O* 1976; *Rosa Luxemburg* 1986; *Wings of Desire* 1987; *Faraway, So Close* 1993

Sanderford, John *The Alchemist* 1981; *My Boyfriend's Back* 1989; *Coins in the Fountain* 1990; *Leprechaun* 1992

Sanders, George *Lloyd's of London* 1936; *Things to Come* 1936; *Lancer Spy* 1937; *Slave Ship* 1937; *Four Men and a Prayer* 1938; *International Settlement* 1938; *Confessions of a Nazi Spy* 1939; *The First Rebel* 1939; *Mr Moto's Last Warning* 1939; *Nurse Edith Cavell* 1939; *The Saint in London* 1939; *The Saint Strikes Back* 1939; *Bitter Sweet* 1940; *Foreign Correspondent* 1940; *Rebecca* 1940; *The Saint Takes Over* 1940; *The Saint's Double Trouble* 1940; *Son of Monte Cristo* 1940; *A Date with the Falcon* 1941; *The Gay Falcon* 1941; *Man Hunt* 1941; *Rage in Heaven* 1941; *The Saint in Palm Springs* 1941; *Sundown* 1941; *The Black Swan* 1942; *The Falcon Takes Over* 1942; *The Falcon's Brother* 1942; *The Moon and Sixpence* 1942; *Quiet Please, Murder* 1942; *Son of Fury* 1942; *Tales of Manhattan* 1942; *Her Cardboard Lover* 1942; *Paris after Dark* 1943; *This Land Is Mine* 1943; *The Lodger* 1944; *Summer Storm* 1944; *Hangover Square* 1945; *The Picture of Dorian Gray* 1945; *The Strange Affair of Uncle Harry* 1945; *The Strange Woman* 1946; *Thieves' Holiday* 1946; *Forever Amber* 1947; *The Ghost and Mrs Muir* 1947; *Lured* 1947; *The Private Affairs of Bel Ami* 1947; *The Fan* 1949; *Samson and Delilah* 1949; *All about Eve* 1950; *I Can Get It for You Wholesale* 1951; *Assignment – Paris* 1952; *Black Jack* 1952; *Ivanhoe* 1952; *Call Me Madam* 1953; *Journey to Italy* 1953; *King Richard and the Crusaders* 1954; *Witness to Murder* 1954; *The Big Tip Off* 1955; *Jupiter's Darling* 1955; *The King's Thief* 1955; *Moonfleet* 1955; *Never Say Goodbye* 1955; *The Scarlet Coat* 1955; *Death of a Scoundrel* 1956; *While the City Sleeps* 1956; *That Certain Feeling* 1956; *From the Earth to the Moon* 1958; *The Whole Truth* 1958; *Solomon and Sheba* 1959; *A Touch of Larceny* 1959; *That Kind of Woman* 1959; *Cone of Silence* 1960; *The Last Voyage* 1960; *The Rebel* 1960; *Village of the Damned* 1960; *In Search of the Castaways* 1961; *Cairo* 1962; *The Cracksman* 1963; *A Shot in the Dark* 1964; *The Amorous Adventures of Moll Flanders* 1965; *The Quiller Memorandum* 1966; *Good Times* 1967; *The Jungle Book* 1967; *Warning Shot* 1967; *The Body Stealers* 1969; *The Candy Man* 1969; *The Kremlin Letter* 1970; *Endless Night* 1971; *Doomwatch* 1972; *Psychomania* 1972

Sanders, Hugh *The Damned Don't Cry* 1950; *Mister 880* 1950; *Storm Warning* 1950; *Boots Malone* 1951; *Sugarfoot* 1951; *That's My Boy* 1951; *The Fighter* 1952; *The Pride of St Louis* 1952; *The Glass Web* 1953; *The Wild One* 1953; *Voice in the Mirror* 1958

Sanders, Jay O *The Prince of Pennsylvania* 1988; *Cold Sassy Tree* 1989; *Meeting Venus* 1990; *Mr Destiny* 1990; *Revealing Evidence* 1990; *Defenseless* 1991; *JFK* 1991; *VI Warshawski* 1991; *My Boyfriend's Back* 1993; *Hostages* 1993; *Angels* 1994; *State of Emergency* 1994; *Nobody's Children* 1994; *The Big Green* 1995; *Down Came a Blackbird* 1995; *Silver Strand* 1995; *Three Wishes* 1995; *Daylight* 1996; *For Richer or Poorer* 1997; *Kiss the Girls* 1997; *The Matchmaker* 1997; *Wrestling with Alligators* 1998; *Earthly Possessions* 1999; *Tumbleweeds* 1999

Sanderson, Martyn *Beyond Reasonable Doubt* 1980; *Bad Blood* 1982; *Sylvia* 1984

Sanderson, William *Coal Miner's Daughter* 1980; *Death Hunt* 1981; *Raggedy Man* 1981; *Blade Runner* 1982; *Black Moon Rising* 1985; *The Defiant Ones* 1986; *The Man Who Broke 1,000 Chains* 1987; *Sometimes They Come Back* 1991; *Skeeter* 1993; *Wagons East!* 1994; *Last Man Standing* 1996

Sandford, Christopher *Deep End* 1970; *Die Screaming Marianne* 1970

Sandler, Adam *Shakes the Clown* 1991; *Airheads* 1994; *Billy Madison* 1995; *Mixed Nuts* 1995; *Bulletproof* 1996; *Happy Gilmore* 1996; *The Waterboy* 1998; *The Wedding Singer* 1998; *Dirty Work* 1998; *Big Daddy* 1999

Sandor, Steve *One More Train to Rob* 1971; *Stryker* 1983

Sandoval, Miguel *Clear and Present Danger* 1994; *Dancing with Danger* 1994; *Fair Game* 1995; *Mrs Winterbourne* 1995

Sandow, Nick *No Looking Back* 1998; *Return to Paradise* 1998

Sandre, Didier *The Lie* 1992; *An Autumn Tale* 1998

Sandrelli, Stefania *Divorce – Italian Style* 1961; *Seduced and Abandoned* 1964; *Partner* 1968; *The Conformist* 1969; *Alfredo Alfredo* 1971; *Somewhere beyond Love* 1974; *We All Loved Each Other So Much* 1974; *1900* 1976; *The Family* 1987; *Mignon Has Left* 1988; *Jamon Jamon* 1992; *Of Love and Shadows* 1994; *Stealing Beauty* 1995

Sandri, Anna-Maria *Le Rouge et le Noir* 1954; *The Black Tent* 1956

Sands, Diana *A Raisin in the Sun* 1961; *The Landlord* 1970; *Doctors' Wives* 1970; *Georgia, Georgia* 1972

Sands, Johnny *aka* **Sands, John** *Till the End of Time* 1946; *Bachelor Knight* 1947; *Blaze of Noon* 1947; *Adventure in Baltimore* 1949; *The Admiral Was a Lady* 1950; *The Lawless* 1950

Sands, Julian *The Killing Fields* 1984; *The Doctor and the Devils* 1985; *Romance on the Orient Express* 1985; *A Room with a View* 1985; *After Darkness* 1985; *Gothic* 1986; *Siesta* 1987; *Vibes* 1988; *Warlock* 1989; *Arachnophobia* 1990; *Night Sun* 1990; *Impromptu* 1991; *Naked Lunch* 1991; *Crazy in Love* 1992; *Tale of a Vampire* 1992; *The Turn of the Screw* 1992; *Boxing Helena* 1993; *Warlock: the Armageddon* 1993; *The Browning Version* 1994; *Witch Hunt* 1994; *The Great Elephant Escape* 1995; *Leaving Las Vegas* 1995; *The Tomorrow Man* 1995; *Circle of Passion* 1996; *The Autumn Heart* 1998; *The Loss of Sexual Innocence* 1999; *The Million Dollar Hotel* 1999; *Vatel* 2000

Sands, Leslie *One More Time* 1970; *The Ragman's Daughter* 1972

Sands, Tommy *Mardi Gras* 1958; *Sing, Boy, Sing* 1958; *Babes in Toyland* 1961; *Love in a Goldfish Bowl* 1961; *Ensign Pulver* 1964; *None but the Brave* 1965; *The Violent Ones* 1967

Sanford, Erskine *Citizen Kane* 1941; *The Magnificent Ambersons* 1942; *Ministry of Fear* 1945; *Angel on My Shoulder* 1946; *Crack-Up* 1946; *Possessed* 1947; *The Lady from Shanghai* 1948; *Macbeth* 1948

Sanford, Garwin *Quarantine* 1989; *Max* 1994; *Maternal Instincts* 1996

Sanford, Isabel *aka* **Sanford, Isabell** *Guess Who's Coming to Dinner* 1967; *Hickey and Boggs* 1972; *Love at First Bite* 1979; *Original Gangstas* 1996; *Sprung* 1997

Sanford, Ralph *Thunderhead – Son of Flicka* 1945; *Copacabana* 1947; *The Glass Menagerie* 1950

Sanford, Stanley *aka* **Sanford, Stanley J** *The Immigrant* 1917; *Modern Times* 1936

Sanipoli, Vittorio *The Great War* 1959; *Three Tough Guys* 1974

Sano, Shiro *Violent Cop* 1989; *The Most Terrible Time in My Life* 1993

Santacroce, Mary Nell *Wise Blood* 1979; *Stolen Babies* 1993

Santiago, Renoly *Dangerous Minds* 1995; *Hackers* 1995

Santini, Pierre *Dirty Hands* 1976; *American Dreamer* 1984; *Polar* 1984

Santon, Penny *Dino* 1957; *Love with the Proper Stranger* 1963; *Moonlight* 1982

Santoni, Reni *Enter Laughing* 1967; *Anzio* 1968; *Dirty Harry* 1971; *I Never Promised You a Rose Garden* 1977; *Dead Men Don't Wear Plaid* 1982; *Bad Boys* 1983; *Brewster's Millions* 1985; *Cobra* 1986

Santos, Joe *The Blue Knight* 1973; *The Friends of Eddie Coyle* 1973; *Shamus* 1973; *Zandy's Bride* 1974; *A Matter of Wife...and Death* 1976; *Fear City* 1984; *The Old Man and the Sea* 1990; *Mo' Money* 1992; *Art Deco Detective* 1994

Santschi, Tom *3 Bad Men* 1926; *Hills of Kentucky* 1927

Sanz, Jorge *Valentina* 1982; *Lovers* 1991; *Belle Epoque* 1992; *A Further Gesture* 1996; *Cha-Cha-Cha* 1998

Sara, Mia *Legend* 1985; *Ferris Bueller's Day Off* 1986; *Apprentice to Murder* 1988; *Daughter of Darkness* 1990; *Any Man's Death* 1990; *A Row of Crows* 1991; *By the Sword* 1992; *A Stranger among Us* 1992; *Blindsided* 1993; *Call of the Wild* 1993; *Someone's Watching* 1993; *Timecop* 1994; *Bullet to Beijing* 1995; *The Maddening* 1995; *The Set Up* 1995; *Black Day Blue Night* 1995; *The Pompatus of Love* 1995; *Undertow* 1996; *Hard Time* 1998

Sarafian, Richard C *aka* **Sarafian, Richard** *Bugsy* 1991; *Sex, Love and Cold Hard Cash* 1993; *Bound* 1996; *Gotti* 1996

Sarandon, Chris *Dog Day Afternoon* 1975; *Lipstick* 1976; *The Sentinel* 1977; *Cuba* 1979; *Broken Promise* 1981; *The Osterman Weekend* 1983; *Protocol* 1984; *Fright Night* 1985; *This Child Is Mine* 1985; *Collision Course* 1987; *Mayflower Madam* 1987; *The Princess Bride* 1987; *Child's Play* 1988; *Farewell Miss Freedom* 1988; *Slaves of New York* 1989; *Forced March* 1989; *The Stranger Within* 1990; *Whispers* 1990; *A Murderous Affair* 1992; *The Resurrected* 1992; *Dark Tide* 1993; *Tim Burton's The Nightmare before Christmas* 1993; *David's Mother* 1994; *Temptress* 1995; *When the Dark Man Calls* 1995; *Danielle Steel's No Greater Love* 1996; *Tales from the Crypt Presents: Bordello of Blood* 1996; *Terminal Justice* 1996; *Edie & Pen* 1996; *American Perfekt* 1997; *The Underworld* 1997; *Little Men* 1998; *Road Ends* 1999

Sarandon, Susan *Joe* 1970; *Lady Liberty* 1971; *The Front Page* 1974; *Lovin' Molly* 1974; *The Great Waldo Pepper* 1975; *The Rocky Horror Picture Show* 1975; *One Summer Love* 1975; *The Great Smokey Roadblock* 1977; *The Other Side of Midnight* 1977; *Pretty Baby* 1978; *King of the Gypsies* 1978; *Something Short of Paradise* 1979; *Atlantic City USA* 1980; *Loving Couples* 1980; *Tempest* 1982; *The Hunger* 1983; *The Buddy System* 1984; *Compromising Positions* 1985; *Women of Valor* 1986; *The Witches of Eastwick* 1987; *Bull Durham* 1988; *Sweet Hearts Dance* 1988; *A Dry White Season* 1989; *The January Man* 1989; *White Palace* 1990; *Light Sleeper* 1991; *Thelma & Louise* 1991; *Bob Roberts* 1992; *Lorenzo's Oil* 1992; *The Client* 1994; *Safe Passage* 1994; *Dead Man Walking* 1995; *Little Women* 1995; *James and the Giant Peach* 1996; *Stepmom* 1998; *Twilight* 1998; *Cradle Will Rock* 1999; *Earthly Possessions* 1999; *Anywhere but Here* 1999

Sarda, Rosa Maria *The Butterfly Effect* 1995; *Actresses* 1996; *Beloved/Friend* 1998; *All about My Mother* 1999

Sardou, Fernand *Marguerite de la Nuit* 1955; *Lunch on the Grass* 1959; *The Little Theatre of Jean Renoir* 1969
Sarelle, Leilani *Checkered Flag* 1990; *Basic Instinct* 1992
Sargent, Dick aka **Sargent, Richard** *Mardi Gras* 1958; *Operation Petticoat* 1959; *Billie* 1965; *The Ghost and Mr Chicken* 1966; *The Private Navy of Sgt O'Farrell* 1968; *Live a Little, Love a Little* 1968; *Hardcore* 1979; *Teen Witch* 1989
Sarkisyan, Rose *Family Viewing* 1987; *The Adjuster* 1991
Sarne, Michael aka **Sarne, Mike** *A Place to Go* 1963; *Every Day's a Holiday* 1964
Sarrazin, Michael *The Doomsday Flight* 1966; *Gunfight in Abilene* 1967; *One Born Every Minute* 1967; *The Sweet Ride* 1967; *Journey to Shiloh* 1968; *Eye of the Cat* 1969; *A Man Called Gannon* 1969; *They Shoot Horses, Don't They?* 1969; *In Search of Gregory* 1970; *Believe in Me* 1971; *Never Give an Inch* 1971; *The Pursuit of Happiness* 1971; *The Groundstar Conspiracy* 1972; *Frankenstein: the True Story* 1973; *Harry in Your Pocket* 1973; *For Pete's Sake* 1974; *The Reincarnation of Peter Proud* 1975; *The Gumball Rally* 1976; *The Loves and Times of Scaramouche* 1976; *Caravans* 1978; *Death Vengeance* 1982; *Joshua Then and Now* 1985; *Keeping Track* 1986; *Mascara* 1987; *Captive Hearts* 1988; *Malarek* 1989; *Lena's Holiday* 1990; *Bullet to Beijing* 1995; *Midnight in St Petersburg* 1995; *The Peacekeeper* 1997; *Midnight Man* 1998
Sarsgaard, Peter *Another Day in Paradise* 1998; *Boys Don't Cry* 1999
Sartain, Gailard *Roadie* 1980; *Hard Country* 1981; *Endangered Species* 1982; *Ernest Saves Christmas* 1988; *Mississippi Burning* 1988; *Blaze* 1989; *Ernest Goes to Jail* 1990; *Fried Green Tomatoes at the Whistle Stop Cafe* 1991; *Stop! or My Mom Will Shoot* 1992; *The Real McCoy* 1993; *Getting Even with Dad* 1994; *Open Season* 1995; *Murder in Mind* 1996; *The Patriot* 1998
Sassard, Jacqueline *The Pirates of Malaysia* 1964; *Accident* 1967; *Les Biches* 1968
Sato, Kei *Onibaba* 1964; *Death by Hanging* 1968
Satton, Lon *The Heroes* 1968; *Hello – Goodbye* 1970
Sauer, Gary *The Unbelievable Truth* 1989; *Trust* 1990
Saunders, Jennifer *The Supergrass* 1985; *Eat the Rich* 1987; *In the Bleak Midwinter* 1995; *Muppet Treasure Island* 1996; *Fanny & Elvis* 1999
Sauvegrain, Didier *Sarraouina* 1986; *Jeanne la Pucelle* 1994
Savage, Ann *Footlight Glamour* 1943; *One Dangerous Night* 1943; *Passport to Suez* 1943; *What a Woman!* 1943; *Detour* 1945
Savage, Ben *Little Monsters* 1989; *Big Girls Don't Cry... They Get Even* 1992
Savage, Brad *The Apple Dumpling Gang* 1974; *No Deposit No Return* 1976; *Echoes of a Summer* 1976; *Return from Witch Mountain* 1978; *Red Dawn* 1984
Savage, Fred *The Boy Who Could Fly* 1986; *The Princess Bride* 1987; *Vice Versa* 1988; *Little Monsters* 1989; *When You Remember Me* 1990; *Christmas on Division Street* 1991; *No One Would Tell* 1996
Savage, John *Bad Company* 1972; *Steelyard Blues* 1973; *The Killing Kind* 1973; *Eric* 1975; *The Deer Hunter* 1978; *Hair* 1979; *The Onion Field* 1979; *Inside Moves: the Guys from Max's Bar* 1980; *The Amateur* 1981; *Cattle Annie and Little Britches* 1981; *The Long Ride* 1984; *Maria's Lovers* 1984; *Nairobi Affair* 1984; *Silent Witness* 1985; *Salvador* 1986; *Hotel Colonial* 1987; *Beauty and the Beast* 1987; *Do the Right Thing* 1989; *Any Man's Death* 1990; *Hunting* 1992; *Primary Motive* 1992; *Killing Obsession* 1994; *Flynn* 1995; *Op Center* 1995; *The Takeover* 1995; *White Squall* 1996; *One Good Turn* 1996; *Amnesia* 1996; *American Strays* 1996; *Before Women Had Wings* 1997; *Hostile Intent* 1997; *Message in a Bottle* 1998; *The Jack Bull* 1999
Saval, Dany *Moon Pilot* 1962; *Boeing Boeing* 1965
Savalas, George *Violent City* 1970; *The Belarus File* 1985
Savalas, Telly *The Young Savages* 1961; *Birdman of Alcatraz* 1962; *Cape Fear* 1962; *The Interns* 1962; *Johnny Cool* 1963; *Love Is a Ball* 1963; *The Man from the Diner's Club* 1963; *Genghis Khan* 1964; *The New Interns* 1964; *The Greatest Story Ever Told* 1965; *The Slender Thread* 1965; *Beau Geste* 1966; *The Dirty Dozen* 1967; *The Karate Killers* 1967; *Buona Sera, Mrs Campbell* 1968; *The Scalphunters* 1968; *Sol Madrid* 1968; *The Assassination Bureau* 1969; *Crooks and Coronets* 1969; *Land Raiders* 1969; *Mackenna's Gold* 1969; *On Her Majesty's Secret Service* 1969; *Kelly's Heroes* 1970; *Violent City* 1970; *Pancho Villa* 1971; *A Town Called Hell* 1971; *Pretty Maids All in a Row* 1971; *Horror Express* 1972; *Inside Out* 1975; *Killer Force* 1975; *Lisa and the Devil* 1976; *Capricorn One* 1978; *Beyond the Poseidon Adventure* 1979; *Escape to Athena* 1979; *Cannonball Run II* 1983; *The Cartier Affair* 1984; *The Belarus File* 1985; *GoBots: Battle of the Rocklords* 1986; *The Dirty Dozen: the Deadly Mission* 1987; *The Dirty Dozen: the Fatal Mission* 1988; *The Hollywood Detective* 1989
Savant, Doug *Trick or Treat* 1986; *Masquerade* 1988; *Paint It Black* 1989; *Shaking the Tree* 1990; *Red Surf* 1990; *The Other Side of Murder* 1991; *Bonnie and Clyde: the True Story* 1992; *Robin Cook's Terminal* 1996
Savelyeva, Lyudmila *War and Peace* 1966; *Sunflower* 1969
Savident, John *Mountains of the Moon* 1989; *Brain Donors* 1992; *Mrs 'arris Goes to Paris* 1992
Savidge, Jennifer *Shootdown* 1988; *Clifford* 1994
Savini, Tom *Martin* 1978; *Knightriders* 1981; *Creepshow 2* 1987
Savoy, Teresa Ann aka **Savoy, Theresa Ann** *Salon Kitty* 1976; *Caligula* 1979
Savvina, Iya *The Lady with the Little Dog* 1960; *Asya's Happiness* 1967; *Private Life* 1982; *Remember Me This Way* 1988
Sawa, Devon *Little Giants* 1994; *The Boys Club* 1996; *The Night of the Twisters* 1996; *Robin of Locksley* 1996; *Wild America* 1997; *A Cool, Dry Place* 1998; *Idle Hands* 1999; *SLC Punk!* 1999; *Final Destination* 2000
Sawalha, Julia *In the Bleak Midwinter* 1995; *The Wind in the Willows* 1996; *Chicken Run* 2000
Sawalha, Nadim *The Wind and the Lion* 1975; *Sinbad and the Eye of the Tiger* 1977; *The Awakening* 1980; *Sphinx* 1980; *Misunderstood* 1984; *Half Moon Street* 1986; *Knights and Emeralds* 1986; *Pascali's Island* 1988; *The Hawk* 1992
Sawyer, Joe aka **Sawyer, Joseph** *I Found Stella Parish* 1935; *Special Agent* 1935; *The Petrified Forest* 1936; *The Black Legion* 1937; *San Quentin* 1937; *Down Mexico Way* 1941; *Two Mugs from Brooklyn* 1942; *Hit the Ice* 1943; *The Outlaw* 1943; *Tarzan's Desert Mystery* 1943; *Gilda* 1946; *Stagecoach Kid* 1949; *Red Skies of Montana* 1952; *Riding Shotgun* 1954
Saxon, John *Running Wild* 1955; *Rock, Pretty Baby* 1956; *The Reluctant Debutante* 1958; *This Happy Feeling* 1958; *The Restless Years* 1958; *The Big Fisherman* 1959; *Portrait in Black* 1960; *The Unforgiven* 1960; *Posse from Hell* 1961; *Mr Hobbs Takes a Vacation* 1962; *War Hunt* 1962; *The Night Caller* 1965; *The Appaloosa* 1966; *The Doomsday Flight* 1966; *Planet of Blood* 1966; *Istanbul Express* 1968; *Mr Kingstreet's War* 1970; *Company of Killers* 1970; *Joe Kidd* 1972; *Enter the Dragon* 1973; *Black Christmas* 1974; *Planet Earth* 1974; *Mitchell* 1975; *The Swiss Conspiracy* 1975; *Moonshine County Express* 1977; *The Glove* 1978; *The Electric Horseman* 1979; *Battle beyond the Stars* 1980; *Blood Beach* 1981; *The Man with the Deadly Lens* 1982; *Tenebrae* 1982; *A Nightmare on Elm Street* 1984; *Fever Pitch* 1985; *Payoff* 1991; *Animal Instincts* 1992; *Beverly Hills Cop III* 1994; *No Escape, No Return* 1994; *Killing Obsession* 1994
Sayer, Diane *Kitten with a Whip* 1964; *The Strangler* 1964
Sayer, Philip *The Green Horizon* 1981; *Slayground* 1983; *Xtro* 1983; *Shanghai Surprise* 1986
Sayers, Jo Ann *Young Dr Kildare* 1938; *The Adventures of Huckleberry Finn* 1939; *Honolulu* 1939
Sayle, Alexei *Gorky Park* 1983; *The Bride* 1985; *Solarwarriors* 1986; *Whoops Apocalypse* 1986; *Siesta* 1987; *Indiana Jones and the Last Crusade* 1989; *Carry On Columbus* 1992; *Reckless Kelly* 1993; *Curacao* 1993; *Swing* 1998
Sayles, John *Return of the Secaucus Seven* 1980; *Lianna* 1983; *Hard Choices* 1984; *Unnatural Causes: the Agent Orange Story* 1986; *Eight Men Out* 1988; *Little Vegas* 1990; *Straight Talk* 1992; *Gridlock'd* 1996
Sbarge, Raphael *Risky Business* 1983; *My Man Adam* 1985; *My Science Project* 1985; *So Proudly We Hail* 1990; *Back to Hannibal: the Return of Tom Sawyer and Huckleberry Finn* 1990; *Final Verdict* 1991; *Murder 101* 1991; *A Message from Holly* 1992; *Carnosaur* 1993; *The Hidden II* 1994; *Deadly Web* 1995; *Quicksilver Highway* 1997
Scacchi, Greta *Heat and Dust* 1982; *Burke and Wills* 1985; *The Coca-Cola Kid* 1985; *Defence of the Realm* 1985; *Good Morning, Babylon* 1987; *A Man in Love* 1987; *White Mischief* 1987; *Three Sisters* 1988; *Presumed Innocent* 1990; *Fires Within* 1991; *Shattered* 1991; *The Player* 1992; *Salt on Our Skin* 1992; *Turtle Beach* 1992; *The Browning Version* 1994; *Country Life* 1994; *Jefferson in Paris* 1995; *Emma* 1996; *Rasputin* 1996; *The Serpent's Kiss* 1997; *The Odyssey* 1997; *The Red Violin* 1998; *Tom's Midnight Garden* 1998; *Cotton Mary* 1999
Scala, Gia *Don't Go Near the Water* 1957; *Tip on a Dead Jockey* 1957; *The Garment Jungle* 1957; *Ride a Crooked Trail* 1958; *The Tunnel of Love* 1958; *The Two-Headed Spy* 1958; *The Angry Hills* 1959; *I Aim at the Stars* 1960; *The Guns of Navarone* 1961
Scales, Prunella *Hobson's Choice* 1953; *Laxdale Hall* 1953; *Waltz of the Toreadors* 1962; *Escape from the Dark* 1976; *The Hound of the Baskervilles* 1977; *The Wicked Lady* 1983; *The Lonely Passion of Judith Hearne* 1987; *A Chorus of Disapproval* 1988; *Consuming Passions* 1988; *Howards End* 1992; *An Awfully Big Adventure* 1994; *Second Best* 1994; *Wolf* 1994; *Stiff Upper Lips* 1997; *Mad Cows* 1999
Scalia, Jack *Fear City* 1984; *Donor* 1990; *With a Vengeance* 1992; *Amore!* 1993; *Casualties of Love: the Long Island Lolita Story* 1993; *Judith Krantz's Torch Song* 1993; *Beyond Suspicion* 1994; *Shadow of Obsession* 1994; *The Silencers* 1995; *T-Force* 1995; *Tall, Dark and Deadly* 1995; *Darkbreed* 1996; *Under Oath* 1996; *Barbara Taylor Bradford's Everything to Gain* 1996
Scarabelli, Michele *Deadbolt* 1992; *Alien Nation: Dark Horizon* 1994; *The Wrong Woman* 1996
Scarano, Tecla *Marriage – Italian Style* 1964; *Shout Loud, Louder... I Don't Understand* 1966
Scardino, Don *Homer* 1970; *The People Next Door* 1970; *Squirm* 1976; *Cruising* 1980; *He Knows You're Alone* 1981
Scardino, Hal *The Indian in the Cupboard* 1995; *Marvin's Room* 1996
Scarfe, Alan *Bay Boy* 1984; *Walls* 1984; *Joshua Then and Now* 1985; *Keeping Track* 1986; *Iron Eagle II* 1988; *Double Impact* 1991; *Jericho Fever* 1993; *Back in Business* 1997; *Sanctuary* 1998
Scarfe, Jonathan *Dead Innocent* 1996; *The Morrison Murders* 1997
Scarpa, Renato *Don't Look Now* 1973; *The Icicle Thief* 1989
Scarpitta, Carmen *Casanova* 1976; *In the Name of the Pope King* 1977; *La Cage aux Folles* 1978
Scarwid, Diana *Inside Moves: the Guys from Max's Bar* 1980; *Mommie Dearest* 1981; *Rumble Fish* 1983; *Silkwood* 1983; *Strange Invaders* 1983; *Extremities* 1986; *Psycho III* 1986; *The Ladies Club* 1986; *After the Promise* 1987; *Heat* 1987; *Brenda Starr* 1989; *Night of the Hunter* 1991; *Labor of Love: the Arlette Schweitzer Story* 1993; *The Cure* 1995; *The Neon Bible* 1995; *Truman* 1995; *Gold Diggers: the Secret of Bear Mountain* 1995; *Critical Choices* 1996; *Before He Wakes* 1998
Schaake, Katrin *Love Is Colder than Death* 1969; *Whity* 1970; *The Bitter Tears of Petra von Kant* 1972
Schaal, Richard *Steelyard Blues* 1973; *Glitz* 1988
Schaal, Wendy *When the Time Comes* 1987; *Out There* 1995
Schade, Doris *The German Sisters* 1981; *Veronika Voss* 1982
Schaech, Johnathon *Sparrow* 1993; *The Doom Generation* 1995; *Poison Ivy II: Lily* 1995; *Invasion of Privacy* 1996; *That Thing You Do!* 1996; *Welcome to Woop Woop* 1997; *Hush* 1998; *Houdini* 1998; *Finding Graceland* 1999
Schaefer, Joshua aka **Schaefer, Josh** *Johns* 1995; *Captain Nuke and the Bomber Boys* 1995; *Eight Days a Week* 1996
Schaeffer, Eric *If Lucy Fell* 1996; *Fall* 1997
Schafer, Natalie *Keep Your Powder Dry* 1945; *Molly and Me* 1945; *Secret beyond the Door* 1948; *Caught* 1949; *Callaway Went Thataway* 1951; *The Girl Next Door* 1953; *Female on the Beach* 1955; *Anastasia* 1956; *Forever, Darling* 1956; *I'm Dangerous Tonight* 1990
Schallert, William *The Man from Planet X* 1951; *The Incredible Shrinking Man* 1957; *Lonely Are the Brave* 1962; *In the Heat of the Night* 1967; *Speedway* 1968; *Colossus: the Forbin Project* 1969; *The Computer Wore Tennis Shoes* 1970; *Mrs Lambert Remembers Love* 1991
Schanz, Heidi *Body Language* 1995; *Mixing Nia* 1998; *Universal Soldier – the Return* 1999
Schanzer, Karl *Tonight for Sure* 1961; *Dementia 13* 1963
Schedeen, Anne *Second Thoughts* 1982; *Cast the First Stone* 1989
Scheider, Roy aka **Scheider, Roy R** *The Curse of the Living Corpse* 1964; *Puzzle of a Downfall Child* 1970; *The French Connection* 1971; *Klute* 1971; *The Seven-Ups* 1973; *Jaws* 1975; *Sheila Levine Is Dead and Living in New York* 1975; *Marathon Man* 1976; *Sorcerer* 1977; *Jaws 2* 1978; *All That Jazz* 1979; *Last Embrace* 1979; *Still of the Night* 1982; *Blue Thunder* 1983; *Tiger Town* 1983; *2010* 1984; *52 Pick-Up* 1986; *The Men's Club* 1986; *Cohen and Tate* 1988; *Listen to Me* 1989; *Night Game* 1989; *The Fourth War* 1990; *The Russia House* 1990; *Somebody Has to Shoot the Picture* 1990; *Naked Lunch* 1991; *Romeo Is Bleeding* 1992; *The Myth of Fingerprints* 1996; *Plato's Run* 1996; *Executive Target* 1997; *Money Plays* 1997; *The Peacekeeper* 1997; *The Rainmaker* 1997; *The White Raven* 1998; *RKO 281* 1999
Scheine, Raynor *Ace Ventura: Pet Detective* 1993; *The Real McCoy* 1993
Schell, Catherine aka **von Schell, Catherina** *Moon Zero Two* 1969; *Madame Sin* 1972; *Callan* 1974; *The Return of the Pink Panther* 1974; *Gulliver's Travels* 1977
Schell, Maria *The Magic Box* 1951; *The Heart of the Matter* 1953; *The Last Bridge* 1954; *The Rats* 1955; *Napoléon* 1955; *Gervaise* 1956; *White Nights* 1957; *The Brothers Karamazov* 1958; *The Hanging Tree* 1959; *Cimarron* 1960; *The Mark* 1961; *The Odessa File* 1974; *Just a Gigolo* 1978; *Samson and Delilah* 1984; *Nineteen Nineteen* 1985
Schell, Maximilian *The Young Lions* 1958; *Judgment at*

Nuremberg 1961; *The Condemned of Altona* 1962; *Five Finger Exercise* 1962; *Topkapi* 1964; *Return from the Ashes* 1965; *The Deadly Affair* 1966; *Counterpoint* 1967; *Krakatoa, East of Java* 1969; *First Love* 1970; *Pope Joan* 1972; *The Odessa File* 1974; *The Pedestrian* 1974; *The Man in the Glass Booth* 1975; *St Ives* 1976; *Cross of Iron* 1977; *Julia* 1977; *A Bridge Too Far* 1977; *Avalanche Express* 1979; *The Black Hole* 1979; *Players* 1979; *The Diary of Anne Frank* 1980; *The Chosen* 1981; *Marlene* 1984; *The Assisi Underground* 1985; *The Rose Garden* 1989; *Labyrinth* 1991; *Miss Rose White* 1992; *Stalin* 1992; *A Far Off Place* 1993; *Little Odessa* 1994; *The Eighteenth Angel* 1997; *Left Luggage* 1997; *Telling Lies in America* 1997; *Deep Impact* 1998; *John Carpenter's Vampires* 1998

Schellenberg, August *Kings and Desperate Men* 1981; *Running Brave* 1983; *Confidential* 1986; *Black Robe* 1991; *Free Willy* 1993; *Geronimo* 1993; *Getting Gotti* 1994; *Iron Will* 1994; *Free Willy 2: the Adventure Home* 1995; *Tecumseh: the Last Warrior* 1995; *The West Side Waltz* 1995; *What Love Sees* 1996; *Free Willy 3: the Rescue* 1997

Schellhardt, Mary Kate *What's Eating Gilbert Grape* 1993; *Apollo 13* 1995; *Free Willy 2: the Adventure Home* 1995

Scherrer, Paul *Children of the Corn II: the Final Sacrifice* 1993; *Fall into Darkness* 1996

Scheydt, Karl *The American Soldier* 1970; *Fear Eats the Soul* 1973

Schiaffino, Rosanna *Two Weeks in Another Town* 1962; *RoGoPaG* 1962; *The Long Ships* 1963; *The Victors* 1963; *Drop Dead Darling* 1966; *The Rover* 1967; *The Heroes* 1972

Schiavelli, Vincent *Taking Off* 1971; *Waiting for the Light* 1989; *The Courtyard* 1995; *Escape to Witch Mountain* 1995; *American Yakuza 2: Back to Back* 1996; *The People vs Larry Flynt* 1996

Schiff, Richard *The Arrival* 1996; *Doctor Dolittle* 1998; *Living Out Loud* 1998; *The Pentagon Wars* 1998

Schiffer, Claudia *The Blackout* 1997; *Black and White* 1999

Schildkraut, Joseph *Orphans of the Storm* 1921; *The Road to Yesterday* 1925; *The King of Kings* 1927; *Cleopatra* 1934; *Viva Villa!* 1934; *The Crusades* 1935; *The Garden of Allah* 1936; *Lancer Spy* 1937; *The Life of Emile Zola* 1937; *Slave Ship* 1937; *Marie Antoinette* 1938; *Suez* 1938; *Idiot's Delight* 1939; *Lady of the Tropics* 1939; *The Man in the Iron Mask* 1939; *Mr Moto Takes a Vacation* 1939; *Pack Up Your Troubles* 1939; *The Three Musketeers* 1939; *The Shop around the Corner* 1940; *Phantom Raiders* 1940; *The Cheaters* 1945; *Flame of the Barbary Coast* 1945; *Monsieur Beaucaire* 1946; *Northwest Outpost* 1947; *The Diary of Anne Frank* 1959

Schiller, Fanny *The Treasure of Pancho Villa* 1955; *Battle Shock* 1956

Schilling, Gus *Citizen Kane* 1941; *Hers to Hold* 1943; *The Lady from Shanghai* 1948; *Bride for Sale* 1949; *Our Very Own* 1950

Schilling, William G *Ruthless People* 1986; *White of the Eye*

1986; *The Great American Sex Scandal* 1990

Schlatter, Charlie *Bright Lights, Big City* 1988; *18 Again!* 1988; *Heartbreak Hotel* 1988; *The Delinquents* 1989; *Stormy Weathers* 1992

Schmid, Helmut *A Prize of Arms* 1961; *The Salzburg Connection* 1972

Schmidtmer, Christiane *Boeing Boeing* 1965; *The Big Doll House* 1971; *The Giant Spider Invasion* 1975

Schnabel, Stefan *The Iron Curtain* 1948; *Diplomatic Courier* 1952; *Houdini* 1953; *The 27th Day* 1957; *Rampage* 1963; *Mr Inside/ Mr Outside* 1973; *Dracula's Widow* 1988

Schnarre, Monika *Waxwork II: Lost in Time* 1992; *Killer* 1994; *Sanctuary* 1998

Schneider, Dan *Hot Resort* 1985; *Happy Together* 1989; *Listen to Me* 1989; *Good Burger* 1997

Schneider, Gary *The Toxic Avenger* 1985; *Class of Nuke 'Em High* 1986

Schneider, John *Eddie Macon's Run* 1983; *The Curse* 1987; *Outback Bound* 1988; *Grand Slam* 1990; *The Night of the Twisters* 1996; *Dukes of Hazzard Reunion* 1997; *Snow Day* 2000

Schneider, Maria *Last Tango in Paris* 1972; *The Passenger* 1975; *A Song for Europe* 1985; *Les Nuits Fauves* 1992; *Jane Eyre* 1996; *Something to Believe In* 1997

Schneider, Michael *Beauty and the Beast* 1987; *Double Edge* 1992

Schneider, Rob *The Beverly Hillbillies* 1993; *Surf Ninjas* 1993; *Judge Dredd* 1995; *The Adventures of Pinocchio* 1996; *Down Periscope* 1996; *Knock Off* 1998; *Susan's Plan* 1998; *Big Daddy* 1999; *Deuce Bigalow: Male Gigolo* 1999

Schneider, Romy *Boccaccio '70* 1961; *Fire and Ice* 1962; *The Trial* 1962; *The Cardinal* 1963; *The Victors* 1963; *Good Neighbor Sam* 1964; *What's New, Pussycat?* 1965; *Triple Cross* 1966; *10:30 PM Summer* 1966; *Otley* 1968; *The Swimming Pool* 1968; *Bloomfield* 1969; *The Things of Life* 1969; *The Assassination of Trotsky* 1972; *César and Rosalie* 1972; *The Last Train* 1972; *Ludwig* 1973; *Loving in the Rain* 1974; *Mado* 1976; *Dirty Hands* 1976; *Une Histoire Simple* 1978; *Bloodline* 1979; *Deathwatch* 1980; *Garde à Vue* 1981

Schober, Andrea *The Merchant of Four Seasons* 1971; *Chinese Roulette* 1976

Schoeffling, Michael *Sixteen Candles* 1984; *Sylvester* 1985; *Vision Quest* 1985; *Belizaire the Cajun* 1985; *Let's Get Harry* 1986; *Mermaids* 1990; *Wild Hearts Can't Be Broken* 1991

Schoelen, Jill *Chiller* 1985; *That Was Then... This Is Now* 1985; *Babes in Toyland* 1986; *Shattered Spirits* 1986; *The Stepfather* 1986; *The Phantom of the Opera* 1989; *Cutting Class* 1989; *Curse II: The Bite* 1989; *Popcorn* 1991; *When a Stranger Calls Back* 1993; *There Goes My Baby* 1994

Schofield, Annabel *Dragonard* 1987; *Solar Crisis* 1990; *Midnight Blue* 1996; *Exit in Red* 1996; *Body Armor* 1996

Schofield, David *An American Werewolf in London* 1981; *Tree of Hands* 1988; *Gladiator* 2000

Schollin, Christina *Dear John* 1964; *Song of Norway* 1970; *Fanny and Alexander* 1982

Scholz, Eva-Ingeborg *The Devil's General* 1955; *The American Soldier* 1970

Schorm, Evald *The Party and the Guests* 1966; *The Joke* 1968

Schorpion, Frank *False Pretense* 1997; *Random Encounter* 1998

Schott, Bob *Gymkata* 1985; *Head of the Family* 1996

Schram, Bitty *A League of Their Own* 1992; *The Pallbearer* 1996; *Caught* 1996

Schrecker, Frederick *Counterspy* 1953; *The Master Plan* 1954

Schreiber, Avery *Swashbuckler* 1976; *Galaxina* 1980; *Caveman* 1981; *Saturday the 14th Strikes Back* 1988

Schreiber, Liev *Party Girl* 1994; *Denise Calls Up* 1995; *Mixed Nuts* 1995; *Scream* 1996; *Walking and Talking* 1996; *Scream 2* 1997; *The Daytrippers* 1998; *Sphere* 1998; *Twilight* 1998; *Phantoms* 1998; *Jakob the Liar* 1999; *Scream 3* 1999; *The Hurricane* 1999; *RKO 281* 1999; *A Walk on the Moon* 1999

Schrier, Paul *Mighty Morphin Power Rangers: the Movie* 1995; *Power Rangers 2* 1997

Schroder, Ernst *The Counterfeit Traitor* 1962; *Heidi* 1965

Schroder, Rick aka **Schroder, Ricky** *The Champ* 1979; *The Last Flight of Noah's Ark* 1980; *The Earthling* 1980; *Little Lord Fauntleroy* 1980; *Something So Right* 1982; *Too Young the Hero* 1988; *Out on the Edge* 1989; *Terror on Highway 91* 1989; *A Son's Promise* 1990; *The Stranger Within* 1990; *Across the Tracks* 1990; *Blood River* 1991; *My Son Johnny* 1991; *Miles from Nowhere* 1992; *Call of the Wild* 1993; *There Goes My Baby* 1994; *To My Daughter with Love* 1994; *Heart Full of Rain* 1997; *Ebenezer* 1998

Schroeder, Barbet *Les Carabiniers* 1963; *Paris Vu Par...* 1965; *Celine and Julie Go Boating* 1974

Schub, Steven *Little Noises* 1992; *Caught* 1996; *The Thirteenth Floor* 1999

Schubert, Karin *Delusions of Grandeur* 1971; *Bluebeard* 1972

Schuck, John *Brewster McCloud* 1970; *McCabe and Mrs Miller* 1971; *Thieves like Us* 1974; *Butch and Sundance: the Early Days* 1979; *Outrageous Fortune* 1987; *Second Sight* 1989; *Four Eyes and Six-Guns* 1992; *Holy Matrimony* 1994

Schull, Rebecca *My Life* 1993; *Mortal Fear* 1994

Schultz, Albert *Web of Deceit* 1994; *Ebenezer* 1998

Schultz, Dwight *Alone in the Dark* 1982; *Shadow Makers* 1989; *A Killer among Us* 1990; *The Long Walk Home* 1990; *Woman with a Past* 1991; *Child of Rage* 1992; *The Temp* 1993; *Victim of Love: the Shannon Mohr Story* 1993; *Star Trek: First Contact* 1996

Schulze, Paul *Laws of Gravity* 1992; *Hand Gun* 1994

Schumann, Erik *The Two-Headed Spy* 1958; *Lili Marleen* 1980; *Veronika Voss* 1982

Schunzel, Reinhold *Notorious* 1946; *Golden Earrings* 1947; *Berlin Express* 1948

Schuster, Tom aka **Schuster, Thomas** *Psycho IV: the Beginning* 1990; *Somebody Has to Shoot the Picture* 1990

Schwartz, Scott *The Toy* 1982; *A Christmas Story* 1983; *A Time to Live* 1985; *Fear* 1988

Schwarzenegger, Arnold aka **Strong, Arnold** *Hercules in New York* 1969; *Stay Hungry* 1976; *Cactus Jack* 1979; *Scavenger Hunt* 1979; *The Jayne Mansfield Story* 1980; *Conan the Barbarian* 1982; *Conan the Destroyer* 1984; *The Terminator* 1984; *Commando* 1985; *Red Sonja* 1985; *Raw Deal* 1986; *Predator* 1987; *The Running Man* 1987; *Red Heat* 1988; *Twins* 1988; *Kindergarten Cop* 1990; *Total Recall* 1990; *Terminator 2: Judgment Day* 1991; *Last Action Hero* 1993; *Junior* 1994; *True Lies* 1994; *Eraser* 1996; *Jingle All the Way* 1996; *Batman and Robin* 1997; *End of Days* 1999

Schweig, Eric *The Last of the Mohicans* 1992; *The Broken Chain* 1993; *The Last Great Warrior* 1994; *Pontiac Moon* 1994; *Follow the River* 1995; *Tom and Huck* 1995

Schweiger, Heinrich *Echo Park* 1985; *Operation Madonna* 1987

Schweiger, Til *The Most Desired Man* 1994; *A Girl Called Rosemarie* 1996; *Knockin' on Heaven's Door* 1997; *The Replacement Killers* 1998; *Judas Kiss* 1998

Schwiers, Ellen *Arms and the Man* 1958; *The Brain* 1962

Schwimmer, David *Crossing the Bridge* 1992; *The Pallbearer* 1996; *Apt Pupil* 1997; *Breast Men* 1997; *Kissing a Fool* 1998; *Six Days Seven Nights* 1998; *Since You've Been Gone* 1998

Schwimmer, Rusty *Jason Goes to Hell: the Final Friday* 1993; *A Little Princess* 1995; *Los Locos* 1997

Schygulla, Hanna *Love Is Colder than Death* 1969; *Gods of the Plague* 1969; *Beware of a Holy Whore* 1970; *Why Does Herr R Run Amok?* 1970; *Whity* 1970; *The Merchant of Four Seasons* 1971; *The Bitter Tears of Petra von Kant* 1972; *Effi Briest* 1974; *The Marriage of Maria Braun* 1978; *The Third Generation* 1979; *Berlin Alexanderplatz* 1980; *Lili Marleen* 1980; *Circle of Deceit* 1981; *Passion* 1982; *La Nuit de Varennes* 1983; *The Delta Force* 1986; *Barnum* 1986; *Forever Lulu* 1987; *Dead Again* 1991; *Golem, the Spirit of Exile* 1992

Sciorra, Annabella *True Love* 1989; *Cadillac Man* 1990; *Reversal of Fortune* 1990; *The Hard Way* 1991; *Jungle Fever* 1991; *Prison Stories: Women on the Inside* 1991; *The Hand That Rocks the Cradle* 1992; *Mr Wonderful* 1992; *Romeo Is Bleeding* 1992; *Whispers in the Dark* 1992; *The Night We Never Met* 1993; *The Addiction* 1994; *The Cure* 1995; *The Innocent Sleep* 1995; *The Funeral* 1996; *Underworld* 1996; *Cop Land* 1997; *Mr Jealousy* 1997; *New Rose Hotel* 1998; *What Dreams May Come* 1998

Scob, Edith *Eyes without a Face* 1959; *Thérèse Desqueyroux* 1962; *Judex* 1963; *The Milky Way* 1968

Scofield, Paul *That Lady* 1955; *Carve Her Name with Pride* 1958; *The Train* 1964; *A Man for All Seasons* 1966; *Tell Me Lies* 1967; *King Lear* 1971; *Bartleby* 1971; *Scorpio* 1973; *A Delicate Balance* 1973; *Anna Karenina* 1985; *Nineteen Nineteen* 1985; *Mr Corbett's Ghost* 1986; *The*

Attic: the Hiding of Anne Frank 1988; *Henry V* 1989; *When the Whales Came* 1989; *Hamlet* 1990; *Utz* 1992; *London* 1994; *Quiz Show* 1994; *The Crucible* 1996; *The Little Riders* 1996; *Robinson in Space* 1997

Scoggins, Tracy *The Great American Sex Scandal* 1990; *The Gumshoe Kid* 1990; *Time Bomb* 1991; *Dead On* 1993; *Jake Lassiter: Justice on the Bayou* 1995; *Dallas: War of the Ewings* 1998

Scolari, Peter *Fire! Trapped on the 37th Floor* 1991; *Ticks* 1993

Scorsese, Martin *Cannonball* 1976; *Taxi Driver* 1976; *The King of Comedy* 1983; *Akira Kurosawa's Dreams* 1990; *The Grifters* 1990; *Guilty by Suspicion* 1990; *Search and Destroy* 1995; *Bringing out the Dead* 1999

Scorsese, Nicolette *Boxing Helena* 1993; *Girls in Prison* 1994; *Ultimate Lie* 1996

Scott, Alex *The Sicilians* 1964; *Darling* 1965; *Fahrenheit 451* 1966; *The Abominable Dr Phibes* 1971; *The Asphyx* 1972; *Sky Pirates* 1986; *Romper Stomper* 1992

Scott, Andrew *Korea* 1995; *Drinking Crude* 1997; *Nora* 1999

Scott, Avis *Waterfront* 1950; *To Have and to Hold* 1951

Scott, Brenda *Johnny Tiger* 1966; *Journey to Shiloh* 1968

Scott, Campbell *From Hollywood to Deadwood* 1989; *Longtime Companion* 1990; *The Sheltering Sky* 1990; *Dead Again* 1991; *Dying Young* 1991; *Singles* 1992; *The Innocent* 1993; *Mrs Parker and the Vicious Circle* 1994; *Big Night* 1996; *The Spanish Prisoner* 1997; *The Daytrippers* 1998; *Hi-Life* 1998; *The Impostors* 1998; *The Tale of Sweeney Todd* 1998; *The Love Letter* 1998; *Let It Be Me* 1998

Scott, Donovan *Zorro, the Gay Blade* 1981; *Savannah Smiles* 1982; *Police Academy* 1984; *Sheena, Queen of the Jungle* 1984; *The Best of Times* 1986; *Splash, Too* 1988

Scott, Douglas *And So They Were Married* 1936; *The Last Gangster* 1937; *Intermezzo* 1939

Scott, Dougray *Another Nine ½ Weeks* 1997; *Regeneration* 1997; *Twin Town* 1997; *Ever After* 1998; *Gregory's Two Girls* 1999; *This Year's Love* 1999; *Mission: Impossible 2* 1999

Scott, Eric *A Day for Thanks on Waltons Mountain* 1982; *Mother's Day on Waltons Mountain* 1982; *A Walton Easter* 1997

Scott, Fred *In Old Montana* 1939; *Knight of the Plains* 1939

Scott, George C *Anatomy of a Murder* 1959; *The Hanging Tree* 1959; *The Hustler* 1961; *Dr Strangelove, or How I Learned to Stop Worrying and Love the Bomb* 1963; *The List of Adrian Messenger* 1963; *The Yellow Rolls-Royce* 1964; *The Bible...in the Beginning* 1966; *Not with My Wife, You Don't!* 1966; *One Born Every Minute* 1967; *Petulia* 1968; *Jane Eyre* 1970; *Patton: Lust for Glory* 1970; *The Hospital* 1971; *The Last Run* 1971; *They Might Be Giants* 1971; *Precinct 45: Los Angeles Police* 1972; *Rage* 1972; *The Day of the Dolphin* 1973; *Oklahoma Crude* 1973; *Bank Shot* 1974; *The Savage Is Loose* 1974; *Fear on Trial* 1975; *The Hindenburg* 1975; *Beauty and the Beast* 1976; *Islands in the Stream* 1977; *The Prince and the*

Pauper 1977; Movie Movie 1978; Hardcore 1979; The Changeling 1980; The Formula 1980; Taps 1981; Oliver Twist 1982; A Christmas Carol 1984; Firestarter 1984; Choices 1986; Last Days of Patton 1986; The Murders in the Rue Morgue 1986; Pals 1986; The Ryan White Story 1989; Descending Angel 1990; The Exorcist III 1990; The Rescuers Down Under 1990; Finding the Way Home 1991; Malice 1993; Curacao 1993; Angus 1995; Tyson 1995; Family Rescue 1997; Twelve Angry Men 1997; Gloria 1998; Inherit the Wind 1999

Scott, Gordon Tarzan's Hidden Jungle 1955; Tarzan and the Lost Safari 1956; Tarzan's Fight for Life 1958; Tarzan and the Trappers 1958; Tarzan's Greatest Adventure 1959; Tarzan the Magnificent 1960; Duel of the Titans 1961; Hero of Babylon 1963

Scott, Jacqueline Macabre 1958; Duel 1971; Charley Varrick 1973; Empire of the Ants 1977

Scott, Janette No Place for Jennifer 1949; No Highway 1951; Background 1953; As Long as They're Happy 1955; The Good Companions 1956; Happy Is the Bride 1958; The Devil's Disciple 1959; School for Scoundrels 1960; Double Bunk 1961; Two and Two Make Six 1961; The Day of the Triffids 1962; The Siege of the Saxons 1963; Paranoiac 1963; The Beauty Jungle 1964; Crack in the World 1965

Scott, Kathryn Leigh House of Dark Shadows 1970; Witches' Brew 1979

Scott, Keith Dot and the Koala 1985; Dot and the Whale 1985; Dot and the Smugglers 1987

Scott, Ken Stopover Tokyo 1957; Beloved Infidel 1959; Woman Obsessed 1959; Five Gates to Hell 1959; Desire in the Dust 1960; The Fiercest Heart 1961; The Second Time Around 1961

Scott, Kimberly The Abyss 1989; Downtown 1990; Flatliners 1990; Caught in the Act 1993

Scott, Larry B A Hero Ain't Nothin' but a Sandwich 1978; Revenge of the Nerds 1984; My Man Adam 1985; That Was Then... This Is Now 1985; SpaceCamp 1986; The Liberators 1987; Fear of a Black Hat 1992

Scott, Lizabeth The Strange Love of Martha Ivers 1946; Dead Reckoning 1947; Desert Fury 1947; I Walk Alone 1947; Pitfall 1948; Easy Living 1949; The Company She Keeps 1950; Dark City 1950; The Racket 1951; Red Mountain 1951; Stolen Face 1952; Scared Stiff 1953; Silver Lode 1954; Bad for Each Other 1954; Loving You 1957; Pulp 1972

Scott, Margaretta Things to Come 1936; The Return of the Scarlet Pimpernel 1937; The Girl in the News 1940; Fanny by Gaslight 1944; The Man from Morocco 1944; The Scamp 1957; Crescendo 1970

Scott, Martha Our Town 1940; The Howards of Virginia 1940; Cheers for Miss Bishop 1941; One Foot in Heaven 1941; War of the Wildcats 1943; The Desperate Hours 1955; Sayonara 1957; Ben-Hur 1959; Thursday's Game 1971; Charlotte's Web 1973; The Turning Point 1977; Adam 1983; Adam: His Song Continues 1986; Doin' Time on Planet Earth 1988

Scott, Pippa Petulia 1968; Cold Turkey 1969

Scott, Randolph Island of Lost Souls 1932; Murders in the Zoo 1933; Supernatural 1933; Roberta 1935; She 1935; So Red the Rose 1935; Follow the Fleet 1936; Go West, Young Man 1936; The Last of the Mohicans 1936; High, Wide and Handsome 1937; Rebecca of Sunnybrook Farm 1938; The Texans 1938; Frontier Marshal 1939; Jesse James 1939; Susannah of the Mounties 1939; My Favorite Wife 1940; Virginia City 1940; When the Daltons Rode 1940; Western Union 1941; Paris Calling 1941; Belle Starr 1941; The Spoilers 1942; To the Shores of Tripoli 1942; Pittsburgh 1942; Bombardier 1943; Corvette K-225 1943; The Desperadoes 1943; Gung Ho! 1943; Belle of the Yukon 1944; Follow the Boys 1944; Abilene Town 1945; Captain Kidd 1945; China Sky 1945; Badman's Territory 1946; Trail Street 1947; Return of the Bad Men 1948; Canadian Pacific 1949; The Doolins of Oklahoma 1949; Fighting Man of the Plains 1949; The Walking Hills 1949; The Cariboo Trail 1950; Colt .45 1950; Fort Worth 1951; Man in the Saddle 1951; Santa Fe 1951; Sugarfoot 1951; Carson City 1952; Thunder over the Plains 1953; The Stranger Wore a Gun 1953; The Bounty Hunter 1954; Riding Shotgun 1954; A Lawless Street 1955; Tall Man Riding 1955; Rage at Dawn 1955; Seventh Cavalry 1956; Seven Men from Now 1956; Decision at Sundown 1957; Shoot-Out at Medicine Bend 1957; The Tall T 1957; Buchanan Rides Alone 1958; Ride Lonesome 1959; Westbound 1959; Comanche Station 1960; Ride the High Country 1962

Scott, Seann William American Pie 1999; Final Destination 2000; Road Trip 2000

Scott, Terry The Night We Got the Bird 1960; What a Whopper! 1961; Carry On Up the Khyber 1968; Carry On Camping 1969; Carry On Loving 1970; Carry On Up the Jungle 1970; Carry On Henry 1971; Bless This House 1972; Carry On Matron 1972

Scott-Taylor, Jonathan The Copter Kids 1976; Damien – Omen II 1978

Scott Thomas, Kristin Under the Cherry Moon 1986; A Handful of Dust 1987; The Tenth Man 1988; Force Majeure 1989; Framed 1990; Spymaker: the Secret Life of Ian Fleming 1990; The Bachelor 1990; Autobus 1991; Bitter Moon 1992; Four Weddings and a Funeral 1994; Angels and Insects 1995; The Confessional 1995; Richard III 1995; The Pompatus of Love 1995; The English Patient 1996; Microcosmos 1996; Mission: Impossible 1996; The Revengers' Comedies 1997; The Horse Whisperer 1998; Up at the Villa 1998; Random Hearts 1999

Scott, Tom Everett That Thing You Do! 1996; An American Werewolf in Paris 1997; Dead Man on Campus 1998; One True Thing 1998; The Love Letter 1999; Boiler Room 2000

Scott, William Lee Before Women Had Wings 1997; The Opposite of Sex 1998; October Sky 1999

Scott, Zachary The Mask of Dimitrios 1944; Mildred Pierce 1945; The Southerner 1945; Cass Timberlane 1947; The Unfaithful 1947; Ruthless 1948; Flamingo Road 1949; South of St Louis 1949; Born to Be Bad 1950; Colt .45 1950; Guilty Bystander 1950; Pretty Baby 1950; Let's Make It Legal 1951; Lightning Strikes Twice 1951; The Secret of Convict Lake 1951; Wings of Danger 1952; Appointment in Honduras 1953; Shotgun 1955; Bandido 1956; The Young One 1960; It'$ Only Money 1962

Scotti, Vito Master of the World 1961; Cactus Flower 1969; The Aristocats 1970; When the Legends Die 1972; I Wonder Who's Killing Her Now? 1975

Scoular, Angela Here We Go round the Mulberry Bush 1967; Doctor in Trouble 1970

Scourby, Alexander Affair in Trinidad 1952; The Big Heat 1953; The Glory Brigade 1953; The Redhead from Wyoming 1953; The Silver Chalice 1954; Me and the Colonel 1958; The Shaggy Dog 1959; Seven Thieves 1960; The Devil at Four o'Clock 1961; Jesus 1979

Scribner, Ronnie The Long Days of Summer 1980; Split Image 1982

Scrimm, Angus Phantasm 1978; Phantasm II 1988; Transylvania Twist 1989; Mindwarp 1992; Deadfall 1993; Phantasm III – Lord Of The Dead 1994; Vampirella 1996; Wishmaster 1997

Seacat, Sandra Country 1984; Promised Land 1988; The Baby Dance 1998

Seaforth, Susan Gunfight at Comanche Creek 1964; Billie 1965

Seagal, Steven Nico 1988; Hard to Kill 1989; Marked for Death 1990; Out for Justice 1991; Under Siege 1992; On Deadly Ground 1994; Under Siege 2 1995; Executive Decision 1996; The Glimmer Man 1996; Fire Down Below 1997; The Patriot 1998

Seagrove, Jenny Local Hero 1983; Savage Islands 1983; Appointment with Death 1988; A Chorus of Disapproval 1988; The Guardian 1990; Don't Go Breaking My Heart 1999

Seal, Elizabeth Town on Trial 1956; Cone of Silence 1960

Seale, Douglas Ernest Saves Christmas 1988; Almost an Angel 1990; Aladdin 1992

Seales, Franklyn The Onion Field 1979; Southern Comfort 1981

Searcy, Nick Nell 1994; About Sarah 1998

Searle, Jackie aka **Searl, Jackie** Huckleberry Finn 1931; Skippy 1931; Topaze 1933; Murder on the Blackboard 1934; No Greater Glory 1934; The Paleface 1948

Sears, Ann Cat and Mouse 1958; The Brain 1962

Sears, Djanet Milk and Honey 1988; April One 1993

Sears, Heather Dry Rot 1956; The Story of Esther Costello 1957; Room at the Top 1958; The Siege of Pinchgut 1959; Sons and Lovers 1960; The Phantom of the Opera 1962; Saturday Night Out 1963; The Black Torment 1964

Seay, James The Face behind the Mask 1941; Miracle on 34th Street 1947; Close to My Heart 1951; Return to Treasure Island 1954; The Amazing Colossal Man 1957; Beginning of the End 1957

Sebanek, Josef A Blonde in Love 1965; The Fireman's Ball 1967

Sebastian, Dorothy Our Dancing Daughters 1928; The Single Standard 1929; Spite Marriage 1929; The Arizona Kid 1939; Rough Riders' Roundup 1939

Sebastian, Tracy On the Air Live with Captain Midnight 1979; Running Cool 1993

Seberg, Jean Saint Joan 1957; Bonjour Tristesse 1958; A Bout de Souffle 1959; The Mouse That Roared 1959; Let No Man Write My Epitaph 1960; In the French Style 1963; Lilith 1964; A Fine Madness 1966; The Looters 1966; Moment to Moment 1966; Paint Your Wagon 1969; Pendulum 1969; Airport 1970; Macho Callahan 1970; Kill! 1972

Secombe, Harry Down among the Z-Men 1952; Forces' Sweetheart 1953; Svengali 1954; Jet Storm 1959; Oliver! 1968; The Bed Sitting Room 1969; Doctor in Trouble 1970; Song of Norway 1970; Sunstruck 1972

Secor, Kyle Inherit the Wind 1988; Shootdown 1988; The Outside Woman 1989; Heart of Dixie 1989; Delusion 1991; Late for Dinner 1991; Sleeping with the Enemy 1991; In the Line of Duty: Siege at Marion 1992; Untamed Heart 1993; Drop Zone 1994; Midwest Obsession 1995

Seda, Jon Gladiator 1992; I Like It like That 1994; Twelve Monkeys 1995; Dear God 1996; Mistrial 1996; Sunchaser 1996; Selena 1997

Sedan, Rolfe The Iron Mask 1929; The Story of Vernon and Irene Castle 1939

Seddon, Margaret Smilin' Through 1932; The Meanest Man in the World 1943

Sedgwick, Edie Vinyl 1965; The Chelsea Girls 1967

Sedgwick, Kyra Tai-Pan 1986; The Man Who Broke 1,000 Chains 1987; Kansas 1988; Born on the Fourth of July 1989; Mr and Mrs Bridge 1990; Pyrates 1991; Women and Men – 2 1991; Miss Rose White 1992; Singles 1992; Heart and Souls 1993; Something to Talk About 1995; The Low Life 1995; Losing Chase 1996; Phenomenon 1996; Montana 1997; Critical Care 1997

Seely, Tim Please Turn Over 1960; Mutiny on the Bounty 1962

Segado, Alberto I, the Worst of All 1990; We Don't Want to Talk about It 1993

Segal, George Act One 1963; The New Interns 1964; Invitation to a Gunfighter 1964; King Rat 1965; Ship of Fools 1965; The Lost Command 1966; The Quiller Memorandum 1966; Who's Afraid of Virginia Woolf? 1966; The St Valentine's Day Massacre 1967; Bye Bye Braverman 1968; No Way to Treat a Lady 1968; The Bridge at Remagen 1969; The Southern Star 1969; Loving 1970; The Owl and the Pussycat 1970; Where's Poppa? 1970; Born to Win 1971; The Hot Rock 1972; Blume in Love 1973; A Touch of Class 1973; California Split 1974; The Terminal Man 1974; The Black Bird 1975; The Duchess and the Dirtwater Fox 1976; Fun with Dick and Jane 1977; Rollercoaster 1977; Who Is Killing the Great Chefs of Europe? 1978; Lost and Found 1979; The Last Married Couple in America 1980; Carbon Copy 1981; Killing 'em Softly 1982; Trackdown: Finding the Goodbar Killer 1983; The Cold Room 1984; Not My Kid 1985; Stick 1985; All's Fair 1989; Look Who's Talking 1989; For the Boys 1991; Me, Myself and I 1992; Army of One 1993; Look Who's Talking Now! 1993; Following Her Heart 1994; The Babysitter 1995; The November Conspiracy 1995; The Cable Guy 1996; Flirting with Disaster 1996; It's My Party 1996; The Mirror Has Two Faces 1996; Houdini 1998

Segal, Gilles Topkapi 1964; Without Apparent Motive 1972

Segal, Zohra Harem 1985; Masala 1991; Bhaji on the Beach 1993

Segall, Pamela aka **Segall Adlon, Pamela** Willy/Milly 1986; After Midnight 1989; Say Anything 1989; Bed of Roses 1995; ...At First Sight 1995; Some Girls 1998

Segura, Santiago The Day of the Beast 1995; Perdita Durango 1997; Dying of Laughter 1999

Seigner, Emmanuelle Detective 1985; Frantic 1988; Bitter Moon 1992; Nirvana 1996; Place Vendôme 1998; The Ninth Gate 2000

Seigner, Françoise L'Enfant Sauvage 1970; Les Misérables 1982

Seiphemo, Rapulana Jump the Gun 1996; Tarzan and the Lost City 1998

Seitz, John Hard Choices 1984; Call Me 1988; Forced March 1989; Out of the Rain 1991; Blood and Wine 1996

Sekka, Johnny Flame in the Streets 1961; The Wild and the Willing 1962; Woman of Straw 1964; Khartoum 1966; The Last Safari 1967; Bloodsuckers 1970; Incense for the Damned 1970; A Warm December 1973; The Message 1976

Selby, David Night of Dark Shadows 1971; Up the Sandbox 1972; The Super Cops 1973; Rich Kids 1979; Raise the Titanic 1980; Rich and Famous 1981; Dying Young 1991; Grave Secrets: the Legacy of Hilltop Drive 1992; D3: the Mighty Ducks 1996

Selby, Nicholas A Midsummer Night's Dream 1969; Macbeth 1971

Selby, Sarah aka **Selby, Sara** Beyond the Forest 1949; Tower of London 1962

Selby, Tony In Search of Gregory 1970; Adolf Hitler – My Part in His Downfall 1972

Seldes, Marian The Big Fisherman 1959; Crime and Punishment, USA 1959; Fingers 1978; Tom and Huck 1995; Affliction 1997; Digging to China 1998; The Haunting 1999

Sellars, Elizabeth Cloudburst 1951; Night Was Our Friend 1951; The Gentle Gunman 1952; Hunted 1952; The Long Memory 1952; The Barefoot Contessa 1954; Desiree 1954; Forbidden Cargo 1954; Three Cases of Murder 1954; Prince of Players 1955; The Shiralee 1957; Law and Disorder 1958; Never Let Go 1960; The Day They Robbed the Bank of England 1960; The Chalk Garden 1964; The Mummy's Shroud 1966; The Hireling 1973

Sellecca, Connie Hotel 1983; Downpayment on Murder 1987; The Last Fling 1987; Turn Back the Clock 1989; Miracle Landing 1990; A House of Secrets and Lies 1992; Passport to Murder 1993; Dangerous Affair 1995; The Surrogate 1995; While My Pretty One Sleeps 1997; Something Borrowed, Something Blue 1997;

Doomsday Rock 1997; *Dangerous Waters* 1999
Selleck, Tom *Myra Breckinridge* 1970; *The Seven Minutes* 1971; *Daughters of Satan* 1972; *Terminal Island* 1973; *Coma* 1977; *Divorce Wars* 1982; *High Road to China* 1983; *Lassiter* 1984; *Runaway* 1984; *Three Men and a Baby* 1987; *Her Alibi* 1989; *An Innocent Man* 1989; *Quigley Down Under* 1990; *Three Men and a Little Lady* 1990; *Christopher Columbus: the Discovery* 1992; *Folks!* 1992; *Mr Baseball* 1992; *Broken Trust* 1995; *Ruby Jean and Joe* 1996; *In & Out* 1997; *Last Stand at Saber River* 1997; *The Love Letter* 1999
Sellers, Peter *Down among the Z-Men* 1952; *Orders Are Orders* 1954; *The Case of the Mukkinese Battle Horn* 1955; *John and Julie* 1955; *The Ladykillers* 1955; *The Naked Truth* 1957; *The Smallest Show on Earth* 1957; *Carlton-Browne of the FO* 1958; *tom thumb* 1958; *Up the Creek* 1958; *I'm All Right Jack* 1959; *The Mouse That Roared* 1959; *The Running, Jumping and Standing Still Film* 1959; *The Battle of the Sexes* 1960; *The Millionairess* 1960; *Never Let Go* 1960; *Two Way Stretch* 1960; *Lolita* 1961; *Mr Topaze* 1961; *Only Two Can Play* 1962; *The Road to Hong Kong* 1962; *Trial and Error* 1962; *Waltz of the Toreadors* 1962; *The Wrong Arm of the Law* 1962; *Dr Strangelove, or How I Learned to Stop Worrying and Love the Bomb* 1963; *Heavens Above!* 1963; *The Pink Panther* 1964; *A Shot in the Dark* 1964; *The World of Henry Orient* 1964; *What's New, Pussycat?* 1965; *After the Fox* 1966; *The Wrong Box* 1966; *The Bobo* 1967; *Casino Royale* 1967; *Woman Times Seven* 1967; *I Love You, Alice B Toklas* 1968; *The Party* 1968; *The Magic Christian* 1969; *Hoffman* 1970; *Simon, Simon* 1970; *There's a Girl in My Soup* 1970; *Where Does It Hurt?* 1971; *Alice's Adventures in Wonderland* 1972; *The Optimists of Nine Elms* 1973; *Soft Beds, Hard Battles* 1973; *The Blockhouse* 1973; *Ghost in the Noonday Sun* 1973; *The Return of the Pink Panther* 1974; *The Great McGonagall* 1974; *Murder by Death* 1976; *The Pink Panther Strikes Again* 1976; *Revenge of the Pink Panther* 1978; *Being There* 1979; *The Prisoner of Zenda* 1979; *The Fiendish Plot of Dr Fu Manchu* 1980; *Trail of the Pink Panther* 1982; *King Lear – Fear and Loathing* 1987
Sellon, Charles *aka* **Sellon, Charles A** *The Monster* 1925; *The Saturday Night Kid* 1929; *Bright Eyes* 1934; *In Old Kentucky* 1935
Selten, Morton *Moscow Nights* 1935; *In the Soup* 1936; *Fire over England* 1937; *The Divorce of Lady X* 1938; *The Thief of Bagdad* 1940
Selwyn, Ruth *Polly of the Circus* 1932; *Speak Easily* 1932
Selzer, Milton *The Legend of Lylah Clare* 1968; *Miss Rose White* 1992
Semmelrogge, Willy *The Enigma of Kaspar Hauser* 1974; *Woyzeck* 1978
Sen, Aparna *The Guru* 1969; *Bombay Talkie* 1970; *The Middleman* 1975; *Hullabaloo over Georgie and Bonnie's Pictures* 1979
Sen, Gita *And Quiet Rolls the Dawn* 1979; *In Search of Famine* 1980
Senda, Koreya *Gate of Hell* 1953; *The H-Man* 1954
Seneca, Joe *Crossroads* 1986; *A Gathering of Old Men* 1987; *School Daze* 1988; *Tarzan in Manhattan* 1989; *Mississippi Masala* 1991; *The Saint of Fort Washington* 1993; *Freedom Road: the Vernon Johns Story* 1994
Sentier, Jean-Pierre *Angel Dust* 1987; *A Strange Place to Meet* 1988
Serato, Massimo *The Man from Cairo* 1953; *The Loves of Three Queens* 1954; *Cartouche* 1954; *Queen of the Pirates* 1960; *El Cid* 1961; *Pontius Pilate* 1961; *The Secret Mark of D'Artagnan* 1962; *Brennus – Enemy of Rome* 1963; *The Tenth Victim* 1965; *The Gamblers* 1969; *Don't Look Now* 1973
Serbedzija, Rade *Before the Rain* 1994; *Broken English* 1996; *The Saint* 1997; *The Truce* 1997; *Mighty Joe Young* 1998; *Polish Wedding* 1998
Serious, Yahoo *Young Einstein* 1988; *Reckless Kelly* 1993
Serkis, Andy *Career Girls* 1997; *Stella Does Tricks* 1997; *Mojo* 1998; *Among Giants* 1998
Serna, Assumpta *Lola* 1986; *Matador* 1986; *I, the Worst of All* 1990; *Wild Orchid* 1990; *Revolver* 1992; *Nostradamus* 1993; *The Shooter* 1994
Serna, Pepe *Shoot Out* 1971; *Walk Proud* 1979; *Joe Dancer: the Monkey Mission* 1981; *Vice Squad* 1982; *Break of Dawn* 1988; *Bad Jim* 1989; *The Rookie* 1990; *American Me* 1992; *A Million to Juan* 1994
Sernas, Jacques *Golden Salamander* 1949; *Helen of Troy* 1955; *The Sign of the Gladiator* 1958; *Duel of the Titans* 1961; *Duel of Champions* 1961; *Hornet's Nest* 1970
Serra, Raymond *aka* **Serra, Ray** *Alphabet City* 1984; *A Deadly Business* 1986; *Forever Lulu* 1987; *Command in Hell* 1988; *Safe Men* 1998
Serrano, Diego *Mixing Nia* 1998; *The 24 Hour Woman* 1999
Serrano, Julieta *Matador* 1986; *Women on the Verge of a Nervous Breakdown* 1988; *Tie Me Up! Tie Me Down!* 1990
Serrano, Nestor *Brenda Starr* 1989; *Hangin' with the Homeboys* 1991; *Girls in Prison* 1994; *Bad Boys* 1995
Serrault, Michel *Les Diaboliques* 1954; *King of Hearts* 1966; *Get out Your Handkerchiefs* 1977; *La Cage aux Folles* 1978; *Buffet Froid* 1979; *La Cage aux Folles II* 1980; *Garde à Vue* 1981; *La Cage aux Folles III: "Elles" se Marient* 1985; *Docteur Petiot* 1990; *The Old Lady Who Walked in the Sea* 1991; *Le Bonheur Est dans le Pré* 1995; *Nelly & Monsieur Arnaud* 1995; *Beaumarchais l'Insolent* 1996; *Artemisia* 1997; *Rien Ne Va Plus* 1997; *The Children of the Marshland* 1998
Serre, Henri *Jules et Jim* 1961; *Fire and Ice* 1962
Serret, John *The Gold Express* 1955; *Rogue's Yarn* 1956; *Scream of Fear* 1961
Servais, Jean *Rififi* 1955; *La Fièvre Monte à el Pao* 1959; *Thomas the Imposter* 1964; *That Man from Rio* 1964; *The Lost Command* 1966; *They Came to Rob Las Vegas* 1968
Servoss, Mary *Youth Runs Wild* 1944; *Beyond the Forest* 1949
Sesay, Mo *Young Soul Rebels* 1991; *Bhaji on the Beach* 1993
Sesselmann, Sabina *Le Bossu* 1959; *Information Received* 1962
Sessions, John *The Bounty* 1984; *Sweet Revenge* 1990; *Freddie as FRO7* 1992; *Princess Caraboo* 1994; *In the Bleak Midwinter* 1995; *The Adventures of Pinocchio* 1996; *The Scarlet Tunic* 1997
Seth, Roshan *Gandhi* 1982; *Indiana Jones and the Temple of Doom* 1984; *My Beautiful Laundrette* 1985; *Little Dorrit* 1987; *1871* 1989; *Not without My Daughter* 1990; *London Kills Me* 1991; *Mississippi Masala* 1991; *Electric Moon* 1992; *Solitaire for 2* 1994; *Street Fighter* 1994; *The Journey* 1997; *Such a Long Journey* 1998
Seton, Bruce *Love from a Stranger* 1936; *Sweeney Todd, the Demon Barber of Fleet Street* 1936; *The Green Cockatoo* 1937; *The Curse of the Wraydons* 1946; *The Blue Lamp* 1949; *Whisky Galore!* 1949; *Eight O'Clock Walk* 1953; *Delayed Action* 1954; *The Crooked Sky* 1957; *Hidden Homicide* 1958; *Undercover Girl* 1958; *Gorgo* 1960
Severance, Joan *See No Evil, Hear No Evil* 1989; *No Holds Barred* 1989; *Bird on a Wire* 1990; *Another Pair of Aces: Three of a Kind* 1991; *The Runestone* 1991; *Lake Consequence* 1992; *Angel of Desire* 1993; *Dangerous Indiscretion* 1994; *Hard Evidence* 1994; *Black Scorpion* 1995; *Black Scorpion: Ground Zero* 1996; *Frequent Flyer* 1996; *Profile for Murder* 1996; *In Dark Places* 1997; *The Last Seduction 2* 1998; *Life of the Party: the Pamela Harriman Story* 1998
Severn, Christopher *Mrs Miniver* 1942; *The Man from Down Under* 1943
Severn, Raymond *We Are Not Alone* 1939; *The Suspect* 1944
Severn, William *Journey for Margaret* 1942; *Son of Lassie* 1945
Severne, Mary Anne *The Adventures of Barry McKenzie* 1972; *Run, Rebecca, Run* 1981
Sevigny, Chloë *kids* 1995; *Trees Lounge* 1996; *Gummo* 1997; *The Last Days of Disco* 1998; *Palmetto* 1998; *Boys Don't Cry* 1999; *julien donkey-boy* 1999; *A Map of the World* 1999; *American Psycho* 2000; *If These Walls Could Talk 2* 2000
Sewell, George *Sparrows Can't Sing* 1962; *Kaleidoscope* 1966; *The Vengeance of She* 1968; *Diamonds on Wheels* 1973
Sewell, Rufus *Twenty-One* 1991; *Dirty Weekend* 1992; *A Man of No Importance* 1994; *Carrington* 1995; *Cold Comfort Farm* 1995; *Victory* 1995; *Hamlet* 1996; *Martha – Meet Frank, Daniel and Laurence* 1997; *The Woodlanders* 1997; *Dark City* 1998; *The Honest Courtesan* 1998
Seweryn, Andrzej *The Conductor* 1980; *Schindler's List* 1993; *Lucie Aubrac* 1997
Sexton III, Brendan *aka* **Sexton Jr, Brendan** *Welcome to the Dollhouse* 1995; *Hurricane Streets* 1997; *Pecker* 1998; *Desert Blue* 1998; *Boys Don't Cry* 1999
Seyferth, Wilfried *aka* **Seyfert, Wilfried** *Decision before Dawn* 1951; *The Devil Makes Three* 1952
Seyler, Athene *Moscow Nights* 1935; *Southern Roses* 1936; *The Franchise Affair* 1950; *Young Wives' Tale* 1951; *Made in Heaven* 1952; *Treasure Hunt* 1952; *The Beggar's Opera* 1953; *Night of the Demon* 1957; *A Tale of Two Cities* 1957; *How to Murder a Rich Uncle* 1957; *Happy Is the Bride* 1958; *The Inn of the Sixth Happiness* 1958; *Make Mine Mink* 1960; *Two and Two Make Six* 1961; *The Girl on the Boat* 1962; *Satan Never Sleeps* 1962; *I Thank a Fool* 1962; *Nurse on Wheels* 1963
Seymour, Anne *All the King's Men* 1949; *The Gift of Love* 1958; *All the Fine Young Cannibals* 1960; *The Subterraneans* 1960; *Good Neighbor Sam* 1964; *Where Love Has Gone* 1964; *Blindfold* 1966; *Triumphs of a Man Called Horse* 1983; *Trancers* 1985
Seymour, Carolyn *Gumshoe* 1971; *Unman, Wittering and Zigo* 1971; *The Ruling Class* 1972; *Steptoe and Son* 1972; *The Bitch* 1979; *Death Ride to Osaka* 1983; *Reform School Girl* 1994
Seymour, Dan *A Night in Casablanca* 1946; *The Searching Wind* 1946; *Intrigue* 1947; *Johnny Belinda* 1948; *Face to Face* 1952; *Abbott and Costello Meet the Mummy* 1955; *Return of the Fly* 1959
Seymour (2), Jane *Back Door to Heaven* 1939; *Remember the Day* 1941; *Tom, Dick and Harry* 1941
Seymour, Jane *Frankenstein: the True Story* 1973; *Live and Let Die* 1973; *Sinbad and the Eye of the Tiger* 1977; *Battlestar Galactica* 1978; *The Four Feathers* 1978; *Somewhere in Time* 1980; *Oh, Heavenly Dog!* 1980; *The Scarlet Pimpernel* 1982; *The Haunting Passion* 1983; *Lassiter* 1984; *Head Office* 1986; *Jack the Ripper* 1988; *Matters of the Heart* 1990; *Sunstroke* 1992; *Are You Lonesome Tonight* 1992; *Praying Mantis* 1993; *Quest for Justice* 1993; *The Absolute Truth* 1997; *The New Swiss Family Robinson* 1999
Seymour, Ralph *Just before Dawn* 1980; *Meatballs 2* 1984; *Killer Party* 1986
Seyrig, Delphine *Pull My Daisy* 1959; *Last Year at Marienbad* 1961; *Muriel* 1963; *Accident* 1967; *The Milky Way* 1968; *Stolen Kisses* 1968; *Daughters of Darkness* 1970; *The Magic Donkey* 1970; *The Discreet Charm of the Bourgeoisie* 1972; *The Day of the Jackal* 1973; *A Doll's House* 1973; *The Black Windmill* 1974; *Jeanne Dielman, 23 Quai du Commerce, 1080 Bruxelles* 1975; *Golden Eighties* 1986
Shaban, Nabil *Born of Fire* 1987; *Wittgenstein* 1993
Shackelford, Ted *Mother of the Bride* 1993; *Sweet Temptation* 1996
Shadix, Glenn *Heathers* 1989; *Nightlife* 1989; *Bingo* 1991; *Meet the Applegates* 1991; *Demolition Man* 1993; *Tim Burton's The Nightmare before Christmas* 1993; *Dunston Checks In* 1996
Shah, Naseeruddin *Junoon* 1978; *Bezubaan* 1981; *Mirch Masala* 1987; *The Perfect Murder* 1988; *Electric Moon* 1992; *Such a Long Journey* 1998
Shakur, Tupac *Juice* 1992; *Poetic Justice* 1993; *Above the Rim* 1994; *Bullet* 1995; *Gridlock'd* 1996; *Gang Related* 1997
Shalhoub, Tony *Barton Fink* 1991; *IQ* 1995; *Big Night* 1996; *Men in Black* 1997; *A Civil Action* 1998; *Paulie* 1998; *The Siege* 1998; *That Championship Season* 1999; *Galaxy Quest* 1999
Shamata, Chuck *aka* **Shamata, Charles** *Running* 1979; *Stone Cold Dead* 1980; *The Devil and Max Devlin* 1981; *Scanners* 1981; *Between Friends* 1983; *Unfinished Business* 1983; *Mafia Princess* 1986; *A Family of Strangers* 1993
Shandling, Garry *Mother Goose Rock 'n' Rhyme* 1990; *Love Affair* 1994; *Mixed Nuts* 1995; *Hurlyburly* 1998
Shane, Gene *Run, Angel, Run* 1969; *The Velvet Vampire* 1971
Shane, Sara *The King and Four Queens* 1956; *Affair in Havana* 1957; *Tarzan's Greatest Adventure* 1959
Shaner, Michael *Bloodfist* 1989; *The Expert* 1994; *Open Fire* 1995
Shankar, Mamata *And Quiet Rolls the Dawn* 1979; *An Enemy of the People* 1989; *Branches of the Tree* 1990; *The Stranger* 1991
Shanks, Don *aka* **Shanks, Donald L** *The Life and Times of Grizzly Adams* 1974; *Down the Long Hills* 1987; *Halloween 5* 1989; *Spirit of the Eagle* 1991; *Wind Dancer* 1991; *3 Ninjas Knuckle Up* 1995
Shannon, Al *The Drifter* 1988; *Out of the Rain* 1991
Shannon, Frank *Flash Gordon* 1936; *The Texas Rangers* 1936
Shannon, Harry *Once upon a Honeymoon* 1942; *Song of Texas* 1943; *The Yellow Rose of Texas* 1944; *San Quentin* 1946; *The Devil Thumbs a Ride* 1947; *Mr Blandings Builds His Dream House* 1948; *Tulsa* 1949; *Cry of the Hunted* 1953; *Witness to Murder* 1954; *The Tall Men* 1955; *The Marauders* 1955; *Written on the Wind* 1956; *Gypsy* 1962
Shannon, Michael J *aka* **Shannon, Michael** *Future Cop* 1976; *The Ted Kennedy Jr Story* 1986; *Royce* 1994; *Night Watch* 1995
Shannon, Molly *Analyze This* 1999; *Never Been Kissed* 1999; *Superstar* 1999
Shannon, Peggy *This Reckless Age* 1932; *Turn Back the Clock* 1933; *The Case of the Lucky Legs* 1935
Shannon, Richard *Arrowhead* 1953; *Pony Express* 1953; *The Bridges at Toko-Ri* 1954; *Alaska Seas* 1954; *Beau James* 1957
Shaps, Cyril *Passport to Shame* 1958; *The Pursuers* 1961; *Operation Daybreak* 1975; *The Lost Son* 1998; *The Clandestine Marriage* 1999
Sharif, Omar *Lawrence of Arabia* 1962; *Behold a Pale Horse* 1964; *The Fall of the Roman Empire* 1964; *Genghis Khan* 1964; *The Yellow Rolls-Royce* 1964; *Doctor Zhivago* 1965; *The Night of the Generals* 1966; *The Poppy Is Also a Flower* 1966; *More than a Miracle* 1967; *The Appointment* 1968; *Funny Girl* 1968; *Mayerling* 1968; *Che!* 1969; *Mackenna's Gold* 1969; *The Burglars* 1971; *The Horsemen* 1971; *The Last Valley* 1971; *Juggernaut* 1974; *The Tamarind Seed* 1974; *Funny Lady* 1975; *Crime and Passion* 1976; *Ashanti* 1979; *Bloodline* 1979; *The Baltimore Bullet* 1980; *Oh, Heavenly Dog!* 1980; *Green Ice* 1981; *Top Secret!* 1984; *Anastasia: the Mystery of Anna* 1986; *The Rainbow Thief* 1990; *Mrs 'arris Goes to Paris* 1992; *The 13th Warrior* 1999
Sharkey, Billy Ray *Dudes* 1987; *After Midnight* 1989

Shellen, Stephen *A Touch of Scandal* 1984; *The Stepfather* 1986; *Casual Sex?* 1988; *Damned River* 1989; *Victim of Beauty* 1991; *A River Runs through It* 1992; *April One* 1993; *Edge of Deception* 1994; *Model by Day* 1994; *The Wrong Woman* 1996
Shelley, Barbara *Blood of the Vampire* 1958; *Bobbikins* 1959; *Village of the Damned* 1960; *Postman's Knock* 1961; *The Shadow of the Cat* 1961; *The Gorgon* 1964; *The Secret of Blood Island* 1964; *Dracula – Prince of Darkness* 1965; *Rasputin, the Mad Monk* 1965; *Quatermass and the Pit* 1967
Shelley, Carole *The Odd Couple* 1968; *The Whoopee Boys* 1986; *The Super* 1991; *Little Noises* 1992
Shelley, Norman *The Silver Darlings* 1947; *The Great Adventure* 1953; *Gulliver's Travels* 1977
Shelley, Paul *Macbeth* 1971; *It Shouldn't Happen to a Vet* 1979; *Caught in the Act* 1996
Shelly, Adrienne *The Unbelievable Truth* 1989; *Trust* 1990; *Big Girls Don't Cry... They Get Even* 1992; *Hold Me, Thrill Me, Kiss Me* 1992; *Hexed* 1993; *Sleep with Me* 1994; *Roadflower* 1994; *Wrestling with Alligators* 1998
Shelton, Anne *King Arthur Was a Gentleman* 1942; *Bees in Paradise* 1943; *Miss London Ltd* 1943
Shelton, Deborah *Body Double* 1984; *Hunk* 1987; *Blind Vision* 1992; *Nemesis* 1993; *Sins of the Night* 1993; *Plughead Rewired: Circuitry Man II* 1994
Shelton, John *Dr Kildare Goes Home* 1940; *A-Haunting We Will Go* 1942; *The Time of Their Lives* 1946
Shelton, Joy *Bees in Paradise* 1943; *Millions like Us* 1943; *Waterloo Road* 1944; *A Case for PC 49* 1950; *Emergency Call* 1952; *Park Plaza 605* 1953; *Impulse* 1955
Shelton, Marley *aka* **Shelton, Marlee** *In the Line of Duty: Ambush in Waco* 1993; *A Secret between Friends* 1996; *Warriors of Virtue* 1997; *Trojan War* 1997; *The Bachelor* 1999
Shelton, Sloane *Jacknife* 1988; *Orpheus Descending* 1990
Shenar, Paul *The Night that Panicked America* 1975; *The Secret of NIMH* 1982; *Deadly Force* 1983; *Dream Lover* 1986; *Raw Deal* 1986; *The Bedroom Window* 1987; *Best Seller* 1987; *Man on Fire* 1987; *The Big Blue* 1988
Shepard, Hilary *aka* **Shepard Turner, Hilary** *Peacemaker* 1990; *Scanner Cop* 1994; *Power Rangers 2* 1997
Shepard, Jan *King Creole* 1958; *Attack of the Giant Leeches* 1960
Shepard, Jewel *Hollywood Hot Tubs* 1984; *Return of the Living Dead* 1985
Shepard, Sam *Days of Heaven* 1978; *Resurrection* 1980; *Raggedy Man* 1981; *Frances* 1982; *The Right Stuff* 1983; *Country* 1984; *Fool for Love* 1985; *Crimes of the Heart* 1986; *Baby Boom* 1987; *Steel Magnolias* 1989; *Bright Angel* 1990; *Defenseless* 1991; *Voyager* 1991; *Thunderheart* 1992; *The Pelican Brief* 1993; *Safe Passage* 1994; *The Good Old Boys* 1995; *Lily Dale* 1996; *Curtain Call* 1998; *Snow Falling on Cedars* 1999; *Purgatory* 1999
Sheperd, Karen *Mission of Justice* 1992; *Operation Golden Phoenix* 1994
Shepherd, Cybill *The Last Picture Show* 1971; *The Heartbreak Kid* 1972; *Daisy Miller* 1974; *At Long Last Love* 1975; *Special Delivery* 1976; *Taxi Driver* 1976; *Silver Bears* 1978; *The Lady Vanishes* 1979; *Seduced* 1985; *Chances Are* 1989; *Alice* 1990; *Texasville* 1990; *Married to It* 1991; *Memphis* 1992; *Once upon a Crime* 1992; *Stormy Weathers* 1992; *There Was a Little Boy* 1993; *Baby Brokers* 1994; *While Justice Sleeps* 1994; *Cosa Nostra: the Last Word* 1995; *Journey of the Heart* 1997
Shepherd, Elizabeth *The Tomb of Ligeia* 1964; *Hell Boats* 1970
Shepherd, Jack *All Neat in Black Stockings* 1969; *The Virgin Soldiers* 1969; *The Object of Beauty* 1991; *Twenty-One* 1991; *Blue Black Permanent* 1992; *Blue Ice* 1992; *No Escape* 1994; *The Scarlet Tunic* 1997; *Wonderland* 1999
Shepherd, Jean *Fame Is the Spur* 1947; *The Silver Darlings* 1947
Shepherd, John *Confessions of a Married Man* 1983; *Friday the 13th: a New Beginning* 1985; *Thunder Run* 1986
Shepherd, Simon *Fire, Ice and Dynamite* 1990; *Wuthering Heights* 1992
Shepherd, Steve John *G:MT Greenwich Mean Time* 1998; *Virtual Sexuality* 1999
Shepherd, Suzanne *The Jerky Boys* 1995; *Lolita* 1997; *Living Out Loud* 1998
Shepley, Michael *A Shot in the Dark* 1933; *Lord Edgware Dies* 1934; *Lazybones* 1935; *Squibs* 1935; *A Place of One's Own* 1944; *Mine Own Executioner* 1947; *Maytime in Mayfair* 1949; *Home at Seven* 1952; *Happy Ever After* 1954; *Where There's a Will* 1955
Sheppard, Delia *Mirror Images* 1991; *Animal Instincts* 1992; *Secret Games* 1992; *Sins of Desire* 1993
Sheppard, Mark *In the Name of the Father* 1993; *Lover's Knot* 1995
Sheppard, Morgan *aka* **Sheppard, W Morgan** *Hawk the Slayer* 1980; *The Keep* 1983; *Elvira, Mistress of the Dark* 1988; *Seduction: Three Tales from the Inner Sanctum* 1992
Sher, Antony *Shadey* 1985; *Erik the Viking* 1989; *The Young Poisoner's Handbook* 1994; *Alive and Kicking* 1996; *Mrs Brown* 1997; *The Miracle Maker* 1999
Sherbedgia, Rade *Eyes Wide Shut* 1999; *Stigmata* 1999
Sheridan, Ann *aka* **Sheridan, Clara Lou** *Murder at the Vanities* 1934; *Mrs Wiggs of the Cabbage Patch* 1934; *Ladies Should Listen* 1934; *Rumba* 1935; *The Black Legion* 1937; *San Quentin* 1937; *Angels with Dirty Faces* 1938; *Letter of Introduction* 1938; *Angels Wash Their Faces* 1939; *Dodge City* 1939; *Naughty but Nice* 1939; *They Made Me a Criminal* 1939; *Indianapolis Speedway* 1939; *Castle on the Hudson* 1940; *City for Conquest* 1940; *It All Came True* 1940; *They Drive by Night* 1940; *Torrid Zone* 1940; *The Man Who Came to Dinner* 1941; *George Washington Slept Here* 1942; *Kings Row* 1942; *Edge of Darkness* 1943; *The Doughgirls* 1944; *Shine On, Harvest Moon* 1944; *Nora Prentiss* 1947; *The Unfaithful* 1947; *Good Sam* 1948; *Silver River* 1948; *I Was a Male War Bride* 1949; *Stella* 1950; *Appointment in Honduras* 1953; *Take Me to Town* 1953; *Come Next Spring* 1956; *The Opposite Sex* 1956
Sheridan, Dan *Bullwhip* 1958; *The Young Captives* 1958; *Ten Who Dared* 1960
Sheridan, Dinah *Get Cracking* 1943; *29 Acacia Avenue* 1945; *The Huggetts Abroad* 1949; *Blackout* 1950; *No Trace* 1950; *Where No Vultures Fly* 1951; *Appointment in London* 1952; *The Sound Barrier* 1952; *Genevieve* 1953; *The Story of Gilbert and Sullivan* 1953; *The Railway Children* 1971
Sheridan, Frank *Danger Lights* 1930; *Washington Merry-Go-Round* 1932
Sheridan, Jamey *Distant Thunder* 1988; *Shannon's Deal* 1989; *Stanley & Iris* 1989; *All I Want for Christmas* 1991; *Talent for the Game* 1991; *A Stranger among Us* 1992; *Whispers in the Dark* 1992; *Killer Rules* 1993; *My Breast* 1994; *All Lies End in Murder* 1997; *Wild America* 1997; *The Echo of Thunder* 1998; *Beauty* 1998
Sheridan, Margaret *The Thing from Another World* 1951; *One Minute to Zero* 1952; *I, the Jury* 1953; *Pride of the Blue Grass* 1954
Sheridan, Nicollette *The Sure Thing* 1985; *Deceptions* 1990; *The Devil's Bed* 1994; *Robin Cook's Formula for Death* 1995; *Silver Strand* 1995; *Spy Hard* 1996; *The People Next Door* 1996; *Beverly Hills Ninja* 1997; *Murder in My Mind* 1997; *Dead Husbands* 1998
Sherman, Bobby *He Is My Brother* 1974; *Get Crazy* 1983
Sherman, Geraldine *Poor Cow* 1967; *There's a Girl in My Soup* 1970; *Take a Girl Like You* 1970
Sherman, Hiram *The Solid Gold Cadillac* 1956; *Mary, Mary* 1963
Sherman, Lowell *Way Down East* 1920; *The Divine Woman* 1928; *Mammy* 1930; *Bachelor Apartment* 1931; *What Price Hollywood?* 1932
Sherrill, David *The Wraith* 1986; *Unhook the Stars* 1996
Sherwood, Madeleine *Cat on a Hot Tin Roof* 1958; *Sweet Bird of Youth* 1962; *Pendulum* 1969
Sherwood, Robin *Tourist Trap* 1979; *Death Wish II* 1981
Sheybal, Vladek *aka* **Sheybal, Wladyslaw** *Kanal* 1957; *Billion Dollar Brain* 1967; *Women in Love* 1969; *Puppet on a Chain* 1970; *The Boy Friend* 1971; *Innocent Bystanders* 1972; *S*P*Y*S* 1974; *The Sellout* 1975; *The Wind and the Lion* 1975; *The Apple* 1980; *After Midnight* 1990
Shields, Arthur *The Plough and the Stars* 1936; *Little Nellie Kelly* 1940; *Confirm or Deny* 1941; *The Gay Falcon* 1941; *The Man from Down Under* 1943; *Youth Runs Wild* 1944; *The Corn Is Green* 1945; *Three Strangers* 1946; *The Verdict* 1946; *The Fabulous Dorseys* 1947; *Seven Keys to Baldpate* 1947; *She Wore a Yellow Ribbon* 1949; *Tarzan and the Slave Girl* 1950; *Apache Drums* 1951; *The River* 1951; *Scandal at Scourie* 1953; *World for Ransom* 1954; *Pride of the Blue Grass* 1954; *Daughter of Dr Jekyll* 1957; *For the Love of Mike* 1960
Shields, Brooke *Pretty Baby* 1978; *Tilt* 1978; *King of the Gypsies* 1978; *Wanda Nevada* 1979; *Just You and Me, Kid* 1979; *The Blue Lagoon* 1980; *Endless Love* 1981; *Sahara* 1983; *Brenda Starr* 1989; *Backstreet Dreams* 1990; *Freaked* 1993; *Stalking Laura* 1993; *Seventh Floor* 1995; *The Almost Perfect Bank Robbery* 1996; *Freeway* 1996; *The Misadventures of Margaret* 1998; *The Bachelor* 1999; *Black and White* 1999
Shiganoya, Benkei *Osaka Elegy* 1936; *Sisters of the Gion* 1936
Shigeta, James *The Crimson Kimono* 1959; *Walk like a Dragon* 1960; *Flower Drum Song* 1961; *Cry for Happy* 1961; *Paradise, Hawaiian Style* 1966; *Nobody's Perfect* 1968; *Lost Horizon* 1973; *The Yakuza* 1975; *The Killer Who Wouldn't Die* 1976; *Die Hard* 1988; *Cage* 1989; *China Cry* 1990; *Cage 2: the Arena of Death* 1994; *Drive* 1997
Shillo, Michael *Dunkirk* 1958; *The Whole Truth* 1958
Shiloach, Joseph *aka* **Shiloah, Joseph,** *aka* **Shiloach, Josef** *Diamonds* 1975; *Jesus* 1979; *The Lion of Africa* 1987
Shiloh, Shmuel *Goodbye New York* 1984; *Double Edge* 1992
Shimada, Teru *Tokyo Joe* 1949; *You Only Live Twice* 1967
Shimada, Yoko *Shogun* 1980; *The Hunted* 1995
Shimerman, Armin *Slaughter of the Innocents* 1993; *Dream Man* 1995
Shimizu, Masao *The Straits of Love and Hate* 1937; *Sanjuro* 1962
Shimizu, Misa *Okoge* 1992; *The Eel* 1997
Shimkus, Joanna *Paris Vu Par...* 1965; *The Adventurers* 1968; *Boom* 1968; *Ho!* 1968; *The Lost Man* 1969; *The Virgin and the Gypsy* 1970; *The Marriage of a Young Stockbroker* 1971; *A Time for Loving* 1971
Shimono, Sab *Come See the Paradise* 1990; *Teenage Mutant Ninja Turtles III* 1992; *Suture* 1993; *The Shadow* 1994; *The Big Hit* 1998
Shimura, Takashi *Sanshiro Sugata* 1943; *Drunken Angel* 1948; *Stray Dog* 1949; *Rashomon* 1950; *The Idiot* 1951; *Ikiru* 1952; *Seven Samurai* 1954; *Godzilla* 1954; *I Live in Fear* 1955; *Throne of Blood* 1957; *The Hidden Fortress* 1958; *The Bad Sleep Well* 1960; *High and Low* 1963; *Ghidrah, the Three-Headed Monster* 1965
Shinas, Sofia *Hourglass* 1996; *Hostile Intent* 1997
Shindo, Eitaro *Sansho the Bailiff* 1954; *The Crucified Lovers* 1954
Shiner, Ronald *Doctor's Orders* 1934; *Trouble Brewing* 1939; *South American George* 1941; *Bees in Paradise* 1943; *Get Cracking* 1943; *George in Civvy Street* 1946; *The Man Within* 1947; *Innocents in Paris* 1953; *Dry Rot* 1956; *Not Wanted on Voyage* 1957; *Girls at Sea* 1958; *The Navy Lark* 1959; *Operation Bullshine* 1959; *The Night We Got the Bird* 1960
Shingler, Helen *Quiet Weekend* 1946; *The Silver Darlings* 1947; *The Rossiter Case* 1950; *Judgment Deferred* 1951; *The Lady with the Lamp* 1951
Shioya, Toshi *Blood Oath* 1990; *Mr Baseball* 1992
Shipman, Nina *Blue Denim* 1959; *The Oregon Trail* 1959
Shipp, John Wesley *The Flash* 1990; *The NeverEnding Story II: the Next Chapter* 1991; *Soft Deceit* 1994; *Deadly Web* 1995; *Lost Treasure of Dos Santos* 1997
Shirakawa, Yumi *The H-Man* 1954; *Rodan* 1956; *Early Autumn* 1961
Shire, Talia *aka* **Coppola, Talia** *The Dunwich Horror* 1970; *Gas-s-s-s, or It Became Necessary to Destroy the World in Order to Save It* 1970; *The Godfather, Part II* 1974; *Foster and Laurie* 1975; *Rocky* 1976; *Kill Me If You Can* 1977; *Rocky II* 1979; *Old Boyfriends* 1979; *Prophecy* 1979; *Rocky III* 1982; *Rocky IV* 1985; *New York Stories* 1989; *The Godfather Part III* 1990; *Rocky V* 1990; *Mark Twain & Me* 1991; *Bed & Breakfast* 1992; *Cold Heaven* 1992; *Father, Son and the Mistress* 1992; *Deadfall* 1993
Shirley, Anne *aka* **O'Day, Dawn** *Anne of Green Gables* 1934; *Steamboat round the Bend* 1935; *Chatterbox* 1936; *Stella Dallas* 1937; *Boy Slaves* 1938; *Condemned Women* 1938; *Law of the Underworld* 1938; *Anne of Windy Poplars* 1940; *Saturday's Children* 1940; *Vigil in the Night* 1940; *Bombardier* 1943; *Government Girl* 1943; *Music in Manhattan* 1944; *Farewell My Lovely* 1945
Shirley, Bill *Abbott and Costello Meet Captain Kidd* 1952; *I Dream of Jeanie* 1952; *Sleeping Beauty* 1959
Shirley, Peg *White Mama* 1980; *Dearly Devoted* 1998
Shoemaker, Ann *Alice Adams* 1935; *My Favorite Wife* 1940; *Strike Up the Band* 1940; *Above Suspicion* 1943; *Conflict* 1945; *House by the River* 1950; *Sunrise at Campobello* 1960
Shoop, Pamela *aka* **Shoop, Pamela Susan** *Empire of the Ants* 1977; *One Man Jury* 1978; *Halloween II* 1981
Shor, Dan *aka* **Shor, Daniel** *Wise Blood* 1979; *Back Roads* 1981; *Tron* 1982; *Strangers Kiss* 1983; *Mesmerized* 1984; *Black Moon Rising* 1985; *Bill & Ted's Excellent Adventure* 1988; *Elvis and the Colonel: the Untold Story* 1993
Shore, Dinah *Thank Your Lucky Stars* 1943; *Belle of the Yukon* 1944; *Up in Arms* 1944; *Follow the Boys* 1944; *Make Mine Music* 1946; *Fun and Fancy Free* 1947
Shore, Pauly *California Man* 1992; *Son in Law* 1993; *In the Army Now* 1994; *Jury Duty* 1995; *Bio-Dome* 1996; *Casper: a Spirited Beginning* 1997
Short, Martin *Lost and Found* 1979; *¡hree Amigos!* 1986; *Cross My Heart* 1987; *Innerspace* 1987; *The Big Picture* 1989; *Three Fugitives* 1989; *Father of the Bride* 1991; *Pure Luck* 1991; *Captain Ron* 1992; *We're Back! A Dinosaur's Story* 1993; *Clifford* 1994; *Father of the Bride Part II* 1995; *The Pebble and the Penguin* 1995; *Mars Attacks!* 1996; *Jungle 2 Jungle* 1997; *A Simple Wish* 1997; *The Prince of Egypt* 1998; *Mumford* 1999
Shorter, Ken *Ned Kelly* 1970; *Sunday Too Far Away* 1974
Shou, Robin *Forbidden Nights* 1990; *Beverly Hills Ninja* 1997; *Mortal Kombat: Annihilation* 1997
Show, Grant *Coopersmith: Sweet Scent of Murder* 1992; *A Woman,*

Her Men and Her Futon 1992; *Between Love and Honor* 1995; *The Price of Heaven* 1997

Showalter, Max aka **Adams, Casey** *Destination Gobi* 1953; *Niagara* 1953; *Naked Alibi* 1954; *Down Three Dark Streets* 1954; *Bus Stop* 1956; *Dragoon Wells Massacre* 1957; *The Monster That Challenged the World* 1957; *How to Murder Your Wife* 1965; *Racing with the Moon* 1984

Shrapnel, John *Testimony* 1987; *How to Get Ahead in Advertising* 1989; *101 Dalmatians* 1996; *Gladiator* 2000

Shroyer, Sonny *The Devil and Max Devlin* 1981; *Scattered Dreams* 1993; *Dukes of Hazzard Reunion* 1997

Shue, Elisabeth *Call to Glory* 1983; *The Karate Kid* 1984; *Link* 1986; *A Night on the Town* 1987; *Cocktail* 1988; *Back to the Future Part II* 1989; *Back to the Future Part III* 1990; *Soapdish* 1991; *Too Hot to Handle* 1991; *Heart and Souls* 1993; *Twenty Bucks* 1993; *Blind Justice* 1994; *Radio Inside* 1994; *Leaving Las Vegas* 1995; *The Underneath* 1995; *The Trigger Effect* 1996; *Cousin Bette* 1997; *Deconstructing Harry* 1997; *The Saint* 1997; *Palmetto* 1998; *Molly* 1999

Shull, Richard B *Slither* 1973; *Ssssss* 1973; *The Fortune* 1975; *Hearts of the West* 1975; *The Pack* 1977; *Dreamer* 1979; *Unfaithfully Yours* 1983; *Splash* 1984; *Seize the Day* 1986; *HouseSitter* 1992; *Trapped in Paradise* 1994

Shvorin, A aka **Shvorin, Aleksandr,** aka **Stewart, Andy** *The Cranes Are Flying* 1957; *Battle beyond the Sun* 1959

Siao, Josephine *The Legend of Fong Sai-Yuk I* 1993; *The Legend of Fong Sai-Yuk II* 1993

Sibbett, Jane *The Resurrected* 1992; *Noah* 1998

Siberry, Michael *Biggles* 1986; *Boundaries of the Heart* 1988; *Teen Agent* 1991

Siddons, Harold *Genevieve* 1953; *The Purple Plain* 1954; *The Baby and the Battleship* 1956

Sidney, George *High Pressure* 1932; *Manhattan Melodrama* 1934

Sidney, Sylvia *An American Tragedy* 1931; *City Streets* 1931; *Street Scene* 1931; *Merrily We Go to Hell* 1932; *Madame Butterfly* 1932; *Jennie Gerhardt* 1933; *Thirty-Day Princess* 1934; *Accent on Youth* 1935; *Fury* 1936; *The Trail of the Lonesome Pine* 1936; *Sabotage* 1936; *Dead End* 1937; *You Only Live Once* 1937; *You and Me* 1938; *The Wagons Roll at Night* 1941; *Blood on the Sun* 1945; *The Searching Wind* 1946; *Les Misérables* 1952; *Violent Saturday* 1955; *Do Not Fold, Spindle or Mutilate* 1971; *Summer Wishes, Winter Dreams* 1973; *Death at Love House* 1976; *God Told Me to* 1976; *Snowbeast* 1977; *Damien – Omen II* 1978; *The Shadow Box* 1980; *A Small Killing* 1981; *Order of Death* 1983; *An Early Frost* 1985; *Pals* 1986; *Beetle Juice* 1988; *Used People* 1992

Siebert, Charles *Deadly Hero* 1976; *White Water Summer* 1987; *A House of Secrets and Lies* 1992

Siedow, Jim *The Texas Chain Saw Massacre* 1974; *The Texas Chainsaw Massacre Part 2* 1986

Siegmann, George *The Birth of a Nation* 1915; *The Three Musketeers* 1921; *Oliver Twist* 1922; *Hotel Imperial* 1927

Siemaszko, Casey *Secret Admirer* 1985; *Stand by Me* 1986; *Three O'Clock High* 1987; *Biloxi Blues* 1988; *Young Guns* 1988; *Breaking In* 1989; *Near Mrs* 1990; *The Chase* 1991; *Of Mice and Men* 1992; *Painted Heart* 1992; *Milk Money* 1994; *Black Scorpion* 1995; *Bliss* 1997; *Limbo* 1999

Siemaszko, Nina *Bed & Breakfast* 1992; *Little Noises* 1992; *The Saint of Fort Washington* 1993; *Airheads* 1994; *Baby Brokers* 1994; *Runaway Car* 1997; *Jakob the Liar* 1999

Sierra, Gregory *The Wrath of God* 1972; *The Thief Who Came to Dinner* 1973; *The Castaway Cowboy* 1974; *Mean Dog Blues* 1978; *Code Name: Dancer* 1987; *The Trouble with Spies* 1987; *Something Is Out There* 1988; *Donor* 1990; *Unspeakable Acts* 1990; *A Low Down Dirty Shame* 1995; *John Carpenter's Vampires* 1998

Signorelli, Tom *Thief* 1981; *Crossover Dreams* 1985; *The Bride in Black* 1990

Signoret, Simone *Against the Wind* 1947; *La Ronde* 1950; *Casque d'Or* 1952; *Thérèse Raquin* 1953; *Les Diaboliques* 1954; *Death in the Garden* 1956; *Room at the Top* 1958; *Le Joli Mai* 1962; *Term of Trial* 1962; *The Sleeping Car Murders* 1965; *Ship of Fools* 1965; *The Deadly Affair* 1966; *Is Paris Burning?* 1966; *Games* 1967; *The Sea Gull* 1968; *L'Armée des Ombres* 1969; *The Confession* 1970; *The Widow Couderc* 1971; *Burnt Barns* 1973; *The Flesh of the Orchid* 1974; *Madame Rosa* 1977

Sihol, Caroline *Confidentially Yours* 1983; *Tenue de Soirée* 1986; *Tous les Matins du Monde* 1992

Sikes, Cynthia *Ladies and Gentlemen, the Fabulous Stains* 1982; *The Man Who Loved Women* 1983; *Love Hurts* 1990; *Possums* 1998

Sikking, James B aka **Sikking, James** *Point Blank* 1967; *Charro!* 1969; *Daddy's Gone A-Hunting* 1969; *Precinct 45: Los Angeles Police* 1972; *Ordinary People* 1980; *Outland* 1981; *The Star Chamber* 1983; *Star Trek III: the Search for Spock* 1984; *Morons from Outer Space* 1985; *Soul Man* 1986; *Bay Cove* 1987; *Too Good to Be True* 1988; *Narrow Margin* 1990; *Final Approach* 1991; *The Pelican Brief* 1993; *Seduced by Evil* 1994; *In Pursuit of Honor* 1995; *Jake Lassiter: Justice on the Bayou* 1995; *Tyson* 1995; *Dare to Love* 1995; *Dead Badge* 1995; *Mutiny* 1999

Silayan, Vic *Daughters of Satan* 1972; *The Children of An Lac* 1980

Siletti, Mario *The Black Hand* 1950; *Kansas City Confidential* 1952; *Bring Your Smile Along* 1955

Silla, Felix *The Black Bird* 1975; *Buck Rogers in the 25th Century* 1979

Sillas, Karen *Simple Men* 1992; *Risk* 1993; *What Happened Was...* 1994; *Female Perversions* 1996; *Sour Grapes* 1998

Sills, Douglas *Justin Case* 1988; *The Swan Princess: The Secret of the Castle* 1997

Sills, Milton *The Sea Hawk* 1924; *The Barker* 1928

Silva, Franco *Hannibal* 1959; *The Mongols* 1961

Silva, Henry *A Hatful of Rain* 1957; *The Tall T* 1957; *The Bravados* 1958; *The Law and Jake Wade* 1958; *Ride a Crooked Trail* 1958; *Green Mansions* 1959; *Cinderfella* 1960; *The Manchurian Candidate* 1962; *Sergeants 3* 1962; *A Gathering of Eagles* 1963; *Johnny Cool* 1963; *The Secret Invasion* 1964; *The Reward* 1965; *Never a Dull Moment* 1968; *The Italian Connection* 1973; *Shoot* 1976; *Love and Bullets* 1978; *Buck Rogers in the 25th Century* 1979; *Thirst* 1979; *Alligator* 1980; *Virus* 1980; *Sharky's Machine* 1981; *The Man with the Deadly Lens* 1982; *Chained Heat* 1983; *Lust in the Dust* 1984; *Code of Silence* 1985; *Allan Quatermain and the Lost City of Gold* 1987; *Bulletproof* 1987; *Nico* 1988; *The Harvest* 1993; *Ghost Dog: the Way of the Samurai* 1999

Silva, Maria *The Awful Dr Orloff* 1962; *As If It Were Raining* 1963; *The Devil's Kiss* 1971

Silva, Simone *Escape by Night* 1953; *Street of Shadows* 1953

Silva, Trinidad *Walk Proud* 1979; *Crackers* 1984; *Stones for Ibarra* 1988; *The Night Before* 1988; *UHF* 1989

Silvani, Aldo *La Strada* 1954; *Nights of Cabiria* 1957

Silveira, Leonor *The Divine Comedy* 1992; *Abraham Valley* 1993; *The Convent* 1995; *Journey to the Beginning of the World* 1997

Silver, Joe *The Apprenticeship of Duddy Kravitz* 1974; *Rhinoceros* 1974; *Shivers* 1975; *Rabid* 1976; *You Light Up My Life* 1977; *Boardwalk* 1979; *The Gig* 1985

Silver, Robert *Eat and Run* 1986; *Dearly Devoted* 1998

Silver, Ron *Semi-Tough* 1977; *Murder at the Mardi Gras* 1978; *The Entity* 1981; *Best Friends* 1982; *Silent Rage* 1982; *Lovesick* 1983; *Silkwood* 1983; *Garbo Talks* 1984; *The Goodbye People* 1984; *Oh, God! You Devil* 1984; *Eat and Run* 1986; *Trapped in Silence* 1986; *A Father's Revenge* 1987; *Enemies, a Love Story* 1989; *Fellow Traveller* 1989; *Blue Steel* 1990; *Reversal of Fortune* 1990; *Forgotten Prisoners: the Amnesty Files* 1990; *Married to It* 1991; *Live Wire* 1992; *Mr Saturday Night* 1992; *Blind Side* 1993; *Lifepod* 1993; *The Good Policeman* 1994; *Timecop* 1994; *Almost Golden: the Jessica Savitch Story* 1995; *Kissinger and Nixon* 1995; *The Arrival* 1996; *Deadly Takeover* 1996; *Danger Zone* 1996; *Skeletons* 1996; *The White Raven* 1998; *Love Is Strange* 1998

Silvera, Frank *The Fighter* 1952; *The Miracle of Fatima* 1952; *White Mane* 1952; *Fear and Desire* 1953; *Killer's Kiss* 1955; *Crime and Punishment, USA* 1959; *The Mountain Road* 1960; *Key Witness* 1960; *The St Valentine's Day Massacre* 1967; *The Stalking Moon* 1968; *Valdez Is Coming* 1971

Silverheels, Jay *Broken Arrow* 1950; *The Battle at Apache Pass* 1952; *Drums across the River* 1954; *Saskatchewan* 1954; *Walk the Proud Land* 1956; *The Lone Ranger* 1956; *The Lone Ranger and the Lost City of Gold* 1958; *Alias Jesse James* 1959; *The Man Who Loved Cat Dancing* 1973; *Santee* 1973

Silverman, Jonathan *Girls Just Want to Have Fun* 1985; *Brighton Beach Memoirs* 1986; *Caddyshack II* 1988; *Stealing Home* 1988; *Traveling Man* 1989; *Weekend at Bernie's* 1989; *Broadway Bound* 1991; *Class Action* 1991; *Age Isn't Everything* 1991; *Father, Son and the Mistress* 1992; *Weekend at Bernie's II* 1992; *Breaking the Rules* 1992; *12:01* 1993; *Little Big League* 1994; *A Feel for Murder* 1995; *...At First Sight* 1995; *Neil Simon's London Suite* 1996; *The Odd Couple II* 1998; *The Inspectors* 1998

Silverman, Robert *Head On* 1980; *Prom Night* 1980

Silvers, Phil *Strike Up the Band* 1940; *Lady Be Good* 1941; *The Penalty* 1941; *Tom, Dick and Harry* 1941; *All through the Night* 1942; *Footlight Serenade* 1942; *My Gal Sal* 1942; *Roxie Hart* 1942; *Coney Island* 1943; *A Lady Takes a Chance* 1943; *Cover Girl* 1944; *Something for the Boys* 1944; *Billy Rose's Diamond Horseshoe* 1945; *A Thousand and One Nights* 1945; *Summer Stock* 1950; *Top Banana* 1953; *Lucky Me* 1954; *Forty Pounds of Trouble* 1962; *It's a Mad Mad Mad Mad World* 1963; *A Funny Thing Happened on the Way to the Forum* 1966; *Carry On Follow That Camel* 1967; *Buona Sera, Mrs Campbell* 1968; *The Boatniks* 1970; *The Strongest Man in the World* 1975; *Won Ton Ton, the Dog Who Saved Hollywood* 1976; *The New Love Boat* 1977; *The Night They Took Miss Beautiful* 1977; *The Chicken Chronicles* 1977; *The Cheap Detective* 1978; *There Goes the Bride* 1979; *The Happy Hooker Goes to Hollywood* 1980

Silvers, Sid *Broadway Melody of 1936* 1935; *Born to Dance* 1936

Silverstone, Alicia *The Crush* 1993; *Scattered Dreams* 1993; *Judith Krantz's Torch Song* 1993; *The Cool and the Crazy* 1994; *The Babysitter* 1995; *Clueless* 1995; *Hideaway* 1995; *Batman and Robin* 1997; *Excess Baggage* 1997; *Blast from the Past* 1998; *Love's Labour's Lost* 1999

Silverstone, Ben *The Browning Version* 1994; *Get Real* 1998

Silvestre, Armando *Apache Drums* 1951; *For the Love of Mike* 1960; *Kings of the Sun* 1963; *Rage* 1966; *The Scalphunters* 1968; *Two Mules for Sister Sara* 1970

Sim, Alastair *A Fire Has Been Arranged* 1935; *The Man in the Mirror* 1936; *Gangway* 1937; *The Squeaker* 1937; *Alf's Button Afloat* 1938; *Climbing High* 1938; *Sailing Along* 1938; *Cottage to Let* 1941; *Waterloo Road* 1944; *Green for Danger* 1946; *Captain Boycott* 1947; *Hue and Cry* 1947; *London Belongs to Me* 1948; *The Happiest Days of Your Life* 1950; *Stage Fright* 1950; *Lady Godiva Rides Again* 1951; *Laughter in Paradise* 1951; *Scrooge* 1951; *Folly to Be Wise* 1952; *Innocents in Paris* 1953; *The Belles of St Trinian's* 1954; *An Inspector Calls* 1954; *Geordie* 1955; *The Green Man* 1956; *Blue Murder at St Trinian's* 1957; *The Doctor's Dilemma* 1958; *Left, Right and Centre* 1959; *The Millionairess* 1960; *School for Scoundrels* 1960; *The Ruling Class* 1972; *Royal Flash* 1975; *Escape from the Dark* 1976

Sim, Gerald *Seance on a Wet Afternoon* 1964; *The Whisperers* 1967; *The Raging Moon* 1970; *Dr Jekyll and Sister Hyde* 1971

Sim, Sheila *A Canterbury Tale* 1944; *Great Day* 1944; *Dancing with Crime* 1946; *The Guinea Pig* 1948; *Pandora and the Flying Dutchman* 1951; *West of Zanzibar* 1954; *The Night My Number Came Up* 1955

Simcox, Tom *Incident at Phantom Hill* 1966; *Istanbul Express* 1968

Simm, John *Boston Kickout* 1995; *Diana & Me* 1997; *Human Traffic* 1999; *Wonderland* 1999

Simmons, Dick aka **Simmons, Richard** *Pilot #5* 1943; *Thousands Cheer* 1943; *Lady in the Lake* 1947; *Undercover Maisie* 1947; *On an Island with You* 1948

Simmons, Gene *Runaway* 1984; *Trick or Treat* 1986; *Wanted Dead or Alive* 1986; *Red Surf* 1990; *Detroit Rock City* 1999

Simmons, J K *The Jackal* 1997; *For Love of the Game* 1999

Simmons, Jean *Give Us the Moon* 1944; *Black Narcissus* 1946; *Great Expectations* 1946; *Hungry Hill* 1947; *Uncle Silas* 1947; *Hamlet* 1948; *Adam and Evelyne* 1949; *The Blue Lagoon* 1949; *Cage of Gold* 1950; *The Clouded Yellow* 1950; *So Long at the Fair* 1950; *Trio* 1950; *Androcles and the Lion* 1952; *The Actress* 1953; *Affair with a Stranger* 1953; *Angel Face* 1953; *The Robe* 1953; *Young Bess* 1953; *Beautiful but Dangerous* 1954; *Desiree* 1954; *The Egyptian* 1954; *A Bullet Is Waiting* 1954; *Footsteps in the Fog* 1955; *Guys and Dolls* 1955; *Hilda Crane* 1956; *Until They Sail* 1957; *This Could Be the Night* 1957; *The Big Country* 1958; *Home before Dark* 1958; *This Earth Is Mine* 1959; *Elmer Gantry* 1960; *The Grass Is Greener* 1960; *Spartacus* 1960; *All the Way Home* 1963; *Life at the Top* 1965; *Mister Buddwing* 1966; *Divorce American Style* 1967; *Rough Night in Jericho* 1967; *The Happy Ending* 1969; *Say Hello to Yesterday* 1971; *Mr Sycamore* 1974; *Dominique* 1978; *A Small Killing* 1981; *Going Undercover* 1984; *The Dawning* 1988; *Inherit the Wind* 1988; *How to Make an American Quilt* 1995; *Barbara Taylor Bradford's Her Own Rules* 1998

Simms, Ginny *Playmates* 1941; *Here We Go Again* 1942; *Seven Days' Leave* 1942; *Hit the Ice* 1943; *Broadway Rhythm* 1944; *Night and Day* 1946

Simms, Larry *Blondie* 1938; *Blondie Meets the Boss* 1939; *Blondie Takes a Vacation* 1939; *The Gay Sisters* 1942; *Footlight Glamour* 1943

Simon, Carly *Taking Off* 1971; *Perfect* 1985

Simon, Josette *Cry Freedom* 1987; *Milk and Honey* 1988

Simon, Michel *The Passion of Joan of Arc* 1928; *La Chienne* 1931; *Boudu, Saved from Drowning* 1932; *L'Atalante* 1934; *Drôle de Drame* 1937; *Le Quai des Brumes* 1938; *The End of the Day* 1939; *La Beauté du Diable* 1949; *Saadia* 1953; *The Train* 1964; *The Two of Us* 1967

Simon, Paul *Annie Hall* 1977; *One-Trick Pony* 1980; *Mother Goose Rock 'n' Rhyme* 1990

Simon, Robert aka **Simon, Robert F** *The Benny Goodman Story* 1955; *Foxfire* 1955; *Bigger than Life* 1956; *The Catered Affair* 1956; *Edge of the City* 1957; *Face of Fire* 1959; *Pay or Die*

RadioTimes ACTORS' INDEX

1960; *The Wizard of Baghdad* 1960
Simon, Simone *Ladies in Love* 1936; *Seventh Heaven* 1937; *La Bête Humaine* 1938; *Josette* 1938; *Daniel and the Devil* 1941; *Cat People* 1942; *And So They Were Married* 1944; *The Curse of the Cat People* 1944; *The Silent Bell* 1944; *La Ronde* 1950; *Le Plaisir* 1951; *The Extra Day* 1956
Simonds, David *Amateur* 1994; *The Book of Life* 1998
Simons, William *Where No Vultures Fly* 1951; *West of Zanzibar* 1954
Simpson, Ivan *The Man Who Played God* 1932; *Trouble for Two* 1936; *The Male Animal* 1942
Simpson, O J *The Klansman* 1974; *The Towering Inferno* 1974; *Killer Force* 1975; *The Cassandra Crossing* 1976; *Capricorn One* 1978; *Firepower* 1979; *Hambone and Hillie* 1984; *Student Exchange* 1987; *The Naked Gun* 1988; *The Naked Gun 2 ½: the Smell of Fear* 1991; *CIA – Codename Alexa* 1992; *No Place to Hide* 1992; *Naked Gun 33⅓: the Final Insult* 1994
Simpson, Raeanin *Wind Dancer* 1991; *Little Heroes* 1992
Simpson, Russell *Annie Laurie* 1927; *Billy the Kid* 1930; *Susan Lenox: Her Fall and Rise* 1931; *Law and Order* 1932; *Way Down East* 1935; *The Grapes of Wrath* 1940; *Wild Geese Calling* 1941; *Along Came Jones* 1945; *Saddle Tramp* 1950; *The Sun Shines Bright* 1953
Sims, Joan *Colonel March Investigates* 1953; *The Square Ring* 1953; *Trouble in Store* 1953; *Will Any Gentleman...?* 1953; *The Young Lovers* 1954; *As Long as They're Happy* 1955; *Dry Rot* 1956; *Carry On Admiral* 1957; *Just My Luck* 1957; *The Naked Truth* 1957; *No Time for Tears* 1957; *The Captain's Table* 1958; *Passport to Shame* 1958; *Carry On Nurse* 1959; *Carry On Teacher* 1959; *Life in Emergency Ward 10* 1959; *Upstairs and Downstairs* 1959; *Carry On Constable* 1960; *Carry On Regardless* 1960; *Doctor in Love* 1960; *Please Turn Over* 1960; *Watch Your Stern* 1960; *Mr Topaze* 1961; *No My Darling Daughter* 1961; *Twice round the Daffodils* 1962; *Nurse on Wheels* 1963; *Carry On Cleo* 1964; *The Big Job* 1965; *Carry On Cowboy* 1965; *Carry On – Don't Lose Your Head* 1966; *Carry On Screaming* 1966; *Doctor in Clover* 1966; *Carry On Follow That Camel* 1967; *Carry On Doctor* 1968; *Carry On Up the Khyber* 1968; *Carry On Again Doctor* 1969; *Carry On Camping* 1969; *Carry On Loving* 1970; *Carry On Up the Jungle* 1970; *Doctor in Trouble* 1970; *Carry On at Your Convenience* 1971; *Carry On Henry* 1971; *Carry On Abroad* 1972; *Carry On Matron* 1972; *Not Now Darling* 1972; *Carry On Girls* 1973; *Don't Just Lie There, Say Something!* 1973; *Carry On Dick* 1974; *Carry On Behind* 1975; *One of Our Dinosaurs Is Missing* 1975; *Love among the Ruins* 1975; *Carry On England* 1976; *Carry On Emmannuelle* 1978; *The Canterville Ghost* 1996
Sims, Warwick *He's My Girl* 1987; *Night Eyes* 1990
Sinatra, Frank *Ship Ahoy* 1942; *Higher and Higher* 1943; *Reveille with Beverly* 1943; *Step Lively* 1944; *Anchors Aweigh* 1945; *Till the Clouds Roll By* 1946; *It Happened in Brooklyn* 1947; *The Miracle of the Bells* 1948; *On the Town* 1949; *Take Me Out to the Ball Game* 1949; *The Kissing Bandit* 1949; *Double Dynamite* 1951; *Meet Danny Wilson* 1952; *From Here to Eternity* 1953; *Suddenly* 1954; *Guys and Dolls* 1955; *The Man with the Golden Arm* 1955; *Not as a Stranger* 1955; *The Tender Trap* 1955; *Young at Heart* 1955; *Around the World in 80 Days* 1956; *High Society* 1956; *Johnny Concho* 1956; *The Joker Is Wild* 1957; *Pal Joey* 1957; *The Pride and the Passion* 1957; *Kings Go Forth* 1958; *Some Came Running* 1958; *A Hole in the Head* 1959; *Never So Few* 1959; *Can-Can* 1960; *Ocean's Eleven* 1960; *Pepe* 1960; *The Devil at Four o'Clock* 1961; *The Manchurian Candidate* 1962; *The Road to Hong Kong* 1962; *Sergeants 3* 1962; *Come Blow Your Horn* 1963; *4 for Texas* 1963; *Robin and the 7 Hoods* 1964; *Paris When It Sizzles* 1964; *Marriage on the Rocks* 1965; *None but the Brave* 1965; *Von Ryan's Express* 1965; *Assault on a Queen* 1966; *Cast a Giant Shadow* 1966; *The Oscar* 1966; *The Naked Runner* 1967; *Tony Rome* 1967; *The Detective* 1968; *Lady in Cement* 1968; *Dirty Dingus Magee* 1970; *The First Deadly Sin* 1980; *Cannonball Run II* 1983; *Young at Heart* 1995
Sinatra Jr, Frank *A Man Called Adam* 1966; *Code Name: Zebra* 1986; *Confessions of a Lady Cop* 1988
Sinatra, Nancy *Get Yourself a College Girl* 1964; *Marriage on the Rocks* 1965; *The Oscar* 1966; *The Wild Angels* 1966; *The Last of the Secret Agents* 1966; *The Ghost in the Invisible Bikini* 1966; *Speedway* 1968
Sinbad *Necessary Roughness* 1991; *Houseguest* 1995; *First Kid* 1996; *Jingle All the Way* 1996; *The Cherokee Kid* 1996; *Good Burger* 1997
Sinclair, Betty *City Streets* 1931; *Something in the City* 1950
Sinclair, Hugh *Our Betters* 1933; *Escape Me Never* 1935; *The Four Just Men* 1939; *The Saint's Vacation* 1941; *Tomorrow We Live* 1942; *The Saint Meets the Tiger* 1943; *They Were Sisters* 1945; *Don't Ever Leave Me* 1949; *The Rocking Horse Winner* 1949; *Trottie True* 1949; *Circle of Danger* 1950; *No Trace* 1950; *Judgment Deferred* 1951; *Mantrap* 1952
Sinclair, Madge *Conrack* 1974; *Leadbelly* 1976; *Convoy* 1978; *Coming to America* 1988; *The Lion King* 1994
Sinclair, Peter *The Man from Morocco* 1944; *The Time of His Life* 1955
Sinclaire, Crystin *Ruby* 1977; *Goin' Coconuts* 1978
Sinden, Donald *The Cruel Sea* 1953; *A Day to Remember* 1953; *Mogambo* 1953; *The Beachcomber* 1954; *Doctor in the House* 1954; *Mad about Men* 1954; *You Know What Sailors Are* 1954; *Above Us the Waves* 1955; *An Alligator Named Daisy* 1955; *Josephine and Men* 1955; *Simba* 1955; *The Black Tent* 1956; *Eyewitness* 1956; *Tiger in the Smoke* 1956; *Doctor at Large* 1957; *The Captain's Table* 1958; *Rockets Galore* 1958; *Operation Bullshine* 1959; *The Siege of Sidney Street* 1960; *Your Money or Your Wife* 1960; *Twice round the Daffodils* 1962; *Decline and Fall... of a Birdwatcher* 1968; *Villain* 1971; *Father Dear Father* 1972; *Rentadick* 1972; *The Day of the Jackal* 1973; *The National Health* 1973; *The Island at the Top of the World* 1974; *That Lucky Touch* 1975; *The Children* 1990; *The Canterville Ghost* 1996
Singer, Campbell *Blackout* 1950; *A Case for PC 49* 1950; *Someone at the Door* 1950; *Conflict of Wings* 1953; *The Square Peg* 1958
Singer, Johnny *Street Song* 1935; *It's Never Too Late to Mend* 1937
Singer, Lori *Footloose* 1984; *The Falcon and the Snowman* 1985; *The Man with One Red Shoe* 1985; *Trouble in Mind* 1985; *Warlock* 1989; *Storm and Sorrow* 1990; *Equinox* 1992; *Sunset Grill* 1992; *Short Cuts* 1993; *FTW* 1994
Singer, Marc *Go Tell the Spartans* 1977; *Something for Joey* 1977; *The Beastmaster* 1982; *Her Life as a Man* 1984; *High Desert Kill* 1989; *Body Chemistry* 1990; *Beastmaster 2: through the Portal of Time* 1991; *Sweet Justice* 1992; *The Sea Wolf* 1993; *Implicated* 1994; *Beastmaster III: the Eye of Braxus* 1995
Singer, Raymond *Feds* 1988; *The Queen of Mean* 1990
Singer, Ritchie *"Crocodile" Dundee* 1986; *Encounter at Raven's Gate* 1988; *Cappuccino* 1989
Singleton, Penny *Blondie* 1938; *Garden of the Moon* 1938; *Hard to Get* 1938; *Blondie Meets the Boss* 1939; *Blondie Takes a Vacation* 1939; *Footlight Glamour* 1943; *Jetsons: the Movie* 1990
Sinise, Gary *My Name Is Bill W* 1989; *A Midnight Clear* 1991; *Of Mice and Men* 1992; *Jack the Bear* 1993; *Forrest Gump* 1994; *Apollo 13* 1995; *The Quick and the Dead* 1995; *Truman* 1995; *Albino Alligator* 1996; *Ransom* 1996; *Snake Eyes* 1998; *That Championship Season* 1999; *Mission to Mars* 1999; *Deception* 2000
Sirico, Tony *Innocent Blood* 1992; *New York Cop* 1995; *The Search for One-Eye Jimmy* 1996
Sirola, Joseph *aka* **Sirola, Joe** *The Super Cops* 1973; *Seizure* 1974; *Love Is a Gun* 1994
Sirtis, Marina *Blind Date* 1984; *Waxwork II: Lost in Time* 1992; *Star Trek: Generations* 1994; *Star Trek: First Contact* 1996; *Star Trek: Insurrection* 1998
Sisti, Michelan *Teenage Mutant Ninja Turtles* 1990; *Teenage Mutant Ninja Turtles II: the Secret of the Ooze* 1991
Sisto, Jeremy *Grand Canyon* 1991; *Hideaway* 1995; *White Squall* 1996; *Suicide Kings* 1997; *Without Limits* 1998; *Some Girls* 1998
Sisto, Rocco *Red Riding Hood* 1987; *Innocent Blood* 1992
Sivero, Frank *The Billion Dollar Hobo* 1978; *Going Ape!* 1981; *GoodFellas* 1990; *Cop and a Half* 1993
Sizemore, Tom *Lock Up* 1989; *Blue Steel* 1990; *Where Sleeping Dogs Lie* 1991; *After the Glory* 1992; *Passenger 57* 1992; *Watch It* 1992; *Heart and Souls* 1993; *Striking Distance* 1993; *Natural Born Killers* 1994; *Devil in a Blue Dress* 1995; *Heat* 1995; *Strange Days* 1995; *The Relic* 1997; *Enemy of the State* 1998; *Saving Private Ryan* 1998; *The Match* 1999; *Bringing out the Dead* 1999; *Play It to the Bone* 2000
Sjöberg, Emma *Taxi* 1998; *Taxi 2* 2000
Sjoberg, Gunnar *The Great Adventure* 1953; *So Close to Life* 1957
Sjöström, Victor *aka* **Seastrom, Victor** *Walpurgis Night* 1935; *To Joy* 1949; *Wild Strawberries* 1957
Skaggs, Jimmie F *aka* **Skaggs, Jimmie** *Ghost Town* 1988; *Oblivion* 1993; *Underworld* 1996
Skaggs, Norm *Decoration Day* 1990; *Shadow of a Doubt* 1991
Skala, Lilia *Lilies of the Field* 1963; *Caprice* 1967; *Charly* 1968; *Deadly Hero* 1976; *Roseland* 1977; *Heartland* 1979; *Flashdance* 1983; *Testament* 1983; *House of Games* 1987
Skarsgård, Stellan *The Simple-Minded Murderer* 1982; *Ake and His World* 1984; *Noon Wine* 1985; *The Perfect Murder* 1988; *The Hunt for Red October* 1990; *Parker Kane* 1990; *The Ox* 1991; *The Democratic Terrorist* 1992; *Wind* 1992; *The Slingshot* 1993; *Zero Kelvin* 1995; *Breaking the Waves* 1996; *Amistad* 1997; *Good Will Hunting* 1997; *My Son the Fanatic* 1997; *Savior* 1997; *Insomnia* 1997; *Ronin* 1998; *Deep Blue Sea* 1999
Skelton, Red *aka* **Skelton, Richard** *Having Wonderful Time* 1938; *Flight Command* 1940; *Dr Kildare's Wedding Day* 1941; *Lady Be Good* 1941; *The People vs Dr Kildare* 1941; *Whistling in the Dark* 1941; *Ship Ahoy* 1942; *Whistling in Dixie* 1942; *DuBarry Was a Lady* 1943; *I Dood It* 1943; *Whistling in Brooklyn* 1943; *Bathing Beauty* 1944; *The Fuller Brush Man* 1948; *A Southern Yankee* 1948; *Neptune's Daughter* 1949; *Three Little Words* 1950; *The Yellow Cab Man* 1950; *Watch the Birdie* 1950; *Lovely to Look At* 1952; *The Clown* 1952; *The Great Diamond Robbery* 1953
Skerritt, Tom *War Hunt* 1962; *Those Calloways* 1964; *MASH* 1969; *Wild Rovers* 1971; *Fuzz* 1972; *Big Bad Mama* 1974; *Thieves like Us* 1974; *The Devil's Rain* 1975; *The Turning Point* 1977; *Ice Castles* 1978; *Cheech & Chong's Up in Smoke* 1978; *Alien* 1979; *A Dangerous Summer* 1981; *Silence of the North* 1981; *Savage Harvest* 1981; *Death Vengeance* 1982; *The Dead Zone* 1983; *Calendar Girl Murders* 1984; *A Touch of Scandal* 1984; *Miles to Go* 1986; *Parent Trap II* 1986; *SpaceCamp* 1986; *Top Gun* 1986; *Opposing Force* 1986; *Wisdom* 1986; *The Big Town* 1987; *Hell Camp* 1987; *Maid to Order* 1987; *Poker Alice* 1987; *Moving Target* 1988; *Nightmare at Bitter Creek* 1988; *Poltergeist III* 1988; *Steel Magnolias* 1989; *The Heist* 1989; *Red King, White Knight* 1989; *Big Man on Campus* 1989; *Child in the Night* 1990; *The China Lake Murders* 1990; *The Rookie* 1990; *She'll Take Romance* 1990; *Getting Up and Going Home* 1992; *Hearts on Fire* 1992; *Knight Moves* 1992; *Poison Ivy* 1992; *A River Runs through It* 1992; *Contact* 1997; *Divided by Hate* 1997; *What the Deaf Man Heard* 1997; *Two for Texas* 1998; *The Other Sister* 1999
Skinner, Claire *Life Is Sweet* 1990; *Naked* 1993; *Clockwork Mice* 1994; *i.d.* 1994; *The Return of the Native* 1994; *You're Dead* 1999
Skinner, Cornelia Otis *The Uninvited* 1944; *The Girl in the Red Velvet Swing* 1955
Skipper, Pat *Demonstone* 1989; *Femme Fatale* 1991; *Memoirs of an Invisible Man* 1992; *Trade-Off* 1995
Skipworth, Alison *Outward Bound* 1930; *Raffles* 1930; *If I Had a Million* 1932; *Sinners in the Sun* 1932; *Night after Night* 1932; *The Song of Songs* 1933; *Tillie and Gus* 1933; *The Captain Hates the Sea* 1934; *Six of a Kind* 1934; *Becky Sharp* 1935; *The Casino Murder Case* 1935; *Dangerous* 1935; *The Devil Is a Woman* 1935; *The Girl from 10th Avenue* 1935; *The Gorgeous Hussy* 1936; *Satan Met a Lady* 1936; *The Princess Comes Across* 1936
Skolimowski, Jerzy *Circle of Deceit* 1981; *White Nights* 1985
Skomarovsky, Vladimir *Black Eagle* 1988; *Martial Outlaw* 1993
Skye, Ione *Stranded* 1987; *River's Edge* 1987; *A Night in the Life of Jimmy Reardon* 1988; *The Rachel Papers* 1989; *Say Anything* 1989; *Mindwalk* 1990; *Gas, Food, Lodging* 1992; *Guncrazy* 1992; *Girls in Prison* 1994; *Dream for an Insomniac* 1996
Slade, Max Elliott *3 Ninja Kids* 1992; *3 Ninjas Kick Back* 1994; *3 Ninjas Knuckle Up* 1995
Slate, Henry *The Belle of New York* 1952; *Bloodhounds of Broadway* 1952; *Somebody Loves Me* 1952; *Hey Boy! Hey Girl!* 1959
Slate, Jeremy *Girls! Girls! Girls!* 1962; *Wives and Lovers* 1963; *I'll Take Sweden* 1965; *Born Losers* 1967; *True Grit* 1969; *Whisperkill* 1988; *The Dream Machine* 1990; *The Lawnmower Man* 1992
Slater, Christian *The Legend of Billie Jean* 1985; *The Name of the Rose* 1986; *Beyond the Stars* 1988; *Gleaming the Cube* 1988; *Tucker: the Man and His Dream* 1988; *Desperate for Love* 1989; *Heathers* 1989; *Pump Up the Volume* 1990; *Young Guns II* 1990; *Kuffs* 1991; *Mobsters* 1991; *Robin Hood: Prince of Thieves* 1991; *Star Trek VI: the Undiscovered Country* 1991; *Tales from the Darkside: the Movie* 1991; *FernGully: the Last Rainforest* 1992; *Where the Day Takes You* 1992; *True Romance* 1993; *Untamed Heart* 1993; *Interview with the Vampire: the Vampire Chronicles* 1994; *Jimmy Hollywood* 1994; *Murder in the First* 1994; *Bed of Roses* 1995; *Broken Arrow* 1996; *Hard Rain* 1997; *Julian Po* 1997; *Very Bad Things* 1998; *Basil* 1998
Slater, Helen *Supergirl* 1984; *The Legend of Billie Jean* 1985; *Ruthless People* 1986; *The Secret of My Success* 1987; *Sticky Fingers* 1988; *Happy Together* 1989; *City Slickers* 1991; *Betrayal of the Dove* 1993; *A House in the Hills* 1993; *12:01* 1993; *Lassie* 1994; *Parallel Lives* 1994; *The Steal* 1994; *No Way Back* 1996; *Best Friends for Life* 1998
Slater, John *Gert and Daisy's Weekend* 1941; *For Those in Peril* 1943; *Against the Wind* 1947; *Conspiracy in Teheran* 1947; *It Always Rains on Sunday* 1947; *Passport to Pimlico* 1949; *The Long Memory* 1952; *Star of India* 1954; *Violent Playground* 1958; *The Night We Got the Bird* 1960; *A Place to Go* 1963
Slattery, Tony *Carry On Columbus* 1992; *The Crying Game* 1992; *Peter's Friends* 1992; *To Die For*

Beret 1953; For Better, for Worse 1954; As Long as They're Happy 1955; Value for Money 1955; It's Never Too Late 1956; The Barretts of Wimpole Street 1957
Stephens, Ann The Upturned Glass 1947; The Franchise Affair 1950
Stephens, Barbara Because He's My Friend 1978; Warming Up 1983
Stephens, Harvey Evelyn Prentice 1934; Let 'em Have It 1935; Murder Man 1935; Whipsaw 1935; After Office Hours 1935; Swing High, Swing Low 1937; The Oklahoma Kid 1939; You Can't Get Away with Murder 1939; Abe Lincoln in Illinois 1940; Our Wife 1941; Joe Smith, American 1942
Stephens, James First Monday in October 1981; The Getaway 1994
Stephens, Martin Count Your Blessings 1959; Village of the Damned 1960; The Innocents 1961; The Battle of the Villa Fiorita 1964
Stephens, Perry Two-Bits and Pepper 1995; Grizzly Mountain 1997
Stephens, Rachel Bigger than Life 1956; The True Story of Jesse James 1957
Stephens, Robert Circle of Deception 1960; The Queen's Guards 1960; A Taste of Honey 1961; Lunch Hour 1962; The Inspector 1962; The Small World of Sammy Lee 1963; Morgan – a Suitable Case for Treatment 1966; The Prime of Miss Jean Brodie 1969; The Private Life of Sherlock Holmes 1970; The Asphyx 1972; Travels with My Aunt 1972; Luther 1974; The Duellists 1977; The Shout 1978; Empire of the Sun 1987; High Season 1987; American Roulette 1988; Henry V 1989; Afraid of the Dark 1991; The Pope Must Die 1991; Century 1993; Innocent Moves 1993; The Secret Rapture 1993
Stephens, Toby Twelfth Night 1996; Sunset Heights 1996; Cousin Bette 1997; Photographing Fairies 1997; Onegin 1999
Stephenson, Henry The Animal Kingdom 1932; A Bill of Divorcement 1932; Cynara 1932; Red-Headed Woman 1932; Little Women 1933; If I Were Free 1933; One More River 1934; The Richest Girl in the World 1934; She Loves Me Not 1934; What Every Woman Knows 1934; Thirty-Day Princess 1934; Mutiny on the Bounty 1935; Reckless 1935; Vanessa, Her Love Story 1935; The Charge of the Light Brigade 1936; Little Lord Fauntleroy 1936; Conquest 1937; The Emperor's Candlesticks 1937; The Prince and the Pauper 1937; When You're in Love 1937; Dramatic School 1938; Marie Antoinette 1938; Suez 1938; The Adventures of Sherlock Holmes 1939; Tarzan Finds a Son! 1939; Down Argentine Way 1940; Little Old New York 1940; Lady from Louisiana 1941; Rings on Her Fingers 1942; This above All 1942; Mr Lucky 1943; Two Girls and a Sailor 1944; The Hour before the Dawn 1944; Tarzan and the Amazons 1945; The Locket 1946; Of Human Bondage 1946; Oliver Twist 1948
Stephenson, James White Banners 1938; We Are Not Alone 1939; King of the Underworld 1939; Devil's Island 1940; The Letter 1940; Shining Victory 1941

Stephenson, Mark Kinsey The Unnamable 1988; The Unnamable Returns 1992
Stephenson, Pamela The Comeback 1977; Stand Up Virgin Soldiers 1977; History of the World Part 1 1981; Scandalous 1983; Superman III 1983; Bloodbath at the House of Death 1983; Finders Keepers 1984; Les Patterson Saves the World 1987
Sterke, Jeannette The Prisoner 1955; The Safecracker 1958; Live Now – Pay Later 1962; A Stitch in Time 1963
Sterling, Ford He Who Gets Slapped 1924; Stage Struck 1925; Her Majesty Love 1931
Sterling, Jan Johnny Belinda 1948; Appointment with Danger 1950; Caged 1950; Mystery Street 1950; Union Station 1950; Ace in the Hole 1951; The Mating Season 1951; Rhubarb 1951; Pony Express 1953; Split Second 1953; The High and the Mighty 1954; The Human Jungle 1954; Alaska Seas 1954; Female on the Beach 1955; Man with the Gun 1955; Women's Prison 1955; 1984 1955; The Harder They Fall 1956; Slaughter on Tenth Avenue 1957; High School Confidential 1958; The Female Animal 1958; Love in a Goldfish Bowl 1961; First Monday in October 1981
Sterling, Mindy Austin Powers: International Man of Mystery 1997; Austin Powers: The Spy Who Shagged Me 1999; Drop Dead Gorgeous 1999
Sterling, Philip The Execution of Raymond Graham 1985; Circle of Violence 1986; The Death of the Incredible Hulk 1990
Sterling, Robert The Gay Caballero 1940; Dr Kildare's Victory 1941; Johnny Eager 1941; The Penalty 1941; Ringside Maisie 1941; Two-Faced Woman 1941; Somewhere I'll Find You 1942; The Secret Heart 1946; Roughshod 1949; Bunco Squad 1950; The Sundowners 1950; Show Boat 1951; Column South 1953; Return to Peyton Place 1961; Voyage to the Bottom of the Sea 1961; A Global Affair 1964
Sterling, Tisha Village of the Giants 1965; Coogan's Bluff 1968; The Defiant 1972; The Killer inside Me 1975
Stern, Daniel Breaking Away 1979; It's My Turn 1980; Diner 1982; I'm Dancing as Fast as I Can 1982; Blue Thunder 1983; Get Crazy 1983; Samson and Delilah 1984; CHUD 1984; Key Exchange 1985; Hannah and Her Sisters 1986; Born in East LA 1987; DOA 1988; Leviathan 1989; Little Monsters 1989; Coupe de Ville 1990; The Court-Martial of Jackie Robinson 1990; Home Alone 1990; City Slickers 1991; Home Alone 2: Lost in New York 1992; City Slickers II: the Legend of Curly's Gold 1994; Bushwhacked 1995; Celtic Pride 1996; Very Bad Things 1998; Tourist Trap 1998
Stern, Isaac Tonight We Sing 1953; Music of the Heart 1999
Stern, Wes The First Time 1969; Up in the Cellar 1970
Sternhagen, Frances Two People 1973; Fedora 1978; Starting Over 1979; Outland 1981; Independence Day 1983; Romantic Comedy 1983; Resting Place 1986; Bright Lights, Big City 1988; Communion 1989; See You in the Morning 1989; Misery 1990; Sibling Rivalry 1990; Doc

Hollywood 1991; Raising Cain 1992; She Woke Up 1992; Labor of Love: the Arlette Schweitzer Story 1993; Reunion 1994
Stevan, Robyn The Stepfather 1986; Bye Bye Blues 1989; Stepping Out 1991; While Justice Sleeps 1994
Stévenin, Jean-François Small Change 1976; Olivier Olivier 1991; Le Bossu 1997
Stevens, Andrew The Oregon Trail 1976; The Boys in Company C 1978; The Fury 1978; Death Hunt 1981; 10 to Midnight 1983; Counterforce 1987; Deadly Innocents 1988; The Terror Within 1988; Night Eyes 1990; Deadly Rivals 1992; Double Threat 1992; Munchie 1992; Illicit Dreams 1994; A Woman Scorned 1994; The Skateboard Kid II 1995
Stevens, Charles aka **Stevens, Charlie** The Three Musketeers 1921; The Black Pirate 1926; Mantrap 1926; Aces and Eights 1936; Warpath 1951
Stevens, Connie Rock-a-Bye Baby 1958; Susan Slade 1961; Parrish 1961; Palm Springs Weekend 1963; Never Too Late 1965; Two on a Guillotine 1965; Way... Way Out 1966; Mister Jerico 1969; Scorchy 1976; Bring Me the Head of Dobie Gillis 1988; Tapeheads 1988; Love Is All There Is 1996
Stevens, Craig The Doughgirls 1944; God Is My Co-Pilot 1945; Night unto Night 1949; Abbott and Costello Meet Dr Jekyll and Mr Hyde 1953; The Deadly Mantis 1957; Buchanan Rides Alone 1958; Gunn 1967; The Snoop Sisters 1972; SOB 1981
Stevens, Dodie Hound Dog Man 1959; Convicts Four 1962
Stevens, Fisher The Burning 1981; The Flamingo Kid 1984; My Science Project 1985; Short Circuit 1986; Short Circuit 2 1988; Reversal of Fortune 1990; Mystery Date 1991; Too Hot to Handle 1991; When the Party's Over 1992; Nina Takes a Lover 1993; Super Mario Bros 1993; Cold Fever 1994; Only You 1994; Hackers 1995
Stevens, Inger The Buccaneer 1958; Cry Terror 1958; The World, the Flesh and the Devil 1959; The New Interns 1964; A Guide for the Married Man 1967; The Long Ride Home 1967; Firecreek 1968; 5 Card Stud 1968; Hang 'em High 1968; House of Cards 1968; Madigan 1968; A Dream of Kings 1969; Run, Simon, Run 1970
Stevens, Joe Lone Star 1995; The Return of the Texas Chainsaw Massacre 1995
Stevens, K T aka **Stevens, Katharine** The Great Man's Lady 1942; Address Unknown 1944; Port of New York 1949; Harriet Craig 1950; Vice Squad 1953; Tumbleweed 1953; Bob & Carol & Ted & Alice 1969; They're Playing With Fire 1984
Stevens, Kay The Man from the Diner's Club 1963; The New Interns 1964
Stevens, Mark The Dark Corner 1946; From This Day Forward 1946; I Wonder Who's Kissing Her Now 1947; The Snake Pit 1948; The Street with No Name 1948; Dancing in the Dark 1949; Oh, You Beautiful Doll 1949; The Lost Hours 1952; Cry Vengeance 1954; Timetable 1956; Gunsight Ridge 1957; White Angel 1993
Stevens, Onslow Counsellor-at-Law 1933; Peg o' My Heart 1933; The Three Musketeers 1935; There Goes the Groom 1937;

Flight from Glory 1937; When Tomorrow Comes 1939; The Man Who Wouldn't Talk 1940; House of Dracula 1945; Angel on My Shoulder 1946; Walk a Crooked Mile 1948; Lorna Doone 1951; Sealed Cargo 1951; The San Francisco Story 1952; Them! 1954; They Rode West 1954; All the Fine Young Cannibals 1960
Stevens, Paul The Mask 1961; Corky 1972
Stevens, Robert Rachel's Man 1975; The Children 1990
Stevens, Ronnie Dentist in the Chair 1960; Dentist on the Job 1961; Nearly a Nasty Accident 1961; Some Girls Do 1969
Stevens, Stella Li'l Abner 1959; Man-Trap 1961; Girls! Girls! Girls! 1962; Too Late Blues 1962; The Courtship of Eddie's Father 1963; The Nutty Professor 1963; Advance to the Rear 1964; Get off My Back 1965; The Secret of My Success 1965; The Silencers 1966; Rage 1966; How to Save a Marriage and Ruin Your Life 1968; Where Angels Go...Trouble Follows 1968; Sol Madrid 1968; The Mad Room 1969; The Ballad of Cable Hogue 1970; A Town Called Hell 1971; The Poseidon Adventure 1972; Slaughter 1972; Arnold 1973; Cleopatra Jones and the Casino of Gold 1975; Nickelodeon 1976; The New Love Boat 1977; The Night They Took Miss Beautiful 1977; The Manitou 1978; Wacko 1981; Chained Heat 1983; Monster in the Closet 1983; The Masterpiece of Murder 1986; Murder in the City of Angels 1988; Jake Spanner, Private Eye 1989; Eye of the Stranger 1993; Hard Drive 1994; Illicit Dreams 1994; Grid Runners 1996
Stevens, Warren The Frogmen 1951; Deadline – USA 1952; Phone Call from a Stranger 1952; Red Skies of Montana 1952; Gorilla at Large 1954; Women's Prison 1955; Forbidden Planet 1956; Intent to Kill 1958; Hot Spell 1958; No Name on the Bullet 1959; Stagecoach to Dancer's Rock 1962; Gunpoint 1966
Stevenson, Charles Hot Water 1924; The Freshman 1925
Stevenson, Cynthia The Player 1992; Watch It 1992; Forget Paris 1995; Live Nude Girls 1995; Air Bud: Golden Receiver 1998
Stevenson, Houseley aka
Stevenson, Housley, aka
Stevenson, Housely Kidnapped 1948; The Lady Gambles 1949; Cave of Outlaws 1951; The Wild North 1952
Stevenson, Juliet Drowning by Numbers 1988; Ladder of Swords 1988; Truly Madly Deeply 1990; The Secret Rapture 1993; The Trial 1993; Emma 1996
Stevenson, Parker Lifeguard 1976; Stroker Ace 1983; That Secret Sunday 1986; Beauty and Denise 1989; Baywatch: Panic at Malibu Pier 1989; Shadow of a Stranger 1992; Are You Lonesome Tonight 1992; Official Denial 1993; Legion 1998
Stevenson, Ray The Return of the Native 1994; The Theory of Flight 1998
Stevenson, Venetia Darby's Rangers 1958; Day of the Outlaw 1959; The City of the Dead 1960; Seven Ways from Sundown 1960; Studs Lonigan 1960
Stewart, Alexandra Tarzan the Magnificent 1960; RoGoPaG 1962; Mickey One 1965; Maroc 7 1967; Only When I Larf 1968; The

Man Who Had Power over Women 1970; Zeppelin 1971; Day for Night 1973; The Marseilles Contract 1974; Black Moon 1974; The Uncanny 1977; Phobia 1980; Agency 1981; The Last Chase 1981; Sans Soleil 1983; Under the Cherry Moon 1986
Stewart, Amy Mark Twain & Me 1991; The Boys Club 1996
Stewart, Athole The Clairvoyant 1934; Accused 1936; Dusty Ermine 1936; Return of a Stranger 1937; The Spy in Black 1939
Stewart, Catherine Mary The Apple 1980; The Last Starfighter 1984; Night of the Comet 1984; With Intent to Kill 1984; Mischief 1985; The Annihilator 1986; Murder by the Book 1986; Nightflyers 1987; World Gone Wild 1988; Weekend at Bernie's 1989; Ordeal in the Arctic 1993; Samurai Cowboy 1993; The Sea Wolf 1993; Number One Fan 1994; Out of Annie's Past 1995
Stewart, Charlotte Eraserhead 1976; Human Highway 1982; Tremors 1989
Stewart, Elaine Everything I Have Is Yours 1952; The Adventures of Hajji Baba 1954; Brigadoon 1954; Night Passage 1957; High Hell 1957; Escort West 1959; The Rise and Fall of Legs Diamond 1960; The Most Dangerous Man Alive 1961
Stewart, Ewan Resurrected 1989; Stella Does Tricks 1997; The Closer You Get 2000
Stewart, French Magic Island 1995; Glory Daze 1995; Love Stinks 1999
Stewart, Jack The Gorbals Story 1949; A Case for PC 49 1950; The Dark Light 1951; Hunted 1952; Ragan 1967
Stewart, James Murder Man 1935; After the Thin Man 1936; Born to Dance 1936; The Gorgeous Hussy 1936; Rose Marie 1936; Wife vs Secretary 1936; Next Time We Love 1936; Small Town Girl 1936; Speed 1936; The Last Gangster 1937; Seventh Heaven 1937; Navy Blue and Gold 1937; Of Human Hearts 1938; The Shopworn Angel 1938; Vivacious Lady 1938; You Can't Take It with You 1938; Destry Rides Again 1939; The Ice Follies of 1939 1939; It's a Wonderful World 1939; Made for Each Other 1939; Mr Smith Goes to Washington 1939; The Mortal Storm 1940; The Philadelphia Story 1940; The Shop around the Corner 1940; No Time for Comedy 1940; Come Live with Me 1941; The Golden Hour 1941; Ziegfeld Girl 1941; It's a Wonderful Life 1946; Magic Town 1947; Call Northside 777 1948; On Our Merry Way 1948; Rope 1948; You Gotta Stay Happy 1948; Malaya 1949; The Stratton Story 1949; Broken Arrow 1950; Harvey 1950; The Jackpot 1950; Winchester '73 1950; No Highway 1951; Bend of the River 1952; The Greatest Show on Earth 1952; Carbine Williams 1952; The Glenn Miller Story 1953; The Naked Spur 1953; Thunder Bay 1953; Rear Window 1954; The Far Country 1955; The Man from Laramie 1955; Strategic Air Command 1955; The Man Who Knew Too Much 1956; Night Passage 1957; The Spirit of St Louis 1957; Bell, Book and Candle 1958; Vertigo 1958; Anatomy of a Murder 1959; The FBI Story 1959; The Mountain Road 1960; Two Rode Together

1961; *X-15* 1961; *How the West Was Won* 1962; *The Man Who Shot Liberty Valance* 1962; *Mr Hobbs Takes a Vacation* 1962; *Take Her, She's Mine* 1963; *Cheyenne Autumn* 1964; *Shenandoah* 1965; *Dear Brigitte* 1966; *The Flight of the Phoenix* 1966; *The Rare Breed* 1966; *Bandolero!* 1968; *Firecreek* 1968; *The Cheyenne Social Club* 1970; *Fools' Parade* 1971; *The Shootist* 1976; *Airport '77* 1977; *The Big Sleep* 1978; *The Magic of Lassie* 1978; *The Green Horizon* 1981; *Right of Way* 1983; *An American Tail: Fievel Goes West* 1991

Stewart, Johnny *Boots Malone* 1951; *Last of the Comanches* 1952

Stewart, Malcolm *For the Love of Aaron* 1993; *Beauty* 1998

Stewart, Marianne *Timetable* 1956; *The Facts of Life* 1960

Stewart, Martha *Daisy Kenyon* 1947; *I Wonder Who's Kissing Her Now* 1947

Stewart, Patrick *Hedda* 1975; *Excalibur* 1981; *Dune* 1984; *Code Name: Emerald* 1985; *Lady Jane* 1985; *Lifeforce* 1985; *Death Train* 1993; *Robin Hood: Men in Tights* 1993; *Gunmen* 1994; *The Pagemaster* 1994; *Star Trek: Generations* 1994; *Jeffrey* 1995; *The Canterville Ghost* 1996; *Star Trek: First Contact* 1996; *Conspiracy Theory* 1997; *Dad Savage* 1997; *Masterminds* 1997; *Safe House* 1997; *The Prince of Egypt* 1998; *Star Trek: Insurrection* 1998; *Let It Be Me* 1998

Stewart, Paul *Citizen Kane* 1941; *Government Girl* 1943; *Mr Lucky* 1943; *Champion* 1949; *Easy Living* 1949; *Twelve O'Clock High* 1949; *The Window* 1949; *Appointment with Danger* 1950; *Edge of Doom* 1950; *Deadline – USA* 1952; *Carbine Williams* 1952; *The Joe Louis Story* 1953; *The Juggler* 1953; *Deep in My Heart* 1954; *Hell on Frisco Bay* 1955; *Kiss Me Deadly* 1955; *Top Secret Affair* 1957; *A Child Is Waiting* 1962; *In Cold Blood* 1967; *Jigsaw* 1968; *Live a Little, Steal a Lot* 1974; *WC Fields and Me* 1976; *Opening Night* 1977; *Revenge of the Pink Panther* 1978; *Seduced* 1985

Stewart, Peggy *That Certain Age* 1938; *Back Street* 1941

Stewart, Penelope *Vigil* 1984; *Boulevard of Broken Dreams* 1988

Stewart, Rob *aka* **Stewart, Robert** *Someone to Die For* 1995; *Operation Delta Force* 1996

Stewart, Robin *The Haunted House of Horror* 1969; *The Legend of the Seven Golden Vampires* 1974

Stewart, Rod *Breaking Glass* 1980; *Play It to the Bone* 2000

Stewart, Roy *Sparrows* 1926; *Zoo in Budapest* 1933

Stewart, Sophie *Maria Marten, or the Murder in the Red Barn* 1935; *The Man Who Could Work Miracles* 1936; *Things to Come* 1936; *As You Like It* 1936; *The Return of the Scarlet Pimpernel* 1937; *Under the Red Robe* 1937; *Nurse Edith Cavell* 1939; *My Son, My Son* 1940; *The Lamp Still Burns* 1943; *Uncle Silas* 1947; *Made in Heaven* 1952; *Escape of the Amethyst* 1956

Stewart, Trish *Mansion of the Doomed* 1975; *Salvage* 1979

Stich, Patricia *aka* **Stich, Pat** *Halls of Anger* 1970; *The Loners* 1971

Stickney, Dorothy *And So They Were Married* 1936; *The Uninvited* 1944; *The Great Diamond Robbery* 1953; *I Never Sang for My Father* 1969; *The Homecoming: a Christmas Story* 1971

Stickney, Phyllis Yvonne *Talkin' Dirty after Dark* 1991; *Tina: What's Love Got to Do with It* 1993

Stidder, Ted *aka* **Stidder, Teddie** *Home Is Where the Hart Is* 1987; *Captive* 1991

Stiers, David Ogden *Magic* 1978; *Harry's War* 1981; *Anatomy of an Illness* 1984; *Better Off Dead* 1985; *Creator* 1985; *Mrs Delafield Wants to Marry* 1986; *J Edgar Hoover* 1987; *The Accidental Tourist* 1988; *Another Woman* 1988; *The Final Days* 1989; *How to Murder a Millionaire* 1990; *Beauty and the Beast* 1991; *Doc Hollywood* 1991; *Falsely Accused* 1993; *Iron Will* 1994; *Past Tense* 1994; *Mighty Aphrodite* 1995; *Pocahontas* 1995; *Steal Big, Steal Little* 1995; *To Face Her Past* 1996; *Beauty and the Beast: the Enchanted Christmas* 1997; *Meet Wally Sparks* 1997; *Krippendorf's Tribe* 1998; *Pocahontas II: Journey to a New World* 1998

Stiglitz, Hugo *Tintorera* 1977; *Naked Lies* 1997

Stiles, Julia *Before Women Had Wings* 1997; *10 Things I Hate about You* 1999; *Down to You* 2000

Still, Aline *A World without Pity* 1989; *Autobus* 1991

Stiller, Ben *Hot Pursuit* 1987; *Fresh Horses* 1988; *Next of Kin* 1989; *Stella* 1990; *Working Trash* 1990; *Highway to Hell* 1992; *Reality Bites* 1994; *The Cable Guy* 1996; *Flirting with Disaster* 1996; *If Lucy Fell* 1996; *Zero Effect* 1997; *Permanent Midnight* 1998; *There's Something about Mary* 1998; *Your Friends & Neighbours* 1998; *Mystery Men* 1999; *Keeping the Faith* 2000

Stiller, Jerry *The Taking of Pelham One Two Three* 1974; *The Ritz* 1976; *Those Lips, Those Eyes* 1980; *Seize the Day* 1986; *Hot Pursuit* 1987; *Nadine* 1987; *Hairspray* 1988; *Little Vegas* 1990; *The Pickle* 1993; *Stag* 1996

Sting *Quadrophenia* 1979; *Radio On* 1979; *Brimstone and Treacle* 1982; *Dune* 1984; *The Bride* 1985; *Plenty* 1985; *Stormy Monday* 1987; *The Adventures of Baron Munchausen* 1988; *The Grotesque* 1995; *Lock, Stock and Two Smoking Barrels* 1998

Stirling, Pamela *Candlelight in Algeria* 1943; *Conspiracy in Teheran* 1947; *Nor the Moon by Night* 1958

Stirner, Brian *All Creatures Great and Small* 1974; *Overlord* 1975

Stock, Barbara *Wizards of the Lost Kingdom* 1985; *Hijacked: Flight 285* 1996

Stock, Nigel *Brighton Rock* 1947; *Eyewitness* 1956; *The Silent Enemy* 1958; *Damn the Defiant!* 1962; *The Password Is Courage* 1962; *The Lion in Winter* 1968; *The Lost Continent* 1968; *Cromwell* 1970; *Bequest to the Nation* 1972; *Young Sherlock Holmes* 1985

Stockdale, Carl *The Fall of Babylon* 1919; *Oliver Twist* 1922

Stockfeld, Betty *The Man Who Changed His Name* 1934; *The Lad* 1935; *I See Ice* 1938; *Guilty?* 1956

Stock-Poynton, Amy *Gunsmoke: the Last Apache* 1990; *Gunsmoke: To the Last Man* 1992; *Beanstalk* 1994

Stockwell, Dean *Anchors Aweigh* 1945; *The Green Years* 1946; *The Arnelo Affair* 1947; *The Boy with Green Hair* 1948; *Down to the Sea in Ships* 1949; *The Secret Garden* 1949; *Kim* 1950; *Stars in My Crown* 1950; *Cattle Drive* 1951; *Gun for a Coward* 1957; *Compulsion* 1959; *Sons and Lovers* 1960; *Long Day's Journey into Night* 1962; *Psych-Out* 1968; *The Dunwich Horror* 1970; *The Last Movie* 1971; *The Loners* 1971; *Tracks* 1977; *Human Highway* 1982; *Alsino and the Condor* 1982; *Dune* 1984; *Paris, Texas* 1984; *The Legend of Billie Jean* 1985; *To Live and Die in LA* 1985; *Blue Velvet* 1986; *Beverly Hills Cop II* 1987; *Gardens of Stone* 1987; *The Time Guardian* 1987; *Married to the Mob* 1988; *Tucker: the Man and His Dream* 1988; *Palais Royale* 1988; *Limit Up* 1989; *Catchfire* 1990; *The Player* 1992; *Shame* 1992; *Bonanza – the Return* 1993; *The Innocent* 1993; *Chasers* 1994; *Hard Evidence* 1994; *In the Line of Duty: the Price of Vengeance* 1994; *Madonna: Innocence Lost* 1994; *Naked Souls* 1995; *Midnight Blue* 1996; *Mr Wrong* 1996; *Unabomber* 1996; *Air Force One* 1997; *The Rainmaker* 1997; *The Shadow Men* 1997; *McHale's Navy* 1997; *Living in Peril* 1997

Stockwell, Guy *The War Lord* 1965; *Beau Geste* 1966; *Blindfold* 1966; *Tobruk* 1966; *And Now Miguel* 1966; *The King's Pirate* 1967; *In Enemy Country* 1968; *It's Alive* 1974; *Santa Sangre* 1989

Stockwell, Harry *All over Town* 1937; *Snow White and the Seven Dwarfs* 1937

Stockwell, John *Christine* 1983; *Losin' It* 1983; *City Limits* 1985; *My Science Project* 1985; *Top Gun* 1986; *Radioactive Dreams* 1986; *Dangerously Close* 1986; *Born to Ride* 1991; *Stag* 1996; *Breast Men* 1997

Stoddard, Malcolm *The Godsend* 1980; *Tree of Hands* 1988

Stoker, Austin *Battle for the Planet of the Apes* 1973; *Abby* 1974; *Assault on Precinct 13* 1976

Stokowski, Leopold *The Big Broadcast of 1937* 1936; *One Hundred Men and a Girl* 1937

Stole, Mink *Multiple Maniacs* 1970; *Mondo Trasho* 1970; *Pink Flamingos* 1972; *Female Trouble* 1974; *Desperate Living* 1977; *Polyester* 1981; *Dark Secrets* 1995; *Lost Highway* 1996; *Pecker* 1998; *But I'm a Cheerleader* 1999

Stoler, Shirley *The Honeymoon Killers* 1969; *Seven Beauties* 1976; *The Deer Hunter* 1978; *Frankenhooker* 1990

Stoll, Gunther *The Castle of Fu Manchu* 1968; *Cold Blood* 1975

Stollery, David *Darling, How Could You!* 1951; *Westward Ho the Wagons!* 1956

Stoltz, Eric *Fast Times at Ridgemont High* 1982; *Running Hot* 1983; *The Wild Life* 1984; *Code Name: Emerald* 1985; *Mask* 1985; *Lionheart* 1986; *Some Kind of Wonderful* 1987; *Haunted Summer* 1988; *The Fly II* 1989; *Say Anything* 1989; *Memphis Belle* 1990; *The Waterdance* 1991; *The Heart of Justice* 1992; *Bodies, Rest and Motion* 1993; *Foreign Affairs* 1993; *Killing Zoe* 1993; *Naked in New York* 1994; *Pulp Fiction* 1994; *Roommates* 1994; *Sleep with Me* 1994; *Don't Look Back* 1995; *Fluke* 1995; *Kicking and Screaming* 1995; *Little Women* 1995; *Rob Roy* 1995; *Grace of My Heart* 1996; *Inside* 1996; *Jerry Maguire* 1996; *Keys to Tulsa* 1996; *Anaconda* 1997; *Mr Jealousy* 1997; *Hi-Life* 1998; *A Murder of Crows* 1998; *Our Guys: Outrage in Glen Ridge* 1999; *The House of Mirth* 2000

Stolze, Lena *Swing* 1983; *The Nasty Girl* 1990

Stona, Winston *The Harder They Come* 1972; *The Lunatic* 1992

Stone, Bobby *Ghosts in the Night* 1943; *Follow the Leader* 1944

Stone, Christopher *The Grasshopper* 1970; *The Howling* 1981; *Cujo* 1983; *Runaway Daughters* 1994

Stone, Doug *Gordy* 1994; *The Swan Princess: The Secret of the Castle* 1997

Stone, Fred *Alice Adams* 1935; *The Trail of the Lonesome Pine* 1936; *Life Begins in College* 1937; *The Westerner* 1940

Stone, George E *Five Star Final* 1931; *Little Caesar* 1931; *Taxi!* 1932; *The Vampire Bat* 1933; *Viva Villa!* 1934; *Frisco Kid* 1935; *The Housekeeper's Daughter* 1939; *Cherokee Strip* 1940; *The Face behind the Mask* 1941; *Road Show* 1941; *Abie's Irish Rose* 1946; *Bloodhounds of Broadway* 1952

Stone, Harold J *The Harder They Fall* 1956; *Somebody Up There Likes Me* 1956; *The Wrong Man* 1956; *House of Numbers* 1957; *The Garment Jungle* 1957; *These Thousand Hills* 1959; *The Man with the X-Ray Eyes* 1963; *Showdown* 1963; *Girl Happy* 1965; *The Big Mouth* 1967; *The Seven Minutes* 1971; *Hardly Working* 1981

Stone, James *Five Guns West* 1955; *Barefoot in the Park* 1967

Stone, Leonard *The Big Mouth* 1967; *Getting Straight* 1970; *Willy Wonka and the Chocolate Factory* 1971; *Once upon a Spy* 1980

Stone, Lewis *The Prisoner of Zenda* 1922; *The Lost World* 1925; *The Private Life of Helen of Troy* 1927; *The Patriot* 1928; *A Woman of Affairs* 1928; *Madame X* 1929; *Wild Orchids* 1929; *The Big House* 1930; *Romance* 1930; *Inspiration* 1931; *Mata Hari* 1931; *The Secret Six* 1931; *The Sin of Madelon Claudet* 1931; *The Mask of Fu Manchu* 1932; *Red-Headed Woman* 1932; *The Wet Parade* 1932; *Bureau of Missing Persons* 1933; *Queen Christina* 1933; *The White Sister* 1933; *Treasure Island* 1934; *The Girl from Missouri* 1934; *China Seas* 1935; *David Copperfield* 1935; *Vanessa, Her Love Story* 1935; *Public Hero No 1* 1935; *Suzy* 1936; *Small Town Girl* 1936; *The Man Who Cried Wolf* 1937; *Bad Man of Brimstone* 1938; *Judge Hardy's Children* 1938; *Love Finds Andy Hardy* 1938; *Out West with the Hardys* 1938; *Yellow Jack* 1938; *You're Only Young Once* 1938; *Andy Hardy Gets Spring Fever* 1939; *The Hardys Ride High* 1939; *The Ice Follies of 1939* 1939; *Judge Hardy and Son* 1939; *Andy Hardy Meets Debutante* 1940; *Andy Hardy's Private Secretary* 1941; *Life Begins for Andy Hardy* 1941; *Andy Hardy's Double Life* 1942; *The Courtship of Andy Hardy* 1942; *Andy Hardy's Blonde Trouble* 1944; *The Hoodlum Saint* 1946; *Love Laughs at Andy Hardy* 1946; *State of the Union* 1948; *Any Number Can Play* 1949; *Key to the City* 1950; *Stars in My Crown* 1950; *Angels in the Outfield* 1951; *The Prisoner of Zenda* 1952; *All the Brothers Were Valiant* 1953

Stone, Marianne *Passport to Treason* 1956; *Lolita* 1961; *The Night of the Prowler* 1962; *Vault of Horror* 1973

Stone, Matt *Orgazmo* 1997; *BASEketball* 1998; *South Park: Bigger, Longer & Uncut* 1999

Stone, Milburn *Branded* 1950; *Roadblock* 1951; *Arrowhead* 1953; *The Siege at Red River* 1954; *Smoke Signal* 1955

Stone, Philip *The Shining* 1980; *Green Ice* 1981; *Indiana Jones and the Temple of Doom* 1984; *The Baby of Macon* 1993

Stone, Sharon *Deadly Blessing* 1981; *Calendar Girl Murders* 1984; *Irreconcilable Differences* 1984; *King Solomon's Mines* 1985; *Allan Quatermain and the Lost City of Gold* 1987; *Police Academy 4: Citizens on Patrol* 1987; *Cold Steel* 1987; *Action Jackson* 1988; *Beyond the Stars* 1988; *Nico* 1988; *Blood and Sand* 1989; *Total Recall* 1990; *He Said, She Said* 1991; *Where Sleeping Dogs Lie* 1991; *Year of the Gun* 1991; *Scissors* 1991; *Basic Instinct* 1992; *Diary of a Hit Man* 1992; *Sliver* 1993; *Intersection* 1994; *The Specialist* 1994; *Casino* 1995; *Last Dance* 1995; *The Quick and the Dead* 1995; *Diabolique* 1996; *Antz* 1998; *Gloria* 1998; *The Mighty* 1998; *Sphere* 1998; *The Muse* 1999; *Simpatico* 1999; *If These Walls Could Talk 2* 2000

Stone, Stuart *Heavenly Bodies* 1985; *The Boys Club* 1996; *What Kind of Mother Are You?* 1996

Stoppa, Paolo *La Beauté du Diable* 1949; *Miracle in Milan* 1950; *The Miller's Wife* 1955; *The Leopard* 1962; *Becket* 1964; *Behold a Pale Horse* 1964; *The Visit* 1964; *After the Fox* 1966

Storch, Arthur *The Strange One* 1957; *Girl of the Night* 1960

Storch, Larry *The Last Blitzkrieg* 1958; *Who Was That Lady?* 1960; *Forty Pounds of Trouble* 1962; *Wild and Wonderful* 1964; *Sex and the Single Girl* 1964; *Bus Riley's Back in Town* 1965; *That Funny Feeling* 1965; *A Very Special Favor* 1965; *The Great Bank Robbery* 1969

Storey, Ruth *The Blue Gardenia* 1953; *Bells Are Ringing* 1960; *The Subterraneans* 1960

Storke, Adam *Mystic Pizza* 1988; *Death Becomes Her* 1992; *Highway to Hell* 1992; *Lifepod* 1993; *Escape from Terror* 1995

Storm, Gale *It Happened on Fifth Avenue* 1947; *The Underworld Story* 1950

Stormare, Peter *Damage* 1992; *Fargo* 1995; *Le Polygraphe* 1996; *Playing God* 1997; *Hamilton* 1998; *8mm* 1999; *Purgatory* 1999; *Circus* 1999; *The Million Dollar Hotel* 1999

Stossel, Ludwig *The Man I Married* 1940; *Great Guns* 1941; *Man Hunt* 1941; *Hers to Hold* 1943; *Hitler's Madman* 1943; *Bluebeard* 1944; *Dillinger* 1945; *House of Dracula* 1945; *The Beginning or the End* 1947; *Escape Me Never* 1947; *The Great Sinner* 1949; *Somebody*

RadioTimes

ACTORS' INDEX RadioTimes

Sykes, Eric *Orders Are Orders* 1954; *Tommy the Toreador* 1959; *Watch Your Stern* 1960; *Very Important Person* 1961; *Kill or Cure* 1962; *Heavens Above!* 1963; *The Bargee* 1964; *Rotten to the Core* 1965; *Those Magnificent Men in Their Flying Machines* 1965; *One Way Pendulum* 1965; *The Liquidator* 1966; *The Spy with a Cold Nose* 1966; *The Plank* 1967; *Shalako* 1968; *Monte Carlo or Bust* 1969; *The Boys in Blue* 1983; *Splitting Heirs* 1993

Sylvester, Harold *Part 2, Sounder* 1976; *Fast Break* 1979; *Uncommon Valor* 1983; *Vision Quest* 1985; *The Reluctant Agent* 1989; *A Cop for the Killing* 1990; *Blind Hate* 1991; *Corrina, Corrina* 1994; *Trippin'* 1999

Sylvester, William *Give Us This Day* 1949; *Appointment in London* 1952; *The Yellow Balloon* 1952; *Albert, RN* 1953; *House of Blackmail* 1953; *A Stranger Came Home* 1954; *Postmark for Danger* 1955; *High Tide at Noon* 1957; *Dublin Nightmare* 1958; *Gorgo* 1960; *Offbeat* 1960; *Information Received* 1962; *Ring of Spies* 1963; *Devil Doll* 1964; *Devils of Darkness* 1964; *The Hand of Night* 1966; *2001: a Space Odyssey* 1968; *Busting* 1974

Sylvie *The End of the Day* 1939; *Les Anges du Péché* 1943; *Thérèse Raquin* 1953; *Ulysses* 1954

Sylwan, Kari *Cries and Whispers* 1972; *Face to Face* 1976

Syms, Sylvia *My Teenage Daughter* 1956; *The Birthday Present* 1957; *The Moonraker* 1957; *No Time for Tears* 1957; *Woman in a Dressing Gown* 1957; *Bachelor of Hearts* 1958; *Ferry to Hong Kong* 1958; *Ice Cold in Alex* 1958; *No Trees in the Street* 1958; *Expresso Bongo* 1959; *Conspiracy of Hearts* 1960; *The World of Suzie Wong* 1960; *Flame in the Streets* 1961; *Victim* 1961; *The Punch and Judy Man* 1962; *The Quare Fellow* 1962; *The World Ten Times Over* 1963; *The Big Job* 1965; *Danger Route* 1967; *Hostile Witness* 1968; *The Desperados* 1969; *Run Wild, Run Free* 1969; *Born to Win* 1971; *Asylum* 1972; *The Tamarind Seed* 1974; *Give Us Tomorrow* 1978; *There Goes the Bride* 1979; *A Chorus of Disapproval* 1988; *Shirley Valentine* 1989; *Dirty Weekend* 1992; *Shining Through* 1992; *Staggered* 1993; *Food of Love* 1997

Szabo, Laszlo *Le Petit Soldat* 1960; *Alphaville* 1965; *Made in USA* 1966; *The Confession* 1970; *Passion* 1982; *L'Amour par Terre* 1984; *L'Eau Froide* 1994

Szapolowska, Grazyna *No End* 1984; *Hanussen* 1988; *A Short Film about Love* 1988

Szarabajka, Keith *Protocol* 1984; *Marie: a True Story* 1985; *Billy Galvin* 1986; *Nightlife* 1989; *A Perfect World* 1993; *One Woman's Courage* 1994

Szekely, Miklos B *Damnation* 1988; *Rothschild's Violin* 1996

Szemes, Mari *Diary for My Children* 1982; *Diary for My Loves* 1987

Szeps, Henri *Run, Rebecca, Run* 1981; *Warming Up* 1983; *Travelling North* 1986; *Les Patterson Saves the World* 1987

Szubanski, Magda *Babe* 1995; *Babe: Pig in the City* 1998

T

Tabakov, Oleg *War and Peace* 1966; *Oblomov* 1980; *Dream Flights* 1983

Tablian, Vic *Sphinx* 1980; *Raiders of the Lost Ark* 1981

Tabori, Kristoffer *Family Flight* 1972; *Journey through Rosebud* 1972

Tabu *Maachis* 1996; *Saajan Chale Sasural* 1997

Taeger, Ralph *X-15* 1961; *The Delta Factor* 1970

Tafler, Sydney *aka* **Tafler, Sidney** *It Always Rains on Sunday* 1947; *Dance Hall* 1950; *Assassin for Hire* 1951; *Hotel Sahara* 1951; *Emergency Call* 1952; *The Glass Cage* 1955; *The Woman for Joe* 1955; *Fire Maidens from Outer Space* 1956; *Booby Trap* 1957; *The Bank Raiders* 1958; *Bottoms Up* 1959; *Light Up the Sky* 1960; *Let's Get Married* 1960; *The Birthday Party* 1968; *The Adventurers* 1970

Tagawa, Cary-Hiroyuki *Spellbinder* 1988; *Kickboxer 2: the Road Back* 1990; *Showdown in Little Tokyo* 1991; *American Me* 1992; *Nemesis* 1993; *Rising Sun* 1993; *Picture Bride* 1994; *Mortal Kombat* 1995; *The Phantom* 1996; *Danger Zone* 1996; *Top of the World* 1997; *Bridge of Dragons* 1999

Taggart, Ben *Before I Hang* 1940; *Man Made Monster* 1941

Taggart, Rita *Wait till Your Mother Gets Home!* 1983; *Torchlight* 1984; *Weeds* 1987; *Splash, Too* 1988; *House III: The Horror Show* 1989; *Coupe de Ville* 1990; *Crossing the Bridge* 1992

Taghmaoui, Saïd *La Haine* 1995; *Hideous Kinky* 1998

Tagore, Sharmila *The World of Apu* 1959; *Devi* 1960; *Waqt* 1965; *Company Limited* 1971; *Mississippi Masala* 1991

Taguchi, Tomoroh *Tetsuo* 1989; *Tetsuo II: Body Hammer* 1991

Tahil, Dalip *The Perfect Murder* 1988; *Baazigar* 1993

Taka, Miiko *Hell to Eternity* 1960; *Cry for Happy* 1961; *A Global Affair* 1964; *Walk, Don't Run* 1966; *The Challenge* 1982

Takakura, Ken *Too Late the Hero* 1970; *Black Rain* 1989; *Mr Baseball* 1992

Takarada, Akira *Godzilla* 1954; *Invasion of the Astro-Monster* 1965; *Ebirah, Horror of the Deep* 1966; *Minbo – or the Gentle Art of Japanese Extortion* 1992

Takashima, Tadao *Frankenstein Meets the Devil Fish* 1964; *Son of Godzilla* 1967

Takei, George *Ice Palace* 1960; *Hell to Eternity* 1960; *Red Line 7000* 1965; *Walk, Don't Run* 1966; *The Green Berets* 1968; *Star Trek: the Motion Picture* 1979; *Star Trek II: the Wrath of Khan* 1982; *Star Trek III: the Search for Spock* 1984; *Star Trek IV: the Voyage Home* 1986; *Return from the River Kwai* 1988; *Star Trek V: the Final Frontier* 1989; *Blood Oath* 1990; *Star Trek VI: the Undiscovered Country* 1991; *Oblivion* 1993; *Kissinger and Nixon* 1995; *Mulan* 1998

Takenaka, Naoto *Shall We Dance?* 1995; *Tokyo Fist* 1995

Talbot, Lyle *Love Is a Racket* 1932; *Three on a Match* 1932; *The Purchase Price* 1932; *The Thirteenth Guest* 1932; *Havana Widows* 1933; *20,000 Years in Sing Sing* 1933; *Ladies They Talk About* 1933; *Mandalay* 1934; *One Night of Love* 1934; *Fog over Frisco* 1934; *The Case of the Lucky Legs* 1935; *Oil for the Lamps of China* 1935; *Our Little Girl* 1935; *Go West, Young Man* 1936; *The Singing Kid* 1936; *Vengeance* 1937; *Westbound Limited* 1937; *Second Fiddle* 1939; *Miracle on Main Street* 1940; *Sensations* 1944; *Glen or Glenda* 1953; *Jail Bait* 1954; *City of Fear* 1959

Talbot, Nita *Bundle of Joy* 1956; *I Married a Woman* 1958; *Who's Got the Action?* 1962; *That Funny Feeling* 1965; *Girl Happy* 1965; *Buck and the Preacher* 1972; *Serial* 1980; *Frightmare* 1981; *The Check Is in the Mail* 1986; *Puppet Master II* 1990; *Amityville 1992: It's About Time* 1992

Talbott, Gloria *Crashout* 1955; *Lucy Gallant* 1955; *We're No Angels* 1955; *The Oklahoman* 1957; *The Cyclops* 1957; *Daughter of Dr Jekyll* 1957; *Cattle Empire* 1958; *I Married a Monster from Outer Space* 1958; *The Oregon Trail* 1959; *Alias Jesse James* 1959; *The Leech Woman* 1960; *Arizona Raiders* 1965; *An Eye for an Eye* 1966

Talbott, Michael *Foolin' Around* 1980; *Deadly Justice* 1995

Tallichet, Margaret *Stranger on the Third Floor* 1940; *It Started with Eve* 1941

Tallier, Nadine *Girls at Sea* 1958; *The Treasure of San Teresa* 1959

Tallman, Patricia *Knightriders* 1981; *Night of the Living Dead* 1990

Talmadge, Constance *Intolerance* 1916; *The Fall of Babylon* 1919

Talman, William *The Woman on Pier 13* 1949; *Armored Car Robbery* 1950; *The Racket* 1951; *One Minute to Zero* 1952; *City That Never Sleeps* 1953; *The Hitch-Hiker* 1953; *Crashout* 1955; *Smoke Signal* 1955; *Big House, USA* 1955; *The Ballad of Josie* 1968

Talton, Alix *aka* **Talton, Alice** *The Great Jewel Robber* 1950; *Rock around the Clock* 1956; *The Deadly Mantis* 1957; *Romanoff and Juliet* 1961

Tamba, Tetsuro *The 7th Dawn* 1964; *You Only Live Twice* 1967

Tamblyn, Russ *Seven Brides for Seven Brothers* 1954; *Hit the Deck* 1955; *Many Rivers to Cross* 1955; *The Fastest Gun Alive* 1956; *The Last Hunt* 1956; *Don't Go Near the Water* 1957; *Peyton Place* 1957; *High School Confidential* 1958; *tom thumb* 1958; *Cimarron* 1960; *West Side Story* 1961; *Follow the Boys* 1963; *The Haunting* 1963; *The Long Ships* 1963; *The Female Bunch* 1969; *War of the Gargantuas* 1970; *Dracula vs Frankenstein* 1970; *The Last Movie* 1971; *Human Highway* 1982; *Running Mates* 1992; *Johnny Mysto* 1996

Tamblyn, Rusty *Samson and Delilah* 1949; *Retreat, Hell!* 1952

Tambor, Jeffrey *...And Justice for All* 1979; *Saturday the 14th* 1981; *Take Your Best Shot* 1982; *No Small Affair* 1984; *Three O'Clock High* 1987; *Brenda Starr* 1989; *A Perfect Little Murder* 1990; *Life Stinks* 1991; *A House in the Hills* 1993; *Big Bully* 1996; *The Man Who Captured Eichmann* 1996; *Weapons of Mass Distraction* 1997; *Doctor Dolittle* 1998; *Meet Joe Black* 1998; *There's Something about Mary* 1998; *Teaching Mrs Tingle* 1999; *Girl, Interrupted* 1999

Tamiroff, Akim *The Big Broadcast of 1936* 1935; *The Gay Deception* 1935; *The Lives of a Bengal Lancer* 1935; *The Last Outpost* 1935; *Anthony Adverse* 1936; *Desire* 1936; *The General Died at Dawn* 1936; *The Adventures of Michael Strogoff* 1937; *High, Wide and Handsome* 1937; *The Buccaneer* 1938; *Spawn of the North* 1938; *Union Pacific* 1939; *Paris Honeymoon* 1939; *The Great McGinty* 1940; *Northwest Mounted Police* 1940; *Texas Rangers Ride Again* 1940; *The Way of All Flesh* 1940; *The Corsican Brothers* 1941; *Tortilla Flat* 1942; *Five Graves to Cairo* 1943; *For Whom the Bell Tolls* 1943; *His Butler's Sister* 1943; *Can't Help Singing* 1944; *Dragon Seed* 1944; *The Miracle of Morgan's Creek* 1944; *Pardon My Past* 1945; *Thieves' Holiday* 1946; *Fiesta* 1947; *The Gangster* 1947; *My Girl Tisa* 1948; *Black Magic* 1949; *They Who Dare* 1953; *Desert Legion* 1953; *You Know What Sailors Are* 1954; *Cartouche* 1954; *Confidential Report* 1955; *Anastasia* 1956; *Escape of the Amethyst* 1956; *The Black Sleep* 1956; *Touch of Evil* 1958; *Me and the Colonel* 1958; *The Bacchantes* 1960; *Ocean's Eleven* 1960; *Romanoff and Juliet* 1961; *The Trial* 1962; *The Black Tulip* 1963; *Topkapi* 1964; *Panic Button* 1964; *Alphaville* 1965; *Lord Jim* 1965; *After the Fox* 1966; *Hotel Paradiso* 1966; *Lt Robin Crusoe, USN* 1966; *The Liquidator* 1966; *Great Catherine* 1968; *The Great Bank Robbery* 1969

Tamm, Mary *Tales That Witness Madness* 1973; *The Odessa File* 1974; *The Likely Lads* 1976

Tamura, Takahiro *Tora! Tora! Tora!* 1970; *Muddy River* 1981

Tan, Philip *Vroom* 1988; *China Cry* 1990; *Showdown in Little Tokyo* 1991; *Bloodsport II: The Next Kumite* 1996

Tanaka, Haruo *The Straits of Love and Hate* 1937; *Good Morning* 1959

Tanaka, Kinuyo *Musashi Miyamoto* 1944; *The Victory of Women* 1946; *Five Women around Utamaro* 1946; *The Love of Sumako the Actress* 1947; *Women of the Night* 1948; *Hen in the Wind* 1948; *My Love Has Been Burning* 1949; *Miss Oyu* 1951; *The Life of Oharu* 1952; *Ugetsu Monogatari* 1953; *Sansho the Bailiff* 1954; *The Ballad of Narayama* 1958; *Equinox Flower* 1958; *Alone on the Pacific* 1963

Tandy, Jessica *The Seventh Cross* 1944; *The Green Years* 1946; *Forever Amber* 1947; *September Affair* 1950; *The Desert Fox* 1951; *The Light in the Forest* 1958; *Hemingway's Adventures of a Young Man* 1962; *The Birds* 1963; *Butley* 1973; *Honky Tonk Freeway* 1981; *Best Friends* 1982; *Still of the Night* 1982; *The World According to Garp* 1982; *The Bostonians* 1984; *Cocoon* 1985; **batteries not included* 1987; *Foxfire* 1987; *The House on Carroll Street* 1987; *Cocoon: the Return* 1988; *Driving Miss Daisy* 1989; *Fried Green Tomatoes at the Whistle Stop Cafe* 1991; *The Story Lady* 1991; *Used People* 1992; *Camilla* 1993; *To Dance with the White Dog* 1993; *Nobody's Fool* 1994

Tani, Yoko *The Wind Cannot Read* 1958; *Piccadilly Third Stop* 1960; *The Savage Innocents* 1960; *Invasion* 1965

Tannen, Charles *The Return of Frank James* 1940; *Careful, Soft Shoulder* 1942

Tanner, Mary *A Billion for Boris* 1984; *Willy/Milly* 1986; *Return to Green Acres* 1990

Tanner, Tony *The Pleasure Girls* 1965; *Stop the World, I Want to Get Off* 1966

Tapley, Colin *The Last Outpost* 1935; *Thank You, Jeeves* 1936; *Cloudburst* 1951; *Wings of Danger* 1952; *The Steel Key* 1953; *The Dam Busters* 1954; *Emergency* 1962

Tarantino, Quentin *Reservoir Dogs* 1991; *Pulp Fiction* 1994; *Sleep with Me* 1994; *Somebody to Love* 1994; *Desperado* 1995; *Destiny Turns on the Radio* 1995; *Four Rooms* 1995; *From Dusk till Dawn* 1995

Tarbuck, Barbara *The Death of the Incredible Hulk* 1990; *The Tie That Binds* 1995; *Before He Wakes* 1998

Tarso, Ignacio Lopez *Macario* 1960; *Under the Volcano* 1984

Tashman, Lilyan *So This Is Paris* 1926; *Camille* 1927; *Bulldog Drummond* 1929; *Gold Diggers of Broadway* 1929; *The Marriage Playground* 1929; *Girls about Town* 1931; *One Heavenly Night* 1931; *Scarlet Dawn* 1932; *Riptide* 1934

Tate, Harry *Happy* 1933; *Wings of the Morning* 1937

Tate, Larenz *Menace II Society* 1993; *No Ordinary Summer* 1994; *Dead Presidents* 1995; *Love Jones* 1997; *The Postman* 1997; *Why Do Fools Fall in Love?* 1998

Tate, Lincoln *Acquasanta Joe* 1971; *On the Third Day Arrived the Crow* 1973

Tate, Nick *The Devil's Playground* 1976; *Summerfield* 1977; *The Gold and Glory* 1984; *The Empty Beach* 1985; *A Cry in the Dark* 1988

Tate, Reginald *The Phantom Light* 1934; *Poison Pen* 1939; *The Man from Morocco* 1944; *Uncle Silas* 1947; *The Secret People* 1951; *Escape Route* 1952; *The Story of Robin Hood and His Merrie Men* 1952; *The Malta Story* 1953

Tate, Sharon *Don't Make Waves* 1967; *The Fearless Vampire Killers* 1967; *Valley of the Dolls* 1967; *Eye of the Devil* 1968; *Twelve plus One* 1969; *The Wrecking Crew* 1969

Tati, Jacques *Jour de Fête* 1947; *School for Postmen* 1947; *Monsieur Hulot's Holiday* 1953; *Mon Oncle* 1958; *Cours du Soir* 1967; *Playtime* 1967; *Traffic* 1972

Tatum, Bradford *The Cool and the Crazy* 1994; *Powder* 1995; *Within the Rock* 1995; *Black Scorpion* 1995

Taube, Aino *aka* **Taube-Henrikson, Aino** *One Single Night* 1939; *Face to Face* 1976

Taube, Sven-Bertil *The Buttercup Chain* 1970; *Puppet on a Chain* 1970; *A Game for Vultures* 1979; *Jerusalem* 1996

Tauber, Richard *Heart's Desire* 1935; *Land without Music* 1936; *Pagliacci* 1936

Taubman, Tiffany *Nowhere to Run* 1992; *See Jane Run* 1995

Tavernier, Nils *Story of Women* 1988; *L.627* 1992; *Mina Tannenbaum* 1993; *D'Artagnan's Daughter* 1994

Taxier, Arthur *The Cover Girl Murders* 1993; *Open Fire* 1995
Tayback, Vic *Door-to-Door Maniac* 1961; *The Blue Knight* 1973; *Alice Doesn't Live Here Anymore* 1974; *The Gambler* 1974; *Lepke* 1975; *Weekend Warriors* 1986; *All Dogs Go to Heaven* 1989; *Knife Edge* 1990; *Treasure Island* 1991
Taylor, Benedict *The Watcher in the Woods* 1982; *Thirteen at Dinner* 1985; *Every Time We Say Goodbye* 1986; *Duel of Hearts* 1990; *Charles & Diana: Unhappily Ever After* 1992
Taylor, Buck *The Wild Angels* 1966; *Pony Express Rider* 1976; *Triumphs of a Man Called Horse* 1983; *Down the Long Hills* 1987
Taylor, Chip *The Catamount Killing* 1974; *Melvin and Howard* 1980
Taylor, Christine *The Brady Bunch Movie* 1995; *Here Come the Munsters* 1995; *The Craft* 1996; *A Very Brady Sequel* 1996; *Overnight Delivery* 1997; *The Wedding Singer* 1998
Taylor, Delores *Billy Jack* 1971; *The Trial of Billy Jack* 1974; *Billy Jack Goes to Washington* 1977
Taylor, Don *The Naked City* 1948; *For the Love of Mary* 1948; *Battleground* 1949; *Ambush* 1949; *Father of the Bride* 1950; *The Blue Veil* 1951; *Father's Little Dividend* 1951; *Flying Leathernecks* 1951; *Japanese War Bride* 1952; *Destination Gobi* 1953; *Stalag 17* 1953; *Men of Sherwood Forest* 1954; *Johnny Dark* 1954; *I'll Cry Tomorrow* 1955; *The Bold and the Brave* 1956
Taylor, Dub *The Bounty Hunter* 1954; *Bonnie and Clyde* 1967; *The Reivers* 1969; *A Man Called Horse* 1970; *The Wild Country* 1971; *Evel Knievel* 1971; *Burnt Offerings* 1976; *Gator* 1976; *Pony Express Rider* 1976; *Moonshine County Express* 1977; *Back to the Future Part III* 1990; *My Heroes Have Always Been Cowboys* 1991; *Falling from Grace* 1992; *Maverick* 1994
Taylor, Elaine *Half a Sixpence* 1967; *The Anniversary* 1968; *Diamonds for Breakfast* 1968; *Lock Up Your Daughters!* 1969; *The Games* 1970
Taylor, Elizabeth *There's One Born Every Minute* 1942; *Jane Eyre* 1943; *Lassie Come Home* 1943; *National Velvet* 1944; *The White Cliffs of Dover* 1944; *Courage of Lassie* 1946; *Cynthia* 1947; *Life with Father* 1947; *A Date with Judy* 1948; *Julia Misbehaves* 1948; *Conspirator* 1949; *Little Women* 1949; *The Big Hangover* 1950; *Father of the Bride* 1950; *Father's Little Dividend* 1951; *A Place in the Sun* 1951; *Love Is Better Than Ever* 1951; *Callaway Went Thataway* 1951; *Quo Vadis* 1951; *Ivanhoe* 1952; *The Girl Who Had Everything* 1953; *Beau Brummell* 1954; *Elephant Walk* 1954; *The Last Time I Saw Paris* 1954; *Rhapsody* 1954; *Giant* 1956; *Raintree County* 1957; *Cat on a Hot Tin Roof* 1958; *Suddenly, Last Summer* 1959; *Butterfield 8* 1960; *Scent of Mystery* 1960; *Cleopatra* 1963; *The VIPs* 1963; *The Sandpiper* 1965; *Who's Afraid of Virginia Woolf?* 1966; *The Comedians* 1967; *Doctor Faustus* 1967; *Reflections in a Golden Eye* 1967; *The Taming of the Shrew* 1967; *Boom* 1968; *Secret Ceremony* 1969; *Anne of the Thousand Days* 1969; *The Only*

Game in Town 1970; *X, Y and Zee* 1971; *Under Milk Wood* 1971; *Hammersmith Is Out* 1972; *Ash Wednesday* 1973; *Night Watch* 1973; *The Driver's Seat* 1975; *The Blue Bird* 1976; *Victory at Entebbe* 1976; *A Little Night Music* 1977; *Winter Kills* 1979; *The Mirror Crack'd* 1980; *Between Friends* 1983; *Malice in Wonderland* 1985; *There Must Be a Pony* 1986; *Poker Alice* 1987; *Young Toscanini* 1988; *Sweet Bird of Youth* 1989; *And the Band Played On* 1993; *The Flintstones* 1994
Taylor, Estelle *The Ten Commandments* 1923; *Don Juan* 1926; *Cimarron* 1931; *The Unholy Garden* 1931; *Street Scene* 1931; *The Southerner* 1945
Taylor, Grigor *Emma's War* 1985; *Afraid to Dance* 1988
Taylor, Holland *Romancing the Stone* 1984; *The Rape of Dr Willis* 1991; *Cop and a Half* 1993; *With Hostile Intent* 1993; *Betrayal of Trust* 1994; *The Counterfeit Contessa* 1994; *Steal Big, Steal Little* 1995; *George of the Jungle* 1997; *The Truman Show* 1998; *Keeping the Faith* 2000
Taylor, Jack *Count Dracula* 1970; *The Female Vampire* 1973; *The Ninth Gate* 2000
Taylor, Joan *Fighting Man of the Plains* 1949; *The Savage* 1953; *Rose Marie* 1954; *Apache Woman* 1955; *Earth vs the Flying Saucers* 1956; *Omar Khayyam* 1957; *20 Million Miles to Earth* 1957
Taylor, Josh *Waltz across Texas* 1982; *The Secret Life of Kathy McCormick* 1988; *Woman on the Ledge* 1993; *Unlikely Suspects* 1996; *A Secret between Friends* 1996; *Stand against Fear* 1996
Taylor, Joyce *The FBI Story* 1959; *Atlantis, the Lost Continent* 1961; *Ring of Fire* 1961; *Twice Told Tales* 1963
Taylor, Kent *I'm No Angel* 1933; *White Woman* 1933; *Mrs Wiggs of the Cabbage Patch* 1934; *I Take This Woman* 1940; *Bomber's Moon* 1943; *The Daltons Ride Again* 1945; *Payment on Demand* 1951; *Playgirl* 1954; *Slightly Scarlet* 1956; *The Iron Sheriff* 1957; *Gang War* 1958; *The Broken Land* 1962
Taylor, Kit *Early Frost* 1981; *Wilde's Domain* 1983; *Mercy Mission: the Rescue of Flight 771* 1993; *Rough Diamonds* 1994
Taylor, Lili *Mystic Pizza* 1988; *Say Anything* 1989; *Bright Angel* 1990; *Arizona Dream* 1991; *Dogfight* 1991; *Watch It* 1992; *Rudy* 1993; *Household Saints* 1993; *The Addiction* 1994; *Cold Fever* 1994; *I Shot Andy Warhol* 1995; *Girls Town* 1996; *illtown* 1996; *Kicked in the Head* 1997; *The Impostors* 1998; *Pecker* 1998; *The Haunting* 1999; *High Fidelity* 2000
Taylor, Marjorie *The Crimes of Stephen Hawke* 1936; *It's Never Too Late to Mend* 1937; *The Ticket of Leave Man* 1937; *The Face at the Window* 1939
Taylor, Mark L *Arachnophobia* 1990; *Murder 101* 1991
Taylor, Meshach *Mannequin* 1987; *How to Murder a Millionaire* 1990; *Mannequin on the Move* 1991; *Class Act* 1992; *Double, Double Toil and Trouble* 1993; *Addicted to Love* 1995
Taylor, Noah *The Year My Voice Broke* 1987; *Flirting* 1989; *Secrets* 1992; *One Crazy Night* 1993; *Shine* 1996; *Simon Magus* 1998

Taylor, Regina *Clockers* 1995; *The Keeper* 1995; *Courage under Fire* 1996; *A Family Thing* 1996; *Hostile Waters* 1996
Taylor, Renee *The Producers* 1968; *The Last of the Red Hot Lovers* 1972; *Lovesick* 1983; *Love Is All There Is* 1996
Taylor (1), Robert *Buried Loot* 1934; *Broadway Melody of 1936* 1935; *Magnificent Obsession* 1935; *The Gorgeous Hussy* 1936; *His Brother's Wife* 1936; *Small Town Girl* 1936; *Broadway Melody of 1938* 1937; *Camille* 1937; *Personal Property* 1937; *This Is My Affair* 1937; *The Crowd Roars* 1938; *A Yank at Oxford* 1938; *Three Comrades* 1938; *Lady of the Tropics* 1939; *Remember?* 1939; *Escape* 1940; *Flight Command* 1940; *Waterloo Bridge* 1940; *Billy the Kid* 1941; *Johnny Eager* 1941; *When Ladies Meet* 1941; *Her Cardboard Lover* 1942; *Stand by for Action* 1942; *Bataan* 1943; *Undercurrent* 1946; *High Wall* 1947; *The Bribe* 1949; *Conspirator* 1949; *Ambush* 1949; *Devil's Doorway* 1950; *Quo Vadis* 1951; *Westward the Women* 1951; *Above and Beyond* 1952; *Ivanhoe* 1952; *All the Brothers Were Valiant* 1953; *Knights of the Round Table* 1953; *Ride, Vaquero!* 1953; *Rogue Cop* 1954; *Valley of the Kings* 1954; *The Adventures of Quentin Durward* 1955; *Many Rivers to Cross* 1955; *D-Day the Sixth of June* 1956; *The Last Hunt* 1956; *The Power and the Prize* 1956; *Tip on a Dead Jockey* 1957; *The Law and Jake Wade* 1958; *Party Girl* 1958; *Saddle the Wind* 1958; *The House of the Seven Hawks* 1959; *The Hangman* 1959; *Killers of Kilimanjaro* 1960; *Miracle of the White Stallions* 1963; *Cattle King* 1963; *The Night Walker* 1964; *Johnny Tiger* 1966; *Where Angels Go...Trouble Follows* 1968
Taylor (2), Robert *Beat Street* 1984; *Steel Justice* 1992
Taylor, Rod *aka* **Taylor, Rodney** *Hell on Frisco Bay* 1955; *World without End* 1955; *The Catered Affair* 1956; *Raintree County* 1957; *Separate Tables* 1958; *Ask Any Girl* 1959; *One Hundred and One Dalmatians* 1960; *The Time Machine* 1960; *Seven Seas to Calais* 1962; *The Birds* 1963; *A Gathering of Eagles* 1963; *Sunday in New York* 1963; *The VIPs* 1963; *Fate Is the Hunter* 1964; *36 Hours* 1964; *Do Not Disturb* 1965; *Young Cassidy* 1965; *The Glass Bottom Boat* 1966; *The Liquidator* 1966; *Dark of the Sun* 1967; *Hotel* 1967; *Chuka* 1967; *Nobody Runs Forever* 1968; *The Hell with Heroes* 1968; *Darker than Amber* 1970; *The Man Who Had Power over Women* 1970; *Zabriskie Point* 1970; *Family Flight* 1972; *The Heroes* 1972; *The Train Robbers* 1973; *The Deadly Trackers* 1973; *A Matter of Wife...and Death* 1976; *The Oregon Trail* 1976; *The Picture Show Man* 1977; *The Treasure Seekers* 1977; *Cry of the Innocent* 1980; *On the Run* 1983; *Palomino* 1991; *Open Season* 1995; *Welcome to Woop Woop* 1997
Taylor, Valerie *Berkeley Square* 1933; *Went the Day Well?* 1942; *Faces in the Dark* 1960; *What a Carve Up!* 1961
Taylor, Vaughn *Meet Danny Wilson* 1952; *It Should Happen to You* 1954; *Jailhouse Rock* 1957;

Cat on a Hot Tin Roof 1958; *The Wizard of Baghdad* 1960
Taylor, Wally *Shaft's Big Score!* 1972; *Hangup* 1973; *Peacemaker* 1990
Taylor-Smith, Jean *Rob Roy, the Highland Rogue* 1953; *It's Never Too Late* 1956; *Ring of Bright Water* 1969; *My Childhood* 1972; *My Ain Folk* 1973
Taylor-Young, Leigh *I Love You, Alice B Toklas* 1968; *The Big Bounce* 1969; *The Adventurers* 1970; *The Buttercup Chain* 1970; *The Horsemen* 1971; *The Gang That Couldn't Shoot Straight* 1971; *Soylent Green* 1973; *Looker* 1981; *Jagged Edge* 1985; *Secret Admirer* 1985; *Who Gets the Friends?* 1988; *Honeymoon Academy* 1990; *Murder or Memory?* 1994; *An Unfinished Affair* 1996; *Stranger in My Home* 1997
Tazaki, Jun *Gate of Hell* 1953; *Ebirah, Horror of the Deep* 1966; *Destroy All Monsters* 1968
Tcherina, Ludmilla *The Red Shoes* 1948; *The Tales of Hoffmann* 1951; *Sign of the Pagan* 1954; *Oh, Rosalinda!!* 1955; *Honeymoon* 1959
Te Wiata, Inia *The Seekers* 1954; *Man of the Moment* 1955
Teagarden, Jack *The Birth of the Blues* 1941; *Glory Alley* 1952
Teague, Marshall *Road House* 1989; *The Colony* 1995
Teakle, Spencer *Cover Girl Killer* 1959; *The Gentle Trap* 1960
Teal, Ray *The Bandit of Sherwood Forest* 1946; *Ace in the Hole* 1951; *Along the Great Divide* 1951; *Distant Drums* 1951; *The Captive City* 1952; *Carrie* 1952; *Ambush at Tomahawk Gap* 1953; *The Wild One* 1953; *The Command* 1954; *Run for Cover* 1955; *The Burning Hills* 1956; *Girl on the Run* 1958
Teale, Owen *War Requiem* 1988; *Robin Hood* 1990; *The Hawk* 1992; *The Cherry Orchard* 1998
Tearle, Conway *Stella Maris* 1918; *Gold Diggers of Broadway* 1929; *The Hurricane Express* 1932
Tearle, Godfrey *The 39 Steps* 1935; *The Last Journey* 1936; *One of Our Aircraft Is Missing* 1942; *Tomorrow We Live* 1942; *The Lamp Still Burns* 1943; *Undercover* 1943; *The Rake's Progress* 1945; *The Beginning or the End* 1947; *White Corridors* 1951; *I Believe in You* 1952; *Mandy* 1952; *The Titfield Thunderbolt* 1952; *Decameron Nights* 1953
Teasdale, Verree *Payment Deferred* 1932; *Roman Scandals* 1933; *Fashions of 1934* 1934; *Madame Du Barry* 1934; *The Milky Way* 1936; *First Lady* 1937; *Fifth Avenue Girl* 1939; *Topper Takes a Trip* 1939; *I Take This Woman* 1940; *Turnabout* 1940; *Come Live with Me* 1941
Tedrow, Irene *Santa Fe Passage* 1955; *A Special Kind of Love* 1978
Teer, Barbara Ann *Slaves* 1969; *The Angel Levine* 1970
Tefkin, Blair *Three for the Road* 1987; *A Sinful Life* 1989
Telezynska, Isabella *The Music Lovers* 1970; *Ludwig* 1973
Teller *My Chauffeur* 1986; *Penn & Teller Get Killed* 1989
Temple, Shirley *Little Miss Marker* 1934; *Mandalay* 1934; *Now and Forever* 1934; *Baby, Take a Bow* 1934; *Bright Eyes* 1934; *Stand up and Cheer!* 1934; *Curly Top* 1935; *The Little Colonel* 1935; *The*

Littlest Rebel 1935; *Our Little Girl* 1935; *Dimples* 1936; *Poor Little Rich Girl* 1936; *Stowaway* 1936; *Captain January* 1936; *Heidi* 1937; *Wee Willie Winkie* 1937; *Little Miss Broadway* 1938; *Rebecca of Sunnybrook Farm* 1938; *Just around the Corner* 1938; *The Little Princess* 1939; *Susannah of the Mounties* 1939; *The Blue Bird* 1940; *Miss Annie Rooney* 1942; *I'll Be Seeing You* 1944; *Since You Went Away* 1944; *Kiss and Tell* 1945; *Bachelor Knight* 1947; *Fort Apache* 1948; *Adventure in Baltimore* 1949; *Mr Belvedere Goes to College* 1949; *The Story of Seabiscuit* 1949; *A Kiss for Corliss* 1949
Tench, John *Dead Ahead* 1996; *The Ticket* 1997
Tengroth, Birgit *Dollar* 1938; *Thirst* 1949
Tennant, David *LA without a Map* 1998; *The Last September* 1999
Tennant, Victoria *The Ragman's Daughter* 1972; *Strangers Kiss* 1983; *All of Me* 1984; *The Holcroft Covenant* 1985; *Best Seller* 1987; *Flowers in the Attic* 1987; *The Handmaid's Tale* 1990; *Whispers* 1990; *LA Story* 1991; *The Plague* 1992
Tenney, Jon *Command in Hell* 1988; *Night Visions* 1990; *Watch It* 1992; *The Twilight of the Golds* 1996; *Fools Rush In* 1997
Tepper, William *Drive, He Said* 1971; *Breathless* 1983; *Bachelor Party* 1984
Ter Steege, Johanna *The Vanishing* 1988; *Vincent and Theo* 1990; *Sweet Emma Dear Böbe* 1992; *Immortal Beloved* 1994
Terajima, Susumu *Hana-Bi* 1997; *After Life* 1998; *Eyes of the Spider* 1999
Terhune, Max *Hit the Saddle* 1937; *Overland Stage Raiders* 1938; *Red River Range* 1938; *Santa Fe Stampede* 1938; *Three Texas Steers* 1939
Terlesky, John *The Allnighter* 1987; *Longarm* 1988; *When He's Not a Stranger* 1989; *Damned River* 1989; *Battling for Baby* 1992
Terranova, Dan *Baby Face Nelson* 1957; *Young Dillinger* 1965
Terrell, Ken *Attack of the 50 Foot Woman* 1958; *The Brain from Planet Arous* 1958
Terrell, Steven *Dragstrip Girl* 1957; *Invasion of the Saucer Men* 1957; *Motorcycle Gang* 1957
Terry, Alice *The Four Horsemen of the Apocalypse* 1921; *The Prisoner of Zenda* 1922; *The Arab* 1924; *Mare Nostrum* 1926; *The Garden of Allah* 1927
Terry, John *Hawk the Slayer* 1980; *Evidence of Love* 1990; *Silhouette* 1990; *Of Mice and Men* 1992; *Seduction: Three Tales from the Inner Sanctum* 1992; *The Resurrected* 1992; *A Dangerous Woman* 1993; *Reflections on a Crime* 1994; *Betrayed: a Story of Three Women* 1995; *The Big Green* 1995; *Kiss and Tell* 1996
Terry, Nigel *The Lion in Winter* 1968; *Excalibur* 1981; *Sylvia* 1984; *Déjà Vu* 1984; *Caravaggio* 1986; *The Last of England* 1987; *War Requiem* 1988; *Edward II* 1991; *Blue* 1993; *The Hunchback* 1997
Terry, Phillip *Music in Manhattan* 1944; *George White's Scandals* 1945; *The Lost Weekend* 1945; *Pan-Americana* 1945; *To Each His Own* 1946; *Lady of Deceit* 1947;

Seven Keys to Baldpate 1947; *The Leech Woman* 1960
Terry, Ruth *Hold That Co-Ed* 1938; *Slightly Honorable* 1939; *Appointment for Love* 1941; *The Cheaters* 1945
Terry, Sheila *Lawyer Man* 1932; *Scarlet Dawn* 1932; *20,000 Years in Sing Sing* 1933; *The Sphinx* 1933; *'Neath the Arizona Skies* 1934; *The Lawless Frontier* 1935
Terry, William *Stage Door Canteen* 1943; *And So They Were Married* 1944
Terry-Thomas *Brothers in Law* 1956; *The Green Man* 1956; *Private's Progress* 1956; *Blue Murder at St Trinian's* 1957; *Lucky Jim* 1957; *The Naked Truth* 1957; *Carlton-Browne of the FO* 1958; *Happy Is the Bride* 1958; *tom thumb* 1958; *Too Many Crooks* 1958; *I'm All Right Jack* 1959; *Make Mine Mink* 1960; *School for Scoundrels* 1960; *Bachelor Flat* 1961; *Kill or Cure* 1962; *It's a Mad Mad Mad Mad World* 1963; *The Mouse on the Moon* 1963; *How to Murder Your Wife* 1965; *Strange Bedfellows* 1965; *Those Magnificent Men in Their Flying Machines* 1965; *You Must Be Joking!* 1965; *Don't Look Now... We're Being Shot At* 1966; *Our Man in Marrakesh* 1966; *The Sandwich Man* 1966; *Munster, Go Home!* 1966; *Arabella* 1967; *Jules Verne's Rocket to the Moon* 1967; *The Karate Killers* 1967; *The Perils of Pauline* 1967; *Danger: Diabolik* 1967; *Don't Raise the Bridge, Lower the River* 1968; *How Sweet It Is!* 1968; *Where Were You When the Lights Went Out?* 1968; *Monte Carlo or Bust* 1969; *Twelve plus One* 1969; *The Abominable Dr Phibes* 1971; *The Heroes* 1972; *Robin Hood* 1973; *Vault of Horror* 1973; *Side by Side* 1975; *The Hound of the Baskervilles* 1977; *The Last Remake of Beau Geste* 1977
Terzieff, Laurent *Kapo* 1959; *Thou Shalt Not Kill* 1961; *The Milky Way* 1968; *Medea* 1970; *Detective* 1985; *Rouge Baiser* 1985; *Germinal* 1993
Tesco, Nicky *Leningrad Cowboys Go America* 1989; *I Hired a Contract Killer* 1990
Tessier, Robert *Born Losers* 1967; *The Glory Stompers* 1967; *The Streetfighter* 1975; *The Deep* 1977; *Billion Dollar Threat* 1979; *One Man Force* 1989
Tester, Desmond *Tudor Rose* 1936; *Sabotage* 1936; *The Drum* 1938
Testi, Fabio *The Garden of the Finzi-Continis* 1971; *One Damned Day at Dawn... Django Meets Sartana* 1971; *Nada* 1974; *The Inheritance* 1976; *China 9, Liberty 37* 1978; *The Ambassador* 1984
Testud, Sylvie *Beyond Silence* 1996; *Karnaval* 1998
Tetzel, Joan *The File on Thelma Jordon* 1949; *Hell below Zero* 1954; *Joy in the Morning* 1965
Tewes, Lauren *The New Love Boat* 1977; *Eyes of a Stranger* 1980; *The China Lake Murders* 1990; *The Doom Generation* 1995; *It Came from Outer Space II* 1996
Texeira, Virgilio aka **Texera, Virgilio** *The Boy Who Stole a Million* 1960; *Return of the Seven* 1966; *The Magnificent Two* 1967
Teynac, Maurice *Night without Stars* 1951; *Bedevilled* 1955; *Paris Holiday* 1958; *Crack in the Mirror* 1960; *In the French Style* 1963; *Ash Wednesday* 1973
Thal, Eric *The Gun in Betty Lou's Handbag* 1992; *A Stranger among Us* 1992; *The Puppet Masters* 1994; *Mixing Nia* 1998
Thalbach, Katharina *The Tin Drum* 1979; *Kaspar Hauser* 1993
Thames, Byron *Johnny Dangerously* 1984; *Blame It on the Night* 1984
Thatcher, Heather *It's a Boy* 1933; *If I Were King* 1938; *Man Hunt* 1941; *The Undying Monster* 1942; *Father's Doing Fine* 1952; *Will Any Gentleman...?* 1953
Thatcher, Torin *The End of the River* 1947; *Affair in Trinidad* 1952; *Blackbeard the Pirate* 1952; *The Crimson Pirate* 1952; *The Snows of Kilimanjaro* 1952; *The Desert Rats* 1953; *Houdini* 1953; *The Robe* 1953; *Bengal Brigade* 1954; *The Black Shield of Falworth* 1954; *Knock on Wood* 1954; *Diane* 1955; *Love Is a Many-Splendored Thing* 1955; *Lady Godiva* 1955; *Band of Angels* 1957; *Witness for the Prosecution* 1957; *Istanbul* 1957; *The 7th Voyage of Sinbad* 1958; *Darby's Rangers* 1958; *The Canadians* 1961; *Jack the Giant Killer* 1962; *Hawaii* 1966
Thaw, John *The Bofors Gun* 1968; *Praise Marx and Pass the Ammunition* 1968; *The Last Grenade* 1970; *Dr Phibes Rises Again* 1972; *Sweeney!* 1976; *Sweeney 2* 1978; *Cry Freedom* 1987; *Business as Usual* 1987; *Chaplin* 1992
Thaxter, Phyllis *Thirty Seconds over Tokyo* 1944; *Bewitched* 1945; *Week-End at the Waldorf* 1945; *The Sea of Grass* 1947; *Living in a Big Way* 1947; *Blood on the Moon* 1948; *Act of Violence* 1949; *The Breaking Point* 1950; *No Man of Her Own* 1950; *Come Fill the Cup* 1951; *Fort Worth* 1951; *Jim Thorpe – All-American* 1951; *She's Working Her Way through College* 1952; *Springfield Rifle* 1952; *Women's Prison* 1955; *The World of Henry Orient* 1964
Thayer, Brynn *Hero and the Terror* 1988; *Triumph over Disaster: the Hurricane Andrew Story* 1993
Theron, Charlize *That Thing You Do!* 1996; *2 Days in the Valley* 1996; *The Devil's Advocate* 1997; *Hollywood Confidential* 1997; *Trial and Error* 1997; *Celebrity* 1998; *Mighty Joe Young* 1998; *The Astronaut's Wife* 1999; *The Cider House Rules* 1999; *Deception* 2000
Thesiger, Ernest *The Old Dark House* 1932; *The Ghoul* 1933; *Night of the Party* 1934; *Bride of Frankenstein* 1935; *The Man Who Could Work Miracles* 1936; *Caesar and Cleopatra* 1945; *Beware of Pity* 1946; *The Ghosts of Berkeley Square* 1947; *The Man Within* 1947; *The Brass Monkey* 1948; *The Man in the White Suit* 1951; *The Robe* 1953; *Father Brown* 1954; *The Adventures of Quentin Durward* 1955; *Value for Money* 1955; *The Battle of the Sexes* 1960; *Sons and Lovers* 1960
Thewlis, David *Vroom* 1988; *Resurrected* 1989; *Life Is Sweet* 1990; *Naked* 1993; *Black Beauty* 1994; *Restoration* 1995; *Total Eclipse* 1995; *DragonHeart* 1996; *The Island of Dr Moreau* 1996; *James and the Giant Peach* 1996; *Seven Years in Tibet* 1997; *American Perfekt* 1997; *Besieged* 1998; *Divorcing Jack* 1998; *Whatever Happened to Harold Smith?* 1999; *The Miracle Maker* 1999; *Gangster No 1* 2000
Thibeau, Jack *Escape from Alcatraz* 1979; *Action Jackson* 1988
Thicke, Alan *Not Quite Human* 1987; *Not Quite Human II* 1989; *The Great American Sex Scandal* 1990; *And You Thought Your Parents Were Weird* 1991; *Still Not Quite Human* 1992; *Betrayal of the Dove* 1993; *Rubdown* 1993
Thiele, Hertha *Girls in Uniform* 1931; *Kühle Wampe* 1931
Thiess, Ursula *Bengal Brigade* 1954; *The Iron Glove* 1954; *The Americano* 1955; *Bandido* 1956
Thiessen, Tiffani-Amber *A Killer among Friends* 1992; *Son in Law* 1993; *She Fought Alone* 1995; *The Stranger beside Me* 1995; *Sweet Dreams* 1996; *Love Stinks* 1999
Thigpen, Lynne *Godspell* 1973; *Fear Stalk* 1989; *Lean on Me* 1989; *Blankman* 1994; *The Paper* 1994; *Cagney & Lacey: the View through the Glass Ceiling* 1995; *Night Ride Home* 1999
Thinnes, Roy *The Manhunter* 1968; *Journey to the Far Side of the Sun* 1969; *Death Race* 1973; *The Hindenburg* 1975; *Blue Bayou* 1990; *Stormy Weathers* 1992; *Robin Cook's Terminal* 1996
Thomas, Damien *Twins of Evil* 1971; *Tiffany Jones* 1973; *The Message* 1976; *Pirates* 1986
Thomas, Danny *Call Me Mister* 1951; *I'll See You in My Dreams* 1951; *The Jazz Singer* 1952; *Journey back to Oz* 1964; *Side by Side* 1988
Thomas (1), Dave aka **Thomas, David** *Strange Brew* 1983; *My Man Adam* 1985; *Love at Stake* 1987; *Moving* 1988; *Cold Sweat* 1993; *Kidz in the Wood* 1996
Thomas, Frank M *Behind the Headlines* 1937; *Criminal Lawyer* 1937; *Danger Patrol* 1937; *Law of the Underworld* 1938; *Smashing the Rackets* 1938; *Among the Living* 1941; *The Great Man's Lady* 1942
Thomas, Frankie *Angels Wash Their Faces* 1939; *One Foot in Heaven* 1941; *The Major and the Minor* 1942
Thomas, Henry *Raggedy Man* 1981; *ET the Extra-Terrestrial* 1982; *Misunderstood* 1984; *Cloak and Dagger* 1984; *Frog Dreaming* 1985; *Valmont* 1989; *Psycho IV: the Beginning* 1990; *A Taste for Killing* 1992; *Fire in the Sky* 1993; *Beyond Obsession* 1994; *Curse of the Starving Class* 1994; *Legends of the Fall* 1994; *Indictment: the McMartin Trial* 1995; *Riders of the Purple Sage* 1996; *Niagara Niagara* 1997; *Bombshell* 1997; *Hijacking Hollywood* 1997
Thomas, Jameson *Piccadilly* 1929; *Three Wise Girls* 1932; *The Moonstone* 1934; *Charlie Chan in Egypt* 1935; *The Last Outpost* 1935
Thomas, Jay *The Gig* 1985; *Miracle Landing* 1990; *Mr Holland's Opus* 1995; *A Strange Affair* 1995; *A Smile like Yours* 1997; *My Date with the President's Daughter* 1998
Thomas, Jonathan Taylor *The Lion King* 1994; *Man of the House* 1994; *Tom and Huck* 1995; *The Adventures of Pinocchio* 1996; *Wild America* 1997; *I'll Be Home for Christmas* 1998
Thomas, Leonard *Bad Lieutenant* 1992; *Dangerous Game* 1993; *DROP Squad* 1994
Thomas, Marlo *Jenny* 1969; *Thieves* 1977; *Nobody's Child* 1986; *In the Spirit* 1990; *Reunion* 1994; *Ultimate Betrayal* 1994
Thomas, Philip Michael aka **Thomas, Philip** *Book of Numbers* 1972; *A Fight for Jenny* 1986; *The Wizard of Speed and Time* 1988; *False Witness* 1989; *Extralarge: Moving Target* 1990
Thomas, Rachel *The Proud Valley* 1940; *Undercover* 1943; *The Captive Heart* 1946; *Blue Scar* 1947; *Valley of Song* 1953
Thomas, Richard *Last Summer* 1969; *Winning* 1969; *The Homecoming: a Christmas Story* 1971; *The Todd Killings* 1971; *You'll Like My Mother* 1972; *9/30/55* 1977; *All Quiet on the Western Front* 1979; *Battle beyond the Stars* 1980; *Go toward the Light* 1988; *Mission of the Shark* 1991; *Yes Virginia, There Is a Santa Claus* 1991; *A Thousand Heroes* 1992; *Lust for Murder* 1993; *Stalking Laura* 1993; *Precious Victims* 1993; *A Walton Thanksgiving Reunion* 1993; *To Save the Children* 1994; *The Christmas Box* 1995; *Death in Small Doses* 1995; *A Walton Wedding* 1995; *What Love Sees* 1996; *Flood: a River's Rampage* 1997; *A Walton Easter* 1997; *Wonder Boys* 2000
Thomas, Robin *About Last Night...* 1986; *Summer School* 1987; *Who Gets the Friends?* 1988; *Memories of Murder* 1990; *The Rape of Dr Willis* 1991; *An Element of Truth* 1995; *Amityville Dollhouse* 1996; *Star Maps* 1997
Thomas, Trevor *Black Joy* 1977; *Sheena, Queen of the Jungle* 1984
Thomassin, Florence *Mina Tannenbaum* 1993; *Elisa* 1994
Thomerson, Tim aka **Thomerson, Timothy** *Remember My Name* 1978; *Carny* 1980; *Fade to Black* 1980; *Take This Job and Shove It* 1981; *Jekyll and Hyde... Together Again* 1982; *Uncommon Valor* 1983; *Rhinestone* 1984; *Iron Eagle* 1985; *Trancers* 1985; *Volunteers* 1985; *The BRAT Patrol* 1986; *Near Dark* 1987; *Cherry 2000* 1988; *The Incredible Hulk Returns* 1988; *Who's Harry Crumb?* 1989; *The Flash* 1990; *Trancers II: The Return of Jack Deth* 1991; *Brain Smasher... a Love Story* 1993; *The Harvest* 1993; *Nemesis* 1993; *Die Watching* 1993; *Fleshtone* 1994; *Hong Kong '97* 1994; *American Yakuza 2: Back to Back* 1996; *When Time Expires* 1997
Thompson, Alina *Dead Cold* 1996; *Marked Man* 1996
Thompson, Beatrix *Dreyfus* 1931; *The Old Curiosity Shop* 1934
Thompson, Bill *Here We Go Again* 1942; *Alice in Wonderland* 1951; *Peter Pan* 1953; *Lady and the Tramp* 1955; *Sleeping Beauty* 1959
Thompson, Brian *You Talkin' to Me?* 1987; *AWOL* 1990; *Moon 44* 1990; *Hired to Kill* 1990; *Life Stinks* 1991; *The Owl* 1991; *Ted & Venus* 1991; *Rage and Honor* 1992; *DragonHeart* 1996
Thompson, Carlos *Fort Algiers* 1953; *Valley of the Kings* 1954; *Magic Fire* 1956; *La Vie de Château* 1965
Thompson, Derek *The Long Good Friday* 1979; *Resurrection Man* 1997
Thompson, Emma *Henry V* 1989; *The Tall Guy* 1989; *Dead Again* 1991; *Impromptu* 1991; *Howards End* 1992; *Peter's Friends* 1992; *In the Name of the Father* 1993; *Much Ado about Nothing* 1993; *The Remains of the Day* 1993; *Junior* 1994; *Carrington* 1995; *Sense and Sensibility* 1995; *The Winter Guest* 1997; *Primary Colors* 1998; *Judas Kiss* 1998; *Maybe Baby* 1999
Thompson, Eric *Private Potter* 1963; *Dougal and the Blue Cat* 1970; *One Day in the Life of Ivan Denisovich* 1971
Thompson, Fred Dalton *Feds* 1988; *Days of Thunder* 1990; *Bed of Lies* 1991; *Curly Sue* 1991; *Thunderheart* 1992; *Barbarians at the Gate* 1993; *In the Line of Fire* 1993; *Baby's Day Out* 1994
Thompson, Jack *Sunday Too Far Away* 1974; *Petersen* 1974; *Caddie* 1976; *Mad Dog* 1976; *Because He's My Friend* 1978; *The Chant of Jimmie Blacksmith* 1978; *Breaker Morant* 1979; *The Club* 1980; *The Earthling* 1980; *Bad Blood* 1982; *The Man from Snowy River* 1982; *Merry Christmas Mr Lawrence* 1982; *Burke and Wills* 1985; *Flesh + Blood* 1985; *Ground Zero* 1987; *Trouble in Paradise* 1989; *Ruby Cairo* 1992; *Turtle Beach* 1992; *Wind* 1992; *A Far Off Place* 1993; *Last Dance* 1995; *The Sum of Us* 1995; *Broken Arrow* 1996; *Excess Baggage* 1997; *Midnight in the Garden of Good and Evil* 1997
Thompson, Kay *Funny Face* 1957; *Tell Me That You Love Me, Junie Moon* 1970
Thompson, Kenan *Heavyweights* 1995; *Good Burger* 1997
Thompson, Lea *All the Right Moves* 1983; *Jaws III* 1983; *Going Undercover* 1984; *Red Dawn* 1984; *The Wild Life* 1984; *Back to the Future* 1985; *Howard, a New Breed of Hero* 1986; *SpaceCamp* 1986; *Some Kind of Wonderful* 1987; *Casual Sex?* 1988; *The Wizard of Loneliness* 1988; *Back to the Future Part II* 1989; *Nightbreaker* 1989; *Back to the Future Part III* 1990; *Montana* 1990; *Article 99* 1992; *The Beverly Hillbillies* 1993; *Dennis* 1993; *Stolen Babies* 1993; *The Substitute Wife* 1994; *The Unspoken Truth* 1995
Thompson, Marshall *The Clock* 1945; *They Were Expendable* 1945; *The Secret Heart* 1946; *Bad Bascomb* 1946; *Words and Music* 1948; *Battleground* 1949; *Devil's Doorway* 1950; *Mystery Street* 1950; *The Tall Target* 1951; *My Six Convicts* 1952; *The Caddy* 1953; *Port of Hell* 1954; *Crashout* 1955; *Good Morning, Miss Dove* 1955; *To Hell and Back* 1955; *Battle Taxi* 1955; *Cult of the Cobra* 1955; *Fiend without a Face* 1957; *First Man into Space* 1958; *It! The Terror from beyond Space* 1958; *Clarence, the Cross-Eyed Lion* 1965; *Around the World under the Sea* 1966; *White Dog* 1981
Thompson, Peter *Santa Fe* 1951; *A Yank in Ermine* 1955
Thompson, Rex *Her Twelve Men* 1954; *The Eddy Duchin Story* 1956; *The King and I* 1956; *The Day They Gave Babies Away* 1957
Thompson, Robert *Patrick* 1978; *Thirst* 1979
Thompson, Ross *The Chain Reaction* 1980; *Boulevard of Broken Dreams* 1988
Thompson, Sada *Desperate Characters* 1971; *The Entertainer* 1975; *My Two Loves* 1986; *Fear Stalk* 1989; *Home Fires Burning* 1989; *Indictment: the McMartin Trial* 1995

Tousey, Sheila *Medicine River* 1992; *Thunderheart* 1992; *Silent Tongue* 1993; *Slaughter of the Innocents* 1993
Toussaint, Lorraine *Breaking In* 1989; *Love, Lies and Lullabies* 1993
Toutain, Roland *La Règle du Jeu* 1939; *Eternal Love* 1943
Tovey, Roberta *The Piper's Tune* 1962; *Dr Who and the Daleks* 1965; *A High Wind in Jamaica* 1965; *Daleks – Invasion Earth 2150 AD* 1966
Towb, Harry *The Sleeping Tiger* 1954; *30 Is a Dangerous Age, Cynthia* 1967; *All Neat in Black Stockings* 1969; *Lamb* 1985
Towers, Constance *Bring Your Smile Along* 1955; *The Horse Soldiers* 1959; *Sergeant Rutledge* 1960; *Shock Corridor* 1963; *The Naked Kiss* 1964; *Sylvester* 1985; *The Next Karate Kid* 1994
Towles, Tom *Henry: Portrait of a Serial Killer* 1986; *High Mountain Rangers* 1987; *The Borrower* 1989; *Night of the Living Dead* 1990; *Blood In Blood Out* 1992; *Mad Dog and Glory* 1992; *Girls in Prison* 1994; *Normal Life* 1995; *Warriors of Virtue* 1997
Towne, Robert *aka* **Wain, Edward** *The Last Woman on Earth* 1960; *Drive, He Said* 1971
Townes, Harry *Screaming Mimi* 1958; *Sanctuary* 1961; *Fitzwilly* 1967; *Santee* 1973; *The Warrior and the Sorceress* 1983
Townsend, Colleen *Chicken Every Sunday* 1948; *When Willie Comes Marching Home* 1950
Townsend, Jill *Sitting Target* 1972; *Alfie Darling* 1975; *The Awakening* 1980
Townsend, Patrice *Sitting Ducks* 1979; *Always* 1985
Townsend, Robert *A Soldier's Story* 1984; *Streets of Fire* 1984; *American Flyers* 1985; *Odd Jobs* 1986; *Ratboy* 1986; *Hollywood Shuffle* 1987; *The Mighty Quinn* 1989; *The Five Heartbeats* 1991; *The Meteor Man* 1993
Townsend, Stuart *Trojan Eddie* 1996; *Resurrection Man* 1997; *Shooting Fish* 1997; *Under the Skin* 1997; *Simon Magus* 1998; *Wonderland* 1999
Toyohara, Kosuke *Godzilla vs King Ghidorah* 1991; *Mr Baseball* 1992
Tozzi, Fausto *The Appointment* 1968; *The Valachi Papers* 1972; *The Valdez Horses* 1973; *The Sicilian Cross* 1976
Tracey, Ian *The Keeper* 1976; *Stakeout* 1987; *The Last Island* 1990; *The Comrades of Summer* 1992; *Trust in Me* 1994; *Man with a Gun* 1995; *The War between Us* 1995; *Dirty Little Secret* 1998
Trachtenberg, Michelle *Harriet the Spy* 1996; *Inspector Gadget* 1999
Tracy, Arthur *Limelight* 1936; *Command Performance* 1937
Tracy, Lee *Born Reckless* 1930; *Doctor X* 1932; *Love Is a Racket* 1932; *Washington Merry-Go-Round* 1932; *The Half Naked Truth* 1932; *The Strange Love of Molly Louvain* 1932; *Advice to the Lovelorn* 1933; *Blonde Bombshell* 1933; *Dinner at Eight* 1933; *Turn Back the Clock* 1933; *The Lemon Drop Kid* 1934; *Behind the Headlines* 1937; *Criminal Lawyer* 1937; *The Spellbinder* 1939; *Betrayal from the East* 1945; *The Best Man* 1964
Tracy, Spencer *Up the River* 1930; *Quick Millions* 1931; *Me and My Gal* 1932; *The Mad Game* 1933; *Man's Castle* 1933; *The Power and the Glory* 1933; *20,000 Years in Sing Sing* 1933; *Dante's Inferno* 1935; *Murder Man* 1935; *Whipsaw* 1935; *Fury* 1936; *Libeled Lady* 1936; *Riffraff* 1936; *San Francisco* 1936; *Big City* 1937; *Captains Courageous* 1937; *Mannequin* 1937; *They Gave Him a Gun* 1937; *Boys Town* 1938; *Test Pilot* 1938; *Stanley and Livingstone* 1939; *Boom Town* 1940; *Edison, the Man* 1940; *I Take This Woman* 1940; *Northwest Passage* 1940; *Dr Jekyll and Mr Hyde* 1941; *Men of Boys Town* 1941; *Keeper of the Flame* 1942; *Tortilla Flat* 1942; *Woman of the Year* 1942; *A Guy Named Joe* 1944; *The Seventh Cross* 1944; *Thirty Seconds over Tokyo* 1944; *Without Love* 1945; *Cass Timberlane* 1947; *The Sea of Grass* 1947; *State of the Union* 1948; *Adam's Rib* 1949; *Edward, My Son* 1949; *Malaya* 1949; *Father of the Bride* 1950; *Father's Little Dividend* 1951; *The People against O'Hara* 1951; *Pat and Mike* 1952; *Plymouth Adventure* 1952; *The Actress* 1953; *Broken Lance* 1954; *Bad Day at Black Rock* 1955; *The Mountain* 1956; *Desk Set* 1957; *The Last Hurrah* 1958; *The Old Man and the Sea* 1958; *Inherit the Wind* 1960; *The Devil at Four o'Clock* 1961; *Judgment at Nuremberg* 1961; *How the West Was Won* 1962; *It's a Mad Mad Mad Mad World* 1963; *Guess Who's Coming to Dinner* 1967
Tracy, William *The Shop around the Corner* 1940; *Strike Up the Band* 1940; *Mr and Mrs Smith* 1941; *Tobacco Road* 1941; *George Washington Slept Here* 1942; *To the Shores of Tripoli* 1942
Train, Jack *It's That Man Again* 1942; *King Arthur Was a Gentleman* 1942; *Miss London Ltd* 1943
Trainor, Mary Ellen *Romancing the Stone* 1984; *Fear Stalk* 1989; *Wings of the Apache* 1990; *Little Giants* 1994; *Congo* 1995; *Seduced and Betrayed* 1995; *Hope* 1997; *Someone to Love Me* 1998
Tran Nu Yen-Khe *The Scent of Green Papaya* 1993; *Cyclo* 1995
Traubel, Helen *Deep in My Heart* 1954; *The Ladies' Man* 1961; *Gunn* 1967
Travanti, Daniel J *aka* **Travanty, Dan** *Who Killed Teddy Bear?* 1965; *St Ives* 1976; *Adam* 1983; *Aurora* 1984; *Adam: His Song Continues* 1986; *Murrow* 1986; *Midnight Crossing* 1988; *Fellow Traveller* 1989; *Making the Case for Murder: the Howard Beach Story* 1989; *Millennium* 1989; *Tagget* 1991; *The Christmas Stallion* 1992; *With Harmful Intent* 1993; *My Name Is Kate* 1994; *Just Cause* 1995
Travers, Bill *The Browning Version* 1951; *Counterspy* 1953; *The Square Ring* 1953; *Street of Shadows* 1953; *Romeo and Juliet* 1954; *Footsteps in the Fog* 1955; *Geordie* 1955; *Bhowani Junction* 1956; *The Barretts of Wimpole Street* 1957; *The Smallest Show on Earth* 1957; *Passionate Summer* 1958; *The Bridal Path* 1959; *Gorgo* 1960; *Invasion Quartet* 1961; *Born Free* 1966; *Duel at Diablo* 1966; *An Elephant Called Slowly* 1969; *Ring of Bright Water* 1969; *The Belstone Fox* 1973
Travers, Henry *The Invisible Man* 1933; *Reunion in Vienna* 1933; *Captain Hurricane* 1935; *After Office Hours* 1935; *The Sisters* 1938; *Dark Victory* 1939; *Dodge City* 1939; *Remember?* 1939; *Stanley and Livingstone* 1939; *You Can't Get Away with Murder* 1939; *Anne of Windy Poplars* 1940; *Edison, the Man* 1940; *Primrose Path* 1940; *Ball of Fire* 1941; *High Sierra* 1941; *The Navy Steps Out* 1941; *Mrs Miniver* 1942; *Random Harvest* 1942; *Madame Curie* 1943; *The Moon Is Down* 1943; *Shadow of a Doubt* 1943; *None Shall Escape* 1944; *The Bells of St Mary's* 1945; *Thrill of a Romance* 1945; *It's a Wonderful Life* 1946; *The Yearling* 1946
Travers, Linden *The Last Adventurers* 1937; *Bank Holiday* 1938; *The Lady Vanishes* 1938; *The Ghost Train* 1941; *South American George* 1941; *Beware of Pity* 1946; *The Master of Bankdam* 1947; *The Bad Lord Byron* 1949; *Christopher Columbus* 1949; *Don't Ever Leave Me* 1949
Travis, June *Ceiling Zero* 1935; *The Case of the Black Cat* 1936; *Go Chase Yourself* 1938; *The Star* 1953
Travis, Kylie *Retroactive* 1997; *Gia* 1998; *Sanctuary* 1998
Travis, Nancy *Three Men and a Baby* 1987; *Air America* 1990; *Internal Affairs* 1990; *Loose Cannons* 1990; *Three Men and a Little Lady* 1990; *Passed Away* 1992; *So I Married an Axe Murderer* 1993; *The Vanishing* 1993; *Greedy* 1994; *Destiny Turns on the Radio* 1995; *Fluke* 1995; *Body Language* 1995; *Bogus* 1996
Travis, Randy *Frank and Jesse* 1995; *Edie & Pen* 1996; *Black Dog* 1998
Travis, Richard *The Man Who Came to Dinner* 1941; *The Big Shot* 1942; *Mission to Moscow* 1943; *Women without Men* 1956
Travis, Stacey *Hardware* 1990; *The Super* 1991; *Only the Strong* 1993; *Suspect Device* 1995
Travolta, Joey *Rosie: the Rosemary Clooney Story* 1982; *The Prodigal* 1983; *Hollywood Vice Squad* 1986; *Amazon Women on the Moon* 1987; *Ghost Writer* 1989; *Round Trip to Heaven* 1992
Travolta, John *The Devil's Rain* 1975; *Carrie* 1976; *Saturday Night Fever* 1977; *Grease* 1978; *Moment by Moment* 1978; *Urban Cowboy* 1980; *Blow Out* 1981; *Staying Alive* 1983; *Two of a Kind* 1983; *Perfect* 1985; *Chains of Gold* 1989; *The Experts* 1989; *Look Who's Talking* 1989; *Look Who's Talking Too* 1990; *Shout* 1991; *Eyes of an Angel* 1991; *Look Who's Talking Now!* 1993; *Pulp Fiction* 1994; *Get Shorty* 1995; *White Man's Burden* 1995; *Broken Arrow* 1996; *Michael* 1996; *Phenomenon* 1996; *Face/Off* 1997; *Mad City* 1997; *She's So Lovely* 1997; *A Civil Action* 1998; *Primary Colors* 1998; *The Thin Red Line* 1998; *The General's Daughter* 1999; *Battlefield Earth* 2000
Traylor, Susan *Sleep with Me* 1994; *Broken Vessels* 1998
Treacher, Arthur *Anything Goes* 1936; *Stowaway* 1936; *Thank You, Jeeves* 1936; *Satan Met a Lady* 1936; *Heidi* 1937; *Step Lively, Jeeves* 1937; *Thin Ice* 1937; *You Can't Have Everything* 1937; *Mad about Music* 1938; *My Lucky Star* 1938; *The Little Princess* 1939; *Irene* 1940; *The Amazing Mrs Holliday* 1943; *Abbott and Costello in Society* 1944; *The Countess of Monte Cristo* 1948; *Love That Brute* 1950
Treacy, Emerson *California Straight Ahead* 1937; *The Prowler* 1951
Treanor, Michael *3 Ninja Kids* 1992; *3 Ninjas Knuckle Up* 1995
Treas, Terri *The Terror Within* 1988; *Rage and Honor* 1992; *Little Miss Millions* 1993; *Alien Nation: Dark Horizon* 1994; *Scene of the Crime* 1996
Trebor, Robert *G.O.R.P.* 1980; *Out of the Darkness* 1985; *52 Pick-Up* 1986; *My Demon Lover* 1987
Tree, David *The Return of the Scarlet Pimpernel* 1937; *The Drum* 1938; *Pygmalion* 1938; *Just William* 1939; *Return to Yesterday* 1940; *Major Barbara* 1941; *Don't Look Now* 1973
Tree, Dorothy *Here Comes the Navy* 1934; *The Woman in Red* 1935; *Abe Lincoln in Illinois* 1940; *Sky Murder* 1940
Treen, Mary *aka* **Treen, Mary Lou** *They Gave Him a Gun* 1937; *Change of Heart* 1943; *I Love a Soldier* 1944; *Let's Live a Little* 1948; *Room for One More* 1952
Tréjan, Guy *Marie Antoinette* 1956; *Piaf: the Early Years* 1974; *The Beast* 1975; *I Married a Dead Man* 1983
Trejo, Danny *Anaconda* 1997; *Los Locos* 1997; *Point Blank* 1997; *The Replacement Killers* 1998
Tremarco, Christine *Under the Skin* 1997; *Hold Back the Night* 1999
Tremayne, Les *Dream Wife* 1953; *I Love Melvin* 1953; *The War of the Worlds* 1953; *A Man Called Peter* 1955; *The Lieutenant Wore Skirts* 1956; *The Monolith Monsters* 1957; *The Perfect Furlough* 1958; *Say One for Me* 1959; *The Angry Red Planet* 1959; *The Gallant Hours* 1960; *Daffy Duck's Movie: Fantastic Island* 1983
Tremblay, Johanne-Marie *Jesus of Montreal* 1989; *Being at Home with Claude* 1992
Trese, Adam *Laws of Gravity* 1992; *Palookaville* 1995; *The Underneath* 1995; *illtown* 1996; *Polish Wedding* 1998
Treves, Frederick *Paper Mask* 1990; *Mad Dogs and Englishmen* 1994
Trevino, George *Captain Scarlett* 1953; *The Brave One* 1956
Trevor, Austin *Lord Edgware Dies* 1934; *Dark Journey* 1937; *Knight without Armour* 1937; *Under Your Hat* 1940; *Champagne Charlie* 1944; *To Paris with Love* 1954; *Konga* 1960; *The Day the Earth Caught Fire* 1961
Trevor, Claire *The Mad Game* 1933; *Baby, Take a Bow* 1934; *Dante's Inferno* 1935; *Human Cargo* 1936; *Dead End* 1937; *The Amazing Dr Clitterhouse* 1938; *The First Rebel* 1939; *Stagecoach* 1939; *Dark Command* 1940; *Honky Tonk* 1941; *Texas* 1941; *Crossroads* 1942; *The Desperadoes* 1943; *Farewell My Lovely* 1945; *Johnny Angel* 1945; *Crack-Up* 1946; *Lady of Deceit* 1947; *Key Largo* 1948; *Raw Deal* 1948; *The Velvet Touch* 1948; *The Lucky Stiff* 1949; *Best of the Badmen* 1951; *Hard, Fast and Beautiful* 1951; *Hoodlum Empire* 1952; *Stop, You're Killing Me* 1952; *The Stranger Wore a Gun* 1953; *The High and the Mighty* 1954; *Lucy Gallant* 1955; *Man without a Star* 1955; *The Mountain* 1956; *Marjorie Morningstar* 1958; *Two Weeks in Another Town* 1962; *The Stripper* 1963; *How to Murder Your Wife* 1965; *Kiss Me Goodbye* 1982; *Norman Rockwell's Breaking Home Ties* 1987
Trevor, Spencer *The Return of Bulldog Drummond* 1934; *The Life and Death of Colonel Blimp* 1943
Trickett, Vicki *Pepe* 1960; *Gidget Goes Hawaiian* 1961; *The Three Stooges Meet Hercules* 1962
Trieste, Leopoldo *The White Sheik* 1951; *I Vitelloni* 1953; *Divorce – Italian Style* 1961; *Seduced and Abandoned* 1964; *The Starmaker* 1994
Trigger, Sarah *Kid* 1990; *Bill & Ted's Bogus Journey* 1991; *The Last to Go* 1991; *Deadfall* 1993; *Politically Correct Party Animals* 1994
Trinder, Tommy *Sailors Three* 1940; *The Foreman Went to France* 1941; *The Bells Go Down* 1943; *Champagne Charlie* 1944; *Fiddlers Three* 1944; *Bitter Springs* 1950; *The Beauty Jungle* 1964; *Barry McKenzie Holds His Own* 1974
Trintignant, Jean-Louis *And God Created Woman* 1956; *Les Liaisons Dangereuses* 1959; *The Seven Deadly Sins* 1961; *Fire and Ice* 1962; *The Easy Life* 1962; *The Sleeping Car Murders* 1965; *A Man and a Woman* 1966; *The Big Silence* 1967; *Les Biches* 1968; *Z* 1968; *The Conformist* 1969; *My Night with Maud* 1969; *And Hope to Die* 1972; *The Last Train* 1972; *Without Apparent Motive* 1972; *Police Story* 1975; *Je Vous Aime* 1980; *La Nuit de Varennes* 1983; *Under Fire* 1983; *Confidentially Yours* 1983; *Long Live Life* 1984; *Rendez-vous* 1985; *A Man and a Woman: 20 Years Later* 1986; *Merci la Vie* 1991; *See How They Fall* 1993; *Three Colours Red* 1994; *A Self-Made Hero* 1995; *Those Who Love Me Can Take the Train* 1998
Trintignant, Marie *Story of Women* 1988; *Wings of Fame* 1990; *Wild Target* 1993; *Les Apprentis* 1995; *Ponette* 1996; *Portraits Chinois* 1996; *News from the Good Lord* 1996
Triola, Anne *Without Reservations* 1946; *Lullaby of Broadway* 1951
Tripp, Louis *The Gate* 1987; *Mama's Going to Buy You a Mockingbird* 1988
Tripplehorn, Jeanne *Basic Instinct* 1992; *The Firm* 1993; *The Night We Never Met* 1993; *Waterworld* 1995; *Sliding Doors* 1997; *Noose* 1997; *'Til There Was You* 1997; *William Faulkner's Old Man* 1997; *Very Bad Things* 1998; *Mickey Blue Eyes* 1999; *Relative Values* 2000
Triska, Jan *Black Eagle* 1988; *Elementary School* 1991
Trissenaar, Elisabeth *Bolwieser* 1977; *In a Year of 13 Moons* 1978; *Berlin Alexanderplatz* 1980
Tristan, Dorothy *End of the Road* 1970; *Klute* 1971; *Isn't It Shocking?* 1973; *Scarecrow* 1973; *Fear on Trial* 1975; *Rollercoaster* 1977
Tritt, Travis *Rio Diablo* 1993; *Outlaw Justice* 1999
Troisi, Massimo *Hotel Colonial* 1987; *Il Postino* 1994
Trooger, Margot *Heidi* 1965; *Pippi Longstocking* 1968
Troughton, David *The Chain* 1984; *Dance with a Stranger* 1984; *Captain Jack* 1998

Apartment 1996; *The Sender* 1997; *BASEketball* 1998
Vaughn, Vince *Swingers* 1996; *Whiskey Down* 1996; *The Locusts* 1997; *The Lost World: Jurassic Park* 1997; *Clay Pigeons* 1998; *A Cool, Dry Place* 1998; *Return to Paradise* 1998; *Psycho* 1998
Vavitch, Michael *Hotel Imperial* 1927; *Two Arabian Knights* 1927
Vawter, Ron *sex, lies, and videotape* 1989; *Empire City* 1991; *Swoon* 1992; *Philadelphia* 1993
Veazie, Carol *A Cry in the Night* 1956; *Baby the Rain Must Fall* 1965
Vedey, Julian *Command Performance* 1937; *The Green Cockatoo* 1937
Vega, Isela *Bring Me the Head of Alfredo Garcia* 1974; *Drum* 1976; *Barbarosa* 1982
Veidt, Conrad *The Cabinet of Dr Caligari* 1919; *Hands of Orlac* 1924; *Waxworks* 1924; *The Man Who Laughs* 1928; *Congress Dances* 1931; *FP1* 1932; *Rome Express* 1932; *I Was a Spy* 1934; *Jew Süss* 1934; *King of the Damned* 1935; *The Passing of the Third Floor Back* 1935; *Dark Journey* 1937; *Under the Red Robe* 1937; *The Spy in Black* 1939; *Contraband* 1940; *Escape* 1940; *The Thief of Bagdad* 1940; *The Men in Her Life* 1941; *A Woman's Face* 1941; *Whistling in the Dark* 1941; *All through the Night* 1942; *Casablanca* 1942; *Above Suspicion* 1943
Velez, Eddie *Repo Man* 1984; *Extremities* 1986; *Rooftops* 1989; *Romero* 1989; *From the Files of Joseph Wambaugh: a Jury of One* 1992; *Bitter Vengeance* 1994; *Under Oath* 1996
Velez, Lauren *I Like It like That* 1994; *Thicker than Blood* 1998
Velez, Lupe *The Gaucho* 1927; *The Squaw Man* 1931; *The Half Naked Truth* 1932; *Hollywood Party* 1934; *Palooka* 1934; *The Girl from Mexico* 1939; *Mexican Spitfire* 1940; *Playmates* 1941; *Ladies' Day* 1943
VelJohnson, Reginald *Die Hard* 1988; *Turner & Hooch* 1989; *The Bride in Black* 1990; *Die Hard 2: Die Harder* 1990; *One of Her Own* 1994; *Deadly Pursuits* 1996
Venable, Evelyn *Death Takes a Holiday* 1934; *Mrs Wiggs of the Cabbage Patch* 1934; *Alice Adams* 1935; *The Little Colonel* 1935; *Pinocchio* 1940
Venables, Bruce *Mortgage* 1989; *Daydream Believer* 1991; *Paperback Hero* 1998
Venantini, Venantino *The Agony and the Ecstasy* 1965; *The Priest's Wife* 1970
Veness, Amy *The Show Goes On* 1937; *Just William* 1939; *This Happy Breed* 1944; *Vote for Huggett* 1948; *The Astonished Heart* 1949
Veninger, Ingrid *The Gate* 1987; *Hush Little Baby* 1993
Vennera, Chick *Thank God It's Friday* 1978; *Yanks* 1979; *High Risk* 1981; *Last Rites* 1988; *Double Threat* 1992
Venocur, Johnny *Savage Streets* 1984; *Exit in Red* 1996
Venora, Diane *Wolfen* 1981; *Terminal Choice* 1983; *F/X* 1985; *Ironweed* 1987; *Bird* 1988; *Heat* 1995; *The Substitute* 1996; *Surviving Picasso* 1996; *William Shakespeare's Romeo + Juliet* 1996; *The Jackal* 1997; *The 13th Warrior* 1999; *The Insider* 1999
Ventham, Wanda *The Blood Beast Terror* 1967; *Mister Ten Per Cent* 1967; *Captain Kronos: Vampire Hunter* 1972
Ventura, Jesse *Predator* 1987; *The Running Man* 1987; *Abraxas* 1991
Ventura, Lino *Honour among Thieves* 1954; *Razzia sur la Chnouf* 1955; *Montparnasses 19* 1958; *The Big Risk* 1960; *Le Deuxième Souffle* 1966; *The Adventurers* 1968; *L'Armée des Ombres* 1969; *The Last Known Address* 1969; *The Sicilian Clan* 1969; *The Valachi Papers* 1972; *The Silent One* 1973; *A Pain in the A...!* 1973; *Happy New Year* 1974; *Three Tough Guys* 1974; *The Trap* 1975; *Illustrious Corpses* 1976; *The Medusa Touch* 1978; *Garde à Vue* 1981; *Les Misérables* 1982; *Sword of Gideon* 1986
Ventura, Viviane *A High Wind in Jamaica* 1965; *Battle beneath the Earth* 1968
Venture, Richard *The Effect of Gamma Rays on Man-in-the-Moon Marigolds* 1972; *The Hunter* 1980; *Missing* 1981; *Scent of a Woman* 1992
Venuta, Benay *Annie Get Your Gun* 1950; *Call Me Mister* 1951; *Stars and Stripes Forever* 1952
Vera-Ellen *Wonder Man* 1945; *The Kid from Brooklyn* 1946; *Three Little Girls in Blue* 1946; *Words and Music* 1948; *Love Happy* 1949; *On the Town* 1949; *Happy Go Lovely* 1950; *Three Little Words* 1950; *The Belle of New York* 1952; *Call Me Madam* 1953; *Big Leaguer* 1953; *White Christmas* 1954
Verdon, Gwen *aka* **Verdon, Gwyneth** *On the Riviera* 1951; *Damn Yankees* 1958; *The Cotton Club* 1984; *Cocoon* 1985; *Nadine* 1987; *Cocoon: the Return* 1988; *Alice* 1990; *Marvin's Room* 1996; *Best Friends for Life* 1998
Verdu, Maribel *Lovers* 1991; *Belle Epoque* 1992; *Golden Balls* 1993; *Goya in Bordeaux* 1999
Verdugo, Elena *Little Giant* 1946; *Thief of Damascus* 1952
Vereen, Ben *Gas-s-s-s, or It Became Necessary to Destroy the World in Order to Save It* 1970; *Funny Lady* 1975; *Louis Armstrong: Chicago Style* 1976; *All That Jazz* 1979; *Buy & Cell* 1988; *Once upon a Forest* 1992; *Why Do Fools Fall in Love?* 1998
Verica, Tom *Donato and Daughter* 1993; *800 Leagues down the Amazon* 1993; *Seeds of Deception* 1993; *Breach of Conduct* 1994; *Not Our Son* 1995
Verley, Bernard *The Milky Way* 1968; *Love in the Afternoon* 1972; *L'Accompagnatrice* 1992; *Hélas pour Moi* 1993; *Six Days, Six Nights* 1994
Vermilyea, Harold *The Big Clock* 1948; *The Miracle of the Bells* 1948; *Born to Be Bad* 1950
Verne, Kaaren *aka* **Verne, Karen** *Ten Days in Paris* 1939; *Sky Murder* 1940; *Underground* 1941; *All through the Night* 1942; *Sherlock Holmes and the Secret Weapon* 1942
Vernier, Pierre *Piaf: the Early Years* 1974; *Romuald et Juliette* 1989
Verno, Jerry *Broken Blossoms* 1936; *Sweeney Todd, the Demon Barber of Fleet Street* 1936; *Old Mother Riley in Paris* 1938
Vernon, Anne *The Love Lottery* 1953; *Beautiful but Dangerous* 1955; *General Della Rovere* 1959; *The Umbrellas of Cherbourg* 1964
Vernon, Glenn *Youth Runs Wild* 1944; *Bedlam* 1946; *The Devil Thumbs a Ride* 1947
Vernon, Howard *Le Silence de la Mer* 1947; *Bob Le Flambeur* 1955; *The Thousand Eyes of Dr Mabuse* 1960; *The Secret Ways* 1961; *The Awful Dr Orloff* 1962; *Alphaville* 1965; *Dracula, Prisoner of Frankenstein* 1972
Vernon, John *Point Blank* 1967; *Tell Them Willie Boy Is Here* 1969; *Topaz* 1969; *Dirty Harry* 1971; *One More Train to Rob* 1971; *Fear Is the Key* 1972; *Charley Varrick* 1973; *The Black Windmill* 1974; *W* 1974; *Brannigan* 1975; *The Outlaw Josey Wales* 1976; *Golden Rendezvous* 1977; *A Special Day* 1977; *National Lampoon's Animal House* 1978; *Herbie Goes Bananas* 1980; *Chained Heat* 1983; *Savage Streets* 1984; *Ernest Goes to Camp* 1987; *Blue Monkey* 1987; *WB, Blue and the Bean* 1988; *Killer Klowns from Outer Space* 1988; *The Woman Who Sinned* 1991; *Wojeck: Out of the Fire* 1992; *Hostage for a Day* 1994; *Sodbusters* 1994; *Malicious* 1995; *Paris or Somewhere* 1995
Vernon, Kate *Roadhouse 66* 1984; *Alphabet City* 1984; *Keys to the Kingdom* 1991; *Malcolm X* 1992; *House of Secrets* 1993; *Dangerous Touch* 1994; *Soft Deceit* 1994; *Bloodknot* 1995; *Flood: a River's Rampage* 1997; *Blackjack* 1998
Vernon, Richard *Hot Enough for June* 1963; *The Servant* 1963; *A Hard Day's Night* 1964; *The Tomb of Ligeia* 1964; *The Early Bird* 1965; *The Intelligence Men* 1965; *The Satanic Rites of Dracula* 1973; *Witness for the Prosecution* 1982; *A Month in the Country* 1987
Vernon, Valerie *Gog* 1954; *The Glass Cage* 1955
Vernon, Wally *Happy Landing* 1938; *Kentucky Moonshine* 1938; *Broadway Serenade* 1939; *Bloodhounds of Broadway* 1952; *Affair with a Stranger* 1953
Verrell, Cec *Hell Comes to Frogtown* 1988; *Mad at the Moon* 1992; *Three of Hearts* 1992
Versois, Odile *A Day to Remember* 1953; *To Paris with Love* 1954; *The Young Lovers* 1954; *Checkpoint* 1956; *Passport to Shame* 1958; *Cartouche* 1961
VeSota, Bruno *Daddy-O* 1959; *Attack of the Giant Leeches* 1960
Vessey, Tricia *The Alarmist* 1997; *Ghost Dog: the Way of the Samurai* 1999
Vetchy, Ondrej *Martha and I* 1990; *Kolya* 1996
Vetri, Victoria *aka* **Dorian, Angela** *Kings of the Sun* 1963; *Chuka* 1967; *When Dinosaurs Ruled the Earth* 1969
Viana, Henrique *Recollections of the Yellow House* 1989; *Here on Earth* 1993
Viard, Karin *Delicatessen* 1990; *La Séparation* 1994; *La Nouvelle Eve* 1999
Vickaryous, Scott *A Champion's Fight* 1998; *Our Guys: Outrage in Glen Ridge* 1999
Vickers, Martha *The Big Sleep* 1946; *The Man I Love* 1946; *Ruthless* 1948; *The Burglar* 1956
Vickers, Yvette *Short Cut to Hell* 1957; *Reform School Girl* 1957; *Attack of the 50 Foot Woman* 1958; *The Mobster* 1958; *Attack of the Giant Leeches* 1960
Vickery, John *Fist of the North Star* 1986; *Promised a Miracle* 1988; *The Boys* 1991
Victor, Charles *My Learned Friend* 1943; *Rhythm Serenade* 1943; *The Silver Fleet* 1943; *Fear in the Night* 1947; *The Calendar* 1948; *The Woman in Question* 1950; *Calling Bulldog Drummond* 1951; *The Frightened Man* 1952; *Made in Heaven* 1952; *The Love Lottery* 1953; *Police Dog* 1955; *Value for Money* 1955; *The Extra Day* 1956; *Home and Away* 1956
Victor, Henry *Freaks* 1932; *Conquest of the Air* 1936
Vidal, Albert *Who Killed Nani?* 1988; *Blood and Sand* 1989
Vidal, Christina *Life with Mikey* 1993; *Welcome to the Dollhouse* 1995
Vidal, Gil *Marianne de Ma Jeunesse* 1955; *Too Many Lovers* 1957
Vidal, Gore *Fellini's Roma* 1972; *Gore Vidal's Billy the Kid* 1989; *Bob Roberts* 1992; *With Honors* 1994; *Shadow Conspiracy* 1996; *Gattaca* 1997
Vidal, Henri *The House on the Waterfront* 1955; *Gates of Paris* 1957; *Too Many Lovers* 1957
Vidal, Lisa *Fall* 1997; *Naked City: a Killer Christmas* 1998; *Hit and Run* 1999
Vidarte, Walter *1919* 1983; *Outrage* 1993
Vidler, Steven *Robbery under Arms* 1985; *The Good Wife* 1986; *Encounter at Raven's Gate* 1988; *Harbour Beat* 1990; *The Territorians* 1996
Vidler, Susan *Naked* 1993; *Trainspotting* 1995; *The Wedding Tackle* 2000
Vidor, Florence *The Marriage Circle* 1924; *The Patriot* 1928
Vidor, King *It's a Great Feeling* 1949; *Love and Money* 1982
Vieira, Asia *The Good Mother* 1988; *Omen IV: the Awakening* 1991
Vigoda, Abe *Newman's Law* 1974; *Plain Clothes* 1988; *Look Who's Talking* 1989; *Joe versus the Volcano* 1990; *Keaton's Cop* 1990; *Batman: Mask of the Phantasm* 1993; *Sugar Hill* 1993; *Jury Duty* 1995; *Underworld* 1996; *Love Is All There Is* 1996; *A Brooklyn State of Mind* 1997; *Good Burger* 1997
Vigran, Herb *Bedtime for Bonzo* 1951; *Go, Johnny, Go!* 1959; *Charlotte's Web* 1973
Viharo, Robert *Villa Rides* 1968; *Return to Macon County* 1975; *Hide in Plain Sight* 1980; *Happy Birthday, Gemini* 1980; *The Night Stalker* 1985
Villagra, Nelson *The Last Supper* 1976; *Amnesia* 1994
Villalonga, Marthe *Ma Saison Préferée* 1993; *Alice et Martin* 1998
Villard, Frank *The Seven Deadly Sins* 1952; *No Exit* 1954; *Guilty?* 1956
Villard, Tom *Parasite* 1982; *Popcorn* 1991
Villechaize, Herve *The Gang That Couldn't Shoot Straight* 1971; *The Man with the Golden Gun* 1974; *Seizure* 1974; *The One and Only* 1978
Villeret, Jacques *Robert et Robert* 1978; *An Adventure for Two* 1979; *Les Uns et les Autres* 1981; *Edith and Marcel* 1983; *Hold-Up* 1985; *Soigne Ta Droite* 1986; *The Favour, the Watch and the Very Big Fish* 1991; *The Children of the Marshland* 1998; *Le Dîner de Cons* 1998
Villiers, Christopher *First Knight* 1995; *Princess in Love* 1996
Villiers, James *Eva* 1962; *Father Came Too* 1963; *Murder at the Gallop* 1963; *King and Country* 1964; *The Nanny* 1965; *Otley* 1968; *Some Girls Do* 1969; *A Nice Girl Like Me* 1969; *Blood from the Mummy's Tomb* 1971; *The Amazing Mr Blunden* 1972; *The Ruling Class* 1972; *Ghost in the Noonday Sun* 1973; *Seven Nights in Japan* 1976; *Saint Jack* 1979; *The Scarlet Pimpernel* 1982; *Under the Volcano* 1984; *Mountains of the Moon* 1989; *King Ralph* 1991
Villiers, Mavis *Suddenly, Last Summer* 1959; *Philadelphia, Here I Come* 1975
Vince, Pruitt Taylor *Shy People* 1987; *Mississippi Burning* 1988; *Jacob's Ladder* 1990; *Dead in the Water* 1991; *Sweet Poison* 1991; *Married for Murder* 1992; *City Slickers II: the Legend of Curly's Gold* 1994; *Nobody's Fool* 1994; *Heavy* 1995; *Under the Hula Moon* 1995; *A Further Gesture* 1996; *The Legend of 1900* 1999; *Mumford* 1999
Vincent, Alex *Child's Play* 1988; *Child's Play 2* 1990
Vincent, Frank *Death Collector* 1976; *Raging Bull* 1980; *Jungle Fever* 1991; *Mortal Thoughts* 1991; *Hand Gun* 1994; *Gotti* 1996
Vincent, Hélène *J'Embrasse Pas* 1991; *Three Colours Blue* 1993; *Ma Vie en Rose* 1997
Vincent, Jan-Michael *Going Home* 1971; *The Mechanic* 1972; *Deliver Us from Evil* 1973; *The World's Greatest Athlete* 1973; *Buster and Billie* 1974; *Bite the Bullet* 1975; *Vigilante Force* 1975; *White Line Fever* 1975; *Damnation Alley* 1977; *Big Wednesday* 1978; *Hooper* 1978; *Defiance* 1979; *Hard Country* 1981; *Last Plane Out* 1983; *Born in East LA* 1987; *Enemy Territory* 1987; *Hit List* 1988; *Tarzan in Manhattan* 1989; *Demonstone* 1989; *Xtro 2: The Second Encounter* 1990; *Haunting Fear* 1990; *The Final Heist* 1991; *Hangfire* 1991; *Raw Nerve* 1991; *Animal Instincts* 1992; *Indecent Behavior* 1993; *Midnight Witness* 1993; *Sins of Desire* 1993; *Orbit* 1996; *Buffalo '66* 1997
Vincent, June *Can't Help Singing* 1944; *Here Come the Co-Eds* 1945; *Black Angel* 1946; *Marry Me Again* 1953
Vincent, Virginia *I Want to Live!* 1958; *The Return of Dracula* 1958; *The Black Orchid* 1959; *Love with the Proper Stranger* 1963; *The Hills Have Eyes* 1978
Vines, Margaret *Open All Night* 1934; *The Vicar of Bray* 1937
Ving, Lee *aka* **Ving James, Lee** *Streets of Fire* 1984; *Black Moon Rising* 1985; *Oceans of Fire* 1986; *Dudes* 1987; *The Taking of Beverly Hills* 1991
Vinovich, Steve *aka* **Vinovich, Stephen** *Jennifer on My Mind* 1971; *The Richest Cat in the World* 1986; *Mannequin* 1987
Vinson, Gary *McHale's Navy* 1964; *Nobody's Perfect* 1968
Vinson, Helen *I Am a Fugitive from a Chain Gang* 1932; *Lawyer Man* 1932; *The Kennel Murder Case* 1933; *The Power and the Glory* 1933; *The Little Giant* 1933; *Broadway Bill* 1934; *The Captain Hates the Sea* 1934; *King of the Damned* 1935; *The Tunnel* 1935; *The Wedding Night* 1935; *Private Worlds* 1935; *Vogues* 1937; *Live,*

Love and Learn 1937; *In Name Only* 1939; *Torrid Zone* 1940; *The Thin Man Goes Home* 1944
Vint, Alan *The Panic in Needle Park* 1971; *Welcome Home, Soldier Boys* 1971; *The Unholy Rollers* 1972; *Badlands* 1973; *Macon County Line* 1973; *The Ballad of Gregorio Cortez* 1983
Vint, Jesse *Silent Running* 1971; *Macon County Line* 1973; *Bug* 1975; *Deathsport* 1978; *Fast Charlie: the Moonbeam Rider* 1978
Vintas, Gustav *Silent Assassins* 1988; *Midnight* 1989
Vinton, Arthur *Washington Merry-Go-Round* 1932; *Dames* 1934
Vinton, Bobby *Big Jake* 1971; *The Train Robbers* 1973
Viscuso, Sal *Max Dugan Returns* 1983; *2 ½ Dads* 1986
Vitale, Joseph *Road to Rio* 1947; *The Paleface* 1948; *Apache Rifles* 1964
Vitale, Milly *The Juggler* 1953; *Seven Little Foys* 1955; *The Flesh Is Weak* 1957; *Hannibal* 1959; *A Breath of Scandal* 1960
Viterelli, Joe *Bullets over Broadway* 1994; *Heaven's Prisoners* 1996; *American Strays* 1996; *Analyze This* 1999; *Mickey Blue Eyes* 1999
Vitez, Antoine *My Night with Maud* 1969; *Ecoute Voir…* 1978; *The Green Room* 1978
Vitold, Michel *La Nuit Fantastique* 1942; *The Testament of Dr Cordelier* 1959; *Judex* 1963; *Thomas the Imposter* 1964; *The Confession* 1970
Vitti, Monica *L'Avventura* 1959; *La Notte* 1961; *Eclipse* 1962; *The Red Desert* 1964; *Modesty Blaise* 1966; *On My Way to the Crusades, I Met a Girl Who…* 1967; *Jealousy, Italian Style* 1970; *The Phantom of Liberty* 1974; *An Almost Perfect Affair* 1979; *Tigers in Lipstick* 1979; *Immortal Bachelor* 1980; *The Oberwald Mystery* 1980
Viva *Bike Boy* 1967; *Lonesome Cowboys* 1968; *Lions Love* 1969; *Sam's Song* 1969; *Cisco Pike* 1971
Vlady, Marina *The Theft of the Mona Lisa* 1965; *Chimes at Midnight* 1966; *Two or Three Things I Know about Her* 1966; *The Thief of Baghdad* 1978; *Tangos, Exilo de Gardel* 1985
Vlahos, Sam *Powwow Highway* 1988; *The Big Squeeze* 1996
Voe, Sandra *Breaking the Waves* 1996; *The Winter Guest* 1997; *Janice Beard 45 WPM* 1999
Vogel, Darlene *Ring of Steel* 1994; *Decoy* 1995
Vogler, Karl Michael *The Blue Max* 1966; *How I Won the War* 1967; *Deep End* 1970
Vogler, Rüdiger *Alice in the Cities* 1974; *Kings of the Road* 1976; *The German Sisters* 1981; *Until the End of the World* 1991; *Faraway, So Close* 1993
Vohs, Joan *Cry Vengeance* 1954; *Sabrina Fair* 1954
Voight, Jon *Frank's Greatest Adventure* 1967; *Hour of the Gun* 1967; *Midnight Cowboy* 1969; *Catch-22* 1970; *The Revolutionary* 1970; *Deliverance* 1972; *The All-American Boy* 1973; *Conrack* 1974; *The Odessa File* 1974; *End of the Game* 1976; *Coming Home* 1978; *The Champ* 1979; *Lookin' to Get Out* 1982; *Table for Five* 1983; *Desert Bloom* 1985; *Runaway Train* 1985; *Eternity* 1990; *Chernobyl: the Final Warning* 1991; *Rainbow Warrior* 1992; *Convict Cowboy* 1995; *Heat* 1995; *The Tin Soldier* 1995; *Mission: Impossible* 1996; *Anaconda* 1997; *The Fixer* 1997; *Most Wanted* 1997; *The Rainmaker* 1997; *Rosewood* 1997; *U Turn* 1997; *Enemy of the State* 1998; *The General* 1998; *Varsity Blues* 1999
Volonté, Gian Maria *aka* **Wells, John** *The Four Days of Naples* 1962; *A Fistful of Dollars* 1964; *For a Few Dollars More* 1965; *A Bullet for the General* 1966; *Face to Face* 1967; *We Still Kill the Old Way* 1967; *Vent d'Est* 1969; *Investigation of a Citizen above Suspicion* 1970; *The Red Circle* 1970; *Sacco and Vanzetti* 1971; *Lucky Luciano* 1973; *Christ Stopped at Eboli* 1979; *The Death of Mario Ricci* 1983; *Chronicle of a Death Foretold* 1987; *Open Doors* 1990
Volter, Philippe *The Music Teacher* 1988; *The Double Life of Véronique* 1991; *Three Colours Blue* 1993
Von Bargen, Daniel *Company Business* 1991; *Scam* 1993; *With Hostile Intent* 1993; *The Gift of Love* 1994; *Lord of Illusions* 1995; *Before and After* 1996; *GI Jane* 1997; *The Postman* 1997; *The General's Daughter* 1999; *Universal Soldier – the Return* 1999
von Brömssen, Tomas *My Life as a Dog* 1985; *All Things Fair* 1995
Von Detten, Erik *Escape to Witch Mountain* 1995; *Top Dog* 1995; *Christmas Every Day* 1996; *Leave It to Beaver* 1997; *Replacing Dad* 1999
Von Dohlen, Lenny *Tender Mercies* 1982; *Electric Dreams* 1984; *Billy Galvin* 1986; *Dracula's Widow* 1988; *Blind Vision* 1992; *Leaving Normal* 1992; *Tollbooth* 1994; *Bird of Prey* 1995; *Entertaining Angels: the Dorothy Day Story* 1996; *One Good Turn* 1996; *Home Alone 3* 1997
von Eltz, Theodore *Four Feathers* 1929; *Confidential* 1935; *Beloved Enemy* 1936; *California Straight Ahead* 1937
von Friedl, Loni *The Blue Max* 1966; *Journey to the Far Side of the Sun* 1969
Von Leer, Hunter *Halloween II* 1981; *Under the Boardwalk* 1988
Von Palleske, Heidi *Dead Ringers* 1988; *Shadows of the Past* 1991; *Sabotage* 1996
von Rezzori, Gregor *A Very Private Affair* 1962; *Viva Maria!* 1965
von Schlettow, Hans Adalbert *Dr Mabuse, the Gambler* 1922; *Asphalt* 1928
von Seyffertitz, Gustav *Sparrows* 1926; *The Gaucho* 1927; *The Student Prince in Old Heidelberg* 1927; *The Docks of New York* 1928; *The Mysterious Lady* 1928; *Canary Murder Case* 1929; *Dishonored* 1931; *The Moonstone* 1934; *She* 1935
von Stroheim, Erich *Hearts of the World* 1918; *Blind Husbands* 1919; *Foolish Wives* 1920; *The Wedding March* 1928; *The Great Gabbo* 1929; *Friends and Lovers* 1931; *As You Desire Me* 1932; *The Lost Squadron* 1932; *La Grande Illusion* 1937; *Pièges* 1939; *I Was an Adventuress* 1940; *So Ends Our Night* 1941; *Five Graves to Cairo* 1943; *The North Star* 1943; *The Great Flamarion* 1945; *Sunset Boulevard* 1950; *Napoléon* 1955
von Sydow, Max *The Seventh Seal* 1957; *So Close to Life* 1957; *The Face* 1958; *The Virgin Spring* 1960; *Through a Glass Darkly* 1961; *Winter Light* 1962; *The Greatest Story Ever Told* 1965; *The Reward* 1965; *Hawaii* 1966; *The Quiller Memorandum* 1966; *The Hour of the Wolf* 1967; *Shame* 1968; *A Passion* 1969; *The Kremlin Letter* 1970; *The Night Visitor* 1970; *The Emigrants* 1971; *The Touch* 1971; *Embassy* 1972; *The New Land* 1972; *The Exorcist* 1973; *Steppenwolf* 1974; *Three Days of the Condor* 1975; *The Ultimate Warrior* 1975; *Illustrious Corpses* 1976; *Voyage of the Damned* 1976; *Exorcist II: The Heretic* 1977; *March or Die* 1977; *Brass Target* 1978; *Hurricane* 1979; *Deathwatch* 1980; *Flash Gordon* 1980; *Escape to Victory* 1981; *She Dances Alone* 1981; *Conan the Barbarian* 1982; *Target Eagle* 1982; *Never Say Never Again* 1983; *Strange Brew* 1983; *Dreamscape* 1984; *Dune* 1984; *Samson and Delilah* 1984; *The Belarus File* 1985; *Code Name: Emerald* 1985; *Quo Vadis?* 1985; *Duet for One* 1986; *Hannah and Her Sisters* 1986; *The Second Victory* 1986; *Pelle the Conqueror* 1987; *The Wolf at the Door* 1987; *Red King, White Knight* 1989; *Awakenings* 1990; *Father* 1990; *Hiroshima: Out of the Ashes* 1990; *The Bachelor* 1990; *Europa* 1991; *A Kiss before Dying* 1991; *The Ox* 1991; *Until the End of the World* 1991; *Best Intentions* 1992; *The Silent Touch* 1992; *Needful Things* 1993; *Citizen X* 1995; *Judge Dredd* 1995; *Jerusalem* 1996; *Private Confessions* 1996; *Hostile Waters* 1996; *Hamsun* 1996; *What Dreams May Come* 1998; *Snow Falling on Cedars* 1999
von Trotta, Margarethe *Gods of the Plague* 1969; *The American Soldier* 1970; *Beware of a Holy Whore* 1970
von Twardowski, Hans *The Cabinet of Dr Caligari* 1919; *The Scarlet Empress* 1934
von Wangenheim, Gustav *Nosferatu, a Symphony of Horrors* 1922; *The Woman in the Moon* 1929
Von Weitershausen, Gila *The Pedestrian* 1974; *Circle of Deceit* 1981; *Trenchcoat* 1983
von Wernherr, Otto *Liquid Sky* 1982; *Blind Alley* 1984
Von Zell, Harry *The Guilt of Janet Ames* 1947; *The Saxon Charm* 1948; *For Heaven's Sake* 1950; *Two Flags West* 1950; *I Can Get It for You Wholesale* 1951; *Son of Paleface* 1952
Von Zerneck, Danielle *My Science Project* 1985; *La Bamba* 1986; *Under the Boardwalk* 1988; *Survive the Savage Sea* 1992; *Living in Oblivion* 1995
Von Zerneck, Peter *Berlin Express* 1948; *A Foreign Affair* 1948
Vonn, Veola *Phantom of the Rue Morgue* 1954; *Hell Bent for Glory* 1957
Voskovec, George *12 Angry Men* 1957; *The 27th Day* 1957; *Wind across the Everglades* 1958; *Barbarosa* 1982
Vosloo, Arnold *The Finishing Touch* 1992; *Hard Target* 1993; *Darkman II – the Return of Durant* 1995; *Diary of a Serial Killer* 1997; *Zeus and Roxanne* 1997; *Progeny* 1998; *The Mummy* 1999
Vosper, Frank *Jew Süss* 1934; *The Man Who Knew Too Much* 1934; *Open All Night* 1934; *Heart's Desire* 1935; *Königsmark* 1935
Vosselli, Judith *The Rogue Song* 1930; *Inspiration* 1931
Votrian, Peter *Big House, USA* 1955; *Crime in the Streets* 1956; *Fear Strikes Out* 1957
Voutsinas, Andreas *The Producers* 1968; *A Dream of Passion* 1978
Voyagis, Yorgo *The Last Valley* 1971; *Chronicle of the Burning Years* 1975; *The Little Drummer Girl* 1984; *Vampire in Venice* 1987; *Frantic* 1988; *Courage Mountain* 1989
Vrana, Vlasta *Scanners II: The New Order* 1991; *Twin Sisters* 1992; *Brainscan* 1994; *Hawk's Vengeance* 1996; *Marked Man* 1996; *The Assignment* 1997
Vriends, Brian *Mortgage* 1989; *Struck by Lightning* 1990
Vroom, Frederick *The Navigator* 1924; *The General* 1927
Vye, Murvyn *Golden Earrings* 1947; *Whispering Smith* 1948; *A Connecticut Yankee in King Arthur's Court* 1949; *Road to Bali* 1952; *Destination Gobi* 1953; *Pickup on South Street* 1953; *Green Fire* 1954; *River of No Return* 1954; *Black Horse Canyon* 1954; *Escape to Burma* 1955; *Pearl of the South Pacific* 1955; *The Best Things in Life Are Free* 1956; *Short Cut to Hell* 1957; *Al Capone* 1959
Vyner, Margaret *Climbing High* 1938; *The Lamp Still Burns* 1943

W

Waddington, Steven *Edward II* 1991; *The Last of the Mohicans* 1992; *Don't Get Me Started* 1994; *Prince of Jutland* 1994; *Carrington* 1995; *Face* 1997; *Tarzan and the Lost City* 1998
Wade, Adam *Gordon's War* 1973; *Claudine* 1974
Wade, Russell *The Ghost Ship* 1943; *The Iron Major* 1943; *The Body Snatcher* 1945; *A Game of Death* 1945
Wadham, Julian *The Madness of King George* 1995; *The English Patient* 1996; *Keep the Aspidistra Flying* 1997; *Preaching to the Perverted* 1997
Wadsworth, Henry *Applause* 1929; *Fast and Loose* 1930; *It Happened One Night* 1934; *The Thin Man* 1934; *Ceiling Zero* 1935
Wager, Anthony *Great Expectations* 1946; *The Hi-Jackers* 1963
Wagner, David *Thrashin'* 1986; *Pet Shop* 1995
Wagner, Fernando *Tarzan and the Mermaids* 1948; *Garden of Evil* 1954
Wagner, Jack *Moving Target* 1988; *Trapped in Space* 1994; *Lady Killer* 1995; *Frequent Flyer* 1996; *Dirty Little Secret* 1998
Wagner, Lindsay *The Paper Chase* 1973; *Two People* 1973; *High Risk* 1981; *Nighthawks* 1981; *Martin's Day* 1984; *Passions* 1984; *This Child Is Mine* 1985; *Convicted* 1986; *Stranger in My Bed* 1986; *Young Again* 1986; *Evil in Clear River* 1988; *Nightmare at Bitter Creek* 1988; *The Taking of Flight 847* 1988; *Bionic Showdown: the Six Million Dollar Man and the Bionic Woman* 1989; *Babies* 1990; *Shattered Dreams* 1990; *Fire in the Dark* 1991; *Ricochet* 1991; *A Message from Holly* 1992; *She Woke Up* 1992; *Nurses on the Line* 1993; *Danielle Steel's Once in a Lifetime* 1994; *Bionic Ever After?* 1994; *Fighting for My Daughter* 1995; *Sins of Silence* 1995; *Contagious* 1997; *Voyage of Terror* 1998
Wagner, Lou *Planet of the Apes* 1968; *Conquest of the Planet of the Apes* 1972; *G.O.R.P.* 1980
Wagner, Robert *Halls of Montezuma* 1950; *The Frogmen* 1951; *Let's Make It Legal* 1951; *Stars and Stripes Forever* 1952; *What Price Glory?* 1952; *With a Song in My Heart* 1952; *Beneath the 12-Mile Reef* 1953; *Titanic* 1953; *Broken Lance* 1954; *Prince Valiant* 1954; *White Feather* 1955; *Between Heaven and Hell* 1956; *A Kiss before Dying* 1956; *The Mountain* 1956; *Stopover Tokyo* 1957; *The True Story of Jesse James* 1957; *The Hunters* 1958; *In Love and War* 1958; *Say One for Me* 1959; *All the Fine Young Cannibals* 1960; *Sail a Crooked Ship* 1961; *The Condemned of Altona* 1962; *The Longest Day* 1962; *The War Lover* 1962; *The Pink Panther* 1964; *The Moving Target* 1966; *How I Spent My Summer Vacation* 1967; *The Biggest Bundle of Them All* 1968; *Don't Just Stand There* 1968; *Winning* 1969; *City beneath the Sea* 1971; *Madame Sin* 1972; *The Affair* 1973; *The Towering Inferno* 1974; *Death at Love House* 1976; *Airport: the Concorde* 1979; *The Curse of the Pink Panther* 1983; *I Am the Cheese* 1983; *To Catch a King* 1984; *There Must Be a Pony* 1986; *Love among Thieves* 1987; *Indiscreet* 1988; *This Gun for Hire* 1991; *Dragon: the Bruce Lee Story* 1993; *Parallel Lives* 1994; *Austin Powers: International Man of Mystery* 1997; *Something to Believe In* 1997; *Overdrive* 1997; *Wild Things* 1998; *Austin Powers: The Spy Who Shagged Me* 1999; *Crazy in Alabama* 1999; *Play It to the Bone* 2000
Wagner, Thomas *Dead On* 1993; *Marilyn and Bobby: Her Final Affair* 1993
Wahl, Ken *The Wanderers* 1979; *Fort Apache, the Bronx* 1981; *Treasure of the Yankee Zephyr* 1981; *Jinxed!* 1982; *Purple Hearts* 1984; *The Dirty Dozen: the Next Mission* 1985; *The Taking of Beverly Hills* 1991; *The Favor* 1994; *Search for Grace* 1994; *Wiseguy* 1996
Wahlberg, Donnie *Bullet* 1995; *Body Count* 1997; *The Sixth Sense* 1999; *Purgatory* 1999
Wahlberg, Mark *The Substitute* 1993; *Renaissance Man* 1994; *The Basketball Diaries* 1995; *Fear* 1996; *Boogie Nights* 1997; *Traveller* 1997; *The Big Hit* 1998; *The Corruptor* 1999; *Three Kings* 1999; *The Perfect Storm* 2000
Wainwright, James *Jigsaw* 1972; *Joe Kidd* 1972; *Killdozer* 1974; *Mean Dog Blues* 1978; *Battletruck* 1982; *The Survivors* 1983
Wainwright III, Loudon *The Slugger's Wife* 1985; *Jacknife* 1988
Waite, Ralph *A Lovely Way to Go* 1968; *Last Summer* 1969; *Five Easy Pieces* 1970; *Kid Blue* 1971; *Chato's Land* 1972; *The Magnificent Seven Ride!* 1972; *Trouble Man* 1972; *The Stone Killer* 1973; *On the Nickel* 1979; *A Day for Thanks on Waltons Mountain* 1982; *Mother's Day on Waltons Mountain* 1982; *Snake Treaty* 1989; *Sparks: the Price of Passion* 1990; *The Bodyguard* 1992; *A Walton Thanksgiving Reunion* 1993; *Keys* 1994; *A*

Radio Times ACTORS' INDEX

Walton Wedding 1995; *Homeward Bound II: Lost in San Francisco* 1996; *A Walton Easter* 1997
Waites, Thomas G *aka* **Waites, Thomas**, *aka* **Waites, Tom** *On the Yard* 1978; *The Warriors* 1979; *The Clan of the Cave Bear* 1986; *Light of Day* 1987; *Blue Jean Cop* 1988
Waits, Tom *The Outsiders* 1983; *Rumble Fish* 1983; *Down by Law* 1986; *Candy Mountain* 1987; *Ironweed* 1987; *Cold Feet* 1989; *Mystery Train* 1989; *At Play in the Fields of the Lord* 1991; *Queens Logic* 1991; *Bram Stoker's Dracula* 1992; *Short Cuts* 1993
Wakabayashi, Akiko *What's Up, Tiger Lily?* 1966; *You Only Live Twice* 1967
Wakao, Ayako *Street of Shame* 1955; *Floating Weeds* 1959; *An Actor's Revenge* 1963
Wakefield, Hugh *The Man Who Knew Too Much* 1934; *Forget-Me-Not* 1936; *Journey Together* 1944; *Blithe Spirit* 1945
Wakeham, Deborah *Middle Age Crazy* 1980; *Stranded* 1989
Walbrook, Anton *The Adventures of Michael Strogoff* 1937; *Victoria the Great* 1937; *Sixty Glorious Years* 1938; *Gaslight* 1940; *Dangerous Moonlight* 1941; *49th Parallel* 1941; *The Life and Death of Colonel Blimp* 1943; *The Man from Morocco* 1944; *The Queen of Spades* 1948; *The Red Shoes* 1948; *La Ronde* 1950; *Lola Montès* 1955; *Oh, Rosalinda!!* 1955; *Saint Joan* 1957; *I Accuse!* 1958
Walburn, Raymond *Broadway Bill* 1934; *The Count of Monte Cristo* 1934; *Lady by Choice* 1934; *She Married Her Boss* 1935; *Thanks a Million* 1935; *Born to Dance* 1936; *The King Steps Out* 1936; *Mr Deeds Goes to Town* 1936; *High, Wide and Handsome* 1937; *Thin Ice* 1937; *Start Cheering* 1938; *Christmas in July* 1940; *Third Finger, Left Hand* 1940; *Confirm or Deny* 1941; *Kiss the Boys Goodbye* 1941; *Louisiana Purchase* 1941; *The Man in the Trunk* 1942; *The Desperadoes* 1943; *Dixie* 1943; *Hail the Conquering Hero* 1944; *Music in Manhattan* 1944; *The Cheaters* 1945; *Rendezvous with Annie* 1946; *Key to the City* 1950; *Mad Wednesday* 1950; *Riding High* 1950; *Golden Girl* 1951; *Beautiful but Dangerous* 1954
Walcott, Gregory *Texas Lady* 1955; *The Lieutenant Wore Skirts* 1956; *Thunder over Arizona* 1956; *Jet Attack* 1958; *Plan 9 from Outer Space* 1959; *The Outsider* 1961; *Prime Cut* 1972; *The Sugarland Express* 1974; *House II: the Second Story* 1987
Walcutt, John *Return* 1985; *Babies* 1990; *Harmful Intent* 1993; *Roseanne* 1994
Walden, Robert *Bloody Mama* 1970; *The Sidelong Glances of a Pigeon Kicker* 1970; *Larry* 1974
Waldis, Otto *The Exile* 1947; *Bird of Paradise* 1951; *Unknown World* 1951; *The Whip Hand* 1951
Waldman, Marian *Black Christmas* 1974; *Deranged* 1974
Waldo, Janet *Waterloo Bridge* 1940; *Fantastic Planet* 1973
Waldron, Charles *Kentucky* 1938; *Stranger on the Third Floor* 1940; *Remember the Night* 1940; *The Big Sleep* 1946
Waldron, Shawna *Little Giants* 1994; *The American President* 1995
Wales, Ethel *The Covered Wagon* 1923; *The Saturday Night Kid* 1929; *Tom Sawyer* 1930
Walken, Christopher *The Anderson Tapes* 1971; *The Happiness Cage* 1972; *Next Stop, Greenwich Village* 1976; *Annie Hall* 1977; *Roseland* 1977; *The Sentinel* 1977; *The Deer Hunter* 1978; *Last Embrace* 1979; *The Dogs of War* 1980; *Heaven's Gate* 1980; *Pennies from Heaven* 1981; *Brainstorm* 1983; *The Dead Zone* 1983; *At Close Range* 1985; *A View to a Kill* 1985; *Witness in the War Zone* 1986; *Biloxi Blues* 1988; *Homeboy* 1988; *The Milagro Beanfield War* 1988; *Communion* 1989; *King of New York* 1989; *The Comfort of Strangers* 1991; *McBain* 1991; *Sarah, Plain and Tall* 1991; *Batman Returns* 1992; *Mistress* 1992; *A Business Affair* 1993; *Day of Atonement* 1993; *Scam* 1993; *Skylark* 1993; *True Romance* 1993; *Wayne's World 2* 1993; *The Addiction* 1994; *The Prophecy* 1994; *Pulp Fiction* 1994; *Nick of Time* 1995; *Things to Do in Denver When You're Dead* 1995; *Search and Destroy* 1995; *The Funeral* 1996; *Last Man Standing* 1996; *Touch* 1996; *Wild Side* 1996; *Excess Baggage* 1997; *Mousehunt* 1997; *Suicide Kings* 1997; *The Prophecy II* 1997; *Antz* 1998; *Blast from the Past* 1998; *New Rose Hotel* 1998; *Vendetta* 1999; *Sleepy Hollow* 1999
Walker, Ally *Universal Soldier* 1992; *The Seventh Coin* 1993; *Bed of Roses* 1995; *Someone to Die For* 1995; *Steal Big, Steal Little* 1995; *Kazaam* 1996; *Happy, Texas* 1999
Walker, Amanda *Heat and Dust* 1982; *Charles & Diana: Unhappily Ever After* 1992
Walker, Arnetia *Scenes from the Class Struggle In Beverly Hills* 1989; *Cast a Deadly Spell* 1991; *Love Crimes* 1991; *Triumph over Disaster: the Hurricane Andrew Story* 1993; *Balloon Farm* 1999
Walker, Clint *Yellowstone Kelly* 1959; *Gold of the Seven Saints* 1961; *Send Me No Flowers* 1964; *None but the Brave* 1965; *The Night of the Grizzly* 1966; *The Dirty Dozen* 1967; *The Great Bank Robbery* 1969; *Sam Whiskey* 1969; *More Dead than Alive* 1969; *Pancho Villa* 1971; *Killdozer* 1974; *Baker's Hawk* 1976; *Snowbeast* 1977; *The White Buffalo* 1977
Walker, Fiona *Far from the Madding Crowd* 1967; *The Asphyx* 1972
Walker, Helen *Abroad with Two Yanks* 1944; *Brewster's Millions* 1945; *Murder, He Says* 1945; *Cluny Brown* 1946; *Murder in the Music Hall* 1946; *Nightmare Alley* 1947; *Call Northside 777* 1948; *My Dear Secretary* 1948; *Impact* 1949; *The Big Combo* 1955
Walker, Jimmie *Water* 1985; *The Guyver* 1992
Walker, Johnnie *The Matinee Idol* 1928; *Ladies of Leisure* 1930
Walker, Johnny *Mr and Mrs '55* 1955; *Chori Chori* 1956; *Kaagaz Ke Phool* 1959
Walker, Kathryn *Rich Kids* 1979; *Family Reunion* 1981; *Neighbors* 1981; *DARYL* 1985
Walker, Kerry *Almost* 1990; *The Piano* 1993
Walker, Lou *Hiding Out* 1987; *The Nightman* 1992; *Quest for Justice* 1993
Walker, Marcy *Hot Resort* 1985; *Babies* 1990; *Midnight's Child* 1992; *Overexposed* 1992
Walker, Martin *Sanders of the River* 1935; *The Vicar of Bray* 1937; *The Drum* 1938; *Love on the Dole* 1941
Walker, Matthew *Intimate Relations* 1995; *Little Women* 1995; *Misbegotten* 1998
Walker, Nancy *Best Foot Forward* 1943; *Girl Crazy* 1943; *Broadway Rhythm* 1944; *Lucky Me* 1954; *Thursday's Game* 1971; *The World's Greatest Athlete* 1973; *Human Feelings* 1978
Walker, Nella *The Woman in Red* 1935; *In Name Only* 1939; *When Tomorrow Comes* 1939; *I Love You Again* 1940; *Hers to Hold* 1943; *Sabrina Fair* 1954
Walker, Paul *Meet the Deedles* 1998; *Varsity Blues* 1999; *She's All That* 1999; *The Skulls* 2000
Walker, Polly *Enchanted April* 1991; *Shogun Warrior* 1991; *Patriot Games* 1992; *Sliver* 1993; *The Trial* 1993; *Restoration* 1995; *Emma* 1996; *Roseanna's Grave* 1996; *The Gambler* 1997; *The Woodlanders* 1997; *Talk of Angels* 1998; *Dark Harbor* 1998; *Curtain Call* 1998; *8½ Women* 1999
Walker, Ray *Baby, Take a Bow* 1934; *Stars on Parade* 1944; *Marry Me Again* 1953
Walker, Robert *Madame Curie* 1943; *Since You Went Away* 1944; *See Here, Private Hargrove* 1944; *Thirty Seconds over Tokyo* 1944; *The Clock* 1945; *The Sailor Takes a Wife* 1945; *Till the Clouds Roll By* 1946; *The Beginning or the End* 1947; *Song of Love* 1947; *The Sea of Grass* 1947; *One Touch of Venus* 1948; *Strangers on a Train* 1951; *Vengeance Valley* 1951; *My Son John* 1952
Walker Jr, Robert *aka* **Walker, Robert** *The Ceremony* 1963; *The Hook* 1963; *Ensign Pulver* 1964; *The Happening* 1967; *The War Wagon* 1967; *Easy Rider* 1969; *Young Billy Young* 1969; *Road to Salina* 1969; *Beware! The Blob* 1971; *Don Juan 73, or If Don Juan Were a Woman* 1973; *Hambone and Hillie* 1984
Walker, Scott *Cahill, United States Marshal* 1973; *Orca* 1977
Walker, Syd *Over She Goes* 1937; *The Gang's All Here* 1939
Walker, Sydney *Love Story* 1970; *Prelude to a Kiss* 1992; *Getting Even with Dad* 1994
Walker, Tippy *The World of Henry Orient* 1964; *Jennifer on My Mind* 1971
Walker, William *The Girl Who Had Everything* 1953; *The Boy Who Caught a Crook* 1961
Walker, Zena *Emergency* 1962; *Sammy Going South* 1963; *One of Those Things* 1970; *The Likely Lads* 1976; *The Dresser* 1983
Wall, Max *The Hound of the Baskervilles* 1977; *Jabberwocky* 1977; *Hanover Street* 1979; *Little Dorrit* 1987; *We Think the World of You* 1988; *Loser Takes All* 1990; *Strike It Rich* 1990
Wall, Robert *The Way of the Dragon* 1973; *Game of Death* 1978
Wallace, Anzac *Utu* 1983; *The Silent One* 1984; *The Quiet Earth* 1985
Wallace, Basil *Marked for Death* 1990; *Return of the Living Dead III* 1993
Wallace, Bill *A Force of One* 1979; *Avenging Force* 1986
Wallace, George D *aka* **Wallace, George** *Six Black Horses* 1962; *Working Trash* 1990; *The Haunted* 1991
Wallace, Ian *Assassin for Hire* 1951; *tom thumb* 1958
Wallace, Jack *The Bear* 1988; *The Killing Jar* 1996
Wallace, Jean *Blaze of Noon* 1947; *Jigsaw* 1949; *The Man on the Eiffel Tower* 1949; *Native Son* 1951; *Star of India* 1954; *The Big Combo* 1955; *The Devil's Hairpin* 1957; *Maracaibo* 1958; *Lancelot and Guinevere* 1963; *Beach Red* 1967
Wallace, Julie T *Hawks* 1988; *The Lunatic* 1992
Wallace, Morgan *Hell's House* 1932; *Confidential* 1935; *Billy the Kid Returns* 1938; *Dick Tracy* 1945
Wallace, Paul *Johnny Trouble* 1957; *Gypsy* 1962
Wallace, Rowena *Relatives* 1985; *Cappuccino* 1989; *Blackwater Trail* 1995
Wallace, Royce *Goodbye, Columbus* 1969; *Green Eyes* 1976; *Thompson's Last Run* 1986
Wallace Stone, Dee *aka* **Wallace, Dee** *The Hills Have Eyes* 1978; *10* 1979; *The Secret War of Jackie's Girls* 1980; *The Howling* 1981; *ET the Extra-Terrestrial* 1982; *Jimmy the Kid* 1982; *Cujo* 1983; *Wait till Your Mother Gets Home!* 1983; *Secret Admirer* 1985; *Legend of the White Horse* 1985; *Critters* 1986; *Shadow Play* 1986; *Addicted to His Love* 1988; *Stranger on My Land* 1988; *I'm Dangerous Tonight* 1990; *Popcorn* 1991; *Rescue Me* 1991; *Alligator II: the Mutation* 1991; *Lightning in a Bottle* 1992; *Huck and the King of Hearts* 1993; *Prophet of Evil* 1993; *Cradle of Conspiracy* 1994; *Runaway Daughters* 1994; *Search and Rescue* 1994; *Witness to the Execution* 1994; *Best of the Best 3: No Turning Back* 1995; *Temptress* 1995; *The Road Home* 1995; *The Skateboard Kid II* 1995; *The Frighteners* 1996; *Skeletons* 1996
Wallach, Eli *Baby Doll* 1956; *The Lineup* 1958; *The Magnificent Seven* 1960; *Seven Thieves* 1960; *The Misfits* 1961; *Hemingway's Adventures of a Young Man* 1962; *How the West Was Won* 1962; *The Victors* 1963; *Act One* 1963; *Genghis Khan* 1964; *Kisses for My President* 1964; *The Moon-Spinners* 1964; *Lord Jim* 1965; *How to Steal a Million* 1966; *The Poppy Is Also a Flower* 1966; *The Good, the Bad and the Ugly* 1967; *The Tiger Makes Out* 1967; *How to Save a Marriage and Ruin Your Life* 1968; *A Lovely Way to Go* 1968; *The Brain* 1969; *Mackenna's Gold* 1969; *The Adventures of Gerard* 1970; *The People Next Door* 1970; *Zigzag* 1970; *The Angel Levine* 1970; *Romance of a Horse Thief* 1971; *Cinderella Liberty* 1973; *The Deep* 1977; *The Domino Principle* 1977; *The Sentinel* 1977; *Girlfriends* 1978; *Firepower* 1979; *Winter Kills* 1979; *The Hunter* 1980; *The Salamander* 1981; *Skokie* 1981; *Anatomy of an Illness* 1984; *Sam's Son* 1984; *Embassy* 1985; *Something in Common* 1986; *Tough Guys* 1986; *Nuts* 1987; *The Godfather Part III* 1990; *The Two Jakes* 1990; *Article 99* 1992; *Legacy of Lies* 1992; *Mistress* 1992; *Night and the City* 1992; *Teamster Boss: the Jackie Presser Story* 1992; *Two Much* 1995; *The Associate* 1996; *Keeping the Faith* 2000
Waller, Eddy *aka* **Waller, Eddy C** *Indian Uprising* 1951; *Man without a Star* 1955
Waller, Fats *King of Burlesque* 1936; *Stormy Weather* 1943
Walley, Deborah *Gidget Goes Hawaiian* 1961; *Bon Voyage!* 1962; *Summer Magic* 1963; *The Young Lovers* 1964; *Beach Blanket Bingo* 1965; *Sergeant Deadhead* 1965; *Ski Party* 1965; *The Ghost in the Invisible Bikini* 1966
Wallis, Shani *Oliver!* 1968; *Terror in the Wax Museum* 1973; *Arnold* 1973; *The Pebble and the Penguin* 1995
Wallraff, Diego *Of Love and Shadows* 1994; *The Perez Family* 1995
Walls, Tom *A Cuckoo in the Nest* 1933; *Fighting Stock* 1935; *Foreign Affaires* 1935; *For Valour* 1937; *Crackerjack* 1938; *Strange Boarders* 1938; *The Halfway House* 1943; *They Met in the Dark* 1943; *Undercover* 1943; *Love Story* 1944; *Johnny Frenchman* 1945; *The Master of Bankdam* 1947; *While I Live* 1947; *Spring in Park Lane* 1948; *The Interrupted Journey* 1949; *Maytime in Mayfair* 1949
Walmsley, Jon *A Day for Thanks on Waltons Mountain* 1982; *Mother's Day on Waltons Mountain* 1982; *A Walton Thanksgiving Reunion* 1993; *A Walton Easter* 1997
Walsh, Dermot *Hungry Hill* 1947; *Jassy* 1947; *Third Time Lucky* 1949; *The Frightened Man* 1952; *Ghost Ship* 1952; *The Blue Parrot* 1953; *Counterspy* 1953; *Sea Fury* 1958; *The Flesh and the Fiends* 1959; *Make Mine a Million* 1959; *The Bandit of Zhobe* 1959; *The Breaking Point* 1961; *Emergency* 1962
Walsh, Dylan *Arctic Blue* 1993; *Nobody's Fool* 1994; *Radio Inside* 1994; *Congo* 1995; *The Almost Perfect Bank Robbery* 1996; *Divided by Hate* 1997; *Changing Habits* 1997
Walsh, Edward *aka* **Walsh, Ed** *California Split* 1974; *Let It Ride* 1989
Walsh, George *Rosita* 1923; *Me and My Gal* 1932; *Black Beauty* 1933; *The Bowery* 1933
Walsh, Gwynyth *Blue Monkey* 1987; *The Crush* 1993; *Falsely Accused* 1993; *The Other Mother* 1995; *Search for Justice* 1996; *Unlikely Suspects* 1996; *The Limbic Region* 1996; *Stand against Fear* 1996
Walsh, J T *Hard Choices* 1984; *Right to Kill?* 1985; *Power* 1986; *Good Morning, Vietnam* 1987; *House of Games* 1987; *Tin Men* 1987; *Tequila Sunrise* 1988; *The Big Picture* 1989; *Dad* 1989; *Wired* 1989; *Crazy People* 1990; *The Grifters* 1990; *Narrow Margin* 1990; *The Russia House* 1990; *Why Me?* 1990; *Backdraft* 1991; *Defenseless* 1991; *Iron Maze* 1991; *True Identity* 1991; *A Few Good Men* 1992; *Hoffa* 1992; *In the Shadow of a Killer* 1992; *Red Rock West* 1992; *Sniper* 1992; *The Last Seduction* 1993; *Morning Glory* 1993; *Needful Things* 1993; *Blue Chips* 1994; *The Client* 1994; *Miracle on 34th Street* 1994; *Silent Fall* 1994; *Charlie's Ghost Story* 1994; *The Babysitter* 1995; *Nixon* 1995; *Black Day Blue Night* 1995; *The Low Life* 1995; *Crime of the Century* 1996; *Gang in Blue* 1996;

Persons Unknown 1996; Sling Blade 1996; Breakdown 1997; Hope 1997; The Negotiator 1998; Pleasantville 1998

Walsh, Joseph aka **Walsh, Joey** Hans Christian Andersen 1952; The Juggler 1953; Anzio 1968; California Split 1974; The Driver 1978

Walsh, Kay Keep Fit 1937; The Last Adventurers 1937; I See Ice 1938; In Which We Serve 1942; This Happy Breed 1944; The October Man 1947; Vice Versa 1947; Oliver Twist 1948; Last Holiday 1950; The Magnet 1950; Stage Fright 1950; Encore 1951; Hunted 1952; Meet Me Tonight 1952; Young Bess 1953; Lease of Life 1954; Cast a Dark Shadow 1957; The Horse's Mouth 1958; The Rainbow Jacket 1958; Greyfriars Bobby 1960; Tunes of Glory 1960; Lunch Hour 1962; Reach for Glory 1962; Dr Syn, Alias the Scarecrow 1963; 80,000 Suspects 1963; The Beauty Jungle 1964; He Who Rides a Tiger 1965; The Witches 1966; Connecting Rooms 1969; The Virgin and the Gypsy 1970; The Ruling Class 1972

Walsh, M Emmet Alice's Restaurant 1969; The Traveling Executioner 1970; The Prisoner of Second Avenue 1974; At Long Last Love 1975; Sarah T: Portrait of a Teenage Alcoholic 1975; Mikey and Nicky 1976; Straight Time 1978; The Jerk 1979; The Fish That Saved Pittsburgh 1979; Ordinary People 1980; Raise the Titanic 1980; Back Roads 1981; Reds 1981; Blade Runner 1982; Cannery Row 1982; The Escape Artist 1982; Fast-Walking 1982; Blood Simple 1983; Scandalous 1983; Grandview, USA 1984; Missing in Action 1984; The Pope of Greenwich Village 1984; Raw Courage 1984; Fletch 1985; Back to School 1986; The Best of Times 1986; Critters 1986; Resting Place 1986; Wildcats 1986; Bigfoot and the Hendersons 1987; Broken Vows 1987; No Man's Land 1987; Clean and Sober 1988; Sunset 1988; Chattahoochee 1989; The Mighty Quinn 1989; Red Scorpion 1989; Narrow Margin 1990; True Betrayal 1990; Deadly Identity 1991; Equinox 1992; Four Eyes and Six-Guns 1992; White Sands 1992; Wild Card 1992; The Music of Chance 1993; Wilder Napalm 1993; Bitter Harvest 1993; Camp Nowhere 1994; Criminal Hearts 1995; Free Willy 2: the Adventure Home 1995; Relative Fear 1995; From the Mixed-Up Files of Mrs Basil E Frankweiler 1995; Dead Badge 1995; Albino Alligator 1996; The Killing Jar 1996; My Best Friend's Wedding 1997; Retroactive 1997; Chairman of the Board 1998; Nightmare in Big Sky Country 1998; Wild Wild West 1999; The Iron Giant 1999; Random Hearts 1999

Walsh, Percy Boys Will Be Boys 1935; King of the Damned 1935; Pastor Hall 1940

Walsh, Raoul Sadie Thompson 1928; It's a Great Feeling 1949

Walsh, Sydney An Early Frost 1985; Trenchcoat in Paradise 1989

Walston, Ray Kiss Them for Me 1957; Damn Yankees 1958; South Pacific 1958; Say One for Me 1959; The Apartment 1960; Portrait in Black 1960; Convicts Four 1962; Who's Minding the Store? 1963; Wives and Lovers 1963; Kiss Me, Stupid 1964; Caprice 1967; Paint Your Wagon 1969; The Sting 1973; Silver Streak 1976; The Happy Hooker Goes to Washington 1977; Popeye 1980; Private School 1983; For Love or Money 1984; Johnny Dangerously 1984; Amos 1985; Driving Academy 1988; Red River 1988; Saturday the 14th Strikes Back 1988; Ski Patrol 1989; Of Mice and Men 1992; Tricks 1997; Addams Family Reunion 1998; My Favorite Martian 1999

Walter, Harriet Turtle Diary 1985; The Good Father 1986; Milou en Mai 1989; The Hour of the Pig 1993; Sense and Sensibility 1995; The Governess 1997; Keep the Aspidistra Flying 1997; Bedrooms and Hallways 1998; Onegin 1999

Walter, Jessica Lilith 1964; Grand Prix 1966; The Group 1966; Bye Bye Braverman 1968; Number One 1969; Three's a Crowd 1969; Play Misty for Me 1971; Black Market Baby 1977; Going Ape! 1981; The Flamingo Kid 1984; The Execution 1985; Tapeheads 1988; Ghost in the Machine 1993; Leave of Absence 1994; Temptress 1995; Doomsday Rock 1997; Slums of Beverly Hills 1998

Walter, Lisa Ann Eddie 1996; The Parent Trap 1998

Walter, Tracey The Hunter 1980; Raggedy Man 1981; Conan the Destroyer 1984; Repo Man 1984; Something Wild 1986; City Slickers 1991; Delusion 1991; Ride with the Wind 1994; In the Line of Duty: Kidnapped 1995; Tell Me No Secrets 1996; Devil's Child 1997; Drive 1997; Wild America 1997

Walters, Jamie aka **Walters, James** Shout 1991; Bed & Breakfast 1992

Walters, Julie Educating Rita 1983; She'll Be Wearing Pink Pyjamas 1984; Car Trouble 1985; Personal Services 1987; Prick Up Your Ears 1987; Buster 1988; Killing Dad 1989; Mack the Knife 1989; Stepping Out 1991; Just like a Woman 1992; Wide Eyed and Legless 1993; Sister My Sister 1994; Intimate Relations 1995; Girls' Night 1997; Titanic Town 1998

Walters, Laurie The Harrad Experiment 1973; The Harrad Summer 1974; The Taking of Flight 847 1988

Walters, Melora Twenty Bucks 1993; Boogie Nights 1997; Los Locos 1997; Twice Upon a Time 1998; Magnolia 1999

Walters, Nancy Monster on the Campus 1958; Blue Hawaii 1961

Walters, Susan A Cop for the Killing 1990; Grand Slam 1990; The Counterfeit Contessa 1994; …At First Sight 1995; Two Came Back 1997

Walters, Thorley Carlton-Browne of the FO 1958; A Lady Mislaid 1958; The Pure Hell of St Trinian's 1960; Suspect 1960; Murder She Said 1961; Petticoat Pirates 1961; The Phantom of the Opera 1962; Ring of Spies 1963; Dracula – Prince of Darkness 1965; Frankenstein Created Woman 1966; Frankenstein Must Be Destroyed 1969; The Man Who Haunted Himself 1970; Trog 1970; Vampire Circus 1971; Bartleby 1971; The Adventure of Sherlock Holmes' Smarter Brother 1975; The People That Time Forgot 1977; The Wildcats of St Trinian's 1980; The Sign of Four 1983

Walthall, Henry B Home, Sweet Home 1914; The Birth of a Nation 1915; The Scarlet Letter 1926; The Road to Mandalay 1926; London after Midnight 1927; The Trespasser 1929; Abraham Lincoln 1930; Tol'able David 1930; Me and My Gal 1932; Strange Interlude 1932; Ride Him, Cowboy 1932; Somewhere in Sonora 1933; The Lemon Drop Kid 1934; Judge Priest 1934; Dante's Inferno 1935; A Tale of Two Cities 1935; China Clipper 1936; The Devil-Doll 1936

Walton, Douglas The Secret of Madame Blanche 1933; Charlie Chan in London 1934; Bride of Frankenstein 1935; Captain Hurricane 1935; Mary of Scotland 1936; Bad Lands 1939; Raffles 1939; Farewell My Lovely 1945; Dick Tracy vs Cueball 1946

Walton, John Undercover 1983; Kangaroo 1986; The Lighthorsemen 1987

Waltz, Lisa Brighton Beach Memoirs 1986; The Odd Couple II 1998

Wanamaker, Sam My Girl Tisa 1948; Give Us This Day 1949; Mr Denning Drives North 1951; The Criminal 1960; Taras Bulba 1962; The Man in the Middle 1964; The Spy Who Came in from the Cold 1965; Danger Route 1967; Warning Shot 1967; The Day the Fish Came Out 1967; The Sellout 1975; Voyage of the Damned 1976; Billy Jack Goes to Washington 1977; Death on the Nile 1978; From Hell to Victory 1979; The Competition 1980; Private Benjamin 1980; Irreconcilable Differences 1984; The Aviator 1985; Embassy 1985; Raw Deal 1986; Baby Boom 1987; Detective Sadie and Son 1987; Superman IV: the Quest for Peace 1987; Judgment in Berlin 1988; Always Remember I Love You 1990; Guilty by Suspicion 1990; Running against Time 1990; Pure Luck 1991; Killer Rules 1993

Wanamaker, Zoë Amy Foster 1997; Wilde 1997

Wang Chung Hsin The Way of the Dragon 1973; Return of the Dragon 1973

Wang, Peter Chan Is Missing 1982; A Great Wall 1985; The Laserman 1988

Wang Xueqi Yellow Earth 1984; The Big Parade 1986

Wanninger, Ashley Europa, Europa 1991; Romance 1998

War Eagle, John The Wild North 1952; The Great Sioux Uprising 1953; When the Legends Die 1972

Waram, Percy Ministry of Fear 1945; The Late George Apley 1947; The Big Hangover 1950; A Face in the Crowd 1957

Warburton, John Nothing but Trouble 1944; Confidential Agent 1945; Saratoga Trunk 1945; Tarzan and the Huntress 1947

Ward, Amelita Clancy Street Boys 1943; The Falcon and the Co-Eds 1943; The Falcon in Danger 1943; Come Out Fighting 1945

Ward, B J Daffy Duck's Quackbusters 1988; Pound Puppies and the Legend of Big Paw 1988

Ward, Fred Escape from Alcatraz 1979; UFOria 1980; Southern Comfort 1981; The Right Stuff 1983; Silkwood 1983; Uncommon Valor 1983; Swing Shift 1984; Noon Wine 1985; Remo – Unarmed and Dangerous 1985; Secret Admirer 1985; Florida Straits 1986; Train of Dreams 1987; Big Business 1988; Saigon 1988; The Prince of Pennsylvania 1988; Tremors 1989; Catchfire 1990; Henry & June 1990; Miami Blues 1990; Cast a Deadly Spell 1991; The Dark Wind 1991; Equinox 1992; Four Eyes and Six-Guns 1992; The Player 1992; Thunderheart 1992; Short Cuts 1993; Two Small Bodies 1993; The Blue Villa 1994; Naked Gun $33\frac{1}{3}$: the Final Insult 1994; Tremors 2: Aftershocks 1995; Chain Reaction 1996; Best Men 1997; First Do No Harm 1997; The Honest Courtesan 1998; Circus 1999

Ward, James Kitten with a Whip 1964; The Night of the Iguana 1964; Red Line 7000 1965; Casper: a Spirited Beginning 1997

Ward, Jonathan White Water Summer 1987; Mac and Me 1988; FernGully: the Last Rainforest 1992

Ward, Kelly Grease 1978; The Big Red One 1980

Ward, Lyman Ferris Bueller's Day Off 1986; Milk and Honey 1988; Sweet Poison 1991; Tagget 1991; Guilty as Charged 1991; No Dessert Dad, Till You Mow the Lawn 1994; The Secret Agent Club 1995; The Wrong Woman 1996

Ward, Mary B aka **Ward, Mary** Playing for Keeps 1986; Surviving Desire 1989; Hangin' with the Homeboys 1991

Ward, Megan Trancers II: The Return of Jack Deth 1991; Amityville 1992: It's About Time 1992; California Man 1992; Arcade 1993; Freaked 1993; Politically Correct Party Animals 1994; Glory Daze 1995; Joe's Apartment 1996; Don't Look Down 1998

Ward, Michael What the Butler Saw 1950; The Frightened Man 1952; Up in the World 1956

Ward, Polly The Old Curiosity Shop 1934; Hold My Hand 1938; It's in the Air 1938

Ward, Rachel Sharky's Machine 1981; Dead Men Don't Wear Plaid 1982; Against All Odds 1984; The Good Wife 1986; Hotel Colonial 1987; How to Get Ahead in Advertising 1989; After Dark, My Sweet 1990; Christopher Columbus: the Discovery 1992; Double Jeopardy 1992; Wide Sargasso Sea 1992; Black Magic 1992; The Ascent 1994; Love, Murder & Deceit 1997

Ward, Richard aka **Ward, Dick** The Learning Tree 1969; Across 110th Street 1972; Cops and Robbers 1973; Mandingo 1975; The Jerk 1979

Ward, Roger Mad Max 1979; Turkey Shoot 1981; Fatal Bond 1991

Ward, Ronald We'll Meet Again 1942; They Met in the Dark 1943

Ward, Sandy The Velvet Vampire 1971; Tank 1984

Ward, Sela The Man Who Loved Women 1983; Nothing in Common 1986; Hello Again 1987; The King of Love 1987; Rainbow Drive 1990; Double Jeopardy 1992; The Fugitive 1993; Killer Rules 1993; Almost Golden: the Jessica Savitch Story 1995; My Fellow Americans 1996; The Reef 1996; Rescuers: Stories of Courage – Two Women 1997; 54 1998

Ward, Simon Frankenstein Must Be Destroyed 1969; I Start Counting 1970; Young Winston 1972; Hitler: the Last Ten Days 1973; All Creatures Great and Small 1974; Dracula 1974; The Four Musketeers 1974; Aces High 1976; Battleflag 1977; Holocaust 2000 1977; Dominique 1978; The Four Feathers 1978; Zulu Dawn 1979; The Monster Club 1980; Supergirl 1984; Leave All Fair 1985

Ward, Skip Easy Come, Easy Go 1967; The Mad Room 1969

Ward, Sophie The Copter Kids 1976; Young Sherlock Holmes 1985; Aria 1987; A Summer Story 1987; Young Toscanini 1988; The Monk 1990; Wuthering Heights 1992; Waxwork II: Lost in Time 1992

Ward, Wally Combat Academy 1986; Thunder Run 1986

Ward, Warwick Vaudeville 1925; The Wonderful Lie of Nina Petrovna 1929; FP1 1932

Warde, Harlan Julie 1956; The Monster That Challenged the World 1957

Warden, Jack From Here to Eternity 1953; The Bachelor Party 1957; Edge of the City 1957; 12 Angry Men 1957; Run Silent, Run Deep 1958; Darby's Rangers 1958; The Sound and the Fury 1959; That Kind of Woman 1959; Wake Me when It's Over 1960; Escape from Zahrain 1962; Donovan's Reef 1963; The Thin Red Line 1964; Bye Bye Braverman 1968; Brian's Song 1971; The Face of Fear 1971; What's a Nice Girl like You…? 1971; Who Is Harry Kellerman, and Why Is He Saying Those Terrible Things about Me? 1971; Welcome to the Club 1971; Billy Two Hats 1973; The Man Who Loved Cat Dancing 1973; The Apprenticeship of Duddy Kravitz 1974; Shampoo 1975; All the President's Men 1976; The White Buffalo 1977; Death on the Nile 1978; Heaven Can Wait 1978; …And Justice for All 1979; Being There 1979; Beyond the Poseidon Adventure 1979; The Champ 1979; Dreamer 1979; Used Cars 1980; Carbon Copy 1981; The Great Muppet Caper 1981; So Fine 1981; Chu Chu and the Philly Flash 1981; The Verdict 1982; Crackers 1984; The Aviator 1985; September 1987; Dead Solid Perfect 1988; The Presidio 1988; Everybody Wins 1990; Problem Child 1990; Problem Child 2 1991; Night and the City 1992; Passed Away 1992; Toys 1992; Guilty as Sin 1993; Bullets over Broadway 1994; Things to Do in Denver When You're Dead 1995; While You Were Sleeping 1995; Problem Child 3 1995; Ed 1996; Chairman of the Board 1998; Dirty Work 1998

Wardwell, Geoffrey The Challenge 1938; Crimes at the Dark House 1939

Ware, Helen The Virginian 1929; Tol'able David 1930

Ware, Herta Cocoon 1985; Crazy in Love 1992

Warfield, Emily The Man in the Moon 1991; Bonanza – the Return 1993; Beyond Obsession 1994

Warfield, Joe Teenager 1974; French Silk 1993

Warfield, Marsha DC Cab 1983; Doomsday Rock 1997

Warhol, Andy Dynamite Chicken 1971; The Driver's Seat 1975

Warlock, Billy aka **Warlock, Bill** Hot Shot 1986; 2 ½ Dads 1986; Baywatch: Panic at Malibu Pier 1989; Honor Thy Father and

Mother: the Menendez Killings 1994
Warnecke, Gordon *My Beautiful Laundrette* 1985; *The Pleasure Principle* 1991
Warner, David *Tom Jones* 1963; *Morgan – a Suitable Case for Treatment* 1966; *The Bofors Gun* 1968; *The Fixer* 1968; *The Sea Gull* 1968; *Work Is a Four Letter Word* 1968; *A Midsummer Night's Dream* 1969; *The Ballad of Cable Hogue* 1970; *Perfect Friday* 1970; *A Doll's House* 1973; *From beyond the Grave* 1973; *Little Malcolm and His Struggle Against the Eunuchs* 1974; *Mister Quilp* 1975; *The Omen* 1976; *Cross of Iron* 1977; *The Disappearance* 1977; *Providence* 1977; *Silver Bears* 1978; *The Thirty-Nine Steps* 1978; *SOS Titanic* 1979; *Time after Time* 1979; *Nightwing* 1979; *The Island* 1980; *Tron* 1982; *The Man with Two Brains* 1983; *A Christmas Carol* 1984; *The Company of Wolves* 1984; *Desperado* 1987; *Hanna's War* 1988; *Mr North* 1988; *Waxwork* 1988; *Mortal Passions* 1989; *Star Trek V: the Final Frontier* 1989; *Spymaker: the Secret Life of Ian Fleming* 1990; *Cast a Deadly Spell* 1991; *Star Trek VI: the Undiscovered Country* 1991; *Teenage Mutant Ninja Turtles II: the Secret of the Ooze* 1991; *The Unnamable Returns* 1992; *Body Bags* 1993; *Necronomicon* 1993; *Quest of the Delta Knights* 1993; *In the Mouth of Madness* 1994; *Tryst* 1994; *Beastmaster III: the Eye of Braxus* 1995; *Naked Souls* 1995; *The Leading Man* 1996; *Rasputin* 1996; *Scream 2* 1997; *Houdini* 1998; *Wing Commander* 1999
Warner, H B *The King of Kings* 1927; *The Divine Lady* 1928; *The Show of Shows* 1929; *The Green Goddess* 1930; *Five Star Final* 1931; *Supernatural* 1933; *Jennie Gerhardt* 1933; *Mr Deeds Goes to Town* 1936; *Lost Horizon* 1937; *Victoria the Great* 1937; *Kidnapped* 1938; *The Toy Wife* 1938; *New Moon* 1940; *The Corsican Brothers* 1941; *Topper Returns* 1941; *Hitler's Children* 1943; *Strange Impersonation* 1946; *High Wall* 1947
Warner, Jack *The Captive Heart* 1946; *Against the Wind* 1947; *Dear Murderer* 1947; *Holiday Camp* 1947; *Hue and Cry* 1947; *Easy Money* 1948; *Here Come the Huggetts* 1948; *My Brother's Keeper* 1948; *Vote for Huggett* 1948; *The Blue Lamp* 1949; *The Huggetts Abroad* 1949; *Train of Events* 1949; *Boys in Brown* 1949; *Scrooge* 1951; *Valley of Eagles* 1951; *Emergency Call* 1952; *Meet Me Tonight* 1952; *Albert, RN* 1953; *The Final Test* 1953; *The Square Ring* 1953; *Bang! You're Dead* 1954; *Forbidden Cargo* 1954; *The Ladykillers* 1955; *The Quatermass Experiment* 1955; *Home and Away* 1956; *Carve Her Name with Pride* 1958; *Jigsaw* 1962; *Dominique* 1978
Warner, Julie *I Want Him Back* 1990; *Doc Hollywood* 1991; *Mr Saturday Night* 1992; *The Puppet Masters* 1994; *Tommy Boy* 1995; *Wedding Bell Blues* 1996; *Mr Murder* 1998
Warner, Malcolm-Jamal *The Father Clements Story* 1987; *Drop Zone* 1994; *The Tuskegee Airmen* 1995; *Tyson* 1995
Warner, Richard *To Have and to Hold* 1951; *Village of the Damned* 1960
Warren, Barry *The Devil-Ship Pirates* 1964; *Frankenstein Created Woman* 1966
Warren, Betty *Variety Jubilee* 1942; *Champagne Charlie* 1944; *Passport to Pimlico* 1949; *So Long at the Fair* 1950; *Tread Softly Stranger* 1958
Warren, C Denier *Good Morning, Boys* 1937; *Keep Fit* 1937; *It's in the Air* 1938; *Strange Boarders* 1938
Warren, E Alyn *Abraham Lincoln* 1930; *Tarzan the Fearless* 1933
Warren, Jennifer *Sam's Song* 1969; *Night Moves* 1975; *Another Man, Another Chance* 1977; *Slap Shot* 1977; *Ice Castles* 1978; *Confessions of a Married Man* 1983; *Mutant* 1984
Warren, Katharine *All the King's Men* 1949; *Tell It to the Judge* 1949
Warren, Katherine *Force of Arms* 1951; *The Prowler* 1951; *The Star* 1953
Warren, Kenneth J *Doctor Blood's Coffin* 1960; *Part-Time Wife* 1961; *I, Monster* 1971; *The Creeping Flesh* 1972; *S*P*Y*S* 1974
Warren, Kiersten *Shadow of the Past* 1995; *Bicentennial Man* 1999
Warren, Lesley Ann *The Happiest Millionaire* 1967; *The One and Only, Genuine, Original Family Band* 1968; *Harry and Walter Go to New York* 1976; *Treasure of the Yankee Zephyr* 1981; *Victor/Victoria* 1982; *A Night in Heaven* 1983; *Choose Me* 1984; *Songwriter* 1984; *Clue* 1985; *Apology* 1986; *A Fight for Jenny* 1986; *Burglar* 1987; *Baja Oklahoma* 1988; *Cop* 1988; *Blind Judgement: Seduction in Travis County* 1991; *Life Stinks* 1991; *Hearts on Fire* 1992; *Pure Country* 1992; *Desperate Justice* 1993; *Color of Night* 1994; *Bird of Prey* 1995; *Joseph in Egypt* 1995; *Murderous Intent* 1995; *Natural Enemy* 1996; *Going All the Way* 1997; *Love Kills* 1998; *The Limey* 1999; *Twin Falls Idaho* 1999
Warren, Marc *Boston Kickout* 1995; *Dad Savage* 1997
Warren, Michael aka **Warren, Mike** *Butterflies Are Free* 1972; *Cleopatra Jones* 1973; *Norman... Is That You?* 1976; *Fast Break* 1979; *Heaven Is a Playground* 1991; *Stompin' at the Savoy* 1992; *Storyville* 1992
Warren, Ruth *Zoo in Budapest* 1933; *Bring Your Smile Along* 1955
Warrender, Harold *Scott of the Antarctic* 1948; *Conspirator* 1949; *Pandora and the Flying Dutchman* 1951; *Where No Vultures Fly* 1951
Warrick, Ruth *Citizen Kane* 1941; *The Corsican Brothers* 1941; *Journey into Fear* 1942; *The Iron Major* 1943; *Guest in the House* 1944; *Secret Command* 1944; *Mr Winkle Goes to War* 1944; *China Sky* 1945; *Driftwood* 1946; *Song of the South* 1946; *Swell Guy* 1946; *Daisy Kenyon* 1947; *Arch of Triumph* 1948; *Let's Dance* 1950; *Ride beyond Vengeance* 1966
Warrington, Don *Rising Damp* 1980; *Bloodbath at the House of Death* 1983; *The Lion of Africa* 1987; *Babymother* 1998
Warshofsky, David *Suffering Bastards* 1989; *GI Jane* 1997
Warwick, Dionne *Slaves* 1969; *Rent-a-Cop* 1988
Warwick, John *The Ticket of Leave Man* 1937; *The Face at the Window* 1939; *Flying 55* 1939; *Spare a Copper* 1940; *Danny Boy* 1941; *The Saint's Vacation* 1941; *Dancing with Crime* 1946; *Conspiracy in Teheran* 1947; *While I Live* 1947; *Escape Route* 1952; *Contraband Spain* 1955; *The Square Peg* 1958
Warwick, Richard *if....* 1968; *Sebastiane* 1976; *The Tempest* 1979; *White Hunter, Black Heart* 1990
Warwick, Robert *Hopalong Cassidy* 1935; *Whipsaw* 1935; *Blockade* 1938; *Devil's Island* 1940; *Sullivan's Travels* 1941; *I Married a Witch* 1942; *The Falcon's Adventure* 1946; *Adventures of Don Juan* 1948; *A Woman's Secret* 1949; *Sugarfoot* 1951; *The Sword of Monte Cristo* 1951; *Against All Flags* 1952; *Silver Lode* 1954; *Chief Crazy Horse* 1955; *Escape to Burma* 1955; *Walk the Proud Land* 1956
Washbourne, Mona *Adventure in the Hopfields* 1954; *Child's Play* 1954; *To Dorothy, a Son* 1954; *It's Great to Be Young* 1956; *A Cry from the Streets* 1957; *Cast a Dark Shadow* 1957; *The Brides of Dracula* 1960; *Billy Liar* 1963; *My Fair Lady* 1964; *Night Must Fall* 1964; *The Collector* 1965; *The Third Day* 1965; *One Way Pendulum* 1965; *if....* 1968; *The Bed Sitting Room* 1969; *Mister Quilp* 1975; *The Driver's Seat* 1975; *The Blue Bird* 1976; *Stevie* 1978
Washburn, Beverly *The Juggler* 1953; *The Lone Ranger* 1956; *Old Yeller* 1957
Washington, Denzel *Carbon Copy* 1981; *A Soldier's Story* 1984; *Power* 1986; *Cry Freedom* 1987; *For Queen and Country* 1988; *Glory* 1989; *The Mighty Quinn* 1989; *Heart Condition* 1990; *Mo' Better Blues* 1990; *Mississippi Masala* 1991; *Ricochet* 1991; *Malcolm X* 1992; *Much Ado about Nothing* 1993; *The Pelican Brief* 1993; *Philadelphia* 1993; *Crimson Tide* 1995; *Devil in a Blue Dress* 1995; *Virtuosity* 1995; *Courage under Fire* 1996; *The Preacher's Wife* 1996; *Fallen* 1998; *He Got Game* 1998; *The Siege* 1998; *The Hurricane* 1999; *The Bone Collector* 1999
Washington, Isaiah *Mr and Mrs Loving* 1993; *Clockers* 1995; *Girl 6* 1996; *Love Jones* 1997; *Mixing Nia* 1998; *True Crime* 1999; *Romeo Must Die* 2000
Wass, Ted *The Curse of the Pink Panther* 1983; *Oh, God! You Devil* 1984; *Sheena, Queen of the Jungle* 1984; *The Longshot* 1986; *Sparks: the Price of Passion* 1990; *Danielle Steel's Star* 1993; *Triumph over Disaster: the Hurricane Andrew Story* 1993
Wasson, Craig *Go Tell the Spartans* 1977; *The Boys in Company C* 1978; *The Outsider* 1979; *Ghost Story* 1981; *Second Thoughts* 1982; *Body Double* 1984; *The Men's Club* 1986; *A Nightmare on Elm Street 3: Dream Warriors* 1987; *Midnight Fear* 1990; *Trapped in Space* 1994; *The Tomorrow Man* 1995; *Deep Family Secrets* 1997
Watanabe, Gedde *Sixteen Candles* 1984; *Volunteers* 1985; *Gung Ho* 1986; *Vamp* 1986; *The Spring* 1990; *Nick and Jane* 1996
Watanabe, Tetsu *Sonatine* 1993; *Hana-Bi* 1997
Waterman, Dennis *The Pirates of Blood River* 1961; *Up the Junction* 1967; *The Smashing Bird I Used to Know* 1969; *The Scars of Dracula* 1970; *Man in the Wilderness* 1971; *Fright* 1971; *The Belstone Fox* 1973; *Sweeney!* 1976; *Sweeney 2* 1978; *Cold Justice* 1991
Waterman, Felicity *Lena's Holiday* 1990; *Thunder In Paradise* 1993; *Unlawful Passage* 1994
Waters, Ethel *Tales of Manhattan* 1942; *Cabin in the Sky* 1943; *Pinky* 1949; *The Member of the Wedding* 1952; *The Sound and the Fury* 1959
Waters, John *The Getting of Wisdom* 1977; *Summerfield* 1977; *Weekend of Shadows* 1978; *Breaker Morant* 1979; *Attack Force Z* 1981; *Passion Flower* 1986; *Grievous Bodily Harm* 1987; *Boulevard of Broken Dreams* 1988; *Heaven Tonight* 1990; *Ebbtide* 1994; *Sweet and Lowdown* 1999
Waters, Russell *Death of an Angel* 1951; *Adventure in the Hopfields* 1954; *Yesterday's Enemy* 1959; *The Wicker Man* 1973; *Black Jack* 1979
Waterston, Sam *Fitzwilly* 1967; *Three* 1969; *Generation* 1969; *Who Killed Mary Whats'ername?* 1971; *The Great Gatsby* 1974; *Rancho Deluxe* 1975; *Capricorn One* 1978; *Eagle's Wing* 1978; *Interiors* 1978; *Friendly Fire* 1979; *Heaven's Gate* 1980; *Hopscotch* 1980; *Sweet William* 1980; *The Killing Fields* 1984; *Warning Sign* 1985; *The Fifth Missile* 1986; *Hannah and Her Sisters* 1986; *Just between Friends* 1986; *Hostile Witness* 1987; *The Room Upstairs* 1987; *September* 1987; *Swimming to Cambodia* 1987; *Crimes and Misdemeanors* 1989; *Welcome Home* 1989; *Mindwalk* 1990; *A Captive in the Land* 1991; *The Man in the Moon* 1991; *Stolen Babies* 1993; *Assault at West Point: the Court Martial of John Whittaker* 1994; *David's Mother* 1994; *The Enemy Within* 1994; *Serial Mom* 1994; *The Journey of August King* 1995; *The Proprietor* 1996; *Shadow Conspiracy* 1996; *Miracle at Midnight* 1998
Watford, Gwen *Never Take Sweets from a Stranger* 1960; *Taste the Blood of Dracula* 1969; *The Ghoul* 1975
Watkin, Pierre *Dangerous* 1935; *Road to Singapore* 1940; *Little Giant* 1946; *The Story of Seabiscuit* 1949
Watkins, Linda *From Hell It Came* 1957; *Because They're Young* 1960
Watling, Dilys *Calculated Risk* 1963; *Two Left Feet* 1963
Watling, Jack *Journey Together* 1944; *The Courtneys of Curzon Street* 1947; *Easy Money* 1948; *Quartet* 1948; *The Winslow Boy* 1948; *Under Capricorn* 1949; *White Corridors* 1951; *Meet Mr Lucifer* 1953; *The Sea Shall Not Have Them* 1954; *The Admirable Crichton* 1957; *The Birthday Present* 1957; *That Woman Opposite* 1957; *The Nanny* 1965; *Father Dear Father* 1972; *11 Harrowhouse* 1974
Watson, Alberta *Best Revenge* 1983; *The Keep* 1983; *White of the Eye* 1986; *Women of Valor* 1986; *Snake Treaty* 1989; *The Hitman* 1991; *Mind of a Killer* 1993; *Spanking the Monkey* 1994; *A Child Is Missing* 1995; *Sweet Angel Mine* 1996; *The Sweet Hereafter* 1997
Watson, Barry *Co-ed Call Girl* 1996; *Teaching Mrs Tingle* 1999
Watson, Bobby aka **Watson, Robert** *Going Hollywood* 1933; *The Paleface* 1948
Watson, Bobs *Blackmail* 1939; *Dr Kildare's Crisis* 1940; *Men of Boys Town* 1941
Watson, Emily *Breaking the Waves* 1996; *The Boxer* 1997; *Metroland* 1997; *Hilary and Jackie* 1998; *Angela's Ashes* 1999; *Cradle Will Rock* 1999
Watson, Jack *Konga* 1960; *The Queen's Guards* 1960; *This Sporting Life* 1963; *The Gorgon* 1964; *Master Spy* 1964; *The Hill* 1965; *The Night Caller* 1965; *Tobruk* 1966; *The Strange Affair* 1968; *The McKenzie Break* 1970; *Every Home Should Have One* 1970; *Tower of Evil* 1972; *11 Harrowhouse* 1974; *The Purple Taxi* 1977; *The Wild Geese* 1978; *North Sea Hijack* 1979
Watson Jr, James A *Halls of Anger* 1970; *The Organization* 1971; *Extreme Close-Up* 1973; *Goldengirl* 1979; *The Killings at Outpost Zeta* 1980
Watson, Lucile *What Every Woman Knows* 1934; *Made for Each Other* 1939; *The Women* 1939; *Florian* 1940; *Waterloo Bridge* 1940; *Footsteps in the Dark* 1941; *The Great Lie* 1941; *Mr and Mrs Smith* 1941; *Rage in Heaven* 1941; *Watch on the Rhine* 1943; *Till We Meet Again* 1944; *The Thin Man Goes Home* 1944; *Uncertain Glory* 1944; *Tomorrow Is Forever* 1945; *My Reputation* 1946; *Song of the South* 1946; *Never Say Goodbye* 1946; *The Emperor Waltz* 1948; *Julia Misbehaves* 1948; *That Wonderful Urge* 1948; *Everybody Does It* 1949; *Little Women* 1949; *Harriet Craig* 1950; *Let's Dance* 1950; *My Forbidden Past* 1951
Watson, Mills *Dirty Little Billy* 1972; *Going Undercover* 1984; *Blood River* 1991; *Gunsmoke: To the Last Man* 1992
Watson, Minor *The Woman I Love* 1937; *Boys Town* 1938; *The Adventures of Huckleberry Finn* 1939; *The Llano Kid* 1939; *Abe Lincoln in Illinois* 1940; *The Big Shot* 1942; *Gentleman Jim* 1942; *Woman of the Year* 1942; *The Falcon Out West* 1944; *Shadows in the Night* 1944; *A Southern Yankee* 1948; *Beyond the Forest* 1949; *Mister 880* 1950; *Bright Victory* 1951; *Face to Face* 1952; *My Son John* 1952; *Untamed Frontier* 1952; *The Star* 1953; *Trapeze* 1956
Watson, Muse *Assassins* 1995; *I Know What You Did Last Summer* 1997; *I Still Know What You Did Last Summer* 1998
Watson, Tom *Another Time, Another Place* 1983; *The Slab Boys* 1997
Watson, Woody *The Last Prostitute* 1991; *Triumph of the Heart* 1991
Watson, Wylie *Please Teacher* 1937; *Jamaica Inn* 1939; *The Saint Meets the Tiger* 1943; *Don't Take It to Heart* 1944; *Brighton Rock* 1947; *London Belongs to Me* 1948; *Whisky Galore!* 1949; *The Magnet* 1950
Wattis, Richard *The Happiest Days of Your Life* 1950; *Appointment with Venus* 1951; *Made in Heaven* 1952; *Blood Orange* 1953; *Colonel March Investigates* 1953; *Hobson's Choice* 1953; *The Intruder* 1953; *Park Plaza 605* 1953; *The Colditz Story* 1954; *An Alligator Named*

Chain Reaction 1996; *Amy Foster* 1997; *Going All the Way* 1997; *The Land Girls* 1997; *I Want You* 1998; *The Mummy* 1999; *Sunshine* 1999

Weitz, Bruce *A Cry for Help: the Tracey Thurman Story* 1989; *A Deadly Silence* 1989; *Rainbow Drive* 1990; *The Liar's Club* 1992; *No Place to Hide* 1992; *Danielle Steel's Mixed Blessings* 1995; *Her Hidden Truth* 1995; *The OJ Simpson Story* 1995; *Search for Justice* 1996

Welch, Bruce *The Young Ones* 1961; *Finders Keepers* 1966

Welch, Elisabeth *Song of Freedom* 1936; *Over the Moon* 1937; *Fiddlers Three* 1944; *The Tempest* 1979

Welch, Raquel *Roustabout* 1964; *Fantastic Voyage* 1966; *One Million Years BC* 1966; *Shout Loud, Louder… I Don't Understand* 1966; *Bedazzled* 1967; *Fathom* 1967; *The Oldest Profession* 1967; *Bandolero!* 1968; *The Biggest Bundle of Them All* 1968; *Lady in Cement* 1968; *The Magic Christian* 1969; *100 Rifles* 1969; *Flareup* 1969; *Myra Breckinridge* 1970; *Hannie Caulder* 1971; *Bluebeard* 1972; *Fuzz* 1972; *Kansas City Bomber* 1972; *Sin* 1972; *The Last of Sheila* 1973; *The Three Musketeers* 1973; *The Four Musketeers* 1974; *The Wild Party* 1975; *Mother, Jugs & Speed* 1976; *The Prince and the Pauper* 1977; *The Legend of Walks Far Woman* 1982; *Right to Die* 1987; *Scandal in a Small Town* 1988; *Trouble in Paradise* 1989; *Tainted Blood* 1993; *Judith Krantz's Torch Song* 1993; *Chairman of the Board* 1998

Welch, Sandy *Chasing the Deer* 1994; *The Bruce* 1996

Welch, Tahnee *Cocoon* 1985; *Night Train to Venice* 1993; *Improper Conduct* 1994; *I Shot Andy Warhol* 1995; *The Criminal Mind* 1995; *Johnny 2.0* 1998

Weld, Tuesday *Rock, Rock, Rock!* 1956; *Rally 'round the Flag, Boys!* 1958; *The Five Pennies* 1959; *High Time* 1960; *Sex Kittens Go to College* 1960; *Because They're Young* 1960; *Bachelor Flat* 1961; *Return to Peyton Place* 1961; *Wild in the Country* 1961; *Soldier in the Rain* 1963; *The Cincinnati Kid* 1965; *I'll Take Sweden* 1965; *Lord Love a Duck* 1966; *Pretty Poison* 1968; *I Walk the Line* 1970; *A Safe Place* 1971; *Looking for Mr Goodbar* 1977; *Who'll Stop the Rain?* 1978; *Serial* 1980; *Thief* 1981; *Author! Author!* 1982; *The Winter of Our Discontent* 1983; *Once upon a Time in America* 1984; *Scorned and Swindled* 1984; *Circle of Violence* 1986; *Something in Common* 1986; *Heartbreak Hotel* 1988; *Falling Down* 1992; *Feeling Minnesota* 1996

Welden, Ben *The Black Abbot* 1934; *The Man Who Changed His Name* 1934; *Smashing the Rackets* 1938; *Shadows in the Night* 1944

Weldon, Charles *Stir Crazy* 1980; *Fast-Walking* 1982

Weldon, Joan *So This Is Love* 1953; *The Stranger Wore a Gun* 1953; *The Command* 1954; *Riding Shotgun* 1954; *Them!* 1954; *Gunsight Ridge* 1957; *Home before Dark* 1958; *Day of the Bad Man* 1958

Welker, Frank *How to Frame a Figg* 1971; *Aladdin* 1992; *The Pagemaster* 1994; *A Goofy Movie* 1995; *Aladdin and the King of Thieves* 1996; *Doug's 1st Movie* 1999; *The Road to El Dorado* 2000

Welland, Colin *Kes* 1969; *Straw Dogs* 1971; *Villain* 1971; *Sweeney!* 1976; *Dancin' thru the Dark* 1989; *Spymaker: the Secret Life of Ian Fleming* 1990

Weller, Mary Louise *The Bell Jar* 1979; *Once upon a Spy* 1980; *Forced Vengeance* 1982

Weller, Peter *Butch and Sundance: the Early Days* 1979; *Just Tell Me What You Want* 1980; *Shoot the Moon* 1982; *Of Unknown Origin* 1983; *The Adventures of Buckaroo Banzai across the 8th Dimension* 1984; *Firstborn* 1984; *A Killing Affair* 1985; *Apology* 1986; *RoboCop* 1987; *Blue Jean Cop* 1988; *Cat Chaser* 1989; *Leviathan* 1989; *RoboCop 2* 1990; *Women and Men: Stories of Seduction* 1990; *Rainbow Drive* 1990; *Naked Lunch* 1991; *Fifty/Fifty* 1991; *Road to Ruin* 1992; *Sunset Grill* 1992; *The New Age* 1994; *The Substitute Wife* 1994; *Beyond the Clouds* 1995; *Decoy* 1995; *Screamers* 1995; *Top of the World* 1997

Welles, Gwen *A Safe Place* 1971; *Hit!* 1973; *California Split* 1974; *Between the Lines* 1977; *Desert Hearts* 1985; *Nobody's Fool* 1986; *Eating* 1990

Welles, Mel *The Undead* 1957; *Attack of the Crab Monsters* 1957; *Little Shop of Horrors* 1960; *Dr Heckyl & Mr Hype* 1980

Welles, Orson *Swiss Family Robinson* 1940; *Citizen Kane* 1941; *Journey into Fear* 1942; *The Magnificent Ambersons* 1942; *Jane Eyre* 1943; *Follow the Boys* 1944; *Tomorrow Is Forever* 1945; *Duel in the Sun* 1946; *The Stranger* 1946; *The Lady from Shanghai* 1948; *Macbeth* 1948; *Black Magic* 1949; *Prince of Foxes* 1949; *The Third Man* 1949; *The Black Rose* 1950; *Return to Glennascaul* 1951; *Othello* 1952; *Trent's Last Case* 1952; *Royal Affairs in Versailles* 1953; *Three Cases of Murder* 1954; *Trouble in the Glen* 1954; *Confidential Report* 1955; *Napoléon* 1955; *Moby Dick* 1956; *Man in the Shadow* 1957; *Ferry to Hong Kong* 1958; *The Long Hot Summer* 1958; *Touch of Evil* 1958; *The Roots of Heaven* 1958; *Compulsion* 1959; *The Battle of Austerlitz* 1960; *Crack in the Mirror* 1960; *King of Kings* 1961; *The Trial* 1962; *RoGoPaG* 1962; *The VIPs* 1963; *Chimes at Midnight* 1966; *Is Paris Burning?* 1966; *A Man for All Seasons* 1966; *Casino Royale* 1967; *I'll Never Forget What's 'Is Name* 1967; *The Sailor from Gibraltar* 1967; *House of Cards* 1968; *The Immortal Story* 1968; *Oedipus the King* 1968; *The Battle of Neretva* 1969; *Twelve plus One* 1969; *The Southern Star* 1969; *Catch-22* 1970; *The Kremlin Letter* 1970; *Waterloo* 1970; *Start the Revolution without Me* 1970; *A Safe Place* 1971; *Ten Days' Wonder* 1971; *Treasure Island* 1972; *Get to Know Your Rabbit* 1972; *F for Fake* 1973; *And Then There Were None* 1974; *Voyage of the Damned* 1976; *Hot Money* 1979; *The Double McGuffin* 1979; *History of the World Part 1* 1981; *Butterfly* 1982; *Slapstick of Another Kind* 1982; *Transformers – The Movie* 1986; *Someone to Love* 1987; *It's All True* 1993

Welles, Virginia *Kiss and Tell* 1945; *To Each His Own* 1946; *A Kiss for Corliss* 1949

Welliver, Titus *The Lost Capone* 1990; *Blind Justice* 1994; *Inflammable* 1994

Wellman Jr, William *Born Losers* 1967; *The Trial of Billy Jack* 1974

Wells, Carole *Come Blow Your Horn* 1963; *The House of Seven Corpses* 1973; *Funny Lady* 1975

Wells, Ingeborg *House of Blackmail* 1953; *Child's Play* 1954

Wells, Jerold *High Hell* 1957; *The Element of Crime* 1984

Wells, John *Rentadick* 1972; *Greystoke: the Legend of Tarzan, Lord of the Apes* 1984; *Revolution* 1985

Wells, Tico *Misplaced* 1989; *The Five Heartbeats* 1991; *Universal Soldier* 1992

Wells, Vernon *Mad Max 2* 1981; *Commando* 1985; *Innerspace* 1987; *Circuitry Man* 1990; *The Shrimp on the Barbie* 1990; *Sexual Response* 1992; *Plughead Rewired: Circuitry Man II* 1994; *T-Force* 1995

Welsh, Jane *Just William's Luck* 1947; *William at the Circus* 1948

Welsh, John *Confession* 1955; *The Birthday Present* 1957; *The Revenge of Frankenstein* 1958; *The Night We Dropped a Clanger* 1959; *Beyond the Curtain* 1960; *Circle of Deception* 1960; *Krull* 1983

Welsh, Kenneth *Of Unknown Origin* 1983; *A Stranger Waits* 1987; *Physical Evidence* 1989; *Perfectly Normal* 1990; *Journey into Darkness: the Bruce Curtis Story* 1991; *Bonds of Love* 1993; *Getting Gotti* 1994; *Dancing in the Dark* 1995; *Margaret's Museum* 1995; *Kissinger and Nixon* 1995

Welsh, Margaret *Smooth Talk* 1985; *Mr and Mrs Bridge* 1990; *Shadow of a Doubt* 1991; *A Killer among Friends* 1992; *Ratchet* 1996

Welter, Ariadna *The Criminal Life of Archibaldo de la Cruz* 1955; *Rage* 1966

Wen Ming-Na *aka* **Ming-Na** *The Joy Luck Club* 1993; *Hong Kong '97* 1994; *Street Fighter* 1994; *Terminal Voyage* 1994; *One Night Stand* 1997; *Mulan* 1998

Wenders, Wim *Long Shot* 1978; *Notebook on Cities and Clothes* 1989

Wendt, George *Dreamscape* 1984; *The Ratings Game* 1984; *Thief of Hearts* 1984; *No Small Affair* 1984; *Fletch* 1985; *Gung Ho* 1986; *House* 1986; *Plain Clothes* 1988; *Guilty by Suspicion* 1990; *Forever Young* 1992; *Hostage for a Day* 1994; *The Little Rascals* 1994; *Man of the House* 1994; *Space Truckers* 1996; *Spice World* 1997; *The Price of Heaven* 1997; *Dennis Strikes Again* 1998; *Outside Providence* 1999

Wengraf, John *The Lovable Cheat* 1949; *5 Fingers* 1952; *Gog* 1954; *The Pride and the Passion* 1957; *Valerie* 1957; *The Return of Dracula* 1958; *Hitler* 1962

Wentworth, Martha *Clancy Street Boys* 1943; *Daughter of Dr Jekyll* 1957; *One Hundred and One Dalmatians* 1960; *The Sword in the Stone* 1963

Wepper, Fritz *The Bridge* 1959; *The Games* 1970; *Cabaret* 1972; *The Last Battle* 1983

Werle, Barbara *Battle of the Bulge* 1965; *Gunfight in Abilene* 1967; *Charro!* 1969; *Krakatoa, East of Java* 1969

Werner, Oskar *Decision before Dawn* 1951; *Lola Montès* 1955; *Jules et Jim* 1961; *The Spy Who Came in from the Cold* 1965; *Ship of Fools* 1965; *Fahrenheit 451* 1966; *Interlude* 1968; *The Shoes of the Fisherman* 1968; *Voyage of the Damned* 1976

Wernicke, Otto *M* 1931; *The Testament of Dr Mabuse* 1932

Werntz, Gary *The Innocent* 1993; *Baby Brokers* 1994

Wert, Doug *By the Sword* 1992; *A Murder of Crows* 1998

Wescott, Helen *Abbott and Costello Meet Dr Jekyll and Mr Hyde* 1953; *God's Little Acre* 1958

Wessel, Dick *Dick Tracy vs Cueball* 1946; *Watch the Birdie* 1950

Wesson, Dick *Destination Moon* 1950; *Force of Arms* 1951; *Jim Thorpe – All-American* 1951; *Calamity Jane* 1953; *The Charge at Feather River* 1953; *The Desert Song* 1953; *The Errand Boy* 1961

West, Adam *Geronimo* 1962; *Soldier in the Rain* 1963; *Tammy and the Doctor* 1963; *The Outlaws Is Coming* 1965; *Batman* 1966; *The Girl Who Knew Too Much* 1969; *The Marriage of a Young Stockbroker* 1971; *The Eyes of Charles Sand* 1972; *Hooper* 1978; *The Happy Hooker Goes to Hollywood* 1980; *One Dark Night* 1982; *Doin' Time on Planet Earth* 1988; *The New Age* 1994; *Drop Dead Gorgeous* 1999

West, Chandra *Tobe Hooper's Night Terrors* 1994; *Into the Arms of Danger* 1997

West, Dominic *True Blue* 1996; *The Gambler* 1997; *Diana & Me* 1997; *William Shakespeare's A Midsummer Night's Dream* 1999; *28 Days* 2000

West, Judi *The Fortune Cookie* 1966; *A Man Called Gannon* 1969

West, Julian *Vampyr* 1932; *X, Y and Zee* 1971

West, Lockwood *The Birthday Present* 1957; *The Leather Boys* 1963

West, Mae *Night after Night* 1932; *I'm No Angel* 1933; *She Done Him Wrong* 1933; *Belle of the Nineties* 1934; *Goin' to Town* 1935; *Go West, Young Man* 1936; *Klondike Annie* 1936; *Every Day's a Holiday* 1937; *My Little Chickadee* 1940; *The Heat's On* 1943; *Myra Breckinridge* 1970; *Sextette* 1978

West, Martin *The Man from Galveston* 1964; *Lord Love a Duck* 1966; *Sweet November* 1968; *Assault on Precinct 13* 1976; *The Price of Survival* 1980; *Mac and Me* 1988

West, Red *Road House* 1989; *The Legend of Grizzly Adams* 1990; *Prey of the Chameleon* 1991

West, Samuel *aka* **West, Sam** *Reunion* 1989; *Howards End* 1992; *Carrington* 1995; *A Feast at Midnight* 1995; *Persuasion* 1995; *Stiff Upper Lips* 1997; *The Ripper* 1997

West, Tamsin *Jenny Kissed Me* 1984; *Frog Dreaming* 1985

West, Timothy *Twisted Nerve* 1968; *The Day of the Jackal* 1973; *Hedda* 1975; *Operation Daybreak* 1975; *The Devil's Advocate* 1977; *Agatha* 1978; *Rough Cut* 1980; *Oliver Twist* 1982; *Cry Freedom* 1987; *The Tragedy of Flight 103: the Inside Story* 1990; *Ever After* 1998

Westbrook, John *Room at the Top* 1958; *The Tomb of Ligeia* 1964

Westcott, Helen *The Gunfighter* 1950; *With a Song in My Heart* 1952; *The Charge at Feather River* 1953; *Hot Blood* 1956; *Monster on the Campus* 1958

Westerfield, James *On the Waterfront* 1954; *Three Hours to Kill* 1954; *The Proud Rebel* 1958; *Wild River* 1960; *That Funny Feeling* 1965; *Hang 'em High* 1968; *A Man Called Gannon* 1969

Westergren, Hakan *Swedenhielms* 1935; *Dollar* 1938

Westerman, Floyd Red Crow *aka* **Westerman, Floyd** *Renegades* 1989; *Dances with Wolves* 1990; *Clearcut* 1992

Westgate, Murray *Class of '44* 1973; *Kavik, the Wolf Dog* 1980

Westley, Helen *Anne of Green Gables* 1934; *Death Takes a Holiday* 1934; *The House of Rothschild* 1934; *The Age of Innocence* 1934; *Captain Hurricane* 1935; *Roberta* 1935; *Splendor* 1935; *Banjo on My Knee* 1936; *Dimples* 1936; *Show Boat* 1936; *Stowaway* 1936; *Heidi* 1937; *I'll Take Romance* 1937; *Alexander's Ragtime Band* 1938; *Rebecca of Sunnybrook Farm* 1938; *Zaza* 1939; *Lillian Russell* 1940; *Adam Had Four Sons* 1941; *Lady from Louisiana* 1941; *Sunny* 1941; *Million Dollar Baby* 1941; *Bedtime Story* 1942; *My Favorite Spy* 1942

Westman, Nydia *Ladies Should Listen* 1934; *When Tomorrow Comes* 1939; *The Swinger* 1966

Weston, Brad *Rough Night in Jericho* 1967; *Barquero* 1970

Weston, Celia *The Road Home* 1989; *Dead Man Walking* 1995

Weston, David *The Beauty Jungle* 1964; *The Masque of the Red Death* 1964; *The Heroes of Telemark* 1965; *The Legend of Young Dick Turpin* 1965

Weston, Jack *All in a Night's Work* 1960; *Please Don't Eat the Daisies* 1960; *The Honeymoon Machine* 1961; *It'$ Only Money* 1962; *Palm Springs Weekend* 1963; *The Incredible Mr Limpet* 1964; *The Cincinnati Kid* 1965; *Mirage* 1965; *Wait until Dark* 1967; *The Thomas Crown Affair* 1968; *The April Fools* 1969; *Cactus Flower* 1969; *A New Leaf* 1971; *Fuzz* 1972; *Deliver Us from Evil* 1973; *Marco* 1973; *Gator* 1976; *The Ritz* 1976; *Cuba* 1979; *The Four Seasons* 1981; *High Road to China* 1983; *The Longshot* 1986; *Dirty Dancing* 1987; *Ishtar* 1987; *Short Circuit 2* 1988

Weston, Jeff *Journey to the Center of the Earth* 1986; *Puppet Master II* 1990

Westwood, Patrick *The Tommy Steele Story* 1957; *Guns in the Heather* 1969

Wettig, Patricia *Guilty by Suspicion* 1990; *City Slickers* 1991; *Silent Motive* 1991; *Taking Back My Life* 1992; *City Slickers II: the Legend of Curly's Gold* 1994; *Nothing but the Truth* 1995; *Nightmare in Big Sky Country* 1998

Wexler, Paul *Timbuktu* 1959; *Doc Savage: the Man of Bronze* 1975

Weyand, Ronald *Child's Play* 1972; *Svengali* 1983

Weyers, Marius *The Gods Must Be Crazy* 1980; *Farewell to the King* 1988; *DeepStar Six* 1989; *Happy Together* 1989; *Bopha!* 1993; *Friends* 1993

Whalen, Michael *The Country Doctor* 1936; *Poor Little Rich Girl* 1936; *White Fang* 1936; *Wee*

RadioTimes ACTORS' INDEX

1950; *The Frogmen* 1951; *Don't Bother to Knock* 1952; *My Pal Gus* 1952; *Red Skies of Montana* 1952; *O Henry's Full House* 1952; *Destination Gobi* 1953; *Pickup on South Street* 1953; *Broken Lance* 1954; *Garden of Evil* 1954; *Hell and High Water* 1954; *The Cobweb* 1955; *A Prize of Gold* 1955; *Backlash* 1956; *The Last Wagon* 1956; *Run for the Sun* 1956; *Saint Joan* 1957; *Time Limit* 1957; *The Law and Jake Wade* 1958; *The Tunnel of Love* 1958; *The Baited Trap* 1959; *Warlock* 1959; *The Alamo* 1960; *Judgment at Nuremberg* 1961; *Two Rode Together* 1961; *The Secret Ways* 1961; *How the West Was Won* 1962; *The Long Ships* 1963; *Cheyenne Autumn* 1964; *Flight from Ashiya* 1964; *The Bedford Incident* 1965; *Alvarez Kelly* 1966; *The Way West* 1967; *Madigan* 1968; *Death of a Gunfighter* 1969; *When the Legends Die* 1972; *Murder on the Orient Express* 1974; *The Sellout* 1975; *To the Devil a Daughter* 1976; *Coma* 1977; *The Domino Principle* 1977; *Rollercoaster* 1977; *Twilight's Last Gleaming* 1977; *The Swarm* 1978; *Bear Island* 1979; *National Lampoon's Movie Madness* 1981; *Hanky Panky* 1982; *Who Dares Wins* 1982; *Against All Odds* 1984; *Blackout* 1985; *A Gathering of Old Men* 1987; *Once upon a Texas Train* 1988; *Cold Sassy Tree* 1989; *True Colors* 1991

Wieman, Mathias *Paracelsus* 1943; *Fear* 1954

Wiesinger, Kai *BackBeat* 1993; *Terror in the Mall* 1998

Wiest, Dianne *It's My Turn* 1980; *I'm Dancing as Fast as I Can* 1982; *Independence Day* 1983; *Falling in Love* 1984; *Footloose* 1984; *The Purple Rose of Cairo* 1985; *Hannah and Her Sisters* 1986; *The Lost Boys* 1987; *Radio Days* 1987; *September* 1987; *Bright Lights, Big City* 1988; *Cookie* 1989; *Parenthood* 1989; *Edward Scissorhands* 1990; *Little Man Tate* 1991; *Bullets over Broadway* 1994; *Cops and Robbersons* 1994; *The Scout* 1994; *Drunks* 1995; *The Associate* 1996; *The Birdcage* 1996; *The Horse Whisperer* 1998; *Practical Magic* 1998; *The Simple Life of Noah Dearborn* 1999

Wieth, Mogens *The Man Who Knew Too Much* 1956; *Private Potter* 1963

Wifstrand, Naima *Dreams* 1955; *The Face* 1958

Wiggins, Chris *King of the Grizzlies* 1970; *The Neptune Factor* 1973; *Why Shoot the Teacher* 1976; *Welcome to Blood City* 1977; *High-ballin'* 1978; *Kavik, the Wolf Dog* 1980; *Bay Boy* 1984; *The Care Bears Movie II: a New Generation* 1986; *Black Fox* 1995; *Evidence of Blood* 1998

Wiggins, Wiley *Dazed and Confused* 1993; *Boys* 1995

Wightman, Robert *A Day for Thanks on Waltons Mountain* 1982; *Impulse* 1984; *Opposing Force* 1986; *Hell Camp* 1987

Wignall, Mark *The Boy Who Had Everything* 1984; *Constance* 1984

Wilbanks, Don *Stagecoach to Dancer's Rock* 1962; *Cry for Me Billy* 1972

Wilbur, George P *Halloween 4: the Return of Michael Myers* 1988; *Halloween 6: the Curse of Michael Myers* 1995

Wilby, James *A Handful of Dust* 1987; *Maurice* 1987; *A Summer Story* 1987; *Conspiracy* 1989; *Immaculate Conception* 1991; *Howards End* 1992; *Regeneration* 1997; *Tom's Midnight Garden* 1998; *Cotton Mary* 1999

Wilcox, Claire *Forty Pounds of Trouble* 1962; *Wives and Lovers* 1963

Wilcox, Frank *Conflict* 1945; *Abbott and Costello Meet the Keystone Cops* 1955; *Go, Johnny, Go!* 1959

Wilcox, Larry *Sky Heist* 1975; *The Last Hard Men* 1976; *The Last Ride of the Dalton Gang* 1979; *The Dirty Dozen: the Next Mission* 1985; *Rich Men, Single Women* 1990

Wilcox, Lisa *A Nightmare on Elm Street 4: The Dream Master* 1988; *A Nightmare on Elm Street 5: The Dream Child* 1989

Wilcox, Paula *The Lovers* 1972; *Man about the House* 1974

Wilcox, Robert *Blondie Takes a Vacation* 1939; *The Man They Could Not Hang* 1939; *The Lone Wolf Strikes* 1940; *Wild Beauty* 1946; *The Vigilantes Return* 1947

Wilcox, Shannon *The Border* 1981; *Six Weeks* 1982; *Hollywood Harry* 1985; *83 Hours till Dawn* 1990

Wilcox-Horne, Collin *The Baby Maker* 1970; *The Revolutionary* 1970

Wilcoxon, Henry *Cleopatra* 1934; *The Crusades* 1935; *The Last of the Mohicans* 1936; *Souls at Sea* 1937; *If I Were King* 1938; *Mysterious Mr Moto* 1938; *Tarzan Finds a Son!* 1939; *The Corsican Brothers* 1941; *That Hamilton Woman* 1941; *Mrs Miniver* 1942; *Unconquered* 1947; *A Connecticut Yankee in King Arthur's Court* 1949; *Samson and Delilah* 1949; *The Greatest Show on Earth* 1952; *Scaramouche* 1952; *Man in the Wilderness* 1971; *Against a Crooked Sky* 1975; *Pony Express Rider* 1976

Wild, Jack *Oliver!* 1968; *Pufnstuf* 1970; *Flight of the Doves* 1971; *Melody* 1971; *The Pied Piper* 1971; *Keep It Up Downstairs* 1976; *Basil* 1998

Wild, Katy *Evil of Frankenstein* 1964; *The Settlement* 1982

Wilde, Brian *We Joined the Navy* 1962; *Rattle of a Simple Man* 1964; *Porridge* 1979

Wilde, Cornel *Life Begins at 8.30* 1942; *Wintertime* 1943; *Leave Her to Heaven* 1945; *A Song to Remember* 1945; *A Thousand and One Nights* 1945; *The Bandit of Sherwood Forest* 1946; *Centennial Summer* 1946; *Forever Amber* 1947; *Road House* 1948; *Shockproof* 1949; *Two Flags West* 1950; *Sons of the Musketeers* 1951; *The Greatest Show on Earth* 1952; *Saadia* 1953; *Treasure of the Golden Condor* 1953; *Passion* 1954; *Star of India* 1954; *Woman's World* 1954; *The Big Combo* 1955; *The Scarlet Coat* 1955; *Hot Blood* 1956; *Omar Khayyam* 1957; *Beyond Mombasa* 1957; *The Devil's Hairpin* 1957; *Maracaibo* 1958; *Edge of Eternity* 1959; *Lancelot and Guinevere* 1963; *The Naked Prey* 1966; *Beach Red* 1967; *The Comic* 1969; *Shark's Treasure* 1975; *The Norseman* 1978; *The Fifth Musketeer* 1979

Wilde, Marty *What a Crazy World* 1963; *Stardust* 1974

Wilder, Gene *Bonnie and Clyde* 1967; *The Producers* 1968; *Quackser Fortune Has a Cousin in the Bronx* 1970; *Start the Revolution without Me* 1970; *Thursday's Game* 1971; *Willy Wonka and the Chocolate Factory* 1971; *Everything You Always Wanted to Know about Sex (But Were Afraid to Ask)* 1972; *Blazing Saddles* 1974; *The Little Prince* 1974; *Rhinoceros* 1974; *Young Frankenstein* 1974; *The Adventure of Sherlock Holmes' Smarter Brother* 1975; *Silver Streak* 1976; *The World's Greatest Lover* 1977; *The Frisco Kid* 1979; *Stir Crazy* 1980; *Hanky Panky* 1982; *The Woman in Red* 1984; *Haunted Honeymoon* 1986; *See No Evil, Hear No Evil* 1989; *Funny about Love* 1990; *Another You* 1991

Wilder, James *Zombie High* 1987; *Prey of the Chameleon* 1991; *Scorchers* 1991; *Night Owl* 1993; *Confessions: Two Faces of Evil* 1994; *Tollbooth* 1994; *The Face* 1996

Wilder, Nick *Caged Hearts* 1995; *Orbit* 1996

Wilder, Yvonne *The Return of Count Yorga* 1971; *Bloodbrothers* 1978; *Seems like Old Times* 1980

Wilding, Michael *Convoy* 1940; *Sailors Three* 1940; *Cottage to Let* 1941; *Kipps* 1941; *In Which We Serve* 1942; *Secret Mission* 1942; *Ships with Wings* 1942; *Undercover* 1943; *English without Tears* 1944; *Carnival* 1946; *The Courtneys of Curzon Street* 1947; *An Ideal Husband* 1947; *Spring in Park Lane* 1948; *Maytime in Mayfair* 1949; *Under Capricorn* 1949; *Stage Fright* 1950; *The Lady with the Lamp* 1951; *Derby Day* 1952; *Trent's Last Case* 1952; *Torch Song* 1953; *The Egyptian* 1954; *The Glass Slipper* 1955; *The Scarlet Coat* 1955; *Zarak* 1956; *Danger Within* 1958; *The World of Suzie Wong* 1960; *The Naked Edge* 1961; *The Best of Enemies* 1962; *A Girl Named Tamiko* 1962; *The Sweet Ride* 1967; *Waterloo* 1970

Wilding Jr, Michael *aka* **Wilding, Michael** *Blame It on the Night* 1984; *Deadly Illusion* 1987

Wildman, John *My American Cousin* 1985; *American Boyfriends* 1989

Wildsmith, Dawn *Terminal Force* 1987; *Surf Nazis Must Die* 1987

Wiles, Jason *Roadracers* 1994; *Kicking and Screaming* 1995

Wilhoite, Kathleen *Private School* 1983; *Murphy's Law* 1986; *Witchboard* 1987; *Dream Demon* 1988; *Bad Influence* 1990; *Everybody Wins* 1990; *Lorenzo's Oil* 1992; *Terror in the Family* 1996; *Breast Men* 1997; *The Edge* 1997

Wilke, Robert J *aka* **Wilke, Robert** *20,000 Leagues under the Sea* 1954; *Shotgun* 1955; *Written on the Wind* 1956; *The Lone Ranger* 1956; *The Tarnished Angels* 1957; *Hot Summer Night* 1957; *Man of the West* 1958; *Tony Rome* 1967; *The Resurrection of Zachary Wheeler* 1971; *Santee* 1973; *Days of Heaven* 1978

Wilker, José *Dona Flor and Her Two Husbands* 1977; *Bye Bye Brazil* 1979; *Prisoner of Rio* 1988; *Medicine Man* 1992

Wilkinson, Tom *Sylvia* 1984; *Parker* 1984; *Wetherby* 1985; *Paper Mask* 1990; *A Business Affair* 1993; *All Things Bright and Beautiful* 1994; *Priest* 1994; *Sense and Sensibility* 1995; *The Ghost and the Darkness* 1996; *The Full Monty* 1997; *The Governess* 1997; *Oscar and Lucinda* 1997; *Wilde* 1997; *Rush Hour* 1998; *Shakespeare in Love* 1998; *Ride with the Devil* 1999; *Essex Boys* 1999; *The Patriot* 2000

Wilkof, Lee *Chattahoochee* 1989; *Addicted to Love* 1997

Willard, Fred *Escape from Bogen County* 1977; *Americathon* 1979; *Roxanne* 1987; *Sodbusters* 1994; *Waiting for Guffman* 1996

Willcox, Toyah *Jubilee* 1978; *The Corn Is Green* 1979; *Quadrophenia* 1979; *The Tempest* 1979; *Anchoress* 1993; *Julie and the Cadillacs* 1997

Willes, Jean *Abbott and Costello Go to Mars* 1953; *All Ashore* 1953; *Invasion of the Body Snatchers* 1956; *The King and Four Queens* 1956; *Desire under the Elms* 1958; *The FBI Story* 1959

William, Warren *Three on a Match* 1932; *Gold Diggers of 1933* 1933; *Lady for a Day* 1933; *The Case of the Howling Dog* 1934; *Cleopatra* 1934; *Imitation of Life* 1934; *Upper World* 1934; *The Secret Bride* 1934; *The Case of the Lucky Legs* 1935; *The Case of the Velvet Claws* 1936; *Go West, Young Man* 1936; *Satan Met a Lady* 1936; *Stage Struck* 1936; *The Firefly* 1937; *Madame X* 1937; *Arsene Lupin Returns* 1938; *Wives under Suspicion* 1938; *The Lone Wolf Spy Hunt* 1939; *The Man in the Iron Mask* 1939; *Lillian Russell* 1940; *The Lone Wolf Strikes* 1940; *Trail of the Vigilantes* 1940; *Arizona* 1940; *The Lone Wolf Keeps a Date* 1941; *The Wolf Man* 1941; *Wild Geese Calling* 1941; *One Dangerous Night* 1943; *Passport to Suez* 1943

Williams, Adam *Vice Squad* 1953; *The Proud and Profane* 1956; *Fear Strikes Out* 1957; *The Badlanders* 1958; *North by Northwest* 1959

Williams, Barbara *The Gentle Rain* 1966; *Thief of Hearts* 1984; *Jo Jo Dancer, Your Life Is Calling* 1986; *Tiger Warsaw* 1988; *Watchers* 1988; *Peter Gunn* 1989; *City of Hope* 1991; *Black Death* 1992; *Oh, What a Night* 1992; *In the Line of Duty: Kidnapped* 1995; *Breach of Faith: Family of Cops II* 1996; *Bone Daddy* 1998; *Naked City: a Killer Christmas* 1998

Williams, Bill *Deadline at Dawn* 1946; *Till the End of Time* 1946; *A Dangerous Profession* 1949; *Fighting Man of the Plains* 1949; *The Stratton Story* 1949; *A Woman's Secret* 1949; *The Cariboo Trail* 1950; *Rose of Cimarron* 1952; *Son of Paleface* 1952; *The Halliday Brand* 1957; *Space Master X 7* 1958; *A Dog's Best Friend* 1960; *Tickle Me* 1965; *Scandalous John* 1971

Williams, Billy Dee *The Last Angry Man* 1959; *Brian's Song* 1971; *Lady Sings the Blues* 1972; *The Final Comedown* 1972; *Hit!* 1973; *The Take* 1974; *Mahogany* 1975; *The Bingo Long Travelling All-Stars and Motor Kings* 1976; *Scott Joplin* 1977; *The Empire Strikes Back* 1980; *Nighthawks* 1981; *Return of the Jedi* 1983; *Marvin and Tige* 1983; *Fear City* 1984; *Courage* 1986; *Oceans of Fire* 1986; *Number One with a Bullet* 1986; *Deadly Illusion* 1987; *Batman* 1989; *Dangerous Passion* 1990; *Percy and Thunder* 1993; *Falling for You* 1995; *Triplecross* 1995; *Hard Time* 1998

Williams, Cara *Happy Land* 1943; *Boomerang!* 1947; *The Saxon Charm* 1948; *Knock on Any Door* 1949; *The Girl Next Door* 1953; *The Great Diamond Robbery* 1953; *Meet Me in Las Vegas* 1956; *The Helen Morgan Story* 1957; *Never Steal Anything Small* 1959; *The Man from the Diner's Club* 1963; *One Man Jury* 1978

Williams, Caroline *The Texas Chainsaw Massacre Part 2* 1986; *Getting Even* 1986; *Stepfather II* 1989; *True Betrayal* 1990; *Flashfire* 1993

Williams, Chuck *Soultaker* 1991; *Double Blast* 1994

Williams, Cindy *Gas-s-s-s, or It Became Necessary to Destroy the World in Order to Save It* 1970; *Travels with My Aunt* 1972; *American Graffiti* 1973; *The Killing Kind* 1973; *The Conversation* 1974; *More American Graffiti* 1979; *UFOria* 1980; *Save the Dog!* 1988; *Tricks of the Trade* 1988; *Rude Awakening* 1989; *Big Man on Campus* 1989; *Menu for Murder* 1990; *Bingo* 1991; *Earth Angel* 1991; *Escape from Terror* 1995; *The Stepford Husbands* 1996; *Meet Wally Sparks* 1997

Williams III, Clarence *The Cool World* 1963; *King: a Filmed Record… Montgomery to Memphis* 1970; *Purple Rain* 1984; *The Last Innocent Man* 1987; *Tough Guys Don't Dance* 1987; *Maniac Cop 2* 1990; *My Heroes Have Always Been Cowboys* 1991; *On the Streets of LA* 1991; *Sugar Hill* 1993; *Against the Wall* 1994; *Tales from the Hood* 1995; *Rebound* 1996; *Hoodlum* 1997; *Sprung* 1997; *The Brave* 1997; *Last Rites* 1998; *Half-Baked* 1998; *Life* 1999; *The General's Daughter* 1999; *Deception* 2000

Williams, Cynda *Mo' Better Blues* 1990; *One False Move* 1992; *Killing Box* 1993; *Erotic Tales* 1994; *Gang in Blue* 1996

Williams, D J *Maria Marten, or the Murder in the Red Barn* 1935; *The Crimes of Stephen Hawke* 1936; *Sweeney Todd, the Demon Barber of Fleet Street* 1936; *Elephant Boy* 1937; *It's Never Too Late to Mend* 1937

Williams, Darnell *Sidewalk Stories* 1989; *How U Like Me Now* 1992

Williams, Dick Anthony *aka* **Williams, Dick** *The Anderson Tapes* 1971; *Who Killed Mary Whats'ername?* 1971; *The Mack* 1973; *An Almost Perfect Affair* 1979; *The Jerk* 1979; *Gardens of Stone* 1987; *Tap* 1989; *Mo' Better Blues* 1990

Williams, Edy *The Pad (and How to Use It)* 1966; *The Secret Life of an American Wife* 1968; *Where It's At* 1969; *Beyond the Valley of the Dolls* 1970; *The Seven Minutes* 1971; *Chained Heat* 1983; *Hollywood Hot Tubs* 1984

Williams, Emlyn *Friday the Thirteenth* 1933; *Evensong* 1934; *The Dictator* 1935; *Broken Blossoms* 1936; *The Citadel* 1938; *Jamaica Inn* 1939; *The Stars Look Down* 1939; *The Girl in the News* 1940; *Hatter's Castle* 1941; *Major Barbara* 1941; *The Last Days of Dolwyn* 1949; *Another Man's Poison* 1951; *Ivanhoe* 1952; *The Deep Blue Sea* 1955; *I Accuse!* 1958; *Beyond This Place* 1959; *The Wreck of the Mary Deare* 1959; *The L-Shaped Room* 1962; *Eye of the Devil* 1968; *The Walking Stick* 1970

Williams, Esther *Andy Hardy's Double Life* 1942; *Bathing Beauty* 1944; *A Guy Named Joe* 1944; *Ziegfeld Follies* 1944; *Thrill of a Romance* 1945; *Easy to Wed*

Ceiling 1995; *Cagney & Lacey: True Convictions* 1996
Ziering, Ian *Endless Love* 1981; *Beverly Hills 90210* 1990; *Welcome to Paradise* 1995
Zima, Madeline *The Hand That Rocks the Cradle* 1992; *Mr Nanny* 1992
Zima, Yvonne *The Long Kiss Goodnight* 1996; *Christmas Every Day* 1996
Zimbalist Jr, Efrem *House of Strangers* 1949; *Band of Angels* 1957; *Bombers B-52* 1957; *The Deep Six* 1958; *Girl on the Run* 1958; *Home before Dark* 1958; *Too Much, Too Soon* 1958; *Violent Road* 1958; *The Crowded Sky* 1960; *By Love Possessed* 1961; *A Fever in the Blood* 1961; *The Chapman Report* 1962; *The Reward* 1965; *Harlow* 1965; *Wait until Dark* 1967; *Airport 1975* 1974; *Hot Shots!* 1991; *Subzero* 1998
Zimbalist, Stephanie *The Magic of Lassie* 1978; *The Awakening* 1980; *The Man in the Brown Suit* 1989; *Caroline?* 1990; *The Killing Mind* 1991; *The Story Lady* 1991; *Breaking the Silence* 1992; *Sexual Advances* 1992; *Incident in a Small Town* 1993; *Jericho Fever* 1993; *Silhouette* 1994; *The Great Elephant Escape* 1995; *Dead Ahead* 1996; *Prison of Secrets* 1997
Zimmer, Kim *Body Heat* 1981; *Trenchcoat in Paradise* 1989; *Hell Hath No Fury* 1991; *The Disappearance of Vonnie* 1994
Zingaretti, Luca *A Private Affair* 1992; *Artemisia* 1997
Zirner, August *Now or Never* 1986; *Voyager* 1991; *The Promise* 1994
Zischler, Hanns *Kings of the Road* 1976; *Dr M* 1989; *The Cement Garden* 1992
Zivojinović, Bata *aka* **Zivojinović, Velimir Bata** *I Even Met Happy Gypsies* 1967; *Pretty Village Pretty Flame* 1996
Zmed, Adrian *Grease 2* 1982; *Bachelor Party* 1984
Zolnay, Pal *Diary for My Children* 1982; *Diary for My Loves* 1987
Zorich, Louis *For Pete's Sake* 1974; *Newman's Law* 1974; *Sunday in the Country* 1975; *Death of a Salesman* 1985; *Young at Heart* 1995
Zorina, Vera *aka* **Zorina** *The Goldwyn Follies* 1938; *On Your Toes* 1939; *I Was an Adventuress* 1940; *Louisiana Purchase* 1941; *Star Spangled Rhythm* 1942; *Follow the Boys* 1944
Zouzou *Love in the Afternoon* 1972; *S*P*Y*S* 1974; *Sky Riders* 1976
Zucco, George *The Bride Wore Red* 1937; *London by Night* 1937; *Arsene Lupin Returns* 1938; *Three Comrades* 1938; *The Adventures of Sherlock Holmes* 1939; *The Cat and the Canary* 1939; *Arise, My Love* 1940; *New Moon* 1940; *The Black Swan* 1942; *My Favorite Blonde* 1942; *Sherlock Holmes in Washington* 1943; *Shadows in the Night* 1944; *Voodoo Man* 1944; *Hold That Blonde* 1945; *Fog Island* 1945; *Desire Me* 1947; *Lured* 1947; *Moss Rose* 1947; *Where There's Life* 1947; *The Pirate* 1948; *Tarzan and the Mermaids* 1948
Zuniga, Daphne *The Initiation* 1984; *Stone Pillow* 1985; *The Sure Thing* 1985; *Vision Quest* 1985; *Spaceballs* 1987; *Last Rites* 1988; *A Cut Above* 1989; *The Fly II* 1989; *Prey of the Chameleon* 1991; *Mad at the*

Moon 1992; *800 Leagues down the Amazon* 1993; *Charlie's Ghost Story* 1994
Zuniga, Jose *Fresh* 1994; *Smoke* 1995; *Hurricane Streets* 1997
Zushi, Yoshitaka *Dodes'ka-Den* 1970; *Akira Kurosawa's Dreams* 1990
Zwerling, Darrell *Chinatown* 1974; *Doc Savage: the Man of Bronze* 1975; *The Ultimate Warrior* 1975

Alternative titles

A

A Chacun Son Enfer To Each His Own Hell
A la Folie Six Days, Six Nights
A la Mode Fausto
A Mezzanotte Va la Ronda del Piacere Immortal Bachelor
A Nos Amours To Our Loves
A Nous Deux An Adventure for Two
Aakaler Sandhane In Search of Famine
Aart and Johtje Vos Rescuers: Stories of Courage: Two Couples
The ABC Murders The Alphabet Murders
Abducted: A Father's Love Fugitive from Justice
Abendland Nightfall
Abgeschminkt Making Up
Able Seaman Brown Sailor of the King
Above the Law Nico
Abraxas, Guardian of the Universe Abraxas
Abre Los Ojos Open Your Eyes
Absinthe Madame X
Absinthe Man on Fire
Abwärts Out of Order
Access Denied When Danger Follows You Home
The Accursed The Traitor
Accused The Mark of the Hawk
The Ace The Great Santini
Acque di Primavera Torrents of Spring
Across the Brooklyn Bridge Over the Brooklyn Bridge
Actors Blood and Woman of Sin Actors and Sin
Actrius Actresses
Acts of Contrition Original Sins
Adalen Riots Adalen 31
Adam and Evalyn Adam and Evelyne
Adamson of Africa Killers of Kilimanjaro
Addict Born to Win
Addio Kira! We the Living
Adios Caballero One after the Other
Adios Ohio He's My Girl
Adiós, Sabata The Bounty Hunters
Admissions How I Got Into College
Adorables Mentiras Adorable Lies
The Adulteress Thérèse Raquin
Advance to Ground Zero Nightbreaker
Adventure for Two The Demi-Paradise
The Adventurer The Rover
Adventures in Babysitting A Night on the Town
The Adventures of a Gnome Named Gnorm Upworld
Adventures of a Young Man Hemingway's Adventures of a Young Man
The Adventures of Baron Munchhausen Baron Münchhausen
The Adventures of Don Quixote Don Quixote
The Adventures of Heidi Courage Mountain
The Adventures of Hercules Hercules II
The Adventures of Pico and Columbus The Magic Voyage
Adventures of Rugby Tom Brown's Schooldays
The Adventures of Sadie Our Girl Friday
The Adventures of St Francis Francis, God's Jester
The Adventures of the Flying Pickle The Pickle
The Adventures of Tintin: Lake of the Sharks Tintin and the Lake of Sharks
The Adventuress I See a Dark Stranger
The Advocate The Hour of the Pig
The Affair at the Villa Fiorita The Battle of the Villa Fiorita
Une Affaire de Femmes Story of Women
L'Affaire Wallraff The Man Inside
Affairs in Versailles Royal Affairs in Versailles
Affairs of Adelaide Britannia Mews
Africa Story The Green Horizon
African Fury Cry, the Beloved Country
After Jenny Died Revenge
After Love Après l'Amour
After Midnight Captain Carey, USA
After the Silence Shattering the Silence
Aftermath Crash: the Mystery of Flight 1501
Aftershock Marshal Law
Agaguk Shadow of the Wolf
Agantuk The Stranger

Agatha Christie's Thirteen at Dinner Thirteen at Dinner
Agent 8¾ Hot Enough for June
L'Aigle à Deux Têtes Eagle with Two Heads
Aimez-Moi Ce Soir! Love Me Tonight
Air Bud 2: Golden Receiver Air Bud: Golden Receiver
Airport '80: the Concorde Airport: the Concorde
AKA: Menace When London Sleeps
Akahige Red Beard
Akaler Sandhaney In Search of Famine
Al Capone in Jail The Revenge of Al Capone
An Alan Smithee Film: Burn, Hollywood, Burn Burn Hollywood Burn
L'Albero degli Zoccoli The Tree of Wooden Clogs
L'Albero delle pere Shooting the Moon
Albino Death in the Sun
The Aldrich Ames Story – The Last Spy Aldrich Ames: Traitor Within
Alexis Zorbas Zorba the Greek
Alferd Packer: the Musical Cannibal! the Musical
Alfred Hitchcock's Aventure Malgache Aventure Malgache
The Algonquin Silent Trigger
Algonquin Goodbye Silent Trigger
Ali: Fear Eats the Soul Fear Eats the Soul
Alias Bulldog Drummond Bulldog Jack
Alien Orders Malaya
Alien Thunder Dan Candy's Law
Alien Warning Without Warning
Alistain MacLean's River of Death River of Death
Alistair MacLean's Death Train Death Train
Alistair MacLean's Night Watch Night Watch
Alistair MacLean's Puppet on a Chain Puppet on a Chain
All Is Well Tout Va Bien
All Mine to Give The Day They Gave Babies Away
All Monsters Attack Godzilla's Revenge
All That Money Can Buy Daniel and the Devil
...All the Marbles The California Dolls
All the Way The Joker Is Wild
All These Women Now about These Women
All Things Bright and Beautiful It Shouldn't Happen to a Vet
All This and Glamour Too Vogues
All This and Money Too Love Is a Ball
Allegheny Uprising The First Rebel
Alley of Nightmares She Freak
All's Fair Weekend Warriors All's Fair
Almost Human Death Corps
Alone Horton Foote's Alone
Alone in the Neon Jungle Command in Hell
Along Came Sally Aunt Sally
Alsino y el Cóndor Alsino and the Condor
Amado Beloved/Friend
L'Amante Milena
L'Amante di Paride The Loves of Three Queens
Amantes Lovers
Amanti A Place for Lovers
Les Amants The Lovers
The Amazing Dr G Dr Goldfoot and the Girl Bombs
The Amazing Legacy of Michael Patrick Smith When You Remember Me
The Amazing Mr Beecham The Chiltern Hundreds
The Amazing Mr Forrest The Gang's All Here
The Amazing Quest of Ernest Bliss Amazing Adventure
The Amazing Spider-Man Spider-Man
Los Ambiciosos La Fièvre Monte à el Pao
Ambush in Waco In the Line of Duty: Ambush in Waco
American Cop Americanski Blues
An American Murder Season of Fear
An American Story After the Glory
The American Way Riders of the Storm
Der Amerikanische Soldat The American Soldier
L'Ami de mon Amie My Girlfriend's Boyfriend
L'Ami retrouvé Reunion

Amigo Beloved/Friend
Amityville 3-D Amityville III: the Demon
The Amorous Adventures of Uncle Benjamin Uncle Benjamin
The Amorous General Waltz of the Toreadors
The Amorous Mr Prawn The Amorous Prawn
L'Amour de Banquier The Maid
Un Amour De Pluie Loving in the Rain
Un Amour de Swann Swann in Love
L'Amour en Embuscade Love in Ambush
L'Amour en Fuite Love on the Run
L'Amour L'Apres-Midi Love in the Afternoon
Les Amours de Toni Toni
Anatahan The Saga of Anatahan
The Anatolian Smile America, America
Anatomy of a Syndicate The Big Operator
And Jenny Makes Three Jenny
And Nothing but the Truth Giro City
And Quiet Rolls the Day And Quiet Rolls the Dawn
And the Third Day Arrived the Crow On the Third Day Arrived the Crow
And Then There Were None Ten Little Indians
An Andalusian Dog Un Chien Andalou
Andy Warhol's Bad Bad
Andy Warhol's Dracula Blood for Dracula
Andy Warhol's Flesh Flesh
Andy Warhol's Frankenstein Flesh for Frankenstein
Andy Warhol's Trash Trash
Angel Cast a Dark Shadow
Angel Farm House of Angels
Angel Farm 2 House of Angels II: The Second Summer
Angel Farm, the Second Summer House of Angels II: The Second Summer
Angel of Death Beyond Forgiveness
Angel of Harlem Rebound
Angel of Vengeance Ms 45
Angel Street Gaslight
Angels and Pirates Angels in the Outfield
Angels in the Outfield Angels
Angels of the Streets Les Anges du Péché
Les Anges Gardiens Guardian Angels
Die Angst Fear
Die Angst des Tormanns beim Elfmeter The Goalkeeper's Fear of the Penalty Kick
Angst Essen Seele Auf Fear Eats the Soul
Angst vor der Angst Fear of Fear
Animas Trujano The Important Man
Ankaemaul Village in the Mist
Anne Boleyn Anna Boleyn
Anne of Windy Willows Anne of Windy Poplars
L'Année Dernière à Marienbad Last Year at Marienbad
Les Années du Mur The Promise
Annie II Annie: a Royal Adventure
The Anti-Extortion Woman Minbo – or the Gentle Art of Japanese Extortion
Antonia Antonia's Line
The Anxious Years Dark Journey
Anyone for Venice? The Honey Pot
Anything for Love Just One of the Girls
Apology for Murder Apology
L'Appât The Bait
The Applegates Meet the Applegates
Appointment with a Shadow The Midnight Story
L'Approche finale Final Approach
Aquarius Stage Fright – Aquarius
Aqui na Terra Here on Earth
The Arab The Barbarian
Arabian Night Arabian Knight
Aranyer Din Ratri Days and Nights in the Forest
L'Arbre de Noël The Christmas Tree
Archie: to Riverdale and Back Again Archie Weekend Reunion
Archy and Mehitabel Shinbone Alley
La Ardilla Roja The Red Squirrel
Are You Alone Tonight? Mind over Murder
L'Argent de poche Small Change
The Arm The Big Town
Armageddon T Redline
The Armour of God II Operation Condor: the Armour of God II
Armoured Command Armored Command
Arms and the Woman Mr Winkle Goes to War

The Army in the Shadows L'Armée des Ombres
Army of Shadows L'Armée des Ombres
Arouse and Beware The Man from Dakota
Arrivederci, Baby! Drop Dead Darling
Arthur the King Merlin and the Sword
L'Ascenseur pour l'Échafaud Lift to the Scaffold
Ascent to Heaven Mexican Bus Ride
The Assassin Venetian Bird
The Assassin Point of No Return
The Assassin The Emperor and the Assassin
Assassins The Emperor and the Assassin
Assault in Waco In the Line of Duty: Ambush in Waco
Assault on Dome 4 Chase Morran
Assault on Paradise Maniac
L'Assedio Besieged
Assignment: Istanbul The Castle of Fu Manchu
Assignment: Kill Castro Cuba Crossing
Assignment Redhead Undercover Girl
Astérix and Obélix vs Caesar Asterix and Obelix Take On Caesar
Asterix and the Stone's Blow Asterix and the Big Fight
Astérix chez les Bretons Asterix in Britain
Astérix et Obéix contre César Asterix and Obelix Take On Caesar
Asterix le Gaulois Asterix the Gaul
The Astral Factor Invisible Strangler
Asylum of Horror The Living Dead
At Dawn We Die Tomorrow We Live
At First Sight Entre Nous
At Sword's Point Sons of the Musketeers
¡tame! Tie Me Up! Tie Me Down!
Atomic Man Timeslip
The Atomic Monster Man Made Monster
Atomic Rocketship Flash Gordon
Attack All Monsters Godzilla's Revenge
Attack from Mars Midnight Movie Massacre
Attack of the Giant Crabs Attack of the Crab Monsters
Au Loin s'en Vont les Nuages Drifting Clouds
Au Travers des Oliviers Through the Olive Trees
Aufzeichnungen zu Kleidern und Städten Notebook on Cities and Clothes
Aus dem Leben der Marionetten From the Life of the Marionettes
Austerlitz The Battle of Austerlitz
Die Austernprinzessin The Oyster Princess
Un Autre Homme, Une Autre Chance Another Man, Another Chance
The Autumn of the Kohayagawa Family Early Autumn
Aux Yeux du Monde Autobus
L'Avare Dandin
The Avengers The Day Will Dawn
Avenging Angels Messenger of Death
Les Aventures Extraordinaires de Cervantes Cervantes
L'Aveu The Confession
Les Aveux les plus doux Sweet Torture
Le Avventure e Gli Amori di Miguel Cervantes Cervantes
L'Avventuriero The Rover

B

Babettes Gaestebud Babette's Feast
The Baby I Don't Want to Be Born
The Baby Web of Deceit
Baby 2000 Cloned
Baby Bump A Sinful Life
The Baby Carriage The Pram
Baby Takes a Bow Baby, Take a Bow
The Baby Vanishes Broadway Limited
Babylon LA Hollywood Confidential
Le Baccanti The Bacchantes
The Bachelor and the Bobby-Soxer Bachelor Knight
Bachelor Bait Adventure in Baltimore
Bachelor Girl Apartment Any Wednesday
Back to Back: American Yakuza 2 American Yakuza 2: Back to Back
Back Track Catchfire
Backstab Back Stab
Backstage Limelight
Backtrack Catchfire

Backwoods Massacre Midnight
Bad Blood The Night Is Young
Bad Day on the Block Under Pressure
The Bad One Sorority Girl
Baiju the Poet Baiju Bawra
Bail Out WB, Blue and the Bean
The Bailiff Sansho the Bailiff
Baisers Volés Stolen Kisses
The Ballad of Joe Hill Joe Hill
Ballad of the Soldier Ballad of a Soldier
Le Ballon Rouge Red Balloon
Balthazar Au Hasard, Balthazar
Bamboo Dolls House The Big Doll House
The Banana Monster Schlock
The Bananas Boat What Changed Charley Farthing?
Band of Gold How to Save a Marriage and Ruin Your Life
Bang, Bang, You're Dead Our Man in Marrakesh
The Bank Breakers Kaleidoscope
The Bank Detective The Bank Dick
Banner in the Sky Third Man on the Mountain
Bare Breasted Countess The Female Vampire
Barnabo delle Montagne Barnabo of the Mountains
Barney Who Says I Can't Ride a Rainbow
Barnvagnen The Pram
Les Bas-Fonds The Lower Depths
Baseball in Black and White Soul of the Game
Basic Deception Deadly Identity
La Bataille de San Sebastian Guns for San Sebastian
Batman & Mr Freeze: Subzero Subzero
The Battle at Elderbush The Battle of Elderbush
Battle Creek The Big Brawl
Battle Creek Brawl The Big Brawl
Battle Flag Battleflag
The Battle for Anzio Anzio
Battle Hell Escape of the Amethyst
The Battle of Elderbush Gulch The Battle of Elderbush
Battle of the Astros Invasion of the Astro-Monster
Battle of the Valiant Brennus – Enemy of Rome
Battle Rage Missing in Action
Battlefront Attack! Attack!
The Battling Bellhop Kid Galahad
Battling Hooper Something to Sing About
Bay Coven Bay Cove
Baywatch: Forbidden Paradise Baywatch the Movie: Forbidden Paradise
Be Prepared Troop Beverly Hills
The Beachcomber Vessel of Wrath
The Beast in Heat The Beast
The Beast of Babylon Against the Son of Hercules Hero of Babylon
The Beast of Morocco The Hand of Night
The Beast of War The Beast
Beastly Christmas The Naked Jungle
The Beasts of Marseilles Seven Thunders
The Beate Klarsfeld Story Nazi Hunter: the Beate Klarsfeld Story
A Beating Heart Your Beating Heart
Beatsville The Rebel Set
Beaumarchais Beaumarchais l'Insolent
Beaumarchais: the Scoundrel Beaumarchais l'Insolent
Beautiful But Deadly The Don Is Dead
The Beautiful Game The Match
The Beautiful Stranger Beautiful Stranger
Beauty and the Devil La Beauté du Diable
Beauty's Revenge Midwest Obsession
The Bed Secrets d'Alcove
Bed Time Story Bedtime Story
Beethoven Abel Gance's Beethoven
Beethoven's Great Love Abel Gance's Beethoven
The Beginners The First Time
The Beginners Three The First Time
Behemoth, the Sea Monster The Giant Behemoth
Behind Every Good Man All Lies End in Murder
Behind the Cellar Door Revenge
Behind the Iron Curtain The Iron Curtain
Behind the Iron Mask The Fifth Musketeer
Behold We Live If I Were Free
Bejeweled Bejewelled
La Bella Mugnaia The Miller's Wife

Bells Murder by Phone
The Beloved Sin
Beloved Milena Milena
Bengal Rifles Bengal Brigade
Berlin Blue Midnight Cop
Berry Gordy's The Last Dragon The Last Dragon
Best Friends Best Friends for Life
Best Intentions Murder without Motive
Best of the Best 4: Without Warning Best of the Best: Without Warning
La Bête The Beast
Between Two Worlds Destiny
Beverly Hills Cowgirl Blues Beverly Hills Connection
Beware of Children No Kidding
Beware the Holy Whore Beware of a Holy Whore
Beyond Consent Trapped and Deceived
Beyond Suspicion Appointment for a Killing
Beyond the Fog Tower of Evil
Beyond the Law Beyond the Walls
Beyond the Law Fixing the Shadow
Beyond the Law – Blue Beyond the Law
Beyond the Limit The Honorary Consul
Beyond the Wall Destiny
The Bible: Jacob Jacob
The Bicycle Thief Bicycle Thieves
Il Bidone The Swindle
The Big Bang Theory Bang
The Big Carnival Ace in the Hole
The Big Feast La Grande Bouffe
The Big Frame The Lost Hours
The Big Grab Any Number Can Win
A Big Hand for a Little Lady Big Deal at Dodge City
The Big Heart Miracle on 34th Street
Big Six Common Law Cabin
The Big Snatch Any Number Can Win
Big Time Operators The Smallest Show on Earth
The Biggest Bank Robbery A Nightingale Sang in Berkeley Square
The Biggest Heist in History The Cops Are Robbers
Billings Not in This Town
Billions Millions
Billy the Kid Gore Vidal's Billy the Kid
Billy the Kid, Sheriff of Sage Valley Sheriff of Sage Valley
Bionic Breakdown Bionic Ever After?
Bird with the Glass Feathers The Bird with the Crystal Plumage
Birds of a Feather La Cage aux Folles
Birthmark The Omen
The Bitch La Garce
The Bitch Drôle de Drame
The Bite Curse II: The Bite
Bitter Blood Bitter Vengeance
The Bitter End Love Walked In
Bitter Reunion Le Beau Serge
Die Bitteren Tränen der Petra von Kant The Bitter Tears of Petra von Kant
Bizarre, Bizarre Drôle de Drame
Bizet's Carmen Carmen
Black Arrow Strikes The Black Arrow
Black Belt Blackbelt
The Black Book Reign of Terror
The Black Buccaneer The Black Pirate
The Black Buccaneer Gordon the Black Pirate
The Black Countess The Female Vampire
Black Eyes Dark Eyes
Black Flowers Wall of Silence
Black Glove Face the Music
Black Peter Peter and Pavla
Black Scorpion II: Aftershock Black Scorpion: Ground Zero
Black Shack Alley Rue Cases Nègres
Black Sunday The Mask of Satan
Black Tuesday The Affair
Black Victory Black and White in Color
Black Widows: the Alabama Twins Separated by Murder
Blackmail Chase Rich and Respectable
Blackout Contraband
Blacula 2 Scream Blacula Scream
Blake Edwards' Son of the Pink Panther Son of the Pink Panther
Blanc de Chine The Chinese Connection
Blank Check Blank Cheque
Blast The Final Comedown
Blast Off Jules Verne's Rocket to the Moon
Der Blaue Engel The Blue Angel
Das Blaue Licht The Blue Light

Blazing Arrows Fighting Caravans
Le Blé en Herbe The Ripening Seed
Die Blechtrommel The Tin Drum
Bleeders Hemoglobin
Die Bleierne Zeit The German Sisters
Blessed Assurance The Price of Heaven
Blind Man's Bluff Cauldron of Blood
Blind Spot Death in the Sun
Block Party Marshal Law
Blokpost Checkpoint
Blonde Bait Women without Men
Blonde Sinner Yield to the Night
Blood Beast from Outer Space The Night Caller
Blood Couple Ganja and Hess
Blood Creature Terror Is a Man
Blood Fiend Theatre of Death
Blood Is My Heritage Blood of Dracula
The Blood Kin Last of the Mobile Hot-Shots
Blood Mad The Glove
Blood Money Requiem for a Heavyweight
Blood Money Under Oath
Blood Moon Bats
Blood of Frankenstein Dracula vs Frankenstein
The Blood of Heroes The Salute Of The Jugger
Blood of the Demon Blood of Dracula
Blood of the Innocent Beyond Forgiveness
Blood on the Streets Borsalino and Co
Blood Ransom Captive Rage
The Blood Seekers Dracula vs Frankenstein
Blood Sisters Sisters
Blood Wedding Les Noces Rouges
Bloodstone Maximum Risk
Bloodstream Daybreak
Bloodwings: Pumpkinhead's Revenge The Revenge of Pumpkinhead – Blood Wings
Bloody Bird ALA Stage Fright – Aquarius
The Bloody Bushido Blade The Bushido Blade
Bloody Friday In the Line of Duty: the FBI Murders
Blowup Blow Up
Blue Three Colours Blue
The Blue and the Gold An Annapolis Story
Blue Jeans Blue Denim
Blue Sierra Courage of Lassie
Blues for Lovers Ballad in Blue
Bluff storia di truffe e di imbroglioni The Con Artists
Boca a Boca Mouth to Mouth
Boda Secreta Secret Wedding
Bodas de Sangre Blood Wedding
Bodily Harm The Operation
Body Beat Dance Academy
Body of a Woman The Big Squeeze
Body of Evidence Blind Judgement: Seduction in Travis County
The Body Politic Quicksilver Highway
Bodycount Body Count
The Bodyguard Yojimbo
Le Boeuf Clandestin The Secret Steak
Bolero Les Uns et les Autres
The Bomber Boys Captain Nuke and the Bomber Boys
Bombshell Blonde Bombshell
Bombsight Stolen Cottage to Let
Bon Appetit, Mama Motherhood
Bonaventure Thunder on the Hill
Bone Housewife
La Bonne Année Happy New Year
Bonnie and Clyde: the Real Story Bonnie and Clyde: the True Story
Bop The Thief
Bordello of Blood Tales from the Crypt Presents: Bordello of Blood
Borderlines The Caretakers
Boredom L'Ennui
Born for Glory Forever England
Born to Be Kissed The Girl from Missouri
Born to Kill Lady of Deceit
Born to Lose Born to Win
Bosambo Sanders of the River
Both Ends of the Candle The Helen Morgan Story
The Bottom of the Bottle Beyond the River
Boudu Sauvé des Eaux Boudu, Saved from Drowning
Bound by Honor Blood In Blood Out
Bounty Tracer Bounty Tracker
Boy of Two Worlds Paw
A Boy Ten Feet Tall Sammy Going South

The Boyfriend from Hell The Shrimp on the Barbie
The Boyfriend School Don't Tell Her It's Me
Boyfriends and Girlfriends My Girlfriend's Boyfriend
Brady's Escape The Long Ride
Brain Candy Kids in the Hall: Brain Candy
The Brainsnatcher The Man Who Changed His Mind
Bram Stoker's The Mummy Bram Stoker's Legend of the Mummy
Brandy Ashore Green Grow the Rushes
Brat Brother
The Brave and the Beautiful The Magnificent Matador
The Brave Young Men of Weinberg Up the Academy
Braving Alaska To Brave Alaska
Breach of Faith A Kidnapping in the Family
Bread and Flower A Moment of Innocence
Bread and Plant A Moment of Innocence
The Break A Further Gesture
Break for Freedom Albert, RN
The Break Up La Rupture
Breakin' Breakdance
Breakin' 2: Electric Boogaloo Breakdance 2 – Electric Boogaloo
Breaking Home Ties Norman Rockwell's Breaking Home Ties
Breaking Point Double Suspicion
Breaking the Silence Shattering the Silence
Breaking the Sound Barrier The Sound Barrier
Breakout Danger Within
The Breakup La Rupture
Breathless A Bout de Souffle
The Bride Comes to Yellow Sky Face to Face
The Bride Is Too Beautiful The Bride Is Much Too Beautiful
Bride of Dragons Bridge of Dragons
Bride of the Atom Bride of the Monster
The Bride Wasn't Willing Frontier Gal
The Bridge Between Two Banks The Bridge
A Bridge Between Two Shores The Bridge
Brighty Brighty of the Grand Canyon
Bring on the Dancing Girls Who's That Knocking at My Door
Brink of Hell Toward the Unknown
Brink of Life So Close to Life
Broken Crown Crowned and Dangerous
Broken Hearts and Noses Crimewave
Broken Lullaby The Man I Killed
Broken Silence Moment of Truth: Race against Fear
Bronco Busters Little Moon & Jud McGraw
Brotherhood of the Yakuza The Yakuza
Brotherly Love Country Dance
Brothers and Sisters Fratelli e Sorelle
Brothers' Destiny The Road Home
Brother's Keeper Stranger in My Home
Brown on Resolution Forever England
Bruce Lee's Game of Death Game of Death
Die Brücke The Bridge
Un Bruit Qui Rend Fou The Blue Villa
The Brute El Bruto
Brute Force The Expert
Brutti, Sporchi e Cattivi Down and Dirty
Die Büchse der Pandora Pandora's Box
Bud the Chud CHUD II: Bud the Chud
The Buddy Factor Swimming with Sharks
Bugs Bunny The Bugs Bunny/Road Runner Movie
Bugs Bunny's Third Movie – 1001 Rabbit Tales Bugs Bunny 1001 Rabbit Tales
A Bullet from God God's Gun
Bullet Proof Bulletproof
Bulletproof Heart Killer
Burial of the Rats Bram Stoker's Burial of the Rats
Burn Burn!
Burn, Baby, Burn Heat Wave
Burn, Witch, Burn Night of the Eagle
Burnin' Love Love at Stake
The Burning Cross The Klansman
The Burning Man A Dangerous Summer
The Burning Question Reefer Madness
The Butcher Le Boucher
Butcher Baker Night Warning
Butter Cream Gang II Secret of Treasure Mountain

The Butterfly Affair Popsy-Pop
The Button-Pinchers Buttoners
The Button-Pushers Buttoners
Buy and Sell Buy & Cell
By Hook or by Crook I Dood It
By Rocket to the Moon Woman in the Moon
By Whose Hand Guilty?
Bye-Bye Brasil Bye Bye Brazil

Ça commence aujourd'hui It All Starts Today
Cabal Nightbreed
Das Cabinett des Dr Caligari The Cabinet of Dr Caligari
Cabiria Nights of Cabiria
Caccia al Maschio Male Hunt
Les Cachetonneurs The Music Freelancers
Cadaveri Eccellenti Illustrious Corpses
Cadence Stockade
La Caduta degli Dei The Damned
Cafe of the Seven Sinners Seven Sinners
La Cage aux Folles III: The Wedding La Cage aux Folles III: "Elles" se Marient
La Cage aux Rossignols A Cage of Nightingales
Caged Females Caged Heat
Cajun Louisiana Story
Call Harry Crown 99 and 44/100% Dead
Call Him Mr Shatter Shatter
Call It Murder Midnight
Call Me a Cab Carry On Cabby
Call Me Genius The Rebel
Call of the Wild Jack London's The Call of the Wild
The Call of the Wild Dog of the Yukon Jack London's The Call of the Wild
El Callejon de los Milagros Midaq Alley
The Calling Murder by Phone
Les Camarades The Organizer
Camille without Camellias La Signora senza Camelie
Campus Justice Silencing Mary
Canaan's Way Blind Justice
Candyman: Farewell to the Flesh Candyman II: Farewell to the Flesh
Cannon Movie Tales: Red Riding Hood Red Riding Hood
Capone The Revenge of Al Capone
Capone in Jail The Revenge of Al Capone
Le Caporal Epinglé The Vanishing Corporal
Captain Blood The Captain
Captain Midnight On the Air Live with Captain Midnight
Captain Moonlight D'Ye Ken John Peel?
Caravan Himalaya
Care of the Spitfire Grill The Spitfire Grill
Carelessly We Love I Met My Love Again
The Carnal Prayer Mat Sex and Zen
Carne Trémula Live Flesh
Carne y Demonio Susana
Les Carnets du Major Thompson The Diary of Major Thompson
Carnival of Terror The Funhouse
Caro Diario Dear Diary
Caroline at Midnight Someone's Watching
The Carolyn Warmus Story A Murderous Affair
Le Carosse d'Or The Golden Coach
Carquake Cannonball
Carrie 2 The Rage: Carrie 2
Carried Away Acts of Love
The Carriers Are Waiting Les Convoyeurs Attendent
Carry On Venus Carry On Jack
The Cars That Eat People The Cars That Ate Paris
Cartagine in fiamme Carthage in Flames
La Carte du Tendre Map of the Human Heart
Le Cas du Docteur Laurent The Case of Dr Laurent
La Casa de Bernarda Alba The House of Bernarda Alba
La Casa dell'Esorcismo Lisa and the Devil
The Case against Paul Ryker Sergeant Ryker
The Case of Jonathan Drew The Lodger
The Case of the Hillside Stranglers The Hillside Stranglers

Case of the Red Monkey Little Red Monkey
Casey For Love of a Child
CASH Whiffs
Cash on Delivery To Dorothy, a Son
Casper and Wendy Casper Meets Wendy
Le Casse The Burglars
Cast Iron The Virtuous Sin
The Castaway The Cheaters
Castle of Doom Vampyr: The Strange Adventure of David Gray
The Castle of the Spider's Web Throne of Blood
Casualty of Love, The Buttafuoco Story Casualties of Love: the Long Island Lolita Story
Catacombs Curse IV: The Ultimate Sacrifice
Catch Fire Catchfire
The Cathedral The Church
Cathedral of Demons The Church
Cathy Tippel Keetje Tippel
Caught in the Act Cosi
I Cavalieri dell'illusione The Loves of Three Queens
The Cave Dwellers Man and His Mate
Cave Man Man and His Mate
La Caza The Hunt
Ce Cher Intrus Once Around
The Celebration Festen
Celine and Julie Vont en Bateau Celine and Julie Go Boating
Cemetery Girls The Velvet Vampire
Central do Brasil Central Station
C'Era una Volta More than a Miracle
C'Eravamo Tanto Amati We All Loved Each Other So Much
Le Cercle Rouge The Red Circle
Le Cerveau The Brain
Cet Obscur Objet du Désir That Obscure Object of Desire
Ceux Qui M'Aiment Prendront le Train Those Who Love Me Will Take the Train
Chained to Yesterday Limbo
Chains of Hate Black Mama, White Mama
Le Chaland Qui Passe L'Atalante
Chamber of Horrors Bedlam
The Chambermaid The Chambermaid on the Titanic
La Chambre Verte The Green Room
Champion for the King The Captain
Champions The Mighty Ducks
Chance Meeting Blind Date
Chance Meeting The Young Lovers
A Change of Heart Two and Two Make Six
Chantons et Choeur Grandeur et Décadence d'un Petit Commerce de Cinéma
Chaos Kaos
Un Chapeau de Paille d'Italie An Italian Straw Hat
Chapter 24 in the Complete Adventures of Indiana Jones: Indiana Jones and the Raiders of the Lost Ark Raiders of the Lost Ark
The Charge Is Murder Twilight of Honor
Charles & Diana: A Palace Divided Charles & Diana: Unhappily Ever After
Charles Dickens' David Copperfield David Copperfield
Charley's American Aunt Charley's Aunt
Charlie at Work Work
Charlie Chan and the Red Dragon The Red Dragon
Charlie Chan in Dangerous Money Dangerous Money
Charlie Chan in Dark Alibi Dark Alibi
Charlie Chan in the Trap The Trap
Charlie on the Farm The Tramp
Charlie the Decorator Work
Charlie the Hobo The Tramp
Charlie the Tramp The Tramp
Charlie's Kids Listen to Me
Charlotte and Lulu An Impudent Girl
Charlotte Bronte's Jane Eyre Jane Eyre
Le Charme Discret de la Bourgeoisie The Discreet Charm of the Bourgeoisie
The Charmer Moonlight Sonata
The Charmer Tall, Dark and Deadly
The Chase for the Golden Needles Golden Needles
La Chasse à l'Homme Male Hunt
The Chastity Belt On My Way to the Crusades, I Met a Girl Who ...
Chattery Teeth Quicksilver Highway

Che? What?
Che Botte, Ragazzi! Shanghai Joe
The Cheaters Les Tricheurs
Cheatin' Hearts Paper Hearts
Checkpoint Trial on the Road
The Cheque Is in the Post The Check Is in the Mail
Chetnik Undercover
Cheval Sauvage White Mane
Chicago, Chicago Gaily, Gaily
La Chiesa The Church
Child of the Night Les Voleurs
Children's Faces Faces of Children
China Blue Crimes of Passion
China Mountain Big Brother The Big Boss
Chinatown Murders: the Man against the Mob Man against the Mob: the Chinatown Murders
Chinchero The Last Movie
The Chinese Box Chinese Box
The Chinese Connection Fist of Fury
The Chinese Portrait Portraits Chinois
Chinese White The Chinese Connection
Chino The Valdez Horses
Chloë in the Afternoon Love in the Afternoon
Le Choc Shock
The Choice Yam Daabo
Choice of Arms Trial by Combat
Le Choix des Armes Choice of Arms
Choke Canyon On Dangerous Ground
The Chosen Holocaust 2000
Les Choses de la Vie The Things of Life
A Christmas Carol Scrooge
Christmas Evil You Better Watch Out
Chronicle of the Years of Embers Chronicle of the Burning Years
Chronicle of the Years of Fire Chronicle of the Burning Years
Chronik der Anna Magdalena Bach Chronicle of Anna Magdalena Bach
Chubby Goes Down Under Chubby Down Under and Other Sticky Regions
Chuck Berry: Hail! Hail! Rock'n'Roll! Hail! Hail! Rock'n'Roll!
CHUD Cannibalistic Humanoid Underground Dwellers CHUD
Ciao Maschio Bye Bye Monkey
A Ciascuno il Suo We Still Kill the Old Way
Le Ciel et la Boue The Sky above, the Mud below
Le Ciel, les Oiseaux et... Ta Mère! Homeboys at the Beach
Il Cielo è Sempre Più Blu Bits and Pieces
Cinderella Rodgers & Hammerstein's Cinderella
Cinderella – Italian Style More than a Miracle
La Ciociara Two Women
The Circle The Vicious Circle
Circle of Love La Ronde
Circus World The Magnificent Showman
Citadel of Crime A Man Betrayed
La Cité des enfants perdus The City of Lost Children
Citizen's Band FM
La Citta delle Donne City of Women
The City Jungle The Young Philadelphians
City Unplugged Darkness in Tallinn
La Ciudad y los Perros The City and the Dogs
Le Clan des Siciliens The Sicilian Clan
The Clansman The Birth of a Nation
La Classe de Neige Class Trip
Classe Tous Risques The Big Risk
Claude The Two of Us
The Cleopatra Arms A Kiss in the Dark
Clickety-Clack Dodes'ka-Den
The Clinic Critical Choices
Clinton and Nadine Blood Money
Clive Barker's Hellraiser Hellraiser
Clive Barker's Lord of Illusions Lord of Illusions
Close to Eden A Stranger among Us
Close to Eden Urga
Closely Watched Trains Closely Observed Trains
The Closer You Come The Closer You Get
Clouds over Europe Q Planes
Clown House Clownhouse
Coach Sunset Park
Coastliner Disaster on the Coastliner
Cobb's Law: Incident in Baltimore Against Her Will

Cobweb Castle Throne of Blood
Cocaine Mixed Blood
Cocaine Kids illtown
Cocktails in the Kitchen For Better, for Worse
Code Name: Trixie The Crazies
Code of Scotland Yard The Shop at Sly Corner
Un Coeur Qui Bat Your Beating Heart
Cold around the Heart Cold Heart
Cold Cash Top of the World
Cold Cuts Buffet Froid
The Cold Heart of a Killer Murder on the Iditarod Trail
Cold Reading Rehearsal for Murder
Cold Water L'Eau Froide
Colder than Death Love Is Colder than Death
Colette Becoming Colette
Colin Nutley's House of Angels House of Angels
La Collina Degli Stavali Boot Hill
Colonel Blimp The Life and Death of Colonel Blimp
The Color of a Hero A Better Tomorrow
The Color of Pomegranates The Colour of Pomegranates
Colossus 1980 Colossus: The Forbin Project
Le combat dans l'île Fire and Ice
Combat High Combat Academy
Comes a Time Silence of the North
Coming Down to Earth Doin' Time on Planet Earth
A Coming-Out Party Very Important Person
Commander Hamilton Hamilton
Comment je me suis disputé... ma vie sexuelle Ma Vie Sexuelle
The Communicants Winter Light
Como Agua para Chocolate Like Water for Chocolate
Como Ser Mujer y no Morir en el Intento How to Be a Woman and Not Die in the Attempt
Company of Cowards? Advance to the Rear
Compartiment Tueurs The Sleeping Car Murders
Computer Killers Horror Hospital
Comrades of 1918 Westfront 1918
Comradeship Kameradschaft
Comstock and Rosemary Keep the Aspidistra Flying
The Con Man The Con Artists
The Con Men The Con Artists
Concerto I've Always Loved You
The Concorde - Airport '79 Airport: the Concorde
The Concrete Jungle The Criminal
Un Condamné à mort s'est échappé A Man Escaped
Condemned to Death Death by Hanging
The Conductor Il Maestro
The Confession Quick, Let's Get Married
The Confessional The Confession
The Confessional House of Mortal Sin
Confessions Private Confessions
Confessions of a Handyman Ups and Downs of a Handyman
Confessions of a Sorority Girl Sorority Girl
Confidential Hollywood Confidential
The Conflict Catholics
Conjugal Cabin Common Law Cabin
The Connecticut Look The Secret Life of an American Wife
A Connecticut Yankee in King Arthur's Court A Knight in Camelot
The Conqueror Worm Witchfinder General
Consider All Risks The Big Risk
Conspiracy of Silence No One Would Tell
Conspiracy of Terror House of Secrets
Conte d'Automne An Autumn Tale
Conte d'Été A Summer's Tale
Contest Girl The Beauty Jungle
The Context Illustrious Corpses
Contract in Blood Shock
Convention City Sons of the Desert
Conviction The Conviction of Kitty Dodds
Conway Body Armor
Coolangatta Gold The Gold and Glory
Cop Killers Order of Death
Cop-Out Stranger in the House
Cop Story Police Story
Copkiller Order of Death
Cops and Robbers The Cops Are Robbers

La Coquille et le Clergman The Seashell and the Clergyman
A Cor do seu Destino The Color of Destiny
Corazon Iluminado Foolish Heart
Le Corbeau The Raven
Cordillera Flight to Fury
El Coronel No Tiene Quien Le Escriba No One Writes to the Colonel
The Corpse Collectors Cauldron of Blood
Corrupt Order of Death
Corrupt Justice Crime Broker
La Corsa dell'Innocente Flight of the Innocent
The Corsican Brothers Cheech & Chong's The Corsican Brothers
I Cosacchi The Cossacks
Cosmic Monsters The Strange World of Planet X
Cosmic Shock Doomsday Rock
Costa Brava Family Album
Count Dracula and His Vampire Bride The Satanic Rites of Dracula
Count Iorga, Vampire Count Yorga, Vampire
The Count of Monk's Bridge The Count of the Old Town
Count Your Bullets Cry for Me Billy
Counted Moments Nick of Time
Counterattack of the Monster Godzilla Raids Again
Country Justice Family Rescue
Coup de Foudre Entre Nous
Le Coup de Menhir Asterix and the Big Fight
Coup de Torchon Clean Slate
Courage Raw Courage
The Courage of Kavik, the Wolf Dog Kavik, the Wolf Dog
La Course du Lièvre à travers les Champs And Hope to Die
Court Martial Carrington VC
The Courtney Affair The Courtneys of Curzon Street
Le Couvent The Convent
The Cover Girl and the Cop Beauty and Denise
Cracking Up Smorgasbord
Cradle to Grave Web of Deceit
Cradle to Rob Web of Deceit
The Craft A Child for Satan
Crash Course Driving Academy
Crash Landing: the Rescue of Flight 232 A Thousand Heroes
The Crash of Silence Mandy
The Crawling Eye The Trollenberg Terror
Crazy For You Vision Quest
The Crazy Ray Paris Qui Dort
Crazy to Kill Dr Gillespie's Criminal Case
The Crazysitter Two Much Trouble
Creative Detour Cool Blue
The Creature, the Kid & Margaret For the Love of Aaron
Creatures From beyond the Grave
The Creatures from beyond the Grave From beyond the Grave
The Creeping Unknown The Quatermass Experiment
Crest of the Wave Seagulls over Sorrento
Cries from the Heart Touch of Truth
Cries in the Night The Awful Dr Orloff
Cries Unheard: the Donna Yaklich Story Victim of Rage
Crime et Châtiment Crime and Punishment
Crime of Honor A Song for Europe
Crime Squad The Man from Cairo
Crime Time Crimetime
Crime Wave The City Is Dark
Crimebroker Crime Broker
The Crimes of Dr Mabuse The Testament of Dr Mabuse
Crimes of Passion: Badge of Betrayal Badge of Betrayal
Crimes of Passion: Nobody Lives Forever Criminal Intent
Crimes of Passion: Victim of Love Victim of Love: the Shannon Mohr Story
Criminal Passion Angel of Desire
The Crimson Blade The Scarlet Blade
Crimson Circle The Red Circle
The Crimson Cult Curse of the Crimson Altar
Crin-Blanc White Mane
Cristo si è Fermato a Eboli Christ Stopped at Eboli
Critical Decision Executive Decision
Critical List Terminal Choice
Cronaca di un Amore Chronicle of a Love
Cronaca di una Morte Annunciata Chronicle of a Death Foretold
Crooks in Clover Penthouse
Cross-Up Tiger by the Tail
Crossed Swords The Prince and the Pauper
Crossfire Quick
Crossing the Line The Big Man
Crosspoint The November Men
Crossroads of Destiny Jailbreak
The Crown Caper The Thomas Crown Affair
Crush Depth Sub Down
Cry Devil Night Visitor
A Cry for Justice A Song for Europe
Crying Out Loud Cotton Queen
Cult of the Damned Angel, Angel Down We Go
La Curée The Game Is Over
The Curious Case of the Campus Corpse The Hazing
The Curse Xala
The Curse of San Michel The Bay of Saint Michel
Curse of the Demon Night of the Demon
Curse of the Golem It!
The Curve Dead Man's Curve
Cutter and Bone Cutter's Way
Cybèle ou les dimanches de Ville d'Avray Sundays and Cybèle
Cyber Space Lawnmower Man 2: Beyond Cyberspace
Cybertech PD Terminal Justice
Cyborg 3: The Creation Cyborg 3: The Recycler
Cyborg Soldier Cyborg Cop II
Czarina A Royal Scandal

D

Da uomo a uomo Death Rides a Horse
Daayraa The Square Circle
Daddy Nostalgia These Foolish Things
Daddy's Little Girl She's Out Of Control
Dad's Week Off National Lampoon's Dad's Week Off
Dal Polo all'Equatore From the Pole to the Equator
Dallas: the Movie Dallas: JR Returns
La Dame dans l'Auto avec des Lunettes et un Fusil The Lady in the Car with Glasses and a Gun
Dance of Death House of Evil
Dance of the Vampires or Pardon Me, but Your Teeth Are in My Neck The Fearless Vampire Killers
Danger Grows Wild The Poppy Is Also a Flower
Danger in the Skies The Pilot
Danger Island Mr Moto in Danger Island
Danger Rides the Range Three Texas Steers
Dangerous Beauty The Honest Courtesan
Dangerous Business Party Girl
A Dangerous Friend The Todd Killings
Dangerous Love Affairs Les Liaisons Dangereuses
Dangerous Obsession Mortal Sins
Danielle Steel's Changes Changes
Danielle Steel's Daddy Daddy
Danielle Steel's Fine Things Fine Things
Danielle Steel's Heartbeat Heartbeat
Danielle Steel's Kaleidoscope Kaleidoscope
Danielle Steel's Palomino Palomino
Danny Boy Angel
Danny's Secret The Secret
Un Danseur: Rudolph Nureyev I Am a Dancer
Dario Argento's Inferno Inferno
Dario Argento's Trauma Trauma
Dark Breed Darkbreed
Dark Empire Dark City
Dark End They Met in the Dark
Dark Family Secrets: The Dawna Kay Wells Story Deep Family Secrets
Dark Goddess Temptress
Dark Matters Normal Life
Dark Obsession Diamond Skulls
Dark of the Night Mr Wrong
Dark Reflection Natural Selection
Dark World Dark City
The Darkest Hour Hell on Frisco Bay
Das Schöne Ende dieser Welt The Beautiful End of This World
A Date with Death The High Bright Sun
A Date with Destiny The Return of October
A Daughter's Courage Her Last Chance
Daughters of Privilege Keys to the Kingdom
A Daughter's Secret: the Traci DiCarlo Story Beyond Obsession
David David: the David Rothenberg Story
Dawandeh The Runner
Dawn Streets
The Day After Up from the Beach
The Day after Tomorrow Strange Holiday
A Day in the Country Une Partie de Campagne
Day of the Badman Day of the Bad Man
Day of the Landgrabbers Land Raiders
The Day the Screaming Stopped The Comeback
A Day to Remember Two Bits
Days of Hope Man's Hope
Daytona Blues Welcome to Paradise
Dead Ahead 36 Hours to Die
Dead Ahead: the Exxon Valdez Disaster Disaster at Valdez
Dead Alive Braindead
Dead Connection Final Combination
Dead End Dogwatch
Dead End False Pretense
Dead End Brattigan The Great Pretender
Dead End: Cradle of Crime Dead End
Dead Image Dead Ringer
Dead on Course Wings of Danger
Dead On: Relentless 2 Relentless 2: Dead On
Dead Suzy The Terror Inside
Dead Waters Dark Waters
Deader than Ever: a Mike Hammer Mystery Come Die with Me
The Deadliest Sin Confession
Deadline Deadline – USA
Deadline Witness in the War Zone
Deadline Midnight –30–
Deadlock Wedlock
Deadly Betrayal: the Bruce Curtis Story Journey into Darkness: the Bruce Curtis Story
Deadly Currents Curacao
Deadly Is the Female Gun Crazy
Deadly Measures Desperate Measures
The Deadly Mr Frost Mister Frost
Deadly Nightshade Fighting for My Daughter
Deadly Outbreak Deadly Takeover
Deadly Roulette How I Spent My Summer Vacation
Deadly Secrets Deadly Family Secrets
Deadly Seduction Blind Date
Deadly Silence Dead Silence
The Deadly Silence Tarzan's Deadly Silence
Deadly Vision Mind over Murder
Dean Koontz's Mr Murder Mr Murder
Dean R Koontz's Servants of Twilight The Servants of Twilight
Dear Emma, Sweet Böbe Sweet Emma Dear Böbe
Dear Mr Grasler The Bachelor
Dearest Love Le Souffle au Coeur
Death and Vengeance Jack Reed: Death and Vengeance
Death Bed Terminal Choice
Death Comes from the Dark Cauldron of Blood
Death Corps Death Corps
Death Has No Sex A Black Veil for Lisa
Death House Silent Night, Bloody Night
Death in Full View Deathwatch
Death in Granada The Disappearance of Garcia Lorca
A Death in Palm Springs Dead Silence
Death List Terminal Choice
Death of a Corrupt Man To Kill a Rat
Death of a Hooker Who Killed Mary Whats'ername?
Death of a San Antonio Cop Shoot First: A Cop's Vengeance
Death of a Yankee Hostile Waters
Death on Everest Into Thin Air: Death on Everest
Death Pays the Sitter The Babysitter's Seduction
Death Scream The Deadly Trap
Death Trap Eaten Alive
Death Watch Deathwatch
Deathbed Terminal Choice
Deathline Redline
Death's Ecstasy The Beast
La Décade Prodigieuse Ten Days' Wonder
Deceiver Liar
Deception Ruby Cairo
Deception Anna Boleyn
La Decima Vittima The Tenth Victim
Dedication Sadhna
Deep in the Heart Handgun
The Defeated The Vanquished
Le Déjeuner sur l'Herbe Lunch on the Grass
Deliria Stage Fright – Aquarius
Deliver Them From Evil: The John List Story Judgment Day: the John List Story
Deliverance Sadgati
Dellamorte Dellamore Cemetery Man
The Delores Donovan Story Locked Up: a Mother's Rage
Les Demoiselles de Rochefort The Young Girls of Rochefort
Demolition Day Captain Nuke and the Bomber Boys
The Demon Onibaba
Demon God Told Me to
The Demon Barber The Tale of Sweeney Todd
The Demon Barber of Fleet Street Sweeney Todd, the Demon Barber of Fleet Street
Demon Cathedral The Church
The Demon Doctor The Awful Dr Orloff
Demon Knight Tales from the Crypt: Demon Knight
Demons 3 The Church
Demons of the Swamp Attack of the Giant Leeches
Dennis the Menace Dennis
Dennis the Menace Strikes Again Dennis Strikes Again
La Dentellière The Lacemaker
Le Dernier Combat The Last Battle
Le Dernier Metro The Last Metro
Des Teufels General The Devil's General
The Descendant of Genghis-Khan Storm over Asia
Descente aux enfers Descent into Hell
Desert Attack Ice Cold in Alex
Desert Nurse Jesse
Desert Patrol Sea of Sand
Desert Tanks The Battle of El Alamein
Il Deserto Rosso The Red Desert
Desire Salt on Our Skin
Los Desperados A Bullet for Sandoval
Desperate Choices: To Save My Child Solomon's Choice
The Desperate Men Cat and Mouse
Desperate Prey Redheads
Después de la tormenta After the Storm
The Destructors The Marseilles Contract
The Detective Father Brown
The Detective Kid The Gumshoe Kid
Deus e o Diabo Na Terra do Sol Black God, White Devil
Deutschland im Herbst Germany in Autumn
Deutschland im Jahre Null Germany, Year Zero
Les Deux Anglaises et le Continent Anne and Muriel
Deux Billets Pour Mexico Dead Run
Deux Hommes Dans La Ville Two against the Law
Deux Hommes dans Manhattan Two Men in Manhattan
The Devil and Daniel Webster Daniel and the Devil
The Devil and the Dead Lisa and the Devil
The Devil and the Flesh Susana
Devil in the Flesh Dearly Devoted
The Devil in the House of Exorcism Lisa and the Devil
The Devil Inside Offbeat
The Devil Never Sleeps Satan Never Sleeps
Devil on Wheels Indianapolis Speedway
The Devil Takes the Count The Devil Is a Sissy
The Devil within Her I Don't Want to Be Born
The Devil Woman Onibaba
The Devil's Bride The Devil Rides Out
The Devil's Brother Bogus Bandits
The Devil's Commandment The Vampires

The Fall of the House of Usher The House of Usher
Fallen Angels Confessions of a Hit Man
Fallen Knight The Minion
Falling from the Sky! Flight 174 Freefall: Flight 174
Die Fälschung Circle of Deceit
False Faces Let 'em Have It
False Witness Zigzag
False Witness Circle of Deceit
Falstaff Chimes at Midnight
La Famiglia The Family
The Family Violent City
Family Affair Life with the Lyons
Family Enforcer Death Collector
Family of Cops II: Breach of Faith Breach of Faith: Family of Cops II
The Family Secret: Incident in a Small Town Incident in a Small Town
Family Secrets The Secret
A Family Torn Apart Sudden Fury
Family without a Dinner Table The Empty Table
The Famous Sword Bijomaru The Famous Sword
Fanatic Die! Die! My Darling
The Fantastic Disappearing Man The Return of Dracula
The Fantastic Invention Invention of Destruction
Le Fantôme de la Liberté The Phantom of Liberty
Faraon Pharaoh
Fargo Wild Seed
The Farm The Curse
Fashions Fashions of 1934
Fat Chance Peeper
Fat Man and Little Boy Shadow Makers
Fatal Attraction Head On
Fatal Chase Nowhere to Hide
The Fatal Passions Dr Mabuse, the Gambler
Fatal Sky Project: Alien
Fate of a Hunter Captive Hearts
Fate of a Man Destiny of a Man
Father Apa
Father and Son On the Streets of LA
Father Master Padre Padrone
Father's on a Business Trip When Father Was Away on Business
The FBI Murders In the Line of Duty: the FBI Murders
Fearless Frank Frank's Greatest Adventure
Federico Fellini's Intervista Intervista
Feiying Gaiwak Operation Condor: the Armour of God II
Les Félins The Love Cage
Fellini Satyricon Satyricon
Fellini's Casanova Casanova
Female and the Flesh The Light Across the Street
The Female Instinct The Snoop Sisters
The Feminine Touch The November Conspiracy
La Femme de Chambre du Titanic The Chambermaid on the Titanic
La Femme de l'Aviateur The Aviator's Wife
Une Femme Douce A Gentle Creature
La Femme du Boulanger The Baker's Wife
La Femme Flic The Lady Cop
La Femme Mariée The Married Woman
La Femme Nikita Nikita
La Femme aux Bottes Rouges The Lady with Red Boots
Femmina The Loves of Three Queens
Fertig The Confession
Fever over Anatahan The Saga of Anatahan
ffolkes North Sea Hijack
Fiddler's Green In Pursuit of Honor
Fielder's Field Girls Can Play
The Fiends Les Diaboliques
The Fifth Chair It's in the Bag
Fight for Freedom Long Road Home
Fighting Back Death Vengeance
The Fighting Pimpernel The Elusive Pimpernel
Figli di Annibale Children of Hannibal
La Fille de D'Artagnan D'Artagnan's Daughter
La Fille sur le Pont The Girl on the Bridge
Filofax Taking Care of Business
Fin Août, Début Septembre Late August, Early September
La Fin du Jour The End of the Day

The Final Crash Steelyard Blues
The Final Option Who Dares Wins
Final Warning Chernobyl: the Final Warning
Finally, Sunday Confidentially Yours
Finding My Way Home Finding the Way Home
Fine and Dandy The West Point Story
A Fine Romance A Touch of Adultery
Fine Snow The Makioka Sisters
Finger of Guilt The Intimate Stranger
The Fingerman Le Doulos
Il Fiore Delle Mille E Una Notte The Arabian Nights
Fire and Ice II Fire, Ice and Dynamite
Fire Birds Wings of the Apache
Fire in the Heart A Son's Promise
The Fire Monster Godzilla Raids Again
Fire Over Africa Malaga
Fire with Fire Captive Rage
The Fire Within Le Feu Follet
The First and the Last 21 Days
The First Emperor The Emperor and the Assassin
The First Hello The High Country
First Strike Jackie Chan's First Strike
Fist in His Pocket Fists in the Pocket
Fist-Right of Freedom Fox and His Friends
A Fistful of Chopsticks They Call me Bruce
Fists of Fury The Big Boss
Fists of Fury Fist of Fury
Fitzwilly Strikes Back Fitzwilly
Five Angles on Murder The Woman in Question
Five Days Home Welcome Home, Soldier Boys
Five Million Years to Earth Quatermass and the Pit
Five Minutes to Live Door-to-Door Maniac
Five Sinister Stories The Living Dead
Flame of My Love My Love Has Been Burning
The Flame of Torment Conflagration
Flame over India North West Frontier
Flames of the Sun Sholay
The Flaming Torch The Bob Mathias Story
Flanagan Walls of Glass
Flare-Up Flareup
La Fleur de Mon Secret The Flower of My Secret
Un Flic Dirty Money
Flic Story Police Story
Flight from Dhahran Escape: Human Cargo
Flight from Terror Satan Never Sleeps
The Flight of Angel 270 Final Descent
The Flight of the White Stallions Miracle of the White Stallions
Flights of Fancy Dream Flights
The Flim-Flam Man One Born Every Minute
Flip Out Get Crazy
Flipper's New Adventure Flipper and the Pirates
La Flor de Mi Secreto The Flower of My Secret
Flower and Fire Hana-Bi
The Flower in His Mouth The Masters
The Flowers of St Francis Francis, God's Jester
FM Citizens Band
Fog A Study in Terror
Folle à Tuer The Evil Trap
Follow That Camel Carry On Follow That Camel
Follow that Guy with the One Black Shoe The Tall Blond Man with One Black Shoe
Follow Your Dreams Independence Day
Fong Sai Yuk II The Legend of Fong Sai-Yuk II
Fontane Effi Briest Effi Briest
For Better or For Worse Honeymoon Academy
For I Have Sinned Shades of Gray
For Love of a Queen The Dictator
For Love or Money The Concierge
For Love or Money Love or Money
For My Daughter's Honor Indecent Seduction
For Richer, For Poorer Father, Son and the Mistress
For Roseanna Roseanna's Grave
For the Children: the Irvine Fertility Clinic Scandal For the Future: the Irvine Fertility Scandal
For the Love of My Daughter While Justice Sleeps

For the Love of My Daughter To Face Her Past
Forbidden Choices The Beans of Egypt, Maine
The Forbidden Dance Lambada! The Forbidden Dance
Forbidden Love Freaks
Forbidden Love Torn Apart
Forbidden Paradise The Hurricane
Forbidden Paradise Hurricane
The Forbidden Street Britannia Mews
Forbidden Subjects Kinjite: Forbidden Subjects
Forbidden Territory: Stanley's Search for Livingstone Forbidden Territory
The Forbin Project Colossus: The Forbin Project
Forever in Love Pride of the Marines
Forever Mozart For Ever Mozart
Forever Young, Forever Free E' Lollipop
Forever Yours Forget-Me-Not
Forget Me Not Sweet Dreams
The Forgiven Sinner Léon Morin, Priest
Forgotten Faces Till We Meet Again
Fork at Devil's Glen What We Did That Night
La Fortuna di Essere Donna Lucky to Be a Woman
Fortune in Diamonds The Adventurers
48 Hours Went the Day Well?
43, the Petty Story Smash-Up Alley
Forward March Doughboys
Four Against Fate Derby Day
Four Dark Hours The Green Cockatoo
Four Desperate Men The Siege of Pinchgut
Four Faces West They Passed This Way
Fourth Horseman Voyage of Terror
Fourth Story Deadly Identity
Fox Fox and His Friends
La Fracture du Myocarde Cross My Heart
Fragments Murder in My Mind
Francesco, Guillare di Dio Francis, God's Jester
Francis, God's Fool Francis, God's Jester
Frank Nitti: the Enforcer Nitti: the Enforcer
Frankenstein Mary Shelley's Frankenstein
Frankenstein and the Giant Lizard Frankenstein Meets the Devil Fish
Frankenstein Conquers the World Frankenstein Meets the Devil Fish
Frankenstein Meets the Giant Devil Fish Frankenstein Meets the Devil Fish
Frankenstein – the Real Story Frankenstein
Frankenstein vs Baragon Frankenstein Meets the Devil Fish
Frankenstein vs the Giant Devil Fish Frankenstein Meets the Devil Fish
Frankenstein vs the Subterranean Monster Frankenstein Meets the Devil Fish
Frankie the Fly The Last Days of Frankie the Fly
Frantic Lift to the Scaffold
Frasier the Lovable Lion Frasier, the Sensuous Lion
Fraternally Yours Sons of the Desert
Frau im Mond Woman in the Moon
Die Frau im Mond Woman in the Moon
Die Frau, nach der Man sich Sehnt Three Loves
Freaks! She Freak
Freddie the Frog Freddie as FRO7
Freefall: the Fate of Flight 174 Freefall: Flight 174
The Freelancers The Music Freelancers
Freeway II: Confessions of a Trickbaby Confessions of a Trickbaby
Freeze-Die-Come to Life Don't Move, Die and Rise Again
French Lesson The Frog Prince
The French They Are a Funny Race The Diary of Major Thompson
French Vampire in America Innocent Blood
A French Woman Une Femme Française
Fresa y Chocolate Strawberry and Chocolate
Fresh Bait The Bait
Freud — the Secret Passion Freud
Die Freudlose Gasse The Joyless Street
Frevel Mischief
Fried Green Tomatoes Fried Green Tomatoes at the Whistle Stop Cafe
A Friend to Die For Death of a Cheerleader
Friends to the End A Killer among Friends

Le Frisson des Vampires Shiver of the Vampires
Frissons Shivers
From beyond the Grave Judge & Jury
From the Heart Dil Se…
From the Mixed-Up Files of Mrs Basil E Frankweiler The Hideaways
Frou-Frou The Toy Wife
Full House O Henry's Full House
Fun Loving Quackser Fortune Has a Cousin in the Bronx
The Funeral Death Japanese Style
Funeral Rites Death Japanese Style
Funny Man The Funny Man
Funny Place for a Meeting A Strange Place to Meet
Fuori dal Mondo Not of This World
The Fury of the Dragon Return of the Dragon
Fuss over Feathers Conflict of Wings
Der Fussgänger The Pedestrian
Future Cop Trancers
FX - Murder by Illusion F/X

G

G I Joe The Story of G I Joe
La Gabbianella e il Gatto Lucky and Zorba
Gadael Lenin Leaving Lenin
Galactic Odyssey Mind Breakers
Galileo Galilei Galileo
The Gallery Murders The Bird with the Crystal Plumage
Game of Danger Bang! You're Dead
The Game of Love The Ripening Seed
Game Pass Jail Bait
Gamera the Invincible Gamera
Gammera, the Invincible Gamera
Gandahar Light Years
Ganesh Ordinary Magic
Gang Walk Proud
Gang War Odd Man Out
The Gangster's Moll Minbo – or the Gentle Art of Japanese Extortion
Garbage Blues Working Trash
Garm Hava Garam Hawa
Garwood: Prisoner of War Prisoner of War
Gaston Leroux's The Wax Mask Wax Mask
Gates of the Night Les Portes de la Nuit
Il Gatto a Nove Code Cat o'Nine Tails
Il Gattopardo The Leopard
The Gay Divorce The Gay Divorcee
The Gay Duellist Meet Me at Dawn
Gay Impostors Gold Diggers in Paris
The Gay Knowledge Le Gai Savoir
The Gay Mrs Trexel Susan and God
Gazon Maudit French Twist
Geliebte Milena Milena
Gemar Gavia Cup Final
Le Gendarme à New York The Gendarme in New York
Le Gendarme de Saint-Tropez The Gendarme de St Tropez
Gendarme et les Extra-Terrestres, Le The Spacemen of St Tropez
A Genius in the Family So Goes My Love
Le Genou de Claire Claire's Knee
Les Gens de la Rizière Rice People
Gente di Rispetto The Masters
The Gentle Touch The Feminine Touch
A Gentle Woman A Gentle Creature
Gentleman for a Day Union Depot
Die Gentlemen Bitten zur Kasse The Great British Train Robbery
Gentlemen Don't Eat Poets The Grotesque
Georges Dandin Dandin
Get Charlie Tully Ooh … You Are Awful
Get On with It Dentist on the Job
Get Your Handkerchiefs Ready Get Out Your Handkerchiefs
Getting Away with Murder End of the Game
Getting Even Utilities
Getting There Father, Son and the Mistress
Gharbar The Householder
Ghare Baire The Home and the World
Ghastly Tales The Living Dead
Ghidora, the Three-Headed Monster Ghidrah, the Three-Headed Monster
Ghidrah: the Greatest Battle on Earth Ghidrah, the Three-Headed Monster

The Ghost The Spectre
Ghost at Noon Le Mépris
The Ghost Brigade Killing Box
The Ghost Creeps Boys of the City
Ghost Mom Bury Me in Niagara
Ghost of Rashmon Hall Night Comes Too Soon
The Ghost Steps Out The Time of Their Lives
Ghosts Spooks Run Wild
Ghosts of Mississippi Ghosts from the Past
Ghosts on the Loose Ghosts in the Night
Ghoulies Go to College Ghoulies III: Ghoulies Go to College
The Giant Leeches Attack of the Giant Leeches
Il Giardino dei Finzi-Contini The Garden of the Finzi-Continis
Gideon of Scotland Yard Gideon's Day
Gift from a Red Planet The Alpha Incident
Gigantis, the Fire Monster Godzilla Raids Again
Gill Woman Voyage to the Planet of Prehistoric Women
Gill Women of Venus Voyage to the Planet of Prehistoric Women
Gina Death in the Garden
Gingerbread House Who Slew Auntie Roo?
Il Giovane Toscanini Young Toscanini
Giovani Mariti Young Husbands
A Girl, a Guy and a Gob The Navy Steps Out
The Girl – an Erotic Thriller The Girl
A Girl Called Katy Tippel Keetje Tippel
A Girl for Joe Force of Arms
The Girl Friends Le Amiche
The Girl from Hanoi Little Girl from Hanoi
The Girl Gets Moe Love To Kill
The Girl-Getters The System
Girl in Distress Jeannie
The Girl in Overalls Swing Shift Maisie
Girl in Pawn Little Miss Marker
The Girl in Room 17 Vice Squad
Girl in the Moon Woman in the Moon
The Girl in the Painting Portrait from Life
Girl in the Street London Melody
The Girl in the Trunk Man in the Trunk
Girl of the Year The Petty Girl
The Girl on the Moon Woman in the Moon
The Girl Swappers Two and Two Make Six
Girl Talk Some Girls
The Girl Who Came Between Them Victim of Innocence
The Girl with the Red Hair The Girl with Red Hair
Girlfriends Les Biches
The Girlfriends Le Amiche
The Girls Les Bonnes Femmes
Girls Gang Easy Wheels
The Girls He Left Behind The Gang's All Here
Girls of the White Orchid Death Ride to Osaka
Girls on the Moon Nude on the Moon
Girly Mumsy, Nanny, Sonny & Girly
Giulietta degli Spiriti Juliet of the Spirits
Give Me a Break Life with Mikey
The Giver The Donor
The Glass Cage Haunted
The Glass Cockpit Final Descent
The Glass Tomb The Glass Cage
Glenorky Magic in the Water
Glitter I Live My Life
Glory at Sea The Gift Horse
A Gnome Named Gnorm Upworld
Go Natalie Strictly Business
Go West Marx Brothers Go West
The Goalie's Anxiety at the Penalty Kick The Goalkeeper's Fear of the Penalty Kick
The God Game The Magus
The Godfather of Harlem Black Caesar
God's Army The Prophecy
God's Payroll Mortal Sins
Godzilla and Mothra: The Battle for Earth Godzilla vs Mothra
Godzilla, King of the Monsters Godzilla
Godzilla 1985 Godzilla
Godzilla on Monster Island Godzilla vs Gigan
Godzilla versus Cosmic Monster Godzilla vs the Cosmic Monster
Godzilla versus Mechagodzilla Godzilla vs the Cosmic Monster
Godzilla vs Monster Zero Invasion of the Astro-Monster
Godzilla versus the Bionic Monster Godzilla vs the Cosmic Monster
Godzilla versus the Sea Monster Ebirah, Horror of the Deep
Godzilla's Counterattack Godzilla Raids Again
Godzilla's Leverage Godzilla's Revenge
Going Places Les Valseuses
Gojira Godzilla
Gojira no Gyakushu Godzilla Raids Again
Gold Coast Elmore Leonard's Gold Coast
Gold Town Barbary Coast Gent
Goldcoast Elmore Leonard's Gold Coast
Golddigger A Robot Called Golddigger
Golden Arrow The Gay Adventure
The Golden Heist Inside Out
Golden Marie Casque d'Or
The Golden Mask South of Algiers
The Golden Virgin The Story of Esther Costello
Golem, l'Esprit de l'Exil Golem, the Spirit of Exile
Der Golem, Wie Er in die Welt Kam The Golem
Golf Punks National Lampoon's Golf Punks
Goliath Hero of Babylon
Golpes a Mi Puerta Knocks at My Door
Gone with the West Little Moon & Jud McGraw
Good Cop, Bad Cop Raw Justice
Good Cops, Bad Cops The Cops Are Robbers
Good Deed Upkaar
A Good Kill Better Off Dead
A Good Marriage Le Beau Mariage
Good Morning, Boys Where There's a Will
The Good-Time Outlaws Smokey and the Good Time Outlaws
The Good Year Happy New Year
Goodbye Bruce Lee: His Last Game of Death Game of Death
Goodbye Children Au Revoir les Enfants
Goodbye, Miss 4th of July Farewell Miss Freedom
A Gorgeous Bird Like Me Une Belle Fille Comme Moi
The Gospel According to Vic Heavenly Pursuits
Gotham The Dead Can't Lie
Götter der Pest Gods of the Plague
Götterdämmerung The Damned
Goya Goya in Bordeaux
Le Graal Lancelot du Lac
The Grace Moore Story So This Is Love
Graced Land The Woman Who Loved Elvis
Graceland The Woman Who Loved Elvis
Graceland Finding Graceland
The Graduate of Malibu High Young Warriors
Graham Greene's The Tenth Man The Tenth Man
The Grail Lancelot du Lac
Gramps Lethal Intent
El Gran Calavera The Great Madcap
Un Grand Amour de Beethoven Abel Gance's Beethoven
Le Grand Blond avec une Chaussure Noire The Tall Blond Man with One Black Shoe
The Grand Duel The Big Showdown
The Grand Maneuver Les Grandes Manoeuvres
Le Grand Meaulnes The Wanderer
Le Grand Pardon II Day of Atonement
Grand Tour: Disaster in Time Timescape
Il Grande Bluff The Con Artists
La Grande Guerra The Great War
Il Grande Silenzio The Big Silence
La Grande Vadrouille Dont Look Now We're Being Shot At
The Grandeur and Decadence of a Small Time Filmmaker Grandeur et Décadence d'un Petit Commerce de Cinéma
Les Granges Brulées Burnt Barns
Grave Indiscretions The Grotesque
Grave Robbers from Outer Space Plan 9 from Outer Space
The Great Adventure The Adventurers
The Great American Bugs Bunny-Road Runner Chase The Bugs Bunny/Road Runner Movie
The Great Bank Hoax The Great Georgia Bank Hoax
Great Charge of All Monsters Godzilla's Revenge
The Great City Syscraper Wilderness The Big City
The Great Feed La Grande Bouffe
The Great Gilbert and Sullivan The Story of Gilbert and Sullivan
The Great Manhunt The Doolins of Oklahoma
The Great Manhunt State Secret
Great Moments in Aviation Shades of Fear
The Great Mouse Detective Basil the Great Mouse Detective
The Great Schnozzle Palooka
The Great Silence The Big Silence
The Great Train Robbery The First Great Train Robbery
The Great Wall Is a Great Wall A Great Wall
The Greatest Love Europa '51
Green-Eyed Woman Take a Letter, Darling
Green Leaves White Death Seeds of Tragedy
Green Monkey Blue Monkey
Greetings From Nantucket One Crazy Summer
Grey Knight Killing Box
The Grey Zone Strong Hands
Grimm's Snow White Snow White: a Tale of Terror
The Grip of Fear Experiment in Terror
Grisbi Honour among Thieves
Gross Anatomy A Cut Above
The Grove The Naked Zoo
G's Trippin Trippin'
Gt Am Movie Book 5 Fingers
La Guerre des Boutons War of the Buttons
La Guerre des Polices The Police War
La Guerre du Feu Quest for Fire
La Guerre sans Nom The Undeclared War
The Guest The Caretaker
La Gueule Ouverte The Mouth Agape
A Guide for the Married Woman The Secret Life of an American Wife
Guilty until Proven Innocent Presumed Guilty
Gumby 1 Gumby: the Movie
Gun for Hire Man with a Gun
Gun Moll Jigsaw
The Gun Runners Santiago
Gunfire China 9, Liberty 37
Gunnar Hedes Saga Gunnar Hede's Saga
Gunpoint At Gunpoint
Guns A' Blazing Law and Order
Guns in the Afternoon Ride the High Country
Guns of Wrath Guns of Hate
Guns of Wyoming Cattle King
Guns, Sin and Bathtub Gin The Lady in Red
Gunslinger The Gunslinger
A Guy and a Gal A Lover and His Lass
Guy with a Grin No Time for Comedy
The Guys The Boys
Gypsy Blood Wild at Heart
Gypsy Girl Sky West and Crooked

H

Halcyon Days Innocent Lies
Hallelujah, I'm a Tramp! Hallelujah, I'm a Bum
Halloween: the Curse of Michael Myers Halloween 6: the Curse of Michael Myers
The Hallucinators The Naked Zoo
Hamam The Turkish Bath
Hamlet Liikemaailmassa Hamlet Goes Business
The Hand Off An Unexpected Family
A Handful of Clouds Doorway to Hell
A Handful of Grain Mother India
Handle with Care Citizens Band
Der Händler der vier Jahreszeiten The Merchant of Four Seasons
Hands Across the City Hands over the City
Hands of a Strangler The Hands of Orlac
The Hands of Orlac Mad Love
Hang Tough Hard Feelings
Hanging Death by Hanging
The Hangover The Female Jungle
The Hank Williams Story Your Cheatin' Heart
Hannibal's Children Children of Hannibal
Hannibal's Sons Children of Hannibal
Happiness Le Bonheur
Happy Go Lucky Hallelujah, I'm a Bum
Happy Gypsies I Even Met Happy Gypsies
Happy Times The Inspector General
Harbour of Desire The House on the Waterfront
Hard City Tales from a Hard City
Hard Cover Best Seller
Hard Driver The Last American Hero
Hard Times The Streetfighter
Hard Vice Vegas Vice
The Hardcore Life Hardcore
Harlequin: Treacherous Beauties Treacherous Beauties
Harmony Parade Pigskin Parade
Harp of Burma The Burmese Harp
Harper The Moving Target
Harry and the Hendersons Bigfoot and the Hendersons
Harry O Smile, Jenny, You're Dead
Harry's Machine Hollywood Harry
Hartbreak Hotel Home Is Where the Hart Is
Hartbreak Motel Home Is Where the Hart Is
Harum Scarum Harem Holiday
Hasards ou Coïncidences Chance or Coincidence
Hasta Morir 'Til Death
Hatchet A Cry in the Wild
The Haunted and the Hunted Dementia 13
Haunted Honeymoon Busman's Honeymoon
The Haunted Strangler Grip of the Strangler
The Haunting of Julia Full Circle
The Haunting of Maurella The Haunting of Morella
Having a Wild Weekend Catch Us If You Can
The Hawaiians Master of the Islands
The Hawk Ride Him, Cowboy
Hawken Hawken's Breed
Hawke's Revenge Hawk's Vengeance
Hawk's Revenge Hawk's Vengeance
Head over Heels Chilly Scenes of Winter
Head over Heels Head over Heels in Love
The Head That Wouldn't Die The Brain That Wouldn't Die
The Heart of New York Hallelujah, I'm a Bum
Heart of Paris Gribouille
Heart of the Matter Body of Influence 2
Heartfarm Middle Age Crazy
The Heart's Dark Side The Dark Side of the Heart
Heartstone Demonstone
Heaven Help Us Catholic Boys
Heaven's a Drag To Die For
The Heavens Call Battle beyond the Sun
A Heidi Adventure Courage Mountain
Heinrich von Kleist's The Prince of Homburg The Prince of Homburg
The Heir to Genghis Khan Storm over Asia
The Heist Hostile Force
Heksen Häxan
Helden Arms and the Man
Helen of Troy The Private Life of Helen of Troy
Hell Fight Magee and the Lady
Hell, Heaven and Hoboken I Was Monty's Double
Hell in Korea A Hill in Korea
Hell's Bells Murder by Phone
Hell's Crossroads Our Daily Bread
Hell's Gate Gate of Hell
Hell's Highway Violent Road
Heloise et Abelard Stealing Heaven
Her Enlisted Man Red Salute
Her Favourite Patient Bedside Manner
Her Final Fury: Betty Broderick the Last Chapter A Woman Deceived
Her Last Best Year The Last Best Year
Her Majesty, Mrs Brown Mrs Brown
Her Man Gilbey English without Tears
Her Own Rules Barbara Taylor Bradford's Her Own Rules
Her Secret Life Code Name: Dancer
Hercules, Samson, Maciste and Ursus Are Invincible Samson and the Mighty Challenge
Hercules: the Movie Hercules in New York
Here Lies Love The Second Woman
Here We Go Again Pride of the Bowery

Here's the Knife Dear, Now Use It Nightmare
L'Héritier The Inheritor
Hero Accidental Hero
The Hero Bloomfield
Hero: The Official Film of the 1986 Fifa World Cup Hero
Heroes Die Hard Mr Kingstreet's War
Heroes of the Regiment Bonnie Scotland
The Heroin Gang Sol Madrid
Les Héroïnes du Mal Heroines of Evil
Heroines of Pain Heroines of Evil
Heroism Eroica
Un Héros Très Discret A Self-Made Hero
Hey Cousin! Salut Cousin!
Hey Sailor Here Comes the Navy
Hidden Assassin The Shooter
Hidden Face Jail Bait
The Hidden Room Obsession
Hidden Vision Night Eyes
Hide and Shriek American Gothic
Hideout in the Alps Dusty Ermine
High and Dry The Maggie
The High Commissioner Nobody Runs Forever
High Encounters Cheech & Chong's Next Movie
High School Honeymoon Too Soon to Love
Higher Laws A Stranger in Town
Highlander: the Final Dimension Highlander III: the Sorcerer
Highlander: the Magician Highlander III: the Sorcerer
Highway to Hell Running Hot
Hijinks Tigers in Lipstick
Der Himmel über Berlin Wings of Desire
Hired for Killing Man with a Gun
His Affair This Is My Affair
His, Hers and Theirs Yours, Mine and Ours
His Other Woman Desk Set
Histoire d'O The Story of O
Une Histoire Immortelle The Immortal Story
La Historia Oficial The Official Version
Historias del Subdesarrollo Memories of Underdevelopment
Hit Parade of 1943 Change of Heart
Hit Radio Dead Air
The Hit Team Company of Killers
Hit Woman Double Edge
Hitler's Gold Inside Out
Hitler's Hangman Hitler's Madman
HMS Defiant Damn the Defiant!
Hoboken Young at Heart
Höhenfeuer Alpine Fire
Hold That Girl Hold That Co-Ed
The Hole Onibaba
Hole in the Sky The Ranger, the Cook and a Hole in the Sky
Holiday in Spain Scent of Mystery
Holiday Week Hindle Wakes
Hollywood Cowboy Hearts of the West
Holy Blood Santa Sangre
Hombres Armados Men with Guns
Home by Midnight Dream Date
Home Fires Burning The Turning
Home Song LaVyrle Spencer's Home Song
Home Video Extreme Close-Up
Homeboys Homeboyz
Homecoming Heimkehr
Un Homme Amoureux A Man in Love
L'Homme de Rio That Man from Rio
L'Homme est une Femme comme les Autres Man Is a Woman
Un Homme et une Femme A Man and a Woman
Un Homme et une Femme: Vingt Ans Déjà A Man and a Woman: 20 Years Later
L'Homme Qui Aimait les Femmes The Man Who Loved Women
Hommes, Femmes, Mode d'Emploi Men, Women: a User's Manual
The Honest Thief Barbary Coast Gent
Honor Guard Honor Guard
The Honourable Mr Wong The Hatchet Man
Hoodwinked Jake Spanner, Private Eye
Hoosiers Best Shot
A Hora da Estrela Hour of the Star
L'Horloger de Saint-Paul The Watchmaker of St Paul
The Horror Chamber of Dr Faustus Eyes without a Face
Horror Hotel The City of the Dead
Horror Hotel Eaten Alive
Horror House The Haunted House of Horror
Horror Maniacs The Greed of William Hart
The Horror of Death The Asphyx
Horror of Dracula Dracula
Horror on Snape Island Tower of Evil
The Horror Star Frightmare
HorrorScope 976-EVIL
A Horse Called Comanche Tonka
The Horse of Pride Le Cheval d'Orgeuil
Horseplayer Knife Edge
The Horse's Mouth The Oracle
Hostage Hostage: the Christine Maresch Story
Hostage: Dallas Getting Even
Hot City Original Gangstas
Hot Money Girl The Treasure of San Teresa
The Hot One Corvette Summer
Hot Shots 2 Hot Shots! Part Deux
Hot Spot I Wake Up Screaming
Hot Toddy White Hot: the Mysterious Murder of Thelma Todd
Hotspot I Wake Up Screaming
Houdini: Believe Houdini
Hounded Johnny Allegro
Hour of Glory The Small Back Room
Hour of Judgment The Hour of the Pig
The House at the End of the World Die, Monster, Die!
The House in Trubnoi Street The House on Trubnaya Square
House of Crazies Asylum
House of Doom The Black Cat
The House of Exorcism Lisa and the Devil
House of Fright The Two Faces of Dr Jekyll
The House of Lost Women Ladies' House of Pleasure
House of Menace Kind Lady
House of Pleasure Le Plaisir
House of 7 Joys The Wrecking Crew
House of the Damned Escape to Nowhere
House of Unclaimed Women The Smashing Bird I Used to Know
House of Usher The Fall of the House of Usher
The House on Chimney Square The House on Trubnaya Square
House on Rubens St Phantom of Death
The House on Sorority Row House of Evil
The House under the Trees The Deadly Trap
House without Windows Seven Alone
The Housekeeper A Judgment in Stone
How Much Loving Does a Normal Couple Need? Common Law Cabin
How Often... That Night Four Times That Night
How to Be a Player Def Jam's How to Be a Player
How to Be a Woman and Survive How to Be a Woman and Not Die in the Attempt
How to Rob a Bank A Nice Little Bank That Should Be Robbed
How to Steal a Diamond in Four Uneasy Lessons The Hot Rock
How to Stuff a Wild Bikini How to Fill a Wild Bikini
How Understanding Comes to Young Girls Mitsou
How You Like Me Now How U Like Me Now
Howard Beach: Making a Case for Murder Making the Case for Murder: the Howard Beach Story
Howard the Duck Howard, a New Breed of Hero
HP Lovecraft's Lurking Fear Lurking Fear
HP Lovecraft's The Resurrected The Resurrected
HR Pufnstuf Pufnstuf
Huckleberry Finn The Adventures of Huckleberry Finn
Huevos de oro Golden Balls
Huis-Clos No Exit
The Human Monster Dark Eyes of London
Humanity L'Humanité
Humanoids from the Deep Monster
The Hunchback Le Bossu
The Hunchback Hairball of UCLA Big Man on Campus
The Hunchback of Notre Dame The Hunchback
Hundred Hour Hunt Emergency Call
Hunt to Kill White Buffalo
Las Hurdes Land without Bread
Hurly Burly Hurlyburly
A Husband, a Wife, and a Lover A Strange Affair
Le Hussard sur le Toit The Horseman on the Roof
Hyperspace Gremloids
The Hypnotist London after Midnight

I

I Accuse J'Accuse
I Am a Fugitive I Am a Fugitive from a Chain Gang
I Became a Criminal They Made Me a Fugitive
I Call First Who's That Knocking at My Door
I Can Read The Sky I Could Read the Sky
I Dance Alone Stealing Beauty
I Dare to Die Dare to Love
I Don't Know What It Means to Say Phoenix, Arizona Smoke Signals
I Don't Want to Talk about It We Don't Want To Talk about It
I Hate Your Guts The Intruder
I Know My Son is Alive Web of Deceit
I Like Money Mr Topaze
I Love You All Je Vous Aime
I Married a Communist The Woman on Pier 13
I Married a Nazi The Man I Married
I, Mobster The Mobster
I-95 Ride
I See Ice! I See Ice
I Shall Return An American Guerrilla in the Philippines
I Stand Alone Seul Contre Tous
I Stand Condemned Moscow Nights
I Want Her Dead W
I Want to Go Back Home I Want to Go Home
I Was a Fireman Fires Were Started
I Was a Teenage Boy Willy/Milly
I Was a Teenage Gorilla Konga
I Was Faithless Cynara
Ich Will Doch Nur, Dass Ihr Mich Liebt I Only Want You to Love Me
Icy Breasts Someone Is Bleeding
Icy Flesh Someone Is Bleeding
Identificazione di una Donna Identification of a Woman
Identikit The Driver's Seat
The Idiot Returns Return of the Idiot
Idioterne The Idiots
Ieri, Oggi, Domani Yesterday, Today and Tomorrow
If Looks Could Kill Teen Agent
If Looks Could Kill Crowned and Dangerous
If You Feel Like Singing Summer Stock
If You Love Me I Live My Life
Il Était une Fois un Flic There Was Once a Cop
Il était une Fois un Pays Underground
Il Faut Vivre Dangereusement You've Got to Live Dangerously
L'île des Chèvres Passionate Summer
I'll Dig Your Grave Sartana, Angel of Death
I'll Get You Escape Route
Ill Town illtown
Illegal Entry Illegal Entry: Formula for Fear
Illicit Interlude Summer Interlude
Im Lauf der Zeit Kings of the Road
The Immaculate Conception of Baby Bump Sinful Life, A
The Immaculate Sword The Famous Sword
Immediate Disaster Stranger from Venus
Immoral Charge Serious Charge
Immortal Battalion The Way Ahead
The Impossible Anhonee
Impossible Object Story of a Love Story
In a Year with 13 Moons In a Year of 13 Moons
In Einem Jahr mit 13 Monden In a Year of 13 Moons
In Evil's Grasp Dream Breakers
In Nome del Papa Re In the Name of the Pope King
In Old Oklahoma War of the Wildcats
In Rosie's Room Rosie the Riveter
In Sickness and in Health Hearts on Fire
In the Best of Families: Marriage, Pride and Madness Bitter Vengeance
In the Body of the Whale In the Belly of the Whale
In the Cold Light of Day The Cold Light of Day
In the Company of a Killer A Taste for Killing
In the Devil's Garden Assault
In the Dog House In the Doghouse
In the Flesh Desperate Measures
In the Heat of Passion II: Unfaithful Behind Closed Doors
In the Line of Duty II – Blood Brothers A Cop for the Killing
In The Line of Duty: A Cop For the Killing A Cop for the Killing
In the Line of Duty: Assault in Waco In the Line of Duty: Ambush in Waco
In the Line of Duty: Blaze of Glory Blaze of Glory
In the Line of Duty: Howard Beach, Making a Case for Murder Making the Case for Murder: the Howard Beach Story
In the Line of Duty: Street War Street War
In the Line of Duty: Time to Kill In the Line of Duty: the Twilight Murders
In the Line of Duty: Trackdown In the Line of Duty: Hunt for Justice
In the Mood The Woo Woo Kid
In the Shadow of the Past Shadows of Our Forgotten Ancestors
In the Shadows With Harmful Intent
In the Woods Rashomon
In Weiter Ferne, So Nah! Faraway, So Close
The Inbetween Age The Golden Disc
Incense for the Damned Bloodsuckers
An Inch over the Horizon Captain Jack
Incident at Deception Ridge Terror at Deception Ridge
Incident at Raven's Gate Encounter at Raven's Gate
The Incredible Invasion Alien Terror
The Incredible Praying Mantis The Deadly Mantis
The Incredibly Strange Creatures The Incredibly Strange Creatures Who Stopped Living and Became Mixed-Up Zombies
The Incredibly Strange Creatures Who Stopped Living and Became Mixed-Up Zombies!!? The Incredibly Strange Creatures Who Stopped Living and Became Mixed-Up Zombies
Indagine su un Cittadino al di Sopra di ogni Sospetto Investigation of a Citizen above Suspicion
L'Inde Fantôme: Réflexions sur un Voyage Phantom India
Indefensible: the Truth about Edward Brannigan A Father's Betrayal
India Indien
Indian Summer Alive and Kicking
Indian Summer The Judge Steps Out
Indiana Jones and the Raiders of the Lost Ark Raiders of the Lost Ark
Indictment Indictment: the McMartin Trial
Das Indische Grabmal The Indian Tomb
Indiscretion Christmas in Connecticut
Indiscretion Terminal Station
The Infernal Idol Craze
Infested Ticks
The Inheritance Uncle Silas
The Inkwell No Ordinary Summer
Inn of the Frightened People Revenge
Innocence Is Bliss Miss Grant Takes Richmond
The Innocent and the Damned Girls' Town
Innocent Victim Tree of Hands
An Innocent War December
Les Innocents aux Mains Sales Dirty Hands
Innocents with Dirty Hands Dirty Hands
L'Inondation The Flood
The Ins and the Outs Les Uns et les Autres
Insatiable Lust The Female Vampire
L' Inspecteur Lavardin ou la Justice Inspecteur Lavardin
Insurgent Mexico Reed: Insurgent Mexico
Intensive Care A Child's Cry for Help
The Interview Intervista
Interview with a Serial Killer White Angel
Intervista Interview Intervista
Into the Fire Sharon's Secret
Intruder Moon 44

Lethal Terminator The Glove
Lethal White Female Dying to Love You
Let's Make Up Lilacs in the Spring
Let's Wash Our Brains RoGoPaG
Der Letze Mann The Last Laugh
Die Letzte Bruecke The Last Bridge
La Ley del Deseo The Law of Desire
Die Liebe der Jeanne Ney The Love of Jeanne Ney
Liebe Ist Kälter als der Tod Love Is Colder than Death
Liebeswalzer The Love Waltz
Das Lied der Gefangene Heimkehr
Les Liens de Sang Blood Relatives
The Lies Boys Tell Take Me Home Again
Le Lieu du crime The Scene of the Crime
A Life Ahead Madame Rosa
The Life and Death of Chico Mendes The Burning Season
The Life and Loves of Beethoven Abel Gance's Beethoven
Life and Nothing More And Life Goes On...
Life before Him Madame Rosa
Life Begins at College Life Begins in College
Life during Wartime The Alarmist
Life Estates Best Friends for Life
Life in the Food Chain Age Isn't Everything
Life Lines Reason for Living: The Jill Ireland Story
Life of Brian Monty Python's Life of Brian
The Life of Jesus La Vie de Jésus
Life on the High Wire Teamster Boss: the Jackie Presser Story
The Light Fantastic Love Is Better Than Ever
Light in the Darkness A Generation
The Light in the Jungle Out of Darkness
Lighthouse Stranded
Lights, Camera... Murder Joe Dancer: the Big Trade
Lights Out Bright Victory
Like a House on Fire The Fireman's Ball
Lili Marlene Lili Marleen
Linda Lust for Murder
Line of Fire Sam's Song
Line of Fire: The Morris Dees Story Blind Hate
The Line of the Horizon The Edge of the Horizon
A Linha do Horizonte The Edge of the Horizon
Lion of Sparta The 300 Spartans
Lionheart AWOL
Lionheart: the Children's Crusade Lionheart
Lisa The Inspector
Liste Noire Hit List
Little Fairground Swing Merry-Go-Round
The Little Girl of Hanoi Little Girl from Hanoi
The Little Kidnappers The Kidnappers
Little Malcolm Little Malcolm and His Struggle Against the Eunuchs
Little Nikita The Sleepers
Little Orphan Annie Annie: a Royal Adventure
Little Red Riding Hood Red Riding Hood
The Little Soldier Le Petit Soldat
The Littlest Horse Thieves Escape from the Dark
Live Bait The Bait
Live for Life Vivre pour Vivre
Living Ikiru
Living Russia or the Man with the Camera Man with a Movie Camera
Lo Que Le Pâso a Santiago What Happened to Santiago
Lock Up Walls
Loco de amor Two Much
Loin du Viêtnam Far from Vietnam
Lola Clubbed to Death
Lola Twinky
Lola Rennt Run Lola Run
Lola und Bilidikid Lola + Bilidikid
Lola's Mistake This Rebel Breed
Lollipop E' Lollipop
Lolly-Madonna XXX The Lolly-Madonna War
The London Scene Tonite Let's All Make Love in London
The Lonely Hearts Killers The Honeymoon Killers
The Lonely Wife Charulata
The Lonely Woman Journey to Italy
Lonesome Gun Stranger on the Run
Long Ago Tomorrow The Raging Moon
Long Corridor Shock Corridor
The Long Dark Night The Pack
The Long Kill Outlaw Justice
The Long Lost Friend Apprentice to Murder
The Long Ride for Justice Outlaw Justice
Long Road Home The Road Home
The Long Walk Home Miles from Nowhere
The Longest Yard The Mean Machine
Look Before You Laugh Make Mine a Million
Look Down and Die Steel
Look See Ecoute Voir...
Lookin' Good Corky
Looking for Eternity Portion d'Eternité
Looking for Larry Criminal Behaviour
Loon Denial
Lorca The Disappearance of Garcia Lorca
A Los Cuatro Vientos To the Four Winds
Loser Takes All Strike It Rich
Loss of Innocence The Greengage Summer
Lost and Found Someone Else's Child
Lost Angels The Road Home
The Lost Illusion The Fallen Idol
Lost Lady The Lady Vanishes
Lost Treasure of the Amazon Jivaro
The Loudest Whisper The Children's Hour
Louis L'Amour's Conagher Conagher
Louis Pasteur The Story of Louis Pasteur
Louisiana Black White Lie
Louisiana Gal Old Louisiana
Love after Death The Marriage Fool
Love and Death in Saigon A Better Tomorrow III
Love and Lies True Betrayal
Love and Money Love or Money
Love and Sacrifice America
Love and War In Love and War
A Love Bewitched El Amor Brujo
The Love Boat III The New Love Boat
Love Eternal Eternal Love
Love in Another Town Barbara Taylor Bradford's Love in Another Town
Love in Las Vegas Viva Las Vegas
Love in Paris Another Nine ½ Weeks
Love is a Weapon Hell's Island
Love Is Forever Comeback
Love Lessons All Things Fair
Love Madness Reefer Madness
The Love Maker Main Street
Love Match Une Partie de Plaisir
Love of a Clown Pagliacci
Love on the Ground L'Amour par Terre
Love Stinks Only You
Love, the Magician El Amor Brujo
Love Trap Let's Get Laid
Love You to Death Deadly Illusion
Lovely to Look At Thin Ice
A Lovely Way to Die A Lovely Way to Go
The Lover Milena
Lover Boy Knave of Hearts
Lover Divine The Unfinished Symphony
Lovers and Liars Travels with Anita
Lovers, Happy Lovers! Knave of Hearts
Lovers Like Us Call Him Savage
Lovers of Deceit A Murderous Affair
The Lovers of Montparnasse Montparnasses 19
Loves and Vendettas The Revengers' Comedies
Loves of a Blonde A Blonde in Love
The Loves of a Dictator The Dictator
The Loves of Ariane Ariane
The Loves of Count Iorga, Vampire Count Yorga, Vampire
The Loves of Count Yorga, Vampire Count Yorga, Vampire
The Loves of Irina The Female Vampire
The Loves of Isadora Isadora
The Loves of Jeanne Ney The Love of Jeanne Ney
The Loyal 47 Ronin of the Genroku Era The Loyal 47 Ronin
Luci del Varietà Variety Lights
Lucky Break Paperback Romance
The Lucky Mascot The Brass Monkey
Lucky Nick Cain I'll Get You for This
Lucky 13 Running Hot
Un Lugar en el Mundo A Place in the World
The Lullaby The Sin of Madelon Claudet
La Lumière D'en Face The Light across the Street
La Lune dans le Caniveau The Moon in the Gutter
Lunga Vita Alla Signora Long Live the Lady!
La Lunga Vita di Marianna Ucria Marianna Ucria
I Lunghi Capelli della Morte The Long Hair of Death
La Lupa Mannara Naked Werewolf Woman
The Lure of the Jungle Paw
Lust For Evil Plein Soleil
The Lust Seekers Good Morning... and Goodbye
Lusts of the Flesh The Love of Jeanne Ney
Lying in Wait Final Appeal

M

M:I 2 Mission: Impossible 2
Ma Nuit chez Maud My Night with Maud
Macabre Serenade House of Evil
MacArthur the Rebel General MacArthur
Maccheroni Macaroni
MacDonald of the Canadian Mounties Pony Soldier
Macon County Jail Jailbreak
Macu, la Mujer del Policia Macu, the Policeman's Wife
Mad Cage La Cage aux Folles
Mad Dog Morgan Mad Dog
Mad Dog Time Trigger Happy
Mad Magazine's Up the Academy Up the Academy
The Mad Monk Rasputin and the Empress
Mad Trapper of the Yukon Challenge to Be Free
Madadayo No, Not Yet
Madagascar Landing Aventure Malgache
Madame Sans-Gêne Madame
Madame Satan Madam Satan
Mädchen in Uniform Girls in Uniform
Das Mädchen Rosemarie A Girl Called Rosemarie
Mademoiselle Fifi The Silent Bell
Mademoiselle France Reunion in France
Madhouse Mansion Ghost Story
Madman Marz Madman
Madonna: Unauthorised Madonna: Innocence Lost
Mafia! Jane Austen's Mafia
Mafia Kid Spike of Bensonhurst
Maggie Invisible Child
Magic Bubble Unbecoming Age
The Magician The Face
The Magnetician's Fifth Winter The Magnetist's Fifth Winter
Mahanagar The Big City
Maid for Murder She'll Have to Go
The Maids of Wilko The Young Ladies of Wilko
Mailbag Robbery The Flying Scot
La Maison des Filles Perdues Ladies' House of Pleasure
La Maison sous les Arbres The Deadly Trap
Le Maître de musique The Music Teacher
Make Me Over But I'm a Cheerleader
Make Mine a Double The Night We Dropped a Clanger
Makica Sisters The Makioka Sisters
Makin' Up! Making Up
Making It Les Valseuses
The Making of "...And God Spoke" ...And God Spoke
La Mala Ordina The Italian Connection
Maladie Contagieuse The Raven
Malaga Moment of Danger
The Maltese Falcon Dangerous Female
Mama Turns a Hundred Mamá Cumple 100 Años
Mamusha Rescuers: Stories of Courage: Two Women
Man against the Mob Murder in the City of Angels
Man against the Mob II Man against the Mob: the Chinatown Murders
Man Bait The Last Page
A Man Called Sullivan The Great John L
The Man From C.O.T.T.O.N. Gone Are the Days
Man from Marrakesh That Man George
Man Hunt Male Hunt
Man in a Cocked Hat Carlton-Browne of the FO
Man in Cement Man against the Mob: the Chinatown Murders
Man in Hiding Man-Trap
A Man in Mommy's Bed With Six You Get Eggroll
A Man Is Ten Feet Tall Edge of the City
Man Looking Southeast Hombre Mirando al Sudeste
Man o' War Men o' War
Man of Affairs His Lordship
Man of Bronze Jim Thorpe – All-American
Man of Evil Fanny by Gaslight
Man of the Hour Colonel Effingham's Raid
Man of the Nile The Barbarian
The Man Who Came Back Swamp Water
The Man Who Lived Again The Man Who Changed His Mind
The Man Who Lost His Way Crossroads
The Man Who Wanted to Live Forever The Only Way Out Is Dead
Man with a Camera Man with a Movie Camera
Man with a Million The Million Pound Note
The Man with 100 Faces Crackerjack
The Man with Rain in His Shoes If Only
The Man with the Flower in his Mouth The Masters
The Man with the Green Carnation The Trials of Oscar Wilde
Man with the Movie Camera Man with a Movie Camera
The Man with Thirty Sons The Magnificent Yankee
The Man with Three Arms The Dark Backward
Man without a Gun Man with the Gun
Mandela: Son of Africa, Father of a Nation Mandela
Maneater Shark!
The Manhattan Project The Deadly Game
Manhunt From Hell to Texas
Manhunt The Italian Connection
Le Mani Forti Strong Hands
Le Mani Sulla Città Hands over the City
Mania The Flesh and the Fiends
Maniacs on Wheels Once a Jolly Swagman
Mannequin Two: On the Move Mannequin on the Move
Männer Men...
Manon of the Springs Manon des Sources
Mao to Mozart: Isaac Stern in China From Mao to Mozart: Isaac Stern in China
Marabunta Legion of Fire: Killer Ants!
March of the Wooden Soldiers Babes in Toyland
Marching Along Stars and Stripes Forever
Marciano Rocky Marciano
Le Mari de la Coiffeuse The Hairdresser's Husband
Maria Candelaria Portrait of Maria
Marianne Marianne de ma Jeunesse
Marianne and Julianne The German Sisters
Marie Marie: a True Story
Marie Antoinette Queen of France Marie Antoinette
Marie Baie des Anges Angel Sharks
Marie Taquet Rescuers: Stories of Courage: Two Couples
Marie Walewska Conquest
La Mariée Est Trop Belle The Bride Is Much Too Beautiful
La Mariée Était en Noir The Bride Wore Black
Marina's Story Fatal Deception: Mrs Lee Harvey Oswald
Marius and Jeanette Marius et Jeannette
Mark of the Beast Fear No Evil
Mark of the Claw Dick Tracy's Dilemma
The Marla Hanson Story Face Value
Marquis de Sade Marquis
Married but Single This Thing Called Love
Married in Haste Consolation Marriage
The Marrying Man Too Hot to Handle
The Marsupials: the Howling III The Howling III
Martha und Ich Martha and I
Martial Law III Mission of Justice
Mary Higgins Clark's Remember Me Remember Me
Mary Higgins Clark's While My Pretty One Sleeps While My Pretty One Sleeps
La Maschera del Demonio The Mask of Satan
Maschera Di Cera Wax Mask
Masculin Féminin Masculine Feminine

The Mask of the Demon The Mask of Satan
Masks Persona
The Massacre at the Rosebud The Great Sioux Massacre
Massacre Hill Eureka Stockade
Master of Dragonard Hill Dragonard
Master of Lassie Hills of Home
Master Swordsman Samurai
Masters of the Universe II: The Cyborg Cyborg
The Match The Gamble
Mathilda Matilda
Matrimonio all'italiana Marriage – Italian Style
A Matter of Conviction The Young Savages
A Matter of Honour The Reckoning
A Matter of Innocence Pretty Polly
Matter of Privacy Absolute Strangers
A Matter of Resistance La Vie de Château
A Matter of Style Andaz
Maurice Sendak's The Nutcracker Nutcracker
Mausoleum One Dark Night
Mauvais Sang The Night Is Young
Les Mauvaises Rencontres The Bad Liaisons
Maximum Force 2 Midnight Witness
Maxwell Smart and the Nude Bomb The Nude Bomb
Maybe Baby Baby Makes Three
Maybe Baby For Keeps
Maybe, Maybe Not The Most Desired Man
Mazel Tov ou le Mariage Marry Me! Marry Me!
The McGherins from Brooklyn Two Mugs from Brooklyn
McGuire, Go Home! The High Bright Sun
McKlusky White Lightning
Me L'Enfance Nue
Me and My Gal For Me and My Gal
The Mechanical Piano An Unfinished Piece for Mechanical Piano
Meet Whiplash Willie The Fortune Cookie
Meia Noite Midnight
Mein Liebster Feind – Klaus Kinski My Best Fiend
Mélodie en Sous-Sol Any Number Can Win
Melody Inn Riding High
Melody of Life Symphony of Six Million
Melody of Youth They Shall Have Music
Mémoire Traquée Lapse of Memory
Memorias del Subdesarrollo Memories of Underdevelopment
Memories of a Marriage Waltzing Regitze
Memory Lapse of Memory
The Memory Expert The Man on the Flying Trapeze
Memory of Evil Forgotten Sins
Men Some Girls
Men in White National Lampoon's Men in White
Men of Destiny Men of Texas
Men of Steel Steel
Men on Her Mind The Girl from 10th Avenue
Menage Tenue de Soirée
Menage à Trois Better Late Than Never
Menschen am Sonntag People on Sunday
Mensonge The Lie
The Mercenaries Cuba Crossing
The Mercenaries Dark of the Sun
The Mercenary A Professional Gun
Meredith Willson's The Music Man The Music Man
Merrily We Go to... Merrily We Go to Hell
A Merry War Keep the Aspidistra Flying
The Messenger: the Story of Joan of Arc Joan of Arc
The Metal Years The Decline of Western Civilization Part II: the Metal Years
Metalbeast Metal Beast
Meteor Monster Teenage Monster
The Metropolis The Big City
Michael Jackson's Moonwalker Moonwalker
Michael's Fright The Peanut Butter Solution
Midnight at the Wax Museum Midnight at Madame Tussaud's
Midnight Auto Supply Love and the Midnight Auto Supply
Midnight Cop Nick Knight
Midnight Lovers Immortal Bachelor
Midnight Pleasures Immortal Bachelor

A Midsummer Night's Dream William Shakespeare's A Midsummer Night's Dream
Midway Battle of Midway
A Midwinter's Tale In the Bleak Midwinter
The Mighty Warrior The Trojan War
Mignon è Partita Mignon Has Left
Mil nove cientos diecinueve Crónica del Alba 1919
Military Policeman Off Limits
The Miller's Beautiful Wife The Miller's Wife
Millie the Non-Stop Variety Girl Friday the Thirteenth
Million Dollar Manhunt Assignment Redhead
Million Dollar Mystery Money Mania
A Million to One A Million to Juan
The Millstone A Touch of Love
Mimi, the Metalworker The Seduction of Mimi
Minbo No Onna Minbo – or the Gentle Art of Japanese Extortion
Mind Games Agency
Mind Games Body Bags
Mind Games Brainwaves
Mind Ripper Wes Craven's Mind Ripper
The Mind Snatchers The Happiness Cage
Minuit Midnight
Minya, Son of Godzilla Godzilla's Revenge
Il Mio Nome è Nessuno My Name is Nobody
A Miracle Can Happen On Our Merry Way
Miracle of Life Our Daily Bread
The Miracle of Our Lady of Fatima The Miracle of Fatima
Miracolo a Milano Miracle in Milan
The Misadventures of Mr Wilt Wilt
Les Misérables du vingtième siècle Les Misérables
Miss Europe Prix de Beauté
Miss Shumway Jette un Sort Rough Magic
Missing Ten Days Ten Days in Paris
Mississippi Summer Murder in Mississippi
Mr Arkadin Confidential Report
Mr Bug Goes to Town Hoppity Goes to Town
Mr Death Mr Death: the Rise and Fall of Fred A Leuchter Jr
Mr Fox of Venice The Honey Pot
Mr Joseph Young of Africa Mighty Joe Young
Mr Lord Says No The Happy Family
Mr Mum Mr Mom
Mr Teas and His Playthings Immoral Mr Teas
Mr Toad's Wild Ride The Wind in the Willows
Mister V Pimpernel Smith
I Misteri della Giungla Nera Kidnapped to Mystery Island
Il Mistero di Oberwald The Oberwald Mystery
Mittelmann's Hardware Finding the Way Home
Mixed Blessings Danielle Steel's Mixed Blessings
The Model Shop Model Shop
Modern Day Houdini The Escapist
The Modern Miracle The Story of Alexander Graham Bell
Modigliani of Montparnasse Montparnasses 19
Mohammed, Messenger of God The Message
The Mole El Topo
The Molester Never Take Sweets from a Stranger
Molly Louvain The Strange Love of Molly Louvain
Moment of Truth: A Mother's Deception Moment of Truth: Cult Rescue
Moment of Truth: A Secret between Friends A Secret between Friends
Moment of Truth: Abduction of Innocence Abduction of Innocence
Moment of Truth: Broken Pledges Broken Pledges
Moment of Truth: Caught in the Crossfire Caught in the Crossfire
Moment of Truth: A Child Too Many A Child Too Many
Moment of Truth: Cradle of Conspiracy Cradle of Conspiracy

Moment of Truth: Cult Rescue Cult Rescue
Moment of Truth: Deceived by Trust Deceived by Trust
Moment of Truth: Eye of the Stalker Eye of the Stalker
Moment of Truth: Fighting Back Moment of Truth: to Walk Again
Moment of Truth: Girls Fight Back Moment of Truth: Stand against Fear
Moment of Truth: Hazing Back Broken Pledges
Moment of Truth: Into the Arms of Danger Into the Arms of Danger
Moment of Truth: Justice for Annie Search for Justice
Moment of Truth Movie: A Champion's Fight A Champion's Fight
Moment of Truth: Murder or Memory? Murder or Memory?
Moment of Truth: Race against Fear Race against Fear
Moment of Truth: Sin of Silence Race against Fear
Moment of Truth: Someone to Love Me Someone to Love Me
Moment of Truth: Stalking Back Stalking Back
Moment of Truth: Stand against Fear Stand against Fear
Moment of Truth: the Other Mother The Other Mother
Moment of Truth: to Sell a Child Cradle of Conspiracy
Moment of Truth: to Walk Again To Walk Again
Moment of Truth: Why My Daughter? Why My Daughter?
Momman, Little Jungle Boy Little Jungle Boy
Momma's Boy Night Warning
Mom's 100 Years Old Mamá Cumple 100 Años
Mon Oncle Benjamin Uncle Benjamin
Monday, Tuesday, Wednesday A Killing Affair
Un Monde sans Pitié World without Pity
Mondo Cane Numero 1 Mondo Cane
Money for Jam It Ain't Hay
Monika Summer with Monika
Monsieur Klein Mr Klein
The Monster I Don't Want to Be Born
The Monster Horror Show Freaks
The Monster of Fate The Golem
Monster of Monsters Ghidrah, the Three-Headed Monster
Monster of Terror Die, Monster, Die!
Monster Zero Invasion of the Astro-Monster
Monsters from the Moon Robot Monster
Montana Mike Heaven Only Knows
Montecarlo The Monte Carlo Story
Monty Python meets Beyond the Fringe Pleasure at Her Majesty's
Monty Python's Holy Grail Monty Python and the Holy Grail
Monument Ave Noose
Mood Indigo Mind of a Killer
Moon Over Miami Off and Running
Moon Valley A Weekend in the Country
The Moondolls Nude on the Moon
Moonlight Becomes You Mary Higgins Clark's Moonlight Becomes You
Moonshot Countdown
Die Mörder Sind Unter Uns The Murderers Are Amongst Us
Morder Unter Uns M
Morgan! Morgan – a Suitable Case for Treatment
Morgan Stewart's Coming Home Home Front
Morituri The Saboteur, Code Name Morituri
The Morning After Her Last Chance
Morris West's The Naked Country The Naked Country
La Mort de Mario Ricci The Death of Mario Ricci
Mort d'un Pourri To Kill a Rat
La Mort en Ce Jardin Death in the Garden
La Mort en Direct Deathwatch
La Mortadella Lady Liberty
Mortal Kombat 2 Mortal Kombat: Annihilation
Moscow Does Not Believe in Tears Moscow Distrusts Tears

Moscow Today Man with a Movie Camera
Moses the Lawgiver Moses
The Most Dangerous Game The Hounds of Zaroff
The Most Dangerous Man in the World The Chairman
The Mother and the Whore La Maman et la Putain
Mother Goose a Go-Go The Unkissed Bride
Mother Joan of the Angels The Devil and the Nun
Mother Knows Best Mother Is a Freshman
Mother Küsters' Trip to Heaven Mother Küsters Goes to Heaven
Mother's Day All She Ever Wanted
A Mother's Right: The Elizabeth Morgan Story Shattered Silence
Motor Mods and Rockers Motor Psycho
Mouse Hunt Mousehunt
Movietone Follies of 1929 Fox Movietone Follies of 1929
Moving In Firstborn
Mowgli and Baloo: Jungle Book II The Second Jungle Book
Mrs Loring's Secret The Imperfect Lady
MST3K: The Movie Mystery Science Theater 3000: The Movie
Mud Honey Mudhoney
Der Müde Tod Destiny
La Muerte de un Burocrata Death of a Bureaucrat
Muertos de Risa Dying of Laughter
Mugsy's Girls Delta Pi
Una Mujer sin Amor A Woman without Love
Mujeres al Borde de un Ataque de Nervios Women on the Verge of a Nervous Breakdown
Münchhausen Baron Münchhausen
Murder at Devil's Glen What We Did That Night
Murder at Malibu Beach The Trap
Murder at the Burlesque Murder at the Windmill
Murder at the PTA Luncheon Menu for Murder
Murder by Confession Absolution
Murder Can Be Deadly The Painted Smile
Murder in the Family Child in the Night
Murder in the Neighbourhood Someone She Knows
Murder in the Old Red Barn Maria Marten, or the Murder in the Red Barn
The Murder in Thornton Square Gaslight
Murder in Three Acts Agatha Christie's Murder in Three Acts
Murder, My Sweet Farewell My Lovely
Murder on Danger Island Mr Moto in Danger Island
Murder on Monday Home at Seven
Murder on the Bayou A Gathering of Old Men
Murder on the Set Death on the Set
Murder 1, Dancer 0... Joe Dancer: the Big Trade
Murder Takes All Mickey Spillane's Mike Hammer: Murder Takes All
Murder Will Out Voice of Merrill
Murder with Mirrors Agatha Christie's Murder with Mirrors
Murderers Among Us The Murderers Are Amongst Us
Muriel, or the Time of Return Muriel
Muriel, Ou le Temps d'un Retour Muriel
Un Muro de Silencio Wall of Silence
Murph the Surf Live a Little, Steal a Lot
The Muse Concert: No Nukes No Nukes
Music in Darkness Night Is My Future
The Mute Bezubaan
Mutronics The Guyver
Mutter Küsters Fahrt Zum Himmel Mother Küsters Goes to Heaven
Mutters Courage My Mother's Courage
My Brother Frankie My Son Johnny
My Crazy Life Mi Vida Loca
My Darling Shiksa Over the Brooklyn Bridge
My Enemy the Sea Alone on the Pacific
My Father, My Master Padre Padrone
My Father's Glory La Gloire de Mon Père
My Father's Shadow: The Sam Sheppard Story Death in the Shadows
My Father's Son Secret Sins of the Father
My Favorite Season Ma Saison Préferée

My Favourite Brunette My Favorite Brunette
My Favourite Martian My Favorite Martian
My Favourite Spy My Favorite Spy
My Favourite Wife My Favorite Wife
My Favourite Year My Favorite Year
My Forgotten Man Flynn
My Friend Frank Frankenstein: the College Years
My Good Fiend My Best Fiend
My Heart Goes Crazy London Town
My Hero A Southern Yankee
My Life Is Yours The People vs Dr Kildare
My Life to Live It's My Life
My Love Burns My Love Has Been Burning
My Love Letters Love Letters
My Man Mon Homme
My Name is Anna Call Me Anna
My Name Is Ivan Ivan's Childhood
My Name Is John Who Fears the Devil?
My New Partner Le Cop
My New Partner II Le Cop II
My Night at Maud's My Night with Maud
My Old Man's Place Glory Boy
My Sex Life … or How I got into an Argument Ma Vie Sexuelle
My Shadow Face of a Stranger
My Sister's Keeper Bad to the Bone
My Son Frankie My Son Johnny
My Stepson, My Lover Love, Murder & Deceit
My Summer Vacation One Crazy Summer
My Two Husbands Too Many Husbands
Les Mystères de Paris The Mysteries of Paris
Mysteries of the Organism WR - Mysteries of the Organism
Mysterious Invader The Astounding She-Monster
Mystery at the Burlesque Murder at the Windmill
The Mystery of Kaspar Hauser The Enigma of Kaspar Hauser
The Mystery of Thug Island Kidnapped to Mystery Island

La Nación Clandestina The Secret Nation
The Nada Gang Nada
Naked Childhood L'Enfance Nue
Naked Island The Island
The Naked Lovers The Naked Zoo
The Naked Night Sawdust and Tinsel
Naked Revenge Cry for Me Billy
Naked Robot 4½ Invader
Naked under Leather The Girl on a Motorcycle
Nam Platoon Leader
The Nanny The Guardian
Napoleone Bonaparte Napoléon
Napoléon vu par Abel Gance Napoléon
Nash's Vision Steel Justice
Nate and Hayes Savage Islands
Nathaniel Hawthorne's "Twice Told Tales" Twice Told Tales
National Lampoon Goes to the Movies National Lampoon's Movie Madness
National Lampoon's Scuba School National Lampoon's Last Resort
National Lampoon's Vegas Vacation Vegas Vacation
Nature Girls on the Moon Nude on the Moon
The Nature of the Beast Hatchet Man
Nature's Mistakes Freaks
Naughty Arlette The Romantic Age
Navigator The Navigator – a Medieval Odyssey
Navy Heroes The Blue Peter
The Nazis: Of Pure Blood Of Pure Blood
Ne Me Demandez Pas Pourquoi Le Testament d'Orphée
Near Misses Near Mrs
Nefertiti, Regina del Nilo Nefertite, Queen of the Nile
Neil Simon's Broadway Bound Broadway Bound
Neil Simon's Lost in Yonkers Lost in Yonkers
Neil Simon's The Odd Couple II The Odd Couple II

Neil Simon's The Slugger's Wife The Slugger's Wife
Neil Simon's The Sunshine Boys The Sunshine Boys
Nelly et Monsieur Arnaud Nelly & Monsieur Arnaud
The Nelson Affair Bequest to the Nation
The Nelson Touch Corvette K-225
Nemesis III: Prey Harder Nemesis 3 – Time Lapse
The Neptune Disaster The Neptune Factor
The Nesting Serpent's Lair
Nettoyage à Sec Dry Cleaning
Neuf Mois Nine Months
Never Cry Devil Night Visitor
Never Ever Circle of Passion
Never Give Up: the Search for Sarah Race against Time: the Search for Sarah
Never Take Candy from a Stranger Never Take Sweets from a Stranger
Never to Love A Bill of Divorcement
Neverever Circle of Passion
The New Adventures of Dr Fu Manchu The Return of Dr Fu Manchu
The New Centurions Precinct 45: Los Angeles Police
The New Enchantment L'Inhumaine
The New Eve La Nouvelle Eve
New Frontier Frontier Horizon
The New Monsters Viva Italia!
New Wave Nouvelle Vague
New York Hallelujah, I'm a Bum
The Newcomers The Wild Country
Newlyweds Young Husbands
Newsboys The News Boys
Newsies The News Boys
Next Time We Live Next Time We Love
Nice Dreams Cheech & Chong's Nice Dreams
A Nice Guy Mr Nice Guy
A Nice, Pleasant, Deadly Weekend The Masterpiece of Murder
Nicht Versöhnt oder "Es Hilft Nur Gewalt, Wo Gewalt Herrscht " Not Reconciled, or Only Violence Helps Where Violence Rules
Nick Carter In Panama Phantom Raiders
Nicky and Gino Dominick and Eugene
The Night La Notte
Night Ambush Ill Met by Moonlight
Night and Fog Nuit et Brouillard
Night Breed Nightbreed
The Night Comers The Nightcomers
The Night Crawlers The Navy vs the Night Monsters
Night Demons Night of the Demons
The Night Fighters A Terrible Beauty
The Night Flier Stephen King's The Night Flier
Night Flight from Moscow The Serpent
Night Hunt Blood Money
A Night in Cairo The Barbarian
Night in the Crypt One Dark Night
The Night Is Ending Paris after Dark
Night Legs Fright
The Night Man The Nightman
Night of Scandal Conspiracy
A Night of Terror Love from a Stranger
Night of the Cyclone Perfume of the Cyclone
Night of the Dark Full Moon Silent Night, Bloody Night
Night of the Demons: Angela's Revenge Night of the Demons 2
Night of the Flesh Eaters Night of the Living Dead
Night of the Laughing Dead The House in Nightmare Park
The Night of the Shooting Stars The Night of San Lorenzo
Night of the Tiger Ride beyond Vengeance
Night Shadows Mutant
The Night the Sun Came Out Watermelon Man
The Night They Invented Striptease The Night They Raided Minsky's
Night Train Night Train to Munich
The Night Watch Le Trou
Night Watch Nightwatch
Night Wind Le Vent de la Nuit
Nightfire Night Fire
Nightfliers Nightflyers
Nightmare Don't Touch My Daughter
Nightmare at Bittercreek Nightmare at Bitter Creek

The Nightmare before Christmas Tim Burton's The Nightmare before Christmas
The Nightmare Cafe Night Visions
Nightmare in Columbia County Victim of Beauty
Nightmare Maker Night Warning
Nightmare on Elm Street 7 Wes Craven's New Nightmare
Nights in a Harem Son of Sinbad
The Nightstalker The Night Stalker
Nina A Matter of Time
Nine Days a Queen Tudor Rose
Nine Hours to Live Nine Hours to Rama
1947 Earth
Ninja I Enter the Ninja
Ninja II Revenge of the Ninja
No Cause for Alarm Project: Alien
No Greater Love Danielle Steel's No Greater Love
No Highway in the Sky No Highway
No Knife The Frisco Kid
No Looking Back Out of the Blue
No Man Walks Alone Black Like Me
No More Mr Nice Guy Mr Nice Guy
No Place Like Homicide What a Carve Up!
No Place to Hide Rebel
No Regrets for My Youth No Regrets for Our Youth
No Sleep Till Dawn Bombers B-52
No Time for Breakfast Doctor Françoise Gailland
No Tree in the Street No Trees in the Street
No Trespassing The Red House
Noah's Ark: The Story of the Deluge Noah's Ark
Nobody Loves a Drunken Indian Flap
Nobody Loves Flapping Eagle Flap
Nobody Makes Me Cry Between Friends
Les Noces de Papier A Paper Wedding
Noi vivi We the Living
Noirs et Blancs en Couleurs Black and White in Color
None but the Brave For the Love of Mike
De Noorderlingen The Northerners
Norman Conquest Park Plaza 605
Norman Mailer's Tough Guys Don't Dance Tough Guys Don't Dance
The North El Norte
The North Avenue Irregulars Hill's Angels
North West Mounted Police Northwest Mounted Police
Un Nos ola Leuad One Full Moon
Nosferatu, a Symphony of Terror Nosferatu, a Symphony of Horrors
Nosferatu a Venezia Vampire of Venice
Nosferatu, eine Symphonie des Grauens Nosferatu, a Symphony of Horrors
Nosferatu, Phantom der Nacht Nosferatu, the Vampire
Nosferatu, the Vampire Nosferatu, a Symphony of Horrors
Nosferatu, the Vampyre Nosferatu, the Vampire
Not in My Family Shattering the Silence
Not on Your Life Island of Love
Not Quite Paradise Not Quite Jerusalem
Not So Quiet Days Quiet Days in Clichy
Not Yet No, Not Yet
A Notebook on Clothes and Cities Notebook on Cities and Clothes
The Noted Sword The Famous Sword
Nothing's Impossible Side by Side
Notorious Gentleman The Rake's Progress
Notre Dame de Paris The Hunchback of Notre Dame
La Notte di San Lorenzo The Night of San Lorenzo
Le Notti Bianche White Nights
Le Notti di Cabiria Nights of Cabiria
N'Oublie Pas Que Tu Vas Mourir Don't Forget You're Going to Die
Des Nouvelles du Bon Dieu News from the Good Lord
Novecento 1900
A Novel Affair The Passionate Stranger
Nowhere to Hide Dangerous Intentions
Nuclear Run The Chain Reaction
Nuclear Terror Golden Rendezvous
La Nuit Américaine Day for Night
Nuit et Jour Night and Day
Nuits Blanches White Nights
Les Nuits de la pleine lune Full Moon in Paris
Nuke Nukie

Nuke 'em High Class of Nuke 'Em High
Numéro Deux Number Two
The Nun La Religieuse
I Nuovi Mostri Viva Italia!
Nuovo Cinema Paradiso Cinema Paradiso
The Nurse The Guardian
Nutcracker: The Motion Picture Nutcracker

OHMS You're In the Army Now
O Que E Isso, Companheiro? Four Days in September
The Oath Keeping the Promise
Obsessed The Late Edwina Black
Obsession Circle of Two
Obsession Obsessed
Oci Ciornie Dark Eyes
The O'Connors Dream Breakers
The Odd Couple: One More Time The Odd Couple: Together Again
Odd Obsession The Key
Of Unknown Origins Black Scorpion
Off Balance Phantom of Death
Off Limits Military Policeman
Off Limits Saigon
The Official Story The Official Version
Offret The Sacrifice
Oh, Charlie Hold That Ghost
Oh Doctor Hit the Ice
Oh! For a Man Will Success Spoil Rock Hunter?
Oh, Woe Is Me Hélas pour Moi
Oil Town Lucy Gallant
The O'Kelley Brothers A Son's Promise
Old and the New The General Line
The Old Capital Twin Sisters of Kyoto
The Old Curiosity Shop Mister Quilp
The Old Dick Jake Spanner, Private Eye
Old Drac Vampira
Old Dracula Vampira
Old Man William Faulkner's Old Man
Old Mother Riley Catches a Quisling Old Mother Riley in Paris
Old New Borrowed Blue With or Without You
Oldest Living Bridesmaid The World's Oldest Living Bridesmaid
O'Leary Night Happy Ever After
Olly, Olly, Oxen Free The Great Balloon Adventure
Olympia Olympiad
Olympiad Berlin 1936 Olympiad
Olympic Visions Visions of Eight
Olympische Spiele 1936 Olympiad
Ombre Bianche The Savage Innocents
L'Ombre du Doute A Shadow of Doubt
Omen 3 The Final Conflict
On Guard Le Bossu
On My Vespa Dear Diary
On the Carpet Little Giant
On the Road Again Honeysuckle Rose
On Wings of Fear Dangerous Intentions
Once a Thief The Happy Thieves
Once Upon a Savage Night Nightmare in Chicago
One against All Seul contre Tous
One Cup of Coffee Pastime
187 One Eight Seven
One Final Hour Five Star Final
One for the Dancer Code Name: Dancer
One Horse Town Small Town Girl
One Hot Summer Night: A Crimes of Passion Movie Crimes of Passion: One Hot Summer Night
One Hour to Doomsday City beneath the Sea
One Man Mutiny The Court-Martial of Billy Mitchell
One Million BC Man and His Mate
One-Piece Bathing Suit Million Dollar Mermaid
One Tough Bastard One Man's Justice
One Way Out Convicted
One Way Out Deadly Care
One Wedding and a Lot of Funerals Leprechaun 2
One Wild Night Career Opportunities
One Woman's Story The Passionate Friends
Only One Night One Single Night
Only the Best I Can Get It for You Wholesale

Only the French Can French Cancan
The Only Woman on Earth The Saga of Anatahan
Open City Rome, Open City
Operation Cicero 5 Fingers
Operation Conspiracy Cloak without Dagger
Operation Disaster Morning Departure
Operation Madball Operation Mad Ball
Operation Masquerade Masquerade
Operation Mermaid The Bay of Saint Michel
Operation Monsterland Destroy All Monsters
Operation Snafu On the Fiddle
Operation Undercover Report to the Commissioner
Opposing Force Hell Camp
Opposing Forces Opposing Force
The Opposite Sex The Opposite Sex and How to Live with Them
Oprah Winfrey Presents: Before Women Had Wings Before Women Had Wings
Oprah Winfrey Presents: David and Lisa David and Lisa
The Optimist Hallelujah, I'm a Bum
The Optimists The Optimists of Nine Elms
Orazi e curiazi Duel of Champions
Orca: The Killer Whale Orca
The Orchestra Conductor The Conductor
Ordinary Heroes: the Sandra Prine Story Hard Evidence
Orfeu Negro Black Orpheus
Les Orgueilleux The Proud Ones
Oriental Dream Kismet
The Original Fabulous Adventure of Baron Munchausen Baron Munchhausen
Orlacs Hände Hands of Orlac
L'Oro di Napoli Gold of Naples
Oro per i Cesari Gold for the Caesars
O'Rourke of the Royal Mounted Saskatchewan
Orson Welles's Ghost Story Return to Glennascaul
Oscar Wilde Wilde
Our Father Padre Nuestro
Our Little Angel Think Big
Our Man in Marrakesh Our Man in Marrakesh
Our Sea Mare Nostrum
L'Ours The Bear
Out of Control Runaway Car
Out of Present Out of the Present
Out of Rosenheim Bagdad Café
Out of the Darkness Teenage Caveman
Out of the Past Build My Gallows High
The Outcast Man in the Saddle
The Outcry Il Grido
The Outing The Lamp
The Outlaws Is Coming The Outlaws Is Coming!
Outpost Wes Craven's Mind Ripper
Outpost in Malaya The Planter's Wife
The Outsider The Guinea Pig
The Outsiders Bande à Part
Over the Bridge Over the Brooklyn Bridge
Overruled In My Daughter's Name
Oxen The Ox

P

P.I. Private Investigations Private Investigations
PJ New Face in Hell
PJ Waters Holy Smoke
P T Barnum's Rocket to the Moon Jules Verne's Rocket to the Moon
PT Raiders The Ship That Died of Shame
The Pad The Pad (and How to Use It)
O Pagador de Promessas The Given Word
Pain in the Neck A Pain in the A...!
The Paint Job Painted Heart
Painted Black Paint It Black
Painted Hero Shadow of the Past
Painting Churches The Portrait
Paisan Paisà
Palle D'Acciaio Head Office
Pane, Amore e Fantasia Bread, Love and Dreams
Panga Curse III: Blood Sacrifice
Panic in Bangkok for Agent OSS 117 Shadow of Evil
Panic in the City Black Death
Panic in the Parlour Sailor Beware!
Panny and Wilka The Young Girls of Wilko
The Paper Cranes of Osen The Downfall of Osen
Paper Flowers Kaagaz Ke Phool
Paper Mansion: the Dottie West Story Big Dreams & Broken Hearts: the Dottie West Story
The Paperhanger Work
Par-delà les Nuages Beyond the Clouds
Paradise Lagoon The Admirable Crichton
Paradise Lost Lost Paradise
Paranoia Brain Dead
Les Parapluies de Cherbourg The Umbrellas of Cherbourg
The Parasite Murders Shivers
Parasites Drag
Paratrooper The Red Beret
Parent Trap III Parent Trap Hawaiian Honeymoon
Paris Brûle-t-il? Is Paris Burning?
Paris Does Strange Things Elena et les Hommes
The Paris Express The Man Who Watched Trains Go By
Paris Was Made for Lovers A Time for Loving
Parisian Belle New Moon
Parisian Encounters Rendez-vous in Paris
Paroles et Musique Love Songs
Parting at Dusk Floating Weeds
La Partita The Gamble
Partners 'n Love Partners in Love
Partyline Party Line
Pas de Problème No Problem!
Pasolini's 120 Days of Sodom Salo, or the 120 Days of Sodom
Pasqualino Settebellezze Seven Beauties
Pasqualino: Seven Beauties Seven Beauties
Pass the Ammunition Pass the Ammo
Le Passager de la Pluie Rider on the Rain
Passe-Passe Quicker than the Eye
Passenger of the Rain Rider on the Rain
Passion and Valour Comeback
Passion Dance Midnight Tease
La Passion de Jeanne d'Arc The Passion of Joan of Arc
The Passion of Anna A Passion
Passion's Way The Reef
Passport to Fame The Whole Town's Talking
Les Patriotes Patriots
El Patrullero Highway Patrolman
Pattern for Plunder The Bay of Saint Michel
Patterns of Power Patterns
Patton Patton: Lust for Glory
Paul et Michelle Paul and Michelle
Paula Framed
Pauline à la Plage Pauline at the Beach
La Paura Fear
Paura e Amore Three Sisters
Pay the Devil Man in the Shadow
PCU Politically Correct Party Animals
The Pear Tree Shooting the Moon
The Pearl Necklace Desire
Peau d'Âne The Magic Donkey
Peccato Che Sia una Canaglia Too Bad She's Bad
The Peddler of Four Seasons The Merchant of Four Seasons
Uma Pedra No Bolso Tall Stories
The Penance Sadhna
The Penguin Pool Mystery The Penguin Pool Murder
Pensioner The Long Way Home
Pentagram The First Power
Penthouse Paradise Laura Lansing Slept Here
The People of France La Vie Est à Nous
Peppermint Soda Diabolo Menthe
Per Qualche Dollaro in Più For a Few Dollars More
Perceval Perceval le Gallois
The Perfect Alibi Alibi
Perfect Stranger Danielle Steel's A Perfect Stranger
Perfect Strangers Blind Alley
Péril Death in a French Garden
Péril en la Demeure Death in a French Garden
The Peril of Being Walter Woods Living in Peril
The Persecution and Assassination of Jean Paul Marat as Performed by the Inmates of the Asylum of Charenton under the Direction of the Marquis de Sade Marat/Sade
Personal Choice Beyond the Stars
Personal Column Lured
Personal Column Pièges
Persons Unknown Big Deal on Madonna Street
La Perversa Caricia de Satan The Devil's Kiss
La Peste The Plague
Peter Rabbit and Tales of Beatrix Potter The Tales of Beatrix Potter
Le Petit Théâtre de Jean Renoir The Little Theatre of Jean Renoir
La Petite Lola Clubbed to Death
Peversion Story Beatrice Cenci
The Phantom Fiend The Lodger
The Phantom Killer The Invisible Ghost
The Phantom Menace Star Wars Episode I: the Phantom Menace
Phantom of Terror The Bird with the Crystal Plumage
Philip Run Wild, Run Free
Philly Private Lessons
Der Philosoph Three Women in Love
Pickup Alley Interpol
Picnic on the Grass Lunch on the Grass
Pie in the Sky Terror in the City
The Pied Piper of Hamelin The Pied Piper
Pigeons The Sidelong Glances of a Pigeon Kicker
Piranha Women in the Avocado Jungle of Death Cannibal Women in the Avocado Jungle of Death
La Piscine The Swimming Pool
The Pistolero of Red River The Last Challenge
Pittsville – ein Safe Voll Blut The Catamount Killing
Pixote: a Lei Do Mais Fraco Pixote
The Pizza Triangle Jealousy, Italian Style
A Place to Be Loved Shattered Family
Planet of Incredible Creatures Fantastic Planet
La Planète Sauvage Fantastic Planet
The Plants Are Watching The Kirlian Witness
Platonov An Unfinished Piece for Mechanical Piano
The Playgirl and the War Minister The Amorous Prawn
Playgirl Gang Switchblade Sisters
The Pleasure Lovers Naked Fury
Pleasure Party Une Partie de Plaisir
The Plot to Kill Roosevelt Conspiracy in Teheran
The Plough that Broke the Plains The Plow that Broke the Plains
Pluck of the Irish Great Guy
Le Plus Vieux Métier du Monde The Oldest Profession
Poe's Tales of Terror Tales of Terror
Point of No Return The Assassin
Poisoned by Love: the Kern County Murders Murder So Sweet
A Poke in the Eye with a Sharp Stick Pleasure at Her Majesty's
Police Force Police Story
Police Story No Margin for Error
Police Story II The Freeway Killings
Police Story IV Project S
Police Story 4: First Strike Jackie Chan's First Strike
Police Story: the Freeway Killings The Freeway Killings
Polly Fulton BF's Daughter
The Polygraph Le Polygraphe
La Pomme The Apple
Un Pont entre Deux Rives The Bridge
Pookie The Sterile Cuckoo
Pornographic Affair Une Liaison Pornographique
Port Chicago Mutiny Mutiny
Le Port du Désir The House on the Waterfront
Port of Shadows Le Quai des Brumes
Porte Aperte Open Doors
Porte des Lilas Gates of Paris
Portrait of a Sinner The Rough and the Smooth
Portrait of Alison Postmark for Danger
Posse 2 – Los Locos Los Locos
Les Possédées Passionate Summer
The Possessed Passionate Summer
The Possession of Michael D Legacy of Evil
The Postman Il Postino
Pot o' Gold The Golden Hour
Potato Fritz Montana Trap
Poulet au vinaigre Cop au Vin
Poussière d'ange Angel Dust
Poussières de vie Dust of Life
Power Jew Süss
Pratidwandi The Adversary
Precious Citizen Ruth
Prehistoric World Teenage Caveman
Prénom Carmen First Name: Carmen
Préparez Vos Mouchoirs Get Out Your Handkerchiefs
The Presence Danger Island
Pretty Kill PrettyKill
Price of Freedom Operation Daybreak
The Price of Passion The Good Mother
The Price of Passion Sparks: the Price of Passion
The Price She Paid Plan of Attack
The Pride of Hollywood Behind the Screen
Pride of Kentucky The Story of Seabiscuit
Prima della Rivoluzione Before the Revolution
O Primeiro Dia Midnight
Prince and the Great Race Bush Christmas
Prince of the Blue Grass Pride of the Blue Grass
Prince of Thieves The Cops Are Robbers
Il Principe di Homburg The Prince of Homburg
La Prise de Pouvoir par Louis XIV The Rise to Power of Louis XIV
Prison The Devil's Wanton
The Prisoner The Cold Room
Prisoners of the Sun Blood Oath
The Prisoners' Song Heimkehr
The Private Life of Oliver the Eighth Oliver the Eighth
The Private Wore Skirts Never Wave at a WAC
Prize of Gold A Prize of Gold
The Prize Pulitzer Roxanne: the Prize Pulitzer
The Proceedings against Hamsun Hamsun
Le Procès de Jeanne d'Arc The Passion of Joan of Arc
Profession: Reporter The Passenger
The Professional Leon
Professione: Reporter The Passenger
Profumo di Donna Scent of a Woman
Profundo Carmesi Deep Crimson
The Programme The Program
Il Proiezionista The Inner Circle
Project: Metalbeast Metal Beast
Project Moon Base Project Moonbase
Project M7 The Net
The Promise Face of a Stranger
The Promise Never Forget
The Promise La Promesse
The Promoter The Card
Protector Valentine's Day
The Protector Body Armor
The Proud and the Beautiful The Proud Ones
Proud, Damned and Dead The Proud and the Damned
The Proud Ones Le Cheval d'Orgeuil
Prova d'Orchestra Orchestra Rehearsal
Psycho-Circus Circus of Fear
Psychotherapy Don't Get Me Started
Psychotic The Driver's Seat
P'tit Con Petit Con
Public Enemies The Public Enemy #1
The Public Eye Follow Me
I Pugni in Tasca Fists in the Pocket
Pulling It Off He's My Girl
Pumpkinhead Vengeance: the Demon
Pumpkinhead 2: Blood Wings The Revenge of Pumpkinhead – Blood Wings
Una Pura Formalità A Pure Formality
The Pure Pakeezah
Pure Heart Pakeezah
The Pure One Pakeezah
Pure Vamp Razor Blade Smile
Purgatory West of the Pecos Purgatory
Purlie Victorious Gone Are the Days
Purple Haze More American Graffiti
Pursuit of the Graf Spee The Battle of the River Plate
Pussycat Alley WUSA
Pussycat Alley The World Ten Times Over

Q

Quatermass The Quatermass Conclusion
Les Quatre Cents Coups The 400 Blows
Quatre Nuits d'un Rêveur Four Nights of a Dreamer
Le Quattro Giornate di Napoli The Four Days of Naples
Que la Bête Meure Killer!
Que Viva Mexico! Time in the Sun
The Queen Margot La Reine Margot
Queen of Blood Planet of Blood
Queen of Destiny Sixty Glorious Years
Queen of Diamonds Popsy-Pop
Queen of the Gorillas The Bride and the Beast
Queen of the Nile Nefertite, Queen of the Nile
Queimada! Burn!
Quentin Durward The Adventures of Quentin Durward
The Quest Frog Dreaming
Quest for Camelot The Magic Sword: Quest for Camelot
Questi Fantasmi Ghosts – Italian Style
Una Questione Privata A Private Affair
Qui Veut Tuer Carlos? Dead Run
Quiet Killer Black Death
A Quiet Little Neighbourhood A Perfect Little Murder
15 faits précis Masculine Feminine
Quirky Gate Hugo Pool

R

Race against Fear: A Moment of Truth Movie Race against Fear
Race against the Dark Nurses on the Line
A Race against Time Nobody's Children
A Race for Life Mask of Dust
Race for the Yankee Zephyr Treasure of the Yankee Zephyr
Race Gang The Green Cockatoo
Race to the Yankee Zephyr Treasure of the Yankee Zephyr
Rachel Cade The Sins of Rachel Cade
Rafferty and the Highway Hustlers Rafferty and the Gold Dust Twins
Rage of the Buccaneers The Black Pirate
The Rage of the Buccaneers Gordon the Black Pirate
Ragged Angels They Shall Have Music
Raid Razzia sur la Chnouf
Raise Ravens Cria Cuervos
Ramatou Hyènes
Ransom Maniac
The Rape of Malaya A Town like Alice
The Rape of Nancy Ziegenmeyer Taking Back My Life
Rape Squad Act of Vengeance
Rappresaglia Massacre in Rome
Rasputin Agony
Die Ratten The Rats
Ravenhawk Raven Hawk
Raw Eddie Murphy Raw
Raw Deal Raw Justice
Raw Meat Death Line
Raw, the Concert Movie Eddie Murphy Raw
Le Rayon Diabolique Paris Qui Dort
Le Rayon Invisible Paris Qui Dort
Le Rayon Vert The Green Ray
Re-Animator 2 Bride of Re-Animator
Re: Lucky Luciano Lucky Luciano
Ready to Wear Prêt-à-Porter
Reasonable Doubt Shadow of Doubt
The Rebel Rebel
Rebel Highway Motorcycle Gang
Rebel Highway Reform School Girl
Rebel Highway Shake, Rattle and Rock
Rebel with a Cause The Loneliness of the Long Distance Runner
Rebound: The Legend of Earl "The Goat" Manigault Rebound
Recollected Memory Forgotten Sins
Record of a Living Being I Live in Fear
Red Three Colours Red
The Red and the Black Le Rouge et le Noir
The Red Baron Von Richthofen and Brown
Red Desert The Red Desert
Red Earth, White Earth Snake Treaty

Red Hot Wheels To Please a Lady
Red Light District Street of Shame
Red Neck Zombies Redneck Zombies
Red Wedding Les Noces Rouges
Redneck County Rape Redneck Zombies
Reed: Mexico Insurgente Reed: Insurgent Mexico
The Ref Hostile Hostages
Regalo di Natale Christmas Present
Regarde les Hommes Tomber See How They Fall
Regina Roma Regina
Rehearsal for a Crime The Criminal Life of Archibaldo de la Cruz
Reindeer Games Deception
Reise der Hoffnung Journey of Hope
Rejuvenatrix The Rejuvenator
Relentless: Mind of a Killer Mind of a Killer
La Religieuse de Diderot La Religieuse
The Remarkable Mr Kipps Kipps
Remembering Satan Forgotten Sins
Remembrance Danielle Steel's Remembrance
Remembrance of Things Past Swann in Love
Remorques Stormy Waters
Renegade Girls Caged Heat
Repeat Performance Turn Back the Clock
Repo Zero to Sixty
A Report on the Party and the Guests The Party and the Guests
Reprieve Convicts Four
Republic of Sin La Fièvre Monte à el Pao
Reputation Lady with a Past
Requiescant Kill and Pray
The Rescue A Father's Revenge
Rescue Me Trojan War
Rest in Peace One Dark Night
Restless Sin
The Resurrection Syndicate Nothing but the Night
Le Retour de Martin Guerre The Return of Martin Guerre
The Return of Godzilla Godzilla Raids Again
The Return of Godzilla Godzilla
The Return of I Spy I Spy Returns
The Return of Maxwell Smart The Nude Bomb
The Return of McCloud The Return of Sam McCloud
The Return of Sandokan Sandokan against the Leopard of Sarawak
The Return of Shanghai Joe Shanghai Joe
The Return of She The Vengeance of She
Return of the Badmen Return of the Bad Men
Return of the Boomerang Adam's Woman
Return of the Corsican Brothers The Bandits of Corsica
The Return of the Dragon The Way of the Dragon
Return of the Six Million Dollar Man and the Bionic Woman Bionic Showdown: the Six Million Dollar Man and the Bionic Woman
The Return of the Vigilantes The Vigilantes Return
Return to the Land of the Demons The Church
The Reunion Forgotten Prisoners: The Amnesty Files
Reunion Reunion in France
Reunion in Hazzard Dukes of Hazzard Reunion
Rêve de Singe Bye Bye Monkey
Revenge Blood Feud
Revenge Is Sweet Babes in Toyland
The Revenge of the Blood Beast The She Beast
Revenge of the Vampire The Mask of Satan
The Revenge of Yuki-No-Jo An Actor's Revenge
Revolution The Love of Jeanne Ney
The Rhinehart Theory Above Suspicion
Riata The Deadly Trackers
Rice Paddy People Rice People
The Rich, Full Life Cynthia
Rich, Young and Deadly Platinum High School
Riches and Romance Amazing Adventure
Ride a Dark Horse Man and Boy
Ride the Whirlwind Ride in the Whirlwind
Ride to Glory The Deserter

Le Rideau Cramoisi The Crimson Curtain
Du Rififi chez les Hommes Rififi
Riget The Kingdom
Ring-a-Ding Rhythm It's Trad, Dad
Ring of Treason Ring of Spies
Ring up the Curtain Broadway to Hollywood
Rio Vengeance Motor Psycho
El Rio y la Muerte The River and Death
Rip Tide Riptide
Les Ripoux Le Cop
Ripoux contre Ripoux Le Cop II
Rise and Fall of a Little Film Company from a Novel by James Hadley Chase Grandeur et Décadence d'un Petit Commerce de Cinéma
The Rise of Catherine the Great Catherine the Great
The Rise of Helga Susan Lenox: Her Fall and Rise
Rising to Fame Susan Lenox: Her Fall and Rise
Riso Amaro Bitter Rice
Rites of Spring White Water Summer
Rites of Summer White Water Summer
The Ritual The Rite
Rive Droite, Rive Gauche Right Bank, Left Bank
The River of Death The River and Death
River of Rage: The Taking of Maggie Keene Murder on the Rio Grande
Road Check Trial on the Road
The Road Home The Long Way Home
The Road Killers Roadflower
Road of Shame Street of Shame
The Road to Graceland Finding Graceland
Road Trip Jocks
The Road Warrior Mad Max 2
Roadgames Road Games
Roads of the South Roads to the South
Roald Dahl's Matilda Matilda
Roaring Timber Come and Get It
Rob Roy Rob Roy, the Highland Rogue
Robert A Heinlein's The Puppet Masters The Puppet Masters
Robert and Robert Robert et Robert
Robin Cook's Harmful Intent Harmful Intent
Robin Cook's Mortal Fear Mortal Fear
Robin Cook's Virus Robin Cook's Formula for Death
Robo Man Who?
Robosaurus Steel Justice
Robot in the Family A Robot Called Golddigger
Robotjox Robot Jox
Rock and Roll High School Rock 'n' Roll High School
Rock around the World The Tommy Steele Story
The Rocket Boys October Sky
Rocket Man Rocketman
Rocket Ship Flash Gordon
Rocket to the Moon Jules Verne's Rocket to the Moon
Rod Serling's A Town Has Turned to Dust A Town Has Turned to Dust
Rod Serling's The Doomsday Flight The Doomsday Flight
Rodon the Flying Monster Rodan
Roger Corman Presents Black Scorpion Black Scorpion
Roger Corman Presents Burial of the Rats Bram Stoker's Burial of the Rats
Roger Corman's Frankenstein Unbound Frankenstein Unbound
Le Roi de Coeur King of Hearts
Le Roi de Paris The King of Paris
Rojin Z Roujin Z
Roller and Violin Katok i Skrypka
Roma Fellini's Roma
Roma, Città Aperta Rome, Open City
Roma Regina Regina
Le Roman de Renard The Tale of the Fox
Le Roman d'un Tricheur The Story of a Cheat
Romance and Rejection So This Is Romance?
Romance and Riches Amazing Adventure
Romance for Three Paradise for Three
Romance Is Sacred The King and the Chorus Girl
Romance on the High Seas It's Magic
Rome Adventure Lovers Must Learn
Romeo and Juliet William Shakespeare's Romeo + Juliet

Romeo in Pyjamas Parlor, Bedroom and Bath
Rommel – Desert Fox The Desert Fox
Romolo e Remo Duel of the Titans
Romp of Fanny Hill Fanny Hill: Memoirs of a Woman of Pleasure
Romuald and Juliette Romuald et Juliette
Rookies Buck Privates
Rookies Come Home Buck Privates Come Home
Room 43 Passport to Shame
The Room Upstairs Martin Roumagnac
Roommates Raising the Wind
Rope Mudhoney
Rope of Flesh Mudhoney
La Rose du Rail La Roue
Roseanne: an Unauthorized Biography Roseanne
The Rosegarden The Rose Garden
Roselyne et les Lions Roselyne and the Lions
The Rosemary Clooney Story Rosie: the Rosemary Clooney Story
Der Rosengarten The Rose Garden
Rosie the Riveter The Life and Times of Rosie the Riveter
Der Rote Kreis The Red Circle
La Roue du Rail La Roue
Le Rouge aux Lèvres Daughters of Darkness
Rough Company The Violent Men
Les Routes du Sud Roads to the South
The Roxanne Pulitzer Story Roxanne: the Prize Pulitzer
Royal Deceit Prince of Jutland
Royal Flush Two Guys from Milwaukee
R.P.M. RPM – Revolutions per Minute
RSVP For Better and for Worse
The Ruby Virgin Hell's Island
Rude Boy Featuring The Clash Rude Boy
Rudyard Kipling's Jungle Book Adventure Jungle Book
Rudyard Kipling's The Second Jungle Book: Mowgli and Baloo The Second Jungle Book
Rue Saint-Sulpice The Favour, the Watch and the Very Big Fish
Rules of Misconduct: the Roy Cohn Story Citizen Cohn
The Ruling Passion The High Price of Passion
The Rumor Mill Malice in Wonderland
The Rumour Mill Malice in Wonderland
A Run on Gold Midas Run
Run Rabbit Run Double X: the Name of the Game
Run, Stranger, Run Happy Mother's Day... Love, George
Runaway Daughter Red Salute
Runaway Girl Moment of Truth: Into the Arms of Danger
The Runaway Train Runaway!
Running Home The Long Way Home
Running Out Mrs Lambert Remembers Love
Running Wild Into the Arms of Danger
Russ Meyer's Up! Up!
Russell Mulcahy's Tale of the Mummy Talos the Mummy

S

SF Shinseiki Lensman Lensman
S.I.S. SIS Extreme Justice
SLC and Me Mark Twain & Me
S.W.A.L.K. Melody
Sabotage When London Sleeps
The Sabre and the Arrow Last of the Comanches
Sabrina Sabrina Fair
Sacco e Vanzetti Sacco and Vanzetti
Sacrificatio The Sacrifice
Sacrifice of Youth Sacrificed Youth
The Sacrilegious Hero New Tales of the Taira Clan
A Sad Comedy Autumn Marathon
Sad Inheritance Love, Lies and Lullabies
Sadhana Sadhna
Sadie and Son Detective Sadie and Son
Sagar Saagar
Saggar Saagar
St George and the Seven Curses The Magic Sword

Saint Maybe Anne Tyler's Saint Maybe
Le Salaire de la Peur The Wages of Fear
Sallah Shabati Sallah
Salo Salo, or the 120 Days of Sodom
Salò, o le 120 Giornate di Sodoma Salo, or the 120 Days of Sodom
Salonique, Nid d'Espions Mademoiselle Docteur
Salt to the Devil Give Us This Day
Saltwater Moose Salt Water Moose
Salut l'Artiste The Bit Player
Salvation! Salvation! Have You Said Your Prayers Today?
Sam & Phyllis Sugartime
Sam Marlow, Private Eye The Man with Bogart's Face
Samantha A New Kind of Love
Same Old Song On Connaît la Chanson
Samurai Force Red Sun
Samurai Musashi Miyamoto Samurai
Samurai Rebellion Rebellion
Sanders Death Drums along the River
The Sandlot Kids The Sandlot
Sandokan Sandokan the Great
The Sandpit Generals The Defiant
Sandra Vaghe Stelle dell'orsa
Le Sang des Autres The Blood of Others
Le Sang d'un Poète The Blood of a Poet
Sangre y Arena Blood and Sand
Sans Douleur The Case of Dr Laurent
Sans Mobile Apparent Without Apparent Motive
Sans Sommation Without Warning
Sans Toit Ni Loi Vagabond
Sansho Dayu Sansho the Bailiff
Santa and Me A Different Kind of Christmas
Santa Claus: the Movie Santa Claus
Santa Fe Satan Catch My Soul
Santiago, the Story of His New Life What Happened to Santiago
Saraband Saraband for Dead Lovers
Sardonicus Mr Sardonicus
Sartana the Gravedigger Sartana, Angel of Death
Sasquatch, the Legend of Bigfoot Sasquatch
Satan's Child A Child for Satan
Satan's Claw Blood on Satan's Claw
Satan's Dog Play Dead
Satan's Skin Blood on Satan's Claw
Satansbraten Satan's Brew
Satellite of Blood First Man into Space
Le Sauvage Call Him Savage
Sauve Qui Peut – la Vie Slow Motion
Savage Attraction Hostage: the Christine Maresch Story
Savage Wilderness The Last Frontier
Saving Grace One Woman's Courage
Scandal in Paris Thieves' Holiday
Le Scandale The Champagne Murders
Scandals George White's Scandals
The Scar Hollow Triumph
SCAR Scarred City
Scar City Scarred City
Scaramouche The Loves and Times of Scaramouche
The Scarlet Buccaneer Swashbuckler
The Scarlet Pen The 13th Letter
The Scarlet Riders Northwest Mounted Police
Scattered Dreams: the Kathryn Messenger Story Scattered Dreams
Scattered Dreams: the Kitty Messenger Story Scattered Dreams
Lo Sceicco Bianco The White Sheik
Das Schiff der Verlorenen Menschen The Ship of Lost Men
Das Schlangenei The Serpent's Egg
Der Schneemann The Snowman
School for Unclaimed Girls The Smashing Bird I Used to Know
The School That Stole My Brain Zombie High
The Schoolmistress and the Devil The Masters
Schrei aus Stein Scream of Stone
Schwestern oder die Balance des Glücks Sisters, or The Balance of Happiness
Scorching Winds Garam Hawa
Scorned A Woman Scorned
Scorpion Rising Scorpion Spring
Scotch on the Rocks Laxdale Hall
Scotland Yard Dragnet The Hypnotist
The Scream Dead on the Money

Scream: The Sequel Scream 2
Screen Kiss Billy's Hollywood Screen Kiss
Screwface Marked for Death
Se Permettete Let's Talk About Women
The Sea Wall This Angry Age
Sea Wyf and Biscuit Sea Wife
The Search for Sarah Race against Time: the Search for Sarah
Search for the Mother Lode Mother Lode
Searching for Bobby Fischer Innocent Moves
Seaside Swingers Every Day's a Holiday
The Seaweed Children Malachi's Cove
Second Best Secret Agent In The Whole Wide World Licensed to Kill
Second Breath Le Deuxième Souffle
Second Family Affair You're Only Young Once
The Secret The Killing Secret
Secret Abduction Visitors of the Night
Le Secret de D'Artagnan The Secret Mark of D'Artagnan
Secret Flight School for Secrets
The Secret Four The Four Just Men
The Secret Four Kansas City Confidential
Secret Interlude The View from Pompey's Head
The Secret Life of Archie's Wife Runaway Heart
The Secret Life of Ian Fleming Spymaker: the Secret Life of Ian Fleming
The Secret of Monte Cristo The Treasure of Monte Cristo
The Secret Passion Freud
The Secret Sharer Face to Face
Secret Weapons Sexpionage
Secret Yearnings Good Luck, Miss Wyckoff
Secrets of G32 Fly by Night
Secrets of the Red Bedroom Sexpionage
Secrets of Women Waiting Women
A Seduction in Travis County Blind Judgement: Seduction in Travis County
See No Evil Blind Terror
See You in Hell, Darling An American Dream
Seeds of Evil The Gardener
Seeing Stars The Decline of Western Civilization Part II: the Metal Years
Seemabaddha Company Limited
Die Sehnsucht der Veronika Voss Veronika Voss
Les Seins de glace Someone Is Bleeding
Sélect Amour Sélect Hôtel
Sensations of 1945 Sensations
La Senyora La Señora
Separate Beds The Wheeler Dealers
The Separation La Séparation
Seppuku Harakiri
Sept fois femme Woman Times Seven
Les Sept Péchés Capitaux The Seven Deadly Sins
September 30, 1955 9/30/55
I Sequestrati di Altona The Condemned of Altona
Sergeant Steiner Breakthrough
Serial Bomber Countdown
Le Serpent The Serpent
The Servile Vidheyan
Sesame Street Presents: Follow That Bird Follow That Bird
Set for Life The Gift of Love
Sette volte donna Woman Times Seven
The Settlers The New Land
Seven Se7en
Seven Bad Men Rage at Dawn
Seven Cities to Atlantis Warlords of Atlantis
The Seven Descents of Myrtle Last of the Mobile Hot-Shots
Seven Different Ways Quick, Let's Get Married
Seven Sisters House of Evil
Seven Waves Away Abandon Ship!
Sex and the Vampire Shiver of the Vampires
Sex Crime of the Century Last House on the Left
Sex Mad I Am Frigid... Why?
Sex on the Run Casanova & Co
Sex through a Window Extreme Close-Up
The Shabby Tiger Masquerade
Shades of Doubt Shadow of a Doubt
Shades of Doubt A Shadow of Doubt
Shades of Grey In Dark Places
The Shadow Army L'Armée des Ombres

Shadow Builder Bram Stoker's Shadowbuilder
Shadow Man Street of Shadows
The Shadow versus the Thousand Eyes of Dr Mabuse The Thousand Eyes of Dr Mabuse
The Shadow Warrior Kagemusha
Shadowbuilder Bram Stoker's Shadowbuilder
Shadowchaser Project: Shadowchaser
Shadows of Desire The Devil's Bed
Shadows of Forgotten Ancestors Shadows of Our Forgotten Ancestors
Shadows of Our Ancestors Shadows of Our Forgotten Ancestors
Shakedown Blue Jean Cop
Shakespeare's Hamlet Hamlet
Shame The Intruder
The Shame of Mary Boyle Juno and the Paycock
Shameless Mad Dogs and Englishmen
The Shaming Good Luck, Miss Wyckoff
Sharon's Baby I Don't Want to Be Born
Shatterbrain The Resurrected
Shattered Hearts A Champion's Fight
Shattered Mind The Terror Inside
She Couldn't Say No Beautiful but Dangerous
She Demons of the Swamp Attack of the Giant Leeches
She Let Him Continue Pretty Poison
She Loved Too Much A House of Secrets and Lies
She Played with Fire Fortune Is a Woman
She Should Have Stayed in Bed I Am Frigid... Why?
Sheba Persecution
Sheena Sheena, Queen of the Jungle
Sheka Zulu The Mark of the Hawk
She'll Be Sweet Magee and the Lady
Sheltered Lady Lady in a Jam
The Sheltered Side Lady in a Jam
Shenanigans The Great Georgia Bank Hoax
Sherlock Bones, Undercover Dog Sherlock – Undercover Dog
Sherlock Holmes and the Scarlet Claw The Scarlet Claw
Sherlock Holmes and the Secret Code Dressed to Kill
A Ship Bound for India A Ship to India
The Ship of Lost Souls The Ship of Lost Men
The Ship Was Loaded Carry On Admiral
Shipwreck! The Sea Gypsies
Shocked Mesmerized
Shocker Town without Pity
Shocker: No More Mr Nice Guy Shocker
Shockwave The Arrival
Shockwave Stranded
Shoeshine Boys Shoeshine
Shogun Island Raw Force
Shoot! Outrage
Shoot First Rough Shoot
Shoot First: a Cop's Vengeance Vigilante Cop
Shoot the Piano Player Tirez sur le Pianiste
Shoot to Kill Deadly Pursuit
The Shop on Main Street The Shop on the High Street
Short Fuse Good to Go
Showdown Top of the World
Showtime Gaiety George
The Shrinking Corpse Cauldron of Blood
Si Versailles M'Etait Conté Royal Affairs in Versailles
Sicarius – the Midnight Party The Female Vampire
Siddharta and the City The Adversary
Sidewalks of London St Martin's Lane
Sidney Sheldon's A Stranger in the Mirror A Stranger in the Mirror
Sidney Sheldon's Bloodline Bloodline
The Siege of Hell Street The Siege of Sidney Street
The Siege of Red River The Siege at Red River
Sierra de Teruel Man's Hope
Le Signe du Lion The Sign of Leo
Signore & Signori The Birds, the Bees, and the Italians
Le Silence Est d'Or Man about Town
Silence Is Golden Man about Town
Les Silences du Palais The Silences of the Palace

Les Silencieux The Silent One
Silent Echoes His Bodyguard
Silent Night, Deadly Night 4: Initiation Bugs
Silent Voice Amazing Grace and Chuck
The Silent Voice The Man Who Played God
Silent Witness The Innocent
Silent Witness: What a Child Saw Blood Brothers
The Silent World Le Monde du Silence
The Silk Noose Noose
Silken Skin La Peau Douce
Silkscreen An Unfinished Affair
Silver Stallion: King of the Wild Brumbies The Silver Brumby
Simoom: A Passion in the Desert Passion in the Desert
A Simple Story Une Histoire Simple
The Sin Good Luck, Miss Wyckoff
Sin compasión No Mercy
The Sin of Harold Diddlebock Mad Wednesday
Sing and Swing Live It Up
The Singing Musketeer The Three Musketeers
Single Dad To My Daughter with Love
Single-Handed Sailor of the King
The Single Standard The Battle of the Sexes
Singleton's Pluck Laughterhouse
The Sinister Invasion Alien Terror
The Sinister Urge Hellborn
The Sinking of the Rainbow Warrier Rainbow Warrior
The Sins of Lola Montès Lola Montès
Sir Gawain and the Green Knight Gawain and the Green Knight
La Sirène du Mississippi Mississippi Mermaid
Sisterhood Addicted to His Love
The Sisterhood Deadly Sins
Situation Normal All Fed Up The Pentagon Wars
Six in Paris Paris Vu Par ...
The Skateboard Kid – A Magical Moment The Skateboard Kid II
The Skating Rink and the Violin Katok i Skrypka
Sketch Artist II: Hands that See A Feel for Murder
The Ski Raiders Snow Job
Skin Making the Case for Murder: the Howard Beach Story
Skinheads So Proudly We Hail
Skipper The Todd Killings
Skirmish All's Fair
Sky Above and Mud Beneath The Sky above, the Mud below
Sky Bandits Gunbus
The Sky Calls Battle beyond the Sun
The Sky Is Calling Battle beyond the Sun
Skylarks on a String Larks on a String
Skyscraper Wilderness Big City
Slapstick Slapstick of Another Kind
Slapstick of a Different Kind Slapstick of Another Kind
Slate & Wyn and Blanche McBride Slate, Wyn & Me
Slaughterday Situation
Slave Coast Cobra Verde
Slithis Spawn of the Slithis
Slow Bleed State of Emergency
The Small Miracle Never Take No for an Answer
Small Time Smalltime
Smart Alec Masterminds
Smilla's Sense of Snow Smilla's Feeling for Snow
Smoke Jumpers Red Skies of Montana
Smoke Jumpers In the Line of Duty: Smoke Jumpers
Smoke Screen Palais Royale
Smokey and the Bandit Ride Again Smokey and the Bandit II
The Smugglers The Man Within
SNAFU The Pentagon Wars
Snake Eyes Dangerous Game
The Snake Goddess Jennifer
Snakes and Ladders A Step toward Tomorrow
Sneakers Hard Feelings
Snitch Noose
The Snout The Informers
Snow White in Happily Ever After Happily Ever After

Snow White in the Black Forest Snow White: a Tale of Terror
Socrates Always Outnumbered
Les Soeurs Brontë The Brontë Sisters
Soft Skin La Peau Douce
Soil Earth
Un Soir Au Music Hall One Night at the Music Hall
Un Soir sur la Plage Violent Summer
El Sol del Membrillo The Quince Tree Sun
Solarbabies Solarwarriors
The Soldier and the Lady The Adventures of Michael Strogoff
Soldier in Love Fanfan la Tulipe
The Soldiers Les Carabiniers
Soldiers of Fortune You Can't Win 'em All
Il Sole Anche di Notte Night Sun
Soleil Rouge Red Sun
I Soliti Ignoti Big Deal on Madonna Street
Solomon a Gaenor Solomon and Gaenor
Some Girls Sisters
Some Kind of Love Breaking the Silence
Some Like It Cool Casanova & Co
Someone's Watching With Harmful Intent
Something Like the Truth The Offence
Something Special Willy/Milly
Sometimes a Great Notion Never Give an Inch
Somewhere Beneath the Wide Sky Somewhere Under the Broad Sky
Somewhere in France The Foreman Went to France
Sommaren med Monika Summer with Monika
Sommarlek Summer Interlude
Les Somnambules Mon Oncle d'Amérique
Son of Blob Beware! The Blob
Sondagsbarn Sunday's Children
Song of Exile Song of the Exile
A Song of Love Un Chant d'Amour
Song of New Life Earth
Song of the Little Road Pather Panchali
Song of the Road Pather Panchali
Sono Sartana, il Vostro Becchino Sartana, Angel of Death
Sons of the Legion Sons of the Desert
Sons of Thunder Walker: Texas Ranger
Sooner or Later Baby Makes Three
La Sorella di Satana The She Beast
Il Sorpasso The Easy Life
Sorrento Beach Hotel Sorrento
Sorrow Floats Floating Away
Sotto gli Occhi dell'assassino Tenebrae
Soul Thief The Killing Mind
The Sound of Trumpets Il Posto
Sounder, Part 2 Part 2, Sounder
Sour Grapes Happy Hour
Sous le Soleil de Satan Under Satan's Sun
The South Sur
South Sea Fury Hell's Island
South: Sir Ernest Shackleton's Glorious Epic of the Antarctic South
Southern Blade The Long Ride Home
Southward on the Quest South
Southwest to Sonora The Appaloosa
Space Avenger Alien Space Avenger
Space Soldiers Flash Gordon
Spacemaster X 7 Space Master X 7
Spaceship to the Unknown Flash Gordon
Special Olympics A Special Kind of Love
Spectre Escape to Nowhere
Spectre Out 1: Spectre
Speed Zone Cannonball Fever
Spellbinders The Spellbinder
Spending Money Small Change
Speriamo che sia femmina Let's Hope It's a Girl
Lo Spettro The Spectre
Spices Mirch Masala
The Spider Earth vs the Spider
Spider Woman Sherlock Holmes and the Spider Woman
Spies from Salonika Mademoiselle Docteur
Spin The Absolute Truth
Die Spinnen The Spiders
Spinster Two Loves
Spirit of the Dead The Asphyx
Spirits of the Dead Histoires Extraordinaires
Spitfire The First of the Few
The Spivs I Vitelloni
The Split Body Count
Spoiled Rotten Battling for Baby
The Spooky Movie Show The Mask
Spoorloos The Vanishing
Spree Survival Run
The Spy Spies
Spy Busters Guns in the Heather
Spy in the Pantry Ten Days in Paris
The Spy Within Flight of the Dove
Spylarks The Intelligence Men
Squanto: A Warrior's Tale The Last Great Warrior
Stacking Season of Dreams
Stagefright Stage Fright – Aquarius
Stairway to Heaven A Matter of Life and Death
Stalking the Judge's Daughter Moment of Truth: Eye of the Stalker
Stampede The Big Land
Stampede Guns of the Timberland
Der Stand der Dinge The State of Things
Stand-Up Tragedy Thicker than Blood
Die Standarte Battleflag
Stanno Tutti Bene Everybody's Fine
Star Danielle Steel's Star
Star Quest Terminal Voyage
Star-Rock The Apple
The Star Said No Callaway Went Thataway
Starflight: the Plane That Couldn't Land Starflight One
Starlight Slaughter Eaten Alive
Staroye I Novoye The General Line
Starquest II Mind Breakers
State of Division Death Race
The Stationmaster's Wife Bolwieser
Steam Heat Immoral Mr Teas
Steamboat Steamboat round the Bend
The Steamroller and the Violin Katok i Skrypka
Steel Force Legion of Iron
The Steel Highway Other Men's Women
Step Mom Stepmom
Stephen King's Silver Bullet Silver Bullet
Stephen King's Sometimes They Come Back Sometimes They Come Back
Stepkids Big Girls Don't Cry... They Get Even
Stiffs Out Cold
Stiletto Cold Steel
Still Smokin Cheech & Chong's Still Smokin'
Die Stille nach dem Schuss The Legends of Rita
Stogies Long Gone
Stolen Hearts Baby Brokers
Stolen Hearts The People Next Door
Stolen: One Husband I Want Him Back
The Stolpa Family Story Snowbound
Stop Me Before I Kill! The Full Treatment
Stop the World – I Want to Get Off Sammy Stops the World
Stories of American Communists Seeing Red
Storm Rider The Big Showdown
The Storm Within Les Parents Terribles
A Story from Chikamatsu The Crucified Lovers
The Story of a Divorce Payment on Demand
Story of a Love Affair Chronicle of a Love
Story of a Marriage Part 3 1918
The Story of Asya Klyachinka Asya's Happiness
The Story of Benjamin Blake Son of Fury
The Story of Dr Ehrlich's Magic Bullet Dr Ehrlich's Magic Bullet
The Story of HMS Amethyst Escape of the Amethyst
Stowaway Girl Manuela
Straight Shootin' Straight Shooting
Stranded Valley of Mystery
Stranded in Paris Artists and Models Abroad
Strange Confession The Impostor
Strange Deception The Accused
Strange Holiday Jules Verne's Strange Holiday
Strange Interval Strange Interlude
The Strange Ones Les Enfants Terribles
A Strange Place for an Encounter A Strange Place to Meet
Strange Skirts When Ladies Meet
Strange Things Happen at Night Shiver of the Vampires
The Stranger The Intruder
Stranger at My Door Dead Run
The Stranger in Between Hunted
Stranger Things For Better or Worse
Strangers Journey to Italy
The Stranger's Gundown Django the Bastard
Strangers in a Small Town Nightmare in Big Sky Country
Strangers in Good Company The Company of Strangers
The Strangler East of Piccadilly
Lo straniero The Stranger
Street Fighters Only the Strong
Street Legal Blue Heat
The Street of Sorrow Joyless Street
Street People Sicilian Cross
Streets of Sorrow Joyless Street
Strictly Confidential Broadway Bill
Strictly for Pleasure The Perfect Furlough
Strike It Rich Loser Takes All
Striker The Night Stalker
The Strikers The Organizer
Striking Back Search and Destroy
Striptease Lady Lady of Burlesque
Strong City Dark City
Stronger than Fear Edge of Doom
Stryker Savage Dawn
The Student Prince The Student Prince in Old Heidelberg
Stützen der Gesellschaft Pillars of Society
Sub-a-Dub-Dub Hello Down There
Subida al Cielo Mexican Bus Ride
The Substitute The Substitute Wife
The Success The American Success Company
Success Confessions of a Married Man
Such a Gorgeous Kid Like Me Une Belle Fille Comme Moi
Such a Lovely Kid Like Me Une Belle Fille Comme Moi
Such Men Are Dangerous The Racers
Such Things Happen Love Is a Racket
Sudden Terror Eyewitness
Sugar Cane Alley Rue Cases Nègres
Sugata Sanshiro Sanshiro Sugata
The Suicide Club Trouble for Two
Suicide Squadron Dangerous Moonlight
A Suitable Case for Treatment Morgan – a Suitable Case for Treatment
The Sullivans The Fighting Sullivans
Sult Hunger
Summer The Green Ray
Summer Dreams: the Story of the Beach Boys The Story of the Beach Boys: Summer Dreams
Summer Fever Delta Fever
Summer Flight Stolen Hours
Summer Fling Last of the High Kings
The Summer Hurricane Senso
Summer Lightning I Met My Love Again
Summer Madness Summertime
Summer Manoeuvres Les Grandes Manoeuvres
Summer of the Seventeenth Doll Season of Passion
Sunless Sans Soleil
Sunset of a Clown Sawdust and Tinsel
Sunshine Club Ikinai
Sunshine Even by Night Night Sun
Suor Omicidio Killer Nun
Super Dude Hangup
SuperChef Mr Nice Guy
Supercop Police Story III: Supercop
Supercop 2 Project S
SuperFantaGenio Aladdin
The Surgeon Exquisite Tenderness
Survival Run Damnation Alley
The Susan Daniels Smith Murder Betrayed by Love
Suzanne The Second Coming of Suzanne
Suzanne Simonin La Religieuse
Suzanne's Profession La Carrière de Suzanne
Svalt Hunger
Swamp of the Blood Leeches The Alien Dead
The Swan Princess: Escape from Castle Mountain The Swan Princess: the Secret of the Castle
Swann's Way Swann in Love
The Swap Sam's Song
The Swashbuckler Sink or Swim
Sweeper Sweepers
Sweet Kill The Arousers
Sweet Violent Tony Cuba Crossing
Sweet Water Redemption The Hired Heart
Sweetheart of the Song Tra Bong A Soldier's Sweetheart
Swept from the Sea Amy Foster
The Swindle Rien Ne Va Plus
The Swindlers The Swindle
Swing, Teacher, Swing College Swing
Swinger's Paradise Wonderful Life
The Swingin' Maiden The Iron Maiden
The Swinging Pearl Mystery The Plot Thickens
Swirl of Glory Sugarfoot
Sword of Lancelot Lancelot and Guinevere
Swords of Blood Cartouche
The Swordsman Musashi Miyamoto
Sympathy for the Devil One Plus One
Symphony of Love Ecstasy
Synanon Get Off My Back
Synapse Memory Run

T

TCM 4 The Return of the Texas Chainsaw Massacre
TR Baskin A Date with a Lonely Girl
Tacones Lejanos High Heels
Das Tagebuch einer Verlorenen Diary of a Lost Girl
The Taira Clan Saga New Tales of the Taira Clan
Tale for All Summer of the Colt
A Tale from Chikamatsu The Crucified Lovers
A Tale of Africa The Green Horizon
A Tale of Summer A Summer's Tale
Tale of the Mummy Talos the Mummy
Tale of the Pale and Silvery Moon after the Rain Ugetsu Monogatari
Tale of the Tiger Tail of a Tiger
Tales of a Pale and Mysterious Moon after the Rain Ugetsu Monogatari
Tales of Erotica Erotic Tales
Tales of Mystery Histoires Extraordinaires
Tales of the Dead Histoires Extraordinaires
Tales of the Taira Clan New Tales of the Taira Clan
Talion An Eye for an Eye
Talking Dirty after Dark Talkin' Dirty after Dark
Tall Tale Tall Tale: the Unbelievable Adventures of Pecos Bill
Tall Tale: the Incredible Adventure Tall Tale: the Unbelievable Adventures of Pecos Bill
Tammy Tammy and the Bachelor
The Tangled Web In the Arms of a Killer
Tangos, the Exile of Gardel Tangos, Exilo de Gardel
Tank Force No Time to Die
Target in the Sun The Man Who Would Not Die
Tartu The Adventures of Tartu
Tarzan and the Jungle Queen Tarzan and the Slave Girl
Tarzan and the Jungle Queen Tarzan's Peril
Tarzan and the Lost Goddess The New Adventures of Tarzan
Tarzan in Guatemala The New Adventures of Tarzan
Tarzan Meets the Vampire Tarzan and the She-Devil
Tarzan the Invincible Tarzan the Fearless
Tashunga North Star
The Taste of Cherries A Taste of Cherry
The Taste of Sunshine Sunshine
Tausend Augen Thousand Eyes
Die Tausend Augen des Dr Mabuse The Thousand Eyes of Dr Mabuse
Un Taxi Mauve The Purple Taxi
Taxi, Mister Two Mugs from Brooklyn
Tchin Tchin A Touch of Adultery
Tea and Rice The Flavour of Green Tea over Rice
Tears and Laughter: the Joan and Melissa Rivers Story Starting Again
Tears for Simon Lost
Tears of Rapture The Game Is Over
Tears of the Yangtse Spring River Flows East
Teenage Dracula Dracula vs Frankenstein
Teenage Lovers Too Soon to Love
Teenage Psycho Meets Bloody Mary The Incredibly Strange Creatures Who Stopped Living and Became Mixed-Up Zombies
Teenage Slumber Party Slumber Party '57
Le Téléphone Rose The Pink Telephone

Tell Laura I Love Her Trapped and Deceived
Tell Me Lies about London Tell Me Lies
Tell Your Children Reefer Madness
Temecula A Weekend in the Country
Le Temps Waati
Le Temps des Amants A Place for Lovers
Le Temps des Loups The Last Shot
Le Temps d'un Retour Muriel
Le Temps Retrouvé Time Regained
Temptation Asphalt
Ten Days That Shook the World October
Ten Little Indians And Then There Were None
Ten Little Niggers And Then There Were None
Tender Flesh Welcome to Arrow Beach
The Tenderfoot Bushwhacked
Tenebre Tenebrae
Tennessee Williams' Orpheus Descending Orpheus Descending
Tentacoli Tentacles
La Tentation de Vénus Meeting Venus
Teorema Theorem
Terminal Station Indiscretion of an American Wife
Terminus Paradis Last Stop Paradise
Terror at the Opera Opera
Terror from under the House Revenge
Terror House The Night Has Eyes
Terror in Copper Valley Wheels of Terror
Terror in Napa Valley Wheels of Terror
Terror in Toyland You Better Watch Out
The Terror of Dr Chaney Mansion of the Doomed
The Terror of Dr Hitchcock The Horrible Dr Hichcock
Terror of Frankenstein Victor Frankenstein
Terror of Sheba Persecution
The Terror of the Vampires Shiver of the Vampires
Il Terrore dei Barbari Goliath and the Barbarians
The Terrorists Ransom
The Terry O'Kelley Story A Son's Promise
A Test of Love Annie's Coming Out
Le Testament du Docteur Cordelier The Testament of Dr Cordelier
The Testament of Orpheus Le Testament d'Orphée
La Teta y la Luna The Tit and the Moon
Texas Chainsaw Massacre 4 The Return of the Texas Chainsaw Massacre
Texas Chainsaw Massacre: The Next Generation The Return of the Texas Chainsaw Massacre
Texas Road Agent Road Agent
Thank You All Very Much A Touch of Love
Thanksgiving Day The Good Family
That Forsyte Woman The Forsyte Saga
That Is the Dawn Cela s'Appelle l'Aurore
That Mad Mr Jones The Fuller Brush Man
That Man Flintstone The Man Called Flintstone
That They May Live J'Accuse
Theatre Royal The Royal Family of Broadway
Their Secret Affair Top Secret Affair
There Goes the Neighborhood Paydirt
Wall of Death Wall of Death
Thérèse Thérèse Desqueyroux
These Are the Damned The Damned
They All Died Laughing A Jolly Bad Fellow
They Came From Within Shivers
They Don't Wear Pajamas at Rosie's The First Time
They Loved Life Kanal
They Were Five La Belle Équipe
They're Coming to Get You Dracula vs Frankenstein
They're Doing My Time Locked Up: a Mother's Rage
Thicker than Water: the Larry McLinden Story Thicker than Blood
The Thief of Bagdad An Arabian Fantasy The Thief of Bagdad
Thieves Les Voleurs
The Thing The Thing from Another World
Think Dirty Every Home Should Have One
Thinner Stephen King's Thinner
The Third Day Arrived the Crow On the Third Day Arrived the Crow
The Third Key The Long Arm
The Thirteen Chairs Twelve plus One
32 Caliber Killer Killer Calibre 32
This Air The Body Stealers
This Is My Affair I Can Get It for You Wholesale
This Is What It Means to Say Phoenix, Arizona Smoke Signals
This Man Must Die Killer!
This Man Reuter A Dispatch from Reuters
This Rebel Age The Beat Generation
This Strange Passion El
This Strange Passion Torments El
Thomas Crown and Company The Thomas Crown Affair
Thomas l'Imposteur Thomas the Imposter
Thoroughbred Run for the Roses
Those Daring Young Men in Their Jaunty Jalopies Monte Carlo or Bust
Those Desperate Men Who Smell of Dirt and Death A Bullet for Sandoval
Those Fantastic Flying Fools Jules Verne's Rocket to the Moon
Those Were the Happy Times Star!
Thou Shalt Honour Thy Wife Master of the House
Though the Sky Falls When the Sky Falls
A Thousand and One Nights Sharaz
A Thousand and One Nights The Arabian Nights
Three Cockeyed Sailors Sailors Three
Three Daughters Teen Kanya
The Three Faces of Fear Black Sabbath
The Three Faces of Terror Black Sabbath
Three Ifs and a Maybe The Big Squeeze
Three Immoral Women Heroines of Evil
Three in the Cellar Up in the Cellar
Three Lives and One Death Three Lives and Only One Death
Three Men and a Girl Kentucky Moonshine
Three Men to Kill Three Men to Destroy
The Three Musketeers Meet the Man in the Iron Mask The Man in the Iron Mask
3 Ninjas 3 Ninja Kids
Three on a Weekend Bank Holiday
Three Shades of Love This Rebel Breed
Three Stooges Meet the Gunslinger The Outlaws Is Coming!
Three Stops to Murder Blood Orange
Three Strange Loves Thirst
Three Ways to Love Cherry, Harry & Raquel
The Threepenny Opera Mack the Knife
Through the Looking Glass The Velvet Vampire
Thunder in the Dust The Sundowners
Thunder in the Valley Bob, Son of Battle
Thunder over Mexico Time in the Sun
Thunderbolt That Man Bolt
Thundercloud Colt .45
Thunderwith The Echo of Thunder
Tierna Es La Noche Tender Is the Night
Tierra Sin Pan Land without Bread
The Ties That Bind All She Ever Wanted
The Tiger Dancer Bagh Bahadur
Tiger in the Sky The McConnell Story
Tiger of Bengal The Tiger of Eschnapur
Tiger of Bengal The Indian Tomb
Tiger of Terror Sandokan Fights Back
Tiger Woods The Tiger Woods Story
Tigerman Bagh Bahadur
Tight Little Island Whisky Galore!
Il Tigre The Tiger and the Pussycat
La Tigre dei Sette Mari Tiger of the Seven Seas
Le Tigre des mers Tiger of the Seven Seas
Til There Was You Till There Was You
Till Death Us Do Part Married for Murder
Till Gladje To Joy
Till Murder Do Us Part A Woman Scorned
Till Murder Do Us Part II A Woman Deceived
Time Flyer The Blue Yonder
Time for Action Tip on a Dead Jockey
A Time for Caring Generation
A TIme for Giving Generation
A Time For Killing The Long Ride Home
Time for Terror Flesh Feast
Time Is on Our Side Let's Spend the Night Together
Time Killer The Night Strangler
Time Lost and Time Remembered I Was Happy Here
The Time of Return Muriel
Time on Target Sabotage
A Time to Live and a Time to Die Le Feu Follet
A Time to Run The Female Bunch
Time Warp The Day Time Ended
Tintin et le Lac aux Requins Tintin and the Lake of Sharks
Tintorera... Bloody Waters Tintorera
Tintorera... Tiger Shark Tintorera
Tirez sur le Pianiste Shoot the Pianist
Tito and I Tito and Me
Titus Andronicus Titus
To Cast a Shadow Always Remember I Love You
To Catch a Spy Catch Me a Spy
To Catch a Spy Catch My Soul
To Each His Own We Still Kill the Old Way
To Elvis, With Love Touched By Love
To Grandmother's House We Go Double, Double Toil and Trouble
To Kill a Dragon That Man Bolt
To Live Ikiru
To Love a Vampire Lust for a Vampire
To Love Again The Seduction of Miss Leona
To Save a Child A Child for Satan
To Save Their Souls Judgment Day: the John List Story
To The Limit Six Days, Six Nights
To the Victor Owd Bob
Todo Sobre Mi Madre All about My Mother
Tom and Jerry Jerry and Tom
Tom & Jerry Jerry and Tom
Tom Cat Dangerous Desire
Tom Waits: Big Time Big Time
Tomato Pummaro
Tomb of the Cat The Tomb of Ligeia
Tonight at 8:30 Meet Me Tonight
Tonight Let's All Make Love in London Tonite Let's All Make Love in London
Tonight's the Night Happy Ever After
Tonight's the Night The Game of Love
Too Dangerous to Love Perfect Strangers
Too Many Chefs Who Is Killing the Great Chefs of Europe?
Too Young a Hero Too Young the Hero
Top Secret The Salzburg Connection
Tops Is the Limit Anything Goes
Torch Song Judith Krantz's Torch Song
Toronto the Good Palais Royale
Torst Thirst
Toto the Hero Toto Le Héros
A Touch of Hell Serious Charge
Touch of the Sun No Secrets
Touch White, Touch Black The Violent Ones
Touchez Pas au Grisbi Honour among Thieves
Toujours les Femmes Near Mrs
Tour of Duty Breach of Conduct
Tout Sur Ma Mère All about My Mother
Toute une Vie And Now My Love
A Town Called Bastard A Town Called Hell
The Town Rat and the Country Rat Town Rat, Country Rat
The Town that Cried Terror Maniac
The Townsend Harris Story The Barbarian and the Geisha
La Tragedia di un Uomo Ridicolo The Tragedy of a Ridiculous Man
La Tragédie de la Mine Kameradschaft
Train de Vie Train of Life
Train of Terror Terror Train
Trained to Kill White Dog
Transatlantic Tunnel The Tunnel
Transit The First Power
The Trap The Baited Trap
Trapped Trouble Shooters: Trapped beneath the Earth
Trauma Terminal Choice
The Traveler Night Visitors
I Tre Fratelli Three Brothers
I Tre Volti della Paura Black Sabbath
Treason Old Louisiana
The Treasure of San Lucas Down Twisted
Treasure of the Piranha Killer Fish
Tree of Liberty The Howards of Virginia
37'2 le Matin Betty Blue
Tri Three
The Trial of Sergeant Rutledge Sergeant Rutledge
Les Tribulations d'un Chinois en Chine Up to His Ears
Trick of the Eye Primal Secrets
A Trip with Anita Travels with Anita
Triple Cross Triplecross
Triple Cross Angel of Fury
Triple Deception House of Secrets
Tristan and Isolde Lovespell
Triumph des Willens Triumph of the Will
Trois Hommes à Abattre Three Men to Destroy
3 Hommes et un Couffin 3 Men and a Cradle
Trois Vies et une Seule Mort Three Lives and Only One Death
The Trojan Horse The Trojan War
A Troll in Central Park Stanley's Magic Garden
Tropicana The Heat's On
Trouble at 16 Platinum High School
Trouble at the Royal Rose The Trouble With Spies
Trouble in the Sky Cone of Silence
The Trouble with Stevenson Curtain Call
The Troubleshooter Man with the Gun
Troubleshooters Trouble Shooters: Trapped beneath the Earth
The True and the Brave Betrayed
True Believer Fighting Justice
True Colors of Hero A Better Tomorrow
The True Story of Barry Seal Double Crossed
Trumps Enormous Changes at the Last Minute
The Truth La Vérité
Truth or Dare In Bed with Madonna
Try and Get Me The Sound of Fury
Tu Ne Tueras Point Thou Shalt Not Kill
Tulipää Flame Top
La Tulipe Noire The Black Tulip
Tune in Tomorrow Aunt Julia and the Scriptwriter
Turbo: A Power Rangers Adventure Power Rangers 2
The Turbulent Man The Most Desired Man
Turks Fruit Turkish Delight
The Turn of the Screw The Haunting of Helen Walker
Turned Out Nice Again It's Turned Out Nice Again
Twelve Miles Out The Second Woman
24/7 TwentyFourSeven
The 21 Carat Snatch Popsy-Pop
Twenty-One Days Together 21 Days
Twice upon a Yesterday If Only
Twilight Women Women of Twilight
Twin Sitters The Babysitters
Twinkle and Shine It Happened to Jane
Twinkle, Twinkle, "Killer" Kane The Ninth Configuration
The Twins Halloween Caper Double, Double Toil and Trouble
Twist of Fate Beautiful Stranger
The Twisted Road They Live by Night
Two Actresses Two Stage Sisters
Two Cops With Hostile Intent
Two Cups of Joe Twice Upon a Time
Two Daughters Teen Kanya
Two English Girls Anne and Muriel
Two Guys Talkin' about Girls ...At First Sight
Two If by Sea Stolen Hearts
Two Men in Town Two against the Law
Two Minds for Murder Someone behind the Door
Two Women Double Edge

U

U-Boat 29 The Spy in Black
Uccellacci e Uccellini Hawks and Sparrows
L'Uccello dalle piume di cristallo The Bird with the Crystal Plumage
Ugly, Dirty and Bad Down and Dirty
Ugly, Dirty and Mean Down and Dirty
La Ultima Cena The Last Supper
Ultimas Imagenes Del Naufragio Last Images of the Shipwreck
Ultimate Action Forgotten Prisoners: The Amnesty Files
The Ultimate Solution of Grace Quigley Grace Quigley
Gli Ultimi Giorni di Pompeii The Last Days of Pompeii
Unchained The Man Who Broke 1,000 Chains
Uncle Harry The Strange Affair of Uncle Harry
Under California Skies Under California Stars

Under My Skin Deadbolt
Under Pressure Deliver Them from Evil: the Taking of Alta View
Under the Clock The Clock
Under the Influence Betrayal of Trust
Under the Olive Trees Through the Olive Trees
Under the Roofs of Paris Sous les Toits de Paris
Under Threat Donato and Daughter
Undercover Johnnie Mae Gibson: FBI
Undercovers Hero Soft Beds, Hard Battles
Undercurrent Desperate Measures
Underground Guerrillas Undercover
An Undersea Odyssey The Neptune Factor
Underworld The Lower Depths
Underworld Informers The Informers
L'Une Chante l'Autre Pas One Sings, the Other Doesn't
An Unfinished Piece for a Player Piano An Unfinished Piece for Mechanical Piano
Unfinished Pieces for Mechanical Piano An Unfinished Piece for Mechanical Piano
Unheimliche Geschichten The Living Dead
The Unholy Four A Stranger Came Home
Unidentified Flying Oddball The Spaceman and King Arthur
The Uninvited Victim of the Haunt
Unknown Deathmask
Unknown Origin The Alien Within
Unnamable II The Unnamable Returns
Uno Dopo l'Altro One after the Other
Unpromised Land Land without Bread
Unreconciled Not Reconciled, or Only Violence Helps Where Violence Rules
Unsane Tenebrae
The Untamed West The Far Horizons
Unto a Good Land The New Land
An Unusual Crime Phantom of Death
Unwanted Attentions Shadow of Obsession
Uomini Duri Three Tough Guys
L'Uomo delle Stelle The Starmaker
Up and Under Up 'n' Under
Up in Smoke Cheech & Chong's Up in Smoke
Upperworld Upper World
The Uprooted Disha
Urban Crossfire Street War
Urban Justice Under Oath
An Urban Legend Suddenly
Urge to Kill With Intent to Kill
Urgent Action: The Amnesty Files Forgotten Prisoners: The Amnesty Files
Urs Al-Jalil Wedding in Galilee
Us Begins with You Don't Go Breaking My Heart
Us Two An Adventure for Two
USS Teakettle You're in the Navy Now
The Usual Unidentified Thieves Big Deal on Madonna Street
Utamaro and His Five Women Five Women around Utamaro

V

Les Vacances de Monsieur Hulot Monsieur Hulot's Holiday
Vacation from Marriage Perfect Strangers
La Vagabonde Vagabond
Vaghe Stelle dell'Orsa Of a Thousand Delights
Valdez the Halfbreed The Valdez Horses
Vale Abraão Abraham Valley
La Valise Man in the Trunk
La Vallée The Valley
The Valley Obscured by Clouds The Valley
The Valley of Abraham Abraham Valley
Valley of the Swords The Castilian
The Vampire-Beast Craves Blood The Blood Beast Terror
Vampire of Venice Vampire in Venice
Vampire Thrills Shiver of the Vampires
Vampires John Carpenter's Vampires
The Vampires Lust of the Vampire
The Vampire's Thrill Shiver of the Vampires
I Vampiri The Vampires
Vampiros en La Habana Vampires in Havana
Il Vangelo Secondo Matteo The Gospel According to St Matthew
Variété Vaudeville
Variety Lights Lights of Variety
Veil Ghunghat
Venere imperiale Imperial Venus
La Venganza del Saxo Curious Dr Humpp
Vengeance The Brain
Vengeance Is Mine Vengeance Is Mine
Vengeance Is Mine A Bullet for Sandoval
Venus impériale Imperial Venus
The Venusian Stranger from Venus
Verbrechen am Seelenleben eines Menschen Kaspar Hauser
Verführung: die Grausame Frau Seduction: The Cruel Woman
Vergesst Mozart Forget Mozart
The Verification Trial on the Road
Die Verlorene Ehre Der Katharina Blum The Lost Honor of Katharina Blum
The Vernon Johns Story Freedom Road: the Vernon Johns Story
Veronica Guerin When the Sky Falls
Versailles Royal Affairs in Versailles
Das Versprechen The Promise
A Very Big Weekend A Man, a Woman and a Bank
A Very Discreet Hero A Self-Made Hero
A Very Shy Hero A Self-Made Hero
The Very Thought of You Martha – Meet Frank, Daniel and Laurence
La Veuve Couderc The Widow Couderc
Viagem ao principio do mundo Journey to the Beginning of the World
Viaggio con Anita Travels with Anita
Viaggio in Italia Journey to Italy
La Victoire en Chantant Black and White in Color
Victory Escape to Victory
La Vida Criminal de Archibaldo de la Cruz The Criminal Life of Archibaldo de la Cruz
La Vie devant Soi Madame Rosa
La Vie Est un Long Fleuve Tranquille Life Is a Long Quiet River
La Vie Est un Roman Life Is a Bed of Roses
La Vie Privée Very Private Affair
La Vie Rêvée des Anges The Dream Life of Angels
La Vie Sexuelle des Belges 1950-1978 The Sexual Life of the Belgians 1950-1978
Le Vieil Homme et l'Enfant The Two of Us
La Vieille Qui Marchait dans la Mer The Old Lady Who Walked in the Sea
El Viento se Llevó lo qué Wind with the Gone
Vier von der Infanterie Westfront 1918
De Vierde Man The Fourth Man
Vigilante Cop Shoot First: A Cop's Vengeance
Vigo Vigo: Passion for Life
Vigo: Histoire d'une Passion Vigo: Passion for Life
The Villain Cactus Jack
Vincent Vincent: the Life and Death of Vincent Van Gogh
Vincent et Moi Vincent and Me
La Vingt-Cinquième Heure The 25th Hour
I Vinti The Vanquished
The Violator Act of Vengeance
The Violent Breed Keoma
Violent Journey The Fool Killer
Violent Midnight Psychomania
Violent Stranger Wetherby
Violent Tradition Once a Thief
Violette Violette Nozière
Violin and Roller Katok i Skrypka
Il Violino Rosso The Red Violin
Le Violon de Rothschild Rothschild's Violin
Virtual Combat Grid Runners
The Virtuous Tramps Bogus Bandits
Virus Robin Cook's Formula for Death
Visages d'Enfants Faces of Children
The Visitors 2: the Corridors of Time Les Visiteurs 2: Les Couloirs du Temps
La Vita È Bella Life Is Beautiful
Vital Contact Orbit
Viva la vie! Long Live Life
Viva Las Vegas! Meet Me in Las Vegas
Vivement Dimanche! Confidentially Yours
Vivre Sa Vie: Film en Douze Tableaux It's My Life
Vladimir and Rosa Vladimir et Rosa
A Voice in the Night Freedom Radio
A Voice in the Night Wanted for Murder
Voices from Within Silhouette
La Voie Lactée The Milky Way
The Volcano Monster Godzilla Raids Again
Volcano Run Eruption
Le Voleur The Thief of Paris
Vortex The Day Time Ended
Voyage au début du monde Journey to the Beginning of the World
The Voyage Home – Star Trek IV Star Trek IV: the Voyage Home
Voyage to Italy Journey to Italy
Voyage to the Beginning of the World Journey to the Beginning of the World
Vulcano Volcano

W

Das Wachsfigurenkabinett Waxworks
Wages and Profit Tarang
Wages of Fear Sorcerer
The Waking Hour The Velvet Vampire
Waking Ned Devine Waking Ned
Walk in the Shadow Life for Ruth
Walker, Texas Ranger Deadly Reunion
Walker: Texas Ranger: Deadly Reunion Deadly Reunion
Walking Down Broadway Hello Sister!
Walking Tall, Part II Part 2 Walking Tall
Waller's Last Trip Waller's Last Walk
Wallers Letzter Gang Waller's Last Walk
Walter Winchell Winchell
Want a Ride, Little Girl? Impulse
The Wanton Contessa Senso
War Correspondent The Story of G I Joe
War Games Suppose They Gave a War and Nobody Came?
War-Gods of the Deep City under the Sea
War of the Monsters Godzilla vs Gigan
War Shock Battle Shock
War Stories A Soldier's Sweetheart
Warlock II Warlock: The Armageddon
Warlords of the 21st Century Battletruck
Warnung vor einer Heiligen Nutte Beware of a Holy Whore
The Warriors The Dark Avenger
Warum läuft Herr R Amok? Why Does Herr R Run Amok?
The Water Boy The Waterboy
The Water Cure The Cure
Waterfront Women Waterfront
The Wave Tarang
The Way of the Dragon Return of the Dragon
Ways of Love L'Amore
Ways of Love: A Day in the Country Une Partie de Campagne
Ways of Love: Jofroi Jofroi
We Are in the Navy Now We Joined the Navy
We Know the Song On Connaît la Chanson
The Weary Death Destiny
Web of Evidence Beyond This Place
Wedding Bells Royal Wedding
Wedding Breakfast The Catered Affair
The Wedding Gift Wide Eyed and Legless
Wedding in Blood Les Noces Rouges
Wednesday's Child Family Life
Wee Geordie Geordie
Welcome to Xanadu Sweet Hostage
The Well-Made Marriage Le Beau Mariage
Wendy Cracked a Walnut Almost
We're in the Army Now Pack Up Your Troubles
Werewolf Woman Naked Werewolf Woman
Wernher von Braun I Aim at the Stars
Wes Craven's Don't Look Down Don't Look Down
Wes Craven's Wishmaster Wishmaster
West Beyrouth West Beirut
West of Montana Mail Order Bride
Western Front 1918 Westfront 1918
What Ever Happened to Aunt Alice? Whatever Happened to Aunt Alice?
What Ever Happened to Baby Jane? What Ever Happened to...?
What Happened to Bobby Earl? Murder in a College Town
What Lola Wants Damn Yankees
What Price Vengeance Vengeance
What She Doesn't Know Shades of Gray
What the Birds Knew I Live in Fear
What's Good for the Gander What's Good for the Goose
What's Love Got to Do with It Tina: What's Love Got to Do with It
What's the Matter with Danny Dunmore? The Secret
Wheel of Fortune A Man Betrayed
When Friendship Kills Moment of Truth: A Secret between Friends
When I Fall in Love Everybody's All-American
When Knighthood Was in Flower The Sword and the Rose
When Somebody Loves You Suddenly
When Strangers Marry Betrayed
When the Bough Breaks 2: Perfect Prey Perfect Prey
When the Door Opened Escape
When the Heavens Fall When the Sky Falls
When Wolves Cry The Christmas Tree
Where the Hart Is Home Is Where the Hart Is
Where the River Bends Bend of the River
Where There's a Will Good Morning, Boys
Where's Mommy Now? Perfect Alibi
Which Witch Is Which? Witches' Brew
While London Sleeps When London Sleeps
The Whipped The Underworld Story
A Whisper Kills Whisperkill
Whispering Death Death in the Sun
White Three Colours White
White Lies Little White Lies
The White Man The Squaw Man
A White, White Boy... Mirror
A White, White Day... Mirror
Whiz Kid Zapped!
Who Do I Gotta Kill? Me and the Mob
Who Is Killing the Stuntmen? Stunts
Who Speaks for Jonathan? Jonathan: the Boy Nobody Wanted
Whoever Slew Auntie Roo? Who Slew Auntie Roo?
Whose Little Girl Are You? Better Late Than Never
Why Bother to Knock Don't Bother to Knock
Why Did Bodhi-Dharma Leave for the East? Why Has Bhodi-Dharma Left for the East?
Why Not! Pourquoi Pas!
Why We Fight, 1 Prelude to War
The Widow of Saint-Pierre La Veuve de Saint-Pierre
The Widower Love and Pain and the Whole Damn Thing
Wild Beds Tigers in Lipstick
The Wild Child L'Enfant Sauvage
Wild Flower Wildflower
Wild for Kicks Beat Girl
Wild Game Jail Bait
The Wild Heart Gone to Earth
Wild in the Sky Black Jack
Wild Orchid III: Red Shoe Diaries The Red Shoe Diaries
The Wild Pack The Defiant
The Wild Reeds Les Roseaux Sauvages
Wild Stallion White Mane
Wildcat The Great Scout & Cathouse Thursday
Wildwechsel Jail Bait
Will It Snow at Christmas? Will It Snow for Christmas?
The Will of Doctor Cordelier The Testament of Dr Cordelier
William Comes to Town William at the Circus
William Peter Blatty's The Exorcist The Exorcist III
The Wind Bloweth Where it Listeth A Man Escaped
Wind from the East Vent d'Est
The Windfall Mr Billion
Window Shopping Golden Eighties
A Window to the Sky The Other Side of the Mountain
The Winged Serpent Q – the Winged Serpent
Wings over the World Rockshow
The Winning Way The All American
The Winston Affair The Man in the Middle
Winter Hawk Winterhawk
Winter Rates Out of Season
Winter Sleepers Wintersleepers
Winterschläfer Wintersleepers
The Wire Caught in the Act
Witch Doctor Men of Two Worlds
Witchboard 3: the Possession Witchboard – The Possession
Witchcraft Curse III: Blood Sacrifice

Witchcraft through the Ages Häxan
Witchery Witchcraft
With All My Heart The Intimate Stranger
With Murdeous Intent Murderous Intent
With Murder in Mind With Savage Intent
Without a Kiss Goodbye Falsely Accused
Without Consent Trapped and Deceived
Without Witnesses A Private Conversation
Wolverine Code Name: Wolverine
Woman L'Amore
A Woman Alone Sabotage
A Woman Destroyed Smash-Up, the Story of a Woman
The Woman Between The Woman I Love
Woman in Hiding Mantrap
The Woman in His House The Animal Kingdom
Woman of Summer The Stripper
Woman of the Dunes Woman in the Dunes
Woman on a Bicycle Rescuers: Stories of Courage: Two Women
The Woman on the Moon Woman in the Moon
The Woman One Longs for Three Loves
The Woman That Men Long for Three Loves
The Woman That Men Yearn for Three Loves
Woman with a Whip Forty Guns
The Woman with Red Boots The Lady with Red Boots
Woman without a Face Mister Buddwing
A Woman's Devotion Battle Shock
The Women Two Women
Women in Chains Black Mama, White Mama
Women in Limbo Limbo
Women of Nazi Germany Hitler
The Women of Spring Break Welcome to Paradise
Women on Wheels Easy Wheels
Women's Penitentiary 1 The Big Doll House
Women's Penitentiary III Women in Cages
Women's Victory The Victory of Women
Wonderful Day I've Gotta Horse
Wonderful to be Young! The Young Ones
The Wonderful Years The Restless Years
Wooden Crosses The Road to Glory
The Word Ordet
The World and His Wife State of the Union
The World of Silence Le Monde du Silence
The World of Yor Yor, the Hunter From the Future
The World's Most Beautiful Woman Beautiful but Dangerous
The Worlds of Gulliver The Three Worlds of Gulliver
Wrecking Crew illtown
Written on the Sand Play Dirty
Wrong Bet AWOL
Wrong Is Right The Man with the Deadly Lens
The Wrong Kind of Girl Bus Stop
Die Wunderbare Lüge der Nina Petrowna The Wonderful Lie of Nina Petrovna

X The Man with the X-Ray Eyes
The X Files Movie The X Files
X: the Man with the X-Ray Eyes The Man with the X-Ray Eyes
Xochimilco Portrait of Maria

Y

Y Aura-t-Il de la Neige à Noël? Will It Snow for Christmas?
Y Mapiwr The Making of Maps
Yacula The Female Vampire
Yang Kwei The Princess Yang Kwei Fei
Yangtse Incident Escape of the Amethyst
A Yank in London I Live in Grosvenor Square
A Yankee in King Arthur's Court A Connecticut Yankee in King Arthur's Court
Year Punk Broke 1991: The Year Punk Broke
Years without Days Castle on the Hudson

Les Yeux sans Visage Eyes without a Face
Yo, la Peor de Todas I, the Worst of All
The Yokel The Captain
Yolanda and the Thief Yolande and the Thief
You Belong to My Heart Mr Imperium
You Can't Sleep Here I Was a Male War Bride
You Can't Steal Love Live a Little, Steal a Lot
You Can't Take Money Internes Can't Take Money
You Don't Know What Love Is Heaven's Burning
You Don't Need Pajamas at Rosie's The First Time
Young and Eager Claudelle Inglish
The Young and the Damned Los Olvidados
The Young and the Immoral Hellborn
The Young and the Passionate I Vitelloni
The Young and the Willing The Wild and the Willing
Young and Willing The Wild and the Willing
The Young Flynn Flynn
The Young Girls of Wilko The Young Ladies of Wilko
Young Hearts Promised Land
The Young Hellions High School Confidential
The Young Invaders Darby's Rangers
Young Man of Music Young Man with a Horn
The Young Rebel Cervantes
Young Scarface Brighton Rock
Young Sherlock Holmes and the Pyramid of Fear Young Sherlock Holmes
The Youngest Spy Ivan's Childhood
Your Mother Wears Combat Boots Mom's Army
Your Past Is Showing The Naked Truth
Youth and Perversion The Vanquished
Yukinojo's Revenge An Actor's Revenge

Z

Zap – Invocation of My Demon Brother Invocation of My Demon Brother
Der Zauber Der Venus Meeting Venus
Zazie in the Metro Zazie dans le Métro
Zee & Co X, Y and Zee
Zendegi Va Digar Hich And Life Goes On…
Zentropa Europa
Zero Degrees Kelvin Zero Kelvin
Zero Hour The Road to Glory
Zero Population ZPG: Zero Population Growth
Zero Tolerance Inflammable
Zig Zag Zigzag
The Zodiac The Limbic Region
Zombie Zombie Flesh Eaters
Zombie 2 Zombie Flesh Eaters
Zombies Dawn of the Dead
Zoo A Zed & Two Noughts
Zooman and the Sign Zooman
Zora Silent Night, Bloody Night
Zormba Zorba the Greek
Zu Time Warrior Zu Warriors
Zu: Warriors from the Magic Mountain Zu Warriors
Zuckerbaby Sugarbaby
Zwei gegen Tod und Teufel Montana Trap
Zwischengleis Yesterday's Tomorrow

Awards

1927/28

Academy Awards

OUTSTANDING PICTURE: **Wings** • *The Last Command* • *The Racket* • *7th Heaven* • *The Way of All Flesh*
UNIQUE AND ARTISTIC PICTURE: **Sunrise** • *The Crowd* • *Chang*
DIRECTING (DRAMATIC PICTURE): **Frank Borzage** *7th Heaven* • King Vidor *The Crowd* • Herbert Brenon *Sorrell and Son*
DIRECTING (COMEDY PICTURE): **Lewis Milestone** *Two Arabian Knights* • Charles Chaplin *The Circus* • Ted Wilde *Speedy*
ACTOR: **Emil Jannings** *The Last Command* • Emil Jannings *The Way of All Flesh* • Charles Chaplin *The Circus* • Richard Barthelmess *The Noose* • Richard Barthelmess *The Patent Leather Kid*
ACTRESS: **Janet Gaynor** *7th Heaven* • Janet Gaynor *Street Angel* • Janet Gaynor *Sunrise* • Louise Dresser *A Ship Comes In* • Gloria Swanson *Sadie Thompson*
WRITING (ORIGINAL STORY): **Ben Hecht** *Underworld* • Lajos Biró *The Last Command* • Rupert Hughes *The Patent Leather Kid*
WRITING (ADAPTATION): **Benjamin Glazer** *7th Heaven* • Anthony Coldeway *Glorious Betsy* • Al Cohn *The Jazz Singer*
WRITING (TITLE WRITING): **Joseph Farnham** *Telling the World* • Joseph Farnham *The Fair Co-Ed* • Joseph Farnham *Laugh, Clown, Laugh* • George Marion Jr *Oh Kay!* • Gerald Duffy *The Private Life of Helen of Troy*

1928/29

Academy Awards

OUTSTANDING PICTURE: **The Broadway Melody** • *Alibi* • *Hollywood Revue* • *In Old Arizona* • *The Patriot*
DIRECTING: **Frank Lloyd** *The Divine Lady* • Harry Beaumont *The Broadway Melody* • Frank Lloyd *Drag* • Irving Cummings *In Old Arizona* • Lionel Barrymore *Madame X* • Ernst Lubitsch *The Patriot* • Frank Lloyd *Weary River*
ACTOR: **Warner Baxter** *In Old Arizona* • George Bancroft *Thunderbolt* • Chester Morris *Alibi* • Paul Muni *The Valiant* • Lewis Stone *The Patriot*
ACTRESS: **Mary Pickford** *Coquette* • Ruth Chatterton *Madame X* • Betty Compson *The Barker* • Jeanne Eagels *The Letter* • Corinne Griffith *The Divine Lady* • Bessie Love *The Broadway Melody*
WRITING: **Hans Kräly** *The Patriot* • Elliott Clawson *The Cop* • Tom Barry *In Old Arizona* • Hans Kräly *The Last of Mrs Cheyney* • Elliott Clawson *The Leatherneck* • Josephine Lovett *Our Dancing Daughters* • Elliott Clawson *Sal of Singapore* • Elliott Clawson *Skyscraper* • Tom Barry *The Valiant* • Bess Meredyth *A Woman of Affairs* • Bess Meredyth *Wonder of Women*

1929/30

Academy Awards

OUTSTANDING PRODUCTION: **All Quiet on the Western Front** • *The Big House* • *Disraeli* • *The Divorcee* • *The Love Parade*
DIRECTING: **George Cukor** *All Quiet on the Western Front* • Clarence Brown *Anna Christie* • Robert Z Leonard *The Divorcee* • King Vidor *Hallelujah* • Ernst Lubitsch *The Love Parade* • Clarence Brown *Romance*
ACTOR: **George Arliss** *Disraeli* • George Arliss *The Green Goddess* • Wallace Beery *The Big House* • Maurice Chevalier *The Big Pond* • Maurice Chevalier *The Love Parade* • Ronald Colman *Bulldog Drummond* • Ronald Colman *Condemned* • Lawrence Tibbett *The Rogue Song*
ACTRESS: **Norma Shearer** *The Divorcee* • Nancy Carroll *The Devil's Holiday* • Ruth Chatterton *Sarah and Son* • Greta Garbo *Anna Christie* • Greta Garbo *Romance* • Norma Shearer *Their Own Desire* • Gloria Swanson *The Trespasser*
WRITING: **Frances Marion** *The Big House* • Maxwell Anderson, George Abbott, Del Andrews *All Quiet on the Western Front* • Julien Josephson *Disraeli* • John Meehan *The Divorcee* • Howard Estabrook *Street of Chance*

1930/31

Academy Awards

OUTSTANDING PRODUCTION: **Cimarron** • *East Lynne* • *The Front Page* • *Skippy* • *Trader Horn*
DIRECTING: **Norman Taurog** *Skippy* • Wesley Ruggles *Cimarron* • Clarence Brown *A Free Soul* • Lewis Milestone *The Front Page* • Josef von Sternberg *Morocco*
ACTOR: **Lionel Barrymore** *A Free Soul* • Jackie Cooper *Skippy* • Richard Dix *Cimarron* • Fredric March *The Royal Family of Broadway* • Adolphe Menjou *The Front Page*
ACTRESS: **Marie Dressler** *Min and Bill* • Marlene Dietrich *Morocco* • Irene Dunne *Cimarron* • Ann Harding *Holiday* • Norma Shearer *A Free Soul*
WRITING (ORIGINAL STORY): **John Monk Saunders** *The Dawn Patrol* • Rowland Brown *Doorway to Hell* • Harry D'Abbadie D'Arrast, Douglas Doty, Donald Ogden Stewart *Laughter* • Kubec Glasmon, John Bright *The Public Enemy* • Lucien Hubbard, Joseph Jackson *Smart Money*
WRITING (ADAPTATION): **Howard Estabrook** *Cimarron* • Fred Niblo Jr, Seton I Miller *The Criminal Code* • Horace Jackson *Holiday* • Robert N Lee, Francis Edward Faragoh *Little Caesar* • Joseph L Mankiewicz, Sam Mintz *Skippy*

1931/32

Academy Awards

OUTSTANDING PRODUCTION: **Grand Hotel** • *Arrowsmith* • *Bad Girl* • *The Champ* • *Five Star Final* • *One Hour with You* • *Shanghai Express* • *The Smiling Lieutenant*
DIRECTING: **Frank Borzage** *Bad Girl* • King Vidor *The Champ* • Josef von Sternberg *Shanghai Express*
ACTOR: **Wallace Beery** *The Champ* • **Fredric March** *Dr Jekyll and Mr Hyde* • Alfred Lunt *The Guardsman*
ACTRESS: **Helen Hayes** *The Sin of Madelon Claudet* • Marie Dressler *Emma* • Lynn Fontanne *The Guardsman*
WRITING (ORIGINAL STORY): **Frances Marion** *The Champ* • Grover Jones, William Slavens McNutt *Lady and Gent* • Lucien Hubbard *The Star Witness* • Jane Murfin, Adela Rogers St John *What Price Hollywood?*
WRITING (ADAPTATION): **Edwin Burke** *Bad Girl* • Sidney Howard *Arrowsmith* • Percy Heath, Samuel Hoffenstein *Dr Jekyll and Mr Hyde*

1932/33

Academy Awards

OUTSTANDING PRODUCTION: **Cavalcade** • *42nd Street* • *A Farewell to Arms* • *I Am a Fugitive from a Chain Gang* • *Lady for a Day* • *Little Women* • *The Private Life of Henry VIII* • *She Done Him Wrong* • *Smilin' Through* • *State Fair*
DIRECTING: **Frank Lloyd** *Cavalcade* • Frank Capra *Lady for a Day* • George Cukor *Little Women*
ACTOR: **Charles Laughton** *The Private Life of Henry VIII* • Leslie Howard *Berkeley Square* • Paul Muni *I Am a Fugitive from a Chain Gang*
ACTRESS: **Katharine Hepburn** *Morning Glory* • May Robson *Lady for a Day* • Diana Wynyard *Cavalcade*
WRITING (ORIGINAL STORY): **Robert Lord** *One Way Passage* • Frances Marion *The Prizefighter and the Lady* • Charles MacArthur *Rasputin and the Empress*
WRITING (ADAPTATION): **Sarah Y Mason, Victor Heerman** *Little Women* • Robert Riskin *Lady for a Day* • Paul Green, Sonya Levien *State Fair*

1934

Academy Awards

OUTSTANDING PRODUCTION: **It Happened One Night** • *The Barretts of Wimpole Street* • *Cleopatra* • *Flirtation Walk* • *The Gay Divorcee* • *Here Comes the Navy* • *The House of Rothschild* • *Imitation of Life* • *One Night of Love* • *The Thin Man* • *Viva Villa!* • *The White Parade*
DIRECTING: **Frank Capra** *It Happened One Night* • Victor Schertzinger *One Night of Love* • W S Van Dyke *The Thin Man*
ACTOR: **Clark Gable** *It Happened One Night* • Frank Morgan *The Affairs of Cellini* • William Powell *The Thin Man*
ACTRESS: **Claudette Colbert** *It Happened One Night* • Bette Davis *Of Human Bondage* • Grace Moore *One*

Night of Love • Norma Shearer *The Barretts of Wimpole Street*
WRITING (ORIGINAL STORY): **Arthur Caesar** *Manhattan Melodrama* • Mauri Grashin *Hide-Out* • Norman Krasna *The Richest Girl in the World*
WRITING (ADAPTATION): **Robert Riskin** *It Happened One Night* • Albert Hackett, Frances Goodrich *The Thin Man* • Ben Hecht *Viva Villa!*

1935

Academy Awards

OUTSTANDING PRODUCTION: **Mutiny on the Bounty** • *Alice Adams* • *Broadway Melody of 1936* • *Captain Blood* • *David Copperfield* • *The Informer* • *Les Misérables* • *The Lives of a Bengal Lancer* • *A Midsummer Night's Dream* • *Naughty Marietta* • *Ruggles of Red Gap* • *Top Hat*
DIRECTING: **John Ford** *The Informer* • Michael Curtiz *Captain Blood* • Henry Hathaway *The Lives of a Bengal Lancer* • Frank Lloyd *Mutiny on the Bounty*
ACTOR: **Victor McLaglen** *The Informer* • Clark Gable, Charles Laughton, Franchot Tone *Mutiny on the Bounty* • Paul Muni *Black Fury*
ACTRESS: **Bette Davis** *Dangerous* • Elisabeth Bergner *Escape Me Never* • Claudette Colbert *Private Worlds* • Katharine Hepburn *Alice Adams* • Miriam Hopkins *Becky Sharp* • Merle Oberon *The Dark Angel*
WRITING (SCREENPLAY): **Dudley Nichols** *The Informer* • Casey Robinson *Captain Blood* • Achmed Abdullah, John L Balderston, Grover Jones, William Slavens McNutt, Waldemar Young *The Lives of a Bengal Lancer* • Jules Furthman, Talbot Jennings, Carey Wilson *Mutiny on the Bounty*
WRITING (ORIGINAL STORY): **Ben Hecht, Charles MacArthur** *The Scoundrel* • Moss Hart *Broadway Melody of 1936* • Gregory Rogers ''G'' *Men* • Stephen Morehouse Avery, Don Hartman *The Gay Deception*

1936

Academy Awards

OUTSTANDING PRODUCTION: **The Great Ziegfeld** • *Anthony Adverse* • *Dodsworth* • *Libeled Lady* • *Mr Deeds Goes to Town* • *Romeo and Juliet* • *San Francisco* • *The Story of Louis Pasteur* • *A Tale of Two Cities* • *Three Smart Girls*
DIRECTING: **Frank Capra** *Mr Deeds Goes to Town* • William Wyler *Dodsworth* • Robert Z Leonard *The Great Ziegfeld* • Gregory La Cava *My Man Godfrey* • W S Van Dyke *San Francisco*
ACTOR: **Paul Muni** *The Story of Louis Pasteur* • Gary Cooper *Mr Deeds Goes to Town* • Walter Huston *Dodsworth* • William Powell *My Man Godfrey* • Spencer Tracy *San Francisco*
ACTRESS: **Luise Rainer** *The Great Ziegfeld* • Irene Dunne *Theodora Goes Wild* • Gladys George *Valiant Is the Word for Carrie* • Carole Lombard *My Man Godfrey* • Norma Shearer *Romeo and Juliet*
ACTOR IN A SUPPORTING ROLE: **Walter Brennan** *Come and Get It* • Mischa Auer *My Man Godfrey* • Stuart Erwin *Pigskin Parade* • Basil Rathbone *Romeo and Juliet* • Akim Tamiroff *The General Died at Dawn*
ACTRESS IN A SUPPORTING ROLE: **Gale Sondergaard** *Anthony Adverse* • Beulah Bondi *The Gorgeous Hussy* • Alice Brady *My Man Godfrey* • Bonita Granville *These Three* • Maria Ouspenskaya *Dodsworth*
WRITING (SCREENPLAY): **Sheridan Gibney, Pierre Collings** *The Story of Louis Pasteur* • Frances Goodrich, Albert Hackett *After the Thin Man* • Sidney Howard *Dodsworth* • Robert Riskin *Mr Deeds Goes to Town* • Morrie Ryskind, Eric Hatch *My Man Godfrey*
WRITING (ORIGINAL STORY): **Sheridan Gibney, Pierre Collings** *The Story of Louis Pasteur* • Norman Krasna *Fury* • William Anthony McGuire *The Great Ziegfeld* • Robert Hopkins *San Francisco* • Adele Comandini *Three Smart Girls*

1937

Academy Awards

OUTSTANDING PRODUCTION: **The Life of Emile Zola** • *The Awful Truth* • *Captains Courageous* • *Dead End* • *The Good Earth* • *In Old Chicago* • *Lost Horizon* • *One Hundred Men and a Girl* • *Stage Door* • *A Star Is Born*
DIRECTING: **Leo McCarey** *The Awful Truth* • Sidney Franklin *The Good Earth* • William Dieterle *The Life of Emile Zola*

• Gregory La Cava *Stage Door* • William A Wellman *A Star Is Born*
ACTOR: **Spencer Tracy** *Captains Courageous* • Charles Boyer *Conquest* • Fredric March *A Star Is Born* • Robert Montgomery *Night Must Fall* • Paul Muni *The Life of Emile Zola*
ACTRESS: **Luise Rainer** *The Good Earth* • Irene Dunne *The Awful Truth* • Greta Garbo *Camille* • Janet Gaynor *A Star Is Born* • Barbara Stanwyck *Stella Dallas*
ACTOR IN A SUPPORTING ROLE: **Joseph Schildkraut** *The Life of Emile Zola* • Ralph Bellamy *The Awful Truth* • Thomas Mitchell *The Hurricane* • H B Warner *Lost Horizon* • Roland Young *Topper*
ACTRESS IN A SUPPORTING ROLE: **Alice Brady** *In Old Chicago* • Andrea Leeds *Stage Door* • Anne Shirley *Stella Dallas* • Claire Trevor *Dead End* • Dame May Whitty *Night Must Fall*
WRITING (SCREENPLAY): **Norman Reilly Raine**, **Heinz Herald**, **Geza Herczeg** *The Life of Emile Zola* • Vina Delmar *The Awful Truth* • Marc Connelly, Dale Van Every, John Lee Mahin *Captains Courageous* • Morrie Ryskind, Anthony Veiller *Stage Door* • Alan Campbell, Robert Carson, Dorothy Parker *A Star Is Born*
WRITING (ORIGINAL STORY): **William A Wellman**, **Robert Carson** *A Star Is Born* • Robert Lord *The Black Legion* • Niven Busch *In Old Chicago* • Heinz Herald, Geza Herczeg *The Life of Emile Zola* • Hans Kräly *One Hundred Men and a Girl*

1938

Academy Awards

OUTSTANDING PRODUCTION: ***You Can't Take It with You*** • *The Adventures of Robin Hood* • *Alexander's Ragtime Band* • *Boys Town* • *The Citadel* • *Four Daughters* • *La Grande Illusion* • *Jezebel* • *Pygmalion* • *Test Pilot*
DIRECTING: **Frank Capra** *You Can't Take It with You* • Michael Curtiz *Angels with Dirty Faces* • Norman Taurog *Boys Town* • King Vidor *The Citadel* • Michael Curtiz *Four Daughters*
ACTOR: **Spencer Tracy** *Boys Town* • Charles Boyer *Algiers* • James Cagney *Angels with Dirty Faces* • Robert Donat *The Citadel* • Leslie Howard *Pygmalion*
ACTRESS: **Bette Davis** *Jezebel* • Fay Bainter *White Banners* • Wendy Hiller *Pygmalion* • Norma Shearer *Marie Antoinette* • Margaret Sullavan *Three Comrades*
ACTOR IN A SUPPORTING ROLE: **Walter Brennan** *Kentucky* • John Garfield *Four Daughters* • Gene Lockhart *Algiers* • Robert Morley *Marie Antoinette* • Basil Rathbone *If I Were King*
ACTRESS IN A SUPPORTING ROLE: **Fay Bainter** *Jezebel* • Beulah Bondi *Of Human Hearts* • Billie Burke *Merrily We Live* • Spring Byington *You Can't Take It with You* • Miliza Korjus *The Great Waltz*
WRITING (SCREENPLAY): **Ian Dalrymple**, **Cecil Lewis**, **W P Lipscomb**, **George Bernard Shaw** *Pygmalion* • John Meehan, Dore Schary *Boys Town* • Ian Dalrymple, Elizabeth Hill, Frank Wead *The Citadel* • Julius J Epstein, Lenore Coffee *Four Daughters* • Robert Riskin *You Can't Take It with You*
WRITING (ORIGINAL STORY): **Dore Schary**, **Eleanore Griffin** *Boys Town* • Irving Berlin *Alexander's Ragtime Band* • Rowland Brown *Angels with Dirty Faces* • John Howard Lawson *Blockade* • Marcella Burke, Frederick Kohner *Mad about Music* • Frank Wead *Test Pilot*

1939

Academy Awards

OUTSTANDING PRODUCTION: ***Gone with the Wind*** • *Dark Victory* • *Goodbye, Mr Chips* • *Love Affair* • *Mr Smith Goes to Washington* • *Ninotchka* • *Of Mice and Men* • *Stagecoach* • *The Wizard of Oz* • *Wuthering Heights*
DIRECTING: **Victor Fleming** *Gone with the Wind* • Sam Wood *Goodbye, Mr Chips* • Frank Capra *Mr Smith Goes to Washington* • John Ford *Stagecoach* • William Wyler *Wuthering Heights*
ACTOR: **Robert Donat** *Goodbye, Mr Chips* • Clark Gable *Gone with the Wind* • Laurence Olivier *Wuthering Heights* • Mickey Rooney *Babes in Arms* • James Stewart *Mr Smith Goes to Washington*
ACTRESS: **Vivien Leigh** *Gone with the Wind* • Bette Davis *Dark Victory* • Irene Dunne *Love Affair* • Greta Garbo *Ninotchka* • Greer Garson *Goodbye, Mr Chips*
ACTOR IN A SUPPORTING ROLE: **Thomas Mitchell** *Stagecoach* • Harry Carey, Claude Rains *Mr Smith Goes to Washington* • Brian Aherne *Juarez* • Brian Donlevy *Beau Geste*
ACTRESS IN A SUPPORTING ROLE: **Hattie McDaniel**, Olivia de Havilland *Gone with the Wind* • Geraldine Fitzgerald *Wuthering Heights* • Edna May Oliver *Drums along the Mohawk* • Maria Ouspenskaya *Love Affair*
WRITING (SCREENPLAY): **Sidney Howard** *Gone with the Wind* • R C Sherriff, Claudine West, Eric Maschwitz *Goodbye, Mr Chips* • Sidney Buchman *Mr Smith Goes to Washington* • Charles Brackett, Walter Reisch, Billy Wilder *Ninotchka* • Ben Hecht, Charles MacArthur *Wuthering Heights*
WRITING (ORIGINAL STORY): **Sidney Buchman** *Mr Smith Goes to Washington* • Felix Jackson *Bachelor Mother* • Mildred Cram, Leo McCarey *Love Affair* • Melchior Lengyel *Ninotchka* • Lamar Trotti *Young Mr Lincoln*

194

Golden Globe Awards

BEST MOTION PICTURE DRAMA: ***Gentleman's Agreement***

1940

Academy Awards

OUTSTANDING PRODUCTION: ***Rebecca*** • *All This, and Heaven Too* • *Foreign Correspondent* • *The Grapes of Wrath* • *The Great Dictator* • *Kitty Foyle* • *The Letter* • *The Long Voyage Home* • *Our Town* • *The Philadelphia Story*
DIRECTING: **John Ford** *The Grapes of Wrath* • Sam Wood *Kitty Foyle* • William Wyler *The Letter* • George Cukor *The Philadelphia Story* • Alfred Hitchcock *Rebecca*
ACTOR: **James Stewart** *The Philadelphia Story* • Charles Chaplin *The Great Dictator* • Henry Fonda *The Grapes of Wrath* • Raymond Massey *Abe Lincoln in Illinois* • Laurence Olivier *Rebecca*
ACTRESS: **Ginger Rogers** *Kitty Foyle* • Bette Davis *The Letter* • Joan Fontaine *Rebecca* • Katharine Hepburn *The Philadelphia Story* • Martha Scott *Our Town*
ACTOR IN A SUPPORTING ROLE: **Walter Brennan** *The Westerner* • Albert Basserman *Foreign Correspondent* • William Gargan *They Knew What They Wanted* • Jack Oakie *The Great Dictator* • James Stephenson *The Letter*
ACTRESS IN A SUPPORTING ROLE: **Jane Darwell** *The Grapes of Wrath* • Judith Anderson *Rebecca* • Ruth Hussey *The Philadelphia Story* • Barbara O'Neil *All This, and Heaven Too* • Marjorie Rambeau *Primrose Path*
WRITING (ORIGINAL SCREENPLAY): **Preston Sturges** *The Great McGinty* • Ben Hecht *Angels over Broadway* • Norman Burnside, Heinz Herald, John Huston *Dr Ehrlich's Magic Bullet* • Charles Bennett, Joan Harrison *Foreign Correspondent* • Charles Chaplin *The Great Dictator*
WRITING (SCREENPLAY): **Donald Ogden Stewart** *The Philadelphia Story* • Nunnally Johnson *The Grapes of Wrath* • Dalton Trumbo *Kitty Foyle* • Dudley Nichols *The Long Voyage Home* • Robert E Sherwood, Joan Harrison *Rebecca*
WRITING (ORIGINAL STORY): **Benjamin Glazer**, **John S Toldy** *Arise, My Love* • Walter Reisch *Comrade X* • Dore Schary, Hugo Butler *Edison, the Man* • Leo McCarey, Bella Spewack, Sam Spewack *My Favorite Wife* • Stuart N Lake *The Westerner*

1941

Academy Awards

OUTSTANDING MOTION PICTURE: ***How Green Was My Valley*** • *Blossoms in the Dust* • *Citizen Kane* • *Here Comes Mr Jordan* • *Hold Back the Dawn* • *The Little Foxes* • *The Maltese Falcon* • *One Foot in Heaven* • *Sergeant York* • *Suspicion*
DIRECTING: **John Ford** *How Green Was My Valley* • Orson Welles *Citizen Kane* • Alexander Hall *Here Comes Mr Jordan* • William Wyler *The Little Foxes* • Howard Hawks *Sergeant York*
ACTOR: **Gary Cooper** *Sergeant York* • Cary Grant *Penny Serenade* • Walter Huston *Daniel and the Devil* • Robert Montgomery *Here Comes Mr Jordan* • Orson Welles *Citizen Kane*
ACTRESS: **Joan Fontaine** *Suspicion* • Bette Davis *The Little Foxes* • Olivia de Havilland *Hold Back the Dawn* • Greer Garson *Blossoms in the Dust* • Barbara Stanwyck *Ball of Fire*
ACTOR IN A SUPPORTING ROLE: **Donald Crisp** *How Green Was My Valley* • Walter Brennan *Sergeant York* • Charles Coburn *The Devil and Miss Jones* • James Gleason *Here Comes Mr Jordan* • Sydney Greenstreet *The Maltese Falcon*
ACTRESS IN A SUPPORTING ROLE: **Mary Astor** *The Great Lie* • Patricia Collinge, Teresa Wright *The Little Foxes* • Sara Allgood *How Green Was My Valley* • Margaret Wycherly *Sergeant York*
WRITING (ORIGINAL SCREENPLAY): **Herman J Mankiewicz**, **Orson Welles** *Citizen Kane* • Norman Krasna *The Devil and Miss Jones* • Abem Finkel, Harry Chandlee, Howard Koch, John Huston *Sergeant York* • Karl Tunberg, Darrell Ware *Tall, Dark and Handsome* • Paul Jarrico *Tom, Dick and Harry*
WRITING (SCREENPLAY): **Sidney Buchman**, **Seton I Miller** *Here Comes Mr Jordan* • Charles Brackett, Billy Wilder *Hold Back the Dawn* • Philip Dunne *How Green Was My Valley* • Lillian Hellman *The Little Foxes* • John Huston *The Maltese Falcon*
WRITING (ORIGINAL STORY): **Harry Segall** *Here Comes Mr Jordan* • Thomas Monroe, Billy Wilder *Ball of Fire* • Monckton Hoffe *The Lady Eve* • Robert Presnell, Richard Connell *Meet John Doe* • Gordon Wellesley *Night Train to Munich*

1942

Academy Awards

OUTSTANDING MOTION PICTURE: ***Mrs Miniver*** • *49th Parallel* • *Kings Row* • *The Magnificent Ambersons* • *The Pied Piper* • *The Pride of the Yankees* • *Random Harvest* • *The Talk of the Town* • *Wake Island* • *Yankee Doodle Dandy*
DIRECTING: **William Wyler** *Mrs Miniver* • Sam Wood *Kings Row* • Mervyn LeRoy *Random Harvest* • John Farrow *Wake Island* • Michael Curtiz *Yankee Doodle Dandy*
ACTOR: **James Cagney** *Yankee Doodle Dandy* • Gary Cooper *The Pride of the Yankees* • Ronald Colman *Random Harvest* • Walter Pidgeon *Mrs Miniver* • Monty Woolley *The Pied Piper*
ACTRESS: **Greer Garson** *Mrs Miniver* • Bette Davis *Now, Voyager* • Katharine Hepburn *Woman of the Year* • Rosalind Russell *My Sister Eileen* • Teresa Wright *The Pride of the Yankees*
ACTOR IN A SUPPORTING ROLE: **Van Heflin** *Johnny Eager* • William Bendix *Wake Island* • Walter Huston *Yankee Doodle Dandy* • Frank Morgan *Tortilla Flat* • Henry Travers *Mrs Miniver*
ACTRESS IN A SUPPORTING ROLE: **Teresa Wright**, Dame May Whitty *Mrs Miniver* • Gladys Cooper *Now, Voyager* • Agnes Moorehead *The Magnificent Ambersons* • Susan Peters *Random Harvest*
WRITING (ORIGINAL SCREENPLAY): **Michael Kanin**, **Ring Lardner Jr** *Woman of the Year* • Michael Powell, Emeric Pressburger *One of Our Aircraft Is Missing* • Don Hartman, Frank Butler *Road to Morocco* • W R Burnett, Frank Butler *Wake Island* • George Oppenheimer *The War against Mrs Hadley*
WRITING (SCREENPLAY): **Arthur Wimperis**, **George Froeschel**, **James Hilton**, **Claudine West** *Mrs Miniver* • Emeric Pressburger, Rodney Ackland *49th Parallel* • Herman J Mankiewicz, Jo Swerling *The Pride of the Yankees* • George Froeschel, Claudine West, Arthur Wimperis *Random Harvest* • Irwin Shaw, Sidney Buchman *The Talk of the Town*
WRITING (ORIGINAL MOTION PICTURE STORY): **Emeric Pressburger** *49th Parallel* • Irving Berlin *Holiday Inn* • Paul Gallico *The Pride of the Yankees* • Sidney Harmon *The Talk of the Town* • Robert Buckner *Yankee Doodle Dandy*

1943

Academy Awards

OUTSTANDING MOTION PICTURE: ***Casablanca*** • *For Whom the Bell Tolls* • *Heaven Can Wait* • *The Human Comedy* • *In Which We Serve* • *Madame Curie* • *The More the Merrier* • *The Ox-Bow Incident* • *The Song of Bernadette* • *Watch on the Rhine*
DIRECTING: **Michael Curtiz** *Casablanca* • Ernst Lubitsch *Heaven Can Wait* • Clarence Brown *The Human Comedy* • George Stevens *The More the Merrier* • Henry King *The Song of Bernadette*
ACTOR: **Paul Lukas** *Watch on the Rhine* • Humphrey Bogart *Casablanca* • Gary Cooper *For Whom the Bell Tolls* • Walter Pidgeon *Madame Curie* • Mickey Rooney *The Human Comedy*
ACTRESS: **Jennifer Jones** *The Song of Bernadette* • Jean Arthur *The More the Merrier* • Ingrid Bergman *For Whom the Bell Tolls* • Joan Fontaine *The Constant Nymph* • Greer Garson *Madame Curie*
ACTOR IN A SUPPORTING ROLE: **Charles Coburn** *The More the Merrier* • Charles Bickford *The Song of Bernadette* • J

Carrol Naish *Sahara* • Claude Rains *Casablanca* • Akim Tamiroff *For Whom the Bell Tolls*

ACTRESS IN A SUPPORTING ROLE: **Katina Paxinou** *For Whom the Bell Tolls* • Gladys Cooper, Anne Revere *The Song of Bernadette* • Paulette Goddard *So Proudly We Hail* • Lucile Watson *Watch on the Rhine*

WRITING (ORIGINAL SCREENPLAY): **Norman Krasna** *Princess O'Rourke* • Dudley Nichols *Air Force* • Noël Coward *In Which We Serve* • Lillian Hellman *The North Star* • Allan Scott *So Proudly We Hail*

WRITING (SCREENPLAY): **Philip G Epstein, Julius J Epstein, Howard Koch** *Casablanca* • Nunnally Johnson *Holy Matrimony* • Robert Russell, Frank Ross, Richard Flournoy, Lewis R Foster *The More the Merrier* • George Seaton *The Song of Bernadette* • Dashiell Hammett *Watch on the Rhine*

WRITING (ORIGINAL MOTION PICTURE STORY): **William Saroyan** *The Human Comedy* • Guy Gilpatric *Action in the North Atlantic* • Steve Fisher *Destination Tokyo* • Robert Russell, Frank Ross *The More the Merrier* • Gordon McDonell *Shadow of a Doubt*

Golden Globe Awards

BEST MOTION PICTURE DRAMA: ***The Song of Bernadette***

BEST PERFORMANCE BY AN ACTOR IN A MOTION PICTURE DRAMA: **Paul Lukas** *Watch on the Rhine*

BEST PERFORMANCE BY AN ACTRESS IN A MOTION PICTURE DRAMA: **Jennifer Jones** *The Song of Bernadette*

BEST PERFORMANCE BY AN ACTOR IN A SUPPORTING ROLE MOTION PICTURE: **Akim Tamiroff** *For Whom the Bell Tolls*

BEST PERFORMANCE BY AN ACTRESS IN A SUPPORTING ROLE MOTION PICTURE: **Katina Paxinou** *For Whom the Bell Tolls*

1944

Academy Awards

BEST MOTION PICTURE: ***Going My Way*** • *Double Indemnity* • *Gaslight* • *Since You Went Away* • *Wilson*

DIRECTING: **Leo McCarey** *Going My Way* • Billy Wilder *Double Indemnity* • Otto Preminger *Laura* • Alfred Hitchcock *Lifeboat* • Henry King *Wilson*

ACTOR: **Bing Crosby** *Going My Way* • Charles Boyer *Gaslight* • Barry Fitzgerald *Going My Way* • Cary Grant *None but the Lonely Heart* • Alexander Knox *Wilson*

ACTRESS: **Ingrid Bergman** *Gaslight* • Claudette Colbert *Since You Went Away* • Bette Davis *Mr Skeffington* • Greer Garson *Mrs Parkington* • Barbara Stanwyck *Double Indemnity*

ACTOR IN A SUPPORTING ROLE: **Barry Fitzgerald** *Going My Way* • Hume Cronyn *The Seventh Cross* • Claude Rains *Mr Skeffington* • Clifton Webb *Laura* • Monty Woolley *Since You Went Away*

ACTRESS IN A SUPPORTING ROLE: **Ethel Barrymore** *None but the Lonely Heart* • Jennifer Jones *Since You Went Away* • Angela Lansbury *Gaslight* • Aline MacMahon *Dragon Seed* • Agnes Moorehead *Mrs Parkington*

WRITING (ORIGINAL SCREENPLAY): **Lamar Trotti** *Wilson* • Preston Sturges *Hail the Conquering Hero* • Preston Sturges *The Miracle of Morgan's Creek* • Richard Connell, Gladys Lehman *Two Girls and a Sailor* • Jerome Cady *Wing and a Prayer*

WRITING (SCREENPLAY): **Frank Butler, Frank Cavett** *Going My Way* • Billy Wilder, Raymond Chandler *Double Indemnity* • Walter Reisch, John L Balderston, John Van Druten *Gaslight* • Jay Dratler, Betty Reinhardt, Samuel Hoffenstein *Laura* • Irving Brecher, Fred F Finklehoffe *Meet Me in St Louis*

WRITING (ORIGINAL MOTION PICTURE STORY): **Leo McCarey** *Going My Way* • Chandler Sprague, David Boehm *A Guy Named Joe* • John Steinbeck *Lifeboat* • Alfred Neumann, Joseph Than *None Shall Escape* • Edward Doherty, Jules Schermer *The Fighting Sullivans*

Golden Globe Awards

BEST MOTION PICTURE DRAMA: ***Going My Way***

BEST DIRECTOR MOTION PICTURE: **Leo McCarey** *Going My Way*

BEST PERFORMANCE BY AN ACTOR IN A MOTION PICTURE DRAMA: **Alexander Knox** *Wilson*

BEST PERFORMANCE BY AN ACTRESS IN A MOTION PICTURE DRAMA: **Ingrid Bergman** *Gaslight*

BEST PERFORMANCE BY AN ACTOR IN A SUPPORTING ROLE MOTION PICTURE: **Barry Fitzgerald** *Going My Way*

BEST PERFORMANCE BY AN ACTRESS IN A SUPPORTING ROLE MOTION PICTURE: **Agnes Moorehead** *Mrs Parkington*

1945

Academy Awards

BEST MOTION PICTURE: ***The Lost Weekend*** • *Anchors Aweigh* • *The Bells of St Mary's* • *Mildred Pierce* • *Spellbound*

DIRECTING: **Billy Wilder** *The Lost Weekend* • Leo McCarey *The Bells of St Mary's* • Clarence Brown *National Velvet* • Jean Renoir *The Southerner* • Alfred Hitchcock *Spellbound*

ACTOR: **Ray Milland** *The Lost Weekend* • Bing Crosby *The Bells of St Mary's* • Gene Kelly *Anchors Aweigh* • Gregory Peck *The Keys of the Kingdom* • Cornel Wilde *A Song to Remember*

ACTRESS: **Joan Crawford** *Mildred Pierce* • Ingrid Bergman *The Bells of St Mary's* • Greer Garson *The Valley of Decision* • Jennifer Jones *Love Letters* • Gene Tierney *Leave Her to Heaven*

ACTOR IN A SUPPORTING ROLE: **James Dunn** *A Tree Grows in Brooklyn* • Michael Chekhov *Spellbound* • John Dall *The Corn Is Green* • Robert Mitchum *The Story of GI Joe* • J Carrol Naish *A Medal for Benny*

ACTRESS IN A SUPPORTING ROLE: **Anne Revere** *National Velvet* • Eve Arden, Ann Blyth *Mildred Pierce* • Angela Lansbury *The Picture of Dorian Gray* • Joan Lorring *The Corn Is Green*

WRITING (ORIGINAL SCREENPLAY): **Richard Schweizer** *Marie-Louise* • Phil Yordan *Dillinger* • Myles Connolly *Music for Millions* • Milton Holmes *Salty O'Rourke* • Harry Kurnitz *See Here, Private Hargrove*

WRITING (SCREENPLAY): **Charles Brackett, Billy Wilder** *The Lost Weekend* • Leopold Atlas, Guy Endore, Philip Stevenson *The Story of GI Joe* • Ranald MacDougall *Mildred Pierce* • Albert Maltz *Pride of the Marines* • Frank Davis, Tess Slesinger *A Tree Grows in Brooklyn*

WRITING (ORIGINAL MOTION PICTURE STORY): **Charles G Booth** *The House on 92nd Street* • Thomas Monroe, Laszlo Gorog *The Affairs of Susan* • John Steinbeck, Jack Wagner *A Medal for Benny* • Alvah Bessie *Objective, Burma!* • Ernst Marischka *A Song to Remember*

Golden Globe Awards

BEST MOTION PICTURE DRAMA: ***The Lost Weekend***

BEST DIRECTOR MOTION PICTURE: **Billy Wilder** *The Lost Weekend*

BEST PERFORMANCE BY AN ACTOR IN A MOTION PICTURE DRAMA: **Ray Milland** *The Lost Weekend*

BEST PERFORMANCE BY AN ACTRESS IN A MOTION PICTURE DRAMA: **Ingrid Bergman** *The Bells of St Mary's*

BEST PERFORMANCE BY AN ACTOR IN A SUPPORTING ROLE MOTION PICTURE: **J Carrol Naish** *A Medal for Benny*

BEST PERFORMANCE BY AN ACTRESS IN A SUPPORTING ROLE MOTION PICTURE: **Angela Lansbury** *The Picture of Dorian Gray*

1946

Academy Awards

BEST MOTION PICTURE: ***The Best Years of Our Lives*** • *Henry V* • *It's a Wonderful Life* • *The Razor's Edge* • *The Yearling*

DIRECTING: **William Wyler** *The Best Years of Our Lives* • David Lean *Brief Encounter* • Frank Capra *It's a Wonderful Life* • Robert Siodmak *The Killers* • Clarence Brown *The Yearling*

ACTOR: **Fredric March** *The Best Years of Our Lives* • Laurence Olivier *Henry V* • Larry Parks *The Jolson Story* • Gregory Peck *The Yearling* • James Stewart *It's a Wonderful Life*

ACTRESS: **Olivia de Havilland** *To Each His Own* • Celia Johnson *Brief Encounter* • Jennifer Jones *Duel in the Sun* • Rosalind Russell *Sister Kenny* • Jane Wyman *The Yearling*

ACTOR IN A SUPPORTING ROLE: **Harold Russell** *The Best Years of Our Lives* • Charles Coburn *The Green Years* • William Demarest *The Jolson Story* • Claude Rains *Notorious* • Clifton Webb *The Razor's Edge*

ACTRESS IN A SUPPORTING ROLE: **Anne Baxter** *The Razor's Edge* • Ethel Barrymore *The Spiral Staircase* • Lillian Gish *Duel in the Sun* • Flora Robson *Saratoga Trunk* • Gale Sondergaard *Anna and the King of Siam*

WRITING (ORIGINAL SCREENPLAY): **Sydney Box, Muriel Box** *The Seventh Veil* • Raymond Chandler *The Blue Dahlia* • Jacques Prévert *Les Enfants du Paradis* • Ben Hecht *Notorious* • Melvin Frank, Norman Panama *Road to Utopia*

WRITING (SCREENPLAY): **Robert E Sherwood** *The Best Years of Our Lives* • Talbot Jennings, Sally Benson *Anna and the King of Siam* • David Lean, Anthony Havelock-Allan,

Ronald Neame *Brief Encounter* • Anthony Veiller *The Killers* • Sergio Amidei, Federico Fellini *Rome, Open City*

WRITING (ORIGINAL MOTION PICTURE STORY): **Clemence Dane** *Perfect Strangers* • Vladimir Pozner *The Dark Mirror* • Jack Patrick *The Strange Love of Martha Ivers* • Victor Trivas *The Stranger* • Charles Brackett *To Each His Own*

Golden Globe Awards

BEST MOTION PICTURE DRAMA: ***The Best Years of Our Lives***

BEST DIRECTOR MOTION PICTURE: **Frank Capra** *It's a Wonderful Life*

BEST PERFORMANCE BY AN ACTOR IN A MOTION PICTURE DRAMA: **Gregory Peck** *The Yearling*

BEST PERFORMANCE BY AN ACTRESS IN A MOTION PICTURE DRAMA: **Rosalind Russell** *Sister Kenny*

BEST PERFORMANCE BY AN ACTOR IN A SUPPORTING ROLE MOTION PICTURE: **Clifton Webb** *The Razor's Edge*

BEST PERFORMANCE BY AN ACTRESS IN A SUPPORTING ROLE MOTION PICTURE: **Anne Baxter** *The Razor's Edge*

Cannes International Film Festival

INTERNATIONAL JURY PRIZE: ***La Bataille du Rail***

DIRECTOR: **René Clément** *La Bataille du Rail*

ACTOR: **Ray Milland** *The Lost Weekend*

ACTRESS: **Michèle Morgan** *La Symphonie Pastorale*

SCREENPLAY: **Boris Tchirkov** *The Turning Point*

1947

British Film Academy Awards

BEST FILM FROM ANY SOURCE, BRITISH OR FOREIGN: ***The Best Years of Our Lives***

BEST BRITISH FILM: ***Odd Man Out***

Academy Awards

BEST MOTION PICTURE: ***Gentleman's Agreement*** • *The Bishop's Wife* • *Crossfire* • *Great Expectations* • *Miracle on 34th Street*

DIRECTING: **Elia Kazan** *Gentleman's Agreement* • Henry Koster *The Bishop's Wife* • Edward Dmytryk *Crossfire* • George Cukor *A Double Life* • David Lean *Great Expectations*

ACTOR: **Ronald Colman** *A Double Life* • John Garfield *Body and Soul* • Gregory Peck *Gentleman's Agreement* • William Powell *Life with Father* • Michael Redgrave *Mourning Becomes Electra*

ACTRESS: **Loretta Young** *The Farmer's Daughter* • Joan Crawford *Possessed* • Susan Hayward *Smash-Up, the Story of a Woman* • Dorothy McGuire *Gentleman's Agreement* • Rosalind Russell *Mourning Becomes Electra*

ACTOR IN A SUPPORTING ROLE: **Edmund Gwenn** *Miracle on 34th Street* • Charles Bickford *The Farmer's Daughter* • Thomas Gomez *Ride the Pink Horse* • Robert Ryan *Crossfire* • Richard Widmark *Kiss of Death*

ACTRESS IN A SUPPORTING ROLE: **Celeste Holm**, Anne Revere *Gentleman's Agreement* • Ethel Barrymore *The Paradine Case* • Gloria Grahame *Crossfire* • Marjorie Main *The Egg and I*

WRITING (ORIGINAL SCREENPLAY): **Sidney Sheldon** *Bachelor Knight* • Abraham Polonsky *Body and Soul* • Ruth Gordon, Garson Kanin *A Double Life* • Charles Chaplin *Monsieur Verdoux* • Cesare Zavattini, Adolfo Franci, Sergio Amidei, Cesare Giulio Viola *Shoeshine*

WRITING (SCREENPLAY): **George Seaton** *Miracle on 34th Street* • Richard Murphy *Boomerang!* • John Paxton *Crossfire* • Moss Hart *Gentleman's Agreement* • Ronald Neame, Anthony Havelock-Allan, David Lean *Great Expectations*

WRITING (MOTION PICTURE STORY): **Valentine Davies** *Miracle on 34th Street* • Georges Chaperot, René Wheeler *A Cage of Nightingales* • Herbert Clyde Lewis, Frederick Stephani *It Happened on Fifth Avenue* • Eleazar Lipsky *Kiss of Death* • Frank Cavett, Dorothy Parker *Smash-Up, the Story of a Woman*

Golden Globe Awards

BEST DIRECTOR MOTION PICTURE: **Elia Kazan** *Gentleman's Agreement*

BEST PERFORMANCE BY AN ACTOR IN A MOTION PICTURE DRAMA: **Ronald Colman** *A Double Life*

BEST PERFORMANCE BY AN ACTRESS IN A MOTION PICTURE DRAMA: **Rosalind Russell** *Mourning Becomes Electra*

BEST PERFORMANCE BY AN ACTOR IN A SUPPORTING ROLE MOTION PICTURE: **Edmund Gwenn** *Miracle on 34th Street*

BEST PERFORMANCE BY AN ACTRESS IN A SUPPORTING ROLE MOTION PICTURE: **Celeste Holm** *Gentleman's Agreement*

BEST SCREENPLAY MOTION PICTURE: **George Seaton** *Miracle on 34th Street*

Cannes International Film Festival

GRAND PRIX PSYCHOLOGICAL AND ROMANTIC FILMS: **Antoine et Antoinette**
GRAND PRIX ADVENTURE AND CRIME FILMS: **Les Maudits**
GRAND PRIX SOCIAL FILMS: **Crossfire**
GRAND PRIX MUSICAL COMEDIES: **Ziegfeld Follies**
GRAND PRIX ANIMATED FILMS: **Dumbo**
GRAND PRIX DOCUMENTARIES: **Inondations en Pologne**

1948

British Film Academy Awards

BEST FILM FROM ANY SOURCE, BRITISH OR FOREIGN: **Hamlet** • *Crossfire* • *The Fallen Idol* • *Four Steps in the Clouds* • *Monsieur Vincent* • *The Naked City* • *Paisà*
BEST BRITISH FILM: **The Fallen Idol** • *Hamlet* • *Oliver Twist* • *Once a Jolly Swagman* • *The Red Shoes* • *Scott of the Antarctic* • *The Small Voice*

Academy Awards

BEST MOTION PICTURE: **Hamlet** • *Johnny Belinda* • *The Red Shoes* • *The Snake Pit* • *The Treasure of the Sierra Madre*
HONORARY FOREIGN LANGUAGE FILM AWARD: **Monsieur Vincent**
DIRECTING: **John Huston** *The Treasure of the Sierra Madre* • Laurence Olivier *Hamlet* • Jean Negulesco *Johnny Belinda* • Fred Zinnemann *The Search* • Anatole Litvak *The Snake Pit*
ACTOR: **Laurence Olivier** *Hamlet* • Lew Ayres *Johnny Belinda* • Montgomery Clift *The Search* • Dan Dailey *When My Baby Smiles at Me* • Clifton Webb *Sitting Pretty*
ACTRESS: **Jane Wyman** *Johnny Belinda* • Ingrid Bergman *Joan of Arc* • Olivia de Havilland *The Snake Pit* • Irene Dunne *I Remember Mama* • Barbara Stanwyck *Sorry, Wrong Number*
ACTOR IN A SUPPORTING ROLE: **Walter Huston** *The Treasure of the Sierra Madre* • Charles Bickford *Johnny Belinda* • José Ferrer *Joan of Arc* • Oscar Homolka *I Remember Mama* • Cecil Kellaway *The Luck of the Irish*
ACTRESS IN A SUPPORTING ROLE: **Claire Trevor** *Key Largo* • Barbara Bel Geddes, Ellen Corby *I Remember Mama* • Agnes Moorehead *Johnny Belinda* • Jean Simmons *Hamlet*
WRITING (SCREENPLAY): **John Huston** *The Treasure of the Sierra Madre* • Charles Brackett, Billy Wilder, Richard Breen *A Foreign Affair* • Allen Vincent, Irmgard von Cube *Johnny Belinda* • Richard Schweizer, David Wechsler *The Search* • Frank Partos, Millen Brand *The Snake Pit*
WRITING (MOTION PICTURE STORY): **Richard Schweizer, David Wechsler** *The Search* • Robert Flaherty, Frances Flaherty *Louisiana Story* • Malvin Wald *The Naked City* • Borden Chase *Red River* • Emeric Pressburger *The Red Shoes*

Golden Globe Awards

BEST MOTION PICTURE DRAMA: **Johnny Belinda • The Treasure of the Sierra Madre**
BEST DIRECTOR MOTION PICTURE: **John Huston** *The Treasure of the Sierra Madre*
BEST PERFORMANCE BY AN ACTOR IN A MOTION PICTURE DRAMA: **Laurence Olivier** *Hamlet*
BEST PERFORMANCE BY AN ACTRESS IN A MOTION PICTURE DRAMA: **Jane Wyman** *Johnny Belinda*
BEST PERFORMANCE BY AN ACTOR IN A SUPPORTING ROLE MOTION PICTURE: **Walter Huston** *The Treasure of the Sierra Madre*
BEST PERFORMANCE BY AN ACTRESS IN A SUPPORTING ROLE MOTION PICTURE: **Ellen Corby** *I Remember Mama*
BEST SCREENPLAY MOTION PICTURE: **Richard Schweizer** *The Search*

1949

British Film Academy Awards

BEST FILM FROM ANY SOURCE: **Bicycle Thieves** • *Berliner Ballade* • *The Last Stage* • *The Set-Up* • *The Third Man* • *The Treasure of the Sierra Madre* • *The Window*
BEST BRITISH FILM: **The Third Man** • *Kind Hearts and Coronets* • *Passport to Pimlico* • *The Queen of Spades* • *A Run for Your Money* • *The Small Back Room* • *Whisky Galore!*

Academy Awards

BEST MOTION PICTURE: **All the King's Men** • *Battleground* • *The Heiress* • *A Letter to Three Wives* • *Twelve O'Clock High*
HONORARY FOREIGN LANGUAGE FILM AWARD: **Bicycle Thieves**

DIRECTING: **Joseph L Mankiewicz** *A Letter to Three Wives* • Robert Rossen *All the King's Men* • William A Wellman *Battleground* • Carol Reed *The Fallen Idol* • William Wyler *The Heiress*
ACTOR: **Broderick Crawford** *All the King's Men* • Kirk Douglas *Champion* • Gregory Peck *Twelve O'Clock High* • Richard Todd *The Hasty Heart* • John Wayne *Sands of Iwo Jima*
ACTRESS: **Olivia de Havilland** *The Heiress* • Jeanne Crain *Pinky* • Susan Hayward *My Foolish Heart* • Deborah Kerr *Edward, My Son* • Loretta Young *Come to the Stable*
ACTOR IN A SUPPORTING ROLE: **Dean Jagger** *Twelve O'Clock High* • John Ireland *All the King's Men* • Arthur Kennedy *Champion* • Ralph Richardson *The Heiress* • James Whitmore *Battleground*
ACTRESS IN A SUPPORTING ROLE: **Mercedes McCambridge** *All the King's Men* • Ethel Barrymore *Pinky* • Celeste Holm, Elsa Lanchester *Come to the Stable* • Ethel Waters *Pinky*
WRITING (STORY AND SCREENPLAY): **Robert Pirosh** *Battleground* • Sidney Buchman *Jolson Sings Again* • Sergio Amidei, Federico Fellini, Roberto Rossellini, Marcello Pagliero, Alfred Hayes *Paisà* • T E B Clarke *Passport to Pimlico* • Helen Levitt, Janice Loeb, Sidney Meyers *The Quiet One*
WRITING (SCREENPLAY): **Joseph L Mankiewicz** *A Letter to Three Wives* • Robert Rossen *All the King's Men* • Cesare Zavattini *Bicycle Thieves* • Carl Foreman *Champion* • Graham Greene *The Fallen Idol*
WRITING (MOTION PICTURE STORY): **Douglas Morrow** *The Stratton Story* • Clare Boothe Luce *Come to the Stable* • Valentine Davies, Shirley W Smith *It Happens Every Spring* • Harry Brown *Sands of Iwo Jima* • Virginia Kellogg *White Heat*

Golden Globe Awards

BEST MOTION PICTURE DRAMA: **All the King's Men**
BEST FOREIGN LANGUAGE FILM: **Bicycle Thieves**
BEST DIRECTOR MOTION PICTURE: **Robert Rossen** *All the King's Men*
BEST PERFORMANCE BY AN ACTOR IN A MOTION PICTURE DRAMA: **Broderick Crawford** *All the King's Men*
BEST PERFORMANCE BY AN ACTRESS IN A MOTION PICTURE DRAMA: **Olivia de Havilland** *The Heiress*
BEST PERFORMANCE BY AN ACTOR IN A SUPPORTING ROLE MOTION PICTURE: **James Whitmore** *Battleground*
BEST PERFORMANCE BY AN ACTRESS IN A SUPPORTING ROLE MOTION PICTURE: **Mercedes McCambridge** *All the King's Men*
BEST SCREENPLAY MOTION PICTURE: **Robert Pirosh** *Battleground*

Cannes International Film Festival

GRAND PRIX: **The Third Man**
DIRECTOR: **René Clément** *The Walls of Malapaga*
ACTOR: **Edward G Robinson** *House of Strangers*
ACTRESS: **Isa Miranda** *The Walls of Malapaga*
SCREENPLAY: **Alfred Werker** *Lost Boundaries*

1950

British Film Academy Awards

BEST FILM FROM ANY SOURCE: **All about Eve** • *The Asphalt Jungle* • *La Beauté du Diable* • *Intruder in the Dust* • *The Men* • *On the Town* • *Orphée*
BEST BRITISH FILM: **The Blue Lamp** • *Chance of a Lifetime* • *Morning Departure* • *Seven Days to Noon* • *State Secret* • *The Wooden Horse*

Academy Awards

BEST MOTION PICTURE: **All about Eve** • *Born Yesterday* • *Father of the Bride* • *King Solomon's Mines* • *Sunset Boulevard*
HONORARY FOREIGN LANGUAGE FILM AWARD: **The Walls of Malapaga**
DIRECTING: **Joseph L Mankiewicz** *All about Eve* • John Huston *The Asphalt Jungle* • George Cukor *Born Yesterday* • Billy Wilder *Sunset Boulevard* • Carol Reed *The Third Man*
ACTOR: **José Ferrer** *Cyrano de Bergerac* • Louis Calhern *The Magnificent Yankee* • William Holden *Sunset Boulevard* • James Stewart *Harvey* • Spencer Tracy *Father of the Bride*
ACTRESS: **Judy Holliday** *Born Yesterday* • Anne Baxter, Bette Davis *All about Eve* • Eleanor Parker *Caged* • Gloria Swanson *Sunset Boulevard*
ACTOR IN A SUPPORTING ROLE: **George Sanders** *All about Eve* • Jeff Chandler *Broken Arrow* • Edmund Gwenn *Mister 880* • Sam Jaffe *The Asphalt Jungle* • Erich von Stroheim *Sunset Boulevard*
ACTRESS IN A SUPPORTING ROLE: **Josephine Hull** *Harvey* • Celeste Holm, Thelma Ritter *All about Eve* • Hope Emerson *Caged* • Nancy Olson *Sunset Boulevard*

WRITING (STORY AND SCREENPLAY): **Billy Wilder, Charles Brackett, D M Marshman Jr** *Sunset Boulevard* • Ruth Gordon, Garson Kanin *Adam's Rib* • Virginia Kellogg, Bernard C Schoenfeld *Caged* • Carl Foreman *The Men* • Joseph L Mankiewicz, Lesser Samuels *No Way Out*
WRITING (SCREENPLAY): **Joseph L Mankiewicz** *All about Eve* • Ben Maddow, John Huston *The Asphalt Jungle* • Albert Mannheimer *Born Yesterday* • Albert Maltz *Broken Arrow* • Albert Hackett, Francis Goodrich *Father of the Bride*
WRITING (MOTION PICTURE STORY): **Edna Anhalt, Edward Anhalt** *Panic in the Streets* • Carlo Lizzani, Giuseppe De Santis *Bitter Rice* • William Bowers, Andre De Toth *The Gunfighter* • Leonard Spiegelgass *Mystery Street* • Sy Gomberg *When Willie Comes Marching Home*

Golden Globe Awards

BEST MOTION PICTURE DRAMA: **Sunset Boulevard**
BEST DIRECTOR MOTION PICTURE: **Billy Wilder** *Sunset Boulevard*
BEST PERFORMANCE BY AN ACTOR IN A MOTION PICTURE DRAMA: **José Ferrer** *Cyrano de Bergerac*
BEST PERFORMANCE BY AN ACTRESS IN A MOTION PICTURE DRAMA: **Gloria Swanson** *Sunset Boulevard*
BEST PERFORMANCE BY AN ACTOR IN A MOTION PICTURE COMEDY OR MUSICAL: **Fred Astaire** *Three Little Words*
BEST PERFORMANCE BY AN ACTRESS IN A MOTION PICTURE COMEDY OR MUSICAL: **Judy Holliday** *Born Yesterday*
BEST PERFORMANCE BY AN ACTOR IN A SUPPORTING ROLE MOTION PICTURE: **Edmund Gwenn** *Mister 880*
BEST PERFORMANCE BY AN ACTRESS IN A SUPPORTING ROLE MOTION PICTURE: **Josephine Hull** *Harvey*
BEST SCREENPLAY MOTION PICTURE: **Joseph L Mankiewicz** *All about Eve*

1951

British Film Academy Awards

BEST FILM FROM ANY SOURCE AND BEST BRITISH FILM: **La Ronde • The Lavender Hill Mob** • *An American in Paris* • *The Browning Version* • *Detective Story* • *Domenica d'Agosto* • *Edouard et Caroline* • *Fourteen Hours* • *The Magic Box* • *The Magic Garden* • *The Man in the White Suit* • *Miss Julie* • *Never Take No for an Answer* • *No Resting Place* • *The Red Badge of Courage* • *The Sound of Fury* • *A Walk in the Sun* • *White Corridors*

Academy Awards

BEST MOTION PICTURE: **An American in Paris** • *Decision before Dawn* • *A Place in the Sun* • *Quo Vadis* • *A Streetcar Named Desire*
HONORARY FOREIGN LANGUAGE FILM AWARD: **Rashomon**
DIRECTING: **George Stevens** *A Place in the Sun* • John Huston *The African Queen* • Vincente Minnelli *An American in Paris* • William Wyler *Detective Story* • Elia Kazan *A Streetcar Named Desire*
ACTOR: **Humphrey Bogart** *The African Queen* • Marlon Brando *A Streetcar Named Desire* • Montgomery Clift *A Place in the Sun* • Arthur Kennedy *Bright Victory* • Fredric March *Death of a Salesman*
ACTRESS: **Vivien Leigh** *A Streetcar Named Desire* • Katharine Hepburn *The African Queen* • Eleanor Parker *Detective Story* • Shelley Winters *A Place in the Sun* • Jane Wyman *The Blue Veil*
ACTOR IN A SUPPORTING ROLE: **Karl Malden** *A Streetcar Named Desire* • Leo Genn, Peter Ustinov *Quo Vadis* • Kevin McCarthy *Death of a Salesman* • Gig Young *Come Fill the Cup*
ACTRESS IN A SUPPORTING ROLE: **Kim Hunter** *A Streetcar Named Desire* • Joan Blondell *The Blue Veil* • Mildred Dunnock *Death of a Salesman* • Lee Grant *Detective Story* • Thelma Ritter *The Mating Season*
WRITING (STORY AND SCREENPLAY): **Alan Jay Lerner** *An American in Paris* • Billy Wilder, Lesser Samuels, Walter Newman *Ace in the Hole* • Philip Dunne *David and Bathsheba* • Robert Pirosh *Go for Broke!* • Clarence Greene, Russell Rouse *The Well*
WRITING (SCREENPLAY): **Michael Wilson, Harry Brown** *A Place in the Sun* • John Huston, James Agee *The African Queen* • Philip Yordan, Robert Wyler *Detective Story* • Max Ophüls, Jacques Natanson *La Ronde* • Tennessee Williams *A Streetcar Named Desire*
WRITING (MOTION PICTURE STORY): **James Bernard, Paul Dehn** *Seven Days to Noon* • Budd Boetticher, Ray Nazarro *The Bullfighter and the Lady* • Oscar Millard *The Frogmen* • Liam O'Brien, Robert Riskin *Here Comes the Groom* • Alfred Hayes, Stewart Stern *Teresa*

Golden Globe Awards

BEST MOTION PICTURE DRAMA: **A Place in the Sun**
BEST MOTION PICTURE COMEDY OR MUSICAL: **An American in Paris**
BEST DIRECTOR MOTION PICTURE: **Laslo Benedek** *Death of a Salesman*

Best Performance by an Actor in a Motion Picture Drama: **Fredric March** *Death of a Salesman*
Best Performance by an Actress in a Motion Picture Drama: **Jane Wyman** *The Blue Veil*
Best Performance by an Actor in a Motion Picture Comedy or Musical: **Danny Kaye** *On the Riviera*
Best Performance by an Actress in a Motion Picture Comedy or Musical: **June Allyson** *Too Young to Kiss*
Best Performance by an Actor in a Supporting Role Motion Picture: **Peter Ustinov** *Quo Vadis*
Best Performance by an Actress in a Supporting Role Motion Picture: **Kim Hunter** *A Streetcar Named Desire*
Best Screenplay Motion Picture: **Robert Buckner** *Bright Victory*

Cannes International Film Festival

Grand Prix: ***Miracle in Milan* • *Miss Julie***
Director: **Luis Buñuel** *Los Olvidados*
Actor: **Michael Redgrave** *The Browning Version*
Actress: **Bette Davis** *All about Eve*
Screenplay: **Terence Rattigan** *The Browning Version*

Berlin International Film Festival

Golden Berlin Bear (Dramatic Films): ***Four in a Jeep***
Golden Berlin Bear (Crime and Adventure Films): ***Justice Est Faite***
Golden Berlin Bear (Comedies): ***Sans Laisser l'Adresse***
Golden Berlin Bear (Musicals): ***Cinderella***

1952

British Film Academy Awards

Best Film from any Source and Best British Film: ***The Sound Barrier*** • *The African Queen* • *Angels One Five* • *The Boy Kumasenu* • *Carrie* • *Casque d'Or* • *Cry, the Beloved Country* • *Death of a Salesman* • *Limelight* • *Los Olvidados* • *Mandy* • *Miracle in Milan* • *Outcast of the Islands* • *Rashomon* • *The River* • *Singin' in the Rain* • *A Streetcar Named Desire* • *Viva Zapata!*
Best Foreign Actor: **Marlon Brando** *Viva Zapata!* • Humphrey Bogart *The African Queen* • Pierre Fresnay *Dieu a Besoin des Hommes* • Francesco Golisano *Miracle in Milan* • Fredric March *Death of a Salesman*
Best Foreign Actress: **Simone Signoret** *Casque d'Or* • Edwige Feuillière *Olivia* • Katharine Hepburn *Pat and Mike* • Judy Holliday *The Marrying Kind* • Nicole Stéphane *Les Enfants Terribles*
Best British Actor: **Ralph Richardson** *The Sound Barrier* • Jack Hawkins *Mandy* • James Hayter *The Pickwick Papers* • Laurence Olivier *Carrie* • Nigel Patrick *The Sound Barrier* • Alastair Sim *Folly to Be Wise*
Best British Actress: **Vivien Leigh** *A Streetcar Named Desire* • Phyllis Calvert *Mandy* • Celia Johnson *I Believe in You* • Ann Todd *The Sound Barrier*

Academy Awards

Best Motion Picture: ***The Greatest Show on Earth*** • *High Noon* • *Ivanhoe* • *Moulin Rouge* • *The Quiet Man*
Honorary Foreign Language Film Award: ***Les Jeux Interdits***
Directing: **John Ford** *The Quiet Man* • Joseph L Mankiewicz *5 Fingers* • Cecil B DeMille *The Greatest Show on Earth* • Fred Zinnemann *High Noon* • John Huston *Moulin Rouge*
Actor: **Gary Cooper** *High Noon* • Marlon Brando *Viva Zapata!* • Kirk Douglas *The Bad and the Beautiful* • José Ferrer *Moulin Rouge* • Alec Guinness *The Lavender Hill Mob*
Actress: **Shirley Booth** *Come Back, Little Sheba* • Joan Crawford *Sudden Fear* • Bette Davis *The Star* • Julie Harris *The Member of the Wedding* • Susan Hayward *With a Song in My Heart*
Actor in a Supporting Role: **Anthony Quinn** *Viva Zapata!* • Richard Burton *My Cousin Rachel* • Arthur Hunnicutt *The Big Sky* • Victor McLaglen *The Quiet Man* • Jack Palance *Sudden Fear*
Actress in a Supporting Role: **Gloria Grahame** *The Bad and the Beautiful* • Jean Hagen *Singin' in the Rain* • Colette Marchand *Moulin Rouge* • Terry Moore *Come Back, Little Sheba* • Thelma Ritter *With a Song in My Heart*
Writing (Story and Screenplay): **T E B Clarke** *The Lavender Hill Mob* • Sydney Boehm *The Atomic City* • Terence Rattigan *The Sound Barrier* • Ruth Gordon, Garson Kanin *Pat and Mike* • John Steinbeck *Viva Zapata!*
Writing (Screenplay): **Charles Schnee** *The Bad and the Beautiful* • Michael Wilson *5 Fingers* • Carl Foreman *High Noon* • Roger Macdougall, John Dighton, Alexander Mackendrick *The Man in the White Suit* • Frank S Nugent *The Quiet Man*
Writing (Motion Picture Story): **Frank Cavett**, **Fredric M Frank**, **Theodore St John** *The Greatest Show on Earth* • Leo McCarey *My Son John* • Martin Goldsmith, Jack Leonard *The Narrow Margin* • Guy Trosper *The Pride of St Louis* • Edward Anhalt, Edna Anhalt *The Sniper*

Golden Globe Awards

Best Motion Picture Drama: ***The Greatest Show on Earth***
Best Motion Picture Comedy or Musical: ***With a Song in My Heart***
Best Director Motion Picture: **Cecil B DeMille** *The Greatest Show on Earth*
Best Performance by an Actor in a Motion Picture Drama: **Gary Cooper** *High Noon*
Best Performance by an Actress in a Motion Picture Drama: **Shirley Booth** *Come Back, Little Sheba*
Best Performance by an Actor in a Motion Picture Comedy or Musical: **Donald O'Connor** *Singin' in the Rain*
Best Performance by an Actress in a Motion Picture Comedy or Musical: **Susan Hayward** *With a Song in My Heart*
Best Performance by an Actor in a Supporting Role Motion Picture: **Millard Mitchell** *My Six Convicts*
Best Performance by an Actress in a Supporting Role Motion Picture: **Katy Jurado** *High Noon*
Best Screenplay Motion Picture: **Michael Wilson** *5 Fingers*

Cannes International Film Festival

Grand Prix: ***Two Pennyworth of Hope* • *Othello***
Director: **Christian-Jaque** *Fanfan la Tulipe*
Actor: **Marlon Brando** *Viva Zapata!*
Actress: **Lee Grant** *Detective Story*
Screenplay: **Piero Tellini** *Guardie e Ladri*

Berlin International Film Festival

Golden Berlin Bear: ***One Summer of Happiness***

1953

British Film Academy Awards

Best Film from any Source and Best British Film: ***Les Jeux Interdits*** • *Genevieve* • *The Bad and the Beautiful* • *Come Back, Little Sheba* • *The Cruel Sea* • *From Here to Eternity* • *The Heart of the Matter* • *Julius Caesar* • *The Kidnappers* • *Lili* • *The Little World of Don Camillo* • *The Medium* • *Mogambo* • *Moulin Rouge* • *Nous Sommes Tous des Assassins* • *Roman Holiday* • *Shane* • *The Sun Shines Bright* • *Two Pennyworth of Hope*
Best Foreign Actor: **Marlon Brando** *Julius Caesar* • Eddie Albert *Roman Holiday* • Van Heflin *Shane* • Claude Laydu *Diary of a Country Priest* • Marcel Mouloudji *Nous Sommes Tous des Assassins* • Gregory Peck *Roman Holiday* • Spencer Tracy *The Actress*
Best Foreign Actress: **Leslie Caron** *Lili* • Shirley Booth *Come Back, Little Sheba* • Marie Powers *The Medium* • Maria Schell *The Heart of the Matter*
Best British Actor: **John Gielgud** *Julius Caesar* • Jack Hawkins *The Cruel Sea* • Trevor Howard *The Heart of the Matter* • Duncan Macrae *The Kidnappers* • Kenneth More *Genevieve*
Best British Actress: **Audrey Hepburn** *Roman Holiday* • Celia Johnson *The Captain's Paradise*

Academy Awards

Best Motion Picture: ***From Here to Eternity*** • *Julius Caesar* • *The Robe* • *Roman Holiday* • *Shane*
Directing: **Fred Zinnemann** *From Here to Eternity* • Charles Walters *Lili* • William Wyler *Roman Holiday* • George Stevens *Shane* • Billy Wilder *Stalag 17*
Actor: **William Holden** *Stalag 17* • Marlon Brando *Julius Caesar* • Richard Burton *The Robe* • Montgomery Clift, Burt Lancaster *From Here to Eternity*
Actress: **Audrey Hepburn** *Roman Holiday* • Leslie Caron *Lili* • Ava Gardner *Mogambo* • Deborah Kerr *From Here to Eternity* • Maggie McNamara *The Moon Is Blue*
Actor in a Supporting Role: **Frank Sinatra** *From Here to Eternity* • Brandon de Wilde, Jack Palance *Shane* • Eddie Albert *Roman Holiday* • Robert Strauss *Stalag 17*
Actress in a Supporting Role: **Donna Reed** *From Here to Eternity* • Grace Kelly *Mogambo* • Geraldine Page *Hondo* • Marjorie Rambeau *Torch Song* • Thelma Ritter *Pickup on South Street*
Writing (Story and Screenplay): **Charles Brackett**, **Walter Reisch**, **Richard Breen** *Titanic* • Betty Comden, Adolph Green *The Band Wagon* • Richard Murphy *The Desert Rats* • Harold Jack Bloom, Sam Rolfe *The Naked Spur* • Millard Kaufman *Take the High Ground*
Writing (Screenplay): **Daniel Taradash** *From Here to Eternity* • Eric Ambler *The Cruel Sea* • Helen Deutsch *Lili* • John Dighton, Ian McLellan Hunter *Roman Holiday* • A B Guthrie Jr *Shane*
Writing (Motion Picture Story): **Ian McLellan Hunter**, **Dalton Trumbo** *Roman Holiday* • Beirne Lay Jr *Above and Beyond* • Alec Coppel *The Captain's Paradise* • Louis L'Amour *Hondo* • Ray Ashley, Morris Engel, Ruth Orkin *The Little Fugitive*

Golden Globe Awards

Best Motion Picture Drama: ***The Robe***
Best Director Motion Picture: **Fred Zinnemann** *From Here to Eternity*
Best Performance by an Actor in a Motion Picture Drama: **Spencer Tracy** *The Actress*
Best Performance by an Actress in a Motion Picture Drama: **Audrey Hepburn** *Roman Holiday*
Best Performance by an Actor in a Motion Picture Comedy or Musical: **David Niven** *The Moon Is Blue*
Best Performance by an Actress in a Motion Picture Comedy or Musical: **Ethel Merman** *Call Me Madam*
Best Performance by an Actor in a Supporting Role Motion Picture: **Frank Sinatra** *From Here to Eternity*
Best Performance by an Actress in a Supporting Role Motion Picture: **Grace Kelly** *Mogambo*
Best Screenplay Motion Picture: **Helen Deutsch** *Lili*

Cannes International Film Festival

Grand Prix: ***The Wages of Fear***
Actor: **Charles Vanel** *The Wages of Fear*
Actress: **Shirley Booth** *Come Back, Little Sheba*

Berlin International Film Festival

Golden Berlin Bear: ***The Wages of Fear***

1954

British Film Academy Awards

Best Film from any Source and Best British Film: ***The Wages of Fear* • *Hobson's Choice*** • *The Adventures of Robinson Crusoe* • *Bread, Love and Dreams* • *The Caine Mutiny* • *Carrington VC* • *The Divided Heart* • *Doctor in the House* • *Executive Suite* • *For Better, for Worse* • *Gate of Hell* • *How to Marry a Millionaire* • *The Maggie* • *The Moon Is Blue* • *On the Waterfront* • *The Purple Plain* • *Rear Window* • *Riot in Cell Block 11* • *Romeo and Juliet* • *Seven Brides for Seven Brothers*
Best Foreign Actor: **Marlon Brando** *On the Waterfront* • Neville Brand *Riot in Cell Block 11* • José Ferrer *The Caine Mutiny* • Fredric March *Executive Suite* • James Stewart *The Glenn Miller Story*
Best Foreign Actress: **Cornell Borchers** *The Divided Heart* • Shirley Booth *About Mrs Leslie* • Judy Holliday *Phffft!* • Grace Kelly *Dial M for Murder* • Gina Lollobrigida *Bread, Love and Dreams*
Best British Actor: **Kenneth More** *Doctor in the House* • Maurice Denham *The Purple Plain* • Robert Donat *Lease of Life* • David Niven *Carrington VC* • John Mills *Hobson's Choice* • Donald Wolfit *Svengali*
Best British Actress: **Yvonne Mitchell** *The Divided Heart* • Brenda de Banzie *Hobson's Choice* • Audrey Hepburn *Sabrina Fair* • Margaret Leighton, Noelle Middleton *Carrington VC*
Best British Screenplay: **Robin Estridge**, **George Tabori** *The Young Lovers* • Jack Whittingham *The Divided Heart* • Nicholas Phipps *Doctor in the House* • David Lean, Norman Spencer, Wynyard Browne *Hobson's Choice* • Hugh Mills, René Clément *Knave of Hearts* • William Rose *The Maggie* • Eric Ambler *The Purple Plain* • Renato Castellani *Romeo and Juliet*

Academy Awards

Best Motion Picture: ***On the Waterfront*** • *The Caine Mutiny* • *The Country Girl* • *Seven Brides for Seven Brothers* • *Three Coins in the Fountain*
Honorary Foreign Language Film Award: ***Gate of Hell***
Directing: **Elia Kazan** *On the Waterfront* • George Seaton *The Country Girl* • William A Wellman *The High and the Mighty* • Alfred Hitchcock *Rear Window* • Billy Wilder *Sabrina Fair*
Actor: **Marlon Brando** *On the Waterfront* • Humphrey Bogart *The Caine Mutiny* • Bing Crosby *The Country Girl* • James Mason *A Star Is Born* • Dan O'Herlihy *The Adventures of Robinson Crusoe*
Actress: **Grace Kelly** *The Country Girl* • Dorothy Dandridge *Carmen Jones* • Judy Garland *A Star Is Born* • Audrey Hepburn *Sabrina Fair* • Jane Wyman *Magnificent Obsession*
Actor in a Supporting Role: **Edmond O'Brien** *The Barefoot Contessa* • Lee J Cobb, Karl Malden, Rod Steiger *On the Waterfront* • Tom Tully *The Caine Mutiny*
Actress in a Supporting Role: **Eva Marie Saint** *On the Waterfront* • Jan Sterling, Claire Trevor *The High and the Mighty* • Nina Foch *Executive Suite* • Katy Jurado *Broken Lance*

Writing (Story and Screenplay): **Budd Schulberg** *On the Waterfront* • Joseph L Mankiewicz *The Barefoot Contessa* • William Rose *Genevieve* • Oscar Brodney, Valentine Davies *The Glenn Miller Story* • Melvin Frank, Norman Panama *Knock on Wood*

Writing (Screenplay): **George Seaton** *The Country Girl* • Stanley Roberts *The Caine Mutiny* • John Michael Hayes *Rear Window* • Billy Wilder, Ernest Lehman, Samuel Taylor *Sabrina Fair* • Albert Hackett, Frances Goodrich, Dorothy Kingsley *Seven Brides for Seven Brothers*

Writing (Motion Picture Story): **Philip Yordan** *Broken Lance* • Ettore Margadonna *Bread, Love and Dreams* • Francois Boyer *Les Jeux Interdits* • Jed Harris, Thomas Reed *Night People* • Lamar Trotti *There's No Business like Show Business*

Golden Globe Awards

Best Motion Picture – Drama: ***On the Waterfront***

Best Motion Picture – Comedy or Musical: ***Carmen Jones***

Best Foreign Language Film: ***Genevieve* • *No Way Back* • *Twenty-Four Eyes* • *La Mujer de las Camelias***

Best Director – Motion Picture: **Elia Kazan** *On the Waterfront*

Best Performance by an Actor in a Motion Picture – Drama: **Marlon Brando** *On the Waterfront*

Best Performance by an Actress in a Motion Picture – Drama: **Grace Kelly** *The Country Girl*

Best Performance by an Actor in a Motion Picture – Comedy or Musical: **James Mason** *A Star Is Born*

Best Performance by an Actress in a Motion Picture – Comedy or Musical: **Judy Garland** *A Star Is Born*

Best Performance by an Actor in a Supporting Role – Motion Picture: **Edmond O'Brien** *The Barefoot Contessa*

Best Performance by an Actress in a Supporting Role – Motion Picture: **Jan Sterling** *The High and the Mighty*

Best Screenplay – Motion Picture: **Billy Wilder, Samuel Taylor, Ernest Lehman** *Sabrina Fair*

Cannes International Film Festival

Grand Prix: ***Gate of Hell***

Berlin International Film Festival

Golden Berlin Bear: ***Hobson's Choice***

1955

British Film Academy Awards

Best Film from any Source and Best British Film: ***Richard III*** • *Bad Day at Black Rock* • *Carmen Jones* • *The Colditz Story* • *The Dam Busters* • *East of Eden* • *The Ladykillers* • *Marty* • *The Night My Number Came Up* • *The Prisoner* • *Seven Samurai* • *Simba* • *La Strada* • *Summertime*

Best Foreign Actor: **Ernest Borgnine** *Marty* • James Dean *East of Eden* • Jack Lemmon *Mister Roberts* • Toshiro Mifune, Takashi Shimura *Seven Samurai* • Frank Sinatra *Not as a Stranger*

Best Foreign Actress: **Betsy Blair** *Marty* • Dorothy Dandridge *Carmen Jones* • Judy Garland *A Star Is Born* • Julie Harris *I Am a Camera* • Katharine Hepburn *Summertime* • Giulietta Masina *La Strada* • Marilyn Monroe *The Seven Year Itch* • Grace Kelly *The Country Girl*

Best British Actor: **Laurence Olivier** *Richard III* • Alfie Bass *The Bespoke Overcoat* • Alec Guinness, Jack Hawkins *The Prisoner* • David Kossoff *A Kid for Two Farthings* • Kenneth More *The Deep Blue Sea* • Michael Redgrave *The Night My Number Came Up*

Best British Actress: **Katie Johnson** *The Ladykillers* • Margaret Johnston *Touch and Go* • Deborah Kerr *The End of the Affair* • Margaret Lockwood *Cast a Dark Shadow*

Best British Screenplay: **William Rose** *The Ladykillers* • Sidney Gilliat, Val Valentine *The Constant Husband* • R C Sherriff *The Dam Busters* • Terence Rattigan *The Deep Blue Sea* • Nicholas Phipps, Jack Davies *Doctor at Sea* • R C Sherriff *The Night My Number Came Up* • Bridget Boland *The Prisoner* • John Baines *Simba* • William Rose *Touch and Go*

Academy Awards

Best Motion Picture: ***Marty*** • *Love Is a Many-Splendored Thing* • *Mister Roberts* • *Picnic* • *The Rose Tattoo*

Honorary Foreign Language Film Award: ***Samurai***

Directing: **Delbert Mann** *Marty* • John Sturges *Bad Day at Black Rock* • Elia Kazan *East of Eden* • Joshua Logan *Picnic* • David Lean *Summertime*

Actor: **Ernest Borgnine** *Marty* • James Cagney *Love Me or Leave Me* • James Dean *East of Eden* • Frank Sinatra *The Man with the Golden Arm* • Spencer Tracy *Bad Day at Black Rock*

Actress: **Anna Magnani** *The Rose Tattoo* • Susan Hayward *I'll Cry Tomorrow* • Katharine Hepburn *Summertime* • Jennifer Jones *Love Is a Many-Splendored Thing* • Eleanor Parker *Interrupted Melody*

Actor in a Supporting Role: **Jack Lemmon** *Mister Roberts* • Arthur Kennedy *Trial* • Joe Mantell *Marty* • Sal Mineo *Rebel without a Cause* • Arthur O'Connell *Picnic*

Actress in a Supporting Role: **Jo Van Fleet** *East of Eden* • Betsy Blair *Marty* • Peggy Lee *Pete Kelly's Blues* • Marisa Pavan *The Rose Tattoo* • Natalie Wood *Rebel without a Cause*

Writing (Story and Screenplay): **William Ludwig, Sonya Levien** *Interrupted Melody* • Milton Sperling, Emmet Lavery *The Court-Martial of Billy Mitchell* • Betty Comden, Adolph Green *It's Always Fair Weather* • Jacques Tati, Henri Marquet *Monsieur Hulot's Holiday* • Jack Rose, Melville Shavelson *Seven Little Foys*

Writing (Screenplay): **Paddy Chayefsky** *Marty* • Millard Kaufman *Bad Day at Black Rock* • Richard Brooks *The Blackboard Jungle* • Paul Osborn *East of Eden* • Daniel Fuchs, Isobel Lennart *Love Me or Leave Me*

Writing (Motion Picture Story): **Daniel Fuchs** *Love Me or Leave Me* • Joe Connelly, Bob Mosher *The Private War of Major Benson* • Nicholas Ray *Rebel without a Cause* • Jean Marsan, Jacques Perret, Raoul Ploquin, Henry Troyat, Henri Verneuil *The Sheep Has Five Legs* • Beirne Lay Jr *Strategic Air Command*

Golden Globe Awards

Best Motion Picture – Drama: ***East of Eden* • *Wichita***

Best Motion Picture – Comedy or Musical: ***Guys and Dolls***

Best Foreign Language Film: ***Eyes of Children* • *Sons, Mothers and a General* • *Ordet* • *Dangerous Curves* • *Stella***

Best Director – Motion Picture: **Joshua Logan** *Picnic*

Best Performance by an Actor in a Motion Picture – Drama: **Ernest Borgnine** *Marty*

Best Performance by an Actress in a Motion Picture – Drama: **Anna Magnani** *The Rose Tattoo*

Best Performance by an Actor in a Motion Picture – Comedy or Musical: **Tom Ewell** *The Seven Year Itch*

Best Performance by an Actress in a Motion Picture – Comedy or Musical: **Jean Simmons** *Guys and Dolls*

Best Performance by an Actor in a Supporting Role – Motion Picture: **Arthur Kennedy** *Trial*

Best Performance by an Actress in a Supporting Role – Motion Picture: **Marisa Pavan** *The Rose Tattoo*

Cannes International Film Festival

Palme d'Or: ***Marty***

Director: **Sergei Vasiliev** *Heroes of Shipka* • **Jules Dassin** *Rififi*

Actor: **Spencer Tracy** *Bad Day at Black Rock*

Berlin International Film Festival

Golden Berlin Bear: ***The Rats***

1956

British Film Academy Awards

Best Film from any Source and Best British Film: ***Gervaise* • *Reach for the Sky*** • *Friends for Life* • *Baby Doll* • *The Battle of the River Plate* • *Le Défroqué* • *The Grasshopper* • *Guys and Dolls* • *The Killing* • *The Man with the Golden Arm* • *The Man Who Never Was* • *Picnic* • *Rebel without a Cause* • *The Shadow* • *Smiles of a Summer Night* • *A Town like Alice* • *The Trouble with Harry* • *War and Peace* • *Yield to the Night*

Best Foreign Actor: **François Périer** *Gervaise* • Gunnar Björnstrand *Smiles of a Summer Night* • James Dean *Rebel without a Cause* • Pierre Fresnay *Le Défroqué* • Karl Malden *Baby Doll* • William Holden *Picnic* • Frank Sinatra *The Man with the Golden Arm* • Spencer Tracy *The Mountain*

Best Foreign Actress: **Anna Magnani** *The Rose Tattoo* • Carroll Baker *Baby Doll* • Eva Dahlbeck *Smiles of a Summer Night* • Ava Gardner *Bhowani Junction* • Susan Hayward *I'll Cry Tomorrow* • Shirley MacLaine *The Trouble with Harry* • Kim Novak *Picnic* • Marisa Pavan *The Rose Tattoo* • Maria Schell *Gervaise* • Jean Simmons *Guys and Dolls*

Best British Actor: **Peter Finch** *A Town like Alice* • Jack Hawkins *The Long Arm* • Kenneth More *Reach for the Sky*

Best British Actress: Virginia McKenna *A Town like Alice* • Dorothy Alison *Reach for the Sky* • Audrey Hepburn *War and Peace*

Best British Screenplay: **Nigel Balchin** *The Man Who Never Was* • Michael Powell, Emeric Pressburger *The Battle of the River Plate* • Sidney Gilliat, Frank Launder *The Green Man* • John Boulting, Frank Harvey *Private's Progress* • Lewis Gilbert *Reach for the Sky* • Moore Raymond, Anthony Kimmins *Smiley* • Hubert Gregg, Vernon Harris *Three Men in a Boat* • WP Lipscomb, Richard Mason *A Town like Alice* • Joan Henry, John Cresswell *Yield to the Night*

Academy Awards

Best Motion Picture: ***Around the World in 80 Days*** • *Friendly Persuasion* • *Giant* • *The King and I* • *The Ten Commandments*

Foreign Language Film: ***La Strada*** • *The Captain from Kopenick* • *Gervaise* • *The Burmese Harp* • *Qivitoq*

Directing: **George Stevens** *Giant* • Michael Anderson *Around the World in 80 Days* • William Wyler *Friendly Persuasion* • Walter Lang *The King and I* • King Vidor *War and Peace*

Actor: **Yul Brynner** *The King and I* • James Dean *Giant* • Kirk Douglas *Lust for Life* • Rock Hudson *Giant* • Laurence Olivier *Richard III*

Actress: **Ingrid Bergman** *Anastasia* • Carroll Baker *Baby Doll* • Katharine Hepburn *The Rainmaker* • Nancy Kelly *The Bad Seed* • Deborah Kerr *The King and I*

Actor in a Supporting Role: **Anthony Quinn** *Lust for Life* • Don Murray *Bus Stop* • Anthony Perkins *Friendly Persuasion* • Mickey Rooney *The Bold and the Brave* • Robert Stack *Written on the Wind*

Actress in a Supporting Role: **Dorothy Malone** *Written on the Wind* • Mildred Dunnock *Baby Doll* • Eileen Heckart *The Bad Seed* • Mercedes McCambridge *Giant* • Patty McCormack *The Bad Seed*

Writing (Screenplay Original): **Albert Lamorisse** *Red Balloon* • Robert Lewin *The Bold and the Brave* • Andrew L Stone *Julie* • Federico Fellini, Tullio Pinelli *La Strada* • William Rose *The Ladykillers*

Writing (Screenplay Adapted): **S J Perelman, James Poe, John Farrow** *Around the World in 80 Days* • Tennessee Williams *Baby Doll* • Michael Wilson *Friendly Persuasion* • Fred Guiol, Ivan Moffat *Giant* • Norman Corwin *Lust for Life*

Writing (Motion Picture Story): **Dalton Trumbo** *The Brave One* • Leo Katcher *The Eddy Duchin Story* • Edward Bernds, Elwood Ullman *High Society* • Jean-Paul Sartre *The Proud Ones* • Cesare Zavattini *Umberto D*

Golden Globe Awards

Best Motion Picture – Drama: ***Around the World in 80 Days***

Best Motion Picture – Comedy or Musical: ***The King and I***

Best Foreign Language Film: ***Before Sundown* • *War and Peace* • *Roses on the Arm* • *The Girl in Black* • *Richard III* • *The White Reindeer***

Best Director – Motion Picture: **Elia Kazan** *Baby Doll*

Best Performance by an Actor in a Motion Picture – Drama: **Kirk Douglas** *Lust for Life*

Best Performance by an Actress in a Motion Picture – Drama: **Ingrid Bergman** *Anastasia*

Best Performance by an Actor in a Motion Picture – Comedy or Musical: **Cantinflas** *Around the World in 80 Days*

Best Performance by an Actress in a Motion Picture – Comedy or Musical: **Deborah Kerr** *The King and I*

Best Performance by an Actor in a Supporting Role – Motion Picture: **Earl Holliman** *The Rainmaker*

Best Performance by an Actress in a Supporting Role – Motion Picture: **Eileen Heckart** *The Bad Seed*

Cannes International Film Festival

Palme d'Or: ***Le Monde du Silence***

Director: **Sergei Yutkevitch** *Othello*

Actress: **Susan Hayward** *I'll Cry Tomorrow*

Berlin International Film Festival

Golden Berlin Bear: ***Invitation to the Dance***

Silver Berlin Bear for the Best Director: **Robert Aldrich** *Autumn Leaves*

Silver Berlin Bear for the Best Actor: **Burt Lancaster** *Trapeze*

Silver Berlin Bear for the Best Actress: **Elsa Martinelli** *Donatella*

1957

British Film Academy Awards

Best Film from any Source and Best British Film: ***The Bridge on the River Kwai*** • *The Bachelor Party* • *A Man Escaped* • *Celui Qui Doit Mourir* • *Heaven Knows, Mr Allison* • *Edge of the City* • *Paths of Glory* • *Pather Panchali* • *Porte des Lilas* • *The Prince and the Showgirl* • *The Shiralee* • *The Tin Star* • *That Night* • *3:10 to Yuma* • *12 Angry Men* • *Windom's Way*

Best Foreign Actor: **Henry Fonda** *12 Angry Men* • Richard Basehart *Time Limit* • Pierre Brasseur *Porte des Lilas* • Tony Curtis *Sweet Smell of Success* • Jean Gabin *A Pig across Paris* • Sidney Poitier *Edge of the City* • Robert Mitchum *Heaven Knows, Mr Allison* • Ed Wynn *The Great Man*

BEST FOREIGN ACTRESS: **Simone Signoret** *The Witches of Salem* • Augusta Dabney *That Night* • Katharine Hepburn *The Rainmaker* • Marilyn Monroe *The Prince and the Showgirl* • Lilli Palmer *Is Anna Anderson Anastasia?* • Eva Marie Saint *A Hatful of Rain* • Joanne Woodward *The Three Faces of Eve*
BEST BRITISH ACTOR: **Alec Guinness** *The Bridge on the River Kwai* • Peter Finch *Windom's Way* • Trevor Howard *Manuela* • Laurence Olivier *The Prince and the Showgirl* • Michael Redgrave *Time without Pity*
BEST BRITISH ACTRESS: **Heather Sears** *The Story of Esther Costello* • Deborah Kerr *Tea and Sympathy* • Sylvia Syms *Woman in a Dressing Gown*
BEST BRITISH SCREENPLAY: **Pierre Boulle** *The Bridge on the River Kwai* • Arthur Laurents *Anastasia* • Jack Whittingham *The Birthday Present* • John Kruse, Cy Endfield *Hell Drivers* • William Rose, John Eldridge *The Man in the Sky* • Terence Rattigan *The Prince and the Showgirl* • William Rose, John Eldridge *The Smallest Show on Earth* • Charles Kaufman *The Story of Esther Costello* • Jill Craigie *Windom's Way* • Ted Willis *Woman in a Dressing Gown*

Academy Awards

BEST MOTION PICTURE: ***The Bridge on the River Kwai*** • *12 Angry Men* • *Peyton Place* • *Sayonara* • *Witness for the Prosecution*
FOREIGN LANGUAGE FILM: ***Nights of Cabiria*** • *The Devil Came at Night* • *Gates of Paris* • *Mother India* • *Nine Lives*
DIRECTING: **David Lean** *The Bridge on the River Kwai* • Sidney Lumet *12 Angry Men* • Mark Robson *Peyton Place* • Joshua Logan *Sayonara* • Billy Wilder *Witness for the Prosecution*
ACTOR: **Alec Guinness** *The Bridge on the River Kwai* • Marlon Brando *Sayonara* • Anthony Franciosa *A Hatful of Rain* • Charles Laughton *Witness for the Prosecution* • Anthony Quinn *Wild Is the Wind*
ACTRESS: **Joanne Woodward** *The Three Faces of Eve* • Deborah Kerr *Heaven Knows, Mr Allison* • Anna Magnani *Wild Is the Wind* • Elizabeth Taylor *Raintree County* • Lana Turner *Peyton Place*
ACTOR IN A SUPPORTING ROLE: **Red Buttons** *Sayonara* • Arthur Kennedy, Russ Tamblyn *Peyton Place* • Vittorio De Sica *A Farewell to Arms* • Sessue Hayakawa *The Bridge on the River Kwai*
ACTRESS IN A SUPPORTING ROLE: **Miyoshi Umeki** *Sayonara* • Hope Lange, Diane Varsi *Peyton Place* • Carolyn Jones *The Bachelor Party* • Elsa Lanchester *Witness for the Prosecution*
WRITING (STORY AND SCREENPLAY WRITTEN DIRECTLY FOR THE SCREEN): **George Wells** *Designing Woman* • Leonard Gershe *Funny Face* • R Wright Campbell, Ivan Goff, Ben Roberts, Ralph Wheelwright *Man of a Thousand Faces* • Joel Kane, Dudley Nichols, Barney Slater *The Tin Star* • Federico Fellini, Ennio Flaiano, Tullio Pinelli *I Vitelloni*
WRITING (SCREENPLAY BASED ON MATERIAL FROM ANOTHER MEDIUM): **Pierre Boulle**, **Carl Foreman**, **Michael Wilson** *The Bridge on the River Kwai* • Reginald Rose *12 Angry Men* • John Huston, John Lee Mahin *Heaven Knows, Mr Allison* • John Michael Hayes *Peyton Place* • Paul Osborn *Sayonara*

Golden Globe Awards

BEST MOTION PICTURE DRAMA: ***The Bridge on the River Kwai***
BEST MOTION PICTURE COMEDY OR MUSICAL: ***Les Girls***
BEST FOREIGN LANGUAGE FILM: ***Woman in a Dressing Gown*** • ***The Confessions of Felix Krull*** • ***Tizoc*** • ***Yellow Crow***
BEST DIRECTOR MOTION PICTURE: **David Lean** *The Bridge on the River Kwai*
BEST PERFORMANCE BY AN ACTOR IN A MOTION PICTURE DRAMA: **Alec Guinness** *The Bridge on the River Kwai*
BEST PERFORMANCE BY AN ACTRESS IN A MOTION PICTURE DRAMA: **Joanne Woodward** *The Three Faces of Eve*
BEST PERFORMANCE BY AN ACTOR IN A MOTION PICTURE COMEDY OR MUSICAL: **Frank Sinatra** *Pal Joey*
BEST PERFORMANCE BY AN ACTRESS IN A MOTION PICTURE COMEDY OR MUSICAL: **Kay Kendall** *Les Girls*
BEST PERFORMANCE BY AN ACTOR IN A SUPPORTING ROLE MOTION PICTURE: **Red Buttons** *Sayonara*
BEST PERFORMANCE BY AN ACTRESS IN A SUPPORTING ROLE MOTION PICTURE: **Elsa Lanchester** *Witness for the Prosecution*

Cannes International Film Festival

PALME D'OR: ***Friendly Persuasion***
DIRECTOR: **Robert Bresson** *A Man Escaped*
ACTOR: **John Kitzmuller** *Dolina Miru*
ACTRESS: **Giulietta Masina** *Nights of Cabiria*

Berlin International Film Festival

GOLDEN BERLIN BEAR: ***12 Angry Men***
SILVER BERLIN BEAR FOR THE BEST DIRECTOR: **Mario Monicelli** *Padri e Figli*
SILVER BERLIN BEAR FOR THE BEST ACTOR: **Pedro Infante** *Tizoc*
SILVER BERLIN BEAR FOR THE BEST ACTRESS: **Yvonne Mitchell** *Woman in a Dressing Gown*

1958

British Film Academy Awards

BEST FILM FROM ANY SOURCE AND BEST BRITISH FILM: ***Room at the Top*** • *Nights of Cabiria* • *Cat on a Hot Tin Roof* • *The Cranes Are Flying* • *The Defiant Ones* • *Ice Cold in Alex* • *Indiscreet* • *No Down Payment* • *Orders to Kill* • *Sea of Sand* • *The Sheepman* • *Aparajito* • *Wild Strawberries* • *The Young Lions*
BEST FOREIGN ACTOR: **Sidney Poitier** *The Defiant Ones* • Marlon Brando *The Young Lions* • Tony Curtis *The Defiant Ones* • Glenn Ford *The Sheepman* • Curt Jurgens *The Enemy Below* • Curt Jurgens *The Inn of the Sixth Happiness* • Charles Laughton *Witness for the Prosecution* • Paul Newman *Cat on a Hot Tin Roof* • Victor Sjöström *Wild Strawberries* • Spencer Tracy *The Last Hurrah*
BEST FOREIGN ACTRESS: **Simone Signoret** *Room at the Top* • Ingrid Bergman *The Inn of the Sixth Happiness* • Anna Magnani *Wild Is the Wind* • Giulietta Masina *Nights of Cabiria* • Tatyana Samoilova *The Cranes Are Flying* • Elizabeth Taylor *Cat on a Hot Tin Roof* • Joanne Woodward *No Down Payment*
BEST BRITISH ACTOR: **Trevor Howard** *The Key* • I S Johar *Harry Black and the Tiger* • Anthony Quayle *Ice Cold in Alex* • Laurence Harvey, Donald Wolfit *Room at the Top* • Michael Craig *Sea of Sand* • Terry-Thomas *tom thumb*
BEST BRITISH ACTRESS: **Irene Worth** *Orders to Kill* • Virginia McKenna *Carve Her Name with Pride* • Hermione Baddeley *Room at the Top* • Karuna Bannerjee *Aparajito*
BEST BRITISH SCREENPLAY: **Paul Dehn** *Orders to Kill*

Academy Awards

BEST MOTION PICTURE: ***Gigi*** • *Auntie Mame* • *Cat on a Hot Tin Roof* • *The Defiant Ones* • *Separate Tables*
FOREIGN LANGUAGE FILM: ***Mon Oncle*** • *Arms and the Man* • *The Road a Year Long* • *Big Deal on Madonna Street* • *La Venganza*
DIRECTING: **Vincente Minnelli** *Gigi* • Richard Brooks *Cat on a Hot Tin Roof* • Stanley Kramer *The Defiant Ones* • Robert Wise *I Want to Live!* • Mark Robson *The Inn of the Sixth Happiness*
ACTOR: **David Niven** *Separate Tables* • Tony Curtis *The Defiant Ones* • Paul Newman *Cat on a Hot Tin Roof* • Sidney Poitier *The Defiant Ones* • Spencer Tracy *The Old Man and the Sea*
ACTRESS: **Susan Hayward** *I Want to Live!* • Deborah Kerr *Separate Tables* • Shirley MacLaine *Some Came Running* • Rosalind Russell *Auntie Mame* • Elizabeth Taylor *Cat on a Hot Tin Roof*
ACTOR IN A SUPPORTING ROLE: **Burl Ives** *The Big Country* • Theodore Bikel *The Defiant Ones* • Lee J Cobb *The Brothers Karamazov* • Arthur Kennedy *Some Came Running* • Gig Young *Teacher's Pet*
ACTRESS IN A SUPPORTING ROLE: **Wendy Hiller** *Separate Tables* • Peggy Cass *Auntie Mame* • Martha Hyer *Some Came Running* • Maureen Stapleton *Lonelyhearts* • Cara Williams *The Defiant Ones*
WRITING (STORY AND SCREENPLAY WRITTEN DIRECTLY FOR THE SCREEN): **Nedrick Young**, **Harold Jacob Smith** *The Defiant Ones* • Paddy Chayefsky *The Goddess* • Melville Shavelson, Jack Rose *Houseboat* • William Bowers, James Edward Grant *The Sheepman* • Fay Kanin, Michael Kanin *Teacher's Pet*
WRITING (SCREENPLAY BASED ON MATERIAL FROM ANOTHER MEDIUM): **Alan Jay Lerner** *Gigi* • Richard Brooks, James Poe *Cat on a Hot Tin Roof* • Alec Guinness *The Horse's Mouth* • Nelson Gidding, Don Mankiewicz *I Want to Live!* • John Gay, Terence Rattigan *Separate Tables*

Golden Globe Awards

BEST MOTION PICTURE DRAMA: ***The Defiant Ones***
BEST MOTION PICTURE MUSICAL: ***Gigi***
BEST MOTION PICTURE COMEDY: ***Auntie Mame***
BEST FOREIGN LANGUAGE FILM: ***A Night to Remember*** • ***The Road a Year Long*** • ***The Girl and the River*** • ***The Girl Rosemarie***
BEST DIRECTOR MOTION PICTURE: **Vincente Minnelli** *Gigi*
BEST PERFORMANCE BY AN ACTOR IN A MOTION PICTURE DRAMA: **David Niven** *Separate Tables*
BEST PERFORMANCE BY AN ACTRESS IN A MOTION PICTURE DRAMA: **Susan Hayward** *I Want to Live!*
BEST PERFORMANCE BY AN ACTOR IN A MOTION PICTURE COMEDY OR MUSICAL: **Danny Kaye** *Me and the Colonel*
BEST PERFORMANCE BY AN ACTRESS IN A MOTION PICTURE COMEDY OR MUSICAL: **Rosalind Russell** *Auntie Mame*
BEST PERFORMANCE BY AN ACTOR IN A SUPPORTING ROLE MOTION PICTURE: **Burl Ives** *The Big Country*
BEST PERFORMANCE BY AN ACTRESS IN A SUPPORTING ROLE MOTION PICTURE: **Hermione Gingold** *Gigi*

Cannes International Film Festival

PALME D'OR: ***The Cranes Are Flying***
DIRECTOR: **Ingmar Bergman** *So Close to Life*
ACTOR: **Paul Newman** *The Long Hot Summer*
ACTRESS: **Bibi Andersson**, **Barbro Hiort Af Ornas**, **Ingrid Thulin**, **Eva Dahlbeck** *So Close to Life*
ORIGINAL SCREENPLAY: **Pier Paolo Pasolini**, **Massimo Franciosa**, **Pasquale Festa Campanile** *Young Husbands*

Berlin International Film Festival

GOLDEN BERLIN BEAR: ***Wild Strawberries***
SILVER BERLIN BEAR FOR THE BEST DIRECTOR: **Tadashi Imai** *Jun-Ai Monogatari*
SILVER BERLIN BEAR FOR THE BEST ACTOR: **Sidney Poitier** *The Defiant Ones*
SILVER BERLIN BEAR FOR THE BEST ACTRESS: **Anna Magnani** *Wild Is the Wind*

1959

British Film Academy Awards

BEST FILM FROM ANY SOURCE AND BEST BRITISH FILM: ***Ben-Hur*** • ***Sapphire*** • *Anatomy of a Murder* • *Ashes and Diamonds* • *The Big Country* • *Compulsion* • *The Face* • *Gigi* • *Look Back in Anger* • *Maigret Sets a Trap* • *North West Frontier* • *The Nun's Story* • *Some Like It Hot* • *Tiger Bay* • *Yesterday's Enemy*
BEST FOREIGN ACTOR: **Jack Lemmon** *Some Like It Hot* • Zbigniew Cybulski *Ashes and Diamonds* • Jean Desailly, Jean Gabin *Maigret Sets a Trap* • Takashi Shimura *Ikiru* • James Stewart *Anatomy of a Murder*
BEST FOREIGN ACTRESS: **Shirley MacLaine** *Ask Any Girl* • Ava Gardner *On the Beach* • Susan Hayward *I Want to Live!* • Ella Lambetti *A Matter of Dignity* • Rosalind Russell *Auntie Mame*
BEST BRITISH ACTOR: **Peter Sellers** *I'm All Right Jack* • Stanley Baker *Yesterday's Enemy* • Richard Burton *Look Back in Anger* • Peter Finch *The Nun's Story* • Laurence Harvey *Expresso Bongo* • Gordon Jackson *Yesterday's Enemy* • Laurence Olivier *The Devil's Disciple*
BEST BRITISH ACTRESS: **Audrey Hepburn**, Peggy Ashcroft *The Nun's Story* • Wendy Hiller *Separate Tables* • Yvonne Mitchell *Sapphire* • Sylvia Syms *No Trees in the Street* • Kay Walsh *The Horse's Mouth*
BEST BRITISH SCREENPLAY: **Frank Harvey**, **Alan Hackney**, **John Boulting** *I'm All Right Jack* • Ben Barzman, Millard Lampbell *Blind Date* • Wolf Mankowitz *Expresso Bongo* • Alec Guinness *The Horse's Mouth* • Nigel Kneale *Look Back in Anger* • Robin Estridge *North West Frontier* • Ted Willis *No Trees in the Street* • Janet Green *Sapphire* • John Hawkesworth, Shelley Smith *Tiger Bay*

Academy Awards

BEST MOTION PICTURE: ***Ben-Hur*** • *Anatomy of a Murder* • *The Diary of Anne Frank* • *The Nun's Story* • *Room at the Top*
FOREIGN LANGUAGE FILM: ***Black Orpheus*** • *The Bridge* • *The Great War* • *Paw* • *The Village on the River*
DIRECTING: **William Wyler** *Ben-Hur* • George Stevens *The Diary of Anne Frank* • Fred Zinnemann *The Nun's Story* • Jack Clayton *Room at the Top* • Billy Wilder *Some Like It Hot*
ACTOR: **Charlton Heston** *Ben-Hur* • Laurence Harvey *Room at the Top* • Jack Lemmon *Some Like It Hot* • Paul Muni *The Last Angry Man* • James Stewart *Anatomy of a Murder*
ACTRESS: **Simone Signoret** *Room at the Top* • Doris Day *Pillow Talk* • Audrey Hepburn *The Nun's Story* • Katharine Hepburn, Elizabeth Taylor *Suddenly, Last Summer*
ACTOR IN A SUPPORTING ROLE: **Hugh Griffith** *Ben-Hur* • Arthur O'Connell, George C Scott *Anatomy of a Murder* • Robert Vaughn *The Young Philadelphians* • Ed Wynn *The Diary of Anne Frank*
ACTRESS IN A SUPPORTING ROLE: **Shelley Winters** *The Diary of Anne Frank* • Hermione Baddeley *Room at the Top* • Juanita Moore *Imitation of Life* • Thelma Ritter *Pillow Talk* • Susan Kohner *Imitation of Life*
WRITING (STORY AND SCREENPLAY WRITTEN DIRECTLY FOR THE SCREEN): **Stanley Shapiro**, **Maurice Richlin**, **Russell Rouse**, **Clarence Greene** *Pillow Talk* • François Truffaut, Marcel Moussy *The 400 Blows* • Ernest Lehman *North by Northwest* • Stanley Shapiro, Maurice Richlin, Paul King, Joseph Stone *Operation Petticoat* • Ingmar Bergman *Wild Strawberries*
WRITING (SCREENPLAY BASED ON MATERIAL FROM ANOTHER MEDIUM): **Neil Paterson** *Room at the Top* • Wendell Mayes *Anatomy of a Murder* • Karl Tunberg *Ben-Hur* •

Robert Anderson *The Nun's Story* • Billy Wilder, IAL Diamond *Some Like It Hot*

Golden Globe Awards

BEST MOTION PICTURE , DRAMA: **Ben-Hur**
BEST MOTION PICTURE , COMEDY: **Some Like It Hot**
BEST MOTION PICTURE , MUSICAL: **Porgy and Bess**
BEST FOREIGN LANGUAGE FILM: **Odd Obsession • The Bridge • Wild Strawberries • Aren't We Wonderful • Black Orpheus**
BEST DIRECTOR , MOTION PICTURE: **William Wyler** *Ben-Hur*
BEST PERFORMANCE BY AN ACTOR IN A MOTION PICTURE DRAMA: **Anthony Franciosa** *Career*
BEST PERFORMANCE BY AN ACTRESS IN A MOTION PICTURE DRAMA: **Elizabeth Taylor** *Suddenly, Last Summer*
BEST PERFORMANCE BY AN ACTOR IN A MOTION PICTURE COMEDY OR MUSICAL: **Jack Lemmon** *Some Like It Hot*
BEST PERFORMANCE BY AN ACTRESS IN A MOTION PICTURE COMEDY OR MUSICAL: **Marilyn Monroe** *Some Like It Hot*
BEST PERFORMANCE BY AN ACTOR IN A SUPPORTING ROLE MOTION PICTURE: **Stephen Boyd** *Ben-Hur*
BEST PERFORMANCE BY AN ACTRESS IN A SUPPORTING ROLE MOTION PICTURE: **Susan Kohner** *Imitation of Life*

Cannes International Film Festival

PALME D'OR: **Black Orpheus**
DIRECTOR: **François Truffaut** *The 400 Blows*
ACTOR: **Dean Stockwell, Bradford Dillman, Orson Welles** *Compulsion*
ACTRESS: **Simone Signoret** *Room at the Top*

Berlin International Film Festival

GOLDEN BERLIN BEAR: **Les Cousins**
SILVER BERLIN BEAR FOR THE BEST DIRECTOR: **Akira Kurosawa** *The Hidden Fortress*
SILVER BERLIN BEAR FOR THE BEST ACTOR: **Jean Gabin** *Archimède the Tramp*
SILVER BERLIN BEAR FOR THE BEST ACTRESS: **Shirley MacLaine** *Ask Any Girl*

1960

British Film Academy Awards

BEST FILM FROM ANY SOURCE AND BEST BRITISH FILM: **The Apartment • Saturday Night and Sunday Morning** • *The Angry Silence • L'Avventura • La Dolce Vita • Elmer Gantry • Hiroshima, Mon Amour • Inherit the Wind • Let's Make Love • Never on Sunday • Black Orpheus • The 400 Blows • Shadows • Spartacus • Le Testament d'Orphée • The Trials of Oscar Wilde • Tunes of Glory*
BEST FOREIGN ACTOR: **Jack Lemmon** *The Apartment* • George Hamilton (CST) *Crime and Punishment, USA* • Burt Lancaster *Elmer Gantry* • Fredric March *Inherit the Wind* • Yves Montand *Let's Make Love* • Spencer Tracy *Inherit the Wind*
BEST FOREIGN ACTRESS: **Shirley MacLaine** *The Apartment* • Pier Angeli *The Angry Silence* • Melina Mercouri *Never on Sunday* • Emmanuelle Riva *Hiroshima, Mon Amour* • Jean Simmons *Elmer Gantry* • Monica Vitti *L'Avventura*
BEST BRITISH ACTOR: **Peter Finch** *The Trials of Oscar Wilde* • Richard Attenborough *The Angry Silence* • Albert Finney *Saturday Night and Sunday Morning* • John Fraser *The Trials of Oscar Wilde* • Alec Guinness, John Mills *Tunes of Glory* • Laurence Olivier *The Entertainer*
BEST BRITISH ACTRESS: **Rachel Roberts** *Saturday Night and Sunday Morning* • Wendy Hiller *Sons and Lovers* • Hayley Mills *Pollyanna*
BEST BRITISH SCREENPLAY: **Bryan Forbes** *The Angry Silence* • Howard Clewes *The Day They Robbed the Bank of England* • John Osborne, Nigel Kneale *The Entertainer* • Val Guest *Hell Is a City* • Bryan Forbes *The League of Gentlemen* • Wolf Mankowitz *The Millionairess* • Alan Sillitoe *Saturday Night and Sunday Morning* • Roger MacDougall, Guy Hamilton, Ivan Foxwell *A Touch of Larceny* • Ken Hughes *The Trials of Oscar Wilde* • James Kennaway *Tunes of Glory*

Academy Awards

BEST MOTION PICTURE: **The Apartment** • *The Alamo • Elmer Gantry • Sons and Lovers • The Sundowners*
FOREIGN LANGUAGE FILM: **The Virgin Spring** • *Kapo • Macario • The Ninth Circle • La Vérité*
DIRECTING: **Billy Wilder** *The Apartment* • Jules Dassin *Never on Sunday* • Alfred Hitchcock *Psycho* • Jack Cardiff *Sons and Lovers* • Fred Zinnemann *The Sundowners*
ACTOR: **Burt Lancaster** *Elmer Gantry* • Trevor Howard *Sons and Lovers* • Jack Lemmon *The Apartment* • Laurence Olivier *The Entertainer* • Spencer Tracy *Inherit the Wind*
ACTRESS: **Elizabeth Taylor** *Butterfield 8* • Greer Garson *Sunrise at Campobello* • Deborah Kerr *The Sundowners* • Shirley MacLaine *The Apartment* • Melina Mercouri *Never on Sunday*

ACTOR IN A SUPPORTING ROLE: **Peter Ustinov** *Spartacus* • Peter Falk *Murder, Inc* • Jack Kruschen *The Apartment* • Sal Mineo *Exodus* • Chill Wills *The Alamo*
ACTRESS IN A SUPPORTING ROLE: **Shirley Jones** *Elmer Gantry* • Glynis Johns *The Sundowners* • Shirley Knight *The Dark at the Top of the Stairs* • Janet Leigh *Psycho* • Mary Ure *Sons and Lovers*
WRITING (STORY AND SCREENPLAY WRITTEN DIRECTLY FOR THE SCREEN): **Billy Wilder, I A L Diamond** *The Apartment* • Bryan Forbes, Michael Craig, Richard Gregson *The Angry Silence* • Norman Panama, Melvin Frank *The Facts of Life* • Marguerite Duras *Hiroshima, Mon Amour* • Jules Dassin *Never on Sunday*
WRITING (SCREENPLAY BASED ON MATERIAL FROM ANOTHER MEDIUM): **Richard Brooks** *Elmer Gantry* • Nedrick Young, Harold Jacob Smith *Inherit the Wind* • T E B Clarke, Gavin Lambert *Sons and Lovers* • Isobel Lennart *The Sundowners* • James Kennaway *Tunes of Glory*

Golden Globe Awards

BEST MOTION PICTURE , DRAMA: **Spartacus**
BEST MOTION PICTURE , COMEDY: **The Apartment**
BEST MOTION PICTURE , MUSICAL: **Song without End**
BEST FOREIGN LANGUAGE FILM: **The Trials of Oscar Wilde • La Vérité • The Virgin Spring**
BEST DIRECTOR , MOTION PICTURE: **Jack Cardiff** *Sons and Lovers*
BEST PERFORMANCE BY AN ACTOR IN A MOTION PICTURE DRAMA: **Burt Lancaster** *Elmer Gantry*
BEST PERFORMANCE BY AN ACTRESS IN A MOTION PICTURE DRAMA: **Greer Garson** *Sunrise at Campobello*
BEST PERFORMANCE BY AN ACTOR IN A MOTION PICTURE COMEDY OR MUSICAL: **Jack Lemmon** *The Apartment*
BEST PERFORMANCE BY AN ACTRESS IN A MOTION PICTURE COMEDY OR MUSICAL: **Shirley MacLaine** *The Apartment*
BEST PERFORMANCE BY AN ACTOR IN A SUPPORTING ROLE MOTION PICTURE: **Sal Mineo** *Exodus*
BEST PERFORMANCE BY AN ACTRESS IN A SUPPORTING ROLE MOTION PICTURE: **Janet Leigh** *Psycho*

Cannes International Film Festival

PALME D'OR: **La Dolce Vita**
ACTRESS: **Melina Mercouri** *Never on Sunday* • Jeanne Moreau *Moderato Cantabile*

Berlin International Film Festival

GOLDEN BERLIN BEAR: **Lazarillo**
SILVER BERLIN BEAR FOR THE BEST DIRECTOR: **Jean-Luc Godard** *A Bout de Souffle*
SILVER BERLIN BEAR FOR THE BEST ACTOR: **Fredric March** *Inherit the Wind*
SILVER BERLIN BEAR FOR THE BEST ACTRESS: **Juliette Mayniel** *Kirmes*

1961

British Film Academy Awards

BEST FILM FROM ANY SOURCE AND BEST BRITISH FILM: **Ballad of a Soldier • The Hustler • A Taste of Honey** • *The Innocents • Judgment at Nuremberg • The Long and the Short and the Tall • Rocco and His Brothers • The Sundowners • Le Trou • Whistle down the Wind • The World of Apu*
BEST FOREIGN ACTOR: **Paul Newman** *The Hustler* • Montgomery Clift *Judgment at Nuremberg* • Vladimir Ivashov *Ballad of a Soldier* • Philippe Leroy *Le Trou* • Sidney Poitier *A Raisin in the Sun* • Maximilian Schell *Judgment at Nuremberg* • Alberto Sordi *The Best of Enemies*
BEST FOREIGN ACTRESS: **Sophia Loren** *Two Women* • Annie Girardot *Rocco and His Brothers* • Piper Laurie *The Hustler* • Claudia McNeil *A Raisin in the Sun* • Jean Seberg *A Bout de Souffle*
BEST BRITISH ACTOR: **Peter Finch** *No Love for Johnnie* • Dirk Bogarde *Victim*
BEST BRITISH ACTRESS: **Dora Bryan** *A Taste of Honey* • Deborah Kerr *The Sundowners* • Hayley Mills *Whistle down the Wind*
BEST BRITISH SCREENPLAY: **Wolf Mankowitz, Val Guest** *The Day the Earth Caught Fire* • **Tony Richardson, Shelagh Delaney** *A Taste of Honey* • Ted Willis *Flame in the Streets* • Carl Foreman *The Guns of Navarone* • Janet Green, John McCormick *Victim* • Keith Waterhouse, Willis Hall *Whistle down the Wind*

Academy Awards

BEST MOTION PICTURE: **West Side Story** • *Fanny • The Guns of Navarone • The Hustler • Judgment at Nuremberg*
FOREIGN LANGUAGE FILM: **Through a Glass Darkly** • *Harry and the Butler • Immortal Love • The Important Man • Placido*

DIRECTING: **Robert Wise, Jerome Robbins** *West Side Story* • J Lee Thompson *The Guns of Navarone* • Robert Rossen *The Hustler* • Stanley Kramer *Judgment at Nuremberg* • Federico Fellini *La Dolce Vita*
ACTOR: **Maximilian Schell** *Judgment at Nuremberg* • Charles Boyer *Fanny* • Paul Newman *The Hustler* • Spencer Tracy *Judgment at Nuremberg* • Stuart Whitman *The Mark*
ACTRESS: **Sophia Loren** *Two Women* • Audrey Hepburn *Breakfast at Tiffany's* • Piper Laurie *The Hustler* • Geraldine Page *Summer and Smoke* • Natalie Wood *Splendor in the Grass*
ACTOR IN A SUPPORTING ROLE: **George Chakiris** *West Side Story* • Jackie Gleason, George C Scott *The Hustler* • Montgomery Clift *Judgment at Nuremberg* • Peter Falk *Pocketful of Miracles*
ACTRESS IN A SUPPORTING ROLE: **Rita Moreno** *West Side Story* • Fay Bainter *The Children's Hour* • Judy Garland *Judgment at Nuremberg* • Lotte Lenya *The Roman Spring of Mrs Stone* • Una Merkel *Summer and Smoke*
WRITING (STORY AND SCREENPLAY WRITTEN DIRECTLY FOR THE SCREEN): **William Inge** *Splendor in the Grass* • Grigori Chukhrai, Valentin Yoshov *Ballad of a Soldier* • Indro Montanelli, Sergio Amidei, Diego Fabbri *General Della Rovere* • Federico Fellini, Ennio Flaiano, Tullio Pinelli, Brunello Rondi *La Dolce Vita* • Stanley Shapiro, Paul Henning *Lover Come Back*
WRITING (SCREENPLAY BASED ON MATERIAL FROM ANOTHER MEDIUM): **Abby Mann** *Judgment at Nuremberg* • George Axelrod *Breakfast at Tiffany's* • Carl Foreman *The Guns of Navarone* • Sidney Carroll, Robert Rossen *The Hustler* • Ernest Lehman *West Side Story*

Golden Globe Awards

BEST MOTION PICTURE , DRAMA: **The Guns of Navarone**
BEST MOTION PICTURE , COMEDY: **A Majority of One**
BEST MOTION PICTURE , MUSICAL: **West Side Story**
BEST FOREIGN LANGUAGE FILM: **Two Women**
BEST DIRECTOR , MOTION PICTURE: **Stanley Kramer** *Judgment at Nuremberg*
BEST PERFORMANCE BY AN ACTOR IN A MOTION PICTURE DRAMA: **Maximilian Schell** *Judgment at Nuremberg*
BEST PERFORMANCE BY AN ACTRESS IN A MOTION PICTURE DRAMA: **Geraldine Page** *Summer and Smoke*
BEST PERFORMANCE BY AN ACTOR IN A MOTION PICTURE COMEDY OR MUSICAL: **Glenn Ford** *Pocketful of Miracles*
BEST PERFORMANCE BY AN ACTRESS IN A MOTION PICTURE COMEDY OR MUSICAL: **Rosalind Russell** *A Majority of One*
BEST PERFORMANCE BY AN ACTOR IN A SUPPORTING ROLE MOTION PICTURE: **George Chakiris** *West Side Story*
BEST PERFORMANCE BY AN ACTRESS IN A SUPPORTING ROLE MOTION PICTURE: **Rita Moreno** *West Side Story*

Cannes International Film Festival

PALME D'OR: **Viridiana • The Long Absence**
DIRECTOR: **Yulia Solntseva** *The Flaming Years*
ACTOR: **Anthony Perkins** *Goodbye Again*
ACTRESS: **Sophia Loren** *Two Women*

Berlin International Film Festival

GOLDEN BERLIN BEAR: **La Notte**
SILVER BERLIN BEAR FOR THE BEST DIRECTOR: **Berhhard Wicki** *The Miracle of Malachias*
SILVER BERLIN BEAR FOR THE BEST ACTOR: **Peter Finch** *No Love for Johnnie*
SILVER BERLIN BEAR FOR THE BEST ACTRESS: **Anna Karina** *Une Femme Est une Femme*

1962

British Film Academy Awards

BEST FILM FROM ANY SOURCE AND BEST BRITISH FILM: **Lawrence of Arabia** • *Billy Budd • The Island • Jules et Jim • A Kind of Loving • The Lady with the Little Dog • Last Year at Marienbad • The Long Absence • Lola • The L-Shaped Room • The Manchurian Candidate • The Miracle Worker • Only Two Can Play • Phaedra • Thou Shalt Not Kill • Through a Glass Darkly • The Vanishing Corporal • West Side Story*
BEST FOREIGN ACTOR: **Burt Lancaster** *Birdman of Alcatraz* • Jean-Paul Belmondo *Léon Morin, Priest* • Franco Citti *Accattone* • Kirk Douglas *Lonely Are the Brave* • George Hamilton *Light in the Piazza* • Charles Laughton *Advise and Consent* • Anthony Quinn *Lawrence of Arabia* • Robert Ryan *Billy Budd* • George Wilson *The Long Absence*
BEST FOREIGN ACTRESS: **Anne Bancroft** *The Miracle Worker* • Harriet Andersson *Through a Glass Darkly* • Anouk Aimée *Lola* • Melina Mercouri *Phaedra* • Jeanne Moreau *Jules et Jim* • Geraldine Page *Sweet Bird of Youth* • Natalie Wood *Splendor in the Grass*
BEST BRITISH ACTOR: **Peter O'Toole** *Lawrence of Arabia* • Richard Attenborough *Trial and Error* • Alan Bates *A Kind*

of Loving • James Mason *Lolita* • Laurence Olivier *Term of Trial* • Peter Sellers *Only Two Can Play*

BEST BRITISH ACTRESS: **Leslie Caron** *The L-Shaped Room* • Virginia Maskell *The Wild and the Willing* • Janet Munro *Life for Ruth*

BEST BRITISH SCREENPLAY: **Robert Bolt** *Lawrence of Arabia* • Peter Ustinov, DeWitt Bodeen *Billy Budd* • Willis Hall, Keith Waterhouse *A Kind of Loving* • Bryan Forbes *Only Two Can Play* • Geoffrey Cotterell, Ivan Foxwell *Tiara Tahiti* • Wolf Mankowitz *Waltz of the Toreadors*

Academy Awards

BEST PICTURE: **Lawrence of Arabia** • *The Longest Day* • *The Music Man* • *Mutiny on the Bounty* • *To Kill a Mockingbird*

FOREIGN LANGUAGE FILM: **Sundays and Cybèle** • *Elektra* • *The Four Days of Naples* • *The Given Word* • *Tlayucan*

DIRECTING: **David Lean** *Lawrence of Arabia* • Frank Perry *David and Lisa* • Pietro Germi *Divorce – Italian Style* • Arthur Penn *The Miracle Worker* • Robert Mulligan *To Kill a Mockingbird*

ACTOR: **Gregory Peck** *To Kill a Mockingbird* • Burt Lancaster *Birdman of Alcatraz* • Jack Lemmon *Days of Wine and Roses* • Marcello Mastroianni *Divorce – Italian Style* • Peter O'Toole *Lawrence of Arabia*

ACTRESS: **Anne Bancroft** *The Miracle Worker* • Bette Davis *What Ever Happened to Baby Jane?* • Katharine Hepburn *Long Day's Journey into Night* • Lee Remick *Days of Wine and Roses* • Geraldine Page *Sweet Bird of Youth*

ACTOR IN A SUPPORTING ROLE: **Ed Begley** *Sweet Bird of Youth* • Victor Buono *What Ever Happened to Baby Jane?* • Telly Savalas *Birdman of Alcatraz* • Omar Sharif *Lawrence of Arabia* • Terence Stamp *Billy Budd*

ACTRESS IN A SUPPORTING ROLE: **Patty Duke** *The Miracle Worker* • Mary Badham *To Kill a Mockingbird* • Shirley Knight *Sweet Bird of Youth* • Angela Lansbury *The Manchurian Candidate* • Thelma Ritter *Birdman of Alcatraz*

WRITING (STORY AND SCREENPLAY WRITTEN DIRECTLY FOR THE SCREEN): **Pietro Germi, Ennio De Concini, Alfredo Giannetti** *Divorce – Italian Style* • Charles Kaufman, Wolfgang Reinhardt *Freud* • Alain Robbe-Grillet *Last Year at Marienbad* • Stanley Shapiro, Nate Monaster *That Touch of Mink* • Ingmar Bergman *Through a Glass Darkly*

WRITING (SCREENPLAY BASED ON MATERIAL FROM ANOTHER MEDIUM): **Horton Foote** *To Kill a Mockingbird* • Eleanor Perry *David and Lisa* • Robert Bolt, Michael Wilson *Lawrence of Arabia* • Vladimir Nabokov *Lolita* • William Gibson *The Miracle Worker*

Golden Globe Awards

BEST MOTION PICTURE DRAMA: **Lawrence of Arabia**
BEST MOTION PICTURE COMEDY: **That Touch of Mink**
BEST MOTION PICTURE MUSICAL: **The Music Man**
BEST FOREIGN LANGUAGE FILM: **The Best of Enemies** • **Divorce – Italian Style**
BEST DIRECTOR MOTION PICTURE: **David Lean** *Lawrence of Arabia*
BEST PERFORMANCE BY AN ACTOR IN A MOTION PICTURE DRAMA: **Gregory Peck** *To Kill a Mockingbird*
BEST PERFORMANCE BY AN ACTRESS IN A MOTION PICTURE DRAMA: **Geraldine Page** *Sweet Bird of Youth*
BEST PERFORMANCE BY AN ACTOR IN A MOTION PICTURE COMEDY OR MUSICAL: **Marcello Mastroianni** *Divorce – Italian Style*
BEST PERFORMANCE BY AN ACTRESS IN A MOTION PICTURE COMEDY OR MUSICAL: **Rosalind Russell** *Gypsy*
BEST PERFORMANCE BY AN ACTOR IN A SUPPORTING ROLE MOTION PICTURE: **Omar Sharif** *Lawrence of Arabia*
BEST PERFORMANCE BY AN ACTRESS IN A SUPPORTING ROLE MOTION PICTURE: **Angela Lansbury** *The Manchurian Candidate*

Cannes International Film Festival

PALME D'OR: **The Given Word**
ACTOR: **Ralph Richardson, Jason Robards Jr, Dean Stockwell** *Long Day's Journey into Night* • **Murray Melvin** *A Taste of Honey*
ACTRESS: **Katharine Hepburn** *Long Day's Journey into Night* • **Rita Tushingham** *A Taste of Honey*

Berlin International Film Festival

GOLDEN BERLIN BEAR: **A Kind of Loving**
SILVER BERLIN BEAR FOR THE BEST DIRECTOR: **Francesco Rosi** *Salvatore Giuliano*
SILVER BERLIN BEAR FOR THE BEST ACTOR: **James Stewart** *Mr Hobbs Takes a Vacation*
SILVER BERLIN BEAR FOR THE BEST ACTRESS: **Rita Gam, Viveca Lindfors** *No Exit*

1963

British Film Academy Awards

BEST FILM FROM ANY SOURCE AND BEST BRITISH FILM: **Tom Jones** • *Billy Liar* • *David and Lisa* • *Days of Wine and Roses* • *Divorce – Italian Style* • *8½* • *The Four Days of Naples* • *Hud* • *Knife in the Water* • *The Servant* • *This Sporting Life* • *To Kill a Mockingbird*

BEST FOREIGN ACTOR: **Marcello Mastroianni** *Divorce – Italian Style* • Howard Da Silva *David and Lisa* • Jack Lemmon *Days of Wine and Roses* • Paul Newman *Hud* • Gregory Peck *To Kill a Mockingbird*

BEST FOREIGN ACTRESS: **Patricia Neal** *Hud* • Joan Crawford, Bette Davis *What Ever Happened to Baby Jane?* • Lee Remick *Days of Wine and Roses* • Daniela Rocca *Divorce – Italian Style*

BEST BRITISH ACTOR: **Dirk Bogarde** *The Servant* • Tom Courtenay *Billy Liar* • Albert Finney, Hugh Griffith *Tom Jones* • Richard Harris *This Sporting Life*

BEST BRITISH ACTRESS: **Rachel Roberts** *This Sporting Life* • Julie Christie *Billy Liar* • Edith Evans *Tom Jones* • Sarah Miles *The Servant* • Barbara Windsor *Sparrows Can't Sing*

BEST BRITISH SCREENPLAY: **John Osborne** *Tom Jones* • Keith Waterhouse, Willis Hall *Billy Liar* • Harold Pinter *The Servant* • David Storey *This Sporting Life*

Academy Awards

BEST PICTURE: **Tom Jones** • *America, America* • *Cleopatra* • *How the West Was Won* • *Lilies of the Field*

FOREIGN LANGUAGE FILM: **8½** • *Knife in the Water* • *Los Tarantos* • *The Red Lanterns* • *Twin Sisters of Kyoto*

DIRECTING: **Tony Richardson** *Tom Jones* • Elia Kazan *America, America* • Otto Preminger *The Cardinal* • Martin Ritt *Hud* • Federico Fellini *8½*

ACTOR: **Sidney Poitier** *Lilies of the Field* • Albert Finney *Tom Jones* • Richard Harris *This Sporting Life* • Rex Harrison *Cleopatra* • Paul Newman *Hud*

ACTRESS: **Patricia Neal** *Hud* • Leslie Caron *The L-Shaped Room* • Shirley MacLaine *Irma la Douce* • Rachel Roberts *This Sporting Life* • Natalie Wood *Love with the Proper Stranger*

ACTOR IN A SUPPORTING ROLE: **Melvyn Douglas** *Hud* • Nick Adams *Twilight of Honor* • Bobby Darin *Captain Newman, MD* • Hugh Griffith *Tom Jones* • John Huston *The Cardinal*

ACTRESS IN A SUPPORTING ROLE: **Margaret Rutherford** *The VIPs* • Diane Cilento, Edith Evans, Joyce Redman *Tom Jones* • Lilia Skala *Lilies of the Field*

WRITING (STORY AND SCREENPLAY WRITTEN DIRECTLY FOR THE SCREEN): **James R Webb** *How the West Was Won* • Elia Kazan *America, America* • Federico Fellini, Tullio Pinelli, Ennio Flajano, Brunello Rondi *8½* • Pasquale Festa Campanile, Massimo Franciosa, Nanni Loy, Carlo Benari, Vasco Pratolini *The Four Days of Naples* • Arnold Schulman *Love with the Proper Stranger*

WRITING (SCREENPLAY BASED ON MATERIAL FROM ANOTHER MEDIUM): **John Osborne** *Tom Jones* • Richard L Breen, Phoebe Ephron, Henry Ephron *Captain Newman, MD* • Irving Ravetch, Harriet Frank Jr *Hud* • James Poe *Lilies of the Field* • Serge Bourguignon, Antoine Tudal *Sundays and Cybèle*

Golden Globe Awards

BEST MOTION PICTURE DRAMA: **The Cardinal**
BEST MOTION PICTURE COMEDY OR MUSICAL: **Tom Jones**
BEST FOREIGN LANGUAGE FILM: **Any Number Can Win**
BEST DIRECTOR MOTION PICTURE: **Elia Kazan** *America, America*
BEST PERFORMANCE BY AN ACTOR IN A MOTION PICTURE DRAMA: **Sidney Poitier** *Lilies of the Field*
BEST PERFORMANCE BY AN ACTRESS IN A MOTION PICTURE DRAMA: **Leslie Caron** *The L-Shaped Room*
BEST PERFORMANCE BY AN ACTOR IN A MOTION PICTURE COMEDY OR MUSICAL: **Alberto Sordi** *The Devil*
BEST PERFORMANCE BY AN ACTRESS IN A MOTION PICTURE COMEDY OR MUSICAL: **Shirley MacLaine** *Irma la Douce*
BEST PERFORMANCE BY AN ACTOR IN A SUPPORTING ROLE MOTION PICTURE: **John Huston** *The Cardinal*
BEST PERFORMANCE BY AN ACTRESS IN A SUPPORTING ROLE MOTION PICTURE: **Margaret Rutherford** *The VIPs*

Cannes International Film Festival

PALME D'OR: **The Leopard**
ACTOR: **Richard Harris** *This Sporting Life*
ACTRESS: **Marina Vlady** *The Conjugal Bed*
SCREENPLAY: **Henri Colpi** *Codine*

Berlin International Film Festival

GOLDEN BERLIN BEAR: **The Devil** • **Bushido Zankoku Monogatari**
SILVER BERLIN BEAR FOR THE BEST DIRECTOR: **Nikos Koundouros** *Mikres Aphrodites*

SILVER BERLIN BEAR FOR THE BEST ACTOR: **Sidney Poitier** *Lilies of the Field*
SILVER BERLIN BEAR FOR THE BEST ACTRESS: **Bibi Andersson** *The Swedish Mistress*

1964

British Film Academy Awards

BEST FILM FROM ANY SOURCE: **Dr Strangelove, or How I Learned to Stop Worrying and Love the Bomb** • *Becket* • *The Pumpkin Eater* • *The Train*

BEST BRITISH FILM: **Dr Strangelove, or How I Learned to Stop Worrying and Love the Bomb** • *Becket* • *King and Country* • *The Pumpkin Eater*

BEST FOREIGN ACTOR: **Marcello Mastroianni** *Yesterday, Today and Tomorrow* • Cary Grant *Charade* • Sterling Hayden *Dr Strangelove, or How I Learned to Stop Worrying and Love the Bomb* • Sidney Poitier *Lilies of the Field*

BEST FOREIGN ACTRESS: **Anne Bancroft** *The Pumpkin Eater* • Ava Gardner *The Night of the Iguana* • Shirley MacLaine *Irma la Douce* • Shirley MacLaine *What a Way to Go!* • Kim Stanley *Seance on a Wet Afternoon*

BEST BRITISH ACTOR: **Richard Attenborough** *Guns at Batasi* • **Richard Attenborough** *Seance on a Wet Afternoon* • Tom Courtenay *King and Country* • Peter O'Toole *Becket* • Peter Sellers *Dr Strangelove, or How I Learned to Stop Worrying and Love the Bomb* • Peter Sellers *The Pink Panther*

BEST BRITISH ACTRESS: **Audrey Hepburn** *Charade* • Edith Evans, Deborah Kerr *The Chalk Garden* • Rita Tushingham *Girl with Green Eyes*

BEST SCREENPLAY FOR A BRITISH FILM: **Harold Pinter** *The Pumpkin Eater* • Edward Anhalt *Becket* • Stanley Kubrick, Terry Southern, Peter George *Dr Strangelove, or How I Learned to Stop Worrying and Love the Bomb* • Bryan Forbes *Seance on a Wet Afternoon*

Academy Awards

BEST PICTURE: **My Fair Lady** • *Becket* • *Dr Strangelove, or How I Learned to Stop Worrying and Love the Bomb* • *Mary Poppins* • *Zorba the Greek*

FOREIGN LANGUAGE FILM: **Yesterday, Today and Tomorrow** • *Raven's End* • *Sallah* • *The Umbrellas of Cherbourg* • *Woman in the Dunes*

DIRECTING: **George Cukor** *My Fair Lady* • Peter Glenville *Becket* • Stanley Kubrick *Dr Strangelove, or How I Learned to Stop Worrying and Love the Bomb* • Robert Stevenson *Mary Poppins* • Michael Cacoyannis *Zorba the Greek*

ACTOR: **Rex Harrison** *My Fair Lady* • Richard Burton, Peter O'Toole *Becket* • Anthony Quinn *Zorba the Greek* • Peter Sellers *Dr Strangelove, or How I Learned to Stop Worrying and Love the Bomb*

ACTRESS: **Julie Andrews** *Mary Poppins* • Anne Bancroft *The Pumpkin Eater* • Sophia Loren *Marriage – Italian Style* • Debbie Reynolds *The Unsinkable Molly Brown* • Kim Stanley *Seance on a Wet Afternoon*

ACTOR IN A SUPPORTING ROLE: **Peter Ustinov** *Topkapi* • John Gielgud *Becket* • Stanley Holloway *My Fair Lady* • Edmond O'Brien *Seven Days in May* • Lee Tracy *The Best Man*

ACTRESS IN A SUPPORTING ROLE: **Lila Kedrova** *Zorba the Greek* • Gladys Cooper *My Fair Lady* • Edith Evans *The Chalk Garden* • Grayson Hall *The Night of the Iguana* • Agnes Moorehead *Hush...Hush, Sweet Charlotte*

WRITING (STORY AND SCREENPLAY WRITTEN DIRECTLY FOR THE SCREEN): **Frank Tarloff, Peter Stone, S H Barnett** *Father Goose* • Alun Owen *A Hard Day's Night* • Raphael Hayes, Orville H Hampton *One Potato, Two Potato* • Mario Monicelli, Scarpelli, Age *The Organizer* • Daniel Boulanger, Ariane Mnouchkine, Jean-Paul Rappeneau, Philippe de Broca *That Man from Rio*

WRITING (SCREENPLAY BASED ON MATERIAL FROM ANOTHER MEDIUM): **Edward Anhalt** *Becket* • Stanley Kubrick, Terry Southern, Peter George *Dr Strangelove, or How I Learned to Stop Worrying and Love the Bomb* • Bill Walsh, Don DaGradi *Mary Poppins* • Alan Jay Lerner *My Fair Lady* • Michael Cacoyannis *Zorba the Greek*

Golden Globe Awards

BEST MOTION PICTURE DRAMA: **Becket**
BEST MOTION PICTURE COMEDY OR MUSICAL: **My Fair Lady**
BEST FOREIGN LANGUAGE FILM: **Girl with Green Eyes** • **Sallah** • **Marriage – Italian Style**
BEST DIRECTOR MOTION PICTURE: **George Cukor** *My Fair Lady*
BEST PERFORMANCE BY AN ACTOR IN A MOTION PICTURE DRAMA: **Peter O'Toole** *Becket*
BEST PERFORMANCE BY AN ACTRESS IN A MOTION PICTURE DRAMA: **Anne Bancroft** *The Pumpkin Eater*

BEST PERFORMANCE BY AN ACTOR IN A MOTION PICTURE COMEDY OR MUSICAL: **Rex Harrison** *My Fair Lady*
BEST PERFORMANCE BY AN ACTRESS IN A MOTION PICTURE COMEDY OR MUSICAL: **Julie Andrews** *Mary Poppins*
BEST PERFORMANCE BY AN ACTOR IN A SUPPORTING ROLE MOTION PICTURE: **Edmond O'Brien** *Seven Days in May*
BEST PERFORMANCE BY AN ACTRESS IN A SUPPORTING ROLE MOTION PICTURE: **Agnes Moorehead** *Hush...Hush, Sweet Charlotte*

Cannes International Film Festival

GRAND PRIX: **The Umbrellas of Cherbourg**
ACTOR: **Antal Pager** *Pacsirta* • **Saro Urzi** *Seduced and Abandoned*
ACTRESS: **Anne Bancroft** *The Pumpkin Eater* • **Barbara Barrie** *One Potato, Two Potato*

Berlin International Film Festival

GOLDEN BERLIN BEAR: **Susuz Yaz**
SILVER BERLIN BEAR FOR THE BEST DIRECTOR: **Satyajit Ray** *The Big City*
SILVER BERLIN BEAR FOR THE BEST ACTOR: **Rod Steiger** *The Pawnbroker*
SILVER BERLIN BEAR FOR THE BEST ACTRESS: **Sachiko Hidari** *The Insect Woman* • **Sachiko Hidari** *Kanajo To Kare*

1965

British Film Academy Awards

BEST FILM FROM ANY SOURCE: **My Fair Lady** • *Hamlet* • *The Hill* • *The Knack ... and How to Get It* • *Zorba the Greek*
BEST BRITISH FILM: **The Ipcress File** • *Darling* • *The Hill* • *The Knack ... and How to Get It*
BEST FOREIGN ACTOR: **Lee Marvin** *The Killers* • **Lee Marvin** *Cat Ballou* • Jack Lemmon *Good Neighbor Sam* • Jack Lemmon *How to Murder Your Wife* • Anthony Quinn *Zorba the Greek* • Innokenti Smoktunovsky *Hamlet* • Oskar Werner *Ship of Fools*
BEST FOREIGN ACTRESS: **Patricia Neal** *In Harm's Way* • Jane Fonda *Cat Ballou* • Lila Kedrova *Zorba the Greek* • Simone Signoret *Ship of Fools*
BEST BRITISH ACTOR: **Dirk Bogarde** *Darling* • Harry Andrews *The Hill* • Michael Caine *The Ipcress File* • Rex Harrison *My Fair Lady*
BEST BRITISH ACTRESS: **Julie Christie** *Darling* • Julie Andrews *The Americanization of Emily* • Julie Andrews *The Sound of Music* • Maggie Smith *Young Cassidy* • Rita Tushingham *The Knack ... and How to Get It*
BEST BRITISH SCREENPLAY: **Frederic Raphael** *Darling* • Ray Rigby *The Hill* • Bill Canaway, James Doran *The Ipcress File* • Charles Wood *The Knack ... and How to Get It*

Academy Awards

BEST PICTURE: **The Sound of Music** • *Darling* • *Doctor Zhivago* • *Ship of Fools* • *A Thousand Clowns*
FOREIGN LANGUAGE FILM: **The Shop on the High Street** • *Blood on the Land* • *Dear John* • *Kwaidan* • *Marriage – Italian Style*
DIRECTING: **Robert Wise** *The Sound of Music* • William Wyler *The Collector* • John Schlesinger *Darling* • David Lean *Doctor Zhivago* • Hiroshi Teshigahara *Woman in the Dunes*
ACTOR: **Lee Marvin** *Cat Ballou* • Richard Burton *The Spy Who Came In from the Cold* • Laurence Olivier *Othello* • Rod Steiger *The Pawnbroker* • Oskar Werner *Ship of Fools*
ACTRESS: **Julie Christie** *Darling* • Julie Andrews *The Sound of Music* • Samantha Eggar *The Collector* • Elizabeth Hartman *A Patch of Blue* • Simone Signoret *Ship of Fools*
ACTOR IN A SUPPORTING ROLE: **Martin Balsam** *A Thousand Clowns* • Ian Bannen *The Flight of the Phoenix* • Tom Courtenay *Doctor Zhivago* • Michael Dunn *Ship of Fools* • Frank Finlay *Othello*
ACTRESS IN A SUPPORTING ROLE: **Shelley Winters** *A Patch of Blue* • Joyce Redman, Maggie Smith *Othello* • Ruth Gordon *Inside Daisy Clover* • Peggy Wood *The Sound of Music*
WRITING (STORY AND SCREENPLAY WRITTEN DIRECTLY FOR THE SCREEN): **Frederic Raphael** *Darling* • Agenore Incrocci, Furio Scarpelli, Suso Cecchi D'Amico, Mario Monicelli, Tonino Guerra, Giorgio Salvioni *Casanova '70* • Jack Davies, Ken Annakin *Those Magnificent Men in Their Flying Machines* • Franklin Coen, Frank Davis *The Train* • Jacques Demy *The Umbrellas of Cherbourg*
WRITING (SCREENPLAY BASED ON MATERIAL FROM ANOTHER MEDIUM): **Robert Bolt** *Doctor Zhivago* • Frank Pierson, Walter Newman *Cat Ballou* • Stanley Mann, John Kohn *The Collector* • Abby Mann *Ship of Fools* • Herb Gardner *A Thousand Clowns*

Golden Globe Awards

BEST MOTION PICTURE DRAMA: **Doctor Zhivago**
BEST MOTION PICTURE COMEDY OR MUSICAL: **The Sound of Music**
BEST FOREIGN LANGUAGE FILM: **Darling** • *Juliet of the Spirits*
BEST DIRECTOR MOTION PICTURE: **David Lean** *Doctor Zhivago*
BEST PERFORMANCE BY AN ACTOR IN A MOTION PICTURE DRAMA: **Omar Sharif** *Doctor Zhivago*
BEST PERFORMANCE BY AN ACTRESS IN A MOTION PICTURE DRAMA: **Samantha Eggar** *The Collector*
BEST PERFORMANCE BY AN ACTOR IN A MOTION PICTURE COMEDY OR MUSICAL: **Lee Marvin** *Cat Ballou*
BEST PERFORMANCE BY AN ACTRESS IN A MOTION PICTURE COMEDY OR MUSICAL: **Julie Andrews** *The Sound of Music*
BEST PERFORMANCE BY AN ACTOR IN A SUPPORTING ROLE MOTION PICTURE: **Oskar Werner** *The Spy Who Came In from the Cold*
BEST PERFORMANCE BY AN ACTRESS IN A SUPPORTING ROLE MOTION PICTURE: **Ruth Gordon** *Inside Daisy Clover*
BEST SCREENPLAY MOTION PICTURE: **Robert Bolt** *Doctor Zhivago*

Cannes International Film Festival

GRAND PRIX: **The Knack ... and How to Get It**
DIRECTOR: **Liviu Ciulei** *The Lost Forest*
ACTOR: **Terence Stamp** *The Collector*
ACTRESS: **Samantha Eggar** *The Collector*
SCREENPLAY: **Ray Rigby** *The Hill* • **Pierre Schoendoerffer** *La 317eme Section*

Berlin International Film Festival

GOLDEN BERLIN BEAR: **Alphaville**
SILVER BERLIN BEAR FOR THE BEST DIRECTOR: **Satyajit Ray** *Charulata*
SILVER BERLIN BEAR FOR THE BEST ACTOR: **Lee Marvin** *Cat Ballou*
SILVER BERLIN BEAR FOR THE BEST ACTRESS: **Madhur Jaffrey** *Shakespeare Wallah*

1966

British Film Academy Awards

BEST FILM FROM ANY SOURCE: **Who's Afraid of Virginia Woolf?** • *Doctor Zhivago* • *Morgan – a Suitable Case for Treatment* • *The Spy Who Came In from the Cold*
BEST BRITISH FILM: **The Spy Who Came In from the Cold** • *Alfie* • *Georgy Girl* • *Morgan – a Suitable Case for Treatment*
BEST FOREIGN ACTOR: **Rod Steiger** *The Pawnbroker* • Jean-Paul Belmondo *Pierrot le Fou* • Sidney Poitier *A Patch of Blue* • Oskar Werner *The Spy Who Came In from the Cold*
BEST FOREIGN ACTRESS: **Jeanne Moreau**, Brigitte Bardot *Viva Maria!* • Joan Hackett *The Group*
BEST BRITISH ACTOR: **Richard Burton** *The Spy Who Came In from the Cold* • Richard Burton *Who's Afraid of Virginia Woolf?* • Michael Caine *Alfie* • Ralph Richardson *The Wrong Box* • Ralph Richardson *Doctor Zhivago* • Ralph Richardson *Khartoum* • David Warner *Morgan – a Suitable Case for Treatment*
BEST BRITISH ACTRESS: **Elizabeth Taylor** *Who's Afraid of Virginia Woolf?* • Julie Christie *Doctor Zhivago* • Julie Christie *Fahrenheit 451* • Lynn Redgrave *Georgy Girl* • Vanessa Redgrave *Morgan – a Suitable Case for Treatment*
BEST BRITISH SCREENPLAY: **David Mercer** *Morgan – a Suitable Case for Treatment* • Bill Naughton *Alfie* • Kevin Brownlow, Andrew Mollo *It Happened Here* • Harold Pinter *The Quiller Memorandum*

Academy Awards

BEST PICTURE: **A Man for All Seasons** • *Alfie* • *The Russians Are Coming, the Russians Are Coming* • *The Sand Pebbles* • *Who's Afraid of Virginia Woolf?*
FOREIGN LANGUAGE FILM: **A Man and a Woman** • *The Battle of Algiers* • *A Blonde in Love* • *Pharaoh* • *Three*
DIRECTING: **Fred Zinnemann** *A Man for All Seasons* • Michelangelo Antonioni *Blow Up* • Claude Lelouch *A Man and a Woman* • Richard Brooks *The Professionals* • Mike Nichols *Who's Afraid of Virginia Woolf?*
ACTOR: **Paul Scofield** *A Man for All Seasons* • Alan Arkin *The Russians Are Coming, the Russians Are Coming* • Richard Burton *Who's Afraid of Virginia Woolf?* • Michael Caine *Alfie* • Steve McQueen *The Sand Pebbles*
ACTRESS: **Elizabeth Taylor** *Who's Afraid of Virginia Woolf?* • Anouk Aimée *A Man and a Woman* • Ida Kaminska *The Shop on the High Street* • Lynn Redgrave *Georgy Girl* • Vanessa Redgrave *Morgan – a Suitable Case for Treatment*
ACTOR IN A SUPPORTING ROLE: **Walter Matthau** *The Fortune Cookie* • Mako *The Sand Pebbles* • James Mason

Georgy Girl • George Segal *Who's Afraid of Virginia Woolf?* • Robert Shaw *A Man for All Seasons*
ACTRESS IN A SUPPORTING ROLE: **Sandy Dennis** *Who's Afraid of Virginia Woolf?* • Wendy Hiller *A Man for All Seasons* • Jocelyn La Garde *Hawaii* • Vivien Merchant *Alfie* • Geraldine Page *You're a Big Boy Now*
WRITING (STORY AND SCREENPLAY WRITTEN DIRECTLY FOR THE SCREEN): **Claude Lelouch, Pierre Uytterhoeven** *A Man and a Woman* • Michelangelo Antonioni, Tonino Guerra, Edward Bond *Blow Up* • Billy Wilder, I A L Diamond *The Fortune Cookie* • Robert Ardrey *Khartoum* • Clint Johnston, Don Peters *The Naked Prey*
WRITING (SCREENPLAY BASED ON MATERIAL FROM ANOTHER MEDIUM): **Robert Bolt** *A Man for All Seasons* • Bill Naughton *Alfie* • Richard Brooks *The Professionals* • William Rose *The Russians Are Coming, the Russians Are Coming* • Ernest Lehman *Who's Afraid of Virginia Woolf?*

Golden Globe Awards

BEST MOTION PICTURE DRAMA: **A Man for All Seasons**
BEST MOTION PICTURE COMEDY OR MUSICAL: **The Russians Are Coming, the Russians Are Coming**
BEST FOREIGN LANGUAGE FILM: **Alfie** • *A Man and a Woman*
BEST DIRECTOR MOTION PICTURE: **Fred Zinnemann** *A Man for All Seasons*
BEST PERFORMANCE BY AN ACTOR IN A MOTION PICTURE DRAMA: **Paul Scofield** *A Man for All Seasons*
BEST PERFORMANCE BY AN ACTRESS IN A MOTION PICTURE DRAMA: **Anouk Aimée** *A Man and a Woman*
BEST PERFORMANCE BY AN ACTOR IN A MOTION PICTURE COMEDY OR MUSICAL: **Alan Arkin** *The Russians Are Coming, the Russians Are Coming*
BEST PERFORMANCE BY AN ACTRESS IN A MOTION PICTURE COMEDY OR MUSICAL: **Lynn Redgrave** *Georgy Girl*
BEST PERFORMANCE BY AN ACTOR IN A SUPPORTING ROLE MOTION PICTURE: **Richard Attenborough** *The Sand Pebbles*
BEST PERFORMANCE BY AN ACTRESS IN A SUPPORTING ROLE MOTION PICTURE; **Jocelyn La Garde** *Hawaii*
BEST SCREENPLAY MOTION PICTURE: **Robert Bolt** *A Man for All Seasons*

Cannes International Film Festival

PALME D'OR: **A Man and a Woman** • *The Birds, the Bees, and the Italians*
DIRECTOR: **Sergei Yutkevitch** *Lenin in Poland*
ACTOR: **Per Oscarsson** *Hunger*
ACTRESS: **Vanessa Redgrave** *Morgan – a Suitable Case for Treatment*

Berlin International Film Festival

GOLDEN BERLIN BEAR: **Cul-de-Sac**
SILVER BERLIN BEAR FOR THE BEST DIRECTOR: **Carlos Saura** *The Hunt*
SILVER BERLIN BEAR FOR THE BEST ACTOR: **Jean-Pierre Léaud** *Masculine Feminine*
SILVER BERLIN BEAR FOR THE BEST ACTRESS: **Lola Albright** *Lord Love a Duck*

1967

British Film Academy Awards

BEST FILM FROM ANY SOURCE: **A Man for All Seasons** • *Bonnie and Clyde* • *A Man and a Woman* • *In the Heat of the Night*
BEST BRITISH FILM: **A Man for All Seasons** • *Accident* • *Blow Up* • *The Deadly Affair*
BEST FOREIGN ACTOR: **Rod Steiger** *In the Heat of the Night* • Warren Beatty *Bonnie and Clyde* • Sidney Poitier *In the Heat of the Night* • Orson Welles *Chimes at Midnight*
BEST FOREIGN ACTRESS: **Anouk Aimée** *A Man and a Woman* • Bibi Andersson *My Sister, My Love* • Bibi Andersson *Persona* • Jane Fonda *Barefoot in the Park* • Simone Signoret *The Deadly Affair*
BEST BRITISH ACTOR: **Paul Scofield** *A Man for All Seasons* • Dirk Bogarde *Accident* • Dirk Bogarde *Our Mother's House* • Richard Burton *The Taming of the Shrew* • James Mason *The Deadly Affair*
BEST BRITISH ACTRESS: **Edith Evans** *The Whisperers* • Barbara Jefford *Ulysses* • Elizabeth Taylor *The Taming of the Shrew*
BEST BRITISH SCREENPLAY: **Robert Bolt** *A Man for All Seasons* • Harold Pinter *Accident* • Paul Dehn *The Deadly Affair* • Frederic Raphael *Two for the Road*

Academy Awards

BEST PICTURE: **In the Heat of the Night** • *Bonnie and Clyde* • *Doctor Dolittle* • *The Graduate* • *Guess Who's Coming to Dinner*
FOREIGN LANGUAGE FILM: **Closely Observed Trains** • *El Amor Brujo* • *I Even Met Happy Gypsies* • *Vivre pour Vivre* • *Portrait of Chieko*

DIRECTING: **Mike Nichols** *The Graduate* • Arthur Penn *Bonnie and Clyde* • Stanley Kramer *Guess Who's Coming to Dinner* • Richard Brooks *In Cold Blood* • Norman Jewison *In the Heat of the Night*
ACTOR: **Rod Steiger** *In the Heat of the Night* • Warren Beatty *Bonnie and Clyde* • Dustin Hoffman *The Graduate* • Paul Newman *Cool Hand Luke* • Spencer Tracy *Guess Who's Coming to Dinner*
ACTRESS: **Katharine Hepburn** *Guess Who's Coming to Dinner* • Anne Bancroft *The Graduate* • Faye Dunaway *Bonnie and Clyde* • Edith Evans *The Whisperers* • Audrey Hepburn *Wait until Dark*
ACTOR IN A SUPPORTING ROLE: **George Kennedy** *Cool Hand Luke* • John Cassavetes *The Dirty Dozen* • Gene Hackman *Bonnie and Clyde* • Cecil Kellaway *Guess Who's Coming to Dinner* • Michael J Pollard *Bonnie and Clyde*
ACTRESS IN A SUPPORTING ROLE: **Estelle Parsons** *Bonnie and Clyde* • Carol Channing *Thoroughly Modern Millie* • Mildred Natwick *Barefoot in the Park* • Beah Richards *Guess Who's Coming to Dinner* • Katharine Ross *The Graduate*
WRITING (STORY AND SCREENPLAY WRITTEN DIRECTLY FOR THE SCREEN): **William Rose** *Guess Who's Coming to Dinner* • David Newman, Robert Benton *Bonnie and Clyde* • Norman Lear, Robert Kaufman *Divorce American Style* • Jorge Semprun *La Guerre Est Finie* • Frederic Raphael *Two for the Road*
WRITING (SCREENPLAY BASED ON MATERIAL FROM ANOTHER MEDIUM): **Stirling Silliphant** *In the Heat of the Night* • Donn Pearce, Frank Pierson *Cool Hand Luke* • Calder Willingham, Buck Henry *The Graduate* • Richard Brooks *In Cold Blood* • Joseph Strick, Fred Haines *Ulysses*

Golden Globe Awards

BEST MOTION PICTURE DRAMA: **In the Heat of the Night**
BEST MOTION PICTURE COMEDY OR MUSICAL: **The Graduate**
BEST FOREIGN LANGUAGE FILM: **Vivre pour Vivre • The Fox**
BEST DIRECTOR MOTION PICTURE: **Mike Nichols** *The Graduate*
BEST PERFORMANCE BY AN ACTOR IN A MOTION PICTURE DRAMA: **Rod Steiger** *In the Heat of the Night*
BEST PERFORMANCE BY AN ACTRESS IN A MOTION PICTURE DRAMA: **Edith Evans** *The Whisperers*
BEST PERFORMANCE BY AN ACTOR IN A MOTION PICTURE COMEDY OR MUSICAL: **Richard Harris** *Camelot*
BEST PERFORMANCE BY AN ACTRESS IN A MOTION PICTURE COMEDY OR MUSICAL: **Anne Bancroft** *The Graduate*
BEST PERFORMANCE BY AN ACTOR IN A SUPPORTING ROLE MOTION PICTURE: **Richard Attenborough** *Doctor Dolittle*
BEST PERFORMANCE BY AN ACTRESS IN A SUPPORTING ROLE MOTION PICTURE: **Carol Channing** *Thoroughly Modern Millie*
BEST SCREENPLAY MOTION PICTURE: **Stirling Silliphant** *In the Heat of the Night*

Cannes International Film Festival

GRAND PRIX: **Blow Up**
DIRECTOR: **Ferenc Kosa** *Tizezer Nap*
ACTOR: **Odded Kotler** *Three Days and a Child*
ACTRESS: **Pia Degermark** *Elvira Madigan*
SCREENPLAY: **Alain Jessua** *Jeu de Massacre* • Elio Petri *We Still Kill the Old Way*

Berlin International Film Festival

GOLDEN BERLIN BEAR: **Le Départ**
SILVER BERLIN BEAR FOR THE BEST DIRECTOR: **Zivojin Pavlovic** *Budjenje Pacova*
SILVER BERLIN BEAR FOR THE BEST ACTOR: **Michel Simon** *The Two of Us*
SILVER BERLIN BEAR FOR THE BEST ACTRESS: **Edith Evans** *The Whisperers*

1968

British Film Academy Awards

BEST FILM: **The Graduate** • *Closely Observed Trains* • *Oliver!* • *2001: a Space Odyssey*
BEST DIRECTOR: **Mike Nichols** *The Graduate* • Lindsay Anderson *if . ...* • Carol Reed *Oliver!* • Franco Zeffirelli *Romeo and Juliet*
BEST ACTOR: **Spencer Tracy** *Guess Who's Coming to Dinner* • Trevor Howard *The Charge of theLight Brigade* • Ron Moody *Oliver!* • Nicol Williamson *The Bofors Gun*
BEST ACTRESS: **Katharine Hepburn** *The Lion in Winter* • **Katharine Hepburn** *Guess Who's Coming to Dinner* • Anne Bancroft *The Graduate* • Catherine Deneuve *Belle de Jour* • Joanne Woodward *Rachel, Rachel*
BEST SUPPORTING ACTOR: **Ian Holm** *The Bofors Gun* • Anthony Hopkins *The Lion in Winter* • John McEnery *Romeo and Juliet* • George Segal *No Way to Treat a Lady*

BEST SUPPORTING ACTRESS: **Billie Whitelaw** *Charlie Bubbles* • Pat Heywood *Romeo and Juliet* • Virginia Maskell *Interlude* • Simone Signoret *Games*
BEST SCREENPLAY: **Calder Willingham, Buck Henry** *The Graduate* • William Rose *Guess Who's Coming to Dinner* • David Sherwin *if . ...* • James Goldman *The Lion in Winter*

Academy Awards

BEST PICTURE: **Oliver!** • *Funny Girl* • *The Lion in Winter* • *Rachel, Rachel* • *Romeo and Juliet*
FOREIGN LANGUAGE FILM: **War and Peace** • *The Boys of Paul Street* • *The Fireman's Ball* • *The Girl with the Pistol* • *Stolen Kisses*
DIRECTING: **Carol Reed** *Oliver!* • Stanley Kubrick *2001: a Space Odyssey* • Gillo Pontecorvo *The Battle of Algiers* • Anthony Harvey *The Lion in Winter* • Franco Zeffirelli *Romeo and Juliet*
ACTOR: **Cliff Robertson** *Charly* • Alan Arkin *The Heart Is a Lonely Hunter* • Alan Bates *The Fixer* • Ron Moody *Oliver!* • Peter O'Toole *The Lion in Winter*
ACTRESS: **Katharine Hepburn** *The Lion in Winter* • **Barbra Streisand** *Funny Girl* • Patricia Neal *The Subject Was Roses* • Vanessa Redgrave *Isadora* • Joanne Woodward *Rachel, Rachel*
ACTOR IN A SUPPORTING ROLE: **Jack Albertson** *The Subject Was Roses* • Seymour Cassel *Faces* • Daniel Massey *Star!* • Jack Wild *Oliver!* • Gene Wilder *The Producers*
ACTRESS IN A SUPPORTING ROLE: **Ruth Gordon** *Rosemary's Baby* • Lynn Carlin *Faces* • Sondra Locke *The Heart Is a Lonely Hunter* • Kay Medford *Funny Girl* • Estelle Parsons *Rachel, Rachel*
WRITING (STORY AND SCREENPLAY WRITTEN DIRECTLY FOR THE SCREEN): **Mel Brooks** *The Producers* • Stanley Kubrick, Arthur C Clarke *2001: a Space Odyssey* • Franco Solinas, Gillo Pontecorvo *The Battle of Algiers* • John Cassavetes *Faces* • Ira Wallach, Peter Ustinov *Hot Millions*
WRITING (SCREENPLAY BASED ON MATERIAL FROM ANOTHER MEDIUM): **James Goldman** *The Lion in Winter* • Neil Simon *The Odd Couple* • Vernon Harris *Oliver!* • Stewart Stern *Rachel, Rachel* • Roman Polanski *Rosemary's Baby*

Golden Globe Awards

BEST MOTION PICTURE DRAMA: **The Lion in Winter**
BEST MOTION PICTURE COMEDY OR MUSICAL: **Funny Girl**
BEST FOREIGN LANGUAGE FILM: **War and Peace • Romeo and Juliet**
BEST DIRECTOR MOTION PICTURE: **Paul Newman** *Rachel, Rachel*
BEST PERFORMANCE BY AN ACTOR IN A MOTION PICTURE DRAMA: **Peter O'Toole** *The Lion in Winter*
BEST PERFORMANCE BY AN ACTRESS IN A MOTION PICTURE DRAMA: **Joanne Woodward** *Rachel, Rachel*
BEST PERFORMANCE BY AN ACTOR IN A MOTION PICTURE COMEDY OR MUSICAL: **Ron Moody** *Oliver!*
BEST PERFORMANCE BY AN ACTRESS IN A MOTION PICTURE COMEDY OR MUSICAL: **Barbra Streisand** *Funny Girl*
BEST PERFORMANCE BY AN ACTOR IN A SUPPORTING ROLE MOTION PICTURE: **Daniel Massey** *Star!*
BEST PERFORMANCE BY AN ACTRESS IN A SUPPORTING ROLE MOTION PICTURE: **Ruth Gordon** *Rosemary's Baby*
BEST SCREENPLAY MOTION PICTURE: **Stirling Silliphant** *Charly*

Berlin International Film Festival

GOLDEN BERLIN BEAR: **Who Saw Him Die?**
SILVER BERLIN BEAR FOR THE BEST DIRECTOR: **Carlos Saura** *Peppermint Frappé*
SILVER BERLIN BEAR FOR THE BEST ACTOR: **Jean-Louis Trintignant** *L'Homme Qui Ment*
SILVER BERLIN BEAR FOR THE BEST ACTRESS: **Stéphane Audran** *Les Biches*

1969

British Film Academy Awards

BEST FILM: **Midnight Cowboy** • *Oh! What a Lovely War* • *Women in Love* • *Z*
BEST DIRECTOR: **John Schlesinger** *Midnight Cowboy* • Peter Yates *Bullitt* • Richard Attenborough *Oh! What a Lovely War* • Ken Russell *Women in Love*
BEST ACTOR: **Dustin Hoffman** *Midnight Cowboy* • **Dustin Hoffman** *John and Mary* • Alan Bates *Women in Love* • Walter Matthau *The Secret Life of an American Wife* • Walter Matthau *Hello, Dolly!* • Nicol Williamson *Inadmissible Evidence*
BEST ACTRESS: **Maggie Smith** *The Prime of Miss Jean Brodie* • Mia Farrow *Secret Ceremony* • Mia Farrow *Rosemary's Baby* • Mia Farrow *John and Mary* • Glenda Jackson *Women in Love* • Barbra Streisand *Funny Girl* • Barbra Streisand *Hello, Dolly!*

BEST SUPPORTING ACTOR: **Laurence Olivier** *Oh! What a Lovely War* • Jack Klugman *Goodbye, Columbus* • Jack Nicholson *Easy Rider* • Robert Vaughn *Bullitt*
BEST SUPPORTING ACTRESS: **Celia Johnson** *The Prime of Miss Jean Brodie* • Peggy Ashcroft *Three into Two Won't Go* • Pamela Franklin *The Prime of Miss Jean Brodie* • Mary Wimbush *Oh! What a Lovely War*
BEST SCREENPLAY: **Waldo Salt** *Midnight Cowboy* • Arnold Schulman *Goodbye, Columbus* • Larry Kramer *Women in Love* • Costa-Gavras, Jorge Semprun *Z*

Academy Awards

BEST PICTURE: **Midnight Cowboy** • *Anne of the Thousand Days* • *Butch Cassidy and the Sundance Kid* • *Hello, Dolly!* • *Z*
FOREIGN LANGUAGE FILM: **Z** • *Adalen 31* • *The Battle of Neretva* • *The Brothers Karamazov* • *My Night with Maud*
DIRECTING: **John Schlesinger** *Midnight Cowboy* • Arthur Penn *Alice's Restaurant* • George Roy Hill *Butch Cassidy and the Sundance Kid* • Sydney Pollack *They Shoot Horses, Don't They?* • Costa-Gavras *Z*
ACTOR: **John Wayne** *True Grit* • Richard Burton *Anne of the Thousand Days* • Dustin Hoffman *Midnight Cowboy* • Peter O'Toole *Goodbye, Mr Chips* • Jon Voight *Midnight Cowboy*
ACTRESS: **Maggie Smith** *The Prime of Miss Jean Brodie* • Geneviève Bujold *Anne of the Thousand Days* • Jane Fonda *They Shoot Horses, Don't They?* • Liza Minnelli *The Sterile Cuckoo* • Jean Simmons *The Happy Ending*
ACTOR IN A SUPPORTING ROLE: **Gig Young** *They Shoot Horses, Don't They?* • Rupert Crosse *The Reivers* • Elliott Gould *Bob & Carol & Ted & Alice* • Jack Nicholson *Easy Rider* • Anthony Quayle *Anne of the Thousand Days*
ACTRESS IN A SUPPORTING ROLE: **Goldie Hawn** *Cactus Flower* • Catherine Burns *Last Summer* • Dyan Cannon *Bob & Carol & Ted & Alice* • Sylvia Miles *Midnight Cowboy* • Susannah York *They Shoot Horses, Don't They?*
WRITING (STORY AND SCREENPLAY BASED ON MATERIAL NOT PREVIOUSLY PUBLISHED OR PRODUCED): **William Goldman** *Butch Cassidy and the Sundance Kid* • Paul Mazursky, Larry Tucker *Bob & Carol & Ted & Alice* • Nicola Badalucco, Enrico Medioli, Luchino Visconti *The Damned* • Peter Fonda, Dennis Hopper, Terry Southern *Easy Rider* • Walon Green, Sam Peckinpah, Roy N Sickner *The Wild Bunch*
WRITING (SCREENPLAY BASED ON MATERIAL FROM ANOTHER MEDIUM): **Waldo Salt** *Midnight Cowboy* • Bridget Boland, John Hale, Richard Sokolove *Anne of the Thousand Days* • Arnold Schulman *Goodbye, Columbus* • James Poe, Robert E Thompson *They Shoot Horses, Don't They?* • Costa-Gavras, Jorge Semprun *Z*

Golden Globe Awards

BEST MOTION PICTURE DRAMA: **Anne of the Thousand Days**
BEST MOTION PICTURE COMEDY OR MUSICAL: **The Secret of Santa Vittoria**
BEST FOREIGN LANGUAGE FILM: **Oh! What a Lovely War • Z**
BEST DIRECTOR MOTION PICTURE: **Charles Jarrott** *Anne of the Thousand Days*
BEST PERFORMANCE BY AN ACTOR IN A MOTION PICTURE DRAMA: **John Wayne** *True Grit*
BEST PERFORMANCE BY AN ACTRESS IN A MOTION PICTURE DRAMA: **Geneviève Bujold** *Anne of the Thousand Days*
BEST PERFORMANCE BY AN ACTOR IN A MOTION PICTURE COMEDY OR MUSICAL: **Peter O'Toole** *Goodbye, Mr Chips*
BEST PERFORMANCE BY AN ACTRESS IN A MOTION PICTURE COMEDY OR MUSICAL: **Patty Duke** *Me, Natalie*
BEST PERFORMANCE BY AN ACTOR IN A SUPPORTING ROLE MOTION PICTURE: **Gig Young** *They Shoot Horses, Don't They?*
BEST PERFORMANCE BY AN ACTRESS IN A SUPPORTING ROLE MOTION PICTURE: **Goldie Hawn** *Cactus Flower*
BEST SCREENPLAY MOTION PICTURE: **John Hale, Bridget Boland** *Anne of the Thousand Days*

Cannes International Film Festival

GRAND PRIX: **if . ...**
DIRECTOR: **Glauber Rocha** *Antonio das Mortes* • Vojtech Jasny *All My Good Countrymen*
ACTOR: **Jean-Louis Trintignant** *Z*
ACTRESS: **Vanessa Redgrave** *Isadora*

Berlin International Film Festival

GOLDEN BERLIN BEAR: **Rani Radovi**

1970

British Film Academy Awards

BEST FILM: **Butch Cassidy and the Sundance Kid** • Kes • M*A*S*H • Ryan's Daughter

BEST DIRECTOR: **George Roy Hill** Butch Cassidy and the Sundance Kid • Ken Loach Kes • Robert Altman M*A*S*H • David Lean Ryan's Daughter

BEST ACTOR: **Robert Redford** Butch Cassidy and the Sundance Kid • **Robert Redford** Tell Them Willie Boy Is Here • **Robert Redford** Downhill Racer • Elliott Gould Bob & Carol & Ted & Alice • Elliott Gould M*A*S*H • Paul Newman Butch Cassidy and the Sundance Kid • George C Scott Patton: Lust for Glory

BEST ACTRESS: **Katharine Ross** Tell Them Willie Boy Is Here • **Katharine Ross** Butch Cassidy and the Sundance Kid • Jane Fonda They Shoot Horses, Don't They? • Goldie Hawn Cactus Flower • Goldie Hawn There's a Girl in My Soup • Sarah Miles Ryan's Daughter

BEST SUPPORTING ACTOR: **Colin Welland** Kes • Bernard Cribbins The Railway Children • John Mills Ryan's Daughter • Gig Young They Shoot Horses, Don't They?

BEST SUPPORTING ACTRESS: **Susannah York** They Shoot Horses, Don't They? • Evin Crowley Ryan's Daughter • Estelle Parsons Watermelon Man • Maureen Stapleton Airport

BEST SCREENPLAY: **William Goldman** Butch Cassidy and the Sundance Kid • Paul Mazursky, Larry Tucker Bob & Carol & Ted & Alice • Ken Loach, Tony Garnett, Barry Hines Kes • James Poe, Robert E Thompson They Shoot Horses, Don't They?

Academy Awards

BEST PICTURE: **Patton: Lust for Glory** • Airport • Five Easy Pieces • Love Story • M*A*S*H

FOREIGN LANGUAGE FILM: **Investigation of a Citizen above Suspicion** • First Love • Hoa-Binh • Paix sur les Champs • Tristana

DIRECTING: **Franklin J Schaffner** Patton: Lust for Glory • Federico Fellini Satyricon • Arthur Hiller Love Story • Robert Altman M*A*S*H • Ken Russell Women in Love

ACTOR: **George C Scott** Patton: Lust for Glory • Melvyn Douglas I Never Sang for My Father • James Earl Jones The Great White Hope • Jack Nicholson Five Easy Pieces • Ryan O'Neal Love Story

ACTRESS: **Glenda Jackson** Women in Love • Jane Alexander The Great White Hope • Ali MacGraw Love Story • Sarah Miles Ryan's Daughter • Carrie Snodgress Diary of a Mad Housewife

ACTOR IN A SUPPORTING ROLE: **John Mills** Ryan's Daughter • Richard Castellano Lovers and Other Strangers • Chief Dan George Little Big Man • Gene Hackman I Never Sang for My Father • John Marley Love Story

ACTRESS IN A SUPPORTING ROLE: **Helen Hayes**, Maureen Stapleton Airport • Karen Black Five Easy Pieces • Lee Grant The Landlord • Sally Kellerman M*A*S*H

WRITING (STORY AND SCREENPLAY BASED ON FACTUAL MATERIAL OR MATERIAL NOT PREVIOUSLY PUBLISHED OR PRODUCED): **Francis Ford Coppola, Edmund H North** Patton: Lust for Glory • Carole Eastman, Bob Rafelson Five Easy Pieces • Norman Wexler Joe • Erich Segal Love Story • Eric Rohmer My Night with Maud

WRITING (SCREENPLAY BASED ON MATERIAL FROM ANOTHER MEDIUM): **Ring Lardner Jr** M*A*S*H • George Seaton Airport • Robert W Anderson I Never Sang for My Father • Renee Taylor, Joseph Bologna, David Zelag Goodman Lovers and Other Strangers • Larry Kramer Women in Love

Golden Globe Awards

BEST MOTION PICTURE . DRAMA: **Love Story**

BEST MOTION PICTURE . COMEDY OR MUSICAL: **M*A*S*H**

BEST FOREIGN LANGUAGE FILM: **Women in Love** • Rider on the Rain

BEST DIRECTOR . MOTION PICTURE: **Arthur Hiller** Love Story

BEST PERFORMANCE BY AN ACTOR IN A MOTION PICTURE DRAMA: **George C Scott** Patton: Lust for Glory

BEST PERFORMANCE BY AN ACTRESS IN A MOTION PICTURE DRAMA: **Ali MacGraw** Love Story

BEST PERFORMANCE BY AN ACTOR IN A MOTION PICTURE COMEDY OR MUSICAL: **Albert Finney** Scrooge

BEST PERFORMANCE BY AN ACTRESS IN A MOTION PICTURE COMEDY OR MUSICAL: **Carrie Snodgress** Diary of a Mad Housewife

BEST PERFORMANCE BY AN ACTOR IN A SUPPORTING ROLE . MOTION PICTURE: **John Mills** Ryan's Daughter

BEST PERFORMANCE BY AN ACTRESS IN A SUPPORTING ROLE . MOTION PICTURE: **Karen Black** Five Easy Pieces • **Maureen Stapleton** Airport

BEST SCREENPLAY . MOTION PICTURE: **Erich Segal** Love Story

Cannes International Film Festival

GRAND PRIX: **M*A*S*H**

DIRECTOR: **John Boorman** Leo the Last

ACTOR: **Marcello Mastroianni** Jealousy, Italian Style

ACTRESS: **Ottavia Piccolo** Metello

1971

British Film Academy Awards

BEST FILM: **Sunday, Bloody Sunday** • Death in Venice • The Go-Between • Taking Off

BEST DIRECTOR: **John Schlesinger** Sunday, Bloody Sunday • Luchino Visconti Death in Venice • Joseph Losey The Go-Between • Milos Forman Taking Off

BEST ACTOR: **Peter Finch** Sunday, Bloody Sunday • Dirk Bogarde Death in Venice • Albert Finney Gumshoe • Dustin Hoffman Little Big Man

BEST ACTRESS: **Glenda Jackson** Sunday, Bloody Sunday • Lynn Carlin Taking Off • Julie Christie The Go-Between • Jane Fonda Klute • Nanette Newman The Raging Moon

BEST SUPPORTING ACTOR: **Edward Fox**, Michael Gough The Go-Between • Ian Hendry Get Carter • John Hurt 10 Rillington Place

BEST SUPPORTING ACTRESS: **Margaret Leighton** The Go-Between • Jane Asher Deep End • Georgia Brown The Raging Moon • Georgia Engel Taking Off

BEST SCREENPLAY: **Harold Pinter** The Go-Between • Neville Smith Gumshoe • Penelope Gilliatt Sunday, Bloody Sunday • Milos Forman, John Guare, Jean-Claude Carriere, John Klein Taking Off

Academy Awards

BEST PICTURE: **The French Connection** • A Clockwork Orange • Fiddler on the Roof • The Last Picture Show • Nicholas and Alexandra

FOREIGN LANGUAGE FILM: **The Garden of the Finzi-Continis** • Dodes'ka-Den • The Emigrants • The Policeman • Tchaikovsky

DIRECTING: **William Friedkin** The French Connection • Stanley Kubrick A Clockwork Orange • Norman Jewison Fiddler on the Roof • Peter Bogdanovich The Last Picture Show • John Schlesinger Sunday, Bloody Sunday

ACTOR: **Gene Hackman** The French Connection • Peter Finch Sunday, Bloody Sunday • Walter Matthau Kotch • George C Scott The Hospital • Topol Fiddler on the Roof

ACTRESS: **Jane Fonda** Klute • Julie Christie McCabe and Mrs Miller • Glenda Jackson Sunday, Bloody Sunday • Vanessa Redgrave Mary, Queen of Scots • Janet Suzman Nicholas and Alexandra

ACTOR IN A SUPPORTING ROLE: **Ben Johnson**, Jeff Bridges The Last Picture Show • Leonard Frey Fiddler on the Roof • Richard Jaeckel Sometimes a Great Notion • Roy Scheider The French Connection

ACTRESS IN A SUPPORTING ROLE: **Cloris Leachman**, Ellen Burstyn The Last Picture Show • Ann-Margret Carnal Knowledge • Barbara Harris Who Is Harry Kellerman, and Why Is He Saying Those Terrible Things about Me? • Margaret Leighton The Go-Between

WRITING (STORY AND SCREENPLAY BASED ON FACTUAL MATERIAL OR MATERIAL NOT PREVIOUSLY PUBLISHED OR PRODUCED): **Paddy Chayefsky** The Hospital • Elio Petri, Ugo Pirro Investigation of a Citizen above Suspicion • Andy Lewis, Dave Lewis Klute • Herman Raucher Summer of '42 • Penelope Gilliatt Sunday, Bloody Sunday

WRITING (SCREENPLAY BASED ON MATERIAL FROM ANOTHER MEDIUM): **Ernest Tidyman** The French Connection • Stanley Kubrick A Clockwork Orange • Bernardo Bertolucci The Conformist • Vittorio Bonicelli, Ugo Pirro The Garden of the Finzi-Continis • Peter Bogdanovich, Larry McMurtry The Last Picture Show

Golden Globe Awards

BEST MOTION PICTURE . DRAMA: **The French Connection**

BEST MOTION PICTURE . COMEDY OR MUSICAL: **Fiddler on the Roof**

BEST FOREIGN LANGUAGE FILM: **The Policeman** • Sunday, Bloody Sunday

BEST DIRECTOR . MOTION PICTURE: **William Friedkin** The French Connection

BEST PERFORMANCE BY AN ACTOR IN A MOTION PICTURE DRAMA: **Gene Hackman** The French Connection

BEST PERFORMANCE BY AN ACTRESS IN A MOTION PICTURE DRAMA: **Jane Fonda** Klute

BEST PERFORMANCE BY AN ACTOR IN A MOTION PICTURE COMEDY OR MUSICAL: **Topol** Fiddler on the Roof

BEST PERFORMANCE BY AN ACTRESS IN A MOTION PICTURE COMEDY OR MUSICAL: **Twiggy** The Boy Friend

BEST PERFORMANCE BY AN ACTOR IN A SUPPORTING ROLE . MOTION PICTURE: **Ben Johnson** The Last Picture Show

BEST PERFORMANCE BY AN ACTRESS IN A SUPPORTING ROLE . MOTION PICTURE: **Ann-Margret** Carnal Knowledge

BEST SCREENPLAY . MOTION PICTURE: **Paddy Chayefsky** The Hospital

Cannes International Film Festival

GRAND PRIX: **The Go-Between**

ACTOR: **Riccardo Cucciolla** Sacco and Vanzetti

ACTRESS: **Kitty Winn** The Panic in Needle Park

Berlin International Film Festival

GOLDEN BERLIN BEAR: **The Garden of the Finzi-Continis**

SILVER BERLIN BEAR FOR THE BEST ACTOR: **Jean Gabin** Le Chat

SILVER BERLIN BEAR FOR THE BEST ACTRESS: **Shirley MacLaine** Desperate Characters • Simone Signoret Le Chat

1972

British Film Academy Awards

BEST FILM: **Cabaret** • A Clockwork Orange • The French Connection • The Last Picture Show

BEST DIRECTOR: **Bob Fosse** Cabaret • Stanley Kubrick A Clockwork Orange • William Friedkin The French Connection • Peter Bogdanovich The Last Picture Show

BEST ACTOR: **Gene Hackman** The French Connection • **Gene Hackman** The Poseidon Adventure • Marlon Brando The Nightcomers • Marlon Brando The Godfather • George C Scott They Might Be Giants • George C Scott The Hospital • Robert Shaw Young Winston

BEST ACTRESS: **Liza Minnelli** Cabaret • Stéphane Audran Le Boucher • Anne Bancroft Young Winston • Dorothy Tutin Savage Messiah

BEST SUPPORTING ACTOR: **Ben Johnson** The Last Picture Show • Max Adrian The Boy Friend • Robert Duvall The Godfather • Ralph Richardson Lady Caroline Lamb

BEST SUPPORTING ACTRESS: **Cloris Leachman** The Last Picture Show • Marisa Berenson Cabaret • Eileen Brennan The Last Picture Show • Shelley Winters The Poseidon Adventure

BEST SCREENPLAY: **Paddy Chayefsky** The Hospital • **Larry McMurtry, Peter Bogdanovich** The Last Picture Show • Jay Presson Allen Cabaret • Stanley Kubrick A Clockwork Orange

Academy Awards

BEST PICTURE: **The Godfather** • Cabaret • Deliverance • The Emigrants • Sounder

FOREIGN LANGUAGE FILM: **The Discreet Charm of the Bourgeoisie** • The Dawns Here Are Quiet • I Love You Rosa • My Dearest Señorita • The New Land

DIRECTING: **Bob Fosse** Cabaret • John Boorman Deliverance • Jan Troell The Emigrants • Francis Ford Coppola The Godfather • Joseph L Mankiewicz Sleuth

ACTOR: **Marlon Brando** The Godfather • Michael Caine, Laurence Olivier Sleuth • Peter O'Toole The Ruling Class • Paul Winfield Sounder

ACTRESS: **Liza Minnelli** Cabaret • Diana Ross Lady Sings the Blues • Maggie Smith Travels with My Aunt • Cicely Tyson Sounder • Liv Ullmann The Emigrants

ACTOR IN A SUPPORTING ROLE: **Joel Grey** Cabaret • James Caan, Robert Duvall, Al Pacino The Godfather • Eddie Albert The Heartbreak Kid

ACTRESS IN A SUPPORTING ROLE: **Eileen Heckart** Butterflies Are Free • Jeannie Berlin The Heartbreak Kid • Geraldine Page Pete 'n' Tillie • Susan Tyrrell Fat City • Shelley Winters The Poseidon Adventure

WRITING (STORY AND SCREENPLAY BASED ON FACTUAL MATERIAL OR MATERIAL NOT PREVIOUSLY PUBLISHED OR PRODUCED): **Jeremy Larner** The Candidate • Luis Buñuel, Jean-Claude Carrière The Discreet Charm of the Bourgeoisie • Chris Clark, Suzanne De Passe, Terence McCloy Lady Sings the Blues • Louis Malle Le Souffle au Coeur • Carl Foreman Young Winston

WRITING (SCREENPLAY BASED ON MATERIAL FROM ANOTHER MEDIUM): **Francis Ford Coppola, Mario Puzo** The Godfather • Jay Presson Allen Cabaret • Bengt Forslund, Jan Troell The Emigrants • Julius J Epstein Pete 'n' Tillie • Lonne Elder III Sounder

Golden Globe Awards

BEST MOTION PICTURE . DRAMA: **The Godfather**

BEST MOTION PICTURE . COMEDY OR MUSICAL: **Cabaret**

BEST FOREIGN LANGUAGE FILM: **The Emigrants** • **The New Land** • **Young Winston**

BEST DIRECTOR . MOTION PICTURE: **Francis Ford Coppola** The Godfather

BEST PERFORMANCE BY AN ACTOR IN A MOTION PICTURE DRAMA: **Marlon Brando** The Godfather

BEST PERFORMANCE BY AN ACTRESS IN A MOTION PICTURE DRAMA: **Liv Ullmann** The Emigrants

BEST PERFORMANCE BY AN ACTOR IN A MOTION PICTURE COMEDY OR MUSICAL: **Jack Lemmon** Avanti!

Best Performance by an Actress in a Motion Picture Comedy or Musical: **Liza Minnelli** *Cabaret*
Best Performance by an Actor in a Supporting Role Motion Picture: **Joel Grey** *Cabaret*
Best Performance by an Actress in a Supporting Role Motion Picture: **Shelley Winters** *The Poseidon Adventure*
Best Screenplay Motion Picture: **Francis Ford Coppola, Mario Puzo** *The Godfather*

Cannes International Film Festival

Grand Prix: ***The Working Class Go to Heaven* • *Il Caso Mattei***
Director: **Miklós Jancsó** *Még Kér a Nép*
Actor: **Jean Yanne** *Nous Ne Vieillirons Pas Ensemble*
Actress: **Susannah York** *Images*

Berlin International Film Festival

Golden Berlin Bear: ***The Canterbury Tales***
Silver Berlin Bear for the Best Director: **Jean-Pierre Blanc** *La Vieille Fille*
Silver Berlin Bear for the Best Actor: **Alberto Sordi** *Detenuto in Attesa di Giudizio*
Silver Berlin Bear for the Best Actress: **Elizabeth Taylor** *Hammersmith Is Out*

1973

British Film Academy Awards

Best Film: ***Day for Night*** • *The Day of the Jackal* • *The Discreet Charm of the Bourgeoisie* • *Don't Look Now*
Best Director: **François Truffaut** *Day for Night* • Fred Zinnemann *The Day of the Jackal* • Luis Buñuel *The Discreet Charm of the Bourgeoisie* • Nicolas Roeg *Don't Look Now*
Best Actor: **Walter Matthau** *Pete 'n' Tillie* • **Walter Matthau** *Charley Varrick* • Marlon Brando *Last Tango in Paris* • Laurence Olivier *Sleuth* • Donald Sutherland *Don't Look Now* • Donald Sutherland *Steelyard Blues*
Best Actress: **Stéphane Audran** *The Discreet Charm of the Bourgeoisie* • **Stéphane Audran** *Juste avant la Nuit* • Julie Christie *Don't Look Now* • Glenda Jackson *A Touch of Class* • Diana Ross *Lady Sings the Blues*
Best Supporting Actor: **Arthur Lowe** *O Lucky Man!* • Ian Bannen *The Offence* • Denholm Elliott *A Doll's House* • Michel Lonsdale *The Day of the Jackal*
Best Supporting Actress: **Valentina Cortese** *Day for Night* • Rosemary Leach *That'll Be the Day* • Delphine Seyrig *The Day of the Jackal* • Ingrid Thulin *Cries and Whispers*
Best Screenplay: **Luis Buñuel, Jean-Claude Carrière** *The Discreet Charm of the Bourgeoisie* • Kenneth Ross *The Day of the Jackal* • Anthony Shaffer *Sleuth* • Melvin Frank, Jack Rose *A Touch of Class*

Academy Awards

Best Picture: ***The Sting*** • *American Graffiti* • *Cries and Whispers* • *The Exorcist* • *A Touch of Class*
Foreign Language Film: ***Day for Night*** • *The House on Chelouche Street* • *The Invitation* • *The Pedestrian* • *Turkish Delight*
Directing: **George Roy Hill** *The Sting* • George Lucas *American Graffiti* • Ingmar Bergman *Cries and Whispers* • William Friedkin *The Exorcist* • Bernardo Bertolucci *Last Tango in Paris*
Actor: **Jack Lemmon** *Save the Tiger* • Marlon Brando *Last Tango in Paris* • Jack Nicholson *The Last Detail* • Al Pacino *Serpico* • Robert Redford *The Sting*
Actress: **Glenda Jackson** *A Touch of Class* • Ellen Burstyn *The Exorcist* • Marsha Mason *Cinderella Liberty* • Barbra Streisand *The Way We Were* • Joanne Woodward *Summer Wishes, Winter Dreams*
Actor in a Supporting Role: **John Houseman** *The Paper Chase* • Vincent Gardenia *Bang the Drum Slowly* • Jack Gilford *Save the Tiger* • Jason Miller *The Exorcist* • Randy Quaid *The Last Detail*
Actress in a Supporting Role: **Tatum O'Neal**, Madeline Kahn *Paper Moon* • Linda Blair *The Exorcist* • Candy Clark *American Graffiti* • Sylvia Sidney *Summer Wishes, Winter Dreams*
Writing (Story and Screenplay Based On Factual Material or Material Not Previously Published or Produced): **David S Ward** *The Sting* • George Lucas, Gloria Katz, Willard Huyck *American Graffiti* • Ingmar Bergman *Cries and Whispers* • Steve Shagan *Save the Tiger* • Melvin Frank, Jack Rose *A Touch of Class*
Writing (Screenplay Based On Material From Another Medium): **William Peter Blatty** *The Exorcist* • Robert Towne *The Last Detail* • James Bridges *The Paper Chase* • Alvin Sargent *Paper Moon* • Waldo Salt, Norman Wexler *Serpico*

Golden Globe Awards

Best Motion Picture . Drama: ***The Exorcist***
Best Motion Picture Comedy or Musical: ***American Graffiti***
Best Foreign Language Film: ***The Pedestrian***
Best Director Motion Picture: **William Friedkin** *The Exorcist*
Best Performance by an Actor in a Motion Picture Drama: **Al Pacino** *Serpico*
Best Performance by an Actress in a Motion Picture Drama: **Marsha Mason** *Cinderella Liberty*
Best Performance by an Actor in a Motion Picture Comedy or Musical: **George Segal** *A Touch of Class*
Best Performance by an Actress in a Motion Picture Comedy or Musical: **Glenda Jackson** *A Touch of Class*
Best Performance by an Actor in a Supporting Role Motion Picture: **John Houseman** *The Paper Chase*
Best Performance by an Actress in a Supporting Role Motion Picture: **Linda Blair** *The Exorcist*
Best Screenplay Motion Picture: **William Peter Blatty** *The Exorcist*

Cannes International Film Festival

Grand Prix: ***Scarecrow* • *The Hireling***
Actor: **Giancarlo Giannini** *Love and Anarchy*
Actress: **Joanne Woodward** *The Effect of Gamma Rays on Man-in-the-Moon Marigolds*

Berlin International Film Festival

Golden Berlin Bear: ***Distant Thunder***

1974

British Film Academy Awards

Best Film: ***Lacombe Lucien*** • *Chinatown* • *The Last Detail* • *Murder on the Orient Express*
Best Director: **Roman Polanski** *Chinatown* • Francis Ford Coppola *The Conversation* • Louis Malle *Lacombe Lucien* • Sidney Lumet *Murder on the Orient Express*
Best Actor: **Jack Nicholson** *The Last Detail* • **Jack Nicholson** *Chinatown* • Gene Hackman *The Conversation* • Albert Finney *Murder on the Orient Express* • Al Pacino *Serpico*
Best Actress: **Joanne Woodward** *Summer Wishes, Winter Dreams* • Cicely Tyson *The Autobiography of Miss Jane Pittman* • Faye Dunaway *Chinatown* • Barbra Streisand *The Way We Were*
Best Supporting Actor: **John Gielgud** *Murder on the Orient Express* • John Huston *Chinatown* • Randy Quaid *The Last Detail* • Adam Faith *Stardust*
Best Supporting Actress: **Ingrid Bergman** *Murder on the Orient Express* • Cindy Williams *American Graffiti* • Sylvia Sidney *Summer Wishes, Winter Dreams* • Sylvia Syms *The Tamarind Seed*
Best Screenplay: **Robert Towne** *Chinatown* • **Robert Towne** *The Last Detail* • Mel Brooks, Norman Steinberg, Andrew Bergman, Richard Pryor, Alan Uger *Blazing Saddles* • Francis Ford Coppola *The Conversation* • Louis Malle, Patrick Modiano *Lacombe Lucien*

Academy Awards

Best Picture: ***The Godfather, Part II*** • *Chinatown* • *The Conversation* • *Lenny* • *The Towering Inferno*
Foreign Language Film: ***Amarcord*** • *Cats' Play* • *The Deluge* • *Lacombe Lucien* • *The Truce*
Directing: **Francis Ford Coppola** *The Godfather, Part II* • Roman Polanski *Chinatown* • François Truffaut *Day for Night* • Bob Fosse *Lenny* • John Cassavetes *A Woman under the Influence*
Actor: **Art Carney** *Harry and Tonto* • Albert Finney *Murder on the Orient Express* • Dustin Hoffman *Lenny* • Jack Nicholson *Chinatown* • Al Pacino *The Godfather, Part II*
Actress: **Ellen Burstyn** *Alice Doesn't Live Here Anymore* • Diahann Carroll *Claudine* • Faye Dunaway *Chinatown* • Valerie Perrine *Lenny* • Gena Rowlands *A Woman under the Influence*
Actor in a Supporting Role: **Robert De Niro**, Michael V Gazzo, Lee Strasberg *The Godfather, Part II* • Fred Astaire *The Towering Inferno* • Jeff Bridges *Thunderbolt and Lightfoot*
Actress in a Supporting Role: **Ingrid Bergman** *Murder on the Orient Express* • Valentina Cortese *Day for Night* • Madeline Kahn *Blazing Saddles* • Diane Ladd *Alice Doesn't Live Here Anymore* • Talia Shire *The Godfather, Part II*
Writing (Original Screenplay): **Robert Towne** *Chinatown* • Robert Getchell *Alice Doesn't Live Here Anymore* • Francis Ford Coppola *The Conversation* • François Truffaut, Suzanne Schiffman, Jean-Louis Richard *Day for Night* • Paul Mazursky, Josh Greenfeld *Harry and Tonto*
Writing (Screenplay Adapted From Other Material): **Francis Ford Coppola, Mario Puzo** *The Godfather, Part II* • Mordecai Richler, Lionel Chetwynd *The Apprenticeship of Duddy Kravitz* • Julian Barry *Lenny* • Paul Dehn *Murder on the Orient Express* • Mel Brooks, Gene Wilder *Young Frankenstein*

Golden Globe Awards

Best Motion Picture . Drama: ***Chinatown***
Best Motion Picture Comedy or Musical: ***The Mean Machine***
Best Foreign Language Film: ***Scenes from a Marriage***
Best Director Motion Picture: **Roman Polanski** *Chinatown*
Best Performance by an Actor in a Motion Picture Drama: **Jack Nicholson** *Chinatown*
Best Performance by an Actress in a Motion Picture Drama: **Gena Rowlands** *A Woman under the Influence*
Best Performance by an Actor in a Motion Picture Comedy or Musical: **Art Carney** *Harry and Tonto*
Best Performance by an Actress in a Motion Picture Comedy or Musical: **Raquel Welch** *The Three Musketeers*
Best Performance by an Actor in a Supporting Role Motion Picture: **Fred Astaire** *The Towering Inferno*
Best Performance by an Actress in a Supporting Role Motion Picture: **Karen Black** *The Great Gatsby*
Best Screenplay Motion Picture: **Robert Towne** *Chinatown*

Cannes International Film Festival

Grand Prix: ***The Conversation***
Actor: **Jack Nicholson** *The Last Detail*
Actress: **Marie-José Nat** *Les Violons du Bal*
Screenplay: **Steven Spielberg** *The Sugarland Express*

Berlin International Film Festival

Golden Berlin Bear: ***The Apprenticeship of Duddy Kravitz***

1975

British Film Academy Awards

Best Film: ***Alice Doesn't Live Here Anymore*** • *Barry Lyndon* • *Dog Day Afternoon* • *Jaws*
Best Director: **Stanley Kubrick** *Barry Lyndon* • Martin Scorsese *Alice Doesn't Live Here Anymore* • Sidney Lumet *Dog Day Afternoon* • Steven Spielberg *Jaws*
Best Actor: **Al Pacino** *The Godfather, Part II* • **Al Pacino** *Dog Day Afternoon* • Richard Dreyfuss *Jaws* • Gene Hackman *French Connection II* • Gene Hackman *Night Moves* • Dustin Hoffman *Lenny*
Best Actress: **Ellen Burstyn** *Alice Doesn't Live Here Anymore* • Anne Bancroft *The Prisoner of Second Avenue* • Valerie Perrine *Lenny* • Liv Ullmann *Scenes from a Marriage*
Best Supporting Actor: **Fred Astaire** *The Towering Inferno* • Martin Balsam *The Taking of Pelham One Two Three* • Burgess Meredith *The Day of the Locust* • Jack Warden *Shampoo*
Best Supporting Actress: **Diane Ladd** *Alice Doesn't Live Here Anymore* • Ronee Blakley *Nashville* • Lelia Goldoni *Alice Doesn't Live Here Anymore* • Gwen Welles *Nashville*
Best Screenplay: **Robert Getchell** *Alice Doesn't Live Here Anymore* • Frank Pierson *Dog Day Afternoon* • Peter Benchley, Carl Gottlieb *Jaws* • Joan Tewkesbury *Nashville*

Academy Awards

Best Picture: ***One Flew over the Cuckoo's Nest*** • *Barry Lyndon* • *Dog Day Afternoon* • *Jaws* • *Nashville*
Foreign Language Film: ***Dersu Uzala*** • *Land of Promise* • *Letters from Marusia* • *Sandakan No 8* • *Scent of a Woman*
Directing: **Milos Forman** *One Flew over the Cuckoo's Nest* • Federico Fellini *Amarcord* • Stanley Kubrick *Barry Lyndon* • Sidney Lumet *Dog Day Afternoon* • Robert Altman *Nashville*
Actor: **Jack Nicholson** *One Flew over the Cuckoo's Nest* • Walter Matthau *The Sunshine Boys* • Al Pacino *Dog Day Afternoon* • Maximilian Schell *The Man in the Glass Booth* • James Whitmore *Give 'Em Hell, Harry!*
Actress: **Louise Fletcher** *One Flew over the Cuckoo's Nest* • Isabelle Adjani *L'Histoire d'Adèle H* • Ann-Margret *Tommy* • Glenda Jackson *Hedda* • Carol Kane *Hester Street*
Actor in a Supporting Role: **George Burns** *The Sunshine Boys* • Brad Dourif *One Flew over the Cuckoo's Nest* • Burgess Meredith *The Day of the Locust* • Chris Sarandon *Dog Day Afternoon* • Jack Warden *Shampoo*
Actress in a Supporting Role: **Lee Grant** *Shampoo* • Ronee Blakley, Lily Tomlin *Nashville* • Sylvia Miles *Farewell, My Lovely* • Brenda Vaccaro *Once Is Not Enough*

WRITING (ORIGINAL SCREENPLAY): **Frank Pierson** *Dog Day Afternoon* • Federico Fellini, Tonino Guerra *Amarcord* • Claude Lelouch, Pierre Uytterhoeven *And Now My Love* • Ted Allan *Lies My Father Told Me* • Warren Beatty, Robert Towne *Shampoo*

WRITING (SCREENPLAY ADAPTED FROM OTHER MATERIAL): **Bo Goldman, Lawrence Hauben** *One Flew over the Cuckoo's Nest* • Stanley Kubrick *Barry Lyndon* • John Huston, Gladys Hill *The Man Who Would Be King* • Ruggero Maccari, Dino Risi *Scent of a Woman* • Neil Simon *The Sunshine Boys*

Golden Globe Awards

BEST MOTION PICTURE DRAMA: **One Flew over the Cuckoo's Nest**

BEST MOTION PICTURE COMEDY OR MUSICAL: **The Sunshine Boys**

BEST FOREIGN LANGUAGE FILM: **Lies My Father Told Me**

BEST DIRECTOR MOTION PICTURE: **Milos Forman** *One Flew over the Cuckoo's Nest*

BEST PERFORMANCE BY AN ACTOR IN A MOTION PICTURE DRAMA: **Jack Nicholson** *One Flew over the Cuckoo's Nest*

BEST PERFORMANCE BY AN ACTRESS IN A MOTION PICTURE DRAMA: **Louise Fletcher** *One Flew over the Cuckoo's Nest*

BEST PERFORMANCE BY AN ACTOR IN A MOTION PICTURE COMEDY OR MUSICAL: **Walter Matthau** *The Sunshine Boys*

BEST PERFORMANCE BY AN ACTRESS IN A MOTION PICTURE COMEDY OR MUSICAL: **Ann-Margret** *Tommy*

BEST PERFORMANCE BY AN ACTOR IN A SUPPORTING ROLE MOTION PICTURE: **Richard Benjamin** *The Sunshine Boys*

BEST PERFORMANCE BY AN ACTRESS IN A SUPPORTING ROLE MOTION PICTURE: **Brenda Vaccaro** *Once Is Not Enough*

BEST SCREENPLAY MOTION PICTURE: **Lawrence Hauben, Bo Goldman** *One Flew over the Cuckoo's Nest*

Cannes International Film Festival

PALME D'OR: **Chronicle of the Burning Years**

DIRECTOR: **Michel Brault** *Les Ordres* • **Costa-Gavras** *Section Spéciale*

ACTOR: **Vittorio Gassman** *Scent of a Woman*

ACTRESS: **Valerie Perrine** *Lenny*

Berlin International Film Festival

GOLDEN BERLIN BEAR: **Adoption**

SILVER BERLIN BEAR FOR THE BEST DIRECTOR: **Sergei Solovyov** *Sto Dnej Possle Detstwa*

SILVER BERLIN BEAR FOR THE BEST ACTOR: **Vlastimil Brodsky** *Jacob the Liar*

SILVER BERLIN BEAR FOR THE BEST ACTRESS: **Kinuyo Tanaka** *Sandakan No 8*

1976

British Academy of Film & Television Arts Awards

BEST FILM: **One Flew over the Cuckoo's Nest** • *All the President's Men* • *Bugsy Malone* • *Taxi Driver*

BEST DIRECTOR: **Ken Kesey** *One Flew over the Cuckoo's Nest* • Alan J Pakula *All the President's Men* • Alan Parker *Bugsy Malone* • Martin Scorsese *Taxi Driver*

BEST ACTOR: **Jack Nicholson** *One Flew over the Cuckoo's Nest* • Robert De Niro *Taxi Driver* • Dustin Hoffman *All the President's Men* • Dustin Hoffman *Marathon Man* • Walter Matthau *The Sunshine Boys* • Walter Matthau *The Bad News Bears*

BEST ACTRESS: **Louise Fletcher** *One Flew over the Cuckoo's Nest* • Lauren Bacall *The Shootist* • Rita Moreno *The Ritz* • Liv Ullmann *Face to Face*

BEST SUPPORTING ACTOR: **Brad Dourif** *One Flew over the Cuckoo's Nest* • Martin Balsam *All the President's Men* • Michael Hordern *The Slipper and the Rose* • Jason Robards Jr *All the President's Men*

BEST SUPPORTING ACTRESS: **Jodie Foster** *Bugsy Malone* • **Jodie Foster** *Taxi Driver* • Annette Crosbie *The Slipper and the Rose* • Vivien Merchant *The Homecoming* • Billie Whitelaw *The Omen*

BEST SCREENPLAY: **Alan Parker** *Bugsy Malone* • William Goldman *All the President's Men* • Lawrence Hauben, Bo Goldman *One Flew over the Cuckoo's Nest* • Neil Simon *The Sunshine Boys*

Academy Awards

BEST PICTURE: **Rocky** • *All the President's Men* • *Bound for Glory* • *Network* • *Taxi Driver*

FOREIGN LANGUAGE FILM: **Black and White in Color** • *Cousin, Cousine* • *Jacob the Liar* • *Nights and Days* • *Seven Beauties*

DIRECTING: **John G Avildsen** *Rocky* • Alan J Pakula *All the President's Men* • Ingmar Bergman *Face to Face* • Sidney Lumet *Network* • Lina Wertmuller *Seven Beauties*

ACTOR IN A LEADING ROLE: **Peter Finch** *Network* • Robert De Niro *Taxi Driver* • Giancarlo Gianini *Seven Beauties* • William Holden *Network* • Sylvester Stallone *Rocky*

ACTRESS IN A LEADING ROLE: **Faye Dunaway** *Network* • Marie-Christine Barrault *Cousin, Cousine* • Talia Shire *Rocky* • Sissy Spacek *Carrie* • Liv Ullmann *Face to Face*

ACTOR IN A SUPPORTING ROLE: **Jason Robards Jr** *All the President's Men* • Burgess Meredith, Burt Young *Rocky* • Ned Beatty *Network* • Laurence Olivier *Marathon Man*

ACTRESS IN A SUPPORTING ROLE: **Beatrice Straight** *Network* • Jane Alexander *All the President's Men* • Jodie Foster *Taxi Driver* • Lee Grant *Voyage of the Damned* • Piper Laurie *Carrie*

WRITING (SCREENPLAY WRITTEN DIRECTLY FOR THE SCREEN BASED ON FACTUAL MATERIAL OR ON STORY MATERIAL NOT PREVIOUSLY PUBLISHED OR PRODUCED): **Paddy Chayefsky** *Network* • Jean-Charles Tacchella, Danièle Thompson *Cousin, Cousine* • Walter Bernstein *The Front* • Sylvester Stallone *Rocky* • Lina Wertmuller *Seven Beauties*

WRITING (SCREENPLAY BASED ON MATERIAL FROM ANOTHER MEDIUM): **William Goldman** *All the President's Men* • Robert Getchell *Bound for Glory* • Federico Fellini, Bernardino Zapponi *Casanova* • Nicholas Meyer *The Seven-Per-Cent Solution* • David Butler, Steve Shagan *Voyage of the Damned*

Golden Globe Awards

BEST MOTION PICTURE DRAMA: **Rocky**

BEST MOTION PICTURE COMEDY OR MUSICAL: **A Star Is Born**

BEST FOREIGN LANGUAGE FILM: **Face to Face**

BEST DIRECTOR MOTION PICTURE: **Sidney Lumet** *Network*

BEST PERFORMANCE BY AN ACTOR IN A MOTION PICTURE DRAMA: **Peter Finch** *Network*

BEST PERFORMANCE BY AN ACTRESS IN A MOTION PICTURE DRAMA: **Faye Dunaway** *Network*

BEST PERFORMANCE BY AN ACTOR IN A MOTION PICTURE COMEDY OR MUSICAL: **Kris Kristofferson** *A Star Is Born*

BEST PERFORMANCE BY AN ACTRESS IN A MOTION PICTURE COMEDY OR MUSICAL: **Barbra Streisand** *A Star Is Born*

BEST PERFORMANCE BY AN ACTOR IN A SUPPORTING ROLE MOTION PICTURE: **Laurence Olivier** *Marathon Man*

BEST PERFORMANCE BY AN ACTRESS IN A SUPPORTING ROLE MOTION PICTURE: **Katharine Ross** *Voyage of the Damned*

BEST SCREENPLAY MOTION PICTURE: **Paddy Chayefsky** *Network*

Cannes International Film Festival

PALME D'OR: **Taxi Driver**

DIRECTOR: **Ettore Scola** *Down and Dirty*

ACTOR: **José Luis Gomez** *Pascual Duarte*

ACTRESS: **Mari Torocsik** *Deryne, Hol Van?* • **Dominique Sanda** *The Inheritance*

Berlin International Film Festival

GOLDEN BERLIN BEAR: **Buffalo Bill and the Indians, or Sitting Bull's History Lesson**

SILVER BERLIN BEAR FOR THE BEST DIRECTOR: **Mario Monicelli** *Caro Michele*

SILVER BERLIN BEAR FOR THE BEST ACTOR: **Gerhard Olschewski** *Verlorenes Leben*

SILVER BERLIN BEAR FOR THE BEST ACTRESS: **Jadwiga Baranska** *Nights and Days*

1977

British Academy of Film & Television Arts Awards

BEST FILM: **Annie Hall** • *A Bridge Too Far* • *Network* • *Rocky*

BEST DIRECTOR: **Woody Allen** *Annie Hall* • Richard Attenborough *A Bridge Too Far* • Sidney Lumet *Network* • John G Avildsen *Rocky*

BEST ACTOR: **Peter Finch** *Network* • Woody Allen *Annie Hall* • William Holden *Network* • Sylvester Stallone *Rocky*

BEST ACTRESS: **Diane Keaton** *Annie Hall* • Faye Dunaway *Network* • Shelley Duvall *3 Women* • Lily Tomlin *The Late Show*

BEST SUPPORTING ACTOR: **Edward Fox** *A Bridge Too Far* • Colin Blakely *Equus* • Robert Duvall *Network* • Zero Mostel *The Front*

BEST SUPPORTING ACTRESS: **Jenny Agutter** *Equus* • Geraldine Chaplin *Welcome to LA* • Joan Plowright *Equus* • Shelley Winters *Next Stop, Greenwich Village*

BEST SCREENPLAY: **Woody Allen, Marshall Brickman** *Annie Hall* • Peter Shaffer *Equus* • Paddy Chayefsky *Network* • Sylvester Stallone *Rocky*

Academy Awards

BEST PICTURE: **Annie Hall** • *The Goodbye Girl* • *Julia* • *Star Wars Episode IV: A New Hope* • *The Turning Point*

FOREIGN LANGUAGE FILM: **Madame Rosa** • *Iphigenia* • *Operation Thunderbolt* • *A Special Day* • *That Obscure Object of Desire*

DIRECTING: **Woody Allen** *Annie Hall* • Steven Spielberg *Close Encounters ofthe Third Kind* • Fred Zinnemann *Julia* • George Lucas *Star Wars Episode IV: A New Hope* • Herbert Ross *The Turning Point*

ACTOR IN A LEADING ROLE: **Richard Dreyfuss** *The Goodbye Girl* • Woody Allen *Annie Hall* • Richard Burton *Equus* • Marcello Mastroianni *A Special Day* • John Travolta *Saturday Night Fever*

ACTRESS IN A LEADING ROLE: **Diane Keaton** *Annie Hall* • Anne Bancroft *The Turning Point* • Jane Fonda *Julia* • Shirley MacLaine *The Turning Point* • Marsha Mason *The Goodbye Girl*

ACTOR IN A SUPPORTING ROLE: **Jason Robards Jr**, Maximilian Schell *Julia* • Mikhail Baryshnikov *The Turning Point* • Peter Firth *Equus* • Alec Guinness *Star Wars Episode IV: A New Hope*

ACTRESS IN A SUPPORTING ROLE: **Vanessa Redgrave** *Julia* • Leslie Browne *The Turning Point* • Quinn Cummings *The Goodbye Girl* • Melinda Dillon *Close Encounters ofthe Third Kind* • Tuesday Weld *Looking for Mr Goodbar*

WRITING (SCREENPLAY WRITTEN DIRECTLY FOR THE SCREEN BASED ON FACTUAL MATERIAL OR ON STORY MATERIAL NOT PREVIOUSLY PUBLISHED OR PRODUCED): **Woody Allen, Marshall Brickman** *Annie Hall* • Neil Simon *The Goodbye Girl* • Robert Benton *The Late Show* • George Lucas *Star Wars Episode IV: A New Hope* • Arthur Laurents *The Turning Point*

WRITING (SCREENPLAY BASED ON MATERIAL FROM ANOTHER MEDIUM): **Alvin Sargent** *Julia* • Peter Shaffer *Equus* • Lewis John Carlino, Gavin Lambert *I Never Promised You a Rose Garden* • Larry Gelbart *Oh, God!* • Luis Buñuel, Jean-Claude Carrière *That Obscure Object of Desire*

Golden Globe Awards

BEST MOTION PICTURE DRAMA: **The Turning Point**

BEST MOTION PICTURE COMEDY OR MUSICAL: **The Goodbye Girl**

BEST FOREIGN LANGUAGE FILM: **A Special Day**

BEST DIRECTOR MOTION PICTURE: **Herbert Ross** *The Turning Point*

BEST PERFORMANCE BY AN ACTOR IN A MOTION PICTURE DRAMA: **Richard Burton** *Equus*

BEST PERFORMANCE BY AN ACTRESS IN A MOTION PICTURE DRAMA: **Jane Fonda** *Julia*

BEST PERFORMANCE BY AN ACTOR IN A MOTION PICTURE COMEDY OR MUSICAL: **Richard Dreyfuss** *The Goodbye Girl*

BEST PERFORMANCE BY AN ACTRESS IN A MOTION PICTURE COMEDY OR MUSICAL: **Marsha Mason** *The Goodbye Girl* • **Diane Keaton** *Annie Hall*

BEST PERFORMANCE BY AN ACTOR IN A SUPPORTING ROLE MOTION PICTURE: **Peter Firth** *Equus*

BEST PERFORMANCE BY AN ACTRESS IN A SUPPORTING ROLE MOTION PICTURE: **Vanessa Redgrave** *Julia*

BEST SCREENPLAY MOTION PICTURE: **Neil Simon** *The Goodbye Girl*

Cannes International Film Festival

PALME D'OR: **Padre Padrone**

ACTOR: **Fernando Rey** *Elisa, Mia Vida*

ACTRESS: **Shelley Duvall** *3 Women* • **Monique Mercure** *JA Martin Photographe*

Berlin International Film Festival

GOLDEN BERLIN BEAR: **The Ascent**

SILVER BERLIN BEAR FOR THE BEST DIRECTOR: **Manuel Gutierrez Aragon** *Camada Negra*

SILVER BERLIN BEAR FOR THE BEST ACTOR: **Fernando Fernan Gomez** *El Anacoreta*

SILVER BERLIN BEAR FOR THE BEST ACTRESS: **Lily Tomlin** *The Late Show*

1978

British Academy of Film & Television Arts Awards

BEST FILM: **Julia** • *Close Encounters ofthe Third Kind* • *Midnight Express* • *Star Wars Episode IV: A New Hope*

BEST DIRECTOR: **Alan Parker** *Midnight Express* • Steven Spielberg *Close Encounters ofthe Third Kind* • Fred Zinnemann *Julia* • Robert Altman *A Wedding*

BEST ACTOR: **Richard Dreyfuss** *The Goodbye Girl* • Brad Davis *Midnight Express* • Anthony Hopkins *Magic* • Peter Ustinov *Death on the Nile*

BEST ACTRESS: **Jane Fonda** *Julia* • Anne Bancroft *The Turning Point* • Jill Clayburgh *An Unmarried Woman* • Marsha Mason *The Goodbye Girl*

BEST SUPPORTING ACTOR: **John Hurt** *Midnight Express* • Gene Hackman *Superman* • Jason Robards Jr *Julia* • François Truffaut *Close Encounters of the Third Kind*

BEST SUPPORTING ACTRESS: **Geraldine Page** *Interiors* • Angela Lansbury, Maggie Smith *Death on the Nile* • Mona Washbourne *Stevie*

BEST SCREENPLAY: **Alvin Sargent** *Julia* • Steven Spielberg *Close Encounters of the Third Kind* • Neil Simon *The Goodbye Girl* • John Considine, Patricia Resnick, Allan Nicholls, Robert Altman *A Wedding*

Academy Awards

BEST PICTURE: **The Deer Hunter** • *Coming Home* • *Heaven Can Wait* • *Midnight Express* • *An Unmarried Woman*

FOREIGN LANGUAGE FILM: **Get out Your Handkerchiefs** • *The Glass Cell* • *Hungarians* • *Viva Italia!* • *White Bim Black Ear*

DIRECTING: **Michael Cimino** *The Deer Hunter* • Hal Ashby *Coming Home* • Warren Beatty, Buck Henry *Heaven Can Wait* • Woody Allen *Interiors* • Alan Parker *Midnight Express*

ACTOR IN A LEADING ROLE: **Jon Voight** *Coming Home* • Warren Beatty *Heaven Can Wait* • Gary Busey *The Buddy Holly Story* • Robert De Niro *The Deer Hunter* • Laurence Olivier *The Boys from Brazil*

ACTRESS IN A LEADING ROLE: **Jane Fonda** *Coming Home* • Ingrid Bergman *Autumn Sonata* • Ellen Burstyn *Same Time, Next Year* • Jill Clayburgh *An Unmarried Woman* • Geraldine Page *Interiors*

ACTOR IN A SUPPORTING ROLE: **Christopher Walken** *The Deer Hunter* • Bruce Dern *Coming Home* • Richard Farnsworth *Comes a Horseman* • John Hurt *Midnight Express* • Jack Warden *Heaven Can Wait*

ACTRESS IN A SUPPORTING ROLE: **Maggie Smith** *California Suite* • Dyan Cannon *Heaven Can Wait* • Penelope Milford *Coming Home* • Maureen Stapleton *Interiors* • Meryl Streep *The Deer Hunter*

WRITING (SCREENPLAY WRITTEN DIRECTLY FOR THE SCREEN): **Nancy Dowd, Robert C Jones, Waldo Salt** *Coming Home* • Ingmar Bergman *Autumn Sonata* • Michael Cimino, Louis Garfinkle, Quinn K Redeker, Deric Washburn *The Deer Hunter* • Woody Allen *Interiors* • Paul Mazursky *An Unmarried Woman*

WRITING (SCREENPLAY BASED ON MATERIAL FROM ANOTHER MEDIUM): **Oliver Stone** *Midnight Express* • Walter Newman *Bloodbrothers* • Neil Simon *California Suite* • Warren Beatty, Elaine May *Heaven Can Wait* • Bernard Slade *Same Time, Next Year*

Golden Globe Awards

BEST MOTION PICTURE DRAMA: **Midnight Express**

BEST MOTION PICTURE COMEDY OR MUSICAL: **Heaven Can Wait**

BEST FOREIGN LANGUAGE FILM: **Autumn Sonata**

BEST DIRECTOR MOTION PICTURE: **Michael Cimino** *The Deer Hunter*

BEST PERFORMANCE BY AN ACTOR IN A MOTION PICTURE DRAMA: **Jon Voight** *Coming Home*

BEST PERFORMANCE BY AN ACTRESS IN A MOTION PICTURE DRAMA: **Jane Fonda** *Coming Home*

BEST PERFORMANCE BY AN ACTOR IN A MOTION PICTURE COMEDY OR MUSICAL: **Warren Beatty** *Heaven Can Wait*

BEST PERFORMANCE BY AN ACTRESS IN A MOTION PICTURE COMEDY OR MUSICAL: **Ellen Burstyn** *Same Time, Next Year* • **Maggie Smith** *California Suite*

BEST PERFORMANCE BY AN ACTOR IN A SUPPORTING ROLE MOTION PICTURE: **John Hurt** *Midnight Express*

BEST PERFORMANCE BY AN ACTRESS IN A SUPPORTING ROLE MOTION PICTURE: **Dyan Cannon** *Heaven Can Wait*

BEST SCREENPLAY MOTION PICTURE: **Oliver Stone** *Midnight Express*

Cannes International Film Festival

PALME D'OR: **The Tree of Wooden Clogs**

DIRECTOR: **Nagisa Oshima** *Ai No Borei*

ACTOR: **Jon Voight** *Coming Home*

ACTRESS: **Jill Clayburgh** *An Unmarried Woman* • **Isabelle Huppert** *Violette Nozière*

Berlin International Film Festival

GOLDEN BERLIN BEAR: **Las Truchas** • *Las Palabras de Max*

SILVER BERLIN BEAR FOR THE BEST DIRECTOR: **Georgi Djulgerov** *Avantage*

SILVER BERLIN BEAR FOR THE BEST ACTOR: **Craig Russell** *Outrageous!*

SILVER BERLIN BEAR FOR THE BEST ACTRESS: **Gena Rowlands** *Opening Night*

1979

British Academy of Film & Television Arts Awards

BEST FILM: **Manhattan** • *Apocalypse Now* • *The China Syndrome* • *The Deer Hunter*

BEST DIRECTOR: **Francis Ford Coppola** *Apocalypse Now* • Michael Cimino *The Deer Hunter* • Woody Allen *Manhattan* • John Schlesinger *Yanks*

BEST ACTOR: **Jack Lemmon** *The China Syndrome* • Woody Allen *Manhattan* • Robert De Niro *The Deer Hunter* • Martin Sheen *Apocalypse Now*

BEST ACTRESS: **Jane Fonda** *The China Syndrome* • Diane Keaton *Manhattan* • Maggie Smith *California Suite* • Meryl Streep *The Deer Hunter*

BEST SUPPORTING ACTOR: **Robert Duvall** *Apocalypse Now* • Denholm Elliott *Saint Jack* • John Hurt *Alien* • Christopher Walken *The Deer Hunter*

BEST SUPPORTING ACTRESS: **Rachel Roberts** *Yanks* • Lisa Eichhorn *The Europeans* • Mariel Hemingway, Meryl Streep *Manhattan*

BEST SCREENPLAY: **Woody Allen, Marshall Brickman** *Manhattan* • Mike Gray, T S Cook, James Bridges *The China Syndrome* • Deric Washburn *The Deer Hunter* • Colin Welland, Walter Bernstein *Yanks*

Academy Awards

BEST PICTURE: **Kramer vs Kramer** • *All That Jazz* • *Apocalypse Now* • *Breaking Away* • *Norma Rae*

FOREIGN LANGUAGE FILM: **The Tin Drum** • *The Young Ladies of Wilko* • *Mama Turns a Hundred* • *Une Histoire Simple* • *To Forget Venice*

DIRECTING: **Robert Benton** *Kramer vs Kramer* • Bob Fosse *All That Jazz* • Francis Ford Coppola *Apocalypse Now* • Peter Yates *Breaking Away* • Edouard Molinaro *La Cage aux Folles*

ACTOR IN A LEADING ROLE: **Dustin Hoffman** *Kramer vs Kramer* • Jack Lemmon *The China Syndrome* • Al Pacino *… And Justice for All* • Roy Scheider *All That Jazz* • Peter Sellers *Being There*

ACTRESS IN A LEADING ROLE: **Sally Field** *Norma Rae* • Jill Clayburgh *Starting Over* • Jane Fonda *The China Syndrome* • Marsha Mason *Chapter Two* • Bette Midler *The Rose*

ACTOR IN A SUPPORTING ROLE: **Melvyn Douglas** *Being There* • Robert Duvall *Apocalypse Now* • Frederic Forrest *The Rose* • Justin Henry *Kramer vs Kramer* • Mickey Rooney *The Black Stallion*

ACTRESS IN A SUPPORTING ROLE: **Meryl Streep**, Jane Alexander *Kramer vs Kramer* • Barbara Barrie *Breaking Away* • Candice Bergen *Starting Over* • Mariel Hemingway *Manhattan*

WRITING (SCREENPLAY WRITTEN DIRECTLY FOR THE SCREEN): **Steve Tesich** *Breaking Away* • Valerie Curtin, Barry Levinson *… And Justice for All* • Robert Alan Arthur, Bob Fosse *All That Jazz* • James Bridges, T S Cook, Mike Gray *The China Syndrome* • Woody Allen, Marshall Brickman *Manhattan*

WRITING (SCREENPLAY BASED ON MATERIAL FROM ANOTHER MEDIUM): **Robert Benton** *Kramer vs Kramer* • Francis Ford Coppola, John Milius *Apocalypse Now* • Marcello Danon, Edouard Molinaro, Jean Poiret, Francis Veber *La Cage aux Folles* • Allan Burns *A Little Romance* • Harriet Frank Jr, Irving Ravetch *Norma Rae*

Golden Globe Awards

BEST MOTION PICTURE DRAMA: **Kramer vs Kramer**

BEST MOTION PICTURE COMEDY OR MUSICAL: **Breaking Away**

BEST FOREIGN LANGUAGE FILM: **La Cage aux Folles**

BEST DIRECTOR MOTION PICTURE: **Francis Ford Coppola** *Apocalypse Now*

BEST PERFORMANCE BY AN ACTOR IN A MOTION PICTURE DRAMA: **Dustin Hoffman** *Kramer vs Kramer*

BEST PERFORMANCE BY AN ACTRESS IN A MOTION PICTURE DRAMA: **Sally Field** *Norma Rae*

BEST PERFORMANCE BY AN ACTOR IN A MOTION PICTURE COMEDY OR MUSICAL: **Peter Sellers** *Being There*

BEST PERFORMANCE BY AN ACTRESS IN A MOTION PICTURE COMEDY OR MUSICAL: **Bette Midler** *The Rose*

BEST PERFORMANCE BY AN ACTOR IN A SUPPORTING ROLE MOTION PICTURE: **Robert Duvall** *Apocalypse Now* • **Melvyn Douglas** *Being There*

BEST PERFORMANCE BY AN ACTRESS IN A SUPPORTING ROLE MOTION PICTURE: **Meryl Streep** *Kramer vs Kramer*

BEST SCREENPLAY MOTION PICTURE: **Robert Benton** *Kramer vs Kramer*

Cannes International Film Festival

PALME D'OR: **The Tin Drum** • *Apocalypse Now*

DIRECTOR: **Terrence Malick** *Days of Heaven*

ACTOR: **Jack Lemmon** *The China Syndrome*

ACTRESS: **Sally Field** *Norma Rae*

SUPPORTING ACTOR: **Stefano Madia** *Caro Papà*

SUPPORTING ACTRESS: **Eva Mattes** *Woyzeck*

Berlin International Film Festival

GOLDEN BERLIN BEAR: **David**

SILVER BERLIN BEAR FOR THE BEST DIRECTOR: **Astrid Henning-Jensen** *Vinterborn*

SILVER BERLIN BEAR FOR THE BEST ACTOR: **Michele Placido** *Ernesto*

SILVER BERLIN BEAR FOR THE BEST ACTRESS: **Hanna Schygulla** *The Marriage of Maria Braun*

1980

British Academy of Film & Television Arts Awards

BEST FILM: **The Elephant Man** • *Being There* • *Kagemusha* • *Kramer vs Kramer*

BEST DIRECTOR: **Akira Kurosawa** *Kagemusha* • David Lynch *The Elephant Man* • Alan Parker *Fame* • Robert Benton *Kramer vs Kramer*

BEST ACTOR: **John Hurt** *The Elephant Man* • Dustin Hoffman *Kramer vs Kramer* • Roy Scheider *All That Jazz* • Peter Sellers *Being There*

BEST ACTRESS: **Judy Davis** *My Brilliant Career* • Shirley MacLaine *Being There* • Bette Midler *The Rose* • Meryl Streep *Kramer vs Kramer*

BEST SCREENPLAY: **Jerry Kosinski** *Being There* • Jim Abrahams, David Zucker, Jerry Zucker *Airplane!* • Christopher de Vore, Eric Bergren, David Lynch *The Elephant Man* • Robert Benton *Kramer vs Kramer*

Academy Awards

BEST PICTURE: **Ordinary People** • *Coal Miner's Daughter* • *The Elephant Man* • *Raging Bull* • *Tess*

FOREIGN LANGUAGE FILM: **Moscow Distrusts Tears** • *Confidence* • *Kagemusha* • *The Last Metro* • *The Nest*

DIRECTING: **Robert Redford** *Ordinary People* • David Lynch *The Elephant Man* • Martin Scorsese *Raging Bull* • Richard Rush *The Stunt Man* • Roman Polanski *Tess*

ACTOR IN A LEADING ROLE: **Robert De Niro** *Raging Bull* • Robert Duvall *The Great Santini* • John Hurt *The Elephant Man* • Jack Lemmon *Tribute* • Peter O'Toole *The Stunt Man*

ACTRESS IN A LEADING ROLE: **Sissy Spacek** *Coal Miner's Daughter* • Ellen Burstyn *Resurrection* • Goldie Hawn *Private Benjamin* • Mary Tyler Moore *Ordinary People* • Gena Rowlands *Gloria*

ACTOR IN A SUPPORTING ROLE: **Timothy Hutton**, Judd Hirsch *Ordinary People* • Michael O'Keefe *The Great Santini* • Joe Pesci *Raging Bull* • Jason Robards Jr *Melvin and Howard*

ACTRESS IN A SUPPORTING ROLE: **Mary Steenburgen** *Melvin and Howard* • Eileen Brennan *Private Benjamin* • Eva Le Gallienne *Resurrection* • Cathy Moriarty *Raging Bull* • Diana Scarwid *Inside Moves: the Guys from Max's Bar*

WRITING (SCREENPLAY WRITTEN DIRECTLY FOR THE SCREEN): **Bo Goldman** *Melvin and Howard* • W D Richter, Arthur Ross *Brubaker* • Christopher Gore *Fame* • Jean Gruault *Mon Oncle d'Amérique* • Nancy Myers, Harvey Miller, Charles Shyer *Private Benjamin*

WRITING (SCREENPLAY BASED ON MATERIAL FROM ANOTHER MEDIUM): **Alvin Sargent** *Ordinary People* • Bruce Beresford, Jonathan Hardy, David Stevens *Breaker Morant* • Tom Rickman *Coal Miner's Daughter* • Christopher de Vore, Eric Bergren, David Lynch *The Elephant Man* • Richard Rush, Lawrence B Marcus *The Stunt Man*

Golden Globe Awards

BEST MOTION PICTURE DRAMA: **Ordinary People**

BEST MOTION PICTURE COMEDY OR MUSICAL: **Coal Miner's Daughter**

BEST FOREIGN LANGUAGE FILM: **Tess**

BEST DIRECTOR MOTION PICTURE: **Robert Redford** *Ordinary People*

BEST PERFORMANCE BY AN ACTOR IN A MOTION PICTURE DRAMA: **Robert De Niro** *Raging Bull*

BEST PERFORMANCE BY AN ACTRESS IN A MOTION PICTURE DRAMA: **Mary Tyler Moore** *Ordinary People*

BEST PERFORMANCE BY AN ACTOR IN A MOTION PICTURE COMEDY OR MUSICAL: **Ray Sharkey** *The Idolmaker*

BEST PERFORMANCE BY AN ACTRESS IN A MOTION PICTURE COMEDY OR MUSICAL: **Sissy Spacek** *Coal Miner's Daughter*

BEST PERFORMANCE BY AN ACTOR IN A SUPPORTING ROLE MOTION PICTURE: **Timothy Hutton** *Ordinary People*

BEST PERFORMANCE BY AN ACTRESS IN A SUPPORTING ROLE MOTION PICTURE: **Mary Steenburgen** *Melvin and Howard*

BEST SCREENPLAY MOTION PICTURE: **William Peter Blatty** *The Ninth Configuration*

Cannes International Film Festival

PALME D'OR: **Kagemusha • All That Jazz**
ACTOR: **Michel Piccoli** Leap into the Void
ACTRESS: **Anouk Aimée** Leap into the Void
SUPPORTING ACTOR: **Jack Thompson** Breaker Morant
SUPPORTING ACTRESS: **Carla Gravina** La Terrazza • **Milena Dravic** Poseban Tretman
SCREENPLAY: **Agenore Incrocci, Furio Scarpelli, Ettore Scola** La Terrazza

Berlin International Film Festival

GOLDEN BERLIN BEAR: **Heartland • Palermo oder Wolfsburg**
SILVER BERLIN BEAR FOR THE BEST DIRECTOR: **István Szabó** Confidence
SILVER BERLIN BEAR FOR THE BEST ACTOR: **Andrzej Seweryn** The Conductor
SILVER BERLIN BEAR FOR THE BEST ACTRESS: **Renate Krössner** Solo Sunny

1981

British Academy of Film & Television Arts Awards

BEST FILM: **Chariots of Fire** • Atlantic City USA • The French Lieutenant's Woman • Gregory's Girl • Raiders of the Lost Ark
BEST DIRECTOR: **Louis Malle** Atlantic City USA • Hugh Hudson Chariots of Fire • Karel Reisz The French Lieutenant's Woman • Bill Forsyth Gregory's Girl
BEST ACTOR: **Burt Lancaster** Atlantic City USA • Robert De Niro Raging Bull • Bob Hoskins The Long Good Friday • Jeremy Irons The French Lieutenant's Woman
BEST ACTRESS: **Meryl Streep** The French Lieutenant's Woman • Mary Tyler Moore Ordinary People • Maggie Smith Quartet • Sissy Spacek Coal Miner's Daughter
BEST SUPPORTING ARTIST: **Ian Holm** Chariots of Fire • Denholm Elliott Raiders of the Lost Ark • John Gielgud Arthur • Nigel Havers Chariots of Fire
BEST SCREENPLAY: **Bill Forsyth** Gregory's Girl • John Guare Atlantic City USA • Colin Welland Chariots of Fire • Harold Pinter The French Lieutenant's Woman

Academy Awards

BEST PICTURE: **Chariots of Fire** • Atlantic City USA • On Golden Pond • Raiders of the Lost Ark • Reds
FOREIGN LANGUAGE FILM: **Mephisto** • The Boat Is Full • Man of Iron • Muddy River • Three Brothers
DIRECTING: **Warren Beatty** Reds • Louis Malle Atlantic City USA • Hugh Hudson Chariots of Fire • Mark Rydell On Golden Pond • Steven Spielberg Raiders of the Lost Ark
ACTOR IN A LEADING ROLE: **Henry Fonda** On Golden Pond • Warren Beatty Reds • Burt Lancaster Atlantic City USA • Dudley Moore Arthur • Paul Newman Absence of Malice
ACTRESS IN A LEADING ROLE: **Katharine Hepburn** On Golden Pond • Diane Keaton Reds • Marsha Mason Only When I Laugh • Susan Sarandon Atlantic City USA • Meryl Streep The French Lieutenant's Woman
ACTOR IN A SUPPORTING ROLE: **John Gielgud** Arthur • James Coco Only When I Laugh • Ian Holm Chariots of Fire • Jack Nicholson Reds • Howard E Rollins Ragtime
ACTRESS IN A SUPPORTING ROLE: **Maureen Stapleton** Reds • Melinda Dillon Absence of Malice • Jane Fonda On Golden Pond • Joan Hackett Only When I Laugh • Elizabeth McGovern Ragtime
WRITING (SCREENPLAY WRITTEN DIRECTLY FOR THE SCREEN): **Colin Welland** Chariots of Fire • Kurt Luedtke Absence of Malice • Steve Gordon Arthur • John Guare Atlantic City USA • Warren Beatty, Trevor Griffiths Reds
WRITING (SCREENPLAY BASED ON MATERIAL FROM ANOTHER MEDIUM): **Ernest Thompson** On Golden Pond • Harold Pinter The French Lieutenant's Woman • Dennis Potter Pennies from Heaven • Jay Presson Allen, Sidney Lumet Prince of the City • Michael Weller Ragtime

Golden Globe Awards

BEST MOTION PICTURE DRAMA: **On Golden Pond**
BEST MOTION PICTURE COMEDY OR MUSICAL: **Arthur**
BEST FOREIGN LANGUAGE FILM: **Chariots of Fire**
BEST DIRECTOR MOTION PICTURE: **Warren Beatty** Reds
BEST PERFORMANCE BY AN ACTOR IN A MOTION PICTURE DRAMA: **Henry Fonda** On Golden Pond
BEST PERFORMANCE BY AN ACTRESS IN A MOTION PICTURE DRAMA: **Meryl Streep** The French Lieutenant's Woman
BEST PERFORMANCE BY AN ACTOR IN A MOTION PICTURE COMEDY OR MUSICAL: **Dudley Moore** Arthur
BEST PERFORMANCE BY AN ACTRESS IN A MOTION PICTURE COMEDY OR MUSICAL: **Bernadette Peters** Pennies from Heaven
BEST PERFORMANCE BY AN ACTOR IN A SUPPORTING ROLE MOTION PICTURE: **John Gielgud** Arthur

BEST PERFORMANCE BY AN ACTRESS IN A SUPPORTING ROLE MOTION PICTURE: **Joan Hackett** Only When I Laugh
BEST SCREENPLAY MOTION PICTURE: **Ernest Thompson** On Golden Pond

Cannes International Film Festival

PALME D'OR: **Man of Iron**
ACTOR: **Ugo Tognazzi** The Tragedy of a Ridiculous Man
ACTRESS: **Isabelle Adjani** Quartet • Isabelle Adjani Possession
SUPPORTING ACTOR: **Ian Holm** Chariots of Fire
SUPPORTING ACTRESS: **Elena Solovei** Grouppa Krovi Nol
SCREENPLAY: **István Szabó** Mephisto

Berlin International Film Festival

GOLDEN BERLIN BEAR: **Deprisa, Deprisa**
SILVER BERLIN BEAR FOR THE BEST ACTOR: **Jack Lemmon** Tribute • **Anatoli Solinitsin** Twenty Six Days in the Life of Dostoevsky
SILVER BERLIN BEAR FOR THE BEST ACTRESS: **Barbara Grabowska** Goraczka

1982

British Academy of Film & Television Arts Awards

BEST FILM: **Gandhi** • ET the Extra-Terrestrial • Missing • On Golden Pond
BEST FOREIGN LANGUAGE FILM: **Christ Stopped at Eboli** • Das Boot • Diva • Fitzcarraldo
BEST DIRECTOR: **Richard Attenborough** Gandhi • Steven Spielberg ET the Extra-Terrestrial • Costa-Gavras Missing • Mark Rydell On Golden Pond
BEST ACTOR: **Ben Kingsley** Gandhi • Warren Beatty Reds • Albert Finney Shoot the Moon • Henry Fonda On Golden Pond • Jack Lemmon Missing
BEST ACTRESS: **Katharine Hepburn** On Golden Pond • Diane Keaton Reds • Jennifer Kendal 36 Chowringhee Lane • Sissy Spacek Missing
BEST SUPPORTING ACTOR: **Jack Nicholson** Reds • Frank Finlay The Return of the Soldier • Edward Fox, Roshan Seth Gandhi
BEST SUPPORTING ACTRESS: **Rohini Hattangady** Gandhi • **Maureen Stapleton** Reds • Candice Bergen Gandhi • Jane Fonda On Golden Pond
BEST SCREENPLAY: **Costa-Gavras, Donald Stewart** Missing • Melissa Mathison ET the Extra-Terrestrial • John Briley Gandhi • Ernest Thompson On Golden Pond

Academy Awards

BEST PICTURE: **Gandhi** • ET the Extra-Terrestrial • Missing • Tootsie • The Verdict
FOREIGN LANGUAGE FILM: **Begin the Beguine** • Alsino and the Condor • Clean Slate • The Flight of the Eagle • Private Life
DIRECTING: **Richard Attenborough** Gandhi • Wolfgang Petersen Das Boot • Steven Spielberg ET the Extra-Terrestrial • Sydney Pollack Tootsie • Sidney Lumet The Verdict
ACTOR IN A LEADING ROLE: **Ben Kingsley** Gandhi • Dustin Hoffman Tootsie • Jack Lemmon Missing • Paul Newman The Verdict • Peter O'Toole My Favorite Year
ACTRESS IN A LEADING ROLE: **Meryl Streep** Sophie's Choice • Julie Andrews Victor/Victoria • Jessica Lange Frances • Sissy Spacek Missing • Debra Winger An Officer and a Gentleman
ACTOR IN A SUPPORTING ROLE: **Louis Gossett Jr** An Officer and a Gentleman • Charles Durning The Best Little Whorehouse in Texas • John Lithgow The World According to Garp • James Mason The Verdict • Robert Preston Victor/Victoria
ACTRESS IN A SUPPORTING ROLE: **Jessica Lange**, Teri Garr Tootsie • Glenn Close The World According to Garp • Kim Stanley Frances • Lesley Ann Warren Victor/Victoria
WRITING (SCREENPLAY WRITTEN DIRECTLY FOR THE SCREEN): **John Briley** Gandhi • Barry Levinson Diner • Melissa Mathison ET the Extra-Terrestrial • Douglas Day Stewart An Officer and a Gentleman • Larry Gelbart, Don McGuire, Murray Schisgal Tootsie
WRITING (SCREENPLAY BASED ON MATERIAL FROM ANOTHER MEDIUM): **Costa-Gavras, Donald Stewart** Missing • Wolfgang Petersen Das Boot • Alan J Pakula Sophie's Choice • David Mamet The Verdict • Blake Edwards Victor/Victoria

Golden Globe Awards

BEST MOTION PICTURE DRAMA: **ET the Extra-Terrestrial**
BEST MOTION PICTURE COMEDY OR MUSICAL: **Tootsie**
BEST FOREIGN LANGUAGE FILM: **Gandhi**
BEST DIRECTOR MOTION PICTURE: **Richard Attenborough** Gandhi

BEST PERFORMANCE BY AN ACTOR IN A MOTION PICTURE DRAMA: **Ben Kingsley** Gandhi
BEST PERFORMANCE BY AN ACTRESS IN A MOTION PICTURE DRAMA: **Meryl Streep** Sophie's Choice
BEST PERFORMANCE BY AN ACTOR IN A MOTION PICTURE COMEDY OR MUSICAL: **Dustin Hoffman** Tootsie
BEST PERFORMANCE BY AN ACTRESS IN A MOTION PICTURE COMEDY OR MUSICAL: **Julie Andrews** Victor/Victoria
BEST PERFORMANCE BY AN ACTOR IN A SUPPORTING ROLE MOTION PICTURE: **Louis Gossett Jr** An Officer and a Gentleman
BEST PERFORMANCE BY AN ACTRESS IN A SUPPORTING ROLE MOTION PICTURE: **Jessica Lange** Tootsie
BEST SCREENPLAY MOTION PICTURE: **John Briley** Gandhi

Cannes International Film Festival

PALME D'OR: **Missing • Yol**
DIRECTOR: **Werner Herzog** Fitzcarraldo
ACTOR: **Jack Lemmon** Missing
ACTRESS: **Jadwiga Jankowska-Cieslak** Another Way
SCREENPLAY: **Jerzy Skolimowski** Moonlighting

Berlin International Film Festival

GOLDEN BERLIN BEAR: **Veronika Voss**
SILVER BERLIN BEAR FOR THE BEST DIRECTOR: **Mario Monicelli** Il Marchese del Grillo
SILVER BERLIN BEAR FOR THE BEST ACTOR: **Michel Piccoli** A Strange Affair • **Stellan Skarsgård** The Simple-Minded Murderer
SILVER BERLIN BEAR FOR THE BEST ACTRESS: **Katrin Sass** Bürgschaft für ein Jahr

1983

British Academy of Film & Television Arts Awards

BEST FILM: **Educating Rita** • Heat and Dust • Local Hero • Tootsie
BEST FOREIGN LANGUAGE FILM: **Danton** • Fanny and Alexander • Confidentially Yours • La Traviata
BEST DIRECTOR: **Bill Forsyth** Local Hero • James Ivory Heat and Dust • Martin Scorsese The King of Comedy • Sydney Pollack Tootsie
BEST ACTOR: **Michael Caine** Educating Rita • **Dustin Hoffman** Tootsie • Michael Caine The Honorary Consul • Robert De Niro The King of Comedy
BEST ACTRESS: **Julie Walters** Educating Rita • Jessica Lange Tootsie • Phyllis Logan Another Time, Another Place • Meryl Streep Sophie's Choice
BEST SUPPORTING ACTOR: **Denholm Elliott** Trading Places • Bob Hoskins The Honorary Consul • Burt Lancaster Local Hero • Jerry Lewis The King of Comedy
BEST SUPPORTING ACTRESS: **Jamie Lee Curtis** Trading Places • Teri Garr Tootsie • Rosemary Harris The Ploughman's Lunch • Maureen Lipman Educating Rita
BEST ORIGINAL SCREENPLAY: **Paul D Zimmerman** The King of Comedy • Bill Forsyth Local Hero • Herschel Weingrod Trading Places • Woody Allen Zelig
BEST ADAPTED SCREENPLAY: **Ruth Prawer Jhabvala** Heat and Dust • Harold Pinter Betrayal • Willy Russell Educating Rita • Larry Gelbart, Murray Schisgal Tootsie

Academy Awards

BEST PICTURE: **Terms of Endearment** • The Big Chill • The Dresser • The Right Stuff • Tender Mercies
FOREIGN LANGUAGE FILM: **Fanny and Alexander** • Le Bal • Carmen • Entre Nous • Job's Revolt
DIRECTING: **James L Brooks** Terms of Endearment • Peter Yates The Dresser • Ingmar Bergman Fanny and Alexander • Mike Nichols Silkwood • Bruce Beresford Tender Mercies
ACTOR IN A LEADING ROLE: **Robert Duvall** Tender Mercies • Michael Caine Educating Rita • Tom Conti Reuben, Reuben • Tom Courtenay, Albert Finney The Dresser
ACTRESS IN A LEADING ROLE: **Shirley MacLaine** Terms of Endearment • Jane Alexander Testament • Meryl Streep Silkwood • Julie Walters Educating Rita • Debra Winger Terms of Endearment
ACTOR IN A SUPPORTING ROLE: **Jack Nicholson**, John Lithgow Terms of Endearment • Charles Durning To Be or Not to Be • Sam Shepard The Right Stuff • Rip Torn Cross Creek
ACTRESS IN A SUPPORTING ROLE: **Linda Hunt** The Year of Living Dangerously • Cher Silkwood • Glenn Close The Big Chill • Amy Irving Yentl • Alfre Woodard Cross Creek
WRITING (SCREENPLAY WRITTEN DIRECTLY FOR THE SCREEN): **Horton Foote** Tender Mercies • Lawrence Kasdan, Barbara Benedek The Big Chill • Ingmar Bergman Fanny and Alexander • Nora Ephron, Alice Arlen Silkwood • Lawrence Lasker, Walter F Parkes WarGames
WRITING (SCREENPLAY BASED ON MATERIAL FROM ANOTHER MEDIUM): **James L Brooks** Terms of Endearment •

Harold Pinter *Betrayal* • Ronald Harwood *The Dresser* • Willy Russell *Educating Rita* • Julius J Epstein *Reuben, Reuben*

Golden Globe Awards

BEST MOTION PICTURE DRAMA: **Terms of Endearment**
BEST MOTION PICTURE COMEDY OR MUSICAL: **Yentl**
BEST FOREIGN LANGUAGE FILM: **Fanny and Alexander**
BEST DIRECTOR MOTION PICTURE: **Barbra Streisand** *Yentl*
BEST PERFORMANCE BY AN ACTOR IN A MOTION PICTURE DRAMA: **Tom Courtenay** *The Dresser* • **Robert Duvall** *Tender Mercies*
BEST PERFORMANCE BY AN ACTRESS IN A MOTION PICTURE DRAMA: **Shirley MacLaine** *Terms of Endearment*
BEST PERFORMANCE BY AN ACTOR IN A MOTION PICTURE COMEDY OR MUSICAL: **Michael Caine** *Educating Rita*
BEST PERFORMANCE BY AN ACTRESS IN A MOTION PICTURE COMEDY OR MUSICAL: **Julie Walters** *Educating Rita*
BEST PERFORMANCE BY AN ACTOR IN A SUPPORTING ROLE MOTION PICTURE: **Jack Nicholson** *Terms of Endearment*
BEST PERFORMANCE BY AN ACTRESS IN A SUPPORTING ROLE MOTION PICTURE: **Cher** *Silkwood*
BEST SCREENPLAY MOTION PICTURE: **James L Brooks** *Terms of Endearment*

Cannes International Film Festival

PALME D'OR: **The Ballad of Narayama**
ACTOR: **Gian Maria Volonte** *The Death of Mario Ricci*
ACTRESS: **Hanna Schygulla** *Storia di Piera*

Berlin International Film Festival

GOLDEN BERLIN BEAR: **Ascendancy** • *La Colmena*
SILVER BERLIN BEAR FOR THE BEST DIRECTOR: **Eric Rohmer** *Pauline at the Beach*
SILVER BERLIN BEAR FOR THE BEST ACTOR: **Bruce Dern** *That Championship Season*
SILVER BERLIN BEAR FOR THE BEST ACTRESS: **Evgenia Glushenko** *Wljubljon Po Sobstvennomu Zhelaniju*

1984

British Academy of Film & Television Arts Awards

BEST FILM: **The Killing Fields** • *The Dresser* • *Paris, Texas* • *A Private Function*
BEST FOREIGN LANGUAGE FILM: **Carmen** • *The Return of Martin Guerre* • *Sunday in the Country* • *Swann in Love*
BEST DIRECTOR: **Wim Wenders** *Paris, Texas* • Peter Yates *The Dresser* • Roland Joffé *The Killing Fields* • Sergio Leone *Once upon a Time in America*
BEST ACTOR: **Haing S Ngor** *The Killing Fields* • Tom Courtenay, Albert Finney *The Dresser* • Sam Waterston *The Killing Fields*
BEST ACTRESS: **Maggie Smith** *A Private Function* • Shirley MacLaine *Terms of Endearment* • Helen Mirren *Cal* • Meryl Streep *Silkwood*
BEST SUPPORTING ACTOR: **Denholm Elliott** *A Private Function* • Michael Elphick *Gorky Park* • Ian Holm, Ralph Richardson *Greystoke: the Legend of Tarzan, Lord of the Apes*
BEST SUPPORTING ACTRESS: **Liz Smith** *A Private Function* • Eileen Atkins *The Dresser* • Cher *Silkwood* • Tuesday Weld *Once upon a Time in America*
BEST ORIGINAL SCREENPLAY: **Woody Allen** *Broadway Danny Rose* • Lawrence Kasdan, Barbara Benedek *The Big Chill* • Bill Forsyth *Comfort and Joy* • Alan Bennett *A Private Function*
BEST ADAPTED SCREENPLAY: **Bruce Robinson** *The Killing Fields* • Julian Mitchell *Another Country* • Ronald Harwood *The Dresser* • Sam Shepard *Paris, Texas*

Academy Awards

BEST PICTURE: **Amadeus** • *The Killing Fields* • *A Passage to India* • *Places in the Heart* • *A Soldier's Story*
FOREIGN LANGUAGE FILM: **Dangerous Moves** • *Beyond the Walls* • *Camila* • *Double Feature* • *Wartime Romance*
DIRECTING: **Milos Forman** *Amadeus* • Woody Allen *Broadway Danny Rose* • Roland Joffé *The Killing Fields* • David Lean *A Passage to India* • Robert Benton *Places in the Heart*
ACTOR IN A LEADING ROLE: **F Murray Abraham** *Amadeus* • Jeff Bridges *Starman* • Albert Finney *Under the Volcano* • Tom Hulce *Amadeus* • Sam Waterston *The Killing Fields*
ACTRESS IN A LEADING ROLE: **Sally Field** *Places in the Heart* • Judy Davis *A Passage to India* • Jessica Lange *Country* • Vanessa Redgrave *The Bostonians* • Sissy Spacek *The River*
ACTOR IN A SUPPORTING ROLE: **Haing S Ngor** *The Killing Fields* • Adolph Caesar *A Soldier's Story* • John Malkovich *Places in the Heart* • Noriyuki "Pat" Morita

---

The Karate Kid • Ralph Richardson *Greystoke: the Legend of Tarzan, Lord of the Apes*
ACTRESS IN A SUPPORTING ROLE: **Peggy Ashcroft** *A Passage to India* • Glenn Close *The Natural* • Lindsay Crouse *Places in the Heart* • Christine Lahti *Swing Shift* • Geraldine Page *The Pope of Greenwich Village*
WRITING (SCREENPLAY WRITTEN DIRECTLY FOR THE SCREEN): **Robert Benton** *Places in the Heart* • Daniel Petrie Jr, Danilo Bach *Beverly Hills Cop* • Woody Allen *Broadway Danny Rose* • Gregory Nava, Anna Thomas *El Norte* • Bruce Jay Friedman, Lowell Ganz, Brian Grazer, Babaloo Mandel *Splash*
WRITING (SCREENPLAY BASED ON MATERIAL FROM ANOTHER MEDIUM): **Peter Shaffer** *Amadeus* • Robert Towne, Michael Austin *Greystoke: the Legend of Tarzan, Lord of the Apes* • Bruce Robinson *The Killing Fields* • David Lean *A Passage to India* • Charles Fuller *A Soldier's Story*

Golden Globe Awards

BEST MOTION PICTURE DRAMA: **Amadeus**
BEST MOTION PICTURE COMEDY OR MUSICAL: **Romancing the Stone**
BEST FOREIGN LANGUAGE FILM: **A Passage to India**
BEST DIRECTOR MOTION PICTURE: **Milos Forman** *Amadeus*
BEST PERFORMANCE BY AN ACTOR IN A MOTION PICTURE DRAMA: **F Murray Abraham** *Amadeus*
BEST PERFORMANCE BY AN ACTRESS IN A MOTION PICTURE DRAMA: **Sally Field** *Places in the Heart*
BEST PERFORMANCE BY AN ACTOR IN A MOTION PICTURE COMEDY OR MUSICAL: **Dudley Moore** *Micki & Maude*
BEST PERFORMANCE BY AN ACTRESS IN A MOTION PICTURE COMEDY OR MUSICAL: **Kathleen Turner** *Romancing the Stone*
BEST PERFORMANCE BY AN ACTOR IN A SUPPORTING ROLE MOTION PICTURE: **Haing S Ngor** *The Killing Fields*
BEST PERFORMANCE BY AN ACTRESS IN A SUPPORTING ROLE MOTION PICTURE: **Peggy Ashcroft** *A Passage to India*
BEST SCREENPLAY MOTION PICTURE: **Peter Shaffer** *Amadeus*

Cannes International Film Festival

GRAND PRIX: **Paris, Texas**
DIRECTOR: **Bertrand Tavernier** *Sunday in the Country*
ACTOR: **Alfredo Landa, Francisco Rabal** *Los Santos Inocentes*
ACTRESS: **Helen Mirren** *Cal*
ORIGINAL SCREENPLAY: **Theo Angelopoulos, Thanassis Valtinos, Tonino Guerra** *Taxidi Sta Kithira*

Berlin International Film Festival

GOLDEN BERLIN BEAR: **Love Streams**
SILVER BERLIN BEAR FOR THE BEST DIRECTOR: **Ettore Scola** *Le Bal*
SILVER BERLIN BEAR FOR THE BEST ACTOR: **Albert Finney** *The Dresser*
SILVER BERLIN BEAR FOR THE BEST ACTRESS: **Inna Tschurikova** *Wartime Romance*

1985

British Academy of Film & Television Arts Awards

BEST FILM: **The Purple Rose of Cairo** • *Amadeus* • *Back to the Future* • *A Passage to India* • *Witness*
BEST FOREIGN LANGUAGE FILM: **Colonel Redl** • *Carmen* • *Dim Sum: a Little Bit of Heart* • *Subway*
BEST ACTOR: **William Hurt** *Kiss of the Spider Woman* • Victor Banerjee *A Passage to India* • Harrison Ford *Witness* • F Murray Abraham *Amadeus*
BEST ACTRESS: **Peggy Ashcroft** *A Passage to India* • Mia Farrow *The Purple Rose of Cairo* • Kelly McGillis *Witness* • Alexandra Pigg *Letter to Brezhnev*
BEST SUPPORTING ACTOR: **Denholm Elliott** *Defence of the Realm* • James Fox *A Passage to India* • John Gielgud *Plenty* • Saeed Jaffrey *My Beautiful Laundrette*
BEST SUPPORTING ACTRESS: **Rosanna Arquette** *Desperately Seeking Susan* • Judi Dench *Wetherby* • Anjelica Huston *Prizzi's Honor* • Tracey Ullman *Plenty*
BEST ORIGINAL SCREENPLAY: **Woody Allen** *The Purple Rose of Cairo* • Robert Zemeckis, Bob Gale *Back to the Future* • Hanif Kureishi *My Beautiful Laundrette* • Earl W Wallace, William Kelley *Witness*
BEST ADAPTED SCREENPLAY: **Richard Condon, Janet Roach** *Prizzi's Honor* • Peter Shaffer *Amadeus* • David Lean *A Passage to India* • Julian Bond *The Shooting Party*

Academy Awards

BEST PICTURE: **Out of Africa** • *The Color Purple* • *Kiss of the Spider Woman* • *Prizzi's Honor* • *Witness*
FOREIGN LANGUAGE FILM: **The Official Version** • *Angry Harvest* • *Colonel Redl* • *3 Men and a Cradle* • *When Father Was Away on Business*
DIRECTING: **Sydney Pollack** *Out of Africa* • Hector Babenco *Kiss of the Spider Woman* • John Huston *Prizzi's Honor* • Akira Kurosawa *Ran* • Peter Weir *Witness*
ACTOR IN A LEADING ROLE: **William Hurt** *Kiss of the Spider Woman* • Harrison Ford *Witness* • James Garner *Murphy's Romance* • Jack Nicholson *Prizzi's Honor* • Jon Voight *Runaway Train*
ACTRESS IN A LEADING ROLE: **Geraldine Page** *The Trip to Bountiful* • Anne Bancroft *Agnes of God* • Whoopi Goldberg *The Color Purple* • Jessica Lange *Sweet Dreams* • Meryl Streep *Out of Africa*
ACTOR IN A SUPPORTING ROLE: **Don Ameche** *Cocoon* • Klaus Maria Brandauer *Out of Africa* • Joseph L Mankiewicz *Forsaking All Others* • Robert Loggia *Jagged Edge* • Eric Roberts *Runaway Train*
ACTRESS IN A SUPPORTING ROLE: **Anjelica Huston** *Prizzi's Honor* • Margaret Avery, Oprah Winfrey *The Color Purple* • Amy Madigan *Twice in a Lifetime* • Meg Tilly *Agnes of God*
WRITING (SCREENPLAY WRITTEN DIRECTLY FOR THE SCREEN): **William Kelley, Earl W Wallace, Pamela Wallace** *Witness* • Robert Zemeckis, Bob Gale *Back to the Future* • Terry Gilliam, Tom Stoppard, Charles McKeown *Brazil* • Aida Bortnik, Luis Puenzo *The Official Version* • Woody Allen *The Purple Rose of Cairo*
WRITING (SCREENPLAY BASED ON MATERIAL FROM ANOTHER MEDIUM): **Kurt Luedtke** *Out of Africa* • Menno Meyjes *The Color Purple* • Leonard Schrader *Kiss of the Spider Woman* • Richard Condon, Janet Roach *Prizzi's Honor* • Horton Foote *The Trip to Bountiful*

Golden Globe Awards

BEST MOTION PICTURE DRAMA: **Out of Africa**
BEST MOTION PICTURE COMEDY OR MUSICAL: **Prizzi's Honor**
BEST FOREIGN LANGUAGE FILM: **The Official Version**
BEST DIRECTOR MOTION PICTURE: **John Huston** *Prizzi's Honor*
BEST PERFORMANCE BY AN ACTOR IN A MOTION PICTURE DRAMA: **Jon Voight** *Runaway Train*
BEST PERFORMANCE BY AN ACTRESS IN A MOTION PICTURE DRAMA: **Whoopi Goldberg** *The Color Purple*
BEST PERFORMANCE BY AN ACTOR IN A MOTION PICTURE COMEDY OR MUSICAL: **Jack Nicholson** *Prizzi's Honor*
BEST PERFORMANCE BY AN ACTRESS IN A MOTION PICTURE COMEDY OR MUSICAL: **Kathleen Turner** *Prizzi's Honor*
BEST PERFORMANCE BY AN ACTOR IN A SUPPORTING ROLE MOTION PICTURE: **Klaus Maria Brandauer** *Out of Africa*
BEST PERFORMANCE BY AN ACTRESS IN A SUPPORTING ROLE MOTION PICTURE: **Meg Tilly** *Agnes of God*
BEST SCREENPLAY MOTION PICTURE: **Woody Allen** *The Purple Rose of Cairo*

Cannes International Film Festival

PALME D'OR: **When Father Was Away on Business**
DIRECTOR: **André Téchiné** *Rendez-vous*
ACTOR: **William Hurt** *Kiss of the Spider Woman*
ACTRESS: **Norma Aleandro** *The Official Version* • **Cher** *Mask*

Berlin International Film Festival

GOLDEN BERLIN BEAR: **Die Frau und der Fremde** • **Wetherby**
SILVER BERLIN BEAR FOR THE BEST DIRECTOR: **Robert Benton** *Places in the Heart*
SILVER BERLIN BEAR FOR THE BEST ACTOR: **Fernando Fernan Gomez** *Stico*
SILVER BERLIN BEAR FOR THE BEST ACTRESS: **Jo Kennedy** *Wrong World*

1986

British Academy of Film & Television Arts Awards

BEST FILM: **A Room with a View** • *Hannah and Her Sisters* • *The Mission* • *Mona Lisa*
BEST FOREIGN LANGUAGE FILM: **Ran** • *Betty Blue* • *Ginger & Fred* • *Otello*
BEST ACHIEVEMENT IN DIRECTION: **Woody Allen** *Hannah and Her Sisters* • Roland Joffé *The Mission* • Neil Jordan *Mona Lisa* • James Ivory *A Room with a View*
BEST ACTOR IN A LEADING ROLE: **Bob Hoskins** *Mona Lisa* • Woody Allen, Michael Caine *Hannah and Her Sisters* • Paul Hogan "Crocodile" Dundee

BEST ACTRESS IN A LEADING ROLE: **Maggie Smith** *A Room with a View* • Mia Farrow *Hannah and Her Sisters* • Meryl Streep *Out of Africa* • Cathy Tyson *Mona Lisa*
BEST ACTOR IN A SUPPORTING ROLE: **Ray McAnally** *The Mission* • Klaus Maria Brandauer *Out of Africa* • Simon Callow, Denholm Elliott *A Room with a View*
BEST ACTRESS IN A SUPPORTING ROLE: **Judi Dench** *A Room with a View* • Rosanna Arquette *After Hours* • Barbara Hershey *Hannah and Her Sisters* • Rosemary Leach *A Room with a View*
BEST ORIGINAL SCREENPLAY: **Woody Allen** *Hannah and Her Sisters* • Paul Hogan, Ken Shadie, John Cornell ''Crocodile'' *Dundee* • Robert Bolt *The Mission* • Neil Jordan, David Leland *Mona Lisa*
BEST ADAPTED SCREENPLAY: **Kurt Luedtke** *Out of Africa* • Hesper Anderson, Mark Medoff *Children of a Lesser God* • Menno Meyjes *The Color Purple* • Akira Kurosawa, Hideo Oguni, Masato Ide *Ran* • Ruth Prawer Jhabvala *A Room with a View*

Academy Awards

BEST PICTURE: **Platoon** • *Children of a Lesser God* • *Hannah and Her Sisters* • *The Mission* • *A Room with a View*
FOREIGN LANGUAGE FILM: **The Assault** • *38* • *Betty Blue* • *The Decline of the American Empire* • *My Sweet Little Village*
DIRECTING: **Oliver Stone** *Platoon* • David Lynch *Blue Velvet* • Woody Allen *Hannah and Her Sisters* • Roland Joffé *The Mission* • James Ivory *A Room with a View*
ACTOR IN A LEADING ROLE: **Paul Newman** *The Color of Money* • Dexter Gordon *'Round Midnight* • Bob Hoskins *Mona Lisa* • William Hurt *Children of a Lesser God* • James Woods *Salvador*
ACTRESS IN A LEADING ROLE: **Marlee Matlin** *Children of a Lesser God* • Jane Fonda *The Morning After* • Sissy Spacek *Crimes of the Heart* • Kathleen Turner *Peggy Sue Got Married* • Sigourney Weaver *Aliens*
ACTOR IN A SUPPORTING ROLE: **Michael Caine** *Hannah and Her Sisters* • Tom Berenger, Willem Dafoe *Platoon* • Denholm Elliott *A Room with a View* • Dennis Hopper *Best Shot*
ACTRESS IN A SUPPORTING ROLE: **Dianne Wiest** *Hannah and Her Sisters* • Tess Harper *Crimes of the Heart* • Piper Laurie *Children of a Lesser God* • Mary Elizabeth Mastrantonio *The Color of Money* • Maggie Smith *A Room with a View*
WRITING (SCREENPLAY WRITTEN DIRECTLY FOR THE SCREEN): **Woody Allen** *Hannah and Her Sisters* • John Cornell, Paul Hogan, Ken Shadie ''Crocodile'' *Dundee* • Hanif Kureishi *My Beautiful Laundrette* • Oliver Stone *Platoon* • Richard Boyle, Oliver Stone *Salvador*
WRITING (SCREENPLAY BASED ON MATERIAL FROM ANOTHER MEDIUM): **Ruth Prawer Jhabvala** *A Room with a View* • Hesper Anderson, Mark Medoff *Children of a Lesser God* • Richard Price *The Color of Money* • Beth Henley *Crimes of the Heart* • Bruce A Evans, Raynold Gideon *Stand by Me*

Golden Globe Awards

BEST MOTION PICTURE DRAMA: **Platoon**
BEST MOTION PICTURE COMEDY OR MUSICAL: **Hannah and Her Sisters**
BEST FOREIGN LANGUAGE FILM: **The Assault**
BEST DIRECTOR MOTION PICTURE: **Oliver Stone** *Platoon*
BEST PERFORMANCE BY AN ACTOR IN A MOTION PICTURE DRAMA: **Bob Hoskins** *Mona Lisa*
BEST PERFORMANCE BY AN ACTRESS IN A MOTION PICTURE DRAMA: **Marlee Matlin** *Children of a Lesser God*
BEST PERFORMANCE BY AN ACTOR IN A MOTION PICTURE COMEDY OR MUSICAL: **Paul Hogan** ''Crocodile'' *Dundee*
BEST PERFORMANCE BY AN ACTRESS IN A MOTION PICTURE COMEDY OR MUSICAL: **Sissy Spacek** *Crimes of the Heart*
BEST PERFORMANCE BY AN ACTOR IN A SUPPORTING ROLE MOTION PICTURE: **Tom Berenger** *Platoon*
BEST PERFORMANCE BY AN ACTRESS IN A SUPPORTING ROLE MOTION PICTURE: **Maggie Smith** *A Room with a View*
BEST SCREENPLAY MOTION PICTURE: **Robert Bolt** *The Mission*

Cannes International Film Festival

PALME D'OR: **The Mission**
DIRECTOR: **Martin Scorsese** *After Hours*
ACTOR: **Michel Blanc** *Tenue de Soirée* • Bob Hoskins *Mona Lisa*
ACTRESS: **Barbara Sukowa** *Rosa Luxemburg* • Fernanda Torres *Eu Sei Que Vou Te Amar*

Berlin International Film Festival

GOLDEN BERLIN BEAR: **Stammheim**
SILVER BERLIN BEAR FOR THE BEST DIRECTOR: **Georgi Schengelaja** *Achalgazrda Kompozitoris Mogzauroba*
SILVER BERLIN BEAR FOR THE BEST ACTOR: **Tuncel Kurtiz** *Hiuh Hagdi*

SILVER BERLIN BEAR FOR THE BEST ACTRESS: **Marcelia Cartaxo** *Hour of the Star* • Charlotte Valandrey *Rouge Baiser*

1987

British Academy of Film & Television Arts Awards

BEST FILM: **Jean de Florette** • *Cry Freedom* • *Hope and Glory* • *Radio Days*
BEST FOREIGN LANGUAGE FILM: **The Sacrifice** • *Jean de Florette* • *Manon des Sources* • *My Life as a Dog*
BEST ACHIEVEMENT IN DIRECTION: **Oliver Stone** *Platoon* • Richard Attenborough *Cry Freedom* • John Boorman *Hope and Glory* • Claude Berri *Jean de Florette*
BEST ACTOR IN A LEADING ROLE: **Sean Connery** *The Name of the Rose* • Gérard Depardieu, Yves Montand *Jean de Florette* • Gary Oldman *Prick Up Your Ears*
BEST ACTRESS IN A LEADING ROLE: **Anne Bancroft** *84 Charing Cross Road* • Emily Lloyd *Wish You Were Here* • Sarah Miles *Hope and Glory* • Julie Walters *Personal Services*
BEST ACTOR IN A SUPPORTING ROLE: **Daniel Auteuil** *Jean de Florette* • Ian Bannen *Hope and Glory* • Sean Connery *The Untouchables* • John Thaw *Cry Freedom*
BEST ACTRESS IN A SUPPORTING ROLE: **Susan Wooldridge** *Hope and Glory* • Judi Dench *84 Charing Cross Road* • Vanessa Redgrave *Prick Up Your Ears* • Dianne Wiest *Radio Days*
BEST SCREENPLAY (ORIGINAL): **David Leland** *Wish You Were Here* • John Boorman *Hope and Glory* • David Leland *Personal Services* • Woody Allen *Radio Days*
BEST SCREENPLAY (ADAPTED): **Gérard Brach, Claude Berri** *Jean de Florette* • Hugh Whitemore *84 Charing Cross Road* • Christine Edzard *Little Dorrit* • Alan Bennett *Prick Up Your Ears*

Academy Awards

BEST PICTURE: **The Last Emperor** • *Broadcast News* • *Fatal Attraction* • *Hope and Glory* • *Moonstruck*
FOREIGN LANGUAGE FILM: **Babette's Feast** • *Au Revoir les Enfants* • *Course Completed* • *The Family* • *Pathfinder*
DIRECTING: **Bernardo Bertolucci** *The Last Emperor* • Adrian Lyne *Fatal Attraction* • John Boorman *Hope and Glory* • Norman Jewison *Moonstruck* • Lasse Hallström *My Life as a Dog*
ACTOR IN A LEADING ROLE: **Michael Douglas** *Wall Street* • William Hurt *Broadcast News* • Marcello Mastroianni *Dark Eyes* • Jack Nicholson *Ironweed* • Robin Williams *Good Morning, Vietnam*
ACTRESS IN A LEADING ROLE: **Cher** *Moonstruck* • Glenn Close *Fatal Attraction* • Holly Hunter *Broadcast News* • Sally Kirkland *Anna* • Meryl Streep *Ironweed*
ACTOR IN A SUPPORTING ROLE: **Sean Connery** *The Untouchables* • Albert Brooks *Broadcast News* • Morgan Freeman *Street Smart* • Vincent Gardenia *Moonstruck* • Denzel Washington *Cry Freedom*
ACTRESS IN A SUPPORTING ROLE: **Olympia Dukakis** *Moonstruck* • Norma Aleandro *Gaby: a True Story* • Anne Archer *Fatal Attraction* • Anne Ramsey *Throw Momma from the Train* • Ann Sothern *The Whales of August*
WRITING (SCREENPLAY WRITTEN DIRECTLY FOR THE SCREEN): **John Patrick Shanley** *Moonstruck* • Louis Malle *Au Revoir les Enfants* • James L Brooks *Broadcast News* • John Boorman *Hope and Glory* • Woody Allen *Radio Days*
WRITING (SCREENPLAY BASED ON MATERIAL FROM ANOTHER MEDIUM): **Bernardo Bertolucci, Mark Peploe** *The Last Emperor* • Tony Huston *The Dead* • James Dearden *Fatal Attraction* • Gustav Hasford, Michael Herr, Stanley Kubrick *Full Metal Jacket* • Pelle Berglund, Brasse Brannstrom, Lasse Hallström, Reidar Jonsson *My Life as a Dog*

Golden Globe Awards

BEST MOTION PICTURE DRAMA: **The Last Emperor**
BEST MOTION PICTURE COMEDY OR MUSICAL: **Hope and Glory**
BEST FOREIGN LANGUAGE FILM: **My Life as a Dog**
BEST DIRECTOR MOTION PICTURE: **Bernardo Bertolucci** *The Last Emperor*
BEST PERFORMANCE BY AN ACTOR IN A MOTION PICTURE DRAMA: **Michael Douglas** *Wall Street*
BEST PERFORMANCE BY AN ACTRESS IN A MOTION PICTURE DRAMA: **Sally Kirkland** *Anna*
BEST PERFORMANCE BY AN ACTOR IN A MOTION PICTURE COMEDY OR MUSICAL: **Robin Williams** *Good Morning, Vietnam*
BEST PERFORMANCE BY AN ACTRESS IN A MOTION PICTURE COMEDY OR MUSICAL: **Cher** *Moonstruck*

BEST PERFORMANCE BY AN ACTOR IN A SUPPORTING ROLE MOTION PICTURE: **Sean Connery** *The Untouchables*
BEST PERFORMANCE BY AN ACTRESS IN A SUPPORTING ROLE MOTION PICTURE; **Olympia Dukakis** *Moonstruck*
BEST SCREENPLAY MOTION PICTURE: **Mark Peploe, Bernardo Bertolucci** *The Last Emperor*

Cannes International Film Festival

PALME D'OR: **Under Satan's Sun**
DIRECTOR: **Wim Wenders** *Wings of Desire*
ACTOR: **Marcello Mastroianni** *Dark Eyes*
ACTRESS: **Barbara Hershey** *Shy People*

Berlin International Film Festival

GOLDEN BERLIN BEAR: **The Theme**
SILVER BERLIN BEAR FOR THE BEST DIRECTOR: **Oliver Stone** *Platoon*
SILVER BERLIN BEAR FOR THE BEST ACTOR: **Gian Maria Volonté** *Il Caso Moro*
SILVER BERLIN BEAR FOR THE BEST ACTRESS: **Ana Beatriz Nogueira** *Vera*

1988

British Academy of Film & Television Arts Awards

BEST FILM: **The Last Emperor** • *Au Revoir les Enfants* • *Babette's Feast* • *A Fish Called Wanda*
FILM NOT IN THE ENGLISH LANGUAGE: **Babette's Feast** • *Au Revoir les Enfants* • *Dark Eyes* • *Wings of Desire*
BEST ACHIEVEMENT IN DIRECTION: **Louis Malle** *Au Revoir les Enfants* • Gabriel Axel *Babette's Feast* • Charles Crichton *A Fish Called Wanda* • Bernardo Bertolucci *The Last Emperor*
BEST ACTOR IN A LEADING ROLE: **John Cleese** *A Fish Called Wanda* • Michael Douglas *Fatal Attraction* • Kevin Kline *A Fish Called Wanda* • Robin Williams *Good Morning, Vietnam*
BEST ACTRESS IN A LEADING ROLE: **Maggie Smith** *The Lonely Passion of Judith Hearne* • Stéphane Audran *Babette's Feast* • Cher *Moonstruck* • Jamie Lee Curtis *A Fish Called Wanda*
BEST ACTOR IN A SUPPORTING ROLE: **Michael Palin** *A Fish Called Wanda* • Joss Ackland *White Mischief* • Peter O'Toole *The Last Emperor* • David Suchet *A World Apart*
BEST ACTRESS IN A SUPPORTING ROLE: **Olympia Dukakis** *Moonstruck* • Maria Aitken *A Fish Called Wanda* • Anne Archer *Fatal Attraction*
BEST ORIGINAL SCREENPLAY: **Shawn Slovo** *A World Apart* • Louis Malle *Au Revoir les Enfants* • John Cleese *A Fish Called Wanda* • John Patrick Shanley *Moonstruck*
BEST ADAPTED SCREENPLAY: **Philip Kaufman, Jean-Claude Carrière** *The Unbearable Lightness of Being* • Gabriel Axel *Babette's Feast* • Tom Stoppard *Empire of the Sun* • Jeffrey Price, Peter S Seaman *Who Framed Roger Rabbit*

Academy Awards

BEST PICTURE: **Rain Man** • *The Accidental Tourist* • *Dangerous Liaisons* • *Mississippi Burning* • *Working Girl*
FOREIGN LANGUAGE FILM: **Pelle the Conqueror** • *Hanussen* • *The Music Teacher* • *Salaam Bombay!* • *Women on the Verge of a Nervous Breakdown*
DIRECTING: **Barry Levinson** *Rain Man* • Charles Crichton *A Fish Called Wanda* • Martin Scorsese *The Last Temptation of Christ* • Alan Parker *Mississippi Burning* • Mike Nichols *Working Girl*
ACTOR IN A LEADING ROLE: **Dustin Hoffman** *Rain Man* • Gene Hackman *Mississippi Burning* • Tom Hanks *Big* • Edward James Olmos *Stand and Deliver* • Max von Sydow *Pelle the Conqueror*
ACTRESS IN A LEADING ROLE: **Jodie Foster** *The Accused* • Glenn Close *Dangerous Liaisons* • Melanie Griffith *Working Girl* • Meryl Streep *A Cry in the Dark* • Sigourney Weaver *Gorillas in the Mist*
ACTOR IN A SUPPORTING ROLE: **Kevin Kline** *A Fish Called Wanda* • Alec Guinness *Little Dorrit* • Martin Landau *Tucker: the Man and His Dream* • River Phoenix *Running on Empty* • Dean Stockwell *Married to the Mob*
ACTRESS IN A SUPPORTING ROLE: **Geena Davis** *The Accidental Tourist* • Joan Cusack, Sigourney Weaver *Working Girl* • Frances McDormand *Mississippi Burning* • Michelle Pfeiffer *Dangerous Liaisons*
WRITING (SCREENPLAY WRITTEN DIRECTLY FOR THE SCREEN): **Ronald Bass, Barry Morrow** *Rain Man* • Gary Ross, Anne Spielberg *Big* • Ron Shelton *Bull Durham* • John Cleese, Charles Crichton *A Fish Called Wanda* • Naomi Foner *Running on Empty*
WRITING (SCREENPLAY BASED ON MATERIAL FROM ANOTHER MEDIUM): **Christopher Hampton** *Dangerous Liaisons* • Frank Galati, Lawrence Kasdan *The Accidental Tourist* • Tab Murphy, Anna Hamilton Phelan *Gorillas in the Mist* •

Christine Edzard *Little Dorrit* • Jean-Claude Carrière, Philip Kaufman *The Unbearable Lightness of Being*

Golden Globe Awards

BEST MOTION PICTURE , DRAMA: **Rain Man**
BEST MOTION PICTURE , COMEDY OR MUSICAL: **Working Girl**
BEST FOREIGN LANGUAGE FILM: **Pelle the Conqueror**
BEST DIRECTOR , MOTION PICTURE: **Clint Eastwood** *Bird*
BEST PERFORMANCE BY AN ACTOR IN A MOTION PICTURE DRAMA: **Dustin Hoffman** *Rain Man*
BEST PERFORMANCE BY AN ACTRESS IN A MOTION PICTURE DRAMA: **Shirley MacLaine** *Madame Sousatzka* • **Jodie Foster** *The Accused* • **Sigourney Weaver** *Gorillas in the Mist*
BEST PERFORMANCE BY AN ACTOR IN A MOTION PICTURE COMEDY OR MUSICAL: **Tom Hanks** *Big*
BEST PERFORMANCE BY AN ACTRESS IN A MOTION PICTURE COMEDY OR MUSICAL: **Melanie Griffith** *Working Girl*
BEST PERFORMANCE BY AN ACTOR IN A SUPPORTING ROLE MOTION PICTURE: **Martin Landau** *Tucker: the Man and His Dream*
BEST PERFORMANCE BY AN ACTRESS IN A SUPPORTING ROLE MOTION PICTURE: **Sigourney Weaver** *Working Girl*
BEST SCREENPLAY , MOTION PICTURE: **Naomi Foner** *Running on Empty*

Cannes International Film Festival

PALME D'OR: **Pelle the Conqueror**
DIRECTOR: **Fernando E Solanas** *Sur*
ACTOR: **Forest Whitaker** *Bird*
ACTRESS: **Barbara Hershey, Jodhi May, Linda Mvusi** *A World Apart*

Berlin International Film Festival

GOLDEN BERLIN BEAR: **Red Sorghum**
SILVER BERLIN BEAR FOR THE BEST DIRECTOR: **Norman Jewison** *Moonstruck*
SILVER BERLIN BEAR FOR THE BEST ACTOR: **Manfred Möck, Jörg Pose** *Einer Trage des Anderen Last*
SILVER BERLIN BEAR FOR THE BEST ACTRESS: **Holly Hunter** *Broadcast News*

1989

British Academy of Film & Television Arts Awards

BEST FILM: **Dead Poets Society** • *My Left Foot* • *Shirley Valentine* • *When Harry Met Sally...*
FILM NOT IN THE ENGLISH LANGUAGE: **Life and Nothing But** • *Pelle the Conqueror* • *Salaam Bombay!* • *Women on the Verge of a Nervous Breakdown*
BEST ACHIEVEMENT IN DIRECTION: **Kenneth Branagh** *Henry V* • Stephen Frears *Dangerous Liaisons* • Peter Weir *Dead Poets Society* • Alan Parker *Mississippi Burning*
BEST ACTOR IN A LEADING ROLE: **Daniel Day-Lewis** *My Left Foot* • Kenneth Branagh *Henry V* • Dustin Hoffman *Rain Man* • Robin Williams *Dead Poets Society*
BEST ACTRESS IN A LEADING ROLE: **Pauline Collins** *Shirley Valentine* • Glenn Close *Dangerous Liaisons* • Jodie Foster *The Accused* • Melanie Griffith *Working Girl*
BEST ACTOR IN A SUPPORTING ROLE: **Ray McAnally** *My Left Foot* • Marlon Brando *A Dry White Season* • Sean Connery *Indiana Jones and the Last Crusade* • Jack Nicholson *Batman*
BEST ACTRESS IN A SUPPORTING ROLE: **Michelle Pfeiffer** *Dangerous Liaisons* • Peggy Ashcroft *Madame Sousatzka* • Laura San Giacomo *sex, lies, and videotape* • Sigourney Weaver *Working Girl*
BEST ORIGINAL SCREENPLAY: **Nora Ephron** *When Harry Met Sally...* • Tom Schulman *Dead Poets Society* • Ronald Bass, Barry Morrow *Rain Man* • Steven Soderbergh *sex, lies, and videotape*
BEST ADAPTED SCREENPLAY: **Christopher Hampton** *Dangerous Liaisons* • Frank Galati, Lawrence Kasdan *The Accidental Tourist* • Shane Connaughton, Jim Sheridan *My Left Foot* • Willy Russell *Shirley Valentine*

Academy Awards

BEST PICTURE: **Driving Miss Daisy** • *Born on the Fourth of July* • *Dead Poets Society* • *Field of Dreams* • *My Left Foot*
FOREIGN LANGUAGE FILM: **Cinema Paradiso** • *Camille Claudel* • *Jesus of Montreal* • *Waltzing Regitze* • *What Happened to Santiago*
DIRECTING: **Oliver Stone** *Born on the Fourth of July* • Woody Allen *Crimes and Misdemeanors* • Peter Weir *Dead Poets Society* • Kenneth Branagh *Henry V* • Jim Sheridan *My Left Foot*
ACTOR IN A LEADING ROLE: **Daniel Day-Lewis** *My Left Foot* • Kenneth Branagh *Henry V* • Tom Cruise *Born on the Fourth of July* • Morgan Freeman *Driving Miss Daisy* • Robin Williams *Dead Poets Society*

ACTRESS IN A LEADING ROLE: **Jessica Tandy** *Driving Miss Daisy* • Isabelle Adjani *Camille Claudel* • Pauline Collins *Shirley Valentine* • Jessica Lange *Music Box* • Michelle Pfeiffer *The Fabulous Baker Boys*
ACTOR IN A SUPPORTING ROLE: **Denzel Washington** *Glory* • Danny Aiello *Do the Right Thing* • Dan Aykroyd *Driving Miss Daisy* • Marlon Brando *A Dry White Season* • Martin Landau *Crimes and Misdemeanors*
ACTRESS IN A SUPPORTING ROLE: **Brenda Fricker** *My Left Foot* • Anjelica Huston, Lena Olin *Enemies, a Love Story* • Julia Roberts *Steel Magnolias* • Dianne Wiest *Parenthood*
WRITING (SCREENPLAY WRITTEN DIRECTLY FOR THE SCREEN): **Tom Schulman** *Dead Poets Society* • Woody Allen *Crimes and Misdemeanors* • Spike Lee *Do the Right Thing* • Nora Ephron *When Harry Met Sally...* • Steven Soderbergh *sex, lies, and videotape*
WRITING (SCREENPLAY BASED ON MATERIAL FROM ANOTHER MEDIUM): **Alfred Uhry** *Driving Miss Daisy* • Ron Kovic, Oliver Stone *Born on the Fourth of July* • Paul Mazursky, Roger L Simon *Enemies, a Love Story* • Phil Alden Robinson *Field of Dreams* • Shane Connaughton, Jim Sheridan *My Left Foot*

Golden Globe Awards

BEST MOTION PICTURE , DRAMA: **Born on the Fourth of July**
BEST MOTION PICTURE , COMEDY OR MUSICAL: **Driving Miss Daisy**
BEST FOREIGN LANGUAGE FILM: **Cinema Paradiso**
BEST DIRECTOR , MOTION PICTURE: **Oliver Stone** *Born on the Fourth of July*
BEST PERFORMANCE BY AN ACTOR IN A MOTION PICTURE DRAMA: **Tom Cruise** *Born on the Fourth of July*
BEST PERFORMANCE BY AN ACTRESS IN A MOTION PICTURE DRAMA: **Michelle Pfeiffer** *The Fabulous Baker Boys*
BEST PERFORMANCE BY AN ACTOR IN A MOTION PICTURE COMEDY OR MUSICAL: **Morgan Freeman** *Driving Miss Daisy*
BEST PERFORMANCE BY AN ACTRESS IN A MOTION PICTURE COMEDY OR MUSICAL: **Jessica Tandy** *Driving Miss Daisy*
BEST PERFORMANCE BY AN ACTOR IN A SUPPORTING ROLE MOTION PICTURE: **Denzel Washington** *Glory*
BEST PERFORMANCE BY AN ACTRESS IN A SUPPORTING ROLE MOTION PICTURE: **Julia Roberts** *Steel Magnolias*
BEST SCREENPLAY , MOTION PICTURE: **Oliver Stone, Ron Kovic** *Born on the Fourth of July*

Cannes International Film Festival

PALME D'OR: **sex, lies, and videotape**
DIRECTOR: **Emir Kusturica** *Time of the Gypsies*
ACTOR: **James Spader** *sex, lies, and videotape*
ACTRESS: **Meryl Streep** *A Cry in the Dark*

Berlin International Film Festival

GOLDEN BERLIN BEAR: **Rain Man**
SILVER BERLIN BEAR FOR THE BEST DIRECTOR: **Dusan Hanak** *Ja Milujem, Ty Milujes*
SILVER BERLIN BEAR FOR THE BEST ACTOR: **Gene Hackman** *Mississippi Burning*
SILVER BERLIN BEAR FOR THE BEST ACTRESS: **Isabelle Adjani** *Camille Claudel* • **Kaipo Cohen, Gila Almagor** *The Summer of Aviya*

1990

British Academy of Film & Television Arts Awards

BEST FILM: **GoodFellas** • *Crimes and Misdemeanors* • *Driving Miss Daisy* • *Pretty Woman*
BEST FILM NOT IN THE ENGLISH LANGUAGE: **Cinema Paradiso** • *Jesus of Montreal* • *Milou en Mai* • *Romuald et Juliette*
BEST ACHIEVEMENT IN DIRECTION: **Martin Scorsese** *GoodFellas* • Giuseppe Tornatore *Cinema Paradiso* • Woody Allen *Crimes and Misdemeanors* • Bruce Beresford *Driving Miss Daisy*
BEST ACTOR IN A LEADING ROLE: **Philippe Noiret** *Cinema Paradiso* • Sean Connery *The Hunt for Red October* • Tom Cruise *Born on the Fourth of July* • Robert De Niro *GoodFellas*
BEST ACTRESS IN A LEADING ROLE: **Jessica Tandy** *Driving Miss Daisy* • Shirley MacLaine *Postcards from the Edge* • Michelle Pfeiffer *The Fabulous Baker Boys* • Julia Roberts *Pretty Woman*
BEST ACTOR IN A SUPPORTING ROLE: **Salvatore Cascio** *Cinema Paradiso* • Alan Alda *Crimes and Misdemeanors* • John Hurt *The Field* • Al Pacino *Dick Tracy*
BEST ACTRESS IN A SUPPORTING ROLE: **Whoopi Goldberg** *Ghost* • Anjelica Huston *Crimes and Misdemeanors* • Shirley MacLaine *Steel Magnolias* • Billie Whitelaw *The Krays*

BEST SCREENPLAY (ORIGINAL): **Giuseppe Tornatore** *Cinema Paradiso* • Woody Allen *Crimes and Misdemeanors* • Bruce Joel Rubin *Ghost* • J F Lawton *Pretty Woman*
BEST SCREENPLAY (ADAPTED): **Nicholas Pileggi, Martin Scorsese** *GoodFellas* • Oliver Stone, Ron Kovic *Born on the Fourth of July* • Alfred Uhry *Driving Miss Daisy* • Carrie Fisher *Postcards from the Edge* • Michael Leeson *The War of the Roses*

Academy Awards

BEST PICTURE: **Dances with Wolves** • *Awakenings* • *Ghost* • *The Godfather Part III* • *GoodFellas*
FOREIGN LANGUAGE FILM: **Journey of Hope** • *Cyrano de Bergerac* • *Ju Dou* • *The Nasty Girl* • *Open Doors*
DIRECTING: **Kevin Costner** *Dances with Wolves* • Francis Ford Coppola *The Godfather Part III* • Martin Scorsese *GoodFellas* • Stephen Frears *The Grifters* • Barbet Schroeder *Reversal of Fortune*
ACTOR IN A LEADING ROLE: **Jeremy Irons** *Reversal of Fortune* • Kevin Costner *Dances with Wolves* • Robert De Niro *Awakenings* • Gérard Depardieu *Cyrano de Bergerac* • Richard Harris *The Field*
ACTRESS IN A LEADING ROLE: **Kathy Bates** *Misery* • Anjelica Huston *The Grifters* • Julia Roberts *Pretty Woman* • Meryl Streep *Postcards from the Edge* • Joanne Woodward *Mr and Mrs Bridge*
ACTOR IN A SUPPORTING ROLE: **Joe Pesci** *GoodFellas* • Bruce Davison *Longtime Companion* • Andy Garcia *The Godfather Part III* • Graham Greene *Dances with Wolves* • Al Pacino *Dick Tracy*
ACTRESS IN A SUPPORTING ROLE: **Whoopi Goldberg** *Ghost* • Annette Bening *The Grifters* • Lorraine Bracco *GoodFellas* • Diane Ladd *Wild at Heart* • Mary McDonnell *Dances with Wolves*
WRITING (SCREENPLAY WRITTEN DIRECTLY FOR THE SCREEN): **Bruce Joel Rubin** *Ghost* • Woody Allen *Alice* • Barry Levinson *Avalon* • Peter Weir *Green Card* • Whit Stillman *Metropolitan*
WRITING (SCREENPLAY BASED ON MATERIAL FROM ANOTHER MEDIUM): **Michael Blake** *Dances with Wolves* • Steven Zaillian *Awakenings* • Nicholas Pileggi, Martin Scorsese *GoodFellas* • Donald E Westlake *The Grifters* • Nicholas Kazan *Reversal of Fortune*

Golden Globe Awards

BEST MOTION PICTURE , DRAMA: **Dances with Wolves**
BEST MOTION PICTURE , COMEDY OR MUSICAL: **Green Card**
BEST FOREIGN LANGUAGE FILM: **Cyrano de Bergerac**
BEST DIRECTOR , MOTION PICTURE: **Kevin Costner** *Dances with Wolves*
BEST PERFORMANCE BY AN ACTOR IN A MOTION PICTURE DRAMA: **Jeremy Irons** *Reversal of Fortune*
BEST PERFORMANCE BY AN ACTRESS IN A MOTION PICTURE DRAMA: **Kathy Bates** *Misery*
BEST PERFORMANCE BY AN ACTOR IN A MOTION PICTURE COMEDY OR MUSICAL: **Gérard Depardieu** *Green Card*
BEST PERFORMANCE BY AN ACTRESS IN A MOTION PICTURE COMEDY OR MUSICAL: **Julia Roberts** *Pretty Woman*
BEST PERFORMANCE BY AN ACTOR IN A SUPPORTING ROLE MOTION PICTURE: **Bruce Davison** *Longtime Companion*
BEST PERFORMANCE BY AN ACTRESS IN A SUPPORTING ROLE MOTION PICTURE: **Whoopi Goldberg** *Ghost*
BEST SCREENPLAY , MOTION PICTURE: **Michael Blake** *Dances with Wolves*

Cannes International Film Festival

PALME D'OR: **Wild at Heart**
DIRECTOR: **Pavel Lounguine** *Taxi Blues*
ACTOR: **Gérard Depardieu** *Cyrano de Bergerac*
ACTRESS: **Krystyna Janda** *Interrogation*

Berlin International Film Festival

GOLDEN BERLIN BEAR: **Music Box** • *Larks on a String*
SILVER BERLIN BEAR FOR THE BEST DIRECTOR: **Michael Verhoeven** *The Nasty Girl*
SILVER BERLIN BEAR FOR THE BEST ACTOR: **Iain Glen** *Silent Scream*
SILVER BERLIN BEAR FOR THE BEST JOINT PERFORMANCE: **Jessica Tandy, Morgan Freeman** *Driving Miss Daisy*

1991

British Academy of Film & Television Arts Awards

BEST FILM: **The Commitments** • *Dances with Wolves* • *The Silence of the Lambs* • *Thelma & Louise*
BEST FILM NOT IN THE ENGLISH LANGUAGE: **The Nasty Girl** • *Cyrano de Bergerac* • *The Hairdresser's Husband* • *Toto Le Héros*
THE DAVID LEAN AWARD FOR THE BEST ACHIEVEMENT IN DIRECTION: **Alan Parker** *The Commitments* • Kevin

Costner *Dances with Wolves* • Jonathan Demme *The Silence of the Lambs* • Ridley Scott *Thelma & Louise*
BEST ACTOR IN A LEADING ROLE: **Anthony Hopkins** *The Silence of the Lambs* • Kevin Costner *Dances with Wolves* • Gérard Depardieu *Cyrano de Bergerac* • Alan Rickman *Truly Madly Deeply*
BEST ACTRESS IN A LEADING ROLE: **Jodie Foster** *The Silence of the Lambs* • Geena Davis, Susan Sarandon *Thelma & Louise* • Juliet Stevenson *Truly Madly Deeply*
BEST ACTOR IN A SUPPORTING ROLE: **Alan Rickman** *Robin Hood: Prince of Thieves* • Alan Bates *Hamlet* • Derek Jacobi *Dead Again* • Andrew Strong *The Commitments*
BEST ACTRESS IN A SUPPORTING ROLE: **Kate Nelligan** *Frankie & Johnny* • Annette Bening *The Grifters* • Amanda Plummer *The Fisher King* • Julie Walters *Stepping Out*
BEST SCREENPLAY (ORIGINAL): **Anthony Minghella** *Truly Madly Deeply* • Richard LaGravenese *The Fisher King* • Peter Weir *Green Card* • Callie Khouri *Thelma & Louise*
BEST SCREENPLAY (ADAPTED): **Dick Clement, Ian La Frenais, Roddy Doyle** *The Commitments* • Jean-Paul Rappeneau, Jean-Claude Carrière *Cyrano de Bergerac* • Michael Blake *Dances with Wolves* • Ted Tally *The Silence of the Lambs*

Academy Awards

BEST PICTURE: **The Silence of the Lambs** • Beauty and the Beast • Bugsy • JFK • The Prince of Tides
FOREIGN LANGUAGE FILM: **Mediterraneo** • Children of Nature • Elementary School • The Ox • Raise the Red Lantern
DIRECTING: **Jonathan Demme** *The Silence of the Lambs* • John Singleton *Boyz N the Hood* • Barry Levinson *Bugsy* • Oliver Stone *JFK* • Ridley Scott *Thelma & Louise*
ACTOR IN A LEADING ROLE: **Anthony Hopkins** *The Silence of the Lambs* • Warren Beatty *Bugsy* • Robert De Niro *Cape Fear* • Nick Nolte *The Prince of Tides* • Robin Williams *The Fisher King*
ACTRESS IN A LEADING ROLE: **Jodie Foster** *The Silence of the Lambs* • Geena Davis *Thelma & Louise* • Laura Dern *Rambling Rose* • Bette Midler *For the Boys* • Susan Sarandon *Thelma & Louise*
ACTOR IN A SUPPORTING ROLE: **Jack Palance** *City Slickers* • Tommy Lee Jones *JFK* • Harvey Keitel, Ben Kingsley *Bugsy* • Michael Lerner *Barton Fink*
ACTRESS IN A SUPPORTING ROLE: **Mercedes Ruehl** *The Fisher King* • Diane Ladd *Rambling Rose* • Juliette Lewis *Cape Fear* • Kate Nelligan *The Prince of Tides* • Jessica Tandy *Fried Green Tomatoes at the Whistle Stop Cafe*
WRITING (SCREENPLAY WRITTEN DIRECTLY FOR THE SCREEN): **Callie Khouri** *Thelma & Louise* • John Singleton *Boyz N the Hood* • James Toback *Bugsy* • Richard LaGravenese *The Fisher King* • Lawrence Kasdan, Meg Kasdan *Grand Canyon*
WRITING (SCREENPLAY BASED ON MATERIAL PREVIOUSLY PRODUCED OR PUBLISHED): **Ted Tally** *The Silence of the Lambs* • Agnieszka Holland *Europa, Europa* • Fannie Flagg, Carol Sobieski *Fried Green Tomatoes at the Whistle Stop Cafe* • Zachary Sklar, Oliver Stone *JFK* • Pat Conroy, Becky Johnston *The Prince of Tides*

Golden Globe Awards

BEST MOTION PICTURE DRAMA: **Bugsy**
BEST MOTION PICTURE COMEDY OR MUSICAL: **Beauty and the Beast**
BEST FOREIGN LANGUAGE FILM: **Europa, Europa**
BEST DIRECTOR MOTION PICTURE: **Oliver Stone** *JFK*
BEST PERFORMANCE BY AN ACTOR IN A MOTION PICTURE DRAMA: **Nick Nolte** *The Prince of Tides*
BEST PERFORMANCE BY AN ACTRESS IN A MOTION PICTURE DRAMA: **Jodie Foster** *The Silence of the Lambs*
BEST PERFORMANCE BY AN ACTOR IN A MOTION PICTURE COMEDY OR MUSICAL: **Robin Williams** *The Fisher King*
BEST PERFORMANCE BY AN ACTRESS IN A MOTION PICTURE COMEDY OR MUSICAL: **Bette Midler** *For the Boys*
BEST PERFORMANCE BY AN ACTOR IN A SUPPORTING ROLE MOTION PICTURE: **Jack Palance** *City Slickers*
BEST PERFORMANCE BY AN ACTRESS IN A SUPPORTING ROLE MOTION PICTURE: **Mercedes Ruehl** *The Fisher King*
BEST SCREENPLAY MOTION PICTURE: **Callie Khouri** *Thelma & Louise*

Cannes International Film Festival

PALME D'OR: **Barton Fink**
DIRECTOR: **Joel Coen** *Barton Fink*
ACTOR: **John Turturro** *Barton Fink*
ACTRESS: **Irène Jacob** *The Double Life of Véronique*
SUPPORTING ACTOR: **Samuel L Jackson** *Jungle Fever*

Berlin International Film Festival

GOLDEN BERLIN BEAR: **La Casa del Sorriso**
SILVER BERLIN BEAR FOR THE BEST DIRECTOR: **Jonathan Demme** *The Silence of the Lambs* • Ricky Tognazzi *Ultrà*
SILVER BERLIN BEAR FOR THE BEST ACTOR: **Maynard Eziashi** *Mister Johnson*
SILVER BERLIN BEAR FOR THE BEST ACTRESS: **Victoria Abril** *Lovers*

1992

British Academy of Film & Television Arts Awards

BEST FILM: **Howards End** • The Crying Game • The Player • Strictly Ballroom • Unforgiven
BEST FILM NOT IN THE ENGLISH LANGUAGE: **Raise the Red Lantern** • Les Amants du Pont-Neuf • Delicatessen • Europa, Europa
THE DAVID LEAN AWARD FOR THE BEST ACHIEVEMENT IN DIRECTION: **Robert Altman** *The Player* • Neil Jordan *The Crying Game* • James Ivory *Howards End* • Clint Eastwood *Unforgiven*
BEST ACTOR IN A LEADING ROLE: **Robert Downey Jr** *Chaplin* • Daniel Day-Lewis *The Last of the Mohicans* • Stephen Rea *The Crying Game* • Tim Robbins *The Player*
BEST ACTRESS IN A LEADING ROLE: **Emma Thompson** *Howards End* • Judy Davis *Husbands and Wives* • Tara Morice *Strictly Ballroom* • Jessica Tandy *Fried Green Tomatoes at the Whistle Stop Cafe*
BEST ACTOR IN A SUPPORTING ROLE: **Gene Hackman** *Unforgiven* • Jaye Davidson *The Crying Game* • Tommy Lee Jones *JFK* • Samuel West *Howards End*
BEST ACTRESS IN A SUPPORTING ROLE: **Miranda Richardson** *Damage* • Kathy Bates *Fried Green Tomatoes at the Whistle Stop Cafe* • Helena Bonham Carter *Howards End* • Miranda Richardson *The Crying Game*
BEST ORIGINAL SCREENPLAY: **Woody Allen** *Husbands and Wives* • Neil Jordan *The Crying Game* • Peter Chelsom, Adrian Dunbar *Hear My Song* • David Webb Peoples *Unforgiven*
BEST ADAPTED SCREENPLAY: **Michael Tolkin** *The Player* • Ruth Prawer Jhabvala *Howards End* • Oliver Stone, Zachary Sklar *JFK* • Baz Luhrmann, Craig Pearce *Strictly Ballroom*

Academy Awards

BEST PICTURE: **Unforgiven** • The Crying Game • A Few Good Men • Howards End • Scent of a Woman
FOREIGN LANGUAGE FILM: **Indochine** • Urga • Daens • A Place in the World • Schtonk!
DIRECTING: **Clint Eastwood** *Unforgiven* • Neil Jordan *The Crying Game* • James Ivory *Howards End* • Robert Altman *The Player* • Martin Brest *Scent of a Woman*
ACTOR IN A LEADING ROLE: **Al Pacino** *Scent of a Woman* • Robert Downey Jr *Chaplin* • Clint Eastwood *Unforgiven* • Stephen Rea *The Crying Game* • Denzel Washington *Malcolm X*
ACTRESS IN A LEADING ROLE: **Emma Thompson** *Howards End* • Catherine Deneuve *Indochine* • Mary McDonnell *Passion Fish* • Michelle Pfeiffer *Love Field* • Susan Sarandon *Lorenzo's Oil*
ACTOR IN A SUPPORTING ROLE: **Gene Hackman** *Unforgiven* • Jaye Davidson *The Crying Game* • Jack Nicholson *A Few Good Men* • Al Pacino *Glengarry Glen Ross* • David Paymer *Mr Saturday Night*
ACTRESS IN A SUPPORTING ROLE: **Marisa Tomei** *My Cousin Vinny* • Judy Davis *Husbands and Wives* • Joan Plowright *Enchanted April* • Vanessa Redgrave *Howards End* • Miranda Richardson *Damage*
WRITING (SCREENPLAY WRITTEN DIRECTLY FOR THE SCREEN): **Neil Jordan** *The Crying Game* • Woody Allen *Husbands and Wives* • Nick Enright, George Miller (2) *Lorenzo's Oil* • John Sayles *Passion Fish* • David Webb Peoples *Unforgiven*
WRITING (SCREENPLAY BASED ON MATERIAL PREVIOUSLY PRODUCED OR PUBLISHED): **Ruth Prawer Jhabvala** *Howards End* • Peter Barnes *Enchanted April* • Michael Tolkin *The Player* • Richard Friedenberg *A River Runs through It* • Bo Goldman *Scent of a Woman*

Golden Globe Awards

BEST MOTION PICTURE DRAMA: **Scent of a Woman**
BEST MOTION PICTURE COMEDY OR MUSICAL: **The Player**
BEST FOREIGN LANGUAGE FILM: **Indochine**
BEST DIRECTOR MOTION PICTURE: **Clint Eastwood** *Unforgiven*
BEST PERFORMANCE BY AN ACTOR IN A MOTION PICTURE DRAMA: **Al Pacino** *Scent of a Woman*
BEST PERFORMANCE BY AN ACTRESS IN A MOTION PICTURE DRAMA: **Emma Thompson** *Howards End*
BEST PERFORMANCE BY AN ACTOR IN A MOTION PICTURE COMEDY OR MUSICAL: **Tim Robbins** *The Player*
BEST PERFORMANCE BY AN ACTRESS IN A MOTION PICTURE COMEDY OR MUSICAL: **Miranda Richardson** *Enchanted April*
BEST PERFORMANCE BY AN ACTOR IN A SUPPORTING ROLE MOTION PICTURE: **Gene Hackman** *Unforgiven*
BEST PERFORMANCE BY AN ACTRESS IN A SUPPORTING ROLE MOTION PICTURE: **Joan Plowright** *Enchanted April*
BEST SCREENPLAY MOTION PICTURE: **Bo Goldman** *Scent of a Woman*

Cannes International Film Festival

PALME D'OR: **Best Intentions**
DIRECTOR: **Robert Altman** *The Player*
ACTOR: **Tim Robbins** *The Player*
ACTRESS: **Pernilla August** *Best Intentions*

Berlin International Film Festival

GOLDEN BERLIN BEAR: **Grand Canyon**
SILVER BERLIN BEAR FOR THE BEST DIRECTOR: **Jan Troell** *Il Capitano*
SILVER BERLIN BEAR FOR THE BEST ACTOR: **Armin Mueller-Stahl** *Utz*
SILVER BERLIN BEAR FOR THE BEST ACTRESS: **Maggie Cheung** *The Actress*

1993

British Academy of Film & Television Arts Awards

BEST FILM: **Schindler's List** • The Piano • The Remains of the Day • Shadowlands
BEST FILM NOT IN THE ENGLISH LANGUAGE: **Farewell My Concubine** • Un Coeur en Hiver • Like Water for Chocolate • Indochine
THE ALEXANDER KORDA AWARD FOR THE OUTSTANDING BRITISH FILM OF THE YEAR: **Shadowlands** • Naked • Raining Stones • Tom & Viv
THE DAVID LEAN AWARD FOR THE BEST ACHIEVEMENT IN DIRECTION: **Steven Spielberg** *Schindler's List* • Jane Campion *The Piano* • James Ivory *The Remains of the Day* • Richard Attenborough *Shadowlands*
BEST PERFORMANCE BY AN ACTOR IN A LEADING ROLE: **Anthony Hopkins** *The Remains of the Day* • Daniel Day-Lewis *In the Name of the Father* • Anthony Hopkins *Shadowlands* • Liam Neeson *Schindler's List*
BEST PERFORMANCE BY AN ACTRESS IN A LEADING ROLE: **Holly Hunter** *The Piano* • Miranda Richardson *Tom & Viv* • Emma Thompson *The Remains of the Day* • Debra Winger *Shadowlands*
BEST PERFORMANCE BY AN ACTOR IN A SUPPORTING ROLE: **Ralph Fiennes**, Ben Kingsley *Schindler's List* • Tommy Lee Jones *The Fugitive* • John Malkovich *In the Line of Fire*
BEST PERFORMANCE BY AN ACTRESS IN A SUPPORTING ROLE: **Miriam Margolyes** *The Age of Innocence* • Holly Hunter *The Firm* • Winona Ryder *The Age of Innocence* • Maggie Smith *The Secret Garden*
BEST SCREENPLAY (ORIGINAL): **Danny Rubin, Harold Ramis** *Groundhog Day* • Jeff Maguire *In the Line of Fire* • Jane Campion *The Piano* • Nora Ephron, David S Ward, Jeff Arch *Sleepless in Seattle*
BEST SCREENPLAY (ADAPTED): **Steven Zaillian** *Schindler's List* • Terry George, Jim Sheridan *In the Name of the Father* • Ruth Prawer Jhabvala *The Remains of the Day* • Bo Goldman *Scent of a Woman* • William Nicholson *Shadowlands*

Academy Awards

BEST PICTURE: **Schindler's List** • The Fugitive • In the Name of the Father • The Piano • The Remains of the Day
FOREIGN LANGUAGE FILM: **Belle Epoque** • Farewell My Concubine • Hedd Wyn • The Scent of Green Papaya • The Wedding Banquet
DIRECTING: **Steven Spielberg** *Schindler's List* • Jim Sheridan *In the Name of the Father* • Jane Campion *The Piano* • James Ivory *The Remains of the Day* • Robert Altman *Short Cuts*
ACTOR IN A LEADING ROLE: **Tom Hanks** *Philadelphia* • Daniel Day-Lewis *In the Name of the Father* • Laurence Fishburne *Tina: What's Love Got to Do with It* • Anthony Hopkins *The Remains of the Day* • Liam Neeson *Schindler's List*
ACTRESS IN A LEADING ROLE: **Holly Hunter** *The Piano* • Angela Bassett *Tina: What's Love Got to Do with It* • Stockard Channing *Six Degrees of Separation* • Emma Thompson *The Remains of the Day* • Debra Winger *Shadowlands*
ACTOR IN A SUPPORTING ROLE: **Tommy Lee Jones** *The Fugitive* • Leonardo DiCaprio *What's Eating Gilbert Grape* • Ralph Fiennes *Schindler's List* • John Malkovich *In the Line of Fire* • Pete Postlethwaite *In the Name of the Father*
ACTRESS IN A SUPPORTING ROLE: **Anna Paquin** *The Piano* • Holly Hunter *The Firm* • Rosie Perez *Fearless* • Winona Ryder *The Age of Innocence* • Emma Thompson *In the Name of the Father*
WRITING (SCREENPLAY WRITTEN DIRECTLY FOR THE SCREEN): **Jane Campion** *The Piano* • Gary Ross *Dave* • Jeff Maguire *In the Line of Fire* • Ron Nyswaner *Philadelphia*

• Jeff Arch, Nora Ephron, David S Ward *Sleepless in Seattle*
Writing (Screenplay Based On Material Previously Produced or Published): **Steven Zaillian** *Schindler's List* • Jay Cocks, Martin Scorsese *The Age of Innocence* • Terry George, Jim Sheridan *In the Name of the Father* • Ruth Prawer Jhabvala *The Remains of the Day* • William Nicholson *Shadowlands*

Golden Globe Awards

Best Motion Picture . Drama: ***Schindler's List***
Best Motion Picture Comedy or Musical: ***Mrs Doubtfire***
Best Foreign Language Film: ***Farewell My Concubine***
Best Director Motion Picture: **Steven Spielberg** *Schindler's List*
Best Performance by an Actor in a Motion Picture Drama: **Tom Hanks** *Philadelphia*
Best Performance by an Actress in a Motion Picture Drama: **Holly Hunter** *The Piano*
Best Performance by an Actor in a Motion Picture Comedy or Musical: **Robin Williams** *Mrs Doubtfire*
Best Performance by an Actress in a Motion Picture Comedy or Musical: **Angela Bassett** *Tina: What's Love Got to Do with It*
Best Performance by an Actor in a Supporting Role Motion Picture: **Tommy Lee Jones** *The Fugitive*
Best Performance by an Actress in a Supporting Role Motion Picture; **Winona Ryder** *The Age of Innocence*
Best Screenplay Motion Picture: **Steven Zaillian** *Schindler's List*

Cannes International Film Festival

Palme d'Or: ***The Piano* • *Farewell My Concubine***
Director: **Mike Leigh** *Naked*
Actor: **David Thewlis** *Naked*
Actress: **Holly Hunter** *The Piano*

Berlin International Film Festival

Golden Berlin Bear: ***The Women from the Lake of Scented Souls* • *The Wedding Banquet***
Silver Berlin Bear for the Best Director: **Andrew Birkin** *The Cement Garden*
Silver Berlin Bear for the Best Actor: **Denzel Washington** *Malcolm X*
Silver Berlin Bear for the Best Actress: **Michelle Pfeiffer** *Love Field*

1994

British Academy of Film & Television Arts Awards

Best Film: ***Four Weddings and a Funeral*** • *Forrest Gump* • *Pulp Fiction* • *Quiz Show*
Best Film Not in the English Language: ***To Live*** • *Belle Epoque* • *Eat Drink Man Woman* • *Three Colours Red*
The Alexander Korda Award for the Outstanding British Film of the Year: ***Shallow Grave*** • *BackBeat* • *Bhaji on the Beach* • *Priest*
The David Lean Award for the Best Achievement in Direction: **Mike Newell** *Four Weddings and a Funeral* • Robert Zemeckis *Forrest Gump* • Quentin Tarantino *Pulp Fiction* • Krzysztof Kieslowski *Three Colours Red*
Best Performance by an Actor in a Leading Role: **Hugh Grant** *Four Weddings and a Funeral* • Tom Hanks *Forrest Gump* • Terence Stamp *The Adventures of Priscilla, Queen of the Desert* • John Travolta *Pulp Fiction*
Best Performance by an Actress in a Leading Role: **Susan Sarandon** *The Client* • Linda Fiorentino *The Last Seduction* • Irène Jacob *Three Colours Red* • Uma Thurman *Pulp Fiction*
Best Performance by an Actor in a Supporting Role: **Samuel L Jackson** *Pulp Fiction* • Simon Callow, John Hannah *Four Weddings and a Funeral* • Paul Scofield *Quiz Show*
Best Performance by an Actress in a Supporting Role: **Kristin Scott Thomas**, Charlotte Coleman *Four Weddings and a Funeral* • Sally Field *Forrest Gump* • Anjelica Huston *Manhattan Murder Mystery*
Best Screenplay (Original): **Quentin Tarantino**, **Roger Avary** *Pulp Fiction* • Stephan Elliott *The Adventures of Priscilla, Queen of the Desert* • Richard Curtis *Four Weddings and a Funeral* • Ron Nyswaner *Philadelphia* • Krzysztof Kieslowski, Krzysztof Piesiewicz *Three Colours Red*
Best Screenplay (Adapted): **Paul Attanasio** *Quiz Show* • Ronald Harwood *The Browning Version* • Eric Roth *Forrest Gump* • Amy Tan, Ronald Bass *The Joy Luck Club*

Academy Awards

Best Picture: ***Forrest Gump*** • *Four Weddings and a Funeral* • *Pulp Fiction* • *Quiz Show* • *The Shawshank Redemption*
Foreign Language Film: ***Burnt by the Sun*** • *Before the Rain* • *Eat Drink Man Woman* • *Farinelli il Castrato* • *Strawberry and Chocolate*
Directing: **Robert Zemeckis** *Forrest Gump* • Woody Allen *Bullets over Broadway* • Quentin Tarantino *Pulp Fiction* • Robert Redford *Quiz Show* • Krzysztof Kieslowski *Three Colours Red*
Actor in a Leading Role: **Tom Hanks** *Forrest Gump* • Morgan Freeman *The Shawshank Redemption* • Nigel Hawthorne *The Madness of King George* • Paul Newman *Nobody's Fool* • John Travolta *Pulp Fiction*
Actress in a Leading Role: **Jessica Lange** *Blue Sky* • Jodie Foster *Nell* • Miranda Richardson *Tom & Viv* • Winona Ryder *Little Women* • Susan Sarandon *The Client*
Actor in a Supporting Role: **Martin Landau** *Ed Wood* • Samuel L Jackson *Pulp Fiction* • Chazz Palminteri *Bullets over Broadway* • Paul Scofield *Quiz Show* • Gary Sinise *Forrest Gump*
Actress in a Supporting Role: **Dianne Wiest**, Jennifer Tilly *Bullets over Broadway* • Rosemary Harris *Tom & Viv* • Helen Mirren *The Madness of King George* • Uma Thurman *Pulp Fiction*
Writing (Screenplay Written Directly for the Screen): **Quentin Tarantino**, **Roger Avary** *Pulp Fiction* • Woody Allen, Douglas McGrath *Bullets over Broadway* • Richard Curtis *Four Weddings and a Funeral* • Peter Jackson, Frances Walsh *Heavenly Creatures* • Krzysztof Kieslowski, Krzysztof Piesiewicz *Three Colours Red*
Writing (Screenplay Based On Material Previously Produced or Published): **Eric Roth** *Forrest Gump* • Alan Bennett *The Madness of King George* • Robert Benton *Nobody's Fool* • Paul Attanasio *Quiz Show* • Frank Darabont *The Shawshank Redemption*

Golden Globe Awards

Best Motion Picture . Drama: ***Forrest Gump***
Best Motion Picture Comedy or Musical: ***The Lion King***
Best Foreign Language Film: ***Farinelli il Castrato***
Best Director Motion Picture: **Robert Zemeckis** *Forrest Gump*
Best Performance by an Actor in a Motion Picture Drama: **Tom Hanks** *Forrest Gump*
Best Performance by an Actress in a Motion Picture Drama: **Jessica Lange** *Blue Sky*
Best Performance by an Actor in a Motion Picture Comedy or Musical: **Hugh Grant** *Four Weddings and a Funeral*
Best Performance by an Actress in a Motion Picture Comedy or Musical: **Jamie Lee Curtis** *True Lies*
Best Performance by an Actor in a Supporting Role Motion Picture: **Martin Landau** *Ed Wood*
Best Performance by an Actress in a Supporting Role Motion Picture; **Dianne Wiest** *Bullets over Broadway*
Best Screenplay Motion Picture: **Quentin Tarantino** *Pulp Fiction*

Cannes International Film Festival

Palme d'Or: ***Pulp Fiction***
Director: **Nanni Moretti** *Dear Diary*
Actor: **Ge You** *To Live*
Actress: **Virna Lisi** *La Reine Margot*
Screenplay: **Michel Blanc** *Grosse Fatigue*

Berlin International Film Festival

Golden Berlin Bear: ***In the Name of the Father***
Silver Berlin Bear for the Best Director: **Krzysztof Kieslowski** *Three Colours Blue*
Silver Berlin Bear for the Best Actor: **Tom Hanks** *Philadelphia*
Silver Berlin Bear for the Best Actress: **Crissy Rock** *Ladybird Ladybird*

1995

British Academy of Film & Television Arts Awards

Best Film: ***Sense and Sensibility*** • *Babe* • *The Madness of King George* • *The Usual Suspects*
Best Film Not in the English Language: ***Il Postino*** • *Les Misérables* • *La Reine Margot* • *Burnt by the Sun*
The Alexander Korda Award for the Outstanding British Film of the Year: ***The Madness of King George*** • *Carrington* • *Land and Freedom* • *Trainspotting*
The David Lean Award for the Best Achievement in Direction: **Michael Radford** *Il Postino* • Mel Gibson *Braveheart* • Nicholas Hytner *The Madness of King George* • Ang Lee *Sense and Sensibility*
Best Performance by an Actor in a Leading Role: **Nigel Hawthorne** *The Madness of King George* • Nicolas Cage *Leaving Las Vegas* • Jonathan Pryce *Carrington* • Massimo Troisi *Il Postino*
Best Performance by an Actress in a Leading Role: **Emma Thompson** *Sense and Sensibility* • Nicole Kidman *To Die For* • Helen Mirren *The Madness of King George* • Elisabeth Shue *Leaving Las Vegas*
Best Performance by an Actor in a Supporting Role: **Tim Roth** *Rob Roy* • Ian Holm *The Madness of King George* • Martin Landau *Ed Wood* • Alan Rickman *Sense and Sensibility*
Best Performance by an Actress in a Supporting Role: **Kate Winslet** *Sense and Sensibility* • Joan Allen *Nixon* • Mira Sorvino *Mighty Aphrodite* • Elizabeth Spriggs *Sense and Sensibility*
Best Screenplay (Original): **Christopher McQuarrie** *The Usual Suspects* • Woody Allen, Douglas McGrath *Bullets over Broadway* • P J Hogan *Muriel's Wedding* • Andrew Kevin Walker *Se7en*
Best Screenplay (Adapted): **John Hodge** *Trainspotting* • George Miller (2), Chris Noonan *Babe* • Mike Figgis *Leaving Las Vegas* • Alan Bennett *The Madness of King George* • Anna Pavignano, Michael Radford, Furio Scarpelli, Giacomo Scarpelli, Massimo Troisi *Il Postino* • Emma Thompson *Sense and Sensibility*

Academy Awards

Best Picture: ***Braveheart*** • *Apollo 13* • *Babe* • *Il Postino* • *Sense and Sensibility*
Foreign Language Film: ***Antonia's Line*** • *All Things Fair* • *Dust of Life* • *O Quatrilho* • *The Starmaker*
Directing: **Mel Gibson** *Braveheart* • Chris Noonan *Babe* • Tim Robbins *Dead Man Walking* • Mike Figgis *Leaving Las Vegas* • Michael Radford *Il Postino*
Actor in a Leading Role: **Nicolas Cage** *Leaving Las Vegas* • Richard Dreyfuss *Mr Holland's Opus* • Anthony Hopkins *Nixon* • Sean Penn *Dead Man Walking* • Massimo Troisi *Il Postino*
Actress in a Leading Role: **Susan Sarandon** *Dead Man Walking* • Elisabeth Shue *Leaving Las Vegas* • Sharon Stone *Casino* • Meryl Streep *The Bridges of Madison County* • Emma Thompson *Sense and Sensibility*
Actor in a Supporting Role: **Kevin Spacey** *The Usual Suspects* • James Cromwell *Babe* • Ed Harris *Apollo 13* • Brad Pitt *Twelve Monkeys* • Tim Roth *Rob Roy*
Actress in a Supporting Role: **Mira Sorvino** *Mighty Aphrodite* • Joan Allen *Nixon* • Kathleen Quinlan *Apollo 13* • Mare Winningham *Georgia* • Kate Winslet *Sense and Sensibility*
Writing (Screenplay Written Directly for the Screen): **Christopher McQuarrie** *The Usual Suspects* • Randall Wallace *Braveheart*
Writing (Screenplay Written Directly for the Screen) Screenplay: Woody Allen *Mighty Aphrodite*
Writing (Screenplay Written Directly for the Screen): Stephen J Rivele, Oliver Stone, Christopher Wilkinson *Nixon* • Joel Cohen, Pete Docter, John Lasseter, Joe Ranft, Alec Sokolow, Andrew Stanton, Joss Whedon *Toy Story*
Writing (Screenplay Based On Material Previously Produced or Published): **Emma Thompson** *Sense and Sensibility* • William Broyles Jr, Al Reinert *Apollo 13* • George Miller (2), Chris Noonan *Babe* • Mike Figgis *Leaving Las Vegas* • Anna Pavignano, Michael Radford, Furio Scarpelli, Giacomo Scarpelli, Massimo Troisi *Il Postino*

Golden Globe Awards

Best Motion Picture . Drama: ***Sense and Sensibility***
Best Motion Picture Comedy or Musical: ***Babe***
Best Foreign Language Film: ***Les Misérables***
Best Director Motion Picture: **Mel Gibson** *Braveheart*
Best Performance by an Actor in a Motion Picture Drama: **Nicolas Cage** *Leaving Las Vegas*
Best Performance by an Actress in a Motion Picture Drama: **Sharon Stone** *Casino*
Best Performance by an Actor in a Motion Picture Comedy or Musical: **John Travolta** *Get Shorty*
Best Performance by an Actress in a Motion Picture Comedy or Musical: **Nicole Kidman** *To Die For*
Best Performance by an Actor in a Supporting Role Motion Picture: **Brad Pitt** *Twelve Monkeys*
Best Performance by an Actress in a Supporting Role Motion Picture; **Mira Sorvino** *Mighty Aphrodite*
Best Screenplay Motion Picture: **Emma Thompson** *Sense and Sensibility*

Cannes International Film Festival

Palme d'Or: ***Underground***
Director: **Mathieu Kassovitz** *La Haine*
Actor: **Jonathan Pryce** *Carrington*
Actress: **Helen Mirren** *The Madness of King George*

Berlin International Film Festival

GOLDEN BERLIN BEAR: **The Bait**
SILVER BERLIN BEAR FOR THE BEST DIRECTOR: **Richard Linklater** Before Sunrise
SILVER BERLIN BEAR FOR THE BEST ACTOR: **Paul Newman** Nobody's Fool
SILVER BERLIN BEAR FOR THE BEST ACTRESS: **Josephine Siao** Xiatian De Xue

1996

British Academy of Film & Television Arts Awards

BEST FILM: **The English Patient** • Fargo • Secrets & Lies • Shine
BEST FILM NOT IN THE ENGLISH LANGUAGE: **Ridicule** • Antonia's Line • Kolya • Nelly & Monsieur Arnaud
THE ALEXANDER KORDA AWARD FOR THE OUTSTANDING BRITISH FILM OF THE YEAR: **Secrets & Lies** • Brassed Off • Carla's Song • Richard III
THE DAVID LEAN AWARD FOR THE BEST ACHIEVEMENT IN DIRECTION: **Joel Coen** Fargo • Anthony Minghella The English Patient • Mike Leigh Secrets & Lies • Scott Hicks Shine
BEST PERFORMANCE BY AN ACTOR IN A LEADING ROLE: **Geoffrey Rush** Shine • Ralph Fiennes The English Patient • Ian McKellen Richard III • Timothy Spall Secrets & Lies
BEST PERFORMANCE BY AN ACTRESS IN A LEADING ROLE: **Brenda Blethyn** Secrets & Lies • Frances McDormand Fargo • Kristin Scott Thomas The English Patient • Emily Watson Breaking the Waves
BEST ACTOR IN A SUPPORTING ROLE: **Paul Scofield** The Crucible • John Gielgud Shine • Edward Norton Primal Fear • Alan Rickman Michael Collins
BEST ACTRESS IN A SUPPORTING ROLE: **Juliette Binoche** The English Patient • Lauren Bacall The Mirror Has Two Faces • Marianne Jean-Baptiste Secrets & Lies • Lynn Redgrave Shine
BEST SCREENPLAY (ORIGINAL): **Mike Leigh** Secrets & Lies • Mark Herman Brassed Off • Ethan Coen, Joel Coen Fargo • John Sayles Lone Star • Jan Sardi Shine
BEST SCREENPLAY (ADAPTED): Anthony Minghella The English Patient • Arthur Miller The Crucible • Alan Parker, Oliver Stone Evita • Ian McKellen, Richard Loncraine Richard III

Academy Awards

BEST PICTURE: **The English Patient** • Fargo • Jerry Maguire • Secrets & Lies • Shine
FOREIGN LANGUAGE FILM: **Kolya** • A Chef in Love • The Other Side of Sunday • Prisoner of the Mountains • Ridicule
DIRECTING: **Anthony Minghella** The English Patient • Joel Coen Fargo • Milos Forman The People vs Larry Flynt • Mike Leigh Secrets & Lies • Scott Hicks Shine
ACTOR IN A LEADING ROLE: **Geoffrey Rush** Shine • Tom Cruise Jerry Maguire • Ralph Fiennes The English Patient • Woody Harrelson The People vs Larry Flynt • Billy Bob Thornton Sling Blade
BEST DIRECTOR: Milos Forman The People vs Larry Flynt
ACTRESS IN A LEADING ROLE: **Frances McDormand** Fargo • Brenda Blethyn Secrets & Lies • Diane Keaton Marvin's Room • Kristin Scott Thomas The English Patient • Emily Watson Breaking the Waves
ACTOR IN A SUPPORTING ROLE: **Cuba Gooding Jr** Jerry Maguire • William H Macy Fargo • Armin Mueller-Stahl Shine • Edward Norton Primal Fear • James Woods Ghosts from the Past
ACTRESS IN A SUPPORTING ROLE: **Juliette Binoche** The English Patient • Joan Allen The Crucible • Lauren Bacall The Mirror Has Two Faces • Barbara Hershey The Portrait of a Lady • Marianne Jean-Baptiste Secrets & Lies
WRITING (SCREENPLAY WRITTEN DIRECTLY FOR THE SCREEN): **Ethan Coen, Joel Coen** Fargo • Cameron Crowe Jerry Maguire • John Sayles Lone Star • Mike Leigh Secrets & Lies • Scott Hicks, Jan Sardi Shine
WRITING (SCREENPLAY BASED ON MATERIAL PREVIOUSLY PRODUCED OR PUBLISHED): **Billy Bob Thornton** Sling Blade • Arthur Miller The Crucible • Anthony Minghella The English Patient • Kenneth Branagh Hamlet • John Hodge Trainspotting

Golden Globe Awards

BEST MOTION PICTURE DRAMA: **The English Patient**
BEST MOTION PICTURE COMEDY OR MUSICAL: **Evita**
BEST FOREIGN LANGUAGE FILM: **Kolya**
BEST DIRECTOR MOTION PICTURE: **Milos Forman** The People vs Larry Flynt
BEST PERFORMANCE BY AN ACTOR IN A MOTION PICTURE DRAMA: **Geoffrey Rush** Shine

BEST PERFORMANCE BY AN ACTRESS IN A MOTION PICTURE DRAMA: **Brenda Blethyn** Secrets & Lies
BEST PERFORMANCE BY AN ACTOR IN A MOTION PICTURE COMEDY OR MUSICAL: **Tom Cruise** Jerry Maguire
BEST PERFORMANCE BY AN ACTRESS IN A MOTION PICTURE COMEDY OR MUSICAL: **Madonna** Evita
BEST PERFORMANCE BY AN ACTOR IN A SUPPORTING ROLE MOTION PICTURE: **Edward Norton** Primal Fear
BEST PERFORMANCE BY AN ACTRESS IN A SUPPORTING ROLE MOTION PICTURE: **Lauren Bacall** The Mirror Has Two Faces
BEST SCREENPLAY MOTION PICTURE: **Scott Alexander, Larry Karaszewski** The People vs Larry Flynt

Cannes International Film Festival

PALME D'OR: **Secrets & Lies**
DIRECTOR: **Joel Coen** Fargo
ACTOR: **Daniel Auteuil, Pascal Duquenne** The Eighth Day
ACTRESS: **Brenda Blethyn** Secrets & Lies
SCREENPLAY: **Jacques Audiard** A Self-Made Hero

Berlin International Film Festival

GOLDEN BERLIN BEAR: **Sense and Sensibility**
SILVER BERLIN BEAR FOR THE BEST DIRECTOR: **Richard Loncraine** Richard III • **Yim Ho** Tai Yang You Er
SILVER BERLIN BEAR FOR THE BEST ACTOR: **Sean Penn** Dead Man Walking
SILVER BERLIN BEAR FOR THE BEST ACTRESS: **Anouk Grinberg** Mon Homme

1997

British Academy of Film & Television Arts Awards

BEST FILM: **The Full Monty** • LA Confidential • Mrs Brown • Titanic
BEST FILM NOT IN THE ENGLISH LANGUAGE: **L'Appartement** • Lucie Aubrac • Ma Vie en Rose • The Tango Lesson
THE ALEXANDER KORDA AWARD FOR THE OUTSTANDING BRITISH FILM OF THE YEAR: **Nil by Mouth** • The Borrowers • The Full Monty • Mrs Brown • Regeneration • TwentyFourSeven
THE DAVID LEAN AWARD FOR THE BEST ACHIEVEMENT IN DIRECTION: **William Shakespeare's Romeo + Juliet** • Peter Cattaneo The Full Monty • Curtis Hanson LA Confidential • James Cameron Titanic
BEST PERFORMANCE BY AN ACTOR IN A LEADING ROLE: **Robert Carlyle** The Full Monty • Billy Connolly Mrs Brown • Kevin Spacey LA Confidential • Ray Winstone Nil by Mouth
BEST PERFORMANCE BY AN ACTRESS IN A LEADING ROLE: **Judi Dench** Mrs Brown • Kim Basinger LA Confidential • Helena Bonham Carter The Wings of the Dove • Kathy Burke Nil by Mouth
BEST PERFORMANCE BY AN ACTOR IN A SUPPORTING ROLE: **Tom Wilkinson**, Mark Addy The Full Monty • Rupert Everett My Best Friend's Wedding • Burt Reynolds Boogie Nights
BEST PERFORMANCE BY AN ACTRESS IN A SUPPORTING ROLE: **Sigourney Weaver** The Ice Storm • Jennifer Ehle Wilde • Lesley Sharp The Full Monty • Zoë Wanamaker Wilde
BEST SCREENPLAY (ORIGINAL): **Gary Oldman** Nil by Mouth • Paul Thomas Anderson Boogie Nights • Simon Beaufoy The Full Monty • Jeremy Brock Mrs Brown
BEST SCREENPLAY (ADAPTED): **Craig Pearce, Baz Luhrmann** William Shakespeare's Romeo + Juliet • James Schamus The Ice Storm • Curtis Hanson, Brian Helgeland LA Confidential • Hossein Amini The Wings of the Dove

Academy Awards

BEST PICTURE: **Titanic** • As Good As It Gets • The Full Monty • Good Will Hunting • LA Confidential
FOREIGN LANGUAGE FILM: **Character** • Beyond Silence • Four Days in September • Secrets of the Heart • The Thief
DIRECTING: **James Cameron** Titanic • Peter Cattaneo The Full Monty • Gus Van Sant Good Will Hunting • Curtis Hanson LA Confidential • Atom Egoyan The Sweet Hereafter
ACTOR IN A LEADING ROLE: **Jack Nicholson** As Good As It Gets • Matt Damon Good Will Hunting • Robert Duvall The Apostle • Peter Fonda Ulee's Gold • Dustin Hoffman Wag the Dog
ACTRESS IN A LEADING ROLE: **Helen Hunt** As Good As It Gets • Helena Bonham Carter The Wings of the Dove • Julie Christie Afterglow • Judi Dench Mrs Brown • Kate Winslet Titanic
ACTOR IN A SUPPORTING ROLE: **Robin Williams** Good Will Hunting • Robert Forster Jackie Brown • Anthony Hopkins Amistad • Greg Kinnear As Good As It Gets • Burt Reynolds Boogie Nights

ACTRESS IN A SUPPORTING ROLE: **Kim Basinger** LA Confidential • Joan Cusack In & Out • Minnie Driver Good Will Hunting • Julianne Moore Boogie Nights • Gloria Stuart Titanic
WRITING (SCREENPLAY WRITTEN DIRECTLY FOR THE SCREEN): **Matt Damon, Ben Affleck** Good Will Hunting • Mark Andrus, James L Brooks As Good As It Gets • Paul Thomas Anderson Boogie Nights • Woody Allen Deconstructing Harry • Simon Beaufoy The Full Monty
WRITING (SCREENPLAY BASED ON MATERIAL PREVIOUSLY PRODUCED OR PUBLISHED): **Curtis Hanson, Brian Helgeland** LA Confidential • Paul Attanasio Donnie Brasco • Atom Egoyan The Sweet Hereafter • Hilary Henkin, David Mamet Wag the Dog • Hossein Amini The Wings of the Dove

Golden Globe Awards

BEST MOTION PICTURE DRAMA: **Titanic**
BEST MOTION PICTURE COMEDY OR MUSICAL: **As Good As It Gets**
BEST FOREIGN LANGUAGE FILM: **Ma Vie en Rose**
BEST DIRECTOR MOTION PICTURE: **James Cameron** Titanic
BEST PERFORMANCE BY AN ACTOR IN A MOTION PICTURE DRAMA: **Peter Fonda** Ulee's Gold
BEST PERFORMANCE BY AN ACTRESS IN A MOTION PICTURE DRAMA: **Judi Dench** Mrs Brown
BEST PERFORMANCE BY AN ACTOR IN A MOTION PICTURE COMEDY OR MUSICAL: **Jack Nicholson** As Good As It Gets
BEST PERFORMANCE BY AN ACTRESS IN A MOTION PICTURE COMEDY OR MUSICAL: **Helen Hunt** As Good As It Gets
BEST PERFORMANCE BY AN ACTOR IN A SUPPORTING ROLE MOTION PICTURE: **Burt Reynolds** Boogie Nights
BEST PERFORMANCE BY AN ACTRESS IN A SUPPORTING ROLE MOTION PICTURE: **Kim Basinger** LA Confidential
BEST SCREENPLAY MOTION PICTURE: **Matt Damon, Ben Affleck** Good Will Hunting

Cannes International Film Festival

PALME D'OR: **The Eel** • **A Taste of Cherry**
DIRECTOR: **Wong Kar-Wai** Happy Together
ACTOR: **Sean Penn** She's So Lovely
ACTRESS: **Kathy Burke** Nil by Mouth
SCREENPLAY: **James Schamus** The Ice Storm

Berlin International Film Festival

GOLDEN BERLIN BEAR: **The People vs Larry Flynt**
SILVER BERLIN BEAR FOR THE BEST DIRECTOR: **Eric Heumann** Port Djema
SILVER BERLIN BEAR FOR THE BEST ACTOR: **Leonardo DiCaprio** William Shakespeare's Romeo + Juliet
SILVER BERLIN BEAR FOR THE BEST ACTRESS: **Juliette Binoche** The English Patient

1998

British Academy of Film & Television Arts Awards

BEST FILM: **Shakespeare in Love** • Elizabeth • Saving Private Ryan • The Truman Show
BEST FILM NOT IN THE ENGLISH LANGUAGE: **Central Station** • Life Is Beautiful • Le Bossu • Live Flesh
THE ALEXANDER KORDA AWARD FOR THE OUTSTANDING BRITISH FILM OF THE YEAR: **Elizabeth** • Hilary and Jackie • Little Voice • Lock, Stock and Two Smoking Barrels • My Name Is Joe • Sliding Doors
THE DAVID LEAN AWARD FOR THE BEST ACHIEVEMENT IN DIRECTION: **Peter Weir** The Truman Show • Shekhar Kapur Elizabeth • Steven Spielberg Saving Private Ryan • John Madden Shakespeare in Love
BEST PERFORMANCE BY AN ACTOR IN A LEADING ROLE: **Roberto Benigni** Life Is Beautiful • Michael Caine Little Voice • Joseph Fiennes Shakespeare in Love • Tom Hanks Saving Private Ryan
BEST PERFORMANCE BY AN ACTRESS IN A LEADING ROLE: **Cate Blanchett** Elizabeth • Jane Horrocks Little Voice • Gwyneth Paltrow Shakespeare in Love • Emily Watson Hilary and Jackie
BEST PERFORMANCE BY AN ACTOR IN A SUPPORTING ROLE: **Geoffrey Rush** Shakespeare in Love • Ed Harris The Truman Show • Geoffrey Rush Elizabeth • Tom Wilkinson Shakespeare in Love
BEST PERFORMANCE BY AN ACTRESS IN A SUPPORTING ROLE: **Judi Dench** Shakespeare in Love • Kathy Bates Primary Colors • Brenda Blethyn Little Voice • Lynn Redgrave Gods and Monsters
BEST SCREENPLAY (ORIGINAL): **Andrew Niccol** The Truman Show • Michael Hirst Elizabeth • Vincenzo Cerami, Roberto Benigni Life Is Beautiful • Marc Norman, Tom Stoppard Shakespeare in Love
BEST SCREENPLAY (ADAPTED): **Elaine May** Primary Colors • Frank Cottrell Boyce Hilary and Jackie • Mark Herman Little Voice • David Mamet, Hilary Henkin Wag the Dog

...y Awards

...T PICTURE: **Shakespeare in Love** • *Elizabeth* • *Life Is
Beautiful* • *Saving Private Ryan* • *The Thin Red Line*
FOREIGN LANGUAGE FILM: **Life Is Beautiful** • *Central Station*
• *The Children of Heaven* • *The Grandfather* • *Tango*
DIRECTING: **Steven Spielberg** *Saving Private Ryan* •
Roberto Benigni *Life Is Beautiful* • John Madden
Shakespeare in Love • Terrence Malick *The Thin Red
Line* • Peter Weir *The Truman Show*
ACTOR IN A LEADING ROLE: **Roberto Benigni** *Life Is Beautiful*
• Tom Hanks *Saving Private Ryan* • Ian McKellen *Gods
and Monsters* • Nick Nolte *Affliction* • Edward Norton
American History X
ACTRESS IN A LEADING ROLE: **Gwyneth Paltrow** *Shakespeare
in Love* • Cate Blanchett *Elizabeth* • Fernanda
Montenegro *Central Station* • Meryl Streep *One True
Thing* • Emily Watson *Hilary and Jackie*
ACTOR IN A SUPPORTING ROLE: **James Coburn** *Affliction* •
Robert Duvall *A Civil Action* • Ed Harris *The Truman
Show* • Geoffrey Rush *Shakespeare in Love* • Billy Bob
Thornton *A Simple Plan*
ACTRESS IN A SUPPORTING ROLE: **Judi Dench** *Shakespeare in
Love* • Kathy Bates *Primary Colors* • Brenda Blethyn
Little Voice • Rachel Griffiths *Hilary and Jackie* • Lynn
Redgrave *Gods and Monsters*
WRITING (SCREENPLAY WRITTEN DIRECTLY FOR THE SCREEN):
Marc Norman, Tom Stoppard *Shakespeare in Love* •
Warren Beatty, Jeremy Pikser *Bulworth* • Roberto
Benigni, Vincenzo Cerami *Life Is Beautiful* • Robert
Rodat *Saving Private Ryan* • Andrew Niccol *The Truman
Show*
WRITING (SCREENPLAY BASED ON MATERIAL PREVIOUSLY
PRODUCED OR PUBLISHED): **Bill Condon** *Gods and
Monsters* • Scott Frank *Out of Sight* • Elaine May
Primary Colors • Thorley Walters *A Simple Plan* •
Terrence Malick *The Thin Red Line*

Golden Globe Awards

BEST MOTION PICTURE . DRAMA: **Saving Private Ryan**
BEST MOTION PICTURE COMEDY OR MUSICAL: **Shakespeare
in Love**
BEST FOREIGN LANGUAGE FILM: **Central Station**
BEST DIRECTOR MOTION PICTURE: **Steven Spielberg** *Saving
Private Ryan*
BEST PERFORMANCE BY AN ACTOR IN A MOTION PICTURE
DRAMA: **Jim Carrey** *The Truman Show*
BEST PERFORMANCE BY AN ACTRESS IN A MOTION PICTURE
DRAMA: **Cate Blanchett** *Elizabeth*
BEST PERFORMANCE BY AN ACTOR IN A MOTION PICTURE
COMEDY OR MUSICAL: **Michael Caine** *Little Voice*
BEST PERFORMANCE BY AN ACTRESS IN A MOTION PICTURE
COMEDY OR MUSICAL: **Gwyneth Paltrow** *Shakespeare in
Love*
BEST PERFORMANCE BY AN ACTOR IN A SUPPORTING ROLE
MOTION PICTURE: **Ed Harris** *The Truman Show*
BEST PERFORMANCE BY AN ACTRESS IN A SUPPORTING ROLE
MOTION PICTURE; **Lynn Redgrave** *Gods and Monsters*
BEST SCREENPLAY MOTION PICTURE: **Marc Norman, Tom
Stoppard** *Shakespeare in Love*

Cannes International Film Festival

PALME D'OR: **Eternity and a Day**
DIRECTOR: **John Boorman** *The General*
ACTOR: **Peter Mullan** *My Name Is Joe*
ACTRESS: **Elodie Bouchez, Natacha Régnier** *The Dream
Life of Angels*
SCREENPLAY: **Hal Hartley** *Henry Fool*

Berlin International Film Festival

GOLDEN BERLIN BEAR: **Central Station**
SILVER BERLIN BEAR FOR THE BEST DIRECTOR: **Neil Jordan**
The Butcher Boy
SILVER BERLIN BEAR FOR THE BEST ACTOR: **Samuel L Jackson**
Jackie Brown
SILVER BERLIN BEAR FOR THE BEST ACTRESS: **Fernanda
Montenegro** *Central Station*

1999

British Academy of Film & Television Arts Awards

BEST FILM: **American Beauty** • *East Is East* • *The End of
the Affair* • *The Sixth Sense* • *The Talented Mr Ripley*
FILM NOT IN THE ENGLISH LANGUAGE: **All about My Mother** •
Buena Vista Social Club • *Festen* • *Run Lola Run*
THE ALEXANDER KORDA AWARD FOR THE OUTSTANDING BRITISH
FILM OF THE YEAR: **East Is East** • *Notting Hill* • *Onegin* •
Ratcatcher • *Topsy-Turvy* • *Wonderland*
THE DAVID LEAN AWARD FOR THE BEST ACHIEVEMENT IN
DIRECTION: **Pedro Almodóvar** *All about My Mother* • Sam
Mendes *American Beauty* • Neil Jordan *The End of the

Affair • M Night Shyamalan *The Sixth Sense* • Anthony
Minghella *The Talented Mr Ripley*
BEST PERFORMANCE BY AN ACTOR IN A LEADING ROLE: **Kevin
Spacey** *American Beauty* • Jim Broadbent *Topsy-Turvy* •
Russell Crowe *The Insider* • Ralph Fiennes *The End of
the Affair* • Om Puri *East Is East*
BEST PERFORMANCE BY AN ACTRESS IN A LEADING ROLE:
Annette Bening *American Beauty* • Linda Bassett *East
Is East* • Julianne Moore *The End of the Affair* • Emily
Watson *Angela's Ashes*
BEST PERFORMANCE BY AN ACTOR IN A SUPPORTING ROLE: **Jude
Law** *The Talented Mr Ripley* • Wes Bentley *American
Beauty* • Michael Caine *The Cider House Rules* • Rhys
Ifans *Notting Hill* • Timothy Spall *Topsy-Turvy*
BEST PERFORMANCE BY AN ACTRESS IN A SUPPORTING ROLE:
Maggie Smith *Tea with Mussolini* • Thora Birch
American Beauty • Cate Blanchett *The Talented Mr
Ripley* • Cameron Diaz *Being John Malkovich* • Mena
Suvari *American Beauty*
BEST SCREENPLAY (ORIGINAL): **Charlie Kaufman** *Being John
Malkovich* • Pedro Almodóvar *All about My Mother* •
Alan Ball *American Beauty* • M Night Shyamalan *The
Sixth Sense* • Mike Leigh *Topsy-Turvy*
BEST SCREENPLAY (ADAPTED): **Neil Jordan** *The End of the
Affair* • Oliver Parker *An Ideal Husband* • Ayub Khan-Din
East Is East • Anthony Minghella *The Talented Mr Ripley*

Academy Awards

BEST PICTURE: **American Beauty** • *The Cider House Rules*
• *The Green Mile* • *The Insider* • *The Sixth Sense*
FOREIGN LANGUAGE FILM: **All about My Mother** • *Himalaya* •
Est-Ouest • *Solomon and Gaenor* • *Under the Sun*
DIRECTING: **Sam Mendes** *American Beauty* • Spike Jonze
Being John Malkovich • Lasse Hallström *The Cider
House Rules* • Michael Mann *The Insider* • M Night
Shyamalan *The Sixth Sense*
ACTOR IN A LEADING ROLE: **Kevin Spacey** *American Beauty* •
Denzel Washington *The Hurricane* • Russell Crowe *The
Insider* • Richard Farnsworth *The Straight Story* • Sean
Penn *Sweet and Lowdown*
ACTRESS IN A LEADING ROLE: **Hilary Swank** *Boys Don't Cry* •
Annette Bening *American Beauty* • Julianne Moore *The
End of the Affair* • Meryl Streep *Music of the Heart* •
Janet McTeer *Tumbleweeds*
ACTOR IN A SUPPORTING ROLE: **Michael Caine** *The Cider
House Rules* • Michael Clarke Duncan *The Green Mile* •
Tom Cruise *Magnolia* • Haley Joel Osment *The Sixth
Sense* • Jude Law *The Talented Mr Ripley*
ACTRESS IN A SUPPORTING ROLE: **Angelina Jolie** *Girl,
Interrupted* • Catherine Keener *Being John Malkovich* •
Chloë Sevigny *Boys Don't Cry* • Toni Collette *The Sixth
Sense* • Samantha Morton *Sweet and Lowdown*
WRITING (SCREENPLAY WRITTEN DIRECTLY FOR THE SCREEN):
Alan Ball *American Beauty* • Charlie Kaufman *Being
John Malkovich* • Paul Thomas Anderson *Magnolia* • M
Night Shyamalan *The Sixth Sense* • Mike Leigh *Topsy-
Turvy*
WRITING (SCREENPLAY BASED ON MATERIAL PREVIOUSLY
PRODUCED OR PUBLISHED): **John Irving** *The Cider House
Rules* • Alexander Payne, Jim Taylor *Election* • Frank
Darabont *The Green Mile* • Eric Roth, Michael Mann *The
Insider* • Anthony Minghella *The Talented Mr Ripley*

Golden Globe Awards

BEST MOTION PICTURE . DRAMA: **American Beauty**
BEST MOTION PICTURE COMEDY OR MUSICAL: **Toy Story 2**
BEST FOREIGN LANGUAGE FILM: **All about My Mother**
BEST DIRECTOR MOTION PICTURE: **Sam Mendes** *American
Beauty*
BEST PERFORMANCE BY AN ACTOR IN A MOTION PICTURE
DRAMA: **Denzel Washington** *The Hurricane*
BEST PERFORMANCE BY AN ACTRESS IN A MOTION PICTURE
DRAMA: **Hilary Swank** *Boys Don't Cry*
BEST PERFORMANCE BY AN ACTOR IN A MOTION PICTURE
COMEDY OR MUSICAL: **Jim Carrey** *Man on the Moon*
BEST PERFORMANCE BY AN ACTRESS IN A MOTION PICTURE
COMEDY OR MUSICAL: **Janet McTeer** *Tumbleweeds*
BEST PERFORMANCE BY AN ACTOR IN A SUPPORTING ROLE
MOTION PICTURE: **Tom Cruise** *Magnolia*
BEST PERFORMANCE BY AN ACTRESS IN A SUPPORTING ROLE
MOTION PICTURE; **Angelina Jolie** *Girl, Interrupted*
BEST SCREENPLAY MOTION PICTURE: **Alan Ball** *American
Beauty*

Cannes International Film Festival

PALME D'OR: **Rosetta**
DIRECTOR: **Pedro Almodóvar** *All about My Mother*
ACTOR: **Emmanuel Schotte** *L'Humanité*
ACTRESS: **Emilie Dequenne** *Rosetta* • **Severine Caneele**
L'Humanité
SCREENPLAY: **Yuri Arabov** *Moloch*

Berlin International Film Festival

GOLDEN BERLIN BEAR: **The Thin Red Line**
SILVER BERLIN BEAR FOR THE BEST DIRECTOR: **Stephen Frears**
The Hi-Lo Country

SILVER BERLIN BEAR FOR THE BEST ACTOR: **Michael Gwisdek**
Night Shapes
SILVER BERLIN BEAR FOR THE BEST ACTRESS: **Maria Schrader,
Juliane Köhler** *Aimée & Jaguar*

2000

Cannes International Film Festival

PALME D'OR: **Dancer in the Dark**
DIRECTOR: **Edward Yang** *A One and a Two*
ACTOR: **Tony Leung** *In the Mood for Love*
ACTRESS: **Bjork** *Dancer in the Dark*
SCREENPLAY: **John C Richards, James Flamberg** *Nurse
Betty*

Berlin International Film Festival

GOLDEN BERLIN BEAR: **Magnolia**
SILVER BERLIN BEAR FOR THE BEST DIRECTOR: **Milos Forman**
Man on the Moon
SILVER BERLIN BEAR FOR THE BEST ACTOR: **Denzel
Washington** *The Hurricane*
JURY PRIZE SILVER BEAR FOR FILM: **The Million Dollar Hotel**